Who's Who in the Midwest

Biographical Reference Works
Published by Marquis Who's Who

Who's Who in America

Who Was Who in America

   Historical Volume (1607-1896)

   Volume I (1897-1942)

   Volume II (1943-1950)

   Volume III (1951-1960)

   Volume IV (1961-1968)

   Volume V (1969-1973)

   Volume VI (1974-1976)

   Volume VII (1977-1981)

Who Was Who in American History—Arts and Letters

Who Was Who in American History—The Military

Who Was Who in American History—Science and Technology

Who's Who in the Midwest

Who's Who in the East

Who's Who in the South and Southwest

Who's Who in the West

Who's Who of American Women

Who's Who in Government

Who's Who in Finance and Industry

Who's Who in Religion

Who's Who in American Law

Who's Who in the World

Who's Who Biographical Record—Child Development Professionals

Who's Who Biographical Record—School District Officials

World Who's Who in Science

Directory of Medical Specialists

Marquis Who's Who Publications/Index to All Books

Travelers' Guide to U.S. Certified Doctors Abroad

Who's Who
in the Midwest ®

Including Illinois, Indiana, Iowa, Kansas,
Michigan, Minnesota, Missouri, Nebraska,
North Dakota, Ohio, South Dakota, and
Wisconsin; and in Canada, Manitoba and
western Ontario

18th edition
1982-1983

MARQUIS
Who'sWho

Marquis Who's Who, Inc.
200 East Ohio Street
Chicago, Illinois 60611 U.S.A.

Library of Congress Catalog Card Number 50-289
International Standard Book Number 0-8379-0718-7
Product Code Number 030255

Distributed in the United Kingdom by
George Prior Associated Publishers
37-41 Bedford Row
London WC 1, England

Manufactured in the United States of America

Table of Contents

Preface

The eighteenth edition of *Who's Who in the Midwest* represents our most recent effort to provide biographical information on men and women of distinction whose influence is concentrated in the midwestern sector of North America. Such individuals are of decided reference interest locally and, to an increasing degree, nationally.

The volume contains more than 18,000 names from the midwestern region of the United States including Illinois, Indiana, Iowa, Kansas, Michigan, Minnesota, Missouri, Nebraska, North Dakota, Ohio, South Dakota, and Wisconsin in the United States and the provinces of Manitoba and western Ontario in Canada. Assiduously reviewed, revised, and amended, the eighteenth edition offers up-to-the-minute coverage of a broad range of Midwesterners based on position or individual achievement.

The persons sketched in this volume represent virtually every important field of endeavor. Included are executives and officials in government, business, education, religion, the press, civic affairs, the arts, cultural affairs, law, and other fields. This edition also includes significant contributors in such fields as contemporary art, music, and science.

In the great majority of cases, the biographees have furnished their own data, thus assuring a high degree of accuracy. In some cases where individuals fail to supply information, Marquis staff members compile the data through careful and independent research. Sketches compiled in this manner are denoted by an asterisk. As in previous editions, biographees are given the opportunity to review prepublication proofs of their sketches to make sure they are correct.

Marquis Who's Who editors exercise the utmost care in preparing each biographical sketch for publication. Occasionally, however, errors do occur despite all precautions taken to minimize such occurrences. Users of this directory are requested to draw the attention of the publisher to any errors found so that corrections can be made in a later edition.

The question often is asked, "How do people get into a Who's Who volume?" Name selection is based on one fundamental principle: reference value.

Biographees of *Who's Who in the Midwest* can be classified in two basic categories: (1) Persons who are of regional reference importance to colleagues, librarians, researchers, scholars, the press, historians, biographers, participants in business and civic affairs, and others with specific or general inquiry needs; (2) Individuals of national reference interest who are also of such regional or local importance that their inclusion in the book is essential.

There is a minimum of duplication of names between this volume and *Who's Who in America*. In recognition of the complementary relationship between the two Marquis publications, this edition of *Who's Who in the Midwest* contains a listing of all those biographees of the midwestern region whose sketches appear in the forty-second edition of *Who's Who in America*.

In the editorial evaluation that resulted in the ultimate selection of the names in this directory, an individual's desire to be listed was not sufficient reason for inclusion; rather it was the person's achievement that ruled. Similarly, wealth or social position was not a criterion; only occupational stature or achievement in a field within the midwestern region of North America influenced selection. Indeed, many of the biographees are engaged in fields marked far more by service than by monetary reward.

The eighteenth edition of *Who's Who in the Midwest* carries on the tradition of excellence established in 1899 with the publication of the first edition of *Who's Who in America*. The essence of that tradition is reflected in our continuing effort to produce reference works that are responsive to the needs of their users throughout the world.

Standards of Admission

The foremost consideration in determining possible biographees of *Who's Who in the Midwest* is the extent of an individual's reference interest. Such reference interest is judged on either of two factors: (1) The position of responsibility held, or (2) The level of significant achievement attained.

Admissions based on the factor of position include:

Members of the U.S. Congress

Federal judges

Governors of states covered by this volume

Premiers of Canadian provinces covered by this volume

State attorneys general

Judges of state and territorial courts of highest appellate jurisdiction

Mayors of major cities

Heads of the major universities and colleges

Heads of leading philanthropic, educational, cultural and scientific institutions and associations

Chief ecclesiastics of the principal religious denominations

Principal officers of national and international businesses

Others chosen because of incumbency, authorship, or membership

Admission based on individual achievement must be decided by a judicious process of evaluating qualitative factors. To be selected on this basis, a person must have accomplished some conspicuous achievement—something that distinguishes the biographee from the vast majority of his contemporaries. The person may scarcely be known in the local community, but may be widely recognized within a special field of endeavor. Such a person may be better known by achievement than by name.

Key to Information in this Directory

❶ BURKE, GEORGE ALLEN, ❷ toy mfg. co. exec.; ❸ b. Highland Park, Ill., Mar. 23, 1926; ❹ s. Miles Benjamin and Thelma (Allen) B.; ❺ B.S., Northwestern U., 1949; ❻ m. Leota Gruber, Jan. 28, 1946; ❼ children—Evangeline Marie Burke Rossett, Joseph Paul, Harvey Edwin. ❽ With Millington Toy Mfg. Co., Peoria, Ill., 1950—, sales mgr., 1955-66, v.p., 1960-69, pres., 1969-76, chmn. bd., 1976—, also dir.; dir. Peoria Title and Trust Co., 1970—; lectr. Peoria Community Coll., 1967-68. ❾ Active Boy Scouts Am.; bd. govs. Lincolnwood Home for the Aged; sec. Ill. Gov.'s Commn. on Pub. Safety, 1972-76; mem. Peoria Heights Bd. Edn., 1956-58. ❿ Served with USNR, 1943-45; PTO. ⓫ Decorated Purple Heart; recipient Silver Beaver award Boy Scouts Am., 1967. ⓬ Mem. AIM, NAM, Beta Theta Pi. ⓭ Democrat. ⓮ Presbyterian. ⓯ Clubs: Masons, Shriners, Peoria Lake Country, Chgo. Athletic. ⓰ Contbr. articles to bus. publs. ⓱ Home: 903 Spring Dr Peoria Heights IL 61613 ⓲ Office: 1912 Main St Peoria IL 61606

The biographical listings in *Who's Who in the Midwest* are arranged in alphabetical order according to the first letter of the last name of the biographee. Each sketch is presented in a uniform order as in the sample sketch above. The abbreviations used in the sketches are explained in the Table of Abbreviations.

Key:

❶ Name
❷ Occupation
❸ Vital Statistics
❹ Parents
❺ Education
❻ Marriage
❼ Children
❽ Career
❾ Civic and political activities
❿ Military record
⓫ Awards and certifications
⓬ Professional and association memberships
⓭ Political affiliation
⓮ Religion
⓯ Clubs (including lodges)
⓰ Writings and special achievements
⓱ Home address
⓲ Office address

Table of Abbreviations

The following abbreviations and symbols are frequently used in this Directory

* (An asterisk) following a sketch indicates that it was researched by the Marquis Who's Who editorial staff and has not been verified by the biographee.

A.A. Associate in Arts
AAAL American Academy of Arts and Letters
AAAS American Association for the Advancement of Science
AAHPER Alliance for Health, Physical Education and Recreation
A. and M. Agricultural and Mechanical
AAU Amateur Athletic Union
AAUP American Association of University Professors
AAUW American Association of University Women
A.B. Arts, Bachelor of
AB Alberta
ABC American Broadcasting Company
AC Air Corps
acad. academy, academic
acct. accountant
acctg. accounting
ACDA Arms Control and Disarmament Agency
ACLU American Civil Liberties Union
A.C.P. American College of Physicians
A.C.S. American College of Surgeons
ADA American Dental Association
a.d.c. aide-de-camp
adj. adjunct, adjutant
adj. gen. adjutant general
adm. admiral
adminstr. administrator
adminstrn. administration
adminstrv. administrative
adv. advocate, advisory, adviser
advt. advertising
A.E. Agricultural Engineeer
A.E. and P., AEP Ambassador Extraordinary and Plenipotentiary
AEC Atomic Energy Commission
aero. aeronautical, aeronautic
aerodyn. aerodynamic
AFB Air Force Base
AFL-CIO American Federation of Labor and Congress of Industrial Organizations
AFTRA American Federation TV and Radio Artists
agr. agriculture
agrl. agricultural
agt. agent
AGVA American Guild of Variety Artists
agy. agency
A&I Agricultural and Industrial
AIA American Institute of Architects
AIAA American Institute of Aeronautics Astronautics
AID Agency for International Development
AIEE American Institute of Electrical Engineers
AIM American Institute of Management
AIME American Institute of Mining, Metallurgy, and Petroleum Engineers
AK Alaska
AL Alabama
ALA American Library Association
Ala. Alabama
alt. alternate
Alta. Alberta
A&M Agricultural and Mechanical
A.M. Arts, Master of
Am. American, America
AMA American Medical Association

A.M.E. African Methodist Episcopal
Amtrak National Railroad Passenger Corporation
AMVETS American Veterans of World War II, Korea, Vietnam
anat. anatomical
ann. annual
ANTA American National Theatre and Academy
anthrop. anthropological
AP Associated Press
APO Army Post Office
apptd. appointed
apt. apartment
AR Arkansas
ARC American Red Cross
archeol. archeological
archtl. architectural
Ariz. Arizona
Ark. Arkansas
Arts D. Arts, Doctor of
arty. artillery
ASCAP American Society of Composers, Authors and Publishers
ASCE American Society of Civil Engineers
ASHRAE American Society of Heating, Refrigeration, and Air Conditioning Engineers
ASME American Society of Mechanical Engineers
assn. association
asso. associate
asst. assistant
ASTM American Society for Testing and Materials
astron. astronomical
astrophys. astrophysical
ATSC Air Technical Service Command
AT&T American Telephone & Telegraph Company
atty. attorney
AUS Army of the United States
aux. auxiliary
Ave. Avenue
AVMA American Veterinary Medical Association
AZ Arizona

B. Bachelor
b. born
B.A. Bachelor of Arts
B. Agr. Bachelor of Agriculture
Balt. Baltimore
Bapt. Baptist
B.Arch. Bachelor of Architecture
B.A.S. Bachelor of Agricultural Science
B.B.A. Bachelor of Business Administration
BBC British Broadcasting Corporation
B.C.,BC British Columbia
B.C.E. Bachelor of Civil Engineering
B.Chir. Bachelor of Surgery
B.C.L. Bachelor of Civil Law
B.C.S. Bachelor of Commerical Science
B.D. Bachelor of Divinity
bd. board
B.E. Bachelor of Education
B.E.E. Bachelor of Electrical Engineering
B.F.A. Bachelor of Fine Arts
bibl. biblical
bibliog. bibliographical
biog. biographical
biol. biological
B.J. Bachelor of Journalism
Bklyn. Brooklyn
B.L. Bachelor of Letters
bldg. building
B.L.S. Bachelor of Library Science

Blvd. Boulevard
bn. battalion
B.&O.R.R. Baltimore & Ohio Railroad
bot. botanical
B.P.E. Bachelor of Physical Education
br. branch
B.R.E. Bachelor of Religious Education
brig. gen. brigadier general
Brit. British, Britannica
Bros. Brothers
B.S. Bachelor of Science
B.S.A. Bachelor of Agricultural Science
B.S.D. Bachelor of Didactic Science
B.S.T. Bachelor of Sacred Theology
B.Th. Bachelor of Theology
bull. bulletin
bur. bureau
bus. business
B.W.I. British West Indies

CA California
CAA Civil Aeronautics Administration
CAB Civil Aeronautics Board
Calif. California
C.Am. Central America
Can. Canada, Canadian
CAP Civil Air Patrol
capt. captain
CARE Cooperative American Relief Everywhere
Cath. Catholic
cav. cavalry
CBC Canadian Broadcasting Company
CBI China, Burma, India Theatre of Operations
CBS Columbia Broadcasting System
CCC Commodity Credit Corporation
CCNY City College of New York
CCU Cardiac Care Unit
CD Civil Defense
C.E. Corps of Engineers, Civil Engineer
CENTO Central Treaty Organization
CERN European Organization of Nuclear Research
cert. certificate, certification, certified
CETA Comprehensive Employment Training Act
CFL Canadian Football League
ch. church
Ch.D. Doctor of Chemistry
chem. chemical
Chem. E. Chemical Engineer
Chgo. Chicago
chirurg. chirurgical
chmn. chairman
chpt. chapter
CIA Central Intelligence Agency
CIC Counter Intelligence Corps
Cin. Cincinnati
Cleve. Cleveland
climatol. climatological
clin. clinical
clk. clerk
C.L.U. Chartered Life Underwriter
C.M. Master in Surgery
C.& N.W.Ry. Chicago & Northwestern Railway
CO Colorado
Co. Company
COF Catholic Order of Foresters
C. of C. Chamber of Commerce
col. colonel
coll. college
Colo. Colorado
com. committee
comd. commanded
comdg. commanding

comdr. commander
comdt. commandant
commd. commissioned
comml. commercial
commn. commission
commr. commissioner
condr. conductor
Conf. Conference
Congl. Congregational
Conglist. Congregationalist
Conn. Connecticut
cons. consultant, consulting
consol. consolidated
constl. constitutional
constn. constitution
constrn. construction
contbd. contributed
contbg. contributing
contbn. contribution
contbr. contributor
Conv. Convention
coop., co-op. cooperative
CORDS Civil Operations and Revolutionary Development Support
CORE Congress of Racial Equality
corp. corporation, corporate
corr. correspondent, corresponding, correspondence
C.&O.Ry. Chesapeake & Ohio Railway
C.P.A. Certified Public Accountant
C.P.C.U. Chartered property and casualty underwriter
C.P.H. Certificate of Public Health
cpl. corporal
CPR Cardiac Pulmonary Resuscitation
C.P.Ry. Canadian Pacific Railway
C.S. Christian Science
C.S.B. Bachelor of Christian Science
CSC Civil Service Commission
C.S.D. Doctor of Christian Science
CT Connecticut
ct. Court
CWS Chemical Warfare Service
C.Z. Canal Zone

d. daughter
D. Doctor
D.Agr. Doctor of Agriculture
DAR Daughters of the American Revolution
dau. daughter
DAV Disabled American Veterans
D.C., DC District of Columbia
D.C.L. Doctor of Civil Law
D.C.S. Doctor of Commercial Science
D.D. Doctor of Divinity
D.D.S. Doctor of Dental Surgery
DE Delaware
dec. deceased
def. defense
Del. Delaware
del. delegate, delegation
Dem. Democrat, Democratic
D.Eng. Doctor of Engineering
denom. denomination, denominational
dep. deputy
dept. department
dermatol. dermatological
desc. descendant
devel. development, developmental
D.F.A. Doctor of Fine Arts
D.F.C. Distinguished Flying Cross
D.H.L. Doctor of Hebrew Literature
dir. director
dist. district
distbg. distributing
distbn. distribution

distbr. distributor
disting. distinguished
div. division, divinity, divorce
D.Litt. Doctor of Literature
D.M.D. Doctor of Medical Dentistry
D.M.S. Doctor of Medical Science
D.O. Doctor of Osteopathy
D.P.H. Diploma in Public Health
D.R. Daughters of the Revolution
Dr. Drive
D.R.E. Doctor of Religious Education
Dr.P.H. Doctor of Public Health, Doctor of Public Hygiene
D.S.C. Distinguished Service Cross
D.Sc. Doctor of Science
D.S.M. Distinguished Service Medal
D.S.T. Doctor of Sacred Theology
D.T.M. Doctor of Tropical Medicine
D.V.M. Doctor of Veterinary Medicine
D.V.S. Doctor of Veterinary Surgery

E. East
E. and P. Extraordinary and Plenipotentiary
Eccles. Ecclesiastical
ecol. ecology, ecological
econ. economic
ECOSOC Economic and Social Council (of the UN)
E.D. Doctor of Engineering
ed. educated
Ed.B. Bachelor of Education
Ed.D. Doctor of Education
edit. edition
Ed.M. Master of Education
edn. education
ednl. educational
EDP electronic data processing
Ed.S. Specialist in Education
E.E. Electrical Engineer
E.E. and M.P. Envoy Extraordinary and Minister Plenipotentiary
EEC European Economic Community
EEG electroencephalogram
EEO Equal Employment Opportunity
EKG electrocardiogram
E.Ger. German Democratic Republic
elec. electrical
electrochem. electrochemical
electrophys. electrophysical
elem. elementary
E.M. Engineer of Mines
ency. encyclopedia
Eng. England
engr. engineer
engring. engineering
entomol. entomological
environ. environmental, environment
EPA Environmental Protection Agency
epidemiol. epidemiological
Episc. Episcopalian
ERA Equal Rights Amendment
ERDA Energy Research and Development Administration
ESEA Elementary and Secondary Education Act
ESSA Environmental Science Services Administration
ethnol. ethnological
ETO European Theatre of Operations
Evang. Evangelical
exam. examination, examining
exec. executive
exhbn. exhibition
expdn. expedition
expn. exposition
expt. experiment
exptl. experimental

F.A. Field Artillery
FAA Federal Aviation Administration
FAO Food and Agriculture Organization (of the UN)
FBI Federal Bureau of Investigation
FCA Farm Credit Administration
FCC Federal Communication Commission
FCDA Federal Civil Defense Administration
FDA Food and Drug Administration
FDIA Federal Deposit Insurance Administration
FDIC Federal Deposit Insurance Corporation
F.E. Forest Engineer
FEA Federal Energy Administration
fed. federal
fedn. federation
fgn. foreign
FHA Federal Housing Administration
fin. financial, finance
FL Florida
Fla. Florida
FMC Federal Maritime Commission
FOA Foreign Operations Administration
found. foundation
FPC Federal Power Commission
FPO Fleet Post Office
frat. fraternity
FRS Federal Reserve System
FSA Federal Security Agency
Ft. Fort
FTC Federal Trade Commission

G-1 (or other number) Division of General Staff
Ga., GA Georgia
GAO General Accounting Office
gastroent. gastroenterological
GATT General Agreement of Tariff and Trades
gen. general
geneal. genealogical
geod. geodetic
geog. geographic, geographical
geol. geological
geophys. geophysical
gerontol. gerontological
G.H.Q. General Headquarters
G.N.Ry. Great Northern Railway
gov. governor
govt. government
govtl. governmental
GPO Government Printing Office
grad. graduate, graduated
GSA General Services Administration
Gt. Great
GU Guam
gynecol. gynecological

hdqrs. headquarters
HEW Department of Health, Education and Welfare
H.H.D. Doctor of Humanities
HHFA Housing and Home Finance Agency
HI Hawaii
hist. historical, historic
H.M. Master of Humanics
homeo. homeopathic
hon. honorary, honorable
Ho. of Dels. House of Delegates
Ho. of Reps. House of Representatives
hort. horticultural
hosp. hospital
HUD Department of Housing and Urban Development
Hwy. Highway
hydrog. hydrographic

IA Iowa
IAEA International Atomic Energy Agency
IBM International Business Machines Corporation
IBRD International Bank for Reconstruction and Development
ICA International Cooperation Administration
ICC Interstate Commerce Commission
ICU Intensive Care Unit
ID Idaho
IEEE Institute of Electrical and Electronics Engineers
IFC International Finance Corporation
IGY International Geophysical Year
IL Illinois
Ill. Illinois
illus. illustrated
ILO International Labor Organization
IMF International Monetary Fund
IN Indiana
Inc. Incorporated
ind. independent
Ind. Indiana
Indpls. Indianapolis
indsl. industrial
inf. infantry
info. information
ins. insurance
insp. inspector
insp. gen. inspector general
inst. institute
instl. institutional
instn. institution
instr. instructor
instrn. instruction
internat. international
intro. introduction
IRE Institute of Radio Engineers
IRS Internal Revenue Service
ITT International Telephone & Telegraph Corporation

J.B. Jurum Baccolaureus
J.C.B. Juris Canonici Bachelor
J.C.L. Juris Canonici Lector
J.D. Juris Doctor
j.g. junior grade
jour. journal
jr. junior
J.S.D. Jurum Scientiae Doctor
J.U.D. Juris Utriusque Doctor
Judge Adv. Gen. Judge Advocate General

Kans. Kansas
K.C. Knights of Columbus
K.P. Knights of Pythias
KS Kansas
K.T. Knight Templar
Ky., KY Kentucky

La., LA Louisiana
lab. laboratory
lang. language
laryngol. laryngological
LB Labrador
lectr. lecturer
legis. legislation, legislative
L.H.D. Doctor of Humane Letters
L.I. Long Island
lic. licensed, license
L.I.R.R. Long Island Railroad
lit. literary, literature
Litt. B. Bachelor of Letters

Litt. D. Doctor of Letters
LL.B. Bachelor of Laws
LL.D. Doctor of Laws
LL.M. Master of Laws
Ln. Lane
L.&N.R.R. Louisville & Nashville Railroad
L.S. Library Science (in degree)
lt. lieutenant
Ltd. Limited
Luth. Lutheran
LWV League of Women Voters

m. married
M. Master
M.A. Master of Arts
MA Massachusetts
mag. magazine
M.Agr. Master of Agriculture
maj. major
Man. Manitoba
M.Arch. Master in Architecture
Mass. Massachusetts
math. mathematics, mathematical
MATS Military Air Transport Service
M.B. Bachelor of Medicine
MB Manitoba
M.B.A. Master of Business Administration
MBS Mutual Broadcasting System
M.C. Medical Corps
M.C.E. Master of Civil Engineering
mcht. merchant
mcpl. municipal
M.C.S. Master of Commercial Science
M.D. Doctor of Medicine
Md., MD Maryland
M.Dip. Master in Diplomacy
mdse. merchandise
M.D.V. Doctor of Veterinary Medicine
M.E. Mechanical Engineer
ME Maine
M.E. Ch. Methodist Episcopal Church
mech. mechanical
M.Ed. Master of Education
med. medical
M.E.E. Master of Electrical Engineering
mem. member
meml. memorial
merc. mercantile
met. metropolitan
metall. metallurgical
Met. E. Metallurgical Engineer
meteorol. meteorological
Meth. Methodist
Mex. Mexico
M.F. Master of Forestry
M.F.A. Master of Fine Arts
mfg. manufacturing
mfr. manufacturer
mgmt. management
mgr. manager
M.H.A. Master of Hospital Administration
M.I. Military Intelligence
MI Michigan
Mich. Michigan
micros. microscopic, microscopical
mil. military
Milw. Milwaukee
mineral. mineralogical
Minn. Minnesota
Miss. Mississippi
M.I.T. Massachusetts Institute of Technology
mktg. marketing
M.L. Master of Laws
MLA Modern Language Association
M.L.D. Magister Legnum Diplomatic

M.Litt. Master of Literature
M.L.S. Master of Library Science
M.M.E. Master of Mechanical Engineering
MN Minnesota
mng. managing
Mo., MO Missouri
moblzn. mobilization
Mont. Montana
M.P. Member of Parliament
M.P.E. Master of Physical Education
M.P.H. Master of Public Health
M.P.L. Master of Patent Law
Mpls. Minneapolis
M.R.E. Master of Religious Education
M.S. Master of Science
MS Mississippi
M.Sc. Master of Science
M.S.F. Master of Science of Forestry
M.S.T. Master of Sacred Theology
M.S.W. Master of Social Work
MT Montana
Mt. Mount
MTO Mediterranean Theatre of Operations
mus. museum, musical
Mus.B. Bachelor of Music
Mus.D. Doctor of Music
Mus.M. Master of Music
mut. mutual
mycol. mycological

N. North
NAACP National Association for the Advancement of Colored People
NACA National Advisory Committee for Aeronautics
NAD National Academy of Design
N.Am. North America
NAM National Association of Manufacturers
NAPA National Association of Performing Artists
NAREB National Association of Real Estate Boards
NARS National Archives and Record Service
NASA National Aeronautics and Space Administration
nat. national
NATO North Atlantic Treaty Organization
NATOUSA North African Theatre of Operations
nav. navigation
N.B., NB New Brunswick
NBC National Broadcasting Company
N.C., NC North Carolina
NCCJ National Conference of Christians and Jews
N.D., ND North Dakota
NDEA National Defense Education Act
NE Nebraska
N.E. Northeast
NEA National Education Association
Nebr. Nebraska
neurol. neurological
Nev. Nevada
NF Newfoundland
NFL National Football League
Nfld. Newfoundland
N.G. National Guard
N.H., NH New Hampshire
NHL National Hockey League
NIH National Institutes of Health
NIMH National Institute of Mental Health
N.J., NJ New Jersey
NLRB National Labor Relations Board
NM New Mexico
N.Mex. New Mexico
No. Northern

NOAA National Oceanographic and Atmospheric Administration
NORAD North American Air Defense
NOW National Organization for Women
N.P. Ry. Northern Pacific Railway
nr. near
NRC National Research Council
N.S., NS Nova Scotia
NSC National Security Council
NSF National Science Foundation
N.T. New Testament
NT Northwest Territories
numis. numismatic
NV Nevada
NW Northwest
N.W.T. Northwest Territories
N.Y., NY New York
N.Y.C. New York City
N.Z. New Zealand

OAS Organization of American States
Ob-Gyn obstetrics-gynecology
obs. observatory
O.D. Doctor of Optometry
OECD Organization of European Cooperation and Development
OEEC Organization of European Economic Cooperation
OEO Office of Economic Opportunity
ofcl. official
OH Ohio
OK Oklahoma
Okla. Oklahoma
ON Ontario
Ont. Ontario
ophthal. ophthalmological
ops. operations
OR Oregon
orch. orchestra
Oreg. Oregon
orgn. organization
ornithol. ornithological
OSRD Office of Scientific Research and Development
OSS Office of Strategic Services
osteo. osteopathic
otol. otological
otolaryn. otolaryngological

Pa., PA Pennsylvania
P.A. Professional Association
paleontol. paleontological
path. pathological
P.C. Professional Corporation
PE Prince Edward Island
P.E. Professional Engineer
P.E.I. Prince Edward Island
PEN Poets, Playwrights, Editors, Essayists and Novelists (international association)
penol. penological
P.E.O. women's organization (full name not disclosed)
pfc. private first class
PHA Public Housing Administration
pharm. Pharmaceutical
Pharm.D. Doctor of Pharmacy
Pharm.M. Master of Pharmacy
Ph.B. Bachelor of Philosophy
Ph.D. Doctor of Philosophy
Phila. Philadelphia
philharm. philharmonic
philol. philological
philos. philosophical
photog. photographic

phys. physical
physiol. physiological
Pitts. Pittsburgh
Pkwy. Parkway
Pl. Place
P.&L.E.R.R. Pittsburgh & Lake Erie Railroad
P.O. Post Office
PO Box Post Office Box
polit. political
poly. polytechnic, polytechnical
P.Q. Province of Quebec
P.R., PR Puerto Rico
prep. preparatory
pres. president
Presbyn. Presbyterian
presdl. presidential
prin. principal
proc. proceedings
prod. produced (play production)
prof. professor
profl. professional
prog. progressive
propr. proprietor
pros. atty. prosecuting attorney
pro tem pro tempore
PSRO Professional Services Review Organization
psychiat. psychiatric
psychol. psychological
PTA Parent-Teachers Association
PTO Pacific Theatre of Operations
pub. publisher, publishing, published
publ. publication
pvt. private

quar. quarterly
q.m. quartermaster
Q.M.C. Quartermaster Corps
Que. Quebec

radiol. radiological
RAF Royal Air Force
RCA Radio Corporation of America
RCAF Royal Canadian Air Force
R.D. Rural Delivery
Rd. Road
REA Rural Electrification Administration
rec. recording
ref. reformed
regt. regiment
regtl. regimental
rehab. rehabilitation
rep. representative
Rep. Republican
Res. Reserve
ret. retired
rev. review, revised
RFC Reconstruction Finance Corporation
R.F.D. Rural Free Delivery
rhinol. rhinological
R.I., RI Rhode Island
R.N. Registered Nurse
roentgenol. roentgenological
ROTC Reserve Officers Training Corps
R.R. Railroad
Ry. Railway

s. son
S. South
SAC Strategic Air Command
SALT Strategic Arms Limitation Talks
S.Am. South America
san sanitary
SAR Sons of the American Revolution

Sask. Saskatchewan
savs. savings
S.B. Bachelor of Science
SBA Small Business Administration
S.C., SC South Carolina
SCAP Supreme Command Allies Pacific
Sc.B. Bachelor of Science
S.C.D. Doctor of Commercial Science
Sc.D. Doctor of Science
sch. school
sci. science, scientific
SCLC Southern Christian Leadership Conference
SCV Sons of Confederate Veterans
S.D., SD South Dakota
SE Southeast
SEATO Southeast Asia Treaty Organization
sec. secretary
SEC Securities and Exchange Commission
sect. section
seismol. seismological
sem. seminary
sgt. sergeant
SHAEF Supreme Headquarters Allied Expeditionary Forces
SHAPE Supreme Headquarters Allied Powers in Europe
S.I. Staten Island
S.J. Society of Jesus (Jesuit)
S.J.D. Scientiae Juridicae Doctor
SK Saskatchewan
S.M. Master of Science
So. Southern
soc. society
sociol. sociological
S.P. Co. Southern Pacific Company
spl. special
splty. specialty
Sq. Square
sr. senior
S.R. Sons of the Revolution
S.S. Steamship
SSS Selective Service System
St. Saint
St. Street
sta. station
statis. statistical
stats. statistics
S.T.B. Bachelor of Sacred Theology
stbizn. stabilization
S.T.D. Doctor of Sacred Theology
subs. subsidiary
SUNY State University of New York
supr. supervisor
supt. superintendent
surg. surgical
SW Southwest

TAPPI Technical Association of Pulp and Paper Industry
Tb Tuberculosis
tchr. teacher
tech. technical, technology
technol. technological
Tel.&Tel. Telephone & Telegraph
temp. temporary
Tenn. Tennessee
Ter. Territory
Terr. Terrace
TESL Teaching English as a Second Language
Tex. Texas
Th.D. Doctor of Theology
theol. theological
Th.M. Master of Theology
TN Tennessee
tng. training

topog. topographical
trans. transaction, transferred
transl. translation, translated
transp. transportation
treas. treasurer
TV television
TVA Tennessee Valley Authority
twp. township
TX Texas
typog. typographical

U. University
UAW United Auto Workers
UCLA University of California at Los Angeles
UDC United Daughters of the Confederacy
U.K. United Kingdom
UN United Nations
UNESCO United Nations Educational, Scientific and Cultural Organization
UNICEF United Nations International Children's Emergency Fund
univ. university
UNRRA United Nations Relief and Rehabilitation Administration
UPI United Press International
U.P.R.R. Union Pacific Railroad
urol. urological
U.S. United States
U.S.A. United States of America
USAAF United States Army Air Force
USAF United States Air Force

USAFR United States Air Force Reserve
USAR United States Army Reserve
USCG United States Coast Guard
USCGR United States Coast Guard Reserve
USES United States Employment Service
USIA United States Information Agency
USIS United States Information Service
USMC United States Marine Corps
USMCR United States Marine Corps Reserve
USN United States Navy
USNG United States National Guard
USNR United States Naval Reserve
USO United Service Organizations
USPHS United States Public Health Service
U.S.S. United States Ship
USSR Union of the Soviet Socialist Republics
USV United States Volunteers
UT Utah

VA Veterans' Administration
Va., VA Virginia
vet. veteran, veterinary
VFW Veterans of Foreign Wars
V.I., VI Virgin Islands
vice pres. vice president
vis. visiting
VISTA Volunteers in Service to America
VITA Volunteers in Technical Service
vocat. vocational
vol. volunteer, volume

v.p. vice president
vs. versus
VT., VT Vermont

W. West
WA Washington
WAC Women's Army Corps
Wash. Washington
WAVES Women's Reserve, U.S. Naval Reserve
WCTU Women's Christian Temperance Union
W. Ger. Germany, Federal Republic of
WHO World Health Organization
WI Wisconsin
Wis. Wisconsin
WSB Wage Stabilization Board
WV West Virginia
W. VA. West Virginia
WY Wyoming
Wyo. Wyoming

YK Yukon
YMCA Young Men's Christian Association
YMHA Young Men's Hebrew Association
YM & YWHA Young Men's and Young Women's Hebrew Association
YWCA Young Women's Christian Association
yr. year

zool. zoological

Alphabetical Practices

Names are arranged alphabetically according to the surnames, and under identical surnames according to the first given name. If both surname and first given name are identical, names are arranged alphabetically according to the second given name. Where full names are identical, they are arranged in order of age—with the elder listed first.

Surnames beginning with De, Des, Du, however capitalized or spaced, are recorded with the prefix preceding the surname and arranged alphabetically, under the letter D.

Surnames beginning with Mac and Mc are arranged alphabetically under M.

Surnames beginning with Saint or St. appear after names that would begin Sains, and are arranged according to the second part of the name, e.g., St. Clair before Saint Dennis.

Surnames beginning with prefix Van are arranged alphabetically under letter V. Surnames containing the prefix Von or von are usually arranged alphabetically under letter V; any exceptions are noted by cross references.

Compound hyphenated surnames are arranged according to the first member of the compound. Compound unhyphenated surnames are treated as hyphenated names.

Parentheses used in connection with a name indicate which part of the full name is usually deleted in common usage. Hence Abbott, W(illiam) Lewis indicates that the usual form of the given name is W. Lewis. In alphabetizing this type name, the parentheses are ignored. However if the name is recorded Abbott, (William) Lewis, signifying that the entire name William is not commonly used, the alphabetizing would be arranged as though the name were Abbott, Lewis.

Who's Who in the Midwest

ABARAY, RAYMOND FRANCIS, retail food chain exec.; b. Pitts., Jan. 31, 1932; s. George and Susan (Pado) A.; B.B.A., U. Pitts., 1953; M.B.A., Duquesne U., 1962; m. Clare M. Gombita, June 25, 1955; 1 son, Terry. With The Kroger Co., Cin., 1959—, acctg. supr., 1959-63, div. controller, 1963-69, asst. corp. controller, 1970-71, controller Kroger Food Stores, Cin., 1971, v.p., corp. controller, 1972-78, v.p. mgmt. info. services, 1978—. Mem. exec. cabinet United Appeal, 1978; group chmn. Bus. Mobilized for Xavier U., 1977-79; mem. bus. adv. council Miami U., 1979-82; trustee Greater Cin. Center for Econ. Edn., 1977-82; mem. adv. council U. Cin., 1982—. Mem. Fin. Execs. Inst. Clubs: Kenwood Country; Bankers. Home: 7950 E Galbraith Rd Cincinnati OH 45243 Office: The Kroger Co 1014 Vine St Cincinnati OH 45201

ABBASI, ALI ABDEL-WAHHAB, physician; b. Safad, Palestine, Feb. 24, 1936; s. Abdel-Wahhab S. and Fattoum (Hadidi) A.; came to U.S., 1964, naturalized, 1976; P.C.B., Damascus U., 1957, M.D., 1963; children—Samer, Basel, Susan. Intern, Damascus U. Hosp., 1962-64; instr. Wayne State U., Detroit, 1969-73, asst. prof., 1973-77, asso. prof., 1977—; staff physician VA Hosp., Allen Park, Mich., 1971—, chief sect. endocrinology and metabolism. 1971—. Recipient AMSA-Eaton Med. Photography award, 1970, 74, 77. Fellow Royal Coll. Physicians Can., A.C.P.; mem. Mich., Wayne County med. socs., AMA, Am. Diabetes Assn., Am. Fedn. Clin. Research, Endocrine Soc. Moslem. Office: VA Hospital Allen Park MI 48101

ABBASY, IFTIKHARUL H., surgeon; b. Pakistan, Oct. 28, 1935; s. Ikramul Haque and Mumtaz Begum; came to U.S., 1964, naturalized, 1970; M.B., B.S., Dow Med. Coll., Karachi, Pakistan, 1961; m. Karen Gaye Hampton, Feb. 14, 1969; 1 dau., Shameem Ara. Intern, Civil Hosp., Karachi, Pakistan, 1961-62, St. Olaves Hosp., London, 1962-63; resident in surgery E. Ham Meml. Hosp., London, 1963, Michael Reese Hosp., Chgo., 1965-69; practice medicine specializing in gen. surgery and peripheral vascular surgery, Villa Park, Ill., 1969—; mem. staff Meml. Hosp., Elmhurst, Ill., McHenry (Ill.) Hosp., Good Samaritan Hosp., Downers Grove, Ill., Harvard (Ill.) Community Hosp. Diplomate Am. Bd. Surgery. Fellow A.C.S., Internat. Coll. Surgeons, Royal Coll. Surgeons Can.; mem. AMA (Physicians's Recognition award 1974-77). Home: 905 Burroak Ct Oak Brook IL 60521 Office: 10 E Central Blvd Villa Park IL 60181

ABBATE, RUTH RUDYS, librarian; b. Chgo., June 2, 1930; d. Joseph F. and Anna (Serbenta) Rudys; B.A., U. Chgo., 1950; M.A. in L.S., Rosary Grad. Sch. Library Sci., 1972; children—Keith A. Krisciunas, Kevin L. Krisciunas, Kenneth M. Krisciunas; stepchildren—Anita L. Abbate, Vincent A. Abbate. Tchr. elementary sch. Westmont, Ill., 1961-63; librarian Dist. 105 pub. schs., La Grange, Ill., 1972—, tchr. gifted students Dist. 105, 1979—. Mem. ALA, Ill. Library Assn., Nat., Ill. Edn. assns., AAUW. Roman Catholic. Home: 5800 Doe Circle Westmont IL 60559 Office: 1001 Spring Ave La Grange IL 60525

ABBOTT, DAVID HENRY, mfg. co. exec.; b. Milton, Ky., July 6, 1936; s. Carl and Rachel (Miles) A.; B.S., U. Ky., 1960, M.B.A., 1961; m. Joan Shefchik, Aug. 14, 1976; children—Kristine, Gina, Beth. With Ford Motor Co., Louisville, also Mpls., Dearborn, Mich., 1961-69; div. controller J.I. Case Co., Racine, Wis., 1970-73, gen. mgr. service parts supply, 1973-75, v.p., 1975—, v.p./gen. mgr. constrn. equipment div., 1975-77, v.p./gen. mgr. Drott div., 1977-79, exec. v.p. worldwide constrn., 1979-81; pres., chief operating officer Portec Inc., Oakbrook, Ill., 1981—. Mem. Constrn. Industry Mfrs. Assn. (past dir.), AED Industry Round table, U.S. C. of C. (constrn. action council). Repubican. Lutheran. Clubs: Kiwanis. Home: 41 Steepleridge Ct Oakbrook IL 60521 Office: 300 Windsor Dr Oakbrook IL 60521

ABBOTT, DONALD FRANKLIN, mfg. co. exec.; b. Sidney, Ohio, Nov. 23, 1941; s. Carl J. and Grace (Davidson) A.; student U. Richmond, 1959-60, Edison State U., 1978; children—Gregg, Ric. With Sidney Oliver Store (IH Trucks), Sidney, 1960-62; machine tool rebuilder Sidney Machine Service, Inc., Sidney, 1962-76, pres., owner, 1977—. Mem. Nat. Tooling and Machining Assn., Dayton Tool and Die Mfrs. Assn., Sidney-Shelby County C. of C., Am. Motorcycle Assn. Republican. Baptist. Club: Moose. Home: 13000 CR 25A Anna OH 45302 Office: PO Box 198 Sidney OH 45365

ABBOTT, JAMES WILLIE, educator; b. Bloodland, Mo., Dec. 29, 1933; s. Mons E. and Stella (Anderson) A.; A.B., Drury Coll., Springfield, Mo., 1956; M.A., U. Mo., 1959; Litt.D. (hon.), Concordia Tchrs. Coll., Seward, Nebr., 1980. Secondary sch. tchr., Lebanon, Mo., 1956-59; asst. dir. lab. schs., instrs. edn. U. Mo., Columbia, 1959-66; dir. Kans. Coop. Urban Tchr. Edn. Program, 1968—; asst. prof., dir. urban edn., chmn. dept. edn. Rockhurst Coll., Kansas City, Mo., 1979—; cons. in field. Adv. bd. Kans. Youth Trust. Mem. Am. Assn. Tchr. Educators, Am. Soc. Curriculum Devel., Phi Delta Kappa. Roman Catholic. Author articles in field. Home: 6375 W 49th St Mission KS 66202 Office: 5225 Troost St Kansas City MO 64110

ABBOTT, JOHN DAVID, clergyman, ch. ofcl.; b. Wyoming, Del., Sept. 29, 1922; s. John Wesley and Mary Mabel (Boggs) A.; Th.B., Eastern Pilgrim Coll., 1943; DD.D. (hon.), Houghton Coll., 1969; m. Gladys Irene Kirkendall, July 22, 1943; children—John David, Kenneth Wayne. Ordained to ministry Wesleyan Ch., 1944; pastor chs. in Chestertown, Pa., 1943, Richeyville and Bentleyville, Pa., 1944, Warren, Pa., 1945, Cambridge, Md., 1950-53; dist. supt. Delmarva dist. The Wesleyan Ch., Denton, Md., 1953-60, gen. sec. Sunday schs. and youth, Indpls., 1960-62, gen. sec.-treas., 1962-66, gen. supt., Marion, Inc., 1966—; v.p. Wesleyan World Fellowship, 1976—; mem. exec. com. World Methodist Council, 1971—, sec. Am. sect., 1971-76, 1st vice chmn. Am. sect., 1977—; mem. exec. com. Gen. Commn. on Chaplains and Armed Forces Personnel, 1977-80. Mem. Christian Holiness Assn. (pres. 1976-78). Editor Sunday Sch. Advance, 1960, Pilgrim Youth News, 1960-62. Home: 1413 Glendale Dr Marion IN 46952 Office: PO Box 2000 Marion IN 46952

ABBOTT, ROBERT PRESTON, real estate appraiser; b. Nashville, Sept. 16, 1951; s. Robert Franklin and Blanch (Sullivan) A.; B.S., Ark. State U., 1975; m. Paulette Cover, Aug. 9, 1975; 1 son, Robert Preston II. Owner, Abbott's Drapery Service, Jonesboro, Ark., 1974-75; asso. Bert Cruse Agy., Jonesboro, 1975; real estate broker and appraiser, 1975—; v.p., chief appraiser for SFS Service Corp. of Security Fed. Savs. and Loan Assn., Sikeston, Mo., 1976-80; staff appraiser Doane Agrl. Service, Inc., Memphis, 1981—. Served with U.S. Army, 1970-73. Mem. Internat. Soc. Real Estate Appraisers, Am. Inst. Real Estate Appraisers, Nat. Assn. Ind. Fee Appraisers, Assn. Govtl. Appraisers, Nat. Assn. Rev. Appraisers, S.E. Mo. Real Estate Appraisers Assn., Am. Legion. Baptist. Club: Sikeston Elks. Home: 7750 Burntwood Cove Southaven MS 38671 Office: 813 Ridge Lake Blvd Memphis TN 38119

ABDNOR, JAMES, senator; b. Kennebec, S.D., Feb. 13, 1923; s. Samuel and Mary (Wehby) A.; B.A. in Bus. Adminstrn., U. Nebr., 1945. High sch. tchr., coach, Presho, S.D., 1948-49; farmer, rancher, Kennebec, 1950—; mem. S.D. Senate, 1956-69; lt. gov. of S.D., 1969-71; mem. 93d-96th congresses from 2d dist. S.D.; mem. U.S. Senate from S.D., 1981—. Chmn., S.D. State Cancer Crusade, 1971-73; S.D. Easter Seal chmn., 1977. Served with AUS, World War II. Mem. Am. Legion, S.D. Stockgrowers, S.D. Wheat Producers, Farm Bur., Farmers Union, Izaak Walton League, Sigma Chi. Methodist. Mason, Elk. Office: 4327 Dirksen Senate Office Bldg Washington DC 20510

ABDULLAH, SAMELLA B. E. P., psychotherapist, educator; b. Chgo., Mar. 9, 1934; d. Samuel Richard and Addie Loraine (Jordan) Berry; B.S., Howard U., 1955, M.S.W. (NIMH grad. stipendee), 1959; Ph.D. in Psychology, Heed U., Fla., 1978; divorced; children—Tracey, Makola Mjasiri, Ghanima Kibibi. Legal aid social worker United Charities Chgo., 1962-64; instr. med. social work Northwestern U. Med. Sch. Clinic, Chgo., 1964-67; dir. social work Near North Children's Center, Chgo., 1967-69; coordinator children adolescent services Englewood Mental Health Center, Chgo., 1972-75; dir. Woodlawn Mental Health Center, Chgo., 1975-77; pvt. practice psychotherapy, Chgo., 1979—; community prof. Governor's State U., Park Forest, Ill.; lectr. Jane Addams Coll. Social Work U. Ill., Chgo.; instr. Central YMCA Community Coll., Chgo.; cons. Mau-Glo Sch. Mentally Retarded, Chgo.; mem. Chgo. City-Wide Community Health Bd.; mem. Ill. Mental Health Planning Bd., 1968-69. Certified social worker, Ill. Mem. Assn. Black Psychologists, League Black Women, Am. Assn. Group Pschotherapists. Home: 7204 S Paxton Ave Chicago IL 60649 Office: 111 N Wabash Ave Suite 1104 Chicago IL 60602

ABDUL RAZEK, MOHAMMAD ZAKI, thoracic surgeon; b. Amga., Palestine, May 1, 1946; came to U.S., 1974; s. Shafic and Ramzieh (Amin) Abdul Razek; B.S., Am. U. Beirut (Lebanon), 1965; m. Hana Emam, Feb. 3, 1974; children—Rula, Rana, Zeina. Intern, Am. U. of Beirut Hosp., 1969-70; resident in gen. surgery Med. Center Am. U. of Beirut, 1970-74; resident in thoracic and cardiovascular surgery U. Calif., Irvine, 1974-76; fellow in pediatric cardiac surgery Deborah Heart and Lung Center, Browns Mills, N.J., 1976-77; practice medicine specializing in thoracic and cardiovascular surgery, Wichita, Kans., 1977—; mem. staffs Wesley Med. Center, St. Francis Hosp., St. Joseph Hosp.; asst. prof. surgery U. Kans. Med. Sch., Wichita. Diplomate Am. Bd. Surgery, Am. Bd. Thoracic Surgery. Fellow Am. Coll. Cardiology, A.C.S.; mem. AMA, Kans. Med. Soc., Med. Soc. Sedgwick County, Wichita Surg. Soc. Office: 905 N Emporia St Wichita KS 67214

ABEC, JAMES MARTIN, clin. psychologist; b. Tangiers, Morrocco, Nov. 4, 1944; came to U.S., 1957, naturalized, 1962; s. Maurice and Margaret A.; B.A., Rutgers U., 1967; Ph.D., Ill. Inst. Tech., 1975. Cons. with Head Start, Yacorzynski, Green, Blechman and Assos., Chgo., 1974-75; mental health supr. DuPage County Health Dept., 1978-80; asst. dir. Chgo. Stress Center, Ltd., 1977—; clin. cons. Elmhurst (Ill.) Sch. Dist., 1978—. Served to capt. U.S. Army, 1968-72. Decorated Bronze Star. Registered psychologist, Ill. Mem. Am. Psychol. Assn., Council for Nat. Register of Health Service Providers in Psychology, Am. Orthopsychiat. Assn. Republican. Condr. research mental health consultation models. Home: 4630 N Virginia Ave Chicago IL 60625 Office: 5214 N Western Ave Chicago IL 60625

ABEL, CHARLES FREDERICK, salt co. exec.; b. Syracuse, N.Y., Oct. 8, 1927; s. Charles F. and Hazel M. (Paul) A.; B.A., Syracuse U., 1954; m. Madeline LaMont, Sept. 16, 1950; children—Diane, Charles Frederick, Timothy. With Bristol Labs., 1950-74, gen. sales mgr. pharms., 1967-70, gen. mgr. med. products div., 1970-74; v.p. sales Wallace Labs. div. Carter-Wallace, Cranbury, N.J., 1974-78; v.p. sales and mktg. Morton Salt div. Morton-Norwich, Chgo., 1978—. Served with U.S. Army, 1944-46. Mem. Nat. Wholesale Grocers Assn., Grocery Mfg. Assn., Salt Inst., Food Merchandiser Internat., Internat. Indsl. Chem. Soc., Water Quality Assn., Food Technologists Internat. Office: Morton Salt 110 N Wacker Dr Chicago IL 60606

ABEL, HAROLD, univ. pres.; b. N.Y.C., July 31, 1926; s. Felix N. and Jennie (Schaefer) A.; A.B., Syracuse U., 1949, M.A., 1951, Ph.D., 1958; m. Iris Tash, Jan. 30, 1949; children—Lawrence William, Matthew Robert. Tchr. advanced mentally retarded Syracuse (N.Y.) Pub. Schs. 1950-51, intermediate mentally retarded Rochester (N.Y.) Public Schs., 1951-52; asst. instr. Sch. Edn. Syracuse U., 1952-54, asst. instr. dept. psychology, 1954-56; asso. prof. to prof. depts. psychology and home econs. and dir. child devel. lab. U. Nebr., 1956-65, chmn. dept. human devel., 1963-65; dir. div. psycho-ednl. studies, prof. edn. U. Oreg., 1965-68, asso. dean, prof. ednl. psychology Coll. Edn., 1968-70; pres. Castleton State Coll., 1970-75, Central Mich. U., Mt. Pleasant, 1975—. Mem. Gov. Nebr. Commn. on Human Relations, 1963-65; vice chmn. Gov. Nebr. Interagy. Com. on Mental Retardation, 1963-65; mem. mayor's com. on phys. handicapped, Lincoln, Nebr., 1963-65; mem. Gov. Oreg. Com. on Aging, 1967-68; mem. nat. adv. com. Project Follow-Through, 1967-69. Served with AUS, 1945-46. Mem. AAAS, Am. Psychol. Assn., Soc. Research in Child Devel., Sigma Xi, Phi Delta Kappa. Home: 524 E Bellows St Mount Pleasant MI 48858 Office: Central Mich U Mount Pleasant MI 48859

ABELE, HOMER EUGENE, judge; b. Wellston, Ohio, Nov. 21, 1916; s. Oscar A. and Margaret (Burke) A.; J.D., Ohio State U., 1953; m. Addie Riggs, Jan. 30, 1938; children—Terrell Ann (Mrs. Robert Smith), Peter Burke, David Anderson. Started as highway patrolman State of Ohio, Van Wert, Findlay, Bellefountaine, 1941-46; admitted to Ohio bar, 1954; practiced in McArthur, Ohio, 1954-66; legislative counsel Ohio Spl. R.R. Transp. Com. Columbus, 1953-57; spl. counsel Ohio atty. gen. McArthur, 1954-58, counsel C.&O. Ry. Co., B.&O. R.R., The Twin States Mining Co., The McArthur Stone & Coal Co.; mem. 88th Congress, 10th dist. Ohio; judge Ct. Appeals 4th Dist. Ohio, 1967—, presiding judge, 1977-78; sec.-treas. Ohio Judges of Ct. of Appeals, 1977, chief justice, 1978. Chmn. ct. sect. Am. Legion Buckeye Boys State. Mem. Ohio Ho. of Reps., 1949-52; asst. to Taft mgr. Republican Nat. Conv., 1952; del. Rep. Nat. Conv., 1956; mem. exec. com. Vinton County Rep. Com., 1952—, chmn. 1954-58; Rep. candidate U.S. Ho. of Reps. from 10th dist. Ohio, 1958. Served with USAAF, 1943-46. Recipient resolution of honor Ohio Senate. Mem. Am. Legion (mem. nat. com. on law and order, dist. exec. officer Ohio Hwy. Patrol sect.; dept. judge adv. 1970-71). Home: Main St McArthur OH 45651 Office: Court House McArthur OH 45651

ABELE, WILLIAM DOUGLAS, lawyer; b. New Haven, Oct. 23, 1949; s. William A. and Joyce G. A.; student Davidson Coll., 1967-68; B.A., Phillips U., 1971; postgrad. U. Mo., Columbia, 1971-72; J.D., U. Mo., Kansas City, 1974; m. Mary Patricia Herlihy, May 22, 1971; 1 dau., Ashley Elizabeth. Admitted to Mo. bar, 1975; partner firm Tisdale & Abele, Boonville, 1975—; city atty., Boonville, 1978—; legal counsel Howard/Cooper County Regional Port Authority, 1978. Recipient Disting. Service award Boonville Jaycees. Mem. Am. Bar Assn., Mo. Bar Assn., Cooper County Bar Assn., Boonville C. of C. (v.p. 1978-80, pres. 1980-81), Friends of Hist. Boonville, Jackson County Hist. Soc., Jaycees (dir. 1976, v.p. 1977, pres. 1978), Mo. Mansion Preservation, Inc., Mo. Heritage Trust, Inc., Kansas City Hist. Found., Lyric Opera Guild, Phi Alpha Delta. Republican. Mem. 1st Christian Ch. (Disciples of Christ) (dir. 1979-81, vice chmn. 1980-81). Club: Boonville Kiwanis (dir. 1976-78). Home: 1119 3d St Boonville MO 65233 Office: United Mo Bank Bldg Boonville MO 65233

ABELL, HARRY WARNER, coll. pres.; b. Brookport, Ill., Dec. 24, 1935; s. William J. and Ruby Lynn A.; B.S., Murray State U., 1958, M.A., 1960; Ph.D., So. Ill. U., 1974; m. Nadine Cagle, Dec. 27, 1958; children—Rick, Kimberly, Jason Andrew. Supt. schs. Brookport (Ill.) Dist. 38, 1961-62, Pope County Unit Dist. 1, Golconda, Ill., 1962-66; dean of student affairs Southeastern Ill. Coll., Harrisburg, 1966-73, pres., 1973—. Trustee Harrisburg-Raleigh Airport Authority, 1976-79; bd. dirs. Doctors Hosp., Harrisburg, 1979, So. Ill. Inc., Christian Ch. Mem. Am. Assn. Higher Edn. Clubs: Masons, Kiwanis (pres. 1977, disting. club pres. dist. II 1977). Office: Southeastern Ill Coll Route 4 College Dr Harrisburg IL 62946

ABELOV, STEPHEN LAWRENCE, uniform co. exec.; b. N.Y.C., Apr. 1, 1923; s. Saul S. and Ethel (Esterman) A.; B.S., N.Y.U., 1945, M.B.A., 1950; m. Phyllis S. Lichtenson, Nov. 18, 1945; children—Patricia C. (Mrs. Marvin Demoff), Gary M. Asst. div. mgr. Nat. Silver Co., N.Y., 1945; sales rep. Angelica Uniform Co., N.Y., 1945-50; asst. sales mgr., 1950-56, western regional mgr., Los Angeles, 1956-66, v.p. Angelica Uniform Co. of Calif., 1958-66, nat. v.p. sales, 1966-72, v.p. Angelica Corp. and Angelica Uniform, 1968—, group v.p. mktg., 1972—, exec. v.p., 1980—. Vis. lectr. marketing N.Y.U. Grad. Sch. Bus. Adminstrn. Vice comdr. Am. Legion; mem. vocational adv. bd. VA.; adv. bd. Woodcraft Rangers; bd. dirs. Univ. Temple. Mem. Am. Assn. Contamination Control (dir.), Am. Soc. for Advancement Mgmt. (chpt. pres.), Sales and Mktg. Execs. Assn., Am. Mktg. Assn., Health Industries Assn. Am. (dir.), various trade assns., St. Louis Council on World Affairs, Los Angeles C. of C. N.Y.U. Alumni Assn., Phi Epsilon Pi (treas.). Mem. B'nai B'rith (past pres.). Clubs: Men's (exec. v.p.); Town Hall, N.Y. U., Aqua Sierra Sportsmen. Contbr. articles to profl. jours. Home: 9821 Log Cabin Ct Ladue MO 63124 Office: 700 Rosedale Ave Saint Louis MO 63112

ABERNATHY, JOANNE KATHLEEN, advt. exec.; b. Topeka, Kans., Jan. 4, 1954; d. Rudolph Leo and Bernice Winifred (Bergmann) Smutny; B.S. in Journalism, William Allen White Sch. Journalism, U. Kans., 1979; m. Darrell Lee Abernathy, Aug. 11, 1979. Adminstrv. asst. Senator Robert B. Madden, Kans., 1975; sales rep. Univ. Daily Kan., Lawrence, 1978-79; advt. mgr. Gibson's Discount Center, Lawrence, 1980; corporate advt. mgr. G.P.K., Inc., Lawrence, 1980—. Winner Am. Advt. Fedn. competition, 1979. Mem. Lawrence C. of C. Democrat. Mem. Eckankar Ch. Home: 211 E 10th St Lawrence KS 66044 Office: PO Box 3286 Lawrence KS 66044

ABERNATHY, K(ENNETH) BROOKS, mfg. co. exec.; b. Missoula, Mont., Aug. 30, 1918; s. Austin Irwin and Evelyn A. (Thompson) A.; B.A., Northwestern U., 1941; postgrad. Harvard Bus. Sch., 1967; m. Susan Koskinen, Mar. 7, 1942; children—Lynn Abernathy Stokoe, Gail Abernathy Dickrell, Kenneth Brooks. Various acctg., mktg. and mfg. assignments Gen. Electric Co., 1941-62; asst. v.p., corp. credit mgr. Brunswick Corp., Skokie, Ill., 1962-63, treas., 1966-69, gen. mgr., 1968-69, v.p. corp., group exec. Marine Power Group, 1969-72, pres., chief operating officer, 1972-76, chmn. bd., chief exec. officer, 1976—, also dir.; dir. Am. Nat. Bank, Stone Container, Nicor, Inc., Walter F. Heller Internat. Corp. Bd. dirs. Goodwill Industries, Inroads, Inc., Northwestern Grad. Sch. Mgmt. Mem. Chgo. Assn. Commerce and Industry, U.S. C. of C. (dir., adv. bd.). Clubs: Econs., Comml., Rotary. Office: One Brunswick Plaza Skokie IL 60077*

ABERNATHY, MEAKOFI JAMES, banker; b. Cin., Apr. 2, 1936; s. William and Alberta (Carter) A.; student U. Cin., Xavier U., Cin. Tech. Coll., Ohio Coll. Applied Sci.; grad. Am. Inst. Banking, 1969, Ohio U. Sch. Banking, 1974, Kent State U. Sch. Banking, 1971; m. Yvonne Verna Stephens, Aug. 23, 1974; children—Ama, Malaika, Ayesha. With The Fifth Third Bank, Cin., 1955—, asst. br. mgr., 1968-69, asst. cashier, mgr., 1969—; realtor, asso. Signature Realtors, Cin., 1974—; sec. Full House, Inc.; lectr. in field. Chmn. labor and industry com. NAACP, 1962-77; founder, pres. African-Am. Cultural Soc., 1967-78; co-chmn. 3d World Forum, Xavier U., 1977-78; co-chmn. Black World Forum U. Cin., 1978; bd. dirs. Big Bros. Greater Cin., 1970-75; mem. Council of Fellows, U. Cin.; mem. City of Cin. Employment Com., 1970; bd. dirs. Journeyman Employment Tng., Preparation Employment, Cin., 1971; mem. Urban League Task Force on Housing, 1977. Mem. Am. Inst. Banking (bd. govs.), Am. Econ. Assn., Nat. Assn. Bus. Economists, Nat. Bankers Assn., Am. Bankers Assn., Ohio Bankers Assn., Cin. Council World Affairs, Real Estate Bd. Ohio, Real Estate Bd. Cin., Nat. Assn. Rev. Appraisers (sr., cert. rev. appraiser), Ohio Sch. Banking Alumni Assn., Internat. Graphoanalysis Soc., Am. Acad. Polit. and Social Sci., NAACP (life), Epsilon Delta Chi. Baptist. Home: 1617 E McMillan St Suite 405 Cincinnati OH 45206 Office: 3407 Montgomery Rd Cincinnati OH 45207

ABINGTON, EUGENE BRYANT, mgmt. and cons. co. exec.; b. Chgo., Aug. 5, 1937; s. Homer Oregon and Petronia Christine (Bryant) A.; B.S., Roosevelt U., 1977; M.S., 1981; m. Michelle Stevens, Jan. 30, 1979; children by previous marriage—Tarra, Carla, Brian, Kimberly. Investigator, Chgo. Police Force, 1964—; chmn. bd. Abington Enterprises, Inc., Chgo., 1978—; pres. AEI Mgmt. & Cons. Co., 1979—. Owner, founder Ida B. Wells Barnett Mus., 1981—. Democrat. Methodist. Office: 4471 S Lake Park Ave Chicago IL 60653

ABLAHAT, NEWTON ANDRE, business cons.; b. Chgo.; s. Haidow and Katie (Samuels) A.; B.S., Northwestern U., 1937; postgrad. U. Chgo., 1940, U. Colo., 1943, Johns Hopkins, 1953-55, Syracuse U., 1961, Am. U., 1965-67; m. Ella May Cason, June 14, 1947; 1 son, Roger Haydon. Mgr. mdse. research, mgr. credit research Spiegel, Inc., Chgo., 1938-41, mgr. market research, 1946-47, dir. policy, 1948-50; economist WPB, Washington, 1941-42; econ. intelligence officer, Yenan, China, 1943-45; exporter Trans World Assos., 1947; cons. Bur. Labor Statistics, Washington, 1950-53; analyst ORO, Johns Hopkins, 1953-56; head ops. research Gen. Electric Co., Phila., 1956-58; cons. Haskins & Sells, Chgo., 1958; cons. Gen. Electric Co., Syracuse, Europe and Washington, 1959-67; v.p. corp. planning dept. Investors Diversified Services, Inc., Mpls., 1967-80; pres. The Stratcon Group Inc., Mpls., 1980—; bus. cons. to fgn. firms; past cons. U.S. Dept. Transp. Bd. dirs. Twin Cities Citizens League, Suburban Community Services. Served with USNR, 1943; CBI. Mem. Am. Finance Assn., Nat. Assn. Bus. Economists, Ops. Research Soc., Inst. Mgmt. Scis., N.Am. Soc. Corp. Planners, Assn. for Corp. Growth. Home: 5200 Chantrey Rd Edina MN 55436 Office: 2240 Dain Tower Minneapolis MN 55402

ABLER, JOYCE LESCELIUS, systems analyst; b. Owosso, Mich., Oct. 13, 1941; d. Toivo Joseph and Agdrina I. (Tahtinen) Lescelius; B.S., Central Mich. U., 1963, M.B.A., 1973. Acct., Dow Chem. Co., Midland, Mich., 1963-64, Sterling Nat. Industries, Milw., 1965; with Molson's Breweries Ont., Ltd. (Can.), 1965-67, B.F. Goodrich Can. Ltd., Kitchener, Ont., 1967-71; systems analyst Central Mich. U., Mt. Pleasant, 1971—; faculty Northwood Inst., Midland, Mich., 1976-78, Central Mich. U., 1978—; sec.-treas. Data Basic Inc., 1980—. Mem. computer adv. com. Mt. Pleasant High Sch., 1976-79; treas. ch. council Zion Luth. Ch., Mt. Pleasant, 1977—. Mem. Data Processing Mgmt. Assn. (sec. 1972-78, v.p. 1978, pres. 1979, newsletter editor 1980), Alpha Sigma Alpha (province dir. 1976—, collegiate sorority advisor 1971-80). Home: 1018 Main St Mount Pleasant MI 48858 Office: 10 Foust Hall Central Mich Univ Mount Pleasant MI 48859

ABLIN, RICHARD JOEL, immunologist; b. Chgo., May 15, 1940; s. Robert Benjamin and Minnie Edith (Gordon) A.; A.B., Lake Forest Coll., 1962; Ph.D. in Microbiology, State U. N.Y., Buffalo, 1967; m. Linda Lee Lutwack; 1 son, Michael David. Grad. asst. dept. biology State U. N.Y., Buffalo, 1963-65, research asst., summer 1963, research fellow, 1965-66, USPHS postdoctoral fellow dept. microbiology Sch. Medicine, lectr., lab. instr., 1966-68; instr., research asst. Rosary Hill Coll., 1965-66; research cons. program med. edn. AID, Paraguay, 1968; dir. div. immunology Millard Fillmore Hosp., Buffalo, 1968-70; head sect. immunology, renal unit, Meml. Hosp. of Springfield (Ill.), 1970-73; dir. sect. immunobiology div. urology dept. surgery Cook County Hosp. and Hektoen Inst. for Med. Research, Chgo., 1973-75, sr. sci. officer div. immunology, 1976—, sr. mem. sci. staff, clin. immunologist Cook County Hosp., 1973-75; asst. prof. medicine So. Ill. U., 1971-73; asso. prof. microbiology Univ. Health Sci./Chgo. Med. Sch., 1973-74. Chief Sangamo Nation Y-Indian Guides, Springfield, 1972-73; mgr. Skokie (Ill.) Indians' Boys' Baseball, 1973-74, 77, 80, 81, bd. dirs., 1979—, exec. v.p., 1981-82; cubmaster N.W. Suburban council Boy Scouts Am., 1974-78, asst. scoutmaster, 1975-77. Recipient Nat. Pres. Leader's Dist. award Boy Scouts Am., 1975; Named Cubmaster of Year, 1977. Fellow Am. Assn. Clin. Immunology, Allergy, Am. Coll. Cryosurgery (adv. bd.); mem. Am. Assn. Cancer Research, AAAS, Am., Chgo. assns. immunologists, Am. Fedn. Clin. Research, Am. Soc. for Immunology of Reproduction, Am. Soc. Microbiology, Brit. Assn. Surg. Oncology (overseas mem.), Comite Internacional de Andrologia, Internat. Soc. Chronobiology, Internat. Soc. Cryosurgery (hon. life pres.), Internat. Soc. Immunology Reprodn., Japan Soc. Low Temperature Medicine, N.Y. Acad. Sci., Reticuloendothelial Soc., Soc. Cryobiology, Soc. Protozoologists, Soc. Study Reprodn., Soc. Exptl. Biology and Medicine, Transplantation Soc., Am. Bd. Clin. Immunology, Allergy (diplomate), Nat. Registry Microbiologists (certified specialist in pub. health and med. lab. microbiology), Cryoimmunotherapeutic Study Group (chmn.), Group d'Etudes de la Cryochirurgis (co-chmn. cryoimmunology sect.), Sigma Xi. Jewish. Contbr. numerous articles to profl. jours. and texts; editor Allergologia et Immunopathologia, 1974—; contbg. editor Current Perspectives in Allergology and Immunopathology, 1974—, Allergologia et Immunopathologia, Seminars in Immunopathology and Oncology, Ill. Med. Jour., 1975—; advisory editor Jour. Cancer, 1976—; asso. editor Low Temperature Medicine, 1975—; internat. editorial staff Medikon, 1974—; editorial bd. Immunology and Allergy Practice, 1979—, Am. Jour. Reproductive Immunology, 1980; sci. bd. TumorDiagnostik, 1980. Home: 5055 Culver St Skokie IL 60076 Office: 1825 W Harrison St Chicago IL 60612

ABNEY, CHARLOTTE MAXINE, sch. counselor, librarian; b. Courtois, Mo., May 9, 1936; d. Grayfer Leo and Isla (Evans) A.; student (Valedictorian scholar, Delta Kappa Gamma scholar) Flat River Jr. Coll., 1953-54; B.S. in Edn. cum laude, SW Mo. State U., 1962, M.S. in Guidance and Counseling, 1970. Mgr., Abneys' Restaurant, Caledonia, Mo., 1954-55; tchr. Grandview R-II Sch., Ware, Mo., 1955-60; tchr., librarian Bismarck (Mo.) R-V Sch., 1960-67, 1969-74, counselor, librarian, 1974—; lectr. edn. and child devel.; tchr. rep. Bd. Edn., 1972-75; cons. to Mo. Dept. Edn. Certified tchr., sch. psychol. examiner, counselor, librarian. Mem. Am. Personnel and Guidance Assn., Am. Sch. Counselors Assn., Mo., SE Mo. Dist. guidance assns., St. Francois County Edn. Assn. (sec. 1965-66), Bismarck R-V Community, Mo. State tchrs. assns. Methodist. Home: Box 707 Bismarck MO 63624 Office: Campus Dr Bismarck MO 63624

ABOULAFIA, ELIE DAVID, vascular surgeon; b. Jerusalem, Israel, June 16, 1928; came to U.S., 1953, naturalized, 1958; s. David and Mathilda (Yeshaya) Aboulafia; B.Sc., U. Geneva, 1949, M.D., 1953; M.Sc., Tufts U., 1960; m. Eileen Helman, May 2, 1965; children—Diane, David, Albert. Intern, Michael Reese Hosp., Chgo., 1953-54; resident surgery Bellevue Med. Center, N.Y.C., 1954-56; resident surgery, fellow vascular surgery Tufts-New Eng. Med. Center, Boston, 1958-61; practice medicine specializing in vascular surgery, Southfield, Mich., 1961—; dir. surg. edn. Highland Park (Mich.) Gen. Hosp., 1974-76; clin. asso. prof. vascular surgery Mich. State U., 1977—. Served with USN, 1956-58. Diplomate Am. Bd. Surgery. Fellow Mass. Heart Assn.; mem. Internat. Coll. Surgeons (v.p.), Maimonides Med. Soc. (past pres.), Sigma Xi. Editorial asso. Internat. Surgery, 1978-80. Home: 27501 W Fourteen Mile Rd Farmington Hills MI 48018 Office: 17000 W Eight Mile Rd Southfield MI 48075

ABRAHAM, BETTE HAVENS, psychotherapist; b. Meriden, Conn., June 19, 1946; d. John Joseph and Abina Dorothy (Walsh) Havens; B.A. with honors, Lake Erie Coll., 1968; M.A., U. N.D., 1970; postgrad. M.B.A. program U. Minn., 1981; m. Alden A. Abraham, Aug. 29, 1970. Tchr., Chgo. Sch. for Retarded, 1971; supr. psychology dept. London Meml. Hosp., Chgo., 1971-75; pvt. practice psychotherapy, Chgo., 1975-77, Mpls., 1977—; cons. Paul Cekan, M.D., 1975-77, Anil Godbole, M.D., 1976-77; asso. Transculture Center for Human Relations, 1974-76, Chgo. Med. Sch. Faculty, 1974-76, Ill. Psychol. Assn., 1974-77; group psychotherapist Abbott Northwestern Hosp., Mpls., 1977-78; family therapist Exodus, St. Paul, 1978; reach coordinator Mental Health Assn. Minn., 1979-81; fin. analyst Pillsbury Corp., 1981—. Mem. U. Chgo. Library Soc., ACLU, Common Cause, Center for Study of Democratic Instns. Minn. Zool. Gardens, Mpls. Inst. Art, Smithsonian Instn., Sci. Mus. Minn., M.B.A. Assn. Home and office: 3526 W 28th St Minneapolis MN 55416

ABRAHAM, ROBERT WILLIAM, controller; b. Chgo., Apr. 29, 1933; s. William H. and Martha (Goura) A.; B.S. in Mgmt., U. Ill., 1963; postgrad. Governors State U., 1979—; m. Louise Marie Spellar, Jan. 28, 1935; children—Robert, Charles. Cost estimator market research Chgo. Bridge & Iron Co., 1957-59; plant acct. Joslyn Mfg. Co., Chgo., 1959-66; cost acct. Velsicol Chem. Co., Chgo., 1966-67; gen. acct. Freeman Coal Co., Chgo., 1967-68; sr. acct. Solo Cup Co., Chgo., 1968-72; cost acctg. mgr. Am. Lock Co., Crete, Ill., 1972-75, controller, 1975—. Sec., Annunciata Baseball League, Chgo., 1969-73. Served with U.S. Army, 1953-55. Roman Catholic. Club: Lions. Home: 10729 Ave E Chicago IL 60617 Office: 3400 W Exchange Rd Crete IL 60417

ABRAHAMSON, LEE MARTIN, former assn. exec., business exec.; b. Indpls., Aug. 31, 1938; s. Arthur Lawrence and Lois Pearl (Kneer) A.; B.S., Ball State U., 1960; M.S. in Bus. Adminstrn., No. Ill. U., 1973; m. Joan Ellen Watkins, May 30, 1960; 1 son, Erik. Dir. mktg. E.C. Seale & Co., Indpls., 1961-63; dir. employee relations and personnel Indpls. Morris Plan, 1963-65; dir. employee relations and devel. AMA, Chgo., 1965-81; cons. Ireland Ednl. Corp., Littleton, Colo., 1973—; pres. Omega Centre for Mgmt., Deer Park, Ill., 1977—, Dunhill of Lincolnshire (Ill.), 1981—; mgmt. practices cons.; mgmt. instr. YMCA Community Coll., 1974—. Mem. Chgo. Jaycees (group v.p. 1973), Am. Soc. Personnel Adminstrs., Am. Soc. Tng. and Devel., Ill. Tng. and Devel. Assn., Am. Soc. Assn. Execs., Am. Assn. Med. Soc. Execs., Soc. Personnel Adminstrs., Chgo. Orgn. Devel. Assn., Human Resource Planning Soc. Democrat. Author: How To Develop Your Personnel Policy Program, 1979; Wage and Salary Administration for Health Care Institutions, 1980. Home: 21166 Pheasant Trail Barrington IL 60010 Office: One Marriott Dr Lincolnshire IL 60015

ABRAHAMSON, SHIRLEY SCHLANGER, justice Wis. Supreme Ct.; b. N.Y.C., Dec. 17, 1933; d. Leo and Ceil (Sauerteig) Schlanger; A.B., N.Y. U., 1953; J.D., Ind. U., 1956; S.J.D., U. Wis., 1962; m. Seymour Abrahamson, Aug. 1953; 1 son, Daniel Nathan. Asst. dir. Legis. Drafting Research Fund, Columbia U. Law Sch., 1957-60; admitted to Wis. bar, 1962; mem. firm Lafollette, Sinykin, Anderson & Abrahamson, Madison, Wis., 1962-76; justice Supreme Ct. Wis., Madison, 1976—; prof. U. Wis. Law Sch., 1966—; mem. Wis. Bd. Bar Commrs.; mem. Madison Mayor's Adv. Com., 1968-70; mem. Wis. Gov.'s Study Com. on Jud. Orgn., 1970-72; mem. adv. bd. Nat. Inst. Justice, U.S. Dept. Justice, 1980—. Bd. dirs. LWV, Madison, 1963-65; bd. dirs. Wis. Civil Liberties Union, 1968-72, chmn. Capital Area chpt., 1969; bd. visitors Ind. U. Law Sch., 1972—. Mem. Am. Bar Assn. (council sect. legal edn. and admissions to bar 1976—), Wis. Bar Assn., Dane County Bar Assn., Am. Law Inst., Order of Coif, Phi Beta Kappa. Editor: Constitutions of the United States (National and State), 2 vols., 1962. Office: State Capitol Madison WI 53702

ABRAMOVICH, LYNNE ROHRICH, advt. agy. exec.; b. Akron, Ohio, Apr. 14, 1951; d. Robert Deuring and Roberta (Dunwiddie) Rohrich; B.A., Hiram Coll., 1973; m. Terry Edward Abramovich, Sept. 14, 1974; 1 son, Robert Thomas. Media supr. Hesselbart & Mitten, Akron, 1973-74; media and prodn. coordinator PR Assos., Akron, 1975-78; account exec. Norman Malone Assos., Akron, 1978—. Mem. Internat. Assn. Printing House Craftsmen, Am. Mktg. Assn., Akron Club of Printing House Craftsmen (bd. govs. 1978—). Republican. Presbyterian. Office: 209 S Main St Akron OH 44308

ABRAMS, ALAN EDWIN, editor, journalist, author, publisher; b. Detroit, Feb. 19, 1941; s. Harry J. and Mildred (Volod) A.; student public schs., Detroit; m. Elizabeth Ann Scala, 1981. Public relations dir. Gale Research Co., Detroit, 1974-76, editor journalism projects, 1976-81; contbg. editor Contemporary Authors, Detroit, 1976-81; book reviewer, religion page and feature writer, paperback columnist The Windsor, (Ont., Can.) Star, 1980—; book reviewer Newsday, L.I., N.Y., 1980-81; appraiser rare books and autographs, IRS, 1978-79. Author: Why Windsor? An Anecdotal History of the Jews of Windsor and Essex County, 1981; Journalist Biographies Master Index, 1979; Media Personnel Guide, 1979. Recipient award of merit U.S. Dept. Labor, 1969; writing grantee Ont. Arts Council, 1980, 81 Mem. Detroit Press Club. Jewish. Office: 794 Chilver Rd Windsor ON N8Y 2K3 Canada

ABRAMSON, HERBERT FRANCIS, supt. schs.; b. Chgo., Dec. 16, 1930; s. Maurice P. and Rose (Harris) A.; B.S., Ind. U., 1953; M.Ed., Loyola U., 1961; postgrad. Roosevelt, Purdue, Ind. univs.; m. Sylvia Linde, June 29, 1958; children—Marcia Beth, Jacquelyn, Rachel. Tchr. pub. secondary schs., Lake Ridge, 1955—, prin. Calumet Jr. High Sch., Lake Ridge Sch. System, 1961-69; prin. Lake Jr. High Sch., 1969-74; supt. Lake Ridge Schs., Gary, 1974—; mem. State Supt. Schs. Adv. Com., 1978—, Ind. Planning Com. for Adult and Community Edn., 1979. Prin. Temple Israel Religious Sch., Gary; dir. Gary Sch. Employee Fed. Credit Union; mem. adv. council Urban League N.W. Ind.; mem. President's Roundtable, Meth. Hosp. Served with AUS, 1953-55; bd. dirs. N.W. Ind. Jewish Welfare Fedn.; bd. dirs. Temple Israel, Gary, 1971-72, pres. 1973-75; cons. Hebrew Acad. N.W. Ind. Mem. Am. Fedn. Tchrs. (past pres. No. 662), Nat. Assn. Secondary Sch. Prins., Lake County Jr. and Sr. High Prins. Assn., Ind. Assn. Pub. Sch. Supts., Ind. Assn. Sch. Bus. Ofcls., N.W. Ind. Public Sch. Supts. Study Council, Am. Assn. Sch. Adminstrs., ACLU. Mem. B'nai B'rith. Contbr. articles to profl. jours. Home: 7210 Polk St Merrillville IN 46410 Office: 6111 W Ridge Rd Gary IN 46408

ABRELL, RONALD LANE, educator; b. Coal City, Ind., Mar. 14, 1934; s. Osce W. and Pauline A. A.; B.S., Ind. State U., 1959, M.S., 1962; Ed.D., Mont. State U., 1972; m. JoAnn Barnhizer, Mar. 31, 1963; 1 son, Lane. Tchr. social scis. Shelbyville (Ind.) High Sch., 1959-62, Broad Ripple High Sch., Inspls., 1962-67, North Putnam Sch. Corp., Bainbridge, Ind., 1967-68; coordinator student teaching in Chgo., Western Ill. U., Macomb, Ill., 1968-73; prof. edn. Coll. Edn., Macomb, 1973—, dir. student teaching, chmn. ednl. field experiences, 1973—. Served with U.S. Army, 1953-55. Mem. Ill. Assn. Tchr. Educators (pres. 1978-79, chmn. legis. com. 1977-78, 79-80), Am. Assn. Sch. Adminstrs., Assn. Supervision and Curriculum Devel., Horace Mann League, N. Am. Soc. Adlerian Psychology, Assn. Tchr. Educators, World Future Soc., Phi Delta Kappa. Democrat. Club: Elks. Author: Strictly for Student Teachers, 1973; contbr. articles to profl. jours. Office: Coll of Education Western Ill Univ Macomb IL 61455

ABROMSON, MARIAN FLEMING (MRS. JAMES J. ABROMSON), civic leader; b. Portland, Ind., Sept. 18, 1907; d. James R. and Jennie (Adair) Fleming; student DePauw U., 1926; m. James J. Abromson, July 15, 1933; 1 dau., Suzanne Fleming Abromson Joiner. Dir. Ft. Wayne Jour.-Gazette. Chmn. vol. blood service program ARC, Portland, 1947—; pres. Jay County Bd. Pub. Welfare, Portland, 1964-80; sec. Earlham Coll. Parents Assn., Richmond, Ind., 1957-58; mem. Jay County Com. Aging, 1951-59; Jay County rep. to NE Ind. Dist. Com. Aging, 1959-60; bd. dirs. Jay County Mental Health Assn., 1958-78; v.p. Jay County ARC; mem. Jay County Hosp. Aux.; chmn. Adopt-a-Patient Program, 1961-73; mem. Ind. Mental Health Bd., 1971—; v.p. bd. Ind. Cultural, Ednl. and Fine Arts Found., Ft. Wayne, 1973—; mem. com. Jay County Hosp. Meml. Trust, 1978—. Del., Democratic Nat. Conv., 1964. Recipient Achievement Service Award, Jay County, 1960; named Woman of Yr., Jay County Bus. and Profl. Women's Club, 1978. Mem. DAR, Daus. Am. Colonists, Delta Theta Tau, Alpha Chi Omega. Presbyterian (deaconess 1960-68, trustee ch. 1969-72). Clubs: Portland Country; Summit (Ft. Wayne). Home: 301 W Race St Portland IN 47371

ABRUZZI, DENNIS MICHAEL, transp. carrier exec.; b. Fountain Hill, Pa., Sept. 26, 1952; s. Alfonso C. and Caroline B. (Sabatino) A.; B.A. in Psychology and Sociology, Bloomsburg (Pa.) State Coll., 1974; m. Eileen B. Adams, June 10, 1972; children—Rachel, Emily, Celeste, Victoria. Social worker Danville (Pa.) State Hosp., 1973; field supr. Custom Deliveries, Inc., Boston and Chgo., 1977-78, asst. mgr., Troy, Mich., 1979, gen. mgr., 1980—. Mem. Bloomsburg State Coll. Alumni Assn., Trucking Mgmt. Inc., Pvt. Carrier Conf., Motor City Traffic Club. Home: 530 S Edison St Royal Oak MI 48067 Office: 30800 Telegraph Rd Suite 4900 Birmingham MI 48010

ABUHL, JEANNE MARIE, retail exec.; b. Des Moines, May 13, 1946; d. Albert James and Marjorie Jeanette (Larson) A.; student Moody Bible Inst., 1966, local community colls. Exec. sec. to v.p. Scripture Press Found., Glen Ellyn, Ill., 1967-73; asst. to nat. field dir. Youth for Christ/USA, Wheaton, Ill., 1973-75; office mgr. Youth for Christ Internat., Geneva, 1975-78; office coordinator Follett Coll. Stores, Elmhurst, Ill., 1978—; cons. Performax Systems. Bd. dirs. campign bd. Fox Valley Youth for Christ, 1981—. Notary public. Mem. Am. Soc. Notaries, Nat. Assn. Female Execs. Republican. Evangelical. Club: Down's Collectors. Home: 2 Wheaton Center #909 Wheaton IL 60187 Office: 103 S Myrtle St Elmhurst IL 60126

ABUZZAHAB, FARUK SAID, SR., psychiatrist; b. Beirut, Lebanon, Oct. 12, 1932; came to U.S., 1953, naturalized, 1978; s. Said Salim and Nimet Mohammad (Muezzin) A.; B.S., Am. U. Beirut, Lebanon, 1955, M.D., 1959; Ph.D., U. Minn., 1968; m. Beverly Elaine Swinter, June 29, 1962; children—Nada Josephine, Mary Jennifer, Faruk Said, Jeffrey Faruk, Mark Faruk. Rotating intern Am. U. Hosp., Beirut, 1958-59; resident psychiatry Johns Hopkins Hosp., Balt., 1959-62; practice medicine specializing in psychiatry and clin. psychopharmacology, Mpls., 1962—; mem. staff U. Minn. Hosps., Fairview, Mpls.; acting med. dir. Hastings (Minn.) State Hosp., 1963-78; mem. staff St. Mary's Hosp., chief psychiatry, 1978-79; chief service Anoka State Hosp., 1978—; research fellow U. Minn., Mpls., 1962-66, instr., 1966-68, asst. prof. psychiatry and pharmacology, 1968-73, clin. asso. prof., 1973-79, clin. prof. psychiatry, pharmacology and family practice, 1979—; cons. psychiatrist St. Croix County Health Center, New Richmond, Wis., 1975-77, Dunn County Health Care Center, Menominee, 1970—. Pres., clin. Psychopharmacology Consultants, 1973—; adminstr. psychopharmacology and pharmacopsychiatry funds, 1969—. Bd. dirs. Minn. Life Care Centers, 1975—. Recipient Faculty Devel. award Pharm. Mfrs. Assn. Found., 1967-69. Fellow Am. Psychiat. Assn., Am. Coll. Clin. Pharmacology; mem. Am. Soc. Clin. Pharmacology and Therapeutics, AMA, Minn. Med. Soc. (subcom. on alcoholism and drug abuse 1970—), Soc. for Biol. Psychiatry, Hennepin County Psychiat. Soc. (pres. 1976-78), Collegium Internat. Neuropsychopharmacologium, Am. Coll. Clin. Pharmacology, Am. Coll. Pharmacology and Exptl. Therapeutics, Sigma Xi, Alpha Omega Alpha. Contbr. articles to profl. jours. Home: 2601 E Lake of the Isles Blvd Minneapolis MN 55408 Office: Suite 818 Fairview-St Mary's Med Bldg 606 S 24th Ave Minneapolis MN 55454 also Box 393 Mayo U Minn Minneapolis MN 55455

ACEY, ROGER ALBERT, biochemist, educator; b. Detroit, July 14, 1946; s. Joseph Albert and Amelia Sarah (Aboud) A.; B.S. in Chemistry, Wayne State U., 1969, Ph.D. in Biochemistry, Sch. Medicine, 1977. Clin. chemist Detroit Osteo. Hosp., 1969-75; chemistry instr. Wayne County Community Coll., Detroit, 1975—; vis. lectr. Calif. State Coll., Bakersfield, summer 1980, 81-82; sci. cons.; research in molecular biology. Mem. Am. Chem. Soc., AAAS, N.Y. Acad. Scis., Sigma Xi. Eastern Orthodox. Contbr. chpt. to book, articles to profl. pubs. in field of developmental biochemistry. Home: 17208 Merryweather Mount Clemens MI 48044 Office: 1001 W Fort Detroit MI 48226

ACHILLES, CHARLES ALBERT, assn. exec.; b. Berwyn, Ill., Sept. 29, 1946; s. Charles Laddie and Mildred Antonette (Volmut) A.; B.S. in Chemistry, No. Ill. U., 1968; M.B.A., Loyola U., Chgo., 1972; m. Sharon Lee Lullo, May 23, 1970; children—Amber Lee, Brylan Charles. Tchr., Woodridge (Ill.) Sch. System, 1968-69, asst. prin., 1969-72; dir. membership services Inst. Real Estate Mgmt., Chgo., 1972-76, staff v.p. membership services and communications, 1976-81, staff v.p. legis. and spl. services, 1981—. Active Community Affairs Com., 1977-79; pres. Oakwood Community Assn., 1978, bd. dirs., 1979; bd. dirs. Oakwood Homeowners Assn., 1979, v.p., 1981; active Community Party of Westmont, 1978, 80. Mem. Am. Mktg. Assn., Am. Soc. Assn. Execs., Community Assns. Inst., Am. Statis. Assn., Assn. MBA Execs., Cavaliers, Phi Eta Sigma. Congregationalist. Clubs: 71; Downtown. Home: 741 Oakwood Dr Westmont IL 60559 Office: 430 N Michigan Ave Chicago IL 60611

ACHTEMEIER, GARY LYNN, atmospheric scientist; b. Wichita, Kans., Mar. 1, 1943; s. Walter John and Phyllis (Norman) A.; B.S., Fla. State U., 1965, M.S., 1969, Ph.D., 1972; m. (Mildred) Sue Dicus, June 15, 1968; children—Cheryl Ann, Scott Alan. NRC grantee Nat. Severe Storms Lab., Norman, Okla., 1972-73; asso. research scientist Ill. State Water Survey, Champaign, 1973—; vis. asso. prof. Lab. for Atmospheric Research, U. Ill., 1981; cons. Nat. Forest Expt. Sta., Macon, Ga., 1975—; proposal reviewer NSF, 1976—. Publicity chmn. Full Gospel Businessmen's Fellowship Internat. Rally, 1979, rally co-chmn., 1981. NSF grantee, 1976-77; NASA grantee, 1982—. Mem. Am. Meteorol. Soc. (com. on severe storms 1980-81), AAAS, Sigma Xi, Chi Epsilon Pi. Republican. Contbr. articles in field to profl. jours.; tech. paper reviewer for three jours., 1976—. Office: Water Resources Bldg 605 E Springfield St PO Box 5050 Champaign IL 61820

ACHTERMAN, JAMES WILLIAM, mgmt. cons.; b. Cin., May 27, 1945; s. Hubert Lewis and Alberta (Moore) A.; B.B.A., U. Cin., 1968; m. Nancy Lee Carroll, June 17, 1967; children—Nicole Lee, Jeffrey

Scott. Mgmt. analyst City of Cin., 1968-70; budget dir. Hamilton County Ohio, Cin., 1970-72, asst. county adminstr., 1972-74; controller Cin. Public Schs., 1974-76; mng. cons. Ernst & Whinney, Cin., 1976-77, mgr. services to local govt., 1977—. Chmn. found. com. United Negro Coll. Fund, 1979-81; councilman City of Wyoming, Ohio, 1979—. Mem. Ohio-Ky.-Ind. Regional Council Govts. (trustee 1971-74), Internat. City Mgmt. Assn., Mcpl. Finance Officers Assn., Ohio Mcpl. Finance Officers Assn. Clubs: Bankers, Wyo. Golf. Home: 36 E Mills Ave Wyoming OH 45215 Office: 1400 DuBois Tower Cincinnati OH 45202

ACKERMAN, JOHN HENRY, state ofcl., physician; b. Fond du Lac, Wis., Feb. 27, 1925; s. Henry Theodore and Clara Frances (Voss) A.; student Cornell U., 1943-44, Ind. U., 1944; M.D., Marquette U., 1948; M.P.H., Johns Hopkins U., 1955; m. Eugenia Ellen Mulligan, May 22, 1948; children—H. John, Mary, Lisa, Paul. Intern, St. Agnes Hosp., Fond du Lac, 1948-49; family practice medicine, Clarksville, Iowa, 1949-51; commd. officer USPHS, 1951-70, dep. chief tng. program Center Disease Control, Atlanta, 1970, ret. as med. dir., 1970; dep. dir. Ohio Dept. Health, Columbus, 1971-75, dir., 1975—; clin. prof. preventive medicine Ohio State U.; cons. WHO. Served with AUS, 1943-46. Fellow Am. Pub. Health Assn., Am. Coll. Preventive Medicine, Royal Soc. Health; mem. Commd. Officers Assn., Ohio Med. Assn., Columbus Acad. Medicine, Alpha Kappa Kappa. Roman Catholic. Home: 4183 Reedbury Ln Columbus OH 43220 Office: 246 N High St Columbus OH 43215

ACKERMAN, LOUISE MAGAW, writer; b. Topeka, July 9, 1904; d. William Glenn and Anna Mary (Shaler) Magaw; B.S., Kans. State U., 1926; M.A., U. Nebr., 1942; m. Grant Albert Ackerman, Dec. 27, 1926; children—Edward Shaler, Anita Louise. Free lance writer, 1930—. Mem. Lincoln Community Arts Council. Mem. Nat. Soc. Daus. Colonial Wars (nat. pres. 1977-80), DAR (past v.p. gen.), Americans of Armorial Ancestry (sec. 1976-82), Nat. Huguenot Soc. (2d v.p. 1977-83), Nebr. Writers Guild (v.p. 1980-81, past sec.-treas.), Nat. League Am. Pen Women, Lincoln C. of C., Phi Kappa Phi. Republican. Club: Nat. Writers. Home: Eastmont Towers III Apt 428 6335 O St Lincoln NE 68510

ACKERMAN, WALTER J., dentist; b. Herreid, S.D., Nov. 1, 1918; s. Henry and Christina (Buckenberger) A.; student U. S.D., 1953-55; B.S., U. Minn., 1957, D.D.S., 1959; m. Viola Elizabeth Papendick, Oct. 9, 1942; 1 son, Michael Alan. With Butler Bros. Mining Co., Nashwauk, Minn., 1941-42, Boeing Aircraft, Seattle, 1942-45; owner Coast to Coast Hardware Store, Dell Rapids, S.D., 1945-47; co-owner Peacock Cafe, Winner, S.D., 1947-50, Men's Clothing store, 1950-53; pvt. dental practice, Rapid City, S.D., 1959—; mem. active staff St. John's Hosp., Rapid City. Mem. Am. Soc. Dentistry for Children (state unit pres. 1964-65, Distinguished Service award S.D. unit 1966), ADA (del. 1980-81), S.D. (v.p. 1975-76, pres. 1977-78), Black Hills dental socs., VMCCA Hist. Auto Club, Soc. Preservation and Encouragement Barbershop Quartet Singing in Am. (pres. Mt. Rushmore chpt. 1976), Delta Sigma Delta (dir. dental chpt. S.D. 1972-73). Elk, Kiwanian (pres. 1972-73). Club: Black Hills Antiques (pres. 1967-68). Home: Rural Route 1 Box 550 Rapid City SD 57701 Office: 2610 Jackson Blvd Rapid City SD 57701

ACOSTA, JULIO BERNARD, obstetrician, gynecologist; b. Loreto, Peru, S. Am., July 29, 1927; came to U.S., 1955, naturalized, 1960; s. Miguel and Flor Maria (Solis) A.; M.D., St. Marcos U. (Peru), 1955; m. Mary Jane Aedinvice, Aug. 30, 1974; children—Raul, Luis-Miguel, Patricia, Silvia, Douglas, Jill. Intern, St. Alexis Hosp., Cleve., 1955-56; resident St. Alexis Hosp., 1956-57, St. Ann Hosp., Cleve., 1957-59; practice medicine specializing in obstetrics and gynecology, Livonia, Mich., 1964—; chief of staff Plymouth Gen. Hosp., Detroit, 1970-73, chief gynecologic sect., 1974—; med. dir. Northland Family Planning Clinic, Southfield, Mich., 1976—; active staff Grace-Harper Hosp., Detroit, 1973—, St. Mary Hosp., Livonia, 1964—. Served to capt., M.C., USAR, 1959-62. Diplomate Am. Bd. Obstetrics and Gynecology. Fellow Am. Coll. Obstetricians and Gynecologists, Am. Fertility Soc., Am. Soc. for Colposcopy and Cervical Pathology, Am. Soc. Abdominal Surgeons, Am. Coll. Internat. Physicians, Mich. Obstetrical-Gynecological Soc.; mem. Detroit Surg. Soc., Peruvian-Am. Med. Soc. Republican. Clubs: Detroit Tennis and Squash, Centaur Racquet. Contbr. articles to profl. jours. Home: 5280 Inkster Rd Bloomfield Hills MI 48013 Office: 27634 Five Mile Rd Livonia MI 48134

ACTON, MELBA JEAN, advt. agy. exec.; b. Monett, Ark., Feb. 1, 1949; d. Luther Woodrow and Doris Clara (Johnson) Covey; student Rockhurst Coll., Kansas City, Mo., 1977—; m. James Thomas Acton, Nov. 25, 1966; children—Lisa Ann, Larry Thomas. Bookkeeper, Grandview (Mo.) Bank, 1968, Barickman Advt. Co., Kansas City, Mo., 1969-72, Treck Photographic, Kansas City, 1972, Fremerman-Papin, Kansas City, 1972-73; asso. media dir. Valentine Radford Advt. Co., Kansas City, 1973—. Baptist. Home: 9829 Shepherds Dr Kansas City MO 64131 Office: 1100 Commerce Tower Kansas City MO 64199

ADAIR, BRUCE JAMES, publishing co. exec.; b. Phila., Apr. 19, 1947; s. Francis and Marion Frances (Kosek) A.; B.A. in Sociology, Eastern Coll., St. David's, Pa., 1969; M.A. in Religious Edn., Eastern Baptist Theol. Sem., Phila., 1971; m. Naomi Lynne Davis, Aug. 2, 1969; children—Kristina Marie, Amy Lynne. Asst. pastor Jacobstown (N.J.) Bapt. Ch., 1966-67; dir. youth Upper Merion (Pa.) Bapt. Ch., 1967-68; minister edn. United Presbyn. Ch. of Manoa, Havertown, Pa., 1969-74; instr. phys. edn., head varsity soccer coach Eastern Coll., 1969-73; field cons., then asst. curriculum product mgr. David C. Cook Pub. Co., Elgin, Ill., 1974-76, curriculum product mgr., 1976-79, curriculum market mgr., 1979—. Recipient Good Citizenship award Phila. Union League, 1968; named Christian Educator of Year, Phila. Sunday Sch. Assn., 1973. Home: 1128 Indian Dr Elgin IL 60120 Office: 850 N Grove St Elgin IL 60120

ADAIR, CHARLES VALLOYD, physician; b. Lorain, Ohio, Apr. 20, 1923; s. Waite and Ella Jane (Robertson) A.; A.B., Hobart Coll., Geneva, N.Y., 1944; M.D., Western Res. U., 1947; m. Constance Dean, Apr. 1, 1944; children—Allen V., Richard D. Intern, then asst. resident in medicine Rochester (N.Y.) Gen. Hosp., 1947-49; fellow in medicine Univ. Hosps., Syracuse, N.Y., 1949-51; practice medicine specializing in internal medicine, Mansfield, Ohio, 1953—; mem. staffs Mansfield Gen. Hosp., Peoples Hosp., Richland Neuropsychiat. Hosp.; mem. Mansfield City Bd. Health; trustee, past pres. Mansfield Meml. Homes. Served to capt. AUS, 1943-46, 51-53. Diplomate Am. Bd. Internal Medicine. Fellow A.C.P.; mem. Am. Soc. Internal Medicine, Am., Ohio med. assns., Richland County Med. Soc. Republican. Congregationalist. Clubs: Our, Westbrook Country, University. Home: 1010 Woodland Rd Mansfield OH 44907 Office: 480 Glessner Ave Mansfield OH 44903

ADAIRE, BRUCE BOWER, beverage co. exec.; b. Providence, Mar. 23, 1937; s. William Roger and Elizabeth M. (Bower) A.; A.B., Princeton U., 1960; M.A., U. Wis., 1961; m. Marilyn Dorothy Miller, Aug. 27, 1960; children—Geoffrey Miller, Jennifer Robin. Mem. faculty Tabor Acad., Marion, Mass., summer 1960, 61; media planner J. Walter Thompson Co., N.Y.C., 1961-62, media supr., 1963-64, in London, 1964-66, account rep., 1966-68, account supr., 1968-71, v.p., 1970-71; mktg. dir. Checkerboard Farms div. Ralston Purina Co., St. Louis, 1971-72; dir. mktg. Seven-Up Internat., Inc., St. Louis, 1972—, v.p., 1973; cons. to mktg. program Washington U., St. Louis, 1973—; dir. internat. devel. Anheuser-Busch Inc., St. Louis, 1979—, v.p., 1981—. Mktg. bd. St. Louis Symphony Soc., 1975—; bd. dirs. Progressive Youth Center, 1980—. Recipient Public Service award Archdiocese of N.Y. Cath. Youth Orgn., 1969; English-Speaking Union Internat. Schoolboy fellow, 1955; Woodrow Wilson fellow, 1960. Mem. Am. Mgmt. Assn., Am. Mktg. Assn., Internat. Advt. Assn., Princeton Alumni Assn. St. Louis (dir. 1980—). Methodist. Clubs: Woodsmill Racquet, Bellerive Country. Home: 13562 Featherstone Dr Saint Louis MO 63131 Office: One Busch Pl Saint Louis MO 63118

ADAM, PAUL JAMES, mech. engr.; b. Kansas City, Mo., Oct. 26, 1934; s. Paul James and Adrienne (Zimmerman) A.; B.S. in Mech. Engring., U. Kans., 1956; m. Barbara Ann Mills, Dec. 18, 1956; children—Paul James III, Blair Dodderidge II, Matthew Mills. Mech. engr. Black & Veatch, Cons. Engrs., Kansas City, Mo., 1956, 59-74, partner, asst. head Power div., 1975-78, exec. partner, head Power div., 1978—; dir. First Continental Bank & Trust Co. Mem. Greater Univ. Fund Adv. Bd., U. Kans., 1964-66. Served to 1st lt., USAF, 1956-59. Registered profl. engr., 13 states. Mem. Nat., Mo. socs. profl. engrs., ASME, Am. Nuclear Soc., Atomic Indsl. Forum, Tau Beta Pi, Sigma Tau, Pi Tau Sigma, Omicron Delta Kappa, Alpha Tau Omega. Episcopalian. Clubs: Mission Hills Country, Saddle and Sirloin. Office: 1500 Meadow Lake Pkwy Kansas City MO 64114

ADAMS, ALLAN WILFRED, bus. cons., lawyer; b. Beloit, Wis., Aug. 23, 1910; s. Harry Wilfred and Prudence Mary (Bennett) A.; A.B., Harvard U., 1932; LL.B., U. Wis., 1935; m. Charlotte Amy Ray, Nov. 26, 1936; children—Allan Wilfred, Prudence B., Polly H., John B. Admitted to Wis. bar, 1935; partner firm Adams & Adams, Beloit, Wis., 1935-61; of counsel firm Hansen, Eggers, Berres & Kelley, Beloit, 1961—; pres. Adams Corp., Beloit, 1946-62; sec. Flakall Corp., Beloit, 1945-61; pres. Dell Foods, Beloit, 1957-61; pres. Adams Internat. div. Beatrice Foods Co., Beloit, 1962-75, cons., 1975-79; corp. sec. Regal-Beloit Corp., 1979—; dir. Heritage Bank Beloit; dir. Regal Beloit Corp., 1955-81, corp. sec., 1979—. Pres., Beloit YMCA, 1955-64, dir., 1950-72; dir. Wis. Taxpayers Alliance, 1963—; bd. dirs. Beloit ARC, 1958-70, United Givers, 1978—, Greater Beloit Steering Com., 1978-81; with OPA-Rent Div., 1942-45; mem. Young Pres. Orgn., 1949-59. Paul Harris Rotary fellow, 1978. Fellow Am. Coll. Probate Counsel, Am., Wis. bar founds.; mem. Rock County Bar Assn. (pres. 1946), Am., Wis. bar assns. Republican. Congregationalist. Clubs: Rotary, Beloit Country, Madison, Elks, Wis. 49ers. Home: 1628 Emerson St Beloit WI 53511 Office: 419 Pleasant St Beloit WI 53511

ADAMS, ARLIE, mfg. co. exec.; b. Louisa, Ky., Oct. 22, 1935; s. George and Effie Josephine (Davis) A.; m. Peggy Jo Branham, Sept. 1, 1956; children—Arlie, James Richard. With Jeffrey Mining Machinery div. Dresser Industries, Columbus, 1956—, mgr. systems adminstrn. services, 1980—. Mem. Hilliard (Ohio) Planning and Zoning Commn., 1978—. Mem. Am. Prodn. and Inventory Control Soc. Home: 5434 Schatz Ln Hilliard OH 43026 Office: 274 E 1st Ave Columbus OH 43216

ADAMS, EENA J. CARLISLE, educator; b. Mt. Hope, Kans.; d. Alfred George and Nora Agnes (Kissick) Carlisle; B.S. in Home Econs., Kans. State U., 1939; M.S. in Foods and Nutrition, 1970; student Ohio U., 1954-61; m. Lawrence D. Adams, Dec. 11, 1940; children—Karen Jean Adams McCarthy, Maureen Janet Adams Mitchell. Tchr., Leonardville, Kans., 1939-40, Jan's Pvt. Sch., Front Royal, Va., 1949-52, Forestdale Sch., McCracken County, Ky., 1952-53, Jackson (Ohio) County and City Schs., 1953-68, Head Start, Jackson, 1965-68; grad. teaching asst. Kans. State U., Manhattan, 1969-70; asst. prof. home econs. Wayne (Nebr.) State Coll., 1970-76; asst. prof. home econs. and dietetics Morehead (Ky.) State U., 1976—, coordinator energy mgmt. asst. program, 1979-80. Mem. Front Royal (Va.) Recreation Council. Delta Kappa Gamma Annie Webb Blanton scholar, 1968. Mem. Am. Dietetic Assn. (registered dietitian), Nutrition Today Soc., Soc. Nutrition Edn., Am. Home Econs. Assn., Inst. Food Tech., W.Va.-Ohio-Ky. Dietetic Assn., Ky. Dietetic Assn., Ohio Edn. Assn., Chi Omega, Delta Kappa Gamma (pres.), Alpha Lambda Delta. Home: Ka-Mel Farms Beaver OH 45613 also Crique Side Apt 4 Morehead KY 40351 Office: Morehead State U Morehead KY 40351

ADAMS, GENE, editor; b. Springfield, Mo., Nov. 3, 1923; s. Charles H. and Marguerite (Kibbe) A.; B.A., Northwestern U., 1950; m. LaVergne Kanara, Apr. 4, 1945; 1 dau., Bonnie Jean. Pub., Midwestern Baker also Chgo. Retail Baker, Chgo., 1950-53; editor, pub. Mobile Homes & Mobile Living, 1953-58; editor Splty. Salesman, Chgo., 1958-67; editor Modern Garden Center, Barrington, Ill., 1967-68; editorial dir. Selling Sporting Goods, Chgo., 1968-72; editor-in-chief Ground Water Age, Elmhurst, Ill., 1972-77; editorial dir. Scott Periodicals, 1977-80; editor Metal Bldg. Rev., Des Plaines, Ill., 1980—. Publ. cons.; graphic and package designer; tchr. ceramics. Active Boy Scouts Am. Served with USN, 1941-45. Mem. Am. Soc. Bus. Press Editors (pres., dir.), Soc. Publ. Designers. Roman Catholic. Club: Chgo. Press. Home: 810 Manchester St Westchester IL 60153 Office: 1800 Oakton St Des Plaines IL 60018

ADAMS, JOHN SMITH, II, leasing exec.; b. Akron, Ohio, Aug. 26, 1930; s. John Smith and Eleanor (Cress) A.; student Fla. State U., 1950-53; children—John Smith III, Randy Cress, Lynn Fontaine, David Scott. Exec. trainee Allied Stores Corp., Tampa, Fla., 1953-54, personnel dir. and selling cost controller, Kansas City, Mo., 1954-58; salaried personnel mgr. Black, Sivalls & Bryson, Kansas City, 1958-60; adminstrv. asst. to pres. Kansas City White Goods, 1960-62; personnel dir., selling cost controller Lamson's, Toledo, 1962-64; asst. personnel dir. Filenes, Boston, 1964-65; v.p., gen. mgr. D.H. Overmyer Co., Tampa and Orlando, Fla., 1965-69; v.p. Furniture Transport Co., Orlando, 1969-71; v.p., partner Bell & Norfleet Enterprises, Tampa, 1971-75; pres. Interstate Distbn. Services, Inc., Toledo, 1975-81; dir. leasing, property mgmt. and personnel Hunger U.S.A., Toledo, 1981—; dir. R.T. Systems, Inc., Interstate Distbn. Services, Inc.; v.p. Manning Telecasting; mgmt. cons. Ohio Compensation Services Co. Trustee, Belle Grove, Inc., Nat. Trust for Historic Preservation; mem. Com. of 100, Tampa, Com. of 200, Orlando. Served with CIC, U.S. Army, 1954-56. Registered real estate broker, Fla. Republican. Episcopalian. Home: 2166 Blackthorn Dr Toledo OH 43614 Office: 302 S Byrne Rd Toledo OH 43615

ADAMS, LEROY SCHURMAN, educator, musician; b. Kilbourne, Wis., Sept. 10, 1904; s. Eli Henry and Helen (Dietzman) A.; student Owasso Bible Sch. (Mich.), 1919-23; Mus.B., People's Bible Coll., Colorado Springs, Colo., 1955; m. Esther Finch, May 20, 1928; children—Leory Schurman, Dale Howell, Joann Katherine; m. 2d, Edith E. Shepherd, July 12, 1972. Tchr., Kingswood Holiness Coll. and Orphanage, 1924-34; tchr. music Colorado Springs Bible Tng. Sch., 1934-36, Immanul Missionary Coll., 1936-41, People's Bible Coll., 1941-47, 50-56, Emmanuel Bible Sch., Salem, Ohio, 1947-50, Beulah Heights Orphanage, 1956-57, Salem (Ohio) Bible Inst., 1957-60; tchr., dean students Kansas City Coll. and Bible Sch., Overland Park, Kans., 1960-68, 70-79, Salem Bible Coll., 1968-69; tchr. Hobe Sound (Fla.) Bible Coll., 1969-70. Mem. Wesleyan Holiness Assn. Chs. Author, composer: Sacred Song Studies for the Guitar, 1939. Home: 7133 Reeds Rd Overland Park KS 66204

ADAMS, LESLIE, composer; b. Clev., 1932; B.Mus., Oberlin (Ohio) Coll., 1955; M.A., Calif. State U., Long Beach, 1967; Ph.D., Ohio State U., 1973. Mem. faculty Kans. U., 1970-78, on leave, 1978-80; composer-in-residence Karamu House, Cleve., 1979-81, Cleve. Music Sch. Settlement, 1981—; Rockefeller Found. fellow, Bellagio, Italy, summer 1979; fellow Yaddo, Saratoga Springs, N.Y., summer 1980; del. Gt. Lakes Assembly for Future Performing Arts, 1980; composer: (ballet) A Kiss in Xanadu, 1954, 73; Piano Concerto, 1974; Ode to Life for Orch., 1979; Symphony No. 1, 1980; also works for piano, horn, cello, brass ensemble, chorus. Winner nat. choral composition competition Christian Arts, 1974; Piano Concerto chosen for performance Houston Symphony Symposium, 1974. Mem. Am. Choral Dirs. Assn., Am. Music Center, Pi Kappa Lambda, Phi Delta Kappa, Phi Mu Alpha Sinfonia, Phi Kappa Phi. Contbr. to profl. jours. Address: 9409 Kempton Ave Cleveland OH 44108

ADAMS, MARK LYNN, state senator; b. Minot, N.D., July 12, 1951; s. Frank F. and Doris B. Adams; A.A.S. in Archtl. Drafting, N.D. State Sch. Sci., Wahpeton, 1972; diploma Western Coll. Auctioneering, Billings, Mont., 1972; m. Julie Piper, June 22, 1974; children—Charles Henry, Tressa Lynn. Draftsman, salesman Kolands of Minot, 1972-73; propr. Adams Constrn. Co., Lansford, N.D., 1977—; co-owner, operator wheat farm, 1971—; partner Border Auction Service, 1977—; dir. Lansford Farmers Elevator; mem. N.D. Senate 6th Dist., 1981—. Supr., Blaine Twp., 1973-81. Mem. N.D. Auctioneers Assn., N.D. Twp. Officers Assn., Lansford Jaycees (charter). Republican. Presbyterian. Clubs: Mohall Gun, Lansford Gun, Elks, Eagles, Masons.

ADAMS, PATRICIA LACY, reading specialist; b. Doniphan, Mo., June 11, 1928; d. James Arthur and Willie Sarah (Miles) Lacy; B.S.Ed., U. Mo., 1949; M.A., Mich. State U., 1966; m. Bill Adams, July 2, 1949; children—Deborah Adams Jung, Jeffrey Miles. Tchr. music, Wardell (Mo.) Public Schs., 1949-50, Braggadocio (Mo.) Public Schs., 1950-51; tchr. music, elem. grades, Evergreen Park, Ill., 1954-55, Dist. 135, Orland Park, Ill., 1955-67; reading specialist Dist. 118, Palos Park, Ill., 1967—. Past pres., sec., treas. Orland Twp. United Way; dir. ch. choir Methodist Ch. Mem. South Suburban Reading Council (pres.), Ill. Reading Council, Internat. Reading Council, Ill. Edn. Assn., Assn. Supervision and Curriculum Devel., Palos Edn. Assn., Lang. Experience Group. Clubs: Quarterly Dance (dir.) Sweet Adelines (asst. dir., v.p.). Home: 10096 W 147th St Orland Park IL 60462 Office: 12700 104th Ave Palos Park IL 60464

ADAMS, RICHARD EDWARD, bldg. materials co. exec.; b. Sullivan, Mo., June 25, 1936; s. Woodrow Carl and Helen Elizabeth A.; student public schs., Normandy, Mo.; m. Janet Marie Vie, Apr. 23, 1955; children—Paul Matthew, Dawn Kathleen, Mark Edward. Salesman, Bevo Realty Co., St. Louis, 1955-61; archtl. draftsman Saul Dien-Architect, Olivette, Mo., 1961-63; prefabrication draftsman County Lumber Co., Hazelwood, Mo., 1963-64; mgr. engring. dept. So. Cross Lumber Co., Hazelwood, 1964-72, prodn. mgr., 1972-75; gen. mgr., sales mgr. Chromalloy Bldg. Products, Hazelwood, 1975—; archtl. cons. Committeeman, Boy Scouts Am., 1975-78, cubmaster, 1976-77; co-chmn. United Way, 1973-78. Recipient Homer award St. Louis Home Builders Assn., 1969, Product Presentation award, 1977, Product Mgmt. award, 1978. Mem. Mid-Am. Lumbermen's Assn. (asso.), Ill. Lumber and Bldg. Material Dealers Assn., Greater St. Louis Lumbermen's Assn., Mid-Mo. Lumbermen's Assn., Cahokia Lumbermen's Assn. Roman Catholic. Home: 2366 Greenberry Hill Ln Chesterfield MO 63017 Office: Chromalloy Bldg Products 131 Byassee Dr Hazelwood MO 63042

ADAMS, ROBERT PAYNE, pub. co. exec.; b. Fargo, N.D., Apr. 29, 1950; s. Edward Thomas and Thelma Mary (Payne) A.; B.A., Macalester Coll., St. Paul, 1972; postgrad. U. Minn., 1973-74. Pres., Forum Pub. Co., Denver, Iowa, 1977—, also dir.; partner Forum Office Products, Denver, 1977—; pres. Horizon Co., Jesup, Iowa, 1978—, also dir. Mem. Nat. Newspaper Assn., Iowa Press Assn. Office: 119 E Main St Denver IA 50622

ADAMS, THOMAS BROOKS, advt. exec.; b. Detroit, Sept. 16, 1919; s. Andrew S. and Louise (Brooks) A.; B.A., Wayne State U., 1941; m. Mary Elizabeth Bryant, Mar. 22, 1945; children—Janis E., Julie A., Kathleen M. With Campbell-Ewald Co., various locations, 1945—, chmn., chief exec. officer, 1968—, pres., 1958-68, chmn. Marschalk Campbell Ewald Worldwide, Warren, Mich., 1976—; dir., exec. com. Interpublic Group of Cos., Inc., McLouth Steel Corp., Kent-Moore Co. Bd. dirs. United Found., Childrens Hosp. Mich., Detroit Renaissance, Boys' and Girls' Clubs Met. Detroit, Detroit Symphony Orch., Menninger Found.; bd. govs. Wayne State U. Served to lt. comdr. USN, 1941-45. Decorated Navy Cross, D.F.C., Air medal; named Outstanding Young Advt. Man of Yr., Assn. Advt. Men and Women N.Y., 1955; recipient Dirs. award Adcraft Club Detroit, 1977; Disting. Alumni award Wayne State U., 1961, Sports Hall of Fame, 1979. Mem. Am. Assn. Advt. Agys, Advt. Council, Adcraft Club Detroit. Clubs: Bloomfield Hills Country, Detroit Athletic, Detroit, Renaissance, Turtle Lake; Whispering Palms (Calif.). Office: 30400 Van Dyke Ave Warren MI 48093

ADAMS, THOMAS TAYLOR, corp. personnel ofcl.; b. Towaco, N.J., Aug. 27, 1920; s. Augustus Hatfield and Agnes Elizabeth (Doyle) A.; B.S. in Agr., Rutgers U., 1942; M.B.A., Harvard U., 1947; m. Virginia Ruth Dayton, May 2, 1942; children—Thomas Taylor, Judith Dayton Adams Meadows, Jonathan Doyle. Orgn. analyst Atlantic Refining Co., Phila., 1947-51; various mgmt. positions Ford Motor Co., Dearborn, Mich., 1951-65; asso. dean Grad. Sch. Bus. Adminstrn., U. Mich., Ann Arbor, 1965-68; dir. tng. First Nat. Bank of Boston, 1968-70; dir. employee relations Procon Internat. Inc., Des Plaines, Ill., 1970-81, UOP Inc., 1981—; edn. chmn. employee relations com. Nat. Constructors Assn. Co-chmn. Plymouth City-Twp. (Mich.) Consolidation Study Com., 1960-61; mem. planning appeals com. City of Plymouth, 1961-68; mem. Jewel Park Utilities Study Com., Barrington, Ill., 1980-81. Served to capt. U.S. Army, 1942-46. Mem. Am. Personnel Assn. (accredited personnel exec.), Phi Beta Kappa, Alpha Zeta. Republican. Presbyterian. Home: 226 Linden Rd Barrington IL 60010 Office: 10 UOP Plaza Des Plaines IL 60016

ADAMS, TIMOTHY RAYMOND, human resource specialist; b. Chgo., July 23, 1951; s. Roy and Norine (Hendrickson) A.; B.S. in Psychology, Loyola U., Chgo., 1973, M.S. in Indsl. Relations, 1977. Employment counselor West Personnel Service, Oak Brook, Ill., 1973-74; personnel asst., human resource rep. Helene Curtis Industries, Inc., Chgo., 1974-78, 78-79; exec. recruiter Ill. Dept. Personnel, Springfield, 1979-80; manpower coordinator Ill. Dept. Mental Health, Chgo., 1980; mgr. personnel resources Chgo. Bd. Options Exchange, 1980—; bus. occupation adv. bd. Dawson Skill Center, Chgo. City Colls., 1975-79; guest lectr. personnel Loyola U., 1976-78. Chmn. 1st aid com. West Cook County dist. ARC, 1978-79, 81—, supr. disaster services, 1980—, instr. 1st aid, 1969—, instr. CPR, 1975—. Recipient service awards ARC, 1974, 79, 81. Mem. Am. Soc. Personnel Adminstrs., Am. Soc. Tng. and Devel., Ill. Tng. and Devel.

Assn., Indsl. Relations Research Assn., Inst. Indsl. Relations Alumni Assn., Soc. Personnel Adminstrs. Greater Chgo. Office: 141 W Jackson Blvd Chicago IL 60604

ADAMS, WAYNE BARRY, public relations exec.; b. Plain City, Ohio, Feb. 20, 1948; s. Paul J. and Ella (Perry) A.; B.S. in Journalism, Ohio U., 1974, M.S. in Internat. Affairs, 1981; postgrad. U. Cin., 1976-77; m. Cheryl Ann Noble, Sept. 2, 1972. Publicity asst., Ohio U. Press, Athens, 1972-74; dir. public relations St. Francis Hosp., Cin., 1975-77; dir. alumni relations Ohio U., Athens, 1977—. dist. public info. officer Ohio Dept. Transp., Marietta, Ohio, 1974-75. Mem. community relations bd. Bleness Meml. Hosp. Served with USN, 1966-70, USNR, 1974-80. Mem. Public Relations Soc. Am., Nat. Geog. Soc., Council Advancement and Support of Edn., Athens Friends Internat. Students. Democrat. Unitarian. Club: Athens Green and White. Home: 155 Morris Ave Athens OH 45701 Office: Konneker Alumni Center U Athens OH 45701

ADAMS, WILLIAM PERRY, govt. ofcl.; b. Danville, Ill., Aug. 2, 1926; s. Grover Dennis and Vesta Mabel (Esworthy) A.; B.A., Mich. State U., 1949; J.D., Georgetown U., 1953; m. Ellen Jane Ross, June 24, 1950; children—Ceryl Adams Harman, Ross Perry, Catherine Jane. Clk., U.S. Senate, 1949-55; asst. legis. counsel Ho. of Reps., 1955-76; v.p. Motion Picture Assn. Am., 1977-78; chmn. U.S. R.R. Retirement Bd., Chgo., 1978—. Served with USAAF, 1945. Mem. Phi Alpha Delta. Methodist. Clubs: Nat. Democratic, University (Washington); Masons. Office: 844 Rush St Chicago IL 60611*

ADAMS, WILLIAM RICHARD, zooarcheologist; b. Bloomington, Ind., Feb. 21, 1923; s. William Baker and Mildred Florence (Dingle) A.; A.B., Ind. U., 1945, M.A., 1949, S.O.P.A., 1980; m. Connie Marie Christie, Oct. 20, 1968; children—William H., James E., Richard B., Margaret E., Scott C., Teresa M. Archeologist, Ind. Hist. Bur., 1945-47; instr., embalmer Sch. Medicine, Ind. U., Bloomington, 1947-49; ethnozoologist Central Miss. Valley Archaeol. Expdn., St. Louis, 1949; field archaeologist Royal Ont. Museum, 1955-56; dir. Ind. Ethnozoological Lab., Bloomington, 1947—; curator Ind. U. Museums, Bloomington, 1949—, instr. ethnozoology, 1956—; pres., chmn. bd. Bloomington Nat. Bank, 1973-80. Mem. Soc. Am. Archaeology, Southwestern Archaeol. Assn., Wilderness Soc., Sierra Club, Audubon Soc., Ind. Hist. Soc., Ind. Acad. Sci., Monroe County Aux. Police. Republican. Clubs: Trowel and Brush, Elks, Ind. Police League, Ind. Chiefs Police. Office: 407 Rawles Hall Bloomington IN 47401

ADAMSON, JAMES CANTWELL, automotive engring. co. exec.; b. Kenosha, Wis., May 21, 1935; s. Harry Richard and Esther Taaffe (Cantwell) A.; B.E.E., Marquette U., Milw., 1959; m. Rita Marie Ruffolo, June 24, 1961; children—Michael, Paula, Gregory, Patrick, Margaret, Catherine (dec.). With Am. Motors Corp., Kenosha, 1959—, sr. product devel. engr., 1967-75, resident engr., 1975—. Served with AUS, 1954-56. Mem. Soc. Automotive Engrs., Wis. Hist. Soc., Kenosha County Hist. Soc., Nat. Rifle Assn., Wis. Sportsman's Assn., Triangle frat. Roman Catholic. Club: Southport Gun. Home: 1518 Harmony Dr Racine WI 53402 Office: 5626 25th Ave Kenosha WI 53140

ADDINGTON, JAMES EDWARD, anthropologist; b. Detroit, Mar. 1, 1947; s. Jack Elwood and Virginia Lucille (Tucker) A.; B.S., Western Mich. U., 1969, M.A., 1972; A.B.D., Ohio State U., 1975; m. Nancy Louise Salchow, Sept. 6, 1969; children—Timothy Finley, Peter Henry. Instr., Ohio State U., Columbus, 1972-75; sr. research asso. Ohio State Mus., Columbus, 1972—; field archaeologist W. Va. Geol. Survey, 1974; cultural resource sect. head Ohio Dept. Transp., Columbus, 1975—; cons. archaeologist Ohio Cultural Resource Cons., Columbus, 1976—; cultural resource cons. Active, Indian Guides, YMCA, Columbus, 1977—. Recipient Cert. of Appreciation, Columbus Public Schs., 1974, Kiwanis, 1978-79, Ohio Transp. Engrs. Assn., 1977, 79; Historic Preservation Survey grantee, 1978-79. Mem. Ohio Archaeol. Council (treas., dir. 1978—), Nat. Trust for Historic Preservation, Am. Assn. Phys. Anthropologists, Soc. Hist. Archaeology, Soc. Indsl. Archaeology, Nat. Hist. Soc., Ohio Hist. Soc., Soc. Am. Archaeology, Central State Anthropol. Assn., Sigma Xi, Alpha Phi Omega. Contbr. articles in field to profl. jours. Home: 2590 Dibblee Ave Columbus OH 43204 Office: Ohio Dept Transp Bur Environ Services 25 S Front St Columbus OH 43215

ADDINGTON, ROBERT EUGENE, II, accountant; b. Evansville, Ind., Sept. 27, 1951; s. Robert Eugene and Margaret Louise (Dower) A.; B.S. in Gen. Mgmt., Purdue U., 1975; m. Stephanie Lynn Darrah, Dec. 15, 1973; children—Darrah Louise, Blythe Marie. Supr. mail dept. Hub States Corp., Indpls., 1975-76; tax examiner Ind. Dept. Revenue, Indpls., 1976-77, field auditor, 1977-79; staff accountant Robert M. Finn & Co., Indpls., 1979—. Mem. Ind. Revenue Auditors Assn. (treas. 1978-79), Kappa Delta Rho. Republican. Mem. Disciples of Christ Ch. Home: 6334 W Bonanza Ln Indianapolis IN 46254

ADDISON, CORNELIUS PHILIP, surgeon; b. Grand Haven, Mich., Aug. 4, 1917; s. Cornelius John and Caroline Anna (Coon) A.; A.B., U. Calif., Berkeley, 1940; M.D., Creighton U., 1943; m. Virginia Ellen Casey, Sept. 24, 1944; children—Sharon, Michael, Brian, Constance, Barbara, Christopher, Ellen, Jon. Intern, St. Mary's Hosp., San Francisco, 1944; resident in surgery Vets. Hosp., Des Moines, 1946-50; staff surgeon Sioux Falls (S.D.) Vets. Hosp., 1950-51; practice medicine specializing in surgery, Ft. Dodge, Iowa, 1951-52, Waterloo, Iowa, 1952—. Served with AUS, 1944-46. Diplomate Am. Bd. Surgery. Fellow A.C.S.; mem. AMA, Iowa Med. Assn., Black Hawk County Med. Soc. Republican. Roman Catholic. Clubs: Elks, K.C., Sunnyside Country. Home: 1128 Ridgemont Rd Waterloo IA 50701 Office: 201 Professional Bldg Saint Francis Dr Waterloo IA 50702

ADDUCCI, ANTHONY JOSEPH, venture capitalist; b. Chgo., Aug. 14, 1937; s. Alexander James and Valeria (Vigna) A.; B.A. in Physics, St. Mary's Coll., Winona, Minn., 1959; postgrad. Ill. Inst. Tech., 1960-64, U. Minn., 1965-72; m. Sandra R. Gordon, Nov. 14, 1965; children—Michael Anthony, Brian Alexander, Alicia Ann. Asso. engr. Jensen Mfg. Co., Chgo., 1960-61; devel. engr. IT&T Kellogg Communications Systems, Chgo., 1961-64; logic design engr. Univac div. Sperry Rand Corp., St. Paul, 1964-66; mgr. sales adminstrn. Medtronic, Inc., Mpls., 1966-72; founder, exec. v.p., dir. Cardiac Pacemakers, Inc., St. Paul, 1972-81; owner, pres. Tech. Enterprises, St. Paul, 1981—; chmn. bd. Check Technology Corp., Med. Graphics Corp.; dir. Horizons Industries Corp. Bd. trustees St. Mary's Coll.; mem. Republican Nat. Com.; chmn. bd. Adducci Family Found.; bd. dirs. St. Paul Chamber Orch. Served with USNR, 1954-62. Decorated Knight Order Holy Sepulchre (Vatican). Mem. Health Industries Mfrs. Assn., IEEE. Contbr. articles to profl. jours.; patentee in field. Office: 3585 N Lexington Ave Saint Paul MN 55112

ADDUCCI, JOSEPH EDWARD, obstetrician, gynecologist; b. Chgo., Dec. 1, 1934; s. Dominee Edward and Harriet Evelyn (Kneppreth) A.; B.S., U. Ill., 1955; M.D., Loyola U., Chgo., 1959; m. Mary Ann Tietje, 1958; children—Christopher, Gregory, Steven, Jessica, Tobias. Intern, Cook County Hosp., Chgo., 1959-60; resident in ob-gyn. Mt. Carmel Hosp., Detroit, 1960-64; practice medicine specializing in obstetrics and gynecology Williston, N.D., 1966—; chief staff, chmn. obstetrics dept. Mercy Hosp., Williston; obstetrician-gynecologist Craven Hagen Clinic, Williston; clin. prof. U. N.D. Med. Sch., 1973—. Mem. N.D. Bd. Med. Examiners, 1974—, past chmn.; project dir. Tri County Family Planning Service; past pres. Tri County Health Planning Council. Chmn., Williams County Welfare Bd., 1966—. Served with M.C., AUS, 1964-66. Diplomate Am. Bd. Obstetrics and Gynecology, Nat. Bd. Med. Examiners. Fellow Am. Soc. Abdominal Surgeons, A.C.S., Am. Coll. Obstetrics and Gynecologists (sect. chmn. N.D.), Internat. Coll. Surgeons (regent 1972-74), Am. Fertility Soc., Am. Assn. Internat. Lazar Soc., Gynecol. Laparopists, N.D. Obstetricians and Gynecologists Soc. (pres. 1966, 76); mem. Am. Soc. for Colposcopy and Colpomicroscopy, Am. Soc. Cryosurgery, Am. Soc. Contemporary Medicine and Surgery, Am. Assn. Profl. Ob-Gyn., Pan Am. Med. Assn. Club: Elk. Contbr. articles to profl. jours. Home: 1717 Main St Williston ND 58801 Office: Med Center Williston ND 58801

ADDY, ALVA LEROY, mech. engr.; b. Dallas, S.D., Mar. 28, 1936; s. Alva Isaac and Nellie Amelia (Brumbaugh) A.; B.S., S.D. Sch. Mines and Tech., 1958; M.S., U. Cin., 1960; Ph.D., U. Ill., 1963; m. Sandra Ruth Turney, June 8, 1958. Engr., Gen. Electric Co., Lancaster, Calif. and Cin., 1958-60; prof. mech. engring. U. Ill., Urbana, 1963—, dir. mech. engring. lab., 1965—, asso. head mech. engring. dept., 1980—; aerodynamics cons. U.S. Army Missile Command, Redstone Arsenal, Ala., summers 1965—; cons. U.S. Army Research Office, 1964—; cons. in high-speed fluid dynamics to indsl. firms, 1963—; vis. research prof. U.S. Army, 1976; lectr. Von Karman Inst. Fluid Dynamics, Brussels, 1968, 75, 76. Asso. fellow Am. Inst. Aeros. and Astronautics; mem. ASME, Soc. Engring. Edn., Sigma Xi, Pi Tau Sigma, Sigma Tau. Home: 1706 Golfview Dr Urbana IL 61801 Office: 208 Mech Engring Lab U Ill Urbana IL 61801

ADE, WALTER FRANK CHARLES, educator; b. Ottawa, Ont., Can., Oct. 24, 1910; s. Leonard Konrad and Bertha Pauline (Rhode) A.; came to U.S., 1949, naturalized, 1954; B.A. (Ellen M. Nickle Meml. fellow), Queen's U., Can., 1933; M.A., U. Toronto, 1939, B.Paed., 1943, M.Ed., 1945; Ph.D., Northwestern U., 1949; M.S. in Edn., Ind. U., 1955, Ed.D., 1960; postdoctoral diplomas, U. Erlangen-Nürnberg, 1955, U. Munich, 1956, U. Heidelberg, 1957; m. Eleanor Anne Schroeder, June 28, 1941 (dec. 1980); children—Virginia Anne (Mrs. Robert Miller), George Leonard. Lectr., U. Toronto, 1933-38, Lisgar Collegiate Inst., Ottawa, 1939-49; asso. prof. Valparaiso (Ind.) U., 1949-58, Ariz. State U., Tempe, 1958-59; prof. modern langs. and edn. Purdue U., Hammond, Ind., 1959-76, prof. emeritus, 1976—, chmn. dept. modern langs., 1959-67. Editor, Agrl. Bulls., Dept. Agr., Toronto, 1934-36; Studienprofessor, Oberrealschule mit humanistischem Gymnasium, Nördlingen/Bavaria/W.Germany, 1956-57; profl. research W.Germany, 1964-65, 67-68; profl. translator, 1966—. Examiner, Coll. Entrance English, Toronto, 1936-39; air raid warden Can., 1940-44; instr. first aid and atomic warfare Can., 1940-44; examiner German and French for naval cadets Fed. Civil Service Commn., Ottawa, 1941-43. Served as flying officer RCAF, 1943-45. P.Q. fellow in French, 1944, Northwestern U. research fellow, 1945-46, Ind. U. grad. research fellow, 1954-55, Fulbright fellow to Germany, 1955-56, Valparaiso U. travel grantee, 1957-58, Purdue Research Found. grantee, 1964-65, Purdue U. travel grantee, 1967-68. Life fellow Internat. Inst. Arts and Letters, Switzerland, Intercontinental Biog. Assn., Cambridge, Eng.; mem. Ind. Fgn. Lang. Tchrs. Assn. (sec.-treas. 1953-57), Am. Assn. Tchrs. German (sec.-treas. Ind. chpt. 1953-55), Sigma Phi Epsilon, Kappa Phi Tau. Club: Canadian (Chgo.). Author numerous books and monographs. Home: 8021 Schreiber Dr Munster IN 46321 Office: Purdue U Classroom-Office Bldg Room 246-E Woodmar at 173d St Hammond IN 46323

ADEGBILE, GIDEON SUNDAY ADEBISI, physician; b. Iree, Nigeria, May 18, 1941; s. John Bimpe and Sarah Oyefunke (Awoyemi) A.; came to U.S., 1962, naturalized, 1974; B.S. cum laude, Va. Union U., 1966; M.D., Meharry Med. Coll., 1971; m. Doris Mae Goodman, June 10, 1966; children—Lisa Aderonke, Titilayo Angel, Babalola Oluwole. Intern, Good Samaritan Hosp., Dayton, Ohio, 1971-72; emergency physician PEG, Inc., Dayton, 1972-75; community health physician Drexel Health Center, Dayton, 1972-73; practice medicine specializing in family medicine Dayton, 1973—; asst. prof. Wright State U. Sch. Medicine, 1975-78, asso. clin. prof., 1978—, chmn. Horizon in Medicine program, 1977—; med. dir. Christel Manor Nursing Home, 1973-80; part-time physician City of Dayton, 1973—; mem. adv. bd. Miami Valley Child Devel. Center, Inc., 1979—. Chmn. bd. Dayton Contemporary Dance Co., 1977-79; mem. bd. Good Samaritan Mental Health Center, 1979—. Recipient cert. of appreciation Christel Manor Nursing Home, 1977. Mem. AMA, Ohio State, Nat. med. assns., Montgomery County Med. Soc., Gem. City Med., Dental and Pharm. Soc. (pres. 1977-80), Am. Coll. Emergency Physicians, NAACP, Alpha Phi Alpha. Democrat. Baptist. Club: Tennis Racket. Research on drug abuse. Home: 1617 Burbank Dr Dayton OH 45406 Office: 2230 Germantown St Dayton OH 45408

ADEGBOYE, OLAWOYE SOLADOYE, statistician; b. Offa, Nigeria, Nov. 20, 1940; s. Soladoye Akano and Ibirinade Abeni (Ajayi) A.; N.C.E., Advanced Tchrs. Coll., 1965; B.S.Ed., Ohio U., 1968, M.S., M.Ed., 1969; m. Ebun Adepoju, Dec. 28, 1969; children—Ademola, Aderike, Mobosede, Olufunke. Math. lectr. Inst. Edn., Ahmadu Bello U., Zaria, Nigeria, 1969-73; math. lectr. dept. math. Kwara State Coll. Tech., Ilorin, Nigeria, head dept. phys. scis.; now scholar dept. math. Bowling Green (Ohio) State U. Mem. Am. Statis. Assn., Am. Math. Soc., Inst. Math. Statistics, Smithsonian Inst. (nat. asso.). Mem. Christian and Missionary Alliance Ch. Home: 300 Napoleon St Apt 83H Bowling Green OH 43402 Office: Bowling Green State U Dept Math and Statistics Bowling Green OH 43403

ADELMAN, FLOYD RANDALL, auto parts co. exec.; b. St. Paul, May 23, 1945; s. Joe H. and Idell M. (Salute) A.; B.A., U. Minn., 1967; m. Andrea Sigal, Jan. 5, 1980; children—Harlan, Barbara. Asst. store mgr. Holiday Auto, Fridley, Minn., 1967-69; store mgr. Skaggs Auto Center, Omaha, 1969-70; mktg. mgr. Empire Warehouse Supply, Edina, Minn., 1970-77; v.p. dirs. Empire-Crown Auto, Inc., Eden Prairie, Minn., 1977—. Bd. dirs. Jewish Community Center, 1977-79; active Fedn. Young Leadership Group; pres. Center Singles, 1978-79, 81-82. Mem. Automotive Parts and Accessories Assn. (dir. 1975-82, v.p. 1980—), Automotive Exec. Club (pres. 1977-78), Automotive Aftermarket Assn. (dir.), Automotive Retailers Group (chmn.). Guest speaker confs. in field. Home: 5347 Beachside Dr Minnetonka MN 55343 Office: 7550 Corporate Way Eden Prairie MN 55344

ADELMAN, LYNN S., state senator; b. Milw., Oct. 1, 1939; B.A. cum laude, Princeton U., 1961; LL.B. cum laude, Columbia U., 1975; married; 2 stepchildren. Mem. Wis. Senate, 1976—. Mem. Waukesha County Mental Health Assn. Democrat. Club: Lions. Contbr. articles to legal jours. Address: Room 40-B South State Capitol Madison WI 53702*

ADELMAN, RAPHAEL MARTIN, physician, hosp. adminstr.; b. Plainfield, N.J., May 4, 1915; s. Samuel and Betty (Taich) A.; D.D.S., U. Pa., 1939; M.Sc., Northwestern U., 1940; B.M., Chgo. Med. Sch., 1943, M.D., 1944; m. Charlotte Mary Koepke, Aug. 25, 1945; children—Karen Rae, Robert John. Intern Norwegian-Am. Hosp., Chgo., 1943-44; asso. in surgery Chgo. Med. Sch., 1945-50; asso. in plastic surgery to Dr. A.M. Brown, Chgo., 1946-50; gen. practice medicine, Wauconda, Ill., 1950—; chief staff St. Therese Hosp., 1963—, chief exec. com., 1965, asst. adminstr., med. dir., 1965—, v.p. med. affairs, 1973, dir., 1974—, also dir. med. edn.; chief sect. ear nose throat Victory Meml. Hosp., Waukegan, 1963, 65-66; clin. asst. prof. family medicine U. Health Scis./Chgo. Med. Sch., 1979—; med. dir. Am. Hosp. Supply Corp.; cons. physician Coll. Lake County Health Services Trust; physician cons. utilization rev. Region V. HEW, 1973-75, cons. quality and standards, 1975; physician cons. Lake County Bd. Health, 1974-76; cons. continuing med. edn. Downey VA Hosp., 1974-76; authorized agt. for Lake County, Ill. Dept. Pub. Health, 1974-76; FAA sr. examiner, 1973—; mem. Am. Bd. Quality Assurance and Utilization Rev. Physicians, 1978—; mem. Ancillary Services Rev., Crescent Counties for Med. Care, 1979—. Mem. exec. com. Lake County chpt. Am. Cancer Soc., 1963—; pres. Wauconda High Sch. Bd. Edn., 1954-60; mem. Wauconda Grade Sch. Bd. Edn., 1952-60; chmn. health and safety N.W. Dist., North Suburban council Boy Scouts Am., 1964-65, vice. chmn. N.W. dist. North Shore council, 1967, 75, mem. exec. com. Northeastern Ill. council; mem. Lake County Health Services Com., 1969—; mem. profl. adv. com. United Community Services Planning Div., 1969—; mem. exec. com., exec. bd. Evanston-North Shore Area Council, 1969; mem. mgmt. com. Lake County Mental Health Clinic, 1967-69; mem. budget and fin. com., 1968-69; group chmn. Regional Conf. on Health Care Costs, Health, Edn. and Welfare, Cleve., 1968; del. Hosp. Planning Council Chgo., 1967-69; chmn. subcom. Ill. Hosp. Licensing Bd. Com., 1969; pres. 1968-69 class U. Ala. Health Service Adminstrs. Devel. Program; chmn. Lake County (Ill.) Health Services Planning Council, Inc.; mem. regional com. Hosp. Admission Surveillance Program, State of Ill., 1972-77; mem. Lake County Drug Commn., 1972-73; mem. Lake County Bd. Health, 1973-77; chmn. orgn. and search com. for exec. dir. Lake County Health Dept.; mem. com. on search for dean univ. health scis. Chgo. Med. Sch., 1975; mem. Lake County Coroner's Adv. Commn., 1977; mem. adv. council health edn. programs Coll. Lake County, 1970-77; bd. dirs. Blumberg Blood Bank; bd. dirs. St. Therese Nurse Scholarship Fund, 1962, Lake County Health Planning Council, 1969-72. Fellow Am. Pub. Health Assn. (life mem., community health edn. accreditation panel 1975-76), AAAS, Chgo. Inst. Medicine, Royal Soc. Health, Am. Acad. Med. Adminstrs., Soc. for Acad. Achievement (life), Am. Coll. Hosp. Adminstrs.; mem. Am., Ill. (state del. 1960-63, dir.), Lake County (past pres.) acads. family practice, AMA, ADA, Assn. Mil. Surgeons of U.S. (life mem.), Ill. Hosp. Assn. (ad hoc com. emergency radio network 1969, state com. safety 1972-77), Ill. Soc. Med. Research, Ill. Med. Soc. (com. physician-hosp. relationship 1974-75), Am. Acad. Dental Radiology, Am. Acad. Family Practice (del. 1974—), Ill. Pub. Health Assn. (exec. council 1976-78), Assn. Hosp. Med. Assn. (resources com. 1976-78), Ill. Found. Med. Care (utilization rev. ednl. accreditation program com. 1973-75, ad hoc com. utilization rev. 1973-75), Am. Coll. Preventive Medicine, Am. Soc. Law and Medicine, Chgo. Acad. Legal Medicine, Ill. Hosp. Attys., Am. Legion (life mem.), Sigma Xi, Alpha Omega, Phi Lambda Kappa. Home: 1202 Oak Trail Dr Libertyville IL 60048 Office: St Therese Hosp Waukegan IL 60085

ADELSTEIN, STANFORD M., corp. exec.; b. Sioux City, Iowa, Aug. 19, 1931; s. Morris E. and Bertha P. (Greenberg) A.; B.S. in Civil Engring., U. Colo., 1953, B.S. in Fin., 1955; D.B.A. (hon.), S.D. Sch. Mines and Tech., 1980; m. Ita Korn, Dec. 19, 1952; children—Daniel J., James D., Jon S. Engr.-estimator Northwestern Engring. Co., Rapid City, S.D., 1957-60, asst. to exec. v.p., 1960-63, v.p., 1963-66, pres., 1966—; pres. Harney Lumber Co., 1969—; pres. Hills Materials Co. div. Northwestern Engring. Co., 1972-81, chmn. bd., 1981—; partner Automobile Bankers S.D., 1952—, Robford Co., 1959—; v.p., treas. Adel Jewelers, Inc., 1969—; adj. prof. S.D. Sch. Mines and Tech., 1981; sec., treas. Black Forest Devel., Inc., 1972-80; dir. Perpetual Savs. & Loan Assn., Rapid City, 1976-81; mem. Nat. Adv. Council on Econ. Opportunity. Nat. v.p. Am. Jewish Com., 1978-81; bd. dirs. Jewish Inst. Nat. Security Affairs, 1980—; del. Jewish Agy. Assembly in Jerusalem, 1975, 76, 77, 78, 79, 80; mem. nat. exec. com. Am. Israel Public Affairs Com., 1981; trustee Rapid City Regional Hosp., 1966-80, officer, 1971-73; alt. del. Rep. nat. convs., 1960, 64; S.D. state central committeeman from Pennington County, 1968—; exec. com. S.D. Rep. Central Com., 1973—, regional chmn. Region 7, 1974—; 5-state regional chmn. Bus. for Reagan/Bush, 1980. Served with C.E., U.S. Army, 1955-57. Recipient Disting. Service award Rapid City Jr. C. of C., 1961, R.A. Pier Good Govt. award, 1970. Mem. Young Presidents' Orgn., Associated Gen. Contractors Am., Associated Gen. Contractors S.D. (pres. 1971), ASCE, Soc. Am. Mil. Engrs. Clubs: Am. Legion, Rapid City Rotary. Office: PO Box 2320 Rapid City SD 57709

ADIARTE, ARTHUR LARDIZABAL, biophysicist; b. San Nicolas, Philippines, Oct. 27, 1943; s. Filomeno Guerrero and Maria (Lardizabal) A.; B.S., U. Philippines, 1963; Ph.D., U. Pitts., 1972; m. Rosario Guerrero, May 6, 1972; children—Alexander, Eric. Instr. physics, math. U. Philippines, 1963-66; research fellow U. Regensburg (W. Ger.), 1972-75; research specialist U. Minn., Mpls., 1975-77; research scientist Minn. Energy Agy., St. Paul, 1977—. Fulbright Hays travel grantee, 1966-72; Alexander von Humboldt research fellow, W. Ger., 1972-75. Mem. N.Y. Acad. Scis., AAAS, Sigma Xi. Home: 743 Parkview Ave St Paul MN 55117 Office: 980 Am Center Bldg 150 E Kellogg Blvd St Paul MN 55101

ADKINS, ROBERT DENNIS, elec. engr.; b. Kansas City, Mo., Aug. 14, 1952; s. Robert Worth, Jr. and Dorothy Lavon (Bundy) A.; B.S. in Elec. Engring., U. Mo., Rolla, 1974; M.B.A., U. Mo., Kansas City, 1979; m. Carolyn Sue Burchfield, Dec. 21, 1974. Power planning engr. Burns & McDonnell Engring. Co., Kansas City, Mo., 1974-79; corp. planning engr. Kansas City Power & Light Co., 1979—. Mem. IEEE, Nat., Mo. socs. profl. engrs., Assn. M.B.A. Execs., Planning Execs. Inst., Phi Kappa Phi, Beta Gamma Sigma. Presbyterian. Clubs: BMW of Kansas City; Mid Am. Rally, Heart of Am. Cursillo. Home: 624 E 74th St Kansas City MO 64131 Office: PO Box 679 1330 Baltimore Ave Kansas City MO 64141

ADKINS, TIMOTHY ARTHUR, ednl. adminstr.; b. Newark, Ohio, May 28, 1945; s. Philip and Thelma A.; A.A., Lorain County Community Coll., 1971; B.S., Ohio State U., 1972, M.Ed., 1978, Ed.S., 1979; postgrad. Bowling Green State U., 1980, Mt. St. Joseph, 1980, Lesley Coll., 1980. Tchr. history, Lorain (Ohio) City Schs., 1972-73; tchr., coordinator occupational work experience Elyria (Ohio) Schs., 1973-75; component coordinator career edn. Parma (Ohio) City Schs., 1978-80, occupational work adjustment coordinator, 1975—; adj. prof. Grad. Sch. Edn., Coll. Mt. St. Joseph, 1980—. Served with USAF, 1965-69; Vietnam. Mem. Am. Vocat. Assn., Ohio Vocat. Assn., NEA, Ohio Edn. Assn., N.E. Ohio Edn. Assn., Parma Edn. Assn., Career Edn. Assn., Ohio Parent Tchrs. Assn., Ohio State Alumni Assn., Kent State U. Alumni Assn. Republican. Methodist. Home: 454 Georgia Ave Elyria OH 44035 Office: Parma City Schools 6726 Ridge Rd Parma OH 44130

ADLER, DAVID LEO, pathologist; b. N.Y.C., Sept. 5, 1913; s. Herman and Rose (Herskovitz) A.; A.B., Ind. U., 1934, M.D., 1938; m. Mary Jane Sanders, June 27, 1939; children—David W., Philip I, Douglas R. Intern, St. Elizabeth Hosp., Dayton, Ohio, 1938-39; instr.

in pathology, Sch. Medicine, U. Tex., Galveston, 1939-40, Sch. Medicine, N.Y. U., N.Y.C., 1946-47; dir. lab. Bartholomew County Hosp., Columbus, Ind., 1947-74; dir. lab. Columbus Med. Lab., 1976—. Dir. ARC, 1950-70; pres. Ind. State Bd. Health, 1960-64; pres. Negro Scholarship Found., 1960-61. Served with M.C. U.S. Army, 1941-46. Recipient commendations, Ind. Gov., Ind. Bd. Health, ARC. Mem. Ind. State, Bartholomew County Med. Socs., Coll. Am. Pathologists, Am. Soc. Clin. Pathologists. Contbr. articles to profl. mags. Home: 4224 N Riverside Dr Columbus IN 47201 Office: Doctors Park Columbus IN 47201

ADLER, MILTON LEON, psychologist; b. Bronx, N.Y., June 11, 1926; s. Siegmund and Josephine (Eppsteiner) A.; B.S., Rutgers U., 1951; M.S., City U. N.Y., 1952; postgrad. N.Y. U., 1952-53; Ph.D., U. Ill., 1963; m. Margrit Klein, Mar. 5, 1948; children—Sandra Ellen, Mark Lawrence. Psychiat. case worker N.J. Neuropsychiat. Inst., Blavenberg, 1953; clin. psychology intern, staff psychologist Manteno (Ill.) State Hosp., 1953-57; regional psychologist Ill. Inst. Juvenile Research, Champaign, 1957-66; sr. psychologist, clin. supr., subregion dir. Herman M. Adler Children's Center, Champaign, 1966-74; cons. psychologist Frederic Chusid and Co., Chgo., 1963-64; lectr. psychology Ill. State U., Normal, 1974-75; instr. psychology Parkland Coll., Champaign, Ill., 1979-80; pvt. practice clin., counseling, cons. psychology, Urbana, Ill., 1965—; presenter growth in groups seminars and workshops on personal growth and interpersonal relationships. Served with USAAF, 1944-47. Registered psychologist, Ill. Mem. Am. Group Psychotherapy Assn. (dir. 1974-76, instr. tng. inst., mem. inst. com.), Ill. Assn. Maternal and Child Health (dir., pres. 1981-82, workshop, seminar presenter), Champaign-Urbana State Employees Assn. (past v.p., pres.), Ill. Group Psychotherapy Soc. (workshop presenter, council rep., award of distinction 1977, v.p., pres.-elect 1980-81), Am. Psychol. Assn., Am. Soc. Psychologists in Pvt. Practice, Acad. of Psychologists in Marital and Family Therapy, Nat. Assn. Sch. Psychologists, Am. Personnel and Guidance Assn., Am. Assn. Mental Health Counselors, Ill. Psychol. Assn., Ill. Acad. Criminology, Ill. Personnel and Guidance Assn., Ill. Assn. Mental Health Counselors, Am. Acad. Psychotherapists, Saab Club Am., N. Am. Hunting Club, Phi Delta Kappa. Democrat. Unitarian. Contbr. workshops on group psychotherapy to profl. insts. Home: 1507 W University Ave Champaign IL 61820 Office: 404 W Green St Urbana IL 61801

ADLER, ROY DOUGLAS, mktg. educator; b. Detroit, Sept. 9, 1943; s. Roy Alvin and Ruth Louise (Potz) A.; A.B., Bucknell U., 1965; M.A., Western Mich. U., 1971; M.B.A., Xavier U., 1973; Ph.D., U. Ala., 1981; m. Cecilia Canales, Mar. 9, 1968; children—Douglas Carlos, Davison Reyes. With William John Upjohn Advt., Kalamazoo, 1965-66, Procter & Gamble, Cin., 1968-70, King's Island, Cin., 1970-71, Levi Strauss, Florence, Ky., 1972-75; faculty Xavier U., Cin., 1973-74, grad. faculty, 1979—; also tchr. Ohio State U., 1976-77, U. Ala., 1977-78, Ga. State U., 1978-79. Served to 1st lt. U.S. Army, 1966-68. Lic. psychologist. Mem. Am. Psychol. Assn., Am. Mktg. Assn., So. Mktg. Assn., Acad. Mktg. Sci., Theta Chi. Republican. Presbyterian. Author: Marketing and Society, 1981; contbr. articles to profl. jours. Home: 1801 Wilaray Ter Cincinnati OH 45230 Office: Xavier Univ Victory Parkway Cincinnati OH 45207

ADLER, SEYMOUR JACK, social work exec.; b. Chgo., Oct. 22, 1930; s. Michael L. and Sarah (Pasnick) A.; B.S., Northwestern U., 1952; M.A., U. Chgo., 1958; m. Barbara Fingold, Mar. 24, 1958; children—Susan Lynn, Karen Sandra, Michelle Lauren. Caseworker, Cook County Dept. Pub. Aid, Chgo., 1955; juvenile officer Cook County Sheriff's Office, 1955-56; U.S. probation-parole officer U.S. Dist. Ct., Chgo., 1958-68; exec. dir. Youth Guidance, Chgo., 1968-73; dir. court services Juvenile ct. Cook County, Chgo., 1973-75; exec. dir. Methodist Youth Services, Chgo., 1975—. Mem. Ill. Law Enforcement Commn., 1969-72; instr. corrections program Chgo. State U., 1972-75; instr. Harper Coll., 1977, St. Joseph's Coll., 1978. Bd. dirs. Child Care Assn. Ill., 1979—. Served to 1st lt. USMCR, 1952-55. Recipient Morris J. Wexler award Ill. Acad. Criminology, 1975, Meritorious Service award Chgo. City Colls., 1968. Mem. Ill. Acad. Criminology (pres. 1972), Nat. Assn. Social Workers (del. Assembly 1977, 79, 81, chmn. Chgo. dist. 1978-80, chmn. group for action planning childrens services 1980—, Disting. Service award Criminal Justice Council 1978), Ill. Probation, Parole and Correctional Assn., Alpha Kappa Delta, Tau Delta Phi. Contbr. articles to profl. jours. Home: 2524 Happy Hollow Rd Glenview IL 60025 Office: 542 S Dearborn St Chicago IL 60605

ADRIAN, PATRICIA LEE GRIMSHAW, assn. exec.; b. Reliance, S.D., July 20, 1938; d. Walter George and Dorthy Veronica (Zastrow) Grimshaw; student Sinte Gleska U., 1973; m. Robert Earl Adrian, Oct. 12, 1957; children—James Robert, Thomas Edward, Kevin Patrick, David Duane. Sec., Cherry Todd Electric, 1956-57; tchr. White River (S.D.) Ind. Sch. Dist., 1970-71; dir. S.D. Beef Industry Council, 1970-73, pres., 1972-73, exec. v.p., 1973—; exec. sec., lobbyist S.D. Livestock Assn., part-time 1977—; dir. Nat. Livestock and Meat Bd. Gov.'s rep. to nutrition symposium Old West Regional Commn., 1979-80; mem. Indsl. Devel. Comm. State of S.D., 1979—; mem. S.D. Agrl. Mktg. Commn., 1980—; S.D. rep. Dist. Export Council, U.S. Dept. Commerce, 1981—. Recipient Disting. Service award S.D. Stockgrowers Assn., 1974, S.D. State U., 1976. Mem. Nat. Fedn. Press Women, Am. Soc. Assn. Execs., Nat. Cattlemen's Assn., S.D. Livestock Assn., Am. Agri-Women, U.S. Meat Export Fedn. (dir. 1980—), S.D. Press Women's Assn., S.D. CowBelles (pres.). Republican. Roman Catholic. Home: Star Route Box 222 White River SD 57579 Office: 110 W Capitol St Pierre SD 57501

ADYE, WALLACE M., JR., physician; b. Newtonville, Ind., Dec. 16, 1928; s. Wallace M. and Opal M. Adye; B.S. in Anatomy and Physiology, Ind. U., 1949, M.D., 1952; m. Wanda Gay Ferguson, Sept. 2, 1951; children—Bruce Alan, Wallace M., Tamara Gayle, Terri Lynn. Intern, St. Elizabeth Hosp., Dayton, Ohio, 1952-53; practice medicine specializing in family practice, Evansville, Ind., 1956—; dir. family practice residency program Deaconess Hosp., 1977—, pres. staff, 1971-72, bd. dirs., 1970-71; med. dir. Parkview Convalescent Center, 1972—; clin. asst. prof. Ind. U. Med. Sch., 1979—; sec. Southwestern Ind. Med. Rev. Orgn., 1978—. Served to capt. M.C., USAF, 1954-56. Diplomate Am. Bd. Family Practice. Fellow Am. Acad. Family Physicians; mem. AMA, Soc. Tchrs. Family Medicine, Ind. Acad. Family Physicians, Ind. State Med. Assn., Vanderburgh County Med. Soc. (pres. 1978-79). Home: 320 Inwood Dr Evansville IN 47711 Office: 611 Harriet St Suite L-100 Evansville IN 47710 also 1307 Stringtown Rd Evansville IN 47711

AESCHLIMANN, DENNIS B., airline exec.; b. St. Louis, Mar. 28, 1943; s. Fernand and Margaret (Kersch) A.; B.S. in Bus. Adminstrn., Northwestern U., Evanston, Ill., 1966; M.B.A., Northwestern U., Chgo., 1967; m. Karen Sprague Benson, June 10, 1967; children—Debra Benson, Robert Benson. Analyst long range and capital planning, distbn. mgr. Tempo designs Standard Oil Co. (Ind.), Chgo., 1967-69; mgr. youth programs, mgr. credit card mktg., mgr. cargo mktg., mgr. mil. and govt. cargo sales, mgr. system postal sales and service United Airlines, Chgo., 1969—. Mem. Air Transport Assn. (chmn. airlines postal affairs com.). Columnist, Schweizer Reklame, 1967-68; reviewer Jour. of Mktg., 1968. Office: United Airlines PO Box 66100 Chicago IL 60666

AGAN, LELAND BARRY, sales rep.; b. Colby, Kans., Dec. 29, 1944; s. Herbert Winfrey and Inez Nell (Allison) A.; student Colby Community Jr. Coll., 1965-66, Seward County Community Coll., 1969-70; m. Loree Jeanine England, Sept. 4, 1971; 1 dau., Erica Janell. Mgr., Hi-Plains Pizza Hut, Inc., Pratt, Kans., 1970-72; club mgr. Holiday Inn, Liberal, Kans., 1972-74; sales rep. Tri-State Office Products, Inc., Liberal, 1974-79; sales rep. Otasco, Inc., Liberal, 1979—. Served with AUS, 1966-69, USMCR, 1966. Mem. Ch. of Nazarene. Clubs: Lions, Liberal Jaycees (dir. 1976-77, pres. 1977-78, state dir. 1978-79). Home: 107 S Pershing St Liberal KS 67901 Office: 1020 S Kansas Liberal KS 67901

AGATHOS, LOUIS JOHN, mfg. co. exec.; b. Brigaton, Mass., Jan. 8, 1933; s. John Agnelo and Evelyn Elnora A.; B.S. with high distinction in Chem. Engring., U. Maine, 1960, M.S. in Chem. Engring., 1961; M.B.A. with high distinction, Harvard U., 1965; m. Barbara Strauther Evans, Oct. 17, 1953; children—Debra Lynn, John Arthur. Vice pres. ops. Brighams, Inc., Arlington, Mass., 1967-69; dir. fast food ops. Skychefs, Inc., N.Y.C., 1969-70; v.p., gen. mgr. Crimsco Inc., Kansas City, Mo., 1970-74; corp. v.p. Sunbeam Corp., Oak Brook, Ill., 1976—; group pres. Sunbeam Mgmt. Services, Oak Brook, 1976—. Served with USNR, 1949-53; Korea. Recipient Ober award, 1959, Hovey award, 1958, Goldman award, 1959; NSF fellow, 1960-61; Wesley Travis fellow, 1964-65. Mem. Am. Inst. Chem. Engrs., Nat. Assn. Food Equipment Mfrs., Nat. Restaurant Assn., Phi Kappa Phi, Tau Beta Pi. Club: Harvard Bus. Sch. Office: Sunbeam Corp 2001 S York Rd Oak Brook IL 60521

AGCAOILI, CLARK REVILLA, mfg. co. exec.; b. Manila, Philippines, July 17, 1947; came to U.S., 1972, naturalized, 1978; s. Claro C. and Simeona R. (Revilla) A.; B.S. in M.E., Mapua Inst. Tech. (Philippines), 1967; M.B.A., Keller Grad. Sch. Mgmt., 1981; m. Melba P. Llanes, Jan. 2, 1972; children—Claudine Dale, Christine Ann, Mark Simon, Michael Clark. Product engr. Westinghouse, Manila, 1967-71; project engr. U.S. Industries, Manila, 1971-72; product devel. engr. Kinkead Industries, Chgo., 1972-77; v.p. product planning and devel. Efron Inc., Chgo., 1977—; design and mfg. cons. Mem. Zoning Bd. Appeals, Glendale Heights, Ill., 1977-78, chmn. planning commn., 1977—; mem. adv. council Bd. of Edn., Glendale Heights, 1978—. Mepua Inst. Tech. acad. scholar, 1965-67; registered profl. engr., Philippines. Mem. Soc. Mfg. Engrs., Soc. Plastics Engrs., Soc. Die Casting Engrs. Roman Catholic. Patentee on carpet kicker, roller and hanger assembly for by-pass doors. Office: 7519 S Greenwood Ave Chicago IL 60619

AGEE, WILLIAM M., mfg. co. exec.; b. Boise, Idaho, Jan. 5, 1938; s. Harold J. and Suzanne (McReynolds); student Stanford, 1956-57; A.A., Boise Jr. Coll., 1958; B.S. with high honors, U. Idaho, 1960; M.B.A. with distinction, Harvard, 1963; D.Sc. in Indsl. Mgmt. (hon.), Lawrence Inst. Tech., 1977; D.Sc. (hon.), Nathaniel Hawthorne Coll., 1977; D.C.S., Eastern Mich. U., 1978; m. Diane Rae Weaver, Sept. 15, 1957; children—Suzanne E., Kathryn D., Robert W. Various positions Boise Cascade Corp., 1963-72, sr. v.p., chief fin. officer, 1969-72; exec. v.p., chief fin. officer The Bendix Corp., Southfield, Mich., 1972-76, pres., 1976-79, chief operating officer, 1976-77, chmn. bd., chief exec. officer, 1977—, also dir.; dir. Equitable Life Assurance Soc. U.S., Dow Jones & Co., Inc., ASARCO, Inc. Bd. dirs. Nat. Council for U.S.-China Trade, Detroit Renaissance, Inc., Detroit Econ. Growth Corp. Recipient Distinguished Alumnus award Boise State U., 1972, Harvard Bus. Sch. Alumni Achievement award, 1977; named to U. Idaho Hall of Fame, 1978. Mem. Am. Inst. C.P.A.s, Idaho Soc. C.P.A.s, Mich. Assn. C.P.A.s, Council Fgn. Relations, Conf. Bd., Council on Fgn. Relations, Bus. Roundtable, Phi Kappa Phi. Republican. Presbyterian. Clubs: Arid (Boise); Economic (dir.), Renaissance (Detroit). Office: The Bendix Corp Bendix Center Southfield MI 48076

AGER, MERLIN FRED, educator; b. Portage, Wis., Nov. 16, 1938; s. Willard Jesse and Marian Evelyn (Stebbins) A.; B.A., Cedarville Coll., 1960; M.S., U. Wis., 1962; Ph.D., Ohio State U., 1967; m. Ruth Ann Himsel, July 31, 1959; children—Minda Lee, Deborah Ann. Tchr., counselor, public schs. Madison, Wis., 1962-64; instr., chmn. edn. dept. Cedarville (Ohio) Coll., 1964-75, dir. student teaching, 1978—; prin. Dayton Christian Schs., 1975-78. Officer, PTA. Mem. Assn. Tchr. Educators, Center for Research on Pvt. Edn., Assn. Supervision and Curriculum Devel., Phi Delta Kappa. Baptist. Home: 192 Walnut St Cedarville OH 45314 Office: PO Box 601 Cedarville OH 45314

AGGARWAL, RAJ KUMAR, educator, business cons.; b. Jagraon, Punjab, India, June 27, 1947; s. Nathu Ram and Pushpa Vati Gupta; B.Tech., Indian Inst. Tech., New Delhi, 1968; M.B.A., Kent State U., 1970, D.B.A., 1975; postgrad. U. Chgo., 1972-73; m. Karen L. Blackburn, May 15, 1976. Tech. dir., dir. Agerson Electronic and Gen. Industries Ltd., New Delhi, 1966-68; grad. appointee, teaching fellow Kent (Ohio) State U., 1968-72; coordinator finance area, faculty lectr. Ind. U., 1972-74; asst. prof. finance Seton Hall U., South Orange, N.J., 1974-76; asso. prof. finance U. Toledo, 1976-79, prof. fin. and internat. bus., 1979—; vis. prof. fin. U. Mich., 1981—; fgn. exchange cons. Dana Corp., Toledo, 1977; internat. strategy cons. Owens-Ill. Inc., Toledo, 1978; asso. cons. Multinat. Computer Models Inc., Montclair, N.J., 1978—; dir. Health Clinics Internat., Toledo. Pres. for Midwest, bd. dirs. Acad. Internat. Bus. Mem. Fin. Mgmt. Assn., Fin. Execs. Inst., Am. Fin. Assn., Acad. Internat. Bus., Inst. Mgmt. Sci., Am. Inst. Decision Scis., So. Internat. Devel., Beta Gamma Sigma, Phi Kappa Phi, Delta Sigma Pi. Author: Financial Policies for the Multinational Company; 1976; International Business Finance: A Selected Bibliography, 1978; The Management of Foreign Exchange, 1980; Applications in Management Science: Cases, 1979; contbr. articles to profl. jours. Home: 2667 Cheltenham Rd Toledo OH 43606 Office: 2801 W Bancroft St Toledo OH 43606

AGGARWAL, SHIV KUMAR, business exec.; b. New Delhi, India; s. Ishwari Prasad and Bhagwati Devi A.; came to U.S., 1956, naturalized, 1975; B.A., U. Delhi, 1953; M.S.W., U. Baroda, India, 1955; M.B.A., U. Mo., 1957. Pres., Imperial Cycle & Motor Co., Bombay, India, 1959-62; dir. neighborhood services East End Neighborhood House, Cleve., 1962-67; founder, exec. dir. Collinwood Community Services Center, Cleve., 1967-80; pres. Century Bus. Systems, Cleve., 1980—. Mem. Gerontol. Soc., India Assn. Greater Cleve. Club: Lions. Home: 2595 Hickory Ln Cleveland OH 44124 Office: 5834 Mayfield Rd Cleveland OH 44124

AGINIAN, RICHARD DICRAN, newspaper pub. co. exec.; b. N.Y.C., Sept. 13, 1941; s. Hrant and Virginia (Solakian) A.; M.B.A., Rutgers U., 1964; Ph.B., Wayne State U., 1963; m. Diane Tashjian, July 31, 1966; children—Dawn, Marla. Audit mgr. Arthur Andersen & Co., Detroit, 1964-75; asst. to pres. Falvey Motors, Troy, Mich., 1975-76; pres., chief exec. officer Suburban Communications Corp., Livonia, Mich., 1976—; dir. Suburban Newspapers of Am., Chgo., 1979—, U.S. Suburban Press, Inc., Chgo., 1979—. Trustee Henry Ford Hosp., West Bloomfield, Mich., 1979—; mem. fin. com. LWV, 1978—. C.P.A., Mich. Mem. Mich. Assn. C.P.A.'s Am. Inst. C.P.A.'s, Young Presidents Orgn. Armenian Orthodox. Clubs: Economic (Detroit); Oakland Hills Country. Home: 835 Westwood St Birmingham MI 48009 Office: 36251 Schoolcraft Rd Livonia MI 48150

AGOOS, LAWRENCE DAVID, psychologist, psychotherapist, forensic psychologist, lawyer; b. Augusta, Ga., Mar. 28, 1947; s. Bernard Samuel and Beatrice (Rosen) A.; B.A., U. Ga., 1969, M.A., 1972, J.D., 1972; postgrad. Tex. A. and M. U.; Ph.D. in Clin. Psychology, Columbia Pacific U.; m. Candace Albert Agoos, Aug. 14, 1974. Asst. to dist. atty., Clarke County, Ga., 1972-73; adminstrv. asst. to v.p., asst. to pres., advisor to dean students, advisor student functions, instr. bus. and communications, Newberry Coll., Newberry, S.C., 1973-74; teaching asst., intern counseling psychology dept. Tex. A. and M. U., Bryan, 1974-75; psychologist Rusk State Hosp., Rusk, Tex., 1975-78; psychol. intern Bur. Prisons, U.S. Dept. Justice. Campaign-office mgr. Jimmy Carter for Gov., Richmond, County, Ga. Environ. and legal researcher for former Sec. of State Dean Rusk. Recipient Edwards Character Award Boy Scouts Am., 1960. Mem. Am. Psychology-Law Soc., Am. Psychol. Assn., Am. Group Psychol. Assn., Am. Mental Health Counselors Assn., Am. Guild of Hypnotherapists, Am. Personnel and Guidance Assn., Am. Assn. Sex Educators, Counselors and Therapists (cert.), Assn. for Humanistic Psychology, Assn. for Specialists in Group Work, Pub. Offender Counselor Assn., Soc. for Advancement of Social Psychology, Tex. Psychol. Assn., Ga. Pub. Relations Student Soc. Am. (founding pres. U. Ga.), Edn. Psychology Student Orgn. (founding treas. Tex. A & M), Domosthenians Lit. Soc. (U. Ga.), Phi Alpha Delta, Tau Epsilon Phi (v.p.), Phi Sigma Epsilon. Co-editor Jacksonville U. Newspaper, 1965-66. Home: 300 S High St Belleville IL Office: Chester Mental Health Center Chester IL 62233

AGRAWAL, DHARMA PRAKASH, computer engr.; b. Balod, India, Apr. 12, 1945; s. Saryoo Prasad and Chandra (Kanta) A.; B.E.E., Ravishankar U., 1966; M.E. with honors, Roorkeee U., 1968; D.Sc.Tech., Fed. Inst. Tech., Lausanne, Switzerland, 1975; m. Purnima Agrawal, May 7, 1971; children—Sonal, Braj Prakash. Mem. faculty M.N.R. Engring. Coll., Allahabad, India, 1968-72, U. Roorkee (India), 1972-73, Fed. Inst. Tech., Lausanne, 1973-75, Univ. Technology, Baghdad, 1976, So. Meth. U., Dallas, 1976-77; asso. prof. elec. and computer engring. Wayne State U., Detroit, 1977—. Mem. IEEE (sr.), Assn. Computing Machinery, Sigma Xi. Contbr. articles to profl. jours. Home: 2318 Parliament Dr Sterling Heights MI 48077 Office: 5050 Anthony Wayne Dr Detroit MI 48202

AGRUSO, VICTOR MICHAEL, JR., psychologist, educator; b. Cin., Nov. 2, 1935; s. Victor Michael and Angelina (Acquaro) A.; A.B., Xavier U., 1965; Ph.D., U. Mo., 1971; m. Ramona R. Mills, Sept. 7, 1957; children—Stephanie, Victor Michael III, Valerie, Natalie. Faculty, Drury Coll., Springfield, Mo., 1967—, prof., chmn. dept. psychology 1974—. Served with USMC, 1953-56; Korea. Mem. Am. Psychol. Assn., N.Y. Acad. Scis. Author: Learning in Later Years, 1978. Home: HSJ Box 8045 Springfield MO 65802 Office: Drury College Springfield MO 65802

AGRUSS, NEIL STUART, physician; b. Chgo., June 2, 1939; s. Meyer and Frances (Spector) A.; B.S., U. Ill., 1960, M.D., 1963; m. Alice Jane Goldberg, Aug. 11, 1965; children—David, Lauren, Michael. Intern, U. Ill. Hosp., Chgo., 1963-64, resident in internal medicine, 1964-65, 67-68; fellow in cardiology, Cin. Gen. Hosp., 1968-70, dir. coronary care unit, 1971-74, dir. echocardiography lab., 1972-74; dir. cardiac diagnostic labs., Central DuPage Hosp., Winfield, Ill., 1974—; asst. prof. medicine, U. Cin., 1970-74, Rush Med. Coll., 1976—. Chmn. coronary care com. Heart Assn. DuPage County, 1974—; active Congregation Etz Chaim, Lombard, Ill. Served to capt. M.C. U.S. Army, 1965-67. Diplomate Am. Bd. Internal Medicine. Fellow A.C.P., Am. Coll. Cardiology, Am. Coll. Chest Physicians, Council Clin. Cardiology, Am. Heart Assn.; mem. AMA, DuPage County, Ill. State Med. Socs., Am. Fedn. Clin. Research, Chgo. Heart Assn. Author and co-author publs. in field. Office: 454 Pennsylvania St Glen Ellyn IL 60137

AGUILAR, CLAYTON NICHOLS, mgmt. cons., educator; b. Escalante, Philippines, Feb. 11, 1934; came to U.S., 1954, naturalized, 1961; s. Serafin Vasquez and Elsie (Nichols) A.; B.S., Silliman U., Dumaguete, Philippines, 1953, B.S. in Chemistry, 1954; M.S., Purdue U., 1956; Ph.D., N.Y. U., 1974; m. Milagro Arenas Santana, Dec. 17, 1964; children—Clayton Nichols Arenas, Paula Margaret Arenas. Chemist, U.S. Rubber, Mishawaka, Ind., 1956-58; internat. salesman, mktg. researcher Union Carbide, N.Y.C., 1961-67; planner Esso Internat., N.Y.C., 1968-69; cons. Roger Williams Tech. and Econ. Services, Princeton, N.J., 1969-72; asst. prof. mgmt. Fordham U., N.Y.C., 1973; asst. prof. adminstrv. scis. Montclair State Coll., Upper Montclair, N.J., 1973-74; asst. prof. mgmt. Rider Coll., Lawrenceville, N.J. 1974-76, 78-79; dean Coll. Bus. Adminstrn., Silliman U., 1976-77; gen. mgr. Aguilar Plantations, Cadiz, Philippines, 1977-78; asst. prof. mgmt. Rider Coll., 1978-79; asso. prof. mgmt. Central Mich. U., Mt. Pleasant, 1979—; pres. Aguilar Assos., Mt. Pleasant, 1979—. Mem. Franklin Twp. (N.J.) Indsl. Devel. Com., 1975-76. Recipient cert. of service Franklin Twp., 1976, cert. of recognition Old Sagay Elem. Sch. Alumni Assn., 1976, cert. of appreciation Leadership Conf., Silliman U., 1976. Mem. Acad. Mgmt., Acad. Internat. Bus., Sigma Xi, Beta Gamma Sigma. Republican. Presbyterian. Club: Rotary (Mt. Pleasant). Research in mgmt., bus. strategy. Home: PO Box 553 Mount Pleasant MI 48858 Office: Central Mich U Mgmt Dept Mount Pleasant MI 48859

AHERN, LAWRENCE FRANK, ins. exec.; b. Cleve., Oct. 23, 1941; s. Martin B. and Caroline Ahern; B.S., Kent (Ohio) State U., 1963; postgrad. Case Western Res. U.; m. Carol S. Cothey, Jan. 31, 1970; children—Shawna Kelly, Justin Patrick. Salesman, Armour & Co., Cleve., 1964-67; ins. agt. Mut. Benefit Life Ins. Co., 1967-74, dir. field personnel, Newark, 1974-76, gen. agt., Akron, Ohio, 1976—; propr. L.F. Ahern Assos.; partner Ahern-Henson and Assos., Cleve. Mem. devel. bd. Greater Newark Hosp., 1974-75; active local Boy Scouts Am., chmn. Gt. Trail Council Explorers, 1976—; bd. dirs. Rotary Camp for Handicapped. Served with USAR, 1963-69. Recipient numerous ins. salesmanship and mgmt. awards; C.L.U. Mem. Gen. Agts. and Mgrs. Assn. (treas. 1978-79, pres. 1979-80), Nat. Assn. Life Underwriters, Cleve.-Akron Estate Planning Council, Gen. Agts. Assn., Akron Life Underwriters Assn. Roman Catholic. Clubs: Edgewood Swim and Tennis; Rotary (dir.) (Akron); Prestwick Country. Office: 829 Centran Bldg Akron OH 44308 also 730 Hanna Bldg Cleveland OH 44115

AHLBERG, CLARK DAVID, univ. pres.; b. Wichita, Kans., May 23, 1918; A.B., U. Wichita, 1939; M.A. (Maxwell fellow), Syracuse U., 1942, Ph.D. in Polit. Sci., 1951, LL.D., 1969; L.H.D. (hon.), St. Lawrence U., 1981. Personnel asst. Panama Canal, 1942; mem. staff adminstrv. mgmt. div. VA, 1946-47; mem. research staff sci. research bd. Exec. Office of Pres., 1947, personnel research staff Nat. Bur. Standards, 1947-48; dir. research Syracuse (N.Y.) U., Washington, 1948-51; asst. dean coll. engring. Syracuse U., 1951-54, v.p. adminstrn. and research, 1959-68, pres. Research Corp., 1959-68; dep. dir. N.Y. State Budget Div., Albany, 1954-57, dir. budget, 1957-59; pres. Wichita State U., 1968—; dir. 4th Nat. Bank & Trust Co., Wichita, Coleman Co., Inc. first dep. controller N.Y. State Dept. Audit and Control, Albany, 1959; cons. N.Y. State CSC, 1959-68, N.Y. State Dept. Audit and Control, 1959-68, USPHS, 1960; mem. adv. com. on arts John F. Kennedy Center for Performing Arts. Served with AUS, 1944-46. Mem. Am. Assn. State Colls. and Univs., Polit. Sci. Assn., Soc. Public Adminstrn., Inst. Logopedics (trustee),

Soc. Engring. Edn., Inst. Indsl. Engring., Phi Eta Sigma, Phi Kappa Phi. Club: Wichita Books and Authors. Author: (with John C. Honey) Attitudes of Scientists and Engineers about Their Government, 1950. Editor: Agency and Departmental Statements on Research and Development Administration, 1947. Contbr. articles to profl. jours. Office: Office of President Wichita State U Wichita KS 67208

AHLENIUS, WILLIAM MATHESON, lawyer; b. Chgo., July 26, 1934; s. William Hilmer and Kathryn Marcella (Trenkle) A.; A.B., U. Ill., 1955, J.D., 1961; postgrad. Georgetown U., 1957-59; m. Jacqueline LaRue Painter, June 15, 1958; children—Lisa Jo, Kristen Sue. Admitted to Ill. bar, 1961, Iowa bar, 1961; asso. firm Betty, Neuman, Heniger & McMahon, Davenport, Iowa, 1961-62; partner firm Swain, Johnson & Gard, Peoria, Ill., 1962—. Mem. faculty Ill. Inst. for Continuing Legal Edn., 1972—. Active Heart of Ill. United Fund. Mem. Peoria County Republican Central Com., 1966-70, 72-79, sec., 1974-79. Served with USN, 1955-59. Mem. Am., Ill., Iowa, Peoria County bar assns., Naval res. Assn., Phi Delta Phi. Episcopalian. Club: Cleve Coeur (Peoria). Home: 1130 Multiflora Ln Peoria IL 61615 Office: 411 Hamilton Blvd Suite 1900 Peoria IL 61602

AHLERS, ANDREW WILLIAM, banker; b. nr. LeMars, Iowa, July 12, 1899; s. Henry Anthony and Wilhelmina (Lewis) A.; student parochial schs.; m. Angela Clare Buckley, June 19, 1934; children—Joan Kathryn (Mrs. Orville Portz), Mary Jean (Mrs. Gerald Portz), Delores Angeles (Mrs. Raphael Portz), Patricia Helen (Mrs. Mike Lovely), Janiece Marie (Mrs. Charles Bohlke). Engaged in farming near Remsen, Iowa, 1934-54; pres. Farmers Savings Bank, Struble, Iowa, 1940—; pres. Andrew W. Ahlers Ins. & Real Estate, Remsen, 1961—. Mem. Service Corps Ret. Execs. Mem. Plymouth County Bankers Assn., Plymouth County Realtors Assn., Remsen C. of C. (dir.). Democrat. Roman Catholic. K.C. Club: Community. Home: 620 Kennedy St Remsen IA 51050 Office: 163 S Washington St Remsen IA 51050

AHLF, GENE DELANE, mfg. co. advt. and sales promotion ofcl.; b. Muscatine, Iowa, Apr. 4, 1947; s. Herman Henry and Sylvia Edna (Blake) A.; B.B.A., U. Iowa, 1973; children—Cara, Justin. With Bandag Inc., Muscatine, 1973—, now mgr. promotion services. Served with USAF, 1966-70. Mem. Meeting Planners Internat., Soc. Corp. Meeting Planners, Nat. Tire Dealers Assn. (young exec. group). Home: 6803 Island Ct Muscatine IA 52761 Office: Bandag Center Muscatine IA 52761

AHLUWALLA, MUNESHWAR SINGH, pathologist; b. Delhi, India, Aug. 5, 1935; s. Rajeshwar and Koshalya Devi (Ahluwalia) Singh; student Hindu Coll., U. Delhi (India), 1951-53; M.B., B.S., Med. Coll., Punjab U., 1958; m. Tarvinder Rekhi, June 13, 1965; children—Arlina, Jasbina, Balrina. Intern, V. J. Hosp., Amritsar also Irwin Hosp., New Delhi, India, 1958-59; instr. microbiology Lady Hardinge Med. Coll., New Delhi, 1959-60; resident pathology All India Inst. Med. Scis., New Delhi, 1960-63; resident, fellowship in hematology Cook County Hosp. also Hektoen Inst. for Med. Research, Chgo., 1963-64; postdoctoral officership in pathology All India Inst. Med. Sci., New Delhi, 1964-66; sr. pathologist Cook County Hosp., Chgo., 1966-70; research asso. in pathology Hektoen Inst. Med. Research, Chgo., 1967-70; asst. prof. pathology Chgo. Med. Sch., 1967-73; clin. asso. prof. pathology U. Ill., Abraham Lincoln Sch. Medicine, Chgo., 1976-81; mem. teaching faculty Cook County Grad. Sch. Medicine, Chgo., 1966-70; asso. prof. pathology Loyola U. Med. Center, Maywood, Ill., 1981—; staff pathologist MacNeal Meml. Hosp., Berwyn, Ill., 1970-79; staff pathologist Morris (Ill.) Hosp., 1974-79; coroner's physician Grundy County, Ill., 1974-79, Pres., Am. Cancer Soc., Berwyn, Ill., 1976-79; dir. labs. Glendale Heights (Ill.) Community Hosp., 1979-80; chief clin. pathology sect. VA Hines (Ill.) Hosp., 1980—; clin. pathologist Foster McGaw Hosp., Maywood, 1981—. Fellow Coll. Am. Pathologists, Am. Soc. Clin. Pathologists, Internat. Coll. Surgeons, Inst. Medicine of Chgo.; mem. Internat. Acad. Pathology, Am. Fedn. Clin. Research, Chgo. Pathol. Soc., Ill. Soc. Anatomic Pathologists, Ill. Soc. Cytology, Am. Assn. Blood Banks, Indian Assn. Pathologists, Indian Med. Assn., South Delhi, Chgo. med. socs., AMA, Ill. State Med. Soc., Chgo. Found. Med. Care. Mason (Shriner). Home: 217 Indian Trail Oakbrook IL 60521 Office: 113 VA Hines Hosp Hines IL 60141

AHMAD, ALTAF, beverage co. exec.; b. Jullundur, India, Oct. 1, 1942; came to U.S., 1972, permanent resident, 1978; s. Aziz and Noor (Bibi) A.; student Sadiq Egerton Coll. (Pakistan), 1957-60; Banking Dip., Agrl. Devel. Bank of Pakistan, 1961-62; B.A., U. Sind (Pakistan), 1964; M.B.A., U. Karachi (Pakistan), 1967; M.B.A. in Acctg., Eastern N.Mex. U., 1973; M.S. in Indsl. Engring. and Econs., Iowa State U., 1976; m. Nusrat Amin, Oct. 31, 1969; children—Saima, Ambreen, Usman. Accountant, Agrl. Devel. Bank of Pakistan, Karachi, 1961-65; fin. analyst Investment Corp. of Pakistan, Karachi, 1967-74; research asst. Iowa State U., Ames., 1974-76; asst. prof. bus. and acctg. Mt. Marty Coll., Yankton, S.D., 1976-78; controller Hart Beverage Co., Inc., South Sioux City, Nebr., 1978—; fin. cons., auditor gen. Image Advt. Agy., Inc., South Sioux City, 1978—, Mitchell-Dennis, Inc., Sioux City, 1979—, Bridgeport Tooling, Sioux City, 1978—, Deltaire, 1980—. Mem. Am. Inst. Indsl. Engrs., Nat. Assn. Accountants, Assn. M.B.A. Execs. Home: 2720 Willow St Sioux City IA 51106 Office: 400 W Colonial Dr South Sioux City NE 68776

AHMAD, SALAHUDDIN, cardiologist, internist; b. Banaras, India, Aug. 1, 1934; s. Mohammad and Amina Athar; came to U.S., 1971, naturalized, 1977; student Dacca U., 1949-51, Dacca (East Pakistan) Med. Coll., 1951-55, King Edward Med. Coll., Lahore, Pakistan, 1955-58; M.B.B.S., U. Punjab (Pakistan), 1958; m. Shahla Sabir, Nov. 26, 1966; children—Akbar Ahmad, Sarah, Ali. Fellow cardiology Jewish Hosp., Washington U. Med. Sch., St. Louis, 1975-77; family practice medicine, Banaras, India, 1958-59; house physician medicine Dacca (East Pakistan) Med. Coll. Hosp., 1959-61; sr. house physician in medicine No. Ireland Hosps. Authority, Belfast, 1961-63, registrar in medicine, 1963-65; physician Beida Hosp., Ministry Health, Libya, 1965-71; rotating intern Mercy Hosp., Buffalo, 1971-72; sr. resident medicine Jamaica (N.Y.) Hosp., 1972-73, chief resident, 1973-74, fellow cardiology, 1974-75; fellow cardiology Jewish Hosp./Washington U. Med. Sch., St. Louis, 1975-77; instr. dept. internal medicine St. Louis U. Med. Sch., 1977—; practice medicine specializing in cardiology and internal medicine, St. Louis, 1977—. Diplomate Am. Bd. Internal Medicine and Cardiovascular Diseases. Fellow Am. Coll. Cardiology; mem. AMA, Ill. State Med. Soc., Madison County Med. Soc. Home: 1939 Windmoor Pl Saint Louis MO 63131 Office: 2120 Madison Ave Suite 404 Granite City IL 62040 also 2105 Vandalia Collinsville IL 62234

AHMED, KHALIL, scientist, educator; b. Lahore, Pakistan, Nov. 30, 1934; s. Abdul and Ghulam (Sughra) Haq; came to U.S., 1960, naturalized, 1965; B.S. with honors, Panjab U., Pakistan, 1954, M.S. with honors, 1955; Ph.D., McGill U., Montreal, Can., 1960; m. Ritva Helena Veikkamo, June 27, 1969; children—Karim, Rehana. Research asso. Wistar Inst., Phila., 1960-63; asst. prof. metabolic research Chgo. Med. Sch., 1963-67; mem. sr. staff Nat. Cancer Inst., Balt., 1967-71; research biochemist, chief toxicology research lab. VA Med. Center, Mpls., 1971—, research career scientist, 1978—; asso. prof. lab. medicine and pathology, U. Minn., Mpls., 1973-77, prof., 1977—; vis. scientist lab. of physiology, Helsinki, Finland, 1962; vis. lectr. Chgo. Med. Sch., 1968-69; mem. pathology B study sect. NIH, 1978-81. Named Outstanding Citizen, Met. Chgo. Citizenship Council, 1966. Mem. Am. Soc. of Pharmacology and Exptl. Therapeutics, AAAS, Am. Soc. of Biol. Chemists, Endocrine Soc., Sigma Xi. Mem. bd. consultants Jour. Urology; contbr. articles to profl. jours. Home: 2011 James Ave S Minneapolis MN 55405 Office: Mpls VA Med Center 54th St and 48th Ave S Minneapolis MN 55417

AHNER, ALFRED FREDRICK, nat. guard officer; b. Huntington, Ind., Nov. 12, 1921; s. Ray C. and Kathryn (Stern) A.; B.A., Ind. Central U., 1947; M.S., Butler U., 1951; m. Betty Young, May 3, 1944; children—Mark, Michael. Joined Army N.G., 1947, advanced through grades to maj. gen., 1974; adj. gen. Ind. Army N.G., Indpls., 1960, 72—. Chmn., Easter Seals, Ind., 1975-76. Served with U.S. Army, World War II; ETO. Mem. N.G. Assn. Ind. (pres. 1965-66), Adjs. Gen. Assn. U.S. (pres. 1979—), Am. Legion. Home: 3719 Lorrain Rd Indianapolis IN 46220 Office: Adjutant Gen's Office PO Drawer AO Indianapolis IN 46241

AHONEN, CLIFFORD JOHN, marketing cons.; b. Ironwood, Mich., Mar. 1, 1934; s. Telfield John and Helen Tina (Kuula) A.; B.B.A., U. Wis., 1959; M.B.A., Roosevelt U., 1963; postgrad. U. Chgo., 1964-65; Ph.D., Calif. Western U., 1980; m. Patricia Ann Doyle, Aug. 20, 1961; children—Helen, Allan, Michael, Mark. Sales engr. Richards-Wilcox Mfg. Co., Aurora, Ill., 1959-61; marketing specialist Link-Belt Co., Chgo., 1961-64; dir. long range planning Joy Mfg. Co., Michigan City, Ind., 1964-69; v.p. mktg. strategy Starcraft Co., Goshen, Ind., 1969-72; exec. v.p. Marketing Cons., Inc., Elkhart, Ind., 1972—, also dir.; faculty Goshen (Ind.) Coll., 1971-74, Southwestern Mich. Coll., Dowagiac, 1974—, Ind. U., 1975—. Chmn. Cherokee dist. Boy Scouts Am., 1975-77. Served with U.S. Army, 1955-57. Mem. Am. Mktg. Assn. (chpt. pres. 1973), Am. Statis. Assn. Republican. Roman Catholic. Club: Sales and Advt. Home: 250 S Main St Goshen IN 46526 Office: 339 Communicana Bldg Elkhart IN 46514

AHRENHOLZ, STEVEN HENRY, indsl. hygienist; b. Milw., May 6, 1954; s. Henry Fredrick and Regina Maria (Langhoff) A.; B.S. summa cum laude in Biology, U. Wis., Stevens Point, 1976; M.S. summa cum laude in Environ. Health, U. Minn., 1978. Commd. ensign USPHS, 1978, advanced to lt. (j.g.), 1979; trainee Nat. Inst. Occupational Safety and Health, Cin., 1978, indsl. hygienist, 1979—; field service instr. Kettering Lab., U. Cin. Coll. Medicine, 1978-79. Mem. Am. Indsl. Hygiene Assn., Am. Conf. Govtl. Indsl. Hygienists, Am. Public Health Assn., Commd. Officers Assn., Nat. Environ. Health Assn., Nat. Audubon Soc., U. Minn. Alumni Assn., Phi Kappa Phi. Lutheran. Home: 2478 Queen City Ave Cincinnati OH 45238 Office: Nat Inst Occupational Safety and Health 4676 Columbia Pkwy Cincinnati OH 45226

AICHER, SHERYL JEAN, occupational therapist; b. Sheboygan, Wis., Sept. 2, 1952; d. Milton John and Carmelita Mae Emma (Maas) Schultz; B.S., Mount Mary Coll., Milw., 1974; m. Fred John Aicher, Aug. 6, 1977. Staff occupational therapist Notre Dame Health Care Center, Elm Grove, Wis., 1975-76; staff occupational therapist Cedar Lake Home, W. Bend, Wis., 1976—, coordinator therapies, 1980—; condr. workshops, 1979—. Mem. Am. Occupational Therapy Assn., Nat. Council Therapy and Rehab. through Horticulture, Wis. Occupational Therapy Assn. Roman Catholic. Home: 1008 Sunset Dr West Bend WI 53095 Office: Cedar Lake Home 5595 Hwy Z West Bend WI 53095

AICHNER, HARRY CLIFFORD, psychologist; b. Erie, Pa., Feb. 19, 1931; s. Harry Clifford and Hattie Angela (Heffinger) A.; A.B., Westminster (Pa.) Coll., 1952; M.S., Pa. State U., 1955. Intern, VA Hosp., Roanoke, Va., 1953-54; psychologist various community mental health facilities, Ohio, 1958—; pvt. practice psychology Springfield, Ohio, 1965-67, Ashtabula, Ohio, 1967-76, Cleve., 1976—; clinic dir., chief psychologist Ohio Mental Health Clinics, 1964-74. Served with AUS, 1956-58. Fellow Internat. Acad. Forensic Psychology; mem. Am., Ohio, Cleve. psychol. assns., AAAS, Ohio Mental Health Forum, Am. Psychology-Law Soc., Phi Kappa Tau. Address: PO Box 129 Ashtabula OH 44004

AIKEN, ROGER GEORGE, energy research analyst; b. Feilding, N.Z., Jan. 12, 1933; s. Henry George and Muriel Christine; came to U.S., 1973; B.Sc., U. Canterbury, Christchurch, N.Z., 1954, B.E. with honours, 1956, M.E. with distinction, 1958; postgrad. in mech. engring., U. Minn., 1973—; m. Susan Graham Hamilton, July 14, 1962; children—Andrew Graham, David George. Energy systems analyst, physics and engring. labs., Dept. Sci. and Indsl. Research, Lower Hutt, N.Z., 1958-59, Collier and Beale Ltd., Wellington, N.Z., 1959-61, Hirst Research Centre, Brit. Gen. Electric Co., Wembley, England, 1961-65, Bell No. Research, Ottawa, Ont., Can., 1965-67, transmission dept. N.Z. Post Office, Wellington, 1968, Communications Research Centre, Canadian Fed. Dept. Communications, Ottawa, Ont., 1968-73; research fellow Center for Studies of Phys. Environment, Inst. Tech., U. Minn., Mpls., 1974-76; energy research analyst research div. Minn. Energy Agy., St. Paul, 1976-78; research fellow Underground Space Center, U. Minn., Mpls., 1978-79, BioEnergy Coordinating Office, 1980; prin. energy systems analyst Synergistic Design and Engring., 1981—. Coordinator, Future Lifestyle Planners Program, U. Minn. YMCA, 1978-80. Mem. Instn. Elec. Engrs. (U.K.), IEEE, Biomass Energy Inst. (Can.), AIAA, Internat. Solar Energy Soc., Minn. Solar Energy Assn. (chmn. policy com. 1978-79), Twin Cities Energy Engrs., Phi Kappa Phi. Presbyterian. Clubs: U. Minn., YMCA. Contbr. articles to profl. jours. and meetings. Home: 1589 Hollywood Ct Saint Paul MN 55108 Office: 1900 Hennepin Ave Minneapolis MN 55403

AIKEN, THOMAS DAVID, food co. exec.; b. Texas City, Tex., Dec. 29, 1953; s. Robert Lawrence and Helen Lee (Beard) A.; B.S., U. Ill., 1976, M.S., 1977; student Moscow State U., 1974, Leningrad State U., 1974. Nutritionist, Animal Nutrition, Inc., Belleville, Ill., 1978-79; asst. mgr. mktg. services Ralston Purina Co., St. Louis, 1979-80, tech. sales rep. for indsl. sales protein div., 1980—. Mem. Inst. Food Technologists. Home: 3864F Provence Saint Louis MO 63125 Office: Checkerboard Sq Saint Louis MO 63188

AILSHIE, ROGER HOWARD, hydraulics mfg. co. exec.; b. Bucklin, Kans., Oct. 25, 1940; s. Howard Edmond and Lois Irene (Speer) A.; B.S., Kans. State U., 1965; A.B.S., Hutchinson Jr. Coll., 1960; m. Jean Florence Servitto, Aug. 16, 1974; children—Gloria, Ronald, Daniel, Roger Allen, Cindy, Kevin. Design engr. Cessna Fluid Power Div., Hutchinson, Kans., 1965-67; successively project engr., mgr. sales and engring., dir. engring. Cross Mfg., Inc., Lewis, Kans., 1967-74; mgr. engring. Power Packer div. Applied Power, Inc., New Berlin, Wis., 1974-76; account sales mgr. Sundstrand Hydro-Transmission Div., Ames, Iowa, 1976-79; successively sales and engring. mgr., v.p. and gen. mgr. Power Packer div. Applied Power, Inc., New Berlin, 1979—; mem. Vocat. Drafting Adv. Bd.; instr. hydraulics seminars. Mem. Lewis City Council, 1970-74; pres., bd. dirs. Lewis Devel., Inc., 1973-74; Peewee baseball coach, 1972-73. Mem. Am. Soc. Agrl. Engring., Soc. Automotive Engrs. Republican. Club: Lewis Lions (pres. 1971). Inventor in field. Home: 680 Forest Grove Ln Brookfield WI 53005 Office: 16901 W Glendale Dr New Berlin WI 53151

AINLEY, JOELYN KAY, tech. inst. adminstr.; b. Monticello, Iowa, Mar. 28, 1947; d. Joseph Leo and Evelyn Mary (Hyde) Staskal; B.S., U. No. Iowa, 1969; M.S. (Univ. grantee), Iowa State U., 1976; m. Ronald Lee Ainley, Aug. 9, 1969; 1 son, Brian David. Acct., pvt. C.P.A. firm, Waterloo, Iowa, 1969-70; tchr. Dubuque (Iowa) Community Schs., 1970-71; instr. N.E. Iowa Tech. Inst., Dubuque, 1971-74, dept. chmn., 1974-80, dir. student services, 1980—. Chmn., Dubuque Scholastic Achievement, Bus. Edn. Industry, 1977-79. Recipient Office Edn. Appreciation cert., 1974; Outstanding Educator of Am. Award, 1974-75. Mem. Am. Vocat. Assn., Iowa Vocat. Assn., Iowa Community Coll. Student Services Assn., Phi Kappa Phi. Home: 1075 Valentine Dr Dubuque IA 52001 Office: NE Iowa Tech Inst Peosta IA 52068

AINSWORTH, BARBARA ARLENE, ednl. services cons., writer; b. Buffalo, N.Y., Aug. 8, 1935; d. Stanley R. and Barbara M. (Price) Fund; B.A., U. Md., 1962, Ed.M., 1967, Ph.D., 1974; m. Peter D. Ainsworth, May 11, 1962; (dec. 1975); children—Peter David II, John, Mary; m. 2d, David H. Trautman, Dec. 29, 1978. Tchr. elem. public schs. Sch. Dist. 50, Washington, Ill., 1960-61; tchr. Prince George's County (Md.) Public Schs., 1962-74, study skills specialist, 1970-72; instr. off-campus div. Coll. Edn., American U., Washington, 1973; grad. asst. Coll. Edn., U. Md., College Park, 1973-74; project editor, writer and cons. Educational Challenges, Inc., Alexandria, Va., 1972—; project coordinator ednl. programs for sr. citizens Iowa Lakes Community Coll., Estherville, Iowa, 1975, instr. sociology, 1975; asst. prof. geography Buena Vista Coll., Storm Lake, Iowa, 1975-76, dir. student teaching, 1975-76; ednl. servies cons. Arrowhead Area Edn. Agy. 5, Fort Dodge, Iowa, 1976-78; free-lance cons. and edn. writer, 1978—; instr. Marshalltown (Iowa) Community Coll., 1978—. Mem. Spirit Lake (Iowa) Bicentennial Com., 1975. Mem. Assn. for Supervision and Curriculum Devel., Coll. and Univ. Faculty Assn., Nat. Council Social Studies, Iowa Council Social Studies, Nat. Assn. for Core Curriculum, Nat. Council Geog. Edn., Iowa Council Tchrs. English, Iowa Assn. for Supervision and Curriculum Devel., AAUW, Phi Delta Kappa (historian Iowa chpt. 1977-78). Democrat. Unitarian. Author: Macmillan Social Studies Series, 1978; Education Through Travel, 1979; Handbook of Ideas for Curriculum Improvement, 1981; Reflections of Yesterday, 1981 producer cassette learning packages, film strips, 1975-81; editor Basic Ideas, 1980-82. Home: 3102 W Lincoln Way Marshalltown IA 50158 Office: Area Edn Agy 6 210 S 12th St Marshalltown IA 50158

AIPPERSPACH, JAMES DANIEL, telephone co. exec.; b. Eureka, S.D., Apr. 4, 1948; s. Daniel F. and Esther (Unruh) A.; B.S. in Indsl. Engring., N.D. State U., Fargo, 1970; Disting. Grad., U.S. Navy Officer Candidate Sch., 1971; m. Roselyn Kay Schaan, Aug. 14, 1971. With Northwestern Bell Telephone Co., 1974—, mgr. customer services, Wahpeton, N.D., 1977-78, dist. mgr. residence/bus., Fargo, 1978—. Bd. dirs. Head of the Red United Way, 1978; div. chmn. United Way Cass Clay, Fargo. Served with USNR, 1971-74. Mem. Am. Inst. Indsl. Engrs., Fargo Downtown Bus. Assn. (dir.), Fargo C. of C. (ex officio dir., pres. Ambassadors), Blue Key. Catholic. Clubs: Kiwanis, Rotary. Office: 105 N 5th St Fargo ND 58102

AKER, FRANK, dentist, naval officer; b. South Bend, Ind., Feb. 17, 1946; s. Frank and Golda Mae (Hudson) A.; B.A., Ind. U., 1970, M.A., 1971; D.M.D., U. Louisville, 1975; M.A. in Hosp. Adminstrn., Webster Coll., 1981. Commd. ensign U.S. Navy, 1975, advanced through grades to lt. comdr., 1979; resident Naval Regional Med. Center, Gt. Lakes, Ill., 1975-76; dental officer Naval Mobile Constrn. Bn. 40, Port Hueneme, Calif., 1976-79; chief facilities support Naval Dental Research Inst., Great Lakes, Ill., 1979—. Fellow Acad. Gen. Dentistry; mem. Am. Dental Assn., Ky. Dental Assn., Louisville Dental Soc., Gt. Lakes Dental Soc., Acad. Gen. Dentistry, Assn. Mil. Surgeons U.S., Am. Security Council, U.S. Naval Inst., Am. Def. Preparedness Assn., Chgo. Council Fgn. Relations, Marine Corps Assn., Assn. U.S. Army, Air Force Assn., U.S. Armor Assn., Delta Sigma Delta, Beta Delta, Omicron Delta Kappa, Kappa Sigma. Ky. Col. Author: Hammer of God: 1973 Yom Kippur War, 1977; The Inflammatory Reaction, 1980. Home: 3377A Beacon St North Chicago IL 60064

AKERLUND, OSCAR OLE, computer co. exec.; b. Chgo., Jan. 13, 1928; s. Carl Oscar and Anne (Jensen) A.; E.E., Ill. Inst. Tech., 1951; B.S., U. Minn., 1971; m. Joyce Merry, Nov. 3, 1951; 1 son, Douglas Paul. Chief engr. Information Systems, Inc., Skokie, Ill., 1948-60; v.p., gen. mgr. Creative Electronics, Charlotte, Mich., 1960-61; with Control Data Corp., Bloomington, Minn., 1962—, v.p. 1977—. Served with U.S. Army, 1946-47. Mem. Am. Soc. for Quality Control, Instrument Soc. Am. (sr.). Home: 5201 Buchanan St NE Minneapolis MN 55421 Office: Control Data Corp 8100 34th Ave S Minneapolis MN 55440

AKERS, ARTHUR, educator; b. Smethwick, Staffordshire, Eng., Mar. 24, 1927; came to U.S., 1975, naturalized, 1981; s. Arthur and Violet May (Davis) A.; B.Sc., U. London, 1953, Ph.D., 1969; M.Sc., Cranfield Inst. Tech., 1955; m. Marcia Lee Pratt, Feb. 25, 1978; children—Andrew, Judith. Sect. leader aerodynamics Armstrong Whitworth, Coventry, Eng., 1955-59; group leader guided weapon design Bristol Aircraft (U.K.), 1959-60; sr. lectr. in aero. engring. Bath (Eng.) U., 1960-64; prin. lectr. fluid mechanics Royal Naval Coll., Greenwich, Eng., 1965-68; prin. lectr. in mech. engring. Ministry of Def., U.K. Royal Mil. Coll. Sci., Shrivenham, 1968-75; vis. prof. U. Va., Charlottesville, 1973-74; asso. prof. engring. sci. and mech. Iowa State U., 1975—; cons. in field. Served with British Army, 1944-48. Blair fellow, 1973-74; registered profl. engr., Iowa; chartered engr., U.K. Fellow Royal Aeronaut. Soc., ASME, Soc. Engring. Sci., Soc. Exptl. Stress Analysis, Soc. Am. Mil. Engrs., Sigma Xi. Patentee coal pyrite separation device; author: Aerodynamics and Hydrodynamics, 1973. Home: 3010 Kellogg Ave Ames IA 50010 Office: 206 ERI Iowa State Univ Ames IA 50011

AKINS, DAVID WAYNE, funeral service exec.; b. Somerville, N.J., Oct. 20, 1955; s. Willie Lee and Allean (Black) A.; B.S. in Criminal Justice, Trenton State Coll., 1976; M.A., U. Detroit, 1979; mortuary sci. cert. Wayne State U., 1981. Community adv. Trenton (N.J.) State Coll., 1974-76; investigator Office of Public Defender, New Brunswick, N.J., 1977; residence hall dir. U. Detroit, 1977-78, residence area coordinator, 1978-79; mortician Barksdale Funeral Homes, Detroit, 1979—. Participant, Community Devel. Workshop, Detroit, 1978; trustee Hartford Meml. Bapt. Ch. Recipient Minority Exec. Council Outstanding Service award, 1976; W.E.B. Dubois award, 1977. Mem. Am. Personnel and Guidance Assn., Am. Coll. Personnel Assn. (adv. council of com. multi-cultural affairs), Assn. Non-White Concerns, Public Offenders Assn. Baptist. Club: Masons. Address: 1120 E State Fair Detroit MI 48203

AKINS, GEORGE TIMOTHY, computer cons. co. exec.; b. Elmhurst, Ill., May 23, 1946; s. Charles Franklin Leonard and Dorothy Irene (Schultz) Leonard; B.S. in Acctg., No. Ill. U., 1975; m. Christine Michelle Wilson, Sept. 11, 1968; children—Jessica Paige, Amanda Leigh. Archtl. draftsman Pence-Schwartz & Assos., Architects, Elmhurst, 1969-73, Arthur G. Jakl, Architect,

Bloomingdale, Ill., 1974; dir. acctg. services Community Unit Sch. Dist. 303, St. Charles, Ill., 1976-78; v.p., sec., treas. Bus. Applications Group, Inc., West Chicago, Ill., 1978—, also dir. Served with USMC, 1964-68. Mem. Beta Gamma Sigma, Phi Kappa Phi. Republican. Lutheran. Club: Nat. Exchange. Home: 324 Fairview Ave West Chicago IL 60185

AKINS, WILLIAM JOHN, security and investigation co. exec.; b. Rockford, Ill., Apr. 26, 1947; s. Donald Leroy and Marion Elizabeth (Drohan) A.; grad. Rock Valley Jr. Coll., Rockford, 1968; m. Lynn Ann Black, May 25, 1973; children—Erin Elizabeth, Kelly Jane. Asst. mgr. Karl Schoening & Sons, Rockford, 1968-70; controller Colonial Builders, Rockford, 1970-71, Fairview Builders, Rockford, 1971; spl. projects cons. Pinkerton's, Inc., Oak Park, Ill., 1971-81; stockholder, dir. public relations and bus. devel. Argus Agy. Inc., Chgo., 1981—; pres. Midwest Indsl. Emergency Planning Group; dir. Unit Systems, Addison, Ill. Served with USAR, 1966-72. Cert. protection profl. Mem. Am. Asso. Bar Assn., Am. Soc. Indsl. Security (editor newsletter 1979-80), Am. Fedn. Police, Ill. Security Conf. Republican. Roman Catholic. Home: 4053 Prairie Schiller Park IL 60176 Office: Argus Agy Inc 25 E Washington Suite 823 Chicago IL 60602

ALANI, MARY KATCHICK, obstetrician, gynecologist; b. Baghdad, Iraq; d. Katchick and Victoria (Sarafian) Mikaelian; M.D., Baghdad U., 1961; m. Hashim M. Alani, Nov. 24, 1961; children—Vickie, Suzanne, Analied. Resident in obstetrics and gynecology St. Luke's Hosp., Bradford, Eng., also Hutzel Hosp., Detroit, 1966-70; fellow in gynecol. endocrinology and infertility William Beaumont Hosp., Royal Oak, Mich., 1972-73; practice medicine specializing in gynecology, obstetrics and infertility, Southfield, Mich., 1974—. Felllow Am. Coll. Obstetrics and Gynecology; mem. Royal Coll. Obstetrics and Gynecology (Eng.), Infertility Soc. Home: 1998 Meadow Ct Bloomfield Hills MI 48013 Office: 20180 Twelve Mile Rd Southfield MI 48076

ALBAN, ROGER CHARLES, constrn. equipment distbn. co. exec.; b. Columbus, Ohio, Aug. 3, 1948; s. Charles Ellis and Alice Jacqueline (Hosfeld) A.; student public schs.; m. 2d, Rebecca Lynn Gallicchio, Aug. 12, 1978; 1 son, Roger, II; 1 dau. by previous marriage, Allison Ann. With Alban Equipment Co., Columbus, 1963—, sales mgr., 1972-75, gen. mgr., 1975—, treas., 1978—, v.p., 1980—. Mem. Grandview Heights Bd. Edn., Columbus, 1978—, pres., 1979, legis. liaison, 1978-79; mem. Met. Ednl. Council. Mem. Associated Equipment Distbrs. (lt. dir. region 6, 1980), Am. Rental Assn., Builders Exchange Central Ohio, Am. Mgmt. Assn., Nat. Right To Work Com., Nat. Fedn. Ind. Bus., Am. Mensa Ltd. (chpt. exec. com. 1979-80). Roman Catholic. Clubs: Sertoma, Downtown Columbus. Home: 1358 Wyandotte Rd Columbus OH 43212 Office: 1825 McKinley Ave Columbus OH 43222

ALBANESE, BUD ROSARIO, editor, pub.; b. Chgo., Nov. 5, 1905; s. Michael and Mary Rachel (Adelizzi) A.; student Chgo. public schs.; m. Anne Ellen Dailey, July 23, 1940; children—Patrick, Mary Ann, Bud Rosario, Michelle Charlene, Don M. Founder, editor North Loop News, Chgo., 1930—; co-founder, 1st editor Civil Service News (Chgo.). Mem. Citizens Save Our Schools Com. Recipient Community Service Citation Chgo. City Council, Ill. Gen. Assembly, Greater N. Michigan Ave. Assn., 3d prize Ill. Press Assn., 1962. Mem. Asso. Community Newspapers Chgo. (past pres.), Chgo. Press Club, Press Vets. Assn. Republican. Roman Catholic. Clubs: Eagles (past pres.), Moose. Office: 800 N Clark St Chicago IL 60610

AL-BEIRUTI, MUHAMMAD SAID, pathologist; b. Damascus, Syria, 1947; came to U.S., 1973; M.D., Damascus U., 1973; m. Basima Dabbas, Nov. 18, 1975; children—Amru, Eiyass. Intern, Marymount Hosp., Cleve., 1973-74; resident in pathology St. Alexis Hosp., Cleve., 1974-78; fellow in hematopathology Henry Ford Hosp., Detroit, 1978-79; pathologist Lapeer County Gen. Hosp., Lapeer, Mich., 1979—. Diplomate Am. Bd. Pathology. Fellow Coll. Am. Pathologists. Office: 1375 N Main St Lapeer MI 48446

ALBERA, VICTOR HAROLD, anesthesiologist; b. Los Angeles, Aug. 1, 1931; s. Elmer and Eaula (Dietrich) A.; student U. Oreg., 1949-50, Denver U., 1950-52; M.D., U. Colo., 1956; m. Nellie Balocca, June 1955; children—Krista, Steven, Teresa, Cynthia, Sylvia, Lisa Jo; m. 2d, Kay Craun, Oct. 2, 1965; 1 adopted dau., Katherine. Intern, Gen. Hosp. Riverside County, Arlington, Calif., 1956-57; gen. practice medicine, Gallup, N.Mex., 1959-65, St. Louis, 1975—; resident anesthesia U. Colo. Med. Center, Denver, 1965-66, U. Mo., Columbia, 1966-68; sr. anesthesiologist Jewish Hosp., St. Louis, 1968-75, Faith West Hosp., 1975—; emergency room physician St. Francis Hosp., Washington, Mo., 1976—; formerly pvt. practice family medicine, St. Clair, Mo., now pvt. practice, Gerald, Mo.; med. examiner Coroner's Office, Franklin County, Mo.; asso. prof. anesthesia Washington U., St. Louis; peer rev. physician Mo. Atty. Gen.'s Office. Mem. com. on security 7 Pines Improvement Assn.; officer Civil Def. St. Louis County Police, 1973-76. Served to capt. M.C., USAR, 1957-59. Fellow Am. Coll. Anesthesiologists, Am. Acad. Family Practioners; mem. Am., Mo., St. Louis County socs. anesthesiologists, Am., Mo. med. assns., St. Louis County Med. Soc. Royal Soc. Medicine (affiliate). Home: Route 2 Box 236 Saint Clair MO 63077

ALBERDING, CHARLES HOWARD, petroleum, hotel exec.; b. Cleyville, N.Y., Mar. 5, 1901; s. Charles and Doris (Roberts) A.; E.E., Cornell U., 1923; m. Bethine Wolverton, May 2, 1930; children—Beth Ann, Mary Katherine, Melissa Linda, Lab. asst., draftsman, operator Producers & Refiners Corp., Parco, Wyo., 1923-25; engr., cracking plant supt. Imperial Refineries, Ardmore Okla., also Eldorado, Ark., 1925-27; head fgn. operating dept. Universal Oil Products Co., London, Eng., Ploesti, Roumania, Rangoon, Burma, Venice, Italy, 1927-33, head operating, service depts., Chgo. hdqrs., 1933-42; pres., dir. Paradise Inn, Inc., Jokake Inn, Inc., Vinoy Park Hotel Co., Holiday Hotel Corp., Alsonett Hotels, Sabine Irrigation Co., Sabine Canal Co., Tides Hotel Corp., Harmony Oil Corp., London Square Corp., Petroleum Spltys., Lincoln Lodge Corp., Peabody Hotel Corp., Memphis, Hermitage Hotel Co., Nashville, Royal Palms Inn, Inc., Torrey Pines Inn, La Jolla, Calif., Charleston First Corp. Petroleum cons. WPB, 1942-43; dist. dir. petroleum refining Petroleum Adminstrn. for War, 1943-45. Mem. Scorpion. Republican. Conglist. Clubs: Valley (Phoenix); Kenilworth, Cornell (Chgo.); Sunset Country, Bath (St. Petersburg, Fla.); Tides Country (pres., dir.). Home: 99 Tudor Pl Kenilworth IL 60043 Office: 9 E Huron Chicago IL 60611

ALBERS, LOIS HELEN, nurse; b. Peotone, Ill., Oct. 30, 1926; d. Carl John and Florence Magdalene (Pries) Schneeweis; R.N., St. Luke's Hosp., 1948; B.S., St. Francis Coll., 1978; m. John Albers, Feb. 14, 1948; children—Steven John, Linda Susan. With Westlake Community Hosp., Melrose Park, Ill., 1948—, dir. nursing services, 1968-76, adminstrv. coordinator for health programming services, 1976—. Mem. Westlake Community Hosp. Women's Guild, Valparaiso U. Women's Guild, Presbyn.-St. Luke's Alumni Assn. Republican. Lutheran. Home: 465 Fairview Ave Elmhurst IL 60126 Office: 1225 Superior St Melrose Park IL 60160

ALBERTS, BARBARA, direct mktg. co. ofcl.; b. Chgo., Dec. 8, 1928; d. Joseph and Mary (Perri) Gironda; student Roosevelt U., 1969-70; m. Joseph L. Alberts, Sept. 1, 1951; 1 dau., Patricia Mary. Various retail positions, Chgo., 1942-46; with Nat. Research Bur., Chgo., 1946-51, Globe Glass Mfg. Co., Chgo., 1961-65, Nat. Communications Corp., Chgo., 1965-66; with Stone & Adler, Inc., Chgo., 1966—, office mgr., asst. to gen. mgr., 1979—. Office: 150 N Wacker Dr Chicago IL 60606

ALBERTS, JOHN HARRY, JR., ins. broker; b. Chgo., Apr. 21, 1950; s. John H. and Monette T. A.; B.A., Knox Coll., 1972; m. Judith C. Zabinski, Sept. 10, 1972; 1 dau., Kathryn Ruth. With William H. Thompson & Co., Chgo., 1972—, sec., treas., 1976—. Vice pres. Crestwood (Ill.) Pub. Library Dist., 1976-78. C.P.C.U. Mem. Chgo. Bd. Underwriters (chmn. personnel lines com. 1977, dir., chmn. comml. lines com. 1978, 79, regional v.p. 1979—, chmn. task force on agts. assistance 1979-80, chmn. steering com. 1979—), Independent Ins. Agents of Ill. (regional v.p. 1979—), Independent Ins Agents Am., ACLU.

ALBERTS, MARION EDWARD, physician; b. Hastings, Nebr., Mar. 14, 1923; s. Eddie and Mary Margaret (Hilbers) A.; B.A., U. Neb., 1944, M.D., 1948; m. Jeannette McDaniel, Dec. 25, 1944; children—Kathryn, Brian, Deborah, Timothy. Intern, Iowa Methodist Hosp., Des Moines, 1948-49; resident in pediatrics Raymond Blank Hosp. Children, Des Moines, 1949-50, 52-53; practice medicine specializing in pediatrics, Des Moines, 1953—; chief pediatrics Mercy Hosp., 1958-78; mem. med. staff Iowa Luth. Hosp., Iowa Meth. Hosp., Broadlawns Polk County Hosp.; instr. clin. pediatrics Coll. Osteo. Medicine and Surgery, 1970—. Served to comdr. USNR, 1943-45, 50-52. Licenciate, Am. Bd. Pediatrics. Fellow Am. Acad. Pediatrics, Internat. Coll. Pediatrics; mem. AMA, Iowa Med. Soc. (sci. editor jour.), Des Moines C. of C. Republican. Presbyterian (elder). Club: Masons. Contbr. articles to profl. jours. Home: 5104 Ashworth Rd West Des Moines IA 50265 Office: 1071 5th Ave Des Moines IA 50314

ALBIN, EDGAR A., artist, educator; b. Columbus, Kans., Dec. 17, 1908; s. Elmer A. and LaVanche (Briggs) A.; B.A., U. Tulsa, 1936; M.A., State U. Iowa, 1946; m. Mildred Mary A.; children—Dick, Judy Albin Lieser. Tchr., Tulsa Public Schs., 1931-39; asso. prof. art U. Tulsa, 1939-47; prof. art U. Ark., 1947-62, chmn. humanities, 1957-62; head art dept., prof. S.W. Mo. State U., Springfield, 1963-74, prof. emeritus, 1974—. Bd. dirs. Springfield Arts Council, 1977-78; mem. adv. bd. Springfield Civic Ballet; mem. acquisitions com. Springfield Art Mus., 1977-81; vis. prof. art Stetson U., 1950-52. Fulbright grantee, India, 1954-55. Mem. AAUP, S.W. Mo. Assn. Architects, Delta Phi Delta, Kappa Delta Pi, Theta Alpha Phi, Sigma Phi Epsilon. Unitarian. Editor Mo. for Art Voices/South, 1978-80; contbg. editor Kansas City Artists Coalition Jour., 1978-79. Contbr. articles to profl. jours.

ALBIN, JOHN SANFORD, farmer; b. Newman, Ill., Oct. 28, 1928; s. Leonard Bruce and Grace Nettie (Herrington) A.; B.S. with honors, U. Ill., 1950; m. Marjorie Ann Martin, Sept. 10, 1949; children—Perry S., David A. Self-employed farmer, Newman, 1951—; operator Albin Farm; pres. Albi Pork Farm, Inc., Plants Pals Inc.; chmn. bd. Longview State Bank (Ill.). Pres., Newman Community Unit 303 Sch. Bd., 1958-66; trustee Parkland Coll., Champaign, Ill., 1968-81, v.p., 1977-81. Recipient Ill. 4H Alumni award, 1968, Master Farmer award Prairie Farmer mag., 1970, award of merit U. Ill. Coll. Agr. Alumni Assn., 1977. Mem. Am. Shropshire Registry Assn. (pres. 1962-65), Ill. Farm Bus. Farm Mgrs. Assn. (pres. 1968-81), E. Central Farm Bus. Farm Mgrs. Assn. (pres. 1965-72), Douglas County Farm Bur. (dir. 1968-81), Top Farmers Assn. Am., Farm House, Alpha Zeta. Republican. Clubs: Villa Grove Country, Masons. Address: PO Box 377 Newman IL 61942

ALBOSTA, DONALD JOSEPH, congressman; b. Saginaw, Mich., Dec. 5, 1925; s. Paul John and Laura (Bennet) A.; ed. public schs.; m. Dorothy Ankoviak, Feb. 10, 1951; children—Christine, Paul. Owner, developer Misteguay Creek Farms, St. Charles, Mich., 1951—; mem. 96th-97th Congresses from 10th Mich. Dist. Twp. trustee, mem. bd. commrs. Saginaw County, 1970-74; former mem. Mich. Ho. of Reps. Served with U.S. Navy, World War II. Mem. Sugar Beet Growers Assn., St. Charles VFW, St. Charles C. of C. Democrat. Roman Catholic. Office: 4400 W Fry Rd Saint Charles MI 48655 also B-1318 Longworth House Office Bldg Washington DC 20515

ALBOTT, WILLIAM LEROY, research clin. psychologists; b. Wichita, Kans., July 6, 1942; s. William Leeroy and Lillian (Humphreys) A.; B.A., Ft. Hays Coll. (Kans.), 1964, M.S., 1965; Ph.D., Ohio U., 1971; m. Carolyn Ramirez, Dec. 2, 1972; children—Cristina Sophia, Andreana Kendra. Clin., psychologist Larned (Kans.) State Hosp., 1965, Osawatomie (Kans.) State Hosp., 1966; sch. psychologist, Kankakee, Ill., 1966-68; grad. teaching asst. Ohio U., Athens, 1968-70; clin. psychol. intern Topeka State Hosp., 1970-71, dir. depts. research and edn., 1972—; pvt. practice, Topeka, 1974—; adj. faculty Wichita State U., Washburn U., Menninger Sch. Psychiatry; cons. Kans. Hwy. Patrol, Kans. Bur. Investigation; former bd. dirs. Central Plains Drug Rehab Center, Inc., Certified psychologist, Kans. Mem. Am. Psychol. Assn., Kans. Psychol. Assn. (gov. 1978—, chmn. com. for continuing edn. 1978-81, pres. 1981-82) Soc. Psychol. Study Social Issues, Internat. Soc. for Non-Verbal Psychotherapy, Soc. Clin. and Exptl. Hypnosis, Internat. Soc. Hypnosis, Sigma Xi. Democrat. Unitarian. Contbr. numerous articles to profl. jours.; reviewer Personality and Social Psychology Bull. Home: 1607 Boswell St Topeka KS 66604 Office: 2700 W 6th St Topeka KS 66606

ALBRECHT, EDWARD DANIEL, metals mfg. co. exec.; b. Kewanee, Ill., Feb. 11, 1937; s. Edward Albert and Mary Jane (Horner) A.; B.S. in Metall. Engring., U. Ariz., 1959, M.S., 1961, Ph.D., 1964, Metal. Engr. (hon.), 1973; m. Mignon Y. Buehler, Jan. 1, 1973; children—Renata E., Deborah J., Paul R. Research metallurgist, U. Calif. Los Alamos Lab., 1959-61; sr. physicist, project mgr. U. Calif. Lawrence Radiation Lab., Livermore, 1964-71; pres. Metall. Innovations Inc., Pleasanton, Calif., 1969-71; gen. mgr. Buehler Ltd. & Adolph I. Buehler, Inc., Evanston, Ill., 1972, v.p., gen. mgr., 1973-76, chmn., pres., 1976, also dir.; dir. Tech Met Canada Ltd., Toronto, Ont., Banner Sci. Ltd., Coventry, Eng. Bd. dirs. Danville (Calif.) Homeowners Inc., 1966-68; trustee Lake Forest Acad. - Ferry Hall Prep Sch., 1977-81; mem. nat. adv. bd. Heard Mus. Anthropology, Phoenix. NDEA fellow, 1959-62. Fellow Am. Soc. Metals (chmn. Tucson 1961); mem. Internat. Metallographic Soc. (pres. 1973-75, dir. 1975-81 chmn. gen. tech. meeting San Francisco 1969, Chgo. 1972, Brighton, Eng., 1980), Sigma Gamm Epsilon, Delta Upsilon. Clubs: Chicago, Onwentsia. Contbr. articles to profl. jours. Patentee in field. Office: PO Box 1 Lake Bluff IL 60044

ALBRECHT, FRANK WAYNE, data processor; b. Bloomington, Ill., May 30, 1936; s. Frank Peter and Ellen May (Middlekauff) A.; A.A. in Computer Sci., Lincoln Land Community Coll., Springfield, Ill., 1972; m. Patsy Ann Florence, Jan. 13, 1958; children—Michelle Rae, Traci Lynn. Computer operator Franklin Life Ins. Co., Springfeld, 1957-61; with State of Ill., 1961—, mgr. data preparation ops. Dept. Public Aid, 1979—; adv. bd. Capitol Area Vocat. Tng. Center, Springfield. Mem. Sangamon County Sheriff's Patrol, 1968-80, Springfield/Sangamon County CD Group, 1968-80. Served with USN, 1954-57; Korea. Mem. Data Entry Mgmt. Assn., Optical Character Reader Users Assn., Ill. Welfare Assn. Roman Catholic. Club: Moose. Office: 931 E Washington St Springfield IL 62762

ALBRECHT, MICHAEL, JR., mgmt. cons.; b. Mediasch, Rumania, Mar. 30, 1940; s. Michael and Elsa (Heihn) A.; came to U.S., 1956, naturalized, 1962; B.S., Ill. State U., 1963; M.B.A., Mich. State U., 1978; m. Kathleen Kay Koerner, Sept. 2, 1961; children—Steven Michael, David Phillip. Asst., Ill. State U., 1963-64; tchr. Aurora (Ill.) Public Schs., 1964-66; quality control engr. Chgo. Aerial Industries, Barrington, Ill., 1966-67; mktg. rep. IBM, Chgo., 1967-74, instr. Customer Exec. Edn. Center, Poughkeepsie, N.Y., 1974-75; asst. to vice chmn. Am. Natural Resources, Detroit, 1975-77; dir. info. systems Mich. Consol. Gas Co., Detroit, 1977-79, exec. dir. corp. info. services, 1978-80; mgmt. cons. M. Albrecht, Jr. & Assos., Inc., Grosse Pointe, Mich., 1980—; cons. corp. planning. Mem. Am. Gas Assn., Advanced Mgmt. Program Club, AAU, Pi Gamma Mu. Office: 12 Lakeside Ct Grosse Pointe MI 48230

ALBRECHT, RONALD FRANK, physician; b. Chgo., Apr. 17, 1937; s. Frank William and Mabel Dorothy (Cassens) A.; A.B., U. Ill., 1958, B.S., 1959, M.D., 1961; m. Joyce Yvonne Burchfield, June 27, 1962; children—Ronald Frank II, Mark Burchfield, Meredith Ann. Intern, Cin. Gen. Hosp., 1961-62; resident anesthesiology U. Ill. Research and Ednl. Hosp., Chgo., 1962-64, attending physician, 1966-73; clin. asso. NIH, Bethesda, Md., 1964-66; practice medicine, specializing in anesthesiology, Chgo., 1966—; mem. med. staff Michael Reese Med. Center, Chgo., chmn. dept. anesthesiology, 1971—; asst. prof. anesthesiology U. Ill. Coll. Medicine, Chgo., 1966-70, clin. asso. prof., 1970-73; prof. anesthesiology U. Chgo. Sch. Medicine, 1973—. Served to lt. comdr. USPHS, 1964-66. Diplomate Am. Bd. Anesthesiology. Fellow Am. Coll. Anesthesiology; mem. AMA, Ill., Chgo. med. socs., Am., Ill. (sec. 1973-78, v.p. 1978-79, pres.-elect 1979-80, pres. 1980-81) socs. anesthesiologists, Chgo. Soc. Anesthesiologists, Assn. Anaesthetists of Gt. Brit. and Ireland, Internat. Anesthesia Research Soc., Am. Physiol. Soc. Presbyterian. Contbr. articles to profl. jours. Home: 28 Salem Ln Evanston IL 60203 Office: Dept Anesthesiology Michael Reese Med Center Chicago IL 60616

ALBRECHTAS, EDMUND, farm machinery co. exec.; b. Kaunas, Luthuania, June 8, 1938; naturalized Can. citizen; s. Joseph and Jadvyca (Osurka) A.; student U. Western Ont., 1958-59; m. Noreen Joyce Williamson, June 24, 1961; children—Lisa Anne, Augustus Joseph John. With Internat. Harvester, 1960—, bus. and products planning mgr. for Latin Am., Chgo., 1979—, dir. mktg. Industria de Maquinas Agricolas Ideal, Santa Rosa, Brazil, 1981—. Served with RCAF, 1956-58. Roman Catholic. Office: International Harvester 401 N Michigan Ave Chicago IL 60611

ALBRIGHT, JUSTIN W., lawyer; b. Lisbon, Iowa, Oct. 14, 1908; B.S.C., U. Iowa, 1931, J.D., 1933; m. Mildred Carlton, 1935; 1 son, Carlton J. Admitted to Iowa bar, 1933; now mem. firm Simmons, Perrine, Albright & Ellwood, Cedar Rapids. Served with AUS, World War II. Mem. Am., Iowa, Linn County bar assns., Cedar Rapids C. of C., Phi Delta Phi. Mason (Shriner), Rotarian. Clubs: Cedar Rapids Country, Pickwick (Cedar Rapids). Editor Iowa Law Rev., 1932-33. Office: 12th Floor Mchts Nat Bank Bldg Cedar Rapids IA 52401

ALBRIGHT, LARRY MCCLURE, mfg. exec.; b. Uniontown, Pa., Oct. 14, 1928; s. Joseph McClure and Dorothy Mae (Herring) A.; B.S., W.Va. U., 1950, postgrad. in indsl. mgmt., 1949-50; m. Madeline Rita Cappellanti, Sept. 24, 1950; children—Larry McClure II, Myra Lynn, Thomas Wayne, Philip William, Michelle, David Eugene. Indsl. engr. Fairmont Foods, Cleve., 1953; successively indsl. engr., br. supr., chief indsl. engring., plant mgr. TRW, Cleve., 1954-62; dir. mfg., exec. v.p. Plasti Kote Co., Medina, Ohio, 1963-69; pres., dir. Aerosol Systems, Inc., Macedonia, Ohio, 1970—. Served with Adj. Gen. Corps U.S. Army, 1951-52. Mem. Chem. Spltys. Mfrs. Assn. (exec. bd.), Nat. Paint and Coatings Assn., U.S. Indsl. Council. Republican. Roman Catholic. Club: Country of Hudson.

ALBY, JAMES FRANCIS PAUL, clergyman, educator; b. Milw., July 16, 1936; s. Francis Joseph and Sara Sophie (Hansen) A.; B.A., Gallaudet Coll., 1963, M.S. in Edn., 1964; M.Div., Va. Theol. Sem., 1971; m. Jan Lorraine Peplinski, Aug. 2, 1980; 1 child. Ordained priest Episcopal Ch., 1971; priest to the deaf St. James Mission of the Deaf, Milw., 1971-76; priest asso. St. Peter's Ch., West Allis, Wis., 1972—. Tchr. high sch. hearing impaired Milw. Pub. Schs., 1972—; instr. interpreting for deaf U. Wis., Milw., 1975-77; sr. high sch. boys dorm supr.-counselor St. John's Sch. for the Deaf, St. Francis, Wis., 1971-72; tchr. lang. of signs Milw. Area Tech. Coll., 1974-75; mem. adv. com. continuing edn. deaf adults, Milw., 1976—, mem. adv. com. on edn. hearing impaired Milw. Pub. Schs., 1977—; mem. sect. 504 com. Southeastern Wis. Disabilities Coalition, 1979—. Mem. Ecumenical Clergy Assn., Evang. and Cath. Mission in Episcopal Ch., Nat., Wis. assns. of deaf, Alpha Sigma Pi. Club: Lions (charter pres. Greater Milw. 1974-76, Lioness Club liaison 1980-81). Contbr. articles to profl. jours. Office: 7729 W Lincoln Ave West Allis WI 53219

ALDEN, DON EDWARD, food co. exec.; b. Long Beach, Calif., Oct. 29, 1937; s. John James and Nathell (Larson) A.; B.S., Okla. State U., 1962; cert., honor grad. Inst. for Mgmt., Ill. Benedictine Coll., 1971; m. Sandra Jean Horn, July 6, 1963; children—Laura Marie, John Vincent. With Swift & Co., Oak Brook, Ill., 1963—, ind. investigator in research, 1963-71, div. head vegetable protein research, 1971-76, research mgr. new product devel., 1978—, grocery product devel., 1980—. Served with M.C., U.S. Army, 1960-66. Mem. Inst. for Mgmt. (v.p. bd. dirs. 1979-81, pres. 1982), Am. Assn. Cereal Chemists, Internat. Food Technologists, Peanut Butter Mfrs. Assn. Democrat. Roman Catholic. Developer texturized vegetable protein, 1971; patentee flavor-free undenatured legume seeds, 1976, vegetable oil extraction, 1980, process for prodn. of flavored protein foods, 1971. Home: 3143 Everglade St Woodridge IL 60517 Office: 1919 Swift Dr Oak Brook IL 60512

ALDEN, HAROLD P., hosp. exec.; b. Omaha, Mar. 31, 1923; s. Harry Carl and Amy Elvira (Granlund) A.; B.A., Augustana Coll., Rock Island, Ill., 1948; M.S. in Hosp. Adminstrn., Columbia U., 1950; m. Mary Catherine Menze, Sept. 22, 1961; children—Marianne, Melanie, Alane, Steven, James, Alison. Adminstrv. asst. St. Francis Meml. Hosp., San Francisco, 1950-51; adminstr. Greens' Eye Hosp., San Francisco, 1951-53; exec. dir. Union Hosp., Dover, Ohio, 1953—. Served with U.S. Army, 1942-46. Fellow Am. Coll. Hosp. Adminstrs.; mem. Am. Hosp. Assn., Ohio Hosp. Assn. (life mem., dir. 1973-75), Ohio Hosp. Mgmt. Services (dir. 1978—, sec. 1979-80, treas. 1980-82), Tuscarawas County (Ohio) C. of C. (treas. 1959-66, dir. 1959-66, 73—, 2d v.p. 1975-76, 1st v.p. 1976-77, pres. 1977-78). Office: Union Hosp 659 Boulevard Dover OH 44622

ALDEN, RAYMOND MACDONALD, telecommunications co. exec.; b. Palo Alto, Calif., Nov. 17, 1921; s. Raymond Macdonald and Barbara (Hitt) A.; A.B. in Engring., Stanford U., 1944; m. Sara Wills, Aug. 30, 1946; children—David Wills, Merritt Ann Alden Booster,

John Lee. Engr., Western Union Telegraph Co., 1946-50; engr. Hawaiian Telephone Co., Honolulu, 1951-62, v.p., 1962-64: exec. v.p. United Telecommunications, Inc., Kansas City, Mo., 1964-73, pres., 1973-80, vice chmn., 1981—, also dir.; dir. C.J. Patterson Co., United Mo. Bank, Kansas City. Served with USNR, 1944-46. Registered profl. engr., Hawaii, Kans. Mem. IEEE (sr.), Nat. Soc. Profl. Engrs. Office: PO Box 11315 Kansas City MO 64112

ALDER, ALTHEA ALICE, mktg. service agy. exec.; b. Wilmore, Kans., Jan. 4, 1933; d. Lloyd Lewis and Margaret Mae (Baldwin) A.; student Ft. Hays State U., 1952-55. Owner, operator 2 beauty shops, 1961-67; quality control mgr., supr. women Solo Cup Co., 1967-70; v.p. purchasing, prodn. and premiums William A. Robinson, Inc., Northbrook, Ill., 1970-79; pres. A-three Services Agy., Ltd., Lake Forest, Ill., 1979—, Lake Forest Tng. Salon, Ltd., 1979—. Served with W.A.C., AUS, 1951-53, 55-61; Korea. Decorated Army Commendation medal. Mem. Purchasing Mgmt. Assn. Chgo., Am. Legion. Clubs: Eastern Star, The Exec. Female. Home: 786 N Oakwood Ave Lake Forest IL 60045 Office: 588 N Western Ave Lake Forest IL 60045

ALDERFER, WILLIAM KENNETH, state historian; b. DuBois, Pa., Nov. 10, 1929; s. Clement Robinson and Katharine (Mayo) A.; B.S., U. Pa., 1951; M.A., U. Rochester (N.Y.), 1956; m. Marilyn Manta Ruth, June 2, 1951; children—W. Kenneth, John M. Asst. supr. gen. acctg. dept. Delco Appliance div. Gen. Motors Corp., Rochester, 1951-55; teaching fellow U. Rochester, 1955-56; teaching asst. U. Wis., 1956-58; supr. Office Field Services, State Hist. Soc. Wis., 1958-64; dir. Mich. Hist. Soc., 1964-67; historian State of Ill., Springfield, 1967—; chancellor Lincoln Acad., Ill., 1970-74, exec. dir., 1974—; mem. Ill. Records Commn., sec., 1967—; sec. Gov. Mich. Com. Restoration State Capitol, 1966-67; chmn. Heritage Day, Mich. Week, 1966-67; mem. Ill. Sesquicentennial Commn., 1967-68, Ill. Bicentennial Commn., 1974-77. Pres., Waubesa Beach Community Center, 1969; mem. Capitol Planning Commn., 1967—. Mem. Am. Assn. State and Local History (council), Am. Lincoln Assn. (sec. 1967—), Ulysses S. Grant Assn. (dir. 1967—), Ill. Hist. Soc. (exec. dir. 1967—), Sangamon County Hist. Soc., Vermillion County Hist. Soc., Chgo. Civil Round Table, ALA. Address: Old State Capitol Springfield IL 62707*

ALDERMAN, ALICE MAE (MRS. DONALD C. ALDERMAN), librarian; b. Westby, Wis.; d. Hjalmar Otto and Agatha Hilda (Mortenson) Rudrud; A.A., North Park Coll., 1945; B.S. magna cum laude, U. Wis., 1965, M.S., 1966, postgrad., 1966—; m. Donald C. Alderman, Dec. 12, 1946; children—Deborah (Mrs. Cecil Rolfe), Andrew, Brent, Marsha. Lab. technician Leaf Brands, Chgo., 1945-46; teaching asst. U. Wis., Madison, 1965-66; with Wis. State Hist. Soc., Madison, 1966—, cataloger documents, 1967-74, asst. documents librarian, 1974—. Mem. ALA, Am. Scandinavian Found., Kappa Delta Phi, Beta Phi Mu. Mem. Modern Woodmen of Am. Author: Organizing Wisconsin Public Documents, 1974; contbr. articles to profl. jours.; co-editor, compiler: Wisconsin Public Documents. Home: 1715 Laurel Crest Madison WI 53705 Office: 816 State St Madison WI 53706

ALDERMAN, ROALDA JENSEN, hosp. adminstr.; b. Rochester, Minn., Apr. 23, 1930; d. Lloyd Bryan and Marvel Dora (Johannesen) Jensen; B.A., U. Chgo., 1949, M.A., 1967; postgrad. Ill. Tchrs. Coll., 1963; m. William Walter Alderman, Nov. 19, 1968; children—Bruce Donald, Karen Laurie, James William. Dietary supr. Billings Hosp., U. Chgo., 1951-53, psychometrist Office Vocation Guidance Counsel, U. Chgo., 1950-51, 53-54; project research specialist div. hosp. and scientific orgn., asst. dir. project new fields sci. inquiry, exobiology Indsl. Relations Center, U. Chgo., 1965-68; dir. tng. Cook County Hosp., Chgo., 1968-69, dir. personnel, 1969-71, asso. hosp. dir. personal services, 1969-70; exec. adminstr. Ill. Dept. Pub. Health Hosp. and Clinics, Chgo., 1971-75; Chgo. region asst. to dep. dir. Ill. Dept. Pub. Aid, 1971-73; supt. div. alcoholism Ill. Dept. Mental Health and D/D, State Alcoholism Authority, 1975-79, asso. dir., 1980—; lectr. Grad. Sch. Pub. Health, U. Ill., 1975—. Co-founder Chel-win South Improvement Assn., 1965, sec., 1966, dir., 1965-67. Recipient State Ill. Gov.'s awards, Superior Achievement certificate, 1972, citation radio sta. WAIT, Chgo., 1975. Mem. Chgo. Hosp. Personnel Mgmt. Assn., Ill. Pub. Health Assn. (mem. membership com. 1971), Am., Ill. hosp. assns., Nat. Assn. State Alcohol and Drug Abuse Dirs., Am. Health Planning Assn., Am. Coll. Hosp. Adminstrs. Home: 28 W 440 Main St Warrenville IL 60555 Office: Room 1500 160 N La Salle St Chicago IL 60601

ALDERTON, HARVEY RANDALL, child psychiatrist; b. Mitcham, Surrey, Eng., Aug. 29, 1927; s. Randall Frederick and Margaret (Bassett) A.; M.B.,B.S., London (Eng.) Hosp. Med. Coll., 1950; Diploma in Psychol. Medicine, Maudsley Hosp., 1957; m. Rae West, Aug. 5, 1954; children—Susan, Jennifer, Gillian. Intern, London Hosp. Med. Coll., 1950-52; resident Inst. Psychiatry, Maudsley Hosp., London, 1954-57; practice medicine specializing in child psychiatry, Toronto, Ont., Can., 1957—; staff psychiatrist Thistletown Regional Centre, Rexdale, Ont., Can., 1957-60, clin. dir., 1961-70, dir. out patient dept., 1967-70, dir. tng. and research, 1970-72, dir. psychiat. tng. and research, 1972-75; sr. staff psychiatrist Hosp. for Sick Children, 1976—; dir. East York-Leaside Child Guidance Clinic, 1960-61; faculty U. Toronto, 1958—, asso. prof. dept. psychiatry, 1970—; cons. psychiatrist North York Bd. Edn., 1972—, Powell-Brown Nursery, 1971—, Earlscourt Children's Home, 1965-80, Stother's Child Care Center, 1978—, Blue Hills Presch. Program, 1981—. Bd. dir. Powell-Brown Nursery, 1972-79, chmn. profl. adv. bd., 1972-79; mem. profl. adv. bd. Earlscourt Childrens Home, 1972-79. Served to capt. M.C., Royal Army, 1952-54. Fellow Royal Coll. Physicians (Can.), Am. Psychiat. Assn., A.C.P., Royal Coll. Psychiatrists; mem. Canadian, Ont. med. assns., Canadian, Ont. (sec. 1969-72) psychiat. assns. Mem. editorial bd. Canadian Psychiat. Assn. Jour., 1965-76. Contbr. articles to profl. jours. Office: PO Box 56 Newmarket ON L3Y 4W3 Canada

ALDIS, HENRY, obstetrician, gynecologist; b. Basim, Berar, India, Nov. 3, 1913; s. Steadman and Ethel Rebecca (Fry) A. (parents Am. citizens); A.B., U. Kans., 1938, M.D., 1941; m. Margaret Elizabeth Warner, June 24, 1941; children—John Warner, Henry Weeks, William Leggett, David Fry. Intern, City Hosp., Winston-Salem, N.C., 1941-42; resident, Gorgas Hosp., C.Z., 1942-43, asst. resident in surgery U. Kans., 1943-44, asst. resident in ob-gyn., Balt. City Hosps., 1954-56, chief resident in ob-gyn., 1956-57; asso. Walter Sheeley, M.D., Shepherdstown, W.Va., 1946-52; gen. practice medicine, Ft. Scott, Kans., 1952-54; practice medicine specializing in ob-gyn., Ft. Scott, 1957—; mem. staff Newman-Young Clinic, Mercy Hosp., Ft. Scott, Bourbon County. Served with AUS, 1944-46; ETO; served to col. M.C. Kans. N.G., 1956-73. Diplomate Am. Bd. Ob-Gyn (also recert.). Mem. AMA, Bourbon County Med. Soc., Kansas City Gynecol. Soc. Republican. Methodist. Home: 501 S Main St Fort Scott KS 66701 Office: Newman-Young Clinic Fort Scott KS 66701

ALDRIDGE, RONALD GORDON, social worker; b. Toronto, Ont., Can., Sept. 16, 1943; s. Gordon James and Gladys Parker (Chapman) A.; came to U.S., 1950, naturalized, 1955; B.A., Mich. State U., 1965, M.S.W., 1967, Ph.D., 1980; m. Cheryl Lee Holmes, Mar. 19, 1966; children—Danielle Marie, Michelle Lee. Social worker Lansing (Mich.) Family Service Agy., 1967-68; commd. 2d lt., U.S. Army, 1968, advanced through grades to maj., 1976; social worker Correctional Tng. Facility, Ft. Riley, Kans., 1968-69; div. social worker 3d Inf. Div., Germany, 1969-73; chief social work service DeWitt Army Hosp., Ft. Belvoir, Va., 1973-77; emergency service social worker Woodburne Center for Community Mental Health, Annandale, Va., 1973-77; dir. Family Problem Center, Dumfries, Va., 1976-77; social worker Mich. Family Inst., Lansing, 1977-80; dir. mental hygiene U.S. Disciplinary Barracks, Ft. Leavenworth, Kans., 1980—; clin. instr. Coll. Osteo. Medicine, Mich. State U., 1979-80; instr. couples communication U. Minn. Mem. exec. bd. Chief Okemos council Boy Scouts Am., 1978-81, mem. nat. com. Nat. Eagle Scout Assn., 1977—. Decorated Army Commendation medal with oakleaf cluster, Meritorious Service medal. Mem. Am. Assn. Sex Educators, Counselors and Therapists, Acad. Cert. Social Workers, Assn. Mil. Social Workers, Nat. Assn. Social Workers, Am. Corrections Assn., Phi Alpha, Alpha Phi Omega, Phi Kappa Phi. Home: 1611 Le Compton Rd Leavenworth KS 66048 Office: DMH US Disciplinary Barracks Fort Leavenworth KS 66027

ALEKSANDROWICZ, FRANK JOHN, photographer; b. Erie, Pa., Sept. 17, 1921; s. John and Julia (Pawski) A.; student St. John Kanty Coll., 1941, U. Pitts., Erie Extension Sch. Journalism, 1941-42; m. Louise Andrianne, July 17, 1945. Newspaper photographer Erie (Pa.) Dispatch, 1941-42, 45-57; photographer Cleve. Press, 1957-67, columnist, 1962; free-lance comml. photography in advt., indsl. pub. relations 1967; one-man shows at Design House, Cuyahoga Savs. and Loan, Broadview Savs. and Loan. Served with AUS, 1943-45; ETO; with AUS, 1950-51; Korea. Recipient advt. photography awards CA. Mag., N.Y. Art Dirs. Show, Chgo. Art Dirs. Show, Cleve. Soc. Communicating Arts. Mem. Nat. Press Photographers Assn., Ohio News Photographers Assn., Am. Soc. Mag. Photographers, Cleve. Soc. Communicating Arts, Sigma Delta Chi. Office: 624 St Clair Ave NW Cleveland OH 44113

ALEVY, MITCHELL ALAN, psychologist; b. N.Y.C., Sept. 1, 1949; s. Alan Norman and Trudy Alevy; B.A., Queens Coll., City U. N.Y., 1971; M.S. (Univ. Psychology Dept. fellow 1971-72, NIMH fellow 1972-73), St. Louis U., 1975, Ph.D., 1977; m. Yael Gris, July 15, 1973. Psychologist, Child Devel. Center, Cardinal Glennon Hosp., St. Louis, 1974-75; instr. Lindenwood Colls., 1976; clin. psychologist St. Louis State Hosp. Youth Center, 1976-78, Christian Hosp. N.W., St. Louis, 1979—; pvt. practice clin. psychology, St. Louis, 1978—; speaker Christian Hosp. N.W. Stop Smoking Seminars and other stop smoking events. Mem. Am. Soc. Clin. Hypnosis, Am. Psychol. Assn., Mo. Psychol. Assn. Jewish. Office: 11916 Kendon Dr Saint Louis MO 63131

ALEXANDER, BARBARA LEAH SHAPIRO, psychiat. social worker; b. St. Louis, May 6, 1943; d. Harold Albert and Dorothy Miriam (Leifer) Shapiro; B.Mus. Edn., Washington U., St. Louis, 1964; postgrad. U. Ill., 1964-66; M.S.W., Smith Coll., 1970; postgrad. Inst. Psychoanalysis, Chgo., 1971-73, Child Therapy Program, 1976-80; certified therapist Sex Dysfunction Clinic, Loyola U., Chgo., 1975; m. Richard E. Alexander. Research asst., NIMH grantee Smith Coll., 1968-70; probation officer Juvenile Ct. Cook County, Chgo., 1966-68, 70; therapist Madden Mental Health Center, Hines, Ill., 1970-72; supr., therapist, field instr. U. Chgo., U. Ill. Grad. Schs. Social Work, also Pritzker Children's Hosp., Chgo., 1972—; therapist, cons., also pvt. practice, 1973—; instr. tng. and advanced tng. Effectiveness Tng. Assos., Chgo., 1974; instr. psychology Northeastern U., Chgo., 1975; intern Divorce Conciliation Service, Circuit Ct. Cook County, 1976-77. Bd. dirs. North Am. Found., Grant Park Concerts Soc. Recipient Sterling Achievement award Mu Phi Epsilon, 1964. Certified social worker, Ill. Mem. Acad. Certified Social Workers, Nat. Assn. Social Workers, Ill. Soc. Clin. Social Work (dir., chmn. services to mems. com.), Am. Assn. Marriage and Family Therapy, Assn. Child Psychotherapists, Am. Assn. Sex Educators and Counselors, Ill. Group Psychotherapy Soc., Chgo. Symphony Soc., Amateur Chamber Music Players Assn., Jewish Geneal. Soc., Smith Coll. Alumni Assn. (dir.). Democrat. Jewish. Contbr. to profl. publns. Home: 179 E Lake Shore Dr Chicago IL 60611 Office: 233 E Erie St Chicago IL 60611

ALEXANDER, BENJAMIN HAROLD, univ. pres.; b. Roberta, Ga., Oct. 18, 1921; s. Bush Monoah and Annie Willie (Flowers) A.; B.A., U. Cin., 1943; M.S., Bradley U., Peoria, Ill., 1950, LL.D. (hon.), 1979; Ph.D., Georgetown U., 1957; m. Mary Ellen Spurlock, Mar. 21, 1948; children—Drew Wilson, Dawn Criket. Adminstr. new health career projects Nat. Center for Health Services Research and Devel., Rockville, Md., 1968-71; acting chief gen. research support br. div. research resources NIH, Bethesda, Md., 1971-74; pres. Chgo. State U., 1974—. Fellow, Acad. of Sci., Washington, 1966—; chmn. research adv. council Water Resources Center, Washington Tech. Inst., 1973-74; chmn. Nelson Com. Workshop, 1973, D.C. Commn. on Arts and Humanities, 1974; mem. adv. com. NSF, 1977. Mem. Washington Bd. Edn., 1966-69; 2d v.p. D.C. Fedn. Civic Assns., 1970-71, pres., 1972-73; mem. Howard U. Commn. on Sch. of Edn., 1973. Trustee, Washington Tchrs. Coll., Bradley U., 1980—. Served with AUS, 1943-47, to maj. Res., 1947-65. Recipient certificate of achievement Dept. of Army, 1967; medal for service to youth D.C. YMCA, 1974; Ann. Alumni Achievement award Georgetown U., 1974, Bradley U., 1977; certificate for distinguished pub. service Washington City Govt., 1974; resolution of appreciation D.C. City Council, 1974; Achiever's award Chgo./South C. of C., 1976; Walter Reuther Humanitarian award, 1978; Internat. Educators award Sigma Gamma Rho, 1978; Outstanding Educators award Am. Tobacco Co., 1978; cert. of appreciation, Dr. Benjamin H. Alexander Day, Mayor of Cin., 1979. Fellow Acad. Scis. (Washington); mem. Chem. Soc. Washington (chmn. symposium on pollution 1970, program chmn. 1971, certificate of appreciation 1970), Am. Chem. Soc. (Community Service award 1967), D.C. Congress Parents and Tchrs. (life), Chgo. Acad. Scis., Am. Bar Assn. (nat. non-lawyer mem. accreditation com.), Alpha Phi Alpha, Beta Kappa Chi. Club: Toastmasters. Contbr. articles to profl. jours. Patentee in field. Office: Chgo State U 95th St at King Dr Chicago IL 60628

ALEXANDER, C. ALEX, physician, educator; b. Kerala, India, Mar. 1, 1935; s. Chandy and Sarah (Yohannan) A.; came to U.S., 1962, naturalized, 1974; M.D., U. Madras (India), 1958; M.P.H., Johns Hopkins U., 1964, Dr.P.H., 1966; m. Chimu Kalaya, Jan. 3, 1960. Intern, Plainfield, N.J., 1962-63; resident in preventive medicine Johns Hopkins U., Balt., 1964-66, asst. to asso. prof. pub. health adminstrn.; 1966-72; dir. med. affairs Provident Hosp., Balt., 1971-73; asso. prof. social and preventive medicine Med. Sch. U. Md., Balt., 1972-75; chief of staff VA Center, Dayton, Ohio, 1975—; clin. prof. community medicine Wright State U., Dayton, 1975—, asst. dean Sch. Medicine, 1975-76; cons. WHO, 1969, USPHS. Lt. col., M.C., U.S. Army Res. Recipient Disting. Service award Community Health Council Md., 1974; Leadership award VA, 1979; diplomate Am. Bd. Preventive Medicine. Fellow Am. Coll Preventive Medicine, Am. Pub. Health Assn., Am. Coll. Internat. Physicians (pres. 1978-79); mem. AMA, Ohio Med. Assn., Montgomery County Med. Soc. Syrian Orthodox. Club: Dayton Racquet. Contbr. articles to profl. jours. Home: 1242 Ashburton Dr Dayton OH 45459 Office: VA Med Center Dayton OH 45428

ALEXANDER, CARL ALBERT, ceramic engr.; b. Chillicothe, Ohio, Nov. 22, 1928; s. Carl B. and Helen E. Alexander; B.S., Ohio U., 1953, M.S., 1956; Ph.D., Ohio State U., 1961; m. Dolores J. Hertenstein, Sept. 4, 1954; children—Carla C., David A. Mem. staff Battelle Columbus Labs., 1956—, research leader, 1974—, mgr. physico-chem. systems, 1976—; mem. faculty Ohio State U., 1963—, prof. ceramic and nuclear engring., 1977—; cons. Dept. Energy. Vice chmn. Grove City (Ohio) City Parks and Recreation Control Bd., 1975—. Served to lt. (j.g.) USNR, 1951-54. Recipient Merit award NASA, 1971; citations Dept. Energy, AEC, ERDA. Mem. Am. Soc. Mass Spectrometry, Keramos, Sigma Xi. Author, patentee in field. Home: 4249 Haughn Rd Grove City OH 43123 Office: 505 King Ave Columbus OH 43201

ALEXANDER, CHARLES FREEMAN, JR., marine propulsion mfg. co. exec.; b. Kansas City, Mo., Nov. 14, 1921; s. Charles Freeman and Marjorie May (Longan) A.; B.S.M.E., B.S. in Naval Architecture and Marine Engring., U. Mich., 1943; student U.S. Navy Midshipman Sch., Columbia U., 1943; postgrad. Advanced mgmt. program Harvard U., 1976; m. Juliet Ruth Lindeman, Nov. 6, 1943; children—Charles Freeman III, Wendy L., Anne K., Lori E. Alexander Michels. Engr., Atlas Imperial Diesel Engine Co., Oakland, Calif., 1946-47, project engr. propulsion lab. U.S. Naval Air Missile Test Center, Pt. Mugu, Calif., 1947-53; asst. to v.p. engring. Mercury Marine div. Brunswick Corp., Fond du Lac, Wis., 1953, chief plant engr., 1953-64, v.p. engring., 1964-77, pres. Mercury Marine, Brunswick Corp.; v.p., group exec. Marine Power, 1977—; dir. Nat. Exchange Bank, Fond du Lac. Bd. dirs. St. Agnes Hosp.; corp. mem. Milw. Sch. Engring. Served to lt. (j.g.) U.S. Navy, 1943-46. Mem. Soc. Automotive Engrs., Am. Soc. Naval Engrs., Soc. Naval Architects and Marine Engrs., ASME, Am. Power Boat Assn. Clubs: South Hills (dir.), Oshkosh Power Boat, Rotary, Elks. Patentee outboard motors and stern drives. Office: 1939 Pioneer Rd Fond du Lac WI 54935

ALEXANDER, CHARLES WILLIAM, psychologist, educator; b. Zanesville, Ohio, Feb. 13, 1951; s. Charles and Doris (Paxson) A.; B.S., Denison U., 1973; M.A., Bowling Green State U., 1975, Ph.D., 1978. Psychol. intern Southwestern Med. Sch., Dallas, 1977-78; asst. prof. psychology Wichita (Kans.) State U., 1978—; pvt. practice clin. psychology, Wichita, 1979—; cons. Roots & Wings Foster Care Project, Mental Health Assn. Sedgewick County, also residential mental retardation facilities. Mem. Am. Psychol. Assn., Soc. Behavioral Medicine, Soc. Psychophysiol. Research, Mental Health Assn. Sedgewck County, Southwestern Psychol. Assn., Wichita Psychol. Assn. Author: (with Richard and Muriel Saunders) The Small Home Handbook: A Kansas Guide to Develop, Fund, and Operate Small Residential Facilities for the DD Adult. Home: 2323 N Woodlawn #433 Wichita KS 67220 Office: Wichita State U Wichita KS 67208

ALEXANDER, CHRISTINE ELLEN, educator; b. Ashland, Ohio, Jan. 19, 1936; d. Myron Lee and Beulah (Grafton) Hootman; student Ohio State U., 1954-55, William Jewell Coll., 1959-64; B.S., Okla. State U., 1966, M.S., 1969; postgrad. Miami U., Oxford, Ohio, 1978-80; m. William S. Alexander, Dec. 21, 1974; children by previous marriage—Laura Lynn Smith Phillips, Mathis Andrew Smith, Rachael Elaine Smith. Dental asst., receptionist, Springfield, Ohio, 1956; clk.-typist Wittenberg U., Springfield, 1957; tech. math. and sci., Perkins, Okla., 1968-69; tchr. home econs. Dayton (Ohio) City Schs., 1969-74, coordinator/tchr. Family Life Program, 1973—; mem. Ohio Council United Services for Effective Parenting. Mem. Am. Vocat. Assn., Ohio Vocat. Assn., Dayton Sch. Mgmt. Assn., Omicron Nu. Home: 3525 Dandridge Ave Dayton OH 45407

ALEXANDER, DON KENNETH, cardiologist; b. Ann Arbor, Mich., July 2, 1932; s. John Byron and Helen Edna (Hammon) A.; B.S. in Pharmacy, U. Mich., 1954, M.D., 1962; m. Caroline Anderson, Aug. 16, 1972; children—Don Kenneth, Renée, Tracy, Donna, Cherie. Intern, St. Joseph Hosp., Ann Arbor, 1962-63, resident in internal medicine, 1963-66; resident in cardiology U. Mich. Med. Center, Ann Arbor, 1966-67; practice medicine specializing in cardiology, Ann Arbor, 1967—; clin. instr. U. Mich. Med. Center. Served with USMC, 1954-56. Mem. AMA, Washtenaw Med. Soc., Mich. State Med. Soc., Am. Heart Assn. Methodist. Home: 1499 Folkstone Ct Ann Arbor MI 48105 Office: St Joseph Mercy Hosp PO Box 995 Ann Arbor MI 48106

ALEXANDER, J(OSEPH) EDWARD, def. industry co. exec.; b. Eugene, Oreg., Mar. 17, 1948; s. Joseph Edward and Opal Marie (Robison) A.; B.S. in Mech. Engring., Oreg. State U., 1970; M.S. in Mech. Engring., Carnegie-Mellon U., 1973; m. Judith Elaine Koharik, July 26, 1980. Mech. design engr. Westinghouse Corp.-Bettis Atomic Power Lab., Pitts., 1970-75, Bettis resident mgr. at FMC Corp., 1976-78; mil. mktg. engr. No. Ordnance div. FMC Corp., Mpls., 1978-79, mgr. concepts devel., 1979—. Registered profl. engr., Pa. Mem. Am. Def. Preparedness Assn., Phi Kappa Phi, Tau Beta Pi, Pi Tau Sigma, Sigma Tau, Phi Eta Sigma. Home: 2633 Natchez Ave S Minneapolis MN 55416 Office: No Ordnance Div FMC Corp 4800 E River Rd Minneapolis MN 55421

ALEXANDER, JAMES, psychoanalyst; b. Galveston, Tex., Sept. 25, 1910; s. Keeton and Daisy (Jeffrey) A.; student U. Tex., 1929-32; M.D., Baylor U., 1936; m. Ann Krumm, Dec. 23, 1939. Intern, Md. Gen. Hosp., Balt., 1936; psychiat. resident Austin (Tex.) State Hosp., 1937-39; practice psychoanalysis, Chgo., 1949—; mem. faculty Northwestern U., Chgo., 1975—, prof. psychiatry, 1975—. Served with AUS, 1942-46. Mem. Assn. Symbolic Logic, Am. Friends Austria, Am. Math. Soc., Am. Psychoanalytic Assn., Internat. Psychoanalytic Assn., Steuben Soc. Am. Club: Germania. Contbr. articles to psychoanalytic jours. Home: 301 S Cuyler St Oak Park IL 60302 Office: 111 N Wabash Ave Chicago IL 60602

ALEXANDER, JOANN SAYRE, nurse, educator; b. Evansville, Ind., Dec. 24, 1934; s. Joseph Sayres and Evelyn Catherine (Schmitt) Coughlin; B.S. in Nursing, St. Louis U., 1956; M.S. in Nursing, U. Evansville, 1976; m. James Edward Alexander, Oct. 11, 1958; children—James Edward, Laurie Ann, Mary E., Jan R. Asst. head nurse Marion (Ill.) VA Hosp., 1956-57; staff nurse Firmin Desloge Hosp., St. Louis, 1957-58; staff nurse Herrin (Ill.) Hosp., 1963-64; staff nurse Byron (Ill.) Clinic, 1966-67; sch. nurse Vanderburgh Sch. Corp., Evansville, Ind., 1968-69; asst. prof. nursing U. Evansville, 1973—; inservice edn. program cons. Welborn Hosp., Evansville; reviewer Ind. Continuing Edn. for Nursing, 1978-79. Tchr., Confraternity of Christian Doctrine, 1973-77, Service award, 1977; active Women's Service Guild, 1968-72; nursing del. Ind. State Conv., 1977, 79. Mem. Am. Nurses Assn., Ind. Nurses Assn., Dist. #4 Nurses Assn. (chmn. nomination com.), Nat. League Nursing, Ind. Citizens League for Nursing, Bus. and Profl. Women's Club (treas. 1958), Beta Sigma Phi. Clubs: Holy Rosary Women's; Horseshoe Bend. Home: 5801 Monroe Ave Evansville IN 47715 Office: Box 329 Evansville IN 47702

ALEXANDER, LEONARD S., advt. exec.; b. N.Y.C., Feb. 9, 1924; s. Nathan and Doris (Solomon) A.; student U. Mich., 1941-43, 46-47; student U. Conn., 1943-44; m. Yvonne S. Schroder, Sept. 28, 1962; 1 dau., Leslie J. Asst. mgr. Cigaret Lighter div. ASR Corp., N.Y.C., 1947-51; asst. retail sales mgr. Belding-Heminway-Corticelli, N.Y.C., 1951-52; asst. engr. Porter-Urquhart, Skidmore, Owings & Merrill,

Morocco, 1952-53; asst. advt. mgr. Mergenthaler Linotype, N.Y.C., 1954-55; dir. communications Miehle-Goss-Dexter, Chgo., 1955-63, 66-68; merchandising mgr. Indsl. Truck div. Clark Equipment Co., Battle Creek, Mich., 1963-66; v.p. mktg. Anderson Bros. Mfg., Rockford, Ill., 1969-72; owner, mgr. Idea Co., Rockford, Ill., 1972-76; mgr. advt. and sales promotion Simplicity Mfg. Co. div. Allis-Chalmers Corp., Port Washington, Wis., 1976-82; gen. mgr. Caldwell-Van Riper, Inc., Fort Wayne, Ind., 1982—. Served with AUS, 1943-46. Home: 11012 Elder Tree Ct Mequon WI 53092 Office: 2827 Rupp Dr Fort Wayne IN 46815

ALEXANDER, ROLAND HAYES, job placement supr.; b. Radford, Va., Sept. 17, 1926; s. Murriel Douglas and Lillie Carmel (Clark) A.; B.S., So. Ill. U., Carbondale, 1971, M.Ed., 1974, Ph.D., 1979; m. Joyce Williams, June 27, 1954; children—Derek A., Robert B. U.S. Air Force, 1948-68; ret., 1968; chmn. electricity, electronics and indsl. arts dept. East St. Louis (Ill.) Sr. High Sch., 1968-74; job placement specialist, 1974—; adj. asst. prof. dept. vocat. edn. studies So. Ill. U., Carbondale, 1979—; module reviewer Nat. Center for Research in Vocat. Edn., 1979-80. Mem. Am. Vocat. Assn., Nat. Council Local Adminstrs., So. Ill. Occupational Edn. Leaders (past pres.), So. Ill. U. Adv. Council for Vocat. Edn. Studies (chmn. 1981-82), Phi Delta Kappa, Iota Lambda Sigma. Club: Masons (33d degree). Home: 47 Montclair Fairview Heights IL 62208 Office: 700 Bond Ave East Saint Louis IL 62207

ALEXANDER, WILLIAM MICHAEL, lawyer; b. Omaha, June 10, 1942; s. Michael Edward and Marie Francie (Roesing) A.; B.A., Creighton U., 1966, J.D., 1972; m. Mary Catherine Wiehl, July 28, 1968; children—Mark Michael, Beth Catherine, Megan Marie. Admitted to Iowa bar, 1972, Nebr. bar, 1972; analyst, underwriter Mutual of Omaha, 1966-69; mem. firm George T. Qualley, Sioux City, Iowa, 1972-75, William M. Alexander, Laurens, Iowa, 1976-81. Mem. Laurens C. of C., Am., Iowa, Nebr. bar assns., Delta Theta Phi. Republican. Roman Catholic. Clubs: Lions, Laurens Country, K.C. Home: 301 S 2d St Laurens IA 50554 Office: 123 3d St N Laurens IA 50554

ALEXANDRE, JEAN CLEHAUT, obstetrician, gynecologist; b. Port-Au-Prince, Haiti, June 12, 1942; came to U.S., 1970; s. Montas and Clara Catherine (Blain) A.; B.S., Instn. St. Louis de Gonzague, 1960; M.D., State U. Haiti, 1967; m. Eve Marie Bruno, Feb. 14, 1970; children—Michelle Jean, Jean Clehaut, Daniel Victor. Intern, Ill. Central Community Hosp., Chgo., 1970-71; resident Loyola U. Med. Center, Chgo., 1971-73, chief resident, 1973-74, clin. instr., 1973—; practice medicine specializing in ob-gyn, Broadview, Ill., 1976—; sr. attending Foster McGaw Hosp.; mem. staffs Westlake Community Hosp., Mt. Sinai Med. Center, Louise Berg Hosp., Glendale Heights Hosp., Northlake Community Hosp.; pres., med. dir. Alma Comprehensive Med. Center, Ltd., Maywood, Ill.; med. dir. Maywood Clinic Family Planning, 1974-76; exec. dir. Council for Health, Info. and Public Service; v.p. bd. dirs. Northlake Community Hosp.; dir. Carribean Devel. Co., S.A.; exec. bd. dirs. Med. Practice Mgmt., Inc. Bd. dirs. Haitian Am. Tb, Inc. Diplomate Am. Bd. Ob-Gyn. Mem. Am. Coll. Ob-Gyn, AMA, Ill. Med. Soc., Chgo. Med. Soc., Internat. Coll. Surgeons, Nat. Assn. Physicians, Cook County Physicians Assn., Am. Assn. Gynecologic Laparoscopists, Am. Fertility Soc., Ill. Family Planning Council, Assocation des Medicins Haitiens a l'Etranger, Ednl. Council Fgn. Med. Grads. Roman Catholic. Office: 2200 W Roosevelt Rd Suite 12 Broadview IL 60153

ALEXIS, MARCUS, educator; b. N.Y.C., Feb. 26, 1932; B.A., Bklyn. Coll., 1953; M.A. (Univ. scholar, Hinman fellow), Mich. State U., 1954; Ph.D. (Univ. fellow), U. Minn., 1959; m.; 3 children. Instr. econs. U. Minn., 1954-57; asst. prof. econs. and mktg. Macalester Coll., 1957-60; asso. prof. mktg. DePaul U., 1960-62; asso. prof. to prof. bus. adminstrn. U. Rochester, 1962-70; prof. econs. Northwestern U., Evanston, Ill., 1970—, chmn. dept., 1975—; mem. ICC, 1979-80, vice chmn., 1981, acting chmn., 1981; vis. prof. U. Calif. at Berkeley, 1969-71. Vis. scholar, Ford Found. fellow Grad. Sch. Bus. Harvard, 1961-62; vis. asso. prof. U. Minn., 1962, 65. Recipient Outstanding Achievement award U. Minn., 1981. Mem. Am. Econ. Assn. (mem. com. to increase supply of minority economists 1971-74, mem. com. on honors and awards 1972—, chmn. com. status of minorities in the profession 1974—, dir. summer program in econs. for minority students 1974-79, mem. nominating com. 1981-82), Am. Mktg. Assn. (dir. 1968-70), Nat. Econ. Assn. (steering com. 1976—, Samuel Z. Westerfield Disting. Achievement award 1979), Caucus Black Economists (chmn. 1969-71, mem. steering com. 1969-73, 76—). Office: Coll Arts and Scis Northwestern U Evanston IL 60201

ALF, JOHN JAMES, chem. co. exec.; b. Aurora, Ill., May 7, 1936; s. Frank Peter and Anne Mary (Urlaub) A.; B.S., St. Mary's Coll., Winona, Minn., 1958; M.B.A., U. Mich., Ann Arbor, 1966; m. Marianne E. Schmidt, Jan. 24, 1959; children—Christine, Julie, Elizabeth, Eric. Chemist, Chemetron Corp., Rockhill Labs., Newport, Tenn., 1960-63, sr. chemist N.W. Chem. div., Detroit, 1963-65; mgr. adminstrv. services Vulcan Labs., Inc., Pontiac, Mich., 1965-68; v.p. ops. water mgmt. div. Clow Corp., Pontiac, 1968—. Mem. Am. Chem. Soc., Mensa. Home: 35306 Lancashire Ct Livonia MI 48152 Office: 408 Auburn Ave Pontiac MI 48058

ALFERINK, LARRY ALLEN, psychologist, educator; b. Holland, Mich., May 26, 1948; s. Benjamin and Dorothy (DeVisser) A.; B.A., Western Mich. U., 1970; M.S., Utah State U., 1973, Ph.D., 1975; m. Laura Rae Lawrence, Aug. 29, 1970; children—Kristine Jennifer, Paul Raymond. Instr. psychology Drake U., Des Moines, 1974, asst. prof. psychology, 1975-79, asso. prof. psychology, 1979—, chmn. dept., 1981—. Exxon Ednl. Found. Impact program grantee, 1978-80. Mem. AAAS, Assn. for Behavior Analysis, AAUP, Am. Psychol. Assn., Midwestern Psychol. Assn. Contbr. articles to profl. jours. Office: Dept Psychology Drake Univ Des Moines IA 50311

ALFORD, RICHARD MICHAEL, psychologist; b. N.Y.C., Feb. 25, 1951; s. David Burton and Helen Virginia (Zalonis) A.; B.A., Central Coll., Pella, Iowa, 1973; M.S., George Williams Coll., Downers Grove, Ill., 1977. Spl. account rep. Burroughs Corp., Oak Brook, Ill., 1973-75; counselor Wholistic Health Center, Hinsdale, Ill., 1976-77; staff psychologist Mercy Center, Aurora, Ill., 1977—; pvt. practice psychology, 1981—; cons., speaker profl., religious and social orgns. Mem. Am. Psychol. Assn., Ill. Psychol. Assn., Fox Valley Psychol. Assn., SAR. Presbyterian. Research on locus of control and adolescent behavior. Home: 305 Lakelawn Blvd Aurora IL 60506 Office: 1325 N Highland Ave Aurora IL 60506 also 1303 W Main St Saint Charles IL 60174

ALFRED, KARL SVERRE, orthopedic surgeon; b. Stavanger, Norway, July 10, 1917; s. Alfred Bjarne Abrahamsen Floen and Thora Garpestad; student U. Va., 1935-38; M.D., L.I. Coll. Medicine, 1942; m. Amalia Leona Bombach, July 26, 1951; children—Patricia (Mrs. Dennis Alleman), Richard Lincoln, Peter Karl. Intern, Mountainside Hosp., Montclair, N.J., 1942-43; resident orthopedics Univ. Hosps., Cleve., 1947-50; practice medicine specializing in orthopedic surgery, Cleve., 1950—; chief orthopedic surgery St. Vincent Charity Hosp., Cleve., 1955—, chief of staff, 1971-75; asso. staff Euclid Gen. Hosp., Cleve.; courtesy staff Univ., St. Luke's hosps., Cleve., Geauga Community Hosp., Chardon, O.; orthopedic cons. Norfolk & Western R.R.; affiliate tchr. orthopedics Bunts Edn. Inst., Cleve. Clinic Found. Trustee St. Vincent Charity Hosp., Cleve. Served with M.C., USNR, 1943-47. Episcopalian. Mason, Rotarian. Contbr. articles to profl. jours. Home: 20 Brandywood Dr Pepper Pike OH 44124 Office: 2475 E 22d St Cleveland OH 44115

ALGUIRE, DONALD EUGENE, product sterilization co. exec.; b. Kalamazoo, June 7, 1927; s. Samuel Isaiah and Catherine Etta (Hennion) A.; B.S. in Chem. Engring., Mich. State U., 1950; m. Frances Maxine Werner, Sept. 10, 1949; children—Mary Frances Alguire Friedman, Catherine Ann. Quality assurance supr. Post div. Gen. Foods, Battle Creek, Mich., 1952-54, research supr., 1954-58; div. tech. services mgr. Borden Co., Elgin, Ill., 1958-62; div. sales mgr. Griffith Labs., Inc., Chgo., 1962-70; pres., gen. mgr. Micro-Biotrol Co., Alsip, Ill., 1970—, also dir. Pres., Young Republican Club, 1960-61; precinct committeeman Republican party, 1962-71, del. state conv., 1969-71, twp. chmn., 1970-71, mem. county central com., 1970-71; mem. exec. com. Hinsdale Caucus Party, 1968-70; U.S. del. 4th UN conf. on peaceful use of atomic energy, 1971; trustee N. Central Coll., 1974—; active United Methodist Ch. Served with USAAF, 1945-46. Mem. Parenteral Drug Assn. (com. chmn. 1974-78), Am. Chem. Soc., Inst. Food Technologists, Assn. Advancement Med. Instrumentation, Internat. Soc. Pharm. Engrs., Chem. Mfrs. Assn. (dir. ethylene oxide industry council), Soc. Cosmetic Chemists, Assn. Governing Bds. Univ. and Colls. Republican. Methodist. Contbr. articles to profl. jours.

ALI, MIR MASOOM, educator; b. Bangladesh, Feb. 1, 1937; s. Mir Muazzam and Azifa Khatoon (Chowdhury) A.; came to U.S., 1969; B.Sc. with honors, U. Dacca, 1956, M.Sc., 1957; M.Sc., U. Toronto, 1967, Ph.D., 1969; m. Firoza Chowdhury, June 25, 1959; children—Naheed, Fahima, Farah, Mir Ishtiaque. Research officer Ministry of Food and Agriculture, Ministry of Commerce, Central Pub. Service Commn., Govt. of Pakistan, 1958-66; teaching asst. U. Toronto (Ont., Can.), 1966-69; asst. prof. math. scis. Ball State U., Muncie, Ind., 1969-74, asso. prof., 1974-78, prof., 1978—; vis. spl. lectr. U. Windsor (Can.), 1972-73; cons., researcher. Grantee Ball State U., 1976-79, Ind. Com. for Humanities, 1976-77. Fellow Royal Statis. Soc. London; mem. Am. Statis. Assn., Inst. Math. Statistics, Am. Math. Soc., Indian Statis. Assn., Am. Inst. for Decision Scis. Moslem. Contbr. articles to profl. jours. Home: 3003 Riverside Ave Muncie IN 47304 Office: Ball State U Dept Mathematical Sciences Muncie IN 47306

ALIBER, ROBERT Z., economist; b. Keene, N.H., Sept. 19, 1930; s. Norman H. and Sophie (Becker) A.; A.B., Williams Coll., 1952; A.B., Cambridge (Eng.) U., 1954; A.M., Yale U., 1958; Ph.D., 1962; m. Deborah Baltzly, Sept. 9, 1955; children—Jennifer, Rachel, Michael. Asst. instr. Yale U., 1958-59; staff economist Commn. on Money and Credit, 1959-61; staff economist Commn. for Econ. Devel., 1961-64; sr. econ. advisor AID, 1964; lectr. internat. econs. Johns Hopkins U., 1964; asso. prof. Grad. Sch. Bus., U. Chgo., 1965-75, prof. internat. econs. and fin., 1975—, chmn. com. on public policy studies, 1978-81, dir. Center for Studies in Internat. Fin., 1975; vis. scholar Fed. Res. Bank, San Francisco, 1975; Nat. Westminster Bank vis. prof. internat. fin. London Grad. Sch. Bus. Studies, 1979; prof. Salzburg Seminar in Am. Studies, 1974; cons. in field. Served with U.S. Army, 1954-56. Mem. Am. Econ. Assn., Acad. Internat. Bus., Can. Econs. Assn., Assn. Policy Analysis and Mgmt. Author numerous books in field including: The International Money Game, 1973, 3d edit., 1978; Exchange Risk and Corporate International Finance, 1979. Editor: National Monetary Policies and the International Financial System, 1976. Home: 5638 S Dorchester Ave Chicago IL 60637 Office: Grad Sch Bus U Chgo 1101 E 58th St Chicago IL 60637

ALIG, FRANK DOUGLAS STALNAKER, constrn. co. exec.; b. Indpls., Oct. 10, 1921; s. Clarence Schirmer and Marjory (Stalnaker) A.; student Mich. U., 1939-41; B.S., Purdue U., 1948; m. Ann Bobbs, Oct. 22, 1949; children—Douglas, Helen, Barbara. Proj. engr. Ind. State Hwy. Commn., Indpls., 1948; pres. Alig-Stark Constrn. Co., Inc., 1949-57, Frank S. Alig, Inc., 1957—; chmn. bd. Concrete Structures Corp., Indpls.; v.p., dir. Bo-Wit Products Corp., Edinburg, Ind.; pres. dir. Home Stove Realty Co.; pres, dir. Home Land Investment Co., Inc. Served with AUS, 1943-46. Registered profl. engr., Ind. Mem. U.S., Ind. socs. profl. engrs., Prestressed Concrete Inst., U.S. Ind. State, Indpls. chambers commerce. Republican. Presbyn. (deacon). Clubs: Woodstock, Dramatic, University, Lambs (Indpls.). Home: 8080 N Pennsylvania St Indianapolis IN 46240 Office: 4849 W 96th St Indianapolis IN 46268

AL-JADDA, SOUHEIL, surgeon; b. Souwera, Iraq, June 27, 1946; came to U.S., 1971; s. Muhammad Aadel and Souheila (Dassouki) Al-J.; M.D., Damascus (Syria) U., 1971; m. Sahar Dassouki, Aug. 5, 1971; children—Souheila, Aadel. Intern, Fairview Gen. Hosp., Cleve., 1971-72, surg. resident, 1972-76; practice medicine, specializing in gen. surgery, Norwalk, Ohio, 1976—; staff, Fisher Titus Meml. Hosp., Norwalk, 1976—. Diplomate Am. Bd. Surgery. Fellow A.C.S., Internat. Coll. Surgeons; mem. AMA, Ohio Med. Assn., Huron County Med. Soc. Home: 115 Sycamore Dr Norwalk OH 44857 Office: 34 Executive Dr Norwalk OH 44857

ALLABASTRO, WARREN ALLEN, architect; b. Elmwood Park, Ill., Apr. 21, 1940; s. Adolph Joseph and Lorraine (Para) A.; B.Arch., U. Ill., 1964; m. Alice Irene Graham, Oct. 22, 1966; children—Claudette, Marjorie, Warren Allen, Matthew. Partner, Anderson Allabastro & Assos., Architects, Northfield, Ill., 1967—; pres. Warren Allen Devel. Co., Northfield, 1965—. Mem. Planning Commn. Deerfield, 1976. Fellow Soc. Am. Registered Architects (dir. Ill. bd. 1972-75, award 1970, 73). Roman Catholic. Home: 80 Lincolnshire Dr Lincolnshire IL 60015 Office: 540 Frontage Rd Northfield IL 60093

ALLBEE, ROBERT GEORGE, justice Iowa Supreme Ct.; b. Muscatine, Iowa, Dec. 14, 1928; s. George Elbert and Ethel Leota (Khone) A.; student Grinnell Coll., 1948-50; A.B., Colo. Coll., 1952; J.D., Drake U., 1955; m. Jennie Johnson, Aug. 13, 1960; children—Susan, Carolyn, Thomas Anne. Admitted to Iowa bar, 1955; practiced law, Des Moines, 1955-75; judge Iowa 5th Dist. Ct., 1975-76; chief judge Iowa Ct. Appeals, 1976-78; justice Iowa Supreme Ct., 1978—. Served with USN, 1946-48. Recipient Disting. Service award Drake U., 1979, Grinnell Coll., 1981. Mem. Am. Coll. Trial Lawyers, Iowa Judges Assn., Iowa Bar Assn., Order of Coif. Republican. Presbyterian. Office: Supreme Ct State Capitol Des Moines IA 50319

ALLEN, BELLE, mgmt. and communications cons. exec.; b. Chgo.; d. Isaac and Clara (Friedman) A.; m. William Karp, May 27, 1961. Pres., Belle Allen Communications, Chgo., 1955—; treas., pres., chmn. bd. William Karp Cons. Co., Inc., Chgo., 1960—; v.p., treas., dir. Cultural Arts Surveys, Inc., Chgo., 1965-80; mem. bd. govs. consumer adv. council Fed. Res. System, 1979—; mem. Ill. Gov.'s Grievance Panel for State Employees, 1979—; mem. adv. gov. bd. Ill. Coalition on Women's Employment, 1979—; Founding mem. United Cerebral Palsy Assn. Chgo., 1954, bd. dirs., 1954-58; mem. Welfare Public Relations Forum, 1958-62; dir. personnel placement Indsl. Relations Research Assos., 1960-61; mem. exec. com., chmn. public relations com. Regional Ballet Ensemble Chgo., 1961-62; cons. City Club Chgo., 1962-65; bd. dirs. Soc. for Chgo. Strings, 1963-64; mem. Ill. State C. of C., 1961-74, Chgo. Hist. Soc., 1962-63, Field Mus. of Natural History, 1966-74; mem. campaign staff Adlai E. Stevenson, 1952, 56, John F. Kennedy, 1960; press conf. staff Eleanor Roosevelt, 1960; pres. Democratic Fedn. Ill., 1958-61; mem. Independent Dem. Coalition, 1968-69; dir. Citizens for Polit. Change, 1969; campaign mgr. City Council Chgo. aldermanic election, 42d Ward, 1969. Recipient Outstanding Service award United Cerebral Palsy Assn. Chgo., 1954; Communications award The White House, 1961. Mem. NOW, Nat. Assn. Inter-Group Relations Ofcls. (nat. conf. program com. 1959), Publicity Club Chgo. (chmn. inter-city relations com. 1960-61, Disting. Service award 1968), Soc. Personnel Adminstrs., Women's Equity Action League, Fashion Group Chgo. (dir. 1981—, editor newsletter 1981—), Chgo. Assn. Commerce and Industry (public relations com. 1961-63), Indsl. Relations Research Assos., Chgo. Area Assn. Affirmative Action and Compliance, Welfare Public Relations Forum. Club: Chicago Press (chmn. women's activities 1969-71). Editor, contbr. to articles and papers in bus. and profl. jours., publs., manuals, book. Office: 900 N Michigan Ave Chicago IL 60611

ALLEN, CARROL VERLE, co. exec., state legislator; b. Royal, Nebr., July 4, 1934; s. Verle Wilton and Gertrude Florance (Scheer) A.; student Yankton Coll.; m. Gladys Herrold, Sept. 20, 1953; children—Bruce, Betty, Charles. Active in profl. baseball, 1956-58; profl. umpire, 1962; owner, pres. Red Allen & Sons Custom Harvesting, Lake Andes, S.D., from 1959; mem. S.D. Senate, 1978—. Vice pres. Restore Lake Andes; mem. S.D. Democratic Central Com.; vol. Lake Andes Vol. Fire Dept. Mem. Lake Andes C. of C. Lutheran. Office: State Legislature State Capitol Pierre SD 57501*

ALLEN, CHARLES EUGENE, educator; b. Burley, Idaho, Jan. 25, 1939; s. Charles William and Elsie Permelia (Fowler) A.; B.S., U. Idaho, 1961; M.S., U. Wis., 1963, Ph.D., 1966; m. Connie Jeanette Block, June 19, 1960; children—Kerry Janelle, Tamara Sue. Research asst. U. Wis.-Madison, 1961-65; NSF fellow Commonwealth Sci. and Indsl. Research Orgn., Div. Food Research, Sydney, Australia, 1966-67; mem. faculty depts. animal sci. and food sci. and nutrition U. Minn., St. Paul, 1967—, prof., 1972—; vis. prof. animal sci. Pa. State U., 1978. Pres., Falcon Heights Parent Tchrs. Assn., 1973-74. Mem. Am. Soc. Animal Sci., Nat. Inst. Food Tech., Am. Meat Sci. Assn., Am. Inst. Nutrition, Minn. Inst. Food Tech., Sigma Xi. Lutheran. Contbr. articles to profl. jours. Office: 1354 Eckles Ave Saint Paul MN 55108

ALLEN, CLYDE EDGAR, JR., state govt. ofcl.; b. Lynn, Mass., Feb. 19, 1935; s. Clyde Edgar and Arlene Wentworth (Parker) A.; B.A. in Polit. Sci., Yale U., 1957; m. Esther Helen Gronhovd, June 22, 1958; children—Cynthia Louise, Scott Parker. Data processing programmer Nat. Security Agy., 1957-59; mgr. data processing Honeywell, Inc., Mpls., 1959-76; research dir. Minn. Taxpayers Assn., 1976-79; commr. revenue State of Minn., 1979—. Mem. Bloomington (Minn.) City Council, 1971-75, Bloomington Housing and Redevl. Authority, 1971-79; pres. Assn. Met. Municipalities, 1975; bd. dirs. League Minn. Cities, 1974-75; mem. met. council chmn.'s adv. com. Met. Transit Commr. Citizens Adv. Com., 1972-79. Republican. Lutheran. Office: Centennial Office Bldg Saint Paul MN 55145*

ALLEN, DELMAS JAMES, anatomist; b. Hartsville, S.C., Aug. 13, 1937; s. James Paul and Sara (Segars) A.; B.S. in Biology, Am. U. of Beirut, Lebanon, 1965, M.S., 1967; postgrad. Med. Coll. Ga., 1968; cert. in Radiation Sci., Colo. State U., 1969; Ph.D., U. N.D., 1974; m. Sarah Bahous, July 5, 1958; children—Carolyn, James, Susan. Teaching fellow dept. biology Am. U. Beirut, 1965-67; instr. dept. biology Clarke Coll., Dubuque, Iowa, 1968-69, asst. prof., 1969-72, chmn. dept. biology, 1969-72; grad. teaching fellow and research asst. U. N.D., Grand Forks, 1972-74; asst. prof. dept. anatomy U. South Ala., Mobile, 1974-75; asst. prof. dept. anatomy Med. Coll. Ohio, Toledo, 1975-77, asso. prof., 1977—, asst. dean Grad. Sch., 1979—; vis. prof., Brazil, 1980, Ryad U. Sch. Medicine, Saudi Arabia, 1981. Recipient A. Rodger Denison award N.D. Acad. Sci., 1973; Ala. Heart Assn. grantee, 1974-75, Am. Cancer Soc. grantee, 1977, Am. Heart Assn. grantee, 1977-80; geriatrics-gerontology grantee, 1980-81; recipient Golden Apple award for Excellence in Teaching, Med. Coll. Ohio, 1977, 78, 79, 80; research award Brazilian Acad. Sci., 1980, Northwestern Ohio Electron Microscopic Soc., 1980. Fellow Ohio Acad. Sci. (membership chmn. med. sci. sect. 1977-78, v.p. med. sect. 1978-79); mem. Soc. for Neurosci., Am. Assn. Anatomists, So. Soc. Anatomists, Am. Soc. Cell Biology, Midwest Assn. Anatomists, Pan Am. Soc. Anatomy, N.Y. Acad. Scis., Am. Heart Assn., European Brain and Behavior Soc. (hon. mem.), Brit. Brain Research Assn. (hon. mem.), Sigma Xi (Thesis Excellence award 1967, Award of Merit 1974, pres. Med. Coll. Ohio club 1978-79). Contbr. articles on neuroanatomy and electron microscopy to sci. jours.; editor: Three-Dimensional Microanatomy; contbr. chpts. in field to various textbooks; co-author neurosci. text. Home: 3341 W Bancroft Toledo OH 43606 Office: Dept Anatomy Med Coll Ohio C S 10008 Toledo OH 43699

ALLEN, DONALD RAY, physician; b. Evansville, Ind., Dec. 6, 1932; s. William Delmar and Mildred Adelaide (Ashworth) A.; A.B. cum laude, U. Evansville, 1957; M.D., Ind. U., 1960. Intern, Marion County Gen. Hosp., Indpls., 1960-61; resident VA Hosp., Louisville, 1963, St. Louis City Hosp., 1964, Washington U. Barnes Hosp., St. Louis, 1965; practice medicine specializing in family practice, Evansville. Diplomate Am. Bd. Family Practice. Fellow Am. Acad. Family Physicians; mem. AMA, Ind. Med. Assn., Vanderburgh County Med. Soc., Alpha Omega Alpha, Phi Chi. Office: VA Outpatient Clinic Evansville IN 47708

ALLEN, ERNIE ALBERT, JR., chem. co. exec.; b. Decatur, Ill., Jan. 16, 1950; s. Ernie Albert and Luise Hefner A.; B.S. in Fin.-Acctg., So. Ill. U., Carbondale, 1972; m. Lynda Ishee, Dec. 1, 1972; children—Christina, Carla, Eric. Jr. acct. Kaiser Agrl. Chems., Inc., Sullivan, Ill., 1972-76, acct. supr. III, 1976-77, regional acctg. mgr., 1978, regional controller, 1978—. Bd. dirs. United Way Moultrie County, 1980—. Mem. So. Ill. U. Alumni Assn., Beta Alpha Psi. Democrat. Methodist. Clubs: Am. Business (v.p. 1979-80, pres.-elect 1980-81, pres. 1981-82), Sno-n-Go Snowmobile. Home: 19 Corey Ave Sullivan IL 61951 Office: Kaiser Agrl Chems Inc 101 W Jefferson St Sullivan IL 61951

ALLEN, EUGENE, JR., mfg. co. exec.; b. Chgo., Nov. 7, 1937; s. Eugene and Pearl (Smith) A.; B.S., Ill. Inst. Tech., 1970; M.B.A., U. Chgo., 1976; m. Ledell Fields, Apr. 16, 1961; children—Sheryl, Karla, Nicole, Eugene M. Chemist, formulator and paint technologist Sherwin-Williams Co., 1963-67; materials engr. Libby, McNeill & Libby, 1967-69; prodn. supr., div. sales mgr. Avon Products Inc., 1969-74; exec. trainee, ops. mgr. Jewel Cos. Inc., Chgo., 1974-75; v.p. mktg. and sales Valeer Industries Inc., Mundelein, Ill., 1975-76; sr. v.p., dir. mktg. and sales HUB States Corp., Indpls., 1976-79; pres., chief operating officer Clinitemp, Inc., Indpls., 1979-81; pres., chief exec. officer Aquamint Labs., Inc., Indpls., 1981—. Pres., Stoney Island Heights Civic Assn., Chgo., 1968-70; bd. dirs. Ivy Hill Civic Assn., Arlington Heights, Ill., 1972-76, Youth for Christ, Indpls.; adv. bd. Lawrence Twp. Sch. Dist., Ind., 1977-78; mem. Dist. Export

Council for Ind., 1979—. Served with U.S. Army, 1961-63. Recipient Paint Technologist award Nat. Paint Industry Ednl. Bur., 1966. Club: Exec. Program (U. Chgo.). Home: 7527 N Cape Cod Ln Indianapolis IN 46250 Office: 6256 La Pas Trail Indianapolis IN 46268

ALLEN, FLORENCE BROTHERTON, cosmetic co. exec.; b. Detroit, Apr. 19, 1918; d. Norton T. and Mary (Kleinow) Brotherton; B. in Design, U. Mich., 1940; postgrad. Chgo. Sch. Design, 1940-41, Eastern Mich. U., 1969-70; m. Arthur W. Allen, Dec. 27, 1940; children—Arthur W., David, Barbara. Asst., Archtl. and Design Library, U. Mich., Ann Arbor, 1969-71; beauty cons. Mary Kay Cosmetics, Ann Arbor, 1971-73, sales dir. mktg. mgmt., 1973-74, sr. sales dir., 1974—; paintings shown at U. Mich. Sch. Architecture, 1970. Recipient Cadillac car award Mary Kay Cosmetics, 1977, 79; named to $250,000 Club, 1980. Mem. U. Mich. Alumni Assn., Bus. and Profl. Women, Women Painters, Washtenaw County Med. Aux. (v.p. 1970), St. Joseph Mercy Hosp. Aux. (co-founder 1946-47), Kappa Kappa Gamma. Republican. Presbyterian. Clubs: Women's City, Faculty Women's. Address: 895 Greenhills Dr Ann Arbor MI 48105

ALLEN, HENRY SERMONES, JR., lawyer, health care cons.; b. Bronxville, N.Y., Aug. 26, 1947; s. Henry S. and Cecelia Marie (Chartrand) A.; A.B. magna cum laude, Washington U., St. Louis, 1969; M.P.A., Cornell U., 1973, J.D., 1974; m. Louann Beckman, June 25, 1976; 1 son, David Beckman. Adminstrv. resident Montefiore Hosp. and Med. Center, Bronx, N.Y., 1971; research trainee Nat. Center Health Services Research, HEW, 1974-75; admitted to Ill. bar, 1974; adj. asst. prof. hosp. law Ithaca (N.Y.) Coll., 1974-75; lectr., adj. asst. prof. health services adminstrn. and law Sangamon State U., Springfield, Ill., 1975—; adj. asst. prof. hosp. law Coll. of St. Francis, Joliet, Ill., 1980-81; asso. firm Vedder, Price, Kaufman & Kammholz, Chgo., 1975-79; ind. practice law, health care cons., Chgo. and Springfield, 1979-81; partner firm Allen & Reed, Chgo. and Springfield, 1981—; lectr. in field. Bd. dirs. Dr. Deepak K. Merchant Found. HUD fellow, 1969-71. Mem. Am. Soc. Hosp. Attys., Ill. Soc. Hosp. Attys., Nat. Health Lawyers Assn., Phi Beta Kappa, Omicron Delta Epsilon. Club: Cornell U. of Chgo. Home: 10421 S Longwood Dr Chicago IL 60643 Office: 134 S LaSalle St Suite 800 Chicago IL 60603 also 1128 S 5th St Springfield IL 62703

ALLEN, HERBERT JOSEPH, social worker; b. Jersey City, May 19, 1922; s. Benjamin James and Jeanetta Gladys (Casey) A.; B.S. in Edn., U. Cin., 1946; M.S. in Social Work, Case Western Res. U., 1948; m. Gwen Cann, July 26, 1949 (div.); 1 dau., Deborah Allen Kane. Dir. social work dept. Barney Children's Med. Center, Dayton, Ohio, 1967; supr. Family and Children's Service, Dayton, 1968; dir. social work dept. Good Samaritan Hosp., Dayton, 1968; field service asso. prof., dir. social work dept. Cin. Gen. Hosp.-U. Cin. Med. Center, 1970—; adj. asst. prof. Thomas More Coll., Ft. Mitchell, Ky., 1978; field service asso. prof. Coll. Community Services, U. Cin., 1979; adj. asso. prof., dir. dept. social work U. Cin. Pres., Central Community Health Bd. Catchment Area 11, 1976, Mt. Auburn Health Center, 1977; lectr. Am. Hosp. Assn., Soc. for Dirs. Hosp. Social Work Depts. Served with U.S. Army, 1942-46. Named Cin. Social Worker of Year, Social Service Assn. Greater Cin., 1952, Nat. Assn. Black Social Workers, 1973; award Pride mag., Cin., 1979. Mem. Soc. Dirs. Hosp. Social Work Depts., Am. Hosp. Assn. (dir. 1975-77), Ohio Hosp. Assn., Child Health Assn., Nat. Conf. Social Welfare, Kappa Alpha Psi. Democrat. Roman Catholic. Home: 144 Dorsey St Cincinnati OH 45210 Office: Cin Gen Hosp-U Cin Med Center 234 Goodman St Cincinnati OH 45229

ALLEN, JAMES CURTIS, mfg. co. exec.; b. Winston, Mo., June 7, 1922; s. Vernon and Carrie Belle (Palmer) A.; grad. Chillicothe Bus. Coll., (Mo.), 1942, Internat. Corr. Schs., 1946; m. Juanita G. Kennedy, Dec. 4, 1944; children—Daryl C., Karen A., Marti L., Jimmie, Randy. Accountant, Nat. Bellas Hess, Kansas City, Mo., 1946-48; controller Lawn-Boy div. Outboard Marine Corp., Lamar, Mo., 1948-63; sec.-treas. EFCO Corp., Monett, Mo., 1963-66; co-owner, sec-treas. F.M. Thorpe Mfg. Co., Lamar, Mo., 1966—; dir. Barton County State Bank. Pres., United Fund, 1970-71; pres. Community Betterment, 1968-70; dist. chmn. Sowemco council Boy Scouts Am., 1964-66, Arrowhead council, 1972, v.p. Mo-Kans Area council, 1975-79, recipient Golden Sun award, Order of Arrow; mem. Lamar Sch. Bd., 1969-71; mem. Lamar Park Bd., 1955—, pres., 1973—. Served with USNR, 1942-45. Recipient Outstanding Leadership award Mo. Municipal League, 1971; Distinguished Service award Kiwanis Club Monett, Mo., 1965; Leadership award Mo. Community Betterment, 1970; Golden Sun award; chpt. farmer award Future Farmers Am., 1979; Boss of Yr. award Am. Bus. Womens Assn., 1980. Mem. Lamar, Mo. chambers commerce. Methodist (chmn. bd. 1971, del. conf. 1968-71, treas. 1966—, supt. 1955-63). Mason (Shriner), Rotarian (pres. 1971-72, Man of Yr. award 1979), Kiwanian (pres. 1968). Home: 400 W 1st St Lamar MO 64759 Office: 1801 Gulf St Lamar MO 64759

ALLEN, JAMES SIDNEY, ophthalmologist; b. Rochester, N.Y., Sept. 25, 1945; s. William Sperry and Mary (Frayer) A.; B.A., Williams Coll., 1967; M.D., U. Oreg., 1972; m. Sharon Smith, Oct. 18, 1977; 1 son, William Sperry. Intern, Santa Clara Valley Med. Center, San Jose, Calif., 1972-73; resident Stanford U., 1973-74, U. Rochester, 1974-77; fellow Wills Eye Hosp., Phila., 1977-78; practice medicine specializing in ophthalmology St. Paul Eye Clinic, 1978—; mem. staffs U. Minn. Hosps., VA Hosp., St. Joseph's Hosp.; clin. asst. prof. U. Minn. Mem. Am. Acad. Ophthalmology, AMA, Am. Assn. Ophthalmology. Presbyterian. Home: 23 Dove Ln Saint Paul MN 55110 Office: 1224 Lowry Med Arts Bldg Saint Paul MN 55102

ALLEN, JULIUS OLU, alcoholism and mental health counselor; b. Cape Coast, Ghana, Feb. 6, 1930; came to U.S., 1962, naturalized, 1970; s. James Akerele and Dorcas Ade (Ejide) Ale; B.A. with high honors, Lewis U., Lockport, Ill., 1975; diploma Chgo. Counseling Center, 1978; M.A., Internat. U., 1979; m. Prudence Addy, Jan. 20, 1957; children—Coni, Moumi, Rotimi, Sonya. Lic. ins. broker, 1965-75; counselor, dir. drug abuse and prevention program Garfield Counseling Center, Chgo., 1977—. Recipient Citizen's award Chgo. Police Dept., 1978. Mem. Am. Assn. Mental Deficiency, Center Counseling and Psychotherapy, Afro-Am. Corrections Officers Movement (pres.). Mormon. Club: Human Growth Book; editor Shegun 1975. Research on mentally health persons, better prison systems. Home: 6959 S Paxton 2E Chicago IL 60649 Office: PO Box 49133 Chicago IL 60649

ALLEN, LOIS ARLENE HEIGHT (MRS. JAMES PIERPONT ALLEN), musician; b. Kenton, Ohio, Sept. 2, 1932; d. Robert Harold and Frances (Sims) Height; B.S., Ohio State U., 1954, M.A., 1958; m. James Pierpont Allen, June 14, 1953; children—Daniel Pierpont, Carole Elizabeth. Tchr. jr. and sr. high music, Upper Arlington High Sch., Columbus, O., 1954-56; high sch. music supr., Westerville, Ohio, 1956-67; tchr. music Ohio State U. Sch., 1957-59; pvt. tchr. music, Columbus, 1960—; ch. organist, choir dir. Mountview Bapt. Ch., Upper Arlington, Ohio, 1960-77; ednl. radio interviewer WOSU, 1970, 71, 72. Mem. Project Hope, Central Ohio, 1967-73; mem. sustaining bd. Maryhaven House for Alcoholic Women, 1969-73, 1st v.p.; mem. women's bd. Columbus Symphony, 1965-79, chmn. youth council, 1965-68, pres.-elect women's assn., 1973, pres., 1974-76; chmn. juried art competition Central Ohio Arts Festival, 1969, 70, chmn. fine and applied arts, 1971, gen. chmn. of festival, 1972; area chmn. United Appeals Franklin County, 1966-68, Heart drive, 1968-75; pres. Ohio State U. Soc. Friends Sch. Music, 1977-78; trustee Columbus Symphony Orch., 1973—, Opera/Columbus, 1981-82; mem. vol. council Am. Symphony Orch. League, 1981—; organist, choir dir. North Congregational Ch., 1979-82; area leader Republican Party, 1966-68. Mem. Am. Guild Organists, Choristers Guild Am., Fedn. Am. Bapt. Musicians, Center Sci. and Industry, Ohio State Hist. Soc., Ohio Orgn. Orchs. (treas. 1976-79, sec. 1979—), Nat. Trust U.S.A., Grange, Tau Beta Sigma, Delta Omicron, Kappa Delta (Central Ohio Woman of Yr. 1970). Mem. Order Eastern Star, White Shrine of Jerusalem. Clubs: Ohio State U. Alumnae of Franklin County (pres. 1962-64, 71-72). Home: 3355 Somerford Rd Columbus OH 43221

ALLEN, LOUIS G., banker; b. 1929; B.B.A., U. Mich., 1951, M.B.A., 1956; married. Fin. analyst Ford Motor Co., Detroit, 1954-58; credit dept. Mfrs. Nat. Bank Detroit, 1958-61, asst. cashier, 1961-63, mortgage dept., 1963-65, v.p. mortgage dept., 1965-66, v.p. adminstrn. mortgage dept., 1966-68, sr. v.p. adminstrn. mortgage dept., 1968-70, exec. v.p., 1970-73, pres., chief adminstrv. officer, 1973—, also dir.; dir. Arnold Home Inc., CBDA Inc.; trustee Citizens Mortgage Investment Trust. Served in U.S. Army, 1951-53. Office: Mfrs Nat Bank Detroit Mfrs Bank Tower Renaissance Center Detroit MI 48243*

ALLEN, MARCIA LEE, sch. counselor; b. Poplar Bluff, Mo., Apr. 14, 1929; d. Marshall Lee and Nola May (Adams) A.; B.M., Central Meth. Coll., Fayette, Mo., 1951; M.S. in Edn., U. Wis., Madison, 1962; M.A. in Edn., Eastern Mich. U., Ypsilanti, 1971; postgrad. U. Hawaii, summers 1964, 71, spring 1969. High sch. tchr., drama coach, volleyball coach, Ellsinore, Mo., 1951-53; high sch. tchr. music, Neelyville, Mo., 1953-56; elem. music tchr. Winship Sch., Detroit, 1956-76; guidance counselor Cerveny Middle Sch., Detroit, 1975-77, acting head counseling dept., 1977-78, guidance counselor, 1978—; Detroit Region 4 counselor rep. A.F.T., 1978. Exec. bd. P.T.O., Winship Sch., Detroit, 1973-74. Recipient cert. of recognition Sch. Vol. Service, Detroit, 1974, cert. achievement Chrysler Group Counseling Tng. Program, 1976. Mem. Guidance Assn. Met. Detroit (exec. council 1978—), Am. Personnel and Guidance Assn., Mich. Personnel and Guidance Assn. (conv. com. 1980—, exec. bd. 1981-82), Am. Sch. Counselors Assn., Mich. Sch. Counselors Assn. (exec. bd. 1981—), Mich. Assn. Measurement and Evaluation in Guidance, Detroit Fedn. Tchrs., Mich. Fedn. Tchrs., A.F.T., AFL-CIO, Cerveny Community Council. Republican. Methodist. Office: 15850 Strathmoor St Detroit MI 48227

ALLEN, MARION CARROLL, clergyman; b. Spartanburg, S.C., Dec. 12, 1914; s. Albert Mayfield and Caroline May (Rogers) A.; B.A., Furman U., 1937; M.Div., Yale, 1940; M.A., Kans. U., 1960; m. Eleanor Earl Burt, July 31, 1943; children—Marian, Burt, Robert, Louise. Ordained to ministry Am. Bapt. Conv., 1940, received into United Ch. of Christ; pastor Bapt. chs., Bristol, Conn., 1940-47, Beaufort, S.C., 1947-50, Clemson, S.C., 1950-56, Lawrence, Kans., 1956-76; pastor First Congregational Ch., Topeka, 1976, Central Congregational Ch., 1977-80, Pilgrim Congregational Ch., Wichita, Kans., 1980—; instr. religion Clemson U., 1951-56, instr. homiletics Central Sem., Kansas City, Kans., 1959-61, English, Kans. U., 1958, 76—. Bd. dirs. YMCA, U. Kans., 1956-60; v.p. Lawrence Friends of Music, 1968-75; sec. adv. bd. Kans. Sch. Religion, 1970-76. Mem. Topeka Ministerial Alliance, Lawrence Ministerial Alliancce, Topeka Council Chs., Consultation of Cooperating Chs. Kans., Kans. Okla. Conf. United Ch. of Christ. Clubs: Masons. Author: A Voice Not Our Own, 1963. Editor: The Springs of Learning, 1969. Editor: Serving in the Armed Forces, monthly 1972-74. Home: 2906 Alabama St Lawrence KS 66044

ALLEN, MARION TURNER, former public health exec.; b. Lansing, Mich., May 18, 1921; d. Howard Elmer and Cora Marie (Lee) Turner; student Mich. State U., 1955, 58, 59, Lansing Community Coll., 1956-57; m. Glenn S. Allen, Jr., Jan. 6, 1979; step-children—Holly Allen (Mrs. Gale Mull), Susan Allen. Sec., office mgr. bur. chief Mich. Dept. Public Health, Lansing, 1948-57, office mgr., 1957-73, adminstrv. analyst, 1973-75, program and personnel coordinator, 1975-79. Mem. Profl. Secs. Internat. Republican. Episcopalian. Club: Lansing City. Home: 13036 Sycamore Dr DeWitt MI 48820

ALLEN, MICHAEL WAKEFIELD, ednl. psychologist; b. Hampton, Iowa, June 6, 1946; s. Eugene Richard and Wilma Mary (Wakefield) A.; B.A., Cornell Coll., 1968; M.A., Ohio State U., 1969, Ph.D., 1971; m. Mary Ann Hoel, Oct. 23, 1976; 1 son, Christopher Wakefield. Dir. research and devel. in computer assisted instrn. Ohio State U., 1970-73; sr. cons. advanced ednl. systems Control Data Corp., Mpls., 1974-78, prin. cons., 1979-80, exec. dir. advanced ednl. systems research and devel., 1980—; mem. faculty dept. curriculum and instructional systems U. Minn., 1981—. Mem. Assn. for Devel. of Computer-Based Instructional Systems (pres. 1980-83), Am. Ednl. Research Assn., Am. Assn. Artificial Intelligence, Assn. for Intelligence Stimulation and Behavior Modeling. Methodist. Founding editor Jour. Computer Based Instrn., 1975-79, mem. editorial rev. bd., 1980—. Home: 8621 Pine Hill Rd Bloomington MN 55438 Office: 511 11th Ave S Minneapolis MN 55415

ALLEN, REVA ILENE, social worker; b. Brownsville, Tex., Jan. 15, 1953; d. Donald Vernon and Helene Irene (Bannert) A.; B.A. in Sociology (fellow), Baylor U., 1974; M.A. in Social Work Treatment, U. Chgo., 1976. Psychol. technician Residential Drug Abuse Center, Heart-of-Tex. Mental Health/Mental Retardation Center, Waco, 1974; psychiat. social worker Family Service & Mental Health Center, Cicero, Ill., 1976-78; psychiat. social worker Children's Rehab. Unit, Family Guidance Center/Community Mental Health Center, St. Joseph, Mo., 1978-80, children's services coordinator, 1980—. Mem. Citizens Adv. Commn., St. Joseph, 1979—. Recipient Community Service award Baylor U., 1974. Bd. dir. Parents and Children Together, 1981—. Mem. Nat. Assn. Social Workers (sec. Mo. chpt., 1980—), Region VII Children's Mental Health Network (chmn. 1980-82), Mo. Child Care Assn. Acad. Cert. Social Workers. Democrat. Mem. Disciples of Christ Ch. Composer: Let Me In, Come to Raise Your Head, Rejoice: We're All Here. Home: 3020 Mayfair Dr Saint Joseph MO 64506 Office: Family Guidance Center/Community Mental Health Center 200 Corby Bldg 5th & Felix Saint Joseph MO 64501

ALLEN, RICHARD BLOSE, lawyer, editor; b. Aledo, Ill., May 10, 1919; s. James Albert and Claire (Smith) A.; B.S., U. Ill., 1941, J.D., 1947; m. Marion Treloar, Aug. 27, 1949; children—Penelope, Jennifer, Leslie Jean. Admitted to Ill. bar, 1947; staff editor Am. Bar Assn. Jour., 1947-48, 63-66, exec. editor, 1966-70, editor, 1970—; pvt. practice law, Aledo, 1949-57; gen. counsel Ill. State Bar Assn., 1957-63. Served from pvt. to maj. Q.M.C., AUS, 1941-46. Mem. Am., Ill. (mem. assembly 1972-74), Chgo. bar assns., Am. Law Inst., Selden Soc., Scribes, Sigma Delta Chi, Kappa Tau Alpha, Phi Delta Phi, Alpha Tau Omega. Clubs: Tower (Chgo.); Mich. Shores (Wilmette). Home: 702 Illinois Rd Wilmette IL 60091 Office: 77 S Wacker Dr Chicago IL 60606

ALLEN, RICHARD JOHN, state senator, veterinarian, farmer; b. Ithaca, Mich., Aug. 6, 1933; s. Lester Jon and Erma (Prichard) A.; B.S., Mich. State U., 1955, D.V.M., 1957; m. Joann Wright, 1963; children—Lester James, Carri Jo, Jotham Mitchell. Owner, veterinarian State Rd. Animal Hosp., Alma, Mich., 1958—; asso. prof. Alma Coll., 1960-69; v.p., treas. Bon Accord Farms, Ithaca, 1962—. Mem. Mich. Ho. of Reps., 1969-72, Mich. State Senate, 1975—. Mem. AAAS, Mich. Vet. Med. Assn., Farm Bur. Presbyterian. Club: Rotary. Address: PO Box 30036 State Capitol Lansing MI 48909*

ALLEN, ROBERT SHAW, chem. engr.; b. Providence, Nov. 12, 1931; s. Ray Spencer and Madeline (Shaw) A.; B.S. in Chem. Engring., Worcester Poly. Inst., 1956; m. Norma Elaine Porter, Nov. 8, 1958; children—Trudi Lynn, Ronald Shaw. With Am. Cyanamid Co., 1956-59; with Dewey & Almy Chem. div. W.R. Grace Co., 1959-62, Monroe Mfg. Co., 1962-67; Neutron Produ- cts, Inc., 1967-68, Continental Oil Co., 1968-72, Allen-Herzog Asso., Framingham, Mass., 1972-73, World-Wide Constrn. Services, Inc., Wichita, Kans., 1973-76; prin. Allen Assos., engrs. and consultants, Wichita, 1976—. Chmn. Sedgwick County Republican Central Com., 1977—. Served with U.S. Army, 1953-55. Mem. Am. Inst. Chem. Engrs., Instrument Soc. Am., Nat. Soc. Profl. Engrs., Kans. Engring. Soc., Wichita Soc. Profl. Engrs., Wichita Area C. of C. Club: Rolling Hills Country. Home: 229 N Westfield St Wichita KS 67212 Office: 9505 W Central Ave Suite 101 Wichita KS 67212

ALLEN, ROSE M., pharmacist; b. Eunice, La., Oct. 13, 1947; d. Clarence Moses and Beatrice (Earl) A.; B.S. in Pharmacy, Tex. So. U., 1971; student U. Houston, 1974-75, Syracuse U., 1975-76. Intern, Quality Pharmacy, Los Angeles, 1969; pharmacist Globe Pharmacies, Inc., Houston, 1971-73; salesperson, cons. Gulfco (now Amfac) Drug Co., Houston, 1973; pharmacist, asst. mgr. Sun Rexall, Alief, Tex., 1973-74; staff pharmacist VA Hosp., Syracuse, N.Y., 1975-76, Cleve., 1976-77; pharmacist in charge outpatient services VA Med. Center, Brecksville, Ohio, 1977-80; clin. pharmacist Univ. Hosps. of Cleve., from 1980; now exec. dir. Allen Enterprises Diversified, Euclid, Ohio; cons. Health, Edn. and Promotion (H.E.A.P.), Drug Info. Services Cons. Second v.p. Young Voter Activists, Inc., Cleve.; del. of People to People Goodwill Tour (Ohio) To People's Republic of China, 1982; trustee young people's congregation Fairmont Temple, Beachwood, Ohio, also chmn. social action com.; chmn. other health agys. sub-com. Am. Cancer Soc.; mem. exec. bd. NAACP, 1978-80, mem. health services com., 1980—, chmn. polit. action com. 1979-80. Recipient, award for outstanding achievement in public edn. Am. Cancer Soc., commendation from city of Euclid council; commendation Bd. County Commrs., Cuyahoga County, Ohio, 1981. Mem. Cleve. Soc. Hosp. Pharmacists (v.p. 1979-80), Fedn. Internationale Pharmaceutique, Am. Soc. Hosp. Pharmacists, Ohio State Pharm. Assn. (chmn. interprofl. relations com.), Greater Cleve. Acad. Pharmacy (chmn. speakers bur., coordinator media and public relations), Nat. Assn. Female Execs. (network dir.), Network Entreprenurial Women, Internat. Platform Assn., Am. Pharm. Assn., Congressional Health Brain Trust, Lambda Kappa Sigma, Delta Sigma Theta, (recipient Pres. Commendation for Outstanding Service 1978). Club: Women's City (Cleve.). Contbr. articles to newspapers; columnist Ask Your Pharmacist, Club Date mag. Home: 26241 Lake Shore Blvd Euclid OH 44132 Office: PO Box 23126 Euclid OH 44132

ALLEN, SANDRA KAE FIRNHABER, educator; b. Red Wing, Minn., Oct. 9, 1938; d. Alfred E. and Dorothy M. (Hack) Firnhaber; B.A., Blackburn Coll., 1961; M.S., So. Ill. U., 1977; children—Elizabeth Anne, Robert Edmund. Tchr., Thomas Edison Jr. High Sch., Springfield, Ill., 1961-63, 1965-67, Lanphier High Sch., Springfield, 1963-64, Nokomis Unit Dist., Fillmore, Ill., 1967; tchr. Hillsboro (Ill.) High Sch., 1967—, chmn. humanities dept., 1974-75, chmn. social studies dept., 1976—; guest speaker Kiwanis, Rotary, and Hillsboro Hist. Socs., 1978-79; partner, part-time operator CtCritic's Choice Bookstore, Hillsboro, 1979—; real estate agt., 1979—. Public relations officer Montgomery County Young Republicans, 1980-81. Recipient Margaretha Klein Ott Honors award in Ednl. Adminstrn., So. Ill. U., 1977. Mem. Assn. Supervision and Curriculum Devel., Hillsboro Unit Edn. Assn. (v.p., mem. exec. bd.). Republican. Lutheran. Home: PO Box 164 Hillsboro IL 62049 Office: 522 E Tremont St Hillsboro IL 62049

ALLEN, THOMAS ERNEST, lawyer; b. Salt Lake City, Sept. 30, 1939; s. Kenneth L. and Joyce Catherine (Thompson) A.; A.B., Dartmouth Coll., 1961; J.D., U. Mich., 1967; m. Elizabeth Harker Curtis, June 26, 1965; children—Kenneth, Susan, Gregory. Admitted to Minn. bar, 1967, Mo. bar, 1976, others; asso. mem. firm Peterson, Peterson & Allen, Albert Lea, Minn., 1967-76, partner, 1970-76; asso. mem. firm Biggs, Curtis, Casserly & Barnes, St. Louis, 1976-77; partner Curtis & Crossen, Clayton, Mo., 1977—. Served with M.I., U.S. Army, 1962-64. Mem. Am., Minn., Mo., St. Louis Met. bar assns., Phi Kappa Psi. Republican. Episcopalian. Clubs: Lions, Mo. Athletic, Masons. Home: 423 Miriam St Kirkwood MO 63122 Office: 230 S Bemiston Suite 410 Clayton MO 63105

ALLEN, THOMAS FRANK, educator; b. Joliet, Ill., June 28, 1950; s. Ambrose and Mary Ann (Dinardo) A.; B.A., Marquette U., 1973; M.A., Sangamon State U., 1974; Ed.S., Iowa State U., 1979; m. Claudia A. McConnell, Aug. 10, 1979; 1 child, Tiffin. Grad. asst. Sangamon State U., 1973-74, Iowa State U., 1977-79; guidance dir. Joliet (Ill.) Cath. High Sch., 1975-77; hall advisor Iowa State U., Ames, 1977-79; prin. East Monona Community Schs., Moorhead, Iowa, 1979-80; supt. Fox Valley Community Schs., Cantril, Iowa, 1980-81, Melcher-Dallas Community Schs., Melcher, Iowa, 1981—; cons. in field. Mem. Iowa Assn. Sch. Adminstrs., Am. Assn. Sch. Adminstrs., Assn. for Supervision and Curriculum Devel., Iowa Assn. for Supervision and Curriculum. Roman Catholic. Club: Lions. Home: Melcher IA 50163 Office: Melcher IA 50163

ALLEN, VERNON EUGENE, mktg. exec.; b. Cleve., Dec. 24, 1919; s. Vernon L. and Beatrice (Figgins) A.; student pub. schs., Cleve.; m. Florence Wilma Stanard, Mar. 5, 1942; children—Vernon William, Carol Jean Allen Holmes, Gregory, Holly L. Allen May. Machine operator, Tinnerman Products Inc., Cleve., 1938-42; devel. engr. Eaton Corp., Cleve., 1946-47, sales supr., 1947-70, sales mgr., 1970-72, div. mktg. mgr., 1972-80, dir. community affairs, 1980—; mem. advisory bd. Investors Heritage Life Ins. Co., 1964-78. Capt. of Ohio Hwy. Patrol Aux., 1968-70. Served with C.E., U.S. Army, 1940-46; PTO, ETO. Decorated Bronze star. Mem. Eaton Soc. Inventors, Home Appliance Mfrs. Assn., Sales Mktg. Execs., Soc. Automotive Engrs., Indsl. Marketers Cleve., Am. Legion, VFW. Republican. Clubs: Wedgewood Country, University. Home: 14181 Cherokee Trail Middleburg Heights OH 44130 Office: 100 Erieview Plaza Cleveland OH 44114

ALLEN, WARREN WILLIAM, JR., brick co. exec.; b. St. Louis, Jan. 2, 1924; s. Warren William and Edith (Eilers) A.; student Purdue U., 1942-43; B.S. in Chem. Engring., Wash. U., 1948; m. Ruth Reddish, June 11, 1949; children—William Reddish, Margaret, John Warren. Sales engr. Presstite Engr. Co., 1948-51; with Hydraulic Press Brick Co., St. Louis, 1951—, sales engr., Cleve., 1951-52, sales mgr., Cleve., 1952-55, mgr. Haydite div., 1955-63, v.p., St. Louis, 1963-67, pres., Cleve., 1967—, also dir.; dir. St. Louis Steel Casting Inc. Dir. Expanded Shale Clay and Slate Inst. Served with AUS,

1943-46. Mem. Am. Ceramic Soc., Am. Concrete Inst., ASTM, Alpha Chi Sigma, Phi Delta Theta. Home: 1690 E Shore Dr Martinsville IN 46151 Office: PO Box 7 Brooklyn IN 46111

ALLEN, WILLIAM CECIL, physician; b. La Belle, Mo., Sept. 8, 1919; s. William H. and Viola O. (Holt) A.; A.B., U. Nebr., 1947, M.D., 1951; M.P.H., Johns Hopkins U., 1960; m. Madge Marie Gebhardt, Dec. 25, 1943; children—William Walter, Linda Diane Allen Deardeuff, Robert Lee, Leah Denise. Intern, Bishop Clarkson Meml. Hosp., Omaha, 1952; practice medicine specializing in family practice, Glasgow, Mo., 1952-59, specializing in preventive medicine, 1960—; dir. sect. chronic diseases Mo. div. health, Jefferson City, 1960-65; asst. med. dir. U. Mo. Med. Center, Columbia, 1965-75, asso. coordinator Mo. Regional Med. Program, 1968-73, coordinator health programs, 1969—, clin. asst. prof. community health and med. practice, 1962-65, asst. prof. community health and med. practice, 1965-69, asso. prof. dept. community health and med. practice, 1969-75, prof., 1975-76, prof. dept. family and community medicine, 1976—; cons. Mo. Regional Med. Program, 1966-76, Norfolk (Va.) Area Med. Sch. Authority, 1965-66; mem. governing body Area II Health Systems Agy., 1977—, mem. coordinating com., 1977—; founding dir. Mid-Mo. PSRO Corp., 1974-75, dir., 1976—. Mem. Gov.'s Adv. Council for Comprehensive Health Planning, 1970-73; trustee U. Mo. Med. Sch. Found., 1976—. Served with USMC, 1943-46. Diplomate Am. Bd. Preventive Medicine, Am. Bd. Family Practice. Fellow Am. Coll. Preventive Medicine, Am. Acad. Family Physicians, Royal Soc. Health; mem. Mo. Acad. Family Physicians (dir. 1956-59, publs. com. 1962—, edn. and sci. assembly com. 1975—), Mo. Med. Assn. (mem. com. on med. edn. and hosps. 1967-70, chmn. com. vol. health agys. 1972-79), Howard County Med. Soc. (pres. 1958-59), Boone County Med. Soc. (pres. 1974-75), Am. Diabetes Assn. (pres. 1978, dir. 1974-77), Mo. Diabetes Assn. (pres. 1972-73), Soc. Tchrs. Family Medicine (mem. com. on constn. and by-laws com. 1971-74), AMA, Mo. Public Health Assn., Mo. Heart Assn. (dir. 1971—, sec. 1979, v.p. 1980). Methodist. Club: Optimist. Contbr. articles to profl. jours. Home: 508 W Briarwood Columbia MO 65201 Office: M304 Medical Center Univ Missouri Columbia MO 65212

ALLEY, LOUIS EDWARD, educator; b. Drexel, Mo., Dec. 9, 1914; B.S. in Edn., Central Mo. State U., 1935; M.S., U. Wis., 1941; Ph.D., State U. Iowa, 1949; m. Mary Lee Brinegar, Nov. 26, 1936; children—Rebecca Ann, Louis William. Tchr. schs., Mo., Iowa and Kans., 1935-43, 45-46; mem. faculty Univ. High Sch., U. Iowa, 1946-54, asso. prof., head dept. phys. edn., 1953-54, vis. prof. under Fulbright program, Burma, 1949-50, mem. faculty U. Iowa, 1953-60, prof., adminstrv. asst. phys. edn., 1959-60, prof. phys. edn., 1960—, head dept. phys. edn. for men, 1960-78; adv. com. Athletic Inst., 1967-72; adv. Ednl. Policies Commn., 1965-68. Served to lt. USNR, 1943-45. Mem. Am. (pres. 1971-72), Central Dist. (pres. 1964-65), Iowa (pres. 1957-58) assns. health, phys. edn. and recreation, Nat. Coll. Phys. Assn. Men (pres. 1966-67), Am. Coll. Sports Medicine, Am. Acad. Phys. Edn. (pres. 1977-78), Nat. Assn. Standard Med. Vocabulary, Phi Sigma Epislon, Phi Kappa Phi, Phi Delta Kappa, Phi Epsilon Kappa. Clubs: Triangle (pres. 1957) (U. Iowa); Iowa City Kiwanis (pres. 1978). Contbr. articles to profl. jours. Home: 1204 Ashley Dr Iowa City IA 52240 Office: Dept Physical Edn Univ Iowa Iowa City IA 52242

ALLEY, ROBERT DALE, educator; b. Allerton, Iowa, Dec. 22, 1935; s. Dale Lane and Clara Leona (Holmes) A.; B.S., Iowa State U., 1957; M.E., U. Mont., 1960; Ed.D., Ariz. State U., 1967; m. Shirley A. Kryder, Aug. 4, 1957; children—Robyn Rene, Darin James. Tchr., Franklin Twp. Sch., Cooper, Iowa, 1957-58, Knoxville (Iowa) High Sch., 1958-61, Scottsdale (Ariz.) Public Schs., 1961-67; mem. faculty Wichita (Kans.) State U., 1967—, prof., asso. dean Coll. Edn., 1980—; cons. in motivation and tchr. behavior. Mem. public relations com. for Historic Cowtown, Wichita, 1978—. Mem. Assn. Tchr. Educators, Assn. Supervision and Curriculum Devel., World Council for Curriculum and Instrn., Phi Delta Kappa. Contbr. articles to profl. lit. Office: Wichita State U Box 28 Wichita KS 67208

ALLEY, WILLIAM J., ins. co. exec.; b. Vernon, Tex., Dec. 27, 1929; s. W. H. and Opal M. (Cater) A.; A.A., Northeastern A. and M. Coll., 1949; B.B.A., U. Okla., 1951, J.D., 1954; m. Deborah Bunn, Dec. 28, 1979; children—Susan Jane, Pamela Jean, Patricia Ann, Sarah Elizabeth, Brayton Bunn. Admitted to Okla. bar, 1954; atty. State Ins. Bd. Okla., 1956-57; asst. v.p. Pioneer Am. Ins. Co., 1957-59, v.p., 1959-60, v.p., agy. dir., 1960-66, dir., 1961, sr. v.p. marketing, 1966; v.p. Franklin Life Ins. Co., Springfield, Ill., 1967-69, sr. v.p., agy. dir., 1969-74, exec. v.p., 1974-75, pres., chief exec. officer, 1976—, chmn. bd., 1977—, also dir.; pres., dir., chmn. bd. Franklin Financial Service Corp.; dir. First Nat. Bank; chmn. bd., pres. Am. Franklin Life Ins. Co., Franklin United Life Ins. Co.; dir. Central Ill. Pub. Service Co., Am. Brands Inc.; chmn. bd., dir. Am. Franklin Co. Bd. dirs. Meml. Hosp., Am. Council Life Ins.; trustee Ill. Coll. Served to capt. USAF, 1954-56. C.L.U. Mem. Springfield Assn. Life Underwriters, Okla. Bar. Assn., Delta Sigma Pi, Phi Kappa Sigma, Phi Alpha Delta. Mason (Shriner). Clubs: Illini Country, Sangamo, Springfield Racquet; Tavern (Chgo.). Home: 2014 Illini Rd Springfield IL 62704 Office: Franklin Sq Springfield IL 62713

ALLI, BILLIAMIN ADE, physician, bus. exec.; b. Lagos, Nigeria, Sept. 12, 1948; s. R.A. and Aj Alli; M.D., St. George Med. Sch., 1979; Ph.D., Columbia U. Union Grad. Sch., 1973. Intern, Parkview Hosp., Toledo, Ohio, Paramount (Calif.) Gen. Hosp.; prof. behavioral scis. York Coll., CUNY, 1972-73; practice medicine specializing in pediatrics and internal medicine; pres., chmn. bd. Dayton Child Devel. Corp. (Ohio), 1978—; med. cons., 1979—; lectr. Grad. Sch. Public and Internat. Affairs. Fellow U. Pitts., 1973. Fellow Royal Soc. Health (Eng.); mem. Am. Public Health Assn., World Med. Council, Assn. Tchrs. Med. Scis., Am. Sociol. Assn., Big Bros. Am., YMCA. Contbr. numerous articles to profl. jours. Address: PO Box 1794 Toledo OH 43603

ALLIN, LAWRENCE CARROLL, historian; b. Independence, Mo., July 17, 1932; s. John Marshall and Josephine Vivian (Luther) A.; A.B., Coll. of Pacific, 1954; M.A. (fellow), Syracuse U., 1967; diplomate (fellow) Frank C. Munson Inst., 1971; Ph.D., U. Maine, 1976; m. Betsy Lee Brackett, June 22, 1977; children by previous marriage—L. Kirk, L. Kyle, L. Kevin, Lisa. Tchr., Cucamonga (Calif.) Jr. High Sch., 1958-69; instr. history U. Maine, Orono, 1970-79; dist. historian Omaha Dist., U.S. Army C.E., 1979—. Bd. dirs. Upland (Ont.) Community Forum, 1963-67; bd. overseers Maine Maritime Mus., 1971—; exec. dir. Maine Gov.'s Com. on Children and Youth, 1976-77; trustee Orono High Sch., 1976-79. Served with USN, 1955-57. Fulbright-Hays fellow Brown U., Am. U., Beirut, 1967; grantee Price Found., 1964, 69, U. Maine, 1976, 79 (with Michael Chaney) Nat. Endowment Humanities, 1977. Mem. Soc. Am. Mil. Engrs., U.S. Naval Inst., Orgn. Am. Historians, Phi Alpha Theta. Club: Lehigh Acres (Fla.) Country. Author: U.S. Naval Institute: Intellectual Forum of the New Navy, 1971; America's Maritime Legacy, 1979; Searsport Master Builders, 1980; contbr. articles to profl. jours. Home: 219-3021 Burt St Omaha NE 68131 Office: 5403 Fed Ct House Omaha NE 68102

ALLINICH, RUTH ANN, nurse; b. Kansas City, Mo., Mar. 16, 1925; d. Joseph Fred and Sylvia Claudia (Simpson) Huard; R.N., Providence Hosp., Leavenworth, Kans., 1947; B.S. in Social Work with honors, Park Coll., Kansas City, Mo., 1976; M.S. in Adult and Occupational Edn., Kans. State U., Manhattan, 1979; m. Samuel J. Allinich, Feb. 7, 1948; children—Michael Dean, Gregory Lynn. Staff nurse and/or head nurse, then inservice instr. Bethany Med. Center, Kansas City, Kans., 1948-73; mem. ednl. staff Providence-St. Margaret Health Center, Kansas City, Kans., 1973—, dir. edn. and tng. dept., coordinator continuing med. edn. programming, 1977—; mem. adv. coms. St. Mary Coll., Leavenworth, U. Mo. Sch. Nursing, Kansas City; mem. N.E. Regional Adv. Com. Continuing Edn. Nurses in Kans. Mem. Am. Soc. Tng. and Devel., Am. Soc. Health, Manpower, Edn. and Tng., Kans. Assn. Hosp. Edn. Coordinators, Am. Bus. Women's Assn. (enrollment chmn. 1981). Home: 71 S 24th St Kansas City KS 66102 Office: 8929 Parallel Pkwy Kansas City KS 66112

ALLISON, DEBRA HUST, systems analyst; b. Cin., Feb. 10, 1951; d. Elmer George and Laverne Marie (Guckiean) Hust; B.A. (Howard White award 1973), Miami U., Oxford, Ohio, 1973; m. Christopher E. Allison, Sept. 3, 1977. Congl. intern, 1972-73; congl. aide, 1973-75; systems analyst Miami U., 1975—. Mem. Am. Personnel and Guidance Assn., Am. Coll. Personnel Assn., Nat. Fedn. Bus. and Profl. Women (named Young Career Woman, Oxford chpt. 1979), Oxford C. of C. (charter). Republican. Presbyterian. Club: Order Eastern Star. Home: 111 Olde Farm Rd Oxford OH 45056 Office: 137 Hoyt Miami U Oxford OH 45056

ALLISON, PATRICIA ANNE, educator; b. Terre Haute, Ind., Aug. 28, 1934; d. Ernest and Leatha M. (Mace) Bailey; B.S. cum laude, Ind. State U., 1972, M.S., 1976; m. Harold E. Allison, June 28, 1953; children—Linda, Betty Jean, Janet, Terry, Michael. Tchr. educable mentally handicapped Crestwood Sch., Paris, Ill., 1972-77, tchr. learning disabilities, 1977-81, tchr. grade 2 transition room, 1981—. Mem. Internat. Reading Assn., Assn. Retarded Citizens (bd. dirs. 1974-79, pres. 1978-79), Council for Exceptional Children, Assn. for Children with Learning Disabilities (founder Edgar County chpt., pres. 1979-80), Ill. Edn. Assn., NEA, Ill. Reading Assn., Delta Kappa Gamma, Lambda Psi Sigma. Republican. Methodist. Home: 1007 Douglas St Paris IL 61944 Office: Route 3 PO Box 160 Paris IL 61944

ALLISON, RICHARD DRING, govt. ofcl.; b. Murphysboro, Ill., Sept. 21, 1944; s. Reuel Dring and Ruby Francis (Jungewaelter) A.; student So. Ill. U., 1973-78, Belleville Area Coll., 1974-78; m. Beverly Lindsey, Oct. 17, 1968; children—Billy Wayne, Jay Dean. Land surveyor R.M. Harrison Co., St. Louis, 1967-70; license examiner Office Sec. of State, Sparta, Ill., 1970-75; corrections clk. Menard (Ill.) Correctional Center, 1975—. Chmn. Bicentennial Wagon Train, Chester, Ill., 1976. Served with U.S. Army, 1965-67. Mem. Ill. Jaycees (John H. Armbruster award 1978, Outstanding Local V.P. 1977-78), Chester Jaycees (pres. 1978-79, mem. internat. senate 1979—). Republican. Roman Catholic. Clubs: K.C., VFW (life), Elks. Home: 1735 Swanwick St Chester IL 62233 Office: Menard Correctional Center Menard IL 62259

ALLMAN, JOHN JOSEPH, social worker; b. Detroit, Aug. 11, 1948; s. John Joseph and Sara Margret (Russell) A.; B.A., Mich. State U., 1970; M.S.W., U. Mich., 1975; m. Barbara Elizabeth De Fazio, May 1, 1971. Caseworker, Oakwood Hosp., Dearborn, Mich., 1970-71, dir. social work, 1971—; field instr. U. Mich. Sch. Social Work, 1976—, Wayne State U. Sch. Social Work, 1977-79. Bd. dirs., v.p. Kings Cove Assn., 1977-79; mem. nursing and health services com. Mich. chpt. ARC, 1981—; mem. planning com. TriState Hosp. Assembly, 1977. Mem. Soc. Hosp. Social Work Dirs. (pres. Mich. chpt. 1977-79, dir. 1975—), Am. Hosp. Assn., Nat. Assn. Social Workers, Mich. League Human Services, Acad. Cert. Social Workers. Office: 18101 Oakwood Blvd Dearborn MI 48124

ALLSUP, GENE DIXON, educator; b. Hurst, Ill., July 7, 1931; s. Brantley Eurie and Mildred Jane (Dixon) A.; B.S. in Edn., So. Ill. U., 1954, M.S. Ed., 1956; M.A. in Spanish, So. Ill. U., 1958, Ph.D., 1966; postgrad. U. P.R., 1960, San Carlos U., Guatemala, 1962; m. Margaret Jane Hester, Oct. 20, 1950; children—Victoria Jane, Michael Alan, Elizabeth Ann, David Gene, Ronald Sean. Tchr., Hurst-Bush Elem. Sch., Hurst, Ill., 1950-53, Hurst-Bush High Sch., 1953-56; supt. schs. Royalton, Ill., 1956-59, Sesser, Ill., 1959-66, Collinsville, Ill., 1966-69; curriculum advisor Ministry of Edn., Honduras, Central Am., 1966-67; prof. edn. adminstrn. and Spanish, So. Ill. U., Edwardsville, 1969—; curriculum cons. Guatemala, Honduras, Calgary, Alta., others. Mem. Assn. for Supervision and Curriculum Devel., MLA, Assn. Tchrs. of Spanish and Portuguese, Phi Delta Kappa. Lutheran. Club: Masons. Author: El Hombre Hispanico, 1971. Home: 11280 Wamsutta Trail Florissant MO 63033 Office: Box 124 So Ill Univ Edwardsville IL 62025

ALM, JAMES, mfg. co. tng. and personnel exec.; b. Hubbard Woods, Ill., May 6, 1937; s. Carl W. and Berith J. A. (Lundstrom) A.; B.A. in English, Cornell U., 1959. Claim negotiator Continental Nat. Am., Chgo., 1960-62; tng. evaluator Allstate Ins. Cos., Northbrook, Ill., 1962-80; dir. corp. tng. and human resource devel. Midas Internat., Chgo., 1980—. Spl. adv. Crusade of Mercy, Chgo., 1964-65; mem. adv. bd. Broader Urban Involvement and Leadership Devel., Chgo., 1965. Served with Submarine Service, USN, 1960-62. Mem. Am. Soc. Tng. and Devel., Am. Soc. Personnel Adminstrn., Human Resources Planning Soc., Orgn. Devel. Inst., Chgo. Orgn. Devel. Assn., Ill. Tng. Dirs. Assn., Nat. Soc. Performance and Instrn. Methodist. Author: Intrinsic Programming: A Primer, 1964; contbr. articles to profl. publs.; subject of profl. articles. Home: 4900 N Marine Dr Chicago IL 60640 Office: 222 S Riverside Plaza Chicago IL 60606

ALMACK, CHARLES ELMER, architect; b. Wellington, Kans., Dec. 12, 1942; s. Virgil Elmer and Isabel Frances (Iddings) A.; B.Arch., State U., 1969, postgrad., 1970-71; m. Rosa Morgan, Apr. 2, 1960. Designer campus planning Kans. State U., Manhattan, 1963-68; prin., designer Phoenix, Inc., Manhattan, 1966-69; instr. Kans. State U., 1968-71, design cons., housing dept., 1969-71; architect, designer Schaefer, Shirmer & Assos., Wichita, 1971-76; prin., architect Almack Assos., Wichita, 1976-78, Almack & Lane Assos., Wichita, 1978-81, The Almack Partnership, 1981—; mem. creative arts bd. Kans. State U. Recipient Gold medal Faenza (Italy) Art Festival, William Frampton Meml. award Am. Soc. Registered Architects, 1968. Mem. Kans. Soc. Architects (dir. 1979, treas. 1980, energy com. 1980-81), AIA (pres. Wichita 1978, mem. interior architecture com. 1979—, membership chmn. Wichita 1981), Inst. Bus. Designers (pres. Mid Am. chpt. 1974-75; nat. dir. 1975), Environ. Design Research Assn., Kans. Solar Energy Soc., Wichita Area C. of C. (energy task force 1980). Club: Ninneschah Yacht. Home: 2243 Bramblewood Apt 603 Wichita KS 67226 Office: 356 N Rock Rd Wichita KS 67206

ALMICH, BRUCE PATRICK, govt. agency adminstr.; b. Cheyenne, Wyo., Jan. 25, 1950; s. Vernon E. and Gertrude J. A.; B.S.E. with high honors (Outstanding Undergrad. Research award 1972), Princeton U., 1972; M.B.A., U. Cin., 1974; M.S. in E.E., Stanford U., 1975. Research engr. USPHS/NIH, Cin., 1972-74; owner Nassau Systems Computer Systems Consulting, Cin., 1972—; group leader Distributed Computer Devel. Group EPA, Cin., 1977-80, chief systems analysis, 1980—; adj. prof. engring. U. Cin. Recipient EPA Bronze medal, 1979. Mem. IEEE, Assn. Computing Machinery, Sigma Xi (recipient book award 1972). Contbr. articles in field to profl. jours. Office: 26 W Saint Clair St Cincinnati OH 45268

ALMONY, ROBERT ALLEN, JR., librarian; b. Charleston, W.Va., Oct. 14, 1945; s. Robert A. and Margaret E. (Morrison) A.; A.A., Grossmont Coll., 1965; B.A., San Diego State U., 1968; M.L.S., U. Calif., Berkeley, 1977; m. Carol Krzmenski, May 6, 1972; children—Robert Allen III, Michael Anthony, Chandra Rene, Rachel Elizabeth. Sr. clk. Humanities Library, San Diego (Calif.) Univ. Library, 1965-68; accountant Calif. Tchrs. Fin. Services, Inc., Orange County, 1968-70, v.p., gen. mgr., 1971-76; reference librarian Oberlin (Ohio) Coll. Library, 1977-79; asst. dir. U. Mo. Ellis Library, Columbia, 1979—. Mem. Am. Library Assn., Mo. Library Assn., Am. Soc. for Information Sci. Home: 301 Rothwell Dr Columbia MO 65201 Office: University of Missouri 104 Ellis Library 9th & Lowry Columbia MO 65201

ALONSO, LOU JOHNSON, educator; b. Mason, Mich.; d. James Reginald and Mabel Elizabeth (Reid) Johnson; B.A., Mich. State U., 1947, M.A., 1950, postgrad., 1951-54; m. Noah Alonso, Dec. 17, 1948; 1 son, Jose Gregory II (dec.). Speech pathologist Flint (Mich.) Pub. Schs., 1947-48; tchr., then asst. prin. Mich. Sch. for Blind, Lansing, 1949-56; prof. spl. edn., coordinator programs preparing personnel for visually handicapped and deaf-blind pupils, dir. Gt. Lakes Region Spl. Edn. Instl. Materials Center, Mich. State U., East Lansing, 1959-80; cons. Office Spl. Edn., U.S. Dept. Edn.; mem. adv. bd. numerous agys. Mem. Council for Exceptional Children, Assn. Ednl. Communication and Tech., Assn. Educators Visually Handicapped, Delta Zeta. Author books, research reports, numerous articles, brochures and instrnl. media. Home: PO Box 1562 East Lansing MI 48823 Office: 336 Erickson Hall Michigan State U East Lansing MI 48824

ALONZO, RONALD THOMAS, mfg. co. exec.; b. Mexico City, June 18, 1942 (mother Am. citizen); s. Rosendo and Alice Jane (Ratcliff) A.; B.A. in Polit. Sci., Tulane U., 1965; B.I.M., Am. Grad. Sch. Internat. Mgmt., 1967-68; m. Denise Angele Rufin, Feb. 10, 1968; children—Rodrigo Joaquin, Micaela Alicia. Adminstrv. asst. Microfilm Humble Oil & Refinery, New Orleans, 1965-67; advt. and sales promotion mgr. Internat. div. Whirlpool Corp., Benton Harbor, Mich., 1968-72, regional sales mgr. Europe, 1972-75, regional sales mgr. Western Markets, 1975-78; mgr. field sales internat. Kohler Co. (Wis.), 1978—; mem. constrn. com. Nat. Council for US-China Trade, Washington. Club: Kohler Sports. Home: 2335 N 3d St Sheboygan WI 53081 Office: Kohler Memorial Dr Kohler WI 53044

ALPER, ALLEN MYRON, carbide mfg. co. exec.; b. N.Y.C., Oct. 23, 1932; s. Joseph and Pauline (Frohlich) A.; B.S., Bklyn. Coll., 1954; Ph.D., Columbia (Univ. fellow, Dyckman Inst. Scholar, Univ. pres.'s scholar), 1957; m. Barbara Marshall, Dec. 20, 1959; children—Allen Myron, Andrew Marshall. Sr. mineralogist Corning Glass Works (N.Y.), 1957-59, research mineralogist, 1959-62, mgr. ceramic research, also sr. research asso., 1962-69; with GET Sylvania Inc., Towanda, Pa., 1969—, chief engr., 1971-72, dir. research and engring., 1972—, 75, dir. research and engring., mgr. aperture mask prodn., 1975-78, mgr. ops., 1978-80; pres. GTE Walmet, 1980—. Mem. Pa. Gov.'s Adv. Panel on Materials, 1971—; mem. materials lab. adv. bd. Pa. State U., 1979—. Grantee N.M. Bur. Mines, 1954-57. Fellow Am. Ceramic Soc., Geol. Soc. Am., Am. Inst. Chemists; mem. British Ceramic Soc., Am. Soc. Metals, Geophy. Union, Am. Chem. Soc., Internat. Platform Assn., Sigma Xi. Presbyterian. Mason. Clubs: Explorers, Towanda Country, Great Oaks Country. Patentee in field. Contbr. to profl. jours. Editor: Phase Diagrams: Materials Science and Technology, 4 vols., 1976; High Temperature Oxides, 4 parts, 1970-71. Editorial bd. High Temperature Sci. jour., 1969—, High Temperature Chemistry, 1973—, Materials Handbook, 1974—; editor Materials Sci. and Tech. Series, Acad. Press, 1972—. Contbr. articles to profl. jours. Home: 880 Great Oaks Blvd Rochester MI 48063 Office: GTE Walmet Royal Oak MI 48068

AL-RASHID, RASHID ABDULLA, physician; b. Bahrain, Manama, Apr. 22, 1934; s. Abdulla R. and Fatima (Anber) Al-Yousif; came to U.S., 1960, naturalized, 1969; B.Sc., Am. U. of Beirut, Lebanon, 1956, M.D., 1960; m. Beverly B. Aubrecht, Sept. 25, 1962; children—Roger, Rodney. Rotating intern Am. U. of Beirut Hosps., 1959-60; resident pediatrics State U. Iowa, Iowa City, 1960-61, D.C. Gen. Hosp., Washington, 1961-62; fellow in hematology Children's Hosp. of Mich. and Child Research Center, Detroit, 1962-64; fellow in cytogenics U. Louisville, Ky., 1966-67; practice medicine specializing in pediatrics and pediatric hematology/oncology Manama, Bahrain, 1964-66, Louisville, Ky., 1966-67, Omaha, 1967—; pediatrician in charge Bahrain Govt. Hosp., 1964-66; instr. dept. pediatrics U. Louisville, 1966-67; research instr. dept. pediatrics U. Nebr., 1967-69, asst. prof., 1969-71, asso. prof., 1971-77, prof., 1977—, dir. hematology and oncology service, 1969—; chemotherapist Tumor Clinic, Children's Meml. Hosp., 1969-72, mem. cons. staff, 1969—. Diplomate Am. Bd. Pediatrics. Mem. Am. Acad. Pediatrics, AMA (Physician's Recognition award 1970), Am. Soc. Clin. Oncology. Author: Pediatric Hematology Case Studies, 1972; Pediatric Oncology Case Studies, 1975; Pediatric Cancer Chemotherapy, 1979; contbr. articles on pediatric oncology and pediatric hematology to profl. jours. Home: 705 N 72nd Ave Omaha NE 68114 Office: Univ Nebr Medical Center Dept Pediatrics 42nd and Dewey Ave Omaha NE 68105

ALSDORF, MARILYNN BRUDER (MRS. JAMES W. ALSDORF), civic worker, export co. exec.; b. Evanston, Ill., Apr. 5, 1926; d. Edward J. and Coramae (Young) Bruder; student Northwestern U. Sch. Journalism; m. James W. Alsdorf, Oct. 3, 1952; children—Gregg, Lynne, Jeffrey, James. Model, John Powers, N.Y.C., 1948, Patricia Stevens, Chgo., 1949-51. Vice pres. A.J. Alsdorf Corp. Exporters, Chgo. Mem. benefit com. Juvenile Protective Assn., Chgo., 1958-60; chmn. art library and exhbn. com. North Shore Country Day Sch., Winnetka, 1960-61; chmn. Benton House Meml. Garden Chgo. 1960-61; publicity com. Winnetka Garden Club, 1961, projects chmn., 1963-64, v.p., 1967; mem. exec. com. World Flower and Garden Show, 1963-64; mem., judge Garden Club Am.; mem. reception com. Arts Club, Chgo., 1961; bd. dirs. Alsdorf Found., Chgo.; governing life mem., vice-chmn. Oriental com., benefactor, pres. women's bd., hon. mem., trustee Art Inst. Chgo., also vice-chmn. classical com.; benefactor John Herron Art Assn., Indpls.; interior design cons. The Goodman Theatre. Trustee Museum of Contemporary Art, Chgo., Ravinia Festival Assn.; mem. woman's bd. U. Chgo.; mem. exec. com. of women's bd. Field Museum, Chgo.; mem. art adv. bd. U. Notre Dame, Martin D'Arcy Gallery Loyola U.; trustee Chgo. Hort. Soc.; community adviser Chgo. Jr. League; dir. Floral Arts Gallery. Recipient horticulture award World Flower Show, 1961; Distinguished Modern award Wedgwood Soc.; Camellia award Loyola U., 1977. Mem. Antiquarians of Art Inst. Chgo., Oriental Ceramic Soc., The Orientals, Sarah Siddons Soc., Compagnons de Beaujolais-Lyons, France, Guild Chgo. Hist. Soc. Gamma Phi Beta. Conglist. Clubs: Sunset Ridge Country (Northfield, Ill.); Bel Aire (Cal.) Country; Post and Paddock (Arlington, Ill.); Art's, Casino, Woman's Athletic (dir.) (Chgo.).

Home: 301 Woodley Rd Winnetka IL 60093 Office: 3200 W Peterson Chicago IL 60645

ALSTERBERG, CARL ERIC, clin. psychologist; b. Detroit, Apr. 30, 1949; s. Carl Edward and Cora Louise (England) A.; B.A., U. Mich., 1971; M.S., Eastern Mich. U., 1974; Ph.D., U.S. Internat. U., 1980; m. Sandra Lee Rosen, May 2, 1980. Program coordinator Southwood House, Chula Vista, Calif., 1974-76, dir., 1976-78, intern Southwood Mental Health Center, 1978; intern Wyandotte (Mich.) Gen. Hosp., 1978-79, staff psychologist, 1979—; pvt. practice clin. psychology, Wyandotte, part-time. Mem. Am. Psychol. Assn., Assn. for Humanistic Psychology, Am. Assn. Marriage and Family Therapy. Home: 911 New York St Lincoln Park MI 48146 Office: Wyandotte Gen Hosp 2333 Biddle Ave Wyandotte MI 48192

ALSTON, FREDDY GENE, plant breeder; b. Temple, Tex., Dec. 2, 1944; s. Herman Buford and Effie Leah (Northam) A.; B.S., Tex. A&M U., 1968, M.S., 1969, Ph.D., 1973; m. Leatrice Sams, Aug. 20, 1965; children—Lori Lynette, Shannon Trae. Research asst. Tex. A&M U., 1968-73; plant breeder, dir. research George Warner Seed Co., Hereford, Tex., 1973-81; product devel. rep., also sorghum breeder Prairie Valley div. Stauffer Seeds, Hutchinson, Kans., 1981—. Sec., Hereford Community Concert Assn., 1977-78. Mem. Am. Soc. Agronomy, Am. Soc. Crop Sci. Home: 4506 Sequoia Hutchinson KS 67501 Office: Box 460 Hutchinson KS 67501

ALT, JANE FULTON, psychiat. social worker; b. Chgo., May 26, 1951; d. Maurice and Muriel (Fantus) Fulton; A.B. with distinction in Edn., U. Mich., 1973; M.A., U. Chgo., 1975; m. Howard Lang Alt, Nov. 27, 1976; 1 dau., Katie Jane. Inpatient psychiat. social worker Inst. Psychiatry, Northwestern Meml. Hosp., Chgo., 1975-76, outpatient psychiat. social worker, 1976-79; pvt. practice psychiat. social work, Chgo., 1979—; cons. mastectomy counseling project Nat. Cancer Inst./Northwestern Meml. Hosp./Northwestern U. Med. Sch., 1981—; research cons. Ill. Gov.'s Commn. To Revise Mental Health Code, 1974; instr. dept. allied health and scis. Northwestern U. Med. Sch., Chgo., 1976—. Registered cert. social worker, Ill. Mem. Acad. Cert. Social Workers, Nat. Assn. Social Workers, Mortar Bd. Home: 2203 Orrington Ave Evanston IL 60201 Office: 645 N Michigan Ave Chicago IL 60611

ALT, STEVEN FRANCIS, cheese co. exec.; b. Cuba City, Wis., Aug. 1, 1956; s. William G. and Margaret (Wiegel) A.; A.A. cum laude, Madison Bus. Coll., 1977; B.S. summa cum laude, Jones Coll., 1978. Accountant, Asso. Hosp., Milw., 1978-79, internal auditor, 1979; acctg. supr. L.D. Schreiber Cheese Co., Green Bay, Wis., 1979-80, acctg. mgr., Monett, Mo., 1980—; tchr. acctg. N.W. Vocat. Tech. Coll., Green Bay, Wis., 1980. Recipient Outstanding Grad. award Madison Bus. Coll., 1977. Mem. Nat. Assn. Accountants, Monett Jaycees. Home: 403 Linden St Monett MO 65708 Office: 10 Dairy St Monett MO 65708

ALTAN, TAYLAN, mech. engr.; b. Trabzon, Turkey, Feb. 12, 1938; s. Seref and Sadife (Baysal) A.; came to U.S., 1963, naturalized, 1970; diploma in mfg. engring. Tech. U. Hannover (W.Ger.), 1962; M.S. in Mech. Engring., U. Calif., Berkeley, 1964, Ph.D., 1966; m. Susan Borah, July 18, 1964; children—Peri, Aylin. Research asst. U. Calif., Berkeley, 1963-66; research scientist DuPont de Nemours Co., Wilmington, Del., 1966-68; sr. research scientist Battelle Inst., Columbus, Ohio, 1968-73, sr. research leader Battelle Columbus Labs., 1973—; adj. prof. indsl. engring. Ohio State U.; cons. in field to U.S. and fgn. cos. Mem. ASME (chmn. div. prodn. engring. 1977), Am. Soc. Metals, Soc. Mfg. Engrs., Internat. Prodn. Engring. Research Instn. Author: (with F.W. Boulger and J.R. Becker) Forging Equipment, Materials and Practices, 1973; contbr. numerous articles to nat., internat. tech. jours.; asso. editor Jour. Mech. Working Tech., 1976. Home: 1380 Sherbrooke Pl Columbus OH 43209 Office: Battelle Labs 505 King Ave Columbus OH 43201

ALTEMUS, JAMES ROY, farm bur. ofcl.; b. West Frankfort, Ill., Jan. 12, 1946; s. Harold and Grace Marie (Chick) A.; B.A. in Edn., Ill. State U., 1969; m. Allida Frisch, Feb. 4, 1967; children—Sarah, Emily. Info. services mgr. Ill. Farm Bur., Bloomington, 1969-73, dir. public relations, 1973-78, dir. public info., 1978—; communications cons. Am. Coll. Testing, Nat. Inst. Fin. Aid. Mem. Dist. 87 Sch. Adv. Com., 1978-79; bd. dirs. Central Ill. Jr. Achievement, 1977-79; bd. dirs. McLean County ARC, 1977-81, 1st v.p., 1979, chmn. bd., 1980-81. Served with Chem. Corps, USAR, 1969-75. Mem. Public Relations Soc. Am. (accredited). Home: 319 Hillside Ln Bloomington IL 61701 Office: 1701 Towanda Ave Bloomington IL 61701

ALTEPETER, GERALD ANTHONY, county ofcl.; b. St. Louis, Apr. 29, 1941; s. Vincent Martin and Marie Ann (Krebs) A.; B.S. in Bus. Adminstrn., So. Ill. U.; m. Joanne C. Friederich, June 22, 1968; children—John Vincent, Nicole Threse, Todd Anthony. Project inspector Asso. Gen. Contractors, Louisville; plant expeditor Contential Iron Works; purchasing mgr. St. Louis Car Co.-Gen. Steel Industries; dir. purchasing and central services St. Clair County, Belleville, Ill.; instr. Belleville Area Coll.; mem. adv. bd. Ill. Sch. Dist. 118, Belleville; bd. dirs. Mo.-So. Ill. Minority Purchasing Council. Served with USN, 1959-63. Nat. Assn. of Counties award, 1973, 74, 75, 77, 79. Mem. St. Louis Regional Purchasing Assn. (pres.), Ill. Public Purchasing Assn. (nat. pres., chmn. bd.), Nat. Inst. Govt. Purchasing, Nat. Purchasing Inst., Pub. Risk and Ins. Mgmt. Assn., Nat. Assn. of Counties. Roman Catholic. Contbr. articles to profl. jours.; contbg. editor Risk Management Manual for Local Government. Home: 400 Hillcrest Dr Belleville IL 62221 Office: 10 Public Sq Belleville IL 62220

ALTER, JAMES M., wholesale co. exec.; b. Chgo., 1922; ed. Lake Forest (Ill.) Coll., 1947, U. Chgo., 1956. Chmn., Harry Alter Co., Chgo. Mem. N. Am. Heating and Air Conditioning Wholesalers Assn. (pres.). Office: 1200 W 35th St Chicago IL 60609*

ALTER, JOANNE HAMMERMAN, elected county ofcl.; b. Chgo., July 3, 1927; d. Sol and Celia (Kagen) Hammerman; B.A. cum laude, Mt. Holyoke Coll., 1949; m. James M. Alter, May 17, 1952; children—Jennifer, Jonathan, Jamie, Harrison. Coordinator fgn. student program Inst. Internat. Edn., 1951-54; commr. Met. San. Dist. Greater Chgo., 1972—, chmn. com. on flood control, com. on research and devel.; Committeewoman, Dem. Nat. Com., 1980; mem. panel Internat. Joint Commn.; mem. Ill. Local Govt. Adv. Council, 1973-76; candidate for lt. gov. Ill., 1976; apptd. Cook County Council of Governments, 1978—. U.S. del. UN Seminar on Civic and Polit. Edn. of Women, Ghana, 1968; Ill. rep. Internat. Women's Year Conf., Mexico City, 1975, Tex., 1977, mem. Ill. Women's Year Com., 1977; trustee, Mt. Holyoke Coll.; bd. dirs. YMCA Met. Chgo.; mem. women's bd. Art Inst. Chgo.; Ill. chmn. UN Day, 1975. Mem. Am. Jewish Com.; mem. art adv. council Mt. Holyoke Coll.; bd. mem. U. Chgo. Bright New Cities; co-convenor Ill. Dem. Women's Caucus, 1971—; co-founder Sta. WIND Call for Action; bd. dirs., founder Internat. Visitors Center. Recipient YWCA Leadership award, 1975, Audubon Soc. award, 1979. Mem. Council Govts. of Cook County, LWV, Chgo. Council Fgn. Relations, Urban League, AAUW, UN Assn., ACLU, Sierra Club, Save the Dunes Council, Lake Michigan Fedn. Club: Arts (Chgo.). Home: 568 W Hawthorne Pl Chicago IL 60657 Office: 100 E Erie St Chicago IL 60611

ALTER, JOSEPH DINSMORE, physician; b. Lawrence, Kans., Apr. 19, 1923; s. David Emmet and Martha (Payne) A.; M.D., Hahnemann Med. Coll., 1950; M.P.H., U. Calif., Berkeley, 1961; m. Marian Elizabeth Wengert, May 31, 1946 (div. Feb. 1981); children—Robert Emmet, Janet Lynn; m. 2d, Joyce Ellen Willis, Apr. 10, 1981. Intern, Huntington Meml. Hosp., Pasadena, Calif., 1950-51; mem. med. staff Group Health Coop. Puget Sound (Wash.), 1951-60, chmn. family practice dept., 1956-57; field dir. Houses for Korea, Coordinated Community Devel. Project, 1953-54; lectr. med. care adminstrn. Sch. Pub. Health, U. Calif., Berkeley, 1961-62; lectr. Sch. Hygiene and Pub. Health, Johns Hopkins U., Balt., 1962-65, asst. prof., 1965-67, dep. dir. rural health research projects, dept. internat. health Sch. Hygiene and Pub. Health, Narangwal Village, Punjab, India, 1962-67, asst. prof. dept. internat. health Sch. Hygiene and Pub. Health, Balt., 1967-68; asso. prof., field prof. community medicine, dept. community medicine Coll. Medicine, U. Ky. Med. Center, 1968-70; med. dir. Pilot City Health Center, Cin., 1970-73, HealthCare of Louisville, 1973-75; chief domiciliary med. service VA Center, Dayton, Ohio, 1975-77, asso. chief staff for extended care, 1977; prof., chmn. dept. community medicine Wright State U. Sch. Medicine, 1977—. Chmn. Dayton regional exec. com., mem. nat. bd. Am. Friends Service Com., 1977-78; trustee Quaker Heights, Waynesville, Ohio. Recipient Physician's Recognition award AMA, 1976, 79; diplomate Am. Bd. Preventive Medicine. Mem. Am. Pub. Health Assn., Am. Acad. Family Physicians, Am. Coll. Preventive Medicine, Gerontol. Soc., Aerospace Med. Assn., Ohio, Montgomery County med. assns. Quaker. Author: Narrowing Our Medical Care Gap, 1972; (with others) The Health Center Doctor in India, 1967, Doctors for the Villages, 1976. Contbr. articles to profl. jours. Home: 6607 Morrow Dr Dayton OH 45415 Office: Dept Community Medicine Wright State U Sch Medicine Box 927 Dayton OH 45401

ALTHEIMER, ALAN MILTON, messenger co. exec.; b. Chgo., July 25, 1940; s. Milton Louis and Rena (Cohen) A.; student Drake U., 1959-61; children—Amy, Marcy. Pres., Altheimer & Baer, Inc., Chgo., 1968-80; pres. v.p. Fast Messenger Service, Inc., Chgo., 1976—. Chmn. Chgo. dist., disaster services ARC, 1972—; bd. dirs. Midwest Epilepsy Center, 1980—. Mem. Ill. Messenger Service Assn. Office: Fast Messenger Service Inc 1015 W Grand Ave Chicago IL 60622

ALTHOFF, JAMES LEWIS, contracting co. exec.; b. McHenry, Ill., June 9, 1928; s. William H. and Eleanora M. Althoff; grad. high sch.; m. Joan Andreen, June 18, 1949; children—Timothy, Betsy, Tod, Katy, Patti, Jim, Karyn. Owner liquefied petroleum gas distbg. co., McHenry, 1952-60; founder, pres. J. Althoff & Assos., McHenry, 1960—, Althoff Industries, Inc., McHenry, 1960—. Pres., Fire Dist., 1966-78, Bd. Edn. Dist. 156, 1969-78; mem. Law Enforcement Commn. Lake and McHenry Counties, 1979—; bd. govs. Ill. Colls. and Univs., 1979—; trustee Plumbers Welfare Fund. Chgo., 1974—. Recipient Service award McHenry High Sch. Dist., 1979, Bradley U., 1976, McHenry Fire Dist., 1978. Mem. Chgo. Contractors Assn., Nat. Plumbing Contractors Assn. Home: 508 Green St McHenry IL 60050 Office: 809 Front St McHenry IL 60050

ALTHOLZ, HERBERT CARL, paper co. exec.; b. Chgo., 1922; grad. Northwestern U., 1943, Inst. Internat. Studies, Geneva, 1961. Chmn., Inlander-Steindler Paper Co., Elk Grove Village, Ill., Gash Paper Co.; treas., dir. PMC Corp.; v.p., dir. I.S.P.-Iowa Inc.; dir. Arrow Blackhawk Paper Co., Schocker Paper Co., Iden Cordage & Twine Co., I.S.P./Weissberger Paper Co., Strauss Paper Corp. Mem. Network Assn. (dir.). Office: 2100 Devon Ave Elk Grove Village IL 60035*

ALTMAN, JOHN STAPLETON, film producer/dir.; b. Kansas City, Mo., Jan. 27, 1947; s. Frank Gerard and Virginia Clara (Aikins) A.; B.A., U. Pa., 1968; postgrad. U. Mo., Kansas City, 1969. Tchr. English lit., dir. curriculum Sunset Hill Sch., Kansas City, Mo., 1968-72; writer, dir. Calvin Communications, Inc., Kansas City, 1972-74; co-founder, producer, dir. Pentacle Prodns., Inc., Kansas City, 1974—; distbn. coordinator Pentacle Films, Inc., Kansas City, 1976—; documentary films include: Thomas Hart Benton's The Sources of Country Music, PBS, 1975, Missouri: Portrait of a People, 1976, Flag: Rita Blitt, 1976, 1976, They Tell It for the Truth: Ozark Storytelling, PBS, 1979; A Question of Duty, 1980. Recipient various nat. film festival awards; Nat. Endowment for Arts grantee, 1974-75, 1978-79; Mo. Arts Council grantee, 1975-76, 1978-79, 80-81; Mid-Am. Arts Alliance grantee, 1977-78. Mem. IFPA, Film and Video Communicators, Am. Film Inst., Mo. Inst. for Film and Video (dir.), Great Alkali Plainsmen, Scion Soc. of Baker Street Irregulars (founder 1963), Phi Delta Theta. Roman Catholic. Home: 1408 W 50th Terr Kansas City MO 64112 Office: 4800 Rainbow Blvd Westwood KS 66205

ALTMAN, JULES, dermatologist; b. Bklyn., June 6, 1931; s. Samuel and Bella (Sherak) A.; M.D., U. Mich., 1958; m. Deborah Levine, Aug. 29, 1956; children—Suzanne, David, Karen. Intern, Univ. Hosp., Ann Arbor, Mich., 1958-59; resident Mayo Clinic, Rochester, Minn., 1959-62; practice medicine specializing in dermatology; mem. staffs Detroit Gen. Hosp., Detroit Meml. Hosp.; clin. asso. prof. dermatology and syphilogy, Wayne State U. Active United Jewish Appeal, Detroit; mem. bd. dirs. Hillel Day Sch., Detroit. Mem. AMA, Mich. State, Macomb County med. socs., Am. Acad. Dermatology, Soc. Investigative Dermatology, Mich. Dermatological Soc., Am. Soc. Dermopathology. Jewish. Club: Wabeek Country. Contbr. articles to med. jours. and texts. Home: 1950 Westlake Ct Bloomfield Hills MI 48013 Office: 11012 E Thirteen Mile Rd Warren MI 48093

ALTMAN, MILTON HUBERT, lawyer; b. Mpls., July 18, 1917; s. Harry Edmund and Lee (Cohen) A.; B.S., U. Minn., 1938, LL.B., 1947; m. Helen Horwitz, May 21, 1942; children—Neil, Robert, James. Admitted to Minn. bar, 1947; partner Altman, Weiss & Bearmon, St. Paul, 1947—. Mem. gov's adv. com. on Constl. Revision, 1950, on Gift and Inheritance Tax Regulations, 1961-65; chmn. atty. gen.'s adv. com. on Consumer Protection, 1961-65. Spl. atty. for Minn. Bd. Med. Examiners, 1963-75; spl. atty. for U. Minn., 1963-75; dir. SPH Hotel Co. Mem. nat. emergency com. Nat. Council on Crime and Delinquency, 1967-69; mem. Minn.-Wis. small bus. adv. council SBA, 1968-70; mem., v.p. Citizens Council on Delinquency and Crime, 1968-76; bd. dirs. Correctional Service Minn., 1968-76; mem. Lawyers Com. for Civil Rights Under Law, 1965-67; mem. U.S. Dist. Judge Nominating Commn., 1979. Chmn. Minn. Lawyers for Johnson and Humphrey, 1968. Bd. dirs. St. Paul Jewish Fund and Council, 1966-69, Minn. Soc. Crippled Children and Adults. Mem. Am., Minn. (chmn. tax sect. 1960-62), Ramsey County (exec. council 1968-71) bar assns., Am. Arbitration Assn. (nat. panel arbitrators), Fgn. Policy Assn. (nat. council 1969), U. Minn. Law Sch. Alumni Assn. (dir. 1967-70), UN Assn. (nat. legacies com. 1967), Am. Law Inst. Clubs: Minn. (dir. 1975-78), Hillcrest Country; St. Paul Athletic. Author: Estate Planning, 1966. Home: 2353 Youngman Ave Saint Paul MN 55116 Office: Degree of Honor Bldg St Paul MN 55101

ALTON, ANN LESLIE, lawyer; b. Pipestone, Minn., Sept. 10, 1945; d. Howard Robert, Jr. and Camilla Ann (DeMong) Alton; B.A., Smith Coll., 1967; J.D., U. Minn., 1970; m. Gerald Russell Freeman, Sr. Admitted to Minn. bar, 1970, U.S. Dist. Ct. bar for Minn., 1972, U.S. Supreme Ct. bar, 1981; asst. county atty., Hennepin County, Mpls., 1970—, felony prosecutor, criminal div., 1970-75, acting chief citizen protection div., 1975-76, chief citizen protection/econ. crime div., 1976—; instr. Hamline U. Law Sch., St. Paul, 1973-76; adj. prof. law William Mitchell Coll. Law, St. Paul, 1977—, U. Minn. Law Sch., 1978—; lectr. in field, 1970—; vice chmn. bd. dirs. Minn. Program on Victims of Sexual Assault, 1974-76; bd. dirs. Physician's Health Plan, Health Maintenance Orgn., 1976-80, exec. com. 1977-80; mem. legal drug abuse subcom. Gov. Minn. Adv. Com. Drug Abuse, 1972; bd. visitors U. Minn. Law Sch., 1979—. Mem. Am., Minn., Hennepin County (ethics com. 1973-76, criminal law com. 1973—, co-chmn. 1979-80, unauthorized practice law com. 1977-78, individual rights and responsibilities com. 1977-78) bar assns., Nat. Dist. Attys. Assn., Minn. County Attys. Assn., Minn. Trial Lawyers Assn., Am. Judicature Soc., Minn. Women Lawyers, U. Minn. Law Sch. Alumni Assn. (dir. 1979—). Author articles, pamphlet, manual. Home: 2105 Xanthus Ln Plymouth MN 55447 Office: 2000 Hennepin County Govt Center Minneapolis MN 55487

ALTVATER, PHILIP C., JR., mktg. exec.; b. Upland, Pa., Jan. 16, 1945; s. Philip C. and Elsie C. (Moore) A.; B.A., Pa. State U., 1966. Sales rep. Westvaco Corp., N.Y.C., 1969-73, Oxford Paper Co., Chgo., 1974; product mgr. Hobart McIntosh Paper Co., Elk Grove, Ill., 1975-76; dist. mktg. mgr. Consol. Papers, Inc., Chgo., 1976—. Served with U.S. Army, 1967-69. Home: 21W 754 Huntington Rd Glen Ellyn IL 60137 Office: 135 S LaSalle St Chicago IL 60603

ALVAREZ, RAQUEL, physician; b. Sagua La Grande, Cuba, Nov. 23, 1928; d. Manuel E. and Adelaida (Santalis) Alvarez; came to U.S., 1970; naturalized, 1976; B.S. U. Havana, 1953, M.D., 1953; m. Orlando Arrom, Sept. 29, (div. Aug. 1966); children—Orlando, Carlos M., Raquel. Gen. practice medicine in Holquin ote, Cuba, 1953-70; intern Augustana Hosp., Chgo., 1972, resident in pathology, 1973; practice medicine specializing in family practice, Chgo., 1973—; mem. staffs Augustana, St. Mary of Nazareth hosps., Chgo. Diplomate Am. Bd. Family Practice. Fellow Am. Acad. Family Practice; mem. A.M.A., Ill., Chgo. med. socs., Am. Women's Med. Assn., Cuban Med. Assn. in Exile. Presbyterian. Home: 9140 Keystone St Skokie IL 60076 Office: 2348 W North Ave Chicago IL 60674

ALVERSON, ROBERT MADISON, agrl. equipment mfg. co. exec.; b. Albertville, Ala., Aug. 4, 1946; s. William Joseph and Mary Helen (Ford) A.; B.S. in Agrl. Engring., Auburn U., 1968; M.S. in Agrl. Engring., Purdue U., 1970; postgrad. in environ. engring. Ohio State U., 1971; M.B.A., U. Chgo., 1979; m. Sandra Marie Pazanin, Aug. 25, 1979. Engring. research asso. Sperry Rand Corp., New Holland, Pa., 1970-73; product research mgr. Agrl. Equipment div. Internat. Harvester, Chgo., 1973-76, mgr. mktg. program devel., 1976-77, mgr. bus. research, corp. planning, 1977-78, mgr. strategy research and devel., corp. planning, 1978-79, mgr. corp. advanced harvesting systems, 1979—; engring./research conferee on maj. agrl. equipment product coms. Registered engr.-in-tng., Ala.; lic. pvt. pilot. Mem. Am. Soc. Agrl. Engrs., Am. Mgmt. Assn., Am. M.B.A. Assn., Aircraft Owners and Pilots Assn., Sigma Xi. Clubs: Chgo. Young Execs., U. Chgo. Execs., 401. Author tech. papers; patentee in field. Office: 401 N Michigan Ave Chicago IL 60611

ALVINE, RAYMOND GUIDO, cons. engr.; b. Burlington, Iowa, Aug. 22, 1926; s. Clark B. and Marcelle (Guerbinot) A.; B.S., Iowa State U., 1949; m. Dorothy Ann Lux, Sept. 1, 1947; children—Mary (Mrs. Jonathan St. Clair), Michael, Joan (Mrs. Albert Pallone), Cynthia, Patricia, Douglas, Suzanne, Steven, Judith, Christine. With Fairmont Foods, Columbus, Ohio, 1949-50, Carl A. Goth, profl. engr., Omaha, 1950-51, Silas Mason Co., Burlington, Iowa, 1951-53; asso. Leo A. Daly Co., Omaha, 1953-61; pres. Raymond G. Alvine & Assos., Inc., mech. and elec. cons. engrs., Omaha, 1961—. Chmn. Omaha Bldg. Bd. Rev., 1973—, Steamfitters Bd. Examiners, 1970—, City of Omaha High Rise Bldg. Ordinance, 1973—; mem. Nebr. State Energy Bd. Registered profl. engr., Iowa, Nebr., S.D., Nev., V.I., Ariz., Kans., Calif. Fellow ASHRAE; mem. Am. Cons. Engrs. Council, ASME, Soc. Am. Mil. Engrs., Nebr. Cons. Engrs. Assn. (pres. 1969), Nebr. Cons. Engrs. Assn. (charter mem., fellow, pres. 1972), Automated Procedures for Engring. Cons. (charter mem., nat. pres. 1974-76), Pi Tau Sigma. Clubs: Toastmasters (pres. 1963), K.C., Exchange, Field; Press (Omaha). Home: 1910 S 32d Ave Omaha NE 68105 Office: 254 Aquila Ct Omaha NE 68102

ALWIN, LEROY VINCENT, JR., mech. engr.; b. Mpls., Sept. 23, 1931; s. LeRoy Vincent and Norma Constance (Hartmuth) A.; B.M.E., U. Minn., 1958; m. Barbara June Hecker, Sept. 23, 1972; children—Elizabeth Ann, Anthony Jay; stepchildren—Pamela Jeanne Bohach, Joel Edward Bohach. Engring. designer, asst. "Linac Project", Dept. Physics, U. Minn., Mpls., 1953-58; weather observer, forecaster, USN, Coco Solo, Canal Zone, 1954-56; design mech. engr. Temperature Control Div., Honeywell, Inc., Mpls., 1958-71; cons. mech. engr., pres. Park Engring., Mpls., 1971—; proprietor Sugar Wood Farm, Mound, Minn., 1959—. Chmn., N. Am. Maple Syrup Council, 1975-77; chmn. Mound, Minn. Park Commn., 1968-71. Served with USNR, 1954-56. Registered profl. engr., Minn., Wis., Iowa, S.D., Mich., N.D. Mem. ASME, Am. Meteorol. Soc. Republican. Club: Engrs. Patentee in field; contbr. articles to profl. jours. Home: Robin Ln Mound MN 55364 Office: 5700 W 36th St Minneapolis MN 55416

ALWOOD, DONALD LEE, motor truck components co. exec.; b. DeKalb County, Ind., Nov. 8, 1938; s. Guy Carlton and Rozella (Mercer) A.; student public schs., Garrett, Ind., 1956; m. Colleen Ann Hoffman, Sept. 5, 1964; children—Dawn Elizabeth, Donald Timothy. Owner, operator Alwood Shell Service, Auburn, Ind., 1957-59; machine operator Dana Corp., Auburn, 1959; salesman Auburn Motor Sales, 1960, 65; with Internat. Harvester Co., Ft. Wayne, Ind., 1965—, gen. foreman inspection, axle transmission div., 1976—. Active Boy Scouts Am., 1971, 72; asst. coach Little League Baseball, 1972-73. Served with U.S. Army, 1961-64. Mem. Am. Mgmt. Assn., Am. Soc. Quality Control. Democrat. Home: 506 S Ijams St Garrett IN 46738 Office: Internat Harvester Co 2710 S Coliseum Blvd Fort Wayne IN 46806

AMACHER, BILL MARSH, mech. constrn. co. exec.; b. Urbana, Ill., Aug. 25, 1955; s. Charles Leslie and Joan Carol A.; B.S., U. Ill., 1977; student Eastern Ill. U., 1978—; m. Bonnie Frohling, Sept. 29, 1979. Controller, R. H. Bishop Co., Champaign, Ill., 1977—. Notary Public. Mem. U.S. C. of C., Ill. State C. of C., Champaign C. of C., Nat. Assn. Purchasing Mgrs., Am. Mgmt. Assn., Am. Inst. Corp. Controllers, U. Ill. Alumni Assn., Phi Gamma Delta. Clubs: Illini Quarterback, Illini Rebounders, Champaign West Rotary. Home: 2511 Sheridan St Champaign IL 61820 Office: 3506 N Mattis St Champaign IL 61820

AMACHER, DONALD LAVERNE, constrn. co. exec.; b. Green County, Wis., Sept. 25, 1941; s. Sindolf Juan and Helen Elizabeth (Disch) A.; m. Donna Jean Waefler, Nov. 22, 1959; children—Debra Marie, Delinda Kay. Asst. mgr. Fullerton Lumber Co., Monroe, Wis., 1965-69; counter salesman Fish Bldg Supply, Monroe, 1969-70; mgr. Hiland Homes, Inc., Monroe, 1970-75; mgr. Amwood Homes, Inc., Brodhead, Wis., 1975-76; pres., owner Home-Craft Constrn. Inc., Monroe, 1976—; owner, mgr. Don Amacher Realty, Monroe, 1973—.

Mem. U.S. C. of C., Green Country Bd. Realtors, Nat. Assn. Realtors. Mem. Ch. of Christ. Club: Marshall Bluff Bowhunters. Home: Route 2 Monroe WI 53566 Office: 1818 1st St Monroe WI 53566

AMADOR, LUIS V., surgeon; b. 1920; M.D., Northwestern U., 1944. Intern, U. Ill., 1944-45, resident in neurology and neurosurgery, 1945-46, 48-50, Rockefeller Found., 1951-52, Guggenheim fellow, 1954, neurosurgeon Children's Meml. Hosp., Northwestern Meml. Hosps. (Wesley and Passavant Pavillions); clin. prof. neurol. surgery U. Ill. Coll. Medicine, Chgo., 1966-78; prof. clin. neurol. surgery Northwestern U., 1978—. Bd. dirs. Spastic Paralysis Research Found. Served to capt. M.C., AUS, 1946-48. Diplomate Am. Bd. Neurosurgeons. Fellow A.C.S., Royal Soc. Medicine; mem. AMA, Congress Neurol. Surgeons, Am. Assn. Neurol. Surgeons, Central Neurosurg. Soc. (pres.), Internat. Soc. Pediatric Neurosurgery, Interurban Neurol. Soc. (dir.), Research Soc. Stereo encephalotomy, AAAS, Sigma Xi. Contbr. articles to books and profl. jours. Office: 707 N Fairbanks Ct Chicago IL 60611

AMANN, ANTON HELMUTH, health care lab. exec.; b. LudwigsBurg, Germany, Dec. 14, 1942; came to U.S., 1955, naturalized, 1966; s. Andreas and Katharine (Eppler) A.; B.S., St. Louis Coll. Pharmacy, 1966; Ph.D., U. Conn., 1970; m. Nancy Lee Burke, June 10, 1967; children—Christopher Matthew, Cameron Cochell, Courtney Michelle. Group leader Abbott Labs., N. Chgo., 1970-75; mgr. new product devel. Adria Labs., Wilmington, Del., 1975-76; sr. scientist Mallinckrodt Labs., St. Louis, 1976-77; dir. pharm. devel. Am. Critical Care, McGaw Park, Ill., 1977-81; v.p. regulatory and tech. affairs K-V Pharm., St. Louis, 1981—. Usher, Little League, Baseball and Soccer coach, 1975—; dir. rules and regulations Libertyville (Ill.) Soccer Assn., 1978-80. Recipient Eli Lilly Achievement award, 1966; Am. Pharm. Assn. Merit award, 1966; McKesson Leadership award, 1966; Pres.'s award, 1972; named Best Soccer Coach Libertyville (Ill.) Soccer Assn., 1979. Mem. Am. Pharm. Assn. (arrangements chmn. 1975, program chmn. Midwestern meeting 1980), Acad. Pharm. Scis., Parenteral Drug Assn., Mo. Pharmacist Assn., Sigma Xi, Rho Chi, Kappa Psi. Roman Catholic. Contbr. articles to profl. jours. Home: 700 Mullady Pkwy Libertyville IL 60048 Office: 2503 S Hanley Rd Saint Louis MO 63144

AMARO, JOHN ANTHONY, chiropractor; b. Kansas City, Mo., Apr. 1, 1947; s. Carl and Virginia (Belmonte) A.; D. Chiropractic, Cleve. Chiropractic Coll., 1970; D. Phys. Therapy, Van Norman U., 1974. Pvt. practice chiropractic N.E. Chiropractic Center, Kansas City, Mo., 1971-75, Metcalf Chiropractic Offices, P.A., Overland Park, Kans., 1975—; fgn. cons. Chinese Med. Inst. Trustee, Nat. Council on Alcoholism. Served with 135th Hosp. Corps, AUS, 1970-73. Fellow Am. Council Applied Clin. Nutrition; mem. Acupuncture Soc. Am. (v.p. 1974—), Mo. Acupuncture Soc. (pres. 1975—), Am., Kans., Mo., Ky. chiropractic assns., Internat. Acad. Clin Acupuncture (pres.), London and County Soc. Physiologists Home: 15310 Melrose Dr Stanley KS 66211 Office: 7203 Metcalf Ave Overland Park KS 66204

AMAROSE, ANTHONY PHILIP, cytogeneticist; b. Oneonta, N.Y., Mar. 17, 1932; B.S., Fordham U., 1953, M.S., 1957, Ph.D. in Cytology, 1959; fellow in gen. pathology Harvard Med. Sch., 1961. Instr., Marymount Coll., Tarrytown, N.Y., 1957-59; resident research asso. Argonne Nat. Lab., 1959-61; cytologic cons., research lab. for mentally retarded Walter E. Fernald State Sch., Waltham, Mass., 1961-62; sr. scientist Cancer Research Inst., New Eng. Deaconess Hosp., Boston, 1961-62, cons. cytogenetics, 1963-67; asst. prof. dept. Ob-Gyn, lectr. dept. pathology Albany (N.Y.) Med. Coll., Union U., 1963-67, research asso. prof. dept. Ob-Gyn, 1966-67; asst. prof. dept. Ob-Gyn, Chgo. Lying-In Hosp., Pritzker Sch. Medicine, U. Chgo., 1967-71, dir. cytogenetic core lab., biol. scis. div. Center for Population Research, U. Chgo., 1972-77, dir. cytogenetics lab., sect. cytology, dept. Ob-Gyn, 1975-78, dir. cytogenetics lab. Chgo. Lying-In Hosp., U. Chgo. Hosps. and Clinics, 1978—, asso. prof. dept. Ob-Gyn, Pritzker Sch. Medicine, 1971—; cons. Inst. Def. Analyses, Arlington, Va., 1965-67. Trustee, Charles A. Berger Scholarship Fund, Fordham U., 1966; mem. med. adv. bd. Barren Found., 1977-78. Served with M.C., U.S. Army, 1953-55, Res., 1955-62. Fellow Royal Micros. Soc. (Gt. Britain); mem. AAAS, Am. Inst. Biol. Scis., Am. Soc. Cell Biology, Am. Soc. Human Genetics, Am. Soc. Law and Medicine, Environ. Mutagen Soc., Inst. Soc., Ethics and the Life Scis., Internat. Acad. Criminology, N.Y. Acad. Scis., Soc. Gynecol. Investigation, AAUP, Sigma Xi. Editorial bd., cons. editor Excerpta Medica, 1963—; reviewer Acta Cytologica, Am. Jour. Ob-Gyn, Archives Gen. Psychiatry, Jour. Reproductive Medicine; contbr. numerous articles to profl. jours. Office: Dept Ob-Gyn Chgo Lying-In Hosp 5841 S Maryland Ave Chicago IL 60637

AMARY, ISSAM BAHJAT, adminstrv. recreation therapist; b. Jerusalem, July 11, 1942; s. Bahjat Kamel and Essaf (El-Khiami) El-Amary; came to U.S., 1962, naturalized, 1972; B.S., Mo. Valley Coll., 1968; M.S., Central Mo. State U., 1974; m. Wilma Jeanne Blinn, Aug. 20, 1967; children—Jason Issam, Jarred Jamal, Dax Tallal. Recreation therapist, dir. activity therapy Marshall (Mo.) State Sch. Hosp., 1969-75, unit dir., 1975—; exec. dir. Mo. Spl. Olympics, 1970-72, chmn. bd. dirs., 1970-73; founding mem. Betterment of Youth Program. Recipient Viki award in dramatic arts. Mem. Nat. Park and Recreation Assn., Nat. Therapeutic Recreation Soc. Clubs: Optimist (dir.), Masons. Author: Creative Recreation for the Mentally Retarded, 1974; A Taste of Lebanon, 1975; Effective Meal Planning and Food Preparation for the Mentally Retarded-Developmentally Disabled, 1979; The Rights of the Mentally Retarded-Developmentally Disabled to Treatment and Education, 1980; Social Awareness, Hygiene, and Sex Education for the Mentally Retarded-Developmentally Disabled, 1980. Home: 711 Plaza Dr Marshall MO 65340 Office: Marshall State School Hospital E Slater St Marshall MO 65340

AMBA, ETIM ANWANA, soil scientist; b. Oron, Nigeria, Aug. 8, 1948; came to U.S., 1977; s. Anwana Mba-Esu Mba and Nkoyo Okpo-Etim Ebito; B.Sc. with honors, U. Nigeria, Nsukka, 1974; M.S., Ohio State U., 1980; m. Aruk Ikpeme Bassey, Sept. 27, 1975; children—Anwana, Ikpeme, Eme. Soil scientist Funtua Agrl. Devel. Project, Funtua, Nigeria, 1974-75; sr. agrl. officer Soil Survey Unit, Fed. Dept. Agr., Umuahia, Nigeria, 1975-80; grad. research asso. dept. agronomy Ohio State U., 1980—. Mem. Soil Sci. Soc. Am., Am. Soc. Agronomy, Internat. Soil Sci. Soc., Am. Soc. Photogrammetry. Methodist. Office: 1885 Neil Ave Columbus OH 43210

AMBELANG, JOEL RAYMOND, social worker; b. Milw., Aug. 23, 1939; s. Raymond Frank and Clara Ottilie (Alft) A.; student Concordia Coll., Milw., 1953-59; B.S., Concordia Sr. Coll., Ft. Wayne, Ind., 1961; M.S. in Community Devel., U. Mo., 1971; m. Lois Jean Yarbrough, Aug. 14, 1964; children—Joel Mark, Kimi Lee, Elizabeth Jean. Chief officer juvenile ct. 11th Jud. Circuit Mo., St. Charles, 1968-74, dir. juvenile ct. services, 1974-76; dir., owner Counseling and Clin. Services, St. Charles, 1976-80; exec. dir. Luth. Family Services N.W. Ind., Inc., Merrillville, 1980—; field instr., part-time asst. prof. dept. social work Valparaiso (Ind.) U., 1981—; instr. sociology and adminstrn. of justice evening coll. Lindenwood Colls., St. Charles, 1975-80; co-founder Youth in Need, Inc., 1973, bd. dirs., 1974-78, pres., 1976-78; cons. Mo. Council on Criminal Justice, Juvenile Tech. Adv. Com., 1973-75; cons., tng. chmn. Mo. Juvenile Justice Assn., 1972-74; mem. St. Charles County Child Welfare Adv. Bd., St. Charles County Child Abuse Task Force; mem. U.S. Cycling Fedn.; chmn. Nat. Bicycle Safety Program, 1979-80. Recipient awards Nat. Dist. Attys. Assn., 1974, Nat. Council Juvenile Ct. Judges, 1979, Juvenile Ct. Services Adminstrn. Nat. Coll. Juvenile Justice, 1971; cert. advanced alcoholism counselor Mo. Dept. Mental Health. Mem. Nat. Council Juvenile and Family Ct. Judges, St. Charles Community Council (award 1978), Nat. Assn. Social Workers, Legal Services Eastern Mo. (adv. com.). Lutheran. Originator, host program Lean On Me, sta. KCLC-FM, 1973-80; participant seminars in field; designer, author courses of study in field. Home: 2606 Sears St Valparaiso IN 46383 Office: 7101 Broadway Merrillville IN 46410

AMBROSE, JERE BRITTON, engr., inventor, automobile industry products mfg. co. exec.; b. Detroit, Mar. 6, 1939; s. Richard Wright and Mary (Van Allsburg) A.; B.S., Trinity U., 1961; m. Norma Jean Nicol, Sept. 8, 1961; children—Joe, Nicole, Richard. Sales engr. No. Fibre Products Co., Holland, Mich., 1961-64, sales mgr., Birmingham, Mich., 1964-66, v.p., 1966-73, exec. v.p., 1973-79, pres., 1979—; dir. 1st Mich. Bank, Zealand, 1980—. Served with U.S. Army, 1962. Recipient Ray S. Erlandson award. Republican. Presbyterian. Patentee in field. Home: 5645 Lakeshore Dr Holland MI 48423 Office: 50 W 3d St Holland MI 49423

AMBROSE, TOMMY W., research exec.; b. Jerome, Idaho, Oct. 14, 1926; s. Fines M. and Advice (Barnes) A.; B.S. in Chem. Engring., U. Idaho, 1950, M.S., 1951; Ph.D., Oreg. State U., 1957; m. Shirley Ball, June 23, 1951; children—Leslie Ann, Julie Lynn, Pamela Lee. With Gen. Electric Co., Richland, Wash., 1951-54, 57-60, supr., 1960-63, mgr. process and reactor devel., 1963-65, mgr. research and engring., 1965; mgr. research and engring. Douglas United Nuclear, Richland, 1965-69; asst. dir. Battelle Meml. Inst., Seattle, 1969-71, exec. dir. Research Center, 1971-75, mgr. W. Jefferson Nuclear Facility, Columbus, Ohio, 1975, dir. research, Richland, 1975, dir. Battelle-N.W. Div., 1975-79, v.p., corp. dir. multicomponent ops., Columbus, 1979—. Mem. engring. adv. bd. U. Idaho, Moscow, 1975—; mem. vis. com. Sch. Engring., U. Wash., Seattle, 1974—. Served with USN, 1944-46. Registered profl. engr., Ohio, Wash. Mem. Am. Inst. Chem. Engrs., Am. Nuclear Soc., Sigma Xi, Phi Lambda Upsilon. Home: 530 Plymouth St Worthington OH 43085 Office: 505 King Ave Columbus OH 43201

AMBROZIAK, SHIRLEY ANN, communication specialist; b. Saginaw, Mich., July 8, 1953; d. John Joseph and Stella Mary (Wasik) A.; B.A. with honors, Mich. State U., 1975; M.A. (grantee), Purdue U., 1977. Speech instr. Purdue U., West Lafayette, Ind., 1975-77, Hammond, Ind., 1977-78; journalism instr. West Side High Sch., Gary, Ind., 1977-78; dir. communications Northwestern U. Transp. Center, Evanston, Ill., 1978, asst. dir., 1978—; speech instr. Northeastern Ill. U., 1979-80. Bd. dirs. Cook County Am. Cancer Soc., 1977-79; chmn. Gov's. Commn. on Higher Edn. Student Adv. Com., East Lansing, Mich., 1973-75. Mem. Women's Transp. Assn. (chmn. seminar and Chgo. program 1980-81), Women in Communications (co-chmn. job placement 1980-82), Transp. Research Forum, Speech Communication Assn. Am., Purdue Alumni Assn. Club: Metro Racquetball. Author: Organizational Communication, 1974; Human Communications, 1975; (with L. Stewart) The Relationship Between Adherence to Traditional Sex Roles and Communication Apprehension, 1976; (with Leon N. Moses) Corporate Planning under Deregulation: The Case of the Airline, 1980; (with Robert P. Neuschel) Managing Effectively under Deregulation, 1981; contbr. articles to profl. jours. and newspapers. Home: 2550 Prairie St Evanston IL 60201 Office: 2001 Sheridan Rd Evanston IL 60201

AMDAHL, DOUGLAS KENNETH, state supreme ct. justice; b. Mabel, Minn., Jan. 23, 1919; s. Olean Knute and Beulah Beth (Franklin) A.; B.B.A., U. Minn., 1946; J.D. summa cum laude, William Mitchell Coll. Law, St. Paul, 1951; m. Phyllis J. Lampland, Apr. 14, 1949; children—Faith Ann, Charles Olean. Admitted to Minn. bar, 1951; pvt. practice, Mpls., 1951-55; asst. county atty. Hennepin County, 1955-61; mcpl. judge City of Mpls., 1961-62; dist. ct. judge, Hennepin County, 1962-80; justice Minn. Supreme Ct., 1980—, chief justice, 1981—; instr. law and judges schs. Served with USAAF, 1942-45. Mem. Am. Bar Assn., Minn. Bar Assn. Lutheran. Office: 230 State Capitol Blvd St Paul MN 55155

AMEN, JOHN MILES, city ofcl.; b. Lincoln, Nebr., Aug. 13, 1950; s. Godfred H. and Evelyn DeVee (Miles) A.; student S.E. Community Coll., 1975; diploma Central Tech. Community Coll., 1979; m. Camelia (Cammy) Jo Deterding, Apr. 9, 1972; children—Dawn Nicole, Travis John. Apprentice printer Lincoln (Nebr.) Jour. Star Printing Co., 1968-72; firefighter Lincoln Fire Dept., 1972-74; waste water plant operator Kawasaki Motor Corp., Lincoln, 1974-77, City of Gothenburg, Nebr., 1977—. Named One of Outstanding Young Men of Am., U.S. Jaycees, 1981; cert. waste water plant operator, Iowa, Colo., Nebr. Mem. Nebr. Water Pollution Control Assn. (chmn. cert. com. 1980—, dir.-at-large 1980—, Scott Wilber award 1978, 79, author corr. course for wastewater treatment plant operators 1980), Am. Water Works Assn. Democrat. Baptist. Club: Masons. Home: 2624 Northaven Dr Gothenburg NE 69138 Office: 409 9th St Gothenburg NE 69138

AMERINE, IVAN ROBERT, sales engr.; b. Galloway, Ohio, Aug. 6, 1930; s. Ivan Robert and Bernice (Fish) A.; B.S., Ohio State U., 1948-51; m. Alice Fulton, July 29, 1949; children—Stephen, David, Brian, Hal. Vice-pres., also dir. Capitol City Mfg. Co., Columbus, Ohio, 1951-56; pres., gen. mgr. Apco Fabricating Co., Columbus, 1956-66; pres., chmn. Columbus Form Tool Co., 1966-70; pres. Isco Inc., Worthington, Ohio, 1970—. Vestry, fin. chmn. St. John's Episcopal Ch., Worthington, 1973-76; vestryman, sr. warden Christ Ch. (Anglican), Columbus, 1978—; chmn. com. for lay vocations Diocese of Mid-West, 1978-79; trustee Anglican Rite Jurisdiction, DIocese of St. Mark. Mem. Soc. Mfg. Engrs. (sr.). Republican. Clubs: Brookside Golf and Country, Columbus Maennerchor; Island Beach (dir., pres. 1979—) (Sanibel Island, Fla.); Elks, Masons, Shriners. Home: 2137 Castlecrest Dr Worthington OH 43085 Office: 893 High St Worthington OH 43085

AMES, CANDICE MARIE ANDERSON, ednl. adminstr.; b. Pine City, Minn., Apr. 29, 1948; d. Lawrence F. and Ruth A. (Teich) Anderson; B.S., St. Cloud State U., 1970, M.S., 1974; postgrad. U. Minn., 1976—; m. Roger Jesse Ames, June 13, 1970; 1 son, Andrew Jesse. Sr. high social studies tchr., Pine City, Minn., 1970-80; curriculum dir. Pine City Public Schs., 1980—. Mem. Pine County Cancer Bd.; chmn. Pine County Democratic Farm Labor Party, 1972. Recipient Outstanding Alumnus award St. Cloud State U., 1980. Mem. NEA, Assn. Supervision and Curriculum Devel., Minn. Edn. Assn. (tchr. of excellence, honor roll tchr. 1978), Minn. Sch. Public Relations Assn., Pine City Edn. Assn. (Tchr. of Yr. 1978). Democrat. Lutheran. Home: 455 7th St Pine City MN 55063 Office: 605 6th St Pine City MN 55063

AMICK, SHIRLEY MARILYN, mktg. services exec.; b. Armour, S.D., Dec. 4, 1925; d. Robert and Bertha Breen; sudent pub. schs. Eastern and Madison, S.D.; children—Sally, Matthew, James, Terry, Darlene. Supr. credit card acquisitions A.J. Wood Corp., Milw., 1968—. Mem. Internat. Traders Guild, Internat. Entrepreneurs Assn. Jehovah's Witness. Home: 2927 S Logan Ave Milwaukee WI 53207 Office: A J Wood Corp 405 E Lincoln Ave Milwaukee WI 53207

AMICK, WILLIAM (BILL) ROBERT, mag. editor; b. Louisville, Feb. 26, 1951; s. Carl Williamson and Mary Davin A.; student Bellarmine Coll., Louisville, 1973; m. Debra Nall, May 17, 1980. Staff sports writer Louisville Courier Jour., 1971-74; racing publicity mgr. Am. Motorcyclist Assn., Westerville, Ohio, 1974-77, editor Am. Motorcyclist mag., 1977-81, mng. editor, 1981—. Mem. Motorcycling Press Assn., Am. Assn. Automobile Racing Writers, Am. Motorcyclist Assn. Office: Box 141 Westerville OH 43081

AMIDON, PAUL CHARLES, pub. co. exec.; b. St. Paul, July 23, 1932; s. Paul Samuel and Eleanor Ruth (Simons) A.; B.A., U. Minn., 1954; m. Patricia Jean Winjum, May 7, 1960; children—Karen, Michael, Susan. Bus. mgr. Paul S. Amidon & Assos., Inc., St. Paul, 1956-66, pres., 1966—. Served with AUS, 1954-56. Home: 1582 Hillcrest Ave Saint Paul MN 55116 Office: 1966 Benson Ave Saint Paul MN 55116

AMIDON, WILLIAM DOUGLAS, retail co. exec.; b. Ashtabula, Ohio, Mar. 23, 1954; s. Douglas B. and Velma J. Amidon; student Kent State U., 1973; B.B.A., U. Toledo, 1976; m. Nancy Ann Kingston, Aug. 26, 1978. With Ashtabula Office Equipment Inc., 1970—, salesman, 1977-78, v.p., 1978—. Mem. Am. Fedn. Musicians, Ashtabula Jr. C. of C. Club: Exchange (pres.). Home: 3582 Austinburg Rd Ashtabula OH 44004 Office: 5402 Main Ave Ashtabula OH 44004

AMIRJAHED, ABDOLREZA KASRA, pharmacist, educator; b. Tehran, Iran, Dec. 15, 1940; s. Mohammad Ali and Khadijeh Kutchak (Bananshahi) A.; came to U.S., 1958; B.S., Am. U. Beirut, 1965; M.S., U. Ill. at Med. Center, Chgo., 1969, Ph.D., 1972. Instr. pharmacy U. Ill. at Med. Center, Chgo., 1969-72, resident in pharmacy research and devel. hosp., 1972; asst. prof. pharmacy U. Toledo, 1972-77, asso. prof., 1977—. Am. Field Service scholar, 1958-59, AID scholar, 1960-65. Mem. Am. Pharm. Assn., Am. Assn. Colls. Pharmacy, Acad. Pharm. Scis., Internat. Transactional Analysis Assn., Sigma Xi, Phi Kappa Phi, Rho Chi. Club: Univ. of Toledo. Office: Coll Pharmacy U Toledo 2801 W Bancroft Ave Toledo OH 43606

AMMAR, RAYMOND GEORGE, physicist, educator; b. Kingston, Jamaica, July 15, 1932; s. Elias George and Nellie (Khaleel) A.; came to U.S., 1961, naturalized, 1965; A.B., Harvard U., 1953; Ph.D., U. Chgo., 1959; m. Carroll Ikerd, June 17, 1961; children—Elizabeth, Robert, David. Research asso. Enrico Fermi Inst., U. Chgo., 1959-60; asst. prof. physics Northwestern U., Evanston, Ill., 1960-64, asso. prof., 1964-69; prof. physics U. Kans., Lawrence, 1969—; cons. Argonne (Ill.) Nat. Lab., 1965-69, vis. scientist, 1971-72; project dir. NSF grant for research in high energy physics, 1962—. Fellow Am. Phys. Soc.; mem. AAUP. Contbr. articles to physics jours. Home: 1651 Hillcrest Rd Lawrence KS 66044 Office: Dept Physics U Kans Lawrence KS 66045

AMMERMAN, JAY NEIL, bar assn. exec.; b. Richmond, Ind., Aug. 21, 1945; s. Francis Andrew and Pollyanna (Kitchel) A.; B.S. in Mathematics, U. Chgo., 1967, M.B.A. in Fin., 1977; M.S. in Mathematics (NSF fellow), Northwestern U., 1968; m. Paula Jean Lorig, Dec. 19, 1969; 1 son, Jason Lorig. Sr. programmer Vapor Corp., Chgo., 1969, systems analyst, 1970, sr. systems analyst, 1970-72, asst. mgr. systems and programming, 1972-75; mgr. systems and programming Am. Bar Assn., Chgo., 1975-77, asst. dir. data processing, 1977-81, dir. data processing, 1981—. Bd. dirs. Hyde Park Co-op Credit Union, 5227 S. Blackstone Corp. Mem. GUIDE, (assn. for large scale IBM computer users), Sigma Xi, Beta Gamma Sigma. Home: 5222 S Blackstone Ave Chicago IL 60615 Office: 1155 E 60th St Chicago IL 60637

AMOR, ROBERT HENRY, architect; b. Chgo., July 23, 1933; s. William Henry and Pearl (Scholten) A.; B.Arch., U. Mich., 1963; m. Alyce Mae Kolence, Aug. 20, 1955; children—Robert Alan, William Andrew, Andrew Gregory, Constance Lynn. Archtl. draftsman Paul Hazelton, Architect, Traverse City, Mich., 1961-62; project architect, designer Gordon Cornwell, Architect, Traverse City, Mich., 1962-65; designer, project architect Daverman Assos., Grand Rapids, Mich., 1965-68; prin., owner Robert H. Amor, Architect, Grand Rapids, Mich., 1968—, Grand Haven, Mich., 1975—; lectr. ch. architecture. chmn. Conf. on Religious Art, Music and Architecture, Grand Haven, 1978-80. Mem. art as worship task force Muskegon Cooperating Chs. Served with AUS, 1953-54. Recipient AIA design award for Bethany Luth. Ch., Kaleva, Mich., 1970. Mem. Interfaith Forum Religion, Art and Architecture, Guild for Religious Architecture, Tau Sigma Delta. Methodist. Architect, United Meth. Ch., Evart, Mich., Manistee, Mich., Bear Lake, Mich., Cath. Info. Center, Grand Rapids, 1st Bapt. Ch., Manistee, Foothills United Meth. Ch., Cameron Park, Calif., Hope United Meth. Ch., Sacramento. Home: 18200 Shore Acres Rd Grand Haven MI 49417 Office: 18200 Shore Acres Rd Grand Haven MI 49417

AMOS, EUNICE CARRIE, home economist, educator; b. Litchfield, Minn., Jan. 20, 1936; d. Arnold and Irene (Martine) Paulson; B.S., U. Minn., 1958; postgrad. Mankato State U., 1979—; m. Marlin Amos, July 19, 1959; 1 son, Paul. Instr. home econs. Lake Crystal (Minn.) Public Schs., 1958-64, dept. head adult evening sch., 1958-64; free-lance work with home econs. occupations and edn., 1964-67; tchr. and supr. home health aides Nicollet County (Minn.) Public Health Nursing Service, 1967-68; tchr. and coordinator home econs. Mankato (Minn.) Area Vocat. Tech. Inst., North Mankato, 1968-75; instr. home econs., dept. lead tchr. St. Peter (Minn.) Public Schs., 1975—, instr. adult tailoring, tutor teenage program for pregnant girls, 1975—, mem. supt.'s adv. council, 1976-78; guest instr. Minn. State Dept. Edn., 1970, 71; mem. Minn. Dept. Vocat. Edn. Evaluation and North Central Assn. Schs. and Colls. teams, 1979-81. Judge, 4-H County Fairs, Minn., 1965-67; sec. exec. bd. St. Peter Play Group for Children, 1967-69; active Cub Scouts, Boy Scouts Am., 1969-70; bd.

dirs. Citizens Scholarship Found., Community Edn. Adv. Council, St. Peter-Kasota area, Minn., 1977-80. Mem. NEA, Minn. Edn. Assn., St. Peter Edn. Assn., Am. Home Econs. Assn., Minn. Home Econs. Assn., Am. Vocat. Assn., Minn. Vocat. Assn., Minn. Home Economists in Edn., Minn., Lake Crystal High Sch., St. Peter High Sch. assns. of future homemakers Am. (hon. mem.), Gustavus Adolphus Coll. Library Assos., Phi Upsilon Omicron. Lutheran. Club: Order Eastern Star (St. Peter, Minn.). Contbr. articles on home econs. to profl. publs. Home: 323 S 7th St Saint Peter MN 56082 Office: Lincoln Dr Saint Peter MN 56082

AMOS, EVERETT R., dentist; b. Kirklin, Ind., Nov. 9, 1901; s. John Henry and Iva Belle (Stephenson) A.; B.A. magna cum laude et cum honore, St. John's Coll., 1929; student Indpls. Sch. Stenotypy; D.D.S. with honors, Ind. U., 1950; m. Martha J. Tilson, Apr. 1, 1944. Served with U.S. Mcht. Marine, 1929-34; tchr. English, typing, until 1942; mem. staff Ind. U. Sch. Dentistry, 1952-57, asst. prof. oral diagnosis, 1954-57; pvt. practice dentistry, Knox, Ind., 1957—; dental cons. Hogar de Niños de Ejercicio Salvaje, Guadalajara, Mex., 1970—. Served with USAAF, 1942-45; CBI. Mem. Soc. Ind. Pioneers, Am. Soc. Guadalajara, Guadalajara Soc. Prevention Cruelty to Animals, Omicron Kappa Upsilon, Psi Omega. Democrat. Methodist (chmn. bd. 1967-68). Kiwanian. Winner Am. Med. Joggers Assn. contigent to Boston Marathon in category of over 70 years of age, 1977, 78, 79; holder record for 15,000 meters for age 76, 77. Home: 309 S Main St Knox IN 46534 also Veracruz Sur 28 No 4 Guadalajara Jalisco Mexico Office: 309 S Main St Knox IN 46534

AMPEL, LEON LOUIS, anesthesiologist; b. Kansas City, Mo., Oct. 29, 1936; s. Joseph and Eva (Resnick) A.; B.A. in Chemistry, U. Mo., 1958, M.D., 1962; m. Jane Lee Isador, June 21, 1959; children—Jill, Ross, Jackie. Intern, Evanston (Ill.) Hosp., 1962-63, resident in anesthesiology, 1965-67, attending anesthesiologist, 1967-74, sr. attending anesthesiologist, 1974—; head dept. anesthesiology Glenbrook Hosp., Glenview, Ill., 1977—; asst. prof. clin. anesthesiology Northwestern U. Active Northbrook (Ill.) Sch. Caucus, 1975-76. Served to lt., M.C., USN, 1963-65. Diplomate Am. Bd. Anesthesiology. Fellow Am. Coll. Anesthesiologists; mem. AMA, Ill. Med. Assn., Chgo. Med. Assn., N. Suburban Med. Soc. (pres., 1974), Am. Soc. Anesthesiology, Ill. Soc. Anesthesiology, Chgo. Soc. Anesthesiology. Clubs: Old Willow, U.S. Lawn Tennis Assn., Chgo. Dist. Tennis Assn. (v.p., dir. 1976—). Contbr. articles to publs. Home: 2701 Oak St Northbrook IL 60062 Office: 2100 Pfingsten St Glenview IL 60025

AMUNDSEN, LOUIS ROALD, phys. therapist, educator; b. Moline, Ill., Aug. 23, 1939; s. Andrew and Helen Ella (Rasmussen) A.; A.A., Moline Community Coll., 1962; B.S., U. Wis., Madison, 1964, Ph.D., 1972; m. Norma Jean Veach, Mar. 29, 1969; children—Andrew Austin, Margery Ellen. Staff phys. therapist Henry Ford Hosp., 1964-65; chief phys. therapist St. Marys Hosp., LaSalle, Ill., 1965-67; asst. prof. Wayne State U., 1973-74, U. Iowa, Iowa City, 1974-80; dir. grad. studies, course in phys. therapy U. Minn., 1980—; cons. Univ. Health Scis., Chgo. Med. Sch. Grad. Program in Phys. Therapy, Sch. Related Health Scis. Served with USAF, 1957-61. Mem. Am. Phys. Therapy Assn. (co-chmn. research com., cardiopulmonary sect.), Am. Coll. Sports Medicine. Contbr. articles to profl. jours. Home: 486 Rolls Rd New Brighton MN 55112

AMUNDSON-EASTER, NANCY ELLEN ANDERSON, occupational therapist; b. Monroe, Wis., Oct. 10, 1936; d. Wallace Lowell and Martha Elizabeth (Burmaster) Anderson; student Kalamazoo Coll., 1954-55; B.S., U. Minn., 1958, postgrad., 1973—; m. Elmo Erickson, May 12, 1957 (dec. 1976); children—Jeffrey Alan, Darcy Lynn; m. 2d, Loren Amundson, 1971 (div. 1974); m. 3d, Douglas King Easter, Aug. 8, 1979. Therapist out-patient rehab. Mpls. Curative Workshop, 1960, outpatient therapy supr., 1961-62, 67-69; cons. Mpls. Nursing Homes, 1965-66; therapist Met. Med. Center, Mpls., 1970; cons. retarded children Didlake Sch., Manassas, Va., 1970-71; propr. Hand Some Things, Mpls., 1974-75; research coordinator Impact Inc., 1975-76; vol. learning disabilities Mpls. Sch. System, 1972—; occupational therapy dir. Sunset Nursing Home, Park Rapids, Minn., 1977—; partner Easterwoods, 1977—. Vol., Vols. Am., 1972-73; leader 4-H, 1973-74; active Boy Scouts Am. Registered occupational therapist. Mem. Am., Minn. occupational therapy assns., Minn. Civil Liberties Union, Children's Home Soc. Minn., Delta Zeta. Democrat. Presbyterian. Home: 21 Kenwood Terr Mora MN 55051 Office: Easterwoods Box 1592 Lake George MN 56458

AMUTA, GERSHON AKOTAOBI, educator; b. Nigeria, June 13, 1945; s. Allison Oriaku and Selinah Nweke (Ogbonna) A.; N.C.E., Advanced Tchrs. Coll., Owerri, 1966; M.Ed., Lincoln U., Mo., 1979; Ph.D., U. Mo., Columbia, 1981; m. Patricia Nkechi Anyanwu, July 16, 1977; children—Eziaku, John, Jeannie. Tchr. high sch., Imo, Nigeria, 1967-71, 74-78; vice prin. high sch. Igedde Oturkpo, Nigeria, 1972; prin. high sch., 1973; dir. Wesley Found., Lincoln U., Jefferson City, Mo., 1979—; dir. A.O. Amuta & Sons, Nigeria. Recipient Curators grant U. Mo., Columbia, 1981. Mem. Assn. Supervision and Curriculum Devel., Assn. Childhood Educators Internat., Nigerian Union Tchrs. (life), Sci. Tchrs. Assn. Nigeria (life), Pi Lambda Theta, Phi Delta Kappa, Kappa Delta Pi. Democrat. Methodist. Home: 1304 Major Dr Jefferson City MO 65101 Office: Wesley Found Box 221 Lincoln U Jefferson City MO 65101

ANANTH, KRISHNAN PADMANABHAN, research inst. exec.; b. Madras, India, Dec. 25, 1945; s. Kavasseri K. and Thangammal Padmanabhan; came to U.S., 1968, naturalized, 1979. Postdoctoral research asso. dept. chem. engring. U. R.I., Kingston, 1972-73; asst. environ. engr. Midwest Research Inst., Kansas City, Mo., 1973-74, asso. environ. engr., 1974-75, program mgr. energy/environ. systems, 1977, head environ. systems sect., 1977-79, asso. dir. energy and materials sci., 1979-80, dir. energy and materials sci. dept., 1980—; research/teaching asst. U. R.I., 1968-72; cons. Owens/Corning Fiberglas, 1972-73. Mem. Am. Inst. Chem. Engrs., Sigma Xi. Contbg. author: Energy and the Environment. Home: 8316 Broadmoor St Overland Park KS 66212 Office: 425 Volker Blvd Kansas City MO 64110

ANDEL, FRED JERRY, computer services exec.; b. Macon, Ga., Feb. 9, 1939; s. Fred John and Ouida (Smith) A.; E.E., Milw. Sch. Engring., 1960; m. Diane Crowbridge, Oct. 15, 1962; children—Jody, Dana, Joel. Developer automated systems inventory control Standard Elec. Co., 1957-60; systems data processing supr. Mortgage Assn., 1960-61; data processing specialist mfg. and mfg. systems Kearney & Trecker, 1961-66; nat. tng. dir. Metro Sch. Bus. and Tech., 1966-72; staff instr. programming and computer sci. Concordia Coll., 1972-73; chief exec. D & F Computer Service, Milw., 1967-81; cons. Wis. Public Edn. of Adminstrv. Systems. Pres., Tanglewood Assn., 1979-80, dir., 1980-81. Mem. Data Processing Mgmt. Assn. Club: Highlander Racquet. Office: 17000 W Cleveland St New Berlin WI 53151

ANDERL, STEPHEN, clergyman; b. Chippewa Falls, Wis., July 13, 1910; s. Henry A. and Katherine (Schneider) A.; B.A. magna cum laude St. John's U., 1932, M.Div., 1974; postgrad. Catholic U. Am., 1940. Ordained priest Roman Catholic Ch., 1936; curate in Wisconsin Rapids, Wis., 1936-37; pastor in Spring Valley, Wis., 1949-52, Hewitt, Wis., 1952-53, Assumption Parish, Durand, Wis., 1953—; tchr., guidance counselor, vice prin. Aquinas High Sch., La Crosse, Wis., 1937-49. Censor books, clergy examiner, vicar for religious Diocese of La Crosse, 1951—; vicar forane Durand Deanery, 1953—; diocesan chaplain Boy Scouts Am., Girl Scouts U.S.A., 1936-49; chaplain XII World Jamboree Boy Scouts, 1967, Nat. Jamboree Boy Scouts Am., 1969, 73; mem. Diocesan Clergy Personnel Bd., 1970-74; exec. sec. Cath. Youth Orgn., Diocese of La Crosse, 1938-49; diocesan dir. Sodality, 1938-49; cons. Central Commn. of Diocese of LaCrosse for Implementation of Vatican Council. Mem. exec. com. Chippewa Valley council Boy Scouts Am., mem. nat. Cath. com. on scouting, 1974—, vice chmn. diocesan Cath. com. on scouting; housing commr., La Crosse, 1948-49; mem. Gov.'s Com. on Children and Youth, 1957-63; adviser Wis. Youth Com., 1960—; mem. State Comprehensive Mental Health and Retardation Planning Com., Durand Community Council; dir. West Central Wis. Community Action Agy., OEO; bd. dirs. La Crosse Diocesan Bd. Edn., La Crosse Diocesan Cath. Social Agy., Inc., Silver Waters council Girl Scouts U.S.A. Created domestic prelate with title of right reverend msgr. by Pope John XXIII, 1962; recipient Silver Beaver award Boy Scouts Am., 1968; St. George award, 1969. K.C. (4 deg., Chaplain). Author: Technique of the Catholic Action Cell, 1942; Papal Teaching on Catholic Action, 1946; The Religious and Catholic Action, 1947; Catholic Action, a Responsibility of the School, 1948; Parish of the Assumption, Life and Times of the Mystical Christ in Durand, 1960. Contbr. articles to religious mags. and jours. Address: 911 W Prospect St Durand WI 54736

ANDERS, LESLIE, educator; b. Admire, Kans., Jan. 22, 1922; s. Ray Leslie and Bertie Mae (Hasson) A.; A.B., Coll. Emporia, 1949; A.M. (Allen Cook White, Jr. fellow), U. Mo., 1950, Ph.D., 1954; m. Mardellya Mary Soles, Oct. 17, 1942; children—Geraldine (Mrs. Robert C. Hunt), Charlotte (Mrs. Alexander Wilson). Historian, Office of Chief of Engrs., Dept. Army, Balt., 1951-55; faculty history Central Mo. State U., Warrensburg, 1955—, prof., 1963—. Hon. commr. Mo. Am. Revolutionary Bicentennial Commn., 1974. Served with AUS, 1940-45. Recipient Merit award Am. Assn. for State and Local History, 1976. Mem. Am. Mil. Inst., State Hist. Soc. Mo., Sons of Union Vets. of Civil War, Scabbard and Blade, Phi Kappa Phi. Republican. Presbyn. Author: The Ledo Road, 1965; The Eighteenth Missouri, 1968; Education for Service, 1971; The Twenty-First Missouri, 1975. Home: 318 Goodrich Dr Warrensburg MO 64093

ANDERSEN, HANS, wholesale trade co. exec.; b. Vancouver, B.C., Can., Sept. 28, 1932; Came to U.S., 1936, naturalized, 1953. s. Hans and Sigrid Andersen; B.S., Wayne U., 1954; M.B.A., U. Mich., 1958; children—Kurt, Karen. Mem. sales staff J.B. Webb Co., Detroit, 1958-59, Rapistan Co., 1959-60; owner, pres., chmn. bd. Andersen & Assos., Inc., Detroit, 1960—. Served with USAF, 1955-56. Mem. Material Handling Equipment Dealers Assn. Office: 24333 Indoplex Circle Farmington MI 48018

ANDERSEN, HARRY EDWARD, oil equipment co. exec.; b. Omaha, Apr. 25, 1906; s. John Anton and Caroline (Ebbensgaard) A.; student pub. schs. and spl. courses, including Ohio State U., 1957, U. Okla., 1959; Ph.D. in Bus. Adminstrn. (hon.), Colo. State Christian Coll., 1972; m. Alma Theora Vawter, June 12, 1931; children—Jeanenne Dee (Mrs. Gaylord Fernstrom) and Maureen Lee (Mrs. Roger Podany) (twins), John Harry. Founder N.W. Service Sta. Equipment Co., Mpls., 1934, pres., treas., 1956—; owner Joint Ops. Co., real estate mgmt.; dir. Franklin Nat. Bank, Mpls. Spl. dep. sheriff Hennepin County, 1951—; hon. fire chief of Mpls., 1951—; pres. Washington Lake Improvement Assn., 1955. Mem. Shrine Directors Assn. (N.W. gov.), Nat. Assn. Oil Equipment Jobbers (pres. 1957-58, dir. 1954-56), C. of C., Upper Midwest Oil Mans Club. Lutheran. Mason (32deg., K.T., Shriner), Jester. Clubs: Viking (pres.), Engineers, Toastmasters, Minneapolis Athletic, Golden Valley Golf, Le Mirador Country (Lake Geneva, Switzerland). Home: 2766 W River Pkwy Minneapolis MN 55406 Office: 2520 Nicollet Ave Minneapolis MN 55404

ANDERSEN, LEONARD CHRISTIAN, polit. worker, real estate investor; b. Waukegan, Ill., May 30, 1911; s. Lauritz Frederick and Meta Marie (Jacobsen) A.; B.A., Huron (S.D.) Coll., 1933; M.A., U. S.D., 1937; m. Charlotte O. Ritland, June 30, 1937; children—Karen (Mrs. Fred Schneider), Paul R., Charlene (Mrs. Kurt Olsson), Mark Luther. Tchr., Onida (S.D.) High Sch., 1934-35; dir. bus. tng. Waldorf Coll., Forest City, Iowa, 1935-39; ins. salesman, 1939-41; tchr. econs., current history Morningside Coll., Sioux City, Iowa, 1941-43; engaged in ins. and real estate, Sioux City, 1943-76; mem. Iowa Ho. of Reps. from Woodbury County, 1961-64, 66-71; mem. Iowa Senate from 26th Dist., 1972-76, chmn. rules and adminstrn. com. Mem. Iowa Commn. on Aging; past mem. Siouxland Council on Alcoholism; bd. regents Augustana Coll., Sioux Falls, S.D., 12 yrs., now mem. Augustana Fellows; chmn. Morningside Lutheran Ch. Mem. Am. Soc. Public Adminstrn., UN Assn. (pres. Siouxland chpt.), Sioux City C. of C., United Comml. Travelers. Republican. Mason, Lion. Home: 712 S Glass St Sioux City IA 51106 Office: 509-A Benson Bldg Sioux City IA 51102

ANDERSEN, RICHARD ROLAND, city ofcl.; b. Omaha, Jan. 17, 1924; s. Alfred C. and Mary D. (Daugaard) A.; B.S., U. Omaha, 1965; M.P.A., U. Nebr., 1974; m. Donna Moore, Dec. 7, 1951. With Police dept. City of Omaha, 1951—, chief of police, 1967—; mem. faculty U. Nebr., 1967-75. Vice chmn. Nebr. Commn. on Law Enforcement and Criminal Justice, 1968—; chmn. police adv. com. Nat. Clearinghouse for Criminal Justice Planning and Architecture, 1974. Mem. Am. Soc. Public Adminstrn. (pres. Nebr. chpt. 1973-74). Office: 505 S 15th St Omaha NE 68102

ANDERSON, ALAN JAMES, corp. safety ofcl.; b. Ft. Dodge, Iowa, June 29, 1941; s. William James and Mabel Josephine (Lind) A.; B.S. in Bus. Adminstrn., U. Minn., 1967; m. Cheryl Ann Zaun, July 24, 1971; 1 dau., Kimberly Ann. Plant safety supr. and mgr. Gillette Co., St. Paul, 1977-79; corp. safety mgr. Control Data Corp., Mpls., 1979—. Chmn., Minn. Safety Council State Conf. Indsl. Sect., 1978, 79, 80, Met. Area Conf. Indsl. Sect., 1979, 80. Cert. safety profl.; cert. hazard control mgr. Mem. Am. Soc. Safety Engrs., Am. Indsl. Hygiene Assn., Nat. Safety Mgmt. Soc., Systems Safety Soc., Nat. Fire Protection Assn., Human Factors Soc. Lutheran. Contbr. articles to publs. in field. Home: 7668 Iverson Ave S Cottage Grove MN 55016 Office: 8100 34th Ave S Box 0 Minneapolis MN 55440

ANDERSON, ARNOLD SEVEREN, pediatrician; b. Mpls., Jan. 11, 1918; s. Arnold Severen and Myrtle (Sholl) A.; B.A., St. Olaf Coll., 1939; M.D., U. Minn., 1944; M.S. in Pediatrics, Mayo Found., Rochester, Minn., 1950; m. Ruth Rusk Dalton, Aug. 31, 1940; children—Renner, Jeffrey, Kimball, Lucinda, Susanna, Whitney, Tyler (dec.), Colin, Amy, Martha. Intern, San Diego (Calif.) County Hosp., 1944, resident, 1944-45; a founder, pediatrician St. Louis Park (Minn.) Med. Center, 1950-67, chief of staff, 1958-60, pres., 1960-66, dir., 1966-69; a founder, mem. staff Children's Health Center & Hosp., Mpls., 1967—, pres., 1972-77, dir. patient care, trustee, 1978—; mem. nutrition edn. tng. com. Minn. Dept. Edn.; clin. prof. pediatrics U. Minn.; mem. Minn. Gov.'s Council on Nutrition; mem. com. scouting for handicapped Viking council Boy Scouts Am.; cons. Met. Council on Pediatric Emergency Med. Care. Served with M.C., U.S. Army, 1945-47. Recipient Dr. Francis E. Harrington award Mpls. Jaycees, 1975; Charles Bolles Bolles-Rogers award Hennepin County Med. Soc., 1978; Disting. Alumnus award St. Olaf Coll., 1979. Mem. Am. Acad. Pediatrics, Ambulatory Pediatric Assn., AMA, Northwestern Pediatric Soc., Minn. Med. Assn., Hennepin County Med. Soc., Mpls. Met. Pediatric Soc. Quaker. Contbr. articles to med. publs. Office: Children's Health Center 2525 Chicago Ave Minneapolis MN 55404

ANDERSON, ARTHUR RODNEY, vocat. educator; b. Oak Park, Ill., Feb. 14, 1930; s. Arthur J. and Hilda Marie (Fauske) A.; B.S., So. Ill. U., 1981; m. Marjorie Raglin, June 23, 1965. Carpenter, Wade Constrn. Co., Itasca, Ill., 1962-72, foreman, 1962-65, supt., 1965-72; tchr. bldg. trades Lockport (Ill.) Twp. High Sch., 1972—, developer vocat. bldg. trades course; lectr. secondary edn. workshops, 1968—. Recipient Outstanding Service award James McKinnon Smith chpt. Nat. Honor Soc., 1975; citation for outstanding contbn. to vocat. edn. studies So. Ill. U., 1981. Mem. Am. Vocat. Assn., Ill. Vocat. Assn., United Brotherhood of Carpenters and Joiners (pres. local 558, Elmhurst, Ill. 1967-76), Iota Lambda Sigma. Lutheran. Club: Sons of Norway. Home: 603 S Dunton Ave Arlington Heights IL 60005 Office: Lockport Twp High School 12th and Jefferson Sts Lockport IL 60441

ANDERSON, AUSTIN GOTHARD, univ. adminstr.; b. Calumet, Minn., June 30, 1931; s. Hugo Gothard and Turna Marie (Johnson) A.; B.A., U. Minn., 1954, J.D., 1958; m. Catherine Antoinette Spellacy, Jan. 2, 1954; children—Todd, Susan, Timothy, Linda, Mark. Admitted to Minn. bar, 1958, Ill. bar, 1962, Mich. bar, 1974; mem. firm Spellacy, Spellacy, Lano & Anderson, Marble, Minn., 1958-62; dir. Ill. Inst. Continuing Legal Edn., Springfield, 1962-64; dir. dept. continuing legal edn. U. Minn., Mpls., 1964-70, asso. dean gen. extension div., 1968-70; mem. firm Dorsey, Marquart, Windhorst, West & Halladay, Mpls., 1970-73; asso. dir. Nat. Center for State Cts., St. Paul, 1973-74; dir. inst. continuing legal edn., U. Mich., Ann Arbor, 1973—; adj. faculty U. Minn., 1974, Wayne State U., 1974-75, William Mitchell Coll. Law, 1973-74; project dir. Select Com. on Judiciary State of Minn., 1974-76; chmn. City of Bloomington (Minn.) Park and Recreation Adv. Commn., 1970-72; pres. bd. King Sch. Parent-Tchr. Orgn., 1977-78; mem. adv. com. Ferris State Coll. Served with USN, 1950-51. Mem. Assn. Legal Adminstrs. (pres. 1969-70), Am. (chmn. sect. of econs. of law practice 1981-82), Mich., Ill., Minn., Washtenaw County bar assns., Am. Mgmt. Assn., Assn. Continuing Legal Edn. Adminstrs. Co-editor, contbg. author: Lawyer's Handbook, 1975. Home: 3617 Larchmont Dr Ann Arbor MI 48105 Office: 432 Hutchins Hall Ann Arbor MI 48109

ANDERSON, BENJAMIN LEE, city ofcl.; b. Washington, Feb. 28, 1944; s. Benjamin Lee A.; B.S. in Polit. Sci., George Washington U., 1966; 1 son, Rafique Omar. Asst. dist. mgr. D.C. Dept. Recreation, 1965-75; personnel dir. Huron-Clinton Metro Authority, Detroit, 1975—; faculty div. recreation Wayne State U. Sch. Edn. Vice-chmn. Detroit Joint Recreation Commn., 1979; active budget and allocation com. United Community Service, Nat. Council for Black Child Devel.; bd. dirs. Detroit Bapt. Youth Home, Boy Scouts Am. Notary public. Mem. Nat. Recreation and Park Assn., Am. Soc. Personnel Adminstrn., Internat. Personnel Mgmt. Assn., Pub. Employee Labor Relations Assn., others. Republican. Baptist. Club: Optimist. Home: One Lafayette Plaisance 304 Detroit MI 48207 Office: 3050 City Nat Bank Bldg Griswold MI 48226

ANDERSON, BERTHA ANNETTE, ednl. adminstr.; b. Edmondson, Ark., Mar. 5, 1932; d. Grandville and Bertha Caroline (Hicks) Ward; B.S., Ind. U., 1954; M.A. in Guidance and Counseling, Roosevelt U., 1976; postgrad. Chgo. State U., 1958-78; m. Robert Henry Anderson, Mar. 10, 1956; children—Cynthia, Robert. Tchr. public schs., Gary, Ind., 1955-56; med. technologist U. Ill. Hosp., 1957-58; with Chgo. Public Schs., 1958—, dean of girls, 1969-76, counselor, 1976-78, asst. prin. for discipline and security, 1978—; owner Personal Services, 1977—. Sec.-Mid-South Mental Health Adv. Council, 1977—. Mem. Am. Fedn. Tchrs. (regional dir. black caucus 1978), Chgo. Tchrs. Union (dist. supr.), Am. Personnel and Guidance Assn., Chgo. Personnel and Guidance Assn. Methodist. Home: 10204 S Eberhart Chicago IL 60628 Office: 180 W Washington Blvd Chicago IL 60602

ANDERSON, BJARNIE R., legis. adminstr.; b. St. Cloud, Minn., Apr. 9, 1947; s. John and Bernice (Anderson) A.; B.S. cum laude, Northwestern U., 1969, M.A., 1972, postgrad. in Mgmt. Sci. and Communication. Asst. to dep. mayor/city adminstr. City of N.Y., 1969-70; urban affairs fellow Center for Urban Affairs, Northwestern U., Evanston, Ill., 1970-72; dir. research and communications Jon Haaven for Congress, 7th Dist., Minn., 1972; research cons. Minn. Ho. of Reps., St. Paul, 1973; dir. adminstrn. office of Hennepin County Atty., Mpls., 1974-81; dir. ops. Office of U.S. Senator Rudy Boschwitz, Washington, 1981—; adj. prof. legal adminstrn. U. Minn., Mpls.; mgmt. cons. tech. assistance program Nat. Dist. Attys. Assn., Chgo. Active Citizens League, Common Cause, Mpls. Soc. Fine Arts, Nat. Trust for Historic Preservation, Am. Swedish Inst., Am. Scandinavian Found., Farmland Trust, Minn. Farm Bur. Prosecution mgmt. study grantee Swedish Ministry of Justice, 1977; recipient Northwestern U. Alumni Service Award, 1981, Mpls. Jaycees service award, 1978. Mem. Am. Soc. for Public Adminstrn., Internat. City Mgmt. Assn., Am. Mgmt. Assn., Nat. Dist. Attys. Assn., Nat. Assn. Legal Adminstrs. Republican. Lutheran. Clubs: Calhoun Beach, Greenway Athletic, Svenska Sällskapet. Home: 4865 E Lake Harriet Pkwy Minneapolis MN 55409 Office: Office of Senator Rudy Boschwitz US Senate Washington DC 20510

ANDERSON, BRIAN EDWARD, editor; b. Mpls., June 13, 1944; s. Bertil Edward and Phyllis May (Johnson) A.; B.A., U. Minn., 1966; m. Theresa Ann McDonald, June 6, 1970; children—David Robert, Elizabeth Marie. Staff writer Mpls. Tribune, 1966-68, 71-73, U.S. Senate Subcom. on Indian Edn., Washington, 1969; legis. asst. to U.S. Senator Walter Mondale, Washington, 1970; account exec. Carl Byoir & Assos., Mpls., 1975-77; editor Mpls. St. Paul mag., Mpls., 1977—. Mem. Phi Beta Kappa, Sigma Delta Chi. Club: Minn. Press (dir.). Office: 512 Nicollet Mall Minneapolis MN 55402

ANDERSON, CHARLENE, home economist, educator; b. Joplin, Mo., Sept. 14, 1920; d. Charles W. and Melissa (Fuel) Cuther; B.S.,

Tuskegee Inst., 1942; M.S., Tchrs. Coll., Columbia U., 1950; m. Chester Robert Anderson, Sept. 23, 1950; 1 dau., Ercelle Anderson Johnson. Tchr. home econs. Joplin (Mo.) public schs., 1942-51; tchr. Kansas City (Mo.) public schs., 1951-55, cons. home econs. 1955-68, vocat. home econs. tchr., 1968-73, Chester R. Anderson Pre-Vocat. Sch., Kansas City, 1973—; cons. to workwhops in home econs. Troop leader Girl Scouts U.S.A., Joplin, 1942-47; bd. dirs. Spofford Home for Disabled Youth, 1981—; active Boys Club Am., ARC and YWCA, Kansas City, Mo. Recipient Cert. of Achievement, Nat. Restaurant Assn., 1972, Cert. of Appreciation, C.R. Anderson Pre-Vocat. Sch., 1978, Cert. of Merit, J.C. Penney Co., 1977, Anniversary Cert. of Appreciation, Soft and Sweet Music Club, 1979; named Home Econs. Tchr. of Yr., Kansas City, Mo., 1975. Mem. Am. Home Econs. Assn., Mo. Home Econs. Assn. (v.p. 1968-69), Mo. Vocat. Assn., Mo. State Tchrs. Assn., Internat. Fedn. Home Econs., Mo. Home Econs. Tchrs. Assn., Home Economist in Edn. (pres. Kansas City 1958-59), Mo. Assn. of Spl. Needs Youth, Am. Vocat. Assn., Mo. Restaurant Assn., Nat. Assn. of Vocat. Home Econs. Tchrs., Tuskegee Inst. Alumni, NAACP. Methodist. Home: 5405 Bellefontaine St Kansas City MO 64130 Office: 1211 McGee St Kansas City MO 64106

ANDERSON, CHARLES SAMUEL, coll. pres.; b. Madison, Wis., Mar. 4, 1930; s. Sam and Guro Anderson; B.A., St. Olaf Coll., 1951; M.A., U. Wis., 1954; B.D., Luther Sem., 1957; Ph.D., Union Sem., 1962; m. Catherine Gregerson, Dec. 23, 1951; children—Eric, Kristin. Ordained to ministry Lutheran Ch., 1957; pastor chs., Wis., N.Y., Minn., 1957—; prof. ch. history Luther Sem., St. Paul, 1961-76; v.p. acad. affairs, dean of coll. Augsburg Coll., Mpls., 1976-80, pres., 1980—. Bd. dirs. Center for Reformation Research, 1980—. Served with USMC, 1951-53. Grantee Am. Assn. Theology Schs., 1967-68, Luth. Brotherhood, 1972-73; Rockefeller Found. and Martin Luther fellow, 1959-61; Bush fellow, 1972-73. Mem. Ebenezer Soc. (dir. 1980—), Soc. for Reformation Research, Renaissance Soc. Am., Soc. for Ch. History, AAUP, Assn. for Higher Edn. Blue Key, Phi Beta Kappa. Clubs: Rotary, Mpls. Author: The Reformation Then and Now, 1966; Augsburg Historical Atlas of Christianity in the Middle Ages and Reformation, 1967; Faith and Freedom: The Christian Faith According to the Lutheran Confessions, 1977. Office: 731 21st Ave S Minneapolis MN 55454

ANDERSON, CLARENCE AXEL FREDERICK, mech. engr.; b. Muskegon, Mich., Dec. 14, 1909; s. Axel Robert and Anna Victoria (Wikman) A.; student Muskegon Jr. Coll., 1929, Internat. Corr. Schs., 1934; m. Frances K. Swem, Apr. 9, 1934; children—Robert Curtis, Clarelyn Christine Anderson Schmelling, Stanley Herbert. With Shaw-Walker Co., Muskegon, Mich., 1928-78, mech. engr., 1940-65, project engr., 1965-70, chief engr., 1970-78; ret., 1978. Mem. Christian edn. bd. Evangel. Covenant Ch., 1959-61, 67-73. Club: Holland (Mich.) Beagle (pres. 1966-68, 70-73, 75—). Home: 5757 E Sternberg Rd Fruitport MI 49415

ANDERSON, DAVID DANIEL, educator; b. Lorain, Ohio, June 8, 1924; s. David and Nora Marie (Foster) A.; B.S., Bowling Green State U., 1951, M.A., 1952; Ph.D., Mich. State U., 1960; m. Patricia Ann Rittenhour, Feb. 1, 1953. From instr. to prof. dept. Am. thought and lang. Mich. State U., East Lansing, 1957—, editor U. Coll. Quar., 1971-80; Fulbright prof. U. Karachi, Pakistan, 1963-64, Am. del. to Internat. Fedn. Modern Langs., and Lit., 1969-78, Internat. Congress Orientalists, 1971-79. Served with USN, 1942-45, AUS, 1952-53. Decorated Silver Star, Purple Heart; recipient Disting. Alumnus award Bowling Green State U., 1976; Disting. Faculty award Mich. State U., 1974. Mem. AAUP, Popular Culture Assn., Modern Lang Assn., Soc. Study Midwestern Lit. (founder, exec. sec.), Assn. Gen. and Liberal Edn. Author: Sherwood Anderson, 1968 (Book Manuscript award 1961); Louis Bromfield, 1964; Critical Studies in American Literature, 1964; Sherwood Anderson's Winesburg, Ohio, 1967; Brand Whitlock, 1968; Abraham Lincoln, 1970; Suggestions for the Instructor, 1971; Robert Ingersoll, 1972; Woodrow Wilson 1978; Ignatius Donnelly, 1980; William Jennings Bryan, 1981; editor: The Black Experience, 1969; The Literary Works of Abraham Lincoln, 1970; Sunshine and Smoke: American Writers and the American Environment, 1971; (with others) The Dark and Tangled Path, 1971; MidAmerica I, 1974, II, 1975, III, 1976, IV, 1977, V, 1978, VI, 1979, VII, 1980, VIII, 1981, IX, 1982; Sherwood Anderson: Dimentions of his Literary Art, 1976; Sherwood Anderson: The Writer at His Craft, 1979; Critical Essays on Sherwood Anderson, 1981; Michigan: A State Anthology, 1982. Home: 6555 Lansdown Dr Dimondale MI 48821 Office: Dept Am Thought and Lang Mich State U East Lansing MI 48824

ANDERSON, DAVID EUGENE, psychologist, educator; b. Artesia, Calif., Apr. 1, 1951; s. Raymond W. and Lois V. (Ingman) A.; B.A. with highest honors, Bethel Coll., 1973; M.A., U. South Fla., 1976, Ph.D., 1980; m. Barbara Bess Buchanan, Feb. 16, 1979. Teaching asst. Bethel Coll., St. Paul, 1972-73; teaching and research asst. dept. psychology U. South Fla., Tampa, 1973-75; instr. (part-time) Hillsborough Community Coll., Tampa, Fla., 1976; clin. intern VA Hosp., Tampa, 1976-77; mem. staff Center for Christian Psychol. Services, St. Paul, 1977—; asso. prof. psychology Bethel Coll., St. Paul, 1977—, mem. counseling staff, 1977—; cons. Mpls. chpt. Salvation Army, 1978; pvt. practice clin. psychology, 1977—. Mem. Am. Psychol. Assn., Minn. Psychol. Assn., Christian Assn. for Psychol. Studies, Am. Council on Alcohol Problems, Assn. for Advancement of Psychology. Mem. Democratic Farm Labor Party. Presbyterian. Home: 210 Rice Creek Blvd Fridley MN 55432 Office: Bethel College Psychology Dept 3900 Bethel Dr St Paul MN 55112

ANDERSON, DONALD NEIL, mgmt. cons.; b. Wagner, S.D., Nov. 16, 1930; s. Neil and Clara Belle (Dufek) A.; student Yale U., 1948-49; B.E.E., S.D. Sch. Mines, 1952; M.B.A., U. Calif., Los Angeles, 1962; m. Fay Spencer, Mar. 6, 1955; children—Karen Fay, Susan Spencer, Mary Elizabeth, Julianne Neil. Mem. tech. staff Bell Telphone Labs., N.Y.C., 1952-54; project mgr. instrumentation Aerojet-Gen. Corp., Covina, Calif., 1958-60, 62-64; mgr. corp. planning So. Calif. Edison, Los Angeles, 1964-70, budget dir., Rosemead, Calif., 1973-77; dep. adminstr. Southwestern Power Adminstrn., U.S. Dept. Interior, Tulsa, 1970-73; v.p. Exec. Action, Inc., Santa Ana, Calif., 1977-78; prin. Oakwood Mgmt. Sers., 1978—; lectr. in field. Treas. Santa Anita Oaks Homeowners Assn., Arcadia, Calif., 1976-77; western co-chmn. Businessmen for Jimmy Carter, 1976; ruling elder Arcadia Presbyn. Ch., 1976-79. Served with C.E., USNR, 1954-57. Named hon. Ky. col.; cert. cost engr. Mem. IEEE, Am. Assn. Cost Engrs., Planning Execs. Inst., Am. Mgmt. Assn., Eta Kappa Nu, Beta Gamma Sigma, Tau Beta Pi. Republican. Contbr. articles in field to profl. jours. Home and Office: 915 8th Ave Brookings SD 57006

ANDERSON, DORRINE ANN PETERSEN (MRS. HAROLD EDWARD ANDERSON), librarian; b. Ishpeming, Mich., Feb. 24, 1923; d. Herbert Nathaniel and Dorothy (Eman) Petersen; B.S. with distinction, No. Mich. U., 1944; postgrad. Northwestern U., summer 1945, U. Wash., summer 1967, U. Mich. Extension, 1958-65; M.S. in L.S., Western Mich. U., 1970; m. Harold Edward Anderson, Aug. 23, 1947; children—Brian Peter, Kent Harold, Bruce Herbert, Timothy Jon. Tchr. English jr. high sch., Eaton Rapids, Mich., 1944-45; tchr. English, speech Arlington Heights (Ill.) High Sch., 1945-48; tchr. English high sch., Nahma, Mich., 1948-49, 54-61, Gladstone, Mich., 1961-62; librarian Gladstone Sch. and Pub. Library, 1962-70; dir. library services Gladstone Area Pub. Schs., 1971—, Bicentennial coordinator, 1975-76. Acting dir. Mid-Peninsula Library Fedn., 1965-66; chmn. Region 21 Media Advisory Council, 1972—; chmn. adv. com. Regional Ednl. Materials Center 21, 1973—; mem. planning com. Upper Peninsula Reading Conf., 1974—; regional del. Mich. White House Conf. on Libraries and Info. Services, 1979. Pres., Delta County League Woman Voters, 1970-72; mem. human resources subcom. Upper Peninsula Com. for Area Progress, 1964—; mem. com. for library devel. Upper Peninsula, chmn. Delta County Library Bd., 1967-76; mem. region 17, Polit. Action Team, 1968-70. County del. Delta County Democratic Com., 1968. Named Tchr. of Year, Region 17 (Mich.), 1969. Mem. N.E.A., Mich. Edn. Assn. (pres. region 17 council 1967-68, chmn. Upper Peninsula dels. to rep. assembly 1966-68), ALA, Mich. Library Assn., Internat. Reading Assn., Mich. Assn. Media in Edn. (state library Week chmn. 1973-74; recipient leadership award 1977), Mich. Assn. Sch. Library Suprs., Am. Assn. U. Women, Assn. Ednl. Communications and Tech., Kappa Delta Pi, Phi Epsilon, Beta Phi Mu, Delta Kappa Gamma (recipient citation for seminars in mgmt. for women 1977). Home: 1723 Montana Ave Gladstone MI 49887 Office: Gladstone Area Sch and Pub Library Gladstone MI 49837

ANDERSON, DOUGLAS MARTIN, coll. adminstr.; b. Flint, Mich., Aug. 10, 1930; s. Axel W. and Clara (Hansen) A.; A.A., Flint Community Coll., 1960; B.A., Mich. State U., 1962, M.A., 1967. Tchr. public schs., Flint, 1962-66; reserach asso. Mich. State U., 1966-67; asso. dean Delta College, University Center, Mich., 1967—. Served with U.S. Army, 1951-53. Recipient meritorious service citation U.S. Army, 1953. Mem. Mich. Library Assn. (chairperson chpt. 1980-81), Saginaw Valley Library Consortium (chmn. 1980-81), Council for Library Planning, ALA, Assn. Ednl. Communication and Tech. Republican. Lutheran. Office: Delta Coll University Center MI 48710

ANDERSON, EARL THEODORE, ednl. pub. co. exec.; b. Chgo., Nov. 7, 1934; s. Earl Oscar and Josephine Marie (Thomsen) A.; B.S. in Journalism, U. Ill., 1956; postgrad. Roosevelt Univ. Sch. Bus., 1976-78; m. Dorothy Murray Marinelli, Nov. 26, 1959; children—Kathleen, Debra, Sharon, Bonnie, Scott; m. 2d, Roselyn DeFrank Ratigan, June 20, 1981. With Fred A. Niles Communication Centers, Chgo., 1958-61; prodn. mgr., producer-dir., account exec. Burt Munk & Co., 1962-67; dir. info. and devel. Lake Bluff (Ill.) Children's Home, 1967-68; with Coronet/Perspective Films/Video/Media, Chgo., 1968—, mgr. mktg., 1980—. Co-founder Glenview Interfaith Council, pres., 1968-69. Served with U.S. Army, 1956-58. Decorated Army Commendation medal. Mem. Assn. Media Producers, Am. Soc. Tng. and Devel., Ill. Tng. and Devel. Assn., Am. Soc. Curriculum and Devel., Internat. Reading Assn., Am. Mktg. Assn. Home: 904 Wesley Dr Park Ridge IL 60068 Office: 65 E South Water St Chicago IL 60601

ANDERSON, ERIC ANTHONY, town mgr.; b. New Orleans, June 2, 1946; s. Eric Albert and Edna (Barrie) A.; B.A., Syracuse U., 1967; M.P.A., SUNY, Albany, 1968; M.A., Maxwell Sch., Syracuse U., 1970; m. Linda Jane Briefstein, June 22, 1967; children—Eric Scott, Stacy Alissa. Adminstrv. intern City of Phoenix, 1970-71; asst. dir. Research and Devel. Center, Internat. City Mgmt. Assn., Washington, 1971-73; asst. town mgr. Town of Windsor (Conn.), 1973-78; town mgr. Munster (Ind.), 1978—. Bd. mgrs. Windsor-Bloomfield YMCA, 1976-78; adv. council Urban League N.W. Ind., 1979. Nat. Endowment for Humanities fellow, 1977. Mem. Ind. Mcpl. Mgmt. Assn. (pres. 1979-80), Conn. City Mgmt. Assn. (treas. 1977-78), Internat. City Mgmt. Assn. Club: Rotary. Home: 9129 Birch Ave Munster IN 46321 Office: 805 Ridge Rd Munster IN 46321

ANDERSON, ERIC EDWARD, psychologist, educator; b. Mpls., Jan. 24, 1951; s. Charles Eric and Elizabeth (Engstrand) A.; B.A. summa cum laude, U. Minn., 1973; M.A. in Theology, Fuller Sem., 1977, Ph.D. in Clin. Psychology, 1978; m. Florence Kaye, June 18, 1978. Asst. prof. Sch. Public Health U. Minn., Mpls., 1979—, coordinator tng. in aging, 1979—; dir. profl. services Kiel Clinic, Edina, Minn., 1980—; cons. on aging, govt. task forces. Lic. cons. psychologist, Minn. Mem. Am. Psychol. Assn., Gerontol. Soc. Am., Minn. Psychol. Assn., Assn. Health Service Providers in Psychology, Phi Beta Kappa. Contbr. articles to profl. jours. Office: Box 717 Mayo U Minn Minneapolis MN 55455

ANDERSON, FLETCHER NEAL, chem. co. exec.; b. Kansas City, Mo., Nov. 5, 1930; s. Chester Gustav and Astrid Cecilia (Crone) A.; B.S.Ch.E., U. Mo., Columbia, 1951; M.S.Ch.E., Washington U., 1956; grad. Stanford exec. program Stanford U., 1972; m. Marilyn Lucille Henke; children—Karl C., Keith F., Susan L. With Mallinckrodt, Inc., St. Louis, 1951—, group v.p. food, drug and cosmetic chems. div., 1974-76, group. v.p.-chem. group, 1976-78, sr. v.p.-chem. group, 1978—, also dir.; mem. adv. council Engring. Sch., U. Mo., Columbia; Mem. Florissant (Mo.) Charter Commn., 1961-63; v.p. Vill. Lutheran. Ch., Ladue, Mo. Recipient Disting. Service to Engring. award U. Mo., Columbia, 1978; registered profl. engr., Mo., Pa. mem. Am. Inst. Chem. Engrs. (mem. nat. vocat. guidance com., rep. Mo. interprofl. council), Engrs. Club St. Louis. Clubs: University, Algonquin. Office: PO Box 5439 Saint Louis MO 63147

ANDERSON, FRANCES SWEM (MRS. CLARENCE A.F. ANDERSON), nuclear med. technologist; b. Grand Rapids, Mich., Nov. 27, 1913; d. Frank Oscar and Carrie (Strang) Swem; student Muskegon Sch. Bus., 1959-60; certificate Muskegon Community Coll., 1964; m. Clarence A.F. Anderson, Apr. 9, 1934; children—Robert Curtis, Clarelyn Christine (Mrs. Roger L. Schmelling), Stanley Herbert. X-ray file clk., film librarian Hackley Hosp., Muskegon, Mich., 1957-59; student refresher course in nuclear med. tech. Chgo. Soc. Nuclear Med. Techs., 1966; radioisotope technologist and sec. Hackley Hosp., 1959-65; nuclear med. technologist Butler Meml. Hosp., Muskegon Heights, Mich., 1966-70, Mercy Hosp., Muskegon, 1970-79; ret., 1979. Mem. Muskegon Civic A Capella choir, 1932-39; mem. Mother-Tch. Singers, PTA, Muskegon, 1941-48, treas. 1944-48; with Muskegon Civic Opera Assn., 1950-51. Soc. Nuclear Medicine Cert. nuclear medicine technologist Soc. Nuclear Medicine. Mem. Am. Registry Radiologic Technologists, Internat. Platform Assn. Mem. Evang. Covenant Ch. (mem. choir 1953-79, choir sec. 1963-69, Sunday sch. tchr. 1954-75, supt. Sunday sch. 1975-78, treas. Sunday sch. 1981—, chmn. master planning council, coordinator centennial com. to 1981). Home: 5757 E Sternberg Rd Fruitport MI 49415

ANDERSON, GARY LEE, state ofcl.; b. Harlan, Iowa, Feb. 3, 1946; s. Lake Nels and Helen Margaret Anderson; A.B., Creighton U., Omaha, 1969; M.P.A., U. Nebr., 1975; m. Jeanne Kwapiszeski, Oct. 15, 1977; 1 son, Gary Lee. Supr., Panganerix, Omaha, 1969-71; asst. adminstr. Doctors' Hosp., Omaha, 1971-73; mem. research team Social Security Adminstrn., Omaha, 1974; dir. Nebr. Dept. Public Instns., Lincoln, 1975-80; systems analyst Mut. of Omaha, Omaha, 1980—. Home: 6006 N 109 Plaza Omaha NE 68164 Office: Mutual of Omaha Mutual Plaza Omaha NE 68175

ANDERSON, GEORGE LEE (SPARKY), profl. baseball team mgr.; b. Bridgewater, S.D., Feb. 22, 1934. Player, Phila. Phillies, from 1959; mgr. Cin. Reds, 1970-78, Detroit Tigers, 1979—. Winner Nat. League championship, 1970, 72, 75, 76; mgr. Nat. League All Star Team, 1971, 73, 76, 77; named Nat. League Mgr. of Year, 1972. Address: Detroit Tigers Tiger Stadium Detroit MI 48216*

ANDERSON, GERALDINE LOUISE, clin. lab. scientist; b. Mpls., July 7, 1941; d. George M. and Viola Julia-Mary (Abel) Havrilla; B.S., U. Minn., 1963; m. Henry Clifford Anderson, May 21, 1966; children—Bruce Henry, Julie Lynne. Med. technologist Swedish Hosp., Mpls., 1963-68; hematology supr. Glenwood Hills Hosp. lab., Golden Valley, Minn., 1968-70; asso. scientist dept. pediatrics U. Minn. Hosps., Mpls., 1970-74; instr. health occupations and med. lab. asst. Suburban Hennepin County Area Vocat. Tech. Center, Brooklyn Park, Minn., 1974-81, St. Paul Tech. Vocat. Inst., 1978—; research med. technologist Miller Hosp., St. Paul, 1975-78; research asso. Children's and United Hosps., Mpls., 1979—; chairperson health occupations adv. com. Hennepin Tech. Centers, 1978-79; mem. hematology slide edn. rev. bd. Am. Soc. Hematology, 1976—. Mem. Med. Lab. Tech. Polit. Action Com., 1978—; resource person lab. careers Robbinsdale Sch. Dist., Minn., 1970—; mem. Luth. Chaplainey Aux. of Mpls., 1978—. Mem. Minn. Soc. for Med. Tech. (sec. 1969-71), Am. Soc. for Med. Tech. (del. to ann. meetings 1972—, chmn. hematology sci. assembly 1976-78), Minn. Public Health Assn., Twin City Soc. Med. Technologists, Twin Cities Hosp. Assn. (speakers bur. 1968-70), Assn. for Women in Sci., Friends of Luth. Campus Ministry Twin Cities (charter), Omicron Sigma (service awards 1969, 70, 79, 81, honors 1978, 80), Sigma Delta Epsilon (corr. sec. Xi chpt. 1980—) Gamma Delta Alumni Assn. Lutheran. Contbr. articles to profl. publs. Home: 8400 33d Pl N Minneapolis MN 55427 Office: United and Children's Hosps Inc Leukocyte Function Research Lab 333 Smith Ave N Saint Paul MN 55102

ANDERSON, GILBERT WERNER, mental health center exec.; b. Fort Wayne, Ind., Apr. 16, 1931; s. Russell Alvin and Opal Madonna (Hardin) A.; B.A., Fort Wayne Coll., 1953; M.Div., Faith Theol. Sem., 1956; M.Ed., U. Del., 1962; Ed.D., U. Ariz., 1969; m. Ellen Bishop Perkins, Oct. 5, 1974; children—Cara, Dane. Dean of students Chesapeake Coll., Wye Mills, Md., 1969-72; dir. Coles County Mental Health Center, Mattoon, Ill., 1972-75; exec. dir. Regional Mental Health Center, Kokomo, Ind., 1975—; asso. instr. psychology Ind. U., Kokomo, 1975—. Pres., Greater Kokomo Assn. Chs., 1977-79; membership capt. YMCA, 1981; mem. membership com. Boy Scouts Am., 1981. Lic. psychologist, Ind. Mem. Nat. Mental Health Assn., Assn. Mental Health Adminstrs., Howard County Mental Health Assn., Ind. Council Mental Health Centers (past officer). Clubs: Rotary (dir. 1980, pres. 1982-83). Elks (Kokomo). Home: 908 James Dr Kokomo IN 46901 Office: Regional Mental Health Center 3500 S Lafountain St Kokomo IN 46902

ANDERSON, GORDON CALDWELL, metals co. exec.; b. Sherbrook, Que., Can., 1920; came to U.S., 1925, naturalized, 1943, B.S., Northwestern U., 1942. Chmn. bd. Fullerton Metals Co., Northbrook, Ill.; dir. Roper Corp. Mem. Nat. Assn. Aluminum Distbrs. (dir.), Copper and Brass Servicenter Assn. (dir.), Steel Service Center Inst. (chmn. exec. com.). Office: 3000 Shermer Rd Northbrook IL 60062

ANDERSON, HARLEY ERIC, obstetrician, gynecologist, educator; b. Omaha, May 7, 1900; s. Charles Hjalmar and Theresa Anna (Ericksson) A.; B.Sc., U. Nebr., 1923, M.D., 1925; m. Jean Louise Hampton, Sept. 20, 1967; children,—John Harley, Georgiana Warburton Anderson Collins, Bruce Franklin. Practice medicine specializing in gynecology, Omaha, 1926—; asst. in bacteriology pathology U. Nebr., Omaha, 1926-31, instr. obstetrics gynecology, 1938-43, asst. prof., 1943-52, asso. prof., 1952-66, sr. cons., 1966—; clin. prof. Creighton U. Med. Sch., Omaha, 1970-74; mem. active staff Nebr. Meth. Hosp., Clarkson Hosp., Immanuel Hosp., U. Nebr. Hosps. Pres. dist. sch. bd., 1948. Diplomate Am. Bd. Obstetrics and Gynecology. Fellow A.C.S., Am. Coll. Obstetricians and Gynecologists, N.Y. Acad. Scis.; mem. Am. Cancer Soc. (pres. Nebr. div. 1962-63, bd. dirs. 1962-74), Am. Fertility Soc. (v.p. 1970), AMA, Omaha-Douglas County Med. Soc. (pres. 1959-60), Alpha Omega Alpha, Phi Delta Theta, Phi Rho Sigma. Republican. Episcopalian. Contbr. articles to med. splty. jours. Office: Physicians Clinic 10060 Regency Circle Omaha NE 68114

ANDERSON, HAROLD EDWARD, dermatologist; b. Battle Creek, Mich., Dec. 1, 1913; s. Olaf Andrew and Ethel Margaret (Stephen) Andersen; B.S., Battle Creek Coll., 1937; M.D., Loma Linda (Calif.) U., 1940; M.S., Wayne State U., Detroit, 1943; m. Mary Vivian Spomer, June 12, 1939; children—Robert, Nancy, Kent. Intern Henry Ford Hosp., Detroit, 1939-40; resident in dermatology Wayne State U., Detroit, 1940-43; practice medicine specializing in dermatology, Long Beach, Calif., 1943-50, Battle Creek, 1950—; mem. staff Leila Y. Post Montgomery Hosp., Community Hosp., Battle Creek Sanitarium Hosp.; cons. VA Hosp., Battle Creek; instr. Loma Linda U. Med. Sch., 1943-50. Diplomate Am. Bd. Dermatology. Mem. Am. Acad. Dermatology, AMA, Mich. Dermatol. Soc., Mich., Calhoun County med. socs., Mich., Central states dermatol. socs. Contbr. med. jours. Home: 951 Riverside Dr Battle Creek MI 49015 Office: 131 E Columbia Ave Battle Creek MI 49015

ANDERSON, HARRY DUANE, educator; b. Clarinda, Iowa, Apr. 7, 1927; s. Harry E. and Thelma A.; B.A., Central Wash. U., 1951; postgrad Drake U., U. S.D., U. No. Iowa; M.A., Clayton U., 1978; m. Marilyn Sue Miller, Nov. 20, 1965; children—Harry L., Edi R., Melissa W., Melissa L., Melanie M., Samuel A. Tchr., coach Central Decatur High Sch., Leon, Iowa, 1951-59, Oelwein (Iowa) Community High Sch., 1959-62, Cedar Falls (Iowa) Community High Sch., 1962—. Served with USAR, 1954-57. Recipient Outstanding Contbn. to Amateur Boxing award Iowa Sec. of State, 1975, Cedar Falls Jaycees Youth award, 1974. Mem. Iowa Edn. Assn., NEA, Nat. Assn. Curriculum Devel., Nat. Assn. Amateur Boxing Coaches, Iowa Football Coaches Assn., Iowa Track Coaches Assn., Cedar Falls Edn. Assn. Democrat. Episcopalian. Home: 1419 State St Cedar Falls IA 50613 Office: 10th and Division Sts Cedar Falls IA 50613

ANDERSON, HOWARD DOUGLAS, health agy. adminstr.; b. Lumpkin, Ga., Feb. 28, 1936; s. James M. and Lila M. (Glenn) A.; B.A., Morehouse Coll., 1968; m. Louise Clapp, Sept. 13, 1958; 1 son, Howard D.; m. 2d, Susan Benson, Oct. 10, 1975; stepchildren—Deborah, Robert Taylor. Postal clk., 1958-66; sales rep. Merck Sharp & Dohme, Chgo., 1969-70; staff writer U. Chgo. Office Pub. Info., 1970-72; exec. dir. Midwest Assn. Sickle Cell Anemia,

Chgo., 1972—. Bd. dirs. Chgo. Regional Blood Program; mem. citizens adv. council U. Chgo. Sickle Cell Center, U. Ill. Sickle Cell Center. Served with U.S. Army, 1958-60. Mem. Nat. Assn. Sickle Cell Disease (founder). Home: 2231 E 67th St Chicago IL 60649 Office: 36 S Wabash Ave Suite 1113 Chicago IL 60603

ANDERSON, JACK FRANCIS, sch. supt.; b. Bagley, Iowa, Feb. 14, 1934; s. John Francis and Grace Lucille (Ferguson) A.; B.S., N.W. Mo. State U., 1961; M.S., Iowa State U., 1974, postgrad., 1975; m. Delores Ellen Faris, June 2, 1957; children—Ann Denise, Jennifer Jill. Teller, Central Nat. Bank, Des Moines, 1955-58; tchr. Menlo (Iowa) Community Sch., 1961-66, E. Greene Community Sch., Grand Junction, Iowa, 1966-75; prin. Jefferson (Iowa) Community Sch., 1975-79; supt. schs. Stuart-Menlo Community Sch., Stuart, Iowa, 1979—; lectr. in field; coll. ofcl. baseball, football, 1966—. Served with U.S. Army, 1953-55. Named Outstanding Prin., Jefferson Tchrs. Assn., 1975. Mem. Am. Assn. Sch. Adminstrs., Iowa Assn. Sch. Adminstrs. Methodist. Clubs: Toastmasters, Masons, Shriners, Lions, Optimists (dir. 1980-81). Home: Grand Junction IA 50107 Office: N 2d and Main Sts Stuart IA 50250

ANDERSON, JAMES DONALD, hosp. adminstr.; b. Rockford, Ill., Apr. 19, 1932; s. Gunnard Arthur and Hannah (Bargren) A.; B.A., Wheaton Coll., 1953; M.S. in Hosp. Adminstrn., Northwestern U., 1957; m. Elaine Karin Johnson, Dec. 11, 1954; children—Elaine Carol, James Richard, Beth Karin, David Charles, Sharon Kay. Adminstrv. asst. Meml. Hosp. of Dupage County, Elmhurst, Ill., 1957-58; asst. exec. dir. Luth. Deaconess Hosp., Chgo., 1958-63; pres. Central DuPage Hosp., Winfield, Ill., 1963—; bd. dirs. Suburban Cook-DuPage County Health Systems Agy.; dir. Bank of Wheaton. Served with U.S. Army, 1953-55. Mem. Ill. Hosp. Assn. (bd. dirs.), Am. Coll. Hosp. Adminstrs. Republican. Club: Lions (past pres. Wheaton). Home: 26W065 Embden Wheaton IL 60187 Office: 0N025 Winfield Rd Winfield IL 60190

ANDERSON, JAMES HARRY, utility engr.; b. Mpls., Aug. 30, 1927; s. Harry Aden and Leilah Betty (Anderson) A.; B. Civil Engring., U. Minn., 1952; m. Marilyn Louise Graaf, Sept. 7, 1951; children—Christine, Richard, Mark, Susan. Cadet engr. Mpls. Gas Co., 1952-54, engr., 1954-56, coordinator suburban div. main and service, 1956-58, asst. chief engr., 1958-68, chief design engr., 1968-72; chief design engr. Minn. Gas Co., Mpls., 1972-76, chief engr., 1977-80, mgr. operating services, 1980—; mem. utility com. Nat. Transp. Research Bd.; lectr. in field. Chmn. Mpls.-St. Paul Met. Utilities Coordinating Com., 1973-80; planning commr. City of Bloomington, 1962-68, city councilman, 1971-75. Chmn. bd. dirs. South Hennepin County Human Service Council. Served with AUS, 1945-47; PTO. Registered profl. engr., Minn., Iowa, S.D., Nebr. Mem. Minn. Pub. Works Assn. (dir. 1966-72), Am. Gas Assn. (chmn. com. distbn. design 1968-69, chmn. com. system protection 1980, gas industry rep. to Am. Pub. Works Assn. 1975-80, operating sect. award of merit 1964), Midwest Gas Assn., Nat., Minn. socs. profl. engrs., Mpls. Engrs. Club (pres. 1966, Engr. of Year award 1976), Internat. Right-of-Way Assn. (pres. Tri State chpt. 1979, internat. liaison com.), Bloomington (Minn.) C. of C. (pres. 1970), ASCE. Contbr. articles to trade mags. Home: 1400 E 100th St Bloomington MN 55420 Office: Minn Gas Co 733 Marquette Ave Minneapolis MN 55402

ANDERSON, JAMES ROBSON, JR., metals co. exec.; b. Kenosha, Wis., 1920; ed. Yale U. Chmn. Chgo. Extruded Metals Co., Oak Brook, Ill., Anchor-Harvey Components, Inc., Tri-Central Maine Terminal, Inc. Office: 600 Hunter Dr Oak Brook IL 60521*

ANDERSON, JERRY MAYNARD, educator, cons.; b. Deronda, Wis., Sept. 16, 1933; s. Jens B. and Mamie P. (Hanson) A.; B.S., Wis. State U., River Falls, 1958; M.S., No. Ill. U., 1959; Ph.D., Mich. State U., 1964; m. Betty Lou Schultz, Feb. 7, 1959; children—Gregory J., Timothy B. Instr. speech U. Maine, 1959-61; asst. prof. speech, dir. forensics Mich. State U., 1961-68; prof., chmn. dept. speech and dramatic arts Central Mich. U., Mt. Pleasant, 1968-72, vice provost, 1972-73; v.p. acad. affairs Western Wash. State Coll., 1973-75; vice chancellor U. Wis.-Oshkosh, 1975-79; pres., prof. speech Ball State U., Muncie, Ind., 1979-81; sr. cons. Am. Assn. State Colls. and Univs. and vis. prof. U. Wis., River Falls, 1981—; Served with USNR, 1952-54. Recipient 1st Sr. Distinguished Professionalism award Central Mich. U., 1971; Sagamore of Wabash Public Service award Gov. Ind., 1980; research fellow Harry S. Truman Found., 1965; fellow Am. Council Edn. Acad. Adminstrn. Internship Program, 1971—. Mem. Central States (pres. 1973; Outstanding Young Tchr. award 1966), Mich. (pres. 1967-68) speech assns., Am. (pres. 1972-74), Midwest (pres. 1969-72) forensic assns., Speech Communication Assn. (legis. council 1967, legis. assembly 1975). Club: Rotary. Author: (with Paul J. Dovre) Readings in Argumentation, 1968; also articles. Office: PO Box 825 Amery WI 54001

ANDERSON, JERRY WILLIAM, JR., electronics co. exec.; b. Stow, Mass., Jan. 14, 1926; s. Jerry William and Heda Charlotte (Petersen) A.; B.S. in Physics, U. Cin., 1949, Ph.D. in Econs., 1976; M.B.A., Xavier U., 1959; m. Joan Hukill Balyeat, Sept. 13, 1947; children—Katheleen, Diane. Research and test project engr. meteorol. equipment, Wright-Patterson AFB, Ohio, 1949-53; project engr., electronics div. AVCO Corp., Cin., 1953-70, program mgr., 1970-73; program mgr. Cin. Electronics Corp. (successor to electronics div. AVCO Corp.), 1973-78; pres. Anderson Industries Unltd., 1978; chmn. dept. mgmt. and mgmt. info. services Xavier U., 1980—; lectr. No. Ky. U., 1977-78; tech. adviser Cin. Tech. Coll., 1971—. Served with USNR, 1943-46. Mem. Madeira (Ohio) City Planning Commn., 1962—; founder, pres. Grassroots, Inc., 1964; active United Appeal, Heart Fund, Multiple Sclerosis Fund; co-founder, tech. Presbyterian Ch., Cin., 1964. Named Man of Year, City of Madeira, 1964. Mem. Assn. Energy Engrs. (charter), Soc. Non-Destructive Testing, Nat. Wood Carvers Assn., Am. Legion (past comdr.), Acad. Mgmt., Madeira Civic Assn. (past v.p.), Omicron Delta Epsilon. Republican. Contbr. articles on lasers, infrared detection equipment, air pollution to govt. publs. and profl. jours. Home and office: 7208 Sycamorehill Ln Cincinnati OH 45243

ANDERSON, JOEL MARK, engring. co. exec.; b. Bronx, N.Y., July 31, 1947; s. Samuel I. and Mildred G. A.; B.S. in Physics, Carnegie-Mellon U., 1969, B.S. in Psychology, 1969; m. Rita M. Meinert, Sept. 27, 1969; children—Michael D., Jason R. Engr., Westinghouse Electric Corp., Balt., 1969-71, Phila., 1971-74; sr. engr. Bechtel Corp., Ann Arbor, Mich., 1974-78, engring. supr., 1978-81, engring. mgr., 1981—; cons. on alt. methods of power generation. NSF grantee, 1968. Inventor gas turbine controls, alt. methods power generation, nuclear and fossil power plant computer simulation. Office: PO Box 1000 Ann Arbor MI 48106

ANDERSON, JOHN FREDRICK, agribus. exec.; b. Scottsbluff, Nebr., Apr. 12, 1924; s. John Fredrick and Larren (Tison) A.; grad. U. Mo., 1949; m. Phyllis Rose Dye, July 13, 1945; children—Marsha Jo Anderson Swainston, Jeffrey Bryan. Process engr. Consumer Coop. Assn. (co. name changed to Farmland Industries, Inc.), Coffeyville, Kans., 1949-58, supt. Coffeyville refinery, 1958-61, v.p. fertilizer mfg., Kansas City, Mo., 1971-74, exec. v.p. mfg. and prodn., 1974-78, pres., chief exec. officer, 1978—; chief engr. CRA subs. Farmland Industries, Inc., Kansas City, 1961-62, plant supt. Coop. Farm Chems. Assn. subs., Lawrence, Kans., 1962-68, v.p., 1968-71; dir. Commerce Bank, Kansas City. Mem. Clay County Devel. Com.; trustee U. Mo., Kansas City, Midwest Research Inst., Kansas City. Served with AC, U.S. Army, 1942-45. Mem. Am. Inst. Chem. Engrs., Nat. Petroleum Refiners Assn., Kansas City C. of C. (dir.). Office: Farmland Industries Inc 3315 N Oak Trafficway Kansas City MO 64118*

ANDERSON, JOHN ROBERT, educator, mathematician; b. Stromsburg, Nebr., Aug. 1, 1928; s. Norris Merton and Violet Charlotte (Stromberg) A.; student Midland Coll., 1945-46; A.A., Luther Jr. Coll., 1949; B.S., U. Nebr., Lincoln, 1951, M.A. in Mathematics, 1954; Ph.D., Purdue U., 1970; m. Bertha Margery Nore, Aug. 27, 1950; children—Eric Jon, Mary Lynn. Tchr. mathematics and coach, Bloomfield (Nebr.) High Sch., 1951-52; control systems analyst, Allison Div. Gen. Motors Corp., Indpls., 1954-60; prof. mathematics Depauw U., Greencastle, Ind., 1960, asst. dean, dir. grad. studies, 1973-76, dir. grad. studies, 1976—, resident dir. W. European Studies Program, W. Ger., France; dir. NSF Coop. Coll. Sch. Sci. Inst., 1969-70, instr. NSF summer inst., 1972; bd. dirs. Law Focused Edn., Indpls., 1975—, Ind. Regional Mathematics Consortium, 1977—; mem. Commn. on Instns. Higher Edn., North Central Assn., 1974-78. Bd. dirs. br. No. 8115 Lutheran Brotherhood. Served with U.S. Army, 1946-48. U. Nebr. regents scholar, 1945-46; Danforth Teacher fellow, 1963-64; NSF sci. faculty fellow, 1964-65; Lilly Found. edn. grantee, summers 1961, 62, 63. Mem. Math. Assn. Am., Nat. Council Teachers of Mathematics, AAHE, Sigma Xi, Pi Mu Epsilon, Kappa Delta Pi, Beta Sigma Psi. Club: Rotary Internat. (sec., 1976-77., v.p. 1977-78, pres. 1978-79). Home: 1560 Bloomington St Greencastle IN 46135

ANDERSON, KARL PAUL, chemist; b. Fergus Falls, Minn., Jan. 10, 1934; s. Paul R. and Irma I. Anderson; B.Sc., Ohio State U., 1958; postgrad. (scholar) U. Göttingen (W.Ger.), 1956; m. Ruby M. Porter, Sept. 7, 1958; children—Ronald Richard, Karen Lynn. Devel. chemist Hanna Chem. Coatings Co., Columbus, Ohio, 1959-65, group leader metal deco. dept., 1965-67, coil coating dept, 1967-69, dir. coil coating div., 1971-81, tech. dir. Atech. chem. coatings, 1981—; group leader coil coating lab. Lilly Indsl. Coatings, Indpls., 1969-70; v.p. Karencraft, Inc., Columbus, 1975—; dir. Corboard, Inc. Asst. scoutmaster Central Ohio council Boy Scouts Am., Columbus, 1969—; head coach N. Columbus Girls Baseball, 1977-79, Univ. Boys Assn., Boys Basketball, 1974-75. Recipient Order of Arrow, Boy Scouts Am., 1976. Mem. Nat. Coil Coaters Assn., Cin. Dayton Indpls. Columbus Soc., Fedn. Socs. Coatings Tech., Nat. Flyers Assn., Scioto Model A Ford Club, North Columbus Ski Club, Buckeye Glider Club, Flying Farmers, Sigma Pi (sec., trustee), Phi Eta Sigma (treas.). Methodist. Clubs: Masons, Shriners. Contbr. articles to profl. jours. Home: 612 E Como Ave Columbus OH 43202 Office: 199 S St Clair St Toledo OH 43602

ANDERSON, KARL STEPHEN, newspaper exec.; b. Chgo., Nov. 10, 1933; s. Karl William and Eleanore (Grell) A.; B.S. in Editorial Journalism, U. Ill., 1955; m. Saralee Hegland, Nov. 5, 1977; children by previous marriage—Matthew, Douglas, Eric. Successively advt. mgr., asst. to pub., plant mgr. Pioneer Press, Oak Park and St. Charles, Ill., 1955-71; asst. to pub., then pub. Crescent Newspapers, Downers Grove, Ill., 1971-73; asso. pub. and editor Chronicle Pub. Co., St. Charles, 1973-80; asso. pub. Chgo. Daily Law Bull., 1981—, also Chicagoland's Condominium Guide. Bd. dirs. Hotel Baker Sr. Living Center, Kane County Republican Central Com. Recipient C.V. Amenoff award dept. journalism No. Ill. U., 1976. Mem. Ill. Press Assn. (Will Loomis award 1977, 80), Nat. Nat. Newspaper Assn., No. Ill. Newspaper Assn., Soc. Profl. Journalists-Sigma Delta Chi, Chi Psi. Club: Chgo. Press. Home: 520 S 12th St Saint Charles IL 60174 Office: 415 N State St Chicago IL 60610

ANDERSON, KENNETH CLIFFORD, trucking co. exec.; b. Sturgeon Bay, Wis., July 18, 1935; s. Roy Clifford and Bel Youngs (Kwapil) A.; B.A., St. Olaf Coll., 1957; M.S., U. Colo., 1966; grad. Indsl. Coll. Armed Forces, 1974; children—Eric Kenneth, Mark Brian. Commd. 2d lt. USAF, 1958, advanced through grades to maj., 1978; stationed Pentagon, 1966-70, command hdqrs., C.Z., 1973-76; ret., 1978; requirements mgr., def. products dept. Oshkosh Truck Corp., (Wis.), 1979—. Decorated Bronze Star; named outstanding hdqrs. command adminstr., USAF, 1974. Mem. Assn. U.S. Army, Ret. Officers Assn., Am. Def. Preparedness Assn., Aircraft Owners and Pilots Assn. Republican. Roman Catholic. Home: 5268 Samers Bay Rd Omro WI 54963 Office: 2307 Oregon St Oshkosh WI 54903

ANDERSON, KENNETH D., cable TV co. exec.; b. Chgo., Jan. 2, 1945; s. William A. and Lola M. (Henrich) A.; B.A., U. Iowa, 1970. Asso., William Kepper Assos., Evanston, Ill., 1972-75; pres. Cable Devel. Corp., Chgo., 1976—. Mem. Nat. Cable TV Assn., Ill.-Ind. Cable TV Assn., Phi Kappa Psi. Club: Bob O'Link Golf (Highland Park, Ill.). Home: 1300 Astor St Chicago IL 60610 Office: 645 N Michigan Ave Suite 834 Chicago IL 60611

ANDERSON, KENNETH OSCAR, film co. exec.; b. Rembrandt, Ia., Dec. 23, 1917; s. Oscar Frank and Ethel Mae (Anderson) A.; student Wheaton Coll., 1936-37, 45-51, Northwestern U., 1947-48; m. Doris Ilene Jones, Nov. 16, 1938; children—Naoma (Mrs. Larry Clark), Margaret (Mrs. T. Landon Mauzy), Donn, Lane, Max, Ken D., Melody. Editor, Campus Life Mag., Wheaton, Ill., 1945-51; with Gospel Films, Muskegon, Mich., 1949-61, exec. producer, 1949-61; pres. Ken Anderson Films, Winona Lake, Ind., 1963—; dir. Master Investments Corp., Warsaw, Ind.; dir. Internat. Films, London, 1969-72, Reach & Teach, London; vis. instr. Haggai Inst., Singapore, 1974—; vis. lectr. St. Xavier's Coll., Bombay, 1979. Mem. pres.'s com. Grace Coll., Winona Lake, 1972—; adv. com. League for the Handicapped, Walworth, Wis., 1965—; bd. dirs. Youth Haven Ranch, Rives Junction, Mich., Crusade Evangelism, London, Ont., Can. Named Evang. Press Assn. Writer of Year, 1962; Nat. Evang. Film Found. award as Dir. of Year, 1970. Mem. Gidions Internat. Presbyterian (elder 1963—). Author: Himalayan Heartbeat, 1966; Stains on Glass Windows, 1969; Adjustable Halo, 1969; Satan's Angels, 1975; (with Tony Mockus) I'm Learning from Protestants How to be a Better Catholic, 1975; producer, dir. film of book Pilgrim's Progress, 1977, film Christiana, 1978, Some Through the Fire (Uganda), 1980, Hudson Taylor, 1981. Home: 720 North Lake St Warsaw IN 46580 Office: PO Box 618 Winona Lake IN 46590

ANDERSON, LAVERNE ERIC, lawyer; b. Rockford, Ill., Feb. 24, 1922; s. Eric J. and Alma M. (Johnson) A.; LL.B., U. Ill., 1944, J.D., 1946; m. Lucille Hardy, Feb. 14, 1954. Admitted to Ill. bar, 1947, admitted to practice U.S. Treasury Dept., Fed. Ct.; individual practice law, Rockford, 1947—; city atty., Rockford, 1947-53, corp. counsel, 1953-57. Mem. Am. Bar Assn., Ill. Bar Assn., Winnebago County Bar Assn., Broadway Bus. Assn., Phi Eta Sigma, Phi Beta Kappa, Phi Kappa Phi. Lutheran. Clubs: Mason, Shriners (rep. Imperial Council, dir., El Hajj Caravanserai No. 4, potentate Tebala Shrine Temple, 1977). Office: 724 Broadway Rockford IL 61108

ANDERSON, LINDA JEAN FULLER, mfg. co. exec.; b. Chgo., Sept. 24, 1948; d. Otmar and Delores (Newman) Fuller; student No. Ill. U., 1966-68; m. John Richard Anderson, Mar. 20, 1971. Budget dir. Leo Burnett Inc., Chgo., 1968-70; controller Leaf Confectionery, Inc., Chgo., 1970—. Mem. Am. Mgmt. Assn. Lutheran. Office: 1155 N Cicero Ave Chicago IL 60651

ANDERSON, LOIS MARILYN, psychologist; b. Cambridge, Minn., Mar. 19, 1934; d. Oliver Ferdinand and Marjorie Constance (Strait) Ledin; m. Malcolm Charles Anderson, July 9, 1960; 1 son, Andrew. B.S., Gustavus Adolphus Coll., 1956; Ph.D., U. Minn., 1969. Intern counseling Student Counseling Bur., Univ. Hosps. dept. of phys. medicine and rehab. U. Minn., 1959-60; research fellow Indsl. Relations Center, U. Minn., 1960-65; research psychologist InterStudy, Mpls., 1969-73; state program mgmt. coordinator Minn. Dept. Adminstrn., St. Paul, 1973-77, projects coordinator Mgmt. Analysis div., 1977-79; staff psychologist Minn. State Services for the Blind, St. Paul, 1979-81, dir. psychol. services, 1981—. Governing mem. YMCA of Met. Mpls., 1971-79; bd. mgmt. Northwest (Mpls.) YMCA, 1970-76; bd. dirs., chmn. Camden Community Theater, 1981—; lectr. U. Minn. Grad. Schs. of Pub. Affairs and Social Work, 1975, 76; mem. Twin City Met. Council Advisory com. on Waste Mgmt. and Water Quality, 1976-78. Mem. Am., Minn. psychol. assns., Psi Chi, Pi Lamdba Theta. Recipient Annual Research award, Am. Rehab. Counseling Assn., 1965. Author: (with others) AFDC Employment and Referral Guidelines, 1973; Impact of Welfare Reform on the Elderly Poor, 1973; Medicaid Cost Containment and Long Term Care, 1976. Home: 4400 Victory Ave Minneapolis MN 55412 Office: 1745 University Ave Saint Paul MN 55104

ANDERSON, LOREN ALBIN, research engr.; b. Fullerton, N.D., May 6, 1927; s. Albin Edwin and Emma Dorothy (Arndt) A.; B.S., U.S. Mil. Acad., 1951; M.S.E., U. Mich., 1957; postgrad. U. Dayton, 1978—; m. Ione Le May Schroeder; children—Loren Albin, Charles Kent. Commd. 2d lt. U.S. Air Force, 1951, advanced through grades to col., 1971, ret., 1978; research engr. U. Dayton (Ohio), 1978—. Trustee, Spicer Heights Neighborhood Assn., 1978-80. Served with U.S. Army, 1946-47. Decorated Legion of Merit, Bronze Star medal, Air medal with 2 oak leaf clusters, Air Force Commendation medal; recipient Student Scholastic award Inst. Aeronautical Sci., 1956. Asso. fellow AIAA; mem. Research Soc. Am., ASME. Republican. Lutheran. Club: Ohio Valley Retriever. Contbr. articles to profl. jours. Home: 3510 Fullerton Ct Dayton OH 45431 Office: 300 College Park Dayton OH 45469

ANDERSON, LOREN DEAN, educator, Realtor; b. Carthage, S.D., July 4, 1934; s. John Edwin and Stella Almer A.; B.S., Dakota State Coll., 1962; M.B.A., U. S.D., 1965; m. Celesta Maybelle Windedahl, July 27, 1955; 1 son, Scott Dean. Tchr., Jefferson (S.D.) High Sch., 1962-64; instr. Yankton Coll., 1965-70; tchr. Fergus Falls (Minn.) Jr. Coll., 1970-72; with Yankton Coll., 1972—, asso. prof. bus. adminstrn. and chmn. social scis. div., 1978—; owner, mgr. Anderson Realty, Yankton, 1978—; owner, dir. Dakota Sch. Real Estate & Bus., Yankton, 1974—. Bd. dirs. Yankton United Fund, 1968, 80-81; chmn. bd. dirs. Yankton United Way, 1981—. Served with USAF, 1954-59. Mem. Nat. Assn. Realtors, Lewis and Clark Bd. Realtors (pres. 1980-81, Realtor of Yr. 1981), Assn. Governing Bds. Univs. and Colls. Republican. Unitarian. Club: Elks. Home: Route 1 Gavins Point Yankton SD 57078 Office: 311 Walnut St Yankton SD 57078

ANDERSON, LOYAL EDWARD, oil jobber, farmer; b. Hugoton, Kans., Aug. 24, 1931; s. Webb Huitt and Lucille Caroline (Flummerfelt) A.; student Mt. Carmel (Ill.) public schs.; m. Mary Ann Baumgart, June 24, 1953; children—Ray, Randy, Ricky, Rose Ann. Pres., Anderson Bros. Oil Co., Mt. Carmel, 1953—; farmer, 1974—; dir. Security Bank & Trust Co. Bd. dirs. Ill. Jaycees, 1953-56; 4-H leader, 1953—; pres. 4-H Youth Found., 1970—; bd. dirs. Wabash County Retarded Children, 1975, Fair Bd., 1954—; pres. Extension Council, 1973—, St. Mary Sch. Bd., 1970-76. Served with USAF, 1950-53. Recipient Community Service award Phillips Petroleum Co., 1975. Mem. Nat. Fedn. Ind. Bus., Am. Legion, Mt. Carmel C. of C. (dir. 1974). Roman Catholic. Clubs: K.C., Elks, Moose. Home: Rural Route 1 Mount Carmel IL 62863 Office: 909 W 9th St Mount Carmel IL 62863

ANDERSON, LUTHER ADOLPH, writer; b. Ironwood, Mich., Oct. 4, 1898; s. Peter Edward and Carolina (Gustafson) A.; B.C.S., DePaul Coll. Commerce, Chgo., 1924; Ph.B., U. Chgo., 1927; m. Ethel Marie Martin, Aug. 1, 1938. Pub. accountant Haskins & Sells, Chgo., 1928-30, Price Waterhouse, Milw., 1931-32; accountant Armour & Co., Ironwood, Mich., 1932-62; writer for hunting, fishing, camping publs., including Field & Stream, Outdoor Life, Sports Afield, Fur-Fish-Game, Ironwood, 1930—. Treas., Bethany Covenant Ch., Ironwood, 1937—, also choir dir.; bd. dirs. Salvation Army, Ironwood, 1961—. Author: Hunting, Fishing and Camping, 1945; Hunting the American Game Field, 1949; Hunting Deer and Small Game, 1959; Guide to Canoe Camping, 1969; How to Hunt American Small Game, 1969; How to Hunt Whitetail Deer, 1968; Hunting the Uplands with Shotgun and Rifle, 1977; Hunting the Woodlands for Small and Big Game, 1980. Home: 139 S Curry St Ironwood MI 49938

ANDERSON, LUTHER ALFRED, assn. exec.; b. Alexandria, Minn., Feb. 24, 1937; s. Alfred C. and Ellen S. (Bjelland) A.; B.A., Augsburg Coll., 1960; M.S., George Williams Coll., 1962; m. Winnie Marie Nordlund, Aug. 19, 1961; children—Mark Courtney, Kari Lynn, Derek Jon. Community youth service dir. Chgo. YMCA, 1962-68; asst. dean students George Williams Coll., Downers Grove, Ill., 1968-70; exec. dir. Knox County YMCA, Galesburg, Ill., 1970-72; asso. regional dir. N.E., Nat. YMCA, N.Y.C., 1972-75; exec. dir. Midway YMCA, St. Paul, 1975-79; v.p. ops. St. Paul Area YMCA, 1979—; planning and mgmt. cons. Media Prodns., Mpls., 1976-77. Mem. adv. com. Ramsey County Juvenile Center Constrn., 1977-78; youth work curriculum advisor Met. State U., Mpls., 1978-79; mem. inter-agy. task force on collaboration St. Paul schs., 1978-79; vice chmn. Congressional Award Adv. Council Minn., 1981—; mem. Roseville Community Edn. Adv. Council, 1981—. Served with USAR, 1960-61. Chgo. YMCA grantee, 1960-61. Mem. Am. Mktg. Assn., Assn. Profl. YMCA Dirs. Lutheran. Home: 2780 Farrington St Saint Paul MN 55113 Office: 475 Cedar St Saint Paul MN 55101

ANDERSON, MAX ELLIOT, TV film prodn. co. exec.; b. St. Charles, Ill., Nov. 3, 1946; s. Kenneth O. and Doris I. (Jones) A.; B.A. in Psychology, Grace Coll., 1973; m. Claudia Lynd, Aug. 21, 1968; children—James Brightman, Sarah Lynd. Cinematographer, Ken Anderson Films, Winona Lake, Ind., 1968-78; partner Q Media Group, Rockford, Ill., 1978—, asso. producer TV, films, 1978—, also cinematographer, since 1963—, advt. exec., 1965—; pres. Philip Lasz Gallery, 1973—. Mem. Summerwood Amphitheater com., Rockford, 1980—. Served with U.S. Army, 1971-73. Recipient Best Cinematography award Christian Film Distbrs. Assn., 1978. Mem. Christian Film Distributor Assn., Christian Booksellers Assn. Republican. Mem. Evang. Free Ch. Home: 4112 Marsh Ave Rockford IL 61111 Office: 610 E State St Rockford IL 61104

ANDERSON, MILADA FILKO, mfg. co. exec.; b. Chgo., Nov. 17, 1922; d. John and Anna (Sianta) Filko; B.S., Northwestern U., 1944, M. Mgmt., 1979; m. George Anderson, Aug. 29, 1945 (div. 1974); children—Mark, Renee, Teri. Tchr. history, Evanston (Ill.) Twp. High Sch., 1946; tchr. social studies, Mt. Prospect (Ill.) Jr. High Sch., 1947-48; dir. F&B Mfg. Co., Chgo., 1965—, corp. sec., 1969-72, pres., 1972—, chmn. bd., 1972—. Mem. Northwestern U. Profl. Womens

Assn., Nat. Assn. Investment Clubs, Execs. Club Chgo., Zeta Tau Alpha. Office: F&B Mfg Co 5480 Northwest Hwy Chicago IL 60630

ANDERSON, MONROE, III, journalist; b. Gary, Ind., Apr. 6, 1947; s. Monroe, Jr. and Norma Jean Anderson; B.A., Ind. U., 1970. Staff writer Nat. Observer, Washington, 1970-72; asst. editor Ebony mag., Chgo., 1972-74; reporter Chgo. Tribune, 1974—. Recipient 1st pl. award for public service Ill. AP, 1976, Chgo. Tribune Edward S. Beck spl. award for outstanding investigative reporting, 1976, 1st pl. award for disting. reporting Inland Daily Press Assn., 1977, Jacob Schwer award for investigative reporting, 1979, 1st pl. award for community service Ill. UP Internat. Editors Assn., 1981. Mem. Chgo. Assn. Black Journalists. Office: 435 N Michigan Ave Chicago IL 60611

ANDERSON, NIKKI-LYNNE, office products co. exec.; b. Indpls., Nov. 11, 1948; d. Nick Kennison and Carolynne (Greenlee) Calloway; student Ball State U., 1966-68, M.A., 1973; B.S., Ind. State U., 1970; postgrad. U. Kans.; m. David Lee Anderson, Apr. 30, 1977; children—Benjamin, Erin, Joseph. Tchr. bus. edn. Marion-Adams High Sch., Sheridan, Ind., 1970-72; tchr., coordinator bus. office edn. and adult edn. Blue River Vocat. Center, Shelbyville, Ind., 1972-74; in service tchr. educator Emporia (Kans.) State U., 1975-76; instr. Kaw Area Vocat. Sch., Topeka, 1976-77; mktg. rep., sales mgr. Vydec Word processors and Savin copiers Seever Systems, Inc., Topeka, 1977-79; sales mgr. Exxon Office Systems, Vydec Word Processors, Oyx Intelligent typewriters, Qwip facsimile systems Modern Office Methods, Inc., Topeka, 1979—. Mem. Internat. Word Processing Assn., Am. Vocat. Assn., Am. Bus. Women's Assn., Nat. Bus. Edn. Assn., NEA, Kappa Delta Pi, Delta Pi Epsilon, Alpha Sigma Alpha. Presbyterian. Office: 3214 W 29th St Topeka KS 66614

ANDERSON, PAUL F., bishop; b. Boston, Apr. 20, 1917; s. Philip Leo and Mary Elizabeth (Doyle) A.; B.A., St. John's Sem., Brighton, Mass., 1943. Ordained priest Roman Cath. Ch., 1943; pastor Sioux Falls (S.D.) Cath. Diocese, 1946-68; coadjutor bishop of Duluth, 1968-69, bishop, 1969—. Home: 2215 E 2d St Duluth MN 55812 Office: 215 W 4th St Duluth MN 55806*

ANDERSON, PHILIP CARLTON, feed co. exec.; b. Lincoln, Nebr., Dec. 12, 1918; s. Carl Louis and Harriet (Barnett) A.; student U. Nebr., 1936-38; m. Norma Gene France, Nov. 4, 1940; children—Mark, Kent, Dale, Sara, Jane, Paul. Pres., founder Feed Service Corp., Crete, Nebr., 1951-76; pres. Tricarbon Corp., Crete, 1976—. Chmn. Saline County (Nebr.) Republican Com., 1964—; del. Rep. Nat. Conv., 1964; Rep. candidate for lt. gov., Nebr., 1966. Mem. Am. Assn. Acads. Sci., Nebr. Acad. Sci., N.Y. Acad. Scis., Soc. Applied Spectroscopy, Internat. Platform Assn., SAR. Author: Spectral Energy Value System of Molecular Structures. Patentee chem. and mech. devices, animal feeding devices. Home: 1225 Jasmine Rd Crete NE 68333 Office: PO Box 242 Crete NE 68333

ANDERSON, PHYLLIS REINHOLD, mgmt. cons., engr., mfg. co. exec.; b. Denver, July 29, 1936; d. Floyd Reinhold and Minerva Eva (Needham) A.; Metall. Engr., Colo. Sch. Mines, 1962; M.B.A., U. Chgo., 1968; children—Kristin Elizabeth, Michele Ann. Mill metallurgist, supr. U.S. Steel Corp., 1962-66; research and devel. sr. metallurgist, supr., planner Continental Can Co., 1966-73; mgr. corp. planning B. F. Goodrich Co., 1973-76; regional asso. Strategic Planning Inst., Cambridge, Mass., 1975-76; project mgr. corp. planning, sales engring., then project mgr. corp. devel. Signode Corp., Glenview, Ill., 1976-80; mgmt. cons., 1974—; pres., prin. cons. Corp. Devel. Assos., Inc., mgmt. cons., strategic planning, mktg., product devel., Oak Brook, Ill., 1980—; initial exec. com., chmn. membership com. Strategic Planning Inst., 1975-76; dir. Quest Assos. Mgmt. and Quality Consultants; instr. bus. analysis methods. Active psychiat. support services, career counseling women's groups and individuals. Recipient leadership award Chgo. YWCA, 1977. Mem. Am. Soc. Metals, Soc. Women Engrs., Am. Mktg. Assn., N.Y. Acad. Scis., Women in Mgmt., Nat. Assn. Women Bus. Owners, AAAS, Mensa. Author: Corporate Strategic Planning: An Integrated Approach, 1981. Home: 2201 S Highland Ave Lombard IL 60148 Office: PO Box 946 Oak Brook IL 60521

ANDERSON, RICHARD HODGSON, computer adv. service exec.; b. Fergus Falls, Minn., Apr. 22, 1937; s. Paul Raymond and Irma Ione A.; B.A., Ohio State U., Columbus, 1959; m. Carolyn Cooper, June 21, 1959; children—Jeffrey Allen, Diana Lynne. Pub. Relations, Western Electric Co., 1959-64; Div. mgr. Universal Guaranty Life Ins. Co., Dayton, Ohio, 1964-66; mktg. asso. IBM, Dayton, 1966-69; v.p. Champion Service Corp., Cleve., 1969-72; mgmt. cons. Mgmt. Horizons Data Systems, Columbus, Ohio, 1972-79; pres. D & C Investors, computer adv. service, Columbus, 1980-81; Nat. accounts Mgr., MCI, Columbus, Ohio, 198—. Chmn., Gettysburg (Ohio) Neighborhood Sch. Coordination Com., 1978—; active Columbus Symphony Orch. Recipient Disting. Sales award Profl. Sales Assos., 1978, Dale Carnegie Sales award, 1966, Nat. Assn. Life Cos., highest award for outstanding performance, 1966, top sales award, 1965. Republican. Methodist. Author: Executive Associates Guide to Successful Selling, 1965. Home: 6005 Winstead Rd Worthington OH 43085 Office: Profl Data Systems 2015 W 5th Ave Columbus OH 43212

ANDERSON, RICHARD IVAN, ednl. psychologist; b. Akron, Iowa, Sept. 14, 1952; s. Ivan Wilfred and Marianne (Kerr) A.; B.S., Iowa State U., 1974; M.S., U. Ill., 1977, postgrad. 1977—; m. Jean Frances Johnson, Aug. 11, 1973. Undergrad. asst. dept. math. Iowa State U., Ames, 1972-74; computer programmer/analyst Standard Oil Co. (Ind.), Chgo., 1974-75; research/teaching asst. dept. computer sci. U. Ill., Urbana, 1975-76, research asst. Center for Study of Reading, 1976-78, teaching asst., dept. ednl. psychology, 1978-80, research asst. Inst. Aviation, 1980—; asst. to FAA designated written test examiner, 1981—. Mem. Am. Ednl. Research Assn., Assn. for Devel. of Computer-based Instructional Systems, Assn. for Ednl. Data Systems, Phi Beta Kappa, Phi Kappa Phi, Phi Delta Kappa, Kappa Delta Pi, Pi Mu Epsilon. Contbr. articles to profl. jours. and meetings. Office: Aviation Research Lab Willard Airport Savoy IL 61874

ANDERSON, ROBERT ARTHUR, author, educator; b. Worcester, Mass., Feb. 27, 1927; s. Louis Fredolph and Ethel Mae (Lowe) A.; A.B., Upsala Coll., 1951; M.A., U. No. Colo., 1953; m. Faye Ella Kroeger, Sept. 15, 1951; children—Jill Anderson, Ned. Tchr., Brighton (Colo.) Jr. High Sch., 1954-59, Duxbury (Mass.) High Sch., 1959-67, Daytona Beach (Fla.) Community Coll., 1967-73, Rich Central High Sch., Olympia Fields, Ill., 1974-77, Rich East High Sch., Park Forest, Ill., 1977—. Mem. City Council South Daytona. Served with USN, 1945-46. Mem. Ill. Edn. Assn., NEA, Nat. Council Tchrs. English. Author: Writers Rhetoric, 1971; A Lexicon of Literary Terms, 1977; Theatre Talk, 1980; also plays, articles in profl. writing mags. Home: 285 Fir St Park Forest IL 60466 Office: Sauk Trail & Westwood Sts Park Forest IL 60466

ANDERSON, ROBERT CHARLES, writer, mag. editor; b. Sault Ste. Marie, Mich., May 22, 1930; s. James Orville and Nesta Grace (Cottle) A.; student Mich. Coll. Mining and Tech., 1954-55; B.A. (Winthrop Burr Chamberlain scholar), U. Mich., 1957; postgrad. Chgo.-Kent Coll. Law, 1969-70; m. Frances Theresa Merimee, July 25, 1952; children—James Russell, Helen Christine Anderson Doepel. Reporter, Evening News, Sault Ste. Marie, 1954-55, Ypsilanti (Mich.) Press, 1957; circulation worker Ann Arbor (Mich.) News, 1956; reporter, TV columnist, mag. editor Chgo. Tribune, 1957-72; mng. editor Oui mag., Chgo., 1972-75; free-lance writer, editor Profl. Photographer, Chgo., 1976-78; editor Success mag., Chgo., since 1978—; lectr. to writers groups, tchr. workshops. Mem. Winnetka (Ill.) Caucus Selection Com., 1968; leader, merit badge counselor Boy Scouts Am. Served with U.S. Army, 1948-52; Korea. Mem. Am. Soc. Journalists and Authors, Midwest Writers (co-chmn.), Kappa Tau Alpha, Phi Eta Sigma. Republican. Unitarian. Author: (with Ray Kroc) Grinding It Out: The Making of McDonald's, 1977; contbr. numerous articles to various mags. Office: 401 N Wabash Ave Suite 530 Chicago IL 60611

ANDERSON, ROBERT HUNTER, data processing and data communications cons.; b. Duluth, Minn., Sept. 17, 1941; s. Herbert Andrew and Mildred May (Hunter) A.; student public schs., Duluth; m. Nancy Jeanne Overland, May 23, 1970; 1 dau., Christina Jeanne. Programmer, Litton Industries, Duluth, 1967-69; programmer/analyst Paper Calmenson & Co., St. Paul, 1970-71, State of Minn., St. Paul, 1971-74, Apache Corp., Mpls., 1974-76; EDP auditor Coopers & Lybrand, Mpls., 1976-78; data communications cons. AT&T, Mpls., 1978—; pres. Creative Computer Solutions, microcomputer systems co., Bloomington, Minn. Served with Minn. Air N.G., 1963-69. Address: 9033 Kell Ave S Bloomington MN 55437

ANDERSON, ROBERT LEROY, educator; b. Wadena, Minn., Nov. 22, 1940; s. Eddie Irvin and Elsie Amelia (Winter) A.; B.S., U. Minn., 1966, in bus. mgmt., 1974. County extension dir. U. Minn., Walker, 1970-71; vets. farm mgmt. instr. Little Falls (Minn.) Community Schs., 1971-74, Area Vo-Tech. Inst., Staples, Minn., 1974-76; adult farm bus. mgmt. instr. Woodland Coop. Center, Staples, 1976—; mgmt. cons. Served with U.S. Army, 1962-64. Mem. NEA, Minn. Edn. Assn., Nat. Agrl. Edn. Instrs. Assn., Minn. Agrl. Educators Assn. Home: PO Box 281 Rural Route 2 Staples MN 56479 Office: Woodland Coop Center Clarissa MN 56440

ANDERSON, ROBERT MILTON, JR., chem. co. exec.; b. Phila., Sept. 27, 1931; s. Robert Milton and Margaret Elizabeth (Mitchell) A.; student Asbury Coll., 1950-52, U. Houston, 1959-63; m. Frances C. Carlock, July 4, 1954; children—Kathryn Elizabeth, Robert Milton. Design draftsman United Carbon, Houston, 1954-63; project engr. Ashland Chem., Houston, 1964-68, project mgr., Speyer, Germany, 1969-70, design engring. mgr., Columbus, Ohio, 1971-74, project mgr., Tampico, Mexico, 1975-77, project mgr., Valencia, Venezuela, 1977-78, mgr. project engring., Columbus, Ohio, 1979—. Served with AUS, 1952-54. Methodist. Club: Masons. Patentee in field. Home: 7080 Rieber St Worthington OH 43085 Office: PO Box 2219 Columbus OH 43216

ANDERSON, ROGER E., banker; b. 1921; B.S., Northwestern U., 1942; married. With Continental Ill. Nat. Bank and Trust Co., Chgo., 1946—, exec. v.p., 1968-73, chmn. bd., 1973—; chmn. bd. Continental Ill. Corp., 1973—, also dir.; dir. Continental Ill. Ltd., Amsted Industries, S.C. Johnson & Son, Inc., Eastman Kodak Co. Served with USNR, 1942-46. Address: care Regina Wells 231 S LaSalle St Chicago IL 60693

ANDERSON, ROLAND GILES, educator; b. Franklin County, Ottawa, Kans., Feb. 27, 1930; s. Arthur Emil and Zona Mae (Porter) A.; B.S., Ottawa U., 1952; M.A., U. Kans., 1954; postgrad. U. Tex., 1954-56, Yale U., 1960; Northwestern U., 1967. Chen. lab. technician Phillips Petroleum Co., Kansas City, Kans., 1956-58; sci. tchr. Olathe (Kans.) Sr. High Sch., 1958-60; chemistry master Kemper Mil. Sch., Bonneville, Mo., 1960-61; biology tchr. San Marino (Calif.) High Sch., 1961-62; chemistry tchr. Dept. Def. Overseas Schs., Okinawa, 1962-63, Libya, 1966-67; chemistry tchr. Center Sr. High Sch., Kansas City, Mo., 1963-66; sci. tchr. DeSoto (Kans.) High Sch., 1967-68; vis. lectr. Univ. Kans., Lawrence, part-time, 1968-70; tchr. sci. Lawrence High Sch., 1968—, named Tchr. of Yr., 1975. NSF grantee 1959, 61, 64, 67, 68, 69, 79. Mem. Am. Chem. Soc., Nat. Sci. Tchrs. Assn., NEA, Kans. Nat. Edn. Assn., Lawrence Edn. Assn., Sigma Xi, Phi Alpha Theta, Phi Delta Kappa, Phi Sigma, Univ. Kans. Alumni Assn. Republican. Mem. Reorganized Ch. of Jesus Christ of Latter-day Saints (priest). Office: 19th and Louisiana Sts Lawrence KS 66044

ANDERSON, RUSSELL DWAYNE, supt. schs.; b. Hendricks, Minn., Aug. 23, 1920; s. Inest Robert and Florence Clara (Olson) A.; student Mankato State Tchrs. Coll., 1938-39; B.A., Gustavus Adolphus Coll., 1942; M.A., U. Minn., 1951, Ed.S., 1957, Ph.D., 1968; m. Genevieve Dolores Quam, May 2, 1943; children—Constance, Steven, Kathleen, Rebecca, Mark. Sci. tchr., coach Balaton High Sch., 1942, Hoffman High Sch., 1946; prin. Cottonwood High Sch., 1946-47; rep. Prudential Ins. Co., Blue Earth, Minn., 1947-48; prin. Delavan High Sch., 1948-51, Park Rapids High Sch., 1951-54, Two Harbors High Sch., 1954-58; asst. supt. schs., West Saint Paul, Minn., 1958-67, supt. schs., 1967—; univ. and seminar instr. and cons. Active Bay Lake Improvement Assn. Served to lt. (s.g.), USNR, 1943-46; PTO. Recipient Outstanding Sch. Adminstrs. award Dakota County, 1979, Adminstrn. Day Recognition plaque Minn. State Fair, 1979. Mem. NEA, Minn. Edn. Assn., Dakota County Area Supts. Assn. (pres. 1980-81), Nat. Acad. Sch. Execs. (Devel. award 1975), Minn. Assn. Sch. Adminstrs. (pres.'s service plaque 1977), Minn. Assn. Sch. Adminstrs. (pres. 1976-77), Sch. Adminstrs. Minn. (pres. 1976-77), Am. Legion. Lutheran. Clubs: Kiwanis, Rotary. Home: 11 E Emerson Ave West Saint Paul MN 55118 Office: 1037 Bidwell St West Saint Paul MN 55118

ANDERSON, RUTH GIBSON, educator; b. Blue Eye, Mo., Apr. 14, 1929; d. Claude Bertrum and Sylvia Jane (Hudson) Gibson; B.S. with high distinction, S.W. Mo. State U., 1951; M.Ed., U. Mo., Columbia, 1962, Ed.D., 1974; m. Lev Zelland Anderson, Aug. 12, 1948; 1 son, Richard Lee. Elem. sch. tchr., Taney County, Mo., 1947-48, Blue Eye, 1951-54, Waynesville, Mo., 1955-58, 60-63, Am. Dependent Schs., Germany, 1958-60; elem. sch. prin., Ft. Wood, Mo., , 1963-65; asst. supt. for instrn. Waynesville-Ft. Wood Schs., 1965-71; teaching fellow U. Mo., 1971; faculty Sch. of Ozarks, Point Lookout, Mo., 1972—, prof. edn., 1977—, chmn. dept., 1979—; ednl. cons., 1972—. Sec., Waynesville USO, 1966-69. Mem. NEA, Mo. State Tchrs. Assn., Internat. Reading Assn. (v.p. elect Mo. State Council 1980-81, editor Newsletter 1980-81), AAUW, Assn. for Supervision and Curriculum Devel., Assn. for Children with Learning Disabilities, Sch. of Ozarks Assos., Delta Kappa Gamma Soc. Internat., Pi Lambda Theta, Phi Delta Kappa, Kappa Delta Pi, Kappa Kappa Iota (state pres. 1965-66). Home: Star Route 1 Box 113 Blue Eye MO 65611 Office: Dept Edn Sch of Ozarks Point Lookout MO 65726

ANDERSON, RUTH NATHAN, columnist, rec. artist; b. N.Y.C., Jan. 28, 1934; d. Solomon and Anna (Cornick) Gans; student N.Y. U., George Washington U., evenings 1952-56; m. Arthur Aksel Anderson, Jr., Sept. 11, 1971; stepchildren—Jack Anderson, Barbara Anderson Stasioski, Terri Anderson. Newsletter editor Washington Post, 1952-53; chief med. writer, press officer Nat. Multiple Sclerosis Soc., N.Y.C., 1953-55; feature editor Crusade for Freedom, Radio Free Europe, N.Y.C., 1955-58; editor jr. TV dept. TV Revue, N.Y.C., 1958-61; feature-series reporter N.Am. Newspaper Alliance, Women's News Service, N.Y.C., 1961-69; writer, originator Doctor's Grapevine column Nat. Features Syndicate, Chgo., 1969-73; author-owner syndicated column VIP Med. Grapevine, Round Lake, Ill., 1973—; feature news corr. Waukegan (Ill.) News-Sun, 1977—; Midwest corr. United Feature Syndicate; Chgo. contbg. editor Music City Entertainer; interviewer/moderator CRIS—Chicagoland Radio Info. Service for the blind; tchr. journalism, creative writing, speech arts Fla. State Bd. Adult Edn., 1968-69; lectr. writing seminars for faculty U. Ill. at Chgo. Circle Campus, 1970—. Trustee, sec. bd. Round Lake Pub. Library, 1977—; Right-to-Read vol. tutor jr. high schs., Round Lake, 1977—; singer ARC entertainment com. Bedside Network, 1974—. Mem. Chgo. Women in Broadcasting, Lake County Assn. Journalists, Nat. Assn. for Female Execs., Chgo. Unltd., Press Vets. Assn., Internat. Platform Assn., Future Physicians Am. (hon.). Clubs: Chgo. Press, Chgo. Advt. Author booklet: How You Can Be a Part of Your United Nations, 1959; contbg. writer Woman's World mag.; contbr. articles to various mags. including Parents, Pageant, Mademoiselle, Science Digest, Reader's Digest, TV Guide, TV Radio Mirror, This Week, Am. Weekly, Am. Home, others; features on U.S. presidents in archives of Hoover, Truman, Eisenhower, Kennedy and Johnson presdl. libraries. Rec. artist mus. comedy songs, country pop for Am. Sound label. Home: 161 Nasa Circle Round Lake IL 60073

ANDERSON, STUART ANTON, educator; b. Mpls., May 17, 1913; s. Alvin Leo and Estelle A.; B.S., U. Wis., Stout, 1935; M.Ed., Marquette U., 1938; Ph.D., U. Wis., Madison, 1948; m. Helen M. Robinson, June 7, 1935; children—Judith Ratcliff, David. Tchr., Milw. Public Schs., 1935-46; asso. prof. edn. U. Wis., Stout, 1946-52; tech. dir. vocat. edn. Fgn. Ops. Adminstrn., IIAA, Lima, Peru, 1952-54; dir. tchr. edn. Eastern Ill. U., Charleston, 1954-56; head UNESCO Tech. Assistance Mission, Manila, Philippines, 1956-57; asso. prof. Sch. Edn., U. Chgo., 1957-58; asst. supt. Niles Twp. High Sch., Skokie, Ill., 1958-62; supt. Riverside-Brookfield Twp. High Sch., Riverside, Ill., 1963-69; prof. adminstrn. Sangamon State U., Springfield, Ill., 1970—; cons. sch. dists., Ill. Assn. Sch. Bds., State Bd. Edn. Mem. Springfield C. of C. (edn. com. 1974-79), Am. Arbitration Assn., Ill. Assn. Sch. Adminstrs., Ill. Conf. Profs. Ednl. Adminstrn., Ill. Congress Parent-Tchrs., Nat. Assn. Secondary Sch. Prins., Nat. Conf. Profs. Ednl. Adminstrn., Nat. Soc. Study of Edn. Home: 213 Circle Dr Springfield IL 62703 Office: Sangamon State U Springfield IL 62708

ANDERSON, THOMAS GRANT, constrn. co. exec.; b. Cedar Rapids, Iowa, Mar. 17, 1948; s. B.L. and Florene (Jolley) A.; student Cornell Coll., Mt. Vernon, Iowa, 1966-69; B.S., Iowa State U., 1972; m. Julianne Eichhorn, Aug. 16, 1969; children—Thomas John, Brittain Leigh. Farm mgr. B.L. Anderson, Inc., Cedar Rapids, 1972—, treas., 1975—; dir. Agra-Partners Ltd. Co-founder, instr. Met. Narcotics Drug Dog Program, 1976-77; mem. Iowa Republican Farm Policy Council, 1979—; bd. dirs. Old Creamery Theater Co., 1980—. Served with U.S. Army, 1970-71; Vietnam. Decorated Air medal, Combat Inf. Badge, Bronze Star, Purple Heart. Named Law and Order Citizen of Yr., Elks., 1976. Mem. Cedar Rapids Agrl. Execs. (pres.-elect), Am. Soc. Farm Mgrs., Iowa Limestone Producers Assn. (chmn. agrl. lime com. 1978-81), Nat. Crushed Stone Assn., Am. Angus Assn., Iowa Soc. Farm Mgrs., Aircraft Owners and Pilots Assn., Profl. Farmers Am., Iowa Farm Bur., DAV. Congregationalist. Clubs: Pickwick, Cedar Rapids Country, Twenty Investment Partners (past pres.), Ducks Unlimited (dir. Eastern Iowa chpt. 1981—). Home: 355 Woodland Dr SE Cedar Rapids IA 52403 Office: PO Box 2007 Cedar Rapids IA 52406

ANDERSON, THOMAS MILBURN, JR., lawyer; b. Ottawa, Ill., Dec. 25, 1934; s. Thomas Milburn and Bessie Mae (Olson) A.; student Am. U., 1955; B.A., Beloit Coll., 1956; J.D., U. Ill., 1959; children—Thomas Milburn III, John D., Mark E. Admitted to Ill. bar, 1959; asst. state's atty., LaSalle County, Ill., 1960-61; magistrate Circuit Ct. LaSalle County, 1963-64; partner firm Anderson & Anderson, Earlville, Ill., 1964—; spl. asst. atty. gen. State of Ill., 1969—. Mem. Ill. Agrl. Export Adv. Commn., 1968-71; zone chmn. Ill. Gov.'s Task Force Mental Health, 1972; mem. Ill. Gov.'s Adv. Council, 1969-72; U.S. rep. European N.Am. Conf. Young Polit. Leaders, Rome, Italy, 1970. Republican candidate for state's atty. of LaSalle County, 1964; mem. LaSalle County Rep. Finance Com., 1965-70, chmn. LaSalle County Rep. Central Com., 1974-76; precinct committeeman, 1969-76; regional campaign mgr. Ralph T. Smith for senator campaign, 1970; vice-chmn. Young Rep. Nat. Fedn., 1969-71, co-chmn. conv., 1969; Ill. 15th Congl. Dist. Rep. State Central committeeman, 1974—; vice chmn. Ill. Rep. Central Com., 1978. Recipient Outstanding Young Rep. of Ill. award, 1969. Mem. LaSalle County Bar Assn. (pres. 1979-80). Elk, Lion. Office: 201 S Ottawa St Earlville IL 60518

ANDERSON, VERGIE LOUISE, real estate broker; b. Jackson, Tenn., Sept. 28, 1947; d. Calvin and Crystal Louise (Matthews) A.; B.A. in Polit. Sci., Loyola U., Chgo., 1977. With Anderson Real Estate, Evanston, Ill., 1973—, v.p., 1973—. Mem. ladies aux. St. Bernard Hosp., Chgo. Recipient various service and recognition awards. Mem. Nat. Assn. Realtors, Nat. Assn. Real Estate Brokers, N.Shore Bd. Realtors, Ill. Assn. Realtors, Operation Push, NAACP, League Black Women, Urban League, Nat. Assn. Negro Bus. and Profl. Women's Clubs, Internat. Orgn. Women Execs. Baptist. Home: 4250 N Marine Dr Chicago IL 60613 Office: 1610 Maple Ave Evanston IL 60201

ANDERSON, WILLIAM MARTIN, coll. adminstr.; b. Detroit, July 12, 1938; s. William Martin and Dorothy (Nichols) A.; B.A., Mich. State U., 1960; M.A., Central Mich. U., 1962; Ph.D., So. Ill. U., 1973; m. Anna Marie Moskowitz, 1977; children—David, Daniel, Susan. Tchr., coach Northwest High Sch., Jackson, Mich., 1965-66; instr., asst. to pres. Southwestern Mich. Coll., Dowagiac, 1966-68; dean of instrn. John A. Logan Coll., Carterville, Ill., 1968-73; v.p. instrn. Carl Sandburg Coll., Galesburg, Ill., 1973-77, coll. pres., 1977—. Lay leader, mem. of council Trinity Luth. Ch., Galesburg, 1978-79; bd. dirs. Knox County (Ill.) YMCA, 1976-79, Galesburg Pioneers Baseball Club, 1978—, Cottage Hosp., 1981—, Knox-Galesburg Symphony, 1981—. Served with U.S. Army, 1962-64; ETO. Mem. Am. Assn. Higher Edn., Galesburg C. of C. (pres., dir.). Club: Galesburg Exchange. Author: They Died to Make Men Free: 19th Michigan Volunteers in the Civil War, 1979. Home: 556 Knollcrest Dr Galesburg IL 61401 Office: Carl Sandburg Coll Galesburg IL 61401

ANDERSON, WILLIAM RHODES, appliance mfg. corp. exec.; b. Fairfield, Ill., Dec. 25, 1921; s. Oscar and Mary Gertrude (Rhodes) A.; student public schs.; m. Shirley Ann Geistwhite, Dec. 27, 1978; children by previous marriage—Donna Anderson Dykstra, William, James. Enlisted USAF, 1942, crew chief, 1942-46, flight engr., 1947-48, quality control insp., 1957-58, maintenance control, 1958-59, instr. aircraft maintenance, flight instr. aircraft systems, 1948-56, non-commd. officer in charge 9 tng. detachments, 1960-65, ret., 1965; supt. maintenance Roper Corp., Kankakee, Ill., 1965-70, project engr., 1971-81; sr. facilities engr. Roper Outdoor Products, Bradley, Ill., 1981—; cons. Occupational Health and Safety Adminstrn., 1971-81, EPA, 1981—. Instl. rep. Rainbow council Boy Scouts Am., 1965-68. Mem. Kankakee Valley Maintenance and

Engring. Assn., Kankakee Mgmt. Assn. Home: 870 Heritage Dr Bourbonnais IL 60914 Office: Roper Outdoor Products Bradley IL 60915

ANDERSON, WILLIAM SUMMERS, business equipment co. exec.; b. Hankow, China, Mar. 29, 1919 (parents Brit. citizens); s. William G. and Mabel (Johnston) A.; ed. public schs., China; m. Janice Elizabeth Robb, Oct. 8, 1947; children—Stephanie Gay, Irene Mabel, Hope Marian. Internal auditor Hongkong & Shanghai Hotels Ltd., 1938-39; auditor Linstead & Davis, Hong Kong, 1940-41; with Nat. Cash Register Co. (now NCR Corp.), 1945—, mgr., Hong Kong, 1946-59, v.p. Far East, also chmn. Nat. Cash Register Japan, 1959-72, corp. pres., dir., Dayton, Ohio, 1972—, chief exec. officer, 1973—, chmn., pres., 1974-76, chmn. bd., chief exec. officer, 1976—; dir. Far East-Am. Council Commerce and Industry, Inc., R.J. Reynolds Industries, Inc., Nat. Council U.S.-China Trade. Mem. adv. council, vice chmn. on Japan-U.S. Econ. Relations; chmn. Dayton Area Progress Council, Brit.-N. Am. Com.; mem. Nat. Com. on U.S. China Relations; mem. council Internat. Exec. Service Corp.; bd. govs. Asian Inst. Mgmt.; chmn. nat. bd. Smithsonian Assos.; chmn. Bus. Council Internat. Understanding; trustee Com. Econ. Devel., Dayton Performing Arts Fund; Eisenhower Exchange Fellowships. Served with U.S. Army, 1941-45. Mem. Assn. Internal Accts., Australian Soc. Accts., Brit.-N. Am. Com., Bus. Council, Conf. Bd., Fgn. Policy Assn. (asso.), Japan Soc. (dir.). Clubs: Dayton Racquet, Moraine Country, The Hundred (trustee) (Dayton); Carmel (Calif.) Valley Golf and Country; 300 Golf (Japan); Links (N.Y.C.); Metropolitan (Chgo.). Office: NCR Corp 1700 S Patterson Blvd Dayton OH 45479*

ANDERT, JEFFREY NORMAN, clin. psychologist; b. Aberdeen, S.D., May 21, 1950; s. Norman Joseph and Irene Eleanor (Olson) A.; B.A. in Psychology, Augsburg Coll., Mpls., 1971; M.A. in Psychology, Mankato State U., 1973; Ph.D. in Clin. Psychology, U. So. Miss., 1976; m. Diane Kay Dunham, May 29, 1971; 1 son, Jason Ryan. Grad. asst. Mankato State U., 1972-73, U. So. Miss., 1974-75; clin. psychology intern Des Moines Child Guidance Center, 1975-76; clin. psychologist Battle Creek (Mich.) Child Guidance and Adult Clinic, 1976-80; pvt. practice clin. psychology, Battle Creek, 1978—; co-owner, dir. Psychol. Consultants of Battle Creek, 1980—; instr. Kellogg Community Coll., Battle Creek, 1976-77. Trustee, Calhoun County (Mich.) Task Force on Child Abuse and Neglect, Inc., 1977—; bd. dirs. Calhoun County Alliance against Sexual Assault, 1981—. Lic. psychologist, Mich. Mem. Am. Psychol. Assn., Am. Assn. Psychiat. Services for Children, Assn. for Advancement Behavior Therapy, Midwestern Psychol. Assn., Mich. Psychol. Assn., Soc. Pediatric Psychology, Psi Chi. Lutheran. Contbr. articles to profl. jours. Home: 319 E Morgan Rd Battle Creek MI 49017 Office: 1407 McKay Tower 25 W Michigan Mall Battle Creek MI 49017

ANDOLSHEK, RICHARD ANDERS, retail stores exec.; b. Crosby, Minn., Mar. 13, 1952; s. Albin Henery and Alice Louise (Arvidson) A.; student U. Minn., 1970-73; m. Lonna Mae Schultz, Dec. 18, 1971; children—Kimberly, Albin. Owner, operator Crosslake IGA Grocery Store (Minn.), 1973—, Dick's Package Liquor Store, Crosslake, 1973—, Andy's Restaurant, Crosslake, 1973—; v.p. Country Printing Enterprises Inc., Pequot Lakes, Minn., 1977-80, LAR, Inc., night club and restaurant, Crosslake, 1977—; pres. Jonable Inc., chain restaurant, Crosslake, 1979—, Richard-Curtis, Inc., Pequot Lakes, 1980—, Brann and Assos., Inc., Brainerd, Minn., 1981—. Mem. Crosslake Planning and Zoning Commn., 1973-74, Region 5 Devel. Commn., 1975-77; mem. Ind. Sch. Dist. 186 Bd. Edn., Pequot Lakes, Minn., 1975—, chmn., 1977. Named Minn. Liquor Retailer of Yr., Midwest Beverage Jour., 1977. Mem. Minn. Food Retailers, Minn. Liquor Retailers (pres.), Midwestern States Fedn. Beverage Licensees (adv. bd.), Crosslake C. of C., Nat. Fedn. Small Bus. Club: Elks. Home and Office: Box 98 Crosslake MN 56442

ANDORFER, DONALD EDWIN, advt. co. artist; b. Clinton, Ia., Jan. 1, 1912; s. Arthur and Mildred Susan (Cram) A.; student Wis. State Coll., 1930-32, Art Inst. Chgo., 1946-47; m. Loretta Adeline Kuhnke, Dec. 24, 1935; children—Donald, Sylvia (Mrs. Gerry Schwindt), Joseph, Virginia (dec.). Free lance artist, Grand Rapids, Mich., 1936-50; artist So. States Coop., Richmond, Va., 1950-60; free lance artist, illustrator, South Bend, Ind., 1960-63; artist Fletcher & Assos., Advt. Inc., St. Joseph, Mo., 1963-67; artist in residence North Mo. area Mo. State Council of Arts; represented in permanent collection at Mo. State Hist. Soc.; commd. to paint mural of Callaway County history, Fulton, Mo., 1978; pvt. instr. in art; propr. Rural Am. Art Gallery, St. Joseph, Mo.; mem. Grand Central Galleries, N.Y.C. Bd. dirs. Albrecht Gallery, 1966-69; founder mem. Mo. Citizens for Arts, St. Louis. Recipient numerous ribbons and trophies in art exhbns.; named one of best artists of Am., Wis. Hist. Soc., 1981. Mem. Internat. Soc. Artists, Am. Artist Profl. League of N.Y., Soc. N. Am. Artists, Greater Kansas City Art Assn., Clinton (Iowa) Art Assn. Methodist (ofcl. bd. 1964-67). Illustrator: Nation of Might, 1942. Home: Rural Route 3 Saint Joseph MO 64505

ANDREAS, BRUCE FREDERICK, pathologist; b. Cleve., May 10, 1925; s. Frederick William and Edna Louise (Buehler) A.; A.B., Heidelberg Coll., 1949; M.D., Ohio State U., 1953; m. Jean Bobbitt, Aug. 28, 1954; children—Karen, Frederick, Patricia, Jonathan; m. 2d, Marie Greder Nimietz, July 4, 1976. Intern, Miami Valley Hosp., Dayton, Ohio, 1953-54, resident in pathology, 1954-58; pathologist, dir. lab., Geauga Community Hosp., Chardon, Ohio, 1959—, chief of staff, 1969-70; pres. Geauga Lab. Services, Inc.; regional dir. Ohio Peer Rev. Orgn., Inc. Charter mem., trustee Met. Health Planning Corp. N.E. Ohio, 1967-76; del. Am. Cancer Soc., 1966-68; v.p. Geauga County Bd. Health, 1966-69; mem. adv. council N.E. Ohio ARC Blood Center, 1966—; mem. adv. bd. med. lab. technologists program Lakeland Community Coll., 1975—; mem. Geauga County Health Adv. Council, 1969-73, pres., 1973; bd. dirs. Geauga County Mental Health Clinic, 1966-69; cons. pathologist to Geauga County coroner, 1962—; bd. dirs., charter mem. Geauga Emergency Med. Services, Inc., 1965-72; field liaison asso. Commn. on Cancer, A.C.S., 1981. Served with U.S. Army, 1943-46. Decorated Bronze Star with two oak leaf clusters. Diplomate Am. Bd. Pathology. Fellow Coll. Am. Pathologists (lab. insp. accreditation program 1976—), Am. Soc. Clin. Pathologists, Am. Coll. Utilization Rev. Physicians; mem. AMA, Ohio Soc. Pathologists, Cleve. Soc. Pathologists (pres. 1971), Ohio Med. Assn. (del.), Geauga County Med. Soc. (pres. 1966), Cleve. Acad. Medicine. Home: 11296 Brookside Rd Chardon OH 44024 Office: Geauga Community Hosp Box 249 Chardon OH 44024

ANDREAS, DWAYNE O(RVILLE), corp. exec.; b. Worthington, Minn., Mar. 4, 1918; s. Reuben P. and Lydia (Stoltz) A.; student Wheaton (Ill.) Coll., 1935-36; m. Bertha Benedict, 1938 (div.); 1 dau., Sandra Ann McMurtrie; m. 2d, Dorothy Inez Snyder, Dec. 21, 1947; children—Terry Lynn Bevis, Michael D. Vice pres., dir. Honeymead Products Co., Cedar Rapids, Iowa, 1936-46; v.p. Cargill, Inc., Mpls., 1946-52; chmn. bd., chief exec. officer Honeymead Products Co. (now Nat. City Bancorp.), Mankato, Minn., 1952-72; chmn. bd., chief exec. officer Archer-Daniels-Midland Co., Decatur, Ill., 1970—; pres. Seaview Hotel Corp., 1958—; Lone Star Industries, Greenwich, Conn.; dir., exec. com. Daniels-Midland Co.; Nat. dir. Boys Club of Am.; dir. Norwestern Nat. Life Ins. Co., Mpls., 1962-73, Phibro Corp., New York, 1982. Mem. Pres.'s Gen. Adv. Com. Fgn. Assistance Programs, 1965-68, Pres.'s Adv. Council on Mgmt. Improvement, 1969-73. Pres., Andreas Found.; trustee U.S. Naval Acad. Found. Mem. Fgn. Policy Assn. N.Y. (dir.). Clubs: Union League (Chgo.); Minneapolis, Minikahda (Mpls.); Indian Creek Country (Miami Beach, Fla.); Links (N.Y.C.); Blind Brook (Port Chester, N.Y.). Home: The Sea View 9909 Collins Ave Bal Harbour Miami Beach FL 33154 Office: Archer Daniels Midland Co Box 1470 Decatur IL 62525

ANDREASEN, GEORGE FREDRICK, dentist, educator; b. Fremont, Nebr., Feb. 16, 1934; s. George T. and Laura Mae (Hynek) A.; B.S. (Regents scholar), U. Nebr., 1959, D.D.S., 1959, M.S. (NIH fellow), 1963; children—Susan, Robin. Research fellow Worcester Coll., Oxford, Eng., 1960-61; asst. prof. orthodontics U. Iowa Coll. Dentistry, Iowa City, 1963-67, asso. prof., acting head dept. orthodontics, 1967, asso. prof., head dept., 1968, prof., head dept. orthodontics, 1968—; practice dentistry, Iowa City, 1963—. Cons. to various dental corps. on dental materials. Named hon. adm. Nebr. Navy, 1972; U. Nebr. Alumnus Master, 1974. Fellow Am. Coll. Dentists, Royal Soc. Health (Eng.); mem. Am. Assn. Orthodontists (chmn. sci. com. 1971-72, nat. com. on research 1976-79, pres. 1980), Iowa Orthodontic Soc. (pres. 1972-73), Am., Iowa dental assns., Univ. Dist. Dental Assn., Iowa Alumni Assn. (life), U. Iowa Med. Center (life), Am. Oxonion, Phalanx Blue Print Key, Sigma Xi, Pi Tau Sigma. Omicron Kappa Upsilon, Delta Tau Delta, Xi Psi Phi. Club: Athletic (Iowa City). Contbr. articles to profl. jours. Patentee in field. Home: 1104 Penkridge Dr Iowa City IA 52240 Office: Room S221 DSB U Iowa Iowa City IA 52240

ANDREJEVICH, MILAN, historian; b. Gary, Ind., Oct. 23, 1953; s. Ivan and Eva (Steidel) A.; B.A., Ind. U. N.W., 1975; postgrad., U. Pitts., 1975-76; Fulbright-Hays, Yugoslav Govt. grantee U. Belgrade, 1976-77; M.A., U. Chgo., 1978; m. Marcia June Nedoff, May 17, 1975. Grad. asst. history dept. U. Ill., Chgo., 1978-79, asst. instr., 1979—, coordinator/lectr. Honor's program, 1981-82, research asso. Summer Research Lab. on Slavic Studies, 1981; instr. Coll. St. Francis, Joliet, Ill., 1980. Mem. Am. Assn. Advancement Slavic Studies, Am. Assn. S.E. European Studies, N.Am. Soc. Serbian Studies, Fulbright Alumni Assn., Yugoslav-Am. Students Assn. (pres. 1980). Contbr. articles to profl. jours. Home: 1229 W 52d Dr Merrillville IN 46410 Office: Dept History Box 4348 U Ill Chicago IL 60680

ANDREOLI, CHARLES ANTHONY, designer, sculptor; b. Kenosha, Wis., Aug. 26, 1928; s. Ralph and Jenny Andreoli; student Am. Acad. Art, 1946-48, DePaul U., 1948-49; student of Alexandre Zlatoff-Mierski, 1947-51; m. Mary Celebre, Nov. 28, 1953. Portrait painter, 1949—; interior designer DaPrato Studio, Chgo., 1954-56, J. Cotey Co., Chgo.; free lance designer to home furnishing trade, including Hillenbrand Industries (Ind.), Sandel Lamps, Chgo., Fuggiti Studios, Chgo., U.S. Industries Lamp div., Chgo., L.C.A. Lamp div., (Ky.), Erie Glass Co., Chgo.; lamp design cons. Prestige Lamp div. McGraw Edison Co., Chgo.; important works include Mayan Room Restaurant, Rockefeller Centre, sculptured arches Emerald Door Restaurant, New Orleans; created Andreoli Porcelaine Sculptures Ltd. Edition. Address: 1340 N Astor St Chicago IL 60610

ANDRES, WILLIAM ALFRED, retail chain exec.; b. Fayette, Iowa, Aug. 9, 1926; s. Alfred G. and Eva Levetta (Eide) A.; B.A., Upper Iowa U., Fayette, 1948, D.B.A. (hon.), 1977; M.A., U. Pitts., 1949; m. Betty Ruth Follett, June 4, 1947; children—Robert A., Charles W., Richard W. With Dayton Hudson Corp., Mpls., 1958—, exec. v.p. retail ops., 1971-74, pres., 1974—, chief exec. officer, 1976—, chmn., 1977—, also dir.; dir. EXXON Corp., 1st Bank Systems, Inc., Internat. Multifoods, The St. Paul Cos. Bd. dirs. United Way, Mpls., 1975—. Served to 2d lt. U.S. Army, 1944-46. Clubs: Minneapolis. Office: 777 Nicollet Mall Minneapolis MN 55402

ANDRESS, SAMUEL COE, lawyer; b. Hayesville, Ohio, June 27, 1906; s. Upton Samuel and Millicent Alma (Coe) A.; A.B., Wittenberg U., 1925; LL.B., U. Cin., 1928. Admitted to Ohio bar, 1928, since practiced in Akron; sr. partner firm Roetzel & Andress. Trustee Akron Beacon Jour. Charity Fund, Akron Community Trusts, Children's Zoo. Served to lt. USNR, 1942-45. Mem. Am., Ohio, Akron bar assns., Akron C. of C. (past pres.), Order of Coif, Lambda Chi Alpha, Delta Sigma Rho, Phi Alpha Delta. Episcopalian. Rotarian. Clubs: City (pres. 1969), University, Portage, Sharon. Home: 161 E Fairlawn Blvd Akron OH 44313 Office: 1 Cascade Plaza Akron OH 44308

ANDREW, ROBERT HARRY, agronomist; b. Platteville, Wis., Aug. 2, 1916; s. Harry Roscoe and Lu (Howery) A.; B.A., U. Wis., Madison, 1938; Ph.D., 1942; m. Nancy H. Wright, Apr. 15, 1944; children—Stephen, Elizabeth, Sarah, Martha, Charles. Agronomist Wis. Expt. Sta., 1942-46; asst. prof. agronomy U. Wis., Madison, 1946-52, asso. prof., 1952-58, prof., 1958—; vis. Fulbright lectr. U. Wageningen (Netherlands), 1953-54. Mem. Am. Soc. Agronomy, Crop Sci. Soc. Am., Sigma Xi, Phi Sigma, Gamma Sigma Delta, Phi Beta Kappa, Gamma Alpha. Methodist. Contbr. articles to profl. jours. Home: 3809 Hillcrest Dr Madison WI 53705 Office: Dept Agronomy U Wis Madison WI 53706

ANDREWS, ALVIN AHO, supts. schs.; b. Cook, Minn., May 4, 1935; s. Andrew Gust and Lydia (Alto) Aho; A.S., Virginia Jr. Coll., 1955; B.S., U. Minn., 1958, M.A., 1963; Ph.D., U. Wis., Madison, 1971; m. Jean Warman, Aug. 6, 1960; children—Steven, Christopher, Todd. Prin., jr.-sr. high sch., Randolph, Minn., 1961-64; prin. high sch., Chetek, Wis., 1964-69; supt. schs. Kettle Moraine Public Schs., Wales, Wis., 1971-78, Bismarck (N.D.) Public Schs., 1978—; instr. U. Wis., 1976-78. State chmn. N.D. Republican. Heritage Council; parliamentarian Dist. Rep. Caucus; bd. dirs. Dakota West Arts Council. Kettering Found. IDEA fellow, 1980, 81. Mem. Bismarck C. of C. (dir.), Am. Assn. Sch. Adminstrs., N.D. Assn. Sch. Adminstrs., Nat. Assn. Parliamentarians. Lutheran (deacon). Clubs: Lions (dir.), YMCA (dir.), Shriners, Masons, Elks. Home: 608 Birchwood Dr Bismarck ND 58501 Office: 400 Ave E Bismarck ND 58501

ANDREWS, ALVIN AHO, ednl. adminstr.; b. Cook, Minn., May 4, 1935; s. Andrew Gust and F. Lydia (Alto) Aho; B.S., U. Minn., St. Paul, 1958, M.A., Mpls., 1963; Ph.D., U. Wis., 1971; m. Jean Warman, Aug. 6, 1960; children—Steven, Christopher, Todd. Jr./sr. high sch. prin., counselor, journalism, sci. tchr., Randolph, Minn., 1961-64; high sch.prin., Chetek, Wis., 1964-69; supt. schs. Kettle Moraine, Wales, Wis., 1971-78, Bismarck, N.D., 1978—; part-time instr. U. Wis., 1976-78; sec. Wilderness Enterprises, Inc., Cook, Minn., 1974—. State pres. N.D. Republican Heritage Group, 1979—; bd. dirs. Dakota West Arts Council, YMCA, Salvation Army. Served with Army NG, 1953-56. Kettering fellow, 1980, 81; Supt.'s Workshop fellow Columbia U., 1979. Mem. Bismarck C. of C. (dir.), Am. Assn. Sch. Adminstrs., N.D. Assn. Sch. Adminstrs., Nat. Assn. Parliamentarians, Assn. Supervision and Curriculum Devel., Phi Delta Kappa. Republican. Lutheran (deacon). Clubs: Lions, Elks, Masons, Shriners, Plainsmen. Office: 400 Ave E East Bismarck ND 58501

ANDREWS, FRANK MEREDITH, social scientist; b. N.Y.C., Apr. 2, 1935; B.A. magna cum laude, Dartmouth Coll., 1957; postgrad. (Rotary Found. internat. fellow) U. Sydney (Australia), 1958, New Sch. Social Research, 1959; Ph.D. (Rackham fellow), U. Mich., 1962. Asst. study dir. Inst. for Social Research U. Mich., Ann Arbor, 1959-61, study dir., 1962-68, sr. study dir., 1968-71, program dir., 1971—, research scientist, 1973—, lectr. dept. psychology, 1963-66, asst. prof., 1967-71, asso. prof., 1971-76, prof., 1976—, prof. population planning, 1979—. Mem. Am. Psychol. Assn., Am. Sociol. Assn., Soc. Internat. Devel., Am. Statis. Assn., Internat. Sociol. Assn., Soc. for Social Studies of Sci., Population Assn. Am., Phi Beta Kappa, Sigma Xi. Author: (with D. Pelz) Scientists in Organizations: Productive Climates for Research and Development, 1966, Japanese edit., 1971, Russian edit., 1973, rev. English edit., 1976; Multiple Classification Analysis, 1967, 2d edit., 1973; Justifying Violence: Attitudes of American Men, 1972, A Guide for Selecting Statistical Techniques for Analyzing Social Science, 1974, Hebrew edit., 1976, French edit., 1977, rev. English edit., 1981; (with R.C. Messenger) Multivariate Nominal Scale Analysis, 1973; (with S.B. Withey) Social Indicators of Well-Being: Americans' Perceptions of Life Quality, 1976; editor: Scientific Productivity: The Effectiveness of Research Groups in Six Countries, 1979; co-editor: Quality of Life: Comparative Studies 1980; other works; contbr. chpts. to books, contbr. articles to profl. jours. Office: Inst for Social Research Univ of Michigan Ann Arbor MI 48109

ANDREWS, JANNA AARESTAD, ednl. adminstr.; b. Crookston, Minn., July 24, 1947; d. Erwin Leo and Eleanor Adeline (Anderson) Aarestad; B.S. summa cum laude (univ. scholar), Moorhead State U., 1968; M.S., St. Cloud State U., 1971; Ph.D., U. Minn., 1980, postgrad. Law Sch., 1981—; m. Larry Thomas Andrews, Oct. 9, 1981; 1 stepdau., Stephanie. Tchr. math., sr. high sch. Ind. Sch. Dist. 279, Osseo, Minn., 1969-78; asst. to supt. schs. Ind. Sch. Dist. 197, West St. Paul, Minn., 1978-79; asst. prin. jr. high sch., Ind. Sch. Dist. 977, Buffalo, Minn., 1979-80; prin. sr. sch. Ind. Sch. Dist. 832, Mahtomedi, Minn., 1980-81; speaker in field. Pres., Sagamore Condominium Assn., Plymouth, Minn.; violinist Mpls. Civic Symphony. Recipient Robert Frost award Moorhead State U., 1968; named to Outstanding Young Women Am., U.S. Jaycees, 1968; N.D. Elks scholar, 1965; Woodrow Wilson fellow, 1968. Mem. Minn. Assn. Supervision and Curriculum Devel. (chairperson polit. action com. 1979-80), Assn. Supervision and Curriculum Devel., Minn. Assn. Secondary Sch. Prins., Nat. Assn. Secondary Sch. Prins., Adminstrv. Women in Edn., Phi Delta Kappa, Kappa Delta Pi, Alpha Lambda Delta. Republican. Clubs: N.W. Racquet, Mid-Am. Karate (Gold Belt). Home: 6338 Xerxes Ave S Edina MN 55424

ANDREWS, LARRY HOWARD, data processing co. exec.; b. St. Peter, Minn., Mar. 28, 1942; s. Howard L. and Anna Mae (Bartak) A.; B.A. in Math. cum laude, Doane Coll., 1965; m. Virginia Faye Rannie, Aug. 4, 1962; children—Kurt, Mark; m. 2d, Carolyn Sue Molnar, July 29, 1978; children—Christina, Emily Lori. Instr. math. Dist. 66 Schs., Omaha, 1965-66; computer systems analyst and programmer Western Electric Co., Omaha, 1966-69; data processing mgr. UNICO, Bellevue, Nebr., 1969-70; pres. ALR Computer Services, Omaha, 1970-77, ALR Systems and Software, Inc., 1977—; treas., dir. K-Kal Products Inc., 1976—. Pres., Meadows Community Assn., 1981. Cert. in data processing. Mem. Assn. Computer Machinery, Data Processing Mgrs. Assn., Omaha C. of C. Republican. Methodist. Clubs: Sertoma. Home: 9002 David Circle Omaha NE 68138 Office: 10334 Ellison Circle Omaha NE 68134

ANDREWS, MARK, farmer, Senator; b. Fargo, N.D., May 19, 1926; s. Mark and Lillian (Hoyler) A.; B.S., N.D. State U., 1949, hon. doctorate, 1978; m. Mary Willming, June 28, 1949; children—Mark III, Sarah Jane, Karen Louise. Farmer, Mapleton, N.D., 1949—; mem. 88th-92d Congresses from 1st. Dist. N.D., 93d-96th Congresses, at-large N.D.; mem. U.S. Senate from N.D., 1981—; mem. Congl. Environ. Study Conf.; ofcl. del. FAO Conf., Rome, 1975; founding mem. Congl. Rural Caucus. Mem. Rep. Nat. Com. for N.D.; Named hon. Am. farmer Future Farmers Am., 1976. Mem. Rep. Nat. Farm Council, N.D. Young Republicans (past chmn.), Farm Bur., Am. Legion, N.D. Stockmen's Assn., N.D. Crop Improvement Assn. (pres.) Greater N.D. Assn., Northwest Farm Mgrs., N.D. Water Users Assn., Nat. Reclamation Assn. (chmn. land limitations com.). Episcopalian. Office: Russell Senate Office Bldg Washington DC 20510

ANDREWS, WILLIAM HENRY, hosp. dir.; b. Wellston, Mo., Oct. 16, 1919; s. William H. and Viola (Williams) A.; B.S. in Edn., Lincoln U., 1941; M.H.A., Washington U., 1954; m. Mildred E. Joyce, Aug. 7, 1943; children—William H., Brenda J. Asst. adminstr. Homer G. Phillips Hosp., 1941-52; adminstr. People's Hosp., 1954-55, George W. Hubbard Hosp., Meharry Med. Coll., 1955-59; adminstr. Forest City Hosp., 1959-64; asst. dir. Cleve. Met. Gen. Hosp., later dep. dir., dir., 1969—; adminstr. Kaiser Permanente Med. Center, Cleve., 1981—. Mem. faculty health services adminstrn. Grad. Sch. Ohio State U.; mem. council Nat. Inst. Arthritis and Metabolic Diseases, 1968-71; mem. physicians clin. asst. adv. com. Cuyahoga Community Coll.; mem. personnel adv. com. and Social Service clearing house com. Cleve. Fedn. for Community Planning. Mem. Catholic Interracial Council, Cleve. Arthritis Found. Trustee Cleve. Hemophilia Found., Hough Norwood Family Health Care Program. Commonwealth Fund fellow, 1952. Fellow Am. Coll. Hosp. Adminstrs. (examiner); mem. Wash. U. Alumni Assn. (treas.), Nat. Assn. Health Services Execs (2d v.p.), Ohio Hosp. Assn. (shared services com. and social work adv. panel), Greater Cleve. Hosp. Assn. (exec. com., blood bank com., house staff com.), Kappa Alpha Psi. Rotarian. Home: 2960 Ripley Rd Cleveland OH 44120 Office: 2475 East Blvd Cleveland OH 44120. *A sincere concern for others will bring with it the energy to do one's best under all circumstances, the courage to withstand adversities and disappointments, a devotion to fairness in dealing with others, and a desire to reach one's full potential.*

ANGELINE, JOHN FREDERICK, mgmt. cons.; b. Somerville, Mass., Sept. 29, 1929; s. Jack L. and Edith (Ciavatti) A.; B.S., Northeastern U., 1952, M.B.A., 1963; m. Doris Helen L'Heureux, Nov. 9, 1957; children—Karen E., Rachel A., Andrea M. Mgmt. cons. Arthur D. Little Inc., Cambridge, Mass., 1952-77; v.p. research and devel. grocery products Quaker Oats Co., 1979-80; prin. Technomic Consultants, Chgo., 1980—. Mem. various town coms. and commns. Topsfield, Mass., 1963-76. Served with U.S. Army, 1954-62. Mem. Inst. Food Technologists, Am. Chem. Soc., N.Y. Acad. Sci., Phi Tau Sigma. Republican. Patentee prodn. odorless carbon. Contbr. articles to profl. jours. Home: 496 Thomas Dr North Barrington IL 60010 Office: 1 N Wacker Dr Chicago IL 60606

ANGELL, MADELINE (MRS. KENNETH F. JOHNSON), writer; b. Devils Lake, N.D., Jan. 6, 1919; d. Bernard Oscar and Evelyn May (Smith) Angell; student Stephens Coll., 1936-37; B.S., U. Minn., 1940; m. Kenneth Frederick Johnson, Aug. 31, 1940; children—Mark Frederick, Randall David. Works include: 120 Questions and Answers about Birds, 1973; America's Best Loved Wild Animals, 1975; The Fantastic Variety of Marine Animals, 1976; Red Wing, Minnesota, Saga of a River Town, 1977; Snakes and Frogs and Turtles and Such, 1979; (with Mary Cavaness Miller) Joseph Woods Hancock: The Life and Times of a Minnesota Pioneer, 1980; contbr. articles to publs. including Parents' Mag., Better Homes and Gardens, Sci. World. Mem. Mayor's Citizens Com. for Red Wing Tng. Sch., co-chmn., 1970-72. Recipient McKnight Found. Humanities award for novel, 1966, Blue Flame Ecology Salute, 1974. Mem. AAUW (co-pres. 1956-58), Audubon Soc., Goodhue County Hist. Soc., Minn. Hist. Soc., Authors Guild, Alpha Chi Omega, Phi Upsilon Omicron, Omicron Nu (pres. 1939-40). Lutheran. Home and office: Route 4 Cardinal Dr Red Wing MN 55066

ANGELO, JENNIFER KAY, occupational therapist, educator; b. Topeka, June 5, 1952; d. Eber Lawrence and Melba May Burgess; B.S., U. Mo., 1975; M.A., Tex. Woman's U., 1978; m. Anil Angelo, May 24, 1975. Occupational therapist Glenwood Nursing Home, Green Bay, Wis., 1975-76, Americana Health Care Center, Appleton, Wis., 1976-77, Tex. Woman's U., 1977-78; clin. asst. prof. U. Wis., Madison, 1978—. clin. asst. prof. U. Wis., Madison, 1978—. Active Madison's Childrens Theatre, 1980—. Mem. Am. Occupational Therapy Assn., Wis. Occupational Therapy Assn., Center for Study Sensory Integrative Dysfunction. Republican. Baptist. Office: 1300 University Ave Madison WI 53706

ANGERMAN, ROBERT BRYON, dentist; b. Gary, Ind., Jan. 18, 1938; s. Robert Ora and Lauretta Illa (Meyer) A.; D.D.S., Ind. U., 1968; m. Sarah Elizabeth Ingram, Sept. 11, 1965; children—Robert Bryon, Devin Elizabeth. Individual practice dentistry, Merrillville, Ind., 1969—; owner, pres. Angerman Dental Corp., 1968—; lectr., Pitts. Dental Sch., 1972; cons. Implants Internat., N.Y.C., 1971—; lectr. throughout U.S., Africa, S.Am. Served with USNR, 1957-61. Recipient numerous profl. awards. Mem. Am. Dental Assn., Am. Acad. Gen. Dentistry (chpt. pres. 1972), Psi Omega. Contbr. articles to profl. publs. Designer America tee shirts worn by Am. hostages in Iran. Home: 13921 80th Pl Dyer IN 46311 Office: 1000 E 80th St Merrillville IN 46410

ANGLE, MARGARET SUSAN, lawyer; b. Lincoln, Nebr., Feb. 20, 1948; d. John Charles and Catherine (Sellers) A.; B.A. with distinction in Polit. Sci., U. Wis., Madison, 1970, M.A. in Scandinavian Studies (tuition scholarship, NDEA fellow), 1972, J.D. cum laude, 1976. Law clk. in Madison and Mpls., then Chgo., 1974-76; admitted to Wis. bar, 1977, Minn. bar, 1978; law clk. U.S. Dist. Ct., Mpls., 1977-78; mem. firm Faegre & Bensen, Mpls., 1978—. Mem. Am. Bar Assn., Minn. Bar Assn., Wis. Bar Assn., Hennepin County Bar Assn; Order of Coif. Note and comment editor U. Wis. Law Rev.; contbr. articles to profl. publs. Home: 221 Loring Way 210 W Grant St Minneapolis MN 55403 Office: 1300 Northwestern Bank Bldg Minneapolis MN 55402

ANGLE, STEPHEN WILLIAM, lawyer; b. Humansville, Mo., Mar. 10, 1948; s. William Milton and Barbara Kay (DeLozier) A.; B.S., U. Mo., Columbia, 1972, M.S., 1975; J.D., U. Mo., Kansas City, 1976; m. Denna Marie Garber, Dec. 13, 1969. Admitted to Mo. bar, 1977; city atty., Warrensburg, Mo., 1978-81; pres. firm Stephen W. Angle, Inc., Warrensburg, 1976—; sec. Grapevine Communications, Inc., Warrensburg, 1980—. Mem. Am. Bar Assn., Mo. Assn. Trial Attys., Assn. Trial Lawyers Am., Mo. Bar Assn., Phi Delta Phi, Phi Delta Kappa. Democrat. Methodist. Home: 809 S Maguire St Warrensburg MO 64093 Office: 105 W Market St Warrensburg MO 64093

ANGLEMIRE, JOYCE MARIE, nursing adminstr.; b. Joliet, Ill., Oct. 7, 1941; d. Peter Steve and Stephanie Mildred (Tomac) Maryanovich; grad. St. Joseph's Hosp. Sch. Nursing, 1962; m. Harold N. Anglemire, Sept. 14, 1963. Pediatric staff nurse St. Joseph's Hosp., Joliet, 1962-64, supr. nursing, 1972-73, coordinator inservice edn., 1973-74, asst. dir. nursing, 1974-78, asso. dir. nursing, 1978—; staff nurse Americana Health Center, 1965-67, dir. nursing, 1967-72. Mem. adv. bd. Joliet Jr. Coll. Nursing. Mem. Nat. League Nursing, Ill. Soc. Nursing Adminstrs. Roman Catholic. Office: 333 N Madison St Joliet IL 60435

ANGLIN, LEO WAYNE, educator; b. Goshen, Ind., Nov. 7, 1946; s. Leo Wayne and Annabelle (Swick) A.; B.S., Manchester Coll., 1969; M.S., Ind. U., Bloomington, 1972; Ph.D., U. Wis., Madison, 1975; m. Joyce Ann Shanahan, Aug. 17, 1969; 1 dau., Katherine Shanahan. Tchr., Elkhart (Ind.) Public Schs.; 1969-73; project asso. U. Wis., Madison, 1973-76; asso. prof. edn. Kent State U. (Ohio), 1976—; cons. Kirschner Assos., Inc., Washington, Sci. Research Assos., Chgo., various sch. dists.; trustee Midwest Tchr. Corps Network. Mem. Am. Edn. Research Assn., Assn. Supervision and Curriculum Devel., Nat. Council Tchrs. Math, Phi Delta Kappa. Contbr. articles to profl. jours. Home: 962 Middleburg Rd Kent OH 44240 Office: Sch Edn Kent State U Kent OH 44242

ANGUS, ROBERT CARLYLE, JR., med. clinic adminstr.; b. Grand Rapids, Mich., July 23, 1946; s. Robert Carlyle and Violet Ileen (Weidman-Deiters) A.; student Grand Rapids Community Coll., 1974; diploma respiratory therapy, St. Mary's Hosp., Grand Rapids Community Coll., 1974; diploma respiratory therapy, St. Mary's Hosp., Grand Rapids. Tech. dir. St. Mary's Hosp., 1970-73; staff therapist Grand Rapids Osteo. Hosp., 1973-74; head dept. respiratory therapy Hackley Hosp., Muskegon, Mich., 1974-76; dept. head cardiovascular lab. and pulmonary div. Am. Internat. Hosp., Zion, Ill., 1976-79; dir. non-invasive diagnostics Mauer Clinic, Zion, Ill., 1978-80; clinic adminstr., 1980—; also physician's asst. in medicine; cons., lectr. in field. Active local Big Bros./Big Sisters, Boy Scouts Am. Served with USAF, 1964-67; Vietnam. Fellow Am. Coll. Respiratory Therapists; mem. Nat. Bd. Respiratory Therapy, Am. Assn. Respiratory Therapy, Nat. Soc. Cardiopulmonary Technologists, Am. Cardiology Technologists Assn., Mich., Ill. socs. respiratory therapy, Ill. Soc. Cardiopulmonary Technologists. Lutheran. Home: 1106 Oak Forest Dr Zion IL 60099 Office: Mauer Clinic 1819 27th St Zion IL 60099

ANICHINI, FRANK JOHN, computer center exec.; b. Lucca, Italy, Oct. 12, 1943; s. Tarcisio Socrate and Celemntina (Paladini) A.; came to U.S., 1955, naturalized, 1963; student U. Ill., 1963, N.C. State U., 1965-67, DePaul U., 1968; A.A.S. in Bus., Elgin Community Coll., 1978; m. Nancy Jo Mrkacek, Sept. 6, 1969; children—Holly Teresa, Steven Vincent. Data processing specialist Playboy Inc., Chgo., 1968-69; data processing specialist, gen. mgr. Alesdan Info. Data Systems, Elk Grove Village, Ill., 1969-76; profl. employment cons., mgr. Computer Centre of Palatine (Ill.), 1976—; mgr., instr. Computer Centre, Inc., Arlington Heights, Ill., 1979—, now group mgr., Arlington Heights and Oak Brook. Served with USAF, 1964-68. Mem. Am. Mgmt. Assn., Nat. Assn. Personnel Cons.'s, Ill. Assn. Personnel Cons.'s. Roman Catholic. Home: 380 Grandview Ct Algonquin IL 60102 Office: Computer Centre Inc 85 W Algonquin Rd Arlington Heights IL 60005

ANICHINI, MARIO, painter; b. Lucca, Italy, Sept. 26, 1941; s. Tarcisio Socrate and Clementina (Paladini) A.; came to U.S., 1955, naturalized, 1963; student public schs., Chgo.; m. Mary Dolores Bernardini, Nov. 26, 1961; children—Mary Ellen, Mario Peter. One-man show: Kenosha (Wis.) Public Mus., 1975; exhibited at Artists/USA, 1977-80; represented in permanent collections: Kenosha Public Museum, Salem (Wis.) Consol. Grade Sch., 1st Nat. Bank of Antioch (Ill.); numerous pvt. collections; paintings include: Stone Age, 1973, Evolution, 1973, 20th Century, 1974, Paul Revere, 1975, Agony and Ecstasy, 1976, Self Portrait, 1977, Spirit of St. Louis, 1978, Perception of Dimension, 1980, Eleven O'Clock in the Afternoon, 1980, transfer of Energy, 1981. Recipient Gold medal Accademia Italia, 1980. Address: 12319 233d Ave Trevor WI 53179

ANNABLE, WILLIAM LAWRENCE, ophthalmologist; b. Grove City, Pa., Mar. 29, 1945; s. William Lawrence and Esther Elizabeth (Cole) A.; B.S. summa cum laude, U. Pitts., 1967; M.D., U. Pa., 1971; m. Mary Louise Mahar, Dec. 26, 1969; children—Gretchen, Raymond J. Intern, Univ. Hosps., Cleve., 1971-72, resident in surgery, 1972-73; fellow in biochemistry Case Western Res. U., 1973-74; resident in ophthalmology Univ. Hosp., Cleve., 1974-77; chief ophthalmology, dir. residency tng. Gorgas Hosp., Panama Canal Zone, 1977-79; asst. prof. ophthalmology Case Western Res. U. Sch. Medicine, Cleve., 1979—; cons. surgeon Cuyahoga County Hosp., Cleve. VA Hosp. Served to maj., U.S. Army, 1977-79. Am. Cancer Soc. fellow, 1975-76; NIH fellow, 1973-74. Mem. AMA, Am. Acad. Ophthalmology, Cleve. Ophthal. Soc., Cleve. Acad. Medicine, Phi Beta Kappa, Alpha Omega Alpha. Home: 2524 Lee Rd Cleveland Heights OH 44118 Office: 1611 S Green Rd Cleveland OH 44121

ANNIS, SPERO, govt. ofcl.; b. Hamilton, Ont., Can., Nov. 2, 1915; s. George and Vasilo (Smerneos) A.; student pub. schs., Tilbury, Ont.; m. Sylvia Jean Jeffrey, Oct. 22, 1943; children—John George, Laurie Jane Annis McQuaig. Asst. mgr. Tilbury (Ont.) Liquor Control Bd., 1943-57, auditor, Windsor and Peterborough, 1957-75, dist. supr., Kitchener-Waterloo, 1975-78, dist. supr., Peterborough, 1978—. Exec. mem. Western Counties Baseball Assn., 1949-54, sec.-treas., bus. mgr., 1954-61; sec.-treas. Ont. Baseball Assn., 1962-76, exec. mem., 1949-62; sec.-treas. Eastern Ont. Baseball Assn., 1964-67; exec. mem. Canadian Fedn. Amateur Baseball, 1967-73, sec.-treas., 1973-75. Recipient Plaque and medal Western Counties Baseball Assn., 1961, Achievement award Govt. Ont., 1969, Plaque, Ont. Baseball Assn., 1976. Anglican. Clubs: Masons (past master), Order Eastern Star (past patron), Liquor Control Bd. Ont., Quarter Centry.

ANNO, JAMES NELSON, scientist, educator; b. Niles, Ohio, Feb. 6, 1934; s. James Nelson and Opal Mae (Gentry) A.; m. Janet Winkel, June 12, 1955; children—James David, Sara Jennifer, Jefferson Nelson. B.S., Ohio State U., 1955, M.S., 1961, Ph.D., 1965. Technician, Battelle Meml. Inst., Columbus, Ohio, 1953-55, supr. research reactor, 1955-60, asst. chief applied nuclear physics div., 1960-65, asst. chief lubrication mechanics div., 1965-67, chief lubrication mechanics div., 1967-70; asso. prof. nuclear engrng. U. Cin., 1970-73, prof., 1973—; pres. Research Dynamics Inc., 1977—. Mem. Am. Phys. Soc., Am. Nuclear Soc., Masons, Sigma Xi, Phi Beta Kappa, Sigma Pi Sigma. Recipient Civic award Columbus Jr. C. of C., 1961; honored by Sat. Evening Post, 1961. Author: Encyclopedia of Draw Poker, 1973; (with J.A. Walowit) Modern Development in Lubrication Mechanics, 1975; Wave Mechanics for Engineers, 1976; Mechanics of Liquid Jets, 1977; contbr. articles to profl. jours. Home: 5882 Ropes Dr Cincinnati OH 45244 Office: 509 Old Chemistry Bldg Cincinnati OH 45221

ANNUNZIO, FRANK, congressman; b. Chgo., Jan. 12, 1915; B.S., M.Ed., DePaul U.; m. Angeline Alesia, Dec. 28, 1935; children—Jacqueline (Mrs. Sal Lato), Linda (Mrs. William O'Donnell), Susan (Mrs. Kevin Tynan). Asst. supr. Nat. Defense Tng. Program Austin Eve. Sch., Chgo.; legislative, ednl. dir. United Steelworkers of Am., Chgo.: mem. 89th-97th Congresses from 11th Dist. Ill. Dir. Ill. Dept. Labor; mem. adv. com. on Unemployment Compensation; mem. adv. com. to Ill. Indsl. Commn. on Health, Safety; mem. adv. bd. Cook County (Ill.) Health and Survey; chmn. Community Services Com.; mem. Chgo. Commn. on Human Relations. Gen. chmn. Villa Scalabrini Devel. Fund; v.p., lay adv. bd. Villa Scalabrini Italian Old People's Home. Mem. Catholic Youth Orgn. K.C. (4 Deg.). Club: City (Chgo.). Office: 2303 Rayburn Bldg Washington DC 20515

ANSALDO, OSCAR PICAR, physician; b. Davao City, Philippines, Jan. 15, 1937; came to U.S., 1964, naturalized, 1979; s. Genaro Salamat and Benigna Picar A.; student (Entrance scholar) U. Philippines, 1954-57; M.D., Far Eastern U., 1963; m. Lilia de la Paz, Jan. 29, 1966; children—Maria Vera, Jean Marie, Lisa Mae. Intern, Mercy Hosp., Hamilton, Ohio, 1964; resident in pathology Swedish Covenant Hosp., Cook County Hosp., Chgo., 1965-69; fellow in pathology Luth. Gen. Hosp., Park Ridge, Ill., 1970-71; staff physician Wis. VA Hosp., King, 1972-79, acting med. dir., 1979—; ind. med. reviewer nursing homes Wis., 1976-80; physician adv. Wis. PSRO, 1976-80; physician cons. Wis. Div. Health, 1980—; med. dir. Wis. Vets. Home, King, 1980—. Diplomate Am. Bd. Family Practice. Fellow Am. Acad. Family Practice; mem. AMA. (Physician's Recognition award 1981), Wis. Med. Soc., Waupaca Med. Soc. Roman Catholic. Home: PO Box 306 King WI 54946 Office: Wis VA Home King WI 54946

ANSBRO, PETER MICHAEL, automobile co. exec.; b. Mt. Vernon, N.Y., Sept. 20, 1938; s. Harold D. and Margaret C. (O'Carolan) A.; B.S. in Elec. Engring., N.Y. U., 1962, M.S. in Elec. Engring., 1964; M.B.A., Mich. State U., 1979; m. Elizabeth C. Smith, Sept. 14, 1963; children—Peter, Kathleen, Jennifer, Megan. Project engr. microelectronics div. Philco-Ford Corp., Lansdale, Pa., 1961-65, supr. automotive electronics Lansdale div., 1965-71; mgr. entertainment systems devel., elec./electronics div. Ford Motor Co., Dearborn, Mich., 1976-78; mgr. advanced engine electronics, elec./electronics div., 1979—. Pres. St. Colettes Men's Club, 1973, 74. Mem. Tau Beta Pi, Eta Kappa Nu. Democrat. Roman Catholic. Home: 18750 Levan St Livonia MI 48152 Office: Ford Motor Co 21500 Oakwood Blvd Box 2053 Dearborn MI 48121

ANSETT, JOHN FREDERICK (JACK), book wholesaler; b. Cornwell Heights, Pa., Sept. 26, 1921; s. Russell L. and Dorothy Martha (Bockius) A.; B.A., Valparaiso U., 1948; postgrad. Northwestern U., 1950-51, Mich. State U., 1968; m. Lois Helen Grote, Nov. 14, 1948; children—John Frederick, Timothy G., Karen L., Kathleen B. With Internat. Packers Ltd., Chgo., 1948-51; treas. Internat. Packers Can. Ltd., Toronto, Ont., 1951-56, pres., 1956-59; dir. mktg. Armour & Co., Ltd. (U.K.), London, 1959-62; pres. Book House, Inc., Jonesville, Mich., 1962—. Served with USAAF, 1942-45; ETO. Mem. ALA, Am. Booksellers Assn. Republican. Lutheran. Home: 105 N Walnut St Jonesville MI 49250 Office: 208 W Chicago St Jonesville MI 49250

ANSHUTZ, WILLIAM MAURICE, radiologist; b. Somerton, Ohio, Sept. 16, 1917; s. Harvey and Atrella (Tomlinson) A.; A.B., Ohio State U., 1942; M.D., 1948; m. Betty Millisor, Sept. 10, 1944; children—Wendy Lee, Cathy Jo. Intern Lima (Ohio) Meml. Hosp., 1949; resident in radiology Henry Ford Hosp., Detroit, 1956-59; gen. practice medicine, Ohio, 1953-56; practice medicine specializing in radiology, Ind., 1959—; mem. staffs St. Francis Hosp., Beech Grove, Ind., 1959-61; radiologist Meth. Hosp., Indpls., 1961-69, Witham Meml. Hosp., Lebanon, Ind., 1959-61, 70, Clinton County Hosp., Frankfort, Ind., 1969-79. Served with U.S. Army, 1942-44; USAF, 1951-53. Decorated Bronze Star. Mem. AMA, Radiol. Soc. N.Am., Am. Coll. Radiology, Ind. Roentgen Soc. Republican. Methodist. Home and office: 6340 Breamore Rd Indianapolis IN 46220

ANSPACH, HERBERT KEPHART, appliance co. exec.; b. Ada, Ohio, Sept. 3, 1926; s. Eldred W. and Della (Kephart) A.; B.S. in M.E., U. Wis., 1947; J.D., U. Mich., 1952; m. Elizabeth McKenzie, June 5, 1952; 1 dau., Heather. Admitted to Ohio bar, 1953, Mich. bar, 1953; indsl. and devel. engr. Goodyear Tire & Rubber, St. Mary's, Ohio, 1947-49; labor. relations rep. Kaiser Motores, Willow Run, Mich., 1953, supr. indsl. relations, 1953; patent examiner U.S. Dept. Commerce, Washington, 1955; patent atty. Whirlpool Corp., Benton Harbor, Mich., 1955-57, dir. patent sect. 1957-59, asst. sec., asst. gen. counsel, 1960-67, v.p. personnel, 1967-74, pres., chief operating officer, 1977—; exec. v.p. Inglis Ltd., Toronto, 1975, pres., chief operating officer, 1975-76, chmn. bd., chief exec. officer, 1976-77. Served with U.S. Navy, 1944-46. Clubs: Met., Union League (Chgo.); Toronto; Point O'Woods (Benton Harbor). Office: 2000 US 33 N Benton Harbor MI 49022

ANTHONY, MICHAEL JAMES, policeman; b. Chgo., Nov. 2, 1950; s. William Richard and Mildred (Rodgers) A.; B.A., Chgo. State U., 1979, M.S., 1980; cert. in police sci. cum laude, Chgo. Police Acad., 1976; married; children—Michael James, Angela, Deborah, Marcus. Investigator, Ill. Service Bur., Chgo., 1971-72; campus police officer U. Chgo., 1972-76; police officer Chgo. Police Dept., 1976-79, detective, 1979-81, dir. security and campus police, 1980—; instr. Chgo. Police Dept., 1979-80; cons. in field. Served with U.S. Army, 1968-71. Mem. Ill. Police Assn., Confedn. Police, Ill. Assn. for Hosp. Security. Office: 707 N Fairbanks Ct Chicago IL 60611

ANTHONY, ROWLAND BARNEY, JR., mfg. co. exec.; b. Chgo., Aug. 31, 1918; s. Rowland B. and Harriet (Pietzsch) A.; student DePauw U., 1937-38, Ill. Inst. Tech., 1939, Grinell Coll., 1940; m. Phyllis Carleton, Dec. 26, 1942; children—Pamela Anthony Cummins, Stephen Carleton. With purchasing dept. Montgomery Ward & Co., Chgo., 1940; asst. sales mgr. Chgo.-Wilcox Mfg. Co., South Holland, Ill., 1945-50, treas., dir., 1951, pres., treas., dir., 1952—, chmn. bd. dirs., 1976—; dir. Smith Victor Corp., Griffith, Ind.; dir., pres. Electric-Aire Corp., South Holland, 1970—; dir. Glenwood (Ill.) Bank. Bd. dirs. Ingalls Meml. Hosp., Harvey, Ill., 1971—; chmn. S. Suburban YMCA, 1972—. Served to lt. comdr. USNR, 1940-46. Mem. Am. Petroleum Inst., Fluid Sealing Assn., Soc. Automotive Engrs. Clubs: Michigan City (Ind.) Yacht; New Buffalo (Mich.) Yacht, Flossmoor (Ill.) Country. Home: 2304 Vardon Ln Flossmoor IL 60422 Office: 16930 State St South Holland IL 60473

ANTOINE, ROBERT FRANK, food co. exec.; b. Sheboygan, Wis., June 8, 1927; s. Alfred F. and Olivia M. (Thill) A.; B.A., Beloit Coll., 1950; m. Jane Staniforth, Nov. 17, 1951; children—Kim, Bret. Mem. sales staff Procter & Gamble, Green Bay, Wis., 1950-51; mdse. mgr. consumer products Am. Can Co., Greenwich, Conn., 1951-67; v.p. mktg. Beatrice Foods, Oconomowoc, Wis., 1967-73; pres. Green Bay Food Co. subs. Dean Food Co., Green Bay, 1973—; group mktg. v.p. Dean Food Co., 1979—; dir. 1st Wis. Bank of Green Bay. Bd. dirs. Jr. Achievement; trustee Beloit Coll. Served with U.S. Army, 1945-47. Mem. Pickle Packers Internat. (pres.), Wis. Mfrs. and Commerce (dir., exec. com.). Unitarian. Clubs: Rotary (past pres.), Oneida Golf and Riding. Home: 3120 Waubenoor Dr Green Bay WI 54301 Office: Green Bay Food Co 857 School Pl Green Bay WI 54303

ANTONIC, JAMES PAUL, internat. mktg. cons.; b. Milw., Mar. 29, 1943; s. George Paul and Betti Ware (Littler) A.; B.S. in Metallurgy, U. Wis., 1964; M.B.A., Boston U., 1976; m. Irene Robson, Dec. 26, 1970; 1 son by previous marriage, Glenn. Owner JPA Supply and Warehouse Co., Milw., 1966-68; product mgr., market mgr. Delta Oil Products, Milw., 1968-74; v.p. internat. ops., Brussels, 1974-76; pres. Internat. Market Devel. Group, Barrington, Ill., 1976—; v.p., dir. J & M, Ltd., Okazaki, Japan, Japan Market Devel. Co., Ltd., Kariya, Japan; lectr. Cast Metals Inst., Am. Mgmt. Assn., Harper Coll., Elgin Coll. Served with U.S. Army, 1964-66. Mem. Licensing Execs. Soc., Internat. Trade Club Chgo. Episcopalian. Home: 9612 Surrey Ln Barrington Hills IL 60010 Office: PO Box 751 Barrington IL 60010

ANURAS, SINN, gastroenterologist; b. Bangkok, Thailand, Apr. 6, 1941; s. Tiang and Ratana (Suppipat) A.; came to U.S., 1967; M.D., Chulalongkorn U., Thailand, 1966; m. Jitra Suppamongkol, Aug. 8, 1969; children—Piyawan, Julia, Sandy. Intern, Resurrection Hosp., Chgo., 1967; resident in internal medicine VA Hosp., Long Beach, Calif., 1968-70; asst. prof. medicine U. Iowa, Iowa City, 1974-80, asso. prof., 1980—. Diplomate Am. Bd. Internal Medicine. Fellow A.C.P.; mem. Am. Gastroenterol. Assn. Buddhist. Research on intestinal motility, clin. liver disease. Home: 55 Arbury Dr Iowa City IA 52240 Office: University of Iowa Iowa City IA 52242

ANVARIPOUR, M.A., lawyer; b. Tehran, Iran, Jan. 23, 1935; s. Ahmed and Monir (Georgie) A.; LL.B., U. Tehran, 1956; B.S., U. San Francisco, 1959; student U. Calif. Hastings Coll. Law, San Francisco; J.D., Ill. Inst. Tech.-Chgo. Kent Coll. Law, 1973; m. Guilda Eshtehardi, Mar. 31, 1978; 1 son, Cyrus Ramsey; 1 dau. by previous marriage, Sandra Monir. Came to U.S., 1957. Asst. field dir. Am. Friends of Middle East, Inc., Iran, 1962-64, field dir., 1964-66; asst. dean students, dean internat. students and faculty affairs Ill. Inst. Tech., Chgo., 1966-81; admitted to Ill. bar, 1973, also fed. cts.; practiced in Chgo., 1973—, ednl. and legal adviser Consulate gen. Iran, Chgo., 1973-80; aux. lawyer NAACP, Chgo., 1973-74; lectr. immigration and law seminar Ill. Inst. Tech.-Chgo.-Kent Coll. Law Sch., 1974. Mem. Am., Iran-Am. (sec.-gen. 1964-66), Ill., Chgo. bar assns., Iran Am. Alumni Assn. (sec. 1964-66), Nat. Assn. Fgn. Student Affairs (Ill. chmn. 1968-69), U. Tehran, U. San Francisco, Idaho State U. (hon.), Ill. Inst. Tech., Chgo.-Kent Coll. Law alumni assns., Am. Immigration Lawyers Assn. (sec.-treas. 1976-78, v.p. 1978-80, pres. 1980-81), Phi Delta Phi. Club: Armour Faculty (pres. 1977-78). Home: 990 N Lake Shore Dr Chicago IL 60611 Office: 20 N Clark St Chicago IL 60602

APA, ALBERT ALEX, assn. exec.; b. Chgo., June 5, 1921; s. Michael and Rose (Tenuta) A.; student schools Chgo.; m. Betty J. Jones, Nov. 6, 1949; 1 dau., Candice Sue Apa Kvitek. Supr. Stewart Warner Corp., 1939-42; sgt. Chgo. Police Dept., 1947-79; exec. dir. Ill. Local Govtl. Law Enforcement Officers Tng. Bd., Springfield, 1979—; chmn. Police of Ill., 1975-78. Pres., Chgo. Police Pension Protective Assn., 1967-78, trustee, 1978-79; mem. Gov.'s Arson Adv. Bd. Served with U.S. Army, 1942-46. Decorated Bronze Star with 3 oak leaf clusters, Purple Heart. Named Man of Year, Chgo. Patrolmen's Assn., 1973; recipient achievement award Ill. Fraternal Order of Police, 1978, Ill. Sheriff's Assn., 1980. Mem. Ill. Police Assn., Internat. Assn. Chiefs of Police, Nat. Assn. State Dirs. of Law Enforcement Tng., Am. Soc. Tng. and Devel. Roman Catholic. Clubs: Fraternal Order of Police, Exchange of Springfield. Author: Handbook on Pensions, 1964; contbr. legis. articles to Ill. Police Jour. Office: 524 S Second St Suite 400 Springfield IL 62706

APILADO, MYRON, univ. adminstr.; b. Chgo., May 18, 1933; s. Inosencio Tadina and Ruth Moselle (Mays) A.; B.A., U. Md., 1971; M.A., Ball State U., 1973; Ed.D., U. S.D., 1976; m. Sherri Ann Mitchell, Oct. 21, 1972; children—Mariano, Kea, Kelli, Anthony, Adam. Mem. exec. com. Community Counseling Program, Torrejon, Spain, 1972; chmn. Ednl. Grad. Orgn. U. S.D., 1974, instr., 1975, asst. prof., 1976; dean for student devel. Peru (Nebr.) State Coll., 1976—; asso. editor AIM Mag., 1975—. Pres., Nemaha County Mental Health Assn., 1980—; mem. adv. com. Region V Mental Health, Alcoholism and Drug Abuse Program, 1981-82. Served with USAF, 1953-73. Decorated Bronze Star. Certified sch. psychologist, Iowa. Mem. Am. Psychol. Assn., Am. Personnel and Guidance Assn., Phi Delta Kappa.

Home: 601 Nebraska Ave Peru NE 68421 Office: Peru State Coll Peru NE 68421

APKE, THOMAS JOSEPH, univ. basketball coach; b. Cin., July 16, 1943; s. Jerome George and Mary Anne (Thuis) A.; B.A., Creighton U., 1965; M.Ed., U. Cin., 1967; m. Eileen F. Blazek, June 26, 1970; children—Michael Steven, Karin Stephanie. Tchr., coach McNicholas High Sch., Cin., 1966-68; asst. basketball coach Creighton U., Omaha, 1968-74, athletic dir., 1974-80, basketball coach, 1974—; mem. basketball rules com., Olympic player Selection com. Nat. Collegiate Athletic Assn. Hon. state chmn. Nat. Heart Assn.'s Run for Life, 1978-79; hon. state chmn. fund dr. Diabetes Assn., 1979. Named Dist. coach of year Nat. Assn. Basketball Coaches, 1978. Mem. Nat. Assn. Basketball Coaches, Nebr. High Sch. Coaches Assn. Roman Catholic. Office: 2400 California St Omaha NE 68178

APKING, WILLIAM TAPPAN, banker; b. Daykin, Nebr., Aug. 31, 1933; s. George F. and Ruth E. (Tappan) A.; student U. Nebr., 1951-58; m. Sharon Anderson, July 3, 1958; children—David Tappan, Elizabeth Ann. With State Bank of Alexandria (Nebr.), 1958—, pres., chmn. bd., 1972—; dir. Packers Nat. Bank, Omaha. County chmn. Republican party, 1960-78; mem. Rep. state central com., 1975-77, mem. exec. com., 1977-79; chmn. Alexandria Village Bd., 1960-80; mem. Alexandria Sch. Bd., 1960-64, Thayer County Sch. Re-orgn. Com., 1974-78; bd. dirs. UN Found., 1979, Nebr. Polit. Action Council, Vision 17. Served with USN, 1953-57. Mem. Nebr. Bankers Assn., Thayer County Bankers Assn., Thayer County Livestock Feeders Assn., Farm Bur. Clubs: Nebr., Fairbury Country. Home: 314 W 5th St Alexandria NE 68303 Office: State Bank of Alexandria Alexandria NE 68303

APPELSON, WALLACE BERTRAND, coll. adminstr.; b. Bklyn., June 9, 1930; B.S., N.Y. U., 1951, M.A., 1952; Ed.D., Columbia U., 1959. Chief X-ray technician Samaritan Hosp., Bklyn., 1951-52; tchr. art White Plains (N.Y.) public schs., 1954-57; research asst. Inst. Adminstrv. Research, Columbia U., 1957-58; asst. prof. ednl. adminstrn. Rutgers U., 1958-60; coordinator terminal program N.J. State Dept. Higher Edn., 1960-65; dean acad. affairs Bucks County Community Coll., Newtown, Pa., 1965-70; pres. Atlantic Community Coll., Mays Landing, N.J., 1970-73; dean faculty LaGuardia Community Coll. CUNY, 1973-76; pres. Truman Coll., Chgo., 1976—. Pres. bd. dirs. North Bus. and Indsl. Council Chgo.; bd. dirs. Ravenswood Hosp. Med. Center, Chgo., Uptown Chgo. Commn. Served with U.S. Army, 1952-54. Mem. Am. Assn. Sch. Adminstrs., Am. Assn. Higher Edn., Am. Assn. Community and Jr. Colls., Uptown C. of C. (dir.), Phi Delta Kappa, Kappa Delta Pi. Editor: Associated Public School System Yearbook, 1958; Toward Higher Education Newsletter, N.J. Div. Higher Education, 1960-65; contbr. articles to profl. jours. Office: 1145 W Wilson Ave Chicago IL 60640

APPLEBY, LESLIE VERE, architect; b. Wichita, Kans., Feb. 17, 1931; s. Vere Griffith and Marie Margaret (McCoy) A.; student Wichita State U., 1949-50; B.Arch., Kans. State U., 1958; children—Vickie Lee Appleby Jones, Bryan Kent, Stephen L. Thyault, Linda G. Thyault; m. 2d, Louise A. Giersch, June 25, 1976. Architect William R. Brown, Ponca City, Okla., 1958-63; architect, mng. partner Shaver & Co., Salina, Kans., 1963-71; architect, sr. partner Appleby & Marsh, Wichita, Emporia, and Salina, 1971—; pres. Lamco Co., Salina, 1972—, 215 Group, Salina, 1974—. Pres. Okla. Jr. Miss Inc., Ponca City, 1961-63. Registered architect Kans., Okla., Mo., Iowa, S.D., Nebr., Tex., Tenn., Nat. Council Archtl. Registration Bds. Mem. AIA (corp.), Kans. State U. Alumni Assn., Salina C. of C., Emporia C. of C. Episcopalian. Elk. Club: Salina Country. Home: 647 Rockview Rd Salina KS 67401 Office: 112 N Santa Fe St Salina KS 67401 also 200 E 1st St Wichita KS 67202 also 15 W 5th St Emporia KS 66801

APPLEGATE, DOUGLAS, Congressman; b. Steubenville, Ohio, Mar. 27, 1928; grad. high sch.; m. Betty Jean Engstrom, 1950; children—Kirk, David. Engaged in real estate bus.; mem. Ohio Ho. of Reps., 1961-69, Ohio Senate, 1969-77; mem. 95th-97th Congresses from 18th Ohio Dist. Mem. Steubenville Community Club, Catholic Community Center, Polish Nat. Alliance. Democrat. Presbyterian. Clubs: Elks, Eagles, Polish Athletic. Office: Room 435 Cannon House Office Bldg Washington DC 20515

APPLEGATE, SARA JOAN, ins. co. exec.; b. Knoxville, Tenn., Aug. 2, 1938; d. Kenneth C. and Elizabeth Winsor (Snead) A.; B.S. in Bus. Adminstrn., Ohio U., 1960; postgrad. U. Cin., 1962. With Hartford Ins. Group, 1960—, property and package underwriting mgr., Cleve., 1974-77, asst. gen. mgr., Milw., 1977—; tchr. profl. courses. Active Cystic Fibrosis Assn., Jerry Lewis Telethon. Mem. C.P.C.U. Soc. (dir. Milw. chpt. 1978—), Ins. Women Milw. (pres.; named Ins. Woman of Yr. 1980), Am. Mgmt. Soc., Nat. Assn. Ins. Women. Home: 4912F S 19th St Milwaukee WI 53221 Office: 111 E Wisconsin Ave Milwaukee WI 53202

APPLETON, ARTHUR I., corp. exec.; b. Chgo., 1915; grad. Dartmouth Coll., 1936, postgrad. Amos Tuck Sch., 1936. Chmn. bd., pres. Appleton Electric Co., Chgo., Oil Corp. Am.; owner Appleton Oil Co., Bridlewood Farm; dir. Gulfstream Park Racing Assn. Office: 1701 W Wellington Ave Chicago IL 60657*

APPOLD, JAMES MARTIN, baking co. exec.; b. Saginaw, Mich., Apr. 10, 1939; s. Martin J. and Louise S. Appold; B.S., Gen. Motors Inst., 1962; M.B.A., U. Toledo, 1977; M.S. in Indsl. Engring., 1978; m. Patricia J. Kirchner, Aug. 20, 1960; children—Jonn, Karen, Melinda, Caitlin, Andrew. Engr., maintenance foreman, maintenance dept. Chevrolet Saginaw (Mich.) Grey Iron, 1957-66; sales engr. Honeywell, Inc., Saginaw, 1966-68; plant supv./engring. mgr. A T. Ferrell & Co., Saginaw, 1968-75; mgr. tech. services The Andersons, Maumee, Ohio, 1975-82; v.p. gen. mgr. Consolidated Biscuit Co., McComb, Ohio, 1982—. Mem. Grain Elevator and Processing Soc. (chmn. environmental com.), Am. Soc. Agrl. Engrs. (mem. air pollution com.), Am. Inst. Plant Engrs., Air Pollution Control Assn., Internat. Maintenance Inst., Nat. Grain and Feed Assn. (mem. energy com.). Republican. Lutheran. Home: 2049 Scottwood Ave Toledo OH 43620 Office: PO Box 847 McComb OH 45858

AQUINO, ROSITA NG, physician; b. Subic, Zambales, Philippines, Apr. 8, 1940; d. Pio and Heng Fong (Kuan) Aquino; came to U.S., 1968, naturalized, 1980; M.D., Far Eastern U., 1966; m. Alexander Wu, Nov. 15, 1975; children—Sabrina Han-Rine, Clarissa Han-Yin. Intern, Niagara Falls (N.Y.) Meml. Med. Center, 1968; resident, St. Joseph Mercy Hosp., U. Mich. Med. Center, Ann Arbor, Mich.; dir. Maternal Infant Care project, Crittenton Gen. Hosp., Detroit, 1973-74, Henry Ford Hosp., Detroit, 1974-79; practice medicine specializing in obstetrics and gynecology, Canton, Mich., 1979—; mem. staff St. Mary's Hosp., Livonia, Mich. Diplomate Am. Bd. Obstetrics and Gynecology. Fellow Am. Coll. Obstetricians and Gynecologists; mem. AMA, Mich. Med. Soc., Mich. Obstetrics and Gynecol. Soc., Wayne County Med. Soc. Roman Catholic. Office: 8594 Canton Center Rd Canton MI 48187

ARABIA, PAUL, lawyer; b. Pittsburg, Kans., Mar. 28, 1938; s. John K. and Melva A. (Jones) A.; B.A. in Speech, Kans. State Coll., 1962; J.D. (fellow) with honors, Washburn U., 1966. Admitted to Kans. bar, 1966; law office and bus. investments, Wichita, Kans., 1966—. Mem. Wichita Traffic Commn., 1966-71, chmn., 1968-69. Mem. Kans., Wichita, Sedgwick County bar assns., Phi Sigma Epsilon (dir. 1962-72), Phi Alpha Delta. Office: 120 S Market St Suite 518 Wichita KS 67202

ARADAS, STEPHEN EFSTRATIOS, county planning exec.; b. Peabody, Mass., Aug. 28, 1928; s. Efstratios Stephen and Barbara Asterope (Kanaracus) A.; student New Eng. Sch. Art, 1948-51; B.A., Youngstown U., 1967; postgrad. in anthropology U. Mass., 1968-70; M.U.A., Boston U., 1976; m. Barbara Jane Sunderlin, July 25, 1959; children—Michael, Stephanie. Sr. planner Merrimack Valley Regional Planning Commn., Haverhill, Mass., 1970-74, asst. dir., 1974-75, dir., 1975-77; dir. McHenry County (Ill.) Dept. Planning, 1977—; mem. planning faculty McHenry County Coll., 1978-80, Northeastern U. Ill., Chgo., 1979-80. Sec. bd. dirs. McHenry County Youth Orch., 1980—; mem. McHenry County Energy Conservation Commn., 1981. Mem. Crystal Lake C. of C. (affordable housing com. 1979—), Am. Planning Assn. (sect. rep. 1979-81, exec. com. Met. Chgo. sect. 1981-83). Greek Orthodox. Active in agrl. lands preservation. Office: 2200 N Seminary Ave Woodstock IL 60098

ARADO, WILLIAM NICHOLAS, business exec.; b. Chgo., Oct. 9, 1945; s. Raymond Francis and Florence Elisabeth (Losch) A.; A.A., Chgo. City Coll., 1967; B.S., So. Ill. U., 1969; m. Mary Anne Gorgos, July 24, 1971; children—Jill Maria, Scott William, Pamela Margret. Sales rep. Mobil Oil Corp., N.Y.C., 1969-73, sr. mktg. rep., 1973-75, sales analyst, 1975-78; in wholesale petroleum sales Tosco Corp., 1978—; pres. Double A Enterprises Inc., residential rentals, Bristal, Wis. Mem. Am. Mktg. Assn., Chgo. Oilmens Assn., Midwest Petroleum Assn., Ill. Petroleum Marketers Assn., Pi Sigma Epsilon. Democrat. Club: Evansville Petroleum. Home: 706 Old Hunt Rd Fox River Grove IL 60021 Office: Tosco Corp 1 Allen Center Suite 3333 Houston TX 77002

ARAI, HAROLD YUTAKA, orthodontist; b. Los Angeles, Feb. 1, 1936; s. Akira B. and Joan Fusako (Fujisawa) A.; B.A., Ohio Wesleyan U., 1957; D.D.S., Loyola U., 1961, M.S., 1966; m. Irene Shigihara, Aug. 27, 1961; children—David Andrew, Shaunna Lynn. Pvt. practice orthodontics, Park Ridge, Ill., 1967—; Lectr. Loyola U., 1966-73, 77, Ind. U., 1975, Emory U., 1975, La. State U., 1977. Pres., U. Chgo. Jarabak Orthodontic Found., 1975-76; v.p. Denver Orthodontic Summer Seminar, 1974, pres., 1975-76; lectr. Fox River Valley Dental Soc. meeting, Greater Miami Midwinter Dental meeting, 1977, Mid-Atlantic Soc. Orthodontists, 1978, Pacific Coast Soc. Orthodontists, 1978, Rocky Mountain Provocative Discussion Seminar, 1979, Cleve. Soc. Orthodontists, 1979, Colo. Orthodontic Assn., 1979. Served to capt. USAF, 1961-63. Mem. ADA (orthodontic chmn. sci. sessions 1974—), Japanese Civic Assn., Am. Assn. Orthodontics (clinician, chmn. round table programs 1979 meeting), Eastern Orthodontic Study Club, Midwestern Orthodontic Soc., Japanese Orthodontic Soc., Southwestern Soc. Orthodontists, Japanese Citizens League, Blue Key, Alpha Sigma Phi, Omicron Delta Kappa, Omicron Kappa Upsilon, Delta Sigma Delta. Author: Welcome to the World of Orthodontics, 1973. Home: 2026 Abbotsford Dr Inverness IL 60010 Office: 101 S Washington Park Ridge IL 60068

ARAIN, MOHAMMED AKRAM, energy corp. exec.; b. Mehrabpur, Pakistan, Mar. 1, 1950; came to U.S., 1975, naturalized, 1978; s. Mohammad Yassen and Kashnood (Akhtar) A.; B.S., U. Sind., Jamshoro, Pakistan, 1973; M.S., Drexel U., 1976; m. Rahila Akram, Nov. 2, 1979. Elec. engr. N.R.T. Corp., Haripur Hazara, Pakistan, 1973-75; research asst. Drexel U., Phila., 1975-78; area field elec. engr. Los Angeles power div. Bechtel Power Corp., Palo Verde, Ariz., 1978-81; area elec. engr. Daniel Internat. Corp., Callaway Nuclear Power Sta., Fulton, Mo., 1981—. Mem. IEEE, Power Engring. Soc., Indsl. Applications Engring. Soc., Tau Beta Pi, Eta Kappa Nu. Moslem. Home: 407 N Sequoia St Columbia MO 65201 Office: Callaway Nuclear Power Sta Daniel Internat Corp PO Box 108 Fulton MO 65251

ARAKAWA, KASUMI, physician, educator; b. Toyohashi, Japan, Feb. 19, 1926; s. Masumi and Fayuko (Hattori) A.; M.D., Tokyo Med. Coll., 1953; m. June Hope Takahara, Aug. 27, 1956; children—Jane Riet, Kenneth Luke, Amy Kathryn. Came to U.S., 1954, naturalized, 1963. Intern Iowa Methodist Hosp., Des Moines, 1954-56; resident U. Kans. Med. Center, Kansas City, 1956-58; practice medicine specializing in anesthesiology; Kansas City, Kans., 1958—; instr. anesthesiology U. Kans. Med. Center, Kansas City, 1961-64, asst. prof., 1964-71, asso. prof., 1971-77, prof., 1977—, chmn. dept. anesthesiology, 1977—; clin. asso. prof. U. Mo.-Kansas City Sch. Dentistry, 1973—. Bd. dirs. Kansas City Health Care, Inc. Fulbright scholar, 1954. Recipient Outstanding Faculty award Student AMA, 1970. Diplomate Am. Bd. Anesthesiology. Fellow Am. Coll. Anesthesiology; mem. Asso. Univ. Anesthesiologists (sec.-treas. 1969—), Acad. Anesthesiology, Japan-Am. Soc. Midwest (v.p. 1965, 71). Home: 7917 El Monte St Shawnee Mission KS 66208 Office: Univ Med Center 39 Rainbow St Kansas City KS 66103

ARASMITH, NEIL HARVEY, state senator, ins. agt.; b. Jewell, Kans., Feb. 23, 1930; s. James H. and Jessie M. (Fields) A.; B.A., U. Kans., 1951; m. Donna Schindler, July 1, 1951; children—David, Jeffrey, Susan, Timothy. Adjustor, Mason Investment Co., Salina, Kans., 1951-54, br. mgr., Garden City, Kans., 1954, Philipsburg, Kans., 1955-68; with Interstate Securities, Philipsburg, 1968-77; ins. agt. Nat. Life Ins. Co., Phillipsburg, 1977—; mem. Kans. State Senate, 1972—. Past chmn. bd. Phillips County Hosp., Phillipsburg Community Found. Served in USAF, 1951. Mem. C. of C. (past dir.). Republican. Methodist. Clubs: Elks, Masons, Shriners. Address: Phillipsburg KS 67661

ARBAUGH, ROBERT BRUCE, data processing exec.; b. Charleston, W.Va., Dec. 31, 1948; s. William Harry and Peggy Jane (Pitts) A.; B.S. in Elec. Engring., Milw. Sch. Engring., 1971; postgrad. (Asso. Western Univs. fellow) U. Ariz., 1971-73. With PolySystems, Inc., Chgo., 1973—, dir. data center, 1974—, v.p. ops., 1978—. Mem. IEEE, Am. Nuclear Soc. Episcopalian. Club: Lake Shore (Chgo.). Office: 400 55 E Jackson Blvd Chicago IL 60604

ARBESMAN, GARY JOHN, mfg. ofcl.; b. Danbury, Conn., Dec. 2, 1943; s. Kenneth A. and Marilyn M. (Miller) A.; A.A.S. in Chem. Engring., Norwalk (Conn.) State Tech. Inst., 1963; B.S. in Mktg., U. Bridgeport (Conn.), 1970; M.B.A. in Mktg., U. New Haven, 1976; m. Heather Jean Mitchell, May 28, 1966; children—Gordon, Kendra. Project mgr. R/M Friction Materials Corp., Bridgeport, 1970-74; mktg. analyst Flygt Corp., Norwalk, 1974-77, mgr. agrl. pump sales, 1977-78, br. mgr., St. Louis, 1979-81, dist. mgr., 1981—. Served with Army NG, 1964-70. Mem. Am. Mktg. Assn. Methodist. Address: 16010 Meadow Oak Dr Chesterfield MO 63017

ARBIT, HARVEY MARVIN, pharm. co. exec.; b. Schenectady, Jan. 17, 1947; s. Joseph Abraham and Ruth (Sherman) A.; B.S. in Pharmacy, Union U., 1970; Pharm.D., Duquesne U., 1972; M.B.A., No. Ill. U., 1979; m. Judith Sue Engel, May 13, 1971; 1 dau., Julie Pamela. Student pharmacist Ellis Hosp., Schenectady, 1967-70; staff pharmacist Homer G. Phillips Hosp., St. Louis, 1970, Mercy Hosp., Pitts., 1970-71, pharmacy resident, 1971-72; sr. clin. research coordinator Travenol Labs., Inc., Deerfield, Ill., 1972-76, supr. regulatory documentation, 1976-79, mgr. regulatory affairs and clin. devel. Hyland Diagnostics, div. Travenol Labs., Inc., 1979—. Bd. dirs. Arlington Heights Community Concert Band. Fellow Am. Coll. Apothecaries (asso.); mem. Am. Pharm. Assn., Am. Soc. Hosp. Pharmacists, AMA (spl. affiliate), Regulatory Affairs Profls. Soc., Assos. Clin. Pharmacology, Rho Pi Phi. Jewish. Clubs: Shriners, Masons, Scottish Rite. Contbr. articles to profl. publs. Office: 1 Baxter Pkwy Deerfield IL 60015

ARBOGAST, FRANCES MARGARETTE, scientist; b. Madisonville, Ky., Nov. 8, 1920; d. Edgar O. and Emma A.; A.B., Western Ky. Tchrs. Coll., 1942; B.S., 1947; M.S., U. Ky., 1950; postgrad. U. Evansville, 1953-54. Tchr., Sturgis (Ky.) High Sch., 1942-43; chem. technologist Chrysler Evansville Ordnance Plant, 1943-44; asst. to chief chemist Beveridge Paper Co., Indpls., 1944-45; chem. technologist Chrysler Evansville Ordnance Plant, 1945; instr. U. Ky., 1947-50, parasitologist, 1950-51; scientist, Mead Johnson Co., Evansville, Ind., 1955—. Mem. AAAS, Am. Bus. Womens Assn., Bus. and Profl. Women, DAR. Presbyterian. Home: 2109 E Gum St Evansville IN 47714 Office: 2404 Pennsylvania St Evansville IN 47721

ARBOR, AUTRY VICTORIA, sch. adminstr.; b. Hughes, Ark., June 23, 1923; d. Albert Morris and Delilah (Crowell) Brown; B.A., LeMoyne Coll., 1947; postgrad. DePaul U., 1949, Chgo. State U., 1972-75; m. Jesse W. Arbor, July 12, 1948; children—Jesse, Deborah Lois, Brenda Melanie. Tchr., Memphis Public Sch. System, 1948-49; tchr. Chgo. Public Schs., 1949-50; tchr. Sch. Dist. 169, East Chicago Heights, Ill., 1960-75, prin. Tidye A. Phillips Elem. Sch., 1975—, coordinator Primary Academic Center, designer dist. flag. Founder, pres. LeMoyne Coll. Edn. Club, 1946. Mem. Assn. Supervision and Curriculum Devel., Ill. Women Adminstrs., Nat. Alliance Black Sch. Educators. Democrat. Roman Catholic. Home: 8922 S Ridgeland Ave Chicago IL 60617 Office: 1401 E 14th Pl East Chicago Heights IL 60411

ARBUCKLE, DOROTHY FRY (MRS. LLOYD ARBUCKLE), business exec., librarian; b. Eldred, Ill., Jan. 23, 1910; d. William George and Sylvia (Mitchell) Fry; student Northwestern U., 1927-28, U. Ill., 1928-30; m. Lloyd Arbuckle, May 13, 1933 (dec. May 1960); children—Kathryn Diane, William Franklin. Freelance reporter, Ind., Ill., 1931; librarian Lake Village Ind. Meml. Twp. Library, 1946—; petroleum jobber, distbr. Lake Village Shell Oil Co., 1960—; pres. Arbuckle Oil Co., Inc., until 1978, now dir.; mem. Key Oil Man's Com., 1976-78; rep. Internat. Oil Seminar, Monte Carlo, 1977. Pres. Lake Village Sch. Corp., 1962—; twp. chmn. Multiple Sclerosis, Newton County, Ind., 1962-65; active George Ade Hosp. Aux. Nat. industry chmn. Laymen's Nat. Bible Assn., 1970, 71. Bd. dirs. Newton County Hist. Soc. Corp., Newton County Mental Health, Newton County Comprehensive Health, Newton County Exec. Com. on Dr. Recruitment, Lake View Retirement Home; chmn. Lake Twp. Bi-Centennial Com., 1975-76; mem. com. Newton County Bicentennial Project, 1976-78; mem. Arrowhead Country Fish and Wildlife Commn., 1976-78. Recipient of George award Lafayette-Courier-Jour., 1964. Mem. Ill. Woman's Press Assn., Nat. Fedn. Press Women, Midland Authors, Children's Reading Roundtable, DAR (co-winner nat. 1st place poetry award 1979, nat. Evelyn Cole Peters poetry award 1979, 80), ASCAP, Ind., Ill., Newton County (vice pres., program chmn. 1966—) hist. socs., Am. Women Composers Inc., Laymen's Nat. Bible Soc. (industry assn. chmn. 1972), Internat. Platform Assn., Grange. Presbyterian (elder 1973—). Mem. Order Eastern Star. Author: The After-Harvest Festival (Disting. Lit. award Ind. U. 1956), 1955; Andy's Dan'l Boone Rifle (cited by Ind. U. 1967), 1965; (anthem, words and music) The Church Wherein I Worship, 1955; (anthem) The Tall Cathedral Windows (award Ind. Composers Assn. 1958); The Hour Will Come, 1962; (ballad) I Never Knew, 1960. Recorded song By the Kankakee River, 1973. Home: Lake Village IN 46349

ARBUCKLE, WILLIAM HEENON, edn. liaison specialist; b. Spooner, Wis., Nov. 21, 1946; s. John and Mina Hazel (Taylor) A.; B.S., U. Wis., Superior, 1970; postgrad. U. Wis., Stout, 1974-75; m. Virginia May Marsh, Jan. 22, 1968; children—Jacquelynn Dawn, Adrian Dare. Weigher, Consol. Printing Inc., St. Paul, 1967-70; instr. Wis. Indianhead Tech. Inst., New Richmond, 1974-75; adminstrv. dir. St. Croix Bd. Chippewa Indians, Webster, Wis., 1975-76; native Am. liaison specialist, dist office Wis. Indianhead Tech. Inst., Shell Lake, 1976—; vice chmn. Black Dirt Constrn. Corp.; vice chmn. St. Croix Tribal Council; tech. advisor Tri-State Indian Community Action Program; home-sch. coordinator Superior (Wis.) Public Sch. System, 1973-74. Served with U.S. Army, 1964-67; Vietnam. Mem. Nat. Indian Edn. Assn., Am. Vocat. Assn., Wis. Assn. Vocat. and Adult Edn., VFW. Office: WITI Dist Office Shell Lake WI 54871

ARCHAMBAULT, BENNETT, mfg. co. exec.; b. Oakland, Calif.; s. Albert Joseph and May (Smales) A.; m. Margaret Henrietta Morgan; children—Suzanne Morgan, Michele Lorraine, Steven Bennett; student Ga. Inst. Tech.; B.S., M.I.T.; LL.D., Ill. Inst. Tech. Vice pres., gen. mgr. M.W. Kellogg Co., N.Y.C., 1946-54; pres. Stewart-Warner Corp., Chgo., 1954—, chmn. bd., 1959—; pres., dir., chmn. bd. Stewart-Warner Corp. of Can., Ltd.; pres., dir. Stewart-Warner Datafax Corp., Thor Power Tool Co., Herramientas Thor de Mexico S.A. de D.V.; dir., chmn. bd. Thor-Fiap, S.p.A.; dir., pres., dir. gen. Stewart-Warner France, S.A.; dir., mem. exec. com. Kemper Corp., Lumbermens Mut. Casualty Co., Am. Motorists Ins. Co., Am. Mfrs. Mut. Ins. Co.; dir. Stewart-Warner, Ltd., Stewart-Warner Internat. Sales Corp., Lawter Internat., Inc.; mem. bd. adminstrn. Stewart-Warner, Alemite GmbH. Mem. Mayor's Com. for Econ. and Cultural Devel., Chgo.; mem. Republican Nat. Finance Com.; bd. govs. United Rep. Fund of Ill.; bd. dirs. Protestant Found. Greater Chgo.; trustee Better Govt. Assn., Ill. Inst. Tech. Research Inst.; trustee, mem. exec. com., chmn. nominating com. Ill. Inst. Tech.; trustee, mem. exec. com., chmn. nominating com. Mus. Sci. and Industry; mem. corp. devel. com. M.I.T. Recipient medal of merit U.S.; His Majesty's medal for service in cause of freedom (U.K.). Mem. U.S. C. of C., Employers Assn. Greater Chgo., Ill. Mfrs. Assn., NAM, Soc. Automotive Engrs., Research Soc. Am., Newcomen Soc. N.Am. Clubs: Chicago, Commercial, Racquet, Saddle and Cycle, Westmoreland Country, Executives, Economics, M.I.T. of Chgo.; Glen View. Home: 3240 Lake Shore Dr Chicago IL 60657 Office: 1826 Diversey Pkwy Chicago IL 60614

ARCHAMBAULT, RENE FRANCIS, surgeon, educator; b. Barre, Vt., Oct. 31, 1911; s. Francois Xavier and Antonia (Pauze) A.; B.A., U. Montreal, 1930; M.D., Creighton U., 1936; M.Sc., U. Pa., 1940; m. Marilyn Miehls, Oct. 13, 1950; children—George, Susan, Rene, Mary Ann. Intern, Mercy Hosp., Council Bluffs, Iowa, 1936-37; resident Sacred Heart Hosp., Allentown, Pa., 1938-40; practice medicine specializing in surgery, Barre, 1940-41, Wayne, Mich., 1951—; adminstr. Nankin Hosp., Wayne, 1951—; adj. asso. prof. anatomy Wayne State U., Detroit, 1957—. Del., Mich. Republican Conv., 1968. Served to maj. AUS, 1941-46. Diplomate Am. Bd. Surgery.

Mem. Pan Am. Med. Assn., Am. Acad. Med. Adminstrs. (regional v.p. 1967). Contbr. articles to profl. jours. Home: 35550 Michigan Ave Wayne MI 48184 Office: 35550 Michigan St Wayne MI 48184

ARCHBOLD, THOMAS JOHN, trust farm exec.; b. Fargo, N.D., July 10, 1947; s. Francis John and Eileen Mary (Fridgen) A.; B.S., N.D. State U., 1969, M.S., 1972; m. Sharon Joan Daub, June 22, 1968; children—Jason Thomas, Kristin Leigh, Kerry Lynn. Research asst. N.D. State U., Fargo, 1969-72; asst. Burleigh County agt. Extension Service, U.S. Dept. Agr., Bismarck, N.D., 1972-73, Ransom County extension agt., Lisbon, 1973-75; farm mgr. 1st Bank of N.D., N.A., Fargo, 1975—; v.p. 1st Trust Co. of N.D. Sec., Ransom County Crop and Livestock Improvement Assn., 1973-75; dir. Extension Staff Devel. Adv. Com., 1974-75; sec. Ransom County Soil Conservation Dist., 1973-75, Ransom County Twp. Officers Assn., 1973-75; bd. dirs. Ransom County Fair Bd., 1973-75. Named Man of Year, Lisbon Jr. C. of C., 1974. Mem. Am. Soc. Farm Mgrs. and Rural Appraisers (pres. N.D. chpt. 1979—), N.W. Farm Mgrs., N.D. Acad. Sci., Lisbon Jr. C. of C. (dir. 1975), Sigma Chi. Roman Catholic. Clubs: Agassiz, Fargo Elks, K.C. Home: 93 23d Ave N Fargo ND 58102 Office: 1st Trust Co of ND Fargo ND 58102

ARCHER, BERNARD THOMAS, radiologist; b. Rock Island, Ill., Dec. 8, 1935; s. Marcus Matthew and Janet Christita (Rank) A.; student St. Ambrose Coll., 1953-56; M.D., U. Iowa, 1960; m. Doreen Mary Smith, Aug. 26, 1961; children—Martha, Amy, Christopher, Stephen, Megan, Matthew. Intern, Milw. County Gen. Hosp., 1960-61; resident Univ. Hosps. Cleve., 1963-66, fellow in radiology, 1966-67; practice medicine specializing in radiology, 1967—; pres. Huron Rd. Radiologists, Cleve., 1970—; dir. dept. radiology Huron Hd. Hosp., East Cleveland, Ohio, 1968—; clin. asst. prof. Case Western Res. U., 1977—. Served with USAF, 1961-63. Certified Am. Bd. Radiology. Mem. Am., Ohio State, Pan-Am. med. assns., Acad. Medicine Cleve., Radiol. Soc. N. Am., Am. Col. Radiology, Ohio State, Cleve. Radiol. Socs. Roman Catholic. Home: 1009 Hillcreek Ln Gates Mills OH 44040 Office: 13951 Terrace Rd Cleveland OH 44112

ARCHER, WESLEY LEA, chemist; b. Marietta, Ohio, Feb. 20, 1927; s. Daniel Wesley and Thelma A. (Marsh) A.; B.A., Kalamazoo Coll., 1950; Ph.D., Ind. U., 1953; m. Mary Susan Walker, May 29, 1971; 1 son, James Wesley. Research chemist Irwin Neisler Co., Decatur, Ill., 1953-56; research asso. Dow Chem. Co., Midland, Mich., 1956—. Served with USNR, 1945-46. Patentee in field. Home: 1117 Scott St Midland MI 48640 Office: Dow Center 2020 Midland MI 48640

ARCY, THOMAS HENRY, educator; b. Detroit, Jan. 22, 1939; s. Henry C. and Mary V. (Kolasa) A.; B.S., Ferris State Coll., 1964; M.A., Mich. State U., 1967, Ed.S., 1970; Ph.D., U. Mich., 1974; m. Judith, Jan. 7, 1962; children—Jeff, Dan, Amy, Matt. Electronics tchr. Saginaw (Mich.) Twp. Community Schs., 1964-67; dir. indsl. arts edn./vocat. edn. Bridgeport (Mich.) Community Schs., 1967-70; cons. vocat. edn. Saginaw Schs., 1970-71; asst. prin. Career Opportunities Center, Saginaw, 1971-73; part time tchr. Bentley High Sch., Livonia, Mich., 1973-74; asso. prof. dept. indsl. edn. Indsl. Vocat.-Tech. Edn., Iowa State U., Ames, 1974—; lectr. in field; coordinator Nat. Occupational Competency Testing Inst. Project, 1974—; pres. Omega Enterprises; owner Tom's Installation. Bd. dirs. Saginaw YMCA Youth Div., 1970-71. Recipient nat. recognition Nat. Occupational Competency Testing Inst., 1979. Mem. Am. Vocat. Assn., (life), Am. Council Indsl. Arts Tchr. Edn. (life), Delta Sigma Phi (charter mem. Ferris State Coll.). Roman Catholic. Club: Kiwanis (dir. N.W. Kiwanis, Saginaw, 1971-72). Author articles and reports in field. Office: 216 I Ed II Ames IA 50011

AREY, LEO BETRAM, clin. psychologist; b. Richfield, N.C., June 19, 1913; s. Nathan Green and Nina (Trexler) A.; m. Jennie Lind Mitchell, Dec. 31, 1941; A.B., Lenoir Rhyne Coll., 1935; Ph.D., U. Chgo., 1952. Registered psychologist, Ill., 1964; diplomate Am. Bd. Profl. Psychology. Psychology intern VA Hosp., Hines, Ill., 1947-51, staff clin. psychologist, 1952-61, research psychologist, 1962-66, asst. chief, psychology service, supervisory psychologist, psychiatry service, 1966-80, pvt. practice, 1981—. Mem. Am., Midwest, Ill. psychol. assns., Assn. Psychophysiol. Study Sleep, Am. Acad. Psychotherapists, Assn. Advancement Psychology, Sigma Xi. Contbr. to psychol. jours. and book. Home: 5532 South Shore Dr Chicago IL 60637

ARGANBRIGHT, AL DEAN, ins. co. exec.; b. Drummond, Wis., July 19, 1930; s. Noel L. and Laura B. (Winkelplick) A.; B.S., Wis. State U., Superior, 1952; M.A., U. Wis.-Madison, 1954; m. Janet M. Gresenz, June 10, 1976; children—Robert, Lynn, Thomas, Donald, Brian, Jane. Mem. actuarial dept. Continental Assurance Co., Chgo., 1954-57; with Wis. Nat. Life Ins. Co., Oshkosh, 1957—, actuary, 1961-66, v.p., 1966, exec. v.p., 1967-71, pres., 1971—; dir. 1st Wis. Nat. Bank of Oshkosh; dir. Wis. Public Service Corp. Pres., dir. U. Wis.-Oshkosh Found., 1980—. Served with USAF, 1952-53. Fellow Soc. Actuaries; mem. Oshkosh C. of C. (past pres.). Republican. Club: Kiwanis (past pres.). Office: 220 Washington Ave Oshkosh WI 54901

ARGANBRIGHT, ESTHER WINDLE, ednl. supr.; b. Wymore, Nebr., Dec. 14, 1920; d. Dean Kenneth and Ruth Esther (Jones) Windle; student Doane Coll., 1938-39; B.S. with distinction, U. Nebr., 1963, M.A., 1969; m. Lawrence Jerald McNulty, Sept. 24, 1940; children—Lawrence Joseph, Susan Kathleen McNulty Bollerup; m. 2d, Donald M. Arganbright, May 4, 1974. Instr. public elem. schs., Wymore, Nebr., 1955-60, McCook, Nebr., 1961-68; lectr. U. Nebr., Lincoln, 1969-71; adminstrv. cons./reading cons. Nebr. Dept. Edn., Lincoln, 1971-73; master tchr., instr. U. Wyo., Laramie, 1973-77; dir. Right to Read program Nebr. Dept. Edn., Lincoln, 1977-79, supr. basic skills, 1980—; reading cons. NDEA scholar Reading Inst., Greeley, Colo., summer 1965. Mem. Snowy Range Council of Internat. Reading Assn. (organizer, pres. 1974-77), Nebr. Reading Council (pres. 1981-82), Phi Lambda Theta, Phi Delta Kappa. Episcopalian. Club: P.E.O. Home: 3421 Allendale Dr Lincoln NE 68516 Office: 301 Centennial Mall S Lincoln NE 68509

ARGRAVES, HUGH OLIVER, poet, artist, playwright; b. Decatur, Ill., July 7, 1922; s. Wendell Oliver and Helen E. (Sax) A.; student Beloit Coll., 1937. Author: Collected Poetry, 1960; contbr. poems to publs.; playwright: Osbert, 1978, The Great Depression, 1978; group shows include: Lynn Kottler Galleries, 1961, 66, Ahda Artz Galleries, N.Y.C., 1962-66, Ligoa Duncan Gallery, 1968 represented in permanent collections: Mus. Modern Art, N.Y.C. Served with U.S. Army, 1943-46. Republican. Presbyterian.

ARGUE, DONALD HARVEY, coll. pres.; b. Winnipeg, Man., Can., July 12, 1939; s. Andrew Watson and Hazel Belle May Argue; M.A., U. Santa Clara, 1967; Ed.D., U. Pacific, 1969; m. Patricia Opheim, Sept. 23, 1961; children—Laurie, Leland, Jonathan. Ordained to ministry Assembly of God Ch., 1964; pastor First Assembly of God, Morgan Hill, Calif., 1965-67; minister of youth Bethel Ch., San Jose, Calif., 1963-65; adminstr. North Central Bible Coll., Mpls., 1974—, pres., 1979—. Mem. Nat. Assn. Evangelicals (mem. bd. adminstrn.), Soc. Pentecostal Studies (past pres.), Am. Psychol. Assn. Club: Rotary. Home: 13081 Herald Circle Apple Valley MN 55124 Office: 910 Elliot Ave S Minneapolis MN 55404

ARKENS, JEAN MARIE, educator; b. Iron Mountain, Mich., Feb. 29, 1948; d. Ruben Herman and Anna Linnea (Branback) Sholander; B.S. Summa cum laude, No. Mich. U., 1970; M.S., Wayne State U., 1981. Sec., Family Enrichment Bur., Escanaba, Mich., 1966-68; sec., Our Own Bakeries, Marquette, Mich., 1969; tchr. Escanaba (Mich.) Area Schs., 1970—, tchr. bus. edn. high sch., 1970—. Recipient Citizenship award Escanaba Lions Club, 1966. Certified tchr. vocat. edn., secondary edn. Mich. Mem. Nat. Bus. Edn. Assn., Upper Peninsula Mich. Bus. Edn. Assn., Mich. Bus. Edn. Assn., NEA, Mich. Edn. Assn., Escanaba Edn. Assn., Delta Kappa Gamma. Lutheran. Clubs: Altrusa, Order Eastern Star, Daus. of Nile. Home: 520 S 29th St Escanaba MI 49829 Office: 500 S Lincoln Rd Escanaba MI 49829

ARKING, ROBERT, geneticist; b. Bklyn., July 1, 1936; s. Henry and Mollie (Levinson) A.; B.S., Dickinson Coll., 1958; Ph.D., Temple U., 1967; m. Lucille Mae Musser, May 8, 1959; children—Henry David, Jonathan Jacob. Sci. tchr. Phila. Public Schs., 1959-61; asst. prof. zoology U. Ky., Lexington, 1968-70; research biologist Center for Pathology, U. Calif., Irvine, 1970-75; asst. prof. biology Wayne State U., Detroit, 1975-81, asso. prof. 1981—. NSF fellow, 1964-66, NIH fellow, 1967-68. Mem. AAAS, Am. Soc. Zoologists, Genetics Soc. Am., Soc. for Developmental Biology, Sigma Xi. Contbr. articles to profl. jours. Office: Wayne State University Dept Biological Sciences Detroit MI 48202

ARKO, ANTHONY CHARLES, metallurgist; b. Loski Potok, Yugoslavia, Sept. 22, 1935; came to U.S., 1949, naturalized, 1956; s. Michael and Paula (Rojc) A.; B.S., Ill. Inst. Tech., 1958; Ph.D. (fellow), Northwestern U., 1965. Research metallurgist Republic Steel Corp., Independence, Ohio, 1965-69, project leader, 1969-73; plant metallurgist Signode Corp., Glenview, Ill., 1973-74; sr. engr./scientist Internat. Harvester Co., Hinsdale, Ill., 1979-80; self-employed, 1980—. Mem. Am. Soc. Metals, Am. Phys. Soc., AIME, Sigma Xi. Roman Catholic. Contbr. articles to profl. jours. Home: 1359 Hillcrest Rd Lemont IL 60439

ARKO, CARL, ednl. adminstr.; b. Detroit, Dec. 19, 1938; B.A., U. Mich., 1968, cert., 1969; M.A., Central Mich. U., 1977; m. Claudia Jean Lemke, Mar. 16, 1962; children—Sally Robin, Jennifer Heather. Tchr. pre-sch., Inkster, Mich., 1969-70; tchr. Am. history and math. Lake Fenton High Sch., Fenton, Mich., 1970-72; tchr. bldg. trades and constrn. tech. Delta-Schoolcraft Area Vocat. Center, 1972-74; adminstrv. intern Delta-Schoolcraft Intermediate Sch. Dist., Edn. Services Center, Escanaba, Mich., 1974-75, state and fed. projects dir., 1975—; cons. and dir. ednl. programs for Mich. Dept. Edn., 1974—, Western Mich. U., 1980-81, Central Mich. U., 1979-80, Mich. State U., 1968; cons. to Hannaville Indian Reservation, Mich., 1980-81; mem. state adv. com. tchr. cert. Mich. Dept. Edn., 1980—; police officer Detroit Police Dept., 1961-69. Served with USAF, 1956-60. Cert. tchr., Mich. Mem. Mich. Assn. Sch. Adminstrs., Assn. Supervision and Curriculum Devel., Am. Soc. Tng. and Devel., Internat. Reading Assn., Council for Exceptional Children, Assn. for Ednl. Communications and Tech., Mich. Profl. Devel. Assn. (pres. 1979—), Mich. Council Vocat. Adminstrs. Contbg. author: Career Education Planning District Handbook, 1976. Home: Star Route Box 20 Cedar River MI 49813 Office: Education Services Center 810 N Lincoln Rd Escanaba MI 49829

ARLINGHAUS, EDWARD JAMES, educator; b. Cin., Jan. 6, 1925; s. Edward A. and Irene (Custer) A.; B.B.A., U. Cin., 1948, Ph.D., 1981; M.B.A., Xavier U., 1958, M.Ed., 1971, M.S., 1973; m. Ilse Denninger, Aug. 10, 1974; 1 dau., Toni Gail. Dir. personnel tng. Mabley & Carew Co., Cin., 1948-51; sales researcher John Shillito Co., Cin., 1951-53; personnel devel. specialist Gen. Elec. Co., Cin., 1953-57; dir. personnel, pub. relations and security Jewish Hosp. of Cin., 1957-66; dir. grad. program in hosp. and health adminstrn. Xavier U., Cin., 1966—; mem. health care sect. Cath. Conf. Ohio; sec. bd. trustees Providence Hosp., 1968-77, St. Francis Hosp., 1968-75, St. Mary's Hosp., 1968-72 (all Cin.); chmn. health manpower com. CORVA, Cin., 1970-75; sec. bd. trustees St. Mary's Hosp., Cin., 1968-72; mem. Ohio Bd. Examiners Nursing Home Adminstrs., 1974-76. Served with AUS, 1943-45; col. Res. (ret.). Fellow Royal Soc. Health; Am. Coll. Hosp. Adminstrs.; mem. Assn. Mental Health Adminstrs., Cath. Hosp. Assn., Am. Public Health Assn., Scarbard and Blade, Phi Delta Kappa. Home: 7568 Trailwind Dr Montgomery OH 45242 Office: Xavier University Cincinnati OH 45207

ARLOOK, THEODORE DAVID, dermatologist; b. Boston, Mar. 12, 1910; s. Louis and Rebecca (Sakansky) A.; B.S., U. Ind. Sch. Medicine, 1932, M.D., 1934; postgrad. dermatology U. So. Calif., 1946-47. Intern, Luth. Meml. Hosp., Chgo., 1934-35; resident in dermatology Indpls. Gen. Hosp., 1947-49; practice medicine specializing in dermatology, Elkhart, Ind., 1950—; mem. staff Elkhart Gen. Hosp.; asso. mem. dermatology dept. Wishard Meml. Hosp., Indpls. Pres., Temple Israel, Elkhart, 1963-64; pres. B'nai B'rith, 1955. Served to capt. M.C. AUS, 1941-46; PTO. Diplomate Am. Bd. Dermatology. Mem. AMA, Am. Acad. Dermatology, Elkhart County Med. Soc. (pres. 1967), Noah Worcester Dermatol. Soc. Contbr. articles to med. jours. Office: 912 W Franklin St Elkhart IN 46516

ARMAGOST, ELSA GAFVERT, computer co. communications cons.; b. Duluth, Minn., Jan. 26, 1917; d. Axel Justus and Martina Emelia (Magnuson) Gafvert; grad. with honors Duluth Jr. Coll., 1936; B.J., U. Minn., 1938; postgrad. in public relations, bus. mgmt., computer tech., 1965-81; m. Byron William Armagost, Dec. 8, 1945; children—David Byron, Laura Martina. Freelance editor, Duluth, 1939-42; procedure editor and analyst U.S. Steel, Duluth, 1942-45; fashion advt. staff Dayton Co., Mpls., 1945-48; systems applications and documentation mgr. Control Data Corp., Mpls., 1969-74, promotion specialist, mktg. editor, 1974-76, corp. staff coordinator info. on edn., 1976-78; instr. communications, publ. specialist, 1978-79, communication cons. peripheral products group, 1979—. Mem. steering com. U.S. Senatorial Bus. Adv. Bd.; bd. dirs. LWV; v.p. Sewickley Valley Hosp. Aux., Sewickley Valley Mental Health Council; dir. publicity Sacred Arts Expo, World Affairs Council radio program, Pitts., 1962-68. Mem. AAUW (1st v.p. Venezuela), Women in Communications (job mart dir.), Nat. Fedn. Press Women, Internat. Platform Assn. Home: 9500 Collegeview Rd Bloomington MN 55437 Office: PO Box 0 Minneapolis MN 55440

ARMENIAN, RAFFI, conductor; b. Cairo, Egypt, June 4, 1942; s. Barour and Marguerite A.; Diploma in Piano, Composition, Conducting, Acad. Music, Vienna, 1969; B.Metallurgy, U. London, 1965; hon. doctorate, U. Waterloo, 1980. Music dir. Kitchener-Waterloo Symphony, Waterloo, Ont., Can., 1971—; resident conductor Can. Opera Co., 1977-78; mem. faculty part time Wilfrid Laurier U., Waterloo. Recipient Silver Jubilee medal, 1977. Office: Box 2 Waterloo ON N2J 3Z6 Canada

ARMES, WALTER SCOTT, educator; b. Okmulgee, Okla., May 15, 1939; s. Ralph Emerson and Lola J. (Hendricks) A.; B.S., Ohio No. U., 1960; M.S., Ind. State U., 1966; postgrad. Ohio State U., 1979-81; m. Jean Ellen Hopkins, June 5, 1965; children—Christina Marie, Rebecca Jean. Tchr., Lykens (Ohio) Local Sch. Dist., 1960-61; tchr. social studies Holmes-Liberty Local Sch. Dist., Bucyrus, Ohio, 1961-63, Painesville (Ohio) Twp. Schs., 1963-64, Weathersfield Twp. Schs., Mineral Ridge, Ohio, 1964-68, Eastland Vocat. Center, Groveport, Ohio, 1968—. Chmn., Whitehall City Bd. Zoning and Bldg. Appeals, 1976—; mem. Franklin County Rep. Central Com., 1976—; pres. Franklin County Council of Edn. Assn., 1977—, negotiator for exchange services agreements with Ohio State U., Otterbein Coll., Capital U. and Ohio Dominican Coll., 1976—; chmn. policy bd. Franklin County Tchr. Center, 1978—; nat. reader U.S. Dept. Edn. Tchr. Center Program, 1981; state reader Ohio State Dept. Edn. Tchr. Center Proposals, 1978; mem. Otterbein Coll. Dept. Edn. adv. com., 1981—; chmn. Franklin County Metro Educators Polit. Action com., 1972-76; trustee East Area Mental Health Services, Columbus, 1981—; pres. exec. bd. Whitehall Community Counseling Center, 1978-81; coach Whitehall Tee-Ball League, 1977-79. Recipient award for outstanding service Whitehall Community Counseling Center, 1981; Mem. Eastland Edn. Assn. (pres. 1980—), Ohio Edn. Assn. (exec. com. 1977-80, legis. com. 1973-77; Service award 1980), Central Ohio Tchrs. Assn. (exec. bd. 1972-80; Service award 1980), NEA, Ohio Vocat. Assn., Phi Delta Kappa, Am. Vocat. Assn., Assn. for Supervision and Curriculum Devel., Nat. Council for Social Studies, Ohio Council for Social Studies. Republican. Methodist. Home: 3975 Virginia Circle E Columbus OH 43213 Office: 4465 S Hamilton Rd Groveport OH 43125

ARMSTRONG, CURTIS E., rehab. adminstr.; b. Martins Ferry, Ohio, Sept. 8, 1946; s. Ralph Edward and Eileen Virginia (Brown) A.; student West Liberty (W.Va.) State Tchrs. Coll., 1964-66, Franklin U., 1970-71; m. Judy Kay Shutt, June 9, 1979. Employment mgr. Grossman & Sons, Inc., Columbus, Ohio, 1976-77; state coordinator handicapped services safety and hygiene div. Indsl. Commn. Ohio, Columbus, 1977-79, dir. public relations rehab. div., 1979-81, acting dir. rehab. div., 1981—; pres. dir. Time, Inc., Columbus, 1979—; adviser Ohio Gov.'s Com. for Employment Handicapped, Nat. Center Research in Vocat. Edn. Ohio; rep. President's Com. on Employment Handicapped, Washington, 1977-78; pres., co-founder Handi-Capable, Inc., 1980—; pres. Central Ohio Employability Awareness Council, 1976-78. Mem. Nat. Assn. Accts., Am. Soc. Personnel Adminstrs. Club: Press of Ohio. Rec. artist Gateway Records, 1962-70. Home: 1054 S James Rd Columbus OH 43227

ARMSTRONG, F(REDRIC) MICHAEL, vehicle rental co. exec.; b. Wichita, Kans., Dec. 20, 1942; s. Frederick Dale and Virginia Pauline Armstrong; B.S. in E.E., M.I.T., 1964; M.B.A., Stanford U., 1966; m. Patricia R. Latif, Dec. 6, 1976. Mgr. capital appropriations Trans World Airlines, N.Y.C., 1966-69; corp. planner Transam. Corp., San Francisco, 1969-70; v.p., dir. Transam. Film Service, Salt Lake City, 1970-73; v.p. fin. Europe Transam. Airlines, Madrid, Spain, 1973-75; v.p. planning and info. services, Oakland, Calif., 1975-77; exec. v.p. fin., dir. Budget Rent a Car Corp., Chgo., 1977—; dir. Compass Computer Services, Inc., Dallas, Transam. Reins. Ltd., Bermuda, Melia Internat. Hotels, Panama. Office: 200 N Michigan Ave Chicago IL 60601

ARMSTRONG, FRANK WILSON, III, health care exec.; b. Brisbane, Australia, Dec. 25, 1944; s. Wilson Frank, Jr. and Gwynedd Maureen (Rawson) A.; came to U.S., 1946; B.S. in Econs., Xavier U., Cin., 1966, M.B.A., 1974, M.H.A. (Equitable Life Assurance scholar), 1974; m. Frances Lynn Gordon, May 20, 1972; children—Daniel Gordon, Brian Gordon. Mktg. rep. Blue Cross S.W. Ohio, Cin., 1971-72; adminstrv. asst. St. Anthony Hosp. Systems, Denver, 1973-74; dir. facilities rev. Orange County Health Planning Council, Tustin, Calif., 1974-76; exec. dir. S.E. Colo. Health Systems Agy., Colorado Springs, 1976-81; mgr. health service relations Goodyear Tire & Rubber Co., Akron, Ohio, 1981—; lectr. Grad. Sch., Calif. State U., Los Angeles, 1975-76; cons. in field. Served with USAR, 1966-70; Vietnam. Decorated D.F.C., Bronze Star, Air medal with oak leaf cluster, Army Commendation medal. Mem. Am. Health Planning Assn. (dir., exec. com.), Am. Hosp. Assn., Am. Hosp. Fin. Mgmt. Assn., Am. Public Health Assn. Democrat. Roman Catholic. Office: 1344 Market St Akron OH

ARMSTRONG, JON STEPHEN, banker; b. Elkhart, Ind., Jan. 23, 1938; s. Lewis and Marcella (Kern) A.; B.S. in Bus., Ind. U., 1960; m. Mary Elizabeth Conrad, June 13, 1959; children—Elizabeth Ann, Wendy Suzanne. Credit analyst Nat. Bank Detroit, 1960-63; asst. v.p. St. Joseph Bank & Trust Co., South Bend, Ind., 1963-64, v.p., 1964-66, sr. v.p., 1966-68; pres., dir. St. Joseph Valley Bank, Elkhart, 1968-73, chmn. bd., 1973—; vice chmn. SJV Corp., Elkhart, 1973—, chmn. bd., 1975—. Mem. pres.'s adv. bd. Goshen Coll., 1969—; mem. dean's adv. council Ind. U., 1977—; mem. adv. council Art Gallery, U. Notre Dame, 1977—; pres. Michiana Pub. Broadcasting Corp., 1976-78; mem. bd. govs. Asso. Colls. Ind., 1973—; campaign chmn. United Way Elkhart County, 1973; pres., trustee Elkhart Community Schs., 1971-73; pres. Greater Elkhart C. of C., 1971-72. Recipient Disting. Service award South Bend Jaycees, 1967, Elkhart Jaycees, 1970; Book of Golden Deeds award Elkhart Exchange Club, 1977. Mem. Am. Bankers Assn. (state v.p.). Contbr. articles to mags. Office: 121 W Franklin St Elkhart IN 46515

ARMSTRONG, NAOMI YOUNG, educator; b. Dermott, Ark., Oct. 17, 1918; d. Allen Wesley and Sarah Elizabeth (Fluker) Young; B.S., Northwestern U., 1961; L.H.D. (hon.), U. Libre, Karachi, Pakistan, 1974; Litt.D. (hon.), Universal Orthodox Coll., Iperu-Remo, Ogun State, Nigeria, 1980; m. Joe Leslie Armstrong, July 17, 1938; 1 dau., Betty-Jo Armstrong Dunbar. Actress, Skyloft Players, also Center Aisle Players, Chgo., 1945-59; silk dress operator Rue-Ann Originals, Chgo., 1947-55; clk. Bur. Pub. Debt, 1955-56, IRS, 1956-59; caseworker Cook County Dept. Pub. Aid, Chgo., 1956-59; tchr. Chgo. pub. schs., 1962—, creative writing instr., 1975-77, instr. Social Center, 1965-67; dramatic instr. Crerar Meml. Presbyn. Ch., Chgo., 1972; real estate salesman Century 21 Maner, 1978—. Mem. exec. bd., membership chmn. Northwestern U. Young Alumni Council, 1971-72; trustee World U., 1973-74. Recipient Hon. Gold diploma, spl. award 3d World Congress Poets, 1976; named Internat. Woman of 1975, United Poets Laureate Internat. others; lic. real estate salesman. Mem. United Poets Laureate Internat. (exec. bd.), Internat. Platform Assn. (life; bd. govs.; 3d Preview winner 1976), World Poets Resource Center, Poetry Soc. London, Centro Studi E. Scambi Internat., World Poetry Soc., Sigma Gamma Rho. Author: A Child's Easter, 1971; Expression I, 1973; Expression III, 1976. Address: 9257 S Burnside Ave Chicago IL 60619

ARMSTRONG, RUTH MILDRED, educator; b. Moulmein, Burma, Aug. 22, 1924; d. Gustaf Adolph and Edna Blanche (Grandin) Sword; parents U.S. citizens; B.A., William Jewell Coll., 1945; postgrad. Northwestern U., 1946, Nat. Coll. Edn., 1960, U. Iowa, 1970; m. Walter Armstrong, Aug. 16, 1975; children from previous marriage—Nancy Ruth Berggren, James Otto Tinzmann. Instr. North Park Jr. Coll., Chgo., 1948-50; tchr. pub. schs., Morton Grove, Ill., 1958-62; instr. psychology Judson Coll., Elgin, Ill., 1964-66; counselor Warrenville (Ill.) Clinic, 1966-68; asst. prof. psychology North Park Coll., Chgo., 1966-78, asso. prof., 1978—; cons. Oak Therapeutic Sch., Chgo., 1972-73. Mem. Niles Township Bd. Spl. Edn., Sch. Bd. Dist. 67, Morton Grove, Ill., 1963-66. Mem. Internat. Council Edn. for Teaching, Am. Assn. Higher Edn., AAAS, AAUP, AAUW, Ill. Assn. Tchr. Educators. Baptist. Contbr. articles to profl. jours. Home: 1746 Good Park Ridge IL 60068 Office: North Park Coll 5125 N Spaulding Chicago IL 60625

ARMSTRONG, THEODORE MORELOCK, corporate exec.; b. St. Louis, July 22, 1939; s. Theodore Roosevelt and Vassar Fambrough (Morelock) A.; B.A., Yale, 1961; LL.B., Duke, 1964; m. Carol Mercer Robert, Sept. 7, 1963; children—Evelyn Anne, Robert Theodore. Admitted to Mo. bar, 1964; with Mo. Pacific Corp. and subsidiaries, St. Louis, 1964—, corporate sec., 1971-75; corporate sec. River Cement Co., 1968-75; asst. v.p. Mississippi River Transmission Corp., 1974-75; v.p. Gas Supply, 1975-79, exec. v.p., 1979—. Mem. Am., Met. St. Louis bar assns., Mo. Bar, So. Gas Assn., Tenn. Soc. St. Louis (dir.), Phi Alpha Delta. Republican. Presbyterian (deacon). Clubs: Bellerive, Clayton, Yale (St. Louis); Yale (N.Y.C.). Home: 307 Woodside Dr Saint Louis MO 63122 Office: 9900 Clayton Rd Saint Louis MO 63124

ARMSTRONG, WILLIAM SANSOM, univ. ofcl.; b. Owensboro, Ky., Nov. 25, 1917; s. William Rhea and Brent (Sansom) A.; B.S. in Edn., Ind. U., 1941; m. Martha Lea Jackson, Apr. 24, 1943; children—Ann L. Hodge, Mary Susan Armstrong Johnson, William Sansom. Sales and advt. mgr. Ideal Pure Milk Co., Owensboro, 1945-52; exec. dir. Ind. U. Found., Bloomington, 1952-69, pres., 1969—, also dir.; dir. Indpls. Indians, TRC Record Co. Chmn. bd. Am. Alumni Council, 1968-69; bd. dirs. Internat. Inst. Sports Sci. and Medicine, Arthur R. Metz Found., Bloomington Unified Funds, Inc., 1970—; Ind. State chmn. Am. Heart Assn. Served to capt. USAAF, World War II. Named Ky. col., 1949, Sagamore of Wabash, 1955, Sachems of Ind., 1970. Mem. Ind. U. Alumni Assn., Sigma Nu (dir. found. 1979, trustee; citation for service 1977), Kappa Kappa Psi, Alpha Kappa Psi. Mem. Christian Ch. (Disciples of Christ). Clubs: Columbia, Meridian Hills Country, Indpls. Athletic (Indpls.); Ocean Reef (Key Largo, Fla.); Ind. Soc. (Chgo.). Office: PO Box 500 Bloomington IN 47402

ARN, KENNETH DALE, city ofcl.; b. Dayton, Ohio, July 19, 1921; s. Elmer R. and Minna Marie (Wannagat) A.; B.A., Miami U., Oxford, Ohio, 1943; M.D., U. Mich., 1946; m. Vivien Rose Fontini, Sept. 24, 1966; children—Christine H. Hulme, Laura P. Hafstad, Kevin D., Kimmel R. Intern, Miami Valley Hosp., Dayton, Ohio, 1947-48; resident in pathology U. Mich., 1948-49, fellow in renal research, 1949-50; fellow in internal medicine Cleve. Clinic, 1950-52; practice medicine specializing in public health and vocat. rehab., 1952—, commr. of health City of Oakwood (Ohio), 1953—; asso. clin. prof. medicine Wright State U., 1975—; mem. staffs Kettering Med. Center, Dayton, Miami Valley Hosp; adj. asso. prof. edn. Wright State U.; field med. cons. Bur. Vocat. Rehab., 1958—, Bur. Services to Blind, 1975—; med. dir. Ohio Rehab. Services Commn., 1979—; mem. Pres's. Com. on Employment of Handicapped, 1971—; chmn. med. adv. com. Goodwill Industries, 1960—; mem., chmn. lay adv. com. vocat. edn. Dayton Public Schs., 1973—; exec. com. Gov.'s Com. on Employment Handicapped; bd. dirs. Vis. Nurses Assn. of Greater Dayton. Named City of Dayton's Outstanding Young Man, Dayton Jr. C. of C., 1957; 1 of 5 Outstanding Young Men of State, Ohio Jr. C. of C., 1958; Physician of Year, Pres's. Com. on Employment of Handicapped, 1971; Bishop's medal for meritorious service Miami U., 1972. Mem. Am., Ohio State (del. 1955-65) med. assns., Montgomery County (Ohio) Med. Soc. (chmn. com. on diabetic detection 1955-65, chmn. polio com. 1954-58), Nat. Rehab. Assn., Am. Diabetes Assn., Am. Profl. Practice Assn., Am. Heart Assn., Am., Ohio public health assns., Aerospace Med. Assn., Nu Sigma Nu, Sigma Chi. Lutheran. Clubs: Dayton Country, Racquet, Masons (33 deg. Scottish Rite, Shriners (past potentate Antioch Shrine), K.T., Order Police, Fraternal Order Police. Home: 167 Lookout Dr Dayton OH 45409 Office: 55 Park Ave Dayton OH 45419

ARNAUT, ARNOLD DOUGLAS, mfg. co. exec.; b. London, Sept. 22, 1920; s. John Oscar and Anna (Joost) A.; came to U.S., 1922, naturalized, 1948; B.Sc., U. Wis., Madison, 1949; m. Claire B. Scanlan, June 25, 1950; children—Kim Nicole, Lynn Yvonne. Phys. metallurgist Sylvania Electric Co., Flushing, N.Y., 1949-52; asst. sales mgr. Denver Equipment Co., N.Y.C., 1952-53; N.E. dist. mgr. Wall Colmonoy Corp., Hicksville, N.Y., 1953-71; pres. Wall Colmonoy (Canada) Ltd., Montreal, Que., 1971—; exec. v.p. Wall Colmonoy Corp., Detroit, also dir. Served with AUS, 1942-45. Registered profl. engr., Que. Mem. Am. Soc. Metals, Am. Welding Soc. Republican. Patentee in electroplating zinc tin. Home: PO Box 809 Birmingham MI 48012

ARNDT, ROBERT GORDON, educator, psychologist; b. Flint, Mich., Apr. 29, 1938; s. Gordon and Charlotte A.; B.S., Carroll Coll., Waukesha, Wis., 1961; M.S., Bradley U., 1962; m. Judith Ann Nissley, June 26, 1965; children—Nicole M., Dean R. In-patient dir. alcoholism unit Singer Zone Center, Rockford, Ill., 1966-68; chief psychologist Stephenson County (Ill.) Mental Health, Freeport, Ill., 1968-74; dir. adult clinic Saginaw County (Mich.) Mental Health, 1974-77; adminstr. Planning for Living, Bay City, Mich., 1977-78; coordinator developmental disability asso. degree Delta Coll., University Center, Mich., 1978—, asst. prof. dept. psychology, 1979—; cons. Saginaw Valley Rehab. Center. Mem. adult edn. com. First Congregational Ch., Saginaw, 1975—; mgr. Little League, 1977-80. Served to lt. (j.g.) USN, 1963-66. Ill. State fellow, 1968-76; cert. psychologist, Ill.; lic. psychologist, Mich. Mem. Am. Psychol.Ass Psychol. Assn., Mich. Psychol. Assn., Mid-Mich. Psychol. Assn. (past pres.). Author tng. manual. Home: 2905 Reppuhn St Saginaw MI 48603 Office: Delta College University Center MI 48710

ARNEAUD, SUSAN EBEL, center ofcl.; b. South Bend, Ind., Nov. 12, 1939; d. Grant and Essie (Ayers) Lewis; B.S., Western Mich. U., 1961; M.A., U. Mich., 1975. Art tchr., Muskegon, Royal Oak and Ann Arbor, Mich., 1961-70; owner Hyperbole, Inc., women's boutique, Detroit, 1966-68; personnel mgr. Little Things Boutique, Ann Arbor, 1970-72; mgr. Circle Book Store, Ann Arbor, 1972-74; counselor, program specialist U. Mich. Center Continuing Edn. for Women, Ann Arbor, 1975-79; asst. dir. tng. and staff devel. Clinton Valley Center, Pontiac, Mich., 1979—; staff and profl. devel. cons. St. Clair Coll., Windsor, Ont., Can., 1975—. Mem. N.Am. Simulation and Gaming Assn., Am. Personnel and Guidance Assn., Am. Soc. for Tng. and Devel., Pi Lambda Theta. Contbr. articles to profl. publs. Home: 20003 Lichfield Detroit MI 48221 Office: 140 Elizabeth Lake Rd Pontiac MI 48053

ARNELL, PAULA ANN YOUNGBERG, pathologist; b. Moline, Ill., Nov. 25, 1938; d. Paul Phillip and Mabel Eleanor (Arnell) Youngberg; B.A. summa cum laude, Augustana Coll., 1960; M.D., U. Iowa, 1964; m. Richard Anthony Arnell, June 28, 1969; children—Carla Ann, Paula Marie, Paul Anthony. Intern, St. Lukes-Mercy Hosp., Cedar Rapids, Iowa, 1964-65; resident pathology U. Iowa, Iowa City, 1965-68; chief resident State U. Iowa Hosp., Iowa City, 1968-69; pathologist, dir. labs. Luth. Hosp., Moline, Ill., 1970—; mem. staffs Moline Pub. Hosp., Franciscan Hosp., Rock Island, Ill. Sec., Rock Island County Blood Bank, 1972-73, v.p., 1973-74; cons. Rock Island Tb Center, 1970-72; profl. del. Am. Cancer Soc., 1971-73; tchr. Luth. Hosp. Sch. Inhalation Therapy, Sch. Nursing, 1970—; med. dir. Royal Neighbors of Am. Ins. Co., Rock Island; asso dir. Met. Med. Lab., Moline, Quad-Cities Pathologists Group Sch. of Med. Tech.; dir. 7th Street Realty Co. Pres. Rock Island County Cancer Soc., 1970-78; mem. alumni bd. Augustana Coll., Rock Island, 1972-75, bd. dirs., 1976—, chmn. bd. dirs., 1977—; sec. med. sect. Nat. Fraternal Congress, 1976—; bd. dirs. Mississippi Valley Regional Blood Bank, 1973—, Ill. div. Am. Cancer Soc., 1980—. Med. dir. Royal Neighbors of Am. Fellow Coll. Am. Pathologists (insp.), Am. Soc. Clin. Pathologists; cons. pathologist, ICON, 1981—; mem. Internat. Acad. Pathologists, Am. Assn. Cytologists, Am. Assn. Blood Banks, Am. Assn. Clin. Scientists, Am. Womans Med. Assn., AMA, Iowa Ill. med. socs., Ill. Pathologists Asso., Rock Island County Hist. Soc., Phi Beta Kappa, Beta Beta Beta. Home: 3904 7th Ave Rock Island IL 61201 Office: Luth Hosp 501 10th Ave Moline IL 61265

ARNELL, RICHARD ANTHONY, radiologist, nuclear medicine physician; b. Chgo., Aug. 21, 1938; s. Tony Frank and Mary Martha (Oberman) Yaki; B.A. (Younker Achievement scholar), Grinnell Coll., 1960; M.D., U. Iowa, 1964; m. Paula Ann Youngberg, June 28, 1964; children—Carla Ann, Paula Marie, Paul Anthony. Intern, Mercy and St. Luke's hosps., Cedar Rapids, Iowa, 1964-65; resident in radiology and nuclear medicine U. Iowa Hosps., 1965-68; practice medicine specializing in radiology and nuclear medicine, Moline, Ill., 1968—; mem. Moline Radiology Assos., 1968—, v.p., 1970-78, sec., 1978—, trustee pension and profit plan, 1979—; mem. staff Luth. Hosp., Moline, dir. continuing med. edn. program for physicians, 1979—, bd. dirs., 1977—; mem. staff Moline Pub. Hosp.; trustee Midstate Found. for Med. Care, 1975-79, exec. com., 1976-79. Supt. Sunday Ch. Sch. St. John's Luth. Ch., Rock Island, Ill., 1974-79, mem. ch. cabinet, 1975-76; del. Chs. United of Scott and Rock Island counties, Ill., 1977; mem. nat. exec. com. Augustana Coll., Rock Island, Ill., 1977-81. Recipient David Theophillus trophy for outstanding athlete Grinnell Coll., 1960; diplomate Am. Bd. Radiology, Am. Bd. Nuclear Medicine. Mem. Am. Coll. Radiology, Ill. Radiol. Soc., Am. Coll. Nuclear Medicine, Soc. Nuclear Medicine, AMA, Ill. (ho. of dels. 1974-79), Rock Island County (exec. com. 1974-79, peer-rev. com. 1975-79), Iowa-Ill. Central (pres.-elect 1977, pres. 1978) med. socs., Central Ill. Med. Assn. (v.p. 1977, pres. 1978), Tri-City Med. Jour. Club (sec.-treas. 1972-77), Am. Coll. Med. Imaging. Club: Short Hills Country. Home: 3904 7th Ave Rock Island IL 61201 Office: 1505 7th St Moline IL 61265

ARNOLD, BOYD EDWARD, radio sta. exec.; b. Mt. Pleasant, Mich., May 16, 1940; s. Thomas E. and Alberta L. (Britton) A.; student Central Mich. U., 1957-59; m. DyAnn Elizabeth Lind, Oct. 31, 1963; children—Michelle E., Thomas B. Dist. mgr. Ency. Brit., Calif. and Mich., 1961-68; account exec. Beck-Ross Communications, Inc., Flint, Mich., 1969-70; sales mgr., 1970-72, gen. sales mgr., 1972-75, asst. gen. mgr., 1975-78, gen. mgr., 1978-79, v.p., gen. mgr., 1980—; Mich. state chmn. govt. relations com., ABC Radio Affiliates, 1981—. Bd. dirs. Jr. Achievement, Flint, 1981—. Mem. Flint C. of C. (dir. 1978—), Mich. Assn. Broadcasters (v.p. 1979-80), Mich. Advt. Ind. Alliance (pres. 1982—), Sales and Mktg. Execs. of Flint (pres. 1977-78). Republican. Baptist. Clubs: Rotary, University (bd. dirs. 1980—). Home: 10574 Runyan Lake Point Fenton MI 48430 Office: G3338 E Bristol Rd PO Box 1470 Flint MI 48501

ARNOLD, CHARLES GREG, swine breeding stock co. exec.; b. Ventura, Calif., Jan. 27, 1953; s. Charles Lewis and Mary Evelyn Arnold; B.S., Tex. A&M U., 1975, M.Agr., 1976; m. Vicky Lynn Twilligear, Apr. 22, 1977; children—Shana Arnold, Shane Arnold, Shylo Arnold. With DeKalb Swine Breeders, Inc., 1976—, asst. mgr. genetic evaluation sta., Quincy, Ill., 1977-78, mgr., 1978-80, supr. nat. genetic evaluation sta., DeKalb, Ill., 1980—. Mem. Am. Mgmt. Assn. Baptist. Club: Jaycees (v.p. 1979-80). Home: Rural Route Sycamore IL 60178 Office: DeKalb Swine Breeders Inc Oak St DeKalb IL 60115

ARNOLD, CHARLES PARKER, telephone co. exec.; b. Salem, Nebr., Apr. 23, 1933; s. L.G. and Dollie E. (Schultz) A.; student U. Mich., 1969; m. Janet Ellen Hook, Mar. 8, 1958; children—John Charles, Andrew Parker. Garage serviceman Lincoln Telephone Co. (Nebr.), 1950-51, frameman, 1951-52, combinationman, 1956-57, comml. rep., 1957, service engr., 1957-62, area sales supr., 1962-65, sales supr., 1965-66, field comml. supr., 1966-67, gen. comml. supt., 1967-73, 2d v.p. comml., 1973-76, v.p. customer services, 1976—. Bd. dirs. Better Bus. Bur., 1968-71; bd. dirs. Better Lincoln Com., 1965-71, pres., 1965; mem. exec. bd. Cornhusker council Boy Scouts Am., 1964-76, pres., 1966, v.p., 1967, 68; bd. dirs. Community Emergency Shop, 1963-72, Contact Center, Inc., 1980-81; pres. Lincoln Center Assn., 1980, dir., 1977-81; unit firm team mem. Lincoln Community Chest, 1964-74; Lancaster County chmn. Nebr. Heart Assn., 1969. Served with USN, 1952-56. Named Lincoln's Young Man of Yr., Lincoln Jaycees, 1964. Mem. Frank H. Woods Telephone Pioneer Assn., U.S. Ind. Telephone Assn. (chmn. comml. subcom. 1979-81, mem. customer services com. 1981), Nebr. Telephone Assn. (pres. 1972-73, dir. 1970-73), Am. Legion, Lincoln C. of C. (dir. 1961-62, 71-74, 81). Republican. Clubs: Hillcrest Country, Lincoln U., Nebraska, Masons, Shriners, Rotary (pres. 1977-78). Home: 1620 Brent Blvd Lincoln NE 68506 Office: 1440 M St Lincoln NE 68508

ARNOLD, DUANE, JR., utility co. exec.; b. Cedar Rapids, Iowa, Apr. 24, 1950; s. Duane and Henrietta (Dows) A.; A.A., Wentworth Mil. Acad., 1970; B.A., Coe Coll., 1971; postgrad. U. Mich., 1981; m. Mary Colleen Geraghty, Aug. 28, 1971; children—Duane Joseph, Mary Brigid, Stephen Richard and Kevin Sutherland (twins). With Iowa Electric Light & Power Co., Cedar Rapids, 1970—, supt. transp., 1977-81, dir. purchasing and stores, 1981—; dir. Dows Real Estate Co., Dows Farms Inc., Dows Manifi Dairys. First aid chmn. local chpt., bd. dirs. ARC, 1976—, Cerebral Palsy, Linn County Emergency Bd., 1976—; dep. sheriff Linn County Sheriff's Office, 1972—; bd. dirs. Cedar Rapids Symphony. Mem. Soc. Automotive Engrs. (governing bd.), Nat. Assn. Fleet Adminstrs., Edison Electric Inst., Jr. C. of C., C. of C., Sports Car Club Am., Porsche Club Am., Am. Biog. Inst. Research Assn. Republican. Presbyterian. Office: Iowa Electric Light & Power Co 200 1st St Cedar Rapids IA 52401

ARNOLD, JOHN M., coal co. exec.; b. Wichita, Kans., Sept. 15, 1925; s. Ransom L. and Millie E. (Erwin) A.; B.S. in Civil Engring., U. Mo., Rolla, 1951; m. Lucy R. Shook, Aug. 16, 1947; children—John P., Pamela A., Tracy L. With Peabody Coal Co., St. Louis, 1951—, field engr., 1951-54, office engr., 1954-56, mine mgr., 1956-60, mine supt., 1960-65, div. engr., 1965-66, dir. engring., 1966-71, v.p. engring. and constrn., 1971—. Served with USAF, 1943-46. Registered profl. engr., Mo., Mont., Colo., Ariz. Mem. Rocky Mountain Coal Mining Inst., Soc. Mining Engrs., Ill. Mining Inst. Office: Peabody Coal Co 301 N Memorial St Saint Louis MO 63102

ARNOLD, LEAH MARY, ednl. adminstr.; b. Port Sanilac, Mich., Oct. 8, 1922; d. James and Mary (Drown) McKenzie; rural teaching cert. Central Mich. U., 1942, B.S., 1960, M.A., 1970; m. Joseph Arnold, May 21, 1946; children—Brenda Ann, Mary Margaret Arnold Hrivnak. Tchr. rural schs., Sanilac County, Mich., 1942-49, 55-61; tchr. Carsonville (Mich.) Public Schs., 1961-73; elem. prin. Carsonville-Port Sanilac Schs., 1973—. Treas., trustee Sanilac Twp. Library, 1953-80. Recipient appreciation award Jaycettes of Port Sanilac, 1980. Mem. Mich. Elem. and Middle Sch. Prins. Assn., Nat. Elem. Prins., Am. Assn. Sch. Adminstrs., Blue Water Reading Council, Mich. Assn. Supervision and Curriculum Devel., Nat. Retired Tchrs., Mich. Reading Assn., Internat. Reading Assn., Delta Kappa Gamma. Methodist. Clubs: Order Eastern Star (past matron), VFW Aux. Office: 4115 E Chandler St Carsonville MI 48419

ARNOLD, LEONARD CHARLES, physician, lawyer; b. Chgo., Aug. 26, 1921; s. Charles L. and Bessie (Schmigelsky) A.; B.S., Northwestern U., 1943, M.B., Chgo. Med. Sch., 1946, M.D., 1947; LL.B., John Marshall Law Sch., 1965, J.D., 1970; m. Janet Lorraine Bloom, Apr. 11, 1943 (div. Dec. 1961); children—Larry I. and Gary R. (twins), Bruce R., Leslie M.; m. 2d, Jeannette G. Zini, Nov. 14, 1962 (dec. July 1971); m. 3d, Dawn J. Cheskes, Apr. 13, 1973; children—Bradley Todd, Chad Douglas. Intern Edgewater Hosp., Chgo., 1946-47; gen. practice medicine, Chgo., 1947—; mem. attending staff Edgewater Hosp.; admitted to Ill. bar, 1965; practice law, Chgo., 1968—; instr. medico-legal seminar DePaul U. Coll. of Law; lectr. medico-legal subjects John Marshall Coll. Law, Chgo. Med. Sch. Served as capt. M.C., AUS, 1952-54. Fellow Am. Coll. Legal Medicine, Am. Acad. Family Practice (charter); mem. AMA, Chgo. Med. Soc., Chgo. Acad. Law and Medicine (co-founder), Acad. Psychosomatic Medicine, Ill. Bar Assn., Chgo. Bar Assn., Tau Delta Phi. Co-editor: Med. Trial Technique Quarterly. Home: 1055 Starr Rd Winnetka IL 60093 Med office: 5701 N Ashland Ave Chicago IL 60660 Legal office: 111 W Washington St Chicago IL 60602

ARNOLD, LYNN ELLIS, engring. mgr.; b. Cin., Nov. 17, 1934; s. Leslie Lee and Emma R. (Betscher) A.; Metall. Engr., U. Cin., 1957; M.S. in Mech. Engring., U. Ill., 1959. Grad. asst. U. Ill., Urbana, 1957-59; with Xtek, Inc., Cin., 1959—, tech. mgr., 1976—. Served with USAF, 1958-59. Registered profl. engr., Ohio. Fellow Am. Soc. Metals (past pres. Cin. chpt.; Wm. H. Eisenman Meml. award 1979), AAAS; mem. Nat. (past chmn. indsl. div., past v.p.), Ohio (past pres. Cin. chpt., Young Engr. award 1965) socs. profl. engrs., ASME (past pres. Cin. sect., past pres. Ohio council), Soc. Mfg. Engrs. (pres. Cin. chpt.), Cin. Tech. and Sci. Socs. Council (past pres.; Community Service award 1979), Engring. Soc. Cin. (past pres.), Cin. Mgmt. Assn. (past pres.), Cin. Editors Assn. (past pres.), Tool Steel Mgmt. Club (past pres.), U. Cin. Engring. Alumni Assn. (past pres.; Disting. Alumnus award 1979), SAR (past pres. Cin. chpt.), Audubon Soc. Ohio (past pres.), Ohio Audubon Council (past pres.), Tau Beta Pi, Alpha Sigma Mu, Alpha Phi Omega, Pi Delta Epsilon, Alpha Chi Sigma. Republican. Methodist. Author articles in field. Home: 5154 Montgomery Rd Cincinnati OH 45212 Office: 211 Township Ave Cincinnati OH 45216

ARNOLD, RICHARD EUGENE, ednl. adminstr.; b. New Kensington, Pa., Dec. 15, 1944; s. Leonard Eugene Hawkins and Dora Jean (Tanner) Hawkins; B.S., Slippery Rock State Coll., 1962; M.A., W.Va. U., 1973; Ph.D., Kent State U., 1978. Dir. econ. devel. North Central W.Va. Community Action Assn., Fairmont, 1972-73; mgmt. analyst Wofac Co., Moorestown, N.J., 1973-75; student adv. Kent State U., 1975-77, program officer KEDS Desegregation Assistance Center, 1977-79; exec. dir. secondary edn. Cleveland Heights (Ohio)-University Heights City Sch. Dist., 1979—. Chmn. community adv. bd. Urban League of Greater Cleve., 1980—. NASA fellow, 1968; NSF fellow, 1968-69. Mem. Assn. Supervision and Curriculum Devel., NAACP, Nat. Alliance of Black Sch. Educators, Slippery Rock Alumni Assn., W.Va. Alumni Assn., Kent State Alumni Assn., Phi Delta Kappa, Kappa Delta Pi. Democrat. Baptist. Home: 4400 Clarkwood Pkwy Warrensville Heights OH 44128 Office: 2155 Miramar Blvd University Heights OH 44118

ARNOLD, WILLIAM, collection agy. exec.; b. Lee County, Ky., Aug. 15, 1944; s. James C. and Anna (Thomas) A.; student public schs., Dallas; m. Joann Swezea, Dec. 3, 1967; children—Jonna Lea, Alicia Lynn. Mgr., Gen. Fin. Corp., Anderson, Ind., 1966-70; pres., Am. Accounts, Inc., Anderson, 1970—. Served with U.S. Army, 1962-65. Mem. Am. Collectors Assn., Nat. Speakers Assn., Ind. Collectors Assn. (dir. 1980-82), Ind. Speakers Assn. (dir. 1980-82), Hosp. Fin. Mgmt. Assn., Anderson C. of C. Mem. Ch. of Christ. Clubs: Exchange, Toastmasters. Office: American Accounts Inc PO Box 1192 Anderson IN 46015

ARNOLDT, ROBERT PATRICK, internat. banking analyst; b. Chgo., Oct. 16, 1944; s. Frederick Werner and Margaret (O'Callaghan) A.; A.A., Chgo. City Coll., 1970; B.A. in History, Elmhurst (Ill.) Coll., 1973; M.A. in History, Northeastern Ill. U., 1979; m. Patricia Ellen Ruh, Dec. 27, 1970; children—Robert Kevin Patrick, James Matthew Patrick, Kathleen Patricia Maureen, Thomas Michael Patrick. Dist. exec. Boy Scouts Am., Oak Park, Ill., 1970-71; supr. trust dept. Continental Ill. Nat. Bank, Chgo., 1972-77, analyst internat. banking dept., 1977—; mil. historian and writer, 1975—. Served with U.S. Army, 1965-68. Decorated Bronze Star medal, Air medal, Combat Infantryman's badge. Home: 1134 S Scoville Ave Oak Park IL 60304 Office: 231 S LaSalle St Chicago IL 60693

ARNOLDY, JAMES PETER, hosp. engr.; b. Rollingstone, Minn., Aug. 18, 1928; s. Theo M. and Margaret O. (Maus) A.; ed. high sch.; m. Johanna Gullickson, Jan. 15, 1954; children—Gilbert, Mary Ann, Jane. Operating engr. Owatonna (Minn.) State Sch., 1956-61; supt. maintenance St. Elizabeth Hosp., Wabasha, Minn., 1961—; tchr. steam engring. course vocat. sch., Winona, Minn., 3 yrs.; lectr. in field. Mem. Wabasha City Council, 1976-78. Served with U.S. Army, 1951-53; Korea. Mem. Nat. Assn. Power Engrs. (pres.'s award 1977, trustee Minn. assn., dir. Minn. assn. 1981—, merit award 1971), So. Minn. Hosp. Engrs. (pres.'s award 1979), Am. Soc. Hosp. Engring., Am. Legion, VFW. Roman Catholic. Home: 124 E Grant Blvd Wabasha MN 55981 Office: St Elizabeth Hosp 1200 5th Grant Blvd W Wabasha MN 55981

ARONOFF, STANLEY J., lawyer, state senator; b. Cin., June 8, 1932; s. Irwin I. and Cecilia (Hyman) A.; B.S. cum laude, Harvard U., 1954, J.D., 1957; m. Gretchen Vicky Schwab, June 15, 1958; children—Traci, Jay, Leslie. Admitted to Ohio bar; partner firm Aronoff & Rosen, L.P.A., Cin., 1959—; mem. Ohio Ho. of Reps., 1960-66; mem. Ohio Senate, 1967—, asst. pres. pro tempore. Trustee, Cin. Playhouse in the Park, Children's Protective Service. Named Senator of Yr., Hamilton County Assn. Twp. Trustees and Clks., 1976. Served in U.S. Army, 1957. Mem. Am. Bar Assn., Ohio Bar Assn., Fed. Bar Assn., Cin. Bar Assn., Nat. Conf. State Legislatures/State Fed. Assembly, Council State Govts., Am. Legis. Exchange Council. Republican. Jewish. Club: Cin. Athletic. Office: 1400 First Nat Bank Center 425 Walnut St Cincinnati OH 45202*

ARORA, GULSHAN K. (JIM), stair treads and walkway products mfg. co. exec.; b. India, Jan. 2, 1941; came to U.S., 1967, naturalized, 1974; s. Ganesh Das and Vidya Wati (Gulati) A.; B.S. in Mech. Engring., U. Jammu and Kashimir, 1965; M.S. in Indsl. Engring., Wayne State U., Detroit, 1968, M.B.A., 1973; m. Urmil Jeirath, Feb. 22, 1970; children—Poonam, Geeta. Indsl. engr. Ford Motor Co., Dearborn, Mich., 1968-75; mgr. cost analysis Premier Indsl. Corp., Wooster, Ohio, 1975-77; mem. corp. staff A-T-O Inc., Willoughby, Ohio, 1977-78; mgr. mfg. engring. Flow Control div. Rockwell Internat. Corp., Barberton, Ohio, 1978-80; pres., chief exec. officer, dir. Wooster Products Inc., 1980—. Mem. Am. Prodn. and Inventory Control Soc. Office: 1000 Spruce St Wooster OH 44691

ARORA, NIGAM, bus. exec.; b. Chandigarh, India, Mar. 24, 1955; came to U.S., 1975; s. Dharam Bir and Prem Kanti (Kumar) A.; B.Sc. in Engring. with honors, Panjab U., 1975; M.S. in Elec. Engring., U. Kans., 1976. Research asst. Center for Research, Inc., Lawrence, Kans., 1975-76; dir. engring. Nuclear Measurements Corp., Indpls.,

1976-81; owner Action Placers, Indpls., 1981—; pres. Val-Yu Products, Indpls., 1981—; asso. faculty Ind. U.-Purdue U., Indpls., 1981—. Mem. Am. Soc. Metals. Home: 845G N Christiana Ln Indianapolis IN 46256 Office: 3020 S Meridian St Indianapolis IN 46217

ARORA, SHIV KUMAR, educator; b. India, Apr. 9, 1939; s. Chiman Lal and Kamla Vati A.; B.Sc., Agra U., India, 1957, B.Chem.E., 60; M.S.E., U. Mich., 1964; M.B.A., Mich. State U., 1971, Ph.D., 1975; m. Shirley Ann Miller, July 30, 1976. Design engr. D.C.M. Chem Works, Delhi, India, 1960-63; chemist duPont Co., Flint, Mich., 1964-70; asst. prof. Phila. Coll. Textile and Sci., 1974-76; asso. prof. Clarion (Pa.) State Coll., 1976-77; asso. prof. Saginaw Valley State Coll., University Center, Mich., 1977-80, prof. mktg., 1980—. U. Mich. sr. fellow, 1964. Mem. Eastern Mich. Bridge League (v.p.), Am. Contract Bridge League, Am. Mktg. Assn., Midwest Mktg. Assn., So. Mktg. Assn., Sigma Iota Epsilon, Delta Sigma Pi, Beta Gamma Sigma. Republican. Club: Rotary. Home: 2164 Marlou Ct Saginaw MI 48603 Office: Dept Bus Saginaw Valley State Coll University Center MI 48710

ARRINGTON, DOROTHY M. CHRISTIAN, dietitian; b. Birmingham, Ala., July 25, 1929; d. Noah and Maggie Louise (Cook) Christian; B.S. (scholar), Tuskegee Inst., 1950; m. W.C. Arrington, Apr. 25, 1950; children—Kathleen Yvonne, William Curtis, Maragret Elaine, Christopher Jay. Dietary technician Michael Reese Hosp., Chgo., 1952-53; library clk. Chgo. Public Library, 1959-61; lunchroom mgr. Chgo. Bd. Edn., 1961-62; dietitian-mgr. St. Peter Lutheran Sch., 1962-64; adminstrv. dietitian Mercy Hosp., Chgo., 1965-77, nutritionist Mercy Hosp. Diagnostic and Treatment Center, 1977—, nutritionist Calorie Anonymous. Mem. parent-tchr. leagues St. Peter Luth. Sch., 1957-76, Luther High Sch. S., 1964-74, Morgan Park High Sch., 1974-76; mem. fund raising com. Whitney Young High Sch. Band Booster Club, 1977-79; active Beverly Area Planning Assn., 1974—. Mem. Am. Dietetics Assn., Ill. Dietetics Assn., South Suburban Dietetic Assn. Cook County, Soc. for Protection Unborn through Nutrition. Democrat. Lutheran. Club: Tuskegee Inst. Alumni. Office: Mercy Hosp Diagnostic and Treatment Center Stevenson Expressway at King Dr Chicago IL 60616

ARROWSMITH, BRIAN G., village ofcl.; b. Wayne, Mich., May 5, 1945; s. Wallace G. and Mildred E. (Bower) A.; B.S., Eastern Mich. U., 1969; m. Patricia A. Dobryden, Nov. 26, 1966; children—Scott, Monica, Alan. Securities clk. Detroit Stock Clearing Corp., Detroit Stock Exchange, 1965-67; traffic clk. Willow Run Airport, Detroit, 1967-69; tchr. Wayne Community Schs., 1969-70; desk clk., bell capt. Stouffers Northland Inn, Detroit, 1971-72; sales mgr. Arrowsmith Campcraft Sales, Detroit, 1971-73; mem. Wayne County Bd. Commrs., 1973-74; chmn. Wayne County Bd. Health, 1973-75; circuit city mgr. Mark Twain Regional Planning Commn., Macon, Mo., 1975; village mgr., Oxford, Mich., 1975—; chmn. 19th chpt. Mich. Alliance Small Communities, 1975—. Dir. 15th Dist. Republican Club. Bd. dirs. Communities United for Action; bd. dirs., v.p. Kiddie Junction Nursery, 1979—. Mem. Mich. Assn. Counties, Internat. City Mgmt. Assn., Eastern Mich. U. Alumni Club. Club: Oxford Rotary (pres. 1980). Home: 416 Thornehill Trail Oxford MI 48051 Office: 22 W Burdick St Oxford MI 48051

ARSENOVIC, ALEXANDAR ILIJA, physician; b. Beograd, Yugoslavia, Dec. 19, 1928; came to U.S., 1969, naturalized, 1975; s. Ilija P. and Ann J. (Muk) A.; M.D., U. Belgrade, 1953; m. Vukosava Dokovic, July 4, 1954; children—Ilija, Nanka. Intern, U. Beograde, 1954-55; ednl. asst. Acad. Sci. Serbia, Inst. Med. Research, 1954, 55; practice medicine specializing in internal medicine, Belgrade, 1955-59; chief lab., Belgrade, Yugoslavia, 1961-68; resident in family practice Edgewater Hosp., Chgo., 1969-70; chief internal medicine dept. Downtown Hosp., Kansas City Med. Center, 1978-80; internist VA Hosp., Topeka, 1980—. Diplomate Am. Bd. Family Practice, Am. Bd. Quality Assurance. Mem. AMA (awards 1974, 78), Am. Geriatrics Soc., Am. Coll. Utilization Physicians. N.Y. Acad. Polit. Sci. Methodist. Author: Viral Cause of Cancer, 1956. Office: Room 145B 2200 Gage Blvd Topeka KS 66622

ARTHUR, JAMES WILLIAM, constrn., fin., devel. co. exec.; b. Akron, Ohio, Jan. 29, 1940; s. William L. and Ethel H. A.; B.A., Kent State U., 1963; m. Nancy L. Sage, June 28, 1964; children—William, Walter, Jennifer. Broker, Merrill Lynch Pierce Fenner & Smith, Akron, 1964-71; owner, pres. Arthur Constrn. Co., Kent, Ohio, 1971-73; pres. Trans Ohio Land Corp., Kent, 1972—; pres. Mahoning River Valley Corp., Kent, 1978—. Mem. Village Council, Sugar Bush Knolls, 1981—. Served with U.S. Army, 1957. Home: 1515 Lake Martin Dr Kent OH 44240 Office: 1640 Franklin Ave Kent OH 44240

ARTHURHULTZ, PHILLIP JAMES, state ofcl.; b. Shelby, Mich., June 16, 1947; s. Earl Franklin and Ruth Efting (Fekken) A.; student Muskegon Community Coll., 1965-67, Albion Coll., 1968-71. Legis. aide Mich. Ho. of Reps., 1967-68; adminstrv. asst. Senator Gary Byker Mich. State Senate, 1971-72, dir. Republican caucus, 1973-78; mem. Mich. State Senate, 1978—, minority whip, 1979—: asst. Congressman Guy VanderJagt, Washington, 1972-73. Mem. Nat. Rifle Assn., Jaycees, Mich. Farm Bur. Clubs: Mich. United Conservation, Old Newsboys, Eagles. Office: State Capitol PO Box 30036 Lansing MI 48909*

ARVIN, CHARLES STANFORD, librarian; b. Loogootee, Ind., Apr. 17, 1931; s. Leland Stanford and Mary Hope (Armstrong) A.; A.B., Wayne State U., 1953, postgrad., 1956-57; M.A. in Library Sci., U. Mich. 1960. Asst. divisional Librarian U. Mich. Natural Sci. Library, 1960-62; head reference Genesee County Library, Flint, Mich., 1962-67, 77—, head central services, 1967-77. Served with AUS, 1953-56. Mem. ALA, Mich. Library Assn., Mich., Ind., Genesee County hist. socs., ACLU. Club: Flint Library. Editor: Flint Geneal. Quar., 1981—. Home: 702 W Oliver St Owosso MI 48867 Office: 4195 W Pasadena St Flint MI 48504

ARZOUMANIDIS, GREGORY G., chemist; b. Thessaloniki, Greece, Aug. 16, 1936; came to U.S., 1964, naturalized, 1976; s. Gerasimos and Sophia A.; B.S.-M.S. in Chemistry, U. Thessaloniki, Greece, 1959; Ph.D. in Inorganic Chemistry, U. Stuttgart (Germany), 1964; M.B.A., U. Conn., 1979; m. Anastasia Anastasopoulos, Jan. 2, 1966; children—Sophia, Alexis. Research asso. M.I.T., Cambridge, 1964-66; research chemist Monsanto, Everett, Mass., 1966-69; sr. research chemist Am. Cyanamid Co., Stamford, Conn., 1969-72, Stauffer Chem. Co., Dobbs Ferry, N.Y., 1972-79, Amoco Chems. Corp., Naperville, Ill., 1979—. Served to 2d lt. Greek Army, 1959-61. Recipient acad. award, Govt. of W. Ger., 1963. Mem. Am. Chem. Soc., Sigma Xi. Greek Orthodox. Inventor comml. catalysts for polypropylene plastics, new processes; U.S. and fgn. patentee; contbr. articles to sci. jours. Home: 7 S 610 Carriage Way Naperville IL 60540 Office: PO Box 400 Naperville IL 60566

ASANTE, KWASI SEITU, artist; b. Jackson, Miss., Feb. 8, 1942; s. Thomas Samuel and Tomuthers (McKee) Harper; degree Coll. Art and Design, U. Detroit, 1965; m. Annette George, May 17, 1969 (div.); children—Ruth, Beradette, Sophia, Kwaku, Kwasi. Comml. artist, illustrator Jam Handy Orgn., 1964-68, Wildings Co., 1968-69; freelance artist, art historian, Detroit, 1969—; rep. permanent collections Johnson Publishing Co., Herbert F. Johnson Mus. at Cornell U., also pvt. collections. Recipient 1st pl. award United Automobile Workers, 1966, Wildings Silver award, 1969, Stax Art award for Expo '72, 1972. Mem. Nat. Conf. Artists.

ASBURY, JEAN ANN, hosp. exec.; b. Charleston, W.Va., Nov. 11, 1947; d. Arnold Crawford and Selma Clara (Bek) A.; B.A., Coll. of Wooster, 1969; student Bowling Green State U., 1976—. Editor, mktg. asst. Toledo Trust Co., 1969-71; campaign asst. for fund devel. campaign Ketchum, Inc., Toledo, 1971; grants asst. St. Vincent Hosp. and Med. Center, Toledo, 1971-73; dir. public relations St. Charles Hosp., Oregon, Ohio, 1973—, mem. adv. bd., 1973—. Pres., Northwest Ohio Regional Alcoholism Council, 1979-81; dist. capt. Am. Cancer Soc. Fund Drive, 1976-80; mem. program operating bd. Info. and Referral Service, United Way agy., 1980—, pres. bd., 1981—. Mem. Hosp. Council Northwest Ohio (chmn. public relations dirs. com. 1976), St. Charles Hosp. Aux., Public Relations Soc. Am., LWV, Ohio Hosp. Assn. (public relations com. 1976-77, 79-80), Am. Soc. Hosp. Public Relations, Ohio Soc. Hosp. Public Relations (charter), Press Club Toledo, Ohio Assn. Hosp. Devel., AAUW. Presbyterian. Club: Zonta (asst. sec.-treas. 1977-78, sec. 1979-80) (Toledo). Home: 2960 W Central Ave Apt 129 Toledo OH 43606 Office: St Charles Hosp 2600 Navarre Ave Oregon OH 43616

ASCHER, JAMES JOHN, pharm. co. exec.; b. Kansas City, Mo., Oct. 2, 1928; s. Bordner Fredrick and Helen (Barron) A.; student Bergen Jr. Coll., 1947-48, U. Kan., 1946-47, 49-51; m. Mary Ellen Robitsch, Feb. 27, 1954; children—Jill Denise, James John, Christopher Bordner. Rep., B. F. Ascher & Co., Inc., Memphis, 1954-55, asst. to pres., Kansas City, Mo., 1956-57, v.p., 1958-64, pres., 1965—. Bd. dirs. Childrens Cardiac Center, 1964—, pres., 1968-70; mem. central governing bd. Children's Mercy Hosp., 1968-80; bd. dirs. Jr. Achievement of Middle Am., 1970—, pres., 1973-76, chmn., 1979—; edn. chmn. Young Presidents' Orgn. 6th Internat. Univ. for Presidents, Athens, 1975. Served to 1st. lt. AUS, 1951-53. Decorated Bronze Star, Combat Infantryman's Badge. Mem. Pharm. Mfrs. Assn., Drug, Chem. and Allied Trades Assn., World Bus. Council, Chief Execs. Forum, Midwest Pharm. Advt. Club, Sales and Advt. Execs. Club, Am. Mgmt. Assn. (pres.'s assn.), VFW, Delta Chi. Rotarian. Clubs: Lotos, N.Y. Athletic; Kansas City; Indian Hills Country (Prairie Village, Kan.). Home: 6706 Glenwood Shawnee Mission KS 66204 Office: 15501 W 109th St Lenexa KS 66219

ASCHOM, DONALD F., univ. ofcl.; b. LaCrosse, Wis., Mar. 24, 1928; s. George C. and Edna D. Aschom; B.A. in Bus. Adminstrn., Luther Coll., Decorah, Iowa, 1950; postgrad. Northwestern U., Mich. State U.: children—Kenneth, Gail, Janet. High sch. tchr., Sanborn, Iowa, 1952-53; asst. to dir. tng. Traffic Inst., Northwestern, 1953-56; mem. adminstrv. staff Mich. State U., 1956-64, dir. civil def. tng. contract, 1964-65, asso. dir. ins. program, 1965-66, dir. ins. program, 1966—. Served with AUS, 1950-52. Mem. Nat. Univ. Extension Assn. Republican. Presbyterian. Clubs: Univ. (Mich. State U.), Masons. Home: 2740 Still Valley Dr East Lansing MI 48823 Office: 56 Kellogg Center Mich State Univ East Lansing MI 48824

ASH, JAMES BOYD, mktg. cons.; b. Ardmore Park, Pa., Feb. 10, 1927; s. Harrison Boyd and Wilda Jane (North) A.; B.S., U. Pa., 1949; M.S., Northwestern U., 1951; m. Iris Gaillard Pond, Mar. 14, 1953; children—Margaret Susan Ash Watkins, Jeffrey Boyd. Mag., newspaper editor, Phila., Lancaster, Coatesville, Pa., 1949-52; asst. mgr. pub. relations Lukens Steel Co., Coatesville, 1952-59; mgr. pub. relations. advt. Borg-Warner Corp., Chgo., 1959-66; dir. pub. info. Perkins & Will Partnership, Chgo., 1966-68; v.p. Crown Center subs. Hallmark Cards, Kansas City, Mo., 1968-69; owner, operator James B. Ash Mktg. Counsel and Service, Shawnee Mission, Kans., 1969—; cons., lectr. in field. Served with inf. and Transp. Corps, U.S. Army, 1945-47; PTO. Mem. Sigma Delta Chi. Methodist. Contbr. articles to profl. archtl., engring., bus. publs., 1969—. Home: 3916 W 58th St Shawnee Mission KS 66205

ASH, RUSSELL HARLOW, wheel mfg. co. exec.; b. Washington, Apr. 7, 1943; s. Ara Russell and Polly (Hymon) A.; B.A., Okla. State U., 1966; M.S., Clemson U., 1971; m. Linda Lou Craig, June 1, 1962; children—Tracy Ellen, Russell Scott, Erin Anne, Colin Craig. Heavy equipment operator/farmhand Keil & Schmidt Constrn. Co., Bessie, Okla., 1956-66; mfg. devel. trainee/indsl. engring. mgr. Allis Chalmers Co., Milw., 1966-68; indsl. engring. mgr. Sangamo Electric Co., West Union, S.C., 1968-71; mfg. mgr. Worthington Pump Co., Shawnee, Okla., 1971-74; plant mgr. Kelsey Hayes Co., Seminole, Okla., 1974-77; ops. mgr. French & Hecht div. Kelsey Hayes Co., Davenport, Iowa, 1977-78, pres., gen. mgr. since 1978—. Ops. mgr. Jr. Achievement of Quad Cities. Mem. Am. Soc. Mfg. Engrs. (cert. mfg. engr.), Am. Prodn. and Inventory Control Soc., Am. Inst. Indsl. Engrs. Presbyterian. Club: Lions. Home: 2536 E George Washington Blvd Davenport IA 52803 Office: French & Hecht 540 E 3rd St Davenport IA 52808

ASH, THOMAS PHILIP, ednl. adminstr.; b. East Liverpool, Ohio, June 4, 1949; s. Bobby and Elizabeth Ann (Ludwig) A.; B.S., Bowling Green State U., 1971; M.S. Ed., Youngstown State U., 1974, postgrad., 1974—; m. Nancy Elizabeth Gauron, June 8, 1973; children—Megan Elizabeth, John Gauron. Tchr., East Liverpool (Ohio) Public Schs., 1971-74, project coordinator, 1974-78, asst. supt. schs., 1978—. Mem. Am. Assn. Sch. Adminstrs., Assn. Supervision and Curriculum Devel., Ohio Assn. Sch. Personnel Adminstrs. East Liverpool Area C. of C. Presbyterian. Club: Kiwanis. Home: 2991 Kingsridge Dr East Liverpool OH 43920 Office: 202 Maplewood Ave East Liverpool OH 43920

ASHBACH, DAVID LAURENCE, internist, nephrologist; b. Chgo., Nov. 17, 1942; s. Sol Henry and Lila Mae A.; A.B., Knox Coll., 1964; M.S., Case Western Reserve U., 1969, M.D., 1970; m. Arlene Rosenthal Nov. 28, 1963; children—Barbara, Deborah, Robert. Intern, Presbyterian-St. Luke's Hosp., Chgo., 1970-71, resident, 1971-73, fellow in nephrology, 1973-75; practice medicine specializing in nephrology, Homewood, Ill., 1975—; mem. staffs St. Margaret's Hosp., Hammond, Ind., Presbyterian-St. Luke's Hosp., Chgo., Meth. Hosp., Gary, Ind., St. Anthony's Hosp., Crown Point, Ind.; instr. Rush Med. Coll.; asst. clin. prof. medicine Ind. U. Diplomate Am. Bd. Internal Medicine. Mem. A.C.P., Am. Internat. socs. nephrology. Jewish. Home: 20457 Ithica St Olympia Fields IL 60461 Office: 18656 Dixie Hwy Homewood IL 60430

ASHBACH, ROBERT O., state senator; b. July 18, 1916; student U. Minn. Chmn. bd. Roseville (Minn.) State Bank; mem. Minn. Ho. of Reps., from 1952, Minn. Senate, 1974—; councilman, mayor Arden Hills. Active numerous civic orgns. Republican. Office: 123B State Office Bldg Saint Paul MN 55155*

ASHBROOK, JOHN MILAN, congressman; b. Johnstown, Ohio, Sept. 21, 1928; A.B. with honors, Harvard U., 1952; J.D., Ohio State U., 1955; LL.D., Ashland Coll., 1963; m. Jean Spencer; children—Barbara, Laura, Madeline. Admitted to Ohio bar, 1955, practiced in Johnstown; pub. Johnstown Ind. weekly, 1953—; mem. 87th-97th Congresses from 17th Dist. Ohio. Mem. 102d-103d Ohio Gen. Assemblies; past chmn. Young Republican Nat. Fedn. Served with USN. Office: 1436 Longworth House Office Bldg Washington DC 20515

ASHBY, DAVID WARD, health care mgmt. cons.; b. Des Moines, Feb. 5, 1946; s. Gerald Joseph and Elizabeth Elaine (Reese) A.; B.A., Willamette U., 1968; M.S., U. Ariz., 1971; M.B.A., Stanford U., 1973; M.S., Stanford Med. Sch., 1974; m. Susan Alice McGeehon, Dec. 28, 1968. Asst. to asst. v.p. med. affairs Stanford (Calif.) Med. Sch., 1973; mgmt. cons. KMB Health Systems, Sunnyvale, Calif., 1974; mgmt. cons., health and med. div. Booz, Allen & Hamilton, San Francisco, 1974-76; dir. health care mgmt. services Arthur Young & Co., Columbus, Ohio, 1976—. Office: Arthur Young Co 100 E Broad St Columbus OH 43215

ASHBY, JOHN ALBERT, advt. agy. exec.; b. Fairmont, W.Va., May 16, 1921; s. William Orr and Emmajean (Ritenour) A.; A.B., Centre Coll., 1943; m. Dolores May Fink, Jan. 13, 1973; children—Jack, Jill, Sharillo, Claudia Meade, Lowell Dillon, Karen Dillon. Editor, Lancaster (Ky.) Central Record, 1943-44; mem. editorial staff Titusville (Pa.) Herald, 1944-45; asst. to pres. Lee Donnelley Corp., 1945-50; v.p. Will Inc., Cleve., 1950-60; pres. Ashby Assos., Inc., Cleve., 1960—; chief exec. officer BP Advt. Assos., 1978—. Pres., Bay Village Bd. Edn., 1956-60. Mem. Am. Assn. Advt. Agys. (gov. 1977-78), First Advt. Agy. Network (past pres.), Pi Kappa Psi, Tau Kappa Epsilon, Omicron Delta Kappa. Republican. Presbyterian. Clubs: Rotary (past pres.), Masons. Office: 525 Terminal Tower Cleveland OH 44113

ASHCOM, JOHN MCCREERY, steel co. ofcl.; b. Pitts., Apr. 7, 1945; s. John M. and Mary Grace (Herron) A.; B.S. in Bus. Adminstrn., Youngstown State U., 1969. Asst. mktg. services mgr. Oisston div. H. K. Porter Co., Pitts., 1970-71; mgr. advt. and sales promotion mcpl. and utility div. Rockwell Internat., Pitts., 1972-77; dir. mktg. communications Sweda Internat. subs. Litton Industries, N.Y.C., 1977-79; mgr. mktg. communications Indsl. Products div. Republic Steel Corp., Canton, Ohio, 1979—. Mem. Bus./Profl. Advertisers Assn., Canton Advt. Club. Office: 1028 Belden Ave NE Canton OH 44705

ASHCRAFT, LAURIE CRAGG, mktg. exec.; b. Washington, May 28, 1945; d. Richard Edwards and Dorothy (Shawhan) Cragg; B.A., Northwestern U., 1967; m. C. Brian Pendleton, May 20, 1972 (div.); m. 2d, W. Dale Ashcraft, Sept. 3, 1977. Psychol. research analyst Allstate Ins. Co., Northbrook, Ill., 1968-70; project supr. Marsteller, Inc., Chgo., 1970-74; mktg. research mgr. corporate mktg. research dept. Internat. Harvester, Chgo., 1974-76; asso dir. mktg. research Libby, McNeill & Libby, Chgo., 1976-78; project mgr. mktg. research S.C. Johnson & Son (Johnson Wax), Racine, Wis., 1978-80; mktg. research mgr. Minnetonka Inc. (Minn.), 1980—; guest lectr. market research various univs. and assns. Mem. Am. Mktg. Assn. (chmn. career conf. 1976—, dir. chpt.), Jr. League, Nat. Orgn. Women, Alliance Francaise, Alpha Delta Pi. Club: Woman's Athletic (Chgo.). Home: 2721 W 47th St Minneapolis MN 55410 Office: Minnetonka Inc PO Box 1A Minnetonka MN 55343

ASHCROFT, JOHN, state ofcl.; b. Springfield, Mo.; grad. Yale U., 1964; J.D., U. Chgo., 1967; married; 3 children. Tchr. bus. law S.W. Mo. State U., Springfield; state auditor Mo., 1972-75, asst. atty. gen., 1975-77, atty. gen., 1977—. Bd. dirs. Greene County chpt. ARC, Sunshine Children's Home, Greater Ozarks chpt. Cystic Fibrosis Found. Mem. Am., Mo., Cole County bar assns., Nat. Assn. Attys. Gen. Republican. Mem. Assembly of God Ch. Author: College Law for Business. Office: Office Atty Gen State Capitol Jefferson City MO 65101

ASHER, JOHN WILLIAM, educator; b. Gary, Ind., Apr. 12, 1927; s. Floyd Gaylord and Ruth Anne (Williams) A.; B.A., DePauw U., 1950; M.S., Purdue U., 1951, Ph.D., 1955; M. Katherine Collyer, Apr. 10, 1955; children—William, Ruth, James, Christopher. Research coordinator U.S. Office Edn., Washington, 1956-60; prof. U. Pitts., 1960-66; prof. edn. and psychol. scis. Purdue U., Lafayette, Ind., 1966—. Served with USNR, 1945-46. Fellow Am. Psychol. Assn., AAAS; mem. Am. Ednl. Research Assn., Interam. Psychol. Assn., Nat. Council Measurement in Edn., Sigma Xi. Republican. Unitarian. Author: Educational Research and Evaluation Methods, 1976. Home: 726 N Chauncey St West Lafayette IN 47906 Office: Dept Edn Purdue U West Lafayette IN 47907

ASHER, STEVEN ROBERT, educator; b. Newark, Feb. 19, 1945; s. Emil and Martha A.; B.A., Rutgers U., 1966; M.A., U. Wis., 1968, Ph.D., 1971; m. Nancy Weinberg, Nov. 30, 1969; children—Matthew, David. Asst. prof. ednl. psychology U. Ill., Urbana-Champaign, 1971-76, asso. prof., 1976-78, asso. prof. ednl. psychology and psychology, 1978—, dir. Bur. Ednl. Research, 1980—. Fellow Am. Psychol. Assn.; mem. Am. Ednl. Research Assn., Soc. Psychol. Study Social Issues, Soc. Research Child Devel. Editor: (with J. M. Gottman) The Development of Children's Friendships, 1981; mem. editorial bd. Child Devel., 1976—; contbr. articles to books and profl. jours. Office: 188 Edn Bldg U Ill 1310 S 6th St Champaign IL 61820

ASHHURST, ANNA WAYNE, educator; b. Phila., Jan. 5, 1933; d. Astley Paston Cooper and Anne Pauline (Campbell) Ashhurst; A.B., Vassar Coll., 1954; M.A., Middlebury Coll., 1956; Ph.D., U. Pitts., 1967; m. Ronald G. Gerber, July 22, 1978. English tchr. Internat. Inst. Spain, Madrid, 1954-56; asst. prof. Juniata Coll., Huntingdon, Pa., 1961-63; asst. prof. Spanish dept. Franklin and Marshall Coll., Lancaster, Pa., 1968-74, acting chmn. Spanish dept., 1972, convenor, fgn. lang. council, 1972-74; asso. prof. dept. modern fgn. langs. U. Mo., St. Louis, 1974-78. Mem. Welcome Wagon Wagon of Lancaster, Pa., 1968-70, 71-74. Fulbright-Hays grantee, Colombia, S.Am., summer 1963; Ford Humanities fellow, summer 1970; Mellon fellow, 1970-71. Mem. Internat. Inst. in Spain, Instituto Internacional de Literatura Iberoamericana, Am. Assn. Tchrs. Spanish and Portuguese, Women's Equity Action League (pres. Mo. div. 1975-76). Author: La literatura hispano-americana en la crítica española, 1980. Home: 2105 Barcelona Dr Florissant MO 63033

ASHLAND, EMELYNE IDA ANDREA, educator; b. Chgo., Oct. 29, 1910; d. Gustav A. and Ida Frances (Alex) A.; B.S., U. Chgo., 1931, S.M., 1933; postgrad. U. Calif. at Berkeley, 1939, U. Colo., 1940. Silhouette artist Century of Progress World's Fair, Chgo., 1933; trade mark artist Colgate-Palmolive Peet Co., Chgo., 1933-34; artist non-verbal Test I.J.R., 1934; med. social worker Unemployment Relief Services, Chgo., 1934-35; tchr. Sterling Twp. (Ill.) High Sch., 1936-37, Chgo. Pub. High Schs., 1937-76; adv., chmn. sci. dept. Gage Park High Sch., 1939-48, Morgan Park High Sch., 1948-54, Senn High Sch., 1954-76; pioneer in traffic safety edn., 1948-51; evaluator sci. materials representing Chgo. South Side schs., 1948-51. Recipient certificate of appreciation Lake County Health Dept., 1976. Mem. Chgo. Tchrs. Union (charter), Soc. Circumnavigators (mem. Marco Polo club). Baptist. Researcher tomato canker incitant: Aplanobactor Michiganese; author (with Tsu-kiang Yen) Devel. of Flower and Fruit of Myrica Rubra, pub. China, 1950. Home: 773 Marion Ave Highland Park IL 60035

ASHLEY, JAMES PHILLIP, ednl. adminstr.; b. Michigantown, Ind., July 31, 1933; s. Jesse Orville and Margaret Susan (Frawley) A.; B.S., Ind. U., 1955, M.S., 1960; postgrad. U. Ill., 1958, U. Colo., 1964, Notre Dame U., 1965; Ph.D., U. Tex., 1967. Tchr., South Bend (Ind.) schs., 1958-62, sci. supr., 1962-65; dir. sci. publications, exec. editor, nat. sci. cons. Ginn and Co., Lexington, Mass., 1966-78; curriculum cons. South Bend Community Sch. Corp., 1979-80, dir. spl. edn. programs, 1980—; instr. St. Mary's Coll., 1961—; cons. in field. Bd. dirs. Tb Assn. of St. Joseph County, 1964; community ambassador Experiment in Internat. Living, Poland, 1962. Served with USAF, 1955-57. Recipient Council for Elem. Sci. Disting. Service award, 1971; Danforth Found. scholar, 1951. Mem. Nat. Sci. Tchrs. Assn., Council for Elem. Sci. Internat., Assn. Supervision and Curriculum Devel., Nat. Council Tchrs. Math., Nat. Council Social Studies, Council Exceptional Children, Phi Delta Kappa. Roman Catholic. Club: Am. Contract Bridge League. Contbr. articles in field. Home: 2025 Waterview Ct South Bend IN 46637 Office: 635 S Main St South Bend IN 46601

ASHLEY, PHYLLIS ALINE, ednl. adminstr.; b. Albion, Ind., Nov. 25, 1918; d. Carna Wilson and Ruth (Myers) Easter; B.S., Ball State U., 1940, M.A., 1965; m. Raymond Wilson Ashley May 31, 1941 (dec.); children—Stephen Ray, Michael Allen. Tchr., LaPorte (Ind.) Schs., 1940-42, Plymouth (Ind.) Schs., 1943-44, Indpls. Schs., 1955-56, 58-62, Winchester (Ind.) Schs., 1956-58; tchr. Muncie (Ind.) Schs., 1962-66, elem. supr., 1967-77, dir. elem. instrn., 1978—. Mem. Assn. Supervision and Curriculum Devel., Ind. Reading Assn., Ind. Assn. Supervision and Curriculum Devel., Nat. Assn. Elem. Sch. Prins., Delta Kappa Gamma. Office: 328 E Washington St Muncie IN 47305

ASHLEY, WAYNE R., clin. psychologist; b. Sublette, Ill., Jan. 5, 1927; s. William M. and Calista (Hurlbut) A.; B.A., Knox Coll., 1950; M.S., U. Okla., 1953, Ph.D., 1960; m. Carolyn Hicks, Jan. 19, 1956; children—Cynthia, Jeff, Julie. Chief psychologist Cerebral Palsy Center of Okla., Norman, 1956-59, Griffin Meml. Hosp., Norman, 1959-64, Five County Mental Health Center, Braham, Minn., 1964-68; pvt. practice psychotherapy, LaSalle, Ill., 1968—; cons. Horizon House Devel. Center (Peru, Ill.). Mem. Senate, Monmouth (Ill.) Coll. Served with AUS, 1945-46. Mem. Am. Psychol. Assn., Ill. Psychol. Assn., Am. Acad. Psychotherapists. Home: Route 1 LaSalle IL 61301 Office: Medical Arts Bldg LaSalle IL 61301

ASHTON, DONALD BRUCE, mfg. co. exec.; b. Grenada, Miss., May 4, 1944; s. Scott Cornell and Nancy (Newlin) A.; student U. Ariz., 1962-63, U. Kans., 1963-66; 1 son, Ian Scott. City editor The Traveler, Arkansas City, Kans., 1972-75; sales mgr., v.p. Brown Cargo Van, Inc., Lawrence, Kans., 1975-78; pres. Ashton Industries div. Brown Cargo Van, Inc., Lawrence, Kans., 1978—. Bd. dirs. Children's Hour Head Start, Jr. Achievement; mem. Homecoming com. U. Kans. Served with U.S. Army, 1967-70. Decorated Bronze Star with oak leaf cluster, Air medal. Mem. Truck Body and Equipment Assn., Nat. Truck Equipment Assn., Lawrence C. of C. (chmn. univ. affairs). Republican. Clubs: Rotary, Cosmopolitan Internat. Home: 2559 Alabama Lawrence KS 66044 Office: 807 E 29th Lawrence KS 66044

ASHTON, RICK JAMES, librarian; b. Middletown, Ohio, Sept. 18, 1945; s. Ralph James and Lydia Marie (Thornbery) A.; A.B., Harvard U., 1967; M.A., Northwestern U., 1969, Ph.D., 1973; M.A., U. Chgo., 1976; m. Marcia K. Zuroweste, Dec. 23, 1966; children—Jonathan Paul, David Andrew. Instr., asst. prof. history Northwestern U., Evanston, Ill., 1972-74; curator local and family history Newberry Library, Chgo., 1974-77; asst. dir. Allen County Public Library, Fort Wayne, Ind., 1977-80, dir., 1980—; cons. Nat. Endowment for Humanities, Nat. Center Edn. Stats., Northwestern U. Office Estate Planning. Bd. dirs. Community Coordinated Child Care, Evanston, 1972-74, Three Rivers Montessori Sch., Fort Wayne, 1977-80; bd. dirs., sec. Allen County-Fort Wayne Hist. Soc., 1977—. Conscientious objector. Nat. Merit scholar, 1963-67; NDEA fellow, 1967-69; Woodrow Wilson fellow, 1971-72. Mem. ALA, Ind. Library Assn., Am. Hist. Assn., Orgn. Am. Historians, Fedn. Geneal. Socs., Bd. for Cert. Genealogists. Clubs: Kiwanis, Fortnightly. Author: The Life of Henry Ruiter, 1742-1819, 1974; The Genealogy Beginner's Manual: A New Edition, 1977. Home: 4617 Calumet Ave Fort Wayne IN 46806 Office: 900 Webster St Fort Wayne IN 46802

ASMAN, ROBERT JOSEPH, lawyer; b. St. Louis, Feb. 7, 1924; s. Robert J. and Anna M. (Spaeth) A.; student Holy Cross Coll., 1941-43; A.B., Cath. U. Am., 1948; LL.B., Georgetown U., 1951; m. Mary Elizabeth Kane, Sept. 8, 1948; children—Kathryn Anne, Robert Joseph III, Peter Kane, Teresa Elizabeth, Suzanne Marie, Elizabeth Jane. Admitted to D.C. bar, 1952, Ohio bar, 1961; asso. firm Cummings, Truitt & Reeves, Washington, 1956; trial atty. anti-trust div. Dept. Justice, 1952-53; asst. U.S. atty. D.C., 1953-60; counsel flight propulsion lab. dept. Gen. Electric Co., 1960-63; v.p., sec., gen. counsel Pneumo Dynamics Corp., Cleve., 1963-70; pres., chief exec. officer Ohio State Bar Assn. Automated Research, Cleve.; mem. firm Van Aken, Bond, Withers, Asman & Smith, Cleve. Mem. Bd. Zoning Appeals, Cleveland Heights, Ohio; mem. Ohio Mental Health and Mental Retardation Adv. Council, 1972—, mem. com. Met. Health Planning Corp.; mem. Cuyahoga County Community Mental Health and Retardation Bd., 1972—. Pres. Hill House, Cleve., 1964; trustee Cleve. Mental Health Assn., 1966-68, St. John's Coll., Hill House. Served with AUS, 1943-45; ETO. Decorated Bronze Star. Mem. Am., Fed., D.C., Ohio bar assns., Greater Cleve. Growth Assn., Phi Delta Phi. Clubs: Clevelander, Skating (Cleve.). Home: 2676 Berkshire Rd Cleveland Heights OH 44106 Office: 1519 Nat City Bank Bldg Cleveland OH 44114

ASPER, BERNICE VICTORIA, newspaper editor; b. Luck, Wis., Apr. 1, 1920; d. Harry Lars and Christine Marie (Hilseth) Johansen; student Mpls. Bus. Coll., 1939; m. Verdie S. Asper, Dec. 23, 1942 (dec.); 1 dau., Vickie Sharon. Bookkeeper, news editor, proofreader Enterprise-Herald, Luck, 1943-44; cashier, sec. Thorp Fin. Corp., Frederic, Wis., 1948-53; bookkeeper Rudell Motor Co., 1953-59, Frederic Telephone Co., 1959-63; editor Inter-County Leader, Frederic, 1963—, also columnist Midweek Musings, As Per Bernice, also editorial writer. Sec., Frederic Citizens Adv. Com., 1970—; bd. dirs. Western Wis. Health Systems Agy., 1976—, Frederic Devel. Corp., 1979—; pres. Polk County Health Forum, 1979; supt. St. Peters Lutheran Sunday Sch., 1947-77. Named Frederic Citizen of Yr., 1980. Author: 75 Years in Frederic, 1976. Home: 302 N Wisconsin Ave Frederic WI 54837 Office: 303 N Wisconsin Ave Frederic WI 54837

ASPEY, WAYNE PETER, zoologist; b. Pitts., Mar. 26, 1946; s. Wayne Stanley and Evelyn Louise (Sardo) A.; A.B. in Psychology, Ohio U., 1968; A.M. (NDEA fellow), Dartmouth Coll., 1971; Ph.D. in Zoology, Ohio U., 1974; m. Lynn Miriam Hirschberg, July 19, 1970; children—Ryan Arnold, Chantelle Erin. Research fellow Marine Biomed. Inst., U. Tex. Med. Br., Galveston, 1974-78; instr. marine biology Moody Coll. of Tex. A&M U., Galveston, 1977-78; asst. prof. zoology Ohio State U., Columbus, 1978—, biology coordinator, 1978—. Mem. Am. Inst. Biol. Sci., Am. Soc. Zoologists, AAAS, AAUP, Nat. Assn. Biology Tchrs., Am. Arachnological Soc., Brit. Arachnological Soc., Animal Behavior Soc., Internat. Soc. Research in Agression, Cambridge Entomol. Club, Sigma Xi. Contbr. articles on animal behavior to sci. jours.; contbr. book revs. to jours. in field. Office: 112 Rightmire Hall Ohio State Univ Columbus OH 43210

ASPIN, LES(LIE), congressman; b. Milw., July 21, 1938; B.A. summa cum laude, Yale, 1960; M.A., Oxford U. (Eng.), 1962; Ph.D. in Econs., Mass. Inst. Tech., 1965. Asst. prof. econs. Marquette U., Milw., 1969-70; mem. 92d-97th Congresses from 1st Dist. Wis.; mem. House Armed Services, Budget, Govt. Ops. coms. Served from 2d lt. to capt. AUS, 1966-68. Mem. Phi Beta Kappa. Office: 442 Cannon House Office Bldg Washington DC 20515

ASRAR, GHASSEM, soil physicist, civil engr.; b. Shiraz, Iran, Oct. 12, 1951; came to U.S., 1976; s. Naser and Masoomeh Asrar (Takesh) A.; B.Sc., U. Shiraz, 1974; M.S., Mich. State U., 1978, 80, Ph.D. (Sage Found. fellow), 1981. Research aide U. Shiraz, 1970-74, lab. instr., 1974; agr. extension specialist, Isfahan, Iran, 1975-76; grad. research asst. Mich. State U., East Lansing, 1976-81; research asso. Kans. State U., Manhattan, 1981—. Mem. Am. Soc. Agronomy, Soil Sci. Soc. Am., Internat. Soil Sci. Soc. Republican. Moslem. Contbr. articles to tech. publs. Home: 525 N Manhattan #4 Manhattan KS 66502 Office: Kans State U Manhattan KS 66506

ATCHISON, BERNARD JAMES, occupational therapist; b. Flint, Mich., Apr. 1, 1952; s. Jack Louis and Audrey Marie (Peltier) A.; B.S. in Occupational Therapy, Western Mich. U., 1975; M.Ed., Ga. State U., 1978; m. Marsha Kmiecik, June 29, 1974; children—Katharine Melissa, Heidi Marie. Instr. dept. occupational therapy Eastern Mich. U., Ypsilanti, 1977-80; occupational therapist Flint Community Schs., 1980—. Mem. adv. bd. Home Health Agy. Served with U.S. Army, 1974-77. Recipient Appreciation certs. Mich. Occupational Therapy Assn., 1980, Home Health Agy., Flint, 1980; Flint Community Schs. grantee, 1981. Mem. Am. Occupational Therapy Assn., NEA, Center for Study Sensory Integrative Dysfuntion, AAUP. Democrat. Roman Catholic. Club: St. Pius X Ushers. Home: 2725 Crestwood Dr Flint MI 48504 Office: Flint Community Schs 1518 W 3d Ave Flint MI 48504

ATHANS, MICHAEL JAMES, psychologist; b. N.Y.C., Jan. 9, 1953; s. Michael and Christine (Georgalas) A.; B.A., St. John's U., 1975; M.A., Columbia U., 1976, M.Ed., 1977; Ph.D., Mich. State U., 1982. Staff therapist LaPorte County Mental Health Center, Michigan City, Ind., Postgrad. Center for Mental Health, N.Y.C.; instr. ednl. psychology Mich. State U., East Lansing; psychol. intern Psychosomatic and Psychiat. Inst., Michael Reese Hosp. and Med. Center, Chgo.; cons. in child psychotherapy and stress mgmt. to schs. and corps. Mem. Am. Psychol. Assn. (asso.), Am. Personnel and Guidance Assn., Am. Rehab. Counseling Assn., Midwest Psychol. Assn., Soc. Personality Assessment, No. Ind. Profl. Psychology Group. Home: 2705 N Mildred St Apt 3D Chicago IL 60614

ATHELSTAN, GARY THOMAS, rehab. psychologist, educator; b. Mpls., Dec. 26, 1936; s. Johann Arnold and Laura Louise A.; B.A., U. Minn., 1960, Ph.D., 1966; m. Helga Matthiesen, May 28, 1960; children—Birgit, Erik. Vocat. rehab. counselor State of Minn., Mpls., 1960-61; counseling psychologist VA Hosp., Mpls., 1962-63; research asst., U. Minn., Mpls., 1961-63, instr., 1964-65, asso. prof., 1970-74, prof. phys. medicine and rehab. and psychology 1975—; research psychologist Am. Rehab. Found., 1965-70. Served with USNR, 1954-55. Mem. Am. Psychol. Assn., Am. Congress Rehab. Medicine. Asso. editor Archives of Physical Medicine and Rehab., 1977—; contbr. articles to profl. jours. Office: University of Minnesota Box 297 860 Mayo Bldg Minneapolis MN 55455

ATKINS, BARBARA ANN, profl. personnel agy. exec.; b. Gary, W.Va., Nov. 11, 1935; d. Charles A. and Beatrice (Wade) Penn; student Mich. State U., 1954-55, Wayne State U., 1963-65, Wayne County Community Coll., 1975-78; m. Will E. Atkins, Mar. 27, 1965; children—Lawrence Douglas, Cheryl Lynn, Brian LeRoy. Sec., Burroughs Corp., Detroit, 1957; office coordinator Wayne State U., 1960-64; adminstrv. asst. U. Detroit, 1967-71; accounts receivable supr. Wayne County Community Coll., 1974; v.p., treas. B.P.A. Enterprises, Inc., Detroit, 1974—; pres. Pica Systems Inc., Detroit, 1980—. Mem. women's com. United Negro Coll. Fund, 1979-80; chmn. Modern Rhymthic Fund, 1978. Mem. Am. Bus. Women's Assn., Founders Soc., Mich. Personnel Assn., Nat. Employment Assn., Am. Soc. Personnel Adminstrs., Women's Econ. Club, NAACP, Urban League, Internat. Word Processing Assn. Mem. A.M.E. Ch. Office: 1700 First Nat Bldg Detroit MI 48226

ATKINS, JAMES ALBERT, food services adminstr., cons.; b. Washington, Apr. 24, 1945; s. James Earl and Dorothy (Mix) A.; A.A. in Applied Sci., Ferris State Coll., 1966; student health care mgmt. program U. Ill., 1978-79; m. Joan Marie Pierce, Nov. 7, 1976; children—James Norman, Katherine Marie. Food service mgr., Fred Harvey Restaurants, Chgo., 1966-69; food and beverage mgr. Quality Motels, Jackson, Mich., 1969-70, St. Louis, 1970; food service mgr. Venture Stores, St. Ann, Mo., 1971; asst. dir. food services St. Francis Hosp., Evanston, Ill., 1971-72; gen. mgr. Food Mgmt. Assos., Glen Ellyn, Ill., 1973; asso. dir. of food services St. Annes Hosp., Chgo., 1973-79, St. Elizabeth's Hosp., Chgo., 1973-79; dir. food and nutrition services U. Chgo. Med. Center, 1979—; instr. (part-time) in food service curriculum Coll. of Du Page, Glen Ellyn, Ill., 1976—, adv. coll. food service curriculum, 1979—; chmn. food service com. Ancilla Domini Health Services, 1977-79; cons. food services, 1975—; pres. Atkins & Assos., 1976—; instr. restaurant mgmt. tng. program Triton Jr. Coll., 1978—; coll. curriculum adv. U. Ill., 1979—; lectr., key speaker at food service and mgmt. seminars, 1978—; chmn. Tri-State Conv. for Health Care Food Service, 1979; seminar leader food service tng. programs. Served with USN, 1967-68; Vietnam. Recipient cert. of recognition Evanston Sch. System and Chgo. Food Service Mktg. Club, 1973; designated disting. healthcare food service adminstr. Mem. Internat. Food Service Execs. Assn. (dir.), Am. Soc. for Hosp. Food Service Adminstrs. (past pres.), Am. Hosp. Assn. (Catering Execs. Roman Catholic. Club: Lion. Home: 1019 Carol St Downers Grove IL 60516 Office: PO Box 81 Clarendon Hills IL 60514

ATKINS, THOMAS LEE, employment exec.; b. Chgo., Dec. 4, 1921; s. Samuel Merritt and Alphonsine Marie (La Londe) A.; B.A., U. Notre Dame, 1943; postgrad. Cath. U. Am., 1947-51; m. Marylin E. Bowman, Dec. 19, 1966; children—Elizabeth Ann, Catherine Marie. Ordained priest, Roman Cath. Ch., 1951; asst. pastor Saginaw (Mich.) Sts. Peter & Paul Ch., 1951-54, St. Helen Ch., Saginaw, 1954-58; chaplain VA Hosp., Saginaw, 1954-58, USNR Training Center, Bay City, Mich., 1958-64; pastor Sebewaing (Mich.) St. Mary's Nativity Ch., 1958-63; tng. specialist Bur. Personnel Services, Mich. Employment Security Commn., 1974—. Bd. dirs. Saginaw Valley Indian Assn., 1972—, pres., 1981—. Served with USNR, 1943-46. Mem. Social Workers Roundtable (pres. 1969-74). Republican. Portrait editor, Notre Dame DOME, 1942; lit. editor Sacred Heart Gothic, 1946-47. Home: 4695 Kingswood Dr Okemos MI 48864 Office: 7310 Woodward St Detroit MI 48202

ATKINS, WILLIAM TAFT, mental health adminstr.; b. Waltham, Mass., Aug. 8, 1944; s. Robert W. and Eleanor W. (Whitman) A.; B.A., So. Ill. U., 1968; M.S.W., St. Louis U., 1971; m. Sharon Sue Moeller, Nov. 17, 1967; children—William Taft, Aaron M. Treatment team leader Madison County Unit, Alton (Ill.) State Hosp., 1967-68, dir. adult psychiat. program, 1968-69, psychologist day treatment center, 1969-71; dir. partial hospitalization program mental health services So. Madison County, Inc., Granite City, Ill., 1971-75, exec. dir., 1975—; adj. asst. prof. St. Louis U., 1976—; adj. instr. So. Ill. U., Edwardsville, 1978—; pres. Council of Community Mental Health Service Providers, region 4, 1978; bd. dirs. Madison County Assn. for Mental Health, 1967-71, pres., 1969-70. Recipient hon. award Community Leader of Am., 1971. Mem. Nat. Assn. Social Workers, Ill. Assn. Community Mental Health Agencies, Am. Assn. Suicidology. Club: Optimist. Co-author: Needs Assessment, A Model for Community Planning; contbr. papers to profl. cons. Home: Rural Route 2 Box 294 Old Carpenter Rd Edwardsville IL 62025 Office: 2024 State St Granite City IL 62040

ATKINSON, ARTHUR JOHN, JR., clin. pharmacologist, educator; b. Chgo., Mar. 22, 1938; s. Arthur John and Inez (Hill) A.; A.B. in Chemistry, Harvard U., 1959; M.D., Cornell U., 1963. Intern and asst. resident in medicine Mass. Gen. Hosp., Boston, 1963-65, chief resident and Howard Carroll fellow in medicine Passavant Meml. Hosp., Chgo., instr. in medicine Northwestern U., Chgo., 1967-68; fellow in clin. pharmacology U. Cin., 1968-69, asst. prof. pharmacology, 1969; vis. scientist dept. toxicology Karolinska Inst., Stockholm, Sweden, 1970; asst. prof. medicine and pharmacology Northwestern U., Chgo., 1970-73, asso. prof., 1973-76, prof., 1976—. Served with NIH, USPHS, 1965-67. Recipient Faculty Devel. award in clin. pharmacology Pharm. Mfrs. Assn., 1970-72; Burroughs Wellcome scholar in clin. pharmacology, 1972-77. Fellow A.C.P.; mem. Am. Fedn. Clin. Research, Central Soc. Clin. Research, Am. Soc. for Clin. Investigation, Am. Soc. Pharmacology and Exptl. Therapeutics, Chgo. Soc. Internal Medicine, Alpha Omega Alpha. Club: Chgo. Yacht. Mem. editorial bd. jours. Rational Drug Therapy, 1972—, Clin. Pharmacology and Therapeutics, 1973—, Pharm. Revs., 1977, Therapeutic Drug Monitoring, 1979. Home: 54 E Division St Chicago IL 60610 Office: 303 E Superior St Chicago IL 60611

ATKINSON, DOROTHY DARLENE SORLIE, educator; b. Eau Claire, Wis., Sept. 10, 1941; d. Walter H. and Clara Lee Sorlie; B.S. cum laude in Edn., U. Wis., Eau Claire, 1963, M.S. in Teaching, 1981; m. Mark Bruce Atkinson, June 22, 1963; children—Thomas Sheridan, Susan Lee, Michael Buffington. Tchr., Waukesha (Wis.) public schs., 1963-65; tchr. English as 2d lang., adult basic edn., speedreading, high sch. credit English, communication skills Study Skills Center, Dist. 1 Tech. Inst., Eau Claire, 1973—; dir. Farmer Store Co., 1975-78; tree farmer, 1980—. Mem. Internat. Reading Assn., Wis. Assn. Vocat. Adult Edn., Wis. Reading Assn., Wis. Assn. Adult Continuing Edn., Eau Claire Reading Council. Republican. Lutheran. Home: 903 Taft Ave Eau Claire WI 54701 Office: 620 W Clairemont Ave Eau Claire WI 54701

ATKINSON, MARK BRUCE, cable co. exec.; b. St. Paul, Aug. 16, 1941; s. Marshall Buffington and Alveretta Irene (Smith) A.; student U. Wis., Madison and Eau Claire; diploma Am. Press Inst., Columbia U., 1971; m. Dorothy Darlene Sorlie, June 22, 1963; children—Thomas Sheridan, Susan Lee, Mike Buffington. Display ad salesman, then retail advt. mgr. Waukesha (Wis.) Freeman, 1963-68; dir. advt. Leader-Telegram, Eau Claire, 1968-82; gen. mgr. Leader Tel-A-Cable, Eau Claire, 1982—; v.p. Eau Claire Press Co.; partner Duerre, Turk & Assos., advt., Eau Claire. Sec.-treas. Waukesha Jaycees, 1964. Mem. Internat. Assn. Newspaper Advt. Execs. (dir.), Wis. Newspaper Advt. Execs. Assn. (Bill Payne Meml. award 1968, 69, 70, 72, 75), Am. Newspaper Pubs. Assn., Internat. Newspaper Promotion Assn., Newspaper Advt. Bur., Eau Claire C. of C. Republican. Lutheran. Clubs: Kiwanis, Indianhead 4-Wheelers. Creator weekly farm newspaper The Country Today, 1978.

ATLAS, MARTHA JANE, media buying service exec.; b. Kansas City, Mo., Dec. 2, 1949; d. Irvin D. and Pearl Gertrude (Gallow) A.; B.S. in Journalism, U. Kans., 1971. Media buyer Fromm, Inc., 1971-72; sales sec. Sta. WDAF, 1972-73; media buyer Brewer Advt., 1973; media buyer, copywriter Siddall Advt., 1973-75; media buyer Bernstein, Rein & Boasberg Advt., 1975-77; focus group moderator New Product Insights, Inc., 1977-78; v.p., media dir. Lane & Assos., Inc., 1978-80; propr. Media Mgmt., Kansas City, 1980—. Campaign chmn. young adults div. Kansas City Jewish Fedn., 1978; treas. Am. Jewish Com., 1980, co-chmn. Viewpoints; sec., asso. bd. dirs. Jewish Geriatric and Convalescent Center; mem. steering com. career and profl. div. Jewish Fedn., 1981; publicity chmn. Bacchus Ball, 1981.

ATTIA, SABRY M., state ofcl.; b. Damanhour, Egypt, Apr. 25, 1927; s. Hassan and Galila A. (El-Sayed) A.; came to U.S., 1970, naturalized, 1975; B.S.W., Cairo Sch. Social Work, 1956; M. Public Adminstrn. U. Detroit, 1979; M.S.W., Wayne State U., 1973; m. Serria Moustafa Rashid, June 9, 1951; children—Mervat, Mona, Madiha, Mayssa. Social planning cons. The Egyptian Govt., 1961-70; instr. social work Cairo Sch. Social Work, 1958-61; unit mgr. Henry Ford Hosp., Detroit, 1970-72; program dir. Catholic Youth Orgn., Detroit, 1972; med. social worker Hutzel Hosp., Detroit, 1973-75; welfare services supr. Dept. Social Service County of Wayne (Mich.), Detroit, 1975-78, program specialist, central adminstr., 1979-81, asst. mgr. med. dist., 1981—; pvt. practice social work, Grosse Pointe, Mich.; dir. Profl. Counseling Services, Inc., Grosse Pointe; dir. The Council Social Agys., Cairo. Recipient Exceptional Achievement award CASE, 1981; cert. social worker, Mich. Mem. Nat. Assn. Social Workers, Acad. Cert. Social Workers, Am. Hosp. Assn., Mich. Unit Mgmt. Assn., Brit. Council Social Workers, Egyptian Assn. Social Workers, Wayne State U. Social Work Alumni Assn. (pres.). Home: 19777 E Ida Ln Grosse Pointe Woods MI 48236 Office: 3107 W Grand Blvd Detroit MI 48202 also 17108 Mack Ave Grosse Pointe MI 48230

ATTWOOD, HOWARD WAYNE, accountant; b. Lincoln, Mo., Mar. 2, 1938; s. John Laverne and Idella May (Henry) A.; B.S. in Acctg., S.W. Mo. State U., 1965; m. Akiko Susan Taira, Aug. 6, 1959; children—Diana Lynn, Jeffrey Wayne. Staff acct. Price Waterhouse & Co., C.P.A.s, Kansas City, Mo., 1965-67; partner Stosberg, Davis, Musgrave & Attwood, C.P.A.s, Higginsville, Mo., 1969—; dir. Am. Bank, Higginsville. Treas., bd. dirs. Grace United Methodist Ch., Higginsville, 1970-77; mem. Higginsville Indsl. Devel. Authority, 1981—; active local Boy Scouts Am. Served with USAF, 1956-60. C.P.A., Mo. Mem. Am. Inst. C.P.A.s, Mo. Soc. C.P.A.s. Clubs: Higginsville Lions (pres. 1980-81), Higginsville Country (treas., dir. 1974). Home: 1906 Pine St Higginsville MO 64037 Office: 312 W 19th St Higginsville MO 64037

ATWATER, H. BREWSTER, JR., food products co. exec.; b. Mpls., 1931; A.B., Princeton U., 1952; M.B.A., Stanford U., 1954; married. With McCullough Corp., 1954-58; with Gen. Mills, Inc., Mpls., 1958—, v.p. consumer foods group, 1969-70, exec. v.p., 1970-76, chief operating officer, 1976-77, pres., chief operating officer, 1977-81, pres., chief exec. officer, 1981—, also dir.; dir. Northwestern Nat. Life Ins. Co., Northwest Bancorp, Donaldson Co. Inc., New Ct. Pvt. Equity Fund, Inc. Trustee, MacAlester Coll., Walker Art Center, Mpls.; mem. adv. council Stanford U. Grad. Sch. Bus. Served to lt. (j.g.) USNR, 1955-58. Office: Gen Mills Inc 9200 Wayzata Blvd Minneapolis MN 55440*

ATWOOD, H(ARRY) MASON, educator; b. Marshfield, Wis., Oct. 19, 1916; s. Henry Harrison and Anna Rosetta (Mason) A.; B.S., U. Wis., Stevens Point, 1940, M.S., Madison, 1953, Ph.D., 1958; m. Opal Thompson Tellman, June 5, 1959; children—Carol Tellman Barngrover, Diane Tellman Baker, Peggy Tellman, Amy Doris. Tchr., Florence (Wis.) High Sch., 1941-42; instr. chemistry U. Wis., Racine, Milw., Green Bay, Wausau, Marinette, 1946-55, grad. asst., Madison, 1955-57; asst. prof. adult edn. Ind. U., 1957-71; prof. adult and community edn. Ball State U., Muncie, Ind., 1971—, dir. Inst. Gerontology, 1976—; mem. Ind. Health Facility Adminstrs. Bd. Registration and Edn., 1976—; cons. in field. Mem. homes for aging div. Ind. Health Facilities Council, 1964—; bd. dirs. Delaware County (Ind.) Council on Aging, 1973-80. Served with AUS, 1942-46. Mem. Adult Edn. Assn. USA, Nat. Assn. Public Continuing and Adult Edn., Gerontol. Soc., Assn. Gerontology in Higher Edn., Adult Edn. Assn. Ind., Inc. (Disting. Service award 1976), Ind. Assn. Public Continuing and Adult Edn. Episcopalian. Clubs: Exchange, Elks. Book rev. editor Adult Leadership, 1973-77, Lifelong Learning: The Adult Years, 1977-78, The AGHE Newsletter, 1978—; contbr. chpts. to books and articles to profl. jours. Home: 220 Alden Rd Muncie IN 47304 Office: Ball State U Muncie IN 47306

ATWOOD, HOWARD WRIGHT, savs. and loan exec., bldg. contractor; b. Tallmadge, Ohio, Feb. 14, 1923; s. Earnest Sackett and Geneva Gertrude (Wright) A.; B.A. cum laude in Bus. Adminstrn., Kent State U., 1948; m. Isabelle Therese Parseghian, Dec. 27, 1953; children—Loraine, Michelle, Diane. Owner, operator Atwood Constrn. Co., Tallmadge, 1948—, Atwood Devel. Co., Tallmadge, 1960—; chmn. Falls Savs. & Loan Assn., Cuyahoga Falls, Ohio, 1973—, dir., 1963—. Trustee Akron Regional Devel. Bd., 1978-83. Served with USAAF, 1943-47. Mem. Nat. Assn. Home Builders (life dir.), Soc. Real Estate Appraisers (asso.), Tallmadge C. of C. Republican. Home: 255 Ernest Dr Tallmadge OH 44278 Office: Falls Savs and Loan Assn 2335 2d St Cuyahoga Falls OH 44222

AUBURN, MARK STUART, educator, univ. adminstr.; b. Cin., Dec. 9, 1945; s. Norman Paul and Kathleen (Montgomery) A.; A.B., S.B., U. Akron, 1967; A.M., U. Chgo., 1968, Ph.D., 1971; m. Sandra Korman, Jan. 25, 1969; children—David Andrew, Benjamin Max Joseph. Mem. faculty Ohio State U., 1971—, asso. prof. English, 1977—, asst. vice provost, sec. arts and scis., 1980—; cons. in field. Trustee, First Unitarian Ch. Columbus, 1976-79, pres., 1977-78, moderator, 1979-80. Grantee Am. Philos. Soc., 1972. Mem. Ohio Humanities Council, Am. Soc. 18th Century Studies, MLA, AAUP, Coll. English Assn. Ohio (mem.-at-large exec. com. 1979), Am. Soc. Theater Research, Lambda Chi Alpha. Club: Ohio State U. Faculty. Author: Sheridan's Comedies, 1977; (with others) Drama Through Performance, 1977. Editor: Marriage a la Mode, 1981; editorial bd. Theatre Ann. Home: 59W Dominion Blvd Columbus OH 43214 Office: 164 W 17th Ave Room 141 Columbus OH 43210

AUER, E. DAVID, mortgage co. exec., real estate developer; b. Fort Wayne, Ind., May 5, 1929; s. Edward D. and Ione (Breeden) A.; B.S., Ind. U., 1951; m. Patricia Ann Dailey, Oct. 13, 1951; children—Denise, Debra, David. Mortgage loan officer Johnstone and Johnstone, Inc., Detroit, 1953-55, Detroit Mortgage & Realty Co., 1955-56; pres. Auer Mortgage Co., Pleasant Ridge, Mich., 1955—. Served as 1st lt. U.S. Army, 1951-53. Mem. Mortgage Bankers Assn. Am., Soc. Real Estate Appraisers, Econ. Club Detroit. Republican. Presbyterian. Clubs: Oakland Hill Country, Bloomfield Open Hunt. Office: 23880 Woodward Ave Pleasant Ridge MI 48069

AUERBACH, MARSHALL JAY, lawyer; b. Chgo., Sept. 5, 1932; s. Samuel M. and Sadie (Miller) A.; student U. Ill.; J.D., John Marshall Law Sch., 1955; m. Carole Landsberg, July 3, 1960; children—Keith Alan, Michael Ward. Admitted to Ill. bar, 1955; pvt. practice law, Evanston, Ill., 1955-72; partner in charge matrimonial law sect., law firm Jenner & Block, Chgo., 1972-80; mem. firm Marshall J. Auerbach & Assos., Ltd., Chgo., 1980—; mem. faculty Ill. Inst. for Continuing Legal Edn. Fellow Am. Acad. Matrimonial Lawyers; mem. Ill. State (chmn. family law sect. 1971-72), Am. (vice-chmn. family law sect. com. for liaison with tax sect. 1974-76) bar assns. Author Ill. Marriage and Dissolution of Marriage Act, enacted into law, 1977; (with Albert E. Jenner, Jr.) Historical and Practice Notes to Illinois Marriage and Dissolution of Marriage Act, 1980; contbr. chpts. to Family Law, Vol. 1. Home: 2314 Orrington Ave Evanston IL 60201 Office: 180 N LaSalle Chicago IL 60601

AUFDENKAMP, JO ANN, lawyer, bank exec., librarian; b. Springfield, Ill., Mar. 22, 1926; d. Erwin C. and Johanna (Ostermeier) Aufdenkamp; B.A., MacMurray Coll. for Women, 1945; B.L.S., U. Ill., 1946; postgrad. U. Chgo., 1964-66; J.D., John Marshall Law Sch., Chgo., 1976. Asst. librarian, commerce library U. Ill., 1946-48; info. mgr. Fed. Reserve Bank of Chgo., 1948-80; adminstr. info. services legal dept. Lincoln Nat. Life Ins. Co., Ft. Wayne, Ind., 1980-81; trust officer Central Trust and Savs. Bank, Geneseo, Ill., 1980—; library cons. Office Nat. Planning, Liberia, 1963. Mem. Am. Bar Assn., Ill. Bar Assn. Republican. Lutheran. Office: PO Box 89 Geneseo IL 61254

AUGHNAY, FRANK WILLIAM, corp. exec.; b. Mandan, N.D., 1923; grad. St. Thomas Coll., 1945. Exec. v.p. Bliss & Laughlin Industries, Inc., Oak Brook, Ill.; dir. Andamios Atlas S.A., Cold Finished Steel Bar Co. Office: 122 W 22d St Oak Brook IL 60521*

AUGSBURGER, JOHN BIRD, state senator; b. Goshen, Ind., Sept. 9, 1934; s. John F. and Dorothy L. (Bird) A.; B.S. in Bus., Ind. U., 1956; m. Oweita F. Tomlinson, May 13, 1980; children—Kimberly Kay, Kerri Ann, Angela Joyce. Pres., owner Augsburgers Inc., supermarkets, Syracuse, Ind., 1956—; dir. Warsaw Fed. Savs. and Loan Assn., Syracuse, 1976—; mem. Ind. Senate from 13th Dist., 1976—, chmn. interstate coop. com., 1980, chmn. natural resources com., 1981—. Mem. Ind. Retail Grocers Assn. (dir.), Milford (Ind.) C. of C. (past pres.). Republican. Mem. Christian Ch. (Disciples of Christ). Clubs: Kiwanis, Masons. Address: Route 4 Box 265D-3 Syracuse IN 46567

AUGUSTIN, ANN SUTHERLAND, author, Realtor; b. Evergreen Park, Ill., Aug. 11, 1934; d. Donald A. and Helen E. (Dorsey) Sutherland; student Iowa State U., 1951-53; m. Edward J. Augustin Jr., Jan. 8, 1955 (div. 1974); children—Edward J. III, Kathryn, Donald J., Suzanne. Exec. sec. Standard Register Co., Chgo., 1953-55; tchr. adult edn. Maine Twp. Sch., Park Ridge, Ill., 1961-68; now realtor Century 21, Schaumburg, Ill., monthly columnist regional Century 21 newsletter; free lance writer. Republican. Roman Catholic. Author: Help! I Want to Remodel My Home, 1975; contbr. articles to Reader's Digest, MacFadden-Bartell, Playboy, Chgo. Daily News, Chgo. Tribune, Mt. Prospect Herald, others. Home: 1100 Randville Dr Palatine IL 60667 Office: Century 21 Country Squire 906 S Roselle Rd Schaumburg IL 60172

AUGUSTIN, CARROLL DARWIN, hardware store exec.; b. Lorain, Ohio, June 6, 1933; s. Arthur Conrad and Edith (Rollason) A.; B.S. in Edn., Miami U., Oxford, Ohio, 1956, M.Ed., 1958; m. Penelope Gifford Tiedjens, Sept. 17, 1955; children—Leslie Gifford, Tracy Carroll, Lindsay Victoria. Tchr., Roosevelt Jr. High Sch., Hamilton, Ohio, 1956-59, Garfield High Sch., Hamilton, 1959-63; dir. adult and vocat. edn., supr. indsl. arts Hamilton Bd. Edn., 1963-66; supr. Miami U. Acad. Center, Hamilton, 1963-67; coordinator fed. study on drop-outs Greater Miami Conf. Schs., 1967; dir. vocat. edn. Butler County (Ohio) Schs., Hamilton, 1968-78; owner Augustin's True Value Hardware Store, Greenwich, Ohio, 1978—. Bd. dirs. Am. Cancer Soc., Hamilton, 1963-65, chmn. edn. com., 1964—; chmn. membership com. Hamilton YMCA, 1966, div. chmn. fund drive, 1970, chmn. gen. fund drive, 1971; bd. mgmt. Hamilton West YMCA, 1971—, chmn., 1974-75. Nat. Def. grad. fellow, 1966-67; recipient Outstanding Layman award YMCA, 1971. Mem. Hamilton Classroom Tchrs. Assn. (pres. 1962-63), Hamilton Assn. trade and industry (chmn. com. 1964), Miami-Hamilton Alumni Assn. (mem. control bd. 1963), Sigma Phi Epsilon, Epsilon Pi Tau, Kappa Phi Kappa, Phi Delta Kappa. Presbyterian. Kiwanian (pres. 1971). Home: Rural Route 2 PO Box 122B New London OH 44851 Office: Augustin's True Value Hardware Store 14 Main St Greenwich OH 44837

AUKAMP, MERLE LOUIS, hosp. adminstr.; b. St. Peter, Ill., Nov. 16, 1932; s. George H. and Lela M. (Niehaus) A.; B.S. in Phys. Edn., U. Ill., 1957; M.H.A., Washington U., St. Louis, 1968; m. Joyce H. Metter, Nov. 16, 1957; children—Regina, Donna, Craig. Coach, tchr. Armstrong (Ill.) Twp. High Sch., 1957-58; recreational dir. Barnes Hosp. Med. Center, St. Louis, 1958-67; mem. adminstrv. staff Meml. Hosp., Belleville, Ill., 1967-72, asso. dir., 1971-72; adminstr. Jane Lamb Meml. Hosp., Clinton, Iowa, 1972-75, Alton (Ill.) Meml. Hosp., 1975—; preceptor health care adminstrn. U. Minn., 1976-78; mem. health adv. council Clinton Community Coll.; mem. part-time faculty Belleville Area Coll.; bd. dirs. Madison County Cancer Soc., Upper Madison County Heart Assn. Served with AUS, 1953-55. Mem. Am. Coll. Hosp. Adminstrs., Am. Hosp. Assn., Am. Assn. Hosp. Planning, Am. Protestant Hosp. Assn., Ill. Hosp. Assn. (regional pres. 1978-79), Southwestern Ill. Hosp. Assn., Greater Alton C. of C. (dir.). Lutheran. Club: Rotary. Office: Alton Meml Hosp Memorial Dr Alton IL 62002

AULABAUGH, NORMAN RICHARD, mfg. co. exec.; b. Geneva, Ill., Oct. 29, 1944; s. Norman Lee and Vivian (Savatson) A.; B.S. in Mgmt., No. Ill. U., 1966, M.B.A. in Mgmt., 1968; m. Carol Grace Topel, June 6, 1970. Systems analyst Parker Pen Co., Janesville, Wis., 1972-77, system and programming mgr., 1978-79, then dir. mgmt. info. Public Expenditure Survey County Budget review chmn., 1978-80. Served with USN, 1968-72. Mem. Assn. for System Mgmt. (pres. Madison chpt.). Republican. Home: Rural Route 4 Janesville WI 53545 Office: 219 E Court St Janesville WI 53545

AULD, FRANK, psychologist; b. Denver, Aug. 9, 1923; s. Benjamin Franklin and Marion Leland (Evans) A.; m. Elinor James, June 29, 1946; children—Mary, Robert, Margaret. A.B., Drew U., 1946; M.A., Yale, 1948, Ph.D., 1950. Certified psychologist Mich., Conn., Ontario. Instr. psychology Yale, 1950-52, asst. prof., 1952-59; asso. prof. Wayne State U., 1959-61, dir. clin. psychology training program, 1960-66, prof. psychology, 1961-67; prof. U. Detroit, 1967-70, dir. psychol. clinic, 1967-69; prof. psychology U. Windsor, Ontario, Canada, 1970—. Chmn. Dearborn (Mich.) Community Council, 1962; mem. advisory com. on college work Episcopal Diocese Mich., 1962-71; cons. in field. Recipient Alumni Achievement award, Drew U., 1965. Fellow Am. Psychol. Assn. (mem. com. on evaluation 1961-66); mem. Can., Mich. psychol. assns. Can. Assn. Univ. Tchrs., Soc. for Psychotherapy Research, Ont. Psychol. Assn. (mem. Edn. and tng. bd. 1976—), Conn. State Psychol. Soc., (pres. 1958), Sigma Xi. Club: Economic (Detroit). Author: Steps in Psychotherapy, 1953; Scoring Human Motives, 1959; contbr. articles to profl. jours. Home: 1340 Pierce St Birmingham MI 48009 Office: Dept Psychology U Windsor Windsor ON N9B 3P4 Canada

AULT, DONNA SHERRILL, educator; b. Effingham, Ill., June 23, 1941; d. Glen Edward and Mary Louise (Harmon) Northway; student Eastern Ill. U., 1959-61; B.S., So. Ill. U., 1963; M.S., Ind. U., 1976; m. Dan Ault, Aug. 20, 1961; 1 dau., Danelle Lynn. Tchr., Bristol (Conn.) Central High Sch., 1964-65, Mattoon (Ill.) Sr. High Sch., 1965-70; tchr. adult night classes Mattoon Area Edn. Extension Center, 1968-71; spl. needs tchr. El-Tip-Wa Area Vocat. Sch., Logansport, Ind., 1976—. Mem. Ind. Assn. Vocat. Edn. Spl. Needs Personnel (exec. dir. 1979-81, treas., membership chair 1980-81), Council Exceptional Children, Am. Vocat. Assn., Ind. Vocat. Assn. (Merit award 1981), Nat. Assn. Vocat. Edn. Spl. Needs Personnel, NEA, Ind. State Tchrs. Assn., Logansport Edn. Assn., Sigma Kappa. Baptist. Clubs: P.E.O., Extension Homemakers. Office: 721 N 6th St Logansport IN 46947

AULT, JAMES LEONARD, cost accountant; b. Monmouth, Ill., Feb. 19, 1947; s. George Leonard and Edna Virginia (Allaman) A.; B.S. in Agrl. Econs., U. Ill., 1969; B.S. in Acctg., Western Ill. U., 1975; postgrad. Bradley U., 1980—; Spl. agt. Prudential Ins. Co., Champaign-Peoria, Ill., 1968-73; tax acct. Coopers & Lybrand, Kansas City, Mo., 1975; cost acct. Gates Rubber Co., Galesburg, Ill., 1976—. Community coordinator United Way, 1970. Mellinger scholar, 1965-69. Mem. Champaign County Life Underwriters, Peoria County Life Underwriters, Nat. Assn. Accts., Nat. Mgmt. Assn., Alpha Gamma Rho. Republican. Home: 2805 W Larchmont St Apt H-3 Peoria IL 61615 Office: Gates Rubber Co Knoxville Rd Galesburg IL 61401

AULT, THOMAS JEFFERSON, III, mfg. co. exec., mgmt. cons.; b. Portland, Ind., June 23, 1911; s. Ross Earl and Olga (Sattler) A.; Asso. in Sci., Cumnock Coll., 1932; B.A. in Econs., UCLA, 1934; student Los Angeles Stock Exchange Inst., 1930-32; m. Mary C. Carr, June 30, 1938; 1 son, Brian Carr. Buyer, Borg-Warner Corp., Chgo., 1937-41, asst. purchasing agt., 1941-51, dir. purchasing, 1951-53, v.p. and asst. gen. mgr. Detroit gear div., 1953-54, pres., 1954-56, pres., gen. mgr. Long mfg. div., Detroit, 1956-58; pres., chief exec. officer Saco-Lowell Shops, Boston, 1958-60, also dir.; pres., gen. mgr. The Budd Co., Detroit, 1960-64, dir. automotive div. Can., Mexico, Argentina, 1960-64; v.p. McCord Corp., Detroit, 1965-68, dir., 1965-70; pres., chief exec. officer Avis Indsl. Corp., Madison Heights, Mich., 1968-70, also dir.; pres., gen. mgr. Flyer Industries Ltd., Winnipeg, Man., Can., 1970-73, chmn. bd., 1972-76, chief exec. officer, 1970-76; chmn. bd., chief exec. officer Saunders Aircraft Corp. Ltd., Gimii, Man., Can., 1972-73; chief exec. officer Superior Kendrick Bearings, Inc., Detroit, 1974-75, also dir.; chief exec. officer Washington Heat Transfer, Inc., Polo, Ill., 1976-79, also dir.; lectr. and exec. in residence Ball State U. Coll. Bus., Muncie, Ind., 1979—; cons. to mgmt. Arthur D. Little Consulting, Inc., 1959—. Bd. dirs. United Found. of Southeastern Mich., 1961-64, ARC, Detroit, 1961-64, Jr. Achievement of Southeastern Mich., 1960-63, Employers Assn. of Detroit, 1955-58, Boston Mus. Sci., 1958-60, Mass. Meml. Hosp., 1958-60. Served to capt. U.S. Army, 1941-45. Recipient Purchasing Progress award Purchasing News, 1953, Outstanding Service award Jr. Achievement of Detroit, 1963. Mem. President's Profl. Assn., Engring. Soc. Detroit, NAM, Mich. Mfrs. Assn., Soc. for Advancement Mgmt., Nat. Safety Council, Acad. of Mgmt., Am. Inst. Mgmt., Nat. Assn. Purchasing Mgmt., Am. Textile Machinery Assn., Automotive Parts Mfg. Assn., Farm Equipment Assn., Am. Ordinance Assn., Am. Soc. for Metals, U.S. C. of C., Air Conditioning and Refrigeration Inst., Econ. Club of Detroit (dir. 1961-64), Ind. Hist. Soc., Am. Security Council, Sigma Nu. Clubs: Elks, Masons, Shriners, Country of Detroit, University; La Coquille (Palm Beach); Delaware Country, Muncie (Muncie); Columbia (Indpls.). Contbr. articles on material control, long range planning and mgmt. to indsl. publs. Home: 4501 N Wheeling St Apt 3-102 Muncie IN 47304 Office: Dept of Mgmt Science College of Bus Ball State Univ Muncie IN 47306

AUSDAL, ROBERT BURNS, investment co. exec.; b. Marshalltown, Iowa, Aug. 25, 1926; s. Peter and Gertrude Celina (Stackhouse) A.; B.A. with high distinction, U. Iowa, 1950; m. June Clark, June 3, 1952; children—Claudia June, Laura Krista, Robert Burns. Vice pres. Quail & Co., Davenport, Iowa, 1950-67, Dain, Kalman & Quail, Inc., Mpls., 1967-74; exec. v.p. Beyer-Ausdal & Co., Davenport, 1974-79; pres. Robert B. Ausdal & Co., Inc., Davenport, 1979—. Served with USNR, 1944-46. Mem. Assn. Investment Brokers, Phi Beta Kappa, Alpha Kappa Psi. Clubs: Davenport Outing, Davenport. Home: 3306 33d Ave Ct Rock Island IL 61201 Office: 805 1st Nat Bldg Davenport IA 52801

AUSTIN, DOROTHY WITTE, journalist; b. Necedah, Wis., Aug. 22, 1918; d. Emil Alfred and Marie (Wake) Witte; B.A. cum laude in Journalism, Marquette U., 1940; m. Harry Russell Austin, Oct. 3, 1953; children—Richard Kirk, Stephen Russell, Christopher. With Cath. Herald Citizen, 1940-43; staff asst. A.R.C., Africa and Italy, 1943-45; advt. copy chief Gimbels, Milw., 1945-50; reporter Milw. Jour., 1950-67; asst. and asso. dir. Summerfest, 1967-69; reporter, feature writer Milw. Sentinel, 1970—; public speaker. Former pres. Women's Overseas Service League, Milw.; former bd. dirs. Milw. County Hist. Soc. Recipient Women in Action award, U. Wis., Milw., 1964, award for women's interest features, Milw. Press Club, 1963, award for features, Wis. Press Women, 1976, staff award for excellence in reporting, Milw. Sentinel, 1977, Headliner award Southeastern Wis. chpt. Women in Communications, 1979, Faith and Humanities award, Nat. Council Jewish Women, Milw., 1979. Mem. Wis. Press Women (past pres.), Washington Press Club, Milw. Press Club (past sec.), Kappa Tau Alpha, Gamma Pi Epsilon. Unitarian. Home: 5858 N Lake Dr Milwaukee WI 53217 Office: 918 N 4th St Milwaukee WI 53201

AUSTIN, JACK KENNETH, banker; b. Anderson, Mo., Sept. 28, 1923; s. Chester Andrew and Edna Sue (Eddins) A.; B.S., U. Denver, 1952, postgrad., 1953; m. Vivian Lenore Bell, July 21, 1966; children—Kathleen, Mary Ann, Debra. Escrow officer, office mgr., acct. Titles Inc., 1954-58; asst. trust officer Am. Nat. Bank, Denver, 1958-65; asst. account adminstr. 1st Nat. Bank, Denver, 1965-69; trust officer Bank of Commerce, Sheridan, Wyo., 1969-73; v.p., trust officer Wyo. Nat. Bank, Casper, 1973-75; v.p., trust officer Central Trust & Savs. Bank, Geneseo, Ill., 1975—; cons. estate planning, taxation. Served with AUS, 1943-46; ETO. Mem. Quad City Estate Planning Council, Rock Island County Assn. Life Underwriters, Am. Bankers Assn., Henry County Bankers Assn., Henry County Bar Assn. Republican. Conglist. Clubs: Elks, Lions, Kiwanis. Home: 26 Geneseo Hills Geneseo IL 61254 Office: 101 N State St Geneseo IL 61254

AUSTIN, LEE SCOTT, civil engr.; b. Albion, Mich., Apr. 27, 1949; s. Carlton Scott and Evelyn Elizabeth (Frisk) A.; B.S. in Civil Engring., U. Mo., Rolla, 1971; postgrad. Sangamon State U., Springfield, Ill., 1976-77; m. Martha Jane Crooks, June 12, 1971; children—Eric Allen, Alexander Lee. Civil engr. III, Ill. Dept. Transp., Peoria, 1971-80; sr. project engr. Randolph and Assos., Inc., Peoria, 1980—. Registered profl. engr., Ill. Mem. ASCE, Ill. Assn. Hwy. Engrs., Ill. Soc. Profl. Engrs. Home: 3011 N University Pl Peoria IL 61604 Office: 8901 N Industrial Dr Peoria IL 61615

AUSTIN, MICHAEL HERSCHEL, lawyer; b. nr. Water Valley, Miss., Nov. 7, 1896; s. Michael Green and Willie C. (Roberson) A.; student U. Miss., 1915-18, LL.B., 1922; postgrad. Akron U., 1919; postgrad. Ohio State U., 1919-21, J.D., 1923; m. Esther Catherine Seebach. Nov. 26, 1920 (dec.); m. 2d, Mary Inez Harpst. Tchr. pub. elementary sch., Miss., 1914-15; admitted to Miss. bar 1922, Ohio bar, 1924, since practiced in Columbus, Ohio; partner firm Pfeiffer and Austin, 1927-30. Franklin County atty. Farmers Home Adminstrn., 1963-70. Mem. chmn.'s council Franklin County Democratic Com., mem. Ohio Dem. Party. Fellow of Harry Truman Library; hon. fellow Truman Library Inst. Served with U.S. Army World War I. Recipient Cross of Honor, UDC, 1944, award for service to Am. Legion and vets. Am. Legion, Lancaster, Ohio, 1969; Golden Circle Certificate Ohio State U. Assn.; named mem. Exec. and Profl. Hall of Fame. Mem. Internat. Platform Assn., Am. Bar Assn. (estate gift tax sect.), Ohio (50 Yrs. Practice award), Columbus (probate ct. com., 50 Yrs. Practice award) bar assns., Am. Judicature Soc., Columbus Real Estate Bd. (asso.). Ohio State U. Alumni Assn., Columbus Area C. of C., Am. Legion (post comdr. 1944-45, county comdr. 1953-54, dist. comdr. 1955-56, state treas. 1958-59, Big Four Vets. Council 1956-57, pres. Past Comdrs. Club 1960-61, judge adv. 12th dist. Ohio, 1967, 68, 69, 75-76, named 12th. dist. Outstanding Legionnaire). Phi Alpha Delta. Mason. Clubs: Columbus Lawyers (past sec.), Franklin County Democratic. Home: 47 Richards Rd Columbus OH 43214 Office: 85 E Gay St Columbus OH 43215

AUSTIN, RICHARD HENRY, sec. state Mich.; b. Ala., May 6, 1913; s. Richard H. and Lelia (Hill) A.: B.S., Detroit Inst. Tech., 1937; LL.D., Detroit Coll. Bus., 1971; LL.D., Detroit Inst. Tech., 1979; m. Ida B. Dawson, Aug. 19, 1939; 1 dau., Hazel. Practice as pub. accountant, Detroit, 1941-71; auditor Wayne County, Mich., 1967-70; sec. of state State of Mich., Lansing, 1971—. Del. Mich. Constl. Conv., 1961-62. Bd. dirs. Harper Hosp., Detroit, Detroit United Found., Mercy Coll., Detroit, Detroit YMCA, Oakland Housing, Inc. Mem. Am. Inst. C.P.A.'s, Mich. Assn. C.P.A.'s (Distinguished Achievement award 1972). Democrat. Office: Treasury Bldg Lansing MI 48918

AUSTIN, ROBERT CRAFT, mfg. co. exec.; b. Portland, Oreg., Mar. 21, 1933; s. Ernest Campbell Edward and Minnie Olive (Craft) A.; 1 son, Craig Randall. Patent draftsman firm Buckhorn, Blore, Klarquist & Sparkman, Portland, 1959-63; project engr. Cranston Machinery Co., Portland, 1963-65, C. Tennant Sons & Co. of N.Y., Warren, Ohio, 1965-67, EPI and Reid Strutt Co., Portland, 1967-68; service engr. Lamb Grays Harbor Co., Hoquiam, Wash., 1968-69; tech. dir. Weld-Loc Systems, Inc., Alliance, Ohio, 1969—. Chmn. bd. dirs. Berlin Reservoir (Ohio) Property Owners Assn. 1975-78. Served with U.S. Army, 1953-59. Mem. Soc. Plastics Engrs. Republican. Methodist. Club: Alliance Country. Designer produ. systems for manufacture of extruded plastic strapping. Home: 2132 Valley Dr Deefield OH 44411 Office: 1469 W Main St Alliance OH 44601

AUSTIN, RONALD CHARLES, mfg. co. exec.; b. Decatur, Ill., Sept. 6, 1948; s. Charles Junior and Reah Margaret (Harrison) A.; B.S.B.A., Millikin U., 1974; m. Janyce Lee Denz, Aug. 18, 1979. Billing clk. Firestone Tire & Rubber Co., Decatur, Ill., 1969-72, analyst rates and routes, 1972-75, supr. pvt. distribution, 1975-79, traffic mgr., 1979—; instr. Richland Community Coll., Decatur. Active fund drives Jr. Achievement, Am. Cancer Soc.; chmn. transp. sect. United Way of Decatur and Macon County, 1981. Served with U.S. Army, 1969. Recipient Cert. of Merit for poem Nashville Newsletter. Club: Transp. Poems pub. in World Treasury of Great Poems, Images of the Mystic Truth, The World's Great

Contemporary Poems. Home: 4794 Redbud Ct Decatur IL 62526 Office: PO Box 1320 Decatur IL 62526

AUSTIN-LETT, GENELLE, educator; b. Chgo.; d. Howard Joseph and Evelyn Gene (Reynolds) Blomquist; B.A., U. Ill., Chgo., 1969; M.A., No. Ill. U., 1972. Teaching and research asst. No. Ill. U., 1970-71; TV prodn. asst. Nat. Coll. Edn. High Sch. Workshop, 1972; prof. mass media and critical consumer Principia Coll., summer 1975; reviewer in interpersonal communication, media and behavioral scis. Houghton Mifflin, Harper & Row, William C. Brown, and Wadsworth Pub., 1972—, also asso. prof. speech communication and media Ill. Central Coll., East Peoria, 1971-79; editorial cons. Concordia Pub. House, 1978—; program dir. Clayton (Mo.) U., 1978—; coordinator performing arts multimedia presentations, publicity and recruitment; lectr. media consumerism, psychopolitics and advt.; instr. communications, cons. crisis intervention Fed. Police Tng., 1974-75. Group leader Community Devel. Council, 1974; organizer 9th Ward Teenage Republicans, Chgo., 1963, coordinator, 1967-69; adviser to Ill. Central Coll. Young Reps., 1971-75; clk., dir. exec. bd., chmn. bd. 1st Ch. of Christ, Scientist, Peoria; nat. advisory bd. Am. Security Council; mem. Rep. Nat. Com. Recipient Honors Day recognition U. Ill., 1968, hon. mention Nat. Arts and Letters playwriting contest, 1972; lic. life ins. agt., Mo. Mem. Ill. Speech and Theatre Assn., Speech Communication Assn., Central States Speech Assn., Internat. Data Speak, Lakeview Center Arts and Scis. Clubs: U.S. Senatorial, Bible Investigation, Racquet. Author: (with others) Instructor's Manual for Mass Communication and Human Interaction, 1977; (with Jan Sprague) Talk to Yourself, 1976; contbr. articles to Christian Sci. periodicals.

AUSTINSON, CARLYLE PALMER, banker, city ofcl.; b. Fillmore, N.D., Oct. 10, 1914; s. Austin K. and Louise (Sterry) A.; student State Sch. Sci., Wahpeton, N.D., 1940; m. Helen Sylvia Rauk, 1941; children—Sharon Sylvia, Kent Carlyle. Asst. cashier First Internat. Bank, Esmond, N.D., 1941-43; cashier Farmers State Bank, Leeds, N.D., 1945-50; cashier Northwood State Bank (N.D.), 1950—, v.p., 1970-75, exec. v.p., 1975-79, chief exec. officer, 1977—, pres., 1979—, dir. 1958—. Alderman, City of Northwood, 1952-56, mayor, 1958—; bd. dirs. Northwood Deaconess Hosp. and Home Assn., pres., 1961—; mem. nat. adv. council Nat. Fedn. Ind. Bus.; mem. corp. United Hosp., Grand Forks, N.D. Served from pvt. to sgt., U.S. Army, 1943-45. Mem. Am. Bankers Assn. (governing council 1981), N.D. Bankers Assn. (pres. N.E. dist. 1955, chmn. bank mgmt. com. 1957, chmn. Northeast dist. Centennial Commn. 1963, chmn. pub. relations 1964, mem. legis. com. 1972, 1st v.p. 1975, pres. 1976), League N.D. Municipalities (regional v.p. 1958, pres. 1961), Am. Legion (comdr. post 92, 1967). Republican. Lutheran. Clubs: Elks, Masons. Office: Northwood State Bank Northwood ND 58267

AUSTRIN, HARVEY ROBERT, clin. psychologist, educator; b. N.Y.C., Nov. 8, 1924; s. Benjamin Ralph and Rose Ruth (Rosen) A.; B.S., CCNY, 1945; M.A., U. Ill., 1946; Ph.D., Ohio State U., 1950; m. Miriam Charlotte Gottschalk, Mar. 28, 1948; children—Diane, Debra, Michael. Psychologist, Columbus (Ohio) Bur. Juvenile Research, 1946-47, Columbus State Sch., 1950-51; chief clin. psychologist VA Mental Hygiene Clinic, Indpls., 1951-55; asst. prof. psychology Ohio State U., Columbus, 1955-57; asso. prof. Temple U., Phila., 1957-63; prof., clin. dir. psychology St. Louis U., 1963-72, prof. psychology, 1963—; cons. psychologist, VA, various state, local mental health programs. USPHS grantee, 1965-72; diplomate Am. Bd. Profl. Psychology. Fellow Am. Psychol. Assn., Mo. Psychol. Assn.; mem. Midwestern Psychol. Assn. Asso. editor Profl. Psychology, 1978-81; contbr. articles to profl. jours. Home: 221 S Warson Rd Ladue MO 63124 Office: 221 N Grand Blvd Saint Louis MO 63103

AUWAERTER, JOHN FRANCIS, mfg. co. exec.; b. Chgo., Aug. 24, 1925; s. Albert Frederick and Frances (Bennington) A.; B.S. in Elec. Engring., Northwestern U., 1948; J.D., DePaul U., 1956; m. Irene McElwain (div. Apr. 1977); 1 dau., Mary Reese. Sales engr., product devel. engr., dir. product devel., v.p. sales and fin. Teletype Corp., Skokie, Ill., 1952-71, v.p. sales and service, 1975-80, v.p. customer service, 1981—; dir. mfg. Western Electric Co., Indpls., 1971-75. Address: 44 Park Ln Apt 223 Park Ridge IL 60068

AVEDISIAN, ARMEN G., corp. exec., investor; b. Chgo., Oct. 28, 1926; s. Karekin Der and Kardovil (Ignatius) A.; B.S., U. Ill., 1949; m. Dorothy D. Donian, Nov. 22, 1952; children—Guy A., Vann A., Donna A. Civil engr. Standard Paving Co., Chgo., 1949; constrn. supt. Gallagher Asphalt Corp., Thornton, Ill., 1950-55; v.p., dir. Am. Asphalt Paving Co., Chgo., 1956-64; chmn. bd., pres. Lincoln Stone Quarry, Inc., Joliet, Ill., 1964—, Avedisian Industries, Inc., Hillside, Ill., 1964—; chmn. bd. Delta Constrn. Corp., Joliet, 1968—, Swenson, Inc., Joliet, 1970—, Midstate Stone Corp., Gillespie, Ill., 1970—; chmn. bd., chief exec. officer Hillside (Ill.) Stone Corp., 1969—, Avedisian Co., 1978—; chmn. bd., chief exec. officer Geneva Capital Corp., Lake Geneva, Wis.; chmn. bd., Citizens Nat. Bank, Geneva. Dir. pres.'s com. Lyric Opera, Chgo., 1968—, dir. Easter Seal Soc.; mem. classical art acquisitions com. Art Inst. Chgo., 1961—; trustee Avery Coonley Sch. (chmn. European Tour Com.), Chgo. Symphony Orch., 1978—; Glenwood (Ill.) Sch. for Boys, Max McGraw Wildlife Found.; v.p. Geneva Lake Water Safety Patrol; mem. exec. bd. Boy Scouts Am., 1978—; gen. com. La Societe des Bains de Herde Monte Carlo World Backgammon championship. Served with AUS, 1944-45. Mem. Nat. Limestone Inst. (chmn. bd. 1971—), Midwest Crushed Limestone Inst. (pres. 1966-67), Nat. Crushed Stone Inst. (bd. govs. 1972—), Ill. Rd. Builders Assn. (dir., treas. 1963), Am., Western socs. civil engrs., Ill. Assn. Aggregate Producers (dir., pres. 1968), Sigma Nu. Clubs: Chicago, Racquet (Chgo.); Butler Nat. Golf (gov. 1978—) (Oak Brook, Ill.); Dunham Woods Riding (Wayne, Ill.); Lake Geneva (Wis.) Country. Patentee impermeable ecol. shale barrier in U.S., Can., U.K., France, West Germany. Home: Hinsdale IL also Lake Geneva WI Office: 900 Jorie Blvd Suite 120 Oak Brook IL 60521

AVEDON, BRUCE, ins. and securities exec.; b. Atlantic City, Dec. 31, 1928; s. N. Jay and Rosalie Ann (Sholtz) A.; B.S., Yale U., 1950; m. Shirlee Florence Young, May 19, 1951; children—Linda Michele, Bruce Frederick. Vice pres. Sholtz Ins. Agy., Inc., Miami, Fla., 1950-51; various positions to dir. planning State Mut. Life Assurance Co. Am., Worcester, Mass., 1953-69, also sec. Am. Variable Annuity Life Assurance Co., Worcester, 1967-69; v.p. equity products Ohio Nat. Life Ins. Co., Cin., 1969—, also v.p., dir. O.N. Equity Sales Co., Cin, 1973—; pres., dir. O.N. Fund, Inc., O.N. Market Yield Fund, Inc. Served to lt. AUS, 1951-53; maj. Finance Corps Res. ret. Mem. Am. Council Life Ins. (chmn. subcom. on state matters), Investment Co. Inst. (pension com.), Life Office Mgmt. Assn. (equity products and annuity com.), Nat. Assn. Securities Dealers (variable contracts com.), Res. Officers Assn., Mil. Order World Wars. Republican. Methodist. Clubs: Yale (Cin.), Masons, Order Eastern Star. Home: 6601 Hitching Post Ln Cincinnati OH 45230 Office: 237 William Howard Taft Rd Cincinnati OH 45219

AVEDON, LINDA MICHELE, profl. fund raiser; b. Worcester, Mass., Sept. 27, 1954; d. Bruce and Shirlee (Young) A.; B.S., Ohio U., 1976, M.A., 1978. Intern, Office of U.S. Senator Robert Taft, Jr. of Ohio, Cin., summers 1973, 74, 75; asst. to fin. dir. 76 Taft for Senate Com., Cin., 1976; grad. asst. Devel./Alumni Office, Ohio U., Athens, 1977; fin. dir. Aronoff for Congress com., Cin., 1978; campaign-communications asso. United Appeal, Cin., 1979—; cons. polit. fund raising. Mem. student govt. reorgn. task force, Ohio U., 1975-76, jud. reorgn. task force, 1975-76, center program bd., 1975-76; campaign staff worker Pres. Nixon, Pres. Ford, Senator Robert Taft Jr., Ohio Senator Stanley J. Aronoff, county commr. Robert Taft II, Senator Howard Baker, Pres. Reagan campaigns. Mem. Greater Cin. Soc. Fund Raising Execs., Women In Communications (treas. Cin. chpt. 1980-81), Hamilton County Young Reps. (v.p. 1982), Hamilton County Rep. Women (dir. 1982), Ohio League Young Rep. Clubs (vice chmn. 1975-76), Ohio U. Alumni Assn. (sec. 1980—), Sigma Sigma Sigma. Republican. Clubs: Hamilton County Rep., Updowntowners of Cin., Order Eastern Star. Home: 2552 Madison Rd Cincinnati OH 45208 Office: 2400 Reading Rd Cincinnati OH 45202

AVELLONE, FRANCIS PAUL, actuarial and pension consulting firm exec.; b. St. Louis, Mar. 5, 1926; s. Salvatore Carmelo and Mary Amanda (Gingrich) A.; B.B.A., Miami U., 1947; M.B.A., Roosevelt U., 1964; m. Elizabeth Therese Byrne, Apr. 26, 1947; children—Mary Eichmann, Richard, William, Francis, Thomas, Anne. Joined U.S. Navy, 1943, commd. ensign, 1945, advanced through grades to comdr.; ret., 1966; with Louis Behr Orgn., Inc., Chgo., 1966—, exec. vice-pres., 1972-76, pres., 1976—. Mem. Am. Acad. Actuaries, Am. Soc. Chartered Life Underwriters, Am. Soc. Pension Actuaries, Am. Legion, Navy League. Roman Catholic. Rotarian. Home: 1290 N Western Lake Forest IL 60045 Office: 401 N Michigan Ave Chicago IL 60611

AVERILL, FRANCES EDWINA CRANE, hosp. ofcl.; b. Saginaw, Mich., Nov. 27, 1923; d. Benjamin Franklin Alonzo and Ethel (Dustin) Crane; student public schs., Saginaw; m. Donald Lewis Averill, Nov. 28, 1942 (dec. May 1978); children—Carole Averill Hernandez, Kathleen Averill Easterling, Donald Edwin, Colleen Averill Beeckman. Central supply aide Saginaw Gen. Hosp., 1958-65, central supply supr., 1965-76, dir. central sterile dept., 1976—. Mem. Internat. Assn. Hosp. Central Service Mgmt., Am. Soc. Hosp. Central Service Personnel, Mich. Soc. Hosp. Central Service Personnel, Mid Mich. Central Service Assn. Methodist. Home: 1512 Durand St Saginaw MI 48602 Office: Saginaw Gen Hosp 1447 N Harrison St Saginaw MI 48602

AVERY, ANNE FORSTER, psychologist; b. N.Y.C., Dec. 23, 1938; d. James Frank and Kathleen (Allen) Forster; B.S., Northwestern U., 1961, Ph.D., 1972; M.A., U. Colo., 1963; postdoctoral studies C.G. Jung Inst., Chgo., 1973-81; m. Cameron S. Avery, Aug. 7, 1965; children—Christopher, Joanne. Tchr., Denver High Sch., 1961-63; tchr., advisor New Trier High Sch., Winnetka, Ill., 1964-68; tchr., counselor North Shore Country Day Sch., Winnetka, Ill., 1969-78; psychotherapist, 1975—; psychologist North Park Clinic, S.C., Park Ridge, Ill., 1979—; mem. profl. staff Forest Hosp., Des Plaines, Ill., 1978—, Old Orchard Hosp., Skokie, Ill., 1979—. Mem. Winnetka Youth Commn., 1976-78. Mem. Nat. Assn. Health Service Providers, Am. Psychol. Assn., Ill. Psychol. Assn., Am. Personnel and Guidance Assn., Chgo. Soc. Jungian Analysts. Address: 323 Rosewood Ave Winnetka IL 60093

AVERY, GUERIN LEE, lawyer; b. Akron, Ohio, Apr. 9, 1940; s. Gerald H. and Barbara J. (Kalinchak) A.; B.S. magna cum laude, John Carroll U., 1961; J.D., Cleve. State U., 1966; m. Catherine Ann Callinan, June 21, 1961; children—Kevin, Karen, Mary Pat, Timothy. Admitted to Ohio bar, 1966; underwriter INA, Cleve. and Phila., 1959-61; sales mgr. W.F. Ryan Corp., Cleve., 1963-66; asst. prof. Cleve. State U., 1966-69; exec. sec., gen. counsel Cuyahoga County Mayors and City Mgrs. Assn., 1968-70; v.p. legal affairs Wright Air Lines, Inc., Cleve., 1970-73; mng. partner firm Avery, & Carbone, Cleve., 1973—; law dir. cities of West View, Ohio, 1967-69, Olmsted Falls, Ohio, 1970-80, Oakwood, Ohio, 1971-72, University Heights, Ohio, 1974-80, Highland Heights, Ohio, 1980, Mayfield Village, Ohio, 1977—; instr. Ohio Peace Officers Tng. Program, 1979-80; instr., cons. police liability Mcpl. Seminars, Inc., 1979— (spl. cons. Indpls. and Macon, 1979-81). Mem. Nat. Inst. Mcpl. Law Officers, Am. Bar Assn., Ohio Bar Assn., Bar Assn. Greater Cleve., Delta Theta Phi, Alpha Sigma Nu. Republican. Roman Catholic. Clubs: Mayfield Village Racquet, Lander Haven Country. Author: Management Techniques for Police Supervisors, 1980. Home: 1007 Roland Rd Lyndhurst OH 44124 Office: 29001 Cedar Rd Suite 333 Lyndhurst OH 44124

AVERY, WILLIAM PAUL, polit. scientist; b. Erwin, N.C., Feb. 7, 1942; s. Sherrill William and Vida (Parker) A.; B.S., U. Tenn., Knoxville, 1968, M.A., 1971; Ph.D., Tulane U., 1975; m. Brenda Kay Davis, Aug. 22, 1966; children—Paul Kevin, Amanda Kay. Instr. polit. sci. Tulane U., New Orleans, 1972-74; asst. prof. polit. sci. U. Nebr., Lincoln, 1974-78, asso. prof., 1978—, vice chmn. dept. polit. sci., 1977-79. Nebr. chmn. Com. of Ams. for Canal Treaties, 1978; U. Nebr. coordinating com. United Way, 1979. Served with USAF, 1960-64. U.S. Office Edn. grantee, 1976-78. Mem. Am. Polit. Sci. Assn., Internat. Studies Assn., Peace Sci. Soc., Midwest Polit. Sci. Assn., So. Polit. Sci. Assn., Latin Am. Studies Assn., Midwest Assn. Latin Am. Studies. Editor: The Process of Rural Transformations, 1979; Rural Change and Public Policy, 1980; contbr. articles to profl. jours. Home: 3245 S St Lincoln NE 68503 Office: Dept Polit Sci U Nebr Lincoln NE 68588

AVISCHIOUS, RAYMOND, food distbn. co. exec.; b. Chgo., Oct. 23, 1931; B.S. in Mktg., U. Ill., 1953; m. Arlene Lentner; children—Tom, Gary. With Kroger Co., 1953; with Shurfine Central Corp., Northlake, Ill., 1955—, pres., gen. mgr., 1971—; dir. Mdse. Nat. Bank, Chgo. Bd. dirs. Aid Assn. Lutherans, Appleton, Wis. Served with U.S. Army, 1953-55. Address: Shurfine Central Corp 2100 N Mannheim Rd Northlake IL 60164

AWAIS, GEORGE MUSA, obstetrician, gynecologist; b. Ajloun, Jordan, Dec. 15, 1929; s. Musa and Meha (Koury) A.; A.B., Hope Coll., 1955; M.D., U. Toronto, 1960; m. Nabila Rizk, June 24, 1970. Intern, U. Toronto Hosps., Ont., Can., 1960-61, resident in obstetrics and gynecology, 1961-64, chief resident, 1965; chief resident Harlem Hosp., Columbia U., N.Y.C., 1966; asst. obstetrician and gynecologist, Cleve. Met. Gen. Hosp., 1967, asso., 1969; instr. obstetrics and gynecology Case Western Res. U., Cleve., 1967-70, asst. obstetrician and gynecologist MacDonald House, 1970, asst. prof., 1970, asst. clin. prof. dept. reproductive biology, 1971, asst. obstetrician and gynecologist Univ. Hosps., 1971; staff dept. gynecology, Cleve. Clinic Found., 1971—; chmn. dept. obstetrics and gynecology King Faisal Specialist Hosp. and Research Center, Riyadh, 1975-76; cons. panel mem. Internat. Corr. Soc. Obstetricians and Gynecologists, 1971. Diplomate Am. Bd. Obstetrics and Gynecology. Fellow A.C.S., Am. Coll. Obstetricians and Gynecologists, Royal Coll. Surgeons Can.; mem. AMA, AAAS, Acad. Medicine of Cleve., Am. Infertility Soc. Contbr. articles to publs. in field, papers, reports to confs., TV appearances, Saudi Arabia. Office: Dept Gynecology Cleveland Clinic Cleveland OH 44106

AWL, CHARLOTTE JANE, nursing educator; b. St. Louis, Apr. 28, 1935; d. Herbert Vincent and Elizabeth Edwards (White) Pate; diploma Presbyn. Hosp. Sch. Nursing, Phila., 1956; student U. Pa., 1957-58; B.S. with distinction in Gen. Nursing, U. Ind., 1960, M.S. in Nursing Edn., 1961; m. Richard Allen Awl, Sept. 2, 1962; children—Deborah Jane, David Allen, Stephen Scott. Team leader Presbyn. Hosp., Phila., 1956-57, head nurse women's surg. ward, 1957-58; staff nurse Bloomington (Ind.) Hosp., part-time 1958-60; pvt. duty nurse Robert Long Hosp., Indpls., spring 1960, Nursing Service Bur. Dist. 5, Ind. State Nurses Assn., Indpls., summer 1962; instr. med.-surg. nursing De Pauw U. Sch. Nursing, Greencastle and Indpls., 1961-63; instr. Meth. Med. Center Sch. Nursing, Peoria, Ill., 1963-64, staff nurse Meth. Med. Center, 1964-66; cons. dept nursing Bradley U., Peoria, 1966-67, asst. prof., 1967-74, asso. prof., 1974—, asso. chmn. dept. nursing, 1972-78, asso. dir. div. nursing, 1978—. Mem. AAUP, Am. Nurses Assn., Nat. League Nursing, Am. Assn. Critical Care Nurses, Assn. Operating Room Nurses, AAUW, Sigma Theta Tau, Pi Lambda Theta, Kappa Delta Pi, Phi Kappa Phi. Presbyterian. Office: Bradley U Peoria IL 61625

AXELROD, BARRY, air force officer; b. Willimantic, Conn., Mar. 23, 1949; s. Samuel and Esther (Steinberg) A.; B.S. in Acctg., U. Conn., 1972; m. Paula J. DesSureault, Aug. 5, 1979. Commd. in USAF, 1972, advanced through grades to capt., 1976; mem. missile combat crew Malmstrom AFB, Mont., 1972-76, jr. officer counsel, v.p., 1973-75; airborne missile ops. comdr. Ellsworth AFB, S.D., 1976-80; airborne launch control system evaluator and emergency war order instr. airborne command post SAC, Offutt AFB, Nebr., 1980—. Mem. Vol. Fire Dept. S.D., 1978—. Mem. Rapid City Jaycees, Big Bros. Assn., Am. Legion. Jewish.

AXELROD, JACK MARTIN, foundry exec.; b. St. Louis, July 16, 1936; s. Sol and Marie Louise (Longo) A.; B.S., Washington U., St. Louis, 1958; postgrad. St. Louis U., 1960; m. Carol Adele Sugerman, June 16, 1957; children—Gary Paul, David Robert, Michael Howard. Ops. mgr. Klines-Franklin-Simon, St. Louis, 1957-60; group leader, fin. analyst McDonnell Aircraft Corp., St. Louis, 1960-64; prin. J. Axelrod, Acct., St. Louis, 1964—; corp. comptroller, v.p. M.P.I., 1975—; gen. partner Dorothy Engel Products, 1979—. Vice pres., bd. dirs. Mo. Delta Amateur Hockey Assn. Mem. Nat. Assn. Public Accountants, Indsl. Acctg. Soc. Mo., Mo. Assn. Tax Practitioners, Credit Mgrs. Assn. Jewish. Clubs: Century (Washington U.); World Trade. Contbr. chpts. to Prentice-Hall Portfolio of Accounting. Home: 13000 Ferncrest Ct Creve Coeur MO 63141 Office: 102 N Cool Springs Dr O'Fallon MO

AXELROOD, HELEN BLAU, psychotherapist, counselor, educator; b. Chgo., Feb. 13; d. Morris and Goldie (Bookstien) Blau; B.A., Roosevelt U., 1951, M.A., 1977; Ph.D., Marquette U., 1982; m. Jack Axelrood, June 27, 1948; children—Lisa, Barney, Larry, Michael. TV and stage actress, 1951-74; actress-writer N.B.C. series Bible Time, 1960, series The Artist Speaks, 1970; actress Second City, Chgo., 1951-53; tchr. Chgo. Bd. Edn., 1958-62; art dir. Temple Emanuel, Chgo., 1957-58; primary supr. Temple Beth El, Chgo., 1965-66; lectr., psychotherapist, counselor, Evanston, Ill., 1976-81; Active Temple Beth Emet, Evanston. Recipient award for Dedicated Service Temple Beth Emet, 1960; Outstanding Service award Temple Beth El, 1970. Mem. Am. Personnel and Guidance Assn., Assn. Specialists in Group Work, Am. Psychol. Assn., Ill. Psychol. Assn., Chgo. Art Inst. Research on drugs, alcohol and food addiction. Home: 2022 Hawthorne Ln Evanston IL 60201 Office: 1601 Sherman Ave Suite 402 Evanston IL 60201

AXFORD, ROY ARTHUR, educator; b. Detroit, Aug. 26, 1928; s. Morgan and Charlotte (Donaldson) A.; B.A., Williams Coll., 1952; B.S., Mass. Inst. Tech., 1952, M.S., 1955, Sc.D., 1958; m. Anne-Sofie Langfeldt Rasmussen, Apr. 1, 1954; children—Roy Arthur, Elizabeth Carole, Trevor Craig. Supr. theoretical physics group Atomics Internat., Canoga Park, Calif., 1958-60; asso. prof. nuclear engring. Tex. A. and M. U., 1960-62, prof., 1962-63; asso. prof. nuclear engring. Northwestern U., 1963-66; asso. prof. U. Ill. at Urbana, 1966-68, prof., 1968—; cons. Los Alamos Sci. Lab., 1963—. Vice-chmn. Mass. Inst. Tech. Alumni Fund Drive, 1970-72, chmn., 1973—. Mem. Am. Nuclear Soc., ASME, Am. Inst. Aeros. and Astronautics, SAR (sec.-treas. Piankeshaw chpt. 1975—), Sigma Xi. Home: 2017 S Cottage Grove Urbana IL 61801

AYARS, JAMES STERLING, editor, author; b. Wilmette, Ill., Nov. 17, 1898; s. Henry Magill and Jeannie (Lord) A.; B.S., Northwestern U., 1922, postgrad. summer 1925, 37; postgrad. U. Chgo., summer 1927, U. Ill., 1938-41; m. Rebecca Caudill, Sept. 8, 1931; children—James Sterling (dec.), Rebecca Jean (Mrs. Carl J. Baker, Jr.). Tchr., Paw Paw (Mich.) High Sch., 1922-25; critic tchr. Western Mich. U., 1925-28; mem. editorial and advt. staff Athletic Jour., Chgo., 1928-37; tech. editor, head sect. publs. and public relations Ill. Natural History Survey, Urbana, 1937-65; author: Basketball Comes to Lonesome Point, 1952; Caboose on the Roof, 1956; Pet Parade, 1960; Happy Birthday, Mom!, 1963; (with Milton W. Sanderson) Butterflies, Skippers and Moths, 1964; Another Kind of Puppy, 1965; John James Audubon, 1966; The Illinois River (Clara Ingram Judson award Soc. Midland Authors, 1969), 1968; (with Rebecca Caudill) Contrary Jenkins, 1969; Track Comes to Lonesome Point, 1973; We Hold These Truths, 1977; editor, contbr. pages Meth. boys' publs., 1930-47; editor: The Ministry of Paul Burt, 1978. Served with U.S. Army, 1918-19. Recipient (with Rebecca Caudill) Disting. Service in Field of Children's Reading award Children's Reading Round Table, Chgo., 1969. Mem. Ill. Acad. Scis. (publicity adviser 1953-60), Conf. Biol. Editors (chmn. com. on form and style, editor of style manual 1972), ACLU, Sigma Delta Chi, Phi Kappa Sigma. Quaker. Home: 101 W Windsor Rd Urbana IL 61801

AYER, MARY JANE, univ. ofcl.; b. Goodman, Wis., May 5, 1930; d. Owen Lee and Alice Nina A.; B.S., U. Wis., 1959, M.S., 1964, Ph.D., 1966. With Univ. Hosps., Madison, Wis., 1952-57; mem. faculty U. Wis.-Madison, 1966, 67—, prof. counseling, 1970—, asso. dean Sch. Edn., 1975—; mem. faculty U. Iowa, Iowa City, 1966-67; adminstr. HEW research grants, 1968-74. Mem. Am. Personnel and Guidance Assn., Nat. Assn. Women Deans, Adminstrs. and Counselors, Am. Psychol. Assn. Editor Rehab. Counseling Bull., 1969-74; contbr. articles on psychol. problems of disabled and mentally retarded to profl. jours. Office: 1000 Bascom Hall Madison WI 53704*

AYERS, EDWARD ROBERT, utility co. exec.; b. Council Bluff, Iowa, May 14, 1948; s. Edward L. and Evelyn B. (Christians) A.; student Kirkwood Community Coll., Cedar Rapids, Iowa, U. Iowa, Hawkeye Inst. Tech., Waterloo, Iowa; m. Mary Ellen Stewart, Nov. 5, 1966; children—Michael Todd, Wendy Lynn. Engring. aide Harlan (Iowa) Mcpl. Utilities, 1967-71; supt. Viola (Wis.) Mcpl. Utilities, 1971-73, Hopkinton (Iowa) Mcpl. Utilities, 1973-76; gen. mgr. Grundy Center (Iowa) Utility, 1976—; exec. dir. N. Iowa Mcpl. Electric Coop. Assn. Pres., Community Club, 1975; sec., 1st trustee Lutheran Ch., 1976; pres. Booster Club, 1977, Emergency Med. Technicians of Grundy, 1978. Cert. water treatment plant operator, Iowa. Mem. Am. Public Power Assn., Iowa Assn. Mcpl. Utilities (dir.), Iowa Firemen's Assn., Iowa Public Employee Retirement Improvement Assn. Home: RFD Holland IA 50642 Office: 506 7th St Grundy Center IA 50638

AYERS, LEONA WESTON, pathologist, physician, educator; b. Garner, N.C., Jan. 14, 1940; d. William Albert and Ida Bertha (Bell) Weston; B.S., Duke, 1962, M.D., 1967; m. James Cordon Ayers, Aug. 1, 1965; children—Ashley Albert, Alan Andrew. Intern, Duke U. Med. Center, Durham, N.C., 1967-68, resident in pathology, 1968-69; resident in pathology Univ. Hosps., Columbus, Ohio, 1969-71; individual practice medicine, specializing in pathology Columbus, Ohio, 1970—; dir. div. clin. microbiology Univ. Hosp., Columbus, 1970—; attending staff, 1971—; asst. prof. allied health professions Ohio State U., Columbus, 1974-78, pathology, 1971-77, asso. prof. pathology, 1977—, allied health professions, 1978—; cons. in field. Diplomate Am. Bd. Pathology. Fellow Am. Soc. Clin. Pathologists (commn. on continuing edn. faculty, cons. nat. com. on affiliate and asso. affairs), Coll. Am. Pathologists; mem. AAUP, Am. Med. Women's Assn., Am. Soc. Microbiology, South Central Assn. Clin. Microbiology (dir.). Contbr. articles to profl. publs.; mem. editorial bd. Lab. Medicine. Home: 3222 Glenellen Ct Columbus OH 43221 Office: 410 W 10th Ave Columbus OH 43210

AYERS, RICHARD WAYNE, elec. mfg. co. exec.; b. Atlanta, Aug. 23, 1945; s. Harold Richard and Martha Elizabeth (Vaughan) A.; B.B.A., Ga. State Coll., 1967; M.B.A., Ind. U., 1969; m. Nancy Katherine Martin, Aug. 9, 1969. Specialist mktg. communications research Gen. Electric Co., Schenectady, 1969-70, copywriter Lamp div., Cleve., 1970-73, supr., distbr. advt. and sales promotion, 1973-75, supr. comml. and indsl. promotional programs Gen. Electric Lighting Bus. Group, 1975-79, mgr. comml. and indsl. market distbr. and promotional programs, 1979—; lectr. in field. Recipient Best Indsl. Promotion award Advt. Age, 1974, Premium Showcase award Nat. Premium Sales Execs., 1975, 76, Gold Key award Nat. Premium Mfrs. Reps., 1976, 77, Golden Key Communicators award Factory mag., 1976. Dir.-at-large Ga. Young Reps., 1966-67. Mem. Blue Key, Delta Sigma Pi, Beta Gamma Sigma. Home: 23951 Lake Shore Blvd Apt 1213B Euclid OH 44123 Office: Nela Park Bldg 308 Cleveland OH 44112

AYERS, THOMAS G., utility exec.; b. Detroit, Feb. 16, 1915; s. Jule C. and Camilla (Chalmers) A.; A.B., U. Mich., 1937; LL.D., Elmhurst Coll., 1966; D.H.L., DePaul U., 1977; m. Mary Andrew, Nov. 25, 1938; children—Catherine Mary Ayers Allen, Thomas G., William Charles, Richard James, John Steven. With Public Service Co. No. Ill., 1938-52, mgr. indsl. relations, 1948-52; asst. v.p. Commonwealth Edison Co., Chgo., 1952, v.p., 1953-62, exec. v.p., 1962-64, pres., 1964-73, chmn., pres., chief exec. officer, 1973-80, also dir.; dir. 1st Nat. Bank Chgo., N.W. Industries, Inc., Tribune Co., Zenith Radio Corp., Gen. Dynamics Corp.; chmn. Breeder Reactor Corp. Chmn., 1969 Met. Crusade of Mercy; chmn. Leadership Council Met. Open Communities, Dearborn Park Corp.; chmn. bd. trustees Northwestern U.; chmn. bd. trustees Chgo. Symphony Orch. Mem. Chgo Assn. Commerce and Industry (past pres., dir.). Clubs: Chicago, Commercial, Tavern, Mid-Day (Chgo.); Glen Oak Country (Glen Ellyn, Ill.). Office: PO Box 767 1 First Nat Plaza Chicago IL 60690

AYLWARD, GLEN PHILIP, pediatric psychologist, educator; b. Hoboken, N.J., July 30, 1950; s. Philip E. and Marian (Attubato) A.; B.A., Rutgers U., 1972; M.A., Fairleigh Dickinson U., 1974; Ph.D., Ga. State U., 1979; m. Deborah E. Bellini, Sept. 9, 1973; children—Shawn Christopher, Megan Beth. Grad. teaching/research fellow Fairleigh Dickinson U., Rutherford, N.J., 1973-74; part-time faculty Ga. State U., Atlanta, 1974-78; intern U. Md. Sch. Medicine, Balt., 1978-79; psychologist dept. pediatrics, div. Newborn Medicine, Emory U. Sch. Medicine and Grady Meml. Hosp., Atlanta, 1977-78; asst. prof. pediatrics and psychiatry So. Ill. U. Sch. Medicine, Springfield, 1979—; cons. NIH, Heart, Lung & Blood Inst. Mem. exec. com., primary cons. team Family Stress Cons. Team, Springfield, 1979—. Ga. State U. Dept. Psychology faculty scholar, 1977. Mem. Am. Psychol. Assn., Nat. Register of Health Service Providers in Psychology, Soc. for Research in Child Devel., Soc. Pediatric Psychology, Ambulatory Pediatric Assn., Southeastern Psychol. Assn., Ill. Psychol. Assn. Roman Catholic. Contbr. articles to profl. jours. Home: 2612 Clifton Dr Springfield IL 62704 Office: So Ill Univ Sch of Medicine Pediatrics Dept PO Box 3926 Springfield IL 62708

AYMOND, ALPHONSE HENRY, lawyer, former public utilities exec.; b. St. Louis, Sept. 27, 1914; s. Alphonse H. and Anne (Putz) A.; A.B., Northwestern U., 1936; J.D., U. Mich., 1939; LL.D., Olivet Coll., 1970; D.Public Service (hon.), Western Mich. U., 1974; m. Elizabeth Shierson, Sept. 30, 1939; children—Charles H., Robert D., William G. Admitted to Ill. bar, 1939, Mich. bar, 1947; asso. firm Miller, Gorham, Wescott & Adams, Chgo., 1939-44; with Commonwealth and So. Corp., N.Y.C., 1946-47; atty. Consumers Power Co., Jackson, Mich., 1947-51, gen. atty., 1951-55, v.p., gen. counsel, 1955-57, exec. v.p., 1957-60, chmn. bd., 1960-79, pres., 1972-75; pres. Mich. Gas Storage Co., 1960-78; dir. City Bank & Trust Co., Nat. Bank Detroit, Am. Seating Co., Kellogg Co., K Mart Corp.; trustee Northwestern Mut. Life Ins. Co., Northwestern Mut. Life Mortgage and Realty Investors. Past pres., mem. exec. bd. Land O'Lakes council Boy Scouts Am.: mem. Mich. Colls. Found., 1965—, pres., 1967-69, chmn., 1969-71; chmn. Mich. Found. for Arts, 1970-75; trustee W.K. Kellogg Found. Served as lt. (j.g.), Supply Corps, USNR, 1944-46. Mem. Am. Bar Assn., State Bar Mich., Assn. Edison Illuminating Cos. (pres. 1976-78), Edison Electric Inst. (pres. 1969-70), Order of Coif, Theta Xi, Phi Delta Phi. Episcopalian. Clubs: Town, Country (Jackson); Detroit; Lost Tree (North Palm Beach, Fla.). Office: 180 W Michigan Ave Jackson MI 49201

AYRES, ALAN LEWIS, advt. agy. exec.; b. Syracuse, N.Y., Mar. 25, 1933; s. William Edward and Julia (Lynch) A.; B.S., Syracuse U., 1960; m. July 12, 1958. Participant exec. tng. program H. J. Heinz Co., Syracuse, 1960-63; account exec. Maxon Inc., Detroit, 1963-66; with various advt. agys., Buffalo, 1966-77; v.p. ops. Byer & Bowman Advt. Inc., Columbus, Ohio, 1977—. Served with U.S. Army, 1953-55. Mem. Buffalo Ad Fedn., Columbus Ad Fedn., Columbus Sales and Mktg. Execs. Republican. Office: 66 S 6th St Columbus OH 43215

AYRES, PAUL JULIUS, ins. co. exec.; b. Lansing, Mich., Jan. 15, 1936; s. Julius S. and Rosalie M. (Ruonavaara) A.; A.A., Mich. State U., 1959; m. Ann M. Edwards, Feb. 22, 1958; children—Robert P., Sandra A., Cheryl L. Mgr. accident and health dept. H.T. Chadwell & Assos., Lansing, 1959-62; group rep. Blue Cross of Mich., Ann Arbor, 1962-65, acting mgr., 1964-65; v.p. Mich. Service Corp., Lansing, 1965-67, sr. v.p., 1967-69, exec. sr. v.p., 1969-71, dir., 1965-71; sec., treas., dir. Electronic Homes, Inc., Okemos, Mich., 1966-69; gen. mgr. Robb-Co, Okemos, 1969-81; pres. Paul Ayres and Assos., Okemos, 1972—, Mich. Programmers Ins. Agy., Inc., Okemos, 1974—; owner, pres. Mich. Service Corp. Inc., Okemos, 1981—. Maj., M.I., Air N.G. Mem. Lansing Life Underwriters, Mich. Employers Assn. (pres. 1966-79), N.G. Assn., Am. Legion. Republican. Club: Eagles. Contbr. articles on ins. to various mags. Office: 1749 Hamilton Rd Okemos MI 48864

AYRES, ROBERT FRANKLIN, supt. schs.; b. nr. Warren, Ind., Apr. 29, 1925; s. James Madison and Dora Evelyn (Lucas) A.; B.S., Butler U., 1949, M.S., 1952; postgrad. Purdue U., 1958-62; m. Helen Denton, Mar. 7, 1947; children—James Michael, Robert William, John David, Christopher Allen, Carolyn Ann. Tchr., Orchard Country Day Sch., Indpls., 1948-50; tchr., dean of boys Frankfort High Sch. (Ind.), 1950-59, prin., 1959-65; asst. supt. schs. Huntington County, Ind., 1965-70; supt. schs. Rensselaer Sch. System, 1970-75; supt. Community Schs. Frankfort, 1975—; instr. Huntington Coll., 1967-70; lectr. Butler U.; dir. Citizen's Savs. and Loan. Exec. bd. Anthony Wayne council Boy Scouts Am.; bd. dirs. Huntington Coll. Found., Rensselaer chpt. Red Cross, Big Bros. Am., Retarded Children's Assn.; mem. Clinton County Area Plan Commn., 1976-78; v.p. and campaign drive chmn. Clinton County United Way. Served to lt. AUS, 1943-46. Nat. Defense Edn. Act fellow, 1960; St. Joseph's Coll. fellow, 1974. Mem. Ind. Assn. Pub. Sch. Supts., N.E.A., Am. Legion, V.F.W., Ind. Schoomen's Club, Am. Assn. Sch. Adminstrs., Clinton County C. of C. (dir. 1977—), Phi Delta Kappa, Lambda Chi Alpha, Tau Kappa Alpha, Alpha Phi Omega. Methodist. Optimist (pres. 1970), Rotarian, Lion. Home: 709 Williams Rd Frankfort IN 46041 Office: 50 S Maish Rd Frankfort IN 46041

AZNEER, J. LEONARD, coll. pres.; b. Roumania, May 26, 1921; s. Morris and Ida (Stein) Azneershansky; B.A., Yeshiva Coll., 1941; grad. Jewish Theol. Sem. Am., 1945, M.H.L., 1949; Ph.D., U. Pitts., 1959; Docteur Osteopathie (hon.), A.T. Still Acad., Lyon, France, 1979; m. Patricia A. Cottrille; children—Jay Barry, Reva Azneer Pearlstein, Ira Brant. Tchr., English, secondary sch., N.Y.C., 1940-41; ordained rabbi, 1945; asso. prof. edn. Youngstown U., 1951-67; sr. mem. grad. faculty Youngstown State U., 1967-70; pres. Coll. Osteo. Medicine and Surgery, Des Moines 1971—, prof. med. humanities, 1971—; pres. U. Osteo. Medicine and Health Scis., Des Moines, 1980—; mem. Adv. Com. Osteo. Edn.; dir. Valley Nat. Bank. Recipient Henry Goode Meml. award Jewish Theol. Sem., 1945. Mem. Am. Osteo. Assn. (vice chmn. task force to study postdoctoral edn.), Am. Assn. Colls. Osteo Medicine (past pres.), Sigma Sigma Phi (hon.). Author: (with others) Diabetic Acidosis: A Programmed Text, 1964; Resuscitation: A Programmed Text, 1965; Passover—A Programmed Text; Sukkot—A Programmed Text. Office: Univ Osteo Medicine and Health Scis 3200 Grand Ave Des Moines IA 50312

BAALMANN, RICHARD FENTON, retail hardware chain exec.; b. St. Louis, Oct. 30, 1935; s. Roderick Oliver and Melba (Bertholdt) B.; student St. Louis U., 1953-57; m. Kathleen Felke, June 12, 1957; children—Richard Fenton, Mary Kathleen, Margaret Grace, Anne Patricia. Vice pres. Mars Enders, Inc., retail hardware, St. Louis, 1956-68, pres., 1968-79; pres. Hardware Center, Inc., retail hardware, St. Louis, 1956-79, Markat, Inc., St. Louis, 1970-79, Bramm, Inc., retail hardware, 1979—. Vol. worker United Fund, 1960; sec. Nat. Cystic Fibrosis Research Found., 1973, chmn., 1981; chmn. St. Louis chpt. Jesuit Program for Living and Learning, nat. chmn., 1979-82; mem. Mo. Air Conservation Commn., 1980-82. Served as 1st lt. USAF, 1958-59. Mem. Brentwood C. of C. (pres. 1966), Young Pres.'s Orgn., St. Louis Regional Commerce and Growth Assn., Advt. Club St. Louis, Delta Sigma Pi. Club: Rotary (pres. 1972). Home: 458 Bambury Way Saint Louis MO 63131 Office: 11767 Manchester Saint Louis MO 63131

BAAR, LILLIAN MARY, bus. exec.; b. Chgo.; d. James and Frances (Stanek) Shuss; student evening sch. J. Sterling Morton Jr. Coll., 1934-36; m. William D. Baar, July 25, 1942; 1 dau., Judy Baar Topinka. Sec. to pres. of Thordarson Mfg. Co., Chgo., 1935-37; sec. to ofcls. of Sears, Roebuck & Co., Chgo., 1937-43; real estate sales, Berwyn, Ill., 1943-44; engaged as realtor and ins. broker with own firm The Baar Realty Co., Berwyn, 1944-69, cons., 1969-75; ins. broker Lillian Baar Ins. Agy., 1944—; real estate cons., 1969-76; owner, operator Baar Baar Realtors, 1976—. Mem. Berwyn-Cicero Gov.'s Council Employment of Handicapped, 1965-73; co-chmn. Berwyn Heart Fund, 1968-72; v.p. Berwyn Community Chest, 1968-70, chmn., 1971-72, bd. dirs., 1970-79; mem. MacNeal Meml. Hosp. Assn., Berwyn, Ladies Aid for Bohemian Home for Aged, Ladies Aux. Bohemian Charitable Assn. Chgo.; dir. DIALOGUE rec. service for blind, 1969-70, 1st v.p., 1971-73, pres., 1972-74, trustee, 1974—; v.p. IN. Council of Real Estate of City of Hope, 1976-77, chmn. bd. dirs., 1978-80; active ARC, Am. Heart Fund. Recipient Rotary Internat. Citizen of Yr. award Berwyn Rotary, 1975-76; honor plaque Grant Works Children's Center, 1981. Mem. Cermak Rd. Bus. Assn. (pres. 1962-64, dir. 1965—), West Towns Bd. Realtors (pres. 1965), Nat. (mem. Nat. Inst. Real Estate Bds. 1968—, mem. Women's council), Ill., assns. real estate bds., Women in Real Estate, Ill. C. of C., Berwyn Business and Profl. Woman's Club (1st v.p. 1972, pres. 1973-75). Clubs: Mothers of Alpha Gamma Delta, Ladies Aux. The Bohemian of Ceska Beseda; West Suburban Exec. Breakfast (dir. 1975—, treas. 1981). Home: Riverside IL 60546 Office: 6335 W Cermak Rd Berwyn IL 60402

BABAI, MASSOOD REZA, psychiatrist; b. Zahedan, Iran, Jan. 27, 1939; s. Gholam Reza and Fatomeh G. B.; came to U.S., 1968; M.D., U. Tehran, 1965; m. Simin Soltanzadeh, May 6, 1963; children—Mojgan, Sarah, Dora. Pvt. practice medicine, Tehran, 1965-66; intern Misericordia Hosp., N.Y.C., 1968-69; resident Rollman Psychiat. Inst., Cin., 1969-72; pvt. practice medicine, specializing in psychiatry, Cuyahoga Falls, Ohio, 1973—; dir. ambulatory services Fallsview Psychiat. Hosp., 1972-74, dir. med. edn., 1974-77; dir., div. psychiatry St. Thomas Hosp., Akron, Ohio, 1976—; tchr. interns and residents St. Thomas Hosp., Fallsview Psychiat. Hosp. Med. Sch.; asso. prof. psychiatry N.E. Ohio U. Coll. Medicine. Served as 2d lt., Health Corps, Iranian Imperial Army, 1966-68. Diplomate Am. Bd. Psychiatry and Neurology. Mem. Am. Psychiat. Assn., Ohio Psychiat. Assn. Translator from English to Persian, Applied Physiology, 1965. Office: 275 Graham Rd Suite 8 Cuyahoga Falls OH 44223

BABBITT, DONALD LEE, mfg. co. exec.; b. Marne, Iowa, Aug. 28, 1932; s. Hubert Merwin and Ruth Winifred (Arp) B.; B.S., U. Minn., 1963; m. Pauline Renee Hickey, Jan. 31, 1959; children—Dee Ann, Curt, Pamela, Patricia. Sales mgr. Ramsey REC Ltd., Richmond Hill, Ont., Can., 1963-68, v.p., 1968-72, pres., 1972-76; v.p., gen. mgr. Ramsey Engring. Co., St. Paul, 1976-80, pres., 1980—, also dir. Served with USN, 1949-53. Mem. Canadian Inst. Mining and Metallurgy, AIME. Roman Catholic. Home: 735 Torchwood Circle New Brighton MN 55112 Office: 1853 W County Rd C Saint Paul MN 55113

BABBITT, DONALD PATRICK, radiologist; b. Oshkosh, Wis., Aug. 24, 1922; s. James Sylvester and Loretta Gertrude (Sensenbrenner) B.; student U. Wis., River Falls, 1939-42; M.D., Med. Coll. Wis., 1946; m. Elizabeth May Gerhard, Apr. 28, 1945 (dec. Nov. 1971); children—Patrick, Ann, James; m. 2d Jill Ann Sieg, Jan. 29, 1975. Intern, Meth. Hosp., Indpls., 1946-47; resident Milw. Hosp. and Milw. Ch Hosp., 1949-52; practice medicine specializing in radiology, Milw.; mem. staff Milw. Children's Hosp., 1952—, chief radiology, 1964—; mem. staff Milwaukee County Gen. Hosp., 1964—; cons. St. Mary's Hosp., Milw., 1968-76; instr. radiology Med. Coll. Wis., 1958, asso. prof. radiology, 1964-70, clin. prof., 1970—, clin. prof. pediatrics, 1979—; asso. clin. prof. radiology U. Wis. Center Health Scis., Madison, 1968-70, clin. prof., 1970—. Served as capt. M.C., AUS, 1947-49; ETO. Named Tchr. of Yr., Milw. Children's Hosp. Dept. Pediatrics, 1980; diplomate Am. Bd. Radiology. Fellow Am. Coll. Radiology (medallion in nuclear medicine 1959), Am. Acad. Pediatrics; mem. Am. Roentgen Ray Soc., European Soc. Pediatric Radiology, Soc. Pediatric Radiology, Radiol. Soc. N. Am., Wis. Radiol. Soc. (pres. 1976), State Wis. Med. Soc., Milw. Surg. Soc. (pres. 1978), Milw. Roentgen Ray Soc. (pres. 1975-77), Milwaukee County Med. Soc. (pres. 1974), Milw. Acad. Medicine 1973), Milw. Pediatric Soc., AMA, Med. Coll. Wis. Alumni Assn., Boy Scouts Am. (century mem.), Alpha Omega Alpha, Phi Chi. Roman Catholic. Clubs: Flying Physicians; Rotary (Milw.). Contbr. numerous articles to profl. jours. Home: 2701 E Beverly Rd Milwaukee WI 53211 Office: 2353 N Lake Shore Dr Milwaukee WI 53211

BABBO, JOSEPH THOMAS, rehab. counselor, social work therapist; b. Chgo., Jan. 24, 1932; s. Angelo and Anna Maria (Cereso) B.; student Loras Coll., 1956-58; Ph.B., Belmont Abbey Coll., 1963; M.S., Ill. Inst. Tech., 1973, postgrad., 1975—; m. Mary Josephine Hamrock, Oct. 29, 1967; children—Angelo Joseph, Mary Immaculata, Martin Francis, Thomas John, Annamaria, Giovanna Carmella. Rehab. counselor Ill. Dept. Rehab. Services, Chgo., 1964—; marriage and family counselor and therapist; union rep., steward AFSCME Local 2000, 1971—; counselor rep. Dept. Vocat. Rehab. Visitor chmn. Christian Outreach, Extraordinary Minister of Holy Communion, Ch. commentator. Served with USN, 1951-55; Korea. Cert. rehab. counselor; cert. social worker. Mem. Nat. Rehab. Assn., Ill. Rehab. Assn., Nat. Rehab. Counselor Assn., Ill. Rehab. Counselor Assn., Am. Psychol. Assn. (asso.). Roman Catholic. Club: Fenwick High Sch. Fathers. Home: 2910 W Meade Ave Chicago IL 60634 Office: 5015 W Lawrence Ave Chicago IL 60630

BABCOCK, DANIEL LAWRENCE, engr., educator; b. Phila., Nov. 25, 1930; B.S., Pa. State U., 1952; M.S., Mass. Inst. Tech., 1953; Ph.D. (N.Am. Rockwell Corp. fellow), U. Calif., Los Angeles, 1970. Chem. engr., tech. writer Dow Corning Corp., Midland, Mich., 1956-59; tech. editor Chem. Propulsion Info. Agy., Johns Hopkins U., 1959-62; supr., project engr., sr. specialist in chem. rocket propulsion Space div. Rockwell Internat. Corp., Downey, Calif., 1963-69; asso. prof. dept. engring. mgmt. U. Mo.-Rolla, 1970-78, prof., 1978—, mem. grad. council, 1981—. Lt. col. USAF Res. Registered profl. engr., Mo. Mem. Am. Soc. Engring. Mgmt. (exec. dir.), Am. Soc. Engring. Edn. (dir., past chmn. engring. mgmt. div.), Am. Soc. Quality Control (certified quality engr.), Joint Engring. Mgmt. Council (sponsors com.), Am. Public Works Assn. (treas. Mo. chpt.), Soc. Am. Mil. Engrs., Tau Beta Pi, Phi Kappa Phi, Phi Lambda Upsilon. Contbr. articles to profl. jours. Home: 1347 California Dr Rolla MO 65401 Office: U Mo-Rolla Dept Engring Mgmt Rolla MO 65401

BABCOCK, MICHAEL WARD, educator; b. Bloomington, Ill., Dec. 10, 1944; s. Bruce W. and Virginia (Neeson) B.; B.S. in B.A., Drake U., 1967; M.A. in Econs., U. Ill., 1972, Ph.D. in Econs., 1973; m. Virginia Lee Brooks, Aug. 4, 1973; children—John, Karen. Teaching asst. U. Ill., Urbana, 1968, 71, research asst., 1972; asso. prof. econs. Kans. State U., Manhattan, 1972—. Served with U.S. Army, 1969-71. Fed. R.R. Adminstrn. grantee, 1976-78; U.S. Army C.E. grantee, 1978-79; U.S. Dept. Agr. grantee, 1978-79, 80-82. Mem. Missouri Valley Econ. Assn., Mid-Continent Regional Sci. Assn., So. Regional Sci. Assn., Kans. Econ. Assn., Transp. Research Forum, Beta Gamma Sigma, Omicron Delta Epsilon. Club: Optimist. Contbr. articles to profl. jours. Home: 720 Harris St Manhattan KS 66502 Office: Econ Dept Kan State Univ Manhattan KS 66506

BABCOCK, ROBERT ALLEN, constrn. co. exec.; b. Indpls., May 4, 1935; s. William Harvey and Beatrice Opal (Durst) B.; student Butler U., 1953-54; m. Virginia Ann Richardson, Sept. 2, 1955; children—Patricia Ann, Debra Sue. With William H. Babcock & Son, Indpls., 1954-70; owner Robert A. Babcock, Gen. Contractor, Indpls., 1970-77; pres. Babcock Constrn., Inc., Indpls., 1977—. Pres., Wayne Twp. Screening Caucus, 1970, pres. Danville Band Parents, 1972; trustee Danville United Methodist Ch., 1980—. Mem. Better Bus. Bur. Republican. Methodist. Clubs: Masons, Shriners, Scottish Rite, Country of Indpls. Home: Rural Route 6 Box 174 Danville IN 46122 Office: 951 Western Dr Indianapolis IN 46241

BABLER, JAMES HAROLD, educator; b. Evanston, Ill., June 14, 1944; s. Bernard Joseph and Berenice A. (Brunk) B.; B.S. magna cum laude, Loyola U. Chgo., 1966; Ph.D. (NIH fellow), Northwestern U., 1971. Asso. prof. chemistry Loyola U. Chgo., 1970—. Mem. Am. Chem. Soc., AAAS, Internat. Platform Assn., Sigma Xi. Patentee in field. Home: 125 Callan Ave Evanston IL 60202 Office: 6525 N Sheridan Rd Chicago IL 60626

BABLITCH, WILLIAM A., state senator; b. Stevens Point, Wis., Mar. 1, 1941; B.S., U. Wis., Madison, 1963, J.D., 1968. Admitted to Wis. bar, 1968; practice law, Stevens Point, Wis., mem. Wis. Senate, 1972—, majority leader, 1977—. Dist. atty. Portage County (Wis.), 1969-72. Mem. Nat. Conf. State Legislators (exec. com. 1979). Democrat. Address: Room 241 South State Capitol Madison WI 53702

BABUDRO, EGIDIO A., med. equipment co. exec.; b. Rijeka, Yugoslavia, Feb. 18, 1936; s. Angelo and Maria (Kisic) B.; B.A., U. Minn., 1963, B.Sc.Ed., 1968; m. Victoria S. Klos, July 11, 1959; children—Pernell T.A., Angelique M.P., Angelica M.P., Parnell T.A. Regional service mgr. Midwest Narco Med. Services, Mpls., 1970-72; coordinator biomedical technology Bown Inst., Mpls., 1972-74; program dir. biomedical equipment technology Sch. Dist. 287, Eden Prairie, Minn., 1974—; founder, pres. Electronic Systems Internat. design and mfg., Mpls., 1972—, Med. Design Instrumentation, sales and service, Mpls., 1974—. Mem. Med. Electronic and Data Soc., Assn. Advancement Med. Instrumentation, Am. Soc. Hosp. Engrs., IEEE (chmn. engring. medicine and biology). Contbr. articles to profl. jours. Home: 10684 Terrace Rd NE Minneapolis MN 55434 Office: 540 Greenhaven Rd Anoka MN 55303

BACH, IRA JOHN, govt. ofcl., city and regional planner; b. Chgo., May 19, 1906; s. Jacob Lester and Rachel (Rose) B.; student U. Ill., 1926-27, Harvard, 1929-30; B.S., Mass. Inst. Tech., 1932; m. Ruth Lackritz, May 22, 1934 (dec. 1961); children—John Lawrence, Caroline Ruth (Mrs. Dennis P. Marandos); m. 2d, Muriel Dunkleman Wolfson, Apr. 14, 1963; 1 step-daughter, Susan Wolfson. Partner archtl. firm Lichtmann and Bach, Chgo., 1935-42; project planner Wash. Terr. Housing Project, Ogden, Utah, 1942-44; dir. Tri-County Regional Planning Commn., Denver, 1944-45; dir. planning Chgo. Housing Authority, 1946-47; exec. dir. Cook County Housing Authority, 1947-48; exec. dir. Chgo. Land Clearance Commn., 1948-57; commr. planning Dept. City Planning, Chgo., 1957-67; exec. dir. Chgo. Dwelling Assn., 1965-69; pres. Urban Assos. of Chgo., Inc., 1969-75; adminstr. Ill.-Ind. Bi-State Commn., 1975-81; sr. project adv. to Mayor of Chgo., 1981—; mem. Chgo. Urban Renewal Bd., Chgo. Comml. Dist. Bd., 1980—; vis. lectr. Yale, 1960—; lectr. in field. Chmn., Commn. Chgo. Hist. and Archtl. Landmarks; mem. Northeastern Ill. Met. Area Local Govt. Services Commn., 1958-62; pres. Northeastern Ill. Met. Area Planning Commn., Chgo., 1968-75; co-chmn. Interstate Planning Commn., 1972-75; cons. renovation Chgo. Pub. Library Cultural Center, Dearborn R.R. Sta. Named Chgo. Man of Year in Architecture and Engring. Chgo. Jr. C. of C., 1960; recipient City Planning award Municipal Art League Chgo., 1960, Honor award Citizens Greater Chicago. Mem. Am. Inst. Cert. Planners (past pres. Chgo. chpt.), AIA, Am. Planning Assn., Nat. Assn. Housing and Redevel. Ofcls., Chgo. Assn. Commerce and Industry (Ind. devel. com.), Lambda Alpha (pres. Ely chpt. 1953-57), Sigma Alpha Mu. Clubs: Tavern, Arts. Author: Uniform Building

Code of Colorado, 1945; Uniform Sub-Division Regulation of Colorado, 1945; A Guide to Chicago's Historic Suburbs, 1981; also papers and articles on housing. Contbr. to Am. Peoples Ency. Arts, Architecture mag. Author 3d edit. Chgo. on Foot, series of archtl. walks; 3d edit. Chicago's Famous Buildings. Office: Room 507 City Hall Chicago IL 60602

BACH, STEVE CRAWFORD, judge; b. Jackson, Ky., Jan. 31, 1921; s. Bruce Grannis and Evelyn (Crawford) B.; A.B., Ind. U., 1943, J.D., 1948; postgrad. Eastern studies U. Mich., 1944, Nat. Trial Judges Coll., 1966, U. Minn. Juvenile Inst., 1967; m. Rosemary Husted, Sept. 6, 1947; children—John Crittenden, Greta Christine. Admitted to Ky., Ind. bars, 1948; atty. Bach & Bach, Jackson, 1948-51; investigator U.S. CSC, Indpls., 1951-54; individual practice law, Mt. Vernon, Ind., 1954-65; judge 11th. Jud. Circuit, Mt. Vernon, 1965—; moderator Ind. Conf. Crime and Delinquency, Indpls., 1968; tchr. seminar on juvenile delinquency Ind. Trial Judges Assn., 1969, del. Internat. Youth Magistrates Conf., Geneva, 1970, Oxford, Eng., 1974, Can., 1977; faculty adviser Criminal Law Inst., Nat. Trial Judges Coll., 1973; treas. Ind. Council Juvenile Ct. Judges, 1975, v.p., 1976, pres., 1978-79, mem. juvenile study com., 1976; bd. dirs. Jud. Conf., Ind. Jud. Center; faculty adv. Nat. Jud. Coll., 1978; mem. faculty Seminar for Inst. for New Judges, State of Ind., 1979. Pres., Greater Mt. Vernon Assn., 1958-59; bd. dirs. Regional Mental Health Planning Commn., Criminal Justice Planning Commn. 8th Region Ind., Evansville, Ind.; mem. Juvenile Justice div. Ind. Jud. Study Commn.; mem. Ind. Gov.'s Juvenile Justice Delinquency Prevention Adv. Bd., 1976-78. Served with intelligence Signal Corps, AUS, 1943-46. Mem. Nat. Council Juvenile Ct. Judges, Am. Legion, Ind. Soc. Chgo., Ind. Bar Assn. (del.), Ind. Judges Assn. (bd. mgrs. 1966-71), Sigma Delta Kappa, Delta Tau Delta. Democrat. Methodist. Mason (Shriner), Kiwanian, Elk. Home: 512 Walnut St Mount Vernon IN 47620 Office: Courthouse Mount Vernon IN 47620

BACHAND, ROMEO THOMAS, JR., physician; b. Springfield, Mass., July 11, 1937; s. Romeo Thomas and Stella Ann (Tremble) B.; B.S., U. Hartford, 1965; Ph.D., Marquette U., 1969; M.D., Med. Coll. Wis., 1972; m. Judith Ann Bice, Jan. 15, 1973; children—Tonya, Trista. Intern, Mayo Clinic, Rochester, Minn., 1972-73, resident, 1973-75; dir. clin. pharmacology Abbott Labs., North Chicago, Ill., 1975-77; med. dir. clin. research Diamond-Shamrock Co., Painesville, Ohio, 1977-80; pres., chief exec. officer Amaric Corp., pharm. research, Concord, Ohio, 1980—; sr. airman med. examiner FAA; mem. affiliate faculty Am. Heart Assn. Served with USAF, 1955-59; flight surgeon Res. Mem. AMA, Am. Soc. Clin. Pharmacology and Therapeutics, Am. Coll. Clin. Pharmacology, Flying Physicians Assn. Home: 10271 Cherry Hill Dr Painesville OH 44077 Office: 9953 Johnny Cake Ridge Rd Concord OH 44060

BACHMAN, NEAL KENYON, sch. adminstr.; b. Iowa City, Aug. 10, 1950; s. Neal and Phyllis Jean (Mattes) B.; B.Mus. in Edn., U. Nebr., 1972, M.Ed., 1978. Tchr. instrumental and vocal music Osceola (Nebr.) Schs., 1972-73; band dir. Elkhorn (Nebr.) Public Schs., 1973-75; retail salesman Musicland, Lincoln, Nebr., 1975-76; media specialist Malcolm (Nebr.) Public Schs., 1978—. Recipient Malcolm Parent-Tchr. Orgn. cert. of recognition, 1981. Mem. Malcolm Edn. Assn. (pres. 1980-81), Assn. Supervision and Curriculum Devel., Nebr. Ednl. Media Assn., Mensa, Phi Delta Kappa. Home: 1503 Superior St Apt 18 Lincoln NE 68521 Office: PO Box 198 Malcolm NE 68402

BACHMANN, MARGARET ALFREDA, bus. exec.; b. Topeka, May 3, 1919; d. Ray Alfred and Mary Alice (Kilbride) Webb; student St. Louis U., 1946, 47; cert. med. records Kans. U., 1946; cert. Purdue U., 1976, cert. advanced bus. ins., 1975; grad. Life Underwriters Tng. Council, 1970; grad. Key Pact Inst. Advanced Studies, 1975; m. T. R. Bachmann, Aug. 31, 1940 (div.); children—Mark Theron, Kent Spencer, Monica Alice. Dep. county clk. Shawnee County (Kans.), 1937-40, auditor, 1943; med. record librarian Starmont Vail Hosp., Topeka, 1945-49; mgr. Trees Orthopedic Clinic, Topeka, 1949-59; owner, operator uniform shop, 1958-60, bridal shop, 1960-64; advt. rep. Consol. Enterprise, Kansas City and Marceline, Mo., 1964-67; ins. broker Woodman A&L, Kansas City, Kans., 1967-72; practice ins. and fin. brokerage, Kansas City, Kans., 1972—; owner, pres. Flock of Lambs, Christian supply mail order co., Overland Park, Kans., 1979—; founder, owner, operator Flock of Lambs To Make a Better Ewe (you), 1979—; pres., chmn. bd. Alfreda's Fin. Devel.; chmn. profl. seminars. Named to Million Dollar Round Table, numerous times; recipient Disting. Salesman award Gov. Kans., 1968, 69; Nat. Quality award Nat. Life Underwriters, 1971, Nat. Sales Achievement award, 1971. Mem. Women's Leaders Round Table (life), Nat. Life Underwriters, Johnson County Wyandotte Life Underwriters, Women's C. of C. Republican. Roman Catholic. Clubs: Zonta Internat. (charter mem., organizer and 1st pres. Johnson County, Kans. club 1972-77), Charismatic Prayer Group. Contbr. articles to mags. Address: PO Box 12547 Shawnee KS 66212

BACHMANN, MONICA, musician; b. Topeka, Kans., Apr. 26, 1948; B.A. in Music Theory, Mt. St. Scholastica Coll., Atchison, Kans., 1969; postgrad. Pittsburg State U., U. Nebr., Lincoln, Bartlesville (Okla.) Wesleyan Coll.; children—John Peter, Simon Jason Howard, Lonna Marceta. Owner Monica's Music Studio, 1981—; part owner Visions Motion Picture Corp., 1981—, Excelsior Prodns., Inc., 1982—. Address: PO Box 359 Excelsior Springs MO 64024

BACHMANN, WILLIAM VINCENT, combustion engine cons.; b. Bozen, S. Tyrol, Italy, Apr. 8, 1913; s. Johann and Franziska (Demetz) B.; student engring. Koenigliche Staatsgewerbeschule, 1929-30, pvt. study art and graphics, 1931-34; m. Diane Thomson, Jan. 3, 1977; children by former marriages—George, Francisca, Vincent. With Massey Ferguson Co., Toronto, Ont., Can., 1953-56; with Dilworth Ewbanks, cons. Can. Air Research Project, Toronto, 1956-58; body A engr. Chrysler Corp., Highland Park, Mich., 1958-70; test engr. cons. Volkswagen Mfg. Corp. Am., Warren, Mich., 1977-78; pres. Bachmann Fire Ring Engine Research Co., St. Clair Shores, Mich., 1979—. Mem. Engring. Soc. Detroit, United Inventors and Scientists Am., Am. Def. Preparedness Assn. Patentee internal combustion engines. Address: 22517 Ten Mile Rd Saint Clair Shores MI 48080

BACKER, DONALD JOSEPH, hosp. adminstr.; b. St. Louis, Dec. 23, 1931; s. Joseph A. and Mable A. (Moore) B.; B.S. in Psychology, St. Louis U., 1957, M.B.A., 1961; m. Irene J. Kustra, Oct. 18, 1958; children—Michele, Mark, Eric, Paul. Dir. indsl. relations Granite City (Ill.) Steel, 1962-70; dir. indsl. relations Gen. Steel Industries, Granite City, 1970-72; dir. employee relations Jewish Hosp. of St. Louis, 1972-74; v.p. personnel and community relations Christian Hosp. Northeast-Northwest, St. Louis, 1974—; lectr. in field. Pres. St. Casimir Sch. Bd., St. Louis; Served with U.S. Army, 1953-55. Mem. Florissant Valley C. of C. (pres. 1980-81), Mo. Hosp. Assn., Hosp. Personnel Mgrs. of Greater St. Louis, Hosp. Assn. Greater St. Louis, Hosp. Public Relations Soc. St. Louis, Indsl. Relations Assn. Greater St. Louis (pres. 1969-70), East Side Indsl. Relations Assn. (pres. 1967-68), Am. Soc. Tng. and Devel., Ill. Mfrs. Assn., C. of C. of Tri-Cities, Nat. Soc. Fund Raisers, Midwest Coll. Placement Assn. Office: 11133 Dunn Rd Saint Louis MO 63136

BACON, GEORGE EDGAR, pediatrician, educator; b. N.Y.C., Apr. 13, 1932; s. Edgar and Margaret Priscilla (Anderson) B.; B.A., Wesleyan U., 1953; M.D., Duke U., 1957; M.S. in Pharmacology, U. Mich., 1967; m. Grace Elizabeth Graham, June 30, 1956; children—Nancy, George, John. Intern in pediatrics Duke Hosp., Durham, N.C., 1957-58; resident in pediatrics Columbia-Presbyn. Med. Center, N.Y.C., 1961-63; instr. U. Mich., Ann Arbor, 1963, asst. prof., 1968, asso. prof., 1971, prof. pediatrics, 1974—, chief pediatric endocrinology service, dept. pediatrics, 1970—; coordinator profl. services C.S. Mott Children's Hosp., 1973—, mem. exec. com. for clin. affairs, 1975-76, 77-79, asso. vice chmn. med. staff, 1978-79; chmn. exec. com. C.S. Mott Children's, Women's, Holden hosps., Ann Arbor, 1973—; mem. Senate Assembly, U. Mich., 1978—; vice chmn. dir.'s adv. council Univ. Hosp., Ann Arbor, 1981—. Served to capt., U.S. Army, 1958-61. Diplomate Am. Bd. Pediatrics, subsplty. Bd. Pediatric Endocrinology. Fellow Am. Acad. Pediatrics; mem. Am. Pediatric Soc., Soc. Pediatric Research (emeritus), Endocrine Soc., Lawson Wilkins Pediatric Endocrine Soc. Republican. Author: A Practical Approach to Pediatric Endocrinology, 1975, 2nd edit. 1981; contbr. articles to med. jours. Home: 3911 Waldenwood Ann Arbor MI 48105 Office: Dept Pediatrics U Mich Ann Arbor MI 48109

BACON, LOLITA SPIVEY, ednl. adminstr.; b. Chgo., Nov. 19, 1935; d. Henry and Mary Jane (Harmon) Spivey; B.Edn., Chgo. Tchrs. Coll., 1956, M.Ed., 1962; Ed.D., Nova U., 1980; m. Ernest George Bacon, May 27, 1956; children—Darrell Ernest, Tanya Lynette. With Chgo. Bd. Edn., 1956—, head tchr. spl. edn. dept. Perry Sch., 1974-76, head tchr. deaf dept. Mahalia Jackson Sch., 1976-77, coordinator hearing impaired programs, 1977—. Trustee, United Meth. Found., U. Chgo., 1960-75, Abraham Lincoln Center, 1978—; mem. gen. council on fin. and adminstrn., legal com. Commn. on Black Colls., 1980—. Mem. Chgo. Tchrs. Hearing Impaired, Ill. Tchrs. Hearing Impaired, Nat. Assn. Sch. Adminstrs., Council Exceptional Children, Nat. Alliance Black Sch. Educators, Stratton Assn., Assn. Curriculum Devel., Phi Delta Kappa. Democrat. United Methodist. Home: 8051 S Yale Ave Chicago IL 60620 Office: 228 N LaSalle St Chicago IL 60601

BACON, WALTER MEREDITH, JR., polit. scientist, educator; b. N.Y.C., June 30, 1946; s. Walter Meredith and Caroline (Dawdy) B.; B.A., Colo. Coll., 1968; M.A., U. Denver, 1972, Ph.D., 1975; m. Lynne Lazier, Aug. 9, 1968. Instr., vis. prof. U. Colo., Colorado Springs, 1974-76; research scholar Hoover Instn. on War, Revolution and Peace, 1975-76; asst. prof. polit. sci. U. Nebr., Omaha, 1976—. Spl. U.S. Rep. to Romanian Observance Am. Bicentennial. Kellogg nat. fellow, 1981-84; Woodrow Wilson nat. dissertation fellow, 1971-72; IREX exchange scholar in Romania, 1971-72. Mem. Internat. Studies Assn., Am. Assn. for Advancement Slavic Studies, Central Slavic Council (pres. 1980-81), Soc. Romanian Studies (v.p. 1979-80). Democrat. Episcopalian. Author: Behind Closed Doors, 1979; contbr. articles to profl. jours. Home: 731 N 58th St Omaha NE 68132 Office: Dept Polit Sci U Nebr Omaha NE 68182

BACON, WILLIAM THOMPSON, JR., investment co. exec.; b. Chgo., Feb. 6, 1923; s. William Thompson and Martha (Smith) B.; grad. Phillips Acad., 1941; B.A., Yale, 1945; m. Margaret Hoyt, Apr. 18, 1942; children—William Thompson III, Catherine (Mrs. Von Stroh), Hoyt Wells, J. Knight, Christopher S. Asst. cashier First Nat. Bank of Chgo., 1946-55; partner Bacon, Whipple & Co., Chgo., 1956—; dir. Walbro Corp., Safecard Services, Inc. Trustee Hadley Sch. for Blind, Winnetka, Ill., Fountain Valley Sch., Colorado Springs, Colo. Served with AUS, 1943-44. Mem. Elihu, Delta Kappa Epsilon. Republican. Episcopalian. Clubs: Yale (pres. 1962-63), Chicago, University (Chgo.); Onwentsia (Lake Forest, Ill.); Shoreacres (Lake Bluff, Ill.); Old Elm (Ft. Sheridan, Ill.); Indian Hill (Winnetka, Ill.); Yale (N.Y.C.); Gulfstream Golf (Delray Beach, Fla.). Home: 1300 N Waukegan Rd Lake Forest IL 60045 Office: 135 S LaSalle St Chicago IL 60603

BADE, PHILLIP EDWIN, cons., tng. and devel. co. exec.; b. Evanston, Ill., July 15, 1934; s. Arthur Carl and Myrtle Elizabeth (Elke) B.; B.S., Bradley U., Peoria, Ill., 1957; m. Frances Ann Fenske, Aug. 17, 1957; children—Richard Phillip, Karl Christopher. Chief tech. tng. center Teletype Corp., Skokie, Ill., 1962-69; mgr. Lake County tng. and edn. Abbott Labs., N. Chicago, Ill., 1969-70, cons. corp. tng. and edn., 1970-72; v.p. program devel. Universal Tng. Systems Co., Northbrook, Ill., 1972—, mng. prin., tng. and devel. group, Prospect Heights, Ill., 1979—. Served with USAF, 1957-62. Mem. Am. Soc. Tng. and Devel., Assn. Edn. Communications and Tech., Nat. Soc. Performance and Instrn. Baptist. Office: 3201 Old Glenview Rd Wilmette IL 60091

BADEER, HENRY SARKIS, physician, educator; b. Mersine, Turkey, Jan. 31, 1915; s. Sarkis and Persape Hagop (Koundakjian) B.; came to U.S., 1965, naturalized, 1971; M.D., Am. U., Beirut, Lebanon, 1938; m. Mariam Mihran Kassarjian, July 12, 1948; children—Gilbert H., Daniel H. Gen. practice medicine, Beirut, 1940-51; asst. instr. Am. U. Sch. Medicine, Beirut, 1938-45, adj. prof., 1945-51, asso. prof., 1951-62, prof. physiology, 1962-65, acting chmn. dept., 1951-56, chmn., 1956-65; research fellow Harvard U. Med. Sch., Boston, 1948-49; prof. physiology Creighton U. Med. Sch., Omaha, 1967—, acting chmn. dept., 1971-72; vis. prof. U. Iowa, Iowa City, 1957-58, Downstate Med. Center, Bklyn., 1965-67; mem. med. com. Azounieh Sanatorium, Beirut, 1961-65; mem. research com. Nebr. Heart Assn., 1967-70. Recipient Golden Apple award Students of AMA, 1975; Rockefeller fellow., 1948-49; grantee med. research com., Am. U. Beirut, 1956-65. Mem. AAAS, Internat. Soc. Heart Research, Am. Physiol. Soc., Alpha Omega Alpha. Contbr. chpts. to books, articles to profl. jours. Home: 2808 S 99th Ave Omaha NE 68124 Office: Creighton U Med Sch 2500 Calif St Omaha NE 68178

BADER, PATRICIA IRENE, physician; b. Paris, Ill., Aug. 26, 1945; d. Eugene J. and Mary A. Englum; B.A. cum laude, DePauw U., 1968; M.D., Ind. U., 1970, M.S. in Genetics, 1974; m. Franklin Joseph Bader, June 14, 1969; children—Jessica Rosemary, Franklin Joseph, Jennifer Katherine. Intern, Ind. Univ. Hosps., Indpls., 1970-71, resident, 1971-74; practice medicine specializing in pediatrics and med. genetics, Indpls. and Bluffton, Ind., 1974—; instr. dept. community health Ind. U. Sch. Medicine, Indpls., 1972, instr. med. genetics, 1973-80, asst. prof. med. genetics, 1980—; asst. dir. clin. research Caylor-Nickel Research Inst., Bluffton, 1973, dir. clin. research, 1974—; genetic counselor 5-County Diagnostic Clinic, Assn. Retarded Citizens Ind., Adams/Wells Tng. Center, Bluffton, 1978—; clin. investigator nutrition studies Mead Johnson & Co., 1978-79; clin. investigator collaborative drug studies Ayerst Labs., N.Y.C., 1978—; med. adviser March of Dimes, Nat. Found., N.E. Ind. chpt., 1976—. NIH fellow, 1972. Diplomate Am. Bd. Pediatrics. Mem. Am. Med. Women's Assn., Am. Acad. Pediatrics, Am. Soc. Human Genetics, Am. Fedn. Clin. Research, AMA, Ind. State Med. Assn., Alpha Lambda Delta. Roman Catholic. Contbr. articles to sci. jours. Home: Badenbower Rural Route 1 Uniondale IN 46791 Office: 311 S Scott St Bluffton IN 46714

BAE, KUN CHAE, pharm. co. exec.; b. Chinjoo, Korea, July 10, 1934; s. Kil Moon and Soo Yeon (Baeck) B.; came to U.S., 1956, naturalized, 1967; B.A. in Chemistry, Millikin U., Decatur, Ill., 1960; m. Myoung Hwa Ok, Feb. 18, 1962; children—Donald, Kevin, Scott. Research chemist Swift & Co., Chgo., 1960-62; chief chemist Oak Park Med. Labs., Inc. (Ill.), 1962-65; quality control dir. Bates Labs., Inc., Chgo., 1965-71; plant mgr. Med. Chem. Corp., Melrose Park, Ill., 1971-73; pres. Bay Labs., Inc., Skokie, Ill., 1973—. Recipient Oil Can award Chgo. Econ. Devel. Corp., 1979. Mem. Chgo. Drug and Chem. Assn. Presbyterian. Club: Korean Y's Men Assn. Home: 6846 N Lorel Skokie IL 60077 Office: 3654 W Jarvis Skokie IL 60076

BAEHR, MELANY ERNA, psychologist; b. Kimberley, Republic South Africa, Oct. 25, 1920; came to U.S., 1948, naturalized, 1953; d. Ernest Horace and Hester Cecilia (Van Niekerk) White; B.S., U. Witwatersrand, Johannesburg, S. Africa, 1940, B.Ed., 1941, M.S., 1946, Ph.D., 1950; postgrad U. Chgo., 1948-49; m. George Otto Baehr, Sept. 9, 1949; children—Alexandra Elaine, Karen Estelle. Research officer South African Council for Sci. and Indsl. Research, 1946-49; project dir. Human Resources Center, U. Chgo., 1950-53, research asso., 1955-57, cons., 1957-62, div. dir., 1962-70, sr. research psychologist, asso. prof. social sci., 1970-78, asso. dir. research, 1979—. Served with South African Air Force, 1939-45. Cert. psychologist, Ill. Fellow Am. Psychol. Assn.; mem. Ill. Psychol. Assn. (past pres. indsl. sect.), Sigma Xi, Psi Chi. Episcopalian. Author psychol. tests and measurement instruments; contbr. articles to profl. jours. Home: 5555 S Everett Av Chicago IL 60637 Office: 1225 E 60th St Chicago IL 60637

BAER, DAVID, JR., lawyer; b. Belleville, Ill., Sept. 24, 1905; s. David and Sunshine (Lieber) B.; LL.B., Washington U., 1928; m. Mary Lynne Cockrell Sweet, Apr. 18, 1938. Partner firm Barnard and Baer, lawyers, St. Louis; dir. Lindell Trust Co.; former pres., dir. Mo.-Lincoln Trust Co.; former dir. Scullin Steel Co., St. Louis. Former mem. St. Louis Boy Scout Endowment Fund Com. Served as sgt. AUS, 1943-45. Mem. Estate Planning Council St. Louis (past pres., dir.), Am., Mo., St. Louis (past chmn. group ins. com.) bar assns., Washington U. Law Alumni Assn., Jr. (life), Ill. Jr. (past pres.), U.S. Jr. (senator) chambers commerce. Mason, De Molay (past master councilor, sr. mem.; mem. Legion of Honor). Club: Mo. Athletic. Home: 701 S Skinker Blvd Saint Louis MO 63105 Office: 818 Olive St Saint Louis MO 63101

BAER, JERRY W., mgmt. cons. firm exec.; b. Chgo., Nov. 3, 1936; s. Jerome W. and Matilda L. Baer; B.S. in Mktg., Ind. U., 1958; M.B.A. (research fellow), U. Chgo., 1963; children—Raji Lynn, Julie Ann. Sr. analyst Ford Motor Co., 1963-66; asst. prof. U. Detroit, 1964; dir. mktg. Cole Nat. Corp., Cleve., 1966-68; pres. Dual Wide Mobile Homes, Los Angeles, 1968-74; group exec. Whittaker Corp., Los Angeles, 1974-76; pres. Wellington Assos., mgmt. cons., Chgo., 1976—. Served to 2d lt. AUS, 1958-59. Writing grantee Hyde Park Coop., Chgo., 1961; recipient Service award Ind. U. YMCA, 1958. Mem. Am. Mktg. Assn. (dir. 1967), Am. Inst. Fin. Analysts (dir. 1964), U. Chgo. Alumni Assn. (dir. 1963-69), Advt. Club Los Angeles. Clubs: Mountaingate Country (Los Angeles); Marina City (Marina Del Rey). Author papers in field. Home: 515 Wellington Chicago IL 60657 Office: 111 E Chestnut Chicago IL 60611 Heights IL 60005

BAER, JULIUS ARTHUR, II, merchant; b. St. Louis, Apr. 18, 1921; s. Arthur B. and Lucile (Calisch) B.; A.B., Duke U., 1943; m. Mary Pauline; children—Julius Arthur, Patricia Anne, Terence Michael. Asst. field dir. ARC, 1943-46; with Stix, Baer & Fuller Co., dept. store, St. Louis, 1946—, div. mdse. mgr., 1955-57, br. store mgr., 1957-59, v.p. charge total store merchandising and publicity, 1959-61, exec. v.p., 1961-63, pres., chief exec. officer, 1963-76, chmn. bd., 1973—, also dir., 1963-76; v.p. Asso. Dry Goods; dir. Union Electric Co., Merc. Trust Co., Boston Store, Ft. Smith, Ark. and Beaumont, Tex., CMC Corp., St. Louis. Chmn., St. Louis Public TV; bd. dirs., former pres. Downtown St. Louis, Inc.; bd. dirs. St. Louis area council Boy Scouts Am., Govtl. Research Inst., Jefferson Nat. Expansion Meml., St. Louis Jewish Hosp., St. Louis Symphony Soc., Dance Concert Soc. St. Louis, Theatre Project Co., Laumeier Park, Herbert Hoover Boys Club of St. Louis, Inc., United Way of Greater St. Louis, Civic Progress; chmn., former pres. St. Louis Mcpl. Opera. Recipient Medal of Honor, Centre Nationale du Commerce Exterieur, French Govt., 1960; Ordre de L'economie French Govt., 1965; Al Mérito Turístico, Spanish Govt., 1968; Am. Legion citation, 1969. Mem. Met. St. Louis Retail Fedn. (dir.), Am. Retail Fedn. (dir.), Nat. Retail Mchts. Assn. (past dir.), St. Louis Council on World Affairs (v.p., dir.), Omicron Delta Kappa, Theta Alpha Phi, Zeta Beta Tau. Office: 500 N Broadway Suite 1547 St Louis MO 63102

BAETZHOLD, HOWARD GEORGE, educator; b. Buffalo, Jan. 1, 1923; s. Howard Kuster and Harriet Laura (Hofheins) B.; student Brown U., 1940-43, Mass. Inst. Tech., 1943-44; A.B. magna cum laude, Brown U., 1944, M.A., 1948; Ph.D., U. Wis., 1953; m. Nancy Millard Cheesman, Aug. 5, 1950; children—Howard King, Barbara Millard. Asst. dir. Veterans Coll., Brown U., Providence, 1947-48, dir., 1948-49, admissions officer, 1948-50; teaching asst. U. Wis.-Madison, 1950-51, asst. to asso. dean Coll. Letters and Sci., 1951-53; asst. prof. English, Butler U., Indpls., 1953-57, asso. prof., 1957-67, prof. English, 1967—, head dept., 1981—, Rebecca Clifton Reade prof., 1981; vis. prof. U. Del., summer 1963. Mem. Indpls. Com. Internat. Visitors, 1965—. Served to 1st lt. AC, AUS, 1943-46. Butler U. faculty fellow, 1957-58, 69-70; Am. Philos. Soc. grantee, 1958; Am. Council Learned Socs. grantee, 1967. Mem. AAUP (v.p. state conf. 1955), Modern Lang. Assn., Am. Studies Assn. (nat. council 1974-76), Midwest Modern Lang. Assn., Ohio-Ind. Am. Studies Assn. (pres. 1967-68), Indpls. Urban League, Art Assn. Indpls., Butler U. Odd Topics Soc., Delta Upsilon. Author: Mark Twain and John Bull: The British Connection, 1970. Contbr. articles to profl. publs. Home: 6723 Riverview Dr Indianapolis IN 46220

BAGBY, MARVIN ORVILLE, chemist; b. Macomb, Ill., Sept. 27, 1932; s. Byron Orville and Geneva Floriene (Filbert) B.; B.S., Western Ill. U., 1957, M.S., 1957; m. Mary Jean Jennings, Aug. 31, 1957; children—Gary Lee, Gordon Eugene. With No. Regional Research Center, U.S. Dept. Agr., Peoria, Ill., 1957—, research leader fibrous products research unit, 1974-80, mgr. No. Agrl. Energy Center, 1980—, also research leader hydrocarbon plants and biomass research unit. Served with AUS, 1953-55. Mem. Am. Chem. Soc., AAAS, TAPPI. Methodist. Contbr. articles to profl. jours. Home: 209 S Louisiana St Morton IL 61550 Office: 1815 N University St Peoria IL 61604

BAGLEY, JAMES EDWARD, hosp. adminstr.; b. Waterloo, Iowa, Sept. 21, 1930; s. William Franklin and Margaret (Craig) B.; grad. pub. schs.; B.Pub. Adminstrn., Upper Iowa U., 1975; credentials advanced hosp. and health care adminstrn. U. Minn., 1976; M. Hosp. Adminstrn., U. Minn., 1977; m. Kathie Rebecca Smith, Nov. 29, 1968; children—Cheryl, Kathleen, Debra, Vicki, Sharri, Lauri. Psychiat. aide U.S. VA Hosp., Knoxville, Iowa, 1952-56; sr. patrolman State Iowa Dept. Public Safety, Iowa Falls, 1956-63; adminstr. Ellsworth Mcpl. Hosp., Iowa Falls, 1963-68; exec. dir. Greene County Med. Center, Jefferson, Iowa, 1968—, dir. Servi-Share of Iowa, Greenwood Homes, Inc. Chmn., Iowa Hosp. Purchasing Council. Served with USN, 1948-52. Named Boss of Yr., Jefferson Jaycees, 1978; lic. nursing home adminstr., Iowa. Fellow Am. Acad. Med. Adminstrs. (nat. sec., chmn.-elect 1981—; Newcomer award Med. Adminstr. of Yr. 1977, Regional Dir. of Yr. 1980); mem. Am., Iowa (chmn. SW region 1971, chmn. div. plant ops. 1969-70, chmn. div. long-term care 1974-75, chmn. div. long term care statistics 1975-76, trustee 1978-80, treas. 1977-78, chmn.-elect 1981-82; James B. Seaman award 1980), hosp. assns., Am. Coll. Hosp. Adminstrs., Am. Coll. Nursing Home Adminstrs., Iowa Assn. Homes for Aging (dir. 1975-76). Methodist (chmn. bd. trustees 1971). Lion, Elk. Home: 507 Rushview Dr Jefferson IA 50129 Office: 1000 W Lincolnway Jefferson IA 50129

BAHNSEN, RONALD RUSSELL, hosp. ofcl.; b. Rockford, Ill., Dec. 2, 1947; s. Wesley and Marjorie E. Bahnsen; B.Pharmacy, Drake U., 1970; M.B.A., U. Ill.; m. Karen Marie Amundson, Dec. 28, 1968; 1 son, Jeffrey. Mgr., Suprex Drug Store, Peoria, Ill., 1970-71; pharmacy mgr. Venture Dept. Store, Peoria, 1971-73; asst. dir. pharmacy Pekin (Ill.) Meml. Hosp., 1973-77, dir. pharmacy, 1977—; mem. part-time staff Ill. Central Coll., East Peoria, 1977—. Mem. Am. Pharm. Assn., Ill. Pharm. Assn., Ill. Council Hosp. Pharmacists (v.p.), Am. Soc. Hosp. Pharmacists, Am. Soc. Parenteral and Nutrition, Assn. M.B.A. Execs., Sigma Iota Epsilon. Republican. Roman Catholic. Club: K.C. Home: 13 Oak Hill Pekin IL 61554 Office: Pekin Meml Hosp Court and 14th Sts Pekin IL 61554

BAHR, MAURICE JAMES, hosp. mgmt. engring. cons.; b. St. Louis, Apr. 3, 1938; s. Maurice Joseph and Agnes Helen (Van Scheltinga) B.; B.I.E., Ga. Inst. Tech., 1962; postgrad. Wayne State U., 1963-67; m. Nancy Isabell Malott, June 10, 1961; children—Mary Louise, James Anthony, Katherine Elizabeth. Indsl. engr. R.C. Mahon Co., Detroit, 1962-64; div. indsl. engr. Wolverine Tube div. U.O.P., Detroit, 1964-69; asso. Community Systems Found., Ann Arbor, Mich., 1969-72; mgr. indsl. engring. St. Joseph Mercy Hosp., Ann Arbor, 1972-79; pres. James Bahr Assos., Ltd., hosp. mgmt. engring. cons., Plymouth, Mich., 1979—. Mem. Am. Inst. Indsl. Engrs., Hosp. Mgmt. Systems Soc., Mich. Hosp. Mgmt. Systems Soc. Home and Office: 10763 Canton Center Rd N Plymouth MI 48170

BAIA, ARLENE VIVIAN SKJEVELAND, nursing educator; b. Duluth, Minn., Aug. 15, 1922; d. Theodore Owen and Pearl Ruby (Thompson) Skjeveland; B.S. in Nursing Edn., U. Minn., 1945; M.S. in Edn., Iowa State U., 1973; children—Barbara Baia Thompson, Gloria Bonnie (dec.). Instr., U. Minn. Sch. Nursing, Mpls., 1945-46; asso. dir. edn. Naeve Hosp. Sch. Nursing, Albert Lea, Minn., 1954-60; instr. St. Joseph Sch. Nursing, Mason City, Iowa, 1960-62, Meth. Kahler Sch. Nursing, Rochester, Minn., 1962-68; instr. nursing North Iowa Area Community Coll., Mason City, 1968-79, chmn. health related div., 1979—. Recipient certificate for distinguished teaching in nursing Rochester C. of C., 1964. Mem. Am. (council advanced practitioners in med.-surg. nursing), Iowa (chmn. rev. panel for continuing edn. 1972-76) nurses assns., P.E.O. Republican. Congregationalist. Club: Order Eastern Star. Home: 417 S Tennessee Pl Apt 6 Mason City IA 50401 Office: 500 College Dr Mason City IA 50401

BAIKERIKAR, KAMALAKAR GHANASHYAM, chemist; b. Halge, India, Apr. 5, 1941; came to U.S., 1971, naturalized, 1975; s. Ghanashyam Ramachandra and Gulabi Dattatray (Revankar) B.; B.S., Karnatak U., 1963, M.S., 1965; Ph.D., Indian Inst. Tech., 1970; m. Vijaya Vernekar, May 25, 1970; 1 child, Kiran. Research fellow Indian Inst. Tech., Bombay, 1965-71; U.S. AEC postdoctoral fellow Ames Lab., Iowa State U., 1971-75, asst. chemist Ames Lab., U.S. Dept. Energy, 1975-80, asso. chemist, 1980—. Mem. Am. Chem. Soc., Electrochem. Soc., Sigma Xi. Hindu. Contbr. articles to profl. jours. Home: 706 24th St Ames IA 50010 Office: 108 O & L Ames Lab Iowa State Univ Ames IA 50011

BAILEY, ANDREA, producer; b. Chgo., Aug. 5, 1945; d. A. Leon and Portia H. (Thomas) Bailey; student Lawrence U., 1961-64, Lake Forest Coll., 1965-66. Tech. dir., producer Thomas Meml. Theatre, Chgo., 1962-65; lit. translator from German, 1969-75; lighting designer, tech. dir. touring Proscenium Players Co., 1971-73; guest dir., theatre prodn. cons.; developer Exptl. Designers Project for Linguistic and Cultural Communication Devel. Corp., 1972-74; cons./demonstrator Skinner Sch. Gifted Program, Chgo., 1974-78; producer, propr. Andrea Bailey Enterprises, Chgo., 1979—; producer Black Independent Cinema USA, film festival, 1981. Mem. U.S. Inst. for Theatre Tech. (vice chairperson Midwest sect.), Am. Soc. Theatre Research, AFTRA, Am. Film Inst., Screen Actors Guild, Nat. Conf. Artists, S. Shore Cultural Council, Chgo. Unltd. Mem. A.M.E. Ch. Editor, Midwest Report, 1978—; pub. Movin' On in Space and Time, 1974-76; author: Greatest of These, 1970; Depth of the Shadow, 1963 (plays); Christophe, One Among the Giants (book); contbr. articles to profl. jours. Office: PO Box 1369 Chicago IL 60690

BAILEY, ANNELL DEANNE, accountant; b. Kansas City, Mo., Aug. 31, 1943; d. Ward Norman and Vida Fae (Votaw) Gibson; B.A. summa cum laude, Mo. Valley Coll., 1966; M.B.A., U. Mo., Kansas City, 1978; m. Willard Lance McGowan, May 28, 1965 (div. 1970); 1 dau., Cherlyn Deanna; m. 2d, Robert Edson Bailey, Dec. 4, 1971. Editor, Hallmark Cards, Inc., Kansas City, Mo., 1967-75; acct. Wolkow & Calys, C.P.A.'s, Fairway, Kans., 1977-79, Craven Wooldridge & Dooley, C.P.A.'s, Kansas City, Mo., 1979-80, Aubrey E. Richardson, C.P.A., Kansas City, Mo., 1980—. Bd. dirs. Jr. Women's Philharm. Assn., 1972-79. C.P.A., Mo. Mem. Dimensions Unlimited, Nat. Assn. Accts., Am. Inst. C.P.A.'s, Kans. Soc. C.P.A.'s, Mo. Soc. C.P.A.'s, Beta Alpha Psi. Presbyterian. Home: 904 Main St Parkville MO 64152 Office: 1020 E 8th St Kansas City MO 64106

BAILEY, EUGENE CARY, cons. engring. co. exec.; b. Chgo., Apr. 7, 1910; s. Alexander Davidson and Alice (Cary) B.; B.S. in M.E., Purdue U., 1932, M.S. in M.E., 1933; m. Marie F. Kerker, Apr. 21, 1931 (dec.); M. 2d Janet L. Sampson, Jan. 24, 1938; children—Willard N., Robert E., Alice (dec.). With Commonwealth Edison Co., Chgo., 1933-75, system mech. and bldg. engr., 1954-62, adminstrv. engr. for v.p., 1962-75; v.p. bus. devel. John Dolio & Assos. (now Dolio and Metz Ltd.), Chgo., 1975—; cons., resource recovery and nuclear and fossil power engring. Trustee Lyons Twp. High Sch. Dist. 204, 1956-69; trustee Coll. of Du Page (Ill.), 1970-77; mem. Ill. Commn. on Atomic Energy. Served from 1st lt. to capt. U.S. Army, 1942-45. Registered profl. engr., Ill. Fellow Am. Soc. Mech. Engrs.; mem. Western Soc. Engrs., Am. Welding Soc., Am. Nuclear Soc., Ill. Soc. Profl. Engrs. Republican. Congregationalist. Clubs: Union League Chgo., Antique Auto Am. Home: 81 S 6th Ave LaGrange IL 60525 Office: 208 S LaSalle St Chicago IL 60604

BAILEY, GWENDOLYN LEE MANNING, educator; b. Dayton, Ohio, Sept. 1, 1930; d. Edgar William and Thelma Evelyn (Doughman) Vahle; B.S. in Edn., U. Dayton, 1963, M.S. in Edn., 1969; m. Charles Sydney Bailey, Aug. 3, 1949; 1 son, Bruce Eugene. Tchr., Northridge Morrison Elementary Sch., Dayton, 1960-63; tchr. Beavercreek Fairbrook Elementary Sch., Xenia, Ohio, 1963-70, counselor Beavercreek High Sch., 1970—. Co-chmn. United Appeal. Recipient Counselor of Yr. award AHEAD, 1980. Mem. Am., Ohio, Miami Valley personnel and guidance assns., NEA, Ohio, Western Ohio edn. assns., Ohio High Sch. Drill Team Assn. (v.p., state dir.), Half-Time U.S.A., Ohio Sch. Counselors Assn., Beavercreek Classroom Tchrs. Assn. Home: 4218 Walbridge Trail Dayton OH 45430 Office: 2940 Dayton-Xenia Rd Xenia OH 45385

BAILEY, IRENE CHAMBERS, aircraft mfg. corp. materials buyer; b. Edwards, Miss., Dec. 2, 1933; d. Alfred Lonzo and Beatrice (Terrell) Chambers; student Wichita State U., 1952-55, Wichita Bus. Coll., 1955-57; m. Sibblitt Shaw, Apr. 20, 1957; children—Sharene, Sherman, Montella, Chevette, Jan. With Boeing Aircraft Corp., Wichita, Kans., 1952-55, 60-63, Avionic div. Lear Jet Corp., Wichita, 1964-65; with Wichita Bd. Edn., 1972-73; sec. Phyllis Wheatley Sch., Wichita, 1973-74; with Beech Aircraft Corp., Wichita, 1974—, now casting, forging buyer raw materials. Mem. Wichita Assn. Colored Women and Girls Clubs (sec. 1967-78, pres. 1980-81). Baptist. Home: 2714 N Spruce St Wichita KS 67219 Office: Beech Aircraft Corp 9709 E Central St Wichita KS 67202

BAILEY, JAMES DAVID, public relations ofcl.; b. Menomonie, Wis., Sept. 3, 1922; s. Paul E. and Ruth (Chickering) B.; B.S., U. Wis., Stout, 1948; M.A., U. Denver, 1950; postgrad. U. Colo., 1962; m. June 9, 1948; children—Dianne Bailey Zemichael, Andrea Bailey Watermann. Printing instr. Keating Jr. High Sch., Pueblo, Colo., 1948-49; instr. communications U. Denver, 1949-50; sales mgr./newscaster/announcer various radio stas., 1950-56; mgr. Northfield (Minn.) C. of C., 1956-64; free lance public relations cons., Northfield, Mpls., 1964-66; public relations/advt. asst. F&M Savings Bank, Mpls., 1966-69; owner James Baily & Assos., Public Relations/Advt. Agy., Mpls., 1969-72; dir. coll. relations St. Norbert Coll., Green Bay/DePere, Wis., 1972-73; public relations officer Wis. Indianhead Vocat.-Tech. Adult Edn. Dist., Shell Lake, 1973—. Mem. Shell Lake planning commn., 1974-81; bd. dirs. UN of Minn., 1969-72; mem. N.G. Citizens Com., Northfield, Minn., 1963-66; safety council chmn. Red Wing, Minn., 1953-56. Recipient cert. of appreciation Shell Lake Bicentennial Com., 1976, Stout U. Found., 1975; commendation cert. Shell Lake, Wis., 1976. Mem. Public Relations Soc. Am., Wis. Newspaper Assn., Nat. Assn. Vocat. Tech. Communicators, Nat. Council for Community Relations, Shell Lake C. of C., Am. Legion (comdr. 1947-48). Republican. Clubs: Minn. Press, Lions (dir. 1974—), Masons Shriners. Contbr. articles to profl. jours. Newsletter editor Minn. Press Club, 1970-72, UN Assn. of Minn., 1971-72; editor Minn. Farm Bur. Tabloid, 1964-65. Home: Route 1 Box 1437 Spooner WI 54801 Office: PO Box B Shell Lake WI 54871

BAILEY, JOHN MAXWELL, mech. engr., cons.; b. Gainesville, Ga., Oct. 31, 1927; s. Francis Livy and Violet Louise (Marlowe) B.; B.S. in Mech. Engring., Purdue U., 1952; m. Judith Joan Hastings, Aug. 12, 1950; children—Marsha, John, Stephen, Eric, Mark, Brett. Research engr. Caterpillar Tractor Co., Peoria, Ill., 1952-58, project engr., 1958-66, staff engr., 1966-69, program mgr., 1969-80, research cons., 1980—. Scoutmaster, Troop 59, Boy Scouts Am., Dunlap, Ill., 1956—, Eagle Scout. Served with USN, 1945-47. Mem. Soc. Automotive Engrs. (energy and materials com.), ASME (vice chmn. fuels and combustion com.), Engine Mfrs. Assn. (chmn. alt. fuels com. 1976-80, Outstanding Achievement award 1978, Oral Presentation award 1979), Alpha Tau Omega. Republican. Contbg. author: Burning A Wide Range of Fuels in Diesel Engines, 1967. Patentee in field. Home: Route 1 Dunlap IL 61525 Office: Research Dept Tech Center Caterpillar Tractor Co Peoria IL 61629

BAILEY, MICHAEL L., state ofcl.; b. Wichita, Kans., Oct. 4, 1948; s. L. C. and W. Jean Baily; B.S., Kans. Newman Coll., 1970; m. Carol A. Andra, Oct. 25, 1969; children—Vaughn, Kelly, Jason. Counselor, Sedgwick County Juvenile Ct., Wichita, 1970-72; field rep. Kans. Commn. Civil Rights, Topeka, 1972-74; dir. compliance Iowa Civil Right Commn., Des Moines, 1974-78; exec. dir. Kans. Commn. Civil Rights, 1978—; cons. YMCA, Kans. Assn. Commerce and Industry. Mem. Internat. Assn. Ofcl. Human Rights Agys., Kans. Human Relations Assn., Regional Exec. Council Civil Rights. Office: 535 Kansas Ave Topeka KS 66603*

BAILEY, NAOMA JUNE, nurse; b. Toledo, July 7, 1923; d. Theo W. and Eunice Lucy (Crown) Harris; L.P.N., Northwestern Ohio Practical Nurse Sch., 1965; A.D.S., Cuyahoga Coll., 1969, R.N., 1969; B.Ed., U. Toledo, 1976, M.Ed., 1981; m. James Arthur Bailey, Sept. 14, 1946; children—Mark Bruce, Paul Kim. Nurse, Maumee Valley Hosp., 1969-71; clin. instr. practical nurses at Mercy Hosp. for Toledo Bd. Edn., 1971-79, coordinator, 1979-80, supr. Practical Sch. Nursing, 1981—; public relations speaker. Vol. counselor Crisis Rescue Service, 1979-80; vol. Republican Party, 1973. Served with WAVES, USNR, 1941-43. Mem. Buckeye State Nurses Orgn., Ohio Orgn. Practical Nurse Educators, Vocat. Edn. Assn., Ohio Nurses Assn., Am. Bus. Women's Assn., Lic. Practical Nurses Orgn. (cons. bd.). Home: 64 Walnut Hills Walbridge OH 43465 Office: 430 Nebraska Ave Toledo OH 43602

BAILEY, RAY VERNON, patent lawyer, property mgr.; b. Royal, Iowa, Dec. 14, 1913; s. George Lewis and Marie (Albers) B.; B.A. cum laude, State U. Iowa, 1935, J.D. cum laude, 1937; m. Velda Maxine Sheldon, June 18, 1938; children—Theron Sheldon, George Bryan. Admitted to Iowa bar, 1937, Ill. bar, 1938; research patent counsel U.S. Gypsum Co., Chgo., 1937-39; asso. Home State Bank, Royal, 1940; partner Dick, Bailey & Fletcher, also Dick and Bailey, Des Moines, 1941-42; investigator U.S. Civil Service Commn., 1942-43; patent adviser Rock Island (Ill.) Arsenal, 1943-45; property mgmt., legal and patent work, Clarion, Iowa, 1945-74, Millers Bay, Milford, Iowa, 1974—; dir., past pres. Okoboji Protective Assn.; owner Century Farm. Past mem. Iowa Ho. Reps., past mem. ethics com., departmental rules review com., banking laws revision com. Mem. adv. bd. Prairie Gold council Boy Scouts Am.; mem. Iowa Bd. Regents, 1969-81, past chmn. banking com.; mem. Iowa Coll. Aid Commn., 1971-81; past bd. dirs. Iowa Student Loan Liquidity Corp., also past chmn. bylaws com. past mem. alumni council U. Iowa; past chmn. public affairs com. Wright County Extension Council, past pres. Clarion Devel. Commn.; past mem. State of Iowa Com. on Mental Hygiene; mem. People to People Higher Edn. Adminstrs. Del. to People's Republic of China, 1978; mem. planning and goals com. World Peace Through Law Center; past bd. dirs. U. Iowa Research Found. Recipient Silver Beaver award Boy Scouts Am. Mem. Am. (patent system policy planning com.), Iowa (com. on patent, trademark and copyright law), Wright County, Dickinson County bar assns., State U. Iowa Alumni Assn. (past pres. Clarion chpt.), Iowa Patent Law Assn., U. Iowa Parents Assn. (past pres.). Lion. Author papers in field. Address: Millers Bay Milford IA 51351

BAILEY, ROBERT L., mfg. co. exec.; b. Akron, Dec. 7, 1916; s. Erna Francis Zeptner Bailey B.S. in Mech. Engring., U. Akron, 1943; postgrad Iowa State U., 1947; m. Henrietta Mae Griffith, May 26, 1943; children—Karen, Debra, Sandra. Sales engr., H.A. Phillips Co., St. Charles, Ill., 1947-49; erection supt. Vilter Sales & Constrn. Co., Chgo., 1949-57; v.p. sales Refrigerating Spltys. Co., Broadview, Ill., 1959—. Served with AUS, 1943-47. Mem. ASHRAE (dir. ednl. com.), Internat. Inst. Ammonia Refrigeration, Refrigerating Machinery Assn. (pres. 1953), Refrigerating Engring. Tech. Assn., Refrigeration Service Engring. Soc. Republican. Home: 223 Middaugh Rd Clarendon Hills IL 60514 Office: 2445 S 25th Ave Broadview IL 60153

BAILEY, WENDELL, Congressman; b. Willow Springs, Mo., July 31, 1940; s. Robert and Ruby (Salisbury) B.; B.S. in Bus. Adminstrn., S.W. Mo. State U., 1962; m. Jane Ann Bray, Nov. 28, 1963; children—Mike, John, Jill. Owner, Bailey Automobile Co., Willow Springs, 1965—; mem. 97th Congress from 8th Dist. of Mo. Mayor, mem. city council, Willow Springs, 1970-72; mem. Mo. Ho. of Reps., 1972-80, chmn. Republican Caucus, 1976-80; mem. Commn. on Student Fin. Assistance, 1981—. Named Disting. Legislator, Mo. Health Care Assn., 1980, Citizen and Man of Yr., Willow Springs C. of C., 1974; numerous other awards. Baptist. Clubs: Lions, Elks. Office: 504 Cannon House Office Bldg Washington DC 20515

BAILEY, WILSON PEASE, pediatrician; b. Waverly, N.Y., Sept. 1, 1929; s. Percival Dee and Ella Marie (Wilson) B.; B.A., Alfred U., 1952; Dr. Osteopathy, Kirksville (Mo.) Coll. Osteo. Medicine, 1959; M.D. (Mead Johnson fellow), Calif. Coll. Medicine, 1962; m. Barbara Ann Miller, Apr. 5, 1958; children—Wilson Pease, John, Valerie, Bruce. Intern, Kirksville Osteo. Hosp., 1959-60, resident, 1960-62, chmn. dept. pediatrics Kirksville Coll. Medicine and Surgery, 1962-68, med. dir. children and youth program, 1966-68, asso. prof., 1965—; practice medicine specializing in pediatrics, Kirksville, 1968—; mem. staff attending pediatric Grim Smith Hosp., Kirksville, chief of staff, 1970-73: cons. OEO programs, rural pediatrics; lectr. N.E. Mo. U., 1962-72. Mem. Sch. Bd. Dist. III, 1972-73, pres., 1972-75; chmn. Head Start Bd., 1966-70. Served to col. M.C., AUS, 1952-55. Diplomate Coll. Osteo. Pediatricians. Mem. Mo. Assn. Osteo. Physicians, Am. Coll. Osteo. Pediatricians, N.E. Mo. Osteo. Physicians, Am. Osteo. Assn. Mason. Club: Kirksville Country. Contbr. articles to profl. jours. Home: RD 3 Kirksville MO 63501 Office: 2905 N Baltimore St Kirksville MO 63501

BAILLON, AUSTIN JOHN, real estate exec.; b. Duluth, Minn., June 22, 1927; s. Austin L. and Marie M. (McDonald) B.; B.A., U. Minn., 1950; B.S., St. Paul Coll. Law, 1952, LL.B., 1954; J.D., William Mitchell Coll. Law, 1969; m. Caroline Myers, Aug. 16, 1958; children—Caroline M., Paul A., Peter M., Catherine G., Alexandra R., Frances E. Claims examiner Minn. Mut. Life Ins. Co., St. Paul, 1950-52, claims mgr., 1952-54, atty. legal dept., 1954-55; sales mgr., appraiser F. M. and E. V. Dolan, Realtors and Appraisers, St. Paul, 1955-56; pres. Baillon Co., Realtors, Real Estate Brokerage and Investment, St. Paul, 1956—; founder, pres. St. Paul Title Ins. Co. subs. St. Paul Cos., Inc., 1963-67; founder Baillon Mortgage Corp., 1964, Bailon Agy., Inc., 1963. Bd. dirs. Minn. Landmarks, 1971-74. Served with USCG, 1945-46; with U.S. Army Res., 1951-54. Mem. Soc. Real Estate Appraisers (past sec.-treas., dir.), Am., Minn. State, Ramsey County bar assns., St. Paul Bd. Realtors (past treas., dir.), St. Paul Bldg. Owners and Mgrs. Assn., Chi Psi, Delta Theta Phi. Clubs: Minn. (dir. 1970-73), Athletic (St. Paul); K.C.; Somerset Country; Biltmore Hunting. Office: 60 W 4th St Saint Paul MN 55102

BAIN, RALPH LEE, chemist, educator; b. Los Angeles, May 8, 1933; s. Edwin Vance and Josephine Louise (Matrisciano) B.; B.S. in chemistry, U. Ill., 1956; Ph.D., Oreg. State U., 1964; 1 dau., Tuvana Louise. Asst. prof. U. Sask. (Can.), 1964-66; mem. faculty So. Ill. U., Edwardsville, 1966—, prof. chemistry, 1976—, chmn. dept., 1970-73, 79-80; health scientist adminstr. NIH, Bethesda, Md., 1980—; spl. projects officer digestive diseases and nutrition program Nat. Inst. Arthritis, Diabetes and Digestive and Kidney Diseases, 1980-81; acting exec. dir. Nat. Digestive Diseases Adv. Bd., 1981—. Mem. Ill. Com. on Water Resources, 1976—. Served with AUS, 1956-58. Univ. Coll. London hon. research fellow, 1973-74; recipient grants NSF, 1969-70, 80-81, NIH, 1976-78, Ill. Office Edn., 1973, Ill. Dept. Mental Health, 1976; Am. Council on Edn. govtl. fellow, 1980-81. Mem. Can. Inst. Chemistry, Am. Chem. Soc., Chem. Soc. London, Ill. Acad. Sci. Contbr. articles to profl. jours. Home: 88 Eastmoor Rd Route 1 East Alton IL 62024 Office: PO Box 65 Edwardsville IL 62026

BAINBRIDGE, WILLIAM LEE, supt. schs.; b. Steubenville, Ohio, Dec. 20, 1945; s. Paul I. and Tillie Bainbridge; B.S., Ohio U., 1967; M.S. in Edn., U. Akron, 1971; Ph.D., Ohio State U., 1980; postgrad. Columbia U., 1981; m. Linda Moffatt, Dec. 22, 1973; 1 son, Adam. Tchr., coach Canton (Ohio) Glenwood High Sch., 1967-72; adminstrv. asst. to Ohio State Supt. Public Instrn., 1972-74; research asso. Ohio State U., Columbus, 1974-75; asst. supt. Rocky River (Ohio) City Sch. Dist., 1975-77; supt. Grandview Heights (Ohio) City Sch. Dist., 1975-77; supt. Newark (Ohio) City Sch. Dist., 1979—. Vice pres. Licking County council Boy Scouts Am., 1980—; Mem. Nat. Acad. Sch. Execs. (state leader), Nat. Center Improvement Learning, Am. Assn. Sch. Adminstrs., Am. Arbitration Assn., State Sch. Supts. Assn. (profl. devel. chmn. 1978—), Central Ohio Schoolmasters (pres. 1981—), Newark C. of C., Phi Delta Kappa. Episcopalian. Club: Newark Rotary. Author articles in field. Office: Newark Sch Dist E Main at 1st St Newark OH 43055

BAINS, DHARM SINGH, clin. psychologist; b. Pajjo-deota, India, Aug. 15, 1935; came to U.S., 1968, naturalized, 1973; s. Gopal Singh and Jawali B.; B.A., Panjab U., India, 1958, B.T., 1960, M.A. in Psychology, 1962; D.M. and S.P. in Med. and Social Psychology, Mysore U., India, 1965; Ph.D. in Counseling Psychology, Kans. State U., 1975; m. Sarnjit Kaur, Jan. 9, 1972; children—Sujeev S., Rushim S. Asst. prof. psychology GHG Tng. Coll., Ludhiana, India, 1962; research asst. India-Internat. Center, New Delhi, 1965-66; asst. prof. psychology Haile Selassie I U., Addis Ababa, Ethiopia, 1966-68; clin. psychologist State Security Hosp., Larned, Kans., 1968-69, Youth Center, Beloit, Kans., 1969-70; clin. psychologist, clin. team leader Larned State Hosp., 1970-75; clin. psychologist, asst. regional dir. N.D. State Hosp., 1975-79; clin. psychologist VA Med. Center, Battle Creek, Mich., 1979—; student rep. All-India Inst. Mental Health, 1963-65; cons. Mem. Kalamazoo India Assn., 1980—. Mem. Am. Psychol. Assn., N.D. Psychol. Assn., Am. Personnel and Guidance Assn., Western Mich. Psychol. Assn., Indian Sci. Congress (life). Sikh. Club: Rotary. Home: 5 Tony Tiger Trail Battle Creek MI 49015 Office: Veterans Administration Medical Center Battle Creek MI 49016

BAIRD, CLYDE RAY, univ. adminstr.; b. Attica, Kans., Jan. 31, 1921; s. Clyde and Elva (Copeland) B.; A.B., Southwestern Coll. (Kans.), 1942; M.A., Columbia U., 1947; Ed.D., U. Okla., 1956; m. Ann Anderson, Oct. 4, 1944; 1 dau., Catherine Ann. Asst. prof. edn., counselor Guidance Bur., Pittsburg (Kans.) State U., 1947-53, dir. admissions, registrar, 1953-68, asso. prof., 1957-58, prof., 1958-66, registrar, 1966-68, exec. v.p., 1968-79, v.p. for adminstrn., 1979—; cons., examiner North Central Assn. Served with USAAF, World War II. Mem. Am. Psychol. Assn., Am. Personnel and Guidance Assn., Am. Assn. Collegiate Registrars and Admissions Officers, Kans. Assn. Collegiate Registrars and Admissions Officers, Pittsburg Area C. of C., Phi Delta Kappa, Omicron Delta Kappa. Methodist. Club: Rotary Internat. Home: Rural Route 5 Pittsburg KS 66762 Office: Pittsburg State U Pittsburg KS 66762

BAIRD, GEORGE HENRY, ednl. adminstr.; b. Rushville, Ill., Sept. 24, 1922; s. George H. and Rose (Cook) B.; B.E., Western Ill. U., 1943; M.A., U. Wyo., 1949; Ed.D., Columbia, 1954; m. Karole V. Litchfield, May 14, 1944; 1 dau., Cheryl Sue Baird Ramsey. Tchr., coach, Alexis, Ill., 1946-47, Dwight, Ill., 1947-48; asst. supt. elementary schs., Worland, Wyo., 1948-53; dir. research spl. services and guidance Shaker Heights, O., 1954-59; exec. dir. Ednl. Research Council of Am., Cleve., 1959-66, pres., exec. dir., 1966—; chmn. bd. Ramsey-Baird Enterprises. Ednl. cons. Jr. Achievement of Greater

Cleve.; mem. regional interviewing com. U.S. Internat. Ednl. Exchange Program. Mem. steering com. Cleve. Energy Center. Served with Inf., AUS, 1944-46. Recipient Disting. Alumnae award Western Ill. U.; Melville Dewey gold medal internat. award for contbn. to edn. in Am. Mem. Greater Cleve. Growth Assn., Am. Assn. Sch. Adminstrs., Phi Delta Kappa, Kappa Delta Pi. Mason (32 deg., Shriner). Club: Union Rotary. Home: 2200 Devonshire Dr Cleveland Heights OH 44106 Office: Rockefeller Bldg Cleveland OH 44113

BAIRD, JAMES NICHOLSON, JR., obstetrician-gynecologist; b. N.Y.C., Feb. 29, 1940; s. James Nicholson and Jean (Sanford) B.; B.S., Ohio State U., 1962, M.D. cum laude (Dean's award), 1966; m. Veronica De Prisco, Aug. 25, 1962; children—Lisa Nicholson, James Nicholson III. Intern, Riverside Methodist Hosp., Columbus, Ohio, 1966-67, resident in obstetrics and gynecology, 1968-71; practice medicine specializing in obstetrics and gynecology, Columbus, 1971—; mem. staff Riverside Meth. Hosp., chmn. dept. Ob-Gyn, 1979-81; mem. staff Ohio State U. Hosp.; asst. clin. prof. Ohio State U. Coll. Medicine. Bd. dirs. Columbus Zool. Gardens. Diplomate Am. Bd. Obstetrics and Gynecology. Mem. AMA, Central Assn. Ob-Gyn, Am. Coll. Obstetrics and Gynecology, Columbus Gynecol. and Obstetric Soc. (treas. 1975, sec. 1976, pres. 1978), Internat. Soc. Aquatic Medicine, Acad. Medicine of Franklin County, Ohio State Med. Assn., Alpha Omega Alpha, Phi Gamma Delta (pres. bd. dirs. 1971-73). Republican. Roman Catholic. Clubs: Rotary, City, Columbus, Scioto Country, Pres.'s of Ohio State U. Home: 4700 Old Ravine Ct Columbus OH 43220 Office: 3545 Olentangy River Rd Columbus OH 43214

BAIRD, JOHN EDWARD, JR., mgmt. cons.; b. Portland, Oreg., July 6, 1948; s. John Edward and Eleanor Grace Baird; B.A., Calif. State U., Hayward, 1969; Ph.D., Ind. U., 1972. Asst. prof. U. N.D., 1973-74, U. Mich., 1974-78; corp. mgr. communication and opinion research Travenol Labs., Inc., Deerfield, Ill., 1978-79; mgmt. cons. Modern Mgmt. Methods, Inc., Bannockburn, Ill., 1980—; cons. editor for various publishers; lectr. and guest prof. communications. U. Mich. research grantee, 1976. Mem. Am. Mgmt. Assn., Speech Communications Assn., Improvement Inst., Central States Speech Communication Assn., Am. Bus. Communication Assn. Author: Workbook for Effective Speaking, 1974; The Dynamics of Organizational Communication, 1977; Communication, 1977; Speaking by Objectives, 1980; contbr. articles to profl. jours. and trade mags. Home: 905 Vose Dr Gurnee IL 60031 Office: Modern Mgmt Methods Inc 2275 Half Day Rd Bannockburn IL 60015

BAIRD, ROBERT DAHLEN, religions scholar, educator; b. Phila., June 29, 1933; s. Jesse Dahlen and Clara (Sonntag) B.; B.A., Houghton Coll., 1954; B.D., Fuller Theol. Sem., 1957; S.T.M., So. Meth. U., 1959; Ph.D., U. Iowa, 1964; m. Patty Jo Lutz, Dec. 18, 1954; children—Linda Sue, Stephen Robert, David Bryan, Janna Ann. Instr. philosophy and religion U. Omaha, 1962-65; fellow Asian religions Soc. for Religion in Higher Edn., 1965-66; asst. prof. religion U. Iowa, Iowa City, 1966-69, asso. prof., 1969-74, prof., 1974—; faculty fellow Am. Inst. Asian Studies, India, 1972. Mem. Am. Acad. Religion, Assn. Asian Studies. Democrat. Presbyterian. Contbr. articles in field to profl. jours.; author: Category Formation and the History of Religions, 1971; (with W. Richard Comstock, et al) Religion and Man: An Introduction, 1971; Indian and Far Eastern Religious Traditions, 1972; editor and contbr. Methodological Issues in Religious Studies, 1975; Religion in Modern India, 1981; book rev. editor Jour. of Am. Acad. Religion, 1979—. Home: Route 1 Box 67 Iowa City IA 52240 Office: School of Religion University of Iowa Iowa City IA 52242

BAISCH, STEPHEN JAMES, cons. engr.; b. Ironwood, Mich., Oct. 28, 1917; s. Michael Carl and Mary A. B.; B.M.E., U. Wis., Madison, 1942; m. Edith Anna Mary Moore, June 6, 1942; children—Michael, James, Timothy. With Thilmany Pulp & Paper Co., Kaukauna, Wis., 1945-58, chief engr., to 1958; pres. S.J. Baisch Assos., Inc., Kaukauna, 1958—; dir. Potsdam Paper Co. (N.Y.). Mem. sch. bd., 1960-63. Served from 2d lt. to maj. U.S. Army, 1942-45. Registered profl. engr., Wis. Mem. ASME, Soc. Profls., TAPPI, Nat., Wis. socs. profl. engrs., C. of C., Scabbard and Blade, Pi Mu Epsilon. Republican. Roman Catholic. Clubs: Butte Des Morts Country, Rotary, Lions, K.C., Elks. Patentee in field. Home: 111 Idlewild St Kaukauna WI 54130 Office: 809 Hyland Ave Kaukauna WI 54130

BAKAN, LLOYD HUGHES, mktg. exec.; b. San Diego, Feb. 21, 1934; s. Theodore George and Estelle Marie (Kreak) B.; B.A., U. Pacific, 1961, M.A., 1965; m. Ellen Louise Hoover, July 1, 1961; children—Michelle D., Pamela D., Lloyd Hughes. Mktg. mgr. Spink Corp., Sacramento, 1973-78; dir. mktg. Howard Needles Tammen & Bergendoff, Kansas City, Mo., 1978—; lectr. in field. Served with USN, 1956-58. Mem. Greater Kansas City C. of C., Am. Mktg. Assn. (workshop chmn. 1979-80), Soc. for Mktg. Profl. Services (pres. 1978-79, dir. 1980), Sales and Mktg. Execs. (exec. v.p. 1981—, bd. dirs. 1981—). Home: 9301 Lee Ct Leawood KS 66206 Office: 1805 Grand Ave Kansas City MO 64108

BAKEN, ROBERT EDWARD, elec. engr.; b. Oak Park, Ill., Feb. 2, 1930; s. Edward Albert and Katherine C. (Schlegal) B.; student DePaul U., 1947-49; B.S., Ill. Inst. Tech., 1958; m. Barbara Marie Marik, Aug. 2, 1975. Draftsman Chgo. Park Dist., 1950-51, Commonwealth Edison, Chgo., 1953-55; with Dept. Pub. Works, City of Chgo., 1955-68, civil engr., 1958-68; with Dept. Water and Sewers, City of Chgo., 1968—, asst. engr. water distbn., 1975-78, engr. water distbn., 1978—. Served with U.S. Army, 1951-53. Mem. ASCE, Western Soc. Engrs. (chmn. community affairs div.), Am. Water Works Assn., Am. Public Works Assn., Chgo. Assn. Commerce and Industry, Art Inst. Chgo. Roman Catholic. Clubs: Elmhurst Country; Union League, Executive (Chgo.). Home: 8629 W Leland Ave Chicago IL 60656 Office: 1000 E Ohio St Chicago IL 60611

BAKER, ALFRED STANLEY, II, computer scientist; b. Hopewell, Va., Oct. 27, 1947; s. Alfred Stanley and Koma Jo (Johnson) B.; B.A. in Math., Ill. Inst. Tech., 1970; m. Janet Marie Borowski, Feb. 15, 1969; children—Jennifer, Nathan. System software designer STAT-TAB, Chgo., 1968-71; supr. system software devel. Standard Oil Co. Ind., 1971-79; v.p., programming dir. Image Producers, Inc., Northbrook, Ill., 1979—; speaker, cons. in field. Mem. Nat. Space Inst. Baptist. Columnist for magazines. Home: 2327 S Westminster St Wheaton IL 60187 Office: 615 Academy Dr Northbrook IL 60062

BAKER, BARNET, civil engr.; b. Boston, Oct. 7, 1898; s. Joseph and Sarah (Bloch) B.; B.S. in Civil Engring., Case Inst. Tech., 1922; m. Florence Kleinman, July 25, 1923; children—Saul Phillip, Melvin. Plant engr. Columbia Chem. Co., Barberton, Ohio, 1922-23; asst. civil engr. City of East Liverpool (Ohio), 1923-24; mem. engring. staff City Cleve., 1924-69, asst. civil engr., sr. asst. civil engr., civil engr., 1924-63, chief civil engr., 1963-69. Mem. social agy. com. Jewish Welfare Fedn. Cleve., 1948-57. Bd. dirs. Ind. Montefiore Shelter Home, pres., 1952-54. Zone warden, Cuyahoga County, Ohio, World War II. Registered profl. engr., Ohio. Fellow ASCE (life); mem. Cleve. (charter, life), Ohio, Nat. socs. profl. engrs., Am. Pub. Works Assn. (life). Mason (Shriner, 32 deg., pres. Sr. Shriners Club 1974-75). Home: 3263 Desota Ave Cleveland Heights OH 44118

BAKER, BETTY LOUISE, mathematician, educator; b. Chgo., Oct. 17, 1937; d. Russell James and Lucille Juanita (Timmons) B.: B.E., Chgo. State U., 1961, M.A., 1964; Ph.D., Northwestern U., 1971. Tchr. math. Harper High Sch., Chgo., 1961-70; tchr. math. Hubbard High Sch., Chgo., 1970—, also chmn. dept. Cultural arts chmn. Hubbard Parents-Tchrs.-Student Assn., 1974-76, 1st v.p., program chmn., 1977-79, pres., 1979-81; organist Hope Lutheran Ch., 1963—. Univ. fellow, 1969-70; cert. tchr. high sch. and elem. grades 3-8 math., Ill. Mem. Nat., Ill. councils tchrs. of math., Math. Assn. Am., Chgo. Tchrs. Union, Nat. Council Parents and Tchrs. (life), Sch. Sci. and Math. Assn., Assn. for Supervision and Curriculum Devel., Luth. Collegiate Assn., Kappa Mu Epislon, Rho Sigma Tau, Mu Alpha Theta (sponsor), Kappa Delta Pi, Pi Lambda Theta, Phi Delta Kappa. Club: Walther League Hiking. Contbr. articles to profl. jours. Home: 3214 W 85th St Chicago IL 60652 Office: 6200 S Hamlin St Chicago IL 60629

BAKER, CHARLES HENRY, JR., seed co. exec.; b. St. Louis, Feb. 27, 1951; s. Charles Henry and Helen Jane (Gendron) B.; B.S.A.E., U. Mo., Columbia, 1971, M.S., 1972, Ph.D., 1974; postgrad. Ohio Agrl. Research and Devel. Center, 1975; m. Gayle Marie, Feb. 22, 1980; children—Shannon John, Cassandra Sue. Research asso. Ohio Agrl. Research and Devel. Center, Wooster, Ohio, 1974-75; with Northrup King Co., Mpls., 1975-79, dir. mgmt. info. systems, 1977-79, hybrid corn product dir., 1979; bus. dir. N.Am. Plant Breeders, Mission, Kans., 1979-80, v.p. bus. ops., 1980—; cons. crop prodn. forecasting. Mem. Am. Soc. Agrl. Engrs., Am. Soc. Agronomy, Soil Sci. Soc., Soc. Computer Simulation, Am. Mgmt. Assn., Sigma Xi, Gamma Sigma Delta. Club: Masons. Contbr. numerous articles to profl. jours. Home: 4305 W 111th Terr Leawood KS 66209 Office: 5201 Johnson Dr Mission KS 66205

BAKER, CLARENCE ALBERT, SR., structural steel constrn. co. exec.; b. Kansas City, Kans., July 2, 1919; s. Earl Retting and Nancy Jefferson (Price) B.; student Kans. U., 1939-40, Finley Engring. Coll., 1937-39, Ohio State U., 1967, 69; m. Marjorie Ellen Yoakum, Mar. 19, 1959; children—Clarence Albert, Jorgeann (Mrs. Harry L. Hiebert); stepchildren—Robert Beale, Barbara Anne Stegner (Mrs. Robert T. Kenney II). With Kansas City (Kan.) Structural Steel Co., 1937—, shop supt., 1959-68, v.p., plant mgr., 1968-73, v.p. plant ops., 1973-77, v.p. engring., 1977—, also dir. Curriculum adv. Kansas City (Mo.) Met. Jr. Coll., 1971-72, Kansas City Vocat. Tech. Sch., 1973—. Committeeman, Republican Party, 1970-72; chmn. City of Mission (Kans.) Rep. Party, 1970-72; councilman, City of Merriam, Kans., 1957-59. Adv. bd. Wentworth Mil. Acad. Served with USNR, 1944-46. Mem. ASTM, Am. Welding Soc. (pres. 1970-71, chmn. 1970, code com. 1976—), Kans. Engring. Soc., Kansas City C. of C. Mason. Home: 6635 Milhaven Dr Mission KS 66202 Office: 21st and Metropolitan Sts Kansas City KS 66106

BAKER, CLORA MAE, educator; b. Bedford, Ind., Jan. 21, 1948; d. Howard Perry and Bethel (Newlin) B.; B.S., Ball State U., 1970, M.A.E., 1971. Sec. to dir. human performance lab. Ball State U., Muncie, Ind., 1967-70; bus. tchr. Carmel (Ind.) High Sch., 1970—; instr. evening div. Ind. U./Purdue U., Indpls., 1979. Mem. Internat. Word Processing Assn. (educator's adv. council 1979-81), Ind. Vocat. Assn., Am. Vocat. Assn., NEA, Ind. Tchrs. Assn., Nat. Bus. Edn. Assn., Delta Pi Epsilon (nat. council rep. 1978-82), Am. Bus. Women's Assn. (named Woman of Yr., Hamilton chpt. 1980). Mem. Christian Ch. Home: 750 Indian Trails Apt B Carmel IN 46032 Office: 520 E Main St Carmel IN 46032

BAKER, DONALD EUGENE, librarian; b. Winamac, Ind., Oct. 8, 1945; s. Willard Jared and Beulah Belle (Taylor) B.; A.B., Ind. U., 1966, A.M., 1968, M.Library Sci., 1976; Asst. editor Indiana Mag. of History, Bloomington, 1972-74; head librarian Willard Library of Evansville (Ind.), 1976—. Former pres. Evansville Arts and Edn. Council; mem. Evansville Museum History Com. Served with USAF, 1968-72. Mem. Vanderburgh County Hist. Soc., Tri State Genealogical Soc. (dir. ex officio), Four Rivers Area Library Services Authority (pres.), Soc. Indiana Archivists, Midwest Archives Conf., Ind. Library Assn., ALA, Adminstrs. Large Pub. Libraries in Ind. Episcopalian. Club: Downtown Kiwanis (Evansville). Home: 219 Oak St Evansville IN 47713 Office: Willard Library 21 1st Ave Evansville IN 47710

BAKER, ELGAN LOUIS, psychologist; b. Lexington, Ky., June 8, 1949; s. Elgan L. and Mary Mildred (Mays) B.; B.A. with honors and highest distinction in Psychology, DePauw U., 1971, B.A. with highest distinction in French, 1971; Ph.D. in Clin. Psychology, U. Tenn., 1976. Staff psychologist Tex. Research Inst. for Mental Scis., Houston, 1976-77; adj. asst. prof. dept. psychology U. Houston, 1976-80; asst. clin. prof. dept. psychiatry U. Tex. Med. Sch., Houston, 1976-80, Baylor Coll. of Medicine, Houston, 1977-80; chief psychologist psychol. therapies Tex. Research Inst. for Mental Scis., Houston, 1977-80, asst. dir. non-med. affairs, 1978-80; cons. and lectr. depts. psychiatry and pediatrics M.D. Anderson Hosp. and Tumor Inst., Tex. Med. Center, Houston, 1979-80; cons. div. psychology VA Hosp., San Francisco, 1977-79, Student Counseling Center, U. Houston, 1977-80; asst. prof. dept. psychiatry Ind. U. Sch. of Medicine, Indpls., 1980—, dir. tng. in clin. psychology, 1980—; cons. dept. neurology Wishard Hosp., Indpls., 1980—, Midtown Mental Health Center, Indpls., 1980—; cons. VA Hosp., Indpls. Mem. Soc. Clin. and Exptl. Hypnosis (recipient Sherry K. and Harold B. Crasilneck award 1979), Am. Psychol. Assn. (mem. continuing edn. com. 1978-79), Am. Soc. Clin. Hypnosis, Nat. Register Health Service Providers in Psychology, Psychologists Interested in Study of Psychoanalysis, Tex. Psychol. Assn., Southeastern Psychol. Assn., Phi Beta Kappa, Phi Eta Sigma. Sigma Xi, Omicron Delta Kappa, Lambda Chi Alpha (named to Hall of Fame 1981). Contbr. articles on clin. psychology to profl. jours. Home: 2921 Horsehill East Indianapolis IN 46224 Office: Dept of Psychiatry Indiana Univ School of Medicine 1100 W Michigan Indianapolis IN 46223

BAKER, GARLAND MAURICE, mktg. exec.; b. Loveland, Colo., May 8, 1953; s. Bill Maurice and Mary Ann (Brungardt) B.; B.S.B.A., Creighton U., 1977. Pres., SMNCO Corp., Omaha, 1976—. Recipient Friendship Force award, 1979, Life Ins. award, 1978, Score award, 1979. Mem. Am. Mgmt. Assn., Assn. M.B.A. Execs. Home: 1254 Downtown Station Omaha NE 68101 Office: 3528 Dodge St Omaha NE 68131

BAKER, JACK, indsl. engr., lawyer; b. Chgo., Mar. 10, 1942; s. Bentley and Margaret Anna (Danek) B.; B.S. in Indsl. Engring., U. Okla., 1965; M.B.A., Oklahoma City U., 1968; J.D., U. Minn., 1972. Project dir. Minn. Teaching Evaluation Project, Mpls., 1973-74; admitted to Minn. bar, 1974; partner firm Wetherbee and Baker, Mpls., 1974-78; propr. Baker Law Assos., Mpls., 1978—; pres. Gopher Critiques, Mpls., 1977—, dir., 1977—; dir. Nat. Gay Archive, 1977—; tchr.-cons. U. Minn. Human Relations Program, 1972-76. Chairing dir. Target City Coalition, 1977-79; candidate Minn. Supreme Ct., 1978, 80. Served with USAF, 1962-66. Registered profl. engr., Okla. Mem. Am. Inst. Indsl. Engrs. (sr.), ASCE. Mem. Ch. of the Chosen People. Author: (with Gail Karwoski) MSA Method of Teaching Evaluation, 1974. Address: 3244 1st Ave South Minneapolis MN 55408

BAKER, JAMES ALLAN, banker; b. Dayton, Ohio, Mar. 4, 1942; s. Wilbur and Lucille (Heck) B.; B.S. in Bus. Adminstrn. (Wall St. Jour. Student Achievement award 1964), Bowling Green (Ohio) State U., 1964; M.B.A., Ind. U., 1966; m. B. Lyn Wallace, Aug. 25, 1962; 3 children. With City Nat. Bank, Columbus, Ohio, 1966-75, banking officer, 1971-75; pres., chief exec. officer Bank One Mansfield (Ohio), 1975—. Chmn., Mansfield United Fund dr., 1976, chmn. allocation com., 1976—; trustee Mansfield Art Center, 1980; bd. dirs., pres. Richland County Growth Corp., 1975—; bd. dirs., treas. Area Indsl. Growth, 1975—, Mansfield Growth Corp., 1977—; pres. Mansfield United Community Service, 1978. Named Boss of Yr., Mansfield Jr. C. of C., 1977. Mem. Am. Banking Assn., Banking Adminstrn. Inst., Young Pres. Orgn., Ohio Bankers Assn., Ohio Citizens Council (v.p. 1980). Republican. Episcopalian. Clubs: Westbrook Country, Brookside Country, 51, Univ. Office: 28 Park Ave W Mansfield OH 44902

BAKER, JAMES EDWARD SPROUL, lawyer; b. Evanston, Ill., May 23, 1912; s. John Clark and Hester (Sproul) B.; A.B., Northwestern U., 1933, J.D., 1936; m. Eleanor Lee Dodgson, Oct. 2, 1937 (dec. Sept. 1972); children—John Lee, Edward Graham. Admitted to Ill. bar, 1936, to practice U.S. Supreme Ct., 1957; practiced in Chgo., 1936—; asso. firm Sidley & Austin and predecessor firms, Chgo., 1936-47, partner, 1948—. Lectr., Northwestern U. Sch. Law, Chgo., 1951-52. Nat. chmn. Stanford Parents Com., 1970-75; bd. visitors Stanford Law Sch., 1976—. Served to comdr. USNR, 1941-46. Fellow Am. Coll. Trial Lawyers (regent 1974—, sec. 1977-79, pres. 1979-80); mem. Am., Ill., Chgo. bar assns., Bar Assn. 7th Fed. Circuit, Order of Coif, Phi Lambda Upsilon, Sigma Nu. Republican. Methodist. Clubs: University, Midday, Legal, Law (Chgo.); Westmoreland Country (Wilmette, Ill.). Home: 1300 N Lake Shore Dr Chicago IL 60610 Office: 1 First Nat Plaza Chicago IL 60603

BAKER, JERRY WAYNE, library adminstr.; b. Hamilton, Ohio, Aug. 25, 1933; s. Broadus and Lucille (Hall) B.; A.B., Murray State U., 1957; M.A., Ind. U., 1966; m. Beverley Anne Leeper, July 9, 1955; children—Carol Elizabeth, Bradley Wayne, Scott David. Tchr. various schs., 1958-63; dir. Owensboro-Daviess County (Ky.) Pub. Library, 1963-65; asst. dir. U. Evansville (Ind.) library, 1965-66, asso. dir., 1966-67; dir. Ohio No. U. Library Ada, 1967—. Active Boy Scouts Am., 1962-63, 68-70. Served to 1st lt. AUS, 1957, 58. Mem. Ohio Library Assn. (chmn. coll. and univ. roundtable 1971-72, chmn. awards and honors com. 1977-78, action counselor acad. and spl. libraries div. 1981-82), Ohio Coll. Assn. (pres. librarian's sect. 1972-73), Acad. Library Assn. Ohio. Home: 224 Grandview Blvd Ada OH 45810 Office: Heterick Meml Library Ohio Northern U 525 S Main St Ada OH 45810

BAKER, JOHN STEVENSON (MICHAEL DYREGROV), author, collector, donor; b. Mpls., June 18, 1931; s. Everette Barrette and Ione May (Kadletz) B.; B.A. cum laude, Pomona Coll., Claremont Colls., 1953; M.D., U. Calif. at Berkeley and San Francisco, 1957. Writer, 1958—; book cataloger Walker Art Center, Mpls., 1958-59; editor, writer neurol. research articles L.E. Phillips Psychobiol. Research Fund, Mpls., 1960-61. Recipient Disting. Service award Minn. State Hort. Soc., 1976; Cert. of Appreciation U.S. Nat. Arboretum, 1978. Mem. Nu Sigma Nu. Contbr. articles and poetry to various publs. in Eng. and U.S.; author 48 published poems and 8 sets of aphorisms. Donor numerous varieties of native plants to Minn. Landscape Arboretum and U.S. Nat. Arboretum, papers of LeRoi Jones and Hart Crane to Yale U., Brahms recs. to Bennington Coll., many others. Office: PO Box 16007 Minneapolis MN 55416

BAKER, MARVIN GLENN, mktg. cons. co. exec.; b. Kokomo, Ind., Oct. 23, 1925; s. Leonard Glenn and Iva Della (Mahres) B.; B.Rel., Marion Coll., 1947, B.S. in Edn., 1949; M.A., Ball State U., 1953, Ed.D. (NDEA fellow 1961-62), 1963; m. Lois Evelyn Jackson, Aug. 11, 1946; children—Evangeline Coleson, Verna Lee, Della Baker. Tchr., Andrews (Ind.) Public Schs., 1949-50; instr. English, music George Fox Coll., 1950-52; tchr. Willamina (Oreg.) Public Schs., 1952-54, Marion (Ind.) Public Schs., 1954-61, 70-79; chmn. div. edn. and psychology Ind. Central U., 1962-67, Marion Coll., 1967-70; provost Newaygo County Campus, Jordan Coll., Fremont, Mich., 1979-80; v.p. Career Mktg., Inc., Birmingham, Mich., 1980—; ordained to ministry, 1949; prin. Marvin G. Baker and Assos., cons., condrs. seminars on career devel.; public relations dir., founder Singing Travelers, Marion, 1969-76; dir. Right Assos., Midwest Career Mktg., Inc.; lectr. in field. Bd. dirs. Urban League, Marion, 1960-62; bd. dirs. Indpls. Youth for Christ, 1963-67, v.p. 1966-67. NDEA postdoctoral fellow Ind. U., 1969-70. Mem. Ind. State Tchrs. Assn., (pres. elem. sect. Eastern div. 1961-62), Nat. Council Tchrs. English, NEA, Am. Personnel and Guidance Assn. Composer and lyricist musical: Peter Marshall, Messenger for the Chief, 1975; author: How To Really Find the Best Jobs, 1981; also The Mighty Miami, Freedom to Read Series, Motivation for the Release of Creativity. Home: 29191 Lancaster Dr Southfield MI 48034 Office: 30600 Telegraph Rd Birmingham MI 48010

BAKER, PAUL LAURENCE, coll. adminstr.; b. Rochester, N.Y., Apr. 27, 1951; s. Laurence Ralph and Evian Finita (Carpenter) B.; B.A., Spring Arbor Coll., 1972; m. Julie Lynn Brown, Nov. 23, 1974; children—Christy, Stephen. Dir. info. services Spring Arbor (Mich.) Coll., 1972-74, dir. public relations, 1974-78, dir. planned giving, 1978—; mem. Estate Planning Council of South-Central Mich. Bd. dirs. Goodwill Industries, 1978—. Mem. Council Advancement and Support Edn., Spring Arbor Alumni Assn. (dir.). Republican. Methodist. Clubs: Lions, Detroit Econ. Home: 140 College Spring Arbor MI 49283 Office: Spring Arbor Coll Spring Arbor MI 49283

BAKER, ROBERT EUGENE, orthodontist; b. St. Paul, Mar. 31, 1923; s. Joseph O. and Eleanor (Morrison) B.; D.D.S., U. Minn., 1945; m. Marillyn June Harris, Sept. 6, 1945; children—Lynn Sandra, Charles Robert, James Harris. Practice dentistry specializing in orthodontics, St. Paul, 1947—; pres. Dr. Robert E. Baker Ltd., 1970—. Mem. City Council Dellwood (Minn.), 1974-76. Served with USN, 1945-47. Diplomate Am. Bd. Orthodontics. Fellow Am. Coll. Dentists; mem. ADA, Minn. Dental Assn., St. Paul Dist. Dental Soc., m. Assn. Orthodontists, Midwestern, Minn. socs. orthodontists, Central Assn. Dentists and Physician, Charles H. Tweed Found. for Orthodontic Research, Upper Midwest Orthodontic Study Club #1, Xi Psi Phi, Sigma Alpha Epsilon. Episcopalian. Club: Rotary. Home: 11 Dellwood Ave White Bear Lake MN 55110 Office: 1044 Lowry Medical Arts Bldg Saint Paul MN 55102

BAKER, ROBERT MAURICE, corp. exec.; b. Odessa, Mo., Feb. 11, 1928; s. William F. and Lillian L. B.; B.S. in Bus. Adminstrn., Central Mo. State Coll., 1951; m. Marilyn D. Strode, Feb. 2, 1979; children—Deborah E., James E., Richard M., Ross A., Michelle L. Audit mgr. Arthur Andersen & Co., 1951-63; with Angelica Corp., St. Louis, 1963—, now treas. Bd. dirs. Boy Scouts Am., 1966-72. Served with U.S. Army, 1946-47. Mem. Tax Execs. Inst. (dir. St. Louis chpt.). Methodist. Office: 10176 Corporate Sq Dr Saint Louis MO 63132•

BAKER, ROGER LORIN, sch. adminstr., mayor; b. Knox County, Ohio, Nov. 29, 1934; s. John Walker and J. Marie (Dalrymple) B.; B.A., Ohio Wesleyan U., 1956; M.A., Ohio State U., 1963; m. Sonia

Ann James, Aug. 21, 1959; children—John M., Nancy A., Jason M. Tchr., South High Sch., Springfield, Ohio, 1959-70, dir. adult edn., 1967-70; prin. Franklin Jr. High Sch., Springfield, 1970-77, Roosevelt Jr. High Sch., Springfield, 1977-80; asst. prin. South High Sch., Springfield, 1980—; city commr. City of Springfield, 1972—, mayor, 1974—. Served with USAF, 1956-59. Mem. Ohio Assn. Secondary Sch. Adminstrs., Springfield Suprs. and Adminstrs. Orgn. Republican. Methodist. Home: 25 Englewood Rd Springfield OH 45504 Office: 700 S Limestone St Springfield OH 45505

BAKER, SAUL PHILLIP, physician; b. Cleve., Dec. 7, 1924; s. Barnet and Florence (Kleinman) B.; B.S. in Physics, Case Inst. Tech., 1945; postgrad. Western Res. U., 1946-47; M.Sc. in Physiology, Ohio State U., 1949, M.D., 1953, Ph D. in Physiology 1957; J.D., Case Western Res. U., 1981. Intern, Cleve. Met. Gen. Hosp., 1953-54; sr. asst. surgeon gerontology br. Nat. Heart Inst., NIH, 1954-56, now Gerontology Research Center, Nat. Inst. Aging; asst. vis. staff physician dept. medicine Balt. City Hosps. and Johns Hopkins Hosp., Balt., 1954-56; sr. asst. resident in internal medicine U. Chgo. Hosps., 1956-57; asst. prof. internal medicine Chgo. Med. Sch., 1957-62; asso. prof. internal medicine Cook County Hosp. Grad. Sch. Medicine, Chgo., 1958-62; practice medicine specializing in geriatrics, cardiology, internal medicine, Cleve., 1962-70, 72—; head dept. geriatrics St. Vincent Charity Hosp., Cleve. 1964-67; cons. internal medicine and cardiology Bur. Disability Determination, Old-Age and Survivors Ins., Social Security Adminstrn., 1963—; cons. internal medicine City of Cleve., 1964—; medicare med. cons. Gen. Am. Life Ins. Co., St. Louis, 1970-71; cons. internal medicine and cardiology Ohio Bur. Worker's Compensation, 1964—; cons. cardiovascular disease FAA, 1973—; cons. internal medicine and cardiology State of Ohio, 1974—. Mem. sci. council Am. Heart Assn. Northeastern Ohio affiliate; adv. com. Sr. Adult div. Jewish Community Center Cleve.; former mem. com. older people Fedn. Community Planning Cleve. Fellow Am. Coll. Cardiology, AAAS, Gerontol. Soc. (former regent for Ohio), Am. Geriatrics Soc., Cleve. Med. Library Assn.; mem. Am. Physiol. Soc., Am., Ohio med. assns., N.Y. Acad. Scis., Chgo. Soc. Internal Medicine, Am. Fedn. Clin. Research, Soc. Exptl. Biology and Medicine, Diabetes Assn. Greater Cleveland (profl. sect.), Am. Heart Assn. (fellow council arteriosclerosis), Nat. Assn. Disability Examiners, Nat. Rehab. Assn., Am. Pub. Health Assn., Assn. Am. Med. Coll., Acad. Medicine Cleve., Internat. Soc. Cardiology (council epidemiology and prevention), Am. Soc. Law and Medicine, Sigma Xi, Phi Delta Epsilon, Sigma Alpha Mu (past pres. Cleve. alumni). Mason (32 deg. Shriner). Club: Cleveland Clinical (past sec.). Contbr. articles to profl. sci. jours. Home: 200 Chatham Way Mayfield Heights OH 44124 Office: 6803 Mayfield Rd Mayfield Heights OH 44124 Mailing Address: PO Box 24246 Mayfield Heights OH 44124

BAKER, SHARON LEE, bldg. products sales rep.; b. Grosse Pointe, Mich., Feb. 26, 1946; d. Robert E. and Doris A. (Madigan) Baker; B.A., Mich. State U., East Lansing, 1975. Office mgr., inside sales Lyons White & Assos., 1970-73, Robert Blair Co., 1974-75; field sales rep. U.S. Gypsum Co., Detroit and Lansing, Mich., 1975—. Active NOW, Common Cause, ACLU, Fund for Animals, Friends of Animals. Mem. AAUW. Democrat. Roman Catholic. Home: 3959 Hunters Ridge Dr Apt 3 Lansing MI 48910

BAKER, WALLACE LEE, mfg. co. exec.; b. Grand Rapids, Mich., Nov. 29, 1931; s. James Edward and Cornelia M. B.; A.B., Calvin Coll., 1957; m. Lucille M. Lantz, Apr. 17, 1954; children—Paul E., Kathleen Ann, Steven L. Salesman, Am. Seating Co., Phila., 1958-60; contracts adminstr. Lear Siegler, Inc., Grand Rapids, 1960-65; regional sales mgr. Weber Tech. Products div. Walter Kidde Corp., Grand Rapids, 1965-72; v.p. Linea Flow Systems Inc. div. Zurn Industries, Grand Rapids, 1972-75; v.p. sales and mktg. Comp-Aire Systems Inc., mfr. contamination controlled environs., Grand Rapids, 1972—. Served with USAF, 1951-55; Korea. Decorated Presdl. citation (Korea). Mem. Inst. Environ. Scis., Assn. Contamination Control Mfrs. (editor Aircom Jour. 1975—, sec. 1975—). Mem. Reformed Ch. America. Clubs: Bay Haven Yacht (Holland, Mich.); Ridgemoore Swim (pres. 1973-74) (Grand Rapids). patentee filtration module. Home: 4505 Hersman St SE Grand Rapids MI 49506 Office: 4160 44th St Grand Rapids MI 49508

BAKEWELL, STANLEY ELLSWORTH, personnel cons.; b. Eagle Bend, Minn., Apr. 10, 1920; s. Benjamin Levis and Eva Mary (Macaulay) B.; B.S. in Fgn. Service, Georgetown U., 1947-49; B.S. in Edn. and Animal Industry, U. Minn., 1943. Econ. asst., vice consul U.S. Fgn. Service, Am. embassy, Mexico City, Mexico, 1949-52; sr. market analyst Kimberly Clark Corp., Neenah, Wis., 1952-60; mgr. market research Forest Products div. Owens-Ill. Glass Co., Toledo, 1960-64; project dir. indsl. research Elrick & Lavidge, Chgo., 1964-66; pres., gen. mgr. Bryant & Bakewell Marketing Personnel div. Bryant Assos., Chgo., 1967—. Trustee Bakewell Investment Trust. Served to lt. (j.g.) USNR, 1944-46. Mem. Chgo. Symphony Soc., Am. Mktg. Assn., Am. Iris Soc., Chgo. Council Fgn. Relations, Alpha Gamma Rho. Republican. Episcopalian. Clubs: Chgo. Athletic Assn., Whitehall, Georgetown (Chgo.); Mason, Shriner, K.T. Author: Bakewell History-Genealogy, 1980. Home: 411 Hickory St Joliet IL 60435 Office: Bryant Assos John Hancock Center 875 N Michigan Ave Chicago IL 60611

BAKKE, GILBERT BENJAMIN, constrn. co. exec., mech. engr.; b. Milw., Sept. 13, 1937; s. Martin A. and Lydia Mary (Wittenberger) B.; B.S. in Mech. Engring., U. Wis., 1961; m. Lorraine Frenz, Aug. 11, 1961; children—Lila, Laura, James, Rebekah. Chief engr., Alby Mfg. Co., Waterford, Wis., 1961-63; design engr. Nomad Equipment, Milw., 1963; design engr. Rex Chainbelt, Milw., 1963-68; mgr. Bakke Electric Co., Waterford, 1968-73, propr., pres., 1973—; propr., pres. Aber Cutters Co., Waterford, 1976—. Chmn. Waterford Fire and Police Commn., 1976-80; mem. Waterford Sch. Bd., 1972-80. Registered profl. engr., Wis. Mem. Am. Soc. for Metals, Tri-County Contractors Assn. (dir. 1974—, treas. 1975—). Lutheran. Club: Lions (pres. 1976). Home: 646 E Main St Waterford WI 53185 Office: 818 W Bakke Ave Waterford WI 53185

BALACEK, THOMAS VINCENT, corp. exec., engr.; b. N.Y.C., Sept. 24, 1937; s. Theodore Vincent and Margaret Alice (Tuohy) B.; student Acad. Aeros., 1956-60; m. Joyce Eldeene Iden, Nov. 19, 1960 (dec. May 5, 1978); children—Thomas Vincent, Valerie Anne, William Theodore, Paul Frederick. Started as engr. Executone, Inc., N.Y.C., 1958-60, U.S. Testing Co., Inc., Hoboken, N.J., 1961; sales engr. Nuclear-Chgo. subsidiary G.D. Searle, Des Plaines, Ill., 1961-65, regional mgr., 1966-67, sales mgr., 1968, advt. mgr., 1969; v.p. sales and marketing Telemed Corp., Hoffman Estates, Ill., 1969-76; founder, pres., chief exec. officer Cardiassist Corp., Hoffman Estates, Ill., 1976-81. Home: 506 N River Rd Fox River Grove IL 60021 Office: 401 Highview Dr Fox River Grove IL 60021

BALADAD, JUANITO TAMOR, physician; b. San Fernando, La Union, Philippines, Sept. 28, 1940; s. Roman U. and Filomena (Tamor) B.; came to U.S., 1966; A.A., Far Eastern U., Manila, 1957-60; M.D., U. Santo Tomas, Manila, 1965; m. Purificacion Rana, Dec. 22, 1968; children—Mary Jane, Michelle Lynn, Juanito. Intern, Resurrection Hosp., Chgo., 1966-67; resident in internal medicine VA Hosp., Hines, Ill., 1967-70; resident in radiology Cook County Hosp., Chgo., 1970-73, attending radiologist, 1973-75; dir. dept. radiology Northlake Community Hosp., Northlake, Ill., 1974—. Mem. Radiol. Soc. N. Am., AMA, Ill. Med. Soc., Chgo. Med. Soc., Philippine Med. Soc. in Chgo. and Midwest. Roman Catholic. Home: 337 Hackberry Ct Wood Dale IL 60191 Office: 365 E North Ave Northlake IL 60164

BALAGOT, REUBEN CASTILLO, anesthesiologist; b. Manila, Philippines, July 28, 1920; s. Pedro G. and Ambrosia (Castillo) B.; B.S., U. Philippines, 1941, M.D., 1944; came to U.S., 1949, naturalized, 1955; m. Lourdes Ramirez, July 10, 1946; children—Joseph, Edgar, Victoria (Mrs. Peter Hermann), Ophelia (Mrs. James Julien). Intern, Philippine Gen. Hosp., Manila, 1943-44; resident U. Ill., Chgo., 1949-50, research fellow, 1951, clin. instr., 1952-54, asst. prof., 1954-56, asso. prof., 1956-60, prof., 1960—, chmn. dept., 1969-71; chmn. Chgo. Med. Sch., Downey, Ill., 1971—; asst. head div. anesthesiology Grant Hosp., 1957, Ill. Masonic Hosp., 1966-67; pres. St. Lukes Hosp., 1967-71, Hines (Ill.) VA Hosp., 1971-75; chmn. dept. anesthesiology Cook County Hosp., Chgo., 1981—. Served with AUS, 1944-46. Named Disting. Physician of Year, Philippine Med. Assn., 1968; Outstanding Filipino Overseas in Med. Research award Philippine Govt., 1977. Diplomate Am. Bd. Anesthesiology. Fellow Am. Fedn. Clin. Research; mem. AMA, A.C.S., AAUP, AAAS, N.Y. Acad. Sci., Ill., Chgo. med. socs., Am. Soc. Anesthesiologists, Ill. Soc. for Med. Research, Am. Writers Research, Am. Assn. for Med. Instrumentation, Sigma Xi. Contbr. articles to profl. jours. Home: 4246 Hazel St Chicago IL 60613 Office: 1825 W Harrison St Chicago IL 60612

BALANOFF, ARNOLD ZELL, pediatrician; b. Des Moines, Aug. 3, 1942; s. Morris Leo and Reva Lenore (Booth) B.; B.A., U. Iowa, 1964, M.D., 1967; m. Diane Sydney Pavlove, July 11, 1965; children—Aaron Saul, Deborah Sue, Brian William. Resident in pediatrics Univ. Hosps., Iowa City, Iowa, 1967-70; practice medicine specializing in pediatrics, Overland Park, Kans., 1972—; chmn. pediatrics Suburban Hosp., Overland Park; pres. Pediatric Specialists, P.A., 1972—; mem. staff Children's Mercy Hosp., St. Joseph Hosp., Shawnee Mission Med. Center. Served with M.C., USAF, 1970-72. Diplomate Am. Bd. Pediatrics. Fellow Am. Acad. Pediatrics; mem. Kansas City S.W. Pediatric Soc., Johnson County Med. Soc., Jackson County Med. Soc., Mo. Med. Soc., Kans. Med. Soc., AMA. Office: 4601 W 109th St Suite 122 Overland Park KS 66211

BALASA, RICHARD WAYNE, pathologist; b. Chgo., Feb. 11, 1946; s. Frank John and Lucille Eleanor (Holsman) B.; B.A. cum laude, Yale U., 1968; M.D., St. Louis U., 1973. Research fellow pathology Rush-Presbyn.-St. Luke's Med. Center, Chgo., 1968-69; research asso. Inst. Molecular Virology, St. Louis U. Med. Sch., 1969-72; acting intern dept. pathology Peter Bent Brigham Hosp., Boston, 1972-73; sr. asst. surgeon USPHS, resident in anatomic pathology Lab. Pathology, Nat. Cancer Inst., 1973-75; fellow surg. pathology, then resident in lab. medicine, then fellow chem. pathology, dept. lab. medicine and pathology, U. Minn. Med. Sch., Mpls., 1975-78; pathologist, dir. dept. clin. biochemistry Lutheran Gen. Hosp., Park Ridge, Ill., 1978—; asst. prof. U. Ill. Coll. Medicine, Chgo., 1978—. Diplomate Nat. Bd. Med. Examiners, Am. Bd. Pathology. Mem. Am. Soc. Clin. Pathologists, Coll. Am. Pathologists, Ill. Soc. Pathologists, Chgo. Pathol. Soc. Clubs: Berzelius (Yale U.); Elizabethan (New Haven); Yale (Chgo.). Home: 2959 N Mason Ave Chicago IL 60634 Office: 1775 Dempster St Park Ridge IL 60068

BALAZS, BILL (BELA) ANTAL, mech. engr.; b. Miercurea-Ciuc, Romania, June 13, 1933; s. Andras and Emilia (Sallo) B.; came to U.S., 1957, naturalized, 1962; B.S., U. Budapest (Hungary), 1955; diploma tool die engring. Acme Tech. Inst., Cleve., 1963; A.P.M., John Carroll U., 1976; m. Vivienne Miskey, Apr. 1, 1960; 1 dau., Corrinne. Instr. tool die engring., machine design, indsl. electronics, Acme Tech. Inst., 1960-65; design engr., heating, ventilating, Morrison Product Inc., Cleve., 1963-65; project engr. Reuter-Stokes, Inc., Cleve., 1965-70, engring. project mgr., 1970-73, engring. mgr., chief engr., 1973—. Pres., Transylvania Hungarian League, 1960—. Registered profl. engr., U.S.A., Can.; cert. cost engring. engr., mfg. mgmt. engr., plant engring. engr. Mem. Am. Inst. Indsl. Engrs., Instrument Soc. Am., Soc. Mfg. Engrs., ASME, Am. Nuclear Soc., Nat., Ohio socs. profl. engrs. Designer nuclear radiation detectors and multi-sensor environ. radiation monitoring systems. Home: 7500 Woodlake Dr Walton Hills OH 44146 Office: 18530 S Miles Pkwy Cleveland OH 44128

BALBACH, DANIEL ROSSWELL, orthodontist; b. Grand Rapids, Mich., Jan. 17, 1938; s. William Rosswell and Clarice J. (Lybart) B.; A.S., Grand Rapids Jr. Coll., Grand Rapids, 1957; D.D.S., U. Mich., Ann Arbor, 1961, M.S. in Orthodontia, 1965; m. Barbara Jean Sands, June 21, 1968; children—Jane Anne, John Daniel. Clin. instr. U. Mich., 1961-62, asst. prof., 1965-69; research asso. Center Human Growth and Devel., U. Mich., 1969-71; spl. lectr. Case Western Res. U., Cleve., 1972-75; lectr. U. Western Ont., 1973—, also pvt. practice specializing in orthodontia, Ann Arbor, 1965—; mem. human subject review com. U. Mich. Sch. Dentistry; mem. research team Found. Orthodontic Research. Sect. leader United Fund, St. Joseph Hosp. Bldg. Fund. Mem. Am., Mich. dental assns., Washtenaw Dist. Dental Soc. (past pres.), Mich. Orthodontic Alumni (pres., sec.-treas.), Am. Soc. Dentistry for Children, Am. Assn. Orthodontics, Great Lakes Soc. Orthodontics, Mich. Soc. Orthodontists, Phi Kappa Phi, Omicron Kappa Upsilon. Republican. Baptist. Clubs: Ann Arbor Rotary (pres.-elect), U. Mich. of Ann Arbor (sec.). Home: 3989 Penberton St Ann Arbor MI 48105 Office: 1303 Packard St Ann Arbor MI 48104

BALCER, CHARLES LEWIS, educator; b. McGregor, Iowa, May 23, 1921; s. Ludvic Frank and Iva Gay (Vaughan) B.; B.S., Winona (Minn.) State Tchrs. Coll., 1942; M.A., State U. Iowa, 1949, Ph.D., 1951; m. M. Elizabeth Belgum, Jan. 9, 1944; children—Mary Balcer Tranberg, Mark, Beth, Brian. Tchr. public schs. Minn. and Iowa, 1943, 46-48; prof. Speech St. Cloud (Minn.) State Coll., 1954-55, 56-61; prof. speech N.Y. State Tchrs. Coll., Oswego, 1955-56; dean acad. adminstrn. St. Cloud State Coll., 1961-65; fellow in coll. adminstrn. U. Mich., 1963; pres. Augustana Coll., Sioux Falls, S.D., from 1965, now Disting. Service prof. Bd. dirs. Sioux Falls Symphony; bd. dirs. McKennan Hosp., Sioux Falls. Served with U.S. Army, 1943-46. Decorated Knight's Cross 1st Class (Norway), 1972; Carnegie Found. grantee, 1963. Mem. NEA, S.D. Edn. Assn., Speech Communication Assn., S.D. Speech Assn., Central States Speech Assn., Am. Assn. Presidents Ind. Colls and Univs. Lutheran. Clubs: Rotary. Author: (with Hugh F. Seabury) Teaching Speech in Today's Secondary Schools, 1965; contbr. articles to profl. jours. Office: Augustana College Sioux Falls SD 57197

BALDRIDGE, RICHARD STANLEY, agronomist; b. Cherry Fork, Ohio, Dec. 8, 1934; s. William Robert and Laura Lucille (Hamilton) B.; B.S., Ohio State U., 1957; m. Betty Jo Tilden, May 18, 1963; children—Brian Keith, Jane Tilden. Insp., Ohio Seed Improvement Assn., Columbus, 1957-58; agronomist Landmark Co-op, Winchester, Ohio, 1959-62; agronomist Texaco, Columbus, Cranberry, N.J., 1963-66; agronomist Sohio Chem. Co., Lima, Ohio, 1966-67; sales mgr. Kenworthy Seed Co., 1967-69; agronomist Occidental Chem. Co., Houston, 1969-73; pres. Baldridge Seed Co., Cherry Fork, Ohio, 1973—; cons. Chem-Lawn. Pres., Adams County Republican Club, 1980—; vice chmn. Adams County Republican Exec. Com., 1980-81; pres. Adams County Hist. Soc., 1976-78. Mem. Am. Soc. Agronomy, Ohio Seed Improvement Assn., Ohio Grain, Feed and Fertilizer Assn., Ohio Soil Improvement Soc. (past pres.), Ohio Turfgrass Found. (past treas.). Presbyterian, Clubs: Masons, Scottish Rite. Address: PO Box 82 Cherry Fork OH 45618

BALDWIN, ARLO CLAYTON, JR., printing co. exec.; b. Hannibal, Mo., Nov. 19, 1939; s. Arlo Clayton and Helen L. (Green) B.; student public schs., Hannibal; m. Nancy Chastain, Apr. 9, 1961; children—Arlo Clayton III, Laura Chastain. With Standard Printing Co., Hannibal, 1958—, sales mgr., 1972-76, v.p., dir. sales, 1976—; v.p. Diversified Display Industries, North Kansas City, Mo.; partner B.F.W. Aero Inc. Served with U.S. Army, 1962-65. Mem. Point-of-Purchase Advt. Inst., Aircraft Owners and Pilots Assn. Republican. Baptist. Home: 11 Coachlight Dr Hannibal MO 63401 Office: 400 S Maple St Hannibal MO 63401

BALDWIN, LLOYD DEANS, computer co. exec.; b. Logan, Utah, Feb. 15, 1936; s. Kelvin Alma and Helen Ann (Deans) B.; student pub. schs., Bountiful, Utah; m. Arlene Ruth Simonis, Oct. 17, 1960; children—Rebecca Ann, Danna Lynn, David Alma, Stefanie Janine, Karina Louise, Emaline Sarah, Carl Nathaniel, Brian Lloyd. Engr., Sperry Engring Co., 1958; missionary Ch. of Jesus Christ Latter-day Saints, 1959-60; engr. IBM, 1960, tech. and mgmt. positions, San Jose, Calif., 1961-69, regional mgr., 1968-69; asst. to v.p. mktg. Info. Storage Systems, Cupertino, Calif., 1969-71; dir. ops. Cincom Systems, Cin., 1971-75; pres. Lloyd Baldwin & Assos., Cin., 1975-76; v.p. Pansophic Systems Inc., Oak Brook, Ill., 1976-78; pres. SDA Products Inc., N.Y.C., 1978-80; dir. ops. Interactive Info. Systems, Inc., Cin., 1980—. Trustee, Deaconess Hosp., Cin., 1974. Served with USN, 1954-58. Mem. Software Industry Assn. (dir. 1970-77, pres. 1975-76), Computer Industry Assn., Am. Mgmt. Assn. Club: Rotary. Home: 6790 N Clippinger Cincinnati OH 45243 Office: 10 Knollcrest Dr Cincinnati OH 45237

BALDWIN, RICHARD LEE, machinery mfg. co. exec.; b. Cherokee, Iowa, Mar. 4, 1941; s. Russel V. and Betty J. (Conley) B.; student in mech. engring. Iowa State U., 1960; m. Suzanne Jo Pudil, Oct. 27, 1962; children—Lisa Ann, Bradley Alan. With Hydrotile Machinery Co. (became subs. of Black Clawson Corp. 1974), Nashua, Iowa, 1960—, mgr. prodn. engring., 1975-78, mgr. engring., 1979—; mem. adv. bd. North Iowa Area Community Coll. Bd. dirs. CD, City of Nashua, 1978—; mem. Nashua City Council, 1979—; mem. com. Nashua Comprehensive Plan Study, Iowa Northland Regional Council Govts., 1978-79; pres. Athletic Booster Club, Nashua, 1976-78; pres. parish council St. Michael's Catholic Ch., Nashua. Mem. Nashua Jaycees (charter). Clubs: Nashua Town and Country, Lions. Home: 910 Greeley St Nashua IA 50658 Office: 65 Maple St Nashua IA 50658

BALDWIN, WILLIAM EDWARD, architect; b. Evergreen Park, Ill., Nov. 5, 1941; s. William Edward and Verda Florence (Cavanaugh) B.; student U. Ill., Urbana, 1959-60, 61-62, Ill. Inst. Tech., 1962-65; m. Georgia Chandler, Oct. 31, 1959; children—Terri Lynn, Patricia Sue, William Edward. With Laramore, Douglass and Popham, Chgo., 1963, Walter H. Sobel and Assos., Chgo., 1963-69, Daniel Comm and Assos., Chgo., 1969-71, Talsma Builders Inc., Alsip, Ill., 1971; founder, pres. William Baldwin and Assos., Oak Brook, Ill., 1972—, Future Environment Co., Oak Brook, 1975—. Mayor's ad-hoc study com. on service stations, Village of Downers Grove, 1974-76; mem. archtl. commn., 1971-76, chmn., 1976; appointee DuPage County Zoning Bd. Appeals, 1981. Cert. architect Ill., Ind., Fla.; recipient awards for archtl. projects, Downers Grove, Ill., LaGrange, Ill., 1973, 75, 79. Mem. Soc. Am. Registered Architects (service award, 1978, 79, pres. Ill. council 1979-80, dir. 1975-77, regent 1977-78, 81, dir. nat. conv. 1981, mem. nat. exec. bd. 1981, 82, editor The Bull., quar. publ. of Ill. council), AIA, Constrn. Specification Inst., Nat. Council Archtl. Registration Bds. Contbr. articles to profl. publs. Office: 1319 Butterfield Rd Downers Grove IL 60515

BALES, DONALD JAMES, mfg. co. exec.; b. Fort Madison, Iowa, Nov. 20, 1934; s. Ellis Doyle and Mary Louise (Benjamin) B.; student Western Ill. U., 1952-53; B.S., Ill. State U., 1963; postgrad. Milliken U., 1972; m. Susan Moore, June 22, 1957; children—Timothy James, Anthony James. Tchr. public schs., Stanford, LeRoy, Ill., 1963-65; mgr. indsl. relations Firestone Tire & Rubber Co., Bloomington, Ill., 1965-71, Decatur, Ill., 1971-73; corp. mgr. labor relations Dayton-Walther Corp., Dayton, Ohio, 1973-77; corp. mgr. personnel, 1977-78; dir. personnel and indsl. relations Minster (Ohio) Machine Co., 1978—. Mem. Western Ohio Personnel Assn., Soc. Advancement Mgrs., Am. Soc. Personnel Adminstrs., Am. Mgmt. Assn. Republican. Episcopalian. Home: Rural Route 2 Box 177 St Marys OH 45885 Office: 240 W 5th Minster OH 45865

BALFOUR, HENRY HALLOWELL, JR., pediatrician, virologist, clin. pathologist, educator; b. Jersey City, Feb. 9, 1940; s. Henry Hallowell and Dorothy Kathryn Dietze B.; A.B. with honors, Princeton, 1962; M.D., Columbia, 1966; m. Carol Lenore Pries, Sept. 23, 1967; children—Henry Hallowell III, Anne Lenore, Caroline Dorothy. Intern, U. Minn. Hosps., Mpls., 1966-67; resident pediatrics Babies Hosp., Columbia-Presbyn. Med. Center, N.Y.C., 1967-68; asst. prof. lab. medicine, pathology, pediatrics U. Minn., 1972-75, asso. prof., 1975-79, prof., 1979—, dir. sect. virology, 1972—, dir. div. clin. microbiology, 1974—; cons. clin. virology VA Hosp., Mpls., 1973—. Served to capt. M.C., USAF, 1968-70. NIH grantee, 1974—. Diplomate Am. Bd. Pediatrics. Fellow Am. Acad. Pediatrics, Infectious Disease Soc. Am.; mem. Am. Fedn. Clin. Research, Am. Soc. Microbiology, Am. Soc. Tropical Medicine and Hygiene, Soc. Exptl. Biology and Medicine, Northwestern Pediatric Soc., Soc. Pediatric Research, Central Soc. Clin. Research, Acad. Clin. Lab. Physicians and Scientists. Contbg. author: Current Therapy, (by Howard F. Conn), 1981; author: Monographs in Virology Series; contbr. clin. and research articles to med. books and jours. Home: 6820 Harold Ave N Minneapolis MN 55427 Office: Box 437 Mayo U Minn Health Scis Center Minneapolis MN 55455

BALKE, VICTOR H., bishop; b. Meppen, Ill., Sept. 29, 1931; s. Bernard H. and Elizabeth A. (Knese) B.; B.A. in Philosophy, St. Mary of Lake Sem., Mundelein, Ill., 1954, S.T.B. in Theology, 1956, M.A. in Religion, 1957, S.T.L. in Theology, 1958; M.A. in English, St. Louis U., 1964, Ph.D., 1973. Ordained priest Roman Catholic Ch., 1958; asst. pastor, Springfield, Ill., 1958-62; chaplain St. Joseph Home Aged, Springfield, 1962-63; procurator, instr. Diocesan Sem., Springfield, 1963-70, rector, instr., 1970-76; ordained, installed 6th bishop of Crookston, Minn., 1976—. Clubs: K.C., Lions. Address: 1200 Memorial Dr PO Box 610 Crookston MN 56716

BALKEMA, CHARLES RICHARD, chem. co. exec.; b. Grand Rapids, Mich., July 10, 1933; s. Jack H. and Kathryn C. (Kidder) B.; student U. Mich., 1951-53; m. Louise D. Kleis, June 10, 1953; children—Charles R., Curtis, Christopher, Cara, Jennifer, Jamison. Salesman, Guardsman Chem. Coatings, Grand Rapids, 1957-64, mgr. packaging coatings div., 1964-68; mktg. mgr. Haviland Products Co., Grand Rapids, 1969-70, dir. mktg., 1970-72, v.p., 1972-73, exec. v.p., 1973-74, vice chmn. bd., 1974—, pres., 1976—; pres., vice chmn. Haviland Enterprises, Inc.; vice chmn. and dir. Haviland Products Co., Haviland Agrl. Chem. Co., Wheaton Chem. Co., Pres. PTA, 1969, Ottawa Hills Neighborhood Assn., 1970-71, Grand Rapids

Neighborhood Alliance, 1971-75; dir. World Affairs Council, 1975—; dir. Econ. Devel. Corp. Grand Rapids. Served with USAF, 1953-57. Mem. World Trade Council, World Affairs Council, Nat. Assn. Chem. Distbrs. (pres.). Congregationalist. Club: Bay Haven Yacht (Holland, Mich.). Patentee method of thermoforming under motion, 1972; mem. adv. bd. Chem. Week Mag. Home: 1572 Alexander Rd SE Grand Rapids MI 49506 Office: 421 Ann St NW Grand Rapids MI 49504

BALKIN, STEVEN MICHAEL, educator; b. Chgo., Mar. 21, 1946; s. David and Sari (Sol) B.; B.S., Wayne State U., 1968, M.A., 1971, Ph.D., 1976; m. Barbara Raikow, June 6, 1974; 1 dau., Melissa. Teaching asst., fellow Wayne State U., 1968-74; asst. prof. dept. criminal justice U. Ill., Chgo., 1974—. NDEA fellow, 1973. Mem. Am. Econs. Assn., Acad. Criminal Justice Sci., Ill. Acad. Criminology. Contbr. articles to profl. jours. Office: Dept Criminal Justice Univ of Ill Chicago Circle Chicago IL 60680

BALL, ARMAND BAER, JR., assn. exec.; b. Dubach, La., Sept. 30, 1930; s. Armand Baer and Lovera (Sanderson) B.; B.A., La. Coll., 1951; M.R.E., Southwestern Bapt. Theol. Sem., 1953; M.S. in Group Work Adminstrn., George Williams Coll., 1958; m. Beverly J. Hodges, Sept. 15, 1957; children—Kathryn Lynn, Robin Armand. Royal Ambassador dir. Fla. Bapt. Conv., Jacksonville, 1953-57; program dir. Woodlawn Boys Club, Chgo., 1957-58; youth and camp dir. YMCA Nashville, 1958-62; exec. Camp Widjiwagan br. and Camp DuNord br. YMCA St. Paul, 1962-74; exec. v.p. Am. Camping Assn., Martinsville, Ind., 1974—; guest lectr. U. Minn., Ind. U. Trustee, Fund for Advancement of Camping; mem. adv. com. Project Reach, U. Ky., 1976-79. Recipient Sue Tinker award, 1975; cert. assn. exec. Mem. Can. Camping Assn. (hon.), Am. Soc. Assn. Execs., Nat. Park and Recreation Soc., Am. Mgmt. Assn., Nat. Park and Conservation Assn., Council on Nat. Cooperation in Aquatics. Presbyterian. Co-author: Basic Camp Management, 1979; contbr. articles to profl. jours. Home: 2812 Fawkes Way Bloomington IN 47401 Office: Bradford Woods Martinsville IN 46151

BALL, CHESTER EDWIN, editor; b. Seth, W.Va., Aug. 19, 1921; s. Roman Harry and Hattie (White) B.; A.B., Marshall U., 1942; M.A., Ohio State U., 1947; m. Betty June Hively, Dec. 29, 1945; children—Beth Elaine (Mrs. John Michael Watkins), Harry Stuart, Chester Edwin. Stringer, Charleston (W.Va.) Daily Mail, 1936-40; reporter, copy editor Huntington (W.Va.) Pub. Co., 1945, 47-48; asso. pub. Wolf Pub. Co., Cin., 1953-55; instr. journalism Marshall Coll., Huntington, W.Va., 1947-51; asst. prof. journalism Ohio State U., Columbus, 1951-56, publs. editor Engring. Expt. Sta., 1956-63; tech. editor, dir. reprographics Ohio State U. Research Found., Columbus, 1963-81, editorial cons. Ednl. Resources Info. Center, 1981—. Mem. Hilliard (Ohio) Charter Commn., 1958-63, vice-chmn., 1958, sec., 1960-61, 62-63; treas. Hilliard chpt. Am. Field Service, 1974-76, pres., 1976-77; mem. Scioto Darby Bd. Edn., Hilliard, 1962-78; bd. dirs. Franklin County Epilepsy Assn., 1976—, treas., 1978-80, pres., 1980-81. Served with AUS, 1942-45; col. Res. (ret.). Decorated Silver Star, Bronze Star medal with one oak leaf cluster, Purple Heart with two oak leaf clusters. Mem. In-Plant Printing Mgmt. Assn. (pres. 1971), Reserve Officers Assn. (sec.-treas., pres. Huntington, W.Va. 1948-50), Sigma Delta Chi. Republican. Methodist (mem. bd. ushers 1956—). Kiwanian. Home: 6174 Sunny Vale Dr Columbus OH 43228

BALL, CLIFFORD NEIL, greeting card co. exec.; b. Olathe, Kans., Jan. 20, 1928; s. Loren Gordon and Edythe Virginia (Woolery) B.; B.S. in Bus., U. Kans., 1950; m. Jo Ann Boyer, June 4, 1948; children—Neila Jo, Malissa, Twila Sue, Mark, Daniel. Merchandiser, Hallmark Card Co., Kansas City, Mo., 1950-53, mdse. control mgr., 1954-64, dir. product promotions, 1965-68, planning mgr., 1969-70, dir. product mgmt. services, 1971-72, sr. product mgr., 1973-78, group product mgr., 1978-80, corp. dir. fixture line mgmt. and visual merchandising, 1981—. Chmn. bd. trustees, ruling elder First United Presbyn. Ch., Olathe, 1970—; pres. Olathe Interchurch Alliance, 1971; v.p. Olathe Arts Council, 1978-79; chmn. ministerial relations crisis com. Kansas City Union Presbytery, 1979—. Served with USN, 1945-46. Recipient Family of Builders award Kans. Kiwanis Found., 1976. Democrat. Home: 605 Edgemere Dr Olathe KS 66061 Office: 25th and McGee Sts Kansas City MO 64141

BALL, JAMES HAMMOND, mech. engr.; b. Milw., Jan. 1, 1942; s. Robert Charles and Margaret Louise (Fass) B.; B.S.M.E., U. Wis., 1965, M.S., 1971, Ph.D., 1975; m. Barbara Ann Sinclair, June 19, 1971. Project engr. Torrington Co. (Conn.), 1965-68; systems engr. Syska-Hennessy, Inc., N.Y.C., 1968; instr. U. Wis., Madison, 1968-71, research asst., 1971-75; cons. Singapore Econ. Devel. Bd., Republic of Singapore, 1970; mgr. blast hole drill devel. Bucyrus Erie Co., Milw., 1975—; session chmn., presenter paper Nat. Conf. on Power Transmission, 1980. NSF grantee, 1972-75; Ford Found. grantee, 1970; registered profl. engr., Wis. Mem. ASME, Soc. Automotive Engrs., Soc. Mfg. Engrs., Am. Soc. Metals, Soc. Mining Engrs., AIME, Sigma Xi, Tau Beta Pi, Pi Tau Sigma, Phi Eta Sigma. Episcopalian. Home: 1835 Tamarack St South Milwaukee WI 53172 Office: PO Box 56 South Milwaukee WI 53172

BALL, LLOYD RICHARD, lawyer; b. Hawarden, Iowa, Feb. 12, 1931; s. Lloyd Ross and Helen (Wells) B.; B.A., State U. Iowa, 1953; LL.B., J.D., U. Nebr., 1956. Admitted to Iowa bar, 1956; since practiced in Hawarden. Mayor City of Hawarden, 1960-62, city atty., 1968-70, 80—. Served to 1st lt. JAG, USAF, 1956-58. Decorated Air Force Commendation medal. Mem. Am., Iowa, Sioux County bar assns., Am. Judicature Soc., Am. Legion, Internat. Platform Assn., Delta Tau Delta, Delta Theta Phi. Congregationalist (deacon). Clubs: Masons (master 1965), Rotary (past pres. Hawarden), Capitol Hill (Washington). Home: 1025 Ave M Hawarden IA 51023 Office: 716 10th St Hawarden IA 51023

BALL, LOUIS ALVIN, ins. co. exec.; b. Kansas City, Mo., Oct. 25, 1921; s. George Rhodom and Frances Mariam (Beals) B.; B.A. in Bus. Adminstrn., Kans. State U., 1947; m. Norma Jane Laudenberger, Jan. 17, 1947. Asst. purchasing agt. Kansas City (Mo.) br. Ford Motor Co., 1942-46; with Farm Bur. Mut. Ins. Co., Inc., Manhattan, Kans., 1947—, claims underwriting mgr., 1956-61, systems and procedures mgr., 1961—, asst. sec., 1977-81, corp. sec., 1981—. Recipient Internat. Achievement award, 1978. Mem. Nat. Assn. Ind. Insurers, Conf. Casualty Cos., Assn. Systems Mgmt. (Internat. Merit award 1971, Internat. Achievement award 1978, Kansas City chpt. Merit award 1970, Kansas City chpt. Diamond Merit award 1977). Club: Manhattan Country. Home: 1101 Pioneer Ln Manhattan KS 66502 Office: 2321 Anderson Ave Manhattan KS 66502

BALL, NEAL, hosp. supply co. exec.; b. Chgo., Oct. 7, 1935; s. C.E. and A. J. Ball; B.Sc. in Communications, U. Ill., 1959; postgrad. Northwestern U., Advanced Mgmt. Inst. Public relations asst. Am. Hosp. Supply Corp., Evanston, Ill., 1960-62, public relations mgr., 1962-65, corp. dir. advt. and public relations, 1965, now v.p. public affairs; dep. press sec. Pres. U.S., 1971-73; vis. exec. U. Iowa, 1976; Neiman fellowship lectr. Harvard U., 1973; lectr. disting. lecture series U. Md., 1973. Mem. primitive art com. Art Inst. Chgo.; vis. com. Center Far Eastern Studies, U. Chgo.; v.p. Internat. Visitors Center for Chgo. Mem. Health Industry Mfrs. Assn. (chmn. public relations sect.), Nat. Health Council (dir., chmn. govt. relations com.), Nat. Investor Relations Inst. (nat. dir., founding mem.), Am. Refugee Com. (founder, chmn.), Chgo. Press Club, Sigma Delta Chi, Headline Club. Clubs: Arts Chgo.; Univ. (Washington). Office: One American Plaza Evanston IL 60201

BALL, TRAVIS, JR., ednl. adminstr.; b. Newport, Tenn., July 13, 1942; s. Travis and Ruth Annette (Duyck) B.; B.A., Carson Newman Coll., 1964; M.A., Purdue U., 1966. Instr., then asst. prof. English, Ill. Wesleyan U., Bloomington, 1966-69; vis. prof. English edn. Millikin U., 1969; asst. headmaster, chmn. English dept. Brewster Acad., Wolfeboro, N.H., 1969-72; dir. admissions, asst. to headmaster Park Tudor Sch., Indpls., 1972—; pres. Travis Ball & Assos., 1980—; mem. commn. on curriculum and grad. requirements Ind. Dept. Public Instrn., 1974-76; mem. adv. council Ednl. Records Bur. Mem. Indiana Non-Public Edn. Assn. (treas., dir.), Independent Schs. Assn. Central States (conf. chmn.), Nat. Council Tchrs. English, Assn. Supervision and Curriculum Devel., Council Advancement and Support Edn. (adv. com. on ind. schs.), Nat. Assn. Ind. Schs., Sigma Tau Delta, Pi Kappa Delta, Phi Delta Kappa (newsletter editor). Baptist. Editor, Tchrs. Service Com. Newsletter for English Tchrs., 1977—; dept. editor English Jour., 1976—; editor/pub. Contact: Newsletter for Admissions Mgmt., 1980—. Home: 6536 Carrollton Ave Indianapolis IN 46220 Office: 7200 N College Ave Indianapolis IN 46240

BALL, WILLIAM JAMES, physician; b. Charleston, S.C., Apr. 16, 1910; s. Elias and Mary (Cain) B.; B.S., U. of South, 1930; M.D., Med. Coll. S.C., 1934; m. Doris Hallowell Mason, July 9, 1938. Intern, Roper Hosp., Charleston, 1934-35; resident dept. pediatrics U. Chgo. Clinics, 1935-37; instr. pediatrics Med. Coll. S.C., 1938-42; practice medicine specializing in pediatrics, Charleston, 1938-42, Aurora, Ill., 1951-70; physician student Health Service No. Ill. U., 1970-72; cons. Mooseheart, Ill.; mem. staff Copley Meml., St. Joseph Mercy hosps.; pediatrician N.W. Clinic, Minot, N.D., 1946-51; asso. prof. Sch. Nursing, No. Ill. U., 1971-72. Mem. Bd. Health, Aurora, Ill., 1958-62; pediatrician, div. services for crippled children U. Ill., 1952—; pediatric cons. sch. dists. 129 and 131, Aurora, 1972—, DeKalb County Spl. Edn. Assn., 1972-81, Dupage County Spl. Edn. Assn., 1980—, Northwestern Ill. Assn. Handicapped Children; med. cons. Aurora Easter Seal Rehab. Center; pres. Kane County sub-area council Health Systems Agy., Kane, Lake, McHenry Counties, 1977-78, sec., 1978-79. Served as capt. M.C., AUS, 1942-46; col. Res., ret. Diplomate Am. Bd. Pediatrics. Fellow Royal Soc. Health, Am. Acad. Pediatrics; mem. AMA, Kane County Med. Soc. (pres. 1962), Am. Heart Assn., Am. Sch. Health Assn., Am. Cancer Soc., Easter Seal Soc., Phi Beta Kappa, Phi Chi, Pi Kappa Phi. Republican. Rotarian. Club: Union League (Aurora). Address: 433 S Commonwealth Ave Aurora IL 60506

BALLARD, JOSEPH GRANT, photographer, photog. co. exec.; b. Greenville, N.C., Nov. 29, 1928; s. Charlie Edgar and Mary Velma (Keel) B.; B.S., Calif. Western U., 1976, M.B.A., 1978; grad. Woodward Sch. of Photography, 1949, Modern Sch. of Photography, N.Y.C., 1950; Ph.D. (hon.), Pacific Coll., 1976; m. Sherry Rae Hall, May 2, 1961; children—Joseph Grant, Don, Patricia, Mike, Ron, Jeffrey Grant, Warren Scott, Vikki Kristine. Exec. v.p. Goldcraft Studios, Cin., 1951-61; pres. Photoland, Inc., Cleve., 1961-71, Nelson's Photography, Inc., Cleve., 1972—; cons. in mktg., promotions, budget controls and fund raising to various bus. firms and orgns., 1975—. Mem. Bicentennial Commn., Cleve., 1975; pres. Recreation Advisory Bd., North Olmsted, Ohio, 1977—; lay Baptist minister; mem. The Chapel in Berea, ordained deacon, 1981, chmn. of deacons, 1981; chmn. com. Child Evangelism Fellowship, Cleve., 1977-79; trustee Child Evangelism Fellowship, Warrenton, Md. Served with USAAF, 1945-47. Recipient numerous awards for portrait photography, 1953—; Joseph G. Ballard Day proclaimed in honor by mayor of Cleve., April 4, 1975. Mem. Profl. Photographers of Am. Assn., Wedding Photographers of Am. Assn., Ohio Assn. Chiefs of Police, Fraternal Order of Police, Cleveland Ad Club, Ohio Profl. Photography Assn. Home: 5612 Allandale Dr North Olmsted OH 44070 Office: 41 Colonial Arcade Cleveland OH 44115

BALLENGER, STEVE GREY, plant breeder; b. Camp Lejune, N.C., Nov. 13, 1953; s. Archie Grey and June Maxine B.; M.S., Purdue U., 1977, Ph.D., 1980. Research sta. mgr. Pfizer Genetics, Inc., Kingston, Ohio, 1980—. Mem. Am. Soc. Agronomy, Crop Sci. Soc. Am., Biometric Soc., Gamma Sigma Delta. Republican. Office: PO Box 816 Kingston OH 45644

BALLOU, RAYMOND JAMES, elec. engr.; b. Rochester, N.Y., July 21, 1945; s. Ivan Oliver and Elizabeth Alida (Barrett) B.; B.E.E., Gen. Motors Inst., 1968; m. Nora Ann Roupe, Nov. 12, 1966; children—Raymond, Kevin, Deanna, Nathan. Sr. research engr. Rochester Products div. Gen. Motors Corp., Rochester, N.Y., 1971-72, supr. mfg. research, 1972-73, gen. supr. mfg. devel., 1973-74, gen. supr. prodn. engring., 1974-77, supt. prodn. engring., 1978-80, supt. tech. services Sioux City ops., 1980—. Adult Leader Otetiana council Boy Scouts Am., 1976—. Cert. mfg. engr. Mem. Rochester Area C. of C. (dir. Greece council 1977-80, pres. 1980). Republican. Roman Catholic. Patentee digital logic test probe, numerical base translator. Home: 4813 Meadow Ln Sioux City IA 51104 Office: 1805 Zenith Dr Sioux City IA 51103

BALLOWE, JAMES, univ. adminstr., educator; b. Carbondale, Ill., Nov. 28, 1933; s. Frank Charles and Wilma Ruth (Maynard) B.; B.A., Millikin U., 1954; M.A., U. Ill., 1956, Ph.D., 1963; children—Jeffrey, Mary. Tchr. public schs., Decatur, Ill., 1954-55; grad. asst. U. Ill., 1955-61; asst. prof. English, Millikin U., 1961-63; mem. faculty dept. English Bradley U., Peoria, Ill., 1963—, prof., 1971—, dean Grad. Sch., 1974—, asso. provost, 1979—. Mem. Ill. Arts Council, 1975—; mem. Ill. State Museums Bd., 1977—. Recipient Ill. Arts Council poetry award, 1975, 78. Mem. Ill. Assn. Grad. Schs. (pres. 1979-80), Commn. on Instns. Higher Edn. (exec. bd. 1980—), Midwestern Assn. Grad. Schs. (pres. 1978-79). Author: (poetry) The Coal Miners, 1979; editor: George Santayana's America, 1967. Office: 1501 W Bradley Ave Peoria IL 61625

BALOGH, JOSEPH DAVID, automobile mfg. co. exec.; b. Detroit, Mar. 12, 1930; s. Joseph and Mary Ann (Koska) B.; grad. Coll. Advanced Traffic, Detroit, 1954; student Henry Ford Community Coll., 1957-62, Washtenaw Community Coll., 1975; m. Mary Caroline Ladd, Dec. 16, 1949; children—Celeste Jeanine, Constance Denice. Traffic supr. Ford Motor Co., Dearborn, Mich., 1959-68; gen. mgr. Fleak Carloading Co., Chgo., 1968; traffic rep. Ford Motor Co., Fin. and Ins. Subs.'s, Dearborn, 1969-78; traffic rep. Climate Control div. Ford Motor Co., Plymouth, Mich., 1978—. Chmn. food services Chelsea (Mich.) Community Fair, 1973; instr. med. self-help course Office CD, Wyandotte, Mich., 1963; mem. Chelsea Village Planning Commn., 1974-77. Served with USMC, 1947-50. Mem. Motor City Traffic Club, Coll. Advanced Traffic Detroit Alumni Assn. Methodist (treas. 1963). Clubs: Moose. Home: 236 E Middle St Chelsea MI 48118 Office: Ford Motor Co 14425 Sheldon Rd Plymouth MI 48170

BALTERS, HENRY LEE, psychologist; b. Omaha, Nov. 15, 1941; s. Steve Anthony and Delores Celia (Pollock) B.; A.A., San Jose City Coll., 1966; B.A., San Jose State Coll., 1968, M.A., 1969; Ph.D., U. Nebr., Lincoln, 1974; m. Sharon Kay Buckles, Oct. 29, 1963; children—Matthew Lee, Marcus Wade. Psychologist, Lincoln (Nebr.) Regional Center, 1974-76, Community Mental Health Center Lancaster County, Lincoln, 1976-78; pvt. practice, Lincoln, 1978—; instr. adult edn. Southeast Community Coll., 1976-78. Served with USMC, 1959-63. Diplomate Am. Bd. Profl. Psychology. Mem. Nebr. Soc. Profl. Psychologists (pres. 1978-79), Nebr. Psychol. Assn. (pres. 1980-81), Am. Psychol. Assn., Assn. Advancement Behavior Therapy, Assn. Advancement Psychology, Midwestern Psychol. Assn., Nebr. Acad. Scis., Assn. Behavior Analysis. Club: Lincoln U. Home: 3025 Sheridan Blvd Lincoln NE 68502 Office: 2221 S 17th St Suite 10 Lincoln NE 68502

BALTHASER, LINDA IRENE, univ. adminstr.; b. Kokomo, Ind., Feb. 25, 1939; d. Earl Isaac and Evelyn Pauline (Troyer) Showalter; B.S. magna cum laude, Ind. Central U., 1961; M.S., Ind. U., 1962; m. Kenneth James Balthaser, June 1, 1963. Tchr. bus. edn. Southport High Sch., Indpls., 1962-63; sec., adminstrv. sec. Office of Pres., Ind. U., Bloomington, 1963-66; with Ind. U.-Purdue U., Fort Wayne, Ind., 1969—, asst. to dean Arts and Letters, 1970—, founding co-dir. Weekend Coll., 1979-80. Bd. dirs. Associated Chs. Fort Wayne, 1980. Ind. Conf. N. Evang. United Brethren Ch. scholar, 1957-61. Mem. Fort Wayne-Allen County Hist. Assn., Embassy Theatre Found., Fort Wayne Mus. Art, Historic Fort Wayne, Fort Wayne Zool. Soc., Am. Assn. Univ. Adminstrs., Internat. Platform Assn., Delta Pi Epsilon, Phi Alpha Epsilon, Epsilon Sigma Alpha, Mensa. Lutheran. Club: Univ. Women's (pres. 1968-69). Home: 2917 Hazelwood Ave Fort Wayne IN 46805 Office: 2101 Coliseum Blvd E Fort Wayne IN 46805

BALTHROPE, JACQUELINE MOREHEAD, educator, author; b. Phila.; d. Jack Walton and Minnie Jessie (Martin) Morehead; B.S. in Edn., Central State U., Wilberforce, Ohio, 1949; M.A. in Edn., Case Western Res. U., 1959; m. Robert Granville Balthrope, Sr.; children—Robert Granville, Yvonne Gertrude, Robin Bernice. Elem. master tchr. Cleve. Bd. Edn., 1950-65, leadership devel. tchr., 1965-69, asst. prin. elem. sch., 1969-77, prin. elem. sch., 1977-80; ednl. cons., 1980—. Mem. AAUW, Cleve. Council Adminstrs. and Suprs., Elem. Sch. Prins., Internat. Reading Assn., Phi Delta Kappa Frat., Delta Kappa Gamma, Alpha Kappa Mu, Zeta Sigma Pi, Pi Lambda Theta, Alpha Kappa Alpha, Phi Delta Kappa, Eta Phi Beta, Gamma Phi Delta (vol., tutor). Methodist. Clubs: Top Ladies of Distinction (local founder, past pres.), Jr. League, Sen Mer Rek. Author: African Boy Comes to America, 1960. Contbr. articles to profl. jours., mags., newspapers. Address: 16220 Delrey Ave Cleveland OH 44128

BALTIS, WALTER STANLEY, property mgmt. exec.; b. Poland, Sept. 19, 1904; s. Matthew and Amelia (Adaszkiewicz) Baltruszajtis; brought to U.S., 1910, naturalized, 1932; student parochial sch., Chgo.; m. Marie Rita Nexdlik, June 22, 1929; children—Phyllis (Mrs. L. James Paul), Joan (Mrs. Joan Lindstrom), Bonnie (Mrs. Robert N. Hutchison), Rita (Mrs. Ralph E. Sheese, Jr.). Sales mgr. Cicero Motor Sales (Ill.), 1926-30; owner Arrow Motor Sales, 1930-35; mgr. Stastny Builders, Berwyn, Ill., 1936-41; pres. Baltis Built Homes, Inc., Westchester, Ill., 1941—, Westchester Savs. and Loan Assn., 1953-60. Trustee Met. San. Dist. of Greater Chgo., 1958-64, pres. credit union, 1960-62. Mem. Cermak Rd. Business men's Assn. (pres. 1932-34). Democrat. Roman Catholic. Elk. Club: Golf (Riverside, Ill.). Home: 306 Downing Rd Riverside IL 60546 Office: 10529 Cermak Rd Westchester IL 60153

BALUNAS, DAVID ALAN, exec. search cons.; b. Chgo., Oct. 14, 1950; s. Vincent J. and Alberta (Soparas) B.; B.A., Loyola U., Chgo., 1972; student U. Md., 1976-77, Georgetown U., 1977-78; m. Selene Van Vleck, Oct. 6, 1973. With Inland Steel Co., Chgo., 1973-75, Van Vleck, Inc., Silver Spring, Md., 1975-77; sr. cons. Ernst & Whinney, Grand Rapids, Mich., 1977—. Mem. Am. Soc. Tng. and Devel., Am. Soc. Personnel Adminstrn. Roman Catholic. Rotarian. Home: 2669 Cascade Springs Dr SE Grand Rapids MI 49506 Office: 900 Michigan Nat Bank Bldg Grand Rapids MI 49502

BAMBERG, ROBERT DOUGLAS, educator; b. Buenos Aires, Argentina, Feb. 6, 1928; s. David Tobias and Hilda B.; B.A., Cornell U., 1951, M.A., 1958, Ph.D., 1961; m. Barbara Berndtsen, Nov., 1975. Instr. English, Cornell U., 1959-60; asst. prof. U. Pa., 1964-68, asso. prof., 1968-70; Charles A. Dana prof. English, dept. chmn. Bates Coll., 1970-72, prof. English, dean of faculty, 1972-75; prof. English, chmn. dept. Kent (Ohio) State U., 1975—. Home: 1258 Greenwood Ave Kent OH 44240 Office: Dept English Kent State Univ Kent OH 44242

BANACH, ART JOHN, graphic art exec.; b. Chgo., May 22, 1931; s. Vincent and Anna (Zajac) B.; grad. Art. Inst. of Chgo., 1955; pupil painting studies Mrs. Melin, Chgo.; m. Loretta A. Nolan, Oct. 15, 1966; children—Heather Anne, Lynnea Joan. Owner, dir. Art J. Banach Studios, 1949—, cartoon syndicate for newspapers, house organs and advt. functions, 1954—, owned and operated advt. agy., 1954-56, feature news and picture syndicate, distbn. U.S. and fgn. countries. Dir. Speculators S Fund. Recipient award 1st Easter Seal contest Ill. Assn. Crippled, Inc., 1949. Chgo. Pub. Sch. Art Soc. Scholar. Mem. Artist's Guild Chgo., Am Mgmt. Assn., Chgo. Assn. of Commerce and Industry, Chgo. Federated Advt. Club, Am. Mktg. Assn., Internat. Platform Assn., Chgo. Advt. Club, Chgo. Soc. Communicating Arts. Clubs: Columbia Yacht, Advertising Executives; Art Directors (Chgo.). Address: 1076 Leahy Circle E Des Plaines IL 60016

BANAS, EMIL MIKE, physicist, educator; b. East Chicago, Ind., Dec. 5, 1921; s. John J. and Rose M. (Valcicak) B.; ed. Ill. Benedictine Coll., 1940-43; B.A. (U.S. Rubber fellow), U. Notre Dame, 1954, Ph.D., 1955; m. Margaret Fagyas, Oct. 9, 1948; children—Mary K., Barbara A. Instr. math. and physics Ill. Benedictine Coll., Lisle, 1946-48, adj. faculty mem., 1971—, trustee, 1959-61; with Civil Service, State of Ind. Hammond, 1948-50; lectr. physics Purdue U., Hammond, 1955-60; staff research physicist Standard Oil Co., Naperville, Ill., 1955-82. Served with USNR, 1943-46. Cert. state tchr., Ill., Ind. Mem. Ill. Benedictine Coll. Alumni Assn. (dir. hon., named alumnus of yr., 1965, pres. 1959-60), Sigma Pi Sigma. Roman Catholic. Clubs: Soc. of Procopians. Contbr. articles to sci. jours. Home: 8 Huntington Circle W Naperville IL 60540 Office: Radiol Safety Officer AMOCO Research Center Naperville IL 60540

BANAS, THOMAS PAUL, pub. affairs exec.; b. Detroit, Apr. 15, 1937; s. Ted J. and Pearl (Danielowicz) B.; Ph.B., U. of Detroit, 1958; M.B.A., Wayne State U., 1964; m. Carolyn Ann Burch, May 23, 1958; children—Scott, Amy, Polly. Gen. tech. aide City of Detroit, 1958-60; market research asst. Micromatic Hone Corp., Detroit, 1960; copywriter Ruben Advt., Detroit, 1960-61; promotion writer The Detroit News, 1961-63; publicity mgr. Sta. WWJ AM-FM-TV, 1963-67; sr. writer G. & D Communications Inc., Detroit, 1967; asst. promotion mgr., Sta. WWJ AM-FM-TV, 1967-73, community relations dir., 1973-76; sr. v.p., P/R Asso., Inc., Detroit, 1976-78; exec. dir. Am. Lung Assn. S.E. Mich., Detroit, 1978—. Instr. Highland Park Coll., 1968-70, U. of Detroit, 1970. Bd. dirs. Royal Oak Boys' Club, 1974—; bd. exec. com. Southeastern Mich. chpt. ARC, 1973-79; mem. exec. bd. met. Detroit chpt. Nat. Found. March of Dimes, 1976-79, Wayne State Fund, 1975—, Comprehensive Health Planning Council S.E. Mich., 1973—, Oakland County Mental Health Bd., 1976—, Pleasant Ridge City Commn., 1973-77; del. S.E. Mich.

Council Govts., 1973-77, Council on Regional Devel., 1973—, Council on Environ. Strategy, 1973—; coordinator Internat. Freedom Festival, 1977. Recipient Mich. Vol. Leadership award, 1972, Spl. Tribute Mich. Ho. Reps., 1973. Mem. Pub. Relations Soc. of Am., Am. Public Health Assn., Detroit Acad. TV Arts and Scis., Mich. Public Health Assn., Assn. Execs. Met. Detroit, Engring. Soc. Detroit. Clubs: Detroit Press, Economic, Adcraft (Detroit). Home: 9 Wellesley Ave Pleasant Ridge MI 48069 Office: 28 W Adams St Detroit MI 48226

BANASIK, ROBERT CASMER, nursing home adminstr., educator; b. Detroit, Dec. 8, 1942; s. Casmer John and Lucille Nathalie (Siperek) B.; B.S. in Mech. Engring., Wayne State U., 1965; M.S. in Indsl. Engring., Tex. Tech. Coll., 1967; M.B.A., Ohio State U., 1973, Ph.D., 1974; m. Jacqueline Mae Miller, Aug. 28, 1965; children—Robert John, Marcus Alan, Jason Andrew. Mgmt. systems engr. Riverside Methodist Hosp., Columbus, Ohio, 1970, 71; owner, mgmt. systems cons. Banasik Assos., Columbus, 1972—; dir. mgmt. systems engring. Grant Hosp., Columbus, 1973-78; owner, mgr. RMJ Investment Enterprises, Columbus, 1975—; pres. Omnilife Systems, Inc., Columbus, 1979—; adminstr. Patterson Nursing Home, Columbus, 1980—; asst. prof. Capital U. Grad. Sch. Adminstrn., Columbus, 1973-79, asso. prof., 1979—; dir. Asset Date Systems, Columbus. Pres. bd. dirs. United Cerebral Palsy Franklin County, 1979-80; mem. founding bd. Support Resources, Inc., 1978—; bd. dirs. Transp. Resources, Inc., 1979-80. Registered profl. engr., Ohio; lic. nursing home adminstr., Ohio. Mem. Am. Hosp. Assn., Am. Inst. Indsl. Engrs., Nat. Soc. Profl. Engrs. (dir. Franklin County chpt. 1976-77), Sigma Xi, Beta Gamma Sigma, Alpha Pi Mu, Phi Kappa Phi. Republican. Lutheran. Editor: Tropics in Hospital Material Management, 1978—; contbr. articles to profl. jours. Home: 2155 Elgin Rd Columbus OH 43221 Office: 71 Woodland Ave Columbus OH 43203

BANDA, ARPAD FREDERIC, educator; b. N.Y.C., June 16, 1928; s. John and Terecia (Varga) B.; B.S. in Social Scis., City Coll. N.Y., 1950; M.B.A., N.Y. U., 1956, Ph.D., 1964, C.F.A., 1977. Instr. econs. Milw.-Downer Coll., 1959-61, Upsala Coll., 1961-62; asst. prof. econs., fin. U. Hartford (Conn.), 1963-66, asso. prof., 1966-68, chmn. dept., 1966-67; asso. prof. fin. U. Akron (O.), 1968-71, prof., 1971—, head dept., 1970-73, 77-78; pres. C.P. Banda & Co. Inc., registered investment advisors). Elder, Hungarian Reformed Ch. Akron; pres. Hungarian Found., Inc.; v.p. Lorantffy Care Center, Inc.; bd. dirs. Am. Hungarian Fedn., 1977-79. Mem. Fin. Mgmt. Assn. (coordinating editor jour. 1970-75), Am., Ohio (pres. 1972-73), Eastern (dir. 1975-78) fin. assns. Home: 2299 Winter Pkwy Apt 295 Cuyahoga Falls OH 44221 Office: 302 E Buchtel Ave Akron OH 44325

BANDLOW, RAY JOHN, supt. schs.; b. Detroit, July 25, 1946; s. Ray John and Mildred Rosetta (Kluge) B.; B.A., Eastern Mich. U., 1969, M.A., 1971; Ph.D., U. Mich., 1975; postgrad. Mich. State U., 1973, Harvard U., 1981; m. Kathleen Ruth Rust, Sept. 2, 1967; children—Matthew, Lisa. Tchr., Allen Park, Mich., 1969-72; adminstrv. asst., community edn. dir., Tecumseh, Mich., 1973-76; supt. schs., Lawton, Mich., 1976-80, Van Buren Intermediate Sch. Dist., Lawrence, Mich., 1980—. Bd. dirs. Van Buren County United Way, Van Buren Council Against Child Abuse. Mem. Am. Assn. Sch. Adminstrs., Am. Mgmt. Assn., Nat. Assn. Sch. Bds., Mich. Assn. Intermediate Sch. Adminstrs., Mich. Assn. Sch. Adminstrs. (region pres.), Mich. Assn. Sch. Bds., Jr. C. of C. Club: Lions. Home: 57 Concord Hills Lawton MI 49065 Office: 701 S Paw Paw St Lawrence MI 49064

BANDY, IRENE GESA, state ofcl.; b. Montgomery, W.Va., Aug. 30, 1940; d. Ernest and Gesa (Koehne) Wolff; B.S.Ed., Ohio U., 1962; M.A., Eastern Ky. U., 1967; Ph.D., Ohio State U., 1979; 1 son, Nicholas. Tchr., pub. schs., Gainesville, Fla., 1962-64, Cin., 1964-65; guidance supr. Eastern Ky. U., Richmond, 1967-68; counselor, jr. high sch., Napoleon, Ohio, 1968-73; cons. Ohio Div. Guidance and Testing, Columbus, 1973-76, asst. dir., 1977-79, exec. dir. adminstrn., 1980—. Mem. Am. (chmn. Midwest region 1977-79, dir. 1979—), Ohio personnel and guidance assns., Assn. Counselor Educators and Suprs. (co editor Newsletter 1976-77), Am. Sch. Counselors Assn., Nat. Vocat. Guidance Assn., Ohio Sch. Counselors Assn., Ohio Assn. Counselor Educators and Supervisors, Buckeye Assn. Sch. Adminstrs., Phi Delta Kappa (pres. 1981-82). Home: 1922 Queensbridge Dr Worthington OH 43085 Office: 65 Front St S Room 808 Columbus OH 43215

BANERJEE, SAMARENDRANATH, orthopaedic surgeon; b. Calcutta, India, July 12, 1932; s. Haridhone and Nihar Bala (Mukherjee) B.; M.B. B.S., R.G. Kar Med. Coll., Calcutta, 1957; postgrad. U. Edinburgh, 1965-66; m. Hima Ganguly, Mar. 1977; 1 son, Rabindranath. Intern R.G. Kar Med. Coll., 1956-58; resident in surgery Bklyn. Jewish Hosp. Med. Center, 1958-60, Brookdale Med. Center, Bklyn., 1960-61, Jersey City Med. Center, 1961-63; research fellow Hosp. for Sick Children, U. Toronto (Ont., Can.), 1968-69; practice medicine specializing in orthopedics, Sault Ste. Marie, Ont.; past pres. med. staff, chmn. exec. com. Gen. Hosp., Sault Ste. Marie, chief dept. surgery, mem. med. adv. com., 1980—; cons. orthopaedic surgeon Gen. Hosp., Plummer Meml. Hosp., Crippled Children Center, Ministry Nat. Health and Welfare, Dept. Vets. Adminstrn.; civilian orthopaedic surgeon to 44th Div. Armed Forces Base Hosp., Kaduna, Nigeria, 1969. Trustee Gen. Hosp., Sault Ste. Marie, 1975-76. Miss Betsy Burton Meml. fellow, 1963-64. Fellow Royal Coll. Surgeons Can., A.C.S., Royal Coll. Surgeons Edinburgh; mem. Can. Orthopaedic Assn., Ont. Orthopaedic Assn., Can. Med. Assn. Home: 50 Alworth Pl Sault Sainte Marie ON P6B 5W5 Canada Office: 125-955 Queen St East Sault Sainte Marie ON Canada

BANFIELD, JAYNE MARIE, foundry exec.; b. Hazel Green, Wis., May 13, 1938; s. Lawrence Frank and Agnes Dorothy (Splinter) Kaiser; student Clarke Coll.; m. Donald J. Banfield, Aug. 17, 1957; children—Klint B. Banfield, Nadine M. Banfield, Jason J. Banfield. Tax accountant Nack, Richardson & Nack, Galena, Ill., 1970-77; accountant John Westwick Foundry, Inc., Galena, treas., 1977—; v.p. JWF Inc., 1981—. Mem. Nat. Accountants Assn., Am. Inst. Corp. Controllers, Am. Foundrymen's Assn., Am. Mgmt. Assn., Bus. Women Am. Assn., Ill. Cast Metals Assn., Am. Soc. Metals. Roman Catholic. Home: 999 S Grandview Ave Dubuque IA 52001 Office: Claude & Meeker Sts Galena IL 61036

BANG, OTTO THEODORE, state senator; b. Madelia, Minn., Sept. 15, 1931; s. Otto and Laura Bertha (Gleason) B.; B.A., U. Minn., 1953; m. Mary Lippman, Sept. 21, 1957; children—Cathy, Rebecca, Thomas, Laurie. With Liberty Mutual Ins. Co., Mpls., 1961-64, Bus. Agy., Consumers, Inc., Mpls., 1964-75, Twin City Ins. Agy., Mpls., 1975-78; salesman Chandler Assos., Ins., Plymouth, Minn., 1978—; dir. Fotomark, Inc., Minn. Vision Services; state senator State of Minn., 1972—, state rep., 1962-72. Mem. Minn. Assn. Ind. Ins. Agts. Republican. Lutheran. Clubs: Exchange (pres. 1972-73), Masons, Shriners. Office: 10000 W Hwy 55 Plymouth MN 55440

BANKIT, PAUL, educator; b. Milw., June 16, 1929; s. Joseph and Sally Josephine B.; student engring., U. Wis., 1946-50; B.G.E., U. Nebr., 1960; M.B.A., Mich. State U., 1966, Ph.D., 1972; m. Esther Lilly Halversen, July 8, 1950; children—Eric J., Paula A.; m. 2d, Judith Beale Watson, Aug. 9, 1980. Commd. 2d lt., U.S. Army, 1952, advanced through grades to col., 1978; armor unit comdr., Ft. Hood, Tex., 1954-57; aviation officer, Germany, 1957-59; instr. Ft. Rucker, Ala., 1959-60, test pilot, 1961-64; combat pilot, Vietnam, 1966-67; div. chief Combat Devels. Command, Ft. Eustis, Va., 1967-70; comdr. Transp. Engring. Agy., Washington, 1973-76; ret., 1978; prof. mgmt. sci. Mich. State U., East Lansing, 1978—; pres., chief operating officer Midwestern Airlines Inc., Lansing, Mich.; cons. Ketron Corp., Washington. Decorated Legion of Merit, Bronze Star, Air Medals; named lectr. of year Army Logistics Mgmt. Center, 1974; recipient achievement award Boy Scouts Am., 1968. Mem. Ops. Research Soc. Am., Am. Mktg. Assn., Acad. Mgmt., Am. Mgmt. Assn. Republican. Lutheran. Club: Masons. Author: Logistics Systems Design, 1972; Logistics Systems Analysis, 1975. Home: 2587 Woodhill Dr Okemos MI 48864 Office: Mich State U East Lansing MI 48824

BANKOFF, SEYMOUR GEORGE, educator; b. N.Y.C., Oct. 7, 1921; s. Jacob and Sarah (Rashkin) B.; B.S., Columbia U., 1940, M.S., 1941; Ph.D., Purdue U., 1952. Research engr. Sinclair Refining Co., East Chicago, Ind., 1941-42; process engr. Manhattan project E.I. du Pont, Richland, Wash., 1942-48; from asst. prof. to prof., head dept. chem. engring. Rose Poly. Inst., 1948-58, with Northwestern U., 1959—, Walter P. Murphy prof. of chem. and nuclear engring., 1973—, chmn. Energy Engring. Council, 1976-80; vis. scientist Centre d' Etudes Nucleaires, Grenoble, France, 1980. Guggenheim fellow, 1966; Fulbright fellow, 1966; NSF fellow, 1958-59. Mem. Am. Inst. Chem. Engrs., ASME, Am. Nuclear Soc. Author articles in field. Office: Dept Chemical Engineering Northwestern U Evanston IL 60201

BANKS, BEVERLY ANN, fast food exec.; b. Hammond, Ind., May 26, 1933; d. Dewey Earl and Inez Irene (Clark) Rodkey; student public schs., St. Francisville, Ill.; children—Elizabeth, Gail. Co-owner St. Joe Drive In, St. Joseph, Mo., 1965—; owner, pres., gen. mgr. Henry's Restaurants, including Pyramid Drive In Inc., St. Joseph, 1971—, Spar Investments Inc., St. Joseph, 1971—, B.E.V. Foods, Inc., St. Joseph, 1978—. Named Mrs. Missouri, 1965. Mem. Mo. Restaurant Assn., Nat. Restaurant Assn., St. Joseph C. of C. (diplomat). Methodist. Home and Office: 8 Dunn Dr Saint Joseph MO 64506

BANKS, DORIS OWEN, hosp. exec.; b. Detroit, Mar. 13, 1928; d. John Lee and Eskaline (Gentry) Owen; student Cleary Coll., Ypsilanti, Mich., 1945, DePaul U.; Chgo., 1956, Kellberg Inst., Chgo., 1958, Wayne State U., 1977; A.A., Wayne County Community Coll., 1976; B.B.A., Mercy Coll., Detroit, 1978; M.A. in Bus. Mgmt. and Public Adminstrn., Central Mich. U., 1981. Sr. sec. Wayne State U., Detroit, 1963-64; sec. to supt. Police/Fire Communications, City of Detroit, 1964-70; sec. Detroit Residential Manpower, 1971; contractor/specialist D.O. Banks Flexile Med. Secretarial Service, Detroit, 1972—; ops. mgr. oncology service Providence Hosp., Southfield, Mich., 1972—; mem. adv. com. Home Health Care Inc., Southfield; mem. adv. bd. Breuer & Hermandez Assos., P.C.-Psychiat. Outpatient Clinic, Southfield. Bd. dirs. Providence Stage Door, Southfield, 1975. Mem. Am. Med. Writers Assn., Detroit Grand Opera Assn., Nat. Secs. Assn., Friends of Belle Isle, Am. Mgmt. Assn. Contbr. articles in field to profl. jours. Home: 39815 Village Wood Rd Novi MI 48050 Office: 16001 W Nine Mile Rd Southfield MI 48075

BANKS, ERNEST (ERNIE), baseball exec.; b. Dallas, Jan. 31, 1931; s. Eddie Banks; grad. high sch. Player with Kansas City Monarchs, Negro Am. League, 1950-51, 53; shortstop, then 1st baseman Chgo. Cubs, 1953-71, then coach, dir. group sales, dir., 1977—; formerly co-owner, v.p. Bob Nelson-Ernie Banks Ford, Inc., Chgo.; now internat. banker Ravenswood Bank, Chgo. Mem. bd. Chgo. Transit Authority, 1969—. Active Boy Scouts Am., YMCA. Served with U.S. Army, 1951-53; Europe. Named most valuable player Nat. League, 1958, 59; played in 13 All Star Games; holds nat. record for Grand Slam home runs; recipient awards from Fans, 1969, Press Club, 1969, Jr. C. of C., 1971; named Nat. League Most Valuable Player award, 1958, 59, to Tex. Sports Hall Fame, 1971, Baseball Hall of Fame, 1977. Republican. Author: (with Jim Enright) Mr. Cub. Office: c/o Chicago Cubs Wrigley Field N Clark and Addison Sts Chicago IL 60613

BANKS, J. B., state senator; b. Hermondale, Mo.; B.S., Lincoln U., Jefferson City; postgrad. St. Louis U., Washington U., St. Louis. Pres. constrn. co.; mem. Mo. Ho. of Reps., 1968-76, Mo. Senate, 1976—; chmn. bd. Masonic Home Loan Assn.; bd. dirs. J.B. (Jet) Banks Info. Center, St. Louis; committeeman 19th Ward Regular Democratic Orgn. Mem. Alpha Kappa Psi. Baptist. Clubs: Shriners, Masons. Author: The Blue Print Planning of the New Negro Market. Office: State Capitol Jefferson City MO 65101*

BANKS, JAMES DAVID, estate planning cons.; b. Boonville, Mo., Sept. 22, 1951; s. Leon F. and Phyllis J. (Linsey) B.; B.S., U. Mo., 1973; postgrad. Lincoln U., 1975; m. Eileen Biesemeyer, Jan. 8, 1972; children—John David, Daleen Michelle. Asst. cashier First Nat. Bank of Callaway County, Fulton, Mo., 1973-76; securities salesman ICH Fin. Services, Kansas City, Mo., 1976—; asst. group mgr. Ozark Nat. Life Ins. Co., Kansas City, Mo., 1977-78, group mgr. for Central Mo., 1979—. Fulton (Mo.) chmn. Jerry Lewis Telethon, 1975. Mem. Fulton Jr. C. of C. (treas. 1974), Nat. Assn. Life Underwriters. Lutheran. Address: 2611 Luan Ct Columbia MO 65201

BANKS, WILLIAM VENOID, broadcasting co. exec.; b. Geneva, Ky., May 6, 1903; s. Richard Dennis and Clara Ann (Barnett) B.; B.A., Detroit Coll. Law, 1929; LL.D., 1968; D.D., Detroit Baptist Coll.; m. Ivy Bird, 1963; children—Tenicia Ann Banks Gregory, Harumi, Alterio Alhanen. Individual practice law, 1929-50; pres., gen. mgr. Sta. WGPR-FM-TV, Detroit, 1962—; guest lectr. Howard U. Delegate Republican Nat. Conv., 1972, 76; pres. 1st Republican Dist. City of Detroit, 1974-77. Recipient Commendation Detroit Common Council; Bus. Service award, Booker T. Washington Businessmen's Assn. Mem. NAACP (recipient outstanding achievement award), Mich. Bar Assn., Wolverine Bar Assn. Republican. Baptist. Club: Mason (internat. supreme grand master 1964). Office: 3140-46 E Jefferson St Detroit MI 48207

BANLEY, THADDEUS JONATHAN, data processing exec.; b. Pine Ridge, S.D., Aug. 15, 1952; s. John Matthew and Stacie Laura (Eagle Staff) B.; B.S., Nat. Coll. Bus., 1980; m. Pamela Faye Poitra, Nov. 26, 1975; children—Thaddeus Jonathan, John Matthew II, Jeremiah Anthony. Salesman, Sears, Roebuck & Co., Rapid City, S.D., 1978-79; acctg. asst., computer operator Cheyenne River Sioux Tribe, Eagle Butte, S.D., 1980; computer programmer/analyst Custom Computer Services, Inc., Rapid City, S.D, 1980-81; systems engr., retail systems div. NCR Corp., Milw., 1981—. Served with U.S. Army, 1972-74. Democrat. Mem. Evang. Free Ch. Office: NCR Corp 10727 W North Ave Milwaukee WI

BANNER, ROBERT GERALD, mfg. co. exec.; b. Youngstown, Ohio, June 19, 1919; s. Josefus and Elsie Marie (Bard) B.; B.S., Ohio U., 1941; m. Elizabeth Jean Anthony, Aug. 15, 1942; children—Richard Michael, Barbara Jean, Robert Scott. With James H. Herron Co., Cleve., 1942; with Diamond Shamrock Corp., Cleve., 1947—, tech. mgr. chromium chems., 1959-77, mgr. research and devel. Soda Products div., 1977—; dir. Western Res. Resources, Cleve. Chmn., Concord Twp. Zoning Commn., 1965-77. Served with U.S. Army, 1943-46. Mem. World Chrome Producers (chmn. health and safety com. 1976—), Mem. Am. Chem. Soc., Am. Soc. Metals, Am. Leather Chemists, Assn., Am. Wood Preservers Assn., Am. Electroplaters Soc. Republican. Club: Rotary. Patentee in field. Home: 6772 Melridge Dr Painesville OH 44077 Office: PO Box 191 Painesville OH 44077

BANNER, THOMAS RICHARD, educator; b. Detroit, Jan. 28, 1947; s. Richard L. and Catherine H. (Schulte) B.; B.A., Lewis U., 1969; M.A., Loyola U., Chgo., 1973; m. Cynthia F. Elden, May 8, 1971; 1 son, Jonathan. Educator, dept. head, coach Montini High Sch., Lombard, Ill., 1969-71; educator, dept. head, coach, counselor St. Benedict High Sch., Chgo., 1971-73; dir. education Archdiocese Chgo., 1973-75; asso. prof. Mallinckrodt Coll., Wilmette, Ill., 1975-76; dir. tng. and devel. St. Francis Hosp., Evanston, Ill., 1975—. Bd. dirs. Oakton Community Coll. Mem. Am. Soc. Tng. and Devel., Am. Mgmt. Assn., Am. Hosp. Assn. Roman Catholic. Home: 931 Michigan Ave Evanston IL 60202 Office: 355 Ridge Ave Evanston IL 60202

BANNES, LORENZ THEODORE, constrn. co. exec.; b. St. Louis, Oct. 24, 1935; s. Lawrence Anthony and Louise Clair (Vollet) B.; B.S. in Civil Engring., St. Louis U., 1957; m. Janet Ann Bruening, Aug. 10, 1957; children—Stephen W., Michael F., Timothy L. From project engr. to exec. v.p. Gamble Constrn. Co. Inc., St. Louis, 1960-69, pres., 1969-72; founder, pres. Bannes-Shaughnessy, Inc., St. Louis, 1972-77, chmn. bd., 1977—; dir., v.p. St. Louis Constrn. Manpower Corp., 1977—. Tchr. civil engring. dept. St. Louis U., 1969—; tchr. contracting and concrete methods U. Mo. Extension Center, 1970—; tchr. constrn. mgmt. Grad. Engring. Center, U. Mo., St. Louis, 1968—, Sch. Architecture, Washington U., St. Louis, 1974—; lectr. So. Ill. U., Edwardsville, 1982; tchr. Nat. Assn. Women in Constrn., 1973. Mem. adv. com. in civil engring. Florissant Valley Community Coll.; mem. adv. com. constrn. tech. Jefferson Coll. Chmn. trustees Aspenhof, 1973; adv. bd. Little Sisters of Poor, 1975—; nat. bd. Living and Learning, Jesuit ednl. program for disadvantaged; mem. Human Rights Commn., Archdiocese of St. Louis, 1980—; trustee Christian Bros. Coll. High Sch., St. Louis, 1980—. Served with USAF, 1957-60. Recipient Alumni Merit award St. Louis U., 1972; named Man of Yr., Exec. Club of St. Louis U., 1978; named to Hall of Fame, Christian Bros. Coll. High Sch., 1981. Mem. Nat. Soc. Profl. Engrs. (recipient Young Engr. of Year award 1971), Mo. Soc. Profl. Engrs. (chmn. Y.E. com.), Concrete Council of St. Louis (pres. 1972-73, Distinguished Service award 1973), Asso. Gen. Contractors Am. (Nat. Build/Am. award 1973), St. Louis (Chmn. of Year 1973), ASCE (nat. com. constrn. research 1973-74), Young Presidents Orgn., Engrs. Club St. Louis (dir. 1975), Nat. Assn. Women in Constrn. (hon., Disting. service award 1974), Xe Chi Epsilon (chpt. hon. mem. 1980). Home: 724 Paschal Dr Saint Louis MO 63125 Office: 6780 Southwest Ave Saint Louis MO 63143

BANNISTER, MARGARET ALICE TRIMBLE, ednl. adminstr.; b. Oklahoma City, Dec. 15, 1924; d. Clyde Waldrop and Mary Melissa (Murray) Trimble; B.A. in Journalism, U. Okla., 1945; teaching cert. U. Mo., St. Louis, 1969, postgrad. extension, 1970-71; postgrad. U. Wash., 1973; m. Lawrence R. Bannister, Jan. 18, 1947 (div. 1968); children—Karen, Barbara Jean, Sally Ann. Reporter, Alva (Okla.) Review-Courier, 1945-46, Clinton (Okla.) Daily News, 1946-47; pub. relations asst. U. Okla., Norman, 1947-51; editorial asst. Consol.-Vultee Aircraft Corp., Ft. Worth, 1951-53; coordinator community relations Berkeley (Mo.) Sch. Dist. (merged with and name changed to Ferguson Sch. Dist. R-2 1975), 1968-72, dir. community relations, 1973-81; editorial cons. Mem. Women in Communications, Nat. Sch. Public Relations Assn. (officer Greater St. Louis chpt. 1969-71, 73-74), Soroptimists Internat. (charter mem. N. St. Louis County chpt.). Methodist (past mem. bd. stewards, youth council). Home: 2040 Argo Dr Florissant MO 63031 Office: 655 January Ave Ferguson MO 63135

BANNON, JOSEPH JOHN, educator; b. Glens Falls, N.Y., May 30, 1931; s. Leo and Elizabeth (Ring) B.; B.S., Ithaca Coll., 1957; M.S., U. Ill., 1958, Ph.D., 1971; postgrad. Columbia U., 1959-63; m. Ann Margaret Carpenter, Mar. 14, 1953; children—Joseph J., Peter L. Phys. edn. instr. U. Ill., 1957-58, chief office of recreation and park resources, 1966-73, prof., head dept. leisure studies, 1973—; supt. Leonia (N.J.) Recreation Commn., 1958-63; lectr. Washburn U., Topeka, 1964-66; gen. supt. Topeka Recreation Commn., 1963-66; pres. Mgmt. Learning Labs. Served with AUS, 1951-53. Recipient Outstanding Service award N.J. Recreation and Park Assn., 1963, Kans. Bd. Health 1965. Disting. fellow Nat. Recreation and Park Assn., Soc. Park and Recreation Educators; mem. Ill. Recreation and Park Assn., Internat. Personnel Mgmt. Assn., Am. Mgmt. Assn., World Leisure and Recreation Assn., Phi Epsilon Kappa. Author: Leisure Resources: Its Comprehensive Planning, 1976; Problem Solving in Recreation and Parks, 1981. Home: 3337 Stoneybrook St Champaign IL 61820 Office: 104 Huff Gym 1206 S 4th St Champaign IL 61820

BANSE, TIMOTHY PAUL, cons., author; b. Clinton, Iowa, Oct. 12, 1951; s. Robert Louis and Helen Leone B.; B.A. in Journalism, U. Iowa, 1981; one son, Christopher Patrick. Pres., Banse and Kelso Assos., Iowa City, 1979—; author articles in mags. including Mechanix Illustrated, Boating, Pick-Up, Van. Served with M.I., U.S. Army, 1969-72. Recipient Wilbur Petersen award U. Iowa Sch. Journalism, 1975, James W. Blackburn award, 1975. Mem. Am. Defense Preparedness Assn., Washington Ind. Writers Group, Writers Guild Am. Home: 3512 N 2d St Clinton IA 52732 Office: 511 Iowa Ave Iowa City IA 52240

BANSER, ROBERT FRANK, JR., journalist; b. Chgo., Aug. 20, 1946; s. Robert Frank and Alice Rita (Proctor) B.; student Chgo. City Coll., 1965-67; B.S., No. Ill. U., 1969; M.A., 1972; m. Lucille Ann Collins, Nov. 7, 1976; children—Robert Ernest, Christopher James. News reporter Paddock Publs., Arlington Heights, Ill., 1968; adminstrv. intern, City of Elgin, Ill., 1969-71; gen. assignment news reporter Star-Tribune, Publs., Chicago Heights, Ill., 1971-76, asso. editor, 1976—. Mem. Internat. City Mgmt. Assn., Soc. Profl. Journalists, Chgo. Headline Club, Sigma Delta Chi, No. Ill. U. Alumni Club, Jaycees. Roman Catholic. Home: 1346 Campbell Ave Chicago Heights IL 60411 Office: 1526 Otto Blvd Chicago Heights IL 60411

BANUELOS, DELMA J., educator; b. Galveston, Tex., Nov. 26, 1947; d. Richard S. and Virginia V. (Nichols) B.; B.A., Tex. Woman's U., 1970, M.Ed., 1974; Ed.D., Wayne State U., 1982. Tchr., Plano (Tex.) Schs., 1971-74; dir. bilingual edn. Region IX Edn. Service Center, Wichita Falls, Tex., 1974-78; instr. dept. spl. edn. Wayne State U., Detroit, 1978—, co-dir. immersion learning project dept. spl. edn., 1980-82. Mem. Phi Delta Kappa, Pi Lambda Theta. Editor, translator: Bilingual Parenting Education Training Manuals, 2 Vols., 1979; contbr. articles to profl. jours. Office: 163-6 Art Edn Bldg Coll Edn Wayne State Univ Detroit MI 48202

BANZHAF, CAROL ROTTIER, civic worker; b. Beaver Dam, Mich., Sept. 16, 1923; d. John A. and Marguerite (Mueller) Rottier; student Calvin Coll., 1942-43; A.B., Kalamazoo Coll., 1946; postgrad. Long Beach State Coll., 1954; M.A., Stetson U., 1959; m. Roger A. Goodspeed, 1946; children—Linn Marie, Carol Rottier; m. 2d, Henry F. Banzhaf, Aug. 6, 1965. Service rep. Mich. Bell Telephone Co.,

Grand Rapids, 1946; receptionist Littles' Studio, Palm Beach, Fla., 1947; tchr. kindergarten Cosa Mesa Union Schs., Calif., 1953-55; directress St. James' Day Sch., Ormond Beach, Fla., 1955-60; dean of girls, tchr. English, Milw. U. Sch., 1960-65; tchr. adult edn. Milw. Area Tech. Coll., 1973-75. Bd. dirs. Vol. Services of Greater Milw., 1963-66, Episcopal Campus Rectory, Milw., 1964-72, Women of St. Mark's Episcopal Ch., 1967-73, St. John's Home, Milw., 1976—, Dept. of Missions, Episcopal Diocese, 1978; bd. dirs. Women of St. Simon the Fisherman, Port Washington, Wis., 1973—, chmn., 1974-76; vol. Lit. Services Wis.; mem. Milw. Children's Hosp. Aux.; pres. St. John's Home Aux. and Assn. Mem. Nat. Women Deans and Counselors, Am. Personnel and Guidance Assn., Herb Soc. Am. Episcopalian. Home: Rural Route 1 5236 Sandy Beach S Belgium WI 53004

BAPTIST, ERROL CHRISTOPHER, pediatrician; b. Colombo, Sri Lanka, Feb. 24, 1945; came to U.S., 1974; s. Egerton Cuthbert and Hyacinth Margaret (Colomb) B.; M.B.,B.S., Faculty of Medicine, U. Ceylon, 1969; m. Christine Rosemary Francke, Aug. 7, 1976; children—Lauren Marianne, Erik Christopher. Intern, Colombo Gen. Hosp. and Children's Hosp., Colombo, Sri Lanka, 1969-70; resident house officer Dist. Hosp., Gampola, Sri Lanka, 1970-71; resident house officer Base Hosp., Kegalle, Sri Lanka, 1971-74; family practitioner, Marawila, Sri Lanka, 1974; resident physician in pediatrics Coll. of Medicine and Dentistry of N.J., Newark, 1975-77; practice medicine specializing in pediatrics, Rockford, Ill., 1977—; asst. prof. pediatrics Rockford Sch. Medicine, Coll. of Medicine, U. Ill., 1977—. Recipient Raymond B. Allen Instructorship award U. Ill., 1979, 80; diplomate Am. Bd. Pediatrics. Mem. Am. Acad. Pediatrics, AMA, Ill. Med. Soc., Boone County Med. Soc. Roman Catholic. Home: 8525 Centaur Dr Belvidere IL 61008 Office: 461 N Mulford Rd Rockford IL 61107

BAPTIST, JEREMY EDUARD, allergist; b. Chgo., Mar. 22, 1940; s. Arthur Henry and Margaret Jane (Beck) B.; B.S. in Physics, U. Chgo., 1960, Ph.D. in Biophysics (USPHS predoctoral fellow), 1966; M.D., U. Mo., Kansas City, 1978; m. Sylvia Evelyn Bonin, July 21, 1962; children—Sarah, Margaret, Catherine. Asst. prof. radiation biophysics U. Kans., 1966-73; claims authorizer Social Security Adminstrn., 1974-75; intern in medicine Northwestern U., 1978-79; allergist Speer Allergy Clinic, Shawnee Mission, Kans., 1979—. Brown-Hazen grantee, 1970. Mem. So. Med. Assn., AMA, Am. Coll. Allergists, Kans. Med. Soc., Johnson County Med. Soc., AAAS, N.Y. Acad. Scis., Am. Assn. Clin. Immunology and Allergy, Internat. Corr. Soc. Allergists, Sigma Xi. Mem. Reorganized Ch. of Jesus Christ of Latter Day Saints. Co-author: Handbook of Clinical Allergy, 1982; contbr. to Britannica Yearbook of Science and the Future, 1973, 74. Home: 3501 W 92d St Leawood KS 66206 Office: 5811 Outlook Dr Shawnee Mission KS 66202

BARADA, PAUL WILLIAM, consultant; b. South Bend, Ind., Oct. 5, 1945; s. Paul Maxwell and Margaret Ruby (Winship) B.; B.S., Ind. U., 1967, postgrad. Law Sch., 1967-68; postgrad. Butler U., 1968; m. Conda Jean Climer, Oct. 10, 1970; children—Paul William, William Climer, Jonathan Winship. Asst. dir. info. div. Ind. Dept. Commerce, Indpls., 1969-71; adminstrv. asst. office of lt. gov., State of Ind., Indpls., 1971-72; exec. sec. Rush County C. of C., Rushville, 1972-79; owner, prin. Barada Cons.'s, bus., communications, govt. cons., Rushville, 1979—; mem. Ind. Area Devel. Council; pres. Barada/Green Advt. and Public Relations, Inc. Apptd. city judge, Rushville, 1973, elected city judge, 1976—; bd. dirs. Arts for Rush County, 1973, Rush County Health, Inc., Rush Meml. Hosp., 1980—. Served with USAR, 1968-74. Completed inst. for orgn. mgmt. U.S. C. of C., Notre Dame U., 1972-78. Mem. Ind. Commerce Execs. Assn., I Men's Assn., Ind. U. Alumni Assn. Republican. Clubs: Columbia of Indpls., Soc. Ind. Pioneers, Old Gentleman's Literary Soc., Elks, Ind. U. Varsity. Author bi-weekly column local newspaper; contbr. feature article to Country Gentleman mag. Home: Route 1 Box 323 Rushville IN 46173 Office: 206 N Main St Rushville IN 46173

BARANCIK, RICHARD M., architect; b. Chgo., Oct. 19, 1924; s. Henry and Carrie (Grawoig) B.; B.S., U. Ill., 1943, B.S. in Architecture, 1948; postgrad. U. Nebr., 1944, U. Cambridge (Eng.), 1946, Beaux Arts (France), 1947; m. Suzanne Hammerman, Jan. 12, 1964; children—Robert, Michael, Cathy, Jill, Ellen. Asst. chief architect Chgo. Housing Authority, 1949; partner Barancik, Conte & Asso., Architects, Chgo., 1950—; cons. in field. Head archtl. com. Greater N. Mich. Ave. Assn., Chgo., 1965; v.p. State, Astor, Lake Shore Dr. Assn., 1968; trustee The Chgo. Latin Sch., 1974-80. Served with U.S. Army, 1943-46. Recipient AIA awards for Interstate Steel Co. bldg., 1962, 332 N. Michigan Ave. bldg., 1958, Ill. Beach State Park, 1961. Mem. AIA, Soc. Am. Registered Architects. Club: Arts. Home: 100 E Bellevue Pl Chicago IL 60611 also 296 Donlea Rd Barrington Hills IL Office: 407 S Dearborn St Chicago IL 60605

BARANEK, ROMAN, textile co. exec.; b. Poland, July 5, 1926; came to U.S., 1956, naturalized, 1961; s. Franciszek and Maria (Byczek) B.; student Nottingham (Eng.) Coll., 1949-52; A.T.I., London Tech. Inst., 1953; m. Helena Szkoda, July 21, 1951. Textile technologist Courtaulds Ltd., Coventry, Eng., 1954-56; with Joanna Western Mills Co., Chgo., 1956—, div. mgr., 1962-72, night supt., 1972-77, div. mgr., 1977—. Served with RAF, 1944-46. Decorated War medal, Air Force medal (Eng.); Disting. medal (Poland). Mem. Textile Inst. (Manchester, Eng.), Textile Assn. U.S.A., Assn. Dyers and Colourists (Eng.), Chem. Assn., Jet Air Force Assn. (sec. Chgo. Wing 1968-73). Roman Catholic. Inventor in field. Home: 5618 N Kenneth Ave Chicago IL 60646 Office: 2141 S Jefferson St Chicago IL 60616

BARBER, CHARLES TURNER, educator; b. Washington, Aug. 30, 1941; s. Charles Turner and Vera Hess (Nolt) B.; B.A. cum laude, W.Va. Wesleyan Coll., 1963; M.A., Am. U., 1965, Ph.D., 1967; m. Sandra Louise Powell, Apr. 18, 1978; children by previous marriage—Gretchen, Katrina; stepchildren—Robin, James, Melissa, Derek Anderson. Asst. prof. polit. sci. E. Tenn. State U., Johnson City, 1967-71; asst. prof. polit. sci. Ind. State U., Evansville, 1971-75, asso. prof., 1975—; panelist Presdl. Debates, Ind. Com. Humanities, 1976; univ. outreach lectr. govt. and family, 1978; TV commentator internat. politics Channel 14, Evansville, 1981; chmn. UN Day observances, Evansville, 1980. Recipient Group Study Exchange award Rotary Found., 1975-76, summer seminar award Nat. Endowment Humanities, U. Tex., 1977. Mem. Internat. Studies Assn., Am. Polit. Sci. Assn., Internat. Polit. Sci. Assn., Ind. Acad. Social Scis. (dir. 1976-79). Democrat. Presbyterian. Clubs: Philatelic Soc., Ind. State U. Evansville Dinner Group, Presbyterian Mariners. Editorial adv. Internat. Studies Notes, 1977—; contbr. articles in field to profl. jours. Home: PO Box 131 Newburgh IN 47630 Office: 8600 University Blvd Evansville IN 47712

BARBER, MARIAN LIN LITTNER, accountant; b. Taiwan, Sept. 14, 1940; d. Hsui-ting and Yueh-O (Shih) Lin; came to U.S., 1969, naturalized, 1980; B.A., Chung-hsing U., Taiwan, 1964; M.B.A., Ind. U., 1973; m. Dennis Barber. Tchr., Tou-wu Middle Sch., Taiwan, 1964-66; payroll clk. Mobil China Allied Chem. Indsl. Ltd., Taiwan, 1966-69; jr. accountant Abbott Labs., North Chicago, Ill., 1973-74; distbn. analyst dept. 291, 1974-76; sr. accountant Square D Co., Milw., 1976—; pres. Marian Fin. Services, 1980—. Gen. chmn. Chinese group Milw. Folk Fair Com., 1979; coordinator Orgn. of Chinese Am. Women; bd. dirs. Chinese-Am. Civic Club of Milw., 1979—. Taiwan Govt. research scholar Nat. Research Inst., Taipei, 1968. Mem. Orgn. Chinese Ams., Chinese-Am. Civic Club Milw. (treas. 1978-79, dir. 1979-80). Author: (in Chinese) You Are What You Eat, 1978. Home: 3985 W College Ave Milwaukee WI 53221

BARBER, SANDRA POWELL, polit. scientist; b. Balt., Dec. 15, 1941; d. Sanford William and Mary Louise (Barry) Powell; B.A. in History (Md. State Tchrs. scholar 1961-63), Mt. St. Agnes Coll., Balt., 1963; M.A. in History, N.Mex. State U., 1970; M.A., in Polit. Sci (Sloan Found. research asst. 1974), Purdue U., 1975; m. Charles Turner Barber, Apr. 18, 1978; children—Robin, James, Melissa, Derek; stepchildren—Gretchen, Katrina. Tchr., Balt. public schs., 1963-64; research asst. N.Mex. State U., 1967-69; acad. adv., instr. polit. sci. Purdue U., 1973-78; lectr. Ind. State U., Evansville, 1979-80, acad. systems analyst, 1980—. Block coordinator Chauncey Neighborhood Assn., West Lafayette, Ind., 1975-76. Mem. Internat. Studies Assn., Am. Polit. Sci. Assn., Center Study Presidency, Am. Acad. Polit. and Social Sci., Midwest Polit. Sci. Assn., So. Polit. Sci. Assn., Ind. Polit. Sci. Assn. (dir. 1978-79), Ind. Acad. Social Scis., Pi Gamma Mu. Presbyterian. Author papers in field. Home: PO Box 131 Newburgh IN 47630 Office: 8600 University Blvd Evansville IN 47712

BARBER, THOMAS LEROY, beverage co. exec.; b. Joliet, Ill., Jan. 27, 1944; s. John Gaylord and Marcella Jane (Black) B.; B.S. in Indsl. Mgmt., So. Ill. U., 1967; m. Marsha Eileen Hursey, June 15, 1968; 1 son, Brett. Tng. specialist Olin Corp., East Alton, Ill., 1968-71; tng. supr. Seven-Up Co., St. Louis, 1971-77; mgr. sales tng. Beverage Mgmt. Inc., Columbus, Ohio, 1977-80, dir. tng., 1980—; instr. Florissant Valley Jr. Coll., 1975-76; mem. vocat. adv. com. Alton High Sch. Ordained elder Presbyterian Ch. Mem. Am. Soc. Tng. and Devel., Nat. Assn. Watch and Clock Collectors, Phi Mu Alpha, Iota Lambda Sigma. Office: 1001 Kingsmill Pkwy Columbus OH 43229

BARBOLINI, ROBERT R., chem. engr.; b. N.Y.C., May 30, 1938; s. Renato J. and Dorothy L. (Curry) B.; B.S., Mass. Inst. Tech., 1959; M.Engring., Yale U., 1962; M.B.A., U. Chgo., 1973; m. Betty M. Halford, Sept. 11, 1976. Chem. engr. Union Carbide Corp., Tonawanda, N.Y., 1959-60; project mgr. Process Plants Corp., N.Y.C., 1961-68; asst. chief engr. Met. San. Dist. Greater Chgo., 1968—. Registered profl. engr., Conn., Ill., N.Y. Mem. Water Pollution Control Fedn., Air Pollution Control Assn., Am. Pub. Works Assn. Home: 2500 Lakeview Ave Chicago IL 60614 Office: 100 E Erie St Chicago IL 60611

BARBU, ROBERT CORNELL, ednl. adminstr.; b. Cleve., Apr. ll, 1937; s. Cornelius Alexander and Flora Jane (Siegler) B.; B.S., Ohio State U., 1959; M.Ed., Kent State U., 1972; m. Janice Marilyn Jacobs, Nov. 28, 1960; children—Scott, Terrance, Troy. Engring. drawing instr. West Tech. High Sch., Cleve., 1960-65; instr. electronics Westlake (Ohio) High Sch., 1965-70; AV-ITV dir. Westlake City Schs., 1970—; v.p. Profl. Computer Services, Inc., Avon Lake, Ohio, 1971, Guidelines, Inc., Fairview Park, Ohio, 1975. Chmn. audio-visual com. Greater Cleve. Sch. Supts. Group Purchasing Council, 1976-77; recreation dir. City of Avon Lake, 1974-75. Mem. Assn. Ednl. Communication Tech., Ohio Ednl. Library Media Assn. (dist. dir. 1978—), Nat., Ohio edn. assns., Northeastern Ohio Tchrs. Assn., Ohio Indsl. Arts Assn., Westlake Tchrs. Assn., Nat. Ski Patrol System, Boy Scouts Am. Writer, producer, host instrnl. TV series Choose It, 1974. Home: 32699 Carriage Ln Avon Lake OH 44012 Office: 27830 Hilliard Rd Westlake OH 44145

BARCH, JAMES JOHN, ednl. adminstr.; b. Manistee, Mich., July 28, 1939; s. Barch Edward Raymond and Myrtle Etta (Anderson) B.; B.S., Central Mich. U., 1965, M.A., 1968; m. Joan Beverly Carr, Aug. 9, 1969; children—James Preston, Jon Craig, Julie Kristin. Tchr. public schs., Bay City, Mich., 1968-69; tchr. public schs., Okemos, Mich., 1969-75, bldg. adminstr., 1976—. Pres., Lakeside Village Homeowners Assn., 1973-75; counselor Boy Scouts Am., 1981—. Served with U.S. Army, 1965-67. Decorated Bronze Star, Purple Heart with oak leaf cluster. Mem. Assn. Supervision and Curriculum Devel., Nat. Assn. Middle Sch. Educators, Nat. Assn. Secondary Sch. Prins., Mich. Assn. Middle Sch. Educators, Mich. Assn. Secondary Sch. Prins., Nat. Geographic Soc., Smithsonian Assos., VFW. Republican. Presbyterian. Home: 2766 Still Valley Ct East Lansing MI 48823 Office: 4406 Okemos Rd Okemos MI 48864

BARCLAY, ALLAN GENE, psychologist, educator; b. Masonville, Iowa, Dec. 22, 1930; s. Otho R. and Marian (Lee) B.; student U. Louisville, 1949-50; A.B. cum laude, U. Tulsa, 1955; postgrad. U. Iowa, 1955-56; Ph.D., Washington U., St. Louis, 1960; children—Lisa, Allan. Clin. psychologist Mental Hygiene Clinic, VA Regional Office, St. Louis, 1959-60; faculty St. Louis U., 1960—, prof. psychology, 1965—, asso. univ. research adminstr., 1968-72, dir. program in developmental psychology, 1965—, dir. Sch. Medicine Child Devel. Clinic, 1972—; chief psychologist dept. pediatrics Cardinal Glennon Meml. Hosp. for Children, St. Louis, 1960—, asso. dean acad. affairs Sch. of Profl. Psychology, Wright State U., Dayton, Ohio, 1979—. Cons. to hosps., govt. agys.; spl. adviser Pres.'s Com. on Mental Retardation; councilor Joint Commn. on Hosps., Accreditation Council on Facilities for Mentally Retarded. Bd. dirs., pres., mem. adv. com. New Hope Found. St. Louis, 1977—; bd. dirs., mem. profl. adv. com. Youth Emergency Services. Served with AUS, 1948-52. Grantee USPHS, 1961-79, U.S. Children's Bur., 1960-68, Joseph P. Kennedy, Jr. Found., 1965, Children's Research Found., 1965, Office Econ. Opportunity, 1965-68, Social Rehab. Service, 1972—; Am. Psychol. Found., 1980; diplomate Am. Bd. Examiners in Profl. Psychology; mem. Nat. Register Health Service Providers in Psychology. Fellow Am. Assn. on Mental Deficiency; Soc. for Rorschach Research and Projective Techniques, Mo. Psychol. Assn., Internat. Council Psychologists; mem. Am. Psychol. Assn. (fellow div. clin. psychology, fellow div. developmental psychology, chmn. bd. profl. affairs, sec.-treas. div. clin. psychology, also div. mental retardation), Ill. Psychol. Assn., Mo. Psychol. Assn., Ohio Psychol. Assn., AAAS, AAUP, Am. Assn. Mental Deficiency, So. Soc. Philosophy and Psychology, Soc. Research in Child Devel. Inter-Am. Soc. Psychology, Internat. Council Psychologists (past pres.), Am. Pub. Health Assn., AMA, Sword and Key, Sigma Xi, Pi Gamma Mu, Psi Chi (nat. pres.), Phi Gamma Kappa. Editor: Jour. Profl. Psychology; contbr. articles to publs. Home: 100 Devonhurst Kettering OH 45429

BARCLAY, DONALD AUDRIE, JR., city ofcl.; b. Arkansas City, Kans., Oct. 22, 1951; s. Donald A. and Eileen L. (Murphy) B.; A.A., Cowley County Community Coll., 1977; B.B.A., Southwestern Coll., 1981; m. Terri J. Young, Dec. 30, 1977. Police officer City of Leavenworth, (Kans.), 1975-76; asst. mgr. Musicland, Leavenworth, 1976; asst. to bus. mgr. Cowley County Community Coll., Arkansas City, 1975-76; disc jockey sta. KSOK, Arkansas City, 1975-76; dep. sheriff Cowley County, Kan., 1977; police officer Arkansas City, 1977-78; fireman City of Arkansas City, 1978—; credit mgr. Sherwin-Williams Co., Arkansas City, 1979—. Served with U.S. Army, 1970-74. Recipient Dean's award for outstanding service to coll. Cowley County Coll., 1977; Cert. of Achievement, City of Leavenworth, 1975. Mem. U.S. Jaycees, Arkansas City Jaycees, Kans. Sheriff's Assn., So. Kans. and No. Okla. Law Enforcement Assn., Kans. Peace Officers Assn. Democrat. Clubs: Spl. Tiger (pres. 1978), Fraternal Order Police. Home: 812 W Linden St Arkansas City KS 67005 Office: City Bldg 1st and Central Sts Arkansas City KS 67005

BARCUS, CHAUNCEY HAROLD, architect, educator; b. Farmersville, Ill., Sept. 9, 1921; s. Chauncey Hobart and Edna Rose (Smith) B.; B.S. in Archtl. Engring., U. Ill., 1947, M.S. in Architecture, 1948; m. Georganne Coon, Dec. 28, 1946; children—Harold Lloyd, David Alan. Grad. asst. U. Ill., 1948; draftsman, archtl. supt. U. Ill. Architect's Office, Urbana, Ill., 1949; architect asso. Small, Wertz, Barcus & Swift, Architects and Engrs., Oxford, Ohio, 1950-78; prof. architecture Miami U., Oxford, Ohio, 1950—; works include library, dining hall, dormitories for Western Coll., Oxford, city recreation bldg., swimming pool and bathhouse, Oxford, several comml. bldgs., chs., frat. houses and residences; cons. architect in energy-efficient bldg. design and solar heating. Served with USN, 1941-45; PTO. Registered architect, Ill., Ohio. Mem. AIA, Assn. Collegiate Schs. Architecture, Illuminating Engring. Soc., Architects Soc. Ohio, ASHRAE, Internat. Solar Energy Soc. Clubs: Oxford Country; Fairfield Glade (Tenn.) Community. Home: 5176 Westgate Dr Oxford OH 45056 Office: Dept Architecture Miami U Oxford OH 45056

BARCUS, FLOYD EUGENE, former ednl. adminstr.; b. Sullivan, Ind., Apr. 13, 1923; s. Floyd C. and Lois E. (Bastaim) B.; B.S. in Edn., Ind. State U., 1951, M.S. in Edn., 1953; postgrad. Kent State U., 1951-53, Ohio U., 1956-57, Ill. State U., 1965; m. Maxine Ray, May 18, 1946; children—Terry, Dan. Tchr. social sci. public high sch., Montpelier, Ohio, 1951-58; head guidance counselor Ashland (Ohio) High Sch., 1958-65; dir. admissions Mansfield (Ohio) Tech. Sch., 1965-67; dir. pupil personnel Pioneer Joint Vocat. Sch., Shelby, Ohio, 1967-80; ret., 1980. Pres. Ashland County Mental Health, 1959-60. Served with USAAF, 1943-46. Recipient Charles H. Weaver award Ohio Sch. Counselors Assn., 1980. Mem. Am. Personnel and Guidance Assn., Am. Vocat. Assn., NEA, Am. Pupil Personnel Adminstrs. Assn. Democrat. Methodist. Clubs: Lions (Ohio chmn. youth com. 1980-81), Masons. Home: 200 Parkview Circle Ashland OH 44803

BARCUS, ROBERT GENE, assn. exec.; b. Monticello, Ind., Oct. 22, 1937; s. Harold Eugene and Marjorie Irene (Dilling) B.; B.P.E. (Alumni scholar 1957), Purdue U., 1959; M.A., Ball State U., 1963; postgrad. Ind. U., summer 1966; supts. license Butler U., 1967; m. Mary Evelyn Shull, Aug. 9, 1959; children—Jennifer Sue, Debra Lynn. Tchr., coach Wabash (Ind.) Jr. High Sch., 1959-63; tchr. Wabash High Sch., 1963-64; tchr., coach North Central High Sch., Indpls., 1964-65; salary cons. Ind. State Tchrs. Assn., Indpls., 1965-67, asst. dir. research, 1967-68, dir. spl. services, 1968-70, exec. asst., 1971-72, adminstrv. asst., 1972-73, asst. exec. dir. spl. services and tchr. rights, 1973—. Mem. NEA, Am. Assn. Sch. Adminstrs., Wabash City (past pres.), Washington Twp. (past pres.) tchrs. assns., Kappa Delta Pi, Pi Delta Kappa. Mem. Ch. of the Brethren (clk. 1966-74, chmn. 1979-80). Clubs: Indpls. Press, Columbia, Indiana Schoolmen's. Home: 2230 Brewster Rd Indianapolis IN 46260 Office: 150 W Market St Indianapolis IN 46204

BARDACH, JANUSZ, plastic surgeon, educator; b. Odessa, Russia, July 28, 1919; came to U.S., 1972; s. Mark and Ottylia (Neuding) B.; Physician, Moscow Med.-Stomatological Inst., 1950, M.D., 1953; 1 dau., Ewa. Resident, Moscow Med.-Stomatological Inst., 1950-54; dept. head, asso. prof. dept. maxillofacial surgery Lodz (Poland) Med. Acad. (Coll. Medicine), 1954-59, docent, 1959-62, prof., 1962-72, dept. head, prof. dept. plastic surgery, 1971-72, asso. dean Coll. Medicine, 1967-71, dir. center for congential facial deformities, 1962-72; vis. prof. dept. otolaryngology and maxillofacial surgery U. Iowa, Iowa City, 1972-73, prof. dept. otolaryngology and maxillofacial surgery, 1973—, prof. plastic surgery, dept. surgery Univ. Iowa Hosps. and Clinics, 1977—, chmn. div. plastic and reconstructive surgery of head and neck, 1973—; vis. prof. dept. plastic surgery Univs. Pekin, Kanton, Shanghai, Tientsin and Kuondiou, China, 1966, Oxford U., Eng., 1968, Haccettepe U., Ankara, U. Istanbul, Turkey, 1971; fellow in gen. plastic surgery, Prague, 1954, Oxford, Eng., 1962. Recipient highest sci. award Ministry of Health, Poland, 1966, 68, Town Council of Lodz, 1970, third prize for clin. research in otolaryngology Am. Assn. Ophthalmology and Otolaryngology, 1977; fed. grantee Maxillofacial Growth Project, 1973-75, 76—. Mem. Internat. Soc. Plastic Surgeons, Brit. Assn. Plastic Surgery, Royal Soc. Medicine (sect. plastic surgery), Internat. Soc. Maxillofacial Surgery, Am. Soc. Plastic and Reconstructive Surgeons (asso.), Turkish Soc. Plastic and Reconstructive Surgery (hon.), AMA, Johnson County Med. Assn., Am. Cleft Palate Assn., Am. Acad. Facial Plastic and Reconstructive Surgery. Club: Rotary Internat. Author six books; contbr. 80 research articles in field to sci. publs. in English, Polish, Czech, Russian, French and German. Home: 328 Highland Dr Iowa City IA 52240 Office: Dept of Otolaryngology and Maxillofacial Surgery University of Iowa Hospitals Iowa City IA 52242

BARDEEN, JOHN, physicist, educator; b. Madison, Wis., May 23, 1908; s. Charles Russell and Althea (Harmer) B.; B.S., U. Wis., 1928, M.S., 1929; Ph.D., Princeton, 1936; D.Sc. (hon.), Union Coll., 1955, U. Wis., 1960; m. Jane Maxwell, July 18, 1938; children—James Maxwell, William Allen, Elizabeth Ann (Mrs. Greytak). Geophysicist Gulf Research & Devel. Corp., Pitts., 1930-33; asst. prof. physics U. Minn., 1938-41; with Naval Ordnance Lab., Washington, 1941-45; research physicist Bell Telephone Labs., Murray Hill, N.J., 1945-51; prof. physics and elec. engring. U. Ill., Urbana, 1951-75, emeritus, 1975—. Mem. Pres.'s Sci. Adv. Com., 1959-62. Recipient Ballantine medal Franklin Inst., 1952; John Scott medal, Phila., 1955; Fritz London award, 1962; Vincent Bendix award, 1964; Nat. Medal Sci., 1966; Michelson-Morley award Case Western Res. U., 1968; co-recipient Nobel prize in physics, 1956, 72; Presdl. Medal of Freedom, 1977. Fellow Am. Phys. Soc. (pres. 1968-69, Buckley prize 1954); mem. Am. Acad. Arts and Sci., Am. Philos. Soc., Nat. Acad. Sci. Nat. Acad. Eng. Home: 55 Greencroft Champaign IL 61820

BARDGETT, JOHN EDWARD, judge Supreme Ct. Mo.; b. St. Louis, Apr. 28, 1927; s. Alfred Latimer and Catherine Cecilia (Heverin) B.; J.D., St. Louis U., 1951; m. Mary Jeanne Branch, Aug. 1, 1953; children—John Edward, Suzanne Marie, Bruce Kevin, Mary Beth. Admitted to Mo. bar, 1951; practiced in St. Louis, 1951-68; mem. firm Morris A. Shenker, 1955-60, Bardgett & Gallagher, 1960-62, Haley & Bardgett, 1962-68; judge St. Louis County Circuit Ct., Clayton, 1968-70; justice Mo. Supreme Ct., Jefferson City, 1970—. Served with USN, 1945-46. Mem. Am. Bar Assn., Mo. Bar Assn. Office: Supreme Ct Supreme Ct Bldg Jefferson City MO 65101

BARDIS, PANOS DEMETRIOS, sociologist, author, editor; b. Lefcohorion, Arcadia, Greece; m. Donna Jean; children—Byron Galen, Jason Dante; B.A. magna cum laude, Bethany (W.Va.) Coll., 1950; M.A., Notre Dame U., 1953; Ph.D., Purdue U., 1955. Prof. sociology, editor Social Sci., U. Toledo, 1959—; cons. Nat. Assn. Standard Med. Vocabulary, 1963—; Am. rep. Internat. Congress Social Scis., Barcelona, Spain, 1965, 66, 71; participant Conf. International de Sociologie de la Religion, Rome, 1969, Strasbourg, 1977, Venice, 1979, Internat. Sci. Congress, Athens, Greece, 1973, 77, Internat. Conf. on Love and Attraction, Swansea, Wales, 1977, Nat. Council on Family Relations, Toronto, Can., 1973, Ohio Acad. Scis., 1975; participant numerous other internat. confs. on peace, sci., philosophy and religion, 1976—. Sec.-treas. World Student Relief, Athens, 1947-48; chmn. crime reduction com. Commn. for Community Devel., Toledo, 1967-68; trustee Marriage Mus., N.Y.C. Fellow AAAS, Am. Sociol. Assn., Institut Internat. de Sociologie (chmn. membership com. 1970—, coordinator for U.S.A. 1974—, participants confs. Rome 1969, Montreal, 1972, Caracas, 1972, Uppsala, 1978, Lisbon, 1980), Internat. Inst. Arts and Letters (life),

World Acad. Scholars; mem. AAUP, Am. Soc. Neo-Hellenic Studies (bd. advisers), Democritos, Group for Study Sociolinguistics, Inst. for Mediterranean Affairs (adv. council), Internat. Sci. Commn. on Family, Internat. Sociol. Assn. (Am. rep., Evian, France 1966, Rome 1969, Varna, Bulgaria 1970, Algiers 1972, Toronto 1974), North Central Sociol. Assn., Modern Greek Soc., Nat. Acad. Econs. and Polit. Sci. (dir.), Nat., Ohio councils on family relations, Nat. Soc. Lit. and Arts, Nat. Writers Club, N.Y. Acad. Scis., Nat. Soc. Published Poets, Sigma Xi, Alpha Kappa Delta, Phi Kappa Phi, Pi Gamma Mu, Kappa Delta Pi. Recipient award for outstanding achievement in edn. Bethany Coll., 1975, Outstanding Teaching award Toledo U., 1975; winner Internat. Lachian Poetry competition, 1981; Kulikowski spl. award in poetry, 1981. Author: Studies in Marriage and the Family, 1975, 78; History of the Family, 1975; The Family in Changing Civilizations, 1967, 69; Ivan and Artemis (novel), 1957; The Future of the Greek Language in the United States, 1976; Encyclopedia of Campus Unrest, 1971; translator On Balances (Archimedes), 1980; co-editor, contbr.: The Family in Asia, 1978, 79; History of Thanatology, 1981; also articles in profl. jours., poetry. Editor, asso. editor or book rev. editor 25 nat. and internat. jours. Composer songs for mandolin: Byron Ballad, 1972; Carnival Dance, 1972; The Gypsy Dreamer, 1973; Jeu de Jason, 1973; Lamentation, 1973; Merlin's Magic, 1973; Minerva Melody, 1973; The Nereid of the North, 1973; Threnody, 1974; Verlaine's Chanson d'Automne, 1974; The Pines of Olympia, 1975; Echoes of Arcadia, 1975; The Dance of the Neutrino, 1975; Multis cum Lacrimis, 1976; Legend of Love, 1978; Death of a Nymph, 1978; The Sorceress of Saturn, 1979; Death of Aphrodite's Dove, 1979; Artemis in the Moonlight, 1979; Cypress Ghosts, 1981. Office: U Toledo Toledo OH 43606

BAREN, JOHN BENNETT, psychiat. social worker; b. San Francisco, July 25, 1944; s. Morton Paul and Juliet (Luton) B.; B.A., U. San Francisco, 1966; M.S.W., Calif. State U., Sacramento, 1968; m. Patricia May Thompson, June 20, 1971; 1 son, Robert John. Psychiat. social worker Bur. Social Work, Sacramento, 1968-70; dir. East Area Community Mental Health Center, div. mental health U. Calif. Davis/Sacramento Med. Center, 1970-77; clin. asst. prof. psychiatry U. Calif. Med. Sch., Davis, 1972-77; pvt. practice psychotherapy, 1968—; exec. dir. Montgomery County (Ohio) Mental Health Bd., Dayton, also clin. asso. prof. psychiatry Wright State U. Med. Sch., 1977—. Mem. Freedom of Choice Coalition, Miami Valley, 1978—. Recipient cert. appreciation Calif. Policewomen's Assn., 1974, Mental Health Assn. Miami Valley, 1979. Mem. Nat. Assn. Social Workers, Acad. Cert. Social Workers, Nat. Assn. Mental Health Adminstrs., Wright State U. Acad. Medicine. Home: 24 Williamsburg Ln Dayton OH 45459 Office: 318 W 4th St Dayton OH 45402

BARG, WILLIAM HENRY, mapping co. exec.; b. Geneva, Ill., June 23, 1930; s. William F. and Theodora H. (Peterson) B.; B.S. in Math., Bradley U., 1954; postgrad. U. Ill., U. Mich., No. Ill. U.; m. Irene Adele Bradshaw, Oct. 11, 1952; children—Scot, Renee, Steven, Michele, Timothy. Mapping maintenance specialist Sidwell Co., West Chicago, Ill., 1950-56, project liaison and coordinator, 1956-59, sales mgr., 1959-64, v.p., mktg. dir., 1964-79, exec. v.p., 1980—. Served with USMC, 1950-52. Fellow Am. Congress Surveying and Mapping; mem. Am. Soc. Photogrammetry (cert. photogrammetrist), Internat. Assn. Assessing Officers, Ill. Assessment Inst., Soc. for Mktg. Profl. Services. Presbyterian. Club: Masons. Contbr. articles in field to profl. jours. Home: 1500 N Morse Wheaton IL 60187 Office: 28W240 North Ave West Chicago IL 60185

BARGER, CHARLES WILLIAM, engring. co. exec.; b. Chgo., Dec. 21, 1938; s. Leslie Donald and Adeline Esther (Schaade) B.; student U. So. Calif., 1957-58; m. Marilyn Ann Brown, Feb. 7, 1959; children—Karen, Angela, Michael. Rodman to v.p. R.W. Petrie & Assos. Inc., Benton Harbor, Mich., 1959-69; pres., owner Barger Engring. Inc., St. Joseph, Mich., 1969—. Chmn. St. Joseph Cath. Parish Council, 1975-77. Registered profl. engr. Mich., Ind., Hawaii. Mem. Mich. (pres. 1975-76), Nat. profl. engrs. in pvt. practice, Mich., Nat. socs. profl. engrs., Am. Cons. Engrs. Council. Home: 4820 Oaklane Stevensville MI 49127 Office: 612 Main St St Joseph MI 49085

BARGER, ROBERT NEWTON, III, educator; b. Peoria, Ill., Oct. 29, 1938; s. Robert Newton and Catherine Marie (O'Brien) B.; B.A., St. Paul Sem., 1961, M.A., 1966, M.Div., 1975; M.A., Coll. St. Thomas, 1966; Ph.D. in Am. Ednl. History (Fred S. Bailey scholar), U. Ill., 1976; m. Josephine Disser, Aug. 6, 1976. Tchr., St. Paul Sch., Danville, Ill., 1965-69; tchr. Schlarman High Sch., Danville, 1965-69; lectr. in religion, adminstr. inter-foundational acad. program, counselor Newman Found., U. Ill., Urbana-Champaign, 1969-75, counselor office student services, 1975-76, instr. dept. ednl. policy studies, 1976-77; asst. prof. philosophy and history of edn. Eastern Ill. U., 1977-79, asso. prof., 1980—; participant Internat. Geophys. Year, Antarctica, 1956-57; observer aboard 1st USAF flight over South Pole, Oct. 26, 1956; vis. counselor Parkland (Community) Coll., 1974-75; pres. Religious Workers Assn. at U. Ill., 1973-74. Com. for a Healing Repatriation, Inc., 1974—; vis. chaplain U.S. Ho. of Reps., 1974; atty. tribunal, mem. bd. consultors Diocese of Peoria, 1974-76. Chmn., Danville Human Relations Commn., 1966-69. Mem. U.S., Midwest history of edn. socs., Midwest Philosophy of Edn. Soc., Am. Ednl. Research Assn., Am. Ednl. Studies Assn., Danforth Assn. Author: A History of the Catholic Cemeteries of the City of Peoria, 1673-1945, 1965; Amnesty: What Does It Really Mean?, 1974; John Lancaster Spalding: Catholic Educator and Social Emissary, 1977; contbg. editor Pvt. Sch. Monitor; mem. editorial bd. Eastern Edn. Jour.; contbr. articles and revs. to profl. publs. Home: 2519 Village Rd Charleston IL 61920 Office: 213 Buzzard Edn Bldg Eastern Ill U Charleston IL 61920

BARGER, WILLIAM MURRAY, machinery bldg. co. exec.; b. Piqua, Ohio, Mar. 6, 1942; s. Thomas William and Dorothy Elizabeth (Reeder) B.; B.S., Ohio No. U., 1964; m. Marian LaRue Shuff, Aug. 24, 1963; children—Heather, Jason, James. With French Oil Mill Machinery Co., Piqua, 1964-79, lab. technician Solvent Extraction Div., 1964-67, mgr. process devel., 1967-72, sales mgr., 1972-75, gen. mgr., 1975-79, v.p. Solvent Extraction div., 1979—; mem. tech. adv. bd. Tex. A&M U. Oilseed Research Lab.; mem. Ohio Trade Del. to China. Mem. health club bd. Miami County YMCA. Registered profl. engr., Ohio. Mem. Am. Oil Chemists Soc. (lectr., chmn. tech. safety and engrs. com.), Nat. Soc. Profl. Engrs., Ohio Soc. Profl. Engrs., Am. Mgmt. Assn., Am. Newcomen Soc. Republican. Episcopalian. Club: Rotary Internat. Developer direct extraction techniques for marigolds and hops. Home: 1324 Stratford Dr Piqua OH 45356 45356

BARICKMAN, JAMES HALL, advt. agy. exec.; b. Mpls., Oct. 5, 1924; s. John B. and Mary Jane (Hall) B.; B.B.A., U. Minn., 1947; m. Mary Mischler, Jan. 28, 1974; children—Nancy, James H.J., Julie K., Robert John, Daniel W. With trust dept. Northwestern Nat. Bank, Mpls., 1947-49; W. Coast advt. mgr. Pillsbury Co., Los Angeles, 1949-52; partner Brewer Advt., Kansas City, Mo., 1952-59; chmn., chief exec. officer Barickman Advt., Kansas City, Mo., 1959-80; chmn. Doyle Dane Bernbach Advt., Inc. (merger with Barickman Advt.), 1980—; dir. Columbia Union Nat. Bank. Pres., Jr. Achievement Kansas City, 1959-60. Served with C.E., U.S. Army, 1943-44. Recipient Am. Advt. Fedn. Silver Medal award, 1976. Mem. Am. Mktg. Assn., Assn. Advt. Agys., Internat. Am. Assn. Advt. Agys. Clubs: Kansas City, Univ., Indian Hills Country, Wolf Creek Country, Carriage, La Quinta Country, Hillcrest Country, Friars, Williams. Home: 6417 Verona Rd Shawnee Mission KS 66208 Office: 421 W 12th St Kansas City MO 64105

BARISAS, BERNARD GEORGE, JR., biochemist; b. Shreveport, La., July 16, 1945; s. Bernard George and Edith (Bailey) B.; B.A., U. Kans., 1965; B.A. (Woodrow Wilson fellow, Rhodes scholar), Oxford U., 1967; M.Ph., Yale U., 1969, Ph.D., 1971. NIH postdoctoral trainee Yale U., 1971-72, research asso., 1972; NIH postdoctoral fellow U. Colo., Boulder, 1973-75, lectr. chemistry, 1975; asst. prof. biochemistry St. Louis U. Sch. Medicine, 1975-80, asso. prof., 1980—. Sec., Mo. Rhodes Scholarship Selection Com., 1976-81. Recipient Research Career Devel. award NIH, 1978. Mem. Am. Soc. Biol. Chemists, Am. Assn. Immunologists, Am. Alpine Club, Biophys. Soc., Am. Chem. Soc., AAAS, AAUP, N.Y. Acad. Scis., Phi Beta Kappa, Sigma Xi, Omicron Delta Kappa, Phi Lambda Upsilon, Pi Mu Epsilon, Delta Phi Alpha. Episcopalian. Contbr. articles to profl. jours. Home: 8341 Big Bend Webster Groves MO 63119 Office: Dept Biochemistry St Louis U Sch of Medicine 1402 S Grand Blvd Saint Louis MO 63104

BARK, MICHAEL AXEL, educator, hist. center ofcl.; b. Menomonie, Wis., Jan. 12, 1947; s. Axel Agustive and Margret Ellen (Solstad) B.; B.S. in Hotel and Restaurant Mgmt., U. Wis., Stout, 1972, Ed.S. in Vocat. Edn., 1975, M.S., 1979; m., June 5, 1971. Mgr., Laural Lodge, and recreation supr., instr., adv. Gt. Oaks Joint Vocat. Sch. Dist., Wilmington, Ohio, 1972-74; instr., adv., supr. Wis. Indianhead Tech. Inst., Ashland, Wis., 1972—, active planning, devel., operation of Tourism Center; supr. Ashland-Bayfield County Hist. Site and Indo. Center, 1976—; corr. tchr. U. Wis., 1980—. Trustee, stewardship mem. Presbyn Ch.; officer, com. mem. Wilmington Sch. Dist.; bd. dirs. New Horizons Developmental Center, Wis. Indian Head Country Inc. Served with U.S. Army, 1966-69. Named Outstanding Young Educator Laurel Oak Joint Vocat. Sch., 1974, recipient Outstanding Hospitality award, 1974. Mem. Am. Vocat. Assn., Wis. Assn. Vocat. Educators, Wis. Vocat. Bus. Edn. Assn., Wis. Fedn. Tchrs., NW Wis. Bus. Tchrs. Council, Bayfield County Recreation Assn., Lake Superior Shorelines Council, Am. Hotel and Motel Assn., Council on Hotel, Restaurant and Instl. Educators, Wis. Innkeepers Assn., Gt. Oaks Sch. Dist. Edn. Assn. Clubs: Cornucopia Yacht, Elks. Author various vocat. ednl. programs in hotel, motel and instl. mgmt. and tourism industry. Home: Route 1 Box 90A1 Washburn WI 54891 Office: 2100 Beaser Ave Ashland WI 54806

BARKATE, JOHN ALBERT, microbiologist, feed co. exec.; b. Sulphur, La., Dec. 4, 1936; s. Antoine and Victoria (Nagmay) B.; B.S. in Math., Northwestern State U., Natchitoches, La., 1959, M.S. in Microbiology, 1963; Ph.D. in Food Microbiology, La. State U., 1967; m. Vickie Ann Vick, Feb. 8, 1964; children—Barbara Anne, Michelle Lee, Marti Lynn, Catherine Jean. Vet. microbiologist Ga. Coastal Plains Experiment Sta., Tifton, Ga., 1964-65; mgr. microbiology dept. Ralston Purina Co., St. Louis, 1967-70; dir. microbiology dept., 1971—, asst. dir. central research, 1979—. Served with U.S. Army, 1959-60. Mem. Am. Mgmt. Assn., Am. Soc. for Microbiologists, Inst. Food Technologists, Indsl. Research Inst. Roman Catholic. Home: 7702 Devonshire St Saint Louis MO 63119 Office: Ralston Purina Co 835 S 8th St Saint Louis MO 63188

BARKER, BEVERLY JEAN, nurse; b. Dayton, Ohio, July 20, 1938; d. Obediah Lester and Frances Louise (Morehead) Brooks; R.N., Good Samaritan Hosp., Dayton, 1960; B.S. in Edn., U. Cin., 1975, M.S. in Edn., 1977; m. William L. Barker, Nov. 25, 1960; children—Stephanie, Terese, Leonard. Staff nurse Good Samaritan Hosp., Dayton, 1960-63, supr. ancillary personnel, 1963-66, asst. dir. nursing, 1966-69, acting dir. nursing, 1969; asst. dir. nursing, 1969-76, adminstrv. dir. nursing service, 1976—; instr. Dayton Sch. Practical Nursing, 1962. Bd. dirs. Heart Assn., 1978—, Hosp. of Dayton, 1979—; mem. Trotwood Citizen Response Com., 1978-79, Task Force Women's Career Devel., 1977-78. Named 1 of 5 Outstanding Career Women in Dayton Area, 1981. Mem. Am. Soc. Hosp. Nursing Service Adminstrs., Kappa Delta Pi. Democrat. Episcopalian. Home: 5012 Heatherton Dr Dayton OH 45426 Office: 2222 Philadelphia Dr Dayton OH 45406

BARKER, HUGH ALTON, electric utility co. exec.; b. Stillwater, Minn., Nov. 26, 1925; s. George Clarence and Minerva (Register) B.; B.B.A. with distinction, U. Minn., 1949; m. Janet M. Breitenbucher, Mar. 18, 1949; 1 dau., Pamela J. Prin., Haskins & Sells, C.P.A.'s, Mpls., 1949-58; asst. to exec. v.p. Pub. Service Ind., Plainfield, Ind., 1958-60, fin. v.p., 1960-68, exec. v.p., 1968-74, pres., 1974-80, chief exec. officer, 1977—, chmn. bd., 1980—, also dir.; dir. 1st Nat. Bank & Trust Co., Plainfield, Am. Fletcher Nat. Bank & Trust Co., Am. Fletcher Corp., Indpls. Mem. Ind. State Commn. on Tax and Financing Policy, 1969-73, chmn., 1971-73; bd. govs. Associated Colls. Ind.; mem. Ind. Local Govt. Property Tax Control Bd., 1973-74, Gov.'s Water Resources Study Commn., 1977-80; trustee Methodist Hosp., Indpls., 1974-81; bd. dirs. Edison Electric Inst., 1978-81. Served with AUS, 1944-45; ETO. C.P.A., Minn. Mem. Nat. Assn. Electric Cos. (dir. 1974-78, chmn. 1978), Ind. Mfrs. Assn. (dir.), Ind. Electric Assn. (dir., past pres.), Am. Inst. C.P.A.'s, Minn. Soc. C.P.A.'s, Ind. C. of C. (dir.), Sigma Alpha Epsilon, Beta Gamma Sigma. Clubs: Columbia, Indpls. Athletic; Union League (Chgo.). Home: Plainfield IN Office: 1000 E Main St Plainfield IN 46168

BARKER, KEITH RENE, investment banker; b. Elkhart, Ind., July 28, 1928; s. Clifford C. and Edith (Hausmna) B.; A.B., Wabash Coll, 1950; M.B.A., Ind. U., 1952; children (by previous marriage)—Bruce C., Lynn K.; m. 2d, Elizabeth S. Arrington, Nov. 24, 1965; 1 dau., Jennifer Scott. Sales rep. Fulton, Reid & Co., Inc., Ft. Wayne, Ind., 1951-55, office, 1955-59, asst. v.p., 1960, v.p., 1960, dir., 1961, asst. sales mgr., 1963, sales mgr., 1964, dir. Ind. ops.; sr. v.p. Fulton, Reid & Co., 1966-75; pres., chief exec. officer Fulton Reid & Staples, Inc., 1975-77; partner William C. Roney & Co., 1977-79; exec. com. Cascade Industries, Inc.; dir. Fulton, Reid & Staples, Inc., Nobility Homes, Inc. Pres. Historic Ft. Wayne, Inc.; cons. to Mus. Hist. Ft. Wayne; mem. Smithsonian Assos.; bd. dirs. Ft. Wayne YMCA, 1963-64. Served to lt. USNR, 1952-55. Recipient Achievement certificate Inst. Investment Banking, U. Pa., 1959. Mem. Ft. Wayne Hist. Soc. (v.p.), Alliance Française, V.F.W. (past comdr.), Co. Mil. Historians, Am. Soc. Arms Collectors, Phi Beta Kappa. Episcopalian. Mason. Clubs: Beaver Creek Hunt, Cleve. Athletic. Home: 351 Cranston Dr Berea OH 44017 Office: 800 Penton Plaza Cleveland OH 44114

BARKER, NANCY LEPARD, educator; b. Owosso, Mich., Jan. 22, 1936; d. Cecil L. and Mary Elizabeth (Stuart) Lepard; B.S., U. Mich. 1957; m. Richard William Barker, Nov. 18, 1972; children by previous marriage—Mary Georgia Cline, Mark Lepard Cline, Melissa Bess Cline, John Charles Cline; stepchildren—Daniel, Richard, Helen Grace, James, Wiley. Instr., U. Mich. Med. Center, Polio Rehab. Center and Burn Units of Hosp. Sch., Ann Arbor, 1958-61; v.p. Med-educator, Chgo., 1967-69; dir. Careers for Women, Northwood Inst., Midland, Mich., 1971-74, dir. spl. services and asst. to chmn., 1974-76, v.p., 1976—. State advisor Mich. Child Study Assn., 1972; chmn. Midland Art Council, 1964-66; bd. dirs. Midland Center for the Arts, 1971-77, active Midland Symphony League, Matrix Midland Festival. Named Midland's Outstanding Young Woman in Community Service, Midland Jr. C. of C., 1967; Disting. Woman, Northwood Inst., 1970. Mem. Nat. Council Women of U.S. (v.p., treas.), Nat. Home Fashions League (pres. Mich. chpt. 1979-81), Mich. Women's Studies Assn. (founding com.), Fashion Group, Career Women's Forum, Phi Gamma Nu, Delta Delta Delta, Phi Beta Kappa, Phi Kappa Phi, Alpha Lambda Delta, Phi Lambda Theta. Republican. Episcopalian. Clubs: Zonta, Contemporary Review, Midland County, Lawyers Wives. Author: (with John F. Welzenbach) Wendy Well and Bill Better series of books, 1970; mem. editorial bd. Woman's Life mag., 1981—. Home: 209 Revere Midland MI 48640 Office: 110 Sugnet Rd Midland MI 48640

BARKER, ROBERT OSBORNE, assn. exec.; b. Cleve., June 13,1932; s. Cecil E. and Barbara O. (Osborne) B.; student Henry Ford Community Coll., 1950; B.A. in Communication Arts and Sci., Mich. State U., 1954; student LaSalle U., 1966-68; children—Debra Jean, Stephen Robert. With public relations dept. Ford Motor Co., Dearborn, Mich., 1953; mgr. Kaiser Aluminum Co., Chgo., 1956-58; adminstrv. mgr. Bastian Blessing Co., Chgo., 1958-59; mgr. Sun Co., Detroit, 1959-71, Goodyear Tire & Rubber Co., Detroit, 1971-72; public affairs dir. NAM, Southfield, Mich., 1972—. Twp. trustee, Findlay, Ohio, 1962; bd. dirs. Dearborn Civic Theater, 1980—; City Beautiful commr., 1970—. Served with USNR, 1954-56. Named Outstanding Jaycee, Findlay, 1963. Mem. Public Relations Soc. Am., Mich. State U. Alumni (past pres.). Republican. Episcopalian. Clubs: Elks; Masons (master); Shriners. Home: PO Box 2231 (24514 Carlysle) Dearborn MI 48123 Office: 801 Northland Towers West Southfield MI 48075

BARKER, S(HIRLEY) HUGH, biol. scientist; b. Beloit, Wis., Nov. 27, 1915; s. Judson Thom and Shirley Brush (Campbell) B.; B.Ed., U. Wis., Whitewater, 1938; Ph.M., U. Wis., Madison, 1940, Ph.D., 1942; m. Dorothy Marian Erickson, Jan. 28, 1944; children—Ellen, Judson, Eldon. With St. Cloud (Minn.) State U., 1946—, prof. biol. scis., 1959-81. Served with AUS, 1942-43, with USAAF, 1943-46. Mem. AAAS, Minn. Gerontol. Soc., Minn. Human Genetics League, Sigma Xi. Office: Saint Cloud State Univ Dept of Biological Scis Saint Cloud MN 56301

BARKER, SUSAN LYNN WEST, psychologist; b. Holden, W.Va., May 3, 1948; s. Lee B. and Vurlia Dean (Hinkle) W.; A.A., Cowley County Community Jr. Coll., 1968; B.A., Emporia State U., 1970, M.S., 1972; children—Sara Allison, Patrick Hinkle. Psychologist alcoholism and drug abuse unit Osawatomie (Kans.) State Hosp., 1973—; tchr. corrections officer tng. Lansing (Kans.) State Penitentiary, 1978-79. Mem. Kans. Orgn. Profl. Psychologists. Democrat. Baptist. Office: Box 500 Osawatomie State Hosp Osawatomie KS 66064

BARKER, WALTER LEE, thoracic surgeon; b. Chgo., Sept. 9, 1928; s. Samuel Robert, M.D., and Esther (Meyerovitz) B.; A.B. cum laude, Harvard U., 1949, M.D., 1953; m. Betty Ruth Wood, Apr. 4, 1967. Intern, resident in gen. and thoracic surgery Cook County Hosp. and Presbyn. St. Luke's Med. Center and affiliated hosps., Chgo., 1953-62; practice medicine specializing in thoracic surgery, Chgo., 1962—; asso. clin. prof. surgery U. Ill.; head sect. thoracic surgery Cook County Hosp. Served with M.C., USNR, 1955-57. Diplomate Am. Bd. Surgery, Am. Bd. Thoracic Surgery. Fellow Am. Coll. Chest Physicians, A.C.S.; mem. Am. Assn. Thoracic Surgery, AMA, Boylston, Chgo., Ill. med. socs., Chest Club, Chgo., Ill., Central surg. socs., Inst. Medicine, Soc. Thoracic Surgeons (founding mem.), Sigma Xi. Author: The Post Operative Chest, 1977. Contbr. articles profl. jours. Research on tuberculosis, pleural infections, lung cancer. Home: 2912 N Commonwealth Ave Chicago IL 60657 Office: 2913 N Commonwealth Ave Chicago IL 60657

BARKIN, BEN, pub. relations cons.; b. Milw., June 4, 1915; s. Adolph and Rose Dora (Schumann) B.; student pub. schs.; m. Shirley Hinda Axel, Oct. 19, 1941; 1 son, Coleman. Nat. field dir. Jr. B'nai B'rith, 1937-41; cons. war finance dept. U.S. Treasury Dept., 1941-45; pub. relations cons. Ben Barkin & Asso., 1945-52; pres. Barkin, Herman, Solochek & Paulsen, Inc. and predecessor firm, Milw., N.Y.C., pub. relations counsel, 1952—; partner, dir. Milw. Brewers Baseball Club, Inc., 1970—. Bd. dirs., v.p., mem. exec. com. Mt. Sinai Med. Center, also chmn. corp. program; pres. Mt. Sinai Med. Center Found.; chmn. bd. trustees Athletes for Youth, Inc.; corp. mem. Milw. Children's Hosp., Columbia Hosp., United Way; mem. mgmt. adv. com. Milw. Urban League, We-Milwaukeeans, Greater Milw. Com.; bd. dirs. Nat. Com. against Discrimination in Housing, Inc., Mus. African Art, Washington; mem. civil rights exec. com. Anti-Defamation League; mem. music adv. panel orch. sect. Nat. Endowment for Arts. Named man of yr., Milw., 1945; recipient Knight of Bohemia award Milw. Press Club, 1978. Mem. Pub. Relations Soc. Am. (Paul Lund award 1978), NCCJ. Mem. B'nai B'rith (nat. chmn. youth commn. 1966-68). Home: 1610 N Prospect Ave Milwaukee WI 53202 Office: 777 E Wisconsin Ave Milwaukee WI 53202

BARKLEY, OWEN HERBERT, photographer; b. Muskegon Heights, Mich., Aug. 9, 1922; s. Kirk Delmont and Mabel Eva (Fowler) B.; student U.S. Navy Photo Sch., 1943, Nat. Camera Repair Sch., 1968; m. Karen Ann Gray, Nov. 13, 1965; children—Matthew Scott, Russell Dean, Jeffrey Wade. Served to chief photographer, USN, 1943-64; mem. photog. sales-service dept. Crescent Camera & Lithography Supply Corp., Kalamazoo, 1965-66; indsl. photographer Clark Equipment Co., Battle Creek, Mich., 1966-80; co-owner K & O Photography, Inc.; works exhibited nat. conv. Profl. Photographers Am., 1975, 79, featured in mag. article, 1976, 80. Pres. Village of Climax, Mich., 1976—. Mem. Profl. Photographers Am., Soc. Photog. Technologists, Am. Legion. Mason (pres. temple bd. assn. 1974); mem. Order Eastern Star (past patron), Order Eagles. Home: 126 N Main St Climax MI 49034 Office: 126 N Main St Climax MI 49034

BARKLEY, RUSSELL ALLAN, neuropsychologist; b. Newburgh, N.Y., Dec. 27, 1949; s. Donald S. and Mildred M. (Terbush) B.; A.A. summa cum laude, Wayne Community Coll., N.C., 1972; B.A. summa cum laude with honors in Psychology, U. N.C., 1973; M.A. in Clin. Psychology, Bowling Green State U., 1975, Ph.D., 1977; m. Patricia Marie Gann, Mar. 15, 1969. Predoctoral intern dept. med. psychology Child Devel. and Rehab. Center, U. Oreg. Med. Sch., Portland, 1976-77; asso. prof. dept. neurology and psychiatry Med. Coll. of Wis., Milw., 1977—; child neuropsychologist Milw. Children's Hosp., 1977—; exec. dir. Willow Glen adv. bd. Willow Glen Acad. for Autistic and Psychotic Children, 1979—. Served with USAF, 1968-72; Vietnam. NSF research grantee, 1974, 76; Med. Coll. Wis. grantee, 1978; NIMH research grantee, 1979; lic. psychologist, Wis. Mem. Am. Psychol. Assn., Midwestern Psychol. Assn., Wis. Psychol. Assn., Milw. County Psychol. Assn., Assn. for Advancement of Behavior Therapy, Soc. Pediatric Psychology, Sigma Xi. Author book on hyperactive children; contbr. numerous articles and revs. on child psychology to sci. jours., chpts. to books. Home: 2837 N 77th St Milwaukee WI 53222 Office: Neuropsychology Sect Med Coll Wis 9001 Watertown Plank Rd Wauwatosa WI 53226

BARLOW, F(RANK) JOHN, mech. contracting co. exec.; b. Milw., July 12, 1914; s. Ernest A. and Alice E. (Norton) B.; B.S. in Mech. Engring., U. Wis., 1937; m. Dorothy M. Marx, Oct. 13, 1935; children—Joyce D., Bonnie M., Joan C., Grace M., Jacqueline S.,

Wendy J., Terri L., Alice M. Engr., Buffalo Forge Co., 1937-40, sales engr., Chgo., 1940-42: plant engr. A.O. Smith Corp., Milw., 1942-44; chief mech. engr. Western Condensing Co., Appleton, Wis., 1944-46. prodn. mgr., 1946-53; owner Azco, Inc., Appleton, 1953—, pres., 1959—, pres. Sanco, Inc., Appleton, 1959—. Baldwin Barlow Corp., Appleton, 1965—, The Downey Co., Milw.; treas. Winagamie Corp., 1965—; dir. First Nat. Bank Appleton. County chmn. March of Dimes, 1957—, state co-chmn., 1958, industry chmn. com. fund dr., 1968-69. Bd. dirs., exec. com. Air Wis.; bd. dirs. Nat. Certified Pipe Welding Bur.; trustee Azco Employees Profit Sharing Trust. Recipient Industry award Wis. Soc. Profl. Engrs., 1967. Mem. Mech. Contractors Assn. Am. (nat. dir., pres. 1974-75), Mech. Contractors Assn. Wis. (pres.), Wis. Soc. Profl. Engrs. (chpt. pres. 1968—), Am. Soc. Heating, Refrigerations and Airconditioning Engrs., Appleton C. of C., ASCE, Flying Engrs., Civil Air Patrol, Nat. Soc. Profl. Engrs. Club: Butte Des Morts Golf (dir., pres. 1961, 62). Mason (Shriner). Rotarian, Elk (past exalted ruler). Home: 178 River Dr Appleton WI 54911 Office: PO Box 567 Appleton WI 54912

BARNARD, ELEANOR BETTY, public relations exec.; b. Chgo., Aug. 16, 1912; d. Harry S. and Lona Ruth (Brill) Spivak; Ph.B., U. Chgo., 1933, postgrad., 1936; m. Morton John Barnard, Aug. 16, 1936; 1 son, James W. Pres. Elbar Assos., public relations and advt., Winnetka, Ill., 1974—; vol., fundraiser law-related edn., 1974—; pres. Nat. Lawyers Wives and Husbands, 1976-77; bd. dirs. Chgo. project Constl. Rights Found.; mem. bd. sch. st. law project Loyola U. Law Sch., Chgo.; mem. standing com. Law-Related Edn. for Public, Ill. State Bar Assn.; mem. Ill. Commn. Edn. Law and Justice; vol. spl. com. youth edn. for citizenship Am. Bar Assn. Mem. LWV (asso. editor county bull. 1972-74), Sigma Delta Tau. Author articles, pamphlets in field; contbg. author: Building Bridges to the Law, 1981. Address: 228 Woodlawn Ave Winnetka IL 60093

BARNARD, KATHLEEN RAINWATER, educator; b. Wayne City, Ill., Dec. 28, 1927; d. Roy and Nina (Edmison) Rainwater; B.S., So. Ill. U., 1949, M.S., 1953; postgrad. Ind. U., 1953; Ph.D., U. Tex., 1959; m. Donald L. Barnard, Aug. 17, 1947 (div. Mar. 1973); children—Kimberly, Jill. Tchr. pub. high sch., Wayne City, Ill., 1946-51; faculty asst., lectr. Vocat. Tech. Inst., So. Ill. U., Carbondale, 1951-53; lectr. bus. edn. Northwestern U., Chgo., 1953-55; chmn. dept. bus. adminstrn. San Antonio Coll., 1955-60; chmn. dept. bus. edn. DePaul U., Chgo., 1960-62; chmn. dept. bus. Loop Coll., City Colls. Chgo., 1962-67, prof., 1968—, exec. sec., bd. dirs. credit union, 1975-78; cons., evaluator Ill. Program for Gifted Children, State Demonstrator Center, Oak Park (Ill.) Pub. Schs.; cons. First Nat. Bank Chgo., 1974; ednl. cons. Ency. Brit., 1969. Cons. edn. and tng. div. Continental Ill. Nat. Bank & Trust Co., Chgo., 1967, Victor Corp., 1965—; cons. IBM, Inc., summer 1968. Mem. Chgo. Assn. Commerce and Industry (edn. com.), North Central Bus. Edn. Assn., Nat. Bus. Edn. Assn., Delta Kappa Gamma, Pi Omega Pi, Alpha Delta Pi (sponsor), Sigma Phi (sponsor), Delta Pi Epsilon (pres. Alpha Theta chpt. 1958). Contbg. author: College Typewriting, 1960; Business Correspondence, 1962. Home: 920 Courtland Ave Park Ridge IL 60068 Office: 64 E Lake St Chicago IL 60601

BARNES, BILL LLOYD, clergyman, sem. ofcl.; b. Kansas City, Mo., July 16, 1926; s. William Lloyd and Augusta (Moore) B.; B.A., Drake U., 1948; M.Div., Christian Theol. Sem., 1952; M.S., Butler U., 1957; m. Shirley Nadine Malone, Oct. 9, 1945; children—Judith Diane (Mrs. Robert Stall), Janis Caryl (Mrs. Kent Barnard). Student minister in Kellogg, Iowa, 1946-48, Indpls., 1948-52; ordained to ministry Disciples of Christ Ch., 1947; minister in St. Louis, 1952-60; dir. devel. Christian Theol. Sem., Indpls., 1960-67, v.p. devel., 1967—. Mem. home and state missions planning council Disciples of Christ 1956-60; sec. Mo. Disciples State Conv., 1954; evangelism rep. St. Louis Met. Ch. Fedn., 1956; pres. St. Louis Ministers, 1957, Disciple Ministers, 1959; substitute tchr. TV program Lessons for Living, Sta. WTTV, Indpls., 1962-65; ministerial enlistment chmn. St. Louis Counseling Center, 1959; mem. Ch. Fedn. New Direction Com., 1973, 74. Mem. bd. higher edn. Disciples of Christ, 1961—, chmn. Ind. inter agy. com., 1971-75, chmn. askings commn., 1972-73; chmn. time place com. Indiana Christian Church Conv., 1964-66. Community relations representative YMCA, St. Louis, 1955; institutional rep. Boy Scouts Am., St, Louis, 1955-60; mem. Indpls. Urban Forum Series Com., 1969-70. Served with USAAF, 1945. A Seminarian of Year Sermon contest winner Pulpit mag., 1951, 52; recipient Distinguished Alumnus award Christian Theol. Sem., 1975. Mem. Sem. Mgmt. Assn. (pres. 1972-74), Hoosier Power Squadron (chaplain 1971—), Theta Phi. Kiwanian. Clubs: Riviera, Indpls. Athletic. Contbr. articles and Sunday Sch. lessons to religious publs. Home: 411 Braeside South Dr Indianapolis IN 46260 Office: 1000 W 42d St Indianapolis IN 46208

BARNES, BRUCE ERNEST, mktg. exec.; b. Lowville, N.Y., June 16, 1949; s. Earle Ernest and Marion L. (Sunderhaft) B.; B.S., Syracuse U., 1972; M.B.A., Fairleigh Dickinson U., 1974; m. Candyce A. Boutin, Oct. 25, 1980. Sales rep. N.Y. area Warner-Lambert Co., Morris Plains, N.J., 1972-74; mktg. staff asst. Colgate Palmolive, Internat. div., N.Y.C., 1974-75, internat. product mgr. Household Products div., 1975-78; product mgr. new products Swift & Co., Chgo., 1978-79, sales planning merchandising mgr., 1979, product mgr. C.P.D. div., 1979, product mgr. Strongheart Pet Products, new products Derby Foods, 1979-81; gen. mgr. Skilcraft div. Monogram Models Inc., Morton Grove, Ill., 1981—. Co-chmn. Syracuse U. ann. fund raising, 1975. Club: Syracuse U. Alumni. Home: 555 W Cornelia Chicago IL 60657 Office: 8601 Waukegan Rd Morton Grove IL 60053

BARNES, BRUCE FRANCIS, cons. engr.; b. Evanston, Ill., Nov. 18, 1926; s. Bruce Francis and Ruth Evelyn (Achuff) B.; B.M.E., Washington U., St. Louis, 1949; m. Gwendolyn Lou Gnaegy, Feb. 17, 1951; children—Sharon Anne Barnes Koch, Steven Bruce. With Fairbanks Morse Engine div. Colt Industries, Beloit, Wis., 1949-68, area sales mgr. St. Louis, 1960-68; asso. Warren & Van Praag, Inc., St. Louis, 1969-72; pres., gen. mgr. Barnes, Henry, Meisenheimer & Gende, Inc., St. Louis, 1972—. Mem. adminstrv. bd. Webster Hills United Meth. Ch., 1968—. Served with USAF, 1944-45. Recipient Order of the Arrow, Boy Scouts Am., 1967. Mem. Nat., Mo. socs. profl. engrs., ASME, Engrs. Club St. Louis. Clubs: Pachyderm, Mo. Athletic. Home: 1503 Azalea Dr Webster Groves MO 63119 Office: 4658 Gravois Ave Saint Louis MO 63116

BARNES, CHARLES MCDONALD, coll. pres.; b. Balt., Oct. 15, 1917; s. Charles McDonald and Florence Margaret (Boyle) B.; B.S., Kans. State U., 1950, M.S., 1950; m. Nellie Ellen Dorsey, July 6, 1940; 1 son, Roger Clifford. Asst. exec. dean Ft. Scott (Kans.) Jr. Coll., 1950-56; exec. dean Pratt (Kans.) Jr. Coll., 1956-59; exec. dean Dodge City (Kans.) Community Coll., 1959-65, pres., 1965—; cons., examiner North Central Assn. Colls. and Schs., 1966—. Served with AUS, 1943-46; ETO. Recipient Phillips award as outstanding alumnus Kans. State U., Pittsburg, 1975. Mich. State U. fellow, 1961; Danforth Found. grantee, 1971. Mem. Council North Central Community Jr. Colls., Kans. Assn. Community Colls. (award of merit 1978). Democrat. Methodist. Club: Dodge City Rotary (pres. 1955-56). Home: 2514 Thompson St Dodge City KS 67801 Office: 14th and By Pass 50 Dodge City KS 67801

BARNES, EARLE B., corp. exec.; b. 1917; m. B.S., Tex. Christian U., 1938; M.S., U. Nebr., 1940. With Dow Chem. Co., 1940—, gen. mgr. Tex. div., 1961-67, dir. corp. mfg., engring. and maintenance, 1967-68, corporate v.p., gen. mgr. U.S. area, 1968-71, mem. corporate exec. com., pres. Dow Chem. U.S.A., 1971-75, corporate exec. v.p., mem. exec. com., 1975-79, chmn., 1979—; dir. Dow Corning Corp. Office: Dow Chem Co 2030 Dow Center Midland MI 48640

BARNES, FRANCES HENRY, educator; b. Norwood, Mo., Dec. 23, 1931; d. Ralph and Alice (Sturgis) Henry; B.S. in Edn., S.W. Mo. State U., 1959; M.A. in Edn., S.E. Mo. State U., 1974; postgrad. So. Ill. U.; m. Clarence E. Barnes; children—Robert E., Carlena Sue, Quentin L., Victoria Kathryn Ann. Recreational therapist St. Vincent's Hosp., St. Louis, 1960; ednl. therapist St. Louis State Hosp., 1961-66; tchr. 2d grade St. John's Luth. Sch., Chester, Ill., 1969-71; remedial reading tchr. Perryville (Mo.) Elementary Sch., 1973-79; adult basic edn. tchr. Menard (Ill.) Correctional Center, 1979—. First v.p. Chester Meml. Hosp. Aux., 1972-74. Mem. Mo. State Tchrs. Assn., Council for Basic Edn., Internat. Reading Assn., Adult and Continuing Educators Assn., Ill. Adult and Continuing Edn. Assn., Internat. Reading Assn., Kappa Delta Pi, Phi Delta Kappa. Developed self checking aids for individualized teaching. Cert. in elem. teaching, lang. art edn., sch. adminstrn., also reading specialist, Ill.; in elementary teaching, art and reading, sch. adminstrn., Mo. Home: PO Box 627 Chester IL 62233 Office: School Bldg Menard Correctional Center Menard IL

BARNES, FRANCIS MERRIMAN, III, state legislator, lawyer; b. St. Louis, July 19, 1918; s. Francis M. and Carlotta (Kimlin) B.; A.B., U. Mo., 1941; LL.B., Washington U., 1948; m. Mary Shore Johnson, Oct. 16, 1948; children—Elizabeth J., Francis Merriman, Barbara Anne. Admitted to Mo. bar, 1947; asst. city counselor City of St. Louis, 1948-49; atty. Southwestern Bell Telephone Co., St. Louis, 1949-51, Gaylord Container Corp., St. Louis, 1951-59; sr. v.p. Crown Zellerbach Corp., San Francisco, 1959-73; state rep. State of Mo., Jefferson City, 1977—. Mem. Gov. Reagan's Com. to Reform Tax Laws, 1968-69; bd. dirs. St. Louis YMCA, 1975—; trustee St. Louis Art Mus., 1976-79, Mo. Hist. Soc., 1978—. Served with U.S. Army, 1941-46. Mem. St. Louis Bar Assn., Mo. Bar Assn., Am. Bar Assn. Republican. Presbyterian. Editor, Kirkwood (Mo.) Hist. Rev., 1980—. Home: 217 S Woodlawn Ave Kirkwood MO 63122 Office: 101 State Capitol Jefferson City MO 65101

BARNES, HYLAND JAY, lock mfg. co. exec.; b. Milw., Mar. 11, 1916; s. Samuel and Lina (Hirschberg) Bernstein; B.A., U. Wis., 1937; m. Shirley Dulberger, Apr. 27, 1941; children—Marsha, Martin. With Master Lock Co., Milw., 1940—, v.p. mktg., 1965-73, pres., 1973-78, chief operating officer, 1973-74, chief exec. officer, 1974—, chmn., 1978—; dir. Am. Brands, Inc. Pres., Milw. Jewish Convalescent Center, 1981—; trustee Citizens Govt. Research Bur., Milw., 1977—. Mem. Mgmt. Resources Assn. (dir. 1974-79, chmn. 1977-78), Hardware Mktg. Council, Nat. Wholesaler Hardware Assn., Nat. Assn. Hardware Mfrs., So. Wholesaler Hardware Assn. Jewish. Mem. editorial adv. bd. Locksmith Ledge Mag., 1977—. Contbr. articles to profl. jours. Office: 2600 N 32d St Milwaukee WI 53210

BARNES, JAMES ALLEN, state legislator; b. Kansas City, Mo., Dec. 4, 1951; s. Lecil H. and Dorris E. (Rawlings) B.; B.A., Rockhurst Coll., 1975; m. Kathleen Ann Hale, Aug. 19, 1977; 1 dau., Jacqueline Celeste. Research analyst Mo. Council for Econ. Devel., Jefferson City, Mo., 1975-78; mem. Mo. Ho. of Reps., 1978—. Vice pres. Raytown (Mo.) Democratic Assn., 1977-78; committeeman Brooking Twp. Dem. Com., 1978-80; mem. hon. bd. dirs. Rockhurst Coll.; bd. govs. Park Lane Hosp. Recipient Disting. Service award Raytown Jaycees, 1980. Mem. Raytown Area C. of C., Nat. Rifle Assn. Democrat. Mem. Christian Ch. Club: Rotary. Office: State Capitol Bldg Jefferson City MO 65101

BARNES, JOHN JAMES INGALLS, utilities co. exec.; b. Detroit, July 4, 1936; s. Russell Curtis and Ruth Constance (Ingalls) B.; A.B. in Econs., Harvard U., 1958; 1 son, Andrew Harrison. Trainee, Ford div. Ford Motor Co., 1961-63; research analyst, copywriter J. Walter Thompson, Detroit, 1963-65; copywriter Gray & Kilgore Advt., 1965-67; sr. copywriter: creative supr. Young & Rubicam Advt., Atlanta and Detroit, 1967-70; creative dir. Detroit News, 1970-74; gen. adminstrv. asst., mgr. advt. and sales promotion Mich. Bell Yellow Pages, Detroit, 1974—. Mem. Friends of Modern Art, Founders Soc. of Detroit Inst. Arts. Episcopalian. Club: Cranbrook Indoor Tennis. Home: 159 Marlborough Dr Bloomfield Hills MI 48013 Office: 882 Oakman Detroit MI 48238

BARNES, JOHN MCGREGOR, geologist; b. Ann Arbor, Mich., July 16, 1929; s. John McGregor and Doris Katherine (Arnold) B.; B.S. in Geology, U. Mich., 1951, M.S., 1953; postgrad. U. Evansville (Ind.), Ind. State U.; m. Catherine Roney, Sept. 6, 1953 (div.); children—James, David, William. Geologist, Carter Oil Co., 1953-58; owner, operator Mid-States Cons. Corp., Evansville, 1958-69; asst. prof. geology-geography Ind. State U., Evansville, 1969—; speaker, cons., adv. in field. Pres. McCutchanville Community Assn., 1960. Mem. Am. Assn. Petroleum Geologists, Fedn. Am. Scientists, Ind.-Ky. Geol. Soc. (pres. 1978), Ind. Sierra Club (exec. com. 1978—), Big Rivers Geol. Soc., Ind. Acad. Scis., Cousteau Soc., Nat. Audubon Soc., Wilderness Soc., Friends of Earth, Sigma Gamma Epsilon. Episcopalian. Author papers in field. Home: 91 Browning Rd Evansville IN 47711 Office: 8600 University Blvd Evansville IN 47712

BARNES, LOIS SANDVEN, govt. ofcl.; b. York, N.D., June 8, 1921; d. Kittle Bernhard and Elvira (Trandum) Sandven; B.A., Concordia Coll., Moorhead, Minn., 1943; M.A. in Public Adminstrn. (HEW grantee), U. Minn., 1970. Bookkeeper various cos., Washington and Rugby, N.D., 1946-56; claims rep. Social Security Adminstrn., Minot, N.D., 1956-68, claims rep., Devils Lake, N.D., 1973—; intern Ramsey County (Minn.) Dept. Welfare, 1969, Minn. State Dept. Welfare, St. Paul, 1969, aging program OEO, Washington, 1970. Mem. AAUW, Am. Acad. Polit. and Social Sci., Nat. Fedn. Bus. and Profl. Women, Beta Sigma Phi. Republican. Lutheran. Clubs: Sons of Norway, 400 of Concordia Coll., 1200 of N.D. Home: Route 1 Box 38 York ND 58386

BARNES, MICHAEL DENNIS, coal mining co. exec.; b. San Antonio, Tex., Jan. 26, 1948; s. William David and Mildred Boatner (Crosley) B.; B.S. in Mech. Engring., Mont. State U., 1972; A. in Mechanics and Welding, No. Mont. Coll., 1969; m. Carol Ann Faller, June 17, 1972; children—Shaina, Ian, Rachel. Mechanic, partsman, engr. Long Constrn. Co., Colstrip, Mont., 1972-77; master mechanic Arch Minerals Corp., Hanna, Wyo., 1977-78; mech. engr., constrn. supt. N.Am. Coal Co., Bismarck, N.D., 1978—. Den leader, com. chmn. Big Sky council Boy Scouts Am., 1972-77; vol. fireman City of Colstrip, 1973—. Mem. Assn. Emergency Care Technicians, Nat. Registry Emergency Med. Technicians. Roman Catholic. Clubs: Elks, Lions. Home: 1021 1st Ave NW Hazen ND 58545 Office: Kirkwood Office Towers North American Coal Bismarck ND 58501

BARNES, MYRON BRUCE, museum dir.; b. Tiffin, Ohio, Oct. 23, 1906; s. Allen and Grace (Tucker) B.; B.A., Heidelberg Coll., Tiffin, 1928, B.Mus., 1931; M.A., Western Res. U., 1939. Tchr. Latin, English and history in pvt. schs., 1934-42; counseling psychologist VA, 1946-64; dir., historian Seneca County Mus., Tiffin, 1976—; a founder, cons. Tiffin Historic Trust. Served with U.S. Army, 1942-46. Mem. Ohio Hist. Soc., Hayes Hist. Soc. Republican. Episcopalian. Author: Bicentennial Sketches, 1976, History of Tiffin and Seneca County, 1880-1976, 1979. Home: 73 Frost Pkwy Tiffin OH 44883 Office: Seneca County Museum 28 Clay St Tiffin OH 44883

BARNES, ROBERT MERTON, artist; b. Washington, Sept. 24, 1934; s. Mahlon Willis and Marjorie (Bain) B.; B.F.A., Art Inst. Chgo., 1956; B.F.A., U. Chgo., 1956; postgrad. Columbia U., 1956, Hunter Coll., 1957-60, U. London Slade Sch., 1961-63; m. Lia Sayers, Sept. 22, 1956 (div. Aug., 1971); children—Catlin Sayers, Forres McKay; m. 2d, Nancy Jean Morgan, June 10, 1972; children—Corby Morgan, Victoria Fabrizia. Exhibited in one man shows at Allan Frumkin Gallery, N.Y.C., 1963, 65, 66-67, 77, 79, Chgo., 1961-64, 71, 75, 78, Gallerie du Dragon, Paris, 1966-67, U. Ill., 1967, Kansas City Art Inst., 1972, Galeria Fanta Spado, Rome, Italy, 1972, 73, Museo Civico Arezzo, 1973, Le Parisina Torino, 1973; exhibited in group shows Art Inst. Chgo., 1955, 58, 60, 61, 63, Exhbn. Momentum, 1952-55, Cliff Dwellers Print Exhbn., Chgo., 1955, U. Chgo., 1956, Rockford Coll., 1956, Boston Arts Festival, 1958, U. Iowa, 1960, U. Colo., 1961, Am. Fedn. Arts Traveling Exhbn., 1961, David Herbert Gallery, N.Y.C., 1961, Ravinia Exhbn., 1961, U. Ind., 1961, Galerie Du Dragon, Paris, 1962, Whitney Mus. Am. Art, 1962-65, Yale U., 1962, Kansas City Art Inst., 1962-63, Allan Frumkin Gallery, Chgo., N.Y.C., 1960, 63, San Francisco Mus. Fine Arts, 1963, Mus. Modern Art, N.Y.C., 1963, 65, Exhbn. Palazzo-D'Accursio, Bologna, 1965, Ind. U. Mus., 1965, Larry Aldrich Mus., 1965, Pa. Acad. Fine Art, 1965, 66, Va. Mus. Fine Arts, 1966, Burpee Art Gallery, 1965, R.I. Sch. Design, 1965, 66, Parrish Art Mus., 1965, Am. Fedn. Arts Exhbn., 1971, Mus. Contemporary Art, Chgo., 1972, Boston U., 1975; represented in permanent collections: Mus. Modern Art, Whitney Mus. Am. Art, Chgo. Art Inst., Pasadena Mus. Art; mem. faculty Ind. U., summer 1960-61, asso. prof., 1965-70, prof., after, 1970—; vis. artist Kansas City Art Inst., 1963-64. Recipient award Copley Found., 1961; Guri Siever award Chgo. Art Inst., 1963; Child Hasaam award Am. Acad. Arts and Letters, 1971. Fulbright grantee, 1961-62, 62-63. Office: Dept Fine Art Indiana Univ Bloomington IN 47401*

BARNES, SAMUEL EDWARD, mech. engr.; b. Somerset, Ky., Oct. 20, 1932; s. Theo A. and Jocie Katherine (Williams) B.; B.S. in Mech. Engring., U. Cin., 1957; m. Florence Ladell Banks, Aug. 30, 1952; children—Douglas Edward, Sandra Lee, Constance Susan, Patricia Ann. Engr., Gen. Electric Aircraft Gas Turbines, Evendale, Ohio, 1952-58; editor Machine Design Mag., Cleve., 1960-69; supr. documentation and promotion Cin. Milacron Co., Lebanon, Ohio, 1969-71; editor Design News Mag., Chgo., 1972; engr. Landco Inc., Worthington, Ohio, 1973-74; pres. Cadmus Constrn. Co., Worthington, 1974-76; systems engr., mgr. tech. support group Div. of Water, City of Columbus (Ohio), 1976—; cons. on water treatment systems, instruments and computer automation. Campaign coordinator Franklin County Engr., 1976. Recipient Meritorious Service award Lakewood Aquamasters, 1968; registered profl. engr., Ohio, Ind., Ky.; lic. broadcaster FCC. Mem. Nat. Soc. Profl. Engrs., Am. Water Works Assn., Instrument Soc. Am. Baptist. Club: Franklin County Forum. Patentee liquid carbon dioxide feeding system; contbr. numerous articles in field to profl. jours.; author/editor: Bearings Book, 1961; Hydraulics Book, 1962. Office: 940 Dublin Rd Columbus OH 43215

BARNETT, BEATRICE ANN, ednl. adminstr.; b. Okeana, Ohio, July 10, 1942; d. Earl Don and Helen Louise (Handy) Loos; B.S., Youngstown State U., 1964; M.Ed., Ohio U., 1978, postgrad., 1979-81; m. David Barnett, Aug. 6, 1966; children—Brian, Beth. Tchr., West Branch Local Sch. Dist., Beloit, Ohio, 1964-67, Jefferson Local Sch. Dist., Gahanna, Ohio, 1968-70, Teays Valley Local Sch. Dist., Ashville, Ohio, 1974-79, Groveport (Ohio) Madison Local Sch., 1979-80; asst. prin. Groveport Freshman Sch., 1980-81, Groveport Madison High Sch., 1981—; cons. individualized instrn. workshop. Mem. Assn. Supervision and Curriculum Devel., Nat. Assn. Secondary Sch. Prins., Ohio Assn. Secondary Sch. Adminstrs. Club: Order Eastern Star (worthy matron 1978). Home: 9698 State Route 752 Ashville OH 43103 Office: 4475 S Hamilton Rd Groveport OH 43125

BARNETT, DON BLAIR, plumbing contractor; b. Mt. Vernon, Ohio, Oct. 21, 1921; s. Homer V. and Bessie (Skeels) B.; student public schs., LaRue, Ohio; m. Virginia V. Ireland, June 24, 1943; children—James, Faye. Maintenance and supervision positions Perfection Steel Body Co., Galion, Ohio, 1942-44; owner, operator Barnett Plumbing and Hearing, Galion, 1948—. Active, Jehovah's Witness Ch., supr. installation and maintenance, nat. and internat. convs., 1950—. Mem. Galion Plumbing Contractors Assn., Christian Labor Union Assn. Home and Office: 127 Wilson Ave Galion OH 44833

BARNETT, JOSEPH H., state legislator; b. Sioux Falls, S.D., Nov. 3, 1931; s. William H. and Julia R. (Gurtel) B.; B.A. magna cum laude, Coll. St. Thomas, 1953; LL.B., U. S.D., 1957; m. Kathleen Bolger, Feb. 23, 1954; children—Joseph P., John, Paul, Sheila, Rita Teresa, William, James, Patricia. Admitted to S.D. bar, 1957; law clk. U.S. Dist. Ct. for S.D., 1957-58; partner firm Siegel, Barnett, Schutz, O'Keefe, Jewett & King, Aberdeen, S.D., 1958—; mem. S.D. Ho. of Reps. from Brown County, 1967—, speaker pro tem, 1971-73, minority leader, 1973-74, speaker, 1975-76, majority leader, 1979—; mem. S.D. Bd. Bar Examiners, 1963-70, chmn., 1967-70. Trustee U. S.D. Law Sch. Found. Served with AUS, 1953-55. Republican. Home: 1411 N 4th St Aberdeen SD 57401 Office: PO Box 1269 Aberdeen SD 57401

BARNETT, MARILYN, advt. agy. exec.; b. Detroit, June 10, 1932; d. Henry and Kate (Boesky) Schiff; B.A., Wayne State U., 1953; children—Rhona, Ken. Supr. broadcast prodn. Northgate Advt. Agy., Detroit, 1968-73; founder, part-owner, exec. v.p. Mars Advt. Co., Southfield, Mich., 1973—. Mem. AFTRA (dir. 1959-67), Adcraft. Women's Adcraft. Office: 18470 W Ten Mile Rd Southfield MI 48075

BARNETT, MARK ALLAN, psychologist; b. Chgo., Sept. 7, 1949; s. Robert and Mona R. (Meyer) B.; B.A., Northwestern U., 1971, Ph.D., 1975; m. Camille Gailani, Mar. 15, 1979. Mem. faculty dept. psychology Kans. State U., Manhattan, 1975—, asso. prof., 1980—. Mem. Am. Psychol. Assn., Midwestern Psychol. Assn., Soc. Research Child Devel., Southwestern Soc. Research Human Devel. Contbr. articles to profl. jours. Cons. editor profl. jours. Office: Dept Psychology Kans State U Manhattan KS 66506

BARNETT, RALPH LIPSEY, mech. engr.; b. Chgo., July 15, 1933; B.C.E., Ill. Inst. Tech., 1955, M.S. in Mechanics, 1958; married; 2 children. Asso. research engr. structural mechanics Armour Research Found., Chgo., 1955-60; evening instr. civil engring. Ill. Inst. Tech.; structural research engr. research and devel. dept. Stanray Corp., Chgo., 1960-62; sr. research engr., group leader Ill. Inst. Tech. Research Inst., Chgo., 1962-68; evening instr. mech. and aerospace engring. Ill. Inst. Tech., 1967-69, mem. faculty full time, 1969—, prof. mech. and aerospace engring., 1969—; dir. research and devel., dir. rubber lab., dir. indsl. chemistry lab. Felt Products Mfg. Co., Skokie,

Ill., 1968-69; chmn. bd. Triodyne, Inc., cons. engr., Skokie, 1972—. CECO Steel Co. scholar, 1953; Armour Research Found. research fellow, 1955. Mem. Am. Acad. Mechanics, ASCE (Collingwood prize 1960, Prize paper Chgo. sect. 1962), ASME, Am. Concrete Inst., Am. Soc. Safety Engrs., Nat. Safety Council, Graphic Arts Tech. Found., Am. Soc. Metals, Am. Nat. Standards Inst., Am. Soc. Engring. Edn., AAUP, Sigma Xi, Chi Epsilon, Pi Tau Sigma, Tau Beta Pi. Author papers, chpts. in books. Address: 2721 Alison Ln Wilmette IL 60091

BARNETT, ROBERT EUGENE, veterinarian; b. Kirksville, Mo., Aug. 18, 1947; s. Cleo Barnett and Ruby Barnett Lindquist; D.V.M., U. Mo., 1971; m. Doris Irene Mauck, Aug. 19, 1967; 1 dau., Martha Jane. Gen. practice veterinary medicine, Fulton, Mo., 1971—, specializing in equine medicine, surgery, Fulton, 1971—; lectr., mem. staff William Woods Coll., Fulton, 1973—. Chmn. Legis. Com. Fulton, 1977—. Mark Morris fellow, 1968; W. Central V.M.A. Leadership award, 1968; Groth Research award, 1970. Mem. AVMA, Am. Animal Hosp. Assn., Am. Assn. Equine Practitioners, Veterinary Med. Assn., Soc. Theriogenology, Assn. Veterinary Anesthesiologists, Am. Assn. Animal Welfare Veterinarians, Veterinary Med. Assn. E. Mo., Mo. C. of C., dir. 1977). Club: Fulton Morning Optimist. Home and Office: Highway 54 S Fulton MO 65251

BARNETT, ROBERT FULTON, JR., radiologist; b. Pitts., Feb. 7, 1929; s. Robert Fulton and Mary Elizabeth (Henry) B.; A.B., Princeton U., 1946-50; M.D., U. Pa., 1954; m. Elizabeth Sherwood McConnel, June 21, 1952; children—Katherine, Robert, William, James. Intern, Henry Ford Hoso., Detroit, 1954-55; communicable disease officer Los Angeles County (Calif.) Health Dept., 1957-58; resident in radiology U. Mich., Ann Arbor, 1958-61; practice medicine specializing in radiology, Grayling, Mich., 1961-69, Cadillac, Mich., 1961—; clin. instr. radiology, U. Mich., 1960-61; cons. in field; dir. radiology, nuclear medicine Mercy Hosp., Cadillac; cons. med. arts. group, Cadillac; dir. 1st Nat. Bank of Evart (Mich.), West Mich. Fin. Corp., Cadillac State Bank. Served with M.C., USN, 1955-57. Diplomate Am. Bd. Radiology. Mem. AMA, Mich. State, Wexford-Missaukee County (sec. 1963-64, pres. 1964-65) med. secs., W. Mich., Mich. radiol. secs., Am. Coll. Radiology, F.J. Hodges Radiology Soc., Phi Beta Kappa. Republican. Presbyterian. Home: 1000 Stimson St Cadillac MI 49601 Office: Mercy Hosp Cadillac MI 49601

BARNETT, WILLIAM A., lawyer; b. Chgo., Oct. 13, 1916; s. Leo James and Anita (Olsen) B.; LL.B., Loyola U., Chgo., 1941; m. Evelyn Yates, June 23, 1945; children—William, Mary Leone (Mrs. John J. Fahey), Therese, Kathleen (Mrs. William D. Norwood). Admitted to Ill. bar, 1941; with U.S. IRS, 1948-54, atty. chief counsel's office, Chgo., 1948-52, dist. counsel penal div., Detroit, 1952-54; chief tax atty. U.S. Atty's Office, Chgo., 1955-60; practitioner before the 6th Circuit Court of Appeals, since 1954, 7th Circuit Ct. Appeals, since 1955, U.S. Supreme Ct., since 1959. Mem. Am., Fed., Ill. and 7th Circuit bar assns., Am. Judicature Soc., Nat. Assn. Criminal Def. Lawyers, Ill. Trial Lawyers Assn. Home: 1448 Norwood St Chicago IL 60660 Office: 135 S LaSalle St Chicago IL 60603

BARNETTE, EMMA CHRISTINE HANSEN (MRS. FOSTER I. BARNETTE), bottling co. cons.; b. Omaha; d. Jens Nielsen and Laurentine C. (Larsen) Hansen; student pub. schs.; m. Foster I. Barnette, Aug. 23, 1930. Dress designer M.E. Smith Co., Omaha, 1917-20, Ely Walker Dry Goods, St. Louis, 1920-33, Carson Pirie Scott Co., Chgo., 1933-35, Lee Garment Co., Chgo., 1935-40; v.p., treas. Pepsi-Cola Bottling Co., Rockford, Ill., 1945-73, cons., 1973—. Presbyterian. Club: Quota. Home: 23 Country Club Beach Rockford IL 61103 Office: 4622 Hydraulic St Rockford IL 61108

BARNETTE, HARRIETTE LOUISE AMOS (MRS. LEWIS FREDERICK BARNETTE), bookseller; b. Chgo., July 20, 1912; d. Gilbert Bitters and Harriette Louise (Medicus) Amos; student Western Mich. U., 1930-32; m. Lewis Frederick Barnette, Aug. 10, 1942; 1 son, William Amos (dec.). Owner Barnette's Books, specializing in antiquarian Americana, South Bend, Ind., 1962—. Mem. Am. Printing History Assn., Bibliog. Soc. Am., Ind. Hist. Soc. Address: 22727 Adams Rd South Bend IN 46628

BARNHART, GENE, lawyer; b. Pineville, W. Va., Dec. 22, 1928; s. Forrest H. and Margaret (Harshman) B.; student W.Va. U., 1946-48; student Coll. Steubenville, 1949-50; J.D., U. Cin., 1953; m. Shirley L. Dunn, Jan. 28, 1952; children—Sheryl Lynne (Mrs. John Dickey), Deborah Lee (Mrs. Kim Orians), Taffie Elise, Pamela Carole, Margaret Melanie. Admitted to Ohio bar, 1953; counsel clothing br. Armed Services Procurement Agy., Washington, Phila., 1953-55; asso. firm Black, McCuskey, Souers & Arbaugh, Canton, Ohio, 1955-60, partner, 1961—; lectr. Ohio Legal Center Inst., Ohio Bar Assn., Am. Inst. Banking. Mem. Jackson Local Bd. Edn., 1966-74, pres., 1970; mem. Jackson Twp. Bd. Zoning Appeals, 1964—, chmn., 1978—; vice-chmn. Jackson Zoning Ordinance Revision Com.; mem. community planning com. United Way of Central Stark County; past pres. Council of Chs. of Central Stark County; past pres. Family Counseling Services Central Stark County; com. chmn. Congressional Action Com., Greater Canton Chamber; trustee United Way of Central Stark County, Canton Preservation Soc., Interfaith Campus Ministry Kent State-Stark Regional Campus, Cancer Edn. and Research Found. Served with USNR, 1948-49. Mem. Stark County (grievance, disputed fee, voluntary pro bond coms.), Ohio State (legal edn. com., com. legal specialization), Am. bar assns., Order of Coif; Phi Alpha Delta. Mem. Calvary Chapel (elder, choir). Home: 2805 Coventry Ln NW Canton OH 44708 Office: 1200 Harter Bank Bldg Canton OH 44702

BARNI, EDWARD JOSEPH, social worker; b. St. Louis, July 24, 1949; s. Edward John and Josephine Marie (Bolazina) B.; B.A., St. Louis U., 1971, M.S.W., 1974. With alcohol-related traffic offender program Div. Adult Probation and Parole, County of St. Louis, Mo., 1974-77, supr., 1976-77; alcohol programs coordinator Safety Council Greater St. Louis, 1977—. Sec. Mut. Activities for Traffic Enforcement, St. Louis, 1978; treas. Alcoholism Coalition of St. Louis, 1979, v.p., 1980; featured speaker Gov.'s Conf. on Hwy. Safety, 1981. Served with Army N.G., 1970-76. Recipient Outstanding Vol. award St. Louis Area chpt. Nat. Council on Alcoholism, 1980; 2-time nominee Helen B. Madden award St. Louis Council on Alcoholism; cert. alcoholism counselor. Mem. Nat. Assn. Social Workers, Acad. Cert. Social Workers, Mo. Assn. Alcoholism Counselors. Democrat. Roman Catholic. Author articles in field. Home: 2832 Hereford Saint Louis MO 63139 Office: 1015 Locust St Saint Louis MO 63101

BARNO, DOUGLAS SANDEN, mfg. co. exec.; b. Berea, Ohio, Aug. 27, 1941; s. Peter Sanden and Janet Campbell B.; B.A., Ohio Wesleyan U., 1963; postgrad. U. Toledo, 1964; children—David Douglas, Christopher Sanden, Mark Andrew. Sr. buyer corp. purchasing Owens-Corning Fiberglas Corp., 1964-66, resident residential constrn. mgr., Columbus, Ohio, 1967-68, indsl. sales mgr., Grand Rapids, Mich., 1969-70, resident mgr., Kansas City, Mo., 1970-71, mgr. market devel., Toledo, Ohio, 1972-77, div. gen. mgr. Stebbins Engring. and Mfg. div., Baton Rouge, 1978-79, group mgr. new corp. ventures, Owens-Corning Fiberglass Tech. Center, Granville, Ohio, 1979-81, project mgr. African-Nigerian ventures, Toledo, 1981—; pres. DSB Assos., Granville, Ohio, 1981—. Mem. Citizens Criminal Justice Adv. Bd.; chmn. Licking County Jail Com. Mem. Soc. Plastics Industry, ASTM. Republican. Methodist. Home: 2300 Lancaster Rd NW Granville OH 43023 Office: Fiberglas Tower Toledo OH 43659

BARNUM, TERRY MARTIN, mfg. co. exec.; b. Canandaigua, N.Y., June 4, 1948; s. Frederik Martin and Shirley (Holden) B.; B.A., Adrian Coll., 1969; M.Div., Garrett Theol. Sem., 1972; M.A.L.S., Rosary Grad. Sch. Library Sci., River Forest, Ill., 1973; Ed.D., No. Ill. U., 1979; m. Sally Carolyn Justis, June 4, 1969. Media technician/studio mgr. Oakton Community Coll., Morton Grove, Ill., 1973-74; dir. instructional media Coll. Podiatric Medicine, Chgo., 1974-76; designer edn. and tng. AM Internat., Schaumburg, Ill., 1979-81, mgr. tng. evaluation, 1981—. Mem. Assn. for Edn. Communications and Tech., Am. Soc. Tng. and Devel., Ill. Tng. and Devel. Assn., No. Ill. Media Assn. Home: 1234 Dewey Ave Evanston IL 60202 Office: 1834 Walden Office Sq Schaumburg IL 60196

BARON, ALMA FAY S., educator; b. Pitts., July 26, 1923; d. Max J. and Emma C. (Aronson) Spann; B.A., U. Pitts., 1943; Ph.D., U. Wis., Madison, 1974; m. Lee A. Baron, Dec. 23, 1944; children—Ellen J., Michael A., Jill S. Advt. mgr. Kaufmann's, Pitts., 1943; head copywriter Levy Bros., Houston, 1945; fashion coordinator Baron's, Madison, Wis., 1946-54; host TV Talent, Sta. WMTV, Madison, 1953-54, Sta. WQED, Pitts., 1954-58, Sta. KORN, Mitchell, S.D., 1958-66, Sta. KELO, Sioux Falls, S.D., 1959-66; co-owner Lee Baron's Women's Store, Madison, 1966-71; instr. U. Wis. Extension, Madison, 1974-77, asso. prof. mgmt., 1978-81, prof. mgmt., 1981—; mem. internat. bd. Inst. Certifying Profl. Secs., 1977—; mem. sr. faculty Am. Soc. Tng. and Devel. Symposium, 1980; vis. faculty La. State U., Pa. State U., U. Okla., Purdue U. Pres., Madison Civic Music Assn., 1971-73; v.p. YWCA, Madison, 1973-76. Recipient Woman of Achievement award This is Madison, 1977; Outstanding Woman award select mag., 1976; Madisonian award Wis. State Jour., 1975; Sales and Mktg. award Sales Mktg. Execs., 1977; Meritorious Ind. Study Course award Nat. Univ. Extension Assn., 1980. Mem. Am. Bus. Communications Assn., Am. Soc. Tng. and Devel., Gen. Semantics Assn., Wis. Acad. Arts and Scis., Assn. Platform Speakers, AAUW, Zeta Phi Eta. Clubs: Blackhawk Country, B'nai B'rith. Author: Assertiveness in the Business Environment, 1979; Nonverbal Communication, 1981; contbr. articles to profl. jours. Home: 3 Honey Locust Trail Madison WI 53717 Office: 432 N Lake St Madison WI 53706

BARONE, NICK, restaurant franchise exec.; b. Volturno, Italy, Oct. 27, 1936; s. Arduino and Adelina (Massucci) B.; came to U.S., 1954, naturalized, 1959; student Wright Coll., Chgo., 1956-57; m. Dec. 12, 1959; children—Adele, Sheila, Edwin. Owner, pres. Barone Inc., La Grange Park, Ill.; cons. in field. Mem. V.F.W. (award 1976), Restaurant Assn. Republican. Roman Catholic. Club: Moose. Home: PO Box 98 Route 2 Barrington Hills IL 60010 Office: 1136 Maple St La Grange Park IL 60525

BARONE, PAUL LOUIS, hosp. adminstr., physician; b. Paterson, N.J., Oct. 11, 1902; s. Joseph and Jennie (Iozia) B.; B.S., Alfred U., 1926; M.D., Royal U., Naples, Italy, 1936; m. Martha Watkins, Jan. 20, 1940; children—Joe A., Jean Ann. Intern, St. Joseph (Mo.) Hosp., 1937, resident, 1938-39; practice medicine, specializing in psychiatry, Nevada, Mo., 1939—; staff physician Mo. State Hosp., 1939—, asst. supt., 1943-48, supt., 1948-70, 72—; clin. dir. Nevada (Mo.) State Hosp., 1970-72, 75-76, supt., 1972-75, 76—. Fellow Am. Geriatric Soc., Am. Psychiat. Assn. (life mem., certified mental hosp. adminstr.); mem. AMA, West Central Mo. Counties Med. Assn., Mo. Med. Assn., Mid Continent Psychiat. Assn. (life), Mo. Internat. Physicians, Western Mo. Psychiat. Assn. (counselor, past pres.). Clubs: Elks, Rotary. Home: 716 S Main St Nevada MO 64772 Office: Nevada State Hosp PO Box 308 Nevada MO 64772

BARR, GINGER ANN, cemetery and memorial co. exec.; b. Kansas City, Mo., Dec. 4, 1947; d. W.M. and Ann (Armstrong) B.; B.S., Baker U., 1969. Mem. news room staff Sta. KTSB-TV, Topeka, Kans., 1969; tchr. Olathe (Kans.) High Sch., 1969-70; adminstrv. asst. Topeka Cemetery 1971-76; v.p. Maplewood/Meml. Lawn Cemeteries, Emporia, Kans., 1973-80; v.p. Graceland/Fairlawn Cemeteries, Decatur, Ill., 1975—; v.p. Security Meml. Presidio Inc., Lenexa, Kans., 1976—; v.p. Lincoln Pet Co. (Ill.), Quality Meml. Co., Decatur, also Lincoln Meml. (Ill.) Co., 1975—; dir. Quantum Inc. Mem. Republican precinct com., Topeka, Kans., 1972—, chmn. Shawnee County Young Republicans, 1973-75, vice-chmn. Kans. Young Reps., 1975-77, chmn., 1977—; bd. dirs. Jr. Achievement. Mem. Am. Cemetery Assn., Kans. Cemetery Assn. (dir., pres. 1979—), Topeka Alumna Baker U. (pres. 1975-76), Ill. Cemetery Assn., Nat. Assn. Cemeteries (sec. 1979), Pre-interment Arrangement Assn., Nat. Monument Builders Assn., Better Bus. Bur. (dir.), Am. Bus. Women Assn., United Daus. Confederacy, Alpha Psi Omega, Beta Sigma Phi. Office: PO Box 1329 Emporia KS 66801

BARR, JOAN HARRIS, career counselor; b. N.Y.C., July 30, 1925; d. William Eber and Rachel Augusta (Sheffield) Harris; B.A., Ohio Wesleyan U., 1947; M.Ed., Kent State U., 1976, Ed.S., 1978; m. Wayne Arthur Barr, 1949 (div. 1969); children—Jacqueline and Jeffrey (twins). Sec. to v.p. Internat. B.F. Goodrich, 1949-54; sec. to headmaster Old Trail Sch., Bath, Ohio, 1969-73; sec. to v.p. pub. affairs Kent State U., 1973-74; aftercare counselor Portage Family Counseling and Mental Health Services, Ravenna, Ohio, 1976-77; asso. Cons.'s for Orgnl. and Personal Effectiveness, Inc., Kent, 1976—; pvt. practice career counseling; psychiat. social worker, vocat. counselor Western Res. Psychiat. Habilitation Center, 1977—. Mem. Am., Ohio personnel and guidance assns., Nat. Vocat. Guidance Assn., Am. Mental Health Counselors Assn., Ohio Mental Health Assn. Counselors Assn. (sec.), Kappa Kappa Gamma, Gertrude Sandford Doll Club. Home and office: 3575 Darrow Rd Stow OH 44224

BARR, JOHN MONTE, lawyer; b. Mt. Clemens, Mich., Jan. 1, 1935; s. Merle James and Wilhelmina Marie (Monte) B.; student Mexico City Coll., 1955; B.A., Mich. State U., 1956; J.D., U. Mich., 1959; m. Marlene Joy Bielenberg, Dec. 17, 1954; children—John Monte, Karl Alexander, Elizabeth Marie. Admitted to Mich. bar, 1959, since practiced in Ypsilanti; mem. firm Ellis B. Freatman, Jr., 1959-61; partner, chief trial atty. Freatman, Barr, Anhut & Moir and predecessor firm, 1961—; city atty. City of Ypsilanti, 1981. Lectr. bus. law Eastern Mich. U., 1968-70. Pres., Ypsilanti Family Service, 1967; mem. Ypsilanti Y Com., 1971; mem. Ypsilanti Public Housing Com., 1980; sr. adviser Explorer law post Portage Trail council Boy Scouts Am., 1969-71, commr. Potawatomi dist., 1973-74, commr. Washtenong dist., 1974-75. Served with AUS, 1959-60. Mem. State Bar Mich. (grievance bd. 1969—, state rep. assembly 1977—), Am., Ypsilanti, Washtenaw County (pres. 1975-76) bar assns., Am., Mich. trial lawyers assns., U.S. (instr. piloting, seamanship, sail), Ann Arbor (comdr. 1972-73) power squadrons. Lutheran. Clubs: Ypsilanti Breakfast Optimist (v.p. 1965), Washtenaw Country, Washtenaw Sportsman's (Ypsilanti). Contbr. articles to boating mags. Home: 1200 Whittier Rd Ypsilanti MI 48197 Office: 105 Pearl St Ypsilanti MI 48197

BARR, KENNETH JOHN, petroleum co. exec.; b. Birmingham, Ala., Aug. 25, 1926; s. Archie and Mable Leona (Griffith) B.; B.S. in Chem. Engring., Auburn U., 1947; postgrad. Inst. Mgmt. Northwestern U., 1964; m. Jeanne Bonner, Jan. 22, 1951; children—Marsha Jeanne, Kenneth John, Darren Clint. With Amoco Prodn. Co., 1948-1973, jr. petroleum engr., Hobbs, N.Mex., 1948-49, chief engr., 1962-65, v.p. and div. mgr., New Orleans, 1970-73, mgr. prodn. and v.p. prodn. Amoco Can. Petroleum Co. (subs.), Calgary, Alta., Can., 1965-70; gen. mgr. supply and coordination dept. Standard Oil Co. Ind., Chgo., 1973-75; exec. v.p. Amoco Internat. Oil Co., Chgo., 1975, Amoco Prodn. Co., 1975—. Served with USAAF, 1945. Mem. Soc. Petroleum Engrs. of AIME, Am. Petroleum Inst., Tex. Mid-Continent Oil and Gas Assn., Phi Lambda Upsilon (hon.). Clubs: Tchefuncta Country, Mid-Am., North River Yacht. Office: 200 E Randolph Dr Chicago IL 60601*

BARR, RODERICK WOOD, communications exec.; b. Oak Park, Ill., Jan. 2, 1931; s. Charles Lee and Aileen (Wood) B.; B.A., Northwestern U., 1952; m. Barbara Bates, July 12, 1952; children—Carolee, Daniel, Diane, Roderick. Sales rep. U.S. Gypsum Co., Chgo., 1955-59, Union Carbide Corp., Chgo., 1959-68; founder, pres. Applied Facsimile Communications Inc., Cin., 1968—, Fleetline Permit Service Inc., Cin., 1974—, Tel-Graphic Products Inc., Cin., 1976—, Fleetline Transp. Service Inc., 1979—; dir. Am. Facsimile Systems Inc. Served with U.S. Army, 1952-54. Roman Catholic. Clubs: Union League (Chgo.); University, Kenwood Country. (Cin.). Home: 7260 Drake Rd Cincinnati OH 45243

BARR, ROY RASSMANN, lawyer; b. Chgo., Sept. 28, 1901; s. Alfred Eugene and Pauline (Rassmann) B.; student Northwestern U., 1918-20; Ph.B., U. Chgo., 1923; J.D., John Marshall Law Sch., Chgo., 1924; m. Katharine Roberts, Sept. 9, 1924 (dec. Sept. 1981); children—Robert Roy (dec.), Barbara Ann (Mrs. Robert E. Newlin), Alfred Eugene II. Admitted to Ill. bar, 1924; in law office of father, 1924, practiced law as Barr & Barr, 1924-26, then Barr, Barr & Corcoran; now individual practice, Chgo. Mem. Am., Ill. State (sr. counselor), Chgo., West Suburban bar assns., Am. Judicature Soc., Phi Sigma Soc., Delta Sigma Phi. Congregationalist. Clubs: Masons, Interfraternity Chgo. Home: 1116 Randolph St Oak Park IL 60302 Office: 10 S La Salle St Chicago IL 60603

BARRETT, CHARLES MARION, physician, ins. co. exec.; b. Cin., Mar. 10, 1913; s. Charles Francis and May (Ryan) B.; A.B., Xavier U., 1934; LL.D., 1974; M.D., U. Cin., 1938; m. May Belle Finn, Apr. 27, 1942; children—Angela (Mrs. Ernest Eynon), Charles, John, Michael, Marian, William. Asso. med dir. Western-So. Life Ins. Co., Cin., 1942, med. dir., 1951-73, exec. v.p., 1965-73, pres., 1973—, also dir.; prof. depts. surgery and radiology U. Cin. Coll. Medicine, 1957—, prof. emeritus, 1974—; dir. Eagle Savs. Assn., Procter & Gamble Co., Cin. Bell, Inc., Eagle-Picher Industries, Inc., So. Ohio Bank. Bd. dirs. Our Lady of Mercy Hosp., U. Cin.; chmn. bd. trustees U. Cin., 1977; mem. Ohio Bd. Regents, 1970-73; mem. Bethesda Hosp. and Deaconess Assn. Recipient Taft medal U. Cin., 1973, Spl. award Ohio Radiol. Soc., 1974; All-Am. award Sports Illus., 1958; Nat. Jewish Hosp. award, 1975. Fellow Am. Coll. Radiology; mem. A.M.A., Life Ins. Assn. Am., Alpha Omega Alpha. Home: 2581 Grandin Rd Cincinnati OH 45208 Office: 400 Broadway Cincinnati OH 45202

BARRETT, EDWARD DUANE, dentist, microbiologist; b. Detroit, July 1, 1925; s. Thomas Joseph and Thelma Louise (Johnson) B.; student Marquette U., 1944-45; B.S., U. Detroit, 1947, M.S., 1949, D.D.S., 1954; postgrad. Wayne State U., 1949-50; m. Evelyn Thelma Trammell, Sept. 2, 1950; children—Heather, Mary Patricia, Theresa, Edward D., Margaret. Microbiologist, Wayne State U., Detroit, 1948-50; practice dentistry, Auburn Heights, Mich., 1955—; mem. microbiology faculty U. Detroit Dental Sch., 1950-57, grad. div., 1965-70, dir. continuing edn., 1977—. Pres. Auburn Heights Boys Club, 1960-66; Active Pontiac (Mich.) United Fund, 1963-65. Bd. mgrs. Rochester (Mich.) YMCA, 1971-77, chmn., 1973-75. Served with USNR, 1944-46. Fellow Internat. Coll. Dentists, Acad. Dentistry International, Am. Acad. Gen. Dentistry (pres. Mich. 1976-78, nat. dir. 1979—); mem. Am. Acad. Oral Medicine, U. Detroit Dental Alumni Assn. (dir.), Oakland County Dental Soc. (pres. 1969-70), Mich. Dental Assn. (trustee 1981—), Am. Legion, Alpha Sigma Nu, Psi Omega. Roman Catholic. K.C., Elk. Club: Auburn Heights Lions (pres. 1960-61). Author: (with Mattman, Barrett) Laboratory Experiments in Nursing Microbiology, 1952; (with Mattman, Barrett) Laboratory Experiments in Medical Microbiology, 1956; (with Mattman, Barrett, Rossmore) Exercises in Introductory Microbiology, 1958. Contbr. articles to sci. and profl. jours. Home: 220 Rochdale St Rochester MI 48063 Office: 3926 Auburn Rd Auburn Heights MI 48057

BARRETT, JAMES THOMAS, microbiologist, educator; b. Centerville, Iowa, May 20, 1927; s. Alfred Wesley and Mary Marjorie (Taylor) B.; B.A., U. Iowa, 1950, M.S., 1951, Ph.D., 1953; m. Barbro Anna-Lill Nilsson, July 31, 1967; children—Sara Joann, Robert Wayne, Annika Lill, Nina Marie. Asst. prof. dept. bacteriology and parasitology U. Ark., Little Rock, 1953-57; asst. prof. dept. microbiology U. Mo., Columbia, 1957-59, asso. prof., 1959-67, prof., 1967—; cons., faculty Chinese Acad. Sci., Taiwan, 1968, U. Lagos, Nigeria, 1974, 79. Served with USN, 1944-45. NIH spl. postdoctoral fellow, 1963-64; Fogarty Sr. Internat. NIH fellow, 1977-78; Exchange Prof. U.S. and Romania Acads. Sci., 1971. Mem. Am. Assn. Immunologists, Am. Soc. Microbiology. Author: Textbook of Immunology, 3rd edit. 1977; Basic Immunology and Its Medical Application, 2nd edit. 1980. Home: 901 Westport Dr Columbia MO 65201 Office: Dept Microbiology Univ Mo Columbia MO 65212

BARRETT, RICHARD HAMILTON, property mgmt. co. exec.; b. Columbus, Ohio, Oct. 30, 1916; s. Starling Heston and Bertha (Aid) B.; B.S., Ohio State U., 1938; m. Jeanne M. Webb, Sept. 9, 1939; children—Phillip H., Patricia L., Deborah A. Accountant, Price, Waterhouse & Co., Detroit, 1938-43, sr. accountant, 1946-47; sr. accountant Keller, Kirschner, Martin and Clinger, Columbus, 1947-48; treas., dir. Gen. Maintenance & Engring. Co., Columbus, 1948-68, sec., 1948-66, exec. v.p., 1966-68; dir., sec.-treas. Werner Constrn. Co., 1960-68, Interstate Maintenance & Engring. Co., 1948-68, Imeco Constrn. Co., Springfield, Ohio, Buckeye Cattle Co., 1962-68; pres., dir. Barrett Corp., Columbus, 1968-70; gen. mgr. Precision/Del. Corp., Delaware, Ohio, 1970-71; nat. exec. v.p. Klingbell Mgmt. Co., Columbus, 1971-74; v.p., gen. mgr. Indiana Mgmt. Co., Indpls., 1974-77; pres., dir. Moynahan, Barrett & Assos., Inc., Indpls., 1977—. Served with AUS, 1943-45; ETO. Decorated Bronze Star, Purple Heart. Mem. Apt. Assn. Ind. (pres. 1977), Ohio State U. Alumni Assn., Sigma Chi. Club: University (Columbus). Home: 4612 Somerset Way S Carmel IN 46032 Office: 8455 Keystone Crossing Indianapolis IN 46240

BARRETT, ROY LEE, computer sales co. exec.; b. Greenwood, Ind., June 24, 1943; s. William H. and Sarah (Jackson) B.; student Los Angeles City Coll., 1964-66, ITT Tech. Inst., 1967-68; m. Paula K. Barrett, May 13, 1971; children—Dawn E., Denise M. With RCA, 1963-64, ITT, 1968-69, Indsl. Nucleonics Co., 1970-73, Decision Data Computer Corp., Phila., 1973-76; pres. Galaxy Used Computer Corp., Indpls., 1976—. Served with USMC, 1960-64. Mem. Computer

Dealers Assn., Computer Multiple Listing Service, Greenwood Jr. C. of C. (past treas.). Clubs: Kiwanis, Optimist. Home: 4701 Citation Circle Indianapolis IN 46227 Office: Galaxy Used Computer Corp PO Box 27354 Indianapolis IN 46227

BARRETT, WILLIAM E., state legislator; b. Lexington, Nebr., Feb. 9, 1929; B.A., Hastings Coll.; student U. Conn., U. Minn., U. Nebr., U. Colo.; m. Else L. Carlson, Nov. 9, 1952; children—William C., Elizabeth A., David H., Jane M. Admissions counselor, then asst. dir. admissions Hastings Coll.; engaged in real estate and ins. bus.; mem. Nebr. Legislature, 1980—; dir. First Savs. Co. Trustee, Hastings Coll.; pres. Dawson County (Nebr.) Young Republicans; mem. Rep. State Exec. Com., 1964-66, 73-79; state coordinator Moblzn. of Rep. Enterprise, 1965-66. Mem. Am. Legion, C. of C., Greater Lexington Devel. Corp., Urban Renewal Corp., others. Presbyterian. Club: Rotary. Office: 507 N Washington St Lexington NE 68850*

BARRETTE, PATRICK EMILE, engineer; b. St. Paul, Mar. 4, 1949; s. Rene L. and Judith (Smolik) B.; student U. Wis., 1967-69, U. Minn., 1974-76. Field engr. LeSueur (Minn.) Foundry, 1977, Schlumberger Well Services, Pleasanton, Tex., 1977-78; with FMC, No. Ordnance, Mpls., 1980—. Served with USAF, 1969-78. Mem. Am. Security Council. Home: PO Box 396 Maiden Rock WI 54750 Office: FMC/NOD 4800 E River Rd Minneapolis MN 55421

BARRIGER, JOHN WALKER, IV, railroad exec.; b. St. Louis, Aug. 3, 1927; s. John Walker and Elizabeth Chambers (Thatcher) B.; B.S., M.I.T., 1949; C.T., Yale U., 1950; m. Evelyn Dobson, Dec. 29, 1955; children—John Walker V, Catherine Brundige. With Santa Fe Ry., 1950-68, 70—, supt. transp., 1965-68, mgr. staff studies and planning, Chgo., 1970-77, asst. v.p. fin., 1977-79, asst. to pres., 1979—; mgr. transp. controls div. Sylvania Info. Systems, Waltham, Mass., 1968-70; mem. vis. com. dept. civil engring. M.I.T., 1972-75; chmn. M.I.T. Mgmt. Conf., Chgo., 1974. Trustee, Village of Kenilworth (Ill.), 1978—, chmn. sts., sanitation and public works. Served with USN, 1946. Recipient Bronze Beaver award M.I.T., 1975, Employee Campaign Chmn. of Yr. award United Way/Crusade of Mercy, 1979. Mem. Am. Assn. R.R. Supts. (dir. 1958-68), Am. Ry. Engring. Assn., Ry. Planning Officers Assn. (chmn. 1971-76), Transp. Research Bd., Transp. Research Forum, Western Ry. Club (pres. 1979-80), Newcomen Soc., M.I.T. Alumni Assn. (dir. 1968-72), Delta Kappa Epsilon. Republican. Roman Catholic. Clubs: Econ. Chgo. Exec. Chgo., M.I.T. Chgo. (pres. 1972-73), Kenilworth, Mich. Shores, Union League Chgo. Home: 155 Melrose Ave Kenilworth IL 60043 Office: 80 E Jackson Blvd Chicago IL 60604

BARRON, FRANCIS HAROLD, educator, broadcast adminstr.; b. Edna, Tex., Apr. 15, 1933; s. Francis Henry and Rosalie (Norcross) B.; B.F.A. in Radio-TV (Sta. KTRH scholar), U. Houston, 1955; M.S. in Edn., Butler U., 1973; grad. basic personnel mgmt. course CSC, 1978, effective exec. course U.S. Army, 1977; postgrad. U. S.C., 1981; m. Gloria J. Bolz, Apr. 20, 1963; 1 dau., Tracy Lynn. Engr., Sta. KTRK-TV, Houston, 1955-56; prodn. mgr. Sta. KETC-TV, St. Louis, 1956-60, Sta. KTVI-TV, St. Louis, 1960-64, Sta. WISH-TV, Indpls., 1966-67; dir. spl. events Sta. WFBM-TV, Indpls., 1964-66; chief instructional TV div. dept. radio-TV, Def. Info. Sch., Ft. Benjamin Harrison, Ind., 1967—; asso. prof. radio-TV dept. Butler U., 1966—. Recipient letter of commendation White House, 1966, 11 Outstanding Ratings, Dept. Army, 1967-81. Mem. Internat. TV Assn., Soc. Broadcast Engrs., Radio TV News Dirs. Assn., Nat. Assn. Ednl. Broadcasters, Nat. Acad. TV Arts and Scis., (charter mem. St. Louis chpt.), Broadcast Edn. Assn., Armed Forces Communications and Electronics Assn., Aircraft Owners and Pilots Assn., Soc. Profl. Journalists. Methodist. Clubs: Officers, Flying, Press. Producer: Missouri Constitution, 1956 (Ohio State Outstanding Ednl. TV award 1956). Home: 10187 Orchard Park W Indianapolis IN 46280 Office: Def Info Sch Fort Benjamin Harrison IN 46216

BARRON, HOWARD ROBERT, lawyer; b. Chgo., Feb. 17, 1930; s. Irving P. and Ada (Astrahan) B.; Ph.B., U. Chgo., 1948; B.A., Stanford U., 1950; LL.B., Yale, 1953; m. Marjorie Ruth Shapira, Aug. 12, 1953; children—Ellen Jean, Laurie Ann. Admitted to Ill. bar, 1953; associate of firm of Jenner & Block and predecessor firms, Chgo., 1957-64, partner, 1964—. Regional rep. Ill., exec. com. Yale Law Sch. Assn., 1971-77; chmn. Chgo. maj. gifts com. Yale Law Sch. Sesquicentennial Campaign. Mem. bd. edn. Lake County Sch. Dist. 107, Highland Park, Ill., 1964-71, pres., 1969-71; chmn. com. on interdistrict cooperation Lake County Sch. Dists. 106-113, 1967-68; pres. Lake County Sch. Bd. Assn., 1970-71; mem. Bd. Edn. Lake County High Sch. Dist. 113, 1973-77. Served to lt. (j.g.) USNR, 1953-57. Mem. Chgo. (grievance com. 1965-73), Ill. (chmn. antitrust sect. 1968-69), Am. bar assns., Yale Law Sch. Assn. Ill. (pres. 1962), Yale Law Sch. Assn. (v.p. 1978-80). Clubs: Legal, Law, Cliff Dwellers, Standard (Chgo.). Contbr. articles to profl. jours. and books. Home: 433 Ravine Dr Highland Park IL 60035 Office: One IBM Plaza Chicago IL 60611

BARRON, ILONA ELEANOR, reading tchr., cons.; b. Mass, Mich., Sept. 19, 1929; B.S. in Elementary Edn., Central Mich. U., Mt. Pleasant, 1961; M.A. in Edn., U. Mich., Ann Arbor, 1966; postgrad. Mich. State U., East Lansing; m. George Barron; 1 son, Fred. Tchr. elem. schs., 1952-67; Title I dir. Saginaw (Mich.) Twp. Community Schs., 1967-68, reading cons., 1971—; elementary internal cons. Mich. State U., 1968-71; elementary reading cons. Saginaw Twp. Public Schs., 1972—. Mem. NEA, Mich., Saginaw Twp. Edn. Assns., Saginaw Area Reading Council. Specialist in reading, methods of teaching developmental reading skills and enrichment. Home: 4891 Hillcrest Dr Saginaw MI 48603 Office: Plainfield Elementary Sch 2775 Shattuck Rd Saginaw MI 48601

BARRON, JOHN MARSHALL, spice co. exec.; b. New Marshfield, Ohio, May 19, 1912; s. Joseph Cephus and Nettie (Stewart) B.; student Mountain State Coll., 1930-32; B.B.A., Ohio U., 1933; m. Evelyn Joan McRill, Mar. 1, 1961; children—Patricia, Virginia, Karen, Beverly, Allona. Tchr., New Marshfield High Sch., 1933-34; sales mgr. F.J. Beasley Co., Athens, Ohio, 1934-38; sales and advt. mgr. David Kirk Sons Co., Findlay, Ohio, 1938-47; dist. mgr. Woolson Spice Co., Toledo, Ohio, 1947-61, v.p. sales, also dir., 1961-66; sales mgr. Baker Importing div. and Mut. Spice div. Hygrade Food Products, Detroit, 1966-69; account exec. Frank Tea & Spice Co., Cin., 1969-74; v.p., sales mgr., dir. Spicecraft, Inc., St. Louis, 1974—. Sec.-treas. Bd. Edn., New Marshfield, 1935-38. Served to lt. comdr. USNR, World War II. Mem. Res. Officers Assn. U.S., Am. Legion. Baptist. Clubs: Masons, (32 deg.), Shriners, Kiwanis, Sertoma (pres. 1940-41). Home: 4981 Archdale Ln Columbus OH 43214 Office: 910 Spruce St Saint Louis MO 63102

BARRON, MARCELLINE ANTOINETTE, educator; b. Detroit, Jan. 27, 1941; d. Joseph A. and Irene L. (Turman) B.; B.S., U. Detroit, 1962, M.A., 1967; Ph.D., U. Mich., 1974. Tchr. mathematics Columbus Jr. High Sch., Detroit, 1962-65; tchr. chemistry, physics and mathematics Edwin Denby High Sch., Detroit, 1965-75; asst. prof. sci. edn. Manhattanville Coll., Purchase, N.Y., 1975-77, prof., acting dir. dept. teacher edn., 1977-78; dir. music and liturgy St. John's U. Parish, Stillwater, Okla., 1978-80; tchr. physics, chemistry, computer assisted instrn. Cin. Public Schools, 1980—; asst. organist Cathedral of St. Peter, Cin., 1980—. Awarded silver medal of distinction and merit by Bishop of Sora, Italy, 1977. Mem. AAUP, Nat. Sci. Tchrs. Assn., AAAS, Assn. Educators of Tchrs. of Sci., Smithsonian Assos., Sch. Sci. and Mathematics Assn. Roman Catholic. Church organist, 1954-58; first chair violinist local community orchestra, 1955-58; contralto soloist, San Moritz Chamber Orchestra and Chorale, Stamford, Conn., concert tours with choirs, Poland, 1976, Italy, 1977, soloist with Phila. Orchestra, 1971, Detroit Symphony, 1970; pvt. voice tchr.; author: Coping with Chemistry Creatively, 1974; editor: Gathering To Praise.

BARRON, PAMELA GURSKY, mktg. exec.; b. N.Y.C., Apr. 23, 1943; d. Aaron Harry and Ruth (Bernstein) G.; student Cornell U., 1959-62; B.A., CCNY, 1963; M.A., Kent State U., 1968, postgrad., 1974; children—Matthew, Seth, Leila. Social worker Canton (Ohio) Welfare Dept., 1964-66; caseworker Info. and Referral Service, 1973-78; founder, exec. dir. Pyramid, Inc., Canton, 1976-79; dir. mktg. services ABS div. Diebold, Inc., North Canton, 1979—; tchr., cons. Kickoff chmn. United Way, 1975-77; media programmer Canton City Schs., 1975-77; program adminstr. Goodwill Industries, 1974-76; bd. dirs. Canton Hometown Affirmative Action Plan, Planned Parenthood; mem. exec. com., chmn. employment com. Canton-Stark-Wayne CETA Adv. Council. Mem. Nat. Personnel and Guidance Assn., Am. Mgmt. Assn., North Central Sociol. Assn., Pi Gamma Mu. Jewish. Clubs: Hadassah (pres. 1974-76), Jr. League. Office: Deibold Inc 5995 Mayfair Rd North Canton OH 47720

BARROWES, STEVEN CLARK, physicist; b. Salt Lake City, Oct. 27, 1940; s. Thayer Clark and Fern Isabella (Rees) B.; B.S., U. Utah, 1963, Ph.D., 1971; m. Hope Richardson, June 14, 1962; children—Wilford, Thomas, Edward, Stephanie, Winston, Benjamin. Vis. asst. prof. dept. physics and astronomy La. State U., 1971-76; vis. asst. prof. physics Miss. State U., 1976-79; asst. prof. physics Ill. State U., Normal, 1979—. Voting dist. chmn., del. Salt Lake County Republican Conv., 1968. Mem. Am. Phys. Soc., Sigma Xi. Mormon. Contbr. articles to profl. jours. Home: 302 E Baker St Bloomington IL 61701 Office: Dept Physics Ill State Univ Normal IL 61761

BARRY, JAMES P(OTVIN), writer, editor, assn. exec.; b. Alton, Ill., Oct. 23, 1918; s. Paul Augustine and Elder (Potvin) B.; m. Anne Elizabeth Jackson, Apr. 16, 1966; B.A. cum laude, with distinction Ohio State U., 1940. Commd. 2d. lt. Arty., U.S. Army, 1940, advanced through grades to col., 1953; served ETO, 1944-46; adviser to Turkish Army, 1951-53; detailed Army Gen. Staff, Washington, 1953-56; ret., 1966; adminstr. Capital U., Columbus, Ohio, 1967-71; freelance writer, editor, Columbus, 1971-77; dir. Ohioana Library Assn., 1977—; editor Ohioana Quar., 1977—; photographer, exhbn. and book illustrator, 1968—; adv. bd. Kenyon Rev., 1980—. Recipient award Am. Soc. State and Local History, 1974. Mem. Gt. Lakes, Marine, Ohio hist. socs., World Ship Soc., Phi Beta Kappa. Clubs: Royal Can. Yacht; Columbus Country, University (Columbus). Author: Georgian Bay: The Sixth Great Lake, 1968, rev. edit., 1978; The Battle of Lake Erie, 1970; Bloody Kansas, 1972; The Noble Experiment, 1972; The Fate of the Lakes, 1972; The Louisiana Purchase, 1973; Henry Ford and Mass Production, 1973; Ships of the Great Lakes (Dolphin Book Club selection), 1973; The Berlin Olympics, 1975; The Great Lakes: A First Book, 1976; Wrecks and Rescues of the Great Lakes (Dolphin Book Club selection), 1981; also booklet on Lake Erie for Ohio EPA, 1980. Home: 353 Fairway Blvd Columbus OH 43213 also Thunder Beach PO Penetanguishene ON Canada Office: 1105 Ohio Depts Bldg 65 S Front St Columbus OH 43215

BARRY, THOMAS HUBERT, pub. co. exec.; b. Phillips, Wis., Mar. 18, 1918; s. John Sumner and Helen (Maloney) B.; student U. Notre Dame, 1936-38; B.A., Marquette U., 1941; m. Rosemary Klein, July 8, 1944; children—Kathleen (Mrs. J. Douglas Ingram), Patricia (Mrs. Thomas Turriff), Mary Beth (Mrs. William O'Donnell), Julie (Mrs. David Carden). Western mgr., welding engr. McGraw Hill Pub. Co., Chgo., 1947-53; Western mgr. Iron Age, Chilton Co., Chgo., 1953-66; Western mgr. Control Engring., Tech. Pub. (a Dun and Bradstreet Co.), Chgo., 1966-69, sales mgr., N.Y.C., 1969-72, asso. pub., Chgo., 1972-76, pub., Barrington, Ill., 1977—. Served with USMC, 1941-47. Decorated Bronze Star medal, Purple Heart medal. Mem. Nat. Indsl. Advertisers Assn., Assn. Indsl. Advertisers (dir. Chgo. chpt. 1963-65), Bus.-Profl. Advtg. Assn., Indsl. Mktg. Club St. Louis, Rockford Advtg. Club, Marine Corps Res. Officers Assn., 1st Marine Div. Assn. (officer, dir. 1954—, pres. 1979—). Roman Catholic. Clubs: K.C., Notre Dame Club of Chgo., Marquette U. Club Chgo., Holy Name Soc. Home: 628 Carriage Hill Dr Glenview IL 60025 Office: 1301 S Grove Ave Barrington IL 60010

BARSHES, WARREN BARRY, corp. compensation mgr.; b. Chgo., July 14, 1943; s. John and Anne (Jonases) B.; B.A. in Psychology, DePaul U., 1965, M.A. in Psychology, 1967; M.S. in Indsl. Relations, Loyola U., 1975; m. Laraine Chorvat, Aug. 10, 1969; children—David Warren, Neal Ryan, Krista Hope. With William Wrigley Jr. Co., Chgo., 1969—, personnel mgr., 1977-81, corp. compensation mgr., 1981—; instr. psychology Moraine Valley Community Coll., Palos Hills, Ill., 1974—. Served to lt. 1st, U.S. Army, 1967-69. Mem. Ill. Psychol. Assn., Indsl. Relations Assn. Chgo. (past dir., sec.), Vietnam Vets. of Am. Office: 410 N Michigan Ave Chicago IL 60611

BART, WILLIAM MARVIN, psychologist; b. Chgo., Nov. 29, 1943; s. Joseph Marvin and Madelynne Joanne (Stroik) B.; B.S., Loyola U., Chgo., 1965; A.M., U. Chgo., 1967, Ph.D., 1969. Asst. prof. ednl. psychology U. Minn., Mpls., 1969-72, asso. prof. ednl. psychology, 1972-80, prof., 1980—. Fulbright-Hays Research scholar, W. Ger., 1974-75. Mem. Am. Psychol. Assn., Am. Ednl. Research Assn., Soc. Research in Child Devel., Jean Piaget Soc. Contbr. articles to Jour. Math. Psychology, Jour. Ednl. Psychology. Home: 609 Jefferson St NE Minneapolis MN 55413 Office: 330 Burton Hall U Minn Minneapolis MN 55455

BARTA, GERALD THOMAS, elec. engr.; b. Milw., May 15, 1921; s. John George and Theresa Anna (Klien) B.; student Marquette U., 1940-43; B.E.E. cum laude, Notre Dame U., 1947; m. Sylvia Helen Wegner, July 13, 1946; children—Kathleen Jean, Patricia Ann, Mary Ellen, Thomas Joseph. Sales engr. Ind. Steel Products Co., Valparaiso, 1947-48, design engr., 1948-52, chief insp., 1952-54; mgr. quality control Ind. Gen. Corp., Valparaiso, 1954-56, sr. devel. engr., 1956-61; v.p. plant mgr. B.L. Downey Co., Chgo., 1961-62; chief product devel. engr. Ind. Gen. Corp., 1962-64, chief engr., 1964-65, mgr. engring., 1965-76, mgr. quality assurance and standards, 1976-77, mgr. customer service, 1977-78; mgr. quality assurance and process control Am. Magnetics Co., Inc., Valparaiso, 1978—. Served with USMCR, 1943-46. Mem. IEEE, C. of C., Pi Mu Epsilon. Roman Catholic. Patentee in field. Home: 128 Williamsburg Manor Valparaiso IN 46383 Office: 342 N County Rd 400 E Valparaiso IN 46383

BARTEL, FRED FRANK, cement co. exec.; b. Milw., Nov. 4, 1917; s. Fred F. and Alma O. (Koppelmeyer) B.; B.S. in Civil Engring., U. Wis., 1940; M.S. (Stanton Walker research fellow), U. Md., 1942; m. Ann E. Staudacher, Oct. 23, 1943; children—Betty Jo, Susan, Mary Jo, Robert. Engring. aid Wis. Highway Dept., 1936-40; asst. dir. engring. Nat. Ready Mixed Concrete Assn., Silver Spring, Md., 1942-49; chief engr., sales mgr. Tews Lime and Cement Co., Milw., 1949-75, pres., chief exec. officer, 1975—. Served to capt. USAAF, 1942-46. Fellow ASCE; mem. ASTM, Am. Concrete Inst., Nat. Ready Mixed Concrete Assn. (chmn. bd. dirs. 1979), Wis. Ready Mixed Concrete Assn. (pres. 1969), Builders Exchange of Milw. (pres. 1966-67). Republican. Roman Catholic. Clubs: Rotary, West Bend Country, Wisconsin. Author book sect. in three editions; contbr. articles to tech. publs. Home: 5421 N Shoreland Ave Milwaukee WI 53217 Office: 6200 W Center St Milwaukee WI 53210

BARTELS, BRYAN DALE, clin. psychologist; b. Seattle, Oct. 16, 1947; s. Dale Edward and Mary Jean (Edison) B.; B.A. (DeWitt Wallace scholar 1965-68), Malcaster Coll., St. Paul, 1969; M.A. (NIMH fellow 1972-74), U. N.D., 1973, Ph.D., 1976; m. Marion Joyce Eastlund, Aug. 14, 1971; children—Joseph Pender, Bethany Bartels. Clin. intern Wichita (Kans.) Collaborative Psychology Internship Program, 1975-76; clin. asst. Psychol. Services Center, U. N.D., 1974-75, therapist /counselor, 1971-75; cons. trainee USPHS, Ft. Totten, N.D., 1974-75; psychologist V, dir. emergency services, clin. outreach, biofeedback, psychology services SE Mental Health and Retardation Center, Fargo, N.D., 1976—; clin. instr. U. N.D. Med. Sch., 1978—; bd. dirs. Centre, Inc., Fargo, 1977-78, adv. bd., 1978—; bd. dirs. Fargo Hotline, Inc., 1978—, Fargo Rape and Abuse Crisis Center, 1979—; adv. bd. occupational therapy program N.D. State Sch. Sci., 1980—. Mem. Am. Psychol. Assn., Am. Soc. Clin. Hypnosis, N.D. Mental Health Assn., N.D. Psychol. Assn. (trustee). Home: 1025 20th Ave S Moorhead MN 56560 Office: 108 S 8th St Fargo ND 58103

BARTER, BRUCE, pediatrician; b. Denver, Nov. 21, 1945; s. Gerson and Maxine (Hoffman) B.; B.A., Washington U., St. Louis, 1967; M.D., U. Colo., 1971; m. Linda Jean Manheim, Sept. 16, 1970; children—David, Michael, Miriam, Steven. Resident in pediatrics U. Iowa Hosps., Iowa City, 1971-74; chief pediatrics Prime Health, Kansas City, Mo., 1976-79, asso. med. dir., 1979—; clin. asso. medicine U. Kans. Med. Sch., 1976—, U. Mo. Kansas City, 1976—. Bd. dirs. United Cerebral Palsy Assn., Kansas City, 1980—; chmn. Concerned Citizens for Handicapped, Leavenworth, 1975-76. Served with AUS, 1974-76. Diplomate Am. Bd. Pediatrics. Fellow Am. Acad. Pediatrics; mem. Kansas City S.W. Pediatric Soc., Jackson County Med. Soc., Mo. Med. Assn. Jewish. Office: 9150 E 51st Terr Kansas City MO 64114

BARTH, EARLE FREDERICK, pharmacist; b. Michigan City, Ind., May 7, 1924; s. Earle Frederick and Amanda Katherine (Helsing) B.; B.S., Purdue U., 1949; m. Lorraine Margaret Murray, Dec. 28, 1944; children—Dennis Eugene, Terrence Lee, Wayne Earle. Pharmacist, Hilbish Drug Store, LaPorte, Ind., Peoples Drug Store, Plymouth, Ind., Muirs Drug Store, Michigan City, Walgreen's Drug Store, Michigan City, Hooks Drug Store, South Bend and Michigan City, Meml. Hosp., Michigan City; pharmacist Walters Hosp., Michigan City, now dir. pharmacy. Vice pres., PTA; active Boy Scouts Am.; sec. City Council Michigan City. Served with USN, 1943-45. Decorated Bronze Star with 4 oak leaf clusters, Presdl. citation. Mem. Nat. Assn. Retail Druggists, Am. Pharm. Assn., Am. Soc. Hosp. Pharmacists, AAAS, Ind. Pharm. Assn., Ariz. Pharm. Assn., LaPorte County Pharm. Assn., Ind. Hosp. Pharmacists Assn., Michigan City Hosp. Pharmacists Assn. Clubs: Kiwanis; Rotary; Moose. Office: Walters Hosp Found 3714 S Franklin St Michigan City IN 46360*

BARTH, FRANCIS, state senator; b. Flasher, N.D., Apr. 2, 1930; s. Phillip F. and Katherine (Leingang) B.; m. Burnetta Gerhardt; children—Dwight, Geisele, Elwood, MaDonna, Leland. Farmer, rancher, Solen, N.D.; mem. N.D. State Senate, 1971—. Democratic committeeman 18th dist., Morton County, N.D., 1951-66; mem. Morton County Dem. Non-partisan League Exec. Com., 1960; del. Dem. State Conv., 1962, 64, 66, 68; del. Dem. Nat. Conv., 1968; sec. dist. 35th N.D. Dem. Non-Partisan League, 1965-66, chmn., 1966—. Mem. Farmers Union, Nat. Farmers Orgn., N.D. Hereford Assn. Roman Catholic. Clubs: KC, Elks. Office: State Capitol Bismarck ND 58505*

BARTH, MELISSA E., educator; b. Chewelah, Wash., Nov. 24, 1948; d. Harold Walter and Thelma Madge (Braker) B.; B.A. magna cum laude, Wash. State U., 1971, M.A., 1974; Ph.D. (David Ross fellow), Purdue U., 1981. Adv. for fgn. study Wash. State U., Pullman, 1972-76; teaching fellow Purdue U., West Lafayette, Ind., 1979-81; asst. prof. English DePauw U., Greencastle, Ind., 1981—; free-lance writer Concept Mktg. Inc., 1980—; cons. Denmark's Internat. Student Com., Lund (Sweden) U.; guest lectr. Wash. State U. Honors Program. Univ. relations staff Pullman Host Family Assn.; mem. Opera de Lafayette; bd. dirs. Act II, Inc. Theatre Co. E.O. Holland grantee, 1969-70; Wash. State U. honors exchange student U. S.Wales, Univ. Coll., Cardiff, 1969-70. Mem. MLA, Am. Bus. Communication Assn., Nat. Assn. Fgn. Student Advs. (cons. regional planning team), Phi Kappa Phi (chpt. sec., 1975-76). Clubs: Audubon Soc., Sierra. Speaker nat. profl. conf.; contbr. to Survey of Modern Fantasy Literature. Office: English Dept DePauw Univ Greencastle IN 46135

BARTHEL, WILLIAM FREDERICK, JR., engr., electronics co. exec.; b. Washington, July 14, 1940; s. William Frederick and Eva (Buday) B.; B.S., McNeese State U., 1972; m. Barbara Joan Adams, Nov. 18, 1961; 1 son, William Frederick III. Shop mgr. Electronics Unlimited, Lake Charles, La., 1968; quality control engr. Rockwell Internat., Cedar Rapids, Iowa, 1974-79, mgr. quality assurance, 1979, sr. engring. scientist, process control devel., 1980—. Served with USAF, 1958-62. Mem. Am. Chem. Soc., Am. Inst. Chemists. Republican. Home: Rural Route 2 Box 105 Mount Vernon IA 52314 Office: Rockwell International EDD 400 Collins Rd NE Cedar Rapids IA 52406

BARTHELMAS, NED KELTON, stock broker; b. Circleville, Ohio, Oct. 22, 1927; s. Arthur and Mary Bernice (Riffel) B.; B.S. in Bus. Adminstrn., Ohio State U., 1950; m. Marjorie Jane Livezey, May 23, 1953; children—Brooke Ann, Richard Thomas. Stock broker Ohio Co., Columbus, 1953-58; pres. First Columbus Securities Corp., stock brokers and investment bankers, 1958—; pres. dir. Ohio Fin. Corp., Columbus, 1960—, United Capital Corp; dir. Conditioned Power Corp., Nat. Foods, 1st Columbus Realty Corp., Franklin Nat. Corp., Lancaster Colony Corp., 1st Nat. Equity Corp., Union Nat. Corp., Midwest Nat. Corp., Am. Nat. Realty Corp., Midwest Equity Corp., Court Realty Co., Medex Inc., Liebert Corp.; chmn., trustee Am. Guardian Fin.; trustee Republic Fin. Trust (all Columbus). Served with Adj. Gen.'s Dept., AUS, 1945-47. Mem. Nat. Assn. Securities Dealers, Nat. Stock Traders Assn., Securities Industry Assn., Nat. Investment Bankers Assn. (pres. 1973), Ohio Investment Dealers (pres. 1973), Columbus Jr. C. of C. (pres. 1956), Ohio Jr. C. of C. (trustee 1957-58), Columbus Area C. of C. (dir. 1956; named an outstanding young man of Columbus, 1962), Am. Mgmt. Assn. (pres.'s council), Young Pres. Orgn. (pres. 1971), Newcomen Soc., Phi Delta Theta. Clubs: Executives, Stock and Bond, Columbus Athletic, Columbus, Scioto Country (Columbus); Crystal Downs Country (Frankfort, Mich.). Home: 1000 Urlin Ave Columbus OH 43212 Office: 1241 Dublin Rd Columbus OH 43215

BARTHOLOMEW, GARY RAY, coll. pres.; b. Kansas City, Mo., July 3, 1947; s. Raymond C. and Dorene (Fornoff) B.; A.A., York Coll., 1967; B.A., Harding U., 1969; M.B.A., U. Denver, 1971; m. Gwen Sims, Dec. 28, 1967; 1 dau., Stacey. Staff accountant Arthur Andersen Co., Denver, 1969-70; asst. prof. bus. adminstrn. Harding U., Searcy, Ark., 1971-76; asst. to pres. York (Nebr.) Coll., 1976-78, pres., 1978—. Mem. City of York Airport Zoning Bd., 1979—. Recipient Wall Street Jour. award Harding U., 1969. C.P.A., Nebr. Mem. Nebr. Soc. C.P.A.'s. Mem. Ch. of Christ. Club: Rotary (chaplain). Home: 1001 Platte Ave York NE 68467 Office: 10th and Kiplinger St York NE 68467

BARTHOLOW, BEVERLY N., social work adminstr.; b. Portage, Utah, Oct. 19, 1932; d. Carl Franz and Elda Mae (Parkinson) Nelson; B.S.W., Utah State U., 1955; M.S.W., U. Nebr., 1974; m. George William Bartholow, June 17, 1955; children—Jeanne, Deborah, Bruce Nelson. Case aide, social service U. Iowa, 1957-59; social worker children's program Jewish Community Center, Omaha, 1974; dir. social service dept. St. Joseph Center for Mental Health, Omaha, 1975—; practicum instr. U. Nebr., Omaha; clin. instr. psychiatry Creighton U.; mem. Mental Health Ad Hoc Task Force for Meeting Needs of Chronically Mentally Ill. Mem. Nat. Assn. Social Workers (pres. Nebr. chpt.), Nebr. Mental Health Assn., Hosp. Social Work Dirs., Methodist. Home: 721 N 57th St Omaha NE 68132 Office: 819 Dorcas St Omaha NE 68108

BARTIMUS, WESLEY, ret. supt. schs.; b. Brownstown, Ill., Dec. 12, 1911; s. Jesse Monroe and Amanda (Warner) B.; B.S. in Edn., So. Ill. U., 1950, M.S., 1954; m. Ethel Rose Loveless, Oct. 26, 1935; children—Derald Wesley, Joanne Ellen (Mrs. James Carrol Sills). Rural sch. tchr., Fayette County, Ill., 1934-42; supt. Brownstown City Schs., 1946-48; asst. supt. Brownstown Community Unit, 1948-54, supt., high sch. prin., 1954-64; asst. supt. schs. Nashville (Ill.) Community Consol. Sch. Dist., 1964-65, supt. schs., 1965-74. Twp. supr., Wheatland. 1940-44. Served with USNR, 1943-46. Mem. Nat. Ret. Tchrs. Assn., Ill. Ret. Tchrs. Assn. (life), Fayette County Ret. Tchrs. Assn. (v.p. 1978, pres. 1979), Am. Legion, PTA (life), Phi Delta Kappa. Mem. 1st Christian Ch. (trustee). Clubs: Masons, Shrine, Lions (club treas., pres., dist. gov. 1963-64, chmn. dist. nominating com. 1964-65, chmn. dist. conv. 1965-66, chmn. dist. care com. 1966-69, chmn. dist. redistricting com. 1968-69, chmn. dist. youth com. 1969-72, dist. chmn. Leo Clubs 1970-73, 2d v.p., dist. rep. Camp Lions 1963-74, dist. chmn. constn. and by laws com. 1976—). Home: 321 W Grandview Dr Vandalia IL 62471

BARTINE, ALLEN RUSSELL, mfg. co. exec.; b. Marshalltown, Iowa, Apr. 2, 1945; s. Edwin Willard and Orpha L. (Froning) B.; B.S., Iowa State U., 1967; M.B.A., Ind. U., 1969; m. Margot Claire Friese, June 8, 1968; children—Todd Allen, Erin Marie. Sr. auditor, cons. Touche Ross & Co., Chgo., 1969-74; corp. controller Am. Tara Corp., Chgo., 1974-75, sec.-treas., 1975-77, v.p. fin., sec.-treas., pension plan adminstr., 1978—. Mem. Am. Inst. C.P.A.'s, Ill. Soc. C.P.A.'s, Internat. Bus. Forms Inst., Nat. Bus. Forms Assn., Printing Industry Am., Chgo. West Central Assn. (mem. urban redevel. com. 1978, now dir. and 2d v.p.). Republican. Presbyterian. Clubs: Lake Bluff Bath and Tennis, Mid-Town Racquet. Office: 1311 W Lake St Chicago IL 60607

BARTLETT, BUD (BYRON ALLAN), TV exec.; b. Las Vegas, Nev., Feb. 14, 1940; s. Byron Edwin and Yvonne (Lodwick) B.; B.A. in Radio-TV, Ariz. State U., 1963; M.A. in Radio-TV-Film, U. Denver, 1967. Producer Sta. KAET-TV, Phoenix, 1963-65; producer, instr. So. Ill. U. Broadcasting Service, stas. WSIU-TV, WUSI-TV, WSIU Radio, Carbondale, 1966-71; instructional TV specialist TV sect. Ill. State Bd. Edn., Springfield, 1971—; pres. Springfield Ednl. Communications Assn., 1977-78, producer, writer 39 public TV programs and ednl. films including Number Please and Sifting the Sands of Time, 1963—. Served with U.S. Army, 1963. Mem. Nat. Assn. Ednl. Broadcasters. Author: By Wave and Wire, 1974. Home: 520 S 2d St Apt 1102 Springfield IL 62701 Office: 100 N 1st St Springfield IL 62777

BARTLETT, PETER GREENOUGH, engring. co. exec.; b. Manchester, N.H., Apr. 22, 1930; s. Richard Cilley and Dorothy (Pillsbury) B.; Ph.B., Northwestern U., 1955; m. Jeanne Eddes, July 8, 1954; children—Peter G., Marta, Lauren, Karla, Richard E. Engr., Westinghouse Electric Co., Balt., 1955-58; mgr. mil. communications Motorola, Inc., Chgo., 1958-60; pres. Bartlett Labs., Inc., Indpls., 1960-63; asso. prof. elec. engring. U. S.C., Columbia, 1963-64; dir. research Eagle Signal Co., Davenport, Iowa, 1964-67; div. mgr. Struthers-Dunn, Inc., Bettendorf, Iowa, 1967-74; pres. Automation Systems, Inc., Eldridge, Iowa, 1974, also dir. Active Boys Scouts Am.; pres. bd. dirs. Save, Inc., 1965-67. Mem. IEEE. Republican. Presbyterian. Patentee in field. Home: 2336 E 11th St Davenport IA 52803 Office: Lancer Park Eldridge IA 52748

BARTLETT, ROBERT CARRICK, pub. exec.; b. Worcester, Mass., Aug. 15, 1915; s. Elwin Irving and Rena Pearl (Carrick) B.; B.A., Williams Coll., 1936; LL.B., Chgo. Kent Coll. Law, 1944, LL.M., 1945; m. Rita Evelyn Fitzgerald, July 24, 1937; children—Beverly A., Robert W., Jeffrey W. Admitted to Ill. bar, 1944; with Commerce Clearing House, Inc., Chgo., 1939—, pres., 1959-80, dir., 1959—; mem. firm Bartlett & Bartlett, Chgo.; dir. Nat. Blvd. Bank, Chgo., Gen. Kinetics, Inc. Mem. Am., Internat., Inter-Am. bar assns., Société de Législation Comparée, Beta Theta Pi. Clubs: Metropolitan, University (Chgo.); Williams, Overseas Press (N.Y.C.); Nat. Lawyers (Washington). Office: 4025 W Peterson Ave Chicago IL 60646

BARTLETT, ROBIN LYNN, educator; b. Muncie, Ind., Nov. 16, 1947; d. Charles Daniel and Marcella Gretchen (Frazier) B.; A.B., Western Coll. Women, 1969; M.A., Mich. State U., 1972, Ph.D., 1974. Reserach asst., summer intern Fed. Res. Bd. Govs., Washington, 1970-72; faculty Denison U., Granville, Ohio, 1974—, asso. prof. econs. since 1979—. Mem. NOW, Am. Econ. Assn. (com. on status of women in econs. profession), Western Econ. Assn., Eastern Econ. Assn., So. Econ. Assn. Author: (with Christine E. Amsler) Be Your Own Economic Analyst, 1980; contbr. articles in field to profl. jours. Home: 410 E Broadway Granville OH 43023 Office: Denison University Dept Economics Granville OH 43023

BARTLETT, VIRGIL LOUIS, educator; b. Roswell, N.Mex., Mar. 20, 1916; s. Brant Louis and Elsie Mert (Allee) B.; B.A., Andrews U., 1944; M.A., Tex. Christian U., 1947; Ed.D. (fellow), Ball State U., 1970; m. Frances Irene May, July 3, 1939; children—Verlyne May, Sandra Ann. Book and Bible house mgr. Texico Conf. of Seventh Day Adventists, 1944-45; head bus. adminstrn. dept. Southwestern Jr. Coll., Keene, Tex., 1945-48; prin. Union Springs (N.Y.) Acad., 1948-51; bus. mgr. Philippine Union Coll., Manila, 1951-52; pres. Mountain View Coll., Malaybalay, Philippines, 1952-55; ordained to ministry Seventh-day Adventist Ch., 1956; ednl. supt., treas. Far Eastern Island Mission, Agana, Guam, 1955-56; prin. Sheyenne River Acad., Harvey, N.D., 1956-59; prin. Ind. Acad., Cicero, 1959-68; ch. pastor, Muncie, Ind., 1968-69; coordinator tchr. edn., dir. student tchrs. Andrews U., Berrien Springs, Mich., 1970—; mem. Deans and Dirs. of Tchr. Edn. in Higher Edn. in Mich.; mem. Com. for Better Utilization of Univ. Resources for Tchr. Edn. in Mich. Mem. Am. Ednl. Research Assn., Assn. for Supervision and Curriculum Devel., Mich. Assn. for Student Teaching, Mich. Assn. Tchr. Educators, Mich. Edn. Assn., Assn. Tchr. Educators, Am. Assn. Colls. for Tchr. Edn., Mich. Assn. Colls. for Tchr. Edn. (treas.), Mich. Assn. Tchr. Edn. (exec. bd., profl. devel. adv. council for SW Mich.), Phi Delta Kappa. Republican. Club: Lions (v.p.). Home: 2719 Willo Dr Berrien Springs MI 49103 Office: Bell Hall Andrews U Berrien Springs MI 49104

BARTLETTE, DONALD LLOYD, social worker, educator, public speaker, writer, human services cons.; b. Walhalla, N.D., Dec. 17, 1939; s. Abraham Bruno and Lily Alice (Houle) B.; Ph.B., U. N.D., 1962; M.A., N.D. State U., 1966; Ph.D., C.P.U., 1981; m. Julie Gay Poer, Feb. 1, 1969; children—Lisa Maaca, Joanna Leigh, Andrea Gay, Marisa Anne, Laura Bethany, Sara Elizabeth. Program dir. Camp Grassick, N.D., 1959-62; Unit supr., counselor Cambridge State Sch. and Hosp., 1963-64; group worker Children's Village, Fargo, N.D., 1964-65; supr. Meth. Children's Village, Detroit, 1966-68; program dir. Mich. Children's Inst., Ann Arbor, 1968-70; exec., program dir. Madison County (Ind.) Assn. for Retarded, 1970-71; dir. program and social work services Outreach Community Center, Mpls., 1972-73; exec. dir. Minn. Epilepsy League, St. Paul, 1974-75; pvt. cons. in retardation, 1972-75; coordinator spl. services, adviser Human Rights Commn. City of Bloomington (Minn.), 1975-78; dir. social services Am. Indian Evang. Ch., Mpls., 1978-79; dir. social services Stark County (Ohio) Bd. Mental Retardation, 1979-80; field work instr. Sch. Social Work, U. Minn., Augsburg Coll., Mpls., 1972-73; off-campus tchr. in retardation and social work Anderson Coll., 1970-71; adj. faculty Univ. Without Walls, U. Minn., 1972-73. Founder Bartlette Scholarship award U. N.D., 1971-75; pres. Nat. Minority Affairs Coalition, 1977-78, sec., 1976-77; mem. Met. Developmental Disabilities Task Force, 1975; chmn. Pub. Info. Coalition Project on Developmental Disabilities, 1974-75; vol. mem. Pres.'s, Minn. Gov.'s coms. on employment handicapped; task force minority affairs Pres.'s Com. Mental Retardation. Bd. dirs. N.W. Hennepin Human Services Council, 1975-76; bd. dirs., chmn. poverty com. Anoka County Assn. for Retarded, 1974-79; bd. dirs. Family and Childrens Services of Greater Mpls., Stark County Mental Health Bd., Citizen Advocacy Program of Stork County; cons. People First of Stark County; adv. Indian children Council for Exceptional Children; patron and com. mem. Lake Center Christian Sch., Hartville, Ohio. Fellow Acad. Ednl. Disciplines; mem. Am. Acad. Mental Retardation, Nat. Assn. Christian Social Workers, Nat. Assn. Retarded Citizens (dir., chmn. com. on poverty and mental retardation 1973-74), Internat. Platform Assn., Assn. Am. Indian Social Workers, Soc. for Protection Unborn through Nutrition (life mem.), Phi Delta Kappa. Author presentation: Macaroni at Midnight. Home: 2602 Ocelot NE North Canton OH 44721

BARTLEY, ROGER ARTHUR, funeral home exec.; b. Canton, Ohio, Apr. 3, 1950; s. Leroy Gilbert and Marilyn Rose (Jackson) B.; B.S., Mount Union Coll., 1972; m. Sherry Lynn Catlett, Apr. 7, 1973; children—Todd Douglas, Corey Andrew. Sports editor, advt. mgr. Minerva (Ohio) Leader, 1973-74; funeral dir. Bartley Funeral Home, Minerva, 1974—. First aid instr. and trainer Minerva chpt. ARC; mem. Minerva Bicentennial Commn., 1975-77; pres., trustee Minerva Public Library, 1978—. Served with AUS, 1972-73. Mem. Ohio Funeral Dirs. Assn. (public edn. com.), Ohio Assn. Emergency Med. Services. Republican. Methodist. Club: Minerva Rotary (v.p.). Editor: Living Out Our Heritage, bicentennial history book, 1976. Home: 203 W Lincolnway Minerva OH 44657 Office: 205 W Lincolnway Minerva OH 44657

BARTMAN, HERBERT MARVIN, elec. engr.; b. Sheboygan, Wis., May 26, 1923; s. John and Lena (Frei) Pluskat; B.S. in Elec. Engring., U. Wis., 1950; postgrad Ohio State U. 1964-72; M.S. in Engring. Mgmt., U. Dayton, 1979; m. Alma A. Glanert, Sept. 3, 1949; children—Douglas M., Debra A., Margarett L. Project scientist communications lab. Wright Patterson AFB, Ohio, 1951-61, sr. project engr. Air Force avionics lab., 1961-70, prin. electronic engr., avionics lab., 1970-79, Air Force aero. lab., 1980—. Active, Asst. scoutmaster, instl. rep. Miami Valley Council Boy Scouts Am., 1962-72; mem. bd. evangelism Concordia Evang. Luth. Ch. Served with AUS, 1943-46, USAF, 1950-51. Mem. IEEE Engring. Mgmt. Soc., Air Force Assn., Sigma Xi. Asso. editor IEEE Electromagnetic Compatibility Transactions, 1971—. Home: 5303 Middlebury Rd Dayton OH 45432 Office: AFWAL/AAAD Wright Patterson AFB OH 45433

BARTOLOME, FRANCISCO MABALAY, food technologist; b. Manila, P.I., Nov. 6, 1939; s. Fruto Feliciano and Emiliana (Mabalay) B.; came to U.S., 1965; B.S. in Chem. Engring., U. Philippines, 1962; M.S., Purdue U., 1968, Ph.D., 1971; m. Dr. Linda Gutierrez, Sept. 3, 1966. Product devel. mgr., packaging engr. Procter & Gamble, Manila, 1962-65; group leader product devel. Hunt-Wesson Foods, Inc., Fullerton, Calif., 1971-75; dir. research and devel. Golden Dipt Co., Millstadt, Ill., 1975-77; mgr. tech. devel. Pillsbury Co., Mpls., 1977—; instr. chem. engring. Manuel L. Quezon U., Manila, 1965-65; research asst. Purdue U., 1966-71. Recipient Dee Chuan grant, 1962. Mem. Inst. Food Technologists, Am. Assn. Cereal Chemists, Phi Tau Sigma. Home: 6501 Vernon Ave S Edina MN 55436 Office: 425 Main St SE Minneapolis MN 55414

BARTON, EDWARD JAMES, educator; b. Monroe, Mich., June 24, 1950; s. Aubrey James and Evelyn Marie (Masserant) B.; B.A., Western Mich. U., 1972, M.A. with honors, 1973; Ph.D., Utah State U., 1978. Child psychologist North Central Mich. Mental Health Center, Cadillac, Mich., 1973-75; behavioral cons. Behavioral Mgmt. Co., Salt Lake City, 1975-76; grad. instr. Utah State U., Logan, 1976-77, research asst., 1976-77, teaching asst., 1976-77; asso. prof. psychology No. Mich. U., Marquette, 1977—. Recipient Faculty Merit awards No. Mich. U., 1978, 79; Utah State U. acad. fellow, 1977; Utah State U. Research Council grantee, 1976, No. Mich. U. Faculty Research Com. grantee, 1979. Mem. Am. Psychol. Assn. (Teaching of Psychology award 1981), AAUP, Assn. Advancement Behavior Therapy, Assn. Behavior Analysis (mem. affiliate com., 1978—, conv. program com. 1979—, area resource person 1978—), Soc. Behavioral Medicine, Soc. Research Child Devel., Midwestern Psychol. Assn., Rocky Mountain Psychol. Assn., No. Mich. U. Child Devel. Adv. Council. Ad hoc editorial cons. Child Behavior Therapy, 1979—, Child Devel., 1979—, Behavior Therapy, 1980—, Jour. Personality and Social Psychology, 1981—; book cons. St. Martin Press, 1980—; contbr. articles to profl. jours., also books. Office: Psychology Dept No Mich U Marquette MI 49855

BARTON, ROBERT, bakery co. exec.; b. Bklyn., Aug. 20, 1936; s. Martin Arthur and Veronica Julia (Keenan) B.; A.A.S., Bklyn. Coll., 1961; B.B.A., St. Francis Coll., 1965; m. Ann C. Whelan, Nov. 12, 1960; children—Robert, Timothy, Jonathan, Brenda. Purchasing agt. Ebingers, Bklyn., 1960-69; commodity analyst Quality Bakers, N.Y.C., 1969; dir. purchasing Sunshine Biscuit Co. div. Am. Brands Corp., N.Y.C., 1969-73; v.p. Am. Bakeries Co., Chgo., 1973—. Served with USMC, 1957-59. Mem. Am. Soc. Bakery Engrs., Am. Bakers Assn., Am. Inst. Baking, Chicago Bakers Club (pres. 1979—). Home: 1531 N King George Ct Palatine IL 60067 Office: Am Bakeries Co 10 S Riverside Plaza Chicago IL 60606

BARTRAM, JOHN GREER, indsl. constrn. co. ofcl.; b. Boulder, Colo., May 17, 1955; s. John Webster and Virginia (Button) B.; B.S.C.E., magna cum laude, U. Mich., 1977; m. Linda Ruth Sessums, Apr. 11, 1981. Engring. trainee Broad Corp., River Rouge, Mich., 1978-79, asst. project mgr., 1979, project mgr., 1979—, estimator, 1979—. Mem. The Player's Theater Group, Tau Kappa Epsilon. Republican. Presbyterian. Home: 843 Nottingham St Grosse Pointe Park MI 48230 Office: 195 Campbell St River Rouge MI 48218

BARTTER, KENNETH LEE, telephone co. exec.; b. Toledo, Oct. 8, 1932; s. Clarence A. and Hazel D. (Watson) B.; B.A., Ohio State U., 1958, M.A., 1961; m. Loretta J. Hurst, June 27, 1953; children—Sheryl Lea, Kathleen Ann, Barbara Lee, Carolyn J. Prodn. mgr. Sta. WOSU-TV, Columbus, Ohio, 1957-60; mgmt. trainee Gen. Telephone Co. of Ohio, Marion, 1960-62, div. public relations rep., 1962-65, gen. office public relations rep., 1965-67, community relations mgr., 1967—; frequent public speaker; speech cons. Mem. exec. bd. Harding Area council Boy Scouts Am., 1968—; bd. dirs. Jr. Achievement of Dover-New Philadelphia, Inc., 1963-65; vice chmn. planning and steering com. for proposed Tuscarawas County Joint Vocat. Sch., 1965; vice chmn. Marion Repeater com., 1979. Served with USN, 1951-55. Named Lion of the Yr., Marion Lions, 1974. Mem. Laser Inst. Am., Ind. Telephone Pioneer Assn. (dir. 1978—), Am. Radio Relay League, Marion Area C. of C., Alpha Epsilon Rho. Republican. Presbyterian. Clubs: Marion Amateur Radio, Marion Racquet, Central Ohio Radio, Masons, Shriners, Lions (pres. 1978-79). Home: 1196 Yorkshire Dr Marion OH 43302 Office: 100 Executive Dr Marion OH 43302

BARUA, SANAT KUMAR, engr.; b. Chittagong, Bangladesh, Nov. 15, 1934; came to U.S., 1969, naturalized, 1977; s. Benoy Bhushan and Premangini B.; I.Sc., Chittagong Coll., 1953; postgrad. Dacca U., 1959, B.S. in Mech. Engring., Ahsanullah Engring. Coll., 1959; m. Indu Prova, Feb. 10, 1965; 1 dau., Shanta. Asst. engr. The Ralph M. Parsons Co., Dacca, Bangladesh, 1960-62, design. engr., 1962-65, sr. engr., 1965-67, chief engr., 1967-68, spl. engring. asst. to project mgr., 1968-69; project engr. Barnhouse Assos., Inc., Columbus, Ohio, 1969-75; sr. sanitary engr. Friedl & Harris, Inc., Columbus, 1975-77; project engr. Burgess & Niple, Ltd., Columbus, 1977-79, project coordinator, 1979—; cons. in field. Pres. Pakistan Buddhist Youth Fedn., Dacca, 1967-69. Registered profl. engr., Ohio, Ind., W.Va. Diplomate Am. Acad. Environ. Engrs.; mem. Nat. Soc. Profl. Engrs., Ohio Soc. Profl. Engrs., ASCE, Water Pollution Control Fedn., Ohio Water Pollution Control Conf., Am. Water Works Assn., Columbus Engrs. Club. Home: 1003 Kelvin Ct Worthington OH 43085 Office: 5085 Reed Rd Columbus OH 43220

BASE, STEVE RICHARD, soil scientist; b. Gooding, Idaho, Apr. 24, 1939; s. Stephen and Lucille (Lewis) B.; B.S., U. Idaho, 1962, M.S., 1969; postgrad. Cornell U., 1976; m. Barbara Lee DeRock, July 1, 1980; children—Daniel, David, Stephen, Michael; stepchildren—Debra Rupe, Douglas DeRock, Dana DeRock, Davis DeRock, Darin DeRock, Daniel DeRock. With Soil Conservation Service, 1962—, leader soil survey party, Grangeville, Idaho, 1970-73, soil correlator, Bismarck, N.D., 1973-77, Lincoln, Nebr., 1977—. Served with U.S. Army, 1957-58. Union Pacific scholar, 1957, Pacific Northwest Plant Food Assn. scholar 1961. Mem. Soil Sci. Soc. Am., Am. Soc. Agronomy, Soil Conservation Soc. Am., Nebr. Soc. Profl. Soil Scientists, Alpha Zeta. Home: 1822 S 56th St Lincoln NE 68506 Office: PO Box 82503 Lincoln NE 68501

BASH, JOHN EDWARD, chem. co. safety supr.; b. Kansas City, Kans., July 27, 1933; s. Earl A. and Laura I. B.; A.S. in Engring., Kansas City Jr. Coll., 1957; also various safety tng. courses; m. Nancy Tracy, May 22, 1955; children—Ronda Lynne, Scott A. With Mobay Chem. Corp. (formerly Chemagro Corp), Kansas City, Mo., 1958—, prodn. foreman, 1958-64, safety supr., 1964—. Served with U.S. Army, 1952-54. Mem. Am. Soc. Safety Engrs. (pres. Heart of Am. chpt. 1968-69), Nat. Agr. Chem. Assn. (nat. pesticide safety area coordinator 1972). Republican. Episcopalian. Home: 3230 NE 47th St Kansas City MO 64117 Office: PO Box 4913 Kansas City MO 64120

BASILE, ABIGAIL JULIA ELLEN HERRON (MRS. JOSEPH BASILE), employment counselor, state ofcl.; b. St. Louis, June 15, 1915; d. Charles Arthur and Abigail (Edwards) Herron; student Kansas City Jr. Coll., 1948-50, U. Kans., 1959; B.S. in Bus. Adminstrn., Rockhurst Coll., 1965; M. Ed., U. Mo., 1967; m. Joseph Basile, Aug. 15, 1939. Employment security dep. Mo. Div. Employment Security, Kansas City, 1945-59, youth coordinator, employment counselor, 1959-65; counselor-supr. Youth Opportunity Center, 1965-66; supr. spl. applicant services Mo. Employment Service. Kansas City, 1966-67, supr. counseling, 1967—. Sec., Inter-Agy. Com. Rehab., 1967-69. Mem. Mo. Assn. Social Welfare. Mem. Am. Personnel and Guidance Assn., Nat. Vocat. Assn., Internat. Assn. Personnel in Employment Security (Mo. pres. 1966-67, internat. sec. 1968), Nat. Rehab. Assn., Am. Legion Aux. Democrat. Episcopalian. Home: 5221 N Wayne St Kansas City MO 64118 Office: 1411 Main St Kansas City MO 64105

BASILE, FRANK MICHEL, property mgmt. co. exec.; b. New Orleans, Oct. 6, 1939; s. Vincent Charles and Ursula Mary (Sendker) B.; B.B.A., Tulane U., 1961; children—Jeffrey, Jason. With Ford Motor Co., 1963-75, gen. field mgr., Indpls., 1971-75; pres. Charisma Publs., Inc., Indpls., 1977—; v.p. Gene Glick Mgmt. Corp., Indpls., 1975—; Vice pres. Indpls. Free U., 1978-81; internat. bd. dirs. Parents Without Partners, 1977-78; mem. Ind. Traffic Safety Council, 1971-74. Cert. property mgr.; cert. Speaking profl. Mem. Nat. Apt. Assn. (v.p. 1980), Nat. Assn. Home Builders, Inst. Real Estate Mgmt. (nat. faculty), Nat. Speakers Assn. (pres. Ind. chpt.), Apt. Assn. Ind. (pres. 1979), Indpls. Sales and Mktg. Execs. (pres. 1981-82), Beta Gamma Sigma. Clubs: Broadmoor Country, Indpls. Racquet, Woodland Springs. Author: Come Fly With Me, 1978; Back to Basics with Basile, 1978; Management Company Reporting Structure, 1978; Beyond The Basics, 1980; Professional Multihousing Management, 1981; Flying to your Success, 1981; also articles. Contbg. editor mgmt. Indpls. Bus. Jour. Office: 9102 N Meridian St Indianapolis IN 46260

BASILE, ROBERT MANLIUS, geographer, soil scientist, educator; b. Youngstown, Ohio, Mar. 12, 1916; s. Giustino G. and Minnie H. (Bailey) B.; B.S., Washington and Lee U., 1938; M.S., Mich. State U., 1940; Ph.D., Ohio State U., 1953; m. Anne Judson Webb, May 23, 1945; children—Elizabeth Anne, L. Lorraine, Karen L. Instr., Northwestern State Coll., Alva, Okla., 1940-42; soil scientist Bur. Reclamation, Huron, S.D., 1947-48, 1950; instr. geography Ohio State Univ., Columbus, 1953-56, asst. prof., 1956-62, asso. prof., 1962-68, prof., 1968-69; prof. geography U. Toledo, 1969—; vis. prof. Ohio U., summer 1952, U. Winnipeg, summer 1960, San Jose State U., summer 1966, U. S.C., summer 1967, U. Wyo., summer 1981. Served with U.S. Navy, 1942-45. NATO grantee, 1966; Nat. Research Inst. grantee, 1966-67. Mem. Assn. Am. Geographers, Soil Sci. Soc. Am., AAAS, Assn. Ohio Pedologists, Smithsonian Instn., Wilderness Soc., Phi Kappa Phi, Gamma Theta Upsilon. Author: A Geography of Soils, 1972; editor: Selected Readings in the Geography of Soils, 1980; contbr. articles to profl. jours. Home: 5929 Angleview Ct Sylvania OH 43560 Office: Univ of Toledo Bancroft St Toledo OH 43606

BASILE, WILLIAM BASIL, mfg. exec.; b. Chgo., Mar 17, 1911; s. Ralph and Carmelia (D'Urso) B.; Ph.B., U. Chgo., 1931, J.D., 1933; research asso. Northwestern U. Law Sch., 1933-34; m. Ruth Rutledge, July 25, 1935; children—Bette Claire, William Basil, Ralph Rutledge. Admitted to Ill. bar, 1933, practiced in Chgo., 1934-43; v.p., dir. indsl. relations Richardson Co., 1943-52, dir. 1944—, exec. v.p., 1952-53, pres. 1953-74, chmn., 1974-79, atty. price adjustment bd. AAF. 1943. Mem. Am., Ill. bar assns., Chgo. Mus. Natural History, Art Inst. Chgo., Phi Alpha Delta, Alpha Sigma Phi. Clubs: Skokie Country (Glencoe); University, Economic (Chgo.). Home: 501 Monroe Ave Glencoe IL 60022 Office: Richardson Co 2400 E Devon Ave Des Plaines IL 60018

BASKIN, JANICE KIMBERLY, coll. ofcl.; b. Pitts., July 19, 1954; d. Norton and Marilyn J. (Weiss) B.; B.A. in Sino-Soviet Fgn. Trade, Ohio State U., 1977. Mktg. researcher Cleve. Survey Center, 1969-74; page to speaker Ohio Ho. of Reps., Columbus, 1975-77; manpower researcher Cuyahoga County Bd. Commrs., Cleve., 1977-78; dir. off-campus credit instrn. Cuyahoga Community Coll., Cleve., 1978—; public relations-promotion cons., Cleve., 1980—. Mem. candidate ratings com. Citizen's League Cleve., 1980—; v.p., public relations dir. UpDowntown, Inc., 1979—; mem. community relations, urban affairs and edn. coms. Cleve. Jewish Community Fedn., 1979—; mem. Nat. Council Jewish Women, 1980—; active state and nat. polit. campaigns, 1968—. Mem. Am. Soc. for Tng. and Devel., Ohio Continuing Edn. Council, Adult Edn. Council Cleve., Sigma Delta Tau. Republican. Jewish. Clubs: Cleve. City (chmn. civic involvement 1980), Womens City (promotion and membership coms., chmn. edn. 1978—) (Cleve.). Home: 4451 University Pkwy University Heights OH 44118 Office: 4250 Richmond Rd Warrensville Twp OH 44122

BASKIN, JOHN ROLAND, lawyer; b. Cleve., Dec. 23, 1916; s. Roland A. and Frances M. (Schwoerer) B.; A.B. magna cum laude, Western Res. U., 1938, LL.B., 1940; m. Madeline Stricker, Feb. 26, 1949 (dec. 1965); d., Barbara Anne; m. 2d, Betty Anne Meyer, May 12, 1967. Admitted to Ohio bar, 1940, FCC, 1949, U.S. Supreme Ct., 1955; practiced in Cleve., 1940—, asso. mem. firm Baker & Hostetler, 1941-54, partner, 1954—. Spl. agt. AUS CIC, U.S. Atomic Bomb project, 1942-46, CIC officer, Armed Forces Spl. Weapons project, 1951-52. Mem. Am., Ohio, Cleve. bar assns., Order of the Coif, Phi Beta Kappa, Delta Tau Delta, Delta Theta Phi, Court of Nisi Prius. Republican. Episcopalian. Clubs: Union, Mayfield Country (Cleve.); University (Washington). Home: 2679 Ashley Rd Shaker Heights OH 44122 also Buttonwood Bay Key Largo FL 33037 also East Chop Martha's Vineyard MA 02557 Office: 3200 National City Center Cleveland OH 44114

BASS, LARRY JUNIOR, clin. psychologist, educator; b. Granby, Mo., Aug. 2, 1944; s. Harold Virgil and Mildred Lucille (Charlton) B.; B.S., U. Mo., 1966, M.S. (NDEA fellow), 1967; Ph.D., Washington U., St. Louis, 1972; m. Meredith Aenone Copeland, Aug. 17, 1968; children—Mark, Darren, Adam. Research asst. Washington U., 1967-68, staff psychologist Child Guidance Clinic, 1970; intern Mt. Zion Med. Center, San Francisco, 1968-69; clin. psychologist Jewish Hosp., St. Louis, 1971-75; asso. prof. Evangel Coll., Springfield, Mo., 1975—; pvt. practice clin. psychology, Springfield, 1975—. Mem. Am., Mo. psychol. assns., Phi Delta Kappa. Home: 936 E Manchester St Springfield MO 65807 Office: 1443 N Robberson St Suite 402 Springfield MO 65802

BASS, ROBERT OLIN, mfg. co. exec.; b. Denver, July 22, 1917; s. Olin R. and Cora Bass; B.S. in Bus. Adminstrn., U. Denver, 1941; m. Isabelle Cantrell, Mar. 22, 1941; 1 dau., Susan. Pres., Eberhardt-Denver Co., 1956; exec. v.p., asst. gen. mgr. Morse Chain Co., Ithaca, N.Y., 1956-58, pres., 1958-66; group v.p. indsl. Borg-Warner Corp., Chgo., 1966-68, exec. v.p., 1968-75, pres., 1975-79, chief operating officer, 1975-80, vice chmn., 1979—, also dir.; dir. SCM Corp., N.Y., Raymond Corp., Greene, N.Y. Mem. bus. adv. council Coll. Bus. Adminstrn. U. Denver, 1976—; trustee Field Mus. of Natural History, Chgo. Recipient Outstanding Alumnus award U. Denver, 1977. Mem. Am. Mgmt. Assn. (v.p. 1977-79, trustee 1979—), Assns. Gen. Mgmt. Council (chmn. 1977-79), Ill. Mfrs. Assn. (dir. 1975). Clubs: Chgo., Univ. (Chgo.). Office: 200 S Michigan Ave Chicago IL 60604

BASSETT, KEITH T., metallurgist, machine co. exec.; b. Leicester, Eng., Apr. 28, 1933; came to U.S., 1974; s. Joseph William and Lillian May (Wightman) B.; B.Sc. in Applied Sci., U. Durham (Eng.), 1954; m. Doris Nicholson, May 14, 1955; children—Martyn John, Peter Richard, Joanne Elizabeth. Metallurgist, Fairey Aviation, Hayes, Eng., 1954-56; mgr. extraction metallurgy Henry Wiggin & Co., Hereford, Eng., 1956-60; sales metallurgist Park Gate Iron & Steel Co., Rotherham, Eng., 1960-62; vacuum degassing service metallurgist English Steel Corp., Sheffield, Eng., 1962-65; sr. service metallurgist Atlas Steels Co., Welland, Ont., Can., 1965-74; mgr. metallurgy Danly Machine Corp., Cicero, Ill., 1974—; seminar lectr.; lectr. Coll. of DuPage; Metals Engring. Inst. course instr., 1969-79, nat. chmn., 1981—. Chmn. Hamilton and Dist. Cricket League, 1968-74, Ont. Cricket Assn., 1972-74; nat. rep. Can. Cricket Assn., 1973-74. Mem. Am. Welding Soc. (nat. subcom. chmn. 1975—), Am. Soc. Metals (nat. com. 1978—, chmn. nat. com. 1981—, chpt. officer 1980—). Office: 2100 S Laramie Ave Cicero IL 60650

BASSETT, MARIAN KAY, telephone co. exec.; b. Dayton, O., May 19, 1945; d. Harry Richard and Lucy Bell (Hetzler) Weikert; B.S., Manchester Coll., 1967; M.S. in Bus. Adminstrn. St. Francis Coll., 1981; m. Ronald William Bassett, June 1, 1974; 1 stepson, Patrick Obrien. Tchr., Concord Community Schs., Elkhart, Ind., 1967-68; mgmt. trainee Gen. Telephone Co. Ind., Fort Wayne, 1968-69, chief operator, 1969-71, coordinator results and budgets, 1972-77; market research adminstr. GTE Services Corp., Stamford, Conn., 1977-79, market research adminstr., No. region, Indpls., 1979-81; gen. operator service mgr. GTE Ind./Mich., Ft. Wayne, Ind., 1981—. Nat. Assn. Female Execs., Inc. Republican. Club: Rathkamp Matchcover Soc. Office: GTE Ind 8001 W Jefferson Blvd Fort Wayne IN 46801

BASSETT, PAUL MERRITT, educator; b. Lima, Ohio, May 28, 1935; s. Paul Gardner and Ruth Abbott (Wiess) B.; B.A., Olivet Nazarene Coll., 1957; B.D., Duke U. Div. Sch., 1960; postgrad. Ohio State U., 1960-62; Ph.D., Duke U., 1967; m. Pearl Ann Householter, Aug. 8, 1958; children—Emilie Ruth, Paul Stephan, Anita Suzanne. Tchr., Southeastern High Sch., Ross County, Ohio, 1961-62; asso. prof. Greek and history Trevecca Nazarene Coll., Nashville, 1965-66; asst. prof. religious studies W. Va. U., Morgantown, 1966-69; asso. prof. history of Christianity, Nazarene Theol. Sem., Kansas City, Mo., 1969-76, prof., 1976—; vis. prof. Point Loma Coll., San Diego, 1969-72, Seminario Nazareno Centroamericana, San Jose, Costa Rica, 1972-76; lectr. U. Mo., Kansas City, others. Rockefeller fellow in religion, 1964-65; Assn. of Theol. Schs. in U.S. and Can. grantee, 1976-77. Mem. Am. Soc. Ch. History, Am. Hist. Assn., Am. Cath. Hist. Soc., Mediaeval Acad. Am., Acad. Religion, Soc. Bibl. Lit., Wesleyan Theol. Soc., Kansas City Soc. for Theol. Studies, Am. Acad. of Research Historians in Medieval Spain. Mem. Ch. of the Nazarene. Author: Keep the Wonder, 1979; contbr. articles to profl. jours. Home: 9930 Linden Ln Overland Park KS 66207 Office: 1700 E Meyer Blvd Kansas City MO 64131

BASSI, SUKH DEV, biologist; b. Kericho, Kenya, East Africa, Feb. 11, 1941; came to U.S., 1963, naturalized, 1975; s. Telu Ram and Vidya Wati (Gug) B.; B.A. (Queens Scout (Eng.) Inst. Internat. Edn. scholar), Knox Coll., 1965; M.S. (grad. fellow), St. Louis U., 1968, Ph.D. (grad. fellow), 1971; m. Jane Gempler, Aug. 21, 1971; children—Neal, Nathan. Tchr., Highland Primary Sch., Kericho, 1960-63; asst. prof. biology Clark Coll., Atlanta, 1970-71; asst. prof. biology Benedictine Coll., Atchison, Kans., 1971-73, asso. prof., 1973-79, prof. biology, 1979—; research biologist Midwest Solvents Co., Atchison. Round Table commr. Boy Scouts Am., 1977, bd. dirs. Pony council, 1979—. Mem. Genetics Soc., Am. Chem. Soc., Am. Inst. Biol. Scis., Kans. Acad. Sci., Sigma Xi. Clubs: Atchison Rotary (v.p. 1977-78, pres. 1978-79), Moose. Contbr. sci. articles to profl. jours. Home: Route 3 Atchison KS 66002 Office: Biology Dept Benedictine Coll Atchison KS 66002

BASSIOUNI, M. CHERIF, educator; b. Cairo, Egypt, Dec. 19, 1937; Came to U.S., 1961, naturalized, 1966. s. Ibrahim and Amina (Khatab) B.; A.B., Coll. Holy Family, Cairo, 1955; postgrad. Dijon U. Sch. Law, France, 1955-57, U. Geneva (Switzerland), 1957; LL.B., U. Cairo (Egypt), 1961; J.D., Ind. U., 1964; LL.M., John Marshall Lawyers Inst., 1966; S.J.D., George Washington U., 1973; m. Rossana Cesari, Dec. 17, 1962. Admitted to Ill., D.C. bars, 1967; practiced in Chgo., 1967—; prof. law DePaul U., 1964—; dean Internat. Inst. Advanced Studies in Criminal Scis., Siracusa, Italy, 1976—; Fulbright-Hays vis. prof. internat. criminal law U. Freiburg (Germany), 1970; vis. prof. law N.Y. U. Sch. Law, 1971; guest scholar Woodrow Wilson Internat. Center for Scholars, Washington, 1972; cons. Chgo. Bd. Edn., 1965-69, chmn. adv. bd. law in Am. soc. project, 1973-75; lectr. in field; spl. cons. Fifth UN Congress Crime Prevention, 1975, 6th UN Congress, 1980; spl. cons. UN; hon. v.p. 5th UN Congress on Crime Prevention and Criminal Justice, 1975; mem. Ill. Commn. on Law and Justice, 1977—. Bd. dirs., sec.-gen. Internat. Assn. Penal Law, 1974—. Decorated Order Merit (Egypt); commendatore Order Merit Italy, also grande ufficiale; recipient Outstanding Citizen of Year award Citizenship Council Met. Chgo., 1967. Mem. World Peace Through Law, Am. Soc. Internat. Law, Am. (chmn. com. internat. legal edn. 1974—), Ill. (chmn. sect. on internat. law 1972-73, sect. council 1970-77), Chgo. (chmn. com. on criminal legislation 1967-69) bar assns., Mid.Am. Arab. C. of C. (chmn. 1973-74, 76-77, sec. gen. counsel 1974-76, pres. 1976—), Assn. Arab-Am. U. Grads. (bd. dirs. 1967-74, pres. 1969-70), Phi Alpha Delta. Author: Criminal Law and Its Processes, 1969; The Law of Dissent and Riots, 1971; (with V.P. Nanda) International Criminal Law, 2 Vols., 1973; (with Eugene Fisher) Storm Over The Arab World, 1972; International Extradition and World Public Order, 1974; International Terrorism and Political Crimes, 1975. Editor: Issues in the Mediterranean, 1976; Citizens Arrest: The Law of Arrest, Search and Seizure, 1977; Substantive Criminal Law, 1978; (with V.V. Savitski) The Criminal Justice System of the USSR, 1979; International Criminal Law: A Draft International Criminal Code, 1981; co-editor-in-chief Revue Internat. de Droit Penal, 1973—; (with Valeri Savitski) The Criminal Justice System of the USSR, 1979; editor The Globe, 1970—, Am. Jour. Comparative Law, 1972—. Office: 25 E Jackson St Chicago IL 60604

BASTIAN, (ROSE) MARIE, banker; b. Belmont, Ohio, Apr. 27, 1940; d. Montraville Sharp and Doris Avanell (Young) Hollingsworth; student Ohio State U., 1959; grad. Ohio Sch. Banking, 1974, Rutgers/Stonier Grad. Sch. Banking, 1980. With Bancohio Nat. Bank, Columbus, 1965—, exec. sec., 1968-71, salary adminstr., 1971-76, asst. v.p., mgr. personnel dept., 1976, v.p., chief personnel officer, 1976-79, sr. v.p. human resources group, 1979—; chmn. bus. adv. com. Franklin U. Bd. dirs. Campfire Girls, Cerebral Palsy of Columbus and Franklin County; mem. Friends of WOSU Devel. Com.; chmn. div. group 4 Heart Fund, 1980, 81; trustee Met. Columbus Learning Community. Nat. Assn. Bank Women scholar, 1972. Mem. Am. Soc. Personnel Adminstrs., Personnel Soc., Am. Inst. Banking, Am. Bankers Assn. (employee relations com.), Nat. Assn. Bank Women, Assn. Bank Women, Adminstrv. Mgmt. Soc. (survey com.), Columbus C. of C. (public relations com.). Club: Columbus Met. Home: 5141 Pebble Ln Columbus OH 43220 Office: 155 Broad St E Columbus OH 43265

BASTILLA, ROBERT FRANCIS, banker; b. Elmira, N.Y., Feb. 2, 1927; s. Francis John and Marjorie Flora (Hoag) B.; m. Shirley Jean Hug, June 7, 1947; children—Robert Michael, Nancy Ann Bastilla Rusick. Owner, operator Bastilla Egg Co., Highland, Ill., 1959-67; sales mgr., broadcaster Sta. WIN-U, Highland, 1967-68; newsman, broadcaster Sta. WRTH, Cottage Hills and Woodriver, Ill., 1968-69; dir. public relations 1st Nat. Bank of Highland, 1969-81, asst. v.p., dir. public relations, 1981—. Alderman, City of Highland, 1957-63; mem. exec. bd. Cahokia Mound council Boy Scouts Am., 1970-75, 79—, dist. chmn., 1979-81; bus. chmn. Highland Cancer Crusade, 1980—; pres. Madison County Fair Assn., 1973-79; mem. Planning Comm., City of Highland, 1979—, now sec.; exec. bd. Faith Countryside Homes, 1980—. Served with USN, 1945-46. Mem. Ill./Mo. Mktg. Assn. (past pres.), Bank Mktg. Assn., Am. Inst. Banking, Highland C. of C., Nat. Rifle Assn., V.F.W. Clubs: Lions (past pres., zone chmn.; Lion of Yr. 1981), Toastmasters (past pres.). Home: 521 Dophin Dr E Highland IL 62249 Office: 1000 Broadway PO Box 10 Highland IL 62249

BASU, ASIT PRAKAS, statistician; b. Jessore, India (now Bangladesh), Mar. 17, 1937; s. Hari Pada and Himansu (Prabha) B.; B.Sc., Calcutta U., 1956, M.Sc., 1958; Ph.D., U. Minn., 1966; m. Sandra J. Bergquist; children—Amit Kumar, Shumit Kumar. Asst. prof. statistics U. Wis., Madison, 1966-68; mem. research staff IBM Research Center, Yorktown Heights, N.Y., 1968-70; asst. prof. indsl. engring. and mgmt. sci. Northwestern U., Evanston, Ill., 1970-71; asso. prof. math. U. Pitts., 1971-74; prof. statistics U. Mo., Columbia, 1974—, chmn. dept., 1976—. Fellow Royal Statis. Soc., mem. Am. Statis. Assn., Inst. Math. Statistics, Calcutta Statis. Assn. Contbr. articles to profl. jours. Home: 3709 W Rollins Rd Columbia MO 65201 Office: Dept Statistics Univ Mo Columbia MO 65211

BATCHELDER, ANNE STUART (MRS. CLIFTON BROOKS BATCHELDER), former publisher, polit. party ofcl.; b. Lake Forest, Ill., Jan. 11, 1920; d. Robert Douglas and Harriet (McClure) Stuart; student Lake Forest Coll., 1941-43; m. Clifton Brooks Batchelder, May 26, 1945; children—Edward, Anne Stuart, Mary Clifton, Lucia Brooks. Clubmobile driver A.R.C., Eng., Belgium, France, Holland and Germany, 1943-45; pub., editor Douglas County Gazette, 1970-75; dir. Omaha Nat. Bank; mem. U.S. Checkbook Com. Mem. Republican Central Com. Nebr., 1955-62, 70—, vice chmn. Central Com., 1959-64, chmn., 1975-79, mem. fin. com., 1957-64; chmn. women's sect. Douglas County Rep. Finance Com., 1955, vice chmn. com., 1958-60; v.p. Omaha Woman's Rep. Club, 1957-58, pres., 1959-60; alternate del. Nat. Conv., 1956, 72; mem. Rep. Nat. Com. for Nebr., 1964-70; asst. chmn. Douglas County Rep. Central Com., 1971—; 1st v.p. Nebr. Fedn. Rep. Women, 1971-72, pres., 1972-74; chmn. Nebr. Rep. Com., 1975-79; chmn. ways and means com. Nat. Fedn. Rep. Women; mem. Nebr. State Bldg. Commn.; Rep. candidate for lt. gov., 1974. Sr. v.p. Nebr. Founders Day, 1958; past trustee Brownell Hall, Vis. Nurse Assn.; trustee Hastings Coll., Nebr. Meth. Hosp. Found. Mem. Mayflower Soc., Colonial Dames, P.E.O., Nat. League Pen Women, Zonta. Presbyterian (elder). Clubs: Omaha Country, Omaha. Home: 6875 State St Omaha NE 68152

BATCHELDER, GEORGE WILSON, marine contractor; b. Danvers, Mass., Jan. 4, 1920; s. Donald Philipp and Aurelia Marie (Begin) B.; student Fgn. Service Sch., Georgetown U., 1939-40, mech. engring. Adamson U., Manila, 1948-51; children—Ann Aurelia, Ruth Elizabeth, Helen Margaret, John Todd. Pilot, instr. comml. airline, Philippines, 1945-48; marine and heavy contractor, Philippines, Hong Kong, Vietnam and Cambodia, 1948-67; engaged in engring. and constrn., U.S., 1967—; pres. Nautilus Constrn. Corp., Highland Park, Ill., 1975; cons. in field. Mem. Lake Forest (Ill.) Symphony chorus, 1981. Served with AUS, also A.C., USNR, 1941-45. Mem. Am. Soc. Mil. Engrs., Marine Tech. Soc., World Dredging Assn., Profl. Assn. Diving Instrs., Internat. Oceanographic Found., Exptl. Aircraft Assn., Lake Mich. Fedn. Episcopalian. Clubs: Manila Yacht (life); American (Hong Kong); S.P.E.B.Q.S.A. Author articles in field. Patentee submersible dredge. Address: 2900 Skokie Valley Hwy Highland Park IL 60035

BATE, CHARLES THOMAS, lawyer; b. Muncie, Ind., Nov. 14, 1932; s. Thomas Elwood and Vina Florence (Jackson) B.; A.B., Butler U., 1955, postgrad., 1955-56; student Christian Theol. Sem., Indpls., 1956-57; J.D., Ind. U., 1962; m. Barbara Kay Dailey, June 17, 1955; children—Charles Thomas, Gregory Andrew, Jeffrey Scott. Admitted to Ind. bar, 1962; staff adjuster State Automobile Ins. Assn., Indpls., 1953-57, claim supr., 1958-59, office mgr., 1960-61, casualty claim mgr., 1961-62, atty., 1962-63; mem. firm Smith & Yarling, Indpls., 1963-67; sr. partner Soshnick, Bate & Harrold, Shelbyville, Ind., 1967—; city atty., Shelbyville, 1981—. Dir., v.p., gen. counsel Discovery Life Ins. Co., Indpls., 1966-70. Bd. dirs. Nat. Pensions Bd. of Ch. of God, 1970-74; trustee Warner Pacific Coll., Portland, Oreg., 1977-79. Recipient Merit award Ind. Jud. Council, 1962, Outstanding Student award Ind. U. Law Week, 1962. Fellow Ind. Bar Found.; mem. Am., Ind. (ho. of dels. 1978-80), Indpls., Shelby County (pres. 1979) bar assns., Am. Judicature Soc., Am. Arbitration Assn. (panel arbitrators), Am., Ind. (dir. 1979—) trial lawyers assns., Republican. Mem. Ch. of God (dir. Glendale Ch. of God Inc. 1958-80, lay speaker 1962—, sec. nat. by-laws com. 1968-72). Club: Shelbyville Elks. Home: Box 26 Shelbyville IN 46176 Office: 24 W Broadway Shelbyville IN 46176

BATEMAN, AARON K., co. fin. exec.; b. Gordon, Nebr., Mar. 11, 1941; s. Francis William and Avis Elizabeth (Conner) B.; B.B.A., Ohio U., 1964; M.B.A., U. Dayton, 1970; m. Mildred Kathryn Wells, June 27, 1964; children—Erin Kathryn, Brian Kendall. Cost engr. Eastman Kodak Co., Rochester, N.Y., 1964-66; controller Lion Uniform Co., Dayton, Ohio, 1968-72; asst. treas. Stearns and Foster Co., Cin., 1972-77; controller Allied Tech., Inc., Dayton, 1977-78, v.p. fin., treas., 1978-80; v.p. fin. and adminstrn., treas. Ziv Steel Co., Livonia, Mich., 1980—. Pres. Dr. John Hole Sch. Interaction Council. Served to 1st lt. U.S. Army, 1966-68. Decorated Bronze Star. Mem. Fin. Execs. Inst., Tax Execs. Inst. Lutheran. Office: Ziv Steel Co 11952 Hubbard Livonia MI 48150

BATES, CHARLES WALTER, personnel exec.; b. Detroit, June 28, 1953; s. E. Frederick and Virginia Marion (Nunneley) B.; B.A. cum laude, Mich. State U., 1975, M. Labor and Indsl. Relations, 1977; postgrad. DePaul U. Law Sch., Chgo., 1979-80, William Mitchell Coll. Law, St. Paul, 1981—. VISTA vol., paralegal Legal Aid Assn. Ventura County, Calif., 1975-76; resource tchr. social studies Lansing, Holt and Okemos (Mich.) sch. systems, 1976-77; job analyst Gen. Mills, Inc., Mpls., 1977-78, plant personnel asst., Chgo., 1978-80, asst. plant personnel mgr., Chgo., 1980—, personnel mgr., mktg. divs., Mpls., 1981—. Asst. scoutmaster Boy Scouts Am., 1971—, Eagle Scout, 1969, Scouter's Tng. award, 1979; active Nat. Eagle Scout Assn., 1st Unitarian Soc., Mpls. Mem. Indsl. Relations Research Assn., Am. Soc. Personnel Adminstrn., Student chpt. Am. Bar Assn., William Mitchell Coll. of Law Student Bar Assn., Mpls. Soc. Fine Arts, Mich. State U. Alumni Assn., Sierra Club, Plymouth Civic League, Phi Alpha Delta. Libertarian. Unitarian-Universalist. Home: 3905 Lancaster Ln Apt 325 Plymouth MN 55441 Office: Gen Mills Inc 3 SW 9200 Wayzata Blvd Golden Valley MN 55426

BATES, DONALD LEE, utilities exec., city ofcl.; b. Bartley, W.Va., Mar. 5, 1940; s. Raymond L. and Marjorie A. (Wolley) B.; grad. public schs., Connersville, Ind.; m. Brenda Clare Morrow, Oct., 1976; children—Donna Louise, Kelley Jo, Nicholas Lee. Various positions in elec. repair, operator in charge water distbn. system utilities supt., street commr., town marshall Town of Sunman, Ind., 1971—; operator in charge Milan (Ind.) Wastewater Treatment Plant, 1973-75, Moores Hill (Ind.) Wastewater Treatment Plant, 1974-76; spl. dep. sheriff Ripley County (Ind.), 1972—. Mem. Sunman Area Life Squad, 1975—; mem. Dreyer Meml. Library Bd., 1976-78. Served with USN, 1957-61. Mem. Water Pollution Control Fedn., Am. Water Works Assn., South Eastern Ind. Treatment Plant Operators Assn., Ripley County Fraternal Order of Police. Democrat. Clubs: Masons (sec. 1977-78, jr. warden 1981), Scottish Rite. Home: Route 2 Box 35 Sunman IN 47041 Office: Town Hall Sunman IN 47041

BATES, GARY DEAN, engring. corp. exec.; b. Covington, Ky., May 10, 1941; s. Harold V. and Anna J. (Crupper) B.; student Anderson (Ind.) Coll., 1959-61; B.S. in Civil Engring., U. Ky., 1964, M.S., 1967; postgrad. U. Cin., 1977-79; postgrad. in real estate Cin. Tech. Coll., 1978-79; m. Joyce Ann Wiedemer, Nov. 14, 1964; children—Cynthia Lynne, Christopher Scott. Design engr. Ky. Dept. Highways, Lexington, 1963-67; project engr. Exxon Corp., Linden, N.J., 1967-69; project mgr. Skilken-Roslovic Design-Build, Inc., Columbus, Ohio, 1969-71; asst. ops. mgr. Miller-Valentine Constrn. Co., Dayton, Ohio, 1971-72; constrn. mgr. Jackson's Realty and Builder's, Indpls., 1972-74; v.p. Fisher-Deyore Constrn. Co., Cin., 1974-75; v.p., dir. tech. services KZF, Inc., Cin., 1975-81; industry mgr. power and mining SDRC, Inc., Milford, Ohio, 1981—; instr. Sch. Architecture U. Ky., 1965-67; instr. constrn. mgmt. program U. Cin., 1975—. Tutor minority children Urban League program, Columbus, 1970-71; v.p. Woodlands Homeowners Assn., Carmel, Ind., 1973-74. Certified fallout shelter analyst U.S. Dept. Def.; registered profl. engr., Ohio, Ky., Ind.; lic. real estate agt., Ohio. Mem. ASCE (chmn. nat. com. on engring. mgmt.), Am. Arbitration Assn., Soc. Advancement Mgmt., Lambda Chi Alpha Alumni. Republican. Methodist. Home: 730 Birney Ln Cincinnati OH 45230 Office: 2000 Eastman Dr Milford OH 45150

BATES, KENNETH FRANCIS, craftsman, educator; b. North Scituate, Mass., May 24, 1904; s. Frank Loring and Winnette Gray (Litchfield) B.; B.S. in Edn., Mass. Sch. Art, 1927; student Fontainebleau Sch. Fine Art (France), 1931; m. Charlotte Young, June 4, 1931; children—Katharine, Cornelia, Benham. Instr. design and enameling Cleve. Inst. Art, 1927-70; instr. summer sessions U. Tenn., 1942-61, U. Notre Dame, 1962-69, Longwood Coll., 1978; group shows include: Cleve. Mus. Art, 1927—, Nat. Ceramic Exhbn., Syracuse, N.Y., 1930-71, Bklyn. Art Mus., 1960, Chgo. Art Inst., 1961, Smithsonian Instn., 1969, Wichita Nat. Ceramics Exhbn., 1968, Am. Craftsmen Council, 1969, Objects U.S.A. exhbns., Europe, 1972, 73, 74, World Fairs, N.Y.C., 1940, San Francisco, 1941, Brussels, 1958. Recipient 41 prizes Cleve. Mus. Art; Cleve. Arts prize, 1963; Ohio Arts Council award, 1976, numerous others. Fellow Am. Crafts

Council, Internat. Inst. Arts and Letters; mem. Microfilm Archives Am. Artists, Internat. Soc. Artists. Republican. Congregationalist. Author: Enameling Principles and Practice, 1951; Basic Design, 1960; The Enamelist, 1967; Salome's Heritage, 1977; contbr. articles to profl. jours. Home: 7 E 194th St Euclid OH 44119

BATES, TED, mayor; b. Detroit, Sept. 30, 1926; s. James and Della (Brown) B.; student Detroit Bus. Inst., 1949-51; m. Eleanor Puzzuoli, Nov. 27, 1948; children—Ted, Barbara, James, Laurie, Cathy. Asst. to supr. Warren Twp. (Mich.), 1950-61; treas. city Warren, 1961-67, mayor, 1967—. Served with USNR, 1943-47. Office: 29500 Van Dyke Ave Warren MI 48093*

BATTEN, JOHN HENRY, mfg. co. exec.; b. Chgo., Jan. 16, 1912; s. Percy H. and Lisa (Stockton) B.; A.B., Yale U., 1935; cert. mech. engring., U. Wis. extension, 1949; m. Katherine Vernet Smith, June 30, 1938; children—Edmund Peter Smith, Michael Ellsworth, Linda Batten Barrington. With Twin Disc, Inc., Racine, Wis., 1935—, dir., 1937—, pres., chief exec. officer, 1948-76, chmn., chief exec. officer, 1976—; dir. Twin Disc Internat., S.A., Twin Disc (Far East) Ltd., Niigata Converter Co., Paragon Gears, M&I Am. Bank & Trust Co., Wausau Ins. Cos., Giddings & Lewis Co., Walker Forge Co. Recipient Citizen of Yr. award VFW. Mem. Soc. Automotive Engrs., Chief Execs. Forum, SAR, Internat. Found. N. Am. Wild Sheep, African Wildlife Leadership Found., Phi Beta Kappa. Republican. Episcopalian. Clubs: Shikar-Safari Internat., Boone and Crockett, Safari. Office: 1328 Racine St Racine WI 53403

BATTISTI, FRANK JOSEPH, fed. judge; b. Youngstown, Ohio, Oct. 4, 1922; s. Eugene and Jennie (Dalesandro) B.; B.A., Ohio U., 1947; LL.B., Harvard U., 1950. Admitted to Ohio bar, 1950; asst. atty gen. Ohio, 1950; atty. Admitted to Ohio bar, 1950; asst. atty gen. Ohio, 1950; atty. adviser C.E., U.S. Army, 1951-52; 1st asst. dir. law, Youngstown, 1954-59; judge Common Pleas Ct., Mahoning County, Ohio, 1959-61; U.S. judge No. Dist. Ohio, Cleve., 1961-69, chief judge, 1969—. Served with C.E., U.S. Army, 1943-45; ETO. Mem. Am., Mahoning County, Cleve. bar assns., Am. Judicature Soc. Roman Catholic. Office: 302 US Courthouse Cleveland OH 44114*

BATTON, CALVERT VORWERK, appliance co. exec.; b. Cuyahoga Falls, Ohio, June 29, 1926; s. Ramsey T. and Mildred B. (Vorwerk) B.; student Bowling Green U., 1946; B.S. in Bus. Adminstrn., Kent State U., 1950, postgrad. Grad. Bus. Sch., 1960-63; m. Edith Sayre Jones, May 18, 1957; children—Susan, Sally, Pamela. With Hoover Co., Canton, Ohio, 1951—, auditor, 1951-53, mgr. br. office, 1953-56, mgr. field accounting, 1956-58, gen. office mgr., 1958-61, asst. budget mgr., 1961-62, mgr. adminstrv. services, 1962-64, asst. v.p., 1964-65, adminstrv. v.p., 1965-75, v.p. adminstrn., 1975—; adv. bd. dirs. Diebold Research, Inc. Bd. dirs. United Way, Canton, Canton Cultural Center, Bowling Green U. Found.; bd. dirs., v.p. Kent U. Found. Served with AUS, 1944-45. Mem. Adminstrv. Mgmt. Soc., Nat. Assn. Accountants, Am. Mgmt. Assn., Sigma Delta Epsilon. Republican. Presbyn. Home: 245 21st St NW Canton OH 44709 Office: Box 2200 North Canton OH 44720

BATTON, EDWARD DEAN, indsl. distbn. co. exec.; b. St. Joseph, Mo., Nov. 2, 1945; s. Dean E. and Jean M. (Schad) B.; B.B.A., U. Miami, Coral Gables, Fla., 1967; m. Janet A. Hosbach, July 15, 1967; children—Jennifer, Jeffrey, Jason. Mgr. mktg. Illini Welding Supplies Inc., Pekin, Ill., 1971-77, pres., 1978—. Served to capt. USAF, 1967-71. Mem. Nat. Welding Supply Assn. (regional chmn.), Am. Welding Soc., Indsl. Distbrs. Assn. Republican. Roman Catholic. Home: Rural Route 1 Box 28 Tremont IL 61568 Office: Illini Welding Supplies Inc 2100 N 8th St Pekin IL 61554

BATTS, WARREN LEIGHTON, mfg. co. exec.; b. Norfolk, Va., Sept. 4, 1932; s. John Leighton and Allie Belle (Johnson) B.; B.E.E., Ga. Inst. Tech., 1961; M.B.A., Harvard U., 1963; m. Eloise Pitts, Dec. 24, 1957; 1 dau., Terri Allison. With Kendall County, Charlotte, N.C., 1963-64; exec. v.p. Fashion Devel. Co., Santa Paula, Calif., 1964-66; dir. mfg. Olga Co., Van Nuys, Calif., 1964-66; v.p. Douglas Williams Assos., N.Y.C., 1966-67; founder Triangle Corp., Orangeburg, S.C., 1967, pres., chief exec. officer, 1967-71; v.p. Mead Corp., Dayton, Ohio, 1971-73, pres., 1973-80, chief exec. officer, 1978-80; pres., dir. Dart Industries, Los Angeles, Ill., 1980—, Dart & Kraft, Inc., 1981—; dir. 1st Nat. Bank Atlanta and Holding Corp. Mem. Dayton C. of C., Author: (with others) Creative Collective Bargaining, 1964. Office: Dart & Kraft Inc 2211 Sanders Rd Northbrook IL 60062

BATY, JACKSON NEAL, educator; b. Chgo., June 18, 1925; s. Eben Neal and Emma Isabel (Jackson) B.; A.B., Stanford U., 1949; M.A., U. No. Iowa, 1968, Ed.S., 1971; Ed.D., Drake U., 1977; m. Jeanette Carlson Kepler, June 29, 1956; children—Corliss Cecil, Jean Annette. Asso. editor, pub. Times-Plain Dealer, Cresco, Iowa, 1949-65; editor, pub. Mitchell County Press-News, Osage, Iowa, 1953-66; asst. prof. edn. U. No. Iowa, Cedar Falls, 1971—, coordinator Profl. Sequence, faculty adv. The No. Iowan; pres. OPC, Inc. Sec.-treas. Bowline Bay Ltd., 1971—. Served with U.S. Army, 1943-46, 50-52. Mem. Assn. Tchr. Educators, NEA, Iowa Higher Edn. Assn., Assn. Supervision and Curriculum Devel., ACLU. Inst. Rational Living, DAV, Am. Legion. Democrat. Clubs: Stanford Buck, Masons. Home: PO Box 510 Cedar Falls IA 50613 Office: Education Center U No Iowa Cedar Falls IA 50614

BAUCOM, WILLIAM ERNEST, advt. display co. exec.; b. Richmond, Va., Jan. 25, 1925; s. Ivey William and Ella (Bradshaw) B.; student U. Ala., 1943; B.M.E., Va. Poly. Inst., 1949; M.B.A., Harvard U., 1952; m. Joyce Nadine Evans, Dec. 30, 1949; children—Dee Evan, Sandra Barbee, Ann Willison. With Gen. Electric Corp., Lynn, Mass., 1949-50; pres., founder E-B Advt. Diplay Co., Massillon, Ohio, 1952—, also dir.; dir. Polygraphic Inc. Served with U.S. Army, 1943-46. Mem. Point of Purchases Inst., Wire Mfrs. Assn. Republican. Clubs: Shady Hollow Country (pres. 1975-77), Massillon. Home: 7819 D Hills & Dale Rd Massillon OH 44646 Office: 2037 Wales Rd NE Massillon OH 44646

BAUDER, GARY LEE, accounting co. exec.; b. Sturgis, Mich., Nov. 28, 1949; s. Ray Orlo, Jr. and Grace Marguerite (Haney) B.; A.A., Glen Oaks Community Coll., 1970; certificate in jr. accounting, State Tech. Inst. and Rehab. Center, 1974. Supervisory trainee Arch Workshop, Inc., Sturgis, 1969-71; mgr. B & F Tax & Accounting Service Corp., Sturgis, 1974-76, pres., dir., 1976—; dir., instr. income tax div. B & F Tax Tng. Inst.; instr. personal income taxes Sturgis Pub. Sch. Sec.-treas. Glen Oaks Community Coll. Circle K, 1968-70; notary pub. Mich.; treas. St. Joseph County (Mich.) Young Democrats, 1968-70; precinct del. St. Joseph County Dem. Party, 1970. Recipient Outstanding Service awards Mich. Assn. Distributive Edn. Clubs Am., 1970, Glen Oaks Community Coll. Boosters, 1970; named Officer of Year, Distributive Edn. Clubs Am., 1970-71. Mem. Distributive Edn. Clubs Am., Glen Oaks Community Coll. alumni assns., Sturgis C. of C., Sturgis Jaycees, Am. Mgmt. Assn., Nat. Small Bus. Assn., St. Joseph County Wheelchair Sports Boosters Assn., Internat. Platform Assn., Nat. Audubon Soc., Smithsonian Assos. Methodist. Office: 221 Susan St Sturgis MI 49091

BAUDER, KENNETH F., assn. exec.; b. Chgo., Sept. 26, 1946; s. Frederick William and Myrtle Emma (Zenke) B.; B.S., So. Ill. U., 1969, M.A., 1971. Founder with E.R. Homewood, The Ontario Press, Chgo., 1971-74, dir., 1972—; dir. Lambda Books; dir. public relations Am. Bar Endowment, Chgo., 1974-75; freelance photographer, journalist, 1975-77; dir. publs. Shoe Service Inst. Am., Chgo., 1977-80, asst. treas., 1977-80. Tchr., Model Cities program, Chgo., 1972-74; bd. dirs. Our Children Found., Chgo., 1980-81; corp. fundraiser Ill. chpt. Nat. Kidney Found. Mem. Chgo. Soc. Assn. Execs. (vice chmn. coll. and univ. relations com. 1978-79), Am. Assn. Assn. Execs., MLA, Am. Public Works Assn. (dir. publs. 1980—). Home: 3619 S Damen Ave Chicago IL 60609 Office: 1313 E 60th Chicago IL 60637

BAUER, CARL FRANCIS, materials scientist; b. Chgo., June 22, 1944; s. Stanley James and Hildagarde C. (Podd) B.; B.E.E., U. Dayton, 1966; M.S., Northwestern U., 1969, Ph.D., 1973; m. Bernadette Bartnik, June 24, 1967; children—Julia, James, Paul. Sr. research materials scientist UOP, Inc., Des Plaines, Ill., 1973-77; supr. metals research Am. Can Co., Barrington, Ill., 1977-81; sect. mgr. sensor prodn. Motorola, Inc., Schaumburg, Ill., 1981—. Mem. IEEE, Am. Ceramic Soc., Am. Soc. Metals, Sigma Xi, Tau Beta Pi. Contbr. articles to profl. jours. Office: 1299 E Algonquin Rd Schaumburg IL 60196

BAUER, EDWARD ALPHONSE, elec. contractor; b. Waite Park, Minn., Aug. 6, 1942; s. Michael Frank and Olive Ann (Lardy) B.; student Drews Bus. Coll., St. Cloud, 1961, Dunwoody Indsl. Sch., Mpls., 1967; grad. in mech. engring., St. Cloud State Coll., 1969; m. Carol Ann Lobb, July 8, 1967; children—Steven J., Gwen Marie, John Edward. Owner, pres. Bauer Inc., elec. contractors, Waite Park, Minn., 1969—; sec., v.p. JAB, Inc., 1975—. Chief, Waite Park Fire Dept., 1980—; scoutmaster Boy Scouts Am. Served with USNR, 1961-62; mem. Res. (ret.). Decorated Naval Meritorious Service medal, Nat. Def. medal; others. Mem. Nat. Assn. Bus. and Ednl. Radio, U.S. C. of C., Minn. Elec. Assn., Waite Park C. of C., Am. Legion. Republican. Roman Catholic. Clubs: Boosters, Rifle (Waite Park); Moose. Home: 149 7th Ave N Waite Park MN 56387 Office: 149 7th Ave N Waite Park MN 56387

BAUER, ELIZABETH HALE WORMAN, mental health services exec.; b. Mpls., Dec. 28, 1937; d. James R. and Virginia H. (Murty) Worman; B.A., Mt. Holyoke Coll., 1959; M.A., Ohio State U., 1975; postgrad. U. Minn., 1959, Wayne State U., 1978, Mich. State U., 1978; m. George Bittner Bauer, Sept. 12, 1959; children—Anna Stuart, Robert Bittner, Virginia Hale, Edward Russell. Speech therapist Morris County Easter Seal Rehab. Center, Morristown, N.J., 1959-60; travel coordinator AFS Internat., N.Y.C., 1960-63; speech therapist St. Barnabas Home, Gibsonia, Pa., 1967-71; tchr. St. Peter's Child Devel. Center, Sewickley, Pa., 1971-72; tchr. cons. spl. edn., Pontiac, Mich., 1975-78; dir. tng. Plymouth Center for Human Devel., Northville, Mich., 1978-80; adminstr. community placement Mich. Dept. Mental Health, Met. Region, 1980-81; exec. dir. Mich. Protection and Advocacy Service for Develmentally Disabled Citizens, Inc., Lansing, 1981—; cons. devel. disabilities tech. assistance system U. N.C., 1974-75; mem. adv. bd. Georgetown U. Child Devel. Center, 1978—. Founder, Montessori in Arlington, Upper Arlington, Ohio, 1973; bd. dirs. Franklin County (Ohio) Assn. Retarded Citizens, 1973-75, Ohio Assn. Retarded Citizens, 1975; bd. dirs. Southfield Youth Symphony Orch., pres., 1978-79; bd. dirs. Epilepsy Center Mich., Detroit, 1975-80, pres., 1978-80; trustee St. Mark's Day Sch., Jackson Heights, N.Y., 1962-67; trustee internat. scholarships Am. Field Service, 1971-73, bd. dirs., 1973—. Named Outstanding Tchr. Sch. Dist. City of Pontiac, 1978. Mem. Am. Speech and Hearing Assn., Council for Exceptional Children, Am. Assn. on Mental Deficiency, Nat. Assn. for Retarded Citizens, Mich. Assn. for Retarded Children, Mt. Holyoke Coll. Alumnae Assn. Episcopalian. Contbr. articles to profl. publs. Home: 1355 Lake Park Birmingham MI 48009 Office: 230 N Washington Sq Lansing MI 48933

BAUER, GRAYDON MILFORD, engring. cons.; b. Galien, Mich., July 4, 1921; s. William Fredrick and Venus (Hanover) B.; B.S. in Elec. Engring., Am. Tech. Inst., Chgo., 1941; postgrad. Acme Sch. Engring., 1948-49, Ind. U., 1957-58; m. Jean A. Ackerman, June 14, 1951; children—Archie A., Kevin L. Project engr. Clark Equipment Co., Buchanan, Mich., 1947; gen. mgr. Berrien Concrete Products Co., Galien, 1954-62: mfg. mgr., corporate engr. Walkden Concrete & Assos. Cos. (merger Berrien Concrete Products Co. and Walkden Cos.), 1956-63; ind. practice as constrn. engring. cons., 1963—; elec. cons. United Indsl. Engring Corp., Madison Heights, Mich., 1964-66; mfg. engr. Dodge Truck div. Chrysler Corp., Detroit, 1966-73, plant environ. control adminstr. Warren Truck Assembly Plants, 1973-75, mfg. facilities engr., 1975—; sec.-treas. Berrie Concrete Products Co., 1954; sec. Towne & Country Pools, Inc., 1962-65. Served with AUS, 1942-46. Mem. Welding Engrs. Soc., IEEE. Lion. Contbg. author: Electrical Standards, 1975. Home: 5895 Burnham Rd Bloomfield Hills MI 48013

BAUER, JANE ELIZABETH, human services aide; b. Enid, Okla., June 5, 1931; d. Richard Herman and Rena Callista (Stanton) Gengelbach; student Mo. Western State Coll., 1949-50, Wichita State U., 1974-77, 80—; m. Robert Ivan Bauer, Mar. 18, 1977; children—Janice Elaine, Jay Douglas, Jill Annette. Clk., Hirsch Bros., St. Joseph, Mo., 1949-51; mem. staff inventory control dept. Quaker Oats, St. Joseph, Mo., 1951-52; IBM operator, gen. office Gen. Motors Parts Dept., Wichita, Kans., 1955-56; supr. care or treatment dept. Sedgwick County, Wichita, Kans., 1967-75, child custody investigator, 1975-80, adminstrv. aide, 1980—. Vice-pres., treas. J-R Assos., Inc. Mem. Epsilon Sigma Alpha. Republican. Home: 9000 Nantucket Circle Wichita KS 67212 Office: Sedgwick County Courthouse 525 N Main St Wichita KS 67203

BAUER, KENNETH WILLIAM, med. center exec.; b. Mission City, B.C., Can., June 2, 1951; s. Albert W. and Ann B. (parents Am. citizens); B.S., Loma Linda U., 1973; M.B.A., Andrews U., 1975; student Newbold Coll. (Eng.), 1970-71; m. Diana M. Weaver, Dec. 17, 1972; 1 dau., Charisa. Unit mgr. Loma Linda (Calif.) U. Med. Center, 1973-74; jr. accountant Roberts C.P.A., Berrien Springs, Mich., 1974-75; internal auditor Kettering (Ohio) Med. Center, 1975-76, asst. treas., 1976-77, treas., chief fin. officer, 1978—; faculty mem., guest lectr. Loma Linda U., 1979—. Charles Weniger fellow, 1974-75; C.P.A., Ohio. Mem. Am. Mgmt. Assn., Hosp. Fin. Mgmt. Assn. Seventh-day Adventist. Club: Kiwanis. Home: 817 Blossom Heath Rd Kettering OH 45419 Office: 3535 Southern Blvd Kettering OH 45429

BAUER, KURT WALTER, civil engr., planning commn. exec.; b. Milw., Aug. 25, 1929; s. Karl Artur and Elisabeth B.; B.S.C.E., Marquette U., 1951; M.S.C.E., U. Wis., Madison, 1955, Ph.D. in Civil Engring., 1961; m. Arlene Vixella English, June 26, 1955; children—Elisabeth, Karoline, Kurt. City planner City of South Milwaukee (Wis.), 1953-55; instr. U. Wis., Madison, 1955-56, Ford Found. research fellow, 1960-61; asso. civil engr. H.C. Webster and Son, Milw., 1956-59; chief current planning Madison City Planning Dept., 1959-60; asst. dir. Southeastern Wis. Regional Planning Commn., Waukesha, 1961-62, exec. dir., 1962—; mem. com. on geodesy Assembly Math. and Phys. Scis., NRC. Served with USAFR, 1953. Recipient Disting. Profl. Achievement award Marquette U., 1973, Assn. Wis. Planners award, 1973, Gt. Lakes Commn. award, 1974, Public Service award Dept. Transp., Fed. Hwy. Adminstrn., 1977, Disting. Service citation U. Wis.-Madison Coll. Engring., 1978. Fellow ASCE; mem. Am. Inst. Planners, Am. Congress Surveying and Mapping, Transp. Research Bd., Soil Conservation Soc., Am. Public Works Assn., Inst. Mcpl. Engring., Sigma Xi, Tau Beta Pi, Chi Epsilon. Contbr. articles to profl. jours., 1961—; dir. numerous Southeastern Wis. Regional Planning Commn. publs. Office: PO Box 769 916 N East Ave Waukesha WI 53187

BAUER, MARILYN DIANE, ednl. adminstr.; b. Chgo., Apr. 19, 1938; d. Steven and Marie (Maodush) Yerkovich; student U. Ill., Navy Pier br., Chgo., 1956-57; B.S. in Biology and Edn., U. Ill., Champaign, 1960; M.S. in Public Adminstrn. and Supervision, Chgo. State U., 1978; m. Jay Allan Bauer, Aug. 18, 1962; children—Jeanne Marie, Steven Jay. Tchr. gen. sci. and biology Thronton Twp. (Ill.) High Sch., Ill. Dist. 205, 1960-67, coordinator student activities, sponsor student council, 1963-67, coordinator family adjustment sch., 1968-71, dean students, 1971-78, adminstrv. asst., 1978-79, asst. prin., 1980—; acad./personal counselor NSF, summers 1961-62. Chmn., Task Force on Teen Sexuality div. Health Partners South Cook County (Ill.), 1977-79; den mother Cub Pack 369, South Cook council Boy Scouts Am., 1978-79; asst. leader South Cook council Girl Scouts U.S.A., 1976-77. Mem. Nat. Assn. Secondary Sch. Prins., Ill. Assn. Women Deans, Adminstrs., and Counselors, Assn. Supervision and Curriculum Devel., Ill. Edn. Assn., NEA, Phi Delta Kappa. Serbian Orthodox. Home: South Holland IL 60473 Office: Thornwood High Sch 170th and S Park South Holland IL 60473

BAUER, NANCY MCNAMARA, TV and radio network exec.; b. Madison, Wis., Mar. 17, 1929; d. Richard Hughes and Lucy Jane (Whitaker) Marshall; B.A., U. Wis., 1950, M.S., 1963; m. J.B. McNamara, Dec. 29, 1952 (div. Mar. 1962); children—Margaret Ann, William Patrick; m. 2d, Helmut Robert Bauer, Mar. 10, 1974. Elementary tchr., Madison, 1963-66; specialist ednl. communications U. Wis., Madison, 1966-71, asst. prof., 1971-72; dir. educative services Ednl. Communications Bd., Wis. Ednl. TV and Radio Networks, Madison, 1972—; dir. Central Ednl. Network, 1973—, exec. com., 1973-74, chmn. Instructional TV Council, 1977—; adv. bd. Instructional TV Co-op., 1972—, exec. com., 1976-77; mem. instrnl. radio adv. com. Nat. Public Radio, 1979—; mem. instrnl. TV adv. com. Public Broadcasting System, 1978-79, service com., 1980—. Ford Found. scholar, 1961-63; recipient Ohio State award, 1975, Am. Bar Assn. Gavel award, 1975, Am. Legion Golden Mike award, 1976. Mem. Nat. Assn. Ednl. Broadcasters. Producer, writer numerous instructional series, as nationally distributed Patterns in Arithmetic and Looking Out Is In, TV, 1967, Inquiry: The Justice Thing, radio, 1973. Home: 127 Kensington Dr Madison WI 53704 Office: 732 N Midvale Blvd Madison WI 53705

BAUER, NORMAN WALTER, educator; b. Stover, Mo., May 5, 1926; s. Walter August and Clara (Luebbert) B.; student public schs., Blackburn, Mo.; m. Margie Bredehoeft, June 6, 1948; children—Patricia Kay, Timothy Keith. Shop mgr. Ziems-Grother Motor Co., Higginsville, Mo., 1949-57; with Jerry Talley Motors, Warrensburg, Mo., 1957-64; body shop mgr. Lenger Chevrolet-Cadillac, Warrensburg, Mo., 1964-73; instr. automotive paint and metals Warrensburg Area Vocat. Tech. Sch., 1973—. Served with USN, 1944-46. Mem. Vocat. Indsl. Clubs Am., Western Sq. Dance Assn. Lutheran. Home: Route 6 Box 429 Warrensburg MO 64093

BAUER, RONALD GUY, personnel exec.; b. Hastings, Mich., Nov. 4, 1938; s. Charles Russell and Alice Ethyl (Hammon) B.; B.S., U. Mich., 1960, M.A., 1966, Ph.D. in Polit. Sci., 1973; m. Nancy Sachiko Abe, June 1, 1968. Corp. mgr. human resources devel., exec. offices Bendix Corp., Southfield, Mich., 1978, corp. mgr. orgn. and assessment, 1978-79, group mgr. human resources Heavy Vehicle Systems Group, Elyria, Ohio, 1979—. Mem., Cherry Home Assn., 1968—, pres., 1974-75. Served as officer USN, 1960-64. Fulbright Overseas Research fellow, 1969-70; NDEA fellow, 1965-70. Mem. Am. Psychol. Assn., Am. Soc. Personnel Adminstrn., Nat. Mgmt. Assn., Nat. Orgn. Devel. Network, Detroit Com. on Fgn. Relations, Midwest Orgn. Devel. Network, Great Lakes Hist. Soc., U. Mich. Alumni Assn., Pi Sigma Alpha. Club: Bendix Management. Recipient 1st Place award Mcpl. Sculpture Competition for City of Ann Arbor (Mich.), 1979. Home: 3715 Charter Pl Ann Arbor MI 48105 Office: 901 Cleveland St Elyria OH 49076

BAUGH, MARYMARGARET MAGDALEN OSADCHY, nurse; b. Minot, N.D., Aug. 1, 1928; d. Nazar and Mary (Paul) Osadchy; B.S. in Nursing, Jamestown Coll., 1971; M.S. in Edn. and Adminstrn., N.D. State U., 1979; postgrad. Minn. State U., Moorhead, 1978—; m. Donald P. Baugh, May 13, 1950; children—Deborah, Seemann, Patrick, MaryBeth, Michael. With N.D. State Hosp., Jamestown, 1961—, staff devel. dir., 1974—; nurse ARC, 1959—. Registered nurse, N.D. Mem. Am., N.D. nurses assns., Am. Soc. Health Edn. Tng. (pres. N.D. 1977-78), AAUW (treas., historian, publicity Jamestown 1975-79). Roman Catholic. Home: 1103 1st Ave N Jamestown ND 58401 Office: Staff Devel Dept ND State Hosp Jamestown ND 58401

BAUGHER, GARY LEE, state senator; b. Davenport, Iowa, Apr. 26, 1942; s. Ray W. and Eula M. (Hackney) B.; B.S. in Edn., B.A. in History, N.E. Mo. U., 1967; M.A. in History, Drake U., 1968; m. Toni Lee Pendergast, Dec. 27, 1964; children—Tirzah Renee, Aaron Henry, Andrew James. Tchr., coach Des Moines public schs., 1968-72; mgr. Mobile Home Park & Sales, 1972-76; owner Mel-Ray Mobile Home Park & Sales, Inc., Ankeny, Iowa, 1976—; mem. Iowa Senate, 1979—. Served with USAR, 1961-63. Mem. Am. Legis. Exchange Council, Iowa Manufactured Housing Assn. (pres. 1976), Ankeny C. of C. Republican. Mem. Federated Ch. Address: Rural Route 1 Ankeny IA 50021

BAUGHMAN, GEORGE WASHINGTON, III, univ ofcl., fin. cons.; b. Pitts., July 7, 1937; s. George W. and Cecile M. (Lytel) B.; B.S. in Psychology, Ohio State U., 1959, M.B.A., 1961, postgrad., 1961-63; 1 dau., Lynn. Pres., Advanced Research Assos., Worthington, Ohio, 1960—; asst. instr. fin. Ohio State U., Columbus, 1961-63, research asso., office of controller, 1964-66, dir. data processing, 1966-68, 70-72, dir. adminstrv. research, 1966-72, asso. to acad. v.p., 1968-70, exec. dir. univ. budget, 1970-72, dir. spl. projects, office of pres., 1972—; chmn. bd. Hosp. Audiences, Inc., 1974—. Founding bd. dirs. Coll. and U. Machine Records Conf., 1971-73; bd. dirs. Uniplan Environ. Groups, Inc., 1970-73, chmn., 1971-73; chmn. Franklin County (Ohio) Republican Demographics and Voter Analysis Com., 1975-80; bd. dirs. Cedar Hill Assn., 1980—; mem. Ohio State Dental Bd., 1980—. Am. Council on Edn. grantee, 1976-77; Nat. Assn. Coll. and Univ. Bus. Officers grantee, 1977-79; NSF grantee, 1980—; Reisman fellow, 1962. Mem. Assn. Instl. Research, Instl. Research Council of Eleven, Coll. and U. Systems Exchange, AAAS, Phi Alpha Kappa, Delta Tau Delta. Republican. Presbyterian. Author: (with D.H. Baker) Writing to People, 1963; (with R.W. Brady) University Program Budgeting, 1968, Administrative Data Processing, 1975; contbr. articles to profl. publs.

Home: 833 Lakeshore Dr Worthington OH 43085 Office: 190 N Oval Mall Columbus OH 43210

BAUGHN, MICHAEL LYNN, educator, mayor; b. Colby, Kans., Apr. 30, 1948; s. James Leslie and Wilma Jean (Burkhead) B.; A.B., Asbury Coll., 1970; M.S., Ft. Hays Kans. State U., 1976. Tchr., Brewster (Kans.) Unified Sch. Dist., 1970-76, instr. secondary social studies, 1970-81, prin., 1976-81; curator Butterfield Trail Mus., 1966-73, elementary supr., 1973-76. Dep. sheriff Thomas County, 1970-81, Logan County, 1970—, dir. Brewster Civil Def., 1971-79; city marshal, Brewster, 1970-74; mem. Brewster City Council, 1974-79, pres., 1979, mayor, 1979—; owner, operator Brewster IGA Store, 1981—; pres., Butterfield Trail Assn., 1974—; chmn. Hi-Plains History Commn., 1971-73, dir. pub. relations, 1973-79; vol. rural fireman, 1975—; vol. city fireman, 1980—; mem. CAP, 1981—; precinct committeeman Republican Party, 1974—; mem. Thomas County Rep. Central Com., 1974—, sec.-treas., 1980—; justice of peace, 1972-74; mem. adv. bd. Ret. Sr. Vol. Program, 1978-81; mem. Thomas County Council on Aging, 1979—; mem. adult edn. adv. bd. Colby Community Coll.; mem. adminstrv. bd. Brewster United Meth. Ch., 1976-79. Mem. Northwestern Plains Am. Revolution Bicentennial Park Assn. (pres. 1974-77), Western Plains Arts Council (sec. 1973-74), Nat. Assn. Secondary Sch. Prins. (dir. 1979—), Kans. Hist. Soc. (dir. 1979—), Phi Delta Kappa (chpt. sec.). Clubs: Masons (past master), Shriners, Lions (pres. 1975, gov. dist. 17NW 1979). Home: PO Box 216 Brewster KS 67732 Office: 325 Kansas Ave Brewster KS 67732

BAUM, DAVID ROY, research psychologist; b. Kings County, N.Y., Feb. 13, 1946; s. John Harold and Sylvia (Adler) B.; B.S., U. Pitts., 1967; M.A., SUNY, Stony Brook, 1969; Ph.D., U. Mich., 1977. Prin. research scientist Honeywell Systems and Research Center, Mpls., 1977—, innovator, dir. human factors internship program, 1978—; cons. to flying tng. div. Air Force Human Resources Lab. Judge, 31st Ann. Sci. and Engring. Fair, St. Paul, 1980. Served with USAF, 1969-73. Mem. Human Factors Soc., Am. Psychol. Assn., AAAS, N.Y. Acad. Scis. Contbr. articles to profl. jours. Office: Honeywell SRC MN17-2318 2600 Ridgway Pkwy Minneapolis MN 55413

BAUM, M(ARY) CAROLYN, occupational therapist; b. Chgo., Mar. 26, 1943; d. Gibson Henry and Nelle (Curry) Manville; B.S., U. Kans., 1966; M.A., Webster Coll., 1979; 1 dau., Kirstin Carol. Staff occupational therapist U. Kans. Med. Center, 1966-67; staff occupational therapist Research Med. Center, Kansas City, Mo., 1967, dir. occupational therapy, 1967-73, dir. phys. medicine and rehab., 1973-76; dir. occupational therapy, clin. services Washington U. Sch. Medicine, St. Louis, 1976—. Coordinator St. Louis Ind. Living Council, 1980-81; mem. nominating com. Greater Kansas City Health Systems Agy., 1974-75; vice-chmn. Village Ch. Accessibility Task Force, 1974-76. Named Employee of Yr., Research Hosp., 1974, Kans. Occupational Therapist of Year, 1975. Fellow Am. Occupational Therapy Assn. (chmn. standards and ethics commn. 1973-77, nat. v.p. 1978—, pres. elect 1981, Eleanor Clarke Slagel Lectureship award 1980); mem. Mo. Occupational Therapy Assn. Contbg. author: Occupational Therapy, 1978; contbr. articles to profl. jours. Office: Dept Occupational Therapy Washington U Sch Medicine 509 S Euclid St Saint Louis MO 63110

BAUMAN, CHARLES LOY, business forms mfg. co. exec.; b. Gatesville, Tex., May 16, 1945; s. Clarence and Margaret Lois (Chandler) B.; B.B.A., N. Tex. State U., Denton, 1968, M.B.A., 1972; m. Lynne C. Witte, Nov. 5, 1966; children—Heath, Lara. With Moore Bus. Forms, Inc., Denton, 1968—, mgr. nat. systems, Glenview, Ill., 1978-79, corp. mgr. info. services data resources, 1979—; pres. Moore Combined Fed. Credit Union. Dist. chmn. Mem. Assn. Systems Mgmt., Soc. Mgmt. Info. Systems, Am. Mgmt. Assn., N. Tex. State U. Alumni Assn. Republican. Methodist. Home: 416 Elm Tree St Vernon Hills IL 60061 Office: 1205 N Milwaukee Ave Glenview IL 60025

BAUMAN, GEORGE DUNCAN, publisher; b. Humboldt, Iowa, Apr. 12, 1912; s. Peter William and Mae (Duncan) B.; student Loyola U., Chgo., 1930-35; J.D., Washington U., St. Louis, 1948; Litt.D. (hon.), Central Methodist Coll.; LL.D. (hon.), Maryville Coll.; L.H.D. (hon.), Mo. Valley Coll.; m. Nora Kathleen Kelly, May 21, 1938. Reporter, Chgo. Herald Examiner, 1931-39; archtl. rep. Pratt & Lambert, Inc., St. Louis, 1939-43; with St. Louis Globe-Democrat, 1943—, personnel mgr., 1951-59, bus. mgr., 1959-67, pub., 1967—; dir. City Bank St. Louis. Bd. dirs. Boys Clubs Am., 1969—, St. Louis YMCA, 1967-72, St. Louis City Welfare Commn., 1967-70, Better Bus. Bur., 1968-72, St. Louis Mcpl. Theatre Assn., 1968—, St. Louis Symphony Soc., 1968—, Arts and Edn. Council, 1972—; mem. lay adv. bd. St. Vincent's Hosp., 1952-75, pres., 1957-58; mem. voting membership bd. Blue Shield, 1968-77; mem. nat. citizens adv. com. Assn. Am. Med. Colls., 1975—; mem. lay adv. bd. DePaul Community Health Center, 1975—; adv. bd. St. Louis Med. Soc., 1976-78; mem. exec. bd. St. Louis council Boy Scouts Am., 1967—, mem. pres.'s council St. Louis U., 1968—; bd. visitors Mo. Mil. Acad., 1970—; mem. adv. bd. Newman Chapel, 1964—, pres., 1968—; bd. dirs. Policemen and Firemen Fund St. Louis, 1959—, sec., 1963-69, pres., 1969-70; bd. dirs. Herbert Hoover Boys Club, St. Louis, 1966—, pres., 1968, 76, 78; bd. dirs. United Way Greater St. Louis, 1964—, mem. exec. com., 1964—, v.p., 1968-71; chmn. exec. com. and regional adv. com. Bi-State Regional Med. Program, 1968-75; bd. dirs. Health and Welfare Council Met. St. Louis, 1960-70, pres., 1965-67; chmn. Mo. Com. Employer Support of Guard and Res., 1981—; sec. Bd. Election Commrs., St. Louis, 1957-61; bd. dirs. Catholic Charities, 1967—, pres., 1969-70; bd. dirs. Child Center Our Lady of Grace, 1965-80, pres., 1965-68; bd. dirs. Jr. Achievement Mississippi Valley, 1953-74, v.p., 1968, pres., 1978-80, nat. bd. dirs., 1979—; mem. Conv. and Visitors Bur. Greater St. Louis, 1968-77, v.p., 1974, pres., 1975-76; bd. dirs. Dismas House, 1964-73, pres., 1968; bd. dirs. Human Life Found., 1973-81, Downtown St. Louis, Inc., 1977—; trustee Mo. Baptist Hosp., 1970—, exec. com., 1974—, treas., 1977—, asst. sec., 1979—; trustee Jefferson Nat. Expansion Meml. Assn., 1968—, Mo. Public Expenditure Survey, 1968—, Freedoms Found. at Valley Forge, 1968-75, David Ranken Jr. Tech. Inst., 1969—, Nat. Jewish Hosp. and Research Center, 1970—, Govtl. Research Inst., 1968—, Laclede Sch. Law, 1981—. Decorated knight of Malta; recipient Disting. Alumnus citation Washington U., 1972, Bus. Leader of Year award Religious Heritage Am., 1973, citation Loyola U. Alumni Assn., 1973; Silver Beaver award Boy Scouts Am., 1978; named to Loyola U. Athletic Hall of Fame, 1976; Right Arm of St. Louis award St. Louis Regional Commerce and Growth Assn., 1980. Mem. Am. Newspaper Pubs. Assn., Am. Soc. Newspaper Editors, Newspaper Personnel Relations Assn. (past pres.), Mo. (dir. 1969-74), St. Louis (exec. com. 1969-73, dir. 1969-73) chambers commerce, Mo. Acad. Squires, Bar Assn. St. Louis, Am., Mo. bar assns., Advt. Club St. Louis (gov. 1972-75). Clubs: Bogey (pres. 1980, 81), Mo. Athletic, Noonday, Racquet, St. Louis, Round Table, Media (dir. 1968—) (St. Louis). Home: 6233 Northwood Ave Saint Louis MO 63105 Office: St Louis Globe-Democrat 710 N Tucker Blvd Saint Louis MO 63101

BAUMAN, WINFIELD SCOTT, fin. analyst, educator; b. Dayton, Ohio, Nov. 7, 1930; s. Carl Louis and Lillian Elizabeth (Limpert) B.; B.B.A., U. Mich., 1953, M.B.A., 1954; D.B.A., Ind. U., 1961; m. Shirlee A.G. Madden, June 20, 1953; children—Dale, Kent, Kimberly, Van. Asso. prof. fin. Coll. Bus. Adminstrn., U. Toledo, 1961-66; prof., head dept. fin. and bus. econs. U. Oreg., 1966-72; exec. dir. Inst. Chartered Fin. Analysts, Charlottesville, Va., 1972-78; exec. dir. Fin. Analyst Research Found., 1972-77; prof. bus. adminstrn. U. Va., Charlottesville, 1972-81; prof. fin., chmn. dept. fin. No. Ill. U., DeKalb, 1981—. Bd. regents Chartered Bank Auditor Program, 1977-80. Served to capt. USAF, 1954-56. Recipient Graham and Dodd Scroll award Fin. Analyst Jour., 1964. Mem. Inst. Quantitative Research in Fin. (dir. 1973—), Portland Soc. FIn. Analysts (pres. 1971-72), Western Fin. Assn. (pres. 1971-72), Am. Fin. Assn., Fin. Mgmt. Assn., N.Y. Soc. Security Analysts, Eastern Fin. Assn., So. Fin. Assn., Beta Gamma Sigma. Presbyterian. Author: Investments: Analysis and Management, 1976; mem. editorial bd., author: The Investment Manager's Handbook, 1980; author: Professional Standards in Investment Management, 1980. Office: Dept Fin No Ill U DeKalb IL 60115

BAUMANN, RICHARD BERNARD, health and human services exec.; b. Sheboygan, Wis., June 11, 1946; s. Bernard E. and Mildred L. (Steffen) B.; diploma Concordia Coll., Milw., 1966; B.A., Carthage Coll., Kenosha, Wis., 1968; M.A., U. Wis., Milw., 1974; postgrad. Goethe Inst., Hong Kong; m. Maj. Charlotte C. Lindblom, Oct. 19, 1971. Tchr. English, Luth. Middle Sch., Kowloon, Hong Kong, 1968-69; research officer analyst, dept. supr. Luth. World Fedn./World Service, Hong Kong, 1969-72; asso. planner Mental Health Planning Council, Milw., 1974-79; dir. community ops. Am. Heart Assn. Wis., Milw., 1979—; research cons. Action Com Against Narcotics, Hong Kong, 1970-71; active Southeastern Wis. Health Systems Agy. Bd. dirs. Swedish Am. Hist. Soc. Wis., vice chmn., 1981-82; active Milw. County Hist. Soc., Internat. Inst. Milw. Mem. Nat. Soc. Fund Raising Execs., Am. Planning Assn. Lutheran. Club: Vasa Order Am. (vice chmn. local lodge 1978-79). Home: 2202 E Newberry Blvd Milwaukee WI 53211 Office: 795 N Van Buren St Milwaukee WI 53202*

BAUMEISTER, CARL F., physician; b. Dolliver, Iowa, May 15, 1907; s. Charles F. and Lida Bard (Moore) B.; B.S.; Chicago U., 1930; M.D., Iowa U., 1933; m. Eleanor Hoskins, Apr. 19, 1930; children—Richard. Physician. internal med., Ind. U. Hosps., 1933-36, Louisville U. Hosps., 1936-37, Council Bluffs Clinic, 1937-43, Berwyn (Ill.) Surburban Med. Center, since 1943; mem. staff MacNeal Meml. Hosp., Berwyn; instr. internal medicine U. Ill., 1943-50, clin. asst. prof., 1950-71, 73—; clin. asst. prof. medicine Stritch Sch. Medicine Loyola U., Maywood, Ill., 1971-73; med. staff Loyola U. Hosp., 1971-73. Fellow Inst. of Medicine Chgo.; member AMA, Am. Heart Assn., Assn. Am. Med. Colls., Am. Med. Writers Assn., Am. Diabetes Assn., S.A.R., N.Y. Acad. Sci. Mason. Contbr. articles to med. jours. Abstract editor on med. education Excerpta Medica of Amsterdam. Author: Computer Diagnosis of the Acute Surgical Abdomen. Research diagnosis and treatment new type vascular headache. Home: 120 S Delaplaine Rd Riverside IL 60546 Office: 3340 S Oak Park Ave Berwyn IL 60402

BAUMEISTER, ELEANOR H. (MRS. CARL F. BAUMEISTER), club woman; b. Lake Linden, Mich., Oct. 2, 1909; d. Thomas and Sarah (Madigan) Hoskins; B.; Music Edn., U. Minn., 1930; m. Carl Frederick Baumeister, Apr. 8, 1929; 1 son, Richard. Co-founder, advt. mgr. The Corn Belt Livestock Feeder trade mag., 1948-51. Publicity dir. Patron's Council, Riverside-Brookfield High Sch., 1951-53; pres. MacNeal Meml. Hosp. Women's Auxiliary, 1956, mem. adv. bd., 1957. Bd. dirs. Riverside Pub. Library, 1961-71, pres., 1967-71; dir. Ill. P.E.O. Home, Knoxville, 1956-58, fin. adviser, 1958-63; vice chmn. bd. dirs. Southwest Suburban chpt. Am. Cancer Soc., 1968-69, chmn. bd. dirs. Central Suburban unit, 1969-71, sec.-treas. Central Suburban unit, 1972—; sec. Dist. 208 Caucus; mem. citizens adv. bd. Morton Coll. Sch. Nursing, 1972—. Mem. Gen. Fedn. Women's Clubs, P.E.O. (pres. Riverside 1955-56, 60-61, Ill. corr. sec., 1956-57, rec. sec. 1957-58). Republican. Presbyterian. Clubs: Chgo. Farmers, Riverside Woman's (pres. 1954-56, chmn. auditing com. 1963). Home: 120 S Delaplaine Rd Riverside IL 60546

BAUMER, BEVERLY BELLE, journalist; b. Hays, Kans., Sept. 23, 1926; d. Charles Arthur and Mayme Mae (Lord) B.; B.S., William Allen White Sch. Journalism, U. Kans., 1948. Summer intern reporter Hutchinson (Kans.) News, 1946-47; continuity writer, women's program dir. Sta. KWBW, Hutchinson, 1948-49; dist. editor Salina (Kans.) Jours., 1950-57; commd. writer State of Kans. Centennial Year, 1961; contbg. author: Ford Times, Kansas City Star, Wichita (Kans.) Eagle, Ojibway Publs., Billboard, Modern Jeweler, Floor Covering Weekly, other bus. mags., 1962-69; owner and mgr. apts., Hutchinson, 1970—; info. officer, maj. Kans. Wing Hdqrs. CAP, 1969-72. Recipient Human Interest Photo award Nat. Press Women, 1956; News Photo award AP, 1952. Mem. Nat. Soc. Magna Charta Dames, Nat. Soc. Daus. Founders and Patriots Am., Nat. Soc. Daus. Am. Colonists, Kans. Soc. Daus. Am. Colonists (organizing regent Dr. Thomas Lord chpt.), Nat. Soc. Sons and Daus. Pilgrims (elder Kans. br.), D.A.R., Ben Franklin Soc. (nat. adv. bd.), Daus. Colonial Wars, Order Descs. Colonial Physicians and Chirurgiens, Colonial Daus. 17th Century, Plantagenet Soc., Internat. Platform Soc. Author book of poems, 1941. Home and Office: 204 Curtis St Hutchinson KS 67501

BAUMGARTNER, ALDEN (FREDERICK), JR., transp. and distbn. cons.; b. Chgo., Nov. 29, 1930; s. Alden F. and Anne R. (Sehocke) B.; A.A., Wilson Jr. Coll., 1947-49; B.A., Roosevelt U., 1949-51; Asso., Coll. Advanced Traffic, 1956-57; m. Rosalie O'Connor, Nov. 13, 1954; children—Diane, Iris, Melissa, Kevin. Dist. mgr. Spector Freight Systems Co., St. Louis, 1961-63; regional mgr. To FC div. Fruehauf Co., Chgo., 1970-76, Acme Fast Freight, 1978-79; v.p. Transp. Cons., Chgo., 1978—; mem. faculty Coll. Advanced Traffic. Mem. com. Ind. Voters Mo. and Ill., 1945-50. Served with USNR, 1945-50; Transp. Corps USAR, 1955-59. Mem. Am. Soc. Traffic, Delta Nu Alpha (pres. St. Louis chpt. 1969-70). Roman Catholic. Clubs: St. Louis Transp., Chgo. Transp., Masons, Shriners.

BAUMGARTNER, ALLEN EDWARD, clergyman, occupational therapist; b. Washington, June 20, 1926; s. Otto and Hazel Laverna (Walston) B.; student Kansas City Jr. Coll., 1946-48; A.B., Baker U., 1950; M.Div., Perkins Sch. Theology So. Methodist U., 1954; B.S. in Occupational Therapy, U. Kans., 1971; m. Kathryn Jane Nichols, Aug. 5, 1951; children—William Allen, David Edward. Ordained to ministry, United Methodist Ch., 1953; pastor Linwood Methodist Ch., 1946-48; pastor Parker-Goodrich Chs., 1948-50, Moran-Mildred-Savonburg Chs., 1954-56, Leawood-Bucyrus Chs., 1956-61; asso. pastor First Methodist Ch., Topeka, 1961-63; pastor Meriden-Pleasant Hill Chs., 1963-70; asst. tchr. occupational therapy U. Kans. Med. Center, 1972-78; upper extremities orthotist Petro's Surg. Supply, Topeka, 1971-72; pastor Soldier-Havensville-Buck's Grove Chs., Kans., 1978—. Served with U.S. Navy, 1944-46. Mem. Am. Occupational Therapy Assn., Kans. Occupational Therapy Assn., Kans. East Conf. of United Methodist Ch. Club: Lions. Home: PO Box 97 Soldier KS 66540

BAUMGARTNER, RICHARD MATHIAS, ins./investments co. exec.; b. Bird Island, Minn., Apr. 3, 1913; s. William and Theresa Baumgartner; B.A. in Bus. Adminstrn., Coll. of St. Thomas, St. Paul, 1937; m. Anne Jane Durkan, May 22, 1943; children—Marcia Sue Baumgartner Wilkowski, Shelley Anne Baumgartner Machacek, Mary Elizabeth Baumgartner Sawdey, Robyn Lynn. With Federated Muts. Co., Mpls., 1937-42; owner, mgr. R.M. Baumgartner Agy., Bemidji, Minn., 1946—; pres. Baumgartner, Inc., Bemidji, 1964—, IPS Inc., Bemidji, 1970—; pres. Valley View, Inc., St. Paul, 1962-67, chmn. bd., 1967—. Bd. dirs. Bemidji State U. Found., 1974-79, Bemidji Devel. Corp. Served with USN, 1942-46. Mem. Nat. Assn. Mut. Agts., Minn. Assn. Ins. Agts. (dir. 1963, cert. of merit 1965), Ind. Ins. Agts. Minn., Minn. Assn. Profl. Ins. Agts., Profl. Ins. Agts. Polit. Action Com., Am. Legion, VFW, Bemidji C. of C. (pres. 1971-72). Republican. Roman Catholic. Clubs: K.C. (grand knight 1951-52), Elks, Moose, Bemidji Blue Line, Presidents (Benidji State U. Found.), Bemidji Town and Country (pres. 1954-55), Leech Lake Yacht, Birchmont Tennis, Bemidji Gun, Bemidji Curling, Ducks Unlimited, Lions. Home: 3042 Birchmont Dr Bemidji MN 56601 Office: 210 Beltrami Ave PO Box 808 Bemidji MN 56601

BAUMHART, RAYMOND CHARLES, univ. pres.; b. Chgo., Dec. 22, 1923; s. Emil and Florence (Weidner) B.; B.S., Northwestern U., 1945; Ph.L., Loyola U., 1952, S.T.L., 1958; M.B.A., Harvard, 1953, D.B.A., 1963; LL.D. (hon.), Ill. Coll., 1977. Ordained priest Roman Catholic Ch., 1957; asst. prof. mgmt. Loyola U., Chgo., 1962-64, dean Sch. Bus. Adminstrn., 1964-66, exec. v.p., acting v.p. Med. Center, 1968-70, pres., 1970—; research fellow Cambridge Center for Social Studies, 1966-68; dir. Continental Ill. Corp. Jewel Cos., Inc. Mem. friends com. Latino Inst. Served to lt. (j.g.) USNR, 1944-46. Decorated Order of Cavalier (Italy); recipient Rôle medal Boston Coll., 1976; John W. Hill fellow Harvard, 1961-62. Mem. Assn. Jesuit Colls. and Univs. (chmn. bd.), Fedn. Ind. Ill. Colls. and Univs. (dir.). Clubs: Commercial, Mid-America, Economic, Tavern (Chgo.). Author: An Honest Profit, 1968; (with Thomas Garrett) Cases in Business Ethics, 1968; (with Thomas McMahon) The Brewer-Wholesaler Relationship, 1969. Corr. editor: America, 1965-70. Home: 6525 N Sheridan Rd Chicago IL 60626

BAURER, JOAN RUTH, investment co. exec., fin. cons.; b. N.Y.C., July 10, 1934; d. Jack Maurice and Elsie Frank (Galkin) Lawson; B.A., Queens Coll., 1955; postgrad. Hunter Coll., 1955-57, Fresno State Coll., 1966-67; postgrad. in fin. Calif. State Coll., Bakersfield, 1973-76; m. Martin E. Baurer, Sept. 23, 1953 (div. May 1979); children—Benjamin Zachary, Valery Suzanne. Tchr. home econs., Astoria, N.Y., 1957-59, New Rochelle, N.Y., 1958-60; tchr. gen. sci., Liverpool, N.Y., 1960; account exec. Internat. Securities Co., Bakersfield, 1975-77, Blunt, Ellis & Loewi Co., Inc., Waukegan, Ill., 1977-79; with All Am. Mgmt., Des Plaines, Ill., 1979—; pres. Joan Baurer & Co. Inc. Vol. dir. menu planning Guild House, restaurant for benefit Child Guidance Clinic, Bakersfield, 1964-66; treas., bd. dirs. McHenry County Estate Planning Council. Mem. Internat. Assn. Fin. Planners, AAUW. Clubs: Women's Network (Crystal Lake); Ski. Home: 54 Silver Tree Circle Cary IL 60013 Office: 451 Coventry Green Suite 94 Crystal Lake IL 60014

BAXTER, JOSEPH DIEDRICH, dentist; b. New Albany, Ind., Sept. 11, 1937; s. James William, Jr. and Beatrice (Diedrich) B.; A.B., Ind. U., 1959, D.M.D., U. Louisville, 1969; m. Carroll Jane Bell, Dec. 23, 1972. Practice dentistry, New Albany, 1969—. Bd. dirs. Floyd County (Ind.) Econ. Opportunity Corp., 1971-76. Served with AUS, 1960-61. Mem. Floyd County Dental Soc. (pres. 1972-74), Am. Dental Assn., Phi Gamma Delta. Republican. Methodist. Home: 36 Bellewood Dr New Albany IN 47150 Office: Professional Arts Bldg New Albany IN 47150

BAXTER, LEON DONALD, indsl. engr.; b. Ft. Madison, Iowa, Jan. 28, 1950; s. Donald Harold and Helen Mary (Meirotto) B.; A.A., Southeastern Community Coll., 1970; B.S. in Indsl. Engring., U. Iowa, 1973. Quality engr. Textron-Sheaffer Eaton, Ft. Madison, 1973-74; chief insp. Keokuk (Iowa) Steel div. Kast Metals, 1974-77; project and indsl. engr. Iowa Army Ammunition Plant, Burlington, 1977—. Mem. Am. Soc. Quality Control (past treas.), Am. Def. Preparedness Assn., Am. Inst. Indsl. Engrs. Roman Catholic. Club: Skiowans. Office: Iowa Army Ammunition Plant Middletown IA 52638

BAXTER, REGINALD (BARNEY) ROBERT, plant food mfg. and distbg. co. exec.; b. Cushman, Ark., May 14, 1925; s. Remmel M. and Mary (Wilson) B.; B.A., U. Ark., 1948; M.S. in Chem. Enging., Iowa State Coll., 1949; m. Jameson Adkins, Jan. 24, 1976; 1 son, Sean Lee. Plant mgr. Anioniaco del Caribe, Colombia, 1961-63; project mgr. Esso Research and Engring. Co., 1963-65; gen. mgr. 1st Nitrogen Corp., Donaldsonville, La., 1965-67; v.p. mfg. CF Industries, Inc., Chgo., 1967-69, exec. v.p., 1969-71, pres., Long Grove, Ill., 1971—; dir. Barnett Banks of Polk County (Fla.). Pres. bd. sponsors Good Shepherd Hosp., Barrington, Ill. Served with U.S. Army, 1944-46. Mem. Nat. Council Farmers Coops. (dir.). Office: Salem Lake Dr Long Grove IL 60047

BAY, JOHN CANTRELL, hosp. adminstr.; b. St. Louis, Feb. 3, 1929; s. Lovell and June (King) B.; B.B.A., U. Mich., 1952, M.H.A., 1957; m. Janet Easum, Aug. 9, 1955; children—James Robert, Nancy June, Judith Carol. Adminstr., Detroit Rehab. Inst., 1957-62, Pennock Hosp., Hastings, Mich., 1962-67, Emma L. Bixby Hosp., Adrian, Mich., 1967-70, Munson Med. Center, Traverse City, Mich., 1970—; vice chmn. Grand Traverse Mental Health Bd., 1976-77. Vice chmn. Traverse Area United Fund, 1976. Served with AUS, 1952-55. Fellow Am. Coll. Hosp. Adminstrs.; Am. Hosp. Assn. (asso.), Mich. Hosp. Assn. (dir. 1972—, chmn. 1978-79), Grand Traverse-Benzie-Leelanau Med. Soc. Club: Traverse City Rotary (pres. 1981). Office: Munson Med Center 6th and Madison St Traverse City MI 49684

BAYER, HARMON SYMOND, mgmt. cons. co. exec.; b. Boston, Sept. 11, 1919; s. Abraham Henry and Miriam (Opp) B.; B.S., U. Mich., 1941; m. Adele Anne Allen, Dec. 20, 1941; children—Edward A., Charles S., Gerald E., Irene S. San. engr. USPHS, Washington, 1941-43; research and devel. engr. Peninsular Grinding Wheel Co., Detroit, 1946-49; head staff quality control engring. Ford div. Ford Motor Co., Dearborn, Mich., 1949-52; pres. Bayer & McElrath, Inc., Mgmt. Cons., Orchard Lake, Mich., 1952-77; pres. Harmon S. Bayer & Assos., W. Bloomfield, Mich., 1978—; vis. lectr. U. Mich., Ann Arbor, 1955-70, Wayne State U., Detroit, 1949-52, Mich. State U., E. Lansing, 1952-55, Marquette U., Milw., 1952-55. Served to capt., San. Corps, AUS, 1943-46. Registered profl. engr., Calif. Fellow Am. Soc. Quality Control, AAAS; mem. Am. Mgmt. Assn. Contbr. articles to profl. jours. Home: 6873 E Knollwood Circle West Bloomfield MI 48033 Office: 6873 E Knollwood Circle West Bloomfield MI 48033

BAYER, WILLIAM LANG, physician; b. N.Y.C., Feb. 14, 1935; s. Bernard and Sylvia (Lang) B.; A.B., Colgate U., 1956; M.D., Albany Med. Coll., Union U., 1962; m. Carol Burns, Feb. 7, 1959; children—Judith Elizabeth, Barbara Rachel. Med. intern and resident Jefferson Med. Coll. Hosp., Phila.; NIH postdoctoral fellow U. Pitts. Sch. Medicine, 1962-66; practice medicine specializing in blood banking and coagulation cons.; instr. dept. medicine U. Pitts. Sch. Medicine, 1966-68, asst. prof., 1968-69; asst. med. dir. Central Blood Bank Pitts., 1966-69; dir. Clin. Coagulation Lab., Pitts., 1966-69; dir. Community Blood Center Greater Kansas City (Mo.), 1969—; WHO adv. Nat. Transfusion Com. of Hungary, 1978; mem. del. U.S.-USSR Exchange Nat. Heart, Lung and Blood Inst., 1978; mem. hemophilia adv. com. Mo. Div. Health, 1976—; mem. Am. Blood Commn. Conf. on Mgmt. and Logistics of Blood Banking, 1977-78, chmn., 1978-79. Mem. Mayor's Corps of Progress, Kansas City, Mo., 1975—; bd. dirs. French Inst., Notre Dame de Sion, 1975—. Mem. Am. Soc. Hematology, Internat. Soc. Thrombosis and Hemostasis, Am. Heart Assn., Heart of Am. Assn. Blood Banks, Am. Assn. Blood Banks, AMA, Mo. Med. Assn., Jackson County Med. Assn., Council Community Blood Centers (pres. 1978-79), N.Y. Acad. Scis. Club: Rotary. Contbr. articles to med. jours. Home: 1256 W 59th St Kansas City MO 64113 Office: Community Blood Center 4040 Main St Kansas City MO 64111

BAYGENTS, ANNA MARY, educator, oil service retail co. exec.; b. Poplar Bluff, Mo., July 13, 1926; d. George Francis and Bertha Louise (Franck) AuBuchon; student U. N.C., 1956, U. Mo., 1972, S.E. Mo. U., 1973-74, Three Rivers Community Coll., 1974-81; m. Roy Emerson Baygents, May 11, 1968 (dec. 1978); 1 son, Ralph George; step-children—Steven Warren, Edris Marie, Roy Emerson, William Michael, Jeffrey Thomas, Timothy Gregory, Patricia Joy. Lab. technician, chairside asst., secretarial asst. to dentist, 1944-68; bookkeeper Baygents Holiday Inn Texaco, Poplar Bluff, 1968-78; instr. dental assisting Three Rivers Community Coll., Poplar Bluff, part-time 1972-76, full time 1976—; owner, bus. mgr., bookkeeper Baygents Mobil Service Co., Poplar Bluff, 1978—. Sec., Butler County United Fund Bd., 1960-61, chmn. budget com., 1959-61; active Butler County Assn. for Retarded Children, 1974—, pres., 1981; troop com. chmn. Boy Scouts Am., Girl Scouts U.S.A., 1979-81. Mem. Am. Dental Assts. Assn. (life, treas. 1963-68, Achievement award 1967), Mo. Dental Assts. Assn. (life, pres. 1956-57, Cooperation award 1974, Achievement award 1976), S.E. Mo. Dental Assts. Soc. (life), Am. Vocat. Assn., Mo. Vocat. Assn., Mo. Dental Assisting Educators, Mo. State Tchrs. Assn., Mo. Assn. Community and Jr. Colls., Butler County Geneal. Soc. (1st v.p. 1980-81), DAR (treas. Poplar Bluff chpt. 1980-81), Mo. Hist. Soc. Democrat. Roman Catholic. Contbr. articles to profl. jours. Home: 725 Kinzer St PO Box 506 Poplar Bluff MO 63901 Office: Three Rivers Community Coll Three Rivers Blvd Poplar Bluff MO 63901

BAYLESS, LAWRENCE GRANT, constrn. machinery co. exec.; b. Crawfordsville, Ind., May 19, 1935; s. Lloyd Richard and Geneice (Patton) B.; B.F.A., Bradley U., 1957; m. Joyce Ann Stribling, June 23, 1957; children—Robert, Michael, John, Ann, Mark, Amy, Joe. Artist, Squires Advt. Agy., Springfield, Ill., 1957-59, Greeley Advt., Springfield, 1959-60; artist, designer Mueller Co., Decatur, Ill., 1960-65; art dir. Evan and Asso., Springfield, 1965-70; head designer Bur. of Design, Public Hearing Services, State of Ill., Springfield, 1970; acting supr. program design, artist edn. center Fiat-Allis, Springfield, 1970-74, supr. multi-media graphics, world-wide publs., 1974—; judge Macon County Art Exhibit, 1964, 67, 71, 73, Town and Country Art Exhibit, U. Ill., 1971; tchr. Bement Art Club. Bd. dirs. Aid to Retarded Citizens, 1968-70; bd. dirs. Lincolnland Pony Baseball, 1972, 73, v.p., 1974-78, coach, 1972-81; mem. com. Boy Scouts Am., 1969-79; bd. dirs. Petersburg Jr. Baseball, 1973-79; coach Thorobred Baseball, 1978, 80-81; coach Little League, 1966-70, Flag football, 1969-71; trustee Methodist Ch.; bd. dirs. Ports Athletic Booster Club, 1974-81, pres., 1975, 79; bd. dirs. Lake Petersburg Assn., 1981. Served with U.S. Army, 1958, 61-62. Recipient art edn. award State of Ill., 1957; award of merit State of Ind. Art Award, 1953. Mem. Advt. and Pub. Relations Club Springfield, Sangamon County Referees Assn., Internat. Graphics Inc. (charter), Nat. Audio-Visual Inst., Am. Amateur Baseball Congress, Bradley U. Alumni Assn., Sigma Phi Epsilon Alumni. Republican. Club: Elks. Home: Rural Route 1 424 Hemlock St Petersburg IL 62675 Office: Fiat-Allis 3000 S 6th St Springfield IL 62710

BAYLESS, ROBERT GORDON, chemist, chem. products co. exec.; b. West Mansfield, Ohio, Feb. 18, 1930; s. Harvey S. and Olivia M. (Hill) B.; B.S. in Chemistry, Central State U., 1956; M.S., U. Cin., 1964; m. Edna Mae Robertson, Jan. 25, 1959; children—Marvin Leroy, Edward Dean, Alaine Jercel. Research asso. in chemistry Antioch Coll., Yellow Springs, Ohio, 1956-58; chemist U.S. Indsl. Chem. Co., Cin., 1960-63; research chemist capsular research NCR Corp., Dayton, Ohio, 1963-67, research chemist in materials research, 1967-73; founder, pres. Capsulated Systems Inc., Yellow Springs, 1973—, also dir. Served with U.S. Army, 1951-53; Korea. Mem. Am. Chem. Soc. Contbr. articles on indsl. chem. processes to profl. jours.; patentee in field. Office: 2076 N Broad St PO Box 1351 Fairborn OH 45324

BAYLISS, LARRY DALE, banker; b. St. Louis, Aug. 19, 1940; s. Arthur Lamoine and Helen Ruth (Balling) B.; B.S.B.A., Washington U., St. Louis, 1968; m. Mariann Stuckenschneider, June 24, 1961; 1 dau., Kathleen Ann. Sales promotion and advt. ofcl. Wagner Elec. Corp., St. Louis, 1958-67; mgr. processing dept. Skinner & Kennedy Co., St. Louis, 1967-68; adminstrv. asst., systems analyst, banking rep., asst. cashier Boatmen's Nat. Bank of St. Louis, 1968-73, asst. v.p. advt. and public relations, 1973-74, v.p. mktg., advt. and public relations, 1975—; pres. B & B Agy., St. Louis, 1977—. Bd. dirs. St. Louis Chamber Orch. and Chorus, 1979—; active corp. solicitations United Way, 1971—. Recipient Clio award Printing Industries Am. award, Flair Award, Fin. World award, St. Louis Soc. Communicating Arts award. Mem. Am. Inst. Banking, Bank Mktg. Assn., Ill.-Mo. Bank Mktg. Assn., Mo. Bankers Assn., Advt. Club Greater St. Louis, St. Louis Press Club. Roman Catholic. Club: Mo. Athletic. Home: 1895 Gerard Park Ln Saint Louis MO 63042 Office: 100 N Broadway Saint Louis MO 63102

BAYM, NINA, educator; b. Princeton, N.J., June 14, 1936; d. Leo and Frances (Levinson) Zippin; B.A., Cornell U., 1957; M.A., Radcliffe Coll.-Harvard U., 1958, Ph.D., 1963; m. Gordon Baym, June 1, 1958; children—Nancy, Geoffrey; m. 2d, Jack Stillinger, May 21, 1971. Asst. in English, U. Calif., Berkeley, 1962-63; instr. English, U. Ill., 1963-67, asst. prof., 1967-69, asso. prof., 1969-72, asso. head dept., 1971-75, prof., 1972—, dir. Sch. Humanities, 1976—. Guggenheim fellow, 1975-76; AAUW fellow, 1975-76; Nat. Endowment Humanities fellow, 1982-83. Mem. MLA, Nathaniel Hawthorne Soc., Robert Frost Soc. Author: The Shape of Hawthorne's Career, 1976; Woman's Fiction: A Guide to novels by and about women in America, 1978; editor: The Awakening and Selected Stories by Kate Chopin, 1981; mem. editorial bd. Am. Quar., Am. Lit. Office: 608 S Wright Urbana IL 61801

BAYMILLER, LYNDA DOERN, social worker; b. Milw., July 6, 1943; d. Ronald Oliver and Marian Elizabeth (Doern) B.; B.A., U. Wis., 1965, M.S.W., 1969; student U. Hawaii, 1962, Mich. State U., 1965. Peace Corps vol., Chile, 1965-67; social worker Luth. Social Services of Wis. and Upper Mich., Milw., 1969-77, contract social worker, 1978-79; dist. supr. Children's Service Soc. Wis., Kenosha, 1977-78; social work supr. Sauk County Dept. Social Services, Baraboo, Wis., 1979—. Bd. dirs. Zoo Pride, Zool. Soc. Milw. County, 1975-77, Sauk County Mental Health Assn., 1979—; mem. Harmony chpt. Sweet Adelines, West Allis, Wis., 1970-75, pres. chpt., 1971; pres. bd. dirs. Growing Pl. Day Care Center, Kenosha, 1977-78. Mem. Nat. Assn. Social Workers, Acad. Cert. Social Workers, Wis. Social Services Assn., AAUW, U. Wis. Alumni Assn. (life mem.), Am. Legion Aux., DAR, Nat. Soc. Magna Charta Dames, Eddy Family Assn. (life mem.), Nat. Soc. Ancient and Hon. Arty. Co. of Mass., Daus. Colonial Wars, Alpha Xi Delta. Author: (with Clara Amelia Hess) Now-Won, A Collection of Feeling (poetry and prose), 1973. Home: 332 4th Ave Baraboo WI 53913

BAZANT, ZDENEK PAVEL, educator, structural engr.; b. Prague, Czechoslovakia, Dec. 10, 1937; came to U.S., 1968, naturalized, 1976; s. Zdenek J. and Stepanka (Curikova) B.; Civil Engr., Czech Tech. U., with highest distinction, 1960, Docent (habilitatis), 1967; Ph.D. in Engring. Mechanics, Czechoslovak Acad. Scis., 1963; diploma in theoretical physics, Charles U., Czechoslovakia, 1966; m. Iva M. Krasna, Sept. 27, 1967; children—Martin Z., Eva S. Bridge engr. Dopravoprojekt, Prague, 1961-63; adj. prof. and scientist Czech Tech. U., Prague, 1963-67; research fellow Centre d'Etude du Bâtiment et des Travaux Publics, Paris, 1966; Ford Sci. Found. fellow U. Toronto, Ont., Can., 1967-68; asso. research engr. U. Calif., Berkeley, 1968-69, vis. scholar, 1978-79; asso. prof. civil engring. Northwestern U., Evanston, Ill., 1969-73, prof., 1973—, coordinator structural engring. program, 1974-78, dir. Center for Concrete and Geomaterials, 1981—; permanent cons. Argonne Nat. Lab.; cons. to various labs. and engring. firms, including Sargent & Lundy, Chgo., Portland Cement Assn., Ont. Hydro, Sandia Labs., Systems Sci. & Software, Oak Ridge Nat. Lab., Babcock & Wilcox, 1973—; vis. prof. Royal Inst. Tech., Stockholm, summer 1977; vis. scholar U. Calif., Berkeley, 1978, Stanford U., 1979, ETH, Zurich, 1979; guest lectr. various univs., 1966—; mem. com. research in cement and concrete in U.S., Nat. Acad. Engring., 1977-80, mem. com. concrete marine structures, 1980—. Served with Czechoslovak Army, 1961. Recipient RILEM gold medal Internat. Union Research Labs. in Materials and Structures, Paris, 1975; named Outstanding New Citizen of 1976, Citizenship Council of Chgo.; Guggenheim fellow, 1978-79; grantee NSF, 1970—, Advanced Research Projects Agy., 1970-71, Oak Ridge Nat. Lab., 1974-75, Air Force Office Sci. Research, 1975-77, Army C.E. Waterways Expt. Sta., 1975, ERDA, 1976-77, Dept. Energy, 1977-78, Los Alamos Sci. Lab., 1978-79; registered structural engr., Ill. Fellow Am. Acad. Mechanics, ASCE (chmn. com. on properties of materials 1975-77, W.L Huber Civil Engring. research prize 1976, T.Y. Lin Prestressed Concrete award 1977), Am. Concrete Inst., Internat. Union Research Labs. in Materials and Structures (chmn. com. on mathematical modeling of creep 1981—); mem. ASTM, AAAS, Internat. Soc. Soil Mechanics and Found. Engring., European Concrete Inst., Am. Ceramic Soc., Internat. Assn. Bridge and Structural Engring., Prestressed Concrete Inst., Internat. Assn. Structural Mechanics in Reactor Tech. (sci. com.), U.S. Olympic Soc., Brit. Concrete Soc. Clubs: Evanston Running, Touhy Tennis. Author: Creep of Concrete in Structural Analysis, 1966; co-author: Analysis of Concrete Structures by Finite Elements, 1978; contbr. numerous articles on structural mechs. and engring. to profl. jours.; editorial bd. Cement and Concrete Research, 1971—, Jour. Engring. Mechanics Div. ASCE, 1973-77, 81—, Internat. Jour. Numerical and Analytical Methods in Geomechanics, 1979—, Archives of Mechanics, 1980—, Materials and Structures, 1981—. Home: 514 Greenwood Ave Kenilworth IL 60043 Office: Dept Civil Engring Northwestern U Evanston IL 60201

BAZARKO, VOLODYMYR OREST, lawyer; b. Myciw, Ukraine, June 14, 1940; s. Ivan and Natalia (Saykewych) B.; came to U.S., 1949, naturalized, 1958; B.S. with honors, Pratt Inst., 1962; M.S., John Carroll U., 1966; J.D. cum laude, Cleve. State U., 1970; m. Lydia Z. Chylak, Aug. 24, 1963; children—Andrew, George. Research engr. NASA, Lewis Research Center, 1962-63, aerospace research engr., 1965-69; v.p. Mural & Son, Inc., 1969-71; admitted to Ohio bar, 1970; partner firm Bazarko, Futey and Oryshkewych, Cleve., 1971—; tchr. real estate law John Carroll U., 1973—. Served with C.E., U.S. Army, 1963-65. Mem. Am., Cleve., Cuyahoga County bar assns., Ukrainian Nat. Republican Fedn. (treas.), Shevchenko Sci. Soc. (v.p.). Contbr. articles to profl. jours. Home: 8400 Oak Knoll Ct North Royalton OH 44133 Office: 5566 Pearl Rd Parma OH 44129

BAZIK, EDNA FRANCES, mathematician; b. Streator, Ill., Dec. 26, 1946; d. Andrew and Anna Frances (Vagasky) B.; B.S.Ed., Ill. State U, 1969; postgrad. Hamilton Coll., summer 1971, Augustana Coll., summer 1973; M.Ed., U. Ill., 1972; Ph.D., So. Ill. U., 1976, gen. adminstrv. cert., 1980. Tchr. math. Northlawn Jr. High Sch., Streator, 1969-74; instr. math. edn. So. Ill. U., 1974-76; asst. prof. math. Concordia Coll., 1976-78; asst. prof. math. Ill. State U., Normal, 1978—; inservice presentations, workshops for tchrs.; cons. to sch. dists. NSF grantee, 1980—. Mem. AAUP, Assn. Tchr. Educators, Ill. Assn. Tchr. Educators, Nat. Council Tchrs. Math., Ill. Council Tchrs. Math. (governing bd., dir. coll. and univ. level), Math. Assn. Am., Nat. Council Suprs. Math., NEA, Ill. Edn. Assn., Sch. Sci. and Math. Assn., U.S. Metric Assn., Am. Ednl. Research Assn., Assn. Supervision and Curriculum Devel., Ill. Assn. Supervision and Curriculum Devel., Assn. Childhood Edn. Internat., Council Exceptional Children, Research Council Diagnostic and Prescriptive Math., Kappa Delta Pi, Phi Delta Kappa (sec. Ill. State U. chpt.), Pi Mu Epsilon, Phi Kappa Phi. Republican. Lutheran. Co-author: Elementary Mathemtical Methods, 1978; Mind Over Math, 1980. Home: 202 Riss Dr Normal IL 61761 Office: Math Dept Ill State U Normal IL 61761

BEACH, OSCAR HARDING, JR., statistician; b. Cottekill, N.Y., Feb. 5, 1929; s. Oscar H. and Edna Mae (Pine) B.; B.S., Syracuse U., 1954, M.B.A., 1961; m. Mary Louise Nisbet, Sept. 1, 1951; 1 dau., Nancy Woodburn. Field rep. Travelers Ins. Co., Conn., Cleve., 1954-58, group supr., Cleve., 1958; sr. research asst. Fed. Res. Bank, Cleve., 1959-61, asst. economist, 1961-63, asso. economist, 1963, statistician, 1963-65, asst. cashier, 1965-71, asst. v.p., 1971—. Served with U.S. Army, 1946-49. Mem. Am. Statis. Assn. Office: Fed Res Bank PO Box 6387 Cleveland OH 44101

BEACHLER, KENNETH CLARKE, univ. adminstr.; b. Battle Creek, Mich., Oct. 11, 1935; s. Hubert Waldo and Nina Kathryn (Eitelbuss) B.; B.A. with high honors, Mich. State U., 1963. Profl. actor and singer, Chgo., 1955-57; radio announcer WKAR-AM/FM, East Lansing, Mich., 1959-62, WSWM-FM, East Lansing, 1962-64; music program dir. WKAR-FM, East Lansing, 1964-70; dir. lecture-concert series Mich. State U., East Lansing, 1971-81, dir. performing arts facilities and programs, 1981—. Host weekly radio program Arts Billboard, 1972—. Chmn. public relations Met. Lansing Arts Council, 1970-72. Bd. dirs. Lansing Symphony Orch., 1971-73, 78—, Okemos Barn Theatre, 1970-71, Opera Co. Greater Lansing, 1978-79, Pashami Dancers, 1976—. Served with AUS, 1957-59. Named Best Actor, Okemos Barn Theatre, 1974, Best Dir., 1969, 71, 76, 80, 81. Mich. State U. Bd. Trustees tuition scholar, 1960, Hinman Broadcasting scholar, 1961-63. Mem. Internat. Soc. Performing Arts Adminstrs. (dir. 1974-77), Assn. Coll., Univ. and Community Arts Adminstrs. Mem. United Ch. of Christ. Rotarian. Club: University of Mich. State U. (dir. 1978—, v.p. 1980—). Home: 1450 Hitching Post Rd East Lansing MI 48823 Office: Mich State U East Lansing MI 48824

BEADLE, GEORGE WELLS, biologist, educator; b. Wahoo, Nebr., Oct. 22, 1903; s. Chauncey Elmer and Hattie (Albro) B.; B.S., U. Nebr., 1926, M.S., 1927, D.Sc. (hon.), 1949; Ph.D., Cornell U., 1931; M.A., Oxford U., 1958, D.Sc. (hon.), 1959; D.Sc. (hon.), Yale U., 1947, Northwestern U., 1952, Rutgers U., 1954, Kenyon Coll., 1955, Wesleyan U., 1956, U. Birmingham, 1959, Pomona Coll., 1961, Lake Forest Coll., 1962, U. Rochester, 1963, U. Ill., 1963, Brown U., 1964, Kans. State U., 1964, U. Pa., 1964, Wabash Coll., 1966, Syracuse U., 1967, Loyola U., Chgo., 1970, Hanover Coll., 1971, Eureka Coll., 1972, Butler U., 1973, Gustavus Adolphus, 1975, Ind. State U., 1976; LL.D. (hon.), U. Calif., Los Angeles, 1962, Miami U., 1963, Brandeis U., 1963, Johns Hopkins U., 1966, Beloit Coll., 1966, U. Mich., 1969; D.H.L., Jewish Theol. Sem. Am., 1966, DePaul U., 1969, U. Chgo., 1969, Canisius Coll., 1969, Knox Coll., 1969, Roosevelt U., 1971, Carroll Coll., 1971; D.Pub. Service (hon.), Ohio No. U., 1970; m. Marion Cecile Hill, Aug. 22, 1928 (div. 1953); 1 son, David; m. 2d, Muriel Barnett, Aug. 12, 1953; 1 stepson, Redmond James Barnett. Teaching asst. Cornell U., 1926-27, experimentalist, 1927-31; NRC fellow Calif. Inst. Tech., 1931-33, instr., 1933-35, prof. biology, chmn. div. biology, 1946-60, acting deal faculty, 1960-61; guest investigator Institut de Biologie Physicochimique, Paris, 1935; asst. prof. genetics Harvard U., 1936-37; prof. biology Stanford U., 1937-46; Eastman vis. prof. Oxford U., 1958-59; pres., trustee, prof. biology U. Chgo., 1961-68, pres. emeritus, William E. Wrather Distinguished Service prof. emeritus, hon. trustee, 1969—; mem. Pres.'s Sci. Adv. Com., 1960. Pres., Chgo. Hort. Soc., 1968-71; bd. dirs. Inst. Biomed. Research, AMA, 1968-70; trustee Mus. Sci. and Industry, Chgo., 1967-68, Nutrition Found., 1969-73, Pomona Coll., 1958-61, Calif. Inst. Tech., 1969-75; mem. sci. adv. bd. Robert A. Welch Found., 1971—. Mem. Nat. Acad. Sci. (council 1969-72), Am. Philos. Soc., Royal Soc., Danish Royal Acad. Sci., Japan Acad. (hon.), Instituto Lombardi di Scienze e Lettre (Milan), AAAS (pres. 1946), Am. Acad. Arts and Scis., Genetics Soc. Am. (pres. 1955), Genetic Soc. (Gt. Britain), Indian Soc. Genetics and Plant Breeding, Indian Nat. Sci. Acad. (hon.), Twelfth Internat. Congress Genetics (hon. pres. 1968), Phi Beta Kappa, Sigma Xi. Clubs: Tavern, Chgo. (Chgo.). Decorated Order St. Olaf; recipient Lasker award, 1950, Dyer award, 1951, Emil Christian Hansen prize (Denmark), 1953, Albert Einstein Commemorative award in sci., 1958, Nobel prize in physiology and medicine, 1958, Am. Cancer Soc. award, 1959, Kimber Genetics award, 1960, Priestley Meml. award, 1967, Edison award for best sci. book for youth, 1967, Donald Jones medal, 1972. Author: (with A.H. Sturtevant) An Introduction to Genetics, 1939; Genetics and Modern Biology, 1953; (with Muriel B. Beadle) The Language of Life, 1966. Home: 1700 E 56th St Chicago IL 60637 Office: Dept Biology U Chgo Chicago IL 60637

BEADLE, MURIEL MCCLURE BARNETT, civic worker, writer; b. Alhambra, Calif., Sept. 14, 1915; d. Richard and Eunice L. (Bothwell) McClure; B.A., Pomona Coll., 1936, LL.D., 1973; D.H.L., Mundelein Coll., 1966; m. Joseph Y. Barnett, July 3, 1941 (dec. Feb. 1951); 1 son, Redmond James; m. 2d, George Wells Beadle, Aug. 12, 1953. Advt. copywriter Carson Pirie Scott & Co., Chgo., 1936-40, Bullock's Pasadena (Calif.), 1945-48; fashion editor, women's editor Los Angeles Mirror-News, 1948-58; free-lance writer newspapers and mags., 1958—. Lectr. on edn. and social welfare, cons. various educator groups, 1957—; v.p. Pasadena Com. on Pub. Edn., 1957-60; mem. Pasadena Library Bd., 1959-61; chmn. Harper Ct. Found., Chgo., 1962-72. Recipient citation City of Pasadena, 1960, citation for service to pub. edn. Pasadena Edn. Assn., 1959, award Chgo. Friends of Lit., 1962, Thomas Alva Edison Found., 1967, Delta Kappa Gamma, 1971. Mem. Phi Beta Kappa. Democrat. Club: Fortnightly (Chgo.). Author: These Ruins Are Inhabited, 1961; (with husband) The Language of Life, 1966; A Child's Mind, 1970; Where Has All the Ivy Gone?, 1972; The Fortnightly of Chicago: The City and Its Women, 1873-1973, 1973; A Nice Neat Operation, 1975; The Cat, 1977. Address: 1700 E 56th St Chicago IL 60637

BEAL, BERT LEONARD, JR., elec. engr.; b. Birmingham, Ala., June 19, 1911; s. Bert Leonard and Catherine (Marks) B.; B.S., Washington U., St. Louis, 1934; m. Josephine Watkins, Feb. 24, 1943; 1 son, Albert G. Asst. mine mgr. So. Coal, Coke & Mining, Belleville, Ill., 1935-36; engr. Carrier Corp., Newark, 1936-37; asst. foreman, foreman tng. supr., engr., asst. gen. mech. supt. St. Joe Minerals Corp., Bonne Terre, Mo. 1937-54. gen. mech. supt., 1954-66, dir. engring., 1966-75; pres. Beal Enterprises, engring. cons. and agribus., 1975—. Active in civic affairs. Trustee Presbyterian Children's Home, bd. chmn., 1973. Served from lt. to lt. col. AUS, 1941-46. Registered profl. engr. Mem. Soc. Mining Engrs., Rivermines Engrs. Club (sec. 1951, v.p. 1952, pres. 1953), St. Francis County Hist. Soc. (pres. 1964), Am. Legion. Presbyterian (deacon, elder). Rotarian (sec. 1955, dir. 1972). Home and Office: 615 W Columbia St Farmington MO 63640

BEAL, ROGER EDWIN, landscape architect; b. Medina, Ohio, July 17, 1952; s. Lawrence Edwin and Donna Marie (Horner) B.; B.S., Ohio State U., 1975; m. Kathleen Grabaskas, Sept. 11, 1976; 1 dau., Ara Grabaskas. Landscape designer Ohio State U., Columbus, 1975-77, coordinator campus graphics, 1977—, instr., 1975, 78. Recipient Exceptional Achievement award Council Advancement and Support Edn., 1978, Columbus Beautification awards, 1975, 76. Mem. Am. Soc. Landscape Architects. Designer Jesse Owens Meml. Plaza, 1980-81. Office: 257 Millikin Rd Columbus OH 43210

BEALS, KENNETH LLOYD, social worker; b. St. Louis County, Mo., Feb. 19, 1935; s. Arthur Loyd and Edna (Dollar) B.; B.S., Washington U., St. Louis, 1961, M.S.W., 1967; postgrad. S.W. Baptist Sem., 1961-62; m. Frances Kay Stricklin, Apr. 18, 1959; children—Michael Lloyd, Rebecca Kay. Cartographer, negative engraver Aero Chart Plant, U.S. Air Force, St. Louis, 1954-61; caseworker Mo. Bapt. Children's Home, St. Louis, 1962-65; protective service caseworker Child and Family Service, State of Ill., East St. Louis, 1965-68; acting dir. Hoyleton (Ill.) Children's Home, 1968-69; dir. residential care Child and Family Service, Muskegon, Mich., 1969-75; exec. dir. Brookview, Inc., Fenton, Mich., 1975-79; supr. Central Bapt. Family Service, Effingham, Ill., 1979-81; adminstr. New Hope Living and Learning Center, Waterloo, Ill., 1981—; pvt. practice, 1981—; mem. faculty Mich. Assn. Child Agys., 1972-74. Ordained to Gospel ministry So. Bapt. Conv., 1963; Explorer leader Boy Scouts Am., 1976-79; recipient 30 Yr. Vet. Scouter award, 1974. Mem. Nat. Assn. Social Workers, Acad. Certified Social Workers. Home: Rural Route 1 Box 290 Waterloo IL 62298 Office: 801 Illinois Ave Waterloo IL 62298

BEAMER, PARKER REYNOLDS, pathologist, educator; b. Centralia, Ill., July 27, 1914; s. Powhatan Reynolds and Bessie Louise (Poole) B.; student U. Louisville, 1931-32; A.B. with high honors, U. Ill., 1935, M.S., 1937, Ph.D., 1940; M.D. cum laude, Washington U., 1943; m. Mary Jo Scovill, 1939; children—Jo Ellen Beamer Zurbrugg, Mary Susan, Grant S(covill). Asst. in bacteriology U. Ill., 1935-39; Jackson Johnson fellow in med. sci. Washington U., 1939-41, lectr. bacteriology Sch. Dentistry, 1941-42, asst. pathol. Sch. Medicine, 1942-44, asst. prof. pathology, 1946-49; asst. pathologist Barnes, St. Louis Children's, St. Louis Maternity and McMillan hosps., 1946-49; attending physician pathology Jefferson Barracks Vets. Hosp., 1947-49; prof. microbiology and immunology, dir. dept., asso. prof. pathology Bowman Gray Sch. Med., 1949-53, asso. dean, 1951-53; bacteriologist, asso. pathologist N.C. Bapt. Hosp., 1949-53; prof. pathology Ind. U. Med. Center, 1953-65, chmn. dept., 1961-65; dir. labs. and pathology, prof. pathology Los Angeles County-U. So. Calif. Med. Center, 1965-70; prof. pathology Chgo Med. Sch., 1970-80, prof. emeritus, 1980—; clin. prof. pathology Stritch Sch. Medicine, Loyola U., Maywood, Ill., 1981—; asso. pathologist, dir. resident tng. West Suburban Hosp., Oak Park, Ill., 1980—; vis. prof. pathology Washington Hosp. Center, 1961. Mem. chancellor's com. of 500, Washington U., 1969—. Served from 1st lt. to lt. col. M.C., AUS, 1943-47; comdg. officer, chief med. bacteriology and parasitology divs. Antilles Gen. Med. Lab., San Juan, P.R., 1945-47. Recipient Gold medal N.C., 1951; Honor medallion Armed Forces Inst. Pathology, 1962; diplomate Am. Bd. Pathology (trustee and bd. dirs., 1961-70, life trustee 1970—). Fellow Am. Soc. Clin. Pathologists, Coll. Am. Pathologists; mem. Am. Assn. Pathologists, Assn. Clin. Scientists (founding fellow), Am. Pub. Health Assn., Am. Soc. Microbiologists, AMA, Am. Soc. Exptl. Biology and Medicine,

AAAS, Assn. Am. Med. Colls., Sigma Xi, Phi Chi, Alpha Omega Alpha, Gamma Alpha. Republican. Baptist. Kiwanian. Author: (with others) Principles of Human Pathology, 1959; Microscopic Pathology, 1964; Microbiology Fundamentals in Relation to Human Diseases, 1982. Editor-in-chief Am. Jour. Clin. Pathology, 1956-65; founding editor Survey of Pathology in Medicine and Surgery, 1964; cons. and contbg. editor (pathology) Stedman's Med. Dictionary, 1958-76, (clin. pathology) Current Med. Digest, 1959-68; co-editor Microbiology-Immunology Series, Year Book Medical Publishers, 1974—. Contbr. numerous articles to profl. jours. Home: 539 N Franklin Ave River Forest IL 60305 Office: Dept Pathology West Suburban Hosp 518 N Austin Blvd Oak Park IL 60302

BEAN, MARVIN DAY, clergyman; b. Tampa, Fla., Sept. 8, 1921; s. Marvin Day and Lillian (Howell) B.; A.B., Fla. So. Coll., 1946, M.S. in Social Work, Vanderbilt U., 1948; postgrad. Ohio State U., 1951-52, Northwestern U., 1950; B.D., Garrett Theol. Sem., 1950; children—Bethany Louise, Thomas Holmes, Carol Sue. Ordained to ministry Methodist Ch., 1950; pastor, Lena Vista, Fla., 1946; asso. pastor San Marcos Meth. Ch., Tampa, 1947; pastor Cedar Lake (Ind.) Meth. Ch., 1948-50, Shepard Meth. Ch., Columbus, Ohio, 1951-68, Stonybrook Meth. Ch., Gahanna, Ohio, 1960-65, Obetz (Ohio) Meth. Ch., 1968-73, Neil Ave. Ch., Columbus, 1973-79, St. Andrew Ch., Columbus, 1979—. Asst. to exec. sec. Meth. Union in Ch. Extension, Columbus, 1965-74; v.p. com. info. and pub. relations Ohio Conf. Meth. Ch., 1964-68, vice chmn. health and welfare ministries, 1968-72, chmn. urban life com. Bd. Missions, 1968-70, asso. sec. Bd. Missions, 1968-72, chmn. Services to Children and Youth, 1962-72; chmn. research Ohio Area Study on Aging, Ohio area Meth. Ch., 1959-64; sec. Columbus dist. conf. Meth. Ch., 1960-68; chmn. sch. religion Columbus area Council Chs., 1953; trustee Meth. Retirement Center Central Ohio, Columbus; trustee United Meth. Children's Home, Worthington, Ohio, 1973-74; chmn. bd. trustees Neil Ave. Found., 1973-79. Served with AUS, 1943-46. Recipient Wolfley Found. recognition award for inner city work, 1961. Mem. Columbus Meth. Ministerial Assn. (pres. 1960-61), Ohio Council Chs. (rep. com. strategy and planning 1965-68). Nat. Assn. Social Workers, Acad. Certified Social Workers. Author: A Guide to United Methodist Building, 1973; You Are on the District Board, 1974; Unto the Least of These, 1981; contbr. articles to profl. jours. Home: 122 W Henderson Rd Columbus OH 43214 Office: 1033 High St Worthington OH 43085

BEAR, SHARON LOUISE, broadcasting co. exec.; b. Dover, Ohio, June 28, 1946; d. Byron Williams and Dicie Edna (Willis) B.; B.A., Malone Coll., 1968; M.A., Bowling Green State U., 1970. Lang.-speech pathologist Montgomery Inst., Akron, 1970-74, Akron Pediatric Neurology, Inc., 1974-80; communication disorders cons., Akron, 1970-82; instr. mass media communications U. Akron, 1981; cons. Group Travel Sales and Incentive Travel Cons., Akron, 1977-82; promotions dir. Sta. WHLO, Susquehanna Broadcasting Co., Akron, 1982—. Mem. Am. Speech Lang. and Hearing Assn. (cert. clin. competence). Club: Akron Woman's City, Jr. League of Akron. Office: 2650 W Market St Akron OH 44313

BEARD, (BARBARA) SUE, coll. adminstr.; b. Logansport, Ind., Nov. 24, 1940; d. James Orma and Gertrude Lucille (Williams) Handy; B.A., Franklin Coll., 1962; M.A., Butler U., 1971; m. John A. Beard, Aug. 26, 1961; children—Kent A., Tracy Lynne. English tchr. Indpls. Public Schs., 1967-70; lectr. Ind. U., Ind. Central U. and Ind. Vocat. Tech. Coll., 1971-79; coordinator extended services Ind. Vocat. Tech. Coll., Indpls., 1979—; cons. English composition; communications seminar and workshop leader. Mem. Lawrence Twp. Sch. Bd. Candidate Selection Com.; dist. chmn. fundraising for ednl. TV, 1971. Mem. Ind. Bus. Communicators, Am. Bus. Communicators, Women in Communications, Ind. Vocat. Assn., Am. Soc. Tng. and Devel., Delta Delta Delta. Club: Women's Dept. (pres. 1974-76). Author: The Counselor's Handbook, 1976. Home: 7222 Brompton Ct Indianapolis IN 46250 Office: 1315 E Washington St Indianapolis IN 46202

BEARD, WARD POWERS, assn. exec.; b. Brookings, S.D., Oct. 4, 1920; s. Ward P. and Marion Elizabeth (Miller) B.; B.A., George Washington U., 1943; m. Lucy Palmer Meade, July 18, 1942; children—Mary, Bill, Russell, James, Tom. Mgr. manpower devel. Mich. Blue Cross Plan, Detroit, 1946-64; cons. Nat. Assn. Blue Cross Plans, N.Y.C., 1960; cons. Florez Inc., Detroit, 1965; dir. of edn. and research Florists Transworld Delivery Assn., Southfield, Mich., 1966—. Served with Air Corps, U.S. Army, 1943-46; PTO. Recipient Nat. Research and Edn. award Mich. State Florists Assn., 1977. Mem. Am. Soc. Tng. and Devel., Mich. Soc. Instructional Tech. Unitarian. Condr. census, compiler FTD Flower Bus. Fact Book, 1970, 75, 81. Home: 1685 Allard Grosse Pointe MI 48236 Office: 29200 Northwestern Hwy Southfield MI 48037

BEARDSLEY, JEFFRY SUMNER, optical mail order co. exec.; b. Elkhart, Ind., Feb. 23, 1948; s. Lehman F. and Virginia J. Beardsley; B.A., U. N.C., 1971; M.B.A., U. Notre Dame, 1973; m. Deborah Dwyer, June 26, 1971; children—Christopher, Gretchen, Andrew. Advt. account exec. MTK & Assos., Wakarusa, Ind., 1973-75; v.p. adminstrn. Partners in Futures, South Bend, Ind., 1975-77; asst. product mgr. consumer products div. Miles Labs., Inc., Elkhart, Ind., 1977-79; pres. Bernell Corp., South Bend, 1979—. Past bd. dirs. Big Bros./Big Sisters; active United Way. Clubs: Elcona Country; Elkhart Racquet. Home: 1704 Lawndale Rd Elkhart IN 46514 Office: 422 E Monroe St South Bend IN 46601

BEARE, GENE KERWIN, co. dir.; b. Chester, Ill., July 14, 1915; s. Nicholas Eugene and Minnie Cole (St. Vrain) B.; B.S. in Mech. Engring., Washington U., 1937; M.B.A., Harvard, 1939; m. Doris Margaret Alt, Dec. 11, 1943 (dec.); children—Gail Kathryn, Joanne St. Vrain; m. 2d, Patricia Pfau Cade, Sept. 12, 1964. With Automatic Electric Co., Chgo., 1939-58, successively asst. to v.p. and gen. mgr., asst. to pres., mgr. internat. affiliated cos., gen. comml. mgr., 1939-54, v.p. prodn., 1954-58, dir., 1956-61; pres., dir. Automatic Electric Internat., Inc., 1958-61; chmn., dir. Automatic Electric (Can.), Ltd., Automatic Electric Sales (Can.), Ltd., 1958-61; pres., dir. Sylvania Internat., 1959-60; pres. Gen. Telephone & Electronics Internat., Inc., 1960-61, dir., 1960-72, also dir. numerous subsidiaries in Colombia, Mexico, Venezuela, Argentina, Switzerland, Panama, Brazil, Belgium, Can., Italy; pres. Sylvania Electric Products, Inc., 1961-69, dir., 1961-72; exec. v.p. mfg., dir. Gen. Telephone & Electronics Corp., 1969-72; exec. v.p., dir. Gen. Dynamics Corp., St. Louis, 1972-77; pres. Gen. Dynamics Comml. Products Co., 1972-77; chmn. Asbestos Corp. Ltd., 1974-77; dir. Arkwright-Boston Mut. Ins. Co., Westvaco Corp., Emerson Electric Co., Stromberg Carlson Corp., 1972-77, Candair Ltd 1972-75, St. Joe Minerals Corp., Am. Maize-Products Corp., Datapoint Corp. Served from ensign to lt. USNR, 1942-45. Registered profl. engr., Ill. Mem. Pan Am. Soc., Nat. Elec. Mfrs. Assn. (bd. govs. 1963-72, v.p. 1964, pres. 1965-66), Armed Forces Communications and Electronics Assn., Nat. Security Indsl. Assn. (trustee 1969-72). Clubs: Wee Burn (gov. 1963-68) (Darien, Conn.); Union League, Economic (N.Y.C.); St. Louis; Old Warson (Ladue, Mo.). Home: 801 S Skinker Blvd Saint Louis MO 63105 Office: Pierre Laclede Center 7701 Forsyth Blvd Suite 545 Saint Louis MO 63105

BEASLEY, ROBERT L., farm supply co. exec.; b. Poplar Bluff, Mo., Mar. 6, 1929; B.A. in Journalism, U. Mo., 1952; m. Betty Beasley; 2 children. With various newspapers, Mo., Iowa, Wis.; with Farmland Industries, Inc., Kansas City, Mo., 1957—, v.p. info. and pub. relations dept., 1971—, mem. exec. council. Vice chmn. bd. govs. Greater Kansas City YMCA; past vice chmn. Kansas City Philharm. Assn.; bd. dirs. Public Broadcasting Channel 19, Kansas City United Way. Mem. Internat. Coop. Alliance, Coop. League U.S.A. (past chmn.), Kansas City C. of C. Office: Farmland Industries Inc PO Box 7305 Kansas City MO 64116

BEASON, JO ANN K., advt. exec.; b. Wichita, Kans., Nov. 20, 1941; d. Joseph H. and Marcella K. (Maechtlen) Zandler; exec. sec. degree Wichita Bus. Coll., 1960; student Friends U., Wichita, 1970-71; m. Donald R. Beason, Oct. 30, 1976. Sec., White Star Machinery & Supply Co., 1960-68; advt. mgr. Berry Cos., Inc., Wichita, 1968—. Recipient Best Used Equipment Campaign award Internat. Harvester Distbr. Advt. Workshop, 1972, 73, 74, Disting. Salesman's award Wichita Sales and Mktg. Execs., 1971. Mem. Nat. Assn. Women in Constrn. (charter mem., pres. Wichita chpt. 1974-75), Wichita Press Women (v.p. 1978, dir.). Democrat. Baptist. Office: 829 N Market St PO Box 829 Wichita KS 67201

BEATON, IAN WILSON, advt. agy. exec.; b. Sydney, N.S., Can., Mar. 10, 1924; s. William Murray and Margaret (MacKenzie) B.; came to U.S., 1924, naturalized, 1945; B.S., Northwestern U., 1950; m. Carol Jean Lindner, Dec. 30, 1950; children—Lynda (Mrs. Roger Freed), Scot. Merchandising mgr. AC Spark Plug Div., Gen. Motors Corp., 1950-56; copywriter Leo Burnett Co. Mich. Inc. (formerly D. P. Brother & Co.), 1956-58, account exec., 1958-61, v.p., gen. account exec., 1961-66, v.p., adminstrn., personnel, 1966-70, v.p., account supr., 1970-74; v.p., sr. account supr. Campbell-Ewald Co., Detroit, from 1975, now sr. v.p., sr. account supr., Warren, Mich. Served with AUS, 1943-45; PTO. Mem. Detroit Advt. Assn., Pi Kappa Alpha. Presbyterian. Clubs: Detroit Adcraft, Great Oaks Country, Recess. Home: 1200 Oakwood Ct Rochester MI 48063 Office: Campbell Ewald Bldg Warren MI 48093

BEATTY, LESTER ROBERT, data processing exec.; b. Natrona Heights, Pa., Sept. 29, 1937; s. Lester R. and Virginia E. (Rumbaugh) B.; B.S., Carnegie Inst. Tech., 1960; M.B.A. magna cum laude, U. Bridgeport, 1970; m. Anita Ruth Ruben, July 27, 1963; children—Virginia, Sandra, Brian. Sci. programmer Carnegie Inst. Tech., Pitts., 1958-60, Allegheny Ludlum Steel, Natrona Heights, Pa., 1960-64; benefits programming project leader U.S. Steel, Pitts., 1964-66; software sr. analyst RCA, Palm Beach Gardens, Fla., 1966-68; applications project leader NASDAQ, Bunker-Ramo, Trumbull, Conn., 1968-70; systems mgr. Champion Internat., Hamilton, Ohio, 1970-79; dir. mgmt. info. and computer systems Cin. Electronics, 1979-81; pres. Phoenix Assos., 1981-82; corp. Systems cons. Armco, Middleton, Ohio, 1982—; data processing cons., 1968—; guest lectr. U. Cin., 1979. County bus. chmn. United Way, Ohio, 1975; county chmn. Young Republicans, 1967-68; data processing chmn. Rep. congressional campaigns, Hamilton County, 1976—; nat. honor guard Rep. Nat. Conv., 1968; pres. Ohio Model Legislature, 1975. Served as 1st lt. Signal Corps, U.S. Army, 1960-61. Cert. data processor. Mem. Assn. Systems Mgmt. (dir. 1981-82), Paper Industry Mgmt. Assn. (nat. EDP com.), Am. Water Ski Assn., SAR, Jaycees (local pres. 1963-64, state chmn. 1967-68, named Outstanding Local Pres. in State, Outstanding State Chmn. in U.S.), Mensa (local editor 1975-76). Presbyterian. Clubs: Kiwanis, Masons (32 deg.), Shriners. Author: One Corporation, One System. Designer NASDAQ securities index widely used in brokerage industry. Home: 10224 Lochcrest Dr Cincinnati OH 45231 Office: 703 Curtis St Middleton OH 45043

BEAUDOIN, GREGORY DAVID, retailer; b. Cadillac, Mich., Feb. 14, 1947; s. William Francis and Flora Jeanette (Sawin) B.; student Northwestern Mich. Coll., 1965-66, No. Mich. U., 1966-67; B.S., Central Mich. U., 1967-69; m. Patricia Agnes Sivak, May 10, 1969 (dec. Feb. 9, 1981); children—Anne-Terese Renee, David Gregory, Daniel Stephen. Tchr. sci. Fowler (Mich.) Pub. Schs., 1969-70; mgr., v.p. Bill's Motor Sales, Cadillac, 1971—; owner Beaudoin Tree Co., 1979—, Vehicle Appraisal Assos., 1979—, Central Excavating Co., 1980—. Chmn., Wexford County Republican Party, 1977-79; mem. Wexford County Rep. Exec. Com., 1976; dir. Wexford County Juvenile Ct. Vols., 1974-78; mem. Haring Twp. Bd. Appeals, 1976-79; chmn. Haring Twp. Bldg. Com., 1976-78; vol. United Way of Wexford County, 1975, 76; trustee Haring Twp. Bd. Suprs., 1976-79; bd. dirs. U.S. 131 Area Devel. Assn., 1974-80. Served with U.S. Army, 1970-71. Mem. Mich. Christmas Tree Growers Assn., Am. Legion. Republican. Roman Catholic. Club: Moose. Home: 4665 E 32d Rd Cadillac MI 49601 Office: 1129 N Mitchell St Cadillac MI 49601

BEAULIEU, RONALD PATRICK, educator; b. Indpls., Mar. 15, 1949; s. Peter Calice and Charlotte Genevieve Beaulieu; B.S., Purdue U., 1972; M.B.A., Ind. U., 1975, D.B.A., 1976. Asso. instr., Ind. U., Bloomington, 1973-76; asst. prof. mgmt. U. Notre Dame (Ind.), 1976-79. Central Mich. U., Mt. Pleasant, 1979—. Mem. Am. Psychol. Assn., Am. Inst. Decision Scis., Acad. Mgmt., Am. Soc. Personnel Adminstrn., Beta Gamma Sigma, Sigma Iota Epsilon. Home: 4965 Bayou Dr Lake MI 48632 Office: Central Michigan Univ School of Business Mt Pleasant MI 48859

BEAVEN, WINTON HENRY, coll. dean; b. Binghamton, N.Y., Jan. 26, 1915; s. student Hamilton Coll., 1933-35; B.S. in History and Internat. Relations, Atlantic Union Coll., 1937; M.A. in History, Clark U., 1938; Ph.D. in Speech, U. Mich., 1950. Instr. history Madison (Tenn.) Coll., 1938-40; instr. speech and English, dean of men Atlantic Union Coll., South Lancaster, Mass., 1940-43; asst. prof. Union Coll., Lincoln, Nebr., 1943-45, asso. prof., 1945-47, prof. speech, 1947-50, chmn. dept. speech, 1943-50; asst. prof. U. Mich., Ann Arbor, 1950-52, asso. prof., 1952-53; asso. sec. Internat. Commn. for Prevention of Alcoholism, Washington, 1953-57; dean Grad. Sch., Potomac U., Washington, 1956-59; dean acad. adminstrn. Columbia Union Coll., Takoma Park, Md., 1959-65, pres., 1965-70; dean Kettering (Ohio) Coll. Med. Arts, 1970—; v.p. edn. Kettering Med. Center, 1972—; v.p., lectr. Internat. Commn. for Prevention of Alcoholism; pres. Nat. Com. for Prevention of Alcoholism; bd. dirs., past chmn. Western Ohio Regional Alcoholism Council; past pres. Dayton Area Council on Alcoholism and Drug Abuse. Pres., Am. Bus. Men's Research Found.; chmn. bd., v.p. Dayton-Miami Valley Consortium; bd. dirs. Miami Valley Health Systems Agy. Inc.; bd. dirs., chmn. health div. United Way. Mem. Assn. Higher Edn., Speech Communication Assn., Religious Speech Communication Assn. Seventh-day Adventist. Club: Rotary. Office: Kettering Med Center 3737 Southern Blvd Kettering OH 45429

BEAVERS, RICHARD ALLEN, dentist; b. Durham, N.C., Oct. 3, 1944; s. William Olive and Eunice Margaret (Brass) B.; B.S. in Biology, Wake Forest U., 1967; M.A. in Biology (Greensboro Wildlife Club scholar), U. N.C., Greensboro, 1975; D.D.S., U. N.C., Chapel Hill, 1979; m. Sharon Jean Mork; 1 dau., Debran Margaret. Grad. teaching asst. U. N.C., Greensboro, 1972-74, instr. in microbiology, 1974; instr. in math. and sci. Guilford Tech. Inst., 1974-75; resident in gen. practice of dentistry Univ. Hosp., Seattle, 1979-80; endodontic resident, clin. instr. U. Mich., Ann Arbor, 1980—; mem. profl. edn. com. Orange County unit, N.C. div. Am. Cancer Soc., 1978-79. Bd. dirs. Univ. Baptist Ch. Kindergarten-Day Care Center, 1975-79. Served with USNR, 1968-72. Recipient Am. Acad. Oral Pathology award, 1979, Pierre Fauchard Acad. award, 1979; Pfeiffer research fellow, 1978; Am. Fund for Dental Health-Dental Tchr. tng. fellow, 1980-82. Mem. ADA, Mich. Dental Assn., Am. Assn. Endodontists, Am. Assn. Dental Schs., Am. Soc. Dentistry for Children, Bapt. Med. Dental Fellowship, Sigma Xi, Omicron Kappa Upsilon, Delta Sigma Delta. Home: 2109 Medford St Apt 29 Ann Arbor MI 48104 Office: Endodontic Dept U Mich Sch Dentistry Ann Arbor MI 48109

BECHERER, RICHARD CONRAD, educator; b. Detroit, Aug. 8, 1945; s. Raymond Paul and Mary Margret (Conrad) B.; B.S., Mich. State U., 1967; M.B.A., U. Ga., 1969; D.B.A., U. Ky., 1974; m. Patricia Lee Foster, Aug. 12, 1967; children—Matthew Alan, Brooke Lindsey. Instr., Central Mo. State U., Warrensburg, 1969-71; adminstrv. asst. U. Ky., Lexington, 1971-74; asso. prof. mktg. Wayne State U., Detroit, 1974—; Independence Health Plan, Southfield, Mich., 1978—; cons. in field. Am. Mktg. Assn. Doctoral Consortium fellow, 1973. Mem. Am. Mktg. Assn., So. Mktg. Assn., Assn. for Consumer Research. Contbr. articles in field to profl. jours.; editorial staff Jour. of Mktg., 1974—. Office: 300 Prentis Bldg Wayne State Univ Detroit MI 48202

BECHTHOLD, GEORGE WALTER, mgmt. cons.; b. Waterloo, Iowa, July 20, 1941; s. Gilbert Fredrick and Calista Ada (Biles) B.; B.S. in Bus. Adminstrn., Northwestern U., 1963; M.B.A. with honors, U. Mich., 1970; m. Margaret June Habicht, Sept. 14, 1963; children—Mary Lee, Jeffrey Todd. Interviewer, Market Facts, Inc., Chgo., 1961-63; transp. analyst, Ford Motor Co., Dearborn, Mich., 1967-70; prin. A.T. Kearney, Inc., Cleve., 1970-74, Los Angeles, 1975-76; pres. The MCS Group, Overland Park, Kans., 1976-80; pres. Mgmt. Perspectives, Inc., Overland Park, Kans., 1980—; spl. advisor to M.B.A. program U. So. Calif., 1974-76. Pack com. chmn. Heart of Am. council Boy Scouts Am., 1976-78; mem. Village Church, Prairie Village, Kans. Served with USN, 1963-67. Mem. Nat. Council Phys. Distbn. Mgmt. (v.p. Kansas City Roundtable). Club: Homestead Country (Prairie Village). Editor, contbr. regular monthly article to Mgmt. Perspectives, Warehouse Distbr. News, 1973-80; editor mgmt. articles Jobber Retailer, 1981—. Home: 3317 W 68th St Mission Hills KS 66208 Office: 9101 W 110th St Overland Park KS 66210

BECHTOL, NANCY JUNE SCHAEFER, artist; b. Chgo., June 24, 1950; d. Leslie Bert and Vera Winifred (Waterloo) Schaefer; B.A., Roosevelt U., 1972; M.A., Loyola U., 1980; m. David Bechtol, Aug. 2, 1975. Tchr. art Chgo. Bd. Edn., 1972—, workshop leader Bur. Staff Devel., 1979—. Counselor, Metro-Help, 1972-73; hostess, council mem. YWCA-USO, 1970-71. Mem. Ill. Creative Artist Registry, Nat. Art Edn. Assn., Ill. Art Assn. Roman Catholic.

BECK, FRANCES JOSEPHINE MOTTEY (MRS. JOHN MATTHEW BECK), educator; b. Eleanora, Pa., July 12, 1918; d. George F. and Mary (Wisnieski) Mottey; B.S., Ind. State Tchrs. Coll., 1939; M.A., U. Chgo., 1955, Ph.D., 1980; m. John Matthew Beck, Aug. 23, 1941. Jr. visitor Pa. Dept. Pub. Assistance, 1940-41; asst. to the sec. dept. edn. U. Chgo., 1952-58, asst. sec., 1958, asst. dean of students Grad. Sch. Edn., 1958-75; asst. to dean Sch. Edn., De Paul U., Chgo., 1975-79, asst. prof., 1979—; reading instr. Central YMCA, Chgo., 1958-6l. Mem. Nat., Ill. assns. women deans and counselors, Internat. Reading Assn., Delta Kappa Gamma. Pi Lambda Theta (nat. v.p. 1966-70, 1st v.p. 1971-74), Sigma Sigma Sigma. Co-author: Extending Reading Skills, 1976; author articles in field. Office: 2323 N Seminary Chicago IL 60614

BECK, GERALD LEE, anchor mfg. co. exec.; b. Grays Lake, Ill., Apr. 22, 1937; s. Alfred Michael and Ruth Ester (Hucker) B.; B.S. in Bus. Adminstrn., No. Ill. U., DeKalb, 1959; M.B.A., Keller Grad. Sch. Mgmt., Chgo., 1979; m. Jennetta A. Nykaza, Jan. 28, 1943. Distbn. mgr. Omark Industries, Portland, Oreg., 1974-75; regional sales mgr. ITT-Phillips Drill Div., Michigan City, Ind., 1975—. Bd. dirs. Trails Sub-div. Homeowners Assn., 1977-78. Served with AUS, 1961-67. Republican. Methodist. Home: 716 Woodfield Trail Roselle IL 60172 Office: Box 364 Michigan City IN 46360

BECK, HELEN J., artist; b. Chgo., July 13, 1908; d. Irwin E. and Anna (Lion) Weil; grad. Prague Art Inst., 1923, Chgo. Inst. Fine Arts, 1927; m. Hugo Beck, Oct. 11, 1931; children—Dolores Ann (dec. 1976), Sandra L. Beck Sabul. Staff advt. artist Wieboldt Stores, Chgo., 1928-31; Chgo. USO; creator Sunshine Rag Doll; lectr. civic, sch. and art groups. Comdr. Emergency and Disaster Corps, Chgo. ARC, 1940-49; nurses' instr. first aid Ill. Masonic Hosp., 1941-46; speaker Am. Cancer Soc.; coordinator Chgo. Tb mobile units, 1940-45. Recipient Meritorious Service medal U.K. War Relief, 1944, Presdl. Life Saving awards ARC, 1945, 46, meritorious service award Kiwanis, 1965. Mem. Am. Assn. Ret. Persons, West Suburban Ostomy Assn. (visitor's program), Chgo. Ostomy Assn. Author travelogues; creator lustrous thread paintings on chiffon.

BECK, JOHN MATTHEW, educator; b. Rogoznig, Austria, Apr. 10, 1913; s. Matthias and Antoinette (Bukowski) B.; came to U.S., 1914, naturalized, 1942; B.S., Ind. State Coll. (Pa.), 1936; M.A., U. Chgo., 1947, Ph.D., 1953; m. Frances Josephine Mottey, Aug. 23, 1941. Tchr., Clymer (Pa.) High Sch., 1937-41; instr. history and philosophy of edn. De Paul U., 1948-53; instr. Chgo. State College, 1953-56, chmn. dept. edn., 1959-60, asst. dean, prof. edn., 1960-66, dean coll., 1966-67; dir. Chgo. Tchr. Corps, 1967—; exec. dir. Chgo. Consortium Colls. and Univs., 1968—; prof. urban tchr. edn. Govs. State U., 1972—; cons. U.S. Office of Edn., 1968—. Mem. Ill. State Advisory Com. on Guidance, 1963—, Citizens Schs. Com., Chgo., 1953—; chmn. curriculum adv. com. Ednl. Facilities Center, Chgo., 1971—; exec. bd. Cook County OEO, 1971—; adv. com. interstate interinstnl. cooperation Ill. Bd. Higher Edn., 1972—; mem. Chgo. Mayor's Adv. Commn. Sch. Bd. Nominations, 1975. Bd. govs. Chgo. City Club, 1961—, v.p., 1962-63, 64-65. Served with AUS, 1941-46. Decorated Bronze Star. Recipient W. Germany grant, 1972. Fellow AAAS, Philosophy of Edn. Soc.; mem. Am. Hist. Assn., Am. Edn. Research Assn., Ill. Edn. Assn. (pres. Chgo. div. 1960-62). Co-author: Extending Reading Skills, 1976. Editor: Chgo. Sch. Jour., 1964-65; co-editor: Teaching the Culturally Disadvantaged Child, 1966; contbr. articles to profl. jours. and encys. Home: 5832 Stony Island Ave Chicago IL 60637 Office: 2235 N Sheffield Ave Chicago IL 60614

BECK, JOSEPH GEORGE, musician, educator; b. Youngstown, Ohio, Feb. 19, 1935; s. George B. and Anna (Eveland) B.; student Youngstown U., 1953-56; Mus.B., Westminster Choir Coll., 1956-59; M.A., Kent State U., 1966; Ed.D., St. Louis U., 1979; m. Sara Louise Ramser, Nov. 17, 1962. Mem., soloist Westminster Choir, Princeton, N.J., 1958-59; pvt. vocal tchr., Youngstown, 1959-62; minister of music, Lowell Ch., Canton, Ohio, 1962-64; instr. music, dir. glee clubs Kent State U., 1964-69; minister music, Main St. Meth. Ch., Akron, 1966-69; vocal dir. Kent State Summer Theater, Kent, Ohio, 1966-68; vocal cons. Kent State U. Theater and Speech Therapy depts.; vis. instr. music dir. chapel choir, voice instr. Mt. Union Coll., Alliance, Ohio, 1968-69; asst. prof., dir. choral activities Webster Coll., St. Louis, 1969-72; mus. dir., cons. dept. theater arts, 1970-72; mus. dir. Repertory Theatre, 1969-70; asst. prof., dir. choral and vocal activities St. Louis U., 1973-78, musical dir. theater dept., 1974-77; asst. prof. Metro Coll., St. Louis U., 1978-80; dir. community relations Spl. Sch. Dist. St. Louis County, 1981—; artist-in-residence, adj. prof. music Maryville Coll., St. Louis, 1981—; cons. in edn. and fine arts Warner Amex Cable of St. Louis, 1980—; master class student John Finley Williamson, choral and voice, 1954-63, Roger Wagner, choral, 1970, Robert Shaw, choral, 1972; producer, musical dir. film O That We Were There, 1979. Served with AUS, 1960-61. Mem. Am. Choral Dirs. Assn. (chmn. local arrangements com. for nat. conv. 1975), AAUP, Assn. Choral Condrs., Nat. Assn. Tchrs. Singing, Music Educators Nat. Conf. Phi Mu Alpha Sinfonia, Alpha Psi Omega. Book reviewer, choral reviewer for Am. Music Teacher mag., 1966-72;

contbr. to The Choral Jour., 1976—. Home: 520 Edgar Ct Saint Louis MO 63119

BECK, LOUIS GEORGE, med. supply co. exec.; b. Bklyn., May 31, 1946; s. Louis and Carmen Mildred (De Rosa) B.; A.A., Temple U., 1969; B.S. in Med. Tech., Cleve. State U., 1971; m. Mary Catherine Manley, Aug. 10, 1974; children—Kelly Ann, Christopher Louis, Michael Joseph. Med. technician Episcopal Hosp., Phila., 1967-69; dir. purchasing Healthco-Schuemann-Jones Co., Cleve., 1969-72; mfrs. rep. Christiansen & Barber Assoc., Chgo., 1972-76; pres. Corpsman Med. Supply Co., Lodi, Ohio, 1976—. Served with USN, 1964-67; Vietnam. Decorated Air medal with 3 oak leaf clusters, D.F.C., Purple Heart with 2 oak leaf clusters, Bronze Star, Navy Cross, Silver Star, Navy Commendation medal, Vietnamese Cross of Gallantry, Vietnamese Army Service medal, others; cert. med. lab. technologist, blood bank technologist, notary public. Mem. Am. Legion, VFW, DAV, Combat Vets. Assn. Republican. Roman Catholic. Club: Medina Kiwanis. Home: 8721 Chippewa Rd Chatham OH 44254 Office: PO Box 179 Lodi OH 44254

BECKER, ALFRED DURRY, pub. co. sales exec.; b. Auburndale, Mass., Feb. 7, 1920; s. Alfred Durry and Laura Charlotte (Birkett) B.; student Dartmouth Coll., 1937-39; B.S. in Chem. Engring., U. Rochester, 1942; m. Sarah E. Norris, Oct. 19, 1944; children—Stephen, Howard, Ralph. Chem. engr. Texaco Oil Co., 1942-43; advt. salesman Chem. Engring. mag. McGraw-Hill, N.Y.C., 1947-50, dist. mgr. Chem. Week, Chgo., 1950—; partner Studio Research Assos. Chmn. Mid-Am. Conf. Indsl. Marketers; owner Chem. Bus. Consultants, 1959-67. Pres. Village House, Kenilworth, Ill., 1970-73; founder, dir. Boy Scout Tree Nursery, 1967-73; Republican precinct capt. 47th Ward, Chgo., 1952. Served to 1st lt., USAAF, World War II. Decorated Air Medal; recipient Trail Blazer award Boy Scouts Am., 1972, hon. mention as top bus. paper rep. Bus. Paper Assn., Chgo., 1970, Community Service award Kenilworth Meml. Day, 1974. Mem. Bus. and Profl. Advertisers Assn., Midwest Chem. Mktg. Assn. (chmn. 1979-81), Chem. Equipment Sales Engrs. Assn. (exec. sec.), Chgo Drug and Chem. Assn., Chgo. Council Fgn. Relations. Republican. Christian Scientist. Clubs: Execs. (Chgo.); Kenilworth; Mpls. Athletic. Home: 467 Provident Ave Winnetka IL 60093 Office: 645 N Michigan Ave Chicago IL 60611

BECKER, BENJAMIN MAX, lawyer; b. Chgo., Feb. 3, 1909; s. Max and Etta (Molschansky) B.; J.D., DePaul U., 1933; m. Jean Merin, Dec. 25, 1930; children—David M., Merle Lynn. Admitted to Ill. bar, 1935; since practiced in Chgo.; partner firm Warden & Becker, 1935-42; asso. mem. firm Levinson Becker Peebles & Swiren, 1942-47; sr. partner firm Becker & Savin, 1947-72; counsel firm Antonow & Fink, Chgo., 1973—. Dir. DePaul Inst. Fed. Taxation, 1952, 53. Chmn. bd., gen. counsel Am. Growth Industries, Inc., Am. Growth Devel. Corp., Burr Ridge Club Co., Oak Brook Club Co., all Oak Brook, Ill.; dir. Traffic Service Corp., Washington, John E. Staren & Co., Chgo.; chmn. bd., gen. counsel Hausske-Harlen Furniture Mfg. Co., Peru, Ind. Mem. Chgo. City Council, 1947-55. Bd. dirs. Chgo. chpt. UN Assn. Recipient distinguished service award Chgo. Life Ins. Underwriters Assn., 1970, several civic awards. Mem. Am., Ill., Chgo. bar assns., Internat. Soc. Law, Decalogue Soc. Author: (with Edward Warden) Illinois Lawyer's Manual (2 vols.) 1939, (with Bernard Savin and David M. Becker), ann. supplements, 1948—; (with David M. Becker) Simplified Estate Planning, 1965; (with Bernard Savin and David M. Becker) Legal Checklists (2 vols.), 1966, ann. supplements, 1967; Is the United Nations Dead, 1969; (with Fred A. Tillman) The Family Owned Business, 1975, 2d edit., 1978; contbr. numerous articles to profl. jours. Home: 342 Charal Ln Highland Park IL 60035 Office: 111 E Wacker Dr Chicago IL 60601

BECKER, BETTIE GERALDINE, artist; b. Peoria, Ill., Sept. 22, 1918; d. Harry Seymour and Magdalene Matilda (Hiller) Becker; B.F.A. cum laude, U. Ill., Urbana, 1940; postgrad. Art Inst. Chgo., 1942-45, Art Student's League, 1946, Ill. Inst. tech., 1948; m. Lionel William Wathall, Nov. 10, 1945; children—Heather Lynn (dec.), Jeffrey Lee. Dept. artist Liberty Mut. Ins. Co., Chgo., 1941-43; with Palenskie-Young Studio, 1943-46; free lance illustrator N.Y. Times, Chgo. Tribune, Saturday Rev. Lit., 1948-50; co-owner, operator Pangaea Gallery/Studio, Fish Creek, Wis.; pvt. tutor, tchr. studio classes. Exhibited one-man show Crossroads Gallery, Art Inst. Chgo., 1973; exhibited group shows including Critics' Choice show Art Rental Sales Gallery Art Inst. Chgo., 1972, Evanston-North Shore exhbns., 1964, 65, Chgo. Soc. Artists, 1967, 71, Union League, 1967, 72; represented in permanent collection Witte Meml. Mus., San Antonio; executed mural (with F. Wiater) Talbot Lab. U. Ill., Urbana, 1940. Active Campfire Girls, Chgo., 1968, 70; art chmn., mem. exec. bd. local PTA, 1959-60; active various art festivals, 1967—. Recipient Newcomb award U. Ill., 1940. Mem. Chgo. Soc. Artists (rec. sec. 1968-77), Artists Guild, Soc. Illustrators, Wis. Arts Council, N.E. Wis. Arts Council (dir.), Alumni Assn. Art Inst. Chgo. Republican. Unity Ch. Contbr. articles, illustrations to mags. and newspapers. Home: Juddville Rd Fish Creek WI 54212

BECKER, DAVID NORBERT, ins. co. exec.; b. St. Louis, July 18, 1945; s. William Paul and Estelle Katherine (Meyer) B.; B.S. cum laude, St. Louis U., 1967, Ph.D. (fellow), 1973; M.A. (fellow) Washington U., St. Louis, 1969, A.S.A., 1977, F.S.A., 1979; m. JoAnn Elizabeth Clark, June 7, 1969. Instr. John Burroughs Sch., Ladue, Mo., 1969-70; instr. math. St. Louis U., 1970-73; asst. prof. math St. Francis Coll., Fort Wayne, Ind., 1973-75; actuarial cons. Lincoln Nat. Life Ins. Co., Ft. Wayne, 1975-79, asst. actuary, 1979-80, dir. group/ind. products, 1980-81; dir. fin. analysis Lincoln Nat. Corp., 1982—. Fellow Soc. Actuaries; mem. Am. Math. Soc., Math. Assn. Am., Pi Mu Epsilon. Contbr. articles to profl. jours. Home: 7102 Woodhue Ln Fort Wayne IN 46804 Office: 1401 S Harrison St Fort Wayne IN 46801

BECKER, LEONARD F., state senator; b. Cicero, Ill., Jan. 15, 1920; ed. Roosevelt U.; m. Georgianne Uher; 1 dau., Debbie. Pres. local Internat. Brotherhood Elec. Workers, Western Electric Co., Chgo.; pres., chmn. Elec. Mfg. Council; now mem. Ill. Senate. Justice of peace, Cicero; Republican precinct committeeman, 1941—. Served with U.S. Army. Mem. Chgo. Fedn. Labor, Ill. State Fedn. Labor, Telephone Pioneers Am., Am. Legion, VFW, Holy Name Soc., Ushers Club St. Frances of Rome Ch. Address: 1849 S 61st Ave Cicero IL 60650*

BECKER, NORMAN OTTO, surgeon; b. Fond du Lac, Wis., Jan. 16, 1918; s. John H. and Otillia A. (Graf) B.; B.A., U. Wis., 1940, M.D., 1943; m. Mildred Murdoch, June 20, 1943; children—Mary Gail, James Murdoch, Julia Brown, Constance Marjorie. Intern, resident, chief resident in surgery Cleve. Met. Hosp., 1943-49; surgeon Asso. Physicians, Fond du Lac, 1949—; asst. clin. prof. surgery U. Wis. Bd. dirs. Med. Coll. Wis.; dir. 1st Wis. Nat. Bank, Fond du Lac. Bd. dirs., exec com. U. Wis. Found.; pres. Citizens Council of U. Wis. Center. Served with USNR, 1944-46; PTO. Diplomate Am. Bd. Surgery. Fellow A.C.S. (bd. govs.); mem. Wis., Fond du Lac County med. socs., AMA, U. Wis. Alumni Assn. (past pres., Distinguished Service award 1976), Wis. Surg. Soc. (past pres.). Lutheran. Club: Fond du Lac Rotary (past pres.). Home: 1022 Mary Hill Park Fond du Lac WI 54935 Office: 505 E Division St Fond du Lac WI 54935

BECKER, R(OY) DAVID, JR., budget analyst; b. Louisville, Dec. 20, 1938; s. Roy David and Faye Ashton (Swartz) B.; student Ind. U., 1956-57; A.B., Hanover Coll., 1961; M.A., Central Mich. U., 1975; M.B.A., U. Dayton, 1977; m. Ann McCrea Roettig, Mar. 18, 1967; children—Mark David, Julia Louise. Mgmt. analyst Avionics lab. U.S. Air Force, Wright-Patterson AFB, Ohio, 1961-63, fin. specialist, budget analyst various programs, 1963-78, staff budget analyst, 1978-81, chief Mission div. Directorate Programs and Budget. comptroller Aero. Systems div., 1981—; lectr. Air Force budget process Air Force Inst. Tech. Active Greater Dayton Big Bros. Assn., 1965-73, YMCA Parent-Child Programs, 1977—; pres. PTA, 1979-80; mem. drug com. Kettering Bd. Edn., 1980-81. Nominee Career Service award Nat. Civil Service League, 1981; recipient outstanding performance and orgnl. excellence awards U.S. Air Force. Mem. Nat. Estimating Soc., Assn. Govt. Accts. (local sec. 1978-79). Methodist. Home: 248 Balmoral Dr Kettering OH 45429 Office: ASD ACBM Wright Patterson Air Force Base OH 45433

BECKER, ROBERT ALLEN, data processing ofcl.; b. Chgo., June 27, 1942; s. Sig and Dorothy (Shaw) B.; B.S. in Indsl. Mgmt., Purdue U., 1964; m. Babette Lee Hefter, Dec. 24, 1964; children—David M., Edie M. Programmer analyst Standard Oil Ind., 1964-67; successively programmer analyst, project leader, supr. computer ops., supr. tech. services R.R. Donnelley & Sons, Chgo., 1967-79; mgr. data processing Chgo. Mercantile Exchange, 1979—; instr. COBOL, Thornton Coll., 1970-71. Recipient cert. of merit U.S. Jaycees, 1970, Spoke award, 1970. Mem. Data Processing Mgmt. Assn., Guide Internat., Chgo. Computer Ops. Mgmt. Assn. Club: Jaycees (Homewood, Ill. Jaycee of month, chpt. service award 1969, 70). Office: 444 W Jackson Blvd Chicago IL 60606

BECKER, WILLIAM DENNIS, health adminstr.; b. St. Louis County, Mo., Oct. 23, 1931; s. Robert James and Virginia Hazel (Windmoeller) B.; B.S., U. Mo., 1953; postgrad. So. Ill. U., Edwardsville, 1974—; m. Mary Ann Hanson, Sept. 27, 1952; one dau., Katherine Ann; one son, William David. Mdse. mgr., asst. mgr. sales Brown Shoe Co., St. Louis, 1953-68; mgr. contract service A.S. Aloe Co., St. Louis, 1968-69; adminstrv. officer health planning Alliance for Regional Community Health, Inc., St. Louis, 1969-73, dep. dir., 1973-76; exec. dir. Mo. Area V Health Systems Agency, Poplar Bluff, 1976—. Pres. Clayton (Mo.) Brownbilt Credit Union, 1964-68; active YMCA. Served as officer USAF, 1953-55; Korea. Mem. Am. Health Planning Assn., Mo. Public Health Assn. Mem. United Ch. Christ. Lion. Home: 2132 Autumn Rd Poplar Bluff MO 63901 Office: 211 S Broadway Poplar Bluff MO 63901

BECKER, WILLIAM HENRY, fed. judge; b. Brookhaven, Miss., Aug. 26, 1909; s. William Henry and Verna (Lilly) B.; m. Geneva Moreton, June 9, 1932; children—Frances Becker Mills, Patricia (Mrs. Richard H. Hawkins), Nancy (Mrs. G. Lemuel Hewes), Geneva Becker Jacks, William Henry III; student La. State U., 1927-28; LL.B., U. Mo., 1932. Admitted to Miss. bar, 1930, Mo. bar, 1932, U.S. Supreme Ct. bar, 1937. Asso. firm Clark & Becker, Columbia, Mo., 1932-36; mem. firm, 1936-44, 46-61; spl. counsel Mo. Ins. Dept., 1936-44; counsel to gov. on Kansas City criminal investigation, 1938-39; spl. asst. to dir. Econ. Stablzn., Office of War Moblzn. and Reconversion, Washington, 1945-46; chmn. Mo. Supreme Ct. Com. to draft Mo. Rules of Civil Procedure, 1952-59; spl. commr. Mo. Supreme Ct., 1954-58; judge U.S. Dist. Ct., Western Dist. Mo., Kansas City, 1961—, chief judge, 1965-77, sr. judge, 1977—; judge Temporary Emergency Ct. Appeals U.S., 1977—; mem. com. on operation of jury system U.S. Jud. Conf., 1966-68, chmn. sub-com. to draft Jury Selection and Service Act of 1968, 1966-67, mem. coordinating com. for multiple litigation, 1962-68, vice chmn., 1967-68; mem. Jud. Panel on Multi-dist. Litigation, U.S. Jud. Conf., 1968-77; faculty Fed. Jud. Center Seminars and Workshops for U.S. Dist. Judges, 1968—. Served as lt. (j.g.) USNR, 1944-45. Decorated Navy commendation medal. Fellow Am. Bar Found., Am. Coll. Trial Lawyers, Am. Coll. Probate Counsel; mem. Am. Judicature Soc., Lawyers Assn. Kansas City, Am., Fed., Mo., Kansas City bar assns., Order of Coif. Bd. editors Manual for Complex Litigation, 1968—, chmn., 1977-81. Office: 741 US Courthouse 811 Grand Ave Kansas City MO 64106

BECKER, WILLIAM KOHL, engr.; b. St. Louis, June 13, 1927; s. William C. and Bessie (Kohl) B.; m. Lois Matthews, Feb. 4, 1951; 1 dau., Joan. B.S., Washington U., 1949; M.S., U. Ill., 1951. Registered profl. engr., Iowa, Mo., Minn., Nebr., Ohio, Pa., Tex., and others. Structural engr. Convair Aircraft Inc., Ft. Worth, 1953-55, William C. E. Becker, St. Louis, 1955-70; pres. Becker, Becker and Pannell, Inc., St. Louis, 1970—. Bd. govs. Washington U., 1975—, chmn. alumni annual giving fund Sch. of Engring. and Applied Sci., 1975—. Mem. ASCE, Am. Concrete Inst., Nat., Mo. socs. profl. engrs., Am. Consulting Engrs. Council, Mo. Athletic Club, Rotary, William Greenleaf Eliot Soc., Theta Xi, Sigma Xi. Office: 411 N 7th St Saint Louis MO 63101

BECKETT, GRACE, educator; b. Smithfield, Ohio, Oct. 7, 1912; d. Roy M. and Mary (Hammond) Beckett; A.B., Oberlin Coll., 1934, A.M., 1935; Ph.D., Ohio State U., 1939. Music supr. Pub. Schs., Kelleys Island, Ohio, 1935-36; grad asst. econs. Ohio State U., 1936-39; asso. prof. econs. and music Ind. Central Coll., 1939-41: with U. Ill., 1941—, asst. prof. econs., 1945-51, asso. prof. econs., 1951-73, asso. prof. emerita, 1973—. Mem. Am., Midwest econ. assns., Music Educators Nat. Conf., Ill. Music Educators Assn., Econ. History Assn., Am. Finance Assn., Am. Hist. Assn., AAAS, N.Y. Acad. Scis., Ohio Acad. History, Bucks County (Pa.) Hist. Soc., Ohio, Md. hist. socs., Winchester-Frederick County (Va.) Hist. Soc., Ohio, Md. geneal. socs., Ill. Music Tchrs. Assn., Music Tchrs. Nat Assn., Interlochen Alumni Assn. (life), Oberlin Friends of Art, Nat. Sch. Orch. Assn., Krannert Art Mus. Assos. (U. Ill.), Met. Mus. Art (N.Y.C.) (nat. asso.), Alpha Lambda Delta (hon.), Phi Beta Kappa, Pi Lambda Theta, Phi Chi Theta (hon.). Methodist. Club: University of Ill. Women's. Author: Reciprocal Trade Agreements Program, 1941, 72· contbr. profl. pubs. Address: PO Box 386 Urbana IL 61801

BECKLEY, BILLIE LEE, bank exec.; b. Jerico Springs, Mo., Feb. 6, 1931; s. Lester Ray and Bernice Irene (Pyle) B.; B.S. in Agr., U. Mo., Columbia, 1953; m. Nellie Dee Jobe, Aug. 24, 1952; children—Sandra Kay, Teresa Ann Beckley Cox. Asst. mgr. Mo. Farmers Assn. Central Coop., Boonville, 1953-55, mgr., Pilot Grove, 1955-61, mgr., Sedalia, 1961-64; mgr. Fed. Land Bank Assn., Memphis, Mo., 1964-71; mgr. Fed. Land Bank Assn. N.E. Mo., Hannibal, 1971-76; regional v.p. Fed. Land Bank of St. Louis, 1976—. Mem. Ill. Soc. Profl. Farm Mgrs. and Rural Appraisers, Mo. Soc. Profl. Farm Mgrs. and Rural Appraisers. Baptist. Office: Fed Land Bank of St Louis 1415 Olive St Saint Louis MO 63166

BECKLEY, THOMAS MALLOY, railroad exec.; b. Mpls., Mar. 2, 1922; s. Miles and Rosemary (Malloy) B.; B.S., Yale U., 1942; LL.B., Harvard U., 1948; m. Nancy M. Arntsen, 1950; children—Rosemary, Margaret, Nancy, Kathryn. Admitted to Minn. bar, 1948, Mich. bar, 1955; practiced law, Mpls., 1948-60; asso. firm Stinchfield, Mackall, Crounse & Moore, 1948-52; gen. counsel, sec. Duluth, South Shore & Atlantic R.R., Mpls., 1953-60; asst. to pres., sec. Soo Line R.R., Mpls., 1961-68, v.p., sec., 1968-78, pres., 1978—. Served to 1st lt. Adj. Gen. Dept., AUS, 1943-46. Clubs: Mpls., Minikahda (Mpls.). Office: Soo Line Bldg Minneapolis MN 55440

BECKWITH, GWENDOLYN CELESTE GAINES, educator; b. St. Louis, Sept. 2, 1939; d. Ferris and Mary Helen Cones (Abron) Gaines; B.A., U. Mo., St. Louis. 1968; M.A., Webster Coll., 1974; married; 1 son, Christopher Lynn. Registered record adminstr. St. Francis Hosp., Chgo., 1961-62, St. Mary's Hosp., St. Louis, 1962-63, Jewish Hosp., St. Louis, 1963-65; tchr. Univ. Forest Sch., University City, Mo., 1970—. Mem. Assn. for Supervision and Curriculum Devel., Internat. Reading Assn., Alpha Kappa Alpha. Home: 7024 Arcadia Ave University City MO 63130 Office: University Forest Sch 1325 Partridge Ave University City MO 63130

BEDELL, BERKLEY, Congressman. Mem. 94th-97th Congresses from 6th Iowa Dist. Office: US House of Representatives Washington DC 20515

BEDELL, EUGENE FRANCIS, corp. exec.; b. N.Y.C., Dec. 12, 1942; s. Eugene James and Jean Veronica (Pershinski) B.; B.S., Poly. Inst. Bklyn., 1964; M.S., N.Y. U., 1966, Ph.D., 1972; m. Laureen Frances Barth, Sept. 5, 1964. Instr. N.Y. U., 1966-69; product mgr. Interactive Data Corp., Waltham, Mass., 1968-72; mgr. systems Morgan Stanley & Co., N.Y.C., 1972-74; asst. v.p. Iowa Beef Processors, Dakota City, Nebr., 1974-75, v.p., 1975, group v.p., 1975-77, dir., 1976-81; dir. Mgmt. Info. Systems, FMC Corp., Chgo., 1978—. Recipient Poly. Inst. Bklyn. award for outstanding service, 1964, N.Y. U. Founders Day award, 1972. NSF fellow, 1964-66. Mem. Alpha Pi Mu. Home: 1550 N State Pkwy Chicago IL 60610 Office: 200 E Randolph Dr Chicago IL 60601

BEDELL, RALPH CLAIRON, psychologist, educator; b. Hale, Mo., June 4, 1904; s. Charles E. and Jennie (Eaton) B.; B.S. in Edn., Central Mo. State U., 1926; A.M., U. Mo., 1929, Ph.D., 1932; m. Stella Virginia Bales, Aug. 19, 1929 (dec. 1968); m. 2d, Ann Barclay Sorency, Dec. 21, 1968 (dec. 1975); m. 3d, Myra Jervey Hoyle, Feb. 14, 1976. Tchr., Hale Pub. Schs., 1922-24; tchr. sci. and math. S.W. High Sch., Kansas City, Mo., 1926-30, 32-33; asst. prof. ednl. psychology N.E. Mo. State U., 1933-34, prof. ednl. psychology, 1934-37, dir. Bur. Guidance, 1934-37; dean, faculty and student personnel Central Mo. State U., 1937-38; freshman counselor, dir. reading labs., asso. prof. ednl. psychology and measurements U. Nebr., 1938-46, prof., 1946-50; chmn. dept., prof. psychology and edn. Sch. Social Scis. and Pub. Affairs, Am. U., Washington, 1950-52; dir. program planning and review br. internat. div. U.S. Office Edn., HEW, 1952-55; sec.-gen. South Pacific Commn. Noumea, New Caledonia, 1955-58; dir. counseling and guidance insts. br. U.S. Office of Edn., Washington, 1959-66; prof. edn., dir. nat. edn. studies U. Mo.-Columbia, 1967 prof. emeritus, 1974—, research asso. Center for Ednl. Improvement, 1974-75; cons. on faculty devel. Lincoln U. of Mo., 1976-77; mem. study group to Surinam, 1954; adviser U.S. delegation UN, 1953, 62, U.S. delegation Caribbean Commn., and West Indian Conf., 1952, 53; cons. Stephens Coll., Columbia, 1974, U. S. Office Edn., 1974; chmn. tech. com. access and retention for master planning Mo. Coordinating Bd. Higher Edn., 1976-78; edn. cons. Prince of Songkla U., Pattani, Thailand, 1980. Vice pres., trustee Sigma Tau Gamma Found., 1972-74; dean Sigma Tau Gamma Leadership Inst., 1973. Served as comdr. USNR, 1942-46. Named Honored Alumnus, Central Mo. State U., 1971; Top Tau, Sigma Tau Gamma, 1970, named to Soc. of the 17, 1980; Outstanding Contbn. certificate Assn. for Counselor Edn. and Supervision, 1967; Award of Merit, Mo. Assn. Sch. Librarians, 1971; U. Mo.-Columbia Alumni Assn. citation for outstanding achievement and meritorious service in edn., 1979. Diplomate Am. Bd. Profl. Psychology. Fellow Am. Psychol. Assn., Royal Soc. Health; mem. NEA (life), Nat. Soc. for Study Edn. (life), Mil. Order of World Wars (perpetual), Am. Personnel and Guidance Assn. (life), Internat. Soc. Polit. Psychology, Am. Assn. for Higher Edn., Am. Ednl. Research Assn., N.Y. Acad. Scis., Mo. Tchrs. Assn., Mo. Guidance Assn. (award of merit 1971), Mo. Personnel and Guidance Assn., Kappa Delta Pi, Phi Kappa Phi, Phi Delta Kappa (life). Clubs: Explorers (N.Y.C.); Army and Navy (Washington); Columbia Country. Author several books in field; also textbooks and standardized achievement exams., articles profl. publs. Home: 106 S Ann St Columbia MO 65201

BEDIER, MARILYN DEE, banker; b. Warrensburg, Mo., Aug. 19, 1939; d. William and Margaret Lee (Drinkwater) Draper; student Central Mo. State Coll., 1958; m. Bruce A. Bedier, July 30, 1978; children by previous marriage—William Allen, Larry Neil, John Byron, Donald James, Knox. With Security Nat. Bank, Kansas City, Kans., 1968—, v.p. ops., sr. ops. officer, 1980—. Mem. Nat. Assn. Bank Women, Women's C. of C., Am. Banking Assn., Assn. Systems Mgmt., Am. Inst. Banking, Bank Adminstrn. Inst., Women's C. of C. (treas. 1977). Democrat. Methodist. Office: Security Nat Bank One Security Plaza Kansas City KS 66117

BEDROSIAN, CLARK DEXTER, mgmt. service co. exec.; b. Seattle, May 11, 1924; s. Celak Der and Arshaluis (Atmadjian) B.; A.B., DePauw U., Greencastle, Ind., 1948; postgrad. Northwestern U., 1949-50; m. Rosemary Carlson, July 5, 1958; children—Lisa Bennett, Marc Der. Mdse. buyer Spiegel, Inc., Chgo., 1948-50; with store mgmt. then mdse. buyer Sears, Roebuck & Co., Chgo., 1950-61; with Service Master Industries Inc., Downers Grove, Ill., 1961—, pres. Health Care div. Midwest, 1976-77, group v.p. franchise group, 1978, pres. materials mgmt. div. health care, 1979—; lectr. in field. Pres. 50th Ward Young Republican Orgn., Chgo., 1951-52; exec. com. Rep. Nat. Com., 1953-55; chmn. chmns. council Chgo. Jr. C. of C., 1954-55; mem. sch. bd. Dist. 30, Northbrook, Ill., 1963-66. Served with USNR, 1943-46. Mem. Am. Mgmt. Assn., Am. Hosp. Assn. Presbyterian.

BEDWELL, TOMMY JOE, mech. engr.; b. Linton, Ind., June 17, 1939; s. Harry Clifford and Mary Teressa (White) B.; B.M.E., Rose Poly. Inst., 1961; m. Freda Faye Speedy, June 16, 1961; 1 dau., Cathy Lynne. Engr., Ind. Pub. Service Co., summer 1960; test engr. truck div. Internat. Harvester, Ft. Wayne, Ind., 1961-64, rotational trainee, 1964-65, devel. engr. research div., 1965-68, sr. devel. engr., 1968-75; staff engr. piston design and devel. Bohn Aluminum and Brass Co. div. Gulf and Western Industries, Inc., South Haven, Mich., 1975—; asst. chief engr. piston design and devel. Bohn Aluminum & Brass Co., 1979-80, chief engr. piston design and devel., 1980—. Registered profl. engr., Ind. Mem. Soc. Automotive Engrs., Am. Soc. for Metals. Republican. Mem. Christian Ch. Club: Masons. Home: 1194 Euna Vista Dr Holland MI 49423 Office: Bohn Aluminum and Brass Co 1310 Kalamazoo St South Haven MI 49090

BEECHER, REXINE ELLEN, civic worker; b. Eldora, Iowa, Aug. 16, 1915; d. Vernon Richard and Gladys Metha (Bateson) Wardman; student U. No. Iowa, 1936-37; B.A., State U. of Iowa, 1939; m. Loyd Giff Beecher, June 15, 1939; 1 dau., Ellen Beth Beecher Feldick. Legal sec. Bateson & Ryan, attys., Eldora, Iowa, 1932, 33-35; asst. bus. mgr. College Eye Newspaper, Cedar Falls, Iowa, 1936-37; sec. econs. dept. Iowa State U., Ames, 1961-62; tchr. English, Union (Iowa) Sch., 1962-63; librarian Union Pub. Library, 1967-69. nat. promoter Children Am. Revolution. Mem. DAR (state registrar 1976-78), DAR State Officers Club, Daus. Colonial Wars, Farm Bur., Iowa Lassies (25-yr. mem. honoree 1981). Republican. Home: Rural Route 1 Union IA 50258

BEEKMAN, STANLEY, podiatrist; b. Bklyn., Aug. 27, 1951; s. David and Sylvia M. (Armel) B.; B.S., CCNY, 1972; D.P.M., N.Y. Coll. Podiatric Medicine, 1976; m. Marion Della Kiefer, June 4, 1978; 1 dau., Amy. Asso. prof. Cleve. Foot Clinic, 1978—; pvt. practice podiatry, Cleve., 1978—; asso. prof. sports medicine Ohio Coll. Podiatric Medicine, 1980—; staff St. John-West Shore Hosp.; cons. podiatry to Cleve. Indians, North Coast Bobsled Team. Recipient award of excellence in orthopedics, 1978; diplomate Am. Bd. Podiatric Orthopedics. Mem. Am. Podiatry Assn., Ohio Podiatry Assn., N.E. Ohio Acad., Am. Soc. Biomechanics, Am. Coll. Podopediatrics, Am. Med. Joggers Assn. Democrat. Jewish. Club: Cleve. West Road Runners. Home: 13601 Saint James Ave Cleveland OH 44135 Office: 2500 Clark Ave Cleveland OH 44109

BEEM, JOHN KELLY, mathematician; educator; b. Detroit, Jan. 24, 1942; s. William Richard and June Ellen (Kelly) B.; A.B. in Math., U. So. Calif., 1963, M.A. in Math. (NSF fellow), 1965, Ph.D. in Math. (NSF fellow), 1968; m. Eloise Masako Yamamoto, Mar. 24, 1964; 1 son, Thomas Kelly. Asst. prof. math. U. Mo., Columbia, 1968-71, asso. prof., 1971-79, prof., 1979—. Mem. Math. Assn. Am., Am. Math. Soc., Phi Beta Kappa. Home: 1906 Garden Dr Columbia MO 65201

BEEMSTER, JOSEPH ROBERT, mfg. co. ofcl.; b. Chgo., Nov. 11, 1941; s. Joseph Z. and Emily (Dehaus) B.; B.A., DePaul U., 1962; postgrad. Ill. Inst. Tech., 1976, 77, U. Minn., 1979, 80; m. Judith L. Scheffers, Sept. 7, 1963; children—David, Susan. Mfg. mgr. Johnson & Johnson, Chgo., 1967-71, mgr. safety and security, 1971-78; div. dir. safety and health Gould, Inc., St. Paul, 1978—. Chmn., Bolingbrook (Ill.) Human Relations Commn., 1971-77. Mem. Am. Soc. Safety Engrs., Am. Indsl. Hygiene Assn. Home: 6908 W 83d St Bloomington MN 55438 Office: PO Box 43140 Saint Paul MN 55164

BEER, BARRETT LYNN, historian; b. Goshen, Ind., July 4, 1936; s. Peter J. and Mabel M. Beer; B.A., DePauw U., 1958; M.A., U. Cin., 1959; Ph.D., Northwestern U., 1965; m. Jill Parker, July 31, 1965; children—Peter, Caroline. Instr. history Kent (Ohio) State U., 1962-65, asso. prof., 1968-76, prof., 1976—; asst. prof. U. N.Mex., Albuquerque, 1965-68, asst. dean Coll. Arts and Scis., 1966-68; dir. Parker Research Ltd., London. Am. Philos. Soc. grantee, 1966; Am. Council Learned Socs. grantee, 1973. Mem. Am. Hist. Assn., Conf. on Brit. Studies, Ohio Acad. History, Phi Beta Kappa (charter mem. Nu of Ohio). Episcopalian. Author: Northumberland: The Political Career of John Dudley, Earl of Warwick and Duke of Northumberland, 1973; editor: (with S.M. Jack) The Letters of William, Lord Paget of Beaudesert, 1547-1563, 1974. Home: 531 Spaulding Dr Kent OH 44240 Office: Dept History Kent State U Kent OH 44242

BEERMANN, ALLEN JAY, state ofcl.; b. Dakota County, Nebr., Jan. 14, 1940; s. Albert and Amanda (Schoenrock) B.; B.A., Midland Luth. Coll., 1962; J.D., Creighton U., 1965; m. Linda Dierking, May 23, 1971; 1 son, Matthew Allen. Newscaster, disc jockey KHUB Radio, Fremont, Nebr., 1960-62; admitted to Nebr. bar, 1965; legal counsel, adminstrv. asst. to Sec. of State, State of Nebr., Lincoln, 1965-67; dep. Sec. of State, State of Nebr., Lincoln, 1967, Sec. of State, 1971—; lectr. in field; dir. Tabitha Devel. Corp. Bd. dirs. Nebraskaland Found., 1967—, Immanuel Med. Center, Omaha, 1976—; mem. exec. bd. Cornhusker council Boy Scouts Am., 1968—; camp dir. Camp Cedars Boy Scouts Camp, Fremont, 1960-65; camp dir. Nat. Boy Scout Jamboree, 1973—. Served to maj. Nebr. N.G., 1965. Recipient Disting. Service plaque Omaha Legal Aid Soc., 1964; Meritorious Service award N.G., 1973; Outstanding Young Man award Nebr. Jaycees, 1974; Meritorious Service Medallion, Nat. Assn. Secs. of State, 1977. Mem. Nat. Assn. Secs. of State (pres. 1976-77), Am. Bar Assn., Nebr. Bar Assn., Am. Judicature Soc., Nebr. Press Assn., Am. Legion, Am. Interprofl. Inst., Pi Kappa Delta, Phi Alpha Delta, Kappa Phi. Lutheran. Club: Internat. Relations (nat. v.p. 1961), Coll. Internat. Relations (pres. 1960). Address: Dept of State Suite 2300 Lincoln NE 68509

BEERY, KENNETH EUGENE, meat and food scientist; b. Lancaster, Ohio, Apr. 30, 1943; s. Robert David and Lucille Ester (Scholl) B.; B.S., Ohio State U., 1965; Ph.D., Pa. State U., 1970; m. Marci Annear, Aug. 22, 1965; children—Kevin, Kendra, Kelli, Kyle. With U.S. Dept. Agr., Berkeley, Calif., 1972-75, Union Carbide Corp., Chgo., 1975-76; dir. research Archer Daniels Midland Co., Decatur, Ill., 1976—. Served with U.S. Army, 1970-72. Recipient Honored Grad. Student award Am. Oil Chemists Soc., 1969. Mem. Inst. Food Technologists (chmn. Iowa sect. 1978-79), AAAS, Am. Meat Sci. Assn., Am. Soc. Animal Sci., Am. Mgmt. Assn., Am. Assn. Cereal Chemists, Research Soc. Am., Sigma Xi, Alpha Gamma Sigma, Gamma Sigma Delta, Alpha Zeta, Phi Tau Sigma. Editorial adv. bd. Food Tech. mag., 1975-78; contbr. articles profl. jours. Office: PO Box 1470 Decatur IL 62525

BEETS, F. LEE, ins. co. exec.; b. Paola, Kans., Apr. 2, 1922; s. William Francis and Nellie (Bryan) B.; B.B.A., Tulane U., 1945; postgrad. Harvard U., 1945, evening sch. U. Kansas City, Rockhurst Coll.; m. Dorothy Loraine Shelton, June 20, 1945; children—Randall Lee, Pamela Lee. Sr. accountant Lunsford Barnes & Co., Kansas City, Mo., 1946-49; v.p., gen. mgr. Viking Refrigerators, 1949-53; v.p., sec.-treas. Equipment Finance Co., 1949-53; exec. v.p., treas., gen. mgr. T.H. Mastin & Co., Consol. Underwriters, Mo. Gen. Ins. Co., Plan-O-Pay, Inc., Mid-Am. Data Co., B O L Assos., Inc., 1953-69; now chmn. bd. chief exec. officer Fin. Guardian Group, Inc., Fin. Guardian Inc., Fin. Compensation Cons., Inc., Worldsurance, Inc., FG Tech. Services, Inc., Financial Guardian Internat. B.V. Served with USNR, 1942-45. C.P.A., Mo. Mem. Mo. Soc. C.P.A.'s, Am. Inst. C.P.A.'s, Soc. C.P.C.U.'s, Pi Kappa Alpha, Sigma Tau Gamma, Phi Mu Alpha Sinfonia. Clubs: Masons, Kansas City. Home: 16 Le Mans Ct Prairie Village KS 66208 Office: 3100 Broadway Kansas City MO 64111

BEHER, LINDA KURTZ, mktg. exec.; b. Canton, Ohio, May 1, 1945; d. Samuel Bowser and Ocie (McAvoy) Kurtz; student Colo. Women's Coll., 1963-64; B.A., McPherson Coll., Kans., 1967; m. John G. Fike. Proofreader, McPherson (Kans.) Daily Sentinel, 1965-67; editorial asst. Ch. of Brethren Gen. Bd., Elgin, Ill., 1967-71, asst. editor, 1971-74; freelance graphic designer, Elgin, 1974; dir. print prodn., distbn. United Meth. Communications, Evanston, Ill., 1974-78; employee services mgr. CNA, 1978-80, sales promotion mgr., 1980—; v.p., dir. New Day Enterprises, Inc., environment/communications co., Chgo., 1976—; Recipient Hinkhouse prize Religious Pub. Relations Council, 1974. Mem. Women in Communications (co-chairperson career conf. Chgo. chpt. 1977-78), NOW, Chgo. Assn. Direct Mktg., Direct Mail Mktg. Assn., Meth. Fedn. for Social Action, Evanston Nuclear Freeze Com. Methodist. Home: 900 Isabella St Wilmette IL 60091 Office: CNA Plaza Chicago IL 60685

BEHFOROOZ, ALI, educator; b. Qum, Iran, May 24, 1942; s. Assadollah and Batool (Poostforoosh) Poostchi; came to U.S., 1970, naturalized, 1976; B.S., Tehran U., 1965, M.S., 1966; M.S., Mich. State U., 1972, M.S., 1973, Ph.D., 1975; m. Farideh Ari, July 1, 1971; 1 son, Amir. Instr. mathematics U. Tehran, 1965-70; research asst. Mich. State U., 1972-74; dir. instl. research Moorhead State U., 1974-76, asst. prof. computer sci., 1974-77, asso. prof., 1978—; vis. prof. U. Calif., Santa Barbara, 1981. Ednl. TV of Iran grantee, 1973-74. NSF grantee, 1978-80. Mem. Assn. Computing Machinery. Contbr. articles in field to profl. jours.; author computer sci. textbook. Home: 401 37th Ave S Moorhead MN 56560 Office: Moorhead State University Moorhead MN 56560

BEHLING, CHARLES FREDERICK, educator; b. St. George, S.C., Sept. 8, 1940; s. John Henry and Floy (Owings) B.; B.A., U. S.C., 1962, M.A., 1964; M.A., Vanderbilt U., 1966, Ph.D., 1969; m. Theresa Diane Swink, Dec. 27, 1963; 1 son, John Charles. Asst. dean of students U. S.C., Columbia, 1962-63; asst. state news editor The State Newspaper, Columbia, S.C., 1963-64; asst. prof. psychology Lake Forest (Ill.) Coll., 1968-74, asso. prof., 1974-77, prof. and chmn. dept. psychology, 1977—; pvt. practice psychotherapy, Lake Bluff, Ill., 1970—. Mem. long-range planning com. Lake Bluff Bd. Edn. Named Outstanding Prof., Underground Guide to Colls.; Outstanding Tchr., Lake Forest Coll., 1981; NASA fellow. Mem. Am. Psychol Assn., Soc. Psychol. Study of Social Issues, Assn. Humanistic Psychology, AAUP, ACLU, U. S.C. Alumni Assn., Psi Chi, Sigma Delta Chi. Democrat. Contbr. articles to profl. jours. Home: 116 E Prospect St Lake Bluff IL 60044 Office: Lake Forest Coll Dept Psychology Lake Forest IL 60045

BEHLMANN, F. LEE, aerospace co. exec.; b. Florissant, Mo., Apr. 24, 1922; s. John H. and Mary A. (Gettemeier) B.; m. Eileen R. Healy, Dec. 31, 1944; 1 dau., Sheila. B.S., DePaul U., 1951. Engring adminstr. to mgr. McDonnell Aircraft Co., St. Louis, 1951-68; dir. engring adminstn. and chmn. performance measurement systems McDonnell Douglas Astronautics, St. Louis, 1968-78, dir. bus. systems and computer applications, 1978—; chmn., pres. Florissant Tire Center, 1963—; dir., v.p. Behlmann GMC Trucks, Florissant, 1971—; pres. Behlmann Investments, Florissant, 1970—; dir., v.p. Behlmann Gas Co., Florissant, 1972—; v.p. Hi-Way Car Wash, Florissant, 1961—, Florissant Broadcasting Co., 1975—. Chmn., Friends of Scouting, Boy Scouts Am., St. Louis. Mem. Am. Legion, Am. Mgmt. Assn., Am. Inst. Aeros. and Astronautics, Am. Inst. Indsl. Engrs., Air Force Assn. Home: 1410 St Louis St Florissant MO 63033 Office: PO Box 516 Saint Louis MO 63166

BEHRENS, CHARLES THOMAS, agronomist; b. Madison, Minn., Aug. 31, 1949; s. Siegfried and Dora Behrens; student S.D. State U., 1968-69; B.S., U. Minn., 1972, M.S., 1974; m. Mary Christine Anderson, June 29, 1974; 1 son, Matthew Thomas. Instr. Canby Area Vocat. Tech. Inst., Canby, Minn., 1975; farmer, Marietta, Minn., 1974-76; agronomist Equity Coop. Feed & Fuel, East Troy, Wis., 1976-77; crop mgmt. agronomist Acco Seed Co., Belmond, Iowa, Mankato, Minn., 1977-80; agronomy dist. coordinator Minn. Dept. Agr., Mankato, 1980-81; regional agronomist Funk Seeds Internat., Bloomington, Ill. and Mankato, Minn., 1981—. Mem. Walworth County Agr. Bicentennial Com. Mem. Am. Soc. Agronomy and Asso. Socs., Am. Soc. Farm Mgrs. and Rural Appraisers, Am. Seed Trade Assn., U. Minn. Alumni Assn. Lutheran. Address: 1223 Warren St Mankato MN 56001

BEHROOZI, CYRUS S., social work educator; b. Tehran, Iran, Sept. 23, 1932; s. Abbas and Nayereh Behroozi; came to U.S., 1956, naturalized, 1966; B.S., U. Wis., Milw., 1960; M.A., Ind. U., 1962; D.S.W., U. Pa., 1974; m. Helga V. Hoffmann, Jan. 30, 1958; children—Jasmin Sonia, Cyrus Armin. Supr. community services Internat. Inst., Milw., 1962-63; asst. prof., clin. social worker U. S.D., Pierre, 1963-65; asst. prof. Sch. Social Work, Ind. U., Indpls., 1965-69, asso. prof., coordinator undergrad. programs, 1971-76, prof., dir. intercampus programs, 1976-77, prof., asso. dean., 1977—; bd. dirs. Internat. Center Indpls., 1977—. Mem. Acad. Cert. Social Workers, Council on Social Work Edn. (site visitor, mem. ann. program com., mem. commn. on accreditation, 1977—), Ind. Assn. Social Work Edn. (pres., 1977-78), Internat. Assn. Schs. of Social Work, Nat. Assn. Social Workers. Home: 4290 N Meridian St Indianapolis IN 46208 Office: 925 W Michigan St Indianapolis IN 46202

BEIDEMAN, RONALD PAUL, chiropractor; b. Norristown, Pa., Mar. 22, 1926; s. Jonas Paul and Bertha May (Cane) B.; student Temple U., 1948; D. Chiropractic, Nat. Coll. Chiropractic, Chgo., 1952; postgrad. Wheaton Coll.; B.A., Lewis U., 1976; m. Lorraine Marian Barrett, Aug. 19, 1950 (dec.); children—Ronald Paul, J. Kirk; m. 2d, Peggy Ann Bartlett, May 31, 1980. Dir. dept. diagnosis Nat. Coll. Chiropractic, Chgo., 1952-66, registrar, 1966-78, dean admissions and records, 1973—; exam. physician Chgo. Gen. Health Service, 1954-65; lectr. in field; pvt. practice chiropractic Chgo., 1954—. Prof., Nat.-Lincoln Sch. Postgrad. Edn., 1964—. Served with USAAF, 1944-46. Fellow Internat. Coll. Chiropractors; mem. Nat. Coll. Chiropractic (corp. sec. 1972—), Nat. Bd. Chiropractic Examiners (chmn. test com. 1967-69), Ill., Chgo. chiropractic socs., Am. Chiropractic Assn., Am. Legion (post comdr. 1957-58), Am., Ill. assns. Collegiate Registrars and Admissions Officers, Ill. Assn. Student Financial Aid Adminstrs., Nat. Assn. Coll. Admissions Counselors, Sigma Phi Kappa, Lambda Phi Delta. Contbr. articles to profl. publs. Office: 200 E Roosevelt Rd Lombard IL 60148

BEIGEL, HERBERT, lawyer; b. Cin., May 10, 1944; s. Alfred and Miriam (Schaechter) B.; B.A. with honors in history, Brandeis U., 1966; J.D. cum laude, U. Pa., 1969; m. Ricki-Beth Horowitz, Dec. 29, 1968; children—Evan Josef, Ethan David. Admitted to D.C. bar, 1969, Ill. bar, 1969; law clk. to Luther Youngdahl, U.S. Dist. Ct., Washington, 1969-70; spl. atty., organized crime sect. U.S. Dept. Justice, Chgo., 1970-72; partner firm Sachnoff, Schrager, Jones, Weaver & Rubenstein, Ltd., Chgo., 1972-78; partner firm Barnett & Beigel, Ltd., Chgo., 1978—. Mem. Am. Bar Assn., Am. Trial Lawyers Assn., Chgo. Bar Assn. Club: Mission Hills Country. Author: Beneath the Badge, 1977. Office: 180 N LaSalle St Suite 1420 Chicago IL 60601

BEILFUSS, BRUCE F., state chief justice; b. Withee, Wis., Jan. 8, 1915; s. Walter W. and Elsie C. (Dodte) B.; B.A., U. Wis., 1936, J.D., 1938; m. Helen Hendrickson; m. 2d, DeEtte Knowlton, Oct. 17, 1961; 1 son, Mark. Admitted to Wis. bar, 1938; dist. atty. Clark County, 1941-48; circuit judge 17th Jud. Circuit, 1948-63; justice Supreme Ct. Wis., 1964-76, chief justice, 1976—. Active Big Bros. Dane County. Served to lt. (j.g.) USNR, 1942-45. Mem. Am., Wis., Dane County bar assns., Am. Judicature Soc., Inst. Jud. Adminstrn., Am. Law Inst. Club: Rotary. Home: 4402 Fox Bluff Rd Middleton WI 53711 Office: Office of Chief Justice Supreme Ct State Capitol Madison WI 53702

BEILMAN, MARK EMIL, architect; b. Nebraska City, Nebr., Feb. 23, 1935; s. Ewald A. and Rose (Sand) B.; B.Arch., U. Nebr., 1966; m. Marlene Maria Freeman, May 11, 1957; children—Eric M., Kurt W., Mark E. Draftsman, Walter, Dorwin, Teague & Assos., Denver, 1957-58; estimator M.W. Anderson Constrn. Co., Lincoln, Nebr., 1966-67; draftsman John J. Flad & Assos., Madison, Wis., 1967-68; designer Daverman & Assos., Madison, Wis., 1968-69; asst. project mgr. State of Wis., Madison, 1970-77, roofing specialist, 1977-81; propr. Mark E. Beilman, Architect, Roofing Cons., 1981—. Served with USAF, 1954-57. Mem. Badger Bonsai Soc. Republican. Roman Catholic. Clubs: Waunona Way Assn., Lake Monona Sailing. Inventor Adjus-to-Fit bicycle handlebar adjuster. Home and office: 2702 Waunona Way Madison WI 53713

BEISEL, DANIEL CUNNINGHAM, ret. newspaper publisher; b. Germantown, Pa., June 30, 1916; s. Fred Cornelius and Margaret Stewart (Cunningham) B.; student U. Mich., 1934-36; m. Catherine E. Turnbull, Nov. 6, 1941; children—Jane Ellen Beisel Quinn, Catherine E. Beisel Arden, Sarah Burnbull Beisel Thulin, Margaret A. Beisel McIlwaine. Traffic rep. Green Bay and Western R.R., 1938-42; with Green Bay Press-Gazette, 1946-80, pub., pres., 1965-80; dir. Peoples Marine Bank, Green Bay Packers. Bd. dirs. Green Bay br. Am. Found. Religion and Psychiatry, Green Bay YMCA. Served with inf. U.S. Army, 1942-45. Mem. Green Bay Area C. of C. (dir. 1962-68, pres. 1966-67). Episcopalian. Clubs: Oneida Golf and Riding (Green Bay); Kiwanis; Delray Dunes Golf and Country (Boynton Beach, Fla.). Office: PO Box 1191 Green Bay WI 54305

BEISSWENGER, NORMAN FREDERICH, office service co. exec.; b. Cleve., Oct. 24, 1918; s. Carl and Emma (Stahl) B.; B.S. in Mech. Engring., Ohio State U., 1942; m. Eleanor Murray, Dec. 25, 1950. Research and devel. engr. Detroit Diesel Allison div. Gen. Motors Corp., Indpls., 1942-57; pres. Standby Office Service, Inc., Indpls., 1957—. Mem. Ind. Assn. Temp. Services (pres. 1976-77), Soc. for Advancement of Mgmt. (pres. 1960-61), Adminstrv. Mgmt. Soc. (pres. 1965-66), Nat. Assn. Accountants (pres. 1971-72), Nat. Assn. Temp. Services (past dir.), Ind. Office Service Inst. (treas.). Republican. Roman Catholic. Clubs: Indpls. Athletic, Columbia. Home: 3137 Melbourne Rd S Dr Indianapolis IN 46208 Office: 130 E Washington St Indianapolis IN 46204

BEITO, GEORGE ANTHONY, banker; b. Thief River Falls, Minn., Jan. 11, 1933; s. George A. and Anne J. (Strande) B.; B.A., St. Olaf Coll., Northfield, Minn., 1955; grad. Rural Banking Sch., 1968; m. Gretchen Urnes, June 29, 1957; children—David A., Kathryn A., Laura E. Asst. cashier No. State Bank, Gonvick, Minn., 1958-60, pres., chmn. bd., 1965—, v.p., Thief River Falls, 1960-65, pres., chmn. bd., 1965—; pres., chmn. bd. Security State Bank, Oklee, Minn., 1st Nat. Bank, McIntosh, Minn., Marshall County State Bank, Newfolden, Minn. Treas. Northland Community Coll. Found.; mem. adv. com. Thief River Falls Area Vocat. Tech. Inst. Served with USNR, 1955-58. Named outstanding young man of Thief River Falls, 1962. Mem. Am. Bankers Assn. (governing council 1978-79), Minn. Bankers Assn. (mem. council 1970-73, pres. 1977-78), Thief River Falls C. of C. (pres. 1963). Clubs: Rotary, Elks, Eagles. Home: 2211 Nelson Dr Thief River Falls MN 56701 Office: 201 E 3d St Thief River Falls MN 56701

BEKKUM, OWEN D, gas co. exec.; b. Westby, Wis., Mar. 2, 1924; s. Alfred T. and Huldah (Storbakken) B.; B.B.A., U. Wis., 1950; postgrad. Northwestern U.; m. Dorothy A. Jobs, Aug. 26, 1950. With Arthur Andersen & Co., 1951-57, Hertz Corp., 1957-62; with No. Ill. Gas Co., 1963—, mgr. tech. acctg., 1964-66, asst. comptroller, 1966-68, comptroller, 1968-70, adminstrv. v.p., 1970-73, exec. v.p., 1973-76, pres., 1976—, chief exec. officer, 1981—, also dir.; dir. NICOR Inc. and all NICOR and NI-Gas subs., New Eng. Energy Co., Andrew Corp. Bd. dirs. Protestant Found. Greater Chgo., 1975—, PACE Inst., 1977—. Served with AUS, 1943-46. C.P.A., Wis., Ill. Mem. Am. Mgmt. Assn., Am. Inst. C.P.A.'s, Am. Gas Assn. (dir. 1978—), Inst. Gas Tech. (trustee 1978—). Clubs: Mid-Day, Economic (Chgo.). Home: 46 Royal Vale Dr Oak Brook IL 60521 Office: PO Box 190 Aurora IL 60507

BELANGER, WILLIAM V., JR., state senator; b. Oct. 18, 1928; student St. Thomas Coll.; m. Lois; 7 children. Sr. program planner Honeywell Def. Systems; mem. Minn. Senate, 1980—. Mem. Bloomington (Minn.) City Council, vice mayor; commr. Bloomington Housing and Redevel. Authority. Served with U.S. Army, 1946-47, 50-51. Recipient WCCO Good Neighbor award. Mem. Bloomington C. of C., Bloomington Hist. Soc. Republican. Office: 129 State Office Bldg Saint Paul MN 55155*

BELBIS, MANUEL EMUSLAN, adhesives co. exec.; b. Pangasinan, Philippines, Apr. 10, 1941; s. Alejandrino Asperilla and Felicidad (Emuslan) B.; came to U.S., 1967, naturalized, 1976; B.S., Mapua Inst. Tech., 1960; m. Rebecca C. Belbis, Sept. 30, 1967; children—Mario, Brian, Jennifer. Research chemist Indsl. Adhesives Co., Chgo., 1967-70; research chemist, quality control mgr., tech. service chemist Armour & Co., Chgo., 1970-72; sales rep. Bostik, USM Corp., Thiokol Chem. Corp., Trenton, N.J., 1972-76; pres. Indsl. Adhesives Co., Chgo., 1976—, Bond-Plus Adhesives & Coatings Corp., Chgo., 1976—. Mem. Am. Chem. Soc., Packaging Inst. U.S.A., Chgo. Rubber Group, Adhesives Mfrs. Assn., Philippines Chem. Soc., Aviation Hall of Fame. Club: Lions. Home: 9748 S Pemberly Ct Palos Hills IL 60465 Office: 2632 W Washington Blvd Chicago IL 60612

BELDEN, GLEN WILLIAM, pub. co. exec.; b. Defiance, Ohio, Feb. 22, 1937; s. Theron and Opal E. B.; B.S. in Elec. Engring., Purdue U., 1965; M.S., U. N.Mex., 1967; postgrad. Stanford U., 1976; m. Patricia Harrold, Sept. 18, 1955; children—Jennifer L., Douglas S. Mem. tech. staff Sandia Corp., Albuquerque, 1965-68; systems performance analyst United Airlines, Chgo., 1968-70, dir. Computer Center, Denver, 1970-73, v.p. computer and communication services, Chgo., 1973-80; exec. v.p. Ofcl. Airline Guides, Inc., Oak Brook, Ill., 1980—. Mem. Am. Mgmt. Assn., IEEE, Execs. Club Chgo., Purdue U. Alumni Assn. Home: 721 S Beverly St Arlington Heights IL 60005 Office: 2000 Clearwater Dr Oak Brook IL 60521

BELDEN, MARSHALL BARBER, oil and gas co. exec.; b. Canton, Ohio, Oct. 2, 1912; s. Henry Seymour and Katherine DeWalt (Barber) B.; student U. Ohio, 1930-33; m. Florence D. McCoy, Dec. 26, 1943; children—Marshall Barber, Timothy Saxton, Katherine, Susan. Various positions in real estate, oil and gas prodn. Canton, 1933-39; laborer Monarch Rubber Co., Canton, 1936-38, Republic Steel Co., Canton, 1937; ind. producer oil and gas Ohio and Mich., 1934-63; partner Belden & Blake, bus. mgmt., Colo., 1955-63; founder, pres. MB Operating Co. Inc., Canton, 1967-78, chmn. bd., chief exec. officer, 1978—. Mem. Ohio Oil and Gas Assn. (dir. 1947-49), Ind. Petroleum Assn. (dir. 1948-49), Am. Petroleum Inst., Am. Gas Assn., AIME, Nat. Oil Scouts and Landmans Assn., Pa. Grade Crude Oil Assn., Am. Forestry Assn., Sigma Pi. Republican. Presbyterian. Club: Elks. Home: RD 1 East Sparta OH 44626 Office: 205 Central Plaza S Canton OH 44702

BELDEN, VINETA DEE SANKEY, nurse; b. Saginaw, Mich., May 3, 1941; d. Virgil Delbert and Alice Capitola (Krohn) Sankey; R.N., Wesley Hosp., Wichita, Kans., 1962; B.S., Marymount Coll., 1973; M.Ed., Wichita State U., 1978. Staff nurse ICU and CCU, Asbury Hosp., Salina, Kans., 1971-72; instr. critical care and leadership St. Joseph's Hosp., Wichita, 1973-75; semester coordinator Wesley Hosp., Wichita, 1975-78; asso. dir. Stormont-Vail Hosp., Topeka, 1978-79, dir. Sch. Nursing, 1980—; adv. council asso. degree nursing program St. Mary's Coll. (Leavenworth, Kans.). Mem. Kans. Master Planning Com. Mem. Kans. Hosp. Schs. Nursing, Kans. League Nursing, Nat. League Nursing, AAUW. Democrat. Lutheran. Office: 635 Clay St Topeka KS 66606

BELDING, ROYCE GLEN, antique furniture restorer; b. Lachine, Mich., Dec. 3, 1922; s. William Arthur and Oleta Oceola (Bishop) B.; student Ohio State U., 1945, Mich. State U., 1948; m. Pauline Mae Linder, May 6, 1950; children—John Arthur, Paul Glenn. Founder, 1953, since propr. Belding's Furniture Restoration, Cedar Rapids, Iowa; frequent lectr., guest on TV programs; restored all antiques for restoration of 1st Iowa State Capitol, 1976, Brackett House antiques, Cornell Coll., Mt. Vernon, Iowa, 1978, also 2 chairs once owned by

George Washington. Active local Boy Scouts Am.; supt. Trinity United Methodist Ch., Cedar Rapids, 1968-70. Served with USN, 1943-46. Mem. Issac Walton League, Am. Legion, VFW, Nat. Rifle Assn. Republican. Office: 2734 Mt Vernon Rd SE Cedar Rapids IA 52403

BELEW, GARY LEE, supermarket exec.; b. Reading, Ohio, Sept. 25, 1947; s. Hilton Lee and Alta Fern (Haubner) B.; B.B.A., U. Cin., 1974; m. Ruth Ann Crumb, Mar. 24, 1973; 1 son, Sean Robert. Mdse. buyer Shillito's Dept. Stores, Cin., 1974-77; sales rep. Magic Marker Corp., Cherry Hill, N.J., 1977-78; sales coordinator, asst. product mgr. Kroger Co., Cin., 1978-80, product mgr., 1980—. Mem. Am. Mgmt. Assn., Delta Sigma Pi. Republican. Home: 3232 Close Ct Cincinnati OH 45208 Office: 1014 Vine St Cincinnati OH 45202

BELEW, JOE EDWARD, obstetrician and gynecologist; b. Lonedell, Mo., Aug. 27, 1931; s. Robert David and Effie Mary (Ueltzen) B.; A.B., Central Methodist Coll., Fayette, Mo., 1953; M.D., St. Louis U., 1957; m. Mary Jane Ash, Aug. 28, 1955; children—Taina Rae, Cynthia, Mark Edward. Intern, St. Louis Hosp., 1957-58; resident in Ob-Gyn, St. Louis Maternity Hosp., 1958-59, St. Louis Hosp., 1959-61; practice medicine specializing on Ob-Gyn, St. Louis, 1964—; mem. staff St. Luke's, Mo. Baptist, Barnes hosps.; pres. Obstetrical Assos. St. Louis Inc., 1970—. Mem. adminstrv. bd. Kirkwood (Mo.) United Methodist Ch. Served as officer M.C., AUS, 1961-64. Mem. Am. Coll. Ob-Gyn, AMA, Willard Allen Residency Soc., Mo. Med. Soc., St. Louis Med. Soc., St. Louis Met. Med. Soc., St. Louis Gynecol. Soc. (pres. 1980), Continental Gynecol. Soc., Washington U. Med. Alumni Assn., St. Louis U. Med. Soc. Clubs: Forest Hills Golf and Country, Shriners. Author papers in field. Home: 221 Lindeman Rd Kirkwood MO 63122 Office: Ballas Med Bldg Room 100 Saint Louis MO 63141

BELIAN, GARABED, dentist; b. Jerusalem, Palestine; s. Sarkis and Haigouhi (Markarian) Behesnilian; student Coll. Des Freres, Jerusalem, 1948, Coll. Des Trois Docteurs, Beirut, Lebanon, 1949; Docteur en Chirugie Dentaire, Universite Saint Joseph, 1953; D.D.S., U. Detroit, 1960; B. Music, Detroit Inst. Musical Arts, 1968; M.A., Wayne State U., 1975; m. Isabelle G. Sapsezian, Nov. 30, 1969; children—Ara Garabed, Lisa S., Raffi Sarkis. Came to U.S., 1956, naturalized, 1962. Active profl. music groups, 1949-53; pvt. practice dentistry, Middle East, 1953-56; bio-chem. researcher Bauer & Black, Chgo., 1956-58; pvt. practice dentistry, Detroit, 1960—. Pres., Art Center Chamber Music Players, 1967-69; chmn. fine arts com. St. John's Armenian Ch., Southfield, Mich., 1978. Mem. Am., Mich. dental assns., Detroit Dental Soc., Founders Soc. Detroit Inst. Arts and the Antiquaries Detroit Inst. Arts. Collector modern art and antiquities. Home: 7297 Kingswood Dr Birmingham MI 48010 Office: 4342 W Vernor St Detroit MI 48209

BELIK, DOBROMIL DAVID, computer cons.; b. Cheb, Czechoslovakia, Dec. 29, 1946; came to U.S., 1970, naturalized, 1978; s. Dobromil and Anna (Kokesova) B.; M.S.E.E., U. Nebr., 1976, Ph.D., 1981. Operator, supr. computer ops. U. Nebr. Computer Network, Lincoln, 1970-73, teaching asst., 1973-80, research fellow, 1980—; computer cons., programmer Universal Systems, Inc., Lincoln, 1975—. Nebr. Public Power Dist. grantee, 1973—. Mem. IEEE, Sigma Xi, Eta Kappa Nu, Tau Beta Pi. Club: Lincoln Legion. Contbr. articles to profl. jours. Home: 1027 Garfield St Lincoln NE 68502 Office: Univ Nebr Lincoln NE 68588 also Universal Systems Inc 1620 E Manor Dr Lincoln NE 68506

BELJAN, JOHN RICHARD, physician, educator; b. Detroit, May 26, 1930; s. Joseph and Margaret Anne (Brozovich) B.; B.S., U. Mich., 1951, M.D., 1954; m. Bernadette Marie Marenda, Feb. 2, 1952; children—Ann Marie, John Richard, Paul Eric. Intern, Univ. Hosp., Ann Arbor, Mich., 1954-55, resident in surgery, 1955-59; dir. med. services Stuart Co., Pasadena, Calif., 1965-66; asst. to asso. prof. surgery U. Calif., Davis, 1966-74, asst. to asso. prof. engring., 1968-74, asst. to asso. dean Sch. Medicine, 1970-74; prof. surgery Wright State U., Dayton, Ohio, 1974—, prof. biomed. engring., 1974—, dean Med. Sch., 1974-81, vice provost univ., 1974-78, v.p. for health affairs, 1978-81, provost, sr. v.p., 1981—; asso. v.p. for med. affairs Central State U., Wilberforce, Ohio, 1976—. Mem. exec. council Miami Valley Health Systems Agy.; trustee Wright State U. Found., Drew Health Center. Served with USAF, 1955-65. NASA grantee, 1968—; NIH grantee, 1967—; diplomate Am. Bd. Surgery. Fellow A.C.S., Royal Soc. Medicine; mem. IEEE, Instrumentation Soc. Am., Biomed. Engring. Soc., AAAS, AAUP, Assn. Acad. Surgery, Civil Aviation Med. Soc., Dayton Surg. Soc., Société Internationale de Chirurgie, Montgomery County Med. Soc., Ohio Med. Assn., AMA, Flying Physicians Assn., Sigma Xi, Phi Beta Kappa, Phi Kappa Phi. Contbr. articles to profl. jours. Home: 1315 Glen Jean Ct Dayton OH 45459 Office: Wright State U Dayton OH 45431

BELKNAP, ELMER CLINTON, ret. social worker; b. Gordon, Nebr., Dec. 24, 1905; s. Elmer Curtis and Kitty Luella (Moss) B.; B.A., Simpson Coll., 1929; M.A., U. Chgo., 1937; m. Mildred Pearl Breniman, May 23, 1932 (dec. June 1978); children—Rowan Curtis, Dean Edward; m. 2d, Mildred Shook Robson, June 7, 1979. Asso. boys' work sec. YMCA, Sioux City, Iowa, 1930-31; jr. boys clubs and handicraft dir. U. Chgo. Settlement House, 1932-33; sr. case worker Cook County Bur. Pub. Welfare, Chgo., 1933-34; dir. Hall County Emergency Relief and Pub. Assistance Adminstrn., Grand Island, Nebr., 1934-44; Nebr. field rep. Nat. Found. Infantile Paralysis, N.Y.C. and Lincoln, Nebr., 1944-65; with Nebr. State Dept. Pub. Welfare, Lincoln, 1965—, dir., 1967-68, med. social work cons., 1969-76; mem. Nebr. Crippled Children Adv. Com., Lincoln, 1947-55, Nebr. Health Planning Com., 1947-52, Nebr. Comprehensive Health Planning Adv. Council, 1967-69. Bd. dirs. Lancaster County chpt. Nat. Found.-March of Dimes, 1965-69. Recipient Distinguished Service citation Nat. Found.-March of Dimes, N.Y.C., 1964. Mem. Am. (nat. bd. dirs. 1968-69), Nebr. (pres. 1937-38) pub. welfare assns., Nebr. Pub. Health Assn. (state sec. 1955-56), Nat. Rehab. Assn. (state dir. 1961-64), Nebr. State Hist. Soc., New Eng. Historic and Geneal. Soc., Pi Kappa Delta. Methodist (chmn. com. edn. 1955-56). Author: A Belknap Genealogy, 1974; A Moss Genealogy, 1977. Home: 2019 Harwood St Lincoln NE 68502

BELL, CHARLES EDWARD, psychologist; b. Galveston, Tex., Feb. 7, 1936; s. Ben Franklin and Johnnie Odet (Rush) B.; B.S., U. Houston, 1962, M.A., 1965; Ed.D., N. Tex. State U., 1977; m. Marvell Marie Mossom, Dec. 20, 1968; children—Charles Butler, Beverly Ann, Laurie Marvell. Asst. prof. Ouachita Bapt. U., Arkadelphia, Ark., 1967-69; staff psychologist Benton (Ark.) State Hosp., 1968-71; staff psychologist Vernon (Tex.) Project for Drug Dependent Youth, 1973-74; staff psychologist S.E. Kans. Mental Health Center, Humboldt, 1974-78; dir. S.E. Kans. Mental Health Assos., Chanute; vis. prof. Vernon Regional Jr. Coll., 1974, Henderson State Coll., 1967-68; teaching fellow U. Houston, 1963-67, N. Tex. State U., 1972-73. Chmn. bd. dirs. Circle B Boys Ranch, Inc. Mem. AAUP, Am., Southwestern psychol. assns., Phi Chi, Phi Delta Kappa. Democrat. Baptist. Clubs: Rotary, Kiwanis, Elks. Author: Transactional Analysis for Classroom Teachers, 1977; A Comparison of Three Techniques for Teaching Oral Hygiene, 1978. Home: 1015 W 3d St Chanute KS 66720 Office: 1013 W 3d St Chanute KS 66720

BELL, CHARLES EUGENE, JR., indsl. engr.; b. N.Y.C., Dec. 13, 1932; s. Charles Edward and Constance Elizabeth (Verbelia) B.; B. Engring., Johns Hopkins U., 1954, M.S. in Engring., 1959; m. Doris R. Clifton, Jan. 14, 1967; 1 son, Scott Charles Bell. Indsl. engr. Signode Corp., Balt., 1957-61, asst. to plant mgr., 1961-63, plant engr., 1963-64, div. indsl. engr., Glenview, Ill., 1964-69, asst. to div. mgr., 1969-76, engring. mgr., 1976—. Served with U.S. Army, 1955-57. Registered profl. engr., Calif. Mem. Am. Inst. Indsl. Engrs. (pres. 1981), Indsl. Mgmt. Club Central Md. (pres. 1964), Nat. Soc. Profl. Engrs., Ill. Soc. Profl. Engrs. Republican. Roman Catholic. Home: 385 Sunset Ln Glencoe IL 60022 Office: 3650 W Lake Ave Glenview IL 60025

BELL, DARRELL EUGENE, broadcasting exec.; b. Lincoln, Nebr., Dec. 22, 1932; s. Frank James and Ila Mae (Johnson) B.; B.S., So. Ill. U., Carbondale, 1960; m. Norma Arleen Zacheis, Sept. 26, 1959; children—David Keith, Sharon Kay, Steven Michael. Engaged in radio broadcasting, 1958—; sales mgr. Sta. WIRL, Peoria, Ill., 1978—. Exec. dir. Miss Heart of Ill. Scholarship Pageant, 1969-73, 79—. Served with USN, 1952-56; Korea. Mem. Am. Mktg. Assn. (dir.), Sales and Mktg. Execs. Internat. (dir.), Peoria Advt. and Selling Club. Presbyterian. Club: Shriners. Home: 9406 N Northview Rd Peoria IL 61615 Office: PO Box 3335 W Glen Sta Peoria IL 61614

BELL, DAVID ARTHUR, advt. agency exec.; b. Mpls., May 29, 1943; s. Arthur E. and Frances (Tripp) B.; B.S., Macalester Coll., 1965; m. Gail G. Bell, June 22, 1968; children—Jenney L., Jennifer L., Jeffrey D. With Leo Burnett Co., Chgo., 1965-67; with Knox Reeves Advt., Mpls., 1967-75, pres., 1974-75; exec. v.p., gen. mgr. Bozell & Jacobs Internat., Mpls., 1975-79, pres. Midwest div., 1979—. Broadcast chmn. Mpls.-St. Paul United Way, 1974, chmn. gen. bus. downtown sect., 1975, chmn. pub. relations, 1976; coordinator United Way Am., 1977-78; chmn. sustaining membership YMCA, Mpls., 1977. Served with Minn. Air N.G., recipient Airman of Yr. award, 1967. Recipient Charter Centennial medallion Macalester Coll., 1974. Presbyterian. Clubs: Minn. Press, Mpls., Mpls. Golf, Minikahda, Omaha. Home: 325 W Fullerton St Chicago IL 60614 Office: 444 N Michigan Ave Chicago IL 60614

BELL, DAVID CURTIS, photo equipment mfg. co. exec.; b. St. Paul, Nov. 5, 1953; s. Dwain Curtis and Aurel Lorna (Waknitz) B.; B.A. summa cum laude with honors, Concordia Coll., 1975; postgrad. Am. U., 1973. Prodn. asst. Pako Photo, Mpls., 1975; sales rep. Pako Corp., Chgo. and eastern Wis., 1976-79; venture plant sales mgr. Pako Corp., Mpls., 1979—; dir. Bell Mfg. & Services, Inc., Mpls. Mem. Photo Mktg. Assn., Am. Mgmt. Assn., North Side Jaycees (officer 1976-78), New Hope Jaycees (pres. 1981-82). Republican. Lutheran. Club: C-400, Kiwanis (Mpls.). Office: 6300 Olson Memorial Hwy Minneapolis MN 55440

BELL, DENIS MICHAEL, entrepreneur cons.; b. Bismarck, N.D., May 1, 1951; s. Theodore, Jr. and Joyce Lillian (Hanson) B.; student public schs. Pres., Am. Venture Resources Inc., entrepreneur cons., Bloomington, Minn., 1979—. Mem. Internat. Entrepreneurs Assn. Lutheran. Home: 920 9th Ave S Apt 8 Hopkins MN 55343 Office: 8200 Stanley Rd # 7 Bloomington MN 55437

BELL, G(EORGE) WILBUR, farmer; b. Saidora, Ill., Sept. 2, 1912; s. Charles Raymond and Eva (Kramer) B.; student Bradley U., 1930-32, U. Ill., 1934; m. Alma Bernadene Malsbury, June 10, 1934. Farmer, Chandlerville, Ill., 1934—; grain dealer, 1940—; v.p., dir. Havana Nat. Bank (Ill.), 1956—. Mem. citizens com. U. Ill. Bd. dirs. K.T. Home for Aged and Infirm; exec. dir. K.T. Eye Found., 1973—. Mem. Mason County Farm Bur., Flying Farmers Prairie Farmer Land, Internat. Flying Farmers, Airplane Owners and Pilots Assn., Bradley U. Nat. Alumni Assn., Philalethes Soc., Acacia (hon.). Methodist. Mason (33 deg., Shriner, Jester, K.T., grand master grand encampment K.T. U.S.A.). Clubs: Union League (Chgo.); Sangamo (Springfield, Ill.). Home: Rural Route 2 Box 10 Chandlerville IL 62627 Office: PO Box 579 Springfield IL 62705

BELL, JAMES ROBERT, agr. co. exec.; b. Bloomington, Ill., Jan. 1, 1932; s. John M. and Marie (Delaney) B.; student public and parochial schs., Bloomington; m. Ruth A. Cates, Nov. 24, 1951; children—James Robert, John W. Owner, pres. Oak Hill Farm Corp., Bloomington, 1969—; co-owner, pres. E. Lynn Corp., Bloomington, 1974—; pres. Agri-Vestors Corp., Bloomington, 1977—; mem. with trading seat organized New Orleans Commodity Exchange, 1979—. Adv. bd. Adult Edn.-Farm Sch., Normal, Ill., 1957-70; mem. exec. bd. Family Services of McLean County, 1969—; adv. bd. dirs. Prodn. Credit Assn., 1974-78; mem. Phil Crane for Pres. nat. adv. com., 1978-80. Served with U.S. Army, 1954-56. Recipient Outstanding Young Farmer award Jr. C. of C., 1963. Mem. McLean County C. of C. (dir. 1977-80), Am. Conservative Nat. Conservative Polit. Action Com. (dir.), Ill. Conservative Union (adv. bd.). Republican. Roman Catholic. Club: K.C. (3 deg.). Address: Route 1 Bloomington IL 61701

BELL, JOHN HENRY, mgmt. cons.; b. Sylacauga, Ala., Apr. 6, 1939; s. John Henry and Lois (Hendrix) B.; B.S., N. Ga. Coll., 1961; m. Diana Kay Sinnen, June 18, 1961; children—Bryan Wayne, Elise Marie. Programmer/analyst Lockheed Aircraft, Marietta, Ga., 1963-66; systems rep. RCA, Atlanta, 1966-67; mgr. software field support RCA, Cherry Hill, N.J., 1967-69, mgr. mktg. programs, Mexico City, 1969-71; cons. asso. Booz, Allen & Hamilton, Washington, 1971-73; dir. Compucare, Chgo., 1973-74; pres., chmn. bd. Consilium, Inc., Chgo., 1974-75; mgr. EDP cons. Coopers & Lybrand, Phila., 1976-79, dir. EDP Cons., Columbus, Ohio, 1979—. Served to 1st lt., U.S. Army, 1961-63. Mem. Am. Mgmt. Assn., World Future Soc., Nat. Geographic Soc. Club: Columbus Athletic. Home: 8875 Braids Ct Dublin OH 43017 Office: 100 E Broad St Columbus OH 43215

BELL, JOHN LEWIS, packaging co. exec.; b. Marion, Ind., June 5, 1942; s. John L. and Lauvonnia C. (Kinder) B.; student Ind. U., 1960-62; B.B.A., U. Miami (Fla.), 1965; M.B.A., Ball State U., 1971, M. in Psychology, 1977; m. Jo-Anne M. Smith, July 27, 1963; children—John, Robert. Asst. cinematographer various TV commls., 1963-65; freelance cinematographer, Miami, Fla.; underwater photographer and actor in Sharks, The Death Machine, NBC-TV film, 1978; pres. Bell Gallery of Photographic Art, Marion, Ind., 1977—; dir. Am. Bank and Trust Co., Marion, 1968—, chmn. bd., 1969—; chief exec. officer Bell Fibre Products Corp., Marion, 1971—, chmn. bd., 1981—, pres., 1968-80; lectr. and cons. bus. orgns., 1970—. Mem. vocat. adv. com. Marion Community Schs., 1970-78, Marion Housing Authority City Planning Council, 1971-79; bd. dirs. Lakeview Wesleyan Ch., 1974—; trustee Taylor U., 1977—. Lic. comml. pilot, lic. scuba diver instr. Mem. Am. Inst. Mgmt., Soc. Advancement Mgmt., Am. Mgmt. Assn., Marion C. of C. (dir. 1975-78), Young Presidents Orgn., Profl. Photographers of Am., Culver Fathers Assn. (v.p. 1978—), Alpha Kappa Psi. Club: Kiwanis; Meshingomesia Country. Home: 1618 W Parkview Dr Marion IN 46952 Office: 3102 S Boots St Marion IN 46952

BELL, JOHN RICHARD, dentist; b. Peoria, Ill., May 18, 1922; s. Ross G. and Frances A. (Seiler) B.; D.D.S., Washington U., St. Louis, 1946; m. Norma Jean Oltmann, June 1979. Gen. practice dentistry, Peoria, Ill., 1946—; mem. hosp. staff St. Francis Hosp., Peoria, Ill. 1953—. Dental cons. Aetna Life & Casualty Co. Bd. dirs., past treas. Peoria County chpt. Am. Cancer Soc. Served to lt. comdr. USNR, 1954-56. Mem. Am. Dental Assn., Ill., Peoria Dist. (treas. 1963-65, pres. 1965-66) dental socs., Sigma Chi, Delta Sigma Delta. Republican. Roman Catholic. Home: 25 Oriole Ln Pekin IL 61554 Office: 1133 N North St Peoria IL 61606

BELL, KATHLEEN ANNE, export agt.; b. Evanston, Ill., Apr. 7, 1941; d. William Bryan and Agnes Patricia (Diederich) Healy; B.S., Northwestern U., 1965; M.B.A., Golden Gate U.; children—Dennis Bell, Amy Bell, Stefanie Bell. Tchr. public schs., Elk Grove, Ill., 1966-76; now internat. export agt. Mem. Republican Nat. Com. Mem. Internat. Visitors, English Speaking Union, Brookfield Zool. Soc., Lincoln Park Zool. Soc., Northwestern U. Library Council, Art Inst., NEA, Council Exceptional Children, Council Fgn. Relations, Adler Planetarium, Chgo. Hist. Soc., Shedd Aquarium, Field Mus. Natural History, Nat. Assn. Female Execs., AAUW, Council Cath. Women, Oriental Inst., Delta Gamma. Air Cargo Assn., Internat. Trade Club, Am. Mgmt. Assn., Northwest Trade Club, Northwestern U. Alumni Assn. Republican. Roman Catholic. Address: 963 Wilshire Ct Vernon Hills IL 60060

BELL, MARILYN ANN, librarian; b. Huxley, Iowa, May 20, 1936; d. Carl Raymond and Ruby Irene (McLaughlin) Reng; B.S. in Edn. cum laude, Ark. State U., 1958, postgrad., 1976; m. Benjamin Joseph Bell, Mar. 22, 1959; children—Beverly, Belinda. Tchr. English, Annie Camp Jr. High Sch., Jonesboro, Ark., 1958-60, Marion (Ark.) High Sch., 1960-64; tchr. spl. edn. Naylor (Mo.) High Sch., 1965; tchr. English, remedial reading, kindergarten, sci. Doniphan (Mo.) Reorganized Dist. 1 Schs., 1966—; librarian Doniphan Sr. High Sch., 1977—. Pres. Doniphan PTA; leader Cotton Boll council Girl Scouts U.S.A.; active Doniphan Booster Club, fund drives Am. Cancer Soc., Heart Fund; youth group leader, Sunday Sch. tchr., choir mem. Meth. Ch. Recipient Wilson award Ark. State U., 1958. Mem. Mo. Tchrs. Assn., Doniphan Classroom Tchrs. Assn. (sr. high rep.), NEA, Ark. Ednl. Assn., Delta Kappa Gamma, Beta Beta Beta, Kappa Delta Pi, Alpha Omicron Pi. Republican. Clubs: Tuesday Reading (pres.), P.E.O. (v.p.), Jr. Fiction (pres.), Modern Homemaker (pres.), Bus. and Profl. Women's (treas.), Lions Aux. (treas.), Bridge. Home: Route 5 Doniphan MO 63935 Office: Ballpark Rd Doniphan MO 63935

BELL, NICHOLAS MONTGOMERY, II, pub. relations exec.; b. St. Louis, May 5, 1921; s. Richard E. and Marjorie Peper (Bell) Hinrichs; A.B., Knox Coll., 1941; postgrad. Northwestern U., 1941-42. Pub. relations and fund raising counsel, Chgo., 1947-51; pres. Nicholas M. Bell II & Assos. Chgo., 1952—. Served as officer AUS, 1942-46; ETO. Mem. Pub. Relations Soc. Am., Chgo. Assn. Commerce and Industry (govt. affairs com. 1968—, ednl. com. 1968—, pub. relations com. 1968—), VFW (comdr. 1953), Sigma Nu. Episcopalian. Clubs: Lions; Minn. (St. Paul). Office: PO Box 1427 Chicago IL 60690

BELL, REGINA JEAN, steel co. exec.; b. Lebanon, Mo., July 27, 1927; d. Stephen S. and Ida M. (Reaves) B.; B.A., Draughens U., 1948; postgrad. Butler U., Ind.-Purdue U., Indpls. Prodn. mgr. Howe Mfg. Co., Inc., Indpls., 1958-64; v.p. budgetary control Howe Engring. Co., Inc., Indpls., 1964-67; mgr. material control Nat. Aluminum Div., Indpls., 1968—. Mem. Purchasing Mgmt. Assn. Office: PO Box 18272 5800 Massachusetts Ave Indianapolis IN 46218

BELL, RODNEY ALLEN, safety engr.; b. Metamora, Ill., Oct. 3, 1932; s. Riley and Fern Josephine (Bohlander) B.; A.A.A.S., Butler Coll., 1974; B.S., So. Ill. U., 1975; M.S., Ill. State U., 1976; m. Ruby Carol Bacon, June 11, 1979; children—Lisa Ann, Eric Von. Commd. 2d lt., U.S. Air Force, 1950; served in Korea and Vietnam; ret., 1972; prof. Coll. Engring. and Tech., So. Ill. U., Carbondale, also pres., owner Expertise Internat. Cons. Engrs., Carbondale, 1976—; presenter profl. meetings. Decorated Air Force Commendation medal, Singman Rhee Citation; registered profl. engr., U.S. and Can.; cert. safety profl., hazard control mgr., mfg. technologist. Mem. Soc. Mfg. Engrs., Am. Soc. Safety Engrs., Nat. Assn. Indsl. Technologists, Nat. Fire Protection Assn., Internat. Hazard Control Orgn., System Safety Soc., Nat. Soc. Profl. Engrs., Ill. Soc. Profl. Engrs., Nat. Assn. Fire Investigators (dir.), Nat. Assn. Arson Investigators, Tactical Air Command Thinkers Club, So. Ill. U. Alumni Assn. (life), Am. Legion, VFW. Republican. Contbr. articles profl. jours. Home: 1306 E Grand St Carbondale IL 62901 Office: Dept of Technology Southern Illinois University Carbondale IL 62901

BELL, TIMOTHY ALEXANDER, state legislator; b. Rock Island County, Ill., Aug. 2, 1942; s. Robert M. and Barbara J. (Johnson) B.; B.A., Western N.Mex. U., 1970, M.S., 1973. Sales, Nabisco, 1964-66; tchr., counselor Moline (Ill.) High Sch., 1970-79; mem. Ill. Ho. of Reps. from 36th Dist., 1979—; vice chmn. revenue com.; mem. exec. and higher edn. coms.; past mem. transp. com. Bd. dirs., past pres. Moline Group Home, Rock River Valley Assn., Rock Island Boosters Club, Upper Rock Island County C. of C.; bd. dirs., past treas. Info. Referral and Assistance Service of Rock Island County (Ill.) and Scott County (Iowa); past pres. Young Republican Club Moline, United Rep. Fund, 1200 Club of United Rep. Fund. Club: Elks. Home: Moline IL Office: 1715 5th Ave Moline IL 61265

BELLA, DANTINA CARMEN QUARTAROLI, psychologist; b. Providence, May 11, 1922; d. Bernardo and Jennie (Zinno) Quartaroli; M.A., Alfred U., 1952, M.S. in Adminstrn., U. Notre Dame, 1973; postgrad. U. Mich., 1977; m. Salvatore J. Bella, Dec. 30, 1946; children—Theresa, Joseph, Jennifer. Rehab. counselor R.I. Dept. Edn., 1942-46; admissions counselor Coll. Bus. Adminstrn., Boston U., 1946-49; asst. to dean Coll. of Ceramics, Alfred (N.Y.) U., 1949-53; dir. pupil personnel services, asst. prin. Marian High Sch., Mishawaka, Ind., 1968-74; registrar, admissions officer Ind. Vocat. Tech. Coll., South Bend, 1974-76; resident counselor, dir. Forever Learning Inst., Harvest House, South Bend, 1977—; textbook cons. South Bend Community Sch. Corp., 1974-77; lectr., workshop coordinator, 1974—. Bd. dirs. Cath. Social Service Center, 1968—, Women Career Center, 1974; pres. South Bend Commn. on Status of Women, 1975-78. Mem. Am. Personnel and Guidance Assn., AAUW, Beta Gamma Sigma. Democrat. Roman Catholic. Author, also producer TV series Pub. Broadcasting System, Older Women and their Needs, 1976, 77; Better Understanding of Self Through Literature, 1978; Mothers of the Depression, 1979. Home: 1029 Clermont Dr South Bend IN 46617 Office: 308 S Scott St South Bend IN 46625

BELLAMY, JOHN, JR., recording co. exec.; b. Chgo., Dec. 15, 1948; s. John Prather and Viola (Miles) P.; student Malcolm X Coll., 1969-72; m. Shannon Vernon, Dec. 23, 1967; children—Angela, Latasha. Driver salesman Capitol Laundry, 1965-67; letter carrier U.S. Postal Service, Chgo., 1969-75; pres. Source Records, Chgo., 1974—; pres., chmn. bd. dirs. Black Arts Celebration, Inc., Chgo., 1975—; adminstrv. asst. Soc. Writers and Editors Am., 1974-75. Adv. bd. Pro and Con Screening Bd., 1977—; bd. dirs. Chgo. Soc. Writers and Editors, 1975-76; 6th Annual Conf. Steering Com. Ill. Commn. on Human Relations, 1979; bd. dirs., exec. com. League Chgo. Theatres, 1981; mem. hypertension subcom. City of Chgo. Health Systems Agy., 1981; coordinator Dick Gregory Run Against Hunger, 1974-76; panelist Nat. Coll. of Edn., 1979; judge Alpha Kappa Internat. Year of the Child, 1979; Ill. caucus treas. Nat. Assn. Community Based Orgns., 1980-81; del. 11th World Festival Youth and Students, Cuba, 1978; active NAACP, Operation PUSH, So. Christian Leadership Conf.; interim bd. dirs. Ill. Arts Alliance, 1981; chmn. Community Cable Com., 1981; mem. adv. com. Chgo. Public Library Cultural Center, 1981—. Served with U.S. Army, 1967-69; Vietnam. Decorated Purple Heart; recipient Image Award, Fred Hampton Scholarship Fund, 1967, Inspiration of Youth Community Achievement Award, 1976, community spotlight award Sta. WVON,

1980, Gov.'s award for arts, 1981. Mem. Lowrey Nickerson Edn. Advancement Inst. Producer Slow Motion Suicide (by Mavis Staples), 1980, Ascension, female vocal group, 1980, 81, First World Symphony, 1980, 81, film/video documentary Dick Gregory Run Against Hunger, 1974, 76.

BELLAS, ROBERT CALDWELL, JR., chem. co. exec.; b. Miami, Fla., Mar. 23, 1942; s. Robert Caldwell and Audrey (Conner) B.; B.S., U.S. Naval Acad., 1966; M.B.A., Stanford U., 1973; m. Terrye Lynn Armstrong, July 1, 1967; children—Tamsinn, Erika. Vice pres. mktg. EMI Therapy Systems, Inc., Sunnyvale, Calif., 1973-78; dir. mktg. Acurex Corp., Mountain View, Calif., 1978-80; gen. mgr. Crystal and Electronic Products div. Harshaw Chem. Co., Solon, Ohio, 1980—. Served to lt. USN, 1966-71; Vietnam. Mem. Am. Mgmt. Assn., Stanford U. Alumni Assn., U.S. Naval Acad. Alumni Assn. Republican. Home: Woodstock Rd Gates Mills OH 44040 Office: 6801 Cochran Rd Solon OH 44139

BELLO-REUSS, ELSA NOEMI, physician; b. Buenos Aires, Argentina, May 1, 1939; d. Jose F. and Julia M. (Hiriart) Bello; came to U.S., 1972; B.S., U. Chile, 1957, M.D., 1964; m. Luis Reuss, Apr. 15, 1965; children—Luis F., Alejandro E. Intern J.J. Aguirre Hosp., Chile, 1963-64; resident in internal medicine U. Chile, Santiago, 1964-66; practice medicine specializing in nephrology Santiago, Chile, 1967-72; Internat. NIH fellow U. N.C., Chapel Hill, 1972-74; vis. asst. prof. physiology U. N.C., Chapel Hill, 1974-75; Louis Welt fellow U. N.C.-Duke U. Med. Center, 1975-76; asst. prof. medicine and physiology Washington U. Sch. of Medicine, St. Louis, 1976—, Jewish Hosp. of St. Louis, 1976—. Mem. Internat., Am. socs. nephrology, Am. Fedn. Clin. Research. Contbr. articles on nephrology and physiology to med. jours.

BELLOW, SAUL, writer; b. Lachine, Que., Can., June 10, 1915; s. Abraham and Liza (Gordon) B.; student U. Chgo., 1933-35; B.S., Northwestern U., 1937, Litt.D., 1962; hon. degrees Bard Coll., 1962, Harvard U., 1972, Yale U., 1972, McGill U., 1973, Brandeis U., 1974, Hebrew Union Coll.-Jewish Inst. Religion, 1976, Trinity Coll., Dublin, 1976; m. Anita Goshkin, Dec. 31, 1937; 1 son, Gregory; m. 2d, Alexandra Tschacbasov, Feb. 1, 1956; 1 son, Adam; m. 3d, Susan Glassman, Dec. 10, 1961; 1 son, Daniel. Tchr., Pestalozzi-Froebel Tchrs. Coll., Chgo., 1938-42; mem. editorial dept. Ency. Britannica, Chgo., 1943-46; faculty mem. Bard Coll., N.Y., 1953-54; faculty Princeton U., N.Y. U., U., Minn.; faculty English dept. U. Chgo., 1963—, mem. Com. on Social Thought, 1963—, chmn., 1970-76, now Raymond W. and Martha Hilpert Gruner Disting. Service prof. Decorated Croix de Chevalier des Arts et Lettres (France); recipient Nat. Inst. Arts and letters award, 1952; Nat. Book Award in Fiction for The Adventures of Augie March, 1954, Herzog, 1965, Mr. Sammier's Planet, 1970; Friends of Lit. Fiction award, 1960; Internat. Lit. prize, 1965; Communicator of Year award, U. Chgo., 1971; Soc. Midland Authors Fiction award, 1976; Nobel Prize for lit., 1976; Guggenheim fellow, 1955-56; Ford Found. grantee, 1959-61. Mem. Am. Acad. Arts and Scis. Author: Dangling Man, 1944; The Victim, 1947; Best Stories of 1950; The Adventures of Augie March, 1953; Seize The Day, 1956; Henderson The Rain King, 1959; Herzog, 1964; (Internat. Lit. prize 1965, James L. Dow award, 1964); Last Analysis (play), 1964; Mosby's Memoirs and Other Stories, 1968; Mr. Sammier's Planet, 1969; Technology and the Frontiers of Knowledge, 1974; Humboldt's Gift, 1975 (Pulitzer Prize 1976); To Jerusalem and Back: A Personal Account, 1976. Contbr. fiction to nat. mags. and lit. quars. Address: care Com on Social Thought U Chicago 1126 E 59th St Chicago IL 60637*

BELLOWS, GLEN LEE, cons. engr.; b. Spencer, Iowa, Jan. 9, 1937; s. Glen LeVern and Virginia Irene (Adams) B.; B.S. in M.E., U. Ill., 1959; m. Sylvia Ruth Dean, June 11, 1959; children—Alice, Ann (dec.), Kevin, Peter. Mech. engr. Brown, Manthei, Davis & Mullins, Champaign, Ill., 1959-65; prin., pres. Buchanan, Bellows & Assos., Ltd., Bloomington, Ill., 1966—; tchr. seminar Am. Mgmt. Assn., 1974. Bd. dirs. McLean County Occupational Devel. Center, 1969-78, treas., 1972-73, 75-78; vice chmn. Bloomington Bldg. Code Review Bd., 1972—; mem. Bloomington Heating and Cooling Bd., 1969-73, Normal (Ill.) Heating and Cooling Bd., 1973—, chmn., 1979—. Registered profl. engr., Ill., Iowa, S.C. Mem. Am. Soc. Heating, Air Conditioning and Refrigeration Engrs., Constrn. Specifications Inst., Nat., Ill. socs. profl. engrs., Ill. C. of C., Nat. Fire Protection Assn., Delta Sigma Omicron (Harold Sharper service award 1959). Republican. Mormon (ward bishop 1977—). Home: 210 Foster Dr Normal IL 61761 Office: 1509 N Clinton Blvd Bloomington IL 61701

BELMONTE, JOHN VIRGIL, surgeon; b. Chgo., Jan. 1, 1938; s. John Virgil and Anne (Izzo) B.; B.S., John Carroll U., 1956; M.D., Loyola U., Chgo., 1963; M.S., U. Ill., 1967; m. Sherill K. Premo, Sept. 26, 1964; children—John, Kristen Ann, Braden, Pamela. Intern, Cook County Hosp., Chgo., 1963-64; resident in surgery Hines (Ill.) VA Hosp., 1964-68; practice medicine specializing in surgery, 1968—; mem. staff Gottlieb Hosp., Central DuPage Hosp., Good Samaritan Hosp., Oak Park Hosp. Served to maj. U.S. Army, 1968-70. Diplomate Am. Bd. Surgeons. Fellow A.C.S.; mem. Ill., Du Page County, Chgo. med. socs., AMA, Am. Trauma Soc., Am. Soc. Abdominal Surgeons, Pan-Pacific Surg. Soc. Roman Catholic. Home: One Pembroke Ln Oak Brook IL 60521 Office: 2340 Highland Ave Suite 280 Lombard IL 60148 also 1440 W North Ave Suite 300-W Melrose Park IL 60160

BELMONTE, STEVEN JOSEPH, hotel chain exec.; b. Oak Park, Ill., Aug. 25, 1952; s. Silvio J. and Vilma (Giannini) B.; B.A. in Hotel Mgmt., Wright Coll., Chgo., 1974; student Holiday Inn U., Memphis, 1974; B.M. in Innkeeping, Harper Coll., Rolling Meadows, Ill., 1981; 1 son, Gino Anthony. With Hyatt Hotels, Inc., 1971; dir. sales Holiday Inns, Chgo., 1974-78, gen. mgr., O'Hare Airport Holiday Inn, regional dir., Schiller Park, Ill., 1978—; speaker Ill. Budget for Tourism, 1978-81. Bd. advisors Wright Jr. Coll.; active fund raiser for various charities and retirement homes. Recipient citation Italo-Am. War Vets. U.S., 1980. Mem. Am. Soc. Travel Agts., Hotel Sales Mgmt. Assn., Soc. Mng. Execs., Am. Automobile Assn., Schiller Park C. of C., Chgo. Innkeepers Assn. (v.p. 1979-81). Home and office: 3801 N Manheim Rd Schiller Park IL 60176

BELSARE, JAYANT VISHNU, physician; b. Sinner, India, Dec. 19, 1938; s. Vishnu Govind and Triveni Vishnu (Khaladkar) B.; came to U.S., 1967; M.B., B.S., U. Poona, 1963; M.S., 1966; m. Vasanti Sakharam Kulkarni, Jan. 26, 1966; children—Shubhada, Geeta Nandini. Intern, CPR Hosp., Kolhapur. India, 1962; resident in gen. surgery Sassoon Hosps., Poona, 1963-64, in anesthesia, 1964-65, in orthopedics, 1965; jr. lectr. B.J. Med. Coll., Poona, 1965-66; hon. surgeon Talegaon Gen. Hosp. (India), 1966-67; resident surgery Watts Hosp., Durham, N.C., 1967-69, Johnston Willis Hosp., Richmond, Va., 1969-71; preceptee surgery Surg. Asso., Mason City, Iowa, 1971-72; pvt. practice surgery, Clarinda, Iowa, 1972-73, Mt. Pleasant, Iowa, 1973—; mem. staff Henry County Health Center, Mt. Pleasant, Burlington (Iowa) Med. Center; med. adviser Henry County Cancer Soc. Diplomate Am. Bd. Surgery. Fellow Royal Coll. Surgeons Can., Internat. Coll. Surgeons; mem. A.C.S., Iowa, Henry County med. socs., AMA, Iowa Acad. Surgery, Mt. Pleasant C. of C. Home: 1107 Linden Ct Mount Pleasant IA 52641 Office: 114 E Monroe St Mount Pleasant IA 52641

BELTER, EDGAR WILLIAM, clergyman, addiction clinic adminstr.; b. Guttenberg, Iowa, Jan. 6, 1929; s. Robert Rudolf and Erna Dora (Teegan) B.; B.A., Carthage Coll., 1948, D.D., 1969; M.Div., N.W. Lutheran Theol. Sem., 1951: m. Deloris Ann Koenig, July 10, 1954; children—Timothy William, Christine Ann. Ordained to ministry Lutheran Ch., 1951; pastor Peace Luth. Ch., Steelville, Ill., 1951-57; asst. to pres. Wartburg Synod, United Luth. Ch. in Am., 1958, 59; sr. pastor Emmanuel Luth. Ch., Racine, Wis., 1959-69; pres., exec. dir. A-Center, Racine, 1969—; dir. Carthage Addiction Inst., 1969—; chmn. legis. com. Alcohol/Drug Problems Assn. N.Am., 1972—, bd. dirs., chmn. bd. mgrs., council of agys., 1977—; chmn. Gov.'s Task Force Alcohol-Drug Ins., 1970-76; cons. Nat. Inst. Drug Abuse, Wis. Bur. Alcohol and Other Drug Abuse; mem. program rev. com. S.E. Wis. Health Systems Agy.; mem. alcohol/drug adv. com. Mission in N. Am. div. Luth. Ch. Am., 1977-78; dir. Wis.-Upper Mich. Synod, Luth. Ch. Am., Strength for Mission Campaign, 1977-78. Pres. Racine County Mental Health Assn., 1969-72; v.p. Wis. Mental Health Assn., 1972-74. Mem. Alcohol/Drug Problems Assn. N. Am. (treas. 1980—), Racine Mfg. and Employers Assn. (dir.). Home: 30 E Four Mile Rd Racine WI 53402 Office: A-Center 2000 Domanik Dr Racine WI 53404

BELTZ, CHARLES ROBERT, engr.; b. Pitts., Feb. 23, 1913; s. Charles Fred and Ester (Johnston) B.; student Greenbrier Mil. Sch., 1930-33; M.E., Cornell U., 1934; B.S. in Aero. Engring., U. Pitts., 1937; m. Amy Margaret Ferguson, Oct. 23, 1935; children—Charles R., A.M. Bonnie (Mrs. Hatch), Homer F., William T., Carol E. (Mrs. Marks), M. Joy (Mrs. O'Keefe). Engr. Crane Co., 1937-39; design engr. Stout Skycraft Corp., 1939-43; project engr. Cycle-Weld Labs., 1943-44; project engr., mgr. Fairchild E & A Corp., Roosevelt Field, 1944-46; corp. engr. Chrysler Corp., 1946-47; pres. Charles R. Beltz & Co., Detroit, 1947—, Beltz Engring. Labs., 1950—, Beltz Parts and Services, Inc., 1954—, Beltemp, Inc., 1969—. Mem. Nat. Aero. Assn. (pres.), Air Conditioning Inst. (pres.), Inst. Aero. Scis. (vice chmn.). Am. Heating, Refrigerating and Air Conditioning Engrs. (contbg. author), N.Y. Acad. Scis., Engring. Soc. Detroit, Detroit Mus. Art Founders Soc., Detroit Hist. Soc., Internat. Plastic Aircraft Soc., Air Force Assn., Detroit Bd. Commerce. Clubs: Aero (dir.), Economic, Curling (Detroit); Grosse Pointe Yacht; Lost Lake Woods. Author: Ice Skating; Skating Weather or Not: ABC's Air-conditioning; Roatable Aircraft. Home: 500 Lakeland Ave Grosse Pointe MI 48230 Office: 15001 Charlevoix Ave Grosse Pointe Park MI 48230

BELZER, FOLKERT OENE, surgeon; b. Soerabaja, Indonesia, Oct. 5, 1930; s. Peter and Jacoba H. (Gorter) B.; came to U.S., 1951, naturalized, 1956; A.B., Colby Coll., Waterville, Maine, 1953; M.A., Boston U., 1954, M.D., 1958; m. Aug. 4, 1956; children—Ingrid J., John B., G. Eric, Paul O. Intern, Grace-New Haven Hosp., 1958-59, asst. resident, 1960-62; chief resident U. Oreg. Med. Sch., 1962-63, instr. surgery, 1963-64; asst. research surgeon U. Calif. Med. Center, San Francisco, 1964, asst. prof. surgery, 1966-69, asst. prof. ambulatory and community medicine, 1966-69, asst. chief Transplant Service, 1967-69, co-chief, 1969-72, chief, 1972-74, asso. prof. surgery, 1969-72, asso. prof. ambulatory and community medicine, 1969-72, prof. surgery, 1972-74, dir. Exptl. Surgery Labs., 1973-74; sr. lectr. Guys Hosp., London, Eng., 1964-66; prof., chmn. dept. surgery U. Wis., Madison, 1974—. Recipient Samuel Harvey award as outstanding resident, 1960. Diplomate Am. Bd. Surgery. Mem. A.C.S., Am., Calif. med. assns., Am. (pres. 1975), Calif. (pres. 1970-72) socs. transplant surgeons, Am., Central surg. assns., Calif. Acad. Medicine, Halsted Soc., Howard C. Naffziger, Madison, Pacific Coast, San Francisco (chmn. program com. 1973-74), Wis. surg. socs., Nat. Kidney Found. (vice chmn. com. on dialysis and transplantation 1974-76), Société Internationale de Chirurgie, Soc. Vascular Surgery, Soc. Surg. Chairmen, Soc. U. Surgeons, Surg. Biology Club III, Transplantation Soc., Whipple Soc. Republican. Contbr. articles to med. jours. Developed method and machine for human kidney preservation. Home: 6105 S Highlands Dr Madison WI 53705 Office: U Wis Center for Health Scis 600 N Highland Ave Madison WI 53706

BELZER, JEFFREY A., lawyer; b. Mpls., Sept. 8, 1941; s. Meyer S. and Kathleen (Bardin) B.; B.A., St. Cloud State U., 1963; J.D., Drake U., 1968; children—Steven, Michael, Anna, Jeffrey. Admitted to Minn. bar, 1968, U.S. Dist. Ct. bar., 1969; mem. firm Henretta, Muirhead, McGinty, Ltd., Mpls., 1968-71; pres., sr. atty. Belzer & Brenner Ltd., Mpls., 1971-80; pres., dir. Walesch Devel. Co., Mpls., 1969—, Walsch Estates, Inc., Mpls., 1971—, Jeff Belzer's Todd Chevrolet Inc., Lakeville, Minn., 1980—. Mem. Am., Hennepin County, Minn. bar assns., Phi Alpha Delta. Staff: Drake Law Rev., 1966-67. Home: 4525 Sedum Ln Minneapolis MN 55435 Office: Hwy 50 and Cedar Ave Lakeville MN 55044

BEMIS, EDWIN LEWIS, pathologist, lab. dir., educator; b. Fond du Lac, Wis., Oct. 11, 1923; s. Edwin Loren and Sophia Marie (Buechner) B.; M.D., Marquette U., Milw., 1950; m. Cecile Adelle Prudell, Aug. 1, 1942; children—Edwin Loren, Catherine Ann, Bridget Mary, William Robert, James Joseph, Peter John, Margaret Clare. Intern, Milw. County Gen. Hosp., Milw., 1950-51; family practitioner, Milw., 1951-56; resident in clin. and anatomic pathology VA Center Hosp., Wood, Wis., 1956-60; asst. dir. labs. St. Francis Hosp., Milw., 1960-61; dep. dir. labs. Deaconess Hosp., Milw., 1961—, vice chief med. staff, 1967-78; asst. clin. prof. pathology Med. Coll. Wis., 1962-79, asso. clin. prof., 1979—; instr. med. tech. Marquette U., 1962—; med. dir. sickle cell center Deaconess Hosp., Milw., 1969-77. Served with U.S. Army, 1942-43, U.S. Navy, 1948-50. Recipient awards for art, photography and sci. exhbts. Fellow Coll. Am. Pathology, Am. Soc. Clin. Pathology, Internat. Acad. Pathologists, Am. Soc. Cytology, Am. Soc. Law and Medicine, Am. Phys. Art Assn. (life; v.p. 1980—; Master's award for oil/acrylics 1979), Alpha Sigma Nu. Author texts for med. technologists; contbr. articles to med. jours. Home: 1540 N 119th St Wauwatosa WI 53226

BEMUS, KARL EUGENE, motor carrier co. exec.; b. Sidney, Ohio, July 18, 1936; s. William Eugene and Pauline Emma (Freytag) B.; B.S., Bowling Green State U., 1959; m. Judith Ann Brown, Aug. 13, 1959; children—Sarah Lynn, David Eugene. Gen. mgr. B & B Warehouses, Inc., 1960-64; v.p. Sidney Truck & Storage, Inc. (Ohio), 1964-71, pres., 1971—; pres. B & B Warehouses, Inc., 1971—; dir. Bank One of Sidney. Chmn. Sidney Civil Service Commn., 1975—. Served with U.S. Army, 1959-61. Mem. Ohio Motor Carrier Freight Tariff Com. (pres.). Clubs: Masons, Shriners, Moose, Elks. Home: 314 Bon Air Dr Sidney OH 45365 Office: 777 W Russell Rd Sidney OH 45365

BENBOW, OLIVET DARICE, advt. sales exec.; b. Winston-Salem, N.C., July 10, 1954; d. Alexander Oliver and Pauline (Lyons) B.; B.A., Smith Coll., 1976; postgrad. Northwestern U., 1977-78. Advt.-account exec. trainee Leo Burnett, Chgo., 1976-78; 1st scholar First Nat. Bank of Chgo., 1978; account exec. Essence Mag., Chgo., 1978—. Nat. Merit Scholar, 1972. Mem. Chgo. Advt. Club, Women's Advt. Club Chgo., Women in Print. Club: Smith Coll. (Chgo.). Home: 5415 N Sheridan Rd Chicago IL 60640 Office: 919 N Michigan Ave Chicago IL 60611

BENDEL, WILLIAM LOUIS, JR., physician; b. Monroe, La., Mar. 1, 1921; s. William Louis and Marie (Gariepy) B.; B.S., Tulane U., 1941, M.D., 1944; Ph.D. in microbiology, Baylor U., 1966; m. Margaret Rose Butler, Feb. 18, 1944 (dec. Jan. 1970); children—Susan Marie, Jan Ann; m. 2d, Kathleen Doris Mabley, Apr. 16, 1971. Intern, Charity Hosp., New Orleans, 1944, resident gen. surgery, 1949-52, resident thoracic surgery, 1952; resident gen. surgery Mt. Carmel Mercy Hosp., Detroit, 1947-48; surgery teaching fellow Tulane U., New Orleans, 1948-49; gen. practice medicine, Monroe, 1953-58; resident pathology Baylor U. Med. Center, Dallas, 1959-63; dir. labs. Unity Hosp., Mpls. Served from 1st lt. to capt., M.C., AUS, 1945-46. Diplomate in anatomic pathology and clin. pathology Am. Bd. Pathology, Am. Bd. Med. Microbiology. Mem. AMA, Minn., Hennepin County med. assns., Holy Name Soc., Alpha Kappa Kappa, Kappa Sigma. Republican. Roman Catholic. Club: K.C. (4 deg.). Contbr. numerous articles to med. jours. Home: 10022 E River Rd NW Coon Rapids MN 55433 Office: Unity Hosp Fridley MN 55432

BENDER, CARL AUGUST, mfg. co. safety and security ofcl.; b. Belleville, Ill., Mar. 27, 1929; s. August Carl and Mattie Elizabeth (DeTienne) B.; A.A. in Engring., Belleville Twp. Jr. Coll., 1950; A.S. in Police Sci., Belleville Area Coll., 1975; B.S. in Bus. Adminstrn., So. Ill. U., Edwardsville, 1978, postgrad., 1979—; m. Olga Eloise Jennings, Jan. 10, 1954; children—Nancy Lee, Janet Lee, Gary Carl, Donald Allen. Patrolman, Belleville Police Dept., 1950-51; served as enlisted man U.S. Air Force, 1951-52, commd. 2d lt., 1952, advanced through grades to lt. col., 1969; served as navigator, bombardier, radar observer, squadron comdr., provost marshal, dir. security and law enforcement, chief of police Travis AFB, Calif., 1968-71, base defense officer Tan Son Nhut AB, Saigon, Vietnam, 1968, ret., 1971; mgr. safety and security Monsanto Co. World Hdqrs., St. Louis, 1971—; instr. Tarkio Coll. Extension, St. Louis, 1980; guest speaker, participant seminars. First aid instr. ARC, 1973—; CPR instr. Am. Heart Assn., 1974—; active Kaskaskia council Boy Scouts Am., 1941-51, 71-75, staff and camp dir., 1946-50, Eagle Scout, Lodge Chief Order of Arrow. Decorated Silver Star, Bronze Star, Air Medal with oak leaf clusters, Purple Heart. Mem. Am. Soc. Indsl. Security (cert. protection profl., chpt. chmn., pub. monthly newsletter St. Louis Chpt. 1972—), Profl. Investigators Council Greater St. Louis, Internat. Assn. Chiefs of Police, Mo. Peace Officers Assn., Law Enforcement Ofcls. of St. Louis County, Ill. Sheriff Assn. Mem. United Church of Christ. Club: Toastmasters (officer, area speech contest winner 1963). Author Security Survey, St. Louis Metropolitan Area, 1978. Office: 800 N Lindbergh Blvd Saint Louis MO 63166

BENDER, CLIFFORD EARL, civil engr., contractor; b. Jamestown, N.Y., May 23, 1935; s. Clifford Lewis and Florence Adeline (Stanton) B.; student Allegheny Coll., 1953-55; B.C.E., Syracuse U., 1962; m. Hildegarde Elsa Groseclose, Aug. 21, 1955; children—William Stanton, Clifford Earl, Jennifer Smiley, Amy Lynette. Project engr. Linde div. Union Carbide Corp., Tonawanda, N.Y., 1963-64, design engr., 1964-66, estimator and cost control, 1966-69; estimator, design engr. Turzillo Contracting Co., Richfield, Ohio, 1969-77, chief engr., chief estimator, 1977—; instr. math. Erie County Tech. Inst.; soils cons. Mem. bd. edn. Highland Local Schs., Medina, Ohio. Registered profl. engr., N.Y., Ohio, Minn., Ga., Fla. Mem. ASCE, Am. Concrete Inst., Ohio Soc. Profl. Engrs. Episcopalian. Home: 1378 Wilbur Rd Medina OH 44256 Office: 3351 Brecksville Rd Richfield OH 44141

BENDER, JOHN HENRY, JR. (JACK), editorial cartoonist; b. Waterloo, Ia., Mar. 28, 1931; s. John Henry and Wilma (Lowe) B.; B.A., U. Ia., 1953; M.A., U. Mo., 1962; postgrad. Art Inst. Chgo., Washington U., St. Louis; m. Jo Ann J. Packey, June 13, 1953; children—Thereza, John IV, Anthony. Art dir., asst. editor Commerce Pub. Co., St. Louis, 1953-58; editor Florissant Reporter, 1958-61; editorial cartoonist Waterloo Courier, 1962—, asso. editor, 1975—; sports cartoons Baseball Digest Mag., U. Iowa, others. Served with USAF, 1954-56, now col. Res. Recipient Best Editorial award Mo. Press Assn., 1960; Grenville Clark Editorial Page award, 1968, Freedoms Found. award, 1969, 71, 75. Mem. Assn. Am. Editorial Cartoonists, Nat. Cartoonists Soc., Sigma Chi. Author: Pocket Guide to Judging Springboard Diving; (with Dick Smith) Inside Diving; (with Ed Gagnier) Inside Gymnastics. Home: 2904 Cottage Row Rd Cedar Falls IA 50613 Office: Box 540 Courier Waterloo IA 50704

BENDER, PAUL L., hosp. adminstr.; b. Bluffton, Ind., Mar. 5, 1918; s. Lawrence L. and Elizabeth A. (Reiff) B.; B.S., Purdue U., 1939; m. Maro L. Bradburn, Apr. 6, 1941; children—Paul L., Linda (Mrs. Carl M. Heuer). With Goodman Mfg. Co., indsl. machinery, Chgo., 1939-47; owner L.L. Bender Co., elec. equipment, Bluffton, Ind., 1947-70; exec. dir., adminstr. Wells Community Hosp., 1970—, pres. hosp. bd., 1953-70. Active Mental Health Assn., United Fund, Cemetary assn., Agrl. Achievement Assn., and other civic groups. Sec., City Plan Commn., Bluffton, Ind., 1953. Mem. exec. bd. Anthony Wayne council Boy Scouts Am., 1962—; bd. dirs. Allen-Wells chpt. ARC, 1979—. Recipient Silver Beaver award Boy Scouts Am., 1966, community service award Wells County, 1971. Mem. Am. Inst. Elec. and Electronic Engrs., Am. Acad. Med. Adminstrs., Hist. Soc. (pres. 1966-70), Bluffton C. of C. (pres. 1954). Methodist. (trustee 1956-58). Clubs: Elks, Lions (dir. 1948—). Home: 506 W Ohio St Bluffton IN 46714 Office: 1100 S Main St Bluffton IN 46714

BENDHEIM, LEONORE CAROLINE, social worker; b. Amsterdam, Holland, Oct. 26, 1921; came to U.S., 1943, naturalized, 1949; d. Martin and Alice S. (Mayer) B.; student Traphagen Sch. Design, N.Y.C., 1943-46; B.A. in Art Edn., Kans. U., 1970; B.A. in Social Work, Washburn U., 1972; M.S. in Clin. Counseling, Emporia State Coll., 1974; postgrad. Kans. State U., 1980—. Interior designer, Mehagian's Home Furnishings, Phoenix, Ariz., 1951-59; prin. Leonore C. Bendheim, interior designer, Phoenix, 1959-63; research asst. Menninger Research Clinic, Topeka, Kans., 1963-64; art therapist Topeka State Hosp., 1966; vol. Vocat. Rehab. Center for the Blind, Topeka, 1967; social worker Kans. Psychiat. Reception and Diagnostic Center, Topeka, 1970-73; social worker VA Hosp. and Med. Center, Topeka, 1973—. Pres., Unitarian Universalist Fellowship, Topeka, 1976-77; active Unitarian Universalist Women's Fedn. and Service Com. Recipient various design awards, 1947-63; lic. social worker, Kans. Mem. Counseling and Guidance Soc., NE Kans. Assn. Social Welfare, Nat. Assn. Humanists, Am. Inst. Interior Designers, Am. Art Therapy Assn., Nat. Assn. Social Workers, Mid-West Weavers Assn., Ashram Soc. Unitarian. Home: 2601 SW James St Topeka KS 66614 Office: 2200 Gage Blvd Topeka KS 66622

BENDIXEN, LEO EMBRO, agronomist; b. Mills, Utah, Oct. 21, 1923; s. James Embro and Sarah (Winter) B.; B.S., Utah State U., 1953; M.S., U. Calif., Davis, 1956, Ph.D., 1960; m. Ellen Hyllen Sorensen, Dec. 10, 1949; children—Christian Leo, Ann Margaret, Steven Embro, Sarah Lynn. Sr. lab. technician U. Calif., Davis, 1955-61; mem. faculty Ohio Agrl. Research and Devel. Center, Ohio State U., Columbus, 1961—, prof. agronomy, 1970—. Bishop, Mormon Ch., 1963-67, counselor stake presidency, 1967-71, high councilor, 1962-63, 71-75, quorum pres., 1954-61, pres. stake Sunday sch., 1976-81. Served with USAAF, 1944-46. Mem. Am. Soc. Agronomy, Am. Soc. Plant Physiologists, Crop Sci. Soc. Am., Internat. Weed Sci. Soc., Weed Sci. Soc. Am., Council Agrl. Sci. and Tech., Sigma Xi, Alpha Zeta, Phi Kappa Phi. Office: 2021 Coffey Rd Columbus OH 43210

BENDIXEN, ROMAINE LEROY, physician; b. Terril, Iowa, Nov. 7, 1937; s. Howard Roy and Ruby Isabelle (Tow) B.; B.A., U. Iowa, 1959, M.D., 1962; m. Amy Elizabeth Bridgmount, Dec. 17, 1966; children—Anne Denise, John Howard, Mary Elizabeth, Amy Catherine. Intern, Nat. Naval Med. Center, Bethesda, Md., 1962-63;

resident in obs.-gyn. San Diego Naval Hosp., 1969-70; commd. ensign U.S. Navy, 1959; flight surgeon, various locations, 1964-72; released from active duty, 1972; pvt. practice family medicine, Denison, Iowa, 1972—; mem. staff Crawford County Meml. Hosp., Denison. Mem. standing com. Episcopal Diocese Iowa. Mem. Flying Physicians Assn. (dir.), AMA, Civil Aeromed. Assn., Phi Beta Kappa, Alpha Omega Alpha, Phi Eta Sigma. Republican. Episcopalian. Clubs: Masons, Shriners. Home: Beggars Roost Fairway Heights Denison IA 51442 Office: 203 N Main St Denison IA 51442

BENEDICT, JOHN ANTHONY, social worker; b. Pittsburg, Kans., June 27, 1943; s. Frances Loriene B.; B.A. in English Lit., St. Meinrad Coll., 1965; M.S. in Counselor Edn., Kans. State Coll., Pittsburg, 1975; m. Marcia Kathleen McCullough, Nov. 22, 1974; 1 stepdau., Amber Peterson; 1 adopted dau., Crystal Kerry. Family social service worker Parsons (Kans.) area office Kans. Social and Rehab. Services, 1965-66, social worker, family services, 1968-69, income maintenance worker, 1969-71, Work Incentive Program social service worker, 1971-77, social worker II, protective service work, youth, 1977—; parenting edn. instr. S.T.E.P. Vice pres. Labette County Cancer Soc., 1969, 70, pres., 1971, 72; mem. Parsons Youth Council, 1969—; mem. community action bd. Labette County Mental Health, 1969, 73; mem. SRS Consortium on Youth; mem. Labette County Coalition on Parenting Edn. Served in U.S. Army, 1966-68. Mem. Am., Kans. personnel and guidance assns., Nat. Vocational Guidance Assn., Pub. Offenders Counselors Assn., Nat. Com. Prevention of Child Abuse, N. Am. Soc. Adlerian Psychology, Internat. Platform Assn. Roman Catholic. Home: 1226 Kimball St Parsons KS 67357 Office: 400 N 32d St PO Box 914 Parsons KS 67357

BENEKE, MILDRED (MILLIE) STONG, civic worker, city ofcl., author; b. Prairie City, Iowa; d. Rueben Ira and Lillian (Garber) Stong; student Wash. U., 1942-43; off-campus student U. Minn., Mankato State Coll., 1951-67; m. Arnold W. Beneke, Aug. 10, 1939; children—Bruce Arnold, Paula Rae, Bradford Kent, Cynthia Jane, Lisa Patrice. Exec. sec. chmn. Vol. Services, ARC, St. Paul, 1940-41; v.p. Pi House, St. Paul, 1972—; founder, bd. dirs. chmn. Project Interaction Boutique, Minn. Correctional Instn. for Women, Shakopee, 1971—, supervising vol., 1970—. Bd. dirs. Mpls. Children's Theatre Co. Republican chairwoman McLeod County (Minn.), 1969-73; mem. Rep. Minn. Platform com., 1970; McLeod County del. Rep. Minn. Central Com., 1969—; bd. dirs. Buffalo Creek Players, 1975—, v.p., 1980-81; mem. Rep. Feminist Caucus; alderman Glencoe City Council, 1974-80. Glencoe elderly housing named Millie Beneke Manor, 1977. Mem. Glencoe Bus. and Profl. Women (Woman of Yr. 1975), Ripon Soc. Lutheran. Author: (play) The Garage Sale, 1978; Politics Unusual, 1979; columnist Council Memos from Millie, Glencoe Enterprise. Home: 330 Scout Hill Dr Glenview Woods Glencoe MN 55336

BENEKE, WILLIAM MICHAEL, psychologist, educator; b. Spokane, July 30, 1945; s. George W. and Dorothy L. (Stewart) B.; B.A., Eastern Wash. U., 1968; M.A. (NIMH trainee), U. N.Mex., 1971, Ph.D. (NIMH trainee), 1972; m. Patricia A. Mark, June 9, 1967; children—Michael R., Jeffrey S. Asst. prof. psychology Lincoln U., 1972-75, asso. prof., research specialist, 1975—, psychology area coordinator, 1979—. Dept. Agr. Sci. and Edn. Adminstrn. grantee, 1975-80, 77-83. Mem. Am. Psychol. Assn., Assn. Advancement Behavior Therapy, Assn. Behavior Analysis, Sigma Xi, Psi Chi. Author: (with others) Eating Slim: A treatment manual for effective weight control through behavior therapy and nutrition education, 1978; contbr. articles to profl. jours. Home: Route 1 Box 117 Henley MO 65040 Office: Dept Psychology Lincoln U Jefferson City MO 65101

BENES, CHARLES JAMES, banker; b. Cleve., May 22, 1904; s. James and Mary (Poskecil) B.; student Dyke Coll. Bus., 1919-20; m. Rose AnnaBelle Jankovsky, July 20, 1950; children—Charles J. Sec., treas. First Fed. Savs. & Loan Assn., Cleve., 1933-78, also dir.; dir. First Fin. Services and Devel. Corp., Cleve. Commr. zoning and planning City of Pepper Pike, Ohio, 1956-69. Mem. Am. Savs. and Loan Inst. (pres. Northeast Ohio chpt. 1951-52). Clubs: Masons (32 deg.), (Shriners; Mentor (Ohio) Yachting; Shaker Heights Country. Home: 29026 Gates Mills Blvd Pepper Pike OH 44124 Office: Park Centre 1255 Superior St Cleveland OH 44114

BENESH, PETER, mfg. co. exec.; b. Toledo, Mar. 24, 1916; s. George Valentine and Eva (Krajsic) B.; student Henry Ford Trade Sch., 1931-34, Ford Apprentice Sch., 1934-37, Ford Engring. Sch., 1937-40; m. Kathryn Macut, Sept. 21, 1935; children—Marijana, Peter Ed, Carolyn L., Eva Kay. Machine builder Ford Motor Co., 1937-39, die designer, 1939-40; machine builder Lemaire Machine Co., 1940-41; supt. Greenfield Machine & Tool Co., 1941-42; machine design checker Allen Engring. Co., 1942-43; founder, mgr. Merit Engring. Co., 1960-78; founder, pres. Benesh Tool & Mfg. Co., Monroe, Mich., 1943—. Pres., Marron Sch. PTA, 1952-54; pres. Marron Sch. Bd. also treas., 1954-58; chmn. Frenchtown Twp. Bd. Zoning Appeals, 1958-63; trustee Frenchtown Twp. Bd., 1963-67. Mem. Soc. Mfg. Engrs. (cert.), Ford Old Timers Club. Republican. Presbyterian. Clubs: Masons. Patentee in human body vertebrate location determiner, chiropractic head support. Home: 100 Cole Rd Monroe MI 48161 Office: 1910 N Telegraph Rd PO Box 906 Monroe MI 48161

BENFORADO, DAVID M., environ. engr.; b. N.Y.C., Nov. 17, 1925; s. Mark Joseph and Mathilde Alton (Abraham) B.; B.S. in Chem. Engring., Columbia, 1948; student Coll. City N.Y., 1942-44; m. Ruth Ann Martin, May 5, 1950; children—Mark Andrew, Marcia Ann, David Dean. Engr., Skelly Oil Co., Eldorado, Kans., 1948-53; applied research engr. Walter Kidde Nuclear Labs., Garden City, N.Y., 1953-56; heat transfer specialist Trane Co., La Crosse, Wis., 1956-61; mgr. application engring. Penn Brass & Copper, Erie, Pa., 1961-65; product mgr. air pollution control equipment Air Preheater Co., Wellsville, N.Y., 1965-69; environ. engring. specialist 3M Co., St. Paul, 1969—; cons. control odorous indsl. emissions Environ. Research & Applications, Inc., Wilton, Conn., 1969—, also fed. govt.; mem. com. odors from stationary and mobile sources NRC, 1978. Active Boy Scouts Am. Registered profl. engr., N.Y. Mem. Air Pollution Control Assn. (dir. 1968—, pres. 1972-73) hon. membership award 1981, Am. Inst. Chem. Engrs., Indsl. Gas Cleaning Inst. Trustee Am. Acad. Environ. Engrs. (diplomate), 1981. Club: Woodbury Lions (sec. 1970, dir. 1971—, pres. 1978). Home: 7100 Glenross Rd Woodbury MN 55119 Office: 3M Co 900 Bush Ave Saint Paul MN 55101

BENFORD, ARTHUR EUGENE, plastics engr.; b. Benton Harbor, Mich., July 21, 1931; s. George Everet and Gladys Irene (Hendrix) B.; student Lake Mich. Coll., 1951, U. Mich., 1952; B.S. in Polymer Chemistry, Western Mich. U., 1957; m. Bernice Irene Kowerdlick, June 29, 1952; children—Lauri Beth, Brice Allen, Blair Ashley. Research materials engr. Whirlpool Research Labs., St. Joseph, Mich., 1956-60, mgr. materials research dept., 1960-72; mgr. plastics research and applications Whirlpool Refrigeration Group, Evansville, Ind., 1972-74, sr. product engr., 1974—. Chmn. Parks Dept., St. Joseph Twp., Mich., 1965-72; mem. Republican County Commn., 1965-72. Served with U.S. Army, 1952-55. Cert. mfg. engr. Mem. Research Soc. Am., Soc. Plastics Engrs., Sigma Xi. Lutheran. Patentee, contbr. articles to various publs. Home: Rural Route 7 Box 216B Evansville IN 47712 Office: US 41 North Evansville IN 47727

BENGTSON, TIMOTHY ANDREW, educator; b. Menominee, Mich., Oct. 30, 1942; s. Gilbert Myron and Gertrude Elizabeth (McGuire) B.; B.B.A., U. Mich., 1964, M.B.A., 1965; M.S. in Journalism, Northwestern U., 1968, Ph.D., 1977; m. Kathryn Ann Ward, Apr. 22, 1972; 1 son, Andrew Ward. Instr. dept. bus. adminstrn. S.E. Mo. State U., Cape Girardeau, 1965-67; instr. Sch. Journalism and Mass Communication, U. Minn., Mpls., 1968-69; instr. Northwestern U., Evanston, Ill., 1969-75; asst. prof. dept. communication U. Utah, Salt Lake City, 1975-79; asso. prof. dept. advt. William Allen White Sch. Journalism, U. Kans., Lawrence, 1979—. Mem. AAUP, Assn. for Edn. Journalism, Am. Acad. Advt., Blue Key, Kappa Tau Alpha. Home: 2704 Lawrence Ave Lawrence KS 66044 Office: Flint Hall The William Allen White School Journalism U Kansas Lawrence KS 66045

BENHAM, ROBERT MILES, JR., retail co. exec.; b. Cin., May 16, 1939; s. Robert Miles and Jean (Murphy) B.; B.S. in Edn., Monmouth (N.J.) Coll., 1966; student Vanderbilt U., 1961-64; m. Ardys Dee Johnson, Nov. 29, 1969; children—Michael Robert, Elizabeth Maren. Buyer menswear, Steinbach Co., Asbury Park, N.J., 1966-69; asst. to exec. v.p. Famous Barr div. May Co., St. Louis, 1970-71, mdse. mgr. May D & F div., Denver, 1971-75; mdse. mgr. I. Magnin div. Federated Dept. Stores, San Francisco, 1976-77; pres. Halls Crown Center div. Hallmark Cards, Inc., Kansas City, Mo., 1978, pres. Hallmark retail div., Kansas City, 1979—, pres., chief exec. officer Halls Merchandising, Inc. subs., 1980-81; dir. Plaza Bank and Trust Co., Kansas City, 1980-81. Active Boy Scouts Am.; mem. mng. bd. Crippled Childrens Nursery Sch., Kansas City, 1980-81. Served with U.S. Army, 1961-64. Mem. Nat. Retail Mchts. Assn., Kansas City Mchts. Assn., Mo. Retail Assn. (dir.), Crown Center Mchts. Assn. (dir.). Republican. Presbyterian. Office: 200 E 25th St Kansas City MO 64108

BENISHEK, BETTY LOU, ins. co. exec.; b. Chgo., Sept. 2, 1931; d. Forrest Bryan and Ruth Warner (Shaw) Brunner; cert. advanced safety Nat. Safety Council, 1973; cert. audiometric technician Ear, Nose and Throat Assos. of Wausau, 1973; student U. Wis., Am. Welding Soc., Harvard U., tech. insts.; m. Albert William Benishek, June 28, 1952; children—Michael A., Lori G. Nurses aide delivery room, technician Meml. Hosp., Manitowoc, Wis., 1956-71; safety technician Aluminum Splty. Co., Manitowoc, 1971-72; safety and health adminstr. Armira Corp., Sheboygan, Wis., 1972-77; safety dir. Universal Foundry Co., Oshkosh, Wis., 1977-80; risk control rep. Comml. Union Ins. Cos., Milw., 1980—. First aid and CPR instr. ARC. Mem. Nat. Safety Council (exec. com.), Wis. Council Safety (exec. com.), No. Wis. Foundry Safety Assn. (founder 1978), Oshkosh Indsl. Safety Council (v.p. 1980), Am. Soc. Safety Engrs., Northeastern Wis. Am. Foundrymens Soc., Am. Indsl. Hygiene Assn., Mgmt. Club (sec.). Lutheran. Contbr. articles to Leather Industry Trade Jour. Home: 4442 Just Ct Manitowoc WI 54220 Office: 10201 W Lincoln St Milwaukee WI 53227

BENJAMIN, ADAM, JR., congressman; b. Gary, Ind., Aug. 6, 1935; s. Adam and Margaret (Marjanian) B.; B.S., U.S. Mil. Acad., 1958; J.D., Valparaiso U., 1966; m. Patricia Ann Sullivan, July 31, 1966; children—Adam III, Alison Louise, Arianne. Commd. 2d lt. U.S. Army, 1958, advanced through grades to 1st lt., 1959; resigned, 1961; zoning adminstr. City of Gary, 1963-65; exec. sec. to mayor Gary, 1965-66; admitted to Ind. bar, 1966, U.S. Supreme Ct. bar; atty. firm Benjamin, Greco & Gouveia, Gary, 1966-76; mem. Ind. Ho. of Reps. from Lake County, 1966-70, Ind. Senate from 4th Dist., 1970-76; mem. 95th-97th Congresses from 1st Dist. Ind.; chmn. transp. subcom. Appropriations Com., mem. Budget Com. Served with USMC, 1952-54. Home: 2106 W 3d Pl Hobart IN 46342 Office: 410 Cannon Bldg Washington DC 20515

BENJAMIN, HARRISON RUSSELL, computer co. ofcl.; b. Hastings, Minn., July 7, 1934; s. Harry Murtice and Florence Elizabeth (Severson) B.; m. Patti Cox, July 16, 1960; children—David, Lisa. B.S. in Engring. with distinction, U. Minn., 1956, postgrad., 1958. Instr., U. Minn. Inst. Tech., 1957-58; electromech. engr. Gen. Mills electronics div., Mpls., 1958-61; engr. mgr. Control Data Corp., Mpls., 1961-68, dir. engring., 1969-71, gen. mgr. terminal devel. div., 1972-75, gen. mgr. small computer devel. div., 1976, gen. mgr. data systems devel., 1977-80, gen. mgr. microcomputer services, 1981—. Bd. dirs. Elbit Inc., Haifa, Israel, 1975-81; mem. Com. for Effective Crime Control. Recipient Honor Student award U. Minn. Mem. Territorial Pioneers Assn. Minn., Hort. Soc. (Minn.), Internat. Wood Collectors Soc., Nat. Rifle Assn., Model T Collectors Assn., Minn. Hist. Soc., Dakota County Hist. Soc., Sci. Mus. Minn., Aircraft Owners and Pilots Assn., Tau Beta Pi. Home: 4805 Eriks Blvd Eagan MN 55122 Office: 8100 34th Ave S Minneapolis MN 55440

BENJAMIN, IVY, pathologist, educator; b. Rajasthan, India, Mar. 25, 1932; d. Thomas and Annamma (Cherian) Thomas; came to U.S., 1966, naturalized, 1969; M.D., Christian Med. Coll., Vellore Madras (India) U., 1956; m. Philip Benjamin, Aug. 18, 1960; children—Ivan, Evan, Bevan, Cyril. Intern, Christian Med. Coll. Hosp., 1956-57, Montreal Children's Hosp., 1962-63, 64-65, Royal Victoria Hosp., 1965-66; resident Mc Gill U., Montreal, Que., Can., 1971-72; asst. pathologist Mt. Sinai Hosp., Cleve., 1972-76; instr. in pathology St. Louis U., 1972-76, asst. prof. pathology, 1976—; co-dir. Medi-Nuclear Inst., St. Louis. St. Louis U. grantee, 1975-76. Mem. St. Louis Soc. Pathologists. Research on human breast cancer heterotransplantation into new born rats. Home: 1418 Old Farm Dr Saint Louis MO 63141 Office: 1402 S Grand Blvd Saint Louis MO 63104

BENJAMIN, NEAL B. H., civil engr.; b. Santa Cruz, Calif., Oct. 24, 1934; s. Charles Hugh and Mildred Emily (Neal) B.; B.S., U.S. Coast Guard Acad., 1956; B.C.E., Renssalaer Poly. Inst., 1962; M.S.C.E., Stanford U., 1967, Ph.D., 1969; m. Mary Louise Schroeder, July 6, 1963; children—Charles Edward, Julia Anne, Kathryn Mary. Served in U.S. Coast Guard, 1956-66; research asst. Stanford U., 1967-69; asst. prof. civil engring. U. Mo., Columbia, 1969-72, asso. prof., 1972-75, prof., 1975—, coordinator Grad. Program in Constrn. Engring. and Mgmt. Registered profl. engr., Mo. Mem. ASCE (chmn. com. on estimating and cost control 1975-78, assn. chmn. 1980-81, exec. com. constrn. div.), Nat., Mo. socs. profl. engrs., Am. Assn. Cost Engrs., Project Mgmt. Inst., Am. Arbitration Assn., Constrn. Specifications Inst. Roman Catholic. Contbr. articles in constrn.-mgmt. to profl. jours. Home: 1108 S Glenwood Columbia MO 65201 Office: 1039 Engring Bldg U Mo Columbia MO 65201

BENNETT, DAVID THOMAS, lawyer; b. Mpls., Aug. 4, 1940; s. Russell Hoadley and Miriam (Fletcher) B.; B.A., Stanford U., 1962; J.D., U. Minn., 1967; m. Sue Ann Schmidt, Nov. 22, 1968; children—Sarah, Ryan, Lesley. Admitted to Minn. bar, 1967; asso. firm Gray, Plant, Mooty, Mooty & Bennett, Mpls., 1967-72, partner, 1972—; instr. U. Minn., 1967-68; dir. Carmichael-Lynch Advt., Inc. Bd. dirs. Guthrie Theatre Found., from 1973, pres., from 1978; trustee Dunwoody Indsl. Inst., from 1968. Served to lt. USNR, 1962-64. Mem. Am. Bar Assn., Minn. Bar Assn., Hennepin County Bar Assn. Club: Minneapolis. Home: 4825 Sheridan Ave S Minneapolis MN 55410 Office: 300 Roanoke Bldg Minneapolis MN 55402

BENNETT, EARLE, advt. exec.; b. Fort Ritner, Ind., Jan. 12, 1910; s. Seibert Everett Newton and Myrtle B.; student Monmouth Coll., 1933-37. Monmouth editor Rock Island (Ill.) Argus, 1935-48; with Galesburg (Ill.) Register-Mail, 1948-52; newscaster WGIL, Galesburg, 1948-52; mem. Agrl. Stabilization Com., 1953-67; dir. advt. The Times Record, Aledo, Ill., 1967—. Mem. Ill. Devel. Council, 1940-48. Mem. Aledo Area C. of C. (sec.), Ill. Press Assn., Christian Scientist. Clubs: Lions, Exchange, Pres., Warren County (Ill.) Young Republican Club, 1934-38. Freelance writer including contbns. to Prairie Farmer, Reader's Digest, Western Stories, Graphic Arts, trade jours. Home: Gerlaw IL 61435 Office: 113 S College Ave Aledo IL 61231

BENNETT, IVAN FRANK, educator, psychiatrist; b. Hartford, Conn., Sept. 6, 1919; s. Frank and Iva (Bacon) B.; B.S., Trinity Coll., 1941, M.D., Thomas Jefferson U., 1944; m. Audrey Poley, Sept. 23, 1944; children—Ivan Stanley, Judith Anne. Intern, Jefferson Hosp., Phila., 1944-45, resident, 1945-46; asst. physician State Hosp., Harrisburg, 1948-50, asst. chief acute intensive treatment service, chief physiol. treatment sect. VA Hosp., Coatesville, Pa., 1950-56; chief psychiat. research, psychiatry and neurology service, dept. medicine and surgery VA, Washington, 1956-58; physician Lilly Lab. for Clin. Research, Eli Lilly & Co., Indpls., 1958-63, sr. physician, 1963-76, clin. investigator, 1976—; instr. psychiatry U. Pa. Sch. Medicine, 1954-56; clin. asst. prof. psychiatry Georgetown U. Sch. Medicine, 1956-58; asst. prof. psychiatry Ind. U. Sch. Medicine, 1958-62, asso. prof., 1962-72, prof., 1972—. Mem. pharmacology and therapeutic study sect., div. research grants NIH, 1956-58, mem. behavioral scis. study sect., div., 1956-58; mem. profl. adv. com. Ind. Mental Health Assn., 1958—; asso. staff physician dept. neuropsychiatry Wishard Meml. Hosp., Indpls., 1958—, dir. Lilly psychiat. clinic, 1959—; mem. sci.-med. adv. bd. Manfred Sakel Inst., 1960-70; mem. adv. com. on alcoholism Ind. Dept. Mental Health, 1961-69, mem. research com., 1962-68, mem. adv. com. div. drug abuse, 1971-72; bd. dirs. Marion County Assn. Mental Health, 1967-73, profl. adv. com., 1967—, exec. com., 1969-73; cons. drug abuse Gen. Bd. Christian Social Concerns of Meth. Ch., 1967—; mem. standing com. to study mental health laws of Ind., 1968-70; mem. Gov.'s Com. Study Mental Health Laws, 1973-76; mem. adv. com. drug edn. Ind. State Health Commr., 1968-74; cons. Indpls. Family Service Assn., 1966—, personnel com., 1969—; mem. project com. drug abuse programs Ind. Dept. Pub. Instrn., 1970-71; mem. sci. adv. com. Nat. Coordinating Council Drug Edn., 1972-76; mem. controlled substances adv. com. State of Ind., 1973-76, mem. exec. com., 1976—; cons. dept. psychiatry Mayo Clinic, Rochester, Minn., 1976—. Bd. dirs., mem. exec. com. Community Addiction Services Agy., Indpls., 1971-78; bd. dirs. U.P. Met. Center, 1974-76; mem. adv. bd. neurosci. program U. Hartford, 1978—; mem. Ind. Bd. Mental Health, 1979—. Served with AUS, 1946-48. Diplomate Am. Bd. Neurology and Psychiatry. Fellow A.C.P., Am. Psychiat. Assn., Am. Coll. Neuropsychopharmacology (charter); mem. AMA, Ind., Marion County med. socs., Ind. Psychiat. Soc. (pres. 1970-71). Contbr. articles to profl. jours. Office: 307 E McCarty St Indianapolis IN 46285

BENNETT, JAMES BENJAMIN, civil engr.; b. Fredericktown, Mo., Jan. 6, 1934; s. Willard Lee and Rebecca Sarah (Barber) B.; B.S. in Civil Engring., U. Mo., Columbia, 1956; children—James Scott, Jon Gregory. Owner, v.p. Bennett-Smith, Inc., Fredericktown, 1958-69; chief engr., asst. sec., v.p. Terre Du Lac, Inc., Bonne Terre, Mo., 1969-79; owner, operator James B. Bennett & Assos., Cons., Farmington, Mo., 1976—. Sec. bd. trustees Madison Meml. Hosp., 1960-68. Served with U.S. Army, 1956-58. Registered profl. engr., Mo.; lic. land surveyor, Mo. Mem. Nat. Soc. Profl. Engrs., Mo. Assn. Registered Land Surveyors, ASCE, Am. Water Works Assn., Am. Congress Surveying and Mapping. Democrat. Club: Elks. Home: Fredericktown MO 63645 Office: Box 232 Farmington MO 63640

BENNETT, JAMES EDWARD, educator, surgeon; b. Burlington, Wis., May 19, 1925; s. John Francis and Florence (Mauer) B.; student Notre Dame U., 1943-44, Mass. Inst. Tech., 1944-45; M.D., Northwestern U., 1950; m. Ellen MacPherson, June 18, 1956; children—David, Martha, Thomas, Jonathan. Intern, Milw. County Hosp., 1949-50; resident surgery U. Mich. Hosp., 1953-58; gen. practice medicine, Burlington, 1950-51; exchange fellow plastic surgery, Wales, 1956-57; resident plastic surgery U. Tex. Sch. Medicine at Calveston, 1958-61; asst. prof. surgery, dir. plastic surgery Ohio State U. Sch. Medicine, 1961-64; prof. surgery, dir. plastic surgery Ind. U. Med. Center, 1964—, Willis D. Gatch prof. surgery, 1981—. Diplomate Am. Bd. Plastic Surgery (dir. 1978—, residency rev. com. 1975-81, chmn. 1978-79). Fellow A.C.S.; mem. Plastic Surgery Research Council (chmn. 1970), Frederick A. Coller Surg. Soc., Am. Soc. Plastic and Reconstructive Surgeons, Am. Assn. Surgery Trauma, Am. Assn. Plastic Surgeons (sec. 1978-81, v.p. 1981—), Am. Surg. Assn., Phi Rho Sigma. Research wound healing, cleft lip-palate. Home: 5865 Hunter Glen Rd Indianapolis IN 46226

BENNETT, JAMES PAUL, radiologist; b. Chgo., Oct. 27, 1896; s. Svante and Hulda Eselia (Johnson) B.; B.S., U. Chgo., 1918, M.S. (Chemistry fellow), 1922; grad. evening sch. Moody Bible Inst., 1923; M.D., Rush Med. Coll., 1927. Intern, Swedish Covenant Hosp., also Cook County Hosp., Chgo., 1927-30; resident in specialties including pathology, ophthalmology, internal medicine, radiology Cook County Hosp., Chgo., 1930-34, asso. roentgenologist, 1934-44, mem. teaching staff in X-ray, 1938-44, cons. in diagnostic X-ray, 1962—; radiologist Bethany Brethren Hosp., Chgo., 1941—, Meth. Hosp., Gary, Ind., 1944-62. Bd. dirs. Evang. Child and Family Welfare Agency, Pacific Garden Mission, Door of Hope Rescue Mission. Recipient Outstanding Service award Cook County Hosp., 1967; diplomate Am. Bd. Radiology. Mem. Christian Med. Soc., AMA, Ill. State, Chgo. med. socs., Ill. Radiological Soc., Am. Coll. Radiology, Am. Roentgen Ray Soc., Radiol. Soc. N.Am., Phi Beta Kappa, Sigma Xi. Contbr. articles in field to profl. jours. Home: 5130 N Albany Ave Chicago IL 60625 Office: 3821 W Washington St Chicago IL 60624

BENNETT, JEROME, mfg. co. exec.; b. Greenwood, Miss., Oct. 20, 1922; s. Harry and Jennie (Arenzon) B.; B.S., La. State U., 1943; postgrad. U. Pa., 1946; m. Julie M. Boyd, Sept. 6, 1947; children—Jerome, Jack, Henry. With Ford Motor Co., Dearborn, Mich., 1950-65, 66-69, dep. dir. Latin ops., 1966-69; dep. comptroller ITT, 1965-66; v.p. Xerox, Stamford, Conn., 1969-75; exec. v.p., chief fin. officer White Motor Corp., Eastlake, Ohio, 1975-76, pres., chief operating officer, 1976—, also dir. Served with U.S. Army, 1943-46. C.P.A., Pa. Mem. Pa. Inst. C.P.A.'s. Clubs: Met. (N.Y.C.); Kirtland Country, Union (Cleve.); Greate Bay (Somers Point, N.J.); John's Island (Fla.). Office: 35129 Curtis Blvd Eastlake OH 44094

BENNETT, JOYCE ARLENE, librarian, educator; b. Madison, Wis., Mar. 25, 1944; d. Ralph Eugene and Florence Marie (Cramer) B.; B.A. in Liberal Arts (scholar), Bradley U., 1966; M.S. in L.S., U. Ill., 1971. Library asst. research library Caterpillar Tractor Co., Peoria, Ill., 1966-67; reference librarian, instr. library tech. Ill. Central Coll., East Peoria, 1967-73; asst. prof. Sangamon State U., Springfield, Ill., 1973-80, asso. prof., 1980—; convenor Council II, Ill. Clearinghouse for Acad. Library Instrn., 1978; presentor 7th Ann. Conf. Acad. Library Instrn., 1977; participant Gt. Lakes Women's Studies Summer Inst., 1981. Pres., Springfield chpt. NOW, 1978-79. Ill. state scholar, 1962-66: recipient Am. Legion citizenship award, 1962; invited Susan B. Anthony luncheon, 1978, 79. Mem. ALA, Ill. Library Assn., Ill. Assn. Coll. and Research Libraries (bibliog. instrn. com.), Am. Fedn. Tchrs., AAUW (chmn. standing com. on women Springfield br., mem. com. on women Ill. state div.), Springfield Art Assn., Beta Phi Mu. Contbr. article in field to publ. Home: 2226 Concord Ct Springfield IL 62704 Office: Sangamon State University Library Springfield IL 62708

BENNETT, LAVERA RITA, educator; b. Seneca, Kans., June 5, 1927; d. John Francis and Rose (Olberding) Dreier; A.A., Highland Jr. Coll., 1965; B.A. magna cum laude, Peru State Coll., 1967; postgrad. Kans. State Tchrs. Coll., U. Kans., Wichita State U., U. Scranton, Ft. Hays State Coll.; m. Oliver O. Bennett, Oct. 6, 1945; children—Oliver O., Mary Ann. Tchr., B&B Unified Sch., Dist., Baileyville, Kans., 1967-69, Sabetha Unified Sch. Dist., Kans., 1969-72, Diller (Nebr.) Community Schs., 1972-75; tchr. English, Downs (Kans.) High Sch. 1975—; cons. Kans. Writing Project. Mem. NEA, Kans. Assn. Tchrs. English, Kans. Authors Club, Sigma Tau Delta, Kappa Delta Phi, Phi Alpha Theta. Republican. Roman Catholic. Clubs: Order of Eastern Star, Quest. Author articles in field. Home: 304 Ross St Downs KS 67437

BENNETT, OLGA, lawyer; b. Viroqua, Wis., May 5, 1908; d. John Henry and Olga (Omundson) Bennett; B.A., U. Wis., 1928, LL.B., 1935. Asst. cashier Farmers Bank, Viroqua, 1929-32; admitted to Wis. bar, 1935; practiced in Viroqua, 1941-70; law clk. to justice Wis. Supreme Ct., Madison, 1936-41; partner firm Bennett & Bennett, 1941-56; individual practice, 1956-70; city atty. City of Viroqua, 1946-48; county judge Vernon County, Viroqua, 1970-76; individual practice law, Viroqua, 1976—; mem. Lower West Central Criminal Justice Planning Council, 1972—, Vernon County Hwy. Safety Commn. Mem. Vernon County Bar Assn., State Bar Wis., Am. Judicature Soc., Nat. Coll. State Judiciary, Vernon County Hist. Soc., Benchers, Kappa Beta Pi. Republican. Lutheran. Home: 322 N Dunlap Ave Viroqua WI 54665 Office: 210 N Main St Viroqua WI 54665

BENNETT, PAMELA JEAN, state ofcl.; b. Balt., July 3, 1943; d. Paul S. and Martha R. Bennett; A.B., Gettysburg Coll., 1965; M.A., Ind. U., 1971, postgrad. in philosophy, 1971-73. Asst. instr. Gettysburg (Pa.) Coll., 1965-67; asst. editor Ind. Mag. History, Ind. U., Bloomington, 1968-72, editorial asst. sesquicentennial history project, 1972-73; editor Ind. Hist. Bur., Indpls., 1973-76, dir., 1976—; mem. Ind. Am. Revolution Bicentennial Commn., 1976—, Ind. Library and Hist. Bd., 1976—; mem. Ind. adv. bd. Nat. Hist. Publs. and Records Commn., 1976—. Mem. Am. Assn. for State and Local History (ethics com. 1980—), Am. Soc. for 18th Century Studies, Soc. Am. Archivists, Orgn. Am. Historians, Nat. Trust for Historic Preservation, Soc. for History of Edn., Assn. for Documentary Editing, Ind. Hist. Soc., Midwest Archives Conf., Assn. Ind. Museums, Soc. Ind. Archivists, Ind. Council for Social Studies. Editor: Fifty Year Index, Mississippi Valley Historical Review, 1914-64, 1973; Progress after Statehood: A Book of Readings, 1974; Ind. Hist. Bull.; contbr. articles to profl. jours., chpts. to books. Office: 140 N Senate Ave Indianapolis IN 46204

BENNETT, RICHARD CARL, social worker; b. Eau Claire, Wis., July 25, 1933; s. Ira Anthony and Marion Rhoda (Johnson) B.; B.A., Hamline U., St. Paul, 1955; M.S., George Williams Coll., 1957; M.S. (Lou Hougttellian fellow, Am. Lutheran Ch. fellow), U. Chgo., 1962; postgrad. Loyola U., Chgo., Roosevelt U., Chgo., Forest Inst., Chgo.; m. Patricia Ann Work, Oct. 27, 1972; children—Matthew, Elizabeth, Kimberly, Timothy. Caseworker, Rock County Welfare Dept., Janesville, Wis., 1957-61; area dir. Luth. Family Service Oreg., Eugene, 1962-67; exec. dir. Family Service Travelers Aid, Fort Worth, 1967-70; mgr. agy. ops. Tarrant County United Way, Fort Worth, 1970-73; exec. dir. Luth. Family Service N.W. Ind., Merrillville, 1973-80; exec. v.p. Listening Inc., 1978—; cons. internat. bd. Parents without Partners. Served with U.S. Army, 1958-62. Mem. Nat. Assn. Social Workers (dir. Ind. chpt.), Acad. Cert. Social Workers, Family Service Assn. Am. (dir. 1969), Assn. Marriage and Family Therapists. Author divorce mgmt. materials and newspaper column, profl. manuals; pub. Step Parent News, 1979—. Home and office: 8716 Pine St Gary IN 46403

BENNETT, ROBERT THOMAS, lawyer, accountant; b. Columbus, Ohio, Feb. 8, 1939; s. Frank Edmund and Mary Catherine (Weiland) B.; B.S., Ohio State U., 1960; J.D., Cleve. Marshall Law Sch., 1967; m. Ruth Ann Dooley, May 30, 1959; children—Robert Thomas, Rose Marie. Admitted to Ohio bar, 1967; C.P.A., Ernst and Ernst, Cleve., 1960-63; with tax assessing dept. Cuyahoga County (Ohio) Auditor's Office, Cleve., 1963-70; mem. firm Bartunek, Bennett, Garofoli and Hill, Cleve., 1975-79; mem. firm Bennett & Klonowski, Cleve., 1979—; mem. bd. Cuyahoga County Port Authority, 1974-80. Exec. vice chmn. Cuyahoga County Rep. orgn. Republican. Roman Catholic. Clubs: Cleve. Athletic, Clevelander, Citizens League, Edgewater Yacht, City Club Cleve., Communicators of Cleve.; Capitol Hill (Washington). Contbr. articles to profl. publs. Home: 4800 Valley Pkwy Fairview Park OH 44126 Office: 800 Standard Bldg 1370 Ontario St Cleveland OH 44113

BENNINGTON, DONALD LEE, purchasing agt.; b. Akron, Ohio, Jan. 21, 1936; s. John Olden and Helen Amanda (Herrin) B.; B.A. in Edn., Ariz. State U., 1969; M.A., John Carroll U., 1976; m. 2d, Judith Lynne Mahnke, Apr. 14, 1973; children by previous marriage—Jeanne, Jesse, Jacques, Jonathan, John. Clk., U.S. Postal Service, Akron, 1957; office mgr. Statewide Contractors, Inc., Glendale, Ariz., 1960-64; cost accountant Meyer & Lundahl Mfg. Co., Phoenix, 1964-67; purchasing agent Standard Oil Co. (Ohio), Cleve., 1970—. Served with USN, 1953-57. Mem. Gamma Theta Upsilon. Home: 6020 Opal St North Ridgeville OH 44039

BENNINK, DUANE EARL, assn. exec.; b. Guthrie County, Iowa, July 21, 1935; s. Lawrence D. and Cora M. Bennink; B.S., Iowa State U., 1959; m. Marlene V. Clark, Aug. 24, 1958; children—Karen C., Kathleen J., David D. Vocat. agr. instr. Marathon (Iowa) Consol. Schs., 1959-63; asst. dir. Iowa Soil Conservation Com., Des Moines, 1963-68; cons. N.W. Iowa Farm Bus. Assn., Sheldon, 1968-79; state coordinator Iowa Farm Bus. Assns., Ames, 1979—. Mem. Iowa Soc. Farm Mgrs. and Rural Appraisers, Am. Soc. Farm Mgrs. and Rural Appraisers, Iowa Consultants Assn. (pres. 1975-77), Nat. Assn. Farm Bus. Analysis Specialists (pres. 1979-80), Iowa State U. Alumni Assn. Methodist. Home: 126 Britson Circle Roland IA 50236 Office: Iowa Farm Bus Assns 137 Lynn St Ames IA 50010

BENSCHNEIDER, RICHARD ALLEN, oil co. exec.; b. Ft. Wayne, Ind., Aug. 11, 1935; s. Ervin W. and A. Lucille (Overmyer) B.; student Miami U., Oxford, Ohio, 1953-54; B.S. in Bus. Adminstrn. and Fin., Internat. Coll., 1956; postgrad. Findlay Coll., 1972-73; P.M.D., Harvard Grad. Sch. Bus., 1976; m. Karen B. Jacobsen, Aug. 8, 1980; children by previous marriage—Brian, Beth, Bradley, Robert. With Marathon Oil Co., Findlay, Ohio, 1956, dept. mgr. refining and mktg. acctg.; controller Marathon Pipe Line Co., Findlay, Marathon Internat. Oil Co., Findlay. Pres., Findlay Music Boosters, Inc., 1978-79. Republican. Lutheran. Clubs: Masons, Elks.

BENSHOFF, DIXIE LEE, psychologist; b. Ravenna, Ohio, Apr. 11, 1950; d. Roy Orrison and Pauline (Gatewood) B.; B.A., Hiram Coll., 1972; postgrad. Cambridge (Eng.) U., 1970, 73; M.Ed., Kent State U., 1973, Ph.D., 1977. Counselor, Hiram (Ohio) Coll., 1973; counselor, counseling and group resources center Kent (Ohio) State U., 1973-74, asst. to sch. counseling program for counseling and personnel services edn. dept., 1974-75; asst. dir. Portage County Mental Health Bd., Kent, 1975-78; psychologist, outpatient dir. Kevin Coleman Mental Health Center, Kent, 1978-81; instr. clin. psychology/family medicine Coll. Medicine, Northeastern Ohio U., 1979—; pres. Portage County Council Health and Social Agys., 1980; dir. transitional services Western Res. Human Services, Akron, Ohio, 1980—; cons. Family Practice Center, Akron City Hosp. Lic. psychologist, Ohio. Mem. Am. Personnel and Guidance Assn., Am. Psychol. Assn., Ohio Psychol. Assn., Assn. Orthopsychiatry, Am. Assn. Marriage and Family Therapists, Nat. Council Tchrs. of English, Nat. Orgn. Legal Problems in Edn., Ohio Assn. Admissions Counselors, Kappa Delta Pi. Contbr. articles in field to profl. jours. Home: 231 Beecher Ave Ravenna OH 44266 Office: Western Reserve Human Services 377 S Portage Path Akron OH 44320 also 1640 Franklin Ave Suite 202 Kent OH 44240

BENSLEY, LOREN B., JR., educator; b. Traverse City, Mich., Apr. 6, 1935; s. Loren B. and Dorothy Helen (Holliday) B.; B.S. in Edn., Central Mich. U., 1958; M.S. in Edn., So. Ill. U., 1959; Ed.D., Boston U., 1969; m. Aug. 9, 1958; children—James, Robert, Karie, William. Tchr. secondary sch., public schs., Portsmouth, N.H., 1959-62; instr. health edn. and health sci. Central Mich. U., 1962-66, asst. prof., 1966-70, asso. prof., 1970-74, prof., 1974—; cons. in field. Leader local Cub Scout Pack, Boy Scouts Am.; parent rep. on local sch. coms. Recipient Disting. Service award Mich. Assn. Sch. Nurses, 1980, Central Mich. U. Dept. Health Edn. and Health Sci., 1981; named Outstanding Tchr., Central Mich. U., 1969. Mem. Am. Sch. Health Assn. (editorial bd. jour. 1976-79, Disting. Service award 1980), Am. Assn. Advancement Health Edn. (editorial bd. Health Edn. 1973-76), Mich. Sch. Health Assn. (Disting. Service award 1981), Eta Sigma Gamma. Contbr. chpts., articles to profl. publs. Office: Pearce 110 Central Mich U Mount Pleasant MI 48859

BENSON, CHRISTINA JANE, registered nurse, educator; b. Gnadenhutten, Ohio, Feb. 25, 1951; d. John Paul and Thelma Elizabeth (Miller-Jones) B.; B.S.N., Ohio State U., 1972; M.S.N., Pa. State U., 1979. Staff nurse Ohio State U. Hosps., Columbus, 1973; psychiat. nursing instr. St. Thomas Hosp. Sch. Nursing, Akron, Ohio, 1973-74; asst. prof. Kent State U. Sch. Nursing, 1974—. Mem. Am. Nurses Assn., Phi Kappa Phi, Sigma Theta Tau. Methodist. Office: Kent State Univ Sch Nursing Kent OH 44242

BENSON, DENNIS KEITH, research cons.; b. Dayton, Ohio, Dec. 20, 1946; s. Charles Prue and Virginia Elizabeth (Zindorf) B.; B.A., Miami U., 1969; M.A. (fellow), Ohio State U., 1972, Ph.D. (fellow), 1976; m. Rose Anne Fredericks, Aug. 30, 1969; 1 son, Kristopher Elliott. Simulation dir. behavioral scis. lab., Ohio State U., Columbus, 1969-73, survey research dir., 1972-73, dep. dir., 1971-73, project dir. Coll. Social Work, 1977; asso. dir. Benchmark program Acad. for Contemporary Problems, Columbus, 1973-74, dir., 1974-75; v.p., treas. C. C. DeJon, Ltd., Columbus, 1976-78; project dir. Capital U., Columbus, 1977-78; pres., chmn. bd. dirs. Appropriate Solutions, Inc., 1978—; cons. in field. Bd. trustees, corr. sec. N.W. Civic Assn., 1972-73; state issues coordinator Ohio Carter Campaign Staff, 1976; mem., chmn. com. Central Ohio Bicentennial Commn., 1975-76. Fellow, Acad. for Contemporary Problems, 1974-75, Nat. Security Edn. Seminar, 1972. Mem. Am. Assn. for Pub. Opinion Research, Am. Soc. for Public Adminstrn., Am. Mgmt. Assn., Ohio, U.S. Capital hist. socs., Nat. Space Inst., Columbus Bus. Devel. Club (past pres.). Democrat. Mem. Am. Bapt. Ch. Author: A Guide to Survey Research Terms, 1975; Social Area Analysis and State Social Policy Management, 1976; A Needs Assessment Survival Kit, 1978; Voluntary Service: A Study of Potential, 1979. Contbg. author: Simulation and Games, 1972, 73; contbr. articles to profl. jours. Home: 94 W Hubbard Ave Columbus OH 43215 Office: 1357 W Lane Ave Suite 207 Columbus OH 43221

BENSON, DOROTHY ANN DURICK (MRS. ROBERT BRONAUGH BENSON), psychologist, business exec.; b. Grand Forks, N.D.; d. William James and Grace (Johnson) Durick; B.S. with distinction, U. N.Mex., 1950; M.A. in Psychology, U. Minn., 1952; m. Robert Bronaugh Benson, May 8, 1954. Research asst. psychology dept., U. Minn., 1950-52; instr., counselor Student Counseling Service, Kans. State Coll., 1952-54; psychometrist, counselor Stephens Coll., 1957-58; officer Benson Bldg. Materials, Inc., Columbia, Mo., 1958—; partner of Koti Krafts from Finland. Active mem. League of Women Voters, Columbia, 1955—, bd. dirs., 1955-61, pres., 1958-59; mem. exec. bd. U. Mo. YWCA, 1962-64. Mem. Phi Kappa Phi, Psi Chi, Phi Sigma. Home: PO Box 3 Columbia MO 65205 Office: Benson Bldg Materials Inc 710 Business Loop 70 W PO Box 3 Columbia MO 65205

BENSON, DUANE DEAN, farmer, state senator; b. Belmond, Iowa, Aug. 5, 1945; s. Dale Floyd and Hazel Mae B.; B.A., Hamline U.; m. Melissa Donehower, June 22, 1968; children—Brooke, Jess. Profl. athlete, 1967-77; farmer, Lanesboro, Minn., 1973—; mem. Minn. State Senate, 1981—. Republican. Office: 131 State Office Bldg Saint Paul MN 55155*

BENSON, EDWARD, prison adminstr.; b. Edina, Liberia, Feb. 8, 1930; s. Joseph A. and Mary A. (Mitchell) B.; B.S., Mich. State U., 1957, M.B.A., 1969, M. Labor and Indsl. Relations, 1971, Ph.D., 1974; M.F., Syracuse (N.Y.) U., 1962; m. Sadye M. Houchins, Dec. 21, 1957; children—Edward L. II, Shaun H. Cons. to Liberian Govt., 1958-60; asso. prof. forestry resources U. Liberia, 1962-64, dean U. Liberia, also co-mgr. UN project, 1964-67; asso. dir. Lansing (Mich.) OEO Human Services Program, 1967-70; research asst. internat. programs Mich. State U., 1969, Indsl. Relations Research Assn., 1971-75, Am. Acad. Polit. and Social Sci., 1971-75; cons., program exec. State of Mich., 1970-74; adminstr. human resources dept. City of Highland Park, Mich., 1974-76; adminstrv. officer Northville (Mich.) Regional Psychiat. Hosp., 1976-80; prison adminstr., Jackson, Mich., 1980—. Pres. bd. dirs. Highland Park Sr. Serenity House, 1976; mem. Mich. Tri-County Regional Manpower Planning Council, 1972-74: ex-officio mem. Lansing Model Cities Policy Bd. and Econ. Planning Task Force, 1972-74; mem. adv. com. substance abuse Wayne County Bd. Commnrs., 1975-76. Mem. Am. Soc. Public Adminstrn. (br. treas. 1968), Am. Soc. Planning Ofcls., Kappa Delta Lambda, Alpha Phi Alpha. Episcopalian. Clubs: Rotary (pres. elect Highland Park chpt. 1975), Masons. Home: 2725 Fireside Dr Lansing MI 48912 Office: 4000 Cooper St Jackson MI 49201

BENSON, ELIZABETH JEAN, dating service exec.; b. Williamson, W.Va., June 11, 1944; d. Thomas Jefferson Bluebaum and Ollie Mae (Moore) Bluebaum Walker (stepfather) Charles B. Walker; m. Wallace Ernest Gall, Dec. 23, 1974. Owner, dir. Chicagoland Register, dating service, Chgo., 1974—; cooking instr. Elizabeth Benson Internat. Cooking Lessons, 1978—; owner Ethnic Party People Catering, 1981—. Home and Office: 6314 N Troy St Chicago IL 60645

BENSON, JAMES LLOYD, banker; b. Bruce, Wis., May 9, 1931; s. Amiel G. and Ethel S. Benson; B.S. in Agrl. Edu., U. Wis., River Falls, 1959; m. Sylvia V. Miniatt, Mar. 14, 1959; children—James A., Susan A. Instr. vocat. agr. Waunakee High Sch., 1959-60; foreman North Star Dairies, 1960-64; br. mgr. Fed. Land Bank Assn., Barron, Wis., 1964-68; county extension agt. U. Wis., Burnett County, 1968-69; county supr. Farm Home Adminstrn., Baldwin, Wis., 1969-72; mgr. Fed. Land Bank Assn., River Falls, 1972-76; v.p., assn. ops. div. Fed. Land Bank St. Paul, 1976—. Served with AUS, 1952-55. Mem. Am. Mgmt. Assn. Congregationalist. Clubs: Masons, Shriners. Home: 1020 Hazel St River Falls WI 54022 Office: 375 Jackson St Saint Paul MN 55101

BENSON, JOSEPH, librarian; b. Chgo., Oct. 9, 1919; s. Charles Edward and Fae (Pritchett) B.; student Wright Jr. Coll., 1947-48; M.A., U. Chgo., 1955; m. Martha J. Kloo, May 24, 1968. Asst. librarian Nat. Soc. Crippled Children and Adults, Chgo., 1951, Wright Jr. Coll., 1951-56; librarian Municipal Reference Library, Chgo., 1956-67, Joint Reference Library of Pub. Administrn. Service, Chgo., 1967-74, Chgo. Transit Authority, 1974—; mem. Commn. on Chgo. Archtl. Landmarks, 1957—; mem. Ill. State Library Adv. Com., 1972-79; affiliates adv. council Chgo. Library System, 1979—, chmn., 1980-81; v.p. bd. dirs. Ill. Regional Library Council, 1971-76; mem. nat. users council Online Computer Library Center. Mem. Am. Soc. Pub. Adminstrn. (pres. Chgo. chpt. 1960-61), Spl. Libraries Assn. (nat. chmn. social sci. div. 1961-62), Am. Assn. Law Libraries (past nat. treas., pres. Chgo. chpt.). Club: Arts. Author various articles pub. in profl. jours. Home: 1366 E Madison Park Chicago IL 60615 Office: Chgo Transit Authority Mdse Mart Chicago IL 60654

BENSON, LAWRENCE EDWARD, ins. co. exec.; b. Mpls., July 31, 1916; s. Linus Edward and Hilma Agnita (Olausson) B.; student Bethel Coll., 1936-37; B.S., U. Minn., 1939; m. Phyllis Elaine Newman, Aug. 23, 1941; children—Laurel, Natalie, Lois, Philip, Kjersti. Underwriter, Employers of Wausau, Mpls., 1940-48; underwriting mgr. Federated Mut. Ins. Co., Owatonna, Minn., 1948-50; underwriting mgr. Mut. Service Ins. Co., St. Paul, 1950-56, dir. underwriting, 1956-61, dir. casualty actuarial dept., 1961-72, v.p. personnel, 1972-76, v.p. casualty, 1976—; dir., chmn. Minn. Ins. Guaranty Fund, Minn. FAIR Plan. Bd. mgmt. YMCA, Mpls., 1955-72, chmn., 1964-66; bd. regents Bethel Coll. and Sem., St. Paul, 1959-64, treas., 1960-62, vice chmn., 1962-64, mem. bd. President's Assos., 1967—; mem. Minn. Central Republican Com., 1966-69; bd. dirs. United Way, St. Paul, 1973-80. Served with U.S. Army, 1942-46. Recipient service award YMCA, 1963, Bethel Coll. and Sem., 1965, Minn. Central Rep. Com., 1966, also various PTA's; cert. Life Office Mgmt. Assn. Mem. Soc. C.P.C.U.'s (cert.), Am. Acad. Actuaries (cert.), Am. Swedish Inst. Republican. Baptist. Club: Midland Hills Country. Contbr. to ins. publs.

BENSON, PAUL, fed. judge; b. Verona, N.D., June 1, 1918; s. Edwin C. and Annie (Peterson) B.; B.S.C., U. N.D., 1942; LL.B., George Washington U., 1949; m. Dec. 29, 1942; children—Santal E. Manos, Polly Benson Diem, Amy Laurel L., Peter. Admitted to N.D. bar; adminstrv. asst. to Senator Milton R. Young, 1946-49; asso. firm H.B. Spiller and Cavalier, 1949-50; mem. firm Shaft, Benson, Shaft and McConn, 1950-71; atty. gen. State of N.D., 1954-55; now chief judge U.S. Dist. Ct., Dist. N.D., Fargo. Tchr. U. N.D. Chmn. Grand Forks County chpt. ARC, 1954-55. Served with USNR, 1942-46. Mem. Am. Bar Assn., Am. Judicature Soc., State Bar Assn. N.D., Am. Legion, V.F.W. Lutheran (pres. congregation Grand Forks 1959). Clubs: Masons, Shriners, Elks. Office: 340 Federal Bldg PO Box 3164 US Courthouse Fargo ND 58102*

BENSON, WARREN STEN, educator; b. Chgo., Aug. 23, 1929; s. Sten Walter and Evelyn Gladys (Arneson) B.; B.A., Northwestern Coll., 1952; Th.M., Dallas Theol. Sem., 1956; M.R.E., Southwestern Bapt. Theol. Sem., 1957; Ph.D., Loyola U., Chgo., 1975; m. Lenore Evelyn Ellis, Aug. 22, 1953; children—Scott Warren, Bruce Ellis. Minister of edn. Winnetka (Ill.) Bible Ch., 1957-62, Lake Ave. Congl. Ch., Pasadena, Calif., 1965-69; minister youth and edn. First Covenant Ch., Mpls., 1962-65; asso. prof. Christian edn. Dallas Thel. Sem., 1974-78; mem. faculty Trinity Evangelical Div. Sch., Deerfield, Ill., 1978—, v.p. acad. adminstrn., 1981—, prof. Christian edn., 1978—; ordained to ministry Ind. Ch., 1959; cons. Gospel Light Publs., 1959—. Mem. Evangelical Theol. Soc., Nat. Assn. Profs. Christian Edn., Midwest History Edn. Soc. Republican. Mem. Evangelical Free Ch. Author: Youth Education in the Church, 1978. Home: 714 Arthur Ct Libertyville IL 60048 Office: 2065 Half Day Rd Deerfield IL 60015

BENTHIN, KEITH VINCENT, civil engr.; b. Thomas, S.D., Apr. 9, 1930; s. Roy S. and Edith V. (Tetzlaf) B.; B.S.C.E., S.D. State U., 1953; m. Avis M. Henderson, Mar. 17, 1956; children—Steven, Michael, Sharon, Douglas. Various engring. positions Minn. Dept. Transp., St. Paul, 1953—, project engr., 1957-65, resident engr., 1965-69, bridge standards engr., 1969-73, state bridge engr., 1973—. Active boy Scouts Am., 1970-75. Served with USN, 1949. Registered profl. engr., Minn. Mem. Am. Assn. State Hwy. and Transp. Ofcls., Transp. Research Bd., ASCE, Minn. Soc. Civil Engrs. (dir. 1977—), Minn. Surveyors and Engrs. Soc., Minn. Govt. Engrs. Council. Lutheran. Clubs: Masons, Shriners. Home: 1768 Pinehurst Ave Saint Paul MN 55116 Office: Minn Dept Transp Transp Bldg St Paul MN 55155

BENTLAGE, RICHARD AUGUST, educator; b. Indpls., June 26, 1936; s. Kurt Fred and Marie (Rossi) B.; grad. summa cum laude Elkhart U., 1955; pre-med. student Ind. U., 1955-58; m. Betty Lynn Thompson, Sept. 6, 1980. Adminstrv. asst. disaster relief ARC, Indpls., 1955-56; X-ray technologist radiol./nuclear St. Vincent's Hosp., Indpls., 1956-57; med./X-ray technologist and dept. head Morgan Health Center, Indpls., 1957-58; med. research technologist, med./surg. staff VA Hosp., Indpls., 1958-61; med. technologist, med. staff White County Meml. Hosp., Monticello, Ind., 1961-64, lab. supr., dept. head, 1964-75; exec. dir. Youth Service Bur. White County, Monticello, 1976-80, coordinator child protection service team, 1978-80; profl. asst. dept. pathology Purdue U., 1980—; cons. microbiologist Ind. Bd. Health; cons., lectr. in field. Treas., Yeoman PTA, 1974-76; mem. adv. bd. Parents Without Partners, Nat. Network of Runaway Youth. Served in USNR, 1953-61. Mem. Am. Med. Technologists, Am., Ind. socs. med. technologists, Nat. Assn. Prevention Profls., Pub. Offender Councilors Assn., Assn. Specialists in Group Work, Am. Personnel and Guidance Assn., Ind. Youth Services Assn., Confrat. Christian Doctrine (cert. instr.), Pi Rho Zeta (life). Roman Catholic. Home: 905 Woodmere Dr Lafayette IN 47905 Office: Purdue U Botany and Plant Pathology Lilly Life Sci Bldg West Lafayette IN 47907

BENTLEY, JAMES HERBERT, elec. engr.; b. Portland, Oreg., May 23, 1935; s. Robert Athy and Helen Louise (Niles) B.; B.S. in Elec. Engring., Mich. Tech. U., 1957; M.S. in Elec. Engring. (Hughes Fellow), U. So. Calif., 1959; m. Elizabeth Anne Willard, Aug. 19, 1958; children—Mary Katherine, John Robert. Elec. engr. Hughes Aircraft Co., Los Angeles, 1957-59, Philco Corp., Palo Alto, Calif.,

1960-64, Bendix Corp., Washington, 1964-65, Univac, St. Paul, 1965-68, Honeywell, Inc., Mpls., 1968-76, 3M Co., St. Paul, 1976-79, Magnetic Peripherals, Inc., Mpls., 1979; dir. Ecology Enterprises, Inc.; adj. prof. elec. engring. U. Minn., Mpls. Mem. Edina Planning Commn.; past chmn. Edina Environ. Quality Commn., 1975-76; mem. exec. com. Dist. 39, Republican Party. Recipient Mayor's commendation award City of Edina, 1976; registered profl. engr., Minn. Mem. Nat., Minn. socs. profl. engrs., IEEE, Tau Beta Pi, Eta Kappa Nu. Presbyterian. Home: 5120 Grove St Edina MN 55436 Office: 7801 Computer Ave Minneapolis MN 55435

BENTLEY, JANICE BABB, librarian; b. Phila., Jan. 13, 1933; d. John William and Janice (Whittier) Babb; A.B., U. Ill., 1954, M.S., 1956; Dir. dept. information Nat. Assn. of Real Estate Bds., Chgo., 1956-63; librarian CNA Financial Corp., Chgo., 1963-76, firm Mayer, Brown & Platt, Chgo., 1976—. Mem. Am. Assn. Law Librarians, Am. Soc. Information Sci. (sec.-treas. Chgo. area chpt. 1963-64, 71-72), Chgo. Assn. Law Libraries (pres. 1978-79), Spl. Libraries Assn. (chmn. housing bldg. and planning sect. 1962-63, chmn. social sci. div. 1965-66, pres. Ill. chpt. 1967-68, chmn. ins. div. 1974-75). Illiniweks (chmn. Chgo. 1959). Author: (with Beverly F. Dordick) Real Estate Information Sources, 1963, Real Estate Appraisal Bibliography, 1965. Home: 1825 N Lincoln Plaza Chicago IL 60614 Office: 231 S LaSalle St Chicago IL 60604

BENTLEY, LAUREL PALESTINE, motel and restaurant exec.; b. Oran, Iowa, Aug. 26, 1917; s. Burton Fay and Mollie Mary (Williams) B.; B.S.C., U. Iowa, 1938; spl. course Iowa State U., 1941; m. Phyllis Marie Lichty, Aug. 9, 1950; children—P. Dawn Bentley Pollitt, Philip Laurel. Sec., B.F. Bentley-Gilt Edge Creamery Co., Plainfield, Iowa, 1938-44; sales trainee Standard Oil Co., Mason City, Iowa, 1946-47; sales rep. to sales mgr. Louden Machinery Co., Fairfield, Iowa, 1947-60; regional mgr. bldgs. and equipment Honeggers & Co., Fairbury, Ill., 1961-63; mfrs. rep., 1963-72; owner, operator Dream Motel, Fairfield, 1972—, Stever House Restaurant, Fairfield, 1976—. Active Boy Scouts Am.; precinct caucus chmn. Jefferson County Republican Party, 1980; fin. chmn. Jefferson County Rep. Central Com., 1980. Served with USNR, 1945-46. Mem. Barn Equipment Assn. (v.p. 1960), Iowa Hotel and Motel Assn. (pres. 1978-79, 79-80, chmn. bd. 1980-81), Am. Hotel and Motel Assn. Clubs: Elks, Masons. Home and Office: Dream Motel Hwy 34W Fairfield IA 52556

BENTLEY, THOMAS HORTON, III, constrn. co. exec.; b. Milw., Aug. 3, 1946; s. Thomas Horton and Virginia M. (Zivney) B.; B.S. in Bus. Adminstrn., Bucknell U., 1969; m. Sally Lynne Ross, Oct. 9, 1971. Sec.-treas. Thomas H. Bentley & Son Inc., Milw., 1970—, dir., 1970—, export mgr., export boxing div., 1969—; bd. dirs., chmn. legis. com. Associated Gen. Contractors, Milw. chpt., 1972—, Allied Constrn. Employers Asso., 1974—; chmn. Nat. A.G.C. Legis. Network, Wis., 1974—; vice chmn. City of Milw. Bd. of Standards and Appeals; advisory mem. Law Related Ed. Project of Wis. Bar Found. Mem. Builders Exchange, Asso. Gen. Contractors, Allied Constrn. Employers Assn. Lutheran. Clubs: Town Tennis, Wis., Sons of Bosses Internat. (pres. Milw. chpt. 1979-81), Milw. North Shore Racquet, Milw. Rotary. Office: 3031 W Mill Rd Milwaukee WI 53209

BENTON, PHYLLIS LORETTA, ednl. adminstr.; b. Omaha, July 2, 1918; d. William Carl and Kathryn Maude (Coiner) Wilson; student Christian Coll., Columbia, Mo., 1935-36, U. So. Calif., 1937-38; B.E., Drake U., 1940; M.A., U. Nebr., 1961, Ed.D., 1965; m. Dudley Benton Conner, Feb. 2, 1941 (dec. Nov. 1967); children—Ellen Kay Conner Leonard, Phillip Douglas; m. 2d, Robert E. Benton, Jan. 2, 1980; stepchildren—Robert K., Harry E. Tchr. sr. high sch., Des Moines, 1939-41; tchr. English and speech, Silver City, Iowa, 1945-47; substitute tchr. sr. high schs., several states, 1941-45; teletype operator Western Union, Los Angeles, 1942-43, Standard Oil Co., 1943; worker family hatchery, feed store Malvern, Iowa, 1930-35, 45-57; tchr., jr. high tchr., jr. high sch. counselor, community counselor Omaha Pub. Schs., 1957—; lectr. adult night sch. Past adv. Rainbow Girls, Boy Scouts Am., Girl Scouts U.S.A. Mem. Greater Omaha C. of C. (pres. women's div. 1976), Pilot Internat. (gov. dist. 12 1976), Nebr. State, Omaha edn. assns., Council for Exceptional Children, AAUW, NEA, Omaha Pub. Schs. Adminstrs. Assn., Am. Legion Aux., Omaha Interclub Council (dir. 1971-72), Kappa Alpha Theta. Republican. Methodist. Clubs: Pilot Omaha pres. 1970-72), Order of Eastern Star (worthy matron 1957). Home: 12519 William Omaha NE 68144 Office: 3819 Jones St Omaha NE 68105

BENTON, ROBERT DEAN, state supt. schs.; b. Guthrie Center, Iowa, July 22, 1929; s. John H. and Luella M. (Rawlings) B.; B.A., U. No. Iowa, 1951, M.A., 1956; Ed.D., U. No. Colo., 1961; m. Rachel Swanson, July 29, 1951; children—Camille, John, Scott. Tchr., Ruthven, Iowa, 1953-56, Mason City, Iowa, 1956-58; dir. public info., coordinator secondary edn., Rapid City, S.D., 1958-61, asst. supt. in charge instrn., 1961-66; supt. schs., Council Bluffs, Iowa, 1966-72; state supt. public instrn. State of Iowa, Des Moines, 1972—; part-time journalism tchr. summer sessions Colo. State Coll., 1959-61; mem. Iowa Adv. Council for Vocat. Edn., 1970—; mem. Commn. on Fed. Paperwork, 1975-77; mem. adv. council on nutrition U.S. Dept. Agr., 1975-78; mem. Fed. Edn. Data Acquisition Council, 1979—. Hon. chmn., mem. founding com. Friends of Music Community Concert Series, 1967; bd. dirs. Chanticleer Community Theater, 1968—, Christian Home, 1968—. Served with USMC, 1951-53. Named Boss of yr., Jaycees, Council Bluffs, 1970; Outstanding Young Man of yr., Jr. C. of C., Rapid City, 1965. Mem. NEA, Council of Chief State Sch. Officers (pres. 1981), C. of C., Phi Delta Kappa, Theta Alpha Phi. Methodist. Rotarian. Office: Grimes Office Bldg Des Moines IA 50319

BENTON, ROBERT WILMER, coll. pres.; b. Guthrie Center, Iowa, Aug. 28, 1931; s. Howard Jasper and Nellie Mae (Gustin) B.; B.A., Northwestern Coll., 1955; Th.M., Dallas Theol. Sem., 1959; postgrad. Simpson Coll., 1963-64; Th.D., Grace Theol. Sem., 1968; postgrad. U. Nebr., Lincoln, 1974—; m. Beryl Edna Anderson, Aug. 20, 1955; children—Gregory, Steven, Sharon, Linda. Ordained to minstry Conservative Bapt. Ch., 1959; pastor Martensdale Community Ch., 1959-64, Tippecanoe Community Ch., 1964-67; instr. O.T. Studies, Grace Coll. of the Bible, Omaha, 1967-71, pres., 1971—. County committeeman Republican party, 1962-64; mem. bd. reference Gospel Missionary Union, Smithville, Mo.; mem. adv. bd. World Impact, Omaha; mem. exec. com. Am. Assn. Bible Colls., Fayetteville, Ark. Home: 93 Jennings Rd Council Bluffs IA 51501 Office: 1515 S 10th St Omaha NE 68108

BENZ, LEO CLARENCE, agrl. engr.; b. Dunn Center, N.D., Jan. 5, 1923; s. Frank Lawrence and Barbara (Unterseher) B.; B.S., N.D. State U., 1952, M.S., 1957; m. Louise Josephine Kyllo, Aug. 19, 1951; children—Linda L., Paul C., Bruce F., L. Jon. Plumbing and irrigation design and sales engr., Shirley Onstad Inc., Fargo, N.D., 1952-53; soil and water conservation engr. U.S. Dept. Interior, Bur. Indian Affairs, Fort Yates, N.D., 1953-56; agrl. engr. USDA Agrl. Research, Mandan, N.D., 1957—. Served with USN, 1943-46; PTO. Recipient Merit cert. USDA, 1958. Registered profl. engr., N.D. Mem. Nat. Soc. Profl. Engrs., Am. Soc. Agrl. Engrs., Am. Geophys. Union, Soil Conservation Soc. Am. Research and numerous publs. on agrl. drainage and irrigation, also reclamation of Saline Soils. Home: 1407 N 23d St Bismarck ND 58501 Office: Box 459 ND Hwy 6 S Mandan ND 58554

BENZON, HONORIO TABAL, anesthesiologist; b. Ilocos Sur, Philippines, Sept. 12, 1946; came to U.S., 1972, s. Alejo Gonzales and Concepcion Tacto (Tabal) B.; B.S., Far Eastern U., Manila, 1966, M.D., 1971; m. Julieta Palpal-latoc, May 30, 1970; children—Barbara Hazel, Hubert Anthony. Intern, Overlook Hosp., Summit, N.J., 1972-73; resident in anesthesia U. Cin. Med. Center, 1973-75, Northwestern U. affiliated hosps., 1975-76; practice medicine specializing in anesthesiology, Chgo., 1976—; asso. dept. anesthesia Northwestern U. Med. Sch., 1976-80, asst. prof., 1980—; asso. staff Northwestern Meml. Hosp., 1976—; asso. dir. Pain Clinic dept. anesthesia, attending staff VA Lakeside Hosp., 1976—; cons. staff Rehab. Inst. Chgo. Diplomate Am. Bd. Anesthesiology. Fellow Am. Coll. Anesthesiologists; mem. AMA, Am. Soc. Anesthesiologists, Internat. Anesthesia Research Soc., Am. Soc. Regional Anesthesia. Roman Catholic. Contbr. numerous articles to med. jours., chpts. to books. Home: 1150 White Mountain Dr Northbrook IL 60062 Office: 303 E Chicago Ave Chicago IL 60611

BERARD, MARJORIE NELSON, health care adminstr.; b. Chippewa Falls, Wis., Aug. 15, 1918; d. Eli William and Emily (Picotte) Nelson; B.A., Coll. St. Benedict, 1940; M.S. in Social Work, St. Louis U., 1942; m. Celse A. Berard, Oct. 5, 1943; children—Sister Maryann, Michele Berard Reardon, Suzanne Berard Parks, Celse A., Renee, Elise, Jeanne. Social worker, dept. of children Cath. Charities of St. Louis, 1941-69; psychiat. social worker, community mental health clinic St. Louis State Hosp., also outpatient clinic St. Francis Mercy Hosp., 1966-74; founder, exec. dir. Profl. Counseling Center, Inc., New Haven, Mo., 1972-78; founder, adminstr. Profl. Home Health Services, Inc., New Haven, 1978—; cons. med. social work to community orgns. Mo. Div. Health grantee, 1974. Mem. Acad. Cert. Social Workers, Nat. Assn. Social Workers (named Social Worker of Yr., Mo. chpt. 1981), Mo. Assn. Social Workers (Social Worker of Yr. award 1981), Nat. Assn. Home Health Agys., Mo. Assn. Home Health Agys., Soc. Hosp. Social Work Dirs. Am. Hosp. Assn., Soc. Hosp. Social Work Dirs. Mo. Hosp. Assn. Roman Catholic. Home: 1508 1st Pkwy Washington DC 63090 Office: Profl Home Health Services Inc 101 Arizona St New Haven MO 63068

BERARDI, ANTHONY LOUIS, psychologist; b. Youngstown, Ohio, Apr. 9, 1945; s. Anthony Domenic and Rose Marie (Nolfi) B.; B.A., U. Notre Dame, 1968; M.S., Ohio U., 1974, Ph.D., 1976; m. Patricia Ann Halasi, May 24, 1969; children—Jessica Erin, Jonathan Paul. Clin. intern Inst. Psychiatry, Northwestern U. Med. Sch., 1975-76; staff clin. psychologist Mental Health Center St. Joseph County, South Bend, Ind., 1976-79; clin. psychologist Family Learning Center, South Bend, 1979—; cons. clin. psychologist Child Abuse and Neglect Coordinating Orgn., South Bend, 1978—; adj. asst. prof. dept. psychology Ind. U., South Bend, 1977—; vol. mem. St. Joseph County Welfare Dept. Child Protection Team, South Bend, 1979—. Served to capt. U.S. Army, 1968-72; Vietnam. Decorated Bronze Star medal. Cert. psychologist, Ind. Mem. Am. Psychol. Assn., Ind. Psychol. Assn. Democrat. Roman Catholic. Home: 1809 Portage Ave South Bend IN 46616 Office: 1513 Miami St South Bend IN 46613

BERBERIAN, H. NICHOLAS, lawyer; b. Phila., Dec. 27, 1952; s. Nicholas H. and Kay (Hamparian) B.; A.B., Kenyon Coll., 1974; M.B.A., U. Chgo., 1975, J.D., 1978; m. Nancy A. Mikaelian. Asst. to dir. research Freehling & Co., Chgo., 1975; mgmt. cons. intern Ernst & Ernst, Chgo., 1975; admitted to Ill. bar, 1978, U.S. Dist. Ct., No. Dist. Ill., 1978; asso. firm Friedman & Koven, Chgo., 1976—; instr. fin. and acctg. Northeastern U., Chgo., 1977—. Chmn. Chgo. admissions program Kenyon Coll. Mem. Am. Bar Assn., Ill. Bar Assn., Chgo. Bar Assn., Omicron Delta Epsilon. Home: 333 E Ontario St Apt 1705B Chicago IL 60611 Office: 208 S LaSalle St Chicago IL 60604

BERDAHL, CLARENCE ARTHUR, educator; b. Baltic, S.D., June 14, 1890; s. Anders J. and Karen (Otterness) B.; A.B., St. Olaf Coll. 1914, LL.D., 1958; A.M., U. S.D., 1917, LL.D., 1961; Ph.D. (fellow), U. Ill., 1920; m. Evelyn Tripp, June 9, 1926. Cik. archives div. War Dept., Washington, 1914-15; asst. in periodicals div. Library of Congress, 1916; instr. polit. sci. U. Ill., 1920-22, asso., 1922-25, asst. prof., 1925-29, asso. prof., 1929-30, prof., 1930-61, prof. emeritus dept. polit sci., 1961—, chmn. div. social scis., 1935-39, chmn. dept. polit. sci., 1942-48; tchr. summers U. Tex., 1920, Tulane U., 1921, Ohio State U., 1923, U. Colo., 1928, Syracuse U., 1929, Columbia U., 1934, Stanford U., 1950; lectr. L'Institut Universitaire de Hautes Etudes Internationales, Geneva, 1932; vis. prof. govt. So. Ill. U., 1958-67; vis. prof. polit. sci. U. Del., 1965; chmn. bd. editors Ill. Studies in Social Scis., 1941-52; cons. U.S. Dept. State 1942-45; on London staff Office Strategic Services, 1944; mem. Internat. Secretariat, UN Conf., San Francisco, 1945; adv. com. on fgn. relations Dept. State, 1957-64, chmn., 1963-64, cons. hist. office, summer 1961; mem. exec. com. Commn. To Study Orgn. of Peace, 1953—; mem. European Conf. Tchrs. Internat. Law and Relations, Carnegie Endowment for Internat. Peace, summer 1926. Served in inf. U.S. Army, 1918. Social Sci. Research Council grantee for study abroad, 1931-32. Mem. Am. Polit. Sci. Assn. (exec. council 1932-35, 3d v.p. 1939, 2d v.p. 1944), Norwegian-Am. Hist. Assn., Am. Soc. Pub. Adminstrn. (council 1944-47), Ill. Hist. Soc., Midwest Polit. Sci. Assn. (pres. 1957-58), Am. Soc. Internat. Law (exec. council 1939-42, 43-46, 52-54), Fgn. Policy Assn., Soc. Advancement of Scandinavian Study, Geneva Research Center (adv. com. 1932-36), Conf. Tchrs. Internat. Law and Related Subjects (exec. com. 1933-42, 47-50), Internat. Studies Assn. (adv. com. 1965-69), Phi Beta Kappa (book award com. Ralph Waldo Emerson award 1966-68). Clubs: Univ., Cosmos (Washington). Author or co-author books including: War Powers of the Executive in the United States, 1921; The Policy of the United States with Respect to the League of Nations, 1932; Aspects of American Government, 1950; Toward a More Responsible Two-Party System, 1950; Presidential Nominating Politics, 1952; also articles. Home: Clark-Lindsey Village 101 W Windsor Rd Apt 4105 Urbana IL 61801

BERE, JAMES FREDERICK, mfg. co. exec.; b. Chgo., July 25, 1922; s. Lambert Sr. and Madeline (Van Tatenhove) B.; student Calvin Coll., 1940-42; B.S., Northwestern U., 1946, M.B.A., 1950; m. Barbara Van Dellen, June 27, 1947; children—Robert Paul, James Frederick, David Lambert, Lynn Barbara, Becky Ann. With Clearing Machine Corp. div. U.S. Industries, Inc., 1946-53, gen. mgr. Clearing Machine Corp., 1953-56, gen. mgr. Axelson Mfg. Co. div., 1956, pres., 1957-61; pres., gen. mgr. Borg & Beck div. Borg-Warner Corp., Chgo., 1961-64, group v.p. 1964-66, exec. v.p. automotive, 1966-68, pres. corp., 1968-75, chief exec. officer, 1972—, chmn. bd., 1975—; dir. Abbott Labs., North Chicago, Continental Ill. Nat. Bank & Trust Co. of Chgo., Continental Ill. Corp. Served as lt. AUS, 1943-45. Mem. Am. Mgmt. Assn., Alpha Tau Omega. Office: Borg-Warner Corp 200 S Michigan Ave Chicago IL 60604

BERENS, LAWRENCE PENINGTON, hosp. adminstr.; b. N.Y.C., June 24, 1943; s. Conrad and Frances Penington (Cookman) B.; B.A., U. N.D., 1969; M.B.A., U. Chgo., 1971; m. Ann Benning Baxter, July 10, 1968; children—Hope Brockett, Amy Lawrence, Emily Wharton, Brooke Van Alstyne. Summer adminstr. Michael Reese Hosp. Med. Center, Chgo., 1970; adminstrv. asst. U. Chgo. Hosp. and Clinics, 1971-72; asst. adminstr. Christ Hosp., Oaklawn, Ill., 1972-75; adminstr. div. medicine Cleve. Clinic Found., Cleve., 1976—; cons. long range planning and health care mgmt.; mem. faculty Webster Coll. Grad. Level Health Facilities. Commodore No. Ohio sea scouts program Boy Scouts Am. Served with USAF, 1964-68. Ray Brown fellow, 1969-70. Mem. Am. Acad. Med. Adminstrs., Am. Coll. Hosp. Adminstrs., Am. Coll. Med. Group Adminstrs., Am. Hosp. Assn., Hosp. Fin. Mgmt. Assn., Hosp. Mgmt. Systems Soc., Internat. Hosp. Fedn., Ill., Ohio hosp. assns., Med. Group Mgmt. Assn., Ohio Med. Group Mgmt. Assn., Pan Am. Health Orgn., Soc. for Computer Medicine, Univ. Med. Practice Adminstrs., Adminstrs. Internal Medicine (founder, dir.), Health Care Adminstrs. Assn. N.E. Ohio (dir.), Greater Cleve. Coalition on Health Care Cost Effectiveness. Clubs: Mentor Harbor Yachting, Shaker Heights Country. Home: Pennhouse 18710 S Woodland Shaker Heights OH 44122 Office: Cleveland Clinic Found 9500 Euclid Ave Cleveland OH 44106

BERENSON, GORDON ARTHUR, profl. hockey player; b. Regina, Sask., Can., Dec. 8, 1939; s. Otto Arthur and Marjorie Patricia (Traynor) B.; B.B.A., U. Mich., 1962, M.B.A., 1966; m. Joy Gwendolyn Cameron, Sept. 5, 1959; children—Kelly, Sandy, Gordie, Rusty. Profl. hockey player Montreal Canadiens, 1962-65, N.Y. Rangers, 1965-67, St. Louis Blues, 1967-71, 75-78, Detroit Red Wings, 1971-75; asst. coach St. Louis Blues, 1979-80, head coach, 1980—. Address: 5700 Oakland Ave St Louis MO 63110

BERETVAS, ANDREW FRANCIS, physicist; b. Los Angeles, Sept. 11, 1939; s. Andor and Helen M. (Sellei) B.; B.S., U. Chgo., 1960, M.S., 1962, Ph.D., 1968. Research asst. Fermi Inst., U. Chgo., 1963-67; asst. prof. physics State U. N.Y., Buffalo, 1968-74; computer cons. U. Chgo., 1974-75; research asso. high energy physics Northwestern U., Evanston, Ill., 1975-76, Argonne (Ill.) Nat. Lab., 1976-77, Fermi Nat. Lab., 1977-78, Rutgers U., 1978—. Mem. Am. Phys. Soc. Address: 6101 N Sheridan Rd Chicago IL 60660

BEREUTER, DOUGLAS KENT, Congressman; b. York, Nebr., Oct. 6, 1939; s. Rupert and Evelyn B.; B.A., U. Nebr., 1961; M.C.P., Harvard U., 1966, M.P.A., 1973; postgrad. Eagleton Inst. Politics, 1975; m. Louise Anna Meyer, 1962; children—Eric David, Kirk Daniel. Residential and comml. devel. cons.; div. dir. Nebr. Dept. Econ. Devel., 1967-68; dir. Nebr. Office Planning and Programming, 1969-71; mem. Nebr. Legislature, 1974-78; mem. 96th Congress from 1st Dist. Nebr. Trustee, Nebr. Wesleyan U. Served to 2d lt. U.S. Army, 1963-65. Mem. Nebr. Crime Commn., 1969-71. Mem. Am. Planning Assn. (dir.), Alumni Assn. John F. Kennedy Sch. Govt. of Harvard U. (exec. council), Phi Beta Kappa. Republican. Office: 1314 Longworth House Office Bldg Washington DC 20515*

BERG, CHARLES, state senator; grad. W. Central Sch. Agr. Farmer; mem. Minn. Senate, 1980—. Mem. Sch. Bd.; bd. dirs. Grace Home, Graceville, Minn. Mem. Minn. Livestock Feeders Assn. (past pres.). Republican. Office: 141 State Office Bldg Saint Paul MN 55155*

BERG, EDNA MARIE, mfg. co. exec.; b. Chgo., Nov. 9, 1906; d. Emil William and Wilhelmina (Adams) B.; student Gregg Bus. Coll., 1921; Stenographer, Reeves Pulley Co., Chgo., 1936-43; sec. J.W. Murphy Co., Chgo., 1943-46; corp. sec. Schrade Batterson Co., Chgo., 1946—. Republican. Lutheran.

BERG, EVELYNNE MARIE, educator; b. Chgo.; d. Clarence Martin and Mildred (Strnad) B.; B.S. with honors, U. Ill., 1954; M.A., Northwestern U., 1959. Geography editor Am. Peoples Ency., Chgo., 1955-57; social studies tchr. Hammond (Ind.) Tech.-Vocat. High Sch., 1958-59; geography tchr. Carl Schurz High Sch., Chgo., 1960-66; faculty geography Morton Coll., Cicero, Ill., 1966—. Asst. leader Cicero council Girl Scouts U.S.A., 1951-53; mem. Greater Chgo. Citizenship Council. Fulbright scholar, Brazil, 1964; NSF scholar, 1963, 65, 71-72; NDEA fellow, 1968-69; fellow Faculty Inst. S. and S.E. Asia, 1980; recipient award Ill. Geog. Soc., 1977. Fellow Nat. Council Geog. Edn. (state coordinator 1973-74, exec. bd. 1973-77); mem. Nat., Ill. (sec.-treas. 1968-69, sec. 1969-70, v.p. 1970-71, pres. 1971-72), De Paul U., Chgo. (exec. bd. 1980-82), geog. socs., Am. Overseas Educators (sec. Ill. chpt. 1974-76, v.p. chpt. 1977-78), AAUW (Chgo. br. rec. sec. 1963-65), Assn. Am. Geographers, Ill., Chgo. acads. sci., AAAS (scholar 1973-74), Nat. Assn. Geology Tchrs., AAUP, Ill. Council Social Studies, Ill. Community Coll. Faculty Assn. (exec. bd.), Sierra Club, Sigma Xi, Gamma Theta Upsilon, Delta Kappa Gamma. Clubs: Order Eastern Star, Bus. and Profl. Women's (acting pres. 1980-81). Contbr. to profl. jours. Home: 3924 N Pioneer Ave Chicago IL 60634 Office: Morton Coll 3801 S Central Ave Cicero IL 60650

BERG, ROBERT STURE, systems analyst; b. Chgo., May 15, 1948; s. Sture John and Josephine Marie (Pitrowski) B.; student U. Ill., Chgo., 1966-68; B.S., U. Ky., 1970. Programmer, U.S. Air Force, Wright Patterson AFB, Ohio, 1970-73, computer specialist, 1973-75; computer specialist VA Hosp., Hines, Ill., 1976; systems analyst Ill. Bell Tel. Co., Chgo., 1976-79; sr. analyst/cons. Gould Inc., Rolling Meadows, Ill., 1979-80; data base analyst/software support Ill. Bell Telephone Co., Chgo., 1980—. Home: 3122 N Clifton Ave Chicago IL 60657 Office: 225 W Randolph St Chicago IL 60606

BERG, SIEGFRIED KURT, electronics engr.; b. Gelsenkirchen, W. Ger., May 4, 1922; s. Adolph Eduard and Ida Hedwig (Matz) B.; came to U.S., 1951, naturalized, 1958; grad. Coll. Behring-Sch., Hohenstein, Ger., 1939, Sch. Communications, Flensburg, Germany, 1941; m. Waltraud Rybak, May 13, 1952. Founder, owner Deutscher Rundfunk Chgo., German radio broadcasting, 1952—, interviewer, program dir., 1952-68; owner Orbit Printing and Advt. Service, Chgo., 1963-68; engring. constrn. technician GTE Automatic Electric, Northlake, Ill., 1968-73, process engr., 1973-77, test engr., 1977—; program dir. Deutscher Rundfunk Chgo. Cert. mfg. technologist Soc. Mfg. Engrs.; cert. profl. mcht. Mem. IEEE. Lutheran. Clubs: Rheinischer Verein, Schlaraffia (Chgo.). Work included Blue Book Am. Photography, 1971-72. Home: 2124 W Giddings St Chicago IL 60625 Office: GTE Automatic Electric E-6 Northlake IL 60164

BERG, STANTON ONEAL, firearms and ballistics cons.; b. Barron, Wis., June 14, 1928; s. Thomas C. and Ellen Florence (Nedland) Silbaugh; student U. Wis., 1949-50; LL.B., LaSalle Extension U., 1951; postgrad. U. Minn., 1960-69; m. June K. Rolstad, Aug. 16, 1952; children—David M., Daniel L., Susan E., Julie L. Claim rep. State Farm Ins. Co., Mpls., Hibbing and Duluth, Minn., 1952-57, claim supt., 1957-66, divisional claim supt., 1966-70; firearms cons., Mpls., 1961—; regional mgr. State Farm Fire and Casualty Co., St. Paul, 1970—; bd. dirs. Am. Bd. Forensic Firearm and Tool Mark Examiners, 1980—; instr. home firearms safety, Mpls.; cons. to Sporting Arms and Ammunition Mfrs. Inst.; lectr. on forensic ballistics. Adv. bd. Milton Helpern Internat. Center for Forensic Scis., 1975—; mem. bd. cons. Inst. Applied Sci., Chgo.; cons. for re-exam. of ballistics evidence in Sirhan case Superior Ct. Los Angeles, 1975. Served with CIC, AUS, 1948-52. Fellow Am. Acad. Forensic Sci.; mem. Assn. of Firearm and Tool Mark Examiners (exec. council 1970-71, Distinguished Mem. and Key Man award 1972, spl. honors award 1976), Forensic Sci. Soc., Internat. Assn. for Identification (mem. firearms subcom. of sci. and practice com. 1961-74), Am. Ordnance Assn., Nat. Rifle Assn., Minn. Weapons, Internat. Cartridge collectors assns. Contbg. editor Am. Rifleman mag., 1973—; mem. editorial bd. Internat. Microform Jour. Legal Medicine and Forensic Sciences, 1979—, Jour. Forensic Medicine and Pathology, 1979—; contbr. articles on firearms and forensic ballistics to profl. pubis. Address: 6025 Gardena Ln NE Minneapolis MN 55432

BERGE, OLE M., union ofcl.; b. Swift Current, Sask., Can., July 22, 1921; s. Thorstein and Thora (Bjorgum) B.; student Trade Union Program, Harvard U., 1963; m. Katherine Ann Anderson; children—Katherine Ann, Linda Maureen, Ola Loraine. Bridge and bldg. helper, carpenter, pipefitter Great No. Railway, 1941; sec.-treas., grievance com. chmn., recording sec., jour. agt. Brotherhood of Maintenance of Way Employes, Lodge 1426, 1953-66, exec. bd. Great No. System div., 1962-66, staff asst. Chgo. office, 1966, grand lodge v.p., 1973, grand lodge pres., Detroit, 1978—. Served with RCAF, 1942-45. Mem. Railway Labor Execs. Assn. Office: 12050 Woodward Ave Detroit MI 48203

BERGE, RICHARD HAROLD, ednl. adminstr.; b. Litchfield, Minn., June 15, 1937; s. Harold A. and Muriel (Slinden) B.; B.A., Augsburg Coll., 1960; M.A., U. Ill., 1968; Ph.D. (Experienced Tchr. fellow), Ohio U., 1977; m. Phyllis D. Raymond, Aug. 6, 1960; children—Robin, Becky, Richard, Betsy. Tchr. English, Clinton (Minn.) Public Schs., 1960-61; tchr. English, social studies Wheaton (Minn.) Public Schs., 1961-63; tchr. econs. Faribault (Minn.) Public Schs., 1963-69, curriculum dir., 1970-72, asst. supt., 1972-80, supt. schs., 1980—. Bd. dirs. YMCA, United Way; pres. Our Saviors Lutheran Ch. Served with Army N.G., 1954-62. NSF fellow, 1964, 66; Bush Found. fellow, 1981. Mem. Minn. Assn. Sch. Adminstrs., Am. Assn. Sch. Adminstrs., Phi Delta Kappa. Club: Sertoma (pres.). Editor: Personal Economics in the Home Economics Curriculum, 1970. Office: 2855 NW 1st Ave Faribault MN 55021

BERGEN, THOMAS JOSEPH, lawyer, nursing homes exec., assn. exec.; b. Prairie du Chien, Wis., Feb. 7, 1913; s. Thomas Joseph and Emma Marilla (Grelle) B.; student U. Wis., 1930-32; J.D., Marquette U., 1937, postgrad., 1937-38; m. Jean Loraine Bowler, May 29, 1941 (dec. Aug. 1972); children—Kathleen Bergen McElwee, Eileen Bergen Bednarz, Patricia Bergen Buss, Thomas Joseph, Patrick Joseph, John Joseph. Admitted to Wis. bar, 1937, U.S. Supreme Ct. bar, 1972; practiced in Milw., 1937—; exec. sec. Wis. Assn. Nursing Homes, 1957-71; legal counsel, exec. dir. Am. Coll. Nursing Home Adminstrs., Milw., 1967-68; sec., dir. Bayside Nursing Home, Milw., 1967—; pres., dir. N.W. Med. Centers, Inc., also Northland Med. Centers, Inc. (both Milw.), 1968—; treas., exec. dir. Nat. Geriatrics Soc., Milw., 1971—; pres., bd. dirs. Senator Joseph R. McCarthy Found., Inc., 1979—; mem. program planning com. Nat. Conf. on Aging, also del. to conf., 1974; panel speaker Nat. Justice Found. conv., 1974. Bd. dirs., treas. Nat. Geriatrics Ednl. Soc., 1971—; bd. dirs., pres. Wis. Justice Found., 1971—. Served with AUS, 1943, 44. Recipient Merit award Wis. Assn. Nursing Homes, 1962, Outstanding Leadership award Nat. Geriatrics Soc., 1976. Mem. Am., Wis., Milw. (pres., exec. dir.) bar assns., Real Estate Profls. Assn. (pres. 1974—), Am. Med. Writers Assn., Delta Theta Phi, Delta Sigma Rho. Roman Catholic. Editor: Silver Threads, Wis. Assn. Nursing Homes publ., 1963-71, News Letter, Am. Coll. Nursing Home Adminstrs., 1967-68, Views and News, Nat. Geriatrics Soc., 1971—; contbr. articles to nursing home publs. Home: 10324 W Vienna Ave Wauwatosa WI 53222 Office: 212 W Wisconsin Ave Milwaukee WI 53203

BERGER, CARL EDWARD, chemist, utility co. engr.; b. Detroit, Mar. 10, 1929; s. Edward Carl and Marie Louise (Campeau) B.; B.S. in Chemistry, U. Detroit, 1952, M.S. in Organic Chemistry, 1955; m. Dolores Evelyn Heleski, July 22, 1961; children—Eric Edward, Thomas Carl, Karen Marie. With central staff Detroit Edison Co., 1957—, now chem. engrng. staff. Treas., advancement chmn. cub and scout troops Detroit Area Council Boy Scouts Am., 1971-77. Cert. chem. engr. Mem. Assn. Analytical Chemists; Detroit Edison rep. ASME (aqueous discharge subcom., 1977—), Am. Water Works Assn. Roman Catholic. Contbr. articles in field to profl. publs., paper to indsl. symposium. Home: 1395 Hampton Rd Grosse Pointe Woods MI 48236 Office: Detroit Edison Co 6100 W Warren (H-2) Detroit MI 48210

BERGER, DAVID GEORGE, state senator; b. Milw., Oct. 27, 1946; B.A., U. Wis., 1969; M.A. in Polit. Sci., Marquette U., 1970; s. Wilford G. and Jean G. (Goodsett) B. Former lectr. Marquette U., Milw.; mem. Wis. Assembly, 1970-74; mem. Wis. Senate, 1974—, co-chmn. Joint Com. for Rev. of Adminstrv. Rules, 1975—; mem. Joint Survey Com. on Tax Exemptions, 1973—; mem. Senate Select Com. on Mining Devel., 1975-77, Motor Vehicle Code Adv. Com., 1975-77, spl. Coms. on Solid Waste Mgmt., 1975-78, mem. Edn. and Revenue Com., 1977-78, Audit, Energy, Ins., Utilities, State and Local Affairs, Taxation cons., 1980—. Mem. Milw. County Library Planning Com., 1971-74; pres. Milw. County Federated Library Bd., 1974—. Mem. Am. Polit. Sci. Assn., Nat. Conf. State Legislators (human resources task force 1975—). Democrat. Club: K.C. Address: 4443 N 82nd St Milwaukee WI 53218

BERGER, JOHN EDWARD, real estate exec.; b. Chgo., Feb. 18, 1929; s. Edward and Marie Dorothy (Mahoney) B.; B.S., Loyola U., 1952; m. Mary Rose Lennon, Nov. 17, 1956; children—John Edward, Michael G., William F., Mary Therese, Joan M., Nancy M. Owner, real estate broker John E. Berger & Co., Chgo., 1954-73 (merger McKey & Poague, Inc., 1973), v.p., 1973—; dir., 1974—, gen. sales mgr., mem. exec. com., 1978—; pres. McKey & Poague Real Estate Sales, Inc., McKey & Poague Services, Inc., Chgo., 1980—. Vice pres. S.E. Community Orgn., Chgo., 1962-64. Served to lt. USMC, 1951-53. Mem. Chgo. Real Estate Bd. (v.p. 1970—, dir. 1968-70, gov. brokers div. 1967-68, chmn. F.H.A. com. 1978-79, Equal Opportunities Com. 1980-81), South Side Real Estate Bd. (pres. 1973—, dir. 1968-70), Beverly Suburban Real Estate Bd. (sec. 1975, treas. 1976), Chgo. Property Mgrs. Assn., Loyola U. Alumni Assn., Ill. Assn. Real Estate Bds. (dist. v.p. 1969-70), Chgo. Athletic Assn. Club: Flossmoor Country. Home: 1266 Berry Ln Flossmoor IL 60422 Office: McKey and Poague Real Estate 10540 S Western Ave Chicago IL 60643

BERGER, KENNETH WALTER, audiologist; b. Evansville, Ind., Mar. 22, 1924; s. Walter P. and Ida (Block) B.; B.A., U. Evansville, 1948; M.A., Ind. State U., 1949; Ph.D., So. Ill. U., Carbondale, 1962; m. Barbara Jane Steadman, Aug. 31, 1946; children—Robert W., Kenna J., Laura M., Karen S. Speech and hearing therapist pub. schs., Carmi, Ill., 1955-61; dir. audiology Kent State U., (Ohio), 1962—, prof., 1967—. Served to capt. U.S. Army, 1943-46, USAF, 1951-55. Fellow Am. Speech and Hearing Assn., Am. Audiology Soc., Acoustical Soc. Am. Author: Speechreading: Principles and Methods, 1971; The Hearing Aid: Its Operation and Development, 1974. Home: 647 Longmere Dr Kent OH 44240 Office: Speech and Hearing Clinic Kent State Univ Kent OH 44242

BERGER, KURT WILHELM, fin. counselor; b. Frankfurt, Germany, Mar. 10, 1912; came to U.S., 1937, naturalized, 1943; s. Walter W. and Bea (Wendel) B.; Ph.D. in Econs., U. Frankfurt, 1936; m. Gudrun M. Wolf, Aug. 24, 1959; 1 dau., Gisela P. Market analyst Merck, Darmstadt & N.J., 1936-37; treas. Express Freight Lines, Inc., Milw., 1943-67; v.p., treas. E.F.L. Motors, Inc., Milw., 1945-67, Transport Services, Inc., Milw., 1945-67; exec. v.p. Nat. Life Ins. Co., Frankfurt, 1968-70; pvt. practice counseling internat. fin. and investments, Koenigstein, W.Ger., 1969-70; ind. mgmt. cons., fin. counselor, 1970—. Mem. Wis. N.G., 1947-49. Mem. Nat. Acctg. and Fin. Council (past v.p., pres., chmn.), Am. Trucking Assn., Motor Carrier Accts. Soc. (past pres.), Personnel Evaluation Inst. (past pres.). Unitarian. Contbr. articles to profl. jours. Home: 4540 N Ardmore Ave Shorewood WI 53211 Office: 12020 W Feerick St Unit J Milwaukee WI 53222

BERGER, MILES LEE, land economist; b. Chgo., Aug. 9, 1930; s. Albert E. and Dorothy (Ginsberg) B.; student Brown U., 1948-50; m. Sally Eileen Diamond, Aug. 27, 1955; children—Albert E., Elizabeth Ann. Engaged in real estate appraisal, research and devel., econs. fields, 1950—; mng. chmn. bd. Berger Fin. Services Corp., Chgo., 1950—; chmn. bd. Mid-Am. Appraisal & Research Corp., (Chgo., 1959-80) also dir.; chmn. bd. Real Estate Services Corp., 1969—; vice chmn. bd., trustee Heitman Fin. Services Ltd., 1970—; prin. econ. cons. Columbia Nat. Bank, Chgo., 1965—; dir. Evans Inc.; trustee Heitman Mortgage Investors. Commr., chmn. Chgo. Plan Commn., 1980—; cons. city Chgo. on Ill. Central Air Rights, 1967—; trustee Latin Sch. Chgo., 1967-73, treas., 1953-55, bd. dirs. Latin Sch. Found.; bd. dirs. Albert E. Berger Found. Mem. Am. Inst. Real Estate Appraisers, Soc. Real Estate Appraisers, Soc. Real Estate Counselors, Am. Right-of-Way Assn., Nat. Assn. Housing and Redevel. Ofcls., Nat. Tax Assn., Internat. Assn. Assessing Officers, Lambda Alpha. Jewish (trustee synagogue). Home: Chicago IL 60610 Office: 180 N LaSalle St Chicago IL 60601

BERGER, PAUL HAROLD, adminstrv. and loan assn. exec.; b. Cleve., Oct. 14, 1924; s. Ted. Ross and Helen (Hirsh) B.; student Tex. A and M. Coll., 1942-43; So. Methodist U., 1946-47, U. Chgo., 1947-51; M.A. in Social Scis., U. Chgo., 1956; m. Phillis Ottem, July 31, 1954; children—Jessica E., Avery Ross. Adminstrv. asst. to Alderman Robert E. Merriam, 1949-51; sales rep. Mich. Steel Supply, Chgo., 1951-53, Abbot Screw & Bolt Co., Chgo., 1953-54; campaign staff Merriam for Mayor Com., 1954-55; ins. broker, Chgo., 1955—; chmn. bd., pres Hyde Park Fed. Savs. & Loan Assn., Chgo., 1961—. Dist. chmn. Boy Scouts Am., 1968-69; treas. Mid South Side Health Planning Orgn., 1969-72, Gateway Houses Found., Inc., 1969-74; bd. dirs. SE Chgo. Commn., 1963—, Woodlawn Hosp., Hyde Park-Kenwood Community Conf., 1964-67; bd. dirs., treas. First Unitarian Soc. Chgo., treas., 1963-64; bd. dirs. Mary McDowell Settlement, 1957-64, v.p., 1960-61; bd. dirs. Chgo. Renewal Efforts Service Corp., 1973-81, chmn., 1976-81; bd. dirs., pres. Hyde Park-Kenwood Devel. Corp., 1974—; bd. dirs. Met. Fair and Expn. Authority, 1975-80, vice chmn. bd., 1978-80; bd. dirs. Community Services and Research Corp., 1975-80. Served with AUS, 1943-46. Life mem. Million Dollar Round Table. Clubs: Economic, Quadrangle (Chgo.). Home: 5816 S Blackstone Ave Chicago IL 60637 Office: 5250 S Lake Park Ave Chicago IL 60615

BERGER, RICHARD WILLIAM, hosp. cons.; b. Arcadia, Wis., Sept. 28, 1939; s. Emil Henry and Luella Elizabeth (Hohmann) B.; B.B.A., U. Wis., Madison, 1963; m. Marjorie Ann Guelzow, Aug. 3, 1963; children—Timothy, Todd, Tara. Acct., IBM Corp., Chgo., 1963; acctg. supr. Zenith Radio Corp., Chgo., 1966-67; chief acct. Madison Gen. Hosp., 1967-68; controller Meth. Hosp., Madison, 1968-75; asst. adminstr. Hosp. Corp. Am., Miami, Fla., 1975-76; exec. dir. Howard Young Med. Center, Woodruff, Wis., 1976-80; prin. The Lakewood Group, Madison, 1980—; steering com. Rock County Health Resource Com. Served with USAF, 1959. Mem. Hosp. Fin. Mgmt. Assn., Am. Coll. Hosp. Adminstrs., Am. Hosp. Assn., Wis. Hosp. Assn. Republican. Lutheran. Home: 16 Paget Rd Madison WI 53704 Office: PO Box 7054 Madison WI 53707

BERGERE, CARLETON MALLORY, contractor; b. Brookline, Mass., Apr. 4, 1919; s. Jason J. and Anna Lillian B.; student Burdett Bus. Coll., 1938, Babsons Sch. Bus., 1940; m. Jean J. Pach, Oct. 1, 1950. Self-employed contractor, Chgo., 1949-57; pres. Permanent Bldg. Supply Co., Inc., Chgo., 1957-62, Gt. No. Bldg. Products, Inc., Chgo., 1962-67, C.M. Bergere Co., Inc., Chgo., 1967—. Served with USN, 1944. Named Man of Yr., Profl. Remodelers Assn. Greater Chgo., 1978. Mem. Profl. Remodelers Assn.(dir., past treas., v.p., sec.), Chgo. Assn. Commerce and Industry, No. Ill. Home Builders Assn., Better Bus. Bur. Met. Chgo., Industry Trade Practice Com. on Home Improvement. Address: 175 E Delaware Pl Chicago IL 60611

BERGERON, ALLEN LLOYD, computer systems ofcl.; b. Kimberly, Wis., June 1, 1951; s. James Bernard and Julietta Ann (Lenz) B.; B.A. in Bus. Adminstrn., U. Wis., Superior, 1973; m. Lori Lee Bergeron. Sales rep. Burroughs Corp., 1973-74, ter. mgr., Duluth, Minn., 1974-80, zone mgr., 1980—. House father Courage House Group Home, 1974-75. Named Man of Year Alpha Xi Delta, 1973, Sigma Tau Gamma, 1972; recipient Legion of Honor, Burroughs Corp., 1975, 78, 79, 80. Mem. U. Wis. Alumni Assn., Sigma Tau Gamma. Clubs: Toastmasters, Icarus Skydiving. Home: 1312 Basin Ave Bismarck ND 58501 Office: 1118 E Superior St Duluth MN 55802

BERGH, GLORIA JEAN, editor; b. Monticello, Minn., Jan. 26, 1941; d. Merle Durb and Frieda Marie (Zum Brunnen) Sutherland; B.S., U. Minn., 1963; m. Owe Martin Gerhard Bergh, Nov. 14, 1964; children—David Martin, Lisa Marie. Staff writer public relations dept. Green Giant Co., LeSueur, Minn., 1964-65; manuscript copy editor C.V. Mosby Co., St. Louis, 1965-71; copywriter, continuity dir. Sta. WQAD-TV, Moline, Ill., 1973; dir. public relations Miss. Valley Girl Scout Council, Bettendorf, Iowa, 1974-81; mng. editor/public relations Modern Woodmen Am., Rock Island, Ill., 1981—. Mem. Davenport C. of C. (public relations com., chmn. publs. subcom. 1978), Bettendorf C. of C. (civic affairs and edn. com. 1978-79), Public Relations Soc. Am. (charter mem. Quad-Cities/Iowa Ill. chpt., pres. 1981, sec., treas. 1980, publicity chmn. 1978-79). Club: Career Women's Network. Home: 20 Century Oaks Ct Bettendorf IA 52722 Office: Mississippi River at 17th St Rock Island IL 61201

BERGHUIS, MELVIN EARL, educator; b. Clara City, Minn., Oct. 19, 1915; s. Jacob Peter and Johanna Elizabeth (Nieuwenhuis) B.; student Northwestern Jr. Coll., 1932-33; A.B., Calvin Coll., 1936; M.A., U. Mich., 1949; Ph.D., Mich. State U., 1964; m. Barbara Jane Heetderks, Sept. 20, 1940; children—Robert Earl, Jane Berghuis Hull, David Melvin. Tchr., prin. Allendale (Mich.) Christian Schs., 1937-39; tchr. Baxter (Mich.) Christian Jr. High Sch., 1939-41, Chgo. Christian High Sch., 1941-45, Grand Rapids (Mich.) Christian High Sch., 1946-48; asst. prof. speech Calvin Coll., Grand Rapids, 1948-57, registrar, 1958-61, dir. student acad. services; 1961-64, v.p. for student affairs, 1964-71, prof. speech, 1971—, chmn. dept. speech, 1952-69, 79-81, instr. Mich. State U., East Lansing, 1957-58. Pres. met. Grand Rapids Adult Edn. Council, 1959; mem. adv. com. Mich. Scholarship Program, 1964-71; mem. scholarship com. Grand Rapids Found., 1967-71. Served with USN, 1945-46. Mem. Speech Communication Assn., Central States, Mich. speech assns., Mich. Intercoll. Speech League (treas. 1950-54, pres. 1960-61), Mich. Assn. Coll. Registrars and Admissions Officers (v.p. 1966-69), Nat. Union Christian Schs. Mem. Christian Ref. Ch. (elder 1952-54, 61, 64-67). Home: 1718 Radcliff Ave SE Grand Rapids MI 49506

BERGLAND, BOB SELMER, govt. ofcl.; b. Roseau, Minn., July 22, 1928; grad. U. Minn. Sch. Agr., 1948; m. Helen Elaine Grohn, 1950; children—Dianne, Linda, Stevan, Jon, Allan, Billy, Franklyn. Mem. 92d to 94th Congresses from 7th Minn. dist.; mem. Agr. Com., mem. Conservation and Credit Subcom., Livestock and Grains Subcom.; mem. Sci. and Astronautics Com.; mem. Select Com. on Small Bus.; sec. Dept. Agr., Washington, 1977—. Mem. Farmers Union, Nat. Farmers Orgn. Mem. Democratic Farm Labor party. Lutheran. Mason, Lion, Eagle. Home: Route 1 Roseau MN 56751*

BERGLIN, LINDA L., state senator; b. Oakland, Calif., Oct. 19, 1944; d. Freeman and Norma (Lund) Waterman; B.F.A., Mpls. Coll. Art and Design, 1967. Graphic designer; mem. Minn. Ho. of Reps., from 1972, Minn. Senate, 1980—. Mem. Council Econ. Status of Women, Council Black Minnesotans. Mem. Democratic-Farmer-Labor party. Office: 303 State Capitol Saint Paul MN 55155*

BERGLUND, ROBERTA LEOLA, educator; b. Freeport, Ill., May 20, 1944; d. Ralph LeRoy and Maxine (Lynch) Hanson; B.S., Ill. State U., 1965; M.S. Ed., No. Ill. U., 1978, postgrad., 1978—; m. David Lee Berglund, June 18, 1966. Tchr. elem. sch. Flanagan, Ill., 1965-69; reading specialist Dixon (Ill.) Public Schs., 1969—, dir. Title I program, 1977—. Mem. Ill. Reading Council (corr. sec. 1981-82), Sauk Valley Reading Council (pres. 1977-78), Ill. Reading Council (dir. 1977-78, 81-82), Internat. Reading Assn., No. Ill. Reading Council, Mid State Reading Council, Assn. Supervision and Curriculum Devel., Title I Dirs. Ill., NEA, Ill. Edn. Assn., Dixon Tchr. Assn., Nat. Council Tchrs. English. Unitarian. Club: PEO. Editor, Reading Unlimited newsletter, 1980—, Ill. Reading Communicator, 1981—; contbr. articles to profl. jours. Home: Rural Route 6 White Oak Estates Dixon IL 61021 Office: 415 S Hennepin Ave Dixon IL 61021

BERGMAN, GREG ALAN, social worker; b. Lorain, Ohio, Feb. 12, 1951; s. Ivan Russell and Marjorie Ann (Yalman) B.; B.A., Ohio State U., Columbus, 1973; M.S.W., U. Nebr., 1975; m. Katherine Holaday, June 24, 1979. Asst. dir., acting dir. social services Dr. Sher Nursing Home, Omaha, 1975-77; social service worker Richard Young Hosp., Omaha, 1974-75; program dir. Social Settlement Assn. Omaha, 1978-80; social service worker Harry S. Truman Meml. Vets. Hosp., Columbia, Mo., 1980—. Lic. nursing home adminstr., Nebr., Mo. Mem. Acad. Cert. Social Workers, Nat. Assn. Social Workers (state dir. 1978-79, regional chmn. 1978-79), Nebr. Welfare Assn. (regional dir. 1979-80), Mo. League of Nursing. Author statistics textbook. Home: 2023 Wolcottwood Columbia MO 65202 Office: 800 Stadium Rd Columbia MO 65201

BERGMAN, JANET LOUISE, flutist, educator; b. St. Louis, June 15, 1920; d. Isadore and Rose (Seidenberg) Marx; student pub. schs., St. Louis; student John F. Kiburz, Laurent Torno; m. Albert Solomon Bergman, June 15, 1947; children—Shelley, Gary Evan, Dana Lynn. Mem. St. Louis Woman's Symphony, 1937-38, St. Louis Opera Co., 1942, St. Louis Symphony, 1943-47; first flutist St. Louis Little Symphony, 1943-47, soloist, 1943-47; flutist Oklahoma City Symphony, 1944-45, soloist, 1944-45; flutist New Orleans Symphony and Opera Co., 1945-47, Chgo. Women's Sinfonietta, 1948, Chgo. Park Band Concerts, 1947—, Chgo. Chamber Orch., 1954-58, Lyric Opera Orch., Chgo., 1964-71; flutist, soloist City Symphony Chgo., 1963—, Aoelian Woodwind Ensemble, Chgo., 1965—; prof. flute Chgo. Conservatory Coll., 1968-78, Northeastern Ill. U., Chgo., 1978—, Am. Conservaory of Music, Chgo., 1978-81; mem. music faculty Niles E. and Niles W. high schs., 1964—, New Trier E. and W. high schs., 1977—; founder, condr. Flute Sinfonietta, 1975—; soloist Artist Assos., 1976-77; adjudicator Ill. High Sch. Solo Assn., 1973-79, Flute Concourse, U. Que., Montreal, 1974-77. Mem. Chgo., St. Louis fedns. musicians, Nat. Flute Assn., Soloist Artists Assn. Chgo., Nat. Health Fedn. (ednl. officer Chgo. chpt. 1975-76, speaker 1976-77), Chgo. Flute Soc. (pres. 1977—), Soc. Am. Musicians. Author: Do's and Don'ts of Flute Playing, 1967. Home: 1817 G W Hood St Chicago IL 60660

BERGMAN, ROBERT SCRIBNER, toy co. exec.; b. Aurora, Ill., Nov. 23, 1934; s. Ross M. and Mary O. (Ochsenschlager) B.; B.S., Ill. Inst. Tech., 1956; postgrad., Stanford U., 1956-58; m. Patricia LeBaron, June 10, 1956; children—David C., Lynne M., Joseph R. With Hughes Aircraft Co., Culver City, Calif., 1956, Gen. Electric Co., Palo Alto, Calif., 1957, Sylvania, Mountain View, Calif., 1958-61; with Processed Plastics, Montgomery, Ill., 1961—, pres., 1969—; pres. Bergman Mfg. & Trading, Montgomery, 1962—; v.p. Moldrite Plastic and Engring., Montgomery, 1962—, Moldrite Tool and Die, Addison, Ill., 1965—; treas. Intertoy, Montgomery, 1977—, Graphic Label Co., Oswego, Ill., 1977—. Mem. Am. Phys. Soc., Toy Mfrs. Am. (dir. 1981—). Republican. Ch. of Christ. Club: Elks. Home: 1330 Monoa Ave Aurora IL 60506 Office: 1001 Aucutt Rd Montgomery IL 60538

BERGMAN, ROY THOMAS, surgeon; b. Cassopolis, Mich., Dec. 20, 1935; s. Roy Edwin and Lois (Townsend) B.; B.S. with high honors, Mich. State U., 1957, D.V.M. with high honors, 1959; M.D., Northwestern U., 1964; m. Sally Jo Proshwitz, June 28, 1958; children—Roy T., Amy Lynn, Samara Edlyn. Rotating intern Evanston (Ill.) Hosp. Assn., 1964-65, resident in gen. surgery, 1967-71; Am. Cancer Soc. clin. fellow in oncological surgery Northwestern U., Chgo., 1970-71; practice medicine specializing in gen. surgery and oncology, Escanaba, Mich., 1972; mem. staff St. Francis Hosp., Escanaba, 1972—, chmn. tumor bd., 1972—, also chief of staff, chief of surgery; instr. surgery U. So. Calif. Med. Center, Los Angeles, 1972-73; asso. prof. surgery Mich. State U. Coll. Human Medicine, East Lansing, 1974—, also surg. coordinator Upper Peninsula med. edn. program; attending physician Nat. Sports Festival, Colorado Springs, 1978, 79, Syracuse, N.Y., 1981, U.S. Olymic Com., Pan Am. Games, P.R., 1979, Summer Games, Russia, 1980; cons. polyclinic U.S. Olympic Com. Winter Games, Lake Placid, N.Y., 1980; attending physician U.S. Olympic Men's Rowing Team, Germany, 1981; mem. Council on Sports Medicine, U.S. Olympic Com. Served to capt. M.C., U.S. Army, 1965-67. Diplomate Am. Bd. Surgery. Fellow A.C.S. (local chmn. com. trauma, chmn. com. on applicants Mich. Dist. 4), Alpha Omega Alpha. Office: Doctors Park Escanaba MI 49829

BERGMAN, SIGRID ELIZABETH, hosp. services adminstr.; b. Lafayette, Ind., June 20, 1940; d. Philip A. and Josephine Elizabeth (Miller) Henderson; B.A., U. Nebr., 1963, M.A., 1970; m. Edward T. Bergman, June 9, 1962; children—Kimberly Kay, Lucinda Sue. Pediatric counselor Nat. Jewish Hosp., Denver, 1962-63; home services rep. Cengas, Lincoln, Nebr., 1963-65; guidance counselor St. Elizabeth Sch. Nursing, Lincoln, 1966-70; dir. social services St. Elizabeth Community Health Center, Lincoln, 1970—; guest lectr. social work and vocat. rehab. U. Nebr. Bd. dirs. Lancaster County Unit Am. Cancer Soc., 1975-78; mem. adv. bd. Tabitha Home Health Care, 1975—, sec. 1975-76; Mem. Cath. Social Services Bd., 1977—; mem. adv. bd. Lincoln Youth Symphony, 1977—, projects chmn., 1978-79, sec., 1979-80, pres., 1980-81. Mem. Soc. for Hosp. Social

Work Dirs. of Am. Hosp. Assn., Nebr. Soc. Hosp. Social Work Dirs. (pres. 1981—), Zeta Tau Alpha. Democrat. Presbyterian. Club: Alpha Chi Omega Mothers (co-chmn. 1981—). Home: 1109 Lancaster Ln Lincoln NE 68505 Office: St Elizabeth Community Center 555 S 70th St Lincoln NE 68510

BERGMANN, ROBERT LEWIS, banker; b. St. Louis, Jan. 21, 1926; s. William G. and Elvera O. (Baum) B.; B.S. in Commerce, St. Louis U., 1949; m. Dorothy E. Thoma, July 24, 1954; children—Laura A., Alice M., Thomas C., Karen S. Sr. auditor Arthur Andersen & Co., St. Louis, 1949-55; mgr. adminstrv. data processing McDonnell Aircraft Corp., St. Louis, 1955-64; v.p. data processing Merc. Trust Co. N.A., St. Louis, 1964-73, sr. v.p., 1973-80, sr. v.p. data processing and ops. depts., 1980—; exec. v.p., chmn. bd. Payment and Adminstrv. Communications Corp./Payment and Telecommunications Services Corp. Served with AC, U.S. Army, 1944-45. C.P.A., Mo. Mem. Assn. for Systems Mgmt. (Merit award 1974), Data Processing Mgmt. Assn., Am. Inst. C.P.A.'s. Clubs: Mo. Athletic, K.C. (St. Louis). Office: PO Box 524 Saint Louis MO 63166

BERGQUIST, BARRY DARRIL, importing co. exec.; b. Cloquet, Minn., Oct. 18, 1945; s. Richard Emil and Margaret (Bengston) B.; B.A. in Bus. Adminstrn., U. Minn., Duluth, 1968; m. Vivian Elizabeth Cook, Nov. 30, 1974. Salesman, mgr. Cades Ltd., Elk Grove, Ill., 1971; dist. mgr. Mass. food equipment div. McGraw Edison Co., 1973; sales mgr., then v.p. Bergquist Imports, Inc., Cloquet, 1977—, pres., owner, 1980—. Vice chmn., chmn. fin. com. 8th Congl. Dist. Republican Party, 1979-81, dist. chmn., 1981—; chmn. Carlton County Rep. Party, 1976-81; bd. dirs. Cloquet chpt. Am. Cancer Soc., 1980—. Served with USAR, 1968-70. Club: Cloquet Kiwanis (dir.). Home: 318 Ave D Cloquet MN 55720 Office: 1412 Hwy 33 S Cloquet MN 55720

BERGSMA, THOMAS ROBERT, marketing exec.; b. Des Moines, Apr. 27, 1945; s. Robert Thomas and Dolores Emma (Fischer) B.; B.S. in Bus. Adminstrn., Drake U., 1970; M.B.A., Loyola U., Chgo., 1977; m. Dixie Ann Overton, May 20, 1967; children—Brenda Kristine, Lisa Kathleen. Programmer analyst, asst. sec. to nat. subcom. Electronic Funds Transfer System, Fed. Res. Bank Chgo., 1970-72; sr. marketing rep. Honeywell, Inc., Des Moines, 1972-74; marketing dir. IMPACT Services div. Pioneer Hibred Internat., Inc., Des Moines, 1974-77; co-founder Midwest Computer Corp., 1977—; v.p. mktg. Midwest Computer Center Co., Johnston, Iowa, 1977—. Former deacon, treas. Highland Park Luth. Ch.; city councilman City of Grimes (Iowa), planning and zoning commr., 1980. Served with USNR, 1966-68; Vietnam. Republican. Home: 115 NW 7th Pl Grimes IA 50111 Office: 5758 Merle Hay Rd Johnston IA 50131

BERGSTRESSER, MELVIN HUBERT, retail co. exec.; b. Frobischer, Sask., Can., June 16, 1932; s. Waldemar and Selma (Kolke) B.; student in Bus. Mgmt., U. Man., 1967-70; student in Theology, N. Am. Bapt. Coll., Edmonton, 1950-52; m. Doreen Laura, June 26, 1954; children—Wayne, Arden, Heather, Kevin. With Gambles Can., Winnipeg, Man., 1956—, buyer major appliances, sporting goods, asst. mgr. sales promotion and advt., group mgr. sporting goods div., 1979—; pres., owner Creative Family Living Assn., 1969—, Parking Lot Marking Services, 1975—, Distinctive Products, 1975—; lectr. family living seminars. Bd. dirs. N.Am. Bapt. Coll., 1967-79; chmn. Man. Bapt. Assn., 1975-78; moderator Grant Park Bapt. Ch., 1972-78, Sunday Sch. tchr., 1959—, capt. Christian Service Brigade Boys, 1964—. Home: 16 Glengarry Dr Winnipeg MB R3T 2J6 Canada

BERGSTROM, BETTY HOWARD, assn. exec.; b. Chgo., Mar. 15, 1931; d. Seward Haise and Agnes Eleanor (Uek) Guinter; B.S. in Speech, Northwestern U., 1952; postgrad U. Nev., Reno, 1974; m. Robert William Bergstrom, Apr. 21, 1979; children by previous marriage—Bryan Scott, Cheryl Lee, Jeffrey Alan. Dir. sales promotion and public relations WLS-AM, Chgo., 1952-56; account exec. E.H. Brown Advt. Agy., Chgo., 1956-59; v.p. Richard Crabb Assos., Chgo., 1959-61; pres., owner Howard Assos., Calif. and Chgo., 1961—; v.p. Chgo. Hort. Soc., 1976—. Del., Ill. Constl. Conv., 1969-70, mem. com. legis. reform, 1973-74, cts. and justice com., 1971-74; apptd. mem. Ill. Hist. Library Bd., 1970, Ill. Bd. Edn., 1971-74. AAUW fellowship grant named in her honor. Mem. Nat. Soc. Fund Raising Execs., Am. Assn. Bot. Garden and Arboreta, Garden Writers Am., AAUW, Northwestern U. Alumni, U. So. Calif. Alumni Assn., LWV. Mem. Glenview Community Ch. Editorial bd. Garden Mag., 1977—; editor Garden Talk, 1976—; contbr. articles on fund devel., horticulture, edn. advt. and agr. to profl. jours.; editor Ill. AAUW Jour., 1966-67. Office: PO Box 400 Glencoe IL 60022

BERGSTROM, RICHARD NORMAN, civil engr.; b. Chgo., Dec. 11, 1921; s. Carl William and Ellen Amanda Victoria (Anderson) B.; B.S. in C.E., Ill. Inst. Tech., 1942, M.S., 1952; m. Patricia Ann Chessman, Apr. 19, 1947; children—George Norman, James Donald. Laura Ann, Martha Jean. Design engr. Carnegie Ill. Steel Corp., Gary. Ind., 1942; structural engr. Sargent & Lundy, Engrs., Chgo., 1946-56, asso., 1956, partner, 1966—, mgr. tech. services dept., 1977—. Mem. nuclear standards mgmt. bd. Am. Nat. Standards Insf., 1975—. Stated clk. Presbyn. Ch. of Barrington (Ill.); bd. dirs. Presbyn. Home, Evanston, Ill. Served to lt., USNR, 1942-46. Decorated Purple Heart. Registered profl. engr., Ariz., Ark., Calif., Colo., Ill., Ind., Iowa, Kans., Ky., La., Mich., N.Y., Ohio, Okla., S.C., Tenn., Tex., Wis. Fellow ASCE, Am. Cons. Engrs. Council; mem. Am. Nuclear Soc., ASME, Am. Concrete Inst., Am. Inst. Steel Constrn., Western Soc. Engrs., Ill. Cons. Engrs. Council (dir.). Presbyn. Clubs: Union League, Barrington Hills Country, Desert Forest Golf, Meadow, Barrington Tennis. Contbr. articles in field to profl. jours. Home: 274 Leeds Dr Barrington Hills IL 60010 Office: 55 E Monroe St Chicago IL 60603

BERGSTROM, ROBERT CARLTON, geologist; b. Highland Park, Ill., Aug. 20, 1925; s. Carl Hilding and Ethel Rose (Hill) B.; B.S., Northwestern U., 1950, M.S., 1954; postgrad. U. Chgo., 1960-61, 67-69; m. Virginia Mae Jensen, June 7, 1952; children—Gary Carlton, Bradley James, Neil Reid. Tchr., Morton High Sch., Cicero, Ill., 1950-53; instr. Morton Coll., Cicero, 1953-63, asso. dean for admissions and records, 1964-74, prof. geology and geography, 1974—. Active, Boys Scouts Am. Served with U.S. Army, 1944-46. NSF fellow, 1960-61. Mem. Ill. State Acad. Sci., Nat. Assn. Geology Tchrs., Soc. Vertebrate Paleontology, Great Lakes Planetarium Assn., Sigma Xi. Luthern. Home: Park Ridge IL 60068 Office: 3801 S Central Ave Cicero IL 60650

BERGSTROM, ROBERT WILLIAM, lawyer; b. Chgo., Nov. 8, 1918; s. C. William and Ellen B. (Anderson) B.; LL.B., Chgo. Kent Coll. Law, 1940, J.D., 1970; M.B.A., U. Chgo., 1947; m. Betty Howard; children—Mark Robert, Philip Alan, Bryan Scott, Cheryl Lee, Jeffrey Alan. Admitted to Ill. bar, 1940, U.S. Supreme Ct. bar, 1950; practiced law in Chgo., 1940—; partner firm Bergstrom, Davis & Teeple, and predecessors, 1951—. Chmn., Glenview (Ill.) Village Caucus, 1961; bd. dirs. Ill. Com. for Constl. Conv., 1969; founding chmn. Com. for Legis. Reform, 1972-75, counsel, 1976-80; founder statewide Com. on Cts. and Justice, exec. com., 1971—. Served to lt. USNR, 1942-46. Named Chicagoan of Year in Law and Judiciary, Chgo. Jaycees, 1969. Mem. Am. Bar Assn. (co-editor antitrust devels. 1965-68), Ill. Bar Assn. (exec. council anti-trust sect. 1967), Chgo. Bar Assn. (sec. 1969-71, editor Chgo. Bar Record 1971-72), Chgo. Assn. Commerce and Industry. Clubs: Execs., Union League (pres. 1971-72, Disting. Public Service award 1981). Author: The Law of Competition in Illinois, 1962; also numerous articles on antitrust law, constl. law, and econs. Office: Bergstrom Davis & Teeple 39 S La Salle St Chicago IL 60603

BERK, BURTON BENJAMIN, optometrist; b. Cleve., Jan. 31, 1930; s. Benjamin C. and Ruth S. (Hirsohn) B.; B.S. in Optometry, Ohio State U., 1953, O.D., 1977; m. Margery A. Rocco, June 17, 1951; children—Deborah L., Bruce C., Michael S., Lawrence R. Practice optometry, Columbus, Ohio, 1953—. Instr. optometry Ohio State U., 1967—. Dir. Corporate Futures, Rochester, N.Y.; sec. Ohio Profl. Investment Corp., 1968—. Pres. Ohio State Bd. Optometry, 1972—. Mem. Nat. Eye Research Found., Optometric Extension Found., Inc., Ohio Vision Service, Better Vision Inst., Vision League of Ohio. Fellow Am. Acad. Optometry; mem. Central Ohio, Ohio, Am. optometric assns., Internat. Orthokeratology Assn., Am. Optometric Found., Phi Sigma Delta. Republican. Clubs: B'nai B'rith, Whitehall Lions, Presidents of Ohio State U. Home: 2775 Brentwood Rd Columbus OH 43209 Office: 5180 E Main St Columbus OH 43213

BERK, JAMES EDWARD, appliance and electronics mfg., wholesale and retail co. exec.; b. Queens, N.Y., Sept. 26, 1945; s. Francis A. and Florence (Jacques) B.; B.B.A., Baruch Coll., CCNY, 1969; M.B.A., City U. N.Y., 1972; m. Laureen Williams, June 30, 1979; children—Kimberly Ann, Deborah Ann, James Joseph. Nat. product mgr. Garland div. Welbilt Corp., Maspeth, N.Y., 1964-71; mktg. mgr. Micro Electronic Products, Inc., Maspeth, 1971-73; v.p. Greenville Products Corp. subs. White Consol. Industries, Greenville, Mich., 1973-78, v.p. mktg. Kelvinator Appliance Co. div., 1978-79; corp. v.p. Midland Internat. Corp. div. Beneficial Fin. Corp., Shawnee Mission, Kans., 1979-80, corp. v.p. mktg. and merchandising Western Auto div., 1980—; educator, speaker in field. Recipient cert. of achievement N.Y.C.'s Mayor's Com., 1963. Mem. Am. Mktg. Assn., Am. Mgmt. Assn. (Disting. Service award 1978), Sales Execs. Club Kansas City, West Mich. Health Systems Agy. Republican. Roman Catholic. Club: Overland Park Racquet, Milburn Country. Home: 13211 W 77th Pl Shawnee Mission KS 66215 Office: 2107 Grand Ave Kansas City MO 64108

BERKBUEGLER, JOHN WILLIAM, health info. specialist, educator; b. Apple Creek, Mo., Nov. 2, 1936; s. August W. and Ida Christine (Kirn) B.; student Maryhurst Normal, 1954-56; A.A., Donnelly Jr. Coll., 1964; B.S. in Med. Records Adminstrn., Southwestern Okla. State U., Weatherford, 1970; M.A., Central Mich. U.; 1 son, John William. Asst. dir. St. Mary's Hosp., Kansas City, Mo., 1959-60, Providence Hosp., Kansas City, Kans., 1960-61; dir. med. record services St. Margaret Hosp., Kansas City, Kans., 1961-64, St. Francis Hosp., Tulsa, 1964-68, St. Anthony Hosp., Oklahoma City, 1968-70; dir., asst. prof. med. records adminstrn. program Ill. State U., Normal, 1970-73, also mem. pres.'s task force on instructional media and tech., dir. med. records Galesburg (Ill.) Cottage Hosp., 1973-74, Columbus-Cuneo-Cabrini Med. Center, Chgo., 1974-76; dir., asst. prof. health data systems U. Wis.-Milw., 1976-79; dir. health info. mgmt. program Stephens Coll., Columbia, Mo., 1979—; surveyor mem. Panel of Accreditation Surveyors, Am. Med. Assn., 1981—; cons. med. record adminstr. health care facilities, Mo., Kans., Okla., Ill., Iowa, Wis.; cons. med. records acad. programs, Okla., Ala., Ill., N.J., Pa., S.D. Mem. bd. edn. St. Eugene Parish, Oklahoma City. Chmn., Human Rights Commn., City of Columbia; eucharistic minister Columbia Cath. Ch. Lic. foster parent, Mo. Mem. Am., Mo., Okla. (past pres.), Ill. (past pres.) med. record assns., Okla. Soc. Tumor Registry Secs. (past pres.). Contbr. articles in field to profl. jours. Home: 3300 Belle Meade Dr Columbia MO 65201 Office: Stephens Coll PO Box 2151 Columbia MO 65215

BERKEBILE, DALE EUGENE, orthopedic surgeon; b. Chgo., Feb. 18, 1935; s. Dale Eugene and Elizabeth Jane (Cook) B.; A.B., DePauw U., 1957; M.S., U. Ind., 1958, M.D., 1962; m. Mary Carroll Jordan, Aug. 25, 1957; children—Charles Jordan, Mary Susan, Sarah Elizabeth. Intern, U. Wis. Hosps., Madison, 1962-63, resident in orthopedic surgery, 1964-66, 68-69; resident in gen. surgery St. Joseph Hosp., Marshfield, Wis., 1963-64; practice medicine specializing in orthopedic surgery, Rapid City, S.D., 1969—; orthopedic surgeon staff Rapid City Regional Hosps., Ft. Meade (S.D.) VA Hosp., 1969—. Served with M.C., U.S. Army, 1966-68. Diplomate Am. Bd. Orthopedic Surgeons. Fellow A.C.S., Am. Acad. Orthopedic Surgeons (bd. councilors). Methodist. Home: 1717 West Blvd Rapid City SD 57701 Office: 725 Meade St Rapid City SD 57701

BERKLEY, RICHARD L., mayor; grad. Harvard U. Sec., treas. Tension Envelope Corp., Kansas City, Mo.; mem. City Council Kansas City (Mo.), mayor, 1979—. Chmn. Jackson County (Mo.) Republican Com. Office: Office of Mayor City Hall 414 E 12th Kansas City MO 64106*

BERKMAN, ARNOLD STEPHEN, clin. psychologist; b. N.Y.C., Sept. 2, 1942; s. Henry and Marion (Lampert) B.; A.B., Oberlin Coll., 1964; M.S., U. Pitts., 1966, Ph.D., 1969; m. Claire Fleet, Apr. 27, 1975; children—Eric, Joshua, Janna. Fellow in clin. psychology U. Chgo. Pritzker Sch. Medicine, Chgo., 1968-69; asst. prof. Counseling Center, Mich. State U., East Lansing, 1969-73, asso. prof., 1973-74; asso. prof. dept. psychiatry, 1974—. UPSHS trainee, 1964-67. Mem. Mich. Psychol. Assn. (v.p. profl. affairs 1978-79, pres. elect 1981, pres. 1982), Am. Psychol. Assn. Jewish. Home: 4780 Arapaho Trail Okemos MI 48864 Office: Dept Psychiatry Mich State U East Lansing MI 48824

BERKOFF, HERBERT ALLEN, physician; b. Buffalo, Oct. 18, 1937; A.B., Columbia Coll., 1959; M.D., N.Y. U., 1963; m.; 2 children. Intern, Bellevue-N.Y. U. Med. Center, N.Y.C., 1963-64; asst. resident in surgery U. Buffalo, 1966-67; resident in surgery U. Mich. Med. Center, Ann Arbor, 1967-70, clin. instr., 1970-72; asst. prof. U. Wis. Med. Center, Madison, 1972-78, asso. prof., 1978—, co-dir. peripheral vascular service, 1976-77, dir., 1977-81, acting dir. div. cardiovascular and thoracic surgery, 1980—. Served to capt. U.S. Army, 1964-66. NIH grantee, 1976-79; Wis. Heart Assn. grantee, 1975-76, 76-77; diplomate Am. Bd. Surgery. Mem. ACS, John Alexander Soc., Madison Surg. Soc., Wis. Surg. Soc. (program chmn. 1979-81), Soc. Thoracic Surgeons, Internat. Study Group for Research in Cardiac Metabolism, Assn. Acad. Surgery, Internat. Coll. Angiology, Central Surg. Assn., Midwest Vascular Soc., Internat. Cardiovascular Soc., Soc. Vascular Surgery, Am. Heart Assn. Council Cardiovascular Surgery. Office: Clin Sci Center 600 Highland Ave Madison WI 53792*

BERKUN, EARL EDWIN, sporting goods mfg. co. exec.; b. Chgo., Aug. 4, 1942; s. Joseph and Sarah (Zoltak) B.; B.S. in Math., U. Ill., 1966, B.S. in Indsl. Design, 1968; m. Toby Sue Stangle, Aug. 26, 1966; children—Sandra Elizabeth, Elana Joy. Jr. project engr. Kenner Products Co., Cin., 1968-70, sr. project engr., 1973-75; project engr. Cosco Co., Indpls., 1970-73; sr. project engr. Wilson Sporting Goods Co., River Grove, Ill., 1976-78, quality assurance mgr., 1979-80, racket sports project mgr., 1980-81, mgr. team sports, 1981, mgr. golf research and devel., 1981-82, v.p. research and devel., 1982—. Mem. Am. Soc. Quality Control. Patentee clothes hamper. Office: 2233 West St River Grove IL 60171

BERLAND, THEODORE, author; b. Chgo., Mar. 26, 1929; s. Samuel and Lena (Siegel) B.; B.S. in Journalism, U. Ill., 1950; A.M. in Sociology, U. Chgo., 1972; postgrad. Bowling Green (Ohio) State U.; m. Cynthia Rich, Dec. 23, 1956; children—Leslie Myra, Elizabeth Ann, David Rueben. Gen. assignment reporter, wire editor Champaign-Urbana (Ill.) Courier, 1950-51; sci. writer Michael Reese Hosp., Chgo., 1955-56, 66—; sci. writer, editor Research Reports, U. Chgo. public relations office, 1956-59; free lance writer, Chgo., 1959—; fgn. corr. Chgo.'s American, Algiers, 1962, Chgo. Daily News, Antarctica, 1963, AMA News, Rotarian Mag., Caribbean, 1965; cons. EPA, 1971—; instr. sci. writing Medill Sch. Journalism, Northwestern U., 1973, 75; instr. nutrition Columbia Coll., Chgo., 1977-80, chmn. dept. journalism, 1980—; vis. asst. prof. journalism Bowling Green State U., 1979-80; lectr. in mass. communication U. Wis., Milw., 1980-81. Pres., North Town Community Council, 1970-73, also Citizens Against Noise; pres. dist. 2 edn. council Chgo. Bd. Edn., 1972-73; v.p. Bernard Horwich Jewish Community Center, 1970-75, pres., 1975-77; pres. Jewish Community Council West Rogers Park, 1975-76; bd. dirs. Ind. Voters Ill., 1974-75, Citizens Schs. Com., 1974-75. Recipient Journalism award Am. Osteo. Assn., 1963; certificate of Recognition med. journalism awards contests AMA, 1964, 66; 8th prize U.S. sect. Internat. Honeywell/Asahi Pentax Photo Contest, 1965; Med. Journalism award Ill. Med. Soc., 1967; Sci. Writers award ADA, 1968, 69; Distinguished Service in Journalism award Am. Optometric Assn., 1973; Distinguished Achievement in Med. Writing award Chgo. chpt. Am. Med. Writers Assn., 1973; Beth Fonda award for excellence in Med. feature writing, 1975, 78. Fellow Am. Med. Writers Assn. (pres. 1981-82); mem. Headline Club Chgo. (treas. 1972-73), Overseas Press Club, Chgo. Press Club, Authors Guild, Nat. Assn. Sci. Writers, Am. Soc. Authors and Journalists, Soc. Midland Authors (pres. 1975-78, treas. 1978-79), Women in Communication, Soc. Profl. Journalists, Chgo. Nutrition Soc. Author: The Scientific Life, 1962; (with Alfred E. Seyler) Your Children's Teeth, 1968; The Fight for Quiet, 1970; (with Mitchell Spellberg) Living with Your Ulcer, 1971; (with Robert Addison) Living with Your Bad Back, 1972; (with Gordon Snider) Living with Your Bronchitis and Emphysema, 1972; (with Richard Perritt) Living with Your Eye Operation, 1973; Rating the Diets, 1974, rev. edits., 1975-81; (with Leslie Sandlow and Richard Shapiro) Living with Your Colitis and Hemorrhoids and Related Disorders, 1976; (with Frank Z. Warren) Acupuncture Diet, 1976; The Fitness Fact Book, 1980, 81; (with Henry A. Jordan) After the Diet . . . Then What?, 1980, The Dieters Calories-Plus Diet, 1981; contbg. author: Stimulus, 1960; Perspectives on Living, 1962; Compact Handbook of College Composition (Maynard J. Brennan), 1964; A Treasury of Tips for Writers, 1965; Great Ideas Today, 1966; World Book Year Book, 1970; Crisis of Survival, 1970; Writing the Magazine Article, 1971; Readings in Health, 1972; The Endangered Environment (Ashley Montagu), 1974; Current Thinking and Writing, 1976; Together, 1977; The Complete Diet Guide for Runners and Other Athletes, 1978; editor: The Medical Importance of Wine; contbr. over 200 articles to major mags. including Parade, Good Housekeeping, Vital, Better Homes and Gardens, Saturday Evening Post, TV Guide, Woman's Day, Family Circle, Today's Health, Family Health, Redbook, Humanitas, New Eng. Jour. Medicine, others; author column The Thin Man, Chgo. Sun-Times, 1978-80, also numerous newspapers through Field News Service, United Feature Syndicate and Enterprise Sci. Service; author documentary movies. Office: PO Box 59170 Chicago IL 60659

BERMAN, ARTHUR LEONARD, state senator; b. Chgo., May 4, 1935; s. Morris and Jean (Glast) B.; B.S. in Commerce and Law, U. Ill., 1956; J.D., Northwestern U., 1958; m. Sondra Ripes, June 22, 1960; children—Adam, Marcy. Admitted to Ill. bar, 1958, since practiced in Chgo.; mem. firm White, White & Berman, Chartered, 1958-74, Maragos, Richter, Berman, Russell & White, Chartered, 1974-81, Chatz, Berman, Maragos, Haber & Fagel, 1981—; spl. atty. Bur. Liquidations, Ill. Dept. Ins., 1962-67; spl. asst. atty. gen. Ill., 1967-68; mem. Ill. Ho. of Reps. from 10th Dist., 1969-72, 11th Dist., 1973-76; mem. Ill. Senate from 11th Dist., 1976—. Adviser dist. edn. council Chgo. Bd. Edn. Bd. dirs. Zionist Orgn. Chgo.; mem. Rogers Park, Edgewater, Northtown communtiy councils. Pres., 50th Ward Young Democrats, 1956-60; v.p. Cook County Young Dems., 1956-60, 50th Ward Regular Dem. Orgn., 1955—; exec. bd. Dem. Party, Evanston, Ill., 1973—. Bd. dirs. Bernard Horwich Jewish Community Center, North Town Community Council; bd. govs. State of Israel Bonds. Mem. Am., Ill., Chgo. (bd. mgrs. 1976-77) bar assns., Decalogue Soc. Lawyers, Am. Trial Lawyers Assn., John Howard Assn., Common Cause, Northwestern U., U. Ill. alumni assns., Phi Epsilon Pi, Tau Epsilon Rho. Office: 140 S Dearborn St Chicago IL 60603

BERMAN, AUBREY, tax cons.; b. Chgo., May 23, 1925; s. William and Ethel (Frankel) B.; B.S., U. Ill., 1948; m. Dorothy Lee Kolodny, Dec. 20, 1949; m. 2d, Penni Maller, July 31, 1977; children—Gordon, Michael, Roberta, Wendy. With IRS, 1949-79, internal revenue agt., Chgo., 1949-58, supervising spl. agt., 1966-70, criminal investigator, 1958-79; self-employed tax cons., security cons., Wilmette, Ill., 1979—. Served with AUS, 1943-46. Mem. U.S. Treasury Agts. Assn., Fed. Criminal Investigators Assn., Chgo. Philatelic Soc. (pres.). Democrat. Jewish. Address: 2443 Cardinal Ln Wilmette IL 60091

BERMAN, HERBERT MARTIN, lawyer, arbitrator, mediator; b. Louisville, Mar. 22, 1936; s. Robert J. and Freda (Baer) B.; B.A., Ind. U., 1958; LL.B., U. Louisville, 1961; m. Sondra Ann Ignatow, Dec. 21, 1958; children—Michael, Frances, Jennifer. Admitted to Ky. bar, 1961, Ill. bar, 1971; asso. firm Shaikun & Helmann, Louisville, 1961-62; field atty. NLRB, Cin., 1962-63; asst. gen. counsel Internat. Brewery Workers Union, Cin., 1963-68; labor relations counselor Brunswick Corp., Chgo., 1968-70; asso. firm Lederer, Fox & Grove, Chgo., 1970-73; partner firm Arnold & Kadjan, Chgo., 1973-76; pres., partner firm Berman & Landrum Ltd., Chgo., 1976-79; prin. firm Herbert M. Berman & Assos., Ltd., Chgo., 1979—. Mem. Am. Arbitration Assn. (panel), Am. Bar Assn., Soc. Profls. in Dispute Resolution. Home: 244 Willow Ave Deerfield IL 60015 Office: 180 N LaSalle St Chicago IL 60601

BERMAN, HOWARD JAMES, assn. exec.; b. Chgo., Feb. 23, 1945; s. Sidney and Mildred B.; B.S. magna cum laude in Fin., U. Ill., 1967; M.H.A., U. Mich., 1969; m. Marilyn Millstone, June 1968; children—Seth, Lindsay. With Commr.'s Office, N.Y.C. Dept. Hosps., 1968-69; asst. prof. hosp. adminstrn. U. Mich., 1970-71; v.p. research and devel. Blue Cross Assn., Chgo., 1971-77; v.p. charge corp. planning, product devel., data processing and research Am. Hosp. Assn., Chgo., 1977-79; group v.p. Health Services Program Group, Am. Hosp. Assn., 1979—; lectr. U. Chgo., 1971—; adj. prof. Govs. State U.; chmn. program policy group Finger Lakes Prospective Payment Experiment, 1976-78; adv. bd. Coop. Info. Center Hosp. Mgmt. Studies, 1972—; mem. ambulatory dental care adv. com. R.W. Johnson Found. Mem. Am. Coll. Hosp. Adminstrs. Co-chmn. editorial bd. Health Services Research; editorial bd. Inquiry, Topics in Hosp. Fin. Mgmt.; author and editor publs. in field. Office: 840 N Lake Shore Dr Chicago IL 60611

BERNACCHI, MICHAEL DENNIS, bus. research cons., educator; b. Kenosha, Wis., May 2, 1944; s. Dino G. and Lola M. (Marcolini) B.; B.A. in Econs., Drake U., 1968, M.A. in Econs., 1970; Ph.D., So. Ill. U., 1973; J.D., U. Detroit, 1977; m. Marilyn Ann Malaney, May 1, 1965; children—Michael Dennis, Dino James, Andria Marie, Amanda Elizabeth, Rocco William, Gabrielli Anthony. Advt. research cons. Home Fed. Savs. and Loan, Des Moines, Iowa, 1968-69, Gerdes Advt. Agy., Des Moines, 1968-69; asso. planner and econ. research analyst Des Moines City Planning and Zoning Commn., 1968-69; mktg. research project leader Joe Schlitz Brewing Co., Milw., 1970; instr. marketing So. Ill. U., Carbondale, 1972-73; marketing cons. Kali Jewelry, Troy, Mich., 1973-76, Consumer Credit Co., Detroit, 1973-76; market researcher Sta. WWJ-TV, 1973-76; asst. prof. marketing Coll. of Bus. and Adminstrn., U. Detroit, 1973-77, market researcher, 1973-77, asso. prof. Schs. of Law and Bus., 1977—; prin. Service Orgn. Consultants, Inc., Berkeley, Mich., 1976—; U. Detroit research coordinator Wayne County (Mich.) Consumer Protection Agy., 1975-76. Mem. adv. com. Troop 1642, Detroit area council Boy Scouts Am., 1978—; instr. Parish Religious Edn. Program, St. Columban Ch., 1978—. Mem. Acad. Mktg. Sci., Am. Acad. Advt., Am. Mktg. Assn., Internat. Communication Assn., Am. Council on Consumer Interest. Roman Catholic. Contbr. numerous articles on consumer protection and marketing research to bus. and legal jours. Home: 127 Elm Park Pleasant Ridge MI 48069 Office: School of Business Univ of Detroit Detroit MI 48221 also Service Orgn Cons Berkeley MI 48072

BERNARD, BURTON CHARLES, lawyer; b. St. Louis, Oct. 19, 1926; s. Adolph and Anne (Koplovitz) B.; A.B., Washington U., 1947; LL.B., Harvard U., 1950. Staff mem. Ill. Commerce Commn., Chgo., 1950-51; practice in Granite City, Ill., also Edwardsville, Ill., also St. Louis, 1951—; asst. states atty. Madison County, Ill., 1957-66. Pres. Jewish Fedn. So. Ill., 1970-72; trustee Jefferson Nat. Meml. Assn.; mem. Tri-City Regional Port Dist., 1975-78. Served from pvt. to sgt., AUS, 1945-46. Mem. Madison County Bar Assn. (chmn. judiciary com. 1963-64), Madison County Hist. Soc. (dir., past pres.), Am. Legion, Am., Ill., Mo., St. Louis, Tri-City, Chgo. bar assns., Ill. Hist. Soc. (bd. dirs. 1960-63), Am. Jewish Hist. Soc. (exec. council 1970-73), Phi Beta Kappa. Democrat. Contbr. articles to legal jours. Office: Bernard Davidson & Kaseberg 3600 Nameoki Rd Granite City IL also Marquette Bldg Saint Louis MO

BERNARD, LOWELL FRANCIS, edni. adminstr.; b. Long Beach, Calif., Dec. 14, 1931; s. Francis M. and Irma V. (Phillips) B.; A.B. in Microbiology, UCLA, 1955, M.S. in Public Health and Preventive Medicine, 1959; postgrad. Ariz. State U., summer 1964, Case Western Res. U., 1966-69; m. Diana Mae Gypson, June 7, 1957; children—Deborah Diana, Steven Lowell, Jocelyn Dawn. Asst. prof. biology SUNY, Poughkeepsie, 1960-66; lectr. Kent (Ohio) State U. 1966-79, U. Akron (Ohio), 1968—; dir. edn. Cleve. Health Mus. and Edn. Center, 1966-69, dir., 1970—; program cons. to Ednl. Research Council Am., Cleve., 1966—; cons. in sex edn. program devel. Lighthouse for the Blind, N.Y.C., 1968; appeared on ednl. TV program Sta. WVIZ-TV, 1967, Sta. WKYC-TV, 1967-79; health cons. to Oak Park (Mich.) Sch. Dist., 1968-72, U.S. Public Health Service Chronic Diseases Program, 1969, El Paso (Tex.) Community Coll., 1977—, Mpls. Cancer Soc., 1977, Lawrence Hall of Sci., U. Calif., Berkeley, 1975—; community curriculum cons. in health edn. Beachwood (Ohio) Sch. Dist., 1970-71; internat. health edn. cons., 1970—; cons. Internat. Center for Artificial Organs and Transplants; asso. in health edn. Case Western Res. U. Sch. Medicine, Cleve., 1969-79, adj. asst. prof., 1979—; guest lectr. various workshops in colls. or univs., 1973-78; chmn. public edn. com. Northeast Ohio Regional Med. Program, 1966-67. Mem. adult edn. council Cleve. Bd. Edn., 1966-69; pres. InterMuseum Council of Northeast Ohio, 1969-70; bd. dirs. Epilepsy Found. of Am., Cleve. chpt., 1972-76, Harris County (Ohio) Dental Museum, 1966-69, Bur. of Drug Abuse, Cleve., 1966-69. Mem. Am. Assn. Museums (chmn. ann. meeting 1979, planning com. ann. meetings 1980, 81), Am. Assn. of Health and Med. Museums (v.p. 1971-73, pres. 1973-75), Assn. of Sci. and Tech. Centers (sec. treas. 1976—, dir. 1976—, chmn. ann. meeting 1979), Acad. of Medicine (health edn. com. 1966—), Fedn. for Community Planning (health planning and devel. com. 1969—). Author: Laboratory Manual in Medical Microbiology, 1967; co-author: Communication in a Health Care Setting, 1980. Home: 244 Monticello Dr Chagrin Falls OH 44022 Office: 8911 Euclid Ave Cleveland OH 44106

BERNARD, MARVIN ROSS, JR., neurosurgeon; b. Mexico, Ind., June 28, 1924; s. Marvin Ross and Irene E. (O'Donnell) B.; M.D., Ind. U., 1951; m. Jean McNeil, Nov. 20, 1971; children—Cameron Ross, Bradford James. Intern Harper Hosp., Detroit, 1951-52; resident N.Y. U. Bellevue Med. Center, 1957; practice medicine specializing in neurosurgery, Gary, Ind., 1958-75, Merrillville, Ind., 1975—; pres. Neuro-Diagnostic Center, 1975—; mem. staff Meth. Hosp., St. Mary Med. Center. Served with AUS, 1942-46. Mem. AMA, Ind. Med. Soc., Ind. Neurosurgery Soc., Inter-urban Neurosurg. Soc., Central Neuro-Surg. Soc. Republican. Methodist. Club: Masons. Home: 6430 Grand Blvd Hobart IN 46342 Office: 5500 E 81st Ave Merrillville IN 46410

BERNARD, ROGER THOMAS, chem. co. exec.; b. St. Louis, May 16, 1953; s. Francis Paul and Ella Mae (Atchison) B.; B.S. in Public Adminstrn. summa cum laude (Univ. scholar, Curator's scholar, H.H. Green Meml. scholar), U. Mo., Columbia, 1975; M.B.A., So. Ill. U., 1981; m. Linda Marie Mann, July 29, 1977. Bank examiner Fed. Deposit Ins. Corp., St. Louis, 1976-79; acct. Monsanto Enviro-Chem Systems, Inc., St. Louis, 1979-80; cost analyst Monsanto, St. Peters, Mo., 1980—. Mem. Am. Mgmt. Assn., Nat. Assn. Accts., Nat. Honor Soc. (Bus. and Public Adminstrn. Top Ten award 1975), Beta Gamma Sigma, Phi Kappa Phi. Club: Forest Park Handball (1st Pl 1977 tournament). Home: 1064 King Carey Saint Louis MO 63141

BERNARDIN, JOSEPH LOUIS, archbishop; b. Columbia, S.C., Apr. 2, 1928; s. Joseph and Maria M. (Simon) B.; A.B. in Philosophy, St. Mary's Sem., 1948; M.A. in Edn., Cath. U. Am., 1952. Ordained priest Roman Catholic Ch., 1952; asst. pastor Diocese Charleston, S.C., 1952-54, vice chancellor, 1954-56, chancellor, 1956-66, vicar gen., 1962-66, dicoesan consultor, 1962-66, adminstr., 1964-65; aux. bishop Atlanta, 1966-68; sec., mem. exec. com. Nat. Conf. Cath. Bishops-U.S. Cath. Conf., gen. sec., 1968-72, pres., 1974-77; archbishop Cin., 1972—. Mem. Sacred Congregation for Bishops, 1973—; del. World Synod of Bishops, 1974, 77, mem. Permanent Council, 1974—; mem. Pontifical Commn. Social Communications, Rome, 1970-72. Mem. Am. Revolution Bicentennial Advisory Council, 1975; mem. Pres.'s Adv. Com. Refugees, 1975. Mem. Nat. Cath. Ednl. Assn. (chmn. bd. 1978). Address: 29 E 8th St Cincinnati OH 45202*

BERNAUER, NORMAN LANG, advt. exec.; b. Pitts., Apr. 19, 1926; s. Norman Leo and Frieda Dorothy (Allmendinger) B.; A.A., Graceland Coll., 1949; B.A., U. Wis., Madison, 1951; cert. TV prodn. Sch. Radio and TV Technic, N.Y.C., 1952; m. Barbara Jean Hands, Sept. 26, 1953; children—Allise Jean, Richard Martin. With Ford Found., WOI-TV, Ames, Iowa, 1952; with Sta. WDAF-TV, Kansas City, Mo., 1952-66; pres. Ber-Raye Prodns. Co., Kansas City, Mo., 1966-68; v.p. Raveill Farley Advt., Independence, Mo., 1968-74; exec. v.p. Everett, Brandt & Bernauer, Inc., Independence, Mo., 1974—. Mem. Kansas City Mayor's Task Force on Airport Commn., 1977—; chmn. Citizens Com. for Eastern Jackson County Airport, 1978; ordained minister Reorganized Ch. Jesus Christ Latter-day Saints, pastor, 1954-61, mem. Stake High Council, 1963—. Served with U.S. Army, 1944-46. Mem. Kansas City Advt. Fin. Club, Advt. Agencies for Action, SIMSA (public relations and public affairs com.). Club: Kiwanis. Home: 427 W 70th St Kansas City MO 64113 Office: 314 W 24 Hwy Independence MO 64050

BERNDT, DAVID JOHN, psychologist; b. Elgin, Ill., July 14, 1950; s. Melvin John and Edith W. B.; B.S. summa cum laude, Coll. of Charleston, 1977; M.A., Loyola U., Chgo., 1979, Ph.D. (NIMH fellow, Doyle fellow), 1981; m. Sheila MacDonald, Mar. 7, 1978. Mental health asst. Charleston (S.C.) County Hosp., 1976-77; intern Michael Reese Hosp. and Med. Center, Chgo., 1979-80, staff psychologist, 1981—. Mem. Assn. Advancement Psychology, Eastern Psychol. Assn., Am. Psychol. Assn., Soc. Personality Assessment. Contbr. articles to profl. jours. Home: 1325 W Addison St 2B Chicago IL 60613

BERNETT, THEODORE BYRON, mgmt. cons.; b. Chgo., Aug. 30, 1924; s. Joseph and Julia (Gorski) B.; B.S. in M.E., U. Ill., 1950; student bus. adminstrn., U. Wis., Milw., 1953-54; m. Helen Brower, Apr. 23, 1949; children—Richard, Michael, James. Julie, Amy. founder T.B. Bernett & Assos., Kenosha, Wis., 1980—. Served with USNR, 1943-46. Mem. ASME. Developed technique to satisfy all theoretical sterility considerations that must be met to process plastic pouches in a retort, also hobbing mechanism to generate mathematically correct involute teeth on any size ellipse. Home: 6622 59th Ave Kenosha WI 53142

BERNFELD, LESTER, textile mfg. co. exec.; b. Chgo., Sept. 15, 1927; s. Benjamin and Dorothy B.; student public schs., Chgo.; m. Shirley Cagan, June 18, 1949; children—Lynn, Jay. Ind. sales rep., Chgo., 1948-50; dir. domestics Cham Tred Industries, Chgo., 1950-56; sales mgr. Purofied Down, Chgo., 1956-68; pres. Jerhart, Inc., Chgo., 1968—, also chmn. bd. Mem. exec. com. Nat. Jewish Hosp.; active Boy Scouts Am. Served with Air Corps, USN, 1944-48. Mem. Am. Arbitration Assn. (panel arbitrators). Home: 7922 Arcadia St Morton Grove IL 60053 Office: 2735 W Armitage Chicago IL 60647

BERNHAGEN, JOHN J., state senator; b. Hutchinson, Minn., Mar. 19, 1934; s. Ed C. and Emma (Malek) B.; grad. cert. program U. Minn., 1954: B.A., Minn. Met. State Coll., 1975; m. Loretta Narr, Oct. 28, 1956; children—Joel, Luann, Paul. Sec., dir. Minn. Assn. Elec. Coops., 1969—; dir. McLeon Coop. Power Assn.; mem. Minn. Ho. of Reps. from 15A Dist., 1969, Minn. Senate from 22d Dist., 1973—. Served with AUS, 1954. Recipient Outstanding Young Farmer award Hutchinson Jr. C. of C., 1965. Republican. Lutheran (pres. congregation 1970). Home: Route 1 Box 122 Hutchinson MN 55350 Office: Room 130 State Office Bldg Saint Paul MN 55101

BERNHARD, JOHN TORBEN, univ. pres.; b. N.Y.C., June 24, 1920; s. Torben Martin and Mary (Nielsen) B.; B.S., Utah State U., 1941; M.A., UCLA, 1949, Ph.D., 1951; LL.D. (hon.), Quincy Coll., 1970; Chungnam Nat. U., Korea, 1975; D.Litt. (hon.), Central Mich. U.; m. Ramona Bailey, June 2, 1941; children—John Gary, Scott Martin, Randall Lee, Julie Ann. Prof. polit. sci. Brigham Young U., 1959-68, dean humanities and social scis., 1962-68; pres., prof. polit. sci. Western Ill. U., Macomb, 1968-74, Western Mich. U., Kalamazoo, 1974—. Served to lt. (j.g.) USCGR. Mem. Am. Assn. Higher Edn., Am. Polit. Sci. Assn., Pi Sigma Alpha, Pi Gamma Mu, Xi Sigma Pi, Sigma Nu, Sigma Iota Epsilon, Phi Delta Kappa, Phi Kappa Phi, Pi Delta Epsilon. Mormon. Office: Western Mich U Kalamazoo MI 49008*

BERNING, KARL, state senator; b. Seattle, June 10, 1911; s. Frank and Clara Berning; A.A., Blackburn Coll., 1933; postgrad., Lake Forest (Ill.) Coll., Northwestern U.; m. Alpha Mikkelsen, Dec. 31, 1939; children—Grant, Penny Berning Schafer, Randall. Constable, W. Deerfield Twp. (Ill.), 1946-53; supr. W. Deerfield Twp. and County Bd., 1953-62; chmn. Lake County (Ill.) Bd. Suprs., 1960-62; pres. Lake County Forest Preserve Dist., 1960; treas. Lake County, 1962-66; mem. Ill. Senate from 32d Dist., 1966—, minority spokesman, past chmn. com. pensions, personnel and vets affairs. Alternate del. Rep. Nat. Conv., 1980; life elder Trinity United Ch. Christ, Deerfield. Recipient numerous service awards. Mem. Nat. Soc. State Legislators, Deerfield, Highland Park and Lake County Hist. Soc., Landmarks Preservation Council. Republican. Clubs: Lions, Mason. Home: 1006 Rosemary Terr Deerfield IL 60015 Office: 625 Deerfield Rd Deerfield IL 60015

BERNSTEIN, ARTHUR, physician; b. Chgo., Aug. 21, 1908; s. Philip and Sarah (Goldstein) B.; B.S., U. Ill., 1931, M.D., 1934; m. Juanita Steman, May 19, 1936; children—Sidney, Henry, Louis. Intern, Cook County Hosp., Chgo., 1933-34, resident in internal medicine, 1935-37; practice medicine specializing in internal medicine, Chgo., 1937—; staff Cook County Hosp., 1937—, asst. med. supt., 1946-69; clin. asso. prof. medicine Coll. Medicine, U. Ill., 1936—; attending physician dept. medicine Columbus-Cuneo-Cabrini Med. Center, 1950—; prof. medicine Cook County Hosp. Grad. Sch. Medicine, 1946—. Served to lt. comdr. M.C., USNR, 1944-46. Fellow A.C.P.; mem. AMA, Chgo. Soc. Internal Medicine, Inst. Medicine Chgo., Am. Diabetes Assn., Am. Heart Assn., Soc. Med. History Chgo., Am. Assn. for History of Medicine. Jewish. Club: Standard of Chgo. Contbr. articles to profl. jours. Editor: Interns Manual, 1954-71. Home: 860 Lake Shore Dr Chicago IL 60611 Office: Suite 1929 25 E Washington St Chicago IL 60602

BERNSTEIN, CHARLES BERNARD, lawyer; b. Chgo., June 24, 1941; s. Norman and Adele (Shore) B.; A.B., U. Chgo., 1962; J.D., DePaul U., 1965; m. Roberta Luba Lesner, Aug. 7, 1968; children—Edward Charles, Louis Charles. Admitted to Ill. bar, 1965, U.S. Supreme Ct. bar, 1972; asso. firm Axelrod, Goodman & Steiner, Chgo., 1966-67, Max & Herman Chill, Chgo., 1967-74, Bellows & Assos., Chgo., 1974-81, Marvin Sacks Ltd., Chgo., 1981; individual practice law, 1981—; basketball press dir. U. Chgo., 1967-74. Vice pres. Congregation Rodfei Zedek, 1979-81, fin. sec., 1981—, bd. dirs., 1978—. Recipient Am. Jurisprudence award, 1963; citation meritorious service Dist. Grand Lodge 6 B'nai B'rith, 1969; My Brothers Keeper award Am. Jewish Congress, 1977. Mem. Chgo., Ill. State bar assns., Chgo. Jewish Hist. Soc. (treas. 1977-79, v.p. 1979—, dir. 1977—), Chgo. Pops Orch. Assn. (treas., exec. com. 1975-81), Am. Jewish Hist. Soc., Art Inst. of Chgo., Chgo. Hist. Soc., Jewish Geneal. Soc. (dir. 1977—), Nu Beta Epsilon. Club: B'nai B'rith. Contbr. articles to profl. jours. and mags. Home: 5400 S Hyde Park Blvd Apt 10-C Chicago IL 60615 Office: 120 W Madison St Chicago IL 60602

BERNSTEIN, HARVEY JAY, fin. systems specialist; b. Detroit, Apr. 16, 1945; s. Morris and Bernice (Rothman) B.; student U. Toledo, 1963-65: A.S., Cuyahoga Community Coll., 1974; B.S. magna cum laude, Dyke Coll., 1977; Sec. of Navy Fin. Mgmt. fellow Weatherhead Sch. Mgmt., Case Western Res. U., 1980-81; m. Irene Harriet Hoffman, Jan. 21, 1968; children—Bradley J., Matthew A. Fiscal acctg. asst. Navy Fin. Center, Cleve., 1971-72, fiscal acct. officer, 1972-73, mil. pay regulation specialist, 1973-79, fin. systems specialist, 1979—; instr. John Carroll U., 1978-79, Cuyahoga Community Coll., 1977—, Dyke Coll., 1981—. Served with USN, 1965-71. Recipient Career Service award Cleve. Fed. Exec. Bd., 1978; lic. real estate broker. Mem. Am. Soc. Mil. Comptrollers (pres. Cleve. chpt. 1976-77), Cleve. Area Bd. Realtors, Am. Contract Bridge League, Mensa. Jewish. Home: University Heights OH 44118 Office: US Navy Finance Center Cleveland OH 44199

BERNSTEIN, MALCOLM ALBERT, ins. agt.; b. Cin., Feb. 18, 1933; s. Herbert B. and Mildred (Abrohams) B.; B.S., U. Pa., 1954; m. Ann Maxine Berkman, Nov. 24, 1960; children—Sarah Elizabeth, Alexander Isaac Joshua. With Isaacs & Bernstein Inc., Cin., 1954-69; v.p. Frederick Rauh & Co., Cin., 1969—; publisher Music & Matter mag., 1958-59; pres. Dimension Cincinnati mag., 1963-65. Bd. dirs. Cin. Jewish Community Relations Council, 1958—, pres., 1980—; bd. dirs. Jewish Family Service, 1965-79, Assn. Home Care Agencies, 1976-79; bd. dirs. Easy Riders, 1975—, pres., 1977-79. CPCU. Mem. Queen City Assn. (dir. 1968-69), Soc. CPCU. Jewish. Club: Losantiville Country. Home: 59 Oliver Rd Cincinnati OH 45215 Office: 3300 Central Pkwy Cincinnati OH 45225

BERNSTEIN, MARTIN STUART, mktg./advt. cons.; b. Omaha, June 5, 1932; s. David B. and Eva (Cohn) B.; B.B.A., U. Tex., 1956; A.B., Del Mar Coll., 1956; postgrad. Harvard U., 1967; m. Martha Gumaer, Sept. 2, 1960; 1 son, Michael David. Advt. dir. U.S. Shoe Corp., Cin., 1962-67; v.p. McManus, John & Adams Advt., Bloomfield Hills, Mich., 1967-68; sr. v.p. Campbell-Ewald Co., Detroit, 1968-72; pres. Sportstats/MCA, Inc., N.Y.C., Universal City, Calif., 1972-75; pres. Mktg. Services Bur., Inc., Southfield, Mich., 1975—. Bd. dirs. Motion Picture Hall of Fame, Los Angeles, 1973-78. Recipient Sec. of Commerce citation for aiding U.S. export sales, 1980. Mem. Am. Mktg. Assn., Am. Footwear Industries Assn. Clubs: Detroit Adcraft, Cin. Advt., N.Y. World Trade, Friars of N.Y., Friars of Calif., Masons. Home: 1560 Brentwood Dr Troy MI 48098 Office: 30555 Southfield Rd Suite 340 Southfield MI 48076

BERNSTEIN, MURRAY M., social worker; b. Milw., July 3, 1938; s. Louis and Rae (Kurzer) B.; B.S., U. Wis., Milw., 1966, M.S.W., 1970; Ph.D., Eastern Nebr. Christian Coll., 1973; m. Nancy Siegel, Jan. 26, 1964; children—David J., Sarah Lynn. Program dir. Milw. Boys Club, 1964-68; social work psychologist VA Hosp., Woods, Wis., 1974—; asst. prof. dept. psychiatry Med. Coll. Wis.; pvt. cons.; dir. Inst. Directive Therapy; cons. therapist Assn. Research and Enlightenment (Edgar Cayce Found.). Pres. Temple Anshe Emeth, Milw., 1979-80. Served with USAF, 1956-60; to capt. M.C., U.S. Army, 1970-74. Cert. Acad. Cert. Social Workers. Mem. Am. Group Psychotherapy Assn., Nat. Assn. Social Workers, Internat. Transactional Analysis Assn. Developer directive therapy method of psycho-social approach to psychotherapy. Home: 8615 W Petersik St Milwaukee WI 53224 Office: Woods Veterans Administration Hospital Woods WI 53193

BERNSTEIN, PHILIP, JR., retail stock brokerage exec.; b. Chgo. Oct. 2, 1933; s. Philip and Mary Elizabeth (Frank) B.; B.S. in Econs., U. Pa., 1955; m. Rita M. Kruger, June 26, 1966; 1 dau., Lynn. Mgmt. trainee Werthan Industries, Nashville, 1955-58; with Freehling & Co., Chgo., 1959—, partner, 1967—. Vol., Michael Reese Hosp., Chgo. Asso. mem. N.Y. Stock Exchange. Clubs: Standard of Chgo., Old Willow Bath & Tennis, Rotary. Designed automated mailing system for brokerage industry. Home: 399 Fullerton Pkwy Chicago IL 60614 Office: 120 S LaSalle St Chicago IL 60603

BERNTSEN, WILLIAM BERNHARD, ednl. adminstr.; b. Chgo., Oct. 6, 1915; s. Bernt and Kristine (Bernhardsen) B.; student Moody Bible Inst., 1934-37; B.A., U. No. Iowa, 1942; M.Mus., Northwestern U., 1944; Ph.C., U. Minn., 1962; D.H., Internat. Coll., 1975; m. Beryl Venette Cutshall, Oct. 5, 1942; 1 dau., Debra Lynn. Ordained minister Baptist Ch.; technician Motorola, 1934-37; asso. pastor Burton Ave. Bapt. Ch., Waterloo, Iowa, 1938-42; asst. pastor Scofield Meml. Ch., Dallas, 1942-43, also dir. religious edn.; asso. pastor Jefferson Park Bible Ch., Chgo., 1943-44; instr. Moody Bible Inst., Chgo., 1943-44; asso. pastor First Bapt. Ch., Denton, Tex., 1944-45, also dir. religious edn.; chmn. div. music Northwestern Coll., Mpls., 1946-65, pres., 1965—. Republican. Author choral compositions and arrangements. Office: 3003 N Snelling St Roseville MN 55113

BERNTSON, STANLEY MARSHALL, savs. and loan assn. exec.; b. Chgo., Aug. 5, 1907; s. Bernard E. and Margurite (Nelson) B.; evening student Northwestern U., 1925-27; m. Lillian Adelaine Johnson, Oct. 14, 1933; children—Gail Lynda, Grant Morgan. Acct., George Reinberg Co., Chgo., 1927-35, George May & Co., 1935-36; exec. sec. Derby Laundry, 1936-40; chmn. bd. Fidelity Fed. Savs., Chgo., 1940—; v.p. Mars Realty Co., 1945—; exec. sec. Samuel Olson Mfg. Co., 1943-56. Bd. dirs. Elmhurst YMCA; chmn. bd. Home of Onesiphorus; trustee Trinity Sem.; bd. dirs. Lydia Children's Home. Mem. Nat. League Insured Assns. (legis. com.), Ill. Savs. and Loan League (legis. com.), Cook County Council Insured Savs. Assn. (pres.), C. of C. (dir.). Mem. Evang. Free Ch. Am. Club: Kiwanis (dir.). Home: 211 Winthrop Ave Elmhurst IL 60126 Office: 5455 W Belmont Ave Chicago IL 60641

BERNZEN, AVRIL MARIE CLARK, microbiologist; b. Quincy, Ill., Jan. 26, 1924; d. Wallace Edward and Marie A. (Recker) Heberling; B.S., Quincy Coll., 1945; voice grad. Quincy Conservatory Music; piano grad. Notre Dame Conservatory Music; student St. John Hosp. Sch. of Med. Tech., 1946-47; 1 dau., Joan Marie Clark Queen. Microbiologist, St. John's Mercy Hosp., St. Louis, 1948-52; med. technologist St. Frances Hosp. Lab., Peoria, Ill., 1956-58; lectr. in microbiology Quincy Coll., 1966-70; adminstrv. technologist, ednl. dir. St. Mary Hosp., Quincy, 1959—. Pres. Altrusa Club, 1974-76; bd. govs. for Dogwood Festival, C. of C., 1975-77; bd. dirs. Quincy Soc. Fine Arts, United Way, 1978—; bd. dirs. Quincy Community Little Theatre, Quincy Art Club, ESA World Center Found., Quincy and Adams County Mus. Named Outstanding Woman of Ill., ESA Orgn., 1968; Outstanding Woman of Quincy, 1970; Outstanding Alumnus, Biology Dept. of Quincy Coll., 1980. Mem. Am. Soc. Med. Tech.; Am. Soc. Clinical Pathologists, Internat. Platform Assn., Epsilon Sigma Alpha (Outstanding Mem. award 1977). Republican. Roman Catholic. Clubs: Elks Aux., Spring Lake Country, Altrusa (Outstanding Mem. 1978-79). Home: 2236 Vermont St Quincy IL 62301 Office: 1415 Vermont St Quincy IL 62301

BEROUNSKY, JOSEPH FRANK, electronics engr.; b. Omaha, Mar. 2, 1930; s. Joseph John and Mary (Kracl) B.; m. Mary Francis Taylor, Apr. 8, 1947; children—Joseph John, Mary Catherne (Mrs. John Whitney), Chris Alan. Radio technician Gen. Communications Co., Inc., Omaha, 1961-66, service mgr., 1966-73, systems engr., 1973-80; sales engr. Omaha Communications Systems Ltd., 1980—. Mem. Ak Sar Ben Radio Club (v.p., pres. 1962-63), Eagles. Home: 9010 Valley St Omaha NE 68124 Office: 827 S 20th St Omaha NE 68108

BERQUIST, THOMAS HENRY, radiologist; b. Bemidji, Minn., Sept. 10, 1945; s. Karl Henry and Audrey (Thomas) B.; B.A. cum laude, Concordia Coll., 1967; B.S., U. N.D., 1969; M.D., Washington

U., St. Louis, 1971; M.S. in Radiology, U. Minn., 1975; m. Kay Ellen McElwain, Sept. 5, 1969; children—Aric, Matthew. Intern, Mayo Grad. Sch. Medicine, Rochester, Minn., 1971-72, resident in radiology, 1972-75; asst. prof. diagnostic radiology Mayo Clinic, 1977— spokesman dept. radiology St. Mary's Hosp.; instr. skeletal anatomy Mayo Med. Sch. Served with U.S. Army, 1976-77. Decorated Legion of Merit. Mem. Am. Coll. Radiology, Am. Roentgen Ray Soc., Minn. Radiol. Soc., Sigma Xi, Alpha Omega Alpha (Lang award 1971). Republican. Methodist. Contbr. articles to profl. jours. Home: 1752 Walden Ln SW Rochester MN 55901 Office: 200 1st St SW Rochester MN 55901

BERREY, ROBERT WILSON, III, lawyer, judge; b. Kansas City, Mo., Dec. 6, 1929; s. Robert Wilson and Elizabeth (Hudson) B.; A.B., William Jewell Coll., 1950; M.A., U. S.D., 1952; LL.B., Kansas City U., 1955; LL.M., U. Mo. at Kansas City, 1972; grad. Trial Judges Coll., U. Nev., 1972; m. Katharine Rollins Wilcoxson, Sept. 5, 1950; children—Robert Wilson IV, Mary Jane, John Lind. Admitted to Mo. bar, 1955, Kans. bar, 1955, since practiced in Kansas City; asso. mem. firm Shugert and Thomson, 1955-56, Clark, Krings & Bredehoft, 1957-61, Terry and Welton, 1961-62; judge 4th Dist. Magistrate Ct., Jackson County, Mo., 1962-79; asso. circuit judge 16th Jud. Circuit Ct., Jackson County, Mo., 1979—, mem. mgmt.-exec. com., 1979—; mem. Supreme Ct. Com. to Draft Rules and Procedures for Mo.'s Small Claims Ct., 1976, 77. Vol. legal cons. Psychiat. Receiving Center. Del. Atlantic Council Young Polit. Leaders, Oxford, Eng., 1965; Kansas City rep. to President's National Conference on Crime Control; del.-at-large White House Conf. Aging, 1972; former pack chmn. Cub Scouts Am.; counselor, com. mem. Boy Scouts Am., sponsor Eagle Scouts; vice chmn. water fowl com. Mo. Conservation Fedn., 1968-69, chmn. water fowl com., 1971-73; v.p. Cook PTA, 1967-68; mem. cts. and judiciary com. Mo. bar, 1969-73; mem. Midwest region adv. com. Nat. Park Service, 1973-78, chmn., 1973-78; mem. Mo. State Judicial Planning Commn., 1977; bd. dirs., founder Kansas City Open Space Found., 1976. Regional dir. Young Rep. Nat. Fedn., 1957-59, gen. counsel, 1959-61, nat. vice-chmn.; chmn. Mo. Young Rep. Fedn., 1960, nat. committeeman, 1959-60, 61-64; Mo. alternate at large Republican Nat. Conv., 1960, asst. gen. counsel, 1964, del. state and dist. convs., 1960, 64, 68. Bd. dirs. Naturalization Council, Kansas City, pres., 1973—; trustee Kansas City Mus., 1972-73. Mem. Mo. Bar (Disting. Service award 1973, agr. law com., com. council 1980-81), Kansas City Bar Assn., Urban League (exec. com., dir.), S.A.R., Kansas City Mus. Natural Sci. Soc. (charter), Alpha Phi Omega, Delta Theta Phi, Pi Gamma Mu, Tau Kappa Epsilon. Mem. Christian Ch. Mason, mem. DeMolay Legion Honor. Clubs: Ward Parkway Country (dir. 1968-69); Leawood Country; Kansas City; Waldo Optimist (v.p. 1967-68); Capitol Hill (Washington); Ducks Unltd. (state com. 1981). Home: 1235 W 58th St Kansas City MO 64113 also summer Route 2 Battle Lake MN Office: Jackson County Ct House Kansas City MO 64106

BERRIO, MARK MANUEL, civil engr.; b. Cordoba, Spain, July 19, 1933; s. Manuel and Serafina Pilar (Benitez) B.; C.E., U. Guatemala, 1962; M.S., U. Mich., 1965; Ph.D., Mich. State U., 1971; m. Margaret Mary Peters, May 1, 1965; 1 dau., Emily Susan. Structural engr. Castillo-Contoux, S.A., Guatemala, 1962-64; structural engr. TIPIC, SA, Guatemala City, 1965-66, Roof Structures, Inc., Rock Hill, St. Louis, 1966-67; prof. civil engring. Tufts U., Medford, Mass., 1971-72, Rose Hulman Inst., Terre Haute, Ind., 1972—; cons. structural engr. NSF grantee, summer 1973. Mem. Historic Archeol. Preservation Com. Terre Haute, Am. Soc. Engring. Edn. (chmn. campus activity), ASCE, Sigma Xi (pres. Ind. State U. chpt.). Club: Camera. Author: Rigidity of Slabless Reinforced Concrete Stairs, 1962; Analysis of Viscoeleastic Frames, 1971. Home: Route 2 Box 314 Greencastle IN 46135 Office: 5500 Wabash St Dept Civil Engring Terre Haute IN 47803

BERRY, CHARLES LEONARD, fin. exec.; b. Granite City, Ill., Sept. 21, 1940; s. P. Louis and Freida (Feltman) B.; B.S., St. Louis U., 1961, M.S., 1972; m. Lynn S. Moore, Oct. 28, 1967; children—Charles Leonard, Catherine, Christopher. With Eastman Kodak Stores, Inc., 1961-70, acct., St. Louis, 1961-63, credit mgr., 1963-66, office supr., San Diego, 1966-70; hosp. controller St. Louis U. Med. Center, 1970-75, adminstrv. controller, 1975-76; asso. controller Normandy Osteo. Hosps., St. Louis, 1977-79; asst. prof. Webster Coll., St. Louis, 1979-80; v.p. fin. McKendree Coll., Lebanon, Ill., 1980—; adj. faculty Maryville Coll., 1975—, Webster Coll., 1974—. Mem. Hosp. Fin. Mgmt. Assn., Alpha Kappa Psi. Home: 280 N Lindbergh Blvd Saint Louis MO 63141 Office: 701 College Rd Lebanon IL 62254

BERRY, JANET PATRICIA, educator; b. Columbus, Ohio, Feb. 12, 1923; d. Maurice Denver and Mary (Funk) B.; B.S., Ohio State U., 1944, postgrad., 1945, 60, 75—; postgrad. Otterbein Coll., 1960-61; M.A., Ohio State U., 1978; m. Escalus E. Elliott, Jr., Apr. 1944 (div. May 1962); 1 son, Escalus E. III; m. 2d, Edward J. Hannon, Jan. 7, 1966 (div. June 1980). Instr. dept. fine arts Ohio State U., 1945-46; art supr., tchr. Gahanna (Ohio) Public Schs., 1960-61; mem. art guide com. Franklin County Bd. Edn., 1960-61; exec. sec. Columbus Town Meeting Assn., producer-dir. Columbus Town Meeting Forum, 1963-72; field services Nat. Center for Vocat. Edn., Ohio State U., 1972-77, 80—. Pres. bd. trustees West Side and Ohio Av. Day Care Centers Assn., 1958-60; gen. chmn. Twigs of Childrens Hosp., 1955-57. Recipient cert. of merit Franklin County Bd. Edn., 1961. Mem. Nat. Assn. for Gifted Children, Pi Lambda Theta, Delta Phi Delta, Kappa Kappa Gamma. Home: 1539 Longeaton Dr Columbus OH 43220 Office: 1960 Kenny Rd Columbus OH 43210

BERRY, LUCILLE MARIE, educator; b. Nameoki, Ill., June 2, 1936; d. P. Louis and Frieda Catherine (Feltman) Berry; B.S., St. Louis U., 1958, M.S. in Commerce, 1963. Supr. cashiers St. Louis U., 1958-64, supr. grants and contracts, 1964-66, chief funds accountant, 1966-71; fin. asst. to provincial treas. Religious of the Sacred Heart, 1971-74, provincial treas., 1974-75; controller Maryville Coll., St. Louis, 1975-76, dir. bus. and fin., 1976-79, adj. instr., 1972-76, adj. asst. prof., 1976-79, asso. prof., 1979—, chmn. mgmt. div., 1979—. Mem. Am. Soc. Women Accountants, Am. Assn. Accountants, Mo. Assn. Accounting Educators, Midwest Bus. Adminstrs. Assn., Pi Lambda Theta. Home: 9616 Old Bonhomme St Louis MO 63132 Office: 13550 Conway Rd St Louis MO 63141

BERRY, RICHARD LEWIS, editor; b. Greenwich, Conn., Nov. 6, 1946; s. John William and Dorothy May (Buck) B.; B.A., U. Va., 1968; M.Sc., York U., 1972; m. Eleanor von Auw, June 7, 1968. Research asst. MacMaster U., Hamilton, Ont., Can., 1973-74; project engr. Toronto (Ont.) Intraspace Internat., 1974-75; editor Astronomy mag., Milw., 1976—; founder, editor Telescope Making mag., Milw. Recipient Clifford Holmes award Astronomy for Am., 1981. Mem. Optical Soc. Am., Milw. Astron. Soc. Office: 625 E St Paul Ave Milwaukee WI 53202

BERRY-CABÁN, CRISTÓBAL SANTIAGO, educator; b. Aguadilla, P.R., Jan. 9, 1953; s. Charles William and María de Lourdes (Cabán) B.; B.A., Coll. Sacred Heart, 1974; M.A., Marquette U., 1976; Ph.D., U. Wis.-Milw., 1981. Tchr. high sch., Liceo Interam. Castro. Rio Piedras, P.R., 1974; curriculum writer Midwest Materials Devel. Center, Milw. Pub. Schs., 1975-76; project specialist, lectr. U. Wis., Milw., 1977—. Mem. Am. Hist. Assn., Ateneo Puertorriqueño, ACLU, Am. Sociol. Assn., Nat. Assn. Bilingual Edn. Roman Catholic. Author: Aromaliris, 1974; (with others) Geografía de Hispano América, 1976; Hispanics in Wisconsin: A Bibliography, 1981. Asso. editor La Guardia, 1974—, Jour. Contemporary Puerto Rican Thought, 1976-78, Puerto Rican Jour., 1981—. Home: PO Box 11854 Shorewood WI 53211 Office: Dept Community Edn U Wis Milwaukee WI 53201

BERRYMAN, ALICE DAVIS (MRS. CECIL WELLS BERRYMAN), concert pianist, composer, educator; b. North Platte, Nebr.; d. George Warren and Alice (Clark) Davis; studied piano with August Borglum, Omaha, Wager Swayne, Paris, Rudolph Ganz, Switzerland, Maine, Denver, N.Y.; mus. analysis with Cecil Berryman; theory, harmony, composition and orchestration with Emile Schvartz, Paris Conservatoire; student music course New Coll. Oxford (Eng.) U., 1969; m. Cecil Wells Berryman (dec. 1960); children—Edward Davis, Warren Leigh, Rudolph Barton. Concert pianist, numerous concerts alone and in joint with husband and three sons, Paris, N.Y. and Midwest, 1912—; debut Princess Theatre, N.Y., 1915; accredited tchr. piano Berryman Piano Conservatory, 1916—, U. Omaha, 1930-57; work shop tchrs. and players courses Presbyn. U., 1929; nat. judge of piano, Tex., Iowa, Ohio, Va., Tenn., Wis., Alaska, Mo., 1939—; judge internat. record contests, 1954-68. Named to Piano Guild U.S.A. Hall of Fame, 1968. Mem. Am. Coll. Musicians (nat. membership com., accredited tchr.), Nat. (certification 1969), Nebr. (exec. com., recipient certificate of profl. advancement, exam. chmn. bd. certification), Omaha (pres. 1977-78) music tchrs. assns., Nat. Soc. Lit. and Arts, Nat. Guild Piano Tchrs. (faculty; chmn. bd. certification State of Nebr.). P.E.O. Presbyterian. Numerous compositions published. Home: 5018 Izard St Omaha NE 68132

BERSCHE, JOSEPH EDWIN, constrn. co. exec.; b. Fairmont, W.Va., Oct. 17, 1931; s. G. Joseph and Jessie Naomi (Darling) B.; student Mich. State Normal Sch., 1949-50, Nyack Coll., 1950-51, U.S. Navy Engring. Sch., 1952; m. Barbara Carol Stegmaier, June 9, 1956; children—Craig, Chris, Kimberly Jo, Curt, Barbi Jo. Pres., Bersche Constrn. Co., Pontiac, Mich., 1956-66; exec. v.p., dir. Hannan Co., Cleve., 1967-77; pres. Inland Constrn., Inc., Chgo., 1977—; dir. Christian Publs. Inc., Harrisburg, Pa.; trustee pension fund Urban Investment and Devel. Co., Chgo. Trustee, Nyack (N.Y.) Coll., Stow Alliance Fellowship, Alliance Theol. Sem., Nyack; bd. mgrs. Christian and Missionary Alliance, Nyack; bd. dirs. Shell Point Village Retirement Home, Ft. Myers, Fla. Served with USN, 1951-55. Mem. Builders Assn. Chgo., Assn. Governing Bds. of Univs. and Colls. Clubs: Hudson Country; Carlton, Execs. (Chgo.). Office: 845 N Michigan Ave Chicago IL 60611

BERST, JANET ROSE, data processing exec.; b. Hammond, Ind., June 25, 1937; d. John Albert and Mary Ruth (Barnes) B.; B.A. in Speech, Taylor U., Upland, Ind., 1959; diploma in programming Internat. Data Processing Inst., Cin., 1967. Lead programmer analyst Midland Mut. Life Ins. Co., Columbus, Ohio, 1969-72, Ohio Dept. Edn., Columbus, 1972-75; sr. programmer analyst Ohio Youth Commn., Columbus, 1975-77; sr. devel. analyst Lincoln Nat. Life Ins., Fort Wayne, Ind., 1977-79; tech. analyst Washington Nat. Ins., Evanston, Ill., 1979—. Active, Evanston Hist. Soc., Chgo. Architecture Found. Life Mgmt. Inst. fellow, 1979. Mem. Assn. Systems Mgmt., Assn. Computing Machinery (pres. Central Ohio chpt.), Internat. Platform Assn., AAUW. Methodist. Club: Photography. Author: Christianity and the Real World. Office: 1630 Chicago Ave Evanston IL 60201

BERTHOLD, JAMES ALFRED, educator; b. Elyria, Ohio, Dec. 26, 1932; s. Alfred William and Mary Agnes (Edwards) B.; B.E., U. Toledo, 1979; m. Sandra Lukens Ludlum, Aug. 25, 1956; children—David, Judith, Jean, Janet, Donald, Douglas, Daniel, Jane, Jennifer, Dale, Daryl. Machine operator Bobdel, Inc., Lorain, Ohio, 1950-51; automobile service technician Slimans Sales & Service, Amherst, Ohio, 1956-74; auto-mechanic tchr. Ehove Joint Vocat. Sch., Milan, Ohio, 1974-80, trades and industry supr., 1980. Served with USAF, 1952-56. cert. automotive technician. Mem. NEA, Am. Vocat. Assn., Ohio Edn. Assn., Ohio Vocat. Assn., Ohio Assn. Trades and Industry Suprs., Phi Eta Sigma. Democrat. Roman Catholic. Home: 631 Jackson St Amherst OH 44001 Office: Ehove Joint Vocational School 316 W Mason Rd Milan OH 44846

BERTING, ROBERT JAMES, advt. agy. exec.; b. Indpls., July 4, 1931; s. Herman Phillip and Vada Melodine (Coleman) B.; student John Herron Art Inst., 1950-52; m. Barbara Jean Freije, Dec. 27, 1975. With Indpls. Times Newspaper, 1950-51, Armour & Co., Indpls., 1951-55, Arthur Murray Dance Studios, Indpls., 1955-58, Hook Drug Co., Indpls., 1958-62, Topics Newspapers, Indpls., 1962-76, Format. Inc., Indpls., 1976-80; pres. Central Ind. Advt., Indpls., 1980—; pres. Advt. Seminars of Ind., 1980—; instr. advt. Ind. U., Indpls., 1981—. Mem. Ind. Bus. Communicators, Central Ind. Suburban Newspapers Assn. (exec. dir. 1977). Club: Advt. of Indpls. Home: 6330 Woburn Dr Indianapolis IN 46250

BERTOG, EUGENE TRACY, educator; b. Chgo., Nov. 29, 1930; s. Frank Carl and Grayce (Tracy) B.; B.S., Loyola U., Chgo., 1952, M.Ed., 1973; m. Elaine Kohl, June 25, 1955; children—Eugene, Elaine, Joseph, Steven, Robert. Dir. edn. and tng. Continental Casualty Co., Chgo., 1955-69; dir. ednl. services CNA Fin. Corp., Chgo., 1969-72; gen. mgr. Lake Shore Club Chgo., 1972-74; prof., chmn. dept. hotel mgmt. Oakton Community Coll., Des Plaines, 1974—. Mem. deans adv. council Loyola U., 1976—; pres. PTA, 1971-73. Served as lt. AUS, 1953-55; Korea. Named Alumnus of Yr., Loyola U., 1967; recipient service to youth through athletics awards. Mem. Hotel Sales Mgmt. Assn. (dir.), Am. Acad. Polit. and Social Sci., Am. Soc. Tng. and Devel., Ins. Co. Edn. Dirs. Soc., U.S. Olympic Soc., Execs. Club Chgo. Clubs: North Shore Country; Lake Shore of Chgo. (pres. dir.); Courtier (Park Ridge); Internat. (Chgo.). Home: 2314 Sussex Ln Northbrook IL 60062 Office: 1600 E Golf Rd Des Plaines IL 60016

BERTRAM, JOSEPH LEO, state senator, farmer; b. Spring Hill, Minn., July 3, 1954; s. Clarence Arnold and Viola Agnes (Gruber) B.; student St. Cloud (Minn.) Area Vocat. Tech. Inst., St. Cloud State U.; m. Mary Lee Imdieke, May 28, 1977; 1 dau., Leah. Congl. staff asst., 1977-80; mem. Minn. Senate from Dist. 16, 1981—. Mem. Stearns County Fair Bd., 1981—; organizer Rural Handicapped Council of Stearns and Meeker Counties; mem. Minn. Citizens Concerned for Life. Mem. Farm Bur., Nat. Farmers Orgn., Farmers Union, Spring Hill Jaycees, Citizens Ednl. Freedom. Mem. Democratic Farmer Labor Party. Roman Catholic. Club: K.C. Office: G-24 State Capitol St Paul MN 55155

BERUBE, PHILLIP, state senator; b. Belcourt, N.D., Apr. 6, 1905; s. Arthur and Victorine (Mongeon) B.; ed. public schs.; m. Alma Casavant, 1929; children—Leonel, Vivian Beruve Cote, Delina Berube Grossal, Loreeta Berube Leanard, Harvey, Julian Berube Lentz, Adrien, Jackie. Farmer, 1927-30; mem. N.D. State Senate, 1952—. Mem. County Sch. Reorgn. Com. N.D., 1947-69. Mem. Farmers Union. Roman Catholic. Club: Commercial. Office: State Capitol Bismarck ND 58505*

BESCHLOSS, MORRIS RICHARD, valve mfg. co. exec.; b. Berlin, Mar. 7, 1929; s. Otto and Manya (Levine) B.; B.S., U. Ill., 1952; m. Ruth Greenwald, Nov. 13, 1954; children—Michael, Steven. Advt. mgr. Hammond Valve Corp. (Ind.), 1956-58, asst. sales mgr., 1958-61, field sales mgr., 1961-62, v.p. sales, 1962-63, pres., 1963-68, chmn. bd., 1968—, also dir.; pres. Conval Corp., 1968—; v.p., dir. Condec Corp.; pres. Plumbing-Heating-Cooling Info. Bur., 1971-72, chmn. bd., 1973—. Pres. Flossmoor-Homewood (Ill.) Area Sch. Bd., 1969-73. Served from 2d lt. to capt. AUS, 1952-54. Recipient Distinguished Eagle award Boy Scouts Am., 1974. Mem. Young Pres.'s Orgn., Valve Mfrs. Assn. (dir., pres. 1971-73), Assn. Industry Mfrs. (charter pres.), World Bus. Council, Tau Delta Phi, Sigma Delta Chi, Alpha Phi Omega. Clubs: Execs., Econ. (Chgo.). Home: Chicago IL 60611 Office: 875 N Michigan Ave Chicago IL 60611

BESS, TIMOTHY ALAN, sch. psychologist; b. Clarksville, Ark., Mar. 30, 1950; s. George William and Angie (Allen) B.; B.A. in Psychology, Butler U., Indpls., 1974, M.S. in Counseling, 1977; m. Nancy Helen Jaracz, Mar. 11, 1977; 1 son, Jonathan. Asso. instr. communication and cognitive devel. Marion County Assn. Retarded Citizens, Indpls., 1975, employment specialist, 1975-76: coordinator psychol. services and spl. edn. Plainfield (Ind.) Community Sch. Corp., 1977-78; coordinator 3-R program emotionally disturbed/behavioral problems students Ind. Sch. Dist. 834, Stillwater, Minn., 1978-79; sch. psychologist Ind. Sch. Dist. 191, Burnsville, Minn., 1979-80, Ind. Sch. Dist. 833, Cottage Grove, Minn., 1980—. Mem. Am. Personnel and Guidance Assn., Assn. Measurement and Evaluation in Guidance, Assn. Specialists Group Work, Marion County Assn. Retarded Citizens, Butler U. Alumni Assn., Phi Delta Kappa. Mem. Baha'i Faith. Home: 705 E Jenks Ave Saint Paul MN 55106 Office: Armstrong Sch 8855 Inwood Ave S Cottage Grove MN 55016

BEST, LINDA LOUISE RICHMER, psychologist; b. Newark, Ohio, Apr. 12, 1934; d. William Raymond and Mary (Price) Richmer; B.S., Ohio U., 1959; M.S., U. Mich., 1963; Ph.D., U. Toledo, 1975; m. James R. Best, Aug. 8, 1959. Tchr., Miamisburg, Ohio, 1955-56, Newark, 1956-59, Inkster, Mich., 1959-60, Livonia, Mich., 1960-62, psychologist Dearborn (Mich.) pub. schs., 1964-66, Mason Consol. Schs., Erie, Mich., 1966-71, U. Toledo, 1971-73, Monroe County (Mich.) Intermediate Sch. dist., 1973-75; pvt. practice as psychologist, Toledo, 1975—. Vol. Toledo Hosp., 1972-73. Mem. Am. Psychol. Assn., Ohio Psychol. Assn., NW Ohio Rehab. Assn. (bd. 1977-80), Kappa Delta Pi. Home: 1685 Wyandotte Blvd Maumee OH 43537 Office: 4346 Secor St Suite 107 Toledo OH 43623

BETOR, GREGORY ALDEN, real estate devel. co. exec.; b. Washington, Dec. 28, 1936; s. Theodore Leroy and Elizabeth (Pelkey) B.; B.S., U. Va., 1959; m. Gwendolyn Swift Althauser, Aug. 23, 1958; children—Marion Tucker, Elizabeth Perkins, Julia Lee. Self-employed developer/builder, Herndon, Va., 1955-60, real estate appraiser, 1964-70; engaged in mortgage banking, Washington, 1960-66; v.p. Newport Corp., Ft. Lauderdale, Fla., 1970-71; dir. Ind. properties Westinghouse Electric Corp., Indpls., 1971-79; v.p. Oxford Devel. Corp., Indpls., 1979—; speaker in field. Bd. dirs. Festival Music Soc., Indpls.; vice precinct chmn. Democratic Party; former vestryman, com. chmn. St. Martins Episc. Ch., Pompano Beach, Fla., Nativity Episcopal Ch., Indpls. Mem. Nat. Assn. Home Builders, Nat. Assn. Realtors, Ind. Assn. Homebuilders, Builders Assn. Greater Indpls., Ind. Assn. Realtors, Met. Indpls. Bd. Realtors, Ind. Collie Club, Collie Club Am., Lafayette Kennel Club. Club: Columbia. Author articles in dog mags. Home: 7835 Allisonville Rd Indianapolis IN 46250 Office: 3939 Meadows Dr Bldg Indianapolis IN 46205

BETSCHMAN, RICHARD FRANK, locksmith, hardware exec.; b. Norwalk, Ohio, May 25, 1932; s. Cyrillus N. and Martha (Egle) B.; m. Dolores Catherine Seifker, Aug. 25, 1951; children—David Paul, Ronald Gerard, Sharon Marie, Kathy Ann, Diane Marie. Foreman outboard finishing line Lyman Boats Co., Sandusky, Ohio, 1953-57; shipping clk. Rotary Printing Co., Norwalk, Ohio, 1957-63; service mgr. appliance repairs P & R Electric Co., Norwalk, 1963-67; purchaser, owner, operator Hess Hardware Co., Monroeville, Ohio, 1970—; lectr. security. Pres. Monroeville Hist. Soc., 1974—; sec. Mayor's Area Devel. Com., Monroeville, Ohio, 1975-76; chmn. Town Meeting Monroeville, 1977; organizer, gen. chmn. Community Picnic Day, 1979, 80, 81. Mem. Asso. Locksmiths Am., Pa.-Ohio Locksmiths Assn., Am., Ohio hardware assns., Am. Hardware Probe Panel, Sentry Hardware Dealer Probe, Huron County (Ohio) Am. Heritage Com. Democrat. Roman Catholic. Clubs: Lockmasters Tru-Center, Kiwanis (sec.-treas. Monroeville 1973-77). Home: 142 E Main St Norwalk OH 44857 Office: 2 N Main St Monroeville OH 44847

BETTS, HENRY BROGNARD, physician; b. New Rochelle, N.Y., May 25, 1928; s. Henry Brognard and Marguerite Meredith (Denise) B.; A.B., Princeton U., 1950; M.D., U. Va., 1954; m. Monika Christine Paul, Apr. 25, 1970; 1 dau., Amanda. Intern, Cin. Gen. Hosp., 1954-55; resident, teaching fellow N.Y. U. Med. Center Inst. Rehab. Medicine, N.Y.C., 1958-63; practice medicine, specializing in phys. medicine and rehab., Chgo., 1963—; staff physiatrist Rehab. Inst. Chgo., 1963-64, asso. med. dir., 1964-65, med. dir., 1965-69, v.p., med. dir., 1969—; Paul B. Magnuson prof., also chmn. dept. rehab. medicine Northwestern U., 1967—, prof., 1968—; chmn. rehab. medicine Northwestern Meml. Hosp.; cons. Chgo. Wesley Meml. Hosp., Passavant Meml. Hosp., Chgo. Mem. United Cerebral Palsy Steering Com., 1967—; mem. med. adv. com., pres. Am. Congress Rehab. Medicine, 1975—; chmn. Govs. Com. for Employment of Handicapped; bd. dirs., mem. Nat. Com. on Arts for Handicapped, 1981—. Served with USNR, 1956-58. Named Physician of Year, Ill. Gov.'s Com., 1964; recipient commendation Ill. Gen. Assembly, 1967, citation for meritorious service Pres.'s Com. on Employment of Handicapped, 1965. Diplomate Am. Bd. Phys. Medicine and Rehab. Mem. Ill. Med. Soc. (chmn. com. on rehab. services), Assn. Academic Physiatrists (pres. 1968-69), Multiple Sclerosis Soc., Am. Assn. for Automotive Medicine. Contbr. articles to profl. jours. Home: 1727 N Orleans St Chicago IL 60614 Office: 345 E Superior St Chicago IL 60611

BETTS, HERMON A., city ofcl.; b. St. Louis, Sept. 8, 1929; s. Andrew Lee and Wille Edna (Love) B.; cert. Hubbard Bus. Sch., 1957, So. Ill. U., Edwardsville, 1975; m. Patsy R. Enge, Nov. 6, 1956; children—Marcia, Sherly, Kathryn, Hermione, Natashia, April; m. 2d, Linda V. Jeter, Nov. 23, 1980. Owner, mgr. Hermon's Beauty Enterprises, East St. Louis, 1957-72; public relations asst. East St. Louis, 1971-72, dir. public relations, 1975-76, asst. to dir. community devel., 1976-77, div. adminstr. Bd. Alderman, 1979—; stockbrokers rep., East St. Louis, 1974; cons. minority enterprises; owner, mgr. Hermon's Assos./Employment Service, 1978—. Campaign coordinator Richard G. Hatcher, mayor of Gary (Ind.), 1967; mem. Democratic Central City Com., East St. Louis, 1974; mem. citizens adv. com. So. Ill. U., 1975; trustee United Way, 1976-77; bd. dirs. St. Clair County Urban League, 1973-75; campaign mgr. Mayor James Williams, 1971, Mayor William E. Mason, 1975; coordinator Mayor Carl E. Officer, 1979; chmn. Edgemont Neighborhood Assn., 1980; sec. citizens for Progress Ward 1, 1979. Served with AUS, 1952-55. Mem. East St. Louis Beauticians Orgn., Allied Cosmetologists Ill., Met. East Businessmens Assn. (dir. 1976—), Ill. Human Relations

Commn. Baptist. Clubs: Elks, Masons. Editor community newsletter The Renaissance, 1976—. Home: 802 Goelz Dr East Saint Louis IL 62203 Office: 7 Collinsville St East Saint Louis IL 62201

BETZ, RONALD PHILIP, pharmacist; b. Chgo., Nov. 26, 1933; s. David Robert and Olga Marie (Martinson) B.; B.S., U. Ill., 1955; m. Rose Marie Marella, May 18, 1963; children—David Christian, Christopher Peter. Asst. dir. of pharmacy U. Ill., Chgo., 1959-62; dir. pharmacy Mt. Sinai Hosp., Chgo., 1962—; teaching asso. Coll. of Pharmacy, U. Ill., Chgo., 1977—; pres. Pharmacy Service and Systems, 1972-81; dir. Ill. Coop. Health Data Systems, 1976-80. Served with U.S. Army, 1956-58. Mem. Am. Pharm. Assn., Am. Soc. Hosp. Pharmacists, Ill. Pharm. Assn. (pres. 1975), Ill. Acad. Preceptors in Pharmacy (pres. 1972), No. Ill. Soc. Hosp. Pharmacists (pres. 1966), Kappa Psi. Democrat. Lutheran. Contbr. articles in field to profl. jours. Home: 7505 N Sheridan Rd Chicago IL 60626 Office: 2750 W 15th Pl Chicago IL 60608

BEUGEN, JOAN BETH, communications exec.; b. Chgo., Mar. 9, 1943; d. Leslie and Janet (Glick) Caplan; B.S. in Speech, Northwestern U., 1965; m. Sheldon Howard Beugen, July 16, 1967. Founder, prin., pres. The Creative Establishment, Chgo. and N.Y.C., 1969—; speaker on entrepreneurship for women at seminars and workshops; del. White House Conf. Small Bus., 1979. Recipient numerous awards for films and multi-media presentations. Mem. Nat. Assn. Women Bus. Owners (pres. Chgo. chpt. 1979), Chgo. Assn. Commerce and Industry, Chgo. Film Council, Chgo. Audio-Visual Producers Assn., Ill. Women's Agenda. Contbr. articles on multi-media to profl. jours. Office: 1421 N Wells St Chicago IL 60610

BEUMER, ORIAN FRANKLIN, med. personnel adminstr.; b. Holland, Ind., Nov. 14, 1926; s. Frank Emil and Lydia Clara (Linstrot) B.; student Butler U., 1947-48; B.A. in English, U. Evansville, 1952, postgrad., 1974—; children—Toni Lynn, Steven Laune. Public relations aide Internat. Harvester Co., Evansville, Ind., 1952-55; employee communications editor Mead Johnson & Co., Evansville, 1955-58, supr. profl. employment, 1958, mgr. new product scheduling and coordination, 1958-66; franchised distbr. Vanda Cosmetics, Evansville, 1966-67; personnel dir. St. Mary's Med. Center, Evansville, 1967—; tchr. nursing home adminstrn. Lockyear Bus. Coll. Pres. bd. dirs. Youth Emergency Service, Inc., Evansville, 1977—. Served with U.S. Navy, 1944-46. Mem. Am. Soc. Personnel Adminstrn. (dist. dir. 1980, accredited exec. in personnel), Ind. Health Careers Inc. (dir. 1972—), Ind. Soc. Hosp. Personnel Adminstrn. (pres. 1969-70, editor newsletter 1971-73), Am. Soc. Hosp. Personnel Adminstrn., Am. Hosp. Assn., Ind. Personnel Assn. (dir. 1981), Evansville Personnel Assn. (pres. 1976-77), Vis. Nurse Assn. Southwestern Ind. (dir. 1976—, v.p. 1979-81, pres. 1981—), Profl. Secs. Internat. (mem. exec. adv. bd. Ind. div.), Ind. State C. of C. (personnel and indsl. relations com. 1981). Office: PO Box 5671 Evansville IN 47715

BEUTEL, ERNEST WILLIAM, surgeon; b. Chgo., Feb. 14, 1946; s. Ernest and Hazel Augusta (Zachow) B.; B.S. magna cum laude, Loyola U., Chgo., 1967; M.D., 1971; m. Anita Paul Harrison, June 11, 1976; children—Ernest Wiley, William Andrew. Intern, St. Joseph Hosp., Chgo., 1971-72, resident in surgery, 1972-76; resident in thoracic surgery Cook County Hosp., 1976-78; commd. lt. comdr. USN, 1978-80; staff thoracic surgeon Naval Regional Med. Center, Great Lakes, 1978-80, cons. thoracic surgeon, 1980—; attending staff thoracic surgery St. Joseph Hosp., Chgo., 1978—, Ravenswood Hosp. Med. Center, Chgo., Resurrection Hosp., Chgo., Gottlieb Meml. Hosp., Melrose Park, Ill., St. Francis Hosp., Evanston, Ill.; surg. asso. Northwestern U. Diplomate Am. Bd. Surgery, Am. Bd. Thoracic Surgery. Fellow Am. Coll. Cardiology (asso.), Am. Coll. Chest Physicians; mem. AMA, Am. Soc. Parenteral and Enteral Nutrition, Alpha Omega Alpha. Address: 2913 N Commonwealth Chicago IL 60657

BEUTLER, ALBERT JACOB, coll. pres.; b. Osceola, Ind., Feb. 20, 1929; s. Jacob Richard and Florence May (Enders) B.; A.B., Bethel Coll., Mishawaka, Ind., 1951; M.A., Winona Lake Sch. Theology, 1959; Ph.D., Mich. State U., 1970; m. Barbara Jean Heeter, Sept. 3, 1950; children—Nancy, Stephen, Amy Jean. Dean of men Bethel Coll., 1951-60, dean of students, 1960-66, pres., 1974—; dean student services Ind. U., South Bend, 1966-74; mem. Ind. Student Assistance Commn. Bd. dirs. United Way of St. Joseph County (Ind.), Jr. Achievement, South Bend-Mishawaka; mem. Michiana Arts and Scis. Council; chmn. Bd. Higher Edn. of the Missionary Ch., Ft. Wayne, Ind., 1969-73; chmn. bd. Salvation Army, Mishawaka, 1971-73; bd. dirs. Urban Coalition St. Joseph County. Named Alumnus of Yr., Bethel Coll., 1966, Top Joe of St. Joseph County, 1977. Mem. Am. Assn. Higher Edn., Council Ind. Colls., Ind. Conf. Higher Edn., Ind. Colls. and Univs. Ind., South Bend-Mishawaka Area C. of C. (dir.), Phi Delta Kappa. Club: Lions (Mishawaka). Author: The Development of a Program of Higher Education in the United Missionary Church, 1959; The Founding and History of Bethel College, 1970. Office: 1001 W McKinley St Mishawaka IN 46545

BEUTLER, CHRISTOPHER JOHN, lawyer, state ofcl.; b. Omaha, Nov. 14, 1944; s. John E. and Dorothy B.; B.A. in Am. Studies, Yale U., 1966; J.D., U. Nebr., 1973; m. Patty Hershey, July 10, 1967; children—Alexa, Erica, Mikahla. Tchr., U.S. Peace Corps, Turkey, 1966-67; researcher Nebr. Crime Commn., 1972; admitted to Nebr. bar, 1973; asso. firm Cline, Williams, Wright, Johnson & Oldfather, Lincoln, Nebr., 1973-78; individual practice law, Lincoln, 1978—; mem. Nebr. Legislature, 1979—. Mem. exec. com. Nebr. Civil Liberties Union, 1976-79. Served to 1st lt. U.S. Army, 1969-71. Mem. Lincoln Bar Assn., Nebr. Bar Assn., Am. Bar Assn. Democrat. Club: Kiwanis. Office: 804 State Capitol Lincoln NE 58509

BEVERLEY, JOHN LOUIS, JR., photographer; b. Phila., July 6, 1930; s. John Louis and Venela Mae (Chapman) B.; B.S. in Elec. Engring., Rutgers U., 1962; M.S., Drexel Inst. Tech., 1964; Ph.D., Oxford U., 1975; D.F.A., U. Paris. Enlisted U.S. Navy, 1947, commd. Warrant Officer, 1967, advanced through grades to lt. comdr., 1973; served in U.S.S. Missouri, 1948-49, Korea, 1950-51; assigned U.S. Naval Air Sta., Pensacola, Fla., 1952-53, Am. embassy, Amman, Jordan, 1960, Saigon, Vietnam, 1967, London, Eng., 1973-75, ret., 1975; owner, operator photography studio, Chgo., 1976—. Decorated Silver Star, Purple Heart with 3 clusters, Air Medal, D.S.C.; Rhodes scholar, 1963; Pres.'s fellow, 1968. Mem. Naval Inst., Ret. Officers Assn., Profl. Photographers Am., Nat. Freelance Photographers Assn., NAACP, Nat. Tech. Assn., Wedding Photographers Internat., Nat. Press Photographers Assn., IEEE, Internat. Platform Assn., ACLU, VFW, Am. Legion. Baptist. Club: Elks. Home and Office: 6030 N Sheridan Rd Chicago IL 60660

BEVIER, JOHN CHARLES, advt. agy exec.; b. Wabash, Ind., Sept. 3, 1951; s. Donald and Ernestine (Smith) B.; B.Arts and Sci., Ind. State U., 1973; m. Donna Sue Vonderheide, Mar. 17, 1973; 1 dau., Jennifer Anne. Art dir. Mathewson Advt., Indpls., 1973; sr. art dir. Danners Inc., Indpls., 1974; creative dir. Shopko, Green Bay, Wis., 1977-79; advt. dir. Art Annex Advt., Jasper, Ind., 1979—; cons. advt. depts. Vincennes U., Ind. State U. Mem. Ind. Art Dirs. Club (Indpls., various awards, 1974, 75, 77). Roman Catholic. Home: Rural Route 1 Box 234 Jasper IN 47546 Office: 402 Mill St Jasper IN 47546

BE VIER, WILLIAM A., ednl. adminstr.; b. Springfield, Mo., July 31, 1927; s. Charles and Erma G. (Ritter) BeV.; B.A., Drury Coll., 1950; Th.M., Dallas Theol. Sem., 1955, Th.D., 1958; M.A., So. Meth. U., 1960; Ed.D., A.B.D., Wayne State U., 1968; m. Jo Ann King, Aug. 11, 1949; children—Cynthia, Shirley. With Frisco Ry., 1943-45, 46-51, John E. Mitchell Co., Dallas, 1952-60; instr. Dallas Theol. Sem., 1958-59; teaching fellow So. Meth. U., Dallas, 1959-60; prof. Detroit Bible Coll., 1960-74, registrar, 1962-66, dean, 1964-73, exec. v.p., 1967-74, acting pres., 1967-68; prof., dean edn., v.p. for acad. affairs Northwestern Coll., Roseville, Minn., 1974—. Bd. dirs. Religious Analysis Service, Mpls., 1979—. Served with USMC, 1945-46, 50-51; col. Army Res. Mem. Res. Officers Assn., Ind. Fund Chs. of Am., Am. Assn. Higher Edn., Huguenot Hist. Soc., Bevier-Elting Family Assn., Phi Alpha Theta. Office: Northwestern Coll Roseville MN 55113

BEVIRT, JOSEPH LLOYD, mgmt. cons.; b. St. Louis, June 22, 1931; s. William John and Jennie Laura (Roehm) B.; B.S., U. Mo.. 1953. M.S. in Biolytical Chemistry, 1956; m. Wilma Leah Evans, Aug. 2, 1953; children—Renee Patrice, Josette Laura, Bruce Joseph. Chemistry instr. U. Mo., 1955-56; chemist Dow Chem. Co., Midland, Mich., 1956-61, market analyst, 1962-66, dir. mktg. research Pacific div., Hong Kong, 1967-70, tech. products mktg. mgr., 1971-72; sales and project dir. Nat. Mktg. Surveys, Midland, 1973-74, sr. mktg. analyst, 1975—; cons. to White House; instr. mktg. Saginaw Valley Coll., 1976—; bus. advisor Chinese U. Hong Kong, 1969-72. Vice pres. Lake Huron Area council Boy Scouts Am., 1973—; bd. dirs. Midland County Cancer Soc., 1976—, Trout Unltd., 1976—; chmn. Mackinac Trail Commn., 1958-67, 76—. Served with U.S. Army, 1953-55. Recipient Mich. Congress Parents Parents and Teachers Distinguished Service award, 1967; Silver Beaver award Boy Scouts Am., 1977. Mem. Am. Chem. Soc.. Chem. Mktg. Research Assn., Am. Mktg. Assn., Market Research Soc. Hong Kong, Sci. Research Soc. Am., MPC Couples Club, Alpha Chi Sigma. Presbyterian. Clubs: Sugar Springs Country, Hong Kong Country, Luzerne. Author: The Determination of Lindane Residues, 1956; contbr. articles, chpts. to tech. jours., texts. Home: 1211 Kingsbury Ct Midland MI 48640 Office: Dow Chemical USA 2020 Dow Center Midland MI 48640

BEY, LOIS AILEEN, info. scientist; b. Chgo., May 8, 1929; d. Leroy Karl and Lillian Dorothy (Johnson) B.; B.S. in Chem. Engring., Ill. Inst. Tech., 1950; M.A. in Library Sci., Rosary Coll., 1967. Asst. engr. Underwriters Labs, Inc., Chgo., 1950-52, Armour Research Found., Chgo., 1952-56; sales engr. F. M. de Beers Assos., Oak Park, Ill., 1956-60; mgr. sci. services Travenol Labs., Inc., Morton Grove, Ill., 1960—. Mem. Am. Inst. Chem. Engrs., Soc. Women Engrs., Am. Soc. Info. Sci., Med. Library Assn., Spl. Libraries Assn., AAAS, Lake Geneva Fresh Air Assn., Tau Beta Pi (woman's badge). Home: 5935 Lincoln Ave Morton Grove IL 60053 Office: 6301 Lincoln Ave Morton Grove IL 60053

BEYER, BALDWIN MARTIN, clergyman, counselor; b. Chgo., Apr. 30, 1926; s. Casimir and Helen (Wozniak) B.; B.A., Mary Immaculate Coll., Garrison, N.Y., 1950; M.A. in Theology, St. Anthony Sem., 1954. Joined Capuchin-Franciscan order Roman Catholic Ch., 1945, ordained priest, 1953; asst. pastor chs., Milw., 1954-58, Appleton, Wis., 1959-61; prof. theology Victory Noll Coll., Huntington, Ind., 1961-65, St. Francis Bros. Sch., Mt. Calvary, Wis., 1967-69; hosp. chaplain, Detroit, 1969-73; alcoholism counselor Sacred Heart Ch., Detroit and Friendship House, Bay City, Mich., 1973-74; dir. Human Aid, Inc., Gladwin, Mich., 1974—; mem. Mich. Certification Bd. for Addiction Specialists; cons. Saginaw Diocesan Health Panel. Cert. hosp. chaplain, alcoholism counselor, social worker, Mich. Mem. Mich. Assn. Alcoholism and Drug Abuse Counselors, Nat. Alcohol and Drug Problems Assn., Nat. Assn. Alcoholism Counselors, Cath. Hosp. Chaplains. Office: 103 N Bowery Box 47 Gladwin MI 48624

BEYER, EMIL E., JR., state legislator; b. Omaha, May 20, 1929; m. Barbara; children—Linda, Diane, Randall, Vicki. Real estate exec.; mem. Nebr. Legislature, 1980—. Bd. dirs. Gretna Parent-Tchr. Orgn.; chmn. Gretna Planning Bd.; pres. Gretna Civic Orng. Club: Optimists (dir.). Address: Gretna NE *

BEYER, KAREN ANN, social worker; b. Cleve., Jan. 30, 1942; d. William Pryor and Evelyn Ann Haynes; B.A., Ohio State U., 1965; M.S.W., Loyola U., Chgo., 1969; cert. Family Inst., Northwestern U., 1979; 1 dau., Jennifer. with Cuyahoga County Div. Child Welfare, Cleve., 1965, Dallas County Child Welfare Unit, Dallas, 1966; with Lutheran Welfare Services Ill., Chgo., 1967-73; pvt. practice clin. social work, Schaumburg, Ill., 1975—; therapist Family Service Assn. Greater Elgin (Ill.), 1973-77, dir. profl. services, 1977—; fieldwork social work instr. for Loyola U., U. Ill., 1977-80; pvt. practice family mediation, 1981—. Mem. Nat. Assn. Social Workers, Acad. Cert. Social Workers, Am. Orthopsychiat. Assn. Unitarian. Home: 1809 Dumont Ln Schaumburg IL 60194 Office: 164 Division St Elgin IL 60120

BEYER, PATRICK WILLIAM, mfg. co. ofcl.; b. St. Paul, Jan. 4, 1947; s. Charles Frederick and June Roxanne Beyer; B.A. in Sociology, St. John's U., Collegeville, Minn., 1967; postgrad. U. Minn., Mpls., 1967-69; m. Mary C. Pallanch, Mar. 15, 1969; children—Michelle, Jeanne, Patrick. Territory mgr. Warner Lambert Co., Santa Ana, Calif., 1970-72, asst. dist. mgr., 1972-73, dist. sales mgr., 1973-75, regional sales mgr., 1975-77, mgr. sales planning and promotion, 1977-78; toiletries specialist Revlon Co., Washington, 1978; sales promotion mgr. Roach, Inc., Columbus, Ohio, 1979-81, mktg. dir., 1981—. Served with USMCR, 1969-75. Mem. Am. Mgmt. Assn. Republican. Roman Catholic. Club: Leatherlips Yacht. Home: 856 Angus Ct Worthington OH 43085 Office: 2255 Westbelt Dr Columbus OH 43228

BEYER, RICHARD ERIK, banker: b. Mt. Clemens, Mich., Oct. 30, 1950; s. Robert Erik and Patricia Ann (Pestel) B.; B.S., U. Kans., 1972; M.B.A., U. Mo., 1976; m. Sarah Jane Crews, Nov. 28, 1970. With Columbia Union Nat. Bank & Trust Co., Kansas City, Mo., 1972—, v.p. personnel, 1975—; lectr. in bus. Rockhurst Coll., Kansas City, 1978—. Mem. mgmt. devel. com. Kans. U., 1978—; Kansas City area treas. Nat. Council on Crime and Delinquency, 1978-79; mem. adv. bd. Salvation Army, 1978—; mem. banking program adv. bd. Sch. Adminstrn., U. Mo., Kansas City, 1979—; mem. edn. com. Greater Kansas City Clearing House, 1975-79. Accredited personnel mgr. Personnel Accreditation Inst. Mem. Am. Inst. Banking (chmn. edn. com. 1978-79), Personnel Mgmt. Assn. (v.p. external affairs 1978-79, dir. 1979—), Am. Soc. Personnel Adminstrn., Delta Chi (sec. alumni bd. 1972—), Alpha Kappa Psi, Beta Gamma Sigma. Republican. Presbyterian. Author article in field. Office: 900 Walnut St Kansas City MO 64106

BEYER, RICHARD WAYNE, agrl. co. exec.; b. Clarion, Iowa, Apr. 28, 1954; s. Harold Frederick and Martha Norma (Bouillon) B.; B.A. in Acctg. and Bus. Adminstrn., Buena Vista Coll., 1975; m. Darlene Evelyn Knutson, July 5, 1975; 1 dau., Gwen Marie. Acct., Hultgrens-Gerlach, Inc., Storm Lake, Iowa, 1974-75; mktg. rep. John Deere Co., Kansas City, Mo., 1976, dealer mgmt. rep., 1976-79, consumer products terr. mgr., 1979—. Recipient Outstanding Performance award, John Deere Acctg. and Mgmt. programs, 1974-75. Mem. Jaycees. Republican. Methodist. Home: 5910 S 25th St Lincoln NE 68512 Office: 3210 E 85th St Kansas City MO 64132

BEYLER, ROGER ELDON, chemist, educator; b. Nappanee, Ind., May 20, 1922; s. Oscar L. and Ethel (Johns) B.; B.A., North Central Coll., 1944; M.A., U. Ill., 1947, Ph.D., 1949; m. Herberta E. Hasewinkel, Aug. 29, 1944; children—Keith, Eric, Jane. Research chemist Merck & Co., Inc., Rahway, N.J., 1949-59; prof. chemistry So. Ill. U., Carbondale, 1959—, acting chmn. dept., 1965-66, dean Coll. Liberal Arts and Scis., 1966-73, dean Coll. Liberal Arts, 1973-74; vis. lectr. U. Minn., summer 1963; OECD fellow U. Strasbourg (France), 1964. Mem. Am. Chem. Soc., AAAS, Ill. Acad. Sci., Sigma Xi, Phi Kappa Phi, Alpha Chi Sigma. Presbyterian. Contbr. articles to profl. jours. Patentee in field. Home: 32 Pinewood Carbondale IL 62901 Office: Dept Chemistry and Biochemistry So Ill Univ Carbondale IL 62901

BEYNEN, GIJSBERTUS KOOLEMANS, bibliographer; b. Surabaya, Indonesia, June 12, 1935; s. G.J.W. and Froukje (de Jong) Koolemans Beijnen; Jur. Cand., Leiden (Netherlands) U., 1957, Lit. Slav. Cand., 1959; Ph.D., Stanford U., 1967; M.L.S., SUNY, Geneseo, 1974; m. Antoinette Reuchlin, June 29, 1963 (div. Dec. 31, 1980); children—Johanna, Margaret, Axel, Sophia, Elisabeth Blake Warner. Asst. prof. Russian, Emporia State U., 1963-66; asst. prof. Fordham U., N.Y.C., 1966-69; asst. prof. U. Rochester (N.Y.), 1969-73; asso. prof. library adminstrn. and Slavic langs., Slavic bibliographer Ohio State U., Columbus, 1974—. Internat. Research and Exchanges Bd. fellow Moscow State U., 1970-71; Nat. Endowment Humanities translation grantee 1981-82; Midwest Consortium for Internat. Affairs exchange fellow Moscow State U., 1981-82; NDEA Title VI fellow, 1962-63. Mennonite. Contbr. articles to profl. jours. Home: 460 E Norwich Apt C Columbus OH 43201 Office: 1858 Neil Ave Columbus OH 43210

BEZNOSKA, NORMAN JOHN, JR., data processing cons.; b. Cleve., Jan. 8, 1941; s. Norman John and Dorothy Marie B.; B.S. in Mgmt., John Carroll U.; m. Bernice Abbott, Aug. 30, 1974; children—Anne Marie, Norman John III. Adminstrv. system ops. specialist IBM, Cleve., 1964-67; systems analyst Central Nat. Bank, Cleve., 1967-69; mgmt. analyst U.S. Navy Fin. Center, Cleve., 1971-74; electronic data processing systems officer Union Commerce Bank, Cleve., 1974-77; mgr. data processing Broadview Savs. & Loan, Cleve., 1977-79; data processing auditor BancSystems Assn., Rocky River, Ohio, 1979-81; EDP cons. Computer Task Group, Cleve., 1981—. Served with USN, 1958-64. Mem. Electronic Data Processing Auditors Assn., Assn. Systems Mgmt. Independent Republican. Author various profl. papers. Home: 18235 Fern Canyon Strongsville OH 44136

BHAKTHAVATHSALAN, AMRUTHA, physician; b. Mysore State, India, Mar. 1, 1933; d. K. and Uma (Devi) Marilingappa; came to U.S., 1966; B.S., Maharani's Coll. for Women, Bangalore, Mysore State, India, 1950; B. Medicine, B. Surgery, Univ. Med. Coll., Mysore, India, 1955. House surgeon, rotating intern Meml. Hosp., Niagara Falls, N.Y., 1966-67; resident obstetrics gynecology, pathology St. Thomas Hosp., Akron, O., 1967; resident obstetrics/gynecology Med. Coll. Ohio at Toledo and Asso. Hosps. Program, Toledo Hosp., 1968, Maumee Valley Hosp., 1969, St. Vincent Hosp., 1969, Toledo Hosp., 1970; chief resident obstetrics/gynecology Maumee Valley Hosp., 1970-71; instr. dept. obstetrics and gynecology Med. Coll. Ohio, Toledo, 1971-73; fellow perinatology Nassau County Med. Center, East Meadow, N.Y., 1973-74; research asso., 1974-75; asst. prof. dept. obstetrics/gynecology State U. N.Y., Stonybrook, 1975-76; physician-in-charge div. obstetrics, dept. obstetrics and gynecology Queens Hosp. Center Affiliation L.I. Jewish-Hillside Med. Center, Jamaica, N.Y., 1975-76; perinatologist N.W. Ohio Regional Perinatal Center, Toledo Hosp., 1976—; clin. asst. prof. dept. obstetrics/gynecology Med. Coll. Ohio, Toledo, 1976-77, clin. asso. prof., 1977-80, clin. prof., 1980—. Diplomate Am. Bd. Obstetrics and Gynecology, subsplty. cert. in Maternal-Fetal Medicine. Fellow Am. Coll. Obstetricians and Gynecologists; mem. Am. Med. Women's Assn., Inc., Ohio State Med. Assn., Toledo Soc. Obstetrics/Gynecology, Toledo Acad. Medicine, Nat. Perinatal Assn., Ohio Perinatal Assn., Soc. Perinatal Obstetricians. Contbr. articles to profl. jours. Office: NW Ohio Regional Perinatal Center Toledo Hosp 2142 N Cove Blvd Toledo OH 43606

BHASIN, KUL B., physicist, mfg. co. ofcl.; b. Kalka, India, June 18, 1949; came to U.S., 1971, naturalized, 1980; s. Sohan L. and Ram D. (Sahani) B.; B.S., Punjab U., India, 1970; M.S. in Physics, Purdue U., 1972; Ph.D. in Physics, U. Mo., Rolla, 1976; m. Charlotte A. Sage, June 14, 1975. Postdoctoral fellow U. Mo., project scientist Gould, Inc., Rolling Meadows, Ill., 1977, quality assurance and devel. mgr. McConnelsville, Ohio, 1978-80, mgr. tech., Cleve., 1981—. Mem. Am. Chem. Soc., Am. Phys. Soc., Am. Vacuum Soc., Am. Electrochem. Soc., Sigma Xi. Club: Kiwanis. Contbr. articles and book revs. to profl. jours.; patentee in field. Office: Gould Inc Foil Div Research and Devel Lab 35129 Curtis Blvd Eastlake OH 44094

BHATIA, SHYAM S(UNDER), geographer, educator; b. Rawalpindi, Pakistan, July 7, 1924; s. Nanak Chand and Lajya (Wati) B.; m. Sushil Bhatia, June 9, 1950; children—Niru, Veena; came to U.S., 1966, naturalized, 1972; M.A., U. Panjab, Lahore, 1947; Ph.D. (Fulbright scholar), U. Kans., 1959. Asso. prof. U. Delhi, 1959-66, chmn. dept. geography, 1959-62; asso. prof., prof. U. Wis., Oshkosh, 1966-70, prof., 1970—; vis. asso. prof. Sch. Internat. Studies, New Delhi, 1960-64; vis. prof. San Diego State U., 1975-76; program chmn. Conf. on S.Asia, 1974. Mem. Assn. Am. Geographers, Population Assn. Am., Alan Gutmacher Inst., Sigma Xi, Candlelight Club. Author: Age and Sex Structure of Wisconsin Population, 1960-70; Age and Sex Structure of Wisconsin Villages, 1970; Age and Sex Structure of Wisconsin Cities, 1970; Population Profile of Fox Valley Region, Wisconsin; contbr. to Ency. Brit., 1960-73. Office: Dept Geography U Wis Oshkosh WI 54901

BHOTE, KEKI RUTTONSHAW, electronic equipment mfg. corp. exec.; b. Madras, India, Feb. 26, 1925; s. Ruttonshaw Byramji and Meherbanoo Dadabhoy B.; came to U.S., 1948, naturalized, 1960; B.Engring., U. Madras, 1947; M.S., (U. research fellow), Harvard U., 1949; m. Mehroo Ardeshir Cursetjee, Dec. 16, 1954; children—Safeena, Shenaya, Adi, Xerxes. With Motorola Co., Chgo., 1950—, mgr. value engring., 1964-69, mgr. quality and value assurance, 1969-75, group dir. quality and value assurance, 1975—; asso. prof. mgmt. scis. Ill. Inst. Tech., 1967—; fgn. corr. Bombay (India) newspapers, 1954—. Pres., Glencoe (Ill.) Bd. Edn., 1971-73; supr., pres. New Trier Twp. Bd. Trustees, 1977—; trustee Ill. Coll. Optometry, 1978—. Named One of Top Ten Young Men of Chgo., Jr. C. of C., 1959, One of Six Outstanding Naturalized Citizens of Chgo., Immigrant Service League, 1965; recipient Zero Defects award U.S. Dept. Def., 1970. Mem. Am. Soc. Quality Control, Soc. Am. Value Engring., Am. Mgmt. Assn., Zoroastrian Assn. Am. (founder, pres. 1965-69), UN Assn. (chmn. nat. council presidents 1973-75, Service to UN award 1975), Chgo. Council on Fgn. Relations. Zoroastrian. Co-author: Value Analysis Methods, 1974; contbr. to Word Book Ency., 1965-71, articles to profl. jours., mags. Home: 493 Woodlawn Ave Glencoe IL 60022 Office: Motorola Co 1299 E Algonquin St Schaumburg IL 60196

BIAGINI, ESTHER PIER, interior designer, retailer, graphoanalyst cons.; b. Chgo.; d. Silvio and Ilia (Paganelli) Nannini; student U. Ill., 1951-52; grad. Harrington Inst. Interior Design; m. Giulio J. Biagini, Oct. 5, 1952; children—Marc, Nannette, Lisa. Graphoanalyst; personal cons. in field; pub. relations cons. Bevmar Co., 1976; pres. E.P. Biagini, interior designs; mgr. Fenco Galleries, Imports. Active PTA; pres. Brookfield (Ill.) Library Bd., 1969-70, 72-73, treas., 1970-71, sec., 1967-68, 73-74. Recipient Am. Legion award, 1950. Mem. ALA, Ill. Library Assn., Ill. Dirs. Library Assn., Brookfield Woman's Club. Home: 4421 S Arthur Ave Brookfield IL 60513

BIBBO, MARLUCE, physician, educator; b. Sao Paulo, Brazil, July 14, 1939; d. Domingos and Yolanda (Ranciaro) Bibbo; M.D., U. Sao Paulo, 1963, Sc.D., 1968. Intern, Hosps. das Clinicas, U. Sao Paulo, 1963, resident in obstetrics and gynecology, 1964-66; instr. dept. morphology and obstetrics and gynecology U. Sao Paulo, 1966-68, asst. prof., 1968-69; asst. prof. sect. cytology dept. obstetrics and gynecology U. Chgo., 1969-73, asso. prof., 1973-77, asso. prof. pathology, 1974-77, prof. obstetrics and gynecology and pathology, 1978—; asso. dir. Cytology Lab., Approved Sch. Cytotech. and Cytocybernetics, AMA-Am. Soc. Clin. Pathologists, 1970—. Mem. research com. Ill. div. Am. Cancer Soc., 1976—. Fellow Internat. Acad. Cytology (chmn. com. lab. cert. 1977—); mem. Am. Soc. Cytology (exec. com. 1972—). Contbr. numerous articles to profl. jours. Home: 400 E Randolph St Apt 2009 Chicago IL 60601 Office: 5841 S Maryland Ave Chicago IL 60637

BIBBY, JOHN ERWIN, banker; b. Brookings, S.D., Nov. 21, 1920; s. Irwin John and Ruth Edith (Erwin) B.; B.S., S.D. State U., 1942; m. Jean Starksen, June 18, 1947; children—Steven, Mary Jo VanderVorste, Nathan. Pres., The Bibby Co., Brookings, 1971-81; v.p., dir. First Nat. Bank, Brookings, S.D., 1979—. Mem. S.D. Ho. of Reps., 1963-75; state senator, S.D., 1975-81. Served to capt., USMC, 1942-46. Decorated Bronze Star medal. Named Outstanding Alumni, S.D. State U., 1975; recipient C. of C. Merit award, 1969. Republican. Methodist. Clubs: Rotary, Elks, Masons (Shriner). Home: 822 8th Ave Brookings SD 57006 Office: PO Box 57 Brookings SD 57006

BIBLER, JOSEPH WADE, banker; b. Rochester, Ind., Dec. 5, 1924; s. Robert Lendon and Marjorie A. (Wade) B.; B.S. in Bus. Adminstrn., Ind. U., 1947; Grad. Sch. Banking, U. Wis., 1958; m. Patricia Elizabeth Hauter, Aug. 21, 1948; children—Jeffrey W., Amy E., Julie A. With Gary (Ind.) Post Tribune, 1947-51; with No. Ind. Bank and Trust Co., Valparaiso, 1951—, pres., 1970-81, chief exec. officer, 1975—, chmn. bd., 1981—. Sec. to bd. Valparaiso U. Served as ensign USNR, 1942-46. Mem. Ind. Bankers Assn. (pres. region II), Ind. Bankers Assn. (v.p.). Republican. Lutheran. Clubs: Valparaiso Golf, Rotary (past pres.) (Valparaiso).

BIBLER, NORMAN WAYNE, distbg. co. exec.; b. Cherokee, Iowa, Dec. 25, 1932; s. Clarence Jacob and Bessie Irene (Mason) B.; m. Lois Jean Reinken, Aug. 23, 1973; children—Lonnie, Barry, Robert, David, Lisa, Lynn. With Electric Line Constrn., Alta, Iowa, 1956-63; elec. supt. City of Waverly, Iowa, 1963-71; salesman truck mounted equipment Telelect Inc., Mpls., 1971-77; pres., partner Utility Sales & Service Corp., Storm Lake, Iowa, 1977—; dir. mcpl. utilities safety div. State of Iowa. Mem. Iowa Assn. Mcpl. Utilities, Minn. Mcpl. Utilities Assn. Inc. Club: Elks. Home: 1306 E 7th St Storm Lake IA 50588 Office: 1403 E 3d St Storm Lake IA 50588

BIBLO, HERBERT, librarian; b. Bklyn., Oct. 17, 1924; s. Philip and Tillie (Levine) B.; B.B.A., Bernard M. Baruch Coll., U. City N.Y., 1949; M.S.L.S., Chgo. State U., 1962; cert. advanced study U. Chgo. Grad. Library Sch., 1970; m. Mary Davidson, Aug. 28, 1951; children—Lisa, David. Pres. Benin Press, Ltd., 1951-60; librarian Chgo. Bd. Edn., 1960-68; reference librarian John Crerar Library, Chgo., 1968-70, asst. librarian, 1970—. Served with U.S. Army, 1943-46. Council on Library Resources fellow, 1974-75. Mem. ALA (treas., exec. bd.), Spl. Libraries Assn. (rep. to biol. and med. libraries sect. of Internat. Fedn. Library Assns.), Ill. Library Assn., Chgo. Library Club. Editor Ill. Assn. Coll. and Research Libraries Newsletter, 1974-78. Office: ALA 50 E Huron St Chicago IL 60611

BICE, DONALD ALLEN, modular housing mfg. co. exec.; b. Flushing, Ohio, Sept. 30, 1929; s. Jacob Leroy and Myrtle Viola (Howard) B.; student Coll. Steubenville, 1953, Cleve. Engring. Inst., 1954, Western Mich. U., 1958, Earlham Coll., 1960, Ind. U., 1964; m. Clara B. Bigger, June 9, 1950; children—Thomas, Ted, William, Donald J., Tamra. Plant mgr. Weather Mate, Inc., Plymouth, Ind., 1965-70; exec. v.p. Benson Mfg. Corp., Menomonee Falls, Wis., 1970-75; v.p. mfg. and engring. Am. Fixture Inc., Joplin, Mo., 1975; pres. Anson & Gilkey Co., Inc., Merrill, Wis., from 1976; now pres. Clairmar Homes, Inc., modular housing mfr., Plymouth, Ind. Served with USN, 1948-52. Mem. Soc. Plastics Engrs., Nat. Woodwork Mfrs. Assn., Nat. Sash and Door Jobbers Assn. Clubs: Merrill Country, Masons. Patentee vinyl hinge, locking mechanism, teaching wall system, shutter and mounting system. Home: 1106A Timber Ln Plymouth IN 46563 Office: 200 Tower St Etna Green IN

BICKEL, ERMALINDA, real estate broker; b. Casole Bruzio Provincia di Cosenza, Italy, Nov. 8, 1919; d. Saverio and Emilia (Fortino) Fortino; came to U.S., 1927, naturalized, 1927; student pub. schs., Italy, Elkhart, Ind.; Grad. Real Estate Inst., Purdue U.; m. William E. Bickel, Aug. 10, 1946; 1 dau., Patricia Ann Heiser. Office clk. Gen. Telephone, Elkhart, 1939-41; sec. to pres. Ames Co. div. Miles Labs., Inc., Elkhart, 1941-52, tech. sec. pharmacy research dept., 1962—; free lance legal sec., 1956-61; owner, founder Blue Chip Realty, Inc., Elkhart, 1968—. Mem. Nat., Ind., Elkhart real estate bds., Delta Theta Tau, Elkhart C. of C. Roman Catholic. Club: Zonta. Office: 26258 Cottage Ave Elkhart IN 46514

BICKEL, FLOYD GILBERT, III, investment counselor; b. St. Louis, Jan. 10, 1944; s. Floyd Gilbert II and Mary Mildred (Welch) B.; B.S. in Bus. Adminstrn., Washington U., St. Louis, 1966; M.S. in Commerce, St. Louis U., 1968; m. Martha Wohler, June 11, 1966; children—Christine Carleton, Susan Marie, Katherine Anne, Andrew Barrett (dec.). With research dept. Yates, Woods & Co., St. Louis, 1966-67; asst. br. mgr. E.F. Hutton & Co., Inc., St. Louis, 1967-70; asst. v.p., resident mgr. Bache & Co., Inc., St. Louis, 1970-72; pres. Donelan-Phelps Investment Advisors, Inc., St. Louis, 1972-80; dir. consulting services E.F. Hutton & Co., Inc., St. Louis, 1980—; founder Brentwood Bancshares, Inc.; pres., dir. Biclan, Inc., Gilmar Realty, Inc.; chmn., dir. Data Research Assos., Inc.; asso. prof. finance Lindenwood Coll.; cons. various television prodns. Mem. City of Des Peres (Mo.) Planning and Zoning Commn., 1975-76; chmn. St. Louis County Bd. Equalization, 1976-79; pub. safety commr. City of Des Peres, 1977-80, mem. audit and fin. com., 1980—; mem. Gov.'s Crime Commn., 1981—. Mem. Internat. Found. Employee Benefit Plan, Am. Mgmt. Assn., St. Louis Soc. Fin. Analysts. Republican. Presbyterian. Clubs: Bellerive Country; St. Louis; Commanderie de Bordeaux. Contbr. bus. articles to mags. Home: 12120 Belle Meade Saint Louis MO 63131 Office: 1034 S Brentwood Blvd Saint Louis MO 63117

BICKFORD, THOMAS EDWARD, civil engr.; b. Newton, Mass., May 22, 1929; s. Edward Milton and Mabel Etta (Eldridge) B.; B.S. in Civil Engring., Northeastern U., 1957; postgrad. Ohio State U., 1960-72; m. Edna Harriett Thompson, Oct. 22, 1955 (div. 1979); children—Douglas Thomas, Linda Kathryn. Civil engr. Columbia Gas System Service Corp., Columbus, Ohio, 1957-60, Scioto Conservancy Dist., Columbus, 1962-64; civil engr. Burgess & Niple, Ltd., Columbus, 1961-62, 64-70, asst. personnel dir., 1966-70, personnel dir., 1971—. Vice-pres. PTA, Columbus, 1969-70, pres., 1971-72; chmn. engrs. group, profl. div. United Way, 1969-70; trustee Forest Park Civic Assn. Registered profl. engr., Ohio, Fla. Mem. Ohio Soc. Profl. Engrs., ASCE, Personnel Soc. Columbus (v.p. 1972, treas. 1977), Am. Soc. Personnel Adminstrn., Nat. Soc. Profl. Engrs. Independent Republican. Home: 6060 Springburn Dr Dublin OH 43017 Office: 5085 Reed Rd Columbus OH 43220

BICKLE, FRANKLIN M., optometrist; b. Newark, Ohio, Dec. 22, 1953; s. Walter K. and Margaret E. (Sepos) B.; D.Optometry, Ohio State U., 1978. Group practice optometry, Newark, 1978—; clin. instr. Ohio State U. Coll. Optometry, Columbus, 1978—; instr. cardio-pulmonary resusitation, 1978—. Ohio State U. undergrad. scholar, 1972-74, Wildermuth Meml. scholar, 1976-78. Mem. Am. Optometric Assn., Nat. Eye Research Found., Am. Public Health Assn., Ohio Optometric Assn., Ohio Public Health Assn., Beta Sigma Kappa, Newark Jaycees. Home: 1519 Wynnewood Dr Newark OH 43055 Office: 305 Deo Dr Newark OH 43055

BICKLEY, JOHN HOWARD, JR., lawyer; b. Chgo., May 12, 1929; s. John H. and Letta (McGraw) B.; student Evanston Twp. Community Coll., 1948; J.D., Chgo. Kent Coll. Law, 1951; children—John H., III, Lisa F., Kathryn M. Admitted to Ill. bar, 1952; partner Peterson, Bogucki & Bickley, Attys., Chgo., 1957-67, individual practice, Chgo., 1968—; mem. firm Bickley & Bickley; spl. asst. atty. gen. Ill., 1968-69; chief environ. control div. Ill. Atty. Gen.'s Office, 1970-71; asst. U.S. atty. No. Dist. Ill., 1955-57; trial atty. Forest Preserve Dist. Cook County; spl. prosecutor Chgo. Police Burglar Scandal, 1961; mem. lecture forum MidWest U.S. Attys. Conf., 1963. Mem. dist. council SBA, 1971-72; legal cons. Ill. State Bd. Elections. Trustee, Village of Mount Prospect (Ill.), 1961-63, 1st v.p. Regular Republican Orgn., Elk Grove Twp., 1961-62; candidate for state's atty. Cook County, 1964. Served with USMCR, now lt. col. (ret.). Named one of Chgo.'s 10 Outstanding Young Men, Chgo. Jaycees, 1964; One of Outstanding Young Men U.S., 1965; named to alumni honor council Chgo. Kent Coll. Law, 1978. Mem. Internat. Acad. Law and Sci., Ill., Chgo., Fed. (pres. Chgo. chpt. 1972-73, nat. v.p. 1973-74) bar assns., Am. Arbitration Assn. (nat. panel arbitrators), Am., Ill. (pres. 1971-72), trial lawyers assns., Trial Lawyers Club Chgo., Soc. Trial Lawyers, Law Club Chgo., Legal Club Chgo., Globe and Anchor Soc. Ill. (past pres.), Chgo. Kent Coll. Law Alumni Assn. (dir.), Am. Legion. Episcopalian. Mason (32 deg., Shriner). Secured conviction of syndicate crime leader Paul (The Waiter) Ricca, 1957. Club: Tavern (Chgo.). Home: 6 Ct of Bucks County Lincolnshire IL 60015 Office: 230 N Michigan Ave Chicago IL 60601

BIDDINGER, JOHN WESLEY, financial exec.; b. Indpls., May 5, 1940; s. Noble L. and Eleanor Jane (Lynch) B.; B.S., Ind. U., 1963; m. Margaret Jo Hunt, Sept. 1, 1962; children—Karen Elizabeth, Katherine Jane. With City Securities Corp., Indpls., 1963—, salesman, 1963-67, v.p., 1967-69, exec. v.p., dir., 1969-79, pres., dir., 1979—; pres. Biddinger Investment Capital Corp.; vice chmn. bd. Anacomp Inc.; dir. Eikon Radiographix, Inc., Media South Inc., Mooney Broadcasting Corp., So. Hospitality Corp. Bd. dirs. Starlight Musicals, Found. Assos. Hon. Ky. col., col. a.d.c. Tenn.; cert. gen. agt., life ins. agt. Mem. Confrerie des Chevaliers du Tastevin, Les Amis du Vin, Confrerie de la Chaine des Rotisseurs, Indpls. Bond Club, Nat. (nominating com., affiliate liaison com., bd. govs. 1978—, chmn. publ. com.), Indpls. (inaugural pres.) security traders assns., Indpls. Jaycees, Well House Soc., Indpls. Mus. Art, Cousteau Soc., Oceanic Soc., Ind. U. Sch. Bus. Alumni Assn., Ind. U. Alumni Assn. (bd. mgrs., chmn. nominating com., mem. dues, ins. and outdoor edn. coms.), Dean's Assos. Ind. U. Bus. Sch., Ind. U. Varsity Club, Ind. U. Hoosier 100, Sigma Chi. Clubs: Masons, Pacesetters, Pointe Golf and Tennis, Meridian Hills Country, Univ., Columbia, Manor House, Andre's. Home: 9121 Spring Hollow Dr Indianapolis IN 46260 Office: 9102 N Meridian St Indianapolis IN 46260

BIDDLE, D. WILLIAM, farmer; b. Hammond, Ind., Apr. 29, 1942; s. Chester Bartee and Edith Mary (Cronwell) B.; degree agrl. econs. Purdue U., 1964; m. Janet Bellows, Aug. 23, 1969; children—C. Bryce, Stephen D. Farmer, Remington, Ind., 1966—; dir. Am. Soybean Assn. Elder, clk. session Presbyterian. Ch.; adv. bd. Benton County Council. Served with AUS, 1964-66. Mem. Acacia (pres. alumni chpt.). Republican. Club: Masons. Home: Route 1 Remington IN 47977*

BIDWELL, EVERETT K., state senator; b. Houston, Minn.; ed. U. Minn.; married. Chmn. bd. bank; farmer; mem. Wis. Assembly, 1952-64, Wis. Senate, 1970—. Mem. County Bd. Republican. Address: Room 140 C South State Capitol Madison WI 53702*

BIDWELL, THOMAS LEROY, controls mfg. co. exec.; b. Greenville, Ohio, July 27, 1932; s. Kenneth Renzie and Catherine Odine (Wilt) B.; grad. high sch.; m. Zita Köbel, Apr. 5, 1979; children—Paula Maria Bidwell Wright, Thomas Christopher. Engr., Stamco Inc., New Bremen, Ohio, 1953-56; with Crown Controls Corp., New Bremen, 1956—, gen. mgr., 1961-72, v.p., 1971—; v.p. Crown Controls Internat., Crown Controls Australia Pty. Ltd.; dir. Industrias Montarcargas S.A. de Mexico. Bd. dirs. Material Handling Inst., Indsl. Truck Assn. Home: 37 Southmoor Shores Saint Marys OH 45885 Office: 40 S Washington St New Bremen OH 45869

BIDWILL, WILLIAM V., football exec. Mng. gen. partner, now pres. St. Louis Cardinals Football Team. Office: Saint Louis Cardinals 200 Stadium Plaza Saint Louis MO 63102*

BIEDERMAN, EARL DONALD, explosive powder mfg. co. exec.; b. Cleve., May 28, 1935; s. Hy and Sally Ann (Simon) B.; B.S., Miami U., 1957; M.S., Purdue U., 1959; m. Marianne Miller, June 13, 1959; children—Scott. Asst. football, basketball, baseball coach Wabash Coll., 1957-58; head football coach, dept. head social studies Toronto (Ohio) Bd. Edn., 1958-60, Mentor (Ohio) Bd. Edn., 1960-63; sales rep. Texaco, Inc., Cleve., 1963-65, dist. sales supr., 1965-70; sales coordinator Ammonium Nitrate sales, West Coast regional mgr. Seismic and Pipeline Explosives div. Austin Powder Co., Cleve., 1970—; area scout Cin. Bengals, 1967—. Recreation commnr., Solon, Ohio, 1972-74; bd. dirs. Grantwood Municipal Golf Course, Solon, 1972-75. Mem. AIME, Soc. Exploration Geophysicists, Permian Basin Geophys. Soc., Geophys. Soc. Alaska, N.Mex. Mining Assn., Calif. Mining Assn., Colo. Mining Assn., Casper Geophys. Soc., Delta Kappa Epsilon. Home: 408 Mill Pond Rd Aurora OH 44202 Office: 3735 Green Rd Beachwood OH 44122

BIEDRON, THEODORE JOHN, newspaper pub.; b. Evergreen Park, Ill., Nov. 30, 1946; s. Theodore John and Ione Margaret B.; B.A. in Polit. Sci., U. Ill., 1968; m. Gloria Anne DeAngelo, Nov. 7, 1970; 1 dau., Jessica Ann. Recruitment advt. mgr. Chgo. Sun-Times, 1968-74; classified advt. mgr. Pioneer Press, Wilmette, Ill., 1974-76; classified mgr., v.p. Lerner Newspapers, Chgo., 1976-79, asso. pub., 1980—; dir. Lerner Cable TV. Mem. Assn. Newspaper Classified Advt. Mgrs. (past bd. advisors), Suburban Newspapers of Am. (award for best classified advt. sect. 1975, cert. of excellence 1979), Ill. Press Assn., Nat. Newspaper Assn. Home: 1130 Lake St Wilmette IL 60091 Office: 7519 N Ashland St Chicago IL 60626

BIELSKI, EWA TERESA MARCEDES, retail clothing store exec.; b. Buenos Aires, Argentina, Aug. 18, 1932; came to U.S., naturalized, 1955; d. Michael A. and Charlotte (Prus-Niewiadomski) Budek; student Wayne State U., 1957-58; m. George Bielski, Jan. 20, 1955; children—Christopher Andre, Andre Christopher. Asst. buyer, then buyer various depts. J.L. Hudson Co., Detroit, 1955-74; mdse. mgr. 15 stores Lane Bryant Co., Ferndale, Mich., 1975-81; pres. Perfect Closet, Grosse Pointe, Mich., 1981—. Chmn., Citizens Commn. on Pension Policy, 1978—. Home: PO Box 36035 Grosse Pointe Farms MI 48236

BIEN, STANLEY DANIEL, accountant; b. Gary, Ind., Nov. 13, 1954; s. Stanley E. and Lillian Bien; B.S., Ferris State Coll., 1977; postgrad. Western Mich. U., 1978—; m. Jean Ann Lotoszinski, Oct. 13, 1979; 1 son, Nicholas James. Program accountant fin. mgmt. sect. Dep. Dir.'s Office, Mich. Dept. Public Health, Lansing, 1977—. Recipient Hoosier State Scholarship award, 1973-74. Mem. Nat. Assn. Accts., State Govtl. Accts. Assn. Mich., Mich. State Employees Assn., Fellowship Christian Athletes, Delta Sigma Pi. Clubs: Canoe, Accounting. Home: 924 Dornell Ave Lansing MI 48910 Office: Mich Dept Public Health Office of Finance and Gen Services 3500 N Logan St Lansing MI 48909

BIETZ, ALAN DEE, zoo dir.; b. Lincoln, Nebr., Feb. 14, 1945; s. Albert D. and Rose D. (Harr) B.; teaching degree in Biology, Union Coll., 1968, B.S. in Phys. Edn., 1968; m. Melody Caroon, July 10, 1968; children—Judd Alan, Allison Deanna. Tchr., Pub. Schs. Houston, 1968-70, Newbery Pauk Acad., Thousand Oaks, Calif., 1970-71, Sheyenne River Acad., Harvey, N.D., 1971-73; dir. Lincoln (Nebr.) Children's Zoo, 1973—. Profl. fellow Am. Assn. Zool. Parks and Aquariums, Am. Assn. Zoo Veterinarians, Am. Assn. Zoo Keepers. Republican. Clubs: Kiwanis, Jaycees. Office: Lincoln Children's Zoo 2800 A St Lincoln NE 68502

BIGELOW, MARTHA MITCHELL, historian; b. Talladega Springs, Ala., Sept. 19, 1921; B.A., Ala. Coll., 1943; M.A., U. Chgo., 1944, Ph.D., 1946; children—Martha Frances, Carolyn. Asso. prof. Miss. Coll., Clinton, 1946-48; asso. prof. Memphis State U., 1948-49; asso. prof. U. Miss., 1949-50; asso. curator manuscripts Mich. Hist. Collections, U. Mich., Ann Arbor, 1954-57; prof. history Miss. Coll., 1957-71, chmn. dept. history and polit. sci., 1964-71; dir. Mich. history div., Mich. Dept. State, sec. Mich. Hist. Commn., state historic preservation officer for Mich., Lansing, 1971—. Julius Rosewald fellow, 1945-46. Mem. Am. Assn. State and Local History (v.p. 1976-78, pres. 1978-80), So. Hist. Assn., Orgn. Am. Historians, Mich. Hist. Soc., Miss. Hist. Soc., Nat. Assn. State Archives and Records Adminstrs. (sec.). Contbr. articles to profl. jours. Office: 208 N Capitol 3d Fl Lansing MI 48918

BIGELOW, PERRY JAMES, home builder; b. Cass City, Mich., June 18, 1940; s. Judson A. and Alta May (Severance) B.; B.A. in Math., Taylor U., Upland, Ind., 1964; B.S. in Civil Engring., Ill. Inst. Tech., 1964; M.B.A., Ohio State U., 1965; m. Nancy Edith Westerberg, Feb. 22, 1964; children—James Perry, Shari Edith. Vice pres. devel. and mktg. Hasbrook Corp., Rolling Meadows, Ill., 1965-73; pres. Barrington Constrn. Co. (Ill.), 1973-76, Bigelow Co., contemporary luxury homes, Hoffman Estates, Ill., 1973—. Chmn. trustees Meadows Baptist Ch., Rolling Meadows, 1973-75, 78-79. Mem. Nat. Assn. Home Builders, ASCE, Am. Mgmt. Assn., Urban Land Inst., Home Builders Assn. Greater Chgo. (Silver Key award 1978, 81). Designer Idea House, 1977, 78, 79, 80, 81. Office: 2200 Stonington St Suite 150 Hoffman Estates IL 60195

BIGGAR, EDWARD SAMUEL, lawyer; b. Kansas City, Mo., Nov. 19, 1917; s. Frank Wilson and Katharine (Rea) B.; A.B., U. Mich., 1938, J.D. with distinction, 1940; m. Susan Bagby, July 9, 1955; children—John Edward, Julie Anne, Nancy Rea, William Bagby, Martha Susan. Admitted to Mo. bar, 1940; asso. firm Stinson Mag, Thomson, McEvers and Fizzell, attys., Kansas City, Mo., 1948-50, partner, 1950—; sec., dir. Russell Stover Candies, Inc., Kansas City, Mo., 1960—; v.p., dir. Ward Paper Box Co., Kansas City, Mo., 1955—; dir. Johnson County Nat. Bank & Trust Co., Kansas City, Western Chem. Co., Kansas City, Cereal Food Processors, Inc., Kansas City. Chmn. Citizens Assn. Kansas City, Mo., 1959-60; bd. dirs. Greater Kansas City YMCA, 1965—, pres., 1979—; chmn. Transp. Planning Commn. Greater Kansas City, 1964-65; mem. Met. Planning Commn., Kansas City Region, 1966-67; pres. Kansas City (Mo.) unit Am. Cancer Soc., 1956-58. Trustee Sunset Hill Sch., Kansas City, Mo., 1971-77; pres. Kansas City (Mo.) Bd. Police Commrs., 1981—. Served to 1st lt. USAAF, 1942-45. Mem. Lawyers Assn. Kansas City (pres. 1966-67), Mo. Bar, Am., Kansas City bar assns., Am. Judicature Soc., Order of Coif, Phi Beta Kappa, Phi Delta Phi, Phi Delta Theta. Republican. Presbyn. Home: 1221 Stratford Rd Kansas City MO 64113 Office: 2100 Charter Bank Center Kansas City MO 64105

BIGGS, BETTY ANN SCHAEFFER, nurse, educator; b. Iola, Kans., Dec. 2, 1931; d. Walter G. and Linda I. (Black) Schaeffer; diploma Halstead Hosp. Sch. Nursing, 1952; B.S., Adams State Coll., 1965, M.A. in Guidance and Counseling, 1969; M. Nursing, U. Kans., 1980; m. Bruce D. Biggs, Dec. 31, 1952; children—Glenn Dale, Jerry Dean, Louann Kay. Supr. surgery Balboa Hosp., San Diego, Calif., 1953; mem. nursing staff Saint Joseph Hosp., Del Norte, Colo., 1954; gen. duty and emergency room nurse Alamosa (Colo.) Community Hosp., 1954-56; office nurse, Alamosa, Colo., 1956-64; sch. nurse (part-time) Alamosa Sch. Dist., 1964-65; sch. nurse, tchr. sci. Sangre de Cristo Sch. Dist., Mosca, Colo., 1965-71; dir. govt. community health pilot project Health Start, Saguache County (Colo.) Community Council Center, 1971-73; instr. nursing U. So. Colo., Pueblo, 1973-74; instr. community health Union Coll., Lincoln, Nebr., 1974-75, 79—, asst. dir. nursing, 1975-77. Instr., chmn. nursing com. ARC, 1974—; mem. Shawnee (Kans.) Fire Dept. Rescue Squad, 1978-79; mem. exec. bd. Lincoln Health Forum, 1975-77, 79-81, chmn. exec. bd., 1980; mem. exec. bd. S.E. Nebr. Health Systems Agy., 1976, 77, edn. com., 1976—. Mem. Am. Nurses Assn. (del. to bi-ann. conv. 1976, 78), Nebr. Nurses Assn. (del. to state conv. 1974, 75, 76, 77, 80, 81, mem. econ. and gen. welfare com. 1976-79), Nebr. Dist. III Nurses Assn. (chmn. ways and means com. 1975-77, 2d v.p. 1979-80), Nebr. League of Nursing, Am. Heart Assn. Seventh Day Adventist. Home: 4511 Lowell St Lincoln NE 68506 Office: 3800 S 48th St Lincoln NE 68506

BIGGS, ROBERT WILDER, JR., mfg. co. exec.; b. Lorain, Ohio, Jan. 21, 1934; s. Robert Wilder and Eleanor (Hughes) B.; B.S. in Bus. Adminstrn., Ind. U., 1958; m. Dolores Bonnadine Ward, July 9, 1955; children—Robert Wilder, Adrienne. In retail industry, 1958-60; asst. purchasing agt. Oglebay Norton Co., Cleve., 1960-64; mgnt. cons. Case & Co., Cleve., 1964-68; with Pickands Mather & Co., Cleve., 1968—, treas., 1974—; v.p., 1981—; mem. adv. bd. Arkwright Boston, 1978—. Trustee, Cleve. Inst. Music, 1979—. Served with U.S. Army, 1954-56. Mem. Fin. Execs. Inst., Nat. Assn. Accts., Am. Iron and Steel Inst., U.S. Power Squadron, Cleve. Treas.'s Club (dir.). Clubs:

Cleve. Athletic, Mid-Day, Sandusky Yacht. Office: 1100 Superior Ave Cleveland OH 44114

BIGHAM, DARREL EUGENE, historian; b. Harrisburg, Pa., Aug. 12, 1942; s. Paul D. and Ethel B.; B.A., Messiah Coll., 1964; postgrad. Harvard Div. Sch., 1964-65; Ph.D., U. Kans., 1970; m. Mary Elizabeth Hitchcock, Sept. 23, 1965; children—Matthew, Elizabeth. Asst. prof. history Ind. State U., Evansville, 1970-75, asso. prof., 1975-81, prof., 1981—. Exec. dir. Leadership Evansville, 1976-79; dir. archives div. Conrad Baker Found., 1971—; chmn. Evansville Bicentennial Council, 1974-77; bd. dirs. Evansville Museum, 1972—, sec., 1977-78, pres., 1979-81; trustee Evansville Vanderburgh County Pub. Library, 1971-80; bd. dirs. Freedom Festival, 1976-77, Met. Evansville Progress Commn., 1981—, Conrad Baker Found., 1971—, Planned Parenthood S.W. Ind., 1978-79. Rockefeller Brothers Theol. fellow, 1964-65; NDEA fellow, 1965-68. Mem. Soc. Ind. Archivists (dir. 1972-75, pres. 1977-79), Am. Hist. Assn., Orgn. Am. Historians, Ind. Hist. Soc., So. Hist. Assn. Mem. United Ch. of Christ. Clubs: Rotary, Petroleum, Oak Meadow Country. Contbr. articles to scholarly jours. Home: 8215 Kuebler Rd Evansville IN 47712 Office: Dept History Ind State Univ Evansville IN 47712

BIGLER, W(ILLIAM) PAUL, corp. exec.; b. nr. Franklin, Pa., Oct. 5, 1904; s. William and Carolin (Gilmore) B.; grad. Perkiomen Sch., 1923; m. Sarah Tate, Dec. 21, 1940; 1 dau., Nancy Ann Bigler Kersey. Mgr. repair parts sales service Joy Mfg. Co., 1926-34, dir. purchases, 1934-37; indsl. purchasing agt. Semet Solvay Engring. Corp., 1937-38; div. mgr. editorial research McGraw-Hill Pub. Co., 1938-40; sales mgr. Mining Machine Parts, Inc., Cleve., 1940-43, gen. mgr., 1943-48, pres., chmn. bd., 1948-67; pres. L. W. Kelley Co., Inc., 1958-67, Compass Equipment Co., Wichita, Kans., 1957-67; pres. Bigler Investment Corp.; v.p. Circle Oil Co., Sage Drilling Co., 1957-67. Mem. Am. Inst. Mining, Metall. and Petroleum Engrs., Am. Mining Congress, Rocky Mountain, W.Va., Ill. mining insts. Clubs: Country; Cleve. Skating; Franklin; United Hunts; Met. (N.Y.C.). Home: 828 Greengate Oval Greenwood Village Northfield OH 44067 also San Remo Club 22871 N Ocean Blvd Boca Raton FL 33431

BIGLEY, JAMES PHILIP, telephone co. exec.; b. Viroqua, Wis., July 28, 1912; s. Lawrence A. and Ellen (McCall) B.; m. Dorothy Bent, Aug. 28, 1948 (dec.); m. Betty Lou Simmons, Nov. 17, 1978. Officer, dir. State Bank of LaCrosse (Wis.), 1930-47; officer, dir. State Bank of Viroqua, 1947-55, 70—, chmn. bd., 1976—; dir. Viroqua Telephone Co., 1948—, sec., treas., mgr., 1954-62, pres., mgr., 1962—; pres. Viroqua Bldg. Corp., 1965—; dir. Capital TransAm. Corp., Capital Indemnity Corp. Chmn. Viroqua Housing Authority, 1969—. Exec. sec. Rep. Party of Wis., 1955-57; bd. dirs. U. Wis.-LaCrosse Found., 1979. Served from pvt. to 1st lt., 32d Div., AUS, 1942-46. Mem. LaCrosse Jr. C. of C. (pres. 1939), 32d Div. Vets. Assn. (nat. pres. 1957-58), Am. Legion, VFW, Wis. Telephone Assn. (pres. 1962), U.S. Ind. Telephone Assn. (dir., v.p. 1974-77, pres. 1977-78). Elk, Eagle (Wis. pres. 1952-53, internat. pres. 1959-60, financial adviser 1962-69, 75-78). Home: 3 S Washington Heights Viroqua WI 54665 Office: 114 E Court St Virogua WI 54665

BILBREY, DAVID MASTON, contracting co. ofcl.; b. Dayton, Ohio, Sept. 25, 1950; s. Percy Bilbrey and Margie Kathryn (Goss) B.; B.B.A., U. Cin., 1972; student Ohio Coll. Applied Sci., Cin., summer 1971; postgrad. Sinclair Community Coll., Dayton, 1973-74; m. Julia Rosario Delgado, Feb. 12, 1977; 1 dau., Jennifer René. Asst. to job supt. and project mgr. B.G. Danis Co. div. Danis Industries Corp., Dayton, 1973-74, equipment scheduler, 1974, field engr., 1974-75, job engr., 1975, office engr., 1975-76, project mgr. In-Plant div., 1976—. Lic. real estate agt., Ohio. Mem. Oakwood Community Jaycees (external v.p. 1978-79). Baptist. Office: BG Danis Co 1801 E 1st St Dayton OH 45403

BILD, FRANK, state senator; b. Romania, Sept. 30, 1911; s. Anton and Katerina (Schiebel) B.; came to U.S., 1913, naturalized, 1937; B.S. in Edn., Ind. U., 1934; J.D., St. Louis U., 1942; m. Flora Huss, Sept. 18, 1937; children—Brian Alan, Karen Ann, Norman Anton, Kathleen Ann. Dir. athletics Southside St. Louis YMCA, 1936-42; admitted to Mo. bar, 1946, since practiced in St. Louis. Republican committeeman Concord (Mo.) Twp., 1956-66; mem. Mo. Ho. of Reps. from 47th Dist., 1963-64, 67-72, Mo. Senate from 15th Dist., 1973—; mem. Mo. Atomic Energy Commn. Served to capt. AUS, 1942-46. Recipient Meritorious award St. Louis Globe Democrat. Lutheran. Club: Concord Village Lions. Home: 7 Meppen Ct St Louis MO 63128 Office: 11648 Gravois Rd Saint Louis MO 63126

BILD, STEPHEN LEV, educator; b. Chgo., May 26, 1955; s. Gerald Sawyer and Harriet Judith (Lev) B.; B.A. in Edn., MacMurray Coll., Ill., 1976; M.A. in Ednl. Supervision and Adminstrn., Roosevelt U., Chgo., 1980; m. Alicia G. Shubart, Aug. 16, 1981. Tchr. hearing impaired Ill. schs., 1976-80; ednl. coordinator hearing impaired program Central Assn. Spl. Edn., Urbana, Ill., 1980—; instr. sign lang. adult edn. classes Coll. DuPage, 1975. Mem. Conv. Am. Instrs. of Deaf, Council Exceptional Children, Assn. Supervision and Curriculum Devel., Alexander Graham Bell Assn. Deaf, Ill. Assn. Deaf, Ill. Tchrs. Hearing Impaired. Office: 1776 E Washington St Urbana IL 61801

BILES, FAY REIFSNYDER, univ. adminstr.; b. Reading, Pa., Mar. 31, 1929; d. Thomas H. and Dora E. (Weaver) Reifsnyder; A.B., Duke U., 1949; M.A., Kent State U., 1956; Ph.D., Ohio State U., 1968; m. Bedford H. Biles, Sept. 7, 1949. Tchr. biology and English, Coventry High Sch., Akron, Ohio, 1950-56; prof. Kent (Ohio) State U., 1956-72, v.p. pub. affairs and devel., prof. health and safety edn., 1972—; cons. Am. Council on Edn., Pres.'s Council Phys. Fitness; pres. FAVA Assos., cons.; dir. City Bank, Kent. Trustee, Council for Advancement and Support of Edn.; chairperson nat. com. Am. Heart Assn. Recipient Disting. Teaching award Kent State U., 1970; Joy of Effort award Nat. Assn. Sport and Phys. Edn., 1978; named Outstanding Woman Collegiate, Delta Phi Rho Alpha, 1949, Outstanding Delta Delta Delta Woman of Year, 1972. Mem. Am. (dist. chmn. phys. edn. sect. Midwest, state v.p. gen. div. Ohio, dir. Pepi project; pres. 1980), Ohio (Meritorious award) assns. health, phys. edn. and recreation, Nat., Midwest (dir., pub. relations chmn., research project chmn.) assns. phys. edn. coll. women, Ohio Coll. Assn. Phys. Edn. for Women (pres.), AAUW, Northeastern Health Assn. (dir.), Am. Coll. Pub. Relations Assn. (nat. dir. 1973-74), Nat. Assn. State Univs. and Land Grant Colls. (chmn. univ. relations council), Omicron Delta Kappa, Delta Psi Rho Kappa, Phi Rho Alpha, Kappa Delta Pi, Alpha Lambda Delta, Delta Kappa Gamma. Home: Kent OH

BILEYDI, SUMER MEHMET, advt. agy. exec.; b. Antalya, Turkey, Feb. 7, 1936; s. Abdurrahman M. and Neriman (Akman) B.; B.A., Mich. State U., 1961, M.A., 1962; m. Lois Elloine Goode, Dec. 30. 1961; children—Can M., Sera N. Mktg. cons. Export Promotion Center, Ankara, Turkey, 1962; planner Gardner Advt. Agy., St. Louis, 1963-65; planning supr. Batten, Barton, Durstine & Osborn, N.Y.C., 1965-69; asso. dir. Ketchum, Macleod & Grove, Pitts., 1969-73; sr. v.p., dir. Carmichael Lynch, Inc., Mpls., 1973—. Pres., Turkish Am. Assn., 1974-75. Mem. Am. Mktg. Assn., Advt. Research Found., Advt. Fedn. Minn. Islam. Club: Minn. Turkish Am. Contbr. articles to profl. jours. Home: 16670 Baywood Terr Eden Prairie MN 55344 Office: 100 22d St E Minneapolis MN 55404

BILKEY, WILLIAM WALTER, JR., mfg. co. exec.; b. St. Louis, Sept. 21, 1943; s. William W. and Romona (Foosey) B.; student S.E. Mo. State U., 1962, Jefferson Coll., 1967-75, Washington U., 1979—. With Carter Carburetor div. A.C.F. Industries, St. Louis, 1963—, gen. foreman carburetor assembly, 1976-78, mgr. tooling and indsl. engring., 1978—. Mem. Am. Inst. Indsl. Engrs. Club: Moo do Kwan. Office: 2840 N Spring St Saint Louis MO 63107

BILLE, DONALD ALLEN, nurse, educator; b. Waupun, Wis., Feb. 10, 1943; s. Arthur and Ada (Wellhouse) B.; grad. St. Luke's Hosp. Sch. Nursing, 1964; B.S.N., U. Wis., Madison, 1966, Ph.D., 1975; M.S.N., Marquette U., 1971. Mem. faculty Coll. Nursing, Marquette U., Milw., 1970-72; coordinator intensive care unit VA Med. Center, Wood, Wis., 1973-74; dir. nursing edn. Mercy Hosp., Chgo., 1975-77; asst. prof. U. Ill. Med. Center, Chgo., 1978-79; asso. prof. nursing DePaul U., Chgo., 1979—, chmn. grad. program, 1980-81. Served with Nurse Corps, U.S. Army, 1966-70. Mem. Ill. League Nursing (chmn. program com., dir.), Nat. League Nursing, Assn. Supervision and Curriculum Devel., Am. Soc. Health Edn. and Tng., Phi Delta Kappa. Congregationalist. Editor: Practical Approaches to Patient Teaching, 1981. Mem. editorial bd. Quality Rev. Bull., Jour. Nursing Edn., Nursing Adminstrn. Quar.; contbr. articles to profl. jours. Home: 3749 N Wilton Ave Chicago IL 60613 Office: DePaul U 2323 N Seminary Ave Chicago IL 60614

BILLICK, L. LARKIN, fin. mktg. co. exec.; b. Des Moines, Sept. 15, 1948; s. Lyle Larkin and Florence Carlson B.; B.S., U. Kans., Lawrence, 1970; grad. Inst. Bank Mktg., U. So. Calif., La. State U., 1978; m. Kathryn Rose Gildner, Aug. 14, 1971; children—Kelly Lynne, Brett Larkin. Group ins. trainee Bankers Life Co., Des Moines, 1970-71; nat. advt. rep. Stoner Broadcasting Co., Des Moines, 1971-74; advt. account supr. Mid-Am. Broadcasting, Des Moines, 1974-75; dir. public realtions and mktg. Iowa Bankers Assn., Des Moines, 1975-77; asst. v.p., advt. mgr. corp. staff Marine Banks, Milw., 1977-79, v.p. advt., 1979-81; pres. Edwards-Billick Fin. Mktg. Group, Milw., 1981—. Bd. dirs. Grad. Inst. Bank Mktg., La. State U., 1978-79; chmn. communications Milwaukee County Performing Arts Center, 1978-79; advt., promotion cons. to polit. candidates; chmn. communications council United Performing Arts Fund Milw., 1978-79; dist. coordinator State Del. for Jimmy Carter, 1972-80; chmn. communications com. Milwaukee County council Boy Scouts Am., 1979-80. Recipient numerous advt. and relations award. Mem. Bank Mktg. Assn. (chmn. nat. advt. conf. 1979, advt. council 1980-81), Am. Bankers Assn. (mem. nat. mktg. conf. com. 1980), Am. Advt. Fedn. (public service com. 1980-81), Am. Mktg. Assn., Milw. Advt. Club (v.p. fin. 1979-81, dir. 1981-82). Democrat. Roman Catholic. Home: 21400 Lower Cambridge Circle Brookfield WI 53005 Office: 350 Bishops Way Brookfield WI 53005 also Box 179 Milwaukee WI 53201

BILLIG, THOMAS CLIFFORD, pub. co. exec., mktg. cons.; b. Pitts., Aug. 20, 1930; s. Thomas Clifford and Melba Helen (Stucky) B.; student Montgomery Jr. Coll., 1948-49, Am. U., 1950-51; B.S. summa cum laude, Northwestern U., 1956; m. Helen Page Hine, May 14, 1951; children—Thomas Clifford III, James Frederick. Asst. ins. mgr. Montgomery Ward & Co., Chgo., 1951-54; ins. mgr., asst. dir. personnel, asst. to chmn. Butler Bros. (now City Products Corp.), Chgo., 1954-59; market research mgr. R.R. Donnelley & Sons, Chgo., 1959-61; pres., dir. Indsl. Fiber Glass Products Corp., Scottville and Ludington, Mich., 1962-68; mass mktg. mgmt. cons., Mpls., 1968-71; v.p. Mail Mktg. Systems & Services, St. Paul and Bloomington, Minn., 1971-74; pres., dir. Nat. Ins. Advt. Regulation Service Corp., Mpls., 1974—, Fins & Feathers Pub. Co., Mpls., 1977—, Billig & Assos., Mpls., 1979—. Mem. Delta Mu Delta, Beta Gamma Sigma. Home: 3445 Zenith Ave Minneapolis MN 55416 Office: Fins & Feathers Pub Co 318 W Franklin Ave Minneapolis MN 55404

BILLINGHAM, DAVID RALPH, psychiat. social worker; b. Rockford, Ill., Apr. 10, 1949; s. Ralph B. and Elfrieda K. (Muehleisen) B.; B.S. in Psychology, Rockford Coll., 1971; M.S.W., U. Ill., Chgo., 1975; m. Jean Caughey, June 2, 1973; 1 son, Matthew David. Social worker Ill. Dept. Children and Family Services, 1971-73; lead social worker Mental Health Advocacy Project, Chgo., 1975-76; forensic psychiatry program social worker Ill. State Psychiat. Inst., Chgo., 1977-80; grant specialist Region II, Ill. Dept. Mental Health, 1980-81; dir. residential services Victor C. Neumann Assn., Chgo., 1981—; mem. human rights com. W.A. Howe Center for Developmentally Disabled. Cert. social worker, Ill. Mem. Acad. Cert. Social Workers, Ill. Acad. Mental Health, Nat. Assn. Social Workers, Am. Assn. Mental Deficiency, Ill. Assn. Retarded Citizens. Office: 3255 W Armitage Chicago IL 60647

BILLINGS, ROGER EVAN, energy research co. exec.; b. Provo, Utah, Jan. 5, 1948; s. Evan A. and Elda Mae (Lewis) B.; B.S. in Systems Engring., Brigham Young U., 1973; m. Tonja Anderson, June 1, 1971; children—Kimberly, Beverly, Stephanie, Natalie, Melanie, Joseph. Program dir. Sta. KIXX, Provo, 1969-70; sr. partner Billings Advt. Spltys., Provo, 1969-70; pres., gen. mgr. Sound Concepts Rec. Studio, Provo, 1970-71; pres. Pollution Control Research Inst., Riverside, Calif., 1972-73, R.B. Sci., Inc., Provo, 1974—; emissions engr. Lear Motor Co., Reno, 1972; pres., chmn. bd. Billings Energy Corp., Independence, Mo., 1973—; chmn. bd. Billings Computer Corp., Provo, 1977—; session chmn. World Hydrogen Energy Conf., Miami, Fla., 1980. Bd. dirs. Utah Valley Health Care Found., Provo. Recipient cert. of achievement U.S. Army, 1964, Mr. Free Enterprise award Sertoma Internat., Provo; named Outstanding Young Man of Yr., Provo Jaycees, 1980; One of 10 Outstanding Young Men of Yr., U.S. Jaycees, 1980; Engring. div. Ford Motor Co. grantee, 1971-72; Kettering Inst. grantee, 1972-73. Mem. IEEE, Soc. Automotive Engrs. (chmn. Salt Lake City), Internat. Assn. for Hydrogen Energy (dir.), Electrochem. Soc., Provo C. of C. (dir.), Independence C. of C. (dir.). Mormon. Contbr. articles to profl. jours.; builder 1st hydrogen-powered automobile, 1965, mass transit vehicle, 1976, home, 1977; patentee in field. Office: 18600 E 37th Terr S Independence MO 64057

BILLINGS, THOMAS MICHAEL, physician; b. Spearville, Kans., Dec. 31, 1939; s. Wayne Gordon and Lillian Rebecca (Horning) B.; B.A., Sterling Coll., 1962; M.D., U. Kans., 1966; m. Nancy McCreery, Aug. 2, 1963; children—Brian Michael, David Allen, John Todd. Intern, Kansas City Gen. Hosp. & Med. Center, 1966-67; USPHS fellow Indian Service, Eagle Butte, S.D., 1967-69; med. missionary Evang. Covenant Ch., Karawa, Zarie (Congo), 1969-71; family practice medicine, McPherson, Kans., 1971—. Served with USPHS, 1967-69. Diplomate Am. Bd. Family Practice. Baptist. Home: 704 Somerset St McPherson KS 67460 Office: 400 W 4th St McPherson KS 67460

BILLINGSLEY, JOHN SMITH, radiologist; b. Newton, Iowa, Jan. 16, 1929; s. John William and Mary Mable (Smith) B.; B.A., Simpson Coll., 1951; M.D., Western Res. U., 1955; m. Cleo Eloise Jones, Aug. 25, 1952; children—John Elliott, James William, Joseph Crane. Intern, Iowa Meth. Hosp., Des Moines, 1955-56; fellow in radiology Mayo Clinic, Rochester, Minn., 1956-59; practice medicine specializing in radiology, Ft. Wayne, Ind., 1961—; asso. Duemling Clinic; staff Luth. Hosp.; asso. faculty Ind. Sch. Medicine, Ft. Wayne Center Med. Edn. Served to capt. M.C., AUS, 1959-61. Mem. Am. Coll. Radiology, AMA, Ind. Med. Assn., Ind., Iowa hist. socs., Am. Def. Preparedness Assn., Nat. Rifle Assn. Club: Ft. Wayne Country. Home: 4720 Crestwood Dr Fort Wayne IN 46807 Office: 2828 Fairfield Ave Fort Wayne IN 46807

BILLMAN, FRED LEO, mfg. co. exec.; b. Hebron, Nebr., June 19, 1941; s. Elsworth Leo and Ruth Marie (Livergood) B.; student Omaha U., 1958-59; B.S. in Chemistry and Math., Fla. State U., 1963; M.S., Wayne State U., 1965, Ph.D., 1969; m. Mary Renee Hagarty, Aug. 7, 1971; children—Thomas Lloyd, Aaron Donald, Ellen Marie. Research asst. Wayne State U., 1963-69; research chemist basic organic research Johnsons Wax, Racine, Wis., 1969-74, sr. research chemist Johnson Wax Internat., 1974-77, research and devel. dir., Mex., 1977-80, Chile, 1980—. Mem. Coledonia Twp. (Wis.) Planning Bd., 1975-76. Mem. Am. Chem. Soc., Mexican Aerosol Soc. Patentee fabric softening agts. Home: 4511 Harvest Ln Racine WI 53402 Office: 1525 Howe St Racine WI 53403

BILLS, EDWIN LYNN, vocat. edn. adminstr.; b. Delaware, Ohio, Dec. 20, 1942; s. Harold Lynn and Lucille (Sharp) B.; B.S. in Edn., U. Cin., 1973, M.Ed., 1975; Ohio Vocat. Edn. Adminstrn. intern, Kent State U., 1977-78; m. Shirlee Costello, June 9, 1972; children—Amylynn, Nathan. Computer ops. shift supr. U.S. Shoe Corp., Cin., 1970-73; communications electronics instr. Great Oaks Joint Vocat. Sch. Dist., Cin., 1973-77, trade and indsl. edn. supr., 1977-80; asso. dir. Scarlet Oaks Career Devel. Center, Cin., 1980—; cons. emergency med. technician-ambulance tng. S.W. Ohio. Bd. dirs. Ripley County Ind. A.R.C., 1978—, Public Service award, 1978; rep. Ripley County Disaster Council. Served with USN, 1962-69. Mem. Ohio Vocat. Assn., Am. Vocat. Assn., Ohio Trade and Indsl. Edn. Suprs. Assn. (charter), Am. Radio Relay League (Public Service award). Roman Catholic. Clubs: Laughery Valley Amateur Radio (past pres.), U. Cin. Vets. (charter, past sec.). Home: Rt 1 Box 195A Sunman IN 47041 Office: 3254 E Kemper Rd Cincinnati OH 45241

BILSKY, EARL, textile/apparel co. exec.; b. Fall River, Mass., Sept. 26, 1928; s. David and Rose (Nulman) B.; B.S., S.E. Mass. U., 1952; M.S. (research fellow), Inst. of Textile Tech., 1954; m. Betty Ann Funk, Dec. 5, 1954; children—Edward Scott, Karen Lee, Matthew Kolman. Engr. specialist Goodyear Aerospace Corp., Akron, Ohio, 1960-62; merchandise mgr. apparel and indsl. Am. Cyanamid Co., N.Y.C. and Wayne, N.J., 1962-71; exec. v.p. Aileen, Inc., N.Y.C. and Abilene, Tex., 1971-76, also dir.; gen. mgr. Eagle Knitting Mills, Milw., 1976—. Bd. dirs. United Way, Abilene, 1975-76, YMCA, Abilene, 1973-76, Abilene Art Mus., 1974-75; planning/zoning commr. City of Abilene, 1975-76. Served with USMC, 1946-48. Patentee in field. Office: 507 S 2d St Milwaukee WI 53204

BINARD, WILLIAM JOHN, research lab. exec.; b. Chgo., June 8, 1938; s. William John and Helen Barbara (Firko) B.; B.Sc., U. Miami, Fla., 1960; postgrad. U. Ill. Coll. Medicine, 1960-62; m. Sylvia G. Neustadt, May 17, 1963; children—Jacqueline Dawn, Anthony Douglas. Dept. head microbiol. assay lab. Dawes Labs., Chgo., 1963-64; head microbiology dept. Indsl. Bio-Test Labs., Northbrook, Ill., 1965-66: sr. scientist toxicology research Life-Stream Labs., Libertyville, Ill., 1966-67; mgr. hosp. research div. Kendall Co., Barrington, Ill., 1968-81; dir. research and new product devel., extracorporeal div. Johnson & Johnson, King of Prussia, Pa., 1981—; instr. physiology U. Miami, 1958-59; 1st aid instr. ARC, 1975-77. Chmn. Barrington United Fund, 1973-74; Merit Badge counselor, pack chmn. Boy Scouts Am., 1978-79. Mem. Assn. Vitamin Chemists, Assn. Advancement Lab. Animal Scis., Soc. Indsl. Microbiology, Internat. Soc. Urodynamics, Soc. Plastic Engrs., Am. Soc. Cytology, Assn. Advancement Med. Instrumentation, Am. Assn. Bio-Materials, Am. Coll. Sports Medicine. Author, patentee in field. Home: 328 Weber Ct Cary IL 60013 Office: Ross and Royal Rd King of Prussia PA 19406

BINDER, CHARLES WILLIAM, options market maker; b. Niagara Falls, N.Y., Oct. 13, 1944; s. William Oakley and Olive (Lauckner) B.; A.B. in Econs., Brown U., 1967; M.B.A., U. Mich., 1969. Investment analyst Harris Trust and Savs. Bank, Chgo., 1969-73, investment analyst Harris Group, Chgo., 1973-75; market maker Chg. Bd. Options Exchange, 1975—. Mem. Market Makers Assn., Chgo. Bd. Options Exchange. Presbyterian. Home and Office: 2020 Lincoln Park W Chicago IL 60614

BINDER, EDWARD CLARENCE, state ofcl.; b. Omaha, Aug. 11, 1923; s. Clarence J. and Myree E. (McNeley) B.; B.S., U. Nebr., 1971; m. Roma Kathleen Chilcutt, Oct. 19, 1946; children—Gary E., Nancy Jo. Commd. 2d lt., Colo. Army Nat. Guard, 1948, Nebr. Army Nat. Guard, 1950; advanced through grades to maj. gen.; chief of staff Nebr. Army N.G., 1968-70, spl. asst. to adj. gen., 1970-74, chief selective service sect., 1976-77, adj. gen. Nebr., 1977—; state dir. CD, state dir. emergency planning, 1977—. Mem. N.G. Assn. U.S., N.G. Assn. Nebr., Peace Officers Assn. Nebr., Am. Legion. Clubs: Masons, Shrines. Home: 6001 Kenwood Circle Lincoln NE Office: 1300 Military Rd Lincoln NE 68508*

BINGAY, JAMES SCLATER, JR., banker; b. Seattle, Aug. 3, 1943; s. James S. and Margaret A. (Blackstock) B.; B.A. in Econs., Brown U., 1965; M.B.A. in Fin., U. Pa., 1967; m. Margaret Jean Meyer, June 14, 1969. Asso. corp. fin. dept. E.F. Hutton & Co., 1970-70; lending officer Citbank, 1970-76; v.p., gen. mgr. Citicorp, San Francisco, 1976-78; v.p., area mgr. Citicorp (U.S.A.), Inc., Cleve., 1978—. Fund raising capt. Musical Arts Assn., 1979-80. Served to lt., Supply Corps, USNR, 1967-69; Vietnam. Recipient Wall St. Jour. achievement award in econs., Brown U., 1965. Mem. Cleve. Growth Assn. Clubs: Olympic Golf, Univ. (San Francisco); Kirtland Country, Union (Cleve.). Office: Citicorp USA Inc 1300 E 9th St Bond Court Bldg Cleveland OH 44114

BINGHAM, MARJORIE JEAN WALL, educator; b. St. Paul, Nebr., May 27, 1936; d. George Richard and Fay Maugerite Wall; B.A., Grinnell Coll., 1958; M.A., U. Minn., 1959, Ph.D., 1969; m. Thomas Egan, Feb. 28, 1975. Tchr. public schs., Davenport, Iowa, 1959-62, St. Louis Park, Minn., 1963-77; dir. women in world area studies St. Louis Park and Robbinsdale (Minn.) schs., 1977—. Woodrow Wilson fellow, 1958-59. Mem. Women Historians of Midwest (pres. 1980—, mem. exec. bd. 1978—), Minn. Hist. Soc. (mem. edn. bd. 1979—), Minn. Council of Social Studies (mem. exec. bd. 1977—), Phi Beta Kappa. Co-author: Women in the U.S.S.R., 1980; Women in Islam, 1980; Women in Israel, 1980; Women in China, 1980; Women in India, 1980. Home: 5732 Lake Rose Dr Minnetonka MN 55343 Office: 6425 W 33d St Saint Louis Park MN 55426

BINGLEY, LEO JULLIAN, JR., physician; b. Shreveport, La., Feb. 10, 1936; s. Leo J. and Laila Laurel (LaFleur) B.; B.S., Hillsdale Coll., 1958; M.D., U. Mich., 1961; m. Nita L. Berry, Aug. 26, 1971; children—Laurel, Leo, Bradley. Intern, USPHS, New Orleans, 1961-62, resident in gen. practice, 1962-64; resident in internal medicine Henry Ford Hosp., Detroit, 1964-67; staff physician Burns Clinic Med. Center, Petoskey, Mich., 1967-73; asso. dir. med. edn., dir. internal med. edn. St. Joseph Hosp., Flint, Mich., 1974-78, dir. med. edn., 1978-80; asso. dir. internal medicine edn. McLaren Gen. Hosp., Flint, 1980—; coordinator undergrad. internal medicine edn. Univ.-Affiliated Hosps. of Flint, 1980—; asso. prof. internal medicine and family practice Mich. State U., 1977—. Pres., Emmett County Heart Assn., 1969-71; bd. dirs. Genesee County Cancer Soc., 1976-79. Served with USPHS, 1961-64. Diplomate Am. Bd. Internal Medicine, Am. Bd. Family Practice. Fellow A.C.P.; mem. Genesee County Med. Soc., Mich. State Med. Soc., Am. Soc. Internal Medicine, Mich. Soc. Internal Medicine, Flint Acad. Medicine. Club: Masons. Office: 302 Kensington Ave Flint MI 48502

BINNING, WILLIAM CHARLES, polit. scientist; b. Boston, Mar. 8, 1944; s. Kenneth William and Josephine Agnes (Crotty) B.; B.A. in Politics, St. Anselm's Coll., 1966; Ph.D. in Govt. and Internat. Relations (NDEA fellow), U. Notre Dame, 1970; m. Maureen G. Fannon, Nov. 26, 1966; children—Patrick, Catherine. Asst. prof. polit. sci. Youngstown (Ohio) State U., 1970-77, asso. prof., chmn. polit. sci., 1977—; project dir. NSF, 1978-79, grant evaluator, 1979. Trustee Internat. Inst., Youngstown, 1972—, Children and Family Services Bd., Mahoning County, 1977—; vice chmn. Mahoning County Republican Central Com., 1973-74. Mem. Am. Polit. Sci. Assn., Internat. Studies Assn., Latin Am. Studies Assn., Midwest Polit. Sci. Assn., AAUP. Home: 2893 Algonquin Dr Poland OH 44514 Office: Dept Polit Sci Youngstown State U Youngstown OH 44555

BINOTTI, DAVID ALLEN, orthodontist; b. Chgo., Apr. 8, 1943; s. Evo Joseph and Anne (DiVita) B.; D.D.S., Loyola U. (Chgo.), 1967, M.S. in Oral Biology, 1969, Certificate Specialty Orthodontics, 1969; m. Barbara J. Rizzo, June 24, 1967; children—Eric David, Nicholas Allen. Practice orthodontics, Oak Lawn, Ill., 1969—, Lombard, Ill., 1971—; asso. with Dr. Ernest Panos, Chgo., 1969-74; clin. instr. dept. orthodontics Sch. Dentistry, Loyola U., 1969-72. Mem. ADA, Chgo. Dental Soc., Am. Assn. Orthodontists, Ill. Soc. Orthodontists. Roman Catholic. Office: 5208 W 95th St Oak Lawn IL 60453 also 805 S Main St Suite 2 Lombard IL 60148

BIPES, ROGER LUELLYEN, mech. engr.; b. Brownton, Minn., Dec. 12, 1936; s. Leullyen L. and Elda M. (Reiter) B.; B.S. in Mech. Engring., Ind. Inst. Tech., 1958; M.B.A., Xavier U., 1979; m. Janice M. Doctor, June 14, 1958; children—Timothy, Thomas, Trisha. Test engr. Ind. and Mich. Electric Co., Lawrenceburg, Ind., 1957-61; sr. indsl. hygienist Nat. Lead Co. of Ohio, Fernald, 1961-66; chief engr. MC & R Mfg. Chemists, Norwood, Ohio, 1966—. Mem. Am. Soc. Safety Engrs., So. Ohio Fire Protection Assn. Republican. Lutheran. Home: 547 Hayes St Lawrenceburg IN 47025 Office: 2909 Highland St Norwood OH 45212

BIRCH, JOHN EDWARD, home builder, Realtor, investor; b. Chgo., Oct. 3, 1917; s. John Edward and Veronica (Motyka) B.; B.A. in Edn., B.A. in Banking and Finance, U. Ill., 1940; M.B.A., Northwestern U., 1942; Ph.D. in Bus. Adminstrn., Colo. State Coll.; children—John Edward, Christopher J., Terrie J., Laurence P. Pres., John Birch & Co. Mem. Ill. Bldg. Authority, 1977—; mem. pres.'s council U. Ill. Trustee, Mid-Am. Hearing Found. of Wesley Meml. Hosp. Served from pvt. to col., USAAF, 1942-46. Ky. Col. Mem. Home Builders Assn. Chicagoland (life dir.), Nat. Assn. Homebuilders, Nat., Ill. assns. real estate bds., DuPage Bd. Realtors, U.S. C. of C., Chgo. Assn. Commerce and Industry (com. mem.), Am. Legion, Art Inst. Chgo., U. Ill. Alumni Assn. (life). Clubs: Moose, Rotary (Oakbrook, Ill.); Torch; Oakbrook Polo.

BIRCH, JOHN RICHARD, archtl. engr.; b. Milw., Nov. 25, 1922; s. Frank Victor and Marion Louise (Yost) B.; B.S. in Civil Engring., Iowa State U., 1947; m. Sophia Janet Oliver, May 18, 1944; children—John Oliver, James Ross, David Richard, Barbara Mary, Mark Denton. Hydrographic surveyor F. H. McGraw & Co., Naval Operating Base, Bermuda, B.W.I., 1942; civil engr. Jensen & Johnson, Elkhorn, Wis., 1947-50; dir. public works City of Whitewater, Wis., 1947-50; city engr. City of Beaver Dam, Wis., 1953-58; dir. engring. Megal Devel. Corp., Brookfield, Wis., 1958-61; prin. Birch-Grisa-Phillips, Inc., Architects-Engrs.-Planners, Brookfield, Wis., 1961—; pres. BGP/CM, Constrn. Mgrs., Brookfield, 1977—; partner BGP Enterprises, Brookfield; partner The GB Partners, Brookfield, New Berlin Assos., Brookfield; mem. Village of Menomonee Falls Archtl. Control Bd. Mem. Wis. Dept. Industry, Labor and Human Relations safety and bldg. code coms. Served to capt. USAAF, 1943-46. Decorated Air medal, Purple Heart; registered Profl. engrs., Wis.; registered surveyor, Wis.; lic. comml. pilot. Mem. Wis. Soc. Profl. Engrs., Nat. Soc. Profl. Engrs., Profl. Engrs. in Pvt. Practice, Wis. Soc. Architects (affiliate), Great Lakes Area Devel. Council, Wis. Soc. Land Surveyors, Beta Theta Pi. Lutheran. Club: Lions (past pres., past dir.). Home: W151 N6963 Glenview Ct Menomonee Falls WI 53051 Office: 3525 N 124th St Brookfield WI 53005

BIRD, BRADLEY WILBUR, savs. and loan exec.; b. Cumberland, Wis., Aug. 31, 1937; s. Wilbur Sameul and Grace Gladys (Shephard) B.; student pub. schs., Cumberland; m. Margaret Lally, Mar. 7, 1964; children—Dean, David, Brian, Jeffrey, Craig. With Sears, Roebuck & Co., Mpls., 1955-56; with proof dept. 1st Nat. Bank, Mpls., 1956-57; with Twin City Fed. Savs. & Loan Assn., Mpls., 1957—, asst. v.p., 1974—, mgr. communications, 1975—. Home and sch. treas. local Catholic Ch., 1975-76, mem. sch. bd., 1977-78; pres. Columbia Heights (Minn.) Jaycees, 1972, state dir., 1971, state treas., 1973. Recipient Disting. Service award Columbia Heights Jaycees, 1975. Home: 4550 6th St Columbia Heights MN 55421 Office: Twin City Fed Savs and Loan Assn 801 Marquette Ave Minneapolis MN 55402

BIRD, GERRY NORMAN, architect, designer; b. Long Beach, Calif., Nov. 11, 1948; s. Harold Arthur and Luisa Mae (Bru) B.; B.Arch., Miami U., Oxford, Ohio, 1971; M.Arch., Ohio State U., Columbus, 1973; postgrad. Capital U., since 1978—; m. Lynn Adair McMakin, June 17, 1972; 1 son, Justin Matthew. Draftsman, design support Tully, Ames, Elzey & Thomas, Architects, Columbus, 1968-70; land planner, designer Ballard H.T. Kirk & Assos., Architects, Columbus, 1970-72; teaching asso. architecture, design critic Ohio State U., 1971-72; land planner, designer, design detailer Ireland Assos., Architects, Columbus, 1972-74; project designer, project architect, mgr. design, v.p. Kellam & Smith, Architects, Engrs. and Planners, Dublin, Ohio, 1974—; mng. partner InterUrban Properties; sec.-treas. Bird Graphics, Inc. partner Contemporary Environments, real estate investment co. Treas., Columbus Architecture Found. Registered architect, Ohio: cert. Nat. Council Archtl. Registration Bds. Mem. AIA (mem. exec. com. and task force environ. edn. Columbus chpt. and nat. com. on continuing edn.), Architects Soc. Ohio. Designer office bldgs., indsl. facilities, schs., univs., labs., banks, residential and govtl. bldgs. Home: 2616 Coventry Rd Columbus OH 43221 Office: 4789 Rings Rd Dublin OH 43017

BIRD, MILFORD GILBERT, mech. engr.; b. Algona, Iowa, Jan. 21, 1917; s. Henry Francis and Verona May (Gilbert) B.; student Chgo. Tech. Coll., 1938-41, U. Minn., 1949-53; m. Bernice Laura Stoeckel, Sept. 9, 1944; children—Ronald Gilbert, Bonnie Laura. With CCC, Grand Rapids, Minn., 1934; asst. to ednl. adviser Roberts-Hamilton Co., Mpls., 1935-38; draftsman Tri-City Roofing & Sheet Metal Works, Whiting, Ind, 1938-41; office mgr. Honeywell, Inc., Mpls., 1944-45; field research engr. Reese Assos., Mpls., 1945-49; v.p. Bird, Bird & Assos., Mpls., 1949-73; sr. mech. engr., pres. U.S. Postal Service Design & Constrn., St. Paul, 1973-81. Served with U.S. Army, 1941-44. Mem. Minn. Assn. Cons. Engrs. (pres. 1966-67), Am. Cons. Engrs. Council (nat. dir. 1970-72), Nat., Minn. socs. profl. engrs., Profl. Engrs. In Govt., Assn. Energy Engrs. Republican. Lutheran. Home: 3200 46th Ave N Robbinsdale MN 55422 Office: 180 E Kellogg Blvd Saint Paul MN 55169

BIRD, RICHARD MERRILL, personnel search co. exec.; b. Ann Arbor, Mich., Apr. 22, 1931; s. Richard Merrill and Nora Louise (Moore) B.; B.S., Mich. State U., 1953, M.B.A., 1954; m. Mary Eckley, Sept. 13, 1952; children—Susan, Gail, Martha, Mary Ann. Div. controller Midwest, Nat. Dairy Products Corp., 1954-60; mem. comml. lending dept. Nat. Bank Detroit, 1961; controller Comstock Foods Co., Newark, N.Y., 1961-64; dir. info. services Nat. Gypsum Co., Buffalo, 1964-68; corp. mgr. info. systems Allis Chalmers, Milw., 1968-69; dir. info. services Standard Register Co., Dayton, Ohio, 1969-70; mgmt. cons. Haskins & Sells, Cin., 1970-71; corp. dir. info. systems Koehring Co., Milw., 1971-72; pres., Robert Half of Wis., Inc., Milw., 1972—. Cert. data processor, cert. employment counselor. Mem. Am. Soc. Personnel Adminstrs., Fin. Execs. Inst., Wis. Assn. Personnel Con.'s, Nat. Assn. Personnel Cons.'s, Data Processing Mgmt. Assn. (pres. 1966-67), Nat. Assn. Accts., Assn. Systems Mgmt. Republican. Episcopalian. Office: Robert Half of Wis Inc 777 E Wisconsin Ave Milwaukee WI 53202

BIRD, THOMAS MONROE, accountant; b. Charlotte, N.C., Nov. 8, 1954; s. Marion Wyle and Edna Virginia (Austell) B.; B.S.B.A., East Carolina U., 1977, M.B.A., 1978; m. Debra Lynne Dickerson, May 27, 1978; 1 dau., Debra Elizabeth. Resident advisor East Carolina U., 1976-78; mfg. supr. Guide div. Gen. Motors Corp., 1978-79, accountant, property sect., Anderson, Ind., 1979—. Scoutmaster, Boy Scouts Am.; mem. Meadowbrook Bapt. Ch. Democrat. Clubs: Masons, Shriners, Scottish Rite. Home: 1811 Roundhill Dr Anderson IN 46013 Office: Pendleton Ave Anderson IN 46013

BIRDWELL, WELDON L., mass transit equipment mfg. co. exec.; b. San Angelo, Tex., Apr. 21, 1950; s. Weldon L. and Billie S.B.: B.A., Mundelein Coll., 1981; m. Linda Crichton, Aug. 27, 1977; 1 son, Christopher. Quality control mgr. Charmglow Products, Bristol, Wis., 1973-78; mgr. regulatory affairs and quality assurance Am. Hosp. Supply Corp., Evanston, Ill., 1978-80; dir. quality assurance, mass transit div. Qonaar Corp., Elk Grove Village, Ill., 1980—. Mem. Am. Soc. Quality Control. Office: Qonaar Corp 751 Pratt Blvd Elk Grove IL 60007

BIRENBAUM, WILLIAM M., coll. pres.; b. Macomb, Ill., July 18, 1923; s. Joseph and Rose (Whiteman) B.; student Iowa State Tchrs. Coll., 1943; J.D., U. Chgo., 1949; L.H.D., Columbia Coll., Chgo., 1970; m. Helen Bloch, Mar. 8, 1951; children—Susan, Lauren Amy, Charles. Dir. student affairs U. Chgo., 1949-54, mem. faculty social scis. coll. of univ., 1950-54, dean students Univ. Coll., 1955-57; dir. research. conf. bd. Asso. Research Councils, Ford Found. project study post-doctoral internat. ednl. exchanges, 19S4-55; asst. v.p. Wayne State U., 1957-61; dean New Sch. Social Research, N.Y.C., 1961-64; v.p., provost Bklyn. Center, L.I. U., 1964-67; pres. Edn. Affiliate. Bedford-Stuyvesant Devel. & Services Corp., Bklyn., 1967-68; pres. S.I. Community Coll., 1968-76, pres. Antioch U., 1976—, also leader study mission to People's Republic China, 1973; mem. faculty N.Y. U. Grad. Sch. Edn., 1969-70. Cons., Austrian Ministry Edn., Vienna, 1969; higher edn. adviser Republic of Zambia, 1972; cons. U. Zambia, 1972; guest lectr. 4th Internat. Congress, for Sci. Edn., Sorbonne, Paris, France, 1973; vis. prof. U. Mass., Amherst, 1974-75. Founder, Nat. Student Assn., 1946-48, chmn. nat. faculty bd., 1950-54; pres. Assn. Community Councils Met. Chgo., 1955-57; chmn. Mich. Cultural Commn.. 1960-61; founder, original dir. Detroit Adventure, vol. assn. cultural instns., 1958-61; mem. Bd. Edn., dists. 21-22, N.Y.C., 1962-64; bd. dirs. Bklyn. chpt. Am. Civil Liberties Union, 1967—, chmn. acad. freedom com., 1967—; chmn. edn. com. Met. council Am. Jewish Congress, 1967—, chmn. acad. freedom com., 1967—; trustee Little Red Schoolhouse on Bleecker St. N.Y.C., 1963—; bd. adv. Bklyn. Acad. Music, 1965—, Bklyn. Inst. Arts and Scis. mem. mass media program com. Religion in Am. Life, 1969—; mem. adv. council Korean Student Assn., N.Y., 1969—; adv. bd. ERIC Clearinghouse for Jr. Coll., Los Angeles, 1970—; mem. commn. on curriculum Am. Assn. Jr. Colls., 1970—; mem. nat. adv. council Eastern Va. Med. Sch., 1971—; bd. govs. Rochdale Inst., 1972—; bd. dirs. Brotherhood-in-Action, 1972—, Regional Plan Assn., 1972—. Trustee Friends World Coll., Westbury, N.Y. Mem. Chgo. Bar Assn., Delta Sigma. Author: Overlive: Power, Poverty and the University, 1968; Something for Everybody is Not Enough: An Educator's Search for His Education, 1971. Contbg. author: Student Personnel Work in Urban Colleges. Office: Antioch U Yellow Springs OH 45387

BIRK, ROBERT EUGENE, physician; b. Buffalo, Jan. 7, 1926; s. Reginald H. and Florence (Diebolt) B.; A.B., Colgate U., 1948; M.D., U. Rochester, 1952; m. Janet L. Davidson, June 24, 1950; children—David Eugene, James Michael, Patricia Jean, Thomas Spencer, Susan Margaret. Intern, resident Henry Ford Hosp., Detroit, 1952-57, chief 2d med. div., 1961-66, asst. to chmn. dept. medicine, 1965-66; practice medicine, specializing in internal medicine, Grosse Pointe, Mich., 1966—; sr. active staff St. John Hosp., 1966—, chief dept. medicine, 1967-70, dir. health edn., dir. grad. med. edn., 1975—, exec. dir. continuing med. edn., 1975—; dir. med. affairs St. Clair Ambulatory Care Corp., St. Clair Home Care Services, 1980—; dir. St. Clair Exec. Diagnostic Services, 1980—; asst. prof. medicine Wayne State U., 1969—. Mem. trustee's council U. Rochester, 1973-75, Med. Center alumni council, 1974-75; corp. mem. bd. Boys Clubs Met. Detroit, 1973—; trustee Mich. Cancer Found., 1980—. Served with Army of U.S., 1943-46. Diplomate Am. Bd. Internal Medicine. Fellow A.C.P.; mem. AMA, Assn. Hosp. Med. Edn., Alpha Tau Omega. Republican. Episcopalian. Clubs: Grosse Pointe (Mich.); Renaissance, Econs., Carleton (Chgo.). Contbr. articles in field to profl. jours. Home: 10 Stratford Pl Grosse Pointe MI 48230 Office: 22151 Moross Rd Suite G33 Detroit MI 48236

BIRKERTS, GUNNAR, architect; b. Riga, Latvia, Jan. 17, 1925; s. Peter and Maria (Shop) B.; came to U.S., 1949, naturalized, 1954; grad. Technische Hochschule, Stuttgart, Germany, 1949; m. Sylvia Zvirbulis, 1950; children—Sven Peter, Andra Sylvia, Erik Gunnar. Designer, Perkins & Will, Chgo., 1950-51, Eero Saarinen & Associates, Bloomfield Hills, Mich., 1951-54; prin. and chief designer Minoru Yamasaki & Associates, Birmingham, Mich., 1955-59; prin. Birkerts & Straub, Birmingham, Mich., 1959-62; pres. Gunnar Birkerts & Associates, Birmingham, Mich., 1962—; prof. arch. U. Mich., Ann Arbor, 1969—. Major works include: U.S. Embassy Bldg., Helsinki, Finland, Law Library Addition, U. Mich., Ann Arbor, IBM Office Bldg., Southfield, Mich., Corning (N.Y.) Glass Mus., Contemporary Arts Mus., Houston, Tex., Fed. Res. Bank, Mpls. and others. Recipient numerous awards including: Gold Medal award Tau Sigma Delta, 1971, Design in Steel award Am. Iron and Steel Inst., 1973, Honor award Cons. Engrs. Council U.S., 1973. Fellow AIA (Honor award 1962, 68, 70, 73, 75, 78, Award of Merit 1963, 67, Gold medal award Detroit chpt. 1975), Graham Found., Latvian Architects Assn.; mem. Mich. Soc. Architects (award of merit 1967, award of honor 1974, 77, 79, 80, Gold Medal award 1980), Brunner Prize in Architecture, Am. Academy and Inst. of Arts & Letters, 1981. Office: 292 Harmon Birmingham MI 48009

BIRKHOLZ, GABRIELLA SONJA ENERSEN, editor; b. Chgo., Apr. 11, 1938; d. Ladislav E. and Sonja (Kosner) Becvar; student U. Wis., 1969-71, Alverno Coll., 1977—; m. 2d, Richard D. Birkholz, Apr. 2, 1975. Editor, owner Fox Lake (Wis.) Rep., 1962-65, McFarland (Wis.) Community Life and Monona Community Herald, 1966-69; bur. reporter Waukesha (Wis.) Daily Freeman, 1969-71; community relations staff Waukesha County Tech. Inst., Pewaukee, Wis., 1971-73; public relations specialist JI Case Co., Racine, Wis., 1973-75, corp. publs. editor, 1975-80; v.p. and dir. publs. Image Mgmt., Valley View Center, Milw., 1980—. Active, Big Sisters Racine County, Inc., 1974—; bd. dirs., public relations chmn. Girl Scouts U.S.A., Racine, 1976-77. Recipient awards Wis. Press Assn., Wis. Press Women, Nat. Fedn. Press Women, Internat. Assn. Bus. Communicators. Mem. Women in Communication, Internat. Assn. Bus. Communicators (accredited mem., v.p. programs S.E. Wis. chpt. 1976-77), Wis. Press Women (treas. 1970-71), Milw. Press Club, Sigma Delta Chi. Contbr. articles in field to profl. jours. Home: 252 Lake View Dr Hartland WI 53029 Office: Valley View Center PO Box 28816 Milwaukee WI 53228

BIRLA, SUSHIL KUMAR, automotive mfg. corp. exec.; b. Sirsa, Haryana State, India, Oct. 1, 1943; came to U.S., 1969, naturalized, 1978; s. Mahabir Prasad and Lalita Devi (Mohunta) B.; B.S.M.E., Birla Inst. Tech. and Sci., Pilani, India, 1965; M.S.E.E., Wayne State U., 1971; m. Pramila Kela, Dec. 14, 1972; children—Jyoti, Asheesh. Mng. partner Madhu Woodcraft Industries, Jaipur, India, 1965-66; supt. prodn. planning and control Hindustan Motors, Uttarpara, India, 1966-69; proposal, controls engr. Cross Co., Fraser, Mich., 1969-73; design engr. Excello Machine Tool Products, Detroit, 1973-76; staff devel. engr. Gen. Motors Mfg. Devel., GM Tech. Center, Warren, Mich., 1976—; mem. Machine Tool Task Force for U.S. Air Force Materials Lab., Dept. Def., 1978-80. Vol. probation aide Macomb County, Mich., 1976-77; vol. probation counsellor Sterling Heights, Mich., 1979—. Recipient Outstanding Contbn. award Dept. Def.; cert. mfg. engr. Mem. Soc. Mfg. Engrs., IEEE (sr.), ASME. Home: 42380 Buckingham Dr Sterling Heights MI 48078 Office: Gen Motors Mfg Devel Gen Motors Tech Center Warren MI 48090

BIRMINGHAM, THOMAS JOSEPH, steel co. ofcl.; b. Balt., Dec. 9, 1922; s. Thomas Joseph and Anna Margaret (Nizer) B.; student McCoy Coll., Johns Hopkins U., 1963-64; m. Pauline Louise Graves, Jan. 7, 1945; 1 dau., Kathleen Cheryl. Gen. Supr. Bethlehem Steel Corp., Sparrows Point, Md., 1941-64, adminstrv. asst., Burns Harbor, Ind., 1964—. Pres. Fullerton Elementary Sch. PTA, Balt., 1959; life mem. Md. Congress Parents and Teachers; mem. Balt. County Youth Recreation Council, Balt., 1959-61. Served with USN, 1942-45. Republican. Lutheran. Clubs: Masons, Scottish Rite (South Bend), Shrine (Porter County, Lake County, South Bend, potentate ORAK Temple, Hammond, 1981), K.T., Royal Order of Jesters. Home: 656 Northview Dr Valparaiso IN 46383 Office: Box 248 Chesterton IN 46304

BIRNBAUM, PHILIP HARVEY, educator; b. San Diego, Jan. 21, 1944; s. Louis and Ruth Laureen (Bay) B.; B.A., U. Calif., Berkeley, 1965; Ph.D., U. Wash., 1975; m. Marlin Sue Van Every, Dec. 26, 1964; 1 son, Brian Philip. Personnel analyst Los Angeles County Civil Service Commn., 1965-67; teaching asso. U. Wash., Seattle, 1972-74; asst. prof. bus. adminstrn. Ind. U., Bloomington, 1975-80, asso. prof., 1980—; vis. scholar Polish Acad. Scis. Served with USAF, 1967-71. NSF fellow, 1974-75; N.Y. Acad. Scis. fellow, 1981; sr. Fulbright scholar, U. Hong Kong, 1981-82; recipient DBA Assn. teaching award Ind. U., 1978. Mem. Acad. of Mgmt., AAAS, Am. Inst. for Decision Scis., Am. Sociol. Assn., Soc. for Social Study of Sci., Inst. of Mgmt. Sci., Internat. Assn. for Study of Interdisciplinary Research, Beta Gamma Sigma, Beta Alpha Psi, Sigma Iota Epsilon. Democrat. Methodist. Co-author: Organization Theory: A Structural and Behavioral Analysis; Modern Management Techniques for Engineers and Scientists; contbr. book reviews, articles to profl. publs., sect. to book, invited papers Germany, Poland, Eng., Canada. Office: Grad Sch Bus Ind Univ Bloomington IN 47405

BIRO, JOHN EDWARD, mgmt. and mktg. analyst; b. Chgo., Sept. 1, 1952; s. Arpad Anthony and Dorothy Jane (Hock) B.; B.S., U. Ill., Chgo., 1974. With United Parcel Service, Northbrook, Ill., 1972-76; dir. Seeker Enterprises, Oak Brook, Ill., 1976—; ops. mgr. Automobile Purchasing Specialists, Chgo., 1977—; pres. Midwest Diversified Services Inc., Oak Brook, 1978—; pres. Affiliated Nat. Systems, Inc., Oak Brook, 1980—; dir. Smart Buyers Shopping Systems Inc., Schaumburg. Mem. Am. Mgmt. Assn. Roman Catholic. Home: 430 N Brainard St LaGrange Park IL 60525 Office: 999 Plaza Dr Schaumburg IL 60195

BIRR, DANIEL HOWARD, interior architect; b. Coffeyville, Kans., Nov. 22, 1951; s. Daniel Harry and Olive Jean (Perkins) B.; B. Interior Arch., Kans. State U., 1974. Designer, G Interiors, Rapid City, S.D., 1974-76; space planner/designer Alpha Techne, Rapid City, 1976-80; project designer Comml. Builders of Kans., Wichita, 1980-81, Pizza Hut Inc., Wichita, 1981—. Episcopalian. Home: 3081 River Park Dr Wichita KS 67203 Office: Pizza Hut Inc 9111 E Douglas Wichita KS

BISEL, HARRY FERREE, physician; b. Manor, Pa., June 17, 1918; s. George Culbertson and Mary Stotler (Ferree) B.; B.S., U. Pitts., 1939, M.D., 1942; m. Sara Louise Clark, Oct. 30, 1954; children—Jane, Clark, Harold. Intern, U. Pitts. Med. Center, 1942-43; resident, U. Pa. Grad. Sch. Medicine, 1948-49, Harvard Med. Sch. (Boston City Hosp.), 1949-50; resident physician Meml. Sloan Kettering Cancer Center, 1951-53; cancer coordinator medicine U. Pitts., 1953-63; chmn. div. med. oncology Mayo Clinic, Rochester, Minn., 1963-72, sr. cons. div. med. oncology, 1972—, prof. oncology Mayo Med. Sch., 1967—; cons. Nat. Cancer Inst. Served to capt. MC USNR, 1943-47. Recipient Philip S. Hench Disting. Alumnus award, U. Pitts. Sch. Medicine, 1972. Mem. Am. Soc. Clin. Oncology (past pres.), Soc. Surg. Oncology, Am. Assn. Cancer Edn., Am. Assn. Cancer Research. Presbyterian. Rotarian. Home: 1223 Skyline Dr Rochester MN 55901 Office: Mayo Clinic Rochester MN 55901

BISENIUS, STEPHEN WILLIAM, state senator, Realtor; b. Monticello, Iowa, June 16, 1947; s. Edwin Joseph and Louise (Savage) B.; student U. Iowa, 1965-67, also U. Plano; B.A., Samford U., 1969. Asso. Dubuque Realty (Iowa), 1972-76; pres. Iowa-Internat. Barter, Inc., Dubuque, from 1979; mem. Iowa Senate, 1976—. Served with U.S. Army, 1969-72; Vietnam. Mem. Iowa Realtors Assn., Am. Legis. Exchange Council (Iowa state chmn. 1979—), Am. Legion, VFW. Republican. Roman Catholic. Clubs: Rotary, K.C. Office: State Senate Office State Capitol Des Moines IA 50319*

BISH, MILAN DAVID, land devel. co. exec., diplomat; b. Harvard, Nebr., July 1, 1929; s. Charles and Mabel Etta (Williams) B.; B.A., Hastings Coll., 1951; m. Allene R. Miller, Mar. 17, 1951; children—Cynthia, Linda, Charles. Pres., Bish Machinery Co., Grand Island, Nebr., 1965-73, Mid-Continent Enterprises, 1974—; dir. Comml. Nat. Bank, Grand Island; state chmn. Nebr. Republican Party, 1971-72; mem. Rep. Nat. Com., 1971-72; mem. Rep. Exec.

Com. Nebr., 1972-74; Nebr. chmn. Citizens for Reagan, 1976; chmn. Nebr. del. Rep. Nat. Conv., 1976; mem. steering com. Citizens for the Republic; Nebr. chmn. Reagan for Pres., 1980; Reagan-Bush polit. dir., fall 1980; mem. presdl. transition team, Dec. 1980-Jan. 1981; U.S. ambassador to Barbados, St. Vincent, St. Lucia, Dominica; spl. rep. for pres. of U.S. to various Caribbean nations; mem. Nebr. Hwy. Commn., 1979—. Named Ambassador of Nebr. Mem. C. of C. (pres. 1977). Mason (32 deg., Shriner), Elk, Eagle, Rotarian (dist. gov. 1970-71). Clubs: Riverside Golf, Liederkranz, Platt Deutsch. Home: 2012 W Louise St Grand Island NE 68801 Office: PO Box 1365 Grand Island NE 68801

BISHARA, SAMIR EDWARD, orthodontist; b. Cairo, Egypt, Oct. 31, 1935; s. Edward Constantin and Georgette Ibrahim (Kelela) B.; B. in Dental Surgery, Alexandria U., Egypt, 1957, diploma in Orthodontics, 1967; M.S., U. Iowa. 1970, certificate in Orthodontics, 1970, D.D.S., 1972; m. Cynthia Jane McLaughlin, July 3, 1975; children—Dina Marie, Dorine Gabrielle, Celine Noelle. Practice gen. dentistry, Alexandria, Egypt, 1957-66, specializing in orthodontics, Iowa City, Iowa, 1970—; fellow in clin. pedodontics Guggenheim Dental Clinic, N.Y.C., 1959-60; resident in oral surgery Moassat Hosp., Alexandria, Egypt, 1960-61, mem. staff, 1961-68; asst. prof. Coll. Dentistry, U. Iowa, Iowa City, 1970-73, asso. prof., 1973-76, prof., 1976—; vis. prof. Alexandria U., 1974-75. Bd. dirs. Am. Cleft Palate Ednl. Found. Mem. ADA, Egyptian Dental Soc., Am. Assn. Orthodontics, Internat. Dental Fedn., AAAS, Internat. Assn. for Dental Research, Am. Cleft Palate Assn., Assn. of Egyptian Am. Scholars, Omicron Kappa Upsilon, Sigma Xi. Contbr. articles on orthodontics to profl. jours. and book chpts. Home: 1014 Penkridge Dr Iowa City IA 52240 Office: Orthodontic Dept College of Dentistry Iowa City IA 52242

BISHOP, ALLEN JOHN, savs. and loan assn. exec.; b. Berwyn, Ill., Feb. 17, 1948; s. John Edward and Mildred Alice (Chovancek) B.; B.S., Eastern Ill. U., 1971, M.B.A., 1972; m. Christine Ann Orbeck, June 8, 1974. With Clyde Savs. and Loan Assn., North Riverside, Ill., 1973—, dir. mktg., 1975-76, asst. v.p., dir. mktg., 1976-80, v.p., dir. mktg., 1980—; instr. Inst. Fin. Edn., Morton Coll., 1973-74. Mem. Savs. Assn. Council (dir.), Savs. Instns. Mktg. Soc. Am. (dir. chpt. 1, v.p. 1981, pres. 1982 Mktg. award 1976), Eastern Ill. U. Alumni Assn. Chgo. Fin. Advertisers, Delta Chi, Delta Mu Delta. Roman Catholic. Home: 9645 W 57th St Countryside IL 60525 Office: 7222 W Cermak Rd North Riverside IL 60546

BISHOP, BUDD HARRIS, mus. ofcl.; b. Canton, Ga., Nov. 1, 1936; s. James Monroe and Eula (Ponder) B.; A.B., Shorter Coll., Rome, Ga., 1958; M.F.A., U. Ga., 1960; m. Julia Crowder, Nov. 30, 1968. Art dir. Ensworth Sch., Nashville, 1961-63; lectr. art history Vanderbilt U., 1962; dir. creative services Transit Advt. Assn., Inc., N.Y.C., 1964-66; dir. Hunter Mus. Art, Chattanooga, 1966-76; dir. Columbus (Ohio) Mus. Art, 1976—; juror, lectr. and cons. in field. Trustee Columbus Acad., 1976—; mem. adv. bd. Jur. League Hist. Restoration Project, 1977—; trustee Franklin Art Fund; chmn. Commn. for Public Art Projects. Recipient Gov.'s award Tenn. Arts Commn., 1971; Alumni award Shorter Coll., 1979. Mem. Assn. Art Mus. Dirs., Ohio Museums Assn., Midwest Museums Assn., Am. Assn. Museums. Clubs: Rotary, Rev., Kit Kat (Columbus). Contbr. articles to profl. jours. Office: 480 E Broad St Columbus OH 43215

BISHOP, DONALD E., state senator; b. Almont, Mich., Feb. 27, 1933; s. G.C. and Jane (Wise) B.; B.A. in Polit. Sci., Oberlin Coll., 1955; J.D., Detroit Coll. Law, 1966; m. Nancy Michael, Aug. 6, 1955; children—Rebecca, Susan, Judy, Martha, Michael. Admitted to Mich. bar, 1967; atty. Martin & Bishop, Rochester, Mich., 1967—; mem. Mich. Ho. of Reps., 1966-70; mem. Mich. Senate, 1970—, mem. com. on corps. and econ. devel., mem. judiciary com., mem. commerce com.; dir. Nat. Bank of Rochester; incorporator Rochester Retirement Homes, Inc. Mem. Mich. Law Revision Commn., 1975—; mem. Uniform State Law Commn. Served with AUS, 1955-57. Home: 2332 W Avon Rd Rochester MI 48063 Office: 103 E 4th St Rochester MI 48063

BISHOP, GEORGE FRANKLIN, polit. social psychologist; b. New Haven, July 26, 1942; s. George Elwood and Mary Bridget (Trant) B.; B.S. in Psychology, Mich. State U., 1966, M.A., 1969, Ph.D., 1973; m. Lucille C. Minervini, Aug. 14, 1971; 1 dau., Kristina Marie. Instr., Multidisciplinary Social Sci. Program, Mich. State U., E. Lansing, 1972-73; asst. prof. Dept. Sociology and Anthropology, U. Notre Dame (Ind.), 1973-75; research asso. behavioral sci. lab. U. Cin., 1975-77, sr. research asso., 1977—. Co-dir. Greater Cin. Survey, U. Cin., 1978—; research cons. Community Mental Health/Mental Retardation bd., Hamilton County, Ohio, 1979—. Served with U.S. Army, 1961-62. NSF grantee, 1977-78, 78-82; Nat. Council Sr. Citizens grantee, 1977-78. Mem. Midwest Assn. for Public Opinion Research (pres. 1977-78), Am. Assn. for Public Opinion Research, Am. Polit. Sci. Assn., Soc. for Advancement of Social Psychology. Sr. editor The Presdl. Debates: Media, Electoral, and Policy Perspectives, 1978; sr. author various articles profl. jours. Home: 459 Karenlaw Ln Cincinnati OH 45231 Office: ML 132 Univ of Cin Cinnati OH 45221

BISHOP, GILBERT CLARE, surgeon; b. Leonard, Mich., Sept. 30, 1899; s. Frank Leo and Genevieve (Thomas) B.; student Oberlin Coll., 1919-21, U. Mich., 1918-23; M.D., U. Chgo. (Rush), 1926; postgrad. U. Pa., 1944-45; m. Jane Lucile Wise, Sept. 22, 1925; children—Robert, Dean, Barbara, Donald, Malcolm, David. Intern, Henry Ford Hosp., Detroit, 1925-26; student surgery Elizabeth Hosp., Vienna, Austria, 1927-28, Allgemeines Krankenhaus, Vienna, 1930-31; founder, adminstr. Bishop Hosp., Almont, Mich., 1935-59; resident in surgery Guthrie Clinic, Sayre, Pa., 1945-46; surgeon-in-chief Community Hosp., Almont, 1959-70; semi-retired, 1973—. Diplomate Am. Bd. Surgery. Fellow A.C.S.; mem. AMA, Mich. Med. Soc., Detroit, Flint acads. surgery. Republican. Congregationalist. Home: 5331 Van Dyke Rd Almont MI 48003 Office: 409 E St Clair St Almont MI 48003

BISHOP, JACK LAWSON, JR., diversified products mfg. co. exec.; b. Rockville Centre, N.Y., Dec. 3, 1939; s. Jack Lawson and Elizabeth Janet (Blee) B.; B.S. in Chem. Engring., U. Colo., 1961; Ph.D., U. Ill., 1972; m. Donna Norine Leavens, June 24, 1962; children—Elizabeth Anona, Jack Lawson III, Kathleen Anne, Caroline Donna Van Alstine. Product devel. engr., mgmt. scis. specialist Dow Corning Corp., Midland, Mich., 1961-72; instr. Central Mich. U., Mt. Pleasant, 1969-70; mgr. mgmt. scis. Ky. Fried Chicken, Louisville, 1972-73; mgr. econ. and gen. research May Dept. Stores Inc., St. Louis, 1973-76; mgr. strategic and econ. planning Brunswick Corp., Chgo., 1976—. Mem. exec. com., community relations com. Midwest regional office Am. Friends Service Com.; bd. dirs., treas. Midwest Friends Housing Corp.; mem. policy com. Friends Com. on Nat. Legislation. Mem. Ops. Research Soc. Am., Chgo Council Fgn. Relations, Inst. Mgmt. Sci.. Econometric Soc., Am. Econ. Assn., Am. Statis. Assn., Nat. Assn. Bus. Economists. Author: Insect, Disease and Weed Control, 1972; Practical Emulsions, 1968. Home: 916 Maple Ave Evanston IL 60202 Office: 1 Brunswick Plaza Skokie IL 60077

BISHOP, JOYCE ANN ARMENTROUT, counselor, educator; b. West Mansfield, Ohio, June 16, 1935; d. Frederic J. and Marjorie Vere (Stephens) Armentrout; A.B., Albion Coll., 1956; B.A., Western Mich. U., 1969; children—Belinda Lee, Thomas James. Tchr. phys. edn. Walled Lake (Mich.) Jr. High Sch., 1956-58; tchr. adult edn. pub. sch., Milw., 1959-65, Lakeview Schs., Battle Creek, Mich., 1966—; dir. student activities, Olivet (Mich.) Coll., 1969-71, also asst. prof., counselor; counselor Kellogg Community Coll., Battle Creek, 1971—. Sec. adult bd. Teens Inc., 1965-68. Mem. Com. to Rev. Articulation Matters (charter), Mich. Assn. Coll. Registrars and Admissions Officers, AAUW, Am., Mich. personnel and guidance assns., Am. Sch. Counselors Assn., Am. Coll. Personnel Assn., Am. Assn. Collegiate Registrars and Admissions Officers (interassn. liaison with Am. Assn. Community and Jr. Colls.), Mich. Assn. Coll. Registrars and Admissions Officers (com. on coll. articulation, pres. 1979-80), Beta Beta Beta, Alpha Chi Omega. Lutheran. Club: Altrusa. Home: 721 Eastfield Dr Battle Creek MI 49015 Office: 450 North Ave Battle Creek MI 49016

BISHOP, MARSHALL EDWARD, educator; b. Amsterdam, N.Y., Aug. 3, 1942; s. Raymond Murle and Muriel Katherine (Johnson) B.; B.A., Oakland U., 1964, M.S., 1967; Ph.D., SUNY, 1975; m. Jacqueline Ann Winter, July 13, 1968; children—Eric Alan, Kathryn Ann. Exptl. spectroscopist Gen. Motors Corp., Pontiac, Mich., 1964-66, 67-69; instr. chemistry Oakland U., Rochester, Mich., 1968; research fellow SUNY, Albany, 1969-75; instr. chemistry Southwestern Mich. Coll., Dowagiac, 1975—; instr. continuing edn. Oakland U., 1968-69. Named Student of Distinction, Oakland U., 1961, 62, 64; NDEA Title IV grad. fellow, 1970-73; cert. profl. chemist Am. Inst. Chemists. Mem. Am. Chem. Soc., Chem. Soc. London, Mich. Coll. Chemistry Tchrs. Assn., Sigma Xi. Republican. Methodist. Club: Grange. Contbr. articles to profl. jours. Home: 54255 Twin Lakes Rd Dowagiac MI 49047 Office: Dept Chemistry Cherry Grove Rd Dowagiac MI 49047

BISHOP, RALPH JOHN, III, educator, bookseller; b. Cleve., July 20, 1944; s. Ralph John and Margaret (Young) B.; B.A., Cornell U., 1966; M.A., Northwestern U., 1971, Ph.D., 1974; m. Leslie Anne Griffin, Sept. 23, 1972. Instr., Roosevelt U., Chgo., 1972-75, 79—; mgr. trade dept. Kroch's & Brentano's, Chgo., 1975-81; founder, pres., Bookchoice, Evanston, Ill., 1981—. Mem. Am. Anthropol. Assn., Am. Booksellers Assn., Council on Anthropology and Edn., Soc. for Applied Anthropology. Episcopalian. Office: Bookchoice PO Box AA1497 Evanston IL 60204

BISHOP, ROBERT DEANE, nuclear engr.; b. Emporia, Kans., June 23, 1946; s. Clarence Dwight and Cora Frances (Foley) B.; m. Sheila Roberts, Dec. 18, 1976; B.S., Kans. State U., 1969; M.B.A., U. Chgo., 1977. Engr. in tng. State of Kans., 1969; nuclear engr. Commonwealth Edison Co., Dresden sta., 1971-75, tech. staff supr. LaSalle County sta., 1975-80, asst. supt. sta., 1980—. Served to 1st lt., inf. U.S. Army, 1970-71. Decorated Bronze Star medal; licensed nuclear reactor operator. Mem. Am. Nuclear Soc. Home: 113 Prairie Dr Minooka IL 60447 Office: LaSalle County Station Box 240 Marseilles IL 61341

BISHOP, WARNER BADER, bus. exec.; b. Lakewood, Ohio, Dec. 13, 1918; s. Warner Brown and Gladys (Bader) B.; A.B., Dartmouth Coll., 1941, M.B.A., Amos Tuck Grad. Sch., 1942; grad. Advanced Mgmt. Program, Harvard U., 1955; m. Katherine Sue White, Dec. 15, 1944; children—Susan, Judith, Katharine, Jennifer; m. 2d, Barrie Osborn, Feb. 4, 1967; children—Wilder, Brooks. With Archer-Daniels-Midland Co., Cleve., 1946-59, successively sales rep., export mgr., sales mgr., divisional gen. mgr., asst. v.p., 1946-56, v.p., 1956-59; pres. Fed. Foundry Supply Co., 1957-59, Wyodak Clay & Chem. Co., 1957-59, Basic, Inc., until 1963; pres. Union Fin. Corp., Cleve., 1963-74; pres. Union Savs. Assn., 1963-74, chmn., 1970—; chmn., pres. Transohio Fin. Corp., Cleve., 1974—; dir. Port Clinton Nat. Bank, Akron Savs. Assn., Cin. Savs. Assn., United Savs. Assn.; trustee Nat. Mortgage Fund, Med. Met. Cleve. Sec. Foundry Ednl. Found., 1956-60; gen. campaign mgr. Cleve. Area Heart Soc., bd. chmn., 1960-61; mem. corp. Fenn Coll.; bd. dirs. Ohio Heart Soc.; chmn. Highland Redevel. Corp., 1963-68; pres. Council High Blood Pressure, 1964-69. Served to lt. USNR, 1942-45; comdg. officer escort vessels. Clubs: Chagrin Valley Hunt; Racquet & Tennis, India House (N.Y.C.); Meadow (Southampton, N.Y.); Dartmouth, Union, Tavern (Cleve.). Contbr. articles to trade jours. Office: Transohio Fin Corp One Penton Plaza Cleveland OH 44114

BISSELL, BRENT JOHN, pub. co. mgr.; b. Dearborn, Mich., July 10, 1950; s. Ernest Ross and Virginia Jane (Pete) B.; B.A., U. Toledo, 1971; m. Libby Schulak, Dec. 4, 1971; children—John, Sarah. Pres., chmn. bd. Bissell Advt. Inc., Toledo, 1976-79; v.p. Communications Concepts, Toledo, 1978-79; creative dir. mktg. dept. Stark Bros. Nurseries & Orchards Co., Louisiana, Mo., 1979-80; nursery and catalog divisional gen. mgr. Consumer Pub. Co., Canton, Ohio, 1980—; musician, rec. artist; pres. B. Urselv Music Prodn. Co., 1979—. Nat. pub. relations dir. Nat. Assn. Congregational Christian Chs., 1979. Club: Toledo. Home: 715 Tell Dr Canal Fulton OH 44614 Office: Consumer Pub Co 401 N Market St Canton OH 44750

BISSELL, STEVEN LEWIS, TV prodn. co. exec.; b. Iowa City, Jan. 30, 1949; s. Lewis Austin and Berniece Margaret (Helmer) B.; B.Gen. Studies, U. Iowa, 1981. Owner Bissell Talent Agency, Iowa City, 1965—; owner, operator Plastic Fantastic, light show, Iowa City, 1969-71; owner New World Entertainment Agy., New World Prodns., Iowa City, 1972—; coordinator Coop. Community Video, Iowa City, 1981— chmn. Jerry Lewis Labor Day telethon com. Iowa City Muscular Dystrophy Assn., 1978; mem. video adv. com. U. Iowa, 1978-81, founder Univ. Broadcast Commn., 1979, exec. asso. Collegiate Assns. Council, 1977-79, 80, founder, chmn., exec. dir. Student Producers Assn./Campus Cable Vision, 1972-80; producer comml. local polit. campaign, 1978; gen. mgr. Campus CableVision, 1979-80; dir., cable programmer, press agt. Iowa Public Interest Research Group, Iowa Meml. Union, 1980-81; dir. mcht. services Consumer/Mcht. Protection Service, Iowa Meml. Union, 1981—; producer, performer cable cartoon show. Recipient Spoke award U.S. Jaycees, 1977. Mem. Public Relations Student Soc. Am., Liberal Arts Student Assn. (congressman 1978-81), New Wave. Democrat. Roman Catholic. Club: Jaycees (dir. Iowa City 1978-79; dir. 1st ann. carnival 1978). Editor, photographer New Liberal Arts Rev., 1980-81. Home: 1030 E Washington St Iowa City IA 52240 Office: Consumer/Mcht Protection Service Iowa Meml Union Iowa City IA 52242

BISSEY, WILLIAM KARL, bank exec.; b. Columbus, Ind., Aug. 18, 1940; s. Harry Carl and Mary M. (Fleming) B.; B.S. (Ford fellow), Ind. U., 1962, M.B.A., 1964. Purchasing agt. Arvin Industries, Inc., Columbus, 1964-68; instr. Ohio No. U., Ada, 1968-73; credit analyst Mchts. Nat. Bank, Indpls., 1974-78; mgr. econ. research Am. Fletcher Nat. Bank, Indpls., 1978—. Served with U.S. Army, 1963-64. Mem. Alpha Kappa Psi, Delta Sigma Phi, Beta Gamma Sigma, Omicron Delta Epsilon. Presbyterian. Home: 8305 Sobax Dr Indianapolis IN 46268 Office: 111 Monument Circle Indianapolis IN 46277

BITELER, CORNELIUS ROYAL, electronic co. exec.; b. Flint, Mich., Oct. 20, 1931; s. Royal Cornelius and Maude Melvia B.; B.S. in Mech. Engring., Purdue U., 1956; grad. Gen. Electric Mfg. Tng. Program, 1959; m. Jean Elaine Moyer, Sept. 27, 1958; children—Mark Christian, Dawn Christina. Mfg. engr., Gen. Electric, 1956-62, Bohn Aluminum, 1962-66; gen. foreman All Steel Equipment, 1966-69; asst. plant mgr. North Electric, Kenton, Ohio, 1969-75; v.p. Gleason Assos., Chgo., 1975-77; ops. analyst GTE Automatic Electric, Northlake, Ill., 1977-78, mgr. mfg. ops. analysis, 1978-80, productivity mgr., 1980—. Active Yokefellows Internat. Home: 141 Joyce Chicago Heights IL 60411 Office: 400 N Wolf Northlake IL 60164

BITKER, MARJORIE MARKS (MRS. BRUNO VOLTAIRE BITKER), writer, editor; b. N.Y.C., Feb. 9, 1901; d. Cecil Alexander and Rachel (Fox) Marks; A.B. magna cum laude (Caroline Duror Meml. fellow), Barnard Coll., 1921; M.A., Columbia U., 1922; m. James C. Jacobson, 1922 (div. 1942); children—Emilie J. Jacobi, Margaret J. Strange, Elizabeth J. Hahn; m. 2d, John C. Mayer, Oct. 24, 1942 (dec. June 1945); m. 3d, Bruno Voltaire Bitker, Oct. 10, 1957. Free lance writer, 1922—; editor Farrar Straus, N.Y.C., 1946-47, G.P. Putnam's Sons, N.Y.C., 1947-53, David McKay Co., N.Y.C., 1953-55; now editorial cons., book reviewer, feature writer. Lectr., Hunter Coll., Coll. City N.Y., 1949-53; Women's Chair for Humanistic Studies, Marquette U., 1972-73. Mem. pres.'s council Alverno Coll., 1975-77; bd. visitors U. Wis., 1962-68; alumnae trustee Barnard Coll., 1964-68, Barnard-in-Milw.; co-founder, past pres., hon. bd. dirs. in perpetuity Bookfellows: Friends Wis. Libraries. Recipient Barnard Alumnae Recognition award, 1978. Mem. AAUW, Women's Nat. Book Assn., Nat. Critics Circle, Women in Communications, Bookfellows Milw. (pres. 1971-73, dir.), Council Wis. Writers (dir. 1971-77), Phi Beta Kappa. Author: (novels) Gold of Evening, 1975, A Different Flame, 1976; contbr. articles, and book revs. to mags. and newspapers. Address: 2330 E Back Bay St Milwaukee WI 53202

BITTING, PHYLLIS DIANE, real estate broker; b. Kosciusko County, Ind., Oct. 11, 1935; d. Earl Vance and Edna Ruth (Powers) Davis; student Ind. U., 1971, 75-77; m. James Duane Bitting, June 26, 1953; 1 son, Andrew Vance. Real estate broker Center Realty, Warsaw, Ind., 1973—; sec., treas. Kosciusko Bd. Realtors, Warsaw, 1975-76, v.p., 1977-78, pres., dir., 1978—; state sec. by law com. Ind. Assn. Realtors, Indpls., 1977—. Trustee, Walnut Creek United Methodist Ch., Warsaw, 1977—. Mem. Nat. Bd. Realtors, Ind. Realtors Assn. (state dir. 1979-82, state public relations and communications com. 1981—), DAR (regent Anthony Nigo chpt. 1974-75). Home: Route 2 Box 88 Warsaw IN 46580 Office: 2304 E Center St Warsaw IN 46580

BITZES, JOHN GEORGE, historian, educator; b. Omaha, Dec. 9, 1926; s. George John and Yasseme (Gillas) B.; B.A. cum laude, U. Nebr., 1954, Ph.D., 1976; m. Helen Loras, Aug. 18, 1963; children—James George, Mark John. Tchr., Am. history Creston (Iowa) Pub. Sch. System, 1959-61; tchr. social studies Omaha Pub. Sch. System, 1961—; lectr. modern European history U. Nebr., Omaha, 1966—; v.p. Built-Rite Corp., Dallas. Recipient James L. Sellers Meml. award, 1971; Maude Hammond Fling dissertation travel fellow, Eng., 1974. Mem. Phi Beta Kappa, Phi Alpha Theta. Republican. Greek Orthodox. Home: 13575 Walnut St Omaha NE 68144

BIVANS, JACK, broadcasting exec.; b. Evanston, Ill., Aug. 30, 1925; s. Walter J. and Edna Mae (Cooney) B.; student DePaul U., 1943-44, Northwestern U., 1946-49; m. Geraldine J. Johnson, July 28, 1962; children—Kirby, Scott, Kathy, Marcia, Kim, Donald, Paul. Freelance radio actor, various Chgo. and network broadcasts, 1938-56; sales rep. Medusa Portland Cement Co., Chgo., 1956-59, Adam Young Inc., Chgo., 1959-61; with CBS-WBBM, Chgo., 1961-68, gen. sales mgr., 1964-68; gen. sales mgr. WFLD-TV, Chgo., 1968-72, v.p., gen. sales mgr., 1972-74; v.p. Field Communications Corp., Chgo., 1972-74; v.p., gen. mgr. Magic City Communications Corp., WCRT/WQEZ, Birmingham, Ala., 1974-76; nat. sales mgr. Century Broadcasting Corp. W-100/FM 100, Chgo., 1976—. Served with USAAF, 1944-46. Decorated Air medal. Mem. Broadcast Advt. Club, Chgo. Advt. Club, Grocery Mfrs. Sales Execs., Broadcast Pioneers, Nat. Acad. TV Arts and Scis., Sigma Alpha Epsilon. Club: Mdse. Execs. Home: 313 Burlington St Western Springs IL 60558 Office: 875 N Michigan Ave Chicago IL 60611

BIXBY, RICHARD WILLIAM, ednl. adminstr.; b. Waterloo, Iowa, June 1, 1941; married, 2 children. B.A. in Phys. Edn. and Secondary Edn., Wartburg Coll., Waverly, 1963; M.A. in Counselor Edn., U. Wis., Platteville, 1970. Tchr., coach, high sch., Manitowoc, Wis., 1963-65, Lancaster, Wis., 1965-69; asst. prof., coach U. Wis., Platteville, 1969-70; dir. guidance Sheboygan Falls (Wis.) Dist. #1, 1970-79; mgr. employee devel. John Deere Product Engring., Waterloo, 1979—. Mem. Am., Wis. personnel and guidance assns., NEA, Wis., Sheboygan Falls edn. assns., Am. Soc. Tng. and Devel., Am. Football Coaches Assn., Wis. Coaches Assn. Certified sch. counselor. Named Football Coach of Year, 1966, 68, 69, Wis. Outstanding Educator of Year, 1975. Home: 220 Angie Dr Cedar Falls IA 50613 Office: PO Box 8000 Waterloo IA 50704

BIXBY, WILLIAM HERBERT, ret. elec. engr.; b. Indpls., Dec. 28, 1906; s. George Linder and Carrie (Tilton) B.; B.S.E., U. Mich., 1930, M.S., 1931, Ph.D., 1933; M.M.E., Chrysler Inst. Engring., 1935; m. Dorothy Bancroft Tibbits, Jan. 17, 1963. Spl. problems engr. Chrysler Corp., Detroit, 1933-36; instr. to prof. elec. engring. Wayne U., 1936-57; v.p. for applied research Power Equipment Co., 1957-61, v.p. research Power Equipment div. North Electric Co., Galion, Ohio, from 1961, now ret.; cons. engr. Power Equipment Co., Detroit, 1937-56. Fellow AAAS, IEEE; mem. Engring. Soc. Detroit, Sigma Xi. Home: 5274 Riverside Dr Columbus OH 43220

BJORK, KENNETH O., ret. educator, editor; b. Enderlin, N.D., July 19, 1909; s. Theodore S. and Martha (Arneson) B.; B.A., St. Olaf Coll., 1930; M.A., U. Wis., 1931, Ph.D., 1935; Ph.D. (hon.), U. Oslo, 1976; m. Thora Lie, Apr. 1, 1960; children—Kenneth T., Arnold L.; children by previous marriage—Herum P., Mark P.; stepchildren—Ellen, Jon T. Asst. prof. history U. Mont., Havre, 1935-37; asst. prof. St. Olaf Coll., Northfield, Minn., 1937-39, asso. prof., 1939-44, prof., 1944-74, prof. emeritus, 1974—, chmn. dept. history, 1960-65; vis. asso. prof. U. Nebr., Lincoln, summers 1938, 40, U. Mich., Ann Arbor, 1940-41, U. Wis., Madison, 1943-44; Rockefeller Found. rep., prof. U. East Africa, 1965-67; editor Norwegian-Am. Hist. Assn., Northfield, 1960-80, editor emeritus, 1980—, pres., 1973-75. Chmn. Gov.'s Com. on Refugee Relief, State of Minn., 1955-58. Decorated knight 1st class Order St. Olav (Norway). Social Sci. Research Council fellow, 1947-48, 51-52; Fulbright scholar, 1959-60. Democrat. Lutheran. Author: Saga in Steel and Concrete, 1947; West of the Great Divide, 1958; editor books; contbr. articles to profl. jours. Address: 500 W Woodley Apt 302 Northfield MN 55057

BJORNDAL, ARNE MAGNE, endodontist; b. Ulstein, Norway, Aug. 19, 1916; s. Martin I. and Anne B.; B.S., State Coll. Volda, 1939; D.D.S., U. Oslo, 1947; D.D.S., U. Iowa, 1954, M.S., 1956; m. Katharine G. Benson, Jan. 12, 1952; children—Katharine, Kari, Lee. Instr., Coll. Dentistry U. Oslo, 1948-50, 51-53; intern Forsyth Dental Infirmary, Boston, 1950-51; mem. faculty U. Iowa, Iowa City, 1954—, prof., 1964—, founder, head dept. endodontics, 1956-80. Served to maj. Army NG, 1963-70. Decorated King Hakon 7th medal (Norway); diplomate Am. Bd. Endodontics; Fulbright scholar, 1950-51. Fellow Am. Coll. Dentistry; mem. ADA (service fgn. countries award 1979), Am. Assn. Endodontics, N.Y. Acad. Sci., Omicron Kappa Upsilon. Republican. Lutheran. Clubs: Optimists,

Elks. Home: 3 Washington Pl Iowa City IA 52240 Office: Coll Dentistry U Iowa Iowa City IA 52242

BJUGAN, LESLIE ARNOLD, social worker; b. Mpls., Mar. 5; s. Leonard Nils and Amanda Jane (Carley) B.; B.S., Moorhead State Coll., 1949; M.A. in Public Adminstrn., U. Minn., 1971, M.S.W., 1980; m. Maxine Lorraine Bolser, Nov. 21, 1945; children—Carley Jo Bjugan Watts, Jody Lynn Everson. Social worker Polk County Welfare Dept., Crookston, Minn., 1949-50; various positions in mental health, child welfare Hennepin County Welfare Dept., Mpls., 1950-77; dir. Crest Homes, Am. Baptist Homes for the Midwest, 1977-78; pre-petition screener Office County Atty., Hennepin County Dept. Community Services, Mpls., 1978—. Mem. Model City Protective Service Adv. Com., 1971-73; adv. U.S. Navy Recruiting Sta., Mpls., 1980; vol. Assn. for Alzheimer's Disease and Related Disorders, 1980. Served with USN, 1942-45. Recipient Outstanding Community Service commendation Am. Acad. Human Services, 1975, citation of honor Hennepin County, 1976. Mem. Nat. Assn. Social Workers, Gerontol. Soc. (charter mem. Minn. chpt.), Nat. Council on Aging. Democrat. Mem. Christian Ch. (Disciples of Christ). Home: 9700 Portland Ave S Bloomington MN 55420 Office: Adult Protection Unit Community Services Div 14A Government Center Minneapolis MN 55467

BLACK, ASA CALVIN, JR., anatomist, educator; b. Clarksville, Tenn., Jan. 2, 1943; s. Asa C. and Josephine Elizabeth Black; m. Cynthia Woods, Apr. 3, 1971; B.A., Vanderbilt U., 1965, Ph.D. in Anatomy (NIH predoctoral fellow), 1974. Asso., U. Iowa, Iowa City, 1973-74, NIH postdoctoral fellow Coll. Medicine, 1974-75, asst. prof. dept. anatomy Coll. Medicine, 1975—; instr. anatomy Vanderbilt U., Nashville, 1972-73. Mem. AAAS, Am. Assn. Anatomists, Am. Chem. Soc., Am. Soc. Neurochemistry, Brit. Brain Research Assn., European Brain Behavior Soc., Internat. Soc. Neurochemistry, Sigma Xi. Contbr. chpts. to books, articles to biol. jours. Home: 801 Woodside Dr Iowa City IA 52240 Office: U Iowa Coll Medicine 1-402 Basic Science Bldg Dept Anatomy Iowa City IA 52242

BLACK, DANIEL ALBERT OLEISKY, mfg. mgr.; b. Mpls., Jan. 17, 1954; s. Albert Samuel and Shirley Jean (Peterson) Oleisky B.; B.Math. with distinction, U. Minn., 1975, M.S. with honors, 1976; m. Vicki Ann Reed, Dec. 18, 1976. Loan collector First Nat. Bank of Mpls., 1975-76; quality control engr. Graco Inc., Mpls., 1976-79, quality assurance engr., 1979; quality assurance mgr. Webster Electric Co. div. Sta-Rite Industries, Inc., Racine, Wis., 1979-80; mfg. planning and prodn. control, 1980-81; mfg. supt. Fairbanks Morse Engine div. Colt Industries, Beloit, Wis., 1981—. Advisor, Jr. Achievement, Mpls., 1977-79; mem. ARC Safety Services, Mpls., 1968-75; trustee Minn. Phi Gamma Delta Ednl. Found., 1975-80; bd. dirs. Phi Gamma Delta House Corp., 1975-80. Named Minn. Young Engr. of Yr., 1978; recipient U. Minn. Outstanding Student Leadership award, 1975; Phi Gamma Delta Weum and Devaney awards, 1975; cert. quality engr., cert. reliability engr., cert. prodn. and inventory mgmt. Mem. Am. Soc. Quality Control, Am. Inst. Indsl. Engrs., Am. Prodn. and Inventory Control Soc. Home: 3737 Bee Ln Beloit WI 53511 Office: 701 Lawton Ave Beloit WI 53511

BLACK, DANIEL GEORGE, communications co. exec.; b. Marion, Ohio, Dec. 1, 1943; s. George F. and Hazel A. Black; student Findlay Coll., 1962-66; B.S., John Jay Coll., 1976; m. Julia C. Lynch, June 19, 1970; children—Heather J., Daniel D., Christopher R. With AT&T, N.Y.C., 1970-79, nat. account exec., 1976-79, account exec. II, 1979, tng. staff supr. Sales and Mktg. Edn. Center, Cin., 1979—; counselor A.T. & T. nat. sales force, 1980-82; profl. fashion model on TV and in newspapers; artist. Served with USN, 1966-70. Cert. account exec. instr. Mem. Am. Mgmt. Assn., Alpha Phi Omega. Roman Catholic. Club: Toastmasters. Contbr. articles to profl. jours. Office: AT&T 15 W 6th St Cincinnati OH 45202

BLACK, DENISE LOUISE, educator; b. Ft. Sill, Okla., Apr. 16, 1950; d. Nelson Arthur and Virginia Mary (Smith) Taber; A.A., Community Coll. of Allegheny County, Boyce campus, 1970; B.S., Slippery Rock State Coll., 1972; M.A., Eastern Mich. U., 1978; m. Robert Paul Black, Aug. 12, 1972; children—Paula Ann, Jennifer Lea. Adult edn. tchr. ecology and physiology Huron Valley Schs., Milford, Mich., 1973-74; tchr. gen. biology and earth sci. Howell (Mich.) Public Schs., 1974-75; adult edn. tchr. life sci. Holly (Mich.) Area Schs., 1978-80, Hartland (Mich.) Consol. Schs., 1978—; tchr. biology Walled Lake (Mich.) Consol. Schs., 1980—. Coach, Milford Youth Athletic Assn., 1972—. Cert. guidance and counselor. Mem. Mich. Personnel and Guidance Assn., Nat. Assn. Biology Tchrs., Mich. Assn. Biology Tchrs., AAAS, Beta Beta Beta, Phi Kappa Phi, Phi Theta Kappa. Methodist. Home: 941 Canal St Milford MI 48042

BLACK, FERNE MAY BEEBE, librarian; b. Cleve., May 16, 1920; d. Harry Jay and Dorothy (Schmidt) Beebe; student Ohio U., 1938-40; A.B., Calif. State U., 1959; M.L.S. cum laude, U. So. Calif., 1961. Research librarian Aeronutronic div. Ford Motor Co., Newport Beach, Calif., 1961-65; info. specialist Battelle Meml. Inst., Columbus, Ohio, 1965-66; supr. library acquisitions group Aerospace Corp., Los Angeles, 1966-67; librarian Cleve.-Seven Counties Land Use/Transp. Study, 1967-69; asst. librarian Parma Heights (Ohio) Pub. Library, 1969-70; head acquisitions Cuyahoga Community Coll., Cleve., 1970-75, mgr. tech. processing div., 1975-77, librarian Met. Campus, 1977—; asst. prof. library-media tech., 1974-77, mem. adv. council, 1975-77; mem. survey team Survey of Sci.-Info. Manpower in Engring. and the Natural Scis., NSF, 1966; vice chmn. com. on library resources Cleve. Area Met. Library System, 1980. Bd. dirs. Cleve. com. for UNICEF, 1978—. Mem. Spl. Libraries Assn. (pres. chpt. 1972-73), AAUP, Beta Phi Mu, Zonta (sec. 1977-78, dir. 1974-75, v.p. 1977-80). Home: 12040 Lake Ave Apt 102 Lakewood OH 44107 Office: 2900 Community Coll Ave Cleveland OH 44115

BLACK, JAMES ROBERT, indsl. engr.; b. Davenport, Iowa, Feb. 17, 1948; s. Robert James and Anne Louise (Johnson) B.; B.S. in Indsl. Engring. (Fisher Governor scholar 1968-69, Maytag scholar 1969-70), Iowa State U., 1970, M.S., 1971; M.B.A., U. Chgo., 1976; m. Mary Ann O'Malley, June 5, 1971; 1 son, Robert Joseph. Indsl. engr. Inland Steel Co., East Chicago, Ind., 1971-76, sr. indsl. engr., 1976-77; indsl. engring. supr. Clark Equipment Co., Jackson, Mich., 1977-78; indsl. engring. mgr. Harrison Plant, Graphic Systems div. Rockwell Internat., Rockford, Ill., 1978—; co-leader, guest lectr. Am. Mgmt. Assn., 1979-80. Cons. Project Business div. Jr. Achievement, 1980; pack com. chmn. Cub Scouts, Boy Scouts Am., 1980-81. Mem. Am. Inst. Indsl. Engrs. (sr. mem.; treas. 1979-80, pres. 1980-81, past pres. 1981-82). Contbr. articles to profl. jours. Home: 5933 Creekside Ln Rockford IL 61111 Office: 2524 11th St Rockford IL 61108

BLACK, JOHN BUNYAN, civil engr.; b. Kansas City, Mo., Dec. 25, 1927; s. Ernest Bateman and Faye Irene (Bunyan) B.; B.S., U. Kans., 1949; m. Marilyn McConnell, Feb. 2, 1957; children—Katherine Faye, Helen Winslow, Robert Winslow II. Asst. resident engr. Black & Veatch, cons. engrs., Los Alamos, 1949-50; engr. Alvord, Burdick & Howson, engrs., Chgo., 1953-65; project mgr. Greeley & Hansen, engrs., 1966-67, asso., 1968-74; owner John B. Black Cons. Engrs., 1975—. Served with AUS, 1951-52. Registered profl. engr., Calif., Iowa, Ill., Mich., Mo., Man., N.Y., Ind., Wis., Va. Fellow ASCE (com. water laws 1977—; dir. Ill. sect. 1977-78, sec. 1979—); mem. Am.

Water Works Assn., Central States Water Pollution Control Assn., Man. Assn. Profl. Engrs., Sigma Alpha Epsilon. Republican. Episcopalian. Club: Colo. Mountain (Boulder). Contbr. articles to profl. publs. Home: 595 Washington Ave Glencoe IL 60022 Office: 2 N Riverside Plaza Chicago IL 60606

BLACK, LOUIS ANTHONY, physician; b. Kenton, Ohio, July 29, 1920; s. Louis Walker and Mary (Lundy) B.; B.A., Ohio State U., 1941, M.D., 1944; student U. Pa. Grad. Sch. Medicine, 1958-59; m. Roberta Mae Johnson, Sept. 29, 1942; children—Linda Ann Black Terwilliger, Thomas J. Intern, Los Angeles County Gen. Hosp., 1944-45; pvt. practice medicine specializing in internal medicine, Kenton, Ohio, 1948-59, specializing in internal medicine and cardiology, Kenton, 1959—; mem. staff Hardin Meml. Hosp., Kenton. Pres., Central Ohio Heart Assn., 1971-72; mem. Kenton Sch. Bd., 1956-60. Served to capt. MC AUS, 1946-47. Diplomate Am. Bd. Internal Medicine. Mem. Ohio State Med. Assn. Office: Philips Med Park 405 N Main St Kenton OH 43326

BLACK, ROBERT STITT, public utility exec.; b. Newport News, Va., Oct. 31, 1951; s. William Holmes and Catherine Louise (Stitt) B.; B.A. cum laude in Econs., Kenyon Coll., 1973; M.B.A. in Fin., U. Mich., 1973-75; m. Christine Carr, Aug. 17, 1974; children—Robert Stitt II, Michael Todd. Regulatory affairs analyst El Paso Natural Gas Co. (Tex.), 1975-76; asst. to pres. Waterville Gas and Oil Co. (Ohio), 1976-77, pres., 1977—; spokesman for gas cos. at legis. and regulatory agy. hearings, 1978—. Mem. Ohio Gas Assn., Assn. M.B.A. Execs., Waterville C. of C. (dir. 1977-78). Republican. Episcopalian. Clubs: Toledo, Belmont Country, Rotary Internat. (bd. dirs. 1981—), Masons. Home: 6204 River Rd Waterville OH 43566 Office: PO Box 40 Waterville OH 43566

BLACK, ROGER LEWIS, physician, hosp. exec.; b. Syracuse, N.Y., Feb. 12, 1924; s. Ernest L. and Ethel M.H. Black; M.D. magna cum laude, Syracuse U., 1946; m. Doris V. Suits, Sept. 22, 1945; children—Gregory Stuart, Geoffrey Scott, Gail Susan. Intern, USPHS Hosp., Balt., 1946-48; resident in internal medicine, 1951-54; fellow in rheumatic disease Johns Hopkins Hosp., Balt., 1954-55; sr. investigator Nat. Inst. Arthritis and Metabolic Diseases, Bethesda, Md., 1955-64, asst. to dir. labs. and clinic NIH, 1964-65, asso. dir. Clin. Center, 1965-76; clin. prof. medicine Georgetown U., Washington, 1971-77; dir. profl. affairs St. Luke's Hosp., Cleve., 1977—; exec. council Sch. Medicine, Case Western Res. U., 1978—. Bd. govs. Rockville (Md.) Nursing Home, 1972-76; trustee Med. Service D.C., 1972-76. Served to rear adml. USPHS, 1946-76. Diplomate Am. Bd. Internal Medicine. Fellow A.C.P.; mem. Acad. Medicine Washington, Acad. Medicine Cleve., Am. Rheumatism Assn., AMA, Ohio Med. Assn., Soc. Mayflower Descs. Episcopalian. Clubs: Army-Navy (Washington); Cleve. Playhouse, Cleve. Skating. Author: (with others) Dermatology in General Medicine, 2d edit., 1979, The Ship's Medicine Chest and Medical Aid at Sea, 1978, International Encyclopedia of Pharmacology and Therapeutics, 1966, others; contbr. articles to profl. jours. Editorial bd. Mil. Surgeon, 1975—. Home: 2913 Torrington Rd Shaker Heights OH 44122 Office: St Luke's Hosp 11311 Shaker Blvd Cleveland OH 44104

BLACK, STEVEN BITTERS, plastic surgeon; b. Rochester, Minn., June 4, 1946; s. Albert Seward and Madge Marie (Bitters) B.; B.S., U. Nebr., Lincoln, 1969, M.D., 1972; m. Joyce Marie Graupmann, July 14, 1979; 1 son, Jonathan Steven; 1 dau. by previous marriage, Michelle Marie. Intern, Mayo Clinic, Rochester, Minn., 1972-73; surg. resident Mayo Grad. Sch. Medicine, Rochester, 1973-77, plastic surgery resident, 1977-79; practice medicine specializing in plastic surgery, Omaha, 1979—; mem. staff Bishop Clarkson Meml., Archbishop Bergan Mercy, Nebr. Meth., Immanuel, Children's, hosps. (all Omaha). Mem. AMA, Nebr. Med. Assn., Met. Omaha Med. Soc. Contbr. articles in field to med. jours. Home: 21467 Brentwood Rd Elkhorn NE 68022 Office: Suite 219 Doctors Bldg 44th and Farnam Sts Omaha NE 68131

BLACK, THOMAS ALEXANDER, JR., dentist; b. Pitts., Jan. 10, 1943; s. Thomas Alexander and Griselda (Best) B.; B.S., Purdue U., 1965; D.M.D., Washington U., St. Louis, 1975; m. Sandra Jean Gredys, May 10, 1969. Prodn. supr. Proctor & Gamble, St. Louis, 1968-69; with Mallinckroft Chem. Works, St. Louis, 1969-71; gen. practice dentistry, Marlborough, Mo., 1976—; clin. instr. dentistry Washington U., St. Louis, 1976-78, asst. prof., 1978—; staff dentist Bethesda Dilworth Meml. Home. Deacon, mem. choir Webster Groves (Mo.) Presbyn. Ch.; pres. York Village Assn. Served to capt. C.E., AUS, 1965-68. Mem. Am., Mo. dental assns., Greater St. Louis Dental Soc., Acad. Gen. Dentistry, Soc. Am. Mil. Engrs., Xi Psi Phi, Alpha Phi Omega. Club: Rotary. Home: 70 York Dr Brentwood MO 63144 Office: 8460 Watson Rd Suite 112 Marlborough MO 63119

BLACK, THOMAS CLAIBORNE, JR., ophthalmologist; b. Norton, Kans., Dec. 11, 1938; s. Thomas Claiborne and Susan Pauline (Terbush) B.; student Duke U., 1955-58; M.D., La. State U., 1962; m. Patricia Louise Cover, Apr. 21, 1969. Intern, Madigan Gen. Hosp., Tacoma, 1962-63; resident U. Kan. Med. Center, Kansas City, 1965-68; practice medicine, specializing in ophthalmology, Kansas City, Mo., 1968—; asso. Kan. U. Med. Center, Kansas City, Kans., 1968—; mem. staff St. Lukes, Bapt. hosps., Kansas City, Mo. Served with AUS, 1962-65. Decorated Air medal with 3 oak leaf clusters. Mem. A.C.S., Am. Acad. Ophthalmology and Otolaryngology, AMA, Jackson County Med. Soc., Sigma Nu. Home: 6411 Belinder Shawnee Mission KS 66208 Office: 1010 Carondelet Dr Kansas City MO 64114

BLACK, THOMAS IGNATIUS, ednl. adminstr.; b. Toledo, Jan. 25, 1935; s. Howard Francis and Catherine Agnes (Leyland) B.; A.B., U. Notre Dame, 1962; M.S. in Edn., U., 1978; m. Myrna May Kipp, Sept. 27, 1958; children—Thomas, Catherine, Terri, Deborah, Karen, Pamela, Paula, Laura. Tchr., Centre Twp. Sch., South Bend, Ind., 1962-63, James Whitcomb Riley High Sch., South Bend, 1963-74; pres., producer, dir. Country Playhouse, South Bend, 1964-69; mgr. Country Playhouse Restaurant, South Bend, 1968-69; prin. Christ the King Sch., South Bend, 1974-81, St. Bernadette Sch., Appleton, Wis., 1981—; dir. community and communications workshops, 1979-81. Diocesan rep. to A.C.T.I.O.N., Inc., South Bend, 1967-68; mem. election bd., adv. planning bd. South Bend Century Center, 1969-70; past pres. South Bend Bd. Edn.; advisor Congregation of Holy Cross, 1980—. Served with U.S. Army, 1956-60. Recipient Ind. Gov.'s award for outstanding support of and service to children, 1979; Prin. of the Month, Today's Cath. Tchr., 1980; K.C. Cath. Man of Yr. nominee, 1980, others. Mem. South Bend Prins. Assn. (pres. 1975-76), Nat. Assn. Elem. Sch. Prins., Assn. Supervision and Curriculum Devel., Nat. Cath. Edn. Assn. Democrat. Roman Catholic. Clubs: Lions, K.C. Home: 1370 Roelke Dr South Bend IN 46614 Office: 2331 E Lourdes Dr Appleton WI 54911

BLACK, WALTER KERRIGAN, lawyer; b. Birmingham, Ala., Jan. 27, 1915; s. Timuel Dixon and Mattie (McConner) B.; A.B., U. Ill., 1939; LL.B., John Marshall Law Sch., 1952; m. Dorothy E. Wickliffe, July 2, 1950. Admitted to Ill. bar, 1952; partner firm McCoy & Black, Chgo., 1952-59; partner firm McCoy Ming & Leighton, Chgo., 1959-64; partner firm McCoy, Ming & Black, Chgo., 1965-77; prin. firm Mitchell & Black, Chgo., 1977—; village atty. Robbins (Ill.),

1952-69, 81—, East Chicago Heights (Ill.), 1954-69, 77—; hearing examiner Ill. Fair Practices Commn.; arbitrator Am. Arbitration Assn., 1971—. Mem. governing bd. Cook County Legal Assistance Found., Inc. Served with AUS, 1942-46. Mem. Ill., Chgo., Cook County bar assns., Kappa Alpha Psi. Mem. A.M.E. Ch. (atty., trustee). Home: 2231 E 67th St Chicago IL 60649 Office: 134 S LaSalle St Chicago IL 60603

BLACKBOURN, JAMES WILLIAM, educator; b. Kenosha, Wis., Mar. 27, 1949; s. Archie William and Thelma La Vonne (Henry) B.; B.A. in Chemistry, U. Wis., 1971, postgrad. in physiology, also in elec. and computer engring.; m. Barbara Lee Davis, June 12, 1970; children—James William, Nancy Lee. Asst. gamma ray spectroscopist dept. chemistry U. Wis., Madison, 1967-71, teaching asst. dept. chemistry, 1971-72, organic chemist sch. pharmacy, 1972-73, NMR spetroscopist, 1973-81. Home: 462 Jean St Madison WI 53703 Office: Elec and Computer Engring U Wis Madison WI 53706

BLACKBURN, DAVID, dancer, educator; b. Dundee, Mich., Feb. 10, 1937; B.A. in Speech and Theatre, Wayne State U., 1963; M.A. in Dance, U. Cin., 1968; postgrad. Severo Sch. Ballet, Schwarz Sch. Dance, U. Cin. Coll.-Conservatory of Music. Prin. dancer Cin. Ballet Co., 1966—; soloist Dayton Civic Ballet, 1963-66, Detroit Ballet Theatre (Severo Ballet), 1958-63, Antioch Area Theatre (Antioch Coll.) Shakespeare 400 Summer Festival, 1964; guest artist Augusta (Ga.) Ballet Co., appeared in Coppelia, 1981; guest dancer Wis. Ballet Co., 1965, Cin. Civic Ballet, 1963, Lima (Oh.) Symphony in Merry Widow (Lehar), 1965, Columbus (Ohio) Civic Ballet, 1966; premier danseur Cin. Summer Opera, 1966; soloist David McLain Dance Theatre for Beaupre Ballet Festival, Stockbridge, Mass., summer 1969; mem. Kenley Players in profl. mus. theatre prodns., Warren, Ohio, Dayton, Columbus, 1966; art instr. Winton Terr. Sch., Cin., 1966-67, Indian Valley Sch., Greene County, Ohio, 1965-66; dir. Lima Sch. Ballet, 1965-66; grad. asst. U. Cin. Coll.-Conservatory of Music Dance div., 1967-68, instr., 1968-70, asst. prof., 1970-74, asso. prof., 1974—; sec.-treas. David McLain Dance Theatre, Inc., 1962-72; asst. artistic dir. Cin. Ballet Co., 1971-75, asso. artistic dir., 1975—; guest instr. U. Tenn., Knoxville, 1981, U. Louisville, summer 1973, W.Va. Ballet Festival, Huntington, 1973, U. Wis., Green Bay, 1973, Eastern Mich. U., Ypsilanti, 1973, U. Ky., Lexington, 1972. *

BLACK-GILBERT, JENNIFER, social worker; b. Plainfield, N.J., Dec. 3, 1950; d. Joseph and Joanna (DeFalco) Black; B.S. in Polit. Sci., Sociology, Drake U., 1968; J.D., DePaul U., 1972; postgrad. Ind. U.-Purdue U., Indpls., 1981—; 1 dau., Nancy Kathleen. Jr. editor Commerce Clearing House, Chgo., 1970-72; mgmt. asso. Community Inter-Faith Housing, Indpls., 1972-74; ops. mgr. for CETA programs Ind. Vocat. Tech. Coll., Indpls., 1974-77; program dir. Near Eastside Sr. Citizens Center, Indpls., 1977-79; head social service dept. Colonial Crest Convalescent Center, Indpls., 1979; social worker Mental Health Assn. Marion County, Indpls., 1980—; asst. prof., project dir. Ind. State U. Project on Adolescent Services, Indpls. Mem. Nat. Assn. Social Workers. Republican. Roman Catholic. Home: PO Box 20215 Indianapolis IN 46220

BLACKLIDGE, KENT HACKLEMAN, II, former newspaper pub.; b. Kokomo, Ind., Dec. 10, 1938; s. Richard Henry and Marian Emmalyn (Reinertsen) B.; B.S. in Indsl. Mgmt., Purdue U., 1961; M.S. in Conservation of Natural Resources, 1975; children—Dawn E., Jill R., Douglas K., Mark R. Instr., Culver (Ind.) Mil. Acad., 1958; apprentice pressman the Kokomo (Ind.) Tribune, 1959, display advt. sales, 1961-62, dispatch mgr., 1962-64, prodn. mgr., 1964-68, bus. mgr., 1968-73, gen. mgr., 1973-76, asso. pub., 1976-78, pub., 1978-81; dir. Kokomo Opalescent Glass Co., Inc. Mem. Mayor's Com. Drug Abuse, 1973; pres. Northwestern Elem. PTO. 1969-70; pres. bd. trustees YWCA, Kokomo, 1977; trustee Congregational Ch., Kokomo, 1968-70. Mem. Inland Daily Press Assn. (prodn. com., mech. and cost and revenue coms.), Inst. Newspaper Controllers, C. of C. (dir.), Phi Kappa Phi, Gamma Sigma Delta, Sigma Delta Chi. Club: Elks. Home: 4018 W Sycamore OONS Kokomo IN 46901 Office: 300 N Union St Kokomo IN 46901

BLACKORBY, EDWARD CONVERSE, historian; b. Hansboro, N.D., May 30, 1911; s. Charles Edward and Clara Ellen (Converse) B.; B.S., Mayville State Tchrs. Coll., 1930; Ph.D., U. N.D., 1958; postgrad. Am. U.; m. Jewel Catherine Barenscheer, Nov. 24, 1937; 1 son, Charles Edward. Tchr. public schs., Russell, Niagara, Pembina and New Rockford, N.D., 1930-49; prof. history Dickinson (N.D.) State Tchrs. Coll., 1949-59; prof. history U. Wis., Eau Claire, 1959—. Mem. City Council Eau Claire, 1966-68, chmn. Cable TV Adv. Com., 1975—; mem. Park Bd.; clk. Sch. Dist. Named Tchr. of Yr., U. Wis., Eau Claire, 1968. Mem. Orgn. Am. Historians, Am. Hist. Assn., State Hist. Soc. Wis., N.D. Hist. Soc., Western History Assn., Agrl. History Assn., Nat. Council Social Studies, AAUP, Wis. Council Social Studies, NEA, Phi Alpha Theta, Phi Delta Kappa, Phi Kappa Phi, Phi Eta Sigma (hon.). Democrat. Congregationalist. Club: Masons. Author: Prairie Rebel: The Public Life of William Lemke; George B. Winship: Progressive Journalist of the Middle Border; contbr. to Ency. Americana, Dictionary of Am. Biography, profl. jours. Home: 2723 Agnes St Eau Claire WI 54701 Office: Dept History U Wis Eau Claire WI 54701

BLACKWELL, KENNETH EMERSON, chem. engr.; b. Clendenin, W.Va., Dec. 13, 1930; s. John Ervin and Ava (Strickland) B.; student N.C. State Coll., 1950-51, Tri-State Coll., 1959-60; B.S., Fla. State Christian Coll., 1972; M.S., Tenn. Christian U., 1977, Ph.D., 1978; m. Harriet Pauline Anderson, Feb. 10, 1953; children—Vicky Jo, Yma Yvonne. Chem. processing supr. Am. Viscose Corp., Nitro, W.Va., 1953-59; chem. processing supr. Purex Corp., St. Louis, 1960-67, sr. project engr., 1967-80, sr. field engr., 1980—. Served with USAF, 1948-52. Mem. Inst. for Cert. of Engring. Technicians. Mem. United Ch. Christ. Home: 12040 Larimore Rd Saint Louis MO 63138 Office: Purex Corp 6506 N Broadway Saint Louis MO 63147

BLACKWOOD, R(OBERT) ROSS, metallurgical co. exec.; b. Windsor, Ont., Can., Sept. 12, 1928; came to U.S., 1929; s. Robert Alexander and Annie (Beecroft) B.; B.S. in Metall. Engring. U. Wis., 1953; m. Beverly Joy Svenson, June 21, 1953; children—Kari Lynn, Scott Andrew. Metall. engr. A.C. Spark Plug Co., Flint, Mich., 1953-54; mgr. T. H. Cochrane Labs., Milw., 1954-60, pres., owner, 1960-74; pres. Tenaxol Inc., Milw., 1965—, chmn. bd., 1967—. Served with U.S. Army, 1946-48; Japan. Recipient Outstanding Engring. award U. Wis., 1977; registered profl. engr., Wis. Mem. Am. Soc. Metals, AIME (chmn. Wis. chpt. 1962-63), Soc. Automotive Engrs., Soc. Mfg. Engrs., Nat. Soc. Profl. Engrs. Republican. Presbyterian. Clubs: Lions (Wauwatosa, Wis.); Masons, Shriners. Patentee metal quenching medium. Home: 2877 N 122d St Wauwatosa WI 53222 Office: 5801 W National Ave Milwaukee WI 53214

BLAGBROUGH, ELIZABETH M. (MRS. HARRY PUTNAM BLAGBROUGH), fine art appraiser; b. Orlando, Fla., Sept. 8, 1926; d. Calvin Burr and Maud Alice (Wagner) McCaughen; B.A., Washington U., 1948; m. Harry Putnam Blagbrough, June 30, 1951; children—Helen Blagbrough Kortkamp, Harry Putnam, Alicia. Apprentice appraiser McCaughen & Burr, Inc., Fine Arts, St. Louis, 1948-70, appraiser, 1970—; pvt. appraisals by referral, 1970—; lectr.

fine arts, art history; instr. Lindenwood Colls., St. Charles, Mo. Fellow Inc. Soc. Valuers and Auctioneers (Gt. Britain); mem. P.E.O., Am. Soc. Appraisers (sr., internat. bd. examiners, sec. St. Louis chpt., chpt. treas. 1974-75, 1st v.p. 1976-77, pres. St. Louis chpt. 1977-78, del. internat. conf., preparator lectr. presentations, chmn. internat. bd. publs.; Appraiser of Year St. Louis 1977-78, mem. internat. recert. bd.), Appraisers Assn. Am. Methodist. Contbr. articles to profl. jours. Home: 340 S Elm Saint Louis MO 63119 Office: 34 N Gore Ave Suite 204 Saint Louis MO 63119

BLAIN, ALEXANDER, III, surgeon; b. Detroit, Mar. 9, 1918; s. Alexander William and Ruby (Johnson) B.; student Washington and Lee U., 1935-37; B.A., Wayne U., 1940, M.D., 1943; M.S. in Surgery, U. Mich., 1948; m. Josephine Woodbury Bowen, May 3, 1941; children—Helen Bowen, Alexander IV, Bruce Scott Murray, Josephine Johnson; m. 2d, Mary E. Mains, 1968. House officer, Halsted fellow in surgery Johns Hopkins, 1943-46; resident surgeon U. Hosp., Ann Arbor, Mich., 1946-50; instr. surgery U. Mich., 1950-57; clin. asst. prof. surgery Wayne State U., 1962—; also surgeon-in-chief Alexander Blain Hosp., Detroit, 1953-78; cons. surgeon Highland Park Gen. Hosp., St. Joseph's Hosp., Blain Clinic; asso. surgeon Detroit Gen. Hosp.; med. dir. The Budd Co., 1977—. Pres., Met. Detroit Family Service Assn., 1962-63, Detroit Museum Soc., 1961-62; staff Harper Hosp., Detroit, Crittenton Hosp., Rochester, Mich., Detroit Deaconess Hosp. Mem. Detroit Zool. Park Commn., 1974—, pres., 1978—; trustee Alexander Blain Meml. Hosp., 1942-67, Ostego Meml. Hosp. Found., Gaylord, Mich., 1976—; bd. dirs. Detroit Zool. Soc., 1972-75. Served as lt. M.C., AUS, 1942-44, maj., 1955-57. Diplomate Am. Bd. Surgery. Fellow A.C.S., N.Y. Acad. Scis.; mem. Internat. Cardiovascular Soc., F.A. Coller Surg. Soc., Am. Fedn. for Clin. Research, Cranbrook Inst. Sci., Soc. Vascular Surgery, Am. Thyroid Assn., Société Internationale de Chirurgie, Mich. Med. Soc. (chmn. surg. section 1963), Assn. Clin. Surgery, Pan-Pacific Surg. Assn., Nu Sigma Nu, Phi Gamma Delta. Clubs: Grosse Pointe, Otsego, Prismatic (pres. 1967), Detroit, Detroit Racquet (pres. 1976-80), Cardio-Vascular Surgeons (pres. 1961-62); Acanthus, Waweatonong. Author: (with F. A. Coller) Indications For and Results of Splenectomy, 1950; Prismatic Papers and an Ode, 1968; Prismatic Haiku Poems (Remembered Voices), 1973; also numerous articles surg. jours. Editorial bd. Review Surgery, 1959-79. Home: 8 Stratford Pl Grosse Pointe MI 48230 Office: 12141 Charlevoix Ave Detroit MI 48215

BLAIN, CHARLOTTE MARIE, physician; b. Meadeville, Pa., July 18, 1941; d. Frank Andrew and Valerie Marie (Serafin) B.; student Coll. St. Francis, 1958-60, DePaul U., 1960-61; M.D., U. Ill., 1965; m. John G. Hamby, June 12, 1971 (dec. May 1976); 1 son, Charles J. Hamby. Intern, resident U. Ill. Hosps., Chgo., 1967-70; practice medicine specializing in internal medicine, Elmhurst, Ill., 1969—; instr. medicine U. Ill. Hosp., 1969-70; asst. prof. medicine Loyola U., 1970-71; mem. staff Elmhurst Meml. Hosp., 1970—; clin. asst. prof. Chgo. Med. Sch., 1978—. U. Ill. fellow in infectious diseases, 1968-69. Diplomate Am. Bd. Family Practice, Am. Bd. Internal Medicine. Fellow A.C.P., Am. Acad. Family Practice; mem. AMA, Am. Med. Women's Assn., Am. Soc. Internal Medicine, Am. Fedn. Clin. Research, Nat. Soc. Residents and Interns, Am. Profl. Practice Assn., AAAS, Am. Soc. Contemporary Medicine and Surgery, Royal Soc. Medicine. Roman Catholic. Club: Univ. (Chgo.). Contbr. articles and chpts. to med. jours. and texts. Home: 320 Cottage Hill Elmhurst IL 60126 Office: 135 Cottage Hill Elmhurst IL 60126

BLAIN, DONALD GRAY, physician; b. Detroit, Feb. 27, 1924; s. Alexander and Ruby (Johnson) B.; ed. Princeton, 1946; M.D., Wayne State U., 1950; m. Grace Carpenter, June, 1954; children—Elizabeth, Ian, Patricia. Intern, Union Meml. Hosp., Balt., 1950-51; gen. surg. resident Ch. Home Hosp., Balt., 1953-55, Henry Ford Hosp., Detroit, 1955-56, Alexander Blain Hosp., Detroit, 1956-58; staff Blain Hosp.; resident urology N.C. Bapt. Hosp. and instr. urology Bowman Gray Sch. Medicine, Winston-Salem, 1962-65; pvt. practice urology, Mount Clemens, Mich., 1965—; pres. Oakland Macomb Profl. Standards Rev. Orgn., 1973-79. Mem. Gov.'s Conf. on Health Manpower, 1973; bd. dirs. Mich. MDPAC. Served to capt. USAF, 1951-53. Diplomate Am. Bd. Urology. Fellow A.C.S.; mem. Macomb County Med. Soc. (past pres.), Am. Assn. Clin. Urologists, Am. Urologic Assn., Detroit Surg. Soc. (council), St. Andrews Soc. Republican. Presbyterian. Clubs: Country of Detroit, Metamora Hunt, Grosse Point Hunt, Detroit, Detroit Racquet, Sedgefield Hunt. Home: 34136 E Jefferson St Clair Shores MI 48082

BLAINE, WILLIAM MCKINLEY, JR., sales exec.; b. Chgo., Apr. 9, 1931; s. William McKinley and Edith Alvina (Charbonnier) B.; A.B. in Sociology/Anthropology, U. Ill., 1954; M.A. in Edn., U. Chgo., 1955; postgrad. U. Wis., 1962-63; M.B.A., Northwestern U., 1980; m. Tokiko Tanabe, Mar. 24, 1956; children—William McKinley III, James. Elem. tchr. Dept. Public Instrn., Territory Hawaii, 1955-56; area mgr. World Book Childcraft Internat., Inc., 1957-58, dist. mgr., 1958-59, div. mgr., 1959-62, div. mgr., Hayward, Calif., 1962-76, asso. sales tng., Chgo., 1976-80, dir. mktg. services/ins. projects, 1980—; guest lectr. Chabot Community Coll., Hayward, 1973. Sec., Oahu Democratic County Com., 1959-60; mem. Sch. Adv. Com., Hayward, 1972; bd. dirs. East Bay Youth Symphony, Hayward, 1973-76; neighborhood commr. Boy Scouts Am., Hayward, 1964-66; pres. Woodland Estates Community Assn., 1973; bd. dirs. Mt. Prospect Public Library, 1979-85. Mem. ALA (mem. library trustee div.), C. of C. Democrat. Methodist. Clubs: Des Plaines Yacht, Rotary. Home: 119 N Emerson St Mount Prospect IL 60056 Office: 510 Merchandise Mart Plaza Chicago IL 60654

BLAIR, ALLAN EDWARD, oral and maxillofacial surgeon; b. Cleve., June 4, 1929; s. Samuel Charles and Rose (Weiss) B.; B.A., Ohio State U., 1951, D.D.S., 1955, M.Sc., 1960; m. Judith Ann Hare, June 11, 1971; children by previous marriage—Bradley, Brian, Scott; stepchildren—Joel, Beth. Intern, Ohio State Univ. Hosp., Columbus, 1957-58, resident oral and maxillofacial surgery, 1958-60; practice dentistry specializing in oral and maxillofacial surgery, Columbus, Ohio, 1960—; asst. prof. physiology Ohio State U. Coll. Medicine, Columbus, 1960—, asso. prof. oral and maxillofacial surgery Coll. Dentistry, 1967—; mem. staff Univ., Children's, St. Anthony hosps.; mem. nat. affiliate faculty advanced life support and extended coronary care Am. Heart Assn. Recipient Outstanding Faculty Mem. award Ohio State U., 1975. Diplomate Am. Bd. Oral and Maxillofacial Surgery. Fellow Am. Dental Soc. Anesthesiology, Am. Assn. Oral and Maxillofacial Surgeons, Internat. Assn. Oral Surgeons; mem. Am., Ohio (pres. 1976-77), Great Lakes socs. oral and maxillofacial surgeons, ADA, Soc. Preservation and Encouragement Barbershop Quartet Singing in Am., Alpha Omega Alpha, Sigma Alpha Mu. Club: Hoover Yacht. Contbr. articles in field to profl. jours. Home: 2526 Stafford Pl Columbus OH 43209 Office: 3242 E Main St Columbus OH 43213

BLAIR, ETCYL HOWELL, chem. co. exec.; b. Wynona, Okla., Oct. 15, 1922; s. Tunice Wilbur and Ruby (Wilson) B.; A.B., Southwestern Coll., Winfield, Kans., 1947, D.Sc. (hon.), 1974; M.S., Kans. State Coll., 1949, Ph.D., 1952; m. Ruth Gross, Sept. 4, 1949; children—David, Ronald, Kevin. Research chemist Dow Chem. Co., Midland, Mich., 1951-56, group leader, 1956-65, div. leader, 1965-66, asst. dir. E.C. Britton Research Lab., 1966-67, dir. lab., 1967-68, mgr. research and devel., agrl. dept., 1968-71, dir. research and devel., ag-organics dept., 1971-73, dir. health and environ. research Dow Chem. U.S.A., 1973-78, v.p., dir. health and environ. scis. Dow Chem. Co., 1978—. Bd. dirs. Chem. Industry Inst. Toxicology; chmn. sci. sub-com. Matrix:Midland, 1978—. Served in USAF, 1943-46. Mem. Am. Chem. Soc. (chmn. Midland sect. 1959; sect. award 1979), Fedn. Am. Scientists, Internat. Acad. Environ. Safety, Research Soc. Am., Am. Inst. Chemists, AAAS, N.Y. Acad. Scis., Soc. Ecotoxicology and Environ. Safety, Soc. Chem. Industry, Sigma Xi. Republican. Methodist. Author: Chlorodioxins—Origin and Fate, 1973. Patentee in field. Home: 4 Crescent Ct Midland MI 48640 Office: 2020 Dow Center Midland MI 48640

BLAIR, JOSEPH SKILES, JR., educator; b. Niles, Ohio, Dec. 16, 1919; s. Joseph Skiles and Elizabeth Leo (Higgins) B.; B.S., Kent State U., 1942; M.A., Columbia U., 1948; Ph.D. (Danforth Found. fellow), Ohio State U., 1962; m. Marjorie Ella Jacot, June 15, 1946; children—Brenda Ruth, Lawrence Paul. Exec. dir. City Coll. N.Y. YM-YWCA and N.Y. U. Med. Students Club, 1948-52; coll. exec. Ohio-W.Va. area YMCA, 1952-59; ednl. services mgr. Nationwide Ins. Co., 1962-68; prof. Franklin U., Columbus, Ohio, 1968—; owner, mgr. Brookside Conf. Center; pres. Vicinia, Inc. Moderator, Univ. Bapt. Ch. Mem. Speech Communication Assn., Am. Mgmt. Assn. Home: 254 E Torrence Rd Columbus OH 43214 Office: 201 S Grant Ave Columbus OH 43215

BLAIR, LACHLAN FERGUSON, urban planner, educator; b. Lakewood, Ohio, Sept. 6, 1919; s. Neil Ferguson and Rebecca Henderson (Gunn) B.; student Cleve. Sch. Architecture, Western Res. U., 1936-40; B.City Planning, M.I.T., 1949; m. Mary Anne Novotny, Dec. 12, 1942; children—Douglas MacLachlan, Marilyn Ruth. Archtl. designer various firms, Cleve., 1940-43; sr. planner Providence City Plan Commn., 1949-51; chief state planning div. R.I. Devel. Council, 1952-56; pres. Blair Assos., Planning Cons., Providence, Syracuse, N.Y., Washington, 1957-66; prof. urban and regional planning U. Ill., Urbana, 1966—. Mem. Ill. Hist. Sites Adv. Council, 1969-77; chmn. Urbana Plan Commn., 1973-80; mem. Champaign County Regional Planning Commn., 1974—. Served with C.E., U.S. Army, 1943-46. EPA public adminstrn. fellow, 1972-73. Mem. Am. Inst. Cert. Planners (past pres. New Eng., Ill. chpts., gov.), Am. Planning Assn., Partners for Livable Places, Nat. Trust for Hist. Preservation, Preservation Action. Democrat. Unitarian. Author: Cape Cod 1980, 1962; College Hill: A Demonstration of Historic Area Renewal, 1959, 67; The Distinctive Architecture of Willemstad, 1961. Home: 506 W Illinois St Urbana IL 61801 Office: 1003 W Nevada Urbana IL 61801

BLAIR, MARVIN SMITH, engr.; b. Killeen, Tex., June 8, 1924; s. Thomas Earle and Margaret Elizabeth (Beaumier) B.; B.B.A., U. Hawaii, 1968; M.A., U. Nebr., 1973; m. Baylor Doris Hale, Feb. 5. 1944; children—Marvin S., Jr., Margaret Baylor. Commd. ensign U.S. Navy, 1942, advanced through grades to capt., 1966; comdr. of Tunny, Daniel Webster, fleet submarine tng. facility, Hawaii, 1957-68; served on 6 submarines and 2 maj. staffs, 1944-73; ret., 1973; nuclear tech. specialist in charge quality assurance Omaha Pub. Power Dist., 1973-74, div. mgr. environ. and regulatory affairs, 1974-77; sr. project engr. Gibbs & Hill, Inc., Omaha, 1977-79, gen. mgr. Midwestern regional office, 1979-80, v.p. and mgr. office, 1980—. Decorated Legion of Merit. Mem. ASME, Subvets World War II. Republican. Baptist. Clubs: Plaza, Fontenelle Hills Country, Happy Hollow Country, Masons. Home: 414 Greenbriar Ct Bellevue NE 68005 Office: 8420 W Dodge Rd Omaha NE 68114

BLAIR, MARY AGNES, cons. spl. edn.; b. Richmond, Mo.; d. Andrew and Lydia (Ward) Blair; B.S., Eastern Mich. U., 1940, Ed.D. (hon.), 1955; M.Ed., Wayne State U., 1946. Tchr., supr. elem. sch. Mich. Sch. Deaf, Flint, 1927-28; tchr., dir. spl. edn. Dearborn (Mich.) Public Sch., 1940-46; cons. spl. edn. Mich. Dept. Edn., Lansing, 1946-76; univ. summer prof. spl. edn. numerous univs. U.S., Can., 1946-76. Bd. dirs. Bay Cliff Camp for Handicapped Children, summer 1947; bd. dirs. Mich. Easter Seal Soc., 1946-75, and Lansing chpt.; vol. Lansing City Council, 1979-80; chmn. publicity com. for Lifeline, Ingham Med. Center Aux., 1981—; mem. community outreach and adult coms. Westminster Presbyn. Ch., Lansing, 1981—. Recipient Eastern Mich. Distinguished Alumni award, 1977, Beekman award, 1977, Mich. State Dept. Edn. award, 1977, award Mich. Suprs. Pub. Sch. Programs for Hearing Impaired, 1977, others. Mem. Eastern Mich. Alumni Assn. (pres. 1962), United Cerebral Palsy Assn (profl. bd. 1949-77), Mich. Speech and Hearing Assn. (award 1976), Council Exceptional Children, Mich. Parents and Tchrs. Hearing Impaired (state cons. spl. edn. 1946-77) Wayne State U. Alumni Assn. (sec. Lansing chpt.). Presbyterian. Home: 1108 W Ionia St Lansing MI 48915

BLAIR, PHILLIP CHARLES, hosp. adminstr.; b. Tulsa, July 6, 1946; s. Victor Charles and Frances Louise Swan (Pugh) B.; B.A., U. Okla., 1968; B.S., U. Md., 1974; M.B.A., Ind. State U., 1976; M.H.A., Ind. U., 1978; m. Sandra Lee Etchison, Jan. 6, 1979: children by previous marriage—Alex Charles, Nancy Lynn; stepchildren—Michael Joseph Etchison, Rebecca Lynn Etchison. Institutional cons. Ind. State Bd. Health, Indpls., 1976-78; hosp. adminstr. Community Hosp., Indpls., 1978—, Major Hosp., Shelbyville. Bd. dirs. Multiple Sclerosis Soc. Ind. Served with U.S. Army, 1969-76. Decorated Bronze Star. Mem. Am. Coll. Hosp. Adminstrs., Am. Hosp. Assn., Indpls. Jaycees (dir. 1977, v.p. 1978) Ind. Jaycees (v.p. 1979), Phi Beta Kappa. Republican. Presbyterian. Home: 1916 Rosedale Dr Indianapolis IN 46227 Office: 150 W Washington Shelbyville IN 46176

BLAIR, RICHARD WILLIAM, state govt. ofcl.; b. Volga, S.D., Oct. 13, 1924; s. Terrace William and Tena I. (Warnes) B.; B.S., S.D. State U., 1949, M.S., 1952; 1 son, Richard William, II. With S.D. Health Dept., 1952-68, 69—, dep. sec. health, 1970-78, sec., 1978—; acting dir. comprehensive health planning Office Gov. S.D., 1968-69. Served with AUS, 1942-44. Decorated Purple Heart. Mem. Am. Public Health Assn., Conf. Public Health Labs. Dirs., Assn. State and Territorial Health Officers, S.D. Public Health Assn. (G.F. Van Heuvelen award), VFW. Republican. Lutheran. Clubs: Elks, Masons. Office: Joss Foss Bldg Pierre SD 57501*

BLAIR, TERRENCE LEE, fin. and data processing cons.; b. LaPorte, Ind., Nov. 23, 1946; s. Stanley F. and Edna (Bluhm) B.; B.B.A., Loyola U., Chgo., 1969; M.B.A., U. Notre Dame, 1971; m. Judy Leigh Johnson, June 20, 1969; children—Tiffany, Holly, Emily, David. Fin. planning asso. Assos. Fin. Planning and Control Co., South Bend, Ind., 1970-71; fin. planning specialist Charles F. Kettering Found., Dayton, Ohio, 1972-78; cons. T.L. Blair & Assos., Dayton, 1974—; mgr. data processing services Flagel, Huber, Flagel & Co., Dayton, 1978-79. Mem. Am. Bus. Club Dayton. Roman Catholic. Club: Notre Dame Alumni (officer) (Dayton). Home: 10280 Grand Vista Dr Dayton OH 45459 Office: Dayton OH

BLAKE, BRUCE DOUGLAS, office furniture mfg. co. exec.; b. Chgo., Mar. 14, 1945; s. Alfred R. and Dorthy M. (Wood) B.; student R.I. Sch. Photography, 1964; B.S.M.E., Tri-State Coll., Angola, Ind., 1971; M.S., Mich. State U., 1975; m. Linda S. Smoker, Sept. 13, 1971; 1 son, Justin N. Sr. product planner Ford Motor Co., Dearborn, Mich., 1971-72; spl. projects engr. Harter Corp., Sturgis, Mich., 1972-75, mgr. engring., 1975-77; sr. product engr. Steelcase, Inc., Grand Rapids, Mich., 1977-79; mgr. engring. Haworth, Inc., Holland, Mich., 1979—. Program adviser Jr. Achievement. Served with USMC, 1965-67. Recipient Merit award City of Holland, 1977. Mem. Soc. Mfg. Engrs. (cert.), Nat. Soc. Profl. Engrs., Am. Soc. Metals, Photog. Soc. Am., U.S. Yacht Racing Union, Lake Michigan Yacht Racing Assn. Home: 1140 Meadowlane Kentwood MI 49508 Office: Haworth Inc 1 Haworth Center Holland MI 49423

BLAKE, DEBORAH ANNE, educator; b. Chgo., Aug. 22, 1954; d. Stan Walter and Maryanne Lois Blake; student DuPage Coll., 1972-74; B.A., De Paul U., 1976, M.Ed., 1980. Tchr. English, Notre Dame High Sch. for Boys, Niles, Ill., 1976-77, Redeemer High Sch., Detroit, 1977-78, Resurrection High Sch., Chgo., 1978-79; grad. asst. De Paul U., Chgo., 1979-80, instr. reading, clinician, 1980—; reading specialist De La Salle High Sch., Chgo., 1980-81, Proviso Twp. High Sch., Hillside, Ill., 1981—. Cert. English tchr. grades 6-12, spl. edn. tchr. grades K-12, Ill. Mem. Nat. Council Tchrs. English, Council for Basic Edn., Chgo. Assn. for Children with Learning Disabilities, Assn. for Supervision and Curriculum Devel., The Learning Exchange (adv. bd.), LWV. Home: 2225 Ridge Ave Evanston IL 60201 Office: S Wolfe Rd and Harrison St Hillside IL also 802 W Belden Ave Chicago IL 60614

BLAKE, FRANK BURGAY, med. record librarian; b. N.Y.C., Feb. 10, 1924; s. Francis Gilman and Marguerite (Burgay) B.; B.S., U. Minn., 1947; M.S., N.Y. U., 1951; diploma Air U., 1960; m. Filomena Yolanda Ciaccio, Dec. 15, 1962; children—Anthony Francis, Robert Burgay. Staff U.S. Army Hosp., Ft. Ord, Calif., 1964-65; med. record librarian County of Tulare, Visalia, Calif., 1966-69, Winnebago (Wis.) Mental Health Inst., 1970—; exec. dir. Medica, Inc., Tulare, Calif., 1968-70. Cons. Brown County Mental Health Center, Green Bay, Wis., 1971-76; cons. Med. record program evaluation Herzing Insts., Inc., Milw., 1971-73, mem. bd. advisers med. stenographer program, 1971-72; bd. advisers med. record technician program Moraine Park Tech. Inst., Fond du Lac, Wis., 1974—. Mem. Northeastern Assn. Med. Record Librarians (v.p. 1970-71). Contbr. articles to profl. jours. Home: 1607 Hazel St Oshkosh WI 54901 Office: Bur Correctional Health Services 110 E Main St Madison WI 53703

BLAKE, PHILIP WAYNE, safety cons.; b. Wichita, Kans., Dec. 26, 1923; s. Charles G.C. and Jessie M. Blake; B.S., U. Kans., 1950; m. Minnie L. Howard, Apr. 8, 1950; children—Sally M., Laura D., Kenneth H. Tchr., head math. dept. Junction City (Kans.) public schs., 1950-52; with Boeing Co., Wichita, 1952-69, program mgr., 1962-69; v.p. Chancellor's Clothing, Wichita, 1969-72; safety cons., 1972-74; v.p. Safety Cons. Inc., Wichita, 1974-77, sr. v.p., 1977—; pres., dir. Beam Tng. Systems, Inc.; mem. faculty Wichita State U., 1977-78. Served with AUS, 1943-46. Mem. Nat. Safety Mgmt. Soc., Nat. Safety Council, Am. Soc. Safety Engrs., Nat. Fire Protection Assn., Am. Indsl. Hygiene Assn., Kans. Safety Assn. Author articles in field. Office: PO Box 4116 Wichita KS 67204

BLAKE, THOMAS GAYNOR, chemist; b. Nashville, Sept. 24, 1917; s. Robert Edwin and Dorothy (Gaynor) B.; student Princeton U., 1935-38; B.A., Central Meth. Coll., Fayette, Mo., 1940; postgrad. Washington U., St. Louis, 1942-44; m. Jane Elizabeth Spore. May 2, 1942; children—Dorothy Gaynor, Thomas Gaynor. Project engr. Explosives div. Olin Mathieson Chem. Corp., East Alton, Ill., 1941-48, head explosives chem. sect., 1948-54, dir. research and devel. explosives div., 1954-56; asst. dir. research and devel. armament div. Universal Match Corp., Ferguson, Mo., 1956-58; pres., dir. research Hanley Industries Inc., St. Louis, 1958—; lectr., cons. in field. Mem. Am. Def. Preparedness Assn. (life), Am. Soc. Indsl. Security, Mo. Athletic Club, Engrs. Club St. Louis, Mo. State Hist. Soc., St. Louis Westerners. Congregationalist. Patentee in field. Home: 16430 Old Jamestown Rd Florissant MO 63034 Office: 3640 Seminary Rd PO Box 1058 Alton IL 62002

BLAKUT, MITCHELL ANTHONY, mfg. co. exec.; b. Chgo., Feb. 15, 1921; s. Anthony and Anna (Ducal) B.; student North Park Coll., 1950; m. May 1, 1943; children—Mary Ann, Charles Mitchell. Process and mfg. engring. Pioneer Tool Co., Chgo., 1958-61; sr. process engr. Pyle Nat. Co., Chgo., 1961-64; quality control supr. Bell & Howell Co., Chgo., from 1964; now with Memorex-Bell & Howell Home Video, Northbrook, Ill. Served with Inf., AUS, 1944-46. Asst. scoutmaster, commr. Chgo. Area council Boy Scouts Am. Mem. Soc. Mfg. Engrs. (v.p., cert. mfg. engr.), Am. Soc. Quality Control, Internat. Biog. Assn. Democrat. Roman Catholic. Registered profl. engr., Calif. Home: 5725 N Marmora St Chicago IL 60646 Office: 720 Landwehr Northbrook IL 60062

BLAMEY, RICHARD LYLE, accountant; b. Fond du Lac, Wis., Dec. 13, 1941; s. Lyle Donald and Lucille Hazel (Immel) B.; B.B.A., U. Wis., 1965; m. Ann-Elizabeth McCallum, Aug. 14, 1977; children—Richard Scott, Heather Lynn. Staff accountant Ronald Mattox & Assos., Madison, Wis., 1965-71, audit mgr., Fond du Lac, 1971-74, partner, 1974-75; partner Alexander Grant & Co., Fond du Lac, 1975—; v.p., treas. Ledgeview Devel. Corp., Fond du Lac, 1971-77, pres., 1977—; partner Mt. Calvary Assos., 1979—. Mem. Fond du Lac Civic Center Com., 1972—; adviser Jr. Achievement, 1974-75; chmn. accountants div. Dane County United Fund drive, 1970-71; first reader First Ch. of Christ Scientist, Fond du Lac, 1975-78, chmn. bd., 1980-81; bd. dirs., treas. Student Center Found., Madison, 1969-71. Mem. Nat. Assn. Accts. (pres. Sheboyan Lakeshore chpt. 1977-78), Wis. Inst. C.P.A.'s, (chmn. practice mgmt. com. and seminar 1972), Fond du Lac Jaycees (v.p. 1974-75), U. Wis. Alumni Assn. (pres. 1977-78). Republican. Clubs: South Hills Country (treas. 1978-81), Wis. Region Classic Car, Antique Auto Club Am., Rotary. Home: Route 4 Ledgeview Springs Fond du Lac WI 54935 Office: 131 S Main St Fond du Lac WI 54935

BLANCHARD, B(IRDSALL) EVERARD, ednl. cons.; b. Chgo., Oct. 19, 1909; s. Birdsall Everard and Mary Alice (Vandervest) B.; B.S., Western Mich. U., 1931; M.S., State U. Iowa, 1932; M.A., U. Chgo., 1946, Ph.D., 1957; m. Ann Quaglia, Nov. 20, 1949; children—Sharon Reyn, David Everard. Ordained to ministry United Meth. Ch., 1936; minister Meth. chs. in Ill., Fla., Va., Nfld., 1936-51; dir. health and phys. edn. jr. high sch., Villa Park, Ill., 1932-36; dir. athletics and phys. edn. McKendree Coll., Lebanon, Ill., 1936-38; asst. supr. adult and vocat. edn. State of Ill., Glen Ellyn, 1938-41; dir. health and phys. edn. jr. high sch., Ft. Myers, Fla., 1941-42; prin. high sch., Cross City, Fla., 1943-46; supt. pub. schs., Minden City, Mich., 1946-47; prof. edn. Elmhurst (Ill.) Coll., 1947-48; prof. edn., dir. tchr. edn. Erskine Coll., Due West, S.C., 1948-49; dean grad. and undergrad. studies Overseas div. U. Md., 1949-51; prof. edn., dir. student teaching Plymouth (N.H.) State Coll., 1951-55; vis. prof. edn. Nat. Coll. Edn., Evanston, Ill., 1961-62; prof. edn. DePaul U., Chgo., 1962-75, dir. Ednl. Field Service, 1962-74, dir. Opinion Poll Survey Center, 1963-69, coordinator grad. programs office, 1966-75; vis. prof. edn. Defiance Coll., 1955-56; pres. Villa Ednl. Research Assos., Villa Park, 1975—; supt. Mil. Dependent Schs., 1949-51; mem. exec. com. Assn. for Field Service in Tchr. Edn., 1963-69. Recipient citation Princeton U., 1973; named hon. Ky. col. Mem. Internat. Assn. for Advancement Ednl. Research, NEA (life mem., citation 1960), Phi Delta Kappa, Kappa Delta Pi, Sigma Theta Gamma. Author:

Destination Teaching, 1960; Introductory Statistics for Student of Education, 1963; A Survey of Illinois Catholic Secondary Schools, 1966; Illinois Index for Selecting Textbooks, 1968; A Profile of Behavioral Characteristics Peculiar to Articulation in American Educational Programs, 1972; contbr. articles to ednl. jours. Home and Office: 303 Astor Ct Villa Park IL 60181

BLANCHARD, JAMES J., Congressman; b. Detroit, Aug. 8, 1942; B.A., M.B.A., Mich. State U., Lansing; J.D., U. Minn.; m. Paula Parker; 1 son, Jay. Admitted to Mich. bar, 1968; legal aide Mich. sec. of state, 1968-69; adminstrv. asst. to atty. gen. State of Mich., 1970-71, asst. dep. atty. gen., 1971-72, asst. atty. gen., 1969-74; mem. 94th-97th congresses from 18th Mich. Dist. Named an Outstanding Young Man Am., U.S. Jaycees, 1978. Mem. Assn. Asst. Attys. Gen., State Bar Mich., Am. Bar Assn. Democrat. Club: Jaycees (Ferndale, Mich.). Office: 2453 Rayburn House Office Bldg Washington DC 20515

BLAND, E. A., moving van co. exec. Pres., chief operating officer Atlas Van Lines, Inc., Evansville, Ind. Office: Atlas Van Lines Inc 1212 St George Rd Evansville IN 47711

BLAND, MURREL WESLEY, publisher; b. Enid, Okla., June 5, 1941; s. Clyde and Tennyson Irene (Welty) B.; B.S. in Journalism, U. Kans., 1963; m. Carol Ann Wilkinson, June 9, 1962; 1 dau., Kimberly Sue. Staff, Kansas City Star, 1964-68; founder, pub. Wyandotte West, Kansas City, Kans., 1968—. Past pres. Family and Children's Service; bd. dirs. Salvation Army, Cancer Action; mem. adv. bd. Bd. Public Utilities, Area Vocat. Tech. Sch. Served in USAF, 1963-64. Recipient Disting. Service award Kansas City Area Jaycees, 1969; Community Service award Kansas City C. of C., 1981. Mem. Kans. Press Assn. (dir.), Nat. Newspaper Assn., Kansas City C. of C. (past vice-chmn.), Sigma Delta Chi. Republican. Episcopalian. Office: 7540 Leavenworth Rd PO Box 12003 Kansas City KS 66112

BLAND, ROBERT DANIEL, educator; b. Terre Haute, Ind., Aug. 23, 1937; s. William Frank and Pearl Averil (Morgan) B.; B.S., Ball State U., 1960, M.S., 1964; Ph.D., U. Minn., 1971; m. Mary Ellen Anderson, July 28, 1968; children—Cynthia, Stephanie. Coordinator gen. biol. program U. Minn., Mpls., 1970-74; chmn. dept. biology Coll. St. Thomas, St. Paul, 1974—. Mem. Minn. Acad. Sci., Am. Inst. Biol. Scis., AAUP, Phycological Soc. Am. Author: General Biology Laboratory Guide, 1973; Freshwater Biology, 1974; Dissertation Abstracts, 1971; contbr. articles to profl. jours. Home: 1639 Ridgewood Ln Saint Paul MN 55113 Office: Dept Biology Coll of St Thomas Saint Paul MN 55105

BLANDFORD, KEITH, steel co. exec.; b. East Chicago, Ind., Jan. 30, 1937; s. Alvin R. and Phyllis E. (Grossman) B.; B.S. in Chem. Engring., U. Ill., 1959; m. Carol McAdoo, Aug. 23, 1958; children—Douglas, Gregory, Jeffrey. Vice-pres. ops. planning Keystone Steel and Wire, Peoria, Ill., 1972-75, v.p. ops., 1975-77, v.p. ops. Keystone Group, 1977-79, pres. Keystone Group, 1979—. Mem. Am. Iron and Steel Inst., Wire Assn. Office: 7000 SW Adams Peoria IL 61641

BLANK, LARRY ALLEN, woodworking tool co. exec.; b. Piqua, Ohio, July 28, 1940; s. Russel Hubert and Pauline Francis (Hershey) B.; B.B.A., Ohio Univ., 1963; m. Joan Jane Borchers, May 17, 1969; children—Amanda Jennifer, Larry Aaron. Accountant Haskins & Sells, Dayton, Ohio, 1964-68; stockbroker Merrill Lynch, Dayton, 1968-73; pres. mktg. div. Shopsmith, Inc., Vandalia, Ohio, 1973—, sr. v.p. sales, 1979—, dir., 1973—; mem. bd. visitors Ohio Univ., Athens, 1980-81. Served with USAF, 1963-64. Named Marketer of Year, Dayton chpt. Am. Mktg. Assn., 1979. Office: 750 Center Dr Vandalia OH 45377

BLANK, MARJORIE KING, coll. dean; b. Kansas City, Mo., June 13, 1925; d. John Charles and Margaret Louise (Huling) King; student U. Mo., Kansas City, 1942-44; B.A., U. Mo., Columbia, 1947, M.Ed., 1951; Ed.D., U. Kans., 1978; m. Donald E. Blank, Aug. 22, 1947; children—Lawrence Dean, Douglas Eugene, Raymond Wayne. Counselor, U. Mo., Columbia, 1949-51; tchr. Kansas City (Kans.) Schs., 1956-57; tchr., counselor Kansas City (Kans.) Community Coll., 1957-65, counselor, 1966-68, dir. admissions, 1968-72, asst. dean student services, 1972-77, asso. dean student services, 1977-81, dean student services, 1981—. Chairperson career devel. com. Kansas City Union Presbytery, 1978—; scholarship chmn. Kaw Valley chpt. March of Dimes, 1979-80, mem. exec. bd., 1979-81, sec., 1981—. Mem. Nat. Assn. Student Personnel Adminstrs., Am. Personnel and Guidance Assn., Am. Coll. Personnel Assn., Nat. Vocat. Guidance Assn., Nat. Assn. Women Deans, Adminstrs. and Counselors, Am. Assn. Collegiate Registrars and Admissions Officers, Kans. Assn. Women Deans, Adminstrs. and Counselors (treas. 1979-81), Kans. Assn. Student Personnel Adminstrs. (pres. 1980-81), Kans. Assn. Collegiate Registrars and Admissions Officers, Kansas City (Kans.) Women's C. of C. (exec. bd. 1980-82), Phi Delta Kappa. Home: 8728 Mackey St Overland Park KS 66212 Office: 7250 State Ave Kansas City KS 66112

BLANK, MICHAEL KENNETH, physician; b. Cape Girardeau, Mo., Oct. 16, 1942; s. Walter E. and Dortha M. (Silsby) B.; A.B., Central Meth. U., 1964; M.D., U. Kans., 1968; m. Kathleen P. Goff, Sept. 6, 1969; children—Jennifer, Michael, Missy. Intern, St. Luke's Hosp., St. Louis, 1968-69; resident in gen. surgery St. John Mercy Med. Center, St. Louis, 1969-73; practice medicine specializing in surgery, De Soto, Mo., 1979—; chief staff Jefferson Meml. Hosp., Festus, Mo., 1979—; asst. prof. Baylor U., Waco, Tex., 1973-74. Vice pres., Dist. 73 Sch. Bd., De Soto, 1974-76, dir., 1976-80; med. adv. nursing program Jefferson Coll., 1976-78; adv. bd. Blue Cross of St. Louis County, 1978-80. Served to maj. M.C., U.S. Army, 1973-75. Diplomate Am. Bd. Surgery. Fellow A.C.S., SW Surg. Congress; mem. Jefferson County Med. Soc. (pres. 1978-79). Republican. Methodist. Club: Elks. Address: 111 Easton St De Soto MO 63020

BLANK, WALLACE JAMES, mfg. co. exec.; b. Neenah, Wis., Apr. 16, 1929; s. Julius August and Caroline Ann (Werner) B.; B.S. in Mech. Engring., U. Wis., 1952; m. Margaret Mary Schultz, June 7, 1958; Staff engr. Fairbanks Morse & Co., Beloit, Wis., 1952-59; sr. engr. Thiokol Chem. Co., 1960, N. Am. Aviation Atomics, internat. div., 1961; dir. mil. engring. FWD Corp., Clintonville, Wis., 1962-68; v.p. engring. Oshkosh Truck Corp. (Wis.), 1974—. Patentee in field. Mem. Soc. Auto Engrs., Am. Def. Preparedness Assn., Assn. U.S. Army. Roman Catholic. Home: 5352 Iahmaytah Rd Oshkosh WI 54901 Office: 2300 Oregon St Oshkosh WI 54903

BLANKENBAKER, RONALD GAIL, physician, educator; b. Rensselaer, Ind., Dec. 1, 1941; s. Lloyd L. and Lovina (Anderson) B.; B.S. in Biology, Purdue U., 1963; M.D., Ind. U., 1968, M.S. in Pharmacology, 1970. Intern, Meth. Hosp. Grad. Med. Center, Indpls., 1968-69, resident in family practice, 1969-71; med. dir. Indpls. Home for Aged, 1971-77, Am. Mid-Town Nursing Center, Indpls., 1974-77, Home Assn., Tampa, Fla., 1977-79; asst. prof. family practice Ind. U., Indpls., 1973-77, clin. prof., 1980—; prof. dept. family medicine U. S. Fla. Coll. Medicine, Tampa, 1977-79, chmn. dept., 1977-79; health commr. State of Ind. and sec. Ind. Bd. Health, Indpls., 1979—; dir. family practice edn. Meth. Hosp. Grad. Med. Center, 1971-77; family practice editor Reference and Index Services, Inc., Indpls., 1976-77, sr. editor, 1977-79; legis. lobbyist Ind. Acad. Family Physicians, 1973-77; med. adv. New Hope Found. of Am., Inc., 1974-79. Bd. dirs. Meals on Wheels, Inc., Peoples Health Center Indpls., Marion County Cancer Soc. Served to maj. USAF Res., 1971—. Decorated Meritorious Service medal; recipient Service to Mankind award Sertoma Club, 1976, Outstanding Alumnus award Mt. Ayr (Ind.) High Sch., 1976; named Sagamore of the Wabash, Gov. Ind., 1980. Diplomate Am. Bd. Family Practice. Fellow Am. Acad. Family Physicians, Am. Coll. Preventive Medicine, Soc. Prospective Medicine (v.p., pres. 1978-80, dir.); mem. AMA, Ind. State Med. Assn., Marion County Med. Soc., Ind. Acad. Family Physicians (v.p. 1977), Ind. Allied Health Assn. (pres. 1973-74), Ind. Acad. Scis., Soc. Tchrs. Family Medicine, Ind. Arthritis Found. (dir.), Ind. Lung Assn. (dir.), Assn. Am. Med. Colls., Assn. Depts. Family Medicine, Fla. Acad. Family Physicians (dir.). Republican. Office: Ind Bd Health 1330 W Michigan Indianapolis IN 46206

BLANKENBAKER, VIRGINIA MURPHY, state senator; b. Indpl., Mar. 29, 1933; d. Charles J. and Francis June (Hesler) Murphy; B.S., Purdue U., 1955; M.S., Butler U., 1979; m. Richard I. Blankenbaker, 1959; children—Susan Bauerle, Sharon Anne, David E., Betty J., James R. Tchr. home econs., Pensacola, Fla., 1955-56, Indpls., 1976—; public relations Colonial Food Stores, 1957-59; sec.-treas. Richard's Market Baskets, Inc., 1961—; mem. Ind. State Senate, 1981—. Mem. Phi Delta Kappa, Omicron Nu, Pi Beta Phi. Methodist. Office: Ind State Senate State Capitol Indianapolis IN 46204

BLANKENSHIP, CAROLE TULLETT, interior designer; b. Newark, May 4, 1944; d. Albert Robert and Marjorie (Buck) Tullett; B.F.A., Ohio State U., 1966; student Ind. U., Purdue U., 1975-76; m. G. Thomas Blankenship, Oct. 27, 1978; children—Kimberly Elaine, Kristina Michele. Interior designer Neil Furniture, Wooster, Ohio, 1966-68; cons. interior designer, Winchester, Va., also Indpls., 1968-77; pres. Caraye Interior Designs, Inc., Indpls., 1977—. Mem. AAUW (pres. Greenwood, Ind. chpt. 1973-74), Nat. Decorating Products Assn., Indpls. Mus. Art, Ohio State U. Alumni Assn., Indpls. Art League, Presbyterian. Home: 600 Valley Lane Ct Greenwood IN 46142 Office: 8212 Madison Ave Indianapolis IN 46227

BLANKENSHIP, MARSHALL LEE, dermatologist; b. Ramsey, Ill., Dec. 10, 1933; s. Merrill F. and Helen G. (Sloan) B.; B.S., U. Ill., 1956, M.D., 1958; m. Barbara K. Kanchier, June 21, 1958; children—Kathryn H., Marshall L., Jr. Intern, Ill. Central Hosp., Chgo., 1958-59; resident Northwestern U., Chgo., 1961-64; asso. in dermatology, 1963-71; practice medicine specializing in dermatology, Oak Lawn, Ill., 1964—; asst. prof. dermatology Rush Med. Coll., 1971-78, asso. prof., 1979—; lectr. dermatology Cook County Grad. Sch., 1966-79. Served with U.S. Army, 1959-61. Mem. Chgo. (treas. 1970-73, sec. 1973-76, pres. 1976), Ill. (sec. 1974-77, pres. 1977) dermatol. socs., Chgo., Ill. State med. socs., AMA, Am. Acad. Dermatology (chmn. adv. bd. council 1977-79), Noah Worchester Dermatol. Soc. Home: 1333 Hillview Rd Homewood IL 60430 Office: 4647 W 103d St Oak Lawn IL 60453

BLANKENSHIP, SAMMY DELANO, computer specialist, educator; b. Chattanooga, Mar. 25, 1936; s. William Doyle and Daisy Irene (Alford) B.; B.S., Murray State U., 1960, M.S. 1968; postgrad. (Bus. Research fellow) Ind. U., 1976-77, Miss. State U., 1978; m. Shirley Elaine Morlock, Sept. 10, 1955; children—Susan Elaine, James Kelley. Systems engr. IBM, Evansville, Ind., 1968-69; tchr. Evansville-Vanderburgh Sch. Corp., 1969-70; systems rep. Honeywell Info. Systems, Evansville, 1970: asst. prof. in bus. Ind. State U., Evansville, 1970-81; sr. applications specialist Gen. Electric Co., 1981—; info. systems cons. to bus., govt. and edn. Precinct committeeman Democratic Party, Vanderburgh County, 1978—; mem. Vanderburgh County Election Bd., 1978-79; candidate Ind. Legislature, 1972. Methodist. Club: Masons. Contbr. articles to newspapers and Midwest Bus. Adminstrn. Assn. Home: Rural Route 1 Box 351C Evansville IN 47712 Office: 1 Lexan Ln Mount Vernon IN 47620

BLANTON, VICTOR LYNN, employee compensation/benefits cons.; b. Gaffney, S.C., Feb. 6, 1941; s. Jonas Bryan and Naoma Virgie (Tipton) B.; B.S., Ind. U., 1967; M.B.A., Bowling Green State U., 1973; children—Scott Victor, Pamela Kaye, Maurice John. Employee relations specialist Marathon Oil Co., Findlay, Ohio, 1967-73; compensation and benefits cons. Findley, Davies & Co., Toledo, Ohio, 1973—; cons. in field; lectr. in field. Mem. Nat. Assn. Pension Cons. and Adminstrs., Internat. Found. Employee Benefit Plans, Internat. Assn. Bus. Communicators, Nat. Assn. Securities Dealers. Contbr. articles to profl. jours. Office: United Savings Bldg Toledo OH 43604

BLASCO, ALFRED JOSEPH, bus. and fin. cons., bank exec.; b. Kansas City, Mo., Oct. 9, 1904; s. Joseph and Mary (Bevacqua) B.; student Kansas City Sch. Accountancy, 1921-25, Am. Inst. Banking, 1926-30; Ph.D. (hon.), Avila Coll., 1969; m. Kathryn Oleno, June 28, 1926; children—Barbara (Mrs. Charles F. Mehrer III), Phyllis (Mrs. Michael R. O'Connor). From office boy to asst. controller Commerce Trust Co., Kansas City, Mo., 1921-35; controller Interstate Securities Co., Kansas City, 1935-45, v.p., 1945-53, pres., 1953—, chmn. bd., 1961-68; sr. v.p. ISC Fin. Corp., 1968-69, hon. chmn. bd., 1970-77, pres., 1979—; chmn. bd. Red Bridge Bank, 1966-72; chmn. bd. Mark Plaza State Bank, Overland Park, Kans., 1973-77; spl. lectr. consumer credit Columbia, N.Y.C., 1956, U. Kans., Lawrence, 1963-64. Mem. Fair Pub. Accomodations Com., Kansas City, Mo., 1964-68; pres. Catholic Community Library, 1955-56; ward committeeman, Kansas City, Mo., 1972-76. Pres. hon. bd. dirs. Baptist Meml. Hosp., 1970-74; chmn. bd. dirs. St. Anthony's Home, 1965-69; chmn. bd. trustees Avila Coll., 1969—. Decorated papal knight Equestrian Order Holy Sepulchre of Jerusalem, 1957, knight comdr., 1964, knight grand cross, 1966, lt. No. Lieutenancy U.S., 1970-77, vice gov. gen., 1977—; named Bus. Man of Year, State of Mo., 1957; named Man of the Year, City of Hope, 1973; recipient Community Service award Rockne Club of Notre Dame, 1959, Brotherhood award NCCJ, 1979, Wisdom award of honor, 1979. Mem. Soc. St. Vincent de Paul (pres. 1959-67), Am. Indsl. Bankers Assn. (nat. pres. 1956-57), Am. Inst. Banking (pres. Kansas City chpt. 1932-33), Bank Auditors and Controllers Assn., Fin. Execs. Inst. Am. (pres. Kansas City chpt. 1928-29), Nat. Assn. Accountants, Kansas City C. of C. Rotarian. Clubs: Kansas City, Hillcrest Country, Serra (pres. 1959-60). Contbr. articles to profl. jours. Home: 11705 Central St Kansas City MO 64114 Office: 8080 Ward Pkwy Kansas City MO 64114

BLASER, PEG ROOS, state ofcl.; b. Ft. Dodge, Iowa, Jan. 19, 1925; d. Carlisle K. and Louise Anna (Klinger) Roos; B.S. in Sociology, Northwestern U., 1945; m. William L. Blaser, June 27, 1945; children—Glenn, Steven, Joan. Owner, Art Mart, Park Forest, Ill., 1952-63; research asso., acting exec. dir. Planning Consortium for Children's Services, 1976-77; dir. bds. and commns., office of gov. of Ill., 1977-78; spl. asst. on women to gov. of Ill., Springfield, 1978-79; dir. Ill. Dept. on Aging, Springfield, 1979—. Village trustee Park Forest, 1968-69; chmn. Ill. ERA Coalition, 1974-76; legis. chmn. Capital City Republican Women's Club. Mem. LWV (lobbyist to Ill. Gen. Assembly 1973-76, mem. state bd. Ill.). Unitarian. Home: 24 Bay Ridge St Springfield IL 62707 Office: Dept on Aging 421 E Capitol Ave Springfield IL 62706

BLATT, MORTON BERNARD, med. illustrator; b. Chgo., Jan. 9, 1923: s. Arthur E. and Hazel B.; student Central YMCA Coll., 1940-42, U. Ill., 1943-46. Tchr., Ray-Vogue Art Schs., Chgo., 1946-51; med. illustrator VA Center, Wood, Wis., 1951-57, Swedish Covenant Hosp., Chgo., 1957-76; med. illustrator Laidlaw Bros., Pubs., River Forest, Ill., 1956-59, cons., artist health textbooks, 1956-59; illustrator health and body charts Standard Edn. Soc., Chgo., 1960; art editor Covenant Home Altar. Served with USAAF, 1943-44. Mem. Art Inst. Chgo., Am.-Scandinavian Found., Asso. Ch. Press, Evangelical Press Assn. Clubs: Chicago Press, Saugatuck Yacht. Illustrator: Atlas and Demonstration Technique of the Central Nervous System, 1961, also numerous med. jours.; illustrator, designer numerous books, record jackets and covenant Hymnal. Art editor Covenant Companion, 1958—. Address: 100 Park St Saugatuck MI 49453

BLATTNER, JOHN FRANCIS, clin. therapist; b. Chgo., Aug. 16, 1948; s. Oscar J. and Marian C. Blattner; B.A., Quincy Coll., 1970; M.A., Ill. State U., Bloomington, 1975; m. Kathy M. Smialek, June 12, 1976; children—Brian, William. Therapist, Leyden Family Service and Mental Health Center, Franklin Park, Ill., 1975-77; therapist alcohol program and edn. center Loretto Hosp., Chgo., 1977-81; coordinator outpatient alcohol center The Roth Group, Northbrook, Ill., 1978-81; cons. Catholic Charities, 1979-81. Mem. subarea council Suburban Health Systems Agy., 1980-81; v.p. Ill. Alcoholism Certification Bd., 1981-82. Served with U.S. Army, 1971-73. Mem. Am. Psychol. Assn., Ill. Psychol. Assn., Nat. Assn. Alcoholism Counselors, Assn. Labor-Mgmt. Adminstrs. and Cons. on Alcoholism (bd. dirs. 1980-82), Ill. Alcoholism Counselors Alliance. Home: 1105 S Wesley Ave Oak Park IL 60304 Office: 500 Skokie Blvd Suite 233 Northbrook IL 60062

BLAUSTEIN, HOWARD YALE, ins. co. exec., painter; b. Hazelton, Pa., May 29, 1930; s. Alan Jacob and Ethel (Gauz) B.; student Syracuse U., 1951; children—Joyce Nancy, Brian. Life ins. agt. Conn. Mut., Utica, N.Y., 1955-59; dist. mgr. Mass. Mut., Utica, 1959-65; gen. agt. Variable Life Ins. Co., Miami, Fla., 1965-67; v.p., also dir. of sales Variable Annuity Mktg. Co., Chgo., 1967-76; pres. Intangible Marketing, Inc., gen. operating partner Public Employees Adminstrn. and Computer Enterprises; sec., dir. Fin. System, Inc.; dir. Polo Stores Inc.; one-man shows paintings, Chgo. galleries, 1974, 75. Chmn. United Jewish Appeal, 1964; trustee Mus. Fine Arts. Served with U.S. Army, 1952-55. Recipient Mass. Mut. Man of the Year award, 1961-64, Variable Annuity Life Ins. Co. Glen Holden Mgmt. award, 1968. Mem. Million Dollar Round Table (life), Chgo. Life Underwriters Assn., Nat. Assn. of Securities Dealers, Chgo. Assn. of Commerce and Industry. Democrat. Jewish (dir. temple). Clubs: Whitehall, Masons, K.P., B'nai B'rith, Covenant; Ravinia Country; Lake Barrington Shores Golf. Home: 1100 Lake Shore Dr Chicago IL 60611 Office: 180 N LaSalle St Chicago IL 60601

BLAZER, SONDRA KAY GORDON, family therapist, writer; b. Middletown, Ohio, June 2, 1937; d. John Charles and Ora Lillie (Stewart) Gordon; A.A. magna cum laude, U. Cin., 1975; m. Ralph J. Bays, Feb. 17, 1956 (dec. 1969); children—Sherry Kay, Cynthia Rae, Robert Jay. Reporter, ch. editor Middletown Jour., 1955-56; mng. editor Warren County Reporter, Lebanon, Ohio, 1966-72; corr. Franklin (Ohio) Chronicle, 1974-78; free lance journalist, 1973—family therapist Mary Haven Youth Center, Lebanon, Ohio, 1981—. Mem. Ohio Gov.'s Traffic Safety Com., 1972—; mem. Warren County Bd. Mental Health and Retardation, 1972-80, chmn., 1974-80; chmn. dist. one planning council Ohio Dept. Mental Health and Mental Retardation; mem. exec. bd. Ohio Community Mental Health Assn., 1979-80; mem. citizens adv. com. Lebanon Correctional Instn., Lebanon, 1971—; sec. Warren County Safety Council, 1972—; mem. citizens com. Ohio Dept. Rehab. and Corrections; bd. dirs. Warren County com. Ohio Easter Seal Soc. for Crippled Children and Adults, 1967—; mem. Warren County Bd. Elections, 1974-80, Warren Profl. Health Adv. Com.; former bd. dirs. Warren United Appeal; asst. to organizer Warren County Disaster Services, 1975; former sec. Warren County Disaster Services Orgn.; sec., Warren County Democratic Women's Club, 1963-67, Warren County Dem. Central and Exec. Com., 1965-80; precinct committeeman Dem. party, 1964-80; mem. land use subcom. Ohio-Ky.-Ind. Council Govts., 1975—; sec. Warren County Interagy. Council, editor newsletter; Sunday sch. tchr. Methodist Ch., 1963-72. Winner 1st pl. Beta Sigma Phi internat. short story contest, 1964, Ohio Dept. Hwy. Safety Media contest, 1970. Mem. Ohio Corrections and Ct. Assn., Am. Police and Fire Reporters Assn., Nat. Council Crime and Delinquency, Internat. Platform Assn., Ohio Assn. Bds. County Visitors (pres. 1981), Phi Kappa Epsilon, Alpha Sigma Lambda. Address: 3730 Beatrice Dr Franklin OH 45005

BLEIER, INGE J., nurse, educator; b. Darmstadt, Germany, Sept. 19, 1925; came to U.S., 1946, naturalized, 1950; d. Julius and Clara (Neu) Joseph; R.N., Michael Reese Hosp. Sch. Nursing, Chgo., 1950; B.S., U. Ill., 1953; M.S., Northwestern U., 1963; m. Frank Bleier, Feb. 25, 1955; 1 dau., Julia Claire. Head nurse Weiss Meml. Hosp., Chgo., 1953-56; obstetrical supr. Louis A. Weiss Hosp., Chgo., 1956-62; instr. maternity nursing Michael Reese Hosp., Chgo., 1964-66; instr. maternity nursing U. Ill., 1966-69; asst. prof. nursing obstetrics DePaul U., 1972-76; instr. expectant parents classes Louis A. Weiss Hosp., Chgo., 1956-62. Recipient Am. Jour. Nursing Mary Roberts scholarship, 1962. Mem. Am. Nurses Assn., Am. Nurses Assn. of Am. Coll. Obstetricians and Gynecologists, German Med. Soc. Club: Northwestern Chgo. Author: Maternity Nursing for the Practical Nurse, 1960, 4th edit., 1979; Workbook of Bedside Maternity Nursing, 3d edit., 1981; Bedside Maternity Nursing, 1979. Address: 3522 Pine Grove Chicago IL 60657

BLESCH, LARRY JOE, real estate exec.; b. Evansville, Ind., Nov. 3, 1944; s. Adolph Henry and Katherine Alma Jean (Weyer) B.; student pub. schs., Evansville; m. Kathy Suzann McBride, Aug. 17, 1974. With Ind. Bell Telephone Co., Evansville, 1964-70; owner Larry's Auto Sales, Evansville, 1970-73; carpenter, Evansville, 1971-73; mgr. Goff Realty, Inc., Evansville, 1973-74; sales asso., sales mgr. Midwest Realty, Evansville, 1974-78; pres. Blesch Realty, Inc., Evansville, 1978—. Pres., Hope of Evansville, Inc., 1977-78. Served with Army N.G., 1962. Mem. Nat. Assn. Ind. Fee Appraisers (v.p. 1979-80), Nat. Assn. Realtors, Ind. Assn. Realtors, Evansville Assn. Realtors, Farm and Land Inst., Womens Council Realtors, Nat. Auctioneers Assn., Ind. Auctioneers Assn., Nat. Assn. Review Appraisers. Republican. Baptist. Clubs: Osseo Haymakers Assn., Eagles, Civitan. Home: 3009 Oak Hill Rd Evansville IN 47711 Office: 3009 Oak Hill Rd Evansville IN 47711

BLETTNER, EDWARD FREDERICK, banker; b. Chgo., Dec. 9, 1907; s. Edward Frederick and Mary (Klaner) B.; A.B., Harvard U., 1928, M.B.A., 1930; J.D., John Marshall Law Sch., 1935; m. Margaret Maw, Mar. 19, 1943; children—Margaret Jean (Mrs. Christopher Angell), Elizabeth Mary. With First Nat. Bank of Chgo., 1930-73, exec. v.p., 1962-67, pres., 1968-69, vice chmn. bd., 1969-73, hon. dir., 1973-78; ret., 1973; dir. Pabst Brewing Co. Life mem. bd. dirs. Lyric Opera of Chgo.; trustee Newberry Library, Chgo.; life trustee Rush-Presbyn.-St. Lukes Med. Center, Chgo.; governing mem. Orchestral Assn. Chgo.; governing life mem. Art Inst. of Chgo. Served from capt. to lt. col., AUS, 1942-45. Congregationalist. Clubs:

Chicago, Commercial, Mid-Day (Chgo.); Indian Hill (Winnetka); Old Elm (Lake Forest, Ill.). Home: 573 Sheridan Rd Winnetka IL 60093

BLETZACKER, RICHARD WELCH, civil engr.; b. Lancaster, Ohio, Jan. 24, 1926; s. Clarence A. and Frances K. (Welch) B.; student Central Mich. Coll., 1944-45, U. Mich., 1945-46; B. Civil Engring., Ohio State U., 1949, M.Sc., 1961; m. Maxine T. Schorr, June 30, 1949; children—Karl R., Joan M. Civil engr. Ohio Dept. Hwys., Columbus and Marietta, 1949-52; sales engr. J.T. Edwards Co., Columbus, 1954-57; research asso. Ohio State U., Columbus, 1957-61, asst. prof., 1961-64, asso. prof. civil engring., 1964-80, dir. bldg. research lab., 1958-80, prof. emeritus, 1980—; pres. Richard W. Bletzacker & Assos., Inc., bldg. system and code cons.'s, Upper Arlington, Ohio, 1980—; cons. indsl. firms, trade assns. and govt. agencies. Exec. com. mem. Columbus and Franklin County CD, 1964-80. Served with USNR, 1944-46, 52-54. Mem. ASCE (Simpson award 1951), Am. Concrete Inst., ASTM (merit award 1977), Nat. Fire Protection Assn., Sigma Xi. Contbr. research articles to profl. jours. Home and Office: 4160 Waddington Rd Upper Arlington OH 43220

BLEWITT, RICHARD FRANCIS, chem. co. exec.; b. Scranton, Pa., Mar. 26, 1947; s. Frank Joseph and Margaret (Kearney) B.; B.S. in Govt. and Politics, U. Md., 1973; M.B.A., U. Chgo., 1981; m. Dec. 7, 1968; children—Mar Lynn and Carrie Ann (twins). Staff writer Scranton Times-Sunday Times, 1966-68; press relations asst. Am. Trucking Assns., Washington, 1970-72; mgr. press relations Mfg. Chemists Assn., Washington, 1972-75; mgr. public relations FMC Corp. Chem. Group, Phila., 1975-78; v.p. public affairs Velsicol Chem. Corp., Chgo., 1978—; pres. Blewitt & Cefalo, Inc., advt./public relations agy., Scranton, Pa., 1981—. Served with USN, 1968-70. Mem. Profl. News Media Assn. Northeastern Pa. (founder, charter pres.), Public Relations Soc. Am., Chgo. Fgn. Relations Council (com. on fgn. affairs), Pennsylvania Soc. Democrat. Roman Catholic. Club: Chgo. Press. Contbg. editor World Book Ency., 1973—. Home: 9459 Drake Ave Evanston IL 60203 Office: 341 E Ohio St Chicago IL 60611

BLINCI, ARTHUR FRANK, ch. orgn. exec.; b. Highland Park, Mich., Feb. 6, 1955; s. Frank Arthur and Cirila Ethel (Sison) B.; B.S. in Bus. Adminstrn., Andrews U., 1977; m. Sharon Janise Hill, Sept. 5, 1976. Bus. intern Mich. Conf. Seventh-day Adventists, Lansing, 1977-78, moving coordinator, 1978, employee services mgr., 1978-81, dir. ops., transport div., 1978—, asst. treas., 1982—. Republican. Seventh-day Adventist. Home: 5525 E Saginaw Hwy Grand Ledge MI 48837 Office: PO Box 19009 Lansing MI 48901

BLISS, CHARLES MELBOURNE, banker; b. Evanston, Ill., Oct. 9, 1921; s. Charles H. and Hazel (Whitmore) B.; A.B. magna cum laude, Harvard, 1943, student Bus. Sch., 1942-43; M.B.A. with distinction, Northwestern U., 1947; m. Margaret Soule, Jan. 1, 1943; children—Charles Melbourne, Marian Bliss White, Emily Bliss Crawford. With Harris Trust & Savs. Bank, Chgo., 1944—, pres., dir., 1976—, chief exec. officer, 1977—, chmn. bd., 1980—; dir. G.D. Searle & Co., Kellogg Co. Trustee Alonzo Mather Found.; bd. dirs. Children's Meml. Hosp.; treas. Chgo. Crusade of Mercy; trustee Chgo. Community Trust, Northwestern U.; bd. dirs. Protestant Found. of Greater Chgo. Served with AUS, 1943. Mem. Assn. Res. City Bankers, Phi Beta Kappa, Beta Gamma Sigma. Episcopalian. Clubs: Casino, Chgo., Comml., Glen View; Metropolitan (Washington). Office: 111 W Monroe St Chicago IL 60603

BLISS, DWIGHT LEWIS, automotive engr.; b. Wellsboro, Pa., Dec. 18, 1946; s. Hugh Dwight and Mary A. (Erway) B.; student Mansfield State Coll., 1965-66; B.M.E., Gen. Motors Inst., 1970. With Chevrolet Motor div. Gen. Motors Corp., Warren, Mich., 1970—, design engr., 1974-76, product planner, 1976-78, engring. contact with Isuzu, Japan, 1978-79, supr. truck systems group, 1979-80, asst. staff engr. driveline dept., 1980—. Served with USAF, 1971. Mem. Soc. Automotive Engrs. Republican. Baptist. Clubs: Racquet, Ski, Cross Country Motorcycle, Environ. Protection. Author: Emission Test Procedure, 1970. Home: 1645 Lakeville Rd Oxford MI 48051 Office: 30003 Van Dyke St Warren MI 48092

BLIXT, ROBERT EDMUND, investment adminstr., lawyer; b. Worthington, Minn., July 9, 1927; s. Edmund Loren and Evelyn (Liljegren) B.; A.A., Worthington Jr. Coll., 1947; B.A. magna cum laude, St. Olaf Coll., 1949, M.S., U. Colo., 1951, J.D., 1953; m. Mary Ellen Cooke, Aug. 3, 1951 (div. Mar. 1976); children—Jerold Robert, Loren Henry, Kathy Ellen (dec.), Kristin Mary, Lisa Jean. Admitted to Minn. bar, 1955; instr. U. Colo., 1950-53; securities analyst, Northwestern Nat. Bank, Mpls., 1953-56; investment counsel, bd. regents U. Minn., 1957-60; exec. sec. Minn. Bd. of Investment, St. Paul, 1960-78; with Dean Witter Reynolds and M.H. Novick and Co., Inc., Mpls., 1978-79; pvt. practice legal and investment counseling, Worthington, Minn., 1979—. Trustee, Baptist Hosp. Fund, 1960—, treas., 1970-78. Mem. Twin Cities Soc. Security Analysts (pres. 1968-69), Inst. Chartered Fin. Analysts (v.p. 1974-75, pres. 1975-76, trustee 1972-78), Financial Analysts Fedn. (dir. 1970-72, 75-76). Home and Office: 406 Olander St Worthington MN 56187

BLIZMAN, PAUL J., lawyer social worker; b. Wyandotte, Mich., June 4, 1940; s. Paul J. and Olga G. (Rudenko) B.; student U. Mich., 1958-62; A.B., Wayne State U., 1966, M.S.W., 1969; J.D., Detroit Coll. Law, 1980; m. Leah Snyder, Sept. 3, 1967; 1 dau., Alexis. Counselor, Reception Center W.J. Maxey Sch., Whitmore Lake, Mich., 1969-71, dir., 1972-74, social work supr., 1971-72; licensing cons. Mich. Dept. Social Services, 1974-78; clin. social worker Health Care Inst., Detroit, 1979-80, Detroit Receiving Hosp., Univ. Health Center, 1980—; pvt. practice social work, Birmingham, Mich., 1975—; field instr. social work Wayne State U., 1979—. Bd. dirs. Youth Living Centers, Inc., Wayne, Mich. Mem. Nat. Assn. Social Workers, Am. Bar Assn., Mich. State Bar, Detroit Bar Assn., Oakland County Bar Assn., Am. Trial Lawyers Assn., Delta Theta Phi. Home: 28700 Herndonwood Dr Farmington Hills MI 48018 Office: 24901 Northwestern Hwy Suite 402 Southfield MI 48075

BLOCH, BARRY STEVEN, lawyer, paper products co. exec.; b. St. Louis, Mar. 23, 1948; s. Gustav and Mildred (Jaffe) B.; B.S. in Bus. Adminstrn., Drake U., 1970; J.D., Northwestern U., 1974; m. Denise Zabrack, Aug. 27, 1972. Tax atty. Jewel Companies, Inc., Chgo., 1974-75; atty. IRS, 1975-76; with Kimberly Clark, Neenah, Wis., 1976—, staff v.p., 1980—. Served with USAR, 1970. Mem. Am. Bar Assn., Ill. Bar Assn., Nebr. Bar Assn., Beta Gamma Sigma. Office: N Lake St Neenah WI 54956

BLOCH, IVAN SOL, realtor; b. Detroit, Nov. 16, 1940; s. Howard and Pauline Betty (Davis) B.; student U. Miami (Fla.), 1958-59, Oakland Community Coll., 1966-68; m. Linda Ehrlich, Oct. 14, 1963; children—Brian, Amy. Partner, Bloch Bros. Corp., land devel., Waterford, Mich., 1962-66; pres. Brian Realty, Birmingham, Mich., 1966—, Waterford Mortgage Co., Birmingham, 1968—, Uniprop/Mich. Mgmt. Co., Birmingham, 1969—. Co-chmn. finance Levin for Gov., 1970, 74, Kelly for Senate, 1972; mem. central finance com. Mich. Democratic party, 1973—; mem. Dem. Nat. Finance Com.; mem. Dem. 500 Club; co-treas. Kennedy for Pres. Com.; co-producer N.Y. Theatre Tintypes. Hon. mem. Boys Town; Antoinette Perry award nominee for best mus. producer, 1980-81. Mem. Nat. Assn. Real Estate Brokers, Real Estate Security and Syndication Inst. Clubs: Detroit Econ., Israel Prime Ministers, Detroit Founders Soc. and Standard, B'nai B'rith (nat. humanitarian award com. 1971-72). Home: 1440 Old Salem Ct Birmingham MI 48009 Office: 480 Pierce St Birmingham MI 48011

BLOCH, THOMAS MORTON, tax preparation co. exec.; b. Kansas City, Mo., Mar. 14, 1954; s. Henry and Marion (Helzberg) B.; B.A. in Econs., Claremont (Calif.) Men's Coll., 1976. With H & R Block, 1976—, pres. tax ops., Kansas City, Mo., 1980—. Office: 4410 Main St Kansas City MO 64111

BLOCH, TIMOTHY PARKER, Realtor; b. Cleve., Apr. 2, 1954; s. Joseph C. and Patricia M. Bloch; student Grand Rapids Jr. Coll., 1973-74, Akron U., 1976-78; grad. Realtors Inst., 1978; m. Phyllis A. Meenas, Mar. 8, 1974; 1 son, Jason. Instr. real estate U. Akron (Ohio), 1979, Wayne Coll., Orrville, Ohio, 1979; mgr., broker Bruce Block Realtors, Medina, Ohio, 1980—. Lic. realtor, Mich., Ohio. Mem. Nat. Assn. Realtors, Ohio Assn. Realtors, Medina County Bd. Realtors, Real Estate Trainers Assn. (charter), Am. Soc. for Tng. and Devel., Medina Area C. of C., Medina Jaycees (dir. 1976-78, Man of Yr. award 1976). Home: 616 E Union St Medina OH 44256 Office: 704 N Court St Medina OH 44256

BLOCHOWSKI, THOMAS KENNETH, mfg. engr.; b. Toledo, Oct. 27, 1942; s. Edmund Eugene and Helen Alice (Sobieralski) B.; Asso. Mfg. Tech., U. Toledo, 1965; m. Judith Ann Gasiorowski, Aug. 24, 1963; children—Kenneth Robert, Cynthia Ann, Kevin Michael. Sales mgr. Block Indsl. Service, Toledo, 1964-69; chief tool engr. Mather Co., Milan, Mich., 1969-71; mfg. engr. machine shop M-S/Tillotson Co., Toledo, 1971-74; sr. lead process engr. Harley Davidson Motor Co., Milw., 1974-75; mfg. engr. corp. staff Prestolite Co., Toledo, 1975-81; pres. Bisel Mfg. Inc., screw machine plant, Toledo, 1981—; mem. faculty Monroe County (Mich.) Community Coll. Registered profl. mfg. engr., Calif. Mem. Soc. Mfg. Engrs. (sr. mem., chmn. Toledo chpt. 1971-72), St. Francis De Sales Alumni Assn., Toledo Jr. C. of C. Roman Catholic. Club: Tamaron Country. Home: 6014 Tetherwood Dr Toledo OH 43613 Office: 1121 Hazelwood St Toledo OH 43605

BLOCK, PAUL, JR., newspaper pub., chemist; b. N.Y.C., May 11, 1911; s. Paul and Dina (Wallach) B.; grad. Hotchkiss Sch., Lakeville, Conn., 1929; A.B. Yale U., 1933; postgrad. Columbia U., 1933-34, Ph.D., 1943; postgrad. Harvard U., 1934-35; m. Eleana Barnes Conley, 1940 (div. 1947); 1 son, Cyrus P.; m. 2d, Marjorie McNab Main, May 26, 1948 (dec. Sept. 1960); children—Allan James, John Robinson; m. 3d, Mary Gall Petok, 1965; 3 children by previous marriage. Reporter Toledo, Blade, 1935, became polit. writer, 1938, asst. editor, 1941, co-pub., 1942; co-pub. Pitts. Post Gazette, 1944—; fellow Mellon Inst. Indsl. Research, Pitts., 1943-44, hon. fellow dept. pharmacology Yale U., 1948-49. Chmn., Toledo Devel. Com., 1975-79; chmn. bd. trustees Med. Coll. Ohio, Toledo, 1964-70; mem. U.S. Metric Bd., 1978-80. Mem. Am. Chem. Soc., Am. Soc. Newspaper Editors, Internat. Press Inst. (chmn. Am. com. 1958-61), Sigma Xi. Home: 4059 River Rd Toledo OH 43614 Office: Toledo Blade 541 Superior St Toledo OH 43660*

BLOCKER, CECIL ARLO, JR., mfg. co. exec.; b. Columbus, Ohio, Feb. 15, 1931; s. Cecil Arlo and Elizabeth Agusta (Davis) B.; B.Mining Engring., B.Petroleum Engring., Ohio State U., 1956, M.B.A., 1964; M.Bus.Mgmt., Frostburg State Coll., 1978; m. Virginia Travis Wakeman, Sept. 2, 1978; children by previous marriage—Debra, Victoria, Craig, Jacqueline. Refinery lab head, petroleum engr. Standard Oil of N.J., Sumatra, Indonesia, 1958-63; mgr. quality assurance Cummins Engine Co., Columbus, Ind., 1965-68; dir. quality assurance Levinson-Hayes, Pitts., 1968-70; plant mgr. Levinson-Levco, Pitts., 1970-73; dir. quality assurance Pullman Trailmobile, Chgo., 1973-75; dir. quality control Pullman-Standard, Chgo., 1975-76; operations mgr., prodn. control mgr., quality control mgr. Frick Co., Waynesboro, Pa., 1976-78; dir. ops. Frick Forest Products, Waynesboro, Pa., 1978; dir., v.p. quality assurance Campbell-Hausfeld Group of Scott Fetzer, Harrison, Ohio, 1978—; cons. in field. Served with USAF, 1956-58. Registered profl. engr., Ohio. Mem. Am. Soc. Quality Control (Cin. chmn. 1979-81, Pitts. chmn. 1972, mem. Chgo. bd. 1974-75. Republican. Unitarian. Club: Elks. Home: 6245 Twinwillow Ln Cincinnati OH 45239 Office: 100 Production Dr Harrison OH 45030

BLODGETT, JOHN WOOD, former lumber exec.; b. Grand Rapids, Mich., May 24, 1901; s. John Wood and Minnie (Cumnock) B.; A.B., Harvard, 1923; m. Sarah Reed Gallagher, Sept. 28, 1939 (div. Dec. 1963); children—Julia Reed (Mrs. John R. Curtis, Jr.), Katherine Blodgett Winter, Sarah Wood (Mrs. Prescott Nelson Dunbar); m. 2d, Edith Irwin Ferris, June 21, 1967. Dir. U.S. Nat. Bank, 1929-52; chmn. Blodgett Co., Ltd., 1932-37; pres. Mich.-Calif. Lumber Co., Camino, Calif., 1936-65; pres. Consol. Timber Co., Portland, Oreg., 1934-49; chmn. Wright-Blodgett Co., Ltd., Grand Rapids, Mich., 1936-47; pres. Western Mgmt. Co., Grand Rapids, 1937-55; sec., mem. bd. mgrs. Hill-Davis Lumber Co., Arcata, Calif., 1937-58; dir. Arcata Redwood Co., 1947-67, sec., 1959-66; dir. Arcata Nat. Corp., 1967-68, Booth-Kelly Lumber Co., 1941-59. Trustee, Blodgett Meml. Hosp., Grand Rapids, 1941—; mem. overseer com. to visit Harvard Library, 1972—, to visit Harvard dept. athletics, 1973—; mem. com. on univ. resources Harvard Coll. Bd. Overseers, 1980—; adv. com. Harvard Fund Council, 1952-55; mem. overseers com. to visit Harvard Forest, 1949-62. Mem. U.S. Naval Inst., USN League, Am. Ordnance Assn., S.A.R. Mason. Clubs: River, Harvard (N.Y.C.); Bohemian (San Francisco); Chicago, Racquet (Chgo.); Kent Country, University, Peninsular (Grand Rapids); University (Portland, Oreg.). Home: 250 Plymouth Rd SE Grand Rapids MI 49506 Office: Peoples Bldg Grand Rapids MI 49503

BLODGETT, VIRGINIA JUNE BALLARD (MRS. RALPH WESLEY BLODGETT), ednl. adminstr.; b. Detroit; d. William King and Marie (Crossley) Ballard; A.B., Asbury Coll., 1935; M.S., Butler U., 1962; postgrad. U. Louisville, Ind. State U., Ball State U., Ohio State U., San Francisco State U.; Ph.D. (hon.), Colo. State Christian Coll.; m. Ralph Wesley Blodgett, Sept. 25, 1935; children—Vivian Sue Shields, Rebecca June Downing, Judith Elaine (Mrs. David Purvis). Tchr. Dependent Schs., Europe, 1951-54, English various high schs., Ind., Va., Fla., 1942—, chmn. English dept. Woodview Sch., Indpls., 1961—, dean girls, 1964—; instr. evening div. Ind. Central Coll., Indpls., 1964-69, adult counselor, 1965—. Active various community drives. Gen. Electric Co. fellow, 1967. Mem. Am., Ind. (sec. 1969) assns. women deans and counselors, NEA, Ind. State Tchrs. Assn., Warren Twp. Classroom Tchrs., Central Ind., Ind. personnel and guidance assns., Alpha Delta Kappa. Methodist (tchr. ch. schs. 1935—). Office: 901 N Post Rd Indianapolis IN 46219

BLOEMER, JOHN WILLIAM, mech. engr.; b. Indpls., June 5, 1935; s. Frank William and Bonnie Grace (Smith) B.; B.S. in Mech. Engring., Purdue U., 1957; M.S. in Mech. Engring., Ohio State U., 1963: M.S. in Mgmt., Case Western Res. U., 1971; m. Sandra A. Updike, Sept. 1, 1956; children—Sherrie, Jennifer, John, Joseph, Kristen. Research engr. Battelle Meml. Inst., Columbus, Ohio, 1957-65; prin. engr. Eaton Corp., Willoughby Hills, Ohio, 1965—. Served with C.E., U.S. Army, 1960. Registered profl. engr., Ohio. Mem. ASME, Inst. Noise Control Engrs. Mem. Church of Christ. Home: 8217 Yorkshire Dr Mentor OH 44060 Office: Eaton Corp 32500 Chardon Rd Willoughby Hills OH 44094

BLOMGREN, HARRY LEROY, advt. agy. exec.; b. Waukegan, Ill., May 7, 1938; s. Robert Leroy and Fay Elizabeth (Rogers) B.; B.A., Beloit Coll., 1960; div.; children—Jeffrey R., Nicole L. Account coordinator Cramer-Krasselt Co., Milw., 1967-69, account exec., 1969-74, v.p., account supr., 1974—. Newsletter editor Centurion's of St. Joseph's Hosp., 1972-74. Served with USNR, 1960-66. Mem. Milw. Advt. Club (pres. 1976-77), Am. Advt. Fedn. (treas. 8th dist. 1980-81). Republican. Presbyterian. Office: 733 N Van Buren St Milwaukee WI 53202

BLOMGREN, HOLTEN EUGENE, assn. exec.; b. Mpls., Mar. 22, 1916; s. Henning Alfred and Jean (Holton) B.; B.A., U. Minn., 1938; M.B.A., Harvard U., 1940; M.A., George Washington U., 1965; grad. Army Command and Gen. Staff Coll., 1956, Army War Coll., 1963; m. Elouise Breckenridge, Nov. 14, 1942; children—Peter Frederick, Donna Lynne (Mrs. Aubrey S. Garrison), Philip Michael, Diane Elizabeth. Joined U.S. Army, advanced through grades to col., 1971; faculty Adj. Gen. Sch., 1942-47; gen. staff Hdqrs. Europe, 1948-51; faculty Army Fin. Sch., 1952-55; comdt., 1967-71; gen. staff Army Hdqrs., Washington, 1956-60, 63-65, Vietnam, 1965-66, ret., 1971; chief exec. Ind. Manufactured Housing Assn., Indpls., 1971-80, pres., Washington, 1980—; exec. dir. Nat. Manufactures Housing Fedn., Washington, 1977-79; fin. advisor Minister Def. Thailand, 1960-62; zoning cons. County Plan Commns. State Ind.; registered lobbyist U.S. Congress; govtl. affairs rep. manufactured housing industry. Decorated Legion Merit with oak leaf cluster, Air medal, Bronze Star medal. Named Sagamore of Wabash, Legion of Hoosier Heroes. Mem. Ret. Officers Assn., Harvard Alumni Assn., Chi Psi. Club: Harvard (Washington). Editor, pub. nat. distributed newsletter; editorial writer nat. trade mag. for manufactured housing industry. Office: 1700 Pennsylvania Ave NW Suite 745 Washington DC 20006

BLOMQUIST, ROGER VINCENT, environ. engring. co. exec.; b. Iron Mountain, Mich., Feb. 11, 1944; s. William Thure and Ellen Dagmar (Johnson) B.; B.S. with honors, Mich. State U., 1966; Ph.D., U. Wis., 1971; exec. devel. program Cornell U., 1976; m. Patricia Ann Beaty, Sept. 6, 1969; children—Jason, Matthew. Agronomist, Internat. Minerals and Chem. Co., Libertyville, Ill., 1966; research asso. U. Wis., Madison, 1966-70; postdoctoral research fellow U. Guelph, Ont., Can., 1971; v.p., treas., dir. Nat. Biocentric Inc., St. Paul, 1971-79; br. mgr. Environ. Research Group, St. Paul, 1979—; mem. adv. com. Rice Creek Watershed Dist.; mem. Ramsey County Engring. and Environ. Adv. Com. Precinct vice chmn. Democratic Farm Labor party, 1976-78, del., dist. conv., 1972, 74, 76, del. county conv., 1972; mem. New Brighton City Council, 1978-81, acting mayor, 1978-81, mem. Park Bd., 1977-79. Bush Found. fellow, 1976; Wis. Alumni Research Found. fellow, 1967-70; Louis Ware scholar, 1966; 4-H scholar, 1962-66. Mem. Nat., Minn. assns. environ. profls., Water Pollution Control Fedn., Air Pollution Control Assn., Izaak Walton League, Am. Soc. Agronomy, Sales and Mktg. Execs., New Brighton Jaycees (v.p. 1973), Sigma Xi, Alpha Zeta. Lutheran. Home: 2023 Pleasant View Dr New Brighton MN 55112 Office: 4663 Chatsworth St Saint Paul MN 55112

BLOOD, GORDON WILLIAM, speech and lang. pathologist; b. Jamestown, N.Y., Aug. 25, 1951; s. Gordon Patrick and Cathleen (Donovan) B.; B.S., SUNY, Buffalo, 1974; M.A. (U.S. Office of Edn. grantee 1975-76), Bowling Green State U., 1976, Ph.D. (teaching fellow 1977-78), 1978; m. Ingrid Maria Unczowsky, Dec. 27, 1975. Dir., Cleft Palate Rehab. Center, Toledo, 1975-77; laryngectomy therapist Mercy Hosp., Toledo, 1977-78; dir. Sandusky (Ohio) Speech and Hearing Clinic, 1977-78, Easter Seals Speech and Hearing Clinic, Napoleon, Ohio, 1977-78; asst. prof. communication disorders Radford (Va.) U., 1978-81; asst. prof. communication disorders Miami U., Oxford, Ohio, 1981—; cons. in field. Recipient Betty Gallagher award as outstanding clinician, 1974; Rotary scholar, W. Africa, 1973; Lilly fellow, 1981-82; lic. speech and hearing tchr., N.Y.; lic. speech and hearing pathologist, Ohio. Mem. Am. Speech and Hearing Assn. (lic. speech and lang. pathologist), Ohio Speech and Hearing. Assn., Council for Exceptional Children. Republican. Roman Catholic. Contbr. articles to profl. jours. Office: Communication and Theatre Miami U Oxford OH 45056

BLOOM, JAMES EDWARD, mgmt. cons.; b. Milw., Aug. 24, 1941; s. Edward Harry and Clarina Louise (Hoppe) B.; B.B.A. with honors, Concordia Coll. Bus., 1968; A.A. with honors, Milw. Area Tech. Coll., 1964; cert. Columbia Hosp. Sch. Radiologic Tech., 1963; postgrad. in mgmt. scis. Marquette U., 1969-72. Radiologic technologist Columbia Hosp., Milw., 1963-69; asst. adminstr. Bel Air Convalescent Center, Inc., Milw., 1969-70; asst. merchandising mgr. Champion Internat., Inc., Milw., 1970-72, tng. dir., personnel mgr., 1972-75; corp. dir. indsl. relations Weyenburg Shoe Mfg. Co., Milw., 1975; gen. mgr. Aqua Spray, Inc., Milw., 1976; mgmt. cons. Bloom & Assos., Milw., 1976—; guest lectr. mgmt. Marquette U., 1975, Milw. Area Tech. Coll., 1974-75, U. Wis., Milw., 1975; adv. bus. devel. State of Wis., 1978—. Mem. Am. Mgmt. Assn., Am. Soc. for Tng. and Devel., Indsl. Relations Research Assn., Am. Soc. for Personnel Adminstrn., Am. Soc. Safety Engrs. Home and Office: 8060 N Navajo Rd Fox Point WI 53217

BLOOM, MAX S., tobacco distbr.; b. Chgo., Aug. 2, 1907; s. Samuel and Mary (Becker) B.; B.A., U. Chgo., 1928; m. Mary F. Bernstein, Apr. 11, 1967; children—Donald, Barbara, Stephen. With S. Bloom, Inc., Chgo., 1928—, pres., now chmn. Mem. Nat., Ill. assns. tobacco distbrs., Nat. Confectionary Wholesalers Assn. Club: Rotary. Home: 2933 Sheridan Rd Chicago IL 60657 Office: 5401 S Dansher Rd Country Side IL 60625

BLOOM, PRESCOTT E., state senator; b. Peoria, Ill., June 18, 1942; ed. Williams Coll., London Sch. Econs. and Polit. Sci., J.D., U. Ill., 1970; m. Dianne Rahmberg. Admitted to Ill. bar; staff intern 76th Ill. Gen. Assembly, 1970-71; spl. asst. to atty. gen. for environ. control, 1971-73; mem. Ill. Senate. Bd. dirs. Peoria County Young Republican Assn. Served with USAR, 1967-73. Mem. Ill., Peoria County bar assns., Ill. Soc. Mayflower Descs., Ill. Wildlife Fedn. Address: Peoria IL 61602*

BLOOM, SAM OLIVER, farmer, state legislator; b. nr. Penock, Minn., June 18, 1915; s. Lars O. and Malene (Blom) B.; student public schs. of N.D.; m. Thora P. Slaaen, Oct. 24, 1936; children—Don O., Roger D., Marjorie Ann. Farmer, Alkabo, N.D., 1936—; owner, mgr. gen. store, 1939-58; mem. N.D. Ho. of Reps., 1958—, chmn. edn. com., 1965; dir. Alkabo Farmers Elevator. Local chmn., bd. dirs. March of Dimes, 1948-55; chmn., bd. dirs. cancer drive, 1945-52; vice chmn. adv. com. Williston Center, U. N.D., mem. adv. com. vocat. edn., 1969—, pres., 1973-75. Mem. Sch. Bd. Alkabo, 1944-59, pres. bd., 1945-59, bd. mem. Divide County reorganized sch. dist., 1962-64, 71-76, pres., 1974-76; Ivy County Sch. Officer, 1975-77; supr., Westby Twp. Bd., 1944-47, chmn., 1945-47; mem. Divide County Redistricting Bd., 1953-59. Mem. Nat. Farm Orgn. (mem. Divide county grain bd. 1968—, chmn. 1968-69), Divide County Hist. Soc. (dir. 1970—), Divide County Sch. Officers Orgn. (pres. 1957-59).

Lutheran (deacon). Club: Toastmasters (pres. 1976—). Address: Grenora ND 58845

BLOOM, STEPHEN JOEL, distbn. vending co. exec.; b. Chgo., Feb. 27, 1936; s. Max Samuel and Carolyn (Gumbiner) B.; B.B.A., U. Mich., 1958; m. Nancy Lee Gillan, Aug. 24, 1957; children—Anne, Bradley, Thomas, Carolyn. Salesman. then gen. mgr. Cigarette Service Co., Countryside, Ill., 1957-65, pres., chief exec. officer, i965—; pres., dir. Intercontinental Cons. Corp., Balt., chmn. bd., 1978—; dir. Ford City Bank & Trust Co. Bd. dirs. Clarendon Hills (Ill.) United Fund, 1975—; finance chmn. DuPage County Republican Com., 1976. Named Man of Year, Chgo. Tobacco Table, 1972. Mem. Nat. Automatic Mdsg. Assn. (Minuteman award 1974), Nat. (Young Exec. of Year award 1973, dir. 1978), Ill. assns. tobacco distbrs. Club: Chgo. Rotary. Home: 3 Hamill Ln Clarendon Hills IL 60514 Office: 5401 S Dansher Rd Countryside IL 60525

BLOOMBERG, RICHARD SAMUEL, finance co. exec.; b. Mpls., June 30, 1929; s. John Nathaniel and Bertha Christine (Ehrenholm) B.; B.B.A., U. Minn., 1951; B. Fgn. Trade, Am. Inst. Fgn. Trade, 1958; m. Oliva Hernandez Betancourt, Feb. 20, 1960; children—Harriet, Gabriella, Erik. Mgr. for So. Caribbean, Pfizer Internat., 1961-64; gen. sales mgr. P.R., Pfizer Corp., 1964-66; product mgr. Syntex Internat., Mexico City, 1966-68; v.p., treas. Bloomberg Companies, Chanhassen, Minn., 1968—. Bd. dirs. Mpls. People to People, 1974—, Am. Dinner Theatre Inst., 1979—. Served to 1st lt. USAF, 1952-56. Mem. Nat. Assn. Accountants, Delta Upsilon. Presbyterian. Home: 1102 Hazeltine Blvd Chaska MN 55318 Office: 501 78th St W Chanhassen MN 55317

BLOOMFIELD, COLEMAN, ins. co. exec.; b. Winnipeg, Man., Can., July 2, 1926; s. Samuel and Bessie (Staniloff) B.; came to U.S., 1952, naturalized, 1958; B.Commerce, U. Man., 1948; m. Shirley Rosenbaum, Nov. 4, 1948; children—Catherine, Laura, Leon, Diane, Richard. With Commonwealth Life Ins. Co., Louisville 1948-51; actuary, sr. v.p. Minn. Mut. Life Ins. Co., St. Paul, 1952-70, exec. v.p., 1970-71, pres., chief exec. officer, 1971—, chmn. bd., 1977—; pres., dir. Fin. Life Ins. Co.; dir. Minn. Title Corp., 1st Nat. Bank St. Paul. Bd. dirs. N. Star Research Inst., Minn. Orch. Assn., United Hosps., Inc.; v.p., bd. dirs. St. Paul United Way. Fellow Soc. Actuaries; mem. St. Paul C. of C., Am. Council Life Ins. (dir.). Office: Minn Mut Life Ins Co 345 Cedar St Saint Paul MN 55101*

BLOOR, HELEN ELIZABETH, county ofcl.; b. Wheeling, W.Va., Nov. 13, 1925; d. Robert Earl and Mary Lucille (Dickerhoff) Foster; grad. high sch.; m. Richard Jesse Bloor, Mar. 22, 1947; children—Rebecca, Bloor Karn, Brower; m. 2d, Robert Francis McKeever, Mar. 26, 1980. Exec. sec. United Methodist Ch., Lisbon, Ohio, 1949-57, Brotherhood Locomotive Firemen and Engineermen, Euclid, Ohio, 1964-66; planning dir. Columbiana County (Ohio), Lisbon, 1966—; speaker. Active local sch. and ch. work. Mem. Ohio Planning Dirs. Assn. Office: 110 Nelson Ave Lisbon OH 44432

BLOSER, DIETER, radiologist; b. Yugoslavia, Aug. 17, 1944; came to U.S., 1947, naturalized, 1954; s. Peter and Eva Helen B.; A.B., Princeton U., 1966; M.D., Case Western Res. U., 1970; m. Deborah Pierce Forbes, Nov. 25, 1967; children—Peter Forbes, Timothy Philip. Intern dept. medicine U. Hosps. of Cleve., 1970-71, resident in radiology, 1971-72, 74-76, chief resident, 1975-76; practice medicine specializing in radiology, Parma, Ohio, 1976—; mem. staff Parma Community Gen. Hosp., 1976—, chief nuclear medicine, 1977—; mem. staff U. Hosps. of Cleve., Cleve. Met. Gen. Hosp. Served to lt. comdr. USN, 1972-74. Diplomate Am. Bd. Radiology. Mem. Am. Coll. Radiology, Radiol. Soc. N. Am., Ohio Radiol. Soc., Cleve. Radiol. Soc., Am. Inst. Ultrasound in Medicine, Cleve. Acad. Medicine, AMA, Ohio Med. Assn., Princeton Alumni Assn. No. Ohio, Phi Beta Kappa, Alpha Omega Alpha. Lutheran. Home: 1251 Oakridge Dr Cleveland Heights OH 44121 Office: 7007 Power Blvd Parma OH 44129 also 18660 Bagley Rd Middleburg Heights OH

BLOUGH, CAROLYN JANE, educator; b. Grandville, Mich., May 30, 1931; married, 4 children. B.S. in Elementary Edn., Western Mich. U., Kalamazoo, 1969, postgrad. in reading. Tchr., Lowell (Mich.) Area Schs., 1961-70, cons. reading, 1970-75, dir. reading, 1975-78, coordinator basic skills, 1978—. Leader, Lowell Area Campfire Girls, 1960-65. Mem. Mich., Internat. reading assns., Kent County Reading Council. Home: 623 N Jefferson St Lowell MI 49331 Office: 700 Elizabeth St Lowell MI 49331

BLOUNT, WILBUR CLANTON, ophthalmologist; b. Columbus, Ohio, Feb. 5, 1929; s. Percy Hammond and Bayetta (Dent) B.; B.Sc. in Bacteriology, Ohio State U., 1951, postgrad., 1951-52, M.D., 1959; m. Elsie M. Paradis; children—Angela Diane, Wilbur S., Elizabeth Rachel, Jacqueline Rebecca. Intern, U. Ill. Research and Ednl. Hosps., Chgo., 1959-60; gen. practice medicine, Williamson, W.Va., 1960-62; resident dept. ophthalmology Coll. Medicine, Ohio State U., Columbus, 1964-67, instr. ophthalmology 1970-71, clin. asst. prof., 1977—; spl. NIH fellow in retinal surgery U. Minn., 1967-69; practice medicine specializing in ophthalmology, especially surgery and diseases of retina; mem. staff U. Ky. Med. Center, Good Samaritan Hosp., Lexington, Ky., Lexington VA Hosp., 1971-77, Grant Hosp., Mt. Carmel Hosp., St. Anthony Hosp., Columbus, Ohio; asst. prof. surgery, dept. ophthalmology U. Ky. Med. Center, Lexington, 1971-77, dir. retinal service. Mem. Friends of Library, Ohio Soc. To Prevent Blindness. Served to 1st lt. USAF, 1954-56. Fellow Aerospace Med. Assn. (asso.), ACS; mem. Nat. Med. Assn., AMA, Ohio Med. Assn., Acad. Medicine Columbus and Franklin County, Soc. USAF Flight Surgeons, Am. Acad. Ophthalmology, Assn. Mil. Ophthalmologists, Pan Am. Soc. Ophthalmology, Air Force Assn., Res. Officers Assn., N.G. Assn. U.S. Club: Rotary. Home: 2820 E Broad St Columbus OH 43209 Office: 300 E Town St Columbus OH 43215

BLUE, ROBERT LEE, educator; b. Columbiaville, Mich., Apr. 23, 1920; s. Arthur Floyd and Elma (Ellis) B.; B.A., Mich. State U., 1941; M.A., U. Mich., 1952; m. Dorothy L. Seward, July 15, 1961. Tchr., Chesaning (Mich.) High Sch., 1941-42, 45-57; prin. Ricker Jr. High Sch., Saginaw, Mich., 1957-59, Buena Vista High Sch., Saginaw, 1960-69; asst. prof. secondary edn. Central Mich. U., Mt. Pleasant, 1969—. Bd. dirs. Hartley Edn. Nature Camp, 1957-69. Served with U.S. Army, 1942-45. Decorated Bronze Star. Mem. NEA (life), Mich. Edn. Assn., Assn. Tchr. Educators, Mich. Assn. Tchr. Educators, Nat. Assn. Secondary Sch. Prins., Mich. Assn. Secondary Sch. Prins., Mich. PTA (hon. life), Am. Legion, Mich. Hist. Soc., Saginaw County Hist. Soc., Lapeer County Hist. Soc., Phi Delta Kappa. Republican. Methodist. Clubs: Optimist, Knife and Fork, Pit and Balcony, Masons. Author: Footsteps Into The Past, A History of Columbiaville, 1979, also articles. Home: 4584 Colonial Dr Saginaw MI 48603 Office: Central Mich U 420 S Warren St Saginaw MI 48607

BLUEMLE, PAUL EDWARD, city ofcl.; b. Springfield, Ohio, Sept. 9, 1926; s. Carl Henry and Mary Ann (Wolbert) B.; B.B.A. magna cum laude, Xavier U. (Ohio), 1951; M.A., U. Oreg., 1953; postgrad. (All-Univ. grantee) Mich. State U., 1957-63; m. Helen Jean Smain, Sept. 13, 1958; children—Joy, Christine, Jude, Laura, Peter. Reporter, Springfield Daily News, 1943-51; exec. sec. Young Christian Students, Chgo., 1952-54; dir. pub. relations Thomas More Coll., Covington, Ky., 1954-55; bus. mgr. Today mag., Chgo., 1955-56; instr. Mich. State U., E. Lansing, 1956-59; editor univ. publs. Bowling Green State U., Ohio, 1959-60; asst. prof., asso. prof., exec. sec., asst. dean Monteith Coll., Wayne State U., Detroit, 1960-76; admissions dir., asst. to v.p. for academic affairs, asst. dean U. Detroit, 1976-80; city clk. Pleasant Ridge (Mich.), 1980—; bd. dirs. Chgo. Research Group Corp., 1956-73. Pres. sch. bd. St. Mary's Parish, Royal Oak, Mich., 1966; mem. Citizens Adv. Commn., Ferndale (Mich.) Sch. Dist., 1972; chmn. com. on community Archdiocese of Detroit, 1972-74. Served with U.S. Army, 1945-46. Mem. Soc. Profl. Journalists, Am. Newspaper Guild (v.p. Springfield 1945), AAUP (sec. Wayne State U. chpt. 1971-72), Kappa Tau Alpha. Roman Catholic. Home: 16 Hanover Rd Pleasant Ridge MI 48069 Office: 23925 Woodward Ave Pleasant Ridge MI 48069

BLUESTEIN, JUDITH ANN, diversified industry exec., educator; b. Cin., Apr. 2, 1948; d. Paul Harold and Joan Ruth (Straus) B.; B.A., U. Pa., 1969; postgrad. Am. Sch. Classical Studies, Athens, Greece, 1968, Vergilian Soc., 1970, 76, 77, 78, Hebrew Union Coll., Jewish Inst. Religion, Jerusalem, 1971, 1979-80, Hebrew Union Coll., Jewish Inst. Religion, Cin., 1980—, Am. Acad. in Rome, 1975; M.A. in Religion (Univ. fellow), Case Western Res. U., 1973, M.A. in Latin, 1973. Sec., Paul H. Bluestein & Co., Cin., 1964—; v.p. Panel Machine Co., 1966—, Blujay Corp., 1966—, Ermet Products Corp., 1966—; partner Companhia Engenheiros Industrial Bluestein do Brasil, Cin., 1971—; tchr. Latin, Cin. Public Schs., 1973-79. Mem. Archeol. Inst. Am., Classical Assn. Middle West and South (v.p. Ohio 1976-79), Am. Classical League, Ohio Classical Conf. (council 1976-79), Vergilian Soc., Soc. Bibl. Lit., Cin. Assn. Tchrs. Classics (pres. 1976-78), Am. Philol. Assn., NEA, Ohio Edn. Assn., Cin. Tchrs. Assn. Address: 3420 Section Rd Cincinnati OH 45237

BLUESTEIN, PAUL HAROLD, mgmt. engr.; b. Cin., June 14, 1923; s. Norman and Eunice D. (Schullman) B.; B.S., Carnegie Inst. Tech., 1946, B. Engring. in Mgmt. Engring., 1946; M.B.A., Xavier U., 1973; m. Joan Ruth Straus, May 17, 1943; children—Alice Sue Bluestein Greenbaum, Judith Ann. Time study engr. Lodge & Shipley Co., 1946-47; adminstrv. engr. Randall Co., 1947-52; partner Paul H. Bluestein & Co., mgmt. cons., 1952—, Seinsheimer-Bluestein Mgmt. Services, 1964—, Companhia Engenheiros Industrial Bluestein do Brasil, 1970—; gen. mgr. Baker Refrigeration Co., 1953-56; pres., dir. Tabor Mfg. Co. 1953-54, Blujay Corp., 1954—, Blatt & Ludwig Corp., 1954-57, Jason Industries, Inc., 1954-57, Hamilton-York Corp., 1954-57, Earle Hardware Mfg. Co., 1955-57, Hermas Machine Co., 1956—, Panel Machine Co., Ermet Products Corp. 1957—, Tyco Labs., Inc., 1968-69, All-Tech Industries, 1969, Del. Tisco Corp., 1970-71; gen. mgr. Hafleigh & Co., 1959-60; sr. v.p., gen. mgr. McCauley Ind. Corp., 1959-60; v.p., gen. mgr. Farmco Machine div. Worden-Allen Co., 1974-75; gen. mgr. Am. Art Works div. Rapid-Am. Corp., 1960-63; sec.-treas., dir. Liberty Baking Co., 1964-65; pres. Duguesne Baking Co., 1964-65, Goddard Bakers, Inc., 1964-65; pub. Merger and Acquisition Digest, 1962—; exec. v.p. Peck, Stow & Wilcox Co., 1976-77; dir. Norameo, Inc., 1964-67. Served from pvt. to tech. sgt. AUS, 1943-46. Registered profl. engr., Ohio. Mem. ASME, Am. Inst. Indsl. Engrs., Joint Engring. Mgmt. Conf., Am. Soc. Engring. Mgmt. Club: B'nai B'rith. Home: 3420 Section Rd Amberley Village Cincinnati OH 45237 Office: 3420 Section Rd Cincinnati OH 45237

BLUHM, MAURICE JOSEPH, Realtor; b. Chgo., Apr. 7, 1916; s. Joseph V. and Rose (Bailey) B.; B.B.A., Northwestern U., 1938; m. Ethel Mary Meyer, July 4, 1940; children—Mark Alan, Barbara Ann. Auditor, Gen. Operating Co., Chgo., 1934-36, supr., 1936-37, gen. mgr., 1937-41; founder Midwest Operating Co., Kansas City, Mo., 1944, now pres.; pres. Maurice J. Bluhm & Co., Realtors, Kansas City, 1945—, Mo., 1962—, Bluhm Investment Co., Inc., Kansas City, 1966—; pres. Plaza Inn Co., Kansas City, Plaza Motor Inn, Inc., Plaza Inn Internat., Inc.; dir., mem. exec. com. Starlight Theatre, Kansas City. Pres., Mayor's Corps of Progress for Greater Kansas City, 1973-76, vice chmn. bd. dirs., 1976-80; commr. Greater Kansas City Sports Commn. Bd. dirs. Conv. and Visitors Bur., 1949—, mem. exec. com., 1971-81; trustee Kansas City Philharmonic Orch.; bd. dirs. Nat. Council on Alcoholism, Country Club Plaza Assn.; bd. govs. Am. Royal Assn. Served with USAAF, 1941-44. Decorated Purple Heart, Air medal with silver oak leaf cluster; named Man of Year Mo. Hotel and Motel Assn., 1972; named Man of Year Fleet Res. Assn., 1972, ann. Humanitarian award, 1976. Mem. Hotel and Motel Greeters Assn. Internat. (bd. govs.), Nat. Assn. Real Estate Bds., Nat. Inst. Real Estate Brokers, Ark.-Mo.-Kans.-Okla. Lodging Assn. (pres. 1971-72), Mo. (v.p. 1966-73, pres. 1973-74), Kansas City (pres. 1969-72, chmn. bd. 1972-75) hotel and motel assns., Mo., Kansas City real estate assns., Nat., Mo. restaurant assns., Am. Legion, Kansas City C. of C., Mo. C. of C. Mason (Shriner, 32 deg.). Clubs: Meadowbrooke Golf and Country (Prairie Village, Kans.); Blue Springs (Mo.) Golf and Country; Question (Independence, Mo.); Mo. Yacht (Lake Lotawana, Mo.). Home: F-3 Route 4 Lake Lotawana Lees Summit MO 64063 Office: 45th and Main Sts care Hilton Plaza Inn Kansas City MO 64111

BLUM, ALBERT ALEXANDER, educator; b. N.Y.C., Apr. 5, 1924; s. Morris and Estelle (Kaplan) B.; B.S., CCNY, 1947; M.A., Columbia U., 1948, Ph.D., 1953; m. Roslyn Silver, Jan. 16, 1949; children—Steven Ephraim, David Joshua. Labor relations specialist Conf. Bd., 1955-57; asst. prof. N.Y. Cornell and Am. U., 1957-60; prof. Mich. State U., East Lansing, 1960-74; research asso. ILO, Geneva, 1966-69; Fulbright research prof. Danish Nat. Inst. Social Research, 1968; research asso. Econ. and Social Research Inst., Dublin, 1970; prof. U. Tel Aviv, 1972; prof., dean Stuart Sch. Mgmt. and Fin., Ill. Inst. Tech., Chgo., 1978—; labor arbitrator Am. Arbitration Assn. and Fed. Mediation and Conciliation Service, 1958—; exec. sec. Com. on Dept. of Labor Manpower Research and Devel., Nat. Acad. Scis., 1973-74; prof., chmn. Sch. Labor and Indsl. Relations, Mich. State U., 1960-74; prof. Lyndon B. Johnson Sch. Public Affairs, U. Tex., Austin, 1974-78. Served with USAF, 1943-45. Social Sci. Research Council Nat. Security Program grantee, 1959-60; Dept. Labor research grantee, 1973-76; Israel Labor Studies grantee, 1972; Lyndon B. Johnson Found. grantee, 1975-76. Mem. Indsl. Relations Research Assn., Am. History Assn., Am. Com. on History-Second World War, S.W. Labor Studies Conf. Author: A History of American Labor Movement, 1972; White Collar Workers, 1971; Teacher Unions and Associations: A Comparative Study, 1969; Drafted of Deferred: Practices Past and Present, 1967; International Handbook of Industrial Relations, 1981; mem. editorial bd. Labor History, 1968-78. Office: 10 W 31st St Chicago IL 60616

BLUM, FRED, librarian; b. N.Y.C., Nov. 27, 1932; s. Henry and Jeanne B.; B.Mus., Oberlin (Ohio) Coll., 1954; M.F.A., Ohio U., Athens, 1955; Ph.D., U. Iowa, 1959; M.S. in L.S., Cath. U. Am., 1968; m. Beula Eisenstadt, Sept. 24, 1967. Reference librarian music div. Library of Congress, 1961-66, editor nat. register of microform masters, 1966-67; head spl. services dept., then head tech. services dept. Cath. U. Am. libraries, 1967-74; dir. Center Ednl. Resources, Eastern Mich. U., Ypsilanti, 1974-79, prof., reference librarian humanities div., 1980—; vis. prof. U. Mich. Sch. Library Sci., Ann Arbor, summer 1979; mem. Coll. and Research Libraries Editorial Bd., 1974-80, Ohio Coll. Library Center Users Council, 1978-79; trustee Mich. Library Consortium, 1974-79. Deutscher Akademischer Austauschdienst, 1959-60; Deutscher Paedagogischer Austauschdienst, 1960-61. Mem. AAUP, ALA, Assn. Coll. and Research Libraries, Music Library Assn., Mich. Acad. Sci., Arts and Letters, Mich. Library Assn., Beta Phi Mu. Author: Music Monographs in Series, 1964; Jean Sibelius: An International Bibliography, 1965; also articles. Home: 3161 Lakehaven Dr Ann Arbor MI 48105 Office: Univ Library Eastern Mich U Ypsilanti MI 48197

BLUME, HERBERT EDWARD, accountant; b. Tripoli, Iowa, Sept. 20, 1917; s. William C. and Hulda D. (Hagenow) B.; student LaSalle Extension U., 1943-44; m. Elvera E. Kelling, Sept. 25, 1938; children—Carol (Mrs. Merlin H. Franzen), Marjorie (Mrs. Arthur F. Maynard), Marilyn (Mrs. Robert F. Seefeld). Farmer, nr. Tripoli, 1938-40; pvt. tax practice, Tripoli, 1944—; pvt. practice accounting, 1945—; treas. Tripoli Devel. Corp., 1959—; pres. Aids for Handicaps, Inc., 1958—; pub. Farm Record. Sec. Bremer County Zoning Commn., 1963-80; pres. Accountants Assn. Iowa, 1970-71; presdl. elector 3d Dist. Iowa, 1980. Accounting practitioner, 1975—. Sec. finance Iowa dist. east Lutheran Ch.-Mo. Synod, 1960-66; chmn. St. John Luth. Ch., Denver, Iowa, 1980. Mem. Nat. Soc. Pub. Accountants (accredited), Assn. of Enrolled Agts., Nat. Assn. Tax Practitioners, Luth. Laymen's League, Farm Bur. Republican. Patentee stairwalking crutches, 1945. Address: Tripoli IA 50676

BLUMENTALS, EDITE, retail mcht. and food processing co. exec.; b. Riga, Latvia; came to U.S., 1950, naturalized, 1955; d. Rolands and Monica (Boka) B.; B.A., U. Minn., 1955. Adminstrv. asst. to dir. Minn. Alumni Assn., U. Minn., Mpls., 1957-60; asst. to field mgr. Mendota Research Group, Englewood, N.J., 1960-61; research supr. Campbell-Mithun, Inc., Chgo., 1961-79; sr. mktg. rep. Peavey Co., Mpls., 1980—. Mem. Am. Mktg. Assn., Am. Mgmt. Assn., U. Minn. Alumni Assn., Imeria. Home: 210 W Grant St Minneapolis MN 55403 Office: Peavey Co 730 S 2d Ave Minneapolis MN 55402

BLUMENTHAL, DAVID LIONEL, psychoanalyst; b. Chgo., Apr. 22, 1926; s. Sol and Ida (Schniederman) B.; B.S. in Mech. Engring., Purdue U., 1948; M.S.W., U. Chgo., 1949, postgrad., 1950; M.A., Butler U., Indpls., 1959; postgrad. Nat. Psychol. Assn. for Psychoanalysis, N.Y.C., 1955-70; M.A., Christian Theol. Sem., 1982; Sc.D. (hon.), Lincoln Coll., Indpls., 1962; m. Patricia Louise Wright, Apr. 19, 1968; 1 dau., Jill Ann. Psychiat. caseworker Ind. U. Med. Center, 1950-51; caseworker, supr., adminstrv. asst. Family Service Assn. Indpls., 1951-54; pvt. practice psychotherapy and psychoanalysis, Indpls., 1954—; psychotherapist, dir. Shelby County Mental Health Center, Shelbyville, Ind., 1955-58; mem. faculty Ind. U., Purdue U., Butler U., Lincoln Coll., 1954-74. Served with USNR, 1944-46. Recipient Public Relations award Family Service Assn. Indpls., 1952, 54. Mem. Acad. Cert. Social Workers, Nat. Assn. Social Workers (charter), Am. Acad. Psychotherapists, Am. Group Psychotherapy Assn., Am. Soc. Group Psychotherapy and Psychodrama, Ind. Soc. Clin. Social Workers, NAACP. Jewish. Author articles in field. Address: 4328 N Park Ave Indianapolis IN 46205

BLUMENTHAL, W. MICHAEL, mfg. co. exec.; b. Germany, Jan. 3, 1926; s. Ewald and Rose Valerie (Markt) B.; B.Sc., U. Calif. at Berkeley, 1951; M.A., M.P.A., Princeton, 1953, Ph.D., 1956; m. Margaret Eileen Polley, Sept. 8, 1951. Came to U.S., 1947, naturalized, 1952. Research asso. Princeton, 1954-57; labor arbitrator State of N.J., 1955-57; v.p. dir. Crown Cork Internat. Corp., 1957-61, also dir. overseas affiliated cos.; became dep. asst. sec. state for econ. affairs Dept. State, 1961; apptd. President's dep. spl. rep. for trade negotiations with rank of ambassador, 1963-67; pres. Bendix Internat., 1967-70; dir. Bendix Corp., 1967-77, vice chmn., 1970-71, pres., chief operating officer, 1971-72, chmn., pres., chief exec. officer, 1972-77; sec. of Treasury, Washington, 1977-79; vice chmn., chief exec. officer Burroughs Corp., Detroit, 1980-81, chmn., chief exec. officer, 1981—, also dir.; dir. Equitable Life Assurance Soc. U.S., 1972-77, 79—, Pillsbury Co., 1979—, Chem. N.Y. Corp. and subs. Chem. Bank, 1979—; U.S. rep. commn. internat. commodity trade UN Econ. and Social Council, 1961, 1962; U.S. adviser spl. meeting Inter-Am. Econ. and Social Council, 1961; chmn. U.S. del. UN Coffee Conf., 1962; bd. dirs. Bus. Com. for Arts; trustee Rockefeller Found. Charter trustee Princeton. Mem. Bus. Council, Am. Econ. Assn., Council Fgn. Relations, Atlantic Council U.S. (dir.), Phi Beta Kappa. Clubs: Princeton, Century (N.Y.C.); Econ. of Detroit (dir.). Office: Burroughs Corp Burroughs Plaza Detroit MI 48232

BLUMSTEIN, RICHARD NORMAN, constrn. co. exec.; b. Chgo., Nov. 14, 1930; s. Jacob and Minnie B.; student Roosevelt U., 1948-52; m. Lila Wood, Feb. 28, 1954; children—Valerie, Howard. Estimator, constrn. supt. Thomas Blondell, Chgo., 1958-62; founder, pres. Statewide Fire Constrn., Chgo., 1962-71; founder, pres. Legacy Homes, Inc., Steger, Ill., 1971—, R.N. Blumstein & Assos., Inc., Steger, 1978—. Vice pres., ritual chmn. Congregation Am Echad, Park Forest, Ill. Served with U.S. Army, 1946-47. Mem. Nat. Assn. Home Builders, South Suburban Home Builders Assn. Club: Birchwood Farm Country (Harbor Springs, Mich.). Home: 1702 Lynwood St Flossmoor IL 60422 Office: Legacy Homes Inc 3411 Chicago Rd Steger IL 60475

BLUNDEN, JERALDYNE, artistic dir.; b. Dayton, Ohio, Dec. 10, 1940; d. Elijah and Winnifred Mildred (Keith) Kilborn; student Conn. Coll. for Women Summer Dance Sch., 1959, Schwarz Sch. Dance, 1948-58, Central State U., Wilberforce, Ohio, 1960, Clark Center for Performing Arts, 1968-74, Alvin Ailey Am. Dance Center, 1971-75, Dance Theatre Harlem, 1968-73, Martha Graham Dance Sch., 1958-59; m. Charles Blunden, Oct. 15, 1959; children—Debra Lynne, Derek Charles. Owner, inst. Jeraldyne's Sch. of the Dance, Dayton, 1961—; instr. Wright State U., Dayton, Ohio, 1975-76; artistic dir. Dayton Contemporary Dance Co., 1961—; adj. instr. Wilberforce U., 1969-73; tchr. dance Sinclair Community Coll.; performing mem. Nat. Assn. Regional Ballet. Mem. arts com. Dayton Bicentennial Commn.; den. mother Boy Scouts Am.; liaison chmn. crafts Choreography Conf., 1975. Recipient Dayton's Ten Top Women award, 1977; dance grantee Ohio Arts Council, 1973, 74, 75, Nat. Endowment grantee, 1975, Dayton Optimist Service certificate, 1973, Tait Found. grantee, 1975, Berman Found. grantee, 1974, Dayton Found. grantee, 1975; Nat. Endowment for Arts fellow, 1980. Choreographer Black History Concerts, 1974, 75, 76, Black Snow, 1976; guest choreographer Dayton Living Arts Center Repertory Co., 1974-75. Mem. N.E. Regional Ballet Assn. (membership chairperson). Home: 1021 Dennison Ave Dayton OH 45408 Office: 136 S Ludlow St Dayton OH 45402

BLYTH, LYNN ALLAN, controls co. lab. exec.; b. Sioux Falls, S.D., Dec. 15, 1942; s. Stanley Wilson and Hazel Merle (Rolfson) B.; B.S. in Physics magna cum laude (Lawrence J. Monville and Lubrizol awards), John Carroll U., 1974, M.S. in Physics, 1976; m. Ann Marie Kacerski, June 26, 1976; children—Breton Alan, Amanda Lynn. Engr., Bailey Meter Co., Wickliffe, Ohio, 1968-72, project engr. research and devel., 1972-73; grad. teaching asst. John Carroll U., Cleve., 1974-76; mgr. quality assurance lab. Bailey Controls Co., Wickliffe, 1976—. Served with AUS, 1962-65. Mem. IEEE, Inst. Environ. Scis., Am. Nuclear Soc., Sigma Pi Sigma. Home: 4138

Ireland Rd Rome OH 44085 Office: 29801 Euclid Ave Wickliffe OH 44092

BOAND, CHARLES W., lawyer; b. Bates County, Mo., Aug. 19, 1908; s. Albert and Edith Nadine (Pipes) B.; A.A., Jr. Coll. Kansas City; J.D. summa cum laude, U. Mo.-Kansas City; M.B.A., LL.B. cum laude, U. Chgo.; m. Phoebe Bard, Aug. 2, 1980; children—Bard, Barbara. Admitted to Mo. bar, 1931, D.C. bar, 1936, Ill. bar, 1937, U.S. Supreme Ct. bar, 1935, U.S. Circuit Ct. Appeals bars; asso. firm Moore & Fitch, St. Louis, 1933; atty. Gen. Counsel's Office, U.S. Treasury Dept., 1933-36; asso. Wilson & McIlvaine, 1937-42, partner, 1945—, chmn. exec. com., 1975—. Mem. council Grad. Sch. Bus., U. Chgo., 1961-68; mem. citizens bd. U. Chgo.; trustee Muskingum Coll., 1965-80. Served as officer USNR, 1942-45; lt. comdr. Res. (ret.). Mem. Am. (litigation Sect., nat. conf. lawyers and C.P.A.'s 1976—), Ill. (chmn. exec. com. corp. securities law sect. 1954-56), Chgo. (chmn. com. corp. law 1963-64), Fed., Seventh Circuit bar assns., U. Chgo. Alumni Assn. (pres. 1975-80, alumni cabinet 1964-70, 72-80, v.p. 1973-74, 1st Alumni Disting. Service award 1981), U. Chgo. Law Sch. Alumni Assn. (pres. 1968-70, dir. 1950-72), Order of Coif, Beta Gamma Sigma, Sigma Chi, Phi Alpha Delta. Presbyterian (stated clk. 1962-65). Clubs: Chgo., Mid-Am., Met., Law, Legal, Execs. (Chgo.); Barrington Hills (Ill.) Country (dir. 1947-55); Los Caballeros Golf (Ariz.); Nat. Lawyers (Washington). Editor: Case Notes, U. Chgo. Law Rev., 1932-33. Home: 250 W County Line Rd PO Box 567 Barrington Hills IL 60010 Office: 135 S LaSalle St Chicago IL 60603

BOBER, MARY LOU, steel co. cons.; b. East Chicago, Ind., July 13, 1955; d. Joseph F. and Myrtle (Bessler) B.; A.B., Ind. U., 1977, M.B.A., 1979. Staff cons. Inland Steel Co., East Chicago, Ind., 1979-81, cons., 1981—. Home: 431 W Barry Apt 424 Chicago IL 60657 Office: Inland Steel Co 30 W Monroe St Chicago IL 60603

BOBINET, LOUIS GEORGE, ins. co. exec.; b. Chelsea, Iowa, Aug. 11, 1937; s. William Antone and Helen Anna (Seidel) B.; B.A., Simpson Coll., 1960; M.S., Drake U., 1968; m. Claire Whinery, Feb. 23, 1974; children—Kyle, Kayla. Jr. high sci. tchr. Indianola (Iowa) Community Sch., 1960-70; adjustor IMT Ins. Co., Des Moines, 1970-71, personnel mgr., 1971—. Mem. Adminstrv. Mgmt. Soc. (v.p. mktg. 1981-82), Sigma Alpha Epsilon (life). Republican. Methodist. Clubs: Kiwanis, Masons, Shriners. Home: 201 N J St Indianola IA 50125 Office: IMT Insurance Co 6000 Grand PO Box 1336 Des Moines IA 50305

BOCK, LEO LOUIS, elec. engr.; b. Poole, Nebr., Jan. 7, 1927; s. Louis Alex and Mary (Heerman) B.; B.S.E.E., U. Nebr., 1951; m. Verona Velma Hafner, Dec. 18, 1951; children—Diane, Gerald, Karen, Michael, Lawrence. Elec. engr. Sperry Univac, 1951-55, engrng. mgr., 1955-61, product planning mgr., 1961-65; sr. engr. IBM Corp., Owego, N.Y., 1965-68; product planning mgr. Mohawk Data Scis., Herkimer, N.Y., 1968-69; coordinator for product Planning Sperry Univac, St. Paul, 1969-70, mktg. mgr., 1970-77, navy systems market planning mgr., 1977-79, staff systems engr., 1979—. Served with USAF, 1945-46. Mem. IEEE. Republican. Lutheran. Home: 10824 York Ave S Bloomington MN 55431 Office: Univac Park Saint Paul MN 55165

BOCKELMAN, J(OHN) RICHARD, lawyer; b. Chgo., Aug. 8, 1925; s. Carl August and Mary (Ritchie) B.; student U. Wis., 1943-44, Northwestern U., 1944-45, Harvard U., 1945, U. Hawaii, 1946; B.S. in Bus. Adminstrn., Northwestern U., 1946; M.A. in Econs., U. Chgo., 1949, J.D., 1951. Admitted to Ill. bar, 1951; atty.-adviser Chgo. ops. office U.S. AEC, 1951-52; asso. firm Schradzke, Gould & Ratner, Chgo., 1952-57, Brown, Dashow & Langeluttig, Chgo., 1957-59, firm Antonow & Weissbourd, Chgo., 1959-61; partner firm Burton, Isaacs, Bockelman & Miller, Chgo., 1961-69; individual practice law, Chgo., 1970—. Prof. bus. law Ill. Inst. Tech., Chgo., 1950—, lectr. econs. De Paul U., Chgo., 1952-53; dir., v.p., sec. Secretaries, Inc., Chgo., Beale Travel Service, Inc., Chgo.; dir., sec. Arlington Engrng. Co., Chgo.; dir., v.p. Universal Distbrs., Inc., Chgo. Served with USNR, 1943-46. Mem. Am., Ill. Chgo. bar assns., Catholic Lawyers Guild Chgo., Phi Delta Theta. Clubs: Lake Point Tower, Barclay Ltd., Whitehall, Internat. (Chgo.); Anvil (East Dundee, Ill.). Home: 1212 Lake Shore Dr Chicago IL 60610 Office: 69 W Washington St Chicago IL 60602

BOCKHOFF, FRANK JAMES, chemist, chem. engr.; b. Tiffin, Ohio, Mar. 26, 1928; s. Cornelius Frank and Helen Odelia (Bormuth) B.; B.S., Case Inst. Tech., 1950; M.S., Case-Western Res. U., 1952, Ph.D., 1959; m. Esther Camperchioli, Jan. 27, 1951; children—Frank M., Susan V., Celia M., James P. Asst. prof. chemistry and chem. engrng. Fenn Coll., 1954-60, asso. prof., 1960-62, asso. prof., chmn. dept. chemistry, 1963-65; prof., chmn. dept. chemistry Cleve. State U., 1965—; cons. in field. Mem. Am. Chem. Soc., Am. Inst. Chemists. Author 2 books on quantum theory and plastics welding; contbr. articles to profl. jours.; patentee on polymer chemistry and applications. Home: 3015 Scarborough Rd Cleveland Heights OH 44118 Office: Cleveland State Univ Cleveland OH 44115

BODE, SANDRA JEAN, ednl. adminstr.; b. Warren, Ohio, Apr. 20, 1941; d. Gilbert Vernon and Clara Helen (Mount) Reed; student Kent (Ohio) State U., 1959-62; B.S. in Edn., Youngstown (Ohio) State U., 1964; postgrad. Purdue U., 1969-70; M.S. in Edn., No. Ill. U., 1977; m. Glen Harold Bode, June 6, 1964. Tchr. elementary sch., Mineral Ridge, Ohio, 1962-66, Kent pub. schs., 1966-68, Duneland Sch. Corp., Chesterton, Ind., 1969-70, Overseas Dependent Schs., Germany, 1971-73; coordinator career edn. Thornton Area Pub. Sch. Corp., 1973-76; dir. DuPage Career Edn. Center, Wheaton, Ill., 1976—; sex equity cons. Ill. Bd. Edn.; mem. teaching staff Nat. Coll. Edn., Evanston, Ill., Governors State U., Park Forest, Ill.; cons. to Cook and DuPage Counties, SBA, U.S. Office of Career Edn., Washington. Home: 726 S Adams St Hinsdale IL 60521 Office: 421 N County Farm Rd Wheaton IL 60187

BODENSTAB, PAUL WILLIAM, life ins. agt.; b. Madrid, Nebr., Apr. 6, 1926; s. Otto August and Alice Mable (Cassels) B.; m. Donna Lee Lewin, June 23, 1972; children by previous marriage—Karen Ann, Brenda Lynn, Rhonda Sue. Gen. agt. Bankers Life Nebr., Lincoln, Nebr., 1950-64; gen. agt. Guarantee Mut. Life Co., Omaha, 1964—. Pres., Lincoln County unit Am. Cancer Soc., 1975-78, state cancer crusade chmn. for Nebr., 1979—, mem. exec. com. state unit, bd. dirs., 1977-79, recipient Vol. of Yr. award, 1979, chmn. unit standards com. state unit, 1980-81. Served with U.S. Army, 1944-46. Mem. North Platte Valley Life Underwriters Assn. (past pres.), Nebr. Life Underwriters Assn. (past v.p.), Am. Soc. C.L.U.'s, Nat. Fedn. Ind. Businessmen (past nat. adv. council, dist. chmn.). Republican. Methodist. Clubs: Toastmasters, Masons. Home: 818 East C St North Platte NE 69101

BODENSTEINER, ROBERT THEODORE, trucking industry exec.; b. Decorah, Iowa, May 14, 1933; s. Cyril Mathew and Acquin Marie (Kilcoin) B.; B.S., Iowa State U., 1955; postgrad. Iowa U., 1957; postgrad. N.Y. City Coll., 1958; m. Amalia Frances Valenti, Nov. 28, 1959; children—Theodore Girard, David Neil, Susan Frances. Internal auditor N.Y. Life Ins. Co., N.Y.C., 1957-59; adminstrv. asst. Ft. Dodge (Iowa) By-Products Co., 1960-63; spl sales agent Lincoln Nat. Life Ins. Co., Ft. Dodge, 1963-67; stock and commodity broker Lamson Bros. and Co., Ft. Dodge, 1967-73, pres., gen. mgr. Center Line, Inc., Ft. Dodge, 1973—; dir. Internat. Mining and Devel., Inc., Ft. Dodge By-Products Co., Webster Rendering Co., Hot Line, Inc., Bowlerama, Inc., Air Lanes, Inc., Center Line, Inc. Pres., Sertoma Club of Ft. Dodge, 1967, gov. W. Iowa dist. Sertoma Internat., 1970-72. Served to lt. j.g. USN, 1955-57. Recipient various sales awards, Lincoln Nat. Life Ins. Co. and Lamson Bros. & Co. Mem. Ft. Dodge C. of C., Nat. C. of C. Republican. Roman Catholic. Club: Barbershoppers. Home: 2209 N 22d St Fort Dodge IA 50501 Office: Box 1275 Fort Dodge IA 50501

BODER, CLARETTA KELSO, ednl. adminstr., psychologist, counselor; b. McDonald, Pa., Nov. 19, 1920; d. William Wallace and Prudence Ann Jane (McEwen) Kelso; B.B.A., Westminster Coll., 1942; postgrad. Washington and Jefferson Coll., summer 1950; M.A., Ohio State U., 1964, Ph.D. in Guidance and Counseling, 1976; m. William Dunbar Boder, Jan. 3, 1942; children—Susan Ann Boder White, Richard Dale, Linda Lee Boder Walters. Tchr., Cecil Twp. Sch. Dist., McDonald, 1943-50; supr. bus. office Beverly Heights United Presbyn. Ch., Mt. Lebanon, Pa., 1951-52; tchr. Claysville (Pa.) Sch. Dist., 1954-55, Southwestern City Sch. Dist., Columbus, Ohio, 1955-61; tchr. and guidance counselor Grandview Heights (Ohio) City Sch. Dist., 1961-69; vocat. guidance coordinator Eastland Joint Vocat. Sch. Dist., Groveport, Ohio, 1969—; instr. psychology Franklin U., Columbus, 1976-77; instr. Ohio State U., 1974; cons. Ohio State U., 1971, Kent State U., 1975; guest lectr. Ohio State U., 1970-75; chmn. in-service programs Eastland Joint Vocat. Sch., 1970-77; counseling psychologist, 1977—; mem. planning com. All Ohio Guidance Conf., 1968-69. Elder, Blvd. United Presbyn. Ch., 1964-67, deacon, 1961-63. Recipient Dwight Arnold Outstanding Counselor award, 1970. Mem. NEA, Ohio Ednl. Assn., Am., Ohio (Distinguished Service award 1975, pres. guidance div. 1974-75) vocat. assns., Ohio Sch. Counselors Assn. (co-editor newsletter 1966), Am. Personnel and Guidance Assn., Ohio Psychol. Assn., Central Ohio Psychol. Assn., Phi Delta Kappa, Delta Kappa Gamma (v.p. 1974-76), Beta Sigma Omicron. Republican. Club: Order Eastern Star. Contbr. articles on guidance and counseling to profl. jours. Home: 1921 Elmwood Ave Columbus OH 43212 Office: 1620 E Broad St Columbus OH 43203

BODEY, HUGH NEWELL, real estate broker; b. Champaign County, Ohio, Oct. 23, 1930; s. Marion Nelson and Mae Irene (Newell) B.; student Franklin U., 1957, Sinclaire Community Coll., 1967, Wright State U., 1973, 74, Edison State Coll., 1976, Real Estate Exchange, 1978, 79; m. Dorothy June Poling, July 5, 1952; children—Terry Lynn, Toni Lee, Todd Lane. Br. mgr. Jerry Oberley Realty, Inc., 1972-73, gen. mgr., 1973-77; v.p. Paul Clark Realty, Inc., 1977-78; pres. Land Office Realty, Inc., St. Paris, Ohio, 1978—; founder, chmn., pres. Champaign Multiple Listing Service; leader home buying and selling seminars. Adult edn. adv. bd. Ohio Hi Point Vocat. Sch.; mem. Nat. Republican Com., Congressional Com. VIP. Served with USN, 1950-54; ETO. Mem. Internat. Exchange Assn., Dayton Traders Club, Ohio Transaction Engr. Group. Home: 8208 Zimmerman Rd Saint Paris OH 43072 Office: 104 S Springfield St Saint Paris OH 43072

BODINE, HAROLD CARL, electric co. exec.; b. Chgo., Mar. 21, 1913; s. Carl David and Emma Charlotte (Anderson) B.; B.S.E.E., Purdue U., 1936; postgrad. Harvard U., M.I.T., 1942; m. Alice Pearl Dann, Mar. 13, 1948; children—Robert William, Debra Lynn, David Carl. With Bodine Electric Co., Chgo., 1936—, now pres., chmn. bd.; dir. Reliance Electric Co., Sola Basic Industries. Served with Armed Forces, 1942-46. Baptist. Address: 2500 W Bradley Pl Chicago IL 60618

BODINUS, PATRICIA KAY, nurse; b. Toledo, Mar. 9, 1952; d. William and Virginia Marie B.; R.N., Mercy Sch. of Nursing, Toledo, 1975; B.S. in Nursing, Mary Manse Coll., Toledo, 1975; postgrad. Siena Heights Coll., Adrian, Mich. Nurse emergency dept. Meml. Hosp., Monroe, Mich., 1975-76; instr. ambulatory nursing St. Vincent Hosp. Sch. of Nursing, Toledo, 1976-80, instr. orthopedic nursing, 1980—; camp nurse Red Pine Camp for Girls, Minocqua, Wis., summer 1979. Disaster nurse, vol. nurse blood program NW Ohio chpt. ARC, mem. nursing and health adv. council. Mem. Toledo Mus. of Art, Nat. League Nursing (Mich. chpt.), Am. Nurses Assn. (sec. public relations com. Toledo dist.), Emergency Dept. Nurses Assn. (Detroit), AAUW (Monroe, Mich.), Med. Coll. Ohio Sch. Nursing Honor Soc. (charter), Ward Found., Nat. Audubon Soc., Nat. Wildlife Soc., Bird Friends Soc. Republican. Episcopalian. Clubs: Am. Chesapeake, Lake Superior State Coll. Unicorn Hunters. Office: St Vincent Hosp Sch Nursing 2201 Cherry St Toledo OH 43608

BODMAN, GERALD RICHARD, cons. engr.; b. Catawissa, Pa., May 22, 1944; s. Gerald Frederick and Betty Mae (Stevenson) B.; B.S., Pa. State U., 1966, M.S., 1968; m. Mary Ellen Ahler, July 21, 1973; children—Lee, Melanie, Julian. Self-employed as irrigation system designer, Catawissa, Pa., 1964-67; instr. Pa. State U., University Park, 1966-68; engr./constrn. supr. New Eng. Pole Builders, Inc., Ludlow, Mass., 1968-70: self-employed in home bldg. and remodeling, Ludlow, Mass., 1970-71; extension agrl. engr., asst. prof. Pa. State U., University Park, 1971-78; pvt. practice cons. agrl. and structural engring. Space Preceptors Assos., State College, Pa., Ludlow, Mass., Lincoln, Nebr., 1970—; specialist on farmstead engring., livestock housing, milking systems and procedures, grain drying; asso. prof., extension agrl. engr. U. Nebr., Lincoln, 1978—; vis. prof. dept. home econs. Ind. U., Bloomington, 1972. Mem. bd. deacons State College Presbyn. Ch., 1974-78, chmn., 1978; deacon Eastridge Presbyn. Ch., Lincoln, 1981—. Registered profl. engr., Pa. N.Y., Mass., Ind., Calif., Maine, N.H., Vt., Md., Colo., Iowa, Kans., Tenn., Del., Conn., Ill., Mo., Nebr., Ohio, N.J., Va., R.I., W.Va.; lic. land surveyor, Pa. Mem. Am. Soc. Agrl. Engrs. (mem. exec. com. North Atlantic region 1975-78, 1st vice-chmn. program 1977-78, chmn. elect Pa. sect. 1977-78, Blue Ribbon awards in Ednl. Aids Competition, 1975, 77, 78, 79, 80, 81), Profl. Engrs. in Pvt. Practice, Nat., Nebr. socs. profl. engrs., ASHRAE, N.E. Dairy Practices Council (chmn. practical plumbing for milking centers subcom.), ASHRAE. Republican. Contbr. 175 articles to profl. jours. and popular publs. Home and Office: 5911 Sunrise Rd Lincoln NE 68510

BOECK, LAVERNE DWAINE, fermentation microbiologist; b. Johnson, Nebr., May 16, 1930; s. Otto Bernhard and Alma Marie (Stutheit) B.; student U. Nebr., 1947-49, Wartburg Coll., 1949-50; B.S. in Biology, Butler U., 1958, M.S. in Microbiology, 1963; m. Fredia Mae Jarrett, Oct. 25, 1953; children—Deborah, Kirk, Bruce, Eric, Gregg, Craig. Clerical engring. analyst Allison div. Gen. Motors Corp., Indpls., 1953-57; asso. microbiologist Eli Lilly & Co., Indpls., 1958-63, microbiologist, 1963-65, asst. sr. microbiologist, 1965-67, asso. sr. microbiologist, 1967-72, sr. microbiologist, 1972—. Served to lt., Anti-aircraft Arty., U.S. Army, 1951-53. Mem. Am. Soc. Microbiology, Soc. Indsl. Microbiology, Am. Chem. Soc., Sigma Xi. Republican. Lutheran. Contbr. articles to profl. jours.; patentee in field. Home: 741 Chapel Hill West Dr Indianapolis IN 46224 Office: Eli Lilly Research Labs Indianapolis IN 46285

BOEKE, ROBERT WILLIAM, mfg. co. exec.; b. Hubbard, Iowa, July 28, 1925; s. John Henry and Elizabeth A. (Schwartz) B.; B.S., Iowa State Coll., 1948, M.S., 1950; postgrad. Columbia U., 1966, Aspen Inst., 1976; m. Roberta Starbuck, Sept. 6, 1947; children—Lee Anne Boeke Burke, Linda Sue Boeke Day, John Robert. Instr., Iowa State U., Ames, 1947-51; with Deere & Co., various locations, 1979—, sr. v.p. components design and mfr., Moline, Ill., 1979—, also dir.; dir. Banks of Iowa. Active Boy Scouts Am., Moline, 1972-81; active United Way of Rock Island and Scott Counties; v.p. Iowa State U. Found., 1977—. Served with USN, 1943-45. Mem. Am. Soc. Quality Control, Farm and Indsl. Equipment Inst. Presbyterian. Home: 2895 W Court Bettendorf IA 52722 Office: Deere & Company John Deere Rd Moline IL 61265

BOELTER, ROBERT IRVIN, advt. agy. exec.; b. Eau Claire, Wis., Nov. 21, 1940; s. Robert H. and La Vyne M. (Sherman) B.; B.S., U. Wis., Madison, 1965; 1 son, Christopher. Art dir. Waldbilling & Besteman, Inc., Madison, 1966-67; creative dir. Stephan & Brady, Inc., Madison, 1967-70; art dir. Hoffman, York, Baker & Johnson, Chgo., 1970-71, Milw., 1971-73; pres. Advt., Boelter & Lincoln, Madison and Milw., 1973—; tchr. Madison Area Tech. Coll., 1966-67, mem. comml. art adv. bd., 1976-81. Recipient numerous awards for advt. creative work, including: Madison Advt. Club, 1967-70, 74-81, Milw. Advt. Club, 1977, Milw. Art Dirs. Club, 1966-71, Milw. Soc. Communicating Arts, 1972-76, Am. Advt. Fedn., 1975-81, Am. Bus. Press Assn., 1972, CLIO, 1979, N.Y. One Show, 1981, Bank Mktg. Assn., 1979-81, Rockford Advt. Club, 1980. Mem. Am. Mktg. Assn. (chpt. pres. 1981), Madison Advt. Club, Madison Art Center, Central Madison Council, Greater Madison C. of C., North Central Briarders (founding pres. 1976-77), Briard Club Am. (v.p.), Nat. Dog Breed Club, Nat. Model Railroaders Assn., Pro-Com. Home: 4383 Windsor Rd Windsor WI 53598 Office: PO Box 1665 123 E Doty St Madison WI 53701

BOEMI, A. ANDREW, banker; b. N.Y.C., Mar. 3, 1915; s. S. and Marietta (Boemi) B.; B.C.E., Coll. City N.Y., 1936, M.C.E., 1938; m. Flora Dorothy DeMuro, Apr. 26, 1941; children—Andrew A., Marcia Rosamond Buchanan. Engr., Gibb & Hill, Cons. Engrs., N.Y.C., 1937; city planner N.Y. Planning Comm., 1938-41; cons. U.S. Bur. Budget, Exec. Office of President, Washington, 1942; asst. loan officer, planning cons., asst. v.p., v.p. First Fed. Savs. & Loan, Chgo., 1946-57; chmn. bd., pres. Madison Bank & Trust Co., Chgo., 1957—; pres., chmn. bd. Madison Financial Corp., Chgo., 1974—; chmn. bd. Madison Nat. Bank of Niles (Ill.), 1976—, 1st Nat. Bank of Wheeling (Ill.), 1978—. Mem. exec. com. Archdiocesan Commn. Human Relations and Ecumenism; mem. Mayor's Commn. Landmarks Preservation Council. Bd. dirs. Met. Housing and Planning Council, 1950—, pres., 1975-76; mem. Elementary Sch. Bd., Park Ridge, Ill., 1953-59, pres., 1956-59; citizens bd. Loyola U., Chgo.; chmn. Joint Action Com. Civic Assns. for location Chgo. campus U. Ill., 1960-61; chmn. Gateway Com., Chgo., 1958-63; bd. dirs. Duncan YMCA, 1964-77. Served to lt. comdr. USNR, 1942-46. Recipient commendation from sec. navy, World War II. Mem. Am. Bankers Assn., Assn. for Modern Banking in Ill. (v.p. 1974-75, dir.), Am. Soc. C.E., Am. Inst. Planners, Assn. Commerce and Industry (chmn. comml. devel. com.), Navy League U.S., Newcomen Soc. N. Am., Am. Legion, Lambda Alpha, Alpha Beta Gamma. Republican. Roman Catholic. Clubs: Economic, Bankers, Metropolitan, University (Chgo.); Park Ridge Country. Home: 1110 N Lake Shore Dr Apt 7-S Chicago IL 60611 Office: 400 W Madison St Chicago IL 60606

BOERGER, WILLIAM GEORGE, oral and maxillofacial surgeon; b. St. Cloud, Minn., May 30, 1941; s. Milton Carl and Geneva Marie (Spaniol) B.; student Crosier Sem., Onamia, Minn., 1959-61, St. Cloud State Coll., 1961-63; B.S., U. Minn., 1965, D.D.S., 1967; m. Hiroko Hamada, Nov. 16, 1968 (div. 1978); 1 son, Jeffrey; m. Theresa M. Wagner, Nov. 3, 1978; children—Megan, John. Resident in oral surgery U. Minn., Mpls., 1969-72; practice oral surgery, Wayzata, Minn., 1972—, also Edina, Minn.; mem. staffs Methodist Hosp., St. Louis Park, Minn., Fairview Southdale Hosp., Edina, Waconia Ridgeview Hosp., also Children's Health Center, Mpls. Served with USNR, 1967-69. Fellow Am. Dental Soc. Anesthesiology, Am. Assn. Oral and Maxillofacial Surgeons; mem. ADA, Minn., Mpls. Dist. dental socs., Mpls., Minn. socs. oral and maxillofacial surgeons, Minnetonka, Bloomington dental study clubs, Southdale Dental Soc., Omicron Kappa Upsilon. Office: 250 N Central Ave #214 Wayzata MN 55391

BOESCHENSTEIN, WILLIAM WADE, glass products mfg. co. exec.; b. Chgo., Sept. 7, 1925; s. Harold and Elizabeth (Wade) B.; B.S., Yale U., 1950; m. Josephine H. Moll, Nov. 28, 1953; children—William W., Michael, Peter, Stephen. With Owens-Corning Fiberglas Corp., 1950—, exec. v.p., 1967-71, pres., 1971—, chief exec. officer, 1972—, also dir.; dir. AEP, Inc., FMC Corp., Hanna Mining Co., Prudential Ins. Co. Am. Trustee Toledo Mus. Art, Phillips Acad., Andover, Mass. Mem. Bus. Council, Conf. Bd. Clubs: Econ. (N.Y.C.); Econ. (Detroit); Inverness (Toledo); Belmont Country (Perrysburg, Ohio); Augusta (Ga.) Nat. Office: Fiberglas Tower Toledo OH 43659

BOESE, GILBERT KARYLE, zoo dir.; b. Chgo., June 24, 1937; s. Carl H. and Winifred A. Boese; B.A., Carthage (Ill.) Coll., 1959; M.S., No. Ill. U., 1965; Ph.D. (NIMH trainee 1970), Johns Hopkins U., 1973; m. Wilma Lou Blenz, Dec. 19, 1959; children—Ann Carroll, Peter Austin. Instr. biology Thornton Community Coll., Harvey, Ill., 1965-67; asst. prof. biology Elmhurst (Ill.) Coll., 1967-69; dep. dir. Chgo. Zool. Park, Brookfield, Ill., 1971-80; dir. Milwaukee County Zool. Gardens, Milw., 1980—; adj. prof. U. Wis., Milw.; bd. dirs. Riveredge Nature Center, 1980—, Greater Milw. Conv. and Visitors Bur. Recipient Disting. Alumni award Carthage Coll., 1981; grantee Elmhust Coll. Alumni Faculty, 1969. Mem. Internat. Crane Found., Am. Assn. Zool. Parks and Aquariums, Am. Mus. Natural History. Clubs: Adventurers; University. Address: L0001 W Bluemound Rd Milwaukee WI 53226

BOESE, ROBERT ALAN, forensic chemist; b. Chgo., Mar. 30, 1934; s. Fred W. and Adeline B. (Kondrad) B.; A.A. in Chemistry, Wright Jr. Coll., 1960; B.S. in Chemistry, Ill. Inst. Tech., 1969, M. Pub. Adminstrn., 1974; m. June C. Franke, Dec. 10, 1955; children—Mark A., Brian A. Patrolman, Chgo. Police Dept., 1956-58, investigator crime lab., 1958-60, firearms examiner, 1960-63, sr. firearms examiner, 1963-65, chemist, crime lab., 1965-71, chief chemist, 1971-74, tech. coordinator, 1974—; pres. B and W Cons. Forensic Chemists, Inc.; part time faculty St. Xavier Coll.; lectr. Northwestern U., Ill. Inst. Tech., U. Notre Dame, Loyola U., Chgo. Police Acad.; state instr. in use of breathalyzer; mem. Task Force for Evaluation of Ill. Crime Lab System, 1974-75. Fellow Am. Acad. Forensic Scis. (criminalistics sect.); mem. Am. Chem. Soc., Midwestern Assn. Forensic Scientists (founder, pres. 1976-77), Am. Firearms and Tool Marks Examiners (charter), Chgo. Gas Chromatography Discussion Group, Am. Soc. Pub. Adminstrn. Clubs: Masons, Shriners. Expert witness in firearms identification and forensic chemistry municipal, county, fed. cts.; contbr. articles to profl. jours. Home: 5657 S Mason Ave Chicago IL 60638 Office: Chicago Police Dept 1121 S State St Chicago IL 60605

BOESE, VIRGINIA ELLEN, curator; b. Troy, Ohio, July 16, 1907; d. William Harry and Virginia Grace (Meeker) Gilbert; student Western Coll. for Women, Oxford, Ohio, 1924-26; B.A., Ohio Wesleyan U., Delaware, 1928; m. Carl Wimmler Boese, Aug. 5, 1929. Tchr. Latin and English, Concord Twp. Sch., Miami County, Ohio, 1928-29; legal sec. to William Harry Gilbert, Troy, 1931-45; dir. Troy

Hist. Soc., 1965-76, archivist-librarian, 1966-76, genealogist, 1966—, dir. hist. room, 1966-76, asst. archivist-librarian, 1976—; dir., curator Overfield Log Tavern Mus., 1966-75, asst. curator, 1975—. Pres., violinist Troy Music Club, 1932-33; pres. Troy Altrurian Club, 1933-34, Current Events Club, 1954-55. Co-recipient (with husband) Community Service award Troy Jaycees, 1972. Mem. DAR, Colonial Dames XVII Century, LWV, Daus. of Founders and Patriots Am., Phi Mu, Kappa Delta Pi. Republican. Presbyn. (deacon). Author: Overfield Genealogy Research Notes, 1968, rev., 1970; Revolutionary Soldiers of Miami County, Ohio, 1976, rev., 1979; Meeker Genealogy, 1975; Genealogy of Knoop Family of Miami County, Ohio, 1981. Compiler, Index to Beers 1880 History, 1973. Home: 106 S Plum St Troy OH 45373 Office: 201 E Water St Troy OH 45373

BOESEL, MILTON CHARLES, JR., lawyer, bus. exec.; b. Toledo, July 12, 1928; s. Milton C. and Florence (Fitzgerald) B.; B.A., Yale U., 1950; LL.B., Harvard U., 1953; m. Lucy Laughlin Mather, Mar. 25, 1961; children—Elizabeth Parks, Charles Mather, Andrew Fitzgerald. Admitted to Ohio bar, 1953, Mich. bar, 1953; counsel firm Ritter, Boesel, Robinson & Marsh, Toledo, 1956—; pres., dir. Michabo, Inc.; dir. First Nat. Bank Toledo. Served to lt., USNR, 1953-56. Episcopalian. Mason. Clubs: Toledo, Toledo Country (Toledo); Leland (Mich.) Country. Home: 2268 Innisbrook Rd Toledo OH 43606 Office: 240 Huron St Toledo OH 43604

BOETGER, LEE WILLIAM, machinery mfg. co. exec.; b. Erie, Pa., Mar. 24, 1917; s. Fred William and Marie Ann B.; B.S. in Acctg., Gannon Coll., 1940; m. Mary Lou Krug, Feb. 22, 1941; children—Robert Owen, Ronald Lee. Supr., Gen. Telephone Co., Erie, 1937-47; asst. controller Boston Store, Erie, 1948-53; auditor Protane Corp., Erie, 1953-56; controller Sealy Mattress Co., Cleve., 1956-58; controller Fasson Products, Inc., Painesville, Ohio, 1958-68; pres. Code Mfg., Inc., Willoughby, Ohio, 1969—. Mem. Fin. Execs. Inst. Clubs: Mayfield Tennis, Riverview Racquet. Office: Code Mfg Inc 4727 E 355th St Willoughby OH 44094

BOETTCHER, ROBERT WALTER, civil engr.; b. Gooding, Idaho, Apr. 3, 1931; s. Walter Alfred and Katherine Benedicta (Hansen) B.; B.S. in Civil Engring., Wash. State U., 1953; m. Marguerite Patricia Warner, Oct. 1, 1960; children—Eric, Edwin, Vanessa. With U.S. Bur. Reclamation, various locations, 1947-52, 55-56; with Joseph K. Knoerle & Assos., Chgo., 1956-63; with Knoerle, Bender Stone & Assos. (now Envirodyne Engrs. Inc.), Chgo., 1963—, project mgr., 1973—, sr. asso., 1976—. Served with U.S. Army, 1953-55. Registered profl. engr., Ill. Mem. ASCE. Designer, planner numerous hwy., bridge, irrigation and drainage projects. Home: 1047 Dell Rd Northbrook IL 60062 Office: 222 W Adams St Chicago IL 60606

BOGAERT, MARGARET JEAN, induction heating mfg. co. exec.; b. Pontiac, Mich., Feb. 24, 1959; d. Albert T. and Christine (Chaney) Bogaert; student Oakland Community Coll., 1978. Head cashier Belk Lindsay Dept. Stores, Maderia Beach, Fla., 1975-76; clk.-typist St. Petersburg Credit Bur., Birmingham, Mich., 1976; v.p. Almar Industries Inc., Hazel Park, Mich., 1976-81, pres., 1981—. Evang. Lutheran. Home: 2811 Griffith St Berkley MI 48072 Office: 21005 Dequindre St Hazel Park MI 48030

BOGDANOR, JANET CAROL, educator; b. St. Louis, Aug. 12, 1941; d. Delo and Charline (Hill) Selig; B.S., U. Mo., Columbia, 1963, M. Elem. Edn., St. Louis, 1979; m. John L. Bogdanor, Apr. 11, 1964; 1 son, John. Tchr., elem. schs. Lindberg Sch. Dist., Mo., 1963-64, Columbia, Mo., 1964-69, Hazelwood (Mo.) Sch. Dist., 1973-74, Francis Howell Sch. Dist., Fairmount Intermediate Sch., St. Peter, Mo., 1980—. Deacon, 1st Presbyn. Ch., Ferguson, Mo., 1981-83. Mem. Mo. Edn. Assn., NEA, Internat. Reading Assn., Assn. Supervision and Curriculum Devel., Delta Delta Delta. Republican. Home: 2204 Rountree St Saint Louis MO 63136 Office: 1725 Thoele Rd St Peters MO 63376

BOGER, GAIL PARSONS GREEN, educator; b. Worthington, Ind., June 8, 1914; d. Byron Tennison and Bula (Taylor) Green; B.S., Ind. U., 1950; M.S. (DuPont fellow), Harvard U., 1959; Ph.D., U. Utah, 1969; m. Alva B. Parsons, June 8, 1935; children—Donald Alva, Robert Bradley, Gail Marie Parsons Michel, Helen Jean Parsons Czuba. Instr., Fresno (Calif.) State Jr. Coll., 1948-54; asst. prof. Purdue U. Extension, Michigan City, Ind., 1955-58; tchr. jr.-sr. high sch., Michigan City, 1954-59; instr. Ind. U., Bloomington, 1959-64; prof. dept. edn. Ohio No. U., Ada, 1964—; chmn. nat. and internat. research coms. Children's Internat. Summer Villages, Inc., chmn. research com. of internat. bd. trustees, 1981—. Dupont fellow, 1957; NSF fellow, 1961, 63; NSF-AEC fellow, 1960. Mem. Am. Assn. Supervision and Curriculum Devel., Am. Assn. Coll. Tchrs. of Edn., AAUP, Nat. Assn. Edn. of Gifted (dir., past v.p.), Nat. Assn. Creative Children and Adults, Ohio Assn. Gifted Children (trustee), NEA, Ohio, N.W. Ohio edn. assns., Ohio Acad. Sci., Kappa Delta Pi, Kappa Sigma Pi. Democrat. Episcopalian. Clubs: Gifted Children's Study, Federated Women's. Contbr. articles to profl. jours. Home: 1703 Wonderlick Rd Lima OH 45805 Office: 315 Dukes Bldg Ohio No U Ada OH 45810

BOGG, RICHARD ALLAN, educator; b. Grosse Pointe, Mich., May 31, 1934; s. Sydney Elmer and Dorothy Marie B.; B.B.A., U. Mich., 1956, Ph.D., 1971; postgrad. U. Exeter (Eng.), 1957-58; M.H.A., Washington U., St. Louis, 1960. Asst. adminstr. Port Huron (Mich.) Hosp., 1960-62; research asso. U. Mich. Sch. Pub. Health, 1965-69; asst. prof. dept. community medicine Faculty Medicine, U. Alta., Edmonton, Can., 1969-72; asst. prof. dept. sociology Ball State U., Muncie, Ind., 1972-77, asso. prof., 1977—. Bd. dirs. Planned Parenthood of Delaware County, 1973-75. USPHS trainee, 1962-65; HEW Childrens Bur. research grantee, 1966-68, Mich. Ho. of Reps. spl. research grantee, 1968. Mem. Am. Sociol. Assn., ACLU. Contbr. articles to profl. jours. Home: Rural Route 2 Daleville IN 47334 Office: Dept Sociology Ball State U Muncie IN 47306

BOGGESS, THOMAS PHILLIP, III, reprographics and graphics arts co. exec.; b. Greenville, Ky., Jan. 22, 1921; s. William C. and Gertrude Lucille (Lumpkins) B.; grad. high sch.; m. Ann Marie Mossner, Sept. 1, 1942; children—Thomas Phillip IV, Nancy L. Vice-pres. Alfred Mossner Co., Chgo., 1945-70, pres., chief operating officer, 1970—, also dir.; treas., dir. Blue Printers Supply Corp., Chgo. Chmn. zoning bd. of appeals, Village of River Forest, Ill., 1950—; mem., past bd. dirs. Westchester (Ill.) Bible Ch. Served with USNR, 1942-45. Decorated Purple Heart. Mem. Blue Print Club of Chgo. (pres. 1957-62). Club: Oak Park Country. Home: 335 Gale Ave River Forest IL 60305 Office: 108 W Lake St Chicago IL 60601

BOGGS, GARY PATRICK, metallurgist; b. Blackey, Ky., Mar. 25, 1946; s. Earl and Mabel (Dixon) B.; student U. Ky., 1964-67; B.S. in Mgmt. Sci., Franklin U., 1979; m. Carol Ann Hamb, Sept. 16, 1967; children—Angela Suzanne, Gary Patrick. Chem. technician N.Am. Rockwell, Winchester, Ky., 1968-72; plant metallurgist Rockwell Internat., Marysville, Ohio, 1972—, supt. quality control, 1980—. Bd. dirs. Union County YMCA, 1976-77, Union County Council on Alcoholism, 1976-77; active Boy Scouts. Mem. Am. Soc. Quality Control, Electroplaters Soc., Am. Soc. Metals. Democrat. Baptist. Home: 307 Elwood Ave Marysville OH 43040 Office: 13311 Industrial Pkwy Marysville OH 43040

BOGINA, AUGUST, JR., state senator; b. Girard, Kans., Sept. 13, 1927; s. August and Mary (Blazic) B.; B.S., Engring., Kans. State U., 1950; m. Velma M. Rank, 1949; children—Kathleen A., August III, Michael E., Mark A. Owner, Bogina & Assos., Lenexa, Kans., 1962-70; pres. Bogina Cons. Engrs., 1970—; former mem. Kans. Ho. of Reps., 1974-80; mem. Kans. Senate, 1980—. Precinct committeeman Kans. Republican party, 1970-74, chmn. city com., 1972-74. Served with U.S. Army, 1946-48. Registered profl. engr., Kans., Mo. Mem. Nat., Mo. socs. profl. engrs., Kans. Engring. Soc., Kans. Soc. Land Surveyors, Mo. Ann. Registered Land Surveyors. Roman Catholic. Address: Lenexa KS

BOGNORE, RONALD JAMES, health care assn. adminstr.; b. Stoneham, Mass., May 7, 1945; s. James C. and Rita (Casey) B.; B.S., Boston Coll., 1967; A.A.S., Coll. Lake County, 1968. Cons. scientist Naval Dental Research Inst., Q.E.I., Inc., Great Lakes, Ill., 1970-73; chief computer facility Research Inst., Am. Dental Assn., Chgo., 1972-73; asst. dir. div. behavioral scis., Am. Dental Assn. Health Found., Chgo., 1973-75; sr. analyst Bur. Economic Research and Statistics, Am. Dental Assn., Chgo., 1975-77, asst. sec. Council on Prosthetic Services and Dental Lab. Relations, 1977—. Recipient Thomasello scholarship, 1963. Mem. Internat. Assn. for Dental Research, Am. Assn. for Dental Research, Am. Assn. Dental Schs., Behavioral Scientists in Dental Research. Home: 317 1/2 Sherman Ave Evanston IL 60202 Office: 211 E Chicago Ave Suite 2001 Chicago IL 60611

BOGOMOLNY, RICHARD JOSEPH, retail exec.; b. Cleve., 1935; grad. Western Res. U., 1957; postgrad. Cleve. State U. Law Sch. Chmn. bd., pres., chief exec. officer First Nat. Supermarket, Maple Heights, Ohio. Office: 17000 Rockside Rd Maple Heights OH 44137*

BOGUE, ANDREW WENDELL, U.S. dist. ct. judge; b. Yankton, S.D., May 23, 1919; s. Andrew S. and Genevieve Bogue; B.S., S.D. State U., 1941; LL.B., U. S.D., 1947; m. Florence Elizabeth Williams, Aug. 5, 1945; children—Andrew Stevenson, Laurie Beth, Scott MacFarlane. Admitted to S.D. bar, 1947; states atty. Turn County (S.D.), from 1952; judge 2d Jud. Circuit S.D., 1967-70; judge U.S. Dist. Ct. Dist. S.D., Rapid City, 1970—, chief judge, 1980—. Mem. Am. Bar Assn., S.D. Bar Assn. Episcopalian. Address: Fed Bldg Room 318 515 9th St Rapid City SD 57701

BOGUSKY, RACHEL M., physician; b. Throop, Pa., Mar. 10, 1939; d. John Paul and Veronica (Farkas) Bogusky; student pvt. schs.; B.S., So. Conn. State Coll.; M.A., U. Conn.; Ed.S., Columbia U., Ed.D.; M.D., Universidad Autonoma de Ciudad Juarez, Mex. Tchr. East Haven (Conn.) Bd. Edn., 1961-62; dir. program for gifted, coordinator sci., master tchr. Greenwich (Conn.) Bd. Edn., 1962-69, 71-72; counseling therapist Psychol. Consultation Center, Columbia U., N.Y.C., 1970-71, instr. applied human devel., 1970-71; asst. prof. edn. U. Mich., Ann Arbor, 1973-76; behavior therapist, assertive tng. cons. Inst. for Behavior Change, Ann Arbor, 1975-76; ednl. psychologist, ednl. mgr. Med. Corp., Ann Arbor, 1976-77; pvt. cons. and counseling practice, Ann Arbor, 1975—. Recipient certificate recognition for ednl. contbns. Greenwich C. of C., 1969. Mem. Am. Psychol. Assn., Am. Personnel and Guidance Assn., Council for Exceptional Children (pres. chpt. 359, Fairfield County 1968-69), Assn. Advancement Behavior Therapy, Am. Soc. Tng. and Devel., Kappa Delta Pi. Author books, monographs and articles. Home and Office: 1 Haverhill Ct Ann Arbor MI 48105

BOHLEY, PAUL BRANCH, pump products mfg. co. exec.; b. Medina, Ohio, Dec. 14, 1923; s. Christian Gotleib and Bessie Louise (Dickerman) B.; student Ohio State U. Coll. Agr., 1941-43, 46-47; m. Dorothy Louise Persons, May 26, 1944; children—Donna Allyn (Mrs. Larry Alan Davis), Keith Persons. Owner-operator Crestview Farms, producers hybrid corn and certified small grain, Medina, 1945-62; gen. sales mgr. O-Y-O Seed Assos., Inc., Marysville, Ohio, 1962-65; sales mgr. agrl. products Gorman Rupp Co., mfr. pumps and associated products, Mansfield, Ohio, 1965—. Mem. Buckeye Consol. Sch. Bd., 1952-64, pres., 1952-53, 61-62. Served with USAAF, 1942-45; lt. col. Res. (ret.). Decorated D.F.C., Air medal with 5 oak leaf clusters. Mem. Nat. Fertilizer Solutions Assn. (dir. 1972, nat. v.p. 1970-73), Sprinkler Irrigation Assn. (chmn. membership com. 1972, chmn. Waste Water resources com. 1973-74, dir. 1974-75, pres. 1978), Ohio Flying Farmers Assn. (dir. 1947-48, 74-76, sec. 1978), Am. Legion, V.F.W., Medina C. of C., Air Force Assn., Ohio Future Farmers Assn. (hon.), Nat. Security Council, Alpha Zeta. Republican. Methodist (lay minister 1955-60). Lion (sec. 1948-52). Contbr. to profl. publs. in field. Home: 5986 Branch Rd Medina OH 44256 Office: 305 Bowman St Mansfield OH 44902

BOHLIM, RICHARD CHARLES, civil engr.; b. Michigan City, Ind., Sept. 5, 1952; s. George A. and Margaret (Elias) B.; B.S.C.E., Ind. Inst. Tech., 1974. Service engr. Combustion Engring., Martins Creek, Pa., 1974, Boston, 1974-75, St. Louis, 1975-76, lead service engr. for combustion engring., Lawrence, Kans., 1976-78, resident service engr., Overland Park, Kans., 1978-80, resident supr. tech. services Kansas City Dist., 1980—, dist. mgr. tech. services, Kansas City, 1981—. Lic. pvt. pilot. Mem. ASCE (citation award 1974), Alpha Sigma Phi. Roman Catholic. Club: Moose. Home: 6301 W 73 Terr Shawnee Mission KS 66204 Office: 6362 College Blvd Overland Park KS 66211

BOHLMANN, MARK PHILIP, state ofcl.; b. West Point, Nebr., Aug. 17, 1947; s. Arthur Erwin and Anne Fredericka (Weeke) B.; B.A. in Polit. Sci., Miami U., 1969; M.A. in Public Adminstrn., Ohio State U., 1974; m. Rebecca Ann Ellwanger, June 8, 1974; children—Eric Arthur, Jeffrey Alan. Legis. fellow Ohio Legis. Service Commn., Columbus, 1969, research asst. to legis. auditor, 1969-71; research asso. Ohio State U., Columbus, 1972-73; legis. asst. Ohio Gen. Assembly, Columbus, 1973; asst. to dir. Ohio Dept. Mental Retardation and Developmental Disabilities, Columbus, 1973-74, asst. commr. adminstr. and planning, 1974—; adj. prof. public adminstrn. Ohio State U., 1980—. Vice chmn. Ohio Bd. of Edn. select task force on spl. edn. fin. and adminstrn., 1977-78. Served with U.S. Army, 1971-72. Cert. qualified mental retardation profl., Ohio. Mem. Assn. Systems Mgmt., Planning Execs. Inst. Author: A Guidebook for Ohio Legislators, 1970; Report on Consumer Protection, 1971. Office: 30 E Broad St Suite 1256 Columbus OH 43215

BÖHM, FRIEDRICH K.M., architect, city planner; b. Krems, Austria, Jan. 27, 1942; came to U.S., 1967; s. Bruno and Luise (Hunger) B.; M.A., U. Vienna, 1966; M.C.P., Ohio State U., 1969; m. Jean-Clare Sims, Sept. 14, 1968; children—Anneliese A., Tyler Clark, Tucker L. Architect, F. Reist, Architekturbureau, Switzerland, 1965-67; lectr. architecture Ohio State U., Columbus, 1967-70; designer Nitschke & Assos., Architects, Columbus, 1969-72; partner, Nitschke-Godwin-Bohm, Architects, Columbus, 1972-76; partner NBBJ Group, Columbus, 1976—; pres. Godwin-Bohm-NBBJ Inc., Columbus, 1976-80; pres. Bohm-NBBJ, 1981—; lectr. Ohio U., Ohio State U., U. Cin., U. Vienna. Mem. Devel. Com. Greater Columbus, 1974—. Fulbright fellow, 1967; Nat. Endowment for Arts research grantee, 1969. Mem. Columbus C. of C., AIA (corp.), Am. Planning Assn., Can. Planning Soc., Austrian Soc. Regional Planning. Roman Catholic. Clubs: Columbus Met. (dir. 1971—), Columbus Athletic. Contbr. articles on urban design and redevel. to profl. jours. Home: 6335 Plesenton Dr Worthington OH 43085 Office: 505 S High St Columbus OH 43215

BOHM, HENRY VICTOR, research adminstr.; b. Vienna, Austria, July 16, 1929; s. Victor Charles and Gertrude (Rie) B.; A.B., Harvard, 1950; M.S., U. Ill., 1951; Ph.D., Brown U., 1958; m. Lucy Margaret Coons, Sept. 2, 1950; children— Victoria Rie, Jeffrey Ernst Thompson. Came to U.S., 1941, naturalized, 1946. Jr. physicist Gen. Electric Co., 1951, 53-54: teaching, research asst. Brown U., 1954-58, research asso., summer 1958; staff mem. Arthur D. Little, Inc., Cambridge, Mass., 1958-59; asso. prof. physics dept. Wayne State U., Detroit, 1959-64, acting chmn. physics dept., 1962-63, prof., 1964—, v.p. for grad. studies and research, 1968-71, v.p. for spl. projects, 1971-72, provost, 1972-75, on leave, 1978—; pres. Argonne Univs. Assn., 1978—. Vis. prof. Cornell U., 1966-67, U. Lancaster (Eng.), summer 1967, Purdue U., spring 1977; cons., examiner commn. on instns. higher edn. N. Central Assn. Colls. and Schs., 1971-80, mem. commn., 1974-78. Bd. dirs. Center for Research Libraries, Chgo, 1970-75, chmn., 1973. Served to lt. (j.g.) USNR, 1951-53. Fellow Am. Phys. Soc. Office: 9700 S Cass Ave PO Box 307 Argonne IL 60439

BOHNERT, WILLIAM PEACE, JR., tech. service specialist; b. Los Angeles, Apr. 27, 1944; s. William Peace and Eleanor (Kohake) B.; B.S. in Agr., U. Mo., 1966, M.S. in Soils, 1967; m. Ann Marie Kramper, Oct. 17, 1980. Area agronomy specialist U. Mo., Plattsburg, 1970-76; tech. service specialist research and devel. Chevron Chem. Co., Omaha, 1976—. Sec., Clinton County Soil and Water Conservation Dist., 1970-76. Served with U.S. Army, 1968-70. Nat. Plant Food Inst. Soil Sci. scholar, 1965. Mem. Am. Soc. Agronomy, Crop Sci. Soc. Am., No-Till Farmer Assn., Gamma Sigma Delta, Alpha Zeta. Democrat. Roman Catholic. Clubs: Dominic (v.p. 1978, treas. 1979), LaSalle. Home: 143 Charles Park Dr Council Bluffs IA 51501 Office: Chevron Chem Co 11244 Davenport St Omaha NE 68154

BOHON, ELLIS G(RAY), public accountant, mgmt. cons., tax cons.; b. LaBelle, Mo., Sept. 1, 1902; s. Frank W. and Lee (Ellis) B.; student Westminster Coll., Fulton, Mo., 1920-21; B.S. cum laude, Knox Coll., Galesburg, Ill., 1924; postgrad. Walton Sch. Commerce, 1927-29, Northwestern U., 1930-33, 1935, 1965-66, YMCA Community Coll., 1963-71, Chgo. Bd. Trade Grain Inst., 1955, 56 (all Chgo.); C.P.A., U. Ill., 1935; m. Joyce L. Finlayson, Apr. 15, 1939; children—Walter Duncan, Ellis Gray, II (dec.). Staff accountant Ernst & Ernst, C.P.A.'s, Chgo., 1927-30; partner R. L. Pearce & Co., C.P.A.s', 1930-36; propr. E. G. Bohon & Co., C.P.A.'s, 1936—; former lectr. Am. Inst. Banking, Walton Sch. Commerce, Ill. Inst. Tech., Chgo., Lake Forest (Ill.) Coll. Former advisor, treas. Lakes chpt. Order DeMolay, bus. men's adv. council Jones Comml. High Sch. (Chgo.). Enrolled as atty. Tax Ct. U.S.A.; C.P.A., Ill., Ky., Iowa, Mo. Member Am. Inst. C.P.A.'s, Am. Accounting Assn., Ill. (past chmn. tech. com.), Ia. socs. C.P.A.'s, Nat. Assn. Accountants, Am. Arbitration Assn., Accounting Research Assn., Am. Inst. Laundering, Ky. Hist. Soc., Midwest Bus. Adminstrn. Assn., Phi Delta Theta. Presbyterian. Clubs: Masons, Shriners (treas. club 1978), Order Eastern Star, Union League, Univ. of Evanston, Swedish Glee. Author papers. Home: 523 E North Ave Lake Bluff IL 60044 Office: 53 W Jackson Blvd Rm 1120 Chicago IL 60604

BOHR, PAUL RICHARD, ednl. instn. adminstr.; b. San Francisco, May 6, 1945; s. Paul Arnold and Lorene Elizabeth B.; B.A. (U. Calif. Regents scholar), U. Calif., Davis, 1967, Ph.D. (Woodrow Wilson fellow), 1978; M.A., Harvard U., 1968, M.Div., 1971; m. Gail Margaret-Rose Chang, June 10, 1972; 1 son, Aaron Anthony. Lay chaplain, tchr., Hong Kong, 1972-74; postdoctoral fellow in East Asian studies U. Calif., Davis, 1978-79, coordinator program for study East Asian culture, 1978-79; asst. prof. Asian history Ohio Wesleyan U., 1979-80; exec. dir. Midwest China Center, St. Paul, 1980—; lectr., cons. in field. Mem. Am. Hist. Assn., Assn. Asian Studies. Episcopalian. Author: Famine in China and the Missionary, 1972. Office: Midwest China Center 308 Gullixson Hall 2375 Como Ave W Saint Paul MN 55108

BOHRMAN, JEFFREY STEPHEN, pharmacologist, physiologist; b. Easton, Pa., Jan. 19, 1944; s. Fred Berger and Rhoda Lucille (Claster) B.; B.S. in Biology, Dickinson Coll., 1967; B.S. in Pharmacy, U. Pitts., 1970; M.S. in Pharmacology, U. Ill., 1972; Ph.D. in Pharmacology, U. Pacific, 1977; m. Evalyn Sue Rudman, Sept. 10, 1970; children—Rebecca Lyn, David Ryan. Pharmacy extern, intern Presbyterian Univ. Hosp., Pitts., 1968-70; teaching asst. U. Ill., 1970-72, U. Pacific, 1972-77; postdoctoral investigator Biology div. Oak Ridge Nat. Lab., 1977-80; research pharmacologist NIOSH, Cin., 1980—. Mem. Am. Pharm. Assn., AAAS, Rho Chi, Phi Kappa Phi. Democrat. Jewish. Home: 3763 Earls Court View Cincinnati OH 45226 Office: ETB 4676 Columbia Pkwy Cincinnati OH 45226

BOILEAU, OLIVER CLARK, aerospace co. exec.; b. Camden, N.J., Mar. 31, 1927; s. Oliver Clark and Florence Mary (Smith) B.; B.S.E.E., U. Pa., 1951, M.S.E.E., 1953; Sc.M. in Indsl. Mgmt. (Sloan fellow), M.I.T., 1964; m. Nan Eleze Hallen, Sept. 15, 1951; children—Clark Edward, Adrienne Lee, Nanette Erika, Jay Marshall. Mgr., Boeing Aerospace Co., Seattle, 1953-66, v.p., 1967-72, mgr. Minuteman, 1966-70, pres., 1972-80; pres. Gen. Dynamics Corp., Clayton, Mo., 1980—, also dir.; dir. 1st Nat. Bank, St. Louis. Served with USN, 1944-46. Mem. AIAA, Navy League, Air Force Assn., Am. Def. Preparedness Assn., Assn. U.S. Army, Armed Forces Communications and Electronics Assn., Nat. Aeros. Assn., Nat. Acad. Engring., Naval War Coll. Found. Club: Nat. Space. Office: 7733 Forsyth Blvd Clayton MO 63105

BOLAZINA, DENNIS ALLEN, architect; b. St. Louis, Aug. 1, 1946; s. Louis Angelo and Katherine B.; B.S., Washington U., St. Louis, 1968, M.Arch., 1970; postgrad. St. Louis U. Sch. Law. Planner, City of St. Louis Beautification Commn., 1968; pvt. practice archtl. design, landscape design, 1970; project architect R.G. McMahon & Assos., architects, St. Louis, 1971-76; prin. Dennis A. Bolazina, Architects, St. Louis, 1976—, Dennis A. Bolazina Realty, St. Louis, 1977—; instr. Washington U., St. Louis, Webster Coll., St. Louis; arbitrator for constrn. industry Am. Arbitration Assn.; expert witness constrn. disputes; cons. to ins. industry on constrn. disputes. Recipient Curators award U. Mo., 1964; Jack Lyons Meml. scholar, 1964; Am. The Beautiful grantee, 1968. Mem. AIA (continuing edn. com.), Am. Inst. Landscape Architects (pres. St. Louis chpt. 1978—), Real Estate Bd. Met. St. Louis (grievance com. 1980-83). Author: Public Art In St. Louis, 1969. Home: 424 Highland Rd Saint Louis MO 63122 Office: 7400 Pershing Ave Saint Louis MO 63130

BOLDON, REGINALD DEWITT, savs. and loan exec.; b. Sparta, Wis., Nov. 2, 1934; s. Dean E. and Amalia (Schneider) B.; student U. Wis., 1952-53; m. Mary Anne Hanson, Nov. 7, 1953; children—Reginald Kim, Terry Lea, Bruce Alan, Bradford Charles. Owner, operator Boldon's Service Sta., 1953-55; field rep. Thorp Finance Corp., Rochester and Richfield, Minn., 1955, South St. Paul, Minn., 1957-62, br. mgr., LaCrosse, Wis., 1962-63; asst. sec.-treas., sec.-treas. Western Fed. Savs. & Loan Assn. (formerly Sparta Fed. Savs. & Loan Assn.), 1963-66, exec. v.p., 1966-72, pres., 1972—, also dir.; pres., dir. Western Service Corp. Chmn., Sparta Ins. Commn., 1971-72; capt. United Fund, Sparta, 1964-65; capt. fund-raising for St.

Marys Hosp. and Methodist Edn. Bldg., 1963-64. Pres., bd. dirs. Sparta Indsl. Found.; pres., bd. govs. St. Mary's Hosp. Recipient Jaycee Spark Plug and Key Man awards, 1966-67, Jaycee Boss of Yr., 1979. Mem. Wis. Savs. and Loan League (dir. Milw. 1972-73, past. pres. N.W. dist.), U.S. League Savs. Assns. (com. on FHLB system), Savs. League Wis. (mgmt. info. com.), Sparta C. of C. Republican. Methodist (fin. com., past chmn. edn. com., past mem. ofcl. bd.). Clubs: Masons (past master), Shriners, Kiwanis (past pres. and dir.), Jaycees (past treas. and v.p.). Home: 611 W Division St Sparta WI 54656 Office: 124 N Court St Sparta WI 54656

BOLEN, CHARLES WARREN, coll. dean; b. West Frankfort, Ill., Sept. 27, 1923; s. William B. and Iva (Phillips) B.; B.M.E., Northwestern U., 1948; M.Mus., Eastman Sch. Music, Rochester, N.Y., 1950; Ph.D., Ind. U., 1954; m. Maxine Sheffler, Aug. 1, 1948; children—Ann, Jayne. Chmn. dept. music, prof. music Ripon (Wis.) Coll., 1954-62; dean Sch. Fine Arts, U. Mont., Missoula, 1962-70; dean Coll. Fine Arts, Ill. State U., Normal, 1970—; chmn. Mont. Arts Council, 1965-70; instr. Interlochen Music Camp, summers 1954-62; v.p. Bloomington-Normal Symphony Soc., 1975—; past mem. adv. bd. J.F. Kennedy Center Arts. Served with USAAF, 1942-46. Decorated Commendation medal; named Outstanding Tchr. of Year, Ripon Coll., 1962. Mem. Internat. Council Fine Arts Deans (chmn. 1969-70). Office: Ill State U Normal IL 61761

BOLGER, T(HOMAS) MICHAEL, lawyer; b. Minocqua, Wis., Dec. 23, 1939; s. Patrick Edward and Mary Frances (McConville) B.; B.A., Marquette U., 1961; M.A., St. Louis U., 1966, Ph.L., 1966; J.D., Northwestern U., 1971; m. Virginia Kay Empey, Aug. 24, 1968; children—John, Jennifer. Admitted to Wis. bar, 1971; mem. firm Quarles & Brady, Milw., 1971—, partner, 1978—; instr. philosophy Marquette U., Milw., 1967-68. Vice chmn. United Performing Arts Fund drive, 1976-77; bd. dirs. Kearney Negro Welfare Found., 1974—, Milw. Repertory Theatre, 1977—, Milw. Ballet Found., Inc., 1981—, Permanent Diaconate Program of Milw. Archdiocese, 1977—; pres. Artreach, Inc., 1979—; pres. bd. trustees Highland Community Sch., 1976—; trustee, sec.). U. Wis.-Milw. Found., 1976—; pres. bd. dirs. Hickory Hollow, 1978—. Mem. Am. Bar Assn., Milw. Bar Assn., Wis. Bar Assn., Fed. Bar Assn., Alpha Sigma Nu, Phi Sigma Tau. Clubs: Univ., The Town. Contbr. articles in field to profl. jours.; editor Northwestern Jour. of Criminal Law, 1970-71. Home: 137 E White Oak Way Mequon WI 53092 Office: 780 N Water St Milwaukee WI 53202

BOLIN, JERRY JOSEPH, state govt. ofcl.; b. Moberly, Mo., May 10, 1933; s. Kenneth L. and Frances S. Bolin; student U. Mo., 1951-52, 65-66, 71, N.E. Mo. State U.; m. Nancy Dreyer, Aug. 2, 1958; children—Mike, Maggie. With Mo. Dept. Corrections, 1966-70, 73-79, asst. dir., 1974-79; asst. dir. Mo. Assn. Social Welfare, 1970-72, Mo. Law Enforcement Council, 1972-73; dir. corrections State of Nebr., 1979—. Served with USMCR, 1957-58. Mem. Am. Correctional Assn., NEA, Nebr. Corrections Assn. Club: Rotary (pres. Moberly 1970). Office: 801 W Van Sorne St Lincoln NE 68509*

BOLIN, RUSSELL LEROY, constrn. co. exec.; b. Edgewood, Ill., Apr. 6, 1918; s. Fred Oscar and Lulu Margaret (Culley) B.; student Ill. Coll., 1936-38; B.S., Ind. State U., 1947; M.S., U. Ill., 1953; m. Anne May Mooney, Nov. 1, 1944; 1 dau., Diane Gege. Coach, Westville (Ill.) High Sch., 1947-51; with R.H. Bishop Co., Champaign, Ill., 1955—, sec., 1963—, v.p., 1970—. Trustee Vance Twp., 1976-81. Served to maj. USAAF, 1941-46; as sr. pilot USAF, 1951-53. Decorated Air medal, D.F.C. Named Basketball Coach of Yr., Vermilion County (Ill.) Coaches, 1951; recipient YMCA award for service to youth, 1968. Mem. Plumbing, Heating and Cooling Assn. Central Ill. (pres. 1962-66, state dir. to Ill. Plumbing and Heating Assn. 1975-81), Am. Legion, V.F.W., Gamma Nu. Club: Moose. Home: Rural Route 1 Box 179 Fairmount IL 61841 Office: 3506 N Mattis Ave Champaign IL 61820

BOLING, CHARLES WALKER, clergyman; b. Greenville, S.C., Aug. 16, 1931; s. John Harold and Mae (Wooten) B.; student North Greenville Jr. Coll., 1951, Furman U., 1953; B.D., Southwestern Bapt. Theol. Sem., 1957, M.Div., 1973; m. Betty Jean Harbin, Aug. 31, 1952; children—Anne Elizabeth, Debra Jean, Charla Kay. Music dir. Lima Bapt. Ch., Greenville, S.C., 1949-51; youth and music dir. Siloam Bapt. Ch., Easley, S.C., 1951-53; summer missionary Home Mission Bd., So. Bapt. Conv., Tulsa, 1954; music educator 1st Bapt. Ch., Springtown, Tex., 1955; ordained to ministry Baptist Ch., 1955; minister La Junta Bapt. Ch., Azle, Tex., 1955-57, 1st Bapt. Ch., Easley, S.C., 1957-68, 1st Bapt. Ch., Pinckneyville, Ill., 1968—; trustee New Orleans Bapt, Theol. Sem., Judson Bapt. Coll., Elgin, Ill. Chmn. Christmas parade, Easley, 1964; chmn. ARC, West Perry County, Ill., 1974-76, fin. chmn., 1976—. Mem. Ill. Bapt. State Assn. (dir.). Republican. Home: 310 W Saint Louis St Pinckneyville IL 62274 Office: 1st Bapt Ch 105 S Mill St PO Box 157 Pinckneyville IL 62274

BOLLAND, ERIC JOHN, state ofcl.; b. Lawton, Okla., Sept. 24, 1947; s. Gerhard Leroy and Eileen Marie (Kelly) B.; B.A. in History, U. Wis., Madison, 1974, M.A. in Public Adminstrn., 1978; m. Mary Ellen Hooyman, June 3, 1972; 1 son, Whitney. Dir., Wis. Registration Drive, 1971-73; legis. analyst Wis. State Senate, 1975-79; exec. dir. Wis. Bd. Aging, 1979—; work supr. U. Wis. social work intern program; founder, dir. elderly advocacy program Wis. Sr. Statesmanship; cons. in field. Mem. Nat. Council Aging. Author articles in field.

BOLLING, RICHARD (WALKER), congressman; b. N.Y.C., May 17, 1916; s. Richard Walker and Florence (Easton) B.; A.B., U. South, Sewanee, Tenn., 1937, A.M., 1939; postgrad. Vanderbilt U., 1939-40; D.C.L. (hon.), U. of South; LL.D., Rockhurst Coll. Dir. student activities, vets. affairs U. Kansas City, 1946-47; nat. vice-chmn. Am. Vets. Com., 1947-48; mem. 81st-97th congresses from 5th Mo. Dist., chmn. house rules com., mem. Democratic steering and policy com. Served to lt. col. AUS, 1941-46; PTO. Recipient Congl. Distinguished Service award Am. Polit. Sci. Assn. Democrat. Episcopalian. Author: House Out of Order, 1965; Power in the House, 1968, rev. edit., 1974. Home: 722 Walnut St Kansas City MO 64106 Office: US Courthouse 811 Grand Kansas City MO 64106 also Rayburn House Office Bldg Washington DC 20515

BOLLMEIER, EMIL WAYNE, mfg. co. exec.; b. Hurst, Ill., Jan. 16, 1925; s. Emil Philip and Flossie Louise (Swain) B.; B.S. in Chem. Engring., U. Nebr., 1947; postgrad. U. Minn., 1949-51; m. Nancy Lee Mercier, Feb. 9, 1972; children—David Wayne, Ann Louise, Paul Wesley. With 3M Co., St. Paul, 1947—, div. v.p. electro products div., 1965-72, group v.p. elec. products group, 1973—, mem. 3M mgmt. com. Mem. Planning Commn., Mendota Heights, Minn., 1960-65; chmn. Republican Party, Dakota County, Minn., 1965-68. Served with USNR, 1945-46. Fellow IEEE; mem. Nat. Elec. Mfrs. Assn. (bd. govs.), Sigma Xi, Sigma Tau, Theta Xi. Presbyterian. Club: White Bear Yacht. Numerous patents in U.S. and fgn. countries spring reserve elec. wire connector, dispensing package for insulating resins, resin injection splicing techniques, self-cleaning, high-tension elec. insulator for contaimated areas, magnetic remote control switch. Office: 3M Center 220-14W Saint Paul MN 55144

BOLTRES, H. WILLIAM, real estate investment cons.; b. Canton, Ohio, Apr. 7, 1936; s. Henry W. and Sarah A. Boltres; student Malone Coll., Ohio State U.; m. Doris Jean Kaufman, Aug. 9, 1958; children—Martin W., Christine A. With Addressograph-Multigraph Corp., Cleve., 1957-63, H.W. Boltres & Assos., Canton, 1963-65, Ohio Dept. Natural Resources, Columbus, 1965-75; pres. The Boltres Co., Newark, Ohio, 1975—; cons. U.S. investments. Mem. fin. com. Licking County Republican party, 1978-80. Served with USMC, 1953-54, U.S. Army, 1954-56. Mem. Nat. Bd. Realtors, Ohio Bd. Realtors, Licking County Bd. Realtors, Nat. Rifle Assn. Methodist. Clubs: Columbus Touchdown, Big Red Touchdown, Ducks Unltd. Home: 123 W Broadway Granville OH 43023 Office: 2112 Cherry Valley Rd Newark OH 43055

BOLYARD, CHARLES WESLEY, behavioral scientist, ins. co. exec.; b. Ft. Wayne, Ind., May 28, 1937; s. Charles Wesley and Virginia Maxine B.; B.B.A., Ind. Central U., 1960: M.A., Ball State U., 1962; Ph.D., Purdue U., 1971; m. Martha E. Hudson, Aug. 14, 1960; children—Mark Gregory, Todd Andrew. Sch. counselor MSD Perry Twp., Indpls., 1963-68; univ. adminstr. Purdue U., 1968-70; prof., univ. adminstr. Ind.-Purdue U., Ft. Wayne, 1970-77; behavioral sci. cons. Lincoln Nat. Life Ins., Ft. Wayne, Ind., 1977—. Mem. adv. bd. Allen County Mental Health Assn., 1979—; mem. adv. bd. Jr. League of Ft. Wayne, 1977—; adminstrv. bd., sec.-treas. Parent Club, Homestead High Sch., 1977-79; mem. adv. com. Ind. Vocat. Services; mem. adv. bd. Nat. Spinal Cord Injury Found., Voluntary Action Center, ARC; mem. Ft. Wayne Area Council on Employment of Handicapped. NDEA fellow, 1964. Mem. Midwest Coll. Placement Assn. (mem. profl. devel. com. 1978-79), Am. Personnel and Guidance Assn., Am. Soc. Personnel Adminstrn., Am. Psychol. Assn., Personnel Assn. Ft. Wayne, World Future Soc. Methodist. Club: Optimists. Author: (with Robert S. Barkhaus) Threads: A Tapestry of Self and Career Exploration, 1979; Career Development in the 1980's: Theory and Practice, 1981; contbr. chpt. to book, article to Mgmt. Quar. Home: 11626 Indigo Dr Fort Wayne IN 46804 Office: 1300 S Clinton St Fort Wayne IN 46801

BOLZ, HARRIETT HALLOCK (MRS. HAROLD A. BOLZ), musician; b. Cleve.; d. Roscoe Scott and Anna (Griffith) Hallock; B.A., Western Res. U., 1933; M.A., Ohio State U., 1958; m. Harold A. Bolz, Aug. 7, 1937; children—William Scott, Everett Arthur, Eric Harold. Composer, pianist numerous compositions; songs with piano, with string accompaniments, religious anthems, sonata for cello and piano, sonata for string and woodwind septet, contata for chorus and orch., sonatina for clarinet and piano; pub. Four Christmas Songs, Carol of the Flowers, 1967; Two Madrigals for Christmas, 1968; That I May Sing, 1970; Episode for Organ, 1979; Narrative Impromptu for Harp, 1979; Sweet Jesus; Two Profiles for Piano, 1980, Floret (piano), 1980, Capitol Pageant (piano), 1980; Polychrome Patterns for Clarinet and Piano performed Lincoln Center, N.Y.C., 1971; Sonic Essay and Fugue for Organ performed at 1st Nat. Congress on Women in Music, N.Y.C. Performances Chgo., Cleve., Indpls., Lafayette, Kokomo, Ind., Columbus, Ohio, Toledo, Miami Beach, Fla., Salt Lake City, Mpls., Cin., Sacramento, Washington, U. Wis., Platteville. Mem. Arlington-Grandview unit Columbus Symphony Orch. Recipient 1st prize for piano composition Nat. Fedn. Music Clubs Adult Contest, 1965; 1st prize religious anthem Nat. League Am. Pen Women, 1970. Mem. Nat. League Am. Pen Women (1st prize, Spl. Bicentennial Music award 1976, Mary Haubiel award 1980), Women's Music Club Columbus (dir.), Nat. Assn. Composers U.S.A., Ohio Fedn. Music Club (dir.), Theta Lambda Phi, Phi Beta (Pi Nu chpt., Rose award). Club: Ohio State University Women's. Composer: Duo Scherzando for trumpet in B-flat and piano, 1976, Pageant for Woodwind Quintet, How Shall We Speak (sacred anthem), 1981. Home: 3097 Herrick Rd Columbus OH 43221

BOMKAMP, LORAINE MARY, educator; b. Cedar Rapids, Iowa, July 9, 1930; d. Frank William and Kathryn (Seifert) Bomkamp; student Clarke Coll., 1948-49; A.A. with distinction, Mt. Mercy Coll., 1950; B.A., U. Iowa, 1958, M.A. in Bus. Edn. and Office Mgmt., 1965. Sec., Simmons, Perrine, Albright, Ellwood and Neff, attys., Cedar Rapids, 1950-51, Century Engring. Corp., Cedar Rapids, 1951-56; tchr. Wausau (Wis.) Tech. Inst., 1958-63, Cedar Rapids Community Sch. Dist., 1964—, coordinator data processing edn., 1964-65. Co-chmn. Donnelly Nursing Edn. Center, Mt. Mercy Coll., Cedar Rapids, 1975; chmn. Sister Immaculata Meml., 1972. Recipient Distinguished Alumni award Mt. Mercy Coll., 1972; Individual Performance award Data Processing Mgmt. Assn., 1978; Women's Equality Day award Cedar Rapids Civic Groups, 1978. Mem. NEA, Nat. Secs. Assn. (award 1967), Am., Iowa (award 1970) vocat. assns., Bus. and Profl. Women's Club (dir. 1967-70, Woman of Year award 1977), AAUW, Cath. Daus. Am., Iowa State, Cedar Rapids edn. assns., Nat., Iowa (award 1969) bus. edn. assns., Iowa Office Edn. Assn., Internat. Fedn. Catholic Alumnae (regent 1968-69), Mt. Mercy, Clarke Coll., U Iowa alumni assns., Delta Kappa Gamma (pres. 1976-78). Roman Catholic. Contbr. articles on bus. edn. to profl. jours. Home: 1352 Hinkley Ave NW Cedar Rapids IA 52405 Office: Jefferson Sr High Sch 1243 20th St SW Cedar Rapids IA 52404

BONACH, LOUISE AHLFORS, hosp. exec.; b. Eveleth, Minn., June 14, 1948; d. George F. and Mary (Gornik) Ahlfors; B.A., U. Minn., Duluth, 1970; m. Joseph V. Bonach, Aug. 27, 1971. Mem. admissions staff Augsburg Coll., Mpls., 1970-71; personnel asst. Fairview Hosp., Mpls., 1971-73, personnel officer, 1973-75, dir. employee relations, 1975-80, dir. human resources, 1980—. Mem. Am. Soc. Tng. and Devel., Am. Soc. Personnel Adminstrs., Am. Soc. Hosp. Public Relations Assn., Minn. Soc. Hosp. Public Relations, Twin Cities Personnel Assn., Am. Hosp. Assn., Mpls. Soc. Fine Arts. Home: 15665 S Woodgate Rd Minnetonka MN 55343 Office: Fairview Hosp 2312 S 6th St Minneapolis MN 55454

BONACKER, GLENN EDWARD, utility co. exec.; b. Sioux Falls, S.D., June 12, 1918; s. William Frederick and Sarah Louise (Gustafson) B.; B.B.A., Nettleton Coll., 1940; m. Bernice Lillian Scott, Dec. 10, 1942; children—Sandra Kay, William Scott. Dist. mgr. Central Electric & Gas Co., Sioux Falls, S.D., 1952-57, asst. utilities mgr., Lincoln, Nebr., 1957-60; div. mgr. Western Power & Gas Co., Lincoln, 1960-62; v.p. Central Telephone and Utilities Corp., Lincoln, 1962-76; v.p. Minn. Gas Co., Lincoln, 1976—; dir. Am. Charter Savs. & Loan, Home Agy., State Realty, Lincoln. Pres., Nebr. Assn. Commerce and Industry, 1981—, Lincoln Chamber Indsl. Devel. Corp., 1977—; pres. Nebr. Resources Found., 1975—; vice-chmn. Lincoln Found., 1977—; v.p. L. L. Coryell & Sons Found., 1980. Served to maj., U.S. Army, 1941-46. Named Nebr. Diplomat of Yr., Gov. Exon, 1976. Mem. Am. Gas Assn., Midwest Gas Assn. (pres. 1968-69), Lincoln C. of C. (pres. 1973—). Republican. Lutheran. Clubs: Lincoln U., Nebr. Country of Lincoln, Candlelight, Crucible, Elks. Home: 1934 S 25th St Lincoln NE 68502 Office: 1201 N St Lincoln NE 68508

BONAVENTURA, LEO MARK, gynecologist; b. East Chicago, Ill., Aug. 1, 1945; s. Angelo Peter and Wanda D. (Kelleher) B.; student Marquette U., 1963-66; M.D., Ind. U., 1970; married; children—Leo Mark, Dena Anne, Angela Lorena. Intern in surgery, Cook County Hosp., Chgo., 1970-71; resident in ob-gyn., Ind. U. Hosps., 1973-76, fellow in reproductive endocrinology and infertility, 1976-78; asst. prof. ob-gyn., Ind. U., 1976—, asst. head sect. reproductive endocrinology and infertility, 1978-80, head sect., 1980—. Served with USN attached to USMC, 1971-73. Named Intern of Yr., Cook County Hosp., 1971. Diplomate Am. Bd. Obstetrics and Gynecology, Am. Bd. Reproductive Endocrinology and Infertility. Mem. Central Assn. Ob-Gyn., Am. Coll. Obstetricians and Gynecologists, Am. Fertility Soc., Can. Fertility Soc. Roman Catholic. Contbr. articles to profl. jours. Office: 1100 W Michigan Ave Indianapolis IN 46223

BOND, CHRISTOPHER SAMUEL, gov. of Mo.; b. St. Louis, Mar. 6, 1939; s. Arthur D. and Elizabeth (Green) B.; B.A. with honors, Princeton U., 1960; LL.B., U. Va., 1963; m. Carolyn Reid, May 13, 1967. Admitted to Mo. bar, 1963, U.S. Supreme Ct. bar, 1967; law clk. to chief judge U.S. Ct. of Appeals, 5th Dist., Atlanta, 1963-64; asso. firm Covington & Burling, Washington, 1965-67; practice law, Mexico, Mo., 1968; asst. atty. gen., chief counsel consumer protection div. State of Mo., 1969-70, auditor, 1971-73; gov. of Mo., 1973-77, 80—; pres. Gt. Plains Legal Found., Kansas City, Mo., from 1978. Chmn., Republican Gov.'s Assn.; vice chmn. Midwestern Gov.'s Assn.; exec. com. Nat. Gov.'s Conf. Republican. Presbyn. Office: Office of Governor State Capitol Jefferson City MO 65101*

BOND, DOROTHY ANN, cartoonist, lectr.; b. Chgo.; d. William George and Helga (Hansen) Peterson; student Chgo. Acad. Fine Arts; m. John Delmar Bond (divorced); children—John Delmar, Raleigh V. Civilian sec. in USN, 1940-44; syndicated cartoonist, 1945—; artist Northwest Hosp., 1970—; portrait artist, 1971—. Sponsor of The Easter Seal Soc. Hon. mem. Nat. Socs. Assn., Toastmistress Club, Chgo. Boys' Clubs, numerous other nat. and local orgns. Author cartoon books: Government Gertie, 1944, Navy Nora, 1945, Office Daze, 1945, The Second Baby, 1946, Life With the Boss, 1947, Mama, The Unsung Heroine, 1948, Meet Me in The Ladies Room, 1948, All Men Are Dogs, 1950, Let's Have a Baby, 1950, Your First or Second Baby?, 1956, Life with the Doctor n' Nurse, 1960, With Love Bobbi Borcherdt, 1961, Bobbi Borcherdt Presents, 1962, Heartwarmers, 1963, Bobbi Borcherdt's 100th Anniversary Booklet, 1968. Creator Dietsticker Cards, 1965; ReaLemon advt. series, 1968; newspaper feature Delightful Dietips, 1966. Address: 2450 N Washtenaw Ave Chicago IL 60647

BOND, EPPERSON ELLIS, chemist; b. Nashville, Apr. 5, 1923; s. Epperson Porter and Margaret (Reed) B.; B.A., Fisk U., 1944, postgrad., 1945; postgrad. DePaul U., 1946; m. Marian Ruth Phillips, June 9, 1950; 1 son, Michael Ellis. Research asso. Glidden Co., Chgo., 1946-47, Med. Sch., U. Ill., Chgo., 1947-50, Northwestern U., Chgo., 1950-53; chemist VA Hosp., Hines, Ill., 1953—, now research chemist. Chmn. credit com. Hines Fed. Credit Union, 1963-73, pres., 1973—; chmn. Hines Hosp. EEO com. Bd. dirs. Roseland Heights Community Assn. Fellow Am. Inst. Chemists; mem. Am. Assn. Clin. Chemists (dir.), Am. Chem. Soc., Ill. Kidney Found., Alpha Phi Alpha. Methodist (vice chmn. bd. stewards). Club: Men's (Chgo.). Home: 9835 Forest Ave Chicago IL 60628 Office: PO Box 41 Hines IL 60141

BOND, LOTTYE LOUISE, social worker; b. Albany, Ga., Mar. 31, 1933; d. Norman Franklin and Cornelia Maecalvin (Martin) Pittman; B.S.W., Madonna Coll., Livonia, Mich., 1977; M.A. in Guidance and Counseling, Eastern Mich. U., 1979; children—Kevin, Kim, Karen, Karla. Various office positions, 1953-57; social worker Neighborhood Service Orgn., Detroit, 1957-67, Family and Neighborhood Service, Inkster, Mich., 1967—; cons. paraprofl. tng., 1973—. Trustee Inkster Sch. Bd., 1974; co-chmn. Inkster's Ednl. Task Force, 1974; chmn. Inkster Police-Community Relations Council, 1971-73, Mayor Inkster Scholarship Com., 1971-74; mem. adv. com. admission and scholarship bd. Madonna Coll., 1975-77, Madonna Achievement Performance Program, 1978. Nat. Bus. and Profl. Women's scholar, 1975. Mem. Nat. Assn. Black Social Workers, Am. Personnel and Guidance Assn., Assn. Non-White Concerns, Nat. Assn. Sch. Bd. Members, Am. Coll. Personnel and Guidance Assn., Gamma Phi Delta. Episcopalian. Home: 1831 Lexington Pkwy Inkster MI 48141 Office: 26807 Michigan Ave Inkster MI 48141

BOND, MORRIS LINDSAY, banker; b. Columbia, S.C., Sept. 30, 1936; s. Lindsay Johnson and Lossie Mae (Johnson) B.; B.S., Clemson U., 1958; M.B.A., St. Louis U., 1967; postgrad. Southwestern Grad. Sch. Banking, So. Meth. U., 1980; m. Patricia Jeanne Hunter, June 14, 1962; children—Stephanie Jane, Michael Morris. Research technologist Corp. Research and Devel. Center, Pet, Inc., Greenville, Ill., 1959-61, supr. project control, 1961-66, sect. chief, 1966-68, mgr. adminstrv. services, 1968-73; ops. improvement officer First Nat. Bank, St. Louis, 1974-76, asst. v.p., 1976-78, v.p. account services div., 1978—; instr. bus. mgmt. Greenville Coll., 1977—, Am. Assn. Indsl. Mgmt., St. Louis, 1977—. Mem. Am. Inst. Indsl. Engrs., Am. Inst. Banking. Methodist. Clubs: Masons, Shriners. Home: 621 Walnut St Greenville IL 62246 Office: 515 Olive St St Louis MO 63101

BOND, ORIEL EDMUND, artist; b. Altus, Okla., July 18, 1911; s. Bert Galen and Bertha Ellen (Hughes) B.; student Rockford Coll., 1930-37; m. Dorothy Olive Swanson, Sept. 5, 1936; children—Bruce Edmund, Judy Kay (Mrs. Jay McCartney Hanson). Comml. artist J.L. Clark Mfg. Co., Rockford, Ill., after 1946; v.p., dir. J.L. Clark Assos., 1948—; one-man shows Burpee Art Gallery, 1956, 59, Belle Keith Gallery, 1959, 67, 72, 78, Rock River Savs. & Loan Co., 1969 (all Rockford), Geneseo (Ill.) Woman's Club, 1970, 71, Geneseo Library, 1978, 79; exhibited in group shows at Burpee Art Gallery, 1937, 38, 56, 58, 60, 68, 76, Wright Art Center, Beloit (Wis.) Coll., 1956, 57, 59, 60, 62, 63, Ill. State Fair, Springfield, 1959, 60, Am. Artists Profl. League, N.Y.C., 1971, 72, Profl. Artists and Designers Guild, Rockford, 1960, 61, 62, Winston-Salem (N.C.) Conv. Center, 1970, Hilton Inn, Williamsburg, Va., 1970, Downtown Gallery, Beloit, 1969, Colonial Village Mall, Rockford, 1962-81, Home Savs. & Loan Co., Rockford, 1962-81, Rockton (Ill.) Art Fair, 1971, 72, 73, 75, Wilhelm Tell Art Fair, New Glarus, Wis., 1972, 73, 75, Sterling (Ill.) Art Fair, 1972, Rock River Savs. & Loan Co., 1966, Greenwich Village Fair, Rockford, 1955-63, 71, 72, 73, 75, Beloit and Vicinity Art Fair, 1963, Janesville (Wis.) Art Fair, 1973; paintings reproduced on Artists of Am. calendars, 1975, 76, 77, 78, 79. Precinct committeeman Rockford Republican Com., 1956-58, 60. Recipient 1st popular award Rockford Art Assn., 1956, 58, 60, Ill. State Fair, 1959, Colonial Village Mall, 1972, Sterling Art Fair, 1972; 1st, 2d and 3d awards Rockton Art Fair, 1971, 72, 75; 2d place award Wilhelm Tell Art Fair, 1972; 2d and 3d place popular award Wright Art Center, 1959, 1st popular award, 1962; tied for popular award Geneseo Art Exhbn., 1981. Mem. Profl. Artists and Designers Guild (sec. 1959-60, v.p. 1961, 1st and 2d popular awards 1961, 62), Am. Artists Profl. League. Home: 7816 Bond Dr Roscoe IL 61073

BONDAR, ANDREW ARTHUR, dentist; b. Manchester, N.H., Oct. 23, 1914; s. Arthur George and Anna (Greneshen) B.; student U. N.H., 1932-34; D.M.D., Tufts U., 1938; diploma U.S. Army Med. Field Service Sch., 1969; certificate Command and Gen. Staff Coll., 1972; m. Ellen Ferguson Stewart, July 24, 1953; 1 dau., Billie Arlene. Pvt. practice dentistry, Manchester, 1939-42, 46-49; dentist VA Hosp., Battle Creek, Mich., 1949—. Lectr., clinician dist. and local dental socs. in N.H., N.Y., Que., Can. Asst. coach Jr. Am. Legion Baseball Team, Manchester, 1947-49; nat. chmn. Nat. German Prisoner of War Meml. Service, Ft. Custer, Mich., 1973-75. Served to capt. AUS, 1942-46, now col. Res. ret. Recipient cert. of commendation United War Vets. Council Battle Creek, 1979. Fellow Am. Acad. Gen. Dentistry, Midwest Acad. Prosthodontics; mem. Am., New Eng. dental assns., Northeastern Dental Soc., Am. Assn. Hosp. Dentists, Assn. U.S. Army, Tufts Coll., U. N.H. alumni assns., Assn. Mil. Surgeons U.S., Am. Soc. Geriatric Dentistry (nat. treas. 1975-81), Fedn. Am. Scientists, AAAS, Fedn. Dentaire Internationale, Am. Legion, VFW, Res. Officers Assn. U.S. (brigade of vols., pres. chpt.; dental surgeon Mich. dept. 1973-77, 79—), 40 and 8. Club: Elks. Home: 519 Alvena Ave Battle Creek MI 49017

BONDE, BRIAN JAMES, radio station exec.; b. Lake Preston, S.D., Nov. 1, 1958; s. John Walfred and Elizabeth Alice (Slocum) B.; student Augustana Coll., 1977-81, U. Ariz., 1978, Higher Edn. Consortium for Urban Affairs, Bogota, Colombia, 1979-80; m. Susan Vivian Greeley, Dec. 29, 1979. Reporter, Moody County Enterprise, Sioux Falls, S.D., 1977; public relations rep. Up With People, Tucson, 1978; program dir. Sta. KAUR-FM, Sioux Falls, 1979, gen. mgr., 1981—; lang. prof. Audio-Visual Center, Bogota, Colombia, 1980; reporter Sta. KIOV-KXRB and UPI, Sioux Falls, 1981; stringer AP, 1981-82; instr., media cons. Augustana Coll., Sioux Falls, 1981—. Mem. Bread for the World, S.D. Peace and Justice Center, S.D. Advt. Fedn., N.W. News Broadcasters Assn., Intercollegiate Broadcasting, Blue Key. Democrat. Methodist. Home: 2408 S Covell Sioux Falls SD 57105 Office: 28th & Summit Sioux Falls SD 57197

BONE, VIDA MARIE, employment cons. co. exec.; b. Vero Beach, Fla., Feb. 14, 1926; d. Raymond Lee and Emma Evangeline (DeFoe) Gore; student schs. Vero Beach; m. Charles Northington Bone, Oct. 11, 1944; children—Charles Raymond, Leonard Olin. With Winn Dixie Grocery Co., Miami, Fla., 1948-59; pvt. practice as beautician, 1960-66; supr. Servomation of Chgo., 1966-67; employment counselor Hallmark Personnel, Chgo., 1967-69; pres., owner, operator Employment Consultants Inc., Lansing, Ill., 1970—. Mem. Nat. (certified), Ill. employment assns. Republican. Lutheran. Club: Lansing Sportsman. Home: 3445 176th St Lansing IL 60438 Office: 2325 177th St Lansing IL 60438

BONEBURG, ANITA STROETZ, educator; b. Hammond, Ind., Feb. 23, 1920; d. Earl S. and Gertrude M. (Willarson) Stroetz; B.S. in Home Econs., Milw. Downer U. (now Lawrence U.), 1942; M.S. in Edn., Cleve. State U., 1978; postgrad. John Carroll U., 1970-75; Kent State U., 1979; m. Chester J. Boneburg, Aug. 25, 1942; children—Katharine D., Thomas J., Peter K. With Gallup-Robinson Opinion Surveys, Cleve. and Princeton, N.J., 1957-59; U.S. census enumataros U.S. Dept. Commerce, Washington, 1960; with Cleve. Public Schs., 1960—, substitute tchr., 1960-63, tchr. Blossom Hill Correctional Facility, 1963-68, tchr. home econs. dept. Lincoln-West High Sch., 1968—; textbook com. Greater Cleve.; participant Martha H. Jennings Econ. Edn. Interface Program, 1981-82. Mem. Future Homemakers Am. Task Force, 1980-82, Ohio regional com. Juvenile protection chmn. PTA, 1964; active West Shore Rep. Club, 1959-64; mem. World Hunger Com., 1979-80; adv. ARC and Human Relations Clubs, 1970-78, Welcome Club, 1980-81, Swords to Plowshares Com. Recipient Martha Holden Jennings tchr. leadership award, 1972; scholar award, 1966; ARC service award, 1975, 80; Quincy Washington Reading award; Sohio award, 1981; Am. Assn. Christians and Jews human relations grantee, 1970. Mem. Am. Vocat. Assn. (public relations com., legis. com. nat. network), Am. Home Econs. Assn., Ohio Vocat. Assn., Greater Cleve. Home Econs. Assn., Cleve. Council on Human Relations, Cleve. Econ. Council, Cleve. Teachers Union (conf. com., del. assembly rep., 1970-75), Lawrence U. Alumni Assn., Cleve. State U. Alumni Assn. Episcopalian. Clubs: Pinehurst Country (Pinehurst, N.C.), Coll. Club West. Active curriculum devel., task forces, research coms. in field; fund raising, Lawrence U., 1973—. Home: 18429 Sloane Lakewood OH 44107 Office: 1380 E Sixth St Cleveland OH 44114

BONÉE, JOHN RAOUL, utility exec.; b. New Orleans, Nov. 11, 1923; s. John Raoul and Lucille Evelyn (Schwarzenbach) B.: student Loyola U., New Orleans, 1940-42; M.A., Aquinas Inst., 1946, 50; Ph.D., U. Fribourg (Switzerland), 1953; m. Mavis Long Heyl, Dec. 22, 1967; children—Mavis Heyl McClung, Larrye Heyl Steldt. Joined Dominican Order, Roman Catholic Ch., 1942, ordained priest, 1949, laicized, 1967; prof. modern and contemporary philosophy Aquinas Inst., River Forest, Ill., 1953-61; prof. communications and homiletics St. Rose Priory, Dubuque, Iowa, 1961-67; mgr. Ill. Bell Tel. Co., Chgo., 1967—, mgr. corp. communications, 1970—; lectr. DePaul U., 1968—; cons. VISCAM, Cameroon, Africa. Mem. Community Relations Commn. Oak Park (Ill.), 1973-74. Mem. Public Relations Soc. Am., Chgo. Press Club. Roman Catholic. Home: 801 S Kenilworth Ave Oak Park IL 60304 Office: 225 W Randolph St Chicago IL 60606

BONES, WALTER I., state legislator; b. Mpls., Jan. 20, 1927; s. Walter I. and Fayetta (Conners) B.; B.S., Iowa State U.; m. Dewenta Gray, 1950; children—Walter III, Cathy Bones Van Hove, Steve, Judy, Jim, John, Susan. Farmer; mem. S.D. Ho. of Reps., 1975—. Named Outstanding Young Farmer, 1961; recipient award Nat. Block and Bridle Club, 1968, Pres.'s award S.D. Stock Growers Assn. Mem. Am. Nat. Cattlemen's Assn. (dir.), Farm Bur. Baptist. Clubs: Elks, Rotary. Office: State Capitol Pierre SD 57501*

BONGIORNO, JOHN ANTHONY, sales mgr.; b. Chgo., Sept. 29, 1951; s. John Anthony and Stephanie Marie (DiTusa) B.; A.S. in Accounting and Bus. Adminstrn., Triton Coll., 1971; student in Mktg., U. Ill., Chgo., 1969-73; m. Sharon Louise Bernath, July 12, 1975. Sales rep. electronic data processing Chgo. office Reynolds & Reynolds Co., Elk Grove Village, 1973-75, sales rep. automotive forms, 1975-81, Eastern div. sales mgr. automotive forms, Dayton, Ohio, 1981—. Named to 300 Club for sales excellence Reynolds and Reynolds Co., 1975-77, 79-80. Mem. Am., Chgo. mktg. assns., Dayton Sales and Mktg. Club. Roman Catholic. Home: 7540 Pelway Dr Dayton OH 45459 Office: 800 Germantown PO Box 1005 Dayton OH 45401

BONHAUS, LAURENCE ALLEN, archtl. lawyer, urban planner; b. Cin., May 27, 1949; s. Alphonse Lawrence and Mary Kathryn (Muchmore) B.; B.S. in Architecture cum laude, U. Cin., 1973, J.D., 1976; m. Jacquelyn Lea Arck, Oct. 11, 1981. Draftsman, designer Arend & Arend Architects, Cin., 1969-72; designer Kral, Zepf, Frietag and Assos., Architects & Engrs., Cin., 1972-73; designer, OSHA specialist offices Robert Harter Snyder, Cin., 1973-76; OSHA and bldg. code specialist, Project Designer AEDES Assos., Inc., 1973-76; admitted to Ohio bar, 1976; individual practice archtl. and planning law, Cin., 1976—; v.p., urban planner Citysystems, Inc., Cin., 1976—; arbitrator Am. Arbitration Assn.; sec. P.D.A., Inc. Co-chmn. Ohio Confederation, 1970-72, lobbyist for state and state affiliated univs.; mem. Gradison Campaign com., N.Avondale Neighborhood Assn.; trustee NAPA; v.p. Fairview/Clifton Heights housing devel. corp.; mem. Greater Cin. Beautiful Com., Contemporary Arts Center; first violinist Cin. Civic Orchestra; treas., bd. dirs., exec. com. Ohio Solar Resources Adv. Panel. Mem. AIA (co-chmn. nat. conv. com. 1980, nat. codes and standards com., Henry Adams cert., 1973, chmn. Cin. chpt. speakers bur.), Am. Bar Assn., Cin. Bar Assn. (chmn. OSHA com., mem. constrn. and engring. law com.), Architects Soc. Ohio, Lawyers Club of Cin., Southwest Ohio Alternate Energy Assn. (founding mem., dir., exec. com.), Ohio Solar Energy Assn. (treas., dir.), SCARAB (v.p., 1970-71), Greater Cin. C. of C. (energy com.), Phi Alpha Delta (alumni justice Cin. chpt., Outstanding Service cert. 1980). Republican (mem. Cin. Charter Party). Methodist (mem. adminstrv. bd.). Clubs: Cin. CINgles (dirs., dir. devel.), Updowntowners, Cincinnatus, Metro. Works include interior design and execution of mosaic panel Forest Chapel United Meth. Ch., 1969, restoration Fleischman mansion, 1974-76, Conroy mansion, 1977-79; new zoning code and land use plan Union Twp., Clermont County, Ohio, 1977-78; handicapped accessibility study Montgomery County, Ohio, 1979-81; urban renewal study Newark, Ohio, 1977-78; ind. living facility Total Living Concepts, Inc., Cin., 1980-81. Home: 948 Dana Ave Cincinnati OH 45229 Office: 18 W 7th St Suite 700 Cincinnati OH 45202

BONIOR, DAVID EDWARD, congressman; b. Detroit, June 6, 1945; s. Edward John and Irene (Gaverluk) B.; B.A., U. Iowa, 1967; M.A., Chapman Coll., 1972. Mem. Mich. Ho. of Reps., 1973-76; mem. 95th-97th Congresses from 12th Mich. Dist. Home: 23500 Denton Bldg R Apt 203 Mount Clemens MI 48043 Office: 1130 Longworth House Office Bldg Washington DC 20515

BONKOFSKY, CHARLES RICKEY, pub. co. exec.; b. Dayton, Ohio, July 15, 1950; s. Charles Louis and Virginia Fern B.; B.S., Bowling Green State U., 1972; m. Christine Ann Oroszi, June 23, 1973; 1 dau., Holly Marie. Salesman, Conn. Mut., 1971-72; salesman, partner Shade Agy., Fairborn, Ohio, 1972-74; mgr., regional mktg. mgr. Continental Cablevision, Springfield, Ohio, 1974-76; with Miami Valley Pub. Co., Fairborn, 1976—, v.p. newspaper ops., 1976—; dir. Herald Square Investments, Fairborn. Sec., Trinity United Ch. Christ, 1973-75; pres. Greene County Priuzte Industry Council, 1979-80. Mem. Advt. Execs. Ohio, Ohio League Home Dailies, Miami Valley Mil. Affairs Assn., Dayton Advt. Club, Fairborn Area C. of C. (pres. 1978-79), Dayton C. of C., Greene County Bd. Realtors (hon.). Republican. Club: Rotary (pres.) (Fairborn). Home: 1340 Red Bud St Fairborn OH 45324 Office: 1 Herald Square Fairborn OH 45324

BONNER, PAUL ANTHONY, med. group exec.; b. Boston, Aug. 19, 1944; s. John Joseph and Adela Ann (Krupovesas) B.; B.S. in Mktg. Mgmt., Boston Coll., 1966; M.P.H. in Hosp. Adminstrn. (Yale scholar), Yale U., 1968; Sc.D. in Health Services Adminstrn., Harvard U., 1976; m. Patricia Ann Kenney, June 22, 1968; children—Alison M., Andrew D. Adminstrv. resident Beth Israel Hosp., Boston, 1968; health center adminstr. Harvard Community Health Plan, Boston, 1968-71; mem. profl. staff health care group Arthur D. Little, Inc., Cambridge, Mass., 1971-76; asst. supt. Wrentham (Mass.) State Sch., 1976-77; v.p. profl. services Greater Cleve. Hosp. Assn., 1977-82; v.p. bd. trustees Central Med. Emergency Dispatch, Inc., Cleve., 1980-82; v.p., chief operating officer Cancer Data System, Inc., Cleve., 1980-82; dir. health systems planning Cleve. Clinic Found., 1982—; trustee Pvt. Accent on Quality, Inc., Cleve., 1981—; USPHS trainees, 1966-67, 73-75. Mem. Am. Hosp. Assn., Am. Public Health Assn., Ohio Hosp. Assn., Ohio Hosp. Planning Assn., Am. Coll. Hosp. Adminstrs. (nominee). Club: Chagrin Valley Athletic. Home: 112 Countryside Dr Chagrin Falls OH 44022 Office: Cleve Clinic Found 9500 Euclid Ave Cleveland OH 44106

BONNER, THOMAS NEVILLE, univ. pres.; b. Rochester, N.Y., May 28, 1923; s. John Neville and Mary (McGowan) B.; A.B., U. Rochester, 1947, M.A., 1948; Ph.D., Northwestern U., 1952; LL.D. (hon.), U. N.H., 1974; m. Carlene Carey Harris, Apr. 19, 1975; children by previous marriage—Phillip Lynn, Diana Joan. Acad. dean William Woods Coll., 1951-54; prof. history, chmn. dept. social sci. U. Omaha, 1955-62; Fulbright lectr. U. Mainz (W. Ger.), 1954-55; prof., head history dept. U. Cin., 1963-68, v.p. acad. affairs, provost, 1967-71; pres. U. N.H., Durham, 1971-74; pres. Union Coll., chancellor Union U., Schenectady, 1974-78; pres. Wayne State U., Detroit, 1978—. Democratic candidate for Congress, 1962; legis. aide to Senator McGovern, 1962-63. Served with Radio Intelligence Corps, AUS, 1942-46; ETO. Guggenheim fellow, 1958-59, 64-65. Mem. Am. Hist. Assn., Orgn. Am. Historians, Phi Beta Kappa, Pi Gamma Mu, Phi Alpha Theta. Author: Medicine in Chicago, 1957; The Kansas Doctor, 1959; (with others) The Contemporary World, 1960; Our Recent Past, 1963; American Doctors and German Universities, 1963. Editor, translator: Journey Through the Rocky Mountains (Jacob Schiel), 1959. Home: 441 W Ferry Detroit MI 48202 Office: Office of Pres Wayne State U Detroit MI 48202*

BONSER, CHARLES FRANKLIN, coll. dean; b. Youngstown, Ohio, Feb. 15, 1933; s. William Harley and Anita (Bromley) B.; B.A., Bowling Green State U., 1954; M.B.A., Ind. U., 1961, D.B.A., 1965; m. Nancy A. Gebhardt, July 3, 1955; children—Catherine, Jeffrey, Andrew. Asst. dir. Bur. Bus. Research, Sch. Bus., Ind. U., Bloomington, 1960-63, dir. state Tax policy, Ind., 1963-65, asso. dir., 1965-69, faculty lectr., 1963-65, asst. prof. bus. adminstrn., 1965-67, asso. prof., 1967-71, prof. bus. adminstrn. and public and environmental affairs, 1971—, asso. dean Sch. Bus., 1969-71, spl. asst. to pres., 1971-72, dean Sch. Public and Environmental Affairs, 1972—; bus. econs. editor Irving Cloud Pub. Co., Chgo., 1966—; mem. Panel to select White House Fellows, 1980-81; mem. U.S. Civil Service Commn. Com. on Career Entry, 1976—; gov's. designee for adminstrn. Fed. Intergovtl. Personnel Act, State Ind., 1972-82; Ind. rep. Midwest Intergovtl. Personnel Council, 1972—; bd. dirs. Nat. Inst. Public Mgmt., Washington, 1976—, chmn. 1981—. Served with USAF, 1959-63. Recipient Sagamore of Wabash award Gov. Ind., 1965, 74; Spl. Citations, U.S. Civil Service Commn., 1974, 78. Mem. Nat. Assn. Schs. Public Affairs/Adminstrn. (pres. 1976-77, mem. exec. council 1973-78), Am. Soc. Public Adminstrn. (mem. exec. council 1975-76, 1981-82), Nat. Acad. Public Adminstrn., Am. Public Works Assn., Ind. Soc. Public Adminstrn. (pres. 1975-76), Beta Gamma Sigma, Pi Alpha Alpha (nat. pres. 1980—). Co-author: Developing Patterns in Indiana Post High School Education, 12 vols., 1971; Indiana Economic Development Study, 3 vols., 1969-71; Indiana Library Needs and Resources Study, 1968-69; Business Taxation In Indiana, 1966; editor Ind. Bus. Rev., 1966-69; asso. editor Bus. Horizons, 1965-68. Home: 4625 Inverness Woods Bloomington IN 47401 Office: Sch Public and Environ Affairs Ind U 400 E 7th St Bloomington IN 47405

BONSETT, GLEN LEO, coll. adminstr.; b. Scott County, Ind., July 29, 1924; s. Leo and Glen Anna (Mahan) B.; student Hanover Coll., 1942-43, Berea Coll., 1943-44; B.S., Ind. U., 1948, M.S., 1949, P.E.D., 1957; postgrad. Mich. State U., 1966-67, U. Calif., Santa Barbara, 1978; m. Melba June Mace, Feb. 21, 1980; children by previous marriage—Sandra Marie, Andrea Lee, Candace Lynn. Tchr., coach Ind. U. Lab. Sch., 1948-53; mem. faculty Hanover (Ind.) Coll., 1953-61, prof., 1955-61, coach intercollegiate athletics, 1953-61, student personnel adminstr., dean of men, 1961-75, v.p. for devel., 1975-81; with Goettler Assos., Columbus, Ohio, 1981—; vis. lectr. Ind. U., 1954-60. Served with USNR, 1943-46. Mem. Council Advancement and Support Edn., Ind. Coll. Personnel Assn. (pres. 1971), Nat. Assn. Student Personnel Adminstrn., Ind. Personnel Guidance Assn., Ind. High Sch. Athletic Assn., AAHPER, Ind. Assn. Health, Phys. Edn. and Recreation (chmn. research sect.), Health, Phys. Edn. and Recreation Alumni Assn. Ind. U. (pres.), Ind. U. Alumni Assn. (dir.), Phi Epsilon Kappa, Lambda Chi Alpha, Phi Delta Kappa, Sigma Pi Sigma, Alpha Phi Omega. Republican. Methodist. Clubs: Masons, Elks, Moose, Scottish Rite, Shriners. Office: 580 S High St Columbus OH 43215

BONSIB, RICHARD EUGENE, mktg. services co. exec.; b. Ft. Wayne, Ind., Nov. 8, 1931; s. Louis William and Marietta Anna (Jacobs) B., Sr.; B.S. in Mktg., Ind. U., 1953; postgrad course Am. Mgmt. Assn., 1966; m. Gretchen Allen, Aug. 23, 1958; children—Gregory Allen, Stephen Richard. Owner, pres. The Century Press, Ft. Wayne, 1948-53; with Bonsib Inc., Ft. Wayne, 1953—, pres., chmn., 1975—; v.p., dir. L.W. Bonsib Found., Inc., Ft. Wayne, 1961-74; v.p. Prodn. Concepts Ltd., Creative Concepts, 1980-81; treas. HPL, Inc., Ft. Wayne, 1965-66; pres. Leemark Tours, Inc., Chgo., 1968-70. Founding dir. Ft. Wayne Horizons Econ. Devel. Council; past v.p., dir. Allen County-Ft. Wayne YMCA; former v.p., dir. fathers bd. Culver (Ind.) Mil. Acad. Served with U.S. Army, 1955-57; Korea. Mem. Ft. Wayne Advt. Club (pres. 1963), Am. Advt. Fedn., Phi Delta Gamma. Republican. Presbyterian. Home: 5511 Covington Rd Fort Wayne IN 46804 Office: The Bonsib Bldg 927 S Harrison St Fort Wayne IN 46802

BONSKOWSKI, CYNTHIA YEWELL, occupational therapist; b. St. Louis, Feb. 6, 1954; d. Robert Johnston and Juanita Louise (Wood) Yewell; student U. Mo., 1972-74; B.S. in Occupational Therapy, Washington U., St. Louis, 1976; m. William John Bonskowski, Jan. 5, 1974. Perceptual-motor specialist Miriam Sch., Webster Groves, Mo., 1976-79; sr. pediatric occupational therapist, outreach and research program St. Louis Children's Hosp., Irene Walter Johnson Rehab. Inst. of Washington U., 1979—; cons., guest lectr. in field. Mem. Am. Occupational Therapy Assn., Mo. Occupational Therapy Assn., Assn. Children with Learning Disabilities, Center for Study Sensory Integrative Dysfunction, Citizens Look at Sch. Priorities, Pediatric Spl. Interest Group St. Louis County (co-chmn. 1979-80, chmn. nominating com. 1980-81). Office: 509 S Euclid Ave Saint Louis MO 63110

BONTRAGER, ROBERT JAMES, banker; b. Kalona, Iowa, May 26, 1925; s. Elmer F. and Magda Lena (Yoder) B.; student LaSalle U. Extension, 1960; m. Jane Kauffman, Apr. 14, 1948; children—Gregory R., Jenifer. Office mgr. Dairy Genetics, Inc., Des Moines, 1948-54; accountant Lewis E. Graf, C.P.A., Fairfield, Iowa, 1954-62; controller Shafer Ford, Inc., Mt. Pleasant, Iowa, 1962-65; with Mt. Pleasant Bank & Trust Co., 1965—, pres., 1979—. Treas., City of Mt. Pleasant, 1975—, City of Mt. Pleasant Library, 1975—, Mt. Pleasant Utilities, 1975—. Served with U.S. Army, 1944-46. Recipient Small Bus. Advocate of Year award State of Iowa, 1976. Republican. Methodist. Club: Kiwanis (pres. 1971). Office: 102 S Main St Mt Pleasant IA 52641

BOOE, JAMES MARVIN, chem. exec.; b. Austin, Ind., Nov. 12, 1906; s. James Ross and Grace (Hesler) B.; B.S., Butler U., 1928; m. Dortha Maud Weaver, July 30, 1938; children—James Marvin, Ann Marie, John Weaver. Chemist, Indpls. Plating Co., 1929; chief chemist P. R. Mallory & Co., 1929-45, dir. electrochem. research, 1945-51, exec. chem. engr., 1951-53, dir. chem. and metall. research corp. labs., 1953-63; dir. chem. labs. Mallory Capacitor Co., Indpls., 1963-72, cons., 1972—. Advisory bd. Am. Security Council; bd. dirs. Irvington Benton House Assn.; pres., bd. dirs. Irvington Hist. Landmarks Found. Accredited profl. chemist Am. Inst. Chemists. Recipient Army-Navy E civilian award, Naval Ordnance Devel. award. Fellow Am. Inst. Chemists; mem. Am. Chem. Soc., Electrochem. Soc., Irvington Hist. Soc., Am. Def. Preparedness Assn., Indpls. Scientech Soc., Smithsonian Instn. (asso.), Indpls. Mus. Art, Goodwill Industries, Ransburg YMCA, Presbyterian (elder, trustee). Kiwanian. Patentee in field (38). Research on electrolytic capacitors, batteries, resistors, semiconductors. Home: 548 N Audubon Rd Indianapolis IN 46219 Office: 3029 E Washington St Indianapolis IN 46201

BOOK, IMOGENE IRIS CLARK (MRS. WILTZ ALONZO BOOK), librarian; b. Mt. Vernon, Ill., Dec. 12, 1924; d. Keith and Mona (Hawkins) Clark; B.S., So. Ill. U., 1946, postgrad., 1955, summer 1956; M.S., U. Ill., 1960, certificate of advanced study in librarianship, 1966; m. Wiltz Alonzo Book, Aug. 18, 1946; children—Douglas Keith, Karen Lynn. Tchr. secondary schs., Bellmont, Ill., 1946-47, Marissa, Ill., 1947-48, Bluford, Ill., 1955-56; tchr. Mt. Vernon Twp. High Sch., 1954-55, 56-57, librarian, 1958-62; librarian Mt. Vernon Community Coll., 1956-67, mem. adv. council, 1961-69; librarian Rend Lake Coll., Mt. Vernon, 1967-70, dir., 1970-79, librarian, 1979—. Cons., Student Ill. Edn. Assn., 1966-69; adviser Rend Lake Coll. Student Edn. Assn., 1956—; mem. adv. council U. Ill. Grad. Sch. Library Sci., 1962-64; mem. Ill. Commn. Tchr. Edn. and Profl. Standards, 1966-69. Mem. Ill. (legis. devel. com. 1965-70), Jefferson County (sec. 1964-65, pres. 1965-66), Mt. Vernon (pres. 1959-60) edn. assns., NEA, ALA, Ill., Mt. Vernon (sec. 1962-63, v.p. 1963-64, pres. 1964-65) library assns., Ill. Audiovisual Assn., Ill. Assn. Sch. Librarians (sec. 1958-59), Ill. Assn. Coll. and Research Librarians (vice chmn. 1974-75, chmn. 1975-76, chmn. community and jr. coll. libraries sect. 1978-79, dir. 1981—), Delta Kappa Gamma (chpt. v.p. 1964-66, rec. sec. 1966-68, pres. 1968-70). Home: 912 S 21st St Mount Vernon IL 62864 Office: Rend Lake Coll Route 1 Ina IL 62846

BOOKER, DEBORAH SHANNON, educator; b. Washington, Apr. 6, 1937; d. Angus R. and Barbara (Stratton) Shannon; B.A., U. Mo., 1959; m. Paul Booker, Nov. 26, 1960; children—Margaret, Sarah, Charles. Psychol. technician U. Mo., Columbia, 1959-61; owner, mgr. The Horse Fair, Columbia, 1965—; asst. prof. equestrian sci. William Woods Coll., Fulton, Mo., 1972—; nat. examiner, mem. instrn. council U.S. Pony Clubs, Inc., 1978—. Mem. Am. Horse Shows Assn. (tech. del. for combined tng. and dressage), U.S. Combined Tng. Assn., U.S. Pony Clubs, Inc. Episcopalian. Home: Route 9 Columbia MO 65201 Office: William Woods Coll Fulton MO 65251

BOOKOUT, WENDELL ROSS, computer analyst; b. Austell, Ga., Dec. 28, 1943; s. Jesse Weymond and Katherin Elizabeth (Messer) B.; m. Mary Ann Konz, Sept. 13, 1978; children by previous marriage—Cynthia Ann, Jonathan Wendell. Asst. engr. EMR Instruments, Warminster, Pa., 1966-69; digital electronics engr. EMR Computer, Mpls., 1969-70; digital systems engr. Copycomposer Corp., Rockville, Md., 1970-71; sr. digital systems engr. AAI Corp., Cockeysville, Md., 1972-77; sr. systems analyst NCR Corp., Wichita, Kans., 1977—. Served with USN, 1961-64. Club: Masons. Home: 125 S Ohio St Benton KS 67017 Office: 3718 N Rock Rd Wichita KS 67226

BOOKWALTER, RICHARD LEROY, aluminum products mfg. co. exec.; b. Mansfield, Ohio, Feb. 6, 1942; s. John Leroy and Leatha Ardella (Lutz) B.; B.S. in Bus. Adminstrn., Franklin U., 1974; m. Beverly Tean Shaarda, Mar. 23, 1961; children—Terri Lynn, Bradley Allen, Derrick Roy. Mgr. mfg. acctg. Faultless Rubber Co., Ashland, Ohio, 1972-76; controller Tubelite Archtl. div. Consol. Aluminum Co. (now Tubelite div. Indal Inc.), Reed City, Mich., 1976-79, plant mgr., 1979-81, v.p. adminstrn. and fin., 1981—. Treas., United Methodist Ch., Reed City, 1980—; mem. Reed City Zoning Bd. Appeals, 1981, W. Central Mich. Pvt. Industry Council, 1981. Mem. Reed City C. of C. Home: 423 W Todd Ave Reed City MI 49677 Office: Tubelite div Indal Inc Old US 131 PO Box 118 Reed City MI 49677

BOONE, DANIEL C., JR., steel co. exec.; b. Mt. Sterling, Ky., Feb. 23, 1920; s. Daniel C. and Grace (Salyer) B.; certificate in accounting, Marquette U., 1947; m. Jayne Deardoff, July 28, 1970; 1 son, Terry. With Superior Lawrence Bag Co., 1937-41, Haskins & Sells, C.P.A.'s, Cin., 1947; with Armco Steel Corp., 1941-42, 47—, controller steel div., 1958-65, corp. controller, 1965-67, v.p. fin., 1967-69, sr. v.p. fin., 1969-73, exec. v.p., 1973-79, pres., chief operating officer, 1979—; dir. Armco Steel Corp., Winters Nat. Bank, Winters Nat. Corp., Duriron Co., Crystal Tissue Corp., Phillips Industries, Am. Life Ins. Co. Served with USAAF, 1942-45. Republican. Home: 2105 Tullis Dr Middletown OH 45042 Office: Armco Steel Corp Middletown OH 45042

BOONE, LESTER VERLIN, agronomist; b. Mount Vernon, Ill., Sept. 5, 1931; s. Charles Lester and Sylvia Mae (Mullinax) B.; B.S., So. Ill. U., 1956; M.S., U. Ill., 1972; m. Norma Jean Anderson, Dec. 22, 1954; children—Andrew V., Dawn E. Boone Barbercheck. Area agronomist for So. Ill., U. Ill., 1956-67, research and extension agronomist, Champaign-Urbana campus, 1967—; evaluator office energy-related inventions Dept. Commerce. Mem. Field Consol. Sch. Bd. Edn., Texico, Ill., 1964-67. Served with USAF, 1950-54. Mem. Am. Soc. Agronomy, Soil Sci. Soc. Am., Internat. Soc. Soil Sci., Council Agrl. Sci. and Tech., Am. Registry Cert. Profls. in Agronomy, Crops and Soils (cert. profl. agronomist and soil scientist). Republican. Baptist. Author: (with others) Producing Farm Crops, 1975; contbr. numerous articles to profl. jours. Home: 2514 Stanford Dr Champaign IL 61820 Office: AW-109 Turner Hall 1102 S Goodwin Ave Urbana IL 61801

BOONKHAM, CHOTCHAI, internist; b. Cheingrai, Thailand, May 29, 1943; s. Boonsing and Homhuon (Yantadilok) B.; came to U.S., 1969; M.D., Siriraj Med. Sch. and Hosp., Bangkok, Thailand, 1968; m. Sumalee Ratanagorn, May 1, 1972; children—Surachade, Monica. Intern, N.Y. Poly-clinic Hosp., N.Y.C., 1969-70; resident in internal medicine Shadyside Hosp., Pitts., 1970-71, St. Mary's Health Center, St. Louis, 1971-73; practice medicine specializing in internal medicine, Overland, Mo., 1973-76, Bridgeton, Mo., 1976—. Diplomate Am. Bd. Internal Medicine. Mem. A.C.P., AMA, Mo., St. Louis med. assns., Am. Soc. Geriatrics, Am., Mo. socs. internal medicine. Buddhist. Home: 15424 Highcroft Dr Chesterfield MO 63017 Office: Suite 220 3466 Bridgeland Dr Bridgeton MO 63044

BOONSTRA, LARRY ALAN, educator; b. Grand Rapids, Mich., May 20, 1951; s. Andrew Peter and Avis Jean Boonstra; B.S. in Biology, Grand Valley State Coll., 1973. Substitute tchr. Kent County Intermediate Sch. Dist., Grand Rapids, 1974; bridge program tchr. aide Upward Bound Program, Hope Coll., Holland, Mich., 1974-75; community edn. tchr. Holland public schs., 1974-75, adult basic edn. tchr., 1980—; adult basic edn. tchr. Kandu Industries, Holland, 1975—; substitute house parent adult foster care home, Holland, 1978—. Mem. Am. Assn. Mental Deficiency. Mem. Reformed Ch. Home: 70 1/2 W 19th St Holland MI 49423 Office: 276 W 13th St Holland MI 49423

BOORAS, NICKOLAS PERICLES, financier; b. Kalamata, Greece, June 23, 1944; s. Peter Pericles and Angelia (Demopolus) B.; came to U.S., 1919, naturalized, 1946; B.A., Mich. Lutheran Coll., 1968; m. Margaret Ferguson, Aug. 27, 1966; children—Heather, Amanda, Nickolas. With mktg. dept. Am. Can. Co., 1967-69, Texaco Inc., 1969-73; pres., chief exec. officer Thalasa Ltd., Birmingham, Mich., 1973—. Mem. Nat. Assn. Credit Mgmt., Builders Exchange, Birmingham, Troy chambers commerce. Greek Orthodox. Clubs: Rotary, Optimists (Troy). Home: 4621 Mill Pond Troy MI 48098 Office: 977 E Big Beaver Troy MI 48098

BOOSALIS, ELSIE, real estate mgmt. exec.; b. Cedar Rapids, Iowa, Dec. 1, 1913; adopted dau. of Peter and Rose (Halleck) B.; student Phoenix Bus. Coll., 1943-44, Northwestern U., 1952-53, U. Minn. Property mgr. Peter Boosalis Bldg. Trust, Mpls., 1953—, trustee, 1960—. Dir., Greater Lake St. Council; sustaining mem. council Girl Scouts U.S.A.; bus. mem. Powderhorn Devel. Corp.; active ARC, YWCA, WAMSO. Mem. Mpls. Soc. Fine Arts, Minn., Hennepin County hist. socs., Mpls. C. of C., Minn. Orchestral Assn. (guarantor), English Speaking Union, Am. Swedish Inst. Home: 4551 Dupont Ave S Minneapolis MN 55409 Office: 2951 Chicago Ave Minneapolis MN 55407

BOOSALIS, HELEN GEANKOPLIS, mayor; b. Mpls., Aug. 28, 1919; d. George A. and Bertha G. (Floeras) Geankoplis; student U. Minn., 1937-39; m. Michael G. Boosalis, Feb. 15, 1945; 1 dau., Mary Beth Boosalis Davis. Mem. City Council, Lincoln (Nebr.), 1959-75, chairperson, 1966-67, 73-75, mayor, Lincoln, 1975—. Pres., League Women Voters, Lincoln, 1957-59. Mem. U.S. Conf. Mayors (adv. council, resolutions com., chairperson human devel. standing com. from 1977), Nebr. Comprehensive Health Bd., Am. Assn. Comprehensive Health Planning Bd. Democrat. Greek Orthodox. Home: 3019 Jackson Dr Lincoln NE 68502 Office: 555 S 10th St Lincoln NE 68508

BOOTH, HARRY LELAND, clergyman; b. Dayton, Ohio, Aug. 29, 1946; s. Harry Robert and Jean Francis (Gebhart) B.; Ph.D., Fla. State Christian U., 1972; 1 dau., Lisa Ann. Founder, 1979, since magister sacrorum First Ch. of Man, Miamisburg, Ohio.

BOOTH, NORMAN JAMES, mental health exec.; b. Hinckley, Ill., Oct. 29, 1923; s. Thomas Judd and Ann Catherine (Watgen) B.; B.A., Aurora Coll., 1947; M.S.W., Loyola U., Chgo., 1955; cert. Chgo. Inst. Psychoanalysis, 1962; Ph.D., So. Ill. U., 1976; m. Marian R. Waclawek, Feb. 14, 1963; children—Michael, Judd, Thomas James. Child welfare worker, child guidance counselor, dir. Child Guidance Clinic, Champaign, Ill., 1951-57; state-wide child guidance cons. Inst. for Juvenile Research, Chgo., 1957-59, dir. child guidance clinic programs, 1959-66; grad. fellow So. Ill. U., Carbondale, 1966-68, instr. health, 1968-70; dir. child and adolescent programs Madden Center, Hines, Ill., 1970—. Served with inf. U.S. Army, 1944-46. Mem. Nat. Assn. Social Workers (chpt. pres. 1966-67), Nat. Assn. Advancement Sci, Acad. Cert. Social Workers, Ill. Child Care Assn., Ill. Welfare Assn. Roman Catholic. Home: 4054 Johnson St Western Springs IL 60558 Office: 1200 1st Ave Hines IL 60141

BORANYAK, SHARON ETZEL (MRS. MARK BORANYAK), writer, editor; b. Topeka, Kans., May 2, 1951; d. Raymond Francis and Julia Elizabeth (Porubsky) Etzel; B.S., Kans. State U., 1973; m. Mark Boranyak, Apr. 20, 1974. Asso. editor Capper's Weekly, Topeka, Kans., 1973-76; pub. info. specialist Stormont-Vail Hosp., Topeka, 1976; informational writer Water Quality Mgmt. sect. Kans. Dept. Health and Environment, Topeka, 1976-77, pub. relations dir. div. environment, 1977-79; editor Kans. Legis. Div. of Post-Audit, 1979—; cons. Topeka Broadcast Council. Mem. Women in Communications (treas. Topeka chpt. 1975-79), Nat. Fedn. Press Women (v.p. Topeka chpt. 1978-79, pres. 1980—), Topeka Home Econs. Assn., People to People. Republican. Roman Catholic. Contbr. articles to profl. jours. Home: 2612 Arrowhead Rd Topeka KS 66614 Office: Kans Legis Div Post Audit Mills Bldg Topeka KS 66612

BORCHERT, STEVEN JOHN, chemist; b. Madison, Wis., Jan. 20, 1950; s. Willard W. and Beatrice N. Borchert; B.A., U. Wis., 1972; A.M. (NSF fellow 1972-74, Standard Oil Co. Calif. scholar 1971), Harvard U., 1973, Ph.D., 1977. Research chemist Upjohn Co., Kalamazoo, 1977—. Mem. Am. Chem. Soc., Parenteral Drug Assn. Home: 1706 Whitby Ave Portage MI 49002 Office: Upjohn Co 7000 Portage Rd Kalamazoo MI 49001

BORCZON, ROBERT STANLEY, hosp. adminstr.; b. Erie, Pa., Feb. 9, 1927; s. Stanley and Julia (Kownacki) B.; M.P.H., U. Pitts., 1957; m. Helen Sufana, Nov. 4, 1950; children—Rebecca, Robin, Roxanne. Asso. dir. Hosp. Counseling Program, Am. Hosp. Assn., Chgo., 1957-62; adminstrv. coordinator for hosps. St. Clare Province, Franciscan Sisters of Poor, Cin., 1963-65; asso. adminstr. Bartholomew County Hosp., Columbus, Ind., 1966-67, exec. dir., 1967—. Served with AUS, 1944-46. Otto M. Ball fellow, 1957. Mem. Ind. Hosp. Assn. (dir. 1971-77), Tri-State Hosp. Assembly (dir. 1974-80), Ind. Rate Rev. Com. Club: Rotary. Home: 2603 Maple St Columbus IN 47201 Office: 2400 E 17th St Columbus IN 47201

BOREN, ARTHUR RODNEY, JR., comml. banker; b. Dayton, Ohio, June 25, 1946; s. A. Rodney and D. Charlotte (Polk) B.; B.A., Washington and Lee U., 1968; M.I.M., Am. Grad. Sch., Phoenix, 1973. Tchr., Miami Valley Sch., Dayton, 1968-70, adminstr., 1970-71; internat. banker Northwestern Nat. Bank, Mpls., 1974-78, nat. banker, 1978-81, v.p. nat. dept., 1980, v.p. treasury div., 1981—. Bd. dirs. Illusion Theater, Mpls. Mem. Am. Inst. Banking, Robert Morris Assos. Republican. Episcopalian. Clubs: Miami Valley Hunt and Polo (Dayton); Minneapolis (Mpls.). Office: Northwestern Nat Bank 7th and Marquette Ave Minneapolis MN 55403

BORENSTINE, ALVIN JEROME, search co. exec.; b. Kansas City, Mo., Dec. 14, 1933; s. Samuel and Ella C. (Berman) B.; m. Roula Alakiotou, Dec. 31, 1976; Ella Marie and Sami (twins). B.S. in Econs., U. Kans., 1956; M.B.A., U. Pa., 1960. Analyst, Johnson & Johnson, New Brunswick, N.J., 1961-62; systems mgr. Levitt & Sons, Levittown, N.J., 1962-66; dir. mgmt. info. services Warren Brothers Co., Cambridge, Mass., 1966-71; mgr. fin. and adminstrv. systems Esmark, Inc., Chgo., 1971-72; pres. Synergistics Assos. Ltd., Chgo., 1972—. Mem. Assn. for Systems Mgmt. (pres. Boston chpt. 1969, Disting. Service award 1970), Soc. Mgmt. Info. Systems, B'nai B'rith. Systems and Procedures Assn. research fellow, 1959-60; Eddie Jacobson Found. scholar, 1958-60. Clubs: Carlton, Whitehall. Home: 6033 N Sheridan Chicago IL 60660 Office: 875 N Michigan Ave Suite 3722 Chicago IL 60611

BORGER, FREDERICK HOWARD, mfg. co. exec.; b. Jamaica, N.Y., Apr. 2, 1946; s. Howard Francis and Irene Albie (Koucky) B.; B.B.A., St. John's U., 1967; M.B.A., N.Y. U., 1970; m. Joan A. Manning, June 24, 1967; children—Kristin, James. Orgn. devel. cons. Western Electric Co., N.Y.C., 1968-72; v.p., cons. Cin. Comml. Cons., Cin., 1972-73; mgr. corp. staffing Borden Inc., Columbus, 1973-78; dir. personnel devel., staffing O.M. Scott & Sons, Marysville, Ohio, 1978—. Vice pres. Homeowners Assn., Norwich, 1974-75; trustee Homeowners Assn., Columbus, Ohio, 1974-76. Mem. Am. Soc. Tng. and Devel., Am. Soc. Personnel Adminstrn., Central Ohio Personnel Assn., Midwest OD Network. Republican. Roman Catholic. Home: 1149 Ashland Ave Columbus OH 43212 Office: 333 N Maple St Marysville OH 43041

BORK, PAUL GEORGE, chem. engr.; b. Akron, Ohio, Oct. 25, 1930; s. Paul Carl and Helen Elma (Hitchcock) B.; B.Chem.Engring., Case Inst. Tech., 1950; M.S. in Chem. Engring., Ohio State U., 1961; m. Emma Louise Stephens, Sept. 17, 1955; children—Susan Louise, Paul Michael, George Fredrick. With E. I. DuPont de Nemours & Co., Inc., Wilmington, Del., 1954-55, Circleville, Ohio, 1956-57, Goodyear Tire & Rubber Co., Akron, Ohio, 1957-60; with Dow Corning Corp., 1961—, reliability engr., 1963-65, mfg. supt., 1967-69, prodn. supt., 1969-72, quality assurance specialist, 1977-79, sr. quality assurance specialist, Hemlock, Mich., 1979-81, sr. mfg. engring. supr., 1981—. Served with Signal Corps, U.S. Army, 1950-52. Mem. Am. Inst. Chem. Engrs., Am. Chem. Soc., Am. Soc. Quality Control, Sigma Xi, Tau Beta Pi, Phi Lambda Upsilon. Club: Lions. Contbr. articles in field to profl. jours.; patentee in field. Office: Dow Corning Med Materials Plant Hemlock MI 48626

BORKHOLDER, FREEMON, bldg. co. exec.; b. Bremen, Ind., Oct. 11, 1932; s. Daniel J. and Emma (Coblentz) B.; student pub. schs.; m. Margaret Hershberger, Apr. 26, 1956; children—Lorene Kaye, Sueetta, Dwayne Alan, Jonathan Jay, Cheryl Elaine. With Coppes Inc., Nappanee, Ind., 1955-62; owner, pres. F.D. Borkholder Co., Nappanee, 1960—; v.p. Borkholder Bldgs., Nunica, Mich., 1967—; sec.-treas. Newmar Industries, Nappanee, 1968—; developer indsl. parks, 1967—. Bd. dirs. No. Youth Programs, Hope Rescue Mission, South Bend, Ind. Mem. Nat. Frame Builders Assn. (pres. 1971-72, dir., pres. Ind. chpt. 1979), Internat. Platform Assn. Mennonite. Home: RD 1 Bremen IN 46506 Office: PO Box 32 Nappanee IN 46550

BORMAN, EDWARD HENRY, assn. exec.; b. Webster Groves, Mo., Sept. 26, 1926; s. Edward Henry and Lillian M. B.; B.S. in Bus. Adminstrn., Washington U., St. Louis, 1950; J.D., St. Louis U., 1965; m. Janet A. Borman, Nov. 19, 1949; children—Anne, Keith, Bethany, Michael. Cashier, Equitable Life Ins. Soc. U.S., St. Louis, 1950-57; dir. Medicare, Gen. Am. Life Ins. Co., St. Louis, 1957-70; admitted to Mo. bar, 1965; exec. dir. Mo. Assn. Osteo. Physicians and Surgeons, Jefferson City, 1970—; dir. Mid-Mo. Med. Found., 1978—; dir. Charles Still Hosp., Mo. Health Data Corp. Chmn., Mo. Health Council, 1971-72; chmn. adv. com. Mo. Center for Health Stats., 1973-75. Served with USNR, 1944-46. Mem. Am. Osteo. Assn. (com. on continuing med. edn.), Assn. Osteo. State Exec. Dirs. (pres.), Mo. Bar Assn., Cole County Bar Assn., Mo. Soc. Assn. Execs., Am. Legion, Phi Alpha Delta, Sigma Nu. Republican. Editor: Jour. of Mo. Osteo. Assn., 1970—. Home: 1610 Greenberry Rd Jefferson City MO 65101 Office: PO Box 748 Jefferson City MO 65102

BORMAN, PAUL, retail exec.; b. Detroit, 1932; s. Abraham B.; ed. Mich. State U. Gen. mgr. Borman's Inc., Detroit, 1959-60, v.p., 1960-65, pres., chief exec. officer, 1965—, also dir. Office: Borman's Inc 18718 Borman Ave Box 446 Detroit MI 48232*

BORNHOEFT, JACK HARRY, constrn. co. exec.; b. Chgo., July 16, 1922; s. Elmer J. and Lilliam M. (Matthias) B.; B.S., Northwestern U., 1947; m. Sept. 6, 1947; children—Nancy, Susan, Gregg. With Gerhardt F. Meyne Co., Chgo., 1945—, chmn., 1978—. Bd. dirs. Chgo. Bldg. Congress, 1978—. Served with USAAF, 1942-45, USAF, 1950-51. Decorated Air medal. Mem. Western Soc. Engrs. Republican. Presbyterian. Clubs: Union League, Tower, Rotary, Germania, East Bank. Office: Gerhardt F Meyne Co 300 W Washington St Chicago IL 60606

BORNHOEFT, JOHN WILLIAM, III, microbiologist; b. Lakewood, Ohio, Apr. 24, 1943; s. John William and Billie Louise (Parshall) B.; B.A., Beloit Coll., 1965; M.S., Chgo. Med. Sch., 1972; Ph.D. (fellow), Loyola U., 1980; m. Margaret Tenesa, June 13, 1971 (dec. 1981); 1 son, John William IV. Research asst. U. Ill. Med. Center, Chgo., 1967-69, Chgo. Med. Sch., 1970-71; clin. instr. Loyola U. Dental Sch., 1974-75; research asst. Loyola U., Chgo., 1976-79, research asso., 1979-81; applied microbiologist, Am. Convertors Co., Evanston, Ill., 1981—; cons. Rapid Med. Services, 1976-77; mem. faculty Mundelein Coll. Chgo., part time 1980; clin. microbiologist Loyola Student Health Services, 1976-81. Mem. Am. Soc. Microbiology, Am. Inst. Biol. Scis., Sigma Xi. Club: Alfa Romeo Owners. Office: 1740 Ridge Ave Evanston IL 60201

BORNSCHLEGL, WILLARD FREDRICK, educator; b. Ohiowa, Nebr., Oct. 21, 1923; s. Jake H. and Malinda B. (Matthies) B.; B.A., Nebr. Wesleyan U., 1949; M.S. in Edn., U. Omaha, 1953; Ed.D., U. Nebr., 1970; m. Harriet Rose Tordsen, June 9, 1946; children—Kay Louise, Rita Marie. Tchr. social studies, coach, public schs., Papillion, Nebr., 1949-52, secondary prin., 1952-54; supt. schs. Arlington (Nebr.) Schs., 1954-63; asst. prof. edn. Bemidji State U., 1965-70, asso. prof., 1970-72, prof., 1972—, head div. edn., 1972-79, acting v.p. acad. affairs, 1979-80, dir. tchr. licensure, 1980—. Served with inf. U.S. Army, 1943-45. Decorated Silver Star. Mem. NEA, Minn. Edn. Assn., Assn. Supervision and Curriculum Devel., Midwest Council Ednl. Adminstrn., Bemidji C. of C., Phi Delta Kappa. Home: Route 9 Box 316 Bemidji MN 55601 Office: 1400 Birchmond Dr Bemidji MN 56601

BOROWITZ, ALBERT IRA, lawyer, author; b. Chgo., June 27, 1930; s. David and Anne (Wolkenstein) B.; B.A. in Classics (Detur award 1948) summa cum laude, Harvard U., 1951, M.A. in Chinese Regional Studies, 1953, J.D. (Sears prize) magna cum laude, 1956; m. Helen Blanche Osterman, July 29, 1950; children—Peter Leonard, Joan, Andrew Seth. Admitted to Ohio bar, 1957; asso. firm Hahn, Loeser, Freedheim, Dean & Wellman, Cleve., 1956-62, partner, 1962—; dir. Bobbie Brooks, Inc. Recipient Cleve. Arts prize for lit., 1981. Mem. Am. Law Inst., Am. Bar Assn., Ohio Bar Assn., Bar Assn. Greater Cleve. Clubs: Union, Rowfant, Ct. of Nisi Prius (Cleve.); Harvard N.Y.C. Author: Fiction in Communist China, 1955; Innocence and Arsenic; Studies in Crime and Literature, 1977; The Woman Who Murdered Black Satin: The Bermondsey Horror, 1981; contbr. articles to profl. jours. Office: 800 National City E 6th Bldg Cleveland OH 44114

BORSAY, FERENC LAJOS, design engr.; b. Parasznya, Hungary, Aug. 4, 1930; s. Ferenc and Jolan (Szatinszky) B.; B.Sc. in Mech. Engring., Tech. U., Budapest, Hungary, 1953; diploma nuclear engring. Borough U. London, 1959; D.Phil., Oxford U., 1970; m. Sylvia Butler, Aug. 15, 1960 (div. 1968). Demonstrator, Tech. U. Budapest, 1952-53; test engr. Ganz Waggon, Budapest, 1953-56; research engr. Associated Elec. Industries, Aldermaston, Eng., 1957-60; project engr. Sci. Research Council, Harwell, Eng., 1960-66; research asso. U. Southampton (Eng.), 1971-72; sr. research asso. Case Western Res. U., Cleve., 1972-78, cons., 1978—; sr. design engr., electrolytic systems div. Diamond Shamrock Corp., Chardon, Ohio, 1978—. Club: Oxford-Cambridge (London). Research in applications of laserlight and ultrasound for investigating thermodynamical, statis. mech. parameters of fluids and properties of electrochem. interfaces. Office: 470 Center St Chardon OH 44024

BORSCH, REUBEN A., lawyer; b. Collinsville, Ill., Mar. 7, 1903; s. Frederick C. and Sarah (Wrigley) B.; A.B., Ill. Wesleyan U., 1925; B.A. in Jurisprudence, Oxford (Eng.) U., 1927, B.C.L., 1928; m. Pearl Irene Houk, May 3, 1930; children—Barbara (Mrs. James Osborn Kaull), Frederick Houk, Jane Robbins Carter. Admitted to Ill. bar, 1929; partner Winston & Strawn, Chgo., 1944-79; dir. Sommer & Maca Industries, Inc., Cicero, Ill. Bd. dirs. Youth Guidance, Chgo.; trustee Episcopal Diocese Chgo. Endowment Fund, Ill. Wesleyan U. Mem. Am., Ill., Chgo. bar assns., Tau Kappa Epsilon. Episcopalian. Republican. Clubs: Law (sec.-treas. 1960-62), Mid-day, Executives (pres. 1955-56) (Chgo.); Hinsdale Golf. Home: 133 E Walnut St Hinsdale IL 60521 Office: One First Nat Plaza Chicago IL 60603

BORST, LAWRENCE MARION, state senator; b. Champaign County, Ohio, July 16, 1927; s. Lawrence M. and Mary (Waldeck) B.; D.Journ., Ohio State U., 1950; m. Edoris, 1947; children—Philip, Elizabeth, David. Mem. Ind. Ho. of Reps., 1967-68, Ind. Senate, 1969—. Del., Republican Nat. Conv., 1968. Office: Ind State Capitol Indianapolis IN 46204*

BORST, RICHARD ALLEN, appraisal and data processing co. exec.; b. Hamburg, N.Y., Dec. 1, 1941; s. George John and Adeline Agnes (Unger) B.; B.E.S. with honors, Cleve. State U., 1964; M.S., SUNY, Buffalo, 1975; m. Nadelle Morteff, Nov. 23, 1967; children—Julia, Sara. Sect. head Calspan Corp., Buffalo, 1973-74; v.p. Cole Layer Trumble Co., Dayton, Ohio, 1974-78, sr. v.p., 1978-80, exec. v.p., 1980-81, pres., 1981—. Mem. Internat. Assn. Assessment Officers, Ops. Research Soc. Am. (asso.). Home: 1801 Quail Hollow Centerville OH 45459 Office: Cole Layer Trumble Co 3535 Salem Ave Dayton OH 45406

BORTOLOTTI, NORMA MAY, investment exec.; b. Omaha, Apr. 8, 1931; d. Isidoro and Michelina (Cominoli) B.; Dickinson Secretarial Sch., Omaha, 1958; B.A., Duchesne Coll., 1954; postgrad. Creighton U., 1957, 58, 77, 78; Typist, W.O.W. Life Ins. Co., Omaha, 1948; with Universal Terrazzo & Tile Co., Omaha, 1949-77, sec., receptionist and acct., 1954-70, v.p., 1964-77; acct., hostess 7301 Corp., night club, Omaha, 1964-69, also dir.; v.p. NND Investment Co., Omaha, 1957—; mgmt. v.p. NND Investment Corp., Omaha, 1957—. Active local ward and precinct work Republican Party, 1975. Recipient Outstanding Service award Republican Party, 1975. Mem. E de M, Catholic Soc. Sacred Heart, Nat. Assn. Female Execs. Home: 9904 Florence Heights Blvd Omaha NE 68112

BORUCKI, WALTER CHESTER, distbg. co. exec.; b. Detroit, June 11, 1916; s. Adam J. and Agata (Hardy) B.; student U. Poznan (Poland), 1937-39; m. Helen Jeza, Jan. 6, 1954; children—Judith Ellen, Mary Elizabeth. Prof. chemistry St. Mary's Coll., Orchard Lake, Mich., 1944-46; pres. Vets. Supply & Distbg. Co., Hamtramck, Mich., 1946—. Served with M.C., U.S. Army, 1941. Clubs: Polish Nat. Alliance, Polish Falcons, Alliance Poles, Amvets, Am. Legion. Author: Historia Stanow Zjednoczonych Ameryki Polnocnej, 1955. Home: 26420 Saint Josaphat Dr Warren MI 48091 Office: 3225 Caniff St Hamtramck MI 48212

BORUFF, DONALD VICTOR, mfg. co. exec.; b. Greene County, Ind.; s. Harvey Victor and Perla Clara (Wonder) B.; ed. Ind. Central U.; m. Berniece Hagaman, 1934; children—Donna Carpenter, Roma Carrick. Personnel dir. Mitts & Merrill, Saginaw, Mich., 1951-65, Am. Hoist Co., Bay City, Mich., 1966-68, KC Engring. & Machine Co., Saginaw, 1969-81; lectr. in field. Active YMCA; bd. dirs. Saginaw City Rescue Mission. Mem. Am. Soc. Personnel Adminstrn. (accredited exec. in personnel, cert. in A.E.P., Superior Merit award 1978), Valley Soc. Personnel Adminstrs. (pres. 1977—). Clubs: Indsl. Exec., Masons. Address: 3358 Nottingham Dr Bay City MI 48706

BORUFF, JOHN DAVID, govt. ofcl.; b. Lakewood, Ohio, July 8, 1930; s. Glenn Tourner and Edith (Weybright) B.; A.B. in Biology, Ind. U., 1953, M.S. in Health and Safety Edn., 1965; m. Martha Lois Myers, June 12, 1953; children—Martha Yvonne Boruff Wyatt, Audrey Elaine, David Paul, Kenneth Edward. Sanitarian, Ind. State Bd. Health, 1957-60, tng. officer Div. Food and Drugs, 1960-63, health edn. cons. Div. Health Edn., 1963-65; health-housing coordinator Associated Migrant Opportunity Services, Inc., Indpls., 1965-66; extension health edn. specialist Purdue U., 1966-69; statistician div. pub. health records, coordinator health data unit pub. health stats. Ind. Bd. Health, 1969—; state data mgr. Nat. Public Health Program Reporting System, Assn. State and Territorial Health Ofcls. Served as hosp. corpsman USCGR, 1953-57; sr. asst. health service officer USPHS Res. Mem. USPHS Commd. Officers Assn., No. Nut Growers Assn., Ind. Nut Growers Assn. (editor bull.), Theta Xi. Presbyterian (elder, past stated clk., asst. ch. organist). Club: Masons (32 deg.; mem. Indpls. Valley Scottish Rite Orch. and Athenaeum Turners Orch.). Author: Health Trends in Indiana 1900-1973; Indiana Health Profile 1968-1978; contbr. Ind. State Bd. Health Bull. Home: RR 1 Box 128 Roachdale IN 46172 Office: 1330 W Michigan St Indianapolis IN 46206

BORYC, NICHOLAS MICHAEL, transp. co. exec.; b. Waukegan, Ill., Oct. 30, 1952; s. Louis J. and Cecile D. B.; B. Applied Scis. with honors, Western Ill. U., 1975; m. Mary C. Rushforth, Nov. 12, 1977. Sales rep. Roadway Express Inc., Chgo., 1976-78, mgr. terminal sales, 1979—. Active Boy Scouts Am. Mem. Better Govt. Assn. Home: 112 Woodstock St Clarendon Hills IL 60514 Office: Roadway Express Inc 3434 W 51st St Chicago IL 60632

BORYSIAK, RALPH ALFRED, environ. cons. co. exec.; b. Munich, Germany, Dec. 7, 1942; came to U.S., 1950, naturalized, 1958; s. Lech Evaryst and Marion (Geigl) B.; B.A., Ind. U., 1966; M.P.H., U. Mich., 1970; m. Judith Veronica Zultanski, Jan. 16, 1964; children—Suzanne Stella, Charles Lech. Insp., Alaska Dept. Health and Welfare, Juneau, 1966-68; insp., educator Greater Anchorage Area Borough, 1968-69; environ. health activities coordinator Alaska Dept. Health and Social Services, Juneau, 1970-73; lectr., cons. Mont. State U., Bozeman, 1973-74; pres. Clean Air Corp., South Bend, Ind., 1974—; mem. pollution control equipment research and devel. bd. advs. Nat. Fedn. Independent Bus. Mem. Assn. Energy Engrs., Energy Conservation Cons. Council, Nat. Environ. Health Assn., Royal Soc. Health (Gt. Britain), Phi Sigma Kappa. Patentee in field. Home: 2101 Oak Park Dr South Bend IN 46617 Office: 1319 N Iowa St South Bend IN 46628

BOSART, EUGENE HALSEY, III, investment banker, stockbroker; b. Springfield, Ohio, Nov. 29, 1942; s. Eugene Halsey, Jr., and Dorothey Jane (Bangert) B.; B.S. in Bus., Miami U., Oxford, Ohio, 1964; m. Sue Ann Simendinger, Apr. 3, 1965; children—Robert Halsey, Earl Bradley, Kristie Sue. Indsl. salesman Goodyear Tire and Rubber Co., Akron, Ohio, 1965-67; stockbroker McDonald and Co., Toledo, 1968-71, Detroit, 1971-72, br. managing partner, Troy, Mich., 1972—. Served with U.S. Army, 1965-68. Mem. Fin. Analysts Soc. Detroit, Bond Club of Detroit. Presbyterian. Clubs: Renaissance of Detroit, Orchard Lake Country, Hundred Club of Mich. Home: 2520 Indian Mound E Birmingham MI 48010 Office: 900 Tower Dr Troy MI 48098

BOSCHWITZ, RUDY, U.S. Senator; b. Berlin, Germany, 1930; came to U.S., 1935; B.S., N.Y. U., 1950, LL.B., 1953; married; children—Gerry, Ken, Dan, Tom. Admitted to N.Y. bar, 1954, Wis. bar, 1959; practiced in N.Y.C., from 1956; founder, operator Plywood Minn., 1963-77; U.S. senator from Minn., 1979—. Del., Minn. Republican Conv., 1968-78; del. Rep. Nat. Conv., 1972, 76. Served with Signal Corps, U.S. Army, 1954-55. Home: Plymouth MN Office: 419 Robert S N Saint Paul MN 55101 also Dirksen Senate Office Bldg Washington DC 20510

BOSHES, LOUIS D., physician, educator; b. Chgo., Oct. 15, 1908; s. Jacob and Ethel (London) B.; B.S., Northwestern U., 1931, M.D., 1936; m. Rhea Amber, Jan. 4, 1942; children—Arlene Phyllis (Mrs. Dennis C. Hirschfelder), Judi Myrl. Intern, Michael Reese Hosp., Chgo., 1935-36, Cook County Hosp., 1936-37; pvt. practice medicine specializing in neurology and psychiatry; fellow psychiatry Ill. Neuro-psychiat. Inst., Chgo., 1941-42, 46-47; sr. attending neurologist and psychiatrist, chief neurology clinic Michael Reese Med. Center, 1958-74; asst. prof. dept. neurology, psychiatry Northwestern U. Sch. Medicine, 1955-63; asso. to clin. prof. neurology Abraham Lincoln Sch. Medicine, U. Ill., Chgo., 1970—; attending neurologist Ill. Research and Ednl. Hosps., 1963—, dir. consultation clinic for epilepsy, 1963-78; asso. and attending neurologist, cons. neurology Cook County Hosp., 1947-63; sr. cons. neurology Downey VA Hosp., 1952-60; prof. neurology Cook County Grad. Sch. Medicine, 1970—. Mem. med. adv. com. Cook County chpt. Nat Found., 1947-55, March of Dimes, 1956—; mem. med. adv. com. Epilepsy Assn. Am., 1964—; bd. dirs., med. adv. com. Epilepsy Found. Am., 1964—; ambassador Internat. Bur. Epilepsy, 1969—; mem. profl. adv. com. Nat. Parkinson Found., 1960—, Nat. Myasthenia Gravis Found., 1972—, profl. adv. bd. United Cerebral Palsy. Served to lt. comdr. M.C., USNR, 1942-46. Diplomate neurology, psychiatry and child neurology Am. Bd. Psychiatry and Neurology. Fellow ACP, Am. Acad. Neurology, Am. Psychiat. Assn., Inst. Medicine Chgo.; mem. AMA (cons. Jour.), Pan-Am. Med. Assn. (pres. sect. neurology, D. of Humanities 1976), Central Neuropsychiat. Assn. (pres. 1973-74), Ill. Psychiat. Soc. (sec.-treas. 1949-50), Chgo. Neurol. Soc. (pres. 1964—, historian), Michael Reese Hosp. and Med. Center Alumni Assn. (pres. 1961—), Assn. for Research in Nervous and Mental Diseases, Internat., Am., Ill. (med. adv. com.) leagues against epilepsy, Ill. (chmn. sect. neurology and psychiatry 1961—), Chgo. med. socs., World Fedn. Neurology, AAAS, Am. Med. Soc. of Vienna (life), Central Assn. Electroencephalography, Phi Delta Epsilon, Sigma Xi, Alpha Omega Alpha. Author, contbr. to books, med. jours. Asso. editor Diseases of the Nervous System, 1962, New Physician, Neuroscis., Internat. Surgery; cons. editor Current Med. Digest, 1962—, Consultant; editor Chgo. Neurol. Soc. Bull., Behavioral Neuropsychiatry; mem. editorial bd. Excerpta Medica, Internat. Jour. Neurosurgery. Home: 3150 N Lake Shore Dr Chicago IL 60657 Office: 30 N Michigan Ave Chicago IL 60602

BOSHINSKI, EDWIN ERNEST, food processing equip. co. exec.; b. Shamokin, Pa., Mar. 10, 1926; s. Edwin Jerome and Bertha Rose (Kulbacki) B.; B.S., Duke U., 1951; postgrad. Washington U., 1951-52; m. Rita Roberta Mackel, Sept. 9, 1950; children—Thomas A., William E., Marilou R., Edwin James. With Hobart Corp., Troy, Ohio, 1952—, mgr. Dayton research, 1964-72, dir. Dayton research, 1972-79, dir. research and engring. for weighing and wrapping, 1979-82, v.p. research and engring., weighing and wrapping, 1982—. Mem. City of Englewood Citizen's Adv. com., 1978; mem. Sch. Bd., St. Rita's Parochial Sch., 1971-73; neighborhood commr. Boy Scouts Am., 1968. Served with USN, 1944-46. Mem. Scale Mfrs. Assn., Nat. Scale Men's Assn., Phi Beta Kappa, Omicron Delta Kappa, Sigma Pi Sigma, Sigma Nu. Republican. Roman Catholic. Club: K.C. Patentee in field. Home: 318 Winterset Dr Englewood OH 45222 Office: 1555 Stanley Ave Dayton OH 45404

BOSLAUGH, LESLIE, judge; b. Hastings, Nebr., Sept. 4, 1917; s. Paul E. and Ann (Herzog) B.; B.B.A., U. Nebr., 1939, LL.B., 1941; m. Elizabeth F. Meyer, Aug. 10, 1943; children—Marguerite Ann, Sarah Elizabeth, Paul Robert. Admitted to Nebr. bar, 1941. Mem. staff Nebr. Statute Revision Commn., 1941-43; pvt. practice law, Hastings, 1946-47; asst. atty. gen. Nebr., 1947-48; mem. firm Stiner & Boslaugh, Hastings, 1949-60; judge Nebr. Supreme Ct., Lincoln, 1961—. Served to lt. AUS, 1943-46. Mem. Am., Nebr. bar assns., Am. Judicature Soc., Inst. Jud. Adminstrn., Appellate Judges Conf., Order of Coif. Office: Supreme Ct Box 4638 Lincoln NE 68509

BOSMA, CHARLES EDWARD, state senator; b. Beech Grove, Ind., Apr. 8, 1922; s. Mitchell C. and Emma (Rodert) B.; B.S., Purdue U., 1970; m. Margaret Pauline Hagge, 1945; children—Janice Irene, Rhonda Jeanne, Brian Charles. Gen. mgr., pres. Bosma Diary Inc., 1945—; mem. Ind. Ho. of Reps., 1962-64, 66-68, Ind. Senate, 1968-82. Republican precinct committeeman, Marion County, Ind., 1961-66. Served with AUS, 1943-46. Mem. Nat. Soc. State Legislators, Luth. Child Welfare Assn. Ind. (dir.), Beech Grove Businessmen's Assn. Lutheran. Club: Kiwanis. Office: Ind Capitol Indianapolis IN 46204

BOSSMAN, KENNETH LEROY, accountant; b. Harrisburg, S.D., Sept. 3, 1939; s. Harvey Joseph and Ethel Lorraine (Radloff) B.; student U. S.D., 1958-60, Nettleton Comml. Coll., 1960, 61, 63, Nat. Coll. Bus., 1967-69; m. Lois Lorraine Stabelfeldt, June 7, 1964; children—Edwin Raymond, Kyla Rachelle, Harlan Joseph, James Kenneth. Engring. aid S.D. Dept. Hwys., Pierre, S.D., 1964-67; accountant Ross Accounting, Mitchell, S.D., 1969-70, E.K. Williams Accounting, Sioux Falls, S.D., 1970-71, Ark. Enterprises for Blind, 1971-72; tax payer service rep. IRS, Aberdeen, S.D., 1972—. Mem. Nat. Treasury Employees Union (1st v.p. 1973-75), S.D. Assn. for Blind (treas. 1966-71, pres. 1972-74), Full Gospel Businessmen's Fellowship Internat. (sec.), Hub City Amateur Radio Club, Aberdeen Area Zool. Soc. Democrat. Mem. Assemblies of God. Clubs: Moose, Elks, Eagles, Lions (past pres.), Masons. Home: 1311 McGovern Ave SE Aberdeen SD 57401 Office: 115 4th Ave SE Aberdeen SD 57401

BOSTER, LAWRENCE WILLIAM, JR., lab. exec.; b. Quincy, Ill., July 7, 1923; s. Lawrence William and Lillian Ann (Bauner) B.; student Boston Coll., 1943; student Quincy Coll., 1941-42, B.S., 1948; postgrad. U. Ill., 1945; m. Marilon McReynolds, June 5, 1948; children—David, Andrew, Mary Elizabeth, Mark. Chief lab technologist Quincy Clinic, 1948—; ednl. coordinator Blessing Hosp., Quincy, 1948—. Pres. Good Samaritan Home, Quincy; bd. dirs. ARC, Quincy, 1975—; sec. Quincy Sch. Bd., 1975-78. Served with U.S. Army, 1942-44, USAF, 1945-46. Decorated Purple Heart. Recipient Selma Southwick Exceptional Children award, 1978; Order of the Arrow, Boy Scouts Am., 1964. Mem. Am. Soc. Clin. Pathology, Navy League, United Comml. Travelers Assn. Republican. Lutheran. Clubs: Shriners, Spring Lake Country. Home: 1631 York St Quincy IL 62301 Office: Blessing Hosp Quincy IL 63301

BOSTIC, JAMES REGAN, mktg. exec.; b. Pipetone, Minn., May 18, 1940; s. Alva A. and May Ellen (Regan) B.; B.A., U. Minn., 1963; M.S.J., Northwestern U., 1964; D.B.A., Pacific Western U., 1976; m. Barbara Ann Williams, Mar. 17, 1980. Research and teaching asst. in consumer motivation Northwestern U., 1963-64; advt. and sales promotion planner Ford Motor Co., 1965-66; asst. mktg. research mgr. General Mills, Inc., 1966-67; advt. account exec. Campbell-Mithun, 1967-68; dir. mktg. Jeep vehicles, dir. advt. and merchandising, dir. mktg., planning Am. Motors, 1968-71; v.p. marketing Starcraft Corp., 1971-73; dir. mktg. Oldsmobile div., Gen. Motors, Lansing, Mich., 1974-79; v.p., gen. mgr. Scout Product div. Internat. Harvester Co., Chgo., 1979—, also v.p. mktg. agrl. equipment group; dir. evening div. advt. program, also lectr. U. Minn., 1966-68. Served to lt. AUS, 1954. Home: 21 W 640 Glen Park Rd Glen Ellyn IL 60137 Office: 401 N Michigan Ave Chicago IL 60611

BOSTLEMAN, FREDERICK WILLIAM, constrn. cons.; b. Toledo, June 25, 1921; s. Frederick Henry and Alice Wilhelmina (Marquardt) B.; student Toledo U., 1940; m. Mary Kathleen Shaner, July 11, 1942; children—Richard L., Bonnie, Mark. Founder Bostleman Corp., Toledo, 1946, inc., 1957, pres., owner, 1957—, chmn. bd., 1975—; owner, pres. Merriweather Realty Co., Toledo, 1958—; governing dir. Bostleman Internat. Ltd., Montserrat, British West Indies, 1968—; project coordinator, cons. Otis Avery Browning Masonic Meml. Home, Waterville, Ohio, 1979—. Trustee Toledo Area Constrn. Workers, Health, Welfare Fund, 1960-74. Chmn., trustee Sylvania Township, 1956-74; chmn. Sylvania Township Zoning Appeals Bd., 1956-64; chmn. Sylvania City, Township Republican Com., 1967-69; mem. exec. com. Lucas County Rep. Com., 1974; trustee Toledo Area Transit Bd. Authority; bd. dirs. Luth. Orphans and Old Folks Soc. Toledo, YMCA Camp Storer. Served with USAAF, 1942-46. Mem. Toledo Home Builders Assn. (pres. 1957), Asso. Gen. Contractors (pres. chpt. 1960-61, sec. Ohio council, 1961-62), Toledo Bldg. Congress (pres. 1962-63), Toledo Small Bus. Assn., (bd. dirs. 1962), Am. Arbitration Assn., Toledo C. of C. (trustee 1962), Toledo Automobile Assn. (dir., trustee). Lutheran (Ch. council 1968—). Mason (Shriner, Jester). Clubs: Inverness Country; Toledo; Montserrat Golf Montserrat Yacht (Montserrat, B.W.I.); Montserrat (Plymouth, B.W.I.), Rotary. Home: 4106 Merriweather Toledo OH 43607 Office: 410 Ryder Rd Toledo OH 43607

BOSWELL, JAMES EDWARD, diversified co. exec.; b. Winona, Mo., Aug. 31, 1910; s. Thomas Walton and Ethel B. (Jamieson) B.; B.S. in Civil Engring., Ga. Sch. Tech., 1933; m. Lois D. Kamerer, June 7, 1936; children—James Edward, Susan Elizabeth, John Joseph. Founder, owner Ind. Stave Co., Inc., Lebanon, Mo., 1934—; pres. Harrison Furniture Mfg. Co.; dir. Mo. Bank. Bd. dirs. Lebanon Community Center; chmn. bd. Bishop of Lebanon. Mem. Mo. (v.p. 1971—), Lebanon chambers commerce, Mo. Forest Products Assn. (dir. 1972—), Asso. Cooperage Industries Am., So. States Indsl. Council (dir.). Clubs: Media, Kiwanis, LOYA. Home: 960 S Jefferson St Lebanon MO 65536 Office: 1078 S Jefferson St Lebanon MO 65536

BOSWELL, NATHALIE SPENCE, speech pathologist; b. Cleve., May 9, 1924; d. Harrison Morton and Nathalie Muriel (Clem) Spence; student Skidmore Coll, 1941-42; Mus.B. in Edn., Northwestern U., 1945; M.A., Western Res. U., 1961; m. June 15, 1946; children—Louis Keith, Donna Spence, Deborah Anne. Speech therapist Highland View Hosp., Cleve., 1961-64; speech pathologist Cleve. VA Hosp., 1964—; chmn. Equal Employment Opportunity Counselors, 1969-74, Fed. Women Speakers Bur., 1968—, Fed. Career Info. Program, 1970-72, Fed. Coll. Relations Council, 1970-74, Fed. Exec. Bd., 1972-73. Mem. Cleve. Orch. Chorus, 1969—; vol. Seamen's Service, 1976—; patron Police Athletic League. Recipient Performance award Equal Employment Opportunities, 1973; Quality Increase award, 1980. licensed speech pathologist, Ohio. Mem. Am. Speech and Hearing Assn. (certificate of clin. competence, speaker confs. 1970, 71, 74), Ohio Speech and Hearing Assn., Aphasiology Assn. Ohio, Chi Omega Alumni Assn., Musical Arts Assn., Western Res. Hist. Soc., Cleve. Mus. Natural History, Cleve. Mus. Art, Smithsonian Assos., Nat. Wildlife Fedn., Audubon Soc., Nat. Trust Hist. Preservation, Am. Heritage Soc. Episcopalian. Club: Lakeside Yacht. Author: Guidelines for EEO Counselors in their Training Program, 1973; co-author: Laryngectomy-Orientation for Patients and Families, 1981. Home: 2946 Berkshire Rd Cleveland Heights OH 44118 Office: 10701 East Blvd Cleveland OH 44106

BOSWELL, ROBERT BOWEN, automobile co. mgr.; b. Washington, Feb. 14, 1920; s. Roscoe Conkling and Ida Blanche (Fowler) B.; B.S. in Metall. Engring., U. Mich., 1942; m. Ruth Ione Capron, Aug. 16, 1942; children—Robert Capron, James Russell, John Richard. Research metallurgist Chrysler Corp., Highland Park, Mich., 1946-50, chief metallurgist Tank Engine div., New Orleans, 1951-54, chief engr. Forge and Foundry div., Highland Park, 1955-60, mgr. product engring. various mfg. divs., Detroit, 1961-75, mgr. material cost analysis, Highland Park, 1975-80, mgr. chassis cost analysis, 1980—; evening sch. instr. Wayne State U., 1948-51. Served to lt. Ordnance, USNR, 1942-45. Mem. Am. Soc. Metals (chmn. Detroit chpt. 1961-62), Soc. Automotive Engrs. (governing bd. Detroit sect. 1964-66). Republican. Presbyterian. Club: C.I.T. (Detroit) Contbr. articles trade jours. Patentee in field. Home: 4332 MacQueen Dr Orchard Lake MI 48033 Office: Chrysler Corp Box 1919 Detroit MI 48288

BOTHWELL, WILBER CLARENCE, educator; b. Kansas City, Mo., May 15, 1910; s. Clarence Harvey and Maud (Wetherby) B.; B.A., Drury Coll., 1931, LL.D. (hon.), 1981; M.A., Washington U., St. Louis, 1933, Ph.D., 1941; m. Marcella Lester, July 4, 1948; children—Alfred, William, Brent Susan, Marcella Roper. Instr. econs. Washington U., 1935-41; sr. staff mem. Govtl. Research Inst., St. Louis, 1941-42; prof. econs., polit. sci. Drury Coll., Springfield, Mo., 1946-58, dir. Breech Sch. Bus. Adminstrn., 1958-61, 65-67, prof. econs. and bus. adminstrn., Ford Found. curriculum study liberal arts program in bus. adminstrn., 1959-60. Mem. panel arbitrators Fed. Mediation and Conciliation Service and Am. Arbitration Assn., Public Employment Relations Bd. Iowa. permanent arbitrator Dayco Corp. and United Rubber Workers, Internat. Paper Co. and United Paperworkers Internat. Union, Zenith Radio and Internat. Brotherhood Elec. Workers, S.W. Bell Telephone and Communication Workers Am. Served from 2d lt. to maj., USAAF, 1942-46; lt. col. res. Mem. Am. Econ. Assn., Nat. Acad. Arbitrators, Phi Beta Kappa. Rotarian. Contbr. articles to profl. jours. Home: 1307 E Meadowmere Springfield MO 65804

BOTINE, KAREN ELIZABETH, home economist; b. Pocahontas County, Iowa, Mar. 21, 1942; d. Lester Ferdinand and Eleanor Barbara (Wiese) B.; B.S. in Home Econs. Edn., Iowa State U., Ames, 1963, M.S. in Home Econs. Edn., 1970. Instr. home econs. Clarion (Iowa) Public Schs., 1963-68; dormitory housemother Iowa State U., 1968-69, 69-70; asst. state supr. home econs. edn. N.D. State Bd. Vocat. Edn., Bismarck, 1970-76, state supr., 1976—; program presenter profl. meetings; cons. FHA/home econs. related occupations, 1980; adult edn. instr., 1978-80. Exec. com. N.D. Commn. Status of Women, 1972, Bismarck-Mandan Lutheran Ch. Coordinating Council, 1978-80, sec.-treas., 1978; sec. N.D. Safety Council, 1979. Mem. NEA, N.D. Edn. Assn., Am. Vocat. Assn., N.D. Vocat. Assn., Nat. Assn. State Suprs. Vocat. Home Econs., Internat. Fedn. Home Econs., Am. Home Econs. Assn., N.D. Home Econs. Assn., Bismarck-Mandan Home Econs. Assn., N.D. Nutrition Council, Bismarck-Mandan Nutrition Council, Mo. Valley Adult Edn. Assn., N.D. Adult Edn. Assn., AAUW, Omicron Nu, Phi Kappa Phi, Delta Kappa Gamma. Office: State Capitol 15th Floor Bismarck ND 58505

BOTKIN, WILLIAM HOWARD, trade assn. exec.; b. Columbus, Ohio, May 18, 1939; s. Fred Emory and Gladys Lorraine (Poole) B.; B.A. in Journalism, Ohio State U., 1962; m. Margaret Anne Harris Wensyel, Feb. 17, 1979; children—Katherine E., William Howard II, Colleen A., Thomas J. Public relations officer Ohio Civil Service Employees Assn., 1969-72; sr. public relations rep. Va. Electric and Power Co., 1972-74; exec. asst. Office Ohio Sec. State, 1974-75; public info. coordinator Ohio Electric Utility Inst., Columbus, 1975—; mem. Ohio Shoreline Adv. Council Coastal Zone Mgmt.; mem. bus./industry adv. group Ohio Council Environ. Edn. Public relations chmn. Franklin County (Ohio) Citizens for Goldwater, 1964; public relations chmn. Central region Assembly Govtl. Employees, 1969-72, nat. public relations co-chmn., 1971-72. Named Ky. Col., 1969, Hon. Citizen, City of Indpls., 1972, Hon. Dep. Sheriff, Hamilton County, Ohio, 1972; recipient key to City of Detroit, 1969. Mem. Ohio Trade Assn. Execs., Internat. Assn. Energy Economists. Republican. Roman Catholic. Clubs: Shriners, Ducks Unlimited. Founder, editor imAGE, 1969-72; editor Public Employee News, 1969-72, Perfecting Security Interest Under the Uniform Commercial Code, 1968, Foreign Corporation Licensing, 1968, proc. Ohio Electoral College, 1968. Home: 2264 Edmonton Rd Columbus OH 43229 Office: 40 S 3d St Suite 335 Columbus OH 43515

BOTSAS, ELEFTHERIOS NICHOLAS, educator; b. Achladine, Greece, Apr. 6, 1931; came to U.S., 1956, naturalized, 1971; s. Nicholas Themistokles and Helen J. (Karabetsos) B.; B.S., U. Detroit, 1960; Ph.D. (grad. fellow 1960-64, Mendelson research fellow 1962, 64), Wayne State U., 1965; m. Chrysoula G. Kyriakou, Dec. 26, 1965; children—Helen G., Nicholas George. Asst. prof. Lafayette Coll., Easton, Pa., 1964-66; asst. prof. Oakland U., Rochester, Mich., 1966-70, asso. prof., 1970-76, chmn. econs. dept., 1972-78, prof. econs. and mgmt., 1978—; mem. Council of Econ. Advisors Oakland County, Mich., 1966-68. Exec. bd. Am. Hellenic Congress, 1974—, chmn. exec. bd., 1979-80; mem. Diocesan Council, Greek Orthodox Ch. of N. Am. and S. Am. Served with Greek Army, 1953-55. Mem. Am. Econ. Assn., AAAS, Am. Assn. for S.E. European Studies, Mich. Acad. Arts, Letters and Scis., Modern Greek Studies Assn. Club: Am. Hellenic Ednl. Progressive Assn. Contbr. writings in field to publs. Home: 2539 Yorkshire Ln Bloomfield Hills MI 48013 Office: Sch Econs and Mgmt Oakland Univ Rochester MI 48063

BOTTUM, EDWARD S., banker; b. Lafeyette, Ind., 1933; ed. Purdue U., 1955, Harvard U., 1959. Exec. v.p. trust and investments Continental Ill. Nat. Bank & Trust Co., Chgo. Address: 231 S LaSalle St Chicago IL 60693*

BOUCHER, JANE, communications cons.; b. Columbus, Ohio, July 4, 1950; d. Roy D. Boucher and Virginia E. Lee; B.S. in Speech and Broadcasting, Ohio State U., 1972, M.A. in Ednl. Communications, 1973, postgrad., 1974—; postgrad. U. South Fla., 1977-79. Program adminstr. Am. Lung Assn., Sarasota, Fla., 1973-74; tchr.-coordinator Sarasota County Vocat. Tech. Center, 1975-77; instr. Kettering Adult Sch., Dayton, Ohio, 1977—; adj. prof. Sinclair Community Coll., Dayton, 1977—, Wright State U., Dayton, 1977—, Clark Tech. Coll., Springfield, Ohio, 1980—; communications cons., Dayton, 1978—. Cert. tchr., Fla., Ohio, Calif. Mem. Am. Soc. Tng. and Devel., Women in Communications, Nat. Speakers Assn., Internat. Transactional Analysis Assn., Personal Dynamics Assn. Home: 27 E Monteray Ave Office: 27 E Monteray Ave Dayton OH 45419

BOUDOULAS, HARISIOS, cardiologist; b. Velvendo, Kozani, Greece, Nov. 3, 1935; came to U.S., 1975; s. Konstantinos and Sophia (Manolas) B.; M.D., U. Salonica, Greece, 1959, doctorate diploma, 1967; m. Olga Paspati, Feb. 27, 1971; children—Sophia, Constantinos. Intern, 401st Gen. Army Hosp., Greece, 1960; resident in cardiology 424th Military Hosp., Salonica, 1961; resident in internal medicine First Med. Clinic, U. Salonica, 1962-64, resident in cardiology, 1964-66, attending physician renal unit, 1966-67, coronary care unit, 1967-69, lectr. in medicine, 1969-70, sr. lectr., head coronary care unit, 1973-75; fellow, instr. div. cardiology Ohio

State U., 1970-73, fellow, 1975, asst. prof. medicine, 1975-78, asso. prof., 1978-80; dir. cardiac non-invasive lab., 1978-80; prof. medicine, chief clin. cardiovascular research, div. cardiology Wayne State U., Detroit, 1980—; chief Cardiovascular Diagnostic and Tng. Center, VA Med. Center, Allen Park, Mich., 1980—. Fellow Am. Coll. Cardiology, Council Clin. Cardiology, Am. Coll. Clin. Pharmacology, Am. Coll. Angiology, A.C.P.; mem. Med. Assn. Salonica, Greek Soc. Biochemistry, Greek Renal Assn., European Dialysis and Transplant Assn., Am. Heart Assn., Greek Heart Assn., Greek Com. Against Hypertension, Am. Fedn. Clin. Research, Central Soc. Clin. Research. Greek Orthodox. Mem. team which performed first successful kidney transplantation in Greece; contbr. numerous articles in field to profl. jours. Home: 22825 Highbank Birmingham MI 48010 Office: Wayne State U Sch Medicine 540 E Canfield Detroit MI 48201

BOUDREAUX, MICHAEL MILES, educator; b. Quincy, Ill., June 9, 1946; s. Miles W. and Martha J. (Ridge) B.; B.A., Quincy Coll., 1968; M.A., U. Mo., Columbia, 1972, Ph.D., 1973, M.B.A., 1976. Asst. prof. bus. adminstrn. Columbia (Mo.) Coll., 1976—, dept. chmn., 1977-81, dir. shopping center mktg. and mgmt. program, 1981. NDEA fellow, 1976-70; named top collegiate chpt. adv. Am. Mktg. Assn. in Midwest, 1978, 80, 81. Mem. Am. Mktg. Assn. (student activities council 1978-80, 81-82, chmn. careers brochures com. 1979-80, chmn. nat. collegiate conf. 1981, chmn. central region student activities council 1980), Midwest Bus. Adminstrn. Assn. (adv. council 1979-81). Author text and workbook: Basic Economics, 1981; Economics: Putting the Pieces Together, 1978; Perspectives: Leadership, Communication and Motivation, 1979; How to Write Cases Reports for Business, 1976. Home: 2309 W Broadway Columbia MO 65201 Office: Columbia College 10th and Rogers Columbia MO 65216

BOULOS, BADI MANSOUR, pharmacologist, physician, educator; b. Alexandria, Egypt, July 3, 1930; s. Nakhla and Olga (Matta) B.; came to U.S., 1960, naturalized, 1972; M.D., U. Alexandria, 1953, diploma in Pharmacology, 1958, diploma in Tropical Medicine, 1960; M.S. with honors in Radiation Research, U. Iowa, 1962; Ph.D. in Med. Pharmacology, U. Mo., 1965; m. Gerda Dorothy Bergen, July 6, 1964; children—Badi Emil, Thomas N., Daniel N., Matthew Henry. Intern, U. Alexandria Hosp., 1953-54; resident Coptic Hosp., Alexandria, 1954-55; practice medicine specializing in Obstetrics and gynecology, Alexandria, 1956-60; med. officer UN Relief and Welfare Agy., Gaza Strip, 1954-56; instr. pharmacology U. Alexandria, 1958-60, asst. prof. pharmacology, 1965-66; asst. scientist Cancer Research Center, Columbia, Mo., 1966-68; asst. prof. pharmacology U. Mo., Columbia, 1968-70; asso. prof. occupational and environ. medicine U. Ill., Chgo., 1972—; prof. community medicine King Faisal U., Dammam, Saudi Arabia, 1978-80; cons. in toxicology to Ill Crime Commn., 1974—, FDA, 1974—, Ill. Inst. of Environ. Quality, 1972—, Nat. Inst. Occupational Safety and Health, U.S. Dept Labor, numerous others; mem. Task Force Toxic Chem. Substances Am. Chem. Assn., 1974—; cons. Ill. Cancer Council, 1974—. USPHS fellow, 1970-72; NIH grantee, 1971-72, 74-75; Fulbright scholar, 1960-64. Mem. Am. Pub. Health Assn., Am. Soc. Pharmacology and Exptl. Therapeutics, Am. Soc. Toxicology, Am. Cancer Soc., N.Y. Acad. Sci., AMA. Episcopalian. Contbr. 300 articles on pharm. and cancer research, environ. and occupational medicine to sci. jours. Home: 812 Heritage Dr Addison IL 60101 Office: School of Public Health Univ of Illinois PO Box 6880 Chicago IL 60680

BOULTON, DALE FREDERICK, mfg. co. exec.; b. Detroit, Dec. 20, 1942; s. Loyal Benjamin and Mildred Lillian (Niedermier) B.; B.A., Olivet Nazarene Coll., 1966; M.B.A., U. Detroit, 1979; m. Helen Ruth Albright, July 28, 1973; 1 son, Jeffrey S.F. Prodn. engr. Chrysler Detroit Tank Plant, Detroit, 1967-68, program engr. Chrysler Def. Engring., 1970-73; controller F.W. Ritter Sons Co., South Rockwood, Mich., 1973-77, chief fin. officer, sec., 1977—, also dir.; dir. Keller Pottery Corp. of Conn. Active Republican Party, Allen Park, Mich. Served with U.S. Army, 1968-70. Mem. Assn. M.B.A. Execs., U.S. Army Armor Assn., U.S. Strategic Inst., Am. Def. Preparedness Assn., U.S. Naval Inst., Econ. Club of Detroit, Sigma Tau Delta. Mem. Ch. of Nazarene. Clubs: Dearborn Republican, Young Republicans, AFV Assn. Home: 9269 Joseph Ave Allen Park MI 48101 Office: 12670 N Dixie Hwy South Rockwood MI 48179

BOUMA, GERALD DALE, educator; b. Orange City, Iowa, Oct. 8, 1944; s. Ralph and Jenny Marjory (Reinsma) B.; student Dordt Coll., 1962-65; A.B., Northwestern Coll., 1967; M.Mus., Ariz. State U., 1969, postgrad., 1973-79; m. Donna Mae Duistermars, July 14, 1966; children—Tonya Nicole, Caron Leigh. Ch. choir dir. Calvary Christian Ref. Ch., Orange City, 1962-66, 72-75; music instr. Unity Christian High Sch., Orange City, 1964-68; prof. music Dordt Coll., Sioux Center, Iowa, 1969—, condr. of bands, 1974—. Mem. fin. bd. Orange City Christian Sch., 1969-72; bd. dirs. Sioux County Concert Series, 1969-72; dir. musicals Sioux County Arts Council, 1976, Orange City Community Prodns., 1968-79. Mem. Music Educators Nat. Conf., Nat. Band Assn., Iowa Bandmasters Assn. Republican. Christian Ref. Ch. Composer: Sonnet for Brass Choir, 1969; March Mae, 1971; Sketch for Euphonium and Band, 1969. Home: 615 Second St SW Orange City IA 51041 Office: Dordt Coll Sioux Center IA 51250

BOUNDS, VERNON MARING, corp. exec.; b. Owing Mills, Md., Aug. 5, 1939; s. Vernon Maring Bounds and Lou Stem (Bennett) Hoover; B.S. in Agrl. Edn., Pa. State U., 1961; M.S. in Agrl. Econs., U. Tenn., 1963; m. Virginia Lee Whitman, Sept. 16, 1961; children—Mark Allan, Stacey Lynn. Grain analyst, editor, Doane Agrl. Service, St. Louis, 1963-65; livestock and grain economist Ralston Purina, St. Louis, 1965-70; dir. commodity research, mgr. corp. hedging accounts, asst. v.p. Shearson Co., Chgo., 1970-72; mgr. grain merchandising and brokerage office, Tabor Co., Decatur, Ill., 1972-74; corp. economist, group mgr. byproduct, export and mil. sales Rath Packing Co., Waterloo, Iowa, 1974-79; pres. VMB Agri-Mktg. Services, Inc., agrl. econ. cons., commodity futures trader, Waterloo, 1979—. Bd. dirs. Russell House Hist. Soc. Club: Elks.

BOURNE, GODFREY RODERICK, wildlife ecologist; b. Georgetown, Guyana, Mar. 20, 1943; came to U.S., 1966, naturalized, 1981; s. Layton George and Edna Rubina (Thompson) B.; B.A., Ohio Wesleyan U., 1971; M.En., Miami U., 1976; postgrad. (fellow 1976-79), U. Mich., 1976-81; m. Carol Elizabeth Mulligan, Dec. 21, 1968. Avian researcher, artist, Guyana, 1962-64; asst. tchr. Christ Ch. Secondary Sch., Guyana, 1964-66; writer-illustrator, U.S., 1971—; cons. LGL Ltd., Ecmonton, Alta., Can., 1975; teaching fellow U. Mich., Ann Arbor, 1976-79, lectr., 1977-79, 81, doctoral candidate wildlife ecology and mgmt., 1977-81; cons. Man and the Biosphere Com., Guyana, 1980. Active Boy Scouts of Guyana, 1952-59, patrol leader, 1957-59; mem. Kamoa Art Group, 1961-65, v.p., 1964-65; mem. Christ Ch. Young People's Movement, 1964-66, pres., 1965-66; mem. Ohio Wesleyan U. Internat. Student Assn., 1967-71, Wheaton Club, 1970-73; hon. mem. Langdon Club, 1975-76. Welder Wildlife Found. fellow, 1973-75, Rackham Block fellow, 1979-81, grantee, 1979-80; research grantee Fred and Jane Stevens, 1974, 80. Chapman Meml. Fund, 1973, 74, 80; recipient Marcia Brady Tucker award Am. Ornithol. Union, 1972. Mem. AAAS, Interciencia Assn., Am. Ornithologists Union, Wilson Ornithol. Soc., Cornell Lab. of Ornithology, Wildlife Soc., Sigma Xi (research grantee, 1979-80), Phi Kappa Phi. Artist, oil painting Abary Wetland, 1961 (Guyana Nat. Mus.); contbr. research papers on ecology of neotropical birds to publs. Home: 1142 Nielsen Ct Apt 9 Ann Arbor MI 48105 Office: School Natural Resources Univ Michigan Ann Arbor MI 48109

BOUSFIELD, ALDRIDGE KNIGHT, educator; b. Boston, Apr. 5, 1941; s. Weston Ashmore and Thelma (Knight) B.; S.B., Mass. Inst. Tech., 1963, Ph.D., 1966; m. Marie Vastersavendts, June 8, 1968. Lectr., Brandeis U., Waltham, Mass., 1966-67, asst. prof., 1967-72; asso. prof. U. Ill., Chgo., 1972-76, prof. math., 1976—; Office of Naval Research research asso., 1966-67. NSF research grantee, 1967—. Mem. Am. Math. Soc., Math. Assn. Am., Sigma Xi. Author: (with D. Kan) Homotopy Limits Completions and Localizations, 1972; (with V. Gugenheim) On PL DeRham Theory and Rational Homotopy Type, 1976; contbr. articles to profl. jours. Home: 400 E Randolph St Apt 2910 Chicago IL 60601 Office: Math Dept U Ill at Chicago Circle Chicago IL 60680

BOUZEK, ROBERT EDWARD, corp. communications exec.; b. Prairie du Chien, Wis., Sept. 24, 1933; s. Edward James and Emma Regina (White) B.; B.S.J., U. Wis.-Madison, 1962; m. Mary Elizabeth Scott, Dec. 20, 1960; children—Michaelle, Elizabeth Mary, Lisa Diane, Jane Ann. Editor, Courier-Press, Prairie du Chien, 1957-58; govtl./bus. reporter Waukesha (Wis.) Freeman, 1958-59; reporter, copy editor Wis. State Jour., Madison, 1959-63; copy editor supr. Milw. Jour., 1963-67; pub. relations specialist Am. Mut. Ins. Alliance, Chgo., 1967-68; pub. relations counsel Carl Byoir & Assos. Inc., Chgo., 1968-70; account supr. Harshe-Rotman & Druck Inc., Chgo., 1970-77, v.p., 1977-79; mgr. media relations Ill. Bell Telephone Co., Chgo., 1979-81, mgr. advt., 1981—. Home: 69 E Quincy St Riverside IL 60546 Office: 225 W Randolph St Chicago IL 60606

BOVEE, EUGENE CLEVELAND, protozoologist, educator; b. Sioux City, Iowa, Apr. 1, 1915; S.s. Earl Eugene and Martha Nora (Johnson) B.; B.A., U. No. Iowa, 1939; M.S., U. Iowa, 1948; Ph.D., UCLA, 1950; m. Maezene B. Wamsley, May 18, 1942; m. 2d Elizabeth A. Moss, May 1968; children—Frances, Gregory, Matthew; stepchildren—Lynne, Lisa. Instr. zoology Iowa U., 1940-41; biology tchr. Greene (Iowa) High Sch., 1941-42; asso. U. No. Iowa, 1946-48, UCLA, 1948-50, research zoologist, 1962-68; asst. prof. biology Calif. Poly. U., 1950-52; asso. prof. zoology, dept. chmn. N.D. State U., 1952-53; asst. prof. biology U. Houston, 1953-55; asso. prof., U. Fla., 1955-62; prof. physiology and cell biology, U. Kans., Lawrence, 1968—, counseling officer div. biol. sci., 1974-80; cons. Am. Type Culture Collection, 1980—, W.C. Brown, Pub., 1978-81. Served to 1st lt. U.S. Army, World War II. Research grantee, NIH, 1957-62, NSF, 1970-74, NIH, NSF, and ONR, 1962-68, Kans. Fed. Water Resources Inst. and U. Kans., 1968-81; recipient Disting. Alumni award, U. No. Iowa, 1980. Mem. Soc. Protozoology (pres. 1979-80, treas. 1977-78, exec. com. 1979-81), Am. Inst. Biol. Sci., Am. Microscopy Soc. (mem.-at-large exec. com. 1959-62), Soc. Systemic Zoology, Western Soc. Naturalists, Iowa Acad. Sci., Kans. Acad. Sci. (life mem., pres. 1979-80, exec. com. 1975-81), Sigma Xi. Editor Kansas Science Bulletin, 1974-79; co-author: How to Know the Protozoa, 2d edit., 1979; contbr. chpts. to books, articles to jours. in field. Office: 154 Snow Hall Univ Kansas Lawrence KS 66044

BOVEE, JOAN GUILDENBECHER, home economist, educator; b. Muncie, Ind., May 8, 1946; d. Robert and Kathryn E. (Bullock) Guildenbecher; B.S., Purdue U., 1968; M.S., St. Francis Coll., 1972; postgrad. Ind. U., 1979-80; m. Norman Alan Bovee, Dec. 28, 1967. Jr. fashion merchandizing cons. Montgomery Wards, Fort Wayne, Ind., 1963-67; clothing and textile lab. technician Purdue U., w. Lafayette, Ind., 1966-67; vocat. home econs. tchr. Prairie Heights Community High Sch., LaGrange, Ind., 1968—, also dir. student activities, 1972—; cons. for local 4-H workshops, 1968—. Mem. adv. com. Prairie Heights Outdoor Community Edn. Center, 1979-81; mem. planning com. Prairie Heights Ann. Fall Farm Festival, 1972-81. Mem. Nat. Assn. Vocat. Home Econs. Tchrs. (state contact person 1980), Am. Home Econs. Assn. (mem. Ho. of Dels. 1978-79), Am. Vocat. Assn. (mem. Ho. of Dels. 1978-80), Ind. Vocat. Assn. (mem. awards com. 1981), Ind. Vocat. Home Econs. Assn. (pres. 1979-80, dist. pres. 1978), Ind. Home Econs. Assn. (mem. public relations com. 1979—), NEA, Ind. State Tchrs. Assn., Prairie Heights Edn. Assn., Nat. Council of Family Relations, Ind. Council of Family Relations, LaGrange County Mental Health Assn., Kappa Delta Pi, Omicron Nu. Mem. Apostolic Christian Ch. Contbg. author: Indiana State Interpersonal Relations Curriculum Guide, 1977, Indiana State Human Development Curriculum Guide, 1979. Home: Rural Route 1 PO Box 320 Wolcottville IN 46795

BOVIS, GEORGE STEVEN, convenience stores co. exec.; b. Chgo., Aug. 3, 1940; s. James Francis and Marian Bernice B.; B.S. in Bus., Ill. Inst. Tech., 1962; M.B.A., U. Chgo., 1968; m. Elizabeth Ann McClurg, Apr. 8, 1967; children—Beth Ann, Christopher Paul. With Jewel Cos., Inc., 1962—, mgr. real estate Jewel Food Stores, Chgo., 1968-71, v.p. store devel. White Hen Pantry, Elmhurst, Ill., 1971-75, v.p. mktg. White Hen Pantry, 1976-77, v.p. market devel. growth planning White Hen Pantry, 1977—. mem. steering com. student exchange program Sch. Dist. 205, 1980. Mem. Nat. Assn. Convenience Stores, Elmhurst C. of C., Sports Club Club Am. (past regional pres.), Delta Tau Delta. Office: Jewel Cos Inc White Hen Pantry 666 Industrial Dr Elmhurst IL 60126

BOWDEN, DOUGLAS IVES, accountant; b. Marceline, Mo., Nov. 4, 1953; s. Homer Ives, Jr., and Betty Jo (Burgener) B.; B.S. in Bus. Adminstrn., U. Mo., Columbia, 1976. Accountant, Dept. Natural Resources, State of Mo., Jefferson City, 1977-78; mgr. acctg. Four Seasons Lakesites, Inc., Lake Ozark, Mo., 1978—. Vol. coll. tutor, tax preparation counselor, disc jockey stas. KLDN-FM, Eldon, Mo., KCOU-FM, Columbia, Mo. Mem. Phi Eta Sigma. Mem. Christian Church (Disciples of Christ). Home: Route 2 Box 179-22 Osage Beach MO 65065 Office: PO Box 408 Lake Ozark MO 65049

BOWDEN, OTIS HEARNE, II, mgmt. cons. firm exec.; b. Stuttgart, Ark., Jan. 2, 1928; s. Otis Hearne and Donna (Trice) B.; B.S. in Bus. Adminstrn., Washington U., 1950, M.B.A., 1953; m. Helen Carol Lamar, June 25, 1949. Financial analyst St. Louis Union Trust Co., St. Louis, 1950-53; dist. mgr. TRW, Inc., Cleve., 1953-63; dir. Mass Transit Center, B.F. Goodrich Co., Akron, Ohio, 1963-67; v.p. E.A. Butler Assos., Inc., Cleve., 1967-71; pres. Bowden & Co., Inc., Cleve., 1972—; guest lectr. Akron U., 1972—. Nat. promotion dir. Laymen's Hour Radio Broadcast, 1959-63; chmn. commerce and industry div. United Fund of Greater Cleve., 1962; pres. Am. Baptist Men of Ohio, 1962-63; trustee Alderson-Broaddus Coll., Philippi, W.Va., 1965-76, Eastern Coll., Phila.; alumni bd. govs. Washington U., St. Louis; bd. dirs. Am. Bapt. Fgn. Mission Soc., 1962-71; regional dir. Project Winsome Internationale; adv. bd. Salvation Army of Greater Cleve., 1979—, also chmn. fin. com. Served with USMCR, 1951. Mem. Am. Mgmt. Assn., Am. Mktg. Assn. Clubs: Rotary (trustee 1975-77, Paul Harris fellow 1978), Union. Home: 1816 Brookshire Rd Akron OH 44313 Office: 5000 Rockside Rd Cleveland OH 44131

BOWDLE, FREDERICK CHARLES, obstetrician, gynecologist; b. Napoleon, Ohio, Mar. 31, 1934; s. Charles P. and Reta Belle (Stuempel) B.; student U. Mich., 1952-55, M.D., 1959; m. Sandra Kay Lowe, June 22, 1963; children—Brian Frederick, Julie Rochelle. Intern, St. Vincent Hosp. and Med. Center, Toledo, 1959-60, resident, 1962-65, now mem. staff, chmn. dept. obstetrics and gynecology, 1971-75, practice medicine specializing in obstetrics and gynecology, Toledo, 1965—; mem. staffs Toledo Hosp., Med. Coll. Ohio; clin. asst. prof. obstetrics and gynecology Med. Coll. Ohio, Toledo, 1972—; mem. profl. edn. com. Lucas County (Ohio) unit Am. Cancer Soc., 1971. Served as capt. M.C. USAF, 1960-62. Diplomate Am. Bd. Obstetrics and Gynecology. Fellow Am. Coll. Obstetrics and Gynecology, A.C.S.; mem. Acad. Medicine of Toledo and Lucas County, Toledo, Mich. socs. obstetrics-gynecology, Central Assn. Obstetrics-Gynecology, AMA, N. Am. Gynecol. Soc., Am. Assn. Gynecologic Laparoscopists, Am. Fertility Soc., U. Mich. Alumni Assn., Ohio State Alumni Assn. Republican. Methodist. Clubs: Royal Order Jesters, Masons, Shriners (potentate 1979). Home: 4629 Beaconsfield Ct Toledo OH 43623 Office: Sunforest Med Bldg 3900 Sunforest Ct Toledo OH 43623

BOWE, CHARLEEN BERNICE, mech. equipment distbr.; b. Peoria, Ill., Aug. 1, 1944; d. Charles Everett and Colleen Esther (Cartwright) Bartholomew; student Ill. Central Coll.; children—Cynthia Lynn White, Thomas Page White. Secretarial positions, West Palm Beach, Fla., 1964-68, Washington, Ill., 1968-69, Linden and Co., Inc., Peoria, 1969-71, Yeomans Distbg. Co., Peoria, 1971-73, Pitney Bowes, Peoria, 1973-74; sec.-treas. Water Power Inc. (formerly Bowe and Assos., Inc.), Peoria, 1974-78, pres., 1978—; mem. Constrn. Action Com. of Peoria. Leader, Girl Scouts U.S.A., 1968-73. Mem. Nat. Assn. Women in Constrn. (past pres. Peoria chpt. 174), Nat. Assn. Women Bus. Owners (pres. Greater Peoria chpt.), Nat. Assn. Female Execs., Greater Peoria Contractors and Builders Assn., Better Bus. Bur. Peoria, Central Ill. Indsl. Assn., Peoria C. of C. Presbyterian. Home: Rural Route 2 Box 273D Chillicothe IL 61523 Office: Water Power Inc 8811 N Pioneer Rd Peoria IL 61615

BOWEN, KEVIN FRANCIS, sporting goods co. exec.; b. Providence, Sept. 1, 1948; s. Francis A. and Katherine (O'Connor) B.; B.A., Brown U., 1970; M.A., Calif. State U., Los Angeles, 1971; Ph.D. (Research fellow), Dartmouth Coll., 1976; M.B.A., U. Chgo., 1979; m. Marianne E. Klinkenberg, Dec. 16, 1972. Sr. research analyst Quaker Oats Co., Chgo., 1976-77, research supr., 1977-78, research mgr., 1978-80; v.p. mktg. services Wilson Sporting Goods, River Grove, Ill., 1980—. Mem. Am. Mktg. Assn., Advt. Research Found. Home: 345 Fullerton Pkwy Chicago IL 60614 Office: 2233 West St River Grove IL 60171

BOWEN, WILLIAM F., state senator; b. Cin., Jan. 30, 1929; s. William F. and Henrietta R. (Washington) B.; student Xavier U., 1952-55; m. Dolores Lee Freeman, 1956; children—William F. III, Keven Braxton, Terrence Samuel. Former mem. Ohio Ho. of Reps.; mem. Ohio Senate, 1970—, minority whip; vice chmn. Hamilton County (Ohio) Dem. Party; mem. Ohio State Exec. Dem. Com., Gov.'s Task Force Corrections; del. Nat. Black Polit. Caucus. Recipient numerous community awards; hon. mention John F. Kennedy Public Service award Ohio League Young Dems. Mem. Hamilton County Black Caucus, NAACP. Baptist. Clubs: Masons, Wayfarers. Office: State Senate Columbus OH 43216*

BOWEN, WILLIAM J., mgmt. cons.; b. N.Y.C.; B.S., Fordham U., 1956; M.B.A., N.Y. U., 1963. Trainee, Smith, Barney & Co., N.Y.C., 1959-61; asst. v.p. investments 1st Nat. City Bank, N.Y.C., 1961-67; instl. salesman Hayden Stone, Inc., N.Y.C., 1967-69; successively v.p. and Eastern regional sales mgr., 1st v.p. and instl. sales mgr. Shearson, Hammill & Co., Inc., N.Y.C., 1969-73; asso. Heidrick & Struggles, Inc., Chgo., 1973-77, v.p., 1977-78, sr. v.p. and mgr., 1978-80, sr. v.p. and central regional mgr., 1980-81, pres. and chief exec. officer, 1981—. Office: Heidrick & Struggles Inc 125 S Wacker Dr Chicago IL 60606

BOWER, DORIS JEAN, ednl. cons.; b. Jackson, Minn., Feb. 28, 1938; d. Edward Joseph and Ethel Dorthea (Madsen) Doyscher; B.S., Mankato State U., 1962, M.S., 1977; m. James P. Bower, June 30, 1979; children—John, Andrew, Joshua. Elementary tchr., St. Louis Park, Minn., 1964-68; reading specialist, Mapleton, Minn., 1968-70; dir. center Ramsey County Head Start, St. Paul, 1970-72; elementary tchr., Inver Grove Heights, Minn., 1972-79; curriculum cons., planner, dir. microcomputer spelling project Ednl. Coop. Service Unit, St. Cloud (Minn.) State U., from 1979; now courseware design, MECC. Fed. grantee, 1979-82, Apple Found. grantee, 1980-81. Mem. Assn. Supervision and Curriculum Devel., Nat. Assn. Ednl. Data Systems, Minn. Assn. Supervision and Curriculum Devel., Minn. Assn. Ednl. Data Systems. Democrat. Home: 1063 Sherren St W Roseville MN 55113 Office: Minn Ednl Computing Consortium 2520 Broadway Dr St Paul MN 55113

BOWER, GLEN LANDIS, state legislator; b. Highland, Ill., Jan. 16, 1949; s. Ray Landis and Evelyn Ferne (Ragland) B.; B.S. in Govt. (President's scholar), So. Ill. U., Carbondale, 1971; J.D. with honors, Chgo. Kent Coll. Law, 1974. Admitted to Ill. bar, 1974; state's atty. Effingham County, 1976-79; mem. Ill. Ho. of Reps. from 54th Dist., 1979—; mem. Nat. Adv. Com. Juvenile Justice and Delinquency Prevention, 1976-80. Trustee McKendree Coll., Lebanon, Ill. Capt. USAF Res. Named Outstanding Freshman Legislator, Ill. Edn. Assn., 1980. Mem. Am. Bar Assn., Ill. Bar Assn., Am. Legis. Exchange Council, Am. Legion. Republican. Methodist. Clubs: Shriners, Kiwanis, Elks. Office: 105 E Jefferson St PO Box 1106 Effingham IL 62401

BOWER, SHIRLEY MAE (MRS. JAY R. BOWER), Realtor; b. Marshfield, Mo., Apr. 2, 1935; d. James Oliver and Ruth Irene (Hyde) Day; B.A. in Speech and Dramatics cum laude, Culver-Stockton Coll., 1957; grad. Ill. Inst. Real Estate Brokers, 1972; m. Jay R. Bower, Aug. 5, 1956; 1 dau., Lisa Lynne. Tchr. speech, drama and English Quincy (Ill.) Jr. High Sch., 1951-58; tchr. speech and drama Central High Sch., Camp Point, Ill., 1958-60, 65—; real estate broker, 1976-78; relocation dir. and co-owner Bower Gallery of Homes, Quincy, Camp Point and Mt. Sterling, Ill., 1967—. Co-dir. Quincy Jr. Theater, 1957-58, bd. dirs.; bd. dirs. Family Service Agy., Quincy, 1967-68, Quincy Jr. High Sch. PTA, 1973; alumni bd. dirs. Culver-Stockton Coll., 1967—, pres., 1965-66. Mem. Quincy Bd. Realtors, Nat. Assn. Real Estate Brokers, Nat. Inst. Real Estate Brokers, Pan-Hellenic Council Quincy, Chi Omega. Mem. Order Eastern Star. Mem. Christian Ch. Club: Spring Lake Country (Quincy). Home: 2828 Southfield Dr Quincy IL 62301 Office: 503 Maine St Quincy IL 62301

BOWER, WILLIAM WALTER, scientist; b. Hammond, Ind., Jan. 9, 1945; s. William Walter and Frances Anita (Good) B.; B.S. in Mech. Engring., Purdue U., 1967, M.S., 1969, Ph.D., 1971. Sr. engr. Propulsion Dept., McDonnell Aircraft Co., St. Louis, 1971-74, scientist Flight Scis. Dept., Research Labs., 1974—; grad. instr. mech. engring. Purdue U., 1970-71. NDEA Title IV fellow, 1967-70; recipient Meritorious Tech. Contbn. award St. Louis sect. AIAA, 1977. Asso. fellow AIAA; mem. ASME. Presbyterian. Club: McDonnell Douglas Corp St Louis Mgmt. Contbr. articles to tech. jours. Home: 4575 Whisper Lake Dr Apt 8 Florissant MO 63033 Office: McDonnell Douglas Corp PO Box 516 Saint Louis MO 63166

BOWERS, MAYNARD CLAIRE, botanist; b. Battle Creek, Mich., Nov. 5, 1930; s. Frederick Claire and Elnora Alice (Hard) B.; A.B., Albion Coll., 1956; M.Ed., U. Va., 1960; Ph.D., U. Colo., 1966; m. Leenamari Kangas, Aug. 16, 1970; children—Maynard Claire, Janet Louise, Piiamari Riikka, Eerik Maynard Johannes. Tchr., Whittier Jr. High Sch., Flint, Mich., 1956-57, Meadowlawn Jr. High Sch., St. Petersburg, Fla., 1957-59; asst. prof. Towson (Md.) State Coll., 1960-62, Catonsville (Md.) Community Coll., 1961-62; prof. botany No. Mich. U., Marquette, 1966—; seasonal naturalist Nat. Park Service, Shenandoah Nat. Park, 1956, Glacier Nat. Park, 1957-66. Served with USAF, 1951-52. U. Colo. scholar, 1965-66; NSF grantee, 1959-60. Mem. Am. Bryological and Lichenological Soc., Internat. Assn. Bryologists, Internat. Assn. Plant Taxonomists, Internat. Orgn. Plant Biosystematists, Mich. Bot. Club, Nordic Bryoloigal Soc., Sigma Xi. Clubs: Am. Legion, Masons. Contbr. articles to profl. jours. Home: 2 Northwoods Ln Marquette MI 49855 Office: Dept Biology No Mich U Marquette MI 49855

BOWERS, THOMAS NEIL, programmer analyst; b. Parkersburg, W.Va., Mar. 30, 1940; s. James David and Genevieve Louis (Ritter) B.; B.S., E. Tenn. State U., 1967, M.S., 1969; m. Marilyn Katherine Meredith, Aug. 27, 1966; children—Katherine Louise, David Thomas. Tchr. public schs., Nashville, 1966-68; grad. asst. E. Tenn. State U., Johnson City, 1968-69; instr. Cin. Milacron, 1969-71, programmer analyst, 1972—; instr. Ohio U., Athens, 1971-72; cons. U. Cin., 1971; tchr. Live Oaks Vocat. Sch., Milford, Ohio, 1979; mem. nat. tech. com. Vocat. Industry Clubs Am., 1976-80. Mem. Epsilon Pi Tau. Served with U.S. Army, 1961-64. Home: 797 Twin Fox Dr Milford OH 45150 Office: Cin Milacron 4710 Marburg Ave Cincinnati OH 45209

BOWERSOX, THOMAS LLOYD, exec. search cons.; b. Troy, Ohio, Aug. 7, 1934; s. Van L. and Julia Fay (Wimmer) B.; B.A. in Bus. Adminstrn. (Danforth Found. fellow), Carthage Coll., Kenosha, Wis., 1957; m. Jeanette Erkert, Aug. 11, 1956; children—Michael, Sue Ann, Kathy Lynn. Asst. dist. traffic mgr. Ill. Bell Telephone Co., Chgo., 1957-61; mgr. labor relations Martin-Marietta Corp., Rapid City, S.D., 1961-63; regional dir. indsl. relations U.S. Envelope Co., Waukegan, Ill., 1963-64; prin. Fry Cons., exec. search, Chgo., 1964-69; owner, pres. Bowersox & Assos., Inc., Des Plaines, Ill., 1969—; lectr. bus. topics. Pres., Civic Assn., Des Plaines, 1958-60; founder Bauersachs Geneal. Soc., 1975, chmn., exec. dir., 1976—. Mem. Am. Soc. Personnel Adminstrn., Am. Mgmt. Assn. (Pres.'s Assn.), Am. Foundrymans Soc. Republican. Lutheran. Clubs: Meadow (Rolling Meadows, Ill.); River Trails Tennis Center (Arlington Heights, Ill.). Author: Executive In-Depth Interview Guide, 1979; contbr. articles to bus. publs. Office: 1025 Margret St Des Plaines IL 60016

BOWLES, GLENN RENO, state ofcl.; b. Agency, Iowa, July 15, 1918; s. E. Glen and Susie A. (Reno) B.; B.S., Simpson Coll., Indianola, Iowa, 1939; M.S., U. Mich., 1950; m. Marietta Litter, June 6, 1948; children—Glenn Reno, Jeanne C., Patricia K., Dorothy L. Instr., coach schs. in Iowa, 1939-41, 46-53; commd. 2d lt. U.S. Army, 1942, advanced through grades to col., 1955; served in N. Africa and Italy; dir. for Iowa, SSS, 1955-71; ret., 1969; civilian ops. mgr. Nat. SSS, Washington, 1971-77; exec. dir. Iowa Commn. Aging, 1977—. Decorated Purple Heart, Bronze Star with 3 oak leaf clusters, Legion of Merit with cluster; Cross of Valor (Italy); recipient Exceptional Service award SSS, 1971, Disting. Service award, 1976; Disting. Alumni award Simpson Coll., 1978; named to Inf. Officers Hall of Fame, 1974; charter mem. Simpson Coll. Basketball Hall of Fame, 1982. Mem. Nat. Assn. Hearing and Speech Activity (pres. 1975), Am. Assn. Ret. Persons, NG Assn., Ret. Officers Assn., Res. Officers Assn. Republican. Presbyterian. Clubs: Sertoma, Shriners. Office: 415 10th St Des Moines IA 50309

BOWLING, DAVID SAMUEL, geophysicist; b. Bennett, Ky., July 10, 1929; s. Reece Madison and Nancy Elizabeth (Knipp) B.; B.A., Berea Coll., 1956; m. Anna Louise Ogle, Dec. 22, 1955; children—Marla Lucille, Theresa Anne, David Reece, John Anthony. Computer trainee Geophys. Service Inc., Dallas, 1956-56, 2d computer, 1956-57, 1st computer, 1957-59, seismologist, 1959-60, party chief, 1960-62; cons. geophysicist Bowling, Roberson and Ward Seismic Assos., Norman, Okla., 1962-63; area supr. explosives product group Monsanto Co., St. Louis, 1963-68; project engr. G.W. Murphy Industries Inc., Houston, 1968-70, ops. mgr., 1970; partner White Engring. Assos. Inc., Joplin, Mo., 1970—, pres., 1972—. Served to sgt., U.S. Army, 1948-52. Registered geophysicist, Calif.; certified geologist Maine; certified profl. geol. scientist Assn. Profl. Geol. Scientists. Mem. Soc. Exploration Geophysicists, AAAS, ASTM, Soc. Am. Mil. Engrs., Seismol. Soc. Am., Am. Assn. Petroleum Geologists (asso.). Methodist. Clubs: Masons, K.T. Home: Route 7 Box 145 Joplin MO 64801 Office: PO Box 1256 Joplin MO 64801

BOWLING, WILLIAM GLASGOW, educator; b. St. Louis, May 7, 1902; s. William Walter and Mary Susan (Glasgow) B.; A.B., Washington U., St. Louis, 1924, A.M., 1925; postgrad. Harvard U., 1930-31; m. Violet Whelen, Aug. 3, 1933; 1 son, Townsend Whelen. Instr., asst. prof., asso. prof. English, Washington U., 1925-70, prof. emeritus, 1970—, asst. to dean, acting dean, dean Univ. Coll., 1925-42; dean Coll. Liberal Arts, 1942-46; dean men, 1942-44; civilian adminstr. Pre-professional Unit of Army Specialized Tng. Program, Washington U., St. Louis, 1943-44, dean admissions, 1946-65, univ. historian, 1965—, univ. grand marshal, 1960-68. Part time drama critic, St. Louis Times, 1929-30; pioneer at Washington U. in radio in edn., alumni insts. and ednl. motion pictures; exec. sec. Washington U. Assn. Lecture Series, 1940-47. Pres., Maryland PTA, Clayton, Mo., 1946-47. Recipient Washington U. Alumni award, 1960. Mem. Greater St. Louis Council Tchrs. of English (pres. 1936-39; exec. sec., 1939-41), Am. Assn. Collegiate Registrars and Admissions Officers (hon.; book rev. editor quarterly jour., College and University 1955-66), St. Louis Audubon Soc. (pres. 1950-52, mem. bd. dir., 1944—), Phi Delta Theta, Omicron Delta Kappa, Phi Delta Kappa. Republican. Episcopalian. Club: University (St. Louis). Contbr. to jours. Address: 7408 Washington Ave Saint Louis MO 63130

BOWMAN, JAMES DALE, indsl. engr.; b. Emporium, Pa., Mar. 25, 1929; s. Andrew D. and Margaret (Narby) B.; B.S., Pa. State U., 1958, M.S., 1964; m. Irene Mary Magagnotti, Aug. 20, 1951. Apprentice, Gen. Electric Co., Erie, Pa., 1947-51, project engr., 1953-54; instr., asst. prof. indsl. engring., head Automation Lab., Pa. State U., 1958-67; tng. and product mgr. Bellows Valvair, Akron, Ohio, 1967-70, dir. tng., 1970-73, mgr. systems engring., Zanesville, Ohio, 1973-74, mktg., sales mgr., 1974-75, dir. tng. Bellows Internat., Akron, 1976, group engring. mgr., 1977-79; sales and engring. mgr. hydraulics Schrader Bellows div. Scovill Mfg. Co., 1979—. Served with AUS, 1951-52. Mem. Soc. Mfg. Engrs., Soc. Advancement Mgmt. (dir. 1959-66), Alpha Pi Mu. Home: 557 Schocalog Rd Akron OH 44320 Office: 200 W Exchange St Akron OH 44309

BOWMAN, MARK DOUGLAS, structural engr.; b. Logansport, Ind., Aug. 9, 1952; s. John Robert and Mabel Louise (Nelson) B.; B.S.C.E. (Elks scholar), Purdue U., 1974, M.S.C.E. (Nellie Munson award), 1975; Ph.D. (C.P. Siess award), U. Ill., 1981; m. Barbara Baerwald, Aug. 6, 1977; 1 dau., Katherine Elaine. Civil engr. Chgo. Bridge & Iron Co., Oakbrook, Ill., summer 1974; teaching and lab. asst. Purdue U., West Lafayette, Ind., 1974-75; structural design engr. Precast/Schokbeton Inc., Kalamazoo, 1975-77; asst. prof. civil engring. Purdue U., 1981—. Mem. ASCE (com. fatigue and fracture of steel structures), Am. Concrete Inst., Nat., Ind. socs. profl. engrs., Nat. Geog. Soc., Sigma Xi, Phi Kappa Phi, Chi Epsilon, Tau Beta Pi, Triangle Frat. Lutheran. Asst. editor Mich. Civil Engr., 1976-77. Home: 16 N 20 St Lafayette IN 47904 Office: Civil Engring Bldg Purdue U West Lafayette IN 47907

BOWMAN, MONROE BENGT, architect; b. Chgo., Aug. 28, 1901; s. Henry William and Ellen Mercedes (Bjork) B.; m. Louise Kohnmann, Nov. 1944; 1 son, Kenneth Monroe; B.Arch., Ill. Inst. Tech., 1924. Registered architect, Ill., Wis., Ind., Ohio, Colo. Asso., Benjamin H. Marshall, Chgo., 1926; exhibited models and photographs of Bowman Bros. comtemporary designs at Mus. Modern Art, N.Y.C., 1931; pvt. practice architecture, Chgo., 1941-44; asso. Monroe Bowman Assos., Chgo., 1945—; cons. Chgo. Dept. City Planning, City of Sparta (Wis.), Alfred Shaw, Architect. Mem. Navy League U.S. Important works include Boeing Aircraft bldgs., Wichita, Kans., Emerson Electric bldgs., St. Louis, Maytag Co., Newton, Iowa, Douglas Aircraft bldgs., Park Ridge, Ill., Shwayder Bros. bldgs., Denver, Clark Equipment Co., Buchannon, Mich., Radio-TV Sta. WHO, Des Moines, Foote, Cone & Belding offices, Chgo., Burridge Devel., Hinsdale, Ill., Yacht Club and recreational facilities, Lake Bemiji, Minn., United Airlines offices downtown Chgo., Automatic Sprinkler Corp., Chgo., King Machine Tool div. Am. Steel Foundries, Cin., Marine Terr. Apts., Chgo., Dorchester Park Apts., Chgo., Manteno (Ill.) State Hosp., No. Ill. Gas Co. bldgs., LaGrange, Joliet, Streator and Morris, 1340 Astor St. Apt. Bldg., Burnham Center, Chgo., NSF, Green Bank, W.Va., Naval Radio Research Sta., Sugar Grove, W.Va., Columbus Boy Choir Sch., Princeton, N.J., office bldg. and hotel, Charleston, W.Va. Home: 730 Ridge Ave Evanston IL 60201

BOWMAN, RICHARD WOOD, health care mgmt. cons.; b. Jacksonville, Ill., Dec. 2, 1939; s. Harold Samuel and Nellie Elizabeth B.; B.B.A., U. Wichita, 1962; M.S. in Bus. Adminstrn. (Univ. teaching fellow), Wichita State U., 1965; m. Sharon Levitt, Sept. 12, 1971; 1 dau., Jennifer Nicole. Teaching fellow Wichita State U., 1963-65; sr. health care cons., project mgr. Cresap McCormick & Paget, Inc., N.Y.C., 1965-71; prin., partner, Midwest regional dir. health care consulting Peat, Marwick Mitchell & Co., Chgo., 1971—; tchr. health care adminstrn. U. Wis.; nat. lectr. Am. Hosp. Assn., Hosp. Fin. Mgmt. Assn.; spl. advisor fed. Health Care Fin. Adminstrn., HEW; mem. tech. com. Chgo. Health Systems Agy. Mem. Hosp. Fin. Mgmt. Assn., Am. Hosp. Assn., Ill. Hosp. Assn., Young Adminstrs. Chgo., Am. Soc. Materials Mgmt. Monthly contbr. to Modern Healthcare Mag., 1977—. Office: Peat Marwick Plaza 303 E Wacker Dr Chicago IL 60601

BOWMAN, SUZZANNE KUHN, phys. therapist; b. Durham, N.C., Sept. 13, 1948; d. Harold Hunter and Beatrice Laura (Hart) Kuhn; student U. Miami, 1966-69; cert. in phys. therapy, Ohio State U., 1971; married. Staff phys. therapist Highland View Hosp., Cleve., 1971-73; chief phys. therapy Sunny Acres Hosp., Cleve., 1973-78; asst. chief phys. therapy Highland View Hosp., Cleve., 1976-78; dir. phys. therapy Friendship Village Health Center, Schaumberg, Ill., 1978; phys. medicine mgr. Good Samaritan Hosp., Downers Grove, Ill., 1978—; chmn. bd., dir. phys. therapy Ill. Therapeutic Assos., Ltd., 1980—; pvt. practice phys. therapy; instr. trainer CPR, 1977—. Recipient Outstanding Service award U. Miami, 1968. Mem. Am. Phys. Therapy Assn. (Ill. quality assurance com. 1979-80, Eastern dist. edn. com. 1979-80), Chicagoland Phys. Therapy Dirs. Forum, Mortar Board. Quaker. Home: 939 Cherry Hills Naperville IL 60540

BOWMAN-DALTON, BURDENE KATHRYN, educator, computer cons.; b. Magnolia, Ohio, July 13, 1937; d. Ernest Mowles and Mary Kathryn (Long) Bowman; B.M.E., Capital U., 1959; M.A. in Edn., Akron U., 1967, postgrad. 1976—; m. Louis W. Dalton, Mar. 13, 1979. Profl. vocalist, various clubs in the East, 1959-60; music tchr. East Liverpool (Ohio) City Schs., 1959-62; music tchr. Revere Local Schs., Akron, Ohio, 1962-75, elem. tchr., 1975-80, elem. team leader/computer cons., 1979-81, tchr. middle sch. math. and gifted-talented, computer cons., 1981—. Mem. Citizen Com., Akron, 1975-76; profl. rep. Bath Assn. to Help, 1978-80; audit com. BATH, 1977-79; volunteer chmn. Antique Car Show, Akron, 1972-81. Martha Holden Jennings Found. grantee, 1977-78; Title IV ESEA grantee, 1977-81. Mem. Assn. for Devel. of Computer-Based Instructional Systems, Assn. Supervision and Curriculum Devel., Ohio Assn. for Gifted Children, NEA, Ohio Edn. Assn., Revere Edn. Assn., Phi Beta. Republican. Lutheran. Home: 353 Retreat Dr Akron OH 44313 Office: 3195 Spring Valley Rd Bath OH 44210

BOWSMAN, MARJORIE ORILLA BURGER, agribusiness exec.; b. Golden, Ill., Apr. 28, 1922; d. William Fremont and Esther (Wright) Burger; student public schs., Ludington and Hillsdale, Mich., 1928-40; m. (Elmer) James Bowsman, Mar. 16, 1941; children—Larry, Mary, Robert, Paul, Leonard, Barbara. Clk., Sears Roebuck and Co., 1940-41; sec.-treas. J Mar Farms, Salem, Ind., 1958-66. Leader 4-H Club. Mem. Washington County Cattlemen's Assn., Washington County Pork Producers, Ind. Beef Cattle Assn., Nat. Cattlemen's Assn., Cowbelles. Republican. Baptist. Club: Home Demonstration. Home and office: Route 6 Box 344 Salem IN 47167

BOXRUCKER, EDWARD JAMES, elec. coop. exec.; b. Dorchester, Wis., July 19, 1925; s. Jake L. and Elizabeth M. (Schumacher) B.; student public schs., Medford, Wis.; m. Jean M. Ziehlke, May 12, 1952; 1 dau., Jill M. Office mgr. Rib Lake Cheese Co., Medford, 1948-57; office mgr. Taylor County Elec. Coop., Medford, 1957-78, mgr., 1978—. Served with U.S. Army, 1944-47. Mem. Medford Area C. of C., Hwy. 13 Businessman Assn., Wis. Elec. Office Mgrs. Assn. Democrat. Roman Catholic. Clubs: K.C. (fin. sec. Medford, 1951-61), Medford Curling (dir.). Home: 405 E Broadway Medford WI 54451 Office: Taylor County Elec Coop Route 5 Box 130 Medford WI 54451

BOYARSKI, ROBERT PHILIP, health services adminstr.; b. Jersey City, Aug. 15, 1936; s. John and Anna (Elling) B.; A.A., Monmouth Coll., 1960; R.N., Monmouth Med. Center Sch. Nursing, 1960; B.S. in Nursing, U. Nev., 1970; M.A. in Nursing Service Adminstrn., U. Iowa, 1971; m. Carole Bergen, Aug. 13, 1967; children—Martin, Michelle, Gary, Shawn. Head nurse Marlboro (N.J.) State Hosp., 1961-64, adminstrv. nursing asst., 1964-67; staff nurse Nev. State Hosp., Reno, 1967, dir. in-service edn., 1968, supr. nurses, 1968-70; dir. nursing Broadlawns Polk County Hosp., Des Moines, 1971-73; dir. nursing Mercy Health Center, Dubuque, Iowa, 1973-77, v.p. profl. services, 1977—. Fellow Am. Acad. Med. Adminstrs.; mem. Nat. League Nursing, Am. Soc. Nursing Service Adminstrs., Cath. Hosp. Assn. (com. nursing 1976-79), Am. Mgmt. Assn., Am. Coll. Hosp. Adminstrs. Club: Masons. Home: 3139 Arbor Oaks Dr Dubuque IA 52001 Office: Mercy Health Center Mercy Dr Dubuque 52001

BOYCE, STANLEY EDMAN, educator; b. Glendale, W.Va., Nov. 11, 1947; s. Marion Stanley and Aurelia Eudoris (Wickham) B.; B.A. in Speech, David Lipscomb Coll., 1970; postgrad. Muskingum Coll., 1975-76, Kent State U., 1975-76, Bowling Green State U., 1980; m. Marlene Ann Maxwell, July 5, 1968; children—Tasha Dawn, Tanya Beth. Jailer, Coshocton County Sheriff's Office, Coshocton, Ohio, 1975; tchr. English Riverview Local Sch. Dist., Warsaw, Ohio, 1976-77; tchr. Licking County Joint Vocat. Sch., Newark, Ohio, 1977-79; tchr. English, Coshocton County Joint Vocat. Sch., 1979—, also advisor student newspaper and yearbook; mem. East Central Uniserv Com. Served with USN, 1971-75. Mem. Ohio Vocat. Assn., Am. Vocat. Assn., NEA, Ohio Edn. Assn., Eastern Ohio Edn. Assn., Coshocton County Joint Vocat. Sch. Edn. Assn. Republican. Mem. Ch. of Christ. Clubs: Coshocton County Sportsmen Assn., Masons. Home: 602 Hill St Coshocton OH 43812 Office: 23640 County Rd 202 Coshocton OH 43812

BOYCE, WILLIAM GEORGE, educator; b. Fairmont, Minn., July 25, 1921; s. William Irving and Nelly Hazel (Goetz) B.; B.S., U. Minn., 1949, M.Ed., 1952; student Mills Coll., 1954-55; m. Joan Palmer, July 29, 1949; children—Todd William, Robyn Jo, Timothy Palmer. Tchr., Worthington (Minn.) public schs., 1949-57; faculty Community Coll., Worthington, Minn., 1949-57; faculty U. Minn., Duluth, 1957—, prof. art, 1970—, dir. Tweed Mus. Art, 1969—. Served with USN, 1942-45. Ford Found. grantee, 1954-55. Mem. Am. Assn. Museums, AAUP, Am. Edn. Assn., Midwest Museums Conf., Midwest Art History Soc., Minn. Mus. Educators Roundtable. Episcopalian. Home: 2700 Minnesota Ave Duluth MN 55802 Office: Tweed Museum of Art U Minn Duluth MN 55812

BOYD, DONALD BRADFORD, research scientist; b. Syracuse, N.Y., Oct. 23, 1941; B.S., Pa. State U., 1963; A.M., Harvard U., 1965, Ph.D., 1968; m. Joanne Patricia Hequembourg, June 12, 1965; children—Susanne Patricia, Cynthia Carole, Douglas Milton. Teaching fellow Harvard U. 1963-65; research asso. Cornell U., Ithaca, N.Y., 1967-68; sr. phys. chemist Lilly Research Labs., Eli Lilly and Co., Indpls., 1968-74, research scientist, 1975—. NIH fellow, 1964-68. Mem. Am. Chem. Soc., Sigma Xi, Phi Lambda Upsilon, Pi Mu Epsilon. Contbr. articles to profl. jours. Office: Lilly Research Labs Eli Lilly and Co Indianapolis IN 46285

BOYD, DOROTHY RUTH, musician, educator; b. Atlantic City, Oct. 20, 1907; d. Herbert C. and Alice Frambes (Boice) Doughty; pvt. student of music, 1923-25; student Progressive Series Piano Inst., Jenkintown, Pa., 1924, Muskingum Coll., summers 1926-30; m. Merton Greer Boyd, June 24, 1930; children—Alys J. Boyd Carpenter, Merilyn J. Boyd Drumm, Merton Greer, Mildred K. Boyd Hibbard. Propr. pvt. music studios in N.J. and Ohio, 1924—, Mansfield, Ohio, 1957—; adjudicator, condr. music workshops; pres. Coshocton (Ohio) Music Club, 1944-45; organist, choir dir. Cambridge (Ohio) First Baptist Ch., 1930-37; organist Newcomerstown (Ohio) Methodist Ch., 1938-41, Coshocton Evang. and Reformed Ch., 1942-46, St. Paul Lutheran Ch., Mansfield, 1958—; choir dir. Bucyrus (Ohio) First Meth. Ch., 1947-57. Active local Camp Fire Girls, Girl Scouts, 4-H Club; mem. bd. Mansfield YWCA, 1960-62, 74-76; mem. women's com. Mansfield Symphony Soc. Mem. Nat. Guild Piano Tchrs., Nat. Organ and Piano Guild, Nat. Guild Auditions (chmn. Mansfield area 1978—), Music Tchrs. Nat. Assn., Ohio Music Tchrs. Assn. (county chmn. 1957-60, vice chmn. N. Central dist. 1976—, chmn. 1961-67), Richland County Music Tchrs. Assn. (sec.-treas. 1980-82), Nat. Fedn. Music Clubs, Independent Music Tchrs. Forum (state chmn. 1977-80), Am. Coll. Musicians, Mansfield Music Study Club (sec. 1972-77). Republican. Lutheran. Club: Order Eastern Star. Address: 86 Bartley Ave Mansfield OH 44906

BOYD, GREGORY ALLAN, aerospace, farming equipment mfg. co. exec.; b. Detroit, Aug. 21, 1951; s. John L. and Frieda R. Boyd; B.S. in Bus. Adminstrn., Wayne State U., Detroit, 1973; M.B.A. in Fin., U. Detroit, 1978. Asst. credit mgr. Hughes & Hatcher, Inc., Detroit, 1973-76; acct. Cadillac div. Gen. Motors Corp., Detroit, 1976-78; credit supr. Fed.-Mogul Corp., Southfield, Mich., 1978-79, credit mgr., 1979-82; group credit and collection mgr., Burroughs Corp., 1982—; membership recruiter Jr. Achievement Southeastern Mich., 1978. Mem. Am. Mgmt. Assn., Nat. Assn. Credit Mgmt., Nat. Black M.B.A. Assn., Assn. M.B.A. Execs., Omega Psi Phi. Home: 30200 Southfield Rd Apt 208 Southfield MI 48076 Office: Burroughs Corp Burrough Pl Detroit MI

BOYD, JAMES CONRAD, mktg. exec.; b. Metropolis, Ill., Jan. 3, 1942; s. James Lee and Rachael Graves (Sammons) B.; B.S.E.E., Ill. Inst. Tech., 1964; B.A., U. Ill., 1966; M.B.A., U. Chgo., 1970; m. Carol Rose Padula, Dec. 18, 1976; 1 son, John Harold; children by previous marriage—James Anthony, Candace Elaine. Political news editor ABC, Indpls., 1971-72; mktg. and pub. relations mgr. Republican Party, State of Ind., Indpls., 1972-73; mgr. nat. pub. relations and fund raising St. Jude's Children's Research Hosp., Memphis and Indpls., 1973-75; internat. dir. mktg. Underwriters Salvage Co., Elk Grove Village, Ill., 1975—, v.p. corp. mktg., 1979—, sec., 1980—; instr. Butler U., Indpls., 1974-75. Served with USAF, 1960-63. Mem. Internat. Sales and Mktg. Execs. Assn., Internat. Assn. Bus. Communications, Ins. Advt. Conf., Pub. Relations Soc. Am., Nat. Pub. Relations Council, Chgo. Council Fgn. Relations. Republican. Episcopalian. Contbr. articles in field to ins. jours. Home: 231 W Walnut St Des Plaines IL 60016 Office: 1400 Busse Rd Elk Grove Village IL 60007

BOYD, JOHN KENT, advt. exec.; b. Portsmouth, Ohio, Oct. 17, 1910; s. Lambert Thomas and Faery Ann (Ritter) B.; student Tulane U., New Orleans, 1927-29; m. Jeanne Marie Dunlap, Dec. 26, 1935; children—John Kent, Barbara Ann. Mem. staff advt. dept. Am. Rolling Mill Co., Middletown, Ohio, 1929-31; advt. mgr. Pitts. and Midway Coal Mining Co., Kansas City, Mo., 1932-35; v.p. Ferry-Hanly Co., 1935-44; partner Bruce B. Brewer & Co., Kansas City and Mpls., 1944-66; pres., chief exec. officer Bruce B. Brewer Co., Inc., 1967-72, chmn. bd., chief exec. officer, 1972-75; dir. Marco Mfg. Co.; past pres., dir. Quivira, Inc.; pres. Kaybee, Inc. Co-chmn. United Funds publicity com., 1953; dir. United Cerebral Palsy Assn. of Kansas City; active Boy Scouts Am.; bd. govs. Starlight Theatre Assn., YMCA, Quiet Birdmen; bd. dirs. Kansas City Crime Commn. Control adv. com. FAA Kanas City Air Traffic. Named Man of Yr. in Gen. Aviation, 1969; recipient silver medal Am. Advt. Fedn., 1972. Mem. AIM, Nat. Aero. Assn., Am. Legion, Kansas City Sr. Golf Assn., Kansas City Promotion Com., Airplane Owners and Pilots Assn. (nat.). Am. Mktg. Assn. (dir. Kansas City chpt.), Am. Royal Assn. (gov.), C. of C., Snipe Class Internat. Racing Assn., Nat. Pilots Assn. (dir.) Am. Bonanza Soc., Air Force Assn., Silver Wings. Clubs: Kansas City, Advt., Sales Execs., Quivira Country, Mission Hills Country, Aero of Kansas City, OX5 of Am.; Capital Hill (Washington); Quivira Sailing (past commodore); Diamondhead Yacht and Country; Bay-Waveland Yacht. Author: Jerry Dalrymple, 1931. Home: 3400 Yacht Club Circle Bay Saint Louis MS 39520 Office: 849 W 52d Terr Kansas City MO 64112

BOYD, RUTH JOYCE, educator; b. Connersville, Ind., Mar. 12, 1934; d. Charles and Isabelle Dickerson; B.S. in Edn., Ball State U., 1966; M.S. in Blind and Partially Seeing, Ohio State U., 1974; children—Teresa, Carolyn. Dental asst. in Richmond (Ind.) offices, 1952-57; sec. H.L. Parsons Inc., Indpls., 1957-63; tchr. vision center Akron (Ohio) Pub. Schs., 1966—; dir. Adult Edn. Sch. Summit County (Ohio) Soc. for Blind, 1974-75. Mem. mgmt. bd. Title VI

Project for Low Incident Handicapped, Ohio. Mem. Council Exceptional Children, Delta Kappa Gamma. Developed curriculum in writing modules for life persisting problems of low incident handicapped children; instrumental in develop. key math. assessment for blind; named Akron Tchr. of Yr., 1976; recipient Wayne County DAR award; cert. in kindergarten-8th grade teaching, teaching blind and partially seeing, Ohio. Home: 55 Waldorf Dr Akron OH 44313 Office: 785 Carnegie Ave Akron OH 44314

BOYD, WILLARD LEE, museum exec.; b. St. Paul, Mar. 29, 1927; s. Willard Lee and Frances L. (Collins) B.; B.S.L., U. Minn., 1949, LL.B., 1951; LL.M. (William W. Cook fellow 1951-52), U. Mich., 1952, S.J.D., 1962; LL.D., Buena Vista Coll., 1969, Coe Coll., 1969, Marycrest Coll., 1974, U. Fla., 1976; L.H.D., Cornell (Iowa) Coll., 1974, U. Iowa, 1981; Litt.D., Simpson Coll., 1976; m. Susan Kuehn, Aug. 28, 1954; children—Elizabeth Kuehn, Willard Lee III, Thomas Henry. Admitted to Minn. bar, 1951, Iowa bar, 1958; asso. firm Dorsey, Windhorst, Hannaford, Whitney & Halladay, Mpls., 1952-54; mem. faculty U. Iowa Coll. law, 1954-81, prof., 1961—, asso. dean Coll. Law, 1964, v.p. academic affairs, dean faculties at univ., 1964-69, pres., 1969-81, pres. emeritus, 1981—; pres. Field Mus. of Natural History, Chgo., 1981—. Vice pres., trustee Iowa Measurement Research Corp.; dir. Cemrel, Inc., Dial Corp.; U.S. del. to Spl. Commn. on Succession of The Hague Conf. Pvt. Internat. Law, 1970-72; mem. commn. on fed. relations Am. Council Edn., 1971-74, bd. dirs., 1978-81; chmn. Iowa Gov.'s Com. for Assemblies on Future of Iowa, 1972-74; chmn. Iowa 2000 Com., 1975-78; mem. Nat. Council on Arts, 1976—; mem. Iowa Coordinating Council for Post High Sch. Edn., 1968-81, chmn., 1976-77; mem. U.S. Senate Commn. on Operation of the Senate, 1975-76; mem. Nat. Com. on Careers for Older Ams., 1978—; mem. Arts, Humanities and Older Ams. Steering Com., 1981—. Bd. dirs. Center for Research Libraries, 1965-68, chmn. 1968; bd. commrs. Nat. Commn. on Accrediting, 1970-74, pres., 1974; bd. dirs. Harry S. Truman Library Inst., 1969-81; bd. dirs. Council Post-secondary Accreditation, 1977-81, exec. com., 1978-81; adv. bd. Met. Opera Assn., 1978—; exec. com. div. baccalaureate and higher degree programs Nat. League Nursing, 1979-81. Served with USNR, 1945-46. Recipient Outstanding Achievement award U. Minn., 1972. Mem. Am. Bar Assn. (past chmn. com. social, labor and indsl. legislation 1963-65, chmn. 1965-66, comparative law sect., chmn. ednl. policy com. legal edn. sect. 1975-78, mem. council 1975—, chmn. 1980-81, mem. clin. legal edn. guidelines project 1977-80, task force on lawyer competency 1978-79), Iowa Bar Assn., Am. Assn. UN, Nat. Assn. State Univs. and Land Grant Colls. (commn. arts and scis. 1969-73, adv. com. Office Advancement Pub. Negro Colls. 1972-79), Assn. Am. Univs. (exec. com. 1977-81, chmn. 1979-80), Order of Coif. Congregationalist. Contbr. articles to profl. jours. Home: 3800 N Lake Shore Dr Apt 3A Chicago IL 60613 Office: Field Mus Natural History Roosevelt Rd at Lake Shore Dr Chicago IL 60605

BOYD, WILLIAM BEATY, found. exec., former univ. pres.; b. Mt. Pleasant, S.C., Feb. 2, 1923; s. Francis Thomas and Eunice (Beaty) B.; A.B., Presbyn. Coll., Clinton, S.C., 1946; M.A., Emory U., 1947; Ph.D., U. Pa., 1954; LL.D., Alma Coll., 1969; m. Louise Philson, June 25, 1945; children—Marcie, Susan. Faculty, Mich. State U., 1953-58; dean of faculty Alma (Mich.) Coll., 1958-65; dir. honors program Coll. Arts and Scis., Ohio State U., 1965-66; vice chancellor student affairs U. Calif., Berkeley, 1966-68; pres. Central Mich. U., Mt. Pleasant, 1968-75; pres. U. Oreg., 1975-80; pres. Johnson Found., Racine, Wis., 1980—. Served with USNR, 1943-46, 51-53. Address: Johnson Foundation Racine WI 53401

BOYDSTON, MICHAEL PAUL, mfg. co. exec.; b. Palo Alto, Calif., Apr. 4, 1945; s. Robert Paul and Billie C. (Dent) B.; B.S. in Public Adminstrn., S.W. Mo. State U., Springfield, 1969; postgrad. U. Mo., Kansas City, 1969, Drake U., 1972; m. Susan Carol Blum, Oct. 9, 1971; children—Mark Christopher, William Robert. Mgmt. intern IRS Midwest Service Center, Kansas City, 1969-71, chief tng. and public affairs br., Des Moines, 1971-74; regional mgr. Robbie Mfg. Co., Lenexa, Kans., 1974, Dallas, 1974-76, Midwest region, Kansas City, 1976-78, nat. sales mgr., 1979, v.p. sales and mktg., Lenexa, 1980-82; mktg. mgr. St. Joseph Packaging, Inc. (Mo.), 1982—. Served with USAF, 1965-68, AUS, 1968-71. Mem. Am. Mgmt. Assn., Nat. Paper Trade Assn., Heart of Am. Paper Assn., Accts. Assn. Iowa (hon.). Office: 4515 Easton Rd St Joseph MO 64503

BOYER, DOROTHY MARGARET, railroad co. exec.; b. Kochville, Mich., Nov. 23, 1910; d. Herbert Adams and Mary Barbara (Gerber) Otto; student U. Mich., 1929-31; B.A., Central State Tchrs. Coll., 1933; m. Harold C. Boyer, Oct. 12, 1940 (dec. May 1965); children—Marjorie J. Boyer Wheaton, Joan B. Boyer Conner, Herbert C. Tchr., Jewett Sch., Kochville, 1933-35, Herig Sch., Saginaw, Mich., 1935-40; chmn. bd. Iowa Terminal R.R. Co., Mason City and Charles City, Iowa, 1965—. Pres. woman's assn. Westminster Presbyn. Ch., Detroit, 1963, elder, 1973-75, sec., 1978, bd. trustees, 1976-78. Club: Lathrup Village (Mich.) Woman's. Home: 18525 Roseland Blvd Lathrup Village MI 48076 Office: PO Box 450 Mason City IA 50401

BOYER, RALPH L., ret. mech. engr.; b. Botkins, Ohio, Aug. 4, 1901; s. Calvin O. and Ethel (Lucas) B.; B.M.E., Ohio State U., 1924, M.E., 1930; m. Doris Dormire, June 7, 1924 (dec. Jan. 1980); 1 dau., Jean Boyer Marshall; m. 2d, Ruth Gibson, May 1981. Diesel engr. Elmer A. Sperry Co., Bklyn., 1922-26; diesel engr. Cooper Bessemer Corp., Mt. Vernon, Ohio, 1926-29, asst. chief engr., 1929-38, chief engr., 1938-50, v.p., chief engr., 1950-56, v.p., dir. engring., 1956-65. Pres. Community Concerts, Mt. Vernon, 1947-58; mem. Mt. Vernon Bd. Edn., 1944-47; trustee Martin Meml. Hosp., chmn. bd., 1959-66; mem. nat. staff ARC, 1963-66. Recipient Lamme Gold medal award Ohio State U. Fellow ASME (Tom Sawyer award for originating aircraft derivative gas turbine 1981); mem. Sigma Xi. Republican. Methodist. Clubs: Masons, Pres.'s Ohio State U. Author: Time Capsules, 1976; contbr. numerous articles on thermodynamics and mech. engring. to profl. jours.; developer of high compression gas engine and originator jet gas turbine. Address: 1011 New Gambier Rd Mount Vernon OH 43050

BOYKE, BRUCE CARL, contractor, concrete and masonry; b. Chgo., May 12, 1930; s. Carl and Elsie Marie (La Ffin) B.; student public schs., Zion, Ill.; m. Kathleen J. McManaman, Sept. 16, 1950;children—Laura, Karen, Bruce, Blair, Kerry. Founder, pres. Bruce Concrete Constrn., Inc., Skokie, Ill., 1959—; formed Bruce Boyke Masonry Corp., Skokie, 1963—. Bruce Boyke Imperial Manor, Waukegan, 1964 (pres.); founder Bruce Boyke's Imperial Towers, Waukegan, 1968—. Spl. mem. Boy Scouts America. Republican committeeman Waukegan, 1951-53; pres. Village of Green Oaks, 1977-81. Served with AUS, 1947-51. Mem. Chgo. Assn. Commerce and Industry (indsl. devel. com.), Lake County Contractors Assn., Zion Benton C. of C., Waukegan-North Chicago C. of C. Home: Green Oaks Libertyville IL 60048 Office: 805 Baldwin Waukegan IL 60085

BOYKIN, WILLIAM GENE, assn. exec.; b. Apperson, Okla., Nov. 10, 1925; s. Jesse Spencer and Mary Jane (Patton) B.; B.A., Okla. State U., 1950; m. Rebecca Louise Burke, Sept. 7, 1974; children by previous marriage—Vicki Lynn, William David, Sherri Lea, Mark Shawn. Publisher, Van Buren County (Ark.) Dem., 1950-51; editor Park Cities (Tex.) News, 1951-53, Capitol Hill (Okla.) Beacon, 1953-55; asst. mgr. Okla. Press Assn., 1955-57; exec. Atkinson Enterprises, Oklahoma City, 1957-63; asso. editor Oklahoma City Jour., 1963-66; exec. dir. Allied Daily Newspapers, Seattle, 1966-69, Fla. Press Assn.; 1970-71, Tex. Press Assn., 1971-74, Inland Daily Press Assn., Chgo., 1974—. Served with USNR, 1944-46. Certified assn. exec. Mem. Newspaper Assn. Mgrs., Inc. (pres. 1975-76), Am. Soc. Assn. Execs., Chgo. Soc. Assn. Execs. (dir.), U.S. C. of C. (bd. regents), Sigma Delta Chi. Methodist. Club: Chgo. Press, Chgo. Headline (pres. 1979-80). Office: 840 N Lakeshore #802-W Chicago IL 60611

BOYLAN, BRIAN RICHARD, author, theatre dir., photographer; b. Chgo., Dec. 11, 1936, s. Francis Thomas and Mary Catherine (Kane) B.; student Loyola U., 1954-58; children—Rebecca, Gregory, Ingrid. Editor, Jour. AMA, Med. World News, The Statesman, 1956-64; author, 1965—; works include: The New Heart, 1969; Infidelity, 1971; Benedict Arnold: The Dark Eagle, 1973; A Hack in a Hurry, 1980; The Last Nazi Hunter, 1981; works include 12 books, 3 plays, 2 screenplays; photographer, 1966—; theatre dir., 1970—; works include 31 plays, videotapes and films. Home: 1530 S 6th St Minneapolis MN 55454

BOYLE, JOHN W., retail exec.; b. 1929; B.B.A., U. Wis., 1950; married. Partner, Arthur Andersen & Co., 1951-71; with The May Dept. Stores Co., St. Louis, 1972—, vice-chmn., 1979-80, chmn. bd., chief fin. officer, 1980—, also dir. C.P.A. Served in U.S. Army, 1951-53. Office: May Dept Stores 611 Olive St Saint Louis MO 63101*

BOYLES, LARRY REX, retail and mail order photog. mktg. co. exec.; b. Whiting, Iowa, Mar. 31, 1936; s. Rex Slater and Dorathy May (Crossley) B.; student Morningside Coll., 1956-60, 62-64; m. Olga Jo Dobler, Aug. 10, 1963; children—Michael Rex, Kimberly Sue Boyles Daniels, Spencer Ryan. Area mgr. Marquette Corp., Sioux City, Iowa, 1965-66; dist. mgr. Continental Albums, Inc., Sioux City, 1967-70, area mgr., Mpls., 1970-72, nat. sales mgr., Omaha, 1972-80; nat. sales mgr. Am. Family Products, Omaha, 1973-80; pres., editor Merit Pubs., Inc., Omaha, 1976-80; pres. C. & B. Enterprises, Sioux City, 1968-81; pres., nat. sales mgr. Am-Fam Corp., Omaha, 1980—; cons. Scherling Corp., 1972-80, A & A Photo Service, 1973-81. Mem. Greater Omaha C. of C. Republican. Clubs: Blair Country, Masons. Editor, pub. bicentennial edit. Who's Who in Nebraska, 1976-77. Home: Route 2 Pioneer Hills Blair NE 68008 Office: PO Box 14075 W Omaha Station Omaha NE 68114

BOYLLS, DIANA KAY, auditor; b. Evansville, Ind., Feb. 1, 1947; d. William Edward and Aura Katherine (Pfettscher) B.; B.S. in B.A., U. Evansville, 1969. With Shane Uniform Co., Evansville, Ind., 1969-70, Pearison Music Co., Poseyville, Ind., 1971-72; advt. rep., writer, editor weekly paper Mt. Vernon (Ind.) Pub. Co., Inc., 1972-75; auditor Posey County, Mt. Vernon, Ind., 1976—; cons. on County Ofcls. Handbook, 1978—. Sec., Posey County Assn. for Retarded Citizens, 1974-75; vice-precinct committeeman Dem. Party, 1970-78, precinct committeeman, 1978—. Mem. Ind. County Auditors Assn., Ind. Fedn. Bus. and Profl. Women's Clubs (dist. dir. 1979—). Democrat. Ch. of Christ. Clubs: Mt. Vernon Bus. and Profl. Women's (pres. 1975-76), Order Eastern Star (matron 1976-77), F.O.P. Home: Rural Route 2 PO Box 256 Mount Vernon IN 47620 Office: Auditors Office Court House Mount Vernon IN 47620

BOYSAW, HAROLD EDWARD, former pub. welfare adminstr.; b. Joliet, Ill., Oct. 28, 1912; s. John and Julia (Fleming) B.; B.A., Ill. Wesleyan U., 1938, L.H.D., 1965; M.A., U. Chgo., 1952; m. Lucille Williams, Aug. 10, 1941. Caseworker, City Chgo. Relief Adminstrn., 1938-41; with Cook County Dept. Pub. Aid, Chgo., 1941-75, supervising caseworker, 1948-52, asst. office supr., 1952-60, office supr., 1960-62, adminstrv. field supr., 1962-69, dep. dir. adminstrv. services, 1969-74, asst. to dir. community services, 1974-75. Mem. Citizens Com. Juvenile Ct. Bd. dirs. Chgo. chpt. Am. Cancer Soc., Big Bros. Met. Chgo., Chgo. Lung Assn.; trustee Ill. Children's Home and Aid Soc. Served with U.S. Army, 1943-45. Mem. Nat. Assn. Social Workers, Acad. Certified Social Workers, Am. Pub. Welfare Assn., Am. Sociol. Assn., Ill. Welfare Assn., Chgo. Urban League, NAACP, Nat. Conf. Social Welfare, Alpha Phi Alpha. Club: City (gov.) (Chgo.). Home: 11360 S Aberdeen St Chicago IL 60643

BOYSEN, A. J., farm mgr.; b. Morning Sun, Iowa, Nov. 1, 1925; s. Boyd August and Margaretha Elizabeth (Dohrman) B.; student Iowa State U., 1946-48, exec. devel. program Iowa Wesleyan Coll., 1964-65; m. Dorothy Ellen Wright, Oct. 17, 1948; children—Robert Boyd, Karen Elaine. Farm owner, operator, Louisa County, Iowa, 1949—; farm mgr., Louisa and Des Moines County, Iowa, 1968—; appraiser Louisa County, 1971—; pres., mgr. Stoney Brook Farms, Inc.; leader, 4-H camp trustee, Iowa; mem. Louisa County extension com. Farm Bur.; leader youth tour People to People Internat. Active United Fund. Served to cpl. USAAF, 1944-46. Recipient 4-H awards. Mem. Iowa Soc. Farm Mgrs. and Rural Appraisers, Louisa County Soy Bean Assn. (charter pres.), Louisa County Beef Producers (dir.), Am. Angus Soc., Pro-Farmers Am. Republican. Methodist. Home and office: 720 S 5th St Wapello IA 52653

BOYSEN, THOMAS J., podiatrist; b. Chgo., Feb. 25, 1946; s. Vernon L. and Irene B.; B.S., No. Ill. U., 1968; D. Podiatric Medicine, Ill. Coll. Podiatric Medicine, 1972; m. Stephanie Hutter, Oct. 9, 1970; 1 dau., Wendi. Resident in surgery St. Bernard Hosp., Chgo., 1972-73; practice podiatry Oak Forest, Ill., 1974—, with J. Allen Chvala, DeKalb, Ill., 1975—; mem. staff Northlake (Ill.) Community Hosp., Mercy Health Center, Justice, Ill. Diplomate Am. Bd. Podiatric Surgery. Mem. Ill. Podiatry Soc., Am. Podiatry Assn., Am. Public Health Assn., Ill. Podiatry Soc. (past pres. Zone 11, del. to bd.). Office: 5601 W Victoria Dr Oak Forest IL 60452

BOZORGI, SIAVOSH, thoracic and cardiovascular surgeon; b. Khoramabad, Iran, Apr. 8, 1938; s. Asadollah and Behjat (Foroughi) B.; student Tehran (Iran) U. Med. Sch., 1962; M.D., U. Pa., 1966; m. Bonnie Hughes, Nov. 5, 1966; children—Darius, Susan. Intern, Norwalk (Conn.) Hosp., 1963, Cleve. Met. Gen. Hosp., 1963-64; resident surgery Grad. Hosp., U. Pa. at Phila., 1964-67, also asst. instr. surgery Med. Sch., 1964-66, instr. surgery, 1967-67; chief resident surgery St. Luke's Hosp., Bethlehem, Pa., 1967-68; chief resident thoracic and cardiovascular surgery Albert Einstein Coll. Medicine, Yeshiva U., N.Y.C., 1968-70, also asst. instr. thoracic surgery; clin. research fellow thoracic and cardiac surgery Mt. Auburn Hosp., Boston, 1970-71, Peter Bent Brigham Hosp., Boston, Harvard Med. Sch.; practice medicine, specializing in thoracic and cardiovascular surgery, Dayton, Ohio, 1971—; mem. staff Good Samaritan Hosp., St. Elizabeth Hosp., Children's Med. Center, Kettering Hosp., Miami Valley Hosp.; asst. clin. prof. surgery Wright State U. Med. Sch., Dayton. Diplomate Am. Bd. Surgery. Fellow A.C.S., Am. Coll. Angiology, Soc. Thoracic Surgeons; mem. Am. Thoracic Soc., Am., Ohio State med. assns., Am. Coll. Chest Physicians, Am. Coll. Cardiology, Montgomery County Med. Soc., Am. Heart Assn., Dayton Surg. Soc. Contbr. articles to profl. jours. Home: 324 Thelma Ave Dayton OH 45415 Office: Miami Valley Tower Room 1790 4th and Ludlow Sts Dayton OH 45402

BRAATEN, KATHLEEN ANN, nurse, educator; b. South Milwaukee, Wis., Sept. 1, 1945; d. Edward S. and Alice F. Weinstock; student Edgewood Coll., Madison, Wis., 1963-64; R.N., St. Marys Sch. Nursing, Madison, 1966; lic. nursing home adminstr., U. Wis., 1976; B.S. (Nursing scholar), Coll. of St. Francis, Joliet, Ill., 1977; m. Lyle D. Braaten, Aug. 6, 1966; children—Todd Allen, Jennifer Lynn, Sara Ann. Staff nurse, supr., dir. nurses, asst. adminstr. Mt. Carmel Nursing Home, Greenfield, Wis., 1966-79; instr. nursing Milw. Tech. Coll., 1979—; operating room nurse St. Marys Hosp., Manhattan, Kans., 1966; staff nurse Irwin Army Hosp., Ft. Riley, Kans., 1967-68; dir. nursing Woodstock Northwest Health Center, 1971-73. Mem. Nat. League for Nursing, Wis. League for Nursing, Am. Fedn. Tchrs. Roman Catholic. Home: W332 N5543 Linden Circle W Nashotah WI 53058

BRABSON, HOWARD VICTOR, social worker, educator; b. Knoxville, Tenn., Sept. 18, 1925; s. Alfred L. and Fannie Ruby Brabson; B.S. in Social Scis., Coll. of Ozarks, 1956; M.S.W. Catholic U. Am., 1962, D. Social Work (fellow), 1975; m. Rudienne Houston, Sept. 13, 1950. Asst. supt. Cedar Knoll Schs., Laurel, Md., 1958-61; supt. vocat. edn. Boys Indsl. Sch., Lancaster, Ohio, 1962-63; dep. commr. Ohio Youth Commn., Columbus, 1963-65; area supr. Vista, Washington, 1965-67, program mgr., Great Lakes region, Chgo., 1967-69; asso. prof. social work U. Mich., Ann Arbor, 1969—; cons. to various community orgns. and schs., 1969—; mem. planning com. Internat. Conf. Social Welfare, 1978. Mem. mayor's Com. for Community Revitalization, Ann Arbor, 1975-76; bd. dirs. Octagon House, 1976-77, chmn., 1977-78. Served to capt. inf., U.S. Army, 1946-58; PTO. Recipient Man of Yr. award Willow Run Adversary Club, 1978; Faculty Recognition award U. Mich., 1981. Mem. Nat. Assn. Social Workers, Acad. Cert. Social Workers, Mich. Assn. Black Social Workers (Outstanding Service award 1978), Assn. Voluntary Action Scholars (dir. 1976-78), Nat. Assn. Black Social Workers (nat. pres. 1978—, mem. steering com. 1971—, founder 1968), Huron Valley Assn. Black Social Workers (pres. 1973—), Zeta Chi Beta. Roman Catholic. Contbr. articles to social work jours. Home: 1325 S Maple St Apt 301 Ann Arbor MI 48103 Office: School of Social Work Univ Michigan 1065 Frieze Bldg Ann Arbor MI 48109

BRACEY, JERE THOMAS, statistician; b. Kennett, Mo., Jan. 15, 1946; s. Ira Dale and Esther Rebecca (Broxon) B.; student DePauw U., 1964-66; B.A., Memphis State U., 1968, M.S., 1970; postgrad. U. Okla., 1973-74; m. Susan Ann Tipton, Aug. 28, 1966; children—Ann Alice, Thomas Adam, Aaron Daniel. Math. statistician New Brunswick Lab., Argonne, Ill., 1974—; math. statistician Internat. Atomic Energy Agy., Vienna, Austria, 1981—. Elder, Christian and Missionary Alliance, Bolingbrook, Ill., 1976—; chmn. exec. bd. Fellowship Chapel, Bolingbrook, 1976-79. Served with USAF, 1970-73. U.S. Dept. Public Health grantee, 1973-74. Mem. Am. Statis. Assn., Technometric Soc., Biometric Soc., U.S. Nat. Guard Assn., Ill. Nat. Guard Assn. Home: 1060 Ridgewood Dr Bolingbrook IL 60439 9800 S Cass Ave Argonne IL 60439

BRACHMAN, MEROM, chem. co. exec.; b. Ft. Worth, Oct. 6, 1936; s. Abraham J. and Sarah (Ruby) B.; A.B. magna cum laude, Harvard, 1958, A.M. in History, 1961; m. Judith Yenkin, Dec. 19, 1957; children—Lavea, Sarai, Shael. Adminstrv. asst. to Senator J.S. Cooper of Ky., Washington, 1963-68; with Yenkin Majestic Paint Corp., Columbus, Ohio, 1968—, dir. mfg. and purchasing, 1969—, v.p., sec., 1970—, gen. mgr. Ohio Polychem. Co. div., 1974—, exec. v.p., 1975—, also dir.; dir. affiliated cos. Majestic Paint Centers, Yenkin Majestic Paint Corp.; pres. Woodland Corp., Columbus; mng. partner Fifth Leonard Co., Wye Co. Ltd., Columbus, Yakima, Wash., 1971—, Ind. Oil Producing Co., Ft. Worth, 1971—. Chmn. regional adv. council Small Bus. Adminstrn., 1971-74; mem. Franklin County Bd. SSS, 1971-75. Republican mem. bipartisan Ohio Ethics Commn., 1975—, chmn., 1976-77, 80-81, vice chmn., 1978-80. Trustee, Columbus Sch. for Girls, 1974—, v.p., mem. exec. com., 1980—; mem. nat. com. Harvard Center Jewish Studies, 1975—. Mem. exec. com. White House Conf. Children and Youth, 1970-71; mem. exec. com. United Community Council Columbus, 1969-74; mem. City of Columbus Campaign Finance and Ethics Commn., 1974—; Reagan-Bush presdl. elector for Ohio 12th Congressional Dist., Electoral Coll., 1980. Served with USAF, 1961-62. Recipient Congl. Staff award Am. Polit. Sci. Assn., 1967. Jewish. Home: 115 S Drexel Ave Columbus OH 43209 Office: 1920 Leonard Ave Columbus OH 43219

BRACKETT, EDWARD BOONE, III, surgeon; b. Fort Worth, Jan. 5, 1936; s. Edward Boone and Bessie Lee (Hudgins) B.; student Tex. Tech. Coll., 1957; M.D., Baylor U., 1961; m. Jean Elliott, July 11, 1959; children—Bess E., Geoffrey, Elliott Mencken, Edward Boone IV, Anneke Gail. Intern, Cook County Hosp., Chgo., 1961-62; resident Northwestern U., Chgo., 1962-66; practice medicine specializing in orthopedic surgery, Oak Park, Ill., 1966—, Westgate Orthopaedics Ltd., Oak Park, 1969—; mem. staff Loyola U., Oak Park Hosp., Loretto Hosp., Rush Med. Sch.; chmn. dept. orthopedics West Suburban Hosp.; clin. asso. prof. orthopedics Loyola U.; chmn. bd. Chgo. Loop Mediclinic, 1973-75; cons. orthopedic surgery City Service Oil Co., 1970. Guarantor Lyric Opera Chgo., 1971-80; guest condr. Chgo. Symphony Orch., 1979, Chgo. Chamber Orch., 1980. Served as lt. comdr. USNR, 1967-69; Vietnam. Recipient Outstanding Tchr. award Dept. Orthopedic Surgery, West Suburban Hosp., 1978, 79. Diplomate Am. Orthopedic Bd. Surgery. Fellow A.C.S., Am. Acad. Orthopedic Surgeons, Inst. of Medicine of Chgo., Am. Acad. Neurol. and Orthopedic Surgeons, Am. Assn. for Hand Surgery; mem. Am. Trauma Soc. (founder), Royal Soc. Medicine, Ill. Orthopedic Soc., Chgo. Orthopedic Soc., AMA, Chgo. Med. Soc. (alt. councilor), Clin. Orthopedic Soc., Internat. Platform Assn., Civil War Round Table, Friends Chgo. Symphony Orch., Chgo. Chamber Orch. Assn. (dir.), Symphonia Musicale (dir.), Sigma Alpha Epsilon, Phi Eta Sigma, Phi Chi, Alpha Epsilon Delta. Cons. orthopedic editor Jour. Indsl. Medicine, 1966-67. Home: 1407 Ashland Ave River Forest IL 60305 Office: 1125 Westgate St Oak Park IL 60301

BRACKHAHN, DONALD GARLAND, univ. adminstr.; b. Kansas City, Mo., Nov. 2, 1936; s. James Alexander and Mary Jeannette (Garland) B.; B.A., U. Mo., Kansas City, 1958, M.A. in History, 1965; m. Nancy Lee Dunbar, Feb. 24, 1962; children—Dawn Renee, Diane Michelle. Grad. asst. history dept. U. Kansas City, 1958-60; social sci. tchr. Kansas City (Mo.) Sch. Dist., 1960-66, athletic dir., tennis coach, 1964-66; asst. dir. devel. U. Mo., Kansas City, 1966-70, dir. devel., alumni and constituent relations, 1970-80, dir. alumni and constituent relations, asst. to pres. for alumni relations, 1980—. Trustee, Kansas City Mus. History and Sci., 1972—, Johnson County (Kans.) Library, 1972-73; mem. Johnson County Charter Commn., 1974-76; bd. dirs. Shawnee Civic Band, 1971—; pres. Johnson County Friends of Library, 1976-78; bd. dirs., pres. Johnson County United Community Services, 1980-81; sec. standing com. Episcopal Diocese of Kans., 1980-81; mem. vestry, lay reader, liturgical asst. Christ Ch., Overland Park, Kans. Served with USNG, 1959-65. Mem. ALA, Kansas City Council for Social Studies (pres. 1965-66), Greater Kansas City Council on Philanthropy (pres. 1980-81), Council for Advancement and Support of Edn., Assn. of Vol. Bds., U. Mo. Kansas City Internat. Alumni Assn. (pres. 1965), Kansas City C. of C., Phi Delta Kappa, Phi Mu Alpha Sinfonia, Tau Kappa Epsilon, Omicron Delta Kappa. Republican. Club: Rockhill Tennis. Home: 6116 Hemlock St Merriam

KS 66202 Office: U Mo Kansas City 5100 Rockhill Rd Kansas City MO 64110

BRACY, JO AHNE C. PENNEY, publisher; b. Detroit, Sept. 25, 1947; d. George S. and Florence W. Penney; B.A. in Speech, Wayne State U., 1974, Cert. in Mortuary Sci., 1980; m. Lonnie Bracy, Oct. 3, 1965; children—Yvette M., Michael A. Jr. copywriter Celeste Advt. & Assos., Detroit, 1965-74; editor Community Bulletin Newspaper, Atlanta, 1975-76; pres. Express Yourself, Atlanta, 1975-76; news reporter Sta. WTVS-TV, Detroit, 1977—; social researcher Merrill Palmer Inst., Detroit, 1978—; editor, publisher Community Business Bulletin, Detroit, 1978—; exec. dir., founder When The Time Comes; cons. in field. Active Detroit Civic and Bus. League, Boy Scouts Am., Boys Club Am. Mem. AFTRA, Nat. Assn. Media Women, Am. Women in Communications, Toastmistress' Internat. Delta Sigma Theta, Sigma Delta Chi. Jewish. Club: Toastmistresses. Author: How To Pass Tests, 1976. Home: 12706 Pickford St Detroit MI 48235 Office: 3269 Webb St Detroit MI 48206

BRADDOCK, CAROL TIPTON, banker; b. Hamilton, Ohio, Sept. 7, 1942; d. Carlace Alpheus and Jimmie Louise Tipton; B.A., U. Cin., 1965, M.A., 1976; grad. Sch. Savs. and Loans, Ind. U., 1980; m. Robert L. Braddock, Aug. 1, 1964; children—Ryan Lawrence, Lauren Patricia Tipton. Buyer, The McAlpin Co., Cin., 1964-69; instr., placement coordinator Vogue Career Coll., 1971; exec. asst. Fed. Home Loan Bank Cin., 1973-76, asst. v.p., 1976-78, v.p., community investment officer, 1978—; pres. Cin. Women Investors, 1981—; cons. Neighborhood Reinvestment Corp., 1973-77. Vice pres. Zoning Bd. Appeals, City of Cin., 1976; mem. exec. com. Sta. WCET-TV, 1974-78, sec. bd., 1981-82; pres. Minority Bus. Devel. Coalition, 1980; bd. advisors Nat. Trust Historic Preservation, 1981-82; mem. Ohio State Hist. Preservation Adv. Bd. Recipient Outstanding Service award Urban Reinvestment Task Force, 1975; Achievement award YMCA, 1979, Career Women of Achievement award, 1981; Disting. Community Service award. Girlfriends, 1980. Mem. Women's Alliance (founder 1966, pres. 1971-73), Joint Underwriting Assn. (gov. 1978-80), Jr. League Cin., Cin. C. of C. (chmn. subcom. 1981-82), Cin. Met. Exchange (v.p.), Delta Sigma Theta. Office: 2500 DuBois Tower Cincinnati OH 45202

BRADEN, BERWYN BARTOW, lawyer; b. Pana, Ill., Jan. 10, 1928; s. George Clark and Florence Lucille (Bartow) B.; student Carthage Coll., 1946-48; student U. Wis., 1948-49, J.D., 1959; m. Barbara Carol Brellenthin, Oct. 15, 1949; children—Scott, Mark, Mathew, Sue, Ralph, Ladd, Brad. Admitted to Wis. bar, 1959, U.S. Supreme Ct. bar, 1965; partner firm Genoar & Braden, Lake Geneva, Wis., 1959-63; individual practice law, Lake Geneva, 1963-68, 72-74; partner firm Braden & English, Lake Geneva, 1968-72, Braden & Olson, Lake Geneva, 1974—; counsel Citizens Nat. Bank, 1959—, also dir.; city atty. Lake Geneva, 1962-64; tchr. Law Sch., U. Wis., 1977. Bd. dirs. Lake Geneva YMCA. Served with USMCR, 1945-46. Mem. Walworth County (pres. 1962-63), Am., Chgo. bar assns., State Bar Wis. (chmn. conv. and entertainment com. 1979—), Bar Assn. 7th Fed. Circuit, Wis. Acad. Trial Lawyers (sec. 1975, treas. 1976, dir. 1977-79), Assn. Trial Lawyers, Phi Alpha Delta. Home: 1175 S Lakeshore Dr Lake Geneva WI 53147 Office: 716 Wisconsin St Lake Geneva WI 53147

BRADEN, ROBERT EDWIN, advt. exec.; b. Vermont, Ill., July 21, 1938; s. Pike Jefferson and Mary Louise (Holmberg) B.; B.S. in Mktg., Millikin U., 1962. Mdse. coordinator Osco Drug, Inc., Oak Brook, Ill., 1966-69, mdse. mgr., 1969-78, advt. mgr., 1978-80, v.p. advt., 1980—. Served with U.S. Army, 1962. Office: 1818 Swift Dr Oak Brook IL 60521

BRADFIELD, HORACE FERGUSON, physician; b. Denver, July 15, 1913; s. George Clarence and Mary Elizabeth (Harris) B.; B.S., U. Mich., 1933, M.S., 1934; M.D., Wayne State U., 1948; m. Mariorie Blackistone, June, 1938; children—David M., Gertrude E. Tchr., Detroit Pub. Schs., 1934-44; intern, sr. intern Detroit Receiving Hosp., 1948-50; resident in psychiatry Wayne County Gen. Hosp., 1968-69; gen. practice medicine, Detroit, 1950—; sr. attending staff Detroit-Hutzel Hosp.; asst. prof. medicine Wayne State U. Coll. Medicine. Mem. Citizens Com. on Equal Ednl. Opportunity, Detroit, 1960-62;trustee Wayne County Community Coll., 1968-76. Recipient awards for service Detroit Urban League, 1967, Wayne County Community Coll., 1977. Diplomate Am. Bd. Family Practice. Mem. Am. Acad. Family Practice, AMA, Nat. Med. Soc., Wayne County Med. Soc., Alpha Phi Alpha. Roman Catholic. Asso. editor Detroit Medical News, 1959-60. Office: 3008 E Grand Blvd Detroit MI 48202

BRADFORD, KIMERLEE JAY, mech. engr.; b. Putnam, Conn., Mar. 22, 1932; s. H. Jay and Dorothy Gertrude (Martin) B.; B.S., U. N.H., 1965; postgrad. U. Ariz., 1970-73; m. Shigeko Shikuma, June 18, 1955; children—Jon Chandler, Karyl Ann, William Jay, Charles Martin. Enlisted USAF, 1950, advanced through grades to maj., 1965; missile ops. officer, N.Mex., W. Ger., 1957-60; missile maintenance officer, W. Ger., 1960-62; program mgmt. specialist, Los Angeles, 1965-70; ret., 1970; reliability engr. Control Data Corp., St. Paul, 1973-81; mgr. receiving insp. No. Telecom Inc.-EOS, 1981—. Committeeman, Boy Scouts Am., 1972-73. Recipient Tech. Excellence award Control Data Corp., 1977. Mem. ASME, Am. Soc. Quality Control, Ret. Officers Assn. Home: 310 107th St W Bloomington MN 55420 Office: 245 E 6 St Saint Paul MN 55101

BRADFORD, WILLIAM STEPHEN, orthodontist; b. Boston, July 23, 1912; s. Joseph S. and Anna (Hogarty) B.; B.S., Harvard U., 1934, postgrad. Engring. Sch., 1934-35; D.D.S., Northwestern U., 1944; M.S., U. Kansas City Dental Sch., 1948; m. Barbara Ann Kennedy, May 30, 1942; children—Martha Ann, William Stephen. Researcher, neurologic unit Harvard Med. Sch., 1935-36; researcher New Eng. Lime Co., Canaan, Conn., 1936-38; chem. rep. for New Eng., Ohio Chem. Co., 1938-41; practice dentistry specializing in orthodontics, Highland Park, Ill., 1948—; prof. orthodontics Loyola U., Chgo., 1969—. Vice pres. Suburban Arts Center; mem. Zoning Bd. Appeals Highland Park. Mem. Harvard Assn. Chemists, Harvard Grads. Soc., Field Museum Natural History, Am. Assn. Orthodontists, ADA, Highland Park C. of C. (dir., pres.), Ill. Doberman Pinscher Club (pres.), Finishing Touch Dog Tng. Group (pres.). Club: Rotary (dir., pres.). Home: 3001 Ridge Rd Highland Park IL 60035 Office: 1964 Sheridan Rd Highland Park IL 60035

BRADLEY, ARNOLD L., ednl. adminstr.; b. Hamburg, Iowa, Jan. 7, 1932; s. E.R. and Irene B.; B.A., Peru State U., 1955; M.S., U. Omaha, 1957; Sp.Ed., U. Nebr., 1970; m. Jeanette Rogers, May 27, 1956; children—Michael, Linda, Jeffrey, Deborah, James, John. Supt., New Monroe (Iowa) Community Schs., 1966-67; supt. Missouri Valley (Iowa) Community Schs., 1967-70; supt. Eagle Grove (Iowa) Community Schs., 1970-79; supt. LeMars (Iowa) Community Schs., 1979—. Served with U.S. Army, 1952-54. Mem. NEA, Am. Assn. Sch. Adminstrs., Iowa Assn. Sch. Adminstrsn., Assn. Supervision and Curriculum Devel. Republican. Club: Rotary. Contbr. articles to profl. jours. Home: 1325 2d Ave SW LeMars IA 51031 Office: 921 3d Ave SW LeMars IA 51031

BRADLEY, CHARLES MACARTHUR, architect; b. Chgo., Sept. 26, 1918; s. Harold Smith and Helen Frances (MacArthur) B.; B.A. in Architecture, U. Ill., 1940; m. Joan Marie Daane, July 27, 1946; children—Mary Barbara, Nancy Ann, Sally Joan, William Charles. With Holabird & Root, architects, Chgo., 1940-41, Giffels & Vallet, architects and engrs., Detroit, 1941-45; partner, corp. pres. Bradley & Bradley, architects and engrs., Rockford, Ill., 1947—; pres. Bradley Bldg. Corp., 1962—; sec.-treas. Security Engring. Co., 1972—; v.p. Westshore Plaza Inc., 1979—. Active, Blackhawk council Boy Scouts Am. Served with C.E., U.S. Army, 1945-46. Decorated Bronze Star; recipient Meritorious Service award Ill. Assn. Sch. Bds., 1976. Mem. AIA (pres. No. Ill. chpt. 1962, treas. Ill. council 1973-74), Ill. Soc. Architects (pres. 1974), Edn. Facilities Planners Inst., Ill. Assn. Sch. Bd. Officers. Republican. Congregationalist. Clubs: Rotary, Shriners; Union League, University, Midday (Chgo.). Prin. works include North Sheboygan (Wis.) High Sch. and addition, 1960-68, J.F. Kennedy Middle Sch., Rockford, 1968, Singer Health Clinic, Rockford, 1964, Jacobs High Sch., Algonquin, Ill., 1976, Atwood plant, Rockford, 1977, Admiral Home, Chgo., 1978, Bushnell (Ill.) Jr. High Sch., 1980. Author papers on life cycling old schs., roofing procedures. Home: 3203 Landstrom Rd Rockford IL 61107 Office: 924 N Main St Rockford IL 61103

BRADLEY, LEON CHARLES, music educator; b. Battle Creek, Mich., Sept. 8, 1938; s. Leon Harvey and Sigrid Pearl (Anderson) B.; B.A., Mich. State U., 1961, M.M. Brass Specialist, 1967; postgrad. U. Okla., summer 1974, U. Wis., summer 1975; m. Mary Elizabeth Bradley, Dec. 23, 1968; children—Kyle Newman, Shannon Sigrid, Karl Norman, Charles Nathan. Band dir. Owosso-St. Paul, Mich., 1958-61, Hopkins (Mich.) Public Schs., 1961-62, Cedar Springs (Mich.) Public Schs., 1962-65; grad. asst. music theory-aural harmony Mich. State U., East Lansing, 1965-67; asst. prof. asst. dir. bands Minot (N.D.) State Coll., 1967-69; asso. prof. instrumental music & music edn., dir. bands Sch. of the Ozarks, Point Lookout, Mo., 1969—; clinician low brass instruments Selmer, Inc., 1979—. Active, Springfield Symphony Orch., 1969-72, 81-82; dir. Abou Ben Adhem Shrine Band, 1978-80. Mem. Coll. Band Dir.'s Nat. Assn., Music Educators Nat. Conf., Nat. Assn. Jazz Educators, Nat. Assn. Wind & Percussion Instrs. (new music reviewer, assn. jour. 1968-71), Mo. Music Edn. Assn., Mo. Bandmasters Assn., Percussive Arts Soc., Music Tchrs. Nat. Assn., Mo. Music Tchrs. Assn. Am. Fedn. Musicians (local 150), Phi Mu Alpha (life). Episcopalian. Clubs: Branson-Hollister Lions, Masons, Joplin Scottish Rite, Ducks Unltd. (mem. com. 1978-81, chmn., 1981. Contbr. articles in field to profl. jours. Home: Box 15 Point Lookout MO 65726 Office: Music Dept Sch of the Ozarks Point Lookout MO 65726

BRADLEY, RONALD HOWARD, neuro-anatomist; b. Detroit, Aug. 21, 1950; s. Clarence Edward and Lorraine Day (Moyers) B.; B.A., Wayne State U., 1973, M.S., 1978; Ph.D., Mich. State U., 1982, med. student 1980—; m. Susan Kay Goebel, June 24, 1973. Chef, Hotel St. Regis. Detroit, 1968-70; chief lab. mgr. Mich. Cancer Found. Electron Microscopy Lab., 1973-76; sr. research asst. anatomy Wayne State U., 1976-80; with neurosci. program Mich. State U., 1980—. Mem. Am. Assn. Cell Biologists, Electron Microscopy Soc. Am., N.Y. Acad. Sci., AAAS, Am. Osteo. Assn., student Osteo. Med. Assn., Sigma Xi, Sigma Sigma Phi, Methodist. Mason. Home: 27000 Franklin Rd Apt 316 Southfield MI 48034 Office: Mich State U 5th Floor Fee Hall East Lansing MI 48824

BRADLEY, WILLIAM ARTHUR, educator; b. Lansing, Mich., Nov. 11, 1921; s. Arthur and Amy F. (Barringer) B.; B.S. in Civil Engring., Mich. State U., 1943; M.S., U. Ill., 1947; Ph.D., U. Mich., 1956; m. Elizabeth G. Ewing, June 29, 1949; children—David, Nancy, Susan. Engr., Douglas Aircraft, El Segundo, Calif., 1943-44; engr. G.M. Foster, Bridge Cons., Lansing, 1945-46; mem. faculty Mich. State U., East Lansing, 1947—, prof. mechanics and civil engring., 1961—; cons. Dow Chem. Corp., 1959-61. Mem. Lansing Orgn. for Schs.; bd. dirs. West Side Neighborhood Assn. Recipient Disting. Faculty award Mich. State U., 1963; Western Electric Fund award, 1966. Mem. ASCE, Am. Concrete Inst., Internat. Assn. Bridge and Structural Engrs., Am. Soc. Engring. Edn., Sigma Xi, Phi Kappa Phi, Tau Beta Pi, Chi Epsilon. Home: 1919 W Kalamazoo St Lansing MI 48915 Office: Coll Engring Mich State U East Lansing MI 48824

BRADSHAW, LAWRENCE JAMES, artist; b. St. Paul, Kans., Sept. 21, 1945; s. James Lawrence and Pauline Marie (Nunnink) B.; B.F.A., Pittsburg (Kans.) State U., 1967, M.A., 1971; M.F.A., Ohio U., Athens, 1973. Designer, Union Oil Co., Honolulu, summer 1967; proofreader, typist CBS-TV, Hollywood, Calif., 1967-69; prodn. artist Writers Service, Hollywood, 1969: advt. mgr. J.C. Penney Co., Pittsburg, 1970-71; teaching asst. Pittsburg State U., 1970-71, Ohio U., 1971-73; instr. Akron (Ohio) Art Inst., summer 1973; asso. prof. art U. Nebr., Omaha, 1973—, dir. univ. galleries, 1974-76; visual arts rep., designer Met. Arts Council, Omaha, 1976; art dir. Akron City Scholarship Program, 1973; juror various art exhbns., 1974—; one-man exhbns. include Hillel House, Athens, Ohio, 1973, U. Nebr., 1974, Pittsburg State U., 1974, 77; group exhbns. in 21 states include Joslyn Art Mus., Omaha, 1974, 78, 80, Fort Hays State U., 1979, 80, U. S.D., Vermillion, 1979, 80, Alice Lloyd Coll. Nat., Pippa Passes, Ky., 1980, Wesleyan Coll., Macon, Ga., 1980, N.C. Mus. Art, Raleigh, 1980. Pres. Catholic Youth Orgn., St. Paul, 1959. Recipient Best of Show award 3d biennial Coll. St. Mary, Omaha, 1978; Purchase award Sioux City Art Center An. Regional Exhbn., 1978; Juror's award Kans. 5th Nat., Hays, 1980; Outstanding Tchr. award U. Nebr., Omaha, 1976, 77, 78; Nebr. Arts Council grantee 1976; NDEA fellow, 1967. Mem. Nat. Coll. Art Assn., Nat. Crafts Council, Mid-Am. Coll. Art Assn., Joslyn Art Mus., Positive Living Found., Internat. Platform Assn., Kappa Pi, Omicron Delta Kappa, Pi Kappa Alpha. Office: Room 391A Adminstrn Bldg Univ Nebr Omaha NE 68182

BRADSHAW, PAUL L., state senator; b. Jefferson City, Mo., July 17, 1930; s. Jean Paul and Catherine Ann (Brandt) B.; A.B., U. Mo., 1952, LL.B., 1954; m. Susan Ward; 1 son, Jean Paul II. Admitted to Mo. bar; partner firm Neale, Newman, Bradshaw & Freeman, Springfield, Mo., 1956—; sr. v.p., gen. counsel Ozark Air Lines, St. Louis, 1968—; mem. Mo. Senate, 1971—, minority floor leader. State coordinator Republican nat. campaign, 1960; chmn. Greene County Rep. Party, 1965-70. Served with USAF, 1954-56. Mem. Greene County Bar Assn., C. of C. Congregationalist. Clubs: Masons, Shriners, Elks. Office: 705 Woodruff Blvd Springfield MO 65806*

BRADT, ACKEN GORDON, ret. banker, educator; b. Wichita, Kan., Sept. 22, 1896; s. Charles Edwin and Nellie (Acken) B.; A.B., Northwestern U., 1920, M.B.A., 1941; m. Aliff Bosier, June 18, 1918; children—Elizabeth Margaret (Mrs. Leonard S. Parsons), Virginia Helen Fullerton, Gordon Edwin. Asst. sec. Bd. Fgn. Missions, Presbyn. Ch. U.S.A., 1920-28; with Continental Ill. Nat. Bank and Trust Co., Chgo., 1928-62, 2d v.p., 1943-59, v.p., 1959-62; mgmt. cons; lectr. mgmt., mem. faculty Northwestern U., 1944—, past mem. adminstrv. com. chmn. bd. mgrs. of Fin. Public Relations; sect. leader, lectr. Sch. Banking, U. Wis., Pacific Coast Sch. Banking, U. Wash., Sch. Public Relations, Northwestern U.; lectr. Bank Public Relations Sch., Princeton, Sch. Banking, South La. State U., Grad. Sch. Banking, So. Meth. U. Chmn., Evanston (Ill.) Mayor's New Generations Service Bd.; mem. council exec. devel. program U. Ill.; past chmn. bus. edn. adv. council Bd. Edn. Chgo.; mem. public sch. com. on policy and curriculum Ill. Bankers Sch.; former sec., mem. exec. com., dir. McCormick Theol. Sem., Chgo.; past mem. exec. com. Evanston Council Chs.; past v.p., dir. Evanston YMCA; former vice chmn. Chgo. Community Fund-Red Cross Joint Appeal; vice chmn. budget com. Chgo. Community Fund; pres. United Community Services of Evanston, Inc.; trustee, dir. Evanston Public Library. Served to sgt. U.S. Army, World War I. Mem. Am. Bankers Assn. (com. banker edn. programs), Am. Inst. Banking (former chmn. and mem. bd. regents Chgo. chpt.), Financial Pub. Relations Assn. (past treas.), Ill. Bankers Assn. (chmn. com. on edn., mem. pub. relations div.), Ill., Evanston (dir.), chambers commerce, Evanston Hist. Soc., Chgo. Assn. Commerce and Industry, Sigma Alpha Epsilon (life mem.). Presbyterian (ruling elder). Clubs: Kickers, Kiwanis, University (Evanston); Union League (2d v.p.) (Chgo.). Author: How to Triple Your Talents and Multiply Your Earning Power, 1963: The Secrets of Getting Results Through People, 1968; Five Keys to Productivity and Profits, 1973; also articles in mgmt. field. Home and Office: 606 Michigan Ave Evanston IL 60202

BRADT, DONA MARY SONTAG, librarian; b. Hastings, Minn., Oct. 18, 1930; d. Edwin Gervase and Maude Marie (Hatten) S.; student Mt. St. Marys Coll., 1948, Library Sch. U. Minn., 1968-70; B.A., Met. State U., 1975; Mt. m. Arnold L. Bradt (div.); children—Michael Edwin, Robert Dana, Jeffrey Arnold, Peter Matthew, Andrew Hatten. Legal sec. Langevin & Langlais, 1964-65; librarian Econs. Lab., Inc., St. Paul, 1965—, head librarian, 1979-80, mgr. corp. info. center, 1980—. Mem. Am. Soc. Info. Sci., Spl. Libraries Assn., ALA, Minn. Library Assn., AAAS. Republican. Roman Catholic. Home: 7981 115th St S Cottage Grove MN 55016 Office: Econs Lab Inc Osborn Bldg Wabasha St Saint Paul MN 55102

BRADTMUELLER, WELDON GOTTLIEB, coll. prof.; b. Fort Wayne, Ind., Dec. 22, 1924; married, 5 children. B.S. in Elementary Edn., Concordia Tchrs. Coll., River Forest, Ill., 1952; M.S. in Ednl. Adminstrn., Ind. U., Bloomington, 1956, Ed.D. in Elementary Edn., 1963. Asst. prof. edn. U. Mich., Ann Arbor, 1963-64; asst. prof. edn. Fla. State U., Tallahassee, 1964-66; cons. adult basic edn. Fla. State Dept. Edn., Tallahassee, 1966-68; asso. prof. edn. No. Ill. U., DeKalb, 1968—. Mem. NEA, Ill. Assn. Higher Edn., Nat. Soc. for the Study of Edn., Internat. Reading Assn., Ill., No. Ill. Reading councils, Coll. Reading Assn., Nat. Reading Conf., Nat., Council Tchrs. English, Ill. Assn., Tchrs. English, Assn. Study of Perception, Internat. (pres. 1975-76), Nat., Ill., DeKalb Area assns. tchr. edn. Author: (with Edwin H. Smith) Individual Reading Placement Inventory, 1969; (with Barney and Starkey) The Process of Teaching Reading, 1970; contbr. articles to profl. jours.; editor Jour. Assn. for Study Perception. Specialist in lang. arts, reading. Home: 1108 S 1st St DeKalb IL 60115 Office: 144 Graham No Ill Univ DeKalb IL 60115

BRADWAY, RAYMOND WILLIAM, JR., surgeon; b. Phila., June 17, 1932; s. Raymond William and Anne (Hannum) B.; student Mansfield State Coll., 1950-52; D.O., Phila. Coll. Osteo. Medicine, 1956; m. Barbara Moffitt, Feb. 25, 1961; children—Beverly Anne, Robert Alan, Karen Denise, Alison Jane. Intern, Detroit Osteo. Hosp., 1956-57, resident in surgery, 1957-61; postgrad. tng. in thoracic surgery, Phila. and Boston, 1961-62; practice medicine specializing in thoracic surgery, Detroit, 1962-63, in gen. and thoracic surgery, Columbus, Ohio, 1963—; sr. attending surgeon, cons. Doctors Hosp., Columbus, 1963—, chmn. div. thor. surgery, 1966—, chmn. dept. gen. surgery, 1979-81; clin. prof. surgery and thoracic surgery Ohio U., 1977—. Trustee, Columbus Acad. Recipient C.L. Ballinger Disting. Osteo. Surgeon award, 1979; diplomate Am. Osteo. Bd. Surgery, Am. Osteo. Bd. Thoracic Surgery. Fellow Am. Coll. Osteo. Surgeons (chmn. continuing surg. edn. com. 1973-80, bd. govs. 1980—, pres. thoracic-cardiovascular sect. 1974); mem. Am. Osteo. Assn. (vice chmn. continuing med. edn. com. 1973-78), Am. Osteo. Bd. Surgery, Ohio Osteo. Assn., Columbus Acad. Osteo. Medicine, Am. Thoracic Soc., Ohio Thoracic Soc., Am. Soc. Contemporary Medicine and Surgery, Am. Soc. Parenteral and Enteral Nutrition, Royal Soc. Medicine. Republican. Presbyterian. Clubs: Scioto Golf and Country, Masons, Shriners. Editorial cons. Jour. Am. Osteopathic Assn., 1966—. Office: 5125 Beacon Hill Rd Columbus OH 43228

BRADY, JOHN EDWARD, nurse; b. Kingston, N.Y., Sept. 4, 1940; s. Owen Francis and Elizabeth (Feeney) B.; A.A.S. in Nursing, Dutchess Community Coll., Poughkeepsie, N.Y., 1975; B.S. in Health Care Adminstrn., St. Francis Coll., Bklyn., 1979; m. Kathie; children—Andrew Francis, Mary Elizabeth. Charge nurse St. Francis Hosp., Roslyn, L.I., 1975-76; nursing supr. No. Dutchess Hosp., Rhinebeck, N.Y., 1976-78; asst. dir. nursing Community Gen. Hosp., Harris, N.Y., 1978-79; dir. nursing Douglas Gen. Hosp., Douglasville, Ga., 1979-81; nursing service adminstr. Marietta (Ohio) Meml. Hosp., 1981—; mem. nursing adv. bd. W. Ga. Coll., 1979-80. Mem. Douglas County Social Services Orgn., 1981—. Mem. Am. Soc. Nursing Service Adminstrs., Ohio Hosp. Assn., Ohio Hosp. Assn. Nursing Service Adminstrs. Home: Mar Ren Manor Apt 2 Tennis Center Rd Marietta OH 45750 Office: Marietta Meml Hosp Marietta OH 45750

BRADY, MARK EDWARD, ins., bus. exec.; b. Minneola, N.Y., Dec. 25, 1931; s. Edward Patrick and Vivian Evelyn (Vizard) B.; B.A., A.A., Passionist Fathers Sem., 1954; postgrad. Yale U., 1956, Hudson Coll., 1957-58, Suffolk U. Sch. Law, 1959; m. Anne M. Sughrue, Feb. 11, 1956; children—Pamela, Kent, Joy, Sean. Mgmt. trainee State St. Trust Co., Boston, 1954-55; with Universal C.I.T., Inc., N.Y.C., 1959-65, br. mgr., 1961-63, dist. mgr., 1963-65; dist. mgr. Yegen Assos., Teaneck, N.J., and Pitts., 1965-67, div. head, 1967-72, v.p., 1972; founder, chmn. Columbus Assos., Inc. (Ohio), 1972—, CAI Inc. (Ohio), 1973—, Brady Ins. Co. (Ohio), 1972—, Nat. Crown Life Ins. Co., 1974—; dir. Britannia Ins. Co. Ltd. (B.W.I.); chmn. Brady Cons. Assos. Inc., N.Y. State, Mass., CAI Acceptance Corp., Tara Cons., Tara Fin. Services. Mem. Pres.'s Council, Georgetown U. Served with USAF, 1955-58. Recipient Freedoms Found Bronze George Washington medal, 1958. Mem. Ohio Mobile Home Assn., U.S. Savs. and Loan League, Ohio Savs. and Loan League, Am. Bankers Assn., Ohio Bankers Assn. Republican. Clubs: Ohio State U. Pres.'s, Rich St., Highlands Golf. Home: Top O' the Mornin' Pataskala OH 43062 Office: 1303 S High St Columbus OH 43206

BRADY, MAUREEN ELIZABETH, educator; b. Chgo., Mar. 15, 1945; d. William James and Gertrude (Hunter) B.; B.S. in Edn., Ill. State U., Normal, 1967, M.S. in Ednl. Media, 1971; postgrad. Nat. Coll. Edn. Librarian, Sch. Dist. 47, Crystal Lake, Ill., 1967-69, Sch. Dist. 155, Crystal Lake, 1969-70; learning center tchr. Rugen Elementary Sch., Glenview, Ill., 1971-73; learning center tchr. Sunny Hill Elementary Sch. Dist. 220, Barrington, Ill., 1974—. Mem. Friends of Minocqua (Wis.) Library; mem. aux. Good Shepherd Hosp., Barrington. Mem. ALA, Ill. Assn. Media in Edn., Assn. Ednl. Communications and Tech., Ill. Assn. Ednl. Communications and Tech. (div. com.), NEA, Ill., Barrington (dir.) edn. assns., Chgo. Suburban Audiovisual Roundtable, No. Ill. Media Assn., AAUW (dir. Barrington area br.), Friends of Barrington Area Library, Elgin Scottish Soc. (pres.), Alpha Beta Alpha, Kappa Delta Pi (dir.). Cert. geography, library sci., ednl. media, Ill. Office: 2500 Helm Rd Carpentersville IL 60110

BRADY, WILLIAM ARTHUR, speech pathologist; b. Titusville, Pa., May 13, 1942; s. Walter Robert and Alma Cecelia B.; B.S. in Speech and Speech Correction, Clarion State Coll., 1966; M.Ed. in Speech Pathology (Office Edn. fellow), Pa. State U., 1967; Ph.D. in Speech Pathology, Kent State U., 1978. Speech therapist Lawrence County (Pa.) Pub. Schs., 1966-68, Titusville (Pa.) Area Schs., summer 1966, Ellwood City (Pa.) Area Schs., 1968; instr. speech pathology dept. Edinboro State Coll., summer 1968, Clarion State Coll., 1968-69, Ill. State U., 1969-70, Allegheny Coll., 1970-71; teaching fellow in speech pathology Kent State U., 1971-74, adj. asso. prof. speech pathology, 1976-77; dir. speech pathology St. Elizabeth Hosp. Med. Center, Youngstown, Ohio, 1974—. Mem. Am. (certified in clin. comptence in speech pathology), Ohio (chmn. com. clin. and hosp. affairs 1976-77), Mahoning Valley (v.p. 1976-77) speech and hearing assns., Aphasiology Assn. Ohio. Contbr. articles to profl. jours. Home: 4521 Washington Sq Apt 2 Youngstown OH 44515 Office: 1044 Belmont Ave Youngstown OH 44501

BRADY, WILLIAM WEBB, lawyer; b. Elgin, Ill., Nov. 9, 1914; s. William Henry and Helen L. (Webb) B.; student U. Ariz., 1932-35; B.S., Northwestern U., 1936. J.D., 1940; m. Barbara M. Rosewater, Sept. 28, 1940; children—Barbara Leslie Brady Karchmer, Nancy Webb Brady Shafer, Katherine Anne, Margaret Louise Brady Safford. Public acct. Arthur Andersen & Co., Chgo., 1936-37; admitted to Ill. bar. 1940; asso. Mayer. Meyer, Austrian & Platt, Chgo., 1940-42; trial atty. Office Contract Settlement, Washington, 1945; practice law, Elgin, 1946—, partner firm Brady, McQueen, Martin, Collins & Jensen; dir. First Nat. Bank, Elgin, Elgin Sweeper Co.; mem. faculty Northwestern U., 1938-79. Trustee Judson Coll., Elgin, 1963-70, chmn., 1963-68; trustee No. Bapt. Theol. Sem., Oakbrook, Ill., 1962—, Bapt. Theol. Union, Chgo., 1975—; pres. adv. bd. St. Joseph Hosp., Elgin, 1972—. C.P.A., Ill. Mem. Am., Ill., Chgo., Kane County, Elgin bar assns. Baptist. Clubs: Union League (Chgo.); Elgin Country. Contbr. to legal books, jours. Home: 332 Vincent Pl Elgin IL 60120 Office: 80 Fountain Sq Plaza Elgin IL 60120

BRAHE, NEIL BENTON, dentist; b. Appleton, Wis., June 21, 1926; s. Ralph Bertrand and Mary Jesse (O'Brien) B.; student Ripon Coll., 1946-49; D.D.S., Loyola Coll., Chgo., 1953; m. Grace Jensen, Oct. 23, 1948; children—Alison Ann, David Carlton, Bruce Benton. Mem. faculty Marquette U., Milw., 1961—, asst. prof. dental practice adminstrn., 1961-65; gen. practice dentistry, Appleton, 1953—; founder, pres. Project D, Appleton, 1961—. Mem. Am. Greater Milw. dental assns., Wis. State, Chgo. (asso.) dental socs., Outagamie Dental Soc., A.V. Purinton Acad., Am. Legion, Appleton C. of C. Clubs: Rotary, Northside Bus., Appleton Yacht, Oshkosh Power Boat, Elks, Masons. Author: Dental Assistants' Self Training Program, 1967; Executive Dynamics in Dental Practice, 1969; We Like These Ideas, 1970, Wonderful World of Modern Dentistry, 1971, Great Ideas for Dental Practice, 1972; (with Alison A. Brahe) Dental Letter Book, 1975. Office: 335 E Wisconsin St Appleton WI 54911

BRAIN, DONALD CHESTER, ins. agt.; b. Beatrice, Nebr.; s. Clinton Chester and Bertha Susan (Jones) B.; B.B.S., U. Kans., 1940; m. Charleen McCann, Sept. 25, 1948; children—Donald Chester, David M. With Retail Credit Co., Kansas City, Mo., 1940-42; spl. agt. Hartford Accident and Indemnity Co., Los Angeles and Kansas City, 1946-48; asso. broker, then gen. partner W.B. Johnson & Co., Kansas City, 1948-63; a founder, 1963, since pres. Brain & Fritson, Inc., Kansas City; trustee Harry J. Loman Found. Ins. Edn., 1964-68, chmn. bd., 1968; tchr. ins. courses U. Kansas City, 1952-56, 79—; elector Ins. Hall of Fame, 1970—; trustee Am. Inst. Property and Liability Underwriters, Inc.; mem. public ins. com. city of Kansas City (Mo.), 1970-76, mem. sch. dist. ins. com., 1963-69; speaker in field, 1969—. Mem. Kansas City Crime Com., 1973—, Mayor Kansas City Prayer Breakfast Com., 1972—. Served with U.S. Army, 1942-45. Recipient citation 100th Ann. Mo. Ins. Dept., 1969; C.P.C.U., 1952. Mem. Soc. C.P.C.U.'s (past nat. pres.), Ind. Ins. Agts. Am. (pres. 1979), Mo. Assn. Ind. Ins. Agts. (past pres., Ins. Man of Yr. award 1976), Kansas City Assn. Ind. Ins. Agts. (past pres.), Kansas City Advt. and Sales Execs. Club, Kansas C. of C., Am. Legion (past post comdr.), 40 and 8, Serra Club (past pres. Kansas City, past dist. gov.). Clubs: Blue Hills Country, University. Address: 1100 United Missouri Bank Bldg Kansas City MO 64106

BRAINERD, GERTRUDE PERKINS, educator; b. Canton, Ill., Feb. 19, 1924; d. Keith Carey and Eva C. (Eggert) Perkins; B.S., Western Ill. U., 1945, M.S., 1955; postgrad. Bradley U., 1950, 62-63, Washington U., 1964, Ind. U., 1965-68; m. Robert W. Brainerd, May 22, 1968. Tchr. Augusta Community High Sch., 1945-47, Canton (Ill.) Jr. and Sr. High Sch., 1948-63, Belleville Twp. High Sch. W., 1963-65; instr. Belleville (Ill.) Area Coll., 1963-66, instr. English, 1970—, chmn. dept., 1977-79; teaching asso. Ind. U., 1966-68. Pres. bd. dirs. YWCA, Canton. Mem. AAUW (Ill. div. dir. 1974-77, 2d v.p. pub. info. 1975-77, corr. sec. 1977, project dir. 1979), AAUP (chpt. v.p. 1974), Pi Lambda Theta. Home: 1411 Princeton Dr O'Fallon IL 62269 Office: Belleville Area Coll Belleville IL 62221

BRAKER, WILLIAM PAUL, aquarium dir.; b. Chgo., Nov. 3, 1926; s. William Paul and Minnie (Wassermann) B.; m. Patricia Reese, Sept. 2, 1950; children—Helen Elizabeth, William Paul, III, Nancy Carol, Gretchen Patricia; B.S., Northwestern U., 1950; M.S., George Washington U., 1953; postgrad. U. Chgo., 1954-58. Aquarist, John G. Shedd Aquarium, Chgo., 1950, asst. curator, 1953-60, asst. dir., 1960-64, dir., 1964—; tissue culture research Nat. Cancer Inst., Bethesda, Md., 1952; cons. various aquariums and marine parks. Auditor, Rich Twp. Govt., 1975—; trustee Prairie State Coll., 1970-74. Mem. Shedd Aquarium Soc. (trustee, sec.), Am. Assn. Zool. Parks and Aquariums (past pres., past chmn. legis. com., past chmn. ethics com.), Internat. Union of Dirs. Zool. Gardens, Am. Soc. Ichthyologists and Herpatologists, Am. Fisheries Soc., Kennicott Club (past pres.). Author, cons. books, columns and encys. on aquatic subjects. Home: RFD 1 Sunset Rd Matteson IL 60443 Office: 1200 S Lake Shore Dr Chicago IL 60605

BRAM, ISABELLE MARY RICKEY MCDONOUGH (MRS. JOHN BRAM), clubwoman; b. Oskaloosa, Ia., Apr. 4; d. Lindsey Vinton and Heddy (Lundee) Rickey; B.A. in Govt., George Washington U., 1947, postgrad., 1947-49; m. Dayle C. McDonough, Jan. 20, 1949. Dep. tax assessor and collector Aransas Pass Ind. Sch. Dist., 1939-41; sec. to city atty., Aransas Pass, Tex., 1939-41; info. specialist U.S. Dept. State, Washington, 1942-48. Treas. Mo. Fedn. Women's Clubs, Inc., 1964-66, 2d v.p., 1966-68, 1st v.p., 1968-70, pres., 1970-72; bd. dirs. Gen. Fedn. Women's Clubs. Mem. steering com. Citizens Com. for Conservation; mem. exec. com. Missourians for Clean Water. Pres., DeKalb County Women's Democratic Club, 1964. Bd. dirs. DeKalb County Pub. Library, pres., 1966; bd. dirs. Mo. Girls Town Found. Mem. AAUW, Nat. League Am. Pen Women, DeKalb County Hist. Soc., Internat. Platform Assn., Zeta Tau Alpha, Phi Delta Delta, Phi Delta Gamma. Democrat. Episcopalian. Mem. Order Eastern Star. Clubs: Tri Arts, Shakespeare, Wimodausis, Gavel, Ledgers. Editor: Mo. Clubwoman mag. Home: Sloan and Cherry Sts Maysville MO 64469

BRAMAN, DONALD WILLIAM, public relations co. exec.; b. Mpls., June 19, 1917; s. Maurice I. and Ida (Garber) B.; B.A. cum laude, U. Minn., 1937; m. Sally Davidson, June 16, 1946; children—Stuart, Sandra, Richard. With Mpls. Star, 1937-41; dir. public relations Manson-Gold Advt. Agy., Mpls., 1946-47; public relations staff, publs. editor Toni Co., St. Paul, 1947-49; asso. dir. public relations Olmsted & Foley, Mpls., 1950-58; co-founder, pres. Don Braman & Assos., Inc., Mpls., 1958-77; v.p. Doremus & Co., Mpls., 1977—; teaching asst., lectr. Sch. Journalism U. Minn.; dir. Minn. Advt. Fedn. Chmn. Mayor's Com. for Employment of Handicapped, 1950's; chmn. Mpls. Symphony Orchestra Guaranty Fund Campaign, 1960's; fin. com. Mpls. LWV, 1970's; dir. Am.-Israel Chamber of Commerce & Industry of Minn., 1980's. Served with USMC, 1941-45. Mem. Public Relations Soc. Am. (dir., pres. Minn. chpt., mem. exec. com. counselors acad., Disting. Service award 1973, accredited), Nat. Investor Relations Inst. (dir., pres. Minn. chpt.), Mpls. Area C. of C. (chmn. coms. various dates), Marine Corps Combat Correspondents Assn., U. Minn. Alumni Assn., Sigma Delta Chi, Zeta Beta Tau. Clubs: Mpls. Athletic, Minn. Press, Masons, Scottish Rite, Shrine. Contbr. articles in field to profl. publs., travel articles to popular publs. Home: 19 S First St B-402 Minneapolis MN 55401 Office: 1500 1st Bank Place W Minneapolis MN 55402

BRAMHALL, ROBERT RICHARD, cons.; b. Ft. Smith, Ark., Oct. 30, 1927; s. Richard Marion and Ima Lucille (Stovall) B.: A.B., Harvard U., 1951, M.B.A., 1960; m. Mary Margaret Bundy, Aug. 10, 1957; children—Robert Richard, Laura Louise. With Gen. Electric Co., N.Y.C., 1954-66, Philco-Ford subs. Ford Motor Co., Phila., 1966-68, Warwick Electronics subs. Whirlpool Corp., Niles, Ill., 1968-70; exec. chmn. Robert R. Bramhall & Assos., Lake Forest, Ill., 1970—; cons. to Rockwell Internat., Bunker-Ramo Corp., Dan River Inc., TRW, Memorex, J.P. Stevens, G.D. Searle, Molex, Spartan Mills, Simpsons-Sears Ltd. (Toronto, Ont., Can.), State of Ill. Pres. Chgo. Tennis Patrons, Inc., 1974-75. Served with U.S. Army, 1946-48. Republican. Baptist. Clubs: Bath and Tennis (Lake Forest); Harvard Bus. Sch. of Chgo. Home: 855 Buena Rd Lake Forest IL 60045 Office: 222 Wisconsin Bldg Lake Forest IL 60045

BRANAGHAN, RICHARD LEROY, SR., health agy. exec.; b. Providence, Feb. 10, 1923; s. Roy and Agnes (Bush) B.; ed. Kent State U.; m. Catherine R. McMahon, May 4, 1946; children—James R., Paula J. Branaghan Suveges, Patricia H. Branaghan Wise, Virginia M. Branaghan Jane, Richard Leroy, Russell J. On-the-job trainer passenger service United Air Lines, Cleve. Hopkins Airport, 1957-65; exec. dir. Nat. Hemophilia Found., No. Ohio chpt., 1965-69, regional dir., 1969-71, dir. field services, asst. exec. dir., N.Y.C., 1971-73; exec. dir. Nat. Commn. to Combat Huntington's Disease, N.Y.C., 1973-75, v.p. N.E. Ohio chpt., 1981; dir. devel. Child Guidance Center, Cleve., 1975—; exec. v.p. Nat. Huntingtons Disease Assn., Cleve., 1975—; pres. B. & R. & Assos. Inc., hearing aid dealers, sales and rental sick room equipment, Parma Heights, Ohio. Dir. vets. affairs, vol. asst. to mayor Pawtucket (R.I.), 1948-53; spl. asst. to U.S. Senator J. Howard McGrath, R.I. office, 1946-48. Served with U.S. Army, 1943-45; ETO. Recipient Vol. awards United Air Lines, 1966, Nat. Hemophilia Found., 1970. Mem. Nat. Soc. Fund Raisers, Ohio Council Fund Raising Execs., Am. Vets. (past state dept. vice comdr. R.I.). Democrat. Roman Catholic. Club: Roadrunner's (exec. sec. 1969-70) (Cleve.). Home: 1545 Elmwood Ave Lakewood OH 44107 Office: Detroit-Warren Bldg 14805 Detroit Ave Lakewood OH 44107

BRANAHL, ERWIN FRED, aerospace co. exec.; b. St. Louis, Mar. 8, 1922; s. Erwin Edward and Mildred Wilhelmina (Kelle) B.; B.S. in Civil Engring., Washington U., St. Louis, 1943, M.S. in Applied Mechanics, 1951; m. Adeline Elizabeth Sweeney, Apr. 15, 1944; children—Sandra Beatrice Branahl Cooper, James Erwin. Stress analyst Curtiss-Wright Corp., 1943-44; with McDonnell Douglas Astronautics Co., St. Louis, 1946—, mgr. space and missile engring. programs, 1961-68, v.p. engring., 1968-74, v.p., gen. mgr., 1974—; v.p., dir. McDonnell Douglas Tech. Services Co.; v.p. McDonnell Douglas Ltd., 1980—; dir. Vitek Systems, Inc. Served to lt. (j.g.) USNR, 1945-46. Registered profl. engr., Mo. Asso. fellow AIAA. Lutheran. Home: 14 Lake Pembroke St Saint Louis MO 63135 Office: PO Box 516 Saint Louis MO 63166

BRANCH, EMANUEL SYLVESTER, clergyman; b. Phila., July 1, 1921; s. Emanuel Sylvestre and Miley Gertrude (Anderson) B.; B.A., Yale U., 1950, M.Div., 1955; Hum. D., Wilberforce U., 1976; m. Gloria Cleo Connolly, Apr. 1, 1950; children—Crystal Alice Branch Parms, Colleen Ann. Ordained to ministry Baptist Ch.; pastor First Bapt. Ch., Milford, Conn., 1947-50, Union Bapt. Ch., Hartford, Conn., 1953-60; asso. exec. dir. Cleve. Council Chs., 1961-64; pastor Antioch Bapt. Ch., Cleve., 1964—. Trustee, Colgate Rochester Div. Sch.; pres. Antioch Apts. Inc., Urban League, Cleve., 1968-69; co-campaign mgr. Carl B. Stokes for Mayor Cleve., 1969; chmn. Greater Cleve. Council Econ. Opportunities, 1968-78. Served with AUS, 1945-46. Recipient Ohio Gov.'s award community action; Edward H. Rhoades award Am. Bapt. Chs. U.S.; named Citizen of Yr., Nat. Assn. Social Workers. Mem. Sigma Pi Phi, Alpha Phi Alpha. Office: 8869 Cedar Ave Cleveland OH 44106*

BRANCH, MARJORIE BEATRICE, ednl. adminstr.; b. Chgo., Mar. 31, 1927; d. Foster Raymond and Josephine Beatrice (Statum) Branch; B.A. in Christian Edn., Wheaton Coll., 1955; M.A. in Edn., U. Chgo., 1959; student Northwestern U., 1946-48; postgrad. Atlanta U., 1956-57, Chgo. Tchrs. Coll., 1959-61. Instr., Carver Bible Inst., 1955-57; tchr. Chgo. Bd. Edn., 1957-66, adminstr. dept. human relations, 1966-72, adminstr. dept. govt. funded programs, 1972-73, prin. Leif Ericson Elementary Sch., 1973—. Instr. community organizing and citizenship tng., 1966-71. Adv. council Met. Comprehensive Health Care Orgn., 1970-71. Bd. dirs. LWV Citizen Info. Service, 1966-72, Tri-Community Day Care Center. Chgo.. 1973-79. Mem. Assn. Adminstrv. Women (dir. Met. Chgo. chpt.), Chgo. Prins. Assn., Phi Delta Kappa (Educator of Yr., 1979). Mem. Christian Ch. (dir. religious edn. 1969-72). Home: 3021 S Michigan Ave Chicago IL 60616 Office: 3600 W 5th Ave Chicago IL 60624

BRANCH, RAYMOND LEE, nursing home adminstr.; b. Balt., Aug. 3, 1928; s. Augustus Lee Branch and Irene Frances (Colbert) Branch Gilmore; B.S. in Health Care Adminstrn., Wichita State U., 1979; m. Idaline Clark, Dec. 27, 1963; children—Joan L. Branch Roberts, Pamela L. Branch Gilyard, Pamela J. Branch Whitaker, Bonnie F. Branch Marshall. Served as enlisted man U.S. Air Force, 1947-74, advanced through grades to master sgt., 1971; various supervisory positions in personnel and records, U.S., Korea, Eng. and Vietnam, 1951-72; personnel supt., chief customer service center 81st Combat Support Group RAF Bentwaters, Eng., 1972-74; ret., 1974; data intern Health Systems Agy. S.E. Kans., Wichita, 1978-79; nursing home adminstr. Medicalodg South of Kansas City (Kans.), 1980—. Decorated Bronze Star medal, Meritorious Service medal, Air Force Commendation medal with oak leaf cluster. Democrat. Baptist. Club: Am. Legion. Home: 615 E Maywood Wichita KS 67216 Office: 6501 Greeley Kansas City KS 66104

BRAND, JOHN, clergyman; b. St. Louis, Apr. 30, 1923; s. William Herman and Mabel Edith (Wimbush) B.; B.S. in Mech. Engring., Mo. Sch. Mines and Metallurgy, 1944; M.Div., Louisville Presbyn. Theol. Sem., 1964; postgrad. U. Ky., 1969-70; m. Virginia May Haggard, Dec. 24, 1970; children—Christy (Mrs. Ghary Akers), Ronald C. Rainey, Donald C., Stephanie Rainey, Virginia, Robin (Mrs. Barry Boston), Elizabeth Carol. Plant engr. Krummrick plant Monsanto Chem. Corp., East St. Louis, Ill., 1944-46, Queeny plant, St. Louis, 1946-53, mech. standards engr. organic div., St. Louis, 1953-55, mgr. mech. standardization, research and engring. div., world hgqrs., St. Louis, 1955-58; ordained to ministry Presbyn. Ch. U.S., 1964 (transferred to Christian Ch. 1970); pastor South Louisville Presbyn. Ch., 1958-60, Eastminister Presbyn. Ch., Lexington, Ky., 1960-69, Cedar Meml. Christian Ch., Davenport, Iowa, 1980—; cons. services adminstr. Ky. Dept. Child Welfare, Frankfort, 1970-72; asst. dir. office occupational programs, bur. health services Dept. for Human Resources, Frankfort, 1972-74, dir., 1974-80. Part time pastor Berea Christian Ch., Henry County, Ky., 1970-80. Bd. deacons Westminister Presbyn. Ch., St. Louis. Mem. Mfg. Chemists Assn. (chmn. mech. tech. com.), Am. Standards Assn., Lexington Assn. Social Professions, Lexington Ministers Assn., Engrs. Club St. Louis, Kappa Sigma. Rotarian. Home: 2020 W 3d St Davenport IA 52802 Office: Cedar Meml Christian Ch 306 Cedar St Davenport IA 52802

BRANDBERG, LAWRENCE CHARLES, food co. exec.; b. Mpls., Oct. 24, 1942; s. Fritz Eric and LaVern Marrion (McCormick) B.; student U. Minn., 1960-63; m. Susan Therese Brandes, Oct. 26, 1963; children—Eric, Christine, Mark, Jonathan. Mem. research staff Pillsbury Co., Mpls., 1964-79; dir. research and tech. Golden Valley Foods, Mpls., 1979—. Mem. Internat. Microwave Power Inst. Patentee in field of microwave foods and hardware. Home: 6280 Rhode Island Ave N Minneapolis MN 55428 Office: Golden Valley Foods 1710 N Douglas Dr Minneapolis MN 55422

BRANDEL, PAUL WILLIAM, lawyer, business exec.; b. Chgo., Oct. 7, 1911; s. Carl P. and Christine (Johnson) B.; grad. North Park Acad., Chgo., 1928; grad. North Park Coll. 1930, LL.D., 1972; J.D., Chgo. Kent Coll. Law, 1933; LL.D., Trinity Coll., 1968, Ill. Benedictine Coll., 1973; m. Bernice Peterson Stege, Jan. 3, 1976; 1 dau., Carola Ruth (Mrs. Loren Anderson). Admitted to Ill. bar, 1933, since practiced in Chgo.; partner firm Brandel, Johnson & Erickson; chmn. bd. Barrington State Bank, Schaumburg State Bank; pres. Paul W. Brandel Enterprises, Inc. Chmn. bd. Stone-Brandel Center; bd. dirs. Am. Found. of Religion and Psychiatry, Interlocken Music Acad., Religious Heritage Am., Ill. Inst. Tech.; adv. bd. Salvation Army, Goodwill Industries. Decorated commandör Kungl. Nordstjärneorden (Sweden). Mem. Am., Ill., Chgo. bar assns., Gideons. Mem. Evang. Covenant Ch. Am. (chmn. bd., benevolence). Kiwanian. Clubs: Union League, Michigan Shores, Svithiod, Nordic Law, Chicago Athletic Assn., Swedish (Chgo.); Lauderdale Yacht; Everglades (Palm Beach, Fla.). Home: 2515 Mayapple Ct Northbrook IL 60062 Office: 500 Skokie Blvd Northbrook IL 60062

BRANDENBURG, GEORGE PAUL, metall. engr., lawyer; b. Lebanon, Ohio, May 2, 1944; B.S. metall. engring., U. Cin., 1970; M.B.A., Xavier U., 1973; J.D., No. Ky. State U., 1978. Chem. technician Battelle Meml. Inst., Columbus, Ohio, 1965-66; phys. metallurgist, nuclear systems programs Gen. Electric Co., Cin., 1966-72, research metallurgist, material and process tech. lab., 1972-73, materials engr., 1974-78, sr. materials application engr., 1978—; admitted to Ohio bar, 1978; sr. partner firm McTigue, Farish & Brandenburg, Cin., 1978—. Registered rpfl. engr., Ohio. Mem. Am. Soc. for Metals, AIME, Nat. Soc. Profl. Engrs., Ohio Soc. Profl. Engrs., Profl. Engrs. in Industry, Tech. Sci. Soc. Cin., Engring. Soc. Cin., Am. Bar Assn., Ohio Bar Assn., Cin. Bar Assn., Fed. Bar Assn., Assn. Trial Lawyers Am., Ohio Acad. Trial Lawyers, Gen. Electric Mgmt. Assn., Phi Alpha Delta. Contbr. articles to profl. jours. Home: 10396 Southwind Dr Cincinnati OH 45242 Office: 602 Gwynne Bldg 6th and Main Sts Cincinnati OH 45202

BRANDENBURG, HENRY LEE, mfg. co. exec.; b. Secaucus, N.J., Feb. 5, 1925; s. Henry Herman and Nathalie Estelle (Ackerman) B.; student Fairleigh Dickinson U., 1946-47, U. Colo., 1947-48, Cleve. State U., 1968-72; m. Sherrill Ann Overton, June 23, 1973; children—Sherry Lee, Henry Lance, Kim Bowen, Kit Archer, Kevin Dixon, Heidi Lalani. Project engr. Gibson Refrigerator Co., Greenville, Miss., 1952-61; mgr. def. products Mueller Brass Co., Port Huron, Mich., 1961-63; mgr. Ordnance Devel. Center, TRW, Cleve., 1964-68; dir. Tech. & Bus. Services, Cleve. State U., 1968-73, also lectr.; pres. Prontour Co., Dennison, Ohio, 1973—; dir. Lashle Enterprises, Dover, Ohio, 1972—. Pres., Small World Credit Union, Dennison, 1981—; indsl. dir. Dennison Growth Assn., 1976—; Served with USAAF, 1943-46. Mem. Cleve. Engring. Soc., AIAA, Buckeye State Sheriff's Assn., Full Gospel Businessmen's Fellowship Internat. Republican. Methodist. Club: Kiwanis. Patentee in field. Home: 635 N Water St Uhrichsville OH 44683 Office: PO Box 269 Dennison OH 44621

BRANDER, MERLE EDWARD, civil engr.; b. Menominee, Mich., Nov. 5, 1939; s. GustaAdolph and Margaret Lillian (Johnson) B.; B.S. with honors, Mich. Coll. Mining and Tech., 1962; m. Shirley Louise Peterson, Jan. 2, 1965; children—Clayton Merle, Kent Edward. Engr., Underwriters Lab., Northbrook, Ill., 1967-68; cons. engr. constrn. materials Wiss, Janney, Elstner & Assos., Northbrook, 1968-74; v.p. constrn. services Soil Testing Services Wis., Inc., Green Bay, 1974-81; pres. Brander Constrn. Technology, Inc., Green Bay, 1981—. Served to capt. USMC, 1962-67. Registered profl. engr., Ill., Wis., Mich., Kans., Minn., N.D. Mem. Am. Concrete Inst., Nat. Soc. Profl. Engrs., Soc. Fire Protection Engrs., ASCE, Prestressed Concrete Inst., VFW, Internat. Platform Assn. Baptist. Author: Introduction to Celestial Navagation and Piloting, 1966. Home: 2527 Oakwood Dr Green Bay WI 54303 Office: 540 Lambeau St Green Bay WI 54303

BRANDER, REYNOLDS A., JR., lawyer; b. Grand Rapids, Mich., Nov. 22, 1937; s. Reynolds A. and Gertrude (Boot) B.; A.B., U. Mich., 1960; J.D., Wayne State U., 1966; m. Janice Ann Lusk, June 29, 1963; children—Gregory, Sara. Admitted to Mich. bar, 1966; mem. staff Kent County Prosecutor's Office, 1966-67; partner law firm Cholette, Perkins & Buchanan, Grand Rapids, Mich., 1967—. Served with USNR, 1960-63. Mem. Am., Mich. State bar assns., Internat. Assn. Ins. Counsel. Home: 634 Plymouth Rd Grand Rapids MI 49506 Office: 755 Old Kent Bank Grand Rapids MI 49503

BRANDES, ANNETTE THERRIEN, educator; b. Cokato, Minn., Nov. 6, 1940; d. Frederick George and Geneva Orcella (Therrien) B.; B.S., U. Minn., 1962, M.A., 1967; postgrad. Ariz. State U., 1969; Ph.D., U. Chgo., 1981. Tchr. phys. edn. Meml. High Sch., Eau Claire, Wis., 1962-64; phys. edn. specialist Stillwater (Minn.) Schs., 1964-66; counselor Centennial High Sch., Circle Pines, Minn., 1966-68, St. Louis Park (Minn.) Schs., 1968-69; dir. counseling Rhein-Main Am. Schs., Frankfurt, West Germany, 1969-71; asst. dean students (dean of women) Westminster Coll., Salt Lake City, 1971-72; head counselor, instr. dept. psychology St. Scholastica Coll., Duluth, Minn., 1972-74; research cons. dept. research and evaluation Chgo. Bd. Edn., 1978-79; asst. to v.p. acad. affairs U. Minn., 1981—; cons. edn. and human relations, Duluth. Leader, Girl Scouts U.S.A, Duluth, 1972-74. Laverne Noyes Found. scholar, 1974-75. Recipient Arrowhead Leadership award U. Minn., Duluth, 1961. Mem. Am. Edn. Research Assn., Am. Sociol. Assn., Pi Lambda Theta. Author novels under pseudonym. Home: 1330 4th Ave S Anoka MN 55303

BRANDIN, DONALD NELSON, bank holding co. exec.; b. N.Y.C., Dec. 28, 1921; s. Nils F. and Dorothy May (Mead) B.; A.B., Princeton U., 1944; children—Robert N., Patricia A., Douglas M. With Bankers Trust Co., N.Y.C., 1946-56; v.p. Boatmen's Nat. Bank, St. Louis, 1956-67, sr. v.p., 1967-68, chmn. exec. com., 1968-70, pres., chief operating officer, 1971-72, pres., 1973-78, chmn. bd., chief exec. officer, 1973—, also dir.; exec. v.p. Boatmen's Bancshares, Inc., St. Louis, 1969-72, chmn. bd., chief exec. officer, 1973—, also dir.; dir. Boatmen's Bank & Trust Co. (Kansas City, Mo.), Boatmen's Union Nat. Bank (Springfield, Mo.), Boatmen's Life Ins. Co. (Phoenix), Mo. Mortgage & Investment Co., Petrolite Corp., William S. Barnickel & Co., Laclede Ave. Real Estate, Inc., Sigma-Aldrich Corp., Laclede Gas Co. (all St. Louis). Bd. dirs. Arts and Edn. Council of Greater St. Louis, St. Louis Symphony Soc., Washington U., St. Louis. Served to capt. U.S. Army, 1943-46. Mem. Assn. Bank Holding Cos., Assn. Res. City Bankers, Am., Mo. bankers assns., Bank Adminstrn. Inst., Robert Morris Assos. Clubs: Old Warson Country, St. Louis, Stadium, Metropolitan (Chgo.); Kansas City; Blind Brook (Purchase, N.Y.); Garden of Gods (Colorado Springs, Colo.). Home: 3 Coach N Four Ln Frontenac MO 63131 Office: 100 N Broadway PO Box 236 Saint Louis MO 63166

BRANDING, DOROTHY MARIE, sch. prin.; b. Granite City, Ill., Dec. 22, 1917; d. Harry William and Georgia Margaret (Schenck) B.; A.B., Harris Tchrs. Coll., 1939; M.A., U. Colo., 1945; postgrad. St. Louis U., U. Hawaii, Washington U. Tchr., Public Schs., St. Louis, 1941-75, prin. Maddox Sch., 1975-80, established, Euclid Montessori Sch., 1980—; mem. nat. adv. com. Social Edn., 1961-69. Blewett scholar, 1959-60, 65-66. Mem. Greater St. Louis Council Tchrs. English (pres. 1961-63), Greater St. Louis Council Social Studies (pres.), Mo. Council Social Studies, Nat. Council Social Studies, St. Louis Adminstrs. Assn., Mo. Tchr. Assn., Assn. Supervision and Curriculum Devel., St. Louis Montessori Assn., Am. Montessori Soc., Delta Kappa Gamma. Roman Catholic. Home: 6537 Oleatha Ave St Louis MO 63139 Office: 1131 N Euclid St Saint Louis MO 63113

BRANDRIET, LEON JOSEPH, newspaper exec.; b. Watertown, S.D., Oct. 18, 1954; s. Charles Loyd and Elizabeth Marie (Lantsberger) B.; B.S. in Mass Communications, Black Hills State Coll., 1976. With Pizza Hut Inc., Spearfish and Pierre, S.D., 1976-77; freelance photographer, Pierre, 1977-78; dir. advt. Daily Capitol Jour., Pierre, 1977—; part-time dir. S.D. Cowboy, Western Heritage Hall of Fame, Ft. Pierre, 1979-81; editor Dakota West mag., 1979-81; advt. dir. Pierre Times, Weekly Sunday Trader, Weekly Reminder Plus, 1981—; adv. sch. yearbook, newspaper staffs. Adv., Pierre Downtown Assn., 1978—, Eagle Flying Club, 1979—, Oahe Divers, 1980—, YMCA Friends, 1979—, Hughes Sherrifs Rescue Squad, 1979—. Mem. Ad Council, S.D. Press Assn., S.D. Newspaper Advt. Assn., Internat. Newspaper Advt. Execs., Pierre C. of C. Republican. Roman Catholic. Clubs: Black Hills Sky Divers, Oahe Divers, Flying, Kiwanis, Elks. Home: 114 Lakeview St Pierre SD 57501 Office: Daily Capitol Jour 415 S Pierre St Pierre SD 57501

BRANDSTETTER, DAVID ALBERT, telephone product sales cos. exec.; b. St. Louis, Apr. 7, 1937; s. Edward Otto and Jeannette Eleanor (Leitner) B.; B.S.B.A., Washington U., St. Louis, 1958; m. Holly Nylander, Dec. 28, 1975; children—Sheri, Scott, Kevin, Jason. Sales rep. S.G. Adams Printing & Stationery, St. Louis, 1958-61; regional mgr. Allied Carbon and Ribbon Mfg. Co., N.Y.C., 1961-65; founder, pres. Electronic Communications Ltd., St. Louis, 1965—, Phone World, St. Louis, 1978--. Recipient Dictaphone Achievement award, 1975, 76, 78, 79, 81. Mem. Adminstrv. Mgmt. Soc., St. Louis Jaycees, Sales and Mktg. Execs., Regional Commerce and Growth Assn. Contbr. articles to Progressive Mgmt. mag., 1979, 80, 81. Home: 1652 Foxleigh Ct Saint Louis MO 63131 Office: Electronic Communications Ltd 5143 Wilson Ave Saint Louis MO 63110 also Phone World 12730 Olive Street Rd Saint Louis MO 63141

BRANDT, KATHLEEN COLE, social worker, advt. agy. exec.; b. Cin., Nov. 22, 1946; d. James Scott and Kathryn Gertrude (Borisch) Cole; B.A., Miami U., 1968; M.S.W., U. Mich., 1972; M.M., Northwestern U., 1978; m. Brian Brandt, Mar. 21, 1970. Social worker Hamilton County Welfare Dept., Cin., 1969-70, Lucas County Children Services Bd., Toledo, 1970-74, East Maine Sch. Dist., Niles, Ill., 1974-77; account exec. Leo Burnett Advt. Agy., Chgo., 1978—; field instr. Loyola U., Chgo., 1976-77. Mem. Acad. Cert. Social Workers, Nat. Assn. Social Workers, Miami U. Alumni Assn. (dir. 1976—), Northwestern U. Profl. Women's Assn. Home: 414 Kelling Ln Glencoe IL 60022 Office: Leo Burnett Advt Agy Prudential Plaza Chicago IL 60601

BRANDT, WILLIAM ARTHUR, JR., cons. co. exec.; b. Chgo., Sept. 5, 1949; s. William Arthur and Joan Virginia (Ashworth) B.; B.A. with honors, St. Louis U., 1971; M.A., U. Chgo., 1972, postgrad., 1972—; m. Patrice Bugelas, Jan. 19, 1980. Asst. to pres. Pyro Mining Co., Chgo., 1972-76; commentator on bus. and polit. affairs Sta. WBBM-AM, Chgo., 1977; with Melaniphy & Asso., Inc., Chgo., 1976-78; pres., cons. Devel. Specialists, Inc., Chgo., 1978—; dir. Lafayette Coal Co., Pyro Mining Co., Black Tam Mining, Pasadena Corp., Harper Sq. Housing Corp., Central Transfer Corp. Mem. adv. bd. Sociological Abstracts, Inc., San Diego, 1979—. LaVerne Noyes scholar, 1971-74. Mem. AAAS, Am. Sociol. Assn., Am. Coll. Real Estate Cons., Internat. Sociol. Assn., Nat. Assn. Housing and Redevel. Ofcls., Nat. Assn. Real Estate Counsellors, Brit. Sociol. Assn., Chgo. Council Fgn. Relations, Ill. Sociol. Assn., Midwest Sociol. Soc., Soc. for Social Research, UN Assn., Aircraft Owners and Pilots Assn. Democrat. Roman Catholic. Clubs: Petroleum (Evansville, Ind.); Amelia Island (Fla.) Plantation. Contbr. articles to profl. jours. Office: 15 Spinning Wheel Rd Suite 426 Hinsdale IL 60521

BRANDZEL, SOL, lawyer, labor union ofcl.; b. Poland, June 5, 1913; s. Benny and Sophie (Grossman) B.; LL.B., J.D., De Paul U., 1938; m. Ruth Cohen, Mar. 2, 1941; children—Merle, Joel, Lisa. With Amalgamated Clothing and Textile Workers Union, 1950—, internat. v.p., asst. gen. sec.-treas., 1966-78, co-mgr. Chgo. and Central States joint bd., 1972-78; mem. exec. bd. Chgo. Fedn. Labor, AFL-CIO, 1972—; dir. Amalgamated Trust and Savs. Bank, Chgo., Amalgamated Bank of N.Y., Amalgamated Cotton Garment and Allied Industries Fund, 1964-79; chmn. Amalgamated Social Benefits Assn., 1973-79, now trustee; chmn. Amalgamated Life and Health Ins. Co., 1972-79, now trustee; pres. Amalgamated Centre, 1972-79, now dir.; pres. Amalgamated Child Day Care and Health Centre, 1972-79, now dir.; labor rep. Ill. Unemployment Compensation Bd., 1956-60; v.p. Labor Coalition on Public Utilities, 1976—. Bd. dirs., treas. Sidney Hillman Found. N.Y., 1962-78; bd. dirs. Jewish Bur. Employment Problems, 1955-60, Israel Histadrut Campaign, 1973—, Music for Westchester Symphony Orch., 1966-72, South East Commn., 1974—, Schwab Rehab. Hosp., 1976—; bd. dirs., v.p. Jewish Manpower Council, 1970—; nat. bd. dirs. Nat. Trade Union Council of Histadrut, 1966-72; chmn. Jewish Labor Com., 1973-76, now dir.; mem. Ill. Council Sr. Citizens Orgns.; mem. adv. bd. TRUST, Inc. (To Reshape Urban Systems Together), 1979—; chmn. Ill. Com. on Health Security, 1974—; commr. Chgo. Health Systems Agy., 1978—, also chmn. project rev. com.; mem. Chgo. Bd. Edn.; trustee Cook County Community Coll. Dist. 508, 1977—. Served from pvt. to maj., Q.M.C., U.S. Army. Mem. Chgo. Jewish Hist. Soc. (dir. 1977—). Office: Amalgamated Clothing and Textile Workers Union 333 S Ashland Blvd Chicago IL 60607

BRANN, EDWARD R(OMMEL), journalist; b. Rostock, Mecklenburg, Germany, May 20, 1920; s. Guenther O.R. and Lilli (Appel) B.; came to U.S., 1938, naturalized, 1966; B.A., Berea Coll., 1945; M.A., U. Chgo., 1946; postgrad. U. Wis., 1948-56; m. Helen Louise Sweet, Dec. 9, 1948; children—Johannes Weidler, Paul George. Asst. membership sec. central YMCA, Chgo., 1946-48; asst. editor Credit Union Mag., Madison, Wis., 1955-65; dir. hist. projects, asst. dir. publs. CUNA Internat., Inc., Madison, 1965-70, staff historian, 1958-65; asst. dir. publs. Credit Union Nat. Assn., Inc., Madison, 1970-72, asst. dir. communications, 1973—, sr. editor Credit Union mag., 1973—, coordinator Innovative Ideas Center, 1980—; dir. hist. projects World Council of Credit Unions, Inc., 1970-79, dir. European relations, 1972—. Active ARC, bd. dirs. Dane County chpt. Recipient Christo et Ecclesiae award Concordia Coll., Milw., 1968, Distinguished Alumnus award Berea Coll., 1977; named Ky. col. Mem. Am. Hist. Assn., Am. Polit. Sci. Assn., NEA, Assn. for Higher Edn., Luth. Laymen's League, Internat. Polit. Sci. Assn., Wis. Hist. Soc., Internat. Raiffeisen Union, Delta Phi Alpha, Pi Gamma Mu. Lutheran. Clubs: Madison Press, Chicago Press. Contbr. articles to profl. jours. Home: PO Box 383 Madison WI 53701 Office: PO Box 431 Madison WI 53701

BRANNON, VICTOR DEWITT, research inst. exec.; b. Des Moines, Aug. 26, 1909; s. Ralph William and Carrie Pearl (Hamblin) B.; A.B., U. Ariz., 1931, A.M., 1932; student U. Wis., 1935-36; Ph.D., U. Mo., 1938; m. Dorothy Ellen Webb, Aug. 20, 1933; children—Vicki Rae, Richard Carlyle. Instr. polit. sci. U. of Ariz., summers 1931, 33; tchr. social scis. San Simon High Sch., 1933-34; research asst. N.Y. Bd. of Regents Inquiry into the cost and character of pub. edn., 1936-37; researcher and statistician Mo. State Highway Dept. and Mo. State Planning Bd., 1938-39; asst. dir. St. Louis Govtl. Research Inst., 1939-46, dir., 1947—; research cons. St. Louis, St. Louis County Bd. Freeholders, 1954, bd. trustees Met. St. Louis Sewer Dist., 1955, St. Louis Charter Bd. Freeholders, 1956-57; research cons. St. Louis Police Dept., 1947-49, 1957-65; sec. Constl. Revision Study Com., 1962; research cons. Com. on Municipalities and Services in St. Louis County, 1958, St. Louis County Charter Com., 1979. Adv. council U. Mo. Sch. Bus. and Pub. Adminstrn., 1965-66. Mem. Govtl. Research Assn. (trustee 1950, 51, pres. 1961-62), Mo. Hist. Soc., Phi Kappa Phi, Phi Delta Kappa. Author articles on polit. sci. Home: 7 Hillard Rd Glendale MO 63122 Office: 915 Olive R 908 Saint Louis MO 63101

BRANNON, VINCENT LEE, concrete constrn. co. exec.; b. Fayetteville, Ark., Mar. 19, 1947; s. Oran Kelly and Wanda Fay B.; student Kans. State U., 1965-66, Mo. So. State Coll., 1966-67; B.S. in Indsl. Tech., Bldg. Design and Constrn., Kans. State Coll., Pittsburg, 1969; m. Joy Lea Carnahan, June 20, 1970; children—Veronica Ann, Matthew Kelly. Draftsman, estimator R.E. Smith Constrn. Co., Joplin, Mo., 1969-71; archtl. draftsman Migdonio Seidler & Assos., Pittsburg, 1973-75; draftsman Allgeier, Martin & Assos., Joplin, Mo., 1971-73, chief archtl. draftsman, project coordinator, 1975-78; founder, pres. Brannon Basement Co., Inc., Galena, Kans., 1978—. Elder, bd. chmn. Southside Christian Ch., Baxter Springs, Kans., 1977—; sec.-treas. bd. dirs. Rural Water Dist. #2, Riverton, Kans., 1978—. Served with Army N.G., 1969-75. Mem. Riverton Jaycees (charter mem., pres. 1978—). Home and Office: Route 1 Box 376 Galena KS 66739

BRANOVAN, LEO, prof. emeritus; b. Kishinev, Romania, Apr. 17, 1895; came to U.S., 1914, naturalized, 1926; s. Itzik and Sophia (Swartz) B.; B.S. in Elec. Engring., U. Wis., 1924; M.S. in Applied Math., U. Chgo., 1927; postgrad. (part-time) Columbia U., 1935-38; m. Pearl Lhevine, July 7, 1933; 1 dau., Rosalind Branovan Turner. Engr., Gen. Electric Co., Ft. Wayne, Ind., 1924-26; instr., cons. math. U. Minn., 1927-31; math. cons. J.D. Goode Co., Chgo., 1932-34; full-time cons. mathematician, N.Y.C., 1935-38; instr., cons. Bklyn. Poly. Inst., 1939-44; mem. faculty Marquette U., Milw., 1944—, asso. prof. math., 1955-70, prof. emeritus, 1970—; math. cons., Milw., 1970—. Mem. Am. Math. Soc., AAUP, Am. Soc. Engring. Edn., AAAS, Wis. Acad. Arts, Letters and Sci., math. socs. Austria, Netherlands, Belgium, Italy, Denmark and Sweden, Pi Mu Epsilon. Clubs: Wis. Alumni, Statesman's; Loyalty, Quarter Century (Marquette U.). Author research paper: Umbilics on Hyperellipsoids in Four Dimensions. Office: 1131 W Wisconsin Ave Milwaukee WI 53233

BRANSDORFER, STEPHEN CHRISTIE, lawyer; b. Lansing, Mich., Sept. 18, 1929; s. Henry and Sadie (Kohane) B.; A.B., Mich. State U., 1951; J.D., U. Mich., 1956; LL.M., Georgetown U., 1958; m. Peggy Ruth Deisig, May 24, 1952; children—Mark, David, Amy, Jill. Admitted to Mich. bar, 1956, U.S. Ct. Appeals D.C., 1959, U.S. Supreme Ct. bar, 1959; trial atty. U.S. Dept. Justice, Washington, 1956-58; spl. asst. U.S. atty. for D.C., 1958-59, also atty.-editor U.S. Dept. Justice, Washington; asso. Miller, Johnson, Snell & Cummiskey, Grand Rapids, Mich., 1959-63, partner, 1963—; vis. instr. Mich. State U., 1973—; lectr. Inst. Continuing Legal Edn., 1973-75; mem. Mich. Supreme Ct. com. on standard jury instructions, 1963-72, com. on rules of evidence, 1975-76; mem. Mich. Civil Service Commn., 1975-78, chmn., 1977-78; Republican candidate for atty. gen. Mich., 1978; trustee Mich. State Bar Found.; pres. Grand Rapids Child Guidance Clinic. Served with AUS, 1951-53. Fellow Am. Bar Found.; mem. Am., Grand Rapids (trustee) bar assns., State Bar Mich. (commr. 1968—, pres. 1974-75), Bar Assn. D.C., 6th Circuit Jud. Conf. (life), Phi Alpha Delta, Delta Chi. Presbyterian (elder, trustee). Club: Rotary. Home: 7250 Bradfield Rd Ada MI 49301 Office: 465 Old Kent Bldg No 1 Vandenberg Center Grand Rapids MI 49503

BRANSON, BYRON MONROE, research physicist; b. Greensboro, N.C., June 24, 1929; s. Byron Russell and Bessie Gilmore (Phipps) B.; B.S. in Physics, Guilford Coll., 1951; m. Wilhelmina Braddock, Sept. 7, 1957; children—Sara Carolyn, Hannah Bess, Christopher Byron. Tchr. public schs., Guilford, N.C., 1952-53; exec. sec. Homewood Friends Meeting (Quakers), Balt., 1953-56; physicist, chief radiometrics Robert A. Taft San. Engring. Center, USPHS, Cin., 1957-66; research physicist, chief radiation protection Nuclear Medicine Lab., Bur. Radiol. Health, FDA, Cin., 1966-78, chief Lab. Adminstrv. Support, 1978-80, asst. to dir. for adminstrn., 1981—; lectr. dept. radiology U. Cin. Coll. Medicine, 1969—. Active Religious Soc. Friends, 1947—; mem. exec. com. Ohio Valley Yearly Meeting, 1966-78, 81—; trustee Friends Home, Inc., 1966-81, v.p., 1972-76, 81, pres., 1976-80; block chmn. North Avondale Neighborhood Assn., chmn. Pupil Enrichment Program, 1973-75. Recipient Superior Work Performance award USPHS, HEW, 1958; High Quality Performance, Quality Increase award FDA, USPHS, HEW, 1971. Mem. Soc. Nuclear Medicine, Health Physics, Soc., Am. Assn. Physicists in Medicine of Am. Inst. Physics, Internat. Radiation Protection Assn., Sigma Xi. Club: Masons. Contbr. articles to sci. jours. Home: 3923 Leyman Dr Cincinnati OH 45229 Office: Nuclear Medicine Lab FDA Cincinnati Gen Hosp Cincinnati OH 45267

BRANSON, JAMES R., bank personnel ofcl.; b. Springfield, Mo., Sept. 18, 1940; s. Ivan Roland and Freida Elizabeth (Baker) B.; student MacMurray Coll., Abilene, Tex., 1961-62; B.A. in Psychology, Drury Coll., 1966; m. Mary Diane Kempker, Nov. 7, 1964; children—Andrew Franklin, Susan Marie. With outting products div. Coleman Co., Wichita, Kans., 1966-67; with ammunition plant Nat. Gypsum Co., Parsons, Kans., 1967-69; dir. personnel Boatmens Union Nat. Bank, Springfield, Mo., 1969—; personnel cons. 7-11 Corp.; instr. Am. Inst. Banking. Exec. advisor Jr. Achievement, 1979-80; chmn. March of Dimes, 1971-77; commr. Ozark council Boy Scouts Am., 1969-71, scoutmaster, 1980—. Served with USAF; 1959-63. Mem. Am. Soc. Personnel Adminstrs., Sierra Club. Republican. Home: 2218 E Cardinal St Springfield MO 65804 Office: PO Box 1157 Southside Station Springfield MO 65807

BRANSTAD, TERRY E., lt. gov. Iowa; b. Leland, Iowa, Nov. 17, 1946; grad. U. Iowa and Drake U. Law Sch.; married Chris Branstad; 2 children. Sr. partner firm Branstad & Schwarm; mem. Ho. of Reps., 1972-74, 74-76, 76-78; mem. House Judiciary and Law Enforcement com., Labor and Indsl. Relations com., Ways and Means Com., Edn. Budget subcom.; lt. gov. State of Iowa, 1979—. Del. to dist. and state Republican convs., 1968, 70, 72, 74, 76, 78, 80; alt. del. Rep. Nat. Conv., 1976, del., 1980. Served with U.S. Army, 1969-71. Recipient Army Commendation medal. Mem. Nat. Conf. Lt. Govs. (intergovtl. relations com.), Farm Bur., Jaycees, Lake Mills C. of C., Am. Legion. Club: Lions. Office: Office of Lt Gov State House Des Moines IA 50319

BRANTLE, THOMAS FRANCIS, statistician; b. Bklyn., Oct. 16, 1951; s. Thomas Francis and Grace Dorothy (Fay) B.; B.S. in Math. cum laude, SUNY, Cortland, 1973; M.S. in Computer Sci. and Stats., U. R.I., 1976; M.A. in Stats. and Ops. Research, Pa. State U., 1979. Research asst. U. R.I., 1974-75, Pa. State U., 1979; instr. math. Asnuntuck Community Coll., Enfield, Conn., 1975-78; research asso. computer sci. and stats. U. R.I., summers 1976, 77; sr. research scientist transp. research dept. Gen. Motors Research Labs., Warren, Mich., 1979—. Mem. Am. Statis. Assn., Ops. Research Soc. Am., Assn. Computing Machinery, IEEE Computer Soc. Club: Mich. Racquetball Assn. Home: 845 Lidlow St Apt E204 Rochester MI 48063 Office: Transp Research Dept Gen Motors Research Labs Warren MI 48090

BRASS, ALAN WILLIAM, hosp. adminstr.; b. Youngstown, Ohio, Mar. 13, 1948; s. William A. and Julia C. (Costarella) B.; A.B., Youngstown State U., 1970; M.S., Ohio State U., Columbus, 1973; m. Deborah A. James, Aug. 22, 1970; children—Mark Alan, Glen Mathew. Adminstrv. asst. Columbus Children's Hosp., 1972-73, asst. adminstr., 1973-77, asso. exec. dir., 1980—; adminstr. Mott Children's, Women's & Holden Perinatal Hosps., U. Mich., Ann Arbor, 1977-78, asso. dir. ops. Med. Center, 1978-80; lectr. Bur. Public Health Adminstrn., 1978-80; faculty hosp. adminstrn. program Ohio State U., 1980—. Trustee ednl. trust fund Ohio State U., 1976-77; co-chmn. exec. com. United Way, 1978-80. Recipient Traineeship award USPHS, 1973, Outstanding Young Man of Yr. award Jr. C. of C., 1978. Mem. Nat. Assn. Children's Hosps. (mem. fin. and legis. com. 1977-80), Am. Coll. Hosp. Adminstrs., Assn. Care of Children in Hosps., Am. Hosp. Assn., Comprehensive Health Planning Council Southeastern Mich., Ohio Hosp. Assn., Mich. Hosp. Assn., Young Adminstrs. Group Central Mich., Ohio State U. Hosp. and Health Services Alumni Assn. (pres. 1977-79). Democrat. Roman Catholic. Home: 6597 Farlook Ct Columbus OH 43229 Office: 700 Children's Dr Columbus OH 43205

BRATAAS, NANCY OSBORN, state senator, mgmt. and data processing cons.; b. Mpls., Jan. 19, 1928; d. John Draper and Flora Lozier (Warner) Osborn; student U. Minn., 1945-47; m. Mark Gerard Brataas, Nov. 27, 1948; children—Mark, Anne. Pres. Nancy Brataas Assos. Inc., cons. charitable and polit. orgns., Rochester, Minn.; mem. Minn. Senate, St. Paul, 1975—. State chairwoman Minn. Republican Com., 1963-69, Minn. Rep. Fin. Com., 1969-71. Mem. AAUW. Episcopalian. Club: Zonta. Office: 139 State Office Bldg Saint Paul MN 55155

BRATTON, EARL ALLEN, trade assn. exec.; b. Oskaloosa, Iowa, Aug. 13, 1921; s. Arthur Allen and Naomi Opal (Wise) B.; student Burlington (Iowa) Community Coll., 1940-42, Ill. Inst. Tech., 1946-47; m. Shirley Lucille Cornelius, Nov. 27, 1943; children—Sandra, Gary, Barry. Western div. mgr. Mobile Homes Mfrs. Assn., Long Beach, Calif., 1950-58; asst. exec. dir. Evanston (Ill.) C. of C., 1958-59; exec. dir. Steel Plate Fabricators Assn., Downers Grove, Ill., 1959—. Served with USMC, 1942-45. Decorated Air medal. Cert. assn. exec. Mem. Am. Soc. Assn. Execs., NAM (nat. indsl. council), U.S. C. of C. (com. of 100), Chgo. Soc. Assn. Execs. (chmn. 1977-78). Home: 4N941 Crane Rd Saint Charles IL 60174 Office: 2901 Finley Rd Downers Grove IL 60515

BRAUDE, ADELE COVY (MRS. JACOB M. BRAUDE), designer; b. Cin.; d. Tobias and Martha (Rosenberg) Covy; student U. Cin. Coll. Music; m. S. Henry Englander, Feb. 10, 1927 (dec. Aug. 1944); children—Ann Englander, Jane E. (Mrs. Berkson); m. 2d, Jacob M. Braude, Feb. 22, 1946 (dec. Dec. 24, 1970). Sec.-treas. The Nordell Co., 1931-44, pres., 1944-47; dir. The Gidding Co., 1946-58. Pres., Cin. chpt. Los Angeles Sanitorium, 1935; v.p. Jr. Council Jewish Women, Cin., 1936; pres. nat. women's com. Greater Chgo. chpt. Brandeis U., 1956; mem. Com. Restoration of Hull House; bd. dirs. Chgo. Women's Aid, Deborah Women's Club; active fund drives A.R.C., Community Fund. Designer, builder miniature rooms done to scale, reprodns. of ancient, period and historic rooms and bldgs. Address: 1000 Lake Shore Plaza Chicago IL 60611

BRAUDE, MICHAEL, banker; b. Chgo., Mar. 6, 1936; s. Sheldon and Nan (Resnik) B.; B.S., U. Mo., 1957; M.S. (Samuel Bronfman fellow), Columbia U., 1958; m. Linda Miller, Aug. 20, 1961; children—Peter, Adam. Vice pres. Merc. Bank, Kansas City, Mo., 1965-70, Commerce Bank of Kansas City, 1970—; exec. v.p. Am. Bank, Kansas City, 1979—; tchr. evening div. U. Kans., 1967-70, Avila Coll., 1974-77. Vice chmn. dean's adv. com. U. Mo. Sch. Bus., 1977-79; v.p. Kansas City Philharmonic Orch., 1977-79; trustee Metro Community Coll. Found., Kansas City, 1978-78. Mem. Bank Mktg. Assn., Mo. Bankers Assn. Jewish. Clubs: Homestead Country (Shawnee Mission, Kans.); Kansas City. Author: Managing Your Money, 1969; author 12 children's books. Home: 5319 Mission Woods Terr Shawnee Mission KS 66205 Office: Am Bank & Trust Co 1 W Armour Blvd Kansas City MO 64111

BRAUER, STEPHEN FRANKLIN, mfg. exec.; b. St. Louis, Sept. 3, 1945; s. Arthur John, Jr., and Jane (Franklin) B.; student Washington and Lee U., 1963-64; B.A., Westminster Coll., 1967; m. Camilla Cary Thompson, June 12, 1971; children—Blackford Fitzhugh, Rebecca Randolph, Stephen Franklin. Sales and mktg. ofcl. Hunter Engring. Co., St. Louis, 1971-78, exec. v.p., 1978-81, pres., 1981—. Served to 1st lt. C.E., AUS, 1968-70. Decorated Army Commendation Medal (U.S.), Cross of Gallantry (Vietnam); recipient Public Works medal Republic of Viet Nam, 1970. Republican. Episcopalian. Club: St. Louis Country. Home: 15 Dromara Rd Saint Louis MO 63124 Office: 11250 Hunter Dr Bridgeton MO 63044

BRAUN, CAROL MOSELEY, state legislator; b. Chgo., Aug. 16, 1947; d. Joseph J. and Edna A. (Davie) Moseley; B.A., U. Ill., 1969; J.D., U. Chgo., 1972; m. Michael D. Braun, 1973; 1 son, Matthew. Legal intern firms in Chgo., 1970, 71; admitted to Ill. bar, 1972; asso. firm Davis, Miner & Barnhill, Chgo., 1972-74; asst. U.S. atty. No. Dist. Ill., 1974-78; mem. Ill. Ho. of Reps. from 24th Dist., 1978—. Bd. dirs. Hyde Park-Kenwood Health Center, Chgo. Recipient Best Legislator award Ind. Voters Ill.-Ind. Precinct Orgn., 1980, Lottie Holman O'Neal 1st Term Legislator award Ill. Women's polit. Caucus, 1980; also numerous certs. appreciation, public service awards. Mem. Am. Judicature Soc., Ill. Bar. Assn., Cook County Bar Assn., Chgo. Council Lawyers, Nat. Assn. Negro Bus. and Profl. Womens Clubs, Nat. Hook-Up Black Women, Chgo. LWV, Hyde Park Hist. Soc., Conf. Women Legislators, Democratic Women's Caucus, Ams. for Dem. Action (dir.). Author newspaper column. Office: 7060 S Merrill St Chicago IL 60649

BRAUN, ROBERT ALEXANDER, psychiatrist; b. Chemnitz, Germany, Dec. 14, 1910; s. Leo and Bertha (Eisenschiml) B.; came to U.S., 1939, naturalized, 1946; M.D., U. Vienna (Austria), 1937; m. Gertrud E. Mittler, Jan. 6, 1946; children—Eleanor, Ronald. Intern, William McKinley Meml. Hosp., Trenton, N.J., 1940-41; resident in psychiatry Rochester (Minn.) State Hosp., 1950-51, staff psychiatrist, 1951-56; resident in psychiatry Lafayette Clinic, Detroit, 1956-58, staff psychiatrist, 1958-60; clin. dir. Clinton Valley Center (formerly Pontiac State Hosp.), Pontiac, Mich., 1960-63, dir. Oakland Div., 1963-80; pvt. practice psychiatry, 1980—; clin. asso. prof. dept. psychiatry Mich. State U., 1969—. Diplomate Am. Bd. Psychiatry. Fellow Am. Psychiat. Assn. Home: 815 Kirts Rd Troy MI 48084 Office: 1777 Axtell Rd Troy MI 48084

BRAUN, ROBERT CLARE, assn. exec.; b. Indpls., July 18, 1928; s. Ewald Elsworth and Lila (Inman) B.; B.S. in Journalism-Advt., Butler U., 1950; postgrad. Ind. U., 1957, 66. Reporter, Northside Topics Newspaper, Indpls., 1949, advt. mgr., 1950; asst. mgr. Clarence E. Crippen Printing Co., Indpls., 1951; corp. sec. Auto-Imports, Ltd., Indpls., 1952-53; pres. O. R. Brown Paper Co., Indpls., 1953-69; Robert C. Braun Advt. Agy., 1959-70, Zimmer Engraving Inc., Indpls., 1964-69; former chmn. bd. O. R. Brown Paper Co., Zimmer Engraving, Inc.; advt. cons. Rolls-Royce Motor Cars, 1957-59; exec. dir., chief exec. officer Historic Landmarks Found., Ind., 1969-73; exec. v.p., purchasing Mgmt. Assn. Indpls., 1974—; pres. A.P.S. Industries, Inc., 1979—; nat. v.p. Associated Purchasing Publs., 1981—; gen. mgr. Midwest Indsl. Show, 1974—, Midwest Office Systems and Equipment Show, 1974—, Grand Valley Indsl. Show, 1974—, Evansville Indsl. Show, 1981. Chmn., Citizens' Adv. Com. to Marion County Met. Planning Dept., 1963; pres. museum com. Indpls. Fire Dept., 1966—; mem. adv. com. Historic Preservation Commn. Marion County, 1967-73; Midwestern artifacts cons. to curator of White House, Washington, 1971-73; mem. Mayor's Contract Compliance Adv. Bd., 1977—; mem. Mayor's Subcom. for Indpls. Stadium, 1981—; mem. Met. Mus. Art, Indpls. Mus. Art. Bd. dirs. Historic Landmarks Found. Ind., 1960-69; dir., sec. Ind. Arthritis and Rheumatism Found., 1960-67, pres., 1969, dir., 1970—, dir. Asso. Patient Services, 1976—; pres. Amanda Wasson Meml. Found., 1961-72, Huggler-Ault Meml. Trust, 1961-72. Recipient Meritorious Service award St. Jude's Police League, 1961; citation for meritorious service Am. Legion Police Post 56, 1962; Nat. Vol. Service Citation, Arthritis Found., 1979; Margaret Egan Meml. award Ind. Arthritis Found., 1980. Mem. Marion County Hist. Soc. (dir. 1964—, pres. 1965-69, 74-76, 1st v.p. 1979), Am. Guild Organists (mem. Indpls. chpt., charter mem. Franklin Coll. br.), Indpls. Humane Soc., Ind. Museum Soc. (treas., dir. 1967-74), Internat. Fire Buff Assos., Indpls. Second Alarm Fire Buffs (sec.-treas. 1967, pres. 1969), Ind. Hist. Soc., Nat. Hist. Soc., Nat. Trust Historic Preservation, Smithsonian Assn., Soc. Archtl. Historians, Am. Heritage Soc., N.A.P.M. Editors Group (nat. sec. 1979-81, nat. chmn./pres. 1981—), Am. Assn. State and Local History, Decorative Arts Soc. Indpls., Ind. Soc. Assn. Execs., Nat. Assn. Purchasing Mgmt., Purchasing Mgmt. Assn. Indpls. (dir. 1974—), Victorian Soc. Am. (nat. sec. 1971-74), Lambda Chi Alpha, Alpha Delta Sigma, Sigma Delta Chi, Tau Kappa Alpha. Club: Indpls. Press, Rolls-Royce Owners. Author: The Mr. Eli Lilly that I Knew, 1977. Editor: Historic Landmarks News, 1969-74; Hoosier Purchasor mag., 1974—. Contbr. articles to profl. jours. Home: 1415 W 52d St Indianapolis IN 46208 Office: 527 Glendale Bldg 6100 N Keystone Ave Indianapolis IN 46220

BRAUN, WARREN D., state senator; b. June 12, 1934; B.S. in Polit. Sci., Marquette U.; M.A. in History, U. Wis., Milw.; 3 children. Tchr., coach Waukesha Meml. High Sch., Milw., Pius XI High Sch., Milw.; dist. alderman, Milw., 1968-76; mem. Wis. State Senate, 1976—; mem. joint com. on fin., chmn. legis. council spl. com. on community correctional programs, mem. judiciary and consumer affairs com. Address: Milwaukee WI *

BRAY, ANDREW MICHAEL, indsl. sales co. exec.; b. Norway, Mich., July 31, 1938; s. Andrew John and Ethel Mary (Cronick) B.; B.S.M.E., Mich. Tech. U., 1960; postgrad. U. Wis., Milw., 1961-63; m. Bethel Barbara Schultz, July 14, 1962; children—Susan Mary, lMark Andrew. Engr., AC Electronics Co., 1960-63; engr. research and devel. Paper Converting Machine Co., Green Bay, Wis., 1963-67; chief engr. Magna-Print Co., Green Bay, 1967-68; sales engr. J.M. Grimstad Inc., Green Bay, 1968-74; pres. OEM Devel. Corp., Oconto Falls, Wis., 1974-77; pres. Tech Draulics Ltd., Oconto Falls, 1975—; instr. mech. engring. U. Wis., Green Bay, 1964-69. Town chmn. Town of Suamico (Wis.), 1974—; sec. Suamico San. Dist., 1972—. Mem. Fluid Power Soc. Roman Catholic. Clubs: K.C., Elks. Contbr. articles to profl. publs. Inventor in field. Home: 3244 Maple Grove St Suamico WI 54173 Office: Tech Draulics Ltd Bowling Green Ln Industrial Park PO Box 164 Suamico WI 54173

BRAY, DAVID LANTZ, SR., electrostatic equipment ofcl.; b. Cleve., Oct. 12, 1952; s. Robert John and Eunice (Lantz) B.; B.S. in Acctg. with distinction, Ind. U., 1976; m. Kristen Marie Oscarson, Jan. 19, 1973; children—Janice Marie, David Lantz. Staff acct. Lester Witte & Co., Indpls., 1976-79; asst. controller Ransburg Electrostatic Equipment, Indpls., 1979—. Guarantor Clowes Hall. C.P.A. Mem. Am. Inst. C.P.A.'s, Ind. C.P.A. Soc., Culver Legion, Ind. U. Alumni Assn., Park Tudor Fathers Assn. Republican. Club: Ind. U. Men's. Home: 7421 Sunset Ln Indianapolis IN 46260 Office: PO Box 88220 Indianapolis IN 46208

BRAY, PIERCE, telephone co. exec.; b. Chgo., Jan. 16, 1924; s. Harold A. and Margaret (Maclennan) B.; B.A., U. Chgo., 1948, M.B.A., 1949; m. Maud Dorothy Minto, May 14, 1955; children—Margaret Dorothy, William Harold, Andrew Pierce. Fin. analyst Ford Motor Co., Dearborn, Mich., 1949-55; cons. Booz, Allen & Hamilton, Chgo. and Manila, 1955-58; mgr. pricing Cummins Engine Co., Columbus, Ind., 1958-61, controller, 1961-66; v.p. fin. Weatherhead Co., Cleve., 1966-67; v.p. Mid-Continent Telephone Corp., Hudson, Ohio, 1967-70, treas., 1967-77, v.p. fin., 1970-81, exec. v.p. fin., 1981—, dir., 1976—, also chmn. various subs.; dir. Cardinal Fund; trustee Cardinal Govt. Securities Trust; instr. fin. and econs. U. Detroit, 1952-54. Trustee Beech Brook, treatment center for disturbed children, Pepperpike, Ohio, 1972—, treas., 1976-79, pres., 1979-81. Served with AUS, 1943-46; PTO. Mem. Fin. Execs. Inst., U.S. Ind. Telephone Assn. (chmn. investor relations com. 1974—), Inst. Public Utilities (exec. com. 1978—, chmn. 1981—), Cleve. Treasurers Club, Delta Upsilon. Presbyterian (elder). Clubs: Downtown Athletic (N.Y.C.); Union, Midday (Cleve.); Walloon Lake (Mich.) Yacht (commodore), Walloon Lake Country. Home: 31173 Northwood Dr Pepper Pike OH 44124 Office: 100 Executive Pkwy Hudson OH 44236

BRAY, RANDALL CHARLES, savs. and loan assn. exec.; b. Waterloo, Iowa, Jan. 22, 1944; s. Russell LaVerne and May Marie (Neipert) B.; B.A., U. No. Iowa, 1967; m. Margaret Jean Dexter, Aug. 12, 1967; children—Sara Kathlyn, Christopher Charles. Asst. loan officer Bohemian Savs. and Loan, Cedar Rapids, Iowa, 1969-71, asst. sec., 1971-72, v.p., 1972-73, adminstrv. asst. to pres., 1973-75, exec. v.p., 1975-76, pres., 1976—. Pres. bd. dirs. YMCA; chmn. fin. com., dir. Mercy Hosp.; bd. dirs. Cedar Rapids Art Center, Am. Cancer Soc.; mem. exec. com. Greater Downtown Assn. Mem. U.S. Savs. and Loan League, Iowa Savs. and Loan League (dir., chmn. mortgage lending com.), Savs. Instns. Mktg. Soc. Am. Republican. Methodist. Club: Rotary (dir., pres. Cedar Rapids 1981-82). Office: 320 3d St SE Cedar Rapids IA 52401

BRAYER, ROGER CHARLES, metallurgist; b. Aubervilliers, Seine, France, July 26, 1923; came to U.S., 1946, naturalized, 1952; s. Jules Ernest and Rachel Eloise (Leloup) B.; B.S., U. Paris, 1944; Certificate d'Etudes Superieures, Sorbonne, 1945; M.S., St. Louis U., 1950; postgrad. Rensselaer Poly. Inst., 1959-63; m. Edith Marie Silies, Dec. 27, 1947; children—Michel Roger, Mark Jean, Patrick Charles, Anne-Marie Suzanne. Spectrographer, analyst, devel. engr. Vickers Electric Div., 1951-58; devel. spectrographer, research chemist, nuclear metallurgist, project engr. Combustion Engring. Nuclear Div., 1958-66; chief metallurgist Vactec, Inc., Maryland Heights, Mo., 1966-69, research and devel. mgr., 1969-73, product mgr., 1973—, safety coordinator, 1976-80, safety dir., 1980—. Mem. disaster team ARC, 1979; scoutmaster Boy Scouts Am., 1979. Served with French Arty., 1945. Chaplain Grady Scholar, 1946. Mem. Am. Chem. Soc., Soc. for Applied Spectroscopy, Am. Soc. for Metals, French Soc. St. Louis (v.p. 1949-50), Sigma Xi. Roman Catholic. Home: 214 Stoneyview Ct Creve Coeur MO 63141 Office: Vactec Inc 10900 Page Blvd Saint Louis MO 63132

BRAZIER, DONN PAUL, museum exec.; b. Dawson, Minn., Oct. 4, 1917; s. William A. and Bessie (Brown) B.; B.S., U. Wis., 1940; postgrad. Marquette U., 1940-41; m. Betty Marion Deppiesse, July 2, 1942; children—Terry Edward, Michael Allan, Liza Lisette, Barry Brooks, Brett Lynn. Ednl. curator Milw. Public Museum, 1946-57; TV tchr. public schs., Milw., 1957-58; ednl. supr. Museum Sci. and Natural History, St. Louis, 1959-61, dir., 1961—. Served with USAAF, 1941-46. Recipient disting. alumnus award U. Wis., Milw., 1967. Fellow AAAS, mem. Am. Assn. Museums, Acad. Sci. St. Louis. Home: 1455 Fawn Valley St Saint Louis MO 63131 Office: Oak Knoll Park Clayton MO 63105

BRECKINRIDGE, DANA WELLS, mgmt. cons.; b. Green Bay, Wis., Aug. 9, 1949; s. William Lewis and Carolyn (Wells) B.; B.S. in Mech. Engring., U. Mo., Rolla, 1972; M.B.A., U. Chgo., 1977. Engr., Caterpillar Tractor Co., 1973-75, Union Electric Co., 1977-78; cons. mfg. planning Internat. Harvester Co., Chgo., 1978-80; mgmt. cons. Case & Co., Inc., 1980—. Served with U.S. Army, 1972-73; capt. Res. Mem. ASME, Soc. Automotive Engrs., Res. Officers Assn. (chpt. sec.-treas. 1978), Civil Affairs Assn. St Louis (v.p. 1978); hon. mem. Tau Beta Pi, Pi Tau Sigma, Phi Kappa Phi. Presbyterian. Address: 9 Woodhaven Rd Webster Groves MO 63119

BRECKON, DONALD JOHN, educator; b. Port Huron, Mich., June 11, 1939; s. Robert Joseph and Margaret Elizabeth (Wade) B.; A.A., Port Huron Community Coll., 1959; B.S., Central Mich. U., 1962, M.A., 1963; M.P.H. (USPHS trainee), U. Mich., 1968; Ph.D., Mich. State U., 1977; postgrad. U. Wis., 1965-66, Western Mich. U., 1968; m. Sandra Kay Biehn, Sept. 4, 1959; children—Lori E., LeeAnne M., Lisa C., Lynanne W. Instr. health edn. Central Mich. U., Mt. Pleasant, 1963-68, asst. prof., 1968-72, asso. prof., 1972-81, prof. health edn., 1978-81, asst. dean health, phys. edn. and recreation, 1981—; cons. hosps. and health agencies. Mem. governing council Health Systems Agy., Region 6, Mich., 1976-79; bd. dirs. Am. Cancer Soc., 1977-79, Community Council on Drug Misuse, 1976-78. Recipient Central Mich. U. Teaching Effectiveness award, 1975; Disting. Service award Mich. Alcoholism and Addiction Assn., 1977; Mich. Dept. Edn. scholar, 1971; Yale U. Drug Dependence Inst. scholar, 1973; Midwest Inst. of Alcohol Studies, Mich. Dept. Public Health scholar, 1974; Am. Council on Edn. Leadership Devel. program fellow, 1979. Mem. Mich. Public Health Assn. (pres. 1976-77), Am. Public Health Assn., Soc. Public Health Edn. (pres. 1978-79), Internat. Soc. Pub. Health Edn., Coalition of Mich. Health Edn. Orgns., Mich. Alcohol and Addiction Assn., Am. Alliance for Health and Phys. Edn. Contbr. articles to profl. jours. Home: 1413 Crosslanes St Mount Pleasant MI 48858 Office: Central Mich Univ Mount Pleasant MI 48859

BREDE, ARDELL FREDERICK, hosp. exec.; b. Austin, Minn., June 23, 1939; s. Fred and Linda Bertha (Scheel) B.; A.Commerce, Austin Jr. Coll., 1957-59; postgrad. U. Minn., 1970-71, Brigham Young U., 1974; m. Judith Ellen Nelson, Mar. 24, 1961; children—Leslie, Scott, Jennifer. With Rochester (Minn.) Methodist Hosp., 1959—, dir. admissions and bus. services, 1975—. Mem. utilization review com. Mayo Clinic, 1970—; chmn. Olmsted County United Way, 1982—; mem. citizens adv. task force Rochester Attraction Center, 1979—. Mem. Hosp. Fin. Mgmt. Assn., Southeastern Minn. Health Systems Agy. Lutheran. Club: Rochester Quarterbacks. Home: 431 14th Ave SW Rochester MN 55901 Office: Rochester Methodist Hospital 201 W Center St Rochester MN 55901

BREDEKAMP, MARRIOTT WARFIELD, chem. engr., educator; b. Jacksonville, Fla., June 7, 1915; s. Herman Henry and Estelle Elizabeth (Warfield) B.; B.S., U. Md., 1938, M.S., 1939, Ph.D. (U.S. Bur. Mines fellow), 1941; m. Mary Elizabeth Klinger, May 30, 1941; children—Judith Ann, David Alan, Susan Jean. Instr. chem. engring. Mich. Coll. Mining and Tech., Houghton, 1941, asst. prof., 1946-51, asso. prof., 1951-58, prof., 1958—; asst. prof. chem. engring. Va. Poly. Inst., Blacksburg, 1942-44; chem. engr. Clinton Engr. Works, Oak Ridge, 1944-46. Mem. Am. Inst. Chem. Engrs., Am. Chem. Soc., Am. Soc. Engring. Edn., Sigma Xi, Delta Sigma Phi, Alpha Chi Sigma, Phi Lambda Upsilon. Republican. Lutheran. Home: 211 East St Houghton MI 49931 Office: Dept Chem Engring Michigan Technol U Houghton MI 49931

BREDENKAMP, NORMAN LOUIS, elec. engr.; b. Peoria, Ill., Jan. 2, 1944; s. John Louis and Dagmar (Soyring) B.; student DeVry Tech. Inst., 1962-64. Self-employed radio technician, Browns, Ill., 1958-62, radio and TV technician, Browns, 1964-65; elec. engr. Pacific Press & Shear, Mount Carmel, Ill., 1967-70; computer analyst RCA, Palm Beach Gardens, Fla., 1967-70; self-employed radio and TV technician, Palm Beach Gardens, 1970-72; radio announcer, program dir. WVMC-WSAB, Mt. Carmel, Ill., 1972-73; self-employed trouble shooter, Grayville, Ill., 1973—. Mem. Grayville Days Com.; vol. Fire Dept.; active Civil Defense. Mem. IEEE, Instrument Soc. Am., C. of C., Am. Sunbathing Assn. Clubs: CB Radio; Traveliers (Lake Geneva, Wis.). Home: Route 1 Grayville IL 62844 Office: Alexander Ln Grayville IL 62844

BREECE, ROBERT WILLIAM, JR., lawyer; b. Blackwell, Okla., Feb. 5, 1942; s. Robert William and Helen Elaine (Maddox) B.; B.S.B.A., Northwestern U., 1964; J.D., U. Okla., 1967; LL.M., Washington U., St. Louis, 1970; m. Elaine Marie Keller, Sept. 7, 1968; children—Bryan, Justin, Lauren. Admitted to Okla. bar, 1967, Mo. bar, 1969, U.S. Supreme Ct. bar, 1976; practice law, St. Louis, 1968—. Mem. Mo. Bar Assn., Am. Bar Assn., Tax Execs. Inst. Inc., Am. Soc. Corp. Secs. Inc. Presbyterian. Clubs: Forest Hills Country (pres. 1978), Mo. Athletic, University. Home: 35 Crown Manor Chesterfield MO 63017 Office: 500 N Broadway Suite 1800 Saint Louis MO 63102

BREED, EILEEN JUDITH, educator; b. Chgo., Sept. 18, 1945; d. John Joseph and Helen Agatha (Hoy) Kennedy; B.A., Northeastern Ill. U., 1966, M.A., 1976, postgrad., 1980-81; postgrad. Nat. Coll. Edn., 1981; m. Harvey Breed, Feb. 3, 1973; 1 dau., Diana Marie Parks. Tchr., Canty Elem. Sch., Chgo., 1967-76; tchr. St. Raymond's Sch., Mt. Prospect, Ill., 1976-78; pvt. practice diagnosis and remediation learning disabilities, cons. spl. edn., Des Plaines, Ill., 1976-78; prin. Angel Town Pvt. Sch., Des Plaines, 1978-79; Title I tchr./coordinator Nipper Sch., spl. edn. facility, Des Plaines, 1979—; tchr. parent-edn. classes; cons. pvt. schs. Mem. Council Exceptional Children, Council on Understanding Learning Disabilities, Nat. Assn. Retarded Citizens, Assn. Supervision and Curriculum Devel. Club: Epilepsy Parent Support Group (pres.). Initiated various spl. edn. programs. Home: 1011 W Grant Dr Des Plaines IL 60016 Office: 1101 E Gregory Des Plaines IL 60016

BREEDLOVE, JAMES GERALD, bus. exec.; b. Opp, Ala., Nov. 7, 1920; s. E. Marvin and Mary (Jeffcoat) B.; B. Ceramic Engring., Ga. Inst. Tech., 1950; m. Carolyn Elizabeth Archer, Nov. 27, 1947; children—Mary Carolyn Breedlove Peacock, Sally Elizabeth Breedlove Byrne, Donna Ellen. Ceramic engr. Tech. Ceramic Products div. 3M Co., Chattanooga, 1950-53, mgr. Titania div. lab., 1953-63, mgr. new product devel. lab., 1963-68, research supr., St. Paul, 1968—. Chief aux. police, Signal Mountain, Tenn., 1964-73. Served to sgt. AUS, 1941-45. Recipient Disting. Community Service award Signal Mountain Lions Club, 1968. Mem. Am. Ceramic Soc., Inst. Ceramic Engrs. Democrat. Episcopalian. Patents and publs. in fields tech. ceramics, dielectrics, procelain enamels. Inventor composite armor plate (ceramic-glass fiber). Home: 88 Walden Burnsville MN 55337 Office: 3M Co Tech Ceramic Products Div St Paul MN 55101

BREEN, BERNARD JOSEPH, def. contracting co. exec.; b. Norwich, Conn., Mar. 9, 1943; s. Arthur Bernard and Eleanor Mary (Kelly) B.; B.S. in Math., Purdue U., 1966; m. Marguerite Ann Piscitello, June 2, 1962; children—Kelly Ann, Traci Lynn. Analyst, Electric Boat Div., Groton, Conn., 1966-75; data systems specialist Eastern Data Systems Center, Groton, 1975-77; corp. cons. Gen. Dynamics Corp., St. Louis, 1977-79, mgr. computer aided design/computer aided mfg. 1979-81, dir. computer aided design and computer aided mfg., 1981—; instr. Thames Valley State Tech. Coll., Norwich, 1970-76. Fin. chmn. Our Lady of Lourdes Ch., Gales Ferry, Conn., 1976. Mem. Com. Research and Engring. Auto and Prodn. in Shipbldg., Assn. Computing Machinery, Soc. Mfg. Engrs., AIAA (chmn. CAD/CAM tech. com.). Roman Catholic. Home: 15305 Country Ridge Dr Chesterfield MO 63017 Office: 12101 Woodcrest Exec Dr Saint Louis MO 63141

BREEN, JOHN GERALD, mfg. co. exec.; b. Cleve., July 21, 1934; s. Hugh Gerald and Margaret Cecelia (Bonner) B.; B.S., John Carroll U., 1956; M.B.A., Case Western Res. U., 1962; m. Mary Jane Brubach, Apr. 12, 1958; children—Kathleen Anne, John Patrick, James Phillip, David Hugh, Anne Margaret. With Clevite Corp., Cleve., 1957-73, gen. mgr. foil div., 1969-73, gen. mgr. engine parts div., 1973-74; group v.p. indsl. group Gould Inc., Rolling Meadows, Ill., 1974-77, exec. v.p., 1977-79; pres. Sherwin Williams Co., Cleve., 1979-81, chmn., pres., chief exec. officer, 1981—, also dir.; dir. Parker-Hannifin Corp., Cleve., Republic Steel, Cleve., Nat. City Bank, Cleve. Served with U.S. Army, 1956-57. Clubs: Pepper Pike, Union, Cleve. Skating, Country. Home: 2727 Cranlyn Rd Shaker Heights OH 44122 Office: Sherwin Williams Co 101 Prospect Ave NW Cleveland OH 44115

BREEN, KATHERINE ANNE, speech and lang. pathologist; b. Chgo., Oct. 31, 1948; d. Robert Stephen and Gertrude Catherine (Bader) Breen; B.S., Northwestern U., 1970; M.A. (U.S. Rehab. Services trainee), U. Mo., Columbia, 1971. Speech/lang. pathologist Fulton (Mo.) pub. schs., 1971-73; co-dir. Easter Seal Speech Clinic, Jefferson City, Mo., summers 1972, 73; speech/lang. pathologist Shawnee Mission (Kans.) pub. schs., 1973—; staff St. Joseph's Hosp., Kansas City, Mo., 1978—; pvt. practice speech therapy; cons. E. Central Mo. Mental Health Center; guest lectr. Fontbonne Coll., St. Louis. Clin. certification in speech pathology. Mem. Am., Kans. speech and hearing assns., NEA, Mo. State Tchrs. Assn., Kansas City Alumni Assn. of Northwestern U. (dir. alumni admissions council, Outstanding Leadership award for work on alumni admissions council 1981), Friends of Art Nelson/Atkins Art Gallery and Museum (vol.), Zeta Phi Eta. Methodist. Home: 6865 W 51st Terr Apt 1C Shawnee Mission KS 66202 Office: 7235 Antioch Shawnee Mission KS 66204

BREGSTEIN, RICHARD FREDRIC, corp. communications exec.; b. N.Y.C., Apr. 25, 1936; s. Samuel Joseph and Muriel (Rubine) B.; B.A., U. Vt., 1957; m. Jane Bell Henning, Dec. 18, 1968; children—Alison Ruth, Jared Joseph. Mgr. community relations Prudential Ins. Co., Newark, 1960-71; mgr. public info. Coll. of Medicine and Dentistry of N.J., Newark, 1971-73; pres. Aspen Group, Inc., Newark, 1973-74; dir. community relations and health info. Martland Med. Center, 1974-76; dir. pub. affairs Ill. Hosp. Assn., Oak Brook, 1976-79; dir. public and profl. relations Joint Commn. on Accreditation of Hosps., Chgo., 1979—; lectr. on health care mktg., public relations and governing bds. Pres. bd. New Well Narcotic Rehab. Center, 1971-72; bd. dirs. Urban League Essex County, 1973-76; bd. dirs. Interracial Council for Bus. Opportunity of N.J., 1965-68; bd. dirs. Am. Lung Assn. of N.J., 1975-76; mem. City of Newark Narcotic Adv. Council, 1971-76; bd. dirs. Newark dist. ARC, 1973-76. Mem. Am. Mktg. Assn., Chgo. Mktg. Assn., N.Y. Acad. Scis., Acad. Hosp. Public Relations. Home: 606 Chippewa Ln Darien IL 60559 Office: 875 N Michigan Ave Chicago IL 60611

BREHM, WILLIAM ALLEN, JR., urban planner; b. Neenah, Wis., Jan. 18, 1945; s. William Allen and Katharine (Gilbert) B.; B.A., Lawrence U., 1967; M.U.P. (Richard King Mellon fellow 1967-68), Mich. State U., 1973; m. Patricia Lee Kelley, Dec. 30, 1967; children—Laura Kelley, William Hunt, Katharine Ann. Dir. planning Charter Twp. of Meridian (Mich.), 1969-72; v.p., treas. Planning Cons. Services, Inc., Lansing, Mich., 1972-76; dir. planning Manson, Jackson, Kane, Architects, Inc., Lansing, 1974-76; dir. planning and devel. City of Appleton (Wis.), 1976—, exec. dir. Redevel. Authority, 1979—. Trustee, Charter Twp of Meridan, 1972-74, supr., 1974-76; dist. chmn. Boy Scouts Am., 1979-81. Lic. profl. community planner, Mich. Mem. Am. Inst. Cert. Planners, Am. Planning Assn., Urban Land Inst., Nat. Trust Historic Preservation, Council Urban Econ. Devel., Assn. Wis. Planners (treas. 1977-79, pres. 1981—), Wis. Econ. Devel. Assn., Mich. Soc. Planning Ofcls., Delta Tau Delta. Mem. United Ch. of Christ. Club: Rotary. Home: 716 S Fidelis Dr Appleton WI 54911 Office: 200 N Appleton St Appleton WI 54911

BREIHAN, EDNA MARIA THIES (MRS. ARMIN HENRY BREIHAN), ret. educator; b. Flossmoor, Ill., Jan. 22, 1911; d. Henry Frederick and Anna (Cohrs) Thies; student Valparaiso U., 1928-30; A.B., Coll. of St. Francis, 1953; M.Ed., De Paul U., 1957; certificate advanced study in reading U. Chgo., 1966; m. Armin Henry Breihan, June 26, 1937; children—Joanne, James. Tchr., Lutheran Parochial Schs., Detroit, Chgo., 1930-37; pvt. tchr. remedial reading, Homewood, Ill., Flossmoor, 1945-51; tchr. Culbertson Sch., Joliet, Ill., 1953-57, Central Sch., Lockport, Ill., 1955-58; reading cons. Lockport Twp. High Sch. 1958-66; reading coordinator Lockport Twp. Sch. Dist. 205, 1966-71, chmn. reading dept., 1971-75. Mem. Lockport Woman's Club (hon.), NEA, Nat. Soc. for Study Edn., Internat. Reading Assn. (past pres. Will County council), Ill. Edn. Assn., Internat. Platform Assn., Lockport Bus. and Profl. Women's Assn., Assn. Supervision and Curriculum Devel., Am. Inst. Mgmt., AAUW, Delta Kappa Gamma, Chi Sigma Xi. Lutheran. Home: 1512 Briggs St Lockport IL 60441

BREIHAN, ERWIN ROBERT, cons. engring. co. exec.; b. nr. St. Louis, Oct. 31, 1918; s. Arthur George and Genevieve Louise (Wolz) B.; B.S. in Civil Engring., Washington U., St. Louis, 1940, postgrad., 1940-41; m. Antoinette V. Corcoran, Nov. 24, 1945; children—John Robert, Patricia Anne, Steve Michael. Structural engr. St. Louis Ordance Plant, 1941-42; with Horner & Shifrin, Inc., St. Louis, 1940—, exec. v.p., 1971-73, pres., chief exec. officer, 1973—. Chmn. Tomahawk dist. Boy Scouts Am., 1978-81. Served to capt. USNR, 1942-71. Fellow ASCE, Am. Cons. Engrs. Council, Royal Soc. Health; mem. Am. Assn. Airport Execs., Am. Soc. Mil. Engrs., Am. Water Works Assn., Nat. Soc. Profl. Engrs., Cons. Engrs. Council Mo. (pres. 1977), Am. Road and Transp. Builders Am., Am. Public Works Assn., Engring. Alumni Assn. Washington U. (pres. 1970), Century Club Engring. (pres. 1969), Mil. Order World Wars, Engrs. Club (St. Louis) (pres. 1976), Cons. Engrs. Council Mo. (pres. 1977), Mo. Soc. Profl. Engrs. (pres. elect 1981). Clubs: Washington U., Mo. Athletic. Office: 5200 Oakland Ave Saint Louis MO 63110

BREITENBECK, JOSEPH M., bishop; b. Detroit, Aug. 3, 1914; s. Matthew J. and Mary A. (Quinlan) B.; student U. Detroit, 1932-35; B.A., Sacred Heart Sem., Detroit, 1938; postgrad. Gregorian U., Rome, Italy, 1938-40; S.T.L., Catholic U., Washington; J.C.L., Lateran U., Rome, 1949. Ordained priest Roman Catholic Ch., 1942; asst. at St. Margaret Mary Parish, Detroit, 1942-44; sec. to Cardinal Mooney, 1944-58; sec. to Cardinal Dearden, 1959; pastor Assumption Grotto, 1959-67; consecrated bishop, 1965; bishop of Grand Rapids, Mich., 1969—. Episcopal adviser Nat. Cath. Laymens Retreat Conf. Mem. Nat. Conf. Cath. Bishops (com. chmn.). Office: 265 Sheldon Ave SE Grand Rapids MI 49502*

BRELSFORD, WILLIAM H., II, mathematician, educator; b. Dayton, Ohio, July 15, 1939; s. William H. Brelsford and Martha Beverly (Bunger) Brelsford Rose; B.S. in Edn., Ashland (Ohio) Coll., 1961; postgrad. Xavier U., 1965; M.A.T. (NSF grantee), Southeastern (Okla.) State Coll., 1966; postgrad. (NSF grantee) U. Kans., 1967, (NSF grantee) Oberlin Coll., 1968, Kent (Ohio) State U., 1973; m. Joanne Rosalie Winfield, July 25, 1959; children—Gregg Lee, Mark Allen, Joel Lance. Tchr. math., athletic coach, Madison Twp. Schs., Dayton, Ohio, 1961-67; asst. prof. math., football coach, Ashland Coll., 1967—. Mem. Nat. Council Tchrs. Math., Math. Assn. Am. Mem. Brethren Ch. Home: 1651 Co Rd 995 RD 6 Ashland OH 44805 Office: Ashland Coll Ashland OH 44805

BREMS, HANS JULIUS, educator; b. Viborg, Denmark, Oct. 16, 1915; came to U.S., 1951, naturalized, 1958; s. Holger and Andrea (Golditz) B.; Ph.D., U. Copenhagen, 1950; hedersdoktor Swedish Sch. Econs., 1970; m. Ulla C. Simoni, May 20, 1944; children—Lisa, Marianne, Karen Joyce. Asst. prof. U. Copenhagen, 1943-51, U. Calif., Berkeley, 1951-54; mem. faculty U. Ill., Champaign, 1954—, prof. econs., 1955—; vis. prof. UCLA, 1953, U. Mich., 1957, U. Calif., Berkeley, 1958, Harvard U., 1960, U. Kiel (W. Ger.), 1961, 72, U. Colo., 1963, Gottingen (W. Ger.) U., 1964, Hamburg (W. Ger.) U., 1967, U. Uppsala (Sweden), 1968, U. Lund (Sweden), 1970, 75, U. Goteborg (Sweden), 1972, U. Copenhagen, 1975, U. Stockholm, 1980. Mem. Royal Danish Acad. Scis. and Letters, Am. Econ. Assn., Royal Econ. Soc., Canadian Econs. Assn., L'Association Canadienne d'Economique. Author: Product Equilibrium under Monopolistic Competition, 1951; Output, Employment, Capital and Growth, 1959; Quantitative Economic Theory, 1968; Labor, Capital and Growth, 1973; A Wage Earners' Investment Fund - Forms and Economic Effects, 1975; Inflation, Interest and Growth, 1980; Dynamische Makrotheorie - Inflation, Zins und Wachstum, 1980. Home: 1103 S Douglas Ave Urbana IL 61801 Office: Commerce W 1206 6th St Champaign IL 61820

BRENGEL, FRED L., bus. exec.; b. Hicksville, N.Y., 1923; B.S.M.E., Stevens Inst. Tech., 1944; married. Test engr. Fairchild Aircraft Co., 1946; with sales staff instrument div. Permutit Co., 1946-47; with Johnson Controls Inc. (formerly Johnson Service Co.), Milw., 1948—, v.p. sales, 1963-65, exec. v.p., 1965-67, pres., chief exec. officer, 1967—, also dir.; dir. First Wis. Co., Heil Co., Sta-Rite Industries, Inc. Served to lt. USN, 1943-46. Office: Johnson Controls Inc 507 E Michigan St Box 423 Milwaukee WI 53201*

BRENIZER, NED WICKLIFFE, mgmt. info. specialist; b. Ft. Wayne, Ind., Oct. 20, 1930; s. Leo Cletus and Hazel Elizabeth (Wickliffe) B.; student Drake U., 1948-50; m. Adeline P. Sylvia, July 15, 1978; children—(by previous marriage) Scott R., Beth A.; stepchildren—Christine, Michael, James. With Capehart-Farnsworth Materials Mgmt., Ft. Wayne, 1951-57; PERT specialist ITT Fed. Div., Ft. Wayne, 1957-65; with Tokheim Corp., Ft. Wayne, Ind., 1965—, mgr. info. systems, mgr. sales adminstrn., 1978—; lectr., cons. in field. Recipient Assn. Systems Mgmt. Merit award, 1974, Achievement award, 1979; Am. Prodn. and Inventory Control Soc. Best Jour. Article of Year award, 1978. Mem. Assn. Systems Mgmt. Presbyterian. Contbr. articles to profl. jours. Home: 6312 Dumont Dr Fort Wayne IN 46815 Office: 1602 Wabash Ave Fort Wayne IN 46802

BRENNAN, DWIGHT JOHN, steel co. exec.; b. Chgo., June 25, 1950; s. John Harvey and Beryl Florence (Gatton) B.; B.A., Loras Coll., 1972; M.B.A., Loyola U. of Chgo., 1975; m. Bonita Jean Fenili, June 19, 1976; children—Emily Jean, Kathryn Marie. Collection mgr. Parker Hannifin Corp., Des Plaines, Ill., 1972-73; spl. agt. Ill. Crime Commn., Chgo., 1975-78; staff analyst Inland Steel Co., E. Chgo., Ind., 1979—. Recipient Letter of Commendation, U.S. Atty. Gen., 1979; Certificate of Appreciation, Ill. Crime Commn., 1978. Mem. Am. Mgmt. Assn., Chgo. Council on Fgn. Relations. Republican. Roman Catholic. Office: 3210 Watling St East Chicago IN 46312

BRENNAN, EDWARD A., retail exec.; b. 1934; B.S., Marquette U., 1955; married. Buyer, Benson Rixon Co., 1955-56; with Sears, Roebuck & Co., Chgo., 1956—, store mgr., Balt., 1967-69, asst. gen. mgr. N.Y. group, 1969-72, gen. mgr. Western N.Y. group, 1972-75, adminstrv. asst. to exec. v.p.-east, 1975-76, gen. mgr. Boston group, 1976-78, exec. v.p.-south, 1978-80, pres., chief operating officer, 1980-81, chmn. bd., chief exec. officer, 1981—, also dir.; dir. Allstate Ins. Co., First Nat. Holding Corp. Office: Sears Roebuck & Co Sears Tower Chicago IL 60684*

BRENNAN, EMMET JAMES, III, personnel cons.; b. St. Louis, Oct. 4, 1945; s. Emmet James and Rita Katherine (Perkinson) B.; student St. Louis U., 1963-65, Washington U., St. Louis, 1965-70, U. Mo., St. Louis, 1975; B.A. with honors in Mgmt., Webster Coll., 1978; m. Elizabeth Jane Webb, Mar. 7, 1970. Personnel specialist Otto Faerber & Assos., St. Louis, 1965-70; indsl. relations personnel mgr. Rexall Drug Co., St. Louis, 1970-71; compensation analyst Dart Industries, Los Angeles, 1971-74; corporate wage and salary adminstr., personnel devel. asso. Mallinckrodt, Inc., St. Louis, 1974-78; dir. St. Louis office Sullivan, Eisemann & Thomsen, St. Louis, 1978-80; pres. Brennan, Thomsen Assos., Inc., Chesterfield, Mo., 1980—; asst. dir. Compensation Inst., 1981—; guest lectr. various univs. and profl. socs. Lector, Incarnate Word Parish. Served with U.S. Army, 1966-68. Mem. Am. Compensation Assn., Am. Soc. for Personnel Adminstrn., Am. Mgmt. Assn., Phi Kappa Theta. Contbr. articles to profl. jours. Office: Brennan/Thomsen Assos Inc 106 Four Seasons Center Chesterfield MO 63017

BRENNAN, SISTER FLORA, artist, educator; b. Toledo, Ohio, Sept. 12, 1918; d. Andrew Philip and Clara Viola (Hartley) B.; B.A., Marygrove Coll., Detroit, 1952; M.E. in Art Edn., Wayne State U., 1961; M.F.A., U. Notre Dame, 1970. Joined Sisters of the Immaculate Heart of Mary, 1935; tchr. Mich. pvt. schs., 1940-53; tchr. fine arts and crafts St. Mary High Sch., Akron, Ohio, 1953-58, St. John High Sch., Jackson, Mich., 1958-62; founder dept. fine arts Cath. U. P.R., Ponce, 1962, chmn., 1962-71, instr. fine arts, 1971-81; tchr. Powers Central High Sch., Flint, Mich., 1981—; exhibited in various shows, including: Wayne State U. Alumni Show, 1962, Ponce Art Mus., 1970, 71, 73, U. P.R. Gallery, Mayaguez, 1970, Biblioteca Encarnacion Valdés of Cath. U., Ponce, 1975, 81; paintings and ceramics in numerous collections in U.S. and P.R.; art dir. Charismatic Renewal Services, Aguas Buenas, P.R., 1975-78; organizer, dir. Apostolate of the Sick, Ponce, 1973. Recipient Tchr. of Tchrs. plaque Ponce Dept. Public Instrn., 1978. Mem. Ponce Museum Club. Art editor Alabare, 1974-78; contbr. articles to profl. jours.

BRENNAN, JOHN JOSEPH, banker; b. Lackawanna, N.Y., Apr. 23, 1941; s. Charles H. and Irene A. (Davis) B.; B.A., Gannon U., 1963; M.B.A., Am. U., 1970; m. Charlotte S. Szymecki, June 1, 1963; children—Patricia, Kathleen, John. Asst. ops. officer Mellon Bank, Pitts., 1970-74, ops. officer, 1975-78; asst. v.p. check processing BancOhio Nat. Bank, Columbus, 1978-80, v.p. corp. services, 1980-81, v.p., mgr. corp. services, 1981—; instr. Am. Inst. Banking, 1976-78. Vice-pres. P.T.A., 1976-77, pres., 1977-78; pres. Westerville Soccer Assn., 1980—. Served to capt. U.S. Army, 1963-70. Decorated Bronze Star medal, Air medals. Mem. Am. Mgmt. Assn., Am. Bankers Assn., Bank Adminstrn. Inst. Office: 770 W Broad St Columbus OH 43215

BRENNAN, LEO JEROME, advt. exec.; b. Detroit, Sept. 19, 1942; s. Leo Jerome and Helen Louis (Wilson) B.; A. Bus., Wayne State U., 1967; spl. courses Macomb Community Coll., 1973, Eastside Sch. Body Design, 1962, Creative Center Design, 1963; m. Margaret Arlene Barr, Apr. 11, 1963; children—Christopher John, Wendy Ann, Stephanie Nicole. Project engr. Paramount Engring., Madison Heights, Mich., 1963-67; art dir., v.p. Van Mourik & Assos., Bloomfield Hills, Mich., 1968-70; pres. Leo Brennan Advt., Inc., Troy, Mich., 1970—. Recipient Liberty Bell award Oakland County, Mich., 1976, award Troy C. of C., 1980, Pyramid award Asso. Splty. Advertisers, 1977, award Indsl. Distbrs. for Gen. Elec., 1975. Mem. Bus. Profl. Advt. Assn., Mich. Advt. Assn. Council, Troy C. of C., Indsl. Marketers of Detroit, Detroit Adcrafters Club. Roman Catholic. Clubs: Warren Rotary, Fraternal Order of Police (Ferndale, Mich.), Garland Golf. Home: 2190 Babcock St Troy MI 48084 Office: 2359 Livernois Rd Troy MI 48084

BRENNAN, MARY THERESE, city ofcl.; b. St. Louis, Apr. 12, 1951; d. Francis Charles and Beulah Mary (Tornatore) B.; student parochial schs., St. Louis. Stenographer, Council on Human Relations, City of St. Louis, 1969-71, sec. Mcpl. Bus. Devel. Commn., 1971-73, exec. sec. to dir. Community Devel. Agy., 1973-80, exec. sec., adminstrv. asst. to mayor's exec. asst. Mayor's Office, 1980—. Home: 3410 McCausland Ave Saint Louis MO 63139 Office: Room 200 City Hall Mayor's Office Market and Tucker Sts Saint Louis MO 63103

BRENNAN, ROBERT LAWRENCE, psychometrician; b. Hartford, Conn., May 31, 1944; s. Robert and Irene Veronica (Connors) B.; B.A., Salem State Coll., 1967; M.A.T., Harvard U., 1968, Ed.D., 1970; m. Sandra Lee Spychala, Aug. 16, 1969; 1 son, Sean Michael. Research asso., lectr. Grad. Sch. Edn. Harvard, Cambridge, Mass., 1970-71; asst. prof. edn. SUNY, Stony Brook, 1971-76; sr. research psychologist Am. Coll. Testing Program, Iowa City, Iowa, 1976-79, dir. measurement research dept., 1979—; adj. faculty Sch. Edn. U. Iowa, 1979—; cons. Office Child Devel., HEW, 1975-79. Harvard prize fellow, 1967. Mem. Am. Ednl. Research Assn. (Div. D award 1980), Am. Statis. Assn., Am. Psychol. Assn., Am. Ednl. Research Assn., Nat. Council Measurement Edn., Psychometric Soc., Phi Delta Kappa. Asso. editor Jour. Ednl. Measurement, 1978—; contbr. articles to profl. jours. Home: 85 N Westminster St Iowa City IA 52240 Office: PO Box 168 Am Coll Testing Program Iowa City IA 52243

BRENNAN, ROBERT WALTER, assn. exec.; b. Chgo., Mar. 12, 1934; s. Walter R. and Grace A. (Mason) B.; B.S., U. Wis., Madison, 1957; m. Mary J. Engler, June 15, 1962; children—Barbara, Susan (twins). Tchr., coach Waukesha (Wis.) High Sch., 1960-63; track coach U. Wis., Madison, 1963-71; exec. asst. to mayor City of Madison, 1971-73; pres. C. of C., Madison, 1973—; dir. Cherokee Park, Inc. Chmn. bd. dirs. Clyde Dupin Reachout Ministries, 1974—; bd. dirs. Bill Glass Evangelistic Assn., 1972—. Named Madison Favorite Son, 1971. Mem. Wis. C. of C. (dir.), Madison Urban League, U. Wis. Alumni Assn., Nat. W Club, Wis. Urban League, C. of C. Execs., Wis. Hist. Soc., Fellowship Christian Athletes, Theta Delta Chi, Phi Epsilon Kappa. Club: Rotary. Midwest corr. Track & Field News, 1963-71; spl. events cons. Letterman Mag., 1971. Home: 5514 Comanche Way Madison WI 53704 Office: PO Box 71 Madison WI 53701

BRENNEMAN, RALPH FRANCIS, mfg. co. exec.; b. Cedar Rapids, Iowa, Feb. 6, 1932; s. Ernest E. and Mary N. (Webster) Brenneman; m. Sandra Lee Matthews, Dec. 10, 1955; children—Brad, Lisa, Scott, Erin, R. David. Buyer, Collins Radio Co., 1954-59; asst. mgr. Deeco Inc., 1959-63; purchasing mgr. Collins Radio Co., 1963-73; founded Brenneman & Asso. Inc., 1973—. Pres., Chs. United, Cedar Rapids/Marion, Iowa; past pres. Lutheran Interparish Ministry, chmn. joint purchasing com.; chmn. task force for aux. funding Luth. Family Service; benevolence rep. Iowa Synod, Luth. Ch. in Am. Mem. Elks, Am. Assn. Small Businessmen, Eastern Iowa Small Indsl. Bus. Assn. (chmn. 1981, 82), IEEE. Home: 1915 McGowan Blvd Marion IA 52302 Office: 201 35th St Marion IA 52302

BRENNEMAN, ROBERT MICHAEL, civil engr.; b. Council Bluffs, Iowa, Nov. 20, 1940; s. Robert Henry and Virginia Ruth (Neumann) B.; B.S. in Civil Engring., U. Nebr., Omaha, 1968, M.S. in Civil Engring., 1971; m. Joan Virginia Schwartz, Nov. 21, 1969; 1 dau., Kathryn Ann. Groundman, Union Pacific R.R., 1960-64; civil technician Leo A. Daly Co., Omaha, 1964-67, U.S. Army Corps Engrs., Omaha, 1967-68; project engr. Leo A. Daly Co., Omaha, 1968-72; sr. design engr. Upland Industries, Omaha, 1972-80, Portland Cement Assn., Omaha, 1980—; part-time pvt. cons.; profl. square dance caller. Registered profl. engr. 12 states; profl. land surveyor, Idaho, Oreg. Mem. Nat. Soc. Profl. Engrs., ASCE Democrat. Roman Catholic. Home: 4615 Spring St Omaha NE 68106 Office: PO Box 6211 Omaha NE 68106

BRENSING, DARRELL DEAN, assn. exec.; b. Great Bend, Kans., Sept. 23, 1935; s. Jacob Franklin and Hulda H. (Teichman) B.; B.S., Ft. Hays Kans. State Coll., 1957; M.S., Kans. State Coll., Pittsburg, 1967; Ph.D., Kans. State U., 1974; m. Patricia Lee Ginder, July 29, 1957; children—Douglas Alan, Kelly Ann. Tchr. indsl. arts Hutchinson (Kans.) public schs., 1957-65; coordinator distributive edn. Hutchinson High Sch., 1965-67; dir. secondary div. Central Kans. Area Vocat. Tech. Sch., Hutchinson, 1967-69; dir. Manhattan (Kans.) Area Vocat. Tech. Sch., 1969-76; v.p. Citizens State Bank and Trust Co., Manhattan, 1976-78; v.p. edn. Am. Inst. Baking, Manhattan, 1978—; cons. Kans. State U., 1979-80. Chmn. human relations bd. City of Manhattan, 1975-76; bd. dirs. Riley County chpt. ARC, 1976-79; bd. dirs. United Way of Riley County, 1978—, pres., 1981; chmn. Airport Adv. Bd., City of Manhattan, 1978—. Mem. Kans. Vocat. Assn. (pres. 1969-70), Am. Soc. Bakery Engrs., Am. Assn. Cereal Chemists, Manhattan C. of C. (v.p. 1975, dir. 1972-75). Mem. Christian Ch. (elder). Clubs: Rotary, Masons, Manhattan Country (pres., bd. dirs. 1974-76). Contbr. articles to profl. jours. Home: 128 S Dartmouth St Manhattan KS 66502 Office: 1213 Bakers Way Manhattan KS 66502

BRENTON, WILLIAM HENRY, banker; b. Dallas Center, Iowa, June 30, 1924; s. Woodward Harold and Etta (Spurgeon) B.; B.S.C., U. Iowa, 1949; grad. Advanced Mgmt. Program, Harvard U., 1975; m. Natalie Graham, June 15, 1948; children—Woodward Graham, Natalie, William Henry. Vice pres. Nat. Bank of Des Moines, 1955-58, pres., chmn., 1958—, dir., 1955—; treas. Brenton Banks, Inc., 1955-64, pres., 1964-69, chmn. bd., 1969—; chmn., dir. Benton Bank & Trust Co., Clarion and Urbandale, Iowa, Brenton Nat. Bank, Des Moines, Dallas County State Bank, Adel, Iowa, Poweshiek County Nat. Bank, Grinnell, Brenton State Bank, Eagle Grove; dir. South Des Moines Nat. Bank, Brenton Bank & Trust Co., Vinton, Brenton Bank & Trust Co. of Cedar Rapids, Brenton State Bank, Dallas Center, 1st Nat. Bank of Perry (Iowa), Fidelity Brenton Bank & Trust Co., Marshalltown, Brenton First Nat. Bank, Davenport, Iowa, N.W. Brenton Nat. Bank, Des Moines, Palo Alto County State Bank, Emmetsburg, Warren County Bank & Trust Co., Indianola, Jefferson State Bank; chmn., pres., treas., dir. Brenco Automation Center, Inc., 1966—; chmn. Brenton Land Co. Trustee, past pres. Des Moines Art Center, 1970-72; trustee Coffin Fine Arts Trust; bd. dirs. Iowa Methodist Hosp., Des Moines; chmn. bd. Brenton Found.; pres., treas. Greater Des Moines Com.; trustee, mem. exec. com. Drake U., Des Moines; bd. dirs., past pres. Iowa Natural Heritage Found.; trustee Iowa Coll. Found. Served with USAAF, 1943-46. Mem. Beta Gamma Sigma, Delta Tau Delta. Republican. Presbyterian. Clubs: Wakonda, Des Moines (Des Moines); Harvard (N.Y.C.); University (Chgo.); Tryall (Jamaica).

BRESKA, GEORGE JOSEPH, agronomist; b. Arcadia, Wis., Feb. 21, 1925; s. Joseph Dominic and Rose (Proxie) B.; B.S., U. Wis., River Falls, 1951, M.S., Madison, 1958; m. Patricia S. Sward, June 22, 1968. Mem. lab. mgmt. staff Olson Labs., Freeport, Ill., 1960-70, DeKalb (Ill.) AgResearch, 1971-72; pres. Farmers Lab. div. Soils Advisory, Inc., Freeport, 1972—. Mem. Am. Soc. Agronomy, Phi Sigma Soc. Roman Catholic. Home and Office: 1039 S Adams Ave Freeport IL 61032

BRESNAHAN, JAMES FRANCIS, educator; b. Springfield, Mass., Dec. 28, 1926; s. James Francis and Margaret Anna (Riley) B.; A.B., Coll. of Holy Cross, 1947; M.A., Weston Coll., 1953; J.D., Harvard U., 1954, LL.M., 1955; S.T.L., 1960; Ph.D., Yale U., 1972. Admitted to Mass. Supreme Jud. Ct. bar, 1955; joined S.J., Roman Catholic Ch., 1949; tchr. Cheverus High Sch., Portland, Maine, 1955-56; asst. prof. religious studies Fairfield U., 1962-66, 69-70; vis. prof. ethics Weston Coll., 1971-72; asso. prof. religious studies Regis Coll., 1972-74; prof. ethics Jesuit Sch. Theology in Chgo., 1975-81; vis. lectr. in med. ethics Northwestern U. Med. Sch., Chgo., 1978-80, in lawyers ethics, Law Sch., 1979, co-dir. ethics program, lectr. ethics Med. Sch., 1980—. Mem. com. to draft code of profl. conduct Canon Law Soc. Am., 1978-79. Fellow Soc. for Values in Higher Edn.; mem. AAUP (v.p. chpt. 1973-74), Soc. Christian Ethics (convenor ethics and law task force 1979-80, dir. 1981—), Council on Religion and Law, Ill. Coalition Against Death Penalty. Contbr. articles to profl. publs. Home: Jesuit House 5554 Woodlawn St Chicago IL 60637 Office: Ward 4-334 Northwestern U Med Sch 303 E Chicago Ave Chicago IL 60611

BRESSETT, KENNETH EDWARD, numismatist, investment cons.; b. Keene, N.H., Oct. 5, 1928; s. George Edward and Florence Elizabeth (Forkey) B.; student Dresser Bus. Sch., 1948; m. Bertha Britton, Oct. 7, 1950; children—Philip Edward, Richard Joseph, Mary Elizabeth. Sr. numismatic editor Western Pub. Co., Inc., Racine, Wis., 1959-69, mgr. numismatic publs., 1969-80; v.p. Kagin's Numismatic Investment Corp., Des Moines, 1980—, cons., lectr. in field; mem. U.S. Assay Commn., 1966. Fellow Am. Numis. Soc., Royal Numis. Soc.; mem. Am. Numis. Assn., Can. Numis. Assn. Roman Catholic. Editor: A Guide Book of U.S. Coins, 1960—; contbr. articles in field to profl. jours. Office: 1000 Insurance Exchange Bldg Des Moines IA 50309

BRETT, CHARLOTTE MAE, genealogist; b. Westport Twp., Dickinson County, Iowa, Nov. 30, 1904; d. John Franklin and Jessie Clara (Cummings) B.; cert. U. No. Iowa, 1927, B.A., 1933; M.A., Columbia U., 1946, postgrad., 1951, 53; postgrad. Western Ill. U., Macomb, 1958, Northwestern U., Evanston, Ill., 1964. Rural sch. tchr., 1924-25; elem. tchr., Guttenberg, Iowa, 1927-30, Mitchell, S.D., 1930-31, Smithland, Iowa, 1933-35, Western Springs, Ill., 1935-40, Hancock, Mich., 1941-44, Blue Island, Ill., 1944-70; ret., 1970; librarian Iowa Lakes Geneal. Soc.; family genealogist; former del. NEA convs.; chmn. cemetery canvass Clay County, Iowa, 1972—; regent Lydia Alden chpt. DAR, 1974-76; state corr. sec. Iowa Soc. Dames of the Ct. of Honor, 1974-78; regent Lakes chpt. Daus. of Am. Colonists, 1978-80, state chaplain Iowa, 1980—. Recipient Buffalo Robe, Camp Fire Girls, 1925; life membership Ill. P.T.A., 1969, cert. Clay County Hist. Soc., 1979. Mem. NEA (life), Chgo. Area Assn. Childhood Edn., Chgo. Art Inst. (life), 1st Families of Ohio, Daus. of War of 1812, Huguenot Soc., U. No. Iowa Alumni Assn. (life), numerous hist. socs. Clubs: Chgo. Doll Collectors, Cherrio Post Card. Author: (with others) Northwest Iowans Share Their Memories, 1978. Home: 218 E 4th St Apt 4A Spencer IA 51301

BRETT, RANDALL PHILIP, mgmt. cons.; b. Balt., June 14, 1950; s. Herbert Saul and Muriel (Berns) B.; B.A., U. Ill., 1972; M.Mgmt., Northwestern U., 1977; m. Deborah L. Lieber, May 20, 1973. Personnel mgr. Interstate Service Corp., Chgo., 1972-74; personnel mgr. Motorola, Inc., Schaumburg, Ill., 1974-77, 79; sr. cons. asso. Drake-Beam & Assos., Inc., Des Plaines, Ill., 1977-79; prin. Employee Relations Assos., Chgo., 1979—; mem. adj. faculty Elmhurst Coll.

Center for Spl. Programs. Mem. Am. Mgmt. Assn., Soc. Personnel Adminstrs. Greater Chgo., Am. Soc. Profl. Cons., Am. Soc. Personnel Adminstrn., Am. Soc. Tng. and Devel. Democrat. Mem. editorial rev. com. Am. Soc. Personnel Adminstrn. Contbr. articles to profl. jours.

BRETT, RICHARD JOHN, speech pathologist; b. Chgo., Sept. 5, 1921; s. Richard J. and Emily (Salter) B.; B.Ed., No. Ill. State Tchrs. Coll., 1943; M.S., U. Ill., 1947; student U. Amsterdam (Holland), 1949, U. Chgo., 1948-49, 62, 66-67, Northwestern U., 1967. Speech supr. Summer Residential Clinic, U. Ill., Urbana, 1948, 50, 52; speech pathologist Waukegan (Ill.) High Schs., 1946—; chmn. Chgo. Regional Interviewing Com. for Exchange of Tchrs., U.S. Dept. Edn., 1962—; del. to Internat. Fedn. of Free Tchr. Unions, Switzerland. 1953. Founder, Pub. Sch. Caucus, Chgo., 1973, chmn., 1973-76. Served with U.S. Army, 1943-45. Fellow Am. Speech and Hearing Assn. (membership com. 1975-77, conv. program com. 1974, 77); mem. Ill. Speech and Hearing Assn. (chmn. legis. com. 1964-65, treas. 1977-78, v.p. bus. affairs 1978-79), Internat. Council Exceptional Children (pres. Chgo. suburban chpt. 1949-50), Am. (co-chmn. internat. relations com. 1952-63), Ill. (chmn. profl. standards com. 1952-57), Lake County (pres. 1949-51, 64-67) fedns. tchrs., UN Assn., Mus. Contemporary Art, ACLU, Common Cause, Art Inst. Chgo., Chgo. Symphony Soc. Club: National Travel. Compiler: World Study and Travel for Teachers, 1952—; editor Five-O-Format, 1951-56, 66-69. Home: 616 4th St Waukegan IL 60085 Office: Waukegan East High School 1011 Washington St Waukegan IL 60085

BREUER, COY LEBURN, civil engr.; b. Phelps County, Mo., Apr. 3, 1924; s. Thomas Franklin and Minnie Mae (Agee) B.; B.S. in Civil Engring., U. Mo., Rolla, 1949; m. Ruby Irene Wycoff, Jan. 19, 1946; children—Rhonda Jean, Randal Coy, Rodney Kent. With Mo. Hwy. and Transp. Dept., and predecessor, 1949—, sr. engr., 1964-69, asst. div. engr., Jefferson City, 1969—. Bd. dirs. Meml. Community Hosp., Jefferson City, Mo., 1979. Served with AUS, 1943-45. Registered profl. engr., Mo. Mem. Acad. Civil Engrs., ASCE, Nat. Soc. Profl. Engrs., Hwy. Engrs. Assn. Mo., Mo. Soc. Profl. Engrs. Office: State Hwy Bldg Jefferson City MO 65102

BREWER, A. KEITH, physicist; b. Richland Center, Wis., Oct. 20, 1893; s. Edward and Hattie (Dove) B.; B.A., U. Wis., 1915, M.S., 1921, Ph.D., 1924; NRC fellow, Calif. Inst. Tech., 1924-27. Physicist, Fixed Nitrogen Research Lab., Washington, 1927-39; chief, mass spectrometer and isotope lab. Nat. Bur. Standards, Washington, 1932-46, chief sci. sect., naval ops., 1946-68; cons. physicist, Washington, 1968—. Co-founder, Richland Jr. Acad. Scis., 1973. Bd. dirs. A. Keith Brewer Found., Inc. Donor A. Keith Brewer Library, Richland Center. Fellow Am. Phys. Soc.; mem. Am. Chem. Soc., N.Y., Washington acads. sci., Washington Philos. Soc., Sigma Xi. Republican. Clubs: Masons, Shriners. Contbr. articles to profl. jours. Address: Sci Room A Keith Brewer Library Richland Center WI 53581

BREWER, ALTEN CLAIR, sci. coordinator, author; b. Hamilton County, Iowa, Dec. 1, 1914; s. Edward W. and Emma (Smith) B.; married, 2 children. B.A. in Sci. and Edn., William Jewell Coll., Liberty, Mo., 1936; M.Ed., U. Ark., Fayetteville, 1955; Ed.D. in Edn., U. Tenn., Knoxville, 1960; m. Margaret (dec.); children—Patricia, Maila; m. 2d, Nell. Instr. William Jewell Coll., Liberty, 1943-45; instr., coach Springfield (Mo.) Sch. Dist. R-12, 1945-55, prin., 1955-60, coordinator sci., 1960—. Bd. dirs. Springfield Airport, 1962-72. Mem. NEA, Nat. Sci. Tchrs. Assn., Nat. Sci. Suprs. Assn. (past pres.), Council Elementary Sci., Internat. (past pres.). Recipient Teaching Excellence Merit award Grade Tchrs. Mag., 1967, Mo. Sci. Educators award, 1969. Author: Exploring and Understanding Light, 1969, Exploring and Understanding Air, 1969, Elementary Science-Learning by Investigation, 1973. Contbr. articles. Home: 2456 S Franklin Springfield MO 65807 Office: 940 N Jefferson Springfield MO 65802

BREWER, GEORGE EUGENE FRANCIS, chem. cons.; b. Vienna, Austria, Jan. 23, 1909; s. Ernest and Sophia (Segalla) B.; A.B., State Coll. Vienna, 1928; M.Sc., U. Vienna, 1930, Ph.D. in Chemistry, 1932; m. Frances Joan Werner, June 29, 1933 (dec. Nov. 1965); m. Maxine R. Levin, Mar. 4, 1967. Came to U.S., 1940, naturalized, 1945. Asst. lectr. U. Vienna (Austria), 1933-36; tech. mgr. S. Wolf & Co. Textile Refining Mill, Erlach, Austria, 1936-38; lectr. Inst. de l'Industrie Textile de Brabant, Brussels, 1939; prof. Rosary Coll., River Forest, Ill., 1940-43; biochemist NRC project Elgin (Ill.) State Hosp., 1943-44; prof. chemistry, head dept. Marygrove Coll., Detroit, 1944-67; cons. Ford Motor Co., Detroit, 1957-67, staff scientist Mfg. Devel. Center, Dearborn, Mich., 1968-72; now coating cons.; Matiello Meml. lectr. Fedn. Socs. Paint Tech., 1973; mem. NRC com. ciphers, codes and punched card techniques, Washington, 1957-59; abstractor Chem. Abstracts, 1948-63. Recipient Midgley medal Detroit sect. Am. Chem. Soc., 1969, Doolittle award div. organic coatings and plastics chemistry, 1969; cert. cons. chemist, profl. chemist, mfg. engr. Fellow Am. Inst. Chemists (chmn. Mich. inst. 1969, pres. 1977—, Chem. Pioneer award 1978), Engring. Soc. Detroit (Engr.'s Week Gold award 1981); mem. Am. Chem. Soc. (councillor 1951—; chmn. Detroit sect. 1960, sec. div. organic coatings and plastics chemistry 1971, chmn. 1974), Met. Detroit Sci. Club (dir. 1948), N.Y. Acad. Sci., Nat. Sci. Tchrs. Assn., Catholic Austrian Confraternity, Chem. Coaters Assn. (program chmn. 1971-73, dir. 1974—, pres. 1976), Assn. Analytical Chemists (pres. 1959), Mich. Coll. Chem. Tchrs. Assn. (pres. 1954), Assn. Cons. Chemists and Chem. Engrs. Contbr. articles to profl. jours. Patentee electrophoretic deposition organic coatings. Home and office: 6135 Wine Lake Rd Birmingham MI 48010

BREWER, GORDON MONTEITH, athletic chmn.; b. Kalamazoo, Mich., May 22, 1923; s. Robert Oscar and Helen Cornelia B.; A.B., Hope Coll., 1948; M.A., U. Mich., 1952; m. Lorraine Virginia Bult, Aug. 14, 1948; children—Robert James, Lawrence Gordon, Daniel Richard, Susan Marie. Tchr., coach Byron Center High Sch., 1948-50; tchr., coach Kelloggsville High Sch., Grand Rapids, Mich., 1950-56; mem. faculty Hope Coll., Holland, Mich., 1956—, dir. athletics, 1960-80, chmn. dept. phys. edn., recreation and athletics, 1980—. Served with USAAF, 1943-45. Mem. Nat. Assn. Collegiate Dirs. Athletics, Nat. Collegiate Track Coaches Assn. Office: Hope Coll Holland MI 49423

BREWER, LAWRENCE THOMAS, dentist; b. Kansas City, Mo., June 23, 1951; s. Lonnie Lawrence and Jo Ann (Botilda) B.; student Center Mo. State U., 1969-71; B.S., Southeastern State U., Durant, Okla., 1973; D.D.S., U. Mo., Kansas City, 1977. Gen. practice dentistry, Orrick, Mo., 1977—, Higginsville, Mo., 1977—. Mem. ADA, Nat. Assn. Residents and Interns, Orrick Jaycees, Higginsville Jaycees. Lutheran. Office: PO Box 67 Creason St and Elm St Orrick MO 64077 also 14 E 18th St Higginsville MO 64037

BREWER, PAUL HUIE, advt. exec.; b. Alexandria, La., Jan. 24, 1934; s. Ralph Wright and Margot (Riviere) B.; B.A., La. Coll., Pineville, 1956; degree in advt. design and Famous Artists Schs., Westport, Conn., 1959; m. Anita Hines, May 16, 1953 (div. 1971); children—Anita Joy (dec.), Laura Riviere; m. 2d, Carole Lynn Kuhrt, July 8, 1972; 1 dau., Nicole Renee. Artist, Ralph Brewer's Studio and Engraving Co., Alexandria, 1952-54; art dir. Sta. KALB-TV, Alexandria, 1954-56; designer New Orleans Public Service Co., 1956; artist King Studio, Chgo., 1957; asst. art dir. Continental Casualty Co., Chgo., 1957-58; designer, art dir. Field Enterprises div. Chgo. Sun-Times, then dir. design; art dir. State Farm Ins. Cos., Bloomington, Ill., 1973, dir. art and design, 1973-77; prodn. mgr. and exec. art dir. U.S. Savs. and Loan League, Chgo., 1977—; one-man shows: La. Coll., 1963, Chgo. Public Library, Chgo. Press Club, 1972; illustrator: Who Am I?, 1973; portraits include: Jack Benny, Danny Kaye, Danny Thomas, Pablo Picasso,; advt. dir. Artists Guild Bull., 1965; chmn. Artists Guild Chgo. Watercolor Show, 1967. Bd. dirs. Artists Guild Chgo. Credit Union, House of Wray Corp. Ill., N. Shore Art League. Recipient awards Am. Newspaper Guild, Artists Guild Chgo., Famous Artists Sch., Graphic Arts Council Chgo.; Hartford Illustration award, 1968; Nat. award Louisville Rotogravure Assn., 1975; SIMSA nat. award, 1977 (3), 1979 (2); award of excellence Hopper Paper Co., 1978, 79; Addy awards State of Iowa, 1980 (2). Mem. Artists Guild Chgo., Famous Artists Sch. Alumni Assn., Am. Watercolor Soc. (asso.), Chgo. Soc. Communicating Arts (dir.), Chgo. Soc. Typographic Arts, N. Shore Art League, La. Coll. Alumni Assn. Presbyterian (elder). Designer and illustrator: New in the City; Count a Lonely Cadence. Home: 41 Red Oak Ln Highland Park IL 60035 Office: 111 E Wacker Dr Chicago IL 60601

BREWER, RUTH RUSSELL (MRS. JOHN I. BREWER), civic worker; b. Great Bend, Kan., June 21, 1904; d. Francis Vernon and Jettie (McBride) Russell; B.A., U. Wis., 1921; M.A., Columbia, 1923; m. John I. Brewer, June 2, 1928; 1 son, John V. Instr., Bradley U., Peoria, Ill., 1923-26; service rep. Trift Inc., Oak Park, Ill., 1927. Head surg. dressing unit ARC, Denver, 1943-44; chmn. women's div. Joint Appeal, Chgo., 1957; mem. woman's planning bd. Crusade of Mercy, 1957-69; treas. Kenwood Social Service Club, Chgo., 1953, 1st v.p., 1954, pres., 1955; treas. women's bd. Women's Aux. of Goodwill Industries, 1962-63. Bd. dirs., corr. sec., 1st v.p. woman's aux. Infant Welfare Soc., Chgo., 1960-63, pres., 1965-66, bd. advisers woman's aux., 1967-69, bd. dirs., 1968-71. Mem. Woman's bd. YWCA-Met. Chgo., 1968—. Mem. Kappa Alpha Theta. Club: Woman's Athletic (Chgo.). Home: 860 Lake Shore Dr Chicago IL 60611

BREWER, WILLIAM FRANCIS, psychologist; b. Pensacola, Fla., Feb. 16, 1941; s. William Francis and Pauline (Neisler) B.; B.A. magna cum laude, Harvard Coll., 1963; Ph.D., U. Iowa, 1967; m. Ellen Jane Furry, June 14, 1963; children—John William, Robert Stephen. Postdoctoral asso. Center for Human Learning U. Minn., 1967-69; asst. prof. psychology U. Ill., Urbana, 1969-75, asso. prof., 1975—, asso. prof. Inst. Communications Research, 1975—, co. dir. Center Study of Reading, 1979-80. USPHS fellow, 1966-67, postdoctoral trainee, 1969; NIMH grantee, 1976-81. Mem. Am. Psychol. Assn., Psychonomic Soc., Soc. Philosophy and Psychology, Linguistic Soc. Am. Coeditor: Theoretical Issues in Reading Comprehension, 1980. Home: 607 W Iowa St Urbana IL 61801 Office: Dept Psychology U Ill 603 E Daniel St Champaign IL 61820

BREWER, WILMA DENELL, educator; b. Riley, Kans., Oct. 18, 1915; d. Benjamin Clarence and Rosetta (James) B.; B.S., Kans. State U., 1935; M.S., Wash. State U., 1939; Ph.D., Mich. State U., 1950. Instr., Simpson Coll., Indianola, Iowa, 1939-40; from instr. to asst. prof. U. N.H., Durham, 1940-43; mem. faculty Mich. State U., East Lansing, 1943-57, prof., nutrition Iowa State U., Ames, 1957—, head dept., 1961-77. Mem. Am. Inst. Nutrition, Am. Dietetic Assn., Am. Home Econs. Assn., Am. Chem. Soc., AAAS. Methodist. Home: 1121 Hyland St Ames IA 50010 Office: Dept Food Nutrition Iowa State Ames IA 50010

BREWSTER, DONALD ELLIOTT, assn. exec.; b. Paterson, N.J., Jan. 29, 1924; s. Benjamin John and Sarah Neille (Elliott) B.; student U. Ill., 1942; B.S., Bradley U., 1950; postgrad. Ind. U., 1968, Washington U., St. Louis, 1971; m. Jerre Owens, Nov. 1958; children—Stephanie, Barbara Jean, Dawn. With Am. Cancer Soc., 1960—, exec. v.p. Mich. Div., Lansing, 1970—; asso. dir. Ketchum, Inc., Pitts., 1956-60. Chmn. fund raising campaign St. Paul Episcopal Ch., 1976, sr. warden vestry, 1978. Served with USN, 1943-46. Mem. Nat. Soc. Fund Raising Execs., U.S. Power Squadron, U.S. Coast Guard Aux. Republican. Clubs: University, Muskegon Yacht, Lansing Racquet. Home: 843 Longfellow Dr East Lansing MI 48823 Office: Am Cancer Soc 1205 E Saginaw St Lansing MI 48906

BREZINSKI, PAUL FRANK, podiatrist; b. Chgo., Mar. 17, 1952; s. I. Frank and Therese V. (Istok) B.; B.S., Bradley U., Peoria, Ill., 1974; D.P.M., Ill. Coll. Podiatric Medicine, 1978; m. Renata Maria Currie, Sept. 5, 1981. Practice podiatric medicine, Chgo., 1978—; mem. staff St. Mary of Nazareth Hosp. Center, 1979—; cons. St. Joseph Home for Aged, 1979—. Mem. Am. Podiatric Assn., Am. Public Health Assn., Ill. Podiatry Soc., Chgo. Soc. Polish Nat. Alliance, Sierra Club. Roman Catholic. Club: Toastmasters Internat. Home: 4442 N Linder St Chicago IL 60630 Office: 5301 W Fullerton Ave Chicago IL 60639

BRICCETTI, THOMAS BERNARD, orch. condr.; b. Mt. Kisco, N.Y., Jan. 14, 1936; s. Thomas Bernard and Joan Therese (Filardi) B.; student of Jean Dansereau, 1948-60, Richart Lert, 1963-64; student U. Rochester Eastman Sch. Music, 1953-54, Columbia Grad. Sch. Fine Arts, 1954-55; m. Billie Lee Mommer, July 10, 1978; children—Katherine Anne, David Clark. Pianist, composer, 1955-62; mus. dir. Pinellas County (Fla.) Youth Symphony, 1962-68, St. Petersburg (Fla.) Philharm. Orch., 1963-68, St. Petersburg Civic Opera Co., 1964-68; asso. condr. Indpls. Symphony Orch., 1968-78; mus. dir. Ft. Wayne (Ind.) Philharm. Orch., 1970-78, Univ. Circle Orch., Cleve. Inst. Music, 1972-75, Omaha Symphony Orch., 1975—, Nebr. Sinfonia, 1977—, Festival 1000 Oaks, 1978—; internat. guest condr., 1972—; prin. guest condr. Nat. Orch., Luxembourg, 1977. Recipient Prix de Rome for mus. composition Italian Govt., 1958-59; Ford. Found. fellow, 1961-62; Yaddo grantee, 1963; named Profl. Artist of Yr., Indpls., 1970. Mem. ASCAP, Phi Mu Alpha Sinfonia. Nat. Endowment for Arts commn. to compose Violin Concerto, 1967; other compositions. Home: 604 N 38th St Omaha NE 68131 Office: 310 Aquila Ct Omaha NE 68102

BRICE, JUANITA CHARLESTINE, educator; b. Bessemer, Ala., Aug. 16, 1928; d. Luther G. and Annie Louise (Craig) B.; B.S., Ala. State U., 1943; M.S., N.Y. U., 1953; postgrad. Miles Coll., Birmingham, Ala., 1962, U. So. Calif., Los Angeles, 1964, U. Ala., 1970. Tchr., Cobb Ave. High Sch., Anniston, Ala., 1943-53, Wenonah Jr. High Sch., Birmingham, 1953-60, Wenonah High Sch., Birmingham, 1960-68, No. High Sch., Flint, Mich., 1968—; sales clk. J. L. Hudson's Dept. Store, Flint, 1970—. Del., Democratic Precinct, Flint, 1977—, conv. del., 1977—. Recipient Civus Optimus, Mich. State U., 1977. Mem. United Tchrs. of Flint (treas. 1973-75), Mich. Edn. Assn., Am. Fedn. Tchrs., NEA, NAACP, Phi Delta Kappa, Alpha Kappa Alpha. Baptist. Clubs: Negro Bus. Women Profl., Order Eastern Star, Elks. Office: No High Sch G-3284 Mackin Rd Flint MI 48504

BRICE, L. RIDER, archtl. designer; b. Toledo, Ohio, Dec. 9, 1943; s. Leonard Rider Brice and Peggy Jean (Neale) Phillips; student Principia Coll., 1961-63; B.F.A., Ohio State U., 1968, B.Arch., 1975; m. Kristine Kay Artopoeus, Sept. 21, 1968; children—Trey, Colin, Tina. Design expeditor Richardson/Smith Inc., Worthington, Ohio, 1965-67, design service salesman, 1967-68; project designer Artolier Lighting & Sound div. Emerson Electric Co., Garfield, N.J., 1971-72; div. sales mgr. Electrolux div. Consol. Foods Corp., Fairfield, N.J., 1971-73, cons. designer, 1971-73; salesman Kenco Security Systems, Columbus, Ohio, 1974-76; archtl. designer Gene Swartz & Assos., Chillicothe, Ohio, 1976-77, C. Curtiss Inscho & Assos., Columbus, 1978—; v.p. Delta Tau Delta House Corp., 1973—; cons. residential design, 1976—. Mem. AIA. Christian Scientist. Home: 2164 Fairfax Rd Upper Arlington OH 43221 Office: 1560 Fishinger Rd Upper Arlington OH 43221

BRICKER, WILLIAM H., chem. co. exec.; b. Detroit, 1932; B.S., Mich. State U., 1953, M.S., 1954. Br. mgr. Ortho div. Calif. Chem. Co., 1954-57; gen. sales mgr. Chemagro, 1957-66; exec. v.p. Velsicot Corp., 1966-69; officer Diamond Shamrock Chem. Co., 1969-72, pres., 1972-74, v.p. Diamond Shamrock Corp., 1972-73, exec. v.p., 1953-75, chief operating officer, 1974-76, pres., 1975-79, chief exec. officer, 1976—, chmn. bd., 1980—, also dir.; dir. Soc. Nat. Bank, Soc. Corp., Lamson & Sessions & Samuel S. Moore & Co. Trustee John Carroll U., Univ. Hosp. Office: Diamond Shamrock Corp 1100 Superior Ave Cleveland OH 44114*

BRICKHOUSE, JOHN B. (JACK), radio, TV sports mgr.; b. Peoria, Ill., Jan. 24, 1916; s. John William and Daisy (James) B.; student Bradley U., Peoria; m. Nelda Teach, Aug. 7, 1939; 1 dau., Jean. Comml., sports announcer Sta. WMBD, Peoria, 1934-40; with WGN, Chgo., 1940-43, 44—, v.p., mgr. sports WGN and WGN TV, 1948—; v.p., mgr. sports WGN Continental Broadcasting Co., 1970—; free lance, comml. announcer, Chgo., 1945; sports announcer, 1947, N.Y. Giants baseball announcer, N.Y.C., 1946. Broadcaster radio and/or TV play-by-play World Series, All Star Baseball Game, All Star Football game, Rose Bowl, Sugar Bowl, Am. Bowl, Orange bowl, Chgo. Cubs, Chgo. White Sox games, Golden Gloves, Louis-Charles and Walcott-Charles fight, Rep. and Dem. nat. convs., Roosevelt Inauguration (1945), Chicago Bears football games, Chgo. Bulls basketball games, Inaugural Ball, Papal audience. Bd. dirs. Chgo. Boys Clubs, City of Hope, Chgo. Wesley Meml. Hosp.; trustee St. Procopius Coll., Bradley U., Peoria, Ill. Served as pvt. USMCR, 1943-44. Recipient numerous Emmy awards, bronze medallions for World Series coverage Look mag., 1954, 59; Man of Year award City of Hope, 1966; Communications award Lincoln Acad., 1968; named Best Sports Announcer, Am. Coll. Radio Arts and Scis.; Nat. Sportscasters and Sportswriters award as outstanding sportscaster of year in Ill. (5 times), Acor award Am. Coll. Radio Arts, Nat. Sportswriters and Broadcasters awards, many others. Mem. Western Golf Assn. (dir.), Acad. Television Arts and Scis. (past pres., gov. Chgo. chpt.). Writer for Chgo. Today, Chgo. Tribune, Ency. Brit. Yearbook, others; pub. Jack Brickhouse's Major League Baseball Record Book, 21 edits. Office: WGN Continental Broadcasting Co 2501 W Bradley Pl Chicago IL 60618*

BRICKLEY, JAMES HENRY, state ofcl.; b. Flint, Mich., Nov. 15, 1928; s. J. Harry and Marie E. (Fischer) B.; B.A., U. Detroit, 1951, LL.B., 1954; LL.M., N.Y. U., 1958; Ph.D. (hon.), Spring Arbor Coll., 1975, Detroit Coll. Bus., 1975, U. Detroit, 1977, Ferris State Coll., 1980, Saginaw Valley State Coll., 1980; children—Janice, James, William, Brian, Kathleen, Kelle. Spl. agt. FBI, 1954-58; admitted to Mich. bar, 1958; pvt. practice law, Detroit, 1959-62; chief asst. prosecutor Wayne County, Mich., 1967-68; pres. Eastern Mich. U., 1975-78; lt. gov. State of Mich., Lansing, 1971-74, 79—; lectr., adj. prof. U. Detroit, Wayne State U., U. Mich., Cooley Law Sch., 1958-62. Supr., Wayne County Bd. Suprs., 1962-66; councilman Detroit City Council, 1962-65, pres. pro-tem, 1966-67; U.S. atty. Eastern Dist. Mich., 1968-69. Mem. Mich. Bar Assn. Republican. Roman Catholic. Home: Okemos MI 48864 Office: 128 Capitol Bldg Lansing MI 48909

BRICKMAN, ROBERT OTTO, landscape co. exec.; b. Chgo., Jan. 22, 1938; s. Theodore William and Amy Edith (Kitzelman) B.; B.A. in Bus. Adminstrn., Lake Forest Coll., 1960; m. Gail Field Walkemeyer, Aug. 29, 1959; children—Jill, Barbara, Cynthia. Sales rep. UARCO, Inc., Chgo., 1960-61; landscape supr. Theodore Brickman Co., Long Grove, Ill., 1961-63, sales mgr., 1964-67, v.p., sec., 1967—. Mem. exec. bd. N.W. Council Boy Scouts Am., 1976-77; trustee Immanuel Ch. New Jerusalem, Glenview, 1971—; bd. dirs. Buehler YMCA. Recipient distinguished service award Countryside Center Handicapped. Mem. Asso. Landscape Contractors Am., Ill. Nurserymen's Assn. (treas.). Republican. Club: Rotary (sec. 1963-65, pres. 1973-74, dist. gov.'s rep. 1974-77 dist. gov. 1981-82). Home: 1025 Gladish Ln Glenview IL 60025 Office: Long Grove Rd Long Grove IL 60047

BRICKMAN, THEODORE W. (DICK), JR., landscape architect; b. Harlingen, Tex., Nov. 17, 1931; s. Theodore William and Amy Edith (Kitzelman) B.; B.A., U. Ill., 1955; m. Sally Gray Barnitz, Aug. 28, 1954; children—Stephen, Scott, Susan, Julie. With Theodore Brickman Co., Long Grove, Ill., 1957—, sec.-treas., until 1973, pres., 1973—; bd. mem. Landscape Architecture Found., 1979—. Mem., chmn. Long Grove (Ill.) Planning Commn., 1960-63; mem. Glenview Appearance Commn., 1973-77; precinct capt. Republican party, 1974-77. Served to 1st lt. Ordinance Corps, U.S. Army, 1955-57. Recipient awards Asso. Landscape Contractors Am., Am. Asso. Nurserymen, Nat. Landscape Assn., Am. Soc. Landscape Architects Ill., Ill. Home Builders Assn. Mem. Asso. Landscape Contractors Am. (past pres., dir.), Am. Soc. Landscape Architects. Republican. Swedenborgian. Club: Tennis (Glenview, Ill.). Contbr. articles in field to profl. jours. Office: Long Grove Rd Long Grove IL 60047

BRIDGEFORTH, JACQUI WEAVER, chemist, info. scientist; b. Indpls., Feb. 2, 1946; d. Richard O. and Norris (Shane) Tanner; B.S., Marian Coll., 1970; children—Patrick Mahaffey, David. With Union Carbide, Indpls., 1965-68; with Eli Lilly & Co., Indpls., 1968—, sr. patent specialist, 1978—. Bd. dirs., hosp. counselor Marion County Victims Advocates Program, 1978—; mem. youth adv. bd. Center for Leadership Devel., 1979—. Mem. Am. Statis. Assn., Assn. Info. Mgrs., Am. Soc. Info. Sci. Roman Catholic. Office: Eli Lilly & Co 307 E McCarty St Indianapolis IN 46285

BRIDGEWATER, BERNARD ADOLPHUS, JR., bus. exec.; b. Tulsa, Mar. 13, 1934; s. Bernard Adolphus and Mary Alethea (Burton) B.; A.B., Westminster Coll., Fulton, Mo., 1955; LL.B., U. Okla., 1958; M.B.A., Harvard, 1964; m. Barbara Paton, July 2, 1960; children—Barrie, Elizabeth, Bonnie. Admitted to Okla. bar, 1958, U.S. Supreme Ct. bar, U.S. Ct. of Claims bar; asst. county atty., Tulsa, 1962; asso. McKinsey & Co., mgmt. cons., Chgo., 1964-68, prin., 1968-72, dir., 1972-73, 75; asso. dir. nat. security and internat. affairs

Office Mgmt. and Budget, Exec. Office Pres., Washington, 1973-74; exec. v.p. Baxter Travenol Labs., Inc., Chgo. and Deerfield, Ill., 1975-79, now dir.; pres. Brown Group, Inc., Clayton, Mo., 1979—; dir. FMC Corp., Chgo., Celanese Corp., N.Y.C., Baxter Travenol, Chgo.; cons. Office Mgmt. and Budget, 1973, 75—. Trustee Rush-Presbyn.-St. Luke's Med. Center, 1974—. Served to lt. USNR, 1958-62. Recipient Rayonier Found. award Harvard, 1963; George F. Baker scholar, 1964. Mem. Beta Theta Pi, Omicron Delta Kappa, Phi Alpha Delta. Clubs: Chgo., Econ. (Chgo.); River (N.Y.C.); Log Cabin (St. Louis); Indian Hill Country (Winnetka, Ill.). Author: (with others) Better Management of Business Giving, 1965. Home: 35 Overhills Dr Ladue MO 63124 Office: 8400 Maryland Ave Clayton MO

BRIDWELL, BERNICE WAYNETTE, nurse; b. Zanesville, Ohio, Feb. 21, 1943; d. Wayne Everett and Marjorie Elsie (Monteith) Fitz; student Wittenberg U., 1960-61; dipl., Springfield City Hosp. Sch. Nursing, 1965; student Ohio State U., 1972; B.S.N., Ohio U., 1979; m. John Robert Bridwell, Jan. 8, 1966; children—Sherry Lu, Robert John. Staff nurse surg. intensive care unit Ohio State U. Hosps., Columbus, 1965; pediatric staff nurse Bethesda Hosp., Zanesville, Ohio, 1966, asst. clin. instr. Sch. Nursing, Zanesville, 1966-67, adult practical nursing instr., 1967-69, instr. pharmacology, 1970-77, jr. instr. high sch. practical nursing, 1972-74, sr. high sch. practical nursing instr., 1978—; instr. practical nursing Muskingum Area Vocat. Sch. Sec., mgr. Girl's Youth Slowpitch Softball League, Zanesville, 1973; tchr. Sun. sch. St. John Luth. Ch., Zanesville, 1967-68, 74-77, planner area Bible Sch., 1977, pres. St. John Luth. Ch. Women, 1973-75, altar chmn., 1977-79, circle leader, 1969-70. Mem. Muskingum Valley Dist. Nurses Assn., Ohio Nurses Assn., Am. Nurses Assn., Muskingum Area Vocational Sch. Edn. Assn., Ohio Edn. Assn., NEA, Ohio Vocat. Assn., Am. Vocat. Assn., Ohio Orgn. Practical Nurse Educators. Clubs: Vocat. Indsl. Clubs of Am. (asst. advisor Muskingum Area chpt. 1980-81), Nat. Vocat. Clubs of Am., Ohio Vocat. Indsl. Clubs of Am. Home: 5585 Kenny Dr Zanesville OH 43701 Office: 400 Richards Rd Zanesville OH 43701

BRIER, JACK HAROLD, state ofcl.; b. Kansas City, Mo., June 25, 1946; s. Marshall W. and M. Pearl (Munden) B.; student U. Kans., 1964-67, 77—; B.B.A., Washburn U., Topeka, 1970. Dep. asst. sec. state for legis. matters State of Kans., Topeka, 1969-70, asst. sec. state, 1970-78, sec. state, 1978—. Nat. v.p. Muscular Dystrophy Assn. Named Outstanding Young Topekan, 1979; Outstanding Young Kansan, 1979. Mem. Kans. Jaycees, Topeka Jaycees, Nat. Assn. Secs. State (exec. com.), Kans. State Hist. Soc. (dir.), Shawnee County Hist. Soc., Sagamore Nat. Honor Fraternity, Blue Key. Republican. Office: Office of Secretary of State Capitol Bldg 2d Floor Topeka KS 66612

BRIERS, JAMES LAURENCE, public utility exec.; b. N.Y.C., Sept. 24, 1923; s. Larry Tennyson and Evelyn (Groeble) B.; student Oberlin Coll., 1941-43; B.S., Ohio State U., (summa cum laude), 1948; M.B.A., Western Res. U., 1965; student Goethe U. (Frankfurt, Germany), 1951-52; m. Evalena Caton, Oct. 7, 1950; 1 dau., Cynthia Katherine. With Ohio Bell Telephone Co., Cleve., 1949—, successively asst. comml. mgr., 1953, comml. mgr., 1954-58, sales mgr., 1959, exec. asst. bus. research, revenue requirements, 1960-62, dist. comml. mgr., 1962-64, named comml. supr. wages and working conditions, 1965, comml. supr. tng., 1972, now comml. supr. personnel; undergrad. asst. Ohio State U., 1948. Cons. ednl. TV, WWIZ; vice chmn. polit. adv. com. 7 County Transp. and Land Use Study; transp. cons. Cleve. Growth Bd.; lectr. Cleve. State U., 1964. Vice chmn. United Appeals, Columbus, Ohio, 1958; pub. relations com. Council Social Agys., 1958; chmn. Bay Village Planning Commn., Cleve., 1963—, Indsl. Devel. Commn., 1963—; chmn. Regional Planning Commn.; co-founder Columbus Youth Found., 1956; dir. Pilot Dogs, 1958-59; dir. Cleve. West Shore YMCA, 1965—. Served with USAAF, 1942-46; served to capt. USAF, 1950-52. Mem. Acad. Mgmt. Am. Econ. Assn., Am. Polit. Sci. Assn., Ohio State U. Alumni Assn., Oberlin Coll. Alumni Assn., Urban League, Beta Gamma Sigma. Republican. Home: 26601 Normandy Rd Bay Village OH 44140 Office: 100 Erieview Plaza Cleveland OH 44114

BRIERTON, DAVID LAWRENCE, housing developer; b. Milw., Sept. 25, 1942; s. Bernard Lawrence and Ruth Margaret (Conway) B.; B.B.A., Wis. State U., Whitewater, 1969; M.S. (HUD fellow), U. Wis., 1970; m. Judith Ann Ruch, Aug. 20, 1966; children—Kristin, Kerry, Kevin, Keely, Kolin, Korey. Project mgr. Gene B. Glick Co., Indpls., 1970-72; pres. Dominion Group Inc., Mpls., 1972—; mem. adv. bd. Ann. Nat. Apt. Builders and Developers Conf. and Exposition, Atlanta, 1978. Served with USAF, 1962-65. Mem. Nat. Leased Housing Assn. (dir. 1979—), Minn. Multi-Housing Assn. (dir. 1979—), Wis. Assn. Housing Authorities. Roman Catholic. Clubs: Rolling Green Country, Calhoun Beach. Home: 3020 Jewel Ln Plymouth MN 55391 Office: 3140 Harbor Ln Plymouth MN 55441

BRIGDEN, ROBERT CAMPBELL, investment broker; b. Cleve., May 19, 1942; s. James H. and A. Margaret (Campbell) B.; B.S. in Indsl. Tech., Ohio U., 1967; m. Nancy Romain Schwarzmann, Feb. 24, 1973. Asst. sales engr. Westinghouse Elec. Co., Columbus, Ohio, 1967-68; securities broker J.N. Russell Co., Cleve., 1969-74, Blyth Eastman Dillon, Cleve., 1974-75, CleveCorp Securities, Cleve., 1975-79, Affiliated Investors Service, 1979—; developer, partner Manor Apts., Alexander Apts.; advisor Newark Wire Cloth Co., Verona Realty. Active Big Bros. Greater Cleve., 1973—; past mem. adv. bd., past dir. Salvation Army, 1977-79; past bd. dirs., v.p. Cleveland Heights Housing Preservation Center, 1977-79. Served as paratrooper AUS, 1962-64. Mem. Theosophical Soc., Jr. C. of C. Presbyterian. Clubs: Cleve. Athletic, Jewish Community Center, Cleve. Rotary, Cleve. Bond. Home: 3455 Edison Rd Cleveland OH 44121 Office: 1701 E 12th St Cleveland OH 44114

BRIGGS, JOHN LAWRENCE, genealogist; b. Battle Creek, Mich., Oct. 6, 1905; s. Mark Roy and Mary Esther (Noyes) B.; m. Ida McCauley, Aug. 20, 1929; 1 son, Stanley John; m. 2d, Glenna Wrate Todd; B.A.S., Chgo. YMCA Coll., 1929; M.A., Mich. State U., 1961; M.A., Western Mich. U., 1962. Asst. exec. Boy Scouts Am., Beloit, Wis., 1929-30, exec., Mt. Clemens, Mich., 1931-37, Ft. Wayne, Ind., 1937-38; caseworker Kalamazoo Welfare Dept., 1939-41; placement specialist War Manpower Commn. and State Employment Service, Kalamazoo, 1942-47; rehab. counselor V.R.S., Kalamazoo, 1947-76; pvt. practice genealogy, Kalamazoo, 1976—; asst. to wife Glenna's Craft Haus, Battle Creek, 1977—. Cert. rehab. counselor. Mem. Nat., Am. rehab. assns., Nat., Mich. rehab. counciling assns., Nat. Vocat. Guidance Assn., Am., Mich., Kalamazoo County personnel and guidance assns., Mich. Psychol. Assn., S.W. Mich. Iris Soc., Kalamazoo Valley Geneal. Soc., Am. Assn. Ret. Persons. Home: 2316 March St Kalamazoo MI 49001

BRIGGS, ROBERT ALFRED, civil engr.; b. Detroit, Aug. 22, 1913; s. Harry B. and Elsa (Neusesser) B.; B.S., Mich. State U., 1937; postgrad. U. Tenn., 1942-43, Lawrence Inst. Tech. Engring., 1945; m. Janet Wilson Bruce, Nov. 26, 1938; children—Harry Alfred, Christine Carole (Mrs. Gerald Campbell), Beryl Ann (Mrs. Timothy O. O'Farrell). Civil engr. Mich. Hwy. Dept., Lansing, 1937-40, TVA, Knoxville, 1941-42; engr. Square Tool & Die Co., Detroit, 1943-44, Monroe Auto Equipment Co. (Mich.), 1945, Mech. Handling System, Detroit, 1946; civil engr. Detroit Edison Co., 1947-64, dir. civil engring. div., 1964-70; cons. engr., 1970-72, dir. archtl. civil engring. div., 1973—. Named Outstanding Civil Engr., Mich., 1972. Registered profl. engr., Mich. Fellow ASCE; mem. Am. Concrete Inst. (dir.), Soc. Am. Mil. Engrs. (dir.), Seismol. Soc. Am., Japanese Soc. Soil Mechanics and Found. Engring., Mich. Engring. Soc., Am. Arbitration Assn., Engring. Soc. Detroit, Internat. Soc. Soil Mechanics and Found. Engring., Internat. Platform Assn. Presbyn. Clubs: Toastmasters, Rivers Edge Marina and Country; Grosse Ile Yacht. Home: 21425 Salisbury Grosse Ile MI 48138 Office: 2000 2d St Detroit MI 48226

BRIGGS, WILLIAM BENAJAH, aero. engr.; b. Okmulgee, Okla., Dec. 13, 1922; s. Eugene Stephen and Mary Betty (Gentry) B.; B.A. in Physics, Phillips U., 1943, D.Sc. (hon.), 1977; M.S. in Mech. Engring., Ga. Inst. Tech., 1947; m. Lorraine Hood, June 6, 1944; children—Eugene Stephen II, Cynthia Anne, Julia Louise, Spencer Gentry. Aero. scientist Nat. Adv. Commn. Aeros., Cleve., 1948-52; propulsion engr. Chance Vought Aircraft/LTV, Dallas, 1952-64; mgr. advanced planning McDonnell Douglas Co., St. Louis, 1964-80, dir. program devel. fusion energy, 1980—; mem. NASA Planetary Quarantine Adv. Panel. Vice chmn. Bd. Christian Bd. Publ., St. Louis, 1974—; chmn. Disciples Council of Greater St. Louis, 1969-73. Served with USN, 1943-46. Asso. fellow AIAA (dir. region 5 1974-77, v.p. mem. services 1978-79); mem. Am. Nuclear Soc. Mem. Disciples of Christ Ch. Club: Masons. Contbr. articles on aero. engring. and energy to profl. jours. Patentee in field. Home: 1819 Bradburn Dr Saint Louis MO 63131 Office: PO Box 516 McDonnell Douglas Astronautics Co Saint Louis MO 63166

BRIGHAM, JAMES BRIAN, retail chain exec.; b. Madison, Wis., Nov. 15, 1949; s. Donald Charles and Mary Etta B.; B.B.A., U. Wis., Eau Claire, 1975; m. Mary Elizabeth Clasen, Aug. 17, 1972; children—Sherry Marie, Brian Henry. Sr. auditor Ernst & Whinney, C.P.A.'s, Milw., 1975-78; nat. audit mgr. F. W. Woolworth Co., Milw., 1978-80, dir. auditing, 1980—. Bd. dirs. Milw. YMCA. Served with U.S. Army, 1968-71. C.P.A., Wis.; cert. internal auditor. Mem. Nat. Retail Mchts. Assn. (dir. internal audit group), Am. Inst. C.P.A.'s, Wis. Inst. C.P.A.'s, Inst. Internal Auditors, Am. Mgmt. Assn., Phi Kappa Phi, Phi Eta Sigma. Home: 9220 N 70th St Milwaukee WI 53223

BRIGHT, NETTIE LOUISE GHERE, food service adminstr.; b. Arcola, Ill., Nov. 12, 1914; d. Roy Andrew and Lillie Elizabeth (Smith) Ghere; student Parkland Coll., 1975-77; m. Earl Bright, Mar. 12, 1938; children—Donna Jean, Ethel Louise, Harry Owen, Lila Lee, Mary Frances, Nancy Sue. Employee, Dr. Fortney, 1932-34; sec. Office of County Supr., 1934-38; cook Arcola (Ill.) pub. schs., 1951-58; mem. staff dietary dept. Jarman Hosp., Tuscola, Ill., 1958-69, food service adminstr., 1969—. Mem. Am. Soc. for Hosp. Food Service Adminstrs. (treas. Central Ill. chpt.). Republican. Methodist. Home: 223 S Pine St Arcola IL 61910 Office: 704 N Main St Tuscola IL 61953

BRIGMAN, CONSTANCE MORGAN, broadcasting exec.; b. Winston-Salem, N.C., July 9, 1952; d. Otis Caston and Carol (Penrose) B.; A.A., Stephens Coll., 1972; B.A., U. Mo., Kansas City, 1974. Disc jockey sta. KCUR-FM, Kansas City, Mo., 1974; with Quastler Advt., Fairway, Kans., 1975; account exec. sta. KAYQ-AM, Kansas City, Mo., 1976-77, KBEQ-FM, Kansas City, Mo., 1977-78, KMBC-TV, Kansas City, Mo., 1978-80; nat. sales rep. Metro TV Sales (Metromedia), Chgo., 1980—. Mem. Am. Women in Radio and TV (chpt. affirmative action chmn. 1979), Advt. Club Kansas City, Alpha Epsilon Rho. Republican. Presbyterian. Home: 1419 N State Pkwy Apt 404 Chicago IL 60610 Office: Wrigley Bldg 410 N Michigan Ave Chicago IL 60611

BRILES, JAMES E., state senator; b. Prescott, Iowa, Mar. 31, 1926; grad. high sch.; m. Lorene Tindall; 3 sons, 2 daus. Former mem. Iowa Ho. of Reps.; mem. Iowa State Senate, 1964—; chmn. Adams County Republican Com.; asso. in auction bus. Served with Armed Forces, 1944-46; PTO. Mem. Am. Legion, VFW. Methodist. Office: State Senate State Capitol Des Moines IA 50319*

BRILL, DAVID MARVIN, food service exec.; b. Chgo., Apr. 30, 1938; s. Marty and Frances (Feder) B.; student U. Ill., 1954-57; B.A., Lake Forest Coll., 1958; M.S. in Food Facilities Engring., Cornell U., 1960; M.B.A., U. Chgo., 1962; m. Carol Mills, Nov. 29, 1959; children—Melinda Sue, Jennifer-Lynn, Andrew Robert. Mem. advt. staff Grubb-Petersen Co., 1959-60; exec. v.p. M. L. Brill & Co., Chgo., 1964-68; asst. to pres. Nat. Tea Co., Chgo., 1968-71; food service exec. Holleb & Co., Bensenville, Ill., 1971—; food cons., 1960—; guest lectr. U. Ill., 1964, 66, 68; pres. Dacar Assos. Ltd., food service cons., Highland Park, Ill., 1965—; lectr. Chgo. Hotel-Motel Assn. Head, Highland Park Jewish United Fund Dr., 1968; bd. dirs. Highland Park Hosp., 1961—, Family Service Bur. S. Lake County. Served with USMCR, 1958-60. Recipient award Chgo. Jewish Appeal, 1966, Instns. award Instns. mag., 1966. Mem. Cornell Soc., Chefs du cuisine, Les Amis des Escoffier, Exec. Chefs. Assn. (hon.), Catering Execs. Club Am., Alpha Delta Sigma, Pi Lambda Phi. Club: Covenant (past pres.). Home: 914 Rolling Wood Rd Highland Park IL 60035 Office: PO Box 34 Highland Park IL 60035

BRILL, RICHARD B(ENJAMIN), public relations co. exec.; b. N.Y.C., Aug. 29, 1944; s. David and Augusta (Harrison) B.; B.S.M.E., Lafayette Coll., 1966; M.B.A., Northwestern U., 1968; m. Marlene Targ, Feb., 1973. Account exec. Anthony M. Franco & Assos., Detroit, 1973-75, Burson-Marsteller, Chgo., 1978; account exec. Selz, Seabolt & Assos., Inc., Chgo., 1975-77, dir. fin. relations, 1979—. Mem. Public Relations Soc. Am., Execs. Club Chgo., Northwestern U. Mgmt. Alumni Assn. Home: 3180 Lake Shore Dr Chicago IL 60657 Office: 221 N LaSalle St Chicago IL 60601

BRILLHART, MAXINE T., physician; b. Coffeyville, Kans., Nov. 11, 1915; d. Forest C. and Rena H. (Huffman) Thornton; M.D., U. Kans., 1950; m. Roy William Brillhart, Nov. 15, 1935; children—Robert Allen, Roy William. Intern, Providence Hosp., Kansas City, Kans., 1950-51, now mem. staff; pvt. practice medicine, Kansas City, 1951—; mem. staff Bethany, St. Margaret, Providence hosps.; dir., sec. Allied Investors, Inc.; dir., v.p., sec. Med. Offices Lab. Mem. Kans. Commn. on Status of Women, 1966. Recipient Matrix award Theta Sigma Phi, 1969. Diplomate Am. Bd. Family Practice. Fellow Am. Acad. Family Physicians; mem. Am., Kans., Wyandotte County med. assns., Kans., Wyandotte County (sec.-treas. 1957-58) acads. gen. practice, World, Am. Women's med. assns., S.W. Clin. Soc., English-Speaking Union, Internat. Personnel Research Soc., Am. Biog. Inst. Methodist. Clubs: Women's City, Soroptimist (pres. Kansas City 1965-66, Woman of Year 1962). Home: 4540 County Line Rd Kansas City KS 66106 Office: 1610 Washington Blvd Kansas City KS 66102

BRIM, PHILLIP LAINE, banker; b. Richmond, Ind., Dec. 27, 1952; s. Joseph Clayton and Constance Fayetta (Palmer) B.; student Sinclair Community Coll., 1974-77, Ind. U. East, 1977, 80, Earlham Coll. Inst. Exec. Growth, 1977. Clk., Richmond Automotive Supply Co., 1970-72; pipefitter Nat. Automatic Tool Co., Richmond, 1972-74; with Second Nat. Bank of Richmond, 1974—, teller mgr., 1976-77, depositor services officer, 1977-78, br. officer, 1978-80, tng. officer, 1980—; instr. bank teller procedures Ind. Vocat. Tech. Inst. Recipient Participation award United Way Wayne County (Ind.), 1975, 76, 77, 78, 79, 80. Mem. Richmond Jaycees (dir. 1974, 78, v.p. 1975, treas. 1976, presdl. asst. 1977, program dir. 1980), Ind. Jaycees (Region 6 Speaking award 1977, ambassador to W.I. 1977, dist. dir. region 6, 1979), U.S. Jaycees. Republican. Roman Catholic. Clubs: Toastmasters, Sertoma, Fraternal Order Police. Office: Second Nat Bank Promenade at Eighth St Richmond IN 47374

BRINDLE, ELWOOD HAROLD, editor; b. Kearny, N.J., Apr. 6, 1917; s. James and Emily (Hunt) B.; student Rutgers U., 1938-39, Columbia U., 1940-41; m. Dorothy Collins, Sept. 6, 1947; children—Paul William, Anne Frances, Ralph Collins. Corr., Prudential Ins. Co., 1934-42; copywriter Gamble-Skogmo, Inc., 1945-47, Batten, Barton, Durstine & Osborn, 1947-67; editor Govt. Product-News, Mpls., 1967-71; editor-in-chief Lakewood Publs., Inc., 1971-72; free-lance editor-writer, 1973—. Co-founder Webfooters Friends, Inc., 1973; dir. Minn. Fellowship of Congregationalists, 1964-67. Served to 2d lt. USAAF, 1942-45. Decorated Air medal with 2 clusters. Mem. League to Uphold Congl. Principles, Minn. Mycological Soc. Co-author: America's Best Garden Flowers; Vegetable Gardening from the Ground Up. Address: 5405 Abbott Pl Edina MN 55410

BRINEGAR, ERNIE JOEL, mfg. co. exec.; b. Sparta, N.C., Mar. 17, 1947; s. Glenn Mack and Lola Ruth (Petty) B.; B.S., Berea Coll., 1969; M.A., Eastern Ky. U., 1972; postgrad mktg. Ohio State U., 1981—; m. Sherry Lynn Sumner, Aug. 12, 1972; 1 son, Danny. Tchr., Rockcastle County Schs., Mt. Vernon, Ky., 1971-73; salesman Coulter Electronics, Cin., 1973-75; account rep. Fisher Sci. Corp., Cin., 1975-81, mktg. mgr. mfg. div., 1981—. Mem. Newark Area Jaycees (dir., sec.), Am. Mgmt. Assn., Am. Chem. Soc., U.S. Jaycees, Ohio Jaycees. Republican. Lutheran. Home: Route 6 Box 262 Indiana PA 15701

BRINGE, BERNARD GLENN, airline exec.; b. Northwood, Iowa, Feb. 11, 1934; s. Melvin Theodore and Gladys Joy (Pangburn) B.; B.S., U. Wis., Whitewater, 1961; M.B.A., Roosevelt U., Chgo., 1968; m. Erna Lynne Tripp, May 29, 1965. Tchr. high sch. bus., Slinger and Salem, Wis., 1961-65; with United Airlines, 1966—, mgr. passenger revenue systems, Chgo., 1978—. Served with U.S. Army, 1955-57. Mem. NEA, Nat. Bus. Edn. Assn., Chgo. Mgmt. Club, Pi Omega Pi. Republican. Presbyterian. Home: 1588 Clover Dr Inverness IL 60067 Office: United Airlines EXOKA PO Box 66100 Chicago IL 60666

BRINGHAM, WILLIAM TALBERT, JR., savs. and loan exec.; b. Hinsdale, Ill., Dec. 13, 1953; s. William Talbert and Ruth Irene (Jaeger) B.; student Kendall Coll., Evanston, Ill., 1971-72; B.A., Albion (Mich.) Coll., 1975; m. Susan Stewart, Sept. 29, 1979. Staff asst. Sigma Chi Fraternity, 1973-75, contbg. editor Sigma Chi mag., 1973—, pres. Albion Coll. chpt., 1974-75; desk mgr. Marriott Hotel Corp., Chgo., 1976-77, personnel mgr., 1977-78; mgr. Telegraph Savs. & Loan Assn., Evanston, Ill., 1978-81; mgr. Highland Park Office, Glenview Guarantee Savs. and Loan Assn., 1981—; faculty Sigma Chi Leadership Sch., 1975—. Precinct capt. Republican Party, 1976-79. Mem. SAR, Evanston Hist. Soc., Am. Mgmt. Assn., Sigma Chi (publs. bd. 1975—). Clubs: Kickers (Evanston); Westmoreland Country (Wilmette, Ill.). Editor: Northfield Twp. Republican Orgn. Newsletter, 1976-77; sr. staff writer Albion Coll. Pleiad, 1974. Home: 1428 Kaywood Glenview IL 60025 Office: Glenview Guarantee Savs & Loan Assn Highland Park IL

BRINGHAM, WILLIAM TALBERT, SR., fraternity exec.; b. Normal, Ill., Dec. 16, 1924; s. Russell Wilson and Sarah E. (Talbert) B.; Ph.B., Illinois Wesleyan University, 1948; J.D., Vanderbilt University, 1951; grad. trust devel. school Northwestern U. Sch. Commerce, 1953; m. Ruth Irene Jaeger, Jan. 10, 1947; 1 son, William Talbert. Spl. agt. FBI, 1951-52; exec. sec. Sigma Chi Frat., 1954—; exec. dir. Sigma Chi Found., 1956—, also sec.; also sec. bd. grand trustee of Sigma Chi, exec. v.p., sec. exec. com., and sec. grand council Sigma Chi Fraternity (name later changed to Sigma Chi Corp.); bd. dirs. Nat. Interfrat. Found. Mem. corp. Kendall Coll.; del. Sch. Bd. Caucus. Del. Ill. Republican Conv., now Northfield Twp. Rep. committeeman, former trustee Wilmette, Ill. Former chmn. and Police Commn., Wilmette, Ill. Served with USNR, 1942-46. Named flying col. Delta Airlines, ambassador Trans World Airlines, admiral Am. Airlines; recipient Grand Consul's Citation, recipient Order of Constantine award. Mem. Am. Personnel and Guidance Assn., Am. Soc. Assn. Execs. (Key award 1973), Wilmette, Evanston hist. socs., Travelers Protective Assn., Am. Legion, Frat. Execs. Assn. (pres., exec. com.), Evanston C. of C. (past dir.), S.A.R., Chgo. Soc. Assn. Execs. (dir., exec. com.), Phi Delta Phi. Mason (Shriner, 33 deg., K.T.) Kiwanian (past pres.), Royal Order Scotland. Clubs: University (pres.) (Evanston). Author booklet on alumni chpts. Sigma Chi. Chmn. com. that edited Visitation Manual for College Fraternities. Address: 4020 Bunker Ln Wilmette IL 60091

BRINK, MARION FRANCIS, assn. exec.; b. Golden Eagle, Ill., Nov. 20, 1932; s. Anton Frank and Agnes Gertrude B.; B.S., U. Ill., 1955, M.S., 1958; Ph.D., U. Mo., 1961. Research biologist U.S. Naval Radiol. Def. Lab., San Francisco, 1961-62; asso. dir. div. nutrition research Nat. Dairy Council, Chgo., 1962-65, dir. div. nutrition research, 1965-70, pres., Rosemont, Ill., 1970—; vice-chmn. human nutrition adv. com. U.S. Dept. Agr., 1980-81. Recipient citation of merit U. Mo. Alumni Assn. Mem. AAAS, Am. Dairy Sci. Assn., Am. Inst. Nutrition, Am. Mgmt. Assn., Am. Soc. Assn. Execs., Am. Soc. Clin. Nutrition, Animal Nutrition Research Council, Dairy Assn. Execs. Conf., Dairy Shrine Club, Dairy Soc. Internat., Harold Brunn Soc. Med. Research, Nutrition Today Soc., Chgo. Nutrition Assn., Sigma Xi, Alpha Tau Alpha, Gamma Sigma Delta. Contbr. articles to profl. jours. Office: 6300 N River Rd Rosemont IL 60018

BRINK, RICHARD EDWARD, lawyer; b. Renwick, Iowa, Apr. 27, 1923; s. John Allyn and Sylvia Lonella (Warman) B.; B.A. in Chemistry with high distinction, State U. Iowa, 1944, B.S. in Chem. Engring. with distinction, 1944; J.D. cum laude, St. Paul Coll., 1952; m. Helen M. Ladwig, Nov. 2, 1946; children—Thomas W., Gretchen K., Sara Jane (dec.), Paul E. (dec.). Admitted to Minn. bar, 1952; with Minn. Mining & Mfg. Co., St. Paul, 1946-59, mgr., 1955-59; mem. firm Carpenter, Abbott, Kinney & Coulter, St. Paul, 1959-70; partner Alexander, Sell, Steldt & DeLaHunt, St. Paul, 1970-76; sr. patent atty. 3M Co., St. Paul, 1976-78, asso. patent counsel, 1978—. Mem. White Bear Lake Sch. Bd., 1960-75, chmn., 1969-75. Served with USNR, 1944-46. Mem. Am. Bar Assn., Minn. Bar Assn., Minn. Patent and Trademark Law Assn. (chmn. public relations com. 1977-80, bd. govs. 1980—), Am. Contract Bridge League, Sons of Norway, Phi Beta Kappa, Tau Beta Pi, Phi Lambda Upsilon, Phi Beta Gamma. Methodist. Author: (with Donald Gipple and Harold Hughesdon) An Outline of U.S. Patent Law, 1959. Home: 27 Oak Knoll Dr White Bear Lake MN 55110

BRINKLEY, GEORGE ARNOLD, JR., educator; b. Wilmington, N.C., Apr. 20, 1931; s. George Arnold and Ida Bell (West) B.; A.B., Davidson Coll., 1953; M.A., Columbia U., 1955, Ph.D., 1964; m. Ann Mae Kreps, Aug. 9, 1959; 1 dau., Heidi Ann. Instr. polit. sci. Columbia U., N.Y.C., 1957-58; with dept. govt. U. Notre Dame, 1958—, prof., 1970—, dir. Program of Soviet & East European Studies, 1969—, chmn. dept., 1969-77, dir. Inst. Internat. Studies, 1975-78. Ford Found. fellow, 1954-57; Internat. Affairs fellow Council on Fgn. Relations, 1968-69. Mem. Am. Assn. Advancement of Slavic Studies (chmn. membership com. 1978-81); Midwest Slavic Assn. (chmn. exec. com. 1979-81), Phi Beta Kappa. Methodist. Author: The Volunteer Army and Allied Intervention in South Russia, 1917-1921, 1966. Office: Dept Govt U Notre Dame Notre Dame IN 46556

BRINKLEY, WILLIAM JOHN, educator; b. Shawneetown, Ill., Dec. 8, 1925; s. William Henry and Frances (Leath) B.; B.S., U. Ill., 1945. Tchr. high sch., McLeansboro, Ill., 1945—, high sch. coordinator vocations, 1968—; owner Brinkley Interiors and Galleries, antique porcelain, McLeansboro. Mem. adv. bd. Ill. Edn. Council, 1967—; mem. Pres.'s Com. 100, 1968; mem. Hamilton County Bicentennial Com.; chmn. rehab. com. McCoy Meml. Library and Hamilton County Hist. Soc. Bldg.; mem. Hamilton County Republican Com., 1950-68. Recipient Tchr. of Year award U. Ill. Edn. Dept., 1963; Merit award Gov. Ill. 1964; Distinguished Service award Future Farmers Am., 1967; George Washington medal honor Freedoms Found. Am., 1966, 69; Outstanding Vocat. Edn. award Ill. State Vocat. Edn. Service, 1981. Mem. NEA, Ill. Edn. Assn., Hamilton County (pres. 1970), Gallatin County hist. socs., Nat., Ill. (Tchr. of Tchrs.) assns. vocat. agr. tchrs., Rend Lake Symphony Soc., Arts and Humanities Soc., SAR, Hereditary Register of U.S., Phi Beta Kappa, Delta Sigma Phi. Presbyn. Mason, Kiwanian, Elk, Lion. Home: 401 Washington St S McLeansboro IL 62859 Office: 200 S Pearl St McLeansboro IL 62859 also 401 S Washington Ave McLeansboro IL 62859

BRINKMAN, JOHN ANTHONY, orientalist, educator; b. Chgo., July 4, 1934; s. A(dam) John and Alice (Davies) B.; A.B., Loyola U. Chgo., 1956, M.A., 1958; Ph.D., U. Chgo., 1962; m. Monique E. Geschier, Mar. 24, 1970; 1 son, Charles E. Research asso. Oriental Inst., U. Chgo., 1963, asst. prof. Assyriology and Ancient History, 1964-66, asso. prof., 1966-70, prof., 1970—, chmn. dept., 1969-72, dir. Oriental Inst., 1972-81; mem. staff of Chgo. Assyrian Dictionary, 1963—; ann. prof. Am. Schs. Oriental Research, Baghdad, 1968-69, chmn. Baghdad Schs. com., 1971—, mem. exec. com., 1971-75 chmn., 1973-75, trustee, 1975—. Mem. vis. com. dept. near Eastern langs. and civilizations Harvard, 1973-80. Fellow Nat. Endowment for the Humanities, 1973-74, Am. Council Learned Socs., 1963-64, Am. Research Inst. Turkey, 1971. Fellow Am. Council Learned Socs.; mem. Am. Oriental Soc. (br. v.p. 1970-71, pres. 1971-72), Brit. Inst. Persian Studies, Brit. Inst. Archaeology at Ankara. Roman Catholic. Author: Political History of Post-Kassite Babylonia, 1968; Materials and Studies for Kassite History, Vol. 1, 1976; mem. editorial bd. Chgo. Assyrian Dictionary, 1977—; editor-in-charge Royal Inscriptions of Mesopotamia Project, Babylonian sect., 1979—. Contbr. articles to profl. jours. Home: 5535 S University Ave Chicago IL 60637 Office: Oriental Inst 1155 E 58th St Chicago IL 60637

BRINKMANN, ARTHUR WILLIAM, labor negotiator, indsl. relations dir.; b. Elizabeth, N.J., Oct. 22, 1934; s. Kurt and Frieda (Schleheck) B.; B.A., Rutgers U., 1956; LL.B., Seton Hall U., 1961, J.S.D., 1971; m. Rose Bette Kosberg, Aug. 16, 1959; children—Alison, Michael, David. Admitted to N.J. bar, 1961; dep. atty. gen. State of N.J., 1961-64; counsel dept. banking and ins. Johnson & Johnson, Chgo., 1964-66, dir. indsl. relations, New Brunswick, N.J., 1966-73; dir. indsl. relations Gen. Public Utilities (nuclear), Middletown, Pa.; arbitrator Am. Arbitration Assn., 1973—; exec. dir. Union County Legal Services, 1967-72, pres., 1973. Pres. Alsip Indsl. Assn., 1977-78, bd. dirs., 1974-78; mem. parole bd. Menlo Park Diagnostic Center, 1963-70. Named Big Brother of Yr., N.J., 1969-70. Mem. TAPPI, Paper Industry Mgmt. Assn., Delta Sigma Phi. Democrat. Lutheran. Clubs: Silver Lake Country, Wimbledon Tennis and Country, Kiwanis (founder Alsip Club). Home: 7920 Laguna Dr Orland Township IL 60462 Office: Middletown PA 17033

BRINKMEYER, LOREN JAY, data processor, coll. adminstr.; b. Udall, Kans., Apr. 21, 1925; s. William Frederick and Verna Christina (Mead) B.; student U. Kans., 1943, 50-51, U. Wis., 1943-44; D. Mus. Dramatics, U. Heidelberg (Germany), 1954; D. Internat. Comml. Law, U. Poitiers (France), 1964; B.S.B. with honors, Emporia State U., 1972, M.S.B. with honors, 1978; also student numerous data processing and computer sci. courses; m. Helen Josephine Walkemeyer, Mar. 10, 1946; 1 son, Karl Phillip. Served as enlisted man U.S. Army, 1943-45, commd. 2d lt., 1945, advanced through grades to lt. col., 1962; data processing supr., Hawaii, 1945-51, W. Ger., 1951-54, U.S., 1955, 60-61, Alaska, 1956-59, France, 1962-64, ret., 1964; dir. data processing Butler County Community Coll., El Dorado, Kans., 1964—; cons. data processing, 1946—. Pres. El Dorado Mcpl. Bd., 1971—; mem. chmn. United Methodist Ch., El Dorado, 1964—; mem. Kans. U. Alumni Band, 1972—. Decorated Army Commendation medal, Bronze Star with two oak leaf clusters, Purple Heart. Mem. NEA, Kans. Higher Edn. Assn., Am. Vocat. Assn., Kans. Vocat. Assn., Kans. Bus. Occupations Assn., Kans. Bus. Edn. Assn., Kans. Bus. Computerized Student Follow-up (adv. bd.), Data Processing Edn. Kans., Assn. Ednl. Data Systems, Data Processing Mgmt. Assn. (cert.), Assn. Computing Machinery, Soc. Data Educators, Internat. Assn. Computer Programmers, Ret. Enlisted Assn., Ret. Officers Assn., 96th Inf. Div. Assn., Nat. Assn. Uniformed Services, Am. Legion, VFW. Independent Republican. Author: Electrical Accounting Machines, 2d edit., 1964; Automated Inventory and Financial Systems, edit., 1976; Punched Card Business Data Processing, 3d edit., 1974. Office: Data Center Butler County Community Coll Haverhill and Towanda El Dorado KS 67042

BRINKMEYER, WILLIS ROBERT, farm corp. exec.; b. Beatrice, Nebr., Jan. 4, 1931; s. Henry and Amelia Marie (Helmke) B.; graduate Bus. Adminstrn., Lincoln (Nebr.) Sch. Commerce; m. Shirley Louis Mitchell, Jan. 1, 1961; children—Renee, Mae Marie. Pres. Brinkmeyer Farms, Inc., Cortland, Nebr., 1972—. Mem. 18th Dist. Jud. Nominating Commn., 1973—. Mem. Top Farmers of Am. Republican. Lutheran. Home: Route 1 Cortland NE 68331

BRINKS, JAMES THOMAS, cons. human resources; b. Quincy, Ill., Feb. 22, 1938; s. Oscar Henry and Margaret Ann (Ott) B.; B.A., St. Mary of Lake Sem., Mundelein, Ill., 1961, M.A., 1963; M.B.A., St. Louis U., 1971; m. Doris Ann Krause, June, 1970; children—René Kendall, Bridget Claudine, Victoria Lyn. Ordained priest Roman Catholic Ch., 1965; priest, Springfield, Ill., 1965-69; mgr. personnel Monsanto Co., St. Louis, 1969-74; mgr. compensation and manpower devel. Fisher Controls Co. subs. Monsanto Co., Marshalltown, Iowa, 1974-78; mgr. human resources cons. Deloitte Haskins & Sells, Chgo., 1978-80; prin. The Wyatt Co., compensation cons., Chgo., 1980—. Precinct committeeman Republican party, Marshalltown, 1975-78. Accredited personnel diplomate; cert. compensation profl. Mem. Am. Compensation Assn., Chgo. Compensation Assn., Am. Soc. Personnel Adminstrn. (compensation and benefits com.), Am. Mgmt. Assn. Republican. Roman Catholic. Home: 300 Bayonne Dr Lake Bluff IL 60044 Office: 233 S Wacker Dr Suite 5600 Chicago IL 60606

BRISCOE, KEITH G., coll. pres.; b. Adams, Wis., Oct. 16, 1933; B.S., U. Wis., La Crosse, 1960; M.Ed., U. N.H., 1968; postgrad. Case Western Res. U., Iowa State U., U. Wis., Okla. State U.; LL.D. (hon.), Coll. Idaho, 1978, Buena Vista Coll., 1979; m. Carmen Irene Schweinler, Aug. 15, 1956; 1 dau., Susan Ann. Asst. dir. Coll. Union, Wis. State U., Stevens Point, 1960-62, U. N.H., 1962-64; dir. Coll. Union, dir. student activities, asst. prof. student life Baldwin Wallace Coll., Berea, Ohio, 1964-70; v.p. Coll. Steubenville (Ohio), 1970-74; pres. Buena Vista Coll., Storm Lake, Iowa, 1974—; higher edn. cons. Cuyahoga Community Coll., Coll. Wooster; v.p., treas. Ednl. Task, Inc., Berea, 1967-69; mem. nat. adv. bd. Coll. Transition Program, Berea, 1967-69; mem. adv. bd. Coll. and Univ. Partnership Program. Bd. dirs., chmn. Council Ind. Colls., 1981-83; bd. dirs., vice chmn. Presbyn. Coll. Union; exec. com., vice chmn. Nexus; adv. to program bd. Presbyn. Ch. U.S.A.; bd. dirs., officer Coll. of Mid-Am.; bd. dirs. Am. Council on Edn., mem. coordinating com., 1981—; co-chmn. Sino-Am. Inst. Higher Edn., Republic of China, 1981. Served with AUS, 1956-58. Mem. Assn. Coll. and Univ. Concert Mgrs. (trustee), UN Assn., Iowa Assn. Ind. Colls. and Univs. (pres., exec. com. 1977—), Iowa Assn. Coll. Presidents (pres. exec. com.), Phi Epsilon Kappa, Phi Delta Kappa. Republican. Methodist. Clubs: Masons, Des Moines, Order of the Arch, Rotary. Author: Directory of College Unions, 1963; An Annotated Bibliography of the College Union, 1967; A Study of Alternatives to Financing Private Higher Private Education, 1973; contbr. articles to profl. jours. Address: Office of Pres Buena Vista Coll Storm Lake IA 50588

BRISLEY, CHESTER LAVOYEN, educator; b. Albion, Pa., Apr. 3, 1914; s. Voyen Francis and Nina May (Dearborn) B.; student Gen. Motors Inst., 1936-39; B.S., Youngstown State U., 1946; M.A., Wayne State U., 1954, Ph.D., 1957; m. Eva Scott, June 19, 1932; Indsl. engr. Packard Electric div. Gen. Motors Corp., Warren, Ohio, 1935-41; supr. indsl. engring. N.Am. Aviation, Dallas, 1942-45; mgr. indsl. engring. Wolverine Tube div. Calumet & Hecla, Inc., Detroit, 1946-58; asst. to dir. ops. Chance Vought Aircraft, Dallas, 1958-59; cons. A.T. Kearney, Chgo., 1960; mgr. indsl. engring. Allis Chalmers, Inc., Milw., 1961-62; mgr. mgmt. services Touche Ross C.P.A., N.Y.C., 1963-64; prof. dept. engring. U. Wis., Milw., 1964—, asso. chmn. dept. engring., 1964—. Fellow Methods Time Measurement Assn. v.p. 1978, Am. Inst. Indsl. Engrs. (past pres. Detroit and Milw. chpts., v.p. Region XI), Soc. Advancement Mgmt. (past pres. Detroit chpts.); mem. Nat. Soc. Profl. Engrs., Wis. Soc. Profl. Engrs. (pres. 1978-79), Hosp. Mgmt. Systems Soc., ASME, Engrs. and Scientists Milw., Inc. (pres. 1974-75), Milw. Council Engring. and Sci. Socs. (pres. 1975-76), Am. Soc. Engring. Edn. (chmn. continuing engring. studies div. 1972-73). Contbr. articles to profl. jours. Home: 1700 Highland Dr Elm Grove WI 53122 Office: 929 N 6th St Milwaukee WI 53203

BRISSEE, WILLIAM MICHAEL, newspaper editor; b. Madison, Wis., Oct. 17, 1933; s. John James and Della Celia (Byreis) B.; B.S., U. Wis., 1955; m. Nancy Margaret Aspinwall, Nov. 29, 1958; children—Nancy, Jane, Stephen, Thomas. Reporter, Seymour (Wis.) Press, 1957-58; reporter Wis. State Jour., Madison, 1958-67, city editor, 1967-74, asso. editor, 1974-76; editor Globe-Gazette, Mason City, Iowa, 1976—. Served with USN, 1955-57. Mem. Asso. Press Mng. Editors Assn. (Iowa chmn.), Iowa Freedom of Info. Council, Soc. for Preservation and Encouragement of Barber Shop Quartet Singing in Am. Roman Catholic. Club: Kiwanis. Office: Globe-Gazette 300 N Washington St Mason City IA 50401

BRISSEY, RUBEN MARION, container co. exec.; b. Auburn, W.Va., July 12, 1923; s. Reuben Marion and Draxie (Meathrell) B.; B.S., Salem Coll., 1943; M.S., W.Va. U., 1948, Ph.D., 1950; m. Helen Catherine McMicken, July 10, 1945; children—Catherine Ann, Gregory Marion. With Gen. Electric Co., 1950-73, lab. mgr., Phila., 1961-66, strategic planning mgr., Phila., 1966-73; dir. research and devel. Lavino div. Internat. Minerals & Chems., Plymouth Meeting, Pa., 1973-74; mgr. research and devel. Nat. Can. Corp., Chgo., 1974-76, v.p. research and devel., 1976—. Mem. Am. Chem. Soc., IEEE, AAAS. Presbyterian. Home: 3410 Hickory Trail Downers Grove IL 60515 Office: 5959 S Cicero Ave Chicago IL 60638

BRISTER, FRANK RAYFIELD, ednl. media specialist, educator; b. Gloucester, Mass., May 8, 1928; s. Frank John and Gladys Mae (Reid) B.; B.A. in Humanities (Rotary scholar), U. Hartford (Conn.), 1965; M.S. in TV-Radio, Syracuse U., 1966, certificate advanced studies, 1969. Coordinator audiovisual services Univ. Coll., Syracuse (N.Y.) U., 1966-69; dir. audiovisual services Ferris State Coll., Big Rapids, Mich., 1969-74, asso. prof. Sch. Edn. Learning Resources, chief instr. media tech. program learning resources careers, 1974—; cons. media utilization modules to improve classroom instruction; author ednl. and community service mediated programs. Home: 403 Maple St Big Rapids MI 49307

BRISTOW, DON H., ednl. adminstr.; b. Centerville, Iowa, May 11, 1947; s. Arthur Harbold and Mary Clarissa (Adams) B.; A.A.S., Centerville Community Coll., 1967; B.S., U. Mo., 1972, M.Ed. cum laude, 1973, specialist degree in vocat. edn., 1980; m. Candace Jean, June 25, 1967; children—Andrea Renee, Benjamin Arthur. Draftsman, A.B. Chance Co., Centralia, Mo., 1967-68, 70-71; instr. vocat. drafting Mexico (Mo.) Area Vocat. Sch., 1972-76, job placement specialist, asst. supr. adult edn., 1975-76, dir. vocat. and adult edn., 1976—; mem. state com. on disadvantaged and handicapped in vocat. edn., statewide job placement in vocat. edn. adv. com. Chmn. bd. Mexico Family YMCA; deacon First Bapt. Ch., Mexico. Served with U.S. Army, 1968-70. Mem. Am. Vocat. Assn., Mo. Vocat. Assn., Mo. Council Local Adminstrs. (sec. N.E. Dist., 1976-80), Mo. State Tchrs. Assn., Mexico Area C. of C. (leadership group). Club: Kiwanis Internat. Home: 1921 Cherry St Mexico MO 65265 Office: 905 N Wade St Mexico MO 65265

BRISTOW, EUGENE KERR, educator; b. Birmingham, Ala., Feb. 12, 1927; s. Eugene B. and Hope (Kerr) B.; A.B., Ind. U., 1950, M.A. 1952; Ph.D., U. Iowa, 1956; m. Norma L. Jones, June 17, 1950; children—Pamela Ruth, Michael Eugene, Carol Jean, Mary Katherine. Tchr. New Albany (Ind.) High Sch., 1950-51, Reitz High Sch., Evansville, Ind., 1952-54; asst. prof. MacMurray Coll., 1956-57; instr. Ind. U., 1957-60, asst. prof. speech and theatre, 1960-68, asso. prof., 1968-71, asso. prof. theatre drama, 1971-79, prof., 1979—, grad. sch. fellow, 1951-52, asso. prof. theatre and drama Russian East European Inst., Ind. U., 1972-79, prof., 1979—; research fellow State U. Iowa, 1955-56; vis. asso. prof. U. Calif., Santa Barbara, 1968-69. Served with USAAF, 1945-46. Recipient Citation for Outstanding Contbn. to Democratic Processes, Mayor of Bloomington, Ind., 1959; named Outstanding Young Speech Tchr., Central States Speech Assn., 1957. Mem. AAUP, Modern Lang. Assn., Speech Communication Assn., Am. Theatre Assn., Am. Assn. Advancement Slavic Studies, Internat. Fedn. for Theatre Research, Am. Soc. for Theatre Research, Theatre Library Assn. Author: Five Plays of Alexander Ostrovsky, 1969; Anton Chekhov's Plays, 1977. Contbr. articles profl. jours. and author several pamphlets. News editor Ednl. Theatre Jour., 1960-63. Home: 604 Staats Dr Bloomington IN 47401

BRITT, RONALD LEROY, mech. engr.; b. Abilene, Kans., Mar. 1, 1935; s. Elvin Elbert and Lona Helen (Conn) B.; B.S.M.E., Wichita State U., 1963; m. Judith Ann Salter, June 29, 1957; children—Brett Gavin, Mark Damon, Melissa. Product engr. to product planner Hotpoint div. Gen. Electric Co., Chgo., 1963-68; product planner Norge Co., Chgo., 1968; product mgr., asst. dir. engring. Leigh Products Inc., Coopersville, Mich., 1968-74; mgr. research and devel. Miami-Carey div. Jim Walter Corp., Monroe, Ohio, 1974—; industry rep. for electric fans Underwriters Labs. Active, Boy Scouts Am., 1970-73, PTA, 1973—. Served with U.S. Army, 1958-60. Recipient Inventor's award Gen. Electric Co., 1967. Mem. ASME, Home Ventilation Inst. (engring. com. 1975—). Republican. Congregationalist. Clubs: Free Blown Glassblowing, Carnival and Art Glass Collectors. Patentee in field. Home: 2605 Central Ave Middletown OH 45042 Office: 203 Garver Rd Monroe OH 45050

BRITTEN, WILLIAM HARRY, editor, pub.; b. Zearing, Iowa, Aug. 25, 1921; s. Harry William and Gertrude Alice (Lehman) B.; B.A., Western Union Coll., 1943; student Iowa State Coll., summer 1942; M.A., State U. Iowa, 1948. Reporter, Worcester (Mass.) Telegram, 1948-55; landscaper John F. Keenen, Leicester, Mass., 1956; sales dept. clk. Reed & Prince Mfg. Co., Worcester, 1957-63, inventory control clk., 1964, chief expeditor, 1965; state editor Marshalltown (Ia.) Times-Republican, 1965-66, staff writer, 1966-67; news editor Denison (Ia.) Bull. and Rev., 1967-68; city editor Boone News Republican, 1968; editor, pub., owner The Tri-County News, Zearing, 1968—; editor, pub. Hubbard (Iowa) Rev., 1969-72; journalism adv. com. Des Moines Area Community Coll. Sec., Young Men's Republican Club, Worcester, 1957; corr. sec. Young People's Rep. Club, 1958; mem. Ward 8 Rep. Com., Worcester, 1960-65; Rep. candidate Mass. state legislature, 1960; ward chmn. to elect Edward W. Brooke atty. gen. Mass., 1962, 64; bd. dirs. Story County Cancer Soc., 1976-81. Served with AUS, 1943-45. Mem. Iowa Press Assn., Nat. Newspaper Assn., Am. Fedn. Arts., Westmar Coll., U. Iowa alumni assns. Mem. Ch. of Christ. Home: 416 S Pearl St Zearing IA 50278 Office: Main St Zearing IA 50278

BRITTON, MORRENE HUGHES, farmer, cattle feeder, comml. pilot; b. Kansas City, Mo., June 24, 1941; d. Morrison and Irene (Arnold) Hughes; student Carleton Coll., 1959-60; B.S. cum laude in Agriculture, U. Mo., 1963; diploma Wilson Flight Tng. Center, 1966; m. Robert Lynn Britton, Jan. 21, 1967; 1 dau., Alison. Co-mgr., Hughes Farms (became Hughes Farms, Inc. 1971), Fayette, Mo., 1963-65, co-mgr., 1969-72, gen. mgr., pres., 1972—; flight instr. Boonville (Mo.) Airport, 1965-66, Wilson Flight Tng. Center, Kansas City, Kans., 1966-69; mem. various agrl. coms. Cert. comml., single and multi-engine aircraft flight instr. Bd. dirs. First Christian Ch., Fayette. Mem. Nat. Assn. Ind. Bus., Am. Farm. Bur. Assn., Nat. Cattlemen's Assn., Gamma Sigma Delta. Club: LTS. Home and Office: Route 3 Fayette MO 65248

BRIXIUS, FRANK JOSEPH, lawyer; b. St. Cloud, Minn., May 23, 1938; s. Albert J. and Mary Kathryn (Thiesen) B.; B.S. (William scholar), U. Minn., 1961; J.D., William Mitchell Coll. Law, 1966; m. Suzanne DeLong, July 14, 1962; children—Elizabeth Ann, Mary Alanah, Frank Joseph. With First Nat. Bank Mpls., 1962-66; admitted to Minn. bar, 1966; asso. firm Hvass, Weisman & King, Mpls., 1966—, partner, 1969—. Mem. Greenwood (Minn.) City Council, 1970-71, 71—, chmn. adv. com., 1970, council rep. to Hennepin County League Municipalities and Met. League Municipalities, 1972—; mayor, Greenwood, 1973—; co-chmn. Hennepin County Criminal Justice Council, 1974-75. Dir. Suburban Rate Authority; dir., mem. exec. com. Suburban League Municipalities, 1974-75, also chmn. pub. safety dept. 1974-75, 77-78, 80-82. Trustee Alpha Nu Trust Fund, 1974—. Recipient West Publishing Outstanding Law Student award, 1965. Fellow Internat. Soc. Barristers; mem. Am., Minn., Hennepin County bar assns., Am., Minn. trial lawyers assns., Assn. Met. Municipalities (dir., exec. com. 1974-75), Am. Judicature Soc., Chi Psi. Home: 21720 Fairview Greenwood MN 55331 Office: 715 Cargill Bldg Minneapolis MN 55402

BROACH, ALGNER EUGENE ADOLPHUS, III, podiatrist; b. Cin., June 2, 1933; s. Algner Eugene Adolphus II and Susie Belle Broach (Lindsey) B.; B.S., Central State U., 1958; D.P.M., Ohio Coll. Podiatric Medicine, 1966; m. Lillie Mae Morton, Aug. 15, 1959; children—Connie M., Charisse M., Cheryl A., Cynthia L., Algner E. A.IV. Practice podiatry, Cin., 1967—; mem. staff, dept. med. dir. Walnut Hills-Evanston Med. Center, 1975-78; mem. staff West End Health Center, 1975—; mem. Cin. Health Dept. Task Force; pres. bd. dirs. Walnut Hills-Evanston Med. Center. Mem. Walnut Hills Community Council, 1980-81. Served with M.C., USAF, 1951-53, U.S. Army Res., 1978—. Mem. Am. Podiatry Assn., Ohio Podiatry Assn., So. Ohio Acad. Podiatry, Jewish Hosp. Assn., Assn. Mil. Surgeons, Am. Assn. Hosp. Podiatrists, Nat. Podiatry Assn., Res. Officers Assn., Greater Cin. Minority Bus. and Profl. Assn., Alpha Phi Alpha, Pi Delta, Phi Alpha Pi. Clubs: Masons. Home: 1139 Cheyenne Dr Cincinnati OH 45216 Office: 2916 Gilbert Ave Ideal Medical Bldg Cincinnati OH 45206

BROCK, RUSSELL OLIVER, JR., coll. dean; b. Ennis, Tex., Dec. 9, 1925; s. Russell and Mary Ellen (Matlock) B.; student Central Mo. State Coll., 1944, U. Tex., 1944-46; B.A., U. Kansas City, 1948, M.A., 1949; Ph.D., U. Colo., 1953; m. Rita Joanne List, Aug. 28, 1949; children—David, Paul, Kevin, Richard. With Army Map Service, 1953-55; mem. faculty No. State Tchrs. Coll., Aberdeen, S.D., 1955—, asso. prof. history, 1958-60, prof., 1960—, chmn. div. social sci., 1963-73, dean div. arts and scis., 1973—. Chmn. bd. trustees Dacotah Prairie Mus., 1979—. Served in USN, 1944-46. Mem. S.D. Social Sci. Assn. (pres. 1968), Brown County Mus. and Hist. Soc. (pres. 1975-77), Am. Hist. Assn., Soc. History Edn., Rocky Mountain Medieval and Renaissance Assn., Am. Conf. Acad. Deans, Council Colls. Arts and Scis., S.D. State Hist. Soc. Home: 1756 S 4th St Aberdeen SD 57401 Office: No State College Aberdeen SD 57401

BROCK, THOMAS WALTER, glass co. adminstr.; b. Marion, Ind., Feb. 15, 1931; s. Richard Mark and Beulah Blanch (Gransinger) B.; B.S., Ball State Tchrs. Coll., 1953; M.S., U. Toledo, 1962; children—Teresa Eileen, William Jeffrey. With Owens Illinois Inc., Toledo, 1953—, materials and process engr., 1966-74, contract adminstr., 1974—. Pres., Mt. Vernon PTA, 1963. Mem. Am. Ceramic Soc., Soc. Glass Tech., Nat. Contract Mgmt. Assn., Sigma Xi. Republican. Methodist. Patentee in glass-ceramic materials and products. Home: 2517 W Village Dr Toledo OH 43614 Office: PO Box 1035 Toledo OH 43666

BROCKERT, KENNETH LEE, hosp. lab. adminstr., med. technologist; b. Springfield, Mo., June 15, 1932; s. Thomas Edward and Lula Rachel (Love) B.; clin. lab. technician certificate U.S. Navy, 1952; A.A. in Liberal Arts, Kent State U., 1973; m. Marilyn Lois Noll, Sept. 29, 1956; children—Ann Marie, Mark Alan, Matthew Lee, Nina Jane. Histology technician U.S. Naval Hosp., North Chicago, Ill., 1956; adminstrv. technologist Timken Mercy Hosp. Lab., Canton, Ohio, 1956-72; lab. dir. Alliance (Ohio) City Hosp., 1972—; mem. nat. lab. panel Market Potential Corp. Bd. dirs. Alliance chpt. ARC, 1972-77; mem. St. Michael's Men's Choir, 1977—; lay dir. Canton Cursillo Center, 1978-80; mem. adv. bd., med. lab. technologists program Stark Tech. Coll., 1980—. Served with USN, 1950-56. Mem. Am. Soc. Clin. Pathologists (certified histology technician), Registry Med. Technologists, Am. Heart Assn. (certified in basic cardiac life support), Am. Soc. Med. Technologists, Citizens Hosp. Assn. Alliance. Democrat. Roman Catholic. Clubs: St. Michaels Men's (sec.); Kiwanis (dir. local club 1974-77, pres. 1977-78, div. chmn. adminstrn. 1978-80) (Alliance). Participant in designing lab. for Alliance City Hosp. Home: 5055 Tralee Circle NW Canton OH 44720 Office: 264 E Rice St Alliance OH 44601

BROD, EVELYN FAY, educator; b. Cin., Apr. 23, 1942; d. Joseph Theodore and Freda Edith (Mandell) B.; B.A. in Spanish, U. Cin., 1964, B.S. in Edn., 1964, M.A. in Spanish, 1966, M.Ed. in Guidance and Counseling, 1975. Teaching asst. U. Cin., 1964-67, 69-70; instr. in Spanish, Mt. Union Coll., Alliance, Ohio, 1967-69; instr. in Spanish, Raymond Walters Coll., Cin., 1970-75, asst. prof. Spanish, 1975-80, asso. prof., 1980—. Mem. Am. Assn. Tchrs. Spanish and Portuguese, AAUP, Am. Council Teaching of Fgn. Langs., Am. Personnel and Guidance Assn., Assn. for Non-White Concerns, Ohio Modern Lang. Tchrs. Assn., Phi Beta Kappa, Alpha Lambda Delta, Sigma Delta Pi, Kappa Delta Pi. Contbr. short stories and poems to coll. lit. mags.; adv. bd. La Reina Press, Cin. Office: Room 346 9555 Plainfield Rd Cincinnati OH 45236

BRODERICK, LEO PATRICK, clergyman; b. Detroit, Mar. 1, 1930; s. James Patrick and Jennie M. (Bergin) B.; B.A., Sacred Heart Sem., 1952; postgrad. St. John's Sem., 1952-56; M.A. in History, Eastern Mich. U., 1969; M.Th., U. Ottawa, 1970; S.T.L., St. Paul U. (Ottawa), 1970. Ordained priest Roman Catholic Ch., 1956; asst. pastor St. Frances Cabrini, Allen Park, Mich., 1956-61, St. John's, Ypsilanti, Mich., 1961-63; Cath. chaplain Eastern Mich. U., Ypsilanti, 1961-69; prof. ch. history St. John's Sem., Plymouth, Mich., 1970-77, dean of students, 1970-77, acting acad. dean, 1973-74; pastor St. William's Ch., Walled Lake, Mich., 1977—. Chaplain VA Hosp., Allen Park. Mem. Am. Cath. Hist. Assn., Mich. Hist. Soc., Detroit Hist. Soc. Author: Detroit's Religious Heritage, 1976. Home and Office: 531 Common St Walled Lake MI 48088

BRODHEAD, JOHN, JR., ins. co. exec.; b. Springfield, Ill., June 12, 1917; s. John and Dorothy (Farish) B.; A.B., Amherst Coll., 1940; postgrad. Washington U., St. Louis, 1949-50; m. Josephine Carr, Aug. 1, 1942; 1 dau., Josephine B. Brodhead Roberts. Partner, George D. Capen & Co., St. Louis, 1945-63; v.p. and mgr. Marsh & McLennan Inc., St. Louis, 1963-71, exec. v.p. and dir., 1969, div. mgr. So. Div., 1969-73; head nat. sales New Bus. Devel., St. Louis, 1973—. Active United Fund St. Louis, 1946—, Arts and Edn. Council, 1963—, Backstoppers, 1965—, St. Louis County Watchdog com., 1969, St. Louis Easter Seals, 1971—; guarantor Municipal Opera, 1967—. Bd. dirs. Rehab. Center St. Louis, St. Louis Assn. Retarded Children, Child Guidance Clinic. Served to lt. comdr. USNR, 1940-45. Decorated Navy Cross medal with Gold Star medal. Clubs: St. Louis Country, Rolling Rock, Log Cabin, Deer Creek, Racquet, Twenty-Nine, Noonday. Home: 4 Town and Country Dr Saint Louis MO 63124 Office: 515 Olive St Saint Louis MO 63101

BRODHEAD, WILLIAM MCNULTY, congressman; b. Cleve., Sept. 12, 1941; s. William McNulty and Agnes (Franz) B.; A.B., Wayne State U., 1965; J.D., U. Mich., 1967; m. Kathleen Garlock, Jan. 16, 1965; children—Michael, Paul. Admitted to Mich. bar, 1968, practiced in Detroit, 1968-74; mem. Mich. Ho. of Reps., 1970-74; mem. 94th-97th Congresses from 17th Mich. dist. Home: 24261 Grand River Ave Detroit MI 48219 Office: 1114 Longworth House Office Bldg Washington DC 20515

BRODKEY, DONALD, state supreme ct. justice; b. Sioux City, Iowa, Jan. 17, 1910; s. Harry Aaron and Fannie Pearl (Gilinsky) B.; student U. S.D., 1928; B.A., U. Iowa, 1931, J.D., 1933; m. Gertrude R. Rothkop, May 30, 1943; children—Bruce Harrison, Amy Catherine, Frank Donald. Admitted to Iowa and Nebr. bars, 1933; individual practice law, 1933-41, 47-56; chief price atty. Omaha Office, O.P.A., 1942-46; mcpl. judge City of Omaha, 1957-60, presiding judge, 1960; dist. judge 4th Jud. Dist. Nebr., 1960-74, presiding judge, 1966; justice Nebr. Supreme Ct., Lincoln, 1974—; adv. com. Revision Nebr. Penal Code, 1972-73. Trustee Goodwill Industries; bd. dirs., trustee Omaha Home for Boys; active PTA, Boy Scouts Am., Cub Scouts; trustee Temple Israel. Kellogg Found. fellow to Nat. Coll. State Trial Judges, 1964. Mem. Inst. Jud. Adminstrn., Am., Nebr. bar assns., Iowa Alumni Assn., Order of Coif, Order of Artus, Phi Beta Kappa. Democrat. Clubs: B'nai B'rith, Eagles, Masons (33 deg.), Shriners. Home: 1301 J St Apt 905 Lincoln NE 68508 Office: Room 2222 State Capitol Bldg Lincoln NE 68509

BRODMAN, ESTELLE, librarian; b. N.Y.C., June 1, 1914; d. Henry and Nettie (Sameth) Brodman; A.B., Cornell U., 1935; B.S., Columbia U., 1936, M.S., 1943, Ph.D., 1953; D.Sc. (hon.), U. Ill., 1974. Asst. librarian N.Y. Hosp. Sch. Nursing, 1936-37; loan desk asst. to acting librarian med. library Columbia, 1937-49; chief reference div. and asst. librarian for reference services Nat. Library of Medicine, 1949-61; librarian, asso. prof. med. history, Washington U. Sch. Medicine, St. Louis, 1961-64, librarian, prof. med. history, from 1964, now librarian and prof. emeritus; instr. Columbia Sch. Library Service, 1946-51; lectr. Cath. U. Dept. Library Sci., 1957; vis. prof. Japan Library Sch., Keio U., Tokyo, Japan, 1962, U. Mo., 1971, 73; expert in documentation Central Planning Inst., New Delhi, Institute, 1967-68, S.-E. Regional Office, WHO, New Delhi, 1970, UN Population div., Bangkok, Thailand, 1973, SE Asia, 1976, UN Fund Population Activities, 1976. Cons. NIMH. Mem. Pres.'s Nat. Adv. Commn. on Libraries; chmn. biomed. communications study sect. NIH, 1973-75. Mem. Am., Med. (pres. 1964-65, dir. 1961-64, editor bull. 1947-57, Noyes award 1971) library assns., Spl. Libraries Assn. (past dir., John Cotton Dana award), Am. Assn. History Medicine, Bibliog. Soc. Am. Author: Development of Med. Bibliography, 1954. Home: 4464 W Pine Blvd St Louis MO 63108 Office: Washington U Sch Medicine St Louis MO 63110

BRODY, MYRON, artist; b. N.Y.C., Apr. 5, 1940; B.F.A., Phila. Coll. Art, 1965; student Nat. Inst. Fine Arts, Mexico City, 1961, Ateneum, Helsinki, 1968-69, U. Va. Sch. Continuing Edn., 1970-71; M.F.A. (scholar), U. Pa., 1968; cert. advanced grad. study in arts adminstrn. Harvard U., 1975; m. Senta Brody; 1 dau., Heather. Substitute tchr. art Phila. Bd. Edn., 1966-67; tchr. Phila. Coll. Art, summer 1968; Total Action against Poverty, Roanoke, Va., 1970-71; mem. faculty U. Va. Sch. Continuing Edn., Charlottesville, 1970-76; tchr., head sculpture program Yeovil (Somerset, Eng.) Tech. Coll., 1973-74; lectr. art dept. Hollins (Va.) Coll., 1975; asst. prof., chmn. art dept. Va. Western Community Coll., Roanoke, 1969-76; prof., chmn. visual art dept. Avila Coll., Kansas City, Mo., 1976—; one-man shows USIA, Helsinki, 1969, Va. Mus. Fine Arts, Richmond, 1975, Roanoke Fine Arts Center, 1976; Bedyk Gallery, Kansas City, Mo., 1982; two-man shows Hollins Coll., 1970, 73, Va. Poly. Inst. and State U., Blacksburg, 1970, 73, Washington and Lee U., 1970, Va. State Coll., Petersburg, 1971, Richard Bland Coll., Petersburg, 1971, Salem Coll., Winston-Salem, N.C., 1971, William and Mary Coll., Williamsburg, 1972; exhibited in numerous group shows, 1968—, including Va. Mus. Fine Arts, Roanoke Fine Arts Center, Philbrook Art Center, Tulsa, Southeastern Center for Contemporary Art, Winston-Salem, Wichita Art Mus., Kansas City Art Inst., Inst. Contemporary Art, Phila.; represented in permanent collections: Prudential Ins. Co. Am., U. Va., Princeton U., State Dept., also others. Founder, mem. steering com., mem. bd. Roanoke Valley Arts Council, 1975-76; founder, mem. steering com. Kansas City Arts Council, 1978—, Arts and Bull Soc., Kansas City, 1979—; vp. bd., chmn. fin. com. Kansas City Artists Coalition, 1979—; ednl. and mktg. cons. Friends of Jazz, Kansas City, 1978—; v.p. bd., chmn. state com. for cultural arts Mo.-U.S.A./Para Brazil, Partners of the Americas, Inc., U. Mo., Rolla, 1978—. Served with U.S. Army, 1961-63. Recipient Dimensional Design award Phila. Coll. Art, 1965, 2d prize for sculpture Piedmont chpt. Va. Mus. Art, Martinsville, 1970, purchase award for sculpture Roanoke Summer Art Festival, 1970, cert. of distinction Va. Mus. Fine Arts, 1973, 75, sculpture prize Festival in Park, Roanoke, 1976, Best in Show award Lynchburg Fine Arts Center, 1976, resolution Kansas City Mcpl. Art Commn., 1979; Fulbright-Hays fellow, 1968-69, 73-74. Mem. Coll. Art Assn. Am., Mid-Am. Coll. Art Assn., Fulbright Alumni Assn. Office: Avila College Kansas City MO

BRODY, ROBERT, physician; b. Cleve., June 15, 1948; s. Melvin and Nancy Elizabeth Brody; A.B. with distinction, Stanford U., 1970; M.D., U. Mich., 1974. Intern in internal medicine, Cleve. Clinic, 1974-75, resident in dermatology, 1975-78; practice medicine specializing in dermatology, Cleve., 1978—; staff physician Kaiser-Permanente Med. Center, 1978—, mem. profl. edn. com., 1978—, chmn., 1980—, also sec. exec. com., 1980; asst. clin. prof. Case Western Res. U. Med. Sch., 1978-80, clin. instr., 1980—, dermatology dept. rep. to gen. faculty, 1980—; asst. physician Univ. Hosps. Cleve., 1979—. Sec., Cleve. Play House Men's Com., 1979—; mem. ann. fund com. Stanford U., 1978—, regional co-chmn., 1981—. Diplomate Am. Bd. Dermatology. Mem. Am. Acad. Dermatology, Cleve. Acad. Medicine. Contbr. articles to med. jours. Club: Cleve. Skating. Home: 13415 Shaker Blvd Cleveland OH 44120 Office: 12301 Snow Rd Cleveland OH 44130

BROECKER, HOWARD WILLIAM, lawyer; b. Chgo., May 16, 1940; s. Wallace Charles and Edith May (Smith) B.; student N. Central Coll., Wheaton Coll., 1959-63; J.D., Ill. Inst. Tech., 1966; m. Candace Balfour, Aug. 19, 1961; children—Peter Jon, Christopher Curtis, Anne Llewellyn. Admitted to Ill. bar, 1966; asso. Ehrlich, Bundesen, Friedman & Ross, Chgo., 1966-67, Ehrlich, Bundesen & Cohn, 1967-70; partner Ehrlich, Bundesen, Broecker, Hoffenberg & Seraphin, P.C., 1970—; prin. Howard William Broecker, P.C., 1980—; lectr. Ill. Inst. Continuing Legal Edn., 1970—, Fox Valley Bd. Realtors, 1975—; instr. Am. Savs. and Loan Inst., 1971-72. Bd. dirs. Sunny Ridge Children's Home, 1975—; pres. Men's Found., Community Hosp., 1977-79. Mem. Am., Ill., Chgo. bar assns., Am. Acad. Matrimonial Lawyers (bd. mgrs. 1977—, v.p. 1981—), Ill. Inst. Tech. Chgo. Kent Alumni Assn. (pres. 1975-77). Baptist. Home: 41 W 391 Fairview Rd Elburn IL Office: 2 N LaSalle St Suite 1808 Chicago IL also 427 S 4th St Geneva IL 60134

BROICH, JAMES DEAN, accountant; b. Adrian, Minn., Sept. 28, 1952; s. Christie Lawrence and Anna Mae (Schneider) B.; B.S., Nat. Coll. Bus., 1978; cert. of completion Am. Automation Tng. Center, 1976; m. Sharon Marie Westphal, Oct. 6, 1973; 1 dau., Tammy Lynn. Accountant, office mgr. Crown Candy Inc., Rapid City, S.D., 1978—. Served with USAF, 1971-75. Mem. Rapid City Jr. C. of C., Nat. Coll. of Bus. Vets. Roman Catholic. Home: 114 Texas St Rapid City SD 57701 Office: 2020 Creek Dr Rapid City SD 57709

BROLANDER, GLEN EARL, ednl. adminstr.; b. Rockford, Ill., Dec. 14, 1929; s. Earl Raymond and Verona (Lindblom) B.; B.S., U. Ill., 1951; M.A., U. Ky., 1956; m. Lois Elaine Nestander, Nov. 7, 1959; children—Randall John, Sheryl Ann. Asst. comptroller Augustana Coll., Rock Island, Ill., 1953-59, comptroller, 1959-61, treas., comptroller, 1961-65, v.p. fin. affairs, treas., 1965—; vice chmn., dir. Black Hawk Fed. Savs. & Loan Assn. Bd. dirs. Swedish Council Am., 1979—; 1st v.p. Swedish Pioneer Hist. Soc., 1978—; pres. bd. dirs. Luth. Hosp., Moline, Ill., 1965-68, 74-75, pres. Sac-Fox and Illowa Councils Boy Scouts Am., 1964-65, 68-70, pres. Am.-Scandinavian Found., 1976-78; pres. ch. council Luth. Ch. Served to 1st lt. U.S. Army, 1951-53. Decorated knight 1st class Order of North Star (Sweden); recipient Silver Beaver award Boy Scouts Am. Mem. Nat. Assn. Coll. and Univ. Bus. Officers, Central Assn. Coll. and Univ. Bus. Officers, Rock Island C. of C. (pres. 1973-74), Phi Gamma Delta, Alpha Phi Omega. Club: Kiwanis. Author geneal. works. Home: 3231 29 Ave Ct Rock Island IL 61201 Office: 639 38 St Rock Island IL 61201

BRONTON, ARNE WIGGO, designer; b. Esbjerg, Denmark, July 31, 1930; came to U.S., 1952, naturalized, 1957; s. Soren Peter and Camilla (Jensen) B.; degree in architecture, Tech. Coll., Esbjerg, 1949; postgrad. U. Chgo., spl. courses; m. Elsa Louise Drenning, Sept. 17, 1960; children—Christian, Allen. Founder, Crown Custom Designs, Inc., Barrington Hills, Ill., 1952—, pres., chief exec. officer, chmn. bd., 1975—; pres. Bank Bldg. Consultants; cons. fin. instns. Past pres., chmn. Danish Nat. Com.; bd. dirs. Royal Danish Guards, Danish Lang. Found., Sovereign Order St. John. Served to 2d lt. Royal Danish Guards, 1950-51. Decorated Knight of Malta, Yugoslav Commemorative War Cross, Knight Order Dannebrog (Denmark), Ordre de la Liberation (France), Badge of Ravna Gora, Royal Order White Eagle III, (Serbia); recipient bronze and gold medal in design, 1949-50. Mem. Pres.'s Assn., Am. Mgmt. Assn., AIA, Am. Soc. Interior Designers, Constrn. Specifications Inst., Exec. Club Chgo., Internat. Assn. Architects. Republican. Lutheran. Clubs: Turnbery Country, Marco Island Country, Marco Island Yacht, Sertoma (life), Masons, Shriners. Office: Crown Custom Design Inc 409 W Countyline Rd Barrington Hills IL 60010

BROOKMAN, JOHN F., assn. pub. relations dir.; b. Chgo., July 31, 1919; s. Roy A. and Helen J. (Tobin) B.; B.A. in Bus., Wright Jr. Coll., 1939; B.S. in Speech, Northwestern U., 1948. Radio and TV writer, radio dir., TV producer NBC, Chgo., 1948-60; v.p. corp. communications United Dairy Industry Assn. and Am. Dairy Assn., Rosemont, Ill., 1960—. Served with USAAF, 1941-46. Decorated D.F.C. with 2 oak leaf clusters, Air Medal with 7 oak leaf clusters. Mem. Pub. Relations Soc. Am. (accredited), Am. Assn. Agrl. Editors, Agrl. Relations Council. Home: 486 Brookside Rd Barrington IL 60010 Office: United Dairy Industry Assn Dairy Center 6300 N River Rd Rosemont IL 60018

BROOKS, ARTHUR VAN NORDEN, lawyer; b. N.Y.C., May 8, 1936; s. Fred Almeron and Marion (Snow) B.; B.S., Cornell U., 1958; LL.B., U. Mich., 1963; children—Lauren, Caryn, Kristin, Tom. Admitted to Ohio bar; asso. firm Baker & Hostetler, Cleve., 1963-72, partner firm, 1972-74, 79—; mem. Ohio. Ho. of Reps., 1975-78; adj. asso. prof. dept. urban affairs Cleve. State U. Chmn., Cleveland Heights Democrats, 1979-82; vice chmn. Ohio Land Use Rev. Com., 1975-77; chmn. Council on Mental Health, 1979-72, Ohio State Budget Coalition, 1981—. Served to lt. USNR, 1958-61. Recipient Civil Liberties award ACLU of Ohio, 1977. Mem. Am. Bar Assn., Ohio Bar Assn. (past gov. real estate sect.), Cleve. Bar Assn. Unitarian. Office: 3200 National City Center Cleveland OH 44114*

BROOKS, BETTY WAGONER, infection control practitioner; b. Balt., May 21, 1925; d. Burton H. and Helen E. (Warren) W.; diplomate, Ch. Home and Hosp. Sch. Nursing, Balt., 1948; B.A. magna cum laude, Baldwin Wallace Coll., 1980; postgrad. U. Cin.; m. John Edward Brooks, Jr., Jan. 26, 1952 (div.); children—John Edward, Michael Paul. Staff nurse hosps., Balt., 1948-51; dep. chief nurse mobile unit ARC, Balt., 1951-53; staff nurse Columbia Hosp., Milw., 1954-55, Presbyn. Hosp., Charlotte, N.C., 1955-60, Deaconess Hosp., Cleve., 1960-66; staff nurse Cleve. Met. Gen. Hosp., 1969-70, head nurse ob-gyn and family planning clinics, 1970-72; nursing supr. Sunny Acres Hosp., Cleve., 1972-74; instr. inservice edn. Deaconess Hosp., Cleve., 1974-75; infection control nurse Deaconess Hosp., 1975-79, infection control coordinator, 1979—. Instr., ARC, Cleve., 1966-69; vol. public TV sta. WVIZ, 1978-81; active Olmsted Players, community theatre, 1979-81. Mem. Assn. Practitioners of Infection Control, Greater Cleve. Hosp. Assn. (ad hoc com. on infection control consortium 1979-80), Cleve. Area Citizens League for Nursing. Unitarian. Home: 5651 Broadview Rd D-10 Parma OH 44134 Office: Deaconess Hosp 4229 Pearl Rd Cleveland OH 44109

BROOKS, GLADYS SINCLAIR, exec.; b. Mpls., June 8, 1914; d. John Franklin and Gladys (Phillips) Sinclair; student U. Geneva, Switzerland, 1935; B.A., U. Minn., 1936; LL.D., Hamline U., 1966; m. Wright W. Brooks, Apr. 17, 1941; children—Diane (Mrs. Roger Montgomery), John, Pamela (Mrs. Jean Marc Perraud). Dir. Farmer's and Mechanics Bank, 1973—; mem. Met. Council, 1975—; lectr. world affairs, 1939—; mem. Mpls. City Council, 1967-73; mem. Met. Airports Commn., 1971-74; pres. World Affairs Center U. Minn., 1976—; instr. continuing edn. for women U. Minn. Lectr. on world tours as Am. specialist U.S. Dept. State; 1959-60; mem. Mpls. Charter Commn., 1948-51; pres. YWCA, 1953-57, mem. nat. bd., del. world meeting, Denmark; pres. Minn. Internat. Center, 1953-63; chmn. Minn. Women's Com. for Civil Rights, 1961-64; mem. U.S. Com. for UNICEF, 1959-68; mem. Gov.'s Adv. Com. Children and Youth, 1953-58, Minn. Adv. Com. Employment and Security, 1948-50; Midwest adv. com. Inst. Internat. Edn.; mem. nat. com. White House Conf. Children and Youth, 1960; chmn. Gov.'s Human Rights Commn., 1961-65; dir. Citizens Com. Delinquency and Crime, 1969-81; chmn. Mpls. Adv. Com. on Tourism, 1976-82; vice chmn. Nat. Community Partnerships Seminars, 1977—; mem. Midwest Selection Panel, White House Fellows, 1981. Del. Rep. Nat. Conv., 1952; state chmn. Citizens for Eisenhower, 1956; founder, pres. Rep. Workshop; co-chmn. Mpls. Bicentennial Commn., 1974-76. Pres. Internat. Center for Fgn. Students; dir. Minn. Alumni Assn.; trustee United Theol. Sem., YWCA, Hamline U. Recipient Centennial Women of Minn. award Hamline U., 1954; Woman of Distinction award AAUW, Mpls. 1956; Woman of Year award YWCA, 1973; Brotherhood award NCCJ, 1975; Service to Freedom award Minn. State Bar Assn., 1976; Community Leadership award YWCA, 1981. Mem. World Affairs Council (pres. 1942-44), Minn. League Women Voters (dir. 1940-45), Mpls. Council Ch. Women (pres. 1946-48), Nat. Council of Chs. (mem. gen. bd., v.p. 1961-69), Minn. Council of Chs. (1st woman pres. 1961-64, Christian service award 1967), Mpls. Council of Chs. (v.p. 1946-48), United Ch. Women (bd. mgrs.), Minn. UN Assn. (dir.), Nat. League Cities (human resources steering com. 1972-73), Am. Acad. Polit. Sci., Mpls. C. of C., Minn. Women's Polit. Caucus, Minn. Women's Econ. Roundtable, AAUW, Women's Symphony Assn. Presbyn. Clubs: Zonta, Women's, Lafayette (Mpls.). Home: 5056 Garfield Ave S Minneapolis MN 55419 Office: Metro Sq Bldg St Paul MN

BROOKS, HENRY PHILIP, mfg. co. exec.; b. Chgo., 1924; grad. U. Chgo., 1940, Ill. Inst. Tech., 1942. Chmn. bd., pres. Prodn. Tool Corp., Chgo.; pres., dir. Compscidata Corp., Egon Machinery Co.; exec., dir. La Sultana Food Products Corp. Office: 1229-41 E 74th St Chicago IL 60619

BROOKS, MICHAEL LYNN, advt. exec.; b. Lafayette, Ind., Feb. 9, 1943; s. Ray Daniel and Velda Deane (Smith) B.; B.S., Ind. State U., 1965; postgrad. Ind. U., 1966. Spl. assignment writer Indpls. News, 1965-68; advt. dir. Eastern Express, Inc., Terre Haute, Ind., 1968-72; pres. CRE, Inc., Brazil, Ind., 1972—. Bd. dirs. Katherine Hamilton Mental Health Center, Inc., Terre Haute, 1980—. Ford Found. grantee, 1966. Mem. Nat. Agri-Mktg. Assn., Bank Mktg. Assn. Club: Advt. of Indpls. Office: PO Box 489 Brazil IN 47834

BROOKS, PHILLIP ASHER, food specialties co. exec.; b. Mpls., July 27, 1954; s. Irving M. and Beverly A. (Plante) B.; B.S., St. Cloud State U., 1976; M.B.A., Coll. St. Thomas, 1979; m. Margot C. Johnson, July 10, 1976; 1 son, Nathan Eric. Various positions H. Brooks and Co., Mpls., part time, 1968-76, full time, 1976—, dir. marketing, 1979—. Knighted Royalty St. Paul Winter Carnival, 1981. Mem. Nat. Family Bus. Council, Minn. Family Bus. Council, St. Cloud State Aero Club (life). Office: H Brooks and Co 2521 E Hennepin St Minneapolis MN 55413

BROOKS, ROGER ALAN, polit. scientist; b. Ann Arbor, Mich., Aug. 9, 1944; s. Warren Wilfred and Sylvia May (Burrell) B.; B.A., U. Mich., 1966; postgrad. U. Strathclyde, Glasgow, Scotland, 1969-70; Ph.D. (NDEA fellow), Mich. State U., 1973; m. Ronnie Lee Durchlag, May 8, 1966; children—Kirsten, Russell. Instr. polit. sci. U. Fla., Gainesville, 1970-71; asst. prof. polit. sci. Macalester Coll., St. Paul, 1971-78; adj. prof. polit. sci. U. Minn., Mpls., 1978-82, Augsburg Coll., Mpls., 1979-82; prin. program evaluator Minn. Office of Legis. Auditor, St. Paul, 1978—. Mem. St. Paul Cable Communications Bd., 1979-81. Woodrow Wilson fellow, 1969-70; European Parliamentary fellow, 1977-78; William Warner Bishop prize U. Mich., 1965. Mem. Am. Polit. Sci. Assn., Minn. Polit. Sci. Assn. (mem. exec. com. 1978-80), Am. Soc. for Public Adminstrn., Evaluation Research Soc. Club: Sierra (vice chmn. Northstar chpt. 1979—). Home: 1671 Pinehurst St Saint Paul MN 55116 Office: 122 Veterans Service Bldg Saint Paul MN 55155

BROOM, ALBERT MOWRY, travel agt.; b. Chgo., May 6, 1929; s. Virgil Marion and Marion (Mowry) B.; B.S., Millikin U., 1953; m. Sandra Chrisman, Mar. 19, 1970. With Dun & Bradstreet, 1953-60, reporting mgr., Davenport, Iowa, 1955-60: spl. rep. Signode Corp., Chgo., 1960-68; owner, mgr. Mid-Am. Travel Agy., Champaign, Ill., 1968—; v.p. Mid-Am. Travel of Monticello, 1976—. Mem. exec. com. Ill. Assn. R.R. Passengers, Chgo., 1977—. Mem. Am. Soc. Travel Agts., Assn. Retail Travel Agts., Campus Businessmen's Assn. Champaign (pres. 1975-77). Democrat. Methodist. Clubs: Lions, Masons. Home: 2003 N Highcross Rd Urbana IL 61801 Office: 703 S Wright St Champaign IL 61820

BROOME, GORDON LEE, electronics educator; b. Alliance, Ohio, June 6, 1938; s. Thorne K. and Genevieve C. (Clarke) B.; B.S., Mt. Union Coll., 1965; M.A., Kent State U., 1975; m. Barbara Kay Brown, June 9, 1968; children—Zane Tyler, Jennifer Noelle. Engr. draftsman Alliance Machine Co., 1965-72; electronics instr. Central-Hower High Sch., Akron, Ohio, 1973—; v.p., treas. T.K. Broome & Son, Inc., Alliance, 1975—. Served with USNR, 1957-62. Mem. Ohio Vocat. Assn., Am. Vocat. Assn., Akron Educators Assn., Iota Lambda Sigma. Mem. United Ch. of Christ. Clubs: Optimist (public service award), Foresters, Community Amateur Radio, Goodyear Amateur Radio, Canton McKinley Rifle and Pistol, Masons. Home: 9647 Louisville St Louisville OH 44641 Office: 123 S Forge St Akron OH 44308 also 1884 Roseland Rd Alliance OH 44601

BROOMFIELD, WILLIAM S., congressman; b. Royal Oak, Mich., Apr. 28, 1922; s. S. C. and Fern (Taylor) B.; student Mich. State U.; m. Jane Smith Thompson, 1951; children—Susan, Nancy, Barbara. Mem. Mich. Ho. of Reps., 1948, 50, 52, speaker pro tem, 1953; mem. Mich. Senate, 1954-56; mem. 85th-97th congresses from 19th Mich. Dist., ranking Republican on Com. Internat. Relations, mem. Small Bus. Com.; U.S. del. NATO Parliamentarians' Conf., Paris, 1960, NATO Conf., Denmark, 1975, U.S.-U.K. Parliamentary Conf., Bermuda, 1962, Can.-U.S. Interparliamentary Conf., 1961-64, 67-69, 72, 74-79, Mex.-U.S. Interparliamentary Group, 1969-74, 22d UN

Gen. Assembly; congressional adviser Conf. of Com. on Disarmament, Geneva, 1970, 71, 72, 73, 74. Pres., Nat. Rep. Club of Capitol Hill, 1970-74; mem. Nat. Fgn. Relations Council of Am. Legion, 1974. Presbyterian. Clubs: Masons, Lions, Odd Fellows, Optimists. Home: Birmingham MI Office: Room 2306 Rayburn House Office Bldg Washington DC 20515

BROSE, MERLE LEVERNE, physician; b. Cedar Falls, Iowa, Aug. 23, 1922; s. Robert Lisle and Amy Belle (Shedd) B.; B.S., U. Wis., 1943; M.D., 1946; m. Phyllis Marie Magill, Jan. 10, 1948; children—Linda (Mrs. Steven Kleinsteiber), Cheryl (Mrs. Clark Kleinheinz), Pamela (Mrs. Thomas Zembal), Sandra (Mrs. Gerald Jackson), William. Intern, Columbia Hosp., Wilkinsburg, Pa., 1946-47, resident in surgery, 1947-48; gen. practice medicine, Irwin, Pa., 1950-63; med. dir. Nat. Union Ins. Co., Pitts., 1962-63; gen. practice medicine, Menomonee Falls, Wis., 1963-65; physician Health Service, U. Wis., Madison, 1965—; faculty U. Wis. Med. Sch., 1965—. Served to capt. USAF, 1948-50. Mem. U.S. Power Squadrons (Madison squadron sec. 1969, treas. 1970, adminstrv. officer 1971, exec. officer, 1972, dist. adminstrv. officer 1972, comdr. 1973, grade Navigator 1970, dist. exec. officer 1974, dist. comdr, 1975). Clubs: Four Lakes Yacht (commodore 1978) (Madison); Masons. Home: 4517 Gregg Rd Madison WI 53705 Office: 1552 University Ave Madison WI 53706

BROSE, PHYLLIS MARIE, nurse; b. Stewartsville, Pa., Sept. 20, 1925; d. George Allan and Roberta Fern (Lintner) Magill; R.N., Columbia Hosp. Sch. Nursing, Wilkinsburg, Pa., 1946; certificate Sch. Anesthesia St. Francis Hosp., Pitts., 1948; m. Merle LaVerne Brose, Jan. 10, 1948; children—Linda Brose Kleinsteiber, Cheryl Brose Kleinheinz, Pamela Brose Zembal, Sandra Brose Jackson, William. Nurse, Columbia Hosp., 1946-47, anesthetist, 1948, staff nurse, 1949-50; nursing supr., coordinator dialysis U. Wis. Hosp., Madison, 1966—. Mem. med. and sci. bd. Kidney Found. Wis., 1970—; mem. adv. council Nat. Center Health Care Tech.; bd. dirs. S. Central chpt. Wis. Kidney Found., 1980-81; mem. Network 13 Coordinating Council End-Stage Renal Disease, Inc. Recipient Exceptional Performance award in nursing U. Wis., 1977. Mem. Am. Assn. Nephrology Nurses and Technicians (pres. Wis. chpt. 1978-79). Club: Four Lakes Yacht. Home: 4517 Gregg Rd Madison WI 53705 Office: 600 Highland Ave Madison WI 53706

BROSNAN, SISTER M. BRIGID (MARGARET ANNE BROSNAN), hosp. exec., nun; b. Cleve.; d. Patrick J. and Mary Loretta (Barrett) B.; B.A., Ursuline Coll., 1951; M.S., St. Louis U., 1953; M.B.A., Kent State U., 1966; J.D., U. Akron, 1971. Joined Sisters of Charity of Saint Augustine, Roman Catholic Ch., 1950; dietician fellow St. Mary Hosp., St. Louis, 1951-53; mem. faculty St. John Coll., Cleve., 1954-62; dir. dietary service St. Vincent Charity Hosp., Cleve., 1953-62; exec. dir. St. Thomas Hosp. Med. Center, Akron, Ohio, from 1962, now pres.; admitted to Ohio bar, 1973; mem. adv. council NE Ohio Regional Med. Program, Health Edn. Network, 1972—. Mem. mayor's com. on a med. sch. in Akron, 1970—; mem. Ohio Planning Commn., 1972—, Akron Planning Commn., 1972—, Akron Historic Preservation Com., 1976—, Summit County Bd. Visitors, 1980. Fellow Am. Coll. Hosp. Adminstrs.; mem. Am. Hosp. Assn., Ohio Hosp. Assn. (mem. various coms. 1968—), Greater Cleve. Hosp. Assn., Akron Regional Health Assn. (pres. 1977-78), Am. Bar Assn., Ohio State Bar Assn., Akron Bar Assn. Contbr. articles on dietetics to profl. jours. Home: 444 N Main St Akron OH 44310 Office: St Thomas Med Center 444 N Main St Akron OH 44310

BROST, EILEEN MARIE, guidance counselor; b. Medford, Wis., July 18, 1909; d. Peter and Pauline (Rudolph) Brost; B.A., Loyola U., 1939; M.A., St. Xavier U., 1954; M.Ed., Loyola U., 1970; postgrad. Alverno Coll., Milw. State Tchrs. Coll., DePaul U., Lewis U., Marquette U., Alfred Adler Inst., Chgo., Marylhurst Coll., Oreg. Joined Sch. Sisters of St. Francis, Roman Cath. Ch., 1925; tchr. various locations, Ill., Oreg. and Wis., 1927-68; religious edn. coordinator St. Anne's Parish, Barrington, Ill., 1968-72; guidance counselor, various schs., Chgo. Public Sch. System and Chgo. Archdiocese, 1972—. Active parish orgns., Pro-Life Orgn. Cert. tchr., Ill., Wis.; Braille cert. Mem. Nat. Ret. Tchrs. Assn., Chgo. Ret. Tchrs. Assn., Am. Guidance and Personnel Assn., Am. Sch. Counselor Assn. Roman Catholic. Home: 1925 Kedvale St Chicago IL 60639 Office: 4131 W Cortland Chicago IL 60639

BROTHERS, BUDD RITTER, business exec.; b. Youngstown, Ohio, Jan. 8, 1931; s. Bern Ritter and Esther Maureen (Newton) B.; B.S., Youngstown Coll., 1948; m. Patricia Susan Jones, Sept. 5, 1952; 1 dau., Bonnie Robin. Stock boy Boardman Roofing Supply, Youngstown, 1946-48, asst. mgr., clerk, 1948-52, gen. mgr., 1954-64; pres. 20th Century Paint Products, Youngstown, 1964-70, chmn. bd., 1971-72; chmn. bd. Century 21, Inc., Youngstown, 1972—. Mem. C.O.E. adv. bd., Mahoning County, Ohio; vice chmn. bd. zoning appeals, Austintown Twp., Mahoning County, 1965—, v.p. bd. edn., 1970-72, pres. bd. edn., 1972; mem. chmn.'s com. U.S. Senatorial Bus. Adv. Bd.; vice chmn. exec. com. Republican Party, 1965-69. Served with AUS, 1952-54. Mem. Austintown Good Govt. League (pres. 1963-68), Ohio Sch. Bds. Assn., Nat. Decorating Products Assn., Alpha Phi Omega Alumni. Mason. Specialist in new paint products research, paint chem. product devel. Home: 3966 Avalon Ct Youngstown OH 44515 Office: 3711 Mahoning Ave Youngstown OH 44515

BROUGH, JOHN HERBERT, occupational therapist, ednl. adminstr.; b. Danville, Ill., June 11, 1945; s. John C. and Elsie B. (Trimby) B.; B.S. in Occupational Therapy, U. Ill., 1968; postgrad. Nat. Coll. of Edn., Evanston, Ill., 1969. Tchr. health edn. Sch. Dist. 303, Ill., 1968-71; remedial specialist Camp Arrowhead, Wis., summers, 1969-71; vocat. evaluator Vermilion County (Ill.) Rehab. Center, 1971-72; dir. remedial program Camp Algonquin, Ill., summers, 1972-79; dir. Brough Learning Center, Danville, Ill., 1972—, dir. occupational therapy Kankakee (Ill.) Area Spl. Edn. Co-op, 1980—; cons. to United Cerebral Palsy, Bur. of Indian Affairs, Children's House, Adolph Meyer Center, Progress Sch., 1974—; mem. adv. com. Area Health Edn. System for Continuing Edn., 1973-79. Bd. dirs. N. Am. Riding for the Handicapped Assn., 1975—. Recipient Vol. Service award VA, 1962, Meritorious Service citation Am. Legion, 1962; James scholar, 1964-68. Mem. Am. Occupational Therapy Assn., Kickapoo Dist. Occupational Therapy Assn. (pres. 1972-76), Ill. Occupational Therapy Assn. (treas. 1976-79), Vermilion Assn. for Learning Disabilities (treas. 1980—), The U.S. Capitol Hist. Soc. (founding mem.). Contbr. articles on therapy to profl. publs. Home: 1774 Georgetown Rd Danville IL 61832 Office: Rural Route 7 Box 339-A Kankakee IL 60901

BROUK, J. JOHN, bldg. and insulation material mfg. co. exec.; b. St. Louis, Apr. 30, 1917; s. Joseph John and Marie (Hilgert) B.; B.S. in Ceramic Engring., U. Ill., 1938: m. Ruthe Garman, Nov. 1, 1946; children—Joseph John, Joanne Marie. Refractory researcher metallurgy dept. Naval Research Lab., Washington, 1943-46; pres. Precast Slab & Tile Co., St. Louis, 1951-54, Perlite Insulation Co., St. Louis, 1951-54; v.p. Fed. Cement Tile Co., Chgo., 1954-57; pres. Brouk Co., St. Louis, 1957—; pres. Perlite Inst., 1950-52; nat. sales agt. perlite ore Great Lakes Carbon Co., 1952-72, Grefco, Inc., 1966-72. Bd. dirs. Mt. St. Rose Hosp., St. Louis Conservatory and Sch. for the Arts, Multiple Sclerosis Soc. Mem. Internat. Vermiculite Assn. (pres. 1976-80), Young Presidents Orgn. (pres. St. Louis chpt. 1959, lectr. mgmt. seminars). Contbr. numerous articles on perlite insulation to profl. and trade jours.; patentee perlite brick veneer wall panel; developer combined perlite and vermiculite concrete and corrugated metal roof-deck system. Office: Brouk Co 1367 S Kingshighway Saint Louis MO 63110

BROWE, WALTER F., ednl. adminstr.; b. Oct. 11, 1927; A.B. in Edn., U. Mich., 1950; M.Ed., Wayne State U., 1954, Ed.D., 1966; postdoctoral student Mich. State U., 1968; m. Jean Hatfield, Jan. 11, 1981; 1 dau. by previous marriage, Judy Lee Browe Rohm. Tchr. Detroit schs., later prin., then adminstr.; dean students Lake Mich. Coll., Benton Harbor, Mich., 1967-69, exec. v.p., 1969-78, pres., 1978—. Bd. dirs. Pvt. Industry Council, 1979, 80, coop. edn. com., 1979, 80; pres. bd. dirs. Twin Cities Symphonic Soc., 1972-75; bd. dirs. Community Concerts Assn., 1977, 78; pres. bd. dirs. Blossomland United Way, 1982, gen. campaign chmn., 1976; mem. state budget com. Mich. United Fund, 1969-71; Mich. State U.-Western Mich. U. Extension Center Adv. Com., 1972-80; program chmn. Twin Cities Community Forum, 1967-69. Served with USMC, World War II. Mem. Am. Assn. Community and Jr. Colls., Am. Assn. Higher Edn., Am. Ednl. Research Assn., Am. Personnel and Guidance Assn., Mich. Community Coll. Personnel Assn., Mich. Community Coll. Assn., Wayne State U. Alumni Assn. (bd. govs.), Twin Cities C. of C. (bus. edn. council 1979, 80, bd. dirs., 1982). Clubs: Rotary (chmn. occupational info. com. 1979, 80, bd. dir., 1981, 82), Mich. Salmon and Steelheaders Fisherman's Assn. (bd. dirs. 1977-78). Office: 2755 E Napier Benton Harbor MI 49022

BROWN, ARVILL BUELL, civil engr.; b. Wetonka, S.D., Aug. 5, 1923; s. Arvill Clay and Anna (Gunderson) B.; B.S., Tri-State U., Angola, Ind., 1946; certificate small homes council course U. Ill., 1954; m. June Strong, Oct. 13, 1944; children—Duane Arvill, LuReign Anne, Anita June. Asst. project engr. Ind. State Hwy. Dept., 1946-47; project engr. Tri-State Coll., Angola, Ind., 1947-48; field engr. James Stewart Corp., Chgo., 1948-50; chief engr., gen. field supt. and estimator Fisher-Stoune, Inc., Decatur, Ill., 1950-60; chief engr. aluminum bldg. products div. Maco Corp., Huntington, Ind., 1960-64; partner B & K Engring. Company, Huntington, 1963-64, v.p., 1964-65, pres. B & K Engring., Inc., Kendallville, Ind., 1966-77, also dir.; pres. Brown Cons. Engrs., Inc., Kendallville, 1977—; owner Arvill B. Brown, profl. engr., Kendallville, 1971—; constrn. mgr., engr. Great Lakes Bible Coll., Lansing, 1971-76; pres. Noble County (Ind.) Plan Commn., 1967-71; hwy. engr. Noble County, 1965-71, surveyor, 1967-71; mem. Noble County Drainage Bd., 1967-71. Active Boy Scouts, Cub Scouts; trustee, sec., forwarding agt. Christian Edn. Assn. of Orient, Inc., 1968—; mem. exec. com. New Chs. Christ Evangelism, 1965—; dir. Lake James Christian Assembly, Angola, Ind., 1970-75; nat. alumni dir. Tri-State Coll., Angola, Ind., 1971-75. Served with USNR, 1944-46. Registered profl. engr., Ill., Ind., Ohio, Mich., Ky., Minn., Wis., Ga.; profl. land surveyor, Ind.; certified fallout shelter analyst U.S. Dept. Def.; certificates on energy-comml. and residential bldgs., Wis. Mem. Nat., Ind. socs. profl. engrs., ASCE (v.p. N.E. Ind. sect. 1971), Ind. Soc. Profl. Land Surveyors, Decatur Contractors Assn. (past sec.-treas.). Mem. Ch. of Christ (elder). Patentee in field. Home: 357 N Main St Kendallville IN 46755 Office: 212 S Main St Kendallville IN 46755

BROWN, BAIRD, ret. ins. co. exec.; b. Chgo., Aug. 8, 1922; s. George Frederic and Irene (Larmon) B.; A.B., Washington and Lee U., 1949; student U. Chgo., 1946-48. Vice pres. Geo. F. Brown & Sons, Inc. Chgo., 1948-52, dir., sec., 1952-70, v.p., 1957-70; exec. v.p., dir. Interstate Nat. Corp., 1970-74; pres. Internat. Visitors Center, 1964-65, Lyric Opera Guild, 1958-59; mem. Ill. Arts Council, 1966-67; mem. Joseph Jefferson Awards Com., 1971-79, 81—. Served with USAAF, 1943-45. Mem. UN Assn. (dir. Chgo. br. 1967-73), Sigma Chi. Club: Arts. Home: 2440 N Lakeview Ave Chicago IL 60614

BROWN, BASIL W., state senator; b. Vandalia, Mich., Mar. 20, 1927; A.B., Western Mich. U.; LL.B., U. Mich., 19—; m. Ermajeanne Seeger, 1950; 1 dau., Lisa Denise. Admitted to Mich. bar, practice law; mem. Mich. State Senate, 1956—, chmn. judiciary com.; mem. Nat. Conf. Commrs. Uniform State Laws. Served in USN. Episcopalian. Office: State Capitol Lansing MI 48909*

BROWN, BRUCE WAYNE, trust co. ofcl.; b. Fairfield, Iowa, Mar. 14, 1950; s. J. Don and Dorothy B. (Osteen) B.; B.S., Iowa State U., 1972; M.P.A., Drake U., 1979; m. Teresa A. Brown, Nov. 11, 1978. Mgr. quality assurance Dept. Public Instruction, State of Iowa, Des Moines, 1972-78; program cons. Midwest Regional Resource Center, Drake U., Des Moines, 1978-80; supr. tng. and devel. specialist Iowa Beef Processors, Inc., Dakota City, Nebr., 1980-81; dir. tng. and devel. Bankers Trust Co., Des Moines, 1981—; dir. Midwest Resources, Inc., Des Moines. Legis. chmn. Iowa Rehab. Assn., 1977-79. Mem. Am. Soc. Tng. and Devel., Pi Alpha Alpha. Home: 1943 NW 80th Pl Des Moines IA 50322 Office: Bankers Trust Co 7th and Locust Sts Des Moines IA 50304

BROWN, CHARLES ASA, lawyer; b. Woodsfield, Ohio, Oct. 17, 1912; s. Charles A. and Anna Miriam (Hayes) B.; A.B. Va. Mil. Inst., 1931-35; student U. Mich., 1937; J.D., Western Reserve U., 1938 children—Charles A. III, Ridgley. Admitted to Ohio bar, 1938, pvt. practice Portsmouth, 1938—; asst. atty. gen. State of Ohio, 1963; owner Raven Rock Farm and Feurt Farm, Scioto River Farm Tract, Winters Farm. Lectr. Indian lore. Active Boy Scouts Am., 1946—, serving as merit badge counsellor, exec. bds. Scioto Area council, Portsmouth dist. commr., scout master troop 12, 1966—, developer, adviser Indian dance team Portsmouth dist., 1964-78, v.p. Scioto Area council, 1967-68, nat. rep. Nat. council, 1967-68; advisory council Girl Scouts of Am., 1947-48; advisory chief Indian Tribes, 1961-63; councilman Western Black Elk Keetowah, Cherokee Nation, 1964—; mem. Cedar River Tulsa Muskogee Band. Bd. dirs. Portsmouth Little League Baseball Assn., 1957-58, Scioto County unit Am. Cancer Soc., 1973—; advisory bd. Practical Nurses Assn., 1960-61; sr. warden Episcopal Ch., lay reader, 1950-76; lay reader Anglican Orthodox Ch., 1976-77, Anglican Ch. N. Am., 1977—. Served from 1st lt. to capt. U.S. Army, 1941-46; lt. col. Res. (ret.). Decorated Bronze Star with oak leaf cluster, Purple Heart, Am. Defense medal, Victory medal, three battle stars, Occupational medal, European theatre ribbon. Named Ky. Col.; recipient Silver Beaver award Boy Scouts Am., 1968, Vigil Order of Arrow, 1971. Mem. Am. Indian, Ohio, Portsmouth (trustee 1966—) bar assns., Am. Legion, VFW, DAV, Nat. Rifle Assn., Ohio Farm Bur., various Am. Indian orgns. Odd Fellow, Redman, Mason (32 deg., master of lodge 1965, Shriner, past comdr.; trustee lodge 1966-71, excellent high priest chpt. 1976-77, illustrious master council 1978-79, pres. 5th dist. Royal Arch Masons 1979, arch adjutant 6th arch council 1979-81, dist. dep. grand high priest 1980—, named high priest R.A.M., recipient silver trowel, Royal Order Scotland, Knight Masons Ireland, Tall Cedars Lebanon, York Cross of Honour, K.T. priest), K.P. (grand tribune Ohio 1961, past chancellor comdr.), Ohio Masonic Vets., Philalethes Soc., Elk, Eagle, Fraternal Order of Police. Mem. Order Eastern Star (patron 1966, trustee 1967-70), White Shrine of Jerusalem. Club: Daniel Boone Muzzle Loading Rifle. Designer flood wall, Portsmouth, Ohio, 1936. Office: 721 Washington St Portsmouth OH 45662

BROWN, CLARENCE J., congressman; b. Columbus, Ohio, June 18, 1927; s. Clarence J. and Ethel (McKinney) B.; B.A. in Econs., Duke U., 1947; M.B.A., Harvard U., 1949; m. Joyce Eldridge, June 11, 1955; children—Elizabeth Ellen (dec. Mar. 1964), Clarence J., Catherine McKinney, Roy E. Editor, Blanchester (Ohio) Star Republican, 1949-53; editor Franklin (Ohio) Chronicle, 1953-57, pub., 1957-59; editor Urbana (Ohio) Daily Citizen, 1957-62, pub., 1959-70; established, mgr. Sta. WCOM-FM, Urbana, 1963-65; pres. Brown Pub. Co., 1965-77, chmn. bd., 1977—; mem. 89th-97th Congresses, 7th Ohio Dist., mem. govt. ops., energy and commerce coms., ranking minority mem. fossil and synthetic fuels subcom., joint econ. com. Past pres. Urbana and Franklin chpts. ARC; past pres. Champaign County Young Republican Club; asst. sgt.-at-arms Rep. Nat. Convs., 1964-64, del., 1972, 76; mem. Champaign County Rep. exec. com., 1963—; bd. visitors Harvard Grad. Sch. Bus. Adminstrn.; adv. council Am. Enterprise Inst. Served to lt. (j.g.) USN, 1944-46, 50-52; Korea. Mem. Nat. Newspaper Assn., Internat. Mgmt. and Devel. Inst., Washington Policy Council, Farm Bur., Blanchester, Franklin, Urbana chambers commerce, Sigma Delta Chi (past pres. Central Ohio chpt.). Presbyterian (trustee). Clubs: Lions, Rotary, Masons (33 deg.), Shriners. Home: 430 Scioto Urbana OH 43078 also 3208 Cleveland Ave NW Washington DC 20008 Office: 2217 Rayburn House Office Bldg Washington DC 20515

BROWN, CLIFFORD F., justice Supreme Ct. Ohio; b. Bronson Twp., Ohio, Jan. 21, 1916; s. Ignatius A. Brown; m. Katherine; children—Charles, Margaret Brown Kramb, Sheila, Ann Brown Playko; A.B. magna cum laude, U. Notre Dame, 1936, LL.B. cum laude, 1938. Admitted to Ohio bar, 1938, Mich. bar, 1939; practice law, Norwalk, Ohio, 1938-64; judge Huron County Ct., 1938-65, Ohio Ct. Appeals, 1965-80; justice Ohio Supreme Ct., 1980—. Served with U.S. Army, World War II. Mem. Am., Ohio, Lucas County, Toledo bar assns., Toledo Old Newsboys Goodfellow Assn., Internat. Inst. Great Toledo, VFW. Democrat. Clubs: Kiwanis, Eagles, YMCA Athletic, Torch. Address: Supreme Court State Capitol Columbus OH 43215*

BROWN, DANIEL H., univ. dean; b. Wisconsin Rapids, Wis., Jan. 14, 1928; s. Wayne Kennon and Josephine (Ibinger) B.; student U. Ill., 1945-46, U. Wis., LaCrosse, 1947-48; B.S., U. Wis., Eau Claire, 1950; M.S., U. Wis., Superior, 1958; Ed.D., U. Kans., 1962; m. Ruth M. Spiering, June 26, 1948; children—Diane, Suzanne, Thomas, Ellen. Thcr., Superior (Wis.) Bd. Edn., 1950-58; prin. elem. sch. Platteville (Wis.) Bd. Edn., 1958-60; instr. U. Kans., 1960-62; prof. U. Wis., River Falls, 1962-71, dean Coll. Edn., 1971—. Served with U.S. Army, 1945-47. Mem. NEA, Phi Delta Kappa. Roman Catholic. Clubs: Lions, Moose. Office: Coll Edn U Wis 410 S 3d St River Falls WI 54022

BROWN, DAVID WAYNE, social worker; b. Chgo., July 29, 1954; s. Byrd Elmer and Lucille Claudette (Shelton) B.; B.S., George Williams Coll., 1976, M.S.W., 1978. Program dir. Near North West Civic Com., Chgo., 1973-75; Big Brother vol. Lombard (Ill.) YMCA, 1972-73; youth minister First Congregational Ch. of Steger (Ill.), 1973-74; tchr. parent-child communication seminar Coll. DuPage, Glen Ellyn, Ill., 1977; co-dir. Downers Grove (Ill.) Twp. Youth Commn., 1976-78; dir. Village of Oak Lawn (Ill.) Youth Commn., 1978—, supr. Champaign region, 1980—. Vol. Cook County Juvenile Ct., 1974-75: bd. dirs. Pilgrim Faith United Ch. Christ Holistic Health Center. Mem. Nat. Assn. Social Workers, Youth Network Council Chgo. (vice chairperson 1979), Ill. Youth Service Bur., Ill. Child Welfare Assn., George Williams Coll. Alumni Assn. Mem. Christian Ch. Clubs: Jaycees Kiwanis (Oak Lawn): rotary.

BROWN, DENNY LEE, glass co. exec.; b. Greenville, Ohio, Nov. 8, 1944; s. James Merrill and Margaret Lucille (Bliss) B.; B.B.A., Ohio State U., 1968; postgrad. U. Toledo, 1973-74; m. Linda Kay Orphal, June 10, 1966; children—Jeffrey Michael, Katherine Ann. With Owens-Ill., Inc., Toledo, Ohio, 1968—, plant comptroller glass container div., Mansfield, Mass., 1974-75, mgr. fin. analysis glass container div., Toledo, 1976, comptroller western hemisphere div., 1979-81, dir. fin. and planning CISPER affiliate, Rio de Janeiro, Brazil, 1981—, adminstrv. mgr. Owens-Ill. de P.R., San Juan, 1977-79. Advisor, Jr. Achievement, 1973-74. Mem. Nat. Assn. Accts., Am. Mgmt. Assn., Am. C. of C. in Rio, Phi Alpha Kappa. Lutheran. Clubs: Am., Brit. Home: 910 Bexton St Perrysburg OH 43551 Office: 405 Madison Ave Toledo OH 43666

BROWN, DON CREAGER, hosp. adminstr.; b. Burbank, Calif., Oct. 9, 1954; s. Robert Creager and Mary Leora (McNeilly) B.; A.A., Allan Hancock Coll., also Asso. Sci., 1974; certificate health facilities mgmt. U. Calif. at Santa Barbara, 1975; B.A., LaVerne Coll., 1975; M.B.A., Golden Gate U., 1977, postgrad., 1977—. Purchasing agt. Lompoc (Calif.) Hosp. Dist., 1975, El Camino Hosp. Dist., Mountain View, Calif., 1975; adminstrv. intern Lompoc Hosp. Dist., 1976; hosp. adminstr., registrar functions David Grant Med. Center, Travis AFB, Calif., 1977-80; chief Health Professions Placement, U.S. Air Force, Los Angeles, 1980-81; chief Health Professions Placement, Midwestern States, 1981—. Chmn. March of Dimes Walk-a-Thon, 1975. Served with Med. Service Corps, USAF, 1976—. Named Jr. Officer of Month, Travis AFB, Calif., 1978; Jr. Officer of Jr., David Grant Med. Center, 1978; Med. Service Corps Jr. Officer of Yr., U.S. Air Force Recruiting Service, 1980; Med. Service Corps Jr. Officer of Yr., U.S. Air Force, 1980; Santa Barbara Found. scholar. Mem. Am. Coll. Hosp. Adminstrs., Am. Hosp. Assn., Health Care Execs., Am. Soc. for Pub. Adminstrs., Am. Assn. Mil. Surgeons, Sacramento Health Care Mgmt. Assn., World Affairs Council No. Calif., Mission Hills Adv. Council, Lompoc-Vacaville Jaycees. Republican. Home: 2503 W Springfield Apt E-10 Champaign IL 61820 Office: 3505 USAF Recruiting Group Chanute AFB IL 61868

BROWN, DONALD L., artist; b. Peoria, Ill., June 1, 1940; s. Noel Wayne and Lillian Mabel (Holland) B.; student Art Inst. Chgo., 1958-60; m. Sherry Stewart, July 29, 1979; children by previous marriage—Stephanie Leann, Stacey Lynn. Art dir., freelance artist, Bloomington, Ill., 1961-66, 68-70; art dir. Fillman Advt., Champaign, Ill., 1966-67; account exec. Graphic Promotions, Indpls., 1967; v.p., art dir. HKC Advt., Hinsdale, Ill., 1970-74; art dir. Ross Advt., Peoria, Ill., 1974-75; freelance artist, designer, Barrington, Ill., 1975-78; lectr. schs. and colls.; works exhibited: Nat. Watercolor Soc., Nat. Sun Carnival Arts (El Paso, Tex.), ISA, Denver, Mcpl. Art League Chgo.; works exhibited Midwest galleries, Mt. St. Mary Coll. (Emmittsburg, Md.), Marshall Jr. High Sch. (Janesville, Wis.), Winona State U., Antioch Ill. State Bank, Mchts. Bank (Watertown, Wis.), Pa. State U.; works rep. public and pvt. collections including: Nat. Archives (Washington), NSF (Washington), The Pentagon, Miami Herald, City of Miami, pvt. collections of individuals and corps. Recipient numerous awards in art including best of show AAUW Art Fair, 1977, Wausau, Wis., 1980, Coconut Grove, Fla., 1981; recipient Charles D. Peacock, III, award Mcpl. Art League Chgo., 1978. Mem. Nat. Watercolor Soc., Watercolor West Soc., Internat. Soc. Artists, Deerpath Art League. Methodist. Home: Rt 1 Box 957 McHenry IL 60050

BROWN, DONALD OWEN, pharm. co. exec.; b. Greeley, Colo., Feb. 24, 1943; s. Robert Van Pelt and Charlma K. (Kurtz) B.; B.A. in Chemistry, B.A. in Biology, U. Denver, 1970; m. Joyce Irene Callison,

June 1, 1963; children—Tracy Lynn, Stephanie Ann. Analytical chemist AMAX Research Labs., Golden, Colo., 1969-72; quality assurance supr. Abbott Labs., North Chicago, Ill., 1972-73; prodn. mgr. Am. Drug & Chem. Co., Sun Valley, Calif., 1973-78; plant mgr. Mead Johnson & Co., Evansville, Ind., 1978—; sterile product processing cons. to several cos., 1974—. Vice pres. PTA, 1980-81. Served with USAF, 1962-66. Mem. Am. Soc. for Quality Control, Am. Chem. Soc., Parental Drug Assns. Lutheran. Home: 3519 Still Meadow Ct Evansville IN 47712 Office: Mead Johnson & Co 2404 W Pennsylvania Ave Evansville IN 47721

BROWN, DOUGLAS RICHARD, businessman; b. Cleve., Mar. 28, 1951; s. Edward Austin and Mary (Westerman) B.; A.S. in Bus. Adminstrn., Rock Valley Coll., Ill., 1976; m. Susan L. Clark, Sept. 18, 1971; 1 son, Kevin Patrick. Dist. sales mgr. Radio Shack div. Tandy Corp., 1972-77; founder, 1977, since gen. mgr. Handi-Fix Stores, Inc., Cleve. and Indpls.; founder, pres. Corp. Personnel, Inc., exec. search firm, Cleve.; speaker in field. Served with U.S. Army, 1969-71. Mem. Am. Mgmt. Assn. Home: 7499 Woodlake Dr Walton Hills OH 44146

BROWN, EDWARD LEE, postal service ofcl.; b. St. Louis, July 5, 1937; s. Rainey A. and Cleola Irene (Shepard) Bernard; B.S. in Bus. Adminstrn., U. Mo., 1973; postgrad. So. Ill. U., 1975-77; m. Allie Stark Crawford, June 4, 1961; children—Stevon A., Byron E., Robin M. Procurement officer U.S. Postal Service, St. Louis, 1967-69, adminstrv. officer, 1969-77, gen. mgr. mgmt. services, 1977—. Bd. dirs. King-Fanon Community Mental Health Center, St. Louis, 1978—; active Mathews Dickey Boys Club. Served with USAF, 1956-60. Mem. St. Louis Assn. of Black Psychologists (fin. sec. 1976—). Mem. African Meth. Episcopal Ch. Home: 1814 Cambridge Ln Saint Louis MO 63147 Office: 1720 Market St Saint Louis MO 63180

BROWN, EDWARD LINUS, patent agt., civil engr.; b. Erie, Pa., July 30, 1906; s. William George and Anna Josephine (Metz) B.; B.S. in Civil Engring., Case Inst. Tech., 1928; m. Doris Anne Maloy, Apr. 11, 1931; children—Anne Brown Manning, Edward Linus, Constance Brown Guild. With Pa. R.R., 1926-35; various position in sales, product design and devel., constrn. Armco Steel Corp., Middletown, Ohio, also Denver, 1936-71; cons. engr., 1971-75; admitted to practice U.S. Patent Office, 1975; patent agt., Middletown, Ohio, 1975—. Chmn. traffic com. Middletown Area Safety Council, 1952; chmn. advancement com. Boy Scouts Am., 1952-60; pres. Friends of Library, 1979-80. Fellow ASCE; mem. Nat. Soc. Profl. Engrs. (life), Ohio Soc. Profl. Engrs. (life, Outstanding Service award 1951, 75), Engrs. Found. Ohio, Sigma Alpha Epsilon. Roman Catholic. Club: Wildwood Golf. Patentee in field of steel products. Home and Office: 3011 Central Ave Middletown OH 45042

BROWN, EDWIN LEWIS, JR., lawyer; b. Parker, S.D., Mar. 15, 1903; s. Edwin Lewis and Lucy Elizabeth (Lowenberg) B.; J.D., U. Nebr., 1926; m. Faye Hulbert, May 8, 1926; children—Betty Lou (Mrs. Philip Trainer), Lewis Charles. Admitted to Nebr. bar, 1926, Ill. bar, 1933, U.S. Supreme Ct., 1960; practice in Chgo., 1933—; partner firm Brown, Stine & Cook (now Brown, Cook & Hanson), 1950—. Mem. wills and bequests com. Shriners Crippled Children's Hosp., Chgo.; bd. dirs. Comml. Law Found. Mem. Am., Ill., Chgo. bar assns., Am. Judicature Soc., Comml. Law League Am. (pres. 1963-64), Phi Alpha Delta. Republican. Presbyterian. Mason (32 deg., K.T., Shriner). Clubs: Union League (Chgo.); Westmoreland Country (Wilmette, Ill.). Home: 2617 Hurd Ave Evanston IL 60201 Office: 135 S La Salle St Chicago IL 60603 also 2114 Central St Evanston IL 60201

BROWN, ELIZABETH MYERS (MRS. KENT LOUIS BROWN), publishing co. exec.; b. Bklyn., Dec. 31, 1915; d. Garry Cleveland and Caroline (Clark) Myers; B.S., Cornell U., 1937; M.A., Case Western Res. U., 1960; m. Kent Louis Brown, June 26, 1940; children—Karen Elizabeth Brown Johnson, Kent Louis, David Stuart, Garry Myers. Tchr., Walden, N.Y., 1937-38, Auburn, N.Y., 1938-39, Cleveland Heights, Ohio, 1939-40; asst. Erie County (N.Y.) home demonstration agt. govt. extension service Cornell U., Ithaca, N.Y., 1940-42; editorial asst. Highlights for Children, Columbus, Ohio, 1962-64, asst. editor, 1964-66, asso. editor, 1966—, asst. sec., 1968—, dir., 1960—; dir. Zaner-Bloser Co. Mem. Metro Writers Workshop, 1970—; trustee New Day Press, 1972-79 (both Cleve.). Bd. dirs. Fedn. Cornell Women's Clubs, 1955-57, Fedn. Women's Clubs of Cleve., 1968-71; bd. dirs. Nutrition Assn. Greater Cleve., 1964-68. Mem. Women's Assn. for Continuing Edn. (treas. 1959-61, pres. 1961-63), Women's Aux. Acad. Med. of Cleve. (pres. 1969-70), Woman's Aux. Ohio Med. Assn. (chmn. mems.-at-large com. 1970-71, dir. 5th dist. 1975—), Women's Nat. Book Assn. (dir. Cleve. chpt. 1978—). Home: 2861 Kersdale Rd Cleveland OH 44124 Office: 803 Church St Honesdale PA 18431

BROWN, EMMA JEAN MITCHELL, educator; b. Marshall, Tex., June 1, 1939; d. Johnnie D. and Elvia L. Mitchell Nickerson; B.S., Bishop Coll., 1961; M.S., Boston State Coll., 1967; postgrad. Boston U., 1963, 66, Howard U., 1974, U. Dayton, 1979, 80, 81, Miami U., Oxford, Ohio, 1980. Tchr. English, N.E. Jr. High Sch., Kansas City, Kans., 1961-62; info.-mail clk. Boston U., 1962-63; service rep. New Eng. Tel. & Tel., Boston, 1963-65; tchr. Harvard Elem. Sch., Boston, 1965-66, Carter Avery Elem. Sch., Needham, Mass., 1966-67; instr. Sinclair Community Coll., 1971-73, Wright State U., 1971-75; vis. lectr. U. Ibadan (Nigeria), 1975-76; tng. coordinator Dayton (Ohio) Job Corps., 1979; reading specialist Colonel White High Sch., Dayton, 1979-81, Int. Alt. Sch., 1981—. Third v.p. Dayton Urban League Guild, 1977. Recipient medallion City of Dayton, 1981. Mem. Internat. Reading Assn., Dayton Edn. Assn., Western Ohio Edn. Assn., Ohio Edn. Assn., NEA, Miami Valley African Assn., City Folk, Ch. Women United, Zeta Phi Beta. Baptist. Author: Come Sit at My Table: A Mini African Cookbook, 1980; contbr. articles to profl. jours. Home: 473 Marathon Dayton OH 45406

BROWN, EVE CAROL, librarian; b. Valparaiso, Ind., Sept. 8, 1947; d. William Henderson and Lydia Emma (Ehrenberg) Philley; B.A., Concordia Tchrs. Coll., 1969; M.A. in Library Sci., U. Mich., 1976; m. Frank Taylor Brown, Sept. 2, 1972; 1 dau., Jacqueline Denise. Tchr., St. Paul Luth. Sch., Flint, Mich., 1969-73; librarian Charles Stewart Mott Found., Flint, 1974-77, records mgmt. supr., 1977—. Mem. Spl. Library Assn. Lutheran. Club: Flint Skating. Office: Mott Found Mott Found Bldg Flint MI 48502

BROWN, FORREST HARRY, environ. engr., home inspection cons.; b. Sedalia, Colo., May 27, 1921; s. Harry Bradford and Katie May (Lange) B.; B.S. in Aero. Engring., U. Colo., 1953; B.D., Lincoln U., 1957; m. Muriel Elizabeth Judd, Nov. 4, 1955. Missionary project engr. U.S. Presbyterian Ch., San Sebastian, P.R., 1957-60; test engr. Beech Aircraft Co., Boulder, Colo., 1961-63, Brown Engring. Co., Huntsville, Ala.. 1963-68, Spaco Co., Huntsville, Ala., 1968-71; environ. engr. Met. San. Dist. of Greater Chgo., 1972-74, L.B. Knight Co., Chgo., 1974-76; home inspection cons., Ala., 1969-72, River Forest, Ill., 1976-78; civil engr. Detroit dist. office constrn. br. C.E., U.S. Army, 1978—. Mem. Huntsville Community Chorus Bd., 1965-72, treas., 1967-72; mem. Bldg. Bd. of Appeals and Water Coms., Village of River Forest, 1977-78. Served with USAAF, 1943-46; PTO. Registered profl. engr., Ala., Ill., Ind. Mem. Nat., Mich. socs. profl. engrs. Republican. Presbyterian. Address: 4176 Kennedy Dr E Windsor ON N9G 1Y2 Canada

BROWN, FRANCES GOLD, nurse, educator; b. Alameda, Calif., Apr. 24, 1913; d. Judel and Sadie (Pivnik) Gold; R.N., Mt. Zion Hosp., San Francisco, 1935; B.S., U. Calif., 1954, M.S., 1956; student Langley Porter Neuopsychiat. Inst., 1954-55; m. Robert Lee Brown, Nov. 27, 1941 (dec. July 1949); 1 son, Robert Lee. Gen. duty and pvt. nurse Alameda County, Calif., 1935-40, gen. duty, pvt. duty nurse, clin. nurse, 1949-56; gen. duty and head nurse Gorgas Hosp., Ancon, C.Z., 1940-42; supervisory nurse Fairmount Hosp., San Leandro, Calif., 1956-59; dir. nursing edn. Oreg. State Hosp., Salem, 1959-62; instr. psychiat. nursing U. Calif. Sch. Nursing, San Francisco, 1962-63; coordinator nursing services H. Douglas Singer Zone Center, Rockford, Ill., 1966-69; nursing adminstr. East Moline (Ill.) Mental Health Center, 1969-80; now health care adminstr. East Moline Correctional Center; sec. Calif. Nurses Assn., 1953-59; mem. Ill. Continuing Edn. Com. Mem. adv. com. Black Hawk Coll., Moline. Mem. Am. Nurses Assn. (vice chmn. inter-group relations com. 1960-62), Ill. Conf. Women Leaders in Traffic Safety (pres. 1979-81), AAUW, League Women Voters, Rock Island County Mental Health Assn., ORT, Pi Lambda Theta. Jewish. Club: Zonta. Author articles in field. Home: 5614B 34th Ave Moline IL 61265

BROWN, GLYNN PRATHER, interior designer; b. Dyersburg, Tenn., Feb. 3, 1940; s. George Wesley and Mamie Charlotte (Prather) B.; student Fullerton Coll.; m. June 1, 1977; 1 son, Sean Hunter Designer, Crossroads Co., Whittier, Calif., 1964-65; owner, designer Diversified Design Co., Orange, Calif., 1965-70, Innerscape Co., Newport Beach, Calif., 1970-76; dir. interior design The Ramos Group Architects, Kansas City, Mo., 1977-79; pres. Glynn Brown, Designer, Inc., Kansas City, Mo., 1978—. Pres. bd. dirs. Woodgate Homes Assn., 1979. Served with USAF, 1960-64. Mem. Am. Soc. Interior Designers (dir. 1979, chmn. program com. 1979, v.p.-elect 1980, pres. 1981). Republican. Office: 20 W 9th St 4th Floor Kansas City MO 64105

BROWN, GORDON MARSHALL, research engr.; b. Detroit, Feb. 17, 1934; s. Everett J. and Agnes (Graig) B.; student Greenville Coll., 1952-54; B.M.E., Gen. Motors Inst., 1958; M.S., U. Mich., 1959; m. Sharla A. Smith, Aug. 16, 1958; children—Gordon C., Julie Marie. Tooling project engr. Fisher Body div. Gen. Motors Corp., Pontiac, Mich., 1954-58; grad. asst. nuclear engring. U. Mich., 1960-61; project engr. nuclear scis. Bendix Aerospace Systems, Ann Arbor, Mich., 1961-67; dir. engring., mgr. mfg. GCO, Inc., Ann Arbor, 1967-73; prin. research engr., mem. engring. and research staff Ford Motor Co., Dearborn, Mich., 1973—; electro-optics cons. Recipient Gen. Motors Grad. fellowships in nuclear engring., 1960-61. Mem. Am. Soc. Non-Destructive Testing (Achievement award 1970), Soc. Photo-Optical Instrumentation, Soc. Automotive Engrs., Optical Soc. Am. Contbr. to Holographic Nondestructive Testing, 1975. Patentee holographic method for testing tires, 1971. Home: 3191 Bluett St Ann Arbor MI 48105 Office: Ford Motor Co Room S-1023 SRL PO Box 2053 Dearborn MI 48121

BROWN, HERBERT CHARLES, chemist; b. London, May 22, 1912; s. Charles and Pearl (Stine) B.; brought to U.S., 1914; A.S.; Wright Jr. Coll., Chgo., 1935; B.S., U. Chgo., 1936, Ph.D., 1938, D.Sc., 1968; m. Sarah Baylen, Feb. 6, 1937; 1 son, Charles Allan. Asst. chemistry U. Chgo., 1936-38; Eli Lilly postdoctorate research fellow, 1938-39, instr., 1939-43; asst. prof. chemistry Wayne U., 1943-46, asso. prof., 1946-47; prof. inorganic chemistry Purdue U., 1947-59, Richard B. Wetherill prof. chemistry, 1959, Richard B. Wetherill research prof., 1960-78, emeritus, 1978—; vis. prof. UCLA, 1951, Ohio State U., 1952, U. Mexico, 1954, U. Calif., Berkeley, 1957, U. Colo., 1958, U. Heidelberg, 1963, SUNY, Stonybrook, 1966, U. Calif., Santa Barbara, 1967, Hebrew U., Jerusalem, 1969, U. Wales, Swansea, 1973, U. Cape Town, South Africa, 1974, U. Calif., San Diego, 1979; Harrison-Howe lectr., 1953; Friend E. Clark lectr., 1953; Freud McCormack lectr., 1954; Centenary lectr. (Eng.), 1955; Thomas W. Talley lectr., 1956; Falk-Plaut lectr., 1957, Julius Stieglitz lectr., 1958, Max Tishler lectr., 1958; Kekule-Couper Centenary lectr., 1958, E.C. Franklin lectr., 1960, Ira Remsen lectr., 1961; Edgar Fahs Smith lectr., 1962; Seydel-Wooley lectr. 1966; Baker lectr., 1969; Chem. Soc. lectr., Australia, 1972; Armes lectr., 1973; Henry Gilman lectr., 1975; Randolph T. Major lectr., 1978; Clifford B. Purves lectr., 1979; chem. cons. to indsl. corps. Served as co-dir. war research projects U. Chgo. for U.S. Army, Nat. Def. Research Com., Manhattan Project, 1940-43. Bd. govs. Hebrew U., 1969—. Recipient Purdue Sigma Xi research award, 1951; Nichols medal, 1959; award Am. Chem. Soc., 1960; S.O.C.M.A. medal, 1960; H.N. McCoy award, 1965; Linus Pauling medal, 1968; Nat. Medal of Sci., 1969; Roger Adams medal, 1971; Charles Frederick Chandler medal, 1973; Chem. Pioneer award, 1975; Madison Marshall award, 1975; Sci. Achievement award medal CCNY, 1976; C.K. Ingold medal, 1978; Elliott Cresson medal, 1978; Nobel prize in chemistry, 1979. Fellow Chem. Soc. (London), Indian Nat. Acad. Sci. (fgn.); mem. Nat. Acad. Scis., Am. Acad. Arts and Scis., Am. Chem. Soc. (chmn. Purdue sect. 1955-56), AAAS, Phi Beta Kappa, Sigma Xi, Alpha Chi Sigma, Phi Lambda Upsilon (hon.). Author: Hydroboration, 1962; Boranes in Organic Chemistry, 1972; Organic Synthesis via Boranes, 1975; The Nonclassical Ion Problem, 1977. Contbr. articles to chem. jours.; awarded patents (with others) on preparation of borohydrides, diborane, hydroboration, synthesis of aliphatic derivatives; research in phys., organic, inorganic chemistry relating chem. behavior to molecular structure; selective reductions, hydroboration; chemistry of organoboranes. Office: Dept Chemistry Purdue Univ West Lafayette IN 47907

BROWN, HOWARD JORDAN, communications co. exec.; b. Chgo., July 31, 1923; s. Isidore and Gladys (Jordan) B.; A.B., Princeton U., 1946; M.S., Columbia U., 1948; m. Elizabeth Kassel, Mar. 2, 1960; children—Lucille, Sally, Amy. Overseas corr. Chgo. Sun Times, 1948-49; advt., circulation, promotion staff Cleve. News-Plain Dealer, 1950-59; with Ottaway Newspapers, Middletown, N.Y., 1959-61; with Kenosha (Wis.) News, 1962—, pub., 1963—; exec. v.p. Sun-Chronicle, Attleboro, Mass., 1969; pres. KEYC-TV, Mankato, Minn., 1977; dir. First Nat. Bank, Kenosha, Wis. Trustee, Kenosha Youth Found., Prairie Sch., Racine, Wis. Served with U.S. Army, 1943-45; ETO. Jewish. Club: Elks. Home: 6926 2d Ave Kenosha WI 53140 Office: 715 58th St Kenosha WI 53140

BROWN, JAMES ANDREW, JR., radio broadcaster; b. Detroit, Apr. 7, 1926; s. James Andrew and Harriet Emma (Tucker) B.; grad. Wayne State U., 1944; m. Joan Ruth Myers, Oct. 28, 1950; children—Mikel, Timothy, Kristin. Announcer, Sta. WKMH, Dearborn, Mich., 1949; media dir. Grant Advt., 1953-59; mgr. Detroit office Venaro, Torbet & McConnell, 1959-68; registered rep. 1st of Mich. Corp., 1968-72; gen. mgr. Sta. WMZK, Detroit, 1972—. Bd. dirs. Jr. Achievement Southeastern Mich.; vice pres. Algonac Sch. Bd., 1970-74; mem. Algonac Planning Commn., 1967-71; treas. Algonac Bldg. Authority, 1978-80. Served with Armed Forces, 1944-46. Mem. Detroit Press Club. Clubs: German Am. Cultural Center, Polish Am. Century, Detroit Swedish. Office: 2056 CNB Bldg Detroit MI 48226*

BROWN, JAMES LEHMON, chem. co. exec.; b. Detroit, Nov. 20, 1929; s. Abram Lehmon and Donnabelle (Chenoweth) B.; A.B., U. Mich., 1951, M.B.A., 1952; m. Judith Marsh Sinclair, June 28, 1952; children—Kirk, Scott, Kim, Carrie, Elizabeth. Propr. constrn. firm, Ann Arbor, Mich., 1955-58; sales mgr. Sinclair Mfg. Co., Toledo, 1958-64, pres., 1964—, also chmn. bd.; chmn. bd. Sinclair Mfg. Assos., WGTE-TV-FM, 1980—; dir. Monroe, Mich., Hunt Chem., Inc., St. Paul. Mem. Toledo Citizens Com. for Effective Govt., 1971-72; pres. Toledo Area Govtl. Research Assn., 1974-75; trustee Toledo Area council Boy Scouts Am., 1971—, exec. bd., 1970—, pres., 1975—; trustee U. Toledo Corp., 1975—, Toledo chpt. ARC, 1977-79. Served with AUS, 1952-55. Mem. Phi Eta Sigma, Theta Delta Chi, Sigma Delta Chi. Club: Toledo. Home: 30 Meadow Ln Toledo OH 43623 Office: 5644 Monroe St Sylvania OH 43560

BROWN, JEFFERSON, III, ins. salesman; b. Sandusky, Ohio, Sept. 30, 1952; s. Jefferson, II, and Rosie (Lee) B.; B.S. in Mktg., W.Va. U., 1974; postgrad. Am. Coll., 1976—; m. Marcie Ann Williams, Apr. 13, 1979; 1 son, Jefferson. Sales rep. Metropolitan Life Ins. Co., Elyria, Ohio, 1975-76, sales mgr., Cleve., 1976-80, sales rep., Beachwood, Ohio, 1980—. Vol. United Cerebral Palsy, Cleve. Foster Children, 1980. Recipient co. nat. sales awards, 1976, 80; C.L.U. (instr.). Mem. Am. Mgmt. Assn., Cleve. Assn. Life Underwriters. Methodist. Clubs: Kiwanis (treas. 1978-79, social com. 1980), Kappa Alpha Psi Alumni (Cleve.). Home: 4671 Dalebridge Apt 409 Warrensville Heights OH 44128 Office: 3659 S Green Rd Beachwood OH 44122

BROWN, JOAN LEE, nurse clinician; b. Jackson, Mich., Oct. 13, 1945; d. Jack Winton and Alma Florence (Gibbard) Brown; B.S. in Nursing, Spalding Coll., Louisville, 1968; M.S. in Nursing, U. N.C., 1972; m. Thomas H. Shultz, Dec. 22, 1975; 1 dau., Jennifer Lee Shultz Brown. Nurse intensive-care units various instns.; instr. med. surg. nursing U. N.C., Chapel Hill, 1972-73; evening supr. Addison (Mich.) Community Hosp., 1973-74; clin. specialist in psychiatry Chelsea (Mich.) Community Hosp., 1976—; psycho-therapist group and individual therapy; lectr. in field. Lic. social worker. Mem. Am. Assn. Critical Care Nurses, U. N.C. Alumni Assn., Spalding Coll. Alumni Assn., Nat. Intravenous Therapy Assn., Sigma Theta Tau. Methodist. Home: PO Box 326 Somerset Center MI 49282 Office: 775 S Main St Chelsea MI 48118

BROWN, JOE EUGENE, state legislator; b. Clinton, Iowa; s. Lewis William and Elizabeth Josephine (Byrnes) B.; A.A., Mt. St. Clare Coll., Clinton, 1971; B.A., William Penn Coll., Oskaloosa, Iowa, 1973; m. Ginger Van Hoever, July 29, 1979; children—Holly, Jeb. Prodn. line supr. Clow Corp., Oskaloosa, 1972-75; tchr. govt. and econs. Montezuma (Iowa) High Sch., 1975-78; mem. Iowa Senate, 1978—. Mem. Iowa State Edn. Assn., Iowa Farm Bur. Democrat. Mem. Assembly of God Ch. Office: State Senate State Capitol Des Moines IA 50319

BROWN, JOHN L., state senator; b. S.D., July 22, 1952; s. Lawrence M. and Helen D. (Davis) B.; B.S. in Animal Sci., S.D. State U., 1974; m. Roberta J. Haskell, Aug. 11, 1979. Engaged in farming and ranching, Buffalo, S.D.; v.p. Cave Hills Cattle Co., Inc.; mem. S.D. Ho. of Reps. from 28th Dist., 1978-80, S.D. Senate from 28th Dist., 1980—. Chmn. Harding County Republican Party, 1974-78. Mem. Rural Fisherman (sec.-treas.), Alpha Zeta, Alpha Psi Omega. Lutheran. Club: Buffalo Lions. Address: PO Box 92 Buffalo SD 57720

BROWN, JOSEPH ANDREW, JR., transp. cons.; b. Bristol, Conn., July 28, 1915; s. Joseph Andrew and Emma Virginia (Robey) B.; student Morse Coll., 1933-35; m. Edythe E. Hill, May 2, 1942 (div.); children—Michael R., Peter D., Stephen J., Kathleen V., Julie Ann, Anthony R. Freight service mgr. Eastern Express Inc., Terre Haute, Ind., 1947-56; v.p. ops., mem. exec. com. Mchts. Motor Freight, Inc., St. Paul, 1957-60; dir. freight claim prevention Spector Freight System, Inc., Chgo., 1960-63; salesman Callner Corp. and Ken-Di Realty Co., Chgo., 1964-70; search cons. Cadillac Assos., Inc., Chgo., 1971—. Mem. transp. adv. com. Richard J. Daley Coll., Chgo., 1979—. Served to lt. col. OSS, AUS, 1941-47. Decorated Legion of Merit; recipient cert. of meritorious service Am. Trucking Assn. Mem. Am. Soc. Traffic and Transp. (a founder), Nat. Council Physical Distbn. Mgmt. Republican. Roman Catholic. Patentee cargo cart conveyor. Home: 445 W Barry St Apt 524 Chicago IL 60657 Office: 32W Randolph St Chicago IL 60601

BROWN, JOSEPH EUGENE, state senator; b. Clinton, Iowa, Apr. 23, 1951; s. Lewis William and Elizabeth J. (Brynes) B.; B.A., William Penn Coll., Oskaloosa, Iowa, 1973; M.A., U. Iowa, 1981; m. Virginia Kaye Van Hoever, July 29, 1979; children—Holly Jayne, Jeb. Prodn. supr. Clow Corp., Oskaloosa, Iowa, 1972-75; tchr. govt. and econs. Montezuma (Iowa) High Sch., 1975-78; mem. Iowa Senate from 35th Dist., 1978—. Mem. Mahaska County Democratic Central Com., 1974-76, Poweshick County Dem. Central Com., 1976-78. Mem. Iowa Edn. Assn., Montezuma Edn. Assn. (past pres.), Common Cause. Office: State Capitol Bldg Des Moines IA 50319

BROWN, LARRY GENE, communications exec.; b. Carbondale, Ill., Oct. 24, 1943; s. Floyd Wilbur and Nellie Mae (Chamness) B.; B.S., U. So. Ill., 1966; postgrad. Golden Gate Sem., 1966-67; m. Pamela Jane McKenzie, Sept. 4, 1964; children—Christopher Lawrence, Meagan McKenzie. Asst. producer KRON-TV, San Francisco, 1966; producer/writer Sta. WAVE-TV, Louisville, 1967-68; cameraman/producer Sta. WPVI-TV, Phila., 1970-74; v.p. Advt. Dynamics, Pleasantville, N.J., 1974; producer Sta. WCAU-TV, Phila., 1975; creative services dir. Sta. WRAU-TV, Peoria, Ill., 1975; v.p. Forward Prodns., Morton, Ill., 1976—; TV cons. Tel-Com Assos., N.Y.C., 1974—; lectr. in field. Cons., Ill. State C. of C., 1980—. Served with U.S. Army, 1968-70. Recipient A.P. Broadcasters of Pa. first pl. award for best TV news, 1973; CINE Golden Eagle award, 1978. Mem. Am. Bus. Clubs. Baptist. Author: (with James Fulbright) Gas, the Inside Story, 1974. Office: 2123 S Main St Morton IL 61550

BROWN, LAWRENCE GILBERT, mgmt. devel. specialist; b. Nashville, Oct. 7, 1946; s. James Earl and Mary Elizabeth (Hankins) B.; B.S., Fisk U., 1973; M.S., U. Ark., 1979; m. Lannie Jewel Pryor, Oct. 6, 1973; children—Ashaki Malkia, Amana Dafina. Mgmt. devel. specialist Sundstrand Corp., Rockford, Ill., 1980—. Dir. tng. Boy Scouts, Cub Scouts, 1981—. Served with USN, 1973-80. Mem. Am. Soc. Tng. and Devel., Rockford Assn. Minority Mgrs., Omega Psi Phi. Seventh-day Adventist. Home: 2218 Pendleton Pkwy Rockford IL 61108 Office: 4751 Harrison Ave Rockford IL 61101

BROWN, LINDA DIANE, sch. prin.; b. Eustis, Fla., May 18, 1948; d. Leicester Hugh and Jean Eloise (Stouffer) B.; student Ball State U., 1966-67; B.S., Manchester Coll., 1970; M.S., Ind. U., 1975, Ed.S., 1977, postgrad., 1977-78. Tchr., Polk County Schs., Lakeland, Fla., 1971-74; admissions counselor Manchester Coll., 1975-76; grad. asst. in ednl. placement office Ind. U., 1976-78; elem. prin. Spencer-Owen Community Sch., Spencer, Ind., 1978-79, Concord Community Sch., Elkhart, Ind., 1979—. Mem. Assn. Supervision and Devel., Am. Assn. Sch. Adminstrs., Nat. Assn. Elem. Sch. Prins., Ind. Assn. Elem. Sch. Prins., Phi Delta Kappa, Pi Lambda Theta. Home: 3621 Beechwood Ct Elkhart IN 46514 Office: Ox Bow Elem Sch 23525 County Rd 45 Elkhart IN 46514

BROWN, MARK GRAHAM, human resource cons.; b. Detroit, Apr. 9, 1955; s. Donald G. and Joan T. Brown; B.A. in Psychology and Communication, Western Mich. U., 1977, M.A. in Applied Behavior Analysis, 1979; m. Marcia A. Rymer, Aug. 16, 1980. Bus. and conv. coordinator Assn. for Behavior Analysis, Kalamazoo, 1978-79; program developer Creative Universal, Inc., Southfield, Mich., 1979—, dir. planning and design, 1981—. Mem. Assn. for Behavior Analysis, Am. Soc. Tng. and Devel., Nat. Soc. for Performance and Instrn., Mich. Soc. for Instructional Tech. Contbr. articles to profl. jours. in field. Home: 4011 Dukeshire Royal Oak MI 48072 Office: 21700 Northwestern Hwy Suite 1200 Southfield MI 48075

BROWN, MARLYS FAYE, educator; b. Cooperstown, N.D., Dec. 6, 1953; d. Milford LuAllen and Sylvia Lorraine (Johnson) Gronneberg; B.A. cum laude (scholar), Concordia Coll., Moorhead, Minn., 1975; m. Mark Owen Brown, June 14, 1975; 1 dau., Kaare Elizabeth. Tchr. vocat. office edn. Sheyenne Valley Multi-Dist. Vocat. Center, Cooperstown, 1976—, also tchr. adult bus. courses. Vice pres. Women's Internat. Bowling Congress, 1979-81. Mem. Am. Vocat. Assn., N.D. Vocat. Assn. (Young educator award Office Edn.), N.D. Bus. and Office Edn. Assn. (sec. 1978-79, treas. 1979-81), Handweavers Guild. Lutheran. Clubs: Elks, Eagles. Home: Box 216 Hannaford ND 58448 Office: Box 505 Cooperstown ND 58425

BROWN, MARVIN, advt. agy. exec.; b. Boston, Mar. 17, 1926; s. Frank A. and Frances (Caplan) B.; student Cornell U., 1943-44, U. Mo., 1946-49; B.J., N.Y. U., 1955; m. Constance Ruth Kaminsky, Sept. 5, 1948; children—Valerie Kay, Mark Kenneth, Randall Craig. Reporter, asst. city editor Shreveport (La.) Times, 1949-53; pub. relations mgr. Glenn Mason Advt., Shreveport, 1953-54; advt. and pub. relations dir. Radio-TV Tng. Assn., N.Y.C., 1954-57; creative services mgr. Nationwide Ins. Cos., Columbus, Ohio, 1957-64; pub. Key Mag., Columbus, 1959—; pres. Marbro Advt., Inc., Columbus, 1965—; dir. Key Mags., Inc., Detroit. Pres., Columbus Quincentennial Expn., 1970—; bd. dirs. Columbus Conv. and Visitors Bur., 1981—. Served with U.S. Army, 1944-46. Mem. Columbus Advt. Fedn. (pres. 1972-73), Columbus Area C. of C. (dir. 1972-73). Clubs: Columbus Athletic, Winding Hollow Country. Home: 180 S Harding Rd Columbus OH 43209 Office: 929 E Broad St Columbus OH 43205

BROWN, MERLE J., surgeon; b. Colo, Iowa, Jan. 16, 1905; s. Jesse J. and Emma (Dolph) B.; B.A., U. Iowa, 1927, M.D., 1933; C.M., U. Pa., 1938; m. Lisette Edith Brooke, June 22, 1933; children—Phyllis Jean Brown Frank, Carolyn Mary Brown Samuels. Instr. sci. Lincoln High Sch., Vinton, Iowa, 1927-29; intern City Hosp. of Akron (Ohio), 1933-34; resident Guthrie Clinic and Robert Packer Hosp., Sayre, Pa., 1936-38; fellow in gen. surgery, 1936-38; practice medicine specializing in surgery, Davenport, Iowa, 1938-42, 46—; pres. med. staff St. Luke's Hosp., Davenport, 1940-41, instr. surgery Sch. Nursing, 1941-42, 46-56, now mem. staff; asst. chief of surgery Mercy Hosp., Davenport, 1947-48, now mem. staff; dir. Jim Samuels Equipment Co., Inc., Denver, 1971-75, Profl. Arts Bldg., Ltd., Davenport, v.p., 1973—. Chmn. awards and gift com. Quad-City Sci. Fair, 1955-57. Served to lt. col., M.C., AUS, 1942-46. Diplomate Am. Bd. Surgery. Fellow A.C.S. (gov. 1962-73); mem. Iowa Acad. Surgery (founder 1953), AMA, Pan Am. Med. Assn., Iowa, Scott County (sec. and program chmn. 1948-56) med. socs., Assn. Mil. Surgeons (life), Collegium Internat. Chirurgie Digestivae, Central Surg. Assn., Soc. Surgery Alimentary Tract, Pan-Pacific Surg. Assn., Internat. Soc. Surgery, Ia. Clin. Surg. Soc., Correspondence Soc. Surgery (charter mem.), Alpha Kappa Kappa, U. Iowa Alumni Assn. Clubs: Davenport, Rock Island Arsenal Golf, Quarterback, Outing. Contbr. articles on surgery to profl. jours. Home: 2247 Fairhaven Rd Davenport IA 52803 Office: 121 W Locust St 307 Professional Arts Bldg Davenport IA 52803

BROWN, MEYER, safety profl.; b. Bklyn., Aug. 18, 1913; s. Nathan and Rebecca (Mendelovitz) B.; B.S. in Commerce, Roosevelt U., 1946; postgrad. No. Ill. U., 1969-72; m. Adele Yanow, Sept. 6, 1942; children—Howard, Brent, Phillip. Safety supt. U.S. Post Office, Chgo., 1957-68; regional safety mgr. Def. Contract Adminstrn. Service, Def. Logistics Agy., Chgo., 1968-73; safety dir. Chgo. Dept. Public Works, 1973-74; mgr. safety IIT Research Inst., Chgo., 1974-75; safety dir., coordinator Ill. Tollway, Oak Brook, 1976-77; pres. Specialized Safety Assos., Inc., 1978—. Lt. col. USAR (ret.). Cert. safety profl., hazard control mgr.; registered profl. engr., Calif. Mem. Am. Soc. Safety Engrs., Constrn. Safety Assn. Am. (v.p. 1972-74), Fed. Safety and Fire Council (chmn. Chgo. 1970-74), Vets. of Safety, Am. Indsl. Hygienists Assn., Am. Conf. Govt. Hygienists (exec. bd.), Nat. Safety Council, Campus Safety Assn. Recipient U.S. Post Office Superior Accomplishment award, 1959, 68; Def. Supply Agency Outstanding Performance award, 1969. Home: 9617 N Tripp Ave Skokie IL 60076

BROWN, MICHAEL JAMES, psychologist; b. Phila., Mar. 14, 1947; s. Richard Lynn and Gertrude May (McTamany) B.; B.A., Mich. State U., 1969, M.A., 1971, Ph.D., 1974; m. Susan Brady, Dec. 30, 1967; children—Jennifer, Emily. Counselor, Lansing (Mich.) Boys Tng. Sch., 1968-71; psychologist Ingham Community Mental Health Center, Lansing, 1971-73; dir. tng. Tri-County Drug Treatment Programs, Lansing, 1973-74; dir. tng. Huron Valley Inst., Ann Arbor, Mich., 1974—; dir. Spectrum Psychol. Services, 1979—; adj. prof. Sch. Community Medicine, Mich. State U., 1972-73; lectr. Oakland U., Rochester, Mich., 1973-74; lectr. social work Mich. State U., 1974-75. Cert. psychol. examiner, cert. psychologist, cert. cons. psychologist, Mich. Mem. Am. Rehab. Counselors Assn. (mem. research com. 1972-73), Internat. Transactional Analysis Assn. (mem. sch. com. 1974-76, mem. tng. standards com. 1976-79, treas. 1979—), Am. Psychol. Assn., Phi Beta Kappa, Phi Eta Sigma. Author: Psychodiagnosis in Brief, 1977; co-author (with Stanley Woollams and Kristyn Huige) Transactional Analysis in Brief, 1974; (with Taibi Kahler) NoTAtions: A Guide to Transactional Analysis Literature, 1977; (with Woollams) Transactional Analysis, 1978; TA: The Total Handbook of Transactional Analysis, 1979. Contbr. to Transactional Analysis jour. Home: 2305 Yorktown St Ann Arbor MI 48105 Office: Huron Valley Inst 6869 Marshall Rd PO Box 123 Dexter MI 48130

BROWN, MIMI OLSEN, nursing adminstr.; b. Chgo., Oct. 13, 1949; d. Cyrus Paul and Faye Mildred O.; R.N., Augustana Hosp., 1970; student Ravenswood Hosp., 1971-73, Barat Coll., 1978-79, Advanced Mgmt. Inst., 1979. Mem. nursing staff Augustana Hosp., 1970-71; staff nurse anesthetist Ravenswood Hosp. and N.W. Hosp., 1973-75; staff anesthetist Forkosh Meml. Hosp., Chgo., 1975-77, supr. operating room services, 1977-79; faculty Sch. Anesthesiology, Ravenswood Hosp. Med. Center, 1979-81; chief anesthesiology Hawthorne Pl. Surg. Center, Libertyville, Ill., 1981—. Mem. Assn. Operating Room Nurses, Am. Assn. Nurse Anesthetists, Ill. Assn. Nurse Anesthetists, Sons of Norway. Republican. Office: 1900 Hollister Dr Libertyville IL 60048

BROWN, NORMAN STEPHEN, artist; b. Chgo., June 21, 1912; s. Norman Charles and Anna (Kirchner) B.; student Art Inst. Chgo., Comml. Art Inst., Chgo., DePaul U.; m. Helen M. Schilf, May 4, 1938 (dec.); children—Mary Ellen, Norman Stephen, Michael, Mark, Edward. Portraits include: Pope Pius XII, Samuel Cardinal Stritch, George Cardinal Meyer, Gov. Dan Walker of Ill., Robert F. Joyce, bishop of Burlington, Vt.; World War II Meml., 103d Gen. Hosp. AUS, Burlintgon. Served with AUS, 1943-46. Recipient medal U.S. Flag Assn. Mem. Artists Guild Chgo., Palette & Chisel Acad., Chgo. Municipal Art League. Home: PO Box 106 Deerfield IL 60015 Studio: 1012 Dearborn St N Chicago IL 60610

BROWN, ORIL IRENE, psychologist; b. Maumee, Ohio, Sept. 16, 1908; d. Edwin J. and L. Irene (Remelsbecker) Brown; student U. Toledo, 1926-28; B.S. cum laude, Northwestern U., 1930; M.A., George Washington U., 1951, Ph.D., 1965. Asst., Medill Sch. Journalism, Northwestern U., 1930-36; copyreader European edit. N.Y. Herald-Tribune, Paris, France, 1936-37; editorial work, free-lance writing, Chgo., 1930-36, 37-42; asst. editor Fgn. Broadcast Intelligence Service, Washington, 1942-51; research asst. Human Resources Research Office, Washington, 1952-53; pub. sch. psychologist, Portsmouth, Va., 1953-54; staff psychologist N.D. State Hosp., Jamestown, 1955-57; instr. psychiatry Med. Coll. of Va., 1957-60; staff psychologist Danville (Pa.) State Hosp., 1960-64; staff psychologist Mental Hygiene Clinic, Toledo, 1964, acting chief psychologist, 1965-68, psychologist dir. I, 1968-70, psychologist dir. II, 1970-77; pvt. practice psychology, Toledo, 1977—. Mem. LWV (dir. 1966-67), Am., Ohio, Midwestern, Southeastern psychol. assns., AAUW (dir. 1973-75), Ohio Hist. Soc., Maumee Valley Hist. Soc., ACLU, Alliance Française, Sigma Xi. Episcopalian. Contbr. articles to profl. jours. Home; 2270 Townley Rd Toledo OH 43614 Office: 2500 W Central Ave Toledo OH 43606

BROWN, PATRICIA LYNN, info. scientist, lab. exec.; b. Lafayette, La., Oct. 1, 1928; d. William Madison and Maude Juanita (Thomas) Brown; B.S. in Chem. Engring., U. Southwestern La., 1947; M.A. in Chemistry, U. Tex., 1949. Instr. analytical chemistry Smith Coll., Northampton, Mass., 1949-50; chemist R&M Labs., Peabody, Mass., 1950; research asso. indsl. toxicology Albany (N.Y.) Med. Coll., 1950-51; mem. info. services staff Ethyl Corp., Ferndale, Mich., 1951-55; sr. tech. writer, editor, staff engr. Westinghouse Atomic Power Div., Pitts., 1955-57; supr., then mgr. info. services, tech. info. cons. Tex. Instruments, Dallas, 1957-66; sr. info. scientist, sr. researcher Battelle Columbus (Ohio) Labs., 1966-76; mgr. sci. services, asso. dir. Travenol Labs., Morton Grove, Ill., 1976—. Loaned exec. United Way Campaign, 1972, 73. Bd. dirs. Engring. Socs. Library, 1961-63, 66-71. Mem. Soc. Women Engrs. (pres. 1961-63), Am. Chem. Soc., Spl. Libraries Assn., Am. Soc. Info. Sci., Soc. Tech. Communication. Author publs. in field. Home: 1109 Skylark Dr Palatine IL 60067 Office: 6301 Lincoln Ave Morton Grove IL 60053

BROWN, PAUL, football exec.; b. Norwalk, Ohio, July 9, 1908; ed. Ohio State U., Miami U. (Ohio). Coach, Severn (Md.) Prep. Sch., 1930-32; coach football and basketball Massillon (Ohio) High Sch., 1932-41; coach Ohio State U., Columbus, 1941-43, Great Lakes Coll., 1944-45; coach profl. football team Cleve. Browns, 1946-62; coach Cin. Bengals, 1968-76, v.p., gen. mgr., 1976—. Office: care Cincinnati Bengals 200 Riverfront Stadium Cincinnati OH 45202*

BROWN, PAUL EDWARD, coll. adminstr.; b. Belleville, Ill., Feb. 4, 1943; s. Glen Edward and Dolores Virginia (Frey) B.; B.S., Quincy Coll., 1965; M.B.A., U. Chgo., 1967; Cost acct. Ryerson Steel Co., Chgo., 1966; instr. Quincy (Ill.) Coll., 1967-68, asst. bus. mgr., 1967-72, asst. to pres., 1972—. Bd. dirs. Quincy Coll. Found., 1976—, pres., 1981—; treas. Salt Lick Found.; sect. co-chmn. United Way. Mem. Soc. Coll. and Univ. Planning Ofcls., Assn. Instl. Research, Am. Ednl. Research Assn., Nat. Assn. Accts. (pres. Quincy chpt. 1974-75), Ill. Act Council, Quincy C. of C. (chmn. legis. com.), Delta Epsilon Sigma (pres. 1964-65). Roman Catholic. Clubs: Kiwanis (pres. Gem City 1981-82), Hawkettes, Solano, Mart Heinen. Office: 1831 College Ave Quincy IL 62301

BROWN, PAUL W., justice Ohio Supreme Ct.; b. Cleve., Jan. 14, 1915; s. William and Mary (Foster) B.; A.B., Ohio State U., 1937, J.D., 1939; m. Helen Page; children—Susan, Julie, Barbara, Mary, Jeffrey, Molly, Daniel. Admitted to Ohio bar, 1939, U.S. Supreme Ct. bar; practiced in Youngstown, Ohio, 1939-40, 46-60; faculty, asst. to pres. Youngstown U.; judge 7th Dis. Appeals of Ohio, 1960-64; atty. gen. state of Ohio, Columbus, 1969-71; asso. justice Supreme Ct. Ohio, 1964-69, 73—. Del., Republican Nat. Conv., 1948. Served with AUS, 1941-45. Decorated Purple Heart, Silver Star. Mem. Ohio, Mahoning County bar assns., Inst. Jud. Adminstrn., Am. Legion, DAV, 1st Armored Div. Assn., Mil. Order Purple Heart. Club: Masons. Home: 2396 Wimbledon Rd Columbus OH 43220 Office: Supreme Ct State Office Tower Columbus OH 43215

BROWN, PHILIP KIMBLE, community action agy. exec.; b. Lorain, Ohio, Nov. 27, 1937; s. Harold August and Hildred Opal (Jones) B.; A.B. in Sociology, Coll. of Wooster, Ohio, 1957; postgrad U. Mich., 1962, (U.S. Dept. Agr. scholar) Nat. Rural Devel. Leaders Sch., Cin., 1976; m. Deborah Ann Manning, Sept. 7, 1976; 1 son, Derek Nolan; children-by previous marriage—Philip Kimble Dane, Stuart Kipling Zane. Mgmt. trainee United Parcel Service, Cleve., 1957-59; mgr. Montgomery Ward, Cin., 1959-61; case worker Lucas County (Ohio) Child Welfare Bd., Toledo, 1961-63; owner, operator farm, Warsaw, Ohio, 1963—; owner, operator Warsaw (Ohio) Milling Co., 1967-75; manpower adminstr. Kno-Ho-Co, Warsaw, 1969-75, exec. dir., 1975—; dir. Corp. for Ohio Appalachian Devel. Bd. dirs. Area Six Health Planning Systems Agy., Marietta, Ohio, 1977. Recipient Govs. award for community action, 1975. Mem. Nat. Assn. Transp. Disadvantaged, Ohio Assn. Community Action Agys. (trustee 1975—), Nat. Assn. Railroad Passengers, Am. Motorcycle Assn. Home: 53192 TR 170 Fresno OH 43824 Office: Rural Route 3 Warsaw OH 43844

BROWN, RICHARD EUGENE, state ofcl.; b. Little Falls, N.Y., June 30, 1937; s. Edward Stanislaus Brown and Mary Elizabeth (Metz) Brown Lynch; A.B. (Coll. scholar), Hope Coll., 1959; M.P.A. (Mich. Fellow), U. Mich., 1960; D.P.A. (Littauer Fellow), Harvard U., 1968; m. Beverly Ann Shaffer, Feb. 25, 1961; children—Kelly Christine, Christopher Richard, Kirsten Marie. Mgmt. analyst Nat. Security Agy., Washington, 1960-61; with TVA, Knoxville, 1961-69, asst. to gen. mgr., 1967-69; dir. audit ops. Legis. Commn. on Expenditure Rev., Albany, N.Y., 1970-75; state auditor Kans. Legislature, Topeka, 1975—; vis. or adj. prof. fin. and adminstrn. William and Mary Coll., U. Kans., U. Tenn., SUNY, Albany; cons. GAO, various state legislatures. Scoutmaster, Boy Scouts Am. Mem. Am. Soc. Public Adminstrn. (chmn. mgmt. sci. sect.), Nat. Conf. State Legislatures (exec. com.), Public Adminstrn. Soc. (pres. Topeka). Mem. United Ch. of Christ. Author: The GAO; Untapped Source of Congl. Power, 1970; editor: The Effectiveness of Legislative Program Review, 1979; contbr. articles to profl. jours.; editorial bd. Midwest Rev. Public Adminstrn., 1979-80, Public Adminstrn. Rev., 1980—. Home: 3017 Campfire Dr Lawrence KS 66044 Office: Mills Bldg Suite 301 Topeka KS 66612

BROWN, RICHARD HENRY, fin. co. exec.; b. Gary, Ind., July 11, 1928; s. Clark Matson and Mary Virginia (Henry) B.; B.A., Valparaiso (Ind.) U., 1951; m. Marguerite L. Park, Dec. 27, 1950; 1 dau., Suzan Renee (Brown) Schweke. With Household Fin. Corp., Chgo., 1951-81, group v.p. personnel, consumer fin. div., Prospect Heights, Ill., 1977—. Past chmn., mem. personnel program com. Community Fund Chgo.; v.p. exec. com., bd. dirs. Gads Hill Center, Chgo., 1970—. Served with USN, 1946-47. Accredited personnel exec. Mem. Am. Soc. Personnel Adminstrs., Soc. Personnel Adminstrs., Chgo. (past dir.). Republican. Lutheran. Clubs: Kenosha Yacht, Mich. Shores. Office: Household Fin Corp 2700 Sanders Rd Prospect Heights IL 60070

BROWN, RICHARD JAY, coll. pres.; b. Council Bluffs, Iowa, Jan. 2, 1922; s. John Howard and Josephine (Decker) B.; B.A., U. Iowa, 1947, M.A., 1948, Ph.D., 1955; m. Barbara Jean Franklin, Sept. 21, 1944; children—Marcia Lynn, Karen Beth. History tchr. Monticello (Iowa) High Sch., 1948-50; prof. history and edn., v.p. U. Wis., Whitewater, 1950-68; exec. dir. Fulbright program, Tehran, Iran, 1965-67; pres. Nicolet Coll., Rhinelander, Wis., 1968—; pres. Council North Central Community Colls., 1977-78. Bd. dirs. St. Mary's Hosp., Rhinelander, Wis., 1975-81; mem. U.S. Nat. Commn. UNESCO, 1973-79. Served with USN, 1941-45. Danforth fellow, 1958-62. Mem. Soc. Iranian Studies, History Edn. Soc., Am. Vocat. Assn., State Hist. Soc. Wis. Club: Rotary (past pres.) (Rhinelander, Wis.). Author: Understanding American Democracy, 2 vols., 1965-66. Home: Route 3 Rhinelander WI 54501 Office: Nicolet Coll PO Box 518 Rhinelander WI 54501

BROWN, RICHARD OSBORNE, physician; b. Detroit, May 20, 1930; s. Richard Wells and Flossie Eva (Osborne) B.; B.A., Wayne State U., 1953; M.D., Howard U., 1959; m. Dolores Debro, Jan. 23, 1954; children—Richard Debro, Kevin Michael; m. 2d, Martha Evelyn McGregor, Oct. 6, 1973; children—Vincent, Tiffany Diane. Intern, Wayne County Gen. Hosp., 1959-60; resident ophthalmology Homer G. Phillips Hosp., St. Louis, 1962-65; staff ophthalmologist CHA-Met. Hosp., Detroit, 1965-67; practice medicine specializing in ophthalmology, Detroit, 1967—; chief med. staff Kirwood Gen. Hosp., 1974-76, now trustee, Cons., Met., SW Detroit, Lakeside, Kirwood, St. Joseph hosps. Mem. Draft Bd., 1971-76. Served with AUS, 1953-55. Mem. Am. Assn. Ophthalmology, Nat. Med. Assn. (2d v.p. 1981—), AMA, Wayne County, Detroit (treas. 1972-78, pres. 1978-80), Mich. State med. socs., Detroit C. of C., Am. Profl. Practice Assn., Council Med. Staffs Mich. (dir. 1971—). Episcopalian. Home: 22854 Newport Southfield MI 48075 Office: 3800 Woodward St Detroit MI 48201

BROWN, ROBERT ORDWAY, food products co. exec.; b. Tyler, Minn., July 31, 1917; s. Peter J. and Ella M. (Hansen) B.; B.Chem. Engring., U. Minn., 1939; m. Margrethe Frederiksen, June 12, 1943; children—Rolf, Linnea (Mrs. Lauren Berg), Karla, Paul, Grete. Sect. head. Pillsbury Mills, Mpls., 1939-56; cons. engr. Robert O. Brown Co., Mpls., 1956—. Mem. Am. Inst. Chem. Engrs., AAAS, Am. Assn. Cereal Chemists, N.Y. Acad. Scis., Inst. Food Technologists, ASHRAE, Am. Chem. Soc., Am. Soc. Cons. Engrs., Nat. Soc. Profl. Engrs., Assn. Energy Engrs. Home: 4500 Morningside Rd Minneapolis MN 55416 Office: 6885 Washington Ave S Suite 200 Edina MN 55435

BROWN, ROBERT VENTON, govt. ofcl.; b. Oklahoma City, June 10, 1936; s. David L. and Grace A. B.; B.A. in Bus., U. Md., 1969, M.B.A., U. Utah, 1971; student Air Command and Staff Coll., 1971-72; sr. exec. fellow, Harvard U., 1980; student U. Okla., 1957-63; m. Barbara Lee Garrett, Sept. 1, 1957; children—Lee-Anita, Jennifer Lynne, Yvonne Kathleen, Denise Ladele. With maintenance and materiel mgmt. Air Force Logistics Command, Okla. and Calif., 1959-66; logistics staff U.S. Air Force in Europe, Germany, 1966-71; chief tech. support sect. Inventory Mgmt. Div., Tex., 1972-77; chief product performance evaluation div., Air Force Acquisition Logistics, Air Force Logistics Command, Wright-Patterson AFB, Ohio, 1977-78, dir. acquisition control Air Force dep. for avionics control, 1978-81, asst. to comdr., 1981; instr. logistics Our Lady of the Lake U., San Antonio, 1973-77; part time faculty local colls. Safety com. PTA; adv. bd. Order of Rainbow for Girls; booster High Sch. Math. and Sci. Club; advisor 4-H Clubs Am. Served with USN, 1954-57. Mem. Soc. Logistics Engrs. (ednl. chmn. Tex. 1975-76), Am. Def. Preparedness Assn., Air Force Assn., Assn. of Grads. Air Force Inst. Tech. (charter). Clubs: VFW, Masons, Scottish Rite, Shrine. Contbr. papers to profl. seminars and symposia. Office: HQ AFALD/CA Wright-Patterson AFB OH 45433

BROWN, ROBERT WINDSOR, coll. pres.; b. Windsor, Ont., Can., Oct. 23, 1925; s. Robert and Susan Marshall (MacFarlane) B.; B.A., Adrian Coll., 1950; M.A., Mich. State U., 1961, Ph.D., 1965; m. Carolyn Louise Berry, June 24, 1956; children—Stephen, Susan, Jennifer. Came to U.S., 1926, naturalized, 1926. Pub. relations trainee Gen. Motors Corp., Detroit, 1950-52; personnel supr. Ferguson Tractor Co., Detroit, 1952-54; admissions dir. Adrian (Mich.) Coll., 1954-60, dir. public relations, 1960-65, v.p., 1965-78; pres. Culver-Stockton Coll., Canton, Mo., 1978—. Pres. Lenowee County YMCA, 1972-74; dir. Mich. council Girl Scouts U.S.A., 1972; bd. dirs. Republican Party, Lenowee County, 1976. Served with U.S. Army, 1944-46; ETO. Recipient Outstanding Alumnus award, Adrian Coll., 1975. Republican. Methodist. Clubs: Rotary (dir. 1963); River Valley Country. Author: College Graduate or Freshman Failure, 1959; Study of Methodist Higher Education, 1965. Home: 800 College St Canton MO 63435 Office: Culver-Stockton College Canton MO 63435

BROWN, ROGER TRUMAN, veterinarian; b. Slater, Iowa, Sept. 2, 1938; s. Truman Mark and Ruth Theressa (Olson) B.; D.V.M., Iowa State U., 1963; m. Nancy Lee Dunham, Dec. 29, 1961. Gen. practice veterinary medicine, Bethesda, Md., 1965-70, Omaha, 1970—; owner Bel Air Animal Clinic, Omaha, 1970—; chmn. bd. dirs., veterinary practice cons. Ancom, Inc.; chmn. bd. dirs. Ornamental Fish Industries, Cartel, Inc., Filing Systems Design, Inc. Served with Veterinary Corps, U.S. Army, 1963-65. Mem. Am., Nebr. veterinary med. assns., Am. Animal Hosp. Assn., Nebr. Acad. Veterinary Medicine, Am. Maltese Assn., Nebr. Kennel Club, Internat. Platform Assn., Kappa Sigma. Republican. Lutheran. Co-author monthly syndicated maltese column Popular Dogs mag., 1973-75, also audio-visual client edn. filmstrips. Home: 1417 S 136th St Omaha NE 68144 Office: 12100 West Center Rd Omaha NE 68144

BROWN, SEYMOUR, anesthesiologist; b. St. Louis, Aug. 26, 1915; s. Adolph S. and Rose (Corson) B.; B.S., Washington U., St. Louis, 1940, M.D., 1940; m. Rose Ann Tropp, Dec. 25, 1941; children—Alvin Richard, Donald Elliott. Intern in pathology Barnes Hosp., St. Louis, 1940; rotating intern Ill. Research Edn. Hosp. U. Ill., Chgo., 1941; fellow in anesthesiology Lahey Clinic, Boston, 1943; clin. asst. prof. anesthesiology St. Louis U., 1952—; practice medicine specializing in anesthesiology, Creve Coeur, Mo.; dir. anesthesiology St. John's Hosp. and St. John's Mercy Med. Center, 1946-75; chief anesthesiology St. Louis County Hosp., 1946-72; cons. VA; mem. exec. bd. St. John's Hosp., St. Louis, St. Louis County Hosp. Bd. dirs. Shaare Emeth Temple, St. Louis. Served from lt. j.g. to lt. comdr. M.C., USNR, 1941-46. Recipient Mercy award St. John's Mercy Hosp., 1970; diplomate Am. Bd. Anesthesiology. Fellow Am. Coll. Anesthesiology; mem. AMA, Am., St. Louis and Mo. socs. anesthesiologists, Internat. Anesthesiology Research Soc., World Fedn. Anesthesiologists, St. Louis Med. Soc., St. Louis Surg. Soc., N.Y. Acad. Scis., Mo. Soc. Medicine, AAAS, Sigma Xi, Alpha Omega Alpha. Republican. Club: Ambassadors. Contbr. articles to med. jours.; anesthesiology editor Clin. Medicine, 1953-65. Home: 2421

Baxton Way Chesterfield MO 63017 Office: 621 S Ballas Rd Creve Coeur MO 63141

BROWN, SORREL (MARTHA), agronomist; b. Frankfurt, Germany, Nov. 5, 1949; parents U.S. citizens; d. Arthur William and Luisa Margarita (Badaracco) B.; student Tex. Christian U., 1967-69, U. Tex., Austin, 1969-70; B.S. in Psychology, Ariz. State U., 1972, M.S. in Soil Sci., 1977. Plant pathologist Ariz. Public Service Utilities Co., Phoenix, 1976, 77; field agronomist Chevron Chem. Co., Des Moines, 1977-80; crop prodn. specialist Iowa State U. Extension, Des Moines, 1980—; speaker in field. Recipient McVickar Agronomy Achievement award Chevron Chem. Co., 1978; Sarah Tyson Bradley Meml. fellow, 1973-74; Laura M. Bohem Found. scholar, 1974-75. Mem. Am. Soc. Agronomy, Soil Sci. Soc. Am., Nat. Assn. County Agrl. Agts. (Career Guidance award 1981), Alpha Zeta. Home: 2806 Adams Des Moines IA 50310 Office: 109 W Winds 1454 30th St West Des Moines IA 50265

BROWN, SPENCER HUNTER, historian; b. Knoxville, Tenn., June 10, 1928; s. John Orville and Edith Frances (Hunter) B.; B.A. in Teaching Social Studies magna cum laude, U. Ill., 1954, M.A. in History (fellow), 1955; Ph.D. in History (African studies fellow), Northwestern U., 1964; m. Doris Lucille Craig, Aug. 4, 1951; 1 dau., Rebecca Lee. Tchr., then tchr./chmn. social scis. dept. Carl Sandburg High Sch., Orland Park, Ill., 1955-59; mem. faculty Western Ill. U., Macomb, 1962—, prof. history, 1971—, chmn. dept., 1976—. Served with USNR, 1945-47. Ford Found. fellow, 1961-62. Mem. African Studies Assn., Am. Hist. Assn., AAUP, Phi Beta Kappa. Gen. editor Jour. Developing Areas, 1965-76, bus. mgr., 1976—. Home: Box 47 Tennessee IL 62374 Office: Dept History Western Ill Univ Macomb IL 61455

BROWN, STEVEN DOUGLAS, psychologist; b. Troy, Ohio, Feb. 17, 1947; s. Irvin Russell and Elma Mae (Lamka) B.; B.A., Muskingum Coll., 1969; M.A., U. Va., 1972; Ph.D., U. Calif., Santa Barbara, 1977. Psychologist, Central State Hosp., Petersburg, Va., 1971-73; mental health cons. San Mateo County (Calif.) Mental Health Services, San Mateo, 1973-74; cons. drug abuse program Fed. Correctional Instn., Lompoc, Calif., 1976-77; fellow dept. psychiatry U. Wis., Madison, 1977-78; dir. counseling psychology clinic, counseling psychology program U. Calif., Santa Barbara, 1978-79; asst. prof. psychology U. Minn., Mpls., 1979—; cons. in field. Cora I. Orr fellow, 1968-69. Mem. Am. Psychol. Assn., Am. Personnel and Guidance Assn., Assn. for Advancement of Behavior Therapy, N.Y. Acad. Scis., Sigma Xi, Psi Chi, Phi Sigma, Kappa Delta Pi. Home: 2224 26th Ave South Minneapolis MN 55406 Office: Dept Psychology N556 Elliott Hall U Minn 75 E River Rd Minneapolis MN 55455

BROWN, SUZANNE WILEY, mus. exec.; b. Cheyenne, Wyo., Aug. 28, 1938; d. Robert James and Catharine Helen (Schroeder) Wiley; B.S. with honors, U. Wyo., 1960, M.S., 1964; postgrad. U. Cin. Med. Sch., 1965-66, U. Ill., 1969-72; m. Ralph E. Brown, July 19, 1968; 1 dau., Nina M. Research asst. Harvard Med. Sch., 1962-63; research asst. U. Cin. Med. Sch., 1964-65; sr. lab. asst. U. Chgo., 1966-67; research asso. U. Colo. Med. Sch., 1968; teaching asst. U. Ill., 1971-73; exec. asst. Chgo. Acad. Scis., 1974—. NDEA fellow, 1960-62. Mem. Mus. Educators of Greater Chgo., Am. Assn. Museums, Internat. Council Museums, Phi Beta Kappa, Sigma Xi, Phi Kappa Phi. Office: 2001 N Clark St Chicago IL 60614

BROWN, THOMAS FRANCIS, village ofcl.; b. Cicero, Ill., Feb. 3, 1923; s. Thomas Francis and Mary Gertrude (McCartin) B.; Ph.B., Loyola U., Chgo., 1947; m. Helen Irene Sauer, June 10, 1944; children—Helen Anne, Thomas Francis, Joachim, Christine, Kathleen, Beth, Timothy, Martin, John. Personnel counselor Western Electric, Chgo., 1947-52; pres. T.F. Brown Co., Chgo., 1952—; trustee Village of LaGrange, Ill., 1966-73, chmn. police and fire com., 1966-73, village pres., 19—; chmn. bd. T.F. Brown Co., 1976. Trustee Plumbers Pension Fund, 1970—; chmn. Selective Service Bd. #111, Ill., 1967-74. Served to lt., USAAF, 1943-46. Decorated D.F.C., Purple Heart, Air Medal with two oak leaf clusters. Recipient distinguished citation, Father of Year award, 1966. Mem. Chgo., Ill., Nat. plumbing contractors assns., W. Central Assn. Chgo., Cook County Community Devel. advisory bd., Cook County Council Govts. (exec. bd.). Roman Catholic. Clubs: Executive of Chgo., K.C., Serra Internat. Author: To Thine Own Self Be True, 1960. Home: 101 N Catherine Ave LaGrange IL 60525 Office: 114 N Halsted St Chicago IL 60606

BROWN, THOMAS JAY, educator; b. Saginaw, Mich., May 22, 1936; s. Jay M. and Mae E. (Uren) B.; B.S., Central Mich. U., 1959, M.A., 1966; m. Patricia Smillie, Aug. 22, 1959; children—Suzanne, Cheryl, Carol, Jeanette. Player, Washington Senators Baseball Club, 1958; tchr. math., coach basketball and baseball Bad Axe (Mich.) High Sch., 1959-62; claims adjuster Sentry Ins. Co., 1962-63; with Northwood Inst., Midland, Mich., 1963—, asst. prof. math., 1976, chancellor, chief operating officer, 1976—, pres., 1979—; evaluator North Central Assn. Program chmn. Midland Nuclear Power Rally, 1972; sec. Tri-City Airport Adv. Com., 1972-76; mem. Midland Long-Range Planning Comm.; alt. mem. Mich. 4 Goal Com. Mem. Assn. Ind. Colls. and Univs. Mich. (past treas., exec. sec., now chmn.). Roman Catholic. Office: 3225 Cook Rd Midland MI 48640

BROWN, (ROBERT) WENDELL, lawyer; b. Mpls., Feb. 26, 1902; s. Robert and Jane Amanda (Anderson) B.; A.B., U. Hawaii, 1924; J.D., U. Mich., 1926; m. Barbara Ann Fisher, Oct. 20, 1934; children—Barbara Ann (Mrs. Neil Maurice Travis), Mary Alice (Mrs. Alfred Lee Fletcher). Admitted to Mich. bar, 1926; Supreme Ct. Mich., U.S. Supreme Ct., 6th U.S. Circuit Ct. of Appeals, U.S. Dist. Ct., Eastern and Western Dists. Mich., U.S. Bd. Immigration Appeals, U.S. Tax Ct.; lawyer firm Routier, Nichols & Fildew, Detroit, 1926, Nichols & Fildew, 1927-28, Frank C. Sibley, 1929, Ferguson & Ferguson, 1929-31; asst. atty. gen. Mich., 1931-32; with legal dept. Union Guardian Trust Co., Detroit, 1933-34; individual practice law, Detroit, 1934—. Legal adviser Wayne County (Mich.) Graft Grand Jury, 1939-40; asst. pros. atty. civil matters Wayne County, 1940; spl. asst. city atty. to investigate Police Dept. Highland Park, Mich., 1951-52. Chmn. citizens com. to form Oakland County (Mich.) Community Coll., 1962-63. Pres. Farmington (Mich.) Sch. Bd., 1952-56; chmn. Oakland County Republican County Conv., 1952; trustee Farmington Twp., Oakland County, 1957-61; pres. Oakland County Lincoln Rep. Club, 1958. Treas., bd. dirs. Friends of Detroit Library, 1943-44; bd. dirs. Farmington Friends of Library, Inc., 1952-58, pres., 1956-57. Hon. mem. Farmington Hist. Soc., 1966, St. Anthonys Guild, Franciscan Friars, 1975. Mem. Detroit Bar Assn. (dir. 1939-49, treas. 1942-44, sec. 1944-46, 2d v.p. 1946-47, 1st v.p. 1947-48, pres. 1948-49, chmn. or mem. various coms. 1935-52, 77-81), State Bar Mich. (chmn. or mem. various coms. 1935-72). Presbyn. (elder). Home: 29921 Ardmore St Farmington Hills MI 48018 Office: 32969 Hamilton Ct Farmington Hills MI 48018

BROWN, WILLARD A., JR., real estate co. exec.; b. Evanston, Ill., Sept. 11, 1931; s. Willard A. and Elaine G. (Grannis) B.; B.S. in Bus. Adminstrn., Western Mich. U., 1953; m. Margaret Elizabeth Drew, May 7, 1960; children—Suzanne, Stacy, Peter. Broker, Arthur Rubloff & Co., Chgo., 1955-60, v.p., 1960-75, exec. v.p., 1975-80, pres., chief exec. officer, 1980—; dir. Ryan Ins. Group. Mem. exec. com. Chgo. council Boy Scouts Am.; mem. Chgo. Revolving Loan Com. Served with USAF, 1953-55. Mem. Soc. Indsl. Realtors, Nat. Assn. Realtors, Urban Land Inst. Republican. Clubs: Union League, Mid-Day (Chgo.); Barrington Hills (Ill.) Country. Office: 69 W Washington St Chicago IL 60602

BROWN, WILLARD AYOTTE, real estate exec.; b. Madison, Wis., May 9, 1909; s. Harry Willard and Ellen (Ayotte) B.; student public schs.; m. Elaine G. Grannis, June 12, 1928; children—Barbara Brown Porter, William Ayotte, Julie Brown Grassly, Harvey G., Donald S., Jill Brown Mattson. Partner, Bolten Realty Co., Park Ridge, Ill., 1929-45; petroleum chemist Buick Motor div. Gen. Motors Corp., 1942-45; regional real estate mgr. Montgomery Ward & Co., 1945-51; with Arthur Rubloff & Co., Chgo., 1952—, sr. v.p. comml. devel. and real estate counseling, 1969-80, exec. v.p., 1981—, also dir.; dir. Evergreen Plaza Bank, Fin N Feather Farms. Mem. Ill. Jr. Coll. Bd., 1967—, Sch. Bd. High Sch. Dist. 211, 1961-67, Park Ridge City Plan Commn., 1935-38. Mem. Am. Soc. Real Estate Counselors (chmn. liaison com. 1972—), Internat. Council Shopping Centers, Am. Arbitration Assn., Nat. Assn. Real Estate Bds., Bldg. Mgrs. Assn. Chgo. (chmn. labor com. 1969—), Chgo. Real Estate Bd., Chgo. C. of C., Park Ridge C. of C. (pres. 1939-41). Clubs: Caxton, Bankers (Chgo.); Lions. Office: 69 W Washington St Chicago IL 60602*

BROWN, WILLIAM BURBRIDGE, justice Ohio Supreme Ct.; b. Chillicothe, Ohio, Sept. 10, 1912; s. Henry Renick and Mabel R. (Downs) B.; B.A., Williams Coll., Williamstown, Mass., 1934; LL.B. Harvard U., 1937; m. Jayne Stone, Aug. 18, 1943; children—Susan Brown Eshbaugh, Henry Renick. Law clk. firm Ritter & Daugherty, Toledo, 1937-39; mem. firm Simpson & Brown, Chillicothe, 1939-42; price atty. consumer goods div., Washington, 1942-43, chief price atty. Hawaii, Honolulu, 1943-44, chief atty., 1944-45; individual practice law, Honolulu, 1945-46; judge Hawaii Ct. of Tax Appeals, 1946-47, 2d Circuit Ct. Ter. of Hawaii, 1951-55; individual practice law, Chillicothe, 1955-57, 67-72; judge Municipal Ct., Chillicothe, 1957-61, Ohio Ct. Appeals 4th Dist., 1961-67, presiding judge, 1965-67; justice Ohio Supreme Ct., 1973—. Mem. Am. Bar Assn., Ohio Bar Assn., Hawaii Bar Assn. (treas. 1947-51), Ross County Bar Assn. (pres. 1966), Am. Judicature Soc., Inst. Judicial Adminstrn. Episcopalian (vestryman 1957-61). Clubs: Columbus Athletic, Chillicothe Country; Pacific (Honolulu); Univ. (Toledo); Rotary, Mason, Shriner, Moose. Office: State Office Tower 30 E Broad St Columbus OH 43215*

BROWN, WILLIAM DARREL, mech. engr.; b. Portland, Oreg., June 2, 1939; s. Charles Frank Lafollette and Mildred Caroline (Bredenbeck) B.; B.S. in M.E., Oreg. State U., 1961; M.S., U. Wash., 1970; m. Sharon Lee Hawley, July 14, 1961; children—Shannon, Ross, Robby. Project engr., Esco Inc., Portland, Oreg., 1961-62; prin. engr. Silver Eagle Co., Portland, 1963-64; design engr. Omark Industries Inc., Portland, 1965-66; mech. engr. Sandwell Intrnat., Inc., Portland, 1967-68; mech. engr. Pacific Rim Inc., Tacoma, Wash., part time 1968-70; mech. engr. Sargent & Lundy, Chgo., 1970-73; sr. nuclear engr. Fluor Pioneer Inc., Chgo., 1973-78; sr. mech. engr. Laramore Douglass and Popham, Cons. Engrs., Chgo., 1978-79; asso. M.W. Brown & Assos., Chgo., 1979—. Cons. Inst. Cultural Affairs. Mem. Village of Oak Park Econ. Devel. Com., 1973; co-founder Beye Neighborhood Council, Oak Park, 1973—; mem. Townmeeting Task Force, 1975-76. Mem. ASME, Am. Nuclear Soc. Democrat. Mem. First Ch. of Religious Science. Home: 426 S Lombard Oak Park IL 60302 Office: 130 S Oak Park Ave Oak Park IL 60302

BROWN, WILLIAM EVERETT, chem. engr.; b. Auburn, N.Y., Nov. 9, 1927; s. Everett Lawton and Helen May (Rasmussen) B.; B.S., Syracuse U., 1951; m. Natalie Smith, Oct. 3, 1953; children—Matthew, Kevin, Paul, Lorraine, Rebecca. With Dow Chem. Co., Midland, Mich., 1951—, head testing sect., 1956-62, head performance and design, 1962-66, sr. sect. head automotive sect., 1967, new applications devel., 1967-70, tech. mgr. new ventures research and devel., 1970-74, research mgr. Saran and Converted Products research, 1974-80, sr. research mgr., 1980—. Chmn. planning com. Bay-Midland OEO, 1970-72; pres. Men of Music, Midland, 1979-80. Mem. ASTM, Sigma Xi. Contbr. articles to profl. jours. Editor: Testing of Polymers, book series, 1965-70. Home: 505 Rodd St Midland MI 48640 Office: Dow Chem USA Saran and Converted Products Research Midland MI 48640

BROWN, WILLIAM JOSEPH, state ofcl.; b. Youngstown, Ohio, July 12, 1940; s. Joseph and Margaret (O'Neil) B.; B.A., Duquesne U.; J.D., Ohio No. U.; m. Cheryl Pocock, May 11, 1974. Former atty. OEO, Youngstown; now atty. gen. Ohio. Chmn. Humphrey for Pres. Com. Columbiana County, Ohio, 1968; mem. jud. council Democratic Nat. Com. Served with AUS. Mem. Mahoning County, Columbiana County bar assns., Nat. Assn. Attys. Gen. (mem. exec. com., chmn. consumer protection com.). Roman Catholic. Address: State Office Tower Columbus OH 43215

BROWN, WILLIAM TERRENCE, accountant; b. Kansas City, Mo., Dec. 6, 1941; s. William Francis and Ninalee (Timmons) B.; B.S., Rockhurst Coll., 1963; J.D., U. Mo., Kansas City, 1969; m. Kathleen Rae Ball, May 28, 1966 (div.); children—Stephen M., Christopher M. Admitted to U.S. Tax Ct. bar, 1972; with Sernes, Chandler, Schupp & Conneally, C.P.A.'s, Kansas City, 1962-64; mng. partner Brown & Co., C.P.A.'s, Kansas City, Mo., 1964—. Lay mem. mediation bd. Jackson County Med. Soc., 1975; treas., bd. dirs., mem. exec. com. Legal Aid of Western Mo., 1974—; bd. dirs. Pre-Trial Diversion Services, Inc., 1975-78, Estate Planning Assn. Kansas City, 1966-68. Mem. Am. Inst. C.P.A.'s. Home: 525 E 129th Terr Kansas City MO 64145 Office: 8080 Ward Pkwy Suite 440 Kansas City MO 64114

BROWNE, ALDIS JEROME, JR., real estate broker; b. Chgo., Mar. 21, 1912; s. Aldis J. and Elizabeth (Cunningham) B.; B.A., Yale U., 1935; m. Bertha Erminger, Oct. 22, 1938; children—Aldis J. III, Howell E., John Kenneth. Vice pres., dir. Browne & Storch Inc., and predecessors, Chgo., 1935-81, dir., 1961-81; with Quinlan & Tyson, Evanston, Ill., 1981—; dir. English Speaking Union, Civic Fedn., Mil. Order World Wars; chmn. Bldg. Review Bd. Lake Forest (certificate appreciation). Vestryman, St. James Episcopalian Ch., 1947-60. Trustee Old Peoples Home, Chgo. Served to capt. USNR. Mem. Chgo. (dir.), Ill., N. Side Chgo. real estate bds., Nat. Realtors Assn., Order Founders and Patriots (gov. Ill. chpt.), Soc. Colonial Wars, Order St. Lazarus, Mil. Order World Wars (comdr. Chgo. br.), Chgo. Art Inst. (governing life), Navy League (past dir.). Republican. Clubs: Chgo., Tavern, Army Navy Washington, Masons. Home: 165 W Onwentsia Rd Lake Forest IL 60045 Office: Quinlan & Tyson 1567 Sherman Ave Evanston IL 60204

BROWNE, WILLIAM SAMUEL, assn. exec.; b. Detroit, Aug. 18, 1932; s. William and Winifred B.; B.S., Wayne State U., 1962, M.A., 1967, Ph.D., 1980; m. Myra L. Clark, Dec. 24, 1965; children—David T. and Kurtis W. (adopted). Prodn. engr. Fisher Body Co. div. Gen. Motors Corp., Warren, Mich., 1956-62; tchr. Warren Consol. Schs., 1962-71; exec. dir. Utica (Mich.) Edn. Assn., 1971—; pres. Browne & Assos., Sterling Heights, Mich., 1976—. Mem. cultural arts and scholarship com. Macomb (Mich.) Community Coll.; active Democratic party. Served with USN, 1952-56. Ford Found. fellow, 1960-63. Mem. Mich. Edn. Assn., Mich. Exec. Dirs. Assn., Mich. Assn. Learning Disabilities Educators, Indsl. Relations Research Assn. Methodist. Office: Utica Edn Assn 51424 Van Dyke St Utica MI 48087

BROWNING, EARL DEAN, sch. adminstr.; b. Annawan, Ill., Jan. 21, 1926; s. Earl F. and Velma L. Browning; B.S., Western Ill. U., 1951; M.A., U. Ill., 1957; advanced cert. of specialist So. Ill. U., 1968; m. Ardythe A. Machesney, June 23, 1951; 1 dau., Lexa Linn. Indsl. arts tchr. Alton (Ill.) Community Sch. Dist., 1951-57, dir. adult edn., 1957-67, adminstrv. asst. vocat. edn., 1967—. Served with U.S. Army, 1944-46. Decorated Bronze Star; recipient Those Who Excel award Ill. Bd. Edn., 1976; named Outstanding Vocat. Adminstr. of Yr., Ill. Council Local Adminstrs., 1981. Mem. Am. Vocat. Assn., Ill. Vocat. Assn., Ill. Indsl. Arts Assn., Nat. Council Local Adminstrs., NEA. Methodist. Home: 5502 Ladue St Godfrey IL 62035 Office: Alton Community School Dist 1854 E Broadway Alton IL 62002

BROWNING, ELEANOR MAY, nurse; b. Toronto, Ont., Can., Aug. 4, 1922; came to U.S., 1944, naturalized, 1947; d. Edwin and Grayce May Tindall; R.N., St. Mary's Hosp., Timmons, Ont., 1943; m. Robert Browning, Aug. 17, 1944; children—Richard, Lynn. Med.-surg. nurse St. Mary's Hosp., New Westminster, B. C., Can., 1943-44; pvt. duty nurse, Port Townsend, Wash., 1944-45; indsl. nurse Link Belt Co., Indpls., 1945; office nurse, 1945-48; mem. nursing staff St. Francis Hosp. Center, Beech Grove, Ind., 1953—, asso. dir. nursing, 1973-78, dir. nursing, 1978—. Mem. Nat. League Nursing, Am. Soc. Nursing Adminstrs. Clubs: Zonta, Toastmasters. Home: 7246 Laurel Dr Indianapolis IN 46227 Office: 1600 Albany St Beech Grove IN 46107

BROWNING, ROBERT DOYLE, constrn. co. exec.; b. Daviess County, Ind., Sept. 30, 1917; s. Ray and Pearl (Browning) B.; grad. high sch.; student Internat. Corr. Sch.; m. Betty Overton, Sept. 2, 1942; children—Sondra Chapman, Larry, Gerald. Farmer, Washington, Ind., 1936-41; asst. engr. roads Ind. State Hwy., 1945-50; with Thompson Constrn. Co., Inc., Indpls., 1950—, field engr., 1961, office engr., estimator, 1961-70, exec. v.p., 1970—, also dir. Bd. dirs. Patton Park. Treas. Young Republicans, Daviess County, Ind., 1946-50; trustee Camby (Ind.) Community Ch. Served to master sgt. USAF, 1941-45. Decorated Bronze Star. Mem. V.F.W., Ind. Constructors Inc. (sec.-treas. 1978-79). Clubs: Masons, K.P. Home: 8641 Camby Rd Camby IN 46116 Office: 3840 Prospect St Indianapolis IN 46203

BROWNING, ROBERT LYNN, educator, clergyman; b. Gallatin, Mo., June 19, 1924; s. Robert W. and Nell J. (Trotter) B.; B.A., Mo. Valley Coll., 1945; M.Div., Union Theol. Sem., 1948; Ph.D., Ohio State U., 1960; postgrad. Columbia U., 1951-53, Oxford (Eng.) U., 1978-79; m. Jean Beatty, Dec. 27, 1947 (dec. 1977); children—Gregory, David, Peter, Lisa; m. 2d. Jackie L. Rogers, Aug. 26, 1979. Ordained to ministry Disciples of Christ Ch., 1949, transferred to United Meth. Ch., 1950; minister edn. Old Stone Ch., Meadville, Pa., 1946-51, Community Ch. at the Circle, Mt. Vernon, N.Y., 1951-53, North Broadway United Meth. Ch., Columbus, Ohio, 1953-59; prof. Christian edn. Meth. Theol. Sch., Delaware, Ohio, 1959-72, William A. Chryst prof. Christian edn., 1972—; pres. Meth. Conf. on Christian edn., 1967-69; exec. dir. Commn. on Role of the Professions in Soc., 1974-76, cons., 1976—. Bd. dirs. Southside Settlement, Columbus, 1968-74, Tray-Lee Center, Columbus, 1955-59, Ohio State U. Wesley Found., 1960-78, vice chmn. 1976-78. Served with USN, 1942-45. Recipient Paul Hinkhouse award Religious Public Relations Council Am., 1971. Mem. Assn. for Profl. Edn. for Ministry (editor proc. 1980—), Religious Edn. Assn., Assn. of Profs. and Researchers in Religious Edn. Author: Communication with Junior Highs, 1968; Guidelines for Youth Ministry, 1970; What on Earth Are You Doing, 1966; (audiotape) (with Charles Foster) Communicating the Faith with Children, 1971; Ways the Bible Comes Alive, 1975; Ways Persons Become Christian, 1976; (with Charles Foster, Everett Tilson) Looking at Leadership with the Eyes of Biblical Faith, 1978; editor: Integration: Objective Studies and Practical Theology, Proc. Assn. Profl. Edn. for Ministry, 1981; contbr. articles on religious edn. to profl. jours. Home: 6613 Hawthorne St Worthington OH 43085 Office: 3081 Columbus Pike Delaware OH 43015

BROWNING, STERLING EDWIN, II, chemist; b. Ardmore, Okla., Aug. 27, 1933; s. Sterling Edwin and Viola Mae (Jones) B.; student Okla. A&M U., 1951-56, Tulsa U., 1961-62; B.A., Okla. State U., 1967; m. Merlene Fox, Sept. 29, 1962; children—Melissa Anne, Sterling Edwin III, Jonathan Brian. Lab. helper Pan Am. Oil Corp., Tulsa, 1956-57; partner Browning's Carpet Co., Tulsa, 1957-61; research asst. chemistry Dowell div. Dow Chem. Co., Tulsa, 1961-63; tech. corr. Fisher Sci. Co., St. Louis, 1963-65; lab. technician Okla. State U., Stillwater, 1965-67; analytic chemist Sci. Assos., St. Louis, 1967-68; chief chemist Sherwood Med. Industries, St. Louis, 1968-74; sr. analytical chemist Sigma Chem. Co., St. Louis, 1974—; staff Applied Sci. Cons.'s, St. Louis, 1972—. Trustee Greenmar Subdiv., Mo., 1972-73; active Boy Scouts Am., Girl Scouts U.S.A., 1975—. Mem. Am. Chem. Soc. (treas. gen. topics group St. Louis sect. 1981-82), St. Louis Soc. Analysts, Soc. for Applied Spectroscopy, Coblentz Soc., St. Louis Chromatography Discussion Group, Sigma Study Group, Sigma Alpha Epsilon. Republican. Presbyterian. Home: 664 Greenbrae Ct Saint Louis County MO 63026 Office: Sigma Chem Co 3500 DeKalb St Saint Louis MO 63118

BROYHILL, ROY FRANKLIN, indsl. turf and agrl. equipment mfg. exec.; b. Sioux City, Iowa, June 20, 1919; s. George Franklin and Effie (Motes) B.; B.B.A., U. Nebr., 1940; m. Arline W. Stewart, Jan. 30, 1943; children—Lynn Diann (dec.), Craig G., Kent Bryan, Bryce Alan. Trainee mgr. Montgomery Ward Co., 1940; semi-sr. acct. L. H. Keightley, 1941-42; chief accountant Army Exchange Service, Sioux City, 1942-46; pres., chmn. Broyhill Co., 1946—; pres., dir. Star Printing & Pub. Co., South Sioux City, 1949—; pres., chmn. Broyhill Corp., 1953—; v.p. Broyhill Mfg. Co., 1978—; pres., chmn. bd. Broyhill Inc.; dir. 1st Nat. Bank, Sioux City. Mem. U.S.A. Exec. Res.; mem. Nebr. dist. adv. council SBA, 1971—. Mayor of Dakota City, 1951-53; mem. Nebr. Republican Central Com., 1954-56. Past mem. local sch. bd. Trustee U. Nebr., U. Nebr. Found. Served with AUS, 1940-41. Mem. Nitrogen Solutions Assn. (dir. 1956-60), Farm Equipment Mfrs. Assn. (dir., pres. 1971-72), Atokad Racing Assn. (past dir.), N.A.M., U.S., South Sioux City chambers commerce, Nebr. Assn. Commerce and Industry (dir. 1972-73), Alumni Assn. U. Nebr. (dir.), Beta Theta Pi, Alpha Kappa Psi. Presbyn. (elder). Mason (Shriner), Kiwanian. Home: 1610 Broadway Dakota City NE 68731 Office: Broyhill Co N Market Sq Dakota City NE 68731

BROZ, THOMAS FRANK, agrl. tech. co. exec.; b. McCook, Nebr., Feb. 4, 1949; s. Vincent C. and Margaret (McLamore) B.; A.A., McCook Community Coll., 1969; B.S., U. Nebr., Lincoln, 1971; m. Nancy A. Eisenhart, June 13, 1970; children—Jenni Rebecca, Jeffrey Scott. Agronomist, area mgr. Agrl. Tech. Co., Wray, Colo., 1971-74, pres., McCook, Nebr., 1974—. Mem. Am. Soc. Agronomy (asso.), Nebr. Ind. Crop Cons. Assn., Nat. Alliance Ind. Crop Cons., Am. Registry Cert. Profls. in Agronomy. Roman Catholic. Clubs: Elks, K.C., Optimist. Home: 1604 W 2d St McCook NE 69001 Office: 206 E 1st St Mc Cook NE 69001

BROZOVIC, RICHARD, mfg. co. exec.; b. Briar Hill, Pa., Apr. 2, 1932; s. Albert Elmer and Emily Louise (Yelinek) B.; student pub. schs., Jefferson, Pa.; m. Jean E. Heverling, Apr. 18, 1953; 1 son, Robert A. Served from pvt. to 1st sgt. U.S. Army, 1947-71, ret., 1971; pres., gen. mgr. Geyer Bros. Brewing Co., Frankenmuth, Mich., 1975—. Decorated Bronze Star medals (2), Purple Heart. Mem. Am. Legion. Roman Catholic. Clubs: Frankenmuth Conservation, Men's of Blessed Trinity Cath. Ch. Home: 448 Sunburst Dr Frankenmuth MI 48734 Office: 425 S Main St Frankenmuth MI 48734

BRUBAKER, CARL H., JR., chemist, educator; b. Passaic, N.J., July 13, 1925; s. Carl Hess and Lillian Alice (Rochow) B.; B.S., Franklin and Marshall Coll., 1949; Ph.D., M.I.T., 1952; m. Mary Ellen Fiske, June 21, 1949; children—Carl, Peter. Mem. faculty dept. chemistry Mich. State U., East Lansing, 1952—, prof., 1961—; Smith-Mundt Fulbright lectr. U. Chile, 1958; cons. in field. Served with AUS, 1943-46. Mem. Am. Chem. Soc., Royal Soc. Chemistry, AAAS. Asst. editor Jour. Am. Chem. Soc., 1964-70, asso. editor, 1970-71, 73—; mem. editorial bd. 3 profl. jours.; contbr. articles to profl. jours. Home: PO Box 128 Okemos MI 48864 Office: Dept Chemistry Mich State Univ East Lansing MI 48824

BRUCE, CAROLYN CORRINGTON, nurse; b. North Vernon, Ind., Apr. 28, 1936; d. Ottis C. and Ruth E. (Davis) Corya; R.N., Methodist Hosp., Indpls., 1956; B.S. in Health Edn., Ind. U., 1975, postgrad., 1976; spl. course in respiratory therapy U. Chgo., 1973; m. Reginald A. Bruce, July 16, 1976; children by previous marriage—Douglas Corrington, Judith Corrington, Carla Corrington. Charge nurse metabolic unit Meth. Hosp., Indpls., 1956-59, head nurse metabolic unit, 1959-63, head nurse ICU, 1968-69, head nurse med. unit, 1969-70, dir. respiratory therapy, 1970-75, asst. dir. nursing, 1975-76; dir. nursing Paris (Ill.) Hosp., 1976-77, Crawford Meml. Hosp., Robinson, Ill., 1978-79; adminstr. Lincolnland Vis. Nurse Assn., 1980—; camp nurse diabetics, office nurse Dr. J.H. Warvel, 1958; indsl. nurse Cummins Engine Co., Columbus, Ind., 1963; head nurse psychiatry, Madison, Ind., 1965-68; former faculty mem. CPR, Ind. Heart Assn. Crawford County sec. Nat. Fedn. Republican Women, 1976-78; co-chairperson com. Crawford County Public Health Dept., 1978; v.p. Health Planning Bd.; vol. ARC, Am. Cancer Soc. Mem. Am. Nurses Assn. (cert. nursing adminstr.), Ill. Nurses Assn. (mem. rev. panel for continuing edn. 1977—), Am. Heart Assn., Am. Soc. Nursing Service Adminstrs., Am. Hosp. Assn., Crawford Meml. Hosp. Aux., AAUW, Meth. Hosp. Nursing Alumnae (pres. 1970-74). Presbyterian. Home: 15 Doral Ct Route 3 Mattoon IL 61938

BRUCE, JAMES FRANKLIN, pub. co. exec.; b. Indpls., Mar. 25, 1930; s. Albert Lee and Myrtle Elizabeth (Horne) B.; B.S., Ind. U., 1953; children—Katherie Stacy, Kevin Thomas. Mgr. consumer affairs dept. Indpls. Better Bus. Bur., Inc., 1958-59; with Ency. Britannica, Chgo., 1959—, dir. specialty mktg. services mktg. dept., 1959-81, dir. co. relations, 1979—. Mem. Spl. Task Force Pres.' Council for Phys. Fitness and Sports, 1973—; mem. spl. adv. group U.S. Bicentennial Adminstrn. Served with USAF, 1953-55. Mem. Wedgewood Soc. Chgo., U.S. C. of C. (mem. bus. consumer council), Chgo. Sales and Mktg. Club, Nat. Premium Advt. Assn. Am., Council Fgn. Relations, Conf. Consumer Orgns., Soc. Consumer Affairs Profls. in Bus. Direct Selling Assn., Ind. U. Alumni Assn., Soc. Consumers and Profls. in Bus. Club: Army-Navy (Washington). Office: 425 N Michigan Ave Chicago IL 60611

BRUCE, TERRY L., state senator; b. Olney, Ill., J.D., U. Ill., 1969; m. Charlotte Roberts; children—Emily Anne, Ellen Catherine. Farm labor staff U.S. Dept. Labor, Washington, mem. staff Congressman George Shipley, Ill. State Senator Philip Benefiel; legis. intern, 1969-70; mem. Ill. Senate, 1970—, asst. majority leader, 1975—. Named Outstanding Legislator of Year, Ill. Edn. Assn., 1973; winner Right to Know award Ill. Press Assn., 1975; award Ill. Community Coll. Trustees Assn. Democrat. Address: Olney IL *

BRUCKER, EDMUND, artist, portrait painter, educator; b. Cleve., Nov. 20, 1912; s. Ludwig and Theresa (Strung) B.; diploma in portrait painting Cleve. Inst. Art, 1934, postgrad., 1934-36; m. Marcelline B. Spencer, Jan. 28, 1939; 1 son, Robert. Instr., Cleve. Inst. Art, 1936-38, John Herron Art Sch., Indpls., 1938-67; lectr. painting Herron Sch. Art, Ind. U., Indpls., 1967-68, asso. prof., 1968-73, prof., 1973—; one-man shows: Herron Art Inst., 1947, 63, Hoosier Art Gallery, Indpls., 1953; groups shows include: Carnegie Art Inst., Pitts., 1941, Library of Congress, 1945, Met. Mus. Art, N.Y.C., 1952, Ind. State Mus., 1979; represented in permanent collections: Eli Lilly & Co., Indpls., Northwestern U., Ind. U., Purdue U., Cleve. Mus. Art, Dartmouth Coll., Evansville (Ind.) Mus. Arts and Scis., City of Cleve. Warner Collection, Scholl Mfg. Co., Chgo., Phillips Oil Co., Bartlesville, Okla., Weir Cook Internat. Airport, Indpls., Indpls. Motor Speedway Hall of Fame Mus., Taylor U.; numerous others; portrait cover artist Ind. Bus. and Industry Mag., 1960-71. Recipient Milliken award Art Assn. Indpls., 1963; named Sagamore of the Wabash, Gov. of Ind., 1965. Mem. Ind. Artists Club, Hoosier Salon Patrons Assn., Indpls. Museum Art. Club: Riviera. Home: 545 King Dr Indianapolis IN 46260 Office: 1701 N Pennsylvania St Indianapolis IN 46202

BRUCKNER, CLARENCE AUGUST, real estate exec.; b. Chgo., Aug. 7, 1931; s. Clarence R. and Elizabeth K. (McCarl) B.; student U. Ill., 1949-51; m. Leta Bruckner; children—Linda, Lisbeth, Paul, Curt. Vice pres. Donald F. Moore, Inc., 1955-67; pres. C.A. Bruckner & Assos., Inc., Oak Brook, Ill., 1967—, Bruckner, Fitts & Assos., Inc. 1977—; sec. Woodsmyth Corp., 1977—; gen. partner Commerce Sq., 1975—. Served with USAF, 1951-52. Mem. Soc. Real Estate Appraisers (past pres. Chgo. chpt.), Am. Inst. Real Estate Appraisers, Am. Soc. Real Estate Counselors, Jr. Real Estate Bd. Chgo. (past pres.). Methodist. Club: Masons (Medinah Temple Shrine). Home: 2408 Shasta Dr Lisle IL 60532 Office: 901 W Liberty Dr Wheaton IL 60187

BRUDZINSKI, ROBERT MICHAEL, indsl. products distbg. co. exec.; b. Phila., Apr. 20, 1947; s. Stanley Francis and Marie Concetta (Boffa) B.; B.S.M.E., Drexel Inst. Tech., 1969; M.E.E.S., Pa. State U., 1974; M.B.A., U. Chgo., 1978; m. Janice Ann Cress, June 20, 1970; children—Michael Robert, Christopher David. Plastics engr. Rohm and Haas Co., Bristol, Pa., 1969-71; mgr. mktg. services, asst. sales mgr. Chein Industries Inc., Burlington, N.J., 1971-75; mgr. mktg. services, merchandising Needlecraft div. Quaker Oats Co., Chgo., 1975-78; mgr. mktg. Packaging div. Lake River Corp., Hinsdale, Ill., 1978-80; mktg. planning mgr. W.W. Grainger, Inc., Chgo., 1980—. Recipient Chmn.'s award for excellence Quaker Oats Co., 1977. Mem. Park Ridge (Ill.) Jaycees (dir. 1979, 80, named Outstanding Jaycee 1978-79, Outstanding Dir. 1979-80). Home: 1317 S Greenwood Ave Park Ridge IL 60068 Office: WW Grainger Inc 5959 W Howard St Chicago IL 60648

BRUE, LESTER DUANE, risk control mgr.; b. Ottawa, Ill., Sept. 19, 1956; s. Reuben L. and Mildred L. (Holloway) B.; B.S., Ill. State U., 1977; m. Claire E. Nowacki, Oct. 21, 1978. Underwriting surveyor Chubb & Son Ins. Co., Chgo., 1978, sr. underwriting surveyor, Indpls., 1978-79; risk control service rep. Comml. Union, Bloomington, Ill., 1979-80, risk control supr., 1980—, territorial risk control mgr., 1981—. Mem. Am. Soc. Safety Engrs., Assn. Casualty Engrs., Sigma Phi Epsilon, Iota Lambda Sigma. Lutheran. Club: ISU Golf. Office: 17W755 Butterfield Rd Oakbrook Terrace IL 60181

BRUENING, WILLIAM PAUL, controls co. exec.; b. St. Louis, Mar, 8, 1935; s. Francis Joseph and Crystal Verda (Baumgartner) B.; B.E.E., U. Dayton, 1957. Sales engr. Cutler-Hammer Inc., St. Louis, 1957-63, O'Brien Equipment Co., St. Louis, 1963-69; v.p., sec. Central Controls Co., Inc., St. Louis, 1969-76; pres. Process Controls Co., Inc., St. Louis, 1976—; dir. Bannes-Sheughnessy Inc. Bd. dirs. St. Louis Area chpt. March of Dimes Birth Defects Found. Served with U.S. Army, 1957-63. Mem. Instrument Soc. Am. (sr.), Confrerie des Chevaliers du Tastevin, Newcomen Soc. N. Am., Commanderie de Bordeaux. Republican. Roman Catholic. Clubs: St. Louis, Mo. Athletic, Rolls-Royce Owners. Home: 6813 Aliceton Ave Saint Louis MO 63123 Office: 20 American Industrial Dr Maryland Heights MO 63043

BRUESKE, FRANK(LIN) HAROLD, assn. exec.; b. Plainview, Minn., Nov. 11, 1936; s. Ray C. and Mary (Yarolimek) B.; B.A., Winona (Minn.) State U., 1958; m. Rose Marie Warner, July 29, 1958; children—John, Christine, Anne. Dir. communications Watkins Products, Inc., Winona, 1965-71; dir. pub. relations Coll. St. Theresa, Winona, Minn., 1971-72; nat. membership dir. Nat. Conf. Cath. Charities, Washington, 1972-74; dir. communications Data Processing Mgmt. Assn., Park Ridge, Ill., 1974-77; mgr. pub. relations and communications div. Lions Internat., Oak Brook, Ill., 1977-80; adminstr. Am. Soc. Contemporary Medicine, Surgery and Ophthalmology, Chgo., 1981—; also publs., communications cons. Active 4-H. Mem. Am. Soc. Assn. Execs., Chgo. Soc. Assn. Execs. Editor Data Mgmt. mag.; mng. editor Lion mag. Home: 12929 60th St Bristol WI 53104 Office: 211 E Chicago Ave Chicago IL 60611

BRUGLER, RICHARD KENNETH, steel and iron mfg. co. exec.; b. Warren, Ohio, Oct. 28, 1928; s. Herman Kenneth and Mildred Marrietta (Fell) B.; B.S. in Mech. Engring., Case Inst. Tech., 1952, B.S. in Elec. Engring., 1954; m. Jean Elizabeth Brooks, Dec. 22, 1951; children—David Kenneth, Diane Jean, Eric Paul, Kurt Ernst. Draftsman, Perfection Stove Co., Cleve., 1951-52; lab. machinist Thompson Products Co., Cleve., 1952-54; with Heltzel Co., Warren, 1954—, chief engr., 1962-65, v.p. engring., 1965-78, v.p. ops., 1978—; chmn. Concrete Plant Mfrs. Bur., 1975-78. Served with USNR, 1946-48. Mem. Nat. Readymix Assn. (dir.), Nat., Trumbull County (sec. 1976-78, pres. 1979) socs. profl. engrs., IEEE (sr.), Nat. Scalemens Assn., Antique Wireless Assn., Palatine Soc. Methodist. Club: Masons. Patentee in field. Home: 1359 Beechcrest St Warren OH 44485 Office: 1750 Thomas Rd Warren OH 44484

BRUHNKE, PAUL EDWARD, appliance mfg. co. exec.; b. Chgo., June 11, 1946; s. Edward G. and Viola Ellen (Krueger) B.; B.S. in Mktg., U. Ill., 1969; M.B.A., DePaul U., Chgo., 1970; m. Joan Mary Murphy, Aug. 29, 1970. Sales rep. Dun & Bradstreet, Inc., 1972-73; account exec. GR Co. div. Kelvinator, Inc., Grand Rapids, Mich., 1973-74; nat. accounts mgr. Kelvinator Appliance Co., Grand Rapids, 1974-75, div. sales mgr., 1975—. Served with U.S. Army, 1970-72. Decorated Army Commendation medal. Office: 930 Ft Duquesne Blvd Pittsburgh PA 15222

BRULL, HANS FRANK, social worker; b. Berlin, Germany, May 17, 1921; s. Victor and Ellen (Berendsen) B.; came to U.S., 1933, naturalized, 1943; B.A., CCNY, 1949; M.S.W., U. Pa., 1951; postgrad. U. Chgo., 1962; m. Rose Weiss, May 3, 1953 (div.); children—Ellen Sandra, Steven Victor; m. 2d, Olive Rue, Dec. 20, 1969. Caseworker Childrens Ct. Clinic, Melbourne, Australia, 1951, Jewish Family and Childrens Service, Mpls., 1951-53, Jewish Children's Bur., Chgo., 1953-56; head sch. social work dept. New Trier High Sch.-W., Northfield, 1963—; clin. asst. prof. Sch. Social Work, Smith Coll., Northampton, Mass., 1975. Pvt. practice as psychiat. social worker, Winnetka. Mem. citizens adv. com. Youth Employment Service, 1965—; pres. Glenview Human Relations Com., 1963-64; mem. bd. Gates House Inc., 1970-73; mem. New Trier Twp. Com. on Youth, 1980—. Served with M.I., AUS, 1943-46. Mem. Nat. Assn. Social Workers (mem. state bd. 1976-77, del. nat. assembly 1977). Contbr. articles to profl. publs. Home: 1416 Edgewood Ln Winnetka IL 60093 Office: 525 Winnetka Ave Winnetka IL 60093

BRUMBACK, CHARLES TIEDTKE, newspaper exec.; b. Toledo, Sept. 27, 1928; s. John Sanford and Frances Hannah (Tiedtke) B.; B.A., Princeton U., 1950; postgrad. U. Toledo, 1953-54; m. Mary Louise Howe, July 7, 1951; children—Charles Tiedtke, Anne V., Wesley W., Ellen P. With Arthur Young & Co., C.P.A.s, 1950-57; bus. mgr., v.p., treas., pres., chief exec. officer, dir. Sentinel Star Co., Orlando, Fla., 1957-81; pres., chief exec. officer Chgo. Tribune, 1981—. Pres., dir. Sentinel Star Community Assn.; mem. Orlando Mcpl. Planning Bd., 1958-63; trustee Orlando Public Library, 1958-63; bd. govs. Orange Meml. Hosp., 1960-76; chmn. bd. dirs. Orlando Regional Med. Center, 1976-78. Served to 1st lt. U.S. Army, 1951-53. Decorated Bronze star. C.P.A., Ohio, Fla. Mem. Ohio, Fla. socs., C.P.A.s, Am. Inst. C.P.A.s, Orlando Area C. of C., Fla. Press Assn. (treas. 1969-76, pres. 1980, dir.), Inst. Newspaper Controllers and Fin. Officers, Clubs: Rotary (hon.), Orlando Country, Citrus, Princeton of N.Y., University. Office: Office of Pres Chgo Tribune Co 435 N Michigan Ave Chicago IL 60611*

BRUMBAUGH, PHILIP SLOAN, quality control cons.; b. St. Louis, Nov. 14, 1932; s. Richard I. and Grace L. (Lischer) B.; A.B., Washington U., St. Louis, 1954, M.B.A., 1958, Ph.D., 1963; postgrad. Univ. Coll. London, 1963-64; m. Bettina Ann Viviano, Feb. 25, 1978. Ops. analyst Humble Oil & Refining Co., Houston, 1961-62; indsl. engr. Falstaff Brewing Corp., St. Louis, 1963; asst. prof. Sch. Engring., Washington U., St. Louis, 1964-70; asso. prof. U. Mo., St. Louis, 1970-74; pres. Qualtech Systems, Inc., Maryland Heights, Mo., 1974—; dir. Palco Equipment, Inc. Mem. indsl. engring. adv. com. St. Louis Community Colls. Served with U.S. Army, 1954-56. Mem. Am. Statis. Assn., Am. Inst. Indsl. Engrs (past nat. dir., past pres. St. Louis chpt.), Am. Soc. for Quality Control (cert. quality engr., past chmn. St. Louis sect.). Clubs: Univ., Engrs. (St. Louis). Home: 1359 Mason Rd Saint Louis MO 63131 Office: Qualtech Systems Inc 100 Progress Pkwy Suite 221 Maryland Heights MO 63043

BRUMMER, GEORGE, ins. co. exec.; b. Vienna, Austria, Nov. 15, 1930; came to U.S., 1940, naturalized, 1947; s. Salomon and Etta B.; B.S. in Math., CCNY, 1954; m. Hannah Israel, Jan. 9, 1949; children—Howard A., Suzanne M. Brummer Berkovits. Asst. sec. U.S. Life Ins. Co., N.Y.C., 1954-60; asst. actuary, v.p. Citizen's Life Ins. Co., N.Y.C., 1960-64; v.p., actuary Gt. No. Mgmt. Co., Inc., Mineola, N.Y., 1965-67; exec. v.p., actuary H.E. Nyhart Co., Inc., Indpls., 1967-71; group actuary, v.p. group life and health Am. United Life Ins. Co., Indpls., 1971-74; partner Wolfman & Moscovitch, cons. actuaries, Chgo., 1974-77; sr. v.p., gen. mgr. life and health div. Zurich Am. Ins. Cos., Schaumburg, 1977—. Fellow Soc. Actuaries, Conf. Actuaries in Public Practice, Can. Inst. Actuaries; mem. Am. Acad. Actuaries. Office: 231 N Martingale Rd Schaumburg IL 60196

BRUMMER, RICHARD H., state legislator; b. Effingham, Ill., June 5, 1942; s. Cletus and Agnes (Grunloh) B.; B.A., Quincy Coll., 1964; postgrad. Inst. European Studies, U. Vienna (Austria), 1963; J.D., U. Ill., 1967; m. Maureen McLean, Aug. 22, 1964; children—Stephen, John, Thomas, Diana, Bonnie, Kathleen, Mary Alice. Admitted to Ill. bar, 1967; partner firm Parker, Brummer, Siemer, Austin & Resch, Effingham, 1968—; mem. Ill. Ho. of Reps. from 54th Dist., 1977—. Chmn. Effingham Mental Health Bd., 1970-72; mem. Democratic Precinct Com., 1970-78. Named Outstanding Man of Year, Effingham Jaycees, 1977; recipient Friend of Edn. award Ill. Bd. Edn., 1977; Public Service award Ill. Electric Coop., 1980. Mem. Am. Bar Assn., Assn. Trial Lawyers Am., Ill. State Bar Assn., Effingham County Bar Assn. Roman Catholic. Clubs: Elks, Rotary, K.C. Office: 307 N 3d St Effingham IL 62401

BRUMMER, ROBERT CRAIG, business exec.; b. Mar. 28, 1945; s. Emmett Anthony and Mary Ellen (Blue) B.; B.B.A., Eastern Mich. U., 1970; m. Jill Sutherland, Feb. 27, 1965; children—Anne Marie, Robert Craig. Ops. asst. mgr., shift leader, also dept. mgr. Interstate Stores, 1969-71, Midwest regional personnel mgr., 1971-72, Eastern regional personnel mgr., 1972-73, store mgr. in tng., 1973, asst. to dir. personnel and employee relations, 1973; dist. personnel mgr. Target Stores, Colo./Okla., 1973-74; regional personnel/ops. mgr. Tex./Okla., 1974-79; mgr. exec. placement and devel. Dayton Hudson Corp., Mpls., 1979—. Mem. Am. Soc. Tng. and Devel. Home: 7153 Willow Rd Maple Grove MN 55369 Office: Dayton Hudson Corp 777 Nicollet Mall Minneapolis MN 55402

BRUMMETT, BARRY J., restaurant chain exec.; b. Waco, Tex., July 30, 1944; s. J.C. and Atheline M. B.; B.S., Tex. A. and M. U., 1966, M.S., 1968, Ph.D., 1972; m. Jane B. Brummett, Sept. 10, 1966; children—Beth, Mark. Dir. food research and devel. and quality assurance Church's Fried Chicken, Inc., San Antonio, 1972-74; v.p. ops. Whip Foods, Inc., San Antonio, 1974-76; sr. dir. research and devel. Pizza Hut, Inc., Wichita, Kans., 1976-81; v.p. Solatrex Industries, Inc., San Antonio, 1981—. Served to capt. USAR. Mem. Inst. Food Technologists, Am. Assn. Oil Chemists, Am. Assn. Cereal Chemists, Tex. Pepper Found., Internat. Connoisseus of Green and Red Chiles, Sigma Xi, Phi Tau Sigma, Phi Sigma Gamma Sigma Delta. Methodist. Club: Elk. Contbr. articles to profl. jours. Office: 9111 E Douglas Wichita KS 67207

BRUMMETT, ROGER STEPHEN, cement co. exec.; b. Great Falls, Mont., June 29, 1945; s. Joseph and Elizabeth (Cox) B.; student U. Minn., 1963-66, Wright State U., 1973-74, 80, Sinclair Coll., 1973-74, 79-80. Dir. community services Salvation Army, 1970-71; coordinator devel. therapy Stillwater Hosp. for Severely and Profoundly Retarded Children, Dayton, Ohio, 1971-72; med. specialist Regional Program for Physically Handicapped, Dayton, 1972-73; safety coordinator Southwestern Portland Cement Co., Fairborn, Ohio, 1973—. Ruling elder Fairborn 1st Presbyterian Ch., 1975—; chmn. task force on ministry with handicapped Ohio Council Chs., 1981—; scoutmaster, chmn. handicapped scouting Boy Scouts Am. Served with USAF, 1966-70. Recipient Service to Mankind award Fairborn Sertoma Club, 1980. Mem. Am. Soc. Safety Engrs., Nat. Assn. Deaf, Ohio Registry Interpreters for Deaf (dist. treas.), Nat. Safety Mgmt. Soc., Dayton Miami Valley Safety Council. Home: 1266 S Central Ave Fairborn OH 45324 Office: PO Box 191 Fairborn OH 45324

BRUMMOND, ROBERT THOMAS, utility exec.; b. Belle Fourche, S.D., Dec. 29, 1950; s. Bruce and Mary Josephine (Waldron) B.; B.S. in Physics, St. Norbert Coll., DePere, Wis., 1973; M.S. in Civil Engring., U. Ill., Champaign-Urbana, 1974. Environ. engr. Lake County Public Works Dept., Waukegan, Ill., 1974-76, supr. ops., 1976—. Cert. wastewater operator, Ill.; registered profl. engr., Ill. Mem. Am. Water Works Assn., Water Pollution Control Fedn., Ill. Soc. Water Pollution Control Operators (1st v.p.). Roman Catholic. Home: 73 Miller Rd Lake Zurich IL 60047 Office: 650 Winchester Rd Libertyville IL 60048

BRUNER, JAMES WILLIAM, JR., lawyer; b. Evansville, Ind., Oct. 15, 1945; s. James William and May Ella (Ritter) B.; B.S.Ch.E., Purdue U., 1967; postgrad. U. Evansville, 1967-68, 70-71; J.D., Ind. U., Bloomington, 1974. Engr., Whirlpool Corp., Evansville, Ind., 1967-68, 70-71; admitted to Ind. bar, 1974; individual practice law, Boonville, Ind., 1974—; dep. prosecutor County of Warrick (Ind.), 1977-78. Bd. dirs. Warrick County Mus. Served with U.S. Army, 1968-70; Vietnam. Decorated Bronze Star; Cross of Gallantry (Vietnam). Mem. Boonville Jaycees (internal v.p. 1976-77), Warrick County Bar Assn. (pres. 1979), Ind. Bar Assn., Am. Bar Assn., Am. Judicature Soc. Republican. Methodist. Club: Kiwanis (pres. Boonville 1976-77, Ind. Dist. lt. gov. Lincoln div. 1978-79). Home: Route 6 Boonville IN 47601 Office: 110 E Main St Boonville IN 47601

BRUNER, JERE WAITE, polit. scientist; b. Akron, Ohio, Mar. 5, 1928; s. Harold Edwards and Evelyn Berenice (Waite) B.; student Harvard U., 1946-48; B.S., Northwestern U., 1962, M.S., 1963; Ph.D. (Woodrow Wilson nat. fellow 1963-64, Univ. dissertation fellow 1965-66, NSF fellow 1966-67), Yale U., 1973; m. Katharina Sabina Kleiner, Aug. 28, 1971; children—Erika Susan, Franziska Renata Corinthia. Tchr., Soc. of Bros., Paraguay, 1951-55, translator, 1951-58, engr., 1949-59, editor, 1954-57; acting asst. prof. govt. Oberlin Coll., 1967-73, asst. prof., 1973-76, asso. prof., 1976—; participant NSF Faculty Workshop, summer 1974. Campaign cons. to state legislator Donald Pease, Ohio (now congressman), 1968-71. Mem. Am. Polit. Sci. Assn., Midwest Polit. Sci. Assn., Internat. Transactional Analysis Assn. Author: (with others) Political Socialization Across the Generations, 1975; editorial bd. Am. Jour. Polit. Sci., 1979—. Office: Govt Dept Oberlin Coll Oberlin OH 44074

BRUNER, PHILIP LANE, lawyer; b. Chgo., Sept. 26, 1939; s. Henry Pfeiffer and Marjorie (Williamson) B.; A.B., Princeton U., 1961; J.D., U. Mich., 1964; M.B.A., Syracuse U., 1967; m. Ellen Carole Germann, Mar. 21, 1964; children—Philip Richard, Stephen Reed, Carolyn Anne. Admitted to Wis. bar, 1964, Minn. bar, 1968; mem. firm Briggs and Morgan, Mpls. and St. Paul, 1967—; adj. prof. William Mitchell Coll. Law, St. Paul, 1970-78, 81; lectr. law seminars U. Minn., 1969—, U. Wis., 1975—, So. Methodist U., 1977—, U. Denver, 1975—, Hamline U., 1978—, Fla. Bar Assn., 1979—, Am. Bar Assn., 1980—, Minn. Bar Assn., 1981—. Bd. dirs., sec. Minn. Protestant Found., 1975—; mem. Bd. Edn., Mahtomedi Ind. Sch. Dist. 832; bd. dirs. St. Paul Chamber Orch. Served to capt. USAF, 1964-67. Recipient Distinguished Service award St. Paul Jaycees, 1974; named One of Ten Outstanding Young Minnesotans, Minn. Jaycees, 1975. Mem. Am., Fed., Minn., Wis., Ramsey, Hennepin bar assns. Club: Mpls. Athletic. Contbr. articles to profl. jours. Home: 8432 80th St N Stillwater MN 55082 Office: 2452 IDS Center Minneapolis MN 55402

BRUNK, SAMUEL FREDERICK, med. oncologist; b. Harrisonburg, Va., Dec. 21, 1932; s. Harry Anthony and Lena Gertrude (Burkholder) B.; B.S., Eastern Mennonite Coll., 1955; M.D. (Mosby scholar) U. Va., 1959; M.S. in Pharmacology, U. Iowa, 1967; m. Mary Priscilla Bauman, June 24, 1976; children—Samuel, Jill, Geoffrey, Heather, Kirsten, Paul, Barbara. Straight med. intern U. Va., Charlottesville, 1959-60; resident in chest diseases Blue Ridge Sanatorium, Charlottesville, 1960-61; resident in internal medicine U. Iowa, Iowa City, 1962-64, fellow in clin. pharmacology (oncology), 1964-65, fellow in clin. pharmacology (oncology), 1966-67, asso. in medicine, 1966, asst. prof. internat. medicine, 1966, asso. prof., 1972-76; fellow in medicine (oncology) Johns Hopkins U., Balt., 1965-66; vis. physician bone marrow transplantation unit Fred Hutchinson Cancer Treatment Center, U. Wash., Seattle, 1975; practice medicine specializing in med. oncology, Des Moines, 1976—; attending physician Iowa Luth. Hosp., 1976—, Iowa Meth. Med. Center, 1976—, NW Community Hosp., 1976—, Mercy Hosp. Med. Center, 1976— (all Des Moines); cons. physician Des Moines Gen. Osteo. Hosp., 1976—; prin. investigator Iowa Oncology Research Assn. in assn. with N. Central Cancer Treatment Group and Eastern Coop. Oncology Group, 1978—. Bd. dirs. Iowa div. Am. Cancer Soc., 1971—, Johnson County chpt., 1968-72. Diplomate Am. Bd. Internal Medicine. Fellow A.C.P., Am. Coll. Clin. Pharmacology; mem. AMA, Iowa Med. Soc., Polk County Med. Soc., Iowa Thoracic Soc., Am. Thoracic Soc., Iowa Clin. Med. Soc., Am. Fedn. Clin. Research, AAAS, Iowa Heart Assn., Am. Assn. Cancer Edn., Am. Soc. Hematology, Am. Soc. Clin. Pharmacology and Therapeutics, Central Soc. Clin. Research. Raven Soc., Alpha Omega Alpha. Roman Catholic. Contbr. articles to med. jours. Home: 3940 Grand Ave West Des Moines IA 50265 Office: 1603 22d St Suite 205 West Des Moines IA 50265

BRUNNER, JULES TERRENCE, lawyer, assn. exec.; B.S., U. Wis.; J.D., Loyola U., Chgo. Exec. dir. Better Govt. Assn., Chgo. Office: 230 N Michigan Ave Better Govt Assn Chicago IL 60601

BRUNNER, KAY LORRAINE, banker; b. Columbus, Ohio, July 17, 1949; d. Clarence Edward and Virginia Belle Yahn; B.S., Bowling Green (Ohio) State U., 1970, M.Ed., 1976; postgrad. U. Toledo, 1977—; m. David W. Brunner, Jr., June 24, 1972. Elem. tchr. public schs., Sylvania, Ohio, 1971-75; adminstrv. masters intern, grad. asst., acad. counselor U. Toledo, 1976-78; asst. employment mgr. Ohio Citizens Trust Co., Toledo, 1978-79, personnel devel. mgr., 1979—. Chmn. bloodmobile ARC, 1979—. Mem. Internat. Assn. Personnel Women, Am. Soc. Tng. and Devel., Toledo Personnel Mgmt. Assn., Bowling Green State U. Alumni Assn., Phi Delta Kappa, Gamma Phi Beta, Pi Lambda Theta, Sigma Alpha Iota, Phi Kappa Phi. Methodist. Office: Ohio Citizens Trust Co 1 Levis Sq Toledo OH 43603

BRUNNER, KIM MARTIN, ins. co. exec.; b. Moline, Ill., Jan. 7, 1949; s. Robert Lee and Vivian Margaret (Jackson) B.; B.A., Augustana Coll., Rock Island, Ill., 1971; J.D., U. Ariz., 1975; m. Donna Jean Huber, Mar. 12, 1977; children—Jonathan Robert, Jeremy Christopher. Admitted to Ill. bar, 1976; instr. U.S. govt. and Am. history adult continuing edn. dept. Black Hawk Coll., Moline, Ill., 1974-75; staff atty. Ill. Dept. Ins., Springfield, 1976-77, asst. chief counsel, 1977-78, chief counsel, 1978-79; dir. govt. relations Nationwide Ins. Co., Columbus, Ohio, 1979-80, govt. relations officer, 1980—. Organizer, pres. Strawberry Farms/Forest Edge Civic Assn., 1981—. Mem. Am. Bar Assn., Ill. State Bar Assn., Columbus C. of C. (state legis. com.). Democrat. Lutheran. Home: 4106 Spring Flower Ct Columbus OH 43230 Office: 1 Nationwide Plaza Columbus OH 43216

BRUNO, LEONARD CARMEN, enzyme Corp. exec.; b. Melrose Park, Ill., Aug. 17, 1923; s. Carmen Emille and Josephine (Pirroni) B.; Sc.B., DePaul U., 1949; m. Olga Kazlauskus, Sept. 3, 1949; children—John Cortelyou, Regina Valeria, Leonard Carmen, Monica Lenore, Jodie Renee, Donna Diane, Mark Matthew. Med. service rep. Baxter Labs., 1950-55; with comml. devel. dept. Rohm & Hass, 1955-64; tech. dir. Sterwin div. Sterling Drug Co., 1964-68; dir. comml. devel. Ventron Corp., Beverly, Mass., 1968-72; mgr. new product devel. Applied Biochemists, Mequon, Wis., 1972-80; gen. mgr. Am. Enzyme Corp., Mequon, 1979—; cons. to tanker cleaner firms, chem. specialist mfrs., 1955—. Served with OSS, AUS, 1942-46. Recipient Chem. Splty. Mfg. award N.Y. Acad. Sci., 1949. Fellow Am. Inst. Chemists; mem. Soc. Cosmetic Chemists, Inst. Food Technologists, Chem. Splty. Mfg. Assn., Comml. Devel. Assn., AAAS. Roman Catholic. Office: Am Enzyme Corp 5300 W County Line Rd Mequon WI 53092

BRUNOW, EDWIN EDWARD, metall. cons.; b. Milw., July 28, 1912; s. John Johann and Anna Henrietta (Radmann) B.; student U. Wis., Milw., 1931-38, Marquette U., 1933-36; m. Grace Gladys Alma De Sham, June 27, 1942; children—Barry W., Nancy G. Brunow Hornsby. Plant metallurgist Sivyer Steel Co., Milw., 1938-59, metall. engr., 1959-63, tech. dir., 1963-69; metall. engr. Ervin Industries, Adrian, Mich., 1969-74, tech. dir., 1974-77; metall. cons., 1977—. Vice-chmn. Potawatomi council Boy Scouts Am.; mem. local sch. bds., 1953-58. Mem. Am. Foundrymen's Soc., Am. Soc. Metals, ASTM, Steel Founders Soc. Am. Research included cast armor plate, early warning system, minuteman silos, nuclear reactors; developed 450 and 250 micron size steel balls for xerography. Home: 1343 Feeman Ct Adrian MI 49221

BRUNS, BILLY LEE, cons. elec. engr.; b. St. Louis, Nov. 21, 1925; s. Henry Lee and Violet Jean (Williams) B.; B.A., Washington U., St. Louis, 1949, postgrad. Sch. Engring., 1959-62; m. Lillian Colleen Mobley, Sept. 6, 1947; children—Holly Rene, Kerry Alan, Barry Lee, Terrence William. Supt., engr., estimator Schneider Electric Co., St. Louis, 1950-54, Ledbetter Electric Co., 1954-57; tchr. indsl. electricity St. Louis Bd. Edn., 1957-71; pres. B.L. Bruns & Assos., cons. engrs., St. Louis, 1963-72; v.p., chief engr. Hosp. Bldg. & Equipment Co., St. Louis, 1972-76; pres., prin. B.L. Bruns & Assos. cons. engrs., St. Louis, 1976—; tchr. elec. engring. U. Mo. St. Louis extension, 1975-76. Mem. Mo. Adv. Council on Vocat. Edn., 1969-76, chmn., 1975-76; leader Explorer post Boy Scouts Am., 1950-57. Served with AUS, 1944-46: PTO, Okinawa. Decorated Purple Heart. Registered profl. engr., Mo., Ill., Wash., Fla., La., Wis., Minn., N.Y., Iowa, Pa., Miss., Ind. Mem. Nat., Mo. socs. profl. engrs., Profl. Engrs. in Pvt. Practice, Am. Soc. Heating, Refrigeration and Air Conditioning Engrs., Illuminating Engrs. Soc., Am. Mgmt. Assn. Baptist. Club: Masons. Tech. editor The National Electrical Code and Blueprint Reading, Am. Tech. Soc., 1959-65. Home: 1243 Hobson Dr Ferguson MO 63135 Office: 10 Adams Suite 111 Ferguson MO 63135

BRUNSDALE, MITZI LOUISA MALLARIAN, educator, book critic; b. Fargo, N.D., May 16, 1939; d. Gregory Starn and Phyllis (Grobe) Mallarian; B.S. with honors (Nat. Merit scholar), N.D. State U., 1959, M.S., 1961; postgrad. Ind. U., 1959-60; Ph.D. (Danforth fellow), U. N.D., 1976; m. John Edward Brunsdale, Dec. 2, 1961; children—Margaret Louisa, Jean Ellen and Maureen Lois (twins). Departmental tchr. N.D. State U., 1958-59, grad. asst., 1960-61, instr. English and French, 1961; grad. asst. Ind. U., 1959-60; book critic Houston Post, 1971—; instr. English, Mayville (N.D.) State Coll., 1975-76, asst. prof., 1976-78, asso. prof., 1978—. Sec., 20th Dist. N.D. Republican Party, 1963-70; chmn. N.D. Humanities Council, 1980, 81-82; grant rev. panelist Nat. Endowment for Humanities. Mem. MLA, Rocky Mountain MLA, D.H. Lawrence Soc. Am., AAUP, Fgn. Lang. Assn. Red River, Linguistic Circle Man. and N.D., P.E.O., Phi Kappa Phi, Sigma Alpha Iota, Kappa Alpha Theta. Republican. Contbr. articles to profl. jours. Home: Rural Route 1 Mayville ND 58257 Office: Dept English Mayville State Coll Mayville ND 58257

BRUSKE, GEORGE WILLIAM, pub. co. exec.; b. Pitts., May 22, 1927; s. Norbert and Marjorie (Glass) B.; B.A., U. Mich., 1951; m. Irene Ann Mooney, June 12, 1946; children—Regina Crosby, George Robert. With Standard Oil Co. Ind., various locations, 1951-67, mktg. dir. Amoco Australia, Sydney, 1961-66; v.p. mktg. Southwest Grease & Oil Co., Inc., Wichita, Kans., 1967-73; dir. sales promotion Farmland Industries, Inc., Kansas City, Mo., 1973-81; regional mgr. High Plains Jour., Dodge City, Kans., 1981—. Mem. advt. com. Universal Coop. Vice pres. mktg. March of Dimes, Wichita, 1971-72; capt. Wesley Hosp. Fund Drive, Wichita, 1970; active United Fund, Wichita, 1971-72. Bd. dirs. New Mark Community Christian Concern. Served with USAAF, 1945-46. Mem. Am. Petroleum Inst., Soc. Automotive Engrs., Am. Soc. Lubrication Engrs., Advt. and Sales Execs. Club, Nat. Agri-Mktg. Assn. (bd. dirs.), Theta Delta Chi, Sigma Delta Chi. Home: 6109 NW Webb Circle Kansas City MO 64151 Office: Box 760 Dodge City KS 67801

BRUXVOORT, KEITH EUGENE, mfg. co. exec. b. Ft. Knox, Ky., June 14, 1953; s. Stanley Harold and Reuvena Marie (Dieleman) B.; B.A. in Bus. Adminstrn. (Coll. scholar), Calvin Coll., 1975; m. Beverly A. Scheeringa, Aug. 8, 1975. Tax intern Seidman & Seidman, Grand Rapids, Mich., 1975; daily ops. mgr. Bills Produce, Inc., Highland, Ind., 1975-76; credit mgr. films packaging Union Carbide Corp., Chgo., 1976-77; cost acct./asst. controller Land O' Frost, Inc., Lansing, Ill., 1977-79, controller Ill. plant, 1979-81, corp. controller, 1981—; pvt. practice acctg., Highland. Comptroller First Christian Ref. Ch., Highland, 1977—, treas., 1978—. C.P.A., Ind., Ill. Mem. Nat. Assn. Accts., Am. Inst. C.P.A.'s, Ind. C.P.A. Soc., Illiana Men's Christian Athletic Assn. (treas. 1978—). Office: 16850 Chicago Ave Lansing IL 60438

BRYAN, A(LONZO) J(AY), service club ofcl.; b. Washington, N.J., Sept. 17, 1917; s. Alonzo J. and Anna Belle (Babcock) B.; student pub. schs.; m. Elizabeth Elfreida Koehler, June 25, 1941 (div. 1961); children—Donna Elizabeth, Alonzo Jay, Nadine; m. 2d, Janet Dorothy Onstad, Mar. 15, 1962; children—Brenda Joyce, Marlowe Francis, Marilyn Janet. Engaged as retail florist, Washington, N.J., 1941-64; now dir. membership devel. Kiwanis Internat., Chgo. Fund drive chmn. ARC, 1952; bd. dirs. Washington YMCA, 1945-55, N.J. Taxpayers Assn., 1947-52; mem. Washington Bd. Edn., 1948-55. Mem. Washington Grange, Sons and Daus. of Liberty, Soc. Am. Florists, Nat. Fedn. Ind. Businessmen, Florists Telegraph Delivery Assn., C. of C. Presbyterian (elder). Clubs: Masons, Tall Cedars of Lebanon, Jr. Order United Am. Mechanics, Kiwanis (pres. Washington (N.J.) 1952, lt. gov. internat. 1953-54, gov. N.J. dist. 1955, sec. N.J. dist. 1957-64, sec. S.E. area Chgo. 1965-74; editor The Jersey Kiwanian 1958-64); Breakfast (pres. 1981-82) (Chgo.). Home: River Plaza Apt 2512 405 N Wabash Ave Chicago IL 60611 Office: Kiwanis Internat 101 E Erie St Chicago IL 60611

BRYAN, ARTHUR ELDRIDGE, JR., lawyer; b. Webster City, Iowa, July 28, 1924; s. Arthur Eldridge and Grace Lillian (Glassburner) B.; B.A., State U. Iowa, 1949, J.D., 1951; m. Elizabeth Ann Stubbings, Oct. 18, 1958; children—Elizabeth Grace, Arthur Eldridge III, John Milner, Daniel Franklin. With U.P. R.R. Co., Omaha, 1942-54; partner, mem. exec. com. McDermott, Will & Emery, Chgo., 1954—; dir. Gits Bros. Mfg., Chgo., 1967-68; dir., v.p., sec. Yuma Mesa Devel. Co., Yuma, Ariz., 1967-79; chmn. bd. dirs., chief exec. officer Lake Arrowhead Devel. Co. (Calif.), 1971-80. Lectr. taxation U. Chgo., Marquette U., No. Ill. U. Mem. com. on legis. action New Trier (Ill.) High Sch., 1974-78; active Boy Scouts Am., Glencoe, Ill., 1968-74; mem. adv. bd. United Settlement Appeal, Chgo., 1962. Bd. dirs., treas., pres. exec. com. Erie Neighborhood House, Chgo., 1958—; trustee N. Central Coll., Naperville, Ill., 1974-79; sec., chmn. bd. trustees, sec. prudential bd. Glencoe Union Ch., 1969-79. Served with inf. AUS, 1942-46; ETO, PTO. Decorated Bronze Star, Combat Inf. badge. Mem. Am. (chmn., spl. adviser sect. taxation com. on comml. banks and financials 1966-74), Ill., Ia., Chgo. bar assns., Ill. C. of C. (chmn. fed. tech. tax com.), Chgo. Assn. Commerce and Industry (fed. appropriations and expenditures com. 1968—). Clubs: Chgo., Mid-Day, Monroe, Executive (Chgo.); Skokie Country. Contbr. articles to profl. jours. Home: 565 Washington St Glencoe IL 60022 Office: 111 W Monroe St Chicago IL 60603

BRYAN, ASHEL GANO, banker; b. Cleveland Heights, Ohio, July 15, 1921; s. Ezra K. and Katherine (Clarke) B.; B.A., Bowling Green State U., 1946; grad. Grad. Sch. Banking, Rutgers U., 1961; D.Econs. (hon.), Hanyang U., Seoul (Korea), 1976; m. Dorothy Jean Uber, Sept. 17, 1943; children—Becky, David, Kathy. Office mgr. Rural Directories, Inc., 1947-51; with Penn Mut. Life Ins., 1951-52; office mgr. Ralph Thayer Chevrolet, 1952; with Mid-Am. Nat. Bank and Trust Co., Toledo, 1952—, chmn., chief exec. officer, 1979—. Trustee Med. Coll. Ohio, 1976—, chmn. bd., 1981—; trustee Bowling Green State U., 1968-76; co-chmn. Bowling Green Republican Com., 1976-77; treas. City of Bowling Green Rep. Com., 1969-73. Served with USAAC, 1939-43. Bryan Recital Hall at Bowling Green State U. named in his honor, 1979. Mem. Ohio Bankers Assn., Am. Bankers Assn., Bank Adminstrn. Inst., Am. Inst. Banking, Bowling Green C. of C. (past pres., trustee), Omicron Delta Kappa (hon.). Clubs: Exchange (past pres.). Mem. editorial bd. Bank Adminstrn. Inst. Mag., 1979—. Office: 222 S Main St Bowling Green OH 43402

BRYAN, HENRY C(LARK), JR., lawyer; b. St. Louis, Dec. 8, 1930; s. Henry Clark and Faith (Young) B.; A.B., Washington U., St. Louis, 1952, LL.B., 1956; m. Sarah Ann McCarthy, July 28, 1956; children—Mark Pendleton, Thomas Clark, Sarah Christy. Admitted to Mo. bar, 1956; law clk. to fed. judge, 1956; asso. firm McDonald & Wright, St. Louis, 1956-60; partner firm McDonald, Bernard, Wright & Timm, St. Louis, 1961-64, McDonald, Wright & Bryan, 1964-81, Wright, Bryan & Walsh, 1981—; v.p., dir. Harbor Point Boat & Dock Co., St. Charles, Mo., 1966-80, Merrell Ins. Agy., 1966-80. Served to 1st lt. AUS, 1952-54. Mem. Am., Mo., St. Louis (past chmn. probate and trust sect., marriage and divorce law com.) bar assns., Kappa Sigma, Phi Delta Phi. Republican. Episcopalian. Elk. Home: 41 Ladue Terr Ladue MO 63124 Office: 11 S Meramec St Saint Louis MO 63105

BRYAN, JOHN HENRY, JR., food co. exec.; b. West Point, Miss., 1936; B.A. in Econs. and Bus. Adminstrn., Southwestern at Memphis, 1958; M.B.A., Miss. State U., 1960. With Consol. Foods Corp., Chgo., 1960—, exec. v.p. ops., 1974-75, pres., chief exec. officer, 1975-76, chmn. bd., chief exec. officer, 1976—, also dir. Office: Consolidated Foods Corp 135 S LaSalle St Chicago IL 60043*

BRYAN, LESLIE A(ULLS), transp. economist; b. Bath, N.Y., Feb. 23, 1900; s. D(aniel) Beach and Anna (Aulls) B.; B.S., Syracuse U., 1923, M.S., 1924, J.D., 1939; Ph.D., Am. U., Washington 1930; Sc.D. (hon.), Southwestern Coll., 1972; m. Gertrude Catherine Gelder, Aug. 22, 1931; children—Leslie A., George G. Prof. bus. adminstrn. Southwestern Coll., Winfield, Kans., 1924-25; asst. coach track Syracuse U., 1925-42, dir. athletics, 1934-37, also instr., 1925-28, asst. prof. transp. and bus. law, 1928-31, asso. prof., 1931-39, prof., 1939-45, Franklin prof. transp., 1945-46; pres. Seneca Flying Sch., Syracuse, N.Y., 1943-46; dir. Inst. Aviation and prof. mgmt. U. Ill., 1946-68, emeritus, 1968—; staff lectr. Air U., 1956-59. Dir. U. Fed. Savs. & Loan Assn., 1960-71, mem. adv. bd., 1971—. Cons. FAA, 1959-61; mem. Pres. Kennedy's Task Force on Nat. Aviation Goals, 1961; mem. Ill. Aerospace Edn. Com., 1961-72, chmn., 1963-64; adv. bd. ATC, 1964, 67-69, cons., 1965-69; acting dir. athletics U. Ill., 1965-66; faculty rep. Intercollegiate Conf. (Big Ten), 1959-68. Pres., Arrowhead council Boy Scouts Am., 1954-60, mem. regional exec. com., 1959-71, nat. council, 1960-71; past mem. aviation adv. bd. Norwich U. Served as lt., inf. U.S. Army, 1917-19; ret. col. USAFR. col. CAP. Chmn. Pres. Eisenhower's Aviation Planning Group, 1957-58; adv. com. Dulles Internat. Airport, 1958-62; dir. aviation N.Y. State 1945; mem. Ill. Bd. Aero. Advisors, 1949-68; transp. cons. Nat. Resources Planning Bd., 1942-44. Pres. Eastern Intercollegiate Boxing Assn., 1936-38; N.Y. State Aviation Council, 1944-46; mem. adv. bd. Ill. State Archives, 1980—. Recipient Brewer Trophy award, 1953; Disting. Service medal CAP, 1954; Sigma Delta Chi award, 1954; Arents Medal, 1955; Air Power award, 1956; Silver Beaver, Boy Scouts Am., 1957, Silver Antelope award, 1959; Tissandier diploma Fedn. Aeronautique International, 1958; Continental Air Command cert. of recognition, 1960; ARC award, 1946; award of merit Air Tng. Command, 1965; Elder Statesman of Aviation award, 1966; Disting. Public Service award FAA, 1965; Patriots medal SAR, 1968, Disting. Alumni award Am. U., 1969; Letterman of Distinction, Syracuse U., 1969; citation Air Force Assn., 1976; elected to Educator's Hall of Fame, Nat. Air and Space Mus., 1979. Fellow U. Aviation Assn. (pres. 1948-49); mem. Nat. Aero. Assn. (v.p. 1953-56, 60, 61, 65, 66, bd. dirs. 1950-52, 57-59, 62-64), Nat. Aerospace Edn. Council (pres. 1952-53, 64-65, dir. 1959-71), Am. Soc. Traffic and Transp. (mem. bd. examiners 1948-61), Am. Assn. Airport Execs. (pres. 1955-56, President's award 1959), Aerospace Writers Assn., Nat. Air Council, AIAA, Newcomen Soc. N.Am., Geneal. Soc. Ill. (pres. 1972-73, Disting. Service award 1974), Nat. Huguenot Soc. (pres. Ill. 1971-73, pres. gen. 1977-79, hon. pres. gen. 1979—, Nat. Disting. Service award 1976), S.A.R. (pres. Ill. 1974-76, genealogist gen. 1973-75, trustee 1975-76, 77—, v.p. gen. 1976-77, Minute Man award 1976, Gold Good Citizen award 1976), Am. U. Alumni Assn. (chmn. bd. govs. 1970), Soc. of Cincinnati, Soc. War of 1812 (asst. adjutant gen. 1975—), Zeta Psi, Phi Delta Phi, Phi Kappa Phi, Phi Kappa Alpha, Alpha Kappa Psi, Alpha Phi Omega, Kappa Phi Kappa, Alpha Delta Sigma, Delta Nu Alpha, Pi Gamma Mu, Alpha Eta Rho, Sigma Alpha Tau, Tau Omega, Beta Gamma Sigma, Scabbard and Blade, Arnold Air Soc., Pershing Rifles. Clubs: University (Urbana); Rotary, Dial; Army and Navy (Washington); Champaign Country. Author: Aerial Transportation, 1925; Industrial Traffic Management, 1929; Principles of Water Transportation, 1939; Air Transportation (with G.L. Wilson), 1949; Aviation Study Manual (with others), 1949; Traffic Management in Industry, 1953; (with others) Fundamentals of Aviation and Space Technology, 1959, rev. edit. 1968; The Aulls Genealogy, 1974; Thomas Bryan Descendants, 1979; Immigrant Ancestors, 1981; also monographs, articles. Contbr. Compton's Ency., World Book Ency., Ency. of Sci. and Tech., Am. Educator Ency., Universal Standard Ency., Our Wonderful World Ency. Adviser, cons. various publs. Address: 34 Fields E Champaign IL 61820

BRYAN, MONK, bishop; b. Blomming Grove, Tex., July 25, 1914; s. Gid. J. and Era (Monk) B.; B.A., Baylor U., 1935; M.Th., So. Meth. U., 1938; D.D., Central Meth. Coll., Fayette, Mo., 1958; L.H.D., Nebr. Wesleyan U., 1978; m. Corneille Downer, July 22, 1941; children—Lucy (Mrs. Samuel S. Barlow, Jr.), James J., Robert M. Ordained to ministry United Meth. Ch., 1939; consecrated bishop, 1976; minister Boyce Circuit, Waxahachie Dist., Central Tex. Conf., 1939-40, St. Lukes Meth. Ch., St. Louis, 1940-47, Centenary Meth. Ch., Bonne Terre, Mo., 1947-49, Meth. Ch., Maryville, Mo., 1949-57, Mo. United Meth. Ch., Columbia, 1957-76; bishop S.Central Jurisdictional Conf., Lincoln, Nebr., 1976—; pres. Coll. of Bishops, S. Central Jurisdiction, 1980-81; mem. World Meth. Council, 1953—, mem. exec. com., participant Confs., Lake Junaluska, N.C., 1956, Oslo, Norway, 1961, London, 1966, Denver, 1971, Dublin, Ireland, 1976, Honolulu, 1981, exchange minister in Eng., 1953; pres. Mo. Conf. Bd. Edn., 1956-64, Mo. Council Chs., 1966-68; chmn. Mo. East Conf. Bd. Christian Social Concerns, 1968-72; mem. Meth. Gen. Bd. Christian Social Concerns, 1964-72; vice chmn. finance com., mem. divs. ecumenical and inter-religious concerns and health and welfare Meth. Gen. Bd. Global Ministries, 1972-76. Bd. dirs. Wesley Found., Columbia, 1957-76, Columbia United Fund, 1964-70; trustee So. Meth. U., 1952-68, 76—, St. Paul Sch. Theology, Kansas City, 1968-72, 76—, Mo. Sch. Religion, Columbia, 1957-76, Philander Smith Coll., Little Rock, 1976—, Lydia Patterson Inst., El Paso, 1976—, pres. bd., 1980—, Mt. Sequoyah Assembly, Fayetteville, Ark., 1976—, Nebr. Wesleyan U., 1976—, Omaha Meth. Hosp., 1976—, Bryan Meml. Hosp., 1976—, Western Nebr. Gen. Hosp., 1976—; mem. adv. council Gt. Rivers council Boy Scouts Am., 1960-76; mem. Gen. Bd. Higher Edn. and Ministry, 1976-80, Gen. Council on Ministries, 1980—, Bicentennial Com. of Am. Methodism, 1980—. Clubs: Masons (K.T., 33 deg.), Rotary. Recipient Silver Beaver award Boy Scouts Am., 1972. Home: 3901 Prescott Ave Lincoln NE 68506 Office: 2641 N 49th St Lincoln NE 68504

BRYAN, WILLIAM ALONZO, univ. ofcl.; b. Valdosta, Ga., July 16, 1938; s. William E. and Lottie Mae (Dees) B.; B.S., Fla. State U., 1960; M.S., Ind. U., 1961; Ed.D., U. Wyo., 1970; m. Marian Eleanor Cooper, Aug. 4, 1963; children—Paige Ellen, Erin Dees, William Ross. Asst. dean men U. Wyo., Laramie, 1968-69, hall dir., 1967-68, dir. student services Coll. Nursing, 1969-71; asso. dean admissions, student personnel, dir. student services Med. Center, U. Ky., Lexington, 1971-73; asso. dean students U. Tex., Austin, 1973-76; dean student devel. U. N.D., Grand Forks, 1976-78, v.p. for student affairs, 1978—. Mem. N.D. Regional Human Services Council, 1981—; bd. dirs. Amigos de las Americas, 1981, United Hosp. Corp., YMCA, 1979-80, Center for Human Devel., Grand Forks, 1980—. Recipient Recognition award Delta Upsilon, 1980; Native Am. Staff Appreciation award, 1981. Mem. Am. Coll. Personnel Assn. (v.p. state divs.), Am. Personnel and Guidance Assn., Nat. Assn. student Personnel Adminstrs., Am. Assn. Higher Edn., Nat. Assn. State Univs. and Land Grant Colls. (v.p. council-student affairs), Am. Assn. U. Adminstrs. (dir. 1981—), N.D. Personnel Deans, N.D. Coll. Personnel Assn., Phi Delta Kappa. Presbyn. Contbr. articles, chpts. to profl. publs. Home: 3615 10th Ave N Grand Forks ND 58201 Office: Office Vice Pres for Student Affairs Box 8132 Grand Forks ND 58202

BRYANT, CAROL, credit exec.; b. Euclid, Ohio, Apr. 27, 1953; d. Albert and Rose F. (Hrovat) Jazbinski; student Baldwin-Wallace Coll., 1977—; m. Richard Alan Bryant, Sept. 28, 1974. Export Order processor TRW Internat. S.A., Cleve., 1971-79; export credit corr. TRW Internat. Trade, Cleve., 1979—. Mem. Nat. Assn. Credit Mgmt. (ednl. com. chmn. 1980-82), Motor and Equipment Mfrs. Assn., Credit Mgrs. Export Group, Am. Bus. Women's Assn. Home: 14315 Shawnee Trail Middleburg Heights OH 44130 Office: 8001 E Pleasant Valley Rd Cleveland OH 44131

BRYANT, DONALD LOYD, JR., ins. exec.; b. Mt. Vernon, Ill., June 30, 1942; s. Donald Loyd and A. Eileen (Galloway) B.; B.A., Denison U., 1964; J.D., Washington U., 1967; M.S.F.S., Am. Coll., 1978; m. Barbara Murphy, July 9, 1981; 1 son, Derek Lawrence. Admitted to Mo. bar, 1967; agt. Equitable Life Assurance Soc. U.S., St. Louis, 1968—; pres. Donald L. Bryant & Assos., 1969-74, Bryant Planning Group, Inc., St. Louis, 1974—. Bd. dirs. St. Louis Area council Boy Scouts Am., 1974—; bd. dirs. United Way, St. Louis. Served with U.S. Navy, 1967. Mem. Am. Bar Assn., Mo. Bar Assn., Assn. Advanced Life Underwriting (dir. 1979-82, asso. v.p. 1979-82), St. Louis Estate

Planning Council, Million Dollar Round Table, Eight Million Dollar Forum. Republican. Presbyterian. Clubs: Bellerive Country, St. Louis, Mo. Athletic. Home: 3 Picardy Ln Saint Louis MO 63124 Office: Suite 1770 100 N Broadway Saint Louis MO 63102

BRYANT, JERRY DOYLE, lawyer; b. Whitley City, Ky., Mar. 12, 1947; s. Fred and Myrtle Roberta (Vanover) B.; B.S., Cumberland Coll., 1969; J.D., Ind. U., 1973; m. Glenna J. Mattingly, Aug. 31, 1968; children—Laura, Jennifer, Jeremy. Mgr., Sears Roebuck & Co., Cin., 1969-70; indsl. relations rep. Westinghouse Co., Bloomington, Ind., 1970-71; admitted to Ohio bar, 1974; individual practice law, Wilmington, Ohio, 1974—; vis. asst. prof. Wilmington Coll., 1975-79; spl. counsel Ohio Atty. Gen., 1975-79. Chmn. Clinton County Bd. Elections, 1976-80; mem. exec. com. Democratic party, Wilmington, 1975-79. Mem. Am. Bar Assn., Am. Trial Lawyers Assn., Ohio Bar Assn., Clinton County Bar Assn., Wilmington C. of C. Democrat. Methodist. Clubs: Eagles, Rotary, Masons, Shriners. Home: 415 Indian Ripple Rd Wilmington OH 45177 Office: 121 W Main St PO Box 470 Wilmington OH 45177

BRYANT, JOE PATRICK, data processing exec.; b. Mansfield, Ohio, Dec. 7, 1933; s. Harry Lee and Ada Viola (Carver) B.; B.S. in B.A., So. Ill. U., 1956; m. Dorothy Ann Johnson Moss, Nov. 20, 1976; children by previous marriage—Kathy, Lori, Elaine; stepchildren—Karen, Joe. Internal cons. and systems and programming mgr. State of Ill., Springfield, 1959-64; programmer/analyst-project leader Monsanto Co., St. Louis, 1964-66; cons. McDonnell Douglas Automation Co., St. Louis, 1966-69; staff specialist systems and procedures McDonnell Douglas Corp., St. Louis, 1969-74; dir. mgmt. info. systems Intertherm Inc., St. Louis, 1974-77; sr. analyst-programmer Srevdrup & Parcel & Assos., Inc., St. Louis, 1977-78; mgr. Systems and programming Store Instrument, St. Louis, 1979-80; mgr. cardholder acctg. Credit Systems Inc., St. Louis, 1979-80; procedures analyst Angelica Corp., St. Louis, 1980—; cons. in data processing. Treas., St. Louis Honeywell Users Group, 1977. Mem. Data Processing Mgmt. Assn. (internal public relations dir. 1959), Systems and Procedures Assn., Assn. System Mgmt. Republican. Baptist. Home: 11555 Criterion Spanish Lake MO 63138 Office: 700 Rosedale Ave Saint Louis MO 63112

BRYANT, MARIE ALENE BOLLINGER, safety edn. broadcast dir.; b. Moran, Kans., Dec. 9, 1900; d. David Asbury and Amy Jeanette (Patterson) Bollinger; B.S., Pittsburg State Tchrs. Coll., 1922; M.A. in English and Speech, Columbia U., 1927; m. Homer Lafayette Bryant, Sept. 21, 1926. Tchr. rural sch., Labette County, 1918; tchr. Parsons High Sch., Mound Valley High Sch., Coffeyville (Kans.) High Sch., 1920-26; speech instr. Hunter Coll. and Jamaica Tchrs. Coll., N.Y.C., 1927-41; office asst. to ophthalmologist, Coffeyville, 1947-49; founder weekly radio safety broadcasts Sta. KGGF, Coffeyville, 1949, producer, dir., dir. safety, 1949—, producer and dir. over 2500 safety broadcasts; organizer, dir. Safety Queen Projects, 1958-68, vehicle safety check, teen weeks, state and nat. workshops; speaker safety confs. Organizer, County Heart Fund, 1956; dir. Circle of Safety grand award for youth-support programs, 1966. Shell Oil grantee, 1959; recipient gold medallion Am. Heart Assn., 1958; Carol Lane plaque, 1959; Allstate Safety Crusade award, 1960; Olin Hwy. Safety award for outstanding safety work in Kans., 1971; Paul Harris fellow award Rotary Internat., 1981; various other state and nat. safety awards. Mem. Nat. Safety Council (citation 1958, bond award 1961), Coffeyville Safety Council (pres. 1951-64, pres. emeritus 1964—), Kans. Citizens Safety Council, Kans. Women for Hwy. Safety, AAUW, Kans. Fedn. Press Women (state and area awards writing contests), Nat. Fedn. Press Women (awards writings contests), Wis. Assn. Women Hwy. Safety Leaders. Republican. Presbyterian. Clubs: Assn. Ret. Tchrs. N.Y.C., Gen. Fedn. Women's Clubs, Nat. Fedn. Bus. and Profl. Women's Clubs (local pres. 1955-56, Kans. Woman of Yr. award 1966), Coffeyville Bus. and Profl. Women's (past pres.), Hosp. Aux. (life), PTA (life). Author first course of study for radio speech, N.Y.C. High Schs., 1937; composer various safety broadcast slogans, prayers, poems. Home: 803 W 9th Coffeyville KS 67337 Office: 306 W 8th Coffeyville KS 67337

BRYANT, RHYS, chem. co. exec.; b. Swansea, Wales, Nov. 28, 1936; s. Sydney Rees and Margaret (Jones) B.; B.Sc. summa cum laude, U. Wales, 1957, Ph.D., 1960; m. Jayne Luise Morgan, Sept. 5, 1960; children—Louise Mary, Timothy Richard Morgan, Daniel Rees. Came to U.S., 1960, naturalized, 1971. Research fellow Yale U., 1960-61; fellow Mellon Inst., Pitts., 1961; research chemist Unilever Research Labs., Bedford, Eng., 1962-63; asst. lectr. U. Manchester (Eng.), 1963-65; group leader Mead Johnson & Co., Evansville, Ind., 1965-67, sect. leader, 1967-68, dir. pharm. quality control, 1968-76; v.p. quality control Plough div. Schering-Plough Corp., Memphis, 1976-78; group dir. quality assurance Searle Pharm.-Consumer Products Group, G.D. Searle & Co., Skokie, Ill., 1978—, including spl. assignments as v.p. quality assurance U.S. Region, 1979-81. Fulbright scholar, 1960-61. Fellow Chem. Soc. (London); mem. Royal Inst. Chemistry (London), Soc. Genealogists (London), Am. Chem. Soc., Research Soc. Am. Methodist. Contbr. articles to profl. jours. Office: PO Box 5110 Chicago IL 60680

BRYANT, TERRY LYNN, counselor; b. Parsons, Kans., Mar. 26, 1952; d. Earl Morris and Neva L. (Sissel) B.; A.A., Labette Com. Jr. Coll., 1972; B.S., Kans. State Coll., 1974, M.S., 1975; Ed.S., Pittsburg (Kans.) State U., 1981; m. Debra Kay Brown, June 14, 1980. Counselor, Kans. State Dept. Human Resources, Pittsburg, 1975—; manpower generalist State of Kans., 1976-77. Mem. Am. Personnel and Guidance Assn., Kans. Assn. Battered Women, Assn. Specialists in Group Work, Internat. Assn. Personnel in Employment Security, S.E. Kans. Assn. Personnel in Employment Security, Phi Theta Kappa. Baptist. Home: PO Box 457 Arma KS 66712 Office: 1st and Pine Sts Pittsburg KS 66762

BRYANT, VIVIAN CHILLIS, educator; b. Detroit, June 25, 1938; d. Ollie and Elizabeth Chillis; B.A., Mich. State U., 1959; M.Ed., Wayne State U., 1965; Ed.S., U. Mich., 1975; m. William Russell Bryant, July 16, 1971; 1 dau., Darmetta Annese. Tchr. Spanish, Inkster (Mich.) High Sch., 1959-62; tchr. English, asst. prin. Carver Jr. High Sch., Los Angeles, 1962-67; guidance counselor, tchr. speech, music Christ the King High Sch., Okinawa, 1967-69; tchr. English, River Rouge (Mich.) High Sch., 1969—, chmn. dept. English, fgn. langs. and art, 1974—. Treas., chmn. Southfield Parent Youth Guidance Commn., 1978—; mem. Southfield Citizens Adv. Bd. on Sex Edn., 1979—; mem. Human Relations Council, 1981. Recipient VFW award, 1976. Mem. Nat. Assn. Women Deans, Adminstrs. and Counselors, Assn. Supervision and Curriculum Devel., Nat. Council Tchrs. English. African Methodist Episcopalian. Clubs: Oak Grove Ensemble (pres.), Ravine's Women's of Southfield. Home: 23100 Staunton Dr Southfield MI 48034 Office: 1411 Coolidge Hwy River Rouge MI 48218

BRYCE, GARY LYNN, educator; b. Detroit, Mar. 28, 1941; s. David and Ingrid (Saastomian) B.; B.S., U. Mich., 1963, M.A., 1975, labor relations certificate, 1975; children—Amy Lynn, David Vincent. Faculty, U. Pitts., 1963-64; tchr. St. Williams Sch., Walled Lake, Mich., 1964-65, Clawson (Mich.) pub. schs., 1965-67; tchr., coach Royal Oak (Mich.) pub. schs., 1967—; clinic organizer Mich. Softball Coaches, 1979. U. Pitts. fellow, 1963-64; named Mich. High Sch. Softball Coach of the Yr., 1979. Mem. Mich. High Sch. Softball Assn. (dir. 1981—), Nat. High Sch. Coaches Assn., Mich. High Sch. Coaches Assn., Mich. Softball Assn., NEA, Mich. Edn. Assn., Am. Security Council, Am. Def. Preparedness Assn. Democrat. Unitarian. Address: 709 N Washington St Royal Oak MI 48067

BRYNICZKA, GREGORY CHARLES, podiatrist; b. Chgo., Apr. 23, 1948; s. William Charles and Beatrice Ann (Carynski) B.; student Western Ill. U., 1966-70; D.P.M., Ill. Coll. Podiatric Medicine, 1974; m. Sherry Steiger, Mar. 12, 1977; children—Adam, Nina. Resident in surgery Northlake (Ill.) Community Hosp. and Children's Meml. Hosp., Chgo. and Hines (Ill.) VA Hosp., 1974-75; practice podiatric medicine with Joseph Blair, Niles and Wheaton, Ill., 1976—; cons. Health Maintenance Orgn.; asso. prof. sports medicine Ill. Coll. Podiatric Medicine. Mem. Ill. Podiatry Soc., Am. Podiatry Soc., Acad. Podiatric Sports Medicine (asso.), Ill. Coll. Podiatric Medicine Alumni Assn., Niles C. of C. Office: 7954 Oakton St Niles IL 60648 also 108 N West St Wheaton IL 60187 also 403 W Irving Park Rd Streamwood IL

BRZECZEK, RICHARD JOSEPH, police chief; b. Chgo., Oct. 8, 1942; B.S., Loyola U., Chgo., 1965; M.P.A., Ill. Inst. Tech., 1968; J.D., John Marshall Law Sch., Chgo., 1972. Admitted to Ill. bar, 1972; practice in Chgo., 1972-80; exec. asst. to supt. Chgo. Police Dept., 1973-80, police chief, 1980—; instr. John Marshall Law Sch., 1973-74. Mem. Am. Bar Assn. (Silver Key award 1971), Ill. Bar Assn., Chgo. Bar Assn. (chmn. police-lawyer relations com. 1975-80), Internat. Assn. Chiefs Police, Advocates Soc. Chgo., Chgo. Assn. Commerce and Industry, Phi Alpha Delta. Office: 1121 S State St Room 400 Chicago IL 60605

BRZEZINSKI, I(GNATIUS) FRANK, dentist; b. Chgo., Nov. 15, 1919; s. Frank Anthony and Mary (Orlowski) B.; D.D.S., Loyola U. (Chgo.), 1944; m. Therese Victoria Istok, Nov. 23, 1950; children—Paul Frank, Daniel Steven, Carol Ann. Practice gen. dentistry, Chgo., 1947—; asso. clin. prof. operative dentistry Sch. Dentistry Loyola U., 1970—. Served to lt. Dental Corps, USNR, 1944-46. Fellow Am. Coll. Dentists, Acad. Gen. Dentistry, Internat. Coll. Dentists; mem. Chgo. Dental Soc. (dir., past pres. N.W. br.), Dental Arts Club Chgo., Am. Prosthodontic Soc., Pierre Fauchard Acad., Omicron Kappa Upsilon. Club: Polish Am. Comml. Home: 5440 N Panama St Chicago IL 60656 Office: 5301 W Fullerton St Chicago IL 60639

BUA, NICHOLAS JOHN, fed. judge; b. Chgo., Feb. 9, 1925; s. Frank and Lena (Marino) B.; J.D., DePaul U., 1953; m. Camile F. Scordato, Nov. 20, 1943; 1 dau., Lisa Annette. Admitted to Ill. bar, 1953; trial atty., Chgo., 1953-63; judge Village Ct., Melrose Park, Ill., 1963-64; asso. judge Circuit Ct. Cook County, Chgo., 1964-71, circuit judge, 1971-76; justice Ill. Appellate Ct.-1st Dist., from 1976; now U.S. dist. judge; northern dist. ILLINOIS vice chmn. exec. com. Jud. Conf. Ill., also mem. supreme ct. rules com., 1970—; lectr. DePaul U.; mem. faculty Def. Tactics Seminar, Ill. Def. Counsel Seminar, 1971. Trustee Goltlieb Meml. Hosp., Schwab Rehab. Hosp. Fellow Nat. Coll. State Trial Judges, U. Nev., 1966. Served with Armed Forces, World War II. Contbr. articles to legal publs. Home: 520 Rose Dr Melrose Park IL 60160 Office: Everett McKinley Dirksen Bldg 219 S Dearborn St Chicago IL 60602

BUBLITZ, JEROME ERNEST, agrl. coop. exec.; b. Montevideo, Minn., Dec. 19, 1948; s. Elmer Ernest and Norma Charlotte (Olson) B.; B.S., U. Chgo., 1970; student (NSF grantee), U. Iowa, 1966. Rebuyer, Western Auto Supply Co., Kansas City, Mo., 1970-71; asst. inventory control mgr. Western Auto Supply Co., Kansas City, Mo., 1971-72, asst. corp. inventory control mgr., 1972-73, asst. to corp. v.p. inventory control, 1973-75; dist. mgr. MFA Livestock Assn., Inc., Marshall, Mo., 1975-78, asst. gen. mgr., 1978—; instr. Nat. Inst. for Coop. Edn., U. Mo., 1979—. Mem. Kansas City-Jackson County Drug Abuse Task Force, 1974-75; mem. Kansas City Mayor's Corps of Progress, 1972-75; mem. Saline County Republican Com., 1976—. Mem. Saline County Hist. Soc. (v.p. 1976-80), Marshall C. of C. (mem. agribus. com.), Am. Swedish Inst., Am. Soc. Tng. and Devel., Am. Inst. Cooperation, Indsl. Mgmt. Soc., Am. Inst. Indsl. Engrs., Psi Upsilon. Republican. Lutheran. Clubs: The Kansas City Club, Vasa Order, Sons of Norway, Germania, Rotary, Optimists. Home: 865 South Salt Pond Marshall MO 65340 Office: PO Box 278 West Hwy 20 Marshall MO 65340

BUCHANAN, BERNARD JAMES, physician; b. Elmhurst, Ill., Oct. 11, 1947; s. Bernard Clifford and Caroline Buchanan; B.A. magna cum laude, Elmhurst Coll., 1970; Ph.D. in Physiology, Loyola U., Chgo., 1975, M.D. cum laude, 1977. Research asso. dept. physiology Loyola U., Chgo., 1974-77; resident in medicine Northwestern U., Chgo., 1977-79; fellow in endocrinology VA Med. Service, Hines, Ill., 1980-82. NSF trainee, 1971-74. Mem. A.C.P., Am. Physiol. Soc., Am. Fedn. Clin. Research, Am. Diabetes Assn., AMA, Reticuloendothelial Soc., Am. Soc. Internal Medicine, Alpha Omega Alpha. Cons. editor Procs. for Soc. Exptl. Biology and Medicine, 1980—. Contbr. articles to profl. jours. Home: 134 N Bloomingdale Rd Bloomingdale IL 60108 Office: Dept Medicine Edward Hines Jr Hosp Hines IL 60141

BUCHANAN, EDWARD ARMSTRONG, clergyman; b. Newark, Aug. 28, 1937; s. Osborne Blunden and Edna Dorothy (Weber) B.; A.B. (Trustees scholar), Rutgers U., 1959; M.R.E., N.Y. Theol. Sem., 1962; Ed.D. (Garrett teaching fellow), So. Bapt. Theol. Sem., 1970; M.L.E., Harvard U., 1981; m. Gladys Jean Heichel, Aug. 28, 1965; children—Roger, Becky. Ordained to ministry Baptist Ch., 1967; tchr. 7th grade lang. arts, Middlesex, N.J., 1963-66; minister of edn. East Bapt. Ch., Louisville, 1966-69; instr. psychology Jefferson Community Coll., Louisville, 1968-69; asso. prof. social sci. and edn. Grand Rapids (Mich.) Bapt. Coll., 1969-74; dir. research and devel. Radio Bible Class, Grand Rapids, 1974-76; acad. dean Lancaster (Pa.) Bible Coll., 1976-78; prof. Christian edn., dir. continuing edn. Bethel Theol. Sem., St. Paul, 1978—. Assn. Theol. Schs. and Lilly Endowment curriculum grantee, 1979-80; alumni grantee Bethel Sem., 1979-80. Mem. Adult Edn. Assn., Assn. Ednl. Communications and Tech., Assn. Supervision and Curriculum Devel., Nat. Soc. Performance and Instrn., Religious Edn. Assn., Nat. Assn. Profs. Christian Edn. Author: Developing Leadership Skills, 1971; contbr. articles to religious jours. Home: 8357 Idaho Ave N Brooklyn Park MN 55445 Office: 3949 Bethel Dr Saint Paul MN 55112

BUCHANAN, GERALD SNYDER, physician; b. Albert Lea, Minn., Jan. 28, 1920; s. Frank Merton and Verian Almeda (Snyder) B.; B.S., Union Coll., 1949; M.D., Loma Linda U., 1949; m. Laura Mae Martin, Sept. 9, 1945 (div. Jan. 1975); children—Gerald Duane, Douglas Lee, Randall Stuart; m. 2d, Edith Ellen Wheelock, Sept. 16, 1977. intern Hurley Hosp., Flint, Mich., 1949-50; practice gen. medicine, Fenton, Mich., 1950-51, Deer River, Minn., 1951-54, Ithaca, Mich., 1956-57, Holly, Mich., 1957—; mem. staff Hurley, McLaren, Genesee Meml. hosps. (all Flint). Pres. North Oakland unit Mich. Cancer Found., 1968-70. Served to capt. USMC, 1954-56. Home: 3258 Grange Hall Rd Holly MI 48442 Office: 3741 Grange Hall Rd Holly MI 48442

BUCHANAN, LARRY DEE, advt. agy. exec.; b. Atlantic, Iowa, Aug. 13, 1937; s. William Howard and Harriet Elizabeth (Simpson) B.; student So. Meth. U., 1958; B.A., N.Tex. State U., 1960; m. Frankie L. Henderson, Mar., 1961 (div.); m. 2d Karen P. Daniels, July, 1975 (div.); 1 dau., Lauri Dee. Writer graphic services dept. Collins Radio Co., Cedar Rapids, Iowa, 1961-63, writer, public relations dept., 1964; co-founder, sec., treas., dir. writer-producer Three Arts, Inc., Cedar Rapids, 1964-70, sr. v.p., dir., creative dir., 1970—. Mem. Cedar Rapids Symphony Orch. Assn., 1967-74, pres., 1970-71; search and rescue pilot CAP, 1969-71. Served with USMCR, 1955-61. Mem. Advt. Fedn. of Cedar Rapids (pres., 1971), Sigma Delta Chi, Phi Mu Alpha Sinfonia. Republican. Office: 501 2nd Ave SE Cedar Rapids IA 52401

BUCHER, HENRY HALE, JR., educator; b. Hainan Island, China, Mar. 7, 1936; s. Henry Hale and Louise Catron (Scott) B. (parents Am. citizens); student Davidson Coll., 1954-56; B.A., Am. U. of Beirut, 1958; postgrad. Univ. Coll., Legon, Ghana, 1960-61, Sorbonne U. Paris, 1962-63; M.Div., Princeton Theol. Sem., 1962; M.A. (Ford fellow), U. Wis., Madison, 1971, Ph.D., 1977; m. Emily Orr Clifford, June 22, 1969; 1 son, Clifford Hale. Ordained to ministry United Presbyterian Ch., U.S.A., 1962; intern service and study project in Gabon, under World Student Christian Fedn. of Geneva, 1962-65; mem. staff dept. higher edn. Nat. Council of Chs., N.Y.C., 1965-68; program dir. Ams. for Middle East Understanding, N.Y.C., 1969; curriculum specialist African studies program U. Wis., Madison, 1977-80; lectr. on So. Africa; mem. Madison Area Com. on So. Africa, 1969—, Madison Friends of Internat. Students, 1975—; Fulbright/Hays Doctoral Dissertation Research Abroad fellow, Gabon, Senegal, France, 1973-74. Mem. Am. Hist. Assn., African Studies Assn., Societe des Africanistes, Societe Francaise d'Histoire d'Outre-Mer, Soc. Intercultural Edn., Tng. and Research, Wis. Council Social Studies. Author: The Third World: Middle East, 1973; contbr. articles on Africa, Middle East to profl. publs. Home: 223 W Oak St Cottage Grove WI 53527 Office: 229 N Main St Cottage Grove WI 53527

BUCHER, OTTO NORMAN, clergyman, educator; b. Milw., June 3, 1933; s. Otto A. and Ida (Smazal) B.; B.A., Capuchin Sem. of St. Felix, Huntington, Ind., 1956; postgrad. Capuchin Sem. of St. Anthony, Marathon, Wis., 1956-60; S.T.L., Catholic U. Am., 1963; S.S.L., Pontifical Bibl. Inst., Rome, 1965. Joined Capuchin Franciscan Order, 1952; ordained priest Roman Catholic Ch., 1959; lector in scripture Capuchin Sem. of St. Anthony, Marathon, 1966-70; asso. prof. Bibl. studies St. Francis Sem., Sch. Pastoral Ministry, Milw., 1970-73; asso. prof. Bibl. studies Sacred Heart Sch. of Theology, Hales Corners, Wis., 1973—, acad. dean, 1979—; mem. exec. com. Midwestern Assn. Theology Schs., 1973-74. Mem. Cath. Bibl. Assn. Am., Soc. Bibl. Lit. Democrat. Home: St Fidelis Friary 528 N 31st St Milwaukee WI 53208 Office: Sacred Heart Sch Theology 7335 S Lovers Lane Rd Hales Corners WI 53130

BUCHHOLZ, RONALD LEWIS, architect; b. Milw., Jan. 14, 1951; s. Raymond LeRoy and Della (Krause) B.; B.S. in Architecture, U. Wis., Milw., 1973; m. Mary Lou Stockhausen, May 20, 1972; children—Lauren Robert, Geoffrey Alan. Archtl. appraiser Am. Appraisal Co., Milw., 1973; plan examiner, bur. bldgs. and structures, div. safety and bldgs. Wis. Dept. Industry, Labor and Human Relations, Madison, 1973-76, staff architect, 1976, architect, adminstrv. code cons., bur. code devel., 1976-80, dep. dir., 1980—; instr. U. Wis., Madison Ext., also state certification courses for bldg. and dwelling insps.; mem. Wis. Bldg. Code Adv. Rev. Bd., 1976—, Fire Prevention Council, 1978—, adv. com. Alternative Energy Tax Credits, 1978, 80; mem. Interagy. Com. on Spills of Hazardous Materials, 1981—. Served with Army N.G., 1970-76. Registered architect, Wis. Mem. Resdl. Facilities Council (exec. sec. 1976-78). Roman Catholic. Author tech. reports. Home: 4925 Knox Ln Madison WI 53711 Office: 201 E Washington Ave Room 101 Madison WI 53702

BUCHSIEB, WALTER CHARLES, orthodontist; b. Columbus, Ohio, Aug. 30, 1929; s. Walter William and Emma Marie (Held) B.; B.A., Ohio State U., 1951, D.D.S., 1955, M.S., 1960; m. Betty Lou Risch, June 19, 1955; children—Walter Charles II, Christine Ann. Pvt. practice dentistry specializing in orthodontics, Dayton, Ohio, 1959—; cons. orthodontist Miami Valley Hosp., Childrens Med. Center, Dayton. Mem. fin. and program com. United Health Found., 1971-73; mem. dean's adv. com. Ohio State U. Coll. Dentistry; bd. dirs. Hearing and Speech Center, 1968—, 2d v.p., 1976-78, pres., 1978—. Served to capt. AUS, 1955-58. Mem. ADA (alt. del. 1968—), Ohio Dental Assn. (sec. council legislation 1969—, v.p. 1978-79, pres.-elect 1979-80, pres. 1980-81), Am. Coll. Dentists, Dayton Dental Soc. (pres. 1970-71), Great Lakes Soc. Orthodontists (sec.-treas. 1972-75, pres. 1977-78), Internat. Coll. Dentists, Am. Assn. Orthodontists (chmn. council legislation 1976, speaker of house-elect 1981), Pierre Fauchard Acad., Ohio State U. Alumni Assn., Delta Upsilon, Psi Omega. Republican. Lutheran (elder 1965-68, v.p. 1974). Clubs: Masons, Rotary (pres. 1973-74). Home: 1101 Viewpoint Dr Dayton OH 45459 Office: 5335 Far Hills Ave Dayton OH 45429

BUCHTEL, FORREST LAWRENCE, coll. dean, musician, composer; b. St. Edward, Nebr., Dec. 9, 1899; s. Charles Stanton and Frances Marian (Stephens) B.; A.B., Simpson Coll., 1921; M.S. in Edn. (scholar), Northwestern U., 1931; B.Mus.Ed., VanderCook Coll. Music, Chgo., 1932, M.Mus.Ed., 1933; m. Jessie Helene Macdonald, June 6, 1925; children—Bonnie Buchtel Cataldo, Helene Buchtel Adams, Beverly Buchtel Platt, Forrest Lawrence. Tchr., South High Sch., Grand Rapids, Mich., 1921-25, Emporia (Kans.) State Coll., 1925-30, Lane Tech. High Sch., Chgo., 1930-34, Amundsen High Sch., Chgo., 1935-54; tchr. VanderCook Coll. Music, Chgo., 1931—, dean of students, 1960; composer, works include: 30 sets of bandbooks, 800 solos and ensembles for sch. bands, 30 marches, 30 overtures. Served with S.A.T.C., 1918. Recipient Alumni award Simpson Coll., 1961, VanderCook Coll., 1965. Mem. Am. Bandmasters Assn., ASCAP, Phi Beta Mu, Phi Mu Alpha Sinfonia, Kappa Kappa Psi, Delta Upsilon. Methodist. Club: Univ. (Chgo.). Home: 1116 Cleveland St Evanston IL 60202 Office: 3209 S Michigan Ave Chicago IL 60616

BUCHTEL, MICHAEL ALFRED, civil engr.; b. Barberton, Ohio, Apr. 22, 1925; s. Ora Percy Elberta and Dortha Opal (Lowery) B.; B.S. in Civil Engring., U. Akron, 1971; m. Pauline Margaret Slee, Dec. 30, 1948; children—Preston Carl, Michele Darlene. Utility boilers Babcock & Wilcox Co., Barberton, 1947-54, draftsman, layout man for power boilers, 1954-73, structural engr., stress analyst on power boilers, from 1974, now performance engr. Active Boy Scouts Am., 1952-56, Jr. Achievement, 1956, Chapel in University Park, Akron, Ohio, 1952-68, Medina Bible Fellowship, 1979—. Served with U.S. Army, 1949-55. Recipient Jr. Achievement award, 1956. Mem. ASCE (pres. Akron sect., award 1978). Republican. Clubs: Hilltoppers, Masons, Gideons Internat. (sec. Medina County camp 1968-78, editor Newsletter 1979—). Home: 875 Andrews Rd Medina OH 44256 Office: Babcock & Wilcox Co 20 Van Buren Ave Barberton OH 44203

BUCK, BERNESTINE BRADFORD, ednl. counselor; b. Altheimer, Ark., July 25, 1926; d. Henry Walker and Dora Lois (Sims) Bradford; B.A., Stowe Tchrs. Coll., 1950; M.Ed., U. Mo., 1973; m. Joseph Wellington Buck, Oct. 1, 1950; children—Stanley W., Linda Carol, Debra Lois. Tchr. pub. schs., St. Louis, 1950-73, sch. counselor, 1973—. Mem. U. Mo. scholarship com., 1954-81. Mem. NEA, Am., Mo. personnel and guidance assns., St. Louis Guidance Assn. (pres. 1979-80), Mo. Guidance Assn. (exec. council 1980-81, v.p. elementary sect.). Baptist.

BUCK, LORRAINE, psychiat. fin. planner, ins. cons.; b. St. Louis, June 10, 1954; d. Willie B. and Lorraine R. Buck; B.S., St. Louis U., 1976, M.S.W., 1977. Intern, St. Louis Juvenile Detention Center, 1977; social worker East Moline (Ill.) Elem. Dist., 1977-80; psychiat. social worker Malcolm Bliss Mental Health Center, St. Louis, 1980-81; cons. in field; with N.Y. Life Ins. Co., St. Louis, 1981—. Mem. edn. and social support com. Rock Island (Ill.) YWCA, 1979-80. Whitney Young Meml. scholar, 1976. Mem. Nat. Assn. Social Workers, Acad. Cert. Social Workers. Home: PO Box 14573 Saint Louis MO 63178 Office: 111 West Port Plaza Suite 500 Saint Louis MO 63141

BUCKINGHAM, ALBERT WILLIAM, coll. exec.; b. Westfield, Iowa, Apr. 1, 1914; s. James W. and Sophie E. (Seamen) B.; B.A., Morningside Coll., 1939; M.A., Stanford U., 1950; postgrad. Notre Dame U., Northwestern U., 1942; m. Marian Marjorie Miller, Oct. 31, 1942; children—Susan Elizabeth, Rosemary, James William. Prin. and coach, Sergeant Bluff, Iowa, 1939-41; athletic dir. and coach, Mapleton, Iowa, 1941-42; basketball coach Morningside Coll., Sioux City, Iowa, 1945-56, dir. phys. edn. and athletics, 1945-69, asst. prof. phys. edn., 1945-55, asso. prof., 1956—, dir. public relations, 1956-68, v.p. estate planning, 1962—. Bd. dirs. U.S. Olympic Com., 1965—, Iowa United Methodist Found., 1975—; pres. U.S. Collegiate Sports Council, 1973-77; chief of missions World Univ. Games, 1977, 79. Served with USN, 1942-45. Named to Hall of Fame, Greater S.C. Athletic Assn., 1970, North Central Intercollegiate Athletic Conf., Helms Hall of Fame, Nat. Assn. Intercollegiate Athletics, 1969. Fellow Am. Sch. Health Assn.; mem. Nat. Assn. Intercollegiate Athletics (pres. 1965-66), Iowa Dirs. Coll. Public Relations (pres. 1955), Sioux City C. of C. (chmn. recreation com. 1954). Republican. Methodist. Clubs: Lions (pres. local club 1954-55), Sioux City Boat, Shriners, Masons (Sioux City). Contbr. articles to phys. edn. mags. Home: 1504 Morningside Ave Sioux City IA 51106 Office: 1501 Morningside Ave Sioux City IA 51106

BUCKINGHAM, EDWIN JOHN, JR., newspaper pub., journalist; b. Spokane, Wash., July 23, 1912; s. Edwin John and Violet Edna (Poole) B.; B.A. in Journalism, U. N.D., 1935; m. Kathryn Ruth Aird, Aug. 31, 1940; 1 son, Edwin John III. Mng. editor, asst. mgr. Dickinson (N.D.) Press, 1940-47, 53-58; mgr. newspapers, Ray, N.D., 1938-39, Culbertson, Mont., 1939-40, New England, N.D., 1947-53; owner, pub. Chamberlain (S.D.) Register, 1958—, Kennebec (S.D.) Advocate-Leader, 1968—; pres. Register Pub. Co., Inc., 1958—. Chmn. Brule County ARC, 1958-59; pres. Chamberlain United Fund, 1971-73. Served with U.S. Army, 1943-46; PTO. Mem. S.D. Comml. Printers (past pres.), S.D. Press Assn. (past pres.), Nat. Newspaper Assn., Soc. Profl. Journalists—Sigma Delta Chi (past pres. S.D.). Republican. Episcopalian. Clubs: Kiwanis, Am. Legion, VFW. Home: 308 E Beebe Ave Chamberlain SD 57325 Office: 218 N Main St Chamberlain SD 57325

BUCKINGHAM, WILLIAM BRICE, physician; b. Chgo., July 25, 1924; s. Brice Albert and Mary (Ahern) B.; student John Carroll U., Cleve., 1942-44; M.D., U. Ill., 1947, B.S., 1956; m. Margery L. Cross, Sept. 15, 1950; children—Cathlin, Megan, Gillian, William Brice, Peter, Michael, John, Maura, Mark, David, Diedre. Intern, Cook County Hosp., Chgo., 1947-49, resident, 1950-52; fellow Northwestern U., 19S1-52. Diplomate Am. Bd. Internal Medicine. Practice medicine, specializing in internal medicine, Chgo., 1952—; attending physician Oak Park Hosp., 1952—, Augustana Hosp., Chgo., 1954-66; staff physician Oak Forest Tb. Hosp.. 1952-55; asso. attending pulmonary disease sect. Cook County Hosp., 1952-56, attending physician, 1956-64, chief pulmonary sect., 1963-64, attending physician dept. medicine, 1964-66; cons. DeKalb County Tb. Hosp. and Clinic, 1954-60; attending physician St. Elizabeths Hosp., Chgo., 1954-65, St. Josephs Hosp., Chgo., 1964-68; attending physician VA Research Hosp., Chgo., 1960-70, cons. pulmonary diseases, 1970; attending physician Northwestern Meml. Hosp., 1966—, dir. pulmonary lab., 1968-75; clin. asst. Northwestern U. Med. Sch., 1952-56, instr., 1956-59, asso. in medicine, 1959-68, asst. prof., 1968-70, asso. prof., 1970—, chief, sect. gen. medicine, 1975—; mem. sci. adv. com. Municipal Tb. Sanitarium, 1968-72; cons. in tb. Ill. Dept. Pub. Health, 1973—; tb. control officer Chgo. Bd. Health, 1974—; vis. prof. medicine Universidad Autonoma de Guadalajara Med. Sch., 1975, 80; cons. med. editor Quality Rev. Bull., Joint Commn. on Accreditation of Hosps., 1975. Fellow A.C.P., Am. Coll. Chest Physicians (pres. Ill. chpt. 1966-67, gen. chmn. First Fall Sci. Assembly, Chgo. 1969), Inst. of Medicine Chgo.; mem. AMA, Am. Soc. Internal Medicine, Ill. Soc. Internal Medicine (exec. council 1965—), Chgo. Soc. Internal Medicine (pres. 1977-78), Am. Thoracic Soc., Ill., Chgo. med. socs., Chgo. Tb. Inst. (dir.), Am. Assn. Inhaalation Therapists (bd. med. advisers 1969-72), Riverside Golf Club. Contbr. articles to profl. jours. Home: 319 Linden Ave Oak Park IL 60302 Office: 222 E Superior St Chicago IL 60611

BUCKLEY, ROBERT MICHAEL, clin. psychologist; b. Chgo., Oct. 20, 1927; s. Michael Francis and Lillian Ruth (Johnson) B.; B.S., Ill. Inst. Tech., 1960, M.S., 1963, Ph.D., 1970; m. Alice Kay Hanson, Oct. 17, 1959; children—Michelle, Tamara, Shawn. Chemist, metallurgist, Nalco, Chgo., 1952-56; psychologist, Chgo. Bur. Child Study, 1964-66, Speed Ednl. Coop., Chicago Heights, Ill., 1966-77; clin. psychologist, pres. Buckley-Long Assos. Ltd., Homewood, Ill., 1974-77. Active Citizens for Congressman Derwinski. Served with USN, 1945-47. Mem. Am., Midwest, Ill. psychol. assns., Biofeedback Socs. Am., Ill. (chmn. instrumentation com). Club: VFW. Contbr. research reports on biofeedback to confs. Home: 4732 W 176th St Country Club Hills IL 60477 Office: 18019 Dixie Hwy Homewood IL 60430

BUCKMAN, CHARLES EDWARD, JR., telephone co. exec.; b. Kansas City, Mo., Sept. 27, 1943; s. Charles Edward and Geraldine Clara (Herold) B.; student Ill. State U., 1961-64; B.S., Quincy Coll., 1966; postgrad. U. Ill., 1967-68; m. Judith Brosi, Nov. 19, 1966; children—Christine Elaine, Erin Noel, Brian Charles. Juvenile parole agent Ill. Youth Commn., 1966-67, regional supr., Springfield, 1967-68; account salesman Ill. Bell Telephone, Moline, 1967-70, communications cons., 1970-72, data communications specialist, 1972-74, account mgr., 1974-76, mgr. data tech. support, Chgo., 1976-77, product mgr., 1977-80, industry mgr., 1980—. Treas. Christian Family Movement, 1975-76; mem. religious edn. bd. Sacred Heart Ch., Moline, 1975-76; mem. curriculum adv. com. Black Hawk Coll., Moline, 1973-76. Mem. Data Processing Mgmt. Assn., Am. Mgmt. Assn. Roman Catholic. Home: 1081 Challdon Ct Naperville IL 60540 Office: 200 W Monroe St Room 500 Chicago IL 60606

BUCKSTEIN, JANET FRANCES, bank mktg. exec.; b. N.Y.C., June 12, 1950; d. Herman and Edna (Goodman) B.; B.A. in Math., Northwestern U., 1972, M.S. with high honors in Mgmt., 1974. Mktg. research analyst Market Facts, Inc., Chgo., 1974-75; project dir. Bozell & Jacobs, Inc., Chgo., 1975-77; sr. mktg. analyst Continental Bank, Chgo., 1977-79, asso. cons. mktg., 1979-81, cons., 1981, 2d v.p., 1981—; guest lectr. mktg. Harper Coll., Northwestern U. Mem. Am. Mktg. Assn., Bank Mktg. Assn., Nat. Assn. Bank Women, Kappa Delta (chmn. adv. bd. Northwestern U. chpt. 1976-79, pres. Chgo. North Suburban Alumnae Assn. 1979-80). Office: 231 S La Salle St Chicago IL 60693

BUCUR, NICHOLAS ANTHONY, III, data processing exec.; b. Managua, Nicaragua, Oct. 11, 1950 (parents Am. citizens); s. Nicholas A. and Jacoba (Galo) B.; student Cuyahoga Community Coll., 1969-71. Propr., Infinity Co., pub., Cleve., 1968—, data processing cons., 1973—; editorialist WZAK Radio, Cleve., 1969-73, dir. pub. affairs, 1975—, moderator, announcer People's Voice program, 1973—; pub. Cleve. Feminist mag., 1973; systems mgr. Systems Info. Services, Cleve., 1976-78; sr. systems analyst Picker Corp., Cleve., 1978—; instr. data processing Cuyahoga Community Coll. Vice pres. Greater Cleve. Young Republican Club, 1971; mem. human relations com. Fedn. for Community Planning, 1973. Cert. computer profl. Mem. Nat. Mgmt. Assn. Mensa. Club: Cleve. City. Home: 10206 Clifton St Cleveland OH 44102 Office: 600 Beta Dr Cleveland OH 44143

BUDDIG, THOMAS ROBERT, meat processing co. exec.; b. Chgo., Mar. 25, 1952; s. Robert Charles and Mary Jane (Brittain) B.; B.S. in Bus. Adminstrn., U. Denver, 1974; m. Alexis C. Evanoff, Nov. 29, 1975. Mem. gen. sales and merchandising staff Carl Buddig & Co., Chgo., 1974-76, new product devel. dept. 1976-77, advt. mgr., 1977-78, nat. sales dir., 1978—. Mem. Am. Mktg. Assn., Am. Mgmt. Assn., Sales and Mktg. Execs. Assn. Chgo., Order of Omega. Presbyterian. Club: Univ. (Chgo.). Office: 11914 S Peoria St Chicago IL 60643

BUDINGTON, WILLIAM STONE, librarian; b. Oberlin, Ohio, July 3, 1919; s. Robert Allyn and Mabel (Stone) B.; B.A., Williams Coll., 1940, L.H.D., 1975; B.S. in L.S., Columbia U., 1941, M.S., 1951; B.S. in Elec. Engring., Va. Poly. Inst., 1946. Reference librarian Norwich U., 1941-42; librarian engring. and phys. scis. Columbia U., 1947-52; asso. librarian John Crerar Library, Chgo., 1952-65, librarian, 1965-69, exec. dir., librarian, 1969—. Mem. U.S.-USSR Spl. Libraries Exchange, 1966; bd. dirs. Center for Research Libraries, 1970-72, chmn., 1972; mem. vis. com. on libraries M.I.T., 1972-77. Served with AUS, 1942-46. Fellow AAAS; mem. ALA, Am. Soc. Info. Sci., Spl. Libraries Assn. (pres. 1964-65), Am. Soc. Engring. Edn., Med. Library Assn., Assn. Research Libraries (dir. 1970-74, pres., 1973), Phi Beta Kappa, Tau Beta Pi, Eta Kappa Nu. Clubs: Caxton, Arts. Office: 35 W 33d St Chicago IL 60616

BUDZAK, KATHRYN SUE (MRS. ARTHUR BUDZAK), physician; b. Racine, Wis., May 6, 1940; d. Raymond Philip and Emma Kathryn (Sorensen) Myer; student Stephens Coll., 1957-58, Luther Coll., 1958-59; B.S. with honors, U. Wis. at Milw., 1962; M.D., U. Wis., 1969; m. Arthur Budzak, Dec. 21, 1961; children—Ann Elizabeth, Lynn Marie. Intern, Madison (Wis.) Gen. Hosp., 1969-70; emergency physician, emergency suite St. Mary's Hosp., Madison, 1971-75; urgent care screening physician Dean Clinic, Madison, 1975—. Recipient Disting. Alumnae award Stephens Coll., 1979. Mem. Am. Coll. Emergency Physicians, Am. Coll. of Sports Medicine, AMA, Am., Wis. (pres. south central chpt. 1979-81), acads. family physicians, Wis., Dane County med. socs., Am. Med. Women's Assn., Wis. Med. Alumni Assn. (dir. 1979—), Sigma Sigma Sigma. Presbyterian. Mem. editorial bd., asst. editor Wis. Med. Alumni Quar. Home: 6110 Davenport Dr Madison WI 53711 Office: 1313 Fish Hatchery Rd Madison WI 53715

BUECHE, WENDELL FRANCIS, mfg. co. exec.; b. Flushing, Mich., Nov. 7, 1930; s. Paul D. and Catherine (McGraw) B.; B.S. in Mech. Engring., U. Notre Dame, 1952; m. Virginia M. Smith, June 14, 1952; children—Denise, Barbara, Daniel, Brian. With Allis-Chalmers Corp., 1952—, utility group sales mgr., Cleve., 1959-62, dist. mgr., Detroit, 1962-64, sales and mktg. mgr., 1964-69, gen. mgr. crushing and screening equipment div., Appleton, Wis., 1969-73, group exec. and v.p. aggregate and coal processing group, West Allis, Wis., 1973-76, exec. v.p. elec. groups, 1976-77, exec. v.p., chief adminstrv. and fin. officer, 1977-80, exec. v.p., head solids process equipment sector and fluids processing group, chief fin. officer, 1980-81, pres., chief operating officer, 1981—, also dir.; dir. Fiat-Allis, Siemens-Allis, M&I Marshall & Ilsley Bank. Mem. Greater Milw. Com., 1981—, Chgo. Com., 1981—. Mem. Am. Inst. Elec. and Electronic Engrs., ASME, Am. Inst. Mining Engrs., Nat. Sand and Gravel Assn. (dir.), Nat. Elec. Mfrs. Assn. (gov.). Clubs: Milw. Country; Westmoor Country. Office: 1205 S 70th St West Allis WI 53201

BUECHLER, ROBERT EUGENE, ret. nat. guard officer, lawyer; b. St. Louis, Jan. 20, 1921; s. George Fred and Frances A. (Neuman) B.; A.B., Washington U., St. Louis, J.D., 1953 and 1956; grad. Air War Coll., 1965; m. Nancy Jane Reisdorff, Nov. 3, 1958; children—Virginia Frances, Anne Carrol, Laura June. Admitted to Mo. bar, 1963, U.S. Supreme Ct. bar, 1968, U.S. Ct. Mil. Appeals, 1968; asso. firm Correnti & Mykins, 1968-74; mgr. edn. and tng. Ralston Purina Corp., St. Louis, 1965-68; jud. hearing officer St. Louis County Juvenile Ct., 1974-77. Commd. maj. Mo. Air N.G., 1953, advanced through grades to maj. gen., 1977; ops. staff officer N.G. Bur., Washington, 1957-60; air N.G. liaison officer Hdqrs. Mil. Airlift Command, Scott AFB, Ill., 1960-64; assigned Air War Coll., 1964-65; dep. chief of staff for air Hdqrs. Mo. Air N.G., 1965-68; comdr. 131st Tactical Fighter Wing of Mo. N.G., 1968-72, adj. gen. State of Mo., 1977-81, ret., 1981. Elder, United Ch. Christ, St. Louis, 1974-77. Decorated D.S.M., Legion of Merit, D.F.C. with 4 clusters, Air medal with four clusters. Served to capt. USAAF, 1942-45; CBI. Mem. Am. Law Sch. Assn. (v.p. 1953-54), Met. Bar Assn. St. Louis, Mo. Integrated Bar, N.G. Assn. U.S., N.G. Assn. Mo., Navy League, Armed Forces Officers Club Greater St. Louis, Delta Theta Phi. Home: 4713 Prague Ave Saint Louis MO 63109

BUEGE, WILLIAM MICHAEL, communications corp. exec.; b. Milw., Jan. 7, 1944; s. Chester Charles and Agnes (Grafenauer) B.; B.S., U. Wis.-Milw., 1965; m. Jill Anne Boeder, Nov. 16, 1966; 1 son, Brian William. With Xerox Corp., 1968—, br. sales mgr., Milw., 1974-75, br. mgr., Chgo., 1976-78, Mpls., 1979—. Served with U.S. Army, 1965-68. Decorated Bronze Star, Silver Star. Home: 8 Oriole Ln North Oaks MN 55110 Office: Xerox Corp 2850 Metro Dr Bloomington MN 55420

BUELL, GRANT DENISON, food co. mktg. ofcl.; b. Seattle, June 18, 1947; s. Ralph Denison and Phyllis Johanna (Adams) B.; B.S., U. Oreg., 1969; M.B.A., Columbia U., 1972; m. Laura Ann Carlson, Mar. 24, 1979; children—Patrick Adams, Johanna Elizabeth. Asst. buyer Lord & Taylor, N.Y.C., 1969; fin. acct. Shell Chem. Co., N.Y.C., 1970; mgr. market devel. Flying Tiger Line, Los Angeles, 1972-73; asst. product mgr. Starkist Foods, Los Angeles, 1974-75; product mgr., mktg. mgr., group mktg. mgr. Pillsbury Co., Mpls., 1976-81; with Kellwood Co., Chesterfield, Mo., 1981—. Mem. Am. Mgmt. Assn., Alpha Kappa Psi. Republican. Presbyterian. Club: NW Racquet and Swim. Participant U.S. Tennis Assn. sanctioned tennis tournaments. Home: 515 Nottingham Dr Ballwin MO 63011 Office: 600 Kellwood Pkwy Chesterfield MO 63017

BUENGER, CLEMENT L., banker; b. Cin., Apr. 27, 1926; s. Clement Lawrence and Estelle (Pelzer) B.; student U. Wis., 1943-44; B.S. in Bus. Adminstrn., Xavier U., 1950; m. Ann McCabe, Apr. 22, 1950. Acct., Kroger Co., Cin., 1950-51; exec. v.p. Selective Ins. Co., Cin., 1951-67, Life Ins. Co. of Ky., Louisville, 1967-69; pres. Fifth Third Bank, Cin., 1969—, also dir.; dir. Fifth Third Bancorp, Hooven & Allison Co. Trustee Boys' Clubs Greater Cin., St. Xavier High Sch.; trustee, mem. pres.'s council Xavier U.; gen. chmn. United Appeal, 1981; bd. dirs. ARC, Boy Scouts Am. Served with USNR, 1943-45. Mem. Assn. Res. City Bankers, Cin. Council on World Affairs, Cin. Bus. Com. Republican. Roman Catholic. Clubs: Cin. Country, Bankers, Comml., Queen City. Home: 1029 Catawba Valley Dr Cincinnati OH 45226 Office: 38 Fountain Sq Plaza Cincinnati OH 45263

BUER, HOWARD HENRY, coll. adminstr.; b. Milw., Jan. 14, 1922; s. Henry William and Hertha Martha (Hinz) B.; B.C.E., M.C.E., U. Wis.; m. Raymir Behrens, Feb. 23, 1946; children—Karen Diane, Scott Howard. Instr. civil engring. U. Wis., Madison, 1948-51; analyst Chance Vought Aircraft Co., Dallas, 1951-52; asst. prof. civil engring. U. Del., Newark, 1952-54; instr. engring. mechanics U. Wis., Madison, 1954-55; asst. to chief structural engr. Mead & Hunt, cons. engrs., Madison, 1955-64; sci. programmer U. Wis. Phys. Scis. Lab., Stoughton, 1964-67; dir. adminstrv. data processing The Principia, St. Louis, 1968-80; dir. Computer Center, Lindenwood Coll., St. Charles, Mo., 1980—; structural engr. mem. City of Madison Bd. Bldg. Examiners and Appeals, 1963-64. Served with C.E., U.S. Army, 1942-46. Registered profl. engr., Wis.; cert. computer programmer, cert. data processor. Mem. Assn. Computer Machinery, Assn. Systems Mgmt., Data Processing Mgmt. Assn., Soc. Preservation and Encouragement of Barber Shop Quartet Singing in Am., Chi Epsilon, Tau Beta Pi. Republican. Christian Scientist. Club: Masons. Home: 3025 Headland Dr Saint Charles MO 63301 Office: Lindenwood Colleges Saint Charles MO 63301

BUERK, HANS GUENTHER, wholesale trade co. exec.; b. Rottweil, Germany, Nov. 23, 1924; s. Christian and Johanna Anna (Martin) B.; M.B.A., U. Tuebingen, 1949; m. Utta Santo-Passo, Aug. 4, 1961; 1 dau., Joan Cristina. Came to U.S., 1961, naturalized, 1967. With Dr. Treude Assn., Stuttgart, West Germany, 1950-54; controller A.G. Messerschmitt, Munich, West Germany, 1955-57; jr. partner Koeck, Baden-Baden, West Germany, 1958-61; cost accountant Harris Trust & Savs. Bank, Chgo., 1962-63; auditor Chemetron Corp., Chgo., 1963-66; with Robert Bosch Corp., Broadview, Ill., 1966—, v.p. finance, 1971-79; v.p. fin., treas., sec. Robert Bosch N. Am. Inc., co. hdqrs., Broadview, 1980—, also dir. Served with German Army, 1942-45. Mem. Am. Mgmt. Assn. (presidents council 1973—). Home: 3400 N Lake Shore Dr Chicago IL 60657 Office: 2800 S 25th Ave Broadview IL 60153

BUERLING, SIEGFRIED FRIEDEL, hist. village ofcl.; b. Essen, Germany, Jan. 29, 1932; s. Friedrich and Bertha Wilhelmiene (Wackermann) B.; came to U.S., 1959, naturalized, 1968; grad. trade sch.; m. Heidi Elisabeth Heid, Aug. 31, 1957; children—Peter Johannes, Curt Tracy. With Buerling Cabinet Shop, Essen, 1945-56; furniture restorer Canadiana Antiques, Montreal, Que., Can., 1956-59; preparator Western Reserve Hist. Soc., Cleve., 1959-62, supr. ops., 1962-66, mgr. ops., 1966-70, mgr. properties, 1970-74, dir. Hale Farm and Village, Bath, Ohio, 1975—, dir. dept. properties and preservation, 1977—; v.p. ops. Cuyahoga Valley Preservation and Scenic R.R. Assn.; restoration cons. Bd. dirs. Hower House Found., Akron, Ohio, 1974—; trustee Northeastern Ohio Inter Museums Council. Recipient Woodrow Wilson award Woodlawn Conf., Nat. Trust for Historic Preservation, 1971; Outstanding Citizen award Nationality Services Center Greater Cleve., 1975. Mem. Internat. Council Crafts and Interpretation. Rotarian (dir. 1975—). Home: 2743 Oak Hill Rd Bath OH 44210 Office: 2686 Oak Hill Rd Bath OH 44210

BUERMAN, RUTH FRANCES, nurse; b. Bancroft, Nebr., Feb. 22, 1927; d. Richard Louis and Ella Christina (Bruning) Stafford; R.N., St. Catherine's Hosp., Omaha, 1947; m. Harlan Buerman, Nov. 15, 1947; children—William, Pamela, Jean. Staff nurse St. Francis Meml. Hosp., West Point, Nebr., 1952-65, supr. central service, 1965-69, purchasing med.-surg. supplies, 1969-71, dir. ancillary services, 1971-74; dir. nurses Hallmark Care Center, Omaha, 1974-78; acting adminstr. Colonial Haven, Beemer, Nebr., 1979. Mem. Omaha Gerontol. Group, Am. Nurses Assn., Am. Hosp. Assn. Purchasing Agents. Republican. Roman Catholic. Home: 5312 S 114th St Omaha NE 68137

BUESSER, ANTHONY CARPENTER, lawyer; b. Detroit, Oct. 15, 1929; s. Frederick Gustavis and Lela (Carpenter) B.; B.A. in English with honors, U. Mich., 1952, M.A., 1953, J.D., 1960; m. Carolyn Sue Pickle, Mar. 13, 1954; children—Kent Anderson, Anthony Carpenter, Andrew Clayton; m. 2d, Bettina Rieveschl, Dec. 14, 1973. Admitted to Mich. bar, 1961; asso firm Chase, Goodenough & Buesser, Detroit, 1961-66; partner firm Buesser, Buesser, Snyder & Blank, Detroit and Bloomfield Hills, 1966—. Trustee, chmn. bd. Detroit Country Day Sch., Birmingham, Mich., 1970—. Served with AUS, 1953-55. Recipient Avery Hopwood award major fiction U. Mich., 1953. Mem. Am., Mich., Detroit (pres. 1976-77), Oakland County bar assns., Am. Judicature Soc., Am. Arbitration Assn. (arbitrator), Alpha Delta Phi, Phi Delta Phi. Clubs: Thomas M. Cooley, Detroit, Detroit Athletic (Detroit). Home and Office: 995 Timberlake Dr Bloomfield Hills MI 48013

BUESSER, FREDERICK GUSTAVUS, III, lawyer; b. Detroit, Apr. 30, 1941; s. Frederick Gustavus and Betty A. (Ronal) B.; B.A., U. Mich., 1964, J.D., 1966; m. Julia Forsyth Guest, June 28, 1963; children—Jennifer, Katherine, Frederick. Admitted to Mich. bar, 1966; asso. firm Buesser, Buesser, Snyder & Blank, Detroit, Bloomfield Hills, 1966, partner, 1967—; lectr. and mem. faculty legal seminars. Mem. Am. Bar Assn., State Bar of Mich., Am. Judicature Soc., Sigma Chi, Phi Delta Phi. Episcopalian. Home: 242 N Glengarry St Birmingham MI 48009 Office: 4190 Telegraph St Bloomfield Hills MI 48013

BUFFARDI, LOUIS JOSEPH, candy mfg. co. exec.; b. Chgo., Mar. 27, 1914; s. Salvatore J. and Carmella (Pagano) B.; student Northwestern U., 1932-35; LL.B., Kent Law Sch., 1938; m. Dorothy Ann Parrillo, Jan. 6, 1940; children—James S., Louis P., Carmellyn R., Donna T. Admitted to Ill. bar, 1938; practiced in Chgo., 1938-40; treas., atty. Ferrara Candy Co., Chgo., 1950-52, treas., atty., 1946—; electronic analyst Motorola, Inc., Chgo., 1942-44; bacteriological chemist Meadowmor Dairy, Chgo., 1944-46. Chgo. area candy industry sect. leader Community Fund, A.R.C., 1942-52. Bd. dirs. Villa Scalabrini, old peoples home. Recipient 10 year service award Red Feather, 1953; 50-Yr. Candy Industry Dean award, 1977. Mem. Ill. Bar Assn., Nat. Confectioners Assn., N.A.M., Nat. Small Bus. Men's Assn., Catholic Lawyers Guild, Chgo. Justinian Soc. Lawyers,

Ill. C. of C., Chgo. Mus. Natural History, Lyric Opera Guild Chgo., Northwestern U. Alumni Assn., Candy Technology Club, Chicago Candy Prodn. Club. Club: Moose. Home: 121 Briarwood Loop Oak Brook IL 60521 Office: 7301 W Harrison St Forest Park IL 60131

BUFFINGTON, IRA, clergyman, educator; b. Halltown, Mo., Apr. 5, 1915; s. Charles William and Jewel Gladys (Fees) B.; B.S., S.W. Mo. State U., 1952; M.Ed., Drury Coll., 1957; postgrad. U. Mo., 1954-70; m. Mamie Malinda Standley, Oct. 21, 1936; children—David, Kathy, Paul, Malinda, Jane, Myra, Robert, Michelle. Tchr. eleme. grades Lawrence County, Mo., 1934-41; prin. elem. grades Greenfield, Mo., 1941-46; tchr. high sch. English and social studies, Dadeville, Mo., 1948-53; tchr. high sch. English, Lockwood, Mo., 1954-55; prin. high sch. Greenfield, 1955-59; asst. prof. edn. and English, S.W. Baptist Coll., Bolivar, Mo., 1959—; ordained minister Baptist Ch., 1936, pastor ch. Dade County (Mo.), 1941-77. Moderator Dade County Baptist Assn., 1953-55. Mem. Nat. Council Tchrs. English, Mo. Philol. Assn. (charter), NEA, Mo. Tchrs. Assn. Democrat. Clubs: Lions, Kiwanis (pres. Bolivar 1976-77). Home: Route 1 Bolivar MO 65613 Office: Southwest Baptist Coll Bolivar MO 65613

BUGBEE, WILLIAM MAYNARD, plant pathologist; b. Clinton, Iowa, May 13, 1935; s. Maynard Vincent and Florence Katherine (Moscrip) B.; B.A., U. Iowa, 1957; M.S., U. Minn., 1962, Ph.D., 1965; m. Joy Mae Bryant, Mar. 15, 1958; children—Pamela Jane, Brian William, William Franklin, Jennifer Louise. Research technician Clinton Foods, Inc., 1957-58; grad. research asst., then research fellow U. Minn., 1960-65; plant pathologist Dept. Agr., Portageville, Mo., 1965-69, plant pathologist, research leader, Fargo, N.D., 1969—; chmn. soil fungicide com. Cotton Disease Council, 1968, sec. council, 1969; adj. prof. N.D. State U., 1970—. Served with U.S. Army, 1958-60. Mem. Am. Phytopathological Soc., AAAS, Am. Soc. Sugarbeet Technologists, Sigma Xi. Lutheran. Club: Elks. Author numerous research papers on diseases of conifer seedlings, cotton, and sugarbeets. Office: 306 Walster Hall ND State U Univ Sta Fargo ND 58105

BUJAKE, JOHN EDWARD, JR., beverage co. exec.; b. N.Y.C., May 23, 1933; s. John E. and Mary (Muzyka) B.; B.S., Manhattan Coll., 1954; M.S., Holy Cross Coll., 1955; Ph.D., Columbia U., 1959; M.B.A., N.Y. U., 1963; m. Gail E. Cruise, Aug. 1, 1964; children—John Edward, Laura, Jacquelyn, William. Research asso. Lever Bros., Edgewater, N.J., 1959-68; dir. research and devel., foods div. Coca Cola Co., Houston, 1968-72; dir. research and devel. Quaker Oats Co., Barrington, Ill., 1972-77; dir. research and devel. Seven Up Co., St. Louis, 1977-78, v.p. research and devel., 1978—. Mem. Indsl. Research Inst., Am. Chem. Soc., Inst. Food Technologists. Mem. editorial bd. Research Mgmt., 1976-77; contbr. articles to profl. jours. Home: 24 Twin Springs Ln Ladue MO 63124 Office: Seven Up Co 121 S Meramec St Saint Louis MO 63105

BUJKO, LESTER GEORGE, petrochem. co. mgr.; b. Hamburg, Germany, June 10, 1947; came to U.S., 1950, naturalized, 1955; m. William and Helena B.; B.S. in Econs., Ill. Inst. Tech., 1972; postgrad. Ill. Inst. Tech., 1973-74, U. Nebr., 1980-81; m. Deborah Susan Saikley, Mar. 26, 1977; 1 dau., Lesley Renae. Fleet mgr. Diversey Chem. Co., 1968; acctg. supr. Atlantic Richfield, 1969-72; mgr. cost and disbursement control InterNorth Corp., Omaha, 1972—. Recipient Exec. Recognition award No. Petrochem., 1979. Mem. Nat. Assn. Accts., Omaha Zool. Soc., Joslyn Art Assn. Republican. Club: Knights of Ak-Sar-Ben. Research on econ. devel. of East and West Germany after World War II, control of contractors in antifreeze ops., mgmt. compliance to Fgn. Corrupt Practices Act of 1977. Office: Northern Natural Gas 2223 Dodge St Omaha NE 68102

BUKER, DAVID WILLIAM, mgmt. cons.; b. Portland, Maine, June 20, 1940; s. Myron William and Harriett Winifred (Bridge) B.; B.A. with honors in Econs., Wheaton Coll., 1966; M.B.A. in Fin., U. Chgo., 1975; m. Marilyn June Watkins, Aug. 4, 1963; children—Michelle Lynette, Bradley David. Material control mgr. Chgo. and Northwestern R.R., 1958-62; corp. materials cons. Hyster Co., 1966-69; dir. prodn. planning Barber-Greene Co., 1969-71; asst. to pres. Desa Industries, 1971-74; dir. materials Dresser Industries, Galion, Ohio, 1974-78; dir. mfg. indsl. edn. Arthur Andersen & Co., St. Charles, Ill., 1978-79; pres. David W. Buker, Inc., Antioch, Ill., 1979—, Fin. Services Co., Antioch, 1974—; chmn. bd. Vacation Island Properties, Sanibel Island, Fla., 1974—; dir., chmn. long-range planning com., chmn. fin. com. Sundial of Sanibel Island, 1980. Cert. practitioner in inventory mgmt. Mem. Am. Prodn. and Inventory Control Soc. (dir. cert. 1978), Internat. Materials Mgmt. Soc. (internat. v.p. 1972), Nat. Assn. Accts., Nat. Assn. Purchasing Mgrs. Republican. Mem. Evangelical Free Ch. Author in field. Home: 24099 Bayview Rd Antioch IL 60002 Office: PO Box 475 Antioch IL 60002

BUKOVAC, MARTIN JOHN, horticulturist; b. Johnston City, Ill., Nov. 12, 1929; s. John and Sadie (Fak) B.; B.S. with honors (William and Sarah E. Hinman scholar), Mich. State U., 1951, M.S., 1954, Ph.D., 1957; NSF postdoctoral fellow, Oxford U., U. Bristol (Eng.), 1965-66; m. Judith Ann Kelley, Sept. 5, 1956; 1 dau., Janice Louise. Asst. prof. horticulture Mich. State U., 1957-61, asso. prof., 1961-63, prof., 1963—; vis. lectr. Japan Atomic Energy Research Inst., 1958; adviser IAEA, Vienna, 1961; Nat. Acad. Scis. exchange lectr. to Council Academies, Yugoslavia, 1971; vis. scholar Va. Poly. Inst., Blacksburg, 1973; guest lectr. Polish Acad. Scis., 1974; disting. vis. prof. N.Mex. State U., 1976; vis. prof. Japan Soc. Promotion of Sci., Osaka Prefecture U., 1977; guest lectr. Serbian Sci. Council, Fruit Research Inst., Cacak, Yugoslavia, 1979; agrl. research adv. com. Eli Lilly Co., Indpls., 1971—; cons. Dept. Agr. Pres. Okemos (Mich.) Music Patrons, 1973-74. Served to 1st lt., AUS, 1951-53. Recipient Joseph Harvey Gourley award, 1969, 76, citation for meritorious research Am. Hort. Soc., 1970, Disting. Faculty award Mich. State U., 1971, Disting. Service award Mich. Hort. Soc., 1974, M.A. Blake award for disting. grad. teaching, 1975. Fellow Am. Soc. Hort. Sci. (Marion Meadows award 1975, citation of appreciation 1975, pres. 1974-75), AAAS; mem. Am. Soc. Plant Physiologists, Bot. Soc. Am., Scandinavian Soc. Plant Physiologists, Japanese Soc. Plant Physiologists, Internat. Soc. Hort. Sci., Soc. Exptl. Biology, Sigma Xi (research award Mich. chpt., pres. 1978-79), Phi Kappa Phi. Club: Mich. State U. Faculty. Contbr. numerous articles to sci. jours. Patentee in field. Home: 4428 Seneca Dr Okemos MI 48864 Office: Dept of Horticulture Michigan State University East Lansing MI 48824

BULKLEY, BETTY LOU COMPTON (MRS. ROY LYMAN BULKLEY), occupational therapist; b. Lawrence, Kan., July 24, 1926; d. James Howard and Florence Mildred (Lemon) Compton; B.S. in Occupational Therapy, U. Kans., 1950, M.A. in Speech Communication, 1975; m. Roy Lyman Bulkley, Oct. 22, 1949; 1 son, Timothy Howard. Occupational therapist Topeka State Hosp., 1949-52, chief occupational therapy, 1961-69, dir. activity therapy dept., 1969—; cons. Topeka Presbyn. Manor, 1970—; lectr. U. Kan. Occupational Therapy Evaluation Techniques, Lawrence, 1973. Sec., Shawnee County Republican Central Com., 1968. Mem. Kans. Occupational Therapy Assn. (pres. 1977-79), Am. Occupational Therapy Assn. (regional audit cons. 1975-77), Kans. Found. for Med. Care (vice chmn. adv. bd. 1979). Home: 3929 Dixie Ct Topeka KS 66614 Office: 2700 W 6th St Topeka KS 66606

BULL, LAWRENCE MYLES, engr.; b. Aliquippa, Pa., Feb. 20, 1931; s. Thomas Leslie and Gertrude Margaret (Miller) B.; B.S.E.E., Ind. Inst. Tech., 1955; m. Emily Jane Antal, June 7, 1958; children—L. Michael, Louis A., Laura A., James C. Transmission corrosion engr. Manufactures Light & Heat Co., Pitts., 1955-64; corrosion engr. Columbia Gas System-Pitts. Group Co., Pitts., 1964-68; project engr. Columbia Gas Systems Service Corp., Marble Cliff, Ohio, 1968-73; mgr. corrosion and leakage control Columbia Gas Distbn. Cos., Columbus, Ohio, 1973—. Served with U.S. Navy, 1948-52. Mem. ASME, ASTM, Nat. Assn. Corrosion Engrs., Nat., Ohio socs. profl. engrs. Republican. Roman Catholic. Clubs: Brookside Civic Assn., Northington Athletic Assn. Home: 6666 McVey Blvd Worthington OH 43085 Office: 99 N Front St Columbus OH 43215

BULL, RICHARD SUTTON, JR., paper co. exec., lawyer; b. Chgo., Jan. 21, 1926; s. Richard Sutton and Sara Rozet (Smith) B.; B.A., Yale U., 1948, J.D., 1951; LL.M., N.Y.U., 1952; m. Lois Karna Werme, July 19, 1950; children—Lois Karna Bull Bouton, Sara Annette Bull Greene, Richard S., Harry Calvin, Mary Ellen Frantz Bull. Instr. econs. Stone Coll., New Haven, 1950-51; admitted to Ill. bar, 1953; atty. Swift & Co., Chgo., 1952-57; with Bradner Central Co., and predecessor, Chgo., 1957—, pres., 1965—, chmn. bd., 1966—; treas., dir. Clearview Farms, 1957—; dir. 1st Security Bank Chgo., 1976—. Bd. dirs. Safer Found., Chgo., 1979—; bd. dirs., vice chmn. Goodwill Industries, Chgo., 1977—; bd. dirs., v.p. Civic and Arts Found., Chgo., 1977—. Served with USNR, 1943-46. Food, Drug and Cosmetic Law Inst. fellow, 1951-52. Mem. Am. Arbitration Assn. (nat. panel arbitrators 1968—), Chgo. Assn. Commerce and Industry (dir. 1973—, sec. 1980—), Paper Converters' Assn., Paper Club Chgo. (past pres., dir.), Chgo. Bar Assn., Chgo. Chpt. Pres.' Assn., Newcomen Soc. Clubs: Econ., Execs.', Chgo., Union League, Chgo. Press, Yale (dir. Chgo. chpt. 1978—), Khyble Bay Yacht (past commodore and mem. bd. govs.), Ruth Lake Country. Home: 4 Countryside Ct Hinsdale IL 60521 Office: Bradner Central 333 S Desplaines St Chicago IL 60606

BULL, ROBERT KEITH, soil scientist; b. Eckert, Colo., Mar. 10, 1927; s. Ernest Atwood and Dorothy (Nelson) B.; B.S. in Agronomy, Colo. State U., 1951, postgrad. in soil sci., 1960; M.S. in Agrl. Econs., N.Mex. State U., 1971; m. Fern Eileen Quiggle, July 21, 1962; children—Karin Elisabeth, Gretchen Louise, Lisa Irene. Soil scientist Soil Conservation Service, U.S., 1951-53; with Morrison Knudsen, Afghanistan, 1953-56, Tams, Iraq, 1956-58; soil scientist Bur. Reclamation, Dept. Interior, 1960-62, Internat. Engring. Co., Bangladesh, 1962-65, Ralph M. Parsons, Saudi Arabia, 1965-67, Internat. Engring. Co., Peru, 1967-69; with Harza Engring. Co., 1971—, Guatemala, Jamaica, Dominican Republic, Haiti, Guyana, Venezuela, Colombia, Honduras, Iran, Thailand, Senegal, Pakistan. Served with U.S. Army, 1945-47. Mem. Am. Soc. Agronomy, Soil Sci. Soc. Am. Home: 1325 E Sanborn Dr Palatine IL 60067 Office: Harza Engring Co 150 S Wacker Dr Chicago IL 60606

BULLARD, MERYL AUDREY, occupational therapist; b. Chgo., Apr. 12, 1933; d. Melville Allan and Helen (Logsdon) Snyder; B.S., U. Wis., Madison, 1955, O.T.R., 1956; postgrad. Drake U., 1979—; children—Linda, Michael, Steven, Alison. Dir. occupational therapy Burlington (Iowa) Med. Center, 1966-74; cons. occupational therapist, Spencer, Iowa, 1975-76; dir. partial hosp. program NW Iowa Mental Health Center, Spencer, 1976-78; cons. Iowa Health Dept., Des Moines, 1978-79; dir. occupational therapy Broadlawns Med. Center, Des Moines, 1980—; chief occupational therapy VA Med. Center, Knoxville, Iowa, 1981—; cons. VA. Bd. dirs. Polk County Public Health Nursing, Des Moines, 1980—. Pres. bd. dirs. Clay County Assn. Retarded Citizens, 1975-79; founder Pre-Sch. for Handicapped, Spencer, Iowa, 1976; bd. dirs. Sunshine Workers, Inc., 1975-79; mem. adv. com. Iowa Found. Med. Care, 1979—. Mem. Iowa Occupational Therapy Assn. (chmn. com. on practice, 1978—), Am. Occupational Therapy Assn., Pi Beta Phi. Congregationalist. Home: 517 NW 9th St Ankeny IA 50021 Office: Broadlawns Med Center 18th and Hickman Sts Des Moines IA 50314

BULLARD, THOMAS ROBERT, retail book exec.; b. Chgo., May 6, 1944; s. Henry M. and Ethel (Munday) B.; B.S., Ill. Inst. Tech., 1966; M.A., Northwestern U., 1968; Ph.D., U. Ill. at Chgo. Circle, 1973. Teaching asst. history U. Ill. at Chgo. Circle, 1969-73; head nautical dept. Owen Davies, bookseller, Chgo., 1973-80, owner, Oak Park, Ill., 1980—; instr. history Sch. Art Inst. Chgo., 1975-77; cons. in field. Nat. Merit scholar, 1961-62, Hon. Ill. State scholar, 1962. Mem. Am. Hist. Assn., Orgn. Am. Historians, U.S. Naval Inst., Internat. Naval Research Orgn., Navy Records Soc. (U.K.), Central Electric Railfans Assn., Electric Railroaders Assn., Chgo., Aurora & Elgin Electric Ry. Hist. Soc., Nat. Ry. Hist. Soc., Ry. and Locomotive Hist. Soc. (dir. Chgo. chpt.). Mem. United Ch. Christ. Home: 228 N Lombard Ave Oak Park IL 60302 Office: Owen Davies Bookseller 200 W Harrison St Oak Park IL 60304

BULLARD, WADE ARTHUR, JR., corp. exec.; b. Wilmington, N.C., Jan. 23, 1931; s. Wade Arthur and Mildred (Anderson) B.; student Columbus U. (Washington), 1949-51; B.B.A., U. Mich., 1957; children—Linda Kay, Cynthia Ann. Pres. gen. mgr. Patterson's, Sturgis, Mich., 1957—, also dir.; v.p., dir. Clark Plastic Engring. Co., Sturgis, 1967-73; pres. dir. Plastek Co., 1968—, Colonial Motor Inn, Inc., 1964-76, Wade Bullard, Inc. chmn. bd. Aronco Plastics, Inc., 1974-75. (all Sturgis), 1969-77. Mem. Sturgis Bd. Zoning Appeals, 1967-77; Sturgis city commr., 1975-77; dir. Bd. Pub. Works, St. Joseph County, 1976-77; pres. Klinger Lake Assn., Sturgis, 1969-71; pres., dir. Sturgis Improvement Assn., 1966—, Sturgis Econ. Devel. Corp., 1978—. Served with CIC, AUS, 1951-54; Korea. Decorated Bronze Star medal, UN Service medal, Nat. Def. Service medal. Episcopalian. Elk. Club: Klinger Lake Country (Sturgis). Home: Klinger Lake Sturgis MI 49091 Office: 1106 W Chicago St Sturgis MI 49091

BULLEN, W(ILLIAM) DEAN, civil engr.; b. Mason, Mich., May 28, 1924; s. Ray L. and Beulah (Dean) B.; B.S. in Civil Engring., Mich. Tech. U., Houghton, 1949. With design div. Bur. Hwys., Mich. Dept. Transp., Lansing, 1949—, design squad leader, 1956-61, spl. assignment engr. structures, 1961—; mem. com. on repair of damaged steel bridges Hwy. Research Bd., 1976—. Treas. St. Augustine of Canterbury Episcopal Ch., Mason, 1964—. Served with U.S. Army, 1942-46. Registered profl. engr., Mich. Mem. ASCE, Nat. Soc. Profl. Engrs. Author: Michigan Bridge Analysis Guide, 1972. Home: 500 VanderVeen Dr Mason MI 48854

BULLER, ALLAN RAY, food co. exec.; b. Morse, Sask., Can., Dec. 2, 1917; came to U.S., 1924; s. Jacob H. and Stella G. (Loewen) B.; B.A., Andrews U., 1941; M.B.A., Ohio State U., 1952; m. Mildred E. Walberg, Sept. 6, 1942; children—Calol E., Janice D., Suzanne E., Allan G. Asst. mgr. Worthington Foods (Ohio), 1946-48, gen. mgr., sec.-treas., 1948-69; exec. v.p. Worthington Food div. Miles Lab., Worthington, 1970—. Trustee, Harding Hosp., 1950—, Andrews U., 1972-76. Served with M.C., U.S. Army, 1941-45. Mem. Am. Mgmt. Assn., Worthington C. of C. (pres. 1960), Worthington Bus. and Profl. Men's Assn. (pres. 1954). Club: Rotary. Office: Worthington Food div Miles Lab 900 Proprietors Rd Worthington OH 43085

BULLMER, KENNETH, psychologist; b. St. Louis, Sept. 14, 1923; s. George and Mildred Bullmer; B.S. in Bus. Adminstrn., Washington U., St. Louis, 1949; A.M., U. Mich., 1967; Ed.D., Ind. U., 1970; m. Carole Marie Hartnett, Jan. 1, 1975; children—Casey, Victoria, Elizabeth, Christina. Dir. admissions Montecello Coll., Godfrey, Ill., 1960-62, Franklin (Ind.) Coll., 1962-64; admissions officer Flint Coll., U. Mich., 1964-67; participant NDEA Inst., Ind. U., 1967-68, counselor counseling and psychol. services, 1968-69, research asso. Inst. Sex Research, 1969-70; asso. prof. psychology Western Mich. U., Kalamazoo, 1970—; pvt. practice psychol. counseling, 1970—; dir. Portage Community Outreach Center, 1978—. Served with AUS, 1943-46; PTO. Decorated Bronze Star. Mem. Am. Psychol. Assn., Am. Soc. Clin. Hypnosis, Am. Assn. Sex Educators, Counselors and Therapists, Mich. Psychol. Assn., Western Mich. Psychol. Assn., Internat. Soc. Hypnosis, Am. Personnel and Guidance Assn., Assn. Counselor Edn. and Supervision. Author: The Art of Empathy, 1975, Empathie, 1978. Home: 6738 Rothbury St Portage MI 49002 Office: 3109 Sangren Hall Western Mich Univ Kalamazoo MI 49008

BULLOCK, JOHN DAVID, ophthalmic surgeon; b. Cin., July 31, 1943; s. Joseph Craven and Emilie Helen (Woide) B.; A.B., Dartmouth Coll., 1965, B.Med. Sci., 1966; M.D., Harvard U., 1968; postgrad. Armed Forces Inst. Pathology, 1970; m. Gretchen Hageman, June 25, 1966; children—John David, Katherine Ann, Richard Joseph. Intern, asst. in medicine Washington U., St. Louis, 1968-69; resident in ophthalmology and plastic surgery Yale U., 1971-74; clin. instr. ophthalmology, 1974; Heed fellow U. Calif., San Francisco, 1974-75; Orbital fellow Mayo Clinic, Rochester, Minn., 1975; clin. instr. ophthalmology Stanford (Calif.) U., 1974-75; practice medicine specializing in ophthalmic surgery, Dayton, Ohio; mem. staff Miami Valley Hosp., Children's Med. Center, Kettering Med. Center, St. Elizabeth Hosp., Good Samaritan Hosp. Trustee, Children's Med. Center, Dayton, 1977-80. Diplomate Am. Bd. Ophthalmology (bd. examiner 1979—). Mem. Am. Assn. Ophthalmology, Am. Acad. Ophthalmology, A.C.S., AMA, Am. Coll. Cryosurgery, Am. Soc. Ophthalmic Plastic and Reconstructive Surgery, Am. Assn. Pediatric Ophthalmology and Strabismus, Assn. for Research Vision and Ophthalmology, Keratorefractive Soc., Am. Soc. Ophthalmic Ultrasound, Am. Intraocular Implant Soc., Orbit Soc., Am. Acad. Facial Plastic and Reconstructive Surgery, Internat. Soc. for Orbital Disorders, Castroviejo Soc., Frank Walsh Soc., Soc. Heed Fellows, Theobald Soc. Clubs: Dayton Country, Bicycle. Contbr. articles to profl. jours. Home: 1155 Ridgeway Rd Dayton OH 45419 Office: 33 W 1st St Suite 590 Dayton OH 45402

BULLOCK, JOHN MCDONELL, bank exec.; b. Cin., June 21, 1932; s. John R. and Marion M. B.; student U. Ky., 1950-51; B.A. in Polit. Sci., U. Mich., 1954; J.D., U. Va., 1959; m. Ann V.; children—Lynn A., John R., II, Amy V. Admitted to Ohio bar, 1959; asso. firm. Taft, Stettinus & Hollister, Cin., 1959-67, partner, 1967-69; sr. v.p. First Nat. Bank Cin., 1969—; dir. Clopay Corp., U.S. Precision Lens, Inc. Trustee, Community Chest and Council of Cin. Area, 1973—, Coll. Mt. St. Joseph, 1978—. Clubs: Ryland Lakes Country, Queen City, Gyro. Office: First Nat Bank Cin PO Box 1118 Cincinnati OH 45201

BULTEMEIER, LARRY WAYNE, sales and mktg. exec.; b. Decatur, Ind., Feb. 28, 1942; s. Clarence and Irene (Buuck) B.; student Ind. Inst. Tech., 1960-61; m. Janice H. Franz, Aug. 26, 1976; children—Marci Rae, Brett Wayne. With Adams Builders Supply, 1962-70, v.p., 1963-74; pres. All Am. Homes, Inc., Decatur, Ind., 1970—. Bd. elders Zion Luth. Ch., 1979-80. Served with USAR, 1963. Mem. Nat. Assn. Home Mfrs. (dir.), Nat. Assn. Home Mfrs. Clubs: Optimist; Otters Swim (pres. 1980-81) (Decatur, Ind.). Home: Rural Route 2 Decatur IN 46733 Office: 309 S 13th St Decatur IN 46733

BUMAGIN, VICTORIA EDITH WEROSUB, social services exec.; b. Free City of Danzig, June 20, 1923; d. Isaac A. and Zinaida (Towbin) Werosub; came to U.S., 1938, naturalized, 1941; B.A., City U. N.Y., 1945; M.S. Social Work, Columbia U., 1969; postgrad. U. Chgo., 1974—; m. Victor I. Bumagin, Mar. 16, 1946; children—Louisa, Susan, Elizabeth, Deborah, Jennifer. Caseworker to intake supr. to case supr. N.J. Bur. Children's Services, 1962-69; sr. social worker Dept. Social Services, Berkshire, Eng., 1970-73; dir. social services Council for Jewish Elderly, Chgo., 1974—; instr. Loyola U., Chgo.; instr. Summer Inst., U. Chgo., univ. sr. clin. asso.; mem. Task Force on Age Discrimination; manifesto for Brit. Nat. Conf. on Aging, 1971-73; mem. tech. adv. com. Protective Service to Aged, 1977—; spl. advisor White House Conf. on Aging, 1981. Mem. Soc. for Life Cycle Psychology, Nat., Brit. (sec., v.p.) assns. social workers, Columbia U. Sch. Social Work Alumni Assn. (dir.), Gerontol. Soc., Acad. Certified Social Workers, Registry Clin. Social Workers. Author: The Appliance Cookbook, 1971; co-author: Aging Is a Family Affair, 1979; also articles in profl. jours. Home: 435 Lake Ave Wilmette IL 60091 Office: 1015 W Howard St Evanston IL 60202

BUMP, MILO SHANNON, info. systems cons.; b. Topeka, Kans., Oct. 26, 1922; s. Wilson Raymond and Pearle Julia (Pickering) B.; m. Reba Mae McCaleb, July 19, 1974; 1 son, Shannon Kevin. Parts and material handler Boeing Airplane Co., Wichita, Kans., 1942-47, expediter, 1947-52, sr. supr., exptl. prodn. control, 1952-55, programmer, analyst, 1955-60; systems analyst Martin-Marietta Co., Denver, 1960-62; mgr. engring. systems Gen. Electric Co., Huntsville, Ala., 1962-66, internal cons. systems, Phoenix, 1967-69; sr. cons. Computer Scis. Corp., St. Louis, Chgo. and London, 1969-71; dir. info. systems Du Quoin Packing Co. (Ill.), 1971-80; cons. info. systems, 1980—. Served with USAAF, 1942-45; ETO. Mem. St. Louis Honeywell Users Group (past treas.). Home: 207 S 3d St Elkville IL 62932 Office: PO Box 306 Elkville IL 62932

BUMP, WILBUR NEIL, lawyer; b. Peoria, Ill., July 12, 1929; s. Wilbur Earl and Mae (Nelson) B.; B.S., State U. Iowa, 1951, J.D., 1958; m. Elaine Bonneval, Nov. 24, 1951; children—William Earl, Jeffrey Neil, Steven Bonneval. Admitted to Iowa bar, 1958; solicitor gen. Iowa Atty. Gen. Office, Des Moines, 1961-64; practiced in Des Moines, 1964—; gen. counsel agrl. industries. Served with USAF, 1951-54. Mem. Am., Iowa (bd. govs. 1976-81), Polk County (pres. 1976-77) bar assns. Club: Kiwanis (pres. 1974-75). Presbyterian (elder). Home: Route 2 Winterset IA 50273 Office: 2 Corporate Pl 1501 42d St West Des Moines IA 50265

BUMPUS, CHARLES PHILIP, pharmacist; b. Clarksville, Tenn., July 31, 1940; s. Estol Ray and Mildred Drusilla (Clendennin) B.; B.A., Asbury (Ky.) Coll., 1962; B.S., U. Ga., 1967; m. Dianne Marie Hage, June 21, 1963; 1 dau., Joanna Dianne. Tchr., Bell High Sch., Hurst, Tex., 1963-64; instr. NSF summer inst. Asbury Coll., 1964; mem. pharmacy staff Athens (Ga.) Gen. Hosp., 1964-66; staff pharmacist Obici Meml. Hosp., Suffolk, Va., 1966-69; dir. pharmacy Hammond-Henry Dist. Hosp., Geneseo, Ill., 1969-73; dir. pharmacy Meml. Hosp., Carthage, Ill., 1973—; instr. pharmacology Carl Sandburg Jr. Coll., Carthage; cons. to nursing homes; high sch. and college football and basketball ofcl. Mem. Am. Soc. Hosp. Pharmacists, Am. Pharm. Assn., Am. Assn. Intravenous Therapy, Ill. Council Hosp. Pharmacists, Spoon River Hosp. Pharmacists Assn. Club: Carthage Kiwanis (dir. 1978-79). Home: 1100 E Wabash Ave

Carthage IL 62321 Office: Memorial Hosp S Adams St Carthage IL 62321

BUNCH, GARY LYNN, supply co. ofcl.; b. Benton Harbor, Mich., Jan. 18, 1950; s. Cecil R.L. and Addie Marie (Powell) B.; A.A.S., Ferris State Coll., Big Rapids, Mich., 1970, B. in Trade Teaching, 1972; m. Vickie Lee Newell, Aug. 31, 1968; children—Scott, Jeremy, Dana. Mechanic, Bunch's Garage, 1964-72; instr. auto mechanics Benton Harbor High Sch., 1971-72, Dowagiac (Mich.) Union High Sch., 1972-73, Southwestern Mich. Coll., Dowagiac, 1972-73; tng. mgr. Whayne Supply Co., Louisville, 1973—; chmn. Ky. Adv. Com. for Staff/Industry Exchange; mem. 10 vocat. sch. adv. coms. Recipient Disting. Service awards for work in Ky. vocat. edn., 1978, numerous recognition awards, 1974-79. Mem. Am. Soc. Tng. and Devel. Mem. Christian Ch. (elder). Home: 304 Biggs Rd Memphis IN 47143 Office: 1400 S 43d St Louisville KY 40211

BUNGE, JOHN ARTHUR, market research co. exec.; b. Elgin, Ill., Mar. 14, 1941; s. Arthur August and Gracia Vinina (Webster) B.; B.S. in Mktg. Mgmt., Northwestern U., 1963; m. Barbara Jean Nall, Aug. 28, 1972; 1 son, Jason Todd. Research analyst Ben Franklin div. City Products Corp., Des Plaines, Ill., 1965-68; mgr. mktg. services Cargill, Wilson & Acree, Richmond, Va., 1968-70; dir. mktg. services Glenn Advt., Dallas, 1970-72; v.p. Message Factors, Inc., Dallas, 1972-74, Atlanta, 1974-75; sr. project dir. Britt and Frerichs, Inc., Chgo., 1975-76, br. mgr. and sr. project dir., Denver, 1976, gen. mgr., Chgo., 1977-78; partner Britt Mktg., Evanston, Ill., 1978-79; pres. Legal Mktg. Research, Inc., Evanston, 1979—; speaker at assn. meetings, seminars. Served with USN, 1963-65. Mem. Am. Mktg. Assn., Mktg. Research Assn., United Comml. Travelers Am. Home and office: 1606 Central St Evanston IL 60201

BUNGE, ROBERT PIERCE, educator; b. Oak Park, Ill., Sept. 24, 1930; s. George Herbert and Caroline Elizabeth (Pierce) B.; M.A., Roosevelt U., 1973; Ph.D., DePaul U., 1975; m. Muriel Perlman, Mar. 17, 1956; step-children—Harmon Berns, Hilary Berns. Tchr. adult evening sch. Maine Twp., Park Ridge, Ill., 1962-74; with Bunge Movers, Evanston, Ill., 1968-72; lectr. Roosevelt U., Chgo., 1971, 73, 75, 77, DePaul U., Chgo., 1974-79; prof. Lakota (Sioux Indian lang.), U. S.D., Vermillion, 1979—; cons. in Indian culture States of S.D., Iowa and Nebr.; ct. interpreter for Lakota lang. Lectr., women's groups, bus. groups; commencement speaker N. Shore Country Day Sch., Winnetka, Ill., 1974. Served with AUS, 1952-54; PTO. Mem. Internat. Platform Assn., Am. Philos. Assn., Theosophical Soc. Author: Sioux Language Phrase Book, 1976. Contbr. articles to profl. jours. Home: 6 Cherrywood Ct Vermillion SD 57069 Office: Dept Modern Langs U SD Vermillion SD 57069

BUNGUM, JOHN LEWIS, economist; b. Kasson, Minn., Dec. 17, 1942; s. Gustav Norman and Elsie Charlotte (Throndson) B.; B.A., Luther Coll., Decorah, Iowa, 1963; M.A. (univ. scholar 1968-69), U. Iowa, 1969; Ph.D. (univ. fellow 1974-76), U. Nebr., 1977; m. Lorna Jean Thiesen, Aug. 13, 1977; children—John Lewis II, Bethany Lorna. From instr. to asso. prof. econs. U. Wis., Platteville, 1969-79; asso. prof. econs. Gustavus Adolphus Coll., St. Peter, Minn., 1979—; instr. U. Wis. Liberal Arts Center, Copenhagen, 1973. Served with USAR, 1964-67; Vietnam. Govt. of Norway scholar, summer 1963. Mem. Am. Econ. Assn., AAUP, Midwest Econ. Assn., Western Econ. Assn., Atlantic Econ. Assn., Minn. Econ. Assn., Mo. Valley Econ. Assn., Atlantic Econ. Assn. Lutheran. Contbr. articles to profl. jours. Home: 841 Church St Saint Peter MN 56082 Office: Dept Econs Gustavus Adolphus Coll Saint Peter MN 56082

BUNT, JAY BROWNLEE, consumer products mfg. co. exec.; b. Paterson, N.J., Sept. 16, 1938; s. James Thomas and Irene (Brownlee) B.; B.A., Monmouth Coll., 1961; m. Barbara Ann Fedor, June 29, 1963; children—James Thomas III (dec.), Michele Ann, Shawn Joseph. Order and traffic man Procter & Gamble, Trenton, N.J., 1963-65, credit man, 1965, adminstrv. asst. Mil. Sales Dept., 1966-72, div. asst. Paper Sales Div., Cin., 1973-79, sales asst. to nat. sales mgr., 1979—. Precinct exec. Republican Party, Hamilton County, Ohio, 1970—; charter mem. Citizens Com. for Community Devel., Forest Park, Ohio, 1974-78, chmn., 1976-78; leader Boy Scouts Am., 1975—; chmn. Com. to Conduct City Census, Forest Park, 1978, Forest Park 2000, 1978; com. mem. Recreation Civic Center, Forest Park, 1978; chmn. com. for sch. issues Greenhills-Forest Park Sch. Dist., 1980—. Served with U.S. Army, 1961-63. Recipient Letters of Appreciation, Forest Park City Council, 1976, 79. Episcopalian. Club: Forest Park Soccer (dir. 1980—). Home: 1415 Kelvin Ct Cincinnati OH 45240 Office: Paper Sales 4C PO Box 599 Cincinnati OH 45201

BUNTE, FREDERICK JOSEPH, univ. pres.; b. Columbus, Ohio, Dec. 19, 1937; s. Fred Joseph and Margaret Louise (Murday) B.; m. Judith Schueneman, June 27, 1964; children—Susan, Rebecca. B.S., Ohio State U., 1959, M.A., 1964, Ph.D., 1972; A.S.B.A., Franklin U., 1974. Chmn., tchr. social studies Upper Arlington Sr. High Sch., Columbus, Ohio, 1959-65; instr. sociology Franklin U., Columbus, 1965-72, prof., chmn. div. social and behavioral sci., 1972-74, dean Gen. Coll., 1974-78, dean acad. affairs, 1975-78, pres., 1978—. Edn. chmn. Clintonville-Beechwold (Ohio) Human Relations Council, 1972-73. Mem. Am. Sociol. Assn., Am. Assn. for Higher Edn., Am. Acad. Polit. and Social Sci., Nat. Council on Family Relations, Newcomen Soc. N. Am. Clubs: Kiwanis, Metropolitan, Torch, Executives, University, Faculty (Ohio State U.). Home: 287 Frontenac Pl Worthington OH 43085 Office: 201 S Grant Ave Columbus OH 43215

BURACK, ELMER HOWARD, educator; b. Chgo., Oct. 21, 1927; s. Charles and Rose (Taerbaum) B.; B.S., U. Ill., 1950; M.S., Ill. Inst. Tech., 1956; Ph.D., Northwestern U., 1964; m. Ruth Goldsmith, Mar. 18, 1930; children—Charles Michael, Robert, Alan Jeffrey. Prodn. supt. Richardson Co., Melrose Park, Ill., 1953-55; prodn. control mgr. Fed. Tool Corp., Lincolnwood, Ill., 1955-59; mgmt. cons. Booz, Allen & Hamilton, Chgo., 1959-60; mem. faculty Ill. Inst. Tech., 1960-78, prof. mgmt., 1978; prof. mgmt., head dept. U. Ill., Chgo. Circle, 1978—; mem. Gov. Ill. Adv. Council Employment and Tng., 1976—, vice chmn., 1978—. Served with USAAF, 1945-47. Research grantee Dept. Labor, 1965-68. Mem. Nat. Acad. Mgmt. (chmn. personnel div., health div. 1976-77), Ill. Mgmt. Tng. Inst. (pres. 1975-77), Indsl. Relations Assn. Chgo. (pres. 1974-75), Am. Soc. Personnel Adminstrn., Personnel Accreditation Inst. (dir.). Club: B'nai B'rith. Author: Manpower Planning, 1972; Personnel Management, 1977; Human Resource Planning, 2 vols., 1980; Growing Careers for Women, 1980. Office: Box 4348 Chicago IL 60680

BURBES, RICHARD H., grocers assn. exec.; b. Allentown, Pa., July 26, 1948; s. Henry L. and Mary R. (Keglovitz) B.; B.S., Pa. State U., 1970; m. Cynthia A. Malouf; 1 dau., Jennifer Lynn. Asst. mgr. Walgreens, Northbrook, Ill., 1970-72, Ponderosa Systems, Chgo., 1972-73; buyer Topco Assos., Skokie, Ill., 1973-77; procurement mgr. IGA, Inc., Chgo., 1977-80; product supr. Shurfine Central Corp., Northlake, Ill., 1980—. Home: 6032 Kit Carson Dr Hanover Park IL 60103 Office: IGA Inc 5725 E River Rd Chicago IL 60631

BURCH, HAROLD DEE, educator; b. Vernon County, Mo., Sept. 9, 1928; s. Harry A. and Florence L. (Coonrod) B.; student Fort Scott (Kans.) Jr. Coll., 1947; B.Music Edn., Pittsburg (Kans.) State U., 1950; M.Music Edn., U. Kans., 1964, Ed.D., 1974; m. Dolores Elaine Reilley, Dec. 20, 1958; children—Stephanie Dee, Angela Kay. Music dir. elem. and secondary public schs., Kans., 1950-66; instr. dept. fine arts Kellogg Community Coll., Battle Creek, Mich., 1966-68; mem. faculty curriculum and instrn. dept. Mankato (Minn.) State U., 1969—, prof., 1979—, co-dir. Center for Personal Devel. in Teaching, 1978—. Faculty research grantee, Mankato U., 1972, 78, 82. Asst. dir., Project HEED (usoe grant project), 1974-77. Mem. Assn. of Tchr. Educators, Assn. for Supervision and Curriculum Devel., Minn. Council on Quality Edn., Minn. Assn. Tchr. Educators (past pres.). Contbg. author: (curriculum handbook) Humanizing Environment and Educational Development, 1975; contbr. articles on edn. to profl. publs. Home: 120 Rita Rd Mankato MN 56001 Office: PO Box 52 Mankato State Univ Mankato MN 56001

BURCH, HOBART ALEXANDER, social worker; b. Appleton, Wis., July 29, 1932; s. Hobart Alexander and Margaret Leone (Marshall) B.; A.B., Princeton U., 1953; M.Div., Union Theol. Sem., N.Y.C., 1956; M.S. in Social Work, Columbia U., 1956; Ph.D. (NIMH fellow 1962-64), Brandeis U., Waltham, Mass., 1965; m. Genevieve Walters, Aug. 29, 1953; children—Juanita, David, Peter. Ordained to ministry United Ch. Christ, 1956; dir. social service dept. Buffalo Council Chs., 1958-62; spl. asst. to manpower adminstr. Dept. Labor, 1964-65; asst. to commr. welfare HEW, 1965-67, dep. chief Office Program Liaison, NIMH, 1967-69; gen. sec. div. health and welfare United Ch. Bd. Homeland Ministries, N.Y.C., 1969-74; exec. dir. Nat. Social Welfare Assembly, N.Y.C., 1974-76; prof., dir. Sch. Social Work, U. Nebr., Omaha, 1976—. Recipient Merit award Dept. Labor, 1965. Mem. Nat. Assn. Social Workers, Council Social Work Edn. Democrat. Clubs: Cosmos (Washington); Princeton (N.Y.C.). Home: 3315 Paddock Rd Omaha NE 68124 Office: Univ Nebr Omaha NE 68182

BURCH, JAMES HENRY, graphic designer; b. Ashtabula, Ohio, Aug. 2, 1938; s. Reed Holtz and Agnes Belle (Shank) B.; student U. Dayton, 1957-59, Miami U., Oxford, Ohio, 1972-78; B.F.A., Dayton Art Inst., 1975; m. Darlene Hazel Samuelson, May 10, 1959; children—Kandy, Lisa, Reed. Advt. artist, designer NCR Corp., Dayton, Ohio, 1961-68; art dir., account rep. Brown & Kroger Pub. Co., Dayton, 1968-70; graphics supr., art dir. Miami U., 1970—; owner, operator James Burch and Assos., Oxford, 1976—. Bd. dirs. Miami U. Fed. Employees Credit Union, 1979—, chmn. fin. and property com., 1979; bd. dirs. Wesley Found. at Miami U., 1976—, treas., 1978-79. Served with USAF, 1956-60. Recipient award of merit for design, silver and bronze award Univ. and Coll. Designers Regional Design Competition, 1977; 1st place award for design of direct mail campaign Dayton Advt. Club, 1968. Mem. Indsl. Graphics Internat. (dir., pres. 1979, award for design excellence, best of show trophy in poster design category), Univ. and Coll. Designers Assn., Graphic Artists Guild. Methodist. Clubs: Art Dirs. (Cin.); Oxford Arts (past pres.). Home: 550 S Main St Oxford OH 45056

BURCHELL, EDWARD V., mfg. co. exec.; b. Chgo., Dec. 26, 1939; s. Edward O. and Marjorie F. (Hathaway) B.; B.A., Hamline U., 1961; m. Mary G. Cossack, Dec. 2, 1961; children—Laurie Ann, Edward R., Susan M. Marketing specialist 3M Co., St. Paul, Minn., 1961-63, sales rep., Louisville, 1963-66, sales rep. converter trades-new products, Cin., 1966-68; mktg./sales specialist Conwed Corp., St. Paul, Minn., 1968-75, sales mgr., 1975-79, mktg. mgr., 1979-81; v.p. Internet, Inc., Mpls., 1981—. Basketball and baseball coach Community Youth Program, 1972-77. Named Outstanding Converter-New Product Salesman, 3M Co., 1967, Outstanding Salesman plastics div. Conwed Corp., 1973, Outstanding Mktg. Contbr., Conwed Corp., 1976. Republican. Methodist. Patentee in field. Office: 770 29th Ave SE Minneapolis MN 55414

BURCHINAL, ALBERT WILLIAM, social work dir.; b. Connellsville, Pa., Oct. 6, 1920; s. John Henry and Anna Eliza (Gaster) B.; B.S. in Econs., Thiel Coll., 1952; M.S.W., U. Pitts., 1954, M.P.H., 1961; m. Katharina Berta Lutz, Nov. 10, 1948; children—John Robert, James Albert, Charles Stephen, William Leighton, David Lutz. Dir. family service dept. Luth. Community Services, Springfield, Ohio, 1954-60; med. social work research asso., birth defects clin. study center Children's Hosp., Columbus, Ohio, 1961-63; instr. Ohio State U. Sch. Social Work, Columbus, 1963-64; research dir. United Community Council, Columbus, 1964-68; project dir. div. adminstrn. on aging Ohio Dept. Mental Hygiene and Corrections, Columbus, 1968-69; coordinator mental retardation services Richland County Mental Health and Mental Retardation Bd., Mansfield, Ohio, 1969-70; dir. social services Mt. Vernon (Ohio) Devel. Center, 1970—; mem. central humanization com. Ohio Dept. Mental Health and Mental Retardation, 1973-75, inst. advocate; Mem. tech. advisory com. Franklin County Regional Planning Commn., 1965-69; mem. Mid-Ohio Health Planning Fedn., 1971—; mem. Columbus Met. Census Tract Com., 1964-69, Knox County Health Planning Adv. Com., 1971—, Knox County Mental Health Assn., 1971—, Knox County Assn. for Retarded Citizens, 1971—; life mem. Parents and Friends Vol. Assn. Mt. Vernon Devel. Center, program chmn., 1972—; mem. program and facilities coms. Columbus Met. Area Community Action Orgn., 1965-66; active Boy Scouts Am.; mem. Clark County com. Gov.'s Commn. on Aging, 1960; mem. Citizens' Advisory Com. Knox County Regional Planning Commn., 1973—, vice chmn., 1976—. Trustee Clark County Mental Health Assn., Planned Parenthood Clinic, Springfield. Served with U.S. Army, 1945-47. Mem. Nat. Assn. Social Workers (register of clin. social workers, state com. Ohio chpt., exec. com., charter, chpt. chmn. med. and health services council 1963—, chpt. treas. 1968-69), Am. Assn. Social Workers, Am. Assn. Med. Social Workers, Acad. Certified Social Workers, Ohio Assn. for Children with Learning Disabilities, Performing Arts for Exceptional Children, Ohio Citizens Council, Ohio State Social Workers Assn., Knox County Community Services Roundtable (1st v.p., treas.), ARC (Knox County chpt.), Am. Legion (post comdr. 1979-80), Am. Assn. Sex Educators, Counselors and Therapists, Luth. Welfare League Cent. Ohio (mem. family service advisory com. 1967-70), Luth. Conf. Social Concern, Nat. Conf. Social Welfare (life), Am. Assn. for Mental Deficiency, Ohio Assn. for Retarded Children, Parents Vol. Assn. Apple Creek Devel. Center (life), Mt. Vernon Area C. of C., Am. Pub. Health Assn. (nat. and Ohio chpt.), Ohio Welfare Conf., Alpha Phi Omega, Club: Rotary. Lutheran (mem. Ohio dist. social service com. 1965-68). Home: 346 Illinois Ave Westerville OH 43081

BURDICK, GARY DEAN, mfg. co. exec.; b. Decatur, Ill., Apr. 22, 1952; s. Charles Dean and Corrine Ruth (Rahn) B.; B.B.A., Western Ill. U., 1974; dipl. pvt. trucking U. Wis. Extension Center, 1978, dipl. Coll. of Advanced Traffic, 1980; m. Deborah Constance Kouzes, July 27, 1974; children—Kelly Corrine, Shelby Irene. Motor corrdinator A.E. Staley Mfg. Co., Decatur, Ill., 1976-78, motor specialist, 1978-80, supr. truck services, 1980-81, supr. Decatur truck services and plantransfer dept., 1981—. Bonded weighmaster, 1976. Mem. Delta Nu Alpha, Phi Beta Lambda. Methodist. Clubs: Transp., A.E. Staley Foreman's. Home: 1855 Burning Tree Dr Decatur IL 62521 Office: 2200 E El Dorado St Decatur IL 62521

BURDICK, MARY LUELLA, hosp. exec.; b. Olean, N.Y., Sept. 22, 1929; d. Leone Leslie and Ida Florence (Tompkins) Sturtevant; student public schs.; m. Kenneth Gerald Burdick, Aug. 31, 1946; children—Ronald Leone, Ann Marie, Gerald Ralph. Bookkeeper, cashier Things Shoe Store, Lockport, N.Y., 1954-55; mgr. trainee Joanlee Dress Shop, Lockport, 1958; supr. Syncro Corp., Hicksville, Ohio, 1960-67; various positions Tribune Printing Co., Hicksville, 1969-77; seamstress, Hicksville, 1976-77; forms coordinator, print shop supr. Parkview Meml. Hosp., Fort Wayne, Ind., 1979—. Treas., Hicksville Missionary Ch., 1970-80, dir. children's group, 1974—. Home: Route 2 Box 12A Hicksville OH 43526 Office: Parkview Meml Hosp 2200 Randallia Dr Fort Wayne IN 46805

BURDICK, QUENTIN NORTHROP, U.S. senator; b. Munich, N.D., June 19, 1908; s. Usher Lloyd and Emma (Robertson) B.; B.A., U. Minn., 1931, LL.B., 1932. Admitted to N.D. bar, 1932, practiced in Fargo, 1932-58; mem. 86th Congress, N.D. at large; member U.S. Senate from N.D., 1960—. Democrat. Home: 1110 S 9th St Fargo ND 58102 Office: 451 Russell Senate Office Bldg Washington DC 20510

BURDON, WILLIAM FONTAINE, advt. agy. exec.; b. Ware, Mass., Dec. 21, 1926; s. Paul P. and Dorothy S. (Schaninger) B.; Asso. B.A., Curry Coll., Boston, 1951; m. Leonora Foronda, Sept. 10, 1954; children—Susan Lee, Linda Marie. With NBC, 1952-54; exec. v.p., creative dir. Marvin Hult & Assos., advt., Peoria, Ill., 1955-61; pres. Burdon Advt., Inc., Peoria, 1962—. Mem. adv. bd. YWCA; bd. dirs. Easter Seal Center, Central Ill. Landmark Found. Served with U.S. Army, 1945-47. Author published poetry. Home: 1827 W Sunnyview Dr Peoria IL 61614 Office: 207 Main St Peoria IL 61602

BURG, JAMES ALLEN, rancher, state legislator; b. Mitchell, S.D., Apr. 22, 1941; s. Albert Leo and Pearl Margaret (Linafelter) B.; B.S. in Agr., S.D. State U., 1963; m. Bernice Marie Kaiser, July 22, 1967; children—Jeff, Cory, Julie, Casey, Lisa. With Fed. Land Bank, Fieldman, Yankton, S.D., 1964-68; rancher, Wessington Springs, S.D., 1968—; mem. S.D. Ho. of Reps., 1974—, asst. minority leader, 1979—. Jerauld County Democratic chmn., 1972-73. Served with S.D. NG, 1963—. Fed. Land Bank scholar, 1963. Mem. S.D. Farm Bur., S.D. Farmers Union, NG Assn. Roman Catholic. Club: Wessington Springs Country. Address: Wessington Springs SD 57382*

BURG, LAWRENCE EDWARD, stock broker; b. LaPorte, Ind., Apr. 2, 1913; s. Clifford Ash and Hazel D. (Russell) B.; student bus. coll., spl. courses Northwestern U., 1946-47; m. Mary Ewing Glickauf, Jan. 10, 1942; children—Kenneth, Bruce, Louise, Mary. Salesman, Commonwealth Edison Co., Chgo., 1931-32, dist. rep., 1937-51; salesman Burg Typewriter Service, 1933, Williams & Meyer Co., 1934-35, Standard Oil Co. (Ind.), 1935-36; owner Minit-Fry Potato Co., 1951-54, pres., 1954-61; mgr. research dept., asst. sec. Wm. H. Tegtmeyer Co., 1961-65; registered rep., research cons., mut. funds specialist Woolard & Co., Chgo., 1965-79, Altorfer, Podesta, Woolard & Co., 1979-81, Stifel, Nicolaus & Co., 1981—; owner Minit Calculator; former partner St. Lawrence Chem. Products Co. Registered rep. Nat. Assn. Security Dealers. Served with AUS, 1941-45. Mem. Am. Security Council (nat. adv. bd.), Am. Contract Bridge League, Internat. Platform Assn., Am. Legion, U.S. Chess Fedn., Aerial Phenomena Research Orgn., Nat. Investigation Com. on Aerial Phenomena. Christian Scientist (1st reader 1959-62, asst. com. on publ. for Ill. 1962—). Clubs: Homewood-Flossmoor Chess, Beverly Social. Home: 820 Elder Rd Apt 214 Homewood IL 60430 Office: 135 S LaSalle St Chicago IL 60603

BURG, RAYMOND HENRY, engr.; b. Hot Springs, S.D., Dec. 17, 1931; s. Henry Albert and Irva (Crinklaw) B.; B.S.M.E., S.D. Inst. Tech., 1954; postgrad. U. Minn., 1961-67; m. Ruth Mary Bazley, Oct. 13, 1956; 1 son, Randall Thomas. Mech. engr. Black Hills Power and Light, Rapid City, S.D., 1954; sect. head Honeywell, Inc., Hopkins, Minn., 1957—. Served with USNR, 1954-57. Mem. Am. Def. Preparedness Assn. Patentee in field. Office: 600 2d St N Hopkins MN 55343

BURGE, JOHN LARRY, exec. staffing cons.; b. Mayfield, Ky., June 18, 1918; s. Edwin and Laura (Staten) B.; B.S., U. Kans., 1941; M.A., Villanova U., 1959; postgrad. in mgmt. Stanford U., 1962, U. Mich., 1977; m. Melva I. Grant, 1938; children—Sharon Gay, Penny Sue. Dir. personnel, public relations and safety Lucky Lager Brewing Co., San Francisco, 1962-66; corp. personnel mgr., dir. pub. relations and safety MJB Coffe Corp., San Francisco, 1966-69; co-owner Ulrich Personnel Agy., Palo Alto, Calif., 1969-70; personnel mgr., area public relations dir. Bechtel Power Corp., Ann Arbor, Mich., 1970-80; exec. Staffing cons. Fluor Corp., Irvine, Calif., 1981—; prof. naval sci. Villanova U., 1956-59. Airport commnr., Ann Arbor, Mich., 1975-77; mem. President's Com. on Handicapped, 1970—; coordinator Explorer Post, Boy Scouts Am. Served to comdr. USN, 1941-62. Decorated Air medal with six oak leaf clusters. Mem. Am. Soc. Personnel Adminstrn., Ann Arbor Personnel Assn. (pres. 1979-80), Navy League, C. of C. (edn. com.). Republican. Baptist. Clubs: Quiet Birdmen, K, Exchange. Middle weight Golden Gloves champion, 1937. Office: Fluor Corp 3333 Michelson Dr Irvine CA 92730

BURGE, JOHN WESLEY, JR., mgmt. cons.; b. Mobile, Ala., Sept. 11, 1932; s. John W. and Mary Jo (Guest) B.; student Centenary Coll., 1955-57, San Antonio Coll., 1958-63, UCLA, 1965; m. Shirley P. Roberts, Mar. 29, 1958; children—John W., Carol Delene, Eric W., Kurt R., Karen K. With ITT Gilfillan, Los Angeles, 1954-69; pres., gen. mgr. RANTEC, Calabasas, Calif., 1969-70; pres. electronics and space div., group v.p. govt. and def. Emerson Electric Co., St. Louis, 1970-80; pres. John W. Burge & Assos., St. Louis, 1981—; mgmt. cons.; adv. dir. Emerson Electric Co.; dir. Emerson Systems, Internat., Emerson Systems Corp.; lectr. in field. Bd. dirs. Progressive Youth Center, St. Louis, 1975-80. Served with USAF, 1950-54. Decorated Grand Cordon of Order of Al-Istiqlal of the 1st order King Hussein of Jordan, 1978. Mem. U.S. Navy League, Am. Mgmt. Assn., Am. Def. Preparedness Assn. Home: 11711 Chanticleer Ct Pensacola FL 32507 Office: 8100 W Florissant St Saint Louis MO 63136

BURGER, MARY LOUISE, psychologist, educator; b. Chgo., Nov. 3; d. Robert Stanley and Margaret Agnes (Brennan) Hirsh; B.A., Mundelein Coll.; M.Ed., Loyola U.; Ed.D. No. Ill. U., 1972; m. William Bronson Burger, Mar. 16, 1968. Tchr., Chgo. Bd. Edn., 1954-68; mem. faculty DePaul U., 1960-61, Roosevelt U., 1967-70; cons. psychologist Worthington-Hurst & Assos., Headstart Program, Chgo., 1972-74; prof. dept. early childhood edn. Northeastern Ill. U., 1968—, chmn. dept., 1968-80, chmn. faculty assembly Coll. Edn.; chmn. subcom. Chgo. region White House Conf. on Children; ednl. dir., owner Childhood Edn. Nursery and Day Care Center, Evanston, Ill.; cons. Chgo. Mayor's Office Child Care Services. Chmn. bd. dirs. Univ. Community Care Center. Mem. Assn. Childhood Edn. Internat. (past pres. Ill. and Chgo. brs., chmn. nominating com. 1980-81), Nat. Assn. Edn. Young Children, Assn. Higher Edn., NW Assn. Nursery Schs., AAUP, Phi Delta Kappa, Delta Kappa Gamma (past pres. Gamma Alpha chpt.). Club: Zonta Internat. Editor bull. and pamphlets Assn. Childhood Edn. Internat., 1975-77. Home: Fairfax Village 1 Kittery on Auburn Rolling Meadows IL 60008 Office: Northeastern Ill U 5500 N St Louis Ave Chicago IL 60025 also Childhood Edn Center 2727 Crawford St Evanston IL 60201

BURGERT, ALFRED LELAND, banker; b. Lawrence, Kans., Mar. 14, 1924; s. Alfred Leander and Myrtle Alma (Atkinson) B.; student Sterling Coll., 1942, Muskingum Coll., 1943; B.S., U. Kans., 1948, J.D., 1950; diploma Stonier Grad. Sch. Banking of Rutgers U., 1964; m. Betty Jane Koontz, Aug. 21, 1946; children—Maretta Kay, Alfred Lee, Philip Lynn. With 1st State Bank & Trust Co., Pittsburg, Kans., 1950—, exec. v.p., chief exec. officer, 1972-73, pres., chief exec. officer, 1973—, trust officer, dir., 1967—. Trustee Pittsburg YMCA, also past pres.; bd. dirs. Mid-Am. YMCA; treas., adv. trustee Mt. Carmel Hosp. Planning Com.; mem., past pres. Pittsburg Pub. Library Bd.; pres. Pittsburg State U. Endowment Assn., 1975-77. Served with AUS, 1943-46. Mem. Kans. Bankers Assn. (bank mgmt. com., past pres. trust div., past exec. com.), Pittsburg C. of C. (pres. 1971-72), Kans., Crawford County bar assns., Phi Alpha Delta. Republican. Presbyterian (elder). Clubs: Lions (pres. Pittsburg 1965-66), Crestwood Country, Kansas City, U. Kans. Chancellors. Home: 1406 S Catalpa St Pittsburg KS 66762 Office: 417 N Broadway Pittsburg KS 66762

BURGESS, JANET HELEN, art gallery dir.; b. Moline, Ill., Jan. 22, 1933; d. John Joseph and Helen Elizabeth (Johnson) B.; student Augustana Coll., Rock Island, Ill., 1950-51, U. Utah, Logan, 1951-52, Marycrest Coll., 1959-60; m. Richard Everett Guth, Aug. 25, 1951; children—John Joseph, Marshall Claude, Linnea Ann Guth Layman; m. Milan Andrew Vodick, Feb. 16, 1980. One-person shows: El Pao, Bolívar, Venezuela, 1952-62; represented in pvt. collections, U.S., Europe, S. Am.; producer, designer Playcrafters Barn Theatre, Moline, Ill., 1963-65; designer, gen. mgr. Grilk Interiors, Davenport, Iowa, 1963—; dir. Fine Arts Gallery, Davenport, 1978—; v.p. Product Handling, Inc., Davenport, 1981—. Bd. dirs. Rock Island Art Guild, 1974—, Quad Cities Arts Council, 1980—; bd. dirs. Village of East Davenport (Iowa) Assn., 1973—, pres., 1981; bd. dirs. Neighborhood Housing Services, Davenport, Davenport Area Conv. and Tourism Bur., 1981; mem. adv. bd. interior design dept. Scott Community Coll., 1975—; mem. Mayor's Com. Historic Preservation, Davenport, Iowa, 1976-77; bd. dir. retail com. Op. Clean Davenport, 1981. Mem. Gift and Decorative Accessories Assn. (nat. merit award 1969), Am. Soc. Interior Designers (asso.), Davenport C. of C., Nat. Trust Historic Preservation, Preservation Group, State Iowa Hist. Soc., Rock Island Arsenal Hist. Soc. Home: 2801 34th Ave Ct Rock Island IL 61201 Office: 2200 E 11th St Davenport IA 52803

BURGESS, WILLIAM CLAYTON, JR., banker; b. Omaha, June 21, 1946; s. William C. and Gertrude M. (Merten) B.; B.S. in Psychology, U. Nebr., Omaha, 1973; m. Sue Ellen Moran, Mar. 15, 1969; children—Jeannie, Laurie, William Clayton. Ops. officer, then personnel officer Omaha Nat. Bank, 1973-77; dir. human resources devel. Fed. Intermediate Credit Bank, Omaha, 1977-81; v.p. human resources Fed. Land Bank, Omaha, 1981—; past pres. Met. Omaha Continuing Edn. Council; mem. part-time faculty Creighton U., U. Nebr., Omaha; cons. in field. Served with USNR, 1967-68; Vietnam. Mem. Am. Soc. Tng. and Devel. (past pres. Nebr. chpt.; Disting. Service award 1979, 80, Outstanding Mem. award 1979, 80), Orgn. Devel. Network. Democrat. Roman Catholic. Office: 206 S 19th St Omaha NE 68102*

BURGESS, WILLIAM ROBERT, power plant personnel instr.; b. Quenemo, Kans., July 30, 1944; s. Merle Auther and Nola Marie (Noll) B.; Asso.Sci. cum laude, Delta Coll., 1978; children—Steven, David. Reactor operator Duane Arnold Energy Center, Palo, Iowa, 1972-76; supr. Midland (Mich.) nuclear power plant Consumers Power Co., 1976-80; plant instr. Palisades Power Plant, Consumers Power Co., Covert, Mich., 1980—. Served with USN, 1963-71. Lic. sr. reactor operator Nuclear Regulatory Commn. Republican. Methodist. Home: Route 1 Box 426 South Haven MI 49090 Office: Palisades Power Plant Consumers Power Co Route 2 Box 154 Covert MI 49090

BURGETTE, JAMES MILTON, dentist; b. Toledo, Aug. 18, 1937; s. James Martin and Louise (Milton) B.; A.B., Lincoln U., 1959; D.D.S., Howard U., 1964; m. Carolyn Harris, Aug. 24, 1963; children—Stephanie, James, Ngina. Practice dentistry, Detroit, 1967—. Sec. Wolverine Polit. Action Com., Detroit, 1971—. Mem. Detroit Pub. Sch. Health Council. Bd. dirs. Comprehensive Neighborhood Health Services; mem. coordinating council Black Christian Nationalist Ch.; mem. deacon bd. Shrine of Black Madonna; trustee Comprehensive Health Planning Council Southeastern Mich. Served to lt. Dental Corps, USNR, 1964-67. Mem. Nat. Dental Assn. (mem. ho. of dels., parliamentarian 1977), Wolverine Dental Soc. Mich. (editor news jour. 1971; recipient meritorious service award 1972, pres. 1976), Acad. Gen. Dentistry, Am. Profl. Practice Com., Orgn. Black Scientists (v.p. 1979), Howard Alumni Assn. (sec. 1969-70), Chi Delta Mu, Omega Psi Phi. Club: Masons. Home: 1660 Lincolnshire Dr Detroit MI 48203 Office: 5050 Joy Rd Detroit MI 48204

BURGHARDT, WILLIAM GEORGE, educator; b. Queens, N.Y., Oct. 17, 1949; s. Edith B.; B.S., Cornell U., 1974; M.B.A., U. Scranton, 1977; M.S., SUNY, Binghamton, 1979; Ph.D. candidate, Mich. State U., 1979—; m. Linda Carol Pastors, July 13, 1975. Gen. mgr. Dairy Ops., Schyler Lake, N.Y., 1973-74; br. mgr. Farm Credit Banks, Binghamton, N.Y., 1974-79; instr. mgmt. and fin. Mich. State U., East Lansing, 1979—. Mem. Am. Agrl. Econs. Assn., Assn. M.B.A. Execs. Republican. Home: 2880 Roseland St East Lansing MI 48823 Office: Mich State U Room 7 Agriculture Hall East Lansing MI 48824

BURGHER, LOUIS WILLIAM, physician, educator; b. Centerville, Iowa, Oct. 31, 1944; s. Wendell and Dorothy (Probasco) B.; B.S., U. Nebr., 1966, M.D. with honors, 1970, M.Med. Sci., 1972, Ph.D. in Med. Sci., 1978; m. Susan Stephens, May 20, 1979; children—Tanya Jo, Tara Lynn, Lucas William. Intern, U. Nebr. Coll. Medicine, 1970-71, resident in internal medicine, 1971-72; practice medicine specializing in pulmonary medicine, Omaha, 1974—; NIH fellow in pulmonary diseases Mayo Grad. Sch. of Medicine, Rochester, Minn., 1972-74, asso. prof., 1981—, chief sect. pulmonary medicine, 1980—; clin. research asso. in pulmonary disease U. Nebr. Coll. of Medicine, 1969-72; med. dir. pulmonary medicine Bishop Clarkson Meml. Hosp., Omaha, 1974—; Tb cons. to Nebr. Dept. Health, 1972—. Med. dir. Nebr. Opportunity for Vols. in ACTION, 1971-72. Recipient Upjohn award Nebr. coll. Medicine, 1970. Diplomate Am. Bd. Internal Medicine, subsplty. bd. pulmonary medicine. Fellow Am. Coll. Chest Physicians; mem. AMA (council on med. edn. 1973-78, mem. liaison com. on med. edn. 1974-79), Nebr. Med. Assn., Am. Thoracic Soc., Zumbro Valley Med. Soc. (exec. com. 1973-74), Univ. Med. Center House Officers Assn. (pres. 1971-72), Mayo Fellows Assn. (pres. 1973-74), Nat. Acad. Scis. (mem. task force study Inst. Medicine), Nebr. Thoracic Soc. (pres. 1980-81). Contbr. articles on pulmonary disease to profl. jours. Home: 139 N Elmwood Rd Omaha NE 68132 Office: Bishop Clarkson Meml Hosp Dewey Ave and 44th St PO Box 3328 Omaha NE 68103

BURGIN, ROBERT AUGUSTUS, transp. co. exec.; b. Rolling Fork, Miss., July 20, 1924; s. Robert Augustus and Jane (Sullivan) B.; B.S., U. Tenn., 1949; m. Sara Porter Shofner, Dec. 4, 1948; children—Sally Burgin Margolis, Robert Augustus III, Christopher. Served with Oak Ridge Inst. Nuclear Studies, Oak Ridge, Tenn., 1949-51; br. chief Dept. of Defense, Washington, and Albuquerque, 1951-56; cons. Stanford Research Inst., 1956-57; with TRW, 1956-78, v.p., asst. to chmn. bd. TRW Systems, 1965-67, v.p., gen. mgr. TRW Automotive Internat., 1967-71, v.p. planning and devel. Automotive Worldwide, 1972-73, v.p., gen. mgr. telecommunications, 1974-78, v.p. planning and devel. TRW Electronics, 1973-78; chmn., chief exec. officer Leaseway Transp. Corp., Cleve., 1978—; dir. E.F. Johnson Co., Waseca, Minn., Storage Tech. Corp., Louisville, Colo., Provident Life and Accident Co., Chattanooga, CFS Continental, Inc., Chgo. Mem. exec. bd. Greater Cleve. council Boy Scouts Am., 1979; mem. exec. com. Hugh O'Brian Youth Found., 1977-79; bd. dirs. Greater Cleve. Growth Assn., 1979; trustee Fuller Theol. Sem., Pasadena, Calif., 1978, The Am. Transp. Assn. Found. Inc., Washington, 1979; mem. devel. council U. Tenn. Served to capt. USAAF, 1943-45, 51-52. Mem. Sigma Phi Epsilon. Clubs: Pepper Pike, Union; Sunrise Country, Desert Horizons Country. Office: 3700 Park East Dr Beachwood OH 44122

BURICK, MARY FRANCES, govt. ofcl.; b. Youngstown, Ohio, Dec. 22, 1952; d. Joseph and Carol Marie (Vlasic) B.; B.A. in Econs., Youngstown State U., 1975; M.A. in Econs., U. Okla., 1981. Fin. analyst examiner Ohio Div. Bank Supervision, Columbus, 1975; liquidator FDIC, Washington, liquidator-in-charge Cleve. Office, 1981—. Mem. Nat. Assn. Bus. Economists, Am. Mgmt. Assn., Am. Soc. Profl. and Exec. Women, Nat. Assn. Female Execs., Internat. Platform Assn. Roman Catholic. Home: 931 Dravis Ave Girard OH 44420 Office: 550 17th St NW Washington DC 20429

BURK, KEITH EUGENE, mgmt. cons.; b. Albion, Mich., May 31, 1941; s. Wilson Eugene and Ruth Elizabeth (Chamberlain) B.; B.S., Western Mich. U., 1969; m. Darlene Carole Nelson, Feb. 2, 1963; children—Linnea Ruth, Eric Eugene. Lab. technician U.S. Plywood (name now Champion Internat.), 1965-67, mgr. tech. engring., 1967-69, tech. service mgr., 1969-70; engring. mgr. Dover Corp., Portage, Mich., 1970-71; engr. A.B. Cassedy & Assos., Ridgefield, Conn., 1971-73, group engr., 1973-74, asst. chief, 1974-76, chief, 1976-80; co-founder KAMACO, Inc., v.p. ops., 1981—. Mem. Kalamazoo Civic Theater, 1973—. Served with U.S. Army, 1961-63. Mem. Am. Mgmt. Assn., AIAA, Am. Inst. Indsl. Engrs., Am. Soc. Profl. Consultants, Am. Security Council. Republican. Christian Scientist. Club: Coterie Dance. Patentee in field.

BURK, WILLIAM CHARLES, railroad pub. relations rep.; b. Beaumont, Tex., Aug. 19, 1921; s. John Leonard and Dona (Robinson) B.; student Central State Coll., Edmond, Okla., 1939-42, Inst. Bus. Econs., U. So. Cal., 1955; m. Mary Irene Meyer, Aug. 19, 1945; children—John Paul, Donald William, Mary Catherine. Newspaper work in Okla. before World War II; system photographer A., T.S.F. Ry., Los Angeles, 1946-47, spl. rep. in Chgo., 1947-53, spl. rep. pub. relations, Topeka, Kans., 1953-61; mgr. pub. relations Santa Fe Ry. System, Chgo., 1961-73, v.p. pub. relations, 1973—. Trustee William Allen White Found. Mem. R.R. Pub. Relations Assn., Pub. Relations Soc. Am. (mem. seminar Cornell U., 1962), Pub. Relation Clinic, Am. Agrl. Editors Assn., Soc. Profl. Journalists, Sigma Delta Chi, Alpha Tau Omega. Republican. Episcopalian. Mason (Shriner). Clubs: Athletic, Press (Chgo.); Western Ry.; Press, Kansas City (Kansas City, Mo.); Press (San Diego); Michigan Shores (Wilmette); Nat. Press (Washington). Home: 923 Cornell St Wilmette IL 60091 Office: 80 E Jackson Blvd Chicago IL 60604

BURKE, ELDON RAY, educator; b. Walkerton, Ind., June 14, 1898; s. Albert Frederick and Lucy May (Freed) B.; A.B. Manchester Coll., 1922; M.A., U. Chgo., 1926, Ph.D., 1936; Litt.D., Manchester Coll., 1977, St. Francis Coll., 1975; m. Cecil Lula Davis, Sept. 18, 1924; 1 dau., Alice Virginia Burke Wend. Tchr., Marshall County (Ind.) pub. schs., 1916-18, 22-24; tchr. Ohio No. U., 1927-31, Shimer Coll., 1932-37, Ball State U., 1937-41; relief worker, dir. Brethren Service Commn., Europe, 1941-46; field rep., dir. CRALOG, Germany, 1946-51; field sec. Iraq Internat. Vol. Services, Inc., 1954-56; field sec. Manchester Coll., 1956-68; prof., chmn. dept. history St. Francis Coll., 1969—. Asia Soc. and Ind. U. grantee, 1960-64. Mem. Assn. Asian Studies, Am., Ind. hist. socs., Ind. Social Sci. Acad. Mem. Ch. of Brethren. Contbr. articles in field to profl. jours. Home: 402 N Mill St North Manchester IN 46962

BURKE, EMMETT CHARLES, educator; b. Montgomery, Ala., Jan. 30, 1920; s. William J. and Ethel (Scott) B.; A.B., B.S., Roosevelt U., 1945; M.A., Loyola U., 1953; M.Ed., DePaul U., 1954; O.D., Ill. Coll. Optometry, 1947; m. Sarah Scott, Aug. 14, 1949. Sr. caseworker Ill. Pub. Aid Commn., Chgo., 1948-56; asst. prin. Wm. Carter Pub. Sch., Chgo., 1957—; asst. prof. Nat. Coll. of Edn., Chgo., 1969—; dir. Washington Pk. YMCA, Afro-Am. Family and Community Services. Active Nat. Urban League, NAACP. Served with USAAF, 1942-45. Certified social worker, Ill. Mem. Nat. Assn. of Black Profs. (dir.), Chgo. African-Am. Tchrs. Assn. (dir.), Chgo. Asst. Prins. Assn. (dir.), Chgo. Council for Exceptional Children (dir.), AAUP, NEA, Phi Delta Kappa, Alpha Phi Alpha. Home: 601 E 32nd St Chicago IL 60616 Office: 5740 S Michigan Ave Chicago IL 60637

BURKE, JAMES DONALD, mus. dir.; b. Salem, Oreg., Feb. 22, 1939; s. Donald James and Ellin Anne (Adams) B.; B.A., Brown U., 1962; M.A., U. Pa., 1966; Ph.D., Harvard U., 1972; m. Diane E. Davies, May 17, 1980. Curator, Allen Art Mus., Oberlin Coll., 1971-72; curator Yale U. Art Gallery, New Haven, 1972-78; asst. dir. St. Louis Art Mus., 1978-80, dir., 1980—. Mem. Am. Assn. Museums, Coll. Art Assn. Am. Author works in field. Office: St Louis Art Mus Forest Park Saint Louis MO 63110

BURKE, JOHN EDWARD, educator; b. Huntington, W.Va., Aug. 10, 1942; s. Charles Joseph and Eloise Marie (Sang) B.; B.A., Marshall U., 1965; M.F.A., Ohio U., 1966, Ph.D., Ohio State U., 1971; children—John Lindsey, Elizabeth Ann. Intern, U.S. Ho. Reps., 1960-61; news writer, editor Sta. WSAZ-TV, Huntington, 1962-65; instr. Kent State U., 1966-69; dir. TV Arts dept. Cleve. Summer Sch. for Arts, 1967-68; asst. to dir. Ohio State U. Telecommunications Center, 1969-71; project dir. Ohio Valley Med. Microwave TV System, Columbus, 1971-73; dir., asso. prof. biomed. communications Ohio State U. Coll. Medicine, asso. prof. communications Coll. Social and Behavioral Scis., 1972—; cons. univs., bus., industry, including U. Tenn., Nat. Med. Audio-Visual Center, Upjohn Co., N. Central Assn. Colls. and Univs. USPHS grantee, 1972-77. Mem. Assn. Biomed. Communications Dirs., Am. Soc. Allied Health Professions, Health Scis. Communications Assn., Am. Med. Writers Assn., Nat. Acad. TV Arts & Scis., Alpha Psi Omega, Alpha Epsilon Rho. Democrat. Roman Catholic. Author: History of Public Broadcasting Act of 1967, 1979; contbr. articles to profl. jours.; editor Jour. Allied Health, 1978—. Home: 1695 Glenn Ave Columbus OH 43212 Office: 1583 Perry St Columbus OH 43210

BURKE, JOHN MICHAEL, chem. physicist; b. Takoma Park, Md., Apr. 27, 1946; s. John Richard and Doris Jean (Waltman) B.; A.B., Thomas More Coll., 1966; Ph.D. (NASA trainee, 1967-69, grad. fellow, 1969-71), Case Western Res. U., 1971; m. Mary Jane Elenewski, May 24, 1975; children—Alexander, Erin. Presdl. intern, Nat. Bur. Standards, Washington, 1972-73; research asso. Princeton (N.J.) U., 1973-77; staff scientist Procter & Gamble, Cin., 1977—. NIH postdoctoral fellow, 1975-76. Mem. Optical Soc. Am., Soc. Mfg. Engrs. Contbr. articles in field to profl. publs. Office: 6300 Center Hill Rd Cincinnati OH 45224

BURKE, KENNETH ANDREW, advt. agy. exec.; b. Cleve., Sept. 9, 1941; s. Frank F. and Margret M. (Tome) B.; B.S. in B.A., Bowling Green State U., 1965; m. Karen Lee Burley, July 1, 1968; children—Allison Leigh, Aric Jason. Account exec. Lang, Fisher, Stashower, Cleve., 1967-69; account supr. Tracy Locke, Dallas, 1969-72, Grey Advt., N.Y.C., 1972-76; v.p. Griswold Eshleman, Cleve., 1976-79; v.p., gen. mgr. Simpson Mktg. Communications Agy., Columbus, Ohio, 1979—; dir. Berkshire Textiles, Cleve., 1979—. Adv. bd. Am. Cancer Soc., Columbus, 1980—. Recipient Navy Achievement in Advt. award, 1975; Cleve. Advt. Club award, 1968. Mem. Am. Mktg. Assn., Columbus Advt. Fedn., Columbus C. of C., Theta Chi. Roman Catholic. Clubs: Rotary, Cleve. Advt., Columbus Athletic, Sawmill Athletic, Agonis Athletic Found. Author: Children's Stories, 1970. Home: 1753 Bedford Rd Upper Arlington OH 43212 Office: 1301 Dublin Rd Columbus OH 43215

BURKE, LARRY KENNETH, mental health adminstr.; b. Louisville, June 12, 1940; s. Harry Kenneth and Jean Ann (Perry) B.; B.A., Georgetown Coll., 1962; M.S.S.W., U. Louisville, 1966; m. Gretchen, N. Hauptli, June 29, 1968; children—Kelly, Christopher, Heather, Jason. Supr., Met. Social Services Dept., Louisville, 1966-68; coordinator Regional Ednl. Diagnostic and Treatment Center, Louisville, 1968-69; coordinator, asst. mgr., personnel dir. and area mgr. River Region Mental Health-Mental Retardation Bd., Inc., Louisville, 1969-76; pres. Burke & Assos., Louisville and Corydon, Ind., 1976-77; dir. St. Louis County Child Mental Health, St. Louis, 1977—; mem. faculty U. Louisville, 1970-71, Vincennes (Ind.) U., 1977, St. Louis U., 1978; project dir. Ind. Com. for Humanities, 1977; program evaluator Ky. Dept. Human Resources, 1975; cons. Harrison County (Ind.) Community Services, 1977, Ky. Mental Health Manpower Commn., 1971; workshop leader Jefferson County Bd. Edn., 1966, Ky. Welfare Assn., 1970-71, Riddick, Flynn and Assos., 1977, United Way Greater St. Louis. Chmn. orgn. structure com., mem. steering com. Childrens Coordinating Council, 1979; bd. dirs., mem. exec. com., co-chmn. edn. com. St. Louis Mental Health Assn. Council on Mental Health and Public Affairs, 1980—; mem. Eastern Mo. Dist. Regional Mental Health coordinating bd., 1977-79; pres. Eastern Mo. Dist. Regional Adv. Council for Comprehensive Psychiat. Services, 1981; mem. exec. com., chmn. nominating com. St. Louis County Child Welfare Adv. Com., 1978—; mem. local impact com. Greater St. Louis Health Systems Agy., 1978-79; chmn. tng. com. Children's Mental Health Services Council, 1978—; resource com. Project Parenting, Sta. KMOX-TV, 1978-79; chmn. planning com. and personnel com., mem. exec. com., v.p. Eastern Mo. Dist. Regional Adv. Council for Comprehensive Psychiat. Services; chmn. planning and budget com. Mo. Adv. Council for Comprehensive Psychiat. Services, 1980—. Recipient Cert. of Appreciation, U. Louisville, 1971; Cert. of Merit, United Way of Greater St. Louis, 1979; State Edn. award Mental Health Assn. Mo., 1981; NIMH grantee, 1964; lic. social worker, Ky. Mem. Nat. Assn. Social Workers (planning com. St. Louis chpt. 1979), Ky. Personnel Assn., Mo. Assn. Social Workers (planning com. 1979), Mo. Assn. for Social Welfare (state dir., co-chmn. mental health task force 1979—). Lutheran. Clubs: Rotary, Order of Ky. Cols. Home: 1974 Claymills Dr Chesterfield MO 63017 Office: 701 S Brentwood Blvd Clayton MO 63105

BURKE, PAUL E, JR., indsl. equipment mfg. co. exec.; b. Kansas City, Mo., Jan. 4, 1934; s. Paul E. and Virginia (Moling) B.; B.S., U. Kans., 1956; m. Patricia Ann Pierson, Dec. 17, 1955; children—Anne Elizabeth, Kelly Patricia, Alice Cathrine, Jennifer Marie. With Webb Belting & Supply Co., Inc., Kansas City, Mo., 1960—, exec. v.p., 1968—, also dir.; mem. Kans. Ho. of Reps., 1973-74; mem. Kans. Senate, 1975—; dir. Forslund Pump Co., Anchor Savs. Assn. Mem. council City of Prairie Village, Kans., 1960-63; chmn. Kans. Turnpike Authority; mem. Citizens Adv. Bd. to Sec. Corrections Kans., 1975-79; mem. citizens ombudsman bd. Kans. Dept. Corrections, 1979—. Served with USAF, 1956-59, to capt. USNR, 1963—. Mem. Kans. Assn. Commerce and Industry, Naval Res. Assn. Republican. Episcopalian. Clubs: Kansas City Navy Aero, Masons, Shriners. Office: 2611 Southwest Blvd Kansas City MO 64108

BURKE, PAUL STANLEY, JR., ins. co. exec.; b. St. Paul, Aug. 5, 1926; s. Paul Stanley and Loretta Josephine (Bertrang) B.; B.B.A., U. Minn., 1956; m. Irene Marie Wagner, Apr. 22, 1950; children—John, Steven, Nancy, Lawrence, Linda, James, Thomas. Regional mgr. Minn. Mutual Life Ins. Co., Los Angeles, 1950-61; pres. Paul Burke & Assos., Inc., ins. consultants and adminstrs., Mpls., 1961-73, Trust Life Ins. Co. Am., Scottsdale, Ariz., 1968-73, Purchase & Discount Buying Service Corp., 1977-80, Am. Reliance Corp., 1967—; chmn. bd. Larson & Burke Inc., 1980—. dir. Lindbom & Assos., Inc., St. Paul. Pres., Boys Clubs of Mpls., 1974-76. Served with USAAF, 1944-47. Mem. Pilots Internat. Assn. (pres. 1966-73). Republican. Roman Catholic. Clubs: Mpls. Athletic, N. Am. Hunting (pres. 1978—). Home: 27 Circle W Edina MN 55436

BURKE, RICHARD T., univ. dean; b. Framingham, Mass., Mar. 27, 1935; s. Russell E. and Reta L. (O'Connell) B.; B.A., Boston U., 1956, M.A., 1957; Ph.D., Northwestern U., 1969; children—David, Carolyn. Indsl. salesman Armstrong Cork Co., Phila., 1959-60; lectr. Northwestern U., 1962-64; instr. history Western Mich. U., Kalamazoo, 1964-70, asst. prof., 1970-71, asso. prof., 1971—, adminstrv. asst. to chmn. dept. history, 1967-71, asso. dean Grad. Coll., 1971-76, dean Div. Continuing Edn., 1977—; cons. Mich. State Bd. Edn. Com. Scholars, 1976-79; chmn. com. on inter-instl. programs Mich. Council Grad. Deans, 1971-76; chmn. bd. dirs. Univ. Consortium Center, Grand Rapids, 1978-80; chmn. Mich. Coordinating Council Continuing Higher Edn., 1980-81, mem. exec. com., 1979-82. Commr., Kalamazoo County Bd. Commrs., 1979-82, vice-chmn., 1981—; bd. dirs. Kalamazoo County Econ. Devel. Corp., 1979-81, Kalamazoo County Conv. and Visitors Bur., 1979-81, Prairie Ronde Found., 1979-83; mem. Kalamazoo City Charter Rev. Com., 1972-73. Served to 1st lt. Transp. Corps, U.S. Army, 1957-59. Mem. Nat. Univ. Continuing Edn. Assn. (dir.-elect 1979-82, mem. Region IV exec. com. 1979-83). Office: Div Continuing Edn Western Mich U Kalamazoo MI 49008

BURKE, THOMAS JOSEPH, civil engr.; b. Grosse Pointe Park, Mich., Sept. 1, 1927; s. Cyril Joseph and Marie Estelle (Sullivan) B.; B.C.E., Villanova U., 1949; m. Elaine Kiefer, Nov. 10, 1951; children—Judy Lee, Kathleen Marie, Maureen Elaine, Thomas P. Pres., Burke Rental Service, Sterling Heights, Mich., 1949—, Cyril J. Burke, Inc., Sterling Heights, Mich., 1949—. Trustee Villanova U., 1980—. Served to lt. USAF, Korea. Mem. ASCE, Detroit Builders Exchange (v.p. 1976-78, dir. 1975-78), Associated Equipment Distbrs. (dir. 1955-58, 75-78), Associated Underground Contractors (dir. 1965-68), Mich. Ready Mix Concrete Assn. (dir. 1960-65), Villanova U. Alumni Assn. (nat. v.p. 1978-79, nat. pres. 1980), Detroit Engring. Soc. Roman Catholic. Clubs: Grosse Pointe Yacht, Otsego Ski, Ocean Reef, Detroit Athletic, Villanova U. of Detroit (pres. 1955-65). Home: 578 Shelden Rd Grosse Pointe Shores MI 48236 also 688 N Lake Shore Rd Port Sanilac MI Office: 36000 Mound Rd Sterling Heights MI 48077

BURKE, THOMAS STEPHEN, sch. adminstr.; b. Chgo., Dec. 13, 1922; s. Patrick Joseph and Bridget Josephine (Murphy) B.; B.Ed., Chgo. Tchrs. Coll., 1945; M.Ed., Loyola U., Chgo., 1955; m. Ruth Ellen Wendt, Aug. 23, 1947; children—Thomas Patrick, James William, John Joseph. Tchr., St. Rita High Sch., Chgo., 1945-47; tchr. Chgo. Pub. Schs., 1947-58, asst. prin. Beale Sch., 1951-61, prin., Deneen Sch., 1961-69, Englewood Evening Sch., 1966-68, Hubbard Evening Sch., 1968-71; pres. Chgo. Prins. Assn., Am. Fedn. Sch. Adminstrs., AFL-CIO, 1969-73; prin. Morgan Park High Sch., Chgo., 1973—. Sec. sch. adminstrs. and suprs. organizing com. AFL-CIO, 1971-76. Mem. Am. Assn. Sch. Adminstrs., Chgo. Prins. Assn., Ill. Prins. Assn., Nat. Assn. Elementary Sch. Prins., Nat. Assn. Secondary Sch. Prins., NEA, Am. Fedn. Sch. Adminstrs. (v.p. 1976—), Nat. Soc. for Study of Edn., Am. Inst. Parliamentarians (chpt. treas. 1977-79), Chgo. State U. Alumni Assn. (pres. 1976-77), St. Thomas More Holy Name Soc., Phi Delta Kappa. Democrat. Roman Catholic. Clubs: Kiwanis, K.C., Elks (Chgo.). Home: 3171 W 83d Pl Chicago IL 60652 Office: 1744 W Pryor Ave Chicago IL 60643

BURKET, GAIL BROOK, author; b. Stronghurst, Ill., Nov. 1, 1905; d. John Cecil and Maud (Simonson) Brook; A.B., U. Ill., 1926; M.A. in English Lit., Northwestern U., 1929; m. Walter Cleveland Burket, June 22, 1929; children—Elaine (Mrs. William L. Harwood), Anne, Margaret (Mrs. James Boyce). Pres. woman's aux. Internat. Coll. Surgeons, 1950-54, now bd. dirs. Mus.; nat. vice chmn. Am. Heritage of DAR, 1971-74; pres. Northwestern U. Guild, 1976-78; sec. Evanston women's bd. Northwestern U. Settlement, 1979-81. Recipient Robert Ferguson Meml. award Friends of Lit., 1973. Mem. Nat. League Am. Pen Women (Ill. state pres. 1952-54, nat. v.p. 1958-60), Soc. Midland Authors, Poetry Soc. Am., Women in Communications, AAUW (pres. N. Shore br. 1961-63), Ill. Opera Guild, Daus. Am. Colonists (state v.p. 1973-76), Colonial Dames Am. (chpt. regent 1974-80), Zonta, Phi Beta Kappa, Delta Zeta. Author: Courage Beloved, 1949; Manners Please, 1949; Blueprint for Peace, 1951; Let's Be Popular, 1951; You Can Write a Poem, 1954; Far Meadows, 1955; This Is My Country, 1960; From the Prairies, 1968. Contbr. articles, poems to lit. publs. Address: 1020 Lake Shore Dr Evanston IL 60202

BURKET, GEORGE EDWARD, JR., physician; b. Kingman, Kans., Dec. 10, 1912; s. George Edward and Jessie May (Talbert) B.; student Wichita State U., 1930-33; M.D., U. Kans., 1937; m. Mary Elizabeth Wallace, Nov. 12, 1938; children—George Edward III, Carol Sue, Elizabeth Christine. Intern, Santa Barbara (Calif.) Gen. Hosp., 1937-38, resident, 1938-39; grad. asst. in surgery Mass. Gen. Hosp., Boston, 1956-57; pvt. practice medicine, Kingman, Kans., 1939-73; preceptor in medicine U. Kans. Med. Sch., 1950-73, asso. prof., 1973-78, clin. prof., 1978—. Mem. Kingman Bd. Edn., 1946-58; mem. Kans. State Bd. Health, 1960-66. Diplomate Am. Bd. Family Practice. Mem. Kans. Med. Soc. (pres. 1966-67), Am. Acad. Family Physicians (pres. 1967-68; John Walsh founders award 1979), Inst. Medicine, A.M.A., Assn. Am. Med. Colls., Soc. Tchrs. Family Medicine, Alpha Omega Alpha. Republican. Episcopalian. Mason (Shriner). Clubs: Leawood South Country, Garden of Gods (Colorado Springs, Colo.), Wichita. Contbr. articles to profl. jours. Home: Spring Lake Route 1 Kingman KS 67068 Office: Rainbow Blvd at 39th St Kansas City KS 66103

BURKETT, EUGENE JOHN, chem. and environ. engr.; b. Cin., Nov. 15, 1937; s. James E. and Amelia A. (Kues) B.; B.S., U. Cin., 1962; m. Patricia Wade, Apr. 15, 1977; 1 son, Matthew. Engring. trainee Hilton Davis Chem. Co., Cin., 1956-61; with Goodyear Tire & Rubber Co., Akron, Ohio, 1962—, sect. mgr. chem. plants engring., 1972-73, mgr. corp. environ. engring., 1974—. Mem. Am. Inst. Chem. Engrs., Rubber Mfrs. Assn., Chem. Mfrs., Ohio Mfrs. Assn., Ohio C. of C. Republican. Roman Catholic. Office: 1144 E Market St Akron OH 44316

BURKEY, LEE MELVILLE, lawyer; b. Beach, N.D., Mar. 21, 1914; s. L. M. and Mina (Horner) B.; B.A., U. Ill., 1936. M.A., 1938; J.D. with honors, John Marshall Law Sch., 1943; m. Lorraine Burghardt, June 11, 1938; 1 son, Lee Melville. Tchr., Princeton, Ill., 1937-38. Harvey, 1938-43; admitted to Ill. bar, 1944; atty. Office of Solicitor. U.S. Dept. Labor, 1944-51; lectr. bus. law Roosevelt Coll., 1949-52; partner law firm Asher, Goodstein, Pavolon, Gittler, Greenfield and Segall, and predecessor firms, 1951—; dir. La Grange Fed. Savs. and Loan Assn. Mem. Northeastern Ill. Planning Commn., 1969-73, pres., 1970—; mem. Employment Security Adv. Bd., 1970-73; life mem. asso. bd. Community Meml. Gen. Hosp., La Grange, Ill.; mem. nat. corp. bd. for homeland ministries United Ch. of Christ, 1977—; bd. dirs. Better Bus. Bur. Met. Chgo., 1975—, Plymouth Place, Inc., 1973-81. Trustee, Village of LaGrange, 1962-68, mayor, 1968-73, village atty., 1973—. Recipient Distinguished Alumnus award John Marshall Law Sch., 1973. Mem. Am., Ill., Chgo., bar assns., Order of John Marshall, SAR (state pres. 1977), S.R. Congregationalist. Mason. Club: LaGrange Country. Author numerous articles on lie detector evidence. Home: 926 S Catherine St LaGrange IL 60525 Office: 228 N LaSalle St Chicago IL 60601

BURKHART, ARDATH, civic worker; b. Vincennes, Ind., Sept. 2, 1905; d. Bert Hall and Fava (Tolbert) Yates; B.S. in Music, DePauw U., 1927; Litt.D., Tri-State Coll., 1974; m. John Burkhart, June 9, 1929 (div. Nov. 1974); children—John (dec.), Gay Burkhart Brown. Tchr., supr. music pub. schs., 1929-35. Mem. nat. devel. com. Girl Scouts U.S.A., 1951-55, mem. Region VII com., 1951-60, vice chmn. region VII, 1953-58, chmn. internat. work Region VII, 1958-60, Friends of Our Cabana Com. (Mexico), 1959-63, mem. bd. dirs. Hoosier Capital council, 1949-63, pres., 1951-54; v.p., mem. exec. com. Women's Affairs Com. of Civic Theatre, 1969-71; founder Women's Council for Ednl. TV Channel 20, 1970, pres., 1970-72, life mem.; mem. Met. Planning Commn., 1963-65; chmn. women's div. United Fund campaign, 1957, bd. dirs., 1957—, mem. exec. com., 1958-80, mem. allocations com., 1958-69, mem. admission com., 1969-73; chmn. women's div. Community Chest, 1950, 51, 56, bd. dirs., 1951-54; founder, pres. United Fund League, 1958-60, 64-65, chmn. selections com., 1961-63, mem. bd., exec. com., 1958—, chmn. individual gifts and founds. campaign, 1977; mem. Bd. Sch. Commns., 1962-63; chmn. Charity Solicitations Commns., 1955-65; bd. govs. Asso. Colls. Ind., 1966—, chmn., 1972-76; bd. dirs. Hoosier Art Salon, 1965, v.p., 1972-78, pres., 1978-81; bd. dirs. 500 Festival, 1967-73, v.p., 1970-73; bd. dirs. Indpls. Day Nursery Assn., 1968-74, St. Mary's Child Center, 1968-71, Civic Theatre, 1970—, Marion County Pub. Library Found., 1972— (also trustee 1972—), Crossroads council Boy Scouts Am., 1975-79, Indpls. Symphony, 1980—; bd. dirs. Jr. Achievement, 1970—, chmn. Capital Funds campaign; bd. dirs., pres. Met. Indpls. Television Assn., 1968-72, pres., 1972-75, del. Pub. Broadcasting Service, 1972—, chmn. bd., 1975-80; mem. bd., com. on human resources Pub. Broadcasting Service, 1977—; trustee Nat. Assn. Public TV Stas., 1980—; bd. dirs. Central Ind. Council on Aging; trustee Wenona Meml. Hosp., 1965-76; trustee, v.p. Civic Theatre, Indpls.; trustee DePauw U., 1955—, life mem., 1978—, nat. alumni co-chmn. fund campaign, 1959-61; trustee Meth. Hosp. Found., 1977—, v.p., 1979—; trustee New Hope Found., 1977—, United Theol. Sem., 1980—; mem. Indpls. Sesquicentennial Commn., 1971, Greater Indpls. Progress Com., 1971-78; mem. arrangements com. NATO Conf. on Cities, 1971; mem. Mayor's Task Force on Aging, 1972, Mayor's Task Force on Women, 1972; mem. advisory com. Kennedy Center for Performing Arts; mem. pres.'s council Greater Indpls. Ch. Fedn., 1972—; pres. Porter Bus. Coll., 1972-74; bd. dirs., chmn. congregational care commn. Meth. Ch., trustee, 1972-80; state chmn. fund dr. Charlene Lugar Endowment Fund for Birth Defects; mem. nat. adv. com. Reagan-1980. Named Woman of Year, B'nai B'rith, 1958; recipient Adminstrv. Service award Girl Scouts U.S.A., 1963; TSP award Theta Sigma Phi, 1968, Woman of Year award, 1971; Distinguished Citizen award 11th dist. Am. Legion, 1970; Ind. Acad. Achievement award, 1973. Mem. Mid-Am. World Trade Assn., Inc. (charter), Nat. Friends Pub. TV, Alpha Chi Omega (past pres. Indpls. Alumni; chmn. Nat. Founders fellowship com. 1946-56, nat. conv. mgr. 1960, chmn. nat. nominating com. 1964, Nat. Achievement award for community service 1960). Home: 8461 Quail Hollow Rd Indianapolis IN 46260

BURKHART, DAMA MARTIN, educator; b. Woodsfield, Ohio, Mar. 16, 1926; d. Wilbert Earl and Carrie Mildred (Doan) Martin; B.S. cum laude, Taylor U., Upland, Ind., 1950; M.S., Butler U., Indpls., 1965; Ph.D. (grad. fellow), Purdue U., 1968; m. George F. Burkhart, Apr. 11, 1981; children by previous marriage—Paige Elizabeth Cofield, Malvin Scott Cofield. Mem. pub. relations dept. Taylor U., 1950-51; tchr., curriculum cons. Howard County (Ind.) Council Chs., 1955-65; staff counselor, psychol. services Purdue U., 1965-68, vis. prof. edn., 1969-70, human devel. specialist, dept. child devel. and family life, 1970-74, staff and program devel. specialist Sch. Home Econs. and Coop. Extension Service, 1974—, asst. dir. Coop. Extension Service, also asst. dean Sch. Consumer and Family Scis.; adult edn. supr. Asso. Migrant Opportunities Services, 1967; v.p. Ind. Council Family Relations, 1972-74, pres., 1980—, bd. dirs., 1975-77; mem. Task Force on Career Devel. for Women, 1975-76; condr. workshops, cons. in field. Recipient Ecumenical citation Howard County, 1965. Council Chs. grantee. Mem. Nat. Council Family Relations, Am. Home Econs. Assn. Republican. Presbyterian. Author articles, bulls. Home: 222 N Main St Woodsfield OH 43793

BURLEIGH, WILLIAM ROBERT, newspaper editor; b. Evansville, Ind., Sept. 6, 1935; s. Joseph Charles and Emma Bertha (Wittgen) B.; B.S., Marquette U., Milw., 1957; LL.D. (hon.), Ind. State U., 1979; m. Catherine Anne Husted, Nov. 28, 1964; children—David William, Catherine Anne, Margaret Walden. From reporter to editor and pres. Evansville Press, 1951-77; editor Cin. Post, 1977—; trustee First Amendment Congress, 1979-81. Chmn. Leadership Cin., 1979-81. Served with AUS, 1957-58. Mem. Am. Soc. Newspaper Editors, Sigma Delta Chi, Alpha Sigma Nu. Roman Catholic. Clubs: Queen City, Cin. Lit. Home: 5925 Ropes Dr Cincinnati OH 45244 Office: 800 Broadway Cincinnati OH 45202

BURLINSON, JOHN JOSEPH, JR., film equipment co. exec.; b. N.Y.C., Dec. 26, 1930; s. John and Alice Grace (Kenny) B.; B.S., Fordham U., 1953, M.A., 1959; m. Martha Marie Quigley, Dec. 29, 1954; children—Alice Gertrude, John Raymond, Monica Marie. Prodn. asst. Breyer Ice Cream Co., N.Y.C., 1954-57; salesman Henry Regnery Co., N.Y.C., Chgo., 1957-64; v.p. Quigley Pub. Co., N.Y.C., 1964-70; mgmt. exec. Nat. Screen Service Co., N.Y.C., 1970-75; gen. mgr. Nat. Theatre Supply, 1975—; v.p., gen. mgr. EPRAD, Inc., Toledo, 1977-80, pres., chief exec. officer, 1980—. Bd. dirs., sec. Found. Motion Picture Pioneers; mem. Cardinal's Com. Cath. Charities N.Y. Mem. Theatre Equipment and Supply Mfrs. Assn. (treas., dir. 1967—), Theatre Equipment Assn. (v.p. 1972—, dir. 1978), Am. Soc. Assn. Execs., So. Soc. Motion Picture and TV Engrs., Brit. Kinematograph Soc. Clubs: Variety of N.Y.; Winged Foot Golf (Mamaroneck, N.Y.); Toledo Country, Rotary (Toledo). Contbr. articles to profl. jours. Home: 2617 Juniper Dr Toledo OH 43614 Office: 123 W Woodruff St Toledo OH 43620

BURMEISTER, EARL HARRY, sheet metal co. exec.; b. Des Moines, Apr. 3, 1918; s. Charles Frederick and Mabel Louise (Kearney) B.; student public schs., Des Moines; m. Helen Louise Collins, Feb. 1, 1946; children—Sally, Susan, Shelly. With Iowa Sheet Metal Contractors, Inc., Des Moines, 1946-69, exec. v.p., until 1969; pres. Universal Sheet Metal, Inc., Ft. Worth, 1970-73; v.p. Broyles & Broyles, Ft. Worth, 1970-73; pres., chief exec. officer Backman Sheet Metal Works, Des Moines, 1973—. Served with USAAC, 1941-45. Decorated Bronze Star. Mem. ASHRAE, Sheet Metal and Air Conditioning Contractors of Am. (chpt. pres. 1980, com. chmn.), Sheet Metal Contractors of Iowa (past pres.). Clubs: Masons, Shriners, Des Moines, Des Moines Golf and Country. Home: 3909 Francrest St Des Moines IA 50265 Office: Backman Sheet Metal Works 1514 Fuller Rd Des Moines IA 50265

BURMEISTER, FLORENCE ESTELLE, librarian, educator; b. Cleve., Apr. 17, 1929; d. William Frederick and Josephine (Kostal) Burmeister; A.B., Western Res. U., 1956, M.S. in L.S., 1958. Library aide Cleve. Pub. Library, 1948-55, asst. childrens librarian E. 131st St. br., 1956-57, childrens librarian Miles Park br., 1958-60, Fleet br., 1960-61; children's books reviewer Booklist and Subscription Books Bull., A.L.A., Chgo., 1962-63; head young peoples and childrens dept. Skokie (Ill.) Pub. Library, 1963—; chmn. children's library services workshop for Bur Oak Library System Joliet, 1968-70; vis. lectr. dept. library sci. Rosary Coll., River Forest, Ill., 1967—. Instr. U.S. Office Edn. Inst. on Library Services for Gifted Children Tex. Woman's U., Denton, summer 1970; asst. prof. pub. library services for children, extension div. U. Ill., spring 1971. Mem. Am. (past com. chmn.; mem., publicity chmn. Newbery Caldecott awards com. 1969-70, chmn. Charles Scribner's Sons awards com. 1971-72, chmn. children's services div. arrangements com. 1972), Ill. (mem. exec. bd., past sect. chmn., del. Ill. Commn. on Children, recipient Davis Cup, Children's Librarians Sect. 1972) library assns., Library Adminstrs. Council No. Ill. (past sect. pres.; chmn. children's reference services workshop 1969), Chgo. Library Club, Childrens Reading Round Table Chgo. (award com. 1968, 74), Case Western Res. U. Sch. Library Sci., Flora Stone Mather Coll. alumni assn., Beta Phi Mu. Unitarian. Home: 201 E Walton St Chicago IL 60611 Office: 5215 Oakton St Skokie IL 60076

BURMEISTER, RAY WILLIAM, internist; b. New Haven, Mo., Nov. 22, 1929; s. William Henry and Ella Caroline (Kissling) B.; B.S. in Biology and Chemistry, St. Louis U., 1950, M.D., 1954; m. Edna Florene Struck, June 6, 1953; children—William Alan, Robert Christian, Brenda Lynn, Brian Edward. Intern, St. Louis U. Hosp., 1954-55; resident in internal medicine St. Louis U. Hosps., 1955-57; chief resident in internal medicine St. Louis City Hosp., 1957-58; trainee in microbiology St. Louis U., 1960-61; asso. dir. unit II med. service St. Louis City Hosp., 1961-71; dir. div. health care adminstrn. St. Louis U. Sch. Medicine, 1971-77; pres. InterMed Med. Consultants, Inc., St. Louis, 1977—, Qual-T-Med, Inc., 1980—; cons. infectious disease St. Louis U. Hosp., 1971-77; med. dir. Mt. St. Rose Hosp. Geriatric Rehab. Center, 1961-80; pres. RTD Med., Inc., 1966—; mem. clin. faculty Joint Commn. Accreditation of Hosps.; dir. Luth. Med. Center. Served to capt. M.C., AUS, 1958-60; col. M.C., USAR. Fellow A.C.P.; mem. N.Y. Acad. Scis., Am. Soc. Internal Medicine, Mo. Soc. Internal Medicine (past pres.), AAAS, Am. Fedn. Clin. Research, AAUP, AMA, Mo. Med. Assn., St. Louis Met. Med. Soc., St. Louis Internists Club (past pres.). Republican. Lutheran. Contbr. articles on internal medicine, infectious disease and patient care rev. to profl. jours. and textbooks. Home: 10834 Forest Circle Dr Saint Louis MO 63128 Office: 3535 Jefferson St Saint Louis MO 63118

BURNETT, HENRY BRUCE, banker; b. Raleigh, Ill., May 25, 1912; s. Rex Corwin and Fayette (Wesley) B.; student U. Ill., 1930-32, U. Wis., 1950-52; m. Virginia Stinson, June 6, 1931; 1 son, Hal Bruce; m. 2d, Joan Stroub, Aug. 23, 1963. Chevrolet dealer, Eldorado, Ill., 1941-58; registered rep. Newhard, Cook & Co., St. Louis, 1960-61; chmn. Norris City State Bank (Ill.), 1962—; pres. C.P. Burnett & Sons, Bankers, Eldorado, Ill., 1969-75, dir., 1950-78; chmn. Egyptian State Bank, Carrier Mills, Ill., 1962-78; chmn. Gallatin County State Bank, Ridgway, Ill., 1975—; dir. So. Ill., Inc. Mayor, Eldorado, 1943-47; former trustee Shrutleff Coll., Alton, Ill.; bd. dirs., v.p. Ferrell Hosp., Eldorado; chmn. Ill. Indsl. Devel. Authority, Marion, 1974-79; bd. dirs. So. Ill. U. Found., 1979—. Served with inf. AUS, 1944-46; ETO. Mem. Eldorado C. of C. (pres. 1957-59). Baptist (chmn. bd. deacons 1957-58, bd. trustees 1950-60). Rotarian (pres. Eldorado 1950-51), Lion (pres. Eldorado 1939-40). Home: 1201 Pine St Eldorado IL 62930 Office: PO Box 450 Norris City IL 62869

BURNETT, JEAN BULLARD (MRS. JAMES R. BURNETT), biochemist; b. Flint, Mich., Feb. 19, 1924; d. Chester M. and Katheryn (Krasser) Bullard; B.S., Mich. State U., 1944, M.S., 1945, Ph.D. (Council fellow), 1952; m. James R. Burnett, June 8, 1947. Research asso. dept. zoology Mich. State U., East Lansing, 1954-59, dept. biochemistry, 1959-61, acting dir. research biochem. genetics, dept. biochemistry, 1961-62, asso. prof., asst. chmn. dept. biomechanics, 1973—; asso. biochemist Mass. Gen. Hosp., Boston, 1964-73; prin. research asso. dermatology Harvard, 1962-73, faculty medicine, 1964-73, also spl. lectr., cons., tutor Med. Sch.; vis. prof. dept. biology U. Ariz., 1979-80. USPHS, NIH grantee, 1965-68; Gen. Research Support grantee Mass. Gen. Hosp., 1968-72; Ford Found. travel grantee, 1973; Am. Cancer Soc. grantee, 1971-73; Internat. Pigment Cell Conf. travel grantee, 1980; recipient Med. Found. award, 1970. Mem. AAAS, Am. Chem. Soc., Am. Inst. Biol. Sci., Genetics Soc. Am., Soc. Investigative Dermatology, N.Y. Acad. Scis., Sigma Xi (Research award 1971), Pi Kappa Delta, Kappa Delta Pi, Pi Mu Epsilon, Sigma Delta Epsilon. Home: PO Box 308 Okemos MI 48864 Office: Dept Biomechanics East Fee Hall Mich State U East Lansing MI 48824

BURNETT, MICHAEL G., newspaper exec.; b. Balt., Nov. 18, 1939; s. George W. and Marion W. (Walker) B.; B.A., Dartmouth Coll., 1961; M.A., Trinity Coll., 1964; M.B.A., Harvard U., 1970; m. Susan Bowie Henry, June 18, 1966; children—Elizabeth, Susan. Tchr. pvt. secondary schs., 1961-67; asst. to dir. of fin. planning Joseph Schlitz Brewing Co., Milw., 1970-72; project mgr. container div., Oak Creek, Wis., 1972-73, mgr. capital expenditures, Milw., 1973-77; controller Mpls. Star and Tribune Co., Mpls., 1977-80, v.p., controller, 1980—. Dir., mem. exec. com. Jr. Achievement of Greater Mpls., 1978—; mem. fin. adv. com. Edina (Minn.) Sch. Bd., 1979—. Mem. Fin. Execs. Inst., Inst. Newspaper Controllers and Fin. Officers. Office: Minneapolis Star and Tribune Co IDS Tower Minneapolis MN 55402

BURNETT, PATRICIA HILL, artist, polit. orgn. ofcl., lectr.; b. Bklyn., Sept. 5, 1920; d. William Burr and Mimi (Uline) Hill; student U. Toledo, 1937-38, Goucher Coll., 1939-40; student Master's program Inst. D'Allende, Mexico, 1967, Wayne State U., 1972; student of John Carroll, Detroit, 1941-44, Sarkis Sarkisian, Detroit, 1956-60, Wallace Bassford, Provincetown, Mass., 1968-72, Walter Midener, Detroit, 1960-63; m. Harry Albert Burnett, Oct. 9, 1948; children—William Hill Lange, Harry Burnett III, Terrill Hill, Hillary Hill. Actress, Lone Ranger program Radio Blue Network, 1941-45; tchr. of painting and sculpture U. Mich. Extension, Ann Arbor, 1965—; lectr. N.Y. Speakers Bur., 1971—; propr. Burnett Studios, Detroit, 1962—, mgr., 1962—. Numerous one-woman shows of paintings and sculpture include: Scarab Club, Detroit, 1971, Midland (Mich.) Art Center, Wayne State U., Detroit, The Gallery, Ft. Lauderdale, Fla., Agra Gallery, Washington, Salon des Artes, Paris; numerous group shows including: Palazzo Pruili Gallery, Venice, Italy, 1971, Detroit Inst. of Arts, 1967, Butler Mus., N.Cleve., 1972, Windsor (Ont., Can.) Art Center, 1973, Weisbaden (Germany) Gallery, 1976; represented in permanent collections: Detroit Inst. of Arts, Wayne State U., Detroit, Wooster (Ohio) Coll., Ford Motor Co., Detroit, Bloomfield Art Assn., Bloomfield Hills, Mich., also private collections; numerous portrait paintings including portraits of Indira Ghandi, Benson Ford, Joyce Carol Oates, Mrs. Edsel Ford, Betty Ford, Roman Gribbs, Princess Olga Mrivani, Lord John Mackintosh, Marlo Thomas, Viveca Lindfois, Betty Freidan, Gloria Steinem, Congresswoman Martha Griffiths. Chairwoman of Mich. Women's Commn., 1972—; pres. Detroit House of Correction Commn., 1975—; treas. Republican Dist. 1 of Mich., 1973—; mem. Issues Com., Republican State Central Com., 1975-76; sec. Republican State Ways and Means Com., 1975—; mem. Mich. State Adv. Council Vocat. Edn.; mem. Mich. Arts in Edn. Council, 1978—; mem. New Detroit Arts Com., 1979—; chmn. World Feminist Commn., 1974—. Recipient Silver Salute award Mich. State U., 1976, Most Popular award San Diego Sculpture Show, 1971, First prize award Cape Cod Artists Show, 1968; named Distinguished Woman of Mich., Bus. and Profl. Women's Orgn., 1974, Distinguished Woman Northwood Inst., 1977. Mem. Detroit Inst. Arts (dir. membership com. 1958—), Nat. Assn. of Commns. for Women (sec., dir. 1976-78), Mich. Acad. of the Arts, Detroit Soc. of Women Painters and Sculptors, Women in the Arts, Scarab Club (dir. 1962-63), Ibex Club (pres. 1951), Nat. Orgn. for Women (nat. bd. 1971-75, del. UN conf., Mex., 1975), Women's Econ. Club, N.Y. Portrait Club (nat. com. 1978—), Alpha Phi. Episcopalian. Club: Zonta Internat. Contbr. articles to art jours. Home: 18261 Hamilton Rd Detroit MI 48203 Office: 217 Farnsworth Detroit MI 48202

BURNISON, JUDITH COATE, assn. exec.; b. Atlanta, Apr. 4, 1944; d. Eugene Russell and Adaline (Carper) Coates; B.S., Ind. U., 1969, M.S., 1976; m. Thomas Burnison, Nov. 16, 1974. Human resources coordinator City of Bloomington (Ind.), 1975-77; program devel. specialist div. continuing edn. Northwestern U., 1977-81; exec. dir. Ill. Library Assn., 1981—; co-chmn. Chgo. '79 Graphic Arts/Communication Show, 1979; cons. in field. Mem. Women in Communications (chmn. career conf. 1979-80, v.p. programs and membership 1980-81). Women in Mgmt., Am. Soc. Assn. Execs., Am. Soc. Tng. and Devel. Office: 425 N Michigan Ave Chicago IL 60611

BURNISTON, KAREN SUE, nurse; b. Hammond, Ind., May 20, 1939; d. George Hubbard and Bette Ruth (Ambler) B.; R.N., Parkview Methodist Hosp., Ft. Wayne, Ind., 1961; B.S. in Nursing, Purdue U., 1974; M.S., No. Ill. U., DeKalb, 1976. Staff nurse Parkview Meml. Hosp., 1961-63, 71-73; physician office and operating room nurse,

1963-67; nurse N.W. Ind. Home Health Services, 1974; mem. faculty Michael Reese Hosp. Sch. Nursing, Chgo., 1977-79; asst. dir. nursing Mt. Sinai Hosp. Med. Center, Chgo., 1977-79; asst. adminstr. patient services St. Margaret Hosp., Hammond, 1980—. Served with Nurse Corps, USAF, 1967-71. Mem. Am. Nurses Assn., Am. Soc. Nursing Service Adminstrs., N.W. Ind. Council Nursing Service Adminstrs., Ind. Nurses Assn., Ind. Soc. Hosp. Nursing Service Adminstrs., Sigma Theta Tau. Mem. Christian Ch. (Disciples of Christ). Club: Altrusa. Home: 1601 Anna St Schererville IN 46375 Office: 5454 Hohman Ave Hammond IN 46320

BURNLEY, WINSTON TOLBERT, ret. graphic co. exec.; b. Atlanta, July 20, 1913; s. Richard Tolbert and Alzie Pearl (Grizzard) B.; student Emory U., 1929-33; m. Gladys Laurene Virgil, Dec. 15, 1973; children—Richard Norman, Linda Kaye, Susan Rebecca, Candace Ann, Rita Jamieson. Staff mgr. real estate dept. Chgo. Herald & Examiner, Los Angeles Times, Georgian Am. and Atlanta Constitution, 1935-42; real estate salesman Gordon Bennett Real Estate Co., also Dimmitt-Rickhoff-Bayer Real Estate Co., 1944-55; sales mgr. Midwest Regions Assos., St. Louis, 1955-66; dir. sales Dynamic Graphics, Inc., Peoria, Ill., 1967-80. Mem. Phi Delta Theta. Republican. Methodist. Home: 2215 Cypress Gardens Blvd Winter Haven FL 33880

BURNS, BRUCE PALMER, psychologist; b. Jamestown, N.Y., Mar. 5, 1922; s. Harold Fletcher and Genevieve Margaret (Erickson) B.; B.A., Coll. Wooster, 1965; M.A., Mich. State U., 1967, Ph.D., 1972. Gen. mgr. Burns Case Goods Corp., Jamestown, 1949-54, 59-64; pres., owner Show Off Inc., Jamestown, 1954-59; asst. program dir. Detroit Substance Abuse Treatment Program, 1972-78; pvt. practice clin. psychology, Detroit, 1976—; dir. Renaissance Psychol. Services, 1978—; vis. lectr. Eastern Mich. U., Ypsilanti, 1971-72; cons. Methadone Clinic, 1975-78. Served to lt. (j.g.) USNR, 1943-46. Cert. health service provider in psychology; lic. psychologist, Mich. Mem. Am., Canadian, Mich. psychol. assns., Am. Rehab. Counselors Assn., Am. Soc. Clin. Hypnosis, Mich. Personnel and Guidance Assn., Soc. Clin. and Exptl. Hypnosis, Mich. Soc. Lic. Psychologists, Mich. Assn. Marriage Counselors, Nat. Registry Health Service Providers in Psychology, SAR, Beta Theta Pi. Club: Renaissance.

BURNS, C(HARLES) PATRICK, hematologist-oncologist; b. Kansas City, Mo., Oct. 8, 1937; s. Charles Edgar and Ruth (Eastham) B.; B.A., U. Kans., 1959, M.D., 1963; m. Janet Sue Walsh, June 15, 1968: children—Charles Geoffrey, Scott Patrick. Intern, Cleve. Met. Gen. Hosp., 1963-64; asst. resident in internal medicine, Univ. Hosps., Cleve., 1966-68, sr. resident in hematology, 1968-69: instr. medicine Case Western Res. U., 1970-71; asst. chief hematology Cleve. VA Hosp., 1970-71; asst. prof. medicine U. Iowa Hosps., Iowa City, 1971-75, asso. prof. medicine, 1975-80, prof. medicine, 1980—, also dir. sect. on med. oncology; cons. U.S. VA Hosp.; mem. study sect. on exptl. therapeutics NIH. Served to capt. M.C., AUS, 1964-66. Am. Cancer Soc. fellow in hematology-oncology, 1968-69; USPHS fellow in medicine, 1969-70; USPHS career awardee, 1978. Diplomate Am. Bd. Internal Medicine, subsplty. bds. hematology, med. oncology. Fellow A.C.P.; mem. Am. Soc. Hematology, Am. Assn. Cancer Research, Internat. Soc. Hematology, Central Soc. Clin. Research, Am. Soc. Clin. Oncology, Soc. Exptl. Biology and Medicine, AAAS, Am. Fedn. Clin. Research, Lambda Chi Alpha, Phi Beta Pi, Alpha Omega Alpha. Research and publs. on tumor lipid biochemistry, leukemia and oncology. Home: 2046 Rochester Ct Iowa City IA 52240 Office: Dept Medicine University Iowa Hospitals Iowa City IA 52242

BURNS, DARRYL EUGENE, podiatrist; b. Balt., Oct. 27, 1949; s. Paul Winfred and Ruby Elizabeth (Baker) B.; B.A., Western Md. Coll., 1971; D.Podiatric Medicine, Pa. Coll. Podiatric Medicine, 1976. Resident, Kern Hosp. for Spl. Surgery, Warren, Mich., 1977-78; pvt. practice podiatry, Detroit, 1978—; instr. Kern Hosp. Foot Clinic, Detroit, 1981—; resident teaching staff Kern Hosp., Warren, Mich., 1978—. Diplomate Am. Bd. Podiatric Surgery, Am. Bd. Podiatric Orthopedics. Fellow Am. Coll. Foot Surgeons, Am. Coll. Foot Orthopedics; mem. Am. Podiatry Assn., Mich. State Podiatry Assn., Civic Hosp. Alumni Residents Assn., Phi Delta. Lutheran. Home: 1768 Northlawn St Birmingham MI 48009 Office: 17333 W 10 Mile Rd Southfield MI 48075

BURNS, DONALD CLARE, community coll. ofcl.; b. Hubbardston, Mich., Jan. 4, 1943; s. Michael Louis and Florence Leona (Hogan) B.; B.A., Aquinas Coll., Grand Rapids, Mich., 1965; M.A. in Guidance and Counseling, Mich. State U., 1969; m. Maureen Ann Empey, Aug. 19, 1967; children—Daniel, Colleen, Donna, Cara. Tchr., coach St. Thomas Sch., Grand Rapids, 1965-68; dir. guidance and admissions Am. Sch. Madrid, 1969-71; counselor, dir. area guidance center Montcalm Community Coll., Sidney, Mich., 1971-74, dean student and community services, 1974-80, v.p. for instrn., 1980—; chmn. Mich. Sch. Counselor Legis. Com., 1973, Career Edn. Planning Dist. 22, 1975-78; vice chmn. Community Action Agy., 1976—; cons. in field. Mem. Am. Assn. for Higher Edn., Am. Personnel and Guidance Assn., Mich. Assn. Community Coll. Instrnl. Adminstrs., Mich. Assn. Community Student Personnel Adminstrs. Roman Catholic. Author articles in field. Office: Montcalm Community Coll Sidney MI 48885

BURNS, HAROLD EDWARD, stockbroker; b. Michigan City, Ind., Aug. 28, 1942; s. Charles Edward and Pearl Margaret (Hanski) B.; student U. Nebr., Omaha, 1960-63; m. Carol Ann Freeman, Feb. 29, 1972; 1 son, Brian Alexander. Regional sales rep. Dadco Diversified Co., 1970-73; mgr. Mgmt. Recruiters, Kalamazoo, 1973-75; stockbroker, br. mgr. Ohio Co., Kalamazoo, 1975-78; stockbroker Smith, Hague & Co., Kalamazoo, 1978—; owner Status Galleries Ltd. Served with USAF, 1960-64. Mem. Am. Assn. Bus. Men, Pilots Internat., Nat. Hist. Soc., Internat. Soc. Registered Reps., Smithsonian Soc. Clubs: Ambucs, Elks. Home: 1815 Thrushwood St Kalamazoo MI 49002 Office: 338 ISB Bldg Kalamazoo MI 49006

BURNS, JERRY FRANK, educator; b. Clio, Iowa, Aug. 11, 1934; s. John William and Maxine Hazel (Rogers) B.; B.S. in Edn., S.W. Mo. State U., 1959; M.Ed., U. Mo., 1962; postgrad. U. Nebr., U. S.D.; m. Phyllis Idell Petty, Feb. 28, 1954. Tchr., asst. prin. Des Moines Public Schs., 1959-67; sch. psychologist Warren and Marion County Bd. Edn., Indianola, Iowa, 1967-75; coordinator spl. edn. Heartland Edn. Agy., Ankeny, Iowa, 1975-78, asst. dir. spl. edn., 1978—. Former sec.-treas., bd. trustees, bd. deacons Assembly of God Ch. Lic. psychologist, Iowa. Mem. NEA (life), Nat. Assn. Sch. Psychologists (charter), Iowa Sch. Psychologists Assn. (charter), Iowa Psychol. Assn., Council Exceptional Children, Des Moines Radio Amateur Assn. Republican. Club: Greater Des Moines FM. Home: 3842 Brinkwood Rd Des Moines IA 50310 Office: 1932 SW 3d St Ankeny IA 50021

BURNS, MARY CLAUDIA, nun, educator; b. Withimsville, Ohio, Mar. 21, 1922; d. Elmer John and Agnes Loretta (McPherson) B.; B.S., Coll. Mount St. Joseph, 1957; M.S. Ed., U. Dayton, 1967; Ed.D., U. Cin., 1981. Joined Order Sisters of Charity of Cin., Roman Catholic Ch., 1938; tchr. of deaf St. Rita Sch., Cin., 1940-47; elem. tchr. St. Mary Sch., Chillicothe, Ohio, 1947-53, St. Joseph Sch., Springfield, Ohio, 1953-54, St. Mary Sch., Albuquerque, 1954-57, Sacred Heart Sch., Denver, 1957-62, St. Marys Cathedral, Lansing, Mich., 1962-64; tchr., Shrine of the Little Flower, Royal Oak, Mich., 1964-69, St. Helens Sch., Saginaw, Mich., 1969-70; prin. Annunciation Sch., Cin., 1970-73; prof. edn., reading specialist Coll. Mt. Saint. Joseph (Ohio), 1973-75, media specialist, dir. audio visuals, 1978—. Mem. Internat. Reading Assn., (pres. 1980-81), Ohio Coll. Council, Ohio Ednl. Library Media Assn., Greater Cin. Library Consortium, Assn. Supervision and Curriculum Devel., Nat. Council Tchrs. English, Ohio Assn. Supervision and Curriculum Devel., Assn. Ednl. Communications and Tech. Address: 5701 Delhi Pike Mount Saint Joseph OH 45051

BURNS, MICHAEL KENT, educator; b. Sarasota, Fla., Jan. 4, 1945; s. Richard Andrew and Lilian Ida (Kent) B.; B.A. (Univ. scholar), Capital U., 1967; M.A., Ohio State U., 1969; ednl. staff personnel adminstrv. specialist cert., Cleve. State U., 1978; m. Brenda Carolyn Bingham, Dec. 24, 1973. Grad. teaching fellow Ohio State U., 1967-69; instr. Wright State U., 1969-70; tchr. Spanish, social studies Euclid (Ohio) High Sch., 1970—, tchr. social studies, 1977—; summer intern Euclid Fisher Body Plant, Gen. Motors Corp., 1978; fellow Taft Inst. Govt., 1978, 79; career guidance inst. intern Cleve. Met. Jobs Council, 1980; tchr. Cleve. State U., 1980-81; group facilitator, drug and alcohol abuse, 1981. Mem. Euclid Tchrs. Assn. (v.p. 1974-76, pres. 1977-78), Ohio Edn. Assn., NEA, Assn. Supervision and Curriculum Devel., World Future Soc., Penticulus, Pi Lambda Theta. Democrat. Unitarian. Home: 19345 Riverview Ave Rocky River OH 44116 Office: 711 E 222d St Euclid OH 44123

BURNS, MICHAEL PAUL, auditor; b. Highland Park, Mich., Dec. 2, 1935; s. Gerald Dennis and Stella Marie Stanislaw B.; A.A. cum laude, Chgo. City Coll., 1961; B.S. in Bus. Adminstrn., cum laude, Roosevelt U., 1962; m. Rosemarie Klem, Aug. 25, 1962; children—Dennis Anthony, Michael Paul, Mary Therese. Mem. staff Peat Marwick Mitchell & Co., C.P.A.'s, Chgo., 1962-65, Pullman Bank & Trust Co., Chgo., 1965-68, Scot Lad Foods Inc., Chgo., 1968-72; auditor I.C. Industries Inc., Chgo., 1972-80, Michael Reese Hosp. and Med. Center, 1980—. Trustee Village of Thornton (Ill.), 1970-72, treas., 1972-77. Served with AUS, 1954-57. Mem. Am. Inst. C.P.A.'s, Ill. State C.P.A.'s, Nat. Acctg. Assn., Hosp. Fin. Mgmt. Assn. Home: 16730 Clyde Ave South Holland IL 60473 Office: 29th St and Ellis Ave Chicago IL 60616

BURNS, NEAL MURRAY, marketing exec.; b. Chgo., July 16, 1933; s. Jack Arnold and Esther (Dinitz) B.; student U. Chgo., 1949-51; B.S., U. Ill., 1955; M.S., McGill U., 1957, Ph.D., 1959; m. Phyllis Syrene Hirsch, Mar. 25, 1974; children—Marc, Scott, Paula Berg, Charles Berg. Head psychopharmacology dept. Parke-Davis Inc., Detroit, 1958; chief environ. stress br. Air Crew Equipment Lab., USN, Phila., 1959-61; dir. life scis. div. Decker Corp., Bala Cynwyd, Pa., 1961-62; dir. mktg. Systems and Research Center, Honeywell, Inc., Mpls., 1962-72; asso. exec. dir Higher Edn. Coordinating Bd., Minn., 1972-76; pres. Marketec, Inc., Mpls., 1976-79; sr. v.p. Hoffman York, Inc., Mpls., 1980—; mktg. cons., 1973-76. USPHS grantee, 1955-58. Mem. Am. Mgmt. Assn., Am. Psychol. Assn., Human Factors Soc., IEEE, Am. Assn. Consultants. Editor: Unusual Environments and Human Behavior (R. Chambers and E. Hendler), 1963. Home: 4633 Sunset Ridge Golden Valley MN 55416 Office: Hoffman York Inc 227 Shelard Plaza Minneapolis MN 55426

BURNS, REALFORD (RALPH) CRAIG, valve mfg. exec.; b. Texarkana, Ark., July 23, 1947; s. Emmett Realford and Pearl (Craig) B.; B.S., Stephen F. Austin State U., 1974, M.A., 1976; m. Judith Stockton, Sept. 12, 1977; children—Julie Marie, Ryan Craig. With W-K-M Valve Co., Houston, 1965-74, Cameron Iron Works, Houston, 1975-77; advt. and sales promotion mgr. DeZurik, unit Gen. Signal Co., Sartell, Minn., 1977—; owner, pres. Tiune Mktg. Cons. Co.; mem. faculty St. Cloud (Minn.) State U. Served with USAF, 1966-70; Vietnam. Teaching grad. asst. Stephen F. Austin State U., 1975. Mem. Bus./Profl. Advt. Assn., AAUP, Am. Mktg. Assn. Democrat. Baptist. Club: SFA Photographic. Home: 706 Kilian Blvd Saint Cloud MN 56301 Office: DeZurik Sartell MN 56377

BURNS, RICHARD DON, orthodontist; b. Leon, Iowa, Nov. 29, 1939; s. Leslie Warren and Ethel (Shafer) B.; D.D.S. summa cum laude, State U. Iowa, 1963; M.S.D. in Dentistry, Ind. U., 1966. Practice orthodontics, Elkhart, Ind., 1967—; founder, pres., treas., dir. OrthoTek, Inc., Elkhart, 1968—, Westwood Realty Elkhart, Inc., 1968—, Lancer Advt. Agy. Inc., Elkhart, 1971—; founding pres. Richard D. Burns Orthodontics, Inc., 1970—. Trustee Richard D. Burns Orthodontics Profit Sharing and Pension Trusts, OrthoTek Profit Sharing and Pension Trust; founder, chmn. trustees Midwest Mus. Am. Art. Served with USPHS, 1963-64, USAF, 1966-67. Mem. Am., Ind. dental assns., Elkhart County Dental Soc. (past pres.), Am. Assn. Orthodontists, Ind. Soc. Orthodontists (past pres., past sec.), Great Lakes Soc. Orthodontists, Am. Soc. Dentistry for Children, Omicron Kappa Upsilon, Psi Omega, Sigma Phi Epsilon. Methodist. Kiwanian. Inventor dental appliance; designer orthodontic pub. relations products. Home: 2413 Greenleaf Blvd Elkhart IN 46514 Office: 1750 Kilbourn St Elkhart IN 46514

BURNS, RICHARD HOWARD, food preparation equipment mfg. co. exec.; b. Ridgewood, N.J., Sept. 26, 1930; s. Robert Orr and Opal May (Shirreffs) B.; B.S. in Applied Art, Auburn U., 1953; m. Beverly Duncan Ritchie, Sept. 9, 1953; children—Richard Howard, Laura Elizabeth. Mgr. indsl. design Hobart Corp., Troy, Ohio, 1955-57, project engr., 1957-66, mgr. indsl. design, 1966—; owner, pres. Richard H. Burns's Assos., indsl. design and engrng. cons. Mem. Miami County Planning Commn., Troy City Council, 1978—. Served with U.S. Army, 1953-55, capt. Res. ret. Mem. Troy C. of C., Am. Def. Preparedness Assn. Republican. Presbyterian (elder). Kiwanian. Patentee in field. Home: 662 Clarendon Rd Troy OH 45373 Office: World Hdqrs Ave Troy OH 45373

BURNS, ROBERT EDWARD, editor, pub.; b. Chgo., May 14, 1919; s. William Joseph and Sara (Foy) B.; student DePaul U., 1937-39; Ph.B., Loyola U., 1941; m. Brenda Coleman, May 15, 1948; children—Maddy F., Martin J. Public relations dir. Cath. Youth Orgn., Chgo., 1943-45, 47-49; exec. dir. No. Ind. Region, NCCJ, South Bend, Ind., 1946; exec. editor U.S. Cath. Mag., gen. mgr. Claretian Pubs., Chgo., 1949—. Chmn. bd. trustees Rosary Coll. Mem. Thomas More Assn. (dir. 1960—). Author: The Examined Life, 1980. Home: 616 High Rd Glen Ellyn IL 60137 Office: 221 W Madison St Chicago IL 60606

BURNS, WILLIAM ARTHUR, hosp. adminstr.; b. Laurens, S.C., Dec. 16, 1943; s. Mason William and Eunice Marie (Braxton) B.; B.A. in Biology, Furman U., Greenville, S.C., 1965; M.H.A., Va. Commonwealth U., 1971; m. Sally Sheldon, Aug. 4, 1978; children—Stephen, Stewart. Adminstr. resident Riverside Hosp., Newport News, Va., 1970-71, asst. adminstr., 1971-77, adminstrv. dir. Community Mental Health Center, 1972-75; adminstr. Patrick Henry Hosp., Inc., Newport News, 1975-77; adminstr. Midlands Community Hosp., Papillion, Nebr., 1977—. Bd. dirs. Youth Emergency Services, 1978. Served with U.S. Army, 1966-68. Decorated Green Hornet Accommodation medal. Licensed nursing home adminstr., Va. Mem. Am. Coll. Hosp. Adminstrs., Nat. Council Community Mental Health Centers (chmn. Va.), Am. Hosp. Assn., Omaha Hosp. Assn. (chmn. emergency med. service com., dir.), Papillion Area C. of C. (co-chmn. Papillion Days 1977, chmn. pub. relations com. 1978). Presbyterian. Clubs: Papillion Lions, Kiwanis. Home: 1797 Kent Circle Papillion NE 68128 Office: Hwy 370 at S 84th St Papillion NE 68046

BURNSIDE, BRADLEY ALLEN, cons.; b. Chgo., Dec. 13, 1921; s. Harry Boland and Gladys (Allen) B.; B.A., Knox Coll., 1946, B.S., 1946; postgrad. Northwestern U., 1943, Purdue U., 1944; m. Nancy Woolger, Feb. 23, 1952; children—Barbara, Bradley, With Time, Inc., Chgo., 1952-62, regional mgr. House & Home mag., 1952-58, mgr., 1958-62; exec. v.p. W.H. Long Marketing Co., Greensboro, N.C., 1962-64; mgr. Chgo. area Am. Builder Mag., 1964-68; exec. dir. Water Conditioning Found., Northfield, Ill., 1968-74; industry cons. Kitchen and Bath Mag., Palm Springs, Calif., 1971-74; fin. and mktg. cons. Jades, S.A., Antigua, Guatemala; sr. cons. Career Mgmt., Inc., 1974-78; now field mktg. mgr. U.S. Gypsum Co. Exec. dir. Water Conditioning Found. Inst., Northfield, 1968-74. Trustee Bus. Inst., Coll. of Desert, Palm Desert, Calif. Served with USMCR, 1944-45. Recipient service award Water Conditioning Found., 1966, Turtle award, 1971. Mem. Water Quality Research Council, Am. Mil. Engrs. Assn., Am. Wood Preservers Assn., ASTM, Iowa Water Conditioning Assn. (life), Tau Kappa Epsilon. Club: Chgo. Knox. Home: 1628 Blackthorn Dr Glenview IL 66025

BURNSIDE, WILLIAM CHARLES, securities co. exec.; b. Edgar County, Ill., Oct. 23, 1936; s. William D. and Juanita W. (Greeson) B.; B.S., Eastern Ill. U., 1959; m. Lola Lafern Trovillion, Oct. 10, 1975; children—Bilinda Cheryl, William Benton, Tyler Thomas; stepchildren—Scott Wesley Trovillion, Mitzi Lynn Trovillion. Jr. exec. trainee Millikin Nat. Bank, Decatur, Ill., 1959-63; salesman acctg. and data processing equipment NCR, Decatur, 1963-65; registered rep. Mid Am. Corp., Paris, Ill., 1965-70, Loewi & Co., Decatur, Ill., 1970-73; owner, pres. William C. Burnside & Co., Inc., Danville, Ill., 1973—; dir. Commn. on State Banks and Trusts, 1978—; sec., dir. Mid-States Railcar Inc., 1979—. Legis. asst., campaign coordinator State Senator Max Coffey, 1976—; legis. asst. State Rep. Max Coffey, 1974-76; treas. 1st United Methodist Ch., 1966-68; mem. bldg. com. Alliance Ch. of Danville, 1980; vice chmn. Ill. Heart Assn., 1966-70, Eastern Ill. U. Found.; pres. Edgar County Heart Assn., 1971-72. Served with USAR, 1955-63. Named Outstanding Young Man Am., Jaycees, 1971. Mem. Securities Investment Protection Corp., Nat. Assn. Securities Dealers (fin. prin.), Internat. Entrepreneurs Assn. Republican. Clubs: Am. Business, Christian Bus. Men's (Danville, Ill.). Home: 322 Fletcher Hills Danville IL 61832 Office: 4 N Vermilion St Danville IL 61832

BURNSTEIN, HAROLD ROBERT, lawyer; b. Chgo., May 28, 1919; s. Samuel and Fay (Fine) B.; B.S.C., Northwestern U., 1940; J.D., DePaul U., 1950; m. Harriet Kahn, May 25, 1946; children—Clifford Nolan, Joan Ellen. Pub. accountant Katz, Wagner & Co., Chgo., 1940-41; tax accountant Consol. Vultee Aircraft Corp., San Diego, 1941-45; tax accountant Hughes and Hughes, Chgo., 1946-50, counsel, 1950-79; of counsel firm Schwartz and Freeman; admitted to Ill. bar, 1950, since practiced in Chgo. Past chmn. Highland Park Voters Assn.; mem. Dist. 108 Sch. Bd., Highland Park, 1967-73, pres., 1972-73; mem. Highland Park Library Bd., 1974-80; bd. dirs. North Suburban Library System, 1976-79, Lay Response Council, 1979-81; bd. dirs. Jewish Children's Bur., 1978—, treas., 1981—. Mem. Am., Chgo. (com. fed. taxation, past chmn.) bar assns., Ill. Soc. C.P.A.'s, Am. Inst. C.P.A.'s, DePaul Bd. Assos., Chgo. Council on Fgn. Relations, Beta Alpha Psi. Jewish. Clubs: Birchwood (past pres.) (Highland Park); Standard, Economic (Chgo.). Contbr. articles on fed. taxation to profl. jours. Home: 510 Ravine Dr Highland Park IL 60035 Office: 401 N Michigan Ave Chicago IL 60611

BURPULIS, EUGENIA G., tel. co. exec.; b. Salem, N.J., Nov. 21, 1942; s. George S. and Thelma (Pirovolos) B.; student Kent State U., 1961-62, Cuyahoga Community Coll., 1977. With Ohio Bell Tel. Co., Cleve., 1961—, Supr., 1964-71, asst. mgr. multi-media, 1971-75, asst. mgr. course devel., 1975-78, mgr. course devel., 1978—. Mem. Nat. Soc. Performance and Instrn., Am. Bus. Woman's Assn. (editor bull.), Ohio Bell Pioneers (editor newsletter), St. Demetrios Philoptochos Soc. Greek Orthodox (mem. choir). Home: 1273 W 108th St Cleveland OH 44102 Office: 100 Erieview Plaza Room 808A Cleveland OH 44114

BURRESS, PROCTOR SHERWOOD, psychologist; b. Louisville, Dec. 27, 1934; s. Proctor Sherwood and Emily Virginia (Koshewa) B.; B.A., U. Ky., 1963, M.A., 1967; m. Shirley Ann Sharp, Nov. 22, 1957; children—Shari Jessica, Mark Proctor. Psychometrist, R.R. Donnelley & Sons, Crawfordsville, Ind., 1963-65; with Cummins Engine Co., Columbus, Ind., 1967—, indsl. personnel counselor, 1967-69, dir. personnel, 1972—; instr. Ind. U./Purdue U., 1969, 81. Bd. dirs. Bartholomew County Mental Health Assn., 1968-70, Pro Musica, 1980—, Laws Scholarship Found., 1970-73. Served with U.S. Army Security Agy., 1958-61. NSF fellow, 1962-63. Mem. Am. Psychol. Assn., Ind. Psychol. Assn. Unitarian-Universalist. Home: 9471 W Youth Camp Rd Columbus IN 47201 Office: 1000 5th St Columbus IN 47201

BURRIS, ROLAND WALLACE, state comptroller; b. Centralia, Ill., Aug. 3, 1937; s. Earl L. and Emma M. (Curry) B.; B.A., So. Ill. U., 1959; postgrad. U. Hamburg (W. Ger.), 1960; J.D., Howard U., 1963; m. Berlean Miller, Dec. 23, 1961; children—Rolanda Sue, Roland Wallace. Admitted to Ill. bar, 1964; nat. bank examiner Dept. Treas., 1963-64; tax cons., Continental Ill. Bank & Trust Co., 1964-66, comml. banking officer, 1966-70, 2d v.p., 1970-73; dir. Dept. Gen. Services, State of Ill., 1973-77; exec. dir. Ops. PUSH, 1977-78; comptroller, State of Ill., 1978—. Co-chmn. Ill. delegation Democratic Nat. Conv., 1980; mem.-at-large Dem. Nat. Com., 1981; mem. exec. bd. Chgo. Area Council Boy Scouts Am. Named Man of Year Goodwill Industries Chgo. and Cook County, 1980; recipient Alumni Achievement award So. Ill. U., 1979, Alumnus of Year award Howard U. Law Sch., 1979. Mem. Nat. State Comptrollers Assn. (pres. 1980-81), Nat. Assn. State Auditors, Comptrollers and Treas. (exec. com.), Am. Bar Assn., Ill. Bar Assn., Cook County Bar Assn., Chgo. Bar Assn., Nat. Bus. League, Alpha Phi Alpha. Baptist. Office: 201 State House Springfield IL 62706

BURRITT, JOHN KERNS, librarian; b. Tomahawk, Wis., May 28, 1923; s. Harry and Mary (Robertson) B.; student U. Wis., 1941-42; B.A., Wartburg Coll., 1949; M.A., U. Ill., 1963; grad. Wartburg Sem., 1952. Ordained to ministry Luth. Ch., 1952; pastor 1st Luth. Ch., Ohio, Ill., 1952-58, St. John's Luth. Ch., Princeton, Ill., 1952-58; interim pastor Perry Luth. Ch., Daleyville, Wis., 1980-81; pastor Trinity Luth. Ch., Oconto, Wis., 1981—; mem. Luth. Hist. Conf.; librarian Wartburg Sem., Dubuque, Iowa, 1958-77; cons. LCA Archives, 1978-79. Mem. Am. Theol. Library Assn. Home: 427 School St Oconto WI 54153

BURROUGHS, MARGARET G., painter, educator; b. St. Rose, La., Nov. 1, 1917; B.A.E., Art Inst. Chgo., 1946, M.A.E., 1948; postgrad. Tchrs. Coll., Columbia U., 1959-61; Ph.D. (hon.), Lewis U. One-woman shows: South Side Art Center, Chgo., 1972, 74, Chgo. YWCA, 1973; group shows include: Atlanta U., 1947-55, Mexico City, 1952, Harvard U., 1957-60, Poland and USSR, 1966; represented in permanent collections: Atlanta U., Howard U., Ala.

A&M U., Jackson State Coll., George Carver Mus., Tuskegee, Ala.; tchr. art Du Sable High Sch., Chgo., 1946-69; tchr. art history Art Inst. Chgo., 1968-69; tchr. humanities Kennedy-King City Coll., Chgo., 1969—. Mem. Gov.'s Commn. to Study Financing of Arts in Ill., 1972-73; Chgo. Council Fine Arts, 1976; Nat. Conf. Artists. Recipient First Watercolor award Atlanta U., 1955; Best in Show, Nat. Conf. Artists, Lincoln U., Jefferson City, Mo., 1963; 3d pl. in sculpture Atlanta U., 1969. Cited by Pres. Carter at White House 1980, apptd. by Pres. Carter to Nat. Commn. on Black History and Culture, 1980. Illustrator: Jasper the Drummer Boy, 1950; What Shall I Tell My Children Who Are Black?, 1965; For Malcolm, 1967; Africa: My Africa (poems), 1969; Did You Feed My Cow?, 1970; Whip Me Whop Me Pudding, 1975.

BURROUGHS, PAULINE HUFF, social worker; b. Carlton, Ga., Mar. 20, 1926; d. Arthur W. and Mattie E. (Huff) Huff; Ph.B., Northwestern U., 1952; M.S.W., Loyola U. Chgo., 1955; M.Ed., DePaul U., 1958; postgrad. U. Chgo. and Smith Coll., 1970-71; m. Stanley A. Burroughs, Mar. 9, 1972. Tchr., Bd. Edn., Chgo., 1956-60, 64; clin. social worker VA Hosp., Buffalo, 1960-62; clin. social worker psychiatry VA Hosp., Tomah, Wis., 1963-65; med. clin. social worker VA Hosp., Hines, Ill., 1965-66; clin. social worker psychiatry VA Hosp., Northport, N.Y., 1966-74; field experience supr. SUNY, VA Hosp., Northport, 1968-74; social worker VA Hosp., Battle Creek, Mich., 1974-76; cons., counseling therapist in pvt. practice, Chgo., 1977—; lectr. in field. Recipient award for superior performance in social work VA Hosp., Northport, 1970, others; cert. social worker, Ill., N.Y. Mem. Nat. Assn. Social Workers (registered clin. social worker), Acad. Social Workers, Council on Social Work Edn., Am. Soc. Profl. and Exec. Women, Nat. Assn. Female Execs., AAUW. Office: PO Box 49365 Chicago IL 60649

BURROWS, GEORGE (BILL), state legislator; b. Adams, Nebr., Oct. 21, 1930; student Nebr. Wesleyan Coll., U. Nebr.; m. Norma Jean Conneally, Dec. 26, 1953; children—Greg, Jay, Mark, Laureen. Farmer; mem. Nebr. Legislature, 1974—. Mem. Gov.'s Adv. Com. State Instns., Dept. Public Welfare; mem. Gage County FHA Adv. Com., Gage County Extension Bd. Home: Rural Route 1 Adams NE 68301*

BURROWS, HAROLD HENRY, investment broker; b. Mpls., Oct. 18, 1942; s. Harold Henry and Emily (Sirotiak) B.; B.S. in Math. and Physics, Iowa State U., 1964; M.S. in Physics, U. Minn., 1967, M.B.A., 1972; m. Renée Ruth Marko, Dec. 18, 1965; children—Jason, Sonja, Suzanne. Research physicist Honeywell Inc., Mpls., 1967-69; account exec. Merrill Lynch Inc., Mpls., 1969-76; investment broker Shearson/Am. Express Inc., Mpls., 1976-81, v.p. investments, 1981—. Ward chmn. Ind. Republican Party. Lutheran. Home: 5135 Fern Dr Loretto MN 55357 Office: 200 Minnesota Fed Bldg Minneapolis MN 55402

BURT, FRANK N., JR., vascular surgeon; b. Freeport, Ill., Apr. 30, 1943; s. Frank N. and Betty N. (Becker) B.; B.S., Northwestern U., 1965, M.D., 1967; m. Connie Grange, Feb. 8, 1969; children—Kristin, Mitchell. Intern LDS Hosp., Salt Lake City, 1967-68, resident, 1968-70; resident St. Agnes Hosp., Balt., 1970-72; fellow in peripheral vascular surgery Providence Hosp., Southfield, Mich., 1975; peripheral vascular surgeon, partner Northland Vascular Clinic, Southfield, 1975-80; asso. Woodland Med. Group, 1980—; med. dir. intensive and spl. care units Providence Hosp., 1976-78, chief sect. vascular surgery, 1979—; guest physician first surg. clinic U. Vienna, 1967; found., chmn. bd. dirs. Data-Med Corp., Southfield, 1976—; lectr. grad. sch. engring. George Washington U., 1976-79. Troop leader Detroit council Boy Scouts Am., 1975-77. Served with USAF, 1972-74. Recipient Michael E. DeBakey research award in vascular surgery, 1977. Diplomate Am. Bd. Surgery. Mem. AMA, Mich. Med. Soc., Oakland County Mich. Med. Soc., Internat. Coll. Angiology, Am. Med. Soc. of Vienna. Mormon. Developer intensive care unit patient data mgmt. system Providence Hosp.; inventor, developer data-med profl. practice mgmt. system; researcher field of vascular surgery. Home: 2178 Coach Way Bloomfield Hills MI 48013 Office: 22341 W Eight Mile Rd Detroit MI 48219

BURTON, CHARLES VICTOR, physician, surgeon; b. N.Y.C., Jan. 2, 1935; s. Norman Howard and Ruth Esther (Putziger) B.; m. Noel Michelle Kleid, Aug. 26, 1961; children—Matthew, Timothy, Andrew; student Johns Hopkins U., 1952-56; M.D., N.Y. Med. Coll., 1960. Intern surgery Yale U. Med. Center, 1961-62; asst. resident neurol. surgery Johns Hopkins Hosp., Balt., 1962-66, chief resident, 1966-67; asso. chief surgery, chief neurosurgery USPHS Hosp., Seattle, 1967-69; vis. research affiliate Primate Center, U. Wash., 1968-69; asst. prof. neurosurgery Temple U. Health Scis. Center, Phila., 1970-73, asso. prof., 1973-74, neurol. research coordinator, 1970-74; dir. dept. neuroaugmentive surgery Sister Kenny Inst., Mpls., 1974-81, 1977-81; med. dir. Low Back Clinic, 1977-81; med. dir. Inst. Low Back Care, Mpls., 1980—; co-chmn. Joint Neurosurg. Com. on Devices and Drugs, 1973-77; chmn. Internat. Standards Orgn., 1974-76, FDA adv. panel on neurologic devices, 1974-77; mem. U.S. Biomed. Instrumentation Del. to Soviet Union, 1974. Research fellow Nat. Polio Found., 1956, HEW, 1958; neurosurg. fellow Johns Hopkins Hosp., 1960-61, 62-67, 69-70; Diplomate Am. Bd. Neurol. Surgery, Nat. Bd. Med. Examiners. Fellow ACS; mem. Congress Neurol. Surgeons (chmn. com. materials and devices 1972-79), Am. Assn. Neurol. Surgeons, Minn. Neurosurg. Soc., AAAS, ASTM (chmn. com. materials 1973-78), Internat. Soc. Study of Lumbar Spine, Am. Nat. Standards Inst. (med. device tech. adv. bd. 1973-78), Philadelphia County Med. Soc. (med.-legal com. 1970-74), Minn. Med. Assn. (Gold medal award for best sci. presentation at 1975 Meeting, subcom. on med. testimony 1978—), Hennepin County Med. Soc. (med.-legal com. 1975—), Mpls. Acad. Medicine, Cor et Manus Soc., Alpha Epsilon Delta. Home: 148 W Lake St Excelsior MN 55331 Office: Inst Low Back Care 2737 Chicago Ave Suite 1750 Minneapolis MN 55407

BURTON, CLELAND PATRICIA, hist. abstractor; b. Detroit, July 15, 1918; d. Fred and Fern Louise (McCloy) B.; student Fairfax Hall, Waynesboro, Va., 1937-39, U. Mich., 1939-40; m. Robert Waller Bragg III, Jan. 25, 1941 (dec.); 1 dau., Melissa. Exec. v.p. Fred Burton Abstract Co., 1947-59; owner Burton Farms for Registered Shetlands, various locations, 1960-64; hist. abstractor Am. Frontier Ltd., Bolar, Va., 1965—; hist. cons. Mason County (W.Va.) Bicentennial Commn., 1974-77, Point Pleasant, W.Va., 1977-79; condr. nat. survey on date and place of 1st battle of Am. Revolution; co-sponsor program commemorating 200th anniversary of death of Andrew Lewis, Bedford County, Va. Recipient award Freedoms Found., 1975. Mem. Nat. Trust Historic Preservation, W.Va. Hist. Soc., W.Va. Press Women, Detroit Hist. Soc. Office: PO Box 1774 Bolar VA 24414

BURTON, COURTNEY, mining and shipping co. exec.; b. Cleve., Oct. 29, 1912; s. Courtney and Sarita (Oglebay) B.; student Mich. Coll. Mining and Tech., 1933-34, B.S., 1956; m. Marguerite Rankin, Sept. 7, 1933 (dec. Apr. 1976); children—Sarita Ann (Mrs. John Limbocker Jr.), Marguerite Rankin (Mrs. George M. Humphrey II); m. Margaret Butler Leitch, Dec. 20, 1978. Dir. E.W. Oglebay Co., Cleve., 1934-57, pres., 1947-57; v.p. Ferro Engring. Co., Cleve., 1950-57; pres. Fortuna Lake Mining Co., Cleve., 1950-57; treas., dir. Columbia Transp. Co., Cleve., 1950-57; v.p. Montreal Mining Co., Cleve., 1950-57; pres. N. Shore Land Co., Cleve., 1950-57; v.p., dir. Brule Smokeless Coal Co., Cleve., 1950-57; chmn. bd., chmn. exec. com. Oglebay Norton Co., Cleve., 1957—; dir. Cleve. Trust Co., 1950-76. Dir. Ohio CD and Rationing, 1941-42; exec. asst. Office Coordinator Inter-Am. Affairs, 1942-44; mem. bd. commrs. Cleve. Met. Park Bd., 1969-74. Mayor, Village of Gates Mills, Ohio, 1948-61; chmn. Ohio Republican Finance Com., 1954-61, Rep. Nat. Finance Com., 1961-64. Trustee Bethany Coll.; past trustee Nat. Park Found.; hon. trustee Univ. Hosp., Cleve., Oglebay Inst., Wheeling, W.Va.; pres. Am.'s Future Trees Found., Cleve. Zool. Soc. (pres. 1968-76). Served to lt. USNR, 1944-46. Mem. Am. Iron and Steel Inst., Nat. Coal Assn. Episcopalian. Clubs: Chagrin Valley Hunt (master of hounds 1946-54) (Gates Mills); Tavern, Union (Cleve.); Rolling Rock (Ligonier, Pa.); Fort Henry (Wheeling); Kirtland, (Willoughby, Ohio). Office: 1100 Superior Ave Cleveland OH 44114

BURTON, DANNY L., state senator; b. Indpls., June 21, 1938; s. Charles W. and Bonnie Lee (Hardisty) B.; ed. Ind. U., 1958, Cin. Bible Sem., 1959-60; m. Barbara J. Logan, 1959; children—Danielle, Kelly, Danny L. Owner, Dan Burton Agy., 1967—; mem. Ind. Ho. of Reps., 1967-69, 77-79, now Ind. Senate. Served with U.S. Army, 1956-57. Office: Ind State Capitol Indianapolis IN 46204*

BURTON, DARRELL IRVIN, engring. exec.; b. Ashtabula, Ohio, Sept. 21, 1926; s. George Irvin and Barbara Elizabeth (Streyle) B.; B.S. in Radio Engring., Chgo. Tech. Coll., 1954; m. Lois Carol Warkentien, Apr. 14, 1951; children—Linda Jean Burton Clinton, Lisa Ann, Lori Elizabeth. Research and devel. engr. Motorola, Inc., Chgo., 1951-60; devel. engr. Hallicrafters, Chgo., 1960-62; chief engr. TRW, Inc., Des Plaines, Ill., 1962-65; devel. engr. Warwick, Niles, Ill., 1965-68; systems mgr. Admiral Corp., Chgo., 1968-76; elec.-electronics lab. mgr. Montgomery Ward & Co., Chgo., 1976—; tchr. electronics and math. Pres. Addison Homeowners Assn., 1958-60, v.p., 1960-62; mem. Addison Plan Commn., 1960-63. Served with USNR, 1944. Mem. IEEE, ASTM. Republican. Lutheran. Patentee in field. Home: 112 Lawndale Ave Elmhurst IL 60126 Office: Montgomery Ward Plaza RD 6 5 Chicago IL 60671

BURTON, DOROTHY HOPE, educator; b. Norwood, Ohio, Apr. 7, 1928; d. Osber Franklin and Ina Belle (Sears) Zachary; student Olivet Nazarene Coll., 1945-49; B.S. in Edn., Ball State U., 1960, M.A. in Edn., 1967; postgrad. Ohio State U., 1977-82; m. Roy Dean Burton, Nov. 28, 1947 (div.); children—Jennifer D., Sally Jo Hunley. Classroom tchr. Aroma Park (Ill.) Sch., 1954-56, Bradley (Ill.) Community Schs., 1957, Crawfordsville (Ind.) City Schs., 1957-58, Muncie (Ind.) City Schs., 1960-77; field placement coordinator, asst. prof. edn. Mount Vernon (Ohio) Nazarene Coll., 1977—; substitute tchr. Kankakee Community Schs. Mem. Assn. Supervision and Curriculum Devel., Nat. Council Tchrs. Math., Am. Assn. Colls. Tchr. Educators, Assn. Tchr. Educators, Nazarene Assn. Colls. Tchr. Edn., Ohio Assn. Tchr. Educators, Kappa Delta Pi. Republican. Nazarene. Home: 9 Claypool Dr Mount Vernon OH 43050 Office: 800 Martinsburg Rd Mount Vernon OH 43050

BURTON, MARY JOAN (MRS. ROBERT E. BURTON), ednl. adminstr.; b. Hamilton County, Ind., July 1, 1918; d. William Nelson and Sybil Anna (Inman) Smith; primary certificate Ball State Tchrs. Coll., Muncie, Ind., 1938; B.S. in Edn., Ind. U., 1942, M.S. in Edn., 1960; m. Robert Ermer Burton, May 26, 1940; children—Ann E. (Mrs. J. Stephen Grimes), John E., Nancy E. (Mrs. Luis A. Morales), William L., James A. Tchr., Union Twp. Schs., Howard County, Ind., 1938-39, Westfield (Ind.) Schs., 1939-40; tchr. Broadview Sch., Bloomington, Ind., 1956-63, tchr. educable retarded, 1963-65; tchr. trainable retarded Headley Sch., Bloomington, 1965-68; dir. Stone Belt Center for Retarded Citizens, Bloomington, 1968—. Sec., Monroe County Health Planning Council, 1972-73, Owen-Monroe County Health Planning Council, 1973-76, Region 10 Health Planning Council, 1973-76; mem. Region 2 Subarea Advisory Council S. Ind. Health Systems Agency, 1977—. Mem. Council for Exceptional Children (pres. S. Central Ind. 1966, 72-73), Am. Assn. Mental Deficiency (sec.-treas. Ind. chpt. 1976-80), Delta Kappa Gamma (pres. Beta Lambda chpt. 1966, corr. sec. Alpha-Epsilon state 1969-71), Pi Lambda Theta (dir. Iota chpt. 1971). Methodist. Club: Altrusa (pres. 1977-78). Home: 501 S Swain Ave Bloomington IN 47401 Office: 2815 E 10th St Bloomington IN 47401

BURTON, WALTER ERVIN, writer; b. McMechen, W.Va., Nov. 18, 1903; s. David William and Mary Lucinda (Yoho) B.; student U. Akron, 1922-23, Johns Hopkins, 1923-24, 27-28. Editorial staffs Evening Times, Times-Press, Herald Pub. Co., Akron, 1922-23, 24-27. Mem. Nat. Assn. Home and Workshop Writers. Club: Portage Camera (Akron). Contbr. numerous articles to mags. including Popular Mechanics, Popular Sci., others. Author: Home-Built Photo Equipment, 1947; The Story of Tire Beads and Tires, 1954, others. Editor: Engineering with Rubber, 1949. Patentee in field. Address: 1032 Florida Ave Akron OH 44314

BUSA, PETER, artist; b. Pitts., June 23, 1914; s. Salvatore and Ernestina (Chrispo) B.; student Carnegie Inst. Tech., 1929-32, Art Students League, N.Y.C., 1933-35, Hans Hofmann Sch. Fine Art, N.Y.C., 1935-36; studied with Alex Kostellero, Ray Simboli, Sam Rosenberg, Thomas Benton; m. Jeanne Juhl, June 26, 1943; children—Christopher, Stephen, Paul, Marianne, Nicholas. One man shows: Peggy Guggenheim Gallery, N.Y.C., 1946, Julius Carlebach Gallery, 1948, Bertha Schaefer Gallery, 1947, 51, 52; group exhibitions include: Whitney Mus., N.Y.C., Retrospective, Chrysler Art Mus., Provincetown, Mass., Parrish Art Mus., 1973; also prof. art U. Minn., Mpls. Yaddo fellow, 1942; Ford Found. award, 1962; Guggenheim fellow, 1976-77. Office: Univ of Minn Dept Art Minneapolis MN 55455

BUSBY, EDWARD OLIVER, univ. dean; b. Macomb, Ill., June 22, 1926; s. Lynn John and Pauline (Hoebel) B.; B.S., U. Wis., 1950, M.S., 1962, Ph.D. (NSF fellow), 1971; m. Lois E. Tehan, June 17, 1950; children—Thomas L., John E., Paula L. Resident engr. Wis. Hwy. Commn., Madison, 1950-51; asst. city engr., La Crosse, Wis., 1951-53; sales engr. Wis. Culvert Co., Madison, 1953-59; lectr. civil engring. U. Wis., Madison, 1959-66; dean Coll. Engring., U. Wis., Platteville, 1966—; v.p. Platteville Area Indsl. Devel. Corp.; mem. Wis. Profl. Engrs. Registration Bd., 1981—. Served with USN, 1944-46. Registered profl. engr., Wis. Fellow ASCE; mem. Nat. Soc. Profl. Engrs. (dir. 1976-81, vice chmn. engrs. in edn. 1971-73), Wis. Soc. Profl. Engrs. (pres. 1972-73, Engr. of Yr. in edn. 1968, Engr. of Yr., S.W. chpt. 1969-70). Republican. Contbr. articles to profl. jours. Home: 940 Mound View Ct Platteville WI 53818 Office: Ottensman Hall U Wis Platteville WI 53818

BUSBY, JACQUELINE GAYLE, univ. adminstr.; b. Olney, Ill., July 31, 1939; d. Gale Lathrop and Dorothy Irene (Kirby) Piper; cert. Sch. Bus., So. Ill. U., Edwardsville, B.S. in Bus. Adminstrn., 1980; m. Aug. 27, 1961; 1 son, Jerry Lynn. Adminstrv. asst. St. Anthony's Hosp., Alton, Ill., 1969-75; research asst. health care mgmt. program So. Ill. U., Edwardsville, 1975-77, asst. dir. Study of Operational Linkages, State of the Art Analysis of CETA Linkages in Ill., 1979, research asso. dept. mgmt., 1980—. Mem. Adminstrv. Mgmt. Soc., Am. Soc. Personnel Adminstrn., Ill. Bus. Edn. Assn., Nat. Bus. Edn. Assn., Am. Vocat. Assn., Pre-Employment and Placement Assn., Pi Omega Pi. Methodist. Home: 239 Wood River Ave East Alton IL 62024 Office: Mgmt Dept PO Box 100 Bldg 2 So Ill Univ Edwardsville IL 62026

BUSCH, AUGUST A., JR., brewing exec.; b. St. Louis, Mar. 28, 1899; s. August A. and Alice (Zisemann) B.; ed. Smith Acad.; LL.D., St. Louis U., 1969; m. Gertrude Buholzer, Mar. 22, 1952. With Mfrs. Ry. Co., Lafayette South Side Bank & Trust Co.; gen. supt. Anheuser-Busch, Inc., 1924-26, 6th v.p., gen. mgr., 1926-31, 2d v.p., gen. mgr., 1931-34, 1st v.p., gen. mgr., 1934-41, pres., 1946-75, chmn. bd., 1956-77, chief exec. officer, 1971-75; pres., chmn. bd., chief exec. officer St. Louis Cardinals, 1953—; chmn. Mfrs. Ry. Co., St. Louis Refrigerator Car Co.; dir. St. Louis Union Trust Co., First Union, Inc., Gen. Am. Life Ins. Co., U.S. Brewers Found., 1st Nat. Bank, St. Louis. Mem. brewing industry adv. com. WPB, 1942; chmn. public relations com. United Fund St. Louis, 1964—. Chmn. bd. Civic Progress, Inc., 13 years, St. Louis U. Devel. Fund drive; bd. dirs. St. Louis Mcpl. Opear; chmn. St. Louis Bicentennial Celebration Com. Served as col. Ordnance Dept., AUS, 1942-45. Recipient Fleur-de-Lis award St. Louis U., 1960; named Man of Year, St. Louis Globe-Democrat, 1961; Man and Boy award Nat. bd. Boys' Clubs Am., 1966; Citizen No. 1 award Press Club Met. St. Louis, 1967; Man of Year award So. Calif. Retail Liquor Dealers Assn., 1971; hon. commodore USCG Aux., 1972. Clubs: St. Louis Country, Racquet, Old Warson, Log Cabin, Bridlespur Hunt (St. Louis); Rolling Rock (Ligonier, Pa.). Home: Grant's Farm 10501 Gravois Ave Saint Louis MO 63123 Office: 721 Pestalozzi St Saint Louis MO 63118

BUSCH, AUGUST ADOLPHUS, III, brewery exec.; b. St. Louis, June 16, 1937; s. August Anheuser and Elizabeth (Overton) B.; student U. Ariz., 1957-59, Siebel Inst. Tech., 1960-61; m. Virginia L. Wiley, Dec. 28, 1974; children—Steven August, Virginia Marie; children by previous marriage—August Adolphus, Susan Marie. With Anheuser-Busch, Inc., St. Louis, 1957—, sales mgr., 1962-64, v.p. mktg. ops., 1964-65, v.p., gen. mgr., 1965-74, pres., 1974—, chief exec. officer, 1975—, also dir.; now also pres., chmn. bd. Anheuser-Busch Cos., Inc.; dir. St. Louis Nat. Baseball Club, Gen. Am. Life Ins. Co., Mfg. R.W. Co., Laclede Gas Co., 1st Nat. Bank St. Louis, Norfolk & Western Ry., Southwestern Bell Telephone Co. Mem. adv. bd. St. John Mercy Med. Center, Busch Center U. Pa.; trustee Washington U.; mem. pres.'s council St. Louis U.; bd. dirs. United Way Greater St. Louis, Nat. Center for Resource Recovery, St. Louis Symphony Soc., Jr. Achievement Mississippi Valley; sponsor Coll. William and Mary, C. of C. U.S.; bd. overseers Wharton Sch., U. Pa.; mem. exec. bd. Boy Scouts Am. Mem. U.S. Brewers Assn. (dir., chmn.). Clubs: St. Louis, Racquet (St. Louis), Log Cabin, Stadium, Noonday, St. Louis Country. Office: One Busch Pl Saint Louis MO 63118

BUSCH, MERRILL JOSEPH, business exec., editor, pub., author; b. Jordan, Minn., July 25, 1936; s. Albert Meinrad and Hildegarde (Bauer) B.; student St. Thomas Coll., St. Paul, 1954-57; B.A. summa cum laude, U. Minn., 1958, postgrad., 1958-59; m. Mary Daphne Meteraud, Oct. 16, 1965; children—Christopher, Jennifer, Amy. Editor, pub. Upper Midwest Investor mag., 1960-62, Mid-Am. Investor mag., 1962-63; editor Minn. mag., 1963-64, editor Cereal Sci. Today and Cereal Chemistry mag., 1965-72, Cereal Industry Newsletter, 1970-72; dir. publs. Am. Assn. Cereal Chemists, 1965-72, Am. Phytopathological Soc., 1968-72, also gen. mgr. both orgns., 1970-72; editor Nematology mag., 1971-72, Phytopathology mag., 1968-72, Phytopathology News, 1968-72, Comml. West mag., 1972-76, Greater Mpls. mag., 1972-80, The Gold Book, 1974—, 9th Fed. Directory Banks, and Nat. Fin. Marketplace, 1974-76; mng. editor mag. div., bus. and fin. editor Sun Newspapers, Inc., 1972-78, dir. spl. publs., 1976-78, dir. promotion, mktg., 1977-78; exec. Bozell & Jacobs Public Relations, 1978-80; pres. Busch & Partners, 1980—; dir. Prime Publs., Inc. Bd. dirs. Butler Sch. Law, Groves Learning Center, Homeward Bound, Inc., De La Salle High Sch., Minn. Motion Picture and TV Devel. Bd.; mem. adv. council Human Growth Found. Served with AUS, 1959-60. Recipient Recognition award Mpls. C. of C., 1975; work included in tricentennial time capsule Minn. Bicentennial Commn., 1976. Mem. Mediaeval Acad. Am., Greater Mpls. C. of C., Phi Beta Kappa. Republican. Roman Catholic. Clubs: Minn. Press; Mpls. Athletic. Author, writer-producer ednl. filmstrips, films, recs. Home: 2120 Girard Ave S Minneapolis MN 55405 also 186 Shorewood Dr St Michael MN 55376 Office: 1111 W 22d St Minneapolis MN 55405

BUSCH, ROBERT MICHAEL, ins. co. exec.; b. Rice Lake, Wis., Nov. 3, 1950; s. Leonard Albert and Rosalie Susan (Schutz) B.; B.S., U. Wis., Eau Claire, 1974, B.S. in Environ. and Public Health, 1976; M.S., U. Wis., Stout, 1978; postgrad in public health U. Minn., 1978-80; m. Leah Ellan Masterson, Dec. 13, 1980. With Wausau Ins. Cos., Mpls., 1980, loss control specialist, Oshkosh, Wis., 1981—; occupational safety and health cons. Mem. Am. Soc. Safety Engrs., Am. Indsl. Hygiene Assn., Oshkosh Indsl. Safety Council, Phi Kappa Phi. Clubs: Wausau Men's, Oshkosh Racquetball, Oshkosh Golf League. Office: PO Box 2644 Oshkosh WI 54903

BUSCH, THEODORE NORMAN, cons. shooting range design; b. Cleve., Dec. 29, 1919; s. Theodore S. and Norma B.; student pub. schs. Cleve.; m. 2d, Sené Rosene, June 30, 1961; 1 dau. by previous marriage, Kathy. Dir. tech. communications DoAll Co., Des Plaines, Ill., 1952-62; v.p. Shooting Equipment, Inc., Chgo., 1962-69; v.p. Caswell Equipment Co., Inc., Mpls., 1969—; v.p. Sente Co. Ind., Mpls., 1976—. Served with USAAF, World War II. Mem. Am. Soc. Quality Control, Soc. Mfg. Engrs., Internat. Assn. Chiefs of Police. Author: Fundamentals of Dimensional Metrology, 1963; Guidelines for Police Shooting Ranges, 1977; Guidelines for Commercial Shooting Ranges, 1979. Contbr. articles to profl. jours. Patentee in field. Home: 410 Groveland St Minneapolis MN 55403 Office: 1221 Marshall St NE Minneapolis MN 55413

BUSCHBACH, THOMAS CHARLES, geologist; b. Cicero, Ill., May 12, 1923; s. Thomas Dominick and Vivian (Smiley) B.; B.S., U. Ill., 1950, M.S., 1951, Ph.D., 1959; m. Mildred Merle Fletcher, Nov. 26, 1947; children—Thomas Richard, Susan Kay (Mrs. Pete Elmer), Deborah Lynn (Mrs. Gary Baker). Geologist, lead and zinc mining stratigraphy, underground storage of natural gas Ill. Geol. Survey, 1951-78; coordinator New Madrid Seismotectonic Study, U.S. Nuclear Regulatory Commn., 1976—; research prof. geology St. Louis U., 1978—. Geologic cons. petroleum, nuclear reactor siting. Served to lt. comdr. USNR, 1942-47. Fellow Geol. Soc. Am.; mem. Am. Assn. Petroleum Geologists (chmn. stratigraphic correlations com. 1970-73), Assn. Engring. Geologists, Am. Geophys. Union. Home: 604 Park Ln Champaign IL 61820 Office: St Louis U PO Box 8099 Laclede Sta Saint Louis MO 63156

BUSCHMAN, THOMAS WESTLAKE, mfg. co. exec.; b. Cleve., May 18, 1949; s. David Riedinger and Peggy Louise (Laughlin) B.; grad. Griswold Inst., 1970; m. Mary Jean McKibben, Mar. 12, 1970; 1 son, Westlake David. Service mgr. Ardac, Willoughby, Ohio, 1972-75; maintenance electrician Fasson, Painesville, Ohio, 1975-78; pres. Buschman Corp., Perry, Ohio, 1978—. Mem. Wire Assn. Internat., Soc. Mfg. Engrs. Republican. Home and Office: 4205 Parmly Rd Perry OH 44081

BUSCHMANN, MARYBETH TANK, anatomist; b. Evanston, Ill., Oct. 10, 1942; d. Marvin H. and Elizabeth Jane (Lind) Tank; diploma with honors Augustana Hosp. Sch. Nursing, 1964; B.S. in Nursing, Augustana Coll., 1965; M.S. in Biology, U. Ill., 1968, Ph.D. in Anatomy, 1975; m. Robert J. Buschmann, Sept. 5, 1970. Staff nurse McKinley U. Hosp., Urbana, Ill., 1966-67, Mercy Hosp., Urbana, 1967; research asst. dept. zoology U. Ill., Urbana, 1968, teaching asst., 1968-69; research dir. Kidney Biopsy Lab., U. Wis. Med. Sch., Madison, 1969-70; teaching asst. dept. anatomy U. Ill. Med. Center, Chgo., 1971-74, asst. prof. dept. gen. nursing, 1975-79, asso. prof., 1979—, asst. prof. dept. anatomy, 1976-81, asso. prof., 1981—. NIH fellow, 1979, Am. Nurses Found. scholar, 1979. Mem. Nat. League for Nursing, Soc. for Neurosci., Am. Soc. for Cell Biology, Gerontol. Soc., Midwest Soc. of Electron Microscopists (dir. 1980-81), Electron Microscopical Soc. Am., Met. Chgo. Coalition on Aging, AAAS, Sigma Xi. Lutheran. Contbr. articles on neurobiology to profl. jours. Home: 943 Monroe River Forest IL 60305 Office: 845 S Damen Ave Chicago IL 60612

BUSEN, KARL MAX, physicist, radio-TV mfg. co. exec.; b. Bonn, Germany, Apr. 19, 1918; s. Heinrich Ferdinand and Hedwig Conradine (Frankowski) B.; B.S., U. Munich (Germany), 1949, Dr. rer. Nat., 1956, postgrad. (German Research Council scholar), 1955-56; m. Johanna Christine Berberich, Jan. 4, 1952. Patent agt. Siemens & Halske, Munich, 1956-58; sr. engr. Sprague Electric Co., North Adams, Mass., 1958-60, sect. head, 1960-63, dept. head, 1963-69; mgr. Zenith Radio Corp., Chgo., 1969—; vis. instr. optics and nuclear physics, Williams Coll., Williamstown, Mass., 1961-69; vis. prof. U. Ill., Chgo., 1977. Mem. Electrochem. Soc., Am. Assn. Physics Tchrs. Contbr. articles to profl. jours. Home: 505 Kingston Terr Deerfield IL 60015

BUSH, DOROTHY JEAN BOHN, counselor; b. Dayton, Ohio, Apr. 18, 1932; d. David William and Carrie May (Tilton) Bohn; A.B., Wittenberg U., 1954, B.S. in Edn., 1954, M.Ed., 1958; postgrad. Miami U., Oxford, Ohio, 1954-55, Antioch Coll., 1963, Wright State U., 1970-74; m. Ralph Royal Bush, Jr., May 23, 1954; children—Rebecca Renee, Cynthia Colette. Tchr., Fairborn (Ohio) City Schs., 1954-61, Beavercreek Twp. Schs., Xenia, Ohio, 1962-65, Dayton (Ohio) City Schs., 1965—; guidance counselor Belmont High Sch., Dayton, 1973—. Clk.-treas. Village of Enon, 1961-62; mem. Bicentennial Com., City of Fairborn. Mem. NEA, Ohio Edn. Assn., Dayton Edn. Assn., DAR, Nat. Soc. Colonial Dames XVII Century, Nat. Soc. Daus. Am. Colonists, Mayflower Descendants in State of Ohio, Soc. Sons and Daus. of the Pilgrims, Nat. Soc. New Eng. Women, Women Descendants of Ancient and Hon. Arty. Guard, Nat. Soc. Children of Am. Revolution (sr. state pres. 1978—), Nat. Soc. Dames of Ct. of Honor, Delta Zeta. Home: 318 Ridgewood Dr Fairborn OH 45324 Office: Belmont High Sch 2323 Mapleview Ave Dayton OH 45420

BUSH, HAROLD, clin. psychologist; b. Chgo., Dec. 27, 1923; s. Herman and Rose Minnie (Weisman) B.; Ph.D., Ill. Inst. Tech., 1971. Part-time instr. Roosevelt U., Chgo., 1967-72; staff psychologist Southeast Mental Health Center, Chgo. Bd. Health, 1968-76; dept. cons. Patient and Family Counseling Center, Little Co. of Mary Hosp., Evergreen Park, Ill., 1974-80; asso. dept. psychiatry, div. psychology Northwestern U. Med. Sch., Chgo., 1981—; pvt. practice psychotherapy, psychol. testing and consultation, Chgo., 1969—. Served with AUS, 1943-46. Licensed psychologist, Ill., Calif. Mem. Ill., Calif., Am. psychol. assns., Nat. Register of Health Service Providers in Psychology. Jewish. Home: 201 E Chestnut St Apt 17B Chicago IL 60611 Office: 30 N Michigan Ave Suite 1024 Chicago IL 60602

BUSH, MARION HAROLD, JR., consultant; b. Joliet, Ill., Sept. 10, 1945; s. Marion Harold and Ella Mae (Deaton) B.; B.S. in Bus. Adminstrn., U. Md., 1969; m. Jeanne Carol Cofran; children—Jason Scott, Amy Sue. Apprentice, Liniger Co., Inc., Marion, Ind., 1964, supt., 1978-80; v.p. B.&M. Tech. Cons., Marion, 1970-72, pres., 1973—. Public safety dir. City of Marion, 1975-76. Served with Spl. Forces U.S. Army, 1966-69; master sgt. U.S. Army N.G., 1972—. Decorated Bronze Star, Combat Inf. badge, Joint Service Commendation medal; recipient commendation Mayor of Marion, 1976, Gov. Bowen, 1978. Mem. Am. Welding Soc., Ind. Vol. Firemen's Assn. (Midwest award, 1978, 79), Spl. Forces Assn., N.G. Assn., Plumbers and Pipefitters Local 166. Democrat. Mem. Bethel Ch. Club: Masons (Ft. Wayne Scottish Rite spl. ops. group).

BUSH, WILLIAM PAUL, petroleum co. exec.; b. Farnhamville, Iowa, June 15, 1920; s. Joseph James and Catherine Josephine (McCorstin) B.; B.S., U. Wyo., 1947; postgrad. U. Pitts., 1959, Am. U., 1965, M.I.T., 1970; m. Mary Elizabeth Burns, Dec. 6, 1947; children—William Paul, Mary Virginia. Engr. supr. Marathon Pipe Line Co., Casper, Wyo., 1948-57, regional mgr., Bridgeport, Ill., 1957-65, pres., dir., Findlay, Ohio, 1968—; dep. mng. dir. Deutsche Marathon Petroleum GmbH, Munich, Germany, 1965-68; past pres., dir. Wolverine Pipe Line Co.; v.p., dir. Cook Inlet Pipe Line Co.; past chmn. bd., dir. LOOP, Inc.; dir. Explorer Pipeline Co. Past mem. exec. bd. Put-Han-Sen Area council Boy Scouts Am. Served to capt., C.E., AUS, 1943-46. Mem. Assn. Oil Pipe Lines (past chmn.; past chmn. exec. com.; past chmn. fed. affairs com.), Am. Petroleum Inst. (past chmn. central com. on pipe line transp., mem. coordinating com. pipe line transp.), Nat. Petroleum Council (mem. coordinating subcom. of com. on emergency preparedness), Findlay C. of C., Sigma Tau, Phi Delta Theta. Republican. Episcopalian. Clubs: Elks; Rotary Internat. (Findlay). Patentee corrosion protection of buried metallic objects. Home: 1000 S Main St Findlay OH 45840 Office: 231 E Lincoln St Findlay OH 45840

BUSHBERG, JERROLD TALMADGE, bionucleonics cons., educator; b. Berkeley, Calif., Nov. 22, 1953; s. Norman T. and Annette L. (Rosenthal) B.; B.S. in Physiology with honors, U. Calif., Davis, 1975; M.S. in Radiol. Physics, Purdue U., 1980, Ph.D. in Bionucleonics, 1981. Lab. technologist dept. pulmonary biochemistry U. Calif., Davis, 1974-75; staff research asso. U. Calif., Palo Alto, also Stanford U., also instr. depts. chemistry and nuclear medicine, 1975-77; lectr. and sr. research asso. Yale U. Sch. of Medicine, New Haven, Conn., 1977-78; radiol. control intern Purdue U., W.Lafayette, Ind., 1978-79, acad. adv., 1979—, grad. instr., 1979—; cons. radiol. health standards U.S. Nuclear Regulatory Commn., 1979—; adv. Health Scis. Club, 1979—; CPR instr. Am. Heart Assn., 1973—; advanced first aid instr. ARC, 1972—; manuscript reviewer Jour. of Nuclear Medicine Tech., 1978—. Dept. Energy Nat. Tng. fellow Yale U. and Mayo Clinic, 1979; recipient Nat. Research Service award HEW, 1979-81, Jenkins Research award Purdue U., 1980; diplomate Am. Bd. Indsl. Hygiene, Am. Bd. Nuclear Medicine Tech. Mem. Am. Nuclear Soc., Soc. of Nuclear Medicine, Am. Soc. of Clin. Pathology, Am. Soc. Med. Tech., Am. Assn. Physics in Medicine, Health Physics Soc., Sigma Xi, Phi Kappa Phi, Rho Chi, Eta Sigma Gamma. Contbr. articles on nuclear medicine to profl. publs. Home: 302 Graduate House E West Lafayette IN 47906 Office: Purdue Univ 156 Pharmacy Bldg West Lafayette IN 47907

BUSHEMI, JOHN PETER, lawyer, state senator; b. Chgo., Apr. 13, 1948; s. Samuel Joseph and Pearl Caroline (Maranto) B.; A.B. in Polit. Sci., Ind. U., 1970, J.D., 1973. Admitted to Ind. bar; atty. Legal Aid Soc. Gary (Ind.), 1974; public defender Lake County Juvenile Ct., 1974-75, Lake County Ct., 1976; individual practice law, Gary, 1974—; instr. bus. law Ind. U. N.W., 1974, 75, 78; mem. Ind. Senate, 1976—; mem. Ind. Commn. Autism, Ind. Rehab. Services Adv. Bd., Ind. Jud. Study Commn., Title XX Adv. Commn. Recipient various certs. appreciation, recognition awards. Mem. Am. Bar Assn., Am. Arbitration Assn., Ind. Bar Assn., Lake County Bar Assn., Ind. U. N.W. Alumni Assn., Italian-Am. Benevolent Soc. Democrat. Roman Catholic. Office: 5847 Broadway Merrillville IN 46410

BUSHING, WILLIAM HENRY, acquisitions and mergers consulting co. exec.; b. Oak Park, Ill., Apr. 12, 1925; s. William G. and Rose (Hilgendorf) B.; student Mont. Sch. Mines, 1943-44; B.S. in Bus. Adminstrn., Northwestern U., 1946; postgrad. Harvard U., 1946; m. Barbara Gallond, Mar. 2, 1946; children—William Walter, Barbara Lee, Judith Ann, Nancy Jean. With A.B. Dick Co., Chgo., 1946-62; nat. sales mgr. Allstate Ins. Co., Northbrook, Ill., 1964-70; pres. W.H. Bushing & Co., Inc., Northbrook, 1970—. Served with U.S. Navy, 1943-46. Office: 1161 Walnut Ln Northbrook IL 60062

BUSKAS, ROBERT JAMES, banker; b. Wetaskiwim, Alta., Can., Aug. 10, 1932; came to U.S., 1956, naturalized, 1965; B.S., Northwestern U., 1964; s. Johann and Susanna (Schmuland) B.; postgrad DePaul U., 1977—. Asst. to pres. George Getz Corp., Chgo., 1959-61; ops. officer Ill. State Bank, Chgo., 1961-68; sr. v.p. Am. Nat. Bank, Chgo., 1968—. Served with U.S. Army, 1957-59. Mem. Loop Systems Assn. Clubs: Tavern, Club Internat. Home: 3200 N Lake Shore Dr Chicago IL 60657 Office: 33 N LaSalle St Chicago IL 60690

BUSKIRK, PHYLLIS RICHARDSON, economist; b. Queens, N.Y., July 19, 1930; d. William Edward and Amy A. Richardson; A.B. cum laude, William Smith Coll., 1951; m. Allen V. Buskirk, Sept. 13, 1950; children—Leslie Ann, William Allen, Carol Amy, Janet Helen. Clk. technician W.T. Grant Co., N.Y.C.; 1948-49; research asst. W.E. Upjohn Inst. for Employment Research, Kalamazoo, 1970-75, research asso., 1976—. Mem. Civil Service bd. City of Kalamazoo, 1977—, chmn., 1981—. Mem. Am. Statis. Assn., Indsl. Relations Research Assn. Presbyterian. Clubs: P.E.O., Kalamazoo Network. Co-editor Business Conditions in the Kalamazoo Area, Quar. Rev., 1979—. Office: 300 S Westnedge Ave Kalamazoo MI 49007

BUSS, DANIEL FRANK, environ. scientist; b. Milw., Jan. 13, 1943; s. Lynn Charles and Pearl Elizabeth (Ward) B.; B.S., Carroll Coll., 1965; M.S. in Biology, U. Wis., 1972, M.S. in Environ. Engring., 1977; m. Ann Makal, Jan. 22, 1977. Dir. limnological studies Aqua-Tech, Inc., Waukesha, Wis., 1969-72; project mgr. environ. studies Point Beach Nuclear Plant, Two Creeks, Wis., 1972-76; dir. aquatic studies environ. sci. div. Camp Dresser & McKee, Inc., Milw., 1977—, dir. indsl. service, 1978—; guest lectr. on nuclear power and the environment. Mem. Am. Nuclear Soc. (sec.-treas. Wis. sect.), Midwest Soc. Electron Microscopists, Internat. Soc. Theoretical and Applied Limnology and Oceanography, Internat. Assn. for Gt. Lakes Research, N.Am. Benthological Soc., Fed. Water Pollution Control Adminstrn. Author: Seasonal Ultrastructural Variations in the Rostral Neurohypophysis of the Alewife in Lake Michigan, 1972; An Environmental Study of the Ecological Effects on Lake Michigan of the Thermal Discharge from the Point Beach Nuclear Plant, 1976. Home: 5543 N Shasta Dr Glendale WI 53209 Office: 6132 W Fond du Lac Ave Milwaukee WI 53218

BUSS, JUDY JOAN, interior designer; b. North Platte, Nebr., Jan. 25, 1948; d. Joseph Walter and June Roseland (Davidson) Brott; B.S., U. Nebr., 1971; m. Jerald Lee Buss, Aug. 18, 1968; children—April Joy, Crystal Jo Ann. Owner, operator Arbor Crest, Lincoln, Nebr., 1974—. Office: 2637 O St Lincoln NE 68510

BUTCHER, JAMES ROBERT, lawyer, state senator; b. Detroit, Mar. 9, 1933; s. James Otis and Beulah Iris (Gammon) B.; B.A., Wittenberg U., Springfield, Ohio, 1955; J.D., Valparaiso U., 1958; m. Marvel Myland, June 27, 1953; children—Kevin, Linda, Jeffery. Admitted to Ind. bar; planning dir. City of Huntington (Ind.), 1958-59, Kokomo (Ind.)-Howard County, 1959-62; gen. counsel Youth for Christ Internat., Wheaton, Ill., 1962-64; individual practice law Ball & Brubaker, Kokomo, 1964—; mem. Ind. State Senate. Founder, 1st pres. Kokomo Christian Businessman Com., 1965, Kokomo Connie Mack Baseball Assn., 1968, Kokomo Area Youth for Christ, 1965; bd. dirs. Kokomo Rescue Mission; chmn. bd. Bible Baptist Ch., alt. del. nat. conv., 1980; del. Republican state conv., 1972-80; pres. Taylor U. Ann. Fund Drive, 1976-77. Named Disting. Parent of Yr., Taylor U., 1976. Mem. Ind. Bar Assn., Howard County Bar Assn., Am. Bar Assn., Christian Legal Soc., Am. Legis. Exchange Council. Baptist. Office: 201 N Buckeye St Kokomo IN 46901*

BUTIN, JAMES WALKER, physician; b. Fredonia, Kans., July 13, 1923; s. James A. and Berenice Marie (Walker) B.; A.B., U. Kans., 1944, M.D., 1947; M.S. in Medicine, U. Minn., 1952; m. Betty Belle Launder, June 29, 1949; children—Richard Edward, Philip Walker, Lucy Elizabeth, John Murray. Intern, U. Kans. Med. Center, 1947-48; resident in pathology, 1948; fellow in internal medicine Mayo Found., 1949-52; practice medicine specializing in internal medicine and gastroenterology, Wichita, Kans., 1952—; mem. staff Wichita Clinic, St. Francis Hosp., Wesley Med. Center; asso. prof. Kans. U. Sch. Medicine, Wichita. Summerfield scholar, 1940-44. Diplomate Am. Bd. Internal Medicine (gastroenterology). Mem. A.C.P., AMA, Am. Gastroenterol. Assn., Am. Assn. History Medicine, Kans. Med. Soc., Sedgwick County Med. Soc. (past pres.) Christian Med. Soc., Wichita Med. Edn. Assn. (chmn. 1973-74), Mayo Alumni Assn., Wichita Audubon Soc. (past pres.), Kans. Ornithol. Soc. (past pres.), Phi Beta Kappa, Alpha Omega Alpha, Nu Sigma Nu, Beta Theta Pi. Republican. Episcopalian. Contbr. articles to med. jours. Home: 38 Mission Rd Wichita KS 67206 Office: 3244 E Douglas Ave Wichita KS 67208

BUTKEWICZ, PETER JOSEPH, air force officer, aerodynamicist; b. Scranton, Pa., June 7, 1936; s. Peter Cyril and Emily Marie (Guzinski) B.; B.S. in Aero. Engring., Parks Coll., 1957; M.S. in Aero. Engring., Air Force Inst. Tech., 1963; Ph.D. in Aerospace Engring., U. Tenn., 1969; grad. Def. Systems Mgmt. Coll.; m. Barbara Anne Juba, Aug. 25, 1962; children—Michael, Gregg, Anne. Commd. 2d lt., U.S. Air Force, 1957, advanced through grades to col., 1979; chief aerodynamics br. Flight Dynamics Lab., Wright-Patterson AFB, Ohio, 1964-73, chief aeromechanics div., 1978-81, dir. flight systems engring. Aero. Systems div., 1981—, asst. chief flight tech. div., directorate flight systems engring., 1974-76; asst. dir. engring. E-4 System Program Office, Hanscom AFB, Mass., 1976-77, chief aircraft engring. div., 1977-78; AF co-chmn. Tactical Aircraft Research and Tech. Conf., 1980; U.S. mem. NATO Adv. Group Study Panel, 1973-74. Decorated Meritorious Service medal with oak leaf cluster, Air Force Commendation medal with oak leaf cluster. Mem. AIAA, Air Force Inst. Tech. Assn. Grads., Sigma Xi. Club: Wright-Patterson Rod and Gun. Home: 1824 Southlawn Dr Fairborn OH 45324 Office: AFWAL FIM Wright Patterson Air Force Base OH 45433

BUTLER, DENNIS ARTHUR, clin. mental health counselor; b. Kansas City, Kans., May 19, 1940; s. Ben Arthur and Naomi Mae (Bernard) B., Jr.; B.S., U. Kans., 1966; M.S., Emporia State U., 1969, Ed.S., 1976; Ph.D., Kans. State U., 1980; m. Reve Marie Gnuse, Sept. 2, 1978; 1 dau. by a previous marriage, Diana Dawn. Accountant, auditor Trans World Airlines, Kansas City, Mo., 1959-63; elem. tchr. Shawnee Mission (Kans.) Sch. Dist., 1966-69, tchr. psychology/anthropology, 1969-75, career devel. cons., 1975—; mental health counselor Inst. for Marriage & Family Counseling, 1979—. Mem. NEA, Nat. Vocat. Guidance Assn., Am. Psychol. Assn., Am. Personnel and Guidance Assn., Am. Mental Health Counselors Assn., Phi Delta Kappa. Republican. Episcopalian. Office: 5800 W 107th St Shawnee Mission KS 66207

BUTLER, GERALDINE HEISKELL (GERRI), designer, artist; b. Detroit, Sept. 6, 1930; d. Artist Kavassel and Geraldine Gentle (Heiskell) B.; student Wright Jr. Coll., 1946; B.E., Chgo. U., 1948; B.A. in Edn. (Delta Sigma Theta Scholar), Chgo. Art Inst., 1949, M.A. in Edn., 1950; postgrad. Harvard U., 1962-64. Tchr. pub. elementary schs., Chgo., 1949-52; tchr. art Chgo. pub. high schs., 1953-61; supr. art Chgo. Bd. Edn., 1962-75; graphic art and media coordinator, dept. instrn. Chgo. Bd. Edn., 1976-77; founder, prin. Gehebu-AK, design cons. services, Chgo., 1976—; founder, prin. Butler Studios, creative designer, Chgo., 1977—; one-man shows include: Saxon Gallery, Chgo., Roosevelt Hotel, N.Y.C., Henri IV Restaurant, Cambridge, Mass., Hilton Trinidad, B.W.I., Goldstein Gallery, Chgo.; group shows include: Triangle Gallery, Chgo., McCormick Pl., Chgo., Hyde Park Art Center, Chgo., Ill. State Fair, Peninsula Exhbts., Door County, Wis.; represented in permanent collections: rental gallery Art Inst. Chgo., Huntington Hartford Collection, N.Y.C.; judge numerous exhbts. and competitions; art cons. and designer. Mem. Ill. wing CAP, 1963—. Huntington Hartford fellow, 1956-58. Mem. Internat., Ill., Nat. art edn. assns., Western Arts Assn., Am. Craftsmen Assn., Alumni Chgo. Art Inst., Soc. Typog. Arts, Artists Guild Chgo., Chgo. Soc. Artists, N. Shore Art League, Hyde Park Art Center, Evanston Art Center, USAF Art Corps, Triangle-Lincoln Park Art Center, Am. Youth Hostels, Delta Kappa Gamma, Delta Sigma Theta. Episcopalian. Office: PO Box 11360 Chicago IL 60611

BUTLER, JAMES MARTIN, educator; b. Freeport, Ill., Apr. 20, 1948; s. Martin Harvey and Elizabeth Ann (Hillebrecht) B.; B.S., U. Ill., 1970, M.S., Northeastern Ill. U., 1978; M.A., Chgo. State U., 1982; m. Ruth Ann Dratwa, Dec. 17, 1972; children—Dawn Marie, Christine Ann, Kimberly Ann, James Martin, Jennifer Lynn. Tchr. sci., chmn. dept. Thornton Fractional North High Sch., Calumet City, Ill., 1979—. Vice pres. Holy Name Soc., St. Andrew Ch., 1979—. Mem. Nat. Assn. Biology Tchrs., Assn. Supervision and Curriculum Devel., Ill. Assn. Biology Tchrs., Ill. Chess Assn., U.S. Chess Fedn., U. Ill. Alumni Assn. (life), Northeastern Ill. U. Alumni Assn. Club: K.C. (4 deg.). Home: 426 155th St Calumet City IL 60409 Office: 755 Pulaski Rd Calumet City IL 60409

BUTLER, JOHN HENRY, city ofcl.; b. McComb, Miss., Feb. 6, 1935; s. Rodgers and Elizabeth (Williams) B.; B.S., Mich. State U., 1957, M.A., 1968, Ph.D., 1975; 1 dau., Natalie Ren ee. Tchr. sci., coach Grand Rapids (Mich.) Central High Sch. 1961-68; asst. prin. Union High Sch., Grand Rapids, 1968-71, Central High Sch., 1971-73, Harrison Park Jr. High Sch., 1974-77; coordinator tng. and services City of Grand Rapids, 1978—. Bd. dirs. Greater Grand Rapids Hosp. Council, 1968-73. Adv. Center for Teens, 1968-73, W. Mich. Health Planning Unit, 1969-73; mem. adv. council bus. and industry Grand Ra pids Bd. Edn., 1978—. Served with USMC, 1958-61. Minority fellow Mich. State U., 1973-74. Mem. Am. Soc. Tng. and Devel. , Western Mich. Soc. Tng. and Devel., Minority Network Am. Soc. Tng. and Devel., NAACP. Home: 2309 Jefferson Dr SE Grand Rapids MI 49507 Office: 300 Monroe Ave NW Grand Rapids MI 49503

BUTLER, JOHN MUSGRAVE, r.r. exec.; b. Bklyn., Dec. 6, 1928; s. John Joseph and Sabina Catherine (Musgrave) B.; B.A. cum laude, St. John's U., 1950; M.B.A., N.Y. U., 1951; m. Ann Elizabeth Kelly, July 9, 1955; children—Maureen, John, Ellen, Suzanne. Sr. acct. Lybrand, Ross Bros. and Montgomery, C.P.A.'s, N.Y.C., 1953-59; sr. auditor ITT, N.Y.C., 1959-62; asst. to controller Dictaphone Corp., Bridgeport, Conn., 1962-63, controller Bridgeport, Conn., Rye, N.Y., 1964-68; v.p. acctg. Chgo. and North Western Ry. Co., Chgo., 1968-69, v.p. fin., 1969-72; v.p. fin. and acctg. Chgo. and North Western Transp. Co., Chgo., 1972-79, sr. v.p. fin. and acctg., 1979—, dir., from 1976, trustee, from 1978. Served with USCGR, 1951-53. C.P.A., N.Y. State. Mem. Assn. Am. Railroads, Am. Inst. C.P.A.'s, Fin. Execs. Inst. Roman Catholic. Office: Chgo and North Western Transp Co One North Western Center Chicago IL 60606

BUTLER, KENNETH B., business exec.; b. Richland, Mich., Aug. 27, 1902; s. Ross S. and Jennie (Blain) B.; B.A., U. Wis., 1925; m. Wilma Steinberg, Nov. 5, 1925; 1 son, Roger Lee; m. Doris Sibigtroth, 1969. Reporter, Madison (Wis.) Capital Times, 1923-25; editor Mendota (Ill.) Sun-Bull., 1925-27; pub. Constantine (Mich.) Advertiser Record, 1927-31; mgr. Conco Press, Mendota, 1931-41; pres. Wayside Press, 1941-78; pres. Kenneth B. Butler and Assos., 1938—; founder Butler Typo-Design Research Center, 1951, Time-Was Village Mus., 1967; lectr. Medill Sch. Journalism, Northwestern U., 1950-75; bus. mgr. P.E.O. Record, 1931-78. Gen. chmn. Mendota Centennial Jubilee, 1953, Mendota Autorama, 1955, 57, 59, 61, Constantine (Mich.) Centennial, 1928; mem. Sweet Corn Festival Com., 1962; chmn. Nat. Glidden Tour., 1963. Bd. dirs. LaSalle County unit Am. Cancer Soc. Named Kiwanis Man of Year, 1953; recipient Community Service award C. of C., 1976. Mem. Mendota Athletic Booster Soc., Ill. State, Mendota (dir. 1947-53) chambers of commerce, Am. Bell Assn., Farm Bur., Ill. Mfrs. Assn., Mark Twain Soc., LaSalle County Hist. Soc., Sigma Delta Chi. Republican. Presbyterian (elder). Elk. Clubs: Horatio Alger (co-founder, pres. 1965-67); Antique Automobile Am. (dir. Ill. region, pres. 1960-61, treas. 1967-68, nat. bd. dirs., dir. activities Central region), Steam Car, Classic Car, Pierce Arrow Society, Rolls Royce Owners, Model T Ford, Horseless Carriage, Men's Garden Am. Author: Headline Design, 1949; Effective Illustration, 1952; 101 Layouts, 1954; Double Spreads, 1955; Back of the Book Makeup, 1957; Ken Butler's Layout Scrapbook, 1958; Display Type Faces, 1959; Back of the Book Makeup, 1960; Borders, Boxes and Ornamentation, 1961; How To Stage an Oldtime Auto Event, 1961. Co-author: Magnificent Whistlestop. Editor Sidelights. Contbr. articles to profl. publs. Speaker and lectr. Home: 1325 W Burlington Rd Mendota IL 61342 Office: 700 14th Ave Mendota IL 61342

BUTLER, KENNETH VAN, lawyer; b. Kansas City, Mo., May 26, 1934; s. George Ellsworth and Mabel (Van Druff) B.; B.A. in Polit. Sci., Yale U., 1956; J.D., U. Chgo., 1959; m. Jean Louise Destler, Aug. 7, 1964; children—John Kenneth, William Destler, Anne Louise. Admitted to Kans. bar, 1959, Mo. bar, 1962; partner firm Gage & Tucker, Kansas City, Mo., Gage, Tucker & vomBaur, Washington and Boston, 1962—; dir. several corps. Bd. dirs. Legal Aid of Western Mo., 1977—; chmn. Shawnee Mission Unitarian Soc., 1970-71, pres., 1978-79, mem. Leawood Planning Commn. Served with U.S. Army, 1959-62. Mem. Lawyers Assn. Kansas City, Kansas City Bar Assn., Mo. Bar Assn., Am. Bar Assn., Estate Planning Assn. Kansas City. Republican. Clubs: Univ., Indian Hills Country, Yale (past pres., dir.), U. Chgo. (dir., sec.) (Kansas City). Home: 10205 Mohawk Ln Leawood KS 66206 Office: 2345 Grand Ave PO Box 23428 Kansas City MO 64141

BUTLER, KERN, constrn. co. exec.; b. Peru, Ind., July 15, 1936; s. M. Auber and Ruth H. Butler, B.S., Ind. U., 1962; m. Anna Mae Greenfield, July 31, 1955; children—Victoria Elizabeth, Roxanne Dawn, Teena Gay. Bookkeeper, M.A. Butler, Spencerville, Ind., 1955-62; gen. mgr. Butler & Butler Constrn. Co., Auburn, Ind., 1962-64, sec., treas., gen. mgr., 1964—; pres. Butler Real Estate, Inc., 1972—; bus. mgr. Vanguard Pub. Co., Auburn, 1968—. Trustee, Eckhart Public Library, 1968—, treas., 1972—; trustee Auburn Presbyterian Ch., 1966-69. Republican. Clubs: Fort Wayne Summit, Gideons. Home: 207 S Dewey St Auburn IN 46706 Office: 207 S West St Auburn IN 46706

BUTLER, LAVONNE RUTH GRASLIE (MRS. WARREN ELMER BUTLER), mayor, former newspaper pub.; b. Faith, S.D., Aug. 22, 1922; d. Ludwig Martin and Lilly Regina (Ness) Graslie; first grade certificate Spearfish Normal Sch., 1942; m. Warren Elmer Butler, Dec. 29, 1942; children—Richard, James. Tchr., Cherry Creek Dist. 2, Ziebach County, S.C., 1943-45; sec. to supr. schs., Faith, 1966-68; editor, pub. Faith Independent, 1969-79; mayor City of Faith, 1981—. Pres., PTA, 1953-54. Mem. Republican State Central Com., 1970—. Mem. Nat. Newspaper Assn., S.D. Press Assn., C. of C. (v.p. 1970—), Beta Sigma Phi. Methodist. Mem. Order Eastern Star. Co-editor Faith Country Book, 1960. Home: Faith SD 57626

BUTLER, OWEN BRADFORD, chem. co. exec.; b. Lynchburg, Va., Nov. 11, 1923; s. James Herbert and Ida Virginia (Garbee) B.; A.B., Dartmouth, 1947; m. Erna Bernice Dalton, Mar. 7, 1945; children—Nancy (Mrs. Wayne Archambault), James. With Procter & Gamble Co., Cin., 1945—, v.p. sales, 1968-70, v.p., group exec., 1970-73, exec. v.p., from 1973, chmn. bd., dir., 1974—; dir. Hosp. Corp. Am., Armco. Chmn. bd. Good Samaritan Hosp. Served with USNR, 1941-45, 50-51. Mem. Phi Beta Kappa. Republican. Club: Queen City (Cin.). Home: 4346-S State Route 123 Morrow OH 45152 Office: PO Box 599 Cincinnati OH 45201

BUTLER, PAUL THURMAN, coll. adminstr.; b. Springfield, Mo., Nov. 17, 1928; s. Willard Drew and Verna Lois (Thurman) B.; Th.B., Ozark Bible Coll., 1961, M.Bibl. Lit., 1973; m. Gale Jynne Kinnard, Nov. 20, 1948; children—Sherry Lynne, Mark Stephen. Non-commd. officer U.S. Navy, 1946-56, mem. staff Amphibious Forces, Pacific, 1947-51, guided missile unit 41, Point Mugu, Calif., 1951-56; ret., 1956; ordained to ministry Christian Ch., 1958; minister Washington Christian Ch., Lebanon, Mo., 1958-60; dean admissions Ozark Bible Coll., Joplin, Mo., 1960—, prof. Bible and philosophy, 1960—. Mem. Am. Legion. Republican. Author: The Gospel of John, 1961; The Minor Prophets, 1968; Daniel, 1976; Isaiah, 3 vols., 1978; Esther, 1979; The Gospel of Luke, 1981; (trans. into Korean, French, Portuguese). Home: 2501 Utica St Joplin MO 64801 Office: 1111 N Main St Joplin MO 64801

BUTLER, WARREN STOCKTON, mech. seal mfg. co. exec.; b. Trenton, N.J., Oct. 31, 1919; student N.C. State U., 1943-44, Newark Coll. Engring., 1947-50, Nazareth Coll., 1978—; m. Alice Elasser, Nov. 19, 1946; children—Jeffrey, Todd. Indsl. engr., Thermmoid Rubber Co., Trenton, 1937-46; chief indsl. engr. Panelyte div. St. Regis Paper Co., Trenton and Kalamazoo, Mich., 1946-55, resident mgr., 1955-61; plant mgr. Spaulding Fibre Co., Tonawanda, N.Y., 1961-63; gen. mgr. Eastern Finishing & Plating Co., Pennsauken, N.J., 1963-65; plant mgr. Wilson Art de Mex., Adhesives Resistol, Mexico City, 1965-70; cons. Sang Mi Ltd., Seoul, S. Korea, 1970-71; v.p. Allied Steel Service Co., Kalamazoo, 1971-72; personnel dir. Durametallic Corp., Kalamazoo, 1972—; dir. Allied Steel Co., Furniture Mfg. Co. Mexico City. Active United Way, Jr. Achievement, Republican party. Served with USAAF, 1942-45; PTO. Decorated Air Medal with oak leaf cluster. Mem. Kalamazoo C. of C., Am. Mgmt. Assn., Am. Inst. Mgmt., Kalamazoo Personnel Assn. (pres. 1976-77). Clubs: Gull Lake Country, Beacon, Elks. Home: 6121 Torrington St Kalamazoo MI 49009 Office: Durametallic Corp 2104 Factory St Kalamazoo MI 49001

BUTLER, WILFORD ARTHUR, JR., assn. exec.; b. Grand Rapids, Mich., Apr. 17, 1937; s. Wilford A. and Dorothy (French) B.; B.A., Western Mich. U., 1961; M.B.A., Fla. Atlantic U. Dir. pub. relations Preferred Ins. Co., Grand Rapids, 1961-62; asst. to chmn. Delta Upsilon fraternity, N.Y.C., 1962, exec. sec., Indpls., 1963-76, exec. dir., 1976—; advisor Mid-Am. Interfrat. Assn., 1965-81. Mem. Am. Coll. Frat. Bicentennial Commn. study, 1975-77. Recipient Salisbury-Scott award Tau Kappa Epsilon, 1975, citation of honor Theta Chi, appreciation citation Delta Chi, 1979. Mem. Assn. Coll. Frats. (pres. 1974), Frat. Execs. Assn. (sec., editor 1974, pres. 1976-77), Commn. on Fraternity Research (treas. 1972-75), Am. Soc. Assn. Execs. (cert.; mem. editors and pubs. sect. adv. bd., chmn. membership dirs. sect. council bd. 1979—, mem. membership promotion com. 1979—), Ind. Soc. Assn. Execs. (chmn. cert. program 1979—, bd. dirs., mem. exec. com. 1980; Disting. Service award 1980), Delta Upsilon (editor monthly Newstrends 1971—, quar. 1973—). Clubs: Indpls. Alumni of Delta Upsilon, Columbia (gen. membership chmn. 1979—, dir. 1980) (Indpls.). Author: Executive Compensation Trends. Editor, Our Record, 1963—, Provision of Leadership corp. officers guide. Office: PO Box 40108 Indianapolis IN 46240

BUTLER, WILLIAM JOSEPH, JR., ins. broker; b. Chgo., Feb. 24, 1942; s. William Joseph and Emily Jane (Mockenhaupt) B.; B.S., Coll. of the Holy Cross, Worcester, Mass., 1964; M.B.A., St. Louis U., 1969; m. Helen Katherine O'Malley, Aug. 28, 1965 (div. 1976); children—Charlotte Anne, Emily Jane. Mgmt. trainee Clinton E. Frank Inc., Chgo., 1969-70; dist. agt. Prudential Ins. Co., Evanston, Ill., 1970-74, spl. agt., Skokie, Ill., 1974—. Mem. fin. com. St. Mary's Ch., Lake Forest, Ill., 1980-81. Served to capt. USAF, 1964-68. C.L.U. Mem. Chgo. Assn. Life Underwriters. Republican. Roman Catholic. Home: 570 N Sheridan Rd Lake Forest IL 60045 Office: Prudential Insurance Co 5150 Golf Rd Skokie IL 60076

BUTSCH, ROBERT STEARNS, zoologist, mus. adminstr.; b. Owatonna, Minn., July 10, 1914; s. Albert Emil and Josephine Thayer (Stearns) B.; B.A., U. Iowa, 1936, M.A., 1941; Ph.D., U. Mich., 1954; m. Miriam Glee Palmer, Dec. 21, 1941; 1 dau., Elizabeth Ann Butsch Cardinal. Curator, Arrowhead Mus., Aurora, Minn., 1936-37; chief preparator Barbados Mus. and Hist. Soc., 1937-39; preparator U. Mich. Mus., 1947-48, asst. to prefect of exhibits, 1948-56, curator exhibits, 1956-75, dir. U. Mich. Exhibit Mus., 1975—. Served with C.E., U.S. Army, 1942-46. Mem. Am. Soc. Mammalogy, Am. Assn. Mus., Mich. Audubon Soc., Sigma Xi. Editor Jack-Pine Warbler, 1960-63. Office: Exhibit Mus Univ Mich Ann Arbor MI 48109

BUTT, DENNIS WILLIAM, motor co. exec.; b. Maquoketa, Iowa, Feb. 4, 1940; s. Henry Morgan and Lois Erma (Guyer) B.; A.A., Palmer Jr. Coll., 1976; B.A., St. Ambrose Coll., 1978; m. Julie Marie Henning, June 11, 1960; children—Yvette Marie, Stacey Jo. With Eagle Signal div. G & W Industries, Davenport, Iowa, 1961-78, supervisory and mgmt. positions, 1965-78; plant mgr. mfg. Kawasaki Motors Corp., Lincoln, Nebr., 1978-81; mem. exec. com., gen. mgr. Timpte Inc., David City, Nebr., 1981—. Mem. Pres.'s Adv. Council U. Nebr. System, 1980-81; bd. dirs. Lincoln Fgn. Trade Zone, 1980-81, Indsl. and Bus. Devel. Corp., David City; mem. chmn.'s com. U.S. Senate Bus. Adv. Bd., 1981—; diplomat Nebr. Dept. Econ. Devel.; chmn. Econ. Devel. Commn., City of Lincoln; mem. Commn. on Future of Nebr. Wesleyan U. Served with USMC, 1957-61. Mem. Inst. Mgmt. Sci. Lincoln C. of C. (bd. dirs.). Home: 5301 S 32d St Lincoln NE 68516 Office: 6600 NW 27th St Lincoln NE 68524

BUTT, JIMMY LEE, orgn. exec.; b. Tippo, Miss., Oct. 13, 1921; s. H.W. and Jimmie O. (Davis) B.; B.S., Auburn U., 1943, M.S., 1949; m. Jane F. Williams, June 23, 1943; children—Janie Lake, Melanie Maryanne, Jimmy Lee. Grad. asst. agrl. engring. dept. Auburn U., 1947-48, asst. 1948-50, asso. agrl. engr., 1950-56; exec. sec. Am. Soc. Agrl. Engrs., St. Joseph, Mich., 1956-74, exec. v.p., 1974—. Trustee, mem. bd., lay leader United Meth. Ch. Served as capt. F.A., AUS, 1943-46. Recipient Disting. Service award Mich. State U., 1975; Ordre du Merite Agricole (France)., 1979; registered profl. engr., Ala. Fellow Am. Soc. Agrl. Engrs.; mem. Nat. Soc. Profl. Engrs., Council Engring. and Sci. Soc. Execs. (pres. 1977-78), Sigma Xi, Tau Beta Pi, Phi Kappa Phi, Gamma Sigma Delta, Alpha Zeta, Omicron Delta Kappa. Clubs: Lions (past pres.), Economic. Office: 2950 Niles Rd St Joseph MI 49085

BUTTARS, MONTE VINCENT, tractor co. exec.; b. Logan, Utah, Nov. 16, 1946; s. Vincent and Della (Palmer) B.; B.S. in Fin., Utah State U., 1974; m. Suzanne Larsen, Aug. 25, 1969; children—Melanie Sue, Kimberlie Jo, Ann Marie, Jonathan Vincent. Salesman, v.p. Buttars Tractor Inc., Logan, 1976-78; dist. mgr. J.I. Case Co., Hutchinson, Kans., 1979—; Adviser 4-H, Logan; precinct chmn. Republican Party, Nibley, Utah. Mormon. Home and Office: 3701 Panorama Dr Hutchinson KS 67501*

BUTTEL, THEODORE LYLE, educator; b. Centerville, Iowa, May 26, 1939; s. Peter George and Matida Maxine (Green) B.; B.A., U. Iowa, 1966; M.A., N.E. Mo. State U., 1970; Ph.D., Walden U., 1979; children—Lisa Michele, Patricia Ann, Denise Kathleen. Tchr. sci., math. English Valley's Schs., North English, Iowa, 1960-67; tchr. sci., chmn. dept. sci. Washington Sch., Ottumwa (Iowa) Public Schs., 1967-72, tchr. sci., interdisciplinary team leader Walsh Sch., 1972-75, tchr. sci., chmn. dept. sci., 1975—; mem. Iowa Instructional and Profl. Devel. Com., 1972-74; trainer for Performance Learning Systems, 1975-81; human relations cons. and tchr. Area Edn. Agy. #15, 1977-81, vice chmn. staff devel. com., 1977-80; county chmn. and mem. Iowa Bd. Polit. Action for Edn., 1966-81; dir. Washington Ednl. Field Trips for Walsh Students, 1972-81; cons., trainer in field. Mem. Nat. TEACH Cadre (charter), U. Iowa Alumni Assn., N.E. Mo. State U. Alumni Assn., Ottumwa Edn. Assn., Iowa State Edn. Assn. (chmn. bd. State Unit 9 Ednl. Div. 1973-75), NEA (life), Nat. Sci. Tchrs. Assn., Iowa Assn. Supervision and Curriculum Devel., Assn. Supervision and Curriculum Devel., Phi Delta Kappa. Democrat. Roman Catholic. Home: 219 1/2 N Marion Ottumwa IA 52501 Office: 2662 Meadowdale Ottumwa IA 52501

BUTTERFIELD, WILLIAM H., univ. chmn.; b. Worland, Wyo., Nov. 11, 1935; s. William Harley and Velma Irene (Enlowe) B.; B.S., U. Nebr., 1960; M.S.W., U. Mich., 1968, Ph.D., 1970; m. Dorothy M. Mack, July 2, 1972; children—Christina, Heather, Lydia. Cons., Wayne State Intermediate Sch. Dist., Detroit, 1968-69; cons., lectr. U. Mich. Sch. Social Work, 1969-70; asst. prof. U. Wis., Madison, 1970-73; chairperson Ph.D. program Washington U., St. Louis, 1973—. Served with USNR, 1954-55. Recipient Leon Levitz An. award, 1966. Mem. Sci. Research Soc. N.Am., Nat. Assn. Social Workers, Assn. Advancement of Behavior Therapy, Am. Psychol. Assn., Behavior Therapy and Research Soc., Council on Social Work Edn., Social Work Group for Study Behavioral Methods, Sigma Xi. Home: 8120 Glen Echo Bel Nor MO 63121 Office: Washington U Lindell and Skinker Sts Saint Louis MO 63130

BUTTERY, JANET LOUISE, movie theatre co. exec.; b. Columbus, Ohio, May 19, 1953; d. Thomas William and Pauline Adelaide (Burgess) B.; B.A., U. Kans., 1975, M.B.A., 1978; Troisième Degré, Université de Bordeaux (France), 1975. Real estate devel. Am. Multi Cinema, Kansas City, Mo., 1978—. Club: Meadowbrook Raquetball. Home: 7510 Lamar St Apt 66 Prairie Village KS 66204 Office: 106 W 14th St Suite 1700 Kansas City MO 64105

BUTTREY, DONALD WAYNE, lawyer; b. Terre Haute, Ind., Feb. 6, 1935; s. William Edgar and Nellie Madaline (Vaughn) B.; B.S., Ind. State U., 1956; J.D., Ind. U., 1961; children—Greg, Alan, Jason. Admitted to Ind. bar, 1961; law clk. to chief judge U.S. Dist. Ct. So. Dist. Ind., 1961-63; mem. firm McHale, Cook & Welch, Indpls., 1963—. Precinct committeeman Indpls. Democratic Com., 1971-74; mem. Slating Conv. Rules Com., 1973, Greater Indpls. Dem. Fin. Com., 1972, 76—. Served with AUS, 1956-58. Mem. Am. (mem. coms. taxation sect.), Ind. (chmn.-elect taxation sect.), Indpls., 7th Circuit bar assns., Ind. Soc. of Chgo., Phi Delta Phi, Theta Chi. Methodist. Clubs: Indpls. Athletic, Univ., Highland Country. Editor Ind. Law Jour., 1960-61. Home: 2215 Rome Dr Indianapolis IN 46208 Office: 1122 Chamber of Commerce Bldg 320 N Meridian St Indianapolis IN 46204

BUTTS, CHARLES LEWIS, state senator; b. Hartford, Conn., Feb. 16, 1942; s. W. Marlin and Jeanne Elizabeth (Beattie) B.; B.A., Oberlin Coll., 1964; m. Alice Gould, Aug. 10, 1963; children—John, Paul, Joanna, Helen. Sec., Civil Service Commn., Cleve., 1967-69; pres. First Class Housing, Cleve., 1969-71, 80—; publisher Franklin Pub. Co., Cleve., 1971-75; mem. Ohio Senate, Cleve., 1974—. Democrat.

BUTZ, BEVERLY GRAHAM, fin. exec.; b. Chgo., Nov. 10, 1948; d. William Otto and Catherine (Graham) B.; student Hollins Coll., 1966-68; B.A., U. Mich., 1970; M.B.A. program, U. Chgo., 1975-78. Programmer trainee No. Trust Co., Chgo., 1970-72; analyst/programmer Zurich Ins. Co., Chgo., 1972-74; programmer/analyst First Nat. Bank of Chgo., 1974-76, lead programmer/analyst, 1976-79, project mgr., 1979—, officer of corp., 1981—. Active, Jr. League of Chgo., 1970-79; vol. Presbyn. St. Luke's Hosp., Chgo., 1970-72, Planned Parenthood, 1980; vol. Una Puerta Abierta, 1972-74, treas. cookbook com., 1975-76; mem. Jr. Bd. of Youth Guidance, 1977-79. Congregationalist. Club: Midtown Tennis. Office: 1 First Nat Plaza Chicago IL 60670

BUZBEE, KENNETH VON, state senator; b. Anna, Ill., Nov. 30, 1937; s. Dellis Pierce and Maude (Pender) B.; B.S., So. Ill. U., 1961, M.A., 1972; m. Betty Ruth Hiller, Dec. 29, 1961; children—Brent, Kendra. In ins. bus., Carbondale, Ill., 1965-70; mem. Ill. State Senate, 1973—, chmn. Appropriations II Com.; chmn. Ill. Energy Resources Commn. Mem. White House Coal Adv. Council; vice chmn. Interstate Coal Task Force. Active Boy Scouts Am., YMCA. Served with USMC, 1961-64; lt. col. Res. Mem. Marine Corps Assn., Marine Corps Res. Officers Assn., Nat. Conf. State Legislators, Am. Legion, VFW. Democrat. Methodist. Club: Elks. Office: 621 W Industrial Park Rd Carbondale IL 62901

BUZZELLI, CHARLOTTE GRACE, educator; b. Akron, Ohio, Mar. 21, 1947; d. Edmund Albert and Sarah Agnes (Russo) B.; B.S., U. Akron, 1969, M.S. in Edn., 1976. Tchr., St. Anthony Sch., Akron, 1969-76; program coordinator, tchr. Akron Montessori Sch. Continuing Edn. Program, Eastwood Center, Akron, 1976-77; dir. edn. Fallsview Psychiat. Hosp., Cuyahoga Falls, Ohio, 1977—; cons. in field. Named Ohio Tchr. of Yr., 1979. Mem. Council Exceptional Children (chpt. pres.), Assn. Supervision and Curriculum Devel., Assn. Children With Learning Disabilities, Internat. Reading Assn., U. Akron Alumni Assn., Pi Lambda Theta (pres.), Phi Delta Kappa, Delta Kappa Gamma, Gamma Beta (pres.). Clubs: Univ., Akron Women's City. Pioneered 1st spl. edn. program in Ohio for adult state psychiat. hosp. Home: 662 Dayton St Akron OH 44310 Office: 330 Broadway East St Cuyahoga Falls OH 44221

BYARS, ANNIE MARIE, educator; b. Decatur, Ala., Nov. 19, 1944; d. Alphonso and Mary Ann (Bevels) B.; B.S., Ala. Agrl. and Mech. U., 1967; M.A., U. Detroit, 1975; postgrad. Wayne State U., 1972-73. Vol., U.S. Peace Corps, Jamaica, West Indies, 1967-69; tchr. Lewis Bus. Coll., Detroit, 1970; life ins. sales agt. Franklin Life Ins. Co., Detroit, 1978-81; tchr. bus. edn. Finney High Sch., Detroit Public Schs., 1970—. Mem. Nat. Bus. Edn. Assn., Am. Vocational Assn., NAACP, North-Central Bus. Edn. Assn., Bus. Tchrs. Club Met. Detroit, Detroit Fedn. Tchrs. Democrat. Office: 17200 Southampton St Detroit MI 48224

BYBEE, RODGER WAYNE, educator; b. San Francisco, 1942; s. Wayne and Genevieve (Mungon) B.; B.A., Colo. State Coll., 1966; M.A., U. No. Colo., 1969; Ph.D., N.Y. U., 1975; m. Patricia Brovsky, May 28, 1966. Sch. tchr. public schs. Greeley, Colo., 1965-66; sci. instr. U. No. Colo., 1966-70; teaching fellow N.Y. U., N.Y.C., 1970-72; instr. in edn. Carleton Coll., Northfield, Minn., 1972-75, asst. prof., 1975-81, asso. prof. edn., dept. chmn. 1981—; cons. D.C. Heath Spl. Edn. for Elem. Sci., Nat. Assessment of Ednl. Progress. Exec. bd. Minn. chpt. Nat. Com. for Prevention of Child Abuse and Neglect. Mem. AAAS, Nat. Sci. Tchrs. Assn., Nat. Assn. Biology Tchrs., Nat. Assn. for Research in Sci. Teaching (exec. bd., publs. adv. bd.), World Future Soc., Assn. for Humanistic Psychology. Editorial bd. Jour. of Research in Science Teaching; co-author: Becoming a Better Elementary Science Teacher, 1975, Becoming a Secondary School Science Teacher, 1981, Violence, Values and Justice in the Schools, 1982; editor, contbr. to Jour. of Social Issues, 1979. Home: 212 Maple Northfield MN 55057 Office: Education Dept Carleton College Northfield MN 55057

BYERS, SANDRA ROBERTS, hosp. ofcl.; b. Rochester, N.Y., Nov. 18, 1937; d. Arthur Eugene and Janet Virginia (Ebert) R.; B.S., Cornell U., 1960; M.S., Ohio State U., 1973; m. Thomas Jones Byers, Aug. 20, 1960; children—Stephen Arthur, Linda Merle. Staff nurse, instr. U. Pa. Hosp., Phila., 1960-63; instr. Maturna Orgn., Washington, 1964-65; staff nurse St. Anthony Hosp., Columbus, Ohio, 1970; asst. dir. staff devel. dept. Ohio State U. Hosp., Columbus, 1973-75; dir. med. nursing services Riverside Methodist Hosp., Columbus, 1975—. Mem. Ohio Nurses Assn., Nat. League for Nursing, Ohio State U. Womens Assn., Sigma Theta Tau. Home: 525 Haymore Ave S Worthington OH 43085 Office: 3535 Olentangy River Rd Columbus OH 43214

BYINGTON, RICHARD PRICE, surg. supply co. exec.; b. Grand Rapids, Mich., July 24, 1940; s. Stanley J. and Constance Y. (Des Noyer) B.; B.S. in Pharmacy, Ferris State Coll., 1962; m. Margaret Ellen Evert, Aug. 26, 1961; children—James, Michael, Connie. Pub. relations rep. Mich. State Pharm. Assn., Lansing, 1962; pharmacist White & White Pharmacy Inc., Grand Rapids, 1962-63; sales rep. White & White Surg. Supply Inc., Grand Rapids, 1963-67, sales mgr., 1967-70, exec. v.p., 1970-74, pres., 1974—; mem. Nursing Home Adminstrs. Licensure Bd., 1970—. Mem. Am. Surg. Trade Assn. (dir., group v.p. govt. relations), Am., Mich. State, Kent County pharm. assns. Roman Catholic. Clubs: Lions, Peninsular. Home: 3341 Ashton Rd SE Grand Rapids MI 49506 Office: 19 La Grave Ave SE Grand Rapids MI 49503

BYRD, DEBORAH ABBOTT, counselor; b. Cleve., Mar. 8, 1952; d. James William and Annie Mae (Evans) Abbott; B.S. in Social Work, Tuskegee (Ala.) Inst., 1975, M.Ed. in Student Personnel (student personnel fellow 1975-76), 1976; postgrad. Kent State U., 1978—; m. Charles Ronald Byrd, July 30, 1977. Admissions clk. John Andrew Hosp., Tuskegee Inst., 1973-75; grad. asst., recruitor admissions office Tuskegee Inst., 1975, grad. asst., dorm dir., 1976; counselor Allied Health Center, Cuyahoga Community Coll., Cleve., 1976-80, counselor Fin. Aid Office, 1980—, also instr. Mem. Am. Coll. Personnel Assn., Am. Personnel and Guidance Assn., AAUW, Northeastern Ohio Personnel and Guidance Assn., Midwest Assn. Student Fin. Aid Adminstrs., Ohio Assn. Student Fin. Aid Adminstrs., Am. Assn. Non-White Concerns, Women of Metro, NAACP, Phi Delta Kappa, Kappa Delta Pi, Alpha Kappa Alpha. Club: Cleve. Tuskegee Inst. Alumni (asst. sec. 1978-79). Office: 2900 Community College Ave Cleveland OH 44115

BYRNE, JAMES JOSEPH, archbishop; b. St. Paul, July 28, 1908; s. Philip J. and Mary (McMonigal) B.; student St. Paul Sem., 1927-33; S.T.B., Cath. U. Am., 1933; summer student U. Minn., 1933; S.T.D., U. Louvain (Belgium), 1937; LL.D., Portland (Oreg.) U., 1960. Ordained priest Roman Cath. Ch., 1933; prof. theology and philosophy St. Thomas Coll., St. Paul, 1937-45; part time prof. theology St. Catharine Coll., St. Paul, 1941-47; prof. theology St. Paul Sem., 1945-47; aux. bishop of St. Paul, 1947-56; bishop of Boise (Idaho), 1956-62; archbishop of Dubuque (Iowa), 1962—. Office: 1105 Locust St Dubuque IA 52001*

BYRNE, JANE M., mayor; b. Chgo., May 24, 1934; d. William and Katharine (Nolan) Burke; B.A., Barat Coll., Lake Forest, Ill.; M.A. in Biol. Scis., U. Ill.; m. William Patrick Byrne, Dec. 31, 1956 (dec. 1959); 1 dau., Katherine; m. 2d, Jay McMullen, Mar. 17, 1978. With Chgo. Anti-Poverty Agy., 1963-68; commr. Chgo. Dept. Consumers Sales, Weights and Measures, 1968-77; mayor City of Chgo., 1979—; past cons. Underwriters Lab. Chmn. resolutions com. Democratic Nat. Com., mem. Com., 1973—; co-chmn. Cook County (Ill.) Dem. Central Com., 1975-76; sec.-treas. presdl. campaign John F. Kennedy, Chgo., 1960; worked in fed. anti-poverty program. Office: Office of the Mayor City Hall 121 N LaSalle St Chicago IL 60602*

BYRNE, MICHAEL JOSEPH, bus. exec.; b. Chgo., Apr. 3, 1928; s. Michael Joseph and Edith (Lueken) B.; B.Sc. in Mktg., Loyola U., Chgo., 1952; m. Eileen Kelly, June 27, 1953; children—Michael Joseph, Nancy, James, Thomas, Patrick, Terrence. Sales engr. Emery Industries, Inc., Cin., 1952-59; with Pennsalt Chem. Corp., Phila., 1959-60; with Oakton Cleaners, Inc., Skokie, Ill., 1960-70, pres., 1960-70; pres. Datatax Inc., Skokie, 1970-74, Dataforms & Midwest Mktg. Assn., 1970—, Metro Tax Service Inc., 1975—, Midwest Synthetic Lubrication Products, 1978—. Served with ordnance U.S. Army, 1946-48. Mem. A.I.M., VFW, Alpha Kappa Psi. Club: Toastmasters Internat. Home: 600 Grego Ct Prospect Heights IL 60070

BYRNS, LOIS ELIZABETH ANNE, educator; b. Lodi, Wis.; d. Daniel and Ellen (Moen) B.; B.A., M.A., Ph.D., U. Wis.-Madison; postgrad. Columbia U., George Washington U., 1954. Asst. prof. Coll. New Rochelle, 1943-46; lectr. Fordham U., 1944-46, Loyola U., 1946-48; asso. prof. Trinity Coll., 1948-52; prof. Manhattanville Coll., 1952-60; prof. English U. Wis.-Menomonie, 1960-77, prof. emeritus, 1977—, chmn. dept., 1962-68. MLA grantee, 1976; Wis. Humanities Com. grantee, 1978-79. Mem. MLA, Midwest MLA, Delta Kappa

Gamma, Pi Lambda Theta. Roman Catholic. Author: Recusant Books in America 1559-1640, 1959; Recusant Books in America 1640-1700, 1961; Recusant Books in America 1700-1829, 1964. Address: West Main St Dane WI 53529

CABLE, GEORGE W., mfg. co. ofcl.; b. St. Louis, Mar. 31, 1924; s. George W. and Clara B. (Herron) C.; B.S., Washington U., 1955; m. Dorothy E. McMahon, Aug. 26, 1945; children—George Alan, Carl Lorenz, Carole Sue. Research investigator C.K. Williams, Inc., East St. Louis, Ill., 1945-50, electron microscopist, 1950-59, head central div. research, 1959-64; mgr. quality control Pfizer, Inc., East St. Louis, 1964-72, mgr. quality control and process devel., 1972-77, mgr. quality assurance, 1977-81, tech. service mgr. product devel., 1981—. Mem. exec. bd. Okaw Valley council Boy Scouts Am. Recipient Disting. Eagle award Boy Scouts Am., 1974. Mem. Electron Microscope Soc., ASTM, Am. Soc. Quality Control, St. Louis Soc. Coatings Tech., Nat. Eagle Scout Assn. Methodist. Club: Moose. Home: 9745 Ridge Heights Fairview Heights IL 62208 Office: 2001 Lynch Ave East Saint Louis IL 62201

CABLE, STEPHEN JAMES, ceramic tile mfr.; b. Canton, Ohio, May 7, 1924; s. Davis Arthur and Gail (Watson) C.; B.S. in Chem. Engring., Case-Western Res. U., 1950; advanced mgmt. tng. Emory U., 1966-67; m. Jane Irwin Purdy, June 24, 1948; children—Nancy Jane, Davis James. Plant engr. Sparta Ceramic Co., 1950-54, plant mgr., 1954-56; successively mgr., sec., group v.p. Spartek, Inc. (formerly U.S. Ceramic Tile Co.), Canton, 1956—, also dir.; pres., dir. Polywood Corp., North Canton, SPR Fund, Inc.; v.p., dir. Joseph A. Locker Co., Canton. Trustee Canton YMCA. Served to 2d lt. Transp. Corps, AUS, 1943-46. Mem. Sigma Xi, Tau Beta Pi, Alpha Chi Sigma. Clubs: Canton (trustee), Congress Lake (Hartville, Ohio). Contbr. articles trade jours. Patentee in field. Home: 44 East Dr Congress Lake Hartville OH 44632 Office: 7801 Freedom Ave North Canton OH 44720

CABOT, JOSEPH, pedodontist; b. Detroit, Oct. 15, 1921; s. Benjamin and Ethel (Gutkovsky) C.; B.S., Wayne State U., 1942; D.D.S., U. Mich., 1945, M.S., 1947; m. Ruth Weiner, Aug. 19, 1945; children—Bonnie (Mrs. James Kaufman), Gary Michael, Elizabeth Ann, Jon Elliott. Mott fellow U. Mich., 1945-46; pedontic fellow Hurley Hosp., Flint, Mich., 1946-47; individual practice pedontics, Detroit, 1947-55, Lathrup Village, Mich., 1969—. Mem. bd. Delta Dental Plan Mich., 1959—, pres., 1963-66; pres., Detroit Dental Aid, 1952-55. Local bd. chmn. Selective Service, 1959-67, appeal bd. chmn., 1969—, dental adviser to state dir., 1968—; assemblyman United Community Services, 1971-77. Served to maj. Dental Corps, AUS, 1955-57. Fellow Internat. Coll. Dentists, Am. Coll. Dentists, Am. Acad. Pedodontics; mem. Am. (ho. of dels. 1965-76, trustee 1977—), Mich. (pres. 1975-76) dental assns., Mich. Soc. Dentistry for Children (pres. 1953-54), Detroit Dist. Dental Soc. (Merit award 1964, pres. 1966-67), Kenneth A. Easlick Grad. Soc. (pres. 1973-75), Pierre Fauchard Acad., Omicron Kappa Upsilon, Alpha Omega. Lion. Home: 3159 Interlaken Rd Orchard Lake MI 48033 Office: 18239 W 12 Mile Rd Lathrup Village MI 48076

CABRAL, GALILEU, internist; b. Minas, Brazil, Feb. 19, 1941; came to U.S., 1969, naturalized, 1976; s. Joaquim Azevedo and Alice Tasca (Sartori) C.; M.D., Univ. Juiz de Fora, Brazil, 1964; postgrad. cert. U. Mo., Columbia, 1973; m. Kathleen Ann Fries, May 10, 1974; children—Anthony Eugene, William Lee. Intern, Mo. Bapt. Hosp., St. Louis County, 1969, resident, 1970-73, chief med. resident, 1973, mem. active staff, 1974—, asso. chief med. staff, 1980—; pres. St. Francois Med. Center, Florissant, Mo., 1979-80; mem. continuing edn. com. Christian Hosp. N.E., 1978—. Served to lt. Brazilian Navy, 1965-68. Diplomate Am. Bd. Internal Medicine. Mem. AMA (Physician Recognition award 1972—), A.C.P., Mo. State Med. Assn., Met. St. Louis Med. Soc., Midwest Internists (v.p.). Roman Catholic. Home: 15244 Lochcrest Ct Ballwin MO 63011 Office: 14377 Woodlake Dr Suite 109 Chesterfield MO 63017

CACANINDIN, VINCENT ARTHUR, podiatrist; b. N.Y.C., Mar. 14, 1944; s. Toribio and Teresa (Teves) C.; B.S. in Chem. Engring., Poly. Inst. Bklyn., 1965; D. Podiatric Medicine, Ill. Coll. Podiatric Medicine, 1978. Chem. engr. Picatinny Arsenal, Dover, N.J., 1965, 68; sr. devel. engr., lab. supr. Pharmaseal Labs. div. Am. Hosp. Supply Corp., Glendale, Calif., 1969-74; resident Henrotin Hosp., Chgo., 1978-79; pvt. practice podiatry, Chgo., 1979—; mem. staff Henrotin Hosp., Mt. Sinai Hosp. Med. Center, Roosevelt Meml. Hosp., Rush Med. Sch., all Chgo. Served with U.S. Army, 1965-67. Decorated Nat. Def. Service medal; recipient Army Res. Components Achievement medal, 1980. Fellow Am. Coll. Foot Orthopedists; mem. Am. Podiatry Assn., Ill. Podiatry Soc., Am. Public Health Assn., Mil. Surgeons U.S. Patentee in field. Home: 563 S Craig Pl Lombard IL 60148 Office: 2720 W 15th St Chicago IL 60608

CACCAMO, NICHOLAS JAMES, accountant; b. Chgo., June 15, 1944; s. Anthony J. and Catherine M. (DiGiovanni) C.; student U. Ill., 1962-64; B.S. in Commerce, DePaul U., 1966, M.B.A., 1969; m. Jane Marie Unger, Nov. 5, 1966; children—Julie Elizabeth, Laurie Therese. Staff auditor Lester Witte & Co., Chgo., 1966-70; staff acct. Pittway Corp., Northbrook, Ill., 1970-74, asst. to fin. v.p., 1974-77, controller, 1977—, asst. sec., 1977-80, sec., 1980—. C.P.A., Ill. Mem. Am. Inst. C.P.A.'s, Ill. C.P.A. Soc. Office: 333 Skokie Blvd Northbrook IL 60062

CADIEUX, EUGENE ROGERS, ins. co. exec.; b. Detroit, Feb. 14, 1923; s. Harold S. and Nadia (Rogers) C.; student U. Detroit Coll. Commerce and Finance, 1941-42, Sch. Law, 1952; m. Leontine R. Keane, May 10, 1975. With bond dept. Standard Accident Ins. Co., Detroit, 1951-54; bond mgr. Am. Ins. Co., Detroit, 1954-65, Fireman's Fund, Cin., 1965-66, Md. Casualty Co., Detroit, 1966-75, Zervos Agency, Inc., 1975; cons. to contractors, 1957—. Asst. dir. boys work Internat Assn. Y's Mens Clubs, 1953; committeeman YMCA, Detroit; mem. citizens council Internat. Inst., 1977—; trustee Joint Meml. Day Assn. Served with AUS, World War II. Mem. Surety Assn. Mich. (sec. 1958), Am. Assn. State and Local History, Mich., Detroit (sec. 1970—, trustee), Cin. (com. on library and acquisitions), Grosse Pointe (pres. 1980—) hist. socs., SAR (pres. Mich. soc. 1961-62, bd. mgrs., nat. Americanism com.), Friends Pub. Library Cin., Friends Pub. Library Grosse Pointe (hist. com.), Delta Sigma Pi, Gamma Eta Gamma. Clubs: Country (Detroit), Algonquin. Home: 208 Ridgemont Rd Grosse Pointe Farms MI 48236 Office: 24724 Farmbrook St Southfield MI 48034

CADOGAN, EDWARD JOHN PATRICK, mfg. co. mktg. exec.; b. London, Dec. 22, 1939; came to U.S., 1959, naturalized, 1964; B.S. in Mktg., L.I. U., 1971; M.B.A., U. Dayton, 1977; m. Wanda Maxine Evans, Dec. 30, 1975. Sr. field engr. Fairchild Camera & Instrument Corp., Syosset, N.Y., in Vietnam and Okinawa, 1964-69; mgr. Honeywell Mut. Alarm Corp., N.Y.C., 1971-72; sales engr. CAI/div. Recon-Optical, Barrington, Ill., 1972-75; mktg. engr. Cin. Electronics Corp., 1977-78; mktg. mgr. electro-optics Electronic Warfare Centre, Systems Research Labs., Dayton, Ohio, 1978—. Mem. Republican Nat. Com. Served with USAF, 1959-63. Mem. Assn. M.B.A. Execs., Assn. Old Crows, Tech. Mktg. Soc. Am., Am. Def. Preparedness Assn., Air Force Assn., Assn. Unmanned Vehicle Systems, Nat. Contract Mgmt. Assn. Home: 5420 Pentland Circle Dayton OH 45424 Office: 2800 Indian Ripple Rd Dayton OH 45424

CAFESJIAN, GERARD LEON, pub. co. exec.; b. N.Y.C., Apr. 26, 1925; s. Leon and Nora (Tashjian) C.; B.A., Hunter Coll., 1950; J.D., St. John's U., 1952; m. Cleo Thomas, July 4, 1947; children—Kathleen, Thomas. Admitted to N.Y. bar, 1952; with West Pub. Co., St. Paul, 1952—, v.p. 1972—; dir. Hudson Products (Wis.). Trustee Minn. Mus. Art, 1979-80, Arts and Sci. Council, St. Paul, 1981—. Served with USN, 1943-46. Mem. Am. Bar Assn. Clubs: Minnesota, Pool and Yacht, Confrerie des Chevaliers du Tastevin. Office: West Publishing Co 50 W Kellogg St Paul MN 55102

CAFFERTY, ELSIE IRENE, home economist; b. Elm Creek, Nebr., Aug. 8, 1934; d. Earl Alvin and Marcella Gwendolyn (Horton) Shuck; B.S. in Home Econs. Edn., Kearney State Coll., 1969, M.S. in Home Econs. Edn., 1971; Ed.D. in Adminstrn., Curriculum and Instrn., U. Nebr., Lincoln, 1980; m. Nov. 11, 1951 (div. 1977); children—Alesia Dianne Cafferty Barelman, Marsha Kay Cafferty Nelson. Grad. asst. instr. in home econs. Kearney State Coll., 1969-71, instr., 1971-72, asso. prof. vocat. edn., 1974—; research instr. Selection Research Inc. at Youth Devel. Center, Kearney, Nebr., 1972-73; microwave oven demonstrator Litton Corp., Kearney, 1973-74, sec. Buffalo County Home Extension Council, 1962-63, 63-64, pres.-elect, 1964-65. Mem. Am. Vocat. Assn., Nebr. Vocat. Assn., Nat. Vocat. Guidance Assn., Am. Personnel and Guidance Assn., Nebr. Personnel and Guidance Assn., Nat. Assn. Vocat. Edn. Spl. Needs Personnel, Nebr. Assn. Vocat. Edn. Spl. Needs Personnel (pres. 1979-80), NEA, Nebr. Edn. Assn., Kearney State Edn. Assn. (sec. 1978-79, 79-80, pres. 1980-81), Assn. Supervision and Curriculum Devel., Assn. Tchr. Educators, Kappa Omicron Phi, Phi Delta Kappa. Republican. Methodist. Club: Order Eastern Star (Worthy Matron, Tuscan chpt. 1971) (Kearney). Home: 3408 3d Ave Kearney NE 68847 Office: Kearney State Coll West Campus Center for Vocat Edn Kearney NE 68847

CAFIERO, EUGENE ANTHONY, automobile co. exec.; b. N.Y.C., June 13, 1926; s. Anthony Eugene and Frances D. (Lauricella) C.; A.B., Dartmouth, 1946; postgrad. Rutgers U., 1947-48, Columbia, 1948-49, U. Mich., 1950-51; M.S. (Sloan fellow), M.I.T., 1959; hon. doctorate Wittenberg U., 1977; m. Nancy Appleton Barnard, Jan. 23, 1960. With David Smith Steel Co., N.Y.C., 194749; with Ford Motor Co., Edgewater, N.J. and Dearborn, Mich., 1949-51; indsl. engr. Briggs Mfg. Co., Detroit, 1951-53; with Chrysler, Detroit, 1953—, v.p. Latin Am. ops., 1968-70, group v.p. U.S. and Can. automotive, 1970-72, group v.p. N.Am. ops., 1972-74, sr. exec. v.p., 1974-75, pres., 1975—, vice chmn., 1978—; pres., chief exec. officer Delorean Motor Co., 1979—. Served with USNR, 1946-47. Mem. Soc. Automotive Engrs., Engring. Soc. Detroit, Nat. Mgmt. Assn., Soc. Sloan Fellows. Presbyterian. Clubs: Oakland Hills Country, Detroit Athletic. Home: 3753 Burning Tree Dr Bloomfield Hills MI 48013 Office: New York NY*

CAGLE, ALBERT WAYNE, engring. cons.; b. High Point, N.C., May 25, 1924; s. Grady Carson and Mary (Davis) C.; B.S., High Point Coll., 1948; M.S., U. Louisville, 1950; m. Bessie Valeria Kivett, Sept. 16, 1949; children—Albert Wayne, Lynne, Deborah, Mark. Research chemist Cone Mills Research, Greensboro, N.C., 1950; with Western Electric Co., Lee's Summit, Mo., 1951—, sr. staff engr., 1970—. Served with U.S. Army, 1943-46. Decorated Bronze Star. Fellow Am. Soc. for Metals; mem. Am. Chem. Soc., Soc. Plastics Engrs., Soc. Mfg. Engrs. Methodist. Clubs: Masons, Shriners. Home: 6622 Englewood Raytown MO 64133 Office: Western Electric Co 777 N Blue Parkway Lee's Summit MO 64063

CAGLE, CHARLES HARMON, educator, author; b. Colorado City, Tex., Sept. 28, 1930; s. William Wallace and Bonnie Belle (Cansler) C.; B.A., Southwestern Okla. State U., 1952; M.A., U. Okla., 1954, postgrad., 1957-58; M.F.A., U. Iowa, 1965. Free lance television writer, N.Y.C., 1956-57; prof. journalism/English, Cameron (Okla.) State U., 1959-60; prof. creative writing Pittsburg (Kans.) State U., 1960—; free lance profl. writer fiction, screenplays. Active Crawford County (Kans.) Hist. Soc., Pittsburg Area Arts and Crafts Players. Served with Signal Corps, U.S. Army, 1952-54; Korea. Recipient citation ALA, 1970. Mem. AAUP, Nat. Assn. Tchrs. English, Kans. Assn. Tchrs. English, Am. Film Inst., Am. Humanist Assn. Democrat. Author: (play) The Sudden Truth, 1957; author eighty paperback novels, 1967—, including The Beast, 1970. Office: English Dept Pittsburg State U Pittsburg KS 66762

CAHILL, MARY FRAN, journalist; b. Milw.; d. Morgan Joseph and Claire Catherine (Warnimont) C.; B.A., M.A., Marquette U. Photojournalist Cedarburg (Wis.) News Graphic, 1965-67; photojournalist Milw. Jour., 1967-76, feature writer, 1976—, mem. unit holders council Jour. Co., 1977-79. Hon. mem. Milw. Fire Dept. Recipient Distinguished Service award Milw. Fire Dept., 1972, 74, 75, 77, 78, 79, 80; cert. of appreciation USCGR, 1975, 77. Mem. Nat. Press Photographers Assn., Wis. News Photographers Assn. (sec. 1973-75), Women in Communications, Milw. Press Club, Zool. Soc. Milwaukee County, Zoo Pride, Wis. Emergency Med. Technicians Assn. (Woman of Yr. award 1975), Nat. Assn. Emergency Med. Technicians, Sigma Delta Chi, Phi Mu, Phi Alpha Theta, Pi Gamma Mu. Club: Nordic Ski. Home: 3318 N 53d St Milwaukee WI 53216 Office: 333 W State St Milwaukee WI 53201

CAHILL, PATRICIA DEAL, broadcasting sta. exec.; b. St. Louis, Oct. 9, 1947; d. Richard Joseph and Dorothy Jane (Deal) C.; B.A., U. Kans., 1969, M.A., 1971; grad. Advanced Mgmt. Devel. Program, Harvard U., 1977; m. Stephen Randal Crump, Apr. 22, 1978; 1 dau., Lindsay Cahill. Continuity dir. Sta. KANU, U. Kans., 1969; audio-reader dir. U. Kans., Lawrence, 1969-73; reporter, Sta. KCUR, Kansas City, Mo., 1973-75, producer, 1973-75; news dir., program dir. Sta. KMUW, Wichita, Kans., 1975-76, mgr. sta., 1976—; instr. Wichita State U., 1975—; bd. dirs. Radio Research Consortium, Inc. Mem. governing bd. Kans. Arthritis Found.; chairperson Wichita Free U., 1977-80, exec. sec., 1981—. Mem. Public Radio in Mid-Am. (pres. 1977-79, dir. 1977-81), Kans. Public Radio Assn. (v.p. 1980—), Wichita Press Women, Alpha Epsilon Rho. Office: 3317 E 17th St Wichita KS 67208

CAIN, JAMES NELSON, concert mgr.; b. Arcadia, Ohio, Jan. 6, 1930; s. Alfred Ray and Gladys Eliza (Cruikshank) C.; B.A., Ohio State U., 1955; m. Marthellen Jones, June 12, 1950; children—Nelson, Jennifer, Richard, Elizabeth. Mgr. Prestige Concerts, Columbus, Ohio, 1948-62; dir. James N. Cain Concert Mgmt., Columbus, 1960-62; exec. dir. Music Assos. of Aspen (Colo.), 1962-68; asst. mgr. St. Louis Symphony Orch., 1968-70, mgr., 1970-80; v.p. St. Louis Conservatory and Schs. for Arts, 1980—. Music critic Columbus Citizen, 1955-62. Home: 2 Nantucket Ln St Louis MO 63132 Office: 560 Trinity at Delmar St Louis MO 63130

CAIN, MARVIN JAMES, veterinarian; b. Dayton, Ohio, Aug. 1, 1931; s. Forrest H. and Loa (Wagaman) C.; D.V.M., Ohio State U., 1955; m. Coralie Lusk, Aug. 6, 1955; 1 dau., Catherine Brett. Asso. veterinarian Jensen Animal Hosp., Cleve., 1955-56, College Hill Animal Hosp., Cin., 1956, Park Hills, Walnut Hills hosps., also Cin. Zoo, 1957; owner, veterinarian Mt. Healthy Animal Hosp., Cin., 1957—; owner thoroughbred farm Liberty Hill Farm, Walton, Ky., 1968—. Mem. AMVA, Ohio, Cin. vet. med. assns., Internat. Vet. Acupuncture Soc., Thoroughbred Breeders Ky. Home: 7474 Greenfarms St Cincinnati OH 45224 Office: 9199 Pippin Rd Cincinnati OH 45239

CAINE, CLIFFORD JAMES, ednl. adminstr.; b. Watertown, S.D., May 28, 1933; s. Louis Vernon and Elizabeth Matilda (Holland) C.; B.A., Macalester Coll., 1955; J.D., U. Minn., 1958, Ph.D., 1975; postgrad. Harvard U., 1976. Admitted to Minn. bar, 1958; dir. men's residence halls and student union Macalester Coll., 1959-63, dir. adminstrv. policies study, 1969-70; lectr. U. Minn., 1966-68, also coordinator Neighborhood Seminar program; asst. headmaster St. Paul Acad. and Summit Sch., St. Paul, 1970—. Bd. dirs. Hallie Q. Brown Community Center, 1972-73, Family Service of St. Paul, 1973-79; ruling elder United Presbyn. Ch., 1962—. Mem. Am. Acad. Polit. and Social Sci., Am. Studies Assn., Nat. Assn. Coll. Admissions Counselors, Minn. Bar Assn., U.S. Profl. Tennis Assn., Minn. Assn. Secondary Sch. and Coll. Admissions Officers (pres. 1978-79). Club: Univ. (St. Paul). Home: 456 Summit Ave Saint Paul MN 55102 Office: 1712 Randolph Ave Saint Paul MN 55105

CAINE, STANLEY PAUL, coll. adminstr., educator; b. Huron, S.D., Feb. 11, 1940; s. Louis Vernon and Elizabeth Mathilda (Holland) C.; B.A., Macalester Coll., 1962; M.S., U. Wis., 1964, Ph.D., 1967; m. Karen Anne Mickelson, July 11, 1964; children—Rebecca, Kathryn, David. Asst. prof. history Lindenwood Colls., St. Charles, Mo., 1967-71; from asst. prof. to asso. prof. history DePauw U., Greencastle, Ind., 1971-77; v.p. acad. affairs and prof. history Hanover (Ind.) Coll., 1977—; mem. Nat. Humanities Faculty. Bd. dirs. Madison Boys' Club. Mem. Orgn. Am. Historians. Presbyterian. Author: The Myth of a Progressive Reform; co-editor: Political Reform in Wisconsin, 1973; contbr. articles and book revs. to scholarly jours. Office: Hanover College Hanover IN 47243

CAIRNS, DONALD FREDRICK, engring. and mgmt. cons.; b. Coulterville, Ill., Sept. 9, 1924; s. Fred Barton and Elsie Loretta (Barbary) C.; B.S., U. Ill., 1950; M.B.A., St. Louis U., 1966, Ph.D., 1972; m. Marion Grace Huey, Sept. 4, 1950; 1 son, Douglas Scott. Asst. engr. Mo. Pacific R.R. Co., St. Louis, 1950-56; project engr., plant engr., asst. to pres., v.p. Granite City Steel Co. (Ill.), 1956-79; pres. Nat. Engrs. and Assos. unit Nat. Steel Corp., St. Louis, 1979—; pres., chmn. bd. Indsl. Waste Control Council; guest lectr. Washington U. Grad. Sch. Bus. Chmn. Webster Groves (Mo.) City Planning Commn., 1958; mem. St. Louis County Traffic Commn., 1960-61, Webster Groves Bus. Devel. Commn., 1962, St. Louis County Charter Commn., 1979; mem., chmn. St. Louis County Planning Commn., 1968-76; pres., dir. Edgewood Children's Center, 1963-72. Served with AUS, 1943-46. Decorated Bronze Star; recipient recognition for control of air pollution Pres.'s Johnson and Nixon, 1970; registered profl. engr., Mo., Ill. Mem. Nat. Soc. Profl. Engrs., Mo. Soc. Profl. Engrs., Am. Iron and Steel Inst., ASCE, Air Pollution Control Assn., Assn. Iron and Steel Engrs., Southwestern Ill. Indsl. Assn. (chmn. bd.). Club: Algonquin Golf. Home: 17 E Swon Ave Webster Groves MO 63119 Office: 7777 Bonhomme Ave Saint Louis MO 63105

CALBERT, JERALD DAVID, lawyer; b. Indpls., Dec. 14, 1937; s. Hildon Robert and Mamie Etheline (Hunt) C.; A.B., Hanover Coll., 1960; J.D., Ind. U., 1966; m. Janet Lorene Hedrick, June 25, 1960; children—Lorilee Ann, Bradley Manson, Eric Hildon. Claims adjuster, claim mgr., ins. cos., 1961-66; admitted to Ind. bar, 1966; partner Houck & Calbert, Greencastle, Ind., 1966-74; now sr. partner firm Calbert & Bremer; instr. bus. law DePauw U., 1970—. Bd. dirs. Coop. Office Edn. Program, Greencastle, 1970-71, Putnam County Health Careers Found., 1970—, West Central Econ. Devel. Commn., State Ind., 1975-78, Ind. U. Sch. Law Indpls. Alumni Assn., 1977—. Served with USAF, 1961, 66. Recipient distinguished service award for community service, 1970; fellow Hanover Coll. Mem. Ind., Putnam County bar assns., Greencastle C. of C. (pres. 1971, dir. 1969-72), Internat. Platform Assn., Phi Delta Theta. Elk. Club: Windy Hill Country. Home: 309 Greenwood Ave Greencastle IN 46135 Office: 7 N College Ave Greencastle IN 46135

CALDARELLI, DAVID DONALD, otolaryngologist; b. Chgo., Nov. 7, 1941; s. David D. and Violet (Angus) C.; student U. Wis., 1961; M.D., U. Ill., 1965, M.S., 1965; m. Janna Sue Nowak, Apr. 1, 1967; children—Leslie Ann, Adam David. Intern, Presbyn. St. Luke's Hosp., Chgo., 1965-66, resident surgery, 1966-67; resident otolaryngology, U. Ill. Eye and Ear Infirmary and Research and Edn. Hosps., Chgo., 1967-70; practice medicine, specializing in otolaryngology, Chgo., 1974—; sr. attending physician, chmn. dept. otolaryngology and bronchoesophagology Rush Med. Coll., Rush-Presbyn.-St. Luke's Med. Center, Chgo., 1974—; attending otolaryngologist Univ. Ill. Research and Edn. Hosps., Chgo., 1970—, St. Francis Hosp., Evanston, Ill., 1974—; otolaryngologist Center for Craniofacial Anomalies, U. Ill., Chgo., 1970—; asst. otolaryngology Coll. Medicine, U. Ill., Chgo., 1967-70, instr. otolaryngology, 1970—; prof., chmn. dept. otolaryngology and bronchoesophagology, Rush Med. Coll., Chgo., 1974—; Cons. Otolaryngologist Chgo. Contagious Disease Hosp., 1975—. Recipient Bordan Found. Undergrad. Research award in medicine, 1965. Nat. Inst. Nervous Diseases and Blindness Research trainee, 1967-70; Ford Found. fellow, 1964; Nat. Inst. Health grantee, 1963, 65. Diplomate Am. Bd. Otolaryngology. Fellow A.C.S.; mem. AMA, Am. Acad. Ophthalmology and Otolaryngology, Am. Council Otolaryngology, Am. Cleft Palate Soc., Chgo. Laryngol. and Otol. Soc., Pan Am. Assn. Oto-Rhino-Laryngology and Broncho-Esophagology, Soc. Acad. Chmn. Otolaryngology, Soc. Univ. Otolaryngologists, Am. Soc. Head and Neck Surgery, Am. Broncho-Esophagological Assn., Triological Soc., Am. Cancer Soc. (unit dir. 1972-75), AAUP. Contbr. articles to profl. jours. and textbooks. Office: 1753 W Congress Pkwy Chicago IL 60612

CALDEIRA, JOSEPH LEONARD, real estate broker; b. Lowell, Mass., Sept. 7, 1944; s. Antonio Goncalves and Mary Suzanne (Sousa) C.; B.A., U. Mass., 1966; m. Chantel Zina Kolar, June 14, 1969; children—J. Leonard, Michael Jason. Real estate salesman Wm. A. White & Sons, N.Y.C., 1969-71; asst. v.p., real estate broker Cushman & Wakefield, Inc., Chgo., 1971-76; v.p., real estate broker LaSalle Partners, Inc., Chgo., 1976—. Served to capt. U.S. Army, 1966-68. Decorated Bronze Star. Mem. Chgo. Real Estate Bd., Nat., Ill. assns. realtors. Roman Catholic. Home: 4333 Johnson Ave Western Springs IL 60558 Office: 208 S LaSalle St Chicago IL 60604

CALDERON, EDUARDO FIEGEHEN, neurologist; b. Santiago, Chile, May 14, 1932; came to U.S., 1974, naturalized, 1979; s. Pedro N. and Teresa F. Calderon; B.Sc., Catholic U. Chile; M.D., U. Chile, 1958; m. Yolanda Urrejola, Nov. 27, 1958; children—Eduardo Tomas, Juan Pablo, M. Alexandra, M. Pauline, Francisco. Intern, Cath. U. Clin. Hosp., Santiago, 1958; gen. practice medicine, Chile, 1958-63; trainee, then instr. in neurology U. Chile, 1963-68, asst. prof. neurology, 1971-74; postdoctoral fellow Stanford U. Med. Sch., 1968-71; practice medicine specializing in neurology, Toledo, 1974—; mem. staff St. Luke's Hosp., Mercy Hosp., Med. Coll. Ohio Hosp.; clin. asso. prof. Med. Coll. Ohio, Toledo; bd. dirs. Multiple Sclerosis Soc. N.W. Ohio, Toledo, 1974—. Diplomate Am. Bd. Psychiatry and Neurology, Am. Bd. EEG Qualification. Mem. Am. Acad. Neurology,

Am. EEG Soc., Ohio Med. Assn., Lucas County Acad. Medicine. Roman Catholic. Home: 5815 Swan Creek Dr Toledo OH 43614 Office: 5757 Monclova Rd Suite 28 Maumee OH 43537

CALDWELL, DANA THOMAS, mfg. co. ofcl.; b. Gallipolis, Ohio, Aug. 13, 1930; s. Elmer E. and Jewel B. (McKean) C.; B.A., Ohio U., 1952; B.S. in Spl. Edn., Rio Grande Coll., 1961; M.A. in Bus. Adminstrn., Central Mich. U., 1975; m. Bernadette T. Dorsey, May 2, 1960; children—Charles, John, Andrew, Christopher. Pilot, Eastern Air Lines, 1957-60; tchr. Columbus (Ohio) Schs., 1961-63; contract adminstr. N.Am. Aviation, Columbus, 1963-71; mgr. contract/program mgr. Owens-Ill. Devel. Center, Toledo, 1971-74, contract specialist, 1974, mgr. contracts, 1976; mgr. contracts and pricing, missile systems div. Rockwell Internat., Columbus, 1979-80, mgr. contracts and proposals, 1980—. Active Civil Assn., Upper Arlington, Ohio. Served with USAF, 1953-57, to col. Res., 1965-81. Mem. Nat. Mgmt. Assn., Nat. Contract Mgmt. Assn. (dir. Central Ohio chpt., cert. profl. contract adminstr.), Res. Officers Assn. (treas. chpt. 5). Home: 2399 Kensington Dr Upper Arlington OH 43221 Office: 4300 E 5th Ave Columbus OH 43216

CALDWELL, JAMES MARSHALL, accountant; b. Chillicothe, Ohio, Aug. 1, 1939; s. Marshall and Emma (Gillette) C.; B.B.A., Ohio U., 1963; m. Pamela Lynne Marsh, June 13, 1963; children—Jennifer Lynne, James Patrick. Dep. auditor Ross County (Ohio), 1960-63, county commr., 1977—; tchr. Jackson (Ohio) City Schs., 1963-64; accountant, Chillicothe, 1961—; pres. Caldwell, Bolt & Co., public accts. City councilman, City of Chillicothe, 1968-74; pres. Ross County Young Republican Club, 1968-69; bd. dirs. Ross County Community Improvement Corp.; trustee Mid-Ohio Health Planning Fedn., 1975-77, Ohio Valley Health Services Found.; pres. Bd. Ross County Commrs., 1979; mem. Ross County Planning Commn.; exec. bd. Ohio Valley Regional Devel. Commn.; mem. citizens policy adv. com. Scioto River Basin, Ohio EPA. Mem. Nat. Soc. Public Accts., Public Acctg. Soc. of Ohio (pres. So. Ohio chpt. 1974-79), Chillicothe-Ross C. of C. (dir. 1970-73, pres. 1973), Chillicothe Jaycees (Citizen of Year 1973). Methodist (mem. adminstrv. bd. 1971-74, chmn. council ministries 1975-76). Kiwanian, Elk. Home: 306 Fairway Ave Chillicothe OH 45601 Office: PO Box 1640 Chillicothe OH 45601

CALDWELL, KENNETH SIMMS, mgmt. cons.; b. Mpls., Oct. 10, 1923; s. Kenneth Simms and Margaret Matilda (Peterson) C.; B.S. in Mech. and Indsl. Engring., U. Calif., 1947; m. Alice Elizabeth Featherstone, Apr. 12, 1952; children—Barbara Catherine, Margaret Elizabeth, Kenneth Simms. Cons., Ernst & Ernst, Los Angeles, 1947-50, 53-54, mgr. in charge mgmt. cons. services, San Francisco, 1954-61, Los Angeles, 1961-63, prin., Cleve., 1963-67, prin., nat. dir. govt. services, Cleve., 1967-76; prin. Nat. Mgmt. Cons. Services, Cleve., 1976—; lectr. Municipal Finance Officers Assn. Past chmn. bd. dirs. Luth. Med. Center, Cleve.; trustee Luth. Med. Center Found.; trustee Nat. History Day; vice-chmn. Greater Cleve. Growth Assn. for Downtown Devel., 1969-71, for Transp., 1971-73; trustee Cotillion Soc., 1971-73. Served as 1st lt. U.S. Army, 1950-53. Registered profl. engr., Calif. Mem. Nat., Ohio soc. profl. engrs., ASME, Am. Inst. of Indsl. Engrs., Cleve. Engring. Soc. (trustee 1969-73). Republican. Lutheran. Clubs: Mayfield Country, Cleve. Athletic, Rotary, Masons. Author: Budgeting for Small Governmental Units, 1976; contbr. articles to profl. jours. Home: 2719 Cranlyn Rd Shaker Heights OH 44122 Office: 1300 Union Commerce Bldg Cleveland OH 44115

CALDWELL, PHILIP, automobile mfg. co. exec.; b. Bourneville, Ohio, Jan. 27, 1920; s. Robert Clyde and Wilhelmina (Hemphill) C.; B.A. in Econs., Muskingum Coll., Concord, Ohio, 1940, L.H.D. (hon.), 1974; M.B.A., Harvard U. Grad. Sch. Bus., 1942; D.B.A. (hon.), Upper Iowa U., 1978; LL.D. (hon.), Boston U., 1979, Eastern Mich. U., 1979, Miami U., Oxford, Ohio, 1980; m. Betsey Chinn Clark, Oct. 27, 1945; children—Lawrence Clark, Lucy Hemphill Caldwell Stair, Desiree Branch Caldwell Armitage. Civilian, Navy Dept., 1946-53, dep. dir. procurement policy div., 1948-53; with Ford Motor Co., Dearborn, Mich., 1953—, v.p., gen. mgr. truck ops., 1968-70, v.p. mfg. group N. Am. automotive ops., 1971-72, exec. v.p. internat. automotive ops., 1973-77, vice chmn. bd., 1977-79, dep. chief exec. officer, 1978-79, pres., 1978-80, chief exec. officer, 1979—, chmn. bd., 1980—, also dir.; pres., dir. Philco-Ford Corp., 1970-71; chmn. chief exec. officer Ford of Europe, Inc., 1972-73; dir. Ford Latin Am., Ford Mid-East and Africa, Ford Asia-Pacific, Ford Motor Credit Co., Ford of Europe, Ford Can.; mem. internat. adv. com. Chase Manhattan Bank; dir. Digital Equipment Corp. Mem. Trilateral Commn.; trustee Com. Econ. Devel.; bd. dirs. Harvard U. Assos. Grad. Sch. Bus. Adminstrn., Detroit Renaissance, Detroit Symphony Orch. European Inst. Bus. Adminstrn.; trustee Muskingum Coll.; vice chmn. bd. trustees New Detroit, Inc. Served to lt. USNR, 1942-46. Recipient 1st William A. Jump Meml. award, 1950, Meritorious Civilian Service award Navy Dept., 1953. Mem. Motor Vehicle Mfrs. Assn. vice chmn., (dir.), Bus. Council, Bus. Roundtable, Conf. Bd. Clubs: Detroit, Detroit Athletic, Renaissance (Detroit); Bloomfield Hills (Mich.) Country. Address: Ford Motor Co American Rd Dearborn MI 48121

CALEB, FRANK, arts adminstr.; b. Fort Smith, Ark., Sept. 13, 1943; s. Phillip Ivor and Frances Irene (Johnston) C.; M.M., Yale U., 1962; m. Victoria Russell, Sept. 5, 1970; children—Vanessa, Phillip. Gen. mgr. Duluth Symphony Orch., 1971-73; asst. mgr., dir. devel. Lyric Opera of Chgo., 1973-78; pres. Milw. Symphony Orch. Trustee Evanston (Ill.) Art Center, 1974—, v.p., 1974-78; trustee St. Paul Opera Co.; bd. dirs. Chgo. Theatre of the Deaf; deacon 1st Presbyn. Ch. of Evanston, 1974-76. Mem. Am. Symphony Orch. League, Opera Am., Old English Sheepdog Club of Am. Clubs: Univ., Tower. Home: 1111 N Astor St Milwaukee WI 53202

CALENDINE, RICHARD HARLEY, coll. adminstr.; b. Parkersburg, W.Va., Oct. 25, 1939; s. Harley William and Margaret Irene (Armstrong) C.; B.A., W.Va. Wesleyan Coll., 1962; M.A., Ohio State U., 1966; m. Georgeann Allard, Aug. 22, 1964; children—Caren Ferree, Michelle Louise. Terminal clk. Am. Bitumals and Asphalt Co., Marietta, Ohio, 1959-61; asst. dir. student financial aids Ohio State U., Columbus, 1964-67, counseling psychologist Counseling Center, 1967-74; financial aids officer Columbus Tech. Inst., 1974—. Individual practice psychology, Columbus, 1973—. Mem. Am., Ohio psychol. assns., Nat., Ohio assns. student financial aid adminstrs., Ohio Geneal. Soc. (v.p. chpt. 1979), Phi Delta Kappa, Omicron Delta Kappa, Psi Chi. Presbyterian (chmn. bd. deacons 1973, elder 1980-83). Club: Masons (pres. club). Author: College Majors as a Guide to Career Planning, 1972. Home: 111 Webster Park Columbus OH 43214

CALES, DWAINE ELMER, dentist; b. Winfield, Kans., Sept. 13, 1948; s. Merle Elmer and Wilma Cales; A.A., Pratt Community Coll., 1966-68; B.A., U. Kans., 1971; D.D.S., Creighton U., 1975; m. Margaret Ann Platt, May 27, 1972; children—Jessica Elizabeth, Joshua Andrew. Gen. practice dentistry, Bolivar, Mo., 1975—. Mem. ADA, Mo. Dental Assn., Springfield Dental Soc., Acad. Gen. Dentistry. Home: Rural Route 3 Bolivar MO 65613 Office: 220 W Jackson St Bolivar MO 65613

CALHOUN, LILLIAN SCOTT, public relations co. exec.; b. Savannah, Ga., June 25, 1925; d. Walter Sanford and Laura (McDowell) Scott; B.A., Ohio State U., 1944; m. Harold William Calhoun, Sept. 20, 1950; children—Laura, Harold, Walter, Karen. Columnist, feature editor Chgo. Defender, 1963-65; asso. editor Jet, Ebony, mags., 1961-63; reporter Chgo. Sun-Times, 1965-68; mng. editor Integrated Edn. mag., 1968-71; info. officer, acting info. dir. Dept. Labor, 1971-73; co-editor Chgo. Reporter, 1973-76; pres., founder Calmar Communications, Inc., Chgo., 1978—; columnist Crain's Chgo. Bus., 1978-80, Chgo. Journalism Rev., 1969-74. Vice-chairperson Ill. Commn. on Human Relations, 1973-75; mem. Gov.'s Commn. on Status of Women, 1965-67, Gov.'s Adv. Council on Manpower, 1973-75. Mem. Soc. Midland Authors, Alpha Gamma Pi. Episcopalian. Clubs: Chgo. Press, Publicity, Arts. Office: 500 N Dearborn St #1115 Chicago IL 60610

CALHOUN, RAYMOND JOSEPH, stone co. exec.; b. Morrison County, Minn., May 9, 1920; s. George Edward and Clara Christine (Portz) C.; student St. John's U., 1938-39; m. Helen Edryce, July 30, 1941 (dec.); children—Robert John, Carol Rae Bolduc, Timothy, Donald; m. 2d, Rose Mary Eidenshink, Aug. 8, 1980. Salesman, Little Falls Granite Works (Minn.), 1941-47, sales mgr., 1947-67, pres, 1967—; pres. subsidiary, St. Cloud Meml. (Minn.), 1969—; pres. CNG Land Holding Co., Little Falls, 1964—; owner Calhoun Rentals Co., Little Falls, 1971—; pres. NW Monument Builders, Little Falls, 1970-74, also dir.; dir. Am. Nat. Bank, Little Falls, First Bank of Little Falls. Pres. St. Mary's Bd. Edn., 1966-70; mem. City of Little Falls City Council, 1969—, pres., 1973—; pres. Little Falls chpt. Am. Cancer Soc., 1962-64; active Boy Scouts Am. Served with USNR, 1942-45; PTO, ATO. Mem. Am. Legion, VFW, Republican. Roman Catholic. Clubs: Little Falls Golf (pres. 1979—), Exchange (pres. Little Falls 1960—), K.C., Moose. Home: 1205 Riverview St Little Falls MN 56345 Office: S Hwy 10 Little Falls MN 56345

CALHOUN, WILLIAM KENNETH, II, retail co. exec.; b. Emporia, Kans., Sept. 4, 1944; s. William Gunn and Dorothy (Crain) C.; B.S., Kans. U., 1966; children—Stephani Kay, Melissa Anne. Buyer, Target Stores, Mpls., 1966-67; sec.-treas. Newman's Inc., Emporia, Kans., 1967—; dir. Citizens Nat. Bank Emporia, 1976—. Bd. dirs., treas. Calhoun Found., 1967—; chmn. Project Pride, 1971-72; pres. bd. United Way Emporia, 1976-77; bd. dirs. Jones Found., 1981—. Mem. Emporia C. of C. (v.p. 1973-74). Clubs: Emporia Country (pres. 1975). Rotary. Office: Box B Emporia KS 66801

CALIHAN, DAVID SCOTT, polit. scientist, educator; b. Dayton, Ohio, Nov. 29, 1944; s. Lawrence William and Sarah (Aydelotte) Calihan; student Otterbein Coll., 1962-64; B.A., Earlham Coll., 1966; J.D., Ohio State U., 1969, M.A., 1970; Ph.D. candidate Miami U., Oxford, Ohio; m. Rebecca Sue Hilty, July 7, 1968; 1 dau., Heather Leigh. Admitted to Ohio bar, 1969; asst. prof. history and polit. sci. Manchester Coll., North Manchester, Ind., 1970-77; teaching fellow Miami U., 1978-79, dissertation fellow, 1979-80; judge North Manchester Town Ct., 1976—; adj. prof. polit. sci. Huntington (Ind.) Coll., 1981. Mem. ACLU, Am. Polit. Sci. Assn., Am. Soc. Public Adminstrn., Midwest Polit. Sci. Assn., Ind. City and Mcpl. Judges Assn. (sec.-treas. 1981), Wabash County Bar Assn. Democrat. Home: 716 N Sycamore North Manchester IN 46962

CALIRI, JOSEPH LOUIS, lawyer, corp. exec.; b. Rochester, N.Y., Mar. 16, 1916; s. Salvatore and Maria Teresa (Bottazzi) C.; A.B., U. Rochester, 1938; LL.B., Cornell, 1941; m. Dorothy Ann McGrath, Aug. 19, 1944; children—Robert Redmond, Barbara Jane. Admitted to N.Y. bar, 1941, Ill. bar, 1974; law dept. Kraft, Inc. (formerly Nat. Dairy Products Corp.), N.Y.C., 1941-51, asst. sec., 1951-52, sec., 1952-71, v.p., 1971—, dir., 1980—; v.p., sec. Dart & Kraft, Inc., 1980-81; ret., 1981. Past pres. Bd. Edn., Union Free Sch. Dist. No. 9, West Islip, L.I. Mem. Am. Judicature Soc., Am. Soc. Corp. Secs., Am., Ill., Chgo. bar assns., Cornell Law Assn., Phi Beta Kappa, Alpha Phi Delta. Clubs: Magoun Landing Yacht (West Islip, N.Y.); Cornell (N.Y.); Mich. Shores, Westmoreland Country (Wilmette, Ill.). Home: 1500 Sheridan Rd Wilmette IL 60091

CALL, JUDITH K., hosp. adminstr.; b. Peoria, Ill., Mar. 30, 1943; d. Emil T. and Erma K. (Miller) C.; B.S., Bradley U., 1965; M.A., U. Iowa, 1970. Asst. dir. Sch. Med. Tech., Presbyn.-St. Lukes Hosp., Chgo., 1965-68; asst. adminstr. McKennan Hosp., Sioux Falls, S.D., 1970-75; sec. of health State of S.D., Pierre, 1975-77; mem. corporate staff Sisters of Mercy Health Corp., Farmington Hills, Mich., 1977-78; pres. Our Lady of Mercy Hosp., Dyer, Ind., 1978—; rural health cons. Mercy Med. Center, Dubuque, Iowa, 1977—; mem. clin. faculty U. S.D. Med. Sch., 1975-77; chmn. bd. Eastern S.D. Community Health Edn. System, 1974-75; mem. S.D. Emergency Med. Services Adv. Council, 1975-77, S.D. Drugs and Substances Adv. Bd., 1975-77. Chmn. preventive health care task force Midwestern Gov.'s Conf., 1976; vice chmn. No. Ind. Found. for Health, 1981. Mem. Am. Coll. Hosp. Adminstrs., Am. Hosp. Assn. (joint com. with Am. Psychiat. Assn. 1981-83), Ind. Hosp. Assn. (bd. dirs. 1982-83), Am. Public Health Assn., Am. Diabetic Assn. (incorporator, mem. bd. S.D. affiliate 1974-77). Democrat. Roman Catholic. Club: Altrusa. Office: Our Lady of Mercy Hosp Dyer IN 46311

CALLAHAN, FRANCIS MICHAEL, pub. co. exec.; b. Chgo., Jan. 14, 1925; s. Michael Francis and Esther Rose (Kirby) C.; B.S., U. Ill., 1950; midg. degree Northwestern U., 1952; m. Jeannine Beacom, Sept. 18, 1954; children—Francis Michael, Brian Gerard, Mary Courtney, Noreen Powers. Midwest sales food div. Proctor & Gamble, Chgo., 1950-54; Midwest sales Sunset Mag., Chgo., 1954-58; southwestern mgr. Ladies Home Jour., Chgo., 1958-72; dir. Midwestern sales Travel & Leisure Mag., Am. Express Pub. Co., Chgo., 1972—. Served with USAAF, 1943-46. Mem. Western Advt. Golf Assn., Agate Club. Republican. Roman Catholic. Clubs: North Shore Country, Mission Hills Country, Chgo. Athletic. Home: 1416 Elizabeth Ln Glenview IL 60025 Office: Travel and Leisure Mag 500 N Michigan Ave Suite 1520 Chicago IL 60611

CALLAHAN, MICHAEL THOMAS, constrn. cons.; b. Kansas City, Mo., Oct. 7, 1948; s. Harry Leslie and Venita June (Yohn) C.; B.A., U. Kans., 1970; J.D., U. Mo., 1973, LL.M., 1979; postgrad. Temple U., 1976-77; m. Stella Sue Paffenbach, Mar. 21, 1970; children—Molly Leigh, Michael Kroh. Admitted to Kans. bar, 1973, N.J. bar, 1975, Mo. bar, 1977; v.p. T.J. Constrn., Inc., Lenexa, Kans., 1973-74; sr. cons. Wagner-Hohns-Inglis, Inc., Mt. Holly, N.J., 1974-77, v.p., Kansas City, Mo., 1977—; arbitrator, lectr. in field. Mem. Am. Bar Assn., N.J. Bar Assn., Mo. Bar Assn., Am. Arbitration Assn., Asso. Builders and Contractors. Congregationalist. Clubs: Kansas City, Indian Hills Country. Author: Desk Book of Construction Law, 1981; contbr. articles to profl. jours. Home: 9011 Delmar St Prairie Village KS 66207 Office: 4420 Madison St Suite 215 Kansas City MO 64111

CALLAHAN, ROBERT SWANSON, JR., restaurant chain ofcl.; b. Martinsville, Va., July 15, 1954; s. Robert Swanson and Ruby Avanell (Conner) C.; B.S. in Sociology and Anthropology, Va. Commonwealth U., 1978. Employee, The Magic Pan, Richmond, Va., 1976-78, asst. mgr., Washington, 1979, midwest regional tng. mgr., Troy, Mich., 1979; Rochester, Mich., 1981—. Mem. Am. Soc. for Tng. and Devel., Nat. Restaurant Assn. Home: 1005 Parker St Detroit MI 48214 Office: 2573 S Rochester Rd Rochester MI 48063

CALLERY, JOHN MICHAEL, fin. exec.; b. Wichita, Kans., July 19, 1948; s. John Eldon and Josephine Marie (Head) C.; B.B.A., Wichita State U., 1974, M.B.A., 1981; 1 son, John Steven. Spl. auditor Santa Fe Trail Transp. Co., Wichita, 1974-76, spl. acct., 1976, asst. to controller, 1976-78; div. acct. Pizza Hut, Inc., Wichita, 1978-79, mgr. fin. policies and procedures, 1979, mgr. spl. projects, 1979—. 1st v.p. bd. dirs. Sheridan W. Townhouses, Wichita, 1978-79. Served with USN, 1968-70; Vietnam. Mem. Nat. Assn. Accts., Am. Mgmt. Assn. Roman Catholic. Author: How to Develop and Write Corporate Policy and Procedure, 1981; A Beginner's Guide to Casino Gambling, 1981. Home: 8803 E Harry St Apt 510 Wichita KS 67207 Office: 9111 E Douglas St Wichita KS 67207

CALLIHAN, HARRIET K., med. soc. adminstr.; b. Chgo., Feb. 8, 1930; d. Harry Louis and Josephine (Olstad) Kohlman; B.A., U. Chgo., 1951, M.B.A., 1953; m. Clair Clifton Callihan, Dec. 17, 1955; 1 dau., Barbara Claire. Personnel dir. Leo Burnett Co., Chgo., 1953-57, John Plain & Co., 1957-62, Follett Pub. Co., 1962-64, Needham, Harper & Steers, N.Y.C., 1966-68, Bell, Boyd, Lloyd, Haddad & Burns, 1964-66; Hume, Clement, Hume & Lee, 1968-70, owner, operator PersD, 1970-75; exec. dir. Inst. Medicine Chgo., 1975—, mng. editor ofcl. med. publ. Proceedings, 1975—. Mem. Chgo. Soc. Assn. Execs., Conf. Med. Soc. Execs. Greater Chgo., Am. Med. Writers Assn., Profl. Conv. Mgrs. Assn., Women in Mgmt., Chgo. Council Fgn. Relations, Execs. Club. Clubs: Westmoreland Country, Michigan Shores. Office: Inst of Medicine of Chicago 332 S Michigan Ave Chicago IL 60604

CALLIS, BRUCE, ins. co. exec.; b. Sedalia, Mo., Dec. 4, 1939; s. George E. and Jo (Trigg) C.; B.S. in Bus. Adminstrn., U. Mo., 1961; m. Nancy Williams, Nov. 14, 1959; children—Cheryl, Kimberly and Kevin (twins). Plant mgr. Boonslick Mfg. Co., Boonville, Mo., 1961-63; claim rep. State Farm Ins., Rolla, Mo., 1963-64, asst. regional personnel mgr., Columbia, Mo., 1964-66, various corp. personnel and mktg. positions, Bloomington, Ill., 1966—, v.p. personnel, 1976—. Mem. McLean County (Ill.) Bd., 1972-78; bd. dirs. Brokaw Hosp.; chmn. McLean County Republican Central Com.; chmn. Normal (Ill.) Human Relations Commn. Recipient Cert. of Appreciation, Am. Compensation Soc., 1970. Mem. Am. Soc. Personnel Adminstrn. (chmn.'s adv. council), Ins. Inst. Hwy. Safety (chmn. personnel adv. com.). Presbyterian. Office: State Farm Ins Co 1 State Farm Plaza Bloomington IL 61701

CALLIS, KENNETH RIVERS, clergyman; b. Louisville, Aug. 26, 1925; s. George Washington and Fannie Lou (Hutcherson) G.; student Berea Coll., 1943-44; B.S. in Mech. Engring., U. Mich., 1947, postgrad. (Margaret Kraus Ramsdell fellow), 1947-48; M.Div., Asbury Theol. Sem., 1950; D.D. (hon.), Albion Coll., 1975; m. Annie Ruth Smith, Sept. 1, 1949; children—Kenneth Rivers, Annette, Cheryl Lynn. Ordained to ministry United Methodist Ch., 1949; minister, Mich., 1950—, sr. minister Ypsilanti 1st Meth. Ch., 1965-72, Court St. Meth. Ch., Flint, 1972-77, Utica United Meth. Ch., Sterling Heights, 1977—; trustee Asbury Theol. Sem., 1979—; pres. bd. trustees United Meth. Retirement Homes, Detroit conf., 1979—; dean Mich. Pastors Sch., 1972-75; mem. World Meth. Council, 1971-76; del. Gen. Conf., 1976. Mem. Sterling Heights Housing Commn., 1978—; exec. bd., council advancement chmn. Clinton Valley council Boy Scouts Am., 1978-80, exec. bd. Tall Pine council, 1974-77; mem. Ypsilanti Housing Commn., 1969-72. Served to ensign USN, 1943-46. Mem. Utica Ministerial Assn. Contbr. articles to religious mag. Home: 8506 Clinton River Rd Sterling Heights MI 48078 Office: Utica United Meth Ch 8650 Canal Rd Sterling Heights MI 48078

CALLOW, WILLIAM GRANT, justice Wis. Supreme Ct.; b. Waukesha, Wis., Apr. 9, 1921; s. Curtis Grant and Mildred G. C.; Ph.B. in Econs., U. Wis., 1943, J.D., 1948; m. Jean A. Zilavy, Apr. 15, 1950; children—William Grant, Christine S., Katherine H. Admitted to Wis. bar, 1948; asst. city atty. City of Waukesha, 1948-52, city atty., 1952-60; judge Waukesha County (Wis.) Ct., 1961-77; justice Supreme Ct. Wis., 1978—; asst. prof. law U. Minn., 1951-52; mem. faculty Wis. Jud. Coll., 1968-75. Served with USMC, 1943-45, USAF, 1948-52; Korea. Recipient Disting. Service award Waukesha Jr. C. of C., 1955, Good Human Relations award Dale Carnegie, Disting. Service award Lawyers Wives of Wis. Assn., Outstanding Alumnus award U. Wis., 1973. Fellow Am. Bar Found.; mem. Am. Bar Assn., State Bar Wis., Dane County (Wis.) Bar Assn., Nat. Conf. Commrs. on Uniform State Laws (Wis. commr., mem. exec. com.). Episcopalian. Author State Bar of Wis. pamphlet for teenagers, used as curriculum for all 9th grade students: You and The Law, 1974; contbr. articles to Am. Bar Jour., S.D. Law Rev. Office: 231 E State Capitol Madison WI 53702

CALVERT, GARY ROSS, ins. co. exec.; b. Columbus, Ohio, Jan. 15, 1947; s. H. Ross and Betty Carol (Wood) C.; B.S., U.S. Mil. Acad., 1969; m. Judith Carolyn Calvert, Nov. 30, 1979; children from previous marriage—Christiana Lynn, Geoffrey Ross. Commd. 2d lt. U.S. Army, 1969, advanced through grades to capt., 1971; ret., 1974; mgr. tng. and devel. Procter and Gamble Paper Products, Mehoopany, Pa., 1974-77; dir. tng. and devel. Arthur Treacher's Fish and Chips, Columbus, 1977-79; dir. tng. and devel. J.C. Penney Casualty Ins., Westerville, Ohio, 1980—. Mem. Am. Soc. Tng. and Devel., Nat. Ins. Cos. Edn. Dirs. Soc., Assn. Grads. U.S. Mil. Acad. Methodist. Home: 1860 Knollridge Ct Columbus OH 43229 Office: 800 Brooksedge Blvd Westerville OH 43081

CAMCAM, GLORIA AMAGO, dietitian; b. Manila, Philippines, Jan. 15, 1929; came to U.S., 1968, naturalized, 1974; d. Emilio N. and Dolores A. (Almendrala) Amago; B.S., U. Philippines, 1953; M.S. in Nutrition, U. Ia., 1954; m. Nicolas G. Camcam, Jr., Apr. 21, 1963; children—Nicolas III, Nathan. Staff dietitian, U. Iowa Hosps., Iowa City, 1954-55; research dietitian Philippine Gen. Hosp., Manila, 1955-68; therapeutic dietitian St. Elizabeth Hosp., Chgo., 1968-71, chief therapeutic dietitian, 1971-79, chief nutritional services, 1980—; 1st chmn. Bd. Examiners for Dietitians, Philippines, 1963-65; cons. dietetic internship Philippine Gen. Hosp., 1965-68. U. Iowa fellow, 1953; 25th Anniversary Certificate of Appreciation as Pres., Dietetic Assn. Philippines, 1957-61. Mem. Ill. Dietetic Assn., Am. Dietetic Assn., Chgo. Dietetic Assn., Am. Soc. Hosp. Food Service Adminstrs. (Chgo.-Midwest chpt.). Mem. Philippine-Am. Ecumenical Ch. Home: 3731 W Windsor St Chicago IL 60625

CAMERON, KAREN JEAN, bank ofcl.; b. Ft. Wayne, Ind., Mar. 10, 1956; d. Samuel James and Dolores Marie (Clark) Himmelhaver; student Sch. Bank Mktg., U. Colo., 1980-81; student Ind. U., Ft. Wayne, 1979—; m. Steven A. Cameron, Apr. 27, 1979. Sec., asst. to dir. mktg. Lincoln Nat. Bank & Trust Co., Ft. Wayne, 1975-79, mktg. asst., 1979-80, mktg. officer, advt. mgr., 1980—. Mem. Am. Inst. Banking, Bank Mktg. Assn., Ind. Bankers Assn., Advt. Assn. Ft. Wayne (dir.), Nat. Assn. Bank Women, U.S. Women's Volleyball Assn. Roman Catholic. Club: Ft. Wayne Turners. Home: 8302 Park State Dr Fort Wayne IN 46815 Office: 116 E Berry St Fort Wayne IN 46802

CAMERON, ROY EUGENE, scientist; b. Denver, July 16, 1929; s. Guy Francis and Ilda Annora (Horn) C.; B.S., Wash. State U., 1953 and 1954; M.S., U. Ariz., 1958, Ph.D., 1961; D.D. (hon.) Ministry of Christ Ch., Delavan, Wis., 1975; m. Margot Elizabeth Hoagland, May 5, 1956 (div. July 1977); children—Susan Lynn, Catherine Ann; m. 2d, Carolyn Mary Light, Sept. 22, 1978. Research scientist Hughes Aircraft Corp., Tucson, Ariz., 1955-56; sr. scientist Jet Propulsion Lab., Pasadena, Calif., 1961-68, mem. tech. staff, 1969-74; dir. research Darwin Research Inst., Dana Point, Calif., 1974-75; dep. dir. Land Reclamation Lab. Argonne (Ill.) Nat. Lab., 1975-77, dir. energy resources tng. and devel. 1977—; cons. Lunar Receiving Lab. Baylor U., 1966-68, Ecology Center Utah State U., Desert Biome, 1970-72, Tundra Biome, 1973-74, U. Maine, 1973-76. Served with U.S. Army, 1950-52; Korea, Japan. Recipient 3 NASA awards for tech. briefs; Paul Steere Burgess fellow U. Ariz., 1959; NSF grantee, 1970-74; Dept. Interior grantee, 1978-80. Mem. AAAS, Soil Scientists Soc. Am., Ecol. Soc. Am., Phycological Soc. Am., Am. Soc. Agronomy, Antarctican Soc., Polar Soc. Am., Am. Scientist Affiliation, World Future Soc., Internat. Soc. Soil Sci., Ariz. Acad. Sci., Am. Inst. Biol. Sci., Sigma Xi. Mem. Christian Ch. Contbr. numerous articles in field to sci. books. 7 Antarctic expdns., 1966-74. Home: 3433 Woodridge Dr Woodridge IL 60517 Office: 9700 S Cass Ave Argonne IL 60439

CAMMA, ALBERT JOHN, neurosurgeon; b. Cleve., Dec. 27, 1940; s. August and Amelia (Catalioti) C.; B.S. cum laude, John Carroll U., 1963; M.D., Western Res. U., 1967; m. Sheryl Virginia Doptis, Aug. 27, 1966; children—August Leon, Albert David. Intern, surg. resident, U. Pitts., 1967-69, resident in neurosurgery 1971-75; practice medicine specializing in neurosurgery, Zanesville, Ohio, 1975—. Bd. trustees Zanesville YMCA, 1976—. Served with M.C. USN, 1969-71. Diplomate Am. Bd. Neurol. Surgeons, Nat. Bd. Med. Examiners. Mem. AMA, Ohio State Med. Assn., Muskingum County Acad. Medicine, Congress Neurol. Surgeons, A.C.S., Am. Assn. Neurol. Surgeons, Ohio State Neurosurg. Soc., Mid-Atlantic Neurosurg. Soc. Office: 2835 Maple Ave Zanesville OH 43701

CAMMA, PHILIP, accountant; b. Phila., May 22, 1923; s. Anthony and Rose (LaSpada) C.; B.S., U. Pa., 1952; m. Anna Ruth Karg, July 21, 1956 (dec. Aug. 1960); 1 son, Anthony Philip. Accountant, Main and Co., C.P.A.'s, Phila., 1952-53; in charge accountant Haskins & Sells, C.P.A.'s, Phila., St. Louis, Cin. and Columbus, Ohio, 1953-60; controller Marvin Warner Co., Cin., 1960-61; controller Leshner Corp., 1961-63; mng. partner Camma & Patrick, C.P.A.'s, 1963-66; founder Philip Camma & Co., C.P.A.'s, Cin., 1966—. Served with USAAF, 1942-45; ETO. Mem. Am. Legion, Am. Inst. C.P.A.'s, Ohio, Ky. socs. C.P.A.'s, Am. Accounting Assn., Nat. Assn. Accountants. Republican. Clubs: Cincinnati; University Pa.; Hamilton City. Home: Phelps Townhouse Cincinnati OH 45202 Office: 712 Gwynne Bldg Cincinnati OH 45202

CAMMARATA, WALTER THOMAS, pub. co. exec.; b. St. Louis, July 2, 1940; s. Walter and Anne (Tucciarello) C.; B.S., St. Louis U., 1964, M.B.A., 1968; m. Gail Ann Leiendecker, Feb. 11, 1961; children—Mark, Dana, Christy. Office mgr. McGraw Hill Book Co., Manchester, Mo., 1967, staff asst., 1968, gen. mgr., 1969, regional v.p., 1980—. Served with U.S. Army, 1962. Mem. Associated Industries of Mo., C. of C., Ballwin Athletic Assn. Republican. Club: Rotary. Home: 651 Tanglewilde Dr Manchester MO 63011 Office: 13955 Manchester Rd Manchester MO 63011

CAMMIN, WILLIAM BENJAMIN, clin. psychologist; b. Saginaw, Mich., Jan. 16, 1941; s. Howard John and Beulah Ione Cammin; B.S., Central Mich. U., 1964; M.A., Western Mich. U., 1966; Ph.D., U. S.C., 1969; m. Joanne Marie Seidel, July 23, 1966; children—Darren William, Kiena Marie, Clane Joseph. Chief psychologist outpatient services Carter Meml. Hosp., Ind. Med. Center, Indpls., 1968-70; cons. clin. psychology Quinco Community Mental Health Center, Columbus, Ind., 1969-70; cons. Community Mental Health Planning, Kokomo, Ind., 1970; exec. dir. Bay-Arenac Community Mental Health Services Bd., Bay City, Mich., 1971—; mem. mental health com. E. Central Mich. Health Systems Agy., 1973—; co-chmn. psychiat. tech. com. Emergency Med. Services Eastern Mich., 1975-78. Mem. Am. Psychol. Assn., Mich. Psychol. Assn., Mich. Assn. Community Mental Health Dirs. (exec. com.). Home: 5578 Mackinaw Rd Saginaw MI 48604 Office: 201 Mulholland St Bay City MI 48706

CAMP, HERBERT LEE, otolaryngologist; b. Saginaw, Mich., May 27, 1940; s. Harper Lee and Agatha (Hardy) C.; B.S., Mich. State U., 1962; M.D., U. Mich., 1966; m. Jacqueline Nelson, June 17, 1961; children—Jeffrey, Susan, Patricia. Intern, Munson Med. Center, Traverse City, Mich., 1966-67; resident in surgery State U. N.Y., Syracuse, 1967-68, resident in otolaryngology, 1968-71; practice medicine specializing in otolaryngology, 1971—; mem. staffs Upstate Med. Center, Syracuse, 1971, Syracuse Meml.-Crous Irving Hosp., 1971, Syracuse Vets. Hosp., 1971, Wilford Hall, Lackland AFB, Tex., 1971-73, Ponce De Leon Infirmary, Atlanta, 1973-74, Grady Meml. Hosp., 1973-74, Midland (Mich.) Hosp. Center, 1974—, Bay Med. Center, Bay City, Mich., 1975—; instr. in otolaryngology State U. N.Y., Syracuse, 1971; adj. asst. prof. Central Mich. U., 1974—. Served with USAF, 1971-73. Fellow Am. Acad. Ophthalmology and Otolaryngology, A.C.S.; mem. AMA, Mich. State, Midland County (Mich.) med. socs., Am. Council Otolaryngology, Soc. Mil. Otolaryngologists. Contbr. articles to profl. jours. Home: 16 Snowfield Ct Midland MI 48640 Office: 4007 Orchard Dr Midland MI 48640

CAMP, LUCILLE E., county ofcl., realtor; b. Goodland, Ind., Aug. 9, 1914; d. Joseph Leonard and Marie (Krintz) Camp; student Internat. Bus. Coll., Ft. Wayne, Ind., 1933, Ind. U. Extension, 1948-49; m. David B. McQuinn, Aug. 11, 1940 (div. Jan. 1946). Cosmetic sales William H. Block Co., Indpls., 1934; sec. Ind. Dept. Edn., 1935-36, Ind. Dept. Agr., Indpls., 1939-40; dental asst. Dr. William J. Stark, Indpls., 1945-47; lab technician, chair asst. Dr. Berkey, Ft. Wayne, 1947-48; surg. asst. Dr. J. B. Shaw, Ft. Wayne, 1948-49; sec. C.T. Foxworthy Co., automobile agy., 1949-51; owner, operator Dairy Queen Ice Cream Stores, Indpls., 1953-59; adminstrv. asst., office mgr. Ind. Commn. for Reorgn. Sch. Corps, Indpls., 1960-66; pvt. sec. to v.p. and dean Ind. Vocat. Tech. Coll., Indpls., 1966; personnel dir. City of Indpls., 1968-71; adminstr. Ind. Office Consumer Affairs, 1972—; ct. reporter Superior Ct. 2, Indpls. Vice committeeman Indpls. Republican Com., 1958, precinct committeeman, 1959-73, ward vice chmn., 1954-73; bd. dirs. Civic Ballet Soc. Indpls. Mem. Am. Bus. Women's Assn. (charter mem.; rec. sec. 1963), Clowes Hall Women's Com., Soc. Ind. Symphony Soc., Internat. Platform Assn., Ind. U. Friends Music, Children's Mus., Indpls. Mus. Art, Indpls. Art Assn., Delta Theta Tau (pres. 1958-59, corr. sec. 1960-62). Methodist. Clubs: Toastmistress (charter), Riviera, Soroptimist Internat. Home: 5928 Devington Rd Indianapolis IN 46226 Office: City-County Bldg Indianapolis IN 46204

CAMPBELL, BRIAN PHILLIP, mfg. co. exec.; b. Oak Park, Ill., Aug. 23, 1940; s. Andrew Frank and Elizabeth (Gabris) C.; B.S.C., DePaul U., 1963; M.B.A., Northwestern U., 1966; M.S. in Fed. Income Taxation, DePaul U., 1973; m. Mary Lucina Lincoln. With No. Trust Co., Chgo., 1963; asst. v.p. Walston & Co., Inc., Chgo., 1963-65; v.p. Glore Forgan Staats, Inc., Chgo., 1965-70; v.p. duPont Glore Forgan Inc., Chgo., 1970-73; v.p. Masco Corp., Taylor, Mich., 1974-77, group v.p., 1977—; lectr. DePaul U., 1972-73. Bd. dirs. Chgo. Boys Clubs, 1972-73, Boys Clubs Met. Detroit, 1974—. Mem. Inst. Chartered Financial Analysts, Financial Execs. Inst., Planning Execs. Inst. Episcopalian. Clubs: Chicago, U. Economics (Chgo.); Chgo., Barton Hills Country. Office: 21001 Van Born Rd Taylor MI 48180

CAMPBELL, CALVIN ARTHUR, JR., mining, tunneling and plastics molding equipment mfg. co. exec.; b. Detroit, Sept. 1, 1934; s. Calvin Arthur and Alta Christine (Koch) C.; B.A. in Econs., Williams Coll., 1956; B.S., MIT, 1959; J.D., U. Mich., 1961; m. Rosemary Phoenix, June 6, 1959; 1 dau., Georgia Alta. With Exxon Co., N.Y.C., 1961-69; chmn. bd., treas. John B. Adt Co., York, Pa., N.Y.C., 1969-70; with Goodman Equipment Corp., Chgo., 1971—, pres., chief exec. officer, 1971—, chmn. bd. Improved Plastics Machinery Corp. subs. Goodman Equipment Corp., 1979—. Mem. Chgo. Econ. Devel. Commn. Mem. Am., N.Y. bar assns., Am. Mining Congress (gov. from 1972, chmn. bd. govs. Mfrs. div. 1980—, dir. 1980—), Ill. Mfrs. Assn. (dir. 1978), Am. Inst. Chem. Engrs., Young Pres.'s Orgn., Newcomen Soc. N.Am., Psi Upsilon, Phi Delta Phi. Clubs: Racquet (Chgo.); Glen View; Skytop (Pa.). Office: 4834 S Halsted St Chicago IL 60609

CAMPBELL, CHARLES EDGAR, co. exec.; b. Evanston, Ill., Jan. 10, 1944; s. Charles Edgar and Martha Burke C.; B.S., No. Ill. U., 1967; M.A., U. Ariz., 1969; m. Jacqueline Joan Howlett, June 24, 1967; children—Courtney Burke, Meegan Hardman. Instr., No. Ill. U., DeKalb, 1969-71; safety dir. Turner Co., Sycamore, Ill., 1971-76; public relation mgr. Wis. Steel div. Internat. Harvester Co., Chgo., 1976-77; asst. to chmn. Envirodyne Industries, Inc., Chgo., 1977-80; pres. Stockbrokers Assn., Inc.; Chgo., 1981—; pres. Charles E. Campbell & Assos., Chgo., 1980—. Dir., Calumet Area Indsl. Commn., Chgo., 1975—; dir. South Chicago YMCA, 1976-77. Mem. Internat. Assn. Bus. Communications. Republican. Episcopalian. Office: 10 S LaSalle St Suite 1251 Chicago IL 60603

CAMPBELL, CHARLES GEORGE, banker; b. Andover, Eng., July 16, 1895; s. William T. and Grace (Calder) C.; came to U.S., 1901, naturalized, 1919; grad. Ind. Bus. Coll., 1916; student U. Chgo., 1920-22; hon. degree Wabash Coll., 1980; m. Helen I. Thompson, June 14, 1926; children—Claire E. (Mrs. David Locke, Jr.), Joyce C. (Mrs. Rodney Beals). Sec.-treas. Kamp Motor Co., Mt. Carmel, Ill., 1923-26, pres., 1926-59; v.p. Vigo Motor Co., Terre Haute, Ind., 1944-50; v.p. Security Bank and Trust Co., Mt. Carmel, 1937-59, pres., 1959-64, chmn. bd., 1969—, also dir.; pres. Am. Savs. & Loan Assn., Mt. Carmel, 1939-59, dir., 1937—; dir. Camray, Inc., Mt. Carmel, Mt. Carmel Area Devel. Corp.; dir. Tri-Country Indsl. Com., 1965-67. Mem. Mt. Carmel City Commn., 1963—; mayor City of Mt. Carmel, 1965-67. Served with U.S. Army, 1917-19; AEF in France. Mem. Mt. Carmel C. of C. (dir. 1959-62, 65-68), Am. Legion (comdr. Wabash post 1937), 40 and 8, Wabash Valley Assn. Presbyterian. Clubs: Masons, Shriners, Elks (lodge trustee 1979-80), Moose, Eagles, Kiwanis (pres. Mt. Carmel 1935, dir. 1936). Home: 323 Cherry St Mount Carmel IL 62863 Office: 400 Main St Mount Carmel IL 62863

CAMPBELL, CHARLES INGALLS, JR., savs. and loan assn. exec.; b. Casper, Wyo., Jan. 9, 1923; s. Charles Ingalls and Ann Marie (Ryan) C.; student U. Mo., 1940-41, U.S. Naval Acad., 1941-43, Marine Corps Schs., 1943, Armed Forces Staff Coll., 1962; m. Kathryn Ryan, Feb. 7, 1953; children—Ann, Charles Ingalls III, Mary Kay, John. Commd. 2d lt. U.S. Marine Corps, 1943, advanced through grades to lt. col., 1970; ret., 1970; asst. sec. dir. personnel and purchasing Safety Fed. Savs. & Loan, Kansas City, Mo., 1971—. Hon. bd. dirs. Rockhurst Coll.; dep. election commr., Kansas City, Mo., 1972-78. Decorated Air medal with three gold stars, Purple Heart, Navy commendation medal. Mem. Mo. Council Retired Officers Assn. (pres. 1975-76), Am. Soc. Personnel Adminstrn., Mil. Order World Wars, U. Mo. Alumni Assn., U.S. Naval Acad. Alumni Assn., Mo. Sheriffs Assn., DAV, Sigma Chi. Democrat. Roman Catholic. Clubs: Army-Navy Country (Washington); Brookridge Country, Homestead Country (dir. 1978-81) (Kansas City, Mo.). Home: 421 Westover Rd Kansas City MO 64113 Office: 910 Grand St Kansas City MO 64106

CAMPBELL, D'ANN MAE, historian; b. Denver, Dec. 30, 1949; d. Bernard Edward and Eleanor Louise (Mahoney) Campbell; B.A., Colo. Coll., 1972; Ph.D. in History, U. N.C., Chapel Hill, 1979; m. Richard Jensen, July 16, 1976. Asst. dir. Family and Community History Center, Newberry Library, Chgo., 1976-78, asso. dir., 1978-79; adj. prof. history U. Ill., Chgo. Circle, 1977—; dean for women's affairs Ind. U., also asst. prof. history. Newberry Library fellow, 1975-76, Nat. Endowment for Humanities grantee, 1976-79; Dept. Edn. grantee, 1979-81. Mem. Am. Studies Assn. (nat. council 1979-81), Orgn. Am. Historians (chair com. status women 1977-79, nominating bd. 1980-82), Am., So., Social Sci. hist. assns., Nat. Hist. Communal Socs. Assn., Quantum Internat. Orgn., Coalition for Women in Humanities and Social Scis., Phi Beta Kappa. Contbr. articles to profl. jours.; editorial bd. Newberry Papers, Teaching History. Home: 1109 Longwood Dr Bloomington IN 47401 Office: Meml Hall E Ind U Bloomington IN 47405

CAMPBELL, DAVID MICHAEL, motion picture co. exec.; b. Columbus, Ohio, June 7, 1949; s. Thurl Garfield and Mary Janice (Thompson) C.; B.S., Fla. State U., 1972; m. Catherine A. Jacobs, Jan. 6, 1979. Studio operator Sta. WPTV, West Palm Beach, Fla., 1968-69; mem. prodn. staff sta. WCTV, Tallahassee, Fla., 1970-71; producer, dir. Sta. KPHO-TV, Phoenix, 1973-74; buyer, semiconductor products div. Motorola, Phoenix, 1972-74; regional dir. Tele-Tronics Corp., Scottsdale, Ariz., 1975; exec. producer Sta. WKEF-TV, Dayton, Ohio, 1975-76; dir. sales Columbia Pictures TV, Chgo., 1976-81; exec. sales dir. Metromedia Producers Corp. Inc., Chgo., 1981—. Mem. Nat. Acad. TV Arts and Scis., Am. Film Inst., Broadcast Advt. Club Chgo., Phi Theta Kappa. Home: 550 Chisholm Court Roselle IL 60172 Office: Metromedia Inc 645 N Michigan Ave Suite 620 Chicago IL 60611

CAMPBELL, F(ENTON) GREGORY, univ. adminstr., historian; b. Columbia, Tenn., Dec. 16, 1939; s. Fenton G. and Ruth (Hayes) C.; A.B., Baylor U., 1960; postgrad. (Fulbright grantee), Philipps U., Marburg/Lahn, W. Ger., 1960-61; M.A. (Woodrow Wilson fellow), Emory U., 1962; postgrad. (Exchange fellow) Charles U., Prague, Czechoslovakia, 1965-66; Ph.D., Yale U., 1967; m. Barbara D. Kuhn, Aug. 29, 1970; children—Fenton H., Matthew W., Charles H. Research staff historian Yale U., New Haven, 1966-68, spl. asst. to acting pres., 1977-78; asst. prof. history U. Wis., Milw., 1968-69; asst. prof. European history U. Chgo., 1969-76, spl. asst. to pres., 1978—, sec. bd. trustees, 1979—; fellow Woodrow Wilson Internat. Center for Scholars, Smithsonian Instn., Washington, 1976-77; mem. E. European selection com. Internat. Research and Exchanges Bd., 1975-78; dir. Vista Homes Bldg. Corp., Chgo., 1979-82. Fulbright grantee, 1973-74; U.S.A.-Czechoslovakia exchange fellow, 1973-74. Mem. Am. Hist. Assn., Am. Assn. for Advancement Slavic Studies, Czechoslovak History Conf. (pres. 1980-82), Conf. Group on Central European History (sec.-treas. 1980-82), Chgo. Council on Fgn. Relations (com. on fgn. affairs 1979—), Phi Beta Kappa. Clubs: Mid-Day, Quadrangle (Chgo.). Author: Confrontation in Central Europe, 1975. Contbr. articles, revs. to profl. jours. Joint editor Akten zur deutschen auswartigen Politik, 1918-45, 1966—. Home: 5830 Stony Island Ave Chicago IL 60637 Office: Office of Pres U Chgo 5801 S Ellis Ave Chicago IL 60637

CAMPBELL, HELEN WOERNER (MRS. THOMAS B. CAMPBELL), librarian; b. Indpls., Oct. 17, 1918; d. Clarence Julius and Gertrude Elizabeth (Colley) Woerner; student Ind. U., 1935-38; B.S., Butler U., 1967; m. Thomas B. Campbell, Jan. 17, 1942; 1 dau., Martha (Mrs. L. Kurt Adamson). Asst. order librarian Ind. U., Bloomington, 1937-42; librarian Ind. U. Sch. Dentistry, Indpls., 1942-46, cataloger, part-time, 1960-65, asst. librarian, 1965-66, librarian, 1966-80. Mem. Am. Assn. Dental Schs., Med. Library Assn., Spl. Libraries Assn. (chpt. pres. 1972-73). Home: 1865 Norfolk St Indianapolis IN 46224

CAMPBELL, JAMES ARTHUR, profl. baseball exec.; b. Huron, Ohio, Feb. 5, 1924; s. Arthur A. and Vanessa (Hart) C.; B.S., Ohio State U., 1949; m. Helene G. Mulligan, Jan. 16, 1954 (div. July 1969). Bus. mgr. Thomasville (Ga.) Baseball Club, 1950, Toledo Baseball Club, 1951, Buffalo Baseball Club, 1952; bus. mgr. Detroit Minor League System, 1953, asst. farm dir. Detroit Baseball Club, 1954-56, v.p., farm dir., 1957-61, v.p., gen. mgr. 1962-65, exec. v.p., gen. mgr. Detroit Tigers, 1965-78, pres., gen. mgr., 1978—. Served with AC, USNR, 1943-46. Named Maj. League Exec. of Year, 1968. Mem. Ohio State U. Varsity O Assn., Delta Upsilon. Presbyterian. Clubs: Detroit Athletic, Detroit Press. Office: Tiger Stadium 2121 Trumbull St Detroit MI 48216

CAMPBELL, MALCOLM DAVID, dentist; b. Detroit, Sept. 23, 1926; s. Malcolm Duncan and Mabel Edith (White) C.; B.A., Wayne State U., 1951, teaching certificate, 1951; D.D.S., U. Detroit, 1955, postgrad., 1962-63; m. Janet Cauhorn, Nov. 14, 1958; children—Mary Catherine, David, Elizabeth, Douglas. Pvt. practice dentistry, Dearborn, Mich.; mem. staff Harper Hosp., Detroit, 1957—; instr. Sch. Dentistry U. Detroit, 1961-65, U. Mich., 1966-74; adviser Wayne County Welfare Dept. Sponsor Detroit council Boy Scouts Am.; bd. dirs. Dearborn Community Health; deacon First Presbyterian Ch. of Dearborn. Fellow Acad. Gen. Dentistry, Acad. Dentistry Internat., Royal Soc. Health; mem. Southwestern Dental Club (treas., corr. sec. 1957, pres. 1960), Dental Aid Commn. (pres. 1959-61), Chgo., Detroit Dist. dental socs., Mich. Soc. Psychosomatic Dentistry (v.p. 1962-63, pres. 1964), Am. Acad. Dental Medicine (pres. Mich. sect. 1964-65), Am. Acad. Oral Medicine, Am. Assn. Dental Schs., Orgn. Tchrs. Dental Practice Adminstrn., Am. Acad. Dental Practice Adminstrn., Mich. Dental Assn. (trustee). Office: 23601 Ford Rd Dearborn MI 48128

CAMPBELL, MAURICE ARNOLD, agronomist; b. Stuart, Iowa, May 23, 1913; s. Clyde Marion and Frances Mabel C.; B.S., Iowa State U., 1938, postgrad., 1978-79; m. Mary Margaret Hill, Dec. 29, 1939; children—James Arnold, Nancy Margaret Campbell Cornish, Paul Thomas. Farmer, Dallas County, Iowa, 1933-35; agt. Iowa State U. Extension, Jasper County, 1938-39, extension dir., Carroll, Iowa, 1940-43, Webster County, 1943-45; asst. prodn. mgr. Garst & Thomas Hybrid Corn Co., Coon Rapids, Iowa, 1945-78; owner, mgr. Campbell Real Estate, 1979—. Chmn. Republican Com. Union Twp., 1948-64; mem. Coon Rapids Public Sch. Bd., 1949-57, pres., 1954-57; mem. Carroll County Bd. Edn., 1961-73; mem. Des Moines Area Community Coll. Bd., 1973-79, pres., 1979. Recipient Service cert. Iowa State U. Alumni Assn., 1968; named (with Mary M. Campbell) Citizens of Yr., Kiwanis, 1978. Mem. Am. Soc. Agronomy, Nat. Assn. Realtors, Iowa Assn. Realtors, C. of C. Methodist. Clubs: Rotary, Masons, Shriners. Home: 705 4th Ave Coon Rapids IA 50058 Office: 106 5th Ave Coon Rapids IA 50058

CAMPBELL, MAXINE ELIZABETH, educator; b. Feb. 26, 1933; d. William Holt and Elizabeth Jane (Napier) Shackelford; A.S. in Elem. Edn., Lees Coll., 1953; B.S. in Elem. Edn., Wright State U., 1969; M.S. in Curriculum and Supervision, 1980; m. Oscar Hobert Campbell, June 5, 1954; children—Venita Kaye, Marc Eugene. Tchr., Talawanda Sch. Dist., Oxford, Ohio, 1954-62; tchr. Northmont Sch. Dist., 1964—, tchr. 6th grade Englewood (Ohio) Elem. Sch.; cons. individualized reading, creative writing; condr. workshops Wright State U. Mem. Assn. Supervision and Curriculum Devel., Northmont Dist. Edn. Assn. (25-Yr. Service pin 1981), Ohio Edn Assn., NEA, Nat. Council Tchrs. English, Internat. Reading Assn., Phi Delta Kappa, Kappa Delta Pi. Methodist. Home: 6425 Noranda Dr Dayton OH 45415 Office: 702 Albert St Englewood OH 45322

CAMPBELL, PATRICIA FORSYTHE, ednl. adminstr.; b. Joliet, Ill., Nov. 29, 1948; d. Donald Joseph and Mary Magdalane (Long) Forsythe; B.S., Coll. St. Francis, 1970; M.S., Mich. State U., 1972; Ph.D., Fla. State U., 1976; m. Gregory Campbell, Aug. 18, 1973; children—David Matthew, Sarah Catherine. Instr. math. Lakeland Community Coll., 1972-73; grad. asst. Mich. State U., 1970-72, Fla. State U., 1973-76; vis. asst. prof. math. and edn. Purdue U., West Lafayette, Ind., 1976-79, coordinator acad. advising dept. computer sci., 1979—; cons. Lafayette Reading Acad.; mem. Ind. Task Force on Adult Edn., 1977-78; HEW grantee Ind. Dept. Public Instrn. Div. Adult Edn., 1976-79. Mem. Am. Ednl. Research Assn., Nat. Council Tchrs. Math., Women and Math. Edn., Ind. Council Tchrs. Math., Research Council for Diagnostic and Prescriptive Math., Spl. Interest Group for Research in Math. Edn. Author: (with G. Kulm) Getting Everything Down: Mathematics, 1981; research, numerous publs. in field. Office: 709 Math Scis Bldg Purdue U West Lafayette IN 47907

CAMPBELL, RICHARD RICE, newspaperman; b. Athens County, Ohio, Mar. 25, 1923; s. Arthur Donald and Marguerite (Rice) C.; A.B. summa cum laude, Ohio U., 1947; M.A., Kent State U., 1977—; m. Margaret Jandes, Feb. 9, 1946; children—Christopher, Constant. With Cleve. Press, 1947-77, asst. city editor, 1959-62, chief editorial writer, 1962-66, asso. editor, 1966-68, mng. editor, 1968-77, on leave Scripps-Howard Newspapers rep. to Newspaper Systems Devel. Group, 1975; editor Columbus (Ohio) Citizen-Jour., E.W. Scripps Co., 1977—. Served with AUS, 1943-46. Recipient Alumni award for outstanding achievement in journalism Ohio U., 1962. Mem. Am. Soc. Newspaper Editors, Phi Beta Kappa, Sigma Delta Chi, Sigma Pi. Methodist. Clubs: Columbus Athletic, Scioto Country. Home: 1243 Kenbrook Hills Dr Upper Arlington OH 43220 Office: Columbus Citizen-Jour 34 S 3d St Columbus OH 43216*

CAMPBELL, ROBERT L., mgmt. cons.; b. Haverford, Pa., Jan. 6, 1943; s. Robert L. and I. Lee (Groah) C.; B.S. in Mktg., Loyola U., Chgo., 1964; M.M., Northwestern U., 1978; m. Elizabeth A. Powers, Dec. 20, 1975; 1 dau., Elisabeth Powers. Mgmt. cons. Quirsfeld, Hussey & Mames, Chgo., 1964-70, Peat, Marwick, Mitchell & Co., Chgo., 1970-73, Booz, Allen & Hamilton, Chgo., 1973-76; owner, mgr. Robert Campbell & Assos., Chgo., 1976—; lectr. Loyola U., part-time, 1976—, Fin. Inst., part-time, 1972—. Bd. dirs. Youth Guidance Chgo., 1977—; chmn. devel. com. Ill. Republican Com., 1970—. Mem. Assn. Bus. Economists, Am. Econometric Assn., Nat. Small Bus. Assn., Am. Prodn. and Inventory Control Soc., Am. Mktg. Assn., Northwestern U. Alumni Assn. (dir. 1978—). Club: University (Chgo.). Contbr. articles on labor econs. to profl. publs. Home: 470 Deming Pl Chicago IL 60614 Office: 18 S Michigan Ave Chicago IL 60603

CAMPBELL, WILLIAM HENRY, geologist; b. Kansas City, Mo., Sept. 20, 1923; s. Myers D. and Wilma (Morris) C.; B.A., Kans. U., 1947; B.S. in Geology, Mo. State U., 1950, M.S., 1960; Ph.D. in Archaeology, U. Biarritz (France), 1965; m. Virginia Hargus, Oct. 8, 1955; children—Constance Lyn, William Arthur. Cons. geologist and oil field operator various locations, 1951-55; mining engr. Batesville, Ark., 1955-57; geologist, v.p. A.R. Jones Oil & Operating Co., Kansas City, Mo., 1957-58, also dir.; pres. Jones & Campbell, Inc., Shawnee Mission, Kans., 1958—, chmn. bd., 1960—; lectr. paleontology Mo. State U., 1960; geologist Lotus & Trojan Oil Co., Kansas City, Mo., 1957-58. Chmn. United Fund, Kansas City, Mo., 1957; mem. Energy Adv. Council, State of Kans., 1976-78; bd. dirs. Gillis Home for Children. Served to capt. U.S. Army, 1943-46; ETO. Decorated Purple Heart, Silver Star, Air Medal, Bronze Star, Legion of Merit; lic. pilot. Mem. Assn. Profl. Geol. Scientists (lic.), Am. Assn. Petroleum Geologists, Soc. Mining Engrs., Smithsonian Assos., Aircraft Owners and Pilots Assn., Air Force Assn., Am. Legion, VFW, Sigma Chi, Phi Sigma Epsilon. Episcopalian. Clubs: University (Kansas City, Mo.), Exchange, Bounders, Masons. Contbr. articles on paleontology and mineralogy to sci. jours.; AAU 3 meter diving champion, 1940; 1st pl. javelin and broad jump Ku Relays, 1947. Office: Prairie Village KS 66208

CAMPION, RUSSELL RICHMOND, food service equipment mfg. co. exec.; b. Milw., Oct. 9, 1930; s. Russell Henry and Anna (Winne) C.; student U. Wis., 1948-49; m. Marguerite Schubert, Sept. 15, 1951; children—Jill Mary, Thomas Richmond, Jon Winne. Sales mgr. F.W. Boelter Co., Milw., 1952-62; sales mgr. Bastian Blessing Co., Chgo., 1962-67, mktg. mgr., Grand Haven, Mich., 1967-76, pres., 1976—, also dir.; dir. Service Action Corp. Mem. Nat. Assn. Food Service Equipment Mfrs. (dir. 1967—, pres. 1974, sec. 1980), West Mich. Mfg. Assn. (dir. 1976—, sec.), Tri-City C. of C. Roman Catholic. Clubs: Century (Muskegon, Mich.); Rotary (Spring Lake, Mich.). Home: 18183 Fruitport Rd Spring Lake MI 49456 Office: 422 N Griffin St Grand Haven MI 49417

CAMPLIN, FORREST RALPH, architect; b. Shirley, Ind., June 28, 1917; s. Russell and Mae C.; ed. pub. schs.; m. Viola Faye Reed, June 15, 1947; children—Gloria Jean, Mary Darlene, Rita Ann. With Russell Camplin, masonry contractor, 1936-42; with Gen. Motors Corp., Anderson, Ind., 1942-50; with Edward D. James, Inc. (now James Assos., Architects-Engrs., Inc.), Indpls., 1951—, architect, 1961—. Served with C.E., U.S. Army, 1942-45. Mem. AIA, Interfaith Forum on Religion, Art and Architecture, Nat. Trust for Historic Preservation, Ind. Hist. Soc., Indpls. Mus. Art Methodist. Mason. Chief archtl. works include Calvary United Meth. Ch., Avilla, 1967, Good Shepherd Luth. Ch., South Bend, 1967, Phi Delta Theta frat. house, Hanover Coll., 1967, St. Thomas Episcopal Ch., Franklin, Ind., 1968, Central Nat. Bank, Greencastle, 1971, Chapel, Ft. Benjamin Harrison, 1976, Morgan County (Ind.) Courthouse, Martinsville, 1976, 1st United Meth. Ch., Crawfordsville, Ind., 1977, Camp Atterbury N.G. Tng. Facilities, 1980. Home: PO Box 27 Wilkinson IN 46186 Office: 2828 E 45th St Indianapolis IN 46205

CAMULLI, STEPHEN JOHN, electronics corp. ofcl.; b. N.Y.C., July 7, 1943; s. Otto and Johanna Maria Elizabeth (Wolters) C.; B.B.A. in Prodn. Mgmt., Hofstra U., 1976; m. Yvette Linda Jacobs, July 26, 1964; children—Elyse Danielle, Eric Ian. Contract adminstr. Electrospace Corp., Glen Cove, N.Y., 1965-66; program adminstr. Hazeltine Corp., Greenlawn, N.Y., 1966-70, mgr. project services, 1970-73, mgr. prodn. planning, 1973-77, mgr. prodn. and inventory control, 1977; asst. nat. parts mgr. Sony Corp. Am., Kansas City, Mo., 1977-. Mem. Am. Prodn. and Inventory Control Soc. (employment chmn. 1974-76, dir. membership retention 1976-77, v.p. membership 1977-78), Japanese Bus. Assn. Greater Kansas City (v.p. 1979-80), Internat. Trade Club of Greater Kansas City. Club: K.P. Office: 8281 NW 107th Terr Kansas City MO 66195

CANADAY, DAYTON WAYNE, state historian; b. Litchfield, Ill., Oct. 30, 1923; s. Ralph and Maybell Dorothy (Kepler) C.; A.B., Ill. Coll., 1948; M.S. in L.S., U. Ill., 1951; m. Olive Mae Wetzel, Sept. 7, 1947; children—Lucy, Liza, Dayton Wayne, Timothy, Sidney. Records mgmt. supr. Union Electric Co., St. Louis, 1952-60, dist. office supr., St. Charles, Mo., 1960-68; state historian of S.D., Pierre, 1968—; mem. Lewis and Clark Nat. Adv. Council, Lewis and Clark Trail Commn., S.D. Lewis and Clark Com. Elder, Presbyn. Ch., 1964—. Served with USMCR, 1943-46, 51-52. Recipient Keyman award St. Louis Jaycees. Mem. Am. Assn. State and Local History, S.D. Hist. Soc., Lewis and Clark Found., S.D. Bicentennial Commn., Mo. Hist. Soc., Ill. Hist. Soc. Author articles in field. Office: Memorial Bldg East Capitol Pierre SD 57501

CANFIELD, ALBERT ALLEN, mgmt. cons., indsl. psychologist; b. Fairmont, Nebr., May 16, 1921; s. Albert Allen and Ada Mae (Wilson) C.; B.Ed., U. Nebr., 1942; M.A., U. So. Calif., 1947, Ph.D., 1949; m. Judith Shep Carr, Aug. 24, 1975; children—Michael Allen, Linda Diane, Neil Edward. Asst. prof. Northwestern U., 1949-51; mem. staff George Fry & Assos., Chgo., 1951-52; asso. prof. Wayne State U., 1952-59; dir. univ. and sci. relations Bendix Corp., Detroit, 1960-65; v.p., instrn. Oakland Community Coll., 1966-68; state dir. community colls. State of Wash., 1968-70; prof. U. Fla., 1970-73; pres. Humanics, Inc., Rochester, Mich., 1974—; cons. IGA, Gen. Motors Corp., J.L. Hudson's, Continental Oil Co. Served with USAAF, 1942-45. Mem. Am. Psychol. Assn., Am. Soc. Curriculum Devel., Acad. of Mgmt. Republican. Patentee study carrel. Address: 473 Timberline Dr Rochester MI 48063

CANFIELD, SHELDON ARTHUR, glass mfg. co. cons.; b. Elmhurst, Ill.; s. Herbert Harvey and Mamie Elizabeth (Hurd) C.; student U. Chgo., 1944-45, 47-49; B.S.E.E., Purdue U., 1954; postgrad. Ohio State U., 1962-64; m. Carol Kathryn Koveleski, Jan. 29, 1949; children—Karl Herbert, Peter Andreas, Benjamin Arthur. Tooler, Alpha Industries, Logansport, Ind., 1946-47; lab. technician Underwriters Lab., Chgo., 1949-50; research asso. Purdue Research Found., West Lafayette, Ind., 1952-54; with Owens Corning Fiberglas, Newark-Granville, Ohio, 1954—, research asso., 1978—. Served with USAAF, 1945-46. Mem. Instrument Soc. Am. (sr.). Republican. Mem. Christian Ch. Clubs: Mason, Apache Trails Riding. Patentee in field. Home: 2041 Hickman Rd NE Newark OH 43055 Office: Owens Corning Fiberglas PO Box 415 SR 16 Granville OH 43023

CANNADY, EDWARD WYATT, JR., physician; b. East St. Louis, Ill., June 20, 1906; s. Edward Wyatt and Ida Bertha (Rose) C.; A.B., Washington U., St. Louis, 1927, M.D., 1931; m. Dixie W. Hill, Oct. 22, 1977; children by previous marriage—Edward Wyatt III, Jane Marie (Mrs. Starr). Intern internal medicine Barnes Hosp., St. Louis, 1931-33, resident physician, 1934-35, asst. physician, 1935—; asst. resident Peter Bent Brigham Hosp., Boston, 1933-34; fellow in gastroenterology Washington U. Sch. Medicine, 1935-36, instr. internal medicine 1935-74, emeritus, 1974—; cons. internal medicine Washington U. Clinics, 1942-74; physician St. Mary's Hosp., East St. Louis, 1935—, pres. staff, 1947-49, chmn. med. dept., 1945-47; physician Christian Welfare Hosp., 1935—, chmn. med. dept., 1939-53, dir. electrocardiography, 1936-77; dir. electrocardiography Centreville Twp. Hosp., East St. Louis. mem. staff Meml. Hosp., Belleville, Ill., St. Elizabeth Hosp., Belleville. Dir. 1st Nat. Bank, East St. Louis; pres. C.I.F. Dir. health service East St. Louis pub. schs., 1936-37; chmn. med. adv. bd. Selective Service, 1941-45; pres. St. Clair County Council Aging, 1961-62; chmn. St. Clair County Home Care Program, 1961-68, St. Clair County Med. Soc. Com. Aging, 1960—; del. White House Conf. Aging, 1961, 71; mem. Adv. Council Improvement Econ. and Social Status Older People, 1959-66; bd. dirs., exec. com. Nat. Council Homemaker Services, 1966-73, chmn. profl. adv. com. 1971-73; bd. dirs. St. Louis Met. Hosp. Planning Commn., 1966-70; mem. Ill. Council Aging, 1966-74; mem. Gov.'s Council on Aging, 1974-76; mem. Ill. Regional Heart Disease, Cancer and Stroke Com.; mem. exec. com. Bi-State Regional Com. on Heart Disease, Cancer and Stroke; pres. Ill. Joint Council to Improve Health Care Aged, 1959-61; dir. Ill. Council Continuing Med. Edn., 1972-77, v.p., 1974-75. Trustee McKendree Coll.; adv. bd. Belleville Jr. Coll. Sch. Nursing, 1970-78; bd. dirs. United Fund Greater East St. Louis, 1953-58. Recipient Disting. Service Award Am. Heart Assn., 1957, Disting. Achievement award, 1957; award Ill. Public Health Assn., 1971; Greater Met. St. Louis award in geriatrics, 1976. Diplomate Am. Bd. Internal Medicine. Fellow Am. Coll. Cardiology, Am. Geriatrics Soc., A.C.P. (gov. 1964-70); mem. AMA (ho. dels. 1961-71, mem. aging com.; editorial adv. bd. Chronic Illness News Letter 1962-70, chmn. Ill. delegation 1964-66, mem. council vol. health agys.), Am. (dir. 1956-62, personnel and personnel tng. com. 1956-60), Ill. (pres. 1950-51) heart assns., St. Clair County (pres. 1952, bd. censors 1953-57), Ill. (sec. cardiovascular sect. 1957, chmn. sect., 1958-59; chmn. com. on aging, 1959-69, speaker Ho. Dels. 1964-68, pres. 1969-70) med. socs., Beta Theta Pi, Nu Sigma Nu, Alpha Omega Alpha. Presbyn. Mason. Clubs: St. Clair Country, Mo. Athletic, Media; Palmbrook Country (Sun City, Ariz.). Contbr. articles to med. jours. Home: 7500 Claymont Ct Apt 2 Belleville IL 62223

CANNING, FRED FRANCIS, drug store chain exec.; b. Chgo., Apr. 1, 1924; s. Fred and Lillian (Popiolek) C.; Registered Pharmacist, Hynes Sch. Pharmacy, 1950; m. Margaret Luby, Nov. 23, 1944; children—Jeanette, Laura, Debbie, Terry, Patrick, Marggie, Timothy, Kathleen. With Walgreen Co., Deerfield, Ill., 1946—, v.p. Drug Store div., 1975-76, sr. v.p., 1976-78, exec. v.p., 1978, pres., 1978—, also chief operating officer, dir. Served with USCG, 1942-45. Mem. Am. Pharm. Assn., Am. Mktg. Assn. Roman Catholic. Office: 200 Wilmot Rd Deerfield IL 60015

CANNING, KATHERINE MARIE BECKMAN, civic leader; b. Des Moines, Aug. 24, 1913; d. Herman Henry and Emily Amelia (Swanson) Beckman; student Grinnell Coll., 1930-31; A.B., Drake U., 1934; postgrad. U. Iowa; m. John Canning, Aug. 22, 1939; children—John Beckman, Emily Jane Canning Blankinship. Pres., Beckman Bros., Inc., Des Moines, 1959—; pres. Homewood (Ill.) PTA, 1954-56; mem. Homewood Elem. Bd. Edn., 1957-68; vol. coordinator Chgo. met. area Am. Field Service program, 1960-80; vol. worker South Suburban Hosp.; mem. resource com. Flossmoor Elem. Schs., 1980—; sec. petition com. for new Homewood-Flossmoor High Sch., 1955; mem. troop com. Girl Scouts U.S.A., 1959-61; den. mother Cub Scouts Am., 1950-52; 2d v.p. Homewood-Flossmoor High Sch. P.T.A., 1964-65; elder, former supt. ch. sch. 1st Presbyterian Ch., Homewood; bd. dirs. YWCA, Chgo., 1966-68, Flossmoor Community Fund. Mem. AAUW, P.E.O. (mem. planning com. Chgo. internat. conv. 1977, treas. Ill. state conv. 1981), LWV, Mortar Bd., Zeta Phi Eta, Delta Gamma, Theta Sigma Phi. Home: 2245 Flossmoor Rd Flossmoor IL 60422

CANNING, WILLIAM MATTHEW, psychologist, educator; b. Chgo., Sept. 14, 1921; s. William J. and Edith E. (Williams) C.; B.S. in Edn., Northwestern U., 1947, M.A., 1948, Ph.D., 1955; m. Marian H. Connor, Apr. 23, 1955; children—David, Paul, Peter. Instr. psychology St. Louis U., 1949-51; asst. dean, dir. student counseling Northwestern U., Evanston, Ill., 1951-54; tchr., asst. dean Chgo. Tchrs. Coll., 1954-56; dir. Bur. Child Study, Chgo. Bd. Edn., 1956-81; pvt. practice psychology, Glenview, Ill., 1960—; cons. VA, univs., Am. Psychol. Assn., city public sch. systems, Mayor's Commn. on Human Relations, Gov.'s Commn. on Mental Retardation, State Dept. Mental Health, Office State Supt. Public Instrn., State Psychol. Adv. Com. Served to capt. Chem. Corps, U.S. Army, 1943-46. Diplomate Am. Bd. Profl. Psychology. Fellow Am. Psychol. Assn. (mem. exec. bd. div. sch. psychology); mem. Midwestern Psychol. Assn., Phi Delta Kappa. Contbr. articles in field to profl. jours. Home: 1425 Blackthorn Dr Glenview IL 60025

CANNON, BENJAMIN WINTON, lawyer; b. Muncie, Ind., Sept. 17, 1944; s. Zane William and Gloria Gene (Phillips) C.; B.A., Western Mich. U., 1965; postgrad. Notre Dame Law Sch., 1966-67; J.D., Wayne State U., 1969; M.B.A., Mich. State U., 1979; m. Diane Joan Koenig, June 24, 1967; children—Matthew Zane, Christine Elizabeth, Leslie Joan. Admitted to Mich. bar, 1970; law clk. labor relations staff Gen. Motors Corp., Detroit, 1966-69; tax atty. Plante & Moran, C.P.A.'s, Southfield, Mich., 1969-71; atty. Burroughs Corp., Detroit, 1971-72; asso. firm Nine and Maister, Attys., Bloomfield Hills, Mich., 1972-73; atty. Chrysler Fin. Corp., Troy, Mich., 1973-78, sr. atty., 1978-80; corp. counsel CF Industries Inc., Long Grove, Ill., 1980-81; asst. gen. counsel, asst. sec. COMDISCO, Inc., Rosemont, Ill., 1981—; asst. sec., gen. counsel Megatron Inc., Bloomfield Hills; instr. law Oakland U., Rochester, Mich., 1980. Mem. State Bar Mich., Ill. State Bar, Chgo. Bar Assn., Am. Bar Assn., Gray's Inn Legal Soc., Omicron Delta Kappa, Kappa Delta Pi. Republican. Presbyterian. Home: 21265 N Pheasant Trail Barrington IL 60010 Office: 6400 Shafer Ct Rosemont IL 60018

CANNON, CHARLES BERNARD, lawyer; b. Superior, Wis., Apr. 3, 1900; s. Dennis M. and Agnes (McCole) C.; B.S. in Chemistry cum laude, Marquette U., 1925; LL.B., Loyola U., Chgo., 1929, B.S.C. in Accounting, 1946; m. Blanche A. Reardon, June 29, 1935 (dec.); 1 dau., Patricia Reardon Willis; m. 2d, Helen O'Toole Meyer, Dec. 27, 1958. Instr. chemistry St. Ignatius High Sch., Chgo., 1925-29, Chgo. Coll. Dental Surgery, 1926-27; lectr. Loyola U. Law Sch., Chgo., 1935-64; of counsel firm FitzGibbon, Roehrig, Greenawalt and Gilhooly, Chgo. Served with U.S. Army, World War I. Recipient medal of Excellence, Loyola U. Law Sch., 1950. Mem. Am. Chem. Soc., Patent Law Assn. Chgo., Am., Ill., N.Y., Chgo. bar assns., Am. Patent Law Assn., Wis. Soc. of Chgo. (pres. 1955-56), Patent Law Assn. N.Y., N.Y. County Lawyers Assn. Clubs: Ill. Athletic, Chgo. Athletic Assn. (Chgo.); Chemists, N.Y. Athletic (N.Y.C.). Home: 860 Lake Shore Dr Chicago IL 60611 Office: Room 1960 135 S LaSalle St Chicago IL 60603

CANNON, CHARLES EARL, research chemist; b. Sylacauga, Ala., Jan. 30, 1946; s. Eugene and Carrie Lue (Clemons) C.; B.S., Ala. A&M U., 1968; postgrad. Vanderbilt U., 1968-69; Ph.D., U. Wis., Milw., 1974. Chemist, Amoco Chems. Corp., Naperville, Ill., 1974-78, Standard Oil Co. Ind., Amoco Research Center, 1978—; career day speaker high schs.; sci. fair judge. Recipient John Phillip Sousa music award, 1967; Pres.'s trophy for acad. excellence Ala. A&M U., 1968; Knapp Dissertation award, 1974; Ford Found. fellow, 1973-74. Mem. Am. Chem. Soc. (vice chmn. Chgo. sect. 1980-81, chmn. 1982-83), Am. Inst. Chemists, Nat. Assn. Negro Musicians, So. Christian Leadership Conf., NAACP, Ala. A&M U. Alumni Assn., Beta Kappa Chi, Alpha Kappa Mu. Democrat. Club: R. Nathaniel Dett Club Music and Allied Arts. Home: 29 W 572 Winchester Circle S Apt 2 Warrenville IL 60555 Office: Standard Oil Co Ind PO Box 400 Naperville IL 60566

CANNON, JOHN LOWER, III, insulation co., monument exec.; b. Cleve., Oct. 30, 1944; s. John Lower, Jr. and Florence Dennis (Fuller) C.; B.S. in Bus. Adminstrn., Tri State U., Angola, Ind., 1967; M.S. in Bus. Adminstrn., St. Francis Coll., Ft. Wayne, Ind., 1970; postgrad. Ind. U.-Purdue U. Extension, Ft. Wayne, 1970; m. Patsy Joan Grooms, Feb. 1, 1969; children—John Lower IV, Collier Fuller. Sr. cost acct. Gen. Telephone Co., Ft. Wayne, 1968; mgmt. trainee Cooper Indsl. Products Co., Auburn, Ind., 1968-70; sr. adminstrv. engr. ITT, Ft. Wayne, 1971; nat. contract coordinator contract sales, supr. warehouse planning Magnavox Co., Ft. Wayne, 1972-75; pres. Heritage Energy Savers, Inc., Auburn, 1973—; owner, pres. Tri State Memls., Auburn, 1976—. Treas. Auburn Community Theatre, 1971, v.p., 1978, pres., 1979-80, bd. dirs., 1979-81, 1971-74; asst. scout master Anthony Wayne council Boy Scouts Am., 1970-72, treas., 1972-79, coordinator, 1978-80; deacon Auburn Presbyterian Ch., 1971-74, elder, 1978-80, trustee, 1981—. Mem. Better Bus. Bur., Monument Builders N.Am., Ind. Monument Builders (v.p. 1979-81), Auburn C. of C. Republican. Club: Rotary (v.p. 1981—). Home: 711 N Main St Auburn IN 46706 Office: 300 E 7th St Auburn IN 46706

CANNON, LEN, toy co. exec.; b. Manchester, Eng., Jan. 12, 1935; came to U.S., 1977; s. John Francis and Isabella C.; student Xavgrian Coll., Manchester; m. Sylvia Fricker, Sept. 5, 1959; children—Michael Leonard Carl, Veronica Louise, Christopher John, Elizabeth Mary. Sales mgr. Brit. Lego Ltd., Wrexham, Wales, 1969-73; mktg. dir. Milton Bradley Europe, London, 1973-75, Milton Bradley Ltd., London, 1976-77; v.p. sales Playskool subs. Milton Bradley Co., Chgo., 1977—. Served with Lancashire Fusiliers. Mem. Inst. Mktg. U.K. Office: Playskool Inc 4501 W Augusta Blvd Chicago IL 60651

CANNON, ZANE WILLIAM, educator; b. Kenyon, Minn., Nov. 18, 1922; s. William Joseph and Floreen (Sanders) C.; student Ball State U., 1940-43; B.S., Western Mich. U., 1960, M.A., 1966; m. Gloria Gene Phillips, July 4, 1943; children—Benjamin W., Russel J., Thomas F. Guest lectr. mktg. Western Mich. U., Kalamazoo, 1963-64, asso. prof. mktg., 1965—; art specialist Portage (Mich.) Pub. Schs., 1964-65; promotion dir. Jour. Advt., 1974-75. Vice-chmn. Kalamazoo Zoning Bd. Appeals, 1967-73. Served in U.S. Army, 1943. Recipient commendation USIS, 1958; Aid Advt. Edn. award, 1969; Bernstein Advisor award, 1971; Direct Mail Spokesman award Direct Mail Mktg. Assn., 1972; Teaching Excellence award, Western Mich. U., 1976; Silver medal award Am. Advt. Fedn., 1977. Mem. Am. Acad. Advt., Am. Advt. Fedn. (dir. 1974-75), AAUP, Am. Mktg. Assn., Am. Assn. Editorial Cartoonists, Direct Mail Advt. Assn., Internat. Assn. Printing House Craftsmen, Point-of-Purchase Advt. Inst., Mktg.-Advt. Roundtable, Kalamazoo Advt. Club, Western Mich. U. Ad Club. Republican. Presbyterian. Designed, illustrated Living in Kalamazoo, 1958. Home: 330 S Drake Rd M-12 Kalamazoo MI 49009 Office: Western Michigan U Coll Bus Mktg Dept Kalamazoo MI 49008

CANTER, MARY EVELYN, city ofcl.; b. St. Louis, June 5, 1935; d. Leland and Eva (Olle) Nichols; student public schs.; m. Robert Canter, July 11, 1953; children—Randall David, Sandra Kay Canter Worthington. Various secretarial and office positions, 1953-62; sec., then office supr. Public Water Supply Dist. 1, Arnold, Mo., 1962-76, office mgr., 1976—; condr. workshops. Mem. Am. Water Works Assn., Mo. Rural Water Assn., Jefferson County Mgrs. Assn. Mem. Assembly of God Ch. Office: 2975 Schneider Dr Arnold MO 63010

CANTON, IRVING DONALD, mgmt. cons.; b. N.Y.C., Feb. 10, 1918; s. Louis and Mollie (Wolf) C.; B.Chem. Engring., Coll. City N.Y., 1940; m. Shelly Terman, Sept. 28, 1958; children—Larry, Diana. Engr., U.S. Navy Dept., 1941-45; research group leader Foster D. Snell Inc., N.Y.C., 1945-49; chem. engring. cons. S.Am., 1949-53; asst. dir. Internat. div. Ill. Inst. Tech., Chgo., 1953-61; founding stockholder, v.p. Indsl. Research Mag., Beverly Shores, Ind., 1961-62; dir. comml. devel. and planning Internat. Minerals and Chem. Co., Skokie, Ill., 1962-67; founder, pres. Strategic Decisions Co. mgmt. cons., Chgo., 1968—. Mem. Am. Mktg. Assn. (dir.; v.p. mktg. mgmt. Chgo.), Midwest Planning Assn. (founding; v.p. 1975), Am. Chem. Soc., World Future Soc. Contbr. articles to profl. jours. Home: 4141 Grove St Skokie IL 60076 Office: 664 N Michigan Ave Chicago IL 60611

CANTONI, LOUIS JOSEPH, psychologist, poet; b. Detroit, May 22, 1919; s. Pietro and Stella (Puricelli) C.; A.B., U. Calif. at Berkeley, 1946; M.S.W., U. Mich., 1949, Ph.D., 1953; m. Lucile Eudora Moses, Aug. 7, 1948; children—Christopher Louis, Sylvia Therese. Personnel mgr. Johns-Manville Corp., Pittsburg, Calif., 1944-46; social caseworker Detroit Dept. Pub. Welfare, 1946-49; counselor Mich. Div. Vocational Rehab., Detroit, 1949-50; conf. leader, tchr. psychology, coordinator family and community relations program Gen. Motors Inst., Flint, Mich., 1951-56; from asso. prof. to prof., dir. rehab. counseling Wayne State U., Detroit, 1956—. Judge Mich., regional and nat. essay and poetry contests, 1965-77. Served to 2d lt. AUS, 1942-44. Recipient award for leadership and service Mich. Rehab. Assn., 1964; South and West Ann. Poetry award, 1970; award for meritorious service Wayne State U., 1971, 81. Fellow AAAS; mem. AAUP, Council of Rehab. Counselor Educators (sec. 1957-58; chmn. 1965-66), Am. Psychol. Assn., Am. Personnel and Guidance Assn., Nat., Mich. (pres. 1963-64, bd. dirs.), Detroit (pres. 1958, dir.) rehab. assns., Detroit Inst. Arts, Poetry Soc. Mich., Acad. Am. Poets, World Poetry Soc., Phi Kappa Phi, Phi Delta Kappa. Democrat. Episcopalian. Author books including: (with Mrs. Cantoni) Counseling Your Friends, 1961; Supervised Practice in Rehabilitation Counseling, 1978; (poetry) With Joy I Called to You, 1969, Gradually the Dreams Change, 1979; editor: Mich. Rehab. Assn. Digest, 1961-63; Grad. Comment, 1963-64; Placement of the Handicapped in Competitive Employment, 1957; contbr. articles and poems to jours. Home: 2591 Woodstock Dr Detroit MI 48203 Office: Wayne State Univ Detroit MI 48202

CANTOR, BERNARD JACK, patent lawyer; b. N.Y.C., Aug. 18, 1927; s. Alexander J. and Tillie (Henzeloff) C.; B. Mech. Engring., Cornell, 1949; J.D., George Washington U., Washington, 1952; m. Judith L. Levin, Mar. 25, 1951; children—Glenn H., Cliff A., James E., Ellen B., Mark E. Examiner U.S. Patent Office, Washington, 1949-52; admitted to D.C. bar, 1952, U.S. Patent Office bar, 1952, Mich. bar, 1953; practice patent law, Detroit, 1952—; partner firm Cullen, Sloman, Cantor, Grauer, Scott & Rutherford, Detroit, 1952—; lectr. in field. Mem. Council Detroit Area Boy Scouts Am., 1972—; trustee Fresh Air Soc. of Detroit; bd. dirs. Jewish Vocat. Service of Detroit. Served with AUS, 1944-46. Recipient Ellsworth award patent law George Washington U., 1952; Shofar award Boy Scouts Am., 1975, Silver Beaver award, 1975. Mem. Am. Technion Soc. (v.p. Detroit 1970—), Am., Mich., Detroit bar assns., Mich. Patent Law Assn., Am. Arbitration Assn., Cornell Engring. Soc., Pi Tau Sigma, Phi Delta Phi, Beta Sigma Rho. Contbr. articles on patent law to profl. jours. Home: 5685 Forman Dr Birmingham MI 48010 Office: 3200 City Nat Bldg Detroit MI 48226

CANTWELL, LOUIS YAGER, lawyer; b. Oak Park, Ill., Nov. 16, 1918; s. Robert Emmett and Anna Harrison (Yager) C.; B.S., Northwestern U., 1940, J.D., 1943; m. Janet Marie Hanssen, Nov. 9, 1956 (div. Sept. 1979); children—Thomas (dec.), Andrea Lee, David Y. Admitted to Ill. bar, 1944; partner firm Cantwell & Cantwell, Chgo., 1946-63. Dir. Faith at Work Inc., N.Y.C., 1965-67, 70—, Ruth Carter Stapleton Ministries, Behold, Inc. Mem. Am. (interstate custody com. 1959-60), Ill. (mem. joint com. with Chgo. bar on codification family law), Chgo. (chmn. matrimonial law com. 1959-60) bar assns., Am. Acad. Matrimonial Lawyers, Phi Delta Phi, Phi Kappa Psi. Contbr. articles to mags. Home: Rancho Santa Fe CA 92067 Office: 1 N LaSalle St Chicago IL 60602

CANTY, MITCHELL RAY, mfg. co. exec.; b. San Diego, Jan. 31, 1952; s. Herbert George and Mildred (Leone) C.; B.S. in Indsl. Engring., Millikin U., Decatur, Ill., 1974; M.B.A., U. Tenn., Chattanooga, 1978; m. Patricia Jane Quinn, Mar. 17, 1978; children—Deana Yvonne, Eric Brandon, Mark Andrew. With Armstrong Cork Co., 1974-79, plant indsl. engr., Winchester, Tenn., 1977-79; product planner Babcock & Wilcox Co., Lancaster, Ohio, 1979-80; advanced venture analyst Owens-Corning Fiberglas Co., Granville, Ohio, 1980—; partner Bus. Educators Inst., 1980—; cons. Mem. Assn. M.B.A. Execs., Kappa Sigma. Republican. Methodist. Club: Optimists. Home: 7106 White Butterfly Ln Reynoldsburg OH 43068 Office: PO Box 415 Granville OH 43023

CAPPO, JOSEPH CARL, journalist, publisher; b. Chgo., Feb. 24, 1936; s. Joseph Victor and Frances M. (Maggio) Cacioppo; B.A. in Philosophy and Econs., De Paul U., 1957; m. Mary Anne Hetterick, May 6, 1967; children—Elizabeth Anne, John Joseph. Dir. advt. and printing prodn. DePaul U., 1957-59; reporter Hollister Publs., Wilmette, Ill., 1961-62; reporter Chgo. Daily News, 1962-68, fin. reporter, 1968-69, bus. columnist, 1969-78; bus. columnist Chgo. Sun-Times, 1978; columnist, pub. Crain's Chgo. Bus., 1978—; v.p. Crain Communications, Inc., 1981—; bus. commentator Sta.-WLOO-FM, 1972—; lectr. mktg.; cons. in field. Founder, Al Weisman Scholarship Fund, Columbia Coll., Chgo. Served with U.S. Army, 1959-61. Recipient awards, including Communications award Justinian Soc. Lawyers, 1978, Page One award Chgo. Newspaper Guild, 1978. Mem. Soc. Am. Bus. and Econ. Writers, Sigma Delta Chi (Peter Lisagor award 1978). Roman Catholic. Office: 740 Rush St Chicago IL 60611

CAPPONE, MARGARET KATHLEEN, psychologist; b. Arnold, Pa., Feb. 26, 1940; d. Theodore Thomas and Josephine Florence (Lilli) C.; B.A., Marymount Coll., 1961; M.A., Fordham U., 1963, Ph.D., 1967. Vocat. counselor Cath. Charities, N.Y.C., 1964, 66; lectr. Pace Coll., Queens Coll., N.Y.C., 1966-67; instr. Marymount Coll., Tarrytown, N.Y., 1964-66; research asso. N.Y. Med. Coll., N.Y.C., 1967-68; chmn. bd. ARCS Corp., Holly, Mich., 1968-76; chmn., prof. psychology Saginaw Valley State Coll. (Mich.), 1976—; dir. Saginaw Psychol. Services, Inc., 1976—, Therapeutic Day-Care Project, Saginaw, 1978—. Trustee Mich. Psychologists for Polit. Action Com., 1977; bd. dirs. Menninger Found. Mem. AAAS, Am. Psychol. Assn., N.Y. Acad. Sci., Soc. Psychol. Study of Social Issues, Mich. Soc. Lic. Psychologists, Sigma Xi. Democrat. Roman Catholic. Office: 714 S Michigan Ave Saginaw MI 48602

CAPRARO, MICHAEL ANTHONY, chem. engr.; b. Detroit, Nov. 19, 1948; s. Anthony and Lucille (Caporosso) C.; B.S., Wayne State U., 1970, M.S., 1974; m. Myrna Lee Bolton, Aug. 28, 1971; children—Ernest Anthony, Rachel Elaine. With BASF Wyandote (Mich.) Corp., 1970—, plant technologist, 1979—. Mem. Am. Inst. Chem. Engrs., Tau Beta Pi. Roman Catholic. Home: 13998 Kingswood St Riverview MI 48192 Office: BASF Wyandotte Corp 1609 Biddle St Wyandotte MI 48192

CAPRINI, JOSEPH ANTHONY, surgeon; b. Upper Darby, Pa., Aug. 20, 1939; s. Joseph G. N. and Teresa C. (Cerra) C.; B.S., Villanova U., 1961; M.D., Hahnemann Med. Coll., 1965; M.S. in Surgery, Northwestern U., 1972; m. Stella Mary Evans, June 12, 1965; children—Michelle, Lara, Carol. Intern, Evanston (Ill.) Hosp., 1965-66; resident Northwestern Univ. Med. Center, Evanston, Chgo., 1966-67, 69-73, Owen L. Coon Found. fellow in surg. hematology, 1973-74; practice medicine specializing in surgery, 1974—; instr. surgery Northwestern U., 1972, clin. asst., 1971, asst. prof., 1973-80, asso. prof., 1980—; mem. staff Evanston Hosp., dir. clin. admissions, 1972-74, asso. attending, 1974-76, attending, 1976-78, sr. attending surgeon, 1978—, dir. blood flow lab., 1975—, dir. surg. research, 1974—, attending surgical ward service, 1973-76, dir. coagulation research lab., 1970—; attending staff VA Research Hosp., Chgo., 1974—; sr. attending surgeon Glenbrook Hosp. Served to capt. USAF, 1967-69. Diplomate Am. Bd. Surgery, Nat. Bd. Med. Examiners. Fellow A.C.S.; mem. AMA (del. council on thrombosis), Ill. State, Chgo. Med. socs., Am. Trauma Soc., Am. Heart Assn. (mem. council on thrombosis), Chgo. Heart Assn., Midwest Blood Club, Central Surg. Assn., Western Surg. Assn., Assn. for Academic Surgery, Am. Fedn. Clin. Research, N.Y. Acad. Scis., Chgo. Inst. Medicine, Chgo. Surg. Soc., MW Surg. Soc., Internat. Soc. Thrombosis Haemostasis, Ill. Surg. Soc. Producer movie: Repair of Giant Epigastric Hernia, 1973; contbr. articles to med. jours. Home: 28 Coventry Rd Northfield IL 60093 Office: 2050 Pfingsten Rd Glenview IL 60025

CAPROON, DOUGLAS MERRITT, pharm. co. exec.; b. Ladysmith, Wis., Mar. 5, 1937; s. Ellsworth Scott and Evelyn Marie (Merritt) C.; student San Francisco City Coll., 1959, 61, Calif. State Coll., Fresno, 1962-63; B.S., U. Ala., 1973; m. Patricia Scherzer, Mar. 17, 1980; children—Kevin Michael, Dana Christopher. Elec. engr. Johnson & Johnson, Chgo., 1964-67, Union Carbide, Chgo., 1967; owner Elec. Control Specialists, Scottsboro, Ala., 1967-72; engring. mgr. Q.E.D., Chgo., 1973-74; asst. chief engr. Nat. Engring., Chgo., 1974-75; project engr. Abbott Lab., North Chicago, Ill., 1975-77; mgr. facility planning G.D. Searle & Co., Skokie, Ill., 1977—; cons. mfg. automation systems. Served with USMC, 1954-58, U.S. Army, 1959-61. Mem. Instrument Soc. Am. (sr.), Soc. Mfg. Engrs. (cert.), AAAS, Ret. Officers Assn. (life), Am. Legion. Republican. Lutheran. Club: Chgo. Health and Tennis. Home: 740 Ardmore Terr Libertyville IL 60048 Office: PO Box 5110 Chicago IL 60680

CARBERRY, JOHN J., clergyman; b. Bklyn., July 31, 1904; D.D., S.T.D., Ph.D., J.C.D., LL.D. Ordained priest Roman Cath. Ch., 1929; apptd. titular bishop of Elis, coadjutor cum lure successionis, 1956; consecrated, 1956, succeeded to See, 1957; bishop of Columbus, Ohio, 1965-68; archbishop St. Louis, 1968-79; created Cardinal, 1969. Address: Chancery Office 4445 Lindell Blvd Saint Louis MO 63108*

CARBINE, MICHAEL ELLIS, public relations exec.; b. Evanston, Ill., Nov. 6, 1939; s. James Edward and Bernice Florence (Ellis) C.; B.S., Loyola U. (Chgo.), 1961; B.A., U. Md., 1977; M.A., U. Chgo., 1980. Dir. pub. relations Mundelein Coll., Chgo., 1964-68; writer, cons. Washington, 1969-72; dir. research Bus. Adv. Council on Nat. Priorities, Washington, 1972-74; writer, cons., Washington, 1974-77; sr. v.p. William A. Throckmorton, Inc., Chgo., 1977—; cons. in field. Served with U.S. Army, 1961-63. Club: Chgo. Press. Contbr. articles to profl. jours. Home: 3520 N Lake Shore Dr Chicago IL 60657 Office: 101 E Ontario St Suite 480 Chicago IL 60611

CARBONE, ALFONSO ROBERT, constrn. exec.; b. Cleve., Jan. 17, 1921; s. Rosario P. and Carmela (Mandalfino) C.; student Sch. Architecture, Western Res. U. and Case Inst. Tech., 1940-42; B.Arch., Western Res. U., 1946; m. Anna Mae Simmons, June 16, 1945; children—Carmela, Florence Roberta, Rosario P. II, Anne Marie. Partner, v.p. estimator R.P. Carbone Constrn. Co., Cleve., 1940-77, owner, pres., 1977—. Alternate builder rep. mem. City of Cleve., Bd. Bldg. Standards and Bldg. Appeals, 1953-64, builder rep. mem., 1964-74, chmn., 1965-74; past chmn. Cleve. Air Pollution Appeals Bd. Mem. Business Men's Club, Central YMCA, Cleve.; mem. Nat. UN Day Com., 1971-80; trustee, past chmn. resources and personnel com. Alta House, pres. bd. trustees, 1981—. Served with U.S. Coast and Geodetic Survey, Washington, 1942-45. Recipient Alpha Rho Chi medal, 1946; decorated cavalier Order Star Solidarity (Italy). Mem. Cleve. Engring. Soc., Asso. Gen. Contractors Am., Builders Exchange Cleve., Holy Name Soc., Ohio Bldg. Insps. Assn., Citizen League Cleve., Greater Cleve. Growth Assn., Order Sons Italy Am. (grand orator, past pres. lodge, grand trustee officer), Epsilon Delta Rho. Roman Catholic (councilman; commd. extraordinary minister for adminstrn. Holy Communion 1974). Home: 3324 Aberdeen Rd Shaker Heights OH 44120 Office: 3185 E 79th St Cleveland OH 44104

CARDA, DANIEL DAVID, geochemist; b. Tyndal, S.D., Sept. 16, 1943; s. Daniel J. and Mildred (Holy) C.; B.S., S.D. Sch. Mines and Tech., 1968, M.S., 1971, Ph.D., 1975. Asst. dir. Expt. Sta., S.D. Sch. Mines and Tech., Rapid City, 1975—. Served with U.S. Army, 1968-70. Mem. Am. Chem. Soc., Nat. Assn. Corrosion Engrs., ASTM, Sigma Xi., Alpha Chi Sigma. Roman Catholic. Home: Route 8 Box 405 Rapid City SD 57701 Office: South Dakota School of Mines and Technology Experiment Station Rapid City SD 57701

CARDEN, TERRENCE STEPHEN, JR., physician; b. Scranton, Pa., Mar. 12, 1938; s. Terrence S. and Jean (McGuire) C.; B.S., U. Scranton, 1960; M.S. in Journalism, Columbia U., 1961; M.D., Jefferson Med. Coll., 1971; m. Corulie Hall; children—Terrence Stephen III, Andrea. Copy editor Phila. Inquirer, 1961-63; wire editor Scranton (Pa.) Times 1963-66; public relations dir. Mercy Hosp., Scranton, 1966-67; copy editor Phila. Bull., 1967-69; intern Duke U. Med. Center, Durham, N.C., 1971-72, resident, 1972; practice medicine specializing in emergency medicine and family practice, Highland Park, Ill., 1973—, Lake Forest, Ill., 1974—, Ingleside, Ill., 1978—, Round Lake, Buffalo Grove and Skokie, Ill., 1980—; dir. emergency services Highland Park Hosp., since 1974—; med. dir. South Lake County Mobile Intensive Care Program, 1974—; dir. emergency services Lake Forest Hosp., 1974-80; pres. Emergency Physicians Group, Ltd., Highland Park, 1974—; clin. asso. prof. dept. surgery Chgo. Med. Sch., Downey, Ill., 1977—; mem. adv. bd. Statewide Mobile Intensive Care, Ill. Dept. Health, 1977-78; dir. First Nat. Bank of Lincolnshire, 1978—. Bd. dirs., chmn. emergency care com. Lake County Heart Assn., 1977—; state conv. publicity aide Pa. Assn. for Retarded Children, 1966. Diplomate Am. Bd. Family Practice, Am. Bd. Emergency Medicine. Mem. Am. Coll. Emergency Physicians, Am. Acad. Family Physicians, Inst. of Medicine Chgo., Ill. Med. Soc., Am. Trauma Soc., Lake County Med. Soc., U. Assn. Emergency Med. Services, Gibbon Surg. Soc., Physicians Nat. Housestaff Assn. (alt. regional rep. 1972-73), U. Scranton Alumni Soc. (nat. sec. 1967), Jefferson Med. Coll. Alumni Assn., Hobart Amory Hare Honor Med. Soc., Alpha Omega Alpha, Alpha Sigma Nu (v.p. Scranton chpt. 1959-60). Roman Catholic. Clubs: Gordon Setter Am., Gordon Highlanders, Fox River Valley Kennel. Author: (with R.H. Daffner and J.A. Gehweiler) Case Studies in Radiology, 1975; contbr. editorials to New Physician publ., 1971-75; contbg. editor Jour. Am. Med. Assn., 1977-80; copy editor Introduction to History of General Surgery, 1968. Home: 23636 N Elm Rd Mundelein IL 60060 Office: 430 Milwaukee Ave Prairie View IL 60069

CARDO, PHILIP THOMAS, mech. engr.; b. Jamaica, N.Y., May 26, 1929; s. Anthony Thomas and Rose (Nunziato) C.; B.S. in M.E., N.Y. U., 1952; m. Gloria R. Jiannette, Apr. 12, 1953; children—Philip A., Gerard P., Susan Mary. Design engr. Babcock & Wilcox Co., N.Y.C., 1952-59; tech. sales engr. Forster Wheeler Co., N.Y.C., 1959-61; regional sales mgr. John Wood Co., Florham Park, N.J., 1961-62, Detroit Stoker Co., Cleve., 1962-68, partner Schmidt Assos., Inc., Cleve., 1968-80; pres., gen. mgr. Consol. Energy Assos., Inc., 1980—; pres. United Consultants, 1981—; asso. lectr. Center for Profl. Advancement. Mem. advisory com. Ohio bd. regents Energy Research Council. Mem. Am. Pub. Works Assn., ASME, Cleve. Engring. Soc. Contbr. articles to profl. jours. Home: 176 Forestwood Dr Northfield OH 44067 Office: PO Box 514 Northfield OH 44067

CARDWELL, JOHN JAMES, food co. exec.; b. N.Y.C., Jan. 3, 1931; s. John Edward and Anne (Boyle) C.; B.S., U.S. Naval Acad., 1953; M.B.A., Harvard U., 1960; m. Mary Jean Carey, June 16, 1956; children—Mary Louise, Michael, Susan, Catherine, Anne, Joseph. With McKinsey & Co., Chgo., 1960-76, dir., mng. dir.; pres. Consol. Foods Corp., Chgo., 1976—, also chief operating officer. Bd. dirs. Northwestern U., Evanston Hosp. Served with USN, 1953-58. Clubs: Chgo., Glen View, Links. Office: 135 S LaSalle St Chicago IL 60603

CARDWELL, MICHAEL STEVEN, obstetrician/gynecologist; b. Salem, Ind., Apr. 3, 1954; s. Carlie and Gladys (Shepard) C.; B.S., Purdue U., 1974; M.D., Ind. U., 1978; m. Debra S. Corbett, Aug. 7, 1976; children—Megan, Zachary. Resident in ob-gyn St. Francis Hosp., Peoria, Ill., 1979—, chief resident, 1981—. Scoutmaster Boy Scouts Am., Livonia, Ind., 1972-74; leader 4-H, Ind., 1970-75. Mem. Am. Public Health Assn., AMA, Am. Inst. Ultrasound in Medicine, Alpha Omega Alpha. Mem. Christian Ch. Home: 2625 W Manor Pkwy Peoria IL 61604 Office: 530 NE Glen Oak Ave Peoria IL 61604

CAREY, BERNARD, lawyer; b., 1934; B.A., St. Mary's Coll., 1956; J.D., De Paul U., 1958. Admitted to Ill. bar, 1958; state's atty. Cook County (Ill.), 1972-80; of counsel firm Isham, Lincoln & Beale, Chgo., 1981—. Office: One 1st National Plaza Chicago IL 60603

CAREY, EDWARD MARSHEL, JR., accounting co. exec.; b. Washington, Pa., June 12, 1942; s. Edward Marshel and Mildred Elizabeth (Bradley) C.; B.S. in Bus. Adminstrn., Greenville (Ill.) Coll., 1964; m. Naomi Ruth Davis, June 1, 1964; children—Martha Ann, Mary Louise. Accountant, Gen. Motors Corp., Anderson, Ind., 1964-68, supr. accounting, 1968-70; staff accountant Carter, Kirlin & Merrill, C.P.A.'s, Indpls., 1970-74, partner, 1974—. C.P.A., Ind. Mem. Am. Inst. C.P.A.'s (mgmt. of accounting practice com. 1976-80, chmn. com. 1978-80, mgmt. adv. services com. 1980—, dir. Indpls. chpt. 1977—, treas. 1978-79, pres. 1979-80), Nat. Assn. Accountants, Am. Mgmt. Assn., Inst. Internal Auditors (dir.), Greenville Coll. Alumni Assn. (dir., treas. Ind. chpt. 1980—). Republican. Methodist. Club: Indpls. Athletic. Home: 215 Royal Oak Ct Zionsville IN 46077 Office: 9102 N Meridian St Indianapolis IN 46260

CAREY, EVANGELINE, See: Gouletas-Carey, Evangeline

CAREY, GERALD EUGENE, veterinarian; b. St. Joseph, Mo., July 12, 1944; s. Earl Victor and Emma Jean (Ensign) C.; B.S., U. Mo.-Columbia, 1966, D.V.M., 1968; m. Donna Louise Graf, June 3, 1967; children—Jeffrey Jay, Mark Christopher, Allison Beth. Unit head dog and cat quarantine unit NIH, Bethesda, Md., 1968-70; individual practice small animal medicine, surgery Kansas City, Mo., 1970-73, Blue Springs, Mo., 1973—. Bd. dirs. Jackson County (Mo.) United Way, 1975-78, Chapel Hill Early Childhood Center; active Boy Scouts Am. Served with commd. corps USPHS, 1968-70. Recipient Pizer award, 1967. Mem. Kansas City (pres. 1977), Mo. (alt. dist. del. 1978—, chmn. small animal disease control com. 1978-79), Am. vet. med. assns. Mo. Acad. Veterinarians. Presbyterian (elder, pres. bd. trustees 1978), Lion. Home: Route 2 Box 58 Blue Springs MO 64015 Office: 938 S 7 Hwy Blue Springs MO 64015

CAREY, HELEN ALLBERY, dietitian cons.; b. Cleve., Oct. 16, 1934; d. Clayton Glen and Emma Blanche (Light) A.; B.S., Baldwin-Wallace Coll., 1961; 1 son, James Clayton Carey. Dietetic intern St. Luke's Hosp., Cleve., 1961-62; asst. food prodn. mgr. Fairview Gen. Hosp., Cleve., 1962-64; asst. dir. Elyria (Ohio) Meml. Hosp., 1964-69; dir. dietetics St. John Hosp., Cleve., 1974-78; dir. dietetics, co-cons. dietitian Asso. Health Care Mgmt., Mayfield Heights, Ohio, 1978—. Pres. Parents without Partners, 1974-75. Mem. Am. Soc. for Hosp. Food Service Adminstrn. (pres. 1977-78), Cleve. Dietetic Assn. (pres. 1968-69), Ohio Dietetic Assn. (pres. 1975-76), Am. Dietetic Assn., Soc. of Mayflower Descendents in State of Ohio. Methodist. Club: Baldwin Wallace Women's. Office: 27601 Westchester Pkwy Westlake OH 44145

CAREY, HENRY G., fin. mgmt. cons.; b. Dunblane, Sask., Can., July 8, 1923; s. George P. and Clara (Amerud) C.; B.S.C., U. Iowa, 1952; m. Marian E. Steninger, Sept. 2, 1950; children—Henry G., James A., Paul R., John R. Mem. audit and systems staff Arthur Andersen & Co., Chgo., 1952-58; dir. systems New Haven R.R., 1958-60; dir. systems, asst. controller telecommunications div. ITT, Chgo., 1960-63; with Chgo. Blue Cross/Blue Shield, Chgo., 1963-81, v.p., controller, 1963-76, asst. treas., 1976-81; prin. Henry G. Carey & Assos., Downers Grove, Ill., 1981—. Pres., Downers Grove Village Forum Bd., 1972-73. Served with USAAF, 1943-46. C.P.A., Ill. Mem. Fin. Execs. Inst., Am. Inst. C.P.A.'s, Ill. Soc. C.P.A.'s. Republican. Home and office: 522 59th St Downers Grove IL 60516

CAREY, JAMES JOSEPH, govt. agy. ofcl.; b. Berlin, Wis., Apr. 9, 1939; s. Robert Emmet Carey and Ruth Margaret (Harrison) Carey Johnson; B.S. in Bus. Adminstrn., Northwestern U., 1960, postgrad. 1969-70; children—Lynn Margaret, Sarah Ann. Pres., Chgo. Offset Printing Co., 1972-74; exec. v.p. Total Graphic Communication, Inc., Addison, Ill., 1974-76; pres. Coordinated Graphics, Inc., Waukegan, Ill., 1976-78; dir. internat. mil. tng. Telemedia, Inc., Chgo., 1978-81; apptd. commr. Fed. Maritime Commn., Washington, 1981—. Candidate for asst. sec. Navy, 1981, for dep. asst. sec. def., 1981. Served as surface warfare officer USN, 1962-65; served to sr. comdr., USNR, 1965—, tng. expert Gt. Lakes, Ill., Washington, San Diego, Pearl Harbor. Life mem. Bluejackets Assn. (nat. pres. 1980-81, mng. editor The Bullhorn 1977—), Navy League of U.S. (dir. 1979-80, v.p. 1980-81), Mil. Order of World Wars (bd. dirs.), U.S. Naval Inst., Am. Def. Preparedness Assn., Fleet Res. Assn., Combat Pilots Assn., Assn. Naval Aviation (v.p. 1981—), Naval Order of U.S., Ret. Officers Assn., Naval Res. Assn. (9th dist. exec. v.p. 1980—), Non-Commd. Officers Assn., Res. Officers Assn., Naval Res. Enlisted Assn. (area advisor); mem. Armed Forces Communication Electronics Assn., N.G. Assn. Ill., Marine Corps League, Res. Enlisted Assn., USAF Assn., Coalition for Peace Through Strength, Nat. Security Council, P.T. Boats Assn., Transport Aircraft Assn., U.S. Naval Sea Cadet Corp. (nat. bd. dirs. 1978-81, regional dir., 1979-81, nat. v.p. 1981—), Zeta Psi (nat. bd. dirs. 1967-71). Republican. Roman Catholic. Clubs: Am. Legion, VFW. Office: Fed Maritime Commn 1100 L St NW Washington DC 20573

CAREY, RAYMOND GEORGE, health care exec.; b. Chgo., Feb. 5, 1929; s. Raymond G. and Elizabeth (Rintelman) C.; grad. St. Mary of the Lake Sem., Mundelein, Ill.; Ph.D. in Social Psychology, Loyola U., Chgo., 1971; m. Rita Caffarello, Nov. 16, 1979; children—Michael, Mark. Advocate, matrimonial tribunal Roman Catholic Archdiocese of Chgo., 1954-76; dir. evaluation and research Luth. Gen. Hosp., Park Ridge, Ill., 1971-80; dir. health care evaluation div. Parkside Med. Services, Park Ridge, 1980—. Mem. Am. Psychol. Assn., Evaluation Network, Evaluation Research Soc., Am. Mgmt. Assn. Club: Elks. Author: (with E. Posavac) Program Evaluation: Methods and Case Studies, 1980; contbr. articles profl. jours.; developer employee and physician attitude survey systems. Home: 1957 Fenton St Park Ridge IL 60068 Office: 1580 Northwest Hwy Park Ridge IL 60068

CAREY, SUSAN FRANCES JARRETT, nurse; b. Manhattan, Kans., Jan. 27, 1945; d. Robert Maxwell and Frances Elizabeth (Jennings) Jarrett; R.N., St. John's Hosp. Sch. of Nursing, Springfield, Ill., 1968; student Lincolnland Community Coll., 1978; M.A. in Human Devel. Counseling, Sangamon State U., 1978—; m. Charles Timothy Carey, Apr. 23, 1966; children—Patrick Blair, Dennis Michael. Staff nurse, charge nurse St. John's Hosp., Springfield, 1968-79, 80—; head nurse Meml. Med. Center, 1979-80. Mem. Springfield Desegregation Monitoring Commn., 1977—; precinct election judge, 1978—; treas. Pack 352 Cub Scouts, Springfield. Recipient Public Service award U.S. Dist. Ct., Springfield, 1978; lic. R.N., Ill. Mem. Am. Personnel and Guidance Assn. (student mem.), Ill. Geneal. Soc., Ind. Hist. Soc., Ill. Congress Parents and Tchrs. (life), Nat. Hist. Soc., St. John's Hosp. Sch. of Nursing Alumni Assn., Ill. Personnel and Guidance Assn., Forum for Death Edn. and Counseling, Prairie Preservation Soc. Ogle County. Democrat. Roman Catholic. Home: 839 Percy Ave Springfield IL 62702

CARHART, JAMES MILTON, internist; b. Youngstown, Ohio, June 7, 1928; s. Clarence Milton and Ruth L. (Sieg) C.; student Adelbert Coll., 1946-48; B.S., Western Res. U., 1949, M.D., Northwestern U., 1952; m. Sally Edith Rutherford, Sept. 9, 1950; children—Katherine Anne, Margaret Susan, John Rutherford. Intern, Wesley Meml. Hosp., Chgo., 1952-53; resident in internal medicine Ohio State U. Hosp., Columbus, 1955-58, Samuel J. Roessler fellow in renal disease, 1958-60; practice medicine specializing in internal medicine, Mt. Vernon, Ohio, 1968—; instr. dept. medicine Ohio State U. Hosp., 1960-63, asst. prof. internal medicine, 1963-66. Served with M.C., U.S. Army, 1953-55. Diplomate Am. Bd. Internal Medicine. Mem. Am., Ohio State, Pan Am. med. assns., Am. Geriatric Soc., Am. Soc. Internal Medicine, Am. Heart Assn., Kidney Found. Central Ohio, AAAS, Knox County Health Council (dir.). Presbyterian. Home: 730 Brookwood Rd Route 3 Mount Vernon OH 43050 Office: 812 Coshocton Rd Mount Vernon OH 43050

CARITHERS, MICHAEL ROBERT, mfg. co. exec.; b. Comer, Ga., Sept. 10, 1942; s. Dorsey and Katherine (Haley) C.; B.S. in Acctg., Wayne State U., Detroit, 1964, M.B.A., 1966; m. Betty Jean Ellis, Oct., 1965; children—Michael, Lorri, Marc. Acct., Gen. Motors Corp., Detroit and Wilmington, Del., 1963-68, fin. analyst, Dearborn, Mich., 1968-70, supr. fin. analysis, 1970-77, controller design center, 1978—. Mem. Nat. Black MBA Assn. (chairperson student affairs com. 1975-76, 1st v.p. 1976-77, pres. 1978-79). Office: 21175 Oakwood Blvd Dearborn MI 48123

CARL, EARL GEORGE, social worker; b. Wooster, Ohio, Sept. 14, 1924; s. Earl George and Effie (Weible) C.; B.S., Ohio U., 1951; M.S., Simmons Coll., 1955; m. Mary J. Sheehan, Dec. 25, 1950;

children—Earl George III, Christopher T., Mary Lisa, Richard S. Boys's supr. Youth Service Bd., State Mass., Boston, 1952-54; psychiat. social worker VA Hosp,, Coatesville, Pa., 1955-57, Family Service Chester County, West Chester, Pa., 1957-59; exec. dir. Family Service Pottstown, Pa., 1959-63; asst. dir. social service dept. Newberry (Mich.) State Hosp., 1963-66, dir. field offices, Marquette, Mich., 1966-70; dir. outpatient dept. Coldwater (Mich.) State Home and Tng. Sch., 1970-73; supr. admissions unit Kalamazoo State Hosp., 1973—; guest lectr. in social work No. Mich. U., supr. field lab. in social work, 1967-69; supr. field lab. in social work Western Mich. U., 1974—. Bd. dirs. McKercher Rehab. Center, Kalamazoo. Served with USNR, 1943-46. Mem. Nat. Assn. Social Work, Am. Assn. Marriage and Family Therapists, Acad. Cert. Social Workers, Cert. Marriage Counselors Mich., Mich. State Employees Assn. Home: 3815 Oakridge Rd Kalamazoo MI 49008 Office: Kalamazoo Regional Psychiat Hosp Kalamazoo MI 49008

CARLEN, ROSALINE ANN, accountant; b. Detroit, July 5, 1938; d. Joseph Aloyious and Hedwig Theresa (Jakubiak) Kowalewski; B.B.A., U. Detroit, 1963; A.Indsl. Engring., Lawrence Inst. Tech., 1973; m. Bernard Albert Carlen, Dec. 31, 1973. Delivery coordinator internat. div. Vickers div. Sperry Rand Corp., 1962-67; supr. prodn. control and inventory control Bryant Computer Products div. Excello Corp., 1968-71; acctg. clk. to sr. fin. analyst, mem. devel. team performance measurement system Vought Corp., 1971-75; sr. fin. analyst EECSG div. Bendix Corp., 1977-78; supr. fin. and cost analysis F. Joseph Lamb Co., Warren, Mich., 1979—. Mem. St. Clair Shores (Mich.) Budget Com., 1979. Lic. real estate broker, Mich. Mem. Am. Mgmt. Assn. Republican. Roman Catholic. Author mil. maintenance manuals. Home: 23221 Doremus Ave Saint Clair Shores MI 48080 Office: 5663 E Nine Mile Rd Warren MI 48091

CARLETON, FREDERICK ONIAS, indsl. psychologist; b. Oneida, N.Y., Apr. 12, 1924; s. Frederick Onias and Eliza May (Vine) C.; A.B., Union Coll., 1947; Ph.D., Syracuse U., 1956; m. Doris Ann Dolphin, Aug. 20, 1955; children—Jeanne, Kristen, Thomas. Research psychologist U.S. Dept. Army, Washington, 1955-57; asso. dir. research and devel. Sci. Research Assn., Chgo., 1957-59; regional mgr. Richardson, Bellows, Henry & Co., New Orleans, 1959-61; indsl. psychologist Sandia Corp., Albuquerque, 1961-66; mgr. psychol. services Standard Oil Co., Cleve., 1966-70; indsl. psychologist So. Railway System, Washington, 1971-72; mgr. psychology, research dir. Personnel Research & Devel. Corp., Cleve., 1972-80; dir. research Ohio Psychol. Cons. to Industry, Inc., Shaker Heights, Ohio, 1980—. Served with USNR, 1943-46. Mem. Am. Psychol. Assn., Ohio Psychol. Assn., Psychometric Soc., Sigma Xi, Phi Delta Kappa. Home: 621 Marygate Dr Bay Village OH 44140 Office: Ohio Psychological Consultants to Industry Inc 3645 Warrensville Center Rd Shaker Heights OH 44122

CARLILE, ROBERT LESLIE, accountant; b. Boswell, Ind., Oct. 2, 1924; s. Jasper Leslie and Mearl (Smith) C.; student Ind. State Tchrs. Coll., 1942-43; B.S., Ind. U. 1946-48; m. Olga E. Gize, Aug. 24, 1952; children—Byron, Bradley. Trainee, Goodyear Tire & Rubber Co., Akron, Ohio, 1948-49, office mgr., Moline, Ill., 1949-51, asst. store mgr., Waterloo, Iowa, 1951-52; cost accountant, chief timekeeper Burgess Battery Co., Freeport, Ill., 1952-55; sr. accountant William T. Bingham, C.P.A., Freeport, 1956-60; self-employed Robert L. Carlile, C.P.A., Freeport, 1960—. Mem. Forestry Commn., Freeport, 1960—. Treas., Freeport Community Chest; mem. adv. com. Highland Community Coll. Treas. Freeport Meml. Hosp. Served with USNR, 1943-46. Mem. No. Ill., Ill. socs. C.P.A.'s, Am. Inst. C.P.A.'s, Delta Sigma Pi. Methodist. Mason (32 deg.). Rotarian. Club: Freeport Country. Home: 1713 Manor St Freeport IL 60132 Office: 905 State Bank Center Freeport IL 61032

CARLIN, CLAIR MYRON, lawyer; b. Sharon, Pa., Apr. 20, 1947; s. Charles William and Carolyn (Vukasich) C.; B.S. in Econs., Ohio State U., 1969, J.D., 1972; m. Cecilia Reis, Aug. 21, 1971 (div.); children—Elizabeth Marie, Alexander Myron. Admitted to Ohio bar, 1973, Pa. bar, 1973, U.S. Supreme Ct. bar, 1976; staff atty. Ohio Dept. Taxation, 1972-73; asst. city atty. City of Warren (Ohio), 1973-75; asso. firm McLaughlin, DiBlasio & Harshman, Youngstown, Ohio, 1975-80; partner firm McLaughlin, Harshman & McNally, Youngstown, 1980—; law dir. City of Newton Falls (Ohio), 1975-79; gen. counsel Newton Falls Petroleum Products, Inc. Vice pres. Trumbull County Services for Aging, Inc., 1976-80. Served with Signal Corps, U.S. Army, 1972; maj. Army N.G., 1972—. Mem. Am. Bar Assn., Ohio Bar Assn., Pa. Bar Assn., Mahoning County Bar Assn., Trumbull County Bar Assn. Democrat. Roman Catholic. Club: Rotary (Warren). Home: 3153 Crescent Dr Warren OH 44483 Office: McLaughlin Harshman & McNally 500 City Centre One Youngstown OH 44503

CARLIN, EDWARD AUGUSTINE, educator; b. Gardiner, N.Y., Sept. 21, 1916; s. Edward A. and Mary (Mulligan) C.; B.S., N.Y. U., 1946, M.A., 1947, Ph.D., 1950; m. Eleanor Helen Bigos, Feb. 20, 1943; children—Mary Ellen, Edward Augustine. Instr. econs. and govt. Packard Bus. Coll., 1946-47; asst. prof. Mich. State U., 1947-51, asso. prof., 1952-56, asst. dean, prof., 1956, dean univ. coll., 1956-77, prof. econs., 1977—; cons. Coll. Gen. Studies U. Nigeria. Served from pvt. to 1st lt., inf. AUS, 1942-46. Decorated Purple Heart. Mem. Am. Econ. Assn., Am. Acad. Polit. and Social Sci., A.A.U.P., Pi Gamma Mu. Author numerous articles in field. Co-editor: Curriculum Building in General Education, 1960. Home: 834 Rosewood St East Lansing MI 48823

CARLIN, JOHN WILLIAM, gov. Kans.; b. Salina, Kans., Aug. 3, 1940; s. Jack W. and Hazel L. (Johnson) C.; B.S. in Agr., Kans. State U., 1962; m. Karen Bigsby Hurley, May 29, 1981; children by previous marriage—John David, Lisa Marie; stepchildren—Patrick Jason Hurley, Marci Lynn Hurley. Farmer, dairyman; mem. Kans. Ho. of Reps. from 92d Dist., 1971-73, from 73d Dist., 1973-79, asst. minority leader, 1975, minority leader, 1975-77, speaker, 1977-79; gov. Kans., 1979—. Democrat. Lutheran. Club: Lions. Office: 2d Floor The Statehouse Topeka KS 66612

CARLIN, PETER PAUL, ednl. adminstr.; b. Cleve., Sept. 20, 1930; s. Michael J. and Catherine (McDonough) C.; B.A., John Carroll U., 1952, postgrad.; postgrad. Case Western Res. U. Grad. Sch. Law, 1952-54; M.Ed., Kent State U., 1960, postgrad.; postgrad. (John Hay fellow) U. Oreg. Inst. Humanities, summer 1965; postgrad. Howard U.; m. Angela Genovese, Sept. 3, 1956; children—Paul Damian, Michael Lawrence. With Cleve. Public Schs., 1954—, coordinator econ. edn. Div. Social Studies, 1967-72, directing supr. Div. Social Studies, 1971-72, asst. supt. schs., 1972-78, supt. schs., 1978—; bd. dirs. Council Gt. City Schs.; mem. adv. council on instrl. TV, Ohio Dept. Edn.; mem. North Central Evaluation Team for High Schs.; mem. Ohio Dept. Ednl. Evaluation Teams for Tchr. Tng. in Colls. and Univs.; master tchr. social studies Princeton U., summer 1966; mem. Educators to Africa, 1971; participant profl. seminars. Trustee, Close-Up, Washington, Rapid Recovery, United Way Services, Real Property Inventory Metro Cleve., Cleve. Scholarship Programs, Univ. Circle, Inc. (all Cleve.). Recipient Samuel H. Elliott award, 1979. Mem. Am. Assn. Sch. Adminstrs., Assn. Supervision and Curriculum Devel. Author: Teaching Urban Youth, 1967; cons., editor: Impact of Our Past; TV tchr. Cleve. Public Schs. Office: 1380 E 6th St Cleveland OH 44114*

CARLIN, THOMAS L., newspaper exec.; b. Bird Island, Minn., Dec. 19, 1921; s. Leo Joseph and Agnes (Hentschell) C.; B.S. in Elec. Engring., U.S. Naval Acad., 1943; m. Dawn Van Eyck, Mar. 31, 1948; children—Thomas, Mark, Paul, Mary, Sara, Andrew. Account exec. Arnold Niemeyer & Assos., 1949-51; sales corr. Am. Hoist & Derrick, 1951-53; advt. rep. St. Paul Pioneer Press Dispatch, 1953-56, asst. prodn. mgr., 1956-57, asst. to pub., 1957-58, bus. mgr., 1958-66, gen. mgr., 1966-73, pub., 1973—; pres. N.W. Publs., Inc., Twin Cities Newspaper Service. Pres. St. Paul Jr. Achievement, 1965; gen. chmn. St. Paul Arts and Sci. Fund drive, 1965; trustee Coll. of St. Catherine, St. Paul, 1974—, chmn., 1976-79. Served with USN, 1943-47. Decorated Silver Star; recipient Outstanding Community Service award St. Paul Jr. C. of C., 1967. Mem. St. Paul Serra Club (pres. 1967), Navy League. Republican. Roman Catholic. Rotarian. Clubs: Minn., St. Paul Athletic, North Oaks Golf (St. Paul). Home: 17 Oak Knoll Dr White Bear Lake MN 55110 Office: 55 E 4th St St Paul MN 55101*

CARLOCK, LANETA L., educator; b. Benkelman, Nebr., May 7, 1943; d. LaVoine T. and Opal R. (Meyer) Collicott; B.S., U. Nebr., 1963, M.Ed., 1968; m. Stanley L. Carlock, June 29, 1963. Bus. edn. tchr. Stamford (Tex.) High Sch., 1963-64, Arbor Heights Jr. High Sch., Omaha, 1965-70; bus. edn. tchr. Westside High Sch., Omaha, 1971—, dir. adult edn., 1977—. Mem. NEA, Nebr. Bus. Edn. Assn. (pres. 1981-82), Nat. Bus. Edn. Assn. (named Secondary Tchr. of Yr. 1978), Am. Vocat. Assn., Nebr. Vocat. Assn., Female Leaders Adminstrn. and Edn., Nebr. State Edn. Assn., Westside Edn. Assn., Mountain Plains Regional Bus. Edn. Assn. (pres. 1981-82), Bus. and Profl. Women's Assn., Phi Delta Kappa, Delta Kappa Gamma, Delta Pi Epsilon (pres. 1969-70, corr. sec. 1980—). Republican. Methodist. Contbr. articles to profl. jours. Office: Westside High School 87th and Pacific Sts Omaha NE 68114

CARLSON, BARTLEY JAMES, data and word processing cons.; b. Rockford, Ill., Mar. 4, 1944; s. Alvin B. and Doris E. (Nelson) C.; B.S., No. Ill. U., 1969; children—Jill C., Barbara J., Brenda J. Customer engr. IBM Corp., Glendale, Calif., Janesville, Wis., and Evanston, Ill., 1962-64; field engr. Xerox Corp., Phoenix, 1964-65; systems coordinator Sundstrand Corp., Rockford, 1965-66; programming mgr. No. Ill. Corp., DeKalb, 1966-68; mem. faculty, dir. computer services Waubonsee Coll., Sugar Grove, Ill., 1968-78; dir. computer services Coll. of DuPage, Glen Ellyn, Ill., 1978-80; sr. cons. Deloitte, Haskins & Sells, Chgo., 1980—; cons. Nat. Systems Labs., Inc.; mem. Nat. Commn. on Software; chmn. Nat. Task Force on Edn. and Tng. of Software Profls., 1981—; chmn. Task Force on Adminstrv. Computing, Ill. Higher Bd. Edn., 1971. Cert. data educator. Mem. Internat. Word Processing Assn., Data Processing Mgmt. Assn., Coll. and Univ. System Exchange (dir.), Word Processing Soc.; Ill. Assn. Ednl. Data Systems (dir. 1973-76), Ill. Community Council of Pres.'s, Nat. Ednl. Computer Network, EDUNET Task Force on Electronic Mail, Coll. and Univ. Machine Records Assn. Club: Country Courts. Home: PO Box 193 Oakbrook IL 60521 Office: Deloitte Haskins & Sells 200 E Randolph Dr Chicago IL 60601

CARLSON, LOREN MERLE, univ. adminstr., lawyer, educator; b. Mitchell, S.D., Nov. 2, 1923; s. Clarence A. and Edna M. (Rosenquist) C.; B.A., Yankton Coll., 1948; M.A., U. Wis., 1952; J.D., George Washington U., 1961; m. Verona Gladys Hole, Dec. 21, 1950; children—Catherine Ann, Bradley Reed, Nancy Jewel. Asst. dir. Govtl. Research Bur., U. S.D., 1949-51; orgn. and methods examiner U.S. Dept. State, Washington, 1951-52; asst. dir. legis. research State of S.D., 1953-55, dir., 1955-59; research asst. to Francis Case, U.S. Senator from S.D., 1959-60, adminstrv. asst., 1960-63; admitted to S.D. bar, 1961, U.S. Supreme Ct. bar, 1976; budget officer State of S.D., 1963-68; dir. statewide ednl. services U. S.D., Vermillon, 1968-74, dean continuing edn., 1974—, asso. prof. polit. sci., 1968-79, prof., 1979—, hwy. laws study dir. Law Sch., 1963; sec. Missouri Valley Adult Edn., 1978-79. Chmn. Model Rural Devel. Commn., Dist. II, State of S.D., 1972-74; chmn. Region VII Planning Commn. on Criminal Justice, S.D., 1969-74; mem. Vermillion City Council, 1980—. Served with USN, 1945-46. Named Outstanding Young Man, Pierre Jaycees, 1959. Mem. S.D. State Bar, Am. Soc. for Public Adminstrn., Nat. U. Continuing Edn. Assn., S.D. Adult Edn. Assn. (chmn. 1973-74), Vermillion C. of C., Am. Arbitration Assn., Am. Legion, Pi Sigma Alpha, Pi Kappa Delta. Republican. Lutheran. Clubs: Lions, Eagles, Author: (with W.O. Farber and T.C. Geary) Government of South Dakota, 1979; contbr. articles to profl. publs. Home: 229 Catalina St Vermillion SD 57069 Office: State Wide Educational Services U South Dakota Vermillion SD

CARLSON, RICHARD FRANK, employee benefit cons. co. exec.; b. Austin, Tex., Nov. 6, 1939; s. Gilbert Frank and Birdie Elaine (Wilt) C.; B.B.A, Tex. Tech U., 1961; M.B.A., U. Dallas, 1974. Bank examiner, Fed. Res. Bank Dallas, 1965-67; mgr. adminstrn. Recognition Equipment Inc., Dallas, 1967-74; v.p. adminstrn. and personnel A.S. Hansen, Inc., Lake Bluff, Ill., 1974—. Chmn., United Fund, Dallas, 1972-73. Served with USNR, 1962-64. Mem. Am. Soc. Personnel Adminstrn., Adminstrv. Mgmt. Soc., Am. Compensation Assn., Sigma Chi, Sigma Iota Epsilon. Republican. Home: 3107 Pheasant Creek Dr Northbrook IL 60062 Office: 1080 Green Bay Rd Lake Bluff IL 60044

CARLSON, RICHARD GEORGE, chem. co. exec.; b. Chgo., Sept. 26, 1930; s. Gustav George and Mildred Elisabeth (Englund) C.; student Purdue U., 1948-49; B.S., Ill. Inst. Tech., 1956; m. S. Diane Russell, Oct. 10, 1948; children—Richard G., Pamela, Kurt D. With Waterway Terminal, Argo, Ill., 1949-56; with Dow Chem. Co., Midland, Mich., 1956—, production mgr. organic chems., 1968-71, bus. mgr. organic chems., 1971-73, dir. process research, 1973—; mem. fossil energy adv. com. U.S. Dept. Energy, 1976—. Pres., Midland Newcomers Club, 1957-58; scoutmaster Paul Bunyon council Boy Scouts Am., 1956-64; adviser Jr. Achievement, 1956-64; program chmn. P.T.A., 1962-63. Mem. adv. group dept. chem. engring. Ill. Inst. Tech., 1974-77. Inst. Gas Tech. scholar, 1954-56. Mem. Am. Inst. Chem. Engrs., Mich. Energy and Resource Research Assn. (trustee 1974-78), Tau Beta Pi. Methodist. Office: Dow Chem Co Midland MI 48640

CARLSON, ROBERT GERALD, thoracic surgeon; b. Mpls., Dec. 22, 1929; s. Henry John and Agnes Emily (Fagerstrom) C.; B.A., U. Minn., 1951, M.D., 1954, M.S., 1969; m. Florence Ilene Fairbairn, Aug. 4, 1951; children—David, James, Diane, Joel. Intern, U. Oreg. Hosps., Portland, 1954-55; gen. practice medicine, Wadena, Minn., 1955-56; resident in gen. surgery Wayne County Gen. Hosp., Eloise, Mich., 1958-62; practice medicine specializing in gen. surgery, Willmar, Minn., 1962-65; resident in cardiovascular surgery U. Minn., Mpls., 1965-68; research fellow, dept. cardiac pathology Charles T. Miller Hosp., St. Paul, 1966; resident in cardiovascular surgery Cornell U., N.Y.C., 1968-69; instr. surgery Cornell U. Med. Center, 1968-69, asst. prof. surgery, 1969-73; practice medicine specializing in cardiovascular and thoracic surgery, Green Bay, Wis., 1974-79; mem. staffs Bellin Meml. Hosp., St. Vincent's Hosp., St. Mary's Hosp., Theda Clark Hosp., Neenah, Wis., 1979—, St. Elizabeth Hosp., Appleton, Wis.; mem. com. on coronary artery surgery Inter-Soc. Commn. for Heart Disease Resources. Publicity chmn. Friends of Garden City Library, 1961; active Boy Scouts Am.; publicity dir. Anoka County Republican Com., 1963; publicity chmn. Rep. Caucus, Anoka, Minn., 1966-67. Served with USAF, 1956-58. Diplomate Am. Bd. Surgery, Am. Bd. Thoracic Surgery, Nat. Bd. Med. Examiners. Fellow A.C.S. (certificate of appreciation 1971), Am. Coll. Cardiology, Soc. Thoracic Surgeons, Soc. Vascular Surgeons, Am. Coll. Chest Physicians (Regents' award 1971, certificate of merit 1971), Am. Coll. Angiology; mem. Am. Heart Assn., N.Y. Cardiol. Soc., Internat. Cardiovascular Soc., Internat. Surg. Soc., AMA (certificate of merit 1971, Billings silver medal 1972), AAAS, Brown County Med. Soc., Audubon Soc., Phi Beta Kappa, Alpha Omega Alpha. Republican. Lutheran. Clubs: Green Bay Downtown Rotary (v.p. elect 1979), Neenah Rotary, Oneida Country. Contbr. articles to profl. jours. Home: 811 Neff Ct Neenah WI 54956 Office: 59 Racine St Menasha WI 54952

CARLSON, ROBERT MARSHALL, hosp. ofcl.; b. Jamestown, N.Y., Oct. 6, 1950; s. Marshall Lawrence and Alice (Christine) C.; B.S., Bowling Green (Ohio) State U., 1972; postgrad. in public health U. Utah, 1972; M.Ed. in Health Edn., U. Toledo, 1977; m. Margaret Swigart, June 10, 1972; children—Todd Marshall, Scott Thomas. Planning analyst, then found. dir. Riverside Hosp., Toledo, 1975-78; hosp. planning coordinator Med. Coll. Ohio, Toledo, 1978-80, asst. hosp. dir. for ambulatory programs, 1980—; planner P.M.S. (Planning & Mgmt. Services) Inc., Bloomington, Minn., 1981—. Active local Boy Scouts Am. Lt. (j.g.), Med. Service Corps, USNR. 1972—. Mem. Am. Coll. Hosp. Adminstrs., Am. Hosp. Assn., Am. Soc. Hosp. Planners, Ohio Hosp. Assn., Res. Officers Assn., Toledo Area C. of C., Phi Kappa Phi, Kappa Sigma. Lutheran. Office: CS 10008 Toledo OH 43699

CARLSON, ROGER MERLE, educator; b. Mitchell, S.D., July 1, 1948; s. Merle Brouwn and Gertrude M. (Van Schaick) C.; B.S., S.D. State U., 1972; m. Laura Lee Irvin, June 10, 1967; children—Michael Lewis, Stephanie Anne, Jason Paul. Instr. agri-bus. tech. Lake Area Vocat. Tech. Inst., Watertown, S.D., 1972-73, dept. head, 1973-79; instr./supr. farm bus. mgmt. Wessington Springs (S.D.) Sch. Dist., 1979—, mem. adv. council agribus. tech. program; mem. S.D. Vocat. Edn. Plan and Accountability Report Devel. Com.; adv. council to S.D. Dept. Agr. Agnet Computer Service; adv. bd. S.D., Am. Coll. Testing; cons. curriculum devel.; mem. various state and regional vocat. program review teams. Chmn. Charolais Show, Watertown Winter Farm Show, 1973-79; chartered Coll. Chpt. Future Farmers Am., Lake Area Vocat. Tech. Inst.; designer agri-bus. salesmanship contest S.D. Future Farmers Am. State Contest, 1975. Named outstanding vocat. agr./agri-bus. instr., S.D., 1978. Mem. Am. Vocat. Assn. (S.D. rep. nat. leadership conf. 1978, 79, 80), S.D. Vocat. Assn. (pres. 1979-80), Nat. Vocat. Agr. Teachers Assn., S.D. Vocat. Agr. Teachers Assn. Republican. Baptist. Contbr. articles to publs. in field. Home: Rural Route 2 Box 101 Wessington Springs SD 57382 Office: Wessington Springs High School Wessington Springs SD 57382

CARLSON, RONALD LEE, lawyer, educator; b. Davenport, Iowa, Dec. 10, 1934; s. Arthur A. and Louise (Sehmann) C.; B.A., Augustana Coll., 1956; J.D. (Clarion DeWitt Hardy law scholar), Northwestern U., 1959; LL.M. (E. Barrett Prettyman law scholar), Georgetown U., 1961; m. Mary Murphy, Feb. 10, 1965; children—Michael, Andrew. Admitted to Ill., Iowa bars, 1959, D.C. bar, 1960, U.S. Supreme Ct. bar, 1966; mem. firm Betty, Neuman, McMahon, Hellstrom & Bittner, Davenport, 1961-65; U.S. commr. So. Dist. Iowa, 1964-65; prof. law U. Iowa, Iowa City, 1965-73, Washington U., St. Louis, 1973—; vis. prof. Wayne State U., Detroit, summers 1974, 76, 77, 79, U. Tex., 1978; cons. Legis. Com. on Criminal Code Revision Iowa, 1969-73; lectr. Nat. Coll. State Judiciary, Reno, 1974, Nat. Coll. Dist. Attys., West Palm Beach, Fla., 1980, Am. Acad. Jud. Edn., 1981; Mason Ladd lectr. Fla. State U., 1981. Vice pres. alumni bd. Augustana Coll., Rock Island, Ill., 1968. Mem. Am. Assn. Law Schs. (chmn. evidence sect., 1973), Fed. (chmn. law sch. div. 1978-79, continuing edn. bd. 1981), Am., Iowa, St. Louis bar assns., Republican. Author: Criminal Justice, 1978; (with M. Ladd) Cases on Evidence, 1972; (with J. Yeager) Criminal Law and Procedure, 1979. Home: 7401 Parkdale St Clayton MO 63105 Office: Sch Law Washington U Saint Louis MO 63130

CARLSON, RUSSELL EDWIN, bank holding co. exec.; b. Detroit, Nov. 29, 1936; s. Elmer Ewald and Alma Charlotte (Anderson) C.; Asso. in Bus., Henry Ford Community Coll., 1957; B.B.A., U. Mich., 1959, M.B.A., 1960; m. Kathryn Margaret Carrington, July 16, 1977; children—Kristin Lara, Erika Nissa. Dist. Sales mgr. Scott Paper Co., 1958-63; trust officer Detroit Bank & Trust Co., 1963-67; mktg. mgmt. coordinator Gen. Motors Co., Gen. Motors Inst., 1967-68; trust and mktg. officer Am. Nat. Bank, Chattanooga, 1968-70; asst. v.p., mktg. officer F & M Corp., Richmond, Va., 1970-74; v.p. mktg. S.E. Banking Corp., Miami, 1974-77; first v.p., dir. corp. mktg. Mfrs. Nat. Corp., Detroit, 1977—. Mem. Bank Mktg. Assn., Am. Mktg. Assn., Am. Mgmt. Assn. Republican. Episcopalian. Clubs: Detroit Athletic, Economic (Detroit). Home: 5648 Aldingbrooke Triangle West Bloomfield MI 48033 Office: 5th Floor 411 W Lafayette St Detroit MI 48226

CARLYON, DON J., coll. pres.; b. Chambers, Neb., Aug. 14, 1924; s. Richard E. and Ruth (Wolters) C.; student Neb. Wesleyan U.; B.S., U. Neb.; LL.D. (hon.), Saginaw Valley State Coll., 1975; m. Betty E. Hunley, June 13, 1946; children—Janette, David, Suzanne, Scott, Richard. Dir., U. Neb. Men's Residence Halls, 1953-56; asst. bus. mgr. U. Kansas City, 1956-57, bus. mgr., 1957-60, instr., 1956-60, acting dean Sch. Bus., 1958; bus. mgr. Delta Coll., Mich., 1960-64, pres., 1964—. Mem. Gov. Mich. Com. Comprehensive State Health Adv. Planning Council; mem. commn. adminstrn. Am. Assn. Jr. Colls.; pres. Mich. Community Coll. Assn. Served with USNR. Mem. Nat. Assn. Ednl. Buyers, Bay County Mental Health Assn., Phi Kappa Tau, Beta Gamma Sigma. Clubs: Torch, Rotary. Methodist. Home: 1980 Hotchkiss Rd Bay City MI 48706 Office: University Center MI 48710

CARMI, SHLOMO, educator, scientist; b. Cernauti, Rumania, July 18, 1937; s. Shmuel and Haia (Marcovici) C.; student Technion, Haifa, Israel, 1958-60; B.S. cum laude, U. Witwatersrand, Johannesburg, South Africa, 1962; M.S., U. Minn., 1966, Ph.D., 1968; m. Rachel Aharoni, Dec. 23, 1963; children—Sharon, Ronen-Itzhak, Lemore. Came to U.S., 1963, naturalized, 1978. Research engr. W. Rand Gold Mining Co., Krugersdorp, South Africa, 1962-63; research asst., research fellow U. Minn., 1963-68; asst. prof. mech. engring. Wayne State U., 1968-70, 72-73, asso. prof., 1973-78, prof., 1978—, chmn. faculty assembly Coll. Engring., 1979-80; sr. lectr. Technion, Israel Inst. Tech., 1970-72, sabbatical, I. Taylor chair, 1977-78; research specialist Ford Motor Co., summer 1973, 74, 76, 77; speaker sci. meetings, Israel, Can. and U.S. Served with Israeli Army, 1956-58. South African Technion Soc. scholar, 1960-62; recipient prize Transvaal Chamber of Mines, 1961, faculty research award Wayne State U., 1970; research grantee U.S. Dept. Energy, U.S. Army Research Office. Mem. Am. Phys. Soc., ASME (com. heat transfer, fluid mechanics), AAUP, Sigma Xi, Tau Beta Pi, Pi Tau Sigma. Asso. editor Jour. Fluids Engring.; contbr. articles and reviews to profl. jours. Home: 5270 Hollow Dr Bloomfield Hills MI 48013 Office: Wayne State University Detroit MI 48202

CARMICHAEL, CHARLES WESLEY, plant engr.; b. Marshall, Ind., Jan 18, 1919; s. Charles Wesley and Clella Ann (Grubb) C.; B.S., Purdue U., 1941; m. Eleanor Lee Johnson, July 2, 1948; one dau., Ann Bromley Carmichael Biada. Owner, operator retail stores, West Lafayette, Ind., 1946-48, Franklin, Ind., 1950-53; mem. staff time study Chevrolet Co., Indpls., 1953-55; indsl. engr. Mallory Capacitor Co., Indpls., 1955-60, Greencastle, Ind., 1960-70, plant engr., 1970—; lectr. in field. Chmn. Greencastle dr. A.R.C., 1962-63; bd. dirs. United Way Greencastle, 1976-79. Served to capt., F.A., U.S. Army, 1941-46; ETO. Decorated Bronze Star Medal, Purple Heart with oak leaf cluster. Mem. Greencastle C. of C. (dir. 1962-64), Am. Inst. Plant Engrs., Putnam County Bd. Realtors, Ind. Hist. Soc. Republican. Methodist. Clubs: Kiwanis (pres. Greencastle 1965), John Purdue, Soc. Ind. Pioneers, Windy Hill Country, Masons, Shriners, Am. Legion. Home: 702 Highwood Ave Greencastle IN 46135 Office: PO Box 489 Greencastle IN 46135

CARMICHAEL, ELEANOR JOHNSON (MRS. CHARLES WESLEY CARMICHAEL), librarian; b. Mooresville, Ind., Aug. 31, 1916; d. Howard Vinson and Cora Alta (Newman) Johnson; B.A., Earlham Coll., 1938; B.L.S., Columbia U., 1941; M.L.S., Ind. U., 1970; m. Charles Wesley Carmichael, July 2, 1948; 1 dau., Ann Bromley (Mrs. George H. Biada, Jr.). Librarian, Coll. Architecture, Cornell U., Ithaca, N.Y., 1942-46; librarian dept. physics Purdue U., Lafayette, Ind., 1946-49; librarian Indpls. Mus. Art, 1956-60; tech. services librarian, asso. prof. Roy O. West Library, DePauw U., Greencastle, Ind., 1960—. Mem. project task force Coop. Bibliographic Center for Ind. Libraries, 1972-74. Mem. AAUW, D.A.R. (regent Washburn chpt. 1977-79), Am., Ind. library assns., Ohio Valley Group Tech. Service Librarians (sec. 1962-63), Beta Phi Mu, Alpha Phi, Tri Kappa. Author: (with K. Lark-Horowitz) A Chronology of Scientific Development, 1848-1948, 1948. Home: 702 Highwood Ave Greencastle IN 46135

CARMICHAEL, VIRGIL WESLY, geologist, engr., coal co. exec.; b. Pickering, Mo., Apr. 26, 1919; s. Ava Abraham and Rosevelt (Murphy) C.; B.S., U. Idaho, 1951, M.S., 1956; Ph.D. in Geol. Engring. and Mgmt., Columbia Pacific U., 1980; profl. geol. engr., U. Idaho, 1967; m. Colleen Fern Wadsworth, Oct. 29, 1951; children—Bonnie Rae, Peggy Ellen, Jacki Ann. Asst. geologist Day Mines, Wallace, Idaho, 1950; mining engr., chief mining engr. De Anza Engring. Co., Troy, Idaho and Santa Fe, 1950-52; hwy. engring. asst. N.Mex. Hwy. Dept., Santa Fe, 1952-53; asst. engr. U. Idaho, also minerals analyst Idaho Bur. Mines, Moscow, 1953-56; mining engr. No. Pacific Ry. Co., St. Paul, 1956-67; geologist N. Am. Coal Corp., Cleve., 1967-69, asst. v.p. engring., 1969-74, v.p., head exploration dept., 1974—. Mem. No. Gt. Plains Resource Council, 1964-67; asst. chief distbn. CD Emergency Mgmt. Fuel Resources for N.D., 1968—. Bd. dirs. Bismarck-Mandan Orch. Assn., 1979—. Served with USNR, 1944-46; PTO. Recipient award 'A' for Sci. writing Sigma Gamma Epsilon, 1957. Registered geologist, Idaho, Calif.; land surveyor, N.Mex., Minn., N.D., Idaho; profl. engr., Idaho, N.Mex., Utah, Minn., N.D. Mem. Am. Inst. Profl. Geologists (past pres. local chpt.), Rocky Mountain Coal Mining Inst. (past v.p.), N.D. Geol. Soc. (past pres.), Am. Inst. Mining Engrs. (pres. local chpt. 1979-80), Am. Mining Congress (bd. govs. western div. 1973—), AAAS, N.Y. Acad. Scis., Internat. Platform Assn., Sigma Xi. Republican. Clubs: Kiwanis (club dir. 1978-80, v.p. 1980-81, pres.-elect 1981-82), Masons, Elks. Office: Kirkwood Office Tower Bismarck ND 58501

CARNAHAN, JOHN ANDERSON, lawyer; b. Cleve., May 8, 1930; s. Samuel Edwin and Penelope (Moulton) C.; B.A., Duke, 1953, LL.B., 1955, J.D., 1955; m. Katherine Halter, June 14, 1958; children—Peter Moulton, Allison Eads, Kristin Alexandra. Admitted to Ohio bar, 1955, pvt. practice law, Columbus, 1955-78; partner firm Knepper, White, Arter & Hadden, 1978—; lectr. Ohio Legal Center Inst., 1969, 73, 74. Chmn. UN Day, Columbus, 1960. Pres. Capital City Young Republicans Club, 1960. Bd. dirs. Columbus Cancer Clinic, pres., 1978-81; bd. dirs. Columbus chpt. ARC; governing bd. Hannah Neil Mission, Inc., 1974-78. Named 1 of 10 Outstanding Young Men of Columbus, 1965. Mem. Am., Ohio (council of dels. 1965-67, exec. com. 1977-81), Columbus (bd. govs. 1970-72, sec.-treas. 1974-75, pres. 1976-77) bar assns., Am. Coll. Probate Counsel, Duke Alumni Admissions Adv. Com. (chmn. 1965-79), Phi Delta Theta, Phi Delta Phi. Presbyn. Clubs: University (Columbus); Worthington (Ohio) Hills. Editor: Duke Law Jour., 1954-55; contbr. to profl. publs. in field. Home: 872 Clubview Blvd N Worthington OH 43085 Office: 180 E Broad St Columbus OH 43215

CARNAHAN, MELVIN EUGENE, lawyer, state ofcl.; b. Birch Tree, Mo., Feb. 11, 1934; s. Albert Sidney Johnson and Mary Kathel (Schupp) C.; B.A. in Bus. Adminstrn., George Washington U., 1954; J.D., U. Mo., 1959; m. Jean Ann Carpenter, June 12, 1954; children—Roger Andrew, Raymond Russell, Robin Colleen, Thomas Sidney. Admitted to Mo. bar, 1959, since practiced in Rolla; mem. Mo. Ho. of Reps., 1963-67, majority floor leader, 1965-67; treas. State of Mo., Jefferson City, 1981—; officer, dir. Rozark Farms, Inc., 1961-76. Bd. dirs. Phelps County chpt. ARC, Rolla Area United Fund; mem. exec. bd. Mo. Bapt. Conv. Served to 1st lt. USAF, 1954-56. Mem. Mo. Bar. Democrat. Office: Room 229 State Capitol Jefferson City MO 65401

CARNEAL, THOMAS WILLIAM, historian, educator; b. Plattsmouth, Nebr., Apr. 8, 1934; s. Glen Thomas and Frances Elizabeth (Wetenkamp) C.; B.A., U. Kansas City, 1963; M.A., U. Mo., Kansas City, 1966; postgrad. U. Mo., 1966-70. Mem. faculty Jr. Coll. program Kemper Mil. Sch., Boonville, Mo., 1965-68; asst. then asso. prof. history N.W. Mo. State U., Maryville, 1968—. Pres., Nodaway County Hist. Soc., 1971—; chmn. Nodaway County Bicentennial Com., 1975-77. Served with U.S. Army, 1953-56. Mem. Orgn. Am. Historians, State Hist. Soc. Mo., Econ. History Assn., Delta Chi. Methodist. Author: A Historic Inventory of Nodaway County, 1977; A Historic Inventory of Andrew County, 1978; A Historic Inventory of the Tri-County Area, 1979; A Historic Inventory of Daviess County, Mo., 1979; Saint Joseph Mo.: Landmarks, 1978; A Historic Inventory of DeKalb County, 1979; A Historic Inventory of Holt County, 1980; A Historic Inventory of Worth County, 1980; A Historic Inventory of Harrison County, 1981; A Historic Inventory of Buchanan County, 1981; Historical and Architectural Landmarks of Nodaway County, 1980; contbr. articles to profl. jours. Home: 418 W 2d St Maryville MO 64468 Office: 306 Colden Hall Northwest Missouri State U Maryville MO 64468

CARNER, WILLIAM JOHN, banker; b. Springfield, Mo., Aug. 9, 1948; s. John Wilson and Willie Marie (Moore) C.; A.B., Drury Coll., 1970; M.B.A., U. Mo., 1972; m. Dorothy Jean Edwards, June 12, 1976. Mktg. rep. 1st Nat. Bank Memphis, 1972-73; asst. br. mgr. Bank of Am., Los Angeles, 1973-74; dir. mktg. Commerce Bank, Springfield, Mo., 1974-76; affiliate mktg. mgr. 1st Union Bancorp., St. Louis, 1976-78; pres. Carner & Assos., Springfield, Mo., 1977—; instr. Drury Coll., 1975. Bd. dirs. Am. Cancer Soc., Greene County, Mo., 1974—, publicity chmn., 1974-78; bd. dirs. Springfield (Mo.) Muscular Dystrophy Assn., 1975-76, Greater Ozarks council Camp Fire Girls, 1980-81. Mem. Bank Mktg. Assn., Savs. Industry Mktg. Assn. (research com. 1980—), Assn. M.B.A. Execs. Democrat. Mem. Disciples of Christ Ch. Clubs: Hickory Hills Country, Kiwanis, Mason, Shrine. Home: 3605 S Parkhill Springfield MO 65807 Office: PO Box 1482 SSS Springfield MO 65807

CARNEY, CLARENCE S., state senator; b. Ossining, N.Y., June 21, 1925; s. Josephine and Clarence G. C.; B.S., Iowa State U., 1951; M.A., U. No. Iowa, 1960; m. Jacquelyn Moore, 1950; 3 children. High sch., coll. tchr., coach, adminstr.; mem. Iowa Senate. Bd. dirs. Prair Gold council Boys Scouts Am., Sioux City Concert Course. Served with USN, World War II. Mem. Phi Delta Kappa. Episcopalian. Clubs: Sertoma (pres.) Masons (master lodge), Shriners, Greater Siouxland Press. Office: State Senate Des Moines IA 50319*

CARNEY, THOMAS PATRICK, med. co. exec.; b. DuBois, Pa., May 27, 1915; s. James Patrick and Margaret Elizabeth (Senard) C.; B.S. in Chem. Engring., U. Notre Dame, 1937, LL.D. (hon.), 1969; M.S. in Chemistry, Pa. State U., 1939, Ph.D., 1941; m. Mary Elizabeth McGuire, Oct. 3, 1942; children—Thomas Patrick, Sheila, James K., Janet. With Reilly Tar & Chem. Corp., Indpls., 1937-38, 41-43; with Eli Lilly & Co., Indpls., 1944-64, v.p., 1954-64; exec. v.p. G. D. Searle & Co., Skokie, Ill., 1964-74; pres. Metatech Corp., Northbrook, Ill., 1975—; dir. Bioferm Corp., Med. Biol. Scis. Trustee, U. Notre Dame, Barat Coll. Recipient Sorin award U. Notre Dame, 1971; award Assn. Cons. Chemists and Chem. Engrs., 1976; Centennial of Sci. award U. Notre Dame, 1972, Centennial of Engring. award, 1974. Fellow N.Y. Acad. Scis., AAAS, Chem. Soc. (London), Am. Inst. Chemists; mem. Am. Chem. Soc., Soc. Chem. Industry (London), Swiss Chem. Soc. Clubs: Onwentsia; Mid-Am.; Met. Author: Laboratory Fractional Distillation, 1949; Instant Evolution: We'd Better Get Good At It, 1980; False Profits: The Decline of Industrial Creativity, 1981; contbr. articles to sci. jours. and popular mags. Office: 910 Skokie Blvd Northbrook IL 60062

CARNICOM, GENE E., clin. social worker; b. Miami, Fla., Nov. 13, 1944; s. Francis Eugene and Kathleen Carnicom; B.A., San Diego State U., 1971, M.S.S.W., 1972; A.B.D., U. Md., 1976; Ph.D., Southeastern U., 1981; m. Lillian Helen Baehr, Mar. 22, 1970; children—Patrick Dylan, Danielle Brooke. Coordinator, Beach Area Free Clinic, San Diego, Calif., 1970-72; exec. dir. RETRED, Inc., San Diego, 1970-72; field instr. U. Md. and Morgan State U., 1973-76; chief social work Balt. City Jail, 1973-76; mem. grad. faculty Webster Coll., St. Louis, 1977-80; commd. 1st lt. U.S. Army, 1976, advanced through grades to capt., 1977; sect. chief behavioral sci. div. U.S. Army, Ft. Sam Houston, Tex., 1976-80; hosp. social work dir. Indian Health Service Hosp., Pine Ridge, S.D., 1980—. Bd. dirs. Inntercity N.W. Neighborhood Corp., San Diego, 1970-72; agy. mem. Community Congress San Diego, 1970-72; mem. site selection com. Community Corrections Task Force, Md. Dept. Corrections, 1976. Served with USNR, 1962-68. Recipient doctoral stipend U. Md., 1972-73; cert. Acad. Cert. Social Workers; registered social worker, Calif. Mem. Council Social Work Edn., Assn. Mil. Surgeons U.S., Am. Sociol. Assn., Nat. Assn. Social Workers, Nat. Council Crime and Delinquency, Undergrad. Social Work Faculty Assn., Assn. Correctional Research and Statistics, Mensa. Democrat. Home: PO Box 841 Pine Ridge SD 57770 Office: Indian Health Service Hosp Pine Ridge SD 57770

CARNS, WILLIAM HULBERT, ins. exec.; b. Central City, Nebr., Apr. 18, 1912; s. James H. and Emma (Hulbert) C.; B.S. in Bus. Adminstrn., U. Nebr., 1933, J.D., 1935; m. Hazel Jane Eldridge, Sept. 10, 1938; children—William E., James O. Admitted to Nebr. bar, 1935; with firm Woods, Aiken & Aiken, Lincoln, Nebr., 1935-37; with Employers Group, Boston, 1937-48, Hartford A & I Co., Chgo., 1948-49; with Zurich-Am. Ins. Cos., Los Angeles, 1949-57, asst. U.S. mgr., sr. v.p., Chgo., 1962-77, chmn. bd., 1977—. Bd. govs. Ins. Crime Prevention Inst. Served to lt. USNR, 1942-45. Mem. Nat. Assn. Ind. Insurers, Phi Delta Phi, Beta Theta Pi. Club: Rolling Green Golf and Country (Arlington Heights, Ill.). Home: 106 S Stratford Rd Arlington Heights IL 60004 Office: 231 N Martingale Rd Schaumburg IL 60196

CAROTHERS, CRAIG HORN, data processing cons.; b. Platte City, Mo., Dec. 2, 1946; s. Victor Lyle and Margaret Helen (Horn) C.; B.A., William Jewell Coll., 1968; M.A., Sangamon State U., 1978; m. Linda Sue Carothers, Feb. 7, 1971; children—Brian, Kevin. Programmer/analyst Nat. Car Rental, Mpls., 1972-75; systems analyst Ill. Dept. Public Aid, Springfield, 1975-76; mgr. systems and program devel. Ill. Dept. Children and Family Services, Springfield, 1976-78; sr. asso. Resource Mgmt. Assos., Springfield, 1978-80; pres. Diversified Systems Services, 1980—. Served to capt., U.S. Army, 1968-72. Cert. data processor. Mem. Ind. Computer Cons. Assn., Am. Public Welfare Assn. Home: 907 Belpre Dr O'Fallon IL 62269

CARPENTER, FRANK DAVID, printing co. exec.; b. Cin., Dec. 10, 1942; s. Frank G. and Joan (Brettschnieder) C.; B.B.A., U. Cin., 1965; M.B.A., U. Louisville, 1971; m. Carole Danbury, Feb. 7, 1964; children—Elizabeth, David. Customer service account exec. Fawcett Printing Co., Louisville, 1965-70, publs. sales mgr., 1970-74; v.p. Midwestern sales World Color Press Inc., Chgo., 1974-79, sr. v.p. mktg., Effingham, Ill., 1979—. Mem. Beta Gamma Sigma, Alpha Kappa Psi, Sigma Alpha Epsilon. Home: Route 5 Box 39M Effingham IL 62401 Office: PO Box 1248 Effingham IL 62401

CARPENTER, IRENE DELLA, educator; b. Wauneta, Nebr., Nov. 15, 1914; d. Dan and Martha (Oyer) Egle; B.S., U. Nebr.; m. Ellis E. Carpenter, Aug. 1, 1936. Tchr. various dists. public schs., Hitchcock County, Nebr. Mem. NEA, Nebr. State Edn. Assn., Assn. Supervision and Curriculum Devel., Internat. Reading Assn., Nebr. Alumni Assn. (life), Delta Kappa Gamma. Club: Community of Stratton. Home: Stratton NE 69043

CARPENTER, JOHN DENNIS, banker; b. Stephen, Minn., Feb. 17, 1933; s. Oscar Dennis and Ingrid Marie (Nilsen) C.; student U. Wis. Sch. Banking, 1967; m. Peggy Eileen Pudil, Dec. 22, 1957; children—Denise, Scott, Daniel. Asst. cashier Grafton Nat. Bank (N.D.), 1956-62; asst. v.p. Northwestern State Bank, Luverne, Minn., 1962-68; v.p. Northwestern State Bank, Slayton, Minn., 1968-71; pres. First Nat. Bank, Hay Springs, Nebr., 1971-73; pres., chmn. bd. Northwestern Bank, Hallock, Minn., 1973—, C-D-L Corp., Hallock. Served with U.S. Army, 1953-55; Korea. Mem. Minn. Bankers Assn., C. of C. (pres., sec.-treas.). Republican. Lutheran. Clubs: Lions (sec.-treas.), Elks, Masons. Home: 217 N 5th St Hallock MN 56728 Office: 302 S 2d St Hallock MN 56728

CARPENTER, VIVIAN LAVERNE THOMAS, state ofcl.; b. Detroit, Nov. 3, 1952; d. Doyal Wilson and Jennie Pettway Thomas; B.S.E., U. Mich., 1973, M.B.A., 1975, postgrad., 1978; m. Alden J. Carpenter, June 22, 1975 (dec.). Research engr. Ford Motor Co., summers 1972-73; sr. cons. Arthur Andersen & Co., 1975-78; instr. acctg. principles U. Mich., 1977-78; dep. state treas. State of Mich., Lansing, 1978—. Ford Found. grantee. Mem. Am. Inst. C.P.A.'s, Mich. Assn. C.P.A.'s, Nat. Assn. Black Accts., Mcpl. Fin. Officers Assn., Nat. State Auditors Council. Office: Treasury Bldg Lansing MI 48922

CARPENTER-REED, CARMEN OLGA, sch. counselor; b. Detroit, Dec. 20, 1937; d. Montgomery O'Neal Tarrant and Nellie Louise (Jackson) Tarrant Tribble; B.S., Wayne State U., 1960, M.Ed., 1975; children—Spencer III, Kevin O'Neal, Brent Dorian; m. 2d, Henry Reed, Oct. 19, 1979. Vocal music tchr. Detroit Bd. Edn., 1960-77; model Hawkins Apparel, Inc., Lynette's Inc., March of Dimes Extravaganza, 1974—; elem. sch. counselor Keidan Sch., Detroit Bd. Edn., 1977—; career edn. liaison com. person Region 3, Detroit Bd. Edn. Pres. Courtis Sch. PTA, 1973-74; public relations chairperson Detroit Council PTA, 1976, 79, corr. sec., 1977-79. Democratic Precinct del., 1976, 78—. Named Woman of Yr., St. Andrews Presbyterian Ch., 1973; Ms. March of Dimes Model, 1977; recipient Outstanding Mich. Citizen award, 1978; Cert. of Appreciation, Wayne County Bd. Commrs., 1980; Cert. of Achievement, Detroit Bd. Edn., Guidance and Counseling Dept., 1981; Appreciation Trophy, God's Humanitarian Garden, 1981. Mem. Detroit Fedn. Tchrs. (bldg. rep. 1969, 73), Am. Personnel and Guidance Assn., Mich. Personnel and Guidance Assn., Mich. Elem. Sch. Counselor Assn., Mich. Non-White Counselors Assn., Guidance Assn. Met. Detroit, Wayne State U. Alumni Assn., Women of Wayne, State Dem. Educators Caucus, Detroit Assn. to Promote Amateur Boxing (rec.-corr. sec. 1979), NAACP, Phi Delta Kappa. Presbyterian. Club: Les Cosmopolites Bridge (pres.). Compiler exhbn., booklet on black scientists and inventors for Afro-Am. Mus., 1974. Office: Keidan Sch 4441 Collingwood St Detroit MI 48204

CARR, ADAM FYFE, indsl. psychologist; b. Urbana, Ill., Dec. 27, 1948; s. Arthur Japeth and Marion Elizabeth (Grudier) C.; B.A. cum laude, Kalamazoo Coll., 1971; M.A., Dalahousie U., 1973, Ph.D. (Killam fellow), 1976. Asst. prof. psychology Trent U., Peterborough, Ont., Can., 1976-77; postdoctoral trainee U. Kans., 1978-79; asst. prof. corrections Ill. State U., Normal, 1979-80; indsl. psychologist Bur. Personnel State of S.D., Pierre, 1980—; cons. Nashville Police Dept. Mem. Am. Psychol. Assn., Phi Beta Kappa. Contbr. articles to profl. jours. Home: 610 W Pleasant Dr Pierre SD 57501 Office: Bur Personnel Capital Bldg Pierre SD 57501

CARR, DAVID ROY, state ofcl.; b. Morris, Ill., Mar. 2, 1946; s. Homer Jay and Geraldine Louise (Lund) C.; student Joliet Jr. Coll., 1971-74; certificate U. Ga., 1978; m. Suzanne R. Collignon, July 16, 1977; children—Heath, Thomas, Heather, Kristen. With Western Electric Co., Chgo., 1965-68; mgr. trainee Household Fin. Co., Aurora, Ill., 1968-69; supt. Ill. and Mich. Canal, Ill. Dept. Conservation, Morris, 1969—; lectr. in field. Vol. weather observer NOAA, Morris, 1971—. Mem. Nat. Recreation and Park Assn., Am. Canal Soc., Ill. Canal Soc. (dir. 1977-78). Club: Morris Camera (chmn. 1978—). Address: PO Box 272 Morris IL 60450

CARR, GENE EMMETT, supt. schs.; b. Madison, S.D., Dec. 6, 1937; s. Emmett A. and Phyllis E. (Heitman) C.; B.S., Dakota State Coll., 1961; M.S., U. Utah, 1964; Edn. Specialist, U. S.D., 1975; m. Carolyn Riley, May 25, 1961; children—Catherine, Robert, Michael, Mark, Patricia, Bradley. Tchr. pub. schs., Garretson, S.D., 1961-63, Dell Rapids, S.D., 1964-70; supt. schs., Oldham, S.D., 1970-76, Hamlin Schs., Hayti, S.D., 1976—. Vice pres. Oldham Fire Dept., 1972-76; mem. agr. com. Sioux Empire Farm Show, 1964-79. Mem. Sch. Adminstrs. S.D., S.D. Sch. Supts. Assn. (dir.), Am. Quarter Horse Assn. Club, Center of Nation Appaloosa Horse Club (pres. 1972-74), Pony of Ams. Club. Contbr. articles to equine mags. Home: PO Box 25 Hayti SD 57241 Office: PO Box 298 Hayti SD 57241

CARR, HAROLD LEE, supt. schs.; b. Thackrey, Ill., Sept. 15, 1934; s. Daniel Lelan and Fanny Elizabeth (Savage) C.; B.S., So. Ill. U., 1956, M.S., 1958; Ph.D., Ohio State U., 1970; m. Patricia Ann Mezo, Mar. 22, 1957; 1 son, Steven Lee. Instr. applied sci. So. Ill. U., 1956-59; instr. machine shop, guidance counselor, asst. supt. East Alton-Wood River High Sch., 1959-67; research asso. Center Vocat. Edn. of Ohio State U., 1967-69; supr. evaluation programs Ohio State Dept. Edn., 1969-70; asst. supt. Hamilton County Joint Vocat. Sch. Dist., 1970-75; supt. Great Oaks Joint Vocat. Sch. Dist., Cin., 1975—; ordained deacon So. Baptist Conv. Mem. Buckeye Assn. Sch. Adminstrs., Ohio Vocat. Assn., Am. Vocat. Assn., Phi Delta Kappa, Phi Kappa Phi, Iota Lambda Sigma. Republican. Club: Wood River Optimists (pres. 1966). Contbr. numerous articles to profl. jours; author: A Program Review Paradigm for Ohio Vocational Education, 1970. Office: 3254 E Kemper Rd Cincinnati OH 45241

CARR, HAROLD NOFLET, airline exec.; b. Kansas City, Kans., Mar. 14, 1921; s. Noflet B. and Mildred (Addison) C.; B.S., Tex. A&M U., 1943; postgrad. Am. U., 1944-46; m. Mary Elizabeth Smith, Aug. 5, 1944; children—Steven Addison, Hal Douglas, James Taylor, Scott Noflet. Asst. dir. route devel. Trans World Airlines, Inc., 1943-47; exec. v.p. Wis. Central Airlines, Inc., 1947-52; mem. firm McKinsey & Co., 1952-54; pres. North Central Airlines, Inc., 1954-69; chmn., 1965-79; chmn. Republic Airlines, Inc., 1979—, also dir.; dir. Dahlberg Electronics, Inc., Ross Industries, Inc., Republic Energy Inc., Governor's Sound, Ltd., Cayman Water Co., Westland Capital Corp. Professorial lectr. in mgmt. engring. Am. U., 1952-62. Trustee, Tex. A&M Research Found.; mem. devel. council Coll. Bus. Adminstrn., Tex. A&M U.; bd. nominations Nat. Aviation Hall of Fame; mem. adv. com. Tex. Transp. Inst., Tex. A&M U. System. Mem. World Bus. Council, Am. Mgmt. Assn., Nat. Def. Transp. Assn., Air Transport Assn., Assn. Local Transport Airlines, Am. Econ. Assn., Minn. Execs. Orgn., Greater Mpls., St. Paul Area chambers commerce, Am. Assn. Airport Execs., Nat. Aero Assn., Smithsonian Assos., Nat. Trust for Historic Preservation, Tex. A&M Former Students Assn., Beta Gamma Sigma. Clubs: Aero, Nat. Aviation (Washington); Stearman Alumnus (Wichita, Kans.); Mpls.; Century, Aggie (dir.) (College Station, Tex.); Briarcrest Country (Bryan, Tex.); Racquet (Miami, Fla.); Wings (N.Y.C.); Gull Lake Yacht (Brainerd, Minn.). Address: 7500 Airline Dr Minneapolis MN 55450

CARR, JAMES CHARLES, physician; b. New Hampton, Iowa, Mar. 28, 1939; s. Hubert B. and Anna Mary (McKone) C.; B.A. in English, Loras Coll., 1957-61; M.D., U. Iowa, 1965; m. Mary Kay Peters, June 17, 1961; children—Barbara, Robert, Jane, Susan, David. Intern, Broadlawns Polk County Hosp., Des Moines, 1965-66; resident in family practice, 1966-67; practice medicine specializing in family medicine Med. Assos., New Hampton, Iowa, 1967—; chief staff St. Joseph's Community Hosp., New Hampton, 1972, 1975, 80; instr. family medicine Mayo Med. Sch., U. Minn., Rochester, 1975—. Bd. dirs. N.E. Iowa Council on Substance Abuse, 1976—. Served to major Iowa N. G., 1966-72. Recipient Distinguished Service Award Jaycees, 1971; recipient Outstanding Young Mem of Am. Award, 1974; diplomate Am. Bd. Family Practice. Fellow Am. Acad. Family Practice; mem. AMA, Chickasaw County, Iowa Med. Socs., N.E. Iowa Emergency Med. Services Assn. (dir., chmn. 1979—). Roman Catholic. Home: 414 N Chestnut Ave New Hampton IA 50659 Office: 201 S Linn Ave New Hampton IA 50659

CARR, LEON CLEMENT, pub. relations exec.; b. lMilbank, S.D., Sept. 11, 1924; s. Frank B. and Laura A. (Kohl) C.; B.A. in Journalism, U. Minn., 1951; m. Donnie M. Cronin, May 19, 1956; 1 son, John. Wire editor St. Cloud (Minn.) Daily Times, 1951-52; staff writer Asso. Press, Sioux Falls, Pierre, S.D., 1952-56; copy editor St. Paul Pioneer Press, 1956-57; copy editor St. Paul Dispatch, 1957-60, asst. news editor, 1960-61; with 3M, St. Paul, 1961—, staff publicist, 1965-71, pub. relations coordinator, 1971-73, supr. media relations, 1973-76, mgr. br. pub. relations, 1976—. Mem. Pub. Relations Soc. Am.

(accredited), U. Minn. Sch. Journalism Mass Communication Alumni Assn. (charter, past pres.), Soc. Profl. Journalists (life). Roman Catholic. Club: Minn. Press (charter). Home: 21 E Logan Ave West Saint Paul MN 55118 Office: 3M Center Box 33600 Saint Paul MN 55133

CARR, ROBERT, lawyer, former congressman; b. Janesville, Wis., Mar. 27, 1943; s. Milton Raymond and Edna (Blood) C.; B.S., U. Wis., 1965, J.D., 1968. Mem. staff Mich. Senate Minority Leader, 1968-69; asst. atty. gen. Mich., 1970-72, adminstrv. asst., 1969-70; counsel Spl. Joint Com. on Legal Edn., Mich. Legislature, 1972; admitted to Mich. bar, 1969; mem. 94th to 96th Congresses from 6th Dist. Mich.; congressional advisor U.S. SALT del., Geneva, 1976-80. Mem. Am. Bar Assn., State Bar Mich., State Bar Wis. Democrat. Contbr. numerous articles to mags. Office: 817 Center St Lansing MI 48906

CARR, ROBERT M., state senator; b. Bernard, Iowa, May 9, 1937; s. M. L. and Mae C.; student Loras Coll., 1954-55; m. Rose T. Connolly, 1960; children—Tim, Mark, Kimberly. Securities rep. Waddell & Reed, Inc., 1967-70, div. mgr., 1970—; mem. Iowa Ho. of Reps., 1973-74, Iowa Senate, 1974—. Precinct worker Dubuque County Dem. Party, 1960-64, precinct committeeman, 1965-72; chmn. Dubuque County Platform Com., 1972. Mem. Nat. Assn. Securities Dealers. Named Outstanding Pres. and Friend of Boys award Dubuque Optimist Club, 1969. Roman Catholic. Office: State Senate Des Moines IA 50319*

CARRAHER, CHARLES JACOB, JR., profl. speaker; b. Cin., Sept. 22, 1922; s. Charles Jacob and Marcella Marie (Hager) C.; grad. pub. schs., Norwood, O.; m. Joyce Ann Root, June 13, 1947; children—Cynthia A., Craig J. With Cin. Enquirer, 1937-72, office mgr., circulation mgr., adminstrv. asst. to exec. v.p., 1947-66, dir. employee community relations, 1966-72; exec. v.p., partner Cin. Suburban Newspapers Inc., 1973-77; asst. dir. devel. WCET-TV, 1977-79; v.p. Garrett Computer Inc., 1979-81; participant numerous symposia. Mem. bd., v.p. Cin. Conv. and Visitors Bur., 1966-72; mem. Cin. Manpower Planning Council, 1972. Bd. dirs. Central Psychiatric Clinic, 1970—, Mental Health Assn., 1970-72, Great Rivers council Girl Scouts U.S.A., 1969-74; v.p. bd. dirs. Neediest Kids of All, 1969-72; bd. dirs. Greater Cin. Urban League, 1971-74, 75-78. Served to lt., USAAF, World War II, ETO. Decorated Air medal with cluster. Mem. Greater Cin. C. of C. (chmn. human resources devel. com. 1972), Beta Gamma Sigma. Republican. Methodist. Author: Chemistry Applied, 1970; Semimicro Qualitative Analysis, 1971; Chemistry in Everyday Life, 1972, rev., 1976; Chemistry in Our World, 1974; (with F. Millich) Interfacial Synthesis, Vol. I, Fundamentals, 1977, Vol. II, Polymer Applications and Technology, 1977, (with J. Preston) Vol. III, Recent Advances, 1982; (with M. Tsuda) Modification of Polymers, 1979, 80; (with Sheats and Pittman) Organometallic Polymers, 1978, Advances in Organometallic Polymer Science, 1981; (with R. Seymour) Polymer Chemistry: An Introductory Textbook, 1981; contbr. numerous articles to profl. jours. Home and Office: 10848 Lake Thames Dr Cincinnati OH 45242

CARRAS, CATHERINE PAPPAS, educator; b. Gary, Ind., Aug. 18, 1930; d. Mike George and Chrisanthy N. (Nicholas) Pappas; B.S. in Edn., Ind. U., 1953; M.S. in Edn., Purdue U., Calumet, Ind., 1973; m. Nathan Angelo Carras, June 20, 1954; children—Evan N., Christine M., Athene Nicolette. Tchr., Tolleston Sch., Gary, 1952-54, Champaign (Ill.) Jr. High Sch., 1954-56; tchr. lang. arts, social studies Scott Middle Sch., Hammond, Ind., 1972—. Troop leader Calumet council Girl Scouts U.S.A., 1964-73; den mother Boy Scouts Am., 1963-64; mem. Citizens Nominating Com. for Sch. Bd., Hammond, Ind., 1970-72; Sunday Sch. tchr. St. Demetrios Greek Orthodox Ch. Mem. Hammond Area Reading Council, Daus. of Penelope, Ladies Philoptochos Sic. St. Demetrios, Living Room Dialogues for Christian Unity. Greek Orthodox. Office: 3635 173d St Hammond IN 46323

CARRELL, TERRY EUGENE, controls co. exec.; b. Monmouth, Ill., July 1, 1938; s. Roy Edwin and Caroline Hilma (Fillman) C.; A.B., Monmouth Coll., 1961; M.B.A., Calif. State U., Los Angeles, 1967; D.B.A., U. So. Calif., 1970; m. Bonnie Lee Clements, July 11, 1964; children—Philip Edwin, Andrew David. Prin. engr. reconnaissance and communications N.Am. Aviation, 1963-67; mgr. avionics analysis and techs. B-1 div. Rockwell Internat., 1967-73, dir. engring. Morse Controls div., 1973-74; gen. mgr. Morse Controls div. Incom Internat. Inc., 1974-78, pres. indsl. div. Morse Controls, 1978-80, pres. Morse Controls, 1980—; cons.; lectr. U. So. Calif., 1967-70. Mem. Hudson (Ohio) Econ. Devel. Com., 1979—; dist. council commr. Boy Scouts Am., 1980—, commr. nat. council, 1981—; mem. service rev. panel United Way of Summit County, 1980. NDEA fellow, 1961-63. Mem. Hudson C. of C. (trustee 1976-78), Boating Industry Assn. (chmn. steering task force 1974—), Am. Boat and Yacht Council (dir. 1980—). Contbr. articles to profl. jours. Patentee in field. Home: 7712 Valley View Hudson OH 44236 Office: 21 Clinton St Hudson OH 44236

CARREÑO, ANTONIO GONZÁLEZ, educator; b. Parada del Sil, Orense, Spain, July 1, 1939; s. Eduardo Pacios and Rosalía Bertólez (González) C.; came to U.S., 1965, naturalized, 1972; M.A., Trinity Coll., Hartford, Conn., 1969; M.A., Yale U., 1973, M. Phil., 1974, Ph.D., 1975; married; children—Marilyn, Tony. Instr. Spanish, Yale U., 1974-75; asst. prof. Spanish, Columbia U., 1975-77; asst. prof. U. Ill., Urbana, 1977-79, asso. prof., 1979—. Recipient Don Ramón Menéndez Pidal prize Royal Spanish Acad., 1978. Mem. Am. Assn. Tchrs. Spanish and Portuguese, MLA, European Assn. Spanish Profs., Assn. Internat. Hispanists. Author: El Romancero lírico de Lope de Vega, 1979; La Persona, la máscara: Ensayos sobre lírica contemporánea, 1981; editor: Luís de Góngora, Romances, 1981; contbr. articles to profl. jours. Home: 2511 Scovill Circle Urbana IL 61801 Office: 4080 Fgn Langs Bldg U Ill Urbana IL 61801

CARRIER, WILFRED PETER, elec. engr.; b. Faulkton, S.D., July 14, 1923; s. Wilfred P. and Mary (Mundy) C.; E.E., Ill. Inst. Tech., 1952; m. Mary M. Mulcahy, July 17, 1943; children—Patrick, Timothy. Dir. quality Standard Coil Products Co., Chgo., 1951-58; dir. quality, reliability Mallory Capacitor Co., Indpls., 1958-74, dir. engring., 1974—. Served with AUS, 1942-46; CBI. Mem. Electronic Industries Assn., Am. Soc. Quality Control (regional award), IEEE, Am. Def. Preparedness Assn., Nat. Security Indsl. Assn. Roman Catholic. Clubs: Indpls. Athletic, K.C. Home: 9861 Chesterton St N Indianapolis IN 46280 Office: 3029 Washington St E Indianapolis IN 46206

CARROLL, CARMAL EDWARD, clergyman, educator; b. Grahn, Ky., Oct. 8, 1923; s. Noah Washington and Jessie Laura (Scott) C.; Ph.B., U. Toledo, 1947, M.A., 1950, B.Edn., 1951; M.L.S., U. Calif. at Los Angeles, 1961; Ph.D., U. Calif., Berkeley, 1969; postgrad. in theology Duke U., Episcopal Div. Sch.; m. Greta E. Seastrom, June 11, 1960; adopted children—Bahram Sabouhi, Mehran Sabouhi. Edn. librarian, U. So. Calif., 1961-62; reference librarian U. Calif. at Berkeley, 1962-65; dir. library So. Oreg. Coll., Ashland, 1965-67; dir. libraries Wichita (Kans.) State U., 1967-70; prof. library sci. U. Mo. at Columbia, 1970—. Named Ky. col. Mem. A.A.U.P., A.L.A., Assn. Am. Library Schs., Mo. Library Assn., N.Y. Acad. Sci., Nat. Micrographics Assn., Internat. Platform Assn., Phi Delta Kappa, Beta Phi Mu. Democrat. Episcopalian. Club: Rotary. Author: Professionalization of Education for Librarianship, 1970. Home: 2001 Country Club Dr Columbia MO 65201

CARROLL, DANIEL THUERING, bus. exec.; b. Burlington, Vt., Mar. 21, 1926; s. Daniel B. and Viola (Thuering) C.; A.B., Dartmouth Coll., 1947; M.A., U. Minn., 1948; student U. Chgo., 1948-50; children—Laura Louise, Lisa Dodge, Daniel Kerr, Grant Thuering; m. Julie A. Virgo, Aug. 20, 1977. Asst. to mgmt. engring. dir. Bur. Yards & Docks, Navy Dept., Washington, 1950-54; cons. Booz, Allen & Hamilton Inc., Chgo., 1954-57, asso., 1957-60, v.p., 1960-63, v.p., Cleve., 1963-66, v.p., region mng. officer, 1966-68, group v.p., dir., 1969, pres. mgmt. consulting div., 1971; pres. Gould Inc., Chgo., 1972-80, also dir.; pres., chief exec. officer, dir. Hoover Universal, Inc., Ann Arbor, Mich., 1980—; dir. Van Straaten Chem. Co., Chgo., Conrac Corp., Stamford, Conn., Wolverine World Wide Inc., Grand Rapids, Mich., Nat. Bank & Trust Co., Ann Arbor, Combined Internat. Corp., Combined Ins. Co. Am., Chgo., Diebold Inc., Canton, Ohio. Trustee, Bexley Hall Sem., Colgate Rochester Divinity Sch.; bd. dirs. Chgo. Urban League; trustee Atlanta U. Center, Union Theol. Sem., N.Y.C., Assn. Governing Bds. Univs. and Univs. Served with USNR, 1944-46. Mem. Chgo. Assn. Commerce and Industry (dir.), Alpha Delta Phi. Office: PO Box 1003 Ann Arbor MI 48106

CARROLL, GEORGE DEEKS, ins. co. exec.; b. Mpls., Mar. 27, 1916; s. Joseph Douglas and Dorothy Elizabeth (Deeks) C.; B.S. in Commerce, Northwestern U., 1937; m. Marguerite Ray, Nov. 19, 1938; children—George Deeks, Judith Ray Carroll Smith. With Spl. Agts. Sch., Employers Liability Assurance Corp., Boston and Chgo., 1938-42; with Marsh & McLennan Inc., Chgo., 1942—, asst. v.p., 1956-58, v.p., 1958—; past pres., dir. Ridge Investors Trust; owner Nawaii Lodge, Lake Tomahawk, Woodruff, Wis. Founder with White Sox, 1st Chgo. Little League, 1952; past pres., bd. dirs. Laguna Woods Home Owners Assn.; mem. exec. bd. Chgo. council Boy Scouts Am., 1962-76. Served with USN, 1942-46. Republican. Congregationalist. Clubs: Union League (Chgo.); Midlothian Country (dir.). Home: PO Box 461 Palos Park IL 60464 also Route 3 Box 58 Woodruff WI 54568 Office: 222 S Riverside Dr Chicago IL 60606

CARROLL, GLADA IROLENE HOUSER, dietitian; b. Carson, Iowa, May 24, 1923; d. Jacob Henry and Sarah Viola (Frain) Houser; B.S., Iowa State U., 1944, M.S., 1977; m. Leo Warren Carroll, Apr. 7, 1945 (dec.); children—Philip, Linda, Daniel, Timothy, Beverly, Rita. Dietitian, Stouffer's Food Corp., Cleve., Chgo., N.Y.C., 1944-46; dietitian, asst. dir. food service Mercy Hosp., Des Moines, 1967-78, dir. food service, 1978—. Mem. Am. Dietetic Assn. (registered dietitian), Iowa Dietetic Assn. (treas. 1979—), Des Moines Dietetic Assn., Am. Soc. for Hosp. Food Service Adminstrs., Omicron Nu. Roman Catholic. Office: Mercy Hosp 6th and University St Des Moines IA 50314

CARROLL, HOWARD WILLIAM, state senator; b. Chgo., July 28, 1942; s. Barney Morris and Lyla (Price) C.; B.S. in Bus. Adminstrn., Roosevelt U., 1964; postgrad. Loyola U., Chgo., 1965; J.D., DePaul U., 1967; m. Eda B. Stagman, Dec. 1, 1973; children—Jacqueline, Barbara. Admitted to Ill. bar, 1967; staff counsel Chgo. Transit Authority, 1967-70; practiced law, Chgo., 1970-74; partner law firm Jann, Carroll, Sain & Dolin, Ltd., Chgo., 1974—; mem. Ill. Ho. of Reps. from 13th Dist., 1971-73; mem. Ill. Senate from 15th Dist., 1973—, chmn. appropriations com.; Democratic ward committeeman, 50th Ward, Chgo.; chmn. legis. Legis. Info. Systems, 1972—, chmn. Jud. Adv. Council. Mem. planning com. met. Chgo. area Jewish United Fund, 1971, chmn. spl. gifts govt. agys. div., 1971, vice chmn. govt. agys. div., 1969, vice chmn. young people's div., 1968; asso. gen. chmn. State Israel Bonds, convener young adults div., 1972, 79, chmn. banking div., co-chmn. public service div., 1979-81; mem. exec. com., bd. dirs. Zionist Orgn. Chgo.; exec. com. B'nai B'rith Council Greater Chgo., 1972, asso. chmn., 1973, chmn. spl. events, 1969-70, chmn. Anti-Defamation League, 1978-80; v.p. Jewish Nat. Fund, 1980—; bd. dirs. Chgo. Assn. Retarded Citizens; mem. Rogers Park-Northtown Mental Health Council, 1969; vice chmn. N. area March of Dimes, 1965, 79; gen. counsel Young Democratic Clubs Am., 1969, 1st v.p., 1971-73; del., mem. exec. bd. Atlantic Alliance Young Polit. Leaders, 1970; mem. youth adv. com. Dem. Nat. Com., 1968; alt. nat. committeeman Young Dems. Ill., 1969, mem. exec. bd., 1966—, treas., 1967, chmn. spl. events, 1967; mem. exec. com. Young Dems. Cook County, 1967; mem. 50th Ward Regular Dem. Orgn., 1959—; pres. 50th Ward Young Dems., 1965; dir. concession Dem. Nat. Conv., 1968, mem. exec. staff, treas. youth activities Chgo. Host Com.; mem. bd. lay advisers Servite Sem.; chmn. bd. lay advs., chmn. festival of leadership Little Flower, 1978-79, chmn. men's bd., 1978-79; vice chmn. Metron Davis Found. Crippling Diseases Children, 1958. Honoree State of Israel Bonds-Budlong Woods lodge B'nai B'rith, 1971; named City Wide B'nai B'rith Jewish Nat. Fund Man of Year, 1974; Outstanding Legislator award Ill. Credit Union League, 1979; numerous other awards. Jewish. Clubs: Masons, Shriners, B'nai B'rith (dir. lodge). Office: 55 E Monroe St Suite 4444 Chicago IL 60603

CARROLL, JAMES LANGTON, telephone co. exec.; b. College Station, Tex., Oct. 22, 1931; s. James Vincent and Mary (Langton) C.; B.S., U.S. Mil. Acad., West Point, N.Y., 1954; B.S.E.E., Washington U., St. Louis, 1963; m. Susannah Myers, Dec. 4, 1954; children—Susannah E. Carroll Card, Francesca J. Carroll Dutton, Elizabeth M. Carroll Cammile. Commd. 2d lt. U.S. Army, 1954, advanced through grades to col., 1975; with Southwestern Bell Telephone Co., Little Rock and El Dorado, Ark., 1959-67, supervising wire chief, 1965-67; div. plant supr. Continental Telephone Service Corp., Wentzville, Mo., 1969-70, asst. v.p. ops. Midwest div., 1970-73, v.p. ops. So. div. Continental Telephone Service Corp., Amherst, Va., 1973-74, v.p. ops. Mid-South div. Tenn. Telephone Co., Knoxville, 1974-75, v.p., gen. mgr. Continental Telephone Co. of Calif., Victorville, 1975-77, v.p., gen. mgr. Central Region, St. Louis, 1977—. Decorated Meritorious Service medal, Army Commendation medal; registered profl. engr., Mo., Kans., N.C., Ill., Calif. Mem. Nat. Soc. Profl. Engrs., Mo. Soc. Profl. Engrs., West Point Soc. St. Louis (pres.). Republican. Roman Catholic. Home: 255 Blackner Pl Webster Groves MO 63119 Office: Continental Telephone Service Corp 502 Earth City Plaza Suite 200 Earth City MO 63045

CARROLL, LOUISE DOLORES, nurse, hosp. adminstr.; b. St. Clairsville, Ohio, Feb. 12, 1924; d. John Joseph and Louise Caritas (Ebbert) C.; R.N., Wheeling (W.Va.) Hosp., 1945; B.S. in Nursing Edn., Catholic U. Am., 1950; M.Ed., Central State U., Wilberforce, Ohio, 1959. Staff nurse Wheeling (W.Va.) Hosp., 1945-46, asst. dir., instr., 1950-55; instr. St. Mary's Hosp., Clarksburg, W.Va., 1946-47; dir. sch. nursing Community Hosp., Springfield, Ohio, 1955-69, v.p., 1969—. Mem. health techs. adv. com. Clark Tech. Coll.; mem. Clark County Chpt. ARC, Community Hosp. Aux. Mem. Nat. League for Nursing (sch. visitor, review bd. for accreditation of hosp. schs., 1957-72), Am. Soc. Nursing Service Adminstrs/,Nat. Forum for Adminstrn. Nursing Service, Ohio Council Diploma Nurse Educators, Ohio Soc. Nursing Service Adminstrs., Ohio Commn. on Nursing Needs and Resources, Ohio League for Nursing (pres.), Am. Hosp. Assn. (del.-at-large, 1972-78, Assembly of Hosp. Schs. of Nursing disting. leadership award 1978). Democrat. Roman Catholic. Home: 3157 Sherwood Park Dr Springfield OH 45505 Office: 2615 E High St Springfield OH 45501

CARROLL, MARY ANN, univ. adminstr.; b. Terre Haute, Ind., Jan. 29, 1929; d. George Charles and Margaret M. (Mountz) C.; B.S., Ind. State U., 1950, M.S., 1955; Ed.D., Ind. U., 1963. Dean girls Sarah Scott Jr. High Sch., Terre Haute, 1955-62, Wiley High Sch., Terre Haute, Ind., 1963-64; asst. dean Sch. Grad. Studies Ind. State U., Terre Haute, 1964-76, dean Sch. Grad. Studies, 1976—; mem. Grad. Record Exams. Bd., 1978-82. Bd. visitors Air Force Inst. Tech., 1981—. Mem. Ind. Assn. Grad. Schs. (chmn.), Midwestern Assn. Grad. Schs. (chmn.), Council of Grad. Schs. in U.S. (dir. 1981—), Phi Kappa Phi, Delta Kappa Gamma, Kappa Delta Pi. Republican. Methodist. Author: Conceptual Tools for Teaching in Secondary Schools, 1970. Office: Parsons Hall Ind State U Terre Haute IN 47809

CARROLL, THOMAS JOHN, assn. exec.; b. St. Paul, Aug. 15, 1929; s. William H. and Neva (Saller) C.; B.A., St. Mary's Coll., Winona, Minn., 1952; m. Eleanor Rose Schmid, Aug. 27, 1955; children—David G., Thomas John, AnnCatherine, Robert G., Paul William. Pharm. salesman A.H. Robins, Davenport, Iowa, 1955-70; in advt. sales Modern Medicine, Chgo., 1970-72; advt. exec. D'Arcy, McManus & Massius, St. Paul, 1972-73; dir. mktg. communications AMA, Chgo., 1973—, editor Synergy monthly, 1975—. Dir. public relations St. Francis Xavier Sch. Bd., LaGrange, Ill., 1977-79; organist St. Francis Xavier Ch., LaGrange, 1964—. Served with AUS, 1952-54; Korea. Cert. Grad. Sch. Mgmt. UCLA, 1977. Mem. Am. Guild Organists (hon.), Pharm. Ad Club, Midwest Pharm. Ad Club (dir.), Med. Mktg. Assos., Chgo. Area Theatre Orgn. Enthusiasts. Republican. Roman Catholic. Clubs: LaGrange Field, LaGrange Tennis Assn. (past pres.), St. Francis Xavier Men's. Home: 333 N Edgewood St LaGrange Park IL 60525 Office: AMA 535 N Dearborn St Chicago IL 60610

CARROLL, VALEREE SUE, speech pathologist; b. Kansas City, Mo., Aug. 29, 1946; d. Middleton Scott and Patricia Pauline (Anderson) C.; B.S. in Edn., U. Kans., 1968, M.A. in Speech Pathology, 1970. Speech/lang. pathologist Clay County Health Dept., Liberty, Mo., 1970-71, Kansas City (Mo.) Pub. Schs., 1971—; mem. spl. edn. placement team Kansas City Public Sch. Dist. U.S. Office Edn. fellow, 1968-70. Mem. Am., Greater Kansas City speech hearing assns., Council for Exceptional Children. Republican. Home: 2115 W 78th St Prairie Village KS 66208 Office: 1211 McGee St Kansas City MO 64106

CARRON, MALCOLM, univ. chancellor, clergyman; b. Detroit, May 15, 1917; s. Harold Gregory and Florence Irene (McLeod) C.; A.B., U. Detroit, 1939; Ph.L., W. Baden Coll., W. Baden Springs, Ind., 1945, S.T.B., 1952; M.A., Loyola U., Chgo., 1949; Ph.D., U. Mich., 1956. Joined Soc. of Jesus, 1939, ordained priest Roman Catholic Ch., 1951; instr. English, St. Ignatius High Sch., Cleve., 1945-48; faculty U. Detroit, 1956—, assoc. prof. dean, dean Coll. Arts and Scis., 1960-63, acad. v.p., 1963-66, pres. univ., 1966-79, chancellor, 1979—; regional chmn. Rhodes Scholarship Selection Com.; dir. City Nat'l Bank, Detroit Edison. Mem. Detroit Police Bd. Commrs.; commr. North Central Accreditation Assn.; Bd. dirs. Else Kolhede Meml. Fund, Met. Fund, New Detroit, Inc., United Found.; bd. dirs. Greater Detroit Round Table of NCCJ. Mem. Assn. Cath. Colls. and Univs., Assn. Jesuit Colls. and Univs., Bus./Edn. Alliance, Newcomen Soc., Blue Key, Alpha Sigma Nu, Phi Delta Kappa, Phi Kappa Phi. Clubs: Engring. Soc., Univ., Econ. (Detroit). Author: The Contract Colleges of Cornell University, A Cooperative Educational Enterprise, 1958; Readings in the Philosophy of Education, 1964. Address: U Detroit Detroit MI 48221

CARSON, CLAUDE MATTESON (KIT), investment counselor; b. Farley, Mo., Sept. 26, 1907; s. Robert Walter and Mirtle Virginia C.; student Advanced Mgmt. Program, Harvard, 1962; m. Helen Long, May 16, 1931. Pres. Hoerner Boxes, Inc., until 1966; sr. v.p. adminstrn., dir. Hoerner Waldorf Corp. (merger Hoerner Boxes, Inc. and Waldorf Paper Products Co.), St. Paul, 1966-73, 76—, also chmn. audit co., mem. exec. com.; dir. Puritan-Bennett Corp., Kansas City, Mo.; v.p., dir. Keokuk Savs. Bank & Trust Co. (Iowa). Mem. Bus. Climate Task Force Com., State of Minn., 1971-73; active Boy Scouts Am. Bd. mgrs. Parker B. Francis Found.; bd. govs. Interlachen. Served with AUS. Fellow Am. Inst. Mgmt. (pres.'s council); mem. Fibre Box Assn. (chmn. bd., past pres.), TAPPI, Fourdrinier Kraft Board Inst., Internat. Corrugated Case Assn. (dir.). Rotarian. Clubs: Union League, Mid-Am. (Chgo.); Interlachen, Question, Mpls., St. Paul Pool and Yacht, Harvard Alumni. Home: 5209 Schaefer Rd Edina MN 55436 Office: Northwestern Financial Center 7900 Xerxes Ave S Suite 106 Minneapolis MN 55431

CARSON, MARY SILVANO, educator; b. Mass., Aug. 11, 1925; d. Joseph and Alice V. (Sherwood) Silvano; B.S., Simmons Coll., Boston, 1947; M.A., U. Chgo., 1961; m. Paul E. Carson, Feb. 21, 1947; children—Jan Ellen, Jeffrey Paul, Amy Jayne. Acting editor Forum Osteopathy, Am. Osteop. Assn., Chgo., 1948; tchr. McKinley Park Sch., 1956-57; mgr. S.W. Youth Opportunity Center, Dept. Labor, Chgo., 1966-67; careers counselor Gordon Tech. High Sch., Chgo., 1971-74; dir. Career and Assessment Center, YMCA Community Coll., Chgo., 1974—; adv. bd. City-Wide Coll. Career Center. Bd. dirs. Loop YWCA, Chgo. Mem. Women's Share in Public Service, Am. Ednl. Research Assn., Am. Personnel and Guidance Assn., Nat. Vocat. Guidance Assn., Bus. and Profl. Women's Club, Pi Lambda Theta (pres. chpt. 1975). Office: 211 W Wacker Dr Chicago IL 60606

CARSON, SANDRA MARIE, sch. counselor; b. Maryville, Mo., Feb. 5, 1948; d. Charles Wesley and Marcia Jean (Martin) Cornell; B.M.E., Kans., U., 1970, M.S.E., 1975; m. David Eugene Carson, July 1, 1973; children—Kyle David, Corey Michael. Instrumental music tchr. elementary and secondary schs. Shawnee Mission (Kans.) Pub. Schs., 1970-73; substitute Manpower tchr., counselor Kansas City (Kans.) Schs., 1974; elementary counselor Title 111 Spice Program, Ottawa (Kans.) Pub. Schs., 1975—; counselor, tutor minority high sch. students. Mem. Am., Kans., N.E. Kans. Area personnel and guidance assns., NEA. Contbr. Career Edn. Learning Packet, 5th grade, 1975. Home: Route 3 Box 56C Lawrence KS 66044

CARSTEN, CALVIN F., state legislator; b. Avoca, Nebr., Nov. 11, 1915; student U. Nebr.; m. Ruth Thelma Ruge, Feb. 2, 1937; children—Sally Carsten Malone, Carroll, Steven. Farmer; mgr. Cass

County Coop. Assn.; sec. Avoca Telephone Co.; mem. Nebr. Legislature, 1970—. Mem. Cass County Sch. Reorgn. Com.; moderator Lincoln Assn. Nebr. Congregational Conf.; sec. Avoca Cemetery Assn.; adv. bd. Good Samaritan Home, Syracuse, precinct committeeman Republican party. Mem. Farm Bur., others. Clubs: Masons, Order Eastern Star. Address: Avoca NE 68307

CARSTENS, PHYLLIS ANN, occupational health nurse; b. Cisco, Ill., June 16, 1936; d. Melvin Elmer and Dorothy Pearl (Evey) Long; diploma St. Joseph's Hosp. Sch. Nursing, Bloomington, Ill., 1958; m. John M. Carstens, Sept. 6, 1958. Staff nurse St. Elizabeth's Hosp., Lafayette, Ind., 1959-60; supr. phys. therapy dept. Ind. Soldiers and Sailers Hosp., West Lafayette, 1960; nursing service St. Joseph's Hosp., 1960-61; occupational health nurse Ill. Agrl. Assn., Bloomington, 1961-71; occupational health nurse Gen. Telephone Co. Ill., Bloomington, 1971—; mem. chem. dependency unit adv. bd. Brokaw Hosp., 1981—, also mem. bylaws and nomination coms.; instr. CPR, ARC, 1977—. Bd. dirs. McLean County Heart Assn., 1973-78, pres., 1976-77; instr. 1st aid ARC, 1976—, bd. dirs., 1977-80. Trustee, Downs Village (Ill.) Bd., 1981-83, also mem. bldg. and fin. com.; active Christian Neighbors Orgn. Cert. audiometric technician; cert. spirometric technician. Mem. Am., Ill. nurses assns., Am., Ill., Central Ill. (v.p., program chmn., chmn. nominating com., dir., pres. 1980-82) assns. occupational health nurses, St. Joseph's Hosp. Alumnae Assn. Home: 307 E Dooley Ave Downs IL 61736 Office: 1312 E Empire St Bloomington IL 61701

CARTER, ANNA CURRY (MRS. E. KEMPER CARTER), civic worker; b. Kansas City, Mo.; d. William Adams and Susan Maud (Machette) Curry; B.S., U. Mo., 1918; M.A., Columbia U., 1930; postgrad. Oxford U., (Eng.), 1935; m. E. Kemper Carter, Feb. 22, 1936 (dec. Dec. 1951); 1 son, E. Kemper (dec.). Tchr., research Kansas City Pub. Schs., 1919-21; dir. speech and dramatics Westport Jr. High Sch., Kansas City, 1921-26; dir. speech and drama S.W. High Sch., Kansas City, 1926-36. Bd. govs. Kansas City Mus. History and Sci., 1960-76; parliamentarian women's div. Kansas City Philharmonic Assn., 1954—; mem. exec. bd., mem. at large Community Children's Theatre, 1955—. Trustee Kansas City Art Inst. and Sch. of Design, Conservatory of Music, U. Mo. at Kansas City, Rockhurst Coll., Kansas City, Mo., Kansas City Philharmonic Assn., Kansas City Museum History and Sci.; hon. dir. Ch. St. Mary Aldenmanburg, Winston Churchill Meml., Fulton, Mo. Sponsor Winston Churchill Meml.; donar Lenox Hill-Skawhegan Art Projects, N.Y.C. Recipient numerous citations and awards including Skowhegan Sch. Art, Kansas City Art Inst., Rockhurst Coll., others. Hon. fellow Harry S. Truman Library Inst.; Soc. fellows William Rockhill Nelson Gallery Art, 1966-76. Mem. AAUW (del. nat. convs.), Alliance Francaise (exec. bd., parliamentarian 1974—), English Speaking Union, Pres. and Past Pres. Gen. Assembly, Sci. Pioneers, Am. Inst. Parliamentarians, ANTA, Speech Assn. Am., Alpha Phi. Baptist. Clubs: University, Woman's City, Carriage, Mission Hills Country, River, Kansas City, Rockhill Tennis; Capitol Hill (Washington). Home: Wornall Plaza 310 W 49th St Apt 507 Kansas City MO 64112

CARTER, ARNOLD NICK, cassette learning systems co. exec.; b. Phila., Mar. 25, 1929; s. Arnold and Margaret (Richter) C.; A.A., Keystone Jr. Coll., 1949; B.S. in Speech and Dramatic Art, Syracuse U., 1951; postgrad. Syracuse U., 1951-52; M.A. in Communications, Am. Univ., 1959; m. Virginia Lucille Polsgrove, Oct. 14, 1955; children—Victoria Lynne, Andrea Joy. Actor Rome (N.Y.) Little Theater, summers, 1951-52; mgr. customer relations Martin Marietta, Orlando, Fla., 1959-70; v.p. communications research Nightingale-Conant Corp., Chgo., 1970—. Served with USNR, 1953-59; Korea. Recipient Continuare Professus Articulatus Excellare award, Nat. Speakers Assn., 1978. Mem. Sales and Mktg. Execs. Chgo. (v.p. 1979-81), Nat. Speakers Assn., Am. Soc. Tng. and Devel., Internat. Platform Assn. Republican. Presbyn. Author: Communicate Effectively, 1978; The Amazing Results-Full World of Cassette Learning, 1980. Home: 1315 Elmwood Ave Deerfield IL 60015 Office: Nightingale-Conant Corp 3730 W Devon Ave Chicago IL 60659

CARTER, CATHLEEN ANN, educator; b. Chappell, Nebr., Jan. 20, 1956; d. Burton Lee and Shirley Ann (Parson) C.; B.S. in Home Econs. Edn., U. Nebr., 1978. Tchr. home econs. Kimball County High Sch., Kimball, Nebr., 1979—; sponsor Future Homemakers Am., 1979—. Youth coordinator Am. Cancer Soc.; youth dir. Trinity United Meth. Ch., Kimball. Mem. Am. Vocat. Assn., Nebr. Vocat. Assn., Nebr. Vocat. Home Econs. Tchrs. Assn. (area chmn.), NEA, Nebr. Edn. Assn., Kimball Edn. Assn., Am. Home Econs. Assn., AAUW. Clubs: Order Eastern Star, Job's Daus. Office: 901 S Nadine St Kimball NE 69145

CARTER, EVERETT FINLEY, mfg. co. exec.; b. Schenectady, N.Y., June 28, 1927; s. E. Finley and Charlotte (Reid) C.; B.S. in Chemistry, St. Lawrence U., 1950; m. Ann Terriberry, Aug. 21, 1948; children—Charles, Terry Ann Carter Close, Stephen, Sandra. Vice-pres., gen. mgr. GTE-Sylvania, Towanda, Pa., 1965-69; asst. to pres. Buckbee-Mears Co., St. Paul, 1969-70, exec. v.p., 1970-76, pres., 1976—, chief exec. exec. v.p., 1970-76, pres., 1976—, chief exec. officer, 1977—, dir.; dir. Northwestern Nat. Bank of St. Paul. Dir., St. Paul Winter Carnival Assn., 1972-78, pres., 1975-76. Served with U.S. Navy, 1945-46. Office: 1150 Am Nat Bank Bldg St Paul MN 55101

CARTER, JAMES EVAN, analytical chemist; b. Calgary, Alta., Can., Oct. 26, 1941; s. Lamonde Lial and Viva (Jones) C.; B.S. in Chemistry, Brigham Young U., 1966, M.S. in Microbiology, 1969; Ph.D. in Medicinal Chemistry, U. Utah, 1975; m. Peggy Irene Keast, Jan. 16, 1965; children—Kerri-Ann, Jeffery Lamonde, Brent Lial, Kimberly. Prin. investigator Utah Community Pesticide Study, Utah State Div. Health, Salt Lake City, 1969-73; research asso. U. Utah, Salt Lake City, 1973-75; group leader analytical devel. Am. Critical Care, McGaw Park, Ill., 1975—. Sci. fair judge Chgo. Public Schs., 1976—; evaluations com. United Way of Lake County, Ill., 1980-81; employee chmn. for Am. Critical Care, United Way, 1979; bishop Mormon Ch. Mem. Am. Chem. Soc., Am. Pharm. Assn. (Midwest conf. analytical chmn., 1980), Assn. Ofcl. Analytical Chemists, Rho Chi. Contbr. writings to profl. publs. in field. Home: 51 Gifford Ct Mundelein IL 60060 Office: 1600 Waukegan Rd McGaw Park IL 60085

CARTER, JERRY RALPH, feed ingredient co. exec.; b. Springfield, Mo., Jan. 11, 1930; s. Lloyd Ralph and Atrelle (Ward) C.; B.S., Drury Coll., 1951; m. Blanchelen Campbell, June 15, 1951; children—Cheri Ellen, Thomas Lloyd, Timmithoy James. Salesman, Nat. Biscuit Co., Springfield, 1954-59; mgr. Southwest Rendering Co., Inc., Springfield, 1959—; mgr. Southwest By-Products, Inc., Springfield, 1959—, pres., 1961—. Served with USAF, 1951-54. Mem. Nat. Renderers Assn. (regional pres. 1971-72), Drury Coll. Alumni (pres. 1975). Episcopalian (vestry 1964-65). Mason (K.T., Shriner, Jester). Home: 2732 E Seminole St Springfield MO 65804 Office: PO Box 2876 CSS Springfield MO 65803

CARTER, JOHN DALE, orgn. devel. cons.; b. Tuskegee, Ala., Apr. 9, 1944; s. Arthur L. and Ann (Bargyh) C.; A.B., Ind. U., 1965, M.S., 1967; Ph.D. (NDEA fellow), Case Western Res. U., 1974; m. Jana Glenn, Aug. 1, 1970. Dir. student affairs Dental Sch., Case Western Res. U., Cleve., 1974-75, asst. prof. applied behavioral sci., 1974—, asst. dean orgn. devel. and student affairs, 1975-78; pres. Carter's Enterprises, Inc., Cleve., 1970-79; chmn. organizational and systems devel. program, dir. program devel. Gestalt Inst. Cleve., 1980—; mem. exec. bd. Nat. Tng. Labs.; bd. dirs. Behavioral Sci. Found. Cleve. Mem. Internat. Assn. Applied Social Scientists. Author: Counselling the Helping Relationship, 1975. Home: 2995 Scarborough Rd Cleveland Heights OH 44118 Office: PO Box 1822 Cleveland OH 44106

CARTER, JOHN PHILLIP, ednl. adminstr.; b. Lansing, Mich., Sept. 30, 1940; s. William Roe and Wanda Virginia Carter; B.B.A., Western Mich. U., 1963; M. Vocat. Edn., Mich. State U., 1967; m. Patricia Ann, Dec. 27, 1977; children—Colleen, Katie, Michael, Kerry. Tchr., adminstr. Grand Blanc (Mich.) Schs., 1963-70; part time extension prof. Mich. State U., 1967—; dir. vocat. edn. Waterford (Mich.) Schs., 1970—; seminar dir. passive solar constrn. Mich. State U. and Mid-Am. Solar Energy Complex, 1980—. Founding pres. bd. dirs. Social Services for Hearing Impaired, Flint, Mich., 1972-74; founding pres. Thread Creek Community Theatre. Recipient joint Mich. Ho. of Reps. and Senate resolution of commendation Solar 80 Project; grantee Office Edn., DOE, CETA, Mich. Dept. Edn. Mem. Am. Vocat. Assn., Mich. Council Vocat. Adminstrs., Mich. Occupational Edn. Assn., Mich. Energy Edn. Forum, Mich. Ind. Edn. Soc., Sigma Tau Gamma, Delta Pi Epsilon. Democrat. Roman Catholic. Contbr. articles to ednl. jours. Home: 631 Estes Ct Pontiac MI 48054 Office: 6020 Pontiac Lake Rd Waterford MI 48095

CARTER, LEE, engring. economist; b. Rock Island, Ill., Sept. 8, 1917; s. Clarence Daniel and Mary Belle (Rowley) C.; B.S., Purdue U., 1940; M.S., Cornell U., 1945; m. Janet Clark, July 27, 1945; children—Robert Clark, Thomas Lee, Margaret Lee. Pilot plant operator Universal Oil Products Co., Chgo., 1940-42; mgr. tech. service Va.-Carolina Chem. Co., Richmond, Va., 1946; research engr. Stone & Webster, Boston, 1946-48; process designer, 1948-60, author proposals and reports, 1947-62, asst. sales mgr., London, 1952-55, regional mgr., Calgary, Can., 1959-62; v.p., mgr. engring. reports R.W. Booker & Assos., Inc., St. Louis, 1963-72; pvt. practice engring.-econs. cons., 1972—. Served with USNR, 1942-46. Mem. AAAS, Am. Econ. Assn., Am. Indsl. Devel. Council, Am. Inst. Chem. Engrs. Anglican Catholic. Address: 622 Belson Ct Kirkwood MO 63122

CARTER, LEONARD MATTHEW, JR., hosp. personnel ofcl.; b. Madera, Calif., Jan. 26, 1953; s. Leonard Matthew and Ruth Chasteen (Brinker) C.; B.A. in Polit. Sci., Tarkio Coll., 1976; M.P.A., Murray State U., 1978. Health planner Lincoln Trail Area Devel. Dist., Elizabethtown, Ky., 1978; dir. Milltown (Ind.) Med. Center, 1978-79; dir. personnel Franklin Hosp., Benton, Ill., 1979—; instr. mgmt. Rend Lake Coll. Active, Lincoln Trail CPR Found., 1978; adv. bd. Rend Lake Coll., 1980—. Served with USMC, 1971-75. Mem. Am. Soc. Hosp. Personnel Adminstrn., Am. Mgmt. Assn., Hosp. Personnel Mgmt. Assn. Greater St. Louis, So. Ill. Hosp. Personnel Assn. Author: Financing Emergency Medical Services and Cost Saving Measures, 1978; Adult Day Care Centers, 1978. Home: 1215 N Main Benton IL 62812 Office: 201 Bailey Ln Benton IL 62812

CARTER, LONNIE TYRONE, psychologist; b. Lynch, Ky., Sept. 30, 1939; s. Lonnie P. and Kathryn E. Carter; B.S., U. Wis., 1962; M.S., Mich. State U., 1963; Ph.D., Marquette U., 1973; m. Emily Louise Wynn, Nov. 28, 1976; children—Nicholas T., Tracey R., Marques J. Tchr., Wells Jr. High Sch., Milw., 1963-65; counselor North High Sch., Milw., 1967-68; psychologist various public schs., Milw. 1968-76; practice, clin. psychology, Milw., 1976—; cons. various ednl., social and indsl. instns. Bd. dirs. YMCA, Milw. Mem. Am. Psychol. Assn., Wis. Psychol. Assn., Am. Soc. Clin. Hypnosis. Home: 2436 W Brantwood St Glendale WI 53209 Office: 1840 N Farwell Ave Milwaukee WI 53202

CARTER, MICHAEL FRANK, urologist; b. Santa Monica, Calif., Sept. 14, 1939; s. Floyd Arthur and Evelyn Elizabeth (Eager) C.; student U. So. Calif., 1957-62; M.D., Georgetown U., 1966; m. Joan Carol Tedford, Aug. 23, 1959; children—Cristen, Timothy, Richard, Gregory. Intern, resident in surgery Harbor Gen. Hosp., Torrance, Calif., 1966-68; resident in urology Johns Hopkins Hosp., Balt., 1968-72; asst. prof. urology Northwestern U., Chgo., 1976—; staff physician Northwestern Meml. Hosp., 1972—, exec. com., 1979—; chief of urology Lakeside VA Hosp.; staff Children's Meml. Hosp. Troop com. chmn. Boy Scouts Am., 1977-79; mem. Wilmette (Ill.) Sch. Bd. Caucus, 1977-79. Named Outstanding Intern, Harbor Gen. Hosp., 1967; Am. Cancer Soc. fellow, 1970-72. Diplomate Am. Bd. Urology. Fellow A.C.S.; mem. Am. Urol. Soc., AMA, Chgo. Urol. Soc. (exec. com. 1979—), Ill. Med. Assn. Episcopalian. Research on uveal micro circulation in rabbits, androgens in cell cycle of prostate gland, prostatic ultrasound, impotence and penile blood pressure. Home: 720 Ashland Ave Wilmette IL 60091 Office: 251 E Chicago Ave Chicago IL 60611

CARTER, PEARLENE, packing co. exec.; b. Coldwater, Miss., Mar. 4, 1943; d. Homer Lawrence and Lue Ella (Vernon) Hill; B.A., Rust Coll., 1963; M.B.A., DePaul U., 1977; m. William L. Carter, Oct. 3, 1964; children—Reginald, Melody. Acct., Chgo. Courier Newspaper, 1963-68, asst. to pub., 1968-74; reconcilement adminstr. Esmark, Inc., Chgo., 1974-77, mgr. acctg., 1977-80, mgr. ops., 1980-81; dir. cash mgmt. Swift Ind. Packing Co., 1981—. Named Rust Coll. Alumnus of the Yr., 1979. Mem. Assn. M.B.A. Execs. Mem. Ch. of Christ. Club: Rust Coll. Alumni (pres. 1980—). Office: 115 W Jackson Blvd Chicago IL 60604

CARTER, ROBERT CORNELIUS, lawyer; b. Chgo., June 4, 1917; s. John Gordon and Ada Christine (Abrahamson) C.; B.S., U. Ill., Champaign, 1946; LL.B., Gonzaga U., Spokane, Wash., 1949, J.D., 1967; m. Georgia R. Richardson, Mar. 9, 1937 (dec. Nov. 3, 1973); m. 2d, Gertrude A. Hetteen, June 3, 1975; 1 son, John M. Admitted to Minn. bar, 1971; individual practice law, Spokane, 1949-51, Roseau, Minn., 1965-81; sr. partner firm Carter & Carter, Roseau, 1980-81; of counsel firm Carter, Mergens, and Hardwick, Roseau, 1980-81. Sec., Minn. Citizens Com. on Natural Resources, 1960-65. Served with USAAF, 1941-46. Decorated Air medal with 7 oak leaf clusters. Mem. Minn. Bar Assn., Wash. Bar Assn., Am. Trial Lawyers Assn., Minn. Trial Lawyers Assn., Am. Judicature Soc., Audubon Soc., Am. Wildlife Assn., Green Peace Soc., Nature Conservancy, Sierra Club, Am. Legion, VFW, Phi Alpha Delta. Home: Beaver Farms Wannaska MN 56761 also 5 Canterbury Dr Grenelefe Golf Club Haines City FL 33844 Office: Carter Mergens and Hardwick 101 Main Ave N Roseau MN 56751

CARTER, SALLY (SOPHIA), art shows cons.; b. Buffalo, Dec. 28, 1914; d. Frank and Caroline Walski; B.A., D'Youville Coll., 1936; postgrad. in Art, So. Ill. U., Edwardsville, 1969-75; m. Thad Robert Carter, Nov. 10, 1945; children—Susan V. Carter Penney, Robert Lloyd. Promoter, cons., curator local art shows, Alton, Ill., 1974—; active Friends of Art, dept. art and design So. Ill. U., Edwardsville, v.p., bd. dirs., 1981—; chmn. ann. art competition Greater Miss. River Art Council., 1981. Served to capt. USAF, 1942-45. Ill. Arts Council Chmn.'s grantee. Mem. Greater Miss. River Art Council. Republican. Roman Catholic. Home: 3750 Aberdeen Ave Alton IL 62002

CARTER, SHIRLEY M. BRYANT, counselor; b. Chgo., Nov. 5, 1949; d. Robert L. and Minnie Ferguson (Amerson) Bryant; B.S. with honors, Chgo. State U., 1974; M.S., 1978; m. Naggie L. Carter, Jr., Nov. 18, 1967; children—Kathryn, Nycole, Tiyaka. Unit leader commn. div. Prudential Ins. Co., Chgo., 1969-71; psychotherapist Jackson Park Hosp., Chgo., 1978; tchr. Chgo. Bd. Edn., 1975—, counselor, 1978—. Pres., St. Elthelreda Sch. Bd., 1978-79; youth coordinator 1st Corinthians Ch., Chgo., 1979; mem. So. Bapt. Assn., 1979—, dir. Vacation Bible Sch., 1981; dir. Christian Pre-Sch. Recipient cert. of honor Black Masters Hall of Fame, Chgo. Mem. Assn. Black Psychologists, Am. Personnel and Guidance Assn., Kappa Delta Pi. Baptist. Club: Brainerd Women's. Home: 8940 S Justine St Chicago IL 60620 Office: 4214 S St Lawrence Chicago IL 60653

CARTER, THOMAS SMITH, JR., railroad exec.; b. Dallas, June 6, 1921; s. Thomas S. and Mattie (Dowell) C.; B.S. in Civil Engring., So. Meth. U., 1944; m. Janet R. Hostetter, July 3, 1946; children—Janet Diane, Susan Jean, Charles T., Carol Ruth. Various positions M.-K.-T. R.R., 1941-44, 46-54, chief engr., 1954-61, v.p. operations, 1961-66; v.p. KCS Ry. Co., L & A Ry. Co., 1966—; pres., dir. K.C.S. Ry., 1973—, chief exec. officer, 1981—; pres., dir. L & A Ry. Co., 1974—, chmn. bd., chief exec. officer, 1981—; dir. Kansas City So. Industries. Served with C.E., AUS, 1944-46. Registered profl. engr., Mo., Kans., Okla., Tex., La., Ark. Fellow ASCE; mem. Am. Ry. Engrs. Assn., Assn. Am. Railroads (dir. 1978—), Nat. Soc. Profl. Engrs. Office: 114 W 11th St Kansas City MO 64105

CARTER, WILLIAM BUTLER, seed co. exec.; b. St. Louis, Nov. 28, 1927; s. Sidney Ernest and Virginia Leah (Butler) C.; student Brown U., 1945-46; A.B., Washington U., 1948; m. Drucilla Davis Bryant, June 20, 1970; children—Nancy, Carolyn, Margaret, Mary, John, Robert, Jason. Pres., Corneli Seed Co., St. Louis, 1965-68; v.p. mktg. Keystone Seed Co., Hollister, Calif., 1968-69; with Asgrow Seed Co., Kalamazoo, Mich., 1969—, group mgr. market devel. and customer services, 1979—. Served with USN, 1945-46. Episcopalian. Home: 96 S Lake Doster Dr Plainwell MI 49080 Office: Asgrow Seed Co 5300 N 28th St Richland MI 49083

CARTEY, MARY LU, ins. agt.; b. Marshall, Mich., Oct. 10, 1931; d. James G. and Mildred Mary (Church) C.; student Marshall public schs. Sec., Calhoun County Health Dept., 1950-53, Belcher Real Estate and Ins. Agy., 1953-64; partner Belcher Ins. Agy., Marshall, 1964-74; owner, agt. Belcher-Cartey Ag., Marshall, 1974—. Mem. Ind. Ins. Agts. Assn. Mich., Ind. Ins. Agts. Assn. U.S., Mich. Profl. Ins. Agts. Assn., Nat. Profl. Ins. Agts. Assn., Marshall C. of C. Episcopalian. Clubs: Bus. and Profl. Women's (past v.p., fashion show dir.), Am. Bus. Women's. Home: 215 N Mulberry St Marshall MI 49068 Office: 221 E Michigan Ave Marshall MI 49068

CARVER, GERFORD CHESTER, mech. engr.; b. Battle Creek, Mich., July 11, 1929; s. Chester Gerford and Gertrude Marguerite (Stock) C.; B.M.E., Mich. Technol. U., 1950; M.S., Chrysler Inst., 1956; m. Eleanor Anne Dunne, June 25, 1955; children—John, James, Marguerite, Elizabeth, William, Sara. Shop liaison engr., detailer Clark Equipment Co., Battle Creek, 1950; test engr. Chrysler Corp., Highland Park, Mich., 1952-55, welding engr., 1955-56; div. project engr. Midland Ross Corp., Cleve., 1956-62; chief engr. R.S.L. Corp., Cleve., 1962; account engr. A.O. Smith Corp., Milw., 1962—. Served in arty. U.S. Army, 1950-52. Registered profl. engr., Ohio. Mem. Soc. Automotive Engrs., Am. Welding Soc., Am. Soc. Metals, Engring. Soc. Milw. Clubs: Snowstar Ski (asst. head instr.) (Milw.); Fairlane (Dearborn, Mich.). Home: 880 E Birch St Milwaukee WI 53217 Office: 3533 N 27th St Milwaukee WI 53216

CARY, JOHN MILTON, physician; b. Ewing, Mo., July 11, 1932; s. Milton Madison and Alice (Sells) C.; A.B., Central Coll. Mo., 1954; M.D., St. Louis U., 1958; m. Barbara Ann Dorsey, June 4, 1955; children—Kimberly Anne, John Madison. Intern, Barnes Hosp., St. Louis, 1958-59, resident in internal medicine, 1959-60, subsequently mem. staff; resident in internal medicine St. Lukes Hosp., St. Louis, 1961-62, subsequently mem. staff; fellow in hematology Washington U., St. Louis, 1960-61; practice medicine specializing in internal medicine, St. Louis, 1962—; mem. staff St. Johns Mercy Med. Center; clin. instr. Washington U., 1966—. Mem. ACP, St. Louis Soc. Internal Medicine, Mo. Med. Assn., St. Louis Med. Soc., Alpha Omega Alpha. Presbyterian. Home: 1541 Arbuckle Dr Saint Louis MO 63017 Office: 224 S Woods Mill Rd Saint Louis MO 63017

CASCINO, MARY DORY, business exec.; b. Chgo., Dec. 21, 1949; d. V. Paul and Vada L. (Tuttle) Dory; A.B., Loyola U., Chgo., 1971; M.A., U. Chgo., 1972; m. Anthony E. Cascino, Jr., July 28, 1973; children—Anthony E. III, Christine Ann, Caroline Stephanie. Asso. planner, local service specialist Northeastern Ill. Planning Commn., 1972-76; self-employed park and recreation planner, Highland Park, Ill., 1976-80; owner Mary Anne Products, Highland Park, Ill., 1981—. Candidate for alderman City of Chgo., 1971. Mem. Am. Planning Assn. Club: Union League Women's Bd. (Chgo.). Author: Bicycle Safety Planning Guide; editor: Montessori Newsletter. Home and Office: 1641 Thornapple Ln Highland Park IL 60035

CASE, KEELA IRENE, mental health counselor; b. Lincoln County, Kans., Apr. 29, 1922; d. Glenn Raymond and Atha Jane (Montgomery) Jones; B.A., Ft. Hays (Kans.) State U., 1970, M.S., 1971; m. Cleo Clarence Case, Feb. 9, 1941; children—Colleen, Colin, C. Wayne. Mental health counselor High Plains Comprehensive Community Mental Health Center br. office, Colby, Kans., 1971-77, dir. br. office, 1977—; cons. in field. Mem. AAUW, Am. Personnel and Guidance Assn., Am. Psychol. Assn., Assn. Humanistic Psychologists, Kans. Personnel and Guidance Assn., Kans. Psychol. Assn., Phi Delta Kappa. Democrat. Episcopalian. Club: Order Eastern Star. Home: 550 S Grant St Colby KS 67701 Office: 210 S Range St Colby KS 67701

CASEY, EDWARD PAUL, mfg. co. exec.; b. Boston, Feb. 23, 1930; s. Edward J. and Virginia (Paul) C.; A.B., Yale, 1952; M.B.A., Harvard, 1955; m. Patricia Pinkham, June 23, 1950; children—Patricia Casey Shepherd, Lucile Tyler Casey Arnote, Jennifer Paul Casey Schwab, Sheila Pinkham, Virginia Louise. With Davidson Rubber Co., Dover, N.H., 1950—, pres., 1965—, dir., 1950—; pres. McCord Corp., Detroit, 1965-78, also dir.; pres., chief exec. officer Ex-Cell-O Corp., Troy, Mich., also dir.; dir. Mfrs. Nat. Bank Detroit. Mem. finance com. Citizens Research Council of Mich.; mem. president's council U. N.H.; trustee Henry Ford Hosp., Detroit; bd. dirs. Detroit Symphony Orch. Mem. Engring. Soc. Detroit, Soc. Automotive Engrs., Chief Execs. Forum, Harvard Bus. Sch. Club Detroit. Clubs: Detroit, Yondotega (Detroit); One Hundred (dir.); Grosse Pointe; Country Club of Detroit (Grosse Pointe Farms, Mich.); Bloomfield Hills (Mich.) Country; Eastern Yacht (Marblehead, Mass.); Union League (N.Y.C.); Wig and Pen (London, Eng.). Home: 4 Rathbone Pl Grosse Pointe MI 48230 Office: Ex-Cell-O Corp 2855 Coolidge Troy MI 48084

CASEY, JACK HESTWOOD, diamond investment counselor; b. Lexington, Va., Dec. 1, 1948; s. John H. and June B. (Broyles) C.; B.A., Bradley U., Peoria, Ill.; m. Angela Suzanne Dolson, Mar. 1, 1979. Owner-operator Nat. Hearing Aid Center, Mattoon, Ill.,

1975-76; pres. House of Hearing Aids, Inc., Mattoon, 1978-80; diamond investment counselor Internat. Diamond Corp., Mattoon, 1978, now dir. tng. and personnel, Great Lakes Region; fin. columnist Suburban Life mags. Served with USMC, 1968-71; Vietnam. Decorated Purple Heart. Mem. Nat. Fedn. Ind. Bus., Internat. Assn. Fin. Planners, Marine Corps League (past trustee Ill.; cert. of merit 1977), Ill. Notary Assn., Am. Legion, VFW. Republican. Methodist. Club: Shriners. Home: 1536 Crimson Ln Palatine IL 60067 Office: 1014 E Algonquin Rd Schaumburg IL 60194

CASEY, JOHN P., educator; b. Pitts., May 26, 1920; s. Patrick F. Casey; B.A., Bethany (W.Va.) Coll., 1949; M.Ed., U. Pitts., 1950; Ed.D. in Secondary Edn., Ind. U., 1963; m. Eileen Casey; children—Charles, Carol. Tchr. Columbus (Ohio) public schs., 1950-59; asst. prof. Ill. State U., Normal, 1959-63; div. chmn. dept. social studies Northwestern Coll., Orange City, Iowa, 1963-64; asst. prof. So. Ill. U., Carbondale, 1964-69, asso. prof. dept. spl. edn. and profl. edn. experiences, 1969-73, prof., 1973—, dir. Talent Retrieval and Devel. Edn. Project (TRADE), 1965-78. Served with U.S. Army. Mem. Ill. Assn. Curriculum Devel., Ill. Assn. Tchr. Educators, Phi Delta Kappa. Certified tchr., Ill., Ohio. Research supervision, research and teaching gifted children. Co-author: Roles in Off-Campus Student Teaching, 1967. Contbr. articles to profl. jours. Home: 623 Glenview Dr Carbondale IL 62901 Office: Coll Edn So Ill U Carbondale IL 62901

CASEY, MURRAY JOSEPH, physician; b. Armour, S.D., May 1, 1936; s. Meryl Joseph and Gladice (Murray) C.; student Chanute Jr. Coll., 1954-55, Rockhurst Coll., 1955-56; A.B., U. Kans., 1958; M.D., Georgetown U., 1962; postgrad. Suffolk U. Law Sch., 1963-64, Howard U., 1965; m. Virginia Anne Fletcher; children—Murray Joseph, Theresa Marie, Anne Franklin, Francis X., Peter Colum. Intern, USPHS Hosp.-Univ. Hosp., Balt., 1962-63; staff physician USPHS Hosp., Boston, 1963-64; staff asso. Lab Infectious Diseases, Nat. Inst. Allergy and Infectious Diseases, NIH, Bethesda, Md., 1964-66; virologist, resident physician Columbia-Presbyn. Med. Center, also Francis Delafield Hosp., N.Y.C., 1966-69; USPHS sr. clin. trainee, 1969-70; fellow gynecol. oncology, resident dept. surgery Meml. Hosp. for Cancer and Allied Diseases, Meml. Sloan-Kettering Cancer Center, N.Y.C., 1969-71, Am. Cancer Soc. fellow, 1969-71; ofcl. observer in radiotherapy U. Tex. M.D. Anderson Hosp. and Tumor Inst., Houston, 1971; vis. scientist Radiumhemmet Karolinska Sjukhuset and Inst., Stockholm, Sweden, 1971; asst. prof. obstetrics and gynecology U. Conn. Sch. Medicine, 1971-75, asso. prof., 1975-80, dir. gynecologic oncology, 1971-80, also mem. med. bd.; prof., asso. chmn. dept. ob-gyn U. Wis. Med. Sch., 1980—; chmn. ob-gyn U. Wis.-Milw. Clin Campus, 1980—; chief Ob-gyn, dir. gynecologic oncology Mt. Sinai Med. Center, Milw., 1980—, also mem. med. exec. com.; chmn. research adv. com., mem. council Conn. Cancer Epidemiology Unit; bd. dirs., mem. exec. com., chmn. profl. edn. com. Hartford unit. Am. Cancer Soc.; mem. med. services 1980 Winter Olympic Games, Lake Placid, N.Y.; mem. med. supervisory team U.S. Nordic Ski Team. Diplomate Am. Bd. Med. Examiners, Am. Bd. Obstetrics and Gynecology. Fellow Am. Coll. Obstetricians and Gynecologists, A.C.S.; mem. AAAS, N.Y. Acad. Scis., Am. Soc. Colposcopy, Am. Fertility Soc., Soc. Gynecologic Oncologists, New Eng. Assn. Gynecologic Oncologists (pres.), Am. Geriatric Soc., Internat. Menopause Soc., Soc. Meml. Gynecologic Oncologists (exec. bd.), lake Placid Olympic Physicians Orgn. (v.p.), Cedarburg C. of C. (Ambassadors Club), St. George Soc. Contbr. articles to profl. jours., chpts. to books. Research in oncogenesis and tumor immunology. Home: Cedarburg WI 53012 Office: Dept Ob-Gyn Mt Sinai Med Center Milwaukee WI 53201

CASEY, PATRICIA MARIE, advt. exec.; b. Chgo., June 8, 1951; d. William James and Mary Lou (Terrill) Mainzer; student So. Ill. U., 1969-74, Harper Coll., 1979—; m. Frank James Casey, May 28, 1977. Graphic artist Lawson Products, Inc., Des Plaines, Ill., 1975-78; advt. coordinator Diversey Chems., Des Plaines, 1978-79, Acco Internat., Inc., Wheeling, Ill., 1979-81; propr. Prism, creative services, Rolling Meadows, Ill., 1982—; account exec. for Images, Des Plaines, Noral Color Corp., Chgo. Sunday sch. tchr. Norwood Gospel Chapel, 1977-80. Nat. Network Women in Sales, Bus. and Profl. Women's Club. Designer/editor monthly bull. Norwood Gospel Chapel, 1976-80. Home: 3209 Kingfisher Ct Rolling Meadows IL 60008

CASEY, PATRICK MICHAEL, computer co. exec.; b. Cazanovia, Wis., Nov. 21, 1930; s. William Robert and Anastasia Veronica (Walsh) C.; grad. Indsl. Mgmt., U. Minn., 1959, Asso. in Adminstrv. Mgmt., 1966; M.B.A., Nat. Coll. Arts and Scis., 1978; m. Donna Rae Robushin, Apr. 13, 1933; children—Michele Ann, Timothy William, Patrick Sean, Kevin Matthew, Kathleen Marie, Colin Brian, Maureen Bridget. With Sperry Univac, St. Paul, 1956—, gen. mgr. Univac Tech. Services Div., 1975—; tchr. adult vocational classes in data processing; cons. on computer aided instrn. systems to sch. dists. Chm. Sch. Dist. 272, 1964-70; dir. Hennepin County Vocational Tech. Dist. 287, 1971-76; mem. Eden Prairie Planning and Zoning Bd., 1974. Served with USN, 1948-52. Republican. Roman Catholic. Club: Lions. Home: 181 Birnamwood Dr Burnsville MN 55337 Office: PO Box 3525 Saint Paul MN 55165

CASEY-MOORE, ROSE ANN, psychologist; b. Des Moines, Sept. 25, 1946; d. Otho Beryl and Mary Edna (McMenamy) Casey; B.S., Drake U., 1972, M.S., 1974; m. Raymond E. Moore, Aug. 14, 1977; 1 dau., Megan Casey; stepchildren—James B., Susan. Counseling psychologist Iowa Methodist Med. Center, Des Moines, 1974-81. Mem. Am. Psychol. Assn., Iowa Psychol. Assn., Iowa Womens Polit. Caucus, NOW, Womens Sports Found., Animal Protection Inst. Am., Des Moines Symphony Guild, Ames Internat. Orch. Festival Assn. Roman Catholic.

CASH, JOSEPH HARPER, coll. adminstr., historian; b. Mitchell, S.D., Jan. 3, 1927; s. Joseph R. and Claudia B. (Harper) C.; B.A., U. S.D., 1949; M.A., 1959; Ph.D., U. Iowa, 1966; m. Margaret Ann Halla, Dec. 18, 1952; children—Sheridan Lisa, Joseph Mark, Meredith Ann. Tchr. public schs., S.D., 1951-62; instr. Black Hills State Coll., summer 1961; grad. asst. U. Iowa, 1962-65; asso. prof. history Eastern Mont. Coll., 1965-68; research asso. Inst. Indian Studies, U. S.D., summer 1967, 68, dir. inst. div. Indian research, 1970-77, acting dir. inst., 1976-77, asso. prof., 1970-74, Duke research prof. history, 1972—, prof., 1974—, dean Coll. Arts and Scis., 1977—; dir. Am. Indian Research Project, State of S.D., 1969-74, dir. S.D. Oral History Project, 1970-74, dir. Oral History Center (merger both projects), 1974-77; chmn. S.D. Bd. Hist. Preservation, 1970-73; chmn. council dirs., cultural pres. div. State S.D., 1975-76; mem. S.D. Council on Humanities, 1975-77, S.D. Hist. Records Adv. Bd., 1976—, S.D. Bd. Cultural Preservation, 1977—, Kampgrounds of Am.-U. Adv. Bd., 1978—. Served with USMCR, 1945-46. Recipient award of merit Am. Assn. State and Local History, 1975. Mem. Am. Hist. Assn., Oral History Assn., Orgn. Am. Historians, S.D. Hist. Soc. (pres. 1977—), Western History Assn., Phi Beta Kappa, Phi Delta Theta. Republican. Author 6 Indian Tribal Series books, 1971-76; author: (with Herbert T. Hoover) To Be An Indian, 1971; Working the Homestake, 1973; The Practice of Oral History, 1974; gen. editor: American Indian Oral History Collection, 1977; bd. editors Rocky Mountain Rev., 1966-68, Midwest Rev., S.D. History. Office: Coll Arts and Scis U SD Vermillion SD 57069

CASHIN, EDWARD ARCHIBALD, controls co. exec.; b. Duluth, Minn., Aug. 22, 1905; s. Francis Martin and Rosemary Katharine (Smith) C.; student U. Chgo., 1923-25; m. Beryl Janice Allen, Sept. 20, 1926; children—Mary Jane Cashin Duryee, Barbara Jo Cashin Rogers. Sec., Internat. Paper & Power Co., N.Y.C., 1930-33; v.p. Barron G. Collier, Inc., N.Y.C., 1933-35; pres. John Panton Co., N.Y.C., 1936-37; exec. v.p., dir. Batten, Barton, Durstine & Osborn, Inc., N.Y.C., 1938-62; chmn. bd. Naegle Advt. Co., 1962-67; exec. v.p., dir. Solid Controls, Inc., Mpls., 1968—; cons. in field. Served to col. Q.M.C., AUS, 1941-44. Clubs: Minikahda, Mpls.; Thunderbird Country (Calif.). Home: 1305 Shoreline Dr Wayzata MN 55391 Office: 6925 Washington Ave S Minneapolis MN 55435

CASKEY, HAROLD LEROY, state senator; b. Bates County, Mo., Jan. 3, 1938; s. James Alfred and Edith Irene (Anderson) C.; A.B., Central Mo. State U., 1960; J.D., U. Mo., Columbia, 1963; m. Kay Head, 1974; children—Kyle James. Pros. atty., Bates County, 1967-72; city atty., Butler, Mo., 1973-76; individual practice law, Butler, Mo.; asst. prof. NE Mo. State U., 1975-76; mem. Mo. Senate, 1977—. Mem. Mo. Bar Assn., Am. Judicature Soc., Fellowship Christian Politicians, Am. Criminal Justice Educators, Order Coif, Acacia, Phi Alpha Delta, Kappa Mu Epsilon, Alpha Phi Sigma. Baptist. Club: Rotary. Office: State Capitol Jefferson City MO 65101*

CASMEY, HOWARD BIRDWELL, state ednl. ofcl.; b. Euclid, Minn., Feb. 4, 1926; s. George and Gladys (Birdwell) C.; B.A., Concordia Coll., 1949; M.A., U. N.D., 1956; m. Eva Mae Lee, Aug. 14, 1949; children—Michael, Kim. Tchr. pub. schs., Plummer, Minn.; supt. schs., Lake Bronson, Minn., Herman, Minn., Ada, Minn., Golden Valley, Minn.; now commr. edn. State of Minn.; dir. Audio Sine Mfg. Co. Served with Armed Forces, World War II. Mem. Chief State Sch. Officers (pres. 1975-76). Office: State Dept Edn Capitol Square Bldg 550 Cedar St St Paul MN 55101*

CASPERS, CARL FREDERICK, civil engr.; b. Hopkinton, Iowa, Dec. 2, 1927; s. Peter Martin and Johanna Elizabeth (Poppi) C.; B.S. in Civil Engring., Iowa State U., 1955; m. Delores J. Adams, Sept. 12, 1953. With Brown Engring. Co., Des Moines, 1955-66; city engr., dir. pub. works, bldg. officer, zoning enforcement officer, mem. planning commn. City of Urbandale (Iowa), 1966-73; village engr. Village of Carpentersville (Ill.), 1973—. Chmn. transp. com. Central Iowa Regional Planning Commn., 1970-73; mem. Iowa hwy. research bd. Iowa State Hwy. Commn., 1971-73. Served with USN, 1945-48, 51-52, Korea. Registered profl. engr., Iowa, Ill. Mem. ASCE (past dir. Iowa sect.), Ill. Soc. Profl. Engrs., Am. Public Works Assn. (past dir. Fox Valley br., sec. 1981-82), Elgin-Aurora Council of Mayors, Am. Legion (past post comdr.). Methodist. Office: Village of Carpentersville 1200 Meadowdale Dr Carpentersville IL 60110

CASS, ROBERT MICHAEL, lawyer, reins. co. exec.; b. Carlisle, Pa., July 5, 1945; s. Robert Lau and Norma Jean (McCaleb) C.; B.A., Pa. State U., 1967; J.D., Temple U., 1971; m. Patricia Ann Garber, Aug. 12, 1967; children—Charles McCaleb, David Lau. Benefit examiner Social Security Adminstrn., Phila., 1967-68; mktg. rep. Employers Comml. Union Ins. Co., Phila., 1968-70; asst. sec. Nat. Reins. Corp., N.Y.C., 1970-77; admitted to N.Y. bar, 1974; asst. v.p. Skandia Am. Reins. Corp., N.Y.C., 1977-80; mgr. Allstate Reins. Co., Northbrook, Ill., 1980—. Mem. Am. Bar Assn. (coms. on internat. ins. law, products, gen. liability, and consumer law, profl. liability law), N.Y. State Bar Assn., Soc. C.P.C.U.s, Conf. Spl. Risk Underwriters. Home: 325 Old Mill Rd Barrington IL 60010 Office: 80 Allstate Plaza S Northbrook IL 60062

CASSANI, JOHN LOUIS, sch. dist. adminstr.; b. Danville, Ill., May 22, 1939; s. Louis C. and E. Cassani; B.S. in Edn., Eastern Ill. U., 1961, M.S. in Edn., 1962; m. Judy R. Jividen, May 2, 1964; children—Christine, Cathleen. Dir. career vocat. edn. DeKalb (Ill.) Dist. 428 Bd. Edn., 1975—; dir. DeKalb Area Migrant Edn. programs, 1976—; dir. N.W. Ill. Career Edn. Service Center, 1979—. Mem. Nat. Assn. Vocat. Tech. Adminstrs., Ill. Assn. Vocat. Tech. Adminstrs., Nat. Career Edn. Assn., Am. Vocat. Edn. Assn., Ill. Vocat. Edn. Assn., Nat. Personnel and Guidance Assn., Ill. Personnel and Guidance Assn., Phi Delta Kappa. Home: 111 Cynthia Pl DeKalb IL 60115 Office: 1515 S 5th St DeKalb IL 60115

CASSELS, DONALD ERNEST, physician, educator; b. Ellendale, N.D., Sept. 9, 1906; s. Ernest Eber and Louise Larsher (Chambers) C.; B.A., U. N.D., 1932; M.D., Harvard U., 1936; m. Isabella Collins, Oct. 8, 1938 (dec. May 1980). Intern, Buffalo Gen. Hosp., 1936-37; resident in pediatrics U. Chgo., Hosps., 1937-38, instr., 1938-39; practice medicine specializing in pediatrics, 1941-43; asst. prof. pediatrics U. Chgo., 1943-48, asso. prof., 1948-54, prof., 1954—; mem. staffs Wyler Children's Hosp., Ill. Services for Crippled Children. Served to maj. M.C., AUS, 1943-46. Decorated Bronze Star; recipient Gold Key U. Chgo. Med. Alumni Assn., 1974. Diplomate Am. Bd. Pediatrics, Bd. Pediatric Cardiology. Mem. Am. Acad. Pediatrics, Am. Pediatrics Soc., Soc. Pediatrics Research, Am. Coll. Cardiology, Am. Coll. Chest Physicians. Clubs: Quadrangle, Sturgeon Bay Yacht. Author: Heart and Circulation in Newborn and Infant, 1966; Electrocardiography in Infants and Children, 1966, others; contbr. articles, papers to med. jours. Home: 5617 Dorchester Ave Chicago IL 60637 Office: 950 E 59th St Chicago IL 60637 Died May 17, 1981

CASSETTARI, LEO JOSEPH, film producer; b. Chgo., Feb. 2, 1931; s. Settimo and Addolorata Cassettari; B.A. in Acctg., Bryant and Stratton Coll., 1952; m. Catheine E. Bohan, Nov. 28, 1959; children—Steven Louis, Dawn Marie. Vice pres. Wilding Inc., Chgo., 1955-69; exec. v.p. Filmmakers Co., Chgo., 1969-72; pres. Studio Seven Inc., Chgo., 1972—, also dir. Bd. dirs. Italian Am. Sports Hall of Fame, 1975—. Mem. Assn. Ind. Comml. Producers, Chgo. Coalition. Roman Catholic. Office: 250 E Illinois St Chicago IL 60611

CASSIDY, DWANE ROY, insulation contracting co. exec.; b. Bedford, Ind., Oct. 20, 1915; s. Leo Clayton and Lilly Fay (Robbins) C.; student Roscoe Turner's Sch. Aviation, 1944; m. Mary Catherine Shrout, Aug. 28, 1937; children—Gail (Mrs. Gordon Everling), Cheryl, Duane, Nina (Mrs. Robert McAnulty). With L. C. Cassidy & Son, Inc., Indpls., 1934—, now v.p.; v.p. L.C. Cassidy & Sons, Inc. of Fla., 1963—. Served with USN, 1944-45; PTO. Mem. Gideons Internat. Methodist. (dir.). Club: Optimists (Indpls.). Home: 644 Lawndale St Plainfield IN 46168 Office: 1918 S High School Rd Indianapolis IN 46241

CASSIDY, GERALD JOSEPH, fast food co. exec.; b. Chgo., Aug. 16, 1941; s. Joseph Patrick and Mary Rita (Gleason) C.; B.S. in Indsl. Econs., Purdue U., 1964; M.B.A., Old Dominion U., 1970; m. Jennie Jones; children—Lisa Kathleen, Mary Elizabeth, Darrin Christopher, Angela Rhonda, Gerald Joseph II. Mdse. mgr. Dave Keen Music, Lafayette, Ind., 1964-66; fin. analyst Gen. Foods Corp., Lafayette, 1971-72; owner/operator 5 McDonald's Restaurants, Cassidy Restaurants, Inc., Tipton, Ind., 1973—, charter mem. McDonald's Corp. Operators' Adv. Bd., 1973, 74; pres. Central Ind. McDonald's Operators Assn., 1975-76; treas. Ronald McDonald House com. Riley Children's Hosp., 1980—; lectr. Purdue U., 1969. Fin. chmn. Tipton County Republican Party, 1976-80, county chmn., 1980-81. Served to lt. USN, 1966-70. Mem. Tipton C. of C., Ind. Restaurant Assn., Sigma Pi. Republican. Roman Catholic. Clubs: Elks, Jaycees.

CASSIDY, KENNETH HOWARD, agrl. products co. ofcl.; b. Fayette, Wis., Oct. 15, 1926; s. Howard Felix and Vera Leola (Ferrell) C.; student Wis. State U., 1945; grad. Rockford Sch. of Bus., 1948; m. Phyllis Rowe, Mar. 15, 1947; children—Linda, Lydell, Louise. Dealer, Farm Craft Feeds, Des Moines, 1951-53, sales mgr., 1956-58, div. mgr., Celina, Ohio, 1958-67, div. mgr. Wis. and Ill., 1968-70, nat. dir. manpower, Cedar Rapids, Iowa, 1979-81; sales trainer Vigortone Agrl. Products, Cedar Rapids, 1979—, bd. dirs., 1978-80. Served with U.S. Navy, 1944-46. Recipient Award of Merit, Vigortone, 1969. Mem. Meeting Planners Internat., Am. Soc. Tng. and Devel., Internat. Assn. Profl. Salesman, V.F.W., Am. Legion. Democrat. Methodist. Clubs: Masons, Shriners, Eagles. Home: 6307 Devonshire Dr NE Cedar Rapids IA 52402 Office: 5264 Council St NE Cedar Rapids IA 52406

CASSOU, JAMES LEON, airline pilot; b. Santa Barbara, Calif., Apr. 2, 1951; s. Leon Joseph and Dorisedna (Forslund) C.; A.A., Santa Barbara City Coll., 1973; postgrad. Calif. State Coll., 1973-74; m. Norita Ellen Besel, Mar. 13, 1976. Ambulance attendant, dispatcher and orderly Santa Ynez Valley Hosp., Solvang, Calif., 1968-73; chief ground instr., asst. chief pilot Gt. Atlantic and Pacific Aeroplane Co., Van Nuys, Calif., 1973-74; personal pilot, adminstrv. asst. to A. Brent Carruth, Counselor at Law, Encino, Calif., 1974-75; v.p. transp. and shipping, head grower Santa Maria Greenhouses, Inc., Nipomo, Calif., 1975-76; chief ground instr. Bud Walen Aviation, Van Nuys, Calif., 1976; flight instr. ATE of Santa Monica (Calif.), 1976; capt. Air Wis., Inc., Appleton, 1976—; ind. distbr. Shaklee Products. Mem. Air Line Pilots Assn. Office: Outagamie County Airport Appleton WI 54911

CASTELLAN, N(ORMAN) JOHN, JR., psychologist, educator; b. Denver, Jan. 21, 1939; s. Norman John and Mary Victoria (Biebl) C.; m. Diane Cecile Swift, July 18, 1964; children—Caryn Lynn, Norman John, III, Tanya Cecile; A.B., Stanford U., 1961; Ph.D., U. Colo., 1965. Prof. psychology Ind. U., Bloomington, 1965—, asso. dean research and grad. devel., 1977—, psychology editor Conduit curriculum com., 1974—; vis. prof. computer sci. U. Colo., summers 1971-73; vis. research asso. Oreg. Research Inst., 1972; mem. steering com. Nat. Conf. on Use of On-Line Computers, 1973-76, conf. chmn., 1974, pres., 1979-80. Active noise subcom. Bloomington Environ. Commn.; mem. Monroe County Edn. Task Force, 1981—; mem. Monroe County Democratic Central Com., 1968-73, 75-78, 80—. Research grantee and fellow NSF, 1971-73, NIMH, 1966—. Fellow AAAS; mem. Am. Psychol. Assn., Am. Statis. Assn., Psychonomic Soc., Assn. Computing Machinery, Sigma Xi. Author: (with Hammond and Householder) Introduction to the Statistical Method, 1970; co-editor, Cognitive Theory, Vol. 1, 1975, Vol. 2, 1977, Vol. 3, 1978; contbr. sci. articles to profl. jours. Home: 703 Ravencrest Bloomington IN 47401 Office: Dept Psychology Ind U Bloomington IN 47405

CASTELLANA, JOHN JOSEPH, architect; b. Glenridge, N.J., June 23, 1948; s. Joseph and Mary Sarah (Petronaci) C.; B.Arch., Kent State U., 1971; M.Arch., U. Ill., 1972; m. Barbara Ann Keefe, Aug. 4, 1973. Archtl. draftsman, designer Port of N.Y. Authority, N.Y.C., summers, 1969, 71; archtl. designer T.P. Bennett & Son, London, summer, 1970; design asso., project designer TMP Assos., Inc., Bloomfield Hills, Mich., 1972—; cons. design architect Brookside Sch. Cranbrook, Bloomfield Hills, Mich., 1977—; works include Plymouth-Canton Elem. Schs. (recipient Honor Design award Detroit AIA), 1977, Detroit Bible Coll., Allied Health Facility/Oakland Community Coll., Oakland County Exec. Office Bldg. Recipient award Young Profl. Competition, Bldg. Design and Constrn. Mag., 1978. Mem. AIA, Mich. Soc. Architects, Kent State Alumni Assn., U. Ill. Alumni Assn. Roman Catholic. Home: 668 Oakland Ave Birmingham MI 48008 Office: 1191 W Square Lake Rd Bloomfield Hills MI 48013

CASTELLINO, FRANCIS JOSEPH, chemist, univ. dean; b. Pittston, Pa., Mar. 7, 1943; s. Joseph Samuel and Evelyn Bonita C.; B.S., U. Scranton, 1964; M.S., U. Iowa, 1966, Ph.D. in Biochemistry, 1968; m. Mary Margaret Fabiny, June 5, 1965; children—Kimberly Ann, Michael Joseph, Anthony Francis. Postdoctoral fellow Duke U., Durham, N.C., 1968-70; mem. faculty dept. chemistry U. Notre Dame (Ind.), 1970—, prof., 1977—, dean Coll. Sci., 1979—. NIH fellow, 1968-70. Fellow N.Y. Acad. Scis.; mem. AAAS, Am. Heart Assn., Am. Chem. Soc., Am. Soc. Biol. Chemistry. Roman Catholic. Contbr. articles to profl. jours. Office: Coll of Science Univ Notre Dame Notre Dame IN 46556

CASTER, RICHARD JOHN, ednl. adminstr.; b. Canton, Ohio, May 12, 1946; s. Peter and Mary Angelantoni) C.; married, 2 children. B.A. in Edn., Walsh Coll., Canton, 1968; M.S. in Tech. Edn., U. Akron (Ohio), 1973, Ed.D., 1979; m. Kathleen Annette; children—Matthew Adam, Scott Michael. Tchr. Columbus (Ohio) City schs., 1968-69; tchr. Canton City schs., 1969-73, coordinator, 1973-74, supr. career edn., 1974-79; asst. prin. Canton McKinley Sr. High Sch., 1979—; mem. Community Task Force for Expanding Minority Opportunities in Tech. Edn. Mem. Am., Ohio vocat. assns., Career Edn. Assn., Ohio Council Local Adminstrs., State Ohio Career Edn. Task Force, Ohio Assn. Secondary Sch. Adminstrs., Canton City Schs. Adminstrs. Assn. (pres.), Phi Delta Kappa. Club: Rotary (Canton). Home: 1854 Spring Valley Dr NW Canton OH 44708 Office: 2323 17th St NW Canton OH 44708

CASTLE, DONALD LAMPERT, lawyer; b. Urbana, Ill., Apr. 18, 1904; s. Charles Bailey and Katherine Elinore (Lampert) C.; A.B., U. Mich., 1926; J.D., Detroit Coll. Law, 1936, LL.D., 1978; m. Edna S. Plageman, Aug. 13, 1932; children—William R., Katherine A. Castle Barth. Admitted to Mich. bar, 1936; with real estate dept. J.L. Hudson Co., Detroit, 1929-40, with personnel relations, 1940-46, asst. personnel dir., 1946-47, exec. dir. Hudson-Webber Found., 1948-69, pension adminstrn. dir., 1948-69; individual practice law, Birmingham, Mich., 1969—; sec.-treas. Hudson-Webber Found., 1958-69. Commr. Detroit Commn. Children Youth, 1956-65; trustee Detroit Coll. Law, 1943—; bd. Detroit YMCA, 1952—, pres., 1954-57, nat. bd., 1969-79, nat. council, 1951-79, Great Lakes regional bd., 1971-78; trustee Webber Founds., 1977—. Mem. State Bar of Mich., Detroit Bar Assn., Am. Judicature Soc., Fin. Analysts Soc. of Detroit. Presbyterian. Clubs: Detroit Athletic, Noontide, Masons, Shriners. Home: 4398 Knightsbridge Ln West Bloomfield MI 48033 Office: 960 E Maple St Suite 120 Birmingham MI 48011

CASTLE, VERNON CHARLES, recording co. exec.; b. Whitewater, Wis., May 17, 1931; s. Erwin Ellesworth and Anne Bertha (Nelson) C.; B.Ed., U. Wis., Whitewater, 1951; m. Jeanette C. Travis, Aug. 4, 1950. Profl. entertainer, musician, 1956-65; pres. Castle Prodns., Inc., Lake Geneva, Wis., 1966-79, Castle Rec., 1972-78, Recreational Recs., Ltd., 1972-77; broadcast advt. cons., 1979—. Served with Adj. Gen. Corps, U.S. Army, 1952-55. Home: 442 Birches Dr Lake Geneva WI 53147 Office: PO Box 628 Lake Geneva WI 53147

CASTLEMAN, RICHARD LAVERN, corp. exec.; b. Taylorville, Ill., Aug. 10, 1934; s. Roy David and Evelyn (Mason) C.; B.S., Millikin U., 1956; 1 dau., Kelly Gale. Clk., Office Ill. Sec. of State, Springfield,

1953-55; sr. accountant firm Gauger & Diehl, C.P.A.'s, Decatur, Ill., 1956-65; pvt. practice as C.P.A., Decatur, 1965—; comptroller Millikin U., Decatur, 1965-66; controller Progress Industries, Inc., Arthur, Ill., 1966-67, v.p. finance, sec., 1967-72; v.p., gen. mgr., dir. Promanco Acceptance Corp., Arthur, 1967-70, exec. v.p., dir., 1970-72; asst. sec. Capital City Casket Co., Little Rock, 1967-72; sec., treas., dir. R.A.S., Inc., Decatur, 1968-76; pres., dir. Comtemporary Leasing Co., Inc., Decatur, 1969—, Contemporary Enterprises, Inc., Decatur, 1970-78; owner Contemporary Vending Amusements, 1972—; pres., dir. Fun Castle Enterprises, Inc., 1978—. Adminstrv. asst. logistics plans and tng. Signal Research and Devel. Labs., U.S. Army, Ft. Monmouth, N.J., 1957-59. Bd. dirs. Smith-Dickerson Found., Decatur. C.P.A. Mem. Am. Inst. C.P.A.'s, Ill. Soc. C.P.A.'s, Ill. Mfgrs. Assn. (legis. com. 1967-72), Amusement and Music Operators Assn., Nat. Automatic Merchandising Assn., Order DeMolay (chpt. adviser 1959-65, Legion of Honor award 1960), Delta Sigma Phi. Republican. Mason, Elk. Office: 10 S Country Club Rd PO Box 1708 Decatur IL 62525

CASTLES, WILLIAM ALBERT, physician; b. Dallas, S.D., Feb. 1, 1911; s. Thomas Ralph and Edna B. (Pabst) C.; student Albia Jr. Coll., 1928-30; M.D., State U. Iowa, 1935; m. Mildred Alyce Owen, Apr. 16, 1932; children—Thomas Ralph, William Albert II. Intern St. Mary's Hosp., Kansas City, Mo., 1935-30; resident Mo. Pacific R.R. Hosp., St. Louis, 1936-37; practice family medicine, Rippey, Iowa, 1939-46, Dallas Center, Iowa, 1946—; mem. staff Iowa Luth. Hosp., Iowa Meth. Hosp., Des Moines; staff physician Midwestern area A.R.C., 1937-39. Dir. Recreational Vehicles Inc., Des Moines, 1972-73. Mem. City Council, Dallas Center, 1948-52. Served from lt. to lt. col. M.C., AUS. 1941-46. Mem. Iowa Med. Soc. (ho. dels. 1952-66), Iowa Acad. Family Practice (dir. 1956-60, pres. 1963-64), Dallas Guthrie County Med. Soc. (pres. 1958), Am. Acad. Family Practice (ho. of dels. 1964-76, commn. membership and credentials). Rotarian (pres. 1959-60). Home: 105 Rhinehart Ave Dallas Center IA 50063 Office: 515 Sycamore St Dallas Center IA 50063

CASTOR, STEPHEN EUGENE, bus. exec.; b. New Castle, Ind., Feb. 4, 1946; s. Ercie Stanton and Helen (Quckenbush) C.; B.A., Adrian Coll., 1971; M.A., U. Mich., 1972; M.B.A., Northwestern U., 1974; J.D., Chgo.-Kent Coll. Law, 1977; m. Esther Marie Olson, Aug. 3, 1974; 1 dau., Stephanie Tara. Banking rep. No. Trust Co., Chgo., 1974-77; v.p., mgr. Asia, Middle East, Africa Northwestern Nat. Bank, Mpls., 1977-81; v.p., gen. mgr. MacLean-Fogg Co., Mundelein, Ill., 1981—; lectr. Coll. Bus., U. Minn.; dir. Am. Equipment Service, Singapore. Mem. edn. bd. Minnetonka Luth. Ch., 1980-81. Served with U.S. Army, 1964-67. Decorated Air medal, Bronze Star, Purple Heart. Mem. World Trade Assn. Minn., Minn. Bankers Assn., Alpha Kappa Psi, Delta Theta Phi. Republican. Lutheran. Clubs: Mpls. Athletic, Tonka Raquette and Swim. Office: 106 Wilmot Rd Suite 210 Deerfield IL 60015

CASTORE, CARL HARRY, psychologist, educator; b. Uniontown, Pa., July 13, 1940; s. George F. and Margaret (Steele) C.; B.S., Pa. State U., 1962; postgrad. U. Tex., 1962-63; M.S., Rutgers U., 1967, Ph.D., 1968; m. Susan E. Tishman, July 29, 1965; children—Anthony D., Collin Andrew. Instr. to asst. prof. psychology Monmouth Coll., West Long Branch, N.J., 1967-68; asst. prof. to asso. prof. psychol. scis. Purdue U., West Lafayette, Ind., 1968—; vis. research scientist USAF Systems Command AFHRL/FT, 1978-79; vis. prof. U. Ill., 1975-76; vis. prof. organizational behavior Ga. Inst. Tech., 1981-82. Adv. bd. Ball Found., 1975-78. NASA research grantee, 1980. Mem. Am. Psychol. Assn., Midwest Psychol. Assn., Acad. Mgmt., Psychonomic Soc., Internat. Assn. Applied Psychology, Public Choice Soc. Contbr. articles on group and individual decision making and risk taking to profl. jours., chpts. in books. Home: 109 Linda Ln West Lafayette IN 47906 Office: Dept of Psychological Sciences Purdue University West Lafayette IN 47902

CASTRANOVA, ANGELO F., bus. safety cons., former fed. safety engr.; b. Lee, Mass., Nov. 17, 1917; s. Giorlando and Giovanna (Duchina) C.; grad. Center for Safety, N.Y. U., 1952, also other tng.; m. Nancy Lucy DiLieto, Sept. 4, 1938; children—George, Frank, Robert, Nancy. Laborer, Bklyn. Navy Yard, 1941, supr., 1941-43, safety coordinator, 1942-43; safety insp., safety engr., 1946-49; safety program specialist and acting safety dir. Mil. Sea Transp. Service, Atlantic, 1950-59; dist. supr. Bur. Labor Standards, U.S. Dept. Labor, St. Louis, 1960-69, area dir. Occupational Safety and Health Adminstrn., 1970-76, ret., 1976; pres. Cass Services, Inc., St. Louis, 1976—. Served with Seabees, USN, 1943-45. PTO. Cert. safety profl. Mem. Am. Soc. Safety Engrs. (profl.). Home and office: 9712 Lynn Town Ct Saint Louis MO 63114

CATALANO, GEORGE DOMINIC, aerospace engr.; b. Syracuse, N.Y., Nov. 8, 1951; s. Dominic and Anella Antoinette (Montuori) C.; B.S., cum laude, La. State U., 1973; M.S., U. Va., 1975, Ph.D., 1977. Research asst. Research Labs. for Engring. Scis., U. Va., Charlottesville, 1973-77; research aerospace engr. USAF, Wright Patterson AFB, Ohio, 1977-81; prof. mech. engring. La. State U., 1981—; prof. Air Force Inst. Tech., 1979-81, Wright State U., 1978-81. Vice-chmn. publicity fund raising activities Dayton Channels 16/14, 1980. Served to capt. USAF, 1977—. La. State U. Alumni Fund fellow, 1969-73; Newcomb fellow, 1973-75; U. Va. Alumni Fund fellow, 1975-77. Mem. AIAA, N.Y. Acad. Sci., Sigma Xi, Cousteau Soc., Fund for Animals, Young Democrats Onandaga County. Democrat. Roman Catholic. Home: 2294 Zink Rd Apt 8 Fairborn OH 45324

CATANIA, FRANCIS J., philosopher, univ. adminstr.; b. Chgo., Mar. 5, 1933; s. Francis P. and Rose F. (Vizza) C.; A.B., Loyola U., Chgo., 1954, M.A., 1958; Ph.D., St. Louis U., 1959; m. Zelda F. Schuman, Aug. 18, 1956; children—Catherine, Francis, Anita, Thomas, Raymond, Robert. Instr., John Carroll U., 1958-60; mem. faculty dept. philosophy Loyola U., Chgo., 1960—, prof., 1977—, dean Grad. Sch., 1977—. Bd. dirs. Edgewater Community Council, 1968-70. Mem. Council Grad. Schs., Am. Acad. Religion, Metaphysical Soc. Am., Am. Cath. Philos. Assn. Office: 820 N Michigan Ave Chicago IL 60611

CATANIA, SUSAN KMETTY, state legislator; b. Chgo., Oct. 12, 1941; d. John and Helen Kmetty; B.A. in Chemistry, St. Xavier Coll., Chgo., 1962; postgrad. Northwestern U., 1962-63; m. Anthony Edward Catania, Dec. 28, 1963; children—Susan, Rachel, Sara Ellen, Melissa, Amy, Annemarie, Margaret. Tech. writer, editor, info. dir. Chgo. Chem. Research Firm, 1963-70; freelance tech. editor, 1970-73; mem. Ill. Ho. of Reps., 1973—; lectr. USIS, 1976. Recipient Liberty Bell award, 1975; named Best Legislator, 1974, 76, 78, 80. Mem. Nat. Order Women Legislators (regional dir.), Am. Chem. Soc., Soc. Tech. Communications (chmn. 1975-76), LWV, Ill. Women's Polit. Caucus (chmn. 1975-76), League Black Women, Ind. Voters Ill., Republican Bus. Women's Club Chgo., NOW, Ill. Status Women Assn. (chmn. 1974—). Roman Catholic. Office: 2043 Stratton Bldg Springfield IL 62707

CATCHINGS, MILDRED WOODARD, nurse educator; b. Dublin, Ga., Nov. 6, 1913; d. James Henry and Lillie Mae (Shellman) Woodard; diploma Provident Hosp. Sch. Nursing, 1935; B.S. in Pub. Health Nursing, (Rosenwald scholar 1939-40), U. Mich. 1945; certificate in phys. therapy (Nat. Found. for Infantile Paralysis scholar 1947-48), Northwestern U., 1948; M.A. in Social Scis., U. Chgo., 1958; m. Lee Catchings, June 29, 1939. Asst. supr. in surgery Provident Hosp., Chgo., 1935-36; Phys. therapist, 1948-51; staff nurse Vis. Nurses Assn., Chgo., 1936-37; pub. health nurse Venereal Disease Control Program, New Orleans, 1937-39, 40-41, Chgo. Bd. Health 1941-43, 45-47; tchr. nurse, tchr. nurse cons. Chgo. Bd. Edn., 1952—; mem. adv. bd. Pupil Personnel Service, Ill. Office Edn.; mem. sch. health tech. com. Nat. Program for Pub. Edn. on Periodontal Disease; mem. statewide com. for Ill., White House Conf. on Children; speaker state sch. nurse workshops. Bd. dirs. Cosmopolitan Community Ch., Chgo. Fellow Am. Sch. Health Assn. (distinguished service award 1975); mem. Am. Nurses Assn., Am. Sch. Health Assn., Ill. Public Health Assn., Ill. Sch. Nurses Assn., Am. Pub. Health Assn., Provident Hosp. Alumni Assn., U. Mich., U. Chgo., Northwestern U. phys. therapy alumni assns.

CATCHINGS, PHILIP MARSHALL, JR., psychologist; b. Chattanooga, Oct. 9, 1951; s. Philip Marshall and Edith Wynn (Applewhite) C.; B.A. (Marian Smith scholar), Millsaps Coll., 1972; postgrad. Vanderbilt U., 1974-75; Ph.D. in Psychology, U. Minn., 1981; m. Kathy Sims, Jan. 3, 1976. Salesman, I-T-E Imperial Corp., 1973-74; psychologist Hudspeth Mental Retardation Center, 1976, dir. psychology, Whitfield, Miss., 1982; research asst. Psychiatry Research Unit, U. Minn., Mpls., 1976—; guest lectr.; cons. non-profit agys. Bd. dirs. Hinds County Community Service Assn., 1970-73, chmn. program and grievance coms., acting chmn. bd. dirs., 1972. Recipient C. Wright Mills award, 1972. Conglist. Home: 1609 W 75th St Richfield MN 55423 Office: Psychiatry Research Unit Univ Minn Box 392 Mayo Minneapolis MN 55455

CATERINE, JAMES MICHAEL, surgeon; b. Milw., Feb. 23, 1935; s. James A. and May Elizabeth (Marasco) C.; student Creighton U., 1952-55; M. D., U. Iowa 1959; m. Barbara Ann Bauer, July 9, 1961; children—Anthony, Rebecca, John Paul, Matthew, Gina. Intern, County Hosp., San Bernardino, Calif., 1959-60; resident Univ. Hosp., VA Hosp., Iowa City, 1960-61, VA Hosp., Des Moines, 1964-66; practice medicine specializing in gen. surgery, Des Moines, 1967—; mem. staffs Mercy, Luth., Meth., N.W., Broadlawns hosps., Des Moines, Mary Greely Hosp., Ames, Iowa; surgery teaching chmn. Mercy Hosp., Des Moines, 1970—, chief surgery, 1976—; asst. clin. prof. surgery Coll. Osteo. Medicine and Surgery, Des Moines, 1970—. Served with USAF, 1961-64. Recipient Excellence in Teaching award Coll. Osteo. Medicine and Surgery, 1974; certificate of recognition Broadlawns Hosp., Des Moines, 1975. Diplomate Am. Bd. Surgery. Fellow A.C.S., Am. Soc. Abdominal Surgeons; mem. Iowa Acad. Surgery, Pan-Am. Med. Assn., Am. Burn Assn., Iowa, Polk County med. socs., AMA (Physicians Recognition award 1977, 80), Med. Forum Club, Am. Med. Tennis Assn. Roman Catholic. Clubs: Embassy, Associates Breakfast. Contbr. articles to med. jours. Home: 7500 Benton Dr Des Moines IA 50322 Office: 1041 5th St Des Moines IA 50314

CATES, WARD MITCHELL, educator; b. Richmond, Va., May 4, 1949; s. Mitchell Dresdner and Marian Granville (Sharwood) C.; B.A., Duke U., 1971, Ed.D., 1979; m. Anne Barnum Sniffen, Nov. 23, 1972; 1 dau., Katherine Sharwood. Tchr. spl. edn. Learning Center, Richmond, Va., 1971-72; tchr. high sch. English, Richmond Public Schs., 1972-73; media specialist Duke U., Durham, N.C., 1973-75; dir. project V-C ESEA, Burlington (N.C.) Public Schs., 1974-75; asso. prof. edn. Pittsburg (Kans.) State U., 1975—. Chmn. United Way, 1979, div. capt. city, 1980; capt. blood drive ARC, 1978. Grantee ESEA, 1974-75, Phi Delta Kappa, 1979-80. Mem. Nat. Council Tchrs. English, Assn. Ind. Video and Filmmakers, Am. Ednl. Research Assn., Kappa Delta Pi, Phi Delta Kappa. Democrat. Rotary. Author: (with R.C. Clinesmith) Exploring New Teaching Strategies, 1978; contbr. articles to profl. jours. Home: 305 W Jefferson St Pittsburg KS 66762 Office: Sch Edn Pittsburg State U Pittsburg KS 66762

CATHCART, SILAS STRAWN, mfg. co. exec.; b. Evanston, Ill., May 6, 1926; s. James A. and Margaret (Strawn) C.; A.B., Princeton U., 1948; m. Corlene Hobbs, Feb. 3, 1951; children—Strawn, James, David and Daniel (twins), Corlene. With Ill. Tool Works, Inc., Chgo., 1948—, exec. v.p., then pres., 1962-72, chmn. bd., 1972—, also dir.; dir. Gen. Electric Co., Am. Hosp. Supply Corp., Jewel Cos., No. Trust Co., Quaker Oats Co., Savs. & Profit Sharing Fund Sears Employees. Bd. dirs. Northwestern Meml. Hosp., Chgo., 1959—. Served with USNR, 1944-46. Mem. Bus. Roundtable. Clubs: Onwentsia, Old Elm (Lake Forest, Ill.); Commercial, Commonwealth, Economic, Chicago (Chgo.); Links (N.Y.C.); Augusta (Ga.) Nat. Golf. Office: 8501 W Higgins Rd Chicago IL 60631

CATRAMBONE, ARTHUR WILLIAM, univ. admintr.; b. Chgo., Jan. 30, 1930; s. Nick and Theresa Catrambone; B.S., St. Benedict's Coll., 1951; exec. devel. program U. Ill., Urbana, summer 1964; m. Harriet M. Classen, Aug. 17, 1957; children—Arthur William, Gerard, Jeffrey, Laura, Nia, Joseph, Mark. With U. Ill., Chgo. campuses, 1951—, asso. dir. bus. Chgo. Circle campus, 1972-74, dir. bus. affairs Med. Center Campus, 1974-76, asst. v.p. fin. affairs, Chgo. campuses, 1976-77, asso. vice chancellor adminstrn., dir. campus planning Chgo. Circle campus, 1977—. C.P.A., Ill. Mem. Ill. Soc. C.P.A.'s, Am. Mgmt. Assn., Nat. Assn. Coll. and Univ. Bus. Officers. Roman Catholic. Club: Lions. Home: 2801 Kensington St Westchester IL 60153 Office: PO Box 4384 Chicago IL 60680

CATTELINO, JOHN ANTHONY, savs. and loan exec.; b. Hurley, Wis., June 24, 1942; s. John Lawrence and Angeline Norma (Patritto) C.; B.S., U. Wis., Whitewater, 1964; M.B.A., No. Ill. U., 1967; m. Derilyn Ruth Dean, June 7, 1969; children—Deborah Dean, Beth Allison, Scott Anthony. Retail mgr. Spurgeon Mercantile Co., Newton, Iowa, 1964-65; mktg. instr. No. Mich. U., Marquette, 1967-71, U. Wis., Platteville, 1971-74; v.p. mktg. Anchor Savs. & Loan Assn., Madison, Wis., 1974—; vis. lectr. U. Wis., Whitewater, 1976—; dir. Anchor Fin. Corp., Craft House '55; mem. adv. bd. mktg. Madison Area Tech. Coll., 1975—; chmn. mktg. com. Wis. Alumni Assn., 1975—. Mem. Savs. League Wis. (chmn. mktg.-public relations com.), Sales and Mktg. Execs. Madison (dir. 1975—), Pi Sigma Epsilon (bus. advisor 1976—), Savs. Instns. Mktg. Soc. Am., AAUP, Assn. M.B.A. Execs., Am. Mktg. Assn., Vilas Park Zool. Soc. (bd. dirs. 1978—). Club: Mendota Boosters. Home: 2710 Mason St Madison WI 53705 Office: 25 W Main St Madison WI 53703

CAUDILL, GEORGE GRAY, pediatric allergist; b. Des Moines, Nov. 15, 1921; s. Wilburn Tyre and Dorothy Margaret (Gray) C.; M.D., U. Iowa, 1952; m. Dorothy May Swendsen, Sept. 5, 1948; children—Kimberly, Marci, Vicki, Catherine, Tammara, George Gray. Intern, Broadlawns Hosp., Des Moines, 1951-53; gen. practice medicine, Newton, Iowa, 1953-54; resident in pediatrics Blank Meml. Hosp., Des Moines, 1954-56; gen. practice pediatrics, Des Moines, 1956-64; fellowship in allergy U. Iowa, Iowa City, 1964-65; individual practice medicine specializing in pediatric allergy, Des Moines, 1965—; chief of pediatrics Blank Meml. Hosp., acting dir. pediatric edn., 1980; guest lectr. Coll. Osteo. Medicine and Surgery, Des Moines; asst. clin. prof. pediatric dept. U. Iowa; dir. South Des Moines Nat. Bank, 1974—. Bd. dirs. Mid-Iowa Computer Center, 1972—, Des Moines Ind. Sch. Dist., 1964-78. Served with USN, 1942-45. Diplomate Am. Bd. Pediatrics, Am. Bd. Allergy and Immunology; recipient awards Cystic Fibrosis Found., 1958, Adult Edn. for the Des Moines Pub. Sch. in Health Edn., 1970, State Dept. Health, 1976. Mem. Am. Acad. Pediatrics (trustee Iowa chpt.), Am. Acad. Allergy, Am. Assn. for Clin. Immunology and Allergy, Iowa, Polk County med. socs., AMA, Iowa Soc. Immunology and Allergy (pres.). Republican. Clubs: Lions. Author revised edit. Better Homes and Gardens Baby Book, 1965-70; contbr. articles to profl. jours. Home: 3900 SW 28th Street Pl Des Moines IA 50321 Office: 1212 Pleasant St Des Moines IA 50309

CAUDILL, RODNEY CHAPPLE CLARK, psychiatrist; b. Morehead, Ky., Sept. 28, 1923; s. Rodney and Eleanor (Kimbrell) C.; student Miami U., 1941-42; M.D., Ohio State U., 1948; m. Vivian Jean Morrison, July 21, 1943; children—Carla Dee, Cristin Morrison, Rodney Curt, Brent Kimbrell. Intern St. Monica Hosp., Phoenix, 1949-50; resident, Topeka VA Hosp., 1962-63, C.F. Menninger Meml. Hosp., Topeka, 1964-65; family practice medicine, Middletown, Ohio, 1950-62; now practice medicine, specializing in psychiatry; staff Menninger Clinic, Topeka, 1962-65; staff psychiatrist Palm Beach Psychol. Clinic, West Palm Beach, Fla., 1965-66; dir. psychiat. services, also tchr., cons. Anderson (Ind.) Coll., 1966-69; founder, dir. Meramec Psychiat. Center, Yorktown, Ind., 1970—; forensic psychiatrist Delaware, Madison and Henry counties, 1972—; tchr., cons. Ball State U., 1972-75; cons. Aquarius House, Muncie, Ind., 1971-74, Family Service of Muncie, 1980—, Blue River Valley Spl. Edn., 1980-81; psychiat. cons. Family Practice Residents, Ball Meml. Hosp., 1973-75. Co-founder Meramec Montessori Childrens' Center, 1972. Served to capt. USAF, 1954-56. Menninger Sch. Psychiatry fellow, 1962-65, NIMH grantee, 1962-65. Mem. AMA, Am., Ind. psychiat. assns., Ohio State, Ind. State med. assns., Sigma Alpha Epsilon, Nu Sigma Nu. Address: Meramec Center PO Box 427 Yorktown IN 47396

CAULFIELD, JOAN, sch. adminstr.; b. St. Joseph, Mo., July 17, 1940; d. Joseph A. and Jane (Lisenby) Caulfield; B.S. in Edn. cum laude, U. Mo., 1963, M.A. in Spanish, 1965, Ph.D., 1963; postgrad. (Mexican Govt. scholar) Nat. U. Mexico, 1963. TV tchr. Spanish, Kansas City (Mo.) pub. schs., 1963-68; tchr. Spanish, French Bingham Jr. High Schs., Kansas City, 1968-78; asst. prin. S.E. High Sch., Kansas City, 1978—; dir. English Inst., Rockhurst Coll., summers, 1972-75. Mem. Sister City Commn., Kansas City, 1980—; ofcl. translator to mayor on trip to Seville, Spain, 1969; cons. Possum Trot (hist. soc.), 1979-80. Delta Kappa Gamma state scholar, 1977-78. Mem. Romance Lang. Assn., Assn. for Supervision and Curriculum Devel., Nat. Assn. Secondary Sch. Prins., Modern Lang. Assn., Am. Assn. Tchrs. Spanish and Portuguese, Westport Hist. Soc., Friends of Seville, Friends of Art, Friends of the Zoo. Phi Sigma Iota, Phi Delta Kappa, Delta Kappa Gamma. Roman Catholic. Home: 431 W 70th St Kansas City MO 64113 Office: 3500 E Meyer St Kansas City MO 64132

CAUSA, ALFREDO GUILLERMO, polymer scientist; b. Montevideo, Uruguay, June 25, 1928; s. Alfredo and Emilia (DeBenedetti) C.; came to U.S., 1959, naturalized, 1975; B.Sc. with honors, Montevideo Sch. Chemistry and Chem. Engring., 1958; M.S., Case Inst. Tech., Cleve., 1962; Ph.D. in Polymer Sci., U. Akron, 1968. Chemist, S.Am. subs. Courtaulds, Ltd., 1952-58; research chemist textile fibres div. Canadian Industries, Ltd., Millhaven Research Lab., Kingston, Ont., 1961-64, Tarrytown, Tech. Center, Union Carbide Corp., Tarrytown, N.Y., 1968-70; prin. chemist Goodyear Tire & Rubber Co., Akron, Ohio, 1970—. Fulbright scholar, 1959-61; Phillips Petroleum fellow, 1964-67. Mem. Am. Chem. Soc., AAAS, Sigma Xi, Alpha Chi Sigma. Contbr. articles to profl. jours. Home: 1255 Ashford Ln Akron OH 44313 Office: 1144 E Market St Akron OH 44316

CAVALIER, DONALD RICHARD, univ. adminstr.; b. Walhalla, N.D., Sept. 28, 1943; s. Amos O. and Francis (McCambridge) C.; B.S., Mayville State Coll., 1965; M.S., Bemidji State U., 1970; m. Mary A. Salisbury, July 23, 1966; children—David Cavalier, Todd. Tchr., coach Warren (Minn.) public schs., 1965-67; tchr., counselor Crookston (Minn.) public schs., 1967-75; edn. dir. N.W. Regional Corrections Center, Crookston, 1975-76; dir. placement, counseling and alumni services U. Minn., Crookston, 1976—; group leader, facilitator, The Social Seminar, Adventures in Attitude Tng., 1975-76; humanistic cons. Moorehead State U., 1973-78. Bd. dirs. S.O.S. Club for Teens, 1976-77; chmn. Family Living Center, Crookston, 1972-73; team leader Crookston Community Drug edn. program, 1975-76. PTO scholar, 1961-62. Mem. Northwestern Minn. Guidance Assn., Minn. Vocat. Guidance Assn., NEA, Nat. Assn. Vocat. Edn. Spl. Needs Personnel, Minn. Coll. Personnel Assn., Minn. Govt. Coll. Council Assn. of Minn. Recruiters and Placement Dirs., Jaycees (pres. 1978-79, named Outstanding Pres. 1979). Democrat. Roman Catholic. Clubs: Lions, K.C., Elks Country, Dance, Town and Country, Eagles, Elks. Home: 614 N Ash Ct Crookston MN 56716 Office: U of Minn Bede Hall Room 107 Crookston MN 56716

CAVANAUGH, GERALD DANIEL, orthodontist; b. Manitowoc, Wis., Sept. 4, 1935; s. William Theodore and Veronica (Bartz) C.; student St. Mary's Coll., 1953-55, U.S. Mil. Acad., 1955-57; B.S. in Math. cum laude, Loras Coll., 1958; D.D.S., U. Minn., 1967, postgrad. in Orthodontics (NIH fellow), 1967-69, Ph.D. in Anatomy (NIH fellow), 1972; m. Grace Pollock Wooten, Aug. 24, 1963; children—Shannon, Michael, Meggan, John Patrick. Asso. engr. ITT, Chgo., 1958-60; engr. Lockheed Missile & Space Co., Sunnyvale, Calif., 1960-61, Philco Western Devel. Lab., Palo Alto, Calif., 1961-63; practice dentistry specializing in orthodontics, Mpls., 1969—; asso. prof. anatomy U. Minn., 1972-73, asso. prof. orthodontics, 1973—; dir. orthodontics Children's Health Center, Mpls., 1973—; dir. 1st Minn. Investment Co. NIH grantee, 1973. Mem. Minn. Internat. assns. dental research, Am., Minn. dental assns., Mpls. Dist. Dental Soc., Am. Assn. Orthodontics, Midwestern, Minn. socs. orthodontics, Gopher State, Minn. Orthodontic, Bloomington (Minn.) study clubs, Delta Sigma Delta, Omicron Kappa Upsilon. Democrat. Roman Catholic. Clubs: St. Anthony Athletic, King's Ct., Madeline Island Yacht, Pres's. of U. Minn., Alumni-St. Mary's Coll., Alumni-Loras Coll., Alumni-U. Minn., K.C., Elks. Office: 3604 Cedar Ave Minneapolis MN 55407 also 3939 W 50th St Edina MN 55414

CAVANAUGH, JOHN J., lawyer, former congressman; b. Omaha, Aug. 1, 1945; s. John J. and Kathleen (Munnelly) C.; B.A., Regis Coll., Denver, 1967; J.D., Creighton U., 1972; m. Kathleen Ann Barrett, Aug. 2, 1969; children—Patrick, Colleen, Maureen, Machaela, John J. Admitted to Nebr. bar, 1972; partner firm Leahy, Washburn, Render & Cavanaugh, 1972-76; mem. Nebr. State Legislature, 1972-76; mem. 95th Congress from 2d Nebr. Dist.; mem. firm Kutak Rock & Huie, Omaha, 1981—. Mem. Omaha Bar Assn., Am. Legion, Jaycees. Clubs: K.C., Eagles, Cornhuskers Cosmopolitan. Recipient James A. Doyle award Creighton U. Sch. Law, 1975; named Outstanding Legislator, Eagleton Inst. Politics, Rutgers U., 1975. Office: Kutak Rock & Huie Omaha Bldg Omaha NE 68102

CAVOSIE, DIANE S., educator, legal sec.; b. Chgo., Dec. 24, 1947; d. Frank E. and Mamie H. (Sand) C.; B.S. in Edn., No. Ill. U., 1969, M.S. in Edn. (Chgo. Area Bus. Educators' Assn. scholar, 1971), 1973, also postgrad.; postgrad. So. Ill. U. Tchr. Morrison (Ill.) High Sch., 1969—; part time instr. Sauk Valley Coll., Dixon, Ill., 1974-80; part time legal sec. firm Pignatelli, Pignatelli & Ripley, Rock Falls, Ill., 1979—. Active polit. campaign for State Rep. Timothy Bell, 1978, 80. Mem. Nat. Bus. Edn. Assn., Ill. Bus. Edn. Assn. (pres. 1979-80), No. Ill. Bus. Edn. Assn. (pres. 1972-73), Ill. Edn. Assn., NEA, Ill. Vocat. Assn., Am. Vocat. Assn., Nat. Legal Secs. Assn., Ill. Legal Secs. Assn., Lee-Whiteside Counties Legal Secs. Assn., Delta Pi Epsilon, Beta Gamma Sigma, Beta Sigma Phi. Republican. Lutheran. Home: 502 S Genesee Ave Morrison IL 61270 Office: 643 Genesee Ave Morrison IL 61270

CAWOOD, THOMAS FRED, music therapist; b. Monroe, Mich., Aug. 29, 1952; s. Fred and Mona Ruth Cawood; student Eastern Mich. U., 1970-72; B.Mus., U. Mich., 1975; B.Music Therapy, Mich. State U., 1977; m. Alice Jane White, Aug. 24, 1974; children—Johannes Fredrick, Amber Diana. Music therapy intern Essex County Hosp. Center, Cedar Grove, N.J., 1977; music therapist Oakdale Regional Center for Devel. Disabilities, Lapeer, Mich., 1978-79, Learning Center, Genessee Ind. Sch. Dist., Flint, Mich., 1979—. State Mich. competitive scholar, 1970-71; Eastern Mich. U. music performance scholar, 1971-72; U. Mich. Sch. Music grantee, 1973-75. Mem. Nat. Assn. Music Therapy, Am. Assn. Mental Deficiency, Mich. State Alumni Assn., U. Mich. Sch. Music Alumni Assn. Episcopalian. Club: Masons, Order Eastern Star. Home: 409 Lou Alice Dr Columbiaville MI 48421 Office: 2413 W Maple St Flint MI 48507

CAYLOR, HAROLD DELOS, surgeon; b. Nottingham, Ind., Aug. 19, 1894; s. Charles E. and Bessie (Ferree) C.; B.S., U. Chgo., 1916; M.D., Rush Med. Coll., 1918; M.S., U. Minn., 1927; m. Ella Leora Carey, Nov. 11, 1919 (dec. Jan. 1969); children—Rebecca (Mrs. Don Meier), Patricia (Mrs. James Niblick); m. Henrietta Louise Noe, Jan. 17, 1972. Intern, Presbyn. Hosp., Chgo., 1918, Evanston (Ill.) Hosp., 1919-20; partner, gen. surgeon Caylor-Nickel Clinic, Bluffton, Ind., 1922-24; asst. prof. surg. pathology Mayo Clinic Found., Rochester, Minn., 1927-29; gen. surgeon Clinic Hosp., Bluffton, Ind., 1929—. Chmn. bd. dirs. Caylor-Nickel Research Found.; trustee Caylor-Nickel Hosp., 1922—, v.p., mem. exec. com., 1972—. Diplomate Am. Bd. Surgery. Mem. A.C.S., Am. Group Practice Assn. (pres. 1962-63), Ind. Lung Assn. (pres. 1951-52), Ind. Bone and Joint Club (pres. 1954), Mpls. Surg. Soc. (hon.), Sigma Xi, Phi Chi, Delta Upsilon. Republican. Methodist. Mason (Shriner), Elk. Clubs: Kiwanis; Sagamore of the Wabash. Home: 24 Columbia Ave Bluffton IN 46714 Office: 303 S Main St Bluffton IN 46714

CAYLOR, TRUMAN E., physician; b. Pennville, Ind., Jan. 10, 1900; s. Charles E. and Bessie (Ferree) C.; student Ind. U., 1917-1919; B.S., Wis. U., 1921; M.D., Rush Med. Coll., 1924; m. Julia Gettle, June 28, 1923 (dec. June 6, 1960); children—Carolyn (Mrs. Herman Wadlington), Charles H., Constance (Mrs. Joseph Carney). m. 2d, Eva Abbott, May 29, 1961 (dec. 1979); m. 3d, Suzanne Black, 1980. Intern, Evanston (Ill.) Gen. Hosp.; practice medicine specializing in urology, Bluffton, Ind., 1924—; co-founder, mem. staff Caylor Nickel Clinic, Bluffton, mem. staff Caylor Nickel Hosp., Bluffton, 1939—, exec. com., 1939-75, also dir.; dir. Mut. Security Life Ins. Co., Ft. Wayne, Ind. Mem. adv. com. Ind. Commn. on Aging, 1972-80; mem. adv. com. Grace Coll., Winona Lake, Ind., 1970—. Bd. dirs. Yorkfellow Inst., Richmond, Ind., Caylor Nickel Research Found. Served with AUS, 1918. Fellow A.C.S.; mem. Ind. Council Sagamores, Ind. State Med. Soc. (50th Year Certificate of Distinction 1974), Am. Urol. Assn., Delta Upsilon. Clubs: Masons, Shriners, Scottish Rite, Rotary (dist. gov. 1965-66). Home: 920 River Rd Bluffton IN 46714 Office: 303 S Main St Bluffton IN 46714

CECALA, AGNES FRICANO, educator; b. Chgo., Mar. 8, 1939; d. Fred E. and Lillian P. (Celano) Fricano; B.S. in Edn., No. Ill. U., 1961, postgrad., 1979-81; m. John James Cecala, Aug. 5, 1961; children—John Joseph, Fred Edward. Secretarial instr. Elmwood Park (Ill.) High Sch., 1964-65; career edn./adult edn. secretarial/communications instr. Triton Coll., River Grove, Ill., 1968-80, word processing/communications instr., 1980—, tng. coordinator, 1980—; cons. word processing, communications and secretarial tng. Mem. Nat. Bus. Edn. Assn., Ill. Bus. Edn. Assn., Internat. Word Processing Assn., Chgo. Bus. Edn. Assn., Am. Bus. Communications Assn., Internat. Soc. Wang Users, Wang Users Assn., Phi Delta Kappa. Author: (Wang tng. texts) Book I Basic, 1980; Wang Advanced Training Text—Book II, 1980; Wang Glossary Training Text III, 1981. Office: Triton Coll 2000 5th Ave River Grove IL 60171

CECIL, HAROLD EVERETT, educator; b. Ft. Wayne, Ind., Dec. 11, 1934; s. Kenneth Everett and Amy Ilene (Leonard) C.; student U. Iowa, 1977-78; m. Anna Mae Hislop, June 19, 1954; children—Thomas Lee, Barbara Ann Cecil Trein, Janis Marie Cecil Hartweg, Brenda Joy, Todd Arthur. Carpenter's helper Bosserman Built Homes, Ft. Wayne, 1950-55, Kurt Hanke Co., Ft. Wayne, 1955-57; owner, operator Harold Cecil Contractor, Ft. Wayne, 1957-63; supt. Engeered Bldgs., Ft. Wayne, 1963-64; constrn. mgr. Surlok Homes, Inc., Ft. Wayne, 1964-66; owner, mgr. Sherlok Homes & Supply, Cissna Park, Ill., 1966-69; supt. Nat. Homes Corp., Lafayette, Ind., 1969-76; carpentry instr. Southeastern Community Coll., Keokuk, Iowa, 1977—; owner, operator Granny Annie's Wash House, Keokuk, 1981—. Mem. adv. com. Iowa Passive Solar House, Iowa Energy Council, 1979-80. Named Employee of Month, Nat. Homes Corp., 1976. Mem. Iowa Vocat. Assn., Am. Vocat. Assn., Keokuk Landlords Assn. Mem. Evangelical Free Ch. Home: 1020 Orleans Ave Keokuk IA 52632 Office: Messenger Rd Keokuk IA 52632

CECIL, ROBERT SALISBURY, electronics co. exec.; b. Manila, Philippines, May 28, 1935 (parents Am. citizens); s. Robert Edgar and Susan Elizabeth C.; B.S., U.S. Naval Acad., 1956; M.B.A., Harvard U., 1962; m. Louise Nuttall Millholland, Nov. 30, 1963; children—Scott Douglass, James Hilliard. Contract negotiator Teledyne, Inc., Los Angeles, 1962-63; br. mgr. IBM, Cleve., 1971-72, regional mktg. mgr., Washington, 1973-75, corp. dir. govt. programs, Washington, 1975-77; v.p., corp. dir. mktg. Motorola Inc., Schaumburg, Ill., 1977—. Served with USAF, 1956-60. Mem. Am. Mktg. Assn. Episcopalian. Club: Bethesda Country. Office: 1303 E Algonquin Rd Schaumburg IL 60196

CELEBREZZE, ANTHONY J., JR., state ofcl.; b. Cleve., Sept. 8, 1941; s. Anthony J. and Anne M. C.; B.S., U.S. Naval Acad., 1963; M.S., George Washington U., 1966; J.D., Cleve. State U., 1973; m. Louisa Godwin, June 19, 1965; children—Anthony J. III, Catherine, Charles, David, Maria. Admitted to Ohio bar, 1973 partner firm Celebrezze and Marco, Cleve., 1975-79; mem. Ohio State Senate, 1975-79; sec. of state State of Ohio, Columbus, 1979—. Pres., Joint Vets. Commn. of Cuyahoga County, Ohio, 1977-79; v.p. Lake Erie Regional Transp. Authority, 1972-74; mem. Gt. Lakes Commn., 1975-78, vice chmn., 1977-78; former bd. dirs. Central br. YWCA, Cleve. Served with USN, 1963-68. Decorated Navy Commendation medal; recipient Jeffersonian Lodge award, 1977, Man of Yr. award Delta Theta Phi; named 1 of 5 Outstanding Legislators by 2 Ohio mags., 1978. Mem. LWV. Democrat. Roman Catholic. Office: 30 E Broad St Columbus OH 43215

CELEBREZZE, ANTHONY JOSEPH, fed. judge; b. Anzi, Italy, Sept. 4, 1910; s. Rocco and Dorothy (Marcoguiseppe) C.; student John Carroll U.; LL.B., Ohio No. U., 1936; D.D., Wilberforce University, 1955; LL.D., Fenn Coll., 1962, Boston Coll., 1963, La Salle coll., 1963, Ohio No. U., 1963; Pd.D., R.I. Coll., 1964; D. Pub. Service, Bowling Green State U., 1964; L.H.D., Miami U., 1965; m. Anne Marco, May 7, 1938; children—Anthony J., Jean Ann, Susan Marie. Admitted to Ohio bar, 1938, engaged in practice of law. Senator Ohio State Legislature, 1952-53; mayor of Cleve., 1953-62; sec. Dept. Health, Edn. Welfare, 1962-65; judge 6th Circuit Ct. of Appeals, 1965—. Mem. President's Adv. Commn. on Intergovtl. Relations 1959—; pres. U.S. Conf. Mayors, 1961-62. Served as seaman USN, World War II. Brotherhood award Nat. Conf. Christians and Jews, 1955, Nat. Human relations award, 1962; Order of Merit of the Republic, Italy, 1955; citation United Negro Coll. Fund, 1956. Nat. Fiorello LaGuardia award, 1961, Nat. Catholic Resettlement Council Ward, 1962, Pub. Service award YMCA, 1962, Gulick award Camp Fire Girls, Inc., 1962, Peter Canisius medal Canisius medal Canisius Coll., 1963, gold medallion City of Rome, 1963; Eleanor Roosevelt Humanities award, 1965. Mem. Am. Municipal Assn. (pres. 1958-59, distinguished service award 1960), Order of Merit. Office: US Post Office and Courthouse Cleveland OH 44114*

CELEBREZZE, FRANK D., justice Ohio Suprene Ct.; b. Cleve., Nov. 13, 1928; s. Frank D. and Mary Delsander Celebrezze; student Ohio State U., 1948-50; B.S., Baldwin-Wallace Coll., 1952; LL.B., Cleve.-Marshall Coll. Law, 1956; m. Mary Ann Armstrong, Jan. 20, 1949; children—Judith, Frank, Laura, David, Brian, Stephen, Jeffrey, Keith, Matthew. Admitted to Ohio bar, 1957; began legal practice, Cleve., 1957; judge Ohio Ct. Common Pleas Cuyahoga County, 1964-72; justice Ohio Supreme Ct., 1972—, now chief justice; mem. Ohio Senate, to 1958. Served with parachute inf. U.S. Army, 1946-47. Recipient Jud. Service award Ohio Supreme Ct., 1972; Outstanding Alumnus award Cleve.-Marshall Coll. Law, 1973; Community Service award AFL-CIO, 1973, Disting. Citizen of Parma award, 1976; Unita Civic award of Youngstown, 1976. Mem. Inst. Jud. Adminstrn. of Bar Assn. Greater Cleve., Am., Cuyahoga County bar assns., Cuyahoga County Joint Vets. Adminstrn. (past pres., past trustee), Cleve. YMCA, Catholic War Vets. Democrat. Roman Catholic. Office: Supreme Ct Ohio State Office Tower 30 E Broad St Columbus OH 43215*

CELY, MONTE ALLAN, telephone co. exec.; b. Houston, July 29, 1952; s. John and Rose Lorraine C.; B.S., Washington U., St. Louis, 1973; m. Linda Ann Coad, Oct. 16, 1976; 1 dau., Angela Marie. Mgmt. trainee Southwestern Bell Telephone Co., St. Louis, 1974-75, acctg. mgr., tech. specialist, 1975-77, mgr. comptrollers ops., tech. specialist, 1977-79, mgr. comptrollers ops. and payroll, 1979—. Mem. Tau Beta Pi, Sigma Alpha Epsilon. Office: 14 S 4th St Saint Louis MO 63102

CENTNER, ROSEMARY LOUISE, chemist; b. Newport, Ky., Sept 23, 1926; d. Alexis F. and Mary Anne (Cloud) Centner; B.A., Our Lady of Cin. Coll., 1947; M.S., U. Cin., 1949. Library asst., tech. library Procter & Gamble Co., 1949-52, br. librarian Miami Valley labs., Cin., 1952-56, tech. librarian, 1956-66, mgr. tech. info. service, 1966-72, mgr. div. info. cons., 1972-73, mgr. NDA coordination, 1973-75, mgr. biomed. communications, 1975-81, mgr. tech. communications, 1981—. Trustee, Edgecliff Coll., 1975—. Mem. Am. Soc. Info. Sci., Am. Chem. Soc., AAAS, Am. Med. Writers Assn. Iota Sigma Pi. Roman Catholic. Home: 2678 Byrneside Dr Cincinnati OH 45239 Office: Winton Hill Tech Center Cincinnati OH 45224

CENTONI, LEONARD GINO, fin. co. exec.; b. Chgo., Oct. 13, 1948; s. Gino Joseph and Agnes Geneva (Pausche) C.; A.S., Triton Coll., 1968. Programming and systems analyst J.L. Simmons Constrn. Co., Chgo., 1973-76; systems analyst Triton Coll., River Grove, Ill., 1976-77; product analyst Am. Valuation Cons., Inc., Des Plaines, Ill., 1977-79; computer applications project leader Chgo. Bd. of Trade, 1979—. Served with USAF, 1969-73. Home: 1306 S Finley St Apt 1K Lombard IL 60148 Office: Chicago Board of Trade 141 W Jackson St Room 1460 Chicago IL 60604

CERNEY, JAMES VINCENT, med. sports injury and health services co. exec.; b. Detroit, Jan. 27, 1914; s. James and Anna (Hein) C.; student Hiram Coll., 1935; A.B., Miami U., 1939; Dr. Podiatric Medicine, Ohio Coll. Podiatric Medicine, 1943; Dr. Mechanotherapy, Central States Coll. Physiatrics, 1948, D. Chiropractic, 1953; m. Martha Elizabeth French, Nov. 2, 1940; children—James F., Lee Carol (Mrs. John Spitler), Patricia Kay (Mrs. Raymond McIntire), Jeffrey Lynn, Kimberle Laine. Leader dance band, 1931-32; dancer Jack Lynch Revue, 1932-33; writer Northwest Sch. of Air series, stas. WLW, WHK, WCLE, 1939; publicity, promotion and merchandising mgr. radio sta. WING, Dayton, 1940; practice podiatric medicine, Dayton, 1943—; pres. Profl. Research, Dayton, 1944—, Sports Injuries Research, Inc., 1978—. Pres. Dayton Triangle Profl. Football Team, 1958. Dir. pub. info. CD, Dayton, 1957-58. Recipient first prize award Nat. Podiatry Assn., 1952, meritorious award Civil Defense, 1954; named Ky. col. Mem. Central States Coll. Physiatrics (pres. 1960-61). Ohio Mechanotherapists (pres. 1960-61), County Podiatry Soc. (pres. 1962), Authors Guild, Nat. Athletic Trainers Assn., Internat. Platform Assn., Am. Coll. Sports Medicine, Acad. Chinese Medicine, C. of C. (various coms. 1958-59), Dayton Purple Mask Theatre (pres. 1958), Dayton Ballet Guild (pres. 1958), Phi Kappa Tau. Mason. Author: Athletic Injuries, 1963; How to Develop a Million Dollar Personality, 1964; Confidence and Power for Successful Living, 1966; Dynamic Laws of Thinking Rich, 1967; Stay Younger-Live Longer, 1968; Talk Your Way to Success with People, 1968; Thirteen Steps to New Personal Power, 1969; Complete Book of Athletic Taping Techniques, 1971; Acupuncture Without Needles, 1974; Modern Magic of Natural Healing with Water Therapy, 1974; A Handbook of Unusual and Unorthodox Healing Methods, 1975; Prevent-System for Football Injuries, 1975; How to Sell Yourself to Others, 1979; Secrets of Chinese Folk Medicine, 1979; (novel) Flame Durrell, 1971; (stage plays) Blues in the Night, 1939, Fury, 1960, History of the Shiloh' Church, 1959. Editor Ohio Podiatry Jour., 1944. Contbr. articles to popular mags. Inventor throw away toothbrush, 1945, whirlpool bath system, 1946. Creator Skip Holiday series for radio, 1957. Home: 5235 N Main St Dayton OH 45415 Office: 5045 N Main St Dayton OH 45415

CERNEY, MARY ELLEN, clin. psychologist; b. Detroit, Apr. 23, 1929; d. Stephen Simon and Mary Anne (Neigoot) Cerney; B.A. summa cum laude, Coll. St. Francis, Joliet, Ill., 1960; M.A., Cath. U. Am., 1962, Ph.D., 1965; grad. Topeka Inst. Psychoanalysis, 1981. Tchr. music pub. and parochial elementary schs., Northwestern Ohio, 1948-62; student Cath. U. Am., Washington, 1963-65, instr. psychology, 1964-67; instr. ednl. psychology Mary Manse Coll., Toledo, Ohio, 1965-66; directress juniorate, Sisters St. Francis, Tiffin, Ohio, 1965-69; instr. ednl. psychology Coll. St. Francis, Joliet, 1966-67; Madonna Coll., Livonia, Mich., 1967-69; postdoctoral clin. psychology Topeka (Kans.) State Hosp., 1969-70; postdoctoral clin. psychology Menninger Found., Topeka, 1970-72, clin. psychologist, psychotherapist, hosp. therapist, supr. psychotherapy vocat. assessment program, 1972—; cons. vocation program, Toledo Diocese, also permanent deacon program. Diplomate Am. Bd. Profl. Psychology; cert. clin. psychologist, Ohio, Kans. Mem. Am. Psychol. Assn., Ohio Psychol. Assn., Soc. Personality Assessment. Contbr. articles to psychol. jours. Home: 900 Lincoln St Topeka KS 66606 Office: Menninger Foundation Box 829 Topeka KS 66601

CERUTTI, EDWARD RAPHAEL, pediatrician; b. Argentina, Dec. 21, 1923; came to U.S., 1963; s. Edward T. and Adella Cerutti; M.D., Buenos Aires (Argentina) Med. Coll., 1950; m. Marilyn Joan Baker, Apr. 18, 1950; children—Edward, Cecily Cerutti-Dole, Daniel. Practice medicine specializing in pediatrics, Mayfield Heights, Ohio,; chief pediatrics Booth Meml. Hosp.; fellow in pediatrics Cleve. Clinic Found., 1963-65; med. asso. La Leche League, 1973; bd. cons. Educated Childbirth, Inc., 1976, mem. profl. adv. bd., 1976-81; asst. clin. prof. pediatrics Case Western Res. U., 1976-81. Diplomate Am. Bd. Pediatrics. Fellow Am. Acad. Pediatrics, Internat. Coll. Pediatrics (Switzerland); mem. Internat. Child Edn. Assn. Office: 6801 Mayfield Rd Mayfield Heights OH 44124

CESARE, ANTHONY GIORGI, JR., writer; b. Chgo., July 31, 1943; s. Anthony Giorgi and Genevieve Stephanie (Lucas) C.; grad. St. John's Mil. Acad., Delafield, Wis., 1961; B.A. in English, Parsons Coll., 1965; m. Margaret Ann Hooks, Sept. 27, 1981. Tech. writer T.M. Pubs., Chgo., 1965-67; copywriter Hilltop Advt., Battle Creek, Mich., 1967-68; mktg. and pub. relations coordinator Ad Art and Design, Kalamazoo, 1968-69; owner Cesare & Assos., Boulder, Colo., 1969-71; freelance writer, 1973-77; tech. editor Chemetron Fire Systems, Monee, Ill., 1971—; sr. tech. writer Allis-Chalmers Corp., 1979-80. Mem. Internat. Platform Assn., Am. Advt. Fedn., Writers Guild. Baptist. Author: The Feathers Technique, 1980. Editor: Chemetron Fire Systems Halon 1301 Design Manual, 1978; inventor card game Snaffle, 1978. Home: Box 407 Route 1 Lake Village IN 46349

CESARI, LAMBERTO, educator; b. Bologna, Italy, Sept. 23, 1910; s. Cesare and Amelia (Giannizzeri) C.; Ph.D. in Math., U. Pisa (Italy), 1933; m. Isotta Hornauer, Apr. 2, 1939. Came to U.S., 1949. Asst., Nat. Research Council Italy, 1935-39; asso. prof. U. Pisa, 1939-42; asso. prof. U. Bologna, 1942-47, prof. math., 1947-48; staff Inst. Advanced Study, Princeton, N.J., 1948; prof. math. U. Calif., Berkeley, 1949, U. Wis., 1950; prof. math. Purdue U., 1950-60; prof. math. U. Mich., Ann Arbor, 1960—, R. L. Wilder prof. math., 1976—. Corr. mem. Accademie delle Scienze di Bologna, Modena, Milano; mem. Math. Assn. Am., Am. Math. Soc. Author: Surface Area, 1955; Asymptotic Properties, 1959; also articles on differential equations, calculus of variations, real analysis. Editorial bd. Applicable Math. Jour., 1970—, Jour. Differential Equations, 1973—, Rendiconti Circolo Matematico di Palermo, 1960—. Home: 2021 Washtenaw Ave Ann Arbor MI 48104

CHA, JAI CHUL, pathologist; b. Seoul, Korea, June 12, 1945; s. Donghwan and Keumyai (Lee) C.; M.D., Seoul Nat. U., 1968; came to U.S., 1971, naturalized, 1978; m. Kwangsoon Nam, Nov. 2, 1970; children—Albert, Jennifer. Teaching fellow, resident in pathology Case Western Res. U., Cleve., 1973-76; asso. pathologist Graham Hosp. Assn., Canton, Ill., 1976—; clin. instr. Peoria Sch. Medicine, 1980—. Mem. Western Counties Subarea Adv. Council, Ill. Central Health System Agy., Inc., 1978—. Served with Korean Air Force, 1968-71. Diplomate Am. Bd. Pathology. Mem. AMA, Ill. Med. Soc., Fulton County Med. Soc. (pres.), Coll. Am. Pathologists, Am. Soc. Clin. Pathologists. Presbyterian. Club: Rotary. Home: 1030 N 1st Ave Canton IL 61520 Office: 210 W Walnut St Canton IL 61520

CHACOS, GREGORY P., structural engr.; b. Coshocton, Ohio, Jan. 30, 1930; s. Pete G. and Kathryn (Varveris) C.; B.S. in Civil Engring., Case Inst. Tech., 1951, M.S. in Civil Engring., 1958; m. Eileen Chacos, Aug. 19, 1956; children—Lori, Katina. Structural engr. Osborn Engring. Co., Cleve., 1958-61; head dept. structural engring. Dalton Dalton Assos., Cleve., 1961-65; asso. R.M. Gensert Assos., Cleve., 1965-67; pres. Chacos & Assos., Inc., Cleve., 1967—; lectr. in field. Served with U.S. Army, 1954-56. Recipient Spl. Citation award Am. Inst. Steel Constrn., 1977; award of excellence in archtl. and engring. design Prestressed Concrete Inst., 1969. Registered profl. engr., Ohio, Colo., Fla., Ga., Idaho, Ill., Md., Mass., Mich., N.J., N.Y., N.C., Pa., W.Va. Mem. ASCE, Cleve. Cons. Engrs. Assn., Nat. Soc. Profl. Engrs., Cleve. Engring. Soc., Am. Concrete Assn., Sigma Xi. Office: 21 Alpha Dr Cleveland OH 44143

CHADDICK, HARRY FRANCIS, real estate developer; b. Chgo., Aug. 27, 1905; s. William Baldwin and Maud M. (LeBlanc) C.; student public schs., Chgo.; m. Elaine M. Torbik, Apr. 27, 1955; 1 dau., Camille Hatzenbuehler. From truck driver to owner, chief exec. officer Am. Transp. Co.-Standard Freight Lines, Chgo., 1931-47; pres., founder Chgo. Indsl. Dist., Inc., 1961-75; developer Ford City Complex, 1961-81; pres., chief exec. officer 1st Am. Realty Co., Chgo., 1964—, parent co. Near South Co., Inc., 1959-67, Harry F. Chaddick Assos., Inc., 1954—, Carnegie Constrn. & Devel., 1961—, Harry F. Chaddick Realty, Inc., 1966—, South Pulaski Corp., 1966—, Forest Park Mall, Inc., 1978—, Palm Springs Country Club and Fair Condominiums (Calif.), 1969—, Andreas Hills, 1972—, Spring Crest Water & Power Co., 1977—, Tennis Club and Hotel, 1961-80 (all Palm Springs); adv., cons. transp. affairs North African invasion to U.S. Govt., 1943; dep. dir. Chgo. CD Corps, 1948. Chmn., Chgo. Zoning Bd. Appeals, 1967-72, Chgo. Mayor's Com. on Rent Control, 1976-78; co-chmn. Chgo. Econ. Devel. Commn., 1976—. Recipient City of Hope award, 1967; Horatio Alger award, 1970, Golden Plate award, 1971; named Chgo.'s Outstanding Real Estate Developer, Little Flower Soc., 1965. Mem. Am. Trucking Assn. (past chmn. bd. govs.), Central Motor Freight Assn. (past pres.), Chgo. Assn. Commerce and Industry, Nat. Assn. Rev. Appraisers, Civic Fedn., Chgo. Real Estate Bd., Better Bus. Bur. Met. Chgo., Ill. C. of C., Chgo. Conv. and Tourism Bur., Am. Truck Hist. Soc., Lambda Alpha. Clubs: City, Hundred of Cook County, Mid-Am., Tower, Traffic, Executive (Chgo.); Whitehall; Ridgemoore Country; O'Donnell Golf; Tennis; Palm Springs Country. Office: 123 W Madison St Chicago IL 60602*

CHAFFEE, ESTHER RIDENOUR (MRS. THOMAS K. CHAFFEE), educator; b. Lima, Ohio; d. Joshua Mechling and Jennie (Hitchcock) Ridenour; student Wittenberg U., 1929-30, Ball State U., 1956-57, Bluffton Coll., 1932-33, U. Mich., 1950-51; B.A. in Music Edn. Lawrence U., 1963; m. David R. Meily, May 23, 1934 (dec. 1972); children—Helen Adelia Chaffee Bayer, Martha Frances (Mrs. Edward C. Senechal), Sara Elizabeth (Mrs. David C. Hayden); m. 2d, Rev. Thomas K. Chaffee, Jr., Aug. 1975. Elementary vocal music tchr., Lima, 1932-34, Morgan Sch., Appleton, Wis., 1963-75; substitute tchr., Washington, 1934-36, Pontiac and Birmingham, Mich., 1945-55; high sch. music tchr., Marion, Ind., 1955-58. Asst. organist Nat. City Christian Ch., Washington, 1934-36; organist, choir dir. First Bapt. Ch., Birmingham, 1950-53, All Sts. Episcopal Ch., Appleton, 1958-64, St. Thomas Episcopal Ch., Menasha, Wis., 1964-75; organist, choir master St. Albans Episcopal Ch., Olney, Ill., and St. Mary's Episcopal Ch., Robinson, Ill., 1975-77, St. Anne's Ch., De Pere, Wis., 1977—. Vol. tchr., programmer Children's Hosp., Detroit, 1950-54; dir. Civic Music Series, Marion, 1952; music tchr. Retarded Children's Sch., Marion, 1954-55; asst. music therapist Winnebago State Hosp., Oshkosh, Wis., 1967-71; music coordinator Opportunity Centers, SE Ill. Daycare Center. Mem. Organ Guild, Wis. Acad. Arts, Nat., Wis. music educators guilds, Am. Contract

Bridge League (life master). Composer: St. Thomas and St. Anne Mass, other sacred works. Home and office: 2600 Riverside Dr Green Bay WI 54301

CHAFIN, DON CARLYLE, elec. co. exec.; b. Logan, W.Va., Aug. 25, 1939; s. Marion R. and Virginia W. (Donevant) C.; B.M.E. with honors, W.Va. U., 1966; M.M.E., Rutgers U., 1968; grad. U.S. Army Engr. Sch., 1972; postgrad. in mech. engring. Ohio State U., 1974—; m. Nancy A. Helton, Dec. 22, 1978; children—Sherrie, Keith, Dawn, Victoria, Marty. Mem. tech. staff Bell Telephone Labs., Holmdel, N.J. and Denver, 1966-72; prin. engr. research and devel. center North Electric Co., Delaware, Ohio, 1972-75, mgr., asst. dir., 1975-78; asst. dir. N. Tech. Center ITT N.Electric Co., Delaware, 1978—; sr. engr., group leader GTE Automatic Electric Labs., Northlake Ill., 1975. Served with U.S. Army, 1961-64. Registered profl. engr., Colo. Mem. ASME (asso.), Soc. Am. Mil. Engrs., Nat. Mgmt. Assn., Res. Officers Assn., Inst. Printed Circuits (ofcl. rep.), Internat. Platform Assn., Pi Tau Sigma, Sigma Nu. Methodist. Clubs: Worthington Hills Country, Continental, Windsong, Olentangy. Home: 256 E Granville Rd Worthington OH 43085 Office: PO Box 20345 Columbus OH 43220

CHAI, WINBERG, educator; b. Shanghai, China, Oct. 16, 1932; came to U.S., 1951, naturalized, 1973; s. Ch'u and Mei-en (Tsao) C.; student Hartwick Coll., 1951-53; B.A., Wittenberg U., 1955; M.A., New Sch. for Social Research, 1958; Ph.D., N.Y. U., 1968; m. Carolyn Everett, Mar. 17, 1966; children—Maria May-lee, Jeffrey Tien-yu. Lectr., New Sch. for Social Research, 1957-61; vis. asst. prof. Drew U., 1961-62; asst. prof. Fairleigh Dickinson U., 1962-65; asso. prof. U. Redlands, 1965-73; prof., chmn. CCNY, 1973-79; disting. prof. polit. sci., v.p. U. S.D., Vermillion, 1979-81; cons. Iowa Assn. Ind. Colls. and Univs., 1981—; cons. Software System & Tech., Inc. Mem. S.D. Com. on Humanities, 1980. Ford Found. humanities grantee, 1968, 69; Haynes Found. fellow, 1967, 68; Pacific Cultural Found. grantee, 1978; NSF grantee, 1970; Hubert Eaton Meml. Fund grantee, 1972-73; Field Found. grantee, 1973, 75; Henry Luce Found. grantee, 1978. Mem. Am. Assn. Chinese Studies (pres. 1978-80), AAAS, AAUP, Am. Polit. Sci. Assn., N.Y. Acad. Sci., Internat. Studies Assn. Democrat. Roman Catholic. Author: (with Ch'u Chai) The Story of Chinese Philosophy, 1961, The Changing Society of China, 1962, rev. edit., 1969, The New Politics of Communist China, 1972, The Search for a New China, 1975; editor: Essential Works of Chinese Communism, 1969; (with James Hsiung) Asia and U.S. Foreign Policy, 1981; co-translator: A Treasury of Chinese Literature, 1965.

CHAIREZ, RUBEN, virologist; b. El Paso, Tex., Apr. 20, 1942; s. Paul and Mary C.; B.A., UCLA, 1965; Ph.D., Oreg. State U., Corvallis, 1970; m. Yolanda Fernandez Andrade, Dec. 23, 1978; 1 son, Paul. Fellow dept. biol. scis. Purdue U., 1970-72; research fellow dept. virology Baylor Coll. Medicine, Houston, 1972-74; asst. prof. biology George Mason U., Fairfax, Va., 1974-77; team leader Abbott Labs., North Chicago, Ill., 1977—. Mem. AAAS, Am. Soc. Microbiology, Sigma Xi, Phi Sigma. Roman Catholic. Contbr. articles to profl. jours. Home: 1045 Linden Ave Deerfield IL 60015 Office: 14th St and Sheridan De North Chicago IL 60064

CHAKIRIS, KENNETH MILTON, marketing exec.; b. Detroit; s. Nicholas and Irene (Cloud) C.; B.A., Mich. State U.; postgrad. Loyola U. (Chgo.); m. Betty June Hughes; children—Kenneth N., James L., Carolyn A. Dir. mktg. TRW Inc., Cleve., 1955-70; v.p. sales Rust-Oleum Internat., Evanston, Ill., 1970-74; sales/mktg. cons. Nat. Gypsum Co., Memphis, 1974-77; mktg. cons. Orgn. Renewal, Inc., Washington, 1977—; exec. v.p. Ill. Bronze Paint Co., Lake Zurich, 1978-80; prin. B.J. Chakiris & Assos., Inc., 1980—. Served with USAF. Decorated Air medal with bronze oak leaf cluster. Mem. Am. Mktg. Assn., Mid-West Planning Assn., Sales and Mktg. Execs. Assn. Chgo., Sales and Mktg. Execs. Assn. Internat., Internat. Cons. Found. Lutheran. Club: Rotary. Address: 755 Lincoln Ave Winnetka IL 60093

CHALGIAN, CHARLES, educator; b. Union City, N.J., July 8, 1930; s. John and Araxe C.; A.B., Antioch Coll., 1958; M.A., Harvard U., 1959; m. Sara Lou Hemenger, Apr. 1, 1955; children—Elizabeth, Douglas, Johanna, Juliet. Tchr. Algonac Community Schs., 1959-61; prof. econs. Macomb County Coll., Warren, Mich., 1961—, active panels; pub. Brown City Banner, weekly newspaper, Sanilac County, Mich. Chmn. Macomb Essentials Transp. Service, 1980-82, mem., 1976—; mem. Macomb County Bd. Commrs., 1976-80; bd. dirs. Southeastern Mich. Transp. Authority, 1978-80. Served with USAF, 1949-53. Decorated UN medal with two stars. Fulbright award, 1965. Mem. Am. Econ. Assn., Democrat. Presbyterian. Author: Current Economic Issues, 1967; contbr. articles to publs. Home: 35290 Moravian St Sterling Heights MI 48077 Office: Macomb County College South Campus Warren MI 48093

CHALKLEY, THOMAS HENRY FERGUSON, ophthalmic surgeon; b. N.Y.C., Nov. 3, 1933; s. Lyman and Katherine (Ferguson) C.; B.A., U. Wis., 1955, M.D., 1958; m. Cynthia Carroll, Nov. 21, 1975; children—Ellen Elizabeth, Deborah Katherine. Intern, E. J. Meyer Hosp., Buffalo, 1958-59; resident physician Northwestern U. Med. Sch., 1960-62; practice medicine specializing in ophthalmic surgery, Chgo., 1962—; attending physician Northwestern Meml., VA Lakeside hosps., Chgo., 1962—; asso. prof. clin. ophthalmology Northwestern U. Med. Sch., 1962—. Bd. dirs. Ill. Soc. Prevention Blindness, 1978-79. Served to comdr. USNR, 1966-68. Recipient Disting. Merit award Hadley Sch. for Blind, 1979. Mem. Internat. Strabismological Soc., Am. Acad. Ophthalmology Pan Am. Ophthal. Soc., Chgo. Ophthal. Soc. (pres. 1977-78), AAUP, Internat. Artists Assn., Wis. Agriculturist. Author: Your Eyes, 1973, 2d edit., 1981; also articles; editorial bd. Am. Jour. Ophthalmology, 1965—. Home: 260 E Chestnut St Chicago IL 60611 Office: 700 N Michigan Ave Chicago IL 60611

CHALMERS, E(DWIN) LAURENCE, JR., museum adminstr.; b. Wildwood, N.J., Mar. 24, 1928; s. Edwin Laurence and Carolyn (Smith) C.; A.B., Princeton U., 1948, M.A., 1950, Ph.D., 1951; m. Hannah Kamp, 1973; 1 son, Timothy Blair; children by previous marriage—Edwin Laurence III, Thomas H. Instr. psychology Princeton U., 1951-52; asst. prof., then prof. psychology, asst. dean faculties Fla. State U., 1962-64, dean Coll. Arts and Scis., 1964-66, v.p. acad. affairs, 1966-69; chancellor U. Kan., Lawrence, 1969-72; pres. Art Inst. Chgo., 1972—. Served to 1st lt. USAF, 1953-56. Mem. Phi Beta Kappa, Sigma Xi, Omicron Delta Kappa. Home: 1301 N Astor St Chicago IL 60610 Office: Art Inst Chgo Chicago IL 60603

CHAMBERLAIN, DONALD SHERWOOD, radiologist; b. Cin., May 21, 1935; s. Sherwood Archibald and Christine Carter (Matthews) C.; B.A., Northwestern U., 1956, M.D., 1960; m. Lillian Joyce Knudsen, June 2, 1956; children—Cheryl Ann, Daniel. Intern, U. Cin. Gen. Hosp., 1960-61, resident in radiology, 1961-64; practice medicine, specializing in radiology, Radiology, Inc., South Bend, Ind., 1966—; med. staff Meml. Hosp., South Bend, 1966—, Elkhart (Ind.) Gen. Hosp., 1966—, Parkview Hosp., Plymouth, Ind., 1966—, South Bend Clinic, 1966—; dir., sec. Ind. Physicians Ins. Co.; dir. X-Ray Equipment Inc., Mishawaka, Ind., Radiology, Inc. Bd. dirs. No. Ind. Health Systems Agy., 1978—, exec. com., 1979—; bd. dirs. Ind. Med. Edn. and Devel. Info. Center, 1978—, Ind. State Wide Profl. Standards Rev. Council, 1978; bd. dirs. Ind. Area 2 PSRO Inc., 1974—, chmn., 1974-79. Served to capt. M.C., U.S. Army, 1964-66. Diplomate Am. Bd. Radiology. Fellow Am. Coll. Radiology; mem. Ind. Med. Soc. (trustee 1978—), St. Joseph County Med. Soc. (pres. 1976-77), AMA, Ind. Roentgen Soc., Radiol. Soc. N.Am., Am. Roentgen Ray Soc., N. Central Ind. Med. Edn. Found., South Bend Med. Found., Am. Radio Relay League, Lambda Chi Alpha, Phi Rho Sigma, Pi Kappa Epsilon. Methodist. Clubs: Profl. Investors, South Bend Country, Masons, Shriners. Contbr. articles to med. jours. Home: 54712 Merrifield Dr Mishawaka IN 46544 Office: 919 E Jefferson Blvd South Bend IN 46622

CHAMBERLAIN, WEBB PARKS, JR., ophthalmologist; b. Cleve., July 19, 1910; s. Webb Parks and Lucy Belle (Libbey) C.; m. Elizabeth Harker Newell, Dec. 4, 1948; children—Marilyn, Ann, Charlotte, Lucy, John. Intern, Univ. Hosps., Cleve., 1936-38; resident N.Y. Eye and Ear Infirmary, N.Y.C., 1938-41; practice medicine specializing in ophthalmology, Cleve., 1946—; ophthalmologist Luth. Med. Center, Cleve., 1946—; clin. prof. ophthalmology, dept. surgery Case Western Res. U. Sch. Medicine, 1958—. Trustee Great Lakes Shakespeare Festival, 1965—, v.p., 1969-72; trustee, pres. Cleve. Met. YMCA, 1977—; pres. Cleve. Med. Library Assn., 1961, trustee; trustee Cleve. Christian Home, 1965—, pres., 1968-69; trustee Hiram (Ohio) Coll., Cleve. Playhouse, 1977—, Cleve. Mus. Natural History, 1978—. Served to maj. M.C., AUS, 1941-46. Fellow Am. Bd. Ophthalmology, Am. Acad. Ophthalmology (honor award 1967), A.C.S. Clubs: Union Hermit, Chagrin Valley Hunt (Gates Mills, O.). Editor: Am. Orthoptic Jour., 1955-71; asso. editor Archives of Ophthalmology, 1961-63. Contbr. articles to various publs. Home: 19100 S Woodland Rd Shaker Heights OH 44122 Office: 1422 Euclid Ave Room 1324 Cleveland OH 44115

CHAMBERLIN, EDNA MAE, bank exec.; b. Dowagiac, Mich., Nov. 16, 1929; d. Michael J. and Mary T. (Luska) Sarabyn; A.A., South Bend Coll. Commerce, 1948; B.S. in Mgmt., Simmons Coll., 1979; postgrad. Nat. Trust Sch., Northwestern U.; m. Donald P. Chamberlin, Sept. 13, 1952. Accountant dept. redevelopment City of Mishawaka (Ind.), 1963-68; cons. City Planning Assos., Mishawaka, 1968-73; trust officer Nat. Bank & Trust Co. of South Bend (Ind.), 1973—. Com. chmn. United Way, 1975-77. Mem. Nat. Assn. Bank Women, South Bend Estate Planning Council, Pilot Club of South Bend. Roman Catholic. Club: Ladies of Elks. Home: 924 W Battell St Mishawaka IN 46544 Office: 112 W Jefferson Blvd South Bend IN 46601

CHAMBERS, BILLY JOE, ch. ofcl.; b. Ft. Worth, Tex., Dec. 13, 1932; s. Joseph Yancy and Bertha Clara (McMillen) C.; B.A., Baylor U., 1955; postgrad. Golden Gate Bapt. Theol. Sem., 1955-58; B.D., Southwestern Bapt. Theol. Sem., 1960; m. Ima Louise Tyson, Aug. 22, 1954; children—Joseph Thurman, Marc William, Carol Lynn. Ordained to ministry, Bapt. Ch., 1956; pastor, So. Bapt. Chs., Ohio, 1960-73; denominational worker Mich. State Baptists, 1973-77; pastor Bapt. Ch., Burton, Mich., 1977-71; denominational worker, dir. ch. services Minn.-Wis. Bapt. Offices, Rochester, Minn., 1981—; associational Sunday sch. dir. World Mission Confs., 1961-75. Trustee Golden Gate Bapt. Sem., 1970-73, Midwestern Bapt. Sem., 1978-81. Mem. Alpha Kappa Delta. Republican. Office: 519 16th St SE Rochester MN 55901

CHAMBERS, EARL RICHARD, personnel adminstr.; b. Wyoming, Ill., Nov. 4, 1916; s. John Thomas and Margaret Jane (Lawless) C.; B.Ed., Ill. State Normal U., 1938; M.A., U. Ill., 1947, postgrad., 1948-53; m. Jane Margaret Petersen, May 8, 1954; 1 son, Robert. Profl. personnel work Ill. Civil Service Commn., 1947-53, chief of exams. adminstrng., employee selection, 1951-53; personnel dir. St. Louis County, Mo., 1953—. Mem. Gov. Mo. Citizens Adv. Council Higher Edn. Act, 1972-73. Served from pvt. to tech. sgt. AUS, 1942-46; Philippines, New Guinea. Mem. Pub. Personnel Assn. (exec. bd. local chapter, 1952-53, regional sec.-treas., 1956-57, regional 1st v.p. 1963-64, regional chmn. 1964-65), Am. Soc. Personnel Adminstrn. (accredited); Am. Soc. Pub. Adminstrn. (exec. bd. local chpt. 1951-52, 59-63, 64-65, 70-71, pres. Met. St. Louis 1963-64), Internat. Personnel Mgmt. Assn. (v.p. St. Louis chpt. 1973-74, pres. 1974-75), Kappa Delta Pi, Pi Gamma Mu. Contbr. articles, abstracts and revs. to profl. jours. Home: 12 Armstrong Dr Glendale MO 63122 Office: 7900 Forsyth Blvd Clayton Mo 63105

CHAMBERS, ERNEST, state legislator; b. Omaha, July 10, 1937; B.A., Creighton U., J.D.; children—Gayla, Mark, Ernie, David. Mem. Nebr. Legislature, 1970—. Address: 3116 N 24th St Omaha NE 68110

CHAMBERS, MARILYN LEE, educator; b. Ashland, Ky., Nov. 20, 1933; d. Bernie Franklin and Hazel Kathryn (Johnson) Patton; B.A., Berea Coll., 1955; postgrad. Ohio State U., summers 1974-77; m. Paul Willard Chambers, Jan. 1, 1961; children—Paula Lynn, Jennifer Lee. Tchr., Princeton (Ohio) City Schs., 1955-63; partner Western Auto Asso. Store, Hillsboro, Ohio, 1968-74; instr. Laurel Oaks Career Devel. Center, Wilmington, Ohio, 1974—; advisor to sch. publs. and clubs. Active Girl Scouts U.S.A., Am. Heart Assn. Mem. NEA, Ohio Vocat. Assn., Am. Vocat. Assn., AAUW. Club: Mardi. Home: 148 Greystone St Hillsboro OH 45133 Office: 2738 Old State Route 73 Wilmington OH 45177

CHAMBERS, RICHARD LEON, investment banker; b. Chgo., July 1, 1943; s. Richard John and Dorothy (Rupe) C.; B.A. with honors, Cornell Coll., 1965; postgrad. Phillips U., 1968-69, N.Y. U., 1970, DePaul U., 1973; m. Karen Lynn Sokody, Apr. 6, 1968; children—Elizabeth Lea, Victoria Lynn. Trading trainee John Nuveen & Co., Chgo., 1965-66, bond trader, Chgo. and N.Y.C., 1966-68, 69; bond trader R.W. Presspich, & Co., N.Y.C. and Chgo., 1969-73; v.p. Loewi & Co., Inc., Chgo., 1973-78; prin., co-founder Barrington Trading Co. (Ill.), 1978—; advisor to Urban Planning Cons., 1980-81. Served with USAF, 1966, 68-69. Named Disting. Grad., USAF Officers Training Sch., San Antonio, 1966. Mem. Cornell Coll. Alumni Assn. Republican. Methodist. Clubs: Barrington Hills Country, Mid Day, Biltmore Country, Lions, Cornell Coll. Pres.'s. Co-creator of taxable bond database, price analysis computer program, 1974. Home: 128 Colony Dr Barrington IL 60010 Office: 200 Applebee St Barrington IL 60010

CHAMBERS, ROBERTA NADINE, organist, educator; b. Arcola, Ill., Oct. 29, 1924; d. Horace Watson and Ethel Irene (Bartholomew) Mulliken; Mus.B., U. Ill., 1947; M.S. in Music, Ill. State U., 1970; m. Mar. 10, 1949; children—Michael Lee, Linda Sue. Asst. instr. keyboard harmony U. Ill., 1946; instr. music Tenn. Wesleyan Coll., Athens, 1947-49; asso. prof. music Lincoln (Ill.) Christian Coll., 1953—; pvt. music tchr.; organist for ch. and service vol. activities. Mem. Am. Guild Organists, Assn. Christian Coll. Music Educators, Nat. Piano Tchrs. Guild, Pi Kappa Lambda, Sigma Alpha Iota. Mem. Christian Ch. Home: 505 Oglesby St Lincoln IL 62656 Office: Lincoln Christian Coll Box 178 Lincoln IL 62656

CHAMBERS, THOMAS EDWARD, priest, educator; b. Cleve., Aug. 1, 1934; s. James Clyde and Mary Celestine (Malone) C.; B.A., U. Notre Dame, 1956, M.A., 1962, Ph.D., 1976; M.A., Holy Cross Coll., 1961. Ordained priest Roman Catholic Ch.; dir. student residence U. Notre Dame, 1970-72, dir. student activities, 1972-74, asst. v.p. for student affairs, 1975-76; v.p. academic affairs Ursuline Coll., Pepper Pike, Ohio, 1976—. Contbr. articles in field to profl. jours. Home: Gilmour Academy Gates Mills OH 44045 Office: Ursuline College 2550 Lander Rd Pepper Pike OH 44124

CHAMBERS, WALTER SCOTT, security cons.; b. Chgo., Mar. 13, 1945; s. Clarence Warren and Helen Eleanor (Anderson) C.; A.A., Kendall Coll., Evanston, Ill., 1968; B.A. in Criminal Justice, Carthage Coll., 1977; m. Kathleen Berg, Jan. 25, 1968; children—Constance, Rebecca, Aaron. Founder, owner, pres. Chambers Agy., Ltd., Libertyville, Ill., 1979—; exec. dir. Chambers Security Inst., 1982—. Mem. Am. Mgmt. Assn., Am. Soc. Tng. and Devel., Am. Soc. Indsl. Security, Am. Soc. Profl. Cons., Meeting Planners Internat., Internat. Assn. Hosp. Security, Acad. Security Educators and Trainers, Council Internat. Investigators, World Assn. Detectives, Nat. Assn. Legal Investigators. Office: 116 Broadway PO Box 561 Libertyville IL 60048*

CHAMBLIN, RODNEY MACK, mfrs. rep.; b. West Union, Ohio, Oct. 8, 1952; s. Paul and Agnes (Bradford) C.; A.S., U. Cin., 1972, B.B.A., 1974. Sales trainee Gen. Box Co., Cin., 1974; profl. sales rep. Winthrop Labs., Cin., 1975-79, Precept div. G.D. Searle, 1979-81, Chamblin Agy./Med. Data Bank, 1981—. Mem. Greater Cin. Jaycees (dir. civic affairs 1977-78, v.p. chpt. mgmt. 1978-79), Delta Sigma Pi. Clubs: Up Downtowners, UCATS, Masons (32d degree Scottish Rite). Office: PO Box 14117 Cincinnati OH 45214

CHAMPAGNE, BRENDA (JEAN) LAMB, occupational therapist; b. Northampton, Mass., Aug. 14, 1951; d. Frank Gilbert and Gertrude Maria (MacArthur) Lamb; student Winthrop Coll., 1969-70, Boston U., 1970; B.S. in Occupational Therapy, Quinnipiac Coll., 1974; m. Clement Henri Champagne, Nov. 9, 1974; 1 dau., Melissa Yolande. Occupational therapist Alexandra Pavilion, Montreal (Que., Can.) Children's Hosp., 1974-75; therapist Area Coop. Ednl. Services, North Haven, Conn., 1975, Trinity Luth. Hosp., Kansas City, Mo., 1976; part time therapist Bethany Med. Center, Kansas City, Kans., 1976-77, dir. occupational therapy, 1977-81; part time asst. prof. dept. occupational therapy, U. Kans., 1977; chmn. Greater Kansas City Occupational Therapy Adminstrv. Council, 1978-79; cons. profl. adv. com. Outreach Rehab. Services, Inc., 1979-80; cons. profl. adv. bd. Crossland Rehab. Agy., Inc., 1980—; council pres. U. Kans. Council on Occupational Therapy Edn., 1980—, chmn. coms., 1978-81. Mem. Am. Occupational Therapy Assn. (registered occupational therapist, elected commn. on edn. 1980—, specialty sect. on devel. disabilities 1978—, on mental health 1978—), Kans. Occupational Therapy Assn. (profl., newsletter editor 1977-79, state long range plan chmn. 1979—, state v.p. 1979-81). Contbg. author, editor: MidTerm Evaluation of Fieldwork Experience, 1979. Home: 8215 Webster St Kansas City KS 66109 Office: 51 N 12th St Kansas City KS 66102

CHAMPAGNE, PAUL JOSEPH, educator; b. Hartford, Conn., Sept. 18, 1947; s. Felix Joseph and Mary Immaculata (Roberts) C.; B.A., Providence Coll., 1969; M.A., U. Hartford, 1973; Ph.D., U. Mass., 1977; m. Natalie Marie Hladky, Aug. 4, 1972; 1 dau., Nora Marie. Asst. underwriter Travelers Ins. Co., Hartford, Conn., 1969-71; instr. N. Adams (Mass.) State Coll., 1976-77; asst. prof. bus. Mich. Technol. U., Houghton, 1977—. Mem. Acad. Mgmt., Soc. for Advancement Mgmt. Contbr. articles in field to profl. jours. Home: 207 Clark St Houghton MI 49931 Office: Sch Bus Mich Technol Univ Houghton MI 49931

CHAMPEAU, BRUCE EDWIN, office adminstr.; b. Mpls., Mar. 11, 1943; s. John Matthew (stepfather) and Alice Marie Wilhelm; B.L.S., U. Okla., 1974. Cost estimator Bartley Sales Co., Inc., Mpls., 1961-63; supr. Midwest Bldg. Services, Inc., Mpls., 1963-68; mgr. gen. services Dorsey, Windhorst, Hannaford, Whitney & Halladay, Mpls., 1968-79; office adminstr. Borgelt, Powell, Peterson & Frauen, S.C., Milw., 1979—; condr. workshops Mpls.-St. Paul chpt. Adminstrv. Mgmt. Soc., 1977, 78. Bd. deacons Emanuel Lutheran Ch., Mpls., 1964-67. Mem. Assn. Legal Adminstrs., Adminstrv. Mgmt. Soc. (past dir.), Acad. Cert. Adminstrv. Mgrs. (cert. 1977), Word Processing Soc., Inc. Home: 1009 N Jackson St Milwaukee WI 53202 Office: Borgelt Powell Peterson & Frauen S C 735 N Water St Suite 1500 Milwaukee WI 53202

CHAMPION, OTELIA ELIZABETH, ednl. counselor; b. Columbus, Ga., Feb. 4, 1914; d. Marshall and Betty E. (Thomas) Simpson; B.S., Northwestern U., 1963, M.A. in Guidance, 1968; student Chgo. Conservatory of Music, 1931-33, Crane Jr. Coll., Chgo., 1929-31; m. William Theodore Champion, Nov. 23, 1960. Tchr. of piano and voice Lemons Conservatory of Music, Indpls., 1936; pvt. tchr. piano and voice, Robbins, Ill., 1937-45, Harvey, Ill., 1937-45, East Chicago, Ind., 1939-54; choir dir. First Bapt. Ch., East Chicago, 1939-54; sec., mgr. Bowles Music House, Chgo., 1939-51; tchr. music Columbus Sch., East Chicago, 1963-70; counselor Block Jr. High Sch., East Chicago, 1971—. Minister of music Zion Bapt. Ch., East Chicago, 1955—; mem. ednl. adv. com. of 1st. Congressional Dist., 1977—. Recipient Dedicated Service award Zion Bapt. Ch., 1966, Disting. Service award Ind. Music Educators Assn., 1970, Cert. of Community Service, Gov. of Ill. 1977, Very Important Citizen award City of East Chicago, 1981, others. Mem. Am. Personnel and Guidance Assn., Ind. Personnel and Guidance Assn., Nat. Assn. of Colored Women's Clubs (pres. 1980—), State Ind. Federated Clubs (1st. v.p. 1978-79, pres. 1979-80), Sigma Gamma Rho. Bapist. Home: 4731 Tod St East Chicago IN 46312 Office: 2700 Cardinal Dr East Chicago IN 46312

CHAMPOUX, ELLEN MILES, educator; b. Prescott, Ariz., May 23, 1920; d. Lyman Fay and Emily Ellen (Fitzpatrick) Barber; B.S. in Edn., No. Ariz. U., 1953; M.A. in Edn., Ariz. State U., 1957; Ed.D. Pa. State U., 1962. Mem. faculty Iowa State Univ., 1961-63, Kans. State Univ., 1963-67, Univ. N.C., Greensboro, 1967-74; Berea (Ky.) Coll., 1974-77; asso. prof. home econs. edn., No. Ill. Univ., DeKalb, 1977—; tchr., cons. Ill. Vocat. Home Econ. Curriculum Com., 1979-81. U. N.C. grantee, 1969-72; named Outstanding Alumna No. Ariz. U., 1974. Mem. Am. Home Econs. Assn., Ill. Home Econs. Assn., Am. Ednl. Research Assn., Am. Vocat. Assn., Ill. Vocat. Assn., NEA, Assn. Tchr. Educators, Ill. Assn. Tchr. Educators, DeKalb Assn. Tchr. Edn., Assn. Supervision and Curriculum Devel., Ill. Assn. Supervision and Curriculum Devel., AAUP, Nat. Assn. Tchr. Edn. Home Econs., Ill. Vocat. Home Econ. Tchrs. Assn., Home Econ. Edn. Assn., Nat. Assn. Coll. Tchrs. Clothing and Textiles, Omicron Nu, Pi Lambda Theta, Phi Kappa Phi. Home: 807 Ridge Dr Apt 904 DeKalb IL 60115 also 707 Albany St Brunswick GA 31520

CHAN, CHUN-WAH, social worker; b. Chao-Young, Kwangtung, China, July 22, 1945; s. Hak-Tang and So-Fong (Yeung) C.; came to U.S., 1969, naturalized, 1978; B.S.Sc. cum laude (scholar) Chinese U. Hong Kong, 1967; M.A. (scholar) U. Chgo., 1971; m. Heidi Kwok-Shun Cheng, June 15, 1968. Social work supr. Family Planning Assn. of Hong Kong, 1967-69; with Cook County Hosp., Chgo., 1971—, divisional dir. psychiat. social service div., 1973—, coordinator staff devel. and quality assurance dept. social service, 1978—; pvt. practice individual and family therapy, Chgo., 1977—. Leader Hong Kong Boy Scout Assn., 1964-69; divisional officer St. John Ambulance Brigade, Hong Kong, 1968-69; bd. dirs. Chinese Am. Service League, Chgo., 1977-78, chmn. nominating com., 1978, pres.

bd. dirs. 1978—. Cert. social worker, Ill. Mem. Nat. Assn. Social Workers, Acad. Cert. Social Workers, Asian Am. Mental Health Research Center. Home: 4946 Sunnyside Dr Hillside IL 60162 Office: Psychiatric Social Service Cook County Hospital 1825 W Harrison St Chicago IL 60612

CHAN, ROBERT JEFFREY, psychologist; b. Rochester, N.Y., Apr. 17, 1954; s. James Tao and Sing Yee (Chong) C.; B.A., Miami U., Oxford, Ohio, 1976; M.A., Central Mich. U., Mount Pleasant, 1979. Data analyst Area IV Profl. Standards Review Orgn. Mich., Saginaw, 1979-80; research asst. dept. psychology Central Mich. U., Mount Pleasant, 1976-78; research analyst Inst. Personal and Career Devel., Mt. Pleasant, 1978; research analyst dept. psychology St. Louis U., 1980; evaluation asso. Center for Application of Behavioral Scis., 1981—. Chue-Jen scholar, 1972-75. Mem. Am. Psychol. Assn., Am. Statis. Assn., Soc. Advancement Social Psychology, Evaluation Research Soc., Midwestern Psychol. Assn. Home: 3863 W Pine St Apt 616 Saint Louis MO 63108 Office: Dept Psychology St Louis U 221 N Grand St Saint Louis MO 63103

CHAN, SHERMAN HSIAW-YUAN, malting co. exec.; b. Hai-Nan Island, China, Apr. 12, 1945; s. Chong-Kow and Wei C.; came to U.S., 1972, naturalized, 1977; B.S., Taiwan U., 1968; M.S., N.D. State U., 1976; m. Amy Ya-Mei Cheng, Sept. 6, 1970; 1 son, Charles Chia-Hua. Research asst., Inst. Botany, Academia Sinica, Taipei, 1969-72; quality control supr. Fleischmann Malting Co., Chgo., 1976-77; prin. research chemist Pabst Brewing Co., Milw., 1978-80; dir. quality assurance Rahr Malting Co., Shakopee, Minn., 1980—, also dir. Mem. Am. Assn. Brewing Chemists, Am. Assn. Cereal Chemists, Inst. Food Technologists. Home: 8224 Nevada Circle Bloomington MN 55438 Office: PO Box 127 Shakopee MN 55379

CHANDEL, MAHENDRA KUMAR, surgeon; b. Dhar, India, Jan. 9, 1944; s. C.K. and Yashodhara (Rathore) C.; came to U.S., 1970, naturalized, 1974; B.S., U. Indore (India), 1961; M.D., M.G.M. Med. Coll., Indore, 1966; m. Carol Ann Lennox, Apr. 29, 1977; children—Leena, Madhur, Michael. Intern, St. Luke's Hosp., Fargo, N.D., 1970-71; resident St. Elizabeth Hosp., Youngstown, Ohio, 1971-72, Highland Park (Mich.) Gen. Hosp., 1972-74; chief of surgery McNamara Community Hosp., Warren, Mich., 1975, Clare (Mich.) Osteo. Hosp., 1977, 79; practice medicine, specializing in gen. surgery, family practice, angiology, proctology, Clare, 1976—. Diplomate Am. Bd. Surgery, Am. Bd. Family Practice, Internat. Bd. Proctology. Fellow Internat. Coll. Surgeons, Am. Soc. Abdominal Surgery, Am. Acad. Family Practitioners, Am. Coll. Emergency Physicians, Am. Coll. Internat. Physicians; asso. fellow Am. Coll. Angiology; mem. AMA, Am. Soc. Contemporary Medicine and Surgery, Wayne County Med. Soc., Mich. Med. Soc., Clare/Isabella County Med. Soc. Office: 212 W 6th St Clare MI 48617

CHANDLER, JAMES THOMAS, police psychologist; b. Pontiac, Mich., June 22, 1934; s. Albert Max and Marian (Thomson) C.; B.A., Wayne U., 1958, M.A., 1962; Ph.D., Holy Cross Coll., 1972; m. Kay Kirby, May 11, 1957; children—Lynn, Mark, Lisa, Eric. Staff clin. psychologist Plymouth State Home and Tng. Sch., Northville, Mich., 1965-66; dir. div. childhood mental illness and health Mich. Soc. Mental Health, Lathrop Village, Mich., 1966-68; psychologist Lincoln Park (Mich.) Public Schs., 1968-69; chief psychologist Kent Oaks Hosp. and Clinic, Grand Rapids, Mich., 1969-71; program coordinator, evaluator Kent County (Mich.) Community Mental Health Services Bd., 1971-72; adolescent care dir. Villa Maria, Grand Rapids, Mich., 1972-75; sch. psychologist, guidance officer Cath. Central High Sch., Grand Rapids, 1976-77; police psychologist Law Enforcement Clarification Center, Western Mich., 1977-79; chief psychologist Ill. Dept. Law Enforcement, Springfield, 1981—; cons. to numerous agys., 1962—. Chmn., Mich. Youth Services Info. System, Statewide Application Adv. Group, 1974-75. Served with USNR, 1956-60; comdr. Res. ret. Fellow Am. Acad. Crisis Interveners; mem. Am. Mental Health Counselors Assn., Am. Personnel and Guidance Assn., Fraternal Order Police, Internat. Assn. Chiefs of Police, Internat. Law Enforcement Stress Assn., Naval Res. Assn., Res. Officers Assn., Ret. Officers Assn., Am. Bus. Clubs. Contbr. articles to various publs. Home: 206 Broadway Apt #6 Springfield IL 62701 Office: State Regional Office Bldg 4500 S 6th St Rd Springfield IL 62706

CHANDLER, JOHN E(DGAR), publisher, state legislator; b. Topeka, July 13, 1915; s. Herbert E. and Ruth (Naylor) C.; A.B., U. Kans., 1937; children—Sara, Lucinda Chandler Koester, Mary Chandler O'Donnell, Leslie Chandler McDaniel. Copywriter, Continental Oil Co., Ponca City, Okla., 1937-40; advt. mgr. Ind. Refiners Service Corp., Wichita, Kans., 1940-41; gen. mgr. Sovereign Service, Inc., Wichita, 1945-48; dist. rep. Fred Eldean Orgn., Kansas City, Mo., 1948-49; advt. mgr. Wood River Oil & Refining Co., Wichita, 1949-50; owner, pub., editor Holton (Kans.) Recorder, 1950—; mem. Kans. Senate, 1977—; dir. Am. Savs. Assn., Wichita. Mem. Kans. Commn. on Assessment Equalization, 1953-54; mem. Holton Bd. Edn., 1959-63; mem. Holton Housing Authority, 1970-74; sec. Jud. Nominating Commn., 2d Jud. Dist. Kans., 1974-76; trustee William Allen White Found. Served to maj. U.S. Army, World War II. Decorated Bronze Star with oak leaf cluster. Mem. Kans. Press Assn. (pres. 1978-79), Sigma Delta Chi, Sigma Chi. Republican. Presbyterian. Clubs: Topeka Press, Rotary (dist. gov. 1961-62). Office: 109 W 4th St Holton KS 66436

CHANDLER, KATHLEEN LEONE, city councilwoman; b. Detroit, Sept. 19, 1932; d. Telford R. and Beatrice L. (Smith) McRae; B.A. cum laude, Mich. State U., 1956, M.S., 1957; postgrad. in public adminstrn. Kent State U., 1980—; m. Charles C. Chandler, July 12, 1958; children—Susan, Beth, Jenny. Tchr. public schs., Macomb County, Mich., 1952-54, Irving, Tex., 1959-60, Marquette, Mich., 1960-62; reading cons., dir. reading clinic Livonia (Mich.) Public Schs., 1957-59; mem. Kent (Ohio) City Council; tchr. summer courses Mich. State U., 1958-61. Bd. dirs. Portage County (Ohio) ARC, 1972—, chairwoman, 1979—; mem. N.E. Ohio council ARC, 1976—, sec., 1977-79; bd. dirs. LWV, Kent, 1976-79, fin. chairperson, 1977, voter service chairperson, 1978-79; chairperson Kent City Cancer Dr., 1977; pres. Univ. Women of Kent State U., 1979; pres. Davey Jr. High Sch. PTA, Kent, 1979; mem. Portage County Council Health and Social Agys. Recipient cert. appreciation, N.E. Ohio ARC, 1979, Portage County ARC, 1979, 80. Mem. Ohio Mcpl. League, Kappa Delta Pi, Phi Kappa Phi, Delta Zeta. Democrat. Clubs: Kent Area Dem., Federated Woman's of Portage County. Home: 455 Dansel Kent OH 44240

CHANDLER, SCOTT STONER, bus. exec.; b. Kansas City, Mo., Dec. 6, 1932; s. Edwin and Sarah (Stoner) C.; B.S. with honors, Kans. State U., 1954, M.S., 1957; postgrad. U. Wis., 1958-60; m. Marjorie Kay Pinther, Sept. 22, 1962; children—Scott Stoner, Holly Ann. Tech. sales Armour Indsl. Chem. Co., Chgo., 1960-62, market devel., 1962-63, industry mgr., 1963-65; sr. mktg. analyst Internat. Minerals & Chem. Corp., Libertyville, Ill., 1965-67, mgr. sales analysis, 1967-68, product mgr., 1968-70, dir. supply and devel., 1970-74, dir. comml. devel., 1974-75, now v.p., gen. mgr. vet. products div.; mem. steering com. Agri-Bus. Adv. Bd. Nat. Am. Indian Cattlemen's Assn.; mem. exec. com. Cattlemen's Action Legis. Fund; bd. dirs. Animal Health Inst., 1977-80; v.p., bd. dirs. Livestock and Meat Industry Council, Kans. State U. Mem. exec. bd. N.E. Ill. council Boy Scouts Am., 1974—. Served to 1st lt. USAF, 1954-56. Fellow Am. Inst. Chemists; mem. Midwest Chem. Mktg. Assn. (chmn. 1968-69, dir. 1969-70), Am. Chem. Soc., Midwest Planning Assn., Nat. Cattleman's Assn. (com. co-chmn., mem. spl. president's com.), U.S. Meat Export Fedn. (dir.), Beta Theta Pi, Gamma Sigma Delta, Alpha Zeta, Alpha Phi Omega. Republican. Mem. Evang. Covenant Ch. Am. Patentee in field. Home: 911 N Glenayre Dr Glenview IL 60025 Office: IMC Plaza Libertyville IL 60048

CHANDRA, GIRISH, steel co. exec.; b. Ballia, Uttar Pradesh, India, July 1, 1941; came to U.S., 1970; s. Vindhyachal Prasad; B.Sc., Banaras Hindu U., India, 1959; M.B.A., Case Western Res. U., Cleve., 1972; m. Chander Kiran Sood, July 8, 1973; children—Ankur, Pravir, Nupur. Prodn. supr. New Central Jute Mills Co., Calcutta, 1964-68; office supr., 1968-69; purchase officer Jaipur Metals and Electricals, Ltd. (India), 1969-70; inventory control analyst Alcan Aluminum Corp., Warren, Ohio, 1972-77; inventory mgr. Wheatland Tube Co. (Pa.), 1978-80, mgr. materials mgmt., 1981—. Mem. Am. Prodn. and Inventory Control Soc. (v.p. communications Youngstown chpt.). Hindu. Home: 9061 Altura Dr Warren OH 44484 Office: 1 Council Ave Wheatland PA 16161

CHANDRA, SATISH MISRA, statis. services co. exec.; b. Bhadaicha, Hardoi, India, Jan. 3, 1945; came to U.S., 1967, naturalized, 1981; s. Shambhu Ratan and Fulwasa Misra (Dwivedi) M.; M.S., U. Chgo., 1969; Ph.D., So. Meth. U., 1971; m. Sheela Misra, Aug. 2, 1974; children—Savita, Kavita. Asso. prof. stats. Tuskegee Inst., 1972-79, dir. Computer Based Edn. Tech., 1976-77; sr. statistician, statis. mgr. Baxter Travenol Labs., Inc., Round Lake, Ill., 1979—; cons. in field. Themis fellow, 1969-71. Mem. Am. Statis. Assn., Biometric Soc., Am. Soc. Quality Control, Nat. Assn. Mathematicians. Home: 1100 Wadsworth Pl Vernon Hills IL 60061 Office: Route 120 and Wilson Rd Round Lake IL 60073

CHANEY, REECE, educator; b. Rowdy, Ky., July 27, 1938; s. Roy and Lola (Hays) C.; B.S., Ohio U., 1962, M.Ed., 1965, Ph.D., 1968; children—Tammy Kaye, Ronald Dean; m. 2d, Mary L. Ross, July 20, 1979; stepchildren—Reid Robert, Erin Leigh. Tchr., Scioto Valley Schs., Piketon, Ohio, 1959-64; NDEA Title IV fellow Ohio U., 1964-68; elementary counselor South Western City Schs., Grove City, Ohio, 1965-66; prof. edn. Ind. State U., Terre Haute, 1968—; cons. career edn. and pupil personnel services Ind. Dept. Pub. Instrn. Cert. psychologist, Ind. Mem. Am., Ind. (pres. 1977-78) personnel and guidance assns., Assn. Counselor Edn. and Supervision, Nat. Vocat. Guidance Assn., Assn. Measurement and Evaluation in Guidance, Am. Sch. Counselor Assn., Phi Delta Kappa. Home: 243 Hudson Ave Terre Haute IN 47803 Office: School of Education Indiana State University Terre Haute IN 47809

CHANG, CHAE HAN JOSEPH, physician, educator; b. Seoul, Korea, July 7, 1929; s. B.I. and E.D. (Min) C.; M.D., Severance Union Med. Coll., Seoul, 1953; Ph.D., Nagoya U., Japan, 1966; m. Chung Sook Chun, Nov. 24, 1956; children—Paul, Marian, Deborah, Linda. Came to U.S., 1954, naturalized, 1963. Intern, St. Joseph's Hosp., Phoenix, 1954-55; resident Emory U. Hosp., Atlanta, 1955-58; practice medicine specializing in radiology, Morgantown, W.Va., 1964-70, Kansas City, Kans., 1970—; asso. prof. radiology W.Va. U. Sch. Medicine, 1964-69, prof., acting chmn. dept. radiology, 1969-70; prof. radiology, head div. roentgenology Kans. U. Med. Center, 1970—. Recipient Excellence in Teaching award W.Va. U. Sch. Medicine, 1970. Fellow Am. Coll. Radiology; mem. Assn. Univ. Radiologists, Soc. Pediatric Radiology, Am. Roentgen Soc., Radiol. Soc. N.Am., AMA, Kans., Wyandotte County med. socs., Kans. Radiol. Soc. (pres. 1979-81). Contbr. articles profl. jours. Home: 2000 W 63d St Shawnee Mission KS 66208 Office: U Kans Med Center 39th and Rainbow Blvd Kansas City KS 66103

CHANG, CHEN-KANG, pathologist; b. Miao-Li, Taiwan, Republic China, Sept. 8, 1945; s. Kai-In and Niemei (Wu) C.; came to U.S., 1972, naturalized, 1979; M.D., Nat. Taiwan U., 1971; m. Julie Huang, July 1, 1973; children—Warren, Peter. Intern, Nat. Taiwan U. Hosp., Taipei, 1970-71; resident in pathology U. Wis. Med. Center, Madison, 1972-76, mem. faculty, 1976—, clin. asst. prof. pathology, 1977—; pathologist St. Mary's Hosp. Med. Center, Madison, Methodist Hosp., Madison, Ft. Atkinson (Wis.) Meml. Hosp., St. Clare's Hosp., Baraboo, Wis., Stoughton (Wis.) Hosp., Richland Hosp., Richland Center, Wis. Served as officer M.C., Chinese Army, 1971-72. Dr. Huang scholar, 1966-69. Mem. Coll. Am. Pathologists, Am. Soc. Clin. Pathologists, Internat. Acad. Pathology, Wis. State Soc. Pathologists. Contbr. articles to med. jours. Home: 21 N Harwood Circle Madison WI 53717 Office: 707 S Mills St Madison WI 53715

CHANG, DAE HONG, educator; b. Nara, Japan, Jan. 9, 1928; s. Chun Bal and Kum I. (Kim) C.; B.A., Mich. State U., 1957, M.A., 1958, Ph.D., 1962; m. Seung Hi Cho, Aug. 20, 1964; children—Morris Bosang, Richard Jaesang. Chmn. dept. sociology Olivet (Mich.) Coll., 1962-66; asst. prof. dept. sociology No. Ill. U., DeKalb, 1966-69, asso. prof., 1968-69; prof., chmn. dept. sociology-anthropology U. Wis.-Whitewater, 1969-74; chmn. dept. adminstrn. justice Wichita (Kans.) State U., 1975—; cons. Ill. Atty. Gen., 1968-69; resource person Mich. State Gov., 1964-66. Smith-Mundt fellow, 1954-55; NSF grantee, 1969-75. Mem. Am. Sociol. Assn., Am. Soc. Criminology, Acad. Criminal Justice Scis., Midwest Sociol. Soc., Wis. Sociol. Assn. Author: Sociology: A Syllabus and Workbook, 1970; The Prison: Voices From the Inside, 1972; Sociology: An Applied Approach, 1973; Criminology: A Cross-Cultural Approach, 1975; Crime and Delinquency Prevention, 1977; Fundamentals of Criminal Justice: A Syllabus and Workbook, 1977; Introduction to Criminal Justice: Theory and Practice, 1979; Critical Issues in Criminal Justice, 1979. Home: 14501 Willowbend Circle Wichita KS 67230 Office: Box 95 Wichita State U Wichita KS 67208

CHANG, HARK CHUN, physician; b. Seoul, Korea, Aug. 14, 1939; s. Soon Gil and Choon Han (Kim) C.; came to U.S., 1967, naturalized, 1976; M.D., Korea U., 1964; m. Sang Yae Lee, Aug. 16, 1968; children—Michael Young Joon, John Young Suk. Intern, resident L.I. Coll. Hosp., Bklyn.; asso. in urology Mass. Gen. Hosp., Boston, 1973-74; clin. instr. surgery and urology Harvard Med. Sch., 1973-74; attending surgeon St. Mary's and St. Luke's hosps., Racine, Wis., 1974—; asso. clin. prof. Med. Coll. Wis., 1978—; cons. in urology VA Hosp., Wood, Wis., 1978—. Served to capt. Korean Air Force, 1964-67. Fellow A.C.S.; mem. AMA, Am. Urol. Assn., Wis. Urology Soc. Home: 363 E Pointview Dr Racine WI 53402 Office: 312 7th St Racine WI 53403

CHANG, JAE CHAN, physician; b. Chong An, Korea, Aug. 29, 1941; s. Tae Whan and Kap Hee (Lee) C.; came to U.S., 1965, naturalized, 1976; M.D., Seoul (Korea) Nat. U., 1965; m. Sue Young Chung, Dec. 4, 1965; children—Sung-Jin, Sung-Ju, Sung-Hoon. Intern, Ellis Hosp., Schenectady, 1965-66; resident in medicine Harrisburg (Pa.) Hosp., 1966-69, fellow in nuclear medicine, 1969-70; instr. in medicine U. Rochester, N.Y., 1970-72; chief hematology sect. VA Hosp., Dayton, Ohio, 1972-75; hematopathologist Good Samaritan Hosp., Dayton, 1975—, dir. oncology unit, 1976—, coordinator of med. edn., 1976-77, dir. oncology-hematology sect., 1976—; asst. clin. prof. medicine Ohio State U., Columbus, 1972-75; asso. clin. prof. medicine Wright State U., Dayton, 1975-80, clin. prof., 1980—; staff St. Elizabeth Med. Center, Dayton, Miami Valley Hosp., Dayton; cons. in hematology VA Hosp. Mem. med. adv. com. Greater Dayton Area chpt. Leukemia Soc. Am., 1977—; trustee Montgomery County Soc. for Cancer Control, Dayton, 1976—. Nat. Cancer Inst. fellow in hematology and oncology, 1970-72; diplomate Am. Bd. Internal Medicine, Am. Bd. Pathology. Fellow A.C.P.; mem. Am. Soc. Hematology, Am. Fedn. Clin. Research, Am. Soc. Clin. Oncologists, Am. Assn. Cancer Research, AAAS, Dayton Oncology Club, Dayton Soc. Internal Medicine. Contbr. articles to profl. med. jours., essays to newspaper columns. Home: 1122 Wycliffe Pl Dayton OH 45459 Office: Good Samaritan Hosp and Health Center 2222 Philadelphia Dr Dayton OH 45406 also 2200 Philadelphia Dr Dayton OH 45406

CHANG, JOHN C. H., chemist; b. Taiwan, China, Sept. 29, 1936; came to U.S., 1964, naturalized, 1976; s. Chin Fu and Lien Kwei (Chen) C.; Ph.D., Ill. Inst. Tech., 1969; m. Shirley H. L. Chen, Dec. 17, 1966; children—Patricia, Julita. Group leader Champion Internat. Corp., Chgo., 1971-77, sect. leader, Hamilton, Ohio, 1977; corp. dir. research Wallace Computer Services, Inc., Hillside, Ill., 1977—. Mem. Am. Chem. Soc. Patentee in field. Office: Wallace Computer Services Inc 4600 W Roosevelt Rd Hillside IL 60162

CHANG, JUNG-CHING, research chemist; b. Taipei, Taiwan, Jan. 13, 1939; came to U.S., 1967; s. Tien-Gen and Mien (Huang) C.; B.S., Tamkang Coll., 1963; M.S., U. P.R., 1969; Ph.D., U. Mo., Kansas City, 1975; m. Mei-Chu, Nov. 12, 1965; 1 dau., Edith. Chem. engr. Taiwan Sugar Corp., 1964-67; research asst. U. P.R., Rio Piedras, 1967-69; research asst., teaching asst., research fellow U. Mo., Kansas City, 1971-75; postdoctoral research asso. U. Oreg., Eugene, 1976-77; postdoctoral fellow U. Cin., 1977-79; chemist ICN Pharmaceuticals, Inc., Cin., 1979-81; research chemist Ashland Chem. Co., Dublin, Ohio, 1981—. Served with Nat. Chinese Air Force, 1963-64. Fisher scholar, 1961-63; NSF research fellow, 1967-69; postdoctoral fellow, 1976-77; U. Kansas City trustees' fellow, 1973-75; U.Mo., Kansas City summer research fellow, 1971-75; Office Naval Research postdoctoral fellow, 1977-79. Mem. Am. Chem. Soc., N.Y. Acad. Scis., Sigma Xi. Contbr. research articles in field to sci. jours. Home: 5245 Portland St Apt 103 Columbus OH 43220 Office: PO Box 2219 Columbus OH 43216

CHANG, UCK IL, engr.; b. Seoul, Korea, Mar. 23, 1941; s. Suk Don and Who Hyun (Kim) C.; B.S.E., Seoul (Korea) Nat. U., 1965; M.S., U. Calif., Berkeley, 1968, Ph.D., 1970; M.B.A., U. Mich., Ann Arbor, 1978; m. Haekyung Park, Mar. 20, 1969; children—Sylvia, Sarah. Mech. engr. Samsung Moolsan Co., Seoul, Korea, 1964-66; research asst. U. Calif., Berkeley, 1966-70; welding devel. engr. mfg. devel. center Ford Motor Co., Detroit, 1971-75, welding devel. engr. engring. and research, 1975-77, mfg. devel. project engr. engring. and research, 1977—. Mem. Am. Welding Soc., Am. Soc. Metals, Laser Inst. Am., Soc. Mfg. Engrs., Korean Scientists and Engrs. Assn. Contbr. articles to profl. publs. Expert in laser material processing. Home: 3053 Bloomfield Park Dr West Bloomfield MI 48033 Office: Ford Motor Co Mfg Processes Lab 24500 Glendale Ave Detroit MI 48239

CHANNER, STEPHEN DYER STANTON, trade assn. exec.; b. Chgo., Nov. 1, 1933; s. George Stanton and Maxine (Dyer) C.; B.A. in Bus. Adminstrn., Colo. Coll., 1956; student U.S. Army Officers Sch., 1957; m. Antoinette Persons, June 29, 1957; children—Stephen Persons, Wyndhan Harvey. Dir. sales Am. Seating Co., Grand Rapids, Mich., 1958-77; with Bus. and Instn. Furniture Mfrs. Assn., Grand Rapids, Mich., 1977—, exec. dir., 1978—. Served to 1st lt., U.S. Army, 1956-58. Mem. Am. Soc. Assn. Execs. Mem. Christian Ch. Club: Grand Rapids Racquet. Contbr. articles to various mags. Office: 2335 Burton St SE Grand Rapids MI 49506

CHAO, BILL KEH-LUNG, mfg. co. exec.; b. China, Apr. 23, 1940; s. C.F. and Ti (Hsuing) C.; B.A., Tunghai U., China, 1962; M.A., U. Wash., 1966; M.B.A., Northwestern U., 1979; m. Shirley C. Chiu, Dec. 14, 1968; children—Jennifer, Kathleen. Data base adminstr. Deere & Co., 1969-72, sr. economist, 1972-74; mgr. bus. econs. dept., chief economist J.I. Case Co., Racine, Wis., 1975-79, dir. corp. planning, 1979—. Pres., Racine Chinese Assn., 1978. Mem. Nat. Assn. Bus. Economists, Am. Econ. Assn. Home: 6 Cherrywood Ct Racine WI 53402 Office: 700 State St Racine WI 53404

CHAO, MARSHALL S., chemist; b. Changsha, China, Nov. 20, 1924; s. Hen-ti and Huey-ying C.; m. Patricia Hu, July 20, 1968; 1 dau., Anita. B.S., Nat. Central U., China, 1947; M.S., U. Ill., 1958, Ph.D., 1961. Teaching asst. Nat. Central U., 1947-49; tech. asst. Taiwan Fertilizer Co., 1949-55; research chemist The Dow Chem. Co., Midland, Mich., 1961-72, research specialist, 1973-79, research leader, 1980—. Deacon First Baptist Ch., Midland, 1974-76. Fellow Am. Inst. Chemists; mem. Am. Chem. Soc., Electrochem. Soc. (chmn. Midland sect. 1973, councilor 1974-76, 81—), Alpha Chi Upsilon, Sigma Xi. Author: Taiwan Fertilizers, 1951; contbr. articles to profl. jours. Patentee in field. Home: 1206 Evamar Dr Midland MI 48640 Office: Inorganic Lab Central Research Dow Chem USA Midland MI 48640

CHAPIN, DWIGHT LEE, publisher, mag. exec.; b. Wichita, Kans., Dec. 2, 1940; s. N. Spencer and Betty June (Helena) C.; student U. So. Calif., 1963; m. Susan Howland, Aug. 18, 1963; children—Kimberly Susan, Tracy Helena. Account rep. J. Walter Thompson Advt. Agy., 1963-66; personal aide to Richard Nixon, 1967-69; appointment sec. The White House, Washington, 1969-73; dir. market planning United Airlines, Chgo., 1973; mktg. cons. W. Clement Stone, Chgo., 1974-76; pres., pub. Success Unlimited Mag. and Co., Chgo., 1976—. Bd. dirs. Santa for the Very Poor; adv. bd. Citizen's Choice. Recipient nat. speakers award, 1977, Milan Hulbert annual human relations award SWAP Club Internat., 1980. Mem. Sales and Mktg. Execs. Assn. Chgo. (award, 1980), Mag. Pubs. Assn., Direct Selling Assn. Republican. Presbyterian. Office: 401 N Wabash Chicago IL 60611

CHAPIN, ROY DIKEMAN, JR., automotive co. exec.; b. Detroit, Sept. 21, 1915; s. Roy Dikeman and Inez (Tiedeman) C.; A.B., Yale, 1937; m. Ruth Mary Ruxton, Oct. 29, 1937 (div.); children—Roy D., Christopher King, William Ruxton, Cicely Penny; m. 2d, Loise Baldwin Wickser, July 17, 1965. With Hudson Motor Car Co. and Hudson Sales Corp., Detroit, 1938-54, dir. 1946-54; asst. treas., dir. Am. Motors Corp., 1954-55, treas., 1955, v.p., treas., 1956, exec. v.p., 1956-67, chmn. bd., chief exec. officer, 1967-78, cons. and dir., 1978—; dir. Whirlpool Corp., Gould, Inc., Am. Natural Resources Co. Mem. exec. com. Detroit Area Council, Boy Scouts Am.; pres. Detroit Sci. Center; adv. bd. Leader Dogs for Blind. Mem. Ruffed Grouse Soc. (dir., pres.), Ducks Unltd. Found. (trustee), Nature Conservancy Mich. (vice chmn.), Chi Psi. Clubs: Elihu Soc. (New Haven); Country, Grosse Pointe, Detroit Fontinalis (Detroit); Links (N.Y.C.); Yale (Mich.); Pacific Union (San Francisco). Address: 333 W Fort St Detroit MI 48226

CHAPMAN, (GEORGE) BRAINERD (III), lawyer; b. Louisville, Oct. 18, 1911; s. George B. and Kathryn (Schneiderhan) C.; B.A., Amherst Coll., 1933; J.D., Harvard, 1936; m. Martha McCaig, June 11, 1948; 1 son, George Brainerd, IV. Admitted to Ill. bar, 1936; asso., then partner Lord, Bissell & Brook, and predecessors, 1936-58; pvt. practice, 1959-62; partner Chapman, Pennington, Montgomery, Holmes & Sloan, Chgo., 1962-70, Vedder, Price, Kaufman & Kammholz, Chgo., 1971—. Dir. various corps., eleemosynary instns. and founds. Former chmn. bd. Presbyn. Home; past bd. dirs., nat. treas. Mil. Tng. Camps Assn. U.S. Served from capt. to col. JAG'S Dept., AUS, 1942-46. Decorated Bronze Star (U.S.); knight officer of Crown (Italy); recipient medal for Eminent Service, Amherst Coll., 1969, Foster and Mary McGaw award, 1977. Mem. Am. Bar Assn., Harvard Law Soc., Beta Theta Pi. Presbyn. (elder, trustee). Author: Dream Cruise, 1980. Clubs: Chgo., University, Law, Ocean Cruising (Great Britain), Glen View (Golf, Ill.); Snowmass (Colo.). Office: 115 S LaSalle St Chicago IL 60603

CHAPMAN, CARL HALEY, anthropologist, educator; b. Steelville, Mo., May 29, 1915; s. William M. and Estelle Madolin (Haley) C.; A.B., U. Mo., 1939; M.A., U. N.Mex., 1946; Ph.D. (Horace H. Rackham fellow), U. Mich., 1959; m. Eleanor Eliza Finley, Mar. 14, 1942; children—Richard Carl, Stephen Finley. Instr. sociology U. Mo., Columbia, 1946-48, instr. sociology and anthropology, 1948-50, asst. prof. anthropology, 1951-56, asso. prof., 1957-60, prof. anthropology, 1960—, research prof. Am. archaeology, 1975—, dir. Mus. of Anthropology, 1949-50, 51-56, dir. Am. archaeology, 1946-65, dir. archaeol. research activities, 1965-75; mem. steering com. Miss. Alluvial Valley Archaeol. Program, 1968-72; chmn. adv. council on archaeology to Mo. State Park Bd., 1959-70; ex-officio mem. Adv. Council on Archaeology and History, 1970-72, Adv. Council on Hist. Preservation, 1977—. Gov.'s rep. to Lewis and Clark Trail Commn. meetings State of Mo., 1966-68; sec. Mo. Lewis and Clark Trail Commn., 1966-67; Democratic committeeman 3rd Ward, Columbia, 1970-72; bd. dirs. Mo. Heritage Trust, 1977—. Served with USAF, 1942-45. Decorated Air medal; Nat. Park Service grantee, 1952-63, NSF grantee, 1961-63; Nat Endowment Humanities grantee, 1971-75. Fellow Am. Anthrop. Assn., AAAS; mem. Soc. Am. Archaeology (Disting. Service award 1975, chmn. com. on public understanding of archaeology 1967-69), Am. Soc. Conservation Archaeology (Conservation award 1980), Soc. Profl. Archaeologists (pres. 1978-79), Mo. Archaeol. Soc. (sec. 1946-50, 51-55, 58—), Soc. Hist. Archaeology, Central States Anthrop. Assn., Assn. Field Archaeology, Am. Ethnol. Soc., Mo. Conservation Fedn., AAUP, Phi Beta Kappa, Sigma Xi. Democrat. Unitarian. Author: (with Eleanor Chapman) Indians and Archaeology of Missouri, 1964; The Origin of the Osage Indian Tribe, 1974; Archaeology of Missouri, Vol. I, 1975, Vol. II, 1980; (with David Evans and John Cottler) Investigation and Comparison of Two Fortified Mississippi Tradition Sites in Southeastern Missouri, 1977; contbg. author: The Indomitable Osage in Spanish Illinois, 1974; Cultural Change and Continuity, 1976; contbr. articles on Am. archaeology to scholarly jours. Home: 211 Edgewood Columbia MO 65201 Office: 205 Swallow Hall U Mo Columbia MO 65211

CHAPMAN, EMILY ELIZABETH, systems analyst; b. Paris, Ont., Can., Jan. 19, 1921; d. Robert Alexander George and Emily Adabelle (Turnbull) Cale; Asso. in Home Econs., Macdonald Inst., Guelph, Ont., 1941; B.S., U. Wis., Madison, 1957, postgrad. Grad. Sch. Computer Scis., 1966-67; m. R. Keith Chapman, Aug. 22, 1942; children—Robert Wayne, Linda Jean, Susan Gay. Research programmer analyst U. Wis., Madison, 1966-70; exec. sec. Sponsors of Sci. Inc., Madison, 1970-74; programmer analyst Higher Ednl. Aids Bd., State of Wis., 1975-78; systems analyst Bur. Info. Devel., Dept. Adminstrn., State of Wis., Madison, 1978-80, project leader, 1980—; cons. programmer analyst, 1970-73. Chmn. Cancer Soc.-Heart Fund Health Drives, Verona, Wis., 1956-57; bd. dirs. Central YWCA, Madison, 1965-66. Recipient Exceptional Performance award Dept. Adminstrn., State of Wis., 1981. Mem. Assn. for Systems Mgmt. (treas. Madison chpt. 1979-81), Entomol. Soc. Am., Council for Agrl. Sci. and Tech., Univ. League Madison, Daus. of Demeter. Home: 1119 Waban Hill Madison WI 53711 Office: State of Wis Dept Adminstrn Gen Exec Facility II Madison WI 53702

CHAPMAN, FRANCES ELIZABETH CLAUSEN (MRS. WILLIAM JAMES CHAPMAN), civic worker; b. Atchison, Kans., Feb. 27, 1920; d. Erwin W. and Helen (Hackney) Clausen; B.A., Wellesley Coll., 1941; m. W. MacLean Johnson, Aug. 31, 1940 (dec. Nov. 1965); children—Stuart MacLean, Duncan Scott, Douglas Hamilton; m. 2d, William James Chapman, Dec. 5, 1970. Project dir. Women in Community Service, Inc., St. Louis, 1965-66; pres. Nursery Found., St. Louis, 1956-58, dir., 1953-59, 65-68; adv. com. Mo. State Children's Day Care, 1963—; chmn. day care com. Mo. Council Children and Youth, 1961, chmn. foster care sect., 1961-63; spl. asst. to the pres. Webster Coll., 1966-68. Bd. dirs. New City Sch., 1967-69, Mid-County YMCA, 1967-70, St. Louis Conservatory and Sch. Arts, 1978—; mem. steering com. Mo. Council on Children and Youth, 1967-69; trustee Jr. Coll. Dist., St. Louis-St. Louis County, 1968-80, pres. bd. trustees, 1971-73, 76-77; trustee John Burroughs Sch., 1973-79, Wellesley Coll., 1976—; bd. dirs. Assn. Governing Bds. Univs. and Colls., 1970-80, v.p., 1977-78, chmn. bd., 1978-79; bd. commrs. Nat. Commn. on Accrediting, 1971-72; bd. overseers Center for Research on Women in Higher Edn. and Professions, Wellesley, Mass., 1977—. Mem. Nat. Soc. Arts and Letters, Wellesley Coll. Alumnae Assn. (sec., dir. 1958-61). Club: Wellesley Coll. (pres. 1965-67). Home: 10 Overbrook Dr St Louis MO 63124

CHAPMAN, RICHARD ALAN, accountant; b. Beatrice, Nebr., Aug. 29, 1947; s. Glenn Ray and Aelcidean Martie (King) C.; student Milw. Sch. Engring., 1968-70; B.S. in Acctg., U. Nebr., 1973; m. Norma Loi-Moi Leung, May 4, 1974. Internal auditor Gen. Telephone & Electronics, Des Plaines, Ill., 1973-75; internal auditor Internat. Minerals & Chem., Des Plaines, 1975-78, fin. analyst chem. group, 1978-79, chief accountant indsl. chems. div., 1979—. Mem. Beta Gamma Sigma. Office: 666 Garland Pl Des Plaines IL 60016

CHAPMAN, ROY WEBSTER, transp. exec.; b. Norfolk, Va., Sept. 26, 1924; s. George W. and Vivian M. (Whitlow) C.; B.S. in Commerce, U. Va., 1949; m. Betty Ann Meredith, June 12, 1948; children—R. Bryan, Carolyn Blair. With Norfolk So. Ry., 1949-64, asst. comptroller, Norfolk, Va. and Raleigh, N.C., 1958-63, comptroller, 1964; v.p., treas. Mfrs. Ry. Co. and St. Louis Refrigerator Car Co., St. Louis, 1965-73, pres. Mfrs. Ry. Co. and St. Louis Refrigerator Car Co., 1974—, also dir. Mfrs. Ry. Co.; dir. Mfrs. Cartage Co., Mfrs Transport Co., Williamsburg Transport, Inc., Fairfield Transport, Inc. Active, United Way Greater St. Louis, Friends of Scouting campaigns. Served to staff sgt. U.S. Army, 1943-46. Club: Traffic St. Louis. Home: 7625 Ravensridge Dr Saint Louis MO 63119 Office: 2850 S Broadway Saint Louis MO 63118

CHAPMAN, WILLIAM FRANCIS, newspaper editor; b. Powersville, Mo., Mar. 28, 1925; s. William Bryant and Esther (Coddington) C.; student jr. coll., St. Joseph, Mo., 1942-43, Central Mo. State Coll., 1946, Wayne State U., 1955; m. Lillian Louise Fyler, Aug. 10, 1945; children—Robert Earl, Karen Louise, Sharon Frances. News editor Warrensburg (Mo.) Daily Star-Jour., 1946-47; mgr. U.P.I., Jefferson City, Mo., 1949, war corr., Korea, 1950-51, mgr. Seattle, 1952-53; asst. city editor Detroit Free Press, 1954-61; exec. editor Daily Times, Chester, Pa., 1961-63; mng. editor The Times, Hammond, Ind., 1964-75, exec. editor, 1975—; editorial dir. Howard Publs., Oceanside, Cal., 1971—. Founding dir. Mid-Am. Press Inst., So. Ill. U. Carbondale (chmn. 1971); mem. Internat. Press Inst. Served with USMCR, 1943-46; PTO. Mem. Am. Soc. Newspaper Editors, A.P. Mng. Editors. Home: 7818 Marshall Pl Merrillville IN 46410 Office: 417 Fayette St Hammond IN 46325

CHAPPELLE, AUSTIN BEMIS, elec. products co. exec.; b. Dierks, Ark., Jan. 28, 1924; s. Case C. and Beatrice V. (Thornton) C.; B.S., U. Ark., 1949, M.S., 1950; postgrad. Mass. Inst. Tech., 1951; m. Patricia Ann Benny, June 29, 1950; children—Tersa Marie, Clifford Austin, Mark Elliott. Asso. prof. Miss. So. U., 1950-51; rocket devel. Hercules Powder Co., Wilmington, Del., 1953-56; research physicist propulsion Gen. Electric Co., Cin., 1956-59; sr. tech. staff Northrop Aircraft Co., Hawthorne, Calif., 1960-64; mgr. product devel. Govt. Electronics div. Motorola, Inc., Scottsdale, Ariz., 1964-74; mgr. WSG-3 programs office, Communications div. Electronic Communications Inc., St. Petersburg, Fla., 1974-75; with govt. telecommunications div. Collins Radio, Cedar Rapids, Iowa, 1975—; dir. Chemseal Corp., 1965. Committeeman, Roosevelt council Boy Scouts Am., 1969-74. Served with USAAF, USAF, 1941-56. Asso. fellow Am. Inst. Aeros. and Astronautics; mem. Am. Inst. Physics, Am. Rocket Soc. (past pres.), Navy League, Old Crow Assn. (charter mem.), Tailhook Assn. Mason. Patentee electronic blasting machine. Home: 6537 Brookview Ln NE Cedar Rapids IA 52402 Office: Govt Telecommunications Group Collins Radio Cedar Rapids IA 52498

CHAREK, ROBERT STANLEY, bus. exec.; b. Cleve., Aug. 8, 1924; s. Stanley Joseph and Lillian Helen (Prosser) C.; grad. St. Ignatius High Sch., 1942; student Center Coll. Ky., 1943, Western Res. U., 1946; m. Hilda Marie Hoffman, Aug. 9, 1944; children—Barbara C. Charek Reesing, Bonita L. Charek McCormick, Ralph K. Prince, Christopher R. Public accountant, 1946-47; Gold Bros. Co., Cleve., office mgr. 1947-49; with Master Builders div. Martin Marietta, Cleve., 1949—, acctg. dept. mgr., 1954-58, dir. acctg., 1959-73, internat. controller, 1974—. Served with USAAF, 1943-45. Mem. Data Processing Mgmt. Assn. (past dir. chpt.). Republican. Roman Catholic. Club: K.C. Home: 21941 Briarwood Dr Fairview Park OH 44126 Office: 23700 Chagrin Blvd Beachwood OH 44122

CHAREWICZ, DAVID MICHAEL, photographer; b. Chgo., Feb. 17, 1932; s. Michael and Stella (Pietrzak) C.; student DePaul U., 1957, Northwestern U., 1952; m. Catherine Uccello, Nov. 8, 1952; children—Michael, Karen, Daniel. Trainee, Merill Chase, Chgo., 1950-51; dark room technician Maurice Seymour, Chgo., 1951-52; photographer Oscar & Assos., Chgo., 1955-63; owner Dave Chare Photography, Park Ridge, Ill., 1963—; pres., owner C&C Duplicating, Inc., 1978—. Pres. Oakton Parent Tchr. Club, 1968-69, del. dist. 64 caucus, 1970, 73; mem. centennial photo com., Park Ridge, Ill., 1973. Served with AUS, 1952-54. Mem. Profl. Photographers Assn., Midstate Indsl. Photographers Assn. (treas. 1981). Home: 739 N Northwest Hwy Park Ridge IL 60068 Office: 1045 N Northwest Hwy Park Ridge IL 60068

CHARLA, KATHLEEN G., advt. sales rep.; b. Holyoke, Mass., Feb. 13, 1942; d. Frank A. and Lena (La Ruffa) Gerace; B.A., Trinity Coll., Washington, 1964; M.A., Stanford U., 1966; Ph.D., Ind. U., 1979; m. Leonard F. Charla, Feb. 3, 1968; children—Larisa, Christopher. Instr., Upsala Coll., 1969-70; free-lance translator Ardis Pubs., Ann Arbor, Mich., Bloomington (Ind.) Translation Group, also McGregor & Werner, Arlington, Va., 1969-75; art cons., Birmingham, Mich., 1976-77; owner, mgr. Kathleen G. Charla Assos., Birmingham, 1976—, advt. sales rep. periodicals Home, Modern Photography, High Fidelity, Los Angeles, San Diego, San Francisco, Palm Springs Life, Chief Executive. Stanford-Warsaw Grad. Exchange fellow, 1965-66; NDEA fellow, 1966-67. Mem. Adcraft Club Detroit, Detroit Mktg. Com., Mag. Pubs. Assn., Am. Assn. Advancement of Slavic Studies, Am. Assn. Tchrs. of Slavic and East European Langs. Contbr. articles and revs. to publs. Address: 21000 W Fourteen Mile Rd Birmingham MI 48010

CHARLES, ANDREW VALENTINE, psychiatrist; b. Chgo., Nov. 5, 1939; s. George and Carol Claire (Goettel) C.; B.A. cum laude, U. Mich., 1961; M.D., U. Ill., 1965. Rotating intern Ill. Masonic Hosp., Chgo., 1965-66; psychiatry resident Presbyn. St. Luke's Hosp., Chgo., 1966-69; practice medicine specializing in psychiatry, Chgo., 1969—; mem. attending staff Presbyn. St. Lukes, Chgo. Lakeshore hosps.; med. dir. Ridgeway Hosp., Chgo., 1976—; instr. psychiatry Rush Med. Sch., Chgo., 1970—; psychiatrist Chgo. Bd. Edn., 1970-77; clin. dir. Exec. Assessment Corp., 1976-78. Diplomate Am. Bd. Psychiatry and Neurology. Mem. A.M.A., Am. Group Psychotherapy Assn., Am., Ill. psychiat. assns., Chgo. Med. Soc., Am. Acad. Med. Dirs., Am. Assn. Utilization Rev. Physicians, Phi Rho Sigma. Contbr. articles to prof. jours. Office: 8 S Michigan Ave Suite 3102 Chicago IL 60603

CHARLES, CONRAD JOSEPH, book publishing co. exec.; b. Chicago Heights, Ill., Aug. 7, 1930; s. Conrad and Isabel (Gayton) C.; student parochial schs.; children—Richard, Michael, Rhonda, Cheryl. Prodn. mgr. Childrens Press Pub., Chgo., 1969-71; v.p. adminstr. Henry Regenry Pub. Co., Chgo., 1971-75, Sheed & Ward Pub. Co., Mission, Kans., 1975-77; dir. prodn. and spl. sales Raintree Pubs., Inc., Milw., 1977—. Active local Big Bros./Big Sisters. Served with AUS, 1951-53. Mem. Printing Industry Wis., Chgo. Book Club. Roman Catholic. Club: Chgo. Press. Home: 1129 N Jackson St Apt 1411 Milwaukee WI 53202 Office: 205 W Highland Ave Milwaukee WI 53203

CHARLES, JAMES HENRY, research and devel. co. exec.; b. Chgo., July 16, 1952; s. Joseph Herman and Frances Wilhelmena (Krause) C.; diploma Devry Inst. Tech., Chgo., 1978. Vice pres. Dollarodeon Theatres, Dundee (Ill.) terr., 1975-77; surveyor crew chief Alan J. Coulson, P.C., Dundee, 1977-79; propr. Common Sense Enterprises, Dundee, 1979—. Mem. Nat. Right to Work Com., 1978. Mem. AAAS. Office: PO Box 162 Dundee IL 60118

CHARLIER, PATRICIA MARY SIMONET, educator; b. Enderlin, N.D., July 12, 1923; d. John Jerome and Sophia Cecelia (Krueger) Simonet; student Coll. of St. Scholastica, 1941-43; B.S., U. Minn., 1944, M.A., 1958; Ph.D. (Pi Lambda Theta scholar), 1960; postgrad. U. Aix-Marseilles (France), summer 1958, U. Paris (France), 1958-59, U. Bordeaux (France), 1971-73; m. Roger Henri L.C.L. Charlier, June 17, 1958; children—Constance Cecelia-Paula, Jean-Armand Leonard. Tchr., Buffalo (Minn.) High Sch., 1944-47; librarian, tchr. Delano (Minn.) High Sch., 1947-49, prin., 1949-56; instr. U. Minn., 1956-57, 57-58, adminstrv. fellow Office Admissions and Records 1959-60; asst. prin. U. Minn. High Sch., 1957-58; asso. prof. ednl. psychology, chmn. secondary edn. dept. Parsons Coll., Fairfield, Iowa, 1960-61; asso. prof. psychology Chgo. State U., 1961-64; asso. prof. edn. and psychology U. Ill., Chgo., 1965—, head div. curriculum, instrn. and evaluation, 1973-78. Asso. dir. div. ednl. travel U. Travel Hdqrs., Inc., Chgo., 1962-69; dir. Edn. Travel Projects, 1954—; vis. prof., asso. dir. Edn. Travel Programs Western N. Mex. U., 1963-68; vis. lectr. psychology Loyola U., Chgo., 1964-65; cons. div. ednl. travel Vacations, Internat., Chgo., 1964-67, ednl. travel div. NEA, 1962-65; vis. prof. U. Autonoma de Baja Calif. (Mexico), 1967; spl. cons. to supr. pub. instrn. Ill., 1969-71; exchange scientist Internat. Research Exchange Commn., 1969-70; vis. prof. Romanian Superior Council on Sci. Research, 1970; co-dir. Sea-Camp '70 Project, 1970; vis. prof. psychology U. Bordeaux, 1971-73; French Ministry Fgn. Affairs cultural exchange scholar, 1973-74; USIA lectr., Asia, Africa and Europe, 1971—; advisor Ministry of Edn., Greek Cyprus Adminstrn.; advisor Office of Edn., Turkish Cypriot Adminstrn. Recipient Silver medal arts, letters and scis., France, 1972, chevalier Ordre des Palmes Académiques (France), 1973; Medal Pro Mundi Beneficio (Brazil), 1975; Fulbright scholar in Cyprus, 1979-80. Mem. Nat. Assn. Supervision and Curriculum Devel., Chgo. Psychol. Assn., Assn. for Higher Edn., Assn. for Student Teaching, Am. Assn. Sci. Teaching, Assn. Francophone pour l'Education Comparée. Phi Kappa Phi, Pi Lambda Theta. Contbr. articles on edn. psychology, sci. teaching, comp. edn. and statistics to profl. jours.

CHARLIER, ROGER HENRI, oceanographer, geographer; b. Antwerp, Belgium, Nov. 10, 1921; came to U.S., 1946, naturalized, 1948; Ph.D., U. Erlangen, 1947; Litt.D., U. Paris, 1956, Sc.D., 1957; m. Patricia Mary Simonet, 1958; children—Jean-Armand, Constance. Prof. geography and history Coll. Baudouin, Brussels, 1941-42; student asst. U. Liège (Belgium), 1943-44; newspaper corr., Europe, 1945-50; dep. dir. assembly centers UNRRA, 1946-48; research analyst Internat. War Crimes Commn., Nuernberg, W. Ger., 1948-49; tchr. Berlitz Sch., Newark, 1950-51; asso. prof. dept. geography, chmn. dept. Polycultural U., Washington, 1951-52; chmn. dept. phys. scis. Finch Coll., N.Y.C., 1952-55; tchr. Brunswick (N.J.) Sr. High Sch., 1955; chmn. dept. geology and geography Hofstra U., N.Y.C., 1955-58; professeur suppléant U. Paris, 1958-59; vis. prof. edn. U. Minn., 1959-60; prof. earth scis. Parsons Coll., Fairfield, Iowa, 1960-61; prof. geology, geography and oceanography Northeastern Ill. U., Chgo., 1961—, research scholar in oceanography, 1962-64, vice chmn. dept. geography, 1964-70, dir. oceanography program, 1962—; prof. extraordinary U. Brussels, 1971—; vis. prof. U. Bordeaux, 1970-74; exec. dir. Inst. Devel. River and Estuary Systems, 1974-76; exchange scientist Internat. Research Exchange Com., 1968-69, Nat. Acad. Sci., 1967-68, 78-79; spl. cons. to Ill. supt. public edn., 1967-69, World Tourism Orgn., UNESCO, 1972—. Served to maj. Belgian Army, World War II. Decorated knight Order Acad. Palms; Médaille du Mérite Touristique; Médaille de vermeil des Arts, Lettrés et Sciences (France); Grande Médaille U. Bordeaux (France); knight Order of Leopold (Belgium); Médaille d'or de l'Encouragement au Progrès (France); Belgian Nat. Found. for Sci. Research grantee, 1977-79; Belgian Govt. grantee, 1976-78; Inst. for River and Estuarine Studies grantee, 1976-78; Fulbright scholar, 1975-76; NATO grantee, 1969-70; French Govt. fellow, 1967-69; Institut Océanographique de Monaco grantee, 1967-68; NSF grantee, 1978, Nat. Acad. Sci. (U.S.) exchange scientist to Rumania, 1968, 79, and Bulgaria, 1979. Fellow Nat. Acad. Sci., Arts et Belles-Lettres (France); mem. profl. assns. Office: Northeastern Ill U 5500 N St Louis Ave Chicago IL 60625

CHARLONS, JULIO IGNACIO, structural engr.; b. Matanzas, Cuba, May 27, 1933; came to U.S., 1969, naturalized, 1974; s. Jose Ignacio and Ana Sofia (Garcia) C.; Land Surveyor, Sch. Land Surveyors, Matanzas, Cuba, 1954; Civil Engr., U. Havana, 1958; M.S., U. Kans., Lawrence, 1975; m. Arminda Zulema Castro, Aug. 18, 1957; children—Arminda Maria Charlons McCallum, Julio Ignacio, Maria de Lourdes. Structural engr., J.A. Vila & Assos., Havana, Cuba, 1957-59. Cuban Ministry Public Works, Havana, Camaguey and Manzanillo, Cuba, 1959-68, Procon Iberica Ltda., Madrid, 1968-69; structural engr. Black & Veatch, Cons. Engrs., Kansas City, Mo., 1969—. Registered profl. engr., Kans., Mo. Mem. ASCE, Am. Concrete Inst., Soc. Am. Mil. Engrs. Home: 13286 W 113th St Overland Park KS 66210 Office: 1500 Meadow Lake Pkwy Kansas City MO 64114

CHARLTON, RICHARD GEORGE, pub. relations exec.; b. Schenectady, N.Y., Mar. 26, 1934; s. Henry C. and Irene F. (DiLallo) C.; B.A., Syracuse U., 1955; m. Diana V. Carver, Aug. 7, 1954; children—Lincoln, Faith, Jennifer. Information specialist Gen. Elec. Co., Utica, Schenectady and Syracuse, N.Y., 1958-62; dir. pub. affairs and information Calspan Corp., Buffalo, 1962-74; dir. communications and pub. affairs J.I. Case Co., Racine, Wis., 1974—. Chmn., Tenn. State U. Cluster, 1978-81; bd. dirs. Racine Urban League. Served with USAF, 1955-58. Mem. Internat. Assn. Bus. Communicators (accredited, pres. 1975-76, Gold Quill award 1970), Farm and Indsl. Equipment Inst., Pub. Relations Soc. Am. (accredited, pres. Niagara Frontier chpt. 1970), Wis. Public Relations Forum, Urban Aesthetics of Racine. Methodist (ofcl. bd.). Author: (with others) Machines of Plenty, 1976. Contbg. editor Pub. Relations Jour., 1968-72. Home: 832 Hialeah Dr Racine WI 53402 Office: 700 State St Racine WI 53404

CHARPENTIER, DONALD ARMAND, psychologist; b. Bklyn., Mar. 8, 1935; s. Joseph Roche and Grace Viola (Adrience) C.; B.A., Hope Coll., 1956; M.A., Ohio U., 1958; Ed.S., George Peabody Coll., 1964; Ph.D., U. Minn., 1972; m. Janice Lee Getting, May 21, 1961; children—Jennifer Diane, Ian Lee. Burke. Asso. dir. Westminster Found. Ohio, 1956-57, acting dir., 1957-58; psychologist, probation officer Cook County Family Court, Chgo., 1961-62; asst. prof. psychology State U. N.Y., Fredonia, 1964-65; asst. prof. U. Wis., River Falls, 1965-72, asso. prof., 1974-80, prof., 1980—. Vis. research fellow, Harvard U., 1973-74. Lic. psychologist, Wis. Mem. AAAS, Am. Assn. Advancement Social Psychology, Am. Psychol. Assn., Am. Sociol. Assn., Internat. Soc. History of Behavioral and Social Scis., Soc. Psychol. Study Social Issues, Soc. for Advancement Am. Philosophy. Home: Rt 4 River Falls WI 54022 Office: Dept Psychology Univ Wis River Falls WI 54022

CHASE, CLINTON IRVIN, educator; b. Reubens, Idaho, Aug. 14, 1927; s. Charles Irvin and Agnes Joanne (Eikum) C.; B.S., U. Idaho, 1950, M.S., 1951; Ph.D., U. Calif., Berkeley, 1958; m. Patricia L. Cronenberger, Aug. 3, 1957; 1 son, Steven Michael. Asst. prof. Idaho State U., Pocatello, 1958-61, Miami U., Oxford, Ohio, 1961-62; mem. faculty Ind. U., Bloomington, 1962—, prof. ednl. psychology 1969—, dir. Bur. Evaluative Studies and Testing, 1970—. Mem. Nat. Council Measurement in Edn., Am. Psychol. Assn., Am. Ednl. Research Assn. Author: Elementary Statistical Procedures, 2d edit., 1976; Measurement for Educational Evaluation, 1978; (with H. Glenn Ludlow) Readings in Educational and Psychological Testing, 1966. Home: 405 Meadowbrook St Bloomington IN 47401 Office: Indiana Univ Bloomington IN 47405

CHASE, ERNEST ARTHUR, accountant; b. Galien, Mich., Apr. 10, 1931; s. Samuel M. and Mildred Irene (Morley) C.; student LaSalle Extension U., 1953-57, Lake Michigan Coll., 1974-75; m. Joyce Elaine Winney, July 21, 1951; children—Ernest L., Arthur M., Robert J., William R., James R. Assembly insp. David Products Co., Niles, Mich., 1951; gen. accountant Warren Featherbone Co., Three Oaks, Mich., 1953-55; cost accountant Bendix Products Co., South Bend, Ind., 1955-56; officer mgr. Babbitt Lumber Co., Niles, 1956-57; cost accountant Curtiss Wright Corp., South Bend, 1957-58; mgr. credit office Am. Home and Gray Aretz Co., South Bend, 1958; chief accountant Millburg Growers Exchange (Mich.), 1958-59; sales mgr. S.W. Mich. dist. Nat. Fedn. Ind. Bus., 1959-60; owner Chase Pub. Accounting Service, Galien, 1958—, Chase Ins. Service Center, Galien, 1960—, Family Everyday Clothing and Shoe Store, Three Oaks, 1963-65; salesman Kiefer Real Estate, Berrien Springs, Mich., 1962—. Leader, Boy Scouts Am., 1957-72; sec., treas., coach Galien

Little League, 1964-76; clk. Village of Galien, 1963-64; mem. adv. com. Galien Twp. Schs., 1963-70, chmn., 1966-70; mem. tax allocation bd. Berrien County, 1971-72, mem. key man com., 1971-72, chmn. finance com., 1971-72, chmn. budget com., 1969-70, county commr., 1969-72, 77-79; mem. regional key man com. Mich. Assn. Counties, 1971-72. Mem. Berrien County Republican Exec. Com., 1969-72. Served with USNR, 1949-50, 52-53. Mem. Ind. Accountants Mich., Mich. Assn. Mut. Ins. Agts., Nat. Soc. Pub. Accountants, Galien Jr. C. of C., Am. Legion. Methodist. Lion. Home: Hwy US 12 E Galien MI 49113 Office: 112 N Main St Galien MI 49113

CHASE, HAROLD WILLIAM, educator; b. Worcester, Mass., Feb. 6, 1922; s. Louis and Bessie (Lubin) C.; A.B., Princeton U., 1943, M.A., 1948, Ph.D., 1954; m. Bernice Mae Fadden, July 3, 1944; children—Bryce Stephen, Eric Lewis. Asst. prof. Princeton U., 1952-57; prof. polit. sci. dept. U. Minn., Mpls., 1957-77, 80—; dep. asst. sec. defense reserve affairs Dept. Def., Washington, 1977-80; vis. prof. Columbia U., 1963-64, U. Chgo., 1966-67, Nat. War Coll., 1965-66; chmn. State Ethical Practices Commn., Minn., 1975-77. Served with USMC, 1943-46, 50-52, 68-69, maj. gen. Res. (ret.). Decorated Legion of Merit (2), Purple Hearts (2); recipient Disting. Teaching award U. Minn., 1962. Mem. Am. Polit. Sci. Assn. Democrat. Club: Cosmos (Washington). Author: Federal Judges, 1972; editor: (with Craig Ducat) Corwin's Constitution and What It Means Today, 1978, Constitutional Interpretation, 1978. Home: 124 Bedford St Minneapolis MN 55414 Office: Polit Sci Dept U Minn Minneapolis MN 55455

CHASE, JOYCE ELAINE, accountant, ins. co. exec.; b. Benton Harbor, Mich., Dec. 4, 1931; d. Richard I. and Evelyn Pauline (Hahn) Winney; student Lake Mich. Coll., 1974-75, Mich. State Ins. Sch., 1974, m. Ernest Arthur Chase, July 21, 1951; children—Ernest L., Arthur M., Robert J., William R., James R. Clk. Gillespie's Drug Store, Benton Harbor, 1945, WoolWorth's Store, Benton Harbor, 1946-47; bookkeeper Reeder's Bookkeeping Service, Benton Harbor, 1949; assembler VM Corp., Benton Harbor, 1950; telephone operator Mich. Bell Co., Benton Harbor, 1951; bookkeeper I & M Electric Co., Buchanan, Mich., 1952, Auto Specialties Co., St. Joseph, Mich., 1953; clk. Galien Drug Store, Galien, Mich., 1955; assembler Electro-Voice Corp., Buchanan, Mich., 1958-62; bookkeeper Chase Bookkeeping & Tax Service, Galien, Mich., 1963-78, sr. tax accountant, 1968—; ins. agt. Chase Ins. Service Center, Galien, Mich., 1974—; emergency med. technician and ambulance driver Galien Vol. Ambulance Service, 1974—. Cub. Scout den mother S.W. Mich. council Cub. Scouts Am., 1963-69; mem. Galien Twp. election bd., 1971-78; mem. Galien Sch. Election Bd., 1971—; pres. Galien Athletic Boosters, 1969; mem. Galien High Sch., PTA, 1966—, adv. com., 1965-68. Mem. Nat. Soc. Pub. Accountants, Mich. Emergency Services Health Council, Am. Legion Aux. Republican. Methodist. Home: US Route 12 East at Garwood Lake Galien MI 49113 Office: 112 N Main St Galien MI 49113

CHASTAIN, CLAUD BLANKENHORN, educator; b. Stamford, Tex., Oct. 12, 1945; s. Claud Harrison and Jean Ida (Blankenhorn) C.; B.S., U. Mo., 1967, D.V.M., 1969; M.S., Iowa State U., 1972; m. Joyce Busche, June 25, 1977; children—Andrea Lee, Danielle Renee. Instr. public health Taiwan Nat. U., 1971-72; instr. Coll. Vet. Medicine, Iowa State U., 1972-75; asst. prof. La. State U., 1975-76; asst. prof. vet. clin. scis. Iowa State U., 1976-77, asso. prof., 1977-81, prof., 1981—. Served to capt. USAF, 1969-71. Mem. Am. Vet. Med. Assn., Am. Acad. Vet. Dermatologists, Am. Assn. Vet. Clinicians, Am. Animal Hosp. Assn., Am. Coll. Vet. Internal Medicine, Iowa Vet. Med. Assn., Nat. Woodcarvers Assn., Nat. Wildlife Fedn., Phi Zeta. Methodist. Office: Iowa State U Ames IA 50011

CHATMAN, DONALD LEVERITT, obstetrician, gynecologist; b. New Orleans, Dec. 27, 1934; s. Aristotle Lorenzo and Eulacie (Shamberger) C.; B.A., Harvard, 1956; M.D., Meharry Med. Coll., 1960; m. Eleanor Mae Scrutchions, Jan. 15, 1957; children—Lynn Ann, Eleanor Louise, Eric Leveritt. Intern, Cooper Hosp., Camden, N.J., 1960-61; gen. practice medicine, Lake Charles, La., 1961-63; resident in ob-gyn Michael Reese Hosp. and Med. Center, Chgo., 1965-69, asst. attending dept. ob-gyn, 1969-74, attending, 1974—; practice medicine specializing in obstetrics gynecology, Chgo., 1969—; clin. asso. prof. Pritzker Sch. Medicine, U. Chgo., 1974—; lectr. Cook County Grad. Sch. Medicine, Chgo., 1978—. Diplomate Am. Bd. Obstetrics Gynecology. Fellow Chgo. Gynecol. Soc., Am. Coll. Obstetricians and Gynecologists; mem. Ill., Chgo. med. socs., AMA, Nat. Med. Assn., Am. Assn. Gynecologic Laparoscopists, Ill. Family Planning Council. Contbr. articles to profl. jours. Home: 9122 S Constance St Chicago IL 60617

CHATTEN, ROGER GERALD, psychologist; b. Quincy, Ill., Feb. 8, 1944; s. Ernest M. and Genevieve D. (Welch) C.; B.A., William Jewell Coll., 1966; M.A., U. Mo., 1968, Ph.D., 1977; m. Carol Ruth Ferril, Apr. 16, 1966; children—Michael, Kimberly. Instr. psychology Donnelly Coll., 1968-69; counseling intern U. Mo., Kansas City, 1971-72, 73-74; clin. dir. Asso. Psychologists and Counselors, Kansas City, Mo., 1978—; adj. prof. Park and Webster Coll., 1973—, Columbia Coll., 1979—, Ottawa U., 1979—; clin. psychology intern Western Mo. Mental Health Center, 1977-78. Lic. psychologist, Mo. Mem. Am. Psychol. Assn. (div. counseling psychology), Biofeedback Soc. Am., Biofeedback Soc. Mo., Greater Kansas City Psychol. Assn., Mo. Psychol. Assn., Profl. Counselors Assn. Home: Kansas City MO Office: Suite 115 4706 Broadway Kansas City MO 64112

CHAUDHRY, DEWAT RAM, psychiatrist; b. Rajasthan, India, Jan. 5, 1942; s. Mallu Ram and Gomti (Siyag) C.; came to U.S., 1970, naturalized, 1978; M.B.B.S., Sardar Patel Med. Coll., Bikaner, India, 1966; m. Lalita Beniwal, May 25, 1967; children—Neena, Suneel. Intern J.L.N. Hosp., Ajmer, India, 1966-67; resident in psychiatry VA and Provincial hosps., St. John, N.B., Can., 1968-70; intern Aultman Hosp., Canton, Ohio, 1970-71; resident in psychiatry Med. Coll. Toledo Hosp., 1971-73; fellow child psychiatry Hawthorn Center, Northville, Mich., 1973-74; child psychiatrist, coordinator children's services Comprehensive Community Mental Health Center Rock Island (Ill.) and Mercer County, 1974-80; practice medicine specializing in psychiatry, Moline, Ill., 1980—. Diplomate Am. Bd. Psychiatry and Neurology. Mem. Am. Psychiat. Assn., Am. Acad. Child Psychiatry, Ill. Psychiat. Soc. Hindu. Office: 2101 47th St Moline IL 61265

CHAVIN, WALTER, biologist; b. U.S., Dec. 6, 1925; s. Isidor and Fanny (Kesch) C.; B.S., CCNY, 1946; M.S., N.Y. U., 1949, Ph.D., 1954. Instr. in biology CCNY, 1946-47, U. Ariz., 1949-51; research specialist Am. Museum Natural History, N.Y.C., 1951-53; asst. prof. biol. scis. Wayne State U., 1953-60, asso. prof., 1960-65, prof., 1965—, prof. radiology Sch. Medicine, 1975-80; research asso. Argonne (Ill.) Nat. Lab., 1955-58; NSF sr. postdoctoral fellow Sorbonne, U. Paris, 1960-61. Pres., Acad. Scholars, Wayne State U., 1979. Recipient Faculty Service award Wayne State U. Alumni, 1975; Presdl. citation Wayne State U., 1977, Disting. Grad. Faculty award, 1978, 25-Yr. award, 1979. Fellow AAAS (sec. sect. biol. scis. 1978—), N.Y. Acad. Sci.; mem. Aerospace Med. Assn., Am. Inst. Biol. Scis., Am. Physiol. Soc., Am. Soc. Cell Biology, Am. Soc. Cancer Research, Am. Soc. Zoologists (chmn. div. comparative endocrinology 1972-74, treas. 1980-82), Endocrine Soc., Internat. Pigment Cell Soc. (editor bull. 1980-82), Societie d'Endocrinologie, Mich. Acad. Arts, Sci., Letters, Mich. Nuclear Soc., Midwest Radioassay Soc. (exec. com. 1972-78), Radiation Research Soc., Soc. Exptl. Biology and Medicine, Sigma Xi (pres. Wayne State U. chpt. 1972-73, Faculty Research award 1968). Author: Responses of Fish to Environmental Changes, 1973; contbr. numerous chpts., articles to profl. publs. Office: 5104 Gullen Mall Wayne State U Detroit MI 48202

CHAZIN, MICHAEL, magazine editor; b. Chgo., July 29, 1948; s. Aaron George and Sonia (Lerman) C.; B.S. in Communications, U. Ill., 1970; M.A. in Psychology, Roosevelt U., Chgo., 1973; m. Helene Susan Blumsack, July 16, 1970; children—Neil Adam, Keith Richard. Public relations asso. Western Electric Co., Inc., Rolling Meadows, Ill., 1973-75; features editor Inland Printer mag., Chgo., 1975-77; editor-in-chief successor mag. Am. Printer and Lithographer, 1977-80; editor Publs. Internat. Ltd., Skokie, Ill., 1980-81; editor Consumer Guide, 1980-81; sr. editor Office Products Dealer mag., Wheaton, Ill., 1981—; tchr. photography Oakton Community Coll., Des Plaines, Ill., 1976—. Office: Hitchcock Pub Hitchcock Bldg Wheaton IL 60187

CHEATHAM, DENNIS HAROLD, banker; b. Madison, Ind., May 27, 1943; s. John Harold and Callie Elizabeth (Hughes) C.; A.B., Ind. U., 1965; m. Quindaro Anne Groth; children—Theodore Chase, Quindaro Elizabeth, John Lester Philip. Sales mgr. charge card div. Indpls. Morris Plan, 1966-67; successively investment officer, asst. v.p., v.p. Am. Fletcher Nat. Bank & Trust Co., Indpls., 1967-72; asst. treas. Am. Fletcher Corp., Indpls., 1970-72; pres., dir., chief exec. officer State Bank Lapel (Ind.), 1972-80, chmn. bd. dirs., 1980—; pres., dir. Pendleton Banking Co. (Ind.), 1973—; pres., dir. Pendleton Co., Inc., 1975—; chmn. bd. dirs. 1st Nat. Bank in New Castle (Ind.), 1979—; dir. Mgmt. Advisers, Inc. and subs.'s, Indpls., 1973—; trustee Underwriters Nat. Assurance Co., Indpls., 1977-80; adviser S. Madison County Bldg. Trades, Inc., 1975. Mem. allocations and rev. com. Madison County United Way, 1973; bd. dirs. Pendleton Festival Symphony, 1976-77; trustee Delta Upsilon Ednl. Found., Columbus, Ohio, 1978—. Mem. Ind. Bankers Assn., League for Econ. Devel. (pres. Indpls. 1979—), Delta Upsilon (nat. treas., dir. 1974, 75, 76, nat. chmn. bd. dirs. 1977—). Clubs: Columbia (Indpls.); Westwood Country (New Castle, Ind.). Home: PO Box 205 Pendleton IN 46064 Office: 100 E State St Pendleton IN 46064

CHEATHAM, WALTER MALCOLM, corporate pub. affairs exec.; b. Toccoa, Ga., May 17, 1932; s. Jess Bailey and Eleanor Irene (Johnson) C.; B.A., Emory U., 1956, J.D., 1956; postgrad. Temple U., 1957-58; student Presbyn. Coll., 1950-51, U. Ga., 1951-54; m. Harriet Ann Craig, Jan. 6, 1973; 1 dau., Elinor Dallas. Mgr. govt. dept. Ga. C. of C., Atlanta, 1958-59; exec. staff rep. The Coca-Cola Co., Atlanta, 1959-62, mgr. mktg., San Antonio, 1962-64, mgr. pub. relations, Chgo., 1964-65; gen. mgr. Southeastern opns. Ruder & Finn Co., Atlanta, 1965-67; prin. Cheatham Pub. Relations/Advt., Atlanta, 1967-71; mktg. cons. N.W. Ayer ABH Internat., Dallas, 1971-74, account exec. Midwest, Chgo., 1974-75; dir. pub. affairs Midwest, Union Carbide Corp., Chgo., 1976-78, Columbus, Ohio, 1978-80; dir. public affairs planning Am. Elec. Power Service Corp., Columbus, 1980—. Trustee Ill. 2000 Found., 1977-78. Mem. advisory bd. Civic Fedn. Chgo., 1976-78; bd. dirs. Pub. Service Communications Council Chgo., 1976-78, Christopher House United Christian Community Services Chgo., 1975-76; dir. Better Govt. Assn. Chgo., 1977-78; mem. steering com. Ohio Alliance for Energy, Growth and Jobs, 1978-80; bd. dirs. Columbus Community Cable Access, Inc., 1980—; ruling elder, mem. session Broad St. Presbyn. Ch., Columbus. Served with U.S. Army, 1956-58. Named One of Georgia's Five Outstanding Young Men, Ga. Jr. C. of C., 1962. Mem. Emory U. Alumni Assn. (v.p. 1967-71), Pub. Relations Soc. Am., Sigma Alpha Epsilon. Club: Athletic (Columbus). Home: 2355 Brentwood Rd Columbus OH 43209 Office: 180 E Broad St Rm 1500C Columbus OH 43215

CHECINSKI, STANLEY STANISLAW, elec. engr.; b. Starokrzepice, Poland, Aug. 30, 1929; came to U.S., 1973, naturalized, 1979; s. Franciszek and Apolonia (Dros) C.; B.S.E.E., U. Wroclaw (Poland), 1956, M.S.E.E., 1958; Sc.D., U. Szczecin (Poland), 1972; m. Jadwiga Wisniewska, July 4, 1954; children—Margaret, George. Design engr. Inst. Electrotechnics, Wroclaw, 1953-64; mgr. automation and measurement labs. Central Mining Inst., Wroclaw, 1964-69; prof. U. Wroclaw, 1969-72; design engr. Inglot Electronics Corp., Chgo., 1973; elec. engr. Lester B. Knight, Chgo., 1974-76; mgr. research and devel. Sweetheart Cup Corp., Chgo., 1976-78; sr. staff scientist Gould, Inc., Rolling Meadows, Ill., 1978—; editor Gornictwo Monthly Mag., U. Wroclaw, 1970-71. Vice pres. Polish-Am. Immigration and Relief com., 1976—; pres. Polish Am. Scholarship Fund, 1976—. UN fellow, 1967. Mem. Instrument Soc. Am., Soc. Mfg. Engrs., Polish Inst. of Arts and Sci. of Am. Roman Catholic. Club: Rolling Meadows. Contbr. articles to profl. jours.; patentee in field. Home: 115 Garland Ct Glendale Heights IL 60137 Office: 40 Gould Center Rolling Meadows IL 60008

CHEFFER, ROBERT GENE, counselor; b. Kankakee, Ill., Aug. 9, 1936; s. Herman Joseph and Cecilia Marie (Dion) C.; B.S., Eastern Ill. U., 1958; M.Ed., Chgo. State U., 1962; m. Patricia Paris, June 25, 1960; children—Christian, Scott. Tchr., Oak Lawn (Ill.) Community High Sch., 1958-70; counselor Maine Twp. High Sch., Park Ridge, Ill., 1970—, Monacep Alt. High Sch. Program, 1976—. Named Outstanding Secondary Educator, 1973. Mem. Am. Personnel and Guidance Assn., Nat. Vocat. Guidance Assn., Am. Sch. Counselors Assn., Ill. Guidance and Personnel Assn. (pres. 1978-79, pres. N.W. Suburban chpt. 1974-75), Ill. Vocat. Guidance Assn. (pres. 1974-75), Ill. Guidance and Personnel Assn., NEA, Ill. Edn. Assn., Ill. Assn. Adult and Continuing Edn. Counselors, Eastern Ill. U. Alumni Assn., Chgo. State U. Alumni Assn., Pupil Personnel Service Consortium. Home: 153 Chandler St Elmhurst IL 60126 Office: 1111 Dee Rd Park Ridge IL 60068

CHEKOURAS, CARL CHRISTOPHER, cons.; b. Beloit, Wis., Apr. 16, 1916; s. George A. and Sophie Theresa (Pierson) C.; student U. Wis. Extension, Beloit Coll., 1943-45; m. Geraldine A. Wolfe, Mar. 2, 1946; children—David, Carl, Susan. Product design and devel. wood-working industry, 1942-54; plant mgr. Agerstrand Corp., Freeport, Ill., 1954-56; organizer, pres. Ackrit Machine Co., Inc., South Beloit, Ill., 1954-56; dist. sales mgr. Atwood, Rockford, Ill., 1963-71; mgmt. staff Morris Midwest, Inc., Wausau, Wis., 1971-74; sales dir. Crown div. Steel King Industries, 1974-81; dir. Thurston Mfg. Co. (Nebr.); cons. Hi-Ton Internat., Birmingham, Eng.; committeeman intercontinental trade shows. Mem. Am. Soc. Agr. Engrs., Farm Equipment Mfg. Assn., Soc. Automotive Engrs., Serra Internat. Contbr. articles to trade publs. Office: 3207 Post Rd Stevens Point WI 54481

CHEN, GILBERT KUO-CHENG, research and devel. exec.; b. Tainan, Taiwan, July 20, 1943; s. Su-Long and Zone (Wang) C.; B.S. in Chem. Engring., Nat. Taiwan U., 1965; M.S. in Chem. Engring., Kans. State U., 1968, Ph.D. in Chem. Engring., 1971; m. Esther Siu-Lan Pan, July 18, 1966; children—Spencer Suh-Ping, Lawrence Suh-Tse. Came to U.S., 1966, naturalized, 1975. Sr. research engr. Monsanto Co., Dayton, Ohio, 1971-73, pilot plant supr., Indpls., 1973, research engring. specialist, St. Louis, 1973-77; dir. research and devel. Koch Engring. Co., Inc., Wichita, Kans., 1977—. Mem. Am. Inst. Chem. Engrs., Air Pollution Control Assn., Sigma Xi, Pi Mu Epsilon. Co-inventor Monsanto's Energy Saving Mist Eliminator, 1977; Koch's Flexigrid, 1979, Reverse Jet Scrubber, 1980. Home: 14230 Timberlakes Rd Wichita KS 67230 Office: 4111 E 37th St North Wichita KS 67207

CHEN, KUN-MU, elec. engr.; b. Taiwan, Feb. 3, 1933; s. Tsa-Mao and Che (Wu) Chen; Ph.D., Harvard U., 1960; m. Shun-Shun Chen, Feb. 22, 1962; children—Maggie, Kathy, Kenneth, George. Research asso. U. Mich., Ann Arbor, 1960-64; asso. prof. Mich. State U., East Lansing, 1964-67, prof. elec. engring., 1967—. Recipient Disting. Faculty award Mich. State U., 1976. Fellow IEEE, AAAS; mem. Internat. Union Radio Sci., Bioelectromagnetics Soc., Sigma Xi, Phi Kappa Phi, Tau Beta Pi. Author numerous papers in areas of electromagnetics, plasma physics, electromagnetic biol. effects. Home: 4608 Tacoma Blvd Okemos MI 48864 Office: Dept Elec Engring Mich State U East Lansing MI 48824

CHEN, PETER FU MING, surgeon; b. Medan, Indonesia, Dec. 3, 1941; s. Ah Sok and Oei Tan; came to U.S., 1968, naturalized, 1977; M.D., Nat. Def. Med. Center, Taiwan, 1968; m. Shueh-Yen Tien, Apr. 9, 1968; children—Vivian, Calvin. Intern, Barberton (Ohio) Citizens Hosp., 1968; resident in surgery Fairview (Ohio) Gen. Hosp., 1969-73; practice medicine specializing in surgery, Mantua, Ohio; staff Robinson Meml. Hosp., Ravenna, Ohio; clin. asst. prof. surgery Neucom (Ohio) U. Recipient Scholar award Chinese Govt., 1968. Diplomate Am. Bd. Surgery. Fellow A.C.S.; mem. Ohio Med. Assn., Cleve. Surg. Soc., Portage County Med. Soc. Baptist. Home: 4692 Streeter Rd Mantua OH 44255 Office: 10683 Maple St Mantua OH 44255

CHEN, SHOEI-SHENG, engr.; b. Taiwan, Jan. 26, 1940; s. Yung-cheng and A-shu (Fang) C.; B.S., Nat. Taiwan U., 1963; M.S., Princeton U., 1966, M.A., 1967, Ph.D., 1968; m. Ruth C. Lee, June 28, 1969; children—Lyrice, Lisa. Research asst. Princeton U., 1965-68; asst. mech. engr. Argonne (Ill.) Nat. Lab., 1968-71, mech. engr., 1971-80, sr. mech. engr., 1980—; cons. to Internat. Atomic Energy Agy. to assist developing countries in research and devel. of nuclear reactor system components, 1977, 79, 80. Mem. ASME, Am. Acad. Mechanics, Acoustical Soc. Am., Sigma Xi. Contbr. numerous articles to profl. jours. Home: 6420 Waterford Ct Willowbrook IL 60521 Office: 9700 S Cass Ave Argonne IL 60439

CHEN, SIMON K., tech. cons. and product devel. co. exec.; b. Peking, China, Oct. 13, 1925; s. Hoshien and Lin Sie (Chao) Tchen; came to U.S., 1948, naturalized, 1955; B.S.M.E., Nat. Chiao-Tung U., Shanghai, 1947; M.S.M.E., U. Mich., 1949; Ph.D. in Mech. engring., U. Wis., 1952; M.B.A., U. Chgo., 1964; m. Rosemary Ho; children—Margaret, Lillian, Vivian, Victor. Div. chief engr. diesel engine div. Internat. Harvester Co., Melrose Park, Ill., 1952-69; v.p., gen mgr. large engine operation, then v.p. engring. and application FM power systems div. Colt Industries, Beloit, Wis., 1969-73; pres. Beloit Power Systems, Am. Laminate Products subs. Tang Industries, Beloit, 1973-79; pres. Power and Energy, Internat., Inc., Beloit, 1979—. Mem. Greater Beloit Com. Recipient Alumni Distinguished Service award U. Wis., 1973, Achievement and Service award Chinese Inst. Engrs., 1976, Arch T. Colwell award, 1966. Mem. Soc. Automotive Engrs. Family Service Assn., ASME, Soc. Naval Architects and Marine Engrs., Sigma Xi, Beta Gamma Sigma. Club: Janesville (Wis.) Indoor Tennis. Home: 325 Racine Delavan WI 53115 Office: PO Box 1064 Beloit WI 53511

CHEN, WAI-KAI, elec. engr., educator; b. Nanking, China, Dec. 23, 1936; s. You-Chao and Shui-Tan C.; came to U.S., 1959, naturalized, 1972; B.S., Ohio U., 1960, M.S., 1961; Ph.D. (fellow), U. Ill., 1964; m. Shirley Shiao Ling, Sept. 1, 1962; children—Jerome, Melissa. Asst. prof. elec. engring. Ohio U., Athens, 1964-67, asso. prof., 1967-71, prof., 1971-78, disting. prof., 1978-81, fellow Research Inst., 1972; prof. and head dept. info. engring. U. Ill., Chgo., 1981—; vis. asso. prof. Purdue U., 1970-71; vis. prof. U. Hawaii, Manoa, 1979. Recipient Baker Fund award Ohio U., 1974; C.T. Loo fellow China Inst. in Am., 1962. Fellow IEEE, AAAS; mem. Math. Assn. Am. (Lester R. Ford award 1967), Am. Soc. Engring. Edn., Soc. Indsl. and Applied Math., Assn. for Computing Machinery, Tensor Soc. Gt. Brit., Sigma Xi, Phi Kappa Phi, Pi Mu Epsilon, Eta Kappa Nu. Author: Applied Graph Theory, 1971; Theory and Design of Broadband Matching Networks, 1976; Applied Graph Theory: Graphs and Electric Networks, 2d edit., 1976; Active Network and Feedback Amplifier Theory, 1980; Linear Networks and Systems, 1982; contbr. articles to profl. jours. Office: Dept Info Engring U Ill at Chgo Box 4348 Chicago IL 60680

CHEN, WEI-TZUOH, nephrologist; b. Taoyuan, Taiwan, Formosa, Apr. 4, 1943; s. Cheng-Chih and Yu-Nu (Chiang) C.; came to U.S., 1972, naturalized, 1978; M.B., Taipei Med. Coll., 1969; m. Shelley R. Yang, June 19, 1973; children—Charles W., Diana. Intern St. Luke's Hosp., Cleve., 1972-73; med. resident VA Hosp., Cleve., 1973-74, Luth. Med. Center, Cleve., 1974-76; nephrology trainee Cleve. Met. Gen. Hosp., 1975-76; nephrology fellow Cleve. Clinic Found., 1976-78; staff physician sect. renal and hypertension VA Hosp., Hines, Ill., 1978—, asst. sect. chief, 1980—; asst. prof. medicine Loyola U., Stritch Sch. Medicine, Chgo., 1978—. Diplomate Am. Bd. Internal Medicine, Am. Bd. Nephrology. Fellow A.C.P.; mem. Am. Soc. Internal Medicine, Am. Soc. Nephrology, Internat. Soc. Artificial Organs, Ill. Soc. Internal Medicine, Taipei Med. Coll. Alumni Assn. N.Am. (mem. exec. com.). Home: 3831 Florence Ave Downers Grove IL 60515 Office: Hines VA Hosp Hines IL 60141

CHEN, WEN FU, otolaryngologist; b. Taiwan, China, Apr. 25, 1942; s. Wainan and Wangchien C.; came to U.S., 1969, naturalized, 1977; M.D., Kaohsiung Med. Coll., Taiwan, 1968; m. Huiying Wu, Sept. 13, 1973; children—David W., Jeffrey W. Intern, Augustana Hosp., Chgo., 1969-70; resident in surgery VA Hosp., Dayton, Ohio, 1970-72; resident in otolaryngology Homer Phillip Hosp., St. Louis, 1972-75; asst. chief otolaryngology VA Hosp., Kansas City, Mo., 1975-77; mem. staff Kansas Med. Center, Kansas City, 1975-77; practice medicine specializing in otolaryngology, Chillicothe, Ohio, 1977—. Diplomate Am. Bd. Otolaryngology. Fellow Am. Acad. Ophalmology and Otolaryngology; mem. AMA, Ohio State Med. Assn. Home: 22 Oakwood Dr Chillicothe OH 45601 Office: Medical Center Hospital Junction 19 and 23 Chillicothe OH 45601

CHEN, WEN-JIA RUSSELL, educator; b. Chungking, China, Mar. 10, 1945; s. Shaw-Pyng and Yu-Zung (Kuo) C.; B.S. in Chem. Engring., Nat. Taiwan U., 1967; M.S. in Chem. Engring., Syracuse U., 1971, Ph.D. in Chem. Engring., 1974. Chem. engr. Allied Chem. Corp., Syracuse, N.Y., 1974-76; research engr. U. N.Mex., Albuquerque, 1976-77; asst. prof. dept. chem. engring. Ohio U., Athens, 1978—. Mem. Am. Inst. Chem. Engrs., Sigma Xi. Office: Chem Engring Dept Ohio U Athens OH 45701

CHEN, YU MIN, biochemist; b. I-shing, Kiangsu, China, Dec. 23, 1922; s. Mu Fan and Yueh Wah (Pan) C.; came to U.S., 1954, naturalized, 1976; B.S., Nat. Chekiang U. China, 1946; M.S., Nat. Taiwan U., 1950; Ph.D., U. So. Calif., 1960; m. Jiachun Nei, July 11, 1964; children—Peter, Plato, Asso. prof. biochemistry Nat. Taiwan

U., 1960-63; fellow Inst. Chemistry, Academia Sinica, Taiwan, 1960-63; research scientist Wayne State U., Detroit, 1963-68, Mich. Cancer Found., Detroit, 1968-73; prin. investigator Wayne State U., Detroit, 1973—. Pres., Chinese Cultural Center, Detroit, 1976. U. So. Calif. scholar, 1954-60; NIH grantee, 1971-74, 75-78. Mem. Am. Assn. Cancer Research, China Chem. Soc., Chinese Assn. Agrl. Chemistry, Sigma Xi. Research in immunochemistry. Home: 30105 High Valley Rd Farmington Hills MI 48018

CHENETTE, LOUIS F(RED), univ. adminstr., musicologist; b. Powersville, Iowa, Apr. 2, 1931; s. Eugene Dow and Freda Anne (Ontjes) C.; B.A. in Music (scholar), Wheaton Coll., 1953; Mus.M., Northwestern U., 1956; Ph.D. in Music Theory, Ohio State U., 1967; m. Emily Louise Scanlan, June 26, 1951; children—David, Jonathan, Nancy, Philip, Holly. Dir. music Antioch (Ill.) Twp. High Sch., 1953-58; instr. Bemidji State Coll., 1958-59; chmn. dept. music Findlay Coll., 1963-65, chmn. div. fine arts, 1965-67; asst. dean, dir. instl. research, 1967-69, asst. to pres., 1969-71, acting pres., 1971-72; dean Jordan Coll., Fine Arts, Butler U., 1972—; trustee Ind. Symphony Soc., Indpls. Civic Ballet Soc., Clowes Hall Adv. Bd., Indpls. Opera Co. Ohio Fedn. Music Clubs scholar, 1963. Mem. Am. Musicol. Soc., Gesellschaft für Musikforschung, Internat. Musicol. Soc., Société Française de Musicologie, Phi Delta Kappa, Phi Kappa Lambda, Phi Kappa Phi. Methodist. Contbr. articles to profl. publs. Office: Butler U 4600 Clarendon Rd Indianapolis IN 46207

CHENEY, DAVID RAYMOND, educator; b. Castle Dale, Utah, Jan. 23, 1922; s. Silas Lavell and Klara (Young) C.; student Snow Coll., 1939-41; B.A., U. Utah, 1948, M.A., 1949; A.M., Harvard U., 1951; Ph.D., U. Iowa, 1955; m. Patricia Anne Snow, Dec. 18, 1948; 1 dau., Pamela. Teaching asst. in English, U. Iowa, 1953-55; instr. English, Lewis and Clark Coll., 1956-58; asso. prof. English, S.W. Mo. State Coll., 1958-63, prof., 1963-65; prof. U. Toledo, 1965—, dir. grad. studies in English, 1968-79. Advisor, youth council NAACP, Springfield, Mo., 1963-65; del. Democratic Nat. Conv., 1976. Served with U.S. Army, 1941-46; PTO. U. Utah research fellow, 1948; U. Toledo research fellow, 1968, 79; U. Iowa grantee, 1966, 68; U. Toledo grantee, 1968, 70, 73, 74, 79. Mem. Modern Humanities Research Assn., Shakespeare Assn. Am., MLA, Central Renaissance Soc. Am., AAUP, Phi Beta Kappa, Phi Kappa Phi. Mormon. Author: The Correspondence of Leigh Hunt and Charles Ollier in the Winter of 1853-54, 1976; editor: Musical Evenings or Selections Vocal and Instrumental (Leigh Hunt), 1964; research on Leigh Hunt letters, Shakespeare. Home: 2833 Goddard Rd Toledo OH 43606 Office: 2801 W Bancroft St Toledo OH 43606

CHENG, CHU YUAN, educator; b. Kwangtung Province, China, Apr. 8, 1927; came to U.S., 1959, naturalized, 1964; s. Hung Shan and Shu Chen (Yang) C.; B.A. in Econs., Nat. Chengchih U., Nanking, China, 1947; M.A., Georgetown U., Washington, 1962, Ph.D., 1964; m. Alice Hua Liang, Aug. 15, 1964; children—Anita Tung I, Andrew Y.S. Research prof. Seton Hall U., 1960-64; vis. prof. George Washington U., Washington, 1963; sr. research economist U. Mich., Ann Arbor, 1964-69; asso. prof. Lawrence U., Appleton, Wis., 1970-71; asso. prof. econs., chmn. Asian studies com. Ball State U., Muncie, Ind., 1971-73, prof. econs., 1974—; cons. NSF, Washington, 1964—. Bd. dirs. Dr. Sun Yat-sen Inst., Chgo., 1978—. Grantee, NSF, 1960-64, Social Sci. Research Council, 1965-67, 74; recipient Outstanding Research award Ball State U., 1976. Mem. Am. Econ. Assn., Assn. Asian Studies, Assn. Comparative Econ. Studies, Am. Acad. Polit. and Social Sci., Ind. Acad. Social Sci., Omicron Delta Epsilon. Author: Scientific and Engineering Manpower in Communist China, 1966; The Machine-Building Industry in Communist China, 1971; China's Petroleum Industry: Output Growth and Export Potential, 1976; China's Economic Development: Growth and Structural Change, 1981; mem. adv. com. Chinese Econ. Studies Quar., 1966—. Home: 1211 Greenbriar Rd Muncie IN 47304 Office: Room 123 Coll Bus Ball State U Muncie IN 47306

CHENG, CRAIG FONG, energy/materials cons.; b. Tientsin, China, Oct. 19, 1917; came to U.S., 1936, naturalized, 1955; s. Yun-Cheong and Mabel (Chow) C.; B.S. in Chem. Engring., M.I.T., 1940; M.S. in Phys. Chemistry, Aurora, U., 1947; m. Fay Nollner, Apr. 20, 1946; children—Peter James, Sloane Marie. Research staff Internat. Nickel Co., N.Y.C., 1955-65; corrosion engring. sect. head Gen. Electric Co., Schnectady, N.Y., 1955-65; mgr. materials engring. Argonne (Ill.) Nat. Lab., 1965-79; pres., dir. ECA, Inc., Energy & Conservation Applications, Lisle, Ill., 1979—; materials cons. Dept. Energy, Nat. Labs., NRC, Commonwealth Edison Co., HPD, Inc., Sci. Applications, Inc., Stone & Webster Engring. Corp., others. Mem. Nat. Assn. Corrosion Engrs., ASTM, Inst. Metals (Eng.). Contbr. articles to profl. jours. Home: 332 Kings Cove Lisle IL 60532

CHENG, FRANCIS SHYUE-TSO, physician; b. Kun-Ming, China, July 8, 1943; s. Wen-Lo and Jane (Young) C.; came to U.S., 1971; M.D., Kaohsiung Med. Coll., Taiwan, 1971; m. Sylvia Yuet-Yu Lam, May, 1973; 1 son, Michael. Intern, U. Ill. Hosp., Chgo., 1971-72, resident, 1972-74; fellow in cardiology Michael Reese Hosp., 1974-75, Rush Presbyn. St. Luke's Hosp., 1975-76; asst. in medicine U. Ill., 1927-74; instr. medicine Rush Med. Sch., Chgo., 1975-76; chief sect. cardiology, dept. internal medicine Alexian Bros. Med. Center, Elk Grove Village, Ill., 1979-81. Bd. dirs. Heart Assn. North Cook County, Ill. Diplomate Am. Bd. Internal Medicine. Fellow Am. Coll. Cardiology; mem. Am. Heart Assn., A.C.P., AMA. Office: 1000 Grand Canyon Pkwy Hoffman Estates IL 60194

CHENG, KUANG LU, educator; b. Yangchow, China, Sept. 14, 1919; s. Fong Wu and Yi Ming (Chiang) C.; came to U.S., 1947, naturalized, 1955; Ph.D., U. Ill., 1951; children—Meiling, Chiling, Hans Christian. Microchemist, Comml. Solvents Corp., Terre Haute, Ind., 1952-53; instr. U. Conn., Storrs, 1953-55; engr., Westinghouse Electric Corp., Pitts. 1955-57; asso. dir. research, metals div. Kelsey Hayes Co., New Hartford, N.Y., 1957-59; mem. tech. staff RCA Labs., Princton, 1959-66; prof. chemistry U. Mo., Kansas City, 1966—. Recipient Achievement award RCA, 1963; N.T. Veatch award for disting. research and creative activity U. Mo.-Kansas City, 1979; cert. of recognition, Office Naval Research, 1979, Tex. A&M U., 1981. Fellow AAAS, Chem. Soc. London; mem. Am. Chem. Soc., Electrochem. Soc., Soc. Applied Spectroscopy, Am. Inst. Physics. Home: 34 E 56th Terrace Kansas City MO 64113 Office: Dept Chemistry Univ Mo Kansas City MO 64110

CHENG, LESTER C., mech. engr., biomed. engring. cons.; b. China, Apr. 20, 1944; s. Chin-Sun and Lu Cheng; came to U.S., 1967, naturalized, 1977; B.S. in Mech. Engring., Nat. Taiwan U., 1965; M.S. in Mech. Engring., N.D. State U., 1968; Ph.D. in Theoretical and Applied Mechanics, U. Ill., 1971; postgrad. San Diego Coll. System, 1974-75; m. Mei Yao, June 1969; children—Gloria, Helen. Research asso. U. Ill., Urbana, 1970-71, Intersci. Research Inst., Champaign, Ill., 1971; engr. analyst Sargent & Lundy Engrs., Chgo., 1971-72, sr. engr., 1972-74; sr. engr. Gen. Atomic Co., San Diego, 1974-76; asst. prof. dept. mech. engring. Wichita (Kans.) State U., 1976-79, asso. prof., 1979—; condr. biomed. engring. program NSF, 1977-80; cons. dept. theoretical and applied mechanics U. Ill., 1974-76, Wichita VA Med. Center, 1978—, Kans. Energy and Environ. Lab., Wichita, 1978—. Registered profl. engr., Kans. Mem. Am. Acad. Mechanics (hon.), ASME, Am. Soc. Engring. Edn., Soc. Automotive Engrs. (Ralph Teetor award 1980), Sigma Xi, Phi Kappa Phi. Contbr. articles fluid mechanics, biomed. engring. and thermal energy studies to sci. jours. Office: Dept Mech Engring Wichita State U Wichita KS 67208

CHENG, PAUL HUNG-CHIAO, civil engr.; b. China, Dec. 1, 1930; s. Yen-Teh and Shu-Yin (Tsou) C.; came to U.S., 1958, naturalized, 1973; B.S. in Civil Engring., Nat. Taiwan U., 1951; M.S. in C.E., U. Va., 1961; m. Lucial Jen Chen, Aug. 1, 1964; children—Maria, Elizabeth, Deborah, Samuel. Structural engr. Swift & Co., Chgo., 1963-67; sr. structural designer P & W Engring., Inc., Chgo., 1967; sr. structural engr. A. Epstein & Son, Inc., Chgo., 1967-68; staff engr. Interlake, Inc., Chgo., 1968-71, supervising engr., 1971-73, chief structural engr., 1973-80, product engring. mgr., 1980—; cons. Kawatetsu/Interlake, Ltd. (Tokyo). Registered structural engr., Ill.; registered profl. civil engr., Calif. Mem. ASCE, Am. Concrete Inst., Am. Mgmt. Assn. Home: 1620 Lawrence Crescent Flossmoor IL 60422 Office: Interlake Inc 100 Tower Dr Burr Ridge IL 60521

CHENG, SYLVIA FAN (MRS. JOHNSON CHU), physician; b. Shangtung, China, June 26, 1918 (came to U.S. 1948, naturalized 1957); d. Stanley C. and Flora C. (Chu) Cheng; B.S., U. Shanghai, 1938; M.D., Woman's Christian Med. Coll., Shanghai, 1942; postgrad. N.Y. U., 1948, Columbia, 1955; m. Johnson Chu, June 11, 1949; children—Stephen Cheng, Timothy Cheng. Rotating intern Margaret Williamson Hosp., 1942-43; resident in medicine, surgery, obstetrics and gynecology St. Luke's and St. Elizabeth Hosp., St. John's U. Hosp., 1943-47; practice medicine specializing in chest diseases, Shanghai, 1947-48, psychiatry and gen. practice, Logansport, Ind., 1956—; chief female service, dir. Tb unit Weston (W.Va.) State Hosp., 1955; chief female service, admission and intensive service, unit dir. Logansport (Ind.) State Hosp., 1956—; cons. physician White County Meml. Hosp., Monticello, Ind., Cass County Meml. hosps., Logansport, Ind., Southeastern Med. Center, Walton, Ind. Recipient award ARC, 1959. Fellow Am. Coll. Chest Physicians, Am. Psychiat. Assn.; mem. AMA, Am. Thoracic Soc., Mental Health Assn., Cass County Med. Soc., Am. Acad. Gen. Practice, Ind. State Med. Assn. Baptist (deaconess 1956-69, 73-76). Home: E 36 Lake Shafer Monticello IN 47960 Office: Southeastern Med Center Walton IN 46994

CHENG, THOMAS TONG, educator; b. Kuk Kong, China, May 14, 1944; Canadian citizen; s. Tsap Hay and Chui Man (Yip) C.; B.Commerce, Sir George Williams U., 1970; M.B.A., Concordia U., 1977; Ph.D., U. Mo., 1981; Teaching asst. U. Mo., Columbia, 1978-79, research asst., 1979-81; at Wharton Sch. Bus., U. Pa., Phila., 1981—. Mem. Can. Inst. Chartered Accts., Inst. Mgmt. Acctg., Inst. Chartered Secs. and Adminstrs., Nat. Assn. Bus. Economists, World Future Soc., Am. Acctg. Assn., Data Processing Mgmt. Assn., Assn. Computing Machinery, Am. Inst. Decision Scis., Am. Statis. Assn., Econometric Soc., Acad. Acctg. Historians. Office: Wharton Sch U Pa Philadelphia PA 19104

CHENG, WILLIAM JEN-PU, chem. co. exec.; b. Changsha, China, Sept. 26, 1915; s. Shao-Chien and Chao (Ling) C.; B.S., Tsing Hua U., 1939; M.S., Washington U., St. Louis, 1951, Heermans fellow, 1952; m. Chuan-Huan Wu, Sept. 25, 1954; children—Elizabeth, James, Nancy, Helen. Came to U.S., 1948, naturalized, 1973. Plant supt. China Vegetable Oil Corp., 1941-44; chem. engr. Chinese Army, 23d Arsenal, 1944-46; with Petrolite Corp., St. Louis, 1952—, head pilot plant, 1960-63, engring. research mgr., 1963-67, dir. engring., 1968-79, v.p. Tretolite div., 1980—. Mem. Am. Inst. Chem. Engrs., Am. Chem. Soc., N.Y. Acad. Sci. Patentee in field. Home: 705 Louwen Dr St Louis MO 63124 Office: 369 Marshall Ave St Louis MO 63119

CHENOWETH, ARLENE JOYCE, constrn. co. exec.; b. Cass City, Mich., Apr. 1, 1941; d. Robert Melvin and Geraldine Thelma (Bell) Milner; grad. Olivet Nazarene Coll., Kankakee, Ill., 1963; postgrad. U. Mich., 1963-65; m. Robert R. Chenoweth, Sept. 1, 1962; children—Timothy, Eric, Gregg. Tchr. bus. edn. Swartz Creek (Mich.) Sr. High Sch., 1963-67, Flushing (Mich.) Sr. High Sch., 1969-74; v.p. A & B Enterprises, Fenton, Mich., 1974—; co-owner, office mgr. Chenoweth Constrn. Co., Inc., Fenton, 1974—, Chenoweth & Assos. Architects, Inc., Fenton, 1978—. Mem. Am. Mgmt. Assn., Nat. Assn. Female Execs., Fenton Area Bus. and Profl. Women's Club (charter mem., treas. 1979), Boynestat Assn. Nazarene. Clubs: Univ. (Flint, Mich.); Spring Meadows Country. Home: 12050 White Lake Rd Fenton MI 48430 Office: Chenoweth Constrn Co Inc 101 N Ally Dr Fenton MI 48430

CHENOWETH, ROBERT DUANE, machinery co. exec.; b. Bedford, Ind., Oct. 10, 1923; s. Henry Carl and Elizabeth Jane (Barrett) C.; engring. student Internat. Corr. Schs., 1946-48; grad. Approved Supply Pastor's Sch., Garrett Theol. Sch., 1959; B.A., Miami U., 1962, postgrad., 1962-64; m. Shirley Ellen Woods, Sept. 17, 1949; children—Steven Carl, Mark Duane, Paula Jane. Cons. engr. J.E. Novotny Co., Dayton, Ohio, 1956-60; ordained elder United Methodist Ch., 1960, ordained to ministry, 1958; pastor Brookville and Miamitown (Ohio) Meth. Chs., 1958-67; chief tool engr. OPW div. Dover Corp., Cin., 1963-64; chief mfg. engr., mgr. mfg. Campbell-Hausfeld Co., Harrison, Ohio, 1964-68; plant mgr. Sheffer Corp., Blue Ash, Ohio, 1968—. Cons. prodn. engring. Helipebs, Ltd., County of Gloucester (Eng.), 1972. Sec., Brookville Planning Com., 1960-63; mem. adv. com. Great Oaks Joint Vocat. Sch., Warren County (Ohio) Joint Vocat. Sch.; mem. adv. council Miami U. Sch. Applied Sci.; mem. Industry Council, Greater Cin. C. of C.; sec. bd. trustees Thomas Meml. Med. Center, Brookville. Recipient Service award City of Brookville, 1963. Mem. Soc. Mfg. Engrs. (past chmn. Dayton chpt., cert. mfg. engr.). Optimist. Home: 1759 Maplewood Dr Lebanon OH 45036 Office: 6990 Cornell Rd Blue Ash OH 45242

CHENOWETH, ROBERT RAY, constrn. co. exec.; b. Columbus, Ohio, July 28, 1942; s. Thurman Ward and Delores Jean (Winget) C.; student Olivet Nazarene Coll., Kankakee, Ill., 1962-63; m. Arlene Joyce Milner, Sept. 1, 1962; children—Timothy, Eric, Gregg. With Case Constrn. Co., 1964-71; gen. supt. Rhoads & Johnson Constrn. Co., 1971-74; pres. Chenoweth Constrn. Co., Inc., Fenton, Mich., 1974—; pres. Chenhen Flying Assos., Inc., Fenton, 1975—; pres. Chenoweth & Assos. Architects, Inc., Fenton, 1978—; dir. Home Mission Aviation, Inc. Tchr. bus. projects Jr. Achievement, Fenton; Mem. bldg. com. Central Ch. of Nazarene, Flint, Mich., also mem. exec. ch. bd., 1974—; donor labor, materials, lay contractor, builder, 5 chs. in Nicaragua, 1977. Named Man of Yr., The Ind., 1978; Bell Ringer award Olivet Nazarene Coll., 1980. Mem. Metal Bldg. Dealers Assn., Airplane Owners and Pilots Assn., Assn. Nazarene Bldg. Profls., Fenton C. of C. (dir. 1974-76, pres. 1977). Clubs: Fellows, Univ., Spring Meadows Country, Genesee Valley Athletic, Boynestat Assn., Kiwanis (dir. 1974-77, pres. 1978—). Office: 101 N Alloy Dr Fenton MI 48430

CHEPP, MARK JOSEPH, mus. adminstr.; b. Milw., July 19, 1948; s. Milton Joseph and Marvel Genevieve (Jacobs) C.; B.S. with high honors, U. Wis., Stevens Point, 1970; M.S. in Art, U. Wis., Milw., 1972, M.A. in Art History, 1974; m. Jean Marie Brindowski, Aug. 14, 1971; children—Andrew Joseph, Valerie Louise. Teaching asst. U. Wis., Milw., 1972-74; sci. aide Milw. Public Mus., 1973; curator visual resources art history dept. U. Wis., Milw., 1974-79, dir. art history gallery, curator of collections, 1979—; cons. visual resources mgmt.; lectr. in field. Mem. Coll. Art Assn. Am., Wis. Fedn. Tchrs., Small Museums Com., Am. Assn. Mus., U. Wis.-Milw. Alumni Assn. (trustee), Athletics Congress. Roman Catholic. Office: Art History Gallery Univ of Wis-Milw Milwaukee WI 53201

CHERKASLY, RONALD L., telephone co. fin. exec.; b. Canton, Ohio, May 28, 1948; s. Albert and Ida (Levin) C.; student Ohio U., 1966-67; B.S. in Acctg., U. Akron, 1971. Acct., audit mgr. J.K. Lasser & Co., merged Touche Ross & Co., Akron, Ohio, 1970-79; v.p. fin. Electronic Engring. Co., Brecksville, Ohio, 1979-81; v.p. fin. Computer Telephone Corp., South Natick, Mass., 1981—. Bd. treas. Fair Housing Contact Service. C.P.A., Ohio. Mem. Am. Inst. C.P.A.'s, Ohio Soc. C.P.A.'s, Akron Jaycees. Home: 213 Owosso Ave Akron OH 44313 Office: 4 Pleasant St South Natick MA 01760

CHERNEY, ARTHUR BERNARD, dentist; b. Milw., Dec. 8, 1911; s. Anthony Benjamin and Frances (Cechal) C.; D.D.S., Marquette U., 1936; m. Doris H. Gronert, Apr. 30, 1938; children—Claudia (Mrs. Frank DeGuire), Mary (Mrs. John McDivitt), Ann (Mrs. Thomas S. Ryder), Michael G. Pvt. practice dentistry, Milw., 1936—. Instr. oral histology and embryology Marquette U., 1937-38, part time lecturer and lab. instr., 1947-53, asst. prof., 1953-58, asso. prof., 1958-65, head oral histology dept., 1956-65, dir. dept. histology, 1958-65, prof. emeritus, 1965—; chief oral medicine St. Michael Hosp., Milw., 1939—, chief dental staff, 1951-62. Adv. bd. St. Charles Home for Boys. Served to lt. USNR, 1943-46. Fellow Am. Coll. Dentists, Royal Soc. Health (Eng.); mem. A.A.A.S., Greater Milw. Dental Assn. (v.p. 1955), Am. Dental Assn., Am. Assn. Hosp. Dentists, Am. Med. Writers, Am. Acad. Oral Medicine, Am. Legion, Omicron Kappa Upsilon. K.C. (4 deg.). Home: 2804 N 98th St Milwaukee WI 53222 Office: 6201 W Center St Milwaukee WI 53210

CHERNICOFF, DAVID PAUL, osteo. physician, educator; b. N.Y.C., Aug. 3, 1947; s. Harry and Lillian (Dobkin) C.; A.B., U. Rochester, 1969; D.O., Phila. Coll. Osteo. Medicine, 1973. Rotating intern Rocky Mountain Hosp., Denver, 1973-74; resident in internal medicine Community Gen. Osteo. Hosp., Harrisburg, Pa., 1974-76; fell in hematology and med. oncology Cleve. Clinic, 1976-78; asst. prof. medicine sect. hematology-oncology Chgo. Coll. Osteo. Medicine, 1978—; co-chmn. tumor task force Chgo. Osteo. Med. Center, 1978—, dir. clin. cancer edn., 1978—; chmn. tumor task force Olympia Fields (Ill.) Osteo. Med. Center. Trustee, Ill. Cancer Council. Diplomate Nat. Bd. Osteo. Examiners, Am. Osteo. Bd. Internat Medicine, also in Hematology-Oncology. Mem. Am. Osteo. Assn., Ohio Osteo. Assn., Am. Coll. Osteo. Internists, Am. Assn. for Cancer Edn., AMA, Ill. Assn. Osteo. Physicians and Surgeons, Ill. Med. Soc., Chgo. Med. Soc., Eastern Coop. Oncology Group (sr. investigator), Am. Soc. Clin. Oncology. Contbr. articles to med. jours. Office: Chgo Coll Osteo Medicine 5200 S Ellis Ave Chicago IL 60615

CHERNISH, STANLEY MICHAEL, physician; b. N.Y.C., Jan. 27, 1924; s. Michael B. and Veronica (Hodon) C.; B.A., U. N.C., 1945; M.D., Georgetown U., 1949; m. Lelia M. Higgins, June 19, 1949; 1 son, Dwight. Intern Washington Gen. Hosp., 1949-51; resident Marion County Gen. Hosp., Indpls., 1953-55; clin. research div. Eli Lilly & Co., Indpls., 1954—, staff physician, 1955-63, sr. physician, 1963-74, clin. pharmacologist, 1974—; clin. research in internal medicine, specializing in gastroenterology; vis. staff Marion County Gen. Hosp., 1965—, also mem. dietary com.; mem. staff Lilly Research Labs.; clin. asso. prof. medicine Ind. U. Sch. Medicine, 1976-80, asso. prof., 1980—. Served with USNR, 1943-45, 50-53; comdr. Res.; commandant's rep. Ind. U. Sch. Medicine, 1965—. Diplomate Nat. Bd. Med. Examiners, Am. Bd. Internal Medicine, also recert. Fellow A.C.P., Am. Coll. Gastroenterology, Am. Coll. Clin. Pharmacology and Therapeutics; mem. AMA (Physicians Recognition award in continuing med. edn.), Ind. (mem. com. conv. arrangements, mem. future planning com., ad hoc data processing com.), Marion County (mem. commn. on ops. and stock ops.) med. socs., Am. Pancreatic Study Group, Assn. Am. Physicians and Surgeons, Am. Fedn. for Clin. Research, Am. Gastroent. Assn., Am. Soc. for Gastrointestinal Endoscopy. Contbr. chpts. to books, articles to profl. jours. Office: 307 E McCarty St Indianapolis IN 46285

CHERRY, JOSEPH, research scientist; b. Chgo., Dec. 19, 1947; s. Joseph Vaughn and Mafalda (DiSomma) C.; B.S. in Math. and Chemistry, Roosevelt U., Chgo., 1975; M.S. in Mgmt., Advanced Mgmt. Inst., Lake Forest, Ill., 1979. Research technician Ill. Inst. Tech. Research Inst., Chgo., 1968-69; med. technician Michael Reese Hosp., Chgo., 1972-74; scientist Continental Can Co., Chgo., 1970—. Mem. Am. Mgmt. Assn., Am. Chem. Soc., Soc. Automotive Engrs., Assn. M.B.A. Execs. Author: Marvin Gaye, 1973; poet: Black King, 1972.

CHERTACK, MELVIN M., internist; b. Chgo., June 19, 1923; s. Nathan and Anna (Wadoplan) C.; B.S., U. Ill., 1944, M.D., 1946, M.S., 1948; m. Orabelle Lorraine Melberg, May 26, 1948; children—Pamela, Craig, Rhonda. Intern, U. Ill. Hosp., Chgo., 1946-47, fellow and resident in internal medicine, 1947-50; practice medicine specializing in internal medicine, Skokie, Ill., 1950—; mem. attending staff Luth. Gen. Hosp., Park Ridge, Ill.; mem. courtesy staff Skokie Valley Hosp.; adj. staff Glenbrook Hosp., Glenview, Ill.; clin. asso. prof. U. Ill. Abraham Lincoln Coll. Medicine; advisor Harper Jr. Coll.; bd. health Skokie. Served with U.S. Army, 1943-45. Recipient Research award Aaron Fox Found. for Diabetes Screening Program, 1976. Diplomate Am. Bd. Internal Medicine. Fellow A.C.P.; mem. Am. Diabetes Assn. (dir. Chgo. chpt., pres. Chgo. and no. Ill. affiliate, com. drugs and therapeutics), Chgo., Ill. med. socs., AMA, Chgo. Soc. Internal Medicine, Chgo., Am. heart assns. Club: Anvil (Dundee). Contbr. articles to profl. jours. Home: 440 Whittier Ln Northfield IL 60093 Office: 64 Old Orchard Skokie IL 60077

CHERUBIM, JUSTIN LAWRENCE SWITHIN, mech. engr.; b. Grenada, W.I., July 15, 1926; s. Edgar Lawrence and Alethea Agnes (John) C.; came to U.S., 1929, naturalized, 1935; B.S. in Mech. Engring., Columbia U., 1951, M.S. in Mech. Engring., 1954; children—J. Lawrence, Krishna R. Asst. research engr. Pitney Bowes, Inc., Stamford, Conn., 1951-54; research engr. Stratos div. Fairchild Corp., Bay Shore, N.Y., 1954-59; chief engr. lubrication div. Analogue Controls, Inc., Hicksville, N.Y., 1959-60; dir. engring., corporate v.p. Fluid Film Bearing div. Indsl. Tectonics, Inc., Hicksville, 1960-65; chief advanced systems Stratos div. Fairchild-Hiller Corp., Bay Shore, 1965-66; prof., chmn. mech. engring. U. W.I., St. Augustine, Trinidad, 1966-69; sr. project engr. Mech. Tech. Inc., Latham, N.Y., 1969-71; asso. prof. mech. engring. dept. Gen. Motors Inst., Flint, Mich., 1971—; founding mem., pres. Condor Enterprises, Inc., N.Y.C., 1963—. Served with U.S. Army, 1944-47; PTO. Registered profl. engr., Trinidad, W.I. Mem. ASME, Trinidad and Tobago Soc. Profl. Engrs. Patentee in field. Home: 3650 Rue Foret Flint MI 48504 Office: Gen Motors Inst 1700 W 3d Ave Flint MI 48502

CHESEN, IRWIN SOMBERG, state ofcl.; b. Lincoln, Nebr., Aug. 22, 1927; s. Jack William and Sara (Somberg) C.; B.S., U. Nebr., 1949; m. Doris Schimmel, Dec. 12, 1951; children—Cathie, Bill, Carrie. Asst. mgr. Hotel Lassen, Wichita, Kans., 1954-57; resident mgr. Hotel Lincoln-Douglas, Quincy, Ill., 1958-63, Cornhusker Hotel, Lincoln, 1964-68; gen. mgr. Villager Motel and Conv. Center, Lincoln,

1969-77; salesman Harleigh Sandler Real Estate Co., Los Angeles, 1977-79; mgr. Pershing Mcpl. Auditorium, Lincoln, 1979; dir. Nebr. Dept. Econ. Devel., Lincoln, 1979—. Served with USN, 1945-47. Mem. Nebr. Hotel-Motel Assn. (pres. 1971-72), Nebr. Lodging Assn. (pres. 1974-75), Internat. Assn. Shrine Motor Corps. (pres. 1970-71), Lincoln C. of C. (life). Republican. Jewish. Clubs: Elks, Rotary (pres. 1973-74) (Lincoln); Masons. Office: 301 Centennial Mall South Lincoln NE 68509

CHESHIER, ROBERT GRANT, library adminstr.; b. Goldendale, Wash., Sept. 28, 1930; s. Wilfred A. and Lillie Pearl (Johnston) C.; B.A., U. Wash., 1960, M.L.S., 1963; postgrad. U. Chgo., 1964-66, Case Western Res. U., 1966—; m. Sylvia Joy Addicoat; children—Laurel Ann, John Treneere, William Grant. Engrng. aide Boeing Co., Seattle, 1958-60, procedures analyst, 1960-61, file cons., 1961, info. specialist, 1961, lit. searcher Central Library, 1961, br. 2 librarian, 1963-64; editor Issues and Ideas, Library Indsl. Relations Center, U. Chgo., 1964; spl. asst. to librarian Chgo. Med. Sch., 1964, acting librarian, 1965, head librarian, 1965-66; dir. Cleve. Health Scis. Library, adj. prof. library sci. Case-Western Res. U., Cleve., 1966—. Served with USAF, 1949-51, U.S. Army, 1951-53. Mem. Med. Library Assn. Contbr. articles to profl. jours. Office: 2119 Abington Rd Cleveland OH 44106

CHESLEY, STANLEY MORRIS, lawyer; b. Cin., Mar. 26, 1936; s. Frank and Rachel (Kinsburg) C.; B.A. in Econs., U. Cin., 1958, LL.B., 1960; m. Suellen Kaufmann, Aug. 15, 1959 (div.); children—Richard Alan, Lauren Beth. Admitted to Ohio bar, 1960; mem. firm Waite, Schneider, Bayless & Chesley, Cin., 1960—; adj. prof. Salmon Chase Law Sch., No. Ky. State, 1973—. Mem. Citizens Com. on Youth, Cin., 1963-64; pres. Camp Livingston, Am. Jewish Com., 1966—. Mem. Am., Ohio, Cin. bar assns., Assn. Trial Lawyers (state committeeman 1968-70; 2d vice chmn. torts sect. 1969-70; vice chmn. torts sect. 1972-73, nat. chmn. torts sect. 1974—, program chmn. 1974—). Jewish (bd. dirs. temple 1964-73). Contbr. articles to various publs. Home: 2930 Belkay Ln Cincinnati OH 45241 Office: 1318 Central Trust Tower Cincinnati OH 45202

CHESNEY, CHESTER ANTON, savs. and loan assn. exec.; b. Chgo., Mar. 9, 1916; s. Anton and Anna C.; B.S., DePaul U., 1939; m. Betty Jane Uetrecht, Feb. 7, 1943; 1 dau., Elizabeth Ann. Mem. 81st Congress from 11th Ill. dist.; fed. liaison officer Fed. Civil Def. Adminstrn., 1950-51; asst. v.p. Advance Mortgage Corp., Chgo., 1952-60; now v.p., dir. Avondale Savs. and Loan, Chgo. Mem. Democratic Com., Elk Grove Twp., 1962-74, alt. del. Nat. Dem. Conv., 1968. Served to maj. USAF, 1941-46. Mem. Soc. Loan Underwriters, N.W. Real Estate Bd. Roman Catholic. Clubs: Rolling Green Country; Marco Island (Fla.) Country. Home: 801 E Golfview Rd Mount Prospect IL 60056 Office: 2965 Milwaukee Ave Chicago IL 60056

CHESS, ROBERT HUBERT, psychiatrist; b. Greenville, Miss., May 20, 1930; s. James and Barbara C.; A.B., Tenn. State U., 1953, M.S., 1954; M.D., Meharry Med. Coll., 1959; M.B.A., Xavier U., 1976; m. Gloria Faye Thompson, Dec. 27, 1960; children—Faye Rosalind, Robert Hubert. Intern, Wayne County Gen. Hosp., Eloise, Mich., 1959-60; resident in psychiatry Rollman Psychiat. Inst., Cin., 1965-68; practice family medicine, Meridian, Miss., 1960-62, Laurel, Miss., 1962-65; resident psychiatrist Rollman Psychiat. Inst., Cin., 1965-68, chief male inpatient service, 1968-71, dir. community services unit, 1971-79, med. dir., 1979—; asst. clin. prof. psychiatry U. Cin., 1972-77, asso. clin. prof., 1977—; individual practice medicine, specializing in psychiatry Cin., 1968—. Bd. dirs. Children's Psychiat. Center, SW Regional Council Alcoholism, Assn. Home Care Agencies. Diplomate Am. Bd. Psychiatry and Neurology. Fellow Am. Psychiat. Assn.; mem. AMA, Nat. Med. Assn., Am. Orthopsychiat. Assn., Am. Assn. Social Psychiatry, Cin. Psychiat. Soc. (pres. 1978-79), Am. Mgmt. Assn., Sigma Pi Phi, Kappa Alpha Psi. Methodist. Clubs: Masons (32 deg.), Shriners. Home: 3280 N Whitetree Circle Cincinnati OH 45236 Office: 3009 Burnet Ave Cincinnati OH 45219

CHESTERFIELD, JAMES STUART, archtl. aluminum mfg. co. exec.; b. Indpls., June 4, 1952; s. John Morris and Erma Jeanne (McKinney) C.; A.B. in Econs., Ind. U., 1974; M.B.A. in Fin. and Mktg., U. Chgo., 1976; m. Gwen Kay Nevins, May 21, 1976. Mktg. rep. The Service Bur. Co. div. Control Data Corp., Chgo., 1976-78; treas., asst. to pres., asst. corp. sec. J-C Products Corp., Indpls., 1978—, exec. v.p., 1981—; v.p. CD Enterprises, Ltd., Chgo., also dir. Vice pres. bd. dirs. The Park of River Oaks Condominium Assn., Calumet City, Ill., 1978; active Marion County (Ind.) Assn. for Retarded Citizens. Mem. Am. Prodn. and Inventory Control. Soc., Lambda Chi Alpha. Club: Econ. (Indpls.). Home: 8030 Warbler Way Indianapolis IN 46256 Office: J-C Products Corp 624 S Belmont Ave Indianapolis IN 46221

CHESTERFIELD, JOHN LAWRENCE, aluminum co. exec.; b. Seattle, Oct. 26, 1942; s. John Morris and Erma-Jeanne C.; B.A. in Math., DePauw U., 1964; children—David Christopher, Daniel Lawrence. With Aluminum Finishing Corp., Indpls., 1968—, v.p. ops., 1970-77, pres., 1977—. Trustee St. Luke's United Methodist Ch., 1971. Served from ensign to lt. j.g. USNR, 1964-68; Vietnam. Mem. Am. Electroplaters Soc., Naval Res. Assn. Republican. Methodist. Office: 1012 E 21st St Indianapolis IN 46202

CHESTON, SHARON HUTSON, counselor; b. Balt., Mar. 19, 1947; d. Hugh Maynard and Margaret Elizabeth (Beck) Hutson; B.A. in Psychology, Roanoke Coll., 1969; M.Ed., N.C. State U., 1975; postgrad. No. Ill. U.; m. James Cheston, Jan. 23, 1969; children—Shannon Elizabeth, Kelly Christine. Counselor, Christ the King Luth. Ch., Cary, N.C., 1975-76; psychol. counselor, cons. Christian edn. Bethany Luth. Ch., Batavia, Ill., 1976; Psychologist, coordinator counseling services Luth. Social Services of Ill. Mem. Am. Personnel and Guidance Assn. Lutheran. Research on marital communications and depression. Home: 1041 Pueblo Dr Batavia IL 60510 Office: 113 N Batavia Ave Batavia IL 60510

CHEW, CHARLES, JR., state senator, safe deposit co. exec.; b. Greenville, Miss., Oct. 9, 1922; s. Charles and Celia (Jenkins) C.; B.S. in Bus., Tuskegee Inst., 1942; postgrad. Harvard U.; 1 son, Lorenzo. Vice-pres., Jackson Mut. Life Ins. Co., 1958; now v.p. South Parkway Safe Deposit Corp., Chgo. Mem. Chgo. City Council, 1963-67, Ill. State Senate, 1966—; del. Democratic Nat. Conv., 1980. Served with USN, 1943-46; PTO. Mem. VFW, NAACP. Baptist. Club: American Friendship. Office: Gen Assembly State Capitol Springfield IL 62706*

CHHABRA, ROSHAN LAL, elec. engr.; b. Gujaranwala, India, Mar. 1, 1941; s. Sardari Lal and Maya (Dora) C.; came to U.S., 1966, naturalized, 1976; B.S., Uttar Pradesh Agrl. U., 1966; M.S., Iowa State U., 1969, Ph.D., 1973. m. Suman Satiya, Nov. 25, 1969; children—Monica K., Paul N. Project engr. Winpower Corp., Newton, Iowa, 1972-73, chief elec. engr., 1973-75, dir. research and devel., 1975-76, dir. engring., 1977-78, asst. gen. mgr., 1979—. Mem. planning com. Des Moines Area Community Coll., 1975-77; tchr. for merit badges Boy Scouts Am. Presdl. scholar, 1962-66. Mem. IEEE, Am. Soc. Agrl. Engrs., Engine Generator Systems Mfrs. Assn., Am. Soc. Quality Control, Sigma Xi, Phi Kappa Phi, Tau Beta Pi, Alpha Epsilon, Gamma Sigma Delta. Contbr. articles to profl. jours. Home: 510 E 4th St S Newton IA 50208 Office: 1207 1st Ave E Newton IA 50208

CHI, RICHARD SEE-YEE, educator; b. Peking, China, Aug. 3, 1918; s. Mi Kang and Pao (Ten) C.; B.S., Nankai U., China, 1937; M.A., Oxford (Eng.) U., 1962, D.Phil., 1964; Ph.D., Cambridge (Eng.) U., 1964. Came to U.S., 1965. Exec. industry China and Hong Kong, 1938-56; inst. Air Ministry, Eng., 1957-60; lectr. Cambridge U., 1960-62, U. London, summer 1961; univ. lectr. Oxford U., 1962-65; curator City Art Gallery, Bristol, Eng., 1965; asso. prof. Ind. U., Bloomington, 1965-71, prof., 1971—, acting chmn., summer 1972; asso. adviser Centro Superiore di Logica e Scienze Comparate, Italy, 1972—; vis. asso. prof. U. Mich., summer 1968; fellow-participant Linguistic Inst., U. Calif., Los Angeles, 1966; contbg. specialist Summer Faculty Seminar on Buddhism, Carleton Coll., Minn., 1968; mem. Workshop on Problems on Meaning and Truth, Oakland U., 1968; adviser for film Buddhism in China, New York, 1972; cons. Inst. Advanced Studies World Religions, 1972—; session chmn. East-West Philosophers' Conf., 1973; panelist Internat. Conf. on Indian Philosophy, U. Toronto, 1974, 5th Internat. Symposium Multiple-valued Logic, Ind. U., 1974, Internat. Seminar on History of Buddhism, U. Wis., 1976, 30th Internat. Congress Human Scis. in Asia, Mexico City, 1976; mem. sub-com. Buddhist philos. materials Nat. Endowment for Humanities, 1974; rep. of State of Ind., Nat. Reconstrn. Conf., China, 1975. Fellow China Acad., 1969. Mem. Cambridge U. Buddhist Soc. (v.p. 1961-62), Royal Asiatic Soc., Aristotelian Soc., Mind Assn., Assn. Brit. Orientalists, Assn. for Symbolic Logic, Linguistic Soc. Am., Soc. for Asian and Comparative Philosophy (bd. mem.-at-large 1975—), Oriental Art Soc. (founding mem.), Kings Coll. Assn. (Eng.), Asian Studies Inst. (mem. adv. com. 1975—), Indpls. Mus. Art. Clubs: Lake Havasu Golf and Country, Univ., Rotary. Author: The Bracket Complex in Chinese Architecture, 1946; A General Theory of Operators, 1967; Buddhist Formal Logic, 1968; A Comparative Study of Propositions in the Western and Indian Logic, 1972; Topics on Being and Logical Reasoning, 1974; A Semantic Study of Propositions, East and West, 1976; The Art of Chinese Calligraphy, 1977. Editor Jour. Buddhist Philosophy, 1978—; reviewer Nat. Endowment for Humanities, 1979—. Home: 3650 E Will Sowders Rd Bloomington IN 47401

CHIANG, EDWARD CHUNG, mech. engr.; b. Shanghai, China, July 4, 1933; came to U.S., 1958, naturalized, 1973; diploma Taipei Inst. Tech., 1954; M.S., Oreg. State U., 1963; Ph.D., Kans. State U., 1966. Plant supr. Taiwan Power Co., 1957-58; research asso. Kans. State U., 1965-66; sr. engr. Cummins Engine Co., from 1967; now prof. mech. engring. Mich. Tech. U., Houghton; cons. in field. NSF fellow; registered profl. engr. Mem. ASME, AAAS, Am. Soc. Engring. Edn., Soc. Automotive Engrs., Sigma Xi, Pi Mu Epsilon. Methodist. Club: Lions. Contbr. articles to profl. jours. Office: Mich Tech U Houghton MI 49931

CHIANG, HUAI CHANG, educator, entomologist; b. Sunkiang, China, Feb. 15, 1915; s. Wentse Chiang and Hsiu Hsiu Chiang; came to U.S. 1945, naturalized 1953; B.S., Tsing Hua U., Peking, China, 1938; M.S., U. Minn. 1946, Ph.D. 1948; D.Sc. (hon.), Bowling Green State U., 1979; m. Zoh Ing Shen, Sept. 8, 1946; children—Jeanne, Katherine, Robert. Asst. instr. entomology Tsing Hua U., Peking, 1938-40, instr. 1940-44; asst. prof. U. Minn., St. Paul, 1954-57, asso. prof. 1957-60, prof. 1960—; cons. FAO, U.S. Dept. Agr.; mem. sci. del. Nat. Acad. Sci.; sci. del. U.S. Dept. Agr./EPA; sci. panel Entomol. Soc. Am., Council Environ. Quality, Nat. Assn. State U. and Land Grant Colls., Internat. Center Insect Physiology and Ecology, U.S. Internat. Communication Agy. Recipient Disting. Service award Am. Inst. Biol. Scis., 1979; named Tchr. of Yr., Student Assn., U. Minn., Duluth, 1961; Guggenheim fellow, 1955. Mem. Am., Canadian, Royal (London) entomol. socs., Am. Ecol. Soc., Am. Inst. Biol. Scis., Japanese Soc. Population Research, Internat. Assn. Ecologists, Internat. Organization Biol. Control, AAAS, Minn. Acad. Sci., Sigma Xi, Gamma Sigma Delta. Editor 3 books; contbr. over 180 research papers to profl. jours. Home: 1896 Carl St St Paul MN 55113 Office: U Minn St Paul MN 55108

CHIARO, A. WILLIAM, mgmt. cons.; b. Chgo., July 12, 1928; s. Anthony Joseph and Marie Anne (Bonario) C.; B.S., U. Ill., 1954; m. Lyne LaVerne Franke, Aug. 27, 1961; children—David Huntington, Caroline Elizabeth. Accountant, IBM, Chgo., 1954-55; with Black & Skaggs Assos., Chgo., 1955—, pres., 1978—; dir. P.M. Chgo., Inc. Served with U.S. Army, 1946-47, USAF, 1950-52. Mem. Soc. Advancement Mgmt., Soc. Profl. Bus. Cons., Nat. Soc. Public Accts. Presbyterian. Clubs: Kenilworth (Ill.); Lake Shore (Chgo.). Contbr. articles to med. and profl. jours. Home: 304 Cumnor Rd Kenilworth IL 60043 Office: 845 N Michigan Ave Chicago IL 60611

CHICHESTER, DOLORES ANN, mfg. co. ofcl.; b. Dixon, Ill., Aug. 1, 1931; s. Harley Russell and Helen Aline (Wimberly) Duncan; cert. mgmt. devel. Albion Coll., 1974; cert. mgmt. Kellogg Community Coll., 1976; m. Willard Lyle Chichester, Nov. 18, 1978; children by previous marriage—Connie Lynn Simmons McElhenie, Penny Sue Simmons. Operator, Ill. Bell Telephone Co., Centralia, Ill., 1948-51; acctg. clk. Montgomery Ward & Co., Centralia, 1953; bookkeeper, sec. Watland Inc., Blue Island, Ill., 1954-57, 59-60; sec. to pres., sales mgr. Brulé Inc., Blue Island, 1961-65; sec. to v.p. engring. Clark Equipment Co., Battle Creek, Mich., 1965-77, supr. staff services, product engring., 1977—. Bd. dirs. Jr. Achievement S. Central Mich., 1980—; chmn. salaried employees Clark United Way, 1974. Mem. Nat. Mgmt. Assn., Battle Creek C. of C., Clark Women's Orgn. (pres. 1968-69), Am. Bus. Women's Assn. (woman of yr. 1972, v.p. 1970), Am. Mgmt. Assn. Club: Minges Creek Racquet. Office: 525 N 24th St Indsl Truck Div Battle Creek MI 49016

CHICKRIS, CHRIS HOMER, cons. engr.; b. East Moline, Ill., July 10, 1924; s. Peter Geroge and Alexandra (Triantos) C.; student St. Ambrose Coll., Davenport, Iowa, 1946-47; B.S. in Elec. Engring., U. Ill., 1950; m. Carol N. Coin, Nov. 28, 1965; 1 dau., Colette A. Engr., Iowa-Ill. Gas & Electric Co., 1950-52; devel. engr. Bendix Aviation Corp., Davenport, Iowa, 1953-55; ordnance engr. Ordnance Weapons Command, Rock Island, Ill., 1955-57; pvt. practice cons. engr., Rock Island, Ill., 1957—; sec. Deka Mgmt. & Investment Co., Inc., Rock Island, 1964—, Rochelle Broadcasting Co., Inc. (Ill.), 1969—; pres. World Charts Co., Rock Island, 1976-81; tech. adv. Rock Island Tech. Sch., 1965-72. Mem. Plumbing Bd. Appeals, City of East Moline, 1964-70; mem. County Bldg. Appeals Bd., Rock Island County, 1967-74, chmn., 1971-74. Served with U.S. Army, 1943-46; ETO. Registered profl. engr., Ill., Iowa, Wis. Mem. Nat. Soc. Profl. Engrs., Illuminating Engring. Soc., ASHRAE, Ill. Soc. Profl. Engrs. Greek Orthodox. Clubs: Rock Island Arsenal Golf (sec. bd. govs.); Ahepa (Moline, Ill.). Contbr. articles to lighting mags. Home: 2924 29th St Rock Island IL 61201 Office: 4200 11th St Rock Island IL 61201

CHIER, MICHAEL DENNIS, mining co. exec.; b. Berlin, Wis., Oct. 25, 1940; s. Leonard Steven and Laura (Maldari) C.; B.B.A., U. Wis., Oshkosh, 1959; postgrad., Spencerian Coll., Milw., 1960-63; m. Georgeanne Farley, May 27, 1961; children—Laurene, Terrence, Margaret, Andrew, Matthew. Office and bus. mgr. Chier Indsl. and Chier St. Marie Sand Co., Berlin, Wis., 1962-79; ops. mgr. Berlin and St. Marie Plants, Badger Mining Corp., Fairwater, Wis., 1979, dir. customer services, 1979, v.p. transp., 1979-80, v.p. adminstrn., treas., 1980—. Mem. Nat. Indsl. Sand Assn., Am. Foundrymen's Soc., Jr. C. of C. (pres., 1973, awards, 1972, 74). Republican. Roman Catholic. Club: Mascoutin Country (dir. 1962-78). Home: 224 Mound St Berlin WI 54923 Office: Badger Mining Corp PO Box 97 Fairwater WI 53931

CHIERICO, RICHARD VINCENT, educator; b. Chgo., Nov. 13, 1939; s. Vincent and Frances (Gambino) C.; A.A., Morton Jr. Coll., 1959; B.Ed., U. Ill., 1961, M.A., 1962; m. Nancy Lois Poch, Oct. 4, 1969; 1 son, Dustin Vincent. Tchr., St. Francis High Sch., Wheaton, Ill., 1962-64; tchr. Palatine (Ill.) High Sch., 1964-66; tchr. Glenbard East High Sch., Lombard, Ill., 1966-67; tchr., coordinator public service practicum Elk Grove (Ill.) High Sch., 1967—; mem. Elk Grove Career Advisory Council, 1975—; pres. Ill. Citizenship Experience; dir. programming Ill. Forum; cons. Public Service Practicum. Mem. Profl. Educators Ill. (pres. 1974, legislative chmn. 1975—), Ill. Vocat. Edn. Assn., Am. Vocat. Assn., Ill. Guidance and Vocat. Services Assn. (legislative chmn., Outstanding tch. award 1980-81), Ill. Cooperative Vocat. Edn. Coordinators Assn., Am. Hist. Assn., Am. Acad. Polit. Sci., Dist. 214 Edn. Assn. (past pres., legislative chmn.), Phi Delta Kappa. Office: 500 W Elk Grove Blvd Elk Grove IL 60007

CHILCOTE, ROBERT RALPH, physician, educator; b. Cleve., Oct. 8, 1941; s. Ralph E. and Margaret A. (Fisher) C.; A.B., Cornell U., 1963; M.D., U. Rochester, 1969; m. Denise Buckley; children—Kelly, Krista, Ryan. Intern in pediatrics Strong Meml. Hosp., U. Rochester (N.Y.), 1969-70, resident in pediatrics, 1970-71, chief resident in pediatrics, 1971-72; fellow in pediatric hematology James Whitcomb Riley Hosp. for Children, Ind. U. Sch. of Medicine, Indpls., 1972-75; practice medicine specializing in pediatric hematology and oncology, Chgo., 1975—; dir. div. pediatric hematology Michael Reese Hosp. and Med. Center, Chgo., 1975-77; co-dir. div. pediatric hematology-oncology Wyler Children's Hosp., 1977—; asst. prof. dept. pediatrics Pritzker Sch. of Medicine, U. Chgo., 1975—. Diplomate Am. Bd. Pediatrics. Mem. Am. Acad. Pediatrics (sect. on oncology-hematology 1974—), Am. Cancer Soc., Am. Soc. Clin. Oncology, Am. Soc. Hematology. Contbr. articles on pediatric hematology and oncology to profl. jours. Office: Wyler Children's Hosp 5801 Ellis Ave Chicago IL 60637

CHILDRES, MARY ROSE, univ. bus. adminstr.; b. Livingston, Ala., Apr. 13, 1936; d. Simon and Mary Magdalene (Sanders) Childress; A.S. in Secretarial Sci., U. Cin., 1973, B.S. in Adminstrv. Mgmt., 1976; m. Robert Walker Greene. Secretarial positions Hamilton County (Ohio) Welfare Dept., 1954-S9, VA Hosp., Cin., 1959-63, Mut. Benefit Life Ins. Co., Cin., 1965-66, Ky. State U., Frankfort, 1966-68; nutrition program asst. W.Va. U., Charleston, 1969-70; with U. Cin., 1970—, bus. adminstr., office of vice provost for continuing edn. and met. services 1978—. Chmn. Cornelius Van Jordan Scholarship Fund, U. Cin. Mem. Nat. Secs. Assn. (charter mem., co-founder Frankfort chpt.), AAUW, United Black Assn. of Faculty, Adminstrs. and Staff U. Cin. (treas.), Mid-Level Mgrs. Assn. U. Cin., Nat. U. Continuing Edn. Assn. (chmn., treas. 1982 conv.), Adminstrv. Women's Assn. U. Cin., Nat. Assn. Female Execs., Delta Tau Kappa. Mem. Ch. of God. Club: Pappa Joe's Private Key. Author: Handbook of Office Procedures, 1973, 75. Home: 838 Crowden Dr Cincinnati OH 45224 Office: 8 McMicken Hall Clifton U Cin Cincinnati OH 45221

CHILDS, GAYLE BERNARD, educator; b. Redfield, S.D., Oct. 17, 1907; s. Alva Eugene and Dora Amelia (Larsen) C.; A.B., Nebr. State Tchrs. Coll., Wayne, 1931; M.A., U. Nebr., 1936, Ph.D., 1949; M.Ed., Harvard, 1938; m. Doris Wilma Hoskinson, Dec. 22, 1930; children—Richard Arlen, George William, Patricia Ann (Mrs. Ronald Bauers). Tchr. sci. Wynot (Nebr.) High Sch., 1928-30; tchr. sci. Wayne (Nebr.) High Sch., 1931-38, prin., 1938-41; supt. Wakefield (Nebr.) pub. schs., 1941-44, West Point (Nebr.) pub. schs., 1944-46; curriculum specialist U. Nebr. extension div., Lincoln, 1946-49, instr. secondary edn. Tchrs. Coll., also curriculum specialist extension div., 1949-51, asst. prof., 1951-53, asso. prof., 1953-56, prof., head class and corr. instrn., 1956-63, prof., asso. dir. extension div., 1963-66, prof., dir. extension div., 1966-74. Nebr. del. White House Conf. on Aging, 1981. Sr. Fulbright-Hays scholar Haile Sellassie I U., Addis Ababa, Ethiopia, 1974. Mem. Nebr. Edn. Assn. (dist. III sec. 1941-42), Nat. U. Extension Assn. (mem. adminstrv. com., div. corr. study 1952-68, chmn. 1963-65, dir. 1963-65, mem. joint com. minimum data and definitions 1965-70, chmn. 1970-73; Walton S. Bittner award 1971; establishment Gayle B. Childs award div. ind. study 1969; Gayle B. Childs award 1973), Internat. Council on Corr. Edn. (chmn. com. on research 1961-69, program com. 9th internat. conf. 1971-72), Assn. Univ. Evening Colls. (program com. 1971-72, membership com. 1971-73), Nebr. Schoolmasters Club, Phi Delta Kappa (dist. rep. 1957-63, dir., 1963-69, mem. commn. on edn. and human rights and responsibilities 1963-74, mem. adv. panel on commns. 1970-72; Disting. Service award 1970). Club: Kiwanis (bd. dirs. 1978-81). Contbr. articles to profl. jours. Home: 4530 Van Dorn St Lincoln NE 68506 Office: 901 N 17th St Lincoln NE 68508

CHILSEN, WALTER J., state senator, TV newscaster; b. Merrill, Wis., Nov. 18, 1923; s. Walter Burt and Margaret (Sullivan) C.; B.S., Lawrence U., 1949; postgrad. in TV, Northwestern U.; m. Roseann Edl, 1952; children—Jon, Anna, Kristine, Elizabeth, Paul, Peter and Patricia (twins), Matthew. Account exec., newscaster Sta. WSAU-TV, Wausau, Wis.; mem. Wis. State Senate, 1966—, minority leader, 1981—, chmn. majority caucus, sec. legis. council, 1975—, mem. senate reapportionment com., others. Mem., vice chmn. Wis. State Rural Devel. Council, exec. com., 1973-76; past pres. Holy Name Soc. and Home and Sch. Assn., Marathon County Workshop for Handicapped. Served to 1st lt. USAAC, 1943-45; PTO. Decorated Purple Heart. Mem. Am. Legion, VFW, DAV. Club: KC. Address: 1821 Town Line Rd Wausau WI 54401

CHIN, PETER PING-SEN, forest product co. exec.; b. Hopei, China, July 1, 1938; came to U.S., 1966, naturalized, 1975; s. Chun Hwa and Tsung (Lan) C.; B.S., Nat. Taiwan U., 1961; M.S., U. Mont., 1969, Ph.D., 1973; m. Helen Chung-i, Nov. 30, 1963; children—Robert, Mark. Jr. specialist Taiwan Forestry Research

Inst., Taiwan, 1963-66; research asst. U. Mont., Missoula, 1966-73, research asso., 1973-77; sr. research chemist Masonite Corp., St. Charles, Ill., 1977-78, sect. mgr., 1978-80, dept. mgr., 1980—. Served with Nat. Chinese Army, 1961-63. Nat. Taiwan U. fellow, 1957-61; Taiwan Bur. Edn. fellow, 1966; Weyerhaeuser Corp. fellow, 1969-71. Mem. Forest Products Research Soc., Am. Chem. Soc., Xi Sigma Pi. Home: 930 W Kane St South Elgin IL 60177 Office: Powis Rd PO Box 379 Saint Charles IL 60174

CHING, JAMES CHRISTOPHER, educator; b. Honolulu, Oct. 12, 1926; s. James I, and Elsie (Ching) Motoyama; B.A., Wabash Coll., 1951; M.A., U. Hawaii, 1953; Ph.D., U. Mo., 1962; m. Won May Lee, Dec. 15, 1950; 1 son, James Michael. Instr. speech U. Mo., 1953-56, U. Hawaii, 1956-58; mgr. C-D Advt. Honolulu, 1958; mng. editor Voice of East Oahu, Honolulu, 1959; asst. prof. speech and theater Wabash Coll., Crawfordsville, Ind., 1960; asst. prof. Tulane U., New Orleans, 1960-64, asso. prof., 1964-67; prof. speech Ill. State U., Normal, 1967; later chmn. dept. speech and theatre arts U. Bridgeport (Conn.); then vis. prof. dept. speech and dramatic art U. Mo., Columbia; now chmn. dept. theatre and communication arts Hamline U., St. Paul. Served with AUS, 1944-46. Mem. Am. Theatre Assn. (dir.), Univ. and Coll. Theatre Assn. (exec. v.p.), Am. Soc. for Theatre Research, Phi Kappa Phi, Tau Kappa Alpha, Phi Kappa Psi, Blue Key. Author: Advanced Public Speaking, 1966.

CHINNERY, WILLIAM THOMAS, fin. planner; b. Kansas City, Kans., July 4, 1935; s. George Willian and Ardyce (Hardy) C.; B.A., Yale U., 1958; m. Wanda M. Shelp, Dec. 22, 1959; 1 dau., Melissa Christine. Gen. agent Bankers Life Nebr. Ins. Co., Kansas City, Mo., 1965-74; area mgr. Physicians Planning Service Corp., Western Mo. and Kans., 1970-77; independent fin. planner, ins. and investments fields, Shawnee Mission, Kans., 1977—; area sales mgr. Firemen's Fund Am. Life Ins. Co., Shawnee Mission, 1978-80. Bd. dirs. St. Paul's Episcopal Day Sch., Kansas City, Mo., 1970-71, Marillac Home for Children, Kansas City, Mo., 1977-78; v.p. Nat. Council on Alcoholism, Kansas City area, 1977-78, trustee; trustee Community Alcohol Programs of Kansas City. Mem. Internat. Assn. Fin. Planners. Episcopalian. Club: Yale of Kansas City (pres. 1967-68). Author: Tax Tangles, 1977; Tax Graffiti by Tax Graffiti, 1979. Home: 2020 W 61st Terr Mission Hills KS 66208 Office: 7721 State Line S-137 Kansas City MO 64114

CHIPAIN, GEORGE CHRIS, orthodontist; b. Oak Park, Ill., Apr. 24, 1935; s. Chris George and Christine (Karales) C.; B.S., U. Ill., 1955; D.D.S., Northwestern U., 1959; M.S.D., Fairleigh Dickinson U., 1969; children—Chris, Georgia. Pres. G. Chipain, D.D.S., M.S.D., Ltd., Elmhurst, Ill., 1969—, Chipain Sports Store, 1974—. Mem. Am. Dental Assn., Ill., Chgo. dental socs., Am. Assn. Orthodontists, Ill. Soc. Orthodontists. Greek Orthodox. Club: Kiwanis (Elmhurst). Office: Thorn Bldg West Suite 3 135 Addison Ave Elmhurst IL 60126 also 1634 S Ardmore Villa Park IL 60181

CHIPMAN, DEBORAH GONDEK, communications exec.; b. Phoenix, Apr. 6, 1953; d. Joseph H. and Dorothy E. (Bradac) G.; B.A. cum laude in Journalism, Duquesne U., 1975; m. John A. Chipman, Oct. 6, 1979. Dir., performer The Young Tamburitzans ensemble, Phoenix, 1968-71; reporter Phoenix Gazette, 1970-71; newswriter, broadcaster Sta. WDUQ, Pitts., 1973-74; ensemble performer Duquesne U. Tamburitzans, nat. folk arts ensemble, Pitts., 1971-75, European tours, 1971-72; communications/planning Chipman Design, Chgo., 1979—; owner Custom Sources, Chgo., 1980—; writer-editor Fairburn Assos., Inc., Phoenix, 1977-79. Recipient Piano Solo Excellence award Nat. Fedn. Musicians, 1971; Quill and Scroll nat. editorial writing award, 1971. Mem. Women in Communications (treas. Phoenix chpt. 1976-77), Internat. Assn. Bus. Communicators Phoenix award of merit 1979, Gold Four award 1981), Am. Planning Assn., Nat. Soc. for Hist. Preservation, Art Inst. Chgo., Sigma Delta Chi (sec. Duquesne chpt. 1974), Kappa Tau Alpha, Duquesne U. Tamburitzans Alumni Assn. Editor Horizons, 1976-77. Home: 400 S Home Ave Park Ridge IL 60068 Office: 5725 E River Rd Suite 515 Chicago IL 60631

CHIPMAN, JOHN SOMERSET, educator; b. Montreal, P.Q., Can., June 28, 1926; s. Warwick Fielding and Mary Somerset (Aikins) C.; student Universidad de Chile, Santiago, 1943-44; B.A., McGill U., Montreal, 1947, M.A., 1948; Ph.D., Johns Hopkins U., 1951; postdoctoral U. Chgo., 1950-51; m. Margaret Ann Ellefson, June 24, 1960; children—Thomas Noel, Timothy Warwick. Asst. prof. econs. Harvard U., Cambridge, Mass., 1951-55; asso. prof. econs. U. Minn., Mpls., 1955-60, prof., 1961—; fellow Center for Advanced Study in Behavioral Scis., Stanford, Calif., 1972-73; vis. prof. econs. various colls. and univs. Fellow Econometric Soc., Am. Statis. Assn., Am. Acad. Arts and Scis.; mem. Am. Econ. Assn., Inst. Math. Stats., Can. Econ. Assn., Royal Econ. Soc. Author: The Theory of Intersectoral Money Flows and Income Formation, 1951; editor (with others) Preferences, Utility, and Demand, 1971; editor Jour. of Internat. Econs., 1977—; asso. editor Econometrica, 1956-69. Office: Dept Econs 1122 Bus Adminstrn Bldg U Minn 271 19th Ave S Minneapolis MN 55455

CHIRON, ROBERT JAY, psychologist; b. Bklyn., Mar. 25, 1948; s. Albert E. and Rose L. Chiron; B.A., Ithaca Coll., 1969; M.A., Columbia U., 1973, M.Ed., 1974; Ph.D., U. Iowa, 1978; m. Linda Rifkin, Jan. 6, 1973. Psychologist, Grant Wood Area Edn. Agy., Iowa City, 1978-80; lectr. U. Iowa, 1978-80, Kirkwood Community Coll., 1978-80; psychologist Diagnostic Center, Elk Grove Village, Ill., 1980-81; pvt. practice psychology, Wheeling, Ill., 1981—; cons. to bus. and industry. Cert. sch. psychologist, Ill. Mem. Am. Psychol. Assn., Nat. Register Health Service Providers in Psychology. Home: 3085 Pheasant Creek Dr Northbrook IL 60062

CHISHOLM, DONALD HERBERT, lawyer; b. Kansas City, Mo., Sept. 25, 1917; s. Herbert C. and Bessie M. (Osborne) C.; A.A., Kansas City Jr. Coll., 1932-35; LL.B., U. Mo., 1938; m. Mildred Ruth Ice, Dec. 1, 1940; children—William L., Nan Elizabeth. Admitted to Mo. bar, 1938, Fed. bar, 1938; since practiced in Kansas City, Mo.; partner firm Stinson, Mag & Fizzell, 1947—. Dir. Park Nat. Bank, Schooley Co., Standard Linen Supply Co., Rockhill Fed. Savs. & Loan Assn., Kansas City Bridge Co. (all Kansas City, Mo.). Bd. dirs. Council on Founds., Washington, Truman Med. Center, Richard Cabot Clinic, Civic Council, Jacob L. and Ella C. Loose Found., Clearing House for MidContinent Founds., Greater Kansas City Community Found.; trustee Edgar Snow Meml. Fund, Kansas City Assn. of Trusts and Founds., Park Coll. Served from pvt. to capt., AUS, 1942-46. Regent Am. Coll. Probate Counsel; mem. Am. Judicature Soc., Am., Kansas City bar assns., The Mo. Bar, Lawyers Assn. Kansas City. Republican. Presbyterian. Clubs: University, Mission Hills. Home: 1015 W 64th Terrace Kansas City MO 64113 Office: 2100 Tenmain Center Kansas City MO 64105

CHISHOLM, GEORGE NICKOLAUS, dentist; b. Pullman, Wash., Sept, 21, 1936; s. Leslie L. and Lila Rene (Cates) C.; D.D.S., U. Nebr., 1960; 1 son, Andrew M. Practice dentistry, Lincoln, Nebr., 1963—; clin. instr. Coll. Dentistry, U. Nebr., 1976—. Mem. S.E. Nebr. Health Planning Agy., 1976—. Served to capt. Dental Corps, USAF, 1960-63. Mem. ADA (del. 1980—), Nebr. Dental Assn. (del. 1974-80, trustee 1980—), Lincoln Dist. Dental Assn. (pres. 1979-80), Sigma Alpha Epsilon, Xi Psi Phi. Mason (32 deg., Shriner). Asst. editor Nebr. State Dental Jour., 1967-69. Home: 1230 Manchester Dr Lincoln NE 68528 Office: 1025 Stuart Bldg Lincoln NE 68508

CHISHOLM, TAGUE CLEMENT, pediatric surgeon, educator; b. E. Millinocket, Maine, Nov. 6, 1915; s. George James and Victoria Mary (Tague) C.; A.B. cum laude, Harvard U., 1936, M.D., 1940; m. Verity Burnett, 1940 (div. 1975); children—Christopher Tague, Penelope Ann, Robin Francis; m. 2d, Johanna Lyon Myers, Aug. 9, 1975. Intern, Peter Bent Brigham Hosp., Boston Children's Hosp., Boston, 1940-41, resident in gen. and pediatric surgery, 1941-46; Arthur Tracy Cabot fellow in surgery Harvard Med. Sch., 1946; practice medicine specializing in pediatric surgery, Mpls., 1947—; mem. faculty U. Minn. Sch. Medicine, Mpls., 1947—, clin. prof. surgery, 1965-81; trustee Mpls. Children's Health Center Hosp. Trustee Bishop Whipple Schs., Faribault, Minn.; bd. dirs. Wells Found., Mpls. Recipient Presdl. award Minn. Med. Assn., 1978; diplomate Am. Bd. Surgery. Recipient Merit medal U. Rio Grande Norte, Brazil, 1976; Charles Bowles Rogers award Hennepin County (Minn.) Med. Soc., 1976. Editorial bd. Jour. Pediatric Surgery, 1965-76, Pediatric Digest, 1962—, Jour. Minn. Med. Assn., 1957—; contbr. articles in pediatric surgery to profl. jours. and books. Home: 16617 Black Oaks Ln Wayzata MN 55391

CHISHOLM, WILLIAM LEE, med. photographer; b. Kansas City, Mo., July 2, 1947; s. Donald Herbert and Mildred Ruth (Ice) C.; student Westminster Coll., 1965-67; B. Profl. Arts, Brooks Inst. Photography, 1973; m. Susan Elizabeth Lilley, Dec. 8, 1974; 1 son, William Alexander. Med. photography intern Parkland Meml. Hosp., Dallas, 1973; dir. photography U. Mo. Sch. Medicine, Kansas City; lectr. photography, 1973—. Served with USNR, 1967-68. Mem. Profl. Photographers of Am., Biol. Photog. Assn., Brooks Inst. Alumni Assn. Home: Lake of the Forest Bonner Springs KS 66012 Office: U Mo at Kansas City Sch Medicine 2411 Holmes Kansas City MO 64108

CHISM, JAMES ARTHUR, data processor; b. Oak Park, Ill., Mar. 6, 1933; s. William Thompson and Arema Eloise (Chadwick) C.; A.B., DePauw U., 1957; M.B.A., Ind. U., 1959. Mgmt. engr. consumer and indsl. products div. Uniroyal, Inc., Mishawaka, Ind., 1959-61, sr. mgmt. engr., 1961-63; systems analyst Miles Labs., Inc., Elkhart, Ind., 1963-64, sr. systems analyst, 1965-69, project supr., distbn. systems, 1969-71, project mgr. systems and programming for corporate finance and adminstrv. depts., 1971-73, mgr. adminstrv. systems and staff services, 1973-79; dir. adminstrn. and staff services Cutter/Miles, 1979-81, dir. adminstrn. and office automation, 1982—; asso. instr. bus. adminstrn. Ind. U., South Bend, 1964-66; mem. systems and data processing curriculum com. Ind. Vocational Tech. Coll., South Bend Campus, 1969-74; mem. systems curriculum adv. com. Southwestern Mich. Coll., 1974—. Bd. dirs. United Way Elkhart County, 1974-75. Served with AUS, 1954-56. Mem. Assn. Systems Mgmt. (chpt. pres. 1969-70, div. dir. 1972-77, recipient Merit award 1975, Achievement award 1977), Am. Mgmt. Assn., Assn. Internal Mgmt. Cons., DePauw U., Ind. U. alumni assns., Delta Kappa Epsilon, Sigma Iota Epsilon. Republican. Episcopalian. Clubs: East Bank Athletic, Morris Park Country, Summit (South Bend, Ind.). Editor: Am. Prodn. Inventory Control Soc. Glossary, 1980. Home: 504 Cedar Crest Ln Mishawaka IN 46544 Office: Miles Labs Inc PO Box 40 1127 Myrtle St Elkhart IN 46515

CHISM, NEAL ASA, economist; b. Humboldt, Nebr., Nov. 5, 1924; s. Ralph Asa and Jessie Ann (Graham) C.; student Weber Coll., Ogden, Utah, 1942, Wabash Coll., Crawfordsville, Ind., 1944-46, U. Ill., 1946; B.S., U. Calif., Berkeley, 1947; certificate d'Etude, U. Grenoble (France), 1949; M.A., U. Nebr., 1951, secondary teaching cert., 1963, Ph.D., 1967; cert. Sch. Banking, U. Wis., 1978; m. Joan Johnson, Feb. 27, 1965; 1 son, John Neal Asa. Export-import salesman Getz Bros. & Co., San Francisco, 1947-48; research officer U.S. Govt., Washington, 1951-53, fgn. service res. officer, 1953-59; asst. to v.p. Am. Express Co., N.Y.C., 1959-62; asst. prof. econs. Nebr. Wesleyan U., Lincoln, 1965—, also head dept. bus. adminstrn./econs., 1977—. Chmn. ednl. com. Nemeco Credit Union, 1967-75; univ. rep. Lincoln Community Concerts, Lincoln Community Chest, 1972, 73; univ. rep. to liaison com. Mayor's Edn. Com., 1971. Served with USN, 1942-46. Recipient Trustee award Nebr. Wesleyan U., 1972. Mem. AAUP (pres. Wesleyan chpt. 1965-69), SAR (pres. Lincoln chpt. 1975-76, pres. Nebr. state soc. 1977), Chism Family Assn. (exec. sec. 1962—), Am. Econs. Assn., Midwest Econs. Assn., Nebr. Bus. and Econs. Assn. (sec.-treas. 1978—), Clan Chisholm Soc. in Am., Scottish Am. Soc., Lincoln Lancaster Geneal. Soc., Delta Phi Epsilon (pres. Alpha chpt. 1977, gov. Nebr. province 1978—), Delta Tau Delta, Tau Kappa Epsilon (faculty adv. Beta Gamma 1969-77, Nat. Advisers award 1974), Omicron Delta Epsilon, Pi Gamma Mu. Republican. Presbyterian (deacon, elder). Clubs: Filson (Louisville); Masons, Shriners. Home: 5243 Huntington Lincoln NE 68504 Office: Nebr Wesleyan U 50th St Paul Lincoln NE 68504

CHITWOOD, JULIUS RICHARD, librarian; b. Magazine, Ark., June 1, 1921; s. Hoyt Mozart and Florence (Umfrid) C.; A.B. cum laude, Quachita Baptist Coll., Arkadelphis, Ark., 1942; M.Mus., Ind. U., 1948; M.A., U. Chgo., 1954; m. Aileen Newsom, Aug. 6, 1944. Music supr. Edinburg (Ind.) pub. schs., 1946-47; music and audio-visual librarian Roosevelt Coll., Chgo., 1948-51; humanities librarian Drake U., 1951-53; spl. cataloger Chgo. Tchrs. Coll., 1953; asst. circulation librarian Indpls. Pub. Library, 1954-57, coordinator adult services, 1957-61; dir. Rockford (Ill.) Pub. Library 1961-79, No. Ill. Library System, Rockford, 1966-76; cons. Evanston (Ill.) System, 1979, Peninsula (Calif.) System, 1979-80; exec. dir. Ill. Regional Library System, Chgo., 1981—. Chmn. subcom. library system devel. Ill. Library Adv. Com., 1965-79; adv. com. Grad. Sch. Library Sci., U. Ill., 1964-68; program adv. com. Sauk Valley Jr. Coll., 1967; cons. in field, participant workshops. Mem. history com. Ill. Sesquicentennial Commn.; mem. Mayor Rockford Com. for UN, 1962-68. Sect. chmn. Rockford United Fund, 1966-70; exec. bd. Rockford Civic Orch. Assn., 1962-70; pres. Rockford Regional Acad. Center, 1974-76. Served to maj., inf. AUS, 1942-45; ETO. Mem. Am. (chmn. standards adult services com., adult services div. 1961-66, chmn. subcom. revision standards of materials, pub. library div. 1965-66, pres. bldg. and equipment sect. library adminstrn. div. 1966-67, chmn. staff devel. com. personnel adminstrn. sect., library adminstr. div. 1964-68, pres. library adminstrn. div. 1969-70), Ill. (v.p. 1964-65, pres. 1965-66, Librarian of Year award 1974) library assns., Rockford C. of C. (mem. bd. Rockford area 1967-69). Unitarian (pres. 1965-67). Rotarian (exec. bd. Rockford 1965-66). Clubs: Professional Men's, Rockford University. Home: 916 Paris Ave Rockford IL 61107 Office: 4036 E State St Rockford IL 61108

CHLEBOWSKI, GERALD JAMES, state ofcl.; b. Green Bay, Wis., Aug. 22, 1936; s. Harry Joseph and Mary Marge Chlebowski; B.S., Wis. State U., Stevens Point, 1958; M.S., Mich. State U., 1961; m. Betty Berg, Aug. 22, 1959; children—Dale, Darryl, Denise. Tchr., Lake Villa (Ill.) Elem. Sch., 1959-60, Two Rivers (Wis.) Public Schs., 1961-67, Ashwaubenon Public Schs., Green Bay, 1967-72; chief supr. program devel. Wis. Bd. Vocat., Tech. and Adult Edn., Madison, 1972—; state adv. com. Wis. Bur. Aging; co-chmn. tech. and vocat. corr. study Task Force Evaluation of Vocat. Edn. NSF fellow, 1964, 65-67, 68, 70; mem. Nat. Internship Program, 1978. Mem. Am. Vocat. Assn., Adult Vocat. Assn., Wis. Assn. Vocat. Edn., Wis. Adult Edn. Assn., Wis. Lyceum. Roman Catholic. Club: Elks. Editor: Chemistry for Beginners (Calvin Midgley), 1960; research on entrocci in agrl. soils. Home: 4717 Anniversary Ln Madison WI 53704 Office: 4802 Sheboygan Ave Madison WI 53702

CHMIELEWSKI, FLORIAN, state senator; student U. Minn. Agrl. Extension, LaSalle Law Extension U.; m. Pat; children—Patty, Florian, Jeffry, Mark. Band dir. Willow River High Sch.; farmer; owner Chmielewski TV Prodns., Chmielewski Bros. Orch. and TV Network; mem. Minn. Senate, 1970—. County commr., 1960-70. Mem. Democratic-Farmer-Labor party. Office: 325 State Capitol Saint Paul MN 55155*

CHNUPA, PEGGY, public sch. adminstr.; b. Gary, Ind., June 10, 1952; d. John Clifton and Dessie Robinson; B.S., Ind. U., 1974; M.S., Purdue U., 1978; cert. in adminstrn. Ind. State U., Terre Haute, 1980; 1 dau., Kathleen Ann. Elem. sch. tchr., then asst. curriculum coordinator Hobart (Ind.) Twp. schs., 1974-79, dir. spl. services, 1980—; cons. Utah Systems Approach to Individualized Learning, 1977—. Mem. Assn. Curriculum and Devel., Phi Delta Kappa. Lutheran. Co-editor curriculum materials. Office: 3334 Michigan St Hobart IN 46342

CHO, CHENG TSUNG, physician, educator; b. Kaohsiung, Taiwan, Dec. 2, 1937; s. R.E. and S.M. (Chou) C.; came to U.S., 1964, naturalized, 1976; M.D., Kaohsiung Med. Coll., 1962; Ph.D., U. Kans., 1970; m. Chiou-shya Chen, Dec. 14, 1968; children—Jennifer, Julie. Intern, Norwegian-Am. Hosp., Chgo., 1964-65; resident U. Kans. Med. Center, 1965-67, fellow, 1967-70, asst. prof. pediatrics, microbiology, 1970-74, asso. prof., 1974-78, prof., 1978—, acting chmn. dept. pediatrics, 1978-79, chief sect. of pediatric infectious disease, dept. pediatrics, 1972—; vis. prof. Tri-Service Gen. Hosp. and Nat. Def. Med. Sch., Taiwan, 1980. Recipient Outstanding Pediatric Teaching award U. Kans. Med. Center, 1975; diplomate Am. Bd. Pediatrics. Fellow Am. Acad. Pediatrics, Infectious Disease Soc. Am.; mem. AAAS, Am. Soc. Microbiology, Soc. Pediatric Research, Soc. Exptl. Biology and Medicine, Kans. Med. Soc., Midwest Pediatric Research Soc., Kaohsiung Med. Coll. Alumni Assn. Am. (pres. 1978). Am. Co-author: Pediatric Infectious Diseases; author articles on virology and infectious diseases. Home: 10215 Howe Ln Leawood KS 66206 Office: Dept Pediatrics U Kans Med Center Kansas City KS 66103

CHOCKLEY, FREDERICK WILSON, JR., lawyer; b. Joliet, Ill., Jan. 23, 1923; s. Frederick W. and Vera (Barrowman) C.; student Duke, 1941-42; B.S., U. Pa., 1947; LL.B., Western Res. U., 1949; m. Nancy Young, July 20, 1945; children—Nancy (Mrs. William R. Seelbach), Lizabeth A., Frederick Wilson III, Laurel Y.; m. 2d, Jean Schilling, June 16, 1972. Admitted to Ohio bar, 1949; mem. firm Walter, Haverfield, Buescher & Chockley, Cleve., 1949—; acting judge Lakewood (Ohio) Municipal Ct., 1968, 69, 70; spl. counsel to atty. gen State of Ohio, 1953. Mem. Ohio Bd. Bar Examiners, 1960-65. Mem. Lakewood Library Bd., 1969-70. Mem. Lakewood City Council, 1953-61, pres., 1960-61. Served with U.S. Army, 1943-45. Mem. Am., Ohio, Cleve. (mem. exec. com. 1964-66) bar assns., Am. Arbitration Assn., Sigma Alpha Epsilon, Phi Delta Phi. Republican. Presbyn. Clubs: Westwood Country, Union, University of Pa. (pres. 1956) (Cleve.). Home: 1443 E Melrose St Westlake OH 44145 Office: Terminal Tower Cleveland OH 44113

CHODOS, DALE DAVID JEROME, physician, pharm. co. exec.; b. Mpls., June 5, 1928; s. John H. and Elvera Isabella (Lundberg) C.; A.B., Carroll Coll., Helena Mont., 1950; M.D., St. Louis U., 1954; m. Joyce Annette Smith, Sept. 8, 1951; children—John, Julie, David, Jennifer. Intern, U. Utah, Salt Lake City, 1954-55, resident in pediatrics, 1955-57; practice medicine specializing in pediatrics, Idaho Falls, Idaho, 1958-62; staff physician Upjohn Co., Kalamazoo, 1962-64, head clin. pharmacology, 1964-65, research mgr. clin. pharmacology, 1965-68, research mgr. clin. services, 1968-73, group research mgr. med. therapeutics, 1973-81, med. dir. domestic med. affairs, 1981—; chief pediatrics Latter-day Saints Hosp., Sacred Heart Hosp., Idaho Falls, 1962; chmn. med. relations operating com. Nat. Pharm. Council, 1977-80, mem. steering com. 1977—, program chmn., 1982-83. Bd. dirs. Family Service Center, Kalamazoo, 1965-71. Served with AUS, 1945-46. Recipient W.E. Upjohn award for Excellence, 1969, Physician's Recognition award, AMA, 1969, 73, 76, 79; NIH fellow, 1957-58; diplomate Am. Bd. Pediatrics. Fellow Am. Acad. Pediatrics; mem. Am. Soc. Clin. Pharmacology and Therapeutics, Am. Coll. Clin. Toxicology, AMA. Contbr. articles to med. and pharm. jours. Home: 619 Aqua View Dr Kalamazoo MI 49009 Office: 7000 Portage Rd Kalamazoo MI 49001

CHOICE, MICHAEL JOHN, securities exec.; b. Chgo., Sept. 12, 1942; s. Herbert John and Josephine (DeVoto) C.; B.A., Beloit Coll., 1965; M.B.A., Roosevelt U., 1969; m. Nancy Lamson, July 10, 1965; 1 dau., Cynthia. Group div. underwriting supr. Continental Casualty Co., Chgo., 1965-70; asst. v.p. Merrill Lynch, Pierce, Fenner & Smith, Inc., Chgo., 1970—. Mem. United Ch. Christ. Home: 510 E Park Ave Elmhurst IL 60126 Office: 33 W Monroe Chicago IL 60603

CHOJNOWSKI, EUGENE FRANCIS, mfg. co. exec.; b. Chgo., Apr. 23, 1929; s. Leo C. and Stella (Werner) C.; m. Jean Kostka, Apr. 16, 1949; children—Robert, Thomas, Barbara, Mark. B.S., Purdue U., 1951. Registered profl. engr., Mich., 1958. Foundry technician Internat. Harvester Co., 1951-53; served with U.S. Army, 1953-55; technician, research metallurgist, chief metallurgist, research and devel. mgr., plant engr. Hayes-Albion Corp., Albion, Mich., 1955-67; partner Heat Transfer Systems Co., Jackson, Mich., 1967-69, pres., 1969—. Chmn. Albion chpt. March of Dimes, 1961-62; chmn. Albion chpt. Red Cross, 1962; asst. advisor explorer scouts Boy Scouts Am., 1958-60. Mem. Am. Soc. Metals (dir. Jackson chpt. 1966-68), Am. Foundrymans Soc., Soc. Automotive Engrs., Purdue Alumni Assn., Jackson Outdoor Club, Mich. Tuberculosis and Respiratory Disease Assn., Arbor Hills Country Club. Recipient Distinguished Service award, 1960. Author: (with others) Am. Soc. for Metals Handbook, Vol. 2, 1965. Home and office: 5891 Picarn Jackson MI 49201

CHOLLAR, ROBERT GANUN, found. exec.; b. Syracuse, N.Y., Feb. 10, 1914; s. Walter Edward and Estelle Augusta (GaNun) C.; student Dartmouth Coll., 1932-33; A.B., Antioch Coll., 1935; D.Sc. (hon.), Ind. Inst. Tech., 1972; m. Thelma Lucille Holt, Sept. 22, 1934; children—Charles Edward, Brian Holt, Richard Robert. With Nat. Cash Register Co., Dayton, Ohio, 1933-71, v.p. research and devel., 1959-64, v.p. and group exec. research, devel. and mfg., 1964-71; chmn. bd., pres. Charles F. Kettering Found., Dayton, 1971-81, chmn., 1981—; dir. Dayton Power & Light Co. Mem. bd. overseers Sloan-Kettering Cancer Center. Recipient Internat. Statesman award Sister Cities, 1974; Ohio Commodore. Mem. Council Fgn. Relations, Internat. Standards Orgn. (chmn. 1961-73), Indsl. Research Inst. (pres. 1960-61), Am. Chem. Soc., Tau Beta Pi, Chi Phi. Clubs: Moraine Country (Dayton); Univ. (N.Y.). Patentee synthetic rubber, plastics, printing. Home: 4472 Lotz Rd Dayton OH 45429 Office: 5335 Far Hills Ave Dayton OH 45429

CHOO, YEOW MING, lawyer; b. Johore Bahru, Malaysia, Aug. 1, 1953; s. Far Tong and Kim Fong (Wong) C.; LL.B. with honors, U. Malaya, 1977; LL.M., Harvard U., 1979; J.D., Chgo.-Kent Coll.,

1980. Admitted to Malaysia bar, 1977, Ill. bar, 1980; lectr. law U. Malaya Law Sch., Kuala Lumpur, Malaysia, 1977-78, Monash U. Law Sch., Melbourne, Australia, 1978; internat. atty. Standard Oil Co. (Ind.), Chgo., 1979-82; partner, law firm of Anderson, Liu and Choo, New York, 1982—. dir. Harvard Bros. Internat. Corp.; Boston; chmn. tax subcom. Nat. Council for US-China Trade, 1980—. Mem. Am. Mining Congress (alt. mem. com. on law of sea 1980—), Am. Bar Assn., Ill. Bar Assn., Chgo. Bar Assn., Malayan Bar Council, U.S. Chess Fedn., Harvard Law Sch. Alumni Assn. Club: Harvard. Home: 1033 S Loyola Ave Chicago IL 60626 Office: 200 E Randolph Dr Chicago IL 60601

CHOP, HELEN ANN, nurse; b. Kansas City, Kans., Mar. 4, 1922; d. Mary B. Sachen; R.N., Providence Sch. Nursing, 1944; B.S., Park Coll., 1976; M.S., Kans. State U., 1979; m. John Chop, Sept. 25, 1948; children—Mary Eileen, Margaret Ann, Rose Marie. Staff nurse Providence Hosp., Kansas City, 1944-47, head nurse, 1947-48, supr., 1948-70, dir. nursing service, 1970-72; dir. nursing service St. Margarets Hosp., 1972-76; dir. nursing service Providence-St. Margarets Health Center, Kansas City, 1976—, now asso. pvt. care services; charge Orthopedic Clinic, Kansas City, 1948. Sec., v.p., pres. Catholic Nurses Archdiocese of Kansas City, 1947-55; Camp Fire leader for St. John Baptist Sch., also Daus. St. Peters Cathedral Sch., 1949-52; pres. Altar Soc., St. Peters Cathedral, 1963; bd. dirs. Cath. Charities, Kansas City, 1965; mem. occupational ednl. adv. council Kansas City Community Coll., 1977; mem. adv. group Kans. Found. for Med. Care, 1978; rep. Liaison Council Organized Profl. Nursing, 1977, Kans. Legislature 1202 Commn., 1978; appointee Bd. of Nursing, State of Kans. Served to 2d lt. U.S. Army, 1945-47. Recipient St. Ann award, 1950. Mem. Am. Hosp. Assn., Am. Soc. Hosp. Nursing Service Adminstrs., Nat. League Nursing, Kans. Soc. Nursing Service Adminstrs. (Dist. 1 rep., dir. 1976, pres. 1979), Kans. Hosp. Assn., Kansas City Area Hosp. Assn. (sec. Dirs. of Nursing Service 1973), VFW. Roman Catholic.

CHOPRA, RAJ KUMAR, supt. schs.; b. India, Mar. 3, 1937; came to U.S., 1969, naturalized, 1976; s. Rajasher Lal and Leela (Wanti) C.; B.A., Punjab U.; M.Ed., Bowling Green State U., 1967, Ph.D., 1971; m. Sukant la Chopra, Feb. 17, 1964; children—Dick, Lucky, Komal. Tchr., then headmaster boarding house Am. Internat. Sch., New Delhi, 1962-68; adminstrv. asst. to asso. dean Bowling Green State U., 1969-70; elem. sch. prin., Ohio, 1969-73; asst. supt. Medina (Ohio) Public Schs., 1973-76; supt. Bellefontaine (Ohio) City Schs., 1976-78; supt. Council Bluffs (Iowa) Community Schs., 1978—; speaker in field. Active Boy Scouts Am.; chmn. United Fund, Council Bluffs, 1981. Recipient various civic and ednl. awards. Mem. Am. Assn. Sch. Adminstrs., Assn. Supervision and Curriculum Devel., Iowa Assn. Sch. Adminstrs., Phi Delta Kappa. Club: Rotary. Author articles in field. Office: 207 Scott St Council Bluffs IA 51501

CHORPENNING, NANCY ELLEN, pub. co. exec.; b. Columbus, Ohio, Nov. 29, 1953; d. Harry Row and Margaret Ellen (Hayes) C.; B.A., Denison U., 1975; postgrad. Northwestern U., 1979—. Ednl. rep. Year Book Med. Pubs. subs. Times Mirror, Chgo., 1975-77, field editor, 1977-79, med. editor, 1979—. Mem. Nat. Assn. Female Execs., Chgo. Women in Pub., Denison U. Alumni Assn., Bus. and Profl. Women's Club of Chgo., Alpha Phi. Republican. Congregationalist. Home: 500 Lake St Evanston IL 60201 Office: Year Book Med Publishers Inc 35 E Wacker Dr Chicago IL 60601

CHOS, LOUIS JOHN, JR., chem. co. exec.; b. Cleve., Sept. 22, 1951; s. Louis John and Ellen Virginia (Carlson) C.; B.S. in Chem. Engring., Case Western Res. U., 1973; m. Diane M. Chos, 1977. Chem. engr. Dow Chem. Co., Midland, Mich., 1972-74, prodn. engr., 1974-77, prodn. supr., 1977-81, project supr., 1980—. Adviser Jr. Achievement, Midland, 1975-76; active Big Brother Orgn., Gladwin-Clare counties, 1975-79; sec. ch. council Good Shepherd Lutheran Ch., 1980-81, pres. ch. council, 1981. Mem. Am. Youth Hostels. Home: 5451 Oak Ridge Dr Beaverton MI 48612 Office: 851 Bldg Dow Chem Co Midland MI 48640

CHOU, CHIEN-ERH E., research engr.; b. Taipei, Taiwan, Jan. 9, 1942; came to U.S., 1967, naturalized, 1981; s. Pau-Chih and Chauh (Pan) C.; B.S., Nat. Taiwan Cheng-Kung U., 1964; M.S., U. Minn., 1969; postgrad. UCLA, 1973-76. Teaching asso. U. Minn., Mpls., 1967-69; metallurgist Gould, Inc., St. Paul, 1969-72, project engr., battery div., 1977—. Mem. Am. Soc. Metals, Chinese-Am. Assn. Minn. Office: Gould Inc 931 N Vandalia St St Paul MN 55114

CHOU, CLIFFORD CHI FONG, research engr.; b. Taipei, Taiwan, Dec. 19, 1940; s. Ching piao and Yueh li (Huang) C.; came to U.S., 1966, naturalized, 1978; Ph.D., Mich. State U., 1972; m. Chu hwei Lee, Mar. 23, 1968; children—Kelvin Lin yu, Renee Lincy. Research asst. Mich. State U., E. Lansing, 1967-70, Wayne State U. Detroit, 1970-72, research asso., 1972-76, research engr. Ford Motor Co., Dearborn, 1976-81, sr. research engr., 1981—; tchr. part-time dynamics, engring. systems analysis; asst. tchr. auto safety related courses; project engr. auto safety research programs. Recipient Safety Engring. Excellence award Nat. Hwy. Traffic Safety Adminstrn., 1980. Soc. Automotive Engrs. grantee. Mem. ASME, AIAA, Sigma Xi. Clubs: Detroit Chinese Am. Assn. Contbr. numerous articles to profl. jours. Home: 45228 Patrick Dr Canton MI 48187 Office: PO Box 2053 Room E 3184 Scientific Research Lab Dearborn MI 48121

CHOU, DAVID HUNG-EN, food scientist; b. Nantou, Taiwan, Dec. 2, 1940; s. Chien-tsai and Shin (Chen) C.; B.S., Nat. Taiwan U., 1966; M.S., U. Minn., 1970, Ph.D., 1973; m. Shuh-Mei Chen, Sept. 18, 1969; children—Cindy, Henry. Research asst., Nat Taiwan U., 1967-68; research asst. U. Minn., 1968-71, research fellow, 1971-73; project leader Ralston Purina Co., St. Louis, 1973-76, sr. project leader, 1976-78, asso. scientist, 1978—. Served to 2d lt. Nationalist Chinese Army, 1966-67. Mem. Chinese Agrl. Chemistry Assn., Inst. Food Technologist, Am. Assn. Cereal Chemists, Soc. Rheology, Am. Chem. Soc., Assn. Chinese Food Scientists and Technologists in Am. (v.p. 1978-79, pres. 1979-80), Sigma Xi, Gamma Sigma Delta. Club: American Formosan. Home: 9250 Arban Dr St Louis MO 63126 Office: Checkerboard Sq St Louis MO 63188

CHOUKAS, NICHOLAS CHRIS, dental educator; b. Chgo., Sept. 5, 1923; s. Chris and Ethel (George) C.; student Wright Jr. Coll., 1941-43, U. Chgo., 1943-44; D.D.S., Loyola U., Chgo., 1950, M.S. in Oral Anatomy, 1958; m. LaVerne Tumosa, Apr. 19, 1951; children—Janet Lynn, Chris Nicholas, Michael John, Nicholas Chris II. Fellow in oral surgery Loyola U., 1953; resident in oral surgery Cook County Hosp., Chgo., 1954-55; practice specializing in oral and maxillofacial surgery, Elmwood Park, Ill., 1956—; asst. prof. Loyola U. Dental Sch., 1957-64, asso. prof., 1964—, chmn. dept. oral surgery, 1962—, asso. prof. oral biology Grad. Sch., 1968-69, prof. dept. oral biology, 1969—, prof. dept. oral and maxillofacial surgery, 1969—; attending oral surgeon Hines (Ill.) VA Hosp., 1958-60; asso. attending surgeon Cook County Hosp., 1959-62; cons. VA Hosp., Hines, Ill., 1960—. Served to lt. (j.g.), USNR, 1951-53. Research grantee NIH, 1961, 62, 63. Diplomate Am. Bd. Oral Surgery. Fellow Internat. Assn. Oral Surgeons, Am. Coll. Dentists, Inst. Medicine of Chgo., Pan Am. Med. Assn., Internat. Coll. Dentists, Internat. Assn. Maxillofacial Surgeons, Am. Coll. Stomatologic Surgeons; mem. Chgo. Soc. Oral Surgeons, Am. Soc. Oral Surgeons, Odontographic Soc., Logan Brophy Meml. Soc., Sigma Xi, Omicron Kappa Upsilon, Delta Sigma Delta. Contbr. articles to profl. jours. Home: 230 Oakdene Rd Barrington Hills IL 60010 Office: 7310 North Ave Elmwood Park IL 60635

CHOW, POO, wood technologist; b. Shanghai, China, Apr. 27, 1934; came to U.S., 1960, naturalized, 1971; s. Kai and Yung-Kwang (Hsieh) C.; M.S. in Forest Products, La. State U., 1961; Ph.D. in Wood Sci. and Tech., Forestry, Mich. State U., 1969; m. Ai-Yu Kuo, July 17, 1965; children—Eugenia, Andrew E. Tech. dir. Pope and Talbot, Inc., Oakridge, Oreg., 1962-67; research grad. Mich. State U., East Lansing, 1967-69; asst. prof. wood sci. U. Ill., Urbana, 1969-74, asso. prof., 1974-80, prof., 1980—, sr. Fulbright scholar, W. Ger., 1976-77; cons. to industry; external examiner U. Ibadan (Nigeria). Served to 2d lt. Nat. Chinese Army, 1957-59. Named Hon. Citizen, State of Nebr., 1979. Mem. Forest Products Research Soc. (award 1976, 78), ASTM, Soc. Wood Sci. and Tech., Ill. Tech. Forestry Assn., Fulbright Assn., Council on Furniture Engring. and Research, TAPPI, Am. Wood Preservatives Assn., Sigma Xi, Gamma Sigma Delta, Xi Sigma Pi, Sigma Lambda Chi. Editor: The Evolution of EPA and OSHA Ruling on Wood Industries; The Optimum Yield, Architectural Design, Marketing, and Metrication of Hardwood, 1976; contbr. articles to profl. jours; patentee. Home: 2406 Burlison St Urbana IL 61801 Office: 110 Mumford Hall 1301 W Gregory U Ill Urbana IL 61801

CHOYKE, ARTHUR DAVIS, JR., luminous ceiling co. exec.; b. N.Y.C., Mar. 13, 1919; s. Arthur Davis and Lillian (Bauer) C.; A.B., Columbia, 1939, B.S., 1940; m. Phyllis May Ford, Aug. 18, 1945; children—Christopher Ford, Tyler Van. With indsl. engring. dept. Procter & Gamble Co., S.I., N.Y., 1940-43; instr. Pratt Inst., Bklyn., 1942-45; chief indsl. engr. M & M, Ltd., Newark, 1943-47; partner Ford Distbg. Co., Chgo., 1947-57; incorporator, pres., treas., dir. Artcrest Products Co., Inc., Chgo., 1951—; dir. Gallery Series, Harper Sq. Press. Clubs: Exec., Arts (Chgo.). Home: 29 E Division St Chicago IL 60610 Office: 401 W Ontario St Chicago IL 60610

CHOYKE, PHYLLIS MAY FORD (MRS. ARTHUR DAVIS CHOYKE, JR.), ceiling systems co. exec.; b. Buffalo, Oct. 25, 1921; d. Thomas Cecil and Vera (Buchanan) Ford; B.S. summa cum laude, Northwestern U., 1942; m. Arthur Davis Choyke, Jr., Aug. 18, 1945; children—Christopher Ford, Tyler Van. Reporter, City News Bur., Chgo., 1942-43, Met. sect. Chgo. Tribune, 1943-44; feature writer OWI, N.Y.C., 1944-45; sec. corp. Artcrest Products Co., Inc., Chgo., 1958—, v.p., 1964—, founder-dir. Harper Sq. Press div., 1966—. Mem. Phi Beta Kappa. Club: Arts (Chgo.). Author: (under name Phyllis Ford) (with others) (poetry) Apertures to Anywhere, 1979; editor: Gallery Series One, 1967; Gal-Series Two—Poems of the Inner World, 1968; Gallery Series Three—Poets: Levitations and Observations, 1970; Gallery Series Four-I am Talking About Revolution, 1973; Gallery Series Five/Poets—To An Aging Nation (with occult overtones), 1977. Home: 29 E Division St Chicago IL 60610 Office: 401 W Ontario St Chicago IL 60610

CHRISOPULOS, JOHN, health care food adminstr., caterer; b. Oak Park, Ill., Jan. 5, 1946; s. Harry and Nicolette (Kappos) C.; student DePaul U., 1964-65; cert., Washburne Trade Sch., 1968; m. Pamela Sue Towsley, Sept. 17, 1978; 1 dau., Amanda Lynn. Sous-chef Racquet Club of Chgo., 1968-69; food service dir. Szabo Food Service, Chgo., 1970-71; owner Markon's Restaurant and Delicatesson, Chgo., 1971-74; mgr. food service Northwestern Meml. Hosp., Chgo., 1974; dir. food service Holy Family Hosp., Des Plaines, Ill., 1975-78; pres. Connoisseurs Caterers, Inc., Barrington, Ill., 1978—; dir. food services Westlake Community Hosp., Melrose Park, Ill., 1979-80; asso. dir. food and nutrition service U. Chgo. Med. Center, 1980—. Mem. Am. Soc. for Hosp. Food Service Adminstrs. (bd. dirs. 1975-76, chmn. 10th annual ednl. conf. 1977, pres.-elect 1977, pres. 1978, mem. nat. nominating com. 1978), Internat. Food Service Execs. Assn., Catering Execs. Club. Am. Greek Orthodox. Home: 752 Whitesail Dr Schaumburg IL 60194 Office: 950 E 59th St Box 431 Chicago IL 60637

CHRISTENSEN, BARLOW FORBES, lawyer; b. Shelley, Idaho, Oct. 21, 1928; s. Joseph Cortez and Lenore Gardner (Forbes) C.; B.S. with high honors Brigham Young U., 1955; J.D., Columbia, 1960; m. Anne Elizabeth Kirk, Aug. 9, 1957; children—Susan Anne, Sharon, Kirk Barlow, Marcia, Joseph, Thomas Arthur. Admitted to Idaho bar, 1960; asso. firm Robert M. Kerr, Jr., Blackfoot, Ida., 1960; law clk. State Idaho Supreme Ct., 1960-62; adminstrv. asst. Am. Bar Assn., Chgo., 1962-65; research atty. Am. Bar Found., Chgo., 1965—. Served with AUS, 1951-53. Mem. Idaho State, Am. bar assns., Phi Kappa Phi. Republican. Mem. Ch. Jesus Christ of Latter-day Saints (missionary 1948-50, patriarch Chicago Heights, Ill. Stake 1975—). Author: Lawyers for People of Moderate Means, 1970; contbr. articles to legal jours. Home: 156 Algonquin St Park Forest IL 60466 Office: 1155 E 60th St Chicago IL 60637

CHRISTENSEN, CHARLES NEIL, pharm. co. exec.; b. Wilmot, S.D., July 27, 1921; s. Charles Hans and Cora B. (Carlson) C.; B.S. in Med. Sci. summa cum laude, U. S.D., 1943; M.D., U. Pa., 1945; m. Florence McCulley, June 22, 1948; children—Charles Neil, Timothy J., Mary, Julie. Intern Hosp. of U. Pa., 1945-46, resident in pediatrics, 1948-50; practice medicine specializing in pediatrics, Springfield, Ill., 1950-55; pediatrician Miners Meml. Hosp., Pikeville, Ky., 1955-57; physician med. dept. Eli Lilly & Co., 1957-63, asst. dir., 1963-67, dir., 1967-69, exec. dir. med. research planning, 1969-73; v.p. Lilly Research Labs., 1973—. Bd. dirs. Indpls. Symphony Orch., 1974-76, Indpls. Opera Co., 1979—. Served with USNR, 1946-48. Mem. Pharm. Mfrs. Assn. (chmn. med. sect. 1970-71), AAAS, Am. Acad. Pediatrics, Author articles in field. Office: 307 E McCarthy St Indianapolis IN 46285

CHRISTENSEN, DON EDWARD, systems design engr.; b. Springfield, Ohio, Aug. 7, 1927; s. Otto M. and Ruth Harriet (Melvin) C.; grad. Machine Accountants Tng. Assn., 1963; student Ind. U.-Purdue U., Indpls., 1974; m. Wanjean Christensen, July 30, 1949; children—Ivan G., Bruce O., Laura M., Phyllis M. With Am. Dist. Telegraph Co., 1944-51, Indpls. Power & Light Co., 1951-56, RCA, Indpls., 1956-59, Acousticon of Indpls. div. Dictograph Corp., 1959-64; systems design engr. RCA, 1964—. Past pres., dir. Marion County chpt. Com. to Restore the Constn.; mem. Commn. on Human Rights of Indpls. and Marion County; chmn. 11th dist. Am. Party, 1973-74, chmn. Am. Party, 1974-76; pres., chief exec. officer Voters for Fiscal Responsibility Inc. Recipient Liberty awards Congress of Freedom Inc., 1975, 76. Mem. IEEE. Republican. Lutheran. Clubs: Ind. Order of Foresters. Patentee TV control circuits. Home: 1016 N Drexel Ave Indianapolis IN 46201 Office: 600 N Sherman Dr Indianapolis IN 46201

CHRISTENSEN, DONN DOUGLAS, lawyer; b. St. Paul, June 30, 1929; s. Jonas Jergen and Hildur Minerva (Lundeen) C.; B.S., U. Minn., 1950, LL.B., 1952; m. Renee E. Pinet, Aug. 31, 1970; children—Keith, Catherine, Eric. Admitted to Minn. bar, 1952, U.S. Fed. Ct., 1955; practiced in St. Paul, 1954-68, 70—; dep. atty. gen. State of Minn., 1968-70; justice of peace, Village of Mendota Heights, Minn., 1961-66; instr. bus. law Macalester Coll., St. Paul, 1960-67. Served with AUS, 1952-54. Mem. Am., Minn. (chmn. environmental law sect. 1972-73), Ramsey County bar assns., Execs. Assn. St. Paul (pres. 1966), Mendota Heights C. of C. (sec. 1965), Delta Theta Phi. Club: Athletic (St. Paul). Home: 676 Schifsky Rd Saint Paul MN 55112 Office: 155 Arden Plaza Office Saint Paul MN 55112 also North Branch MN 55056

CHRISTENSEN, JERRY MELVIN, agrl. engr.; b. Volga, S.D., May 5, 1949; s. Melvin Nicholi and Louise (Werner) C.; B.S., S.D. State U., 1972. Engr., Morton Bldgs., Spencer, Iowa, 1972-73, Morton, Ill., 1973—, livestock housing products mgr., 1981—. Mem. vocat. adv. council Morton High Sch. Registered profl. engr., Ill., S.D. Mem. Am. Soc. Agrl. Engrs. Democrat. Lutheran. Home: Prairie Village Unit 10 Morton IL 61550 Office: Morton Bldgs Inc 252 W Adams St Morton IL 61550

CHRISTENSEN, MARGUERITE ALICE, librarian; b. Trout Lake, Wis., Aug. 24, 1917; d. Peter Carl and Alice (Cady) Christensen; B.A., U. Wis., 1938, B.L.S., 1939. Librarian, high sch. and Pub. Library, Bloomer, Wis., 1939-41; asst. librarian Wis. State U., Superior, 1941-43, Carroll Coll., Waukesha, Wis., 1943-45; asst. reference librarian U. Wis.-Madison, 1945-66, head gen. reference dept., 1967—. Mem. ALA, Assn. Coll. and Research Libraries. Home: 4469 Hillcrest Dr Madison WI 53705

CHRISTENSEN, ORLA JUNE, educator; b. Clarkfield, Minn., June 5, 1934; d. Clifford Arnold and Clara Theoline (Stokke) C.; B.A. in Health and Phys. Edn., Augsburg Coll., Mpls., 1956; M.S. in Counseling (NDEA fellow), Purdue U., 1966; Ed.D. in Counseling and Personnel Services in Higher Edn. (Delta Kappa Gamma scholar), Mont. State U., 1972. Tchr. health and phys. edn. Appleton (Minn.) Pub. Schs., 1956-58, Alexandria (Minn.) Pub. Schs., 1958-65; counselor Irvington (N.Y.) High Sch., 1966-67, Tacoma (Wash.) Pub. Schs., 1967-73; prof. ednl. psychology and human services U. S.D., Vermillion, 1973—; coordinator, participant workshops in communications, human relations, cultural awareness, career devel. Mem. Am., S.D. psychol. assns., Am., S.D. personnel and guidance assns., Nat. Vocat. Guidance Assn., Assn. Counselor Edn., N.Am. Soc. Adlerian Psychology, Delta Kappa Gamma Internat., Phi Delta Kappa. Contbr. articles in field to profl. jours. Office: Dezell Edn Center U SD Vermillion SD 57069

CHRISTENSEN, RAYMOND A., state legislator; b. Morris, Ill., May 11, 1922; s. Einer and Margaret (Broderick) C.; student public schs., Morris; m. Norma Fiori, Sept. 18, 1948; children—Guy, Gary, Gregg. Owner, operator Lisbon Locker Plant; animal insp. State of Ill., 1975-76; mem. Ill. Ho. of Reps. Pres., Morris Community High Sch. Dist. 101 Bd. Edn., 1971-72; alderman Morris City Council, 1971-75. Served with USAAF, 1942-45. Mem. Am. Legion, VFW. Democrat. Roman Catholic. Clubs: KC, Eagles. Office: 424 Liberty St Morris IL 60450*

CHRISTENSEN, RUTH KOCH, business adminstr.; b. Seward, Nebr., Sept. 1, 1919; d. Ernest Karl and Lydia (Schneider) K.; student U. Nebr., 1937-39; B.S., Elmhurst Coll., 1970; M.S., George Williams Coll., Downers Grove, Ill., 1981; m. Delbert L. Christensen, June 10, 1944; children—Ingrid, Connie Jo, Mark, David. Tchr. elem. sch., 1939-42; founder RE:AL, Inc., personal devel. program, Elmhurst, Ill., 1976, bus. adminstr., from 1976. Bd. dirs. YMCA, 1967-77; Christian edn. chmn. Chgo. Presbytery, Mission 6, 1968-70. Mem. Am. Personnel and Guidance Assn., AAUW. Author: Pinky Pig Sprouts Feather, 1959; contbr. stories to children's mags., 1956-70. Home: 360 Ridgeland Ave Elmhurst IL 60126 Office: RE:AL Inc 367 Spring Rd Elmhurst IL 60126

CHRISTENSON, CHRIS, photographer; b. Bedford, O., Nov. 13, 1925; s. Chris and Ilah (Fivecoate) C.; grad. high sch.; m. Eunice McAdoo, Sept. 1, 1957; children—Jeffrey, Joan, Susan. Photographer, Bedford Pictorial Studio, 1948-58; pres., Chris Christenson Photographer, Inc., Bedford, 1958—; track photographer, Thistledown, Randall Park, Cranwood, Summit, 1961—; staff photographer Ohio Thoroughbred mag., 1971—. Home: 719 Johnson St Bedford OH 44146 Office: 39 Woodrow St Bedford OH 44146

CHRISTIAN, EDWARD KIEREN, radio sta. exec.; b. Detroit, June 26, 1944; s. William Edward and Dorothy Miriam (Kieren) C.; student Mich. State U., 1962-64; B.A., Wayne State U., 1966; M.A., Central Mich. U., 1980; m. Judith Dallaire, Nov. 21, 1966; children—Eric, Dana. Mgr., John C. Butler Co., Detroit, 1968-69; nat. sales mgr. WCAR Radio, Detroit, WSUN Radio, St. Petersburg Fla., 1969-70; v.p., gen. mgr. WCER Radio, Charlotte, Mich., 1970-74; exec. v.p. Josephson Internat./Radio div. WNIC, WNIC-FM, Detroit, WNOR, WNOR-FM, Norfolk, Va., WVKO, WVKO-FM, Columbus, Ohio, 1974—; vice chmn. Mut. Broadcasting Affiliates Council, 1977-79; chmn. Arbitron Radio Adv. Council, 1978-79; bd. dirs. All Industry Music Licensing Com. Pres., United Way, Charlotte, 1973-74; del. Republican State Conv., 1974; bd. dirs. Greater Detroit Safety Council; bd. dirs. Alpha Epsilon Rho Nat. Adv. Council, 1980—. Mem. Dearborn C. of C. (dir.). Kiwanian. Home: 795 Lakeland St Grosse Pointe MI 48230 Office: 15001 Michigan Ave Dearborn MI 48126

CHRISTIAN, RICHARD CARLTON, advt. exec.; b. Dayton, Ohio, Nov. 29, 1924; s. Raymond A. and Louise (Gamber) C.; B.S. in Bus. Adminstrn., Miami U., Oxford, O., 1948; M.B.A., Northwestern U., 1949; student Denison U., The Citadel, Biarritz Am. U.; m. Audrey Bongartz, Sept. 10, 1949; children—Ann Carra, Richard Carlton. Mktg. analyst Nat. Cash Register Co., Dayton, 1948, Rockwell Mfg. Co., Pitts., 1949-50; exec. v.p. Marsteller Inc., Chgo., 1951-60, pres., 1960-75, chmn. bd., 1975—; dir., chmn. Bus Publs. Audit of Circulation, Inc., 1969-75; dir. Wilmette Bank; speaker, author mktg., sales mgmt., mktg. research and advt. Trustee Nat. Coll. Edn., Northwestern U., 1970-74; chmn. exec. com. James Webb Young Fund Edn., U. Ill., 1962-75; adv. bd. Sch. Journalism U. Ga. Served with inf., AUS, 1942-46; ETO. Decorated Bronze Star, Purple Heart; recipient Gov.'s award State of Ohio, 1977; 1st Disting. Service award Am. Acad. Advt., 1979, adv. council J.L. Kellogg Grad. Sch. Mgmt., Northwestern U. Mem. Am. Mktg. Assn. (dir. 1953-54), Indsl. Mktg. Assn. (founder, chmn. 1951), Bus./Profl. Publs. Advt. Assn. (life mem. Chgo.; pres. Chgo. 1954-55, nat. v.p. 1955-58, G.D. Crain Jr. award 1977), Northwestern U. Bus. Sch. Alumni Assn. (founder, pres.), Am. Mgmt. Assn., Am. Assn. Advt. Agys. (dir., chmn. 1976-77), Nat. Advt. Rev. Council (pres. 1976-77), Northwestern U. Alumni Assn. (nat. pres. 1968-70), Better Bus. Bur. Chgo. (council, dir.), Chgo. Assn. Commerce and Industry, Council Fgn. Relations, Alpha Delta Sigma, Beta Gamma Sigma, Delta Sigma Pi, Phi Gamma Delta. Baptist (trustee). Clubs: Sky (N.Y.C.); Chicago, Mid-America, Executives, Economic (Chgo.); Kenilworth; Westmoreland Country (Wilmette, Ill.); Pine Valley Golf (Clementon, N.J.). Home: 132 Oxford Rd Kenilworth IL 60043 Office: Marsteller Inc 1 E Wacker Dr Chicago IL 60601

CHRISTIAN, THOMAS MICHAEL, real estate developer; b. Detroit, July 3, 1945; s. Frank B. and Mary Helen (Winand) C.; B.S., U. Mich.; 1 dau., Lauren E. With Peat, Marwick, Mitchell & Co., Detroit, 1968-72, Flair Devel. Co., Dearborn, Mich., 1973-78; v.p. fin. T.J. Parrent, Inc., Dearborn, 1978—. Served with AUS, 1969-70. C.P.A., Mich. Mem. Am. Mgmt. Assn., Am. Inst. C.P.A.'s, Mich.

Assn. C.P.A.'s, Detroit Econ. Club. Republican. Presbyterian. Clubs: Plaza (Chgo.), Detroit Yacht. Office: 1014 Parklane Towers W Dearborn MI 48126

CHRISTIAN, WILLIAM LAMAR, clin. psychologist; b. Chattanooga, June 27, 1941; s. Eugene Lee and Thelma Alice (Howard) C.; B.S. magna cum laude, U. Tenn., Chattanooga, 1974; M.S., Auburn U., 1976, Ph.D., 1978. Psychology grad. asst. East Ala. Mental Health Center, Opelika, 1975-76; intern in psychology Central State Hosp., Milledgeville, Ga., 1977-78; clin. psychologist Moccasin Bend Mental Health Inst., Chattanooga, 1978-80, VA Med. Center, Marion, Ind., 1980—. Served with USAF, 1959-61. Mem. Am. Psychol. Assn., Southeastern Psychol. Assn., Chattanooga Psychol. Assn. Contbr. articles in field to profl. jours. Home: 1713 Quarry Rd Apt 224 Williamsburg Manor Marion IN 46952 Office: Veterans Administration Medical Center Marion IN 46952

CHRISTIANSEN, PAUL ALGER, business exec.; b. Detroit, July 3, 1928; s. Alger Cornelius and Gladys Marie (Volz) C.; B.S., Wayne State U., 1948, M.A., 1949; postgrad. U. Minn., 1950-60, Harvard U., 1978-79; m. Irene A. Adams, July 16, 1954; children—Paul Alger II, John Adams. Instr., Va. Poly. Inst. and State U., Blacksburg, 1949-51; accountant Arthur Andersen & Co., Kansas City, Mo., 1952-55; sr. tax accountant Arthur Young & Co., Kansas City, 1956-58; prof. acctg. U. Mo., Kansas City, 1958-80; owner Paul A. Christiansen, C.P.A., Kansas City, 1958—; pres. Metal Engineered Structures, Inc., Kansas City, 1963—, Paul A. Christiansen & Co., Blue Springs, Mo., 1966—, Lake Village Corp., Blue Springs, 1975—, Oak Grove Med Center, Inc. (Mo.), 1979—. Mem. Jackson County Bond Adv. Commn., 1967-73; chmn. 4th Congl. Dist. Republican Com., 1968; mem. Jackson County Rep. Com., 1968-72; pres. Independence Rep. Club, 1968-72. Decorated King Fredrik II Medal (Norway); C.P.A., Mo. Mem. Am. Inst. C.P.A.'s, Mo. Soc. C.P.A.'s, AAUP (chpt. pres. 1964-65), Nat. Assn. Home Builders, Eastern Jackson County Builders and Developers Assn., Beta Alpha Psi. Contbr. articles to profl. jours. Home: 3333 Lake Shore Dr Blue Springs MO 64015 Office: 333 Lake Village Blvd Blue Springs MO 64015

CHRISTIANSON, ELIN BALLANTYNE, librarian, civic worker; b. Gary, Ind., Nov. 11, 1936; d. Donald B. and Dorothy May (Dunning) Ballantyne; B.A., U. Chgo., 1958, M.A., 1961, certificate advanced studies, 1974; m. Stanley David Christianson, July 25, 1959; children—Erica, David. Asst. librarian, then librarian J. Walter Thompson Co., Chgo., 1959-68; library cons., 1968—; part-time lectr. Grad. Library Sch., U. Chgo., 1981—. Chmn. Hobart Am. Revolution Bicentennial Commn., 1974-76; bd. dirs. Hobart Hist. Soc., 1973—, pres., 1980—; pres. League Women Voters, Hobart, 1977-79. Recipient Laura Bracken award Hobart Jaycees, 1976; certificate achievement Ind. Am. Revolution Bicentennial Commn., 1975. Mem. Am. Assn. Info. Sci., Am., Ind. library assns., Spl. Libraries Assn. (chmn. advt. and mktg. div. 1967-68), Am. Assn. State and Local History, AAUW (pres. Hobart br. 1975-77), U. Chgo. Grad. Library Sch. Alumni Assn. (v.p. 1971-74, 76-77, pres. 1977-79). Unitarian. Author: Non-Professional and Paraprofessional Staff in Special Libraries, 1973; Directory of Library Resources in Northwest Indiana, 1976; Old Settlers Cemetery, 1976; New Special Libraries: A Summary of Research, 1980; Daniel Nash Handy and the Special Library Movement, 1980; co-author: Subject Headings in Advertising, Marketing and Communications Media, 1964; Special Libraries: A Guide for Management, 1981. Address: 141 Beverly Blvd Hobart IN 46342

CHRISTIE, ADRIAN JOSEPH, pathologist; b. Cardiff, Wales, Dec. 1, 1940; s. Maxwell and Sonia (Samuel) C.; came to U.S., 1975; M.D., Welsh Nat. Sch. Medicine, 1964; m. Mynetta Ann Michaelson, Dec. 12, 1965; children—Helen, Leona, Gavin. Resident in pathology Mt. Sinai Hosp., N.Y.C., 1967-68; asst. lectr. pathology Middlesex Hosp. Med. Sch., London, 1968-69; sr. registrar Southmead Hosp., Bristol, Eng., 1970-73; pathologist Grace and I.O.D.E. hosps., Windsor, Ont., Can., 1973-75, Detroit-Macomb Hosps. Assn., Detroit, 1976, Cottage Hosp., Grosse Pointe, Mich., 1976—, Kern Hosp., Detroit, 1979—; clin. asst. prof. Wayne State U. Med. Sch., Detroit. Diplomate Am. Bd. Pathology. Fellow Royal Coll. Physicians and Surgeons (Can.), Am. Soc. Clin. Pathologists, Coll. Am. Pathologists, Internat. Acad. Pathology; mem. Royal Coll. Pathologists, AMA, Wayne County Med. Soc., Mich. Soc. Pathologists (med. care ins. com.). Jewish. Club: H.M.C.S. Hunter (Windsor). Author papers complications silicone joint implants. Home: 1010 W Lincoln St Birmingham MI 48009 Office: 11800 E 12 Mile Rd Warren MI 48093

CHRISTIE, JOHN EDWIN, constrn. co. exec.; b. Ridgewood, N.J., July 11, 1929; s. Wallace Thurston and Marion Isabel (Baker) C.; B.A. cum laude in Math., Amherst Coll., 1951. Various positions in heavy constrn., 1954-74; chief estimator, Pa. constrn. mgr. John J. Dunn Constrn. Co., Runnemede, N.J., 1974-76; owner Christie and Sandy Co., Mickleton, N.J., 1976-77; v.p. S.J. Groves Overseas, Nigeria, 1977-78; sr. estimator S.J. Groves & Sons, Mpls., 1978-80, v.p., area mgr., Plymouth, Minn., 1980—. Served with AUS, 1952-54. Mem. Am. Mgmt. Assn., Asso. Gen. Contractors. Republican. Presbyterian. Home: 15725 County Rd 15 Plymouth MN 55447 Office: 10000 Hwy 55 West Plymouth MN 55441

CHRISTIE, WALTER SCOTT, state ofcl.; b. Indpls., 1922; s. Walter Scott and Nina Lilian (Warfel) C.; B.S. in Bus. Adminstrn., Butler U., 1948. With Roy J. Pile & Co., C.P.A.'s, Indpls., 1948-56, Howard E. Nyhart Co., Inc., actuarial consultants, Indpls., 1956-62; with Ind. Dept. Ins., Indpls., 1962—, dep. commr., 1966-74, adminstrv. officer, 1974-79, sr. examiner, 1979—. Bd. dirs. Delt House Corp., Butler U. Served with AUS, 1942-45. Named Ky. Col.; C.P.A., Ind.; certified fin. examiner. Mem. Ind. Assn. C.P.A.'s, Soc. Fin. Examiners, Indpls. Acturarial Club, Nat. Assn. Ins. Commrs. (chmn. Zone IV life and health com. 1970-75). Episcopalian (asso. vestryman 1948-60). Club: Optimist (dir.). Home: 620 E 53d St Indianapolis IN 46220 Office: 509 State Office Bldg 100 N Senate Ave Indianapolis IN 46204

CHRISTIN, VIOLET MARGUERITE, ret. banker; b. Chgo., Oct. 4, 1903; d. Charles A. and Eva M. (Bosse) Christin; student Northwestern U., 1936-37, Am. Inst. Banking, 1955-75; Ph.D., Colo. State Christian Coll. With Nat. Bank Austin, 1922-76, asst. sec., 1953-57, sec., 1957-65, sec., asst. v.p., 1965-75, also cons., sec. mktg. com., 1977-79. Mem. Am. Inst. Banking, Ill. Bankers Assn. (50 yr. club), Assn. Chgo. Bank Women, Nat. Assn. Bank Women, Ill. Group. Nat. Assn. Bank Women, Chgo. Financial Advertisers (life mem.; Eagle award 1977, dir., treas.). Clubs: Executives, Advertising, Press (Chgo.). Home: 805 N Grove Ave Oak Park IL 60302

CHRISTMAS, GEORGIA LEE, educator; b. Pittsburg, Kans., July 16, 1945; d. George Abraham and Vivian Marie (Nickell) Hull Gehrer; B.S., Kans. State Tchrs. Coll., Emporia, 1967; M.S. Ed., No. Ill. U., 1974; m. Philip Lee Christmas, Nov. 24, 1965; children—Susan Leann, Laura Jean. Tchr., Unified Sch. Dist. 259 Wichita, Kans., 1967-69, York Community High Sch., Elmhurst, Ill., 1970-74; instr. Sauk Valley Community Coll., Dixon, Ill., 1974-76; food service edn. coordintor Wichita Area Vocat. Tech. Sch., 1976-80; coordinator support service, food service Wichita Public Schs., 1980—; tchr. USD 259, 1981—; mem. Govs. Adv. Com. Food Service and Lodging Standards, 1979—. Sec., state senatorial campaign, 1980. Mem. Kans. Culinary Assn. (culinarian of yr. 1979), Am. Culinary Fedn. (sec. treas. 1977-80), Am. Sch. Food Service Assn., Am. Vocat. Assn., Kans. Public Health Assn., Jaycee Jaynes. Democrat. Mem. Ch. of Christ. Home: 717 Atherton St Maize KS 67101 Office: Dept Home Econs Wichita High Sch North 1437 Rochester Wichita KS 67203

CHRISTOPHER, NORMAN FRANKLIN, physicist; b. Irvine, Ky., Sept. 23, 1930; s. Thomas Ashcraft and Anna Maude (Turner) C.; m. Jane Anne Dean, June 16, 1952; children—Paula, Phyllis. B.A., Ky. Wesleyan Coll., 1952; M.S., Ohio U., 1969. Shift chemist Liberty Powder Def. Corp., Baraboo, Wis., 1952-54; shift supr. Goodyear Atomic Corp., Piketon, Ohio, 1954-57, sect. head mass spectrometry dept., 1957-79, asst. gen. mgrs.' staff, 1979—. Mem. Am. Soc. Mass Spectrometry. Home: 406 S Market St Waverly OH 45690 Office: PO Box 628 Piketon OH 45661

CHRISTOPHERSEN, EDWARD R., psychologist, educator; b. Oak Park, Ill., July 15, 1940; s. Walter and Vivian Christophersen; B.A., So. Ill. U., 1964; M.A., Mich. State U., 1965; Ph.D., U. Kans., 1970; m. Miki Richardson, Dec. 30, 1971; children—Hunter, Catherine. Asst. prof. dept. human devel. U. Kans., Lawrence, 1970-75, asso. prof., 1975-80, asso. prof. dept. pediatrics, 1975-80; prof. U. Kans. Med. Center, Kansas City, 1980—. USPHS fellow, U. Kans., 1967-69. Mem. Soc. Pediatric Research, Soc. Behavioral Medicine, Am. Psychol. Assn., Ambulatory Pediatrics Assn., Physicians for Automotive Safety. Author: Little People: Guidelines for Common Sense Child Rearing, 1977. Office: Univ Kansas Med Center Dept Pediatrics 39th and Rainbow Blvd Kansas City KS 66103

CHRISTOPHERSON, WESTON, retail chain co. exec.; b. Walum, N.D., May 5, 1925; s. Carl and Ermie (Larsen) C.; B.S., U. N.D., 1949, J.D., 1951; m. Myrna Christensen, June 8, 1951; children—Mia Karen, Mari Louisa, Kari Marie. Admitted to N.D. bar, 1951, Ill. bar, 1952; with Jewel Cos., Inc., Chgo., 1951—, v.p., gen. mgr. Jewel Home Shopping Service, 1963-67, exec. v.p., gen. mgr. Osco Drug, Inc., 1965-67, pres. Jewel Home Shopping Service, Osco Drug, Inc., 1967-70, pres. Jewel Cos., Inc., 1970-80, Chief exec. officer, 1970—, chmn. bd., 1980—, also dir.; dir. Ill. Tool Works, Borg-Warner, Aurrera, S.A., Mexico City, Ill. Bell Telephone Co., GATX Corp., Continental Ill. Corp., Continental Ill. Nat. Bank & Trust Co. Vice chmn. bd. trustees U. Chgo.; mem. Chgo. Com., Chgo. United, Met. Chgo. United Way/Crusade of Mercy. Mem. Northwestern U. Assos., U. Ill. Found. Presbyn. Clubs: Economic, Chicago, Casino, Onwentsia, Old Elm, Commercial, Commonwealth. Home: 1696 S Oak Knoll Dr Lake Forest IL 60045 Office: 5725 E River Rd Chicago IL 60631

CHRON, GUSTAV NICHOLAS, ednl. adminstr.; b. Chgo., June 6, 1926; s. Nicholas Constantine and Jennie (Athans) C.; B.A., DePaul U., 1952; M.A., Northwestern U., 1954; B.A. in Aeros., Stanton U., 1965, Ph.D., 1976; M. Ed., Loyola U., Chgo., 1969; J.D. (hon.), Clinton U., 1971; D.Phil., Met. Coll. Inst., London, 1974; m. Helen Hoegerl, Sept. 18, 1948; children—Edward, Karen, Timothy. Mem. staff Chgo. Better Bus. Bur., 1954-58; tchr. Northbrook (Ill.) elementary schs., 1958-60, Northbrook Jr. High Sch., 1960-63, Glenbrook South High Sch., Glenview, Ill., 1963-64; adminstrv. asst. Comsat div. Trust Dept. Continental Ill. Nat. Bank, Chgo., 1964-65; prin. Westmoor Sch., Northbrook, 1966—; dir. Northbrook Dist. 28 Summer Sch., 1971, 77; asst. prof. aeros. Grad. Research Inst., East Coast U., 1975—. Mem. adv. bd. Am. Security Council. Served with USNR, 1943-46. Decorated Air medal, Purple Heart, Navy Commendation medal; named to Aviation Hall of Fame. Mem. Nat., Ill. sch. prins. assns., Am. Security Council, Navy League, Navy Inst., Am. Legion, Assn. Naval Aviation, Tailhook Assn., Am. Mil. Inst., Nat. Rifle Assn., Am. Def. Preparedness Assn., Vets. OSS, Assn. Former Intelligence Officers, Nat. Intelligence Study Center, U.S. Parachute Assn., 82d Airborne Div. Assn., Nat. Eagle Scout Assn., Air Force Assn., Am. Philatelic Soc., Phi Delta Kappa, Delta Theta Phi, Pi Gamma Mu. Club: Moose. Home: Chicago IL Office: 2500 Cherry Ln Northbrook IL 60062

CHRONIC, JANET ELIZABETH, restaurant chain exec.; b. Robinson, Ill., Oct. 12, 1953; d. Floyd W. and Cora E. (Coulter) C.; B.S., So. Ill. U., 1975; postgrad. Ind. U.-Purdue U., Indpls. High sch. bus. tchr., Lawrenceville, Ill., 1976-77; asst. restaurant mgr. Burger Chef Restaurant, Robinson, 1977-78, Zionsville, Ill., 1978-79, restaurant mgr., Carmel, Ind., 1979, mktg. services mgr. Burger Chef Systems, Indpls., 1979-81, mgr. systems mktg., 1981—. Active Big Sisters Indpls. Mem. Am. Mgmt. Assn., Nat. Restaurant Assn., Sigma Kappa (founder Gamma Kappa chpt. So. Ill. U. 19—). Office: Burger Chef Systems PO Box 927 College Park Indianapolis IN 46206

CHRONISTER, HARRY B., state legislator; b. Schuyler, Nebr., Sept. 30, 1922; ed. Spartan Sch. Aeros., Tulsa; m. Katherine Coufal, Oct. 12, 1946; children—Mary Christine Chronister Sinieski, Mark, Janet. Sec.-treas. Wagner Mills, Inc.; mem. Nebr. Legislature, 1979—. Former mem. Schuyler City Council, Schuyler Sch. Bd., 19—; former sec. treas. Colfax County Republican party; former mem. Nebr. Rep. Central Com.; alt. del. Rep. Nat. Conv., 1976. Served with USAAF, World War II. Mem. Am. Legion. Roman Catholic. Club: K.C., Rotary. Office: 1303 Colfax St Schuyler NE 68661*

CHU, ALBERT, motel exec.; b. China, July 10, 1933; came to U.S., 1976, naturalized, 1976; s. Hsi-Drin and Bau-Tsen C.; B.A., Nat. Taiwan U., 1959; m. Chia-Ling Sun, June 15, 1966; children—Bob, Jaime, Sabrina. Supr., gen. agt. Korean Nat. Airlines, Far Eastern Airlines, Taiwan, 1959-61; sales agt. Civil Air Transport, Taiwan, 1961-66; mgr. Chen Chang Wood Industry, Taiwan, 1966-75; pres. Chen Chang Internat. Corp., Taiwan, also Cleve., 1975-77; owner Sheridan and Gateway Motels, Dayton, Ohio, 1977-79; pres. Chu's Dayton Motels, Inc., 1979—. Mem. Dayton C. of C., Hotel Motel Assn. Office: Chu's Dayton Motels Inc 1891 Harshman Rd Dayton OH 45424

CHU, JOHNSON CHIN SHENG, physician; b. Peiping, China, Sept. 26, 1918; s. Harry S. P. and Florence (Young) C.; M.D., St. John's U., 1945; m. Sylvia Cheng, June 11, 1949; children—Stephen, Timothy. Came to U.S., 1948, naturalized, 1957. Intern U. Hosp., Shanghai, 1944-45; resident, research fellow N.Y.U. Hosp., 1948-50; resident, physician in charge State Hosp. and Med. Center, Weston, W.Va., 1951-56; chief services, clin. dir. State Hosp., Logansport, Ind., 1957—. Fellow Am. Psychiat. Assn., Am. Coll. Chest Physicians; mem. A.M.A., Ind. Med. Assn., Cass County Med. Soc., A.A.A.S. Research in cardiology and pharmacology. Contbr. articles profl. jours. Home: E 36 Lake Shafer Monticello IN 47960 Office: Southeastern Medical Center Walton IN 46994

CHUA, CHENG LOK, educator; b. Singapore, Jan. 5, 1938; s. Yew Cheng and Kuo Hui (Tan) C.; came to U.S., 1956, naturalized, 1965; B.A., DePauw U., 1960; M.A., U. Conn., 1962, Ph.D., 1968; m. Gretchen Taeko Sasaki, July 26, 1965; children—Iu-Hui Jarrell, Poh-Pheng Jaime. Part-time instr. English, U. Conn., Storrs, 1960-65; asst. prof. English, U. Mich., Ann Arbor, 1965-72; lectr., sr. lectr. English, U. Singapore, 1972-74; lectr. English, Calif. State U. at Fresno, 1974-76; Nat. Endowment Humanities postdoctoral fellow Yale U., 1976-77, vis. fellow comparative lit., 1976-77; asso. prof. Moorhead (Minn.) State U., 1977-81. Australasian Univs. Lang. and Lit. Assn. grantee, 1975; Am. Council Learned Socs. grantee, 1978; Nat. Endowment Humanities summer fellow, 1980. Mem. MLA, Nat. Council Tchrs. English, Multi-Ethnic Lit. of U.S., AAUP, Nat. Assn. Interdisciplinary Ethnic Studies. Home: 1102 S 16th St Moorhead MN 56560

CHUANG, RICHARD YO, educator; b. Shanghai, China, Mar. 9, 1939; came to U.S., 1962; s. Han K. and Rose C.; LL.B., Nat. Taiwan U., 1961; M.A. (fgn. student scholar), U. Minn., 1964, Ph.D. (fgn. student scholar), 1970; cert. (scholar) Parker Sch. Fgn. and Comparative law, Columbia U., 1973; m. Elsie Yao Chuang, Sept. 4, 1965; children—Erik, Cliff, Fleur. Vis. asso. prof. law Nat. Taiwan U., 1971-72; vis. asso. prof. polit. sci. Nat. Chung Hsin U., Taipei, Taiwan, 1973-74; asst. prof. No. State Coll., Aberdeen, S.D., 1968-71, asso. prof., 1971-76, prof. polit. sci., 1976—, acting chmn. dept. social sci., 1979—, chmn. dept. social sci., 1981; NSF vis. prof. Republic of China, 1973-74; participant, scholar Diplomat Seminars, U.S. Dept. State, 1981; cons. Mem. Am. Polit. Sci. Assn., Am. Soc. Internat. Law. Democrat. Buddhist. Club: Mason. Author: The International Air Transport Association, 1972; editor No. Social Sci. Rev., 1975—; contbr. articles to profl. jours. Home: 216 21st Ave NE Aberdeen SD 57401 Office: No State Coll Aberdeen SD 57401

CHUBICK, LESLEY IRWIN, advt. exec.; b. Clinton, Iowa, Nov. 17, 1943; s. Delvin Dow and Anna Belle (Nichols) C.; B.S., Central Mo. State U., 1967; m. Markey Lou Ewing, July 11, 1980; children by previous marriage—Lesley Irwin, Jeannette Louise; 1 stepchild, Carol Ann. Lay-out artist/copywriter Sears, Roebuck & Co., Kansas City, Mo., 1973-75; advt. artist/copy writer Medco Jewelry Corp., Overland Park, Kans., 1975-78; free-lance work in advt., Merriam, Kan., 1978-79; advt. mgr. Knit-Rite Inc., Kansas City, Mo., 1979—. Bd. dirs. Quail Valley Coop., 1980—, sec., 1980—, editor bi-weekly Quail Valley Newsletter, 1980—. Recipient Award of Excellence, Advt. Artists Guild of Kansas City, Mo., 1970; cert. of completion Avila Coll. Seminar in Coop. Mgmt., 1980. Mem. Plains Assn. Clubs: Ad of Kansas City, Art Dirs., Sportscar. Home: 10914 Haskins Lenexa KS 66210 Office: PO Box 208 2020 Grand Ave Kansas City MO 64141

CHUCK, KENNETH CHARLES, restaurant exec.; b. Sheboygan, Wis., Jan. 28, 1927; s. Charles and Jessie (Spendal) C.; student pub. schs.; m. Mary Ann Susan, Apr. 15, 1950; children—Karen, Nancy, Kenneth L. Formed Chuck's Supper Club, Oconomowoc, Wis., 1947—, pres., 1968—; pres. Hospitality Industry Inc., 1975—, So. Gateway Inc., 1973—. Town constable Town of Summit, 1965-73, mem. Planning Bd., 1968-77; officer Summit Vol. Fire Dept., 1971, 72, 73. Served with AUS, 1945-47. Recipient Golden Knife award Am. Dairy Assn., 1976. Mem. U.S. Trotting Assn., Tavern League Wis., Nat., Wis. (dir.) restaurant assns., Oconomowoc C. of C. (dir.), Wis. Fans for Auto Racing (pres.). Roman Catholic. Club: Kiwanis. Home: 37304 Valley Rd Oconomowoc WI 53066 Office: 37238 Valley Rd Oconomowoc WI 53066

CHUNG, HYUNG DOO, neuropathologist; b. Kyung-Nam, Korea, Nov. 15, 1940; came to U.S., 1970, naturalized, 1976; m. Jae Yul and Yuh Ah (Park) C.; M.D., Pusan Nat. U., 1965; m. Jeung Hie Choi, Apr. 12, 1968; children—Sung Chung, Steven Chung, Cindy Chung. Intern, Bronx-Lebanon Hosp. & Med. Center, Bronx, N.Y., 1970-71; resident, Montefiore Hosp. & Med. Center, Bronx, 1971-75; staff neuropathologist VA Med. Center, St. Louis, 1975—; cons. neuropathologist Firmin Desloge Hosp., Cardinal Glenon Children's Hosp., St. Louis, 1980—; asst. clin. prof. pathology St. Louis U. Med. Sch., 1979-80, asst. prof. pathology, 1980—. Served with Korean Army, 1965-68. Diplomate Am. Bd. Pathology. Mem. Internat. Acad. Pathology, Am. Assn. Neuropathologists, Internat. Soc. Neuropathology. Home: 14350 Rainey Lake Dr Chesterfield MO 63017 Office: 915 N Grand Blvd Saint Louis MO 63125

CHUNG, OKKYUNG KIM, chemist; b. Seoul, Korea, Apr. 11, 1936; came to U.S., 1959, naturalized, 1972; d. Changshik and Yoonam (Hahn) Kim; B.S., Ewha Womens U., Korea, 1959; M.S., Kans. State U., 1965, Ph.D., 1973; m. Do Sup Chung, Nov. 22, 1961; children—Clara K., Josephine K. Grad. teaching asst. Kans. State U., Manhattan, 1961-64, research asst., 1964-66, 68-71, postdoctoral research asso., 1973-74, adj. asso. prof., 1975—; research chemist U.S. Grain Mktg. Research Lab., U.S. Dept. Agr., Manhattan, 1974—; lectr. in field. Recipient Gold Medal award Ewha Women's U., 1959; W.E. Long Merit award So. Bakers Assn., 1971. Mem. Am. Assn. Cereal Chemists (sect. chmn. 1977-78), Am. Chem. Soc., Am. Oil Chemists Soc., Sigma Xi, Phi Lambda Upsilon, Gamma Sigma Delta. Contbr. articles to profl. jours.; asso. editor Cereal Chemistry, 1978—. Home: 200 Carlisle Terr Manhattan KS 66502 Office: 1515 College Ave Manhattan KS 66502

CHUNG, TAE SOO, physician; b. Kyungsan, Korea, Mar. 3, 1943; s. Doo Pyo and Jung Sook (Suh) C.; came to U.S., 1972; M.D., Kyungpook Nat. U., (Korea), 1967; m. Chung Wha Rhim, Dec. 5, 1969; children—Sung Joon, Young Joon. Intern, West Suburban Hosp., Oak Park, Ill., 1972-73; resident in therapeutic radiology VA Med. Center, Hines, Ill., 1974-76, staff therapeutic radiologist, 1977—, chief of resident tng., 1977—; clin. asst. prof. radiology U. Health Scis., Chgo. Med. Schs., 1981—. Served to capt. Korean Army, 1968-71. Diplomate Am. Bd. Radiology. Mem. Am. Soc. Therapeutic Radiologists, Radiol. Soc. N.Am. Korean Presbyterian. Home: 12954 Shawnee Rd Palos Heights IL 60463 Office: 1st Ave and Roosevelt Rd Hines IL 60141

CHURCH, IRENE ZABOLY, personnel services co. exec.; b. Cleve., Feb. 18, 1947; d. Bela Paul and Irene Elizabeth (Chandas) Zaboly; student public schs.; children—Irene Elizabeth, Elizabeth Anne. Personnel cons., Cleve., 1965; sec., Cleve., 1966-68; personnel cons., Cleve., 1968-70; owner, pres. Oxford Personnel, Euclid, Ohio, 1973—; chmn. bd. Oxford Temporaries, Inc., Euclid, 1979—; guest lectr. in field. Fund raiser Better Bus. Bur., 1973; troop leader Lake Erie council Girl Scouts Am., 1980—; mem. Christian action com. Federated Ch., 1981—, also mem. Martha Mary Circle. Mem. Nat. Assn. Personnel Consultants (co-chmn. ethics com. 1977-78), Ohio Assn. Personnel Consultants (trustee 1975-80, 1st v.p., chmn. bus. practices and ethics 1976-78, chmn. resolutions com. 1981—), Greater Cleve. Assn. Personnel Consultants (1st v.p., chmn. bus. practices and ethics 1974-76, pres., recipient Vi Pender award 1976-77, adv., chmn. Vi Pender award 1977-78, chmn. award 1980, chmn. arbitration 1980—, chmn. fund raising 1980—, state trustee 1975-80), Euclid C. of C. (small bus. com. 1981—), Am. Bus. Women's Assn. Home: 8 Ridgecrest Dr Chagrin Falls OH 44022 Office: Oxford Personnel 711 Babbitt Rd Euclid OH 44123

CHURCH, JAY KAY, psychologist, educator; b. Wichita, Kans., Jan. 18, 1927; s. Kay Iverson and Gertrude (Parrish) C.; B.A., David Lipscomb Coll., 1948; M.A., Ball State U., 1961; Ph.D., Purdue U., 1963; m. Dorothy Agnes Fellerhoff, May 21, 1976; children—Karen Patrice Church Edwards, Caryn Annice Church Casey, Rex Warren, Max Roger. Chemist, Auburn Rubber Corp., 1948-49; salesman Midwestern United Life Ins. Co., 1949-52; owner, operator Tour-Rest Motel, Waterloo, Ind., 1952-66; tchr., guidance dir., public schs., Hamilton, Ind., 1955-61; counselor Washington Twp. (Ind.) Schs., Indpls., 1961-62; asst. prof. psychology Ball State U., 1963-67, asso.

prof., 1967-71, prof., 1971—, chmn. dept. ednl. psychology, 1970-74, dir. advanced grad. programs in ednl. psychology, 1978—; pvt. practice psychology, 1963—. Mem. Am. Psychol. Assn., Midwest Psychol. Assn., Ind. Psychol. Assn., Nat. Assn. Sch. Psychologists. Home: 8501 N Ravenwood Dr Muncie IN 47302 Office: Ball State U Muncie IN 47306

CHURCH, MARGARET, educator; b. Boston, Apr. 8, 1920; d. Joseph W. and Sophy (Phillips) Church; A.B., Radcliffe Coll., 1941, Ph.D., 1944; M.A., Columbia U., 1942. Instr. English, Temple U., 1944-46, Duke U., 1946-53; asst. prof. English Purdue U., Lafayette, Ind., 1953-61, asso. prof. English, 1961-65, prof. English, 1965—, also chmn. comparative lit. Mem. Am. Comparative Lit. Assn., Midwest MLA (pres. 1977), MLA, Phi Beta Kappa (hon.). Episcopalian. Author: Time and Reality: Studies in Contemporary Literature, 1963; Don Quixote, The Knight of La Mancha, 1971; also articles in field. Editorial bd. Modern Fiction Studies, 1968, co-editor, 1971—. Home: 808 N Rd 400 W West Lafayette IN 47906

CHURCHILL, DENNIS WILLIAM, monument mfg. co. exec.; b. Dubuque, Iowa, Aug. 23, 1944; s. Willis Bernard and Rita Marie (Miller) C.; asso. Lansing Bus. U., 1964; student Lansing Community Coll., 1963-64; m. Sally Jill Scheidt, Jan. 16, 1965; children—Catherine Anne, Christina Marie, Jared Andrew. Partner, div. Churchill Enterprises, C & B Trucking Co., Lansing, Mich., 1964-67; sales mgr. Yunker Memls., Inc., Lansing, 1967-69, asst. v.p., 1969-80, pres., owner, 1980—. Pres., P.T.A., Wainwright Sch., Lansing, Mich., 1971; chief Indian Guide program YMCA, Owosso, Mich., 1979-80. Mem. Monument Builders N. Am. (dir. Mich. div.), Lansing C. of C., Lansing Philatelic Soc. Democrat. Roman Catholic. Clubs: Rosicrucians. Inventor door lock and key-less locking device for automobiles. Home: 12463 Spruce Ln Forest Green Estates Perry MI 48872 Office: 1116 E Mount Hope Ave Lansing MI 48910

CHURCHILL, LEE CALDWELL, educator; b. N.Y.C., Feb. 23, 1925; d. William Edward and Hortense (Storer) Caldwell; B.A., N.J. Coll. for Women, 1947; M.A. in English, U. Wis., 1952, M.S.Ed., 1955; M.S. Adult Edn., Ind. U., 1977; children—Andrew, John, David. Test writer Ednl. Testing Service, Princeton, N.J., 1949-51; tchr. secondary English, Masters Sch., Dobbs Ferry, N.Y., 1952-54; tchr. jr. English, West High Sch., Madison, Wis., 1955-56; fiction editor Saturday Evening Post, Indpls., 1973; instr. in English, Ind. U.-Purdue U., Indpls., 1975—, Ind. Vocat. Tech. Coll., Indpls., 1978—; leader Gt. Books, Seattle, Cin., and Phila. Condr. workshops on leadership LWV. Mem. Am. Bus. Communications Assn., Phi Beta Kappa. Republican. Episcopalian.

CHURCHILL, RUEL VANCE, mathematician; b. Akron, Ind., Dec. 12, 1899; s. Abner Cain and Meldora (Friend) C.; B.S., U. Chgo., 1922; Ph.D., U. Mich., 1929; m. Ruby Sicks, 1922 (dec. 1969); m. 2d, Alice Baldwin Warren, 1972; children—Betty Churchill McMurray, Eugene S. Instr. to prof. U. Mich., Ann Arbor, 1922-65, prof. emeritus, 1965—; researcher U. Freiburg, Germany, 1936; researcher Calif. Inst. Tech., 1950; vis. lectr. U. Wis., Madison, 1941; mathematician USAF, 1944. Mem. Math. Assn. Am., Am. Math. Soc., Phi Beta Kappa. Author: Complex Variables and Applications, 3d edit., 1974; Fourier Series, 3d edit., 1978; Operational Mathematics, 3d edit., 1972. Home: 1231 Wisteria Dr Ann Arbor MI 48104 Office: U Mich Dept Math Ann Arbor MI 48109

CHURLIN, LAURENCE, systems programmer; b. Chgo., Feb. 23, 1944; s. Dewey Thomas and Mary (Hanslick) C.; A.A.S., Prairie State Coll., 1978; m. Georgia Stewart, July 5, 1969; children—Christine, Scott. Supr. computer ops. Field Enterprises Ednl. Corp., Chgo., 1967-70; mgr. computer ops. Systems Data Processing Center, Chgo., 1970-76; mgr. computer ops. Mercy Hosp. and Med. Center, Chgo., 1976-79; systems programmer Mercy Center for Health Care Services, 1979—, pres. Mercy Center Fed. Credit Union. Publicity chmn. Woodgate PTO, 1976-77. Served with USAF, 1963-67. Mem. Matteson Jaycees (sec., Cert. of Merit 1979, Jaycee of Yr. 1979). Roman Catholic. Home: 155 Central St Matteson IL 60443 Office: 1325 N Highland Aurora IL 60506

CHUSID, MICHAEL THOMAS, architect, product designer; b. Chgo., Dec. 8, 1952; s. Frederick M. and Ruth Elaine (Sacks) C.; B.A. in Design, So. Ill. U., 1974; M.Arch., U. Ill., 1977; m. Charlotte Francis Dunn, June 12, 1976; children—Aaron Jacob, Andrew Warren. Designer engring. bldg. products Inryco, Inc., Milw., 1977-79; architect Stubenrauch Assos., Architects and Engrs., Sheboygan, Wis., 1979—; instr. Moraine Park Tech. Inst., Fond du Lac, Wis.; corr. Wis. Jewish Chronicle. Mem. bldg. com., bd. dirs. Congregation Beth El, Sheboygan; mem. John Michael Kohler Arts Center, Sheboygan. Registered architect, Wis. Mem. Sheboygan County Landmarks (dir.), Alpha Rho Chi. Jewish.

CHUTE, ROBERT DONALD, elec. engr., educator; b. Detroit, Nov. 29, 1928; s. George Maynard and Josephine Chute; B.S. in Elec. Engring., U. Mich., 1950; M.S., Wayne State U., 1966; m. Marion Louise Price, June 17, 1950; children—Janet Louise, Lawrence Robert. Control engr. indsl heating div. Gen. Electric Co., Shelbyville, Ind., 1950-57; group leader Chrysler Corp., Warren, Mich., 1957-59; chief product engr. internat. div. Burroughs Corp., Detroit, 1959-73; asso. prof. elec. engring. Lawrence Inst. Tech., Southfield, Mich., 1973—; cons. in indsl. controls, 1969—. Instl. rep. Detroit Met. Area council Boy Scouts Am., 1964-68. Registered profl. engr., Mich., Ind. Mem. IEEE, Am. Soc. Engring. Edn., Nat. Soc. Profl. Engrs., Engring. Soc. Detroit. Presbyterian. Clubs: Just Right, Economic of Detroit. Author: (with George M. Chute) Electronics in Industry, 1971, 5th edit., 1979; patentee in field. Office: 21000 W Ten Mile Rd Southfield MI 48075

CHUTIS, LAURIEANN LUCY, social worker; b. Detroit, Nov. 30, 1942; d. Paul J. and Helen Marie (Shilakes) C.; A.B., U. Mich., 1964, M.S.W., 1966. Community worker Tuskegee (Ala.) Inst., 1966; social worker Catholic Sch. Bd. Head Start, Chgo., 1966; community worker Cath. Charities, Chgo., 1966-70; asst. to dir. Ravenswood Hosp. Community Mental Health Center, Chgo., 1970-72, coordinator consultation and edn. dept., 1972, dir. consultation and edn. dept., 1972—, also cons., trainer therapist; instr. Chgo. Bd. Edn., Northeastern Ill. U., 1974—; guest lectr. various profl. assn. groups, corps., 1975—; pvt. practice individual group and family therapy; 1976—; cons. NIMH, mental health centers, bus. and industry, 1977—. Coordinator Nat. Consultation and Edn. Net working; mem. Salvation Army Community Services Bd., 1978—; mem. com. Chgo. Health Systems Agy., 1980—; mem. Ill. Alcohol Prevention Task Force, 1980—. Mem. Nat. Assn. Social Work, Acad. Certified Social Work, World Fedn. Mental Health, Registry Clin. Social Workers, Nat. Council Community Mental Health Centers (council on Prevention 1977-79), Assn. Consultation-Edn: Service Providers (pres. 1978-79). Contbg. author: To Your Good Health. Contbr. articles to profl. jours. Office: 4550 N Winchester Chicago IL 60640

CHWISTEK, FRANK CHARLES, constrn. co. exec.; b. Cook County, Ill., Dec. 25, 1946; s. Frank Joseph and Julia Chwistek; student Washburn Sch., 1970, Ill. Inst. Tech.; m. Marie Chwistek, Apr. 15, 1974. Cabinetmaker, Vincent Cabinet Co., Chgo., 1979; machine operator/engr. Victor Products Corp., Chgo., 1979—. Served with U.S. Army, 1966-67. Mem. Carpenters Council. Republican. Roman Catholic.

CIANCIO, LARRY G., mfg. co. exec.; b. McAllen, Tex., Aug. 15, 1943; s. Jacob J. and Helen (Sassi) C.; B.A., SUNY, New Platz, 1965; m. Wanda G. Lack, June 18, 1977; children—Brandon, Judson, Matthew, Michael. Asst. mgr. advt. Delaval Separator Co., Poughkeepsie, N.Y., 1969-71; advt. mgr. Norton Co., Troy, N.Y., 1971-73; advt. and sales promotion mgr. PPG Industries, Southfield, Mich., 1974-79, dir. advt., Troy, Mich., 1979—. Mem. Auto Advertisers Council, Adcraft Club Detroit, Bus. Profl. Advt. Assn., Sportscasters of Detroit, Automotive Service Industries Assn., Young Exec. Forum, U.S. Auto Club. Roman Catholic. Home: 22019 Shadybrook Rd Novi MI 48050 Office: 2155 W Big Beaver Rd Troy MI 48084

CIATTEO, CARMEN THOMAS, psychiatrist; b. Clifton Heights, Pa., May 25, 1921; s. Ralph and Grace (Manette) C.; A.B. in Chemistry, U. Pa., 1947; M.D., Loyola U., Chgo., 1951; m. Lucille Dolores Ranum, Nov. 1, 1957; children—William, Jane, Thomas. Intern, Mercy Hosp., Chgo.; resident Fitzsimons Army Hosp., Denver, 1952-53, Hines (Ill.) VA Hosp., 1957-59; practice medicine specializing in psychiatry, Joliet, Ill., 1959-72; cons. Ill. Dept. Corrections, Joliet, correctional and forensic psychiatrist, 1966, psychiatrist VA hosps., 1959; cons. Dept. Vocat. Rehab., 1959-72, Matrimonial Tribunal Diocese Joliet, 1959-76; cons. Fed. Prison System, U.S. Dept. Justice, Chgo., 1975-76, 77—, correctional and forensic psychiatrist, 1977—; tchr. nursing tng. Hines VA Hosp., 1957-59. Served with USAF, 1942-46, 51-56. Diplomate Am. Bd. Psychiatry and Neurology. Mem. Ill. Psychiat. Soc., Am. Psychiat. Assn., Am. Acad. Psychiatry and Law, Am. Correctional Assn. Democrat. Roman Catholic. Home: Rt #2 135 Little Creek Lockport IL 60441

CICCONE, WILLIAM, data processing exec.; b. St. Louis, Apr. 11, 1937; s. Gerardo and Frances (Caputo) C.; student parochial schs., St. Louis; children—Anna Maria, Anthony William, Mary Frances, Mark Olan. Data processing mgr. Comml. Union-N. British Group, Kansas City, Mo., Chgo., 1958-61; data processing mgr. Electronic Pub. Co., Inc., Chgo., 1961; data processing cons. Mgmt. Assistance, Inc., Chgo., 1961-62; data processing mgr. Cruttenden Podesta & Miller, Chgo., 1962-63; v.p. Data Systems Training Corp., Hammond, Ind., 1963; pres., chmn. Illiana Data Processing Services, Inc., Tinley Park, Ill., 1963—. Trustee Twp. of Orland (Ill.), 1977—, collector, 1976-77, chmn. youth commn., 1976—, youth service bur. adv. bd., 1978—; Ill. State rep. legis. aide, 1977—; bd. dirs. Cath. Grad. Sch. Conf., 1975-78; chmn./pres. Cath. Central Parochial Basketball League, 1966-78; chmn. Sch. Dist. 135 Sch. Bd. Caucus, 1978; sec. Village of Orland Park Planning Commn., 1965-69. Served with USAF, 1955-58. Cert. data processor. Mem. Twp. Ofcls. of Ill. (2d v.p. collector div. 1976-77, dir. 1979—), Twp. Ofcls. of Cook County (dir. 1979—, sec. 1981—). Democrat. Roman Catholic. Home: PO Box 174 Orland Park IL 60462 Office: 16860 Oak Park Ave PO Box 399 Tinley Park IL 60477

CICIRELLI, VICTOR GEORGE, psychologist; b. Miami, Fla., Oct. 1, 1926; s. Felix and Rene (DeMaria) C.; B.S. in Chemistry, U. Notre Dame, 1947; M.A. in Philosophy, U. Ill., 1950; M.Ed. in Counseling, U. Miami, 1958; Ph.D. in Ednl. Psychology (Univ. fellow), U. Mich., 1964; Ph.D. in Devel. Psychology, Mich. State U., 1971; m. Jean Solveson, Aug. 9, 1953; children—Anna, Michael, Gregory. Asst. prof. ednl. psychology U. Mich., 1963-65; dir. student teaching U. Pa., 1965-67; asso. prof. early childhood edn. Ohio U., 1967-69; prof. devel. and aging psychology Purdue U., West Lafayette, Ind., 1970—, dir. devel. psychology program, 1977-78, 80-81; cons. in field. Office Edn. fellow Inst. Cognitive Learning, U. Wis., 1969-70; Adminstrn. on Aging postdoctoral fellow Portland State U., 1979; NSF summer inst. scholar, 1956, 59, 60; OEO grantee, 1968-69, 71-73; Office Edn. grantee, 1972, 73; Nat. Inst. Edn. grantee, 1973-74; Office Child Devel. grantee, 1973-74; Nat. Ret. Tchrs. Assn.-Am. Assn. Ret. Persons Andrus Found. grantee, 1978-81. Fellow Am. Psychol. Assn.; mem. Soc. Research Child Devel., Am. Ednl. Research Assn., Gerontol. Soc., Phi Kappa Phi. Contbr. numerous articles, chpts. to profl. publs. Home: 1221 N Salisbury St West Lafayette IN 47906 Office: Dept Psychol Scis Purdue U West Lafayette IN 47907

CIEMINSKI, LEO JOHN, clin. psychologist; b. Chgo., Oct. 11, 1916; s. Leo Joseph and Joan Pauline (Marek) C.; B.S., Ill. Inst. Tech., 1940; M.A., U. Chgo., 1941. Psychologist Ill. State Tng. Sch. for Boys, St. Charles and Sheridan, 1943-44; civilian psychologist U.S. Armed Forces Induction and Recruiting Stas., Milw. and Chgo., 1944-46, Fort Sheridan, Ill., 1946-47; clin. psychologist VA Hosp., Milw., 1948-49; instr. Chgo. Bd. Edn., 1949-58, 61-80; psychologist Veit Clinic, Milw., 1958-60; pvt. practice clin. psychology, Chgo., 1961—. Mem. Am. Psychol. Assn. Roman Catholic. Home: 2034 N Wolcott Ave Chicago IL 60614

CIKO, JOHN DANIEL, health care products mfg. co. exec.; b. Detroit, Apr. 9, 1945; s. John and Mary (Augustine) C.; B.A., Wayne State U., 1968, M.A., 1975; m. Patricia Jane McHugh, June 8, 1968; children—John Alexander, Nicholas Andrew. Staff chemist BASF Wyandotte (Mich.) Corp., 1968-76; sr. analyst, cons. Abbott Lab., North Chicago, Ill., 1976—. Chmn., St. Nicholas Orthodox Ch. Council, 1981—. Mem. Am. Statis. Assn., Am. Chem. Soc. Patentee in field. Home: 2500 Thornwood Dr Lindenhurst IL 60046 Office: Abbott Labs 14th and Sheridan Rd North Chicago IL 60064

CILLEY, JANE YEARSLEY, educator; b. Camden, N.J., 1914; widowed, 2 children. Certificate in Elementary Edn., Glassboro (N.J.) State U., 1935; B.S. in Edn., Kent (Ohio) State U., 1960, M.S. in Reading Specialist, 1968. Coaching class Medford (N.J.) pub. schs., 1935-38; tchr. Kenston Local Sch. Dist., Chagrin Falls, Ohio, 1953-70, reading specialist, 1970—. Leader Rutherford (N.J.) council Girl Scouts U.S.A., 1950-53. Mem. Internat. Reading Assn., Ohio Council Internat. Reading Assn., NEA, Delta Kappa Gamma, Kappa Delta Pi. Home: 8815 Tanglewood Trail Chagrin Falls OH 44022 Office: 17870 Chillicothe Rd Chagrin Falls OH 44022

CILLIE, JOHN JAMES, car rental agy. ofcl.; b. Martins Ferry, Ohio, Jan. 4, 1940; s. John Peter and Margaret C.; student Cleve. State U.; m. Janice Kudley, Sept. 30, 1961; children—Sheila, John James. With City Loan and Savs., Cleve., 1961-65, Avco Delta Corp., Cleve., 1965-70, Bobbie Brooks Inc., Cleve., 1970-74, Allstate Ins., Cleve., 1974-76; accounts receivable mgr. Rent-a-Car Agy., Bedford, Ohio, 1976—. Ky. Colonel. Office: 466 Northfield Rd Bedford OH 44146

CIMPERMAN, JOHN D., city ofcl.; b. Cleve., Feb. 15, 1935; s. John J. and Frances Cimperman; B.A., Cleve. State U.; m. Mary, July 28, 1962; children—John, James, Joseph, Julie. Dir., Cleve. Landmarks Commn.; pres. Interstate Planning Corp.; lectr. govt. and city planning, cons. hist. preservation and renovation. Mem. Cleve. City Council, 1961-71. Recipient Design Arts award Nat. Endowment Arts, also various spl. civic awards. Mem. Am. Assn. Hist. Preservationists, Nat. Trust Hist. Preservation, Am. Assn. State and Local History, Cleve. Bd. Realtors, Early Settlers Assn. Western Res. (pres.), Cleve. Restoration Soc. (trustee), Friends of Landmarks Commn. (pres.). Author books, articles in field; asso. editor: Undiscovered Ohio; co-editor Facade. Office: Room 28 City Hall 601 Lakeside St Cleveland OH 44114*

CINCIRIPINI, PAUL MICHAEL, clin. psychologist, educator; b. Pitts., Dec. 17, 1953; s. Joseph Paul and Helen Marie (Sperduto) C.; B.S. cum laude in Psychol. Biology, Pa. State U., 1974; M.S. in Clin. Psychology, Auburn U., 1976, Ph.D. in Clin. Psychology, 1978; m. Doreen Dora Dobrenich, Dec. 14, 1974; 1 dau., Carlina Marie. Psychol. intern Western Psychiat. Inst. and Clinic, U. Pitts. Sch. Medicine, 1977-78; asst. prof. dept. behavioral sci. Sch. Medicine, U. Minn., Duluth, 1978—, asst. prof. clin. psychology and physiology dept. physiology, 1979—; dir. research chronic pain unit Miller-Dwan Hosp., Duluth, 1979—; dir. research Family Practice Center, Duluth, 1980—. Minn. Med. Found. grantee, 1978-79; Paul F. Dwan Found. grantee, 1979-81. Mem. Am. Psychol. Assn., Assn. for Advancement Behavior Therapy, Soc. Behavioral Medicine, Soc. for Psychophysiol. Research, AAAS. Contbr. articles to profl. jours. Office: U Minn Sch Medicine Duluth MN 55812

CINDRIC, JOHN FRANCIS, JR., organizational devel. cons.; b. Lima, Ohio, Oct. 6, 1947; s. John F. and Margorie S. C.; B.S., Miami U., 1970; M.A. (Univ. fellow), Bowling Green State U., 1972; Ed.D., U. Toledo, 1981; postgrad. Ohio State U., 1974; m. Jean Heringhaus, Aug. 22, 1970; children—Chelsey Ann, John F. III. Spl. edn. tchr., Findlay, Ohio, 1970-71; spl. edn. coordinator Hancock County Schs., 1972-74; Title III spl. edn. coordinator, Northwest, Ohio, 1974-75; edn. cons. State Ohio, Toledo, 1975-79; organizational devel. cons. Marathon Oil Co., Findlay, 1979—. Pres., Hancock County Community Center, 1976—; exec. sec., chmn. planning com. Hancock County Mental Health and Retardation Bd., 1979—; mem. planning com. Blanchard Valley Mental Retardation Sch., 1979—; active Hancock County Mus. Jr. Assn., Findlay Art Mus. Assn., Findlay Art Council. Mem. Am. Soc. Tng. and Devel., N.W. Ohio Supr. and Work-Study Assn., Miami U. Alumni Assn., Bowling Green U. Alumni Assn., Sigma Alpha Epsilon. Roman Catholic. Clubs: Rotary, Black Swamp Supper and Game, Elks. Home: 118 1st St Findlay OH 45840 Office: 539 S Main St Findlay OH 45840

CIOCIOLA, MELVIN JEROME, advt. agy. exec.; b. Phila., Sept. 25, 1944; s. Salvador Joseph and Charlotre B. (Krasny) C.; student Temple U., Phila., 1965-66; m. Camille Disclafani, Apr. 6, 1979; children—Heather Blair, Shana Rebecca, Ryan Paul. Copywriter advt. agencies in Phila. and N.Y.C., 1966-69; copywriter, supr. Young & Rubicam, Inc., N.Y.C., 1970-73; group creative dir. Cunningham & Walsh, Inc., N.Y.C., 1973-74; asso. partner The Project Group, N.Y.C., 1974-75; v.p., asso. creative dir. BBDO, Inc., N.Y.C., 1975-80, exec. v.p., exec. creative dir., Chgo., 1980—. Served with USN, 1962-65. Recipient Clio award, 1972, 77, 78, 80, Andy award, 1976, Internat. Broadcast award, 1975, 100 Best award, 1974; also awards of merit. Office: 410 N Michigan Ave Chicago IL 60611

CIPOLLA, LAWRENCE JOHN, human resources devel. services co. exec.; b. Hartford, Conn., Nov. 30, 1943; s. Anthony Francis and Rose Marie (Alesi) C.; A.A. with honors, Manchester Community Coll., 1968; B.A. with high honors, U. Conn., 1970; M.A. with honors (Regent's Fund scholar), U. Minn., 1972; m. Judith L. Peterka, June 24, 1972. Spencer Found. research fellow U. Minn., Mpls., 1971-72; cons., sr. instructional analyst 3M Co., St Paul, 1972-74, supr., 1974-76; pres. Cipolla Cos., Inc., Mpls., 1979—; cons. in sales and mgmt. performance systems, productivity systems, behavior modeling, communication skills; lectr., author in field. Served with USAF, 1961-65. Mem. Am. Soc. Tng. and Devel., Am. Soc. for Performance Improvement, Sales and Mktg. Execs. Internat., Am. Soc. Mag. Photographers, Profl. Photographers Am., Phi Beta Kappa. Club: Sports and Health (Mpls.). Home: 7021 Comanche Ct Edina MN 55435

CIRCLE, SYBIL JEAN, psychiatrist; b. Peoria, Ill., July 2, 1945; d. Sidney Joseph and Sydell C.; B.A., Northwestern U., 1967, M.D., 1971. Intern, Passavant Meml. Hosp., Chgo., 1971-72; resident in psychiatry Northwestern U. Med. Sch., Chgo., 1972-74; practice medicine specializing in psychiatry, Maywood, Ill., 1975—; mem. faculty Loyola U. Med. Sch., Chgo., 1975—, asst. prof., 1977-81, clin. asst. prof., 1981—, dir. undergrad. edn., dept. psychiatry, 1977—. Diplomate Am. Bd. Psychiatry and Neurology. Mem. AMA, Am. Psychiat. Assn., Ill. Psychiat. Soc., Chgo. Med. Soc. Office: 2160 S 1st St Maywood IL 60153

CIRIACY, EDWARD WALTER, physician, educator; b. Phila., Feb. 12, 1924; s. William Frederick and Elizabeth Jane (McGettigan) C.; B.S., Pa. State Coll., 1948; M.D., Temple U., 1952; m. Adele Large Wallis, Sept. 9, 1942; children—Adele, Edward Walter, Deborah, Melissa Jane, Timothy. Intern, Frankford Hosp., Phila., 1952-53, surg. resident, 1953-54; surg. resident Temple Hosp., Phila., 1953-54; practice medicine specializing in family practice, Ely, Minn., 1954-57, 58-71, Miami, Fla., 1957-58; mem. staffs Ely-Bloomenson Community Hosp.; prof. U. Minn., 1971—, chmn. dept. family practice, 1971—. Mem. adv. panel for subcom. on patient care Cancer Coordinating Com. for Health Scis. Served with USAAF, 1944-46. Recipient Merit award Minn. Acad. Gen. Practice, 1963. Diplomate Nat. Bd. Med. Examiners, Am. Bd. Family Practice (chmn. recertification com. 1972-76). Fellow Am. Acad. Family Physicians (charter); mem. Minn. Acad. Family Physicians (pres. 1967-68, com. on med. sch. relations and tng. programs), AMA, Pan Am. Med. Assn., Soc. Tchrs. of Family Medicine (pres. 1975—), Minn. Med. Assn. (mem. com. med. services 1970—), Range Med. Soc. (pres. 1961), Babcock Surg. Soc., Assn. Am. Med. Colls., Alpha Omega Alpha. Mason. Contbr. numerous articles to med. jours. Home: 17 E Beacon Hill Rd Ely MN 55731 Office: Phillips-Wangensteen Bldg U Minn Minneapolis MN 55455

CISLAK, PETER JOHN, computer co. exec.; b. Indpls., June 26, 1931; s. Francis Edward and Jeannette Grace (Huling) C.; student Swarthmore Coll., 1952; B.S., Purdue U., 1958, M.S., 1958; m. Margaret Frances Noble, June 6, 1953; children—Gregory Noble, Carol Margaret, David John, Susan Marie. Instr., Purdue U., 1958-62; statistician Reilly Tar & Chem. Corp., Indpls., 1962-64, data processing mgr., 1964-69, prodn. mgr. chem. div., 1969-77, sr. mgr. chems., 1977-81; chmn., chief exec. officer Alpha Comp Inc., 1981—; dir. Reilly Chems., Reilly Chem. S.A., Belgium; lectr. Ind. U.-Purdue U., Indpls., 1970. Asst. dist. commr. Boy Scouts Am., 1963—. Served with AUS, 1953-57. Mem. Am. Mgmt. Assn. (chmn. seminar), Am. Statis. Assn., Assn. Computing Machinery, Ops. Research Soc. Am., Soc. Chem. Industry, Am. Inst. Chem. Engrs. (chmn. Indpls. sect. 1978), Ind. Soc. Mayflower Descs. (dep. gov. 1974-79). K.C. (4 deg.). Home and office: 8065 Morningside Dr Indianapolis IN 46240

CISZEWSKI, JOSEPH ANTHONY, brewery co. exec.; b. Milw., Feb. 12, 1924; s. Joseph M. and Anna C.; student public schs., Milw. With, Joseph Schlitz Brewing Co., Milw., 1942—, mgr. brand adminstrn. and packaging devel., 1967—. Mem. Packaging Inst., Brewers and Beverage Packaging Assn., Master Brewers Assn. Republican. Roman Catholic. Office: Joseph Schlitz Brewing Co 235 W Galena St Milwaukee WI 53201

CITIPITIOGLU, ERGIN, research engr.; b. Ankara, Turkey, Feb. 18, 1937; s. Mehmet Ali and Belkis (Pornek) C.; came to U.S., 1962; M.C.E., Istanbul Tech. U., 1960; Ph.D., Okla. State U., 1965; m. Gul Ataman, Mar. 11, 1971; children—Lale, Ahmet. Bridge design engr. Turkish State Hwy. Directorate, 1960-62; asst. prof. civil engring. U. Louisville, 1965-67, asso. prof., 1967-68; research asso. mech. engring. dept. U. Cin., 1968-69; tech. v.p. Hypermation, Inc., 1969-70; asso. prof. civil engring. Middle East Tech. U., 1970-74; mem. tech. staff Structural Dynamics Research Corp., Cin., 1975-79; prof. civil engring. Purdue U., Indpls., 1979—. Registered profl. engr., Ind., Ohio, Ky. Mem. Am. Acad. Mechanics, ASCE, Am. Concrete Inst., Am. Soc. Engring. Edn. Club: Masons. Home: 3323 Eden Way Circle Carmel IN 46032 Office: 1201 E 38th St Indianapolis IN 46205

CITRIN, PHILLIP MARSHALL, lawyer; b. Chgo., Nov. 1, 1931; s. Mandel Hirsch and Birdie (Gulman) C.; B.S., Northwestern U., 1953, J.D., 1956; m. Judith Goldfeder, Dec. 23, 1967; 1 son, Jeffrey Scott Levin. Admitted to Ill. bar, 1957; partner firm Davis, Jones & Baer, Chgo., 1961-80; individual practice law specializing in domestic relations, Chgo., 1980—. Republican candidate judge circuit ct., Cook County, Ill., 1976, 78. Served with USNR, 1956-58. Fellow Am. Acad. Matrimonial Lawyers (founding); mem. Chgo. (bd. mgrs. 1974-76, co-author ann. satire program 1963—), Ill. (mem. assembly of dels. 1972-73), Am. (gavel awards com.) bar assns., Phi Delta Phi. Clubs: Arts (Chgo.). Home: 423 Greenleaf Ave Wilmette IL 60091 Office: 30 N LaSalle St Chicago IL 60602

CLAFLIN, JAMES FRED, aggregates co. exec.; b. Mason City, Iowa, June 11, 1921; s. James L. and Minnie B. (Brooking) C.; student public schs., Fairfax and Cedar Rapids, Iowa; m. Florence I. Cope, Jan. 10, 1947; children—James Allen, John Frederick. Stock clk. John Blaul & Sons Co., Cedar Rapids, Iowa, 1939-40; timekeeper Martin Marietta Aggregates, Cedar Rapids, 1940-42, asst. purchasing agent, 1946-52, purchasing agent, 1952-68, dir. purchasing, 1968—. Served with USMC, 1942-46. Mem. Purchasing Mgmt. Assn. Republican. Club: Optimist. Home: 1346 Highwood Dr Cedar Rapids IA 52405 Office: Martin Marietta Aggregates 4096 First Ave NE Cedar Rapids IA 52406

CLAGGETT, CHARLES EVANS, JR., advt. agy. exec.; b. St. Louis, Dec. 30, 1947; s. Charles Evans and Blanche Elliot (Fischel) C.; B.A., U. Denver, 1970; m. Katherine McBride Mullins, May 17, 1975; children—Elisabeth Mahaffey, Julia McBride. Writer, producer D'Arcy-MacManus & Masius, 1972-77, asso. creative dir., 1977-79, v.p., creative dir., 1979-81, sr. v.p., group creative dir., 1981—. Recipient Clio, N.Y. Art Dirs. award, 1980. Author: The Salesman, 1972. Home: 6 Town and Country Ln Saint Louis MO 63124 Office: Marcy-MacManus & Masius 1 Memorial Dr Saint Louis MO 63102

CLAMPITT, RICHARD ROY, psychologist; b. New Providence, Iowa, Dec. 7, 1925; s. Roy Justin and L. Pauline (Felt) C.; B.S., Iowa State U., 1951, M.S., 1954; Ph.D. (USPHS fellow), State U. Iowa, 1955; m. Joan Lucile Utzinger, June 30, 1956; children—Christopher Alan, Carolyn Elaine, Susan Lucinda. Clin. psychologist, asst. prof. Columbus (Ohio) Psychiat. Inst., Ohio State U. Med. Sch., 1956-61; clin. psychologist Central Minn. Mental Health Center, St. Cloud, 1961—. Coordinator, Counselin Services to Clergy, Minn. Conf. United Meth. Ch., 1969—. Chmn. Civil Service Bd., City of St. Cloud, Minn., 1968-69, 71-72, 74-75, 77-78, 80-81; bd. dirs. Family Planning Center, 1971-76, chmn. founding bd., 1971-73; bd. dirs. United Cerebral Palsy Central Minn., 1965-80, chmn., 1969-70. Diplomate Am. Bd. Profl. Psychology. Fellow Am. Psychol. Assn. (Minn. rep. council reps. 1974-76, 79-81, pres. div. state assns. 1977); mem. Minn. Psychol. Assn. (mem. exec. council 1970-76), Common Cause, St. Cloud Area C. of C. (chmn. municipal affairs div. 1966), N. Am. Gladiolus Council, Sigma Xi, Phi Kappa Phi, Phi Mu Alpha Sinfonia, Pi Mu Epsilon, Psi Chi. Democrat. Methodist (mem. adminstrv. bd. 1963—). Home: 39 Pandolfo Pl St Cloud MN 56301 Office: 1321 13th St N St Cloud MN 56301

CLANCY, DANIEL FRANCIS, journalist; b. Logansport, Ind., May 8, 1918; s. Joseph Francis and Daisy C. (Strecker) C.; student pub. schs.; m. Okodell Glads Salyer, Apr. 12, 1947; children—Cassandra Sue, Holly Eve. Reporter Logansport Press, 1942-46, Springfield (Ohio) Daily News, 1946-47, Springfield Sun, 1947-56; reporter, Columbus (Ohio) Dispatch, 1956-80, ret. 1980. Dir. Nat. Com. Against Limiting the Presidency, 1949-54; trustee More Agrl. Prodn. Served to lt. col. Ohio Def. Corps. Decorated French Nat. Merit, Gold medal, La Renaissance Francaise, medal Honor and Merit, knight Order of Lion of Ardennes, Cross of Lorraine and Compains of Resistance, Soc. Encouragement Arts, Scis., Letters Silver medal (France); knight Order of Crown of Stuart (Eng.); Assn. Am. Friendship Bronze medal, Trieste; count Ho. of Deols (Italy); knight Delcassian Order (Ireland); medal Institute of Libertador Ramon Castilla (Peru); medal Internat. Eloy Alfaro Found. (Panama); silver medal spl. membership Japanese Red Cross Soc.; Ohio Faithful Service ribbon; recipient Nat. Headliner award, 1948, 49; 1st place award for editorial columns Nat. Found. for Hwy. Safety, 1970; cert. of appreciation Ohio Vets. World War I, 1971; Appreciation plaque Ohio N.G., 1976; Meritorious service medal SSS; spl. recognition award Ohio VFW, 1981; named hon. Ky. col., hon. adm. Nebr. Navy, hon. col., hon. adm. Tex. Navy, hon. N.Mex. col., hon. Miss. col., hon. lt. col. Ala., Ga., lt. gov. Ohio, Ind. Sagamore; commodore Okla., Ohio. Mem. Am. Mil. Inst., Orders and Medals Soc. Am., Ohio Def. Officers Assn., Nat. Flag Found., Ohio Valley Mil. Soc., Am. Internat. Acad., Brazilian Acad. Polit. and Social Sci., Nat. Citizens for State 51; (P.R.), Inst. Heraldry (Spain), Internat. Inst. Study and Devel. Human Relations, Brazilian Acad. Econs. and Adminstrv. Scis., Sons Union Vets. Civil War (past state comdr.), Nat. Council Encouragement of Patriotism, Patriotic Edn. Inc., Continental Confedn. Adopted Indians (v.p. 1954—), Assn. U.S. Army, Am. Indian Lore Assn. (hon.), My Country Soc. Clubs: National Headliners; Honolulu Press. Author: Two Term Tradition, 1940; Collected Poems, 1937-47, 1948. Contbr. articles to mags. Home: 2420 Zollinger Rd Columbus OH 43221

CLANCY, LENA LEA TRENT, dietitian; b. Atoka, Okla., Feb. 19, 1931; d. Roy G. and Edith L. (Wilson) Trent; B.S., Okla. State U., 1952; M.S., Kans. State U., 1969; m. James N. Clancy, July 27, 1952; children—Patricia, Michael. Mem. faculty, dir. dietary dept. Sch. of Nursing, West Nebr. Gen. Hosp., Scottsbluff, 1952-55; cons. dietitian, vocat. home econs. tchr. Lewellen High Sch., Western, Nebr., 1957-65; dir. food services Mitchell County Hosp., Beloit, Kans., 1966-68; vocat. home econs. tchr. Beatrice (Nebr.) Sr. High Sch., 1968-70; asst. food dir. Univ. Student Union, U. Nebr., Lincoln, 1971-76; dir. dietary dept. Lincoln Gen. Hosp., 1976-80; asst. prof. dept. foods and nutrition, clin. faculty dietetic internship U. Nebr., 1972—; chmn. dept. home econs. Southeast Community Coll., 1980—; gen. chmn. food service div. Midwest Health Congress, 1978-79; chmn. food adv. bd. Lancaster County Health Dept., 1977—. Mem. adv. bd. for food services S.E. Community Tech. Coll., Lincoln, 1973-78. Named Woman of Yr., Beta Sigma Phi, 1967; Outstanding Dietitian, Nebr., 1980; registered dietitian. Mem. Am. Dietetic Assn., Nebr. Dietetic Assn., Lincoln Dietetic Assn., Nat. Restaurant Assn., Nebr. Restaurant Assn., Am. Sch. Food Service, Am. Soc. for Hosp. Food Service Adminstrs., AAUW, Food Service Systems Edn. Council, Alpha Delta Kappa, Bus. and Profl. Women's Club, Omicron Nu. Democrat. Roman Catholic. Clubs: Altrusa, Order of Eastern Star. Home: 7200 Pine Lake Rd Lincoln NE 68516 Office: 8800 East O St Lincoln NE 68520

CLANCY, THOMAS G., newspaper co. exec.; b. Chgo., Apr. 9, 1934; s. Frank J. and Hellen (Brady) C.; student Loyola U., 1957; m. Carol A. Drexler, July 28, 1962; children—Thomas, John, Erin, Tara. With Chicago Tribune Co., 1959—, salesman classified advt., 1959-72, mgr. New York Advt. div., N.Y.C., 1972-73, gen. advt. mgr., Chgo., 1973-74, home delivery sales promotion mgr., 1974-75, mgr. suburban circulation, 1975-76, dir. circulation, 1976-80, v.p., 1978—, dir. mktg., 1980—. Mem. exec. adv. bd. St. Joseph's Hosp., 1980-81; mem. citizen's adv. bd. Loyola U., 1978-81; trustee Fed. Defender, 1980; bd. dirs. Chgo. Athletic Assn., 1979. Served with USMC, 1957-59. Club: Economic. Home: Winnetka IL 60093 Office: 435 N Michigan Ave Chicago IL 60611

CLAPP, THOMAS REID, concrete co. exec.; b. Washington, June 11, 1947; s. Roger Alvin and Harriet (Reid) C.; student Monmouth Coll.; m. Linda Mae Kinkaid, Apr. 14, 1967; children—Thomas Charles, Barbara Ellen. Asst. dist. mgr. Atlantic Mobile Corp., Chgo., 1971-75; pres. Anchor Concrete Service, Inc., Chillicothe, Ill., 1975—, also dir. Served with U.S. Army, 1969-71. Decorated Bronze Star medal, Army Commendation medal. Mem. Am. Rental Assn., Chillicothe C. of C., Asso. Builders and Contractors, Am. Concrete Inst., Mobile Concrete Assn. (dir.), Nat. Ready Mixed Concrete Assn., Am. Soc. for Concrete Constrn., Poured Concrete Wall Contractors Assn. Home: 907 Santa Fe Chillicothe IL 61523 Office: PO Box 482 Route 29 Chillicothe IL 61523

CLARDY, JESSE V., educator; b. Olney, Tex., Feb. 15, 1929; s. Jesse Ellis and Tiny (Pringle) C.; B.S., Tex. Arts and Industries U., 1949, M.S., 1951; Ph.D., U. Mich., 1961. Faculty, U. Tex., Arlington, 1961-62; faculty U. Mo., Kansas City, 1963—, asso. prof. Russian history, 1964-68, prof., 1968—. Served with AUS, 1951-54. Mem. S.W. Slavic Assn. (pres. 1964-65), Bi-Slavic Assn. (sec. 1970-71), Assn. for Advancement Slavic Studies. Republican. Author: Philosophical Ideas of Alexander Radishchev, 1964; G.R. Derzhavin a Political Biography, 1967; The Superfluous Man in Russian Letters, 1980. Home: 1004 Broad St Warrensburg MO 64093 Office: Dept History U Mo Kansas City MO 64110

CLARE, STEWART, educator, research biologist; b. nr. Montgomery City, Mo., Jan. 31, 1913; s. William Gilmore and Wardie (Stewart) C.; B.A., U. Kans., 1935; M.S., Iowa State U., 1937; Ph.D., U. Chgo., 1949; m. Lena Glenn Kaster, Aug. 4, 1936. Student asst. entomology, also William Volker scholar U. Kans., 1931-35; Rockefeller Research fellow Iowa State U., 1935-36, teaching fellow, 1936-37; Univ. fellow zoology U. Chgo., 1937-40; dist. survey supr. entomology U.S. Civil Service Commn. Bur. Entomology and Plant Quarantine, 1937-40, tech. cons., 1941-42; instr. meteorology USAAF Weather Sch., 1942-43; research biologist Midwest Research Inst., Kansas City, Mo., 1945-46; spl. study, research Kansas City Art Inst., U. Mo., 1946-49; instr. zoology U. Alta., 1949-50, asst. prof. zoology, lectr.-instr. sci. color, dept. fine arts, 1950-53; research grantee Alberta Research Council, 1951-53; asst. prof. Kansas City Coll., 1953; lectr. zoology U. Adelaide, S. Australia, 1954-55; sr. research officer entomology Sudan Govt. Ministry Agr., Khartoum, Sudan and Gezira Research Sta., Wad Medani, Sudan, N.Africa, 1955-56; sr. entomologist Klipfontein Organic Products Corp., Johannesburg, Union S.Africa, 1957; prof., head dept. biology Union Coll., 1958-59, chmn. sci. div., prof., head biology, 1959-61, spl. study grantee, 1960; prof., head dept. biology Mo. Valley Coll., Marshall, 1961-62, research grantee, 1961-62; lectr., instr. biology, meteorology, sci. of color Adirondack Sci. Camp div. edn. N.Y. State U. Coll. summers 1962-66, dir. acad. program 1963-66, research facilities grantee, 1963-66; Buckbee Found. prof. biology Rockford (Ill.) Coll., lectr. biology eve. coll., 1962-63, spl. research grantee, 1962-63; prof., chmn. dept. biochemistry, mem. research div. Kansas City (Mo.) Coll. Osteopathy and Surgery, 1963-67, also NIH basic research grantee, 1963-67; prof. biology Coll. of Emporia (Kans.), 1967-74, dir. biol. research, 1972-74, prof. emeritus, 1974—, research study grantee, 1967-74, research biologist, cons., 1974—, spl. research grantee Coll. of Emporia and U. Alaska, 1970, No. Research Survey, Arctic Inst. N. Am., 1970, 72, Coll. of Emporia Central Am. and Mexico, 1973; cons. to Vols. for Internat. Tech. Assistance, 1962—, Adirondack Research and Field System, 1962-66, Nat. Referral Center for Science and Technology, 1970—. Mem. adv. bd. Fine Art Registry, Soc. N.Am. Artists, 1971—. Served with USNR, 1943-45. Recipient certificate service Vols. Internat. Tech. Assistance, 1970; creativity recognition award Internat. Personnel Research, 1972; Outstanding Educator award Coll. of Emporia, 1973; Distinguished Achievement and Service awards for edn. and research in biology, Certificate of Merit in Art, Internat. Biog. Centre, 1968, 72, 73, 76 numerous other awards. Fellow Intercontinental Biog. Assn. (life), Am. Biog. Inst., Explorers Club, Anglo-Am. Acad. (hon.); mem. Brit. Assn. Adv. Sci. (life), Am. Entomol. Soc. (life), Nat. Assn. Biology Tchrs., Arctic Inst. N.Am., Am. Polar Soc., N.Y. Acad. Scis. (life), Inter-Soc. Color Council, Sigma Xi, Phi Sigma, Psi Chi, numerous others. Contbr. monographs in capillary movement in porous materials, physiology and biochemistry of anthropoda; research on sci. and designing of color; numerous local, nat. and internat. exhibits; also articles to profl. jours. Home: 405 NW Woodland Rd Indian Hills in Riverside Kansas City MO 64150

CLARENBACH, FRED A., polit. scientist; b. Jefferson City, Mo., Apr. 27, 1909; s. Louis Adolph and Julia Helen (Schaper) C.; B.A., U. Mo., 1930, M.A., 1932; Ph.D., Cornell U., 1941; m. Laura Belle McGaffey, Aug. 28, 1930; children—Ann Louise, Lois Elinor. Instr. econs. Cornell U., 1936-39; economist U.S. Dept. Agr., 1939-45; asst. prof. agrl. econs. and polit. sci. U. Wis., 1945-46, asso. prof., 1946-48, asso. prof. polit. sci., 1948-51, prof. polit. sci., 1951-62, prof. urban and regional planning, 1962-72, prof. emeritus, 1972—, dir. U. Wis. Grad. Tng. Program in Water Resources Mgmt.; cons. USPHS, Nat. Planning Council, Govt. of Ceylon, Wis. Dept. Resource Devel., Water Resources Center U. Calif., Berkeley, Wis. Dept. Local Affairs and Devel., City of Madison Water Utility, N.W. Wis. Regional Planning Commn., Dept. Agr., Dept. Interior, Food and Agrl. Orgn. of UN. Mem. Am. Polit. Sci. Assn., Am. Planning Assn., AAUP. Unitarian. Contbr. articles to profl. jours. Office: Dept Urban and Regional Planning Univ of Wis Madison WI 53706

CLARITY, TIMOTHY BALDWIN, advt. exec.; b. Des Moines, July 10, 1951; s. James Archibald and Georgia (Baldwin) C.; B.S. in Advt., Iowa State U., 1977. Press intern on staff gov. Iowa, Des Moines, 1977; advt. rep. Webb Co., St. Paul, 1977-79; founder, chief exec. officer Clarity Coverdale Advt., Inc., Mpls., 1979—. Recipient cert. of appreciation Iowa Exec. Dept. Mem. Minn. Advt. Fedn., Nat. Agri-Mktg. Assn. Home: 2800 Girard Ave S Minneapolis MN 55408 Office: 10 S 5th St Minneapolis MN 55401

CLARK, C. KENNETH, JR., lawyer; b. Youngstown, Ohio, Mar. 11, 1930; s. C. Kenneth and Katharine (Griswold) C.; A.B., Oberlin Coll., 1951; J.D., Harvard U., 1954. Admitted to Ohio bar, 1954; partner firm Harrington, Huxley & Smith, Youngstown, 1963—; dir. WKBN Broadcasting Corp., Youngstown, others. Pres. Vol. Service Bur. Youngstown, 1965-68; Trustee Youngstown Health and Welfare Council, Youngstown Playground Assn., Asso. Neighborhood Centers Youngstown, pres., 1969. Mem. Am., Ohio State bar assns., U.S. Jud. Conf. for Sixth Circuit, Youngstown Area C. of C. Presbyn. Clubs: Torch (Youngstown, dir.), Cambium (pres. 1967-68), Youngstown. Home: 1637 Tanglewood Dr Youngstown OH 44505 Office: Mahoning Bank Bldg Youngstown OH 44503

CLARK, CHARLES EDWARD, arbitrator; b. Cleve., Feb. 27, 1921; s. Douglas John and Mae (Egermayer) C.; student Berea Coll., 1939-41, King Coll., 1945; LL.B., U. Tex., 1948; m. Nancy Jane Hilt, Mar. 11, 1942; children—Annette S. (Mrs. Paul Gernhardt), Charles Edward, John A., Nancy P., Paul R., Stephen C., David G. Admitted to Tex. bar, 1948, Mass. bar, 1956, U.S. Supreme Ct. bar, 1959; practice law, San Antonio, 1948-55; writer legal articles, editor NACCA Law Jour., Boston, 1955-58; legal asst. to vice chmn., chief voting sect. U.S. Commn. on Civil Rights, Washington, 1958-61; spl. counsel Pres.'s Com. on Equal Employment Opportunity, 1961-65; sr. compliance officer Office Fed. Contract Compliance, 1965-66; regional dir. Equal Employment Opportunity Commn., Kansas City, Mo., 1966-79; arbitrator, 1979—; prof. law, asst. dean St. Mary's U. Sch. Law, 1948-55. Active Boy Scouts Am. Served with AUS, 1943-44. Mem. Am. Trial Lawyers Assn., State Bar Tex., Am. GI Forum (D.C. vice chmn. 1962-63), Indsl. Relations Research Assn. (exec. bd. Kansas City 1976—, treas. chpt. 1979), Internat. Platform Assn., Phi Delta Phi (province pres. 1951-55). Contbr. articles to legal jours. Home and Office: 6418 Washington St Kansas City MO 64113

CLARK, CLESTEEN ABRAHAM, nutritionist; b. Pineville, La., June 11, 1953; d. James and Mary Lamell Abraham; B.S. in Food and Nutrition (scholar), So. U., Baton Rouge, La., 1975; M.S. in Nutrition, Iowa State U., 1977; m. Leon Clark, Jr., Dec. 23, 1977. Iowa State Home Econs. Assn. scholar food and nutrition dept. Iowa State U., Ames, 1975-77; asst. dietitian Pinecrest State Sch., Pineville, La., summer 1975; nutritionist public affairs dept. Kellogg Co., Battle Creek, Mich., 1977-78, mgr. nutrition communications, 1978-80, mgr. print media services, 1980—. Mem. Iowa State U. Home Econs. Adv. Council, 1978—; steward Mt. Zion African Meth. Episcopal Ch., 1979-81; grad. counselor Commn. Christian Edn., 1980-81. Mem. Am. Home Econs. Assn., Soc. Nutrition Edn., Home Econs. in Bus., Calhoun County Nutrition Council, Mich. Home Econs. Assn., Am. Dietetics Assn., Omicron Nu, Psi Upsilon Omicron, Pi Gamma Mu. Office: 235 Porter Battle Creek MI 49016

CLARK, DAVID WILLARD, hosp. adminstr.; b. Rockford, Ill., May 17, 1930; s. Willard Wilbur and Arline Marie (Anderson) C.; m. Barbara Ardel Boyd, June 18, 1955; children—Deborah Jean, Alan Boyd; B.S., Beloit Coll., 1952; M.B.A., U. Chgo., 1955. Adminstrv. resident Univ. Hosps. of Cleve., 1955-56, adminstrv. asst., 1956-60, asst. adminstr., 1960-66, asso. adminstr., 1966-67, adminstr., 1967-78, sr. v.p., 1979—; pres. Hosp. Finance Corp., Med. Center Co. Chmn. hosp. div. United Torch, 1976. Mem. Am., Ohio (trustee, dist. chmn.), Greater Cleve. (chmn.) hosp. assns., Am. Coll. Hosp. Adminstrs., Univ. Hosps. Exec. Council, Council Teaching Hosps., Phi Beta Kappa. Club: Masons. Recipient Kate Baron Service award, 1952. Home: 18906 Scottsdale Blvd Cleveland OH 44106 Office: 2065 Adelbert Rd Cleveland OH 44106

CLARK, DONALD, sch. adminstr.; b. Kewanna, Ind., Aug. 22, 1923; s. Ora Robert and Lela Juanita (Overmeyer) C.; B.S., Ind. U., 1948; M.S., Ind. State U., 1955; M.S. (Inland Steel fellow), Purdue U., 1961; m. Lorene Mutti, July 27, 1950; children—Daniel and David (twins). Elem. tchr., Kewanna, Bremen and Highland, Ind., 1949-57; high sch. math. tchr., Highland, 1957-61, chmn. dept. math., 1957-70; dir. data processing Sch. Town of Highland, 1970—; guest lectr. computer sci. Purdue U., Calumet; part-time instr. data processing Ind. Tech. Vocat. Sch. Served with AUS, 1943-45. NSF fellow U. Notre Dame, 1957, Knox Coll., 1964, Pa. State U., 1967; Shell Merit fellow Cornell U., 1963. Mem. Highland Classroom Tchrs. (past pres.), Ind. Tchrs. Assn. (past pres.), N.W. Assn. Ednl. Data Systems. Methodist. Home: 395 Greendale St Valparaiso IN 46383 Office: 9145 Kennedy St Highland IN 46322

CLARK, DONALD CAMERON, diversified co. exec.; b. Bklyn., Aug. 9, 1931; s. Alexander and Sarah (Cameron) C.; B.B.A., Clarkson Coll., Potsdam, N.Y., 1953; M.B.A., Northwestern U., 1961; m. Jean Ann Williams, Feb. 6, 1954; children—Donald C., Barbara Jean, Thomas Robert. With Household Internat., Prospect Heights, Ill., 1955—, treas., 1972-74, sr. v.p., 1974-76, exec. v.p., chief fin. officer, 1976-77, pres., 1977—; dir. The Burch Co., Square D Co. Bd. dirs. Evanston (Ill.) Hosp.; trustee Clarkson Coll., Northwestern U. Served with U.S. Army, 1953-55. Mem. Chgo. Assn. Commerce and Industry, Econ. Club (dir.). Clubs: Westmoreland Country, Mid-Am., Econ. Office: 2700 Sanders Rd Prospect Heights IL 60070

CLARK, EDWARD MAURICE, tax accountant; b. Kansas City, Mo., Apr. 24, 1947; s. Eugene M. and Mabel M. Clark; B.S., Central Mo. State U., 1969. Owner, operator Edward M. Clark Acctg. & Tax Service, Raytown, Mo., 1974—; tchr. Project Bus. div. Jr. Achievement. Treas., Landlords of Kansas City, 1976-79. Real estate broker, Mo.; notary pub. Mem. Nat. Soc. Pub. Accountants, Mo. Assn. Tax Practitioners, Ind. Accountants Soc. Mo. (Kansas City chpt.). Methodist. Club: Blue Ridge Kiwanis (treas.). Author: Clark's Mileage Minders; The Easy To Keep Mileage Book, 1979. Office: 6115 Blue Ridge Blvd Raytown MO 64133

CLARK, ELIZABETH ANN, nurse; b. Alton, Ill., Dec. 10, 1950; d. Angelo Thomas and Josephine Ann (Lombardo) Alben; grad. St. Joseph's Sch. Nursing, Alton, 1971; student nursing McKendree Coll., 1981—; m. Gary Daniel Clark, Aug. 20, 1970; children—Nicole Leigh, Jason Andrew. Staff nurse obstetrics-gynecology S.W. Tex. Meth. Hosp., San Antonio, 1971; staff nurse operating room Kansas City (Mo.) Gen. Hosp., 1971-73; staff nurse obstetrics, recovery room, med.-surg. Spelman Meml. Hosp., Smithville, Mo., 1974-76; staff nurse operating room Alton Meml. Hosp., 1976—; sec. Anestat, Inc., 1975-76. Roman Catholic. Home: 2915 Gilbert Ln Alton IL 62002

CLARK, EMMA JEAN, ednl. adminstr.; b. Independence, Mo., Oct. 20, 1925; d. Dennis and Lelia (Harrison) Hambright; B.S. in Edn., Lincoln U., 1946; M.A., U. Mich., 1948; postgrad U. Chgo., 1966, Kans. State Tchrs. Coll., U. Mo., Kansas City; m. Robert Newton Clark, July 23, 1950; children—Carole Patrice, Robert Newton. Tchr., public schs., Tucson, 1946-47, Kansas City, Mo., 1948-65, reading specialist, 1965-66; reading cons., 1966-68, dir. and elem. edn. specialist, coop. urban tchr. edn. program, Mid Continent Regional Ednl. Lab., 1968-75, elem. curriculum specialist, 1975-79, dir. elem. instrn., curriculum, in service, 1979—. Bd. dirs. Fellowship House, Learning Exchange; past bd. dirs. NAACP; mem. council Camp Fire Girls; pres. Jack and Jill of Am.; mem. YWCA. Recipient Freedoms Found. at Valley Forge award, 1965, Boys Club award, 1975, 78, Black Woman on the Move award So. Christian Leadership Conf., 1975, Outstanding Educator plaque Elem. Tchrs. Community Assn., 1967. Mem. Assn. Supervision and Curriculum Devel., Internat. Reading Assn., Kans. City Mus. Assn., Kansas City Sch. Adminstrs. Assn., U. Mich. Alumni Assn., Lincoln U. Alumni Assn., Women's C. of C., Women's Ednl. Network, Menninger Found., Phi Delta Kappa. Lutheran. Clubs: Impromptu, Tallyettes, Bids, No-Name. Home:

3328 N 36th St Kansas City KS 66104 Office: 1211 MGee St Room 810 Kansas City MO 64106

CLARK, ERNEST LYNN, real estate investor; b. St. Louis, May 12, 1947; s. John C. Clark and Ella Mae (Baker) Clark; A.A., St. Louis Jr. Coll. Dist., 1973; B.S. in Bus. Adminstrn., B.S. in Law Enforcement and Corrections, N.E. Mo. State U., 1975. Dep. clk., then asst. chief clk. Ct. Criminal Causes, St. Louis, 1969-70; cons. Ct. Adminstrv. Office, St. Louis, 1971-72; computer operator Gen. Bancshares Service Corp., St. Louis, 1971-75, N.E. Mo. State U., Kirksville, 1973-74; research analyst Mo. Ho. of Reps., Jefferson City, 1975-76, 76-77; statewide campaign coordinator candidate for lt. gov. Mo., 1976; personnel specialist Bi-State Devel. Agency, St. Louis, 1977-80; real estate investor, 1980—; cons. data processing, fed. funding, mgmt. and personnel relations; fed. funding specialist Mo. Ho. of Reps., 1975. Co-organizer 1st Nat. Alliance of Businessmen's Job Fair for Vets., St. Louis, 1971; mem. revised policy manual com. St. Louis Jr. Coll. Dist., 1971. Served with USCG, 1965-69. Recipient letter of commendation for community service St. Louis Mayor, 1972; citation Mo. Ho. of Reps., 1977. Mem. Collegiate Vets. Mo. (founder), St. Louis Council Collegiate Vets. (a founder), Am. Criminal Justice Assn., Am. Mgmt. Assn., Mo. Sheriff's Assn. Home: 2929 Magnolia Ave Saint Louis MO 63118

CLARK, GLENN THOMAS, broadcasting exec.; b. Watertown, Wis., Feb. 27, 1947; s. Gaylord James and Jeanette Ida (Froemming) C.; student U. Wis., Whitewater, 1970-71; m. Karen Marie Conners, June 13, 1970; 1 dau., Angenette Lynn. Mgr. data processing to v.p. Robert S. Block Advt., Milw., 1973-77; mgr., broker Robert W. Baird, Milw., 1977-78; mgr. facilities mgmt. Oconomowoc Canning Co. (Wis.), 1978-79; dir. SELECTV Wis., Milw., 1979—, v.p., gen. mgr., 1981—. Served with U.S. Army, 1966-68. Mem. Am. Mgmt. Assn., VFW, Data Processing Mgmt. Assn. Lutheran. Home: 1530 Riverdale Dr Oconomowoc WI 53066 Office: SELECTV 4085 N 128th St Brookfield WI 53005

CLARK, JAMES GORDON, cons. engr.; b. Kansas City, Mo., Dec. 23, 1913; s. John Arthur and Stella (Wright) C.; A.S., Kansas City Jr. Coll., 1933; B.S. with honors, U. Ill., 1935, M.S., 1939; m. Jeannette Hazel McKinstry, May 8, 1937 (dec. Dec. 2, 1951); children—Nannette Kay, Diana Jean; m. 2d, Janice Elizabeth Winters, Nov. 28, 1952; children—Mary Elizabeth, Jane, James. Instr. civil engring. Ore. State Coll., 1935; jr. engr. U.S. Bur. Reclamation, Denver, 1936; from instr. to prof. civil engring. U. Ill., 1936-55; interim profl. work structural engring. Am. Bridge Co., Bethlehem Steel Co., Howard, Needles, Tammen & Bergendoff, Curtiss Wright Corp.; structural engr. Consol. Vultee Aircraft Corp., 1944-45; partner Balke & Clark, 1953-54; asso. Harry Balke Engrs., 1955; partner Clark & Daily, 1956, partner Clark, Daily & Dietz, 1957-63; pres. Clark, Dietz & Assos., engrs., Urbana, Ill., Memphis, Sanford, Fla., Jackson, Miss., Carbondale, Ill., Chgo. and St. Louis, 1963-75, cons., 1975-80; part owner ESCA Consultants, Inc., Urbana, 1981—; partner Clark, Altay & Assos., 1965-76. Mem. profl. engrs. license com. State Ill.; chmn. James F. Lincoln Arc Welding Found. Award Programs, 1949, 50, 52, 58. Trustee Ill. Bapt. Student Found., 1954—. Mem. Nat., Ill. socs. profl. engrs., Am. Soc. C.E. (past pres. Central Ill. sect.), Am. Soc. Engring. Edn., Am. Ry. Engring. Assn., Am. Soc. Testing Materials, Am. Welding Soc., Hwy. Research Bd., Am. Ry. Bridge and Bldg. Assn., Sigma Xi, Tau Beta Pi, Chi Epsilon. Author: Elementary Theory and Design of Flexural Members (with J. Vawter), 1950; Welded Deck Highway Bridges, 1950; Welded Highway Bridge Designs, 1952; Comparative Bridge Designs, 1954; Welded Interstate Highway Bridges, 1959. Home: 716 W Florida Ave Urbana IL 61801 Office: 302 W Elm St Urbana IL 61801

CLARK, JAMES LEROY, ret. plastic products mfg. co. exec.; b. Ottawa, Kans., Sept. 26, 1913; s. William Everett and Charlotte Daisy (Horn) C.; student Carnegie Inst. Tech., 1931-35; m. Harriet Elizabeth Janda, Nov. 24, 1937; children—Mary Elizabeth Clark Parsons, Virginia Lee. Sales mgr. Wis. Cuneo Press, Milw., 1937-41; divisional sales mgr. Milprint, Inc., Milw., 1941-43; pres. Clarvan Corp., Milw., 1943-53, Mark-Clark, Inc., Milw., 1953-62; chmn., pres., chief exec. officer Plastronics, Inc., Milw., 1962-79; dir. Mgmt. Resources Assos., Inc., 1977-80, Five Star Industries. Vice pres., dir. Met. Milw. Civic Alliance, 1976-80, pres., 1980-81; bd. dirs. Milw. Hearing Soc., De Paul Rehab. Hosp., Milw., 1976—; chmn. bicentennial com. Greater Milw. Service Clubs, 1976—; chmn. DePaul Sertoma Industries, 1979-81. Mem. Soc. Plastics Industry, Am. Mgmt. Assn., Wis. Mfrs. Assn., Health Industry Mfrs. Assn. (chmn. engring. com.), Friends of Mus., Milw. Art Center, Riveredge Found., Milw. Soc. Clubs: Milw. Athletic, Sertoma. Patentee health care and other plastic products.

CLARK, JOHN ROBERT, mgmt. psychologist; b. Pitts., Oct. 23, 1943; B.A., U. Notre Dame, 1965; M.B.A., Loyola U., 1974; Ph.D., Ill. Inst. Tech., 1979; m. Mary Diorio, Nov. 24, 1966. Supr. manpower procurement Hyster Co., Portland, Oreg., 1967-70, sales rep., Chgo., 1970-79; v.p. Mark Silber Assos. Ltd., 1979-81; sr. cons. Witt and Dolan Assos., Inc., Oak Brook, Ill., 1981—. Mem. Am. Psychol. Assn., Am. Theatre Organ Soc. Roman Catholic. Club: Notre Dame (Chgo.). Home: 1457 Davine Dr Glendale Heights IL 60137 Office: 1415 W 22d St Oak Brook IL 60521

CLARK, LARRY DALTON, civil engr.; b. Sask., Can., May 12, 1942; s. Albert Ray and Christina Emily (Marum) C.; B.S. in Civil Engring., S.D. Sch. Mines, Rapid City, 1971; m. Janice Martina Kettleson, Aug. 16, 1969; children—Tamara Dayrie, Laura Janelle, Jennifer Lynette. Engr. in tng. Iowa Hwy. Commn., Ames, 1971-75; asst. resident engr. Iowa Dept. Transp., New Hampton, 1975-79, acting resident engr., 1977-78; county engr. Black Hawk County, 1979—. Active local United Way campaign, 1976-77. Registered profl. engr., Iowa; registered land surveyor. Mem. ASCE, Nat., Iowa socs. profl. engrs., Sigma Tau. Lutheran. Home: 4224 Spruce Hills Dr Cedar Falls IA Office: Black Hawk County Courthouse Waterloo IA 50703

CLARK, LINDA MARIE, cons.; b. Chgo., June 9, 1940; d. Harold Dean and Edith M. (Nystrom) C.; B.S., U. Mich., 1962; M.B.A., U. Chgo., 1969. Analyst, Biol. Scis. Computation Center, Billings Hosp., U. Chgo., 1962-65; dir. math. and statis. services Armour & Co., Chgo., 1965-68; pvt. practice cons., Chgo., 1968-69; pres. LMC Cons. Co., Flossmoor, Ill., 1969—; dir. Internat. Computer Edn. Corp., Ill., 1971-75. Bd. govs. Internat. House, U. Chgo., 1976—; sec.-treas. U. Chgo. Alumnae Council Exec. Com., 1976-77; del. White House Conf. Small Bus., 1980; mem. Pvt. Industry Council Suburban Cook County, 1980—. Mem. Am. Statis. Assn. (pres. Chgo. chpt. 1972-73, bd. dirs. 1971-74), Optical Soc. Am. (mem. nat. com. on computers 1976-77), AAAS, Ill. Delegation on Small Bus., Ind. Bus. Assn. Ill., Chgo. Assn. Commerce and Industry (bd. dirs. 1974-79), U. Chgo. Women's Bus. Group, Alpha Chi Omega. Club: P.E.O. (pres. chpt. HH 1981—). Contbr. articles to profl. jours. Pub. Met. Chgo. Maj. Employer's Directory, 1977. Home: 1127 Dartmouth Rd Flossmoor IL 60422

CLARK, M.R., supt. schs.; b. Union, Iowa, Aug. 10, 1904; s. Fred C. and Elizabeth Frances (Hansen) C.; A.B., Iowa State Tchrs. Coll., 1931; M.A., State U. Iowa, 1936; LL.D., Upper Iowa Coll., 1967; m. Dorothy A. Cunliffe, June 20, 1931; 1 dau., Barbara Ann. Classroom instr., Randalia, Iowa, 1925-31, supt. schs., 1931-37, West Branch, Iowa, 1937-40, Sac City, Iowa, 1940-46, Dubuque, Iowa, 1946-66; supt. Area One Vocational Tech. Sch. Dist., Calmar, Iowa, 1966-75. Dir. Iowa High Sch. Ins. Co. Pres. Cummunity Chest, 1952-53; Ia. Community Chests and Councils, 1953; pres. N.E. Iowa Boy Scout Council (Silver Beaver award). Bd. dirs. Dubuque County Mental Health, Dubuque Cancer Soc., A.R.C., United Fund Iowa. Recipient Alumni Service award State Coll. Iowa; classroom and lab. named in his honor. Mem. N.E.A., Am. Assn. Sch. Adminstrs., Am., Iowa assns. adult edn., Iowa Edn. Assn. (past pres. N.E. dist.), Iowa Supts. Club (pres. 1956-57), Iowa Area Sch. Adminstrs. (pres. 1971-73), Dubuque C. of C. (dir.), Epsilon Pi Tau, Phi Delta Kappa. Republican. Methodist. Mason (32 deg., Shriner); mem. Order Eastern Star. Clubs: Rotary (pres.; dist. gov. 1957-58), Dubuque Auto (dir.). Contbr. to jours. Home: 102 Sunset Dr Decorah IA 52101

CLARK, MARY JANE, assn. adminstr.; b. Kokomo, Ind., Apr. 10, 1922; d. Benjamin Harrison and Mary A. (Richards) Wineinger; student Stephens Coll., 1940-41, Butler U. Coll. of Bus., 1941-43; children—Katherine E. Clark Redding, Barbara Ann Clark Schneider. Sec. to prin. Westlane Jr. High Sch., Indpls., 1958-66; sec. to dir. of guidance North Central High Sch., Indpls., 1966-68; sec. to pres. Nat. Assn. Mut. Ins. Cos., Indpls., 1968-78, sec. to v.p. legislation, 1968-71, office mgr., 1972-78, asst. to pres., dir. adminstrn., 1979—. Mem. Adminstrv. Mgmt. Soc., Nat. Secs. Assn., P.E.O., Kappa Kappa Kappa. Republican. Clubs: Am. Legion Aux., Kappa Kappa Gamma. Home: 2005 Seaport Dr Indianapolis IN 46240 Office: 3707 Woodview Trace PO Box 68700 Indianapolis IN 46268

CLARK, MARY ROMAYNE SCHROEDER (MRS. DONALD ARTHUR CLARK), educator, civic worker; b. Fergus Falls, Minn.; d. Christian Frederick and Dorothy Genevieve (Miller) Schroeder; B.A., Coll. St. Teresa, 1944; diploma fine arts Conservatory St. Cecelia, 1944; M.A., Marquette U., 1978; postgrad. U. Salzburg (Austria); m. Donald Arthur Clark, Aug. 24, 1946 (dec. Jan. 1975); children—Donald Arthur, Anne Elizabeth, Christopher John. Instr., Ottumwa (Iowa) Heights Coll., 1944-46; instr. U. N.D., Grand Forks, 1946-48, Marquette U., Milw., 1948-52, Milw. Area Tech. Coll., 1962-66, Mt. Mary Coll., Milw., 1976—; communications cons. 1st Bank Milw., 1978-80, coordinator community relations, 1980—. Mem. com. on edn. U.S. Cath. Conf., Washington, 1971-75; state vol. adviser Nat. Found., 1971—; mem. adv. bd. Sickle Cell Disease Center, Deaconess Hosp., Milw., 1970-73; mem. nat. alumnae bd. Coll. St. Teresa, Winona, Minn., 1970—; mem. bd. edn. Archdiocese Milw., 1965-71, pres., 1967-71. Named Wis. Woman of Year, Wis. Cath. War Vets., 1963, Alumna of Year, Coll. St. Teresa, 1969, Outstanding Vol. Nat. Found., 1974, Vol. Activist Germaine Monteil, 1974. Mem. Archdiocesan Confraternity Christian Mothers (pres. 1961-63), Archdiocesan League Cath. Home and Sch. Assns. (pres. 1963-65), Archdiocesan Council Cath. Women (dist. pres. 1965-67), Nat. Forum Cath. Parents Orgns. (v.p. 1979), Internat. Fedn. Cath. Alumnae, AAUW, Marquette U. Women's (pres. 1959). Home: 317 N Story Pkwy Milwaukee WI 53208

CLARK, MAXINE, retail exec.; b. Miami, Fla., Mar. 6, 1949; d. Kenneth and Anne (Lerch) Kasselman; B.A. in Journalism, U. Ga., 1971. Exec. trainee Hecht Co., Washington, 1971, hosiery buyer, 1971-72, misses sportswear buyer, 1972-76; mgr. mdse. planning and research May Dept. Stores Co., St. Louis, 1976-78, dir. mdse. devel., 1978-80, v.p. mktg. and sales promotion Venture Stores div., 1980-81, sr. v.p. mktg. and sales promotion Venture Stores div., 1981—. Sec., Lafayette Sq. Restoration Com., 1978-79. Mem. Nat. Assn. Female Execs., St. Louis Women's Commerce Assn., Advt. Club Greater St. Louis. Home: 1912 Rutger St Saint Louis MO 63104 Office: 615 Northwest Plaza Saint Ann MO 63074

CLARK, MONTAGUE GRAHAM, JR., coll. pres.; b. Charlotte, N.C., Feb. 25, 1909; s. Montague G. and Alice C. (Graham) C.; student Ga. Inst. Tech. Sch. Engring.; LL.D., Drury Coll., 1957; Ed.D., S.W. Baptist Coll., 1972; Litt.D., Sch. of the Ozarks, 1975; D.D., Missouri Valley Coll., 1977; m. Elizabeth Hoyt, May 2, 1933; children—Elizabeth (Mrs. Joe Embser), Alice (Mrs. Harold Davis), Margaret (Mrs. William Miller), Julia (Mrs. Cecil Hampton). Vice pres. Hoyt & Co., Atlanta, 1934-46; v.p. Sch. of Ozarks, Point Lookout, Mo., 1946-52, pres., 1952-81, sec. bd. trustees, 1957-71, now chmn.; ordained to ministry Presbyn. Ch., 1950; dir. Bank of Taney County; dir., mem. exec. com., sec. corp. Blue Cross. Past mem. Commn. on Colls. and Univs., North Central Assn. Colls. and Secondary Schs.; former moderator Lafayette Presbytery and Synod of Mo., Presbyn. Ch. of U.S. Past mem. nat. adv. council on health professions edn. NIH; mem. Nat. council Boy Scouts Am., also mem. adv. bd. Ozarks Empire Area council; mem. Wilson's Creek Battlefield Nat. Commn., 1961—; hon. mem. Mo. Am. Revolution Bicentennial Commn.; former v.p. Am. Heart Assn., also dir.; mem. exec. com., chmn. fund raising adv. and policy com., Gt. Plains regional chmn.; chmn. Mo. Heart Fund, mem. adv. council Council on Am. Affairs. Chmn. bd. Mo. Heart Assn.; trustee Patriotic Edn., Inc.; mem. South Central/Lakes County Med. Services System; v.p. Thomas Hart Benton Homestead Meml. Commn.; bd. dirs. St. Louis Scottish Towers Residence Found.; chmn. burns prevention com. Shrine of N. Am.; hon. edn. chmn. for So. Mo. div. Am. Cancer Soc. Served to maj. Internal Security, World War II. Named Ark. traveler, 1962; recipient Silver Beaver award Boy Scouts Am.; Gold Heart award Am. Heart Assn.; George Washington certificate Freedoms Found., 1974, 78; In God We Trust award Family Found.; Disting. Service award Am. Legion, Mo.; numerous other awards; named to Ozark Hall of Fame. Mem. SAR (past pres. gen. nat. soc., hon. v.p. Mo. Soc.; Nat. Soc. Good Citizenship medal, Patriot medal, Minute Man award, Va. Soc. medal), Navy League U.S., Mo. C. of C., Branson C. of C. (econ. devel. com.), Mo. Pilots Assn. (1st chmn. bd.), Civil Air Patrol (dir., adv. bd.), White River Valley Hist. Soc. (past pres.), Soc. Colonial Wars, Acad. Mo. Squires, Order Founders and Patriots Am., Air Force Assn., Assn. U.S. Army, Mo. Assn. State Troopers Emergency Relief Soc., Internat. Assn. Chiefs of Police. Clubs: Mason (33 deg., Shriner, K.T., Red Cross of Constantine, York Rite, past imperial chaplain Imperial Council, Nobles of Mystic Shrine of N. Am.; grand chaplain Grand Lodge Mo.; honoree various ceremonies), Rotary (past local pres., dist. gov. 1966-67), De Molay. Address: The Sch of the Ozarks Point Lookout MO 65726

CLARK, MONTE DALE, profl. football club coach; b. Fillmore, Calif., Jan. 24, 1937; s. Doley Guy and Lorene (Couch) C.; B.A. in Edn., U. So. Calif.; postgrad. San Francisco State U.; m. Charlotte D. Clark; children—Bryan, Randy, Eric. Profl. football player Cleve. Browns, 1959-69; asst. coach Miami (Fla.) Dolphins, 1970-76; head coach San Francisco 49er's, 1976, Detroit Lions, 1978—, also dir. football ops.; sec. Far West Restaurants Corp., San Jose, Calif., Membership chmn. Oakland County YMCA. Presbyterian. Home: 1482 Cochridge Rd Bloomfield Hills MI 48013 Office: 1200 Featherstone St Pontiac MI 48057

CLARK, PATRICIA IRENE, mfg. co. exec.; b. Toledo, Ohio, June 23, 1939; d. Edward Frank and June Daisy (Budd) Gorka; student Mary Manse Coll., 1968, U. Toledo, 1979-80; m. Jack L. Clark, Mar. 30, 1978; children by previous marriage—Cathleen, Kevin, Michael Stapleton. Sec. to pres. Heating Trades Supplies, Inc., Toledo, 1957-66; exec. sec. to pres. Toledo Beaver Tools, 1966-68; sec./contract coordinator/adminstrv. technician Teledyne CAE, Toledo, 1968-79, price adminstr., Toledo, 1979—. Advisor, Jr. Achievement of N.W. Ohio, 1977-78. Mem. Nat. Mgmt. Assn., Nat. Contract Mgmt. Assn., Tech. Mktg. Assn., Delta Chi Sigma (internat. sec. 1978-79). Methodist. Home: 4037 Wise St Northwood OH 43619 Office: 1330 Laskey Rd Toledo OH 43612

CLARK, PATSY SUE, pub. relations dir.; b. Vernon, Tex., Aug. 6, 1934; d. Henry Devrick and Christine B. (Barrett) Hays; B.A. in Communications, Baylor U., 1955; m. John D. Clark; children—Russell Devrick, Susan Patricia. Copy writer Alexander McKenzie Advt., Dallas, 1966-67; concept dir. Vic Lundberg, Inc., Advt., Grand Rapids, Mich., 1967-70; ex-officio dir. Williams & Works, Inc., Cons. Engrs., Planners, Architects, Surveyors, Geologists, Grand Rapids, 1970—; vis. lectr. public relations Aquinas Coll., Grand Valley State Colls. Recipient Excellence awards Advt. Council Grand Rapids, 1969, Rockford, Ill., 1969, Springfield, Ohio, 1969, Midwest Advt. Council, 1969. Mem. Soc. Tech. Communications (dir., Merit award 1974), Am. Cons. Engrs. Council (public relations com.), Cons. Engrs. Council Mich. (public relations com., dir. polit. action com.), Public Relations Soc. Am. (exec. bd. govt. sect.). Republican. Club: Press (Grand Rapids). Home: 4243 Greenbrier Ct SE Grand Rapids MI 49506 Office: 611 Cascade West Pkwy SE Grand Rapids MI 49506

CLARK, PAUL EDWARD, publisher; b. Metropolis, Ill., Mar. 7, 1941; s. Paul E. and Lillie Jean (Melcher) C.; B.A., So. Ill. U., 1963, M.A., 1965; M.Div., Northwestern U., 1970; D.Mus., Inst. Musical Research (London), 1973; Ph.D., U. Ill., 1978. Staff accompanist The Story (TV series) and White Sisters (Word Records), 1959-62; staff accompanist voice faculty So. Ill. U., Carbondale, 1961-65; ordained to ministry, Meth. Ch., 1966; pastor Stockland (Ill.) United Meth. Ch., 1966-70; minister of music First United Meth. Ch., Watseka, Ill., 1972-76; dir. choral activities Unit 3, Donovan (Ill.) schs., 1970-79; studio musician Chgo., Nashville, Los Angeles, 1966—; pres. Clark Music Pub. and Prodn., Watseka, 1973—; adminstrv. asst., bus. mgr. Community Unit 3 Schs., 1980—; cons. for workshops, univs. Named Piano Tchr. of the Year, So. Ill. U., 1970; Gospel Music Instrumentalist award, 1971; Ill. Chess Coach award, 1973, 74; U. Calif. at Los Angeles fellow, 1971. Mem. Am. Choral Dirs. Assn. (dist. chmn. 1977-80), Am. Fedn. Musicians, Music Educators Nat. Conf., Ill. Music Educators Assn., U.S. Chess Fedn., So. Ill. U. Alumni Assn., NEA, Broadcast Music Inc., Phi Mu Alpha, Mu Alpha Theta. Republican. Methodist. Contbr. articles in field to profl. jours. music reviewer, critic, columnist The Illiana Spirit (newspaper), 1976—; composer; The Voice That Calls His Name, 1961; Jesus Dear Jesus, 1971; Spring Was But A Child, 1977; Country Living, 1976; Losing is the Hurting Side of Love, 1977; Use Me Lord, 1978; Come On In, 1978; All I Ask of You, 1979. Home: 115 W Locust St Watseka IL 60970 Office: PO Box 299 Watseka IL 60970

CLARK, PAUL THOMAS, hosp. ofcl.; b. Ironton, Ohio, Oct. 13, 1943; s. Charles Nelson and Lucille May (Dudley) C.; B.A. in Journalism, Ohio State U., 1969, postgrad., 1971-73; m. Janice M. Merrill, Oct. 16, 1965; children—Colin, Sean. Editor, Ohio Petroleum Marketers Assn., Columbus, 1969; dir. public relations Otterbein Coll., Westerville, Ohio, 1970-72, Riverside Meth. Hosp., Columbus, 1972-77, Bronson Meth. Hosp., Kalamazoo, Mich., 1977—. Spl. events chmn. Kalamazoo United Way, 1978; pub. affairs Kalamazoo County C. of C., 1977—. Served with AUS, 1961-64. Recipient McEach- ern award Am. Hosp. Assn., 1974, awards Ohio Hosp. Assn., 1974, 75, 76, awards Columbus Advt. Fedn., 1975, 76. Mem. Public Relations Soc. Am. (Silver Anvil award 1981), Am. Acad. Hosp. Public Relations, Am. Soc. Hosp. Public Relations Dirs. Club: Kalamazoo Rotary. Home: 1713 Suffolk Ave Kalamazoo MI 49002 Office: 252 E Lovell St Kalamazoo MI 49007

CLARK, PERCY, JR., ednl. adminstr.; b. Chgo., July 21, 1942; s. Percy and Mary (Carson) C.; B.A., Western Mich. U., 1964, M.A., 1969; Ph.D., U. Mich., 1978; m. Carol Sue Christophersen, Mar. 19, 1964; children—Mark, Michelle, Nicole. Elementary and secondary classroom tchr. Portage (Mich.) pub. schs., 1964-68; inservice coordinator Kalamazoo Valley Intermediate Sch. Dist., 1968-69; prin. Northglade Elementary Sch., Kalamazoo, 1969-72; dir. student services Kalamazoo pub. schs., 1972-78; asst. supt. Shaker Heights (Ohio) City Sch. Dist., 1978—; cons. in field. Bd. dirs. Northside Assn. Community Devel., Jr. Achievement, Boys Club Am., County Vol. Services Program, Kalamazoo Goodwill Industries, Child Guidance Clinic, Family Health Center, NAACP; mem. outreach com. Boy Scouts Am. Recipient various certificates of appreciation. Mem. Am., Mich. personnel and guidance assns., Assn. Supervision and Curriculum Devel., Nat. Assn. Pupil Personnel Adminstrs., Ohio Assn. Elem. Sch. Prins., Mich. Soc. Mental Health, Am. Assn. Sch. Adminstrs. Home: 3052 Huntington Rd Shaker Heights OH 44120 Office: 15600 Parkland Dr Shaker Heights OH 44120

CLARK, PETER BRUCE, newspaper exec.; b. Detroit, Oct. 23, 1928; s. Rex Scripps and Marian (Peters) C.; B.A., Pomona Coll., 1952, LL.D. (hon.), 1972; M.P.A., Syracuse U., 1953; Ph.D., U. Chgo., 1959; H.H.D. (hon.), Mich. State U., 1973; LL.D. (hon.), U. Mich., 1977; m. Lianne Schroeder, Dec. 21, 1952; children—Ellen, James. Research asso., then instr. polit. sci. U. Chgo., 1957-59; asst. prof. polit. sci. Yale U., 1959-61; with Evening News Assn., Detroit, 1960—, sec., v.p., 1961-63, pres., pub. Detroit News, 1963—, chmn. bd., 1969—, also dir.; chmn. Fed. Res. Bank Chgo., 1975-77. Bd. dirs. United Found. Met. Detroit, Harper-Grace Hosps. Detroit. Served with AUS, 1953-55. Mem. Am. Newspaper Pubs. Assn. (dir. 1966-74), Am. Polit. Sci. Assn., Am. Soc. Newspaper Editors, Adcraft Club Detroit, Econ. Club Detroit, Pi Sigma Alpha. Clubs: Detroit Country, Detroit, Detroit Athletic. Office: 615 Lafayette Blvd Detroit MI 48231*

CLARK, RICHARD ALLEN, mfg. co. exec.; b. Holmes County, Ohio, Feb. 27, 1950; s. Howard Allen and Lois Maxine C.; B.S. in Bus. Adminstrn., Mt. Union Coll., Alliance, Ohio, 1972; m. Betty Lou Mullet, Aug. 18, 1972; children—Kelly Joe, Joshua Allen, Laura Elizabeth. With Wayne Door Co., Mt. Hope, Ohio, 1972—, asst. to pres., 1977—, corporate officer, 1978—. Youth Sponsor Berlin (Ohio) Mennonite Ch., 1974-75, tchr. Sunday sch., 1976-77, asst. supt., 1979-80. Office: Box 67 Mount Hope OH 44660

CLARK, ROBERT EUGENE, educator; b. Cheyenne, Wyo., Aug. 19, 1931; s. Glen E. and Anna W. (Shaw) C.; B.A., Wheaton Coll., 1961; M.S., U. Nebr., Omaha, 1965; Ed.D., U. Denver, 1968; m. Marian A. Anderson, June 13, 1954; children—Kathleen, Kevin, Kristine, Karen, Ken, Kraig. Dir. Christian edn. Bethel Bible Ch., Hammond, Ind., 1954-58; tchr. Faith Bapt. Bible Coll., Ankeny, Iowa, 1958-59, chmn. Christian edn. dept., 1961-69; prof. Christian edn. faculty Moody Bible Inst., Chgo., 1969—. Baptist. Author: (with others) Understanding People, 1972; editor Childhood Education in the Church, 1975; contbr. to publs. in field. Home: 1044 Garner Ave Wheaton IL 60187 Office: Moody Bible Inst 820 N LaSalle St Chicago IL 60610

CLARK, ROBERT LOY, human services adminstr.; b. Kansas City, Mo., July 2, 1937; s. Robert William and Donna Lavonna (Loy) C.; A.B., No. Colo. U., 1959; postgrad. Syracuse U., 1959; M.S. in

Psychology, Ft. Hays (Kans.) State U., 1963; postgrad. U. Nebr., 1963; m. Connie Lou Davis, Sept. 3, 1960; children—Vicki Marie, Robert Scott, Angie Linn. Vocational rehab. counselor Hays (Kans.) Div. Rehab. Services, 1960-62, Lincoln (Nebr.) Div. Rehab. Services, 1964-65, Glenwood (Iowa) Hosp.-Sch. for Mentally Retarded, 1965-66; exec. dir. Greater Omaha Assn. Retarded Citizens, 1966-71; dir. Douglas County (Nebr.) Dept. Mental Health Resources, Omaha, 1971-74; asst. dir. human services Eastern Neb. Human Services Agy., Omaha, 1974-75; adminstr. human services Lincoln-Lancaster County (Nebr.), 1975—. Community services cons. U. Nebr. Coll. Medicine, 1971-74, instr. med. psychology, dept. psychiatry, 1975-79; adv. mem. governing bd. Eastern Nebr. Community Office of Retardation, 1970-74; mem. Nebr. Gov.'s Citizens' Study Com. Mental Retardation, 1967-69; mem. Lincoln-Lancaster County Emergency Med. Services Council, 1975-78; bd. dirs. Nebr. Assn. Mental Health, 1972—, treas., 1974-76; bd. dirs. Lincoln Action Program, 1976-80. Mem. Rehab. Assn. Nebr. (past dir., treas. 1964-72). Democrat. Home: 1681 Woodsview Lincoln NE 68502 Office: 555 S 10th St Lincoln NE 68508

CLARK, SAMUEL SMITH, physician, educator; b. Phila., Sept. 2, 1932; s. Horace E. and Jane (Mullin) C.; B.S., McGill U., 1954, M.D. C.M., 1958; m. Heather Jean Ogilvy, June 21, 1957; children—Ross Angus, Erin, Brian Mullin. Intern, Bethesda (Md.) Naval Hosp., 1958-59; resident Royal Victoria Hosp., Montreal, Que., Can., 1962-67; practice medicine, specializing in urology, Munster, Ind., 1967-68, Chgo., 1969-76, Wheaton, Ill., 1976—; attending urologist St. Catherine's Hosp., East Chicago, Ind., 1967, Our Lady of Mercy Hosp., Dyer, Ind., 1967, St. Margarets Hosp., Hammond, Ind., 1967, Central DuPage Hosp., Winfield, Ill., 1976—, Delnor Hosp., St. Charles, Ill., 1976—, Glendale Heights Hosp., 1979—, VA Hines Hosp., 1980—; chief urology West Side VA Hosp., Chgo., 1969-77, U. Ill. Hosp., Chgo., 1971-77; cons. urology Kankakee State Hosp., 1969-75, Ill. State Pediatric Inst., 1970—, Dixon State Sch., 1971—, Chgo. Read Mental Health Center, 1972-77; asst. prof. urology Abraham Lincoln Sch. of Medicine, U. Ill., Chgo., 1968-71, asso. prof., 1971-73, prof., 1973-80, head div. urology, 1971-77; clin. prof. Loyola U., Chgo., 1980—; med. dir. Crescent Counties Found. for Med. Care, 1979—. Bd. dirs. Marianjoy Rehab. Hosp., Wheaton, Ill., 1979—. Served to lt. M.C., USN, 1958-62. Diplomate Am. Bd. Urology, Fellow A.C.S., Inst. of Medicine of Chgo.; mem. Am. Urol. Assn. (exec. com. North Central sect. 1974-77), Canadian Urol. Assn., Ill. Urol. Assn. (pres. 1979-80), Soc. Univ. Urologists, AAUP, DuPage Med. Soc. (councilor 1977-78, 80-82), AMA, Warren H. Cole Soc., Chgo. Urol. Soc. (sec. treas. 1974-79, pres. 1979-80). Episcopalian. Clubs: Chicago Athletic, Glen Oak Country. Contbr. articles to profl. jours. Home: 592 Turner St Glen Ellyn IL 60137 Office: 399 Schmale Rd Wheaton IL 60187

CLARK, STEPHEN RUSSELL, lawyer; b. St. Louis, Apr. 12, 1949; s. William Albert and Eileen (Seibert) C.; B.A., St. Louis U., 1971, J.D., 1974; m. Dianne Elizabeth Davis, Jan. 27, 1978; 1 son, Kyle William. Admitted to Ill. bar, 1974; atty. firm McRoberts, Sheppard, McRoberts & Wimmer, P.C., East St. Louis, Ill., 1974-77; partner firm Montalvo & Clark, Belleville; Ill., 1977—. Treas., bd. dirs. Children, Family and Youth Advocacy Council, Belleville, 1978—; chmn. Young Republican Orgn. Ill., 1977-79; vice chmn. Young Rep. Nat. Fedn., 1979—; pres. St. Clair County Young Rep. Club, 1976—. Recipient resolution award State of Ill., 1977, Man of Year award Young Rep. Orgn. Ill., 1978. Mem. Am. Bar Assn., Am. Trial Lawyers Assn., Conf. Personal Fin. Law, Ill. Bar Assn., Ill. Trail Lawyers Assn., St. Clair County Bar Assn. Roman Catholic. Club: Elks. Home: 1404 Cumberland Ct Belleville IL 62221 Office: 9425 W Main St Belleville IL 62223

CLARK, THOMAS RALPH, ins. co. exec.; b. Des Moines, Dec. 3, 1940; s. Thomas McKinstry and Vivian Irene (Lewis) C.; B.A., Drake U., 1980; m. Suzanne David, Aug. 25, 1975; children—Thomas Lewis, Karen Sue, Michelle Patterson, Todd Patterson. With Mass. Mut. Life Co., Asso. Ins. Services, Inc., Des Moines, 1966—, salesman, 1981—. C.L.U. Mem. Internat. Assn. Fin. Planners, Iowa Assn. Life Underwriters (pres. 1975-76, nat. committeeman 1976-83), Des Moines Assn. Life Underwriters (pres. 1980-81), Am. Soc. C.L.U.'s, Polk County Estate Planners, Million Dollar Round Table (life), Des Moines C. of C. Republican. Mem. Christian Ch. (Disciples of Christ). Club: Des Moines. Home: 3007 Mary Lynn Dr Urbandale IA 50322 Office: 1100 UCB Bldg Des Moines IA 50309

CLARK, THOMAS ROLFE, clin. psychologist; b. Detroit, Oct. 30, 1947; s. Edward Rolfe and Ruth Ann (Spurr) C.; m. Mary Franzen, July 15, 1972. A.B. magna cum laude, Greenville Coll., 1963; Ph.D. (Robards Doctoral fellow), U. Windsor (Can.), 1972; intern Wayne County Psychiat. Hosp., Detroit, mem. staff, 1972-77; chief psychologist Heritage Hosp., 1978-81; dir. mental health Marian Manor Med. Center, 1981—; pvt. practice clin. and med. psychology and psychotherapy, Detroit, 1972—; faculty Henry Ford Community Coll., Dearborn, Mich., 1972-76; dir. clin. services Met. Guidance Center, Livonia, Mich., 1978—; mental health cons. People's Community Hosp. Authority, various police depts. Organist 1st United Meth. Ch., Dearborn, 1965—; concert organist, 1975—; bd. dirs. Meth. Children's Home Soc., Livonia, Mich., 1974—. Fellow Am. Orthopsychiat. Assn., Masters and Johnson Inst., Christian Assn. Psychol. Studies; mem. Am., Southeastern, Western, Mich. psychol. assns., Internat. Therapy Behavior Assn., Am. Assn. Sex Edn. Counselors, Acad. of Psychologists in Marital, Sex, and Family Therapy, Mich. Soc. Lic. Psychologists, Mich. Alcoholism and Addiction Assn., Am. Guild Organists, Internat. Council Psychologists, Mich. Profl. Police Assn. Contbr. articles to profl. jours.; rec. artist. Recipient awards in music, psychology. Home: 26347 Sims Dr Dearborn Heights MI 48127 Office: Suite 112 29865 W Six Mile Rd Livonia MI 48152

CLARK, THOMAS WEBSTER, kitchen cabinet co. exec.; b. Chgo., Aug. 29, 1947; s. Robert Ohmer and Clare Adeline (Webster) C.; A.A., U. S.D., 1969; B.A. Governors State U., 1976, M.B.A., 1977; m. Madonna Marie Becker, July 14, 1971; children—Thomas Webster II, Robert James, Cristen Clare. With Homewood (Ill.) Industries Inc., 1972—, trainer dealers, mktg. consultants, 1976—; with Cabinetpak, Inc., 1976—, owner, partner Cambinetpak of Homewood, Inc., 1977—. Mem. Better Bus. Bur., 1976—; supporter Purple Heart Vets., 1972—; mem. Republican Nat. Com., 1978—. Served with U.S. Army, 1970-72. Mem. VFW, Homewood C. of C. (dir. 77-80), Governors State U. Alumni Assn., Tau Kappa Epsilon Alumni Assn. Club: Chgo. Wergamers Assn. Home: Rural Route 1 Box 134 Monee IL 60449 Office: Cabinetpak of Homewood Inc 17641 S Ashland St Homewood IL 60430

CLARK, THREESE ANNE, occupational therapist; b. Bath, N.Y., Jan. 16, 1946; d. Frank G. and Belulah Irene (Harris) Brown; B.S. (O'Connor scholar) magna cum laude in Occupational Therapy, U. N.D., 1967, M.S. in Counseling and Guidance, 1977; one child by previous marriage. Mem. staff occupational therapy U. N.D., Grand Forks, 1968; chief occupational therapy developer Corning Hosp., Corning, N.Y., 1968-69, Arnot-Ogden Hosp., Elmira, N.Y., 1969-71; mem. staff occupational therapy Bath (N.Y.) VA Center, 1971-74; instr. dept. occupational therapy U. N.D., Grand Forks, 1974-77; cons. Grafton (N.D.) State Sch. for the Retarded, 1975-76, Heart of Am. Rehab. Center, Rugby, N.D., 1976-77; prin. investigator/instr. vocat. content, occupational therapy dept. Ohio State U., 1977-79; occupational therapist Regional Ednl. Assessment and Consultation Team, Hillsboro, Ohio, 1979—. Chairperson U.S. Govt. Youth Adv. Com., Bath (N.Y.) VA Center, 1972-74; chairperson family life and human relations Northtown Elem. Sch. PTA, Columbus, Ohio, 1978. Lic. occupational therapist, Ohio; cert. spl. edn. tchr., Ohio. Mem. Am. Occupational Therapy Assn. (mem. council on edn. 1974-76), Ohio Occupational Therapy Assn., Nat. Rehab. Assn. Baptist. Home: 211 W South Hillsboro OH 45133 Office: 5799 W New Market Rd Hillsboro OH 45133

CLARK, WALTER HILL, savs. and loan exec.; b. Athens, Ga., June 5, 1928; s. John Quincy and Beulah Bernice (Hill) C.; B.B.A., So. Ill. U., 1951; M.B.A., De Paul U., 1958; grad. Advanced Mgmt. Program Harvard, 1971; m. Juanita E. Dillard, July 13, 1957; children—Hilton Pierre, Jaunine Charise. With First Fed. Savs. and Loan Assn. Chgo. (Ill.), 1962—, treas., 1967—, v.p., 1969-74, sr. v.p., group mgr., 1974-75, exec. v.p., 1975—. Vice pres. Travelers Aid Soc.-Immigration Service League, Chgo., 1967-76, pres., 1976—, bd. mem., 1967—; bd. dirs. Community Renewal Soc., Chgo., 1961—. Bd. dirs. adv. council bus. adminstrn. U. Ill., Chgo. campus, 1969—. Served with AUS, 1952-54. Mem. Nat. Soc. Controllers and Financial Officers Savs. Instns., Alpha Phi Alpha. Conglist. (financial sec. 1956—, trustee). Clubs: Economic, Union League, (Chgo.), 71. Home: 1235 E Madison Park Chicago IL 60615 Office: 1 S Dearborn St Chicago IL 60603

CLARK, WILLIAM GEORGE, judge; b. Chgo., July 16, 1924; s. John S. and Ita (Kennedy) C.; student Loyola U., Chgo., 1942-43, 44; J.D., DePaul U., 1946; J.D. (hon.), John Marshall Law Sch., Chgo., 1962; m. Rosalie Locatis, Nov. 28, 1946; children—Merrilee, William George, Donald, John Steven, Robert. Admitted to Ill. bar, 1947; mem. firm Crane, Kearney, Korzen, Phelan & Clark, and predecessor, Chgo., 1947-56; atty. for Pub. Adminstr. Ill., 1949-53; mem. Ill. Ho. of Reps. from Austin Dist. of Chgo., 1952-54, 56-60, mem. Senate, 1954-56, majority leader, 1959; atty. gen. Ill., 1960-69; partner firm Arvey, Hodes & Mantynband, Chgo.; justice Supreme Ct. Ill., 1976—. Served with AUS, 1942-44. Mem. Am., Fed., Ill., Chgo., West Suburban bar assns., AMVETS, Celtic Legal Soc., Am. Legion, Ancient Order Hibernians, Irish Fellowship Club (pres. 1961-62), Catholic Lawyers Guild Chgo., Am. Judicature Soc., Nat. Lawyers Club, Delta Theta Phi. Clubs: Moose, Elk, K.C. Office: Ill Supreme Ct Richard J Daley Center Chicago IL 60602

CLARK, WILLIAM MERLE, baseball scout; b. Clinton, Mo., Aug. 18, 1932; s. Merle William and Beulah (Wilson) C.; student George Barr Umpire Sch., 1950, Central Mo. State U., 1950-51; B.J., U. Mo., 1958; postgrad. Somers Umpire Sch., 1962; m. Dolores Pearl Denny, Aug. 11, 1955; children—Patrick Sean, Michael Seumas, Kelly Kathleen, Kerry Maureen, Casey Connor. Umpire, Central Mexican League, Neb. State League, 1956; sportswriter, Lexington (Ky.) Leader, 1958, Columbia (Mo.) Missourian, 1958-60, Columbia (Mo.) Tribune, 1963—; recreation dir. City of Columbia, Mo., 1962-68. Umpire, Pioneer League, 1962; partner J.C. Stables, Columbia, Mo., 1965—; scouting supr. Pitts. Pirates, 1968, Seattle, 1969, Milw., 1970, Cin., 1971—. Served with AUS, 1951-54. Mem. Amateur Athletic Union (life), Mo. Sportswriter's Assn. (pres. 1958), Mo. Archeol. Soc., Mo. Hist. Soc., Columbia Audubon Soc. Unitarian-Universalist. Address: 3906 Grace Ellen Dr Columbia MO 65201

CLARKE, CHARLES FENTON, lawyer; b. Hillsboro, Ohio, July 25, 1916; s. Charles F. and Margaret (Patton) C.; A.B. summa cum laude, Washington and Lee Coll., 1938; LL.B., U. Mich., 1940; LL.D., Cleve. State U., 1971; m. Virginia Schoppenhorst, Apr. 3, 1945; children—Elizabeth, Margaret, Jane, Charles Fenton IV. Admitted to Mich. bar, 1940, Ohio bar, 1946; pvt. practice law, Detroit, 1942; asso. Squire, Sanders & Dempsey, Cleve., 1946-57, partner, 1957—. Dir. Found. Equipment Corp., W.M. Brode Co. Trustee Legal Aid Soc., 1959-67; pres. Nat. Assn. R.R. Trial Counsel, 1966-68; pres. Alumni bd. dirs. Washington and Lee U., 1970-72; pres. bd. dirs. Free Med. Clinic Greater Cleve., Inc.; life mem. Sixth Circuit Jud. Conf.; chmn. legis. com. Cleve. Welfare Fedn., 1961-68; trustee Cleve. Citizens League, 1956-62; dir. Citizens adv. bd. Cuyahoga County Juvenile Ct., 1970-73; dir. George Jr. Republic, Greenville, Pa., 1970-73; vice chmn. Cleve. Crime Commn., 1974-75. Mem. exec. com. Cuyahoga County Rep. Orgn., 1950—; councilman, Bay Village, Ohio, 1948-53. Pres., trustee Cleve. Hearing and Speech Center, 1957-63; trustee Laurel Sch.; bd. dirs. Bowman Tech. Sch. Served to 1st lt. C.I.C., AUS, World War II. Fellow Am. Coll. Trial Lawyers; mem. Cleve. Civil War Round Table (pres. 1968), Cleve. Zool. Soc. (dir. 1970), Phi Beta Kappa. Republican. Presbyn. (sec. bd. trustees 1965-74, elder). Clubs: Skating, Union (Cleve.); Tavern. Home: 2262 Tudor Dr Cleveland Heights OH 44106 Office: Union Commerce Bldg Cleveland OH 44115

CLARKE, CHARLES JOSEPH, III, educator, mgmt. cons.; b. Columbus, Ohio, Sept. 14, 1943; s. Charles Joseph, Jr., and Helen (Pryor) C.; B.A., Miami U., Ohio, 1966; B.S., Parsons Coll., 1967; M.A. (Castle and Cooke grad. scholar), U. Hawaii, 1968; postgrad. U. Md., 1968-70, U. Ariz., 1970-72; m. Kaye Anne Intlekofer; children—Tamara Lee, Tiffany Catherine, Charles Joseph IV. Asst. Office of Placement and Career Planning, U. Hawaii, 1967-68; instr. Ft. Ritchie Mil. Base, 1969, U. Md., 1969-70; teaching asso. U. Ariz., 1970-72; faculty asso. Ariz. State U., 1971; instr. sociology Kirkwood Community Coll., summer 1973, Coe Coll., summer 1976; real estate investment counselor R.L. Smith Realtors, 1978-81; pres. Clarke Investments, Inc., Cedar Rapids, Iowa, 1978—; prof. sociology and real estate, chmn. dept. sociology Mt. Mercy Coll., Cedar Rapids, 1972-79. Mem. AAUP, Nat. Assn. Realtors, Iowa Assn. Realtors, Cedar Rapids Assn. Realtors, Am. Sociol. Assn., Midwest Sociol. Soc., Iowa Sociol. Assn. (pres. 1976-77), SAR, Cedar Rapids Jaycees (v.p. 1977-78, dir., 1976-77), Alpha Kappa Delta, Psi Chi. Author: The Real Estate Experiment, 1981. Home: 2144 Grande Ave SE Cedar Rapids IA 52403

CLARKE, CHARLES PATRICK, electronics co. exec.; b. Chgo., Oct. 3, 1929; s. James Patrick and Elizabeth (McLaughlin) C.; student U. Ill., 1948-50; B.S., DePaul U., 1953. Auditor, Baumann Finney Co., C.P.A.'s, Chgo., 1953-55; with Cuneo Press, Inc., Chgo., 1955-66, successively asst. gen. accounting supr., asst. chief corp. accountant, gen. auditor, 1955-61, systems, procedures and audit mgr., 1961-64, asst. to treas., 1964-66; comptroller Internat. Couriers Corp. (formerly Bankers Utilities Corp.), Chgo., 1966-69, treas., 1969-72, financial v.p., 1972-75; pres. C.P. Charles & Assos., 1975-76; treas., corp. controller DC Electronics, Inc., Aurora, Ill., 1976—. C.P.A., Ill. Mem. Am. Inst. C.P.A.'s, Ill. Soc. C.P.A.'s, Nat. Assn. Accountants, Financial Execs. Inst. Democrat. Roman Catholic. Home: 36 Parliament Dr W Palos Heights IL 60463 Office: 544 N Highland Aurora IL 60506

CLARKE, OSCAR WITHERS, physician; b. Petersburg, Va., Jan. 29, 1919; s. Oscar Withers and Mary (Reese) C.; B.S., Randolph Macon Coll., 1941; M.D., Med. Coll. Va., 1944; m. Susan Frances King, June 18, 1949; children—Susan Frances, Mary Elizabeth, Jennifer Ann. Intern Boston City Hosp., 1944-45; resident internal medicine Med. Coll. Va., 1945-46, 48-49, fellow in cardiology, 1949-50; practice medicine specializing in internal medicine, cardiology Gallipolis (Ohio) Holzer Med. Center, 1950—. Dir. Ohio Valley Devel. Co., Gallipolis, Community Improvement Corp. Vice pres. Tri-State regional council Boy Scouts Am., 1957. Pres. Gallipolis City Bd. Health, 1955—, Gallia County Heart Council, 1955—. Trustee, Med. Meml. Found., Holzer Hosp. Found.; v.p. Ohio State Med. Bd. Served as capt. M.C., AUS, 1946-48; ETO. Recipient John Stewart Bryant pathology award Med. Coll. Va., 1943. Fellow A.C.P., Royal Soc. Medicine; mem. Gallia County Med. Soc. (pres. 1953), A.M.A., Am., Central Ohio (recipient medal of merit 1960, trustee) heart assns., Ohio Med. Assn. (pres. 1973-74), Am., Ohio (trustee) socs. internal medicine, Tri-State Community Concert Assn. (pres. 1957-59), Alpha Omega Alpha, Sigma Zeta, Chi Beta Phi. Presbyn. Rotarian (pres. 1953-54). Contbr. articles in field to profl. jours. Home: Spruce Knoll Gallipolis OH 45631 Office: Box 344 Holzer Med Clinic Gallipolis OH 45631

CLARKE, WILLIAM RILEY, physician; b. Newbern, Ala., Dec. 10, 1921; s. Henry A. and Delia W. (Hatch) C.; B.S., Ala. State Coll., 1941; postgrad. U. Sheffield, Eng., 1945-46, Ohio State U., 1946-47; M.D., Meharry Med. Coll., 1951; postgrad. Cook County Sch. Grad. Medicine, 1962, U. Calif., San Francisco, 1969; children by previous marriage—William Riley, Gregory C., Clifton B. Intern, Mt. Sinai Hosp., Chgo., 1951-52, resident in internal medicine, 1953-56; practice medicine specializing in internal medicine, Chgo., 1957—; attending physician Cook County Hosp., Mt. Sinai Hosp., Bethany-Garfield Hosp.; attending physician Roosevelt Meml. Hosp., dir. med. studies, 1959-76, pres. med. staff, 1973-76; instr. Chgo. Med. Sch., 1957-66, asst. prof., 1966-72, asso. prof., 1972—; dir. Hyde Park Bank & Trust Co. Mem. exec. council Boy Scouts Am., Chgo., Ill., 1957—; bd. dirs. Better Boys Found., 1958—, Step Sch. of Retarded Children, 1975—, Adlai Stevenson Inst. Internat. Studies, 1972-76; mem. Ill. Gov.'s Commn. on Health Planning, 1976-77. Served to 1st lt. Chem. Corps, U.S. Army, 1943-46. Mem. Am. Soc. Internal Medicine, Nat. Med. Assn., Ill. Mfed. Soc., Chgo. Med. Soc., Prairie State Med. Assn., AMA. Office: 111 N Wabash Ave Suite 1518 Chicago IL 60602

CLARY, JACK RAY, lawyer; b. Piggort, Ark., Sept. 8, 1932; s. Shella R. and Audra (Binkley) C.; B.S. cum laude, Central Mich. U., 1954; J.D., U. Mich., 1959; m. Joellen K. Donnelly, June 11, 1955;children—Jack C., John R., Jennifer J. Admitted to Mich. bar, 1960, since practiced in Grand Rapids; clk. for labor arbitrator David A. Wolfe, 1956-59; asso. firm Warner, Norcross & Judd, 1959-64, partner, 1964-69; partner Clary, Nantz, Wood, Hoffius, Rankin & Cooper, 1970—. City commnr., East Grand Rapids, 1973-78. Chmn. devel. bd. Central Mich. U. Served with AUS, 1954-56. Mem. Central Mich. U. Alumni Assn. (past pres.), Am., Mich., Grand Rapids bar assns. Contbr. articles to profl. jours. Home: 336 Manhattan SE Grand Rapids MI 49502 Office: 700 Commerce Bldg Grand Rapids MI 49502

CLARY, ROSALIE BRANDON STANTON, timber farm exec., civic worker; b. Evanston, Ill., Aug. 3, 1928; d. Frederick Charles Hite-Smith and Rose Cecile (Liebich) Stanton; B.S., Northwestern U., 1950, M.A., 1954; m. Virgil Vincent Clary, Oct. 17, 1959; children—Rosalie Marian, Frederick Stanton, Virgil Vincent, Kathleen Elizabeth. Tchr., Chgo. Public Schs., 1951-55, adjustment tchr., 1956-61; faculty Loyola U., Chgo., 1963; v.p. Stanton Enterprises, Inc., Adams County, Miss., 1971—; author Family History Record, genealogy record book, Kenilworth, Ill., 1977—. Leader, Girl Scouts, Winnetka, Ill., 1969-71, 78—, Cub Scouts, 1972-77; badge counselor Boy Scouts Am., 1978—; election judge Republican party, 1977—. Mem. Nat. Soc. D.A.R. (Ill. rec. sec. 1979-81, nat. vice chmn. program com. 1980—), Am. Forestry Assn., Forest Farmers Assn., North Suburban Geneal. Soc. (v.p. 1979—), Winnetka Hist. Soc. (governing bd. 1978—), Delta Gamma. Roman Catholic. Home: 509 Elder Ln Winnetka IL 60093 Office: PO Box 401 Kenilworth IL 60043

CLAUER, CALVIN ROBERT, cons. engr.; b. South Bend, Ind., Sept. 8, 1910; s. Calvin Kingsley and Etta (Fiddick) C.; B.S. in Civil Engring., Purdue U., 1932; postgrad. Columbia U., 1944-45; m. Rosemary Y. Stultz, June 23, 1934; 1 son, Calvin Robert. Project engr. Ind. State Hwy. Commn., 1932-35; engr. Erie R.R. Co., 1935-36; dist. chief engr. Truscon Steel Co., Indpls., 1936-42; chief engr. United Steel Fabricators, Inc., 1945-55, div. sales mgr., 1955-57; pres. Clauer Assos., Engrs. for Industry, Wooster, Ohio, 1957-60, chief product engr. Mfg. group Republic Steel Corp., Youngstown, Ohio, 1960-75; prin. Clauer Assos., Youngstown, 1975-79; prin. Midgley-Clauer & Assos., Youngstown, 1979—. Chmn. civil engring. tech. indsl. adv. com. Youngstown State U., 1971-76. Served to col. USAR, 1932-60. Fellow ASCE; mem. Internat. Assn. for Bridge and Structural Engring., ASTM, Am. Iron and Steel Inst., Am. Concrete Inst., Internat. Materials Mgmt. Soc., Soc. Profl. Journalists-Sigma Delta Chi. Republican. Christian Scientist. Clubs: Rotary, Tippecanoe Country, Masons, Shriners. Holder patent on sheet metal box beam. Home: 7401 W Parkside Dr Youngstown OH 44512 Office: 860 Boardman Canfield Rd Youngstown OH 44512

CLAUSIUS, GERHARD PAUL, optometrist; b. Chgo., Dec. 18, 1907; s. Robert Adolph and Margaret (Reutlinger) C.; Dr. Optometry, Ill. Coll. Optometry, 1932; m. Ella Marie Carlson, July 22, 1933; children—Gerhard Paul, Donald Robert, Doris Constance (Mrs. Donald Allan Mosser). Practice optometry, Belvidere, Ill., 1932—; lectr., writer on Lincoln and Civil War, 1948—. Mem. Belvidere Bd. Edn., 1939-42; mem. Ill. Sesqui-Centennial Commn. Mem. Am. Optometric Found., Am., Ill. (dir. 1948) optometric assns., No. Ill. Optometric Soc. (v.p. 1958-59), Ill. (v.p.), Vicksburg-Warren County, Boone County (life), Chgo. hist. socs., Chgo. Civil War Round Table (past pres.), Wis. Lincoln Fellowship (speaker 1979), Phi Theta Upsilon. Lutheran. Rotarian (past pres. Belvidere). Club: Buena Vista (past dir., v.p.) (Fontana, Wis.). Home: 929 Garfield Ave Belvidere IL 61008 Office: 601 S State St Belvidere IL 61008

CLAUSSEN, VERNE EVERETT, JR., optometrist; b. Wilson, Kans., Aug. 10, 1944; s. Verne E. and Dorothy Louise (Soukup) C.; student (Santa Fe scholar, Union Pacific scholar), 1962-65; B.S., U. Houston Coll. Optometry, 1966, certificate in optometry, 1968; certificate (Gesell fellow) in pediatrics, 1969; D.Optometry, U. Houston, 1970; m. Patricia Mary Williams, Aug. 26, 1966; children—Verne Everett III, Mary Chris. Practice optometry U. Houston Coll. Optometry, mem. clin. staff, 1970; optometrist, Wamego and St. Mary's, Kans., 1970—. Lectr. optometry Eastern Seaboard Conf., Washington, U. Houston, 1969; vision cons. Briarwood Sch. for learning problems, Houston, 1967-69. Councilman, Alma City (Kans.), 1971-73. Bd. dirs. Optometric Extension Program Found. Recipient Contest award Kans. Optometric Jour., 1971. Mem. Am., Kans. optometric assns., Heart of Am. Contact Soc., Alma, Wamego (dir.), St. Mary's (pres.) chambers commerce, Farm House Assn. (v.p. 1976-77), Phi Theta Upsilon, Farm House Frat. (dir.). Republican. Methodist. Club: Dutch Mill Swingers Square Dance. Home: Route 2 Alma KS 66401 Office: 5th and Elm Wamego KS 66547

CLAVIN, TERRY JOHN, SR., distillery exec.; b. Mpls., Mar. 13, 1927; s. Bernard James and Frances Marcella (Harrington) C.; student St. Thomas Coll., 1947-48, U. Minn., 1948-49; m. Sally Arlet Beach, Sept. 18, 1947; children—Terry John II, Candace, Jayme, Timothy, Melisa. Owner, Midwest Industries, Inc., Long Prairie, Minn., 1947-55; partner Jet Oil Co., Long Prairie, 1956-70; with Northeastern Refinery, St. Paul Park, Minn.; owner, pres. Minn. Distillers, Inc., Long Prairie, 1970—; Minn. coordinator J.F. Kennedy campaign, 1960, Hubert H. Humphrey campaign, 1964. Served with USNR, 1945-46. Decorated Bronze Star medal. Mem. V.F.W., Am. Legion, K.C., Elk. Home: 212 3d St N Long Prairie MN 56347 Office: 609 6th St NE Long Prairie MN 56347

CLAWSON, ROBERT WAYNE, educator; b. Glendale, Calif., Dec. 21, 1939; s. Charles Vernor and Ada Fern (Hower) C.; student Tex. A&M U., 1957-58; A.B., UCLA, 1961, M.A. (Charles Fletcher Scott fellow 1961-64), 1964, Ph.D., 1969; Exchange Scholar U.S. Def. Lang. Inst., 1963-64, State U. Moscow, USSR, 1966; m. Judith Louise Lisy, June 25, 1961; children—Deborah Marie, Gregory Scott. Research asst. Russian and East European Studies Center, UCLA, 1961-65; asst. prof., asso. prof. polit. sci. Kent (Ohio) State U., 1966—, dir. center for internat. and comparative programs; v.p. research, internat. trade INTERTAG INC., 1973-75; cons. editor Houghton Mifflin; cons. BDM Corp., McLean, Va. Acad. year research fellow Kent State U., spring 1971. Mem. Am. Assn. for Advancement Slavic Studies, Am. Polit. Sci. Assn., Am. Acad. Internat. Bus., AAUP (pres. Kent State chpt. 1975). Democrat. Presbyterian. Club: Sigma Nu. Contbr. articles to profl. publs. Home: 7336 Westview St Kent OH 44240 Office: Center for International Programs Kent State University Kent OH 44242

CLAY, LOREN PAUL, electronics co. exec.; b. Wauseon, Ohio, Oct. 4, 1955; s. Ricahrd Louis and Marilyn Bernice (Falor) C.; Asso. in Engring. and Electronics, Valparaiso Tech. Inst. of Electronics, 1976. Electronics technician Swiss Controls, Michigan City, Ind., 1976-77, field engr., Northlake, Ill., 1977-78, quality control technician, Michigan City, 1978, quality control mgr., 1978-80, sales engr., 1980-81, mgr. engring. services, 1981—. Democrat. Club: Am. Taekwondoe Assn. Home: PO Box 901 Michigan City IN 46360 Office: PO Box 567 Michigan City IN 46360

CLAYBURG, JOHN FRANKLIN, veterinarian; b. Carroll, Iowa, June 28, 1946; s. Frank Thomas and Claribel J. (Anderson) C.; D.V.M., Iowa State U., 1971; m. Karen S. Fenney, July 13, 1968; children—Gary, Roger, Kathy, Tom, Michael. Practice veterinary medicine, Coon Rapids, Iowa, 1971—; mem. faculty Des Moines (Iowa) Community Coll., 1977—; cons. to local swine farms, 1974—. Mem. Coon Rapids Bd. Adjustment, 1977, mem. Planning and Zoning Commn., 1975-78, chmn., 1977-78; vol. ambulance attendent, Coon Rapids, 1974—, mem. Vol. Fire Dept., 1974-78; instr., coordinator CPR program, Coon Rapids; mem. council on ministries United Meth. Ch., Coon Rapids, 1973-77, pres., 1975-77, mem. adminstrv. bd., 1971—; v.p. adv. council to local vocat. agr. program, 1979—. Mem. Am., Iowa veterinary med. assns., Am. Assn. of Swine Practitioners, Coon Rapids C. of C., Tomahawk, Gamma Sigma Delta, Phi Zeta. Club: Rotary (pres. 1979-80). Home: Route 3 Box 170 Coon Rapids IA 50058 Office: 114 6th Ave Coon Rapids IA 50058

CLAYCAMP, HENRY JOHN, mfg. co. exec.; b. Ogallah, Kans., Mar. 12, 1931; s. Henry John and Jenny Katherine (Armbruster) C.; B.A. in Econs. magna cum laude, Washburn U., 1956; M.A., U. Ill., 1957, Ph.D., 1961; m. Joanne Hillman, Aug. 20, 1950; children—Eric, Gregg, Jan, Jill. Asst. prof. mktg. M.I.T., 1961-65; asso. prof. Stanford U., 1965-69; vis. prof. IMEDE Mgmt. Devel. Inst., Lausanne, Switzerland, 1969-70; sr. v.p. advanced methods and research N.W. Ayer & Son, N.Y.C., 1970-73, also dir., v.p. corporate mktg. Internat. Harvester, Chgo., 1973-77, v.p. corporate planning, 1977—. Chmn. Coll. Mktg. Instn. of Mgmt. Scis., 1973. Mem. Am. Mktg. Assn. (v.p. 1975-76). Mem. editorial bd. Jour. Mktg. Research, 1975-79, Research on Consumer Behavior Jour., 1977; Strategic Mgmt. Jour., 1979; contbr. articles to profl. jours. Office: 401 N Michigan Ave Chicago IL 60611

CLAYTON, AURELIUS THOMAS, health cons.; b. McAlester, Okla., Dec. 27, 1937; s. Joseph and Ira (Vincent) C.; B.A., Langston (Okla.) U., 1960; M.P.H., U. Mich., 1968; m. Christine Coleman, Sept. 25, 1962; children—Adrienne Michele, Andrea Deneen. Career devel. officer, health educator Miles Sq. Health Center, Chgo., 1968-70; dir. health Black Strategy Center for Community Devel., Chgo., 1970-71; regional cons. family planning Nat. Center for Family Planning, USPHS, HEW, Chgo., 1978, regional program cons. Appalachian health, 1978—; adj. instr. health adminstrn. Central YMCA Coll., Chgo., 1971—. Recipient Key to City of Benton Harbor (Mich.), 1976; USPHS trainee, 1967-68. Mem. Soc. Public Health Edn. (pres. Ill. chpt. 1973), Am. Public Health Assn., Nat. Assn. Health Services Execs. Presbyterian. Club: Lions. Office: Primary Care Cluster Appalachian Health USPHS HEW 33d Floor 300 S Wacker Dr Chicago IL 60606 also PO Box 8522 Chicago IL 60680

CLAYTON, BRUCE DAVID, educator; b. Grand Island, Nebr., Mar. 9, 1947; s. John David and Eloise Regnier (Camp) C.; student Hastings Coll., 1965-67; B.S., U. Nebr., 1970; D.Pharmacy, U. Mich., 1973; m. Francine Evelyn Purdy, June 19, 1971. Asst. prof. clin. pharmacy Creighton U., Omaha, 1974-77; asso. prof. and vice chmn. dept. pharmacy practice Coll. Pharmacy, U. Nebr. Med. Center, Omaha, 1978—; unit coordinator perinatal pharmacy services Univ. Hosps., Omaha, 1978-80; Ciba-Geigy vis. prof., Australia and N.Z., 1979. Recipient Bristol award for professionalism, 1970; named Nebr. Hosp. Pharmacist of Yr., 1978. Mem. Nebr. Soc. Hosp. Pharmacists (pres. 1978-79, dir. 1979-80), Am. Soc. Hosp. Pharmacists (council on organizational affairs 1979-82, com. on nominations 1980-82, ho. of dels. 1980-82), Am. Pharm. Assn., Nebr. Pharm. Assn., Am. Assn. Colls. of Pharmacy, Great Plains Perinatal Orgn., Rho Chi. Author: (with S.A. Ryan): Handbook of Practical Pharmacology, 1977, 2d edit., 1980; (with J.E. Squire) Basic Pharmacology for Nurses, 7th edit., 1981; contbr. articles to profl. jours. Home: 5717 Tucker St Omaha NE 68152 Office: 42d and Dewey St Omaha NE 68105

CLAY-TURLEY, PAMELA ANN, telephone co. exec.; b. Ames, Iowa, Apr. 22, 1944; d. Roger Leon and Barbara Ruth (Hunt) Clay; B.A., Grinnell Coll., 1966; m. Jack Turley, Sept. 13, 1980. With, Gen. Telephone Co. Ill., Bloomington, 1966—, dir. tng., 1980—. Bd. dirs., chmn. public relations McLean County YWCA, 1980—. Mem. Am. Soc. for Tng. and Devel., Bus. and Profl. Women's Club. Home: 1305 Schroeder Normal IL 61761 Office: Gen Telephone Co Ill 404 Brock Dr Bloomington IL 61701

CLEARY, PATRICK JAMES, newspaper editor; b. Momence, Ill., Jan. 20, 1929; s. James Augustine and Nellie DeWitt (Liston) C.; student U. Chgo., 1946-48; m. Alice Marie Duval, Oct. 1, 1955; children—Mary Elizabeth, James Augustine, Michael John. Reporter, wire editor, city editor Kankakee (Ill.) Daily Jour., 1945-52; reporter Gary (Ind.) Post-Tribune, 1952-53; staff asst. Ill. Senate, 1953-57; dir. pub. relations Plumbing Contractors Assn. Chgo. Cook County (Ill.), 1957-59; city clk. City of Kankakee, 1955-57, clk., county and probate cts. County of Kankakee, 1959-63; editor Farmers Weekly Rev., Joliet, Ill., 1963—; editor Compass Newspapers Inc., Kankakee, 1977, Herscher (Ill.) Rev., 1963-69; editor Crete (Ill.) Record, Steger (Ill.) News, 1963-64; chmn. bd. rev. Ill. Dept. Labor, 1969-73. Office: 100 Manhattan Rd Joliet IL 60433

CLEARY, ROBERT EMMET, gynecologist, infertility specialist; b. Evanston, Ill., July 17, 1937; s. John J. and Brigid (O'Grady) C.; M.D., U. Ill., 1962; m. June 10, 1961; children—William Joseph, Theresa Marie, John Thomas. Intern, St. Francis Hosp., Evanston, 1962-63, resident, 1963-66; practice medicine specializing in gynecology and infertility, Indpls., 1970—; head Sect. of Reproductive Endocrinology and Infertility, Chgo. Lying-In Hosp., U. Chgo., 1968-70; head Sect. of Reproductive Endocrinology and Infertility, Ind. U. Med. Center, Indpls., 1970-80; prof. ob-gyn Ind. U., Indpls., 1976-80, clin. prof. ob-gyn, 1980—. Recipient Meml. award Pacific Coast Obstetrical and Gynecol. Soc., 1968; diplomate Am. Bd. Ob-Gyn, Am. Bd. Reproductive Endocrinology and Infertility. Fellow Am. Coll. Ob-Gyn, Am. Fertility Soc.; mem. Endocrine Soc., Central Assn. Obstetricians and Gynecologists (award, 1974, 79), Soc. Gynecol. Investigation, Pacific Coast Fertility Soc., Sigma Xi. Roman Catholic. Contbr. articles in field to med. jours. Home: 7036 Dubonnet Ct Indianapolis IN 46278 Office: 2020 W 86th St Indianapolis IN 46260

CLEBERG, HAROLD DEAN, feed mfg. co. exec.; b. Redfield, S.D., Sept. 2, 1938; s. Harry B. and Grace A. (Rasmussen) C.; B.S., No. State Coll., Aberdeen, S.D., 1960; m. Clara M. Niemann, May 30, 1959; children—Brian A., Renae G. With S.D. Wheat Growers Assn., 1959-68; with Farmland Industries, Kansas City, Mo., 1968—, exec. dir. feed sales adminstrn., 1975-77, v.p. feed sales and mfg., 1977—; bd. dirs. Boone Valley Coop. Assn., Eagle Grove, Iowa. Pres., Brown County Young Democrats, 1961; bd. dirs. Brown County Fair, 1965-68, Indsl. Devel., Aberdeen, S.D., 1965-68. Mem. Nat. Feed Ingredients Assn. (past pres.), Am. Feed Mfrs. Assn. (dir.). Democrat. Methodist. Clubs: Shriners, Masons. Office: 3315 N Oak Trafficway Kansas City MO 64116*

CLEEK, JOHN EARL, profl. inst. pres.; b. Wynona, Okla., Feb. 7, 1935; s. Earl L. and Mary Ruth C.; B.A., Okla. Bapt. U., 1956; B.D., M.Div., So. Bapt. Theol. Sem., 1960; M.A., U. Ky., 1963, Ph.D., 1967; m. Bernadine Gayle Durkfelt, Oct. 22, 1955; children—Karla Kay, John Alan. Ordained to ministry Baptist Ch., 1956; pastor Millville Bapt. Ch., Frankfort, Ky., 1958-64; instr. U. Ky., 1963-65; research asso. Ky. Council on Higher Edn., Frankfort, 1964-65; asst. to chancellor Okla. State System Higher Edn., Oklahoma City, 1965-69, 74-75; dir. customer services Sequoyah Industries, Oklahoma City, 1970-71; pres. South Oklahoma City Jr. Coll., 1971-74, Johnson County Community Coll., 1975-81; pres. Inst. for Profl. Mgmt., 1981—; vice chmn. Kansas City Regional Council for Higher Edn.; mem. adj. grad. faculty U. Mo., Kansas City; host weekly public affairs TV program. Named Outstanding Citizen South Oklahoma City C. of C. Mem. Am. Assn. Advancement Humanities, AAUP, Am. Mgmt. Assn., Soc. Coll. and Univ. Planning, Assn. Am. Colls. (dir.), Am. Assn. Community and Jr. Colls. (chmn. internat/intercultural consortium), Overland Park (Kans.) C. of C. (dir.), Phi Delta Kappa. Democrat. Presbyterian. Office: 6009 W 89th Terr Overland Park KS 66207

CLELLAND, ROD, hosp. adminstr.; b. Imperial, Calif., Oct. 17, 1916; s. George Andrew and Laura (Miller) C.; B.F.A. with high distinction, U. Ariz., 1937; M.B.A., Ariz. State U., 1966; postgrad. U. Ga., 1970-73, U. Ala., 1975; postgrad. in public adminstrn. Nova U.; m. Nathel Stapley, Dec. 21, 1936; children—Jean Boghossian, Rick A., Michael Dow, Marty Kathleen (Mrs. Michael Abercrombie), Jacquelyn Dee McDonald, Christine Anne Archer, Jeffrey George, Shelly Gay. Exec. sec. Ariz. Council Assns., Phoenix, 1947-52; bus. adminstr. Ariz. State Hosp., Phoenix, 1952-64; adminstr. Maryvale Community Hosp., Phoenix, 1964-67; adminstrv. supt. Central State Hosp., Milledgeville, Ga., 1967-72; supt. Bryce State Hosp., Tuscaloosa, Ala., 1972-75; supt. Larned (Kans.) State Hosp., 1975-79, Massillon (Ohio) State Hosp., 1979—. Mem. bd. Bapt. Hosp., Scottsdale, Ariz., 1962-63. Served with USNR, World War II. Fellow Am. Coll. Hosp. Adminstrs., Assn. Mental Hosp. Adminstrs. (past pres.), Nat. Assn. Hosp. Purchasing Agts. (past pres.), Am. Hosp. Assn., Nat. Assn. Purchasing Agts. (past dir.), Iota Sigma Alpha, Alpha Mu Gamma, Delta Psi Omega. Mem. Ch. of Jesus Christ of Latter-day Saints. Author: The Human Side of Hospital Administration, 1974; contbr. articles to profl. jours. Home: Box 540 Massillon OH 44648

CLEM, ALAN LELAND, polit. scientist; b. Lincoln, Nebr., Mar. 4, 1929; s. Remey Leland and Bernice (Thompson) C.; B.A., U. Nebr., 1950; M.A., Am. U., 1957, Ph.D., 1960; m. Mary Louise Burke, Oct. 24, 1953; children—Andrew, Christopher, Constance, John, Daniel. Copywriter, research dir. Ayres Advt. Agy., Lincoln, Nebr., 1950-52; pres. sec. Congressman Carl Curtis, Nebr., 1953-54, Congressman R. D. Harrison, Nebr., 1955-58; info. specialist Fgn. Agrl. Service, Dept. Agr., 1959-60; asst. prof. polit. sci. U. S.D., 1960-62, asso. prof., 1962-64, prof., 1965—, asso. dir. govtl. research bur., 1962-76, chmn. dept. polit. sci., 1976-78; state analyst U. N.C. Comparative State Elections Project, Rockefeller Found. grant, 1968-73; partner Opinion Survey Assos., 1964—; mem. U.S. Census Bur. Adv. Com. on State and Local Govt. Statistics, 1970-74. Mem. Vermillion (S.D.) City Council, 1965-69; sr. warden St. Paul's Episcopal Ch., Vermillion, 1971-73. Ford Found. Nat. Conv. faculty fellow, 1964. Mem. Am. Polit. Sci. Assn., M.W. Polit. Sci. Assn. (exec. council 1979-82), Mensa, Phi Beta Kappa, Phi Alpha Theta, Pi Sigma Alpha, Sigma Delta Chi. Republican. Author books, including: South Dakota Political Almanac, 1962, 2d, edit., 1969; The Nomination of Joe Bottum, 1963; Prairie State Politics, 1967; The Making of Congressmen: Seven Campaigns of 1974, 1976; American Electoral Politics: Strategies for Renewal, 1981; contbr. articles to profl. jours.; editor: Contemporary Approaches to State Constitutional Revision, 1969; editorial bd. Am. Jour. Polit. Sci. 1972-73. Office: Dept Polit Sci U SD Vermillion SD 57069

CLEM, PAUL MILTON, coll. ofcl.; b. Lincoln, Nebr., Aug. 16, 1953; s. Oliver Douglas and Fern Elaine (Bockmann) C.; B.A., Mid-Am. Nazarene Coll., Olathe, Kans., 1975; M.S. in Edn., U. Kans., 1981; m. Susan Joyce Lunn, June 5, 1976; 1 son, Carter Paul. With Capitol Fed. Savs. and Loan Assn., Shawnee, Kans., 1973-74; dir. student recruitment and publicity Mid-Am. Nazarene Coll., 1975—; mem. staff HELP, cons. firm, Olathe, 1980—. Mem. Assn. Christian Schs. Internat., Council for Advancement Secondary Edn., Nat. Assn. Coll. Admissions Counselors, Olathe C. of C. (edn. com.). Republican. Office: PO Box 1776 Olathe KS 66061

CLEMANS, THEODORE VAUGHN, personnel and labor relations cons.; b. Springfield, Ohio, Dec. 29, 1946; s. Frank E. and Norma M. (Smith) Wells; A.A., Urbana Coll., 1969; B.S. in Bus. Adminstrn., Wright State U., 1970, postgrad., 1971-72; student Capital U. Law Sch., 1972-73; m. Karen Sue Roach, June 21, 1969. Field rep. Ohio Assn. Pub. Sch. Employees, Columbus, 1972-73; internat. rep., state coordinator Am. Fedn. State, County and Municipal Employees, Columbus, 1973-75; dir. elections Ind. Employment Relations Bd., Indpls., 1975; exec. dir. Physicians Alliance div. State Med. Soc. Wis., Madison, 1976; pres. Clemons, Nelson & Assos., Columbus, 1976—; instr. United Auto Workers Family Edn. Center, Black Lake, Mich., 1970-71; guest speaker, lectr. at various univs. on labor relations, 1971-81; participant, panel mem. Labor-Mgmt. Arbitration Conf., 1974, 75, 76, 78, 80, 81. Mem. Indsl. Relations Research Assn., Am. Soc. for Personnel Adminstrn., Am. Arbitration Assn. (mem. labor panel), Soc. of Profls. in Dispute Settlement, Am. Soc. Tng. and Devel., Internat. Personnel Mgmt. Assn., Am. Inst. Profl. Consultants. Democrat. Lutheran. Editor Mgmt. Negotiators Digest, 1976-77. Home: 2329 Pawnee Dr London OH 43140 Office: 1889 Fountain Square Ct Suite 326 Columbus OH 43224

CLEMENS, BRYAN TILLMAN, clergyman; b. Beckum County, Okla., Jan. 22, 1934; s. Ben Tillman and Lou Ella (Thornton) C.; B.S., Wayland Bapt. Coll., Plainview, Tex., 1959; M.S. (NDEA fellow 1962-63), Purdue U., 1963, Ph.D., 1969; m. Odessa Louise Wilson, Dec. 14, 1952; children—Daniel Clay, Kathy Kay, Sharon Sue, Ben Tillman. Public sch. tchr., Tex., 1959-62; asst. dean Purdue U., 1964-67; dean of students Wayland Bapt. Coll., 1967-69; asst. dean of men, then dean of men Purdue U., 1969-74; counselor Southeastern Sch. Corp., 1974-78; ordained to ministry Am. Bapt. Ch., 1964; pastor Blue Ball Ch., Walton, Ind., 1971-78, Metea Bapt. Ch., Lucerne, Ind., 1979—. Club: Grass Creek Lions. Author articles in field. Address: Rural Route 1 Box 54E Lucerne IN 46950

CLEMENT, PAUL PLATTS, JR., edn. devel. co. exec.; b. Geneva, Ill., Aug. 30, 1935; s. Paul P. and Vera Elizabeth (Dahlquist) C.; A.B., Coe Coll., 1957; m. Susan Alice Aikins, June 7, 1958; children—Paul Platts IV, Kathleen Elizabeth. Sales tech. rep. Burroughs Corp., Chgo., 1960-63; mgr. EDP, Harding-Williams Corp., Chgo., 1963-65; edn. coordinator Standard Oil Co., Chgo., 1965-69; mgr. product planning Edutronics Systems Internat., Chgo., 1969-71; dir. interactive tng. products Advanced Systems Inc., Chgo., 1971—; cons. in field. Served to capt. USAF, 1958-60. Mem. Assn. Computer Machinery, Nat. Soc. Performance and Instrn. Home: 4942 Linscott Ave Downers Grove IL 60515 Office: 2340 S Arlington Heights Rd Arlington Heights IL 60005

CLEMENTE, JAVIER LARRANGA, physician; b. Lima, Peru, Oct. 5, 1940; came to U.S., 1968; s. Hilario and Sabina Clemente; student Nat. Mayor U. San Marcos, Lima, 1959-60; M.D., San Marcos U., Lima, 1967; m. Barbara Pelegrin, May 30, 1970; children—Michael, Daniel, Deanna, Jonathan. Resident, Cayetano Heredia U., Lima, 1967-68; intern Carney Hosp., Boston, 1968-69, resident, 1969-71; fellow in nephrology U. Chgo. Hosp. and Clinics, 1971-72; sr. resident in nephrology VA Hosp., Hines, Ill., 1972-73, staff physician renal sect., 1973-77, physician-in-charge assisted dialysis, 1974-76, physician-in-charge assisted and ltd. care dialysis, 1976-77; practice medicine specializing in internal medicine and nephrology, Cleve., 1977—; clin. instr. medicine Loyola U., Maywood, Ill., 1973-77, asst. prof., 1977. Diplomate Am. Bd. Internal Medicine, Am. Bd. Nephrology. Mem. AMA (Physician recognition award 1976-79), Cleve. Acad. Medicine, Ohio Med. Assn. Contbr. articles and abstracts to med. jours. Office: 18099 Lorain Ave Suite 316 Cleveland OH 44111

CLEVELAND, DONALD LESLIE, assn. exec., ins. broker; b. Omaha, Nebr., July 16, 1938; s. Albert Leslie and Lucille Arlene (Fancher) C.; B.S. in Polit. Sci. and Journalism, Creighton U., 1961; M.A. in Polit. Sci., U. Nebr., 1968; m. Christa Anita Wahl, Oct. 9, 1965; children—Christopher Leslie, Stephan Donald. Adminstrv. asst. Clarkson Hosp., Omaha, 1965-67; adminstrv. asst. Assn. Minn. Counties, St. Paul, 1967-68; asst. dir. house research dept. Minn. Ho. of Reps., St. Paul, 1968-71; exec. dir. Iowa State Assn. Counties, Des Moines, 1971—; chmn. Cleveland Research and Devel. Corp.; v.p. domestic ops. GIF Ins. Co. Ltd.; chief exec. officer Multi-County Services Agy., Joint County Unemployment Compensation Fund, County Liability Indemnification Fund, Local Govt. Research Found., 1975-80. Pres., St. Paul Beautiful Coordinating Com., 1970-71; county rep. Mid Continent Fed. Regional Council, Kansas City, 1977-80. Served to capt. U.S. Army, 1961-66. Mem. Am. Soc. Assn. Execs., Am. Soc. Public Adminstrn., Acad. Polit. Sci., Council Fgn. Relations, Internat. Personnel Mgmt. Assn., Nat. Assn. Counties, Nat. Assn. County Assn. Execs. (sec.-treas. 1978—, 2d v.p. 1979-80, 1st v.p. and pres. 1980). Democrat. Roman Catholic. Editor The County, 1971-80. Office: Iowa State Assn Counties 730 E 4th St Des Moines IA 50316

CLEVELAND, (JAMES) HARLAN, polit. scientist; b. N.Y.C., Jan. 19, 1918; s. Stanley Matthews and Marian Phelps (Van Buren) C.; A.B. in Politics with high honors, Princeton U., 1938; Rhodes scholar Oxford (Eng.) U., 1938-39; LL.D. (hon.), Rollins Coll., 1956, Franklin and Marshall Coll., 1969, Middlebury Coll., 1962, Kent State U., 1962, Ariz. State U., 1968, Willamette U., 1976, L.H.D. (hon.), Alfred U., 1938, Kenyon Coll., 1966; Litt.D., U. Pitts., 1968, Brandeis U., 1971; Boston U., 1968, Korea U., 1972, Monterey Inst. Fgn. Studies, 1976; D.C.L. (hon.), Am. U., 1966; m. Lois W. Burton, July 12, 1941; children—Carol Zoe Cleveland Palmer, Anne Moore Cleveland Kalicki, Alan Thorburn. Intern, Nat. Inst. Public Affairs, 1939-40; writer info. div. Farm Security Adminstrn., 1940-42; ofcl. Bd. Econ. Warfare, and successor Fgn. Econ. Adminstrn., 1942-44; exec. dir. econ. sect. Allied Control Commn., Italy, 1944-45, acting v.p. charge econ. sect., 1945-46; mem. U.S. del. 3d session UNRRA Council, London, 1945, dept. chief Italian mission, 1946-47, dir. China office, Shanghai, 1947-48; dir. China aid program FCA, 1948-49, dep. asst. adminstr., 1949-51; asst. dir. for Europe, Mut. Security Agy., 1951-53; exec. editor The Reporter, N.Y.C., 1953-56, pub., 1955-56; prof. polit. sci., dean Maxwell Grad. Sch. Citizenship and Public Affairs, Syracuse (N.Y.) U., 1956-61; asst. sect. orgn. affairs Dept. State, 1961-65; ambassador, rep. to NATO, 1965-69; pres. U. Hawaii, Honolulu, 1969-74; dir. program internat. affairs Aspen Inst. Humanistic Studies, Princeton, N.J., 1974-80; chmn. Weather Modification Adv. Bd., 1977-78; disting. vis. Tom Slick prof. world peace LBJ Sch. Public Affairs, U. Tex., 1979; prof. public affairs, dir. Hubert M. Humphrey Inst. Public Affairs, U. Minn., Mpls., 1980—. Del. Democratic Nat. Conv., 1960. Decorated Medal of Freedom, 1946; grand knight officer Order Crown Italy; gold star Order Brilliant Star (China); recipient Woodrow Wilson prize Princeton, 1968; Prix de Talloires, 1981. Mem. Am. Polit. Sci. Assn., Am. Soc. Public Adminstrn. (pres. 1970-71), Phi Beta Kappa. Clubs: Waikiki Yacht (Honolulu); Century, Princeton (N.Y.C.); Internat. (Washington). Author: The Obligations of Power, 1966; NATO: The Transatlantic Bargain, 1970; The Future Executive (Louis Brownlow Book award 1975), 1972; China Dairy, 1976; The Third Try at World Order, 1977; (with others) Humangrowth: An Essay on Growth, Values and The Quality of Life, 1978; The Overseas Americans, 1960. Editor: The Promise of World Tensions, 1971; Energy Futures for Developing Countries, 1980; The Management of Sustainable Growth, 1981; co-editor: The Art of Overseasmanship, 1957; The Ethic of Power, 1962; Ethics and Bigness, 1962; Bioresources for Development, 1980. Office: Hubert H Humphrey Inst Public Affairs 909 Social Sci Bldg 267 19th Ave S U Minn Minneapolis MN 55455

CLEVELAND, HELEN BARTH, teaching cons., civic worker; b. Alliance, Ohio, Aug. 28, 1904; d. Luther Martin and Ella Mae (Forest) Barth; A.B., Mt. Union Coll., 1927; postgrad. Kent State U., 1929-32, Akron U., 1946-48, N.Y. U., 1950-53; M.A., Syracuse U., 1955, Ph.D., 1958; postgrad. London Acad. Arts, 1970, U. San Juan, 1972, Acad. Arts Honolulu, 1973; m. Harold J. Cleveland, Oct. 26, 1946; children—Carol, Ronald, Marilyn, George, Donald. Tchr., cons. Alliance Public Schs., 1927-74; instr. crafts Syracuse U., 1953-60; instr. art, Sierra Leone, 1963-64; pres., dir. Chautauqua (N.Y.) Art Gallery, 1963-76, pres. emeritus, bd. dirs., 1977—; bd. dirs., cons. adminstr. Mabel Hartzel Mus., Alliance, 1974—; bd. dirs. Lighthouse Gallery, Tequesta, Fla., 1970-72, Canton (Ohio) Culture Center, 1970—; trustee Alliance Art Center; mem. Keating (Mich.) Antique Village. Recipient Bronze plaque Community Alliance Bi-Centennial Com., 1976, Community Service award Am. Legion Aux., 1975. Mem. Am. Assn. Ret. Persons (pres.), Am. Fedn. Art, Ohio Fedn. Art; life mem. NEA, Ohio Edn. Assn. Republican. Methodist. Clubs: Mt. Union College Women, Alliance Woman, Chautauqua Woman, Univ. Women, Order Eastern Star, K.T. Ladies, Shrine Ladies, DeMolay-Rainbow (Mom of Year 1959). Author: Arts and Crafts, 1955; Art in Poetry, 1959; Creativity in Elementary Schools, 1963. Home: 1192 Parkside Dr Alliance OH 44601

CLEVELAND, JERRY LESTER, hosp. ofcl.; b. Ft. Dodge, Iowa, Nov. 1, 1949; s. Lester Jessie and Maxine Evelyn (Burch) C.; A.A., Area XI Community Coll., Ankeny, Iowa, 1977; m. Adella Lynn Lara, Dec. 19, 1970; children—Michael, Timothy, Frank. Asst. chief, then chief supply, processing and distbn. VA Hosp., Des Moines, 1973-77; dir. central service St. Luke's Methodist Hosp., Cedar Rapids, 1977—, chmn. safety com., 1979, chmn. products improvement com., 1980-82, chmn. associated activities com., 1980. Served with USN, 1969-73. Mem. Am. Soc. Hosp. Central Service Personnel (membership com. 1980-81, dir. region II 1982—), Central Service Assn. Iowa (chmn. membership 1978, pres. 1979-81), Am. Legion. Roman Catholic. Club: Los Amigos (v.p. 1978-79 pres. 1980-81) (Cedar Rapids). Office: 1026 A Ave NE Cedar Rapids IA 52402

CLEVELAND, LELA JEANNE, comptroller; b. Sallisaw, Okla., Nov. 13, 1927; d. P.J. and Delia (Cagle) Garich; m. widow; children—Victoria Lynne, Monte Ral, Jonnie Marie. Operator, Ill. Bell Telephone Co., Salem, 1946-49; payroll clk. Brown Shoe Co., Salem, 1958-59; accountant P.J.'s Machine Shop, Salem, 1959-70; comptroller, corp. sec., credit mgr. Wisniewski Bros. Music, Salem, 1980—. Roman Catholic. Home: 328 S Vincent Salem IL 62881 Office: Wisniewski Bros Music Inc 115 E Main St Salem IL 62881

CLEVELAND, ROBERT RAHLYN, communications mfr.; b. Searcy, Ark., Nov. 22, 1948; s. Thomas Chester and Jennie Marie (Griffin) C.; student Tallulah (La.) public schs., spl. engring. courses; m. Beatriz Santiago, Nov. 25, 1968; children—Robert Michael, Shiela Michelle, Kenneth Eric. Broadcast engr. Am. Forces Radio and TV Service, Taiwan and Philippines, 1967-73; v.p. contracting and systems div., dir. Alexander Electronics, Inc., St. Louis and Kansas City, Mo., 1973-76; pres., chmn. bd. Video Masters, Inc., Kansas City, Mo., 1976—; dir. Video Systems Research, Inc. Sec., Home Owners Assn. Kansas City North, 1977-78. Served with USAF, 1967-73. Decorated Meritorious Service medal; registered profl. engr., Mo.; cert. elec. supr. City of Kansas City. Mem. Nat. Assn. Broadcasters, Am. Assn. R.R.'s, Ry. System Suppliers, Inc., Better Bus. Bur. Kansas City, Mo. City C. of C., Smithsonian Instn., Elec. Assn. Kansas City. Contbr. articles to Progressive Railroading, Ry. Age. Patentee rail car identification system using TV. Office: 1616 Broadway Kansas City MO 64108

CLEVEN, DONALD LE ROY, constrn. co. exec.; b. Kendall, Wis., Mar. 11, 1931; s. Morris Edward and Anne Marie (Preuss) C.; Master of Accounts, Madison (Wis.) Bus. Coll., 1950; postgrad. Madison Area Tech. Coll., 1968-73, U. Wis., Madison, 1973-77; m. Maxine Eileen Schuchmann, May 18, 1958; children—Gina, Paul, Ruth. Acct. trainee, distbr. sales acct. Borden Co., Madison, Wis., 1950-57, internal auditor, Chgo., 1958; acct. Vogel Bros. Bldg. Co., Madison, 1958-69, treas., 1969—; dir., Vogel Bros. Bldg. Co., Madison, R. J. Lederer Co., Milw., Profl. Contractors, Inc., Lakeland, Fla. C.P.A. Mem. Nat. Assn. Accts., Am. Inst. C.P.A.'s, Wis. Inst. C.P.A.'s. Lutheran. Home: 1706 Wendy Ln Madison WI 53716 Office: 2701 Packers Ave PO Box 7696 Madison WI 53707

CLEVENGER, HORACE MARSHALL, operations research analyst; b. Manhattan, Kans., Dec. 21, 1913; s. Charles Henry and Edna (Warren) C.; B.S.A., Purdue U., 1938; M.S., Ohio State U., 1952; postgrad. Harris Tchrs. Coll., St. Louis, 1956-57, So. Ill. U., Alton, 1961, Washington U., 1962-71; m. Roberta Walter, June 8, 1941; children—John Walter, Robert Marshall, Donna Jean. Clk., Bur. Census, Washington, 1940-41; agrl. statistician Bur. Agr. Econs., Trenton, N.J., 1941-42; analytical statistician Bur. Agrl. Econs., Columbus, 1942-52, Doane Agrl. Service, St. Louis, 1953-54; acting asst. traffic mgr. Stix, Baer & Fuller, St. Louis, 1954-56; tchr. St. Louis Bd. Edn., St. Louis, 1956-57; analytical statistician U.S. Army Transp. Materiel Command, St. Louis, 1957-60, operations research analyst, 1960-64; math. statistician U.S. Army Aviation Systems Command, 1964-69; ops. research analyst U.S. Army Troop Support and Aviation Materiel Readiness Command, 1969-79; ret., 1979. Mem. Ops. Research Soc. Am., Am. Soc. Quality Control, Am. Statis. Assn., Am. Econ. Assn. Contbr. articles to profl. jours. Home: 21 Almeda Pl Ferguson MO 63135

CLEVENGER, ROBERT VINCENT, lawyer; b. Hancock, Mich., July 23, 1921; s. Arthur W. and Yolande (Elwood) C.; student Earlham Coll., Richmond, Ind., 1939-41; A.B., U. Ill., 1942, J.D., 1947; m. Dorothy Jean Marsh, Sept. 18, 1943; children—Arthur Eugene, Darley Yolande, Mary Marsha. Admitted to Ill. bar, 1947, since practiced in Pekin; asst. state's atty., Tazewell County (Ill.), 1951-52, spl. asst. state's atty., 1956-57; public guardian, conservator of Tazewell County, 1961-69; dir., sec. Pekin Devel. Corp., 1970-74, Future Horizons, Inc., Pekin, 1972-80; sec. Celestial Investors, Pekin, 1966—. Vice chmn. Tomahawk Dist., Creve Coeur council Boy Scouts Am., 1967-68, dean of merit badge counselors, 1969—, explorer adviser Explorer Post 1776, 1976-77; chmn. Tazewell Citizens Com. on Human Relations, 1967; chmn. Tri-County Anti-Crime Project, 1977-79; pres. Pekin Edison Sch., PTA, 1954-55, 62-63, Pekin council, 1955-56; pres. Greater Peoria area chpt. World Federalists, U.S., 1967-69, 81—, sec., 1969-81; pres. Pekin Safeguard Against Crime Com., 1976-78, sec., 1979—; v.p. Greater Peoria Area Crime Stoppers, Inc., 1981—; mem. Town Bd. of Pekin Twp., 1949-53; pres. Champaign County (Ill.) Young Democrats, 1946-47; Tazewell County chmn. Ill. Com. for Constl. Revision, 1950; Pekin Twp. chmn. Dem. Com., 1950-52; Dem. precinct committeeman, 1972-74; mem. Tazewell County Dem. Central Com., 1972-74. Served as master sgt. AUS, 1942-46, 50-53. Recipient Citation for Outstanding Contbn. to Human Relations, Tazewell Citizens Com. on Human Relations, 1968; Order of Arrow, Boy Scouts Am., 1960, Silver Beaver award, 1967. Mem. Am., Ill., Tazewell County (pres. 1955-56, chmn. legal aid com. 1971-72, chmn. ethics com. 1979—) bar assns., Fedn. Local Bar Assns. (pres. 3d dist. 1963), Assn. Trial Lawyers Am., World Federalists (v.p. Midwest 1969), Pekin C. of C. (chmn. edn. com. 1955-56, chmn. local affairs com. 1959-60, chmn. legis. reform com. 1979-80), Tri-County Urban League, Internat. League for Rights of Man, World Peace Through Center (com. on regional orgns. and devel. internat. law 1970, spl. com. on rev. of UN 1970), Alpha Kappa Lambda, Phi Alpha Delta. Methodist (chmn. Christian social concerns commn. 1967-70). Clubs: Kiwanis (pres. 1956, sec. 1963-64, lt. gov. Ill.-Eastern Iowa dist. 1965, mem. internat. relations com. Ill.-Eastern Iowa dist. 1967, chmn. support chs. in spiritual aims Ill.-Eastern Iowa dist. 1966, chmn. citizenship services com. Pekin club 1976-77, 79-80), Pekin Boat (judge advocate 1957—). Home: 1011 Monroe St Pekin IL 61554 Office: 342 St Mary Pekin IL 61554

CLIFFORD, JAMES MICHAEL, JR., mfg. co. exec.; b. Great Lakes, Ill., Nov. 9, 1951; s. James M. and Eleanore M. (Racz) C.; B.B.A., St. Norbert Coll., 1973. With Electro-Motive Div., Gen. Motors, Chgo., 1973; asst. transp. mgr., overseas buyer Chgo. Bridge & Iron Co., 1973-77; supr. fgn. traffic Rockwell Internat., Des Plaines, Ill., 1977-79; supr. Distbn. Scis. Inc. audit Travenol Labs., Deerfield, Ill., 1979—. Mem. Am. Mgmt. Assn. Roman Catholic. Home: 7708 Chestnut Dr Orland Park IL 60642 Office: 1 Baxter Pkwy Deerfield IL 60015

CLIFTON, DONALD O., psychol. research co. exec.; b. Butte, Nebr., Feb. 5, 1924; s. Kem A. and Pearl (Hoscheit) C.; B.S., U. Nebr., 1948, M.A., 1949, Ph.D., 1953; m. Shirley May Roush, Oct. 15, 1945; children—Connie, James, Mary, Jane. Prof. U. Nebr., Lincoln, 1950-69; pres. Selection Research, Inc., Lincoln, 1969—; asso. dir. Nebr. Human Resources Research Found., Inc. Bd. dirs. Father Flanagan's Boys Town. Served with USAF. Decorated D.F.C., Air Medal. Certified psychologist, Nebr. Mem. Am., Nebr. psychol. assns., Newcomen Soc. Republican. Methodist. Clubs: Rotary (pres. NE Lincoln, dist. gov.). Author: The Magnificence of Management, 1970; The Agent Perceiver, 1971. Home: 630 Cottonwood Dr Lincoln NE 68510 Office: 2646 S 48th St Lincoln NE 68506

CLINE, CHARLES WILLIAM, poet; b. Waleska, Ga., Mar. 1, 1937; s. Paul Ardell and Mary Montarie (Pittman) C.; A.A., Reinhardt Coll., 1957; student Conservatory of Music, U. Cin., 1957-58; B.A., George Peabody Coll. for Tchrs., 1960; M.A., Vanderbilt U., 1963; m. Sandra Lee Williamson, June 11, 1966; 1 son, Jeffrey Charles. Asst. prof. English, Shorter Coll., Rome, Ga., 1963-64; instr. English, W. Ga. Coll., Carrollton, 1964-68; manuscript procurement editor Fideler Co., Grand Rapids, Mich., 1968; asso. prof. English, Kellogg Community Coll., Battle Creek, Mich., 1969-75, prof. English and resident poet, 1975—; condr. poetry readings and workshops; chmn. creative writing sect. Midwest Conf. on English, 1976. Recipient poetry awards from Weave Anthology, 1974, Modus Operandi, 1975, Internat. Belles-Lettres Soc., 1975, Poetry Soc. of Mich., 1975, N.Am. Mentor, 1976, 77. Founding fellow Internat. Acad. of Poets; fellow Internat. Biog. Assn.; mem. Tagore Inst. Creative Writing Internat. (life), Nat. Council of Tchrs. of English, Midwest Conf. on English, Soc. for Study of Midwestern Lit., Nat. Mich. edn. assns., Mich. Assn. of Higher Edn., World Poetry Soc. Intercontinental, Centro Studi e Scambi Internazionali (Poet Laureate award and Diploma di Benemerenza), Accademia Leonardo da Vinci, Poetry Soc. Am. Presbyterian. Author: Crossing the Ohio, 1976; Questions for the Snow, 1979. Editor: Forty Salutes to Mich. Poets, 1975. Contbr. poems to jours. and anthologies. Home: 9866 S Westnedge Ave Kalamazoo MI 49002 Office: 450 North Ave Battle Creek MI 49016

CLINE, DOROTHY MAY STAMMERJOHN (MRS. EDWARD WILBURN CLINE), educator; b. Boonville, Mo., Oct. 19, 1915; d. Benjamin Franklin and Lottie (Walther) Stammerjohn; grad. nurse U. Mo., 1937; B.S. in Edn., 1939, postgrad., 1966-67; M.S., Ark. State U., 1964; m. Edward Wilburn Cline, Aug. 16, 1938 (dec. May 1962); children—Margaret Ann (Mrs. Rodger Orville Bell), Susan Elizabeth (Mrs. Gary Lee Burns), Dorothy Jean. Dir. Christian Coll. Infirmary, Columbia, Mo., 1936-37; asst. chief nursing service VA Hosp., Poplar Bluff, Mo., 1950-58; tchr.-in-charge Tng. Center No. 4, Poplar Bluff, 1959-66, State Sch. No. 53, Boonville, 1967—; instr. U. Mo., Columbia, 1973-74; cons. for workshops for new tchrs., curriculum revision Mo. Dept. Edn. Mem. Butler County Council Retarded Children, 1959-66; v.p. Boonslick Assn. Retarded Children, 1969-72; sec.-treas. Mo. chpt. Am. Assn. on Mental Deficiency, 1973-75. Mem. NEA, Mo. Tchrs. Assn., Am. Assn. on Mental Deficiency, Council for Exceptional Children, AAUW (v.p. Boonville br. 1968-70, 75-77), Mo. Writers Guild, Creative Writer's Group (pres. 1974—), Columbia Creative Writers Group, Eastern Center Poetry Soc., Laura Speed Elliott High Sch. Alumni Assn., Bus. and Profl. Women's Club, Smithsonian Assn., U. Mo. Alumni Assn., Ark. State U. Alumni Assn., Internat. Platform Assn., Mo. Hist. Soc., Boonslick Hist. Soc., Friends Historic Boonville, Delta Kappa Gamma. Mem. Christian Ch. Home: 603 E High St Boonville MO 65233

CLINE, JAYSON HOWARD, coin dealer; b. Richlands, Va., Sept. 21, 1934; s. George Henry and Rachael Elizabeth (Ray) J.; student public schs., Richlands; m. Vicki Ann Coleman Hyer, Jan. 30, 1981; children by previous marriage—Carlotta Cline Bernard, Quinton, Carmellia; stepchildren—Brian Hyer, Keith Hyer. Apprentice, Sunshine Biscuit Co., Dayton, Ohio, 1954-55; with Nat. Cash Register Co., Dayton, 1955-65; owner, operator Cline's Rare Coins, Dayton, 1955—; lectr. numismatics Wilberforce Coll. Cedarville Coll. Mem. Am. Numismatic Assn. (life), Blue Ridge Numismatic Assn. (life), Penn-Ohio Gt. Eastern Numismatic Assn. (life), So. Calif. Numismatists, Tex. State Numismatists, Tenn. State Numismatists, Mich. State Numismatists, Central States Numismatists, Fla. United Numismatists. Republican. Mem. Brethren Ch. Club: Green County Coin. Author: Standing Liberty Quarters, 1976; contbr. articles to profl. publs. Office: 4421 Salem Ave Dayton OH 45416

CLINE, RICHARD GORDON, retail distbn. co. exec.; b. Chgo., Feb. 17, 1935; s. William R. and Katherine A. (Bothwell) C.; B.S., U. Ill., 1957; m. Carole J. Costello, Dec. 28, 1957; children—Patricia, Linda, Richard, Jeffrey. With Jewel Cos., Inc., 1963—, pres. Osco Drug, Inc. subs., 1970-79, sr. exec. v.p., 1979, vice chmn., Chgo., from 1979, now pres., chief operating officer, also dir.; dir. NICOR, Inc., No. Ill. Gas Co., Aurrera, S. A., Mexico City (alt.); bd. dirs. Nat. Assn. Chain Drug Stores, Inc. Bd. dirs. United Way Met. Chgo., Inc.; trustee Rush-Presbyterian-St. Luke's Med. Center; gov. and former chmn. bd. Central DuPage Hosp.; mem. adv. council Coll. Commerce and Bus. Adminstrn., U. Ill. Clubs: Econ., Chgo., Comml., Commonwealth, Chgo. Golf, Butler Nat. Office: Jewel Cos Inc 5725 East River Rd Chicago IL 60631

CLINE, RICHARD LEE, lawyer; b. Muncie, Ind., June 14, 1942; s. Woodrow C. and Lelia Florence (Lanning) C.; B.A., Ball State U., 1964; J.D., Ind. U., 1968; m. Christina Kay Kennedy, June 19, 1965; children—Karen Elizabeth, Kristin Lee. Admitted to Ind. bar, 1968, Ill. bar, 1973; dep. adminstr. inheritance tax div. State of Ind., Indpls., 1966-68; asst. sec., atty. Burger Chef Systems, Inc., Indpls., 1968-72; atty. Ceco Corp., Chgo., 1972—, sec., 1977—. Mem. Am. Soc. Corp. Secs., Am. Bar Assn., Ind. Bar Assn., Ill. Bar Assn., Chgo. Bar Assn., Phi Delta Phi, Sigma Chi. Presbyterian. Home: 1041 Alder Ln Naperville IL 60540 Office: 1400 Kensington Rd Oak Brook IL 60521

CLINE, WILBUR JAMES, ednl. adminstr.; b. Centerville, Iowa, May 28, 1918; s. Thomas C. and Nadie (Maring) C.; B.S., Iowa Wesleyan Coll., 1940; M.S. in Edn., Drake U., 1954; Specialists Degree, U. Colo., 1959; m. Olive Lucille Jones, Oct. 25, 1942; 1 dau., Marjorie Anne Cline Holland. Tchr. Centerville (Iowa) Pub. Schs., 1939-41, Ottumwa (Iowa) Pub. Schs., 1941-42, Mason City (Iowa) Pub. Schs., 1942-43; tng. officer VA, Des Moines, Iowa, 1946-53; guidance counselor Davenport High Sch., Iowa, 1954-60; dir. guidance services Davenport (Iowa) pub. schs., 1960-63; dir. data processing services Scott County (Iowa) schs., 1963-66; dir. Area 9 Schs. Info. Center, Bettendorf, Iowa, 1966-70; v.p. Kempton-Cline Data Systems, Davenport, Iowa, 1970-74; asst. to dir. Bi-State Met. Computer Commn., 1974-75; guidance counselor Pleasant Valley Community Schs., Pleasant Valley, Iowa, 1975-80; vocat. cons. to Social Security Adminstrn., 1963-64. Mem. citizens adv. com. Scott County Mental Health Center, 1977, 1978-79; elder Newcomb Presbyn. Ch., Davenport, 1957-60. Served with USAAF, 1942-46; CBI, with USAF, 1950-52; lt. col. Res. ret. Mem. Iowa Edn. Assn. (life), Ret. Officers Assn., Res. Officers Assn., Air Force Assn., Am. Assn. Ret. Persons, Nat. Ret. Tchrs. Assn., Beta Beta Beta. Clubs: Masons (32 deg.), Moose, Shriners. Home: 1555 W Garfield St Davenport IA 52804

CLINE, WILLIAM RUSSELL, JR., profl. sports exec.; b. Ft. Walton Beach, Fla., Oct. 15, 1943; s. William Russell and Virginia Frances (Kirkland) C.; B.S. in Psychology, William Jewell Coll., 1972; m. Melanie Jean Griffin, Jan. 22, 1981; children by previous marriage—Lisa Lee, Lori Lynn. Dir. counseling and youth edn. Morgan Ave. Bapt. Ch., 1965-66, Swope Park Bapt. Ch., Kansas City, Mo., 1966-75; dir. promotions and game prodn. Kansas City (Mo.) Chiefs, 1975—; mktg. com. Nat. Football League; guest prof. Midwestern Sem. Bds. dirs. Heart of Am. United Way, Big Brothers; exec. Sunday Sch. Bd., So. Bapt. Conv., 1969-75. Served with USAF, 1962-65. Cited by Pres. Nixon for outstanding youth work; recipient vol. award United Way, 1980, mktg. excellence award Am. Mktg. Assn., 1979. Mem. Advt. and Execs. Club (seminars). Democrat. Musical composer, 1968-75; recording artist, 1965-75; contbr. articles on youth work to publs. Home: 700 La Costa Lee Summit MO 64063 Office: 1 Arrowhead Dr Kansas City MO 64063

CLINGAN, MELVIN HALL, lumber exec., publisher; b. Atchison, Kans., July 12, 1929; s. Frank E. and Hazel Ellen (Hall) C.; B.S. in Bus. (Summerfield scholar), U. Kans., 1951; m. Athelia Roberta Sweet, Apr. 7, 1956; children—Sandra, Scott, Kimberly, Marcia. Pres., Holiday Homes, Inc. and Clingan Land Co., Shawnee Mission, Kans., 1956—; pres. Johnson County Pubs., Inc., pub. Gardner News, De Soto News and Spring Hill New Era, 1965—; dir. R.L. Sweet Lumber Co. and subs.'s, Kansas City, Kans., 1959—, exec. v.p., 1973-80, pres., 1981—. Vice pres. Westwood View Sch. Bd., 1965-68; Republican congl. dist. chmn., mem. state exec. com., 1966-72; bd. dirs. Johnson County Community Coll. Found., 1973—. Served with USAF, 1951-55. Mem. Home Builders Assn. Greater Kansas City (past pres.), Home Builders Assn. Kans. (past pres.), Nat. Assn. Home Builders (nat. life dir.), Mission C. of C. (pres. 1971), Sigma Nu (grand officer 1961-68, ednl. found. 1980—), Omicron Delta Kappa, Beta Gamma Sigma, Republican. Mem. Disciples of Christ Ch. Club: Mission Hills Country; Mo. Yacht. Home: 5345 Mission Woods Rd Shawnee Mission KS 66205 Office: 4500 Roe Blvd Kansas City KS 66103

CLINTON, FRANK LEE, assn. exec.; b. Chgo., July 29, 1937; s. Francis Ring and Eva (Strohl) C.; B.S., U. Ill., 1960. Credit analyst Marshall Field & Co., Chgo., 1961-62; with trust dept. Edgar County Nat. Bank, Paris, Ill., 1962-64; purchasing mgr., accountant Bastian-Blessing Co., Chgo., 1965-71; production mgr. McCann Engring. & Mfg. Co., Glendale, Calif., 1971-74; exec. v.p. Paris (Ill.) C. of C., 1975-80; pres. Charleston (Ill.) Area C. of C., 1980-81. Bd. dirs. Edgar County Fair Assn., 1966-78, v.p., 1970-73; bd. dirs. Covered Bridge council Girl Scouts U.S., 1977—; pres. Young Republican Orgn., Edgar County, 1964. Served to sgt. Army N.G., 1960-66. Mem. Ill. Assn. of C. of C. Execs. Presbyterian. Clubs: U.S. Auto, Masons, Rotary (dir. 1976-80) Sports announcer for Paris Broadcasting Corp., 1953-79. Home: 1002 S Main St Paris IL 61944

CLINTON, LAWRENCE M., state supreme ct. justice; b. Sidney, Nebr., Mar. 21, 1915; s. Frank and Mary (Mikkelsen) C.; LL.B., Creighton U., 1940; m. Virginia Martin, Nov. 27, 1948; children—Lawrence M., Kathryne Ann, Marie, Mark. Admitted to Nebr. bar, 1940; practice law, Sidney, 1946-71; county atty. Cheyenne County (Nebr.), 1947-51; city atty. Sidney, 1953-71; justice Nebr. Supreme Ct., 1971—. Served in U.S. Army, 1941-46. Decorated Bronze Star; recipient Alumni Achievement citation Creighton U., 1980. Mem. Am. Bar Assn., Nebr. Bar Assn., Am. Legion. Roman Catholic. Club: KC. Co-author: Practitioners' Handbook for Appeals in the Courts of Nebraska, 1979. Office: 2207 State Capitol Bldg Lincoln NE 68509

CLINTON, WILLIAM CHRISTOPHER, physicist; b. Dubuque, Iowa, Aug. 19, 1937; s. William Milford and Mary Avo (Thorpe) C.; B.A., William Jewell Coll., 1966; student Ill. Inst. Tech., 1967, M.I.T., 1968; m. Lisa DeWandel, July 8, 1978. Med. lab. technician U.S. Air Force, Aeromed. Research Lab., Holloman AFB, N.Mex., 1961-65; physicist U.S. Bur. Mines, Rolla (Mo.) Metallurgy Research Center, 1966—. Chmn., Rolla Combined Fed. Campaign, 1976-78; bd. dirs. Rolla Civic Theatre, 1976-78, Alamogordo (N.Mex.) Players Workshop, 1963-65; bd. govs. Eye Research Found. Mo., 1979—. Mem. Microbeam Analysis Soc., Internat. Metallographic Soc., Sigma Xi. Club: Rolla Lions (treas. 1971-77, sec. 1977—, dist. gov. 1979-80). Contbr. articles to tech. jours. Home: PO Box 1125 Rolla MO 65401 Office: Bur Mines PO Box 280 Rolla MO 65401

CLIPSON, ADDISON HENDRICKSON, JR., architect; b. Sandusky, Ohio, Apr. 3, 1932; s. Addison Hendrickson and Mildred Leona (Stickreth) C.; B.S., U. Cin., 1953; m. Jeraldyne Mae Beets, Dec. 19, 1953; children—Randall, Brian. Engr., Mead Corp., Cin., 1952-55; designer, Elliston & Hall-McAllister-Stockwell, Cin., 1957-63; partner, Fisk-Rinehart & Hall-McAllister-Stockwell, Cin., 1970-75; pres. Addison Clipson Architects, Cin., 1975—; partner No. Ky. Architects Consortium, 1975—; bldg. commr., Woodlawn, Ohio, 1979—, Loveland, Ohio, 1980—. Mem. adv. bd. Indian Hill Historic Mus. Assn., 1974—; v.p. Glendale (Ohio) Heritage Preservation, Inc., 1974—. Served with CIC, AUS, 1955-57. Recipient Honor award A.I.A., 1974, 76. Mem. Nat. Assn. Watch and Clock Collectors (sec. Buckeye chpt. 1973-74), Early Am. Industries Assn., Am. Clock and Watch Mus., Nat. Trust Historic Preservation, Miami Purchase Assn. (trustee 1980—), A.I.A., Ohio Geneal. Soc., Ohio Soc. Architects, English Speaking Union, Huguenot Hist. Soc., Cin. Hist. Soc., Scarab, Caledonian Soc. (historian 1977—, pres. 1978-79, Ohio Tool Collectors Soc. Club: Glendale Lyceum. Home: 905 Greenville Ave Glendale OH 45246 Office: 24 Village Sq Cincinnati OH 45246

CLOE, MICHAEL EARL, hosp. adminstr.; b. Indpls., June 27, 1946; s. Earl and Gertrude Antoinette (Duncan) C.; student IRS Spl. Agts. Sch., Washington, 1973, U.S. Treasury Criminal Investigators Sch., Glynco, Ga., 1976; B.S., Ind. U., 1979; m. Cathy Cheryll Fitzerald, Oct. 30, 1970; children—Michael Andrew, Brittany Nicole. Mdse. mgr. Hook's Drug Co., Indpls., 1964-66; insp. Retail Credit Co., Indpls., 1969; computer programmer, comml. corr. Aero Mayflower Transit Co., Indpls., 1969-71; property mgr., equipment fund acct. VA Hosp., Indpls., 1971-73; spl. agt. intelligence div. IRS, Indpls., 1973-77; asst. chief supply processing and distbn. VA Med. Center, Indpls., 1977, chief, 1977—. Served with Intelligence Corps, U.S. Army, 1966-69. Recipient Time/Life award, 1964. Mem. Fed. Criminal Investigators Assn., NEA, Ind. State Tchrs. Assn. Office: VA Medical Center 1481 W 10th St Indianapolis IN 46212

CLOKE, THOMAS HENRY, mech. engr.; b. Chgo., Oct. 17, 1921; s. Thomas Henry and Lillian Clara (Krez) C.; B.S., U. Ill., 1943; m. Frances Irene Fox, Dec. 19, 1942; children—Deborah (Mrs. Wayne R. Kalbow), Thomas Myron. With Shaw, Naess & Murphy and Naess & Murphy, architects, Chgo., 1946-62, chief mech. engr., 1954-62; chief engr. Jensen & Halstead, architects, Chgo., 1962-64; prin. Neiler, Rich & Bladen, Inc., cons. engrs., Chgo., 1964-68, Gritschke & Cloke, Inc., cons. engrs., Chgo., 1968-79, Loebl Schlossman & Hackl, architects, Chgo., 1979—. Cons. engr. U.S. Air Force in Japan, 1963. Mem. Glen Ellyn (Ill.) Park Bd., 1957-60, pres., 1961; mem. Recreation Commn., Village of Glen Ellyn, 1965-74, chmn., 1974-75, mem. Bldg. Bd. of Appeal, 1973-77. Served to capt. AUS, 1943-46. Decorated Bronze Star medal. Registered profl. engr., Ill. Fellow ASHRAE (mem. research promotion com. 1969-75, research and tech. com. 1976-77, chmn. 1977-78, Disting. Service award); mem. Air Pollution Control Assn., Nat. Fire Protection Assn., Am. Mgmt. Assn., Soc. Am. Mil. Engrs., Am. Gas Assn., U.S. Power Squadron, U.S. Naval Inst., U. Ill. Alumni Assn., Theta Chi. Home: 950 Roslyn Rd Glen Ellyn IL 60137 Office: 845 N Michigan Ave Chicago IL 60611

CLOKEY, SHARON ANN, ins. agt.; b. Thief River Falls, Minn., Nov. 12, 1946; d. Erling and June Anne (Lawrence) Sovde; student Detroit Lakes Bus. Coll., 1964-65, Univ. Minn., 1976, Am. Mgmt. Sch., 1977; m. Philip L. Clokey, Jan. 6, 1968; children—Shawn Lee, Renee Michelle, Rechelle Katrice. Clk.-stenographer FAA, Mpls., 1965-68; loan sec. First Nat. Bank, Wayzata, Minn., 1969-71; profl. sec. M & M Exec. Services, Inc., Mpls., 1971-72; sales rep. Avon Products, Inc., Morton Grove, Ill., 1973-75; with Resource Agy., Inc., Long Lake, Minn., 1975—, ins. agy. mgr., since 1976—, agt., 1976—, risk mgr., 1978—. Sunday Sch. tchr. Our Father's Luth. Ch. Mem. Rockford Area Bus. Assn., Risk Mgmt. Soc. Mpls., Big I Independent Ins. Agts. Assn. Home: 6540 Edgewood St Rockford MN 55373 Office: 2685 Wayzata Blvd Box 159 Long Lake MN 55356

CLONINGER, FRANKLIN DALE, plant breeder; b. Hartshorn, Mo., Sept. 25, 1938; s. George Franklin and Patsy Jane (Derryberry) C.; B.S., U. Mo., Columbia, 1960, M.S., 1968, Ph.D., 1973; m. Marion Ruth Haas, May 19, 1962; children—Carla Sue, Mary Jane. Materials insp. Mo. Hwy. Dept., Kirkwood, 1964-65; research asst. P.A.G. Seeds Co., Carrollton, Mo., 1965-66; grad. asst. in agronomy U. Mo., Columbia, 1966-68, research specialist, 1968-74; plant breeder Golden Harvest, J.C. Robinson Seed Co., Waterloo, Nebr., 1974—. Chmn. Christian edn. Faith Christian Ch., Omaha, 1978-81. Served with AUS, 1960-63. Mem. Am. Soc. Agronomy, Crop Sci. Soc. Am., Genetics Assn. Am., Sigma Xi, Gamma Sigma Delta. Mem. Disciples of Christ Ch. Home: 602 Westridge St Elkhorn NE 68022 Office: JC Robinson Co Waterloo NE 68069

CLOONAN, JAMES BRIAN, educator, cons.; b. Chgo., Jan. 28, 1931; s. Bernard V. and Lauretta D. (Maloney) C.; student Northwestern U., 1949-52, B.A., 1957, Ph.D., 1972; M.B.A., U. Chgo., 1964; m. Edythe Adrianne Ratner, Mar. 26, 1970; children—Michele, Christine, Mia; stepchildren—Carrie Madorin, Harry Madorin. Prof., Sch. Bus., Loyola U., Chgo., 1966-71; pres. Quantitative Decision Systems, Inc., Chgo., 1972-73; chmn. bd. Heinold Securities, Inc., Chgo., 1974-77, 71-74; prof. Grad. Sch. Bus., DePaul U., Chgo., 1978—; cons. Computer Based Decision Systems, Chgo.; pres., founder Am. Assn. Individual Investors, 1979—. Served with U.S. Army, 1951-54. Mem. Ops. Research Soc., Inst. for Mgmt. Sci., Am. Fin. Assn., Am. Mktg. Assn., An. Inst. for Decision Scis., Assn. for Consumer Research. Author: Estimates of the Impact of Sign and Billboard Removal Under the Highway Beautification Act of 1965, 1966; Stock Options - The Application of Decision Theory to Basic and Advanced Strategies, 1973; An Introduction to Decision-Making for the Individual Investor, 1980. Home: 70 E Walton Chicago IL 60611 Office: 612 N Michigan Ave Chicago IL 60611

CLOSE, ALAN JEAN, accountant; b. St. Joseph, July 11, 1949; s. Donald Dean and Evelyn May (Sears) C.; B.S., U. Mo., Columbia, 1971; m. Eleanor Jane Henderson, July 1, 1972. Contract auditor Mo. Hwy. Dept., Jefferson City, 1972-75; supr. cost acctg. ONC Freight Systems, St. Joseph, Mo., 1975-78, spl. projects, clerical procedures analyst, 1978-79; plant accounting mgr. Pittsburgh Corning Corp., Sedalia, Mo., 1979—. Mem. Fed. Govt. Accts. Assn., Nat. Assn. Accts., Sedalia C. of C. Club: Rotary. Home: 1811 W 5th St Sedalia MO 65301

CLOSE, JAMES JOSEPH, printing-pub. co. exec.; b. Chgo., Apr. 14, 1936; s. Sylvester R. and Catherine J. (Hernon) C.; B.A., St. Mary of Lake, 1963; M.A., U. Notre Dame, 1981. Ordained priest, Roman Cath. Ch., 1963; pastor chs., Chgo., 1963-73; supt. mission of Our Lady of Mercy Orphanage and Social Service Programs, Chgo., 1973-81, dir., chmn. bd. Mission of Our Lady of Mercy, 1973—; pres. Mission Press, Chgo., 1973-81; pres. Nat. Cath. Devel. Conf., 1978-81. Bd. dirs. Boys Hope of Ill., 1979—; founder, bd. dirs. Mercy Mission Learning Center Chgo., 1974—; bd. dirs. Misericordia Homes Chgo., 1978—. Mem. West Central Assn. Child Care Assn. Ill., Cath. Press Assn., Nat. Cath. Devel. Conf. Clubs: Lake Point Tower, Whitehall, Center. Editor Waif's Messenger Monthly mag., 1973—. Home: 222 E Chestnut St Chicago IL 60601 Office: 1140 W Jackson Blvd Chicago IL 60607

CLOSSER, THOMAS A(NTHONY), community devel. exec.; b. Martins Ferry, Ohio, Nov. 22, 1937; s. Dominic and Amelia (Letroy) C.; student Belmont County br. Ohio U., 1958-59, indsl. devel. tng. program, planning and devel. technicians program Ga. Inst. Tech., 1971, Nat. Rural Devel. Leaders Sch., Dept. Agr., 1974; m. Loretta R. Pata, Oct. 2, 1965; children—Leslie Ann, Cynthia Marie. Asst. supt. water and sewer dept. Village Yorkville (Ohio), 1958-69; coordinator community devel., 1966-69; dep. dir. community devel. Buckeye Hills-Hocking Valley Regional Devel., Marietta, Ohio, 1969-74, exec. dir., 1974—; chmn. fin. com. Ohio U. Public Broadcast Adv. Council, 1975-79. Served with U.S. Army, 1961-62. Recipient award of appreciation Corp. Health Edn. in Appalachian Ohio, 1980. Mem. Nat. Assn. Regional Councils (exec. dirs. adv. com.), Nat. Assn. Devel. Orgns., Appalachian Devel. Dist. Assn. (v.p.). Democrat. Roman Catholic. Clubs: Lions, K.C. (past Grand Knight) Am. Legion. Office: Suite 410 215 Putnam St Marietta OH 45750

CLOUD, JACK LESLIE, gallery exec., pub.; b. Fremont, Ohio, Mar. 15, 1925; s. Wesley James and Mildred Elizabeth (Miller) C.; grad. Walsh Coll. Acctg., 1948; m. Janet Sorg, Apr. 1, 1944; children—Jack Leslie, Charles Robert. With Nat. Lithograph Co., Detroit, 1946-57; with Shelby Lithograph Co., Detroit, 1957-62; with Calvert Lithograph Co., Detroit, 1962-70; with Litho-Graphics, Detroit, 1970-75; with Odyssey Internat. Gallery, Livonia, Mich., 1975-79, pres., chmn. bd. dirs., 1975-80; with Candle-lite Inc., Birmingham, Mich., 1977-79, pres., chmn. bd. dirs., 1977-80; chmn. bd. dirs. Litho-Graphics, Inc. Realtor, Birmingham, Mich., 1980—. Served with AUS, 1943-46. Mem. Rockport Art Assn., Internat. Platform Assn., Am. Printing History Assn., U. Mich. Artist Guild. Espicopalian (sr. warden 1977-78, trustee endowment trust 1979—). Clubs: Elks (chmn. bd. trustees 1966-67), Detroit Athletic. Home: 4253 Brandywyne Dr Troy MI 48098 Office: 1821 W Maple Rd Birmingham MI 48009

CLOUSE, JOHN DANIEL, lawyer; b. Evansville, Ind., Sept. 4, 1925; s. Frank Paul and Anna Lucille (Frank) C.; A.B., U. Evansville, 1950; J.D., Ind. U., 1952; m. Georgia L. Ross, Dec. 7, 1978; 1 son, George Chauncey. Admitted to Ind. bar, 1952; asso. law firm James D. Lopp, Evansville, 1952-56; pvt. practice law, Evansville, 1956—; guest editorialist Community Comment, Evansville Courier, 1978—, Focus, Radio Sta. WGBF, 1978—; 2d asst. city atty. Evansville, 1954-55. Pres., Civil Service Commn. of Evansville Police Dept., 1961-62; pres. Ind. War Memls. Com., 1963-69; mem. jud. nominating com. Vanderburgh County, Ind., 1976—. Served with U.S. Army, 1943-46. Decorated Bronze Star medal. Fellow Ind. Bar Found.; mem. Evansville Bar Assn. (v.p. 1972), Ind. Bar Assn., Selden Soc., Pi Gamma Mu. Republican. Club: Travelers Century. Home: 819 S Hebron St Evansville IN 47715 Office: 1004 Hulman Bldg Evansville IN 47708

CLYDE, GRACE KATHERINE, employment counselor; b. Oak Park, Ill., Jan. 31, 1919; d. Joel Albert and Cora Myrtle (Hinds) Johnson; B.A. in Sociology, Beloit (Wis.) Coll., 1941; postgrad. Am. Acad. Art, 1942-60, Ohio State U., 1973; m. Henry B. Clyde, Jr., Sept. 13, 1947; children—Henry B., Bruce William, Carol Diane. Admissions counselor Beloit Coll., 1942-44; fashion store mgr. Montgomery Ward & Co., Ann Arbor Mich., 1944; asst. buyer, mgr. infants and children's wear The Fair Store, Oak Park, 1945-49; adminstrv. asst. GI Builders, Downers Grove, Ill., 1952-62; rep., cons. Scholastic Mag., Inc., N.Y.C., 1963-66; social worker Franklin County Welfare Dept., Columbus, Ohio, 1967-68; employment counseling supr. Ohio Bur. Employment Services, Columbus, 1968-80; job placement specialist Rehab. Services Commn., Bur. Vocat. Rehab., Columbus, 1980—; vocat. expert Bur. Hearings and Appeals, Social Security Adminstrn., Washington, 1977—; mem. Gov.'s Com. on Employment of Handicapped, Columbus Met. Area Com. Employment of Handicapped; pub. speaker on employment counseling. Adv. com. Columbus Pub. Schs. Adult Edn.; mem. Linkage Com. for Developmentally Disabled; ednl. dir. Lima (Ohio) PTA Council; trustee Epilepsy Assn. Franklin County. Mem. Am., Ohio (commn. licensure of counselors) personnel and guidance assns., Nat. Employment Counselors Assn. (Ohio sec.), Ohio Vocat. Guidance Assn. (sec.-treas.), Internat. Assn. Personnel in Employment Services, Central Ohio Weavers Guild, Delta Gamma. Editor: (with John Rowe and Valerie Wickham) Midwest Colleges and Universities: Data and Entry Requirements, 1943; (with others) Let's Talk, 1965. Home: 634 Morning St Worthington OH 43085 Office: 899 E Broad St Columbus OH 43205

CLYDE, PAYSON JAMES, civil engr.; b. Columbus, Ohio, Sept. 6, 1930; s. Paul Hibbert and Mildred Rebecca (Smith) C.; B.S. in Civil Engring., Pa. State U., 1952; m. Marilyn Jean Ashley, Nov. 19, 1965; 1 dau. by previous marriage, Alberta Ann Sanders. Sales engr. Armco Drainage & Metal Products, Inc., Detroit, Tucson, 1957-63; exec. sec., dir. engring. Wis. Concrete Pipe Assn., Madison, 1963-66; project engr., customer service engr., safety engr., aircraft engine group Gen. Electric Co., Cin., 1966—, now mgr. marine and indsl. spare parts sales; expert witness; vocat. sch. counselor. Served with USN, 1952-55. Registered profl. engr., Wis., Ind., Calif. Fellow ASCE; mem. Am. Pub. Works Assn., Naval Res. Assn., Res. Officers Assn. Republican. Roman Catholic. Club: Elks. Author: OSHA and the Safety Engineer, 1977; OSHA and Its Impact, 1978. Home: 11269 Marlette Dr Cincinnati OH 45242 Office: Gen Electric Co Mail Drop N-133 Cincinnati OH 45215

COAD, WILLIAM JAMES, III, computer cons.; b. Omaha, July 25, 1939; s. William James and Ethel (Worthington) C.; student Trinity Coll., 1959-62, Omaha U., 1962-64; M.B.A., U. Nebr., 1967. Cons., Booz, Allen & Hamilton, Chgo., 1968, Peat, Marwick & Mitchell, Chgo., 1969; sr. cons. Leasco, Chgo., 1972; prin. Coad and Assos., Chgo., 1973—; instr. Roosevelt U., 1974. Mem. Mensa. Republican. Episcopalian. Office: 44 W Fountainhead Dr 1G Westmont IL 60559

COAN, WARREN RONALD, bus. cons. exec.; b. Oak Park, Ill., Nov. 29, 1941; s. Warren A. and Charlotte C. (Sigler) C.; student Ill. Inst. Tech., Chgo., 1971; m. Janis Ruth Plapp, June 17, 1961; children—David, Robert, Sharon. Project leader Consol. Foods Corp., Chgo., 1972-73; systems designer Kennecott Copper Corp., Salt Lake City, 1973-75; systems analyst Fuller Brush Co., Chgo., 1975; systems analyst Infotek Corp., Milw., 1975-76; pres. R. Coan & Assos., Inc., Tampa, Fla., 1976—; cons in field. Cub master Boy Scouts Am., Waukesha, 1975-77. Lutheran. Office: 8013 Hibiscus Dr Tampa FL 33617

COASH, RONALD JAMES, elec. engr.; b. Clifton, Kans., May 15, 1939; s. Russell Francis and Hazel Marie (Scouten) C.; B.S., Kans. State U., 1972, A.M.; m. Linda Ann Dieker, June 26, 1965; children—Russell E., Jennifer M., Christopher J. Engring. technician environ. research Kans. State U., 1968-70; chief engr. Raincat Engring. Co., Greeley, Colo., 1974, Reinke Mfg. Co., Deshler, Nebr., 1974—; applications, service and mfg. engr. IC/MIDWEC, 1978. Served with USAR, 1961-63. Mem. Am. Soc. Agrl. Engrs., Internat. Brotherhood Elec. Workers, Am. Legion. Roman Catholic. Club: K.C. Author handbook, articles in field. Patentee control circuit. Home: 1027 Union St Hebron NE 68370 Office: Box 566 Deshler NE 68340

COATES, GLENN RICHARD, lawyer; b. Thorp, Wis., June 8, 1923; s. Richard and Alma (Borck) C.; student Milw. State Tchrs. Coll., 1940-42, N.M. A. and M.A., 1943-44; LL.B., U. Wis., 1948, D.Juridicial Scis., 1951; m. Dolores Milburn, June 24, 1944; children—Richard Ward, Cristie Joan. Admitted to Wis. bar, 1949; atty. Mil. Sea Transp. Service, Dept. Navy, 1951-52; pvt. law practice, Racine, Wis., 1952—; dir. Pioneer Savings & Loan Assn., Racine Federated, Inc. Lectr., U. Wis. Law Sch., 1955-56. Chmn. bd. St. Luke's Meml. Hosp., 1973-76; pres. Racine Area United Way, 1979-81. Served with AUS, 1943-46. Mem. State Bar Wis. (bd. govs. 1969-74, chmn. bd. 1973-74), Wis. Jud. Council (chmn. 1969-72), Am. Bar Assn., Am. Law Inst., Order of Coif. Methodist (chmn. finance com. 1961-67). Mason. Club: Racine Country. Contbr. to profl. publs. in field. Author: Chattel Secured Farm Credit, 1953. Home: 2830 Michigan Blvd Racine WI 53402 Office: 840 Lake Ave Racine WI 53403

COATES, ROGER SPENCER, sch. psychologist; b. Ann Arbor, Mich., June 26, 1955; s. Randall Fitzgerald and Pauline Rosanna (Rogers) C.; B.A., Western Mich. U., 1976, M.A., 1978. Psychologist, Van Buren Intermediate Sch. Dist., Lawrence, Mich., 1978—; resource person Schoocraft Schs., Western Mich. U., 1976-78. Mem. Mich. Assn. Sch. Psychologists, Assn. Behavior Analysis. Office: 701 S Paw Paw St Lawrence MI 49064

COATS, DANIEL R., congressman; b. Jackson, Mich., May 16, 1942; B.A., Wheaton (Ill.) Coll., 1965; J.D., Ind. U., 1971; m. Marcia Anne Crawford, 1965; children—Laura, Lisa, Andrew. Admitted to Ind. bar, 1972; congressional dist. rep., 1976-80; mem. 97th Congress from 4th Ind. Dist. Pres. Big Bros./Big Sisters Ft. Wayne, 1978-80; elder Community Christian Reformed Ch., Ft. Wayne; bd. dirs. Anthony Wayne Raheb. Center, Historic River Cruises Ft. Wayne. Served with USAR, 1966-68. Mem. Allen County Bar Assn. Republican. Club: Quest. Address: 1427 Longworth House Office Bldg Washington DC 20515

COATS, JOANNE, speech pathologist; b. Mpls., Apr. 9, 1936; d. John Arnold and Rachel Marguerite (Marten) Johnson; B.S., U. Minn., 1957; M.A., Southeast Mo. State U., 1974; m. Ms. Johnson; children—Steven, Suzanne. Tchr., Bethel Lutheran Sch., Burbank, Calif., 1959-61, Schs. Overseas, 1961-63; speech pathologist Cochise County Schs., Bisbee, Ariz., 1976-78, Northeast R-IV Sch., Cairo, Mo., 1978-79, Moberly public schs., 1979—. Cert. clin. competence in speech pathology. Mem. Am. Speech and Hearing Assn., Mo. Speech and Hearing Assn. Methodist. Home: 515 Greenbrier Rd Moberly MO 65270

COBLE, PAUL ISHLER, advt. co. exec.; b. Indpls., Mar. 17, 1926; s. Earl and Agnes Elizabeth (Roberts) C.; A.B., Wittenberg U., 1950; postgrad. Case-Western Res. U., 1950-53; m. Marjorie M. Trentanelli, Jan. 27, 1951; children—Jeff, Sarah Anne, Doug. Reporter, Springfield (Ohio) Daily News, 1944; reporter, feature writer Rockford (Ill.) Register-Republic, 1947-48; account exec. Fuller & Smith & Ross, Inc., Cleve., 1949-57; dir. sales promotion McCann Erickson, 1957-63; dir. sales devel. Marschalk Co., 1963-65, v.p., 1965-70, sr. v.p., 1970-73; pres. Coble Group, 1973—; chmn. bd., sec.-treas. Hahn & Coble. Inc., advt., mktg. and pub. relations, 1977—; pub. Islander mag., Hilton Head Island, S.C., 1973—. Chief instr. Cleve. Advt. Club Sch., 1961-73. Active fund raising drives for various charitable and youth orgns. Served with AUS, 1944-46. Mem. Sales and Marketing Internat., Assn. Indsl. Advertisers, Cleve. Advt. Club, Newcomen Soc. Clubs: River Oaks Racquet; Sea Pines (Hilton Head Island, S.C.); Cleve. Rotary. Contbr. articles to profl. pubs. Home: 22683 Meadowhill Ln Rocky River OH 44116 Office: Hanna Bldg Cleveland OH 44115

COBLER, LOIS BEULAH, educator; b. Garrett, Ind., June 1, 1899; d. Thomas C. and Ida M. (Van Zile) C.; grad. Tri State U., 1923; B.S., Ind. U., 1937; postgrad. Manchester Coll., Clark U., Western Mich. U., Ball State U., Ind. U., 1938-58. Tchr. public schs., Garrett-DeKalb County, Ind., 1918-56, Garrett Jr. High Sch., 1927-28; librarian J.E. Ober Elem. Sch., Garrett, 1956-66; now librarian, organist Garrett Ch. of Christ. Bd. dirs., monthly radio commentator Garrett Hosp. Aux.; chmn. nat. projects Northeastern Ind. Garden Clubs, 1970—, parliamentarian, 1972—; co-chmn. steering com. DeKalb County Internat. Christian Leadership Prayer Breakfast, 1972, sec., chmn. public relations county prayer breakfast, 1973, chmn. county breakfast, 1974; bd. dirs. Garrett Community Hosp. Aid Found., 1974—; chmn. nominations com. Ind. Mother of Year, 1974. Named Bus. and Profl. Hoosier Lady of Year, 1965; Alumni Disting. Service award Tri State Coll. and Alumni Assn., 1969; Sr. Citizen Queen, DeKalp County (Ind.), 1976-77; Citizen of Yr., Garrett C. of C., 1979. Mem. Nat., Ind. ret. tchrs. assns., DeKalb County Ret. Tchrs., Garrett Hosp. Assn., Ind. Sch. Librarians Assn., Ind. State Tchrs. Assn. (life), Garrett Hist. Soc., Bus. and Profl. Women's Club (hon.; pres. 1932-34, 65-66), Delta Kappa Gamma, Tri Kappa (pres. 1974-76). Club: Garrett Roadside Garden (sec.). Author: History of Garrett Church of Christ, 1967; contbr. biographies of Nancy Hanks Lincoln and Gene Stratton Porter to Mothers of Achievement in American History, 1776-1976, 1976. Co-editor: So Grows A City—Greater Garrett Centennial 1875-1975. Contbr. articles to profl. jours. Columnist Garrett Clipper, 1981-82. Home: 301 W King St Garrett IN 46738

COCHIN, ALAN, hosp. exec.; b. Bklyn., Dec. 19, 1936; s. Mark and Goldie (Siegelman) C.; B.S. in Chemistry, Roosevelt U., Chgo., 1969, M.S. in Biochemistry, 1972; m. Rita R. Gang, Dec. 31, 1960; 1 dau., Gayle. Lab. instr. biochemistry Roosevelt U., 1968-72; asst. prof. surg. research U. Ill., Chgo., 1971-76; dir. surg. research Hektoen Inst., Chgo., 1976-77; asst. to pres. South Shore Hosp., Chgo., 1977—; cons. chem. research Cook County Hosp.; civilian guest scientist U.S. Naval Research Inst., Bethesda, Md., 1970. Founding mem. Hoffman Estates United Party, 1981. Served with AUS, 1961-63. Mem. AAAS, Am. Public Health Assn., Chgo. Area Health Planning Assn., N.W. Suburban Pistol League. Club: Burnham Park Yacht (Chgo.). Contbr. chpt. to Neuro-Humoral and Metabolic Disease, 1973; contbr. articles to sci. jours. Home: 1595 W Oakmont Rd Hoffman Estates IL 60194 Office: South Shore Hosp 8015 S Luella Ave Chicago IL 60617

COCHRAN, DWIGHT EDWIN, II, veterinarian; b. East Chicago, Ind., May 18, 1948; s. Dwight Edwin and Laura Eileen (Meyer) C.; student Baylor U., 1966-68; D.V.M., Purdue U., 1973; m. Glenda Kay Boyd, May 19, 1973. Gen. practice veterinary medicine, herd health cons., Boswell, Ind., 1973—; cons. Ind. Dairy Goat Assn. Recipient Leadership award 4-H Clubs, 1978. Mem. Ind. Acad. Veterinary Medicine, Acad. Vet. Cons., Am. Assn. Swine Practitioners, Am. Assn. Sheep, Goat Practitioners, Am. Assn. Bovine Practitioners, Am., Ind., West Central Ind. veterinary med. assns., Am. Registry Cert. Animal Scientists, Am. Soc. Agrl. Cons. Presbyterian. Club: Rotary Internat. (dir. Boswell chpt.). Author: Common Diseases of Dairy Goats, A Guide to Their Prevention, Treatment, and Control For the Herdsman, 1977. Home: 402 E North St Boswell IN 47921 Office: 104 E Main St Boswell IN 47921

COCHRAN, HOWARD HENRY, banker; b. Detroit, Aug. 24, 1933; s. Marion and Florence R. (Henderson) C.; ed. Bowling Green U., Walsh Coll., U. Wis.; postgrad. Harvard Sch. Bus.; m. Hattie A. Trapold, Mar. 16, 1955; children—Howard Henry, Harold, Hugh. Collection supr. Mich. Bank, Detroit, successively br. mgr., comml. loan dept., credit analyst, asst. v.p., v.p. ops. div.; sr. v.p. Mich. Nat. Bank, Pt. Huron, 1971, chief exec. officer, to 1975; sr. v.p. Mich. Nat. Bank, Flint, 1975—, now chief exec. officer, chmn. bd.; dir. Mich. Nat. Leasing Corp., Indsl. Devel. Corp., Pt. Huron. Bd. dirs. United Found. St. Clair County; bd. dirs., v.p. United Way, Flint Area Conf. Served with USAF, 1951-55. Recipient commendation Pres. U.S., 1976. Mem. Midland C. of C., Nat. Alliance Bus. (chmn.), Detroit Inst. Arts, Econ. Club Detroit. Baptist. Clubs: Rotary; Warwick Hills Country; Univ., Flint City. Home: 8101 Irish Rd Grand Blanc MI 48439 Office: 519 S Saginaw St Flint MI 48502

COCHRAN, JULIENNE VRADENBURGH, librarian; b. San Anselmo, Calif., June 19, 1907; d. Preston Hickok and Juliet Burroughs (Cochran) Vradenburgh; A.B., Mills Coll. 1930; M.A., Stanford U., 1946; M.L.S., Case Western Reserve U., 1960; postgrad. U. Ill., 1972—; m. Dennis G. McQuade, June 19, 1932; m. 2d Stefan A. Wade, Jan. 4, 1971. Librarian, Pasadena (Calif.) Star-News and Post, 1932-42; safety engr. U.S. Naval Air Sta., Moffatt Field, 1944-46; librarian Stanford (Calif.) U., 1948-50, Tacoma (Wash.) Pub.

Library, 1950-52; instr. Coll. Puget Sound (Wash.), summer 1952; librarian Miss Hall's Sch. for Girls, Pittsfield, Mass., 1953-54; documents librarian Whitman Coll., 1954-55; asst. librarian S.D. Tchrs. Coll., Aberdeen, 1956-57; law librarian U. Ida., Moscow, 1957-58; ref. librarian Case Western Res. U., Cleve., 1958-60; law librarian Akron (Ohio) Law Library, 1960-62, Cook County Law Library, Chgo., 1966-68; Ill. Research Librarian, Champaign, Ill., 1972—; library cons. Ill. Continuing Edn., 1972—. Recipient Certificate of Achievement, No. Ill. U., 1971, 72; Social Sci. Research Council grantee, 1946, 52, 58-60, 68-72, 74—; Ill. State grantee, 1980—. Mem. Women in Communication, DAR, Theta Sigma Phi, Sigma Delta Chi, Sigma Iota Epsilon, Delta Gamma Sigma, Phi Beta Lambda, Alpha Phi Omega, Kappa Delta Phi. Republican. Clubs: Order Eastern Star, Women's, Allied Arts. Author: Guaranteed Annual Wage, 1946; State Sources to School Libraries, 1965; Internat. Ednl. Orgn., 1952; Guide to Thomas Beer 1962, 77, 81; Paul Monroe Writings, 1966, 81; Books on Financial History of U.S., 1970; Guide for Business Research, 1975; Civil Disturbances and Civil Disorders, 1976, 80. Home: 1107 W Green St Urbana IL 61801 Office: PO Box 2979 Sta A Champaign IL 61820

COCHRAN, MALCOLM LOWELL, psychologist; b. Crawfordsville, Iowa, Oct. 17, 1941; s. Vaun Wesley and Pearl Ida (Robertson) C.; B.A., Iowa Wesleyan Coll., 1963; M.S., Municipal U. of Omaha, 1965; m. Barbara Sue Stotts, Apr. 17, 1966; children—Teresa Marie, Gary Lowell, Debra Sue, Patricia Diane. Intern sch. psychometrist, Child Study Service Municipal U. of Omaha, 1963-64; research psychometrist, sch. psychologist Glenwood State Hosp.-Sch., Glenwood, Iowa, 1964-68, cons. psychologist, diagnostic and evaluation clinic, 1968-74, dir. employee testing program, 1968-72, dir. psychol. testing center, 1974—, lectr.,-in-service training, child devel., 1968-72. Cubmaster Boy Scouts Am., Glenwood, 1976-77. Served with Army N.G., 1961. Recipient Explorer Scouts Silver Award Boy Scouts Am., 1958; certified sch. psychologist, Iowa; licensed psychologist, Iowa. Fellow Am. Assn. Mental Deficiency. Republican. Methodist. Contbr. articles to profl. jours. Home: 225 W Florence Ave Glenwood IA 51534 Office: 711 S Vine St Glenwood IA 51534

COCHRAN, MARY LEE BROWN, educator; b. Clifton Hill, Mo., Jan. 28, 1931; d. Aubrey E. and Mary Margaret (Asbell) Brown; B.S. in Elem. Edn., Northwest Mo. State U., Kirksville, 1971; M.Ed. in Reading, U. Mo., Columbia, 1974; m. Ralph H. Cochran; children—Mary Alice Cochran Rosenbloom, Ralph Michael, Clinton F. Tchr. kindergarten Renick (Mo.) Sch. Dist., 1968-70; tchr. Macon (Mo.) R1 Sch., 1971-74, tchr. learning disabilities, dept. head, 1974—. Mem. Mo. State Tchrs. Assn., Macon Community Tchrs. Assn. (sec. treas. 1974-76), Macon Community Tchrs. Assn. (pres. 1977-78), N.E. Mo. chpt. Council Exceptional Children (sec. 1980-81), Pi Lambda Theta. Home: Box 145 Jacksonville MO 65260 Office: Hwy 63 Macon MO 63552

COCHRAN, MORRIS WAYNE, assn. exec.; b. Columbus, Ind., Aug. 30, 1941; s. Carl M. and Elfreda M. (Stillinger) C.; B.F.A., U. Cin., 1963; M.S. (Univ. Scholar), U. Ill., 1964; postgrad. Mich. State U., 1968, Syracuse U., 1969, John Marshall Law Sch., 1970-72, Washington U., 1970-72; m. Mary-Ellen Skeen, July 29, 1963; children—Justine Della, Morris Wayne. News dir. WLTH Radio, Gary, Ind., 1964-65; exec. sec., mgr. Better Bus. Bur. N.W. Ind., Gary, 1965—, pres. ednl. found., 1975—; founder, dir. N.W. Ind. Credit Counseling, 1974—. Bd. dirs. Gary Urban Coalition, 1969-70; chmn. town formation Ross Park, Ind., 1973—; bd. dirs. Gary Jr. Achievement, 1978-81; mem. Conf. of Social Concern, 1981. Recipient U.P.I. News award, 1965; State Broadcaster of Month award, 1967. Mem. Gary Jaycees (dir. 1965-66), Gary Exchange (dir. 1972-74). Office: 2500 W Ridge Rd Gary IN 46408

COCHRAN, RICHARD MORRISON, biologist; b. West Plains, Mo., July 24, 1941; s. Russell Van and Dulcie Anona (Morrison) C.; student U. Mo., 1959-61; B.S.E., Ark. State U., 1963, M.S.E., 1965; postgrad. Okla. State U., summers 1968-70; m. Connie Lee Garner, Oct. 12, 1963; children—Richard Garner, Gretchen Hallie. Lookout, U.S. Forest Service, Boise (Idaho) Nat. Forest, 1960, 62; tchr. biology Sandia High Sch., Albuquerque, 1963-64; grad. asst. Ark. State U., 1964-65; tchr. Trumann (Ark.) High Sch., 1965-66; instr. biology S.W. Mo. State U., West Plains, 1966-81, asst. prof. life scis., 1981—; owner, operator Rick's Music Shop, West Plains, 1974—; lectr. wild turkey behavior; profl. musician. Pres., Downtown Mcht.'s Assn., West Plains, 1978-79. Recipient Curators award U. Mo., 1959. Mem. Nat. Wild Turkey Fedn. Club: Rotary. Research in wild turkey behavior; contbr. articles to local publs. Home: PO Box 11A D Cr Route West Plains MO 65775 Office: SW Mo State U West Main St West Plains MO 65775

COCHRAN, RICHARD TIMOTHY, investment banker; b. Newark, Ohio, Mar. 12, 1939; s. Jacque P. and Lena H. (DeVito) C.; B.A., Ohio U., Athens, 1966; m. Annetta Marie Giesy, Oct. 31, 1972; children—Sean P. (dec.), Richard Sean, Scott Ellwood. Salesman, Wheeling Steel Co. (W.Va.), 1966-67, Anchor Hocking Glass Co., Lancaster, Ohio, 1967; with Merrill Lynch, Pierce, Fenner & Smith Inc., Columbus, Ohio, 1968—, sr. account exec., then asst. v.p., 1973-77, v.p., 1977—, leading options broker, 1980—; leader option seminars. Mem. fin. com. Broad St. United Methodist Ch., Columbus, 1979-80. Mid-Am. Conf. scholar-athlete, 1965. Mem. Columbus Stock and Bond Club, Phi Beta Kappa. Republican. Clubs: Brookside Country, Columbus Athletic. Office: 180 E Broad St Columbus OH 43215

COCKRELL, RONALD SPENCER, scientist, educator; b. Kansas City, Mo., June 26, 1938; s. Robert Spencer and Jean (Hammond) C.; B.S., U. Mo., 1960, B.Med.Sci., 1964; Ph.D., U. Pa., 1968; m. Florence Barbara Hanline, June 17, 1960; children—Richard, Synthia. Asst. prof. biochemistry St. Louis U. Sch. Medicine, 1969-74, asso. prof., 1974—. Nat. Cancer Inst. grantee, 1970—. Mem. Am. Soc. Biol. Chemists. Home: 9540 Hale Dr St Louis MO 63123 Office: 1402 S Grand St Louis MO 63104

COCKS, RICHARD ERNEST, chem. engr.; b. Coldwater, Mich., Aug. 1, 1917; s. Harry A. and Harriette Nina (Hall) C.; A.B., Western Mich. U., 1939, B.S. in Chem. Engring., U. Ill., 1942; m. Anna Pearl Rhodes, June 20, 1943; children—Valerie A. (Mrs. Ronald Roughton), Margaret (Mrs. Michael A. Row). Supr., Hercules Powder Co., Radford, Va., 1942-45; research chem. engr. Victor Chem. Works, Chicago Heights, Ill., 1945-48, div. supt., Nashville, 1948-49; dept. head Panelyte div. St. Regis Paper Co., Kalamazoo, 1950-53, plant mgr. plant food div. Farm Bur. Services, Kalamazoo, 1953-55; with Miles Labs., Inc., Elkhart, Ind., 1955—, adminstr. engring. services and real estate, 1968-75, mgr. corp. real estate and facilities planning, 1976—. Adviser, Jr. Achievement, 1962-63; active United Way. Registered profl. engr., Ohio, Ind. Mem. Ind. Soc. Profl. Engrs., Nat. Soc. Profl. Engrs., Am. Chem. Soc., Am. Inst. Chem. Engrs., ASTM, Indsl. Devel. Research Council, Nat. Assn. Corp. Real Estate Execs. Episcopalian. Mason (32 deg.), Lion. Home: 1622 Victoria Dr Elkhart IN 46514 Office: 1227 Myrtle St Elkhart IN 46514

CODDINGTON, THOMAS TUCKER, automotive co. exec.; b. Columbus, Ohio, Jan. 1, 1938; s. Gilbert Harold and Louise (Hazen) C.; B.M.E., Ohio State U., 1961; M.Automotive Engring., Chrysler Inst., Highland Park, Mich., 1964; m. Cecelia Ann McLaughlin, Aug. 31, 1968; children—Maureen Louise, Kevin Ward. With Chrysler Corp., Detroit, 1961—, engring. coordinator, spl. vehicle devel., 1969-74, supr. fuel metering systems, engring. office, 1974-78, product planner, truck produce planning, 1978-80; partner, v.p. engring. Specialize Vehicles, Inc., Troy, Mich., 1980—. Served in USAF, 1961-62. Mem. Soc. Automotive Engrs., Ohio State U. Alumni Assn., SAR. Club: Economic (Detroit). Patentee fuel filter, rollover valve, emergency fuel line closure. Home: 6179 Herbmoor St Troy MI 48098 Office: 2468 Industrial Row Troy MI 48084

CODY, JOHN CARDINAL, cardinal, archbishop Chgo.; b. St. Louis, Dec. 24, 1907; s. Thomas Joseph and Mary (Begley) C.; grad. St. Louis Prep. Sem., 1926; Ph.D., N.Am. Coll., Rome, 1928, S.T.D., 1932, D.Canon Law, 1938. Ordained priest Roman Catholic Ch., Dec. 8, 1931; aux. bishop Diocese St. Louis, 1947-54; co-adjutor with right of succession to bishop St. Joseph, Mo., 1954; bishop St. Joseph, 1955; coadjutor to Bishop Kansas City-St. Joseph, 1956, bishop, Oct. 1956; coadjutor with right of succession to Archbishop of New Orleans, 1961, apostolic adminstr., 1962-64, archbishop, 1964-65; archbishop Chgo., Aug. 24, 1965—; elevated to cardinalate, June 26, 1967. Mem. Nat. Conf. Cath. Bishops, Sacred Congregation for Clergy; chancellor Cath. Ch. Extension Soc.; mem. regional bd. Boy Scouts Am.; nat. chaplain Nat. Cath. Soc. Foresters; high spiritual dir. Cath. Order Foresters. Died April 25, 1982.

COE, JOHN WILLIAM, retail store exec.; b. Highland Park, Mich., Oct. 2, 1924; s. C. Leroy and Grace Lamont C.; B.S. in Indsl.-Mech. Engring., U. Mich., 1949; m. Sally Childs, Oct. 24, 1953; children—John Childs, Daniel William. Acct., Charles L. Coe and Assos., 1949; buyer J.L. Hudson Co., Detroit, 1950-58, div. mdse. mgr., 1959-68, v.p., gen. mgr. stores, 1968—; dir. Champion Home Builders. Dist. chmn. United Found., 1971-72; bd. dirs. Planned Parenthood League, Inc. Served to lt. (j.g.) USNR, 1943-46. Mem. Am. Mgmt. Assn., Northland-Eastland Mchts. Assn. (dir., past pres.), Phi Alumni Assn. Psi Upsilon (dir.). Republican. Anglican. Clubs: Detroit Athletic, Country of Detroit; Pere Marquette Rod and Gun; Univ. (Ann Arbor, Mich.); Rotary (past pres.)(Harper Woods, Mich.); Players. Home: 488 Lakeland Grosse Pointe MI 48230 Office: J L Hudson Co 1206 Woodward St Detroit MI 48226

COE, RALPH TRACY, mus. ofcl.; b. Cleve., Aug. 27, 1929; s. Ralph M. and Dorothy T. C.; B.A., Oberlin Coll., 1953; M.A., Yale U., 1957. Asst. curator Nat. Gallery Art, Washington, 1957-59; curator paintings and sculpture Nelson Gallery Art, Kansas City, Mo., 1959, asst. dir., 1965-77, dir., 1977—. Lectr. art history U. Kans., Lawrence, 1969—; vis. research asst. Victoria and Albert Mus., London, Eng., 1956-57. Mem. IRS commr. art adv. panel, Washington, 1973-77, NEA Mus. Panel, 1977—; trustee Am. Fedn. Arts, 1977—. Mem. Coll. Art Assn. Am., Am. Assn. Mus., Soc. Archtl. Historians, Assn. Art Mus. Dirs. (trustee, 1979, v.p. 1980). Club: River (Kansas City, Mo.). Author: Dale Eldred: Sculpture into Environment, 1978; co-editor: American Architecture and Other Writings, 1961; contbr. articles to profl. jours., exhbn. catalogs. Office: 4525 Oak St Kansas City MO 64111

COE, ROBERT WILLIAM, state ofcl.; b. Johnston City, Ill., Feb. 19, 1927; s. Myron John and Lola Oneida (Cothern) C.; B.S., No. Ill. U., 1965, M.S., 1966; m. Dorothy L. Thorson, June 8, 1947; children—Sandra Coe Freedman, Ronald, Cheryl Coe Gray, Dena. Sanitarian, Ill. Dept. Public Health, Carbondale, 1950-54, Rock Island, 1954-64, Aurora, 1964-71, Springfield, 1971-72, exec. adminstr., Chgo., 1972—; prof. mgmt. No. Ill. U. at DeKalb, 1966-67. Asst. scoutmaster Cub Scouts Am., 1957-59; asst. scoutmaster Boy Scouts Am., 1959-61, scoutmaster, 1961-64, dist. commr., 1964-66. Served with AUS, 1945-47. Mem. Ill. Pub. Health Assn., Assn. Ill. Milk, Food and Environmental Sanitarians (sec., treas. 1968-80), AAUP. Author: A Study to Determine the Effect of Appropriations Upon Program Administration, 1966. Editor: Office Management (Clarence Sims), 1965. Home: 206 Boulder Hill Pass Montgomery IL 60538 Office: Ill Dept Public Health 2121 W Taylor St Chicago IL 60612

COELHO, RICHARD JOSEPH, univ. ofcl.; b. Newark, Ohio, July 26, 1913; s. Joseph Arthur and Marguerite (Kuster) C.; A.B., Denison U., 1935; M.A., U. Denver, 1954, Ph.D., 1955; m. Helen C. Lindquist, June 4, 1945; children—Joseph R., David F., Christine A., Carl A. Chief clk. freight traffic dept. Pa. R.R., Pitts., 1935-41; gen. office mgr. Lucien Lelong, Inc., Chgo., 1946-48; credit, traffic mgr. Robbins Incubator Co., Denver, 1950-52; dir. conf. leadership tng. Ford Motor Co., Dearborn, Mich., 1956-57; communications cons. nursing staff Sparrow Hosp., Lansing, Mich., 1957-58; faculty Mich. State U., East Lansing, 1955—, dir. residence halls acad. programs, 1962-71, asso. dean U. Coll., 1971—; dir. Binational Cultural Center, Juiz de Fora, Brazil on grant from USIA, 1960-61. Commr., East Lansing council Boy Scouts Am., 1962-64; lay rep. edn. div. Mich. Catholic Council Bishops, 1962—. Served to col. AUS, 1941-46. Decorated Bronze Star medal with cluster. Mem. Speech Assn. Am., Assn. Gen. and Liberal Studies, Am. Assn. Univ. Adminstrs., Sigma Alpha Epsilon, Pi Delta Epsilon, Omicron Delta Kappa, Phi Mu Alpha. Republican. Home: 1103 Old Hickory Ln East Lansing MI 48823

COFFEE, JAMES FREDERICK, lawyer; b. Decatur, Ind., Mar. 6, 1918; s. Claude M. and Frances N. (Butler) C.; B.C.E., Purdue U., 1939; J.D., Ind. U., 1947; m. Jeanmarie Hackman, Dec. 29, 1945 (dec. 1978); children—James, Carolyn, Susan, Sheila, Kevin, Richard, Elizabeth, Thomas, Claudia; m. 2d, Marjorie Hansen Masterson, Oct. 4, 1980. Admitted to Wis. bar, 1947, Ill. bar, 1952; patent atty. Allis Chalmers Mfg. Co., Milw., 1947-51; mem. firm Anderson, Luedeka, Fitch, Even & Tabin, and predecessors, Chgo., 1951-64, partner, 1956-64; individual practice law, Chgo., 1964-71; partner law firm Coffee & Sweeney, Chgo., 1971-76; partner, gen. counsel design firm Marvin Glass & Assos., Chgo., 1973—. Served to capt. AUS, 1941-46. Mem. Am., Ill., Chgo. (chmn. com. patents, trademark and unfair trade practices 1967) bar assns., Am. Patent Law Assn., Patent Law Assn. Chgo. (chmn. com. copyrights 1969), Am. Judicature Soc. Home: 320 Earls Ct Deerfield IL 60015 Office: 815 N La Salle St Chicago IL 60610

COFFELT, JOHN J., univ. pres.; b. Neosho, Mo., Dec. 26, 1924; s. Roscoe John and Estella Matilda (Turner) C.; B.S., U. Denver, 1948; M.A., Northeastern State U., Greeley, Colo., 1951; Ed.D., U. Colo., 1962; m. Anna Marie Nelson, Feb. 27, 1945; children—Susan Ann (Mrs. Robert Lyon), Margaret Jean (Mrs. Duane Spatar), Janet Lee (Mrs. Robert Bannon), John Byron. Aircraft mechanic Boeing Aircraft Corp., Seattle, 1942-43; bookkeeper Colo. Nat. Bank, Denver, 1946-48; dir. accounts and records, registrar, instr. State Tchrs. Coll., Dickinson, N.D., 1948-52; dir. research Colo. Dept. Edn., Denver, 1952-56; dir. Colo. Legis. Com. on Edn., dir. Colo. Sch. Bd. Assn., Boulder, 1958-62; coordinator research, Okla., 1962-65; vice chancellor research and planning Okla. State Regents for Higher Edn., Oklahoma City, 1965-68; v.p. adminstrv. affairs Youngstown (Ohio) State U., 1968-73, pres., 1973—. Mem. exec. com. Mahoning Area council Boy Scouts Am.; trustee Youngstown Hosp. Assn., N.E. Ohio U. Coll. Medicine, N.E. TV of Ohio, Butler Inst. Am. Art. Served with USAAF, 1943-45. Decorated Air medal, D.F.C. Mem. Assn. for Higher Edn., Am. Assn. State Colls. and Univs., Youngstown C. of C. (dir., exec. com.), Alpha Kappa Psi, Phi Delta Kappa, Phi Kappa Phi. Clubs: Masons (32 deg.), Lions. Home: 1010 Colonial Dr Youngstown OH 44505 Office: Youngstown State U Youngstown OH 44555*

COFFEY, JOHN LOUIS, state supreme ct. justice; b. Milw., Apr. 15, 1922; s. William Leo and Elizabeth Ann (Walsh) C.; B.A., Marquette U., 1943, LL.B., 1948, LL.D., 1948; M.B.A. (hon.), Spencerian Coll., 1963; m. Marion Kunzelmann, Feb. 3, 1951; children—Peter Lee, Elizabeth Mary Coffey Robbins. Admitted to Wis. bar, 1948, U.S. Fed. Ct. bar, 1948, U.S. Supreme Ct. bar, 1980; asst. city atty., Milw., 1949-54; judge Civil Ct., Milw., 1954-60; judge Milw. Mcpl. Ct., 1960-61; judge Br. 12 Circuit Ct., Milw., 1964-78, sr. felony judge Circuit Ct., Milwaukee County, 1974-77; justice Wis. Supreme Ct., Madison, 1978—; mem. Wis. Bd. Criminal Ct. Judges, 1960-78, Wis. Bd. Circuit Ct. Judges, 1962-78; lectr. on causes and remedies of crime, dental and med. malpractice. Chmn. adv. bd. St. Joseph's Home for Children, 1958-64; mem. adv. bd. St. Mary's Hosp., 1964-70; mem. Milw. County council Boy Scouts Am.; chmn. St. Eugene's Sch. Bd., 1967-72, St. Eugene's Parish Council, 1974; mem. vol. services adv. com. Milwaukee County Dept. Public Welfare; bd. govs. Marquette U. High Sch. Served with USNR, 1943-46. Named Outstanding Young Man of Yr., Milw. Jr. C. of C., 1951; One of Five Outstanding Young Men in State, Wis. Jr. C. of C., 1957; recipient Disting. Service award Am. Legion, 1973; named Marquette U. Law Alumnus of Year, 1980. Fellow Am. Bar Found.; mem. Alpha Sigma Nu. Roman Catholic. Clubs: M (past dir.), Woolsack (dir.). Office: 206 E Capital Madison WI 53702

COFFEY, MAX E., state senator; b. Vermilion County, Ill., 1939; ed. public schs.; 2 children. Farmer, 1957-61; asst. mgr. feed and fertilizer bus., 1961-64; owner, operator Coffey's Flower Shop, 1965-75, also Coffey Apts.; former mem. Ill. Ho. of Reps.; Ill. Senate, 1976—. Mem. Coles County Bd., 1971-74; supr. Charlestown Twp. (Ill.), 1971-74. Mem. C. of C. Clubs: Elks, Moose, Kiwanis. Office: PO Box 625 1504 20th St Charleston IL 61920*

COFFMAN, KENNETH MORROW, mech. contractor; b. Ann Arbor, Mich., Aug 3, 1921; s. Harold Coe and Aletha (Morrow) C.; B.S., Lawrence U., 1943; m. Barbara Ann Porth, Dec. 30, 1943; children—Gregory, Deborah Coffman Greene, Jenifer. Exec. v.p. Stanley Carter Co. Ohio, Toledo, 1957-59; v.p. sales Wenzel & Henoch Co., Milw., 1959-64; exec. v.p. Milw. W & H Inc., 1964-70; exec. v.p. Azco Downey Inc., Milw., 1970-76, pres., 1977-81. Bd. dirs. YMCA, Milw., 1968-72, Tri County, 1973-78; chmn. bd. mgrs. Camp Minikani, 1965-81. Served with USMC 1943-46. Named Layman of year, Tri County YMCA, 1973. Mem. Nat. Certified Pipe Welders Bur. Wis. (dir. 1973-81), Mech. Contractors Assn. South East Wis. (dir. 1970-80), Mech. Contractors Devel. Fund. (dir., pres. 1972-73), Wis. Constrn. Employers Council (dir. 1973-81), MCA of Wis. (dir. 1977-81), Nat. Fire Protection Assn., Nat. Assn. Plumbing, Heating, Cooling Contractors, Sheet Metal and Air Conditioning Contractors Nat. Assn. Congregationalist. Home: 925 E Wells St Milwaukee WI 53202 Office: Box 1155 Milwaukee WI 53201

COFFMAN, PHILLIP HUDSON, educator; b. Lincoln, Nebr., Nov. 27, 1936; s. Rowland Francis and Elberta (Hudson) C.; B. Music Edn., U. Nebr., 1958; M. Music, U. Idaho, 1962; Ph.D., U. Toledo, 1971; m. Karen M. Preston, Aug. 14, 1958; children—Phillip C., Catherine L. Tchr. pub. schs., Rushville, Neb., 1958-59; instr. Doane Coll., Crete, Nebr., 1959-60; teaching asst. U. Idaho, Moscow, 1960-62, instr., 1962-65; asso. prof., chmn. dept. music Jamestown (N.D.) Coll., 1965-68; adminstrv. intern U. Toledo, 1968-71; asso. prof., head dept. music U. Minn., Duluth, 1971-76, prof., dean Sch. Fine Arts, 1976—. Mem. Lincoln Symphony, 1954-60, Toledo Symphony, 1969-71; guest artist Ednl. TV, 1964; instr. Internat. Music Camp, 1967-68. Pres. Civic Music Assn., 1967, Campus Ministry Bd., 1972-75, Minn. Coll. and Univ. Council for Music, 1976; music adjudicator, interviewer Bush Leadership Fellows Program, 1977—; chmn. bd. Duluth Festival of Arts, 1979-81. F.E. Olds scholar, 1963, Bush Found. fellow, 1973. Mem. Internat. Council Fine Arts Deans, Theta Xi, Phi Mu Alpha, Pi Kappa Lambda, Kappa Kappa Psi. Home: 4601 Woodland Ave Duluth MN 55803

COFFMAN, THOMAS MILES, athletic dir.; b. Winchester, Ind., Nov. 4, 1952; s. Robert J. and Evelyn J. C.; B.A., Heidelberg Coll., 1974; M.Ed., Bowling Green State U., 1976; m. Deborah Lynne Buchman, July 24, 1976. Athletic dir. Tiffin (Ohio) U., 1974—, dean of men, 1980—, dir. devel. and alumni affairs, 1981—; sales rep. Focht Bros. Constrn., summer 1978; pres. Mid-Ohio Conf., 1977. Chmn. Seneca County Easter Seals, 1977-78, bd. dirs., 1978—; bd. dirs. Tiffin Community YMCA. Mem. Nat. Assn. Athletic Dirs. Mem. United Church of Christ. Clubs: Seneca County H Assn., Alumni H Assn. (v.p., 1978—), Elks. Home: 281 Melmore Tiffin OH 44883 Office: 155 Miami Tiffin OH 44883

COFRIN, DOUGLASS, radio sta. exec.; b. Chgo., Dec. 12, 1942; s. John Paige and Barbara Louise (Hauxhurst) C.; B.A., Cornell U., 1965; J.D., U. Wis., 1968; m. Regina Marie Longo (div.); 1 dau., Regina Louise. Admitted to Wis., N.Y. bars; individual practice law, Green Bay, Wis., 1968-70; announcer Sta. WNEW, N.Y.C., 1971; copywriter, radio voice Korvettes, N.Y.C., 1971-72; announcer Sta. WAUN-FM, Kewaunee, Wis., 1973-76; owner, mgr. Sta. WFMR-FM, Milw., 1976—, also pres.; pub. Milw. Mag., 1979—, owner, 1978—; lectr. in field. Trustee, Wis. Conservatory of Music; Rep. candidate U.S. Senate from Wis., 1980. Mem. State Bar N.Y., State Bar Wis. Republican. Contbr. articles to mags. Office: 711 W Capitol Dr Milwaukee WI 53206

COGAN, THOMAS PATRICK, clin. psychologist; b. Chgo., Mar. 9, 1948; s. Robert K. and Agnes V. (Vargo) C.; B.A., Lewis U., 1970; Ph.D., Ill. Inst. Tech., 1977; m. Bette Herbert, Sept. 3, 1971. Staff psychologist Mercy Hosp. and Med. Center, Chgo., 1977—; pvt. practice clin. psychology, Chgo., 1977—. Recipient Aquinas award Lewis U., 1970. Mem. Am. Psychol. Assn. Condr. research on risk taking in psychotherapy, friendship in psychotherapy. Home: 3282 W Wrightwood Ave Chicago IL 60647 Office: 30 N Michigan Ave Chicago IL 60602

COGNATA, DONALD JASPER, police officer; b. St. Louis, Oct. 20, 1941; s. Frank and Francine (Caldwell) C.; A.S., Forest Park Community Coll., 1965; B.S., U. Mo., 1971; M.A., St. Louis U., 1974; grad. Nat. Crime Prevention Inst., 1973, Mo. U. Crime Prevention Workshop, 1974; m. Eileen Beverly Schultz, July 17, 1965; children—Donald Antoin, Christina Lee, Troy Dominic. With St. Louis Met. Police Dept., 1965—, precinct sgt., 1975, project coordinator geo-coding system, 1975-77, supr. mgmt. service sect., 1977—; lectr., cons. geo-coding, computer security, police mgmt., crime prevention, psychodeterence; bd. dirs. Aid to Victims of Crime; bd. advisers South St. Louis Alcoholism Council; mem. exec. bd. Spl. Offenders Council, Life Crisis Services. Comml. exec. vol. SBA. Served with USMC, 1958-62. Certified probation and parole bd. vol., Mo. Mem. Internat. Assn. Police Officers, St. Louis Police Officers

Assn., Am. Statis. Soc. Home: 6964 Marquette St Saint Louis MO 63139 Office: 1200 Clark St Saint Louis MO 63103

COHEN, ALLAN RICHARD, lawyer; b. Chgo., Feb. 25, 1923; s. Louis and Ruth (Cohen) C.; B.A., U. Wis., 1947, J.D., 1949; postgrad. Northwestern U., 1953-54; m. Audrey Doris Levy, Oct. 14, 1960; children—Joseph, David, Gale. Admitted to Ill. bar, 1950, since practiced in Chgo. Served with AUS, 1943-45. Decorated Presdl. citation with oak leaf cluster. Mem. Fed., Ill. (vice chmn. sect. comml. bankruptcy and banking laws 1977-78), Chgo. (vice chmn. com. bankruptcy 1972-73, chmn. 1973-74; panelist seminar on bankruptcy, 1968, 72, 74) bar assns., Zeta Beta Tau, Tau Epsilon Rho. Clubs: Lions, Covenant of Ill., Elms Swim and Tennis (Highland Park, Ill.). Home: 1986 Dale St Highland Park IL 60035 Office: 55 W Monroe St Chicago IL 60603

COHEN, BURTON DAVID, franchising exec., lawyer; b. Chgo., Feb. 12, 1940; s. Allan and Gussy (Katz) C.; B.S. in Bus. and Econs., Ill. Inst. Tech., 1960; J.D., Northwestern U., 1963; m. Linda Rochelle Kaine, Jan. 19, 1969; children—David, Jordana. Admitted to Ill. bar, 1963; staff atty. McDonald's Corp., Oak Brook, Ill., 1964-69, asst. sec., 1969-70, asst. gen. counsel, 1970-76, asst. v.p., 1976-78, dir. legal dept., 1978-80, v.p. licensing, asst. gen. counsel, asst. sec., 1980--; lectr. Practising Law Inst. Served with AUS, 1963-64. Mem. Am. Bar Assn., Ill. Bar Assn., Chgo. Bar Assn., Internat. Franchise Assn., Assn. Nat. Advertisers, Chgo. Council Fgn. Relations, Tau Epsilon Phi, Phi Delta Phi. Club: Execs. (Chgo.). Author: Franchising: Second Generation Problems, 1969. Office: McDonalds Plaza Oak Brook IL 60521

COHEN, CARL MORDECAI, chem. co. exec.; b. Boston, Jan. 17, 1954; s. Arthur I. and Harriet P. (Morrison) C.; B.A., U. Chgo., 1975; M.B.A., U. Mich. 1979. Adminstrv. asst. Wholesale Electric Distbrs., Chgo., 1975-77; asst. to pres. Ross Chem. Co., Detroit, 1979-80, product mgr., 1981—. Home: 8121 Agnes St Detroit MI 48214 Office: Ross Chem Co 8485 Melville St Detroit MI 48209

COHEN, JEROME, electronic bus. equipment co. exec.; b. Kansas City, Mo., Oct. 9, 1913; s. Rueben and Helen (Silverstein) C.; grad. Kansas City (Mo.) Jr. Coll., 1931; student Huffs Bus. Coll., 1932, Central Bus. Coll., 1933; m. Jeannette Baier, Nov. 25, 1934; children—Rosalyn Jean, Elaine Marie. Asst. mgr. Burts Shoe Store, Kansas City, Mo., 1932-34; sec. to State Senator of Mo., 1934-35; chief clk. Mo. Old Age Assistance Div., 1935-37, Jackson County (Mo.) Welfare Office, Kansas City, 1937-38; founder Tempo Co., Kansas City, Mo., 1938, pres., 1938—, chief exec. officer, 1938—; pres., chief exec. officer Electronic Bus. Equipment, Inc., Kansas City, Mo., 1957—, Jefferson City, Mo., 1960—, Saint Joseph, Mo., 1961—; commr. Kansas City (Mo.) Park Bd., 1955-72. Vice pres. Am. Humanics Found., Kansas City, Mo., 1956-80; chmn. Kansas City (Mo.) Jewish Chautauqua Drive, 1962-64; mem. Nat. Com. for Support of Public Schs., 1967-78; mem. exec. com. Kansas City Safety Council, 1958-81; chmn. Mayor's Christmas Tree Assn., Kansas City, 1955-81; mem. adv. bd. Met. Jr. Coll., 1972-78; Kansas City chmn. Richards Gebaur AFB Community Council, 1960-61; mem. Kansas City Bus. and Indsl. Commn., 1955-62; pres. Temple B'nai Jehudah Brotherhood; mem. exec. bd. Sr. Citizens Corp. of Kansas City, 1954-65, Kansas City Recreation Commn., 1955-70, Citizens Assn., 1940-70, Child's World, 1969-81, Camp Fire Girls, 1956-66, Starlight Theatre, 1950—, v.p., 1978-80; chmn. Kansas City Soap Box Derby, 1947-64; bd. dirs. U. Kans. Sch. of Religion, 1971-76, Scottish Rite Found. of Mo., 1969—; hon. trustee Heart of Am. council Boy Scouts Am., 1960—. B'nai Jehudah Brotherhood Hall of Fame Honoree, 1976; named Kansas City (Mo.) Mktg. Exec. of Year, 1981. Hon. fellow Harry S. Truman Library Inst.; mem. Mo. C. of C., Kansas City (Mo.) C. of C., Kansas City (Kans.) C. of C., Native Sons of Kansas City (Mo.), Conservation Fedn. of Mo., Mo. U. Assos., Bus. Dist. League (pres. 1963-65), Jackson County Execs. (exec. council), Jackson County Hist. Soc., Audubon Soc., Am. Assn. of Zoos and Aquariums, Bus. Products Council Assn. (pres. 1970-72), Mid-Town Assn. (v.p. 1964-65), Friends of the Zoo (pres. 1973-74), Navy League, Kansas City (Mo.) Lyric Theatre Guild, Japan Am. Soc., Jewish Chautauqua Soc., Hebrew Acad. of Kansas City, Hyman Brand Hebrew Acad., Piscator's Soc. (pres. 1970-71), Sci. Pioneers, Friends of Art, NCCJ, Air Force Assn., U.S. China Friendship Assn., Am. Royal Assn. (bd. govs. 1955-81). Clubs: Masons (33 degrees), Shriners, Kansas City Athletic, Meadowbrook Country, Elmers Fishing (pres. 1968-69). Home: 6616 Ward Parkway Kansas City MO 64113 Office: 1500 Grand Ave Kansas City MO 64108

COHEN, LESLIE JAY, personnel exec.; b. Chgo., June 19, 1931; s. Jack and Sylvia Thelma (Sanders) C.; B.S. in Commerce, Roosevelt U., 1952. Asst. to pres. Jay Mills Co., Chgo., 1954-60; founder EDP Personnel, Inc., Chgo., 1960, pres., 1960-64; founder, pres. Secretaries Inc., Chgo., 1964—; mem. industry liaison com. Better Bus. Bur., 1970—. Served with U.S. Army, 1952-54. Decorated Bronze Star. Mem. Nat. (Pres.'s award 1973, treas. 1973-74, dir. 1972—), Ill. (Lincoln Meml. award 1976, treas. 1970, dir. 1971-72) employment assns., Temporaries Ind. Profl. Soc. (treas. 1977—, pres. 1978-79), Nat., Chicagoland assns. temporary services. Jewish. Home: 20 E Cedar St Chicago IL 60611 Office: 808 N Dearborn St Chicago IL 60610

COHEN, LIONEL, radiation oncologist; b. Johannesburg, S. Africa, Jan. 6, 1918; came to U.S., 1972; s. Moshe and Bella F. (Segal) C.; M.B., BCh., U. Witwatersrand (S. Africa), 1942, Ph.D., 1960; children—David Aaron, Benjamin Victor, Eugene Morton. Intern, Johannesburg Gen. Hosp., 1943-44; resident Bellevue Hosp., N.Y.C., 1946-47, Royal No. Hosp., London, 1948-49; radiation therapist Johannesburg Gen. Hosp., 1950-55; prof. therapeutic radiology U. Witwatersrand, Johannesburg, 1956-71; chmn. radiation oncology Michael Reese Med. Center, Chgo., 1972—; dir. cancer therapy facility Fermi Nat. Accelerator Lab., Batavia, Ill. Mem. Brit. Inst. Radiology, Radiation Research Soc., Am. Soc. Therapeutic Radiologists. Office: 29th St and Ellis Ave Chicago IL 60616

COHEN, MELVIN SAMUEL, mfg. co. exec.; b. Mpls., Jan. 16, 1918; s. Henry Benjamin and Mary (Witebsky) C.; B.S. in Law, U. Minn., 1939, J.D., 1941; m. Eileen Phillips, Aug. 16, 1947; children—Amy Rebecca, Mary-Jo Rose. Admitted to Minn. bar, 1941, U.S. Supreme Ct. bar, 1944; practiced in Mpls. until 1942; with legal div., rationing sect. OPA, Washington, 1942-43; pub. counsel CAB, 1943-44; with Nat. Presto Industries, Inc., Eau Claire, Wis., 1944—, treas., 1950-51, v.p., adminstr., treas., 1951-54, exec. v.p., 1954-60, pres., 1960-75, chmn. bd., 1975—; also dir.; chmn. bd., dir. Century Metalcraft Corp., Los Angeles, Guardian Service Security Systems, Los Angeles, Presto Mfg. Co., Jackson, Miss., Johnson Printing, Eau Claire, United Truck Leasing, Inc., Mpls., Lawrence Motors, Inc., Red Wing, Minn., Red Wing Transp. Co., Red Wing Truck Rental, Inc., World Aerospace Corp., Mpls., 1963—; pres., dir. Master Corp. Tex., Abilene, 1965, Jackson Sales & Storage Co. (Miss.), Presto Parts and Service Corp., Mineola, N.Y., Presto Parts and Service, Inc., Los Angeles, Presto Parts & Service Corp., Atlanta, Nat. Presto Industries Export Corp., Eau Claire, Presto Internat. Ltd., Hong Kong, Canton Mfg. Co. (Miss.); v.p., dir. Nat. Pipeline Co., Cleve. Nat. Automatic Pipeline Ops., Inc., Escanaba, Mich.; dir. 1st Wis. Nat. Bank, Eau Claire. Mem. industry advisory com. for aluminum industry and internat. combustion engine industry Nat. Prodn. Authority, Korean War. Club: Eau Claire Country. Editor Minn. Law Rev., 1939-41. Home: 1703 Drummond St Eau Claire WI 54701 Office: Presto Area Eau Claire WI 54701

COHEN, MILLARD STUART, diversified mfg. co. exec.; b. Chgo., Jan. 17, 1939; s. Lawrence Irmas and Myra Paula (Littmann) C.; B.S. in Elec. Engring., Purdue U., 1960; m. Judith E. Michel, Aug. 2, 1970; children—Amy Rose, Michele Lauren. Design engr. GTE Automatic Electric Labs., Northlake, Ill., 1960-66; chief elec. engr. Nixdorff Krein Industries, St. St. Louis, 1966-68, dir. data processing, 1968-72, treas., 1970—, v.p., 1980—, exec. v.p. Nixdorff Chain, 1972-76, pres. Grape Expectations, 1976—, also dir. Dist. commr. Boy Scouts Am., 1968-72; judge Mo. State Fair. Recipient award of merit French Wine Commn., 1972. Mem. Nat., Mo. restaurant assns., Assn. Computing Machinery, IEEE, Mensa, Les Amis du Vin, Chaine des Rotisseurs, Commanderie de Bordeaux. Jewish (trustee temple). Clubs: Mo Athletic, St. Louis. Home: 561 Bonhomme Forest Olivette MO 63132 Office: PO Box 27479 Saint Louis MO 63141

COHEN, MYRON AARON, musician; b. Denver, Mar. 28, 1918; s. Goodman and Rose (Cohen) C.; student De Paul U. Sch. Music, 1936-38, Am. Conservatory of Music, Chgo., 1939-42, Juilliard Sch. Music, 1947; B.A., U. Omaha, 1947; Mus.M., U. Nebr., Lincoln, 1960; violin student with Richard Czerwonky, Scott Willits, Louis Persinger, others. Concertmaster following orchs.: Omaha Symphony Orch., 1947-77, Omaha Opera Co. Orch., 1959-79, Lincoln (Nebr.) Symphony Orch., 1951-60; organized String Quartet, 1978; asst. condr. Omaha Youth Orch., 1958-66; part-time faculty U. Omaha, 1951-52, U. Nebr., Lincoln, 1958-59, Coll. St. Mary, 1980—; soloist radio, TV; pvt. violin tchr., Omaha, 1946—. Served with AUS, 1943-45. Winner commencement contest for violinists Am. Conservatory Music, 1940. Mem. Omaha Musicians Assn. (mem. exec. bd.), Neb. Music Tchrs. Assn. (past pres.), Am. String Tchrs. Assn., Pi Kappa Lambda. Democrat. Jewish religion. Author: The Beginning Violinist's Left Hand Technique, 1956; Finger Relationships through Patterns and Keys for Violin, 1964; also revs. and articles. Home: 3925 S 24th St Omaha NE 68107

COHEN, PAUL G(ERSON), mgmt. cons.; b. N.Y.C., July 23, 1938; s. Henry A. and Esther (Reiner) C.; B.A., Union Coll., Schenectady, 1960; m. Jeanne A. Hurwitz, June 17, 1962; children—David Mark, Deborah Esther. With Northwestern Bell Tel. Co., Omaha, 1966-74, revenue supr. long distance and WATS, 1971-74; asst. v.p., sec. S. Riekes & Sons, Inc., Omaha, 1974-75, gen. ops. mgr., 1975-76; v.p. ops., Riekes Crisa Corp., Omaha, 1976-81; pres. Mid-Am. Bus. Advisors, Omaha, 1981—. Treas., youth sports program Omaha Suburban Athletic Assn., 1976-77; bd. dirs. Cystic Fibrosis Assn. Nebr., 1977-79; bd. dirs. Jewish Fedn. Omaha, 1973-76, v.p., 1977-81, pres., 1982—; trustee Nat. Jewish Hosp./Nat. Asthma Center, Denver. Served with USAF, 1960-66; lt. col. Nebr. Air N.G., 1967—. Mem. Air Force Assn., Nebr. N.G. Assn. (dir. 1973-76, pres. 1979), Internat. Platform Assn. Jewish. Clubs: B'nai B'rith (past pres.; regional pres. 1974-75, dist. bd. govs., 1976-78), Rotary. Home: 1855 S 130th St Omaha NE 68144

COHEN, PENNIE MYERS, psychologist; b. Phila., Aug. 16, 1939; d. William Lee and Roberta B. (Appel) Myers; B.A. magna cum laude, Wichita State U., 1973, M.A., 1975; children—Susan Lee, Robert Lewis. Counselor, Wichita (Kans.) State U., 1975-78, coordinator consulting, 1978—. Chairperson Wichita Sedgewick County Women's Task Force on Alcohol Abuse, 1979; mem. Wichita Sedgewick County Task Force on Drug Abuse, 1976-79; bd. dirs. Residential Homes for Boys, Mid-Kans. Jewish Welfare Fedn., Family Consultation Service. Mem. Am. Psychol. Assn., Am. Assn. Marriage and Family Therapists, Kans. Psychol. Assn., Kans. Alcoholism Counselors Assn. Office: Box 91 Wichita State Univ Wichita KS 67208

COHEN, PHILIP EDWARD, social worker; b. Chgo., May 26, 1948; s. Morris and Miriam Ann (Wolfson) C.; student Parsons Coll., 1966-67; B.S., Murray State U., 1970; m. Elaine E. Biegacz, Oct. 8, 1972; 1 dau., Miriam Esther. Clk., Bur. of Census, U.S. Dept. Commerce, Jeffersonville, Ind., 1970-71; social work asso. VA Med. Center, Chillicothe, Ohio, 1971—; mem. supervisory com. Chivaho Fed. Credit Union, 1976-80, chmn., 1978. VA Med. Center rep. Internat. Yr. of Child, 1979; mem. ad hoc com. Internat. Yr. of Disabled Persons, VA Med. Center; trustee Beth Jacob Congregation, 1981—. Recipient Superior Performance award VA Med. Center, 1978. Mem. Nat. Assn. Social Workers, VA Employees Assn. (pres. 1977-79, dir. 1979-80), Central Ohio Diabetes Assn., Murray State U. Alumni Assn. (life), Fraternal Order Police Assos., Ky. Col. Democrat. Jewish. Club: B'nai B'rith (Pres.'s award 1973, Community Service award 1975, historian 1973-74, v.p. membership 1975-76, 78-79), Beth Jacob Brotherhood, Beth Jacob Young Couples. Home: 5114 Teddy Dr Columbus OH 43227 Office: VA Medical Center 17273 State Route 104 Chillicothe OH 45601

COHEN, ROBERT, physician; b. Easton, Pa., Feb. 6, 1925; s. Joseph Samuel and Dorothy (Shaffer) C.; A.B., Lafayette Coll., 1944; M.D., U. Pa., 1948; M.P.H., U. Calif., Berkeley, 1967; m. Barbara Frese, June 23, 1973; children—Joseph Samuel, Diane Sharon, Jeffrey Robert, Jennifer Lynn. Intern Einstein Med. Center, Phila., 1948-49; resident Children's Hosp., Phila., 1949-50, 52-53; practice medicine specializing in pediatrics, Easton, 1950-65; asst. commr. Tenn. Dept. Mental Health, Nashville, 1967-69; dep. commr. mental health State of N.C., 1969-71; exec. physician Ill. Dept. Public Health, Springfield, 1971-72; asst. chief staff Hosp. of U. Ill. Med. Center, Chgo., 1973-80, asso. chief of staff, 1980—; asso. prof. pediatrics and asso. prof. preventive medicine and community health Abraham Lincoln Sch. Medicine, U. Ill., Chgo., 1973—, cons. health maintenance orgn. for quality of care and health delivery services Ill. Dept. Public Health, 1974—; mem. regional com. on patient care evaluation studies for Chgo. PSRO, 1977-80, mem. data com., 1980—. Children's Bur. fellow U. Calif. Sch. Public Health, Berkeley, 1965-67. Diplomate Am. Bd. Pediatrics. Mem. Am. Acad. Pediatrics, Am. Public Health Assn., Am. Coll. Utilization Rev. Physicians, Am. Bd. Quality Assurance and Utilization Rev. Physicians. Contbr. articles in field to profl. jours. Home: 728 Wisconsin Ave Oak Park IL 60304 Office: PO Box 6998 Chicago IL 60680

COHEN, STEVEN RICHARD, govt. ofcl.; b. Haverhill, Mass., Dec. 14, 1940; s. Kaufman and Cilia (Richer) C.; B.S. cum laude, U. Mass., Amherst, 1962, postgrad., 1962-63; m. Carole Simons, Mar. 21, 1970; children—Scott Michael, Lisa Michelle. With U.S. Office Personnel Mgmt. (formerly U.S. Civil Service Commn.), 1962—, investigator, varied personnel mgmt. and staffing positions, Boston region, 1962-68, adminstrv. officer, bur. recruiting and examining, Washington, 1968-70, mgr. Norfolk (Va.) Area Office, 1970-73, asst. to dep. exec. dir., Washington, 1973-75, dep. regional dir. Great Lakes Region, Chgo., 1975-81, regional dir., 1981—, also mem. numerous coms., task forces, 1975—. Chmn., Cub Scout Pack, DuPage council Boy Scouts Am., 1980—. Served with AUS, 1963. Mem. Internat. Personnel Mgmt. Assn., Am. Soc. Public Adminstrs., Chgo. Fed. Exec. Bd., Chgo. Fed. Personnel Council, Tau Epsilon Phi. Jewish. Home: 1542 Orth Ct Wheaton IL 60187 Office: 230 S Dearborn St Chgo IL 60604

COHILL, DONALD FRANK, surgeon; b. Darby, Pa., Dec. 1, 1934; s. Raymond Harris and Agnes Mae (Smith) C.; A.B. in Chemistry, Haverford (Pa.) Coll., 1956; M.D., U. Pa., 1960; m. Lorna Westcott, Feb. 15, 1957; children—Karen Lea, Linda Lea, Julie Lea, Andrew Scott. Intern, U. Pa.-Presbyn. Hosp., Phila., 1960-61; surg. resident Abington (Pa.) Meml. Hosp., 1966-70, asso. surgeon, 1969-70; practice medicine specializing in gen. surgery, Racine, Wis., 1970—; surgeon St. Mary's, St. Luke's hosps.; dir. med. edn. St. Mary's Hosp.; exec. com. Kurten Med. Group; adv. bd. Life Line, Racine. Served with M.C., USAF, 1962-64. Decorated Commendation medal; named Flight Surgeon of Yr., SAC, USAF, 1963-64. Fellow A.C.S., Milw. Acad. Surgery; mem. AMA, Wis., Racine County med. socs., Racine Acad. Medicine, Wis. Surg. Soc. Mem. Evang. Ch. Home: 1902 Crestwood Dr Caledonia WI 53108 Office: 2405 Northwestern Ave Racine WI 53404

COHN, EARL, coffee roasting co. exec.; b. Chgo., Oct. 16, 1917; s. Harry and Sadie (Silverstone) C.; B.A., U. Ill., 1939; m. Madelyn Lois Burger, June 29, 1941; children—Steven Jay, Marcie Beth Cohn Berk. With Superior Tea & Coffee Co., Chgo., 1939—, pres., 1960—, exec. employee, dir. 1980—. Bd. dirs. Culinary Inst., Hyde Park, N.Y. Mem. Tau Epsilon Phi. Clubs: Twin Orchard Country, Canyon Country, Tamarisk Country (Palm Springs, Calif.). Home: 3200 N Lake Shore Dr Chicago IL 60657 Office: Douwe Egberts Superior Co 990 Supreme Dr Bensenville IL 60106

COHU, LINDA KAY, chemist, oil refining corp. exec.; b. Geneva, Ill., Mar. 8, 1954; d. Alfred Earnest and Suzanne Jean (Dettman) Schudel; B.S., Loyola U., Chgo., 1976; postgrad. Iowa State U., 1976-77; m. Alvin D. Cohu, Nov. 18, 1978. Analytical chemist Harvey Tech. Center, Atlantic Richfield Co., (Ill.), 1977-79, chemist engine oils research and devel., 1979—. Mem. Citizen Action Program, 1977—. Republican. Lutheran. Home: Homewood IL 60430 Office: Atlantic Richfield Co 400 E Sibley Blvd Harvey IL 60426

COIL, ROBERT MACK, mfg. co. exec.; b. Flora, Ill., July 28, 1943; s. Harold Frederick and Zelma Aileen (Smith) C.; student Ohio U., 1961, 62-65, 66; m. Judith Lynn Slater, Mar. 24, 1979; children—Robert Frederick, Stephanie Ann. With Gen. Electric Co., Columbus, Ohio, 1966-67; owner, operator motel and restaurant, Trenton, Ill., 1967-70; sales mgr. Indsl. Silo div. Marietta Concrete Co. (Ohio), 1971-77; v.p. Marietta (Ohio) Tecktonics, Inc., 1978-81; exec. v.p. Mar Tec, Inc., Marietta, 1980—, dir., 1980—; sr. partner Boord & Coil, mgmt. investment firm. Chmn. masonry com. Washington County Vocat. Sch., 1976-81, chmn. levy com., 1980. Served with U.S. Army, 1962-65. Mem. Southeastern Ohio Ceramic Soc., Washington County Homebuilders Assn. (sec. 1972-80), Am. Legion. Republican. Congregationalist. Club: Elks. Home: 202 Clark Dr Marietta OH 45750 Office: Marietta Tecktonics Inc 215 Fearing St Marietta OH 45750

COIN, SHEILA REGAN, mgmt. cons.; b. Columbus, Ohio, Feb. 17, 1942; d. James D. Regan and Jean M. (Hodgson) Evers; B.S., U. Iowa, 1964; m. Tasso Harry Coin, Sept. 17, 1967; children—Tasso Harry, Alison Regan. Staff nurse VA Hosp., Boston, 1964-66; field rep. health services program devel. ARC, Chgo., 1966-67, adminstr. blood program, 1967; asst. div. dir. Am. Hosp. Assn., also sec. Am. Soc. for Hosp. Dirs. of Nursing Service, Chgo., 1967-69; propr., mgmt. cons. Sheila Regan Coin & Assos., Chgo., 1975-77; partner, mgmt. devel. cons. Coin, Newell & Assos., Chgo., 1977—; instr. dept. continuing edn. Loyola U. Chgo., 1975-77, Rock Valley Coll. Mgmt. Inst., Rockford, Ill., 1978—, Ill. Central Coll. Inst. for Personal and Profl. Devel., Peoria, Ill., 1979—. Vol., Art Inst. Chgo., 1968-69; mem. Chgo. Beautiful Com., 1968-73; mem. jr. bd. Girl Scouts Assn., 1975-76; chmn. Mayor Daley's Chgo. Beautiful Awards Project, 1972; mem. jr. governing bd. Chgo. Symphony Orch., 1971—, pres., 1977-78, governing mem. Orchestral Assn. of Chgo. Symphony Orch.; bd. dirs. ARC, Mid-Am. chpt., 1979—, Chgo. dist., 1981—, mem. fin. devel. com., 1980—; bd. dirs. Com. for Thalassomia, 1981—; mem. Chgo. women's bd. Nat. Com. for Prevention Child Abuse, 1981—. Mem. Am. Mgmt. Assn., Am. Soc. for Tng. and Devel., Chi Omega. Mem. Greek Orthodox Ch. Home: 1037 W North Shore Ave Chicago IL 60626 Office: 919 N Michigan Ave Suite 2506 Chicago IL 60611

COLBER, RUSSELL HOWARD, pub. relations exec.; b. Milw., June 21, 1938; s. Ralph Howard and Margaret Marie (Hoppens) C.; B.A. (WLOL Broadcasting scholarship), U. Minn., 1965; M.S. (Nat. Acad. of TV Arts and Scis. fellowship), Syracuse U., 1966; m. Bonita Elizabeth Cheesebrough, Sept. 1, 1963; children—Newell Howard II, Geoffrey Howard, Charles Howard Page. Asst. to v.p. corp. communications Dayton Hudson Corp., Mpls., 1966-70; v.p., Advertisers Diversified Services, Mpls., 1970-73; chmn. communications div. The Mpls. Inst. of Arts, 1973-75; pres., Russ Colber & Assos., Mpls., 1975—; convenor, Twin Cities Journalism Conf.; chmn. communications com. Nat. Model Cities Conf.; instr. journalism Normandale Community Coll. Bd. dirs. Minn. Dance Theatre; arts com. chmn. Twin Cities Ednl. TV Fund-Raising, 1972, 73. Accredited in Pub. relations. Mem. Pub. Relations Soc. of Am. (counselors and health sects.), Minn. Arts Forum, Walker Art Center, Lowry Hill Residents Assn., The Nat. Trust (Gt. Britain). Pantheist. Clubs: Minn. Press. Editorial bd. MPLS. Mag., 1974—; contbr. articles and stories to Minn. newspapers and mags. Home: 1805 Irving Ave S Minneapolis MN 55403 also North Shore Dr Waverly MN 55390

COLBERT, JAMES, utility co. exec.; b. Waverly, Ill., Feb. 14, 1920; s. James R. and Ura R. (Reichard) C.; student Ill. Comml. Coll., 1938, Milliken U., Decatur, Ill., 1940-41, IBM Schs., Chgo., 1941-46, Ill. Corr. Sch., Chgo., 1949-55; cert. Grad. Sch. Bus. Adminstrn., U. Mich., 1963; m. Marjorie Lane Patton, Apr. 3, 1937; children—James Barry, John William, Cathy Lane. Supr., IBM dept. Ill. Power Co., Decatur, 1939-43; spl. rep. IBM Corp., Chgo., 1943; with Iowa-Ill. Gas and Electric Co., 1943—, mgr. bus. machine dept., Davenport, Iowa, 1943-54, dist. mgr., Cedar Rapids, Iowa, 1954-65, exec. analyst communication and control study unit, Davenport, 1966-68, mgr. customer service, 1968-75, v.p. adminstrn., 1975—; mem. adv. com. Inst. Public Utilities, Mich. State U., 1979—. Chmn., United Crusade, 1970; pres. Indsl. Comml. Fund Rock Island, 1975—; bd. dirs. Rock Island C. of C., 1975—, pres., 1979—; bd. dirs. St. Anthony's Continuing Care Center, 1975—; v.p. Quad-City Council Chambers, 1980. Served with USNR, 1944-46. Mem. Black Hawk Fed. Savs. and Loan Assn. (dir.), Quad-Cities Electric League (pres. 1979, dir.), Nat. Machine Accts. Assn. (chpt. pres. 1953; nat. dir. 1953). Republican. Presbyterian. Clubs: Rock Island Arsenal Golf; Davenport; Masons (Blue Lodge). Office: Iowa Ill Gas Electric Co 206 E 2nd St Davenport IA 52808

COLBY, MICHAEL PRESTON, data processing co. exec.; b. Des Moines, Sept. 7, 1954; s. Charles I., Jr. and Patty E. (Luin) C.; B.A., Drake U., Des Moines, 1977; m. Linda S. Farnham, July 16, 1977; 1 son, Michael Preston. Founder, 1978, since pres., owner Landmark Data Processing Co., West Des Moines; founder, 1976, since pres., owner Landmark West Corp., West Des Moines. Bd. dirs. West Des Moines YMCA, 1972. Mem. Sigma Alpha Epsilon. Republican. Mem. Ch. of Christ. Office: 1001 Office Park Rd West Des Moines IA 50265

COLBY, ROBERT LESTER, psychologist; b. N.Y.C., Jan. 21, 1941; s. Allen M. and Beatrice D. (Kalkut) C.; B.A., N.Y. U., 1963; M.S., L.I. U., 1965. Psychiat. technician St. Vincent's Hosp., N.Y.C., 1963-64; psychometrist Vocational Service Center, N.Y.C., 1964-65; counselor N.Y. State Dept. of Labour, div. of employment, N.Y.C., 1965; ednl. counselor, vocational counselor Vocat. Service Centre, N.Y.C., 1965-66; teaching fellow, research asst. U. Waterloo (Ont., Can.), 1966-67; lectr. Wellington Coll., U. Guelph (Ont.), 1967-69, clin. and research fellow Centre for Ednl. Disabilities, 1967-69; chief behavioral cons. Brant County Bd. of Edn., Brantford, Ont., 1969—; pvt. practice, Vancouver, B.C.; cons. Assn. Children with Learning Disabilities. Rep. Ont. Anti-Poverty Coalition, 1975—. Bd. dirs. Workers Task Force, 1974-75; chmn. Inter-Agy. Coordinating Com., 1975-77. Mem. Am., Can. psychol. assns., Assn. for Psychol. Study Social Issues, Adminstrv. Psychologists in Edn., Regional Assn. Profls. in Psychology (treas. 1975-76), Assn. Psychologists N.S., B.C. Psychol. Assn., Can. Mental Health Assn. (chmn. sci. adv. com. 1973-75, dir. 1969—, pres. 1975-76), Ont. Assn. Cons.'s, Counselors, Psychometrists and Psychotherapists (community youth services com.). Home: 50 Blenheim Rd Cambridge ON N1S 1E8 Canada Office: 349 Erie Ave Brantford ON N3S 2H7 Canada

COLE, A(NNA) RUTH, former educator; b. Eaton, Ohio; d. George Washington and Esther (Akel) Cole; student U. Colo., summer 1937, B.S., Miami U., Oxford, Ohio, 1939; M.A., Ohio State U., 1953, postgrad., 1963. Tchr., Morris Sch., Hamilton, Ohio, 1921-23, 24-25, Edison Elem. Sch., Columbus, Ohio, 1925-26, Robert Louis Stevenson Sch., Columbus, 1926-71. Mem. Buckeye Fed. Savs. & Loan Assn. Mem. mission work area Trinity United Meth. Ch., 1973-76; mem. Upper Arlington Srs. Activities, 1975—. Martha Holden Jennings scholar, 1968-69. Mem. Republican Womens' Clubs. Mem. Grandview Heights Tchrs. Assn. (pres. 1954-56, profl. activities com. 1966-67), Franklin County Hist. Soc., Center Sci. and Industry, Assn. for Childhood Internat. (pres. 1958-60), NEA (life), Ohio Edn. Assn., Central Ohio Tchrs. Assn., Wesleyan Service Guild (pres. 1943-45, 62-65, dist. sec. 1957-61, v.p., program chmn. 1968-69), Ohio Ret. Tchrs. Assn. (life), Am. Assn. Ret. Persons, Kappa Phi (life), Phi Delta Gamma (pres. 1955-57; life), Delta Kappa Gamma (membership chmn. 1962-64; mem. initiation com. 1966-68, 69—, chmn. initiation com. 1973—, rec. sec. chpt. 1978-80), Am. Contract Bridge League. Methodist (mem. edn. commn. 1966-68, dist. sec. program resources United Meth. Women 1973-77, chmn. Christian Global Concerns 1974-78, mem. adminstrv. bd. 1978—, coordinator prayer circles 1978-79, mem. Bible study group 1978—, v.p., past dist. officer 1979-81). Home: 1314 W 7th Ave Columbus OH 43212

COLE, CECIL RAY, oil co. exec.; b. Laurel, Miss., Sept. 28, 1941; s. Albert and Seather Mae Cole; B.S. in Bus. Adminstrn., Nat. Coll. Bus., 1977; M.B.A., Central Mich. U., 1978; children—Raye Marie, Cecil Anthony, Byron Stephan. Stock distbr., inventory specialist Amoco Oil Co., Council Bluffs, Iowa, 1972-73, accountant, Kansas City, Mo., 1973-77, supr. gen. acctg., 1977-80; internal auditor Standard Oil of Ind., 1980—; instr. acctg. Omaha Opportunities Industrialization Center, 1972—, Nat. Coll. Bus., Kansas City, Mo., 1979—; customer service rep. Levitz Furniture Co., Lenexa, Kans., 1979—. Served with USAF, 1962-69; Viet Nam. Mem. So. Christian Leadership Conf. Democrat. Baptist. Home: 10808 W 90th Terr Overland Park KS 66212 Office: PO Box 1099 Kansas City MO 64141

COLE, CHARLES STEVEN, bank exec.; b. Poplar Bluff, Mo., July 29, 1947; s. Harry Newell and Wanda Jean C.; B.S. in Acctg., S.W. Mo. State U., 1969; student U. Mo., Kansas City, 1977-78; m. Faith Adele Brown, July 14, 1967; children—Kelli Renée, Karen Lehann, Leah Elizabeth. Staff acct. Arthur Andersen & Co., Kansas City, Mo., 1970-71; asst. comptroller United Missouri Bancshares, Inc. Kansas City, 1971-75, asst. auditor, 1975-76; asst. cashier United Mo. Bank of Kansas City, N.A., 1977-78; pres. United Mo. Bank of Hickman Hills, Kansas City, 1978-81; pres. United Mo. Bank of Jefferson County, 1981—; guest lectr. S.W. Mo. State U., Springfield, Rockhurst Coll., Kansas City, 1978-79. Coach, Little League Baseball, 1970; scoutmaster, Boy Scouts Am., 1975-78, dist. com. Three Rivers Dist., 1981. Recipient Woodbadge cert. Boy Scouts Am., 1975. Mem. Am. Inst. Banking (chmn. bank audit report seminar 1975-76), Bank Adminstrn. Inst., Mo. Bankers Assn., Am. Bankers Assn., Robert Morris Assos. Republican. Mem. Assemblies of God Ch. Clubs: Arnold Rotary, South St. Louis Lions. Office: 1384 Jeffco Blvd Arnold MO 63010

COLE, DONALD WHEELER, mgmt. psychologist; b. Cleve., Dec. 30, 1929; s. Lawrence Chester and Mabel Louise (Wheeler) C.; A.B., U. R.I., 1950; M.S., Boston U., 1952; 3d year cert. Smith Coll., 1955; D.S.W., Washington U., St. Louis, 1964; m. Norma Gale Skoog, July 11, 1953; 5 children. Mgr. mgmt. devel. TRW, Inc., Cleve., 1963-71; mgmt. psychologist, cons., pres. Don Cole & Assos., Cleve., 1968—; dir. personnel and orgn. devel. Bobbie Brooks, Cleve., 1974-76; mem. sci. and tech. council Am. Industries Corp., Cleve., 1969-71; mem. faculty Cleve. State U., 1966-73; dir. Orgn. Devel. Inst., 1968—; pres. Internat. Registry Orgn. Devel. Profls., Cleve., 1968—, pub., 1974—. Lic. psychologist, Ohio. Fellow Am. Orthopsychiat. Assn.; mem. Société Internationale pour le Développement des Organisations (N. Am. dir. 1977—), Am. Psychol. Assn., Cleve. Psychol. Assn., Orgn. Devel. Network (trustee 1978-81). Author: Professional Suicide, 1981; editor Orgns. and Change, 1974—; asso. editor Leadership and Orgn. Devel. Jour., 1979—. Home: 11234 Walnut Ridge Rd Chesterland OH 44026 Office: 6151 Wilson Mills Rd Suite 107 Cleveland OH 44143

COLE, EDYTH LUTICIA, state govt. ofcl.; b. Chgo., Dec. 3, 1942; d. Alfred Jackson and Helen Louise (Dixon) Cole; B.S., Wilberforce U., 1967; M.Ed., U. Ill., 1969; 2 adopted children, Cary Calvin, Cessley Louise. Asst. dean of students LeMoyne-Owen Coll., Memphis, 1969-70; field rep. Ill. Fair Employment Commn., Chgo., 1970-72; affirmative action officer Sangamon State U., Springfield, Ill., 1972-75; personnel dir. Ill. Bd. Edn., Springfield, 1975—. Rehab. fellow, 1967-69. Mem. Am. Personnel and Guidance Assn., Ill. Affirmative Action Officers Assn. (v.p. 1979), Nat. Assn. Affirmative Action Officers (dir.), Delta Sigma Theta (2d v.p. 1976-78, fin. sec.). Methodist. Home: 856 Independence Ridge Springfield IL 62702 Office: 100 N 1st St Springfield IL 62777

COLE, EUGENE ROGER, clergyman, author; b. Cleve., Nov. 14, 1930; s. Bernard James and Mary Louise (Rogers) C.; B.A., St. Edwards Sem., 1954; student John Carroll U., 1957; M.Div., Sulpician Sem. N.W., 1958; A.B., Central Wash. U., Ellensburg, 1960; M.A., Seattle U., 1970. Ordained priest Roman Catholic Ch., 1958; Newman moderator and cons. Central Wash. U., Ellensburg, 1958-59; bus. mgr. Experiment Press, Seattle, 1959-60; chaplain St. Elizabeth Hosp., Yakima, Wash., 1959-61; chmn. English dept. Yakima Central Cath. High Sch., 1959-66, Marquette High Sch., Yakima, 1966-68; poetry critic Nat. Writers Club, Denver, 1969-72; poet in service Poets & Writers Inc., N.Y.C., 1974—; instr. contract bridge, Ind., 1975; freelance writer, editor, researcher, 1958—; researcher Harvard, 1970; religious counselor. Recipient Poetry Broadcast award, 1968; Musical Expertise award, 1970; Lorraine Harr Haiku award, 1974; Ann. Mentor Poetry award, 1974; Pro Mundi Beneficio award, 1975; Readers Union award, 1976. Mem. Authors Guild, Poetry Soc. Am. (judge 1970), Western World Haiku Soc., Acad. Am. Poets, World-Wide Acad. Scholars, Internat. Poetry Soc., Internat. Platform Assn., Expt. Group Soc. for Study of Midwestern Lit., Nat. Fedn. State Poetry Socs., Poetry Soc. (London), Am. Contract Bridge League, Kappa Delta Pi. Composer: Werther, 1948; Chronicle for Tape, 1960. Author: Which End, the Empyrean?, 1959; April Is the Cruelest Month, 1970; Falling Up, 1979; Act & Potency (poems), 1980; editor: Grand Slam: 13 Great Short Stories about Bridge, 1975; In the Beginning, 1978; asso. editor: The Harvester, 1955; guest editor Experiment: An Internat. Rev., 1961; author religious monograph, also contbr. articles, poetry and drama to numerous lit. jours. and anthologies. Home and office: PO Box 272 Whiting IN 46394

COLE, FRANK CRUNDEN, mfg. co. exec.; b. St. Paul, May 14, 1922; s. Wallace H. and Mary (Crunden) C.; B.A., Williams Coll., 1943; m. Ardath Starkloff, May 23, 1959; children—Maria C., Catherine L., Wendy F., Mary C., Caroline B. Vice pres. Crunden Martin Mfg. Co., St. Louis, 1954-64, pres., 1964—, chmn. bd., 1971—; mng. partner Riverfront Realty Co. Bd. dirs. Jefferson Expansion Meml., 1965—; mem. project rev. com. Health Services Agy., 1977—. Served to lt. (j.g.), USNR, 1943-46. Clubs: St. Louis Country, Noonday, Deer Creek, Stadium. Office: Crunden Martin Mfg Co PO Box 508 Saint Louis MO 63166

COLE, FRANKLIN ALAN, bank holding co. exec.; b. Park Falls, Wis., May 20, 1926; s. David A. and Elizabeth S. Cole; B.A., U. Ill., 1947; J.D., Northwestern U., 1950; m. Joan Lauter; children—Todd, Andrew, Robert, Mary, Ellen, Peter. Admitted to Ill. bar, 1950; asso. firm Lederer, Livingston, Kahn & Adsit, Chgo., 1950-55; sr. partner firm Cole, Wishner, Epstein & Manilow, Chgo., 1955-63; with Walter E. Heller Internat. Corp., Chgo., 1963—, chmn. bd., chief exec. officer, 1971—, also dir.; dir. Am. Nat. Bank and Trust Co. Chgo., Peoples Energy Co., Diebel Mfg. Co., Oak Industries, Inc. Trustee, United Way of Met. Chgo., Crusade of Mercy/United Way, Northwestern U., Michael Reese Hosp. and Med. Center. Mem. Chgo. Com., Am. Bar Assn., Chgo. Bar Assn. Clubs: Comml., Chgo., Met., Carlton, Econ. (dir. 1979—), Lake Shore Country (Chgo.). Office: 105 W Adams St Chicago IL 60603

COLE, KENNETH DUANE, architect; b. Ft. Wayne, Ind., Jan. 23, 1932; s. Wolford J. and Helen Francis (McDowell) C.; student Ft. Wayne Art Inst., 1950-51; B.S. in Arch., U. Cin., 1957; m. Carolyn Lou Meyer, Apr. 25, 1953; children—David Brent, Denelle Hope, Diana Faith, Dawn Love. Draftsman/intern Humbrecht Asso., Ft. Wayne, Ind., 1952-57; designer/draftsman Humbrecht Asso., Ft. Wayne, 1957-58; partner/architect Cole-Matott, Architects/Planners, Ft. Wayne, 1959—; mem. adv. bd. Gen. Services Adminstrn., Region 5, 1976, 78. Bd. dirs. Ft. Wayne Art Inst., 1969-74, Arch, Inc., Ft. Wayne, 1975-77, Downtown Ft. Wayne Assn., 1977—, Izaak Walton League Am., Ft. Wayne, 1970-76. Recipient Citation, Ind. Soc. of Architects for remodeling of Bonsib Bldg., 1978. Mem. Ft. Wayne C. of C., AIA (bd. dirs. No. Ind. 1971-74, pres. 1974), Ind. Soc. Architects (bd. dirs. 1973-76, sec. 1976), Ft. Wayne Soc. Architects (pres. 1970-71), Am. Arbitration Assn. (panel of arbitrators 1980—). Lutheran. Archtl. works include: Weisser Park Jr. High Sch., 1963, Brandt Hall, 1965, Bonsib Bldg., 1967, Lindley Elem. Sch., 1969, Young Elem. Sch., 1972, Study Elem. Sch., 1975, Old City Hall Renovation, 1978, Peoples Trust Bank Adminstrv. Services Center, 1979. Home: 1321 Maple Ave Fort Wayne IN 46807 Office: 123 1/2 W Wayne St Fort Wayne IN 46802

COLE, LARRY GENE, nursing home adminstr.; b. Neosho, Mo., Nov. 1, 1949; s. Gerald W. and Verna Lou (Randal) C.; Asso. in Edn., Crowder Coll., 1969; postgrad. U. Mo., Columbia, 1976-77; m. Katherine Lee Turner, Aug. 28, 1969; 1 son, Jason William. Residential dir. Big Bros. Inc. Children's Home, Joplin, Mo., 1969-76; adminstr. Fair Acres Nursing Home, Carthage, Mo., 1976-79; adminstr. Elmhurst Nursing Home, Webb City, Mo., 1979—; adminstrv. dir. Jasper County Assn. for Social Service, Inc., 1979—. Mem. Carthage Council of Social Agys. 1976—; bd. dirs. Sunshine Children's Home, Carthage, Innovative Industries, Ozark Mental Health Center, Joplin, Crisis Intervention Inc., Joplin, Big Bros., Joplin; minister music College View Bapt. Ch., Joplin, 1981—. Lic. nursing home adminstr., lic. funeral dir. Mo. Mem. Mo. League Nursing Home Adminstrs. Home and Office: Route 1 Box 100C Webb City MO 64870

COLE, PATRICIA ANN SHANNON, ednl. adminstr.; b. Trenton, Mich., Sept. 5, 1948; d. James Norman and Virginia Ruth (Davis) Shannon; B.S., U. Mich., 1970, Ph.D., 1981; M.A., Eastern Mich. U., 1974. Jr. high sch. bus. edn. tchr. Wyandotte (Mich.) Schs., 1970-72, adult edn. tchr. bus. edn., 1970-72, bus. edn. tchr. Roosevelt High Sch., 1972-78, dir. vocat. and career edn., 1978—; instr. secretarial sci. Detroit Coll. Bus., Dearborn, Mich., 1974. Cert. profl. sec., 1975; recipient certificates of appreciation for service in field; named outstanding bus. edn. student U. Mich., 1970. Mem. Mich. Council Vocat. Adminstrs. (rep. to Vocat. Edn. Study Task Force, 1980-81), Am. Vocat. Assn., Mich. Occupational Edn. Assn., Vocat. Edn. Planning Com. (chmn. Wayne County, Mich. chpt.), S.E. Regional Vocat. Educators, Mich. Assn. Career Edn., Mich. Bus. Edn. Assn., Nat. Bus. Edn. Assn., Nat. Secs. Assn., AAUW, Delta Pi Epsilon, Pi Omega Pi. Club: Bus. and Profl. Women. Guest speaker profl. confs.; contbr. articles to profl. publs. in field. Home: 3301 Biddle St Apt 2D Wyandotte MI 48192 Office: 540 Eureka Ave Wyandotte MI 48192

COLEBROOK, KIM EDWARD, radio broadcaster; b. Bedford, Ohio, June 18, 1946; s. Ralph Franke and Leneigha (Thesan) C.; B.A., Baldwin Wallace Coll., 1969; M.A., Kent State U., 1979; m. Wendy Dunnett, Aug. 2, 1969; children—Kelly Lyn, Allison Lee. High sch. tchr. speech, theatre and English, Pepper Pike, Ohio, 1969-71; salesman stas. WERE-AM and WGEL-FM, Cleve., 1972-76, sales mgr., 1976-79, v.p., gen. mgr., 1979-81, pres., gen. mgr., 1981—. Trustee, Downtown Bus. Council, Greater Cleve. Growth Assn.; bd. dirs. Am. Cancer Soc. Mem. Cleve. Assn. Broadcasters (dir.). Office: 1500 Chester Ave Cleveland OH 44114*

COLEMAN, C. JOSEPH, state senator, farmer; b. Clare, Iowa, Mar. 14, 1923; student Iowa State U., Bradley U.; m. Polly Pflanz, 1954; children—Joe, Kevin, Kerry. Farmer, Clare; former technician U.S. Dept. Agr.; mem. Iowa State Senate, 1956—, minority whip, 1956—. Mem. Am. Soybean Assn. (dir.), Am. Soybean Inst. (v.p.). Office: State Senate State Capitol Des Moines IA 50319*

COLEMAN, CLARENCE WILLIAM, banker; b. Wichita, Kans., Mar. 24, 1909; s. William Coffin and Fanny Lucinda (Sheldon) C.; degree U. Kans., 1928-32; LL.D. (hon.), Ottawa U., 1973; m. Emry Regester Ingrham, Oct. 2, 1935; children—Rochelle, Pamela, Kathryn Sheldon. Dir., The Coleman Co., Inc., Wichita, 1932—, v.p. mfg., 1944-51, asst. gen. mgr., 1951-54, vice chmn. bd., 1971—; pres. Union Nat. Bank of Wichita, 1957-72, vice chmn. bd., 1972—; chmn. bd. Cherry Creek Inn, Denver, 1961-69. Bd. dirs. Found. for Study of Cycles, Pitts., 1966—; bd. dirs. Inst. Logopedics, Wichita, 1940-74, chmn. bd., 1947-48; bd. dirs. Wichita Symphony Soc., Inc., 1965—; trustee Wichita Symphony Soc. Found., 1966—; bd. dirs. United Fund Wichita and Sedgwick County, 1957-70; trustee Friends U., 1956-65; bd. dirs. Wichita Crime Commn., 1953—, pres., 1958-59. Mem. NAM, Wichita C. of C. (dir. 1947-60, pres. 1956), Phi Kappa Psi. Club: Rotary. Home: 530 Broadmoor Ct Wichita KS 67206 Office: 1005 Union Center Wichita KS 67202

COLEMAN, DONALD PATRICK, constrn. co. exec.; b. Buffalo, N.Y., Sept. 10, 1939; s. L.C. and A.M. (Heiderman) C.; student Cornell U., 1957-59; B.S. (Maytag scholar in Commerce), U. Mo., 1964; m. Diane J. De Luca, Fab. 1, 1964. Sr. v.p., gen. mgr. Garney Co's, Inc., Kansas City, Mo., 1970-77; pres. Weatherby Lake Improvement Co., Kansas City, Mo., 1977-80, treas., 1972-74, v.p., 1974-77, chmn. environ. protection com., 1973-75, dir., 1970-79; pres. Coleman Indsl. Constrn. Inc., 1979—. Mem. adv. bd. Rockhurst Coll. Mgmt. Center; dir. Platte County (Mo.) Indsl. Devel. Commn., 1980-81. Mem. Asso. Bldg. Contractors (dir. Gt. Plains chpt. 1980-81), Kansas City Heavy Contractors Assn., Kansas City Mech. Contractors Assn., Kansas City C. of C. Centurions. Home: 7902 NW Scenic Dr Kansas City MO 64152

COLEMAN, E. THOMAS, congressman; b. Kansas City, Mo., May 29, 1943; s. Earl T. and Marie (Carlson) C.; A.B. in Econ., William Jewell Coll., 1965; M.P.A., N.Y. U., 1969; J.D., Washington U., 1969; m. Marilyn Anderson, June 8, 1968; children—Julie Anne, Emily Catherine, Megan Marie. Admitted to Mo. bar, 1969; practiced in Gladstone, 1973-76; asst. atty. gen. Mo., 1969-73; mem. Mo. Ho. of Reps., 1973-77; mem. 95th-97th Congresses for 6th Mo. Dist. Home: 2919 NE Russell Rd Kansas City MO 64117 Office: US House of Representatives Washington DC 20515

COLEMAN, GEORGE HUNT, chemist; b. San Gabriel, Calif., Oct. 15, 1928; s. Thomas and Grace Muriel (Love) C.; A.B., U. Calif., Berkeley, 1950; Ph.D., UCLA, 1958; m. Lois Mae Tarleton, Feb. 14, 1953; children—David Howe, Thomas George, Margaret Rose. Microanalyst, U. Calif., Berkeley, 1950-51; nuclear chemist Calif. Research and Devel. Corp., 1951-53; sr. nuclear chemist Lawrence Livermore Lab., 1957-69; asso. prof. chemistry Nebr. Wesleyan U., Lincoln, 1969-78, prof., 1979—, acting head dept., 1976-78, head dept. chemistry, 1978-80. Mem. Am. Chem. Soc., AAAS, AAUP. Democrat. Presbyterian. Home: 5920 Margo Dr Lincoln NE 68510 Office: Nebr Wesleyan U 50th and St Paul St Lincoln NE 68504*

COLEMAN, JANICE ROSE, educator; b. Pitts., Jan. 1, 1949; d. Joseph T. and Alma Joann (Drenevich) C.; B.S. cum laude in Edn., St. Bonaventure U., 1971, M.S. in Edn., 1975, S.A.S.Edn., 1976; Ed.D., SUNY, Buffalo, 1979. Elem. tchr. Bradford (Pa.) Area Schs., 1971-80; dir. elem. edn. Marymount Coll., Salina, Kans., 1980—; co-sponsor student NEA, 1980—. Recipient NEA Service award, 1981; Nat. Press Day awards, 1964-66; Rotary Club grantee, 1979-80. Mem. Marymount Faculty Orgn. (sec. 1980-81), NEA, Assn. Supervision and Curriculum Devel., AAUW, Am. Assn. Colls. Tchr. Edn., Internat. Reading Assn., Phi Delta Kappa. Contbr. articles to profl. jours. Home: 2310 Applewood Ln Salina KS 67401 Office: E Iron and Marymount Rd Salina KS 67401

COLEMAN, LESTER EARL, chem. co. exec.; b. Akron, Ohio, Nov. 6, 1930; s. Lester Earl and Ethel Angeline (Miller) C.; B.S., U. Akron, 1952; M.S., U. Ill., 1953, Ph.D., 1955; m. Jean Goudie Moir, Aug. 31, 1951; children—Robert Scott, Kenneth John. With Goodyear Tire & Rubber, Akron, 1951-52; with Lubrizol Corp., Cleve., 1955—, asst. div. head research and devel., 1968-72, v.p. internat. ops., asst. to pres., 1972-74, exec. v.p., 1974-76, pres., 1976—, chief exec. officer, 1978—, also dir.; dir. Society Corp., Society Nat. Bank, Cleve., Norfolk and Western Ry. Co., Roanoke, Va., S.C. Johnson & Son, Inc., Racine, Wis. Pres., exec. bd. East Central region Boy Scouts Am.; mem. Euclid Gen. Hosp. Assn.; bd. dirs. Lake County YMCA. Served to capt. USAF, 1955-57. Mem. Am. Chem. Soc. (local chmn. 1973), Chem. Mfrs. Assn., Greater Cleve. Growth Assn., Sigma Xi, Alpha Chi Sigma, Phi Lambda Upsilon, Phi Delta Theta. Methodist. Contbr. articles to profl. jours. Patentee organic and polymer chemistry. Office: 29400 Lakeland Blvd Wickliffe OH 44092

COLEMAN, MARILYN RUTH ADAMS, poultry scientist, educator; b. Lancaster, S.C., Mar. 27, 1946; d. Coyte and Jill J.D. (Lyon) Adams; B.S., U. S.C., 1968; postgrad. U. Va., 1971, 72, Va. Poly. Inst., 1972; Ph.D. in Physiology, Auburn U., 1976; m. George Edward Coleman III, Jan. 27, 1968; children—Jill Ann Marie, George Edward. Teaching asst. U. S.C., 1967-68; research technician Va. Poly. Inst. and State U., 1968; tchr. biology, basketball coach Brunswick County Schs., 1968-69; teaching asst. biology Va. Poly. Inst. and State U., 1970-72; research asst. poultry sci. Auburn U., 1973-76; asst. prof. poultry sci. Ohio State U.-Ohio Agr. Research and Devel. Center, Columbus, 1977—; owner MAC Assos., 1974—. Resource person Upper Arlington Sch. Bd., 1977—; mem. research com. Columbus Zoo, 1979—. NSF grantee, 1967, 71, 72. Mem. Poultry Sci. Assn., World Poultry Sci. Assn. (life), Am. Physiol. Soc., Southeastern Poultry Sci. Assn. (session chmn. 1980), Auburn U. Alumni Assn., U. S.C. Alumni Assn., Va. Poly. Inst. Alumni Assn., Sigma Xi, Gamma Sigma Delta, Phi Sigma. Contbr. articles to profl. jours. Office: 674 W Lane Ave Columbus OH 43210*

COLEMAN, MARVIN GRANVILLE, air force officer; b. Washington, Nov. 16, 1949; s. Marvin Gifford and Ruby Virginia (Keys) C.; B.S. in Chem. Engring., U. S.C., 1971; M.S. in Meteorology, U. Utah, 1978; m. Linda Colette Trudeau, Jan. 26, 1979; 1 son, Timothy Albert. Commd. 1st lt. U.S. Air Force, 1971; advanced through grades to capt., 1975; detachment weather forecaster, Eglin AFB, Fla., 1927-73, Howard AFB, Panama Canal Zone, 1973-76, environ. analyst, Scott AFB, Ill., 1978-79, asst. chief spl. projects sect., 1979—. Mgr. Koury League Baseball Team, Belleville, Ill. Allied Chem. Corp. grantee, 1967-68; Air Force Res. Officer Tng. Corps grantee, 1968-71. Mem. Am. Meteorol. Soc., Air Force Assn., Sigma Xi, Chi Epsilon Pi. Presbyterian. Home: 21 Morrison Dr Belleville IL 62221 Office: Scott AFB IL 62225

COLEMAN, MARY STALLINGS, state chief justice; b. Tex.; d. Leslie C. and Agnes B. (Huther) Stallings; B.A., U. Md., 1935; J.D., George Washington U., 1939; H.H.D., Nazareth Coll., 1973; LL.D., Olivet Coll., 1973, Alma Coll., 1973, Eastern Mich. U., 1974, Western Mich. U., 1974, Detroit Coll. Law, 1975, Adrian Coll., 1976, U. Md., 1977, Saginaw Valley State Coll., 1979, N.Y. Sch. Law, 1982; D.Public Adminstrn. (hon.), Albion Coll., 1982; m. Creighton R. Coleman, June 24, 1939; children—Leslie (Mrs. Donald Jackson Hagan), Carol. Admitted to D.C. bar, 1940, Mich. bar, 1950; practice law, Washington, 1940-46; partner Wunsch & Coleman, attys., Battle Creek, Mich., 1950-61; probate and juvenile ct. judge, Calhoun County, Mich., 1961-73; justice Mich. Supreme Ct., from 1973, now chief justice. Mem. Mich. Gov.'s Commn. on Crime, 1964-68, Gov.'s Commn. on Delinquency, 1968-70, Gov.'s Commn. on Youth, 1964-70, Gov.'s Commn. on Law Enforcement and Criminal Justice, 1968-72; mem. Pres.'s Commn. Internat. Women's Year, 1975. Trustee, Albion Coll. Recipient awards Calhoun County Assn. Sch. Bds., 1964, Frat. Order Police, 1967, Enquirer and News, 1969, Young Adult Council, NAACP, 1969; Disting. mem. Phi Kappa Phi, 1973; Profl. Achievement award George Washington U. Alumni Council, 1973, Disting. Alumna award, 1980; Outstanding Woman Mich. Bus. and Profl. Women, 1973; Disting. Alumna award U. Md., 1973; Religious Heritage Am. award, 1974; Woman of Yr. award Mich. Assn. Professions, 1976; Woman of Yr. award Soroptomists, 1976; Disting. Citizen award Mich. State U., 1977; Resolution, Mich.

Legislature, 1977; DAR Medal of Honor, 1978; 1 of 10 Top Michiganians award Detroit News, 1980; Disting. Service award Mich. Juvenile Detention Assn., 1980; Merit award Am. Judges Assn., 1980; Disting. Vol. Leadership award March of Dimes, 1981; Law Day award Mich. Pine and Dunes council Girl Scouts U.S.A., 1981; Disting. Woman award Northwood Inst., 1981. Fellow Am. Bar Found.; mem. Am., Mich., Calhoun County bar assns., Am. Judicature Soc., Nat. Assn. Juvenile Ct. Judges, Nat., Mich. assns. women lawyers, AAUW (Disting. Service award Mich. chpt. 1979), Mich. Probate and Juvenile Ct. Judges Assn. (award 1973, pres. 1971-72), Altrusa Internat., Bus. and Profl. Women, Jr. League, P.E.O., Am. Legion Aux., Order of Coif (hon.), Beta Sigma Phi, Alpha Delta Kappa, Alpha Omicron Pi (Outstanding Alumni award 1975). Episcopalian. Club: Battle Creek Country. Home: 355 E Hamilton Ln Battle Creek MI 49015 Office: Law Bldg Box 30052 Lansing MI 48909

COLEMAN, RICHARD WALTER, educator; b. San Francisco, Sept 10, 1922; s. John Crisp and Reta (Walter) C.; B.A., U. Calif., Berkeley, 1945, Ph.D., 1951; m. Mildred Bradley, Aug. 10, 1949, (div. Oct. 1951); 1 dau., Persis C. Research asst. div. entomology and parasitology U. Calif., Berkeley, 1946-47, 49-50; ind. research, 1951-61; prof. biology, chmn. dept. Curry Coll., Milton, Mass., 1961-63; chmn. div. scis. and math. Monticello Coll., Godfrey, Ill., 1963-64; vis. prof. biology Wilberforce U., Ohio; 1964-65; prof. sci. Upper Iowa U., Fayette, 1965—; collaborator natural history div. Nat. Park Service, 1952; spl. cons. Arctic Health Research Center, USPHS, Alaska, 1954-62; apptd. explorer Commr. N.W. Ty., Yellowknife N.W. Ty., Can., 1966. Mem. Iowa Acad. Sci., Geol. Soc. Iowa (affiliate), AAAS, AAUP, Am. Inst. Biol. Scis., Nat. Sci. Tchrs. Assn., Ecol. Soc. Am., Am. Soc. Limnology and Oceanography, Am. Bryological and Lichenological Soc., Arctic Inst. N.Am., N.Am. Benthological Soc., Am. Malacological Union, Assn. Midwestern Coll. Biology Tchrs., Société de Biologie de Montréal, Nat. Assn. Biology Tchrs., Sigma Xi. Methodist. Contbr. articles to profl. reports. Home: PO Box 156 Fayette IA 52142

COLEMAN, ROBERT EDWARD, orthodontist; b. Detroit, Jan. 16, 1915; s. Edward M. and Kathryn J. (Bolton) C.; B.S., U. Detroit, 1936, D.D.S., 1937; M.S., U. Mich., 1939; m. Marion Purdy, Nov. 30, 1940; children—Carolyn Coleman Sieffert, Edward Michael, Mary Coleman Scarfone, Janet Coleman Palombit. Practice orthodontics, Detroit, 1937—; head dept. orthodontics Dental Sch., U. Detroit, 1951-63. Served as capt. Dental Corps, AUS, 1943-46. Diplomate Am. Bd. Orthodontics. Fellow Am. Coll. Dentistry (pres. Mich. chpt. 1974); mem. Am. Dental Assn., Mich., Detroit Dist. dental socs., Am. Assn. Orthodontists, Great Lakes Soc. Orthodontists (pres. 1964), Edward H. Angle Soc. Orthodontists (pres. Midwest chpt. 1962), A.A.A.S., Charles H. Tweed Found. Orthodontic Research, U. Detroit Alumni Assn. (past dir.), U. Detroit Dental Alumni Assn. (past pres., sec. 1939-49), U. Mich. Orthodontic Alumni Soc. (pres. 1966), Omicron Kappa Upsilon (past pres.), Delta Sigma Delta (past grand master). Lion (past dir.). Clubs: Detroit Dental Clinic (past dir.), Downtown Dental (past pres.), Detroit Athletic, Country of Detroit. Contbr. articles to profl. jours. Home: 69 Webber Pl Grosse Pointe Shores MI 48236 Office: 20166 Mack Ave Grosse Pointe MI 48236

COLEMAN, STEVEN LAURENCE, hosp. adminsr., air force officer; b. Ft. Wayne, Ind., June 20, 1940; s. Laurence Ferguson and Lois Virginia (McMaken) C.; B.S.B.A., Ohio State U., 1966; M.H.A., Baylor U., 1975; m. Lela Ann Tidwell, Sept. 5, 1964; 1 son, Scott A. Enlisted in USAF, 1962, advanced through grades to maj. 1978; adminstr. 20th Aeromed. Staging Flight, Tachikawa Air Base, Japan, 1970-71; asst. adminstr. resource mgmt. USAF Hosp., Tachikawa Air Base, 1971-73; hosp. adminstr. USAF Hosp., Kincheloe AFB, Mich., 1975-77; dir. base med. services, comdr.. USAF Clinic, Ankara, Turkey, 1977-79; chief health care affairs Hdqrs. SAC, Offutt AFB, Nebr., 1979—. Decorated Air Force Commendation medal. Mem. Am. Coll. Hosp. Adminstrs., Am. Hosp. Assn. Mem. Christian Ch. (Disciples of Christ). Clubs: Masons, Shriners. Home: 13008 S 35th St Omaha NE 68123 Office: HQS SAC/SGHXX Offutt AFB NE 68113

COLEMAN, THOMAS CHARLES, lawyer; b. Streator, Ill., Aug. 7, 1932; s. Glenn Alfred and Anne Jane (Fox) C.; B.A., Yale U., 1954; J.D., Washington U., St. Louis, 1961; m. Georgea Flynn Schneider, Jan. 11, 1962; children—George, Thomas Charles, Stephen. Admitted to Mo. bar, 1961; partner firm Green, Hennings, Henry, Evans & Arnold, St. Louis, 1961-67; atty. Ralston Purina Co., St. Louis, 1967-69, counsel consumer products group, 1969-81, corp. food and drug counsel, 1981—; lectr. Am. Mgmt. Assn. Music cons., soloist Opera Theatre of St. Louis; soloist St. Louis Symphony. Mem. Am. Bar Assn., Mo. Bar, Bar Assn. Met. St. Louis. Episcopalian. Clubs: Racquet, Whiffenpoofs. Office: Ralston Purina Co 835 S 8th St Saint Louis MO 63188

COLEMAN, THOMAS JAMES, physician; b. Wichita, Kans., June 3, 1918; s. Thomas James and Marguerite (Crummey) C.; student Kans. State U., 1940-41, U. Va, 1946-47; M.D., U. Rochester, 1951; m. Amy Desmond Jones, Aug. 27, 1949; children—Thomas James, Pamela Jane, Patricia Lynn, Richard Cahill, Martha Sue, Robert Bruce. Intern, U. Kans. Med. Center, 1951-52, resident, 1952-55; practice medicine specializing in internal medicine; mem. staffs St. Francis Hosp., Wesley Med. Center, St. Joseph Hosp. and Rehab. Center; clin. asst. prof. medicine Wichita State U. br. U. Kans. Sch. Medicine, 1977—; NIH fellow in endocrinology U. Kans., 1954-55. Served to capt. USAAF, 1942-46. Decorated D.F.C., Air medal with oak leaf cluster. Diplomate Am. Bd. Internal Medicine, Nat. Bd. Med. Examiners. Mem. A.C.P., Am. Coll. Cardiology, AMA, Flying Physicians Assn., Am. Heart Assn. (dir. Kans, affiliate), Kans. Heart Assn. (pres. 1974-75), Am. Soc. Internal Medicine. Republican. Club: Wichita State U. Shocker. Home: 155 N Crestway Wichita KS 67208 Office: 959 N Emporia St Wichita KS 67214

COLL, DENNIS RAYMOND, investment cons. co. exec.; b. Pitts., Aug. 18, 1943; s. Edward G. and Alice V. (Ebeling) C.; B.S., U.S. Mil. Acad., 1965; M.B.A., U. Chgo., 1973; m. Judith L. Buchanan, June 4, 1966; children—Brian, Shannon, Gavin, Brandon. Sales positions IBM, Chgo., 1969-72, account mgr., 1972-73; pres. Arlington Fin. Services, Arlington Heights, Ill., 1974-75; pres. Murdoch & Coll, Arlington Heights, 1975—; dir. 1st. Nat. Bank Lincolnshire (Ill.). Mem. Assn. Grads. admission com. U.S. Mil. Acad. Served to capt. U.S. Army, 1965-69. Decorated Bronze Star. Registered real estate broker, prin., registered securities dealer, prin., registered ins. broker. Mem. West Point Soc. Chgo. (pres. 1978-81), other orgns. Republican. Roman Catholic. Office: 3233 N Arlington Heights Rd Arlington Heights IL 60004

COLLEN, SHELDON ORRIN, lawyer; b. Chgo., Feb. 7, 1922; s. Jacob Allen and Ann (Andalman) C.; B.A. cum laude, Carleton Coll., 1944; J.D., U. Chgo., 1948; m. Ann Blager, Apr. 8, 1946; 1 son, John O. Admitted to Ill. bar, 1949, Minn. bar, 1976, U.S. SUpreme Ct., 1965; practiced in Chgo., 1949—; asso. Adcock, Fink & Day, 1948-51; mem. firm Simon & Collen, 1952-57, Friedman & Koven, 1958—; specialist fed. antitrust litigation; sec. Jupiter Industries, Inc., Chgo., 1961—. Mem. bd. edn. U. Chgo. Law Rev., 1948-49. Bd. dirs. Lower Northcenter, Chgo. Youth Centers, Union League Found. for Boys, Oak Park (Ill.) Theatre Festival, Contemporary Arts Workshop, Edward P. Martin Soc., Center for Study of Multiple Births; sec., bd. dirs. 3750 Lake Shore Dr., Inc.; sr. counselor Union League Civic and Arts Found. Served with AUS, 1943-46. Mem. Am., Chgo. (antitrust law and securities law coms., chmn. antitrust 1976-77), Ill. (counsel corp. and securities law sect.) bar assns., Bar Assn. 7th Circuit, Am. Judicature Soc., Art Inst. Chgo., Mus. Contemporary Art, Chgo. Council Fgn. Relations. Clubs: Union League (Chgo); Lafayette (Minnetonka Beach, Minn.). Mem. adv. bd. Antitrust Bull. and Jour. Reprints for Antitrust Law and Econs. Home: 3750 Lake Shore Dr Chicago IL 60613 also Meadville Rd Excelsior MN Office: 208 S LaSalle St Chicago IL 60604

COLLEY, LYNN ALLAN, ins. co. agt.; b. Sanford, Maine, Oct. 31, 1945; s. Leonard V. and Phyllis A. (Treadwell) C.; student S.E. Mo. U., 1963-67; m. Saundra L. Cumpton Brunke, Dec. 14, 1974; 1 dau., Brooke Anne. Owner, Sikeston (Mo.) Coin & Stamp Co., 1965-68; agt. Met. Life Ins. Co., Sikeston, 1968—; owner C & C Stationery Supply, Sikeston, 1968—, Statewide Pest Control, Sikeston, 1979—. Chmn., Scott County Rep. Com., 1968-74, vice chmn., 1966-68; treas. bd. dirs. Sikeston Activity Center, 1975—; mem. Channey-Harris Meml. Com., Sikeston, 1978—. Recipient Am. Legion History award, 1962; Dr. Tom L. Chidester award Sikeston Little Theatre, 1965; Nat. Assn. Life Underwriters Nat. Quality award, 1974, 78, 79, Nat. Health Quality award, 1976, Nat. Sales Achievement award, 1976. Mem. Sikeston Assn. Life Underwriters (sec.-treas. 1975—), Mo. Assn. Life Underwriters, Nat. Assn. Life Underwriters, Sikeston Little Theatre (pres. 1966-82), Mo. Arts Council (adv. com. 1981), Sikeston Arts and Edn. Council (treas. 1975—), St. Louis Symphony in Sikeston Com. (treas. 1976—). Jehovah's Witness. Home: 916 Alexander St Sikeston MO 63801 Office: PO Box 789 Sikeston MO 63801

COLLIE, JOHN, JR., insurance agt.; b. Gary, Ind., Apr. 23, 1934; s. John and Christina Dempster (Wardrop) C.; student Purdue U., 1953; A.B. in Econs., Ind. U., 1957; m. Jessie Fearn Shaw, Aug. 1, 1964; children—Cynthia Elizabeth, Douglas Allan Hamilton, Jennifer Fearn. Operator, Collie Optical Lab., Gary, 1957-62; owner, operator Collie Ins. Agy., Merrillville, Ind., 1962—. Lt. col. U.S. Army Res., 1957—; instr. Command and Gen. Staff Coll., 1973-77. Mem. Profl. Ins. Agts. Assn. Ind. (dir.), Internat. Platform Assn., Mil. Order World Wars, Res. Officers Assn. (sec., v.p. Ind. chpt.), Phi Kappa Psi. Republican. Presbyterian. Clubs: Masons (32 deg.), Shriners, Elks. Home: 717 W 66th Pl Merrillville IN 46410 Office: 5600 Broadway PO Box 8049 Merrillville IN 46410

COLLIE, ROBERT MORRIS, pastoral counselor; b. Eastland, Tex., Dec. 15, 1929; s. Turner Morris and Zula (Overbey) C.; B.S., Tex. Wesleyan Coll., 1951; B.D., So. Meth. U., 1954; Th.D., Grad. Theol. Union, 1971; m. Annelie Moxter, Aug. 26, 1977; children—Crista, Robert, Felix Moxter. Ordained to ministry United Methodist Ch., 1952; pastor various chs. in Central Tex. and La. Ann. Confs.; dir. Office of Pastoral Care, West Ohio Conf., United Meth. Ch., 1969-78; dir. North Area Guidance Center, Children's Mental Health Service, Columbus, Ohio, 1978-79; dir. Samaritan Pastoral Counseling Center, Ft. Wayne, Ind., 1979—; bd. dirs. MidWest Career Devel. Center, Columbus. Pastoral counseling fellow Pacific Sch. Religion; Berkeley Center for the Study of Alcoholism fellow; diplomate Am. Assn. Pastoral Counselors. Mem. Am. Psychol. Assn. Author: Matthias, 1975. Home: 7219 Tanbark Ln Fort Wayne IN 46825 Office: 300 W Wayne St Fort Wayne IN 46802

COLLIER, B. BRUCE, jewel co. exec.; b. Mumford, Tex., Apr. 3, 1928; s. Hosea Oscar and Percy Virginia (Moore) C.; B.S., Baylor U., 1948; postgrad., Ohio State U., 1948-49, Purdue U., 1949-50; m. Mary Carollene Gardner, Sept. 9, 1949; children—Suzanne, Rachel, Bryan, Holly. Partner, Gardner-Collier Jewelry Co., Kirksville, Mo., 1950-66; pres. Gardner-Collier Inc., Kirksville, 1966—; pres., chmn. bd. Kirksville Savs. & Loan Assn., 1970—. Pres., Adair County Credit Bur., 1960; fund raising chmn. group to bring industries to Kirksville, 1960-72. Named outstanding young man Kirksville Jaycees, 1957. Mem. Kirksville C. of C. (pres. 1957), Retail Jewelers Am., Mo. Jewelers Assn. Republican. Baptist. Clubs: Kirksville Country, Masons, Shriners. Home: 1302 E Patterson St Kirksville MO 63501 Office: 111 W Washington St Kirksville MO 63501

COLLIER, HELEN VANDIVORT, counseling psychologist; b. Nagpur, India; d. William Boardley and Stephena Ruth (Hecker) C.; A.B., Ohio Wesleyan U., 1950; M.Ed., U. Toledo, 1968, Ed.D., 1974; children—Keith Vandivort, Daniel Vandivort, Heidi Vandivort. Tchr. elem. schs., Itasca, Ill., 1950-53; ednl. cons. Toledo Bd. Edn., 1960-67; elem. counselor Toledo Pub. Schs., 1968; counseling psychologist, asst. prof. U. Toledo, 1968-74; asst. dir. adult counseling project Sch. Continuing Studies, Ind. U., Bloomington, 1975-76; pvt. practice psychotherapy and counseling, cons., Bloomington, 1974—; cons. orgnl. devel.; grad. San Diego Gestalt Tng. Center. Women's Ednl. Equity Act, Office of Edn. grantee, 1977—; licensed psychologist, Ohio. Mem. Am. Psychol. Assn., Assn. for Women in Psychology, Am. Personnel and Guidance Assn., Nat. Vocat. Guidance Assn., Assn. for Counselor Edn. and Supervision, Am. Soc. Tng. and Devel., Women's Equity Action League, Nat. Women's Polit. Caucus. Co-editor: Meeting the Educational and Occupational Planning Needs of Adults, 1975; author: Free Ourselves: Removing Internal Barriers to Equality, 1979; also articles. Home: 3801 Morningside Dr #6 Bloomington IN 47401 Office: Box 464 Bloomington IN 47402

COLLIER, ROBERT GEORGE, educator; b. Stockton, Calif., Aug. 23, 1944; s. Laurence Donald and Dorothy Louise (Braghetta) C.; A.A., San Joaquin Delta Coll., 1965; B.A. in Psychology, U. Calif., Riverside, 1967; M.A. in Elem. Edn., Calif. State U., Los Angeles, 1973; Ph.D. in Edn., Claremont Grad. Sch., 1978; m. Sandra LaVaughn Haller, July 22, 1972; children—Steven Edward, Brian James. Asst. football coach U. Calif., Riverside, 1967-68, instr. univ. extension, 1979; elem. tchr. Riverside Unified Sch. Dist., 1968-74, 75-79; research asst. Claremont Grad. Sch., 1974-75; tchr. Lovett's Presch., Riverside, summer 1979; asst. prof. early childhood edn. Western Ill. U., 1979—; mem. rev. com. Erikson Inst., Chgo.; mem. McDonough County Council Child Devel.; mem. governing bd. Wee Care Center, Macomb, Ill. Served with USAR, 1968-74. Recipient Peter L. Spencer award Phi Delta Kappa at Claremont Grad. Sch., 1978; Western Ill. U. Faculty Devel. Office mini grantee, 1980; Western Ill. U. Research Council grantee, 1981; cert. elem. tchr., Calif. Mem. Assn. Childhood Edn. Internat., Assn. Supervision and Curriculum Devel., Assn. Anthropol. Study Play, Council Exceptional Children, Nat. Assn. Edn. Young Children, Phi Delta Kappa (v.p.-elect. Western Ill. U. chpt. 1981-82). Home: 30 Briarwood Pl Macomb IL 61455 Office: Elem Edn Dept Western Ill U Macomb IL 61455

COLLIER, WILLIAM JEWELL, physician; b. Albany, Mo., Apr. 25, 1925; s. Ora and Mabel (Adkisson) C.; student U. Chgo. Sch. Medicine, 1945-46; B.S., Tulane U., 1947; M.D., Bowman Gray Sch. Medicine, Wake Forest U., 1949; m. Mary Evelyn Fisher, Mar. 29, 1952; children—William Jewell II, Sherry Lynn, Terri Lee, Linda Lorraine. Intern, U.S. Naval Hosp., Great Lakes, Ill., 1949-50; resident internal medicine VA Hosp., Wadsworth, Kans., 1950-51, resident gen. surgery, 1951-52, 54-57; asst. chief surgery VA Hosp., Wichita, Kans., 1957-58; pvt. practice gen. and thoracic surgery, McPherson, Kans., 1958—. Dir. Home State Bank & Trust. Former mem. aviation adv. bd. McPherson City-County Airport. Served from lt. (j.g.) to lt. M.C., USNR, 1952-54. Diplomate Am. Bd. Surgery. Fellow Southwestern Surg. Congress, A.C.S., Internat. Coll. Surgeons; mem. C. of C. Mem. Christian Ch. Rotarian. Home: 302 S Walnut St McPherson KS 67460 Office: 400 W 4th St McPherson KS 67460

COLLINS, CARDISS, Congresswoman; b. St. Louis; ed. Northwestern U.; m. George W. Collins (dec.); 1 son, Kevin. Stenographer, Ill. Dept. Labor; sec. Ill. Dept. Revenue, then accountant, revenue auditor; mem. 93d-97th Congresses from 7th Ill. Dist., mem. Govt. Ops. com., Energy and Commerce com.; chmn. Manpower and Housing com., former majority whip-at-large; past chmn. Congressional Black Caucus; former chmn. Mems. of Congress for Peace through Law. Bd. dirs. Greater Lawndale Conservation Commn., Chgo. Mem. NAACP, Nat. Council Negro Women, Chgo. Urban League, Alpha Kappa Alpha. Baptist. Democrat. Office: 2438 Rayburn House Office Bldg Washington DC 20515

COLLINS, DAVID RAYMOND, educator, author, lectr.; b. Marshalltown, Iowa, Feb. 29, 1940; s. Raymond Amby and Mary Elizabeth (Brecht) C.; B.S., Western Ill. U., 1962, M.S., 1966. Instr. English, Woodrow Wilson Jr. High Sch., 1962—; founder, dir. Miss. Valley Writers Conf., 1973—, Children's Lit. Festival, 1979—; Sec., Quad Cities Arts Council, 1971-75; pres. Friends of Moline Pub. Library, 1965-66. Recipient writing award Writer's Digest, 1967, writer of the year award Writers' Studio, 1971, award Bobbs-Merrill Pub. Co., 1971, writer of the year award Quad-Cities Writers Club, 1972, writing awards Judson Coll., 1971. Mem. Nat., Ill., Moline (dir. 1964-67) edn. assns., Ill. PTA (life; Outstanding Ill. Educator award 1975), Ill. Hist. Soc., Black Hawk Div. Tchrs. English (pres. 1967-68), Writers Studio (pres. 1967-71), Children's Reading Roundtable, Authors Guild, Soc. Children's Book Writers, Juvenile Forum, Quad-Cities Writers Club (pres. 1973-75, 77-78), Am. Amateur Press Assn., Western Ill. U. Alumni (dir. 1968-74, Outstanding Achievement award 1973), Kappa Delta Pi, Sigma Tau Delta, Alpha Delta, Delta Sigma Phi. Democrat. Roman Catholic. Author: Kim Soo and His Tortoise, 1970; Great American Nurses, 1971; Walt Disney's Surprise Christmas Present, 1972; Linda Richards, America's First Trained Nurse, 1973; Harry S. Truman, People's President, 1975; Football Running Backs, 1975; I, Abraham Lincoln, 1976; Illinois Women: Born to Serve, 1976; Joshua Poole Hated School, 1977; Charles Lindbergh, Hero Pilot, 1978; A Spirit of Giving, 1978; If I Could, I Would, 1979; Joshua Poole and Sunrise, 1979; The Wonderful Story of Jesus, 1980; A Special Guest, 1980; The Only Thing Wrong with Birthdays, 1980; George Washington Carver, 1981. Home: 3403 45th St Moline IL 61265 Office: 1301 48th St Moline IL 61265

COLLINS, DON CARY, lawyer; b. Christopher, Ill., Sept. 10, 1951; s. Everett Hugh, Jr. and Evelyn Loriene (Wootton) C.; student Western Ky. U., 1969-70; B.A., Ill. State U., Normal, 1972; J.D., So. Ill. U., 1976. Admitted to Ill. bar, 1976, Mo. bar, 1977, U.S. Dist. Ct. bar, 1978, U.S. Supreme Ct. bar, 1980; partner firm Kaucher, Collins & Ligman, Belleville and Highland, Ill. Public relations/media chmn. S.W. Ill. Regional Spl. Olympics, 1979. Mem. Am., Ill., Mo., St. Clair County, East St. Louis, Met. St. Louis bar assns., Am. Trial Lawyers Assn., Ill. Trial Lawyers Assn., Am. Judicature Soc. Home: 920 E B St Belleville IL 62221 Office: 4715 W Main St Belleville IL 62223 also 1115 Washington St Highland IL 62249

COLLINS, EARLEEN, state senator; b. Miss.; B.A. in Sociology and Edn., U. Ill.-Chgo. Formerly child welfare exec. Ill. Dept. Children and Family Services; mem. Ill. State Senate from 21st dist. Mem. Sch. Dist. 19 Parent Adv. Com., Commn. Youth Welfare; bd. dirs. Lawndale Mental Health Clinic, Op. Brotherhood. Mem. Chgo. Assn. Edn. Young Child, Black Child Devel. Assn., NAACP. Office: State Capitol care Gen Assembly Chicago IL 60644*

COLLINS, EDWARD JAMES, JR., assn. exec.; b. Lawrence, Mass., Mar. 17, 1933; s. Edward James and Mary Elizabeth (Rogers) C.; m. Dorothy Jane McCann, Sept. 19, 1964; 1 son, Edward James, III; 1 stepdau., Dorothy Lorraine; A.B. in Journalism, U. Calif., Berkeley, 1959. Mng. editor Brawley (Calif.) Daily News, 1959-62; asso. exec. dir. Calif. Veterinary Med. Assn., Moraga, Calif., 1962-65; exec. dir. Marin Med. Soc., San Rafael, Calif., 1965-66; asst. dir., prof., pub. relations Calif. Med. Assn., San Francisco, 1966-68; v.p. Assn. Western Hosps., San Francisco, 1968-76; exec. dir. Am. Assn. Med. Soc. Execs., Chgo., 1977-81; pres., chief exec. officer Am. Econ. Devel. Council, Chgo., 1981—. Mem. Am., No. Calif. (pres. 1973), Chgo. socs. assn. execs., Recipient Agrl. Writers award, 1961, Key Man award Oakland (Calif.) Jaycees, 1964. Home: 617 Indian Hill Rd Deerfield IL 60015 Office: 4849 N Scott St Suite 10 Schiller Park IL 60176

COLLINS, EVA MAE LOMERSON, ins. agency exec.; b. Lake Orion, Mich., July 10, 1930; d. J.M. and Thelma Marie (Kimmery) Lomerson; student U. Mich., 1948-49, Wayne State U., 1954-55; m. John Armstrong Collins, Feb. 24, 1968. Divisional mgr. Sears Roebuck & Co., Pontiac, Mich., 1951-69; underwriter personal lines Bingham & Bingham Inc., Birmingham, Mich., 1970-73, comml. lines, 1973-74, agency mgr., 1974-77, v.p. InterCEDE Group, 1977—; v.p., office mgr. Bingham & Bingham, Inc., 1979—. Mem. Founders Soc. of Detroit Inst. Arts. Named woman of year Land-O-Oak chpt. Am. Bus. Women's Assn., 1965. Mem. DAR (chpt. regent 1967-69, state chmn. pages and jr. membership 1967-70, state outstanding jr. mem. 1966, state chmn. Good Citizens 1982-85), Detroit Soc. Geneal. Research, Hist. Soc. Mich., Nat. Assn. Female Execs., Ins. Women Met. Detroit (rec. sec. 1977-78, corr. sec. 1978-79, treas. 1979-80, 2d v.p. 1980-81, 1st v.p. 1981-82, pres. 1982-83), U. Mich. Alumni Assn. (life), Daus. Colonial Wars, Nat. Trust Historic Preservation, Nat. Audubon Soc., Friends of Detroit Public Library, Nat. Wildlife Fedn. Republican. Clubs: Club on Hill, Gt. Oaks Country (Rochester, Mich.). Home: PO Box 734 Rochester MI 48063 Office: 30700 Telegraph Rd S-4535 Birmingham MI 48010

COLLINS, JAMES HAROLD LEE, personnel mgr.; b. Moline, Ill., Feb. 1, 1946; s. Alphonso and Mattie Lucille (Pennington) C.; B.A. in Sociology, St. Ambrose Coll., 1969; m. Karen Jean Raebel, Jan. 2, 1965; children—James Harold Lee, Kimberly Dianne, Candace Sue, Anthony Joseph, Kevin Michael. Exec. dir. Project N.O.W., Rock Island County, Ill., 1968-71; instr. Augustana Coll., Rock Island, 1971; indsl. relations rep., supr., EEO coordinator, mgr. personnel John Deere, Milan, Ill., 1964—. Chmn. Human Rights Commn. Dubuque, Iowa, 1973; pres. Quad Cities Council Crime and Delinquency, 1978-79; bd. dirs. Quad Cities United Way, 1975-78; bd. Scott and Rock Island Councils of Churches; mem. Metro-Com Br. NAACP; v.p. Quad City Merit Employment Council, 1975; counselor Big Brothers and Jr. Achievement; den leader Cub Scouts Boy Scouts Am. Recipient Am. Legion award, 1961, Rotary award, 1964. Mem. Milan C. of C. (bd. dirs., 2d. v.p.). Roman Catholic. Home: 2706 E 28 Ct Davenport IA 52803 Office: 1600 1st Ave E Milan IL 61264

COLLINS, JAMES SLADE, II, lawyer; b. St. Louis, June 9, 1937; s. James S. and Dolma Ruby (Nielsen) C.; B.S. in Bus. Adminstrn., Washington U., 1958, J.D., 1961; m. Neva Frances Guinn, June 27,

1959; children—Shari Lynn, Camala Ann. Admitted to Mo. bar, 1961, U.S. Supreme Ct., 1969, U.S. Dist. Ct. for Eastern Mo., 1972; asso. Whalen, O'Connor, Grauel & Sarkisian, St. Louis, 1961-70; partner Whalen, O'Connor & Byrne, 1970-72; partner Whalen, O'Connor, Collins, & Danis, 1972-75; asso. Hullverson, Hullverson & Frank, Inc., 1975-78; individual practice law, St. Louis, 1979—. Trustee, Village of Hanley Hills, Mo., 1966-69, mayor, 1967, municipal judge, 1967-68, 69-70. Mem. Am. Bar Assn., Bar Assn. Met. St. Louis, Lawyers Assn. St. Louis, Am. Trial Lawyers Assn., Mo. Assn. Trial Lawyers, Phi Delta Phi. Republican. Baptist. Home: 916 Parkwatch Dr Saint Louis County MO 63011 Office: 1015 Locust St Saint Louis MO 63101

COLLINS, JAY WILSON, hosp. adminstr.; b. Cleve., Dec. 30, 1917; s. Charles H. and Alice A. (Murray) C.; A.B., Fenn Coll., 1940; M.A., Ohio State U., 1941; m. Ileene J. Lustic, July 11, 1969; 1 son, Grant L. Regional dir. FSA, Youngstown, Ohio, 1941; mem. faculty Fenn Coll., Cleve., 1942; adminstrv. asst. U. Hosp. of Cleve., 1945-46; asst. dir. Samaritan Hosp., Troy, N.Y., 1946-47; pres. Euclid (Ohio) Gen. Hosp., 1947—; v.p. Regional Health Data Services, Inc., 1977-79; pres. Hosp. Fin. Corp., 1974-79; v.p. exec. div. Euclid Devel. Corp., 1977—. Mem. adv. bd. Lakeland Community Coll., 1971-76, Villa Angela Acad., 1975—; councilman City of Euclid, 1971-73; pres. Euclid Community Relations Council, 1968-73; city leader Republican Party, 1975-80; pres. Community Improvement Corp., 1980—; v.p. Fenn Ednl. Commn., 1980—; trustee Euclid YMCA, pres., 1966-68; trustee Fenn Coll., 1954-57, Greater Cleve. Red Cross, 1962-66, Greater Cleve. YMCA, 1970—, Euclid Red Cross, 1961-66, Euclid Civic Orch., 1961-64, Euclid Cultural Council, 1967-68; trustee Early Settlers Assn. of Western Res., 1976—, v.p., 1980—. Served to capt., M.C., U.S. Army, 1942-45. Recipient Disting. Service awards City of Euclid, 1977, YMCA, 1963, Fenn Coll., 1958. Fellow Am. Coll. Hosp. Adminstrs.; mem. Ohio Hosp. Assn. (trustee 1950-58, pres. 1955-56), Greater Cleve. Hosp. Assn. (pres. 1977-79, trustee 1951-79), Am. Hosp. Assn., Internat. Hosp. Fedn., Royal Soc. Health, Soc. Mayflower Descs., SAR, Newcomen Soc. N.Am., Euclid C. of C. (pres. 1978-81), U.S. C. of C. Republican. Presbyterian. Clubs: Kiwanis (pres. 1964-65); Mayfield Village Racquet; Riverview Racquet. Contbr. articles on hosp. adminstrn. to profl. jours. Office: East 185th St and Lake Erie Euclid OH 44119

COLLINS, JOYCE OLIVIA, ednl., nutritional, bus. mgmt. cons.; b. Chicago, Mar. 22, 1948; d. Prince A. and Olivia (Smith) McMorris; student Ill. Inst. Tech., 1970-73; B.Ph., U. Healing, Campo, Calif., 1978, M.Ph., 1981; B.S., Internat. Inst. Natural Health, 1978; m. Carley E. Lowe, Sept. 13, 1967 (div.); 1 son, Anthony; m. 2d, Orville A. Collins, Dec. 14, 1974 (div.). Adminstr., Sch. Data Processing, Seymore Systems Inc., Chgo., 1972-74; data base adminstr., sr. programmer Signode Corp., Glenview, Ill., 1975-78; computer data processing dept. coordinator, data processing instr. Central YMCA Community Coll., Chgo., 1979-80; dir., data processing cons. Eduteach Inst. Computer Sci., Chgo., 1979—; v.p., dir. methodology Action Concentrated Tng. Inst., Chgo., 1980—; mgmt. and ednl. cons. Roseland Community Edn. Center, Chgo., 1981—; data processing lectr., ednl. cons. Malcolm X Coll., Chgo., 1981; mgmt. and nutritional cons., 1977—; ordained to ministry God Unltd. Ch., 1978. Recipient Merit award Central YMCA Community Coll., 1980. Mem. Nat. Tech. Assn., Systems Programmers Soc. (G. Calvin Comer meml. award 1975), Learning Exchange, Universal Found. for Better Living, United Women for Positive Community Ideas, Alliance for Human Devel. Clubs: Rosicrucians, Better Boys Found. Women's Aux. Office: Action Concentrated Tng Inst 155 N Harbor Dr Suite 3111 N Chicago IL 60601

COLLINS, LAWRENCE TURNER, educator; b. Livingston, Tex., Mar. 1, 1937; s. Theodore E. and D. Eleanor (Turner) C.; B.S., Stephen F. Austin Coll., 1959; M.S. (Research fellow 1966), Tex. Technol. Coll., 1966; Ph.D., U. Wis., 1973; m. Pansy R. Hillin, July 25, 1958; children—Lawrence Turner, Jr., David A., Sarah A. Prin., Shepherd (Tex.) High Sch., 1959-64; instr. botany Tex. Tech. Inst., Lubbock, 1967; mem. faculty Evangel Coll., Springfield, Mo., 1971—, asso. prof. biology, 1976—. Mem. Solid Waste Disposal Com., Springfield, Mo., 1973; mem. Environ. Adv. Bd., 1974-80, chmn., 1978-79; chmn. Resource Recovery Task Force, 1978; mem. Resource and Energy Adv. Panel, 1980—. Sigma Xi grantee, 1968; recipient Hatcher Meml. award U. Wis., 1970. Mem. Am. Bot. Soc., Southwestern Assn. Naturalists, Am. Sci. Affiliation, Nature Conservancy, Sigma Xi. Contbr. articles to various manuals; research in botany, ecology, parasitic flowering plants. Home: 2169 E Monroe Terr Springfield MO 65802 Office: Dept Sci and Tech Evangel Coll Springfield MO 65802

COLLINS, MARVA DELOISE NETTLES, educator; b. Monroeville, Ala., Aug. 31, 1936; d. Alex L. and Bessie Maye (Knight) Nettles; B.A., Clark Coll., Atlanta, 1957; postgrad. Chgo. Tchrs. Coll. and Columbia Coll., 1965-67; hon. degrees, Howard U., Wilberforce U., 1980; m. Clarence Collins, Sept. 2, 1961; children—Eric Tremayne, Patrick, Cynthia. Tchr., Monroeville, 1957-59, Chgo. Public Schs., 1960-75; founder Westside Prep. Sch., Chgo., 1975—; featured on Phil Donahue Show, Good Morning America, 60 Minutes, mags., newspapers throughout U.S.; subject of film The Marva Collins Story, 1981; condr. workshops U.S. and Europe; dir. local Right to Read Program. Recipient Watson Washburne award, 1979, West Garfield Image award, 1980, United Negro Coll. Fund award, 1980, Sears Week of the Child award, 1980, Sojourner Truth award, 1980, West Garfield Park award, 1980, Educator of Yr. award, 1981. Mem. Internat. Platform Assn., Alpha Kappa Alpha. Baptist. Contbr. articles to newspapers and mags. Office: 4146 W Chicago Ave Chicago IL 60624

COLLINS, MARY ALICE, psychiat. social worker; b. Everett, Wash., Apr. 20, 1937; d. Harry Edward and Mary (Yates) Caton; B.A. in Sociology, Seattle Pacific Coll., 1959; M.S.W., U. Mich., 1966; Ph.D., Mich. State U., 1974; m. Gerald C. Brocker, Mar. 24, 1980. Dir. teenage, adult and counseling depts. YWCA, Flint, Mich., 1959-64, 66-68; social worker Catholic Social Services, Flint, 1969-71, Ingham Med. Mental Health Center, Lansing, Mich., 1971-73; clin. social worker Genesee Psychiat. Center, Flint, 1974—; instr. social work Lansing Community Coll. and Mich. State U., 1974; vis. prof. Hurley Med. Center, 1979—; cons. Ingham County Dept. Social Services, 1971-73. Advisor human relations Youth League, Flint Council Chs., 1964-65; sec. Genesee County Young Democrats, 1960-61. Mem. Nat. Assn. Social Workers, Acad. Certified Social Workers, Registry Clin. Social Workers, Registry Health Care Workers, Phi Kappa Phi, Alpha Kappa Sigma. Contbr. articles to profl. jours. Home: 5945 Round Lake Rd Laingsburg MI 48848 Office: PO Box 7179 Flint MI 48507

COLLINS, OAKLEY C., state senator; b. Lawrence County, Ohio, 1916; B.S., Ohio U., 1938. Sch. adminstr.; former mem. Ohio Ho. of Reps.; mem. Ohio Senate, 1952-72, 75—. Mem. Ohio Republican State Exec. Com., 1968—; del. Rep. Nat. Conv., 1980. Office: State Senate Columbus OH 43216*

COLLINS, RICHARD ANTHONY, data processing exec.; b. Lake Forest, Ill., Sept. 19, 1931; s. Anthony D. and Alice A. (Luedke) Czaikowski; B.A. magna cum laude, Augustana Coll., 1956; M.B.A., U. Wis., 1957, postgrad., 1966-70; m. Joan V. Krapfel, Apr. 17, 1965; children—Craig R., Clark A. Econ. statistician Eastman Kodak, Rochester, N.Y., 1957-59; mgr. mktg. research Ritter Co., mfr. dental and med. equipment, Rochester, N.Y., 1959-63; mktg. research supr. Oscar Mayer & Co., meat packing, Madison, Wis., 1964-66; mktg. program coordinator U. Wis. Extension, Madison, 1966-68; prof. U. Wis., Whitewater, 1968-72; marketing exec. Anchor Savs. & Loan Assn., Madison, 1972-73; EFTS project dir. Fed. Home Loan Bank Bd., 1973-74; dir. EFT projects Credit Union Nat. Assn., Madison, 1974-76, v.p. fin. systems, 1976-78; exec. v.p. Cunadata Corp., Madison, 1978-80; v.p. mktg. services Clark Sutton Assos. Inc., Washington, 1980—; v.p. MDI Thrift Services, Madison, Wis., 1980—; ad hoc prof. mktg. programs for small bus. U. Wis. Extension, 1970-73; instr. Savings and Loan Inst. courses, 1965-72; Served with AUS, 1949-53. Mem. Am. Mktg. Assn. (chpt. seminar chmn. 1972-73). Author: (with George L. Herpel) Specialty Advertising in Marketing, 1972. Home: 2812 Waunona Way Madison WI 53713 Office: 802 W Broadway Suite L8-A Madison WI 53713

COLLINS, RICHARD JOHN, sales exec.; b. Gary, Ind., June 24, 1921; s. Frank H. and Aileen Mary (Cary) C.; student Gary Coll., 1939-42; B.S., Ind. U., 1947; m. Betty Ann Cogswell, Sept. 21, 1946; children—Cary, Thomas, Libby A., Timothy, Theodore, Cathleen. Sales cons. Met. Life Ins. Co., 1960-70; field mgr. mgmt. sales Commonwealth Life & Accident & Ins., 1967-69; cons. sales engr. Batestor (now Batesco), Gary, 1969-75, field sales engr., research and devel., 1975—; cons. Mespeco, Inc., v.p., 1978—; v.p. Melt Spltys. Co., 1978—. Treas. Gary Republican Central Com., 1966-70; precinct capt. Gary Rep. Com., 1964-70, Crown Point (Ind.) Rep. Com., 1971-75. Served with USMC, 1942-46. C.L.U. Mem. Am. Foundry Soc., Metall. Soc. and Iron and Steel Soc. of AIME, N.W. Ind. Ceramic Engring. Soc., Molten Metals Testing Assn., Research and Devel. Guild, Am. Legion. Roman Catholic. Patentee. Home: 306 Northeast St Crown Point IN 46307 Office: PO Box 8115 Gary IN 46410

COLLINS, WILLIAM JAMES, mfg. co. exec.; b. Grand Rapids, Mich., Dec. 1, 1915; s. Frank C. and Aileen (Cary) C.; B.S., U. Mich., 1939; m. Margery Aileen McDevitt, Nov. 23, 1942; children—Margaret Totin, William Jeffrey, C. Casey. With Batesco, Inc., Gary, Ind., 1964—, pres., sales mgr., 1981—; pres., sales mgr. Melt Specialties Co., Gary, 1976-81. Served with AC, U.S. Army, 1942-45, USAF, 51-52. Mem. AIME, Am. Foundrymen's Soc., U. Mich. Alumni Assn., Am. Legion, 8th AF Hist. Soc., 486th Bomb Group Assn. Club: Lions. Patentee in field. Home: 7005 Madison St Merrillville IN 46410 Office: PO Box 8115 Gary IN 46410

COLLINS, WILLIAM THOMAS, pathologist; b. Omaha, Feb. 21, 1922; s. John Maurice and Elizabeth (Ewing) C.; B.S., U. Ky., 1942; M.D., U. Mich., 1944; m. Ann E. Adams, May 30, 1942; children—William Thomas, Carol Ann, John Mark, Donald Brian. Intern, Good Samaritan Hosp., Cin., 1944-45; resident in pathology Cin. Gen. Hosp., 1945-46, asst. attending pathologist, 1948-51; pathologist, dir. labs. Good Samaritan Hosp., Cin., 1952-56; fellow in exfoliative cytology Free Hosp. for Women, Brookline, Mass., 1949; asso. pathologist Blodgett Meml. Hosp., Grand Rapids, Mich., 1956-57; asso. pathologist Lima (Ohio) Meml. Hosp., 1957-58, pathologist, dir. lab., 1958—; asso. clin. prof. pathology Med. Coll. Ohio, Toledo, 1972—; instr. in pathology Coll. Medicine, U. Cin., 1948-51, asst. prof. pathology, 1951-56; pres. med. staff Lima Meml. Hosp., 1968-70; chmn. adv. group Northwestern Ohio Regional Med. Program, 1970-71; mem. exec. com., bd. dirs., sec.-treas. Gt. Lakes Regional Quality Assurance Assn.; mem. certified lab. assts. com. Nat. Accrediting Agy. for Clin. Lab. Scis., 1974-76; chmn. bd. dirs. Ohio Region III PSRO, 1977-80; mem. Ohio Statewide Profl. Standards Rev. Council, 1980—. Bd. dirs. Allen County chpt. ARC, pres., 1972-73; bd. dirs. Allen County unit Am. Cancer Soc., pres., 1973-75, mem. exec. com. Ohio div., sec., 1979-80, v.p., 1980-81, pres., 1981-82; mem. exec. com. N.W. Ohio Cancer Network; bd. dirs. Lima Area C. of C., 1962-65, Lima Symphony Orch., 1963-69, United Fund of Greater Lima, 1970-72. Served to lt. (j.g.) M.C., USNR, 1946-48. Diplomate Am. Bd. Pathology. Mem. Lima and Allen County Acad. Medicine (sec.-treas. 1972-79), Ohio Med. Assn., AMA, Ohio Soc. Pathologists (pres. 1970-71), Am. Assn. Pathologists, Am. Soc. Clin. Pathologists, Coll. Am. Pathologists (rep. to ho. of dels.), Internat. Acad. Pathology, AAAS, Sigma Xi. Republican. Presbyterian. Clubs: Rotary (pres. 1964-65), Elks. Home: 1524 Fairway Dr Lima OH 45805 Office: Lima Meml Hosp Lima OH 45804

COLLOTON, JOHN WILLIAM, hosp. adminstr.; b. Mason City, Iowa, Feb. 20, 1931; B.S., Loras Coll.; M.S., U. Iowa. With U. Iowa Hosps. and Clinics, Iowa City, 1956—, dir. and asst. to univ. pres., 1971—; chmn. Nat. Council Teaching Hosps., Assn. Am. Med. Colls., 1979-80. Served with Armed Forces, 1953-55. Mem. Am., Iowa (dir., pres. 1977) hosp. assns. Contbr. articles to profl. jours. Office: U Iowa Hosps and Clinics Newton Rd Iowa City IA 52242

COLON, RONALD WARREN, advt. exec.; b. Elmwood Park, Ill., Dec. 10, 1931; s. Leroy Lewis and Sylvia Gwendolyn (De Prey) C.; B.A., Oberlin Coll., 1953; postgrad. U. Mich., 1955-56. Broadcast dir. Beeson-Reichert Advt., Toledo, 1959-63; writer-producer W.B. Doner Advt., Detroit, 1963-70; broadcast dir. Creative House Advt., Detroit, 1970-74; advt. mgr. Art Van Furniture Warren, Mich., 1975-78; pres. Colon & Assos., 1979-80; asst. to exec. v.p. N.Y. Carpet World, Southfield, Mich., 1980—; free-lance TV producer; speaker advt. conf. of rotogravure Sunday mags., 1976. Corp. rep. Council Christians and Jews, 1964-65; asst. chief, historian YMCA Indian Princesses, 1972-74. Served with Armed Forces, 1953-55. Recipient Retailer of Year award Brand Names Found., 1976. Mem. NAACP (council 1965-66), Adcraft Club Detroit. Home: 23840 Ithaca St Oak Park MI 48237 Office: NY Carpet World Southfield MI

COLONESE, JOSEPH SAL, architect, engr.; b. Cleve., Dec. 22, 1921; s. Vincent and Irene (Ross) C.; B.S., Kent State U., 1950; m. Jean Melick, Sept. 16, 1950; children—Mark Gary, Jo-Ean. Engr., architect, Union Carbide & Carbon, Cleve., 1950-51; engr., architect N.Y. Central R.R., Cleve., 1951-53; architect, engr. Chrolet Gen. Motors Corp., Cleve., 1953-65, sr. project engr., architect-engr. Gen. Motors World Hdqrs., Detroit, 1965-81; architect-engr. Arabian Am. Oil Co., Ras Tanura, Saudi Arabia, 1981—; past pres. Exec-U-World; engring. cons., 1974—. Active in Unreached Youth, 1955-75; chief engr. Soap Box Derby, 1955-65. Served with USN, 1942-45, U.S. Army, 1945-58. Recipient Best Design awards Mfrs. Assn., 1955-64. Mem. Detroit Engring. Soc. Author 3 books in field, including Plant Engineering Manual. Home: 4894 Haddington Dr Bloomfield Hills MI 48013 Office: ARAMCO Ras Tanura Saudi Arabia

COLOSIMO, ANTONIO, architect; b. Dayton, Ohio, Apr. 3, 1949; s. Joseph Antonio and Maria Antoinette (Guerri) C.; B.S., Ohio State U., 1974. Founder, pres., owner 3D/Group, Inc., Architects, Columbus, Ohio, 1978—, 3D/Constrn. Co., Inc., 1980—; lectr. Sch. Architecture, Sch. Engring. Ohio State U., 1978—. Registered architect, Ohio, Ky., Tenn., Ga. Mem. AIA, Architects Soc. Ohio, Constrn. Specifications Inst., Am. Assn. Cost Engrs., Internat. Council Shopping Centers, Nat. Council Architects Registration Bds. Club: Ohio State U. Pres.'s. Office: 6076 Busch Blvd Columbus OH 43229

COLSTON, FREDDIE CHARLES, polit. scientist; b. Gretna, Fla., Mar. 28, 1936; s. Henry Bill and Willie Mae (Taylor) C.; B.A., Morehouse Coll., 1959; M.A., Atlanta U., 1966; Ph.D., Ohio State U., 1972; m. Doris Marie Suggs, Mar. 13, 1976; 1 dau., Deirdre Charisse. Teaching asso. Ohio State U., 1968-71; asso. prof. polit. sci. So. U., Baton Rouge, La., 1972-73; asso. prof. polit. sci. and black studies U. Detroit, 1973-76; chmn. div. social scis. Dillard U., New Orleans, 1976-78; asst. prof. polit. sci. Delta Coll., University Center, Mich., 1978—. Mem. bd. mgmt. Northwestern br. YMCA Met. Detroit, 1976; mem. govt. subcom. Task Force 2000, City of Midland (Mich.), 1979. Internat. Studies summer fellow, 1967; So. Fellowships Fund fellow, 1968-71. Mem. Am. Polit. Sci. Assn., Midwest Polit. Sci. Assn., Nat. Conf. Black Polit. Scientists, Center for Study of the Presidency, Policy Studies Orgn., AAUP, Omega Psi Phi, Pi Sigma Alpha, Alpha Phi Gamma. Home: 1703 Wildwood St Midland MI 48640

COLTER, ELIZABETH ANN, nurse; b. Norristown, Pa., Jan. 26, 1931; d. Lewis J. and Nancy (Hardy) Coffey; diploma Sacred Heart Hosp., Allentown, Pa., 1951; Asso. Applied Sci., Meramec Community Coll., St. Louis, 1976; B.S. in Mgmt. Maryville Coll., St. Louis, 1979—; m. Norman C. Colter, July 4, 1952 (div. Sept. 1979); children—Gregory, Marianne. Nurse, Mercy Hosp., Jackson, Mich., 1954-56, Madigan Meml. Hosp., Houlton, Maine, 1956-59; staff nurse to asst. head nurse operating room Mercy Hosp., Jackson, 1959-69; staff nurse St. Lawrence Hosp., Lansing, Mich., 1969-70; nurse Barnes Hosp., St. Louis, 1970-80, head nurse operating room, 1971-74, asst. dir. operating room, 1974-80; dir. operating rooms U. Mich., Ann Arbor, 1980—. Mem. Assn. Operating Room Nurses (pres. St. Louis 1973-74), Phi Theta Kappa. Democrat. Roman Catholic. Home: 2124 Pauline Blvd Apt 307 Ann Arbor MI 48103 Office: U Mich Hospital 1405 E Ann St Ann Arbor MI 48109

COLVIN, GEORGE WILLIAM, elec. contracting co. exec.; b. Springfield, Ill., Nov. 2, 1931; s. Earl George and Mae Belle (Hall) C.; m. Mary Alice Schlitt, Feb. 24, 1962; children—George William, Julia Marie. Elec. apprentice Kelly Rachford Electric Co., Springfield, 1951-55; pres. Colvin Electric Co. Inc., Springfield, 1965—. Served with U.S. Army, 1952-53. Mem. Nat. Elec. Contractors Assn. Lutheran. Clubs: Masons, Shriners, Jesters. Home: 1314 N 6th St Springfield IL 62702 Office: 1935 S 10 1/2 St Springfield IL 62703

COLVIN, WAYNE SCOTT, personnel adminstr.; b. Boston, Apr. 2, 1951; s. Kenneth Crawford and Gem (Moore) C.; B.A., Ohio Wesleyan U., 1974; M.A., Ohio State U., 1976; m. Cynthia J. Chapman, Aug. 18, 1979. Dir. small group housing and Greek life Bowling Green (Ohio) State U., 1976—; exec. dir. Mid-Am. Interfrat. Council Assn., 1981—; pres. Ohio Epsilon Alumni Assn., ednl. found., 1974-80. Mem. Am. Personnel and Guidance Assn., Am. Coll. Personnel Assn., Nat. Assn. Student Personnel Adminstrs., Ohio Assn. Student Personnel Adminstrs., Nat. Assn. Frat. Advisors (nat. dir. 1977-79, chmn. profl. devel. com. 1980-81, v.p. 1981—), Sigma Phi Epsilon. Office: 425 Student Services Bldg Bowling Green State Univ Bowling Green OH 43403

COMAN, EDWARD JOHN, JR., financial-accounting exec.; b. Chgo., Dec. 7, 1939; s. Edward John and Agnes (Martin) C.; B.S., Walton Sch. Commerce, 1961; C.P.A., U. Ill., 1964; M.B.A., U. Chgo., 1969; m. Maxine M. Mikols, Dec. 29, 1962; children—Martin, Daniel, Timothy, Amy. Sr. accountant Glenn Ingram & Co., C.P.A.'s, Chgo., 1962-67; mgr. internal cons. Jewel Food Stores, Melrose Park, Ill., 1967-68, controller mfg. and distbn., 1968-69; pres. Edward J. Coman & Assos. - C.P.A.'s, 1969—. Mem. faculty U. Ill. at Circle Campus, 1970-72. Scoutmaster Boy Scouts Am., Glen Ellyn. Mem. Am. Inst. C.P.A.'s, Ill. Soc. C.P.A.'s, Am. Mgmt. Assn., Accounting Research Assn., Am. Accounting Assn. C. of C. Rotarian. Office: 1100 S Main St Lombard IL 60148

COMATY, JOSEPH EDWARD, JR., psycho-pharmacologist; b. Trenton, N.J., Dec. 31, 1949; s. Joseph Edward and Mary Jane (Mooney) C., Sr.; A.B., Villanova U., 1971, M.S., 1976; m. Claire Diane Advokat, July 8, 1978. Research scientist N.Y. State Research Inst. Neurochemistry and Drug Addiction, Ward's Island, 1973-74, research scientist dept. pharmacology, 1974-76; research asso. pharmacology Chgo. Med. Sch., 1976-78. Sigma Xi grantee, 1977-78. Mem. Am., Eastern, Ill. psychol. assns., AAAS, N.Y. Acad. Sci., Soc. Neurosci. Roman Catholic. Club: K.C. Contbr. numerous articles in field to profl. jours., chpts. to textbooks; author 24 abstracts. Home: 1471 Brown St Apt 1 Des Plaines IL 60016 Office: Ill State Psychiat Inst 1601 W Taylor St Chicago IL 60612

COMBS, CLARENCE MURPHY, anatomist; b. Louisville, Apr. 13, 1925; s. C.H. and Mary (Murphy) C.; A.B., Transylvania U., 1946; M.S., Northwestern U., 1948, Ph.D., 1950; m. Virginia Lee Thompson, Aug. 24, 1946 (div. Oct. 1964); children—Jeanne Marie, Stephen Murphy, Nancy Clare. Instr., W.Va. U. Med. Sch., 1948; Ward fellow Northwestern U. Med. Sch., 1946-50, faculty, 1950-66, prof. anatomy, 1963-66; prof., chmn. dept. anatomy Chgo. Med. Sch., 1966-76, acting dean Sch. Grad. and Postdoctoral Studies, 1975-76, prof. anatomy, 1966—; asso. prof. U. P.R. Med. Sch., 1958-60; chief sect. perinatal physiology Nat. Inst. Neurol. Disease and Blindness, San Juan, P.R., 1958-60, spl. cons., 1958. Spl. lectr. Ill. State Psychopathic Inst., 1954-58. USPHS Sr. Research fellow, 1959-61; recipient Research Career Devel. award USPHS, 1961-64; Outstanding Basic Sci. Prof. award Chgo. Med. Sch., 1970, 81, 82. Mem. Am. Assn. Anatomists, Soc. for Neurosci., Internat. Brain Research Orgn., AAUP, AAAS, Biol. Stain Commn., Sigma Xi. Editorial bd. Dorland's Med. Dictionary, 1965, revision of Parr's Med. Ency., 1976. Research, publs. on relationships between cerebellum and other parts of central and peripheral nervous systems, interconnections between cerebral cortex and diencephalon, gross structure of spinal cord segments, neurophysiol. regulation lingual movement. Home: 1706 Washington St Evanston IL 60202 Office: 3333 Green Bay Rd North Chicago IL 60064

COMBS, JANET CONSTANCE, social worker; b. Birmingham, Ala., Nov. 25, 1949; d. Eugene Columbus and Lillian Odessa (Bunn) Combs; B.A. in Sociology/Anthropology, Morgan State Coll., Balt., 1971; M.S.W. in Casework (Social Rehab. Services trainee), U. Utah, 1973; cert. John Marshall Law Sch., 1979. Clin. social worker Levinson Center for Mentally Handicapped Children, Chgo., 1974-75; VA West Side Med. Center, Chgo., 1975—; preceptor social work students U. Ill., Chgo., 1976-79. Active choir Bapt. Ch. Recipient choir award for outstanding performance Morgan State Coll., 1970-71. Mem. Nat. Assn. Social Workers, Ill. Continuity of Care Orgn. Baptist. Home: 505 N Lake Shore Dr Apt 807 Chicago IL 60611

COMBS, MAXINE CLARA, educator, real estate salesperson, artist; b. Belington, W.Va., May 13, 1922; d. Ernest Lee and Ocie Norma (Talbott) Turner; B.S. in Elem. Edn., Alderson Broaddus Coll., 1941; student U. Akron, 1967; m. Elwood Combs, July 26, 1941; children—Sheridan Lee, Sheron Maureen. Elem. tchr. Milroy Sch., Akron, Ohio, 1953-79; salesperson Wm. Kay Realty Co., Akron, 1957—. Recipient award Martha Holden Jennings Found., 1966; Valley Forge Freedom Found. award, 1978. Mem. NEA (life), Ohio Edn. Assn. (life), Internat. Reading Assn. (life), Am. Bus. Women's

Assn. (pres. 1979-80, Summit chpt. Woman of Year 1980), AAUW, Am. Golf Assn., Women's Internat. Bowling Congress, Kappa Kappa Iota (local pres. 1972, state pres. 1973, 74, nat. officer 1976). Presbyterian. Clubs: Coll. (Akron); Univ. Home: 652 Lakemont Ave Akron OH 44314

COMISKEY, JOHN ANTHONY, hosp. adminstr.; b. Chgo., Dec. 15, 1931; s. Edwin A. and Peggy C.; B.S. in Commerce, Loyola U., Chgo., 1957; M.H.A., U. Mich., 1963; m. Beverly Ann Olson, Mar. 27, 1954; children—Catherine, Stephen, Daniel, Jean, Marie. Resident, Rockford (Ill.) Meml. Hosp., 1962-63; asst. adminstr. St. Joseph Mercy Hosp., Ann Arbor, Mich., 1963-67, asso. adminstr., 1967-72, adminstr., 1972-74; pres. St. Michael Hosp., Inc., Milw., 1974—; instr. U. Mich., 1969-74; v.p. Met. Detroit Hosp. Services, Inc.; chmn. bd. Purchasing Council, Sisters of Mercy, Detroit Province; lectr. Wayne State U. Chmn. bd. dirs. CCD Program, St. Francis Ch.; pres. Health Care Council Franciscan Sisters of Wheaton, 1977—; also profl. artist. Served with USAF, 1951-55. Recipient Alumni Thesis award U. Mich., 1963. Fellow Am. Coll. Hosp. Adminstrs.; mem. Am. Hosp. Assn., Catholic Hosp. Assn., Wis. Hosp. Assn., Alumni Assn. U. Mich. (exec. bd.), Ozaukee Art Center Assn. Home: 3418 W Clubview Ct Mequon WI 53092 Office: 2400 W Villard Ave Milwaukee WI 53209

COMITO, RICHARD LE, pharmacist, state senator; b. Des Moines, Feb. 11, 1939; s. Frank M. and Rose Marie (Greco) C.; B.S., Drake U., 1961; m. Margaret Ann Miller, Feb. 6, 1960; children—Ellen Marie, Juanita Ann, Carmela Star, Rachelle, Richard Le. Owner, pharmacist Hurdle Drug Co., Waterloo, Iowa, 1966—; owner AC Meat Market, Knoxville, Iowa; mem. Iowa Senate, 1978—. Served with U.S. Navy, 1956. Mem. Blackhawk County Pharmacy Assn. (past pres.), Iowa Pharm. Assn., Am. Pharm. Assn., Pi Kappa Alpha. Republican. Roman Catholic. Clubs: K.C., Elks. Office: State Senate Office State Capitol Des Moines IA 50319*

COMPANIK, PAUL JAMES, psychologist; b. East Chicago, Ind., Sept. 5, 1946; s. Albert William and Ann May (Adamec) C.; B.A., Ind. U., N.W., 1969; M.S., U. Wis., Milw., 1972, Ph.D., 1977; m. Katherine Howell Kircher, May 17, 1975; children—Jennifer Toy, Christopher Paul. Head tchr. Southwell Inst., Olympia Fields, Ill., 1971-73; asso. prof. psychology S.W. Mo. State U., Springfield, 1974—; pvt. practice psychology, 1975—; psychol. cons. Springfield Epilepsy Found., 1976—, Greene County Bd. for Devel. Disabled, 1978—. Cons., bd. dirs. Mo. Region VI Devel. Disabilities Coordinating Com., 1975—. Mem. Am. Personnel and Guidance Assn., Midwest Psychol. Assn., Psi Chi. Contbr. psychol. articles to profl. jours. Home: 2769 W Vincent Springfield MO 65807 Office: S W Mo State U 901 S National Springfield MOO 65802

COMPTON, EDITH MARIE, educator; b. Summersville, Mo., Nov. 13, 1938; d. Elmer Ollie and Hildred P. (Smith) Hines; B.S. in Edn., Kans. State Tchrs. Coll., Pittsburg, 1960, M.S., 1963; Ed.S., Pittsburg State U., 1979; m. Jack A. Compton, June 9, 1957; children—Rachele Jean, Denise Ellen. Sec. grain div. Mo. Farmers Assn., Lamar, Mo., 1959-65; tchr. bus. Liberal (Mo.) public schs., 1960-67; mem. faculty Mo. So. State Coll., Joplin, 1967—, asst. prof. bus. adminstrn., 1972—; instr., seminar leader Ozark chpt. Profl. Secs. Internat., recipient certs. appreciation Secs. Internat., 1978. Mem. Nat. Bus. Edn. Assn., Am. Bus. Communications Assn., North Central Bus. Edn. Assn., Mo. Vocat. Assn., Mo. Tchrs. Assn., Delta Pi Epsilon. Mem. Christian Ch. Home: Box 116 Route 4 Lamar MO 64759 Office: Mo So State Coll Newman and Duquesne Rds Joplin MO 64801

COMSTOCK, LARRY DEWAYNE, steel co. exec.; b. Wichita, Kans., Aug. 26, 1951; s. Jerome D. and Betty Aldene (Wright) C.; B. in Mktg. Mgmt., Mo. So. State Coll., 1980. With Nat. Steel Service Center, Joplin, Mo., 1972—, gen. mgr., 1977—. Regiment comdr. United Way, Joplin. Served with U.S. Navy, 1971-72. Mem. Joplin Jaycees. Republican. Methodist. Club: Exchange. Developed real estate sales course for coll. Home: 2032 E 24th St Joplin MO 64801 Office: 727 Schifferdecker St Joplin MO 64801

CONARD, JOHN JOSEPH, state ofcl.; b. Coolidge, Kans., June 30, 1921; s. Joseph Harvey and Jessie May (Shanstrom) C.; B.A., U. Kans., 1943, M.A., 1947; D.Internat. Law, U. Paris, 1951; m. Virginia Louise Powell, Sept. 13, 1947; children—Joseph Harvey II (dec.), James Powell, Spencer Dean, John Joseph. Instr. polit. sci. U. Kans., 1946-49, asst. to chancellor, 1970-75; spl. asst. U.S. Mut. Security Agy., Paris, 1951-54; editor, pub. Kiowa County Signal, Greensburg, Kans., 1955-70; exec. officer Bd. Regents, State of Kans., Topeka, 1976—; dir. Haviland State Bank (Kans.). Mem. Kans. Ho. of Reps., 1959-69, mem. State Fin. Council, 1961-69, speaker of House, 1967-69; exec. asst. to gov. of Kans., 1975-76; trustee William Allen White Found., 1959—. Served to ensign USNR, 1943-45. Summerfield scholar, 1939-42; Rotary Found. fellow, 1949-50. Mem. VFW, Phi Beta Kappa, Sigma Delta Chi, Pi Sigma Alpha, Tau Kappa Epsilon. Republican. Congregationalist. Clubs: Masons; Rotary. Home: Route 1 Lecompton KS 66050 Office: 1416 Merchants Nat Bank Tower Topeka KS 66612*

CONBOY, JANET ELIZABETH, devel. disabilities mgr.; b. Birmingham, Ala., Apr. 8, 1947; d. Faris Lyndle and Thelma Maude (Bolin) C.; B.A., Birmingham-So. Coll., 1968; M.A., U. Mo., Columbia, 1971, M.Ed., 1972. Tchr. secondary English, Decatur (Ala.) City Schs., 1968-70; sch. counselor Rock Port (Mo.) Schs., 1972-77; successively mental health counselor, br. office mgr. Albany Regional Center Devel. Disabilities, Mo. Dept. Mental Health, Maryville, 1977-79, asst. center dir. for treatment, 1979-81, regional center dir., 1981—; cons. Regional Developmental Disabilities Adv. Council. Mem. Am. Assn. Mental Deficiency, Assn. Children with Learning Disabilities, Council Exceptional Children, Nat. Assn. Developmental Disabilities Mgrs., Nat. Assn. Retarded Citizens. Episcopalian. Home: 4204 N 31st St Apt C Saint Joseph MO 64506 Office: Rt 1 Albany MO 64402

CONDON, BETTY JEAN, occupational therapist; b. Akron, Ohio, May 20, 1931; d. Samuel D. and Virginia P. Stanson; B.Sc. in Occupational Therapy, Ohio State U., 1956; M.A. in Edn., Kent State U., 1963; m. Robert Edward Condon, Aug. 13, 1966; 1 son, Douglas Alan. Staff occupational therapist Highland View Hosp., Cleve., 1956-59; dir. occupational therapy Arthritis Found. and Multiple Sclerosis Soc., Akron, Ohio, 1959-61; sr. occupational therapist VA Hosp., Brecksville, Ohio, 1962-63; mem. faculty U. N.H., Durham, 1963-64, McGill U., Montreal, Que., Can., 1964-66; lectr. in occupational therapy Kings Coll. Hosp., London, Eng., 1967; spl. instr., tutor U. Liverpool, Eng., 1968; part-time staff Rehab. Center, Akron, 1971-73; cons. in edn. Western Res. Psychiat. Hosp., Northfield, Ohio, 1980-81; occupational therapy cons. and dir. occupational therapy Fallsview Psychiat. Hosp., Cuyahoga Falls, Ohio, 1976-81; part time instr. Cuyahoga Community Coll., Cleve., 1978-81. Mem. women's bd. Akron Gen. Med. Center, 1978—, bazaar com., 1981-82, pres. Hudson League for Service, 1981-82, chmn. fund raising, 1979-81, hospitality com., 1978-79. Rancho Los Amigos fellow, 1965; lic. occupational therapist, Ohio. Mem. Am. Occupational Therapy Assn. (cert.), Ohio Occupational Therapy Assn., Akron Occupational Therapy Assn., P.E.O. Sisterhood, Pi Gamma Mu, Kappa Delta. Episcopalian. Club: Establishment. Home: 1912 Stoney Hill Hudson OH 44236 Office: Western Reserve Psychiat Habilitation Center Northfield OH

CONDON, GAYLE DEAN, wholesale trade exec.; b. nr. Hampton, Nebr., Feb. 26, 1919; s. Walter S. and Emma E. (Kaeding) C.; student U. Nebr., 1938-41; m. Vivian Splain, June 1, 1941; children—Carolyn Gail (Mrs. Walden), William Dean. Mechanic, Chris Beck Tire & Rubber Co., Lincoln, Nebr., 1945-48; pres., owner Condon Auto Electric Co., Lincoln, 1949—. Cons. J.C. Distbg. Co. Served with USAAF, 1942-45. Decorated Bronze Star medal. Mem. United Automobile Assn., Automotive Service Industry Assn., United Comml. Travelers, Woodmen of the World, V.F.W., Am. Legion. Lutheran. Mason (32 deg., Shriner). Home: 4520 Vandorn St Lincoln NE 68506 Office: 1821 N St Lincoln NE 68508

CONFORTI, JAMES ANTHONY, podiatrist; b. N.Y.C., June 10, 1921; s. James Vincent and Bridget C.; student John Carroll U., 1939-42; D. Podiatric Medicine, Ohio Coll. Podiatric Medicine, 1944; m. Frances Jeanette Marconi, May 18, 1946; children—James Michael, Stephen Paul, Bruce Charles, Douglas Mark. Pvt. practice podiatry, Bedford, Ohio, 1945-65; dir. clinics Ohio Coll. Podiatric Medicine, Cleve., 1966-72, v.p. for planning, govtl. and community affairs, 1972-79, exec. v.p., 1970—, prof. community podiatry; staff podiatrist Hawthornden State Hosp., 1950-68. Active Health Plan Com., Met. Health Planning Corp.; mem. Commn. on Health Concerns, Fedn. for Community Planning, Cleve. Recipient disting. alumnus award Ohio Coll. Podiatric Medicine, 1976. Mem. Am. Podiatry Assn. (pres., 1964-65), Northeast Ohio Acad. Podiatric Medicine (pres. 1950-51), Ohio Podiatry Assn. (pres., 1953-54, spl. recognition award, 1965, man of year award, 1957), Alumni Assn. John Carroll U. of University Heights, Ohio (trustee), Foot health columnist Cleve. Plain Dealer, 1970-71. Home: 18214 Van Aken Blvd Shaker Heights OH 44122 Office: 10515 Carnegia Ave Cleveland OH 44106

CONFORTI, MICHAEL DOMINIC, JR., metal fabrication co. exec.; b. Torrington, Conn., Sept. 27, 1929; s. Michael Dominic and Elizabeth M. (Downey) C.; B.S. in Mech. Engring., U. Conn., 1952; m. Mary T. Stolicny, Feb. 26, 1949; children—Mary Beth (Mrs. David Hale), Donna (Mrs. David Moore), Michael Dominic III. Mech. engr. Torin Mfg. Co., Torrington, 1952-58, sales engr., 1958-60, regional tech. service mgr., Chgo., 1960-65; product mgr. Medart div. Jackes Evans Mfg. Co., St. Louis, 1965-67, gen. mgr., 1967-76, v.p., 1970-74, exec. v.p. Jackes Evans, 1974-76; pres. Medart, Inc., Rosemont, Ill., 1976-77; pres. Hydro Air Engring., Inc., St. Louis, 1977—. Served with AUS, 1946-48. Mem. ASME, Am. Soc. Heating, Refrigeration and Air Conditioning Engrs., Sons of Italy (pres. 1960-61). Home: 686 Applewood St Kirkwood MO 63122 Office: 1210 S Vandeventer St Saint Louis MO 63110

CONGER, CARL CLARENCE, farmer; b. Albia, Iowa, Apr. 17, 1907; s. Jacob Israel and Isabel C.; B.S. in Agr., Kans. State U., 1933; m. Mary Alice Tilton, May 6, 1933; children—Gordon O., David L., Carleen A. With Kans. Ext. Service, Kans. State U., 1934-44; county agrl. agt. Soil Conservation Service, U.S. Dept. Agr., 1945-66; owner, operator Triple C Farms, Iola, Kans., 1939—; dir. Mid regional Milk Advt. and Promotion Agy., 1973—; mem. Gov.'s Task Force Kans. Water Resources, 1977-78; chmn. Com. Kans. Farm Orgns., 1978; dir. Kans. Farm City Days, 1972—; mem. budget rev. com. Kans. State U., 1977; chmn. Allen County Planning Com., 1974-77. Recipient Disting. Service award Gov. Kans., 1978. Mem. Kans. Rural Water Assn. (pres. 1965-76, legis. dir. 1976-79), Soil Conservation Soc. Am., Holstein-Friesian Assn. Am., Kans. Farm Bur., Kans. Livestock Assn., Iola C. of C., Alpha Gamma Rho. Club: Rotary. Address: Triple C Farms Rural Route 2 Iola KS 66749

CONGER, DUANE HENRY, hydrologist; b. Oxford, Wis., Feb. 5, 1930; s. Henry Fern and Lena Emma (Groskreutz) C.; B.S. in Civil Engring., U. Wis., 1954; m. Joanne Rose Anderzon, Aug. 26, 1967; 1 son, Dennis Duane. Hydrologist, U.S. Geol. Survey, Madison, Wis., 1954, 1956—. Served with USAF, 1954-56. Registered profl. engr., Wis. Fellow ASCE. Home: 4321 Herrick Ln Madison WI 53711 Office: 1815 University Ave Madison WI 53706

CONKLIN, REBECCA ANNE, nurse adminstr.; b. Knoxville, Tenn., June 27, 1942; d. John William and Rebecca Ernest Coleman; R.N., U. Tenn. Hosp., 1963; children—Erin Leigh, Kelly Wynne. Office nurse for Donald E. Wallis, Knoxville, 1964-67; staff nurse West Acton (Mass.) Nursing Home, 1967-68; office nurse Dr. Freddie N. Pederson, Wayland, Mass., 1968-69; staff nurse Livonia Nursing Center (Mich.), 1976, nursing dir., 1976-77; nursing dir. Edgewater Convalescent Center, Detroit, 1977-78, Applewood Nursing Center, Woodhaven, Mich., 1978-80; owner, pres., chief exec. officer Nurses T.I.D., 1980—; mem. steering com. Downriver Area Hosp. Nursing Home; lectr. in field. Supt. nursery Ward Presbyn. Ch., Livonia, 1975-77; mem. adv. com., mem. spl. needs assessment com. Downriver Area Vocat. Consortium. Mem. Nat. League Nurses, Mich. League Nurses (long term patient care com.), Novi (Mich.) Jaycees Aux. (sec. 1971-72, outstanding new mem. 1972). Office: 18336 Huntley Wyandotte MI 48192

CONLEE, JAMES KENT, corp. exec.; b. White Hall, Ill., Jan. 2, 1934; s. Thomas Harrison and Gussie (DeHart) C.; B.S., Western Ill. U., 1956; postgrad. in organic chemistry Washington U., St. Louis, 1956-57; m. Joan Cardwell, June 28, 1953; children—Teresa, Mark, Michael, Andrew, John. Research chemist Alton Box Board Co. (Ill.), 1956-58, Universal Match Corp., Ferguson, Mo., 1958-61; process engr. and project mgr. Union Starch & Refining Co., Granite City, Ill., 1961-66; chief engr. milling div. Cargill, Inc. and Corn Starch & Syrup Co., Cedar Rapids, Iowa and Dayton, Ohio, 1966-73; pres., dir. Modern Process Design, Inc., Dayton, 1973—; v.p., dir. NEMCO, S.A. (Mexico City), Midwest Mfg., Inc. Registered profl. engr., Ohio. Mem. Nat., Ohio socs. profl. engrs., Order of Engrs., Am. Assn. Oil Chemists, Dayton Engrs., Full Gospel Businessmen's Fellowship Internat. (dir.). Mem. Ch. of God. Developed new methods for producing corn syrups and starches. Home: 6437 Westford Rd Dayton OH 45426 Office: 4977 Northcutt Pl PO Box 1400E Dayton OH 45414

CONLEY, HAROLD DEAN, state legislator; b. Paintsville, Ky., Apr. 15, 1946; s. Eucker and Melba (Martin) C.; B.A. in Communications, Ohio State U., 1969; m. Karen Elaine Habib, June 16, 1978. Substitute tchr. Columbus (Ohio) Sch. System, 1972; mktg. rep. Ohio Bell Telephone Co., Columbus, 1972-78; mem. Ohio Gen. Assembly, Columbus, 1979—. Bd. dirs. Sr. Companion Program of Catholic Social Services, 1977-79. Served as lt. (j.g.) USN, 1969-71. Winner Ohio State U. Intercollegiate debate championship, 1969. Mem. Internat. Assn. Bus. Communicators, Naval Res. Assn., Am. Legion, U.S. Chess Fedn., North Columbus Jr. C. of C. (dir. 1975). Home: 5553-E Chatford Dr Columbus OH 43227 Office: Ohio Ho of Reps Columbus OH 43215

CONLEY, PATRICIA ANN, home economist; b. Carroll County, Ga., Sept. 15, 1949; d. Willie and Minnie Ruth (Carten) C.; B.S. in Home Econs. Edn., Morris Brown Coll., 1972; M.A. in Home Econs. Edn., Tenn. State U., 1973, M.A. in Adult Edn., 1976; postgrad. U. Ark., 1974-75; Ph.D. in Adult and Occupational Edn., Kans. State U., 1979. Designer, interior decorator Conley's Originals, Atlanta, 1968; grad. tchr. clothing and textiles, Nashville, 1972; counselor residence center Tenn. State U., Nashville, 1973-76; research investigator Clothing Research Project, Pine Bluff, Ark., also instr. dept. home econs. U. Ark., 1974-78; community relations specialist Kans. State U. Midwest Sex and Race Desegregation Assistance Center; Manhattan, 19 - ; cons. to community groups on modeling tips and charm clinics. Recipient Sterling Silver award in home econs. S.W. High Sch., 1968, trophy in home econs., 1966; finalist World Stylemaker Sewing Contest, 1969; runner-up for title of Miss Black Atlanta, 1969. Mem. Assn. Coll. Profs. Textiles and Clothing, Am. Home Econs. Assn., Ark. Home Econs. Assn., Kans. Home Econs. Assn., Kappa Delta Pi, Delta Sigma Theta. Mem. Ch. of God in Christ. Home: V12 Jardine Terr Manhattan KS 66502 Office: Kans State U Manhattan KS 66502

CONLIN, JAMES CLYDE, real estate broker; b. Ft. Dodge, Iowa, Aug. 12, 1940; s. Clyde Elwin and Evelyn (Olson) C.; student Wentworth Mil. Acad., 1959-61; grad. Nat. Real Estate Inst.; m. Roxanne Elizabeth Barton, Mar. 21, 1964; children—Jacalyn Rae Alice, James Barton, Debra Ann, Douglas Klein. Agt., Cooper Realty Inc., Des Moines, 1966-68, Stanbrough Realty, Des Moines, 1968-72; v.p., sales mgr. Iowa Realty Comml. Brokers div. Iowa Realty Co., Inc., 1972-81; pres. The Conlin Co., Brokers; pres. Mid-Iowa Mgmt. Co., Inc.; mng. partner West Des Moines Med. Center Partnership, Adventureland Village, Stephens Bldg.; pres. Southbrook Green Inc., Indianola Village Ltd.; gen. partner Alpha Partners; pres. Mid-Iowa Mgmt. Co. Mem. Nat. Assn. Realtors, Nat. Inst. Real Estate Brokers, Realtors Nat. Mktg. Inst., Farm and Land Inst., Nat. Assn. Home Builders, Real Estate Securities and Syndication Inst., Polk/Des Moines Taxpayers Assn. (dir.), Greater Des Moines Bd. Realtors. Home: 6116 SW 48th Ave Des Moines IA 50321 Office: The Conlin Co Brokers 424 Stephens Bldg Des Moines IA 50309

CONLIN, ROXANNE BARTON, lawyer, former U.S. atty.; b. Huron, S.D., June 30, 1944; d. Marion William and Alyce (Muraine) Barton; B.A., Drake U., 1964, J.D., 1966, M.P.A., 1979; LL.D., U. Dubuque, 1975; m. James C. Conlin, Mar. 21, 1964; children—Jacalyn, James. Admitted to Iowa bar, 1966, practice in Des Moines, 1966-67; dep. indsl. commnr. Iowa Indsl. Commn., 1967-68; asst. atty. gen. Iowa dir. civil rights div., Des Moines, 1969-76; U.S. atty. So. Dist. Iowa, 1977-81; guest lectr. Midwest colls. and univs. Mem. Iowa Commn. on Status of Women, 1972-78; chmn. for Iowa, Women's Polit. Caucus, 1973-75, mem. nat. steering com., 1974-77; nat. committeewoman Iowa Young Democrats, 1965-66, state vice chmn., 1964-65, chmn. Polk County div., 1963-65; del. Iowa Dem. Conv., 1972. Reader's Digest scholar, 1962-64; Fisher Found. scholar, 1965-66; recipient Ser. award Chi Omega, 1964; award Iowa Civil Liberties Union, 1974; named Outstanding Young Woman Iowa, 1974; admitted to Iowa Women's Hall of Fame, 1981. Mem. Am., Iowa bar assns., Common Cause, Phi Beta Kappa, Alpha Lambda Delta. Office: 122 US Courthouse Des Moines IA 50309

CONN, ARTHUR LEONARD, chem. engr.; b. N.Y.C., Apr. 5, 1913; s. Nathan Avram and Jennie (Harmel) C.; S.B. in Chem. Engring., MIT, 1934, S.M. (Thorp fellow), 1935; postgrad. Inst. Mgmt. Northwestern U., 1959; m. Bernice Robbins, Sept. 2, 1937 (dec. May 1970); children—Robert Harmel, Elizabeth (Mrs. J. Geoffrey Magnus), Alex Paul; m. 2d, Irene Sekely Farkas, June 10, 1972. Chem. engr. Blaw-Knox Co., Pitts., 1936; exptl. chemist Alco products div. Am. Locomotive Co., Dunkirk, N.Y., 1936-39; with Standard Oil Co. (Ind.) and Amoco Oil Co. subs., 1939-78, various mgmt. positions including div. dir. pilot plants, div. dir. process design and econs., supt. tech. service, dir. process devel., dir. govt. contracts; pres. Arthur L. Conn & Assos., cons. firm in new energy and info. techs., Chgo., 1978—; cons. AEC, 1951-53, Office Coal Research, 1969-75, ERDA, 1975-77; mem. indsl. adv. com. U. Ill., Chgo., 1973-76, mem. com. on coal liquefaction Nat. Acad. Engring., 1975-77, chmn. com. on refining coal and shale liquids, 1977-80. Fellow AAAS (dir. 1970-73), Am. Inst. Chem. Engrs. (dir. 1966-71, v.p. 1969, pres. 1970, Founders award); mem. Am. Chem. Soc., Tau Beta Pi. Contbr. articles to profl. jours. Patentee in field. Home and office: 1469 E Park Pl Chicago IL 60637

CONN, EDGAR LEONARD, mfg. co. exec.; b. East Chicago, Ind., Apr. 10, 1918; s. Earl and Edna Alice (Welch) C.; B.S.M.E., Purdue U., 1941; m. Betty Lorraine Smyers, Aug. 16, 1941; children—Pamela J. Conn Chambers, Jack Earl. Mech. engr. Fairbanks-Morse & Co., Beloit, Wis., 1941-52; works mgr., 1952-55; mgr. mfg. South Wind div. Stewart-Warner Corp., Indpls., 1955-64, asst. gen. mgr., 1964, gen. mgr., 1964-67, v.p., gen. mgr. South Wind div., 1967—. Chmn., Central Ind. Safety Council, 1963, v.p., 1971; active Boy Scouts Am. Mem. Indpls. C. of C., Soc. Automotive Engrs. (dir. Milw. sect. 1953-55). Presbyterian (elder 1968-72, treas. bd. deacons 1962-68). Club: Kiwanis. Office: 1514 Drover St Indianapolis IN 46221

CONNELL, CHARLES RICHARD, agrl. co. exec.; b. Storm Lake, Iowa, July 13, 1930; s. Charles Joseph and Nora Ann (O'Boyle) C.; student Iowa State U., 1948-52; m. Louise Joanne Pierre, Aug. 2, 1954; children—Scott Richard, Laurie Louise, Kathleen Lisa. Dairy farmer, Storm Lake, 1955-63; with Farmland Industries, 1964—, dist. mgr., 1969-76, div. gen. mgr., Bloomington, Ill., 1976—. Chmn., Ill. Young Farmers Adv. Com., 1972, chmn. Ill. Coop. Coordinating Com., 1977. Served with U.S. Army, 1952-54. Mem. Iowa State U. Alumni Assn. Roman Catholic. Club: Bloomington Agr. Office: Farmland Industries 503 Four Seasons Rd Suite 3A Bloomington IL 61701

CONNELL, CONNIE ELIZABETH, airline corp. exec.; b. Augusta, Ga., July 21, 1943; d. Troy William and Mary Louise (Green) C.; B.A., Ohio State U., 1965. Flight attendant TWA, 1966-69, supr. flight attendants, 1969-72, dir. customer services, Chgo., 1972-74, supr. ticket counter, Chgo., 1974-75, mgr. public telephone sales (reservations), Chgo., 1975—; instr. Dale Carnegie, part-time 1968-69. Home: 516 Yosemite Ct Roselle IL 60172 Office: TWA 128 S State St Chicago IL 60603

CONNELLAN, THOMAS KENNEDY, JR., business exec.; b. Wyandotte, Mich., June 15, 1942; s. Thomas Kennedy and Florence Irene (Rhea) C.; B.B.A., U. Mich., 1964, M.B.A., 1966, Ph.D., 1973; m. Sandra J. Sherlock, Dec. 27, 1969; 1 dau., Avis Murphy. Program dir., research asso. Bur. Indsl. Relations, Grad. Sch. Bus. Adminstrn., U. Mich., 1966, editorial dir., div. mgmt. edn., 1968-73; pres. The Mgmt. Group, Inc., Ann Arbor, Mich., 1973—; dir. Standard Realty Corp; cons. Hudson's Bay Co., Kellogg-Salada Co., Clark Equipment Co., Gould Inc., Gen. Motors Corp., IBM, AT&T, Honeywell Ltd. Served with U.S. Army, 1966-68. Named one of leading organizational devel. thinkers Am. Mgmt. Assn. Mem. Acad. Mgmt. Author: The Brontosaurus Principle: A Manual for Corporate Survival, 1976; How to Improve Human Performance: Behaviorism in Business and Industry, 1978; How to Grow People Into Self-Starters, 1980. Office: 2200 Fuller Rd Suite 201 West Tower Ann Arbor MI 48105

CONNELLAN, WILLIAM WESLEY, univ. adminstr.; b. Detroit, Apr. 25, 1945; s. Thomas Kennedy and Florence Irene (Rhea) C.; B.A., Oakland U., 1967; M.A., U. Mich., 1971; postgrad. U. Americas, Mexico City, 1966; Ph.D., U. Mich., 1981; 1 son, Brian Patrick. Reporter, Detroit News, 1965-70; faculty Oakland U., Rochester, Mich., 1970—, adminstrv. asst. to pres., 1970-74, asst. to pres., dir. public relations, 1974-78, dir. public relations and info. services, 1978-81, asst. provost, 1981—, adj. asst. prof. communications arts, 1974—. Bd. dirs., v.p. Oakland County Tourist and Conv. Bur., 1975-79; Dem. precinct del., 1974-78; bd. dirs., mem. exec. com. Met. Detroit Conv. and Visitors Bur., 1980—; mem. Avon Twp. Bldg. Authority, 1980—; mem. Mich. Super Bowl com., 1979—. Mem. Am. Assn. Higher Edn., Council for Advancement and Support of Edn., Oakland U. Alumni Assn. Democrat. Presbyterian. Contbr. articles to profl. jours. Home: 236 Ann Maria St Rochester MI 48063 Office: 520 O'Dowd Hall Oakland Univ Rochester MI 48063

CONNELLY, JOHN PETER, physician, educator; b. Boston, May 12, 1926; s. Thomas J. and Bridget (Finnigan) C.; B.S., Boston Coll., 1951; M.D., Georgetown U., 1955; m. Martha T. Cronin, June 24, 1950; children—Maureen, Martha, Eileen, Marie, Cathleen, John, Michael. Intern, Royal Victoria Hosp., Montreal, Que., Can., 1955-56; jr. resident children's service Mass. Gen. Hosp., Boston, 1956-57, asst. resident, 1957-58, chief resident, 1964-68, co-dir., 1968-73, chief pediatric resident Mass. Gen. Hosp., sr. resident in pediatrics Johns Hopkins Hosp., Balt., 1957-58; practice medicine, specializing in pediatrics, Boston, 1958-73; asst. pediatrician children's service Mass. Gen. Hosp., Boston, 1962-64, chief children's ambulatory clinic, 1963-64, chief ambulatory div., 1964-69, pediatrician, 1967-73, med. dir. pediatric nurse practitioner program, 1964-73, exec. dir. Bunker Hill Health Center, 1967-73; vis. physician Lying-In div. Boston Hosp. for Women, 1961-69, cons. maternal and child health, 1968-69; teaching fellow pediatrics Harvard, 1957-58, 61-62, instr., 1962-64, asso. in pediatrics, 1964-67, asst. clin. prof. pediatrics, 1967-69, asso. prof. pediatrics, 1969-73; chief pediatrics Foster McGaw Hosp., Loyola U., Maywood, Ill., 1972-76, prof., chmn. dept. pediatrics Loyola U. Stritch Sch. Medicine, Maywood, 1972-76; sr. lectr. Sch. Social Adminstrn. and Policy, U. Chgo., 1979—; chmn. dept. health services devel. Am. Acad. Pediatrics, Evanston, Ill., 1976—; dep. asst. commr. health City of Boston, 1969-73; cons. Boston Children's Service Assn., 1966-73; cons. Nat. Center for Health Services Research and Devel., HEW, and Welfare, 1970-72; cons. Office Asst. Sec. Health and Sci. Affairs, HEW, 1971-73; civilian cons. pediatrics U.S. Naval Hosp., Chelsea, Mass. Dir. Mass. Dental Service Corp., 1971-73. Mem. Mass. Gov.'s Adv. Council, Comprehensive Health Planning Agy., 1971-73; mem. Harvard Center for Community Health and Med. Care, 1968-73; bd. dirs. Mass. Soc. Prevention Cruelty Children, 1967-73, Orphans of Italy, Inc., 1962-73; bd. dirs. Catholic Charitable Bur., Boston, 1968-70, cons., 1970-73; bd. adv. B.S. in Pediatrics program, U. Colo., Denver, 1969-70; mem. community resources com. Interinstl. Cardiovascular Center, Chgo., 1973-75; mem. Ill. Sudden Infant Death Syndrome Study Commn., 1975—. Served with AUS, 1944-45; to capt. M.C., USAF, 1958-61; rear-Admiral M.C., USNR. Decorated Knight Order of Malta. Diplomate Am. Bd. Pediatrics. Mem. Mass., Chgo. med. socs., New Eng., Chgo. pediatric socs., Am. Fedn. for Clin. Research, Am. Acad. Pediatrics (council on practice, chmn. liaison com. with Am. Nurses Assn. 1970-72), Assn. for Ambulatory Pediatric Services, Logan-Brophy Soc. Oral Surgery (hon.), Am., New Eng. diabetes assns., Royal Coll. Medicine (London), Irish and Am. Pediatric Soc. (sec.-treas. 1968-70, exec. council 1970—, pres. 1976-77), D.A.V., U.S. Naval Inst., Am. Legion, Alpha Omega Alpha. Clubs: Union Boat, Appalachian Mountain (Boston); Harvard; Chicago Athletic. Author: (with L. Berlow) You're Too Sweet—A Manual for Juvenile Diabetics, 1969; (with J.D. Stoeckle, R.M. Farrisey) The Nurse Clinician, 1974. Contbr. numerous articles in field to profl. jours., chpts. to books. Home: 147 Herrick Rd Riverside IL 60546 Office: 1801 Hinman Ave Evanston IL 60204

CONNELLY, RILEY WILLIAM, lawyer; b. Yankton, S.D., Oct. 1, 1926; s. Riley Cornelius and Florence Lucille (Thompson) C.; student Augustana Coll., 1946-47, N.D. State Coll., 1947-48; LL.B., Creighton U., 1952; m. Suzanne Marie Ament, Dec. 29, 1956; children—Todd R., Craig J., Cheryl Ann, JoAnne M. Admitted to S.D. bar, 1961; claims mgr. Security Gen. Ins. Co., Sioux Falls, S.D., 1955-62; partner Zimmer & Connelly, attys., Parker, S.D., 1962-67; prin. Riley W. Connelly, Atty., Parker, 1967—. Dep. states atty., Turner County, S.D., 1962-66, states atty., 1966-76; city atty., Parker, 1968-76; law trained magistrate 1st Circuit, 1976-80. Bd. dirs. Problems in Living Center, 1972—, pres., 1975-76. Served with USAAF, 1945. Mem. S.D. Bar Assn., S.D. States Attys. Assn. (pres. 1976-77), S.D. Claims Assn. (pres. 1961-62), Delta Theta Phi. Republican. Lutheran. Mason (Shriner). Home: Box 337 Parker SD 57053 Office: Madsen Bldg Parker SD 57053

CONNELLY, THOMAS JOSEPH, lawyer; b. Kansas City, Mo., Jan. 31, 1940; s. Edward Joseph and Mary Costello (McCallum) C.; A.B., U. Detroit, 1963, J.D., 1970; m. Barbara Marciniak, Aug. 1, 1964; children—Catherine, Jennifer. Admitted to Mich. bar, 1970; individual practice law, Plymouth, Mich., 1970-74; partner firm Connelly, Jacques, Ziem & Reilly, Walled Lake, Mich., 1974—; prosecutor, city atty., Wixom, Mich., Milford (Mich.) Village and Twp., Wolverine Lake, Mich., Lyon Twp., Mich., 1974—. Pres. parish council St. Mary's Ch.; mem. exec. com. Oakland County Republicans. Mem. Am. Judicature Soc., Am., Mich. (rep. assembly), Oakland County bar assns., Mich. Arabian Horse Assn., Milford C. of C., Blue Key. Home: 1635 Garner Rd Milford MI 48042 Office: 2410 S Commerce Rd Walled Lake MI 48088

CONNER, DONALD GENE, banker; b. Muncie, Ind., Aug. 7, 1936; s. Chalmer Amos and Alpha Mae (Corkwell) C.; student Bank Adminstrn. Inst., Am. Inst. Banking; m. Donna Sue Scott, Jan. 25, 1975; children—Bruce Allen, David Wayne. With Farmers State Bank, Mooreland, Ind., 1956-58; with Indsl. Trust & Savs. Bank, Muncie, 1958—, asst. cashier, 1962-65, auditor, 1965-76, comptroller, 1976—, v.p., 1981—; instr. bank adminstrn. various univs., 1971—. Pres. bd. dirs. Children's Home, 1972-78; bd. dirs. Yorktown (Ind.) Jr. Athletic Assn., 1972-73. Mem. Bank Adminstrn. Inst. (chartered bank auditor, pres. E. Central Ind. 1970-71, state dir. 1978-80), Inst. Internal Auditors (cert.; gov. Indpls. chpt. 1977-78), C. of C. Clubs: Lions (pres. Yorktown 1970-71, zone chmn. 1971-72), Elks. Home: Rural Route 2 Box 570B Yorktown IN 47396 Office: 220 Walnut Plaza Muncie IN 47305

CONNER, EUNICE EILEEN, writer; b. Germantown, Ohio, Sept. 13, 1929; d. George Washington and Mable Marguerite (Hoyt) Crickmore; student Newspaper Inst. Am., 1963-64, Ohio U., 1964-66, Miami Jacobs Bus. Coll., Dayton, Ohio, 1960; m. Charles Richard Conner, Dec. 20, 1975; stepchildren—Linda Johnson, Thomas Conner, Roger Conner, Mary Conner Jager. Telephone operator Germantown Ind. Telephone, 1948; clk. Dayton Police Dept., 1949, Merica Detective Agy., 1950; with News Tribune, Dayton, 1966-69; freelance reporter, 1966-69; clk., presiding judge Montgomery County Bd. Elections, 1970-72; sec. Ohio Dept. Liquor Control, Dayton, Ohio, 1972-80; freelance writer, 1980—. Sec., Montgomery County Democratic Women, 1969-70. Recipient hon. mention John C. Klein Meml. award Newspaper Inst. Am., 1964; Presdl. citation Nat. Amateur Press Assn., 1970. Mem. LWV (sec. 1965-68), Air Force Mus. Found. (charter). Clubs: Order Eastern Star, Ladies of Oriental Shrine (Dayton). Author books including: (poetry) Scenarios of Life, 1970; The Man, 1970; New Voices in American Poetry, 1980; (jour.) Haliksai, Vol. I, 1969, Vol. II, 1970; (cookbook) Peaches, Pine and Wine, 1971; (fiction) Star Buck, 1982. also articles. Home: 321 Ashwood Ave Dayton OH 45405

CONNER, JERRY DOUGLAS, advt. agy. exec.; b. Spring Valley, Ill., July 5, 1948; s. Leonard Jerome and Thelma (Baker) C.; B.S. in Fin., No. Ill. U., 1970; M.Internat. Mgmt., Am. Grad. Sch. Internat. Mgmt., 1973; m. Judith Massey Arnold, June 14, 1970; children—Jennifer, Carolyn. Account exec. Leo Burnett Co., Chgo., 1976-78, account supr., 1979-80, v.p., account supr., 1980—. Served with U.S. Army, 1970-72. Home: 9249 Avers St Evanston IL 60203 Office: Leo Burnett Co Prudential Plaza Chicago IL 60601

CONNER, LAURENCE MICHAEL, educator; b. Hannibal, Mo., July 11, 1939; s. Woodrow W. and Mildred M. (Morris) C.; B.S., Carthage Coll., 1961; M.S., Western Ill. U., 1967; Ph.D., So. Ill. U., 1973; m. Patricia Striegel, Nov. 23, 1961; children—Christopher, Daniel, Leslie. Dir. theatre Cardinal Stritch High Sch., Keokuk, Iowa, 1960-62; dir. theatre Keokuk High Sch., 1962-67; dir. theatre Keokuk Coll., 1965-67; chairperson div. fine arts and communications Marycrest Coll., Davenport, Iowa, 1967—; head drama program U. So. Calif., Idyllwild, 1976—; cons. in field. Mem. Ednl. Drama Assn., Am. Theatre Assn., Speech Communication Assn. Roman Catholic. Dir. numerous plays, musicals and operas. Home: 2503 Fairhaven Rd Davenport IA 52803 Office: 1607 W 12th St Davenport IA 52806 or PO Box 38 Idyllwild CA 92349

CONNER, WARREN J., market research co. mktg. exec.; b. Woodbury County, Iowa, June 2, 1938; s. Warren Thomas and Evelyn Francis (Petersen) C.; B.A., Morningside Coll., 1960; M.S.T., Drew U, 1963; m. Doris May Sadler, June 14, 1959 (dec.); children—Stephen Andrew, Sheryl Lynn. Ordained to ministry United Meth. Ch., 1963; pastor chs., Iowa, 1963-70; prodn. mgr. Majers Corp., Omaha, 1970-76, mktg. dir., 1976—. Democrat. Home: 2298 Country Club Ave Omaha NE 68104 Office: 10202 F St Omaha NE 68137

CONNOLLY, L. WILLIAM, lawyer; b. Gary, Ind., June 14, 1923; s. Leo W. and Lauretta E. (Feely) C.; student Miss. State U., City U N.Y.; Ph.B., Marquette U., 1948, J.D., 1951; m. Suzanne M. Irving, Sept. 2, 1950; children—Thomas A., Charles D., Alicia M., James J., Charlene, Susan, John J., Robert P. With Am. Automobile Ins. Co., Milw., 1951-52; admitted to Wis. bar, 1952, U.S. Supreme Ct. bar, 1967; practiced in Milw.; mem. firms Rummel & Connolly, 1952-55, Spence, Rummel & Connolly, 1955-59, Spence & Connolly, 1959-64. Trustee Village of Thiensville, Wis., 1957-61. Served with AUS, 1943-46. Fellow Internat. Acad. Lex et Scienta; mem. Am., Wis., Milw. bar assns., Am. Arbitration Assn. (nat. panel arbitrator 1973—), Am. Judicature Soc., Delta Theta Phi. Home: 830 Wood Dr Oconomowoc WI 53066 Office: 3106 W 80th St Milwaukee WI 53222

CONNON, CHARLES KENNETH, sch. fin. exec.; b. Mishawaka, Ind., July 30, 1934; s. William Alexander and Zella May (Smith) C.; student Southeastern Bible Coll., 1954-56, No. Bapt. Sem., 1956-58; m. Patricia Ann Phillips, Mar. 10, 1956; children—Charles Ronald, Kathleen Ann, David Phillips, James Christian, Kristin Jean. Insp., Western Electric Co., Chgo., 1956-58; meat cutter IGA and Pick'N Save, 1958-70; accountant, tax cons. Byrne & Co., Westmont, Ill., 1970-73; asst. controller Moody Bible Inst., Chgo., 1973-76, dir. acctg., 1976-78, controller, 1978—. Baptist. Home: Route 1 Box 164 Plainfield IL 60544 Office: 820 N La Salle St Chicago IL 60610

CONNOR, ARTHUR CHARLES, orthopaedic surgeon; b. Chgo., Mar. 1, 1920; s. Harry Duncan and Anna Elizabeth (Peet) C.; B.S., U. Chgo., 1941, M.D., 1943; M.Sc., Ohio State U., 1949; m. Selma Irene Renstrom, Apr. 15, 1945; children—Barbara, Arthur Michael, Eric, Catherine, Margaret, Dory, William. Intern, Hurley Hosp., Flint, Mich., 1944; resident in surgery Ohio State U., Columbus, 1947-52; practice medicine specializing in orthopaedic surgery; mem. staffs Palos Community Hosp., St. James Hosp.; prof. orthopaedic surgery Loyola U., Chgo., 1970—; adj. prof. Chgo. Osteopathic Hosp., 1980—. Served to lt. M.C., USNR, 1944-46, 52-53. Diplomate Am. Bd. Orthopaedic Surgery. Fellow A.C.S.; mem. World Med. Assn. (U.S. com.), AMA, Am. Acad. Orthopaedic Surgery, Internat. Arthroscopy Assn., Pan Pacific Surg. Soc. Roman Catholic. Club: Lake Michigan Yacht. Office: 6450 W College Dr Palos Heights IL 60463

CONNOR, JAMES RUSSELL, automotive ofcl.; b. Lima, Ohio, Oct. 30, 1940; s. Russell Thurman and Esther Mae (Rowe) C.; student Bowling Green State U., 1969-71; B.S. in Bus., Defiance Coll., 1972; M.B.A. in Prodn. Mgmt., Ind. U., 1974; m. Beryl Anna Dixon, Aug. 25, 1973; children—Steven Eric, Jeffrey Allen. Corp. responsibility mgr. Cummins Engine Co., Columbus, Ind., 1975-76; gen. supr. Ford Motor Co., Lima, Ohio, 1976-78, shift supt., 1978-79, area supt., 1979-80, quality control supt., 1980—. Chmn. Urban Bus. Assn., 1980—; mem. Human Rights Commn., 1976; minority placement advisor, 1973-74; active Jr. Achievement, 1976. Served with USMC, 1961-66. Consortium Grad. Study in Mgmt. fellow, 1973-74; Ednl. Opportunity fellow, 1974. Mem. Am. Soc. Quality Control, Am. Mgmt. Assn., Assn. M.B.A. Execs., Beta Gamma Sigma. Baptist. Home: 301 E Parkwood St Sidney OH 45365 Office: Bible Rd and Sugar St Lima OH 45802

CONNOR, JOANN, desegregation specialist; b. Pitts., May 19, 1947; d. Charles Melvin Connor and Millicent (Reed) Jackson; B.A. in Music Theory, Oakwood Coll., 1970; B.M., Mich. State U., 1973, M.A. in Curriculum, 1973, M.A. Edn. Adminstrn., 1978. Music tchr. Beecher Pub. Schs., Flint, Mich., 1970-71; music therapist Little City Found., Palatine, Ill., 1972-73; adv. specialist in sex desegregation Lansing (Mich.) Sch. Dist., 1975-76, Emergency Sch. Aid Act dir., 1976-80; exec. dir. Ronnoc Ednl. Cons., 1980—. Ingham County Equal Opportunity commr., 1977-79. Recipient Certificate of Recognition, Internat. Yr. of the Child, Lansing Schs. and Community Edn., 1979; Emergency Sch. Aid Act grantee, 1976-80; Title IV grantee, 1977-81. Mem. Equal Ednl. Opportunity Network, Mich. Assn. Black Sch. Educators, Nat. Com. Sch. Desegregation, Nat. Assn. Affirmative Action Officers, Am. Assn. Affirmative Action Officers, Mich. Assn. State and Fed. Program Officers, Mich. Out-State Chpt. of Human Rights Workers, NAACP. Office: 514 S Chestnut Suite 1 Lansing MI 48933

CONNOR, JOHN THORP, II, accountant; b. Omaha, Feb. 6, 1944; s. John Thorp and Margaret M. (Hensley) C.; B.S., U. Nebr., 1966, J.D., 1969; m. Janice Kay Blazek, Aug. 27, 1967; children—Meredith Ann, John Thorp, III. Admitted to Nebr. bar, 1969, Kans. bar, 1970; tax supr. Touche Ross & Co., Kansas City, Mo., 1969-72, dir. tax ops., partner, Omaha, 1972-77, asso. partner-in-charge, 1977-78, partner-in-charge, 1978—. Bd. dirs. Children's Hosp., Jr. Achievement, Omaha Indsl. Found., Brounell-Talbot Sch.; chmn. bd. dirs. Econ. Devel. Council. C.P.A., Nebr., Iowa, Kans., La., Mo. Mem. Am. Inst. C.P.A., Nebr. Soc. C.P.A.'s (pres.), Nebr. Diplomats, Nebr. Bar Assn., Am. Bar Assn., Omaha C. of C. (v.p., dir.). Home: 711 N 56 St Omaha NE 68132 Office: 2000 First National Center Omaha NE 68102

CONNOR, LARRY JEAN, agrl. economist, educator; b. North Platte, Nebr., Nov. 7, 1934; s. John and Ida B. Connor; B.S., U. Nebr., 1956; M.S., Okla. State U., 1960, Ph.D., 1964; m. Dee Ann Stephens, May 22, 1965; children—Noelle, Kevin. Agrl. economist U.S. Dept. Agr., 1956-61, 64-66; research asst. Okla. State U., 1961-64; prof. agrl. econs. Mich. State U., East Lansing, 1966—, chmn. dept. agrl. econs., 1978—. Served as 2d lt. U.S. Army, 1957. Mem. Internat. Assn. Agrl. Economists, Am. Agrl. Econs. Assn., Mich. Assn. Farm Mgrs. and Rural Appraisers, Sigma Xi, Alpha Zeta, Pi Gamma Mu. Lutheran. Contbr. numerous articles on agrl. econs. to profl. jours.; contbr. chpts. to books on agrl. econs. Home: 3870 Sheldrake St Okemos MI 48864 Office: Dept of Agrl Econs Mich State Univ East Lansing MI 48824

CONNOR, LAWRENCE STANTON, journalist, editor; b. Indpls., Aug. 31, 1925; s. Nicholas John and Agnes (Peelle) C.; student Butler U., summers, 1943, 47, U. Ky., 1943; Miss. State U., 1944; A.B., U. Notre Dame, 1949; postgrad. Fordham U., 1949; m. Patricia Jean Alandt, Nov. 3, 1956; children—Carolyn, Julia, Lawrence Stanton, Maureen, Janet, Michael Connor. With Indpls. Star, 1949—, chief copy desk, news editor, city editor, 1963-79, editor and mng. editor, 1979—. Bd. dirs. Indpls. chpt. ARC, Cath. Social Services. Served with USAAF, 1943-46. Mem. Am. Soc. Newspaper Editors, A.P. Mng. Editors Assn., Roman Catholic. Club: Indpls. Press. Office: Indianapolis Star 307 N Pennsylvania St Indianapolis IN 46206

CONNORS, DORSEY (MRS. JOHN E. FORBES), TV and radio commentator, newspaper columnist; b. Chgo.; d. William J. and Sara (MacLean) Connors; B.A. cum laude, U. Ill.; m. John E. Forbes; 1 dau., Stephanie. Appeared on Personality Profiles, WGN-TV, Chgo., 1948, Dorsey Connors Show, WMAQ-TV, Chgo., 1949-58, 61-63, Armchair Travels, WMAQ-TV, 1952-55, Home Show, NBC, 1954-57, Haute Couture Fashion Openings, NBC, Paris, France, 1954, 58, Dorsey Connors program, WGN, 1958-61, Tempo Nine, WGN-TV, 1961, Society in Chgo., WMAQ-TV, 1964; floor reporter WGN-TV, Republican Conv., Chgo., 1960, Democratic Conv., Los Angeles, 1960; writer column Hi! I'm Dorsey Connors, Chgo. Sun Times, 1965—. Founder Ill. Epilepsy League; mem. exec. bd. Chgo. Beautiful Com.; mem. woman's bd. Ill. Children's Home and Aid Soc. Mem. AFTRA, Screen Actor's Guild, Nat. Acad. TV Arts and Scis., Soc. Midland Authors, Chgo. Hist. Soc., Chi Omega. Author: Gadgets Galore, 1953; Save Time, Save Money, Save Yourself, 1972. Address: care Chgo Sun Times 401 N Wabash Chicago IL 60611

CONNORS, JOHN MICHAEL, actuarial cons. exec.; b. Chgo., Feb. 5, 1932; s. John Thomas and Mary Agnes (Moxley) C.; B.S., Ind. U., 1954; m. Martina Ann McMullen, Dec. 5, 1953; children—Shawn Michael, Bret Patrick, Kelly Ann, Megan Kathleen. Tchr., coach St. Patrick's High Sch., Chgo., 1954-56; sales rep. Blue Cross/Blue Shield, Chgo., 1956-58; sales rep. group div. Mass. Mut. Life Ins. Co., Battle Creek, Mich., 1958-64, life ins. agt. John E. Bromley gen. agy., Battle Creek, 1964-65; founder, pres., gen. mgr. Pension & Group Services, Inc., Kalamazoo, 1965—; dir. Indsl. State Bank and Trust Co., Kalamazoo, Fed. Disclosure Reporting, Inc., Kalamazoo, Profl. Sales Assn., Inc., Kalamazoo. Spl. fund raising com. Kalamazoo Coll. Mem. Nat. Assn. Accountants, Internat. Found. Employee Benefits, Soc. Profl. Benefit Adminstrs., Am. Soc. Pension Actuaries, Ind. U. Alumni Assn., Nat. Wrestling Coaches Assn., Delta Sigma Pi. Roman Catholic. Clubs: Kalamazoo Country, Gull Lake Country, Ind. U. I Men's. Author manuals in field, 1978. Home: 1016 Cohasset Ln Kalamazoo MI 49008 Office: 161 E Michigan Haymarket Bldg Kalamazoo MI 49007

CONOMY, JOHN PAUL, physician; b. Cleve., July 31, 1938; s. John James and Marie Elizabeth (Bimbea) C.; B.S., John Carroll U., 1960; M.D., St. Louis U., 1964; m. Jeanette Melchior, Oct. 19, 1963; children—John, Lisa, Christopher. Intern, St. Louis U. Hosps., 1964; resident in neurology Univ. Hosps. Cleve., 1965-68; fellow in neuropathology Case Western Res. U., 1968; postdoctoral research fellow U. Pa., 1970-71; clin. instr. neurology U. Tex. Southwestern Med. Sch., 1971-72, also sr. staff neurologist Scott and White Clinic & Hosp.; asst. prof. neurology Case Western Res. U., 1972-75; practice medicine specializing in neurology; mem. staff Cleve. Met. Gen. Hosp., Univ. Hosps. Cleve., Cleve. VA Hosp.; chmn. dept. neurology Cleve. Clinic Found., 1975—; asso. prof. Case Western Res. U., 1976—; health care systems cons. Served with USAF, 1968-70. Recipient grants Mary B. Lee Fund, Reinberger Found., NIH, Mellen Fund. Fellow A.C.P., Am. Acad. Neurology (chmn. membership com., chmn. ethics com., asst. sec.-treas.); mem. Am. Neurol. Assn. (chmn. public relations 1980—), Soc. Neurosci. (pres. Cleve.), AMA (vice chmn. sect. neurology), Am. Assn. History Medicine, Assn. Research in Nervous and Mental Diseases, Assn. Univ. Profs. Neurology, Council Med. Spltys. Socs. (chmn. health care delivery), Alpha Omega Alpha. Roman Catholic. Contbr. articles to profl. jours., chpts. to books.

CONRAD, CARL EUGENE, mktg., advt. co. exec.; b. Wilmington, Del., Nov. 17, 1931; s. Carl and Susie Delina (Troyer) C.; B.S., Ohio U., 1957, M.S., 1958; m. J. Elaine Ferguson, July 11, 1954; children—Leslie Sue, Carl Kurtis. Public relations dir. Muskingum Coll., New Concord, Ohio, 1958-62; adminstrv. asst. Ohio State U., Columbus, 1962-64; v.p. J.W. Tolly & Assos., Columbus, 1964-68; pres. Carl E. Conrad & Assos., Columbus, 1968—; pres., chmn. bd. Conrad, Phillips & Vutech, Columbus, 1980—. Served with U.S. Army, 1952-54. Mem. Nat. Assn. for Hosp. Devel., Am. Coll. Public Relations Assn., Columbus Advt. Fedn., Ohio Hosp. Assn., Columbus C. of C., Sigma Delta Chi, Kappa Tau Alpha. Lutheran. Black Belt, Taekwondo. Home: 385 Jackson St Columbus OH 43206

CONRAD, JEROME CHARLES, facility mgmt., planning and design cons.; b. Chgo., Mar. 20, 1947; s. William George and Patricia Theresa (Gieser) C.; B.F.A., No. Ill. U., 1976; A.A., Chgo. City Coll., 1973; m. Judith B. Brudek, Dec. 11, 1971; children—Matthew Jerome, Daneen Judith. Sr. acctg. analyst Libby McNeil & Libby,

Chgo., 1967-73; prin., owner JC Designs, Sycamore, Ill., 1974-76; asst. to chief exec. officer EMCO, Chgo., 1976; asso. partner Fulton & Partners, Toledo, 1977-80, v.p., gen. mgr. facility mgmt. and planning div., 1980—; project dir. Environ. Design Inst., Purdue U., West Lafayette, Ind., 1980—; guest lectr. design, bus. and restaurant design; instr. upholstered furniture design; space planning cons. Active, Ohio Arts Council Environ. Arts Panel, Toledo Zool. Soc., Toledo Mus. Art; mem. environ. design program adv. council Purdue U. Served with USNR, 1968-70. Cert. load master; lic. sr. parachute rigger FAA. Mem. Nat. Trust Hist. Preservation, Inst. Bus. Designers, Indsl. Design Soc. Am., Constrn. Specifications Inst., Orgn. Faculty Mgrs. and Planners, Open Landscape Users Group, Phi Theta Kappa. Republican. Club: Rotary. Home: 2055 South Ave Toledo OH 43609 Office: 505 Jefferson Ave Toledo OH 43604

CONRAD, JOHN JOSEPH, editor; b. Red Bud, Ill., Mar. 3, 1950; s. Roy Peter and Georganne Louise (Ries) C.; B.A. in Mass Communications, So. Ill. U., Edwardsville, 1974; 1 dau., Sarah. With Clarion Printing Co., Columbia, Ill., 1969—, news editor, 1971-75, partner, 1975—, editor publs. Columbia Star and Monroe County Clarion, 1975—, sec.-treas., 1975—; v.p. Conrad Press, Ltd. Founding mem. Columbia Bus. Dist. Devel. and Redevel. Commn.; pres. bd. dirs. Monroe County (Ill.) Mental Health Services, Inc. Served with USAR, 1969-75. Recipient Am. Press certificate of appreciation U.S. Jaycees, 1976, 77. Mem. So. Ill. Editorial Assn. (dir., sec.-treas. 1978-79, 1st v.p. 1980-81, pres. 1981-82), Ill. Press Assn., Nat. Newspaper Assn., Columbia Gymnastic Assn., Columbia C. of C. (dir., treas.), Am. Legion. Roman Catholic. Clubs: Lions (Columbia); K.C. Home: Route 2 Box 6 Gilmore Lakes Columbia IL 62236 Office: 212 W Locust St Columbia IL 62236

CONRAD, JOHN R., electric co. exec.; b. Chgo., Dec. 3, 1915; s. Nicholas J. and Irene (Billups) C.; student Yale U., 1934-36; B.S., U. Chgo., 1937; postgrad. Boeing Sch. Aeros., 1938; m. Arlys M. Streitmatter, Apr. 11, 1958; children by previous marriage—Lynn, Catherine (Mrs. Bruce Anglin), Joanne. Properties mgr. engring. and mfg. divs. Douglas Aircraft Co., 1938-45; v.p. S&C Electric Co., Chgo., 1945-52, pres., 1952—, chmn. bd. S&C Electric Can. Ltd.; dir. SyC-Selmec, S.A. Trustee, Ill. Inst. Tech.; bd. overseers Ill. Inst. Tech. Armour Coll. Engring.; mem. Citizens Adv. Bd., U. Chgo.; mem. City of Chgo. Hazardous Materials Cons. Com.; mem. City of Chgo. Air Quality Adv. Council; trustee and governing mem. Orchestral Assn.; mem. pres.'s council Mus. Sci. and Industry. Mem. IEEE. Clubs: Mid-Am., Chgo. Yacht. Office: 6601 N Ridge Blvd Chicago IL 60626

CONRAD, KARL EDWARD, educator; b. Lancaster, Ohio, Aug. 13, 1948; s. Ned Salem and Mary Vivian (Fox) C.; A.S., Hocking Tech. Coll., 1976; teaching cert. Ohio State U., 1980; m. Dianna Lynn Johnson, Jan. 23, 1973; 1 son, Ryan Patrick. Tchr. graphic arts Paul C. Hayes Tech. Sch., Grove City, Ohio, 1979—; owner, mgr. Conradis Printing Service, Lancaster, 1977-79; mgr. Kwik Kopy, Columbus, 1976-77. Served with AUS, 1968-70. Mem. Vocat. and Indsl. Clubs Am. Republican. Methodist. Club: Moose. Home: 901 Reese Ave Lancaster OH 43130 Office: 4436 Haughn Rd Grove City OH 43130

CONRAD, LORETTA JANE, sch. prin.; b. Wooster, Ohio, Aug. 9, 1934; d. Donald William and Celia Irene (Smith) C.; B.Mus.Edn. cum laude, Coll. of Wooster, 1956; M.Mus.Edn., U. Colo., 1969; postgrad. cert. supervision/adminstrn. (Univ. scholar), John Carroll U., 1978. Tchr., Avon Lake (Ohio) public schs., 1956-61, Dept. Def., Europe and Far East, 1961-64, Bay Village (Ohio) Bd. Edn., 1964-73, Elyria (Ohio) public schs., 1973-78; asst. prin. Bay Village Bd. Edn., Bay High Sch., 1978—; music clinician, adjudictor; pvt. tchr. piano; accompanist, dir. Ch. Choir, Luth. Ch., 1966-80. Presser scholar, 1955-56; Annie Webb Blanton scholar, Delta Kappa Gamma, 1968. Mem. Ohio Assn. Secondary Sch. Prins., Nat. Assn. Secondary Sch. Prins., Assn. Secondary Curriculum Devel., Phi Delta Kappa, Delta Kappa Gamma. Democrat. Lutheran. Club: Quota. Home: 1650 Cedarwood St Westlake OH 44145 Office: 29230 Wolf Rd Bay Village OH 44140

CONRAD, MARY MAGDALENE, lawyer; b. Chgo., Oct. 12, 1944; d. James Edward and Magdalen Conrad; B.S.C. summa cum laude, DePaul U., 1968, J.D. cum laude (Lex Legio scholar), 1970; LL.M., U. Ill., 1973. Admitted to Ill. bar, 1970; individual practice law, Chgo., 1970-71; law clk., legal analyst to Chief Judge of Circuit Ct. of Cook County, Chgo., 1972-73; sr. counsel Atty. Registration and Disciplinary Commn., Supreme Ct. Ill., Chgo., 1973—; mem. faculty Loyola U. Sch. Law, 1976-77, Am. Bar Assn. Disciplinary Workshop, 1978, 80, DePaul U. Sch. Law, 1979—; mem. rev. bd. Multistate Profl. Responsibility Exam., Nat. Conf. Bar Examiners. Asso. Rehab. Inst. Chgo., 1977—. Recipient Arthur Young Accounting award, 1967; Maurice Weigle award Chgo. Bar Found., 1979; NDEA fellow, 1971. Mem. Nat. Orgn. Bar Counsel, Ill. Bar Assn., Women's Bar Assn., Ill. Appellate Lawyers Assn., Lex Legio of DePaul U., Delta Zeta. Office: 203 N Wabash Ave Chicago IL 60601

CONRAD, WILLIAM RAPHAEL, JR., mgmt. cons.; b. Pitts., Mar. 26, 1932; s. William Raphael and Esther Feilbach (Kamerer) C.; B.A., Hiram Coll., 1954; M.S., George Williams Coll., 1960; m. Helen A. Semenek, May 28, 1966. Youth work sec. Cleve. YMCA, 1957-59; with Chgo. Boys' Clubs, 1959-75, asst. dir. devel., 1969-75; chmn. bd., pres. IVO Press, Inc., Chgo., 1978—; pres. Inst. for Vol. Orgns., Chgo., 1975—; adj. asst. prof. George Williams Coll., 1974—. Mem. Downers Grove (Ill.) Sch. Bd., 1973-75; trustee Hiram (Ohio) Coll., 1979—. Served with U.S. Army, 1954-56. Mem. Am. Soc. Tng. and Devel., Assn. Voluntary Action Scholars, Social Welfare Council, World Future Soc., Hiram Coll. Alumni Assn. (pres. 1979-79), George William Coll. Alumni Council. Author works in field. Home: 4800 Prince Downers Grove IL 60515 Office: Suite A1703 175 W Jackson Blvd Chicago IL 60604

CONRATH, RICHARD CRANMER, educator, clergyman; b. Cambridge, Ohio, June 23, 1937; s. Carl W. and Marguerite (Doughty) C.; B.A., St. John Vianney Coll., 1959; B.S. in Edn., Coll. of Steubenville, 1965; Licentiae Sacrae Theologiae, Catholic U. of Am., 1963; Ed.M., Kent State U., 1970, Ph.D., 1975; m. Jan. 21, 1967 (div. Feb. 1975); children—Christine Marie, Carrie Margaret, Cathleen Mary; m. 2d, Karyn Nelson, June 6, 1981. Ordained priest Roman Catholic Ch., 1963, later laicized; asst. pastor St. Mary's Ch., Shadyside, Ohio, 1963-65, Ohio U., Athens, 1965-66; tchr. English Allen East High Sch., Lafayette, Ohio, 1966-67, Mentor (Ohio) pub. schs., 1967-69; instr. philosophy Lakeland Community Coll., Mentor, 1969-72, asst. prof. philosophy 1972-74, asso. prof., 1974-77, prof., 1977—, chmn. depts. of philosophy, music, humanities, 1979—; pres. Conrath Assos., 1978—; tennis coach, 1975-79. Bd. dirs. Lake County Youth Fedn., 1969-71. Am. Studies fellow, 1967. Mem. Ohio, Tri-State philos. assns., Nat. Orgn. on Legal Problems of Edn., Am. Classical League, Ohio Assn. of Two-Year Colls. (dir. 1970-73), Phi Delta Kappa. Democrat. K.C. Contbr. poetry and articles to various publs. Home: 1932 Bromton Dr Lyndhurst OH 44124 Office: Lakeland Community College Mentor OH 44060

CONROY, ROBERT JOSEPH, mgmt. info. systems dir.; b. Toledo, May 6, 1931; s. Martin John and Ethelyn Nina (McGill) C.; B.B.A. with honors, U. Toledo, 1955; grad. Ind. Exec. Program; m. Wanda J. Conroy; 1 dau., Cathleen Ann Conroy Shirley. Orgn. and methods examiner Army Ordnance, Rossford Ordnance Depot, 1955-57, computer programmer, 1957-59; with Owens Corning Fiberglas, Inc., Toledo, 1959—, beginning as computer programmer, successively sr. programmer, EDP methods supr., systems and procedures mgr., mgr. computer systems, dir. corporate data processing services, 1973-76, dir. mgmt. info. systems planning and control, 1976-79, dir. corp. mgmt. info. systems ops. and support, 1979-81, dir. corp. computer and telecommunication services, 1981—; v.p. Gourmet Curiosities, Inc., Toledo; data processing adv. com. U. Toledo Community and Tech. Coll.; former lectr. Am. Mgmt. Assn.; past speaker RCA Users Assn. Served with USNR, 1951-53; Korea. Cert. data processor. Mem. Data Processing Mgmt. Assn., Internat. Communicators Assn., Am. Legion, U. Toledo Alumni Assn. (trustee), Toledo Mus. Art, Toledo Humane Soc., Toledo Zool. Soc., Toledo Orch. Assn. Republican. Episcopalian. Club: Toledo. Reviewer quar. publ. Soc. Mgmt. Info. Systems. Home: 2704-2 Westcastle Dr Toledo OH 43615 Office: Fiberglas Tower Toledo OH 43659

CONROY, THOMAS HYDE, lawyer; b. Beloit, Kans., Feb. 6, 1922; s. Thomas Emmett and Ida Ruth (Hyde) C.; A.B., U. Kans., 1945, LL.B., 1949; m. Helen Regina Supple, Nov. 27, 1952; children—Thomas William, Sheila Anne, Regina Marie, Joseph Patrick. Admitted to Kans. bar, 1949; asso. Ralph H. Noah, Beloit, 1949-52; city atty., City of Beloit, 1953-55; county atty., County of Mitchell, 1957-65; partner Hamilton & Conroy, 1965; practice, 1965—; city atty., Beloit, 1967-81; owner, developer Conroy Place, 1965—; dir. First Nat. Bank, Beloit. Bd. dirs. Mitchell County Hist. Soc., Inc., 1972—, 1st v.p., 1972-75, pres., 1975-77; trustee Mitchell County Hosp., 1965—, pres., 1965-73. Mem. Am. Legion, Phi Kappa, Phi Delta Phi. K.C. (state adv. 1958-59), Elk, Lion. Home: 721 E 3d St Beloit KS 67420 Office: 209 E Main St Beloit KS 67420

CONROYD, W. DANIEL (WALTER FRANCIS), univ. ofcl., lawyer; b. Oak Park, Ill., Oct. 1, 1920; s. Walter Earl and Lucille Mary (McCabe) C.; B.S. in Bus., Loyola U., Chgo., 1942; J.D., DePaul U., 1947; m. Margaret Ann McAuliff, Feb. 13, 1943; children—Colleen (Mrs. Michael C. Strening), Maureen (Mrs. Thomas Fitzgerald), Michael, Sheila (Mrs. William Hogan), Alicia (Mrs. Louis W. Smith). Clk., FBI, 1942-44; wage adminstr. Montgomery Ward & Co., 1944-45; with Loyola U., Chgo., 1945—, dir. pub. relations, 1945-50, dir. fulfillment fund, 1950-55, asst. to pres., 1955-59, v.p. devel. and pub. relations, 1959—; admitted to Ill. bar, 1947. Sec. lay bd. trustees Loyola U.; bd. dirs. St. Francis Hosp. Served with USNR, 1943. Mem. Pub. Relations Soc. Am., Am., Chgo. bar assns., Am. Coll. Pub. Relations Assn., Pub. Relations Clinic, Am. Alumni Council, Delta Theta Phi, Tau Kappa Epsilon. Clubs: Met., Econ., Chgo. Athletic Assn., Whitehall (Chgo.); North Shore Country (Glenview, Ill.). Home: 3108 Walden Ln Wilmette IL 60611 Office: 820 N Michigan Ave Chicago IL 60611

CONSIDINE, FRANK WILLIAM, container corp. exec.; b. Chgo., Aug. 15, 1921; s. Frank Joseph and Minnie (Regan) C.; Ph.B., Loyola U., Chgo., 1943; m. Nancy Scott, Apr. 3, 1948. Partner, F. J. Hogan Agy., Chgo., 1945-47; asst. to pres. Graham Glass Co., Chgo., 1947-51; pres. F.W. Considine Co., Chgo., 1951-55; v.p. Metro Glass div. Kraftco, Chgo., 1955-60; v.p., dir. Nat. Can Corp., Chgo., 1961-67, exec. v.p., 1967-69, pres., 1969—, chief exec. officer, 1973—, also mem. fin. com., chmn. exec. com., mem. corp. devel. com.; dir. Allis Chalmers Corp., 1st Chgo. Corp., 1st Nat. Bank Chgo., Maytag Co., Internat. Minerals & Chem. Corp., Tribune Co. Mem. governing bd. Ill. Council Econ. Edn.; chmn. U.S.-Egypt Bus. Council; trustee Loyola U., Chgo.; exec. com., trustee Mus. Sci. and Industry of Chgo.; bd. dirs. Can Mfrs. Inst., Evanston Hosp., Lyric Opera of Chgo., Jr. Achievement Chgo., Econ. Devel. Com. Chgo.; bd. dirs. Com. Ill. Indsl. Devel. Authority. Served to lt. USNR, 1943-46. Mem. U.S. Brewers Assn. (asso. dir.), Econ. Club Chgo., Am. Inst. Food Distbrn. (bd. trustees, chmn.), Chgo. Assn. Commerce and Industry (past pres.). Clubs: Chgo., Econ., Comml., Mid Am. (Chgo.); Glenview. Office: 8101 Higgins Rd Chicago IL 60631

CONSOLAZIO, PETER CARMINE, food co. exec.; b. Mt. Vernon, N.Y., May 30, 1944; s. A. Nino and Lola A. (Manzione) C.; B.S., Fordham U., 1968, M.B.A., 1971; m . Emily Norris, June 26, 1965; children—Lori Ann, Amy Patricia. Fin. analyst Gen. Foods Corp., White Plains, N.Y., 1968-70, fin. mgr., 1970-73, asso. mgr. promotion, 1973-76; group mgr.-promotions U.S. Grocery Products, Quaker Oaks Co., Chgo., 1976—. Mem. Promotion Mktg. Assn. Am. (dir. 1976—). Club: Premium Industry. Home: 602 S Knollwood Dr Wheaton IL 60187 Office: Mdse Mart Plaza Suite 345 Chicago IL 60654

CONTARSY, GEORGE SULTAN, holding co. exec.; b. Oak Park, Ill., Oct. 1, 1932; s. Edward Eli and Sara (Berkson) C.; student U. Ill., 1950-52, John Marshall Law Sch., 1952-54; B.A. in Applied Behavioral Sci., Nat. Coll. Edn., 1981; m. Carole Ruth Freed (dec.); children—Laurence, Elise T.; m. 2d, Joyce Koransky, May 30, 1976. Credit mgr. Fairbanks Morse Co., Chgo., 1954-57; gen. mgr. Marshalls Inc., Gary, Ind., 1957-61; v.p. Comml. Discount Corp., Chgo., 1961-69; v.p., treas. LIBCO Corp., Lincolnwood, Ill., 1969-73, pres., 1973—, also dir.; v.p. Bank of Lincolnwood (Ill.), 1980—; dir. Teleo Mktg. Services. Mem. bd. edn. dist. 219 Niles Twp., 1977. Democrat. Jewish. Home: 4712 Greenwood St Skokie IL 60076 Office: 625 N Michigan Ave Chicago IL 60611

CONTI, ANTHONY J., grocery store franchise co. exec.; b. 1919. With Conti & Freeman, Inc., 1958-61; with Scott Lad Foods, Inc., 1961-81, v.p., dir., to 1981; chmn. bd., pres., chief exec. officer Convenient Food Mart, Inc., Meadowmoor Dairies Group. Address: Convenient Food Mart Inc 875 N Michigan Ave Chicago IL 60611. *Died Nov. 19, 1981.**

CONTOS, RICHARD FRANCIS, pharmacist; b. Duluth, Minn., Sept. 22, 1933; s. Robert Leo and Florence Julia (LaPlante) C.; student U. Minn., Duluth, 1951-52; B.S., N.D. State U., 1960, NSF scholar, 1960; m. Vivian Spray, June 17, 1975; children—Michael, Michele, Christopher, Aaron Bartsch, Daniel Bartsch, Matthew Bartsch. Stock boy Lion Drug Store, Duluth, 1949-51; with Ramsey Drug Co., Devils Lake, N.D., 1960-63; chief pharmacist, dir. pharmacy Northwestern Hosp., Thief River Falls, Minn., 1963—. Founder, pres. Falls Day Activity Center, ARC, 1966-67; chmn. Pennington County Republican Party, 1967-69, Local Bicentennial Celebration, 1974-76; mem. scholastic and curriculum adv. com. Coll. Pharmacy, U. Minn., area coordinator continuing edn., 1975—; chmn. drug utilization rev. Minn. Dept. Public Welfare, 1979-80. Served with U.S. Army, 1954-57. Recipient Scouter's Key, 1969, Scouter's award, 1975, 30 Yr. Vet.'s award, 1979 (all Boy Scouts Am.), Wood Badge, Boy Scouts Can., 1975. Mem. Am. Pharm. Assn., Am. Soc. Hosp. Pharmacists (preceptor), Minn.-Dak. Soc. Hosp. Pharmacists (past pres.), Minn. Pharm. Assn., Minn. Soc. Hosp. Pharmacists, Am. Legion (1st and 2d vice comdr., adj.), Minn. Jaycees (local pres., state dir., state chmn., Bronze Key award 1966, Disting. Service award 1967). Home: Route 1 Box T-25 Thief River Falls MN 56701 Office: 120 S LaBree Ave Thief River Falls MN 56701

CONVERSE, JAMES LEONARD, illustrator; b. Jackson, Mich., Jan. 19, 1937; s. Orrin Leonard and Clara Estella (Snow) C.; student Am. Acad. Art Chgo., 1956-57, Art Center Coll. Design, Los Angeles, 1963-64; m. Gloria Jean Stevens, July 3, 1956; children—Errol B., Jennifer D. Illustrator, Pacific Press Pub. Assn., Mountain View, Calif., 1960-63; owner, art dir. Converse Illustrations, Los Angeles, 1963-67, Columbus, Ohio, 1967-70, Midland, Mich., 1970—; illustrator Dow Chem. Co., Midland, 1969-73; art dir. Worthington Foods (Ohio), 1967-69; illustrator books, mags., filmstrips, slides. Executed numerous sci. and ednl. art projects, also artwork in conjunction with Walt Disney for movie Mary Poppins, 1964. Home: 213 Sinclair St Midland MI 48640

CONWAY, JOAN ESTHER, merchandise systems exec.; b. Chgo., Jan. 9, 1953; d. Paul Francis and Esther Mae (Smith) Winkler; B.S. in Math., U. Ill., 1975; m. James Francis Conway, June 28, 1974. Programmer, Natural Gas Pipeline, Chgo., 1975-76; project mgr. B. Dalton Bookseller, Mpls., 1976—. Home: 10201 Wildwood Rd Bloomington MN 55437 Office: 7505 Metro Blvd Minneapolis MN 55435

CONWAY, ROBERT MARTIN, banker; b. St. Louis, July 9, 1933; s. Alphonses Henry and Leota (Martin) C.; B.B.A., St. Mary's U., 1955; M.S. in Commerce, St. Louis U., 1967; m. Patricia A. Forrestal, June 27, 1959; children—Kathy, Robert, Carolyn. Salesman Johnson Foil Co., St. Louis, 1957-60, Dolan Co., realtors, St. Louis, 1960-61; sr. investment analyst Prudential Ins. Co. Am., St. Louis, 1961-70; exec. v.p., sr. loan officer Tower Grove Bank & Trust Co., St. Louis, 1971-76, pres., chief exec. officer, 1976-78; pres. Robert M. Conway & Assos., St. Louis, 1978—; asst. prof. fin. jr. coll. dist., St. Louis. Bd. dirs. Landmarks Assn. Greater St. Louis, United Student Aid Fund. Served with AUS, 1955-57. Mem. Mo. Realtors Inc., Nat. Realtors Inc., St. Louis Realtors Inc., Mortgage Bankers Assn., Homebuilders Assn. Home: 40 Midpark Ln Saint Louis MO 63124 Office: 11 S Meramec St Saint Louis MO 63105

CONYERS, JOHN, JR., Congressman; b. Detroit, May 16, 1929; s. John and Lucille (Simpson) C.; B.A., Wayne State U., 1957, LL.B., 1958. Admitted to Mich. bar, 1959; legis. asst., State of Mich., 1958-61; practice law, Detroit, 1962-64; referee Mich. Workmen's Compensation Dept., Detroit, 1962-64; mem. 89th-97th congresses from 1st Mich. Dist., chmn. criminal justice subcom. of judiciary com. Trustee, Martin Luther King, Jr. Center for Nonviolent Social Change. Mem. NAACP (dir. Detroit chpt.), ACLU (Mich. adv. bd.). Served to 2d lt., C.E., U.S. Army, 1951. Baptist. Office: 2313 Rayburn House Office Bldg Washington DC 20515

COOHON, DONALD BURNS, veterinarian; b. Sturgis, Mich., May 14, 1921; s. Leo G. and Velva (Burns) C.; D.V.M., Mich State U., 1943; M.P.H., U. Mich., 1954; m. Ruthmary Veen, Sept. 11, 1943; children—Carolyn Boyd, William James, Claudia Ann Nightingale, Catherine Louise Baird. Practice vet. medicine, Dowagiac, Mich., 1944-46; veterinarian Grand Rapids Health Dept., 1946-51, Kalamazoo County Health Dept., 1951-55, Mich. Dept. Pub. Health, Lansing, 1955—. Vis. lectr. epidemiology U. Mich., 1963. Mem. exec. com. orgn. and extension, area council Boy Scouts Am., Kalamazoo, 1955. Mem. Am., Mich. (certificate appreciation 1966), Midstate vet. med. assns., Mich. Pub. Health Assn. (pres. 1963-65), Conf. Pub. Health Vets., Assn. State and Territorial Pub. Health Vets., AAAS, Mich. Health Officers Assn., Alpha Tau Omega. Lutheran. Contbr. articles to profl. pubs. Home: 3641 E Arbutus Dr Okemos MI 48864 Office: 3500 N Logan St Lansing MI 48914

COOK, ALEXANDER BURNS, educator; b. Grand Rapids, Mich., Apr. 16, 1924; s. Gorell Alexander and Harriette Florence (Hinze) C.; B.A., Ohio Wesleyan U., 1949; M.S., Case Western Res. U., 1967. Editorial cartoonist, artist Cleve. Plain Dealer, 1949-55; account exec. Edward Howard & Co., Cleve., 1955-61; spl. art tchr. Cleve. Pub. Schs., 1964—; curator exhibits Gt. Lakes Mus., Vermilion, Ohio, 1970-78, curator, 1978—, chmn. mus. operating com., 1977—. Served with AUS, 1943-45. Recipient award of honor Ohio Wesleyan U., 1955; Distinguished Achievement award Gt. Lakes Hist. Soc., 1973; 1st pl. award for editorial cartoons Union Tchr. Press Assn., 1980. Mem. Gt. Lakes Hist. Soc. (exec. v.p. 1959-64, v.p. 1964—, trustee, mem. exec. com. 1959—), Ohioana Library Assn., Akron Art Inst., Cleve. Mus. Art, Am. Soc. Marine Artists, Delta Tau Delta, Pi Delta Epsilon, Pi Sigma Alpha. Republican. Episcopalian. Contbr. editorial cartoons to Reid Cartoon Collection, U. Kans. Jour. Hist. Center, The Critique, 1975—; editorial adviser, numerous articles to Inland Seas, 1957—, The Chadburn, 1976—; cover illustrations for Ohioana Quar., 1979—. Paintings represented in pvt. collections, 1960—; executed mural depicting Gt. Lakes shipping Gt. Lakes Mus., 1969. Home: 11820 Edgewater Dr Lakewood OH 44107

COOK, DAVID LEE, accountant; b. Dayton, Ohio, July 5, 1943; s. Norbert Ashby and Mary Elizabeth (Curtis) C.; student U. Dayton, 1961-65, Sinclair Coll., 1965-67, Wright State U., 1967-70; m. Betty Jayne Rich, Nov. 23, 1972; 1 dau., Robin Elizabeth. Bookkeeper, Norbert A. Cook, P.A., Dayton, 1957-65; asst. paymaster B.G. Danis Co., Inc., Dayton, 1965-67; acct. Kleckner & Cole, C.P.A.'s, Dayton, 1967-69; supr. Alexander Grant & Co., Dayton, 1969-72; supr. Fehrman & Cook, Dayton, 1972-73; supr. Norbert A Cook & Assos., Dayton, 1973-75; pres. Bookkeeping Services, Inc., Dayton, 1975—. Pres., United Health Services of Dayton Area; adv. com. Montgomery County (Ohio) Joint Vocat. Sch. Roman Catholic. Club: Miami Valley Orchid Soc. (past treas.). Home: 7790 Peters Pike Dayton OH 45414 Office: 63 Grafton Ave Dayton OH 45406

COOK, DAVID RAY, engr.; b. Tulsa, June 19, 1936; s. Artie Wrothal and Nellie Mae (Miller) C.; m. Benetta Borne, May 26, 1959; children—Kathryn, Karlene, Kristine. B.M.E., Okla. State U., 1959; M.S. in Systems Mgmt., Fla. Inst. Tech., 1969, M.S. in Contract Mgmt., 1970. Registered profl. engr., Ala. Design engr. Douglas Aircraft Co., Santa Monica, Calif., 1959-60; sr. design engr. Gen. Dynamics, Omaha, 1960-62; design engr. Boeing Co., Huntsville, Ala., 1962-65; mgr. Bendix Corp., Troy, Mich., 1965—; v.p. Profl. Consultants, Inc., 1974—. Pres. Brevard Symphony Orch., Cocoa, Fla., 1973-74. Mem. ASME (chmn. plant engrs. div.), Nat. Soc. Profl. Engrs., Soc. Automotive Engrs. Club: Masons (32 deg.). Contbr. articles to profl. jours. Home: 2551 Armstrong Dr Lake Orion MI 48035 Office: 900 W Maple St Troy MI 48084

COOK, EMIL NORWOOD, sanitary engr.; b. Paris, Ky., Apr. 18, 1948; s. Norwood Thomas and Thelma Rankin (Sharon) C.; student Eastern Ky. U., 1966-67; B.S. in C.E., U. Ky., 1971, M.S., 1972; m. Martha Van Deren Brown, June 5, 1977. Project mgr. Crawford, Murphy & Tilly, Inc., Springfield, Ill., 1972—. Adv. council Springfield area Vocat. Center, 1974-75; chmn. bd. deacons West Side Christian Ch., Springfield, 1979—. Served with USAR, 1971-77. Decorated Army Commendation medal. Named Outstanding Civil Engring. Student, U. Ky., 1971. Mem. Nat. Soc. Profl. Engrs., Ill. Soc. Profl. Engrs., ASCE, Water Pollution Control Fedn., Tau Beta Pi, Chi Epsilon. Contbr. articles in field to profl. jours. Home: 420 Yeoman Dr Springfield IL 62704 Office: 2750 W Washington Rd Springfield IL 62702

COOK, JACK, computer specialist, indsl. engr.; b. Pitts., July 20, 1937; s. John Joseph and Mary Josephine (Schmitt) C.; student Duquesne U., 1955-57; B.S., U. Pitts., 1959; M.S. in Indsl. Engring., U. Toledo, 1979, cert. in data processing, 1976; m. Barbara Ann Kahn,

Oct. 25, 1969; children—Joe, Judy, Jann, Jerry, Doug, Steve. Programmer analyst Republic Steel Corp., Cleve., 1960-63; senior systems rep. Honeywell EDP, Cleve., 1963-64; data processing mgr. Tel. Services Inc., Lima, Ohio, 1964-67; computer services mgr. Nat. Family Opinion, Toledo, 1967-78; adminstrv. and planning mgr. The Andersons, Maumee, Ohio, 1978—; chmn. bus. adv. com. Penta County Vocat. Sch., 1978-79. Republican precinct committeeman, 1970-73. Mem. Computer Mgmt. Assn. (dir. 1976—, treas. 1979), Am. Inst. Indsl. Engrs. Roman Catholic. Club: Sylvania Country. Home: 4206 Gilhouse Rd Toledo OH 43623 Office: PO Box 119 Maumee OH 43537

COOK, JULIAN ABELE, JR., judge; b. Washington, June 22, 1930; s. Julian Abele and Ruth Elizabeth (McNeill) C.; B.A., Pa. State U., 1952; J.D., Georgetown U., 1957; m. Carol Annette Dibble, Dec. 22, 1957; children—Julian Abele, Peter Dibble, Susan Annette. Law clk. to Judge Arthur E. Moore, 1957-58; mem. firm Bledsoe, Ford and Bledsoe, 1958-60; mem. firm Taylor, Patrick, Bailor and Lee, 1960-61; mem. firm Cook and Hooe, 1961-65; mem. firm Hempstead, Houston, McGrath and Cook, 1965-68; individual practice law, 1968-75; partner firm Cook, Wittenberg, Curry and Magid, 1975; partner firm Cook and Curry, 1976-78; judge U.S. Dist. Ct. Eastern Dist. Mich., Detroit, 1978—; adj. prof. law U. Detroit Sch. Law, 1971-74; gen. counsel WTVS, Public Broadcasting TV, 1973-78; mem. Mich. State Bd. Ethics, 1977-78; labor arbitrator Am. Arbitration Assn. and Mich. Employment Relations Commn., 1975-78; mem. Mich. Law and Media Commn., 1978—. Mem. exec. bd. dirs. Child and Family Services Mich., also pres.; bd. dirs. Todd-Phillips Children's Home, Inc., Camp Oakland, Inc., Franklin-Wright Settlement, Inc., Pontiac Opportunities Industrialization Center; mem. Oak Park (Mich.) Compensation Commn.; bd. advisors East Mich. Environ. Action Council; bd. dirs. Oakland Youth Symphony; chmn. Mich. Civil Rights Commn., 1968-71; bd. dirs., treas. Oakland Livingston Econ. Devel. Corp.; bd. dirs. Mich. ACLU, Mich. United Way; chmn. citizens com. Project Twenty Com., Oakland U.; pres., dir. Pontiac Area Urban League. Served with U.S. Army, 1952-54. Recipient Disting. Citizen of Year award NACCP, 1970; Merit citation Pontiac Urban League, 1971; resolution Mich. Ho. of Reps., 1971; Service award Todd Phillips Children's Home, 1978; Pathfinders award Oakland U., 1977. Mem. Am. Bar Assn., Mich. Bar Assn. (chmn. constl. law com. 1969, vice chmn. civil liberties com. 1970), Nat. Bar Assn., Oakland Bar Assn. (chmn. continuing legal edn. com. 1968-69, vice chmn. dist. ct. com. 1977), Wolverine Bar Assn., Fed. Bar Assn., Indsl. Relations Research Assn. Office: 277 United State Courthouse Detroit MI 48226

COOK, KATHLEEN ANN, dietitian; b. Valley City, N.D., June 11, 1946; d. John Nickolos and Christine Mary (Knutson) C.; B.S. in Nutrition, Dietetics and Edn., U. N.D., 1968; student Valley City (N.D.) State Coll., summers, 1965, 66. Intern, staff dietitian St. Mary's Hosp., Mayo Clinic, Rochester, Minn., 1968-69; staff dietitian Kenosha (Wis.) Meml. Hosp., 1970-72; dir. dietary Riverview Hosp. Assn., Crookston, Minn., 1973-79, Valley Meml. Nursing Homes, Grand Forks, N.D., 1979—; cons. McVille (N.D.) Hosp., Warren (Minn.) Hosp., Karlstad (Minn.) Hosp. and Nursing Home; instr. food service mgmt. U. Minn. (Crookston), also adv. bd. dietary technician program; mem. exec. and adv. bd. Crookston Home Delivered Meals; adv. bd. U. N.D. dietetic assts. corr. course, Agassiz Valley Vocat. Edn. Program. Mem. Am. Dietetic Assn., N.D. Dietetic Assn., Am. Home Econs. Assn., Nutrition Today Soc. Roman Catholic. Home: 1626 Earl Circle Grand Forks ND 58201 Office: Valley Meml Nursing Homes Grand Forks ND

COOK, KENNETH TYLER, JR., food processing co. exec.; b. Denver, Dec. 22, 1930; s. Kenneth Tyler and Lillian Iowa (Burke) C.; grad. Coll. Advanced Traffic, 1957; student Oakland City Coll., 1959-61, U. Houston, 1970-71, Northwestern U., 1975; m. Carol Anne Hardesty, Nov. 24, 1950; children—Tamara Anne, Crystal Hope, Diane Elaine. Statistician, So. Pacific Co., Salt Lake City, 1953-59; freight audit supr. Stokely Van Camp, Oakland, Calif., 1959-62; traffic mgr. Idaho Potato Processors, 1962-64; successively mgr. prodn. planning, gen. mgr. prodn. and inventory control, gen. mgr. distbn. Ore-Ida Foods, Boise, Idaho, 1964-78; v.p. distbn. Hubinger Co., Keokuk, Iowa, 1978—. Local pres. PTA, 1965-66, Library Bd., 1981—. Served with USN, 1952-53; Korea. Mem. Am. Prodn. and Inventory Control Soc. (cert. practitioner, past v.p.), Delta Nu Alpha. Republican. Home: 211 Hickory Ct Hamilton IL 62341 Office: 601 Main St Keokuk IA 52632

COOK, MICHAEL H., editor; b. Kankakee, Ill., Oct. 25, 1949; s. Harold A. and Anne E. (Hamlin) C.; B.S. in Communications, No. Ill. U., DeKalb, 1972. Editorial asst., then asst. editor Tng. and Devel. Jour., ofcl. publ. Am. Soc. Tng. and Devel., Madison, Wis., 1972-74, editor, 1974—; cons. editor Jour. Instructional Devel., publ. Assn. Ednl. Communications and Tech.; bd. dirs. W. Madison Bus. Assn. Mem. Internat. Assn. Bus. Communicators, Am. Soc. Tng. and Devel., Wis. Assn. Bus. Communicators. Club: Masons. Office: PO Box 5307 Madison WI 53705*

COOK, MORREECE ELAINE, social worker; b. Owosso, Mich., June 17, 1946; d. Charles and Freda Saunders, B.S.N., Mercy Coll. of Detroit, B.S.W., 1971; M.S.W., Wayne State U. Asst. adminstr. Four Chaplins Convalescent Center, Detroit, 1971-72, dir. social services Medicenter of Am., Detroit, 1970; med. social worker Sinai Hosp. of Detroit, 1972—. Mem. Nat. Assn. Social Workers (sec.-treas. 1976—, med. council Mich. chpt.), Social Workers Club Met. Detroit (v.p. 1976, pres. 1977). Home: 8712 Kenberton St Oak Park MI 48237 Office: 6767 W Outer Dr Detroit MI 48235

COOK, NOEL ROBERT, mfg. co. exec.; b. Houston, Mar. 19, 1937; s. Horace Berwick and Leda Estelle (Houghton) C.; student Iowa State U., 1955-57; B.S. in Indsl. Engring., U. Mich., 1960; children—Laurel Jane, David Robert. Engr. in tng. Eaton Mfg., Saginaw, Mich., 1960-61; mgr. mfg. and contracting J. N. Fauver Co., Madison Heights, Mich., 1961-65; pres. Newton Mfg., Royal Oak, Mich., 1965—; soc. Indsl. Piping Contractors, Birmingham, Mich., 1969-75; pres. RNR Metal Fabricators, Inc., Royal Oak, Mich., 1974-78; chmn. bd. Kim Internat. Sales Co., 1978—; pres. Newton Sales Co., Royal Oak, 1978—, Power Package Windsor Ltd., Windsor, Ont., Can., 1981—. Served with U.S. Army, 1960-61. Registered profl. engr., Mich. Mem. Fluid Power Soc., Nat. Fluid Power Assn., Birmingham Jr. C. of C. (past bd. dirs.). Patentee in field. Home: 1903 Wickham Rd Royal Oak MI 48073 Office: 4249 Delemere Blvd Royal Oak MI 48073

COOK, RICHARD BORRESON, architect; b. Harvard, Ill., May 23, 1937; s. Ernest Keller and Clara Matilda (Borreson) C.; B.Arch., U. Ill., 1962; m. Shirley Antrup, June 13, 1959; children—Alan, Elizabeth, Rebecca. Staff, Skidmore, Owings & Merrill, Chgo., 1962-64, Ulrich Franzen & Assos., N.Y.C., 1964-65, I.W. Colburn & Assos., Chgo., 1965-70, Metz Train Olson & Youngren, Chgo., 1970-78; prin.-in-charge Orput Assos. Inc., Wilmette, Ill., 1978—, Green Cook Ltd., Chgo., 1980—. Chmn., Chgo. Office Practice Commn., 1976—. Mem. Am. Arbitration Assn. (panel), AIA (pres. Chgo. chpt. 1981), Greater North Michigan Ave Assn. Chgo. Home: 1330 Wesley Ave Evanston IL 60201 Office: 1200 Central Ave Wilmette IL 60091

COOK, ROBERT WILCOX, educator, lawyer; b. Providence, Dec. 1, 1943; s. Irving Howes and Joyce (Wilcox) C.; B.E.E., Rensselaer Poly. Inst., 1968, M.S., 1968; Ph.D., Northwestern U., 1970; J.D. with honors, Chgo. Kent Coll. Law, 1977; m. Elizabeth Stoneman, Apr. 11, 1976; children—Paul Wilcox, Peter DeVaney. Tech. staff Bell Telephone Labs., Naperville, Ill., 1966-73, mem. patent staff, 1973-76; vis. asst. prof. Roosevelt U., Chgo., 1976-77; asst. prof. econs. and bus. North Central Coll., Naperville, Ill., 1977—, chmn. computer sci. discipline, 1979—; admitted to Ill. bar, 1977; individual practice law, Naperville, 1977—. Village trustee Village of Weston (Ill.), 1967-69, chmn. planning commn., 1967-69. Mem. IEEE, Assn. Computing Machinery, Am. Bar Assn. Mem. Reorganized Ch. of Jesus Christ of Latter Day Saints. Patentee in field; also articles, chpt. in book. Home: PO Box 72 Naperville IL 60566 Office: North Central Coll Naperville IL 60566

COOK, RONALD JAMES, nuclear engr.; b. Niles, Ohio, May 24, 1934; s. Robert Alex and Ellen (Cunningham) C.; B.M.E., Ohio State U., 1967, M.S., 1974; m. Leona Baird, July 21, 1960; children—Dian, Dawna, Rebecca. Apprentice, N.Y.C. R.R., 1952; reactor operator NASA, Sandusky, Ohio, 1962-63; ops. supr. reactor lab. Ohio State U., Columbus, 1964-71; reactor insp. AEC (now Nuclear Regulatory Commn.), Region III, Glen Ellyn, Ill., 1971-78, resident insp. pilot program nuclear plant, Midland, Mich., 1978—; cons. design engr.; lectr. in field. Active Boy Scouts Am. Served with USN, 1953-62, now Res., mem. crew, prototype Navy nuclear program. Lic. fallout shelter analyst; cert. shelter monitor instr.; cert. CPR instr. Mem. ASME. Author profl. papers; patentee in field. Home: 204 Chesterfield Ct Midland MI 48640

COOK, STANTON R., newspaper pub.; b. Chgo., July 3, 1925; s. Rufus Merrill and Thelma Marie (Bogerson) C.; B.S. in Mech. Engring., Northwestern U., 1949; m. Barbara Wilson. Dist. sales rep. Shell Oil Co., 1949-51; prodn. engr. Chgo. Tribune, 1951-60, asst. prodn. mgr., 1960-65, prodn. mgr., 1965-67, prodn. dir., 1967-70, dir. ops., 1970, v.p. Chgo. Tribune Co., 1967-70, exec. v.p., gen. mgr., 1970-73, pres., 1973—, pub., 1973—, chief exec. officer, from 1974, chmn., 1974—; v.p., dir. Tribune Co., Chgo., 1973-74, pres., chief officer, 1974—; dir. Newspaper Advt. Bur., Inc., AP. Trustee U. Chgo., Mus. Sci. and Industry, Chgo., Orchestral Assn. (Chgo. Symphony), Field Mus. Nat. History, Chgo., Am. Newspaper Pubs. Assn. Found., Robert R. McCormick Trusts and Founds. Mem. Am. Newspaper Pubs. Assn. (dir.). Office: 435 N Michigan Ave Chicago IL 60611

COOK, THOMAS EDWARD, environ. control cons., chem. engr.; b. Fresno, Calif., Jan. 10, 1925; s. Francis William and Josephine Agatha (Sakalauskas) C.; student Bradley U., 1946-47, 51; B.S. in Chem. Engring., Columbia, 1949; postgrad. Ohio State U., 1961, 67; m. Shirley Caroline Mackie, May 30, 1943. Phys. technologist Caterpillar Tractor Co., Peoria, Ill., 1949-52; prin. chem. engr. Battelle Meml. Inst., Columbus, Ohio, 1952-61; project engr., chief chemist Tectum Corp., Columbus, 1961-63; self-employed in cons. and fundamental research, Columbus, 1963-66; design and sales engr. Harrop Precision Furnace Co., Columbus, 1966-68; cons. energy conservation and environ. control processes, Columbus, 1968-79, Nuclear Cons. Services, Columbus, 1979—; customer service rep. Swift Chem. Co., Columbus, 1971-76. Merit badge counselor Boy Scouts Am., 1963—; pres. Cat Welfare Assn., 1970-71. Mem. Greater Clintonville Community Council, 1967—, pres., 1974. Served with USNR, 1942-45. Mem. Am. Chem. Soc. (pub. relations and community affairs chmn. 1975-76), Am. Inst. Chem. Engrs. (mem. exec. com. 1967-68), Engrs. Found. Ohio (council continuing profl. edn.), Am. Chem. Soc., Air Pollution Control Assn., No. Bus. and Profl. Assn. (pres. 1980—), Ind. Profl. Cons.'s Assn., Ohio Acad. Scis., Bradley Fedn. Scholars. Patentee in field. Address: 3570 Maize Rd Columbus OH 43224

COOK, WELLS FRANKLIN, educator; b. Ovid, Mich., May 20, 1928; s. Wayne Baldwin and Beatrice Cecelia (Stuart) C.; B.S., Central Mich. U., 1950; M.A., U. Mich., 1955; Ph.D., Mich. State U., 1973; m. Lois Arlene Anderson, June 20, 1952; children—Natalie Ruth Cook Hermes, Annette Jean, Wayne Earl. Bus. tchr. Fenton (Mich.) High Sch., 1953-57; tchr. coordinator, placement dir. coop. edn. Royal Oak (Mich.) Public Schs., 1957-67; faculty Central Mich. U., Mt. Pleasant, 1967—, prof. bus. edn. 1981—, asst. dean Sch. Bus. Adminstrn., 1981—. Served with U.S. Army, 1951-53. Mem. NEA, Nat. Bus. Edn. Assn., Mich. Bus. Edn. Assn., Mich. Vocat. Coordinators Assn., Mich. Edn. Assn., Mich. Assn. Career Edn., Mich. Occupational Tchr. Edn. Assn., North-Central Bus. Edn. Assn., Phi Delta Kappa, Delta Pi Epsilon. Methodist. Home: 1002 Glenwood Pl Mount Pleasant MI 48858 Office: Central Michigan University 112 Grawn Hall Mount Pleasant MI 48859

COOKE, EVELYN KATHLEEN CHATMAN, educator; b. Jackson, Tenn.; d. Charles Elijah and Josie (Bond) Chatman; B.A. cum laude, Lane Coll., 1955; M.Ed., Xavier U.; m. James T. Cooke, Apr. 21, 1954 (div. Aug. 1970); 1 dau., Madelyn LaRene. Tchr. public schs., Chattanooga, 1957-67, Cin., 1967—; cons. career edn. Public Schs., Cin. Pres., Harriet Tubman's Black Women's Democratic Club; mem. upper grade sch study council. Recipient Spirit of Detroit award, 1981. Mem. Fellowship United Meth. Musicians, NAACP, Council for Co-op Action, Am., Ohio Fedn. Tchrs. Cin. Fedn. Tchrs., Nat. Council Negro Women, Top Ladies of Distinction (outstanding service award 1981, nat. corr. sec., chmn. info. com., pres. Cin. chpt.), Sigma Gamma Rho (nat. constn. and by-laws com.), Gamma Theta, Sigma Rho Sigma. Methodist (dir. music ch.). Home: 6748 Elwynne Dr Cincinnati OH 45236

COOKE, THORNTON, II, ins. co. exec.; b. Kansas City, Mo., May 22, 1928; s. Sidney Merritt and Thelma (Rossner) C.; student U. Kans., 1945-48; m. Joan Davis, Oct. 4, 1952 (dec.); children—Helen Darlington, Caroline Davis. Vice-pres. Universal Underwriters Ins. Co., Kansas City, Mo., 1951-70; pres. First Am. Ins. Co., Kansas City, Mo., 1971—; dir. Columbia Union Nat. Bank, Kansas City, First Am. Fin. Corp., Kansas City. Chmn. bd. trustees Sunset Hill Sch.; dir. Kansas City Art Inst. Club: Kansas City Country, Kansas City. Home: 631 W 56th St Kansas City MO 64113 Office: 3100 Broadway Kansas City MO 64111

COOLEY, ADELAIDE NATION, artist; b. Idaho Falls, Idaho, Apr. 18, 1914; d. Carl DeLos and Ivo Ethel (Miller) Nation; student Stephens Coll. Women, 1931-33; B.S., U. Wis., 1935; m. William Cooley, Jr., Aug. 24, 1937; children—Marcia Jean, Susan Adelaide, William Carl. One-woman shows (11), Chgo., Springfield, Quincy, Peoria, Ill., 1958-74, Peoria Art Guild, 1979; numerous group shows, Ill., Mich., Calif., Iowa, N.Y., Mass.; juror, art exhbns., 1971—; pres. Peoria Art Center, 1962-63; art cons. exhibits Carson Pirie Scott Co., Peoria, 1967-68; writer daily art news Sta. WIVC-FM (now WIRL Radio), E. Peoria, 1968; founder pub. art com., Peoria, 1974. Recipient Outstanding Woman in Art award Peoria YWCA, 1973, Leadership in Art award, 1976. Author published biographies of two sculptors. Home: 808 Chalon St Peoria IL 61614

COOLEY, CALVIN EDWIN, pub. co. exec.; b. Downs, Kans., Jan. 14, 1926; s. Miles Webb and Mabel Caroline (Hull) C.; B.S., U. Kans., 1959; M.B.A., U. Houston, 1960; m. LaVerla Dell Harris, Aug. 7, 1950 (div. 1972); children—Edwin, Marc; m. 2d, Gloria Sanders Telander, June 20, 1972. Dir. surplus property disposal State of Kans., Topeka, 1952-54; sales engr. Westinghouse Electric Co., Houston, 1955-63; dir. mktg. training Cessna Aircraft, Wichita, Kans., 1963-66; owner/mgr. Cons., Inc., Wichita, 1966-71; v.p. mktg., treas. Print Media Services, Ltd. pub. of Wheelers Guides, Elk Grove Village, Ill., 1972—; v.p. mktg. Chgo. Sport Scene mag., 1980—. Served with USMC, 1944-46. Mem. Recreation Vehicle Industries Assn., Recreation Vehicle Dealers Assn., Warehouse Distbrs. Assn., Nat. Campground Owners Assn. Club: Masons. Home: 5451 N East River Rd Apt 300 Chicago IL 60656 Office: 1521 Jarvis Ave Elk Grove Village IL 60007

COOLEY, FLETCHER EARL, counselor; b. Montgomery, Ala., May 25, 1935; s. William Edward and Frankie (Armstead) C.; B.S., Ala. State U., 1961; M.Ed., Tuskegee Inst., 1965; certificate Urban Edn., U. Chgo., 1970; postgrad. U. Minn., 1975—. Recreational dir. Ft. Bragg (N.C.), 1966-67, Ft. Gordon (Ga.), 1967-68; counselor Ralph Bunche Sch., Canton, Ga., 1965-66, Clam Lake (Wis.) Civilian Job Corps Center, 1968, Central High Sch., Mpls., 1968—. Active Bancroft Neighborhood Assn.; mem. ednl. task force Mpls. Urban League. Served with USN, 1953-58, USNR, 1958—. Recipient YMCA Century Club Award, 1976; Minn. Masonic Meritorious Award for Counselors, 1975; named Central High Sch. Counselor of Year, 1972; Gen. Elec. fellow vocat. guidance U. Louisville, 1972. Mem. Am. Personnel and Guidance Assn., Am. Sch. Counselor Assn., Am. Coll. Personnel Assn., Minn., Mpls. edn. assns., Phi Delta Kappa. Democrat. Roman Catholic. Clubs: Tuskegee Minn., Holy Name Soc., K.C., Knights of Peter Claver. Home: 3924 Elliot Ave S Minneapolis MN 55407 Office: 3416 4th Ave S Minneapolis MN 55408

COOLEY, MARION SHERMAN, artist; b. St. Paul, Jan. 3, 1930; d. Harold Curtis and Verda Ethel (Garringer) Sherman; A.B., Central Methodist Coll., Mo., 1951; student Washington U., St. Louis, 1949; M.Ed. (AAUW fellow), Miami U., Ohio, 1969; postgrad. U. Cin., 1974; m. William E. Cooley, June 5, 1952; children—Charles, Marilyn, Harold, Noele. Tchr. art high sch., St. Louis, 1951-52; art supr., Arcola, Ill., 1952-53; instr. art Thomas More Coll., Ft. Mitchell, Ky., 1969-70; instr. art edn. Miami U., Oxford, Ohio, 1970—; pres. Coolver Studios, Wyoming, Ohio; design cons., lectr. metal jewelry making. Mem. Nat. Art Edn. Assn., Phi Beta. Republican. Clubs: Wyoming Women's, Wyoming Book. Editor: The Report of Women's Caucus of Nat. Art Edn. Assn., 1977-79, Jour. Ohio Art Edn. Assn., 1980—; contbr. articles on art, art edn. and jewelry making to profl. jours. Patentee process for imparting dark patina to low-melting metal articles. Home: 531 Chisholm Trail Wyoming OH 45215 Office: 105 Van Voorhis Miami U Oxford OH 45056

COOMBES, CLAUDE JOHN, advt. agy. exec.; b. San Francisco, Nov. 27, 1950; s. C. Gren and Flora Marie (Tonazzo) C.; grad. Kendall Sch. Design, 1971. Owner, operator C. John Coombes Studios, 1974-78; co-owner, art dir. Jason Blair Advt., Grand Rapids, Mich., 1978—; owner Congenealfiles, 1980—; asso. Hunter Bart Coombes Assos., 1981—; designer Amway Corp., 1982—; art dir. O & O Communications, 1982—. Served with U.S. Army, 1971-74. Grand Rapids MI 49508

COONEY, GEORGE AUGUSTIN, lawyer; b. Detroit, July 12, 1909; s. Augustin W. and Mary (McBride) C.; A.B., U. Detroit, 1932, J.D., 1935; m. Julia Grace Starrs, Oct. 26, 1940; children—George Augustin, Michael Edward, Timothy John. Admitted to Mich. bar, 1935; since practiced in Detroit. Lectr., U. Mich. Inst. Continuing Legal Edn. Recipient Tower award U. Detroit, 1972. Fellow Am. Coll. Probate Counsel; mem. Am., Mich., Fed., Detroit bar assns., Am. Judicature Soc., Cath. Lawyers Soc. Detroit (dir.), Inc. Soc. Irish-Am. Lawyers, Selden Soc., Mich. Assn. Professions, State Bar Mich. (dir. probate and trust law sect., editor sect. publ. Probate Alert). Served as warrant officer USAAF, 1943-46. K.C. Clubs: Detroit Golf, Nat. Lawyers (Washington); Stoney Point (Ont.) Sportsmen. Home: 17177 Parkside Ave Detroit MI 48221 Office: 2329 Commonwealth Bldg Detroit MI 48226

COONS, CATHERINE CASTLE, med. social worker; b. Sitka, Ky., Feb. 3, 1942; d. Edwardand Arthie (Daniels) Castle; B.A. in Sociology, Berea (Ky.) Coll., 1966; M.Ed. in Psychology, Xavier U., Cin., 1970; 1 son, Erik Chandler. Juvenile counselor Ky. Dept. Child Welfare, 1966-67; tchr. Dixie Heights High Sch., Erlanger, Ky., 1967; dir. social service dept. Bethesda North Hosp., Cin., 1970—. Mem. Mental Health Services East Bd., 1972-75; allocations com. United Appeal, 1977-78. Mem. Am. Hosp. Assn., Nat. Assn. Social Workers, Urban Appalachian Council, Council on Aging, Ohio Hosp. Assn., Ohio Valley Hosp. Assn. Social Work Dirs. (sec. 1977-78), Ohio Citizens Council, Social Service Assn. Cin. Unitarian. Author articles in field. Home: 10869 Lakehurst Ct Cincinnati OH 45242 Office: 10500 Montgomery Rd Cincinnati OH 45242

COONS, ELDO JESS, JR., recreational vehicle mfg. co. exec.; b. Corsicana, Tex., July 5, 1924; s. Eldo Jess and Ruby (Allison) C.; student engring. U. Calif., 1949-50; m. Betty June Muntz, June 1, 1954; children—Roberta Ann, Valerie, Cheryl. Owner C & C Constrn. Co., Pomona, Calif., 1946-48; sgt. traffic div. Pomona Police Dept., 1948-54; nat. field dir. Nat. Hot Rod Assn., Los Angeles, 1954-57; pres. Coons Custom Mfg., Inc., Oswego, Kans., 1957-68; chmn. bd. Borg-Warner Corp., 1968-71; pres. Coons Mfg., Inc., Oswego, 1971—. Mem. Kans. Gov.'s Adv. Com. for State Architects Assn. Served with C.E., AUS, 1943-46. Named to Exec. and Profl. Hall Fame, Recreational Vehicle/Mobile Homes Hall of Fame; recipient Paul Abel award Recreation Vehicle Industry Assn., 1978. Mem. Oswego C. of C. (dir.), Nat. Juvenile Officers Assn., Municipal Motor Officers Assn., Am. Legion, AIM (fellow pres.'s council), Young Pres.'s Orgn. Mason (K.T., Shriner), Rotarian (pres. Oswego 1962-63). Originator 1st city sponsored police supervised dragstrip. Home: 1315 North St Oswego KS 67356 Office: 2300 W 4th St Oswego KS 67356

COONS, HAROLD MEREDITH, lawyer; b. Montgomery County, Ind., July 31, 1911; s. Merle Fuson and Clara Leona (Van Cleave) C.; A.B., Wabash Coll., 1932; J.D., Ind. U., 1936; m. Margaret Louise Richman, Apr. 9, 1938; children—Stephen M., Philip M. Admitted to Ind. bar, 1936; individual practice law, Crawfordsville, Ind., 1936-37; claims atty. Aetna Casualty & Surety Co., Indpls., 1937-43; claims atty., partner firm Pruyn & Coons, Indpls., 1946-59; claims atty., pres. Coons & Horton, New Albany, Ind., 1960-68; individual practice law, New Albany, 1968—; dir. Farmers State Bank, New Market, Ind., 1940-68. Chmn. Floyd County Republican Party, 1968-77, del. Ind. Rep. state convs., 1968-80, alt. del. Rep. nat. conv., 1972, del., 1976; judge Floyd County Superior Ct., 1978; mem. Falls of the Ohio Interstate Park Commn. Served with U.S. Army, 1943-46. Named Sagamore of the Wabash, 1969, 75. Fellow Ind. State Bar Assn.; mem. Floyd County Bar Assn., Am. Legion, Beta Theta Pi, Phi Delta Phi. Presbyterian. Club: Rotary. Home: 1312 Riddle Rd New Albany IN 47150 Office: 412 E Main St New Albany IN 47150

COOPER, C(HARLES) E(DWARD), artist, photographer; b. Chgo., Nov. 5, 1922; s. Sam and Rose (Achtman) C.; student Corcoran Gallery Art, 1944-45, Inst. Design, 1946-47, Roosevelt Coll., 1948-52, Sch. Art Inst. Chgo., 1948-51; B.Art Edn., Loyola U. Chgo,

1964; I.D., Ill. Inst. Tech. 1966. With Jan Smith Gallery, 1950-51, House of Arts, 1952-56, Robert North Gallery, 1958-60, Kerrigan Hendrick Gallery, 1961 (all Chgo.); exhibited one-man shows Club St. Elmo, Morris B. Sachs North Side, 1949, Northwestern U. Hillel Found., Evanston, Ill., 1960, 64, Fisher Hall Gallery, Chgo., Alpha Gallery, 1977; exhibited in group shows Momentum shows, 1948, 49, 51, 52, 54, Am. Jewish Art Club, 1951—, Ill. Inst. Tech., 1963, Navy Pier No-Jury Show, Chgo., 1957, Art Inst. Chgo. Vicinity shows, 1947, 52, 53, 58, 63, Art Inst. Chgo. Rental Gallery, 1960—, Chgo. Soc. Artist Gallery, 1967-69, 70—, Alpha Gallery, 1977, 78, Metanatural Dream Gallery, 1981; represented in permanent collection Spertus Mus. of Judaica, Chgo.; high sch. art tchr. Chgo. Pub. Sch. System, 1952—; lectr. art pvt. orgns.; art cons. Bd. Jewish Edn., Chgo.; cons. pvt. collectors. Mem. planning com. for arts Am. Jewish Com.; exec. bd. Lane Tech. PTA. Served with USMC, 1942-45; PTO. Recipient Raymond Schiff Realtors award, 1961; Morris DeWoskin award 1965; Bekker-Stein award, 1980; Leon Garland award Spertus Mus., 1981. Mem. Chgo. Soc. Artists (dir., 1st v.p.), Artists Guild Chgo., Chgo. New Art Assn. (dir.), Am. Jewish Arts Club (Maurice Spertus award 1964, Nathan A. Schwartz award 1970, exhbn. chmn. 1965, 69, rec. sec. 1963, v.p. 1972, 73, co-chmn.), Chgo. Artists Coalition (dir., chmn. fair practices com., internal dir. 1981—), Artists Equity. Studio: 216 W Ontario St Chicago IL 60610 Office: care Lane Technical High School Chicago IL 60618

COOPER, CALVIN GORDON, constrn. co. exec.; b. Richland County, Wis., Sept. 10, 1925; s. William Ray and Edna Florence (Adams) C.; B.S., U. Wis., 1950; m. Avadele Thompson; children—Vicki Lynn, Scott William. Elec. engr. Underwriters Labs., 1950-52; project engr. Askania Regulator Co., 1952-54; elec. engr. Revere Copper & Brass Co., 1954-56; with Kelso-Burnett Electric Co., Chgo., 1956—, v.p., 1968-75, exec. v.p., 1975-76, pres., 1976—, also dir.; pres., dir. Mech. Systems, Inc., Rockford, Ill., 1972—. Served with USNR, 1943-46. Mem. Nat. Electric Contractors Assn., Rock River Valley Electric Assn., Fed. Elec. Contractors. Home: 9809 Partridge Ln Crystal Lake IL 60014 Office: 5200 Newport Dr Rolling Meadows IL 60008

COOPER, CHARLES G., toiletries and cosmetics mfg. exec.; b. Chgo., Apr. 4, 1928; s. Benjamin and Gertrude C.; B.S. in Journalism, U. Ill., 1949; m. Miriam Meyer Cooper, Feb. 11, 1951; children—Deborah, Ruth, Janet, Benjamin. With sales promotion dept. Maidenform, N.Y.C., 1949-51; with circulation promotion dept. Esquire Mag., Chgo., 1951-52; with Helene Curtis, Chgo., 1953—, pres. salon div., 1971-75, pres. consumer products div., 1975—. Served with U.S. Army, 1952-53. Mem. Nat. Wholesale Druggists' Assn., Nat. Assn. Chain Drug Stores. Club: Mid-Am. (Chgo.). Office: 4401 W North Ave Chicago IL 60639

COOPER, CLAUDE ALTON, mfg. co. exec.; b. Eaton County, Mich., Sept. 8, 1905; s. Perl William and Matie (Fraise) C.; student Ebersole Bus. Coll., Lansing, Mich., 1928-29; m. Agnes May Hockenberry, July 30, 1928; children—J. Allen, Charlotte Ann. With Thompson Airlines, 1929-31, mgr. automotive service dept., 1932-43; operator Charlotte (Mich.) Airport, 1943-55; owner, pres., mgr. Automatic Screw Products, Inc., Charlotte, 1955—. Mem. Charlotte Bd. Tax Rev., 1956-57; former officer CAP. Congregationalist. Clubs: Charlotte Yacht, Charlotte Country, Charlotte Rotary; Lansing City, Elks (Lansing); OX5 Aviation (hon. gov. Mich. wing). Home: 344 S Sheldon St Charlotte MI 48813 Office: 205 S Lincoln St Charlotte MI 48813

COOPER, GUY MAC, brokerage exec.; b. Oklahoma City, May 26, 1947; s. Guy N. and Betty M. Cooper; B.A. in Econs. with honors, Yale U., 1969; M.B.A., Stanford U., 1972. With Merrill Lynch Pierce Fenner & Smith, 1972—, instl. salesman modern portfolio theory, Milw., 1974-76, instl. office mgr., 1976—, now asst. United Performing Arts Fund, Milw., 1974—. Served with U.S. Army, 1969-74. Mem. Milw. Soc. Security Analysts, Stanford Bus. Sch. Assn., Milw. Bond Club. Democrat. Clubs: Milw., Univ. (Milw.). Home: 1630 E Hampton Rd Whitefish Bay WI 53217 Office: 270 E Kilbourn Ave Milwaukee WI 53202

COOPER, IRMA MARGARET, musician; b. Sturgis, S.D., Sept. 28, 1912; d. Harold Miles and Edna (Anderson) C.; B.M., Grinnell (Iowa) Coll., 1934; M.M., Am. Conservatory of Music, Chgo., 1937. Winner Chicagoland Music Festival, 1940; profl. singer, Chgo., 1939-43, N.Y.C., 1943-52; appearances include Handel and Haydn Soc., Boston, Lindsborg, Kans. Easter Festival, Miami Opera Guild, Manhattan Opera Co.; opera in Germany, performing 30 leading roles in 600 performances, 1952-64; prof. voice Ohio State U., Columbus, 1964—; chmn. bd. Am. Inst. Musical Studies Service, 1978. Recipient Disting. Teaching award, Ohio State U., 1968. Mem. Met. Opera Nat. Council, Nat. Assn. Tchrs. of Singing, Music Tchrs. Nat. Assn., Nat. Assn. Tchrs. of Singing Found. (bd. dirs.) Opera/Columbus (bd. dirs.), Ohio State U. Friends and Alumni of Sch. of Music, (bd. dirs.), Delta Omicron, Pi Kappa Lambda. Home: 2825 River Park Dr Columbus OH Office: School of Music Ohio State U Columbus OH 43210

COOPER, JAMES CLINTON, social worker; b. Brinson, Ga., Feb. 3, 1929; s. James C.; B.S., Savannah State Coll., 1956; M.S.W., Atlanta U., 1958; postgrad. U. Pitts., 1977-79; m. July 14, 1959. Dir., Residential Treatment Center, Cleve., 1964-67; exec. dir. Goodrich-Bell Center, Cleve., 1967-69; dir. social services Cleve. State Hosp., 1969-74; dir. social services Fairhill Mental Health Center, Cleve., 1974—; lectr. Case Western Res. U., 1968, Cuyahoga Community Coll., West, 1970. Bd. dirs. Hough Area Devel. Corp., 1967-77, 1st vice chmn., 1976-77; adv. bd. Mt. Pleasant Community Center, 1974-77, treas., 1975-77. Served with U.S. Army, 1951-53. Council Social Work Edn. fellow, 1977-79. Mem. Nat. Assn. Social Workers, Acad. Cert. Social Workers (charter), Soc. Hosp. Social Work Dirs. Home: 3602 Glencairn Rd Shaker Heights OH 44122 Office: 12200 Fairhill Rd Cleveland OH 44120

COOPER, JAY JOSEPH, educator; b. Chgo., June 15, 1936; s. Homer Jay and Florence (Murray) C.; B.A., U. Ill., 1956; M.A., U. Alta., 1971; Ph.D., Northwestern U., 1976. Asst. dir. personnel Hart Schaffner & Marx, 1966-69; recruitment officer Portland Cement Assn., Skokie, Ill., 1969-70; sr. personnel analyst City of Chgo., 1971-75; asso. prof. English lit. DePaul U., 1974—; tng. officer VA, Chgo., 1975-79; chief tng. and career mgmt. C.E., U.S. Army, Chgo., 1979—. Bd. dirs. SSS, Chgo.; mem. exec. bd. Chgo. Urban League, 1975-81. Served with U.S. Army, 1953-55. Mem. Am. Mgmt. Assn., Smithsonian Assos. Home: 6101 N Sheridan Rd Chicago IL 60660 Office: 219 S Dearborn St Chicago IL 60604

COOPER, KENNETH CARLTON, tng. cons. co. exec.; b. St. Louis, May 2, 1948; s. George Carlton and Mary Frances (Kavanaugh) C.; B.S., U. Mo. Columbia, 1970, M.S. in Indsl. Engring., 1971; Ph.D. in Communications, Internat. U., 1977; m. Susan Ann Bujnak, Sept. 6, 1969; children—Jeffrey Carlton, Daniel Stephen, Mara Elizabeth. Mktg. rep. IBM, St. Louis, 1971-76; account exec. Downtowner Newspaper, St. Louis, 1976; pres. KCA Assos., Ellisville, Mo., 1976—; adj. faculty St. Louis U., 1972-73, Columbia Coll., 1976-79, Webster Coll., 1977-79; speaker in field. Roy P. Hart Scholar-Athlete grantee, 1970-71; registered profl. engr., Mo.; cert. adminstrv. mgr. Mem. ASTD, Nat. Writers Club, Nat. Speakers Assn., Mensa. Republican. Methodist. Author: Nonverbal Communication For Business Success, 1979; (with Lance Humble) The World's Greatest Blackjack Book, 1980; Body Business, 1981. Home: 1541 Froesel Dr Ellisville MO 63011 Office: PO Box 1205 Ballwin MO 63011

COOPER, MARTIN, electronics co. exec.; b. Chgo., Dec. 26, 1928; s. Arthur and Mary Cooper; B.S.E.E., Ill. Inst. Tech., 1950, M.S.E.E., 1957; children—Scott David, Lisa Ellen. Research engr. Teletype Corp., Chgo., 1953-54; with Motorola, Inc., Schaumburg, Ill., 1954—, ops. mgr., 1967-71, div. mgr., 1977-78, v.p., corp. dir. research and devel., 1978—; mem. computer-telecommunications bd. NRC, 1979-81; mem. indsl. adv. bd. U. Ill. Served with USN, 1950-54. Fellow IEEE (pres. vehicular tech. soc. 1973-74, award for contbns. to radiotelephony, mem. telecommunications policy com. 1978—), Radio Club Am. Patentee in field. Office: 1303 E Algonquin Rd Schaumburg IL 60196

COOPER, REGINALD RUDYARD, orthopaedic surgeon, educator; b. Elkins, W.Va., Jan 6, 1932; s. Eston H. and Kathryn (Wyatt) C.; B.A. with honors, W.Va. U., 1952, B.S., 1953; M.D., Med. Coll. Va., 1955; M.S., U. Iowa, 1960; m. Jacqueline Smith, Aug. 22, 1954; children—Pamela Ann. Douglas Mark, Christopher Scott, Jeffrey Michael. Orthopedic surgeon U.S. Naval Hosp., Pensacola, Fla., 1960-62; asso. in orthopedics U. Iowa Coll. Medicine, Iowa City, 1962-65, asst. prof. orthopaedics, 1965-68, asso. prof., 1968-71, prof., 1971—, chmn. dept., 1973—; research fellow orthopedic surgery Johns Hopkins Hosp., Balt., 1964-65; exchange fellow to Britain for Am. Orthopedic Assn., 1969. Served to lt. comdr. USNR, 1960-62. Diplomate Am. Bd. Orthopedic Surgeons (examiner 1968—). Mem. Iowa, Johnson County med. socs., Orthopedic Research Soc. (sec.-treas. 1970-73, pres. 1974-75), Am. Acad. Orthopedic Surgeons (Kappa Delta award for outstanding research in orthopedics 1971), Canadian, Am. orthopedic assns., Am. Acad. Orthopedic Surgeons (dir. 1973-74, sec.-elect 1981, sec. 1982), N.Y. Acad. Sci., Assn. Bone and Joint Surgeons, AMA, Am. Rheumatism Assn., Am. Fedn. Clin. Research. Home: 201 Ridgeview Ave Iowa City IA 52240

COOPER, WYLOLA, counselor, educator; b. Cleve., Feb. 12, 1926; d. William and Leola (Anderson) Wilkins; B.E., Chgo. State U., 1967; M.A., Roosevelt U., 1974; m. Henry Julius Cooper, Apr. 4, 1948; children—Henry Julius, Wylola, Antigone, Yolanda Lee. Tchr., counselor Southwest Coop. for Spl. Edn., Chgo., 1967—, Dist. 117 Pub. Schs., Chgo., 1967—. Mem. Am. Fedn. Tchrs., NEA, Ill. Educators Assn., Am. Personnel and Guidance Assn., Council Exceptional Children, Chgo. State, Roosevelt U. alumni assns. Roman Catholic. Home: Chicago IL

COOPERRIDER, TOM SMITH, botanist; b. Newark, Ohio, Apr. 15, 1927; s. Oscar Harold and Ruth Evelyn (Smith) C.; B.A., Denison U., 1950; M.S., U. Iowa, 1955, Ph.D. (NSF fellow), 1958; m. Miwako Kunimura, June 13, 1953; children—Julie Ann, John Andrew. With Kent (Ohio) State U., 1958—, instr. biol. scis., 1958-61, asst. prof., 1961-65, asso. prof., 1965-69, prof., 1969—, dir. exptl. programs, 1972-73, curator herbarium, 1968—, dir. Bot. Gardens and Arboretum, 1972—, mem. editorial bd. Univ. Press, 1976-79; on leave as asst. prof. dept. botany U. Hawaii, 1962-63; NSF researcher Mountain Lake Biol. Sta., U. Va., summer 1958; faculty mem. Iowa Lakeside Lab., U. Iowa, summer 1965; cons. endangered and threatened species U.S. Fish and Wildlife Service, Dept. Interior, 1976—; cons. Davey Tree Expert Co., 1979—. Served with AUS, 1945-46. NSF research grantee, 1965-72. Fellow Ohio Acad. Scis. (v.p. 1967); mem. Am. Soc. Plant Taxonomists, Internat. Assn. Plant Taxonomists, AAAS, Bot. Soc. Am., Nature Conservancy, Wilderness Soc., Explorers Club, Blue Key, Sigma Xi. Author: Ferns and Other Pteridophytes of Iowa, 1959; Vascular Plants of Clinton, Jackson and Jones Counties, Iowa, 1962. Home: 548 Bowman Dr Kent OH 44240

COOPERSMITH, BERNARD IRA, physician, surgeon; b. Chgo., Oct. 19, 1914; s. Morris and Anna (Shulder) C.; B.S. cum laude, U. Ill., 1936, M.D. cum laude, 1938; m. Beatrice Klass, May 26, 1940; children—Carol, Cathie. Intern, Michael Reese Hosp., Chgo., 1938-39, resident in obstetrics and gynecology, 1939-42; practice medicine specializing in obstetrics and gynecology, Chgo., 1942—; mem. staff Prentice Women's Hosp. of Northwestern Meml. Hosp., Michael Reese Hosp., Mt. Sinai Hosp., Chgo. Maternity Center; asst. prof. obstetrics and gynecology Northwestern U. Med. Sch., Chgo., 1948—. Pres. Barren Found. Chgo., 1971-73. Diplomate Am. Bd. Obstetrics and Gynecology, also recert. Recipient Service awards Michael Reese Hosp., 1972, Northwestern U. Med. Sch., 1973, Chgo. Maternity Center, 1968. Fellow A.C.S.; mem. Chgo., Ill. med. socs., AMA, Chgo. Gynecol. Soc., Central Assn. Obstetrics and Gynecology, Am. Coll. Obstetrics and Gynecology, Alpha Omega Alpha. Jewish. Clubs: Bryn Mawr Country, Carleton. Contbr. articles to profl. jours. Home: 1110 N Lake Shore Dr Chicago IL 60611 Office: 333 E Superior St Suite 444 Chicago IL 60611

COOPWOOD, CARNEY FERMANDO, detail tooling draftsman; b. Gary, Ind., Oct. 27, 1948; s. Theodore Roosevelt and Lillier Anna (McNeil) C.; student Chgo. Urban Skills Inst., 1972, Chgo. Tech. Coll., 1973-75, Chgo. City Colls., 1976-79; m. Marjorie Bradley, Dec. 29, 1978; 1 son, Carney Fermando. Draftsman, Amphenol Indsl. Div., Cicero, Ill., 1972-75, Chicago-Allis Mfg. Corp., Chgo., 1975; detail draftsman Am. Screen Process, Chgo., 1977, Pettibone Mfg. Corp., Chgo., 1978-80, Channan Corp., 1980-81, Guardian Electric Mfg. Corp., Chgo., 1981—. Served with USAF, 1966-69. Mem. Nat. Splty. Merchandisers Assn. Home: 323 S Franklin St Suite 804 Box H 7D Chicago IL 60606 Office: 1550 W Carroll St Chicago IL 60607

COORTS, GERALD DUANE, educator; b. Emden, Ill., Feb. 3, 1932; s. Ralph Albert and Hannah Tena (Wubben) C.; B.S. (Danforth fellow), U. Mo., 1954, M.S., 1958; Ph.D., U. Ill., 1964; m. Annette Bosman, Sept. 14, 1957; children—David Jonathan, Charles Frederick, Cynthia Anne. Instr. horticulture Purdue U., 1959-61; asst. prof. horticulture U. R.I., 1964-68; asso. prof. plant and soil sci. So. Ill. U., Carbondale, 1968-72, prof., 1972—, chmn. dept., 1973—. Bd. dirs. Jackson County YMCA, Green Earth, Inc. Served to 1st lt., Chem. Corps, AUS, 1954-56. Recipient Obelisk award for Outstanding Teaching, 1972. Mem. U.S. Jr. C. of C. (chpt. v.p. 1966-67), Am. Soc. Hort. Sci., Am. Soc. Agronomy, Am. Hort. Soc., Council for Agrl. Sci. and Tech., Plant Growth Regulator Soc. of Am. Soc. Am. Florists, Sigma Xi, Alpha Zeta, Gamma Sigma Delta, Pi Alpha Xi, Phi Mu Alpha, Phi Sigma, Phi Kappa Phi, FarmHouse. Home: 1714 Colonial Dr Carbondale IL 62901

COPE, RON, state legislator; b. Pawnee County, Nebr., Feb. 23, 1911; student Peru State Coll.; m. Carol Schrepel, 1939. Farmer, Kearney, Nebr.; mem. Nebr. Legislature, 1974—. Former chmn. Kearney City Planning Commn., Tri-City Coordinating Council; former chmn. bd. dirs. ARC; former mem. Nebr. Republican Central Com. Mem. Kearney C. of C., Buffalo County Livestock Feeders Assn., Buffalo County Hist. Soc. Clubs: Elks, KC. Address: 20 Hillcrest Dr Kearney NE 68847*

COPE, RONALD WAYNE, ednl. adminstr.; b. St. Louis, Nov. 11, 1946; s. Emmette Lowell and Dorothea Elizabeth (Witt) C.; B.S., U. Mo., 1968, M.Ed., 1971, Ed.S., 1977, Ed.D., 1981; m. Phyllis Ann Albart, June 8, 1968; children—Tara Ann, Nicole Ann, Jessica Ann. Tchr., Fort Zumwalt Sch. Dist., O'Fallon, Mo., 1968-71, prin. elementary sch., 1971-74; disabilities determination examiner Mo. Dept. Elem. and Secondary Edn., St. Louis, 1974-75; coordinator fed. programs North Callaway Sch. Dist., Kingdom City, Mo., 1975-78; supt. schs., Maries County R-II Sch. Dist., Belle, Mo., 1978—. Mem. Citizens Adv. Council Sta. KETC-TV, St. Louis, 1974-75; chmn. citizens adv. com. Family and Children's Services of Greater St. Louis, 1972-74; mem. Meramec Regional Planning Commn. Public Transp. Com., 1979-81. Mem. Assn. Supervision and Curriculum Devel., Mo. Assn. Sch. Adminstrs., South Central Assn. Sch. Adminstrs., Mo. State Tchrs. Assn., Maries County Community Tchrs. Assn. Roman Catholic. Clubs: Lions, Belle Country. Office: PO Box AC Belle MO 65013

COPELAND, ELAINE JOHNSON, ednl. adminstr.; b. Catawba, S.C., Mar. 11, 1943; d. Aaron Jasper and Roberta Lucille (Hawkins) Johnson; B.S., Livingstone Coll., 1964; M.A. in Teaching, Winthrop Coll., 1971; Ph.D., Oreg. State U., 1974; m. Robert M. Copeland, Sept. 26, 1964; 1 son, Robert. Tchr. sci. Florence (S.C.) Pub. Schs., 1964-65; tchr. biology York (S.C.) Pub. Schs., 1965-70; counselor Oreg. State U., 1970-74; research asso. U. Ill., Champaign, 1974-75, asst. dean, dir. minority affairs grad. coll., 1975—; project supr. Title 1, Black Elderly Project, 1974-75; co-organizer Black Elderly Conf. of Champaign County, 1975. Chmn. bd. dirs. Univ. YWCA, 1976-77; bd. dirs. Ill. Children's Home and Aid, 1975—; pres. Champaign-Urbana Girls' Club, 1978—. Recipient award for service to elderly Telecare, 1975. Mem. Am. Psychol. Assn., Nat. Assn. Women Deans, Adminstrs. and Counselors, Am. Personnel and Guidance Assn., Assn. for Non-White Concerns in Personnel and Guidance, Coll. Student Personnel Assn., Phi Kappa Phi, Delta Sigma Theta. Methodist. Clubs: Urban League Guild, Champaign County. Home: 34 Ashley Ln Champaign IL 61820 Office: 337 Administration Bldg University of Illinois Urbana IL 61801

COPELAND, JESSE WARREN, JR., educator; b. Norfolk, Va., July 18, 1929; s. Jesse Warren and Bertna (Grey) C.; B.S., Va. State Coll., 1959; M.S., Wayne State U., 1971; postgrad. U. Mich., summer 1960, Mich. State U. summer 1961, Eastman Sch. Music, summer 1962; cert. in human sexuality Merrill Palmer Inst., Detroit, 1976. Tchr., William C. Taylor High Sch., Warrenton, Va., 1959-62; tchr.-counselor Boys Tng. Sch., Lansing, Mich., 1962-65; tchr. music Highland Park (Mich.) Sch. Dist., 1965-78, tchr. social studies, 1978—, chmn. dept. high sch. social studies, 1979—; bd. dirs. Head Start, Teen Father and Mother Program; mem. Mighty Voices of Thunder male chorus Greater New Mt. Moriah Baptist Ch., Detroit. Served with U.S. Army, 1948-55. Decorated Purple Heart. Mem. Assn. Supervision and Curriculum Devel., Mich. Council Social Studies, Council Exceptional Children, NAACP. Home: 2725 W McNichols St Apt 205 Detroit MI 48221 Office: 15900 Woodward Highland Park MI 48203

COPELAND, RICHARD ALLAN, environ. cons. corp. exec.; b. Los Angeles, May 30, 1942; s. Charles Sallaz and Marjorie Helen (Stemsrud) C.; B.S. in Geology and Chemistry, U. Calif., Berkeley, 1964; Ph.D. in Environ. Chemistry, M.I.T., 1969; postgrad. U. Mich., 1969; m. Ida Michi Yamanaka, July 1, 1967; 1 dau., Caroline. Asst. research chemist U. Mich., Ann Arbor, 1970; pres. Environ. Research Group Inc., Ann Arbor, 1971—, chief operating officer, 1971-77, chief exec. officer, 1977—, also dir.; guest lectr. U. Mich.; guest speaker in field civic and public interest groups. Recipient fed. and state grants; fed. and state lic. lab. dir. Mem. ASTM, Water Pollution Control Fedn., AAAS, Mich. C. of C., Sigma Xi. Republican. Contbr. writings in field to profl. publs. Home: 2730 W Ellsworth Rd Ann Arbor MI 48104 Office: 117 N First St Ann Arbor MI 48104

COPELAND, WILLIAM EDGAR, physician; b. Huntington, W.Va., Nov. 22, 1920; s. Orville Edgar and Clara Gertrude (Naylon) C.; M.D., Med. Coll. Va., 1945; m. Carolyn Ann Varin, Jan. 31, 1948; children—William Edgar, Christopher Marsh, Stephen Jeffrey. Intern, Stuart Circle Hosp., Richmond, Va., 1945-46; resident in obstetrics gynecology Hosp. U. Pa., Phila., 1948-51; practice medicine specializing in obstetrics and gynecology, Phila., 1951-53, Columbus, Ohio, 1953—; mem. staff Ohio State U. Hosp., Columbus, Childrens Hosp., VA Hosp., Dayton, Riverside Meth. Hosp., Columbus, Wright Patterson AFB Hosp., Dayton; mem. faculty Ohio State U., 1953—, prof. obstetrics and gynecology, 1970—, dir. clin. div., dept., 1971-73. Mem. adv. com. Planned Parenthood, YMCA. Served with USN, 1943-47. Fellow Am. Coll. Obstetricians and Gynecologists, ACS, Am. Soc. Study Fertility; mem. Central Assn. Obstetricians and Gynecologists, AMA, N. Am. Obstet. and Gynecol. Soc., Ohio Med. Soc., Ohio State U. Health Center Med. Soc., Assn. Am. Med. Colls. Clubs: Scioto Country, Faculty, Zanesfield Rod and Gun, Grand Hotel Hunt, Ohio State U. Pres., League Ohio Sportsmen. Contbr. articles to profl. jours. Home: 2495 Sherwin Rd Columbus OH 43221 Office: 1800 Zollinger Rd Columbus OH 43221

COPELAND, WILLIAM MACK, hosp. adminstr., lawyer; b. Harriman, Tenn., Jan. 21, 1937; s. John Hyder and Margaret Elizabeth (Gardner) C.; B.A., So. Colo. State U., 1965; M.S., U. Colo., 1969; J.D., No. Ky. State U., 1977; m. Barbara Ann Leurck, 1980; children—Elizabeth, William, Brian, George, Carolyn. Commd. 2d lt. U.S. Air Force, 1954, advanced through grades to capt., 1968, ret., 1975; asso. adminstr. St. George Hosp., Cin., 1976-77, adminstr., 1977-78; pres. St. Francis-St. George Hosp., Inc., Cin., 1978—; lectr. Patients Right Inst.; admitted to Ohio bar, 1978, Fed. Dist. Ct. bar, 1978; v.p. Greater Cin. Hosp. Council; charter pres. Dayton Area Adminstrs. Group; adj. faculty Xavier U. and InterAm. U. Vice chmn. dept. health affairs Ohio Cath. Conf., chmn. inst. plan com. and legis. com. Decorated Meritorious Service medal, Air Force Commendation medal with oak leaf cluster; recipient Monsignor Griffin award Ohio Hosp. Assn., 1979. Fellow Am. Coll. Hosp. Adminstrs., Am. Acad. Health Adminstrs. (pres.-elect Ohio chpt.), Nat. Health Lawyers Assn., Am. Soc. Hosp. Attys., Cath. Health Assn. U.S. (govt. legis. com., health planning com.), Am. Soc. Law and Medicine, Am. Bar Assn., Ohio Bar Assn., Cin. Bar Assn. Club: Kiwanis. Contbr. articles to profl. jours. Office: 3098 Queen City Ave Cincinnati OH 45238

COPENHAVER, LLOYD FRANKLIN, mech. engr.; b. Palmyra, Mo., June 5, 1948; s. Arthur Lloyd and Greta (Hustead) C.; B.S.M.E., U. Mo., Columbia, 1971, M.S.M.E., 1972; m. Mary Beth Loesing, Dec. 30, 1972. Research engr. Carrier Corp., 1972-73, devel. engr. Day and Night Payne div., 1973-75; sr. devel. engr. to mgr. gas furnace devel. BDP Co. div. Carrier Corp., Indpls., 1975—. Lic. profl. engr., Ind. Mem. ASHRAE. Home: 6438 Columbine Dr Indianapolis IN 46224 Office: BDP Co 7310 W Morris St Indianapolis IN 46231

COPES, MARVIN LEE, ednl. adminstr.; b. Connersville, Ind., Sept. 19, 1938; s. Kenneth Edward and Frances Gertrude (Bean) C.; B.S., Purdue U., 1961, M.S., 1962, Ph.D., 1975; postgrad. Ind. State U., 1967-68, Ind. U., 1967-68; m. Luretta Ann Grenard, Aug. 26, 1961; children—Bradley Alan, Brian Keith, Brent Lee. Grad. asst. agr. edn. Purdue U., 1961-62, grad. instr., 1968-69; tchr. vocat. agr. Tri-County Sch. Corp., Walcott, Ind., 1964-65; vocat. dir. Met. Sch. Dist. Vernon Twp., Crothersville, Ind., 1965-68, also dir. Ind. Vocat. Agr. Demonstration Center; asst. exec. sec. Kappa Delta Pi Hdqrs., West

Lafayette, Ind., 1969-70; dir. Blue River Vocat.-Tech. Center, Shelbyville, Ind. 1970-79; nat. curriculum devel. coordinator ITT Ednl. Services, Indpls., 1979-80, nat. dir. edn., 1980—. Pres., Loper Parent Tchr. Orgn., 1974—; leader 4-H, 1964—; adviser Future Farmers Am., 1964—; cubmaster Cub Scouts Am., 1976; scoutmaster, commr. Boy Scouts Am.; bd. dirs. Shelbyville Boys Club Am., 1976, Northeast India Christian Mission, 1974. Served to 1st lt., AUS, 1962-64. Mem. Am., Ind. vocat. assns., Ind., Nat. councils local adminstrs., Future Farmers Am. Alumni Assn., Shelby County C. of C., Pershing Rifles, Gideons Internat., Alpha Tau Alpha, Kappa Delta Pi, Phi Delta Kappa, Delta Pi Epsilon. Mem. Christian Ch. (elder). Mason; mem. Order Eastern Star. Author: A Curriculum Guide for Training in Agricultural Supply, 1968, Student Handbook for Cooperative Progress in Agricultural Occupations, 1968, A Predictability of Career Choices of High School Seniors, 1975. Home: Rural Route 2 Box 370 Fairland IN 46126 Office: 3750 Guion Rd Indianapolis IN 46222

COPLEY, PATRICK O'NEIL, univ. dean; b. Seneca, Mo., Feb. 4, 1933; s. Charles Milton and Lorraine Lida (McCoy) C.; B.A., Grand Canyon Coll., Phoenix, 1958; M.A., Ariz. State U., 1959, Ed.D., 1967; m. Elizabeth Ann Wheeler, Nov. 8, 1953; children—Chazell, Charlene, Patrice. Dir. edn. and music Parkview Baptist Ch., Phoenix, 1955-59; tchr. Central High Sch., Phoenix, 1959-65; asst. dean Sch. Edn., U. Mo., St. Louis, 1965-67; dean Sch. Edn., S.W. Mo. State U., Springfield, 1967—. Bd. dirs. Springfield United Cerebral Palsy, Mo. Bapt. Children's Home, St. Louis. Served with USAF, 1951-55. Grantee HEW, 1977-81. Mem. Am. Assn. Colls. Tchrs. Edn. (council state reps., dir., exec. com.), Mo. Assn. Colls. Tchr. Edn. (pres. 1977-79), Tchr. Edn. Council of State Colls. and Univs. (pres. 1980-81), Mo. State Tchrs. Assn., Phi Delta Kappa, Kappa Delta Phi, Alpha Phi Omega. Author articles in field. Office: 901 S National St Springfield MO 65802

CORAN, ARNOLD GERALD, pediatric surgeon, educator; b. Boston, Apr. 16, 1938; s. Charles and Anne (Cohen) C.; B.A. cum laude, Harvard U., 1959, M.D. cum laude, 1963; m. Susan Williams, Nov. 17, 1960; children—Michael, David, Randi Beth. Intern, Peter Bent Brigham Hosp., Boston, 1963-64, resident in surgery, 1964-68, chief surg. resident, 1969; resident in surgery Children's Hosp. Med. Center, Boston, 1965-66, sr. surg. resident, 1966, chief surg. resident, 1968; instr. surgery Harvard, Cambridge, Mass., 1967-69; asst. clin. prof. surgery George Washington U., Washington, 1970-72; head physician pediatric surgery Los Angeles County-U. So. Calif. Med. Center, 1972-74; asst. prof. surgery U. So. Calif., 1972-73, asso. prof., 1973-74; prof. surgery U. Mich., Ann Arbor, 1974—, head sect. pediatric surgery U. Mich. Hosp., 1974—. Served to lt. comdr. M.C., U.S. Navy. Diplomate Am. Bd. Surgery, Am. Bd. Thoracic Surgery. Fellow A.C.S.; mem. Am. Acad. Pediatrics, Soc. Univ. Surgeons, Am. Pediatric Surg. Assn., Western, Central surg. assns. Contbr. numerous articles in field to profl. jours. Home: 3450 Vintage Valley Rd Ann Arbor MI 48105 Office: Mott Children's Hosp Ann Arbor MI 48109

CORBALLY, JOHN EDWARD, educator; b. South Bend, Wash., Oct. 14, 1924; s. John Edward and Grace (Williams) C.; B.S., U. Wash., 1947, M.A., 1950; Ph.D., U. Calif. at Berkeley, 1955; LL.D. (hon.), U. Md., 1971, Blackburn Coll., 1972, Ill. State U., 1977, Ohio State U., 1980; Litt.D. (hon.), Akron U., 1979; m. Marguerite B. Walker, Mar. 12, 1946; children—Jan Elizabeth, David William. Tchr., Clover Park High Sch., Tacoma, 1947-50; prin. Twin City High Sch., Stanwood, Wash., 1950-53; asst. prof. edn., asso. prof. Ohio State U., Columbus, 1955-61, prof., 1961-69, dir. personnel budget and exec. asst. to pres., 1961-64, v.p. adminstrn., 1964-66, provost, v.p. acad. affairs, 1966-69; chancellor, also pres. Syracuse U., 1969-71; pres. U. Ill., Chgo. and Urbana, 1971-79, pres. emeritus and Disting. prof. higher edn., 1979—; pres., dir. John D. and Catherine T. MacArthur Fund; dir. Ill. Bell Telephone Co., Bankers Life and Casualty Co., 1st Nat. Bank, Champaign. Mem. governing bd. Joint Council Econ. Edn.; chmn. nat. council ednl. research Nat. Inst. Edn., 1973-79. Bd. dirs. Council for Fin. Aid to Edn., 1975-79, Found. for Teaching of Econs.; acad. trustee Lincoln Acad. Ill. Served to lt. (j.g.) USNR, 1943-46. Recipient Disting. Eagle Scout award, 1978. Mem. Phi Beta Kappa, Phi Kappa Sigma, Phi Delta Kappa, Phi Kappa Phi, Omicron Delta Kappa, Chi Gamma Iota, Beta Gamma Sigma. Clubs: Mid-Day, Tavern (Chgo.); Champaign (Ill.) Country. Author: Introduction to Educational Administration, 4th edit., 1971; Educational Administration: The Secondary School, 2d edit., 1965; School Finance, 1962. Home: PO Box 441 Urbana IL 61801 Office: 333 Education Bldg U Ill Urbana IL 61801

CORBAN, DOUGLAS MAC, data processing cons. and mgr.; b. Cin., Oct. 7, 1946; s. Wilbur Hall and Faith Marion C.; B.B.A., Kent State U., 1968; M.B.A., U. Utah, 1973; m. Mary Katherine Gerring, July 11, 1970; children—Jeffrey Wilbur, Lori Ann. Account mgr. Burroughs Corp., Salt Lake City, 1973-76; project leader, data processing mgr. J.R. Simplot Corp., Pocatello, Idaho, 1976-78; mgr. data processing cons. McGladrey Hendrickson & Co., Elkhart, Ind., 1978—. Served to capt., USAF, 1968-72. Decorated Air Force commendation medal. Mem. Data Processing Mgmt. Assn., Am. Production and Inventory Control Soc. Mem. Assembly of God Ch. Home: 50915 Hill Dr Elkhart IN 46515 Office: Main and Franklin PO Box 99 Elkhart IN 46515

CORBETT, DENNIS DALE, advt. exec.; b. Evansville, Ind., Apr. 11, 1944; s. Cecil W. and Gertrude M. (Jackson) C.; B.S. in Bus., U. Evansville, 1966; B.S. in Econs., Henry George Sch., 1969; theol. certificate Ambassador Coll., 1970; m. Dwana Sue Yates, Jan. 27, 1973; 1 dau., Koelle Kristen. Spl. investigator Research Assos., 1963-65; detective Internat. Films, 1968-71; owner Corbett Enterprises, Evansville, Ind., 1963—. Probation counselor Vanderburgh County Vol. Probation Counselors Program, 1972—; campaign dir. March of Dimes, 1968; mem. nat. adv. com. Am. Security Council; mem. citizens adv. com. for Right to Keep and Bear Arms; founder Archtl. Barriers Research. Bd. dirs. Evansville Area Council Chs., mem. mass media com.; asst. lay leader Seventh Day Adventist Ch.; bd. dirs. Concern for Haiti (orphanage); mem. Republican Citizens Finance Com. Ind.; chmn. Title I parents adv. council Harwood Sch., 1980-81; spl. advisor troop 505 Boy Scouts Am., 1980—. Recipient Key Man award Jr. C. of C., 1966. Mem. Am. Mgmt. Assn. (presidents assn.), Nat. Rifle Assn., Nat. Wildlife Fedn., ACLU, Direct Selling Legion, Internat. Speakers Network, Ams. Against Union Control of Govt., Council on Religion and Internat. Affairs, Conservative Caucus, Security and Intelligence Fund, Council Inter-am. Security, Interam. Soc. OAS, Nat. Right to Work Com., Am. Film Inst., Assn. Supervision and Curriculum Devel., Inst. Soc., Ethics and Life Scis., Inst. Am. Relations, Target '76, Jr. C. of C., Evansville Mus., Evansville Zool. Soc. Home: 1311 Northbrook Ct Evansville IN 47710 Office: 150 Broadway New York NY 10038 also 1639 N California St Chicago IL 60647

CORBIN, GARY GEORGE, state legislator; b. Bedford, Ind., Dec. 13, 1941; s. George and Mamie (Saltz) C.; B.A., Anderson Coll., 1963, M.Div., 1967; m. Sheila Buck, 1962; children—Susan, Sally. Ordained to ministry Ch. of God, Anderson, Ind., 1968; pastor Community Ch. of God, Clio, Mich., 1967-74; county commr. Dist. 12 Genesee County (Mich.), 1970-74; mem. Mich. Senate, 1975—, asst. majority leader, 1976—; mem. ethics and elections com. Nat. Council State Legislatures, 1977—; mem. agr. and edn. coms. Council State Govts., 1977—. Trustee Olivet Coll., 1979—. Recipient Disting. Service award Assn. Ind. Colls. and Univs., 1977, award for services to Mich. higher edn. Mich. AAUP, 1977, Goodwill Industries award, 1978. Democrat. Office: PO Box 30036 Lansing MI 48909

CORBIN, WILLIAM NEWTON, educator; b. Vanderlip, W.Va., Aug. 28, 1915; s. Reuben Heitt and Catherine Miranda (Cosner) C.; B.B.A., St. Mary's U., 1952, B.A., 1952; M.A., U. Denver, 1953; m. Aileen Frances Stichnot, Sept. 9, 1942. Personnel supr. U.S. Civil Service, San Antonio, 1945-49; tchr. Classen High Sch., Oklahoma City, 1953-55; with Idaho State U., Pocatello, 1955-80, asso. prof. speech, 1969-80, prof. emeritus, 1980—; vis. asso. prof. debate NE Mo. State U., 1980—. Served with AUS, 1940-45; ret. chief master sgt. USAF, 1975. Named Ronald Regan Coach of Yr., Sacramento, Calif., 1977; Outstanding Forensics Dir., Eastern Mont. State Coll., 1979; recipient Cert. of Appreciation, UCLA, 1979, Idaho State Bd. Regents, 1980. Mem. Am. Inst. Parliamentarians (accrediting com. 1974-78, dir. 1976, 78, fin. com. 1976-80, membership com. 1980), Am. Arbitration Assn., Speech Communication Am., Western Speech Communication Assn., Am., Western forensic assns., Noncommd. Officers Assn. (trustee), Phi Kappa Phi. Roman Catholic. Club: K.C. Home: 901 E Orchard Kirksville MO 63501

CORBOY, PHILIP HARNETT, lawyer; b. Chgo., Aug. 12, 1924; s. Harold Francis and Marie (Harnett) C.; student St. Ambrose Coll., 1942-43, U. Notre Dame, 1945; J.D., Loyola U., 1949; m. Doris Marie Conway, Nov. 26, 1949; children—Philip Harnett, Joan Marie, John Richard, Thomas Michael. Admitted to Ill. bar, 1949; asst. corp. counsel City Chgo., 1949-50; individual practice, 1950—; lectr. schs. and profl. assns. Trustee Roscoe Pound Found. Served with AUS, 1943-45. Fellow Am. Coll. Trial Lawyers; mem. Am. (chmn. litigation sect. 1979-80), Ill., Chgo. (pres. 1972-73) bar assns., Law Sci. Acad., Am. Judicature Soc., Am., Ill. (pres. 1963-64) trial lawyers assns., Nat. Inst. Trial Advocacy (vice chmn. 1971-72), Internat. Acad. Trial Lawyers, Internat. Soc. Barristers, Inner Circle Advs. Clubs: Evanston Golf, Covenant, Chgo. Athletic Assn. Contbr. articles to profl. jours. Home: 180 E Pearson St Chicago IL 60611 Office: Suite 630 33 N Dearborn St Chicago IL 60602

CORCORAN, JAMES MARTIN, JR., lawyer; b. Evanston, Ill., Nov. 12, 1932; s. James M. and Ethel M. (Fitzgerald) C.; A.B., U. Notre Dame, 1955, J.D., 1956; m. Catherine F. Howland, Aug. 6, 1955; children—Mary Carol, John Kevin, Lawrence T., Rosemary C., Pauline M., Moira E., Daniel P. Admitted to Ill. bar, 1956, practiced in Evanston, 1956-78; partner Corcoran & Corcoran, attys., Evanston, 1957-63, sr. partner, 1964-72; pres. Corcoran & Corcoran, P.C., Evanston, 1973-78; partner firm D'Ancona, Pflaum, Wyatt & Riskind, Chgo., 1979—; lectr. in field. Mem. sch. bd. St. Mary's Sch., 1969-72. Recipient Harrison Tweed award Assn. Continuing Legal Edn. Adminstrs., 1975; Disting. Service award Chgo. Estate Planning Council, 1975. Fellow Am. Coll. Probate Counsel (editorial bd. Probate Notes 1975-78); mem. Am., Ill. (bd. govs. 1972-75), Chgo. bar assns. Roman Catholic. Author: Alternatives to Probate, 1972; Suggested Will and Trust Clauses, 1973; In the Office—A Form Book for Lawyers, 1974; Estate, Gift and Generation-Skipping Taxation for the General Practitioner, 1979, supplement, 1980; Probate Forms for Estates of Minors, Incompetents and Decedents, 1977; (with others) Drafting Wills and Trust Agreements, rev., 1982; editor estate planning, probate and trust law questions Ill. Bar Jour., 1965—. Contbr. chpts. to continuing legal edn. books, 57 articles to profl. jours. Home: 929 Sheridan Rd Evanston IL 60202 Office: 30 N LaSalle St Chicago IL 60602

CORCORAN, MAURICE FRIDOLIN, elec. engr.; b. New Bedford, Mass., Dec. 15, 1926; s. Charles S. and Norma (Bartholomeus) C.; B.S. in Elec. Engring., Tufts U., 1951; m. Irene Helen McDonald, June 17, 1951; children—Christine, Valerie, Sandra, Gregory. With Allis Chalmers, various locations, 1951-73, field engr., Cleve., 1953-59, sr. engr. indsl. systems, Milw., 1959-62, sr. elec. engr. project ops., Milw., 1962-66, mgr. elec. engring. project ops., Milw., 1966-73; staff cons. engr. Doyen & Assos., Inc., Chgo., 1973—. Served with AUS, 1945-46. Registered profl. engr., Wis. Mem. IEEE (sr.), Assn. Iron and Steel Engrs. Home: 2833 Fern Ave Northbrook IL 60062 Office: 222 W Adams St Room 381 Chicago IL 60606

CORCORAN, TOM, Congressman; b. Ottawa, Ill., May 23, 1939; s. Thomas F. C.; m. Helenmarie Anderson; children—Camilla, Evan, Philip, Steven, Monica; grad. U. Notre Dame, 1961; postgrad. U. Ill., 1961-62, Northwestern U., 1966-68, U. Chgo., 1962-63. Legis. asst. Ill. Senate Pres. Pro Tem W. Russell Arrington, 1966-69; dir. State of Ill. Office, Washington, 1969-72; v.p. Chgo. & North Western Transp. Co., 1974-76; mem. 95th-97th Congresses from 15th Ill. Dist. Home: Ottawa IL 61350 Office: 1107 Longworth House Office Bldg Washington DC 20515

CORDIN, WALTER WOLFE, banker; b. Hinsdale, Ill., Mar. 22, 1943; s. Nicholas S. and Ruth A. (Wolfe) C.; A.B. in Econs., U. Mich., 1965; m. Evelyn A. Butler, Dec. 7, 1973; children—Sara, Alison, Michael, Nichole. Gen. mgr. freight consolidation Cordin & Co., Detroit, 1965-67; asst. trust officer 1st Nat. Bank of West Chicago (Ill.), 1968-69, v.p., 1970-73, v.p., cashier, 1973-74, pres., 1975—; dir. Cordin Motor Freight, Inc. Treas., United Way West Chicago, 1968—; founder Community Coordinating Council West Chicago, 1978; chmn. citizens com. Community Redevel. Commn., 1980; trustee St. Mary's Ch. Mem. Am. Bankers Assn., Bank Adminstrn. Inst., Ind. Bankers Assn. Am., West Chicago C. of C. (pres.). Republican. Roman Catholic. Club: Lions. Office: 101 Main St West Chicago IL 60185

CORFIAS, JOHN CHRYST, coll. adminstr.; b. Youngstown, Ohio, Sept. 30, 1929; s. Chryst John and Mary C.; B.A., Case Western Res. U., 1951, M.A., 1959, Ed.D., 1967; m. Dolores Jean Burden, Jan. 31, 1953; children—John Michael Christopher, Stephen Peter Lowell. Asst. mgr. prodn. control Gen. Motors Corp., 1955-62; dir. admissions and records Cuyahoga Community Coll., Cleve., 1962-64, asso. prof., 1965-67, dean bus. adminstrn. and technologies, 1967-71, acting dean arts and scis., 1968-69, interim campus pres., 1969-70; pres. Dyke Coll., Cleve., 1971—. Trustee, Ohio Council on for Econ. Edn.; trustee, pres. Cleve. Restoration Soc.; trustee Greater Cleve. Ethnographic Mus., Inc., Goodwill Industries of Greater Cleve.; mem. exec. com. Cleve. Golden Gloves Assn.; mem. Cleve. Commn. on Higher Edn.; mem. community liaison council Cleve. Playhouse; mem. admissions com. United Way Services; mem. County Commrs.' Adv. Com. on Shelters for Victims of Domestic Violence; sec. Pvt. Industry Council-CETA, Cuyahoga-Parma-Geauga. Recipient Outstanding Service award Shaker Boys League, 1973; Boss of Yr. award Am. Bus. Women's Assn. Cleve. chpt. 1978-79; Downtown Recognition award Greater Cleve. Growth Assn., 1979; Citizen of Yr. award Cleve. Area Bd. Realtors, 1981. Mem. Ohio Coll. Assn., Newcomen Soc., English Speaking Union. Clubs: Case Res. Athletic, Rotary, Cleve. Athletic, City, 13th St Racquet. Office: Dyke Coll 1375 E 6th St Cleveland OH 44114

CORLETT, CYNTHIA LOUISE, microbiologist; b. Cleve., Aug. 11, 1954; d. Donald F. and Elizabeth Louise (Grande) C.; B.S., Ashland Coll., 1976; student Cleve. Clinic Sch. Med. Tech., 1975-76; postgrad. Cleve. State U.; m. K. Brad Knapp, July 29, 1978. Med. technologist, microbiol. researcher, Cleve. Clinic Hosp., 1976—. Mem. Am. Soc. Microbiology, Am. Soc. Clin. Pathology (cert.). Republican. Episcopalian. Co-author abstracts, contbr. articles in field to profl. publs. Office: 9500 Euclid Ave Cleveland OH 44106

CORLEY, WILLIAM GENE, research and devel. co. exec.; b. Shelbyville, Ill., Dec. 19, 1935; s. Clarence William and Mary Winifred (Douthit) C.; B.S., U. Ill., 1958, M.S., 1960, Ph.D., 1961; m. Jenny Lynd Wertheim, Aug. 9, 1959; children—Anne Lynd, Robert William, Scott Elson. Research and teaching asst. U. Ill., Urbana, 1958-61; devel. engr. Portland Cement Assn., Skokie, Ill., 1964-66, mgr. structural devel. sect., 1966-74, dir. engring. devel. div., 1974—. Mem. adv. panels NSF; pres. caucus Glenview (Ill.) Sch. Bd., 1971-72; elder United Presbyn. Ch., 1975-79; sec. bd. dirs. Assn. House, Chgo., 1976, treas., 1977, pres., 1978-79. Served to 1st lt., C.E., U.S. Army, 1961-64. Recipient Wason medal for Research, 1970; Bloem award Am. Concrete Inst., 1978; Martin Korn award Prestressed Concrete Inst., 1978; registered profl. engr. several states. Fellow Am. Concrete Inst., ASCE (T.Y. Lin award 1979); mem. Nat. Soc. Profl. Engrs., Earthquake Engring. Research Inst. (chpt. sec.-treas. 1980—), Internat. Assn. Bridge and Structural Engring., RILEM, Post-Tensioning Inst., Chgo. Com. High-Rise Bldgs. (vice-chmn. 1978—). Presbyterian. Contbr. articles to tech. and profl. jours. Home: 744 Glenayre Dr Glenview IL 60025 Office: Portland Cement Assn 5420 Old Orchard Rd Skokie IL 60077

CORN, ROBERT MARION, mech. engr.; b. Emington, Ill., Feb. 12, 1940; s. William Prentice and Viola Helen (Hewson) C.; B.M.E., Bradley U., 1962; m. Nancy Ann Carlson, June 6, 1964; 1 son, Dennis Robert. Engring. trainee Ford Motor Co., Dearborn, Mich., 1962-64, design analyst, 1964-67, design engr., 1967-79, sr. design engr., 1969-74, prin. engr., 1974-78, engring. supr., 1978-81; owner Engine and Control Systems, Inc., cons. firm, Livonia, Mich., 1981—. Registered profl. engr., Mich. Mem. Soc. Automotive Engrs. Home: 33824 Tawas Westland MI 48185 Office: 12319 Levan Livonia MI 48150

CORNELIUS, RICHARD DEAN, chemist, educator; b. Chgo., Sept. 18, 1947; B.A. in Chemistry, Carleton Coll., 1969; Ph.D. in Inorganic Chemistry, U. Iowa, 1974; postdoctoral study U. Wis., 1974-77. Research and teaching asst. dept. chemistry U. Iowa, 1969-74; research asso. U. Wis., Madison, 1974-77; asst. prof. chemistry Wichita (Kans.) State U., 1977—. Mem. Am. Chem. Soc., Sigma Xi. Contbr. articles on inorganic chemistry to sci. publs. Home: 209 N Fountain St Wichita KS 67208 Office: Dept Chemistry Wichita State Univ Wichita KS 67208

CORNELIUS, THOMAS PAUL, cert. public accountant; b. Hubbard, Ohio, Sept. 17, 1950; s. Paul Myron and Carol Alice (Dittmer) C.; B.S. in Bus. Adminstrn., Youngstown (Ohio) State U., 1972; m. Ellen Louise Rung, Dec. 29, 1971. Staff acct. Touche, Ross & Co., Cleve., 1971-72; gen. acct. Standard Transformer Co., Warren, Ohio, 1972; staff acct. Packer, Deislinger & Co., Warren, 1972-74; gen. acct. Edward J. DeBartolo Corp., Youngstown, 1974-75, asst. mgr. gen. acctg., 1975, gen. acctg. mgr., 1975-76, asst. controller, 1977-80; partner Ross, Cornelius & Assos., Hubbard, 1980—. Pres., Oak Tree Men's Assn., 1979-81; trustee Hubbard Public Library, 1980—. C.P.A., Ohio. Mem. Am. Inst. C.P.A.'s, Ohio Soc. C.P.A.'s, Estate and Gift Tax Planning Council of Manoning-Shenango Valleys. Club: Oak Tree Country (West Middlesex, Pa.). Research on shopping center operations, operational audits of shopping centers. Office: Eight Walnut Pl Hubbard OH 44425

CORNELIUS, WILLIAM FRANK, accountant; b. Chgo., May 18, 1946; s. Clarence William and Helen Sarah C.; B.S. in Acctg., DePaul U., 1968; m. Patricia Marie Cronin, June 1, 1980; 1 dau., Karen Marie; 1 stepdau., Kelly Marie Cronin. Acct., Alexander Grant, C.P.A., Chgo., 1968-70; bus. mgr. Gordon Tech. High Sch., Chgo., 1971-76; pres., prin. William F. Cornelius & Assos., Niles, Ill., 1976—; br. mgr., cons. TLS Co. Computer Services; acting controller Internat. Travel Tng. Courses, Inc., 1980—. Served with U.S. Army, 1969-71. Mem. Nat. Soc. Public Accts., Ill. Soc. Public Accts. Presbyterian. Clubs: Niles Lions (1st v.p. 1974—, chmn. Candy Day 1980), Suburban Bowlers 300. Home: 7745 Neva St Niles IL 60648 Office: 7788 Milwaukee St Niles IL 60648

CORNELL, FRED ALLEN, JR., sch. adminstr.; b. Youngstown, Ohio, May 22, 1923; s. Fred Allen and Matilda Jane (McGlen) C.; student Youngstown State U., 1941-42; m. Ruth Hope Raub, Mar. 25, 1944; children—Gary A., Linda R., Marilyn J., Richard L. With Pa. R.R., 1942-46, Cook Coffee Co., 1946-47, Foy Labs., Wernersville, Pa., 1947-50, 54-58, U.S. Steel Co., Youngstown, 1950-56, Watson Standard Paints, Pitts., 1958-70; supr. bldgs., grounds and maintenance Boardman Local Schs., Youngstown, 1970—. Served with USN, 1943-45. Mem. Ohio Assn. Pub. Sch. Employees, DAV. Republican. Clubs: Masons (past master lodge, 32 deg.); Shriners; Order Eastern Star (past patron). Home: 56 Ohlin Dr New Middletown OH 44442 Office: 7410 Market St Youngstown OH 44512

CORNELL, LARRY ROBERT, med. diagnostic equipment mfg. co. exec.; b. Mt. Pleasent, Pa., July 8, 1947; s. Walter Edward and Iva Mae (Uphouse) C.; Asso. Electronic Tech., Donora Manpower Devel. Tng., 1967; student Cuyahoga Coll., 1974-78, Thomas A. Edison Coll., 1978—, m. Marie Agnes Ranker, Sept. 24, 1966; children—Larry Robert, Jennifer Lee, Dustin Patrick. Tech. tng. specialist Picker Corp., Cleve., 1971-73, sr. tech. tng. specialist, 1973-75, dir. media and TV, 1975-76, tng. supr. nuclear, ultrasound and clin. labs., 1976-79, corp. tng. mgr., 1979—. Served with U.S. Army, 1967-70; Vietnam. Mem. Am. Soc. for Tng. and Devel. (nat. spl. interest chmn. 1976, nat. appreciation cert. 1976), Nat. Mgmt. Assn. (chpt. exec. v.p. 1978-79, Outstanding Contbn. award 1977, 78). Democrat. Roman Catholic. Home: 2619 Winchell Rd Aurora OH 44202 Office: Picker Corp 1020 London Rd Cleveland OH 44110

CORNELL, WILLIAM DANIEL, mech. engr.; b. Valley Falls, Kans., Apr. 19, 1919; s. Noah P. and Mabel (Hennessy) C.; B.S. in Mech. Engring., U. Ill., 1942; m. Barbara L. Ferguson, Aug. 30, 1942; children—Alice Margaret, Randolph William. Research engr. Linde Air Products Co., Buffalo, 1942-48, cons. to Manhattan Dist. project, 1944-46; project engr. devel. of automatic bowling machine Am. Machine and Foundry, Buffalo, 1948-55; cons. to Gen. Electric Co., Hanford, Wash., 1949-50; project engr. Brunswick Corp., Muskegon, Mich., 1955-59, mgr. advanced engring., 1959-72; mgr. advanced concepts and tech. Sherwood Med. Industries div. Brunswick Corp., St. Louis, 1972—; mem. faculty Coll. Engring., U. Buffalo, 1946-47. Recipient Navy E award, 1945, Manhattan Project Recognition award, 1945, Award of Merit, Maritime Commn., 1945; registered profl. engr., N.Y. Republican. Presbyterian. Holder 30 patents, including automatic golf and bowling game apparatus, med. instruments and developer new method of measuring hemoglobin. Home: 907 Camargo Dr Ballwin MO 63011 Office: 11802 Westline Ind Dr Saint Louis MO 63141

CORNIEA, ROBERT EDWARD, motor parts co. exec.; b. South St. Paul, Minn., Sept. 19, 1907; s. Edward Henry and Anna Marie (Munson) C.; public schs., St. Paul; m. Dorothea Ada Townsend, June 18, 1932; children—Robert Edmond, Nancy Rose Ann, Raymond Leo, Donald George, James John. Clk., St. Paul Book and Stationery, 1924-25, Montgomery Ward & Co., 1925-27, Nat. Bushing and Parts Co., 1927-34; owner, operator Motor Parts Service Co., Inc., South St. Paul, 1943-79, pres., 1979—; pres. Motor Parts of Shakopee, Inc. (Minn.), 1956—; owner, pres. Motor Parts of Farmington (Minn.), 1964—; owner, pres. Motor Parts of Hastings (Minn.), 1978—. Mem. Motor and Equipment Wholesalers Assn., C. of C. (past v.p.), Coast Guard Aux. Roman Catholic. Clubs: Kiwanis (past pres.), Moose (gov. South Saint Paul 1941, Minn. pres. 1943, dist. dep. supreme gov. 1946, 47, Pilgrim Degree of Merit 1951); Southview Country, St. Paul Yacht, Pool and Yacht. Home: 1450 Hwy 110 Inver Grove Heights South Saint Paul MN 55075 Office: Motor Parts Service Co Inc 1111 S Concord St South Saint Paul MN 55075

CORNING, BLY ARGLE, mfg. co. exec.; b. nr. Buckley, Mich., Feb. 22, 1917; s. Clark E. and Nina B. (Milliman) C.; student Eastern Mich. U., 1937-40; m. Audrey Tuttle, Sept. 27, 1940; 1 dau., Jenifer Blye. With AC Spark Plug div. Gen. Motors, Flint, Mich., 1940-45; owner Corning Mfg. Co., Swartz Creek, Mich., 1949—. Bd. govs. William C. Clements Lib-Assos., U. Mich. Served with AUS, 1946-47. Mem. Music Library Assos., Sheet Music Collectors Assn., Sonneck Soc., Kappa Phi Alpha. Mason. Clubs: Presidents (U. Mich.); Flint Golf. Home: 1902 Hampden Rd Flint MI 48503

CORNWELL, LEROY EUGENE, data processor; b. Bushong, Kans., Nov. 18, 1930; s. Raymon Ensign and Villa Rosetta (Duncan) C.; diploma Kansas City (Kans.) Jr. Coll., 1950; B.B.A., U. Mo., Kansas City, 1956; m. Laura Ellen Jesse, Mar. 31, 1956; children—Lynn E., Larry E. EDP auditor United Mo. Bancshares, Kansas City, 1970-71; EDP supr. Combustion Engring. Inc., Enterprise, Kans., 1973-74; mgr. application systems Mo. State Hwy. Patrol, Jefferson City, Mo., 1974-75; programmer/analyst Kansas City (Mo.) Mcpl. Ct., 1978—. Sunday sch. dir., Sunday sch. tchr., ch. trustee. Served with USAF, 1950-54. Cert. in data processing. Mem. Data Processing Mgmt. Assn., Assn. for Systems Mgmt. Republican. Baptist. Home: 11805 Troost St Kansas City MO 64131

CORNYN, JOHN EUGENE, accounting co. exec.; b. San Francisco, Apr. 30, 1906; s. John Eugene and Sara Agnes (Larkin) C.; B.S., St. Mary's Coll., 1935; M.B.A., U. Chgo., 1936; m. Virginia R. Shannahan, Sept. 10, 1938 (dec. Dec. 1964); children—Virginia R., Kathleen R. Cornyn Arnold, John Eugene, Madeleine A. Cornyn Stanley, Carolyn G. Cornyn Clemons; m. 2d, Marian C. Fairfield, Aug. 21, 1965. Partner, John E. Cornyn & Co., C.P.A.'s, Winnetka, Ill., 1951-73; pres. John E. Cornyn & Co. Ltd., 1973—. Exec. sec. North Shore Property Owners Assn., 1953—. C.P.A., Ill. Mem. Am. Inst. C.P.A.'s, Ill. Soc. C.P.A.'s, Am. Acctg. Assn., Am. Tax Assn., Fellowship Cath. Scholars. Catholic (Byzantine Rite). Home: 126 Bertling Ln Winnetka IL 60093

CORONA, DAVID ANTHONY, pub. co. exec.; b. Chgo., Mar. 5, 1949; s. Leonard John and Shirley Emily (Frey) C.; B.F.A. magna cum laude, U. Ill., 1971. Graphic designer U. Chgo. Press, Chgo., 1971-74; design dir. William C. Brown Co. Pubs., Dubuque, Iowa, 1974-77, dir. prodn. devel. and design, 1977—, asst. v.p., officer, 1981—. Recipient numerous profl. design awards. Mem. Chgo. Book Clinic, Soc. Typographic Arts, U. Ill. Alumni Assn., Phi Gamma Delta, Phi Kappa Phi. Roman Catholic. Clubs: Rotary, Dubuque Golf and Country. Home: 409 Lowell Dubuque IA 52001 Office: 2460 Kerper Blvd Dubuque IA 52001

CORONADO, ROSA, restaurant and food mfg. co. exec.; b. St. Paul, July 27, 1938; d. Arthur Morquecho and Elvira (Gamez) C.; B.A. in Pub. Relations, U. Mexico, 1960. With La Casa Coronado Restaurant, Mama Coronado Food Products, Mpls., 1960—, sec., 1973—, owner, 1974—; cons. food; mem. adv. bd. Dakota County Vocat. Trade Sch. Food Dept.; vol. tchr. fgn. foods Mpls. Sch. System; profl. cooking instr.; condr. seminar on Mexican foods Gen. Mills. Co., 1977. Mem. Mpls. Downtown Council, 1968-73, adv. bd. City Center Redevel., City of Mpls.; bd. dirs. Met. Econ. Devel. Assn., Mpsl; mem. Minn. Small Bus. Task Force; mem. ch. council, pres. soc. Our Lady of Guadalupe' Ch., St. Paul. Recipient Letter of Merit, Amoco Co., 1976, spl. listing C. of C. Mag.'s Women in Bus. Sect., 1979. Mem. Internat. Geneva Assn. (ann. trophies for food displays 1970-77, plaque spl. recognition 1979), Geneva Exec. Chef Assn. (dir.), Nat. Assn. Cooking Sch. Instrs., Midwest Chefs Soc. (rec. sec. bd. dirs.), Minn. Restaurant Assn., Nat. Restaurant Assn. Democrat. Author: Cook in Mexico. Home: 2733 France Ave S Minneapolis MN 55416

CORRADI, VALENTINE, marketing exec.; b. Newburgh, N.Y., Nov. 29, 1922; s. Valentine and Helen Gertrude (Farina) C.; B.S., Rider Coll., 1942; M.S., Northwestern U., 1947; m. Mary Virginia Roberts, Jan. 28, 1950; 1 dau., Jo Ann. Vice pres., account exec. D. P. Brother & Co., Detroit, 1947-67; v.p., account supr. Leo Burnett Co., Detroit, 1967-77; v.p. automotive mktg. Newspaper Advt. Bur., Birmingham, Mich., 1977—. Served with USCG, 1942-45. Mem. Internat. Newspaper and Mktg. Execs., Newspaper Advt. Sales Assn., Detroit Advt. Assn., Adcraft Club Detroit. Republican. Presbyterian. Clubs: Oakland Hills Country, Recess, Cascade. Home: 5122 Woodlands Dr Bloomfield Hills MI 48013 Office: 280 N Woodward Ave Birmingham MI 48011

CORRIGAN, EARL JAMES, ednl. adminstr.; b. Carroll, Iowa, June 25, 1931; s. William Joseph and Lillian Veronica (Duffy) C.; B.A., U. No. Iowa, 1966; M.A., Roosevelt U., 1973; m. Lavon Marie Martin, Mar. 28, 1969. In sales and managerial positions with Brady Motorfrate, Inc., Iowa, Nebr., Mass., Fla., Ill., 1951-64; tchr. bus. edn. Oak Park-River Forest (Ill.) High Sch., 1966-76, dir. career edn., 1976—; planner-specialist Equal Employment Opportunity Program, 1975—. Mem. Mem. Am. Personnel and Guidance Assn., Ill. Guidance Assn., Ill. Council Local Adminstrs., Bus. Leaders Am., Phi Delta Kappa, Phi Beta Lambda. Author: Your Job Application, 1977, rev., 1979; author high sch. materials. Home: 228-C S Maple Ave Oak Park IL 60302 Office: 201 N Scoville Ave Oak Park IL 60302

CORRY, ROBERT JOHN, surgeon; b. Cleve., Dec. 3, 1934; s. Robert Milton and Isabel Catherine (Gledhill) C.; student Univ. Sch., 1951-53; A.B. magna cum laude, Yale, 1957; M.D., Johns Hopkins, 1961; m. Linda Sally Selin, June 5, 1965; children—Robert, Sara, Catherine. Intern, Johns Hopkins Hosp., 1961-63; surg. asst. resident Mass. Gen. Hosp., Boston, 1965-67, chief resident, 1968-69, asst. surgery, 1969-73; attending surgeon, asso. prof. surgery U. Iowa Coll. Medicine, Iowa City, 1973-76, prof. surgery, 1976—, dir. transplantation, 1973—. Teaching fellow Harvard Med. Sch., 1968-69, instr., 1969-72, asst. prof. surgery, 1972-73; cons. Iowa City VA Hosp., 1973—. Bd. dirs., chmn. med. adv. com. Kidney Found. Iowa, 1973—. Diplomate Am. Bd. Surgery. Mem. A.M.A., A.C.S., Transplantation Soc., Am. Soc. Transplant Surgeons, Soc. U. Surgeons, Assn. for Acad. Surgery, Soc. Surgery of Alimentary Tract, Mass., Iowa Johnson County med. socs., Iowa Acad. Surgery, Iowa Clin. Surg. Soc., Central Surg. Assn., Collegium Internationale Chirurgiae Digestivae, Internat. Coll. Surgeons, Am. Assn. Tissue Banks. Contbr. articles to profl. jours. Home: 319 Hutchinson Ave Iowa City IA 52240 Office: Univ Hosps Iowa City IA 52242

CORSER, DAVID HEWSON, pediatrician; b. Mpls., Aug. 4, 1930; s. John and Mary (Griswold) C.; A.B., Washington U., 1951, M.D., 1954; m. Bettyrose Nerlich, June 10, 1954; children—William, Diana, Joan, Carolyn, Bonnie, Jennifer. Intern, Mpls. Gen., 1954-55; resident U. Minn. Hosps., Mpls., 1955-57; practice medicine specializing in pediatrics Skemp Clinic, LaCrosse, Wis., 1959-69, Skemp-Grandview Clinic, LaCrosse, 1969-79; chief pediatrics Skemp-Grandview-LaCrosse Clinic, 1979—; also clin. asst. prof. pediatrics U. Wis., Madison; staff St. Francis, LaCrosse Coustesy, LaCrosse Lutheran. Served with U.S. Army, 1957-59. Diplomate Am. Bd. Pediatrics. Mem. Am. Acad. Pediatrics, La Crosse County Med. Assn., Wis. Med. Assn., AMA. Roman Catholic. Club: Optimist. Home: 1615 Sunset Dr LaCrosse WI 54601 Office: 815 S 10th St LaCrosse WI 54601

CORSON, THOMAS HAROLD, recreational vehicle mfg. co. exec.; b. Elkhart, Ind., Oct. 15, 1927; s. Carl W. and Charlotte (Keyser) C.; student Purdue U., 1945-46, Rensselaer Poly. Inst., 1946-47, So. Meth. U., 1948-49; m. Dorthy Claire Scheide, July 11, 1948; children—Benjamin Thomas, Claire Elaine. Chmn. bd., chief exec. officer Coachmen Industries, Inc., Middlebury, Ind., 1965—; dir. St. Joseph Valley Bank, Elkhart, First State Bank; chmn. bd., sec. Greenfield Corp. Viking Boat Co. Inc., Middlebury; chmn. bd., Henco Enterprises, Inc., Niles, Mich.; chmn. bd. Space Age Camper Co., Inc., Middlebury. Chmn. Elkhart County Rep. Finance Com. Bd. dirs., v.p. Michiana Econ. Devel. Found.; trustee Interlochen Arts Acad. and Nat. Music Camp; mem. adv. bd. Goshen (Ind.) Coll. Served with USNR, 1945-47. Mem. Ind. Mfrs. Assn. (dir.). Methodist. Mason (Shriner). Club: Elcona Country (past dir.). Home: PO Box 504 Skyview Dr Middlebury IN 46540 Office: Coachmen Dr PO Box 30 Middlebury IN 46540

CORTESE, THOMAS ANTHONY, surgeon; b. Mesoraca, Italy, Feb. 20, 1908 (parents Am. citizens); s. Joseph and Mary (Schipani) C.; A.B., Ind. U., 1930, B.S., 1931, M.D., 1933. Intern, resident in surgery Columbus Hosp., Chgo., 1933-34; intern St. Francis Hosp., Indpls., 1932-33; practice medicine specializing in surgery, Indpls., 1934—; mem. staff St. Francis, Community, Univ. Heights hosps.; mem. Pres. Johnson's Commn. on Cardiovascular Disease, 1966-67. Mem. Pres. Johnson's Council on Youth Opportunity, 1966-67. Served with M.C., U.S. Army, World War II. Recipient Cavaliere di Merito, Republic of Italy, also commendatore. Diplomate Am. Bd. Surgery, Am. Bd. Abdominal Surgery, Internat. Coll. Surgeons. Fellow Internat. Fertility Assn.; mem. Indpls., Marion County med. socs., Am. Soc. Contemporary Medicine and Surgery, Am. Soc. Study of Sterility, Am. Fedn. Scientists, N.Y. Acad. Scis., Am. Assn. Clinics, AAAS, World Med. Assn. (founder), Ind. State Med. Assn., AMA, Fedn. of Italian Am. Socs. Ind. (pres., founder), Am. Legion, St. Francis Pathol. Soc., Am. Atomic Scientists. Club: Indpls. Athletic. Author: Hiatus Hernia, 1947; contbr. articles to profl. jours. Home: 3525 Payne Dr Indianapolis IN 46227 Office: 3901 SE St Indianapolis IN 46227

CORTNER, KAY LAMARR, computer hardware specialist, army officer; b. Kansas City, Mo., July 28, 1944; d. Robert Lee and Pearle Emogene (Willis) C.; B.A., Kans. State Coll., 1966; M.A., U. Tex., 1969; postgrad. U. Mo., 1976-78. Commd. 2d lt. U.S. Army, 1966, advanced through grades to maj., 1977; personal affairs officer, Ft. Jackson, S.C., 1967; comdr., Ft. Knox, Ky., 1968; computer specialist U.S. Forces, Korea, 1972, III Corps, Ft. Hood, Tex., 1973; personnel officer U.S. Retrograde Force, S.E. Asia, 1973; automatic data processing officer 1st Inf. Div., Ft. Riley, Kans., 1978; personnel and adminstrn. officer Saudi Arabian Nat. Guard Modernization Program, Riyadh, 1979-81; mil. personnel officer Hdqrs. U.S. Army Armament Readiness Command, Rock Island, Ill., 1981—. Decorated Meritorious Service Medal, 3 Army Commendation Medals; recipient award for leadership DAR, 1971. Mem. Assn. U.S. Army, Promotion Research Com. Democrat. Home: 444 E Cedar St Olathe KS 66061 Office: NQ ARRCOM Rock Island IL 61299

CORUSY, PAUL VINCENT, assn. exec.; b. Canton, Ohio, May 20, 1925; s. Paul and Mary (Kufta) C.; B.Sc., Ohio U., 1949; J.D., Cleve. State U., 1961; m. Maxine Joyce McKellips, Aug. 30, 1947; children—Lynne Denise Corusy Conlan, Paul Martin, Mark Allyn. With Glidden Co., Cleve., 1949-60, mgr. local taxes, until 1960; mgr. local taxes Minn. Mining & Mfg. Co., 1960-64; exec. dir. Interat. Assn. Assessing Officers, Chgo., 1964—. Trustee Pub. Adminstrn. Service, 1964-75, Govt. Affairs Inst. Served with USNR, 1943-46. Mem. Chgo. Soc. Assn. Execs. (vice chmn., chmn. 1977-79), Am., Ill., Chgo. bar assns. Home: 5520 Grand Ave Western Springs IL 60658 Office: 1313 E 60th St Chicago IL 60637

CORWELL, ANN E., automobile co. exec.; b. Battle Creek, Mich.; d. James A. and Marion (Shertzer) Corwell; B.A., Mich. State U., 1971, M.B.A., 1981. Communications specialist Ford Mktg. Corp., Dearborn, Mich., 1971-72; sr. publicist City of Dearborn, 1972-76; sr. staff asst. Gen. Motors Corp., Detroit, N.Y.C., 1976-77; community relations mgr. Pontiac Motor div. Gen. Motors Corp., Detorit, 1977-81, internal communications mgr., 1981—. Mem. devel. council and communications alumni bd. Mich. State U., 1979—; mem. Mich. Council for Arts; mem. Bus., Industry, Labor Adv. Bd., 1980—. Mem. Public Relations Soc. Am., Women in Communications, Oakland County (Mich.) C. of C. (dir. 1980—, vice chmn. 1980-81, chmn.-elect 1982, chmn. 1983). Club: Civitan. Office: General Motors Corp Pontiac Motor Div 1 Pontiac Plaza Pontiac MI 48053

CORWIN, ROBERT GILBERT, dermatologist; b. Dayton, Ohio, July 27, 1942; s. Charles Frederick Snyder and Josephine Harshman (Kiefaber) C.; A.B. cum laude, Princeton U., 1964; M.D., Case Western Res. U., 1968; m. Marilyn Louise Nagare, June 21, 1969; children—Robert Phillip, Michael Thomas. Intern, Univ. Hosp., Cleve., 1968-69, resident in internal medicine, 1969-70; resident in dermatology Cleve. Met. Gen. Hosp., 1972-75; practice medicine specializing in dermatology, Middleburg Heights, Ohio, 1975—; mem. staff Cleve. Met. Gen. Hosp.; mem. courtesy staff S.W. Gen. Hosp.; asst. clin. prof. dermatology Case Western Res. U. Served with M.C., USAF, 1970-72. Diplomate Am. Bd. Dermatology. Fellow Am. Acad. Dermatology; mem. Alpha Omega Alpha. Home: 9409 Kings Ct Brecksville OH 44141 Office: Southland Profl Bldg 6867 Pearl Rd Middleburg Heights OH 44130

COSCIA, RICHARD ANTHONY MCKOIN, microbiologist; b. Flint, Mich., Aug. 3, 1949; s. Anthony John and Julia Verrenness (McKoin) C.; B.S., Mich. State U., 1972; m. Wendy Sue Symons, Jan. 3, 1970; 1 dau., Lisa Marie. Tech. asst. nursing service Hurley Med. Center, Flint, 1968-72; coordinator infection control McLaren Gen. Hosp., Flint, 1972—; instr. Mott Community Coll., Flint, 1971-72; cons. Genessee, Lapeer, Shiawassee County Area 5 Planning Group for Health Care Facilities. Served with USAF, 1972-73. Center for Disease Control grantee, 1972. Mem. Mich. Soc. Infection Control (founder, recipient Certificate of Merit 1973, program chmn.), Flint Soc. Infection Control, Assn. Practitioners of Infection Control, Am. Mgmt. Assn., Mich. State U. Alumni Assn. Roman Catholic. Editor news bull. Mich. Soc. Infection Control, 1974-76. Home: 707 Country Club Ln Flint MI 48507 Office: McLaren Gen Hosp 401 Ballenger Hwy Flint MI 48502

COSENTINO, LOUIS CIRO, bioengr.; b. Bklyn., Mar. 23, 1944; s. Louis J. and Lucy Cosentino; B.S. in Elec. Engring., Poly. Inst. Bklyn., 1965, M.S., 1967, Ph.D. in Bioengring., 1972; m. Judith Ann Reiss, Sept. 5, 1965; 4 children. Biomed. engr. biophys. research dept. Hoffman-La Roche, Nutley, N.J., 1967-69; mgr. product devel. Datascope Corp., Saddle Brook, N.J., 1969-70; biomed. engr. Roche Med. Electronics, Cranberry, N.J., 1970-72; dir. advanced research and devel. Medtronic, Inc., Mpls., 1972-74; pres. Renal Systems, Inc., Mpls., 1974—. Mem. exec. com. Minnetonka chpt. U.S. Power Squadron, 1980-81. Named Outstanding Citizen of Plymouth (Minn.), 1979, One of 10 Outstanding Minnesotans, 1979, One of 10 Outstanding Young Men of Am., 1980 (all U.S. Jaycees). Mem. IEEE, Assn. Advancement Med. Instrumentation. Contbr. articles on med. instrumentation and biomed. engring. to profl. jours.; patentee biomed. instruments. Office: 14905 28th Ave N Minneapolis MN 55441

COSGRIFF, ROBERT P., fund raising cons.; b. Iowa City, Feb. 16, 1926; s. Harold F. and Elizabeth (Phelan) C.; student Washington U., St. Louis, 1946-48; B.S.C., U. Iowa, 1950; postgrad. St. Louis U., 1950-51; children—Kevin, Ann, Jean, Joan. Mem. Beaver Assos., Chgo., 1954-60; founder, pres. Cosgriff Co., Omaha, 1960—. Served with USMC, 1944-46. Mem. Nat. Soc. Fund Raising Execs., Am. Public Relations Assn., Iowa C. of C. Execs. Assn., Omaha C. of C., Am. Fund Raising Council (dir.), Am. Legion. Clubs: Omaha, Happy Hollow Country, Lake Shore Country. Office: 1480 1st Nat Center Omaha NE 68102

COSGROVE, WILLIAM M., bishop; b. Canton, Ohio, Nov. 26, 1916; student John Carroll U. Ordained priest, Roman Cath. Ch., 1943; titular bishop of Trisipa and aux. bishop of Cleve., 1968-76; bishop of Belleville, Ill., 1976—. Office: Chancery Office 5312 W Main St Box 896 Belleville IL 62223*

COSKEY, RALPH JOSEPH, dermatologist; b. Detroit, July 29, 1929; s. Leo A. and Hedwig D. (Fellner) C.; B.A., U. Mich., 1951; M.D., Wayne State U., 1955; m. Carol Goldenberg, July 6, 1952; children—Laura, Larry. Intern Sinai Hosp., Detroit, 1955-56; resident in dermatology Henry Ford Hosp., Detroit, 1958-61; practice medicine specializing in dermatology, 1961—; mem. staff Sinai, Providence, Detroit Receiving hosps.; clin. asso. prof. dermatology Wayne State U., 1975—; mem. self-assessment com. Am. Bd. Dermatology. Bd. dirs. Fresh Air Soc.; sec. Drawing and Print Club, Detroit Inst. Art. Served with USAF, 1956-58. Mem. AMA, Mich. State., Oakland County med. socs., Am. Acad. Dermatology, Soc. Investigative Dermatology, Mich. Dermatol. Soc., Noah Worcester Dermatologic Soc. (dir.), Wayne State U. Sch. Medicine Alumni Assn. (dir.), Wayne State U. Alumni Assn. (dir.). Republican. Jewish. Contbr. articles to med. jours. Mem. editorial bd. Jour. Dermatology and Allergy. Office: 23133 Orchard Lake Rd Farmington MI 48024

COSSABOOM, EWING ORVILLE, lawyer, farm mgr.; b. Millersburg, Ky., Mar. 17, 1917; s. Charles O. and Lillian (Young) C.; A.B., Transylvania U., 1939; J.D., U. Cin., 1942; m. Joy G. Ferdon, July 20, 1962. Chief purchase and claims sect., real estate div. Ohio River div. U.S. Army Engrs., 1942-45; practiced law in Cin., 1945—; mem. firm Dickerson, Ahrens, Cossaboom & Burns, 1954—; farm mgr. J.M. Ewing Farm, Morgan, Ky., 1952-73; sec., treas. College Hill Realty Co., 1950-77; v.p. Whitney Corp., 1965—, treas., 1967—; dir. Mt. Healthy Savs. & Loan Co. Chmn., Mt. Healthy Civil Service Commn., 1968—. Mem. Christian Ch. Contbr. articles to profl. jours. Home: 1623 Madison Ave Mount Healthy OH 45231 Office: Am Bldg 30 E Central Pkwy Cincinnati OH 45202

COSTELLO, MARGARET ANN, psychologist; b. Scranton, Pa., July 8, 1952; d. John Nicholas and Ann Annette (Prinzo) C.; student U. Salamanca (Spain), 1973; B.S. in Psychology, Pa. State U., 1974; M.A. in Rehab. Adminstrn., So. Ill. U., 1975; M.A. in Psychology (Gamma Phi Beta Founder's fellow 1975, USPHS fellow 1975-76), U. Mich., 1976, postgrad. in edn. and psychology, 1978. Psychology intern A. L. Bowen Children's Center, Harrisburg, Ill., 1974-75; counselor Summer Employment Program for Disadvantaged Youth, Howell, Mich., summers 1976-77; teaching fellow in psychology U. Mich., 1976-78; intern in psychology and spl. edn. Inst. for Study Mental Retardation and Related Disabilities, Ann Arbor, 1977-78; psychologist Southgate (Mich.) Regional Center for Devel. Disabilities, 1977-79; instr., coordinator tng. grant Ellsworth Community Coll., 1979-80; psychologist Mich. Services for Developmentally Disabled, Southfield, 1980—. Cert. psychologist, Mich.; cert. in postsecondary edn., Iowa. Mem. Council Exceptional Children, Assn. Behavior Analysts, Am. Assn. Mental Deficiency, Assn. for Severly Handicapped, Am. Assn. Behavior Therapists, Nat. Assn. Retarded Citizens, Am. Psychol. Assn., Nat. Soc. Autistic Children, Nat. Women's Polit. Caucus, Gamma Phi Beta, Phi Beta Kappa. Democrat. Roman Catholic. Home: 2923 Roundtree Blvd Apt C-1 Ypsilanti MI 48197 Office: One Northland Plaza Suite 104 Southfield MI 48075

COSTELLO, MICHAEL THOMAS, county ofcl.; b. East St. Louis, Ill., Oct. 9, 1945; s. Daniel Edward and Elsa Lenora (Moore) C.; student Belleville Coll., 1970-72; m. Judith Elaine O'Guinn, Oct. 9, 1965. Instrument man H.W. Lochner Engring., E. St. Louis, 1963-66; electrician Alton & So. R.R., E. St. Louis, 1966-67; laborer Gen. Steel Co., Granite City, Ill., 1966-67; patrolman National City (Ill.) Police Dept., 1968; chmn. mapping, platting and bldg. depts. St. Clair County, Belleville, Ill., 1968-74, mem. Bd. Rev., 1974-79, 80— chmn., 1979-80. Owner Becherer's Jewelers, Belleville, 1976—; pres. Mike Costello, Inc., Belleville, 1976—. Precinct committeeman Democratic party. Mem. Ill. Retail Jewelers Assn., Belleville C. of C., Belleville Jr. C. of C. Roman Catholic. Clubs: Eagles, Moose, K.C. Home: 1908 E C St Belleville IL 62221 Office: St Clair County Building 10 Public Sq Belleville IL 62220

COSTELLO, PAUL JAMES, steel co. exec.; b. Grand Island, Nebr., Dec. 15, 1946; s. James Thomas and Dorothy Irene (Leslie) C.; B.S. in Bus. Adminstrn., So. Ill. U., Edwardsville, 1972; m. Karen Lynne LaPeire, Apr. 18, 1969; children—Trisha Lynne, Matthew Paul. Acct., R.C. Fietsam and Co., C.P.A.'s, Belleville, Ill., 1972-73; internal auditor Nat. Steel Corp., Pitts., 1973-75, gen. supr. acctg. Granite City (Ill.) steel div., 1975-79, mgr. acctg. Granite City steel div., 1979—. Adviser Jr. Achievement, 1977—; chmn. budget and allocations Tri-City Area United Way, 1978, pres., 1979; mem. St. Margaret Mary's Catholic Ch. Parish Council, 1978; mem. Bishop's Pastoral Council, Springfield, Ill., 1980; bd. dirs. Madison County Cancer Soc. Served to 1st lt. U.S. Army, 1966-69; Vietnam. Decorated Silver Star, Bronze Star with oak leaf cluster, Air medal. Mem. Inst. Internal Auditors, Assn. Iron and Steel Engrs., Assn. U.S. Army, Res. Officers Assn., Am. Security Council, Alumni Assn. So. Ill. U., VFW. Republican. Club: Torch (asst. treas. 1975—). Home: 48 Villa Dr Granite City IL 62040 Office: Nat Steel Corp 20th and Madison Ave Granite City IL 62040

COSTELLO, RUSSELL THOMAS, JR., urologist; b. Detroit, Dec. 22, 1937; s. Russell Thomas and Evelyn (Adams) C.; B.A., Wayne State U., 1959, M.D., 1963; m. Sandra Wilson, June 24, 1961; children—Jeffrey Robert, Kathryn Ann. Intern, Detroit Receiving Hosp., 1963-64; resident in urology, Wayne County Gen. Hosp., 1964-69; practice medicine, specializing in urology, St. Joseph and Benton Harbor, Mich., 1970—; instr. urology U. Mich., 1969-70; adj. clin. prof. Western Mich. U., 1976—; chmn. dept. surgery Mercy Hosp., Benton Harbor, 1974, Meml. Hosp., St. Joseph, 1975, chmn. combined depts. surgery, pres. Cedarwood Med. Center, St. Joseph, 1971-76, chmn. bd. dirs., 1971—. Diplomate Am. Bd. Urology. Fellow A.C.S.; mem. Reed Nesbitt Soc. Home: 1227 Harriet St Saint Joseph MI 49085 Office: Cedarwood Med Center 820 Lester St Saint Joseph MI 49085

COSTIGAN, JAMES IVAN, educator; b. Bloomington, Ill., May 27, 1936; s. Thomas Ivan and Josephine Harriet (Boone) C.; B.S., Ill. State U., 1958; M.S., So. Ill. U., 1959, Ph.D., 1970; m. Nancy Jane McQuilliam, Aug. 10, 1963; children—James Thomas, Jane Marie, Jennifer Anne, Jean Catherine. Television announcer Sta. WBLN-TV, 1958-59; tchr. Petersburg (Ill.) High Sch., 1959-60; mem. faculty dept. communications Fort Hays State U., Hays, Kans., 1960—, prof., 1970—, chairperson dept., 1970—; cons. in field. Mem. Speech Communication Assn. Democrat. Roman Catholic. Author: Interpersonal Communication: Influences and Alternatives, 1975. Office: Communication Dept Fort Hays State Univ Hays KS 67601

COTHRAN, ANDREW NEILSON, coll. pres.; b. Kreole, Miss., Oct. 6, 1929; s. John Austin and Ruby Viola C.; A.B., Baylor U., 1951; M.A., Columbia U., 1952; Ph.D., U. Md., 1966; m. Frances Denson, Aug. 22, 1955; children—Leslee Elaine, John Neilson, Benjamin Andrew. Tchr. public schs., Mobile, Ala., 1951-53; asst. to pres. Judson Coll., Marion, Ala., 1954-55; asst. dir. pupil personnel Louisville Public Schs., 1955-58; instr. U. Louisville, 1957-60, asst. prof. Am. studies, 1960-63, asso. prof., 1966-67; chmn. div. humanities Prince George's Community Coll., Largo, Md., 1963-66; cultural attache Am. Embassy, Oslo, Norway and chmn. U.S. Ednl. Found. Norway, 1967-69; pres. Tusculum Coll., Greeneville, Tenn., 1969-72; pres. Kendall Coll., Evanston, Ill., 1972—. Served with U.S. Army, 1947-48. Mem. Am. Council Edn., Fedn. Ind. Ill. Colls., Am. Studies Assn. Republican. Episcopalian. Clubs: Sheridan Shores Yacht (Wilmette, Ill.); Chgo. Econ., Rotary. Office: 2408 Orrington Ave Evanston IL 60201

COTMAN, IVAN LOUIS, state ofcl.; b. Detroit, Apr. 4, 1940; B.A. in English and Social Sci., Ky. State U., 1962; M.A. in Social Work, Atlanta U., 1964; postgrad. in med. care orgn. U. Mich. Sch. Public Health, 1969-70; cert. in urban and social planning U. Manchester (Eng.), summer 1972; Ed.D., Wayne State U., 1975; m. Jeanetta Hawkins, Aug. 18, 1964; children—Ivan Louis, Arthur, Amir. Sch. social worker, dept. evaluative services Detroit Bd. Edn., 1964-69; agy. program cons./asst. budget dir. United Community Services Met. Detroit, 1969-72; dir. employment New Detroit, Inc., 1972-73; area adminstr. Bur. Rehab., Mich. Dept. Edn., Oak Park, 1973-79, asso. supt. for rehab., Lansing, 1979—. Bd. dirs. Narcotics Addiction Rehab. Coordinating Orgn., Urban Alliance; mem. adv. bd. dept. social work and psychology clinic U. Detroit; vice-chmn. Alpha Phi Alpha Edn. Found., 1962—. Cert. tchr., Mich.; cert. disability examiner. Named in resolution of tribute Mich. State Senate, 1973; recipient Vocat. Rehab. award, 1974, Disting. Citizen award Mich. Ho. of Reps., 1977. Mem. Nat. Rehab. Assn., Phi Delta Kappa. Club: Econ. (Detroit). Editorial bd. Phylon: The Atlanta U. Jour. Race and Culture, 1968-79; contbr. articles to profl. jours. Office: Mich Dept Edn Lansing MI 48909

COTNER, DOUGLAS MONROE, econ. geographer; b. Hawthorne, Calif., Sept. 15, 1942; s. Monroe and Vergie Jeanette (Montfort) C.; A.A., El Camino Coll., 1965; B.A., Calif. State U., Long Beach, 1967; postgrad. Central Mich. U., 1975; m. Margaret Ann Cotner, Sept. 30, 1967; children—Margaret Lyn, David Morrison. Tchr., Los Angeles City Schs., 1967-69; corp. planner/analyst Robert Stone & Assos., Woodland Hills, Calif., 1969; tech. librarian TRW, Inc., Redondo Beach, Calif., 1970; br. locations analyst United Calif. Bank, Los Angeles and San Francisco, 1970-72; sr. planner Saginaw County Met. Planning Commn., Saginaw, Mich., 1973-78; pres., chief exec. officer Econ. Research and Data Corp., Saginaw, 1978—; guest lectr. Delta Community Coll., University Center, Mich., 1974-78; spl. econs. cons. local small bus. groups in Mich., 1978—. Mem. Gamma Theta Upsilon. Republican. Jewish. Clubs: B'nai B'rith, De Molay (life). Contbr. articles to profl. jours. Office: 1203 Gratiot Rd Saginaw MI 48602

COTTELEER, MICHAEL ALEXANDER, lawyer; b. Chgo., Feb. 4, 1944; s. Alexander Charles and Helen Lucille (Schmitt) C.; B.A., No. Ill. U., 1968; J.D. (Alumni scholar), Loyola U., Chgo., 1971; m. Nancy McKeating, Apr. 4, 1977; children—Jennifer, Amy, Kevin. Admitted to Ill. bar, 1971; atty. Chgo. Title & Trust Co., 1971-72; atty. firm Herrick, McNeill, McElroy & Peregrine, Chgo., 1972-74, Daniels, Hancock & Faris, Elmhurst, Ill., 1974-75; asst. dean, asso. prof. law No. Ill. U. Coll. Law, Glen Ellyn, 1975-78; individual practice law, Wheaton, Ill., 1978-81; partner firm Borenstein, Cotteleer, Greenberg & Young, Chgo. and Wheaton, 1981—. Bd. dirs. No. Ill. U. Found., 1979—, mem. pres.'s legis. action com., 1978—; bd. dirs., producer Festival Theater, Oak Park, Ill., 1981—. Served with U.S. Army, 1962-65. Recipient award for service Ill. Bd. Regents, 1979. Mem. Am. Bar Assn., Ill. State Bar Assn. (vice chmn. sect. council on corps. and securities law), Chgo. Bar Assn., DuPage County Bar Assn., No. Ill. U. Alumni Assn. (v.p., bd. dirs. 1977—), Sigma Alpha Epsilon. Roman Catholic. Office: 35 E Wacker Dr Chicago IL 60601 also 209 N Washington St Wheaton IL 60187

COTTER, PATRICK DAVID, med. psychologist; b. Brewster, Minn., Jan. 29, 1947; s. Vincent Richard and Dorothy (Tibodeau) C.; B.A., U. S.D., 1969, M.A., 1971, Ph.D., 1973; m. Kay Delores Lillig, Aug. 18, 1972. Intern, then resident in psychology U. Oreg. Med. Sch., Portland, 1973-75; med. psychologist Children's Meml. Hosp., Chgo., 1975-81; asso. psychology Northwestern U. Med. Sch., 1977-81; pvt. practice psychology, Chgo., 1976-81; pvt. practice Pediatric Psychology Services, Mpls., 1981—. Mem. Am., Ill. psychol. assns., Am. Assn. Mental Deficiency, Midwestern Assn. Behavior Analysis, Soc. Pediatric Psychology, Psi Chi. Democrat. Roman Catholic. Home: 2400 W 102 St Bloomington MN 55431 Office: 2222 Park Ave S Minneapolis MN 55404

COTTINGHAM, JOHN ELMER, agrl. economist; b. Fennimore, Wis., Aug. 5, 1938; s. Elmer John and Dorothy Lucile (Knappmiller) C.; B.S., U. Wis., Platteville, 1961; M.S., U. Wis., Madison, 1963, Ph.D., 1965; m. Katherine Kreul, July 10, 1960; children—Steven, David, Robert. Mem. faculty U. Wis., Platteville, 1964—, prof. agrl. econs., 1967—, chmn. dept., 1966—. Sec. bd. dirs. S.W. Vocat. Tech. Inst., 1978-81. Served with U.S. Army, 1957. Mem. Wis. Agri-Bus. Council (dir. 1971-74), Am. Agrl. Econs. Assn., Assn. Coop. Educators, Nat. Assn. Tchrs. Agr. Methodist. Club: Kiwanis (past pres.). Home: 960 Williams St Platteville WI 53818 Office: Dept Agrl Econs U Wis Platteville WI 53818

COTTINGHAM, SHERMAN, ednl. adminstr.; b. Arcadia, La., Feb. 11, 1936; s. Ellis and Essie (Stover) C.; B.S. (Scholar), Grambling State U., 1958; M.Ed. N.E. State U., 1968; Ed. Sp., Wayne State U., 1976, Ed.D., 1979; m. Williette Foster, Mar. 28, 1970; children—Debra Kay, Jill Renee. Tchr. jr. high sch. Tensas Parish (La.) Sch. Dist., 1959-65, elem. prin., 1965-68, high sch. prin., 1969-70, jr. high sch. prin., 1970-71; high sch. asst. prin. Mt. Clemens (Mich.) Sch. Dist., 1971-80, asst. supt., 1980—; cons. edn. Bd. dirs. Waterproof council Boy Scouts Am., 1959-66; brother, Phi Beta Sigma, Detroit; bd. dirs. United Community Services, Detroit, YMCA, Mt. Clemens; trustee Greater Morning Star Bapt. Ch., Mt. Clemens. Cert. tchr., La. Mem. Assn. Supervision and Curriculum Devel., Mich. Assn. Supervision and Curriculum Devel., Macomb County Personnel Assn., Am. Assn. Sch. Personnel Adminstrs., NAACP, Phi Delta Kappa (editorial bd. jour.). Home: 37456 Charter Oaks Mount Clemens MI 48043 Office: 167 Cass Ave Mount Clemens MI 48043

COTTRELL, RICHARD ROSS, data processing cons.; b. Grant City, Mo., June 12, 1942; s. Lorin G. and Frances E. Cottrell; B.S., No. Ariz. U., 1966; M.A. (NDEA fellow), U. Ariz., 1969; m. Nina Kenerson, June 3, 1964. Accountant, Shell Chem. Co., Pittsburg, Calif., 1966-67; mgr. employee performance appraisal Minn. State Dept. Personnel, St. Paul, 1973-76, mgr. planning and data services, 1976-79; mgr. human resource planning No. Telecom Systems, Mpls., 1979—; sr. cons. Integral Systems Inc., Walnut Creek, Calif. Methodist. Office: 39 Quail Ct Walnut Creek CA 94596

COTTRELL, ROBERT LYMAN, retail food chain exec.; b. Cin., Sept. 11, 1932; s. William Frederick and Annice (Lyman) C.; B.S. summa cum laude, Miami U., 1954; m. Nancy Sohngen, June 8, 1954; children—Philip, Robert, Richard. With The Kroger Co., 1954—, v.p. distbn. adminstrn., Cin., 1979—; dir. Citizens Bank, Hamilton, Ohio, 1974-79. Mem. adv. council Miami U. Sch. Applied Sci., 1974-78, chmn., 1978; mem. adv. council Miami U. Sch. Bus., 1979—; trustee Miami U. Fund, 1980—, trustee Ft. Hamilton-Hughes Meml. Hosp., 1975—, treas., 1977-79. Served with USAF, 1954-57. Mem. AIIE. Republican. Presbyterian. Office: 1014 Vine St Cincinnati OH 45202

COUCH, HOWARD JOSEPH, food co. exec.; b. South Bend, Ind., Dec. 9, 1927; s. Fred John and Cecilia Mary (Gooley) C.; student Mich. State U., 1955-56; m. Joan Mary Obergfell, May 22, 1965; children—Anne, Andrew, Sarah. Mgr., Gilmer Park Supermarket, South Bend, 1946-48, owner, mgr., 1948-51; mgr. night stocking Kroger Store, South Bend, 1953, checker, dairy trainee, 1954-55, sales asst., Fort Wayne, 1956-57, asst. buyer, 1957, grocery buyer, 1957-60; exec. v.p., gen. mgr. Dilgard Frozen Foods, Inc., Fort Wayne, 1960-78, pres., chief exec. officer, 1978—, also dir. Mem. Citizens com. Allen County Democratic Com., 1977—; bd. dirs. Youth Super stars, 1977—. Served with US Army, 101st Airbourne Inf. div., 1951-53. Mem. Fort Wayne C. of C., U.S. C. of C., Frozen Foods Assn., Nat. Distbn. Food Assn. Roman Catholic. Clubs: Orchard Ridge Country, K.C., Elks. Home: 6710 Sky Blue Dr Fort Wayne IN 46804 Office: 830 Hayden St Fort Wayne IN 46803

COULTER, JAMES EDWARD, hosp. adminstr.; b. Reading, Mich., Apr. 28, 1940; s. Thomas Weldon and Hilda E. (Keefer) C.; B.S., Hillsdale Coll., 1963; M.A., Western Mich. U., 1971. Tchr., Pittsford (Mich.) Area Schs., 1963-75; asst. to pres. Hillsdale Foundry (Mich.), 1963-70; instr. Hope Coll., Holland, Mich., summer 1974, 75; dir. edn. Holland Community Hosp., Holland, 1975—; prin. Coulter and Assos., Inc., Holland, 1979—. Bd. dirs. Upward Bound Hope Coll., 1975-79, pres., 1978-79. Mem. Lake Michigan Soc. Health Manpower Edn. and Tng. (pres. 1981-82), Mich. Soc. Health Manpower Edn. and Tng., Am. Soc. Health Edn. and Tng., ASTD. Home: 138 Bel Air Holland MI 49423 Office: 602 Michigan Ave Holland MI 49423

COULTER, THOMAS H(ENRY), former assn. exec., mgmt. cons.; b. Winnipeg, Man., Can., Apr. 21, 1911; s. David and Sarah Anne (Allen) C.; B.S., Carnegie Inst. Tech., 1933; M.A., U. Chgo., 1935; m. Mary Alice Leach, Nov. 24, 1937; children—Sara, Anne, Jane, Thomas II. Investment analyst Shaw & Co., Chgo., 1935-36; sales engr. Universal Zonolite Insulation Co., Chgo., 1936-39, sales promotion mgr., 1939-40, gen. sales mgr., 1940-41, v.p., 1941-45; mgr. devel. div. Booz, Allen & Hamilton, Chgo., 1945-48, partner, 1948-50; pres. Am. Bildrok Co., 1950-54; chief exec. officer Chgo. Assn. Commerce and Industry, 1954-81; exec. v.p. Lester B. Knight & Assos., Chgo., 1981—; pub. Commerce mag.; lectr. mktg., exec. program U. Chgo.; dir. Chgo.-Tokyo Bank. Mem. State Dept.'s Top Mgmt. Seminar Team, Israel, 1956, Japan, 1958; mem. Dist. Export Council. Mem. Mayor's Commn. Rehab. Persons; mem. Chgo.-Cook County Criminal Justice Commn., Cook County Real Estate Tax Study Commn., Ill. Gov.'s Council on Health and Fitness, Chgo. Dept. Human Services Bd. dirs. Chgo. Crime Commn.; bd. dirs. Chgo. chpt. ARC, 1953-59, USO of Chgo.; mem. citizens bd., council Sch. Bus. Assn.; bd. govs. Internat. House, U. Chgo.; mem. citizens com. U. Ill.; exec. council Chgo. Civil Def. Corps; exec. com. Ill. Council Econ. Edn.; hon. trustee Skokie Valley Community Hosp., pres., 1955-57, 66-70; bd. dirs. Better Bus. Bur. Met. Chgo., Hosp. Planning Council Met. Chgo., Chgo. Council Fgn. Relations; mem. Northwestern U. Assos.; trustee Village of Golf (Ill.), 1951-55; mem. nat. adv. bd. Am. Security Council Edn. Found.; mem. adv. bd. Chgo. Area council Boy Scouts Am.; mem. Cook County Home Rule Commn.; mem. Rehab. Inst. Chgo. Assos.; mem. adv. com. U. Chgo. Met. Inst.; mem. nat. adv. council Nat. Legal Center for Pub. Interest; mem. Cook County Econ. Devel. Adv. Com. Decorated comdr.'s cross Order of Merit (Germany); knight Order of Merit (Italy); knight Order of Lion (Finland); knight 1st class Royal Order of Vasa, comdr. Royal Order Vasa (Sweden); chevalier Nat. Order of Merit (France); 3d class Order of Sacred Treasure (Japan); recipient Silver Ann. All-American award Sports Illustrated, 1957; Outstanding Civilian Service medal U.S. Army, 1961; Gold Badge of Honor for Merits (Austria), 1962, (Province of Vienna), 1971; citation pub. service U. Chgo.; Alumni merit award for outstanding profl. achievement Carnegie Inst. Tech.; Indsl. Statesman award U.S.-Japan Trade Council, 1976; Citizen Fellowship award Inst. Medicine, 1976. Mem. Nat. Sales Execs., Newcomen Soc. N.Am., U.S. C. of C. (banking, monetary and fiscal affairs com.), Nat. Planning Assn., U.S. Olympians (dir. Midwest chpt.), Internat. Bus. Council, Midwest-Japan Assn., Japan-Am. Soc. Chgo. (dir.), French-Am. C. of C. in U.S. (dir. Midwest chpt.), Am. Austrian Soc. of Midwest, Finnish Am. C. of C. of Midwest, Ill. Assn. C. of C. Execs., Am. Mgmt. Assn., Royal Hort. Soc., Chgo. Hist. Soc., Chgo. Architecture Found, Field Mus. Natural History, Art Inst. Chgo., Mus. Sci. and Industry, Chgo. Council on Fgn. Relations (Chgo. com.), Mid-Am. Swedish Trade Assn., Lambda Alpha. Clubs: Mid-Am., Comml., Execs. (pres. 1950-51), Sales and Mktg. Execs. (pres. 1953-54, award 1979), Internat. Trade, Canadian Univ., Economic (Chgo.); Glenview (Golf, Ill.).

COULTON, MARTHA JEAN GLASSCOE (MRS. MARTIN J. COULTON), librarian; b. Dayton, Ohio, Dec. 11, 1927; d. Lafayette Pierre and Gertrude Blanche (Miller) Glasscoe; student Dayton Art Inst., 1946-47; m. Martin J. Coulton, Sept. 6, 1947; children—Perry Jean, Martin John. Dir. Milton (Ohio) Union Public Library, 1968—. Named Outstanding Woman, Jaycees, 1979. Mem. cable TV com., West Milton. Mem. ALA, Ohio Library Assn., Miami Valley Library Orgn. (sec.), West Milton C. of C., Internat. Platform Assn., DAR. Home: 1910 N Mowry Rd Pleasant Hill OH 45359 Office: 560 S Main St West Milton OH 45383

COULTON, MARTHA JEAN GLASSCOE (MRS. MARTIN J. COULTON), librarian; b. Dayton, Ohio, Dec. 11, 1927; d. Lafayette Pierre and Gertrude Blanche (Miller) Glasscoe; student Dayton Art Inst., 1946-47; m. Martin J. Coulton, Sept. 6, 1947; children—Perry Jean, Martin John. Dir. West Milton (Ohio) Union Public Library, 1968—. Active, West Milton (Ohio) Cable TV Com. Named Outstanding Woman Jaycees, 1978-1979. Mem. ALA, Ohio Library Assn., Miami Valley Library Orgn. (sec. 1981, v.p. 1982), Internat. Platform Assn., DAR. Home: 1910 N Mowry Rd Pleasant Hill OH 45359 Office: 560 S Main St West Milton OH 45383

COUNSELL, LEE ALBERT, dentist; b. Neillsville, Wis., July 5, 1923; s. Clarion and Henrietta (Clemens) C.; D.D.S., Northwestern U., 1948; B.A., U. Wis., Madison, 1949; diploma grad. pedodontics Forsyth Dental Center, Boston, 1949; M.P.H., U. Mich., 1967. Commd. lt. Dental Corps, U.S. Navy, 1950, discharged, 1952, rejoined, 1955, advanced through grades to comdr., 1961, ret., 1972; intern staff Naval Hosp., Gt. Lakes, Ill., 1950; asst. dir. dept. pedodontics Marquette U., 1952-54; practice pedodontics, Washington, 1954-55; house staff Naval Hosp., Boston, 1959-62; dir. dental dept. Naval Constrn. Bn. Center, Davisville, R.I., 1964-66; head preventive dentistry program Naval Base, Gt. Lakes, Ill., 1968-70; asst. chief clin. investigations div. Naval Dental Research Inst., 1971, chief, 1972; asst. dir. Bur. Dental Health, Div. Health, State of Fla., 1972-73; fellow U. Dundee (Scotland), 1973; research asso. Am. Dental Assn., Chgo., 1973-74; asso. prof. So. Ill. U., Carbondale, 1974-77; cons. dental health edn., vital stats., 1977—. Decorated Navy Commendation medal. Fellow Am. Assn. Endodontists; mem. ADA, Am. Guild Organists (voting mem.), Xi Psi Phi (life). Episcopalian. Contbr. numerous articles to profl. publs. Home and Office: 204 Pine Ln Carbondale IL 62901

COUPER, DAVID CORTLAND, city ofcl.; b. Little Falls, Minn., Apr. 5, 1938; s. John V. and Elsa D. Couper; B.A., U. Minn., 1968, M.A. (NIMH fellow), 1970; children—Peter, Catherine, Sarah, Michael, Matthew, Jennifer. Officer, Edina (Minn.) Police Dept., 1960-62; officer, detective Mpls. Police Dept., 1962-69; dir. Burnsville (Minn.) Public Safety Dept., 1969-72; chief police City of Madison (Wis.), 1972—; instr. sociology-criminology U. Minn., 1970-71, U. Wis., 1974-77. Bd. dirs. Group Health Coop., Madison, 1979-81. Served with USMC, 1957-60. U. Minn. grantee to study European police, 1971. Mem. Police Exec. Research Forum, Internat. Assn. Chiefs of Police. Club: Rotary. Contbr. numerous articles to profl. publs. Office: 211 S Carroll St Madison WI 53710

COUPLIN, JAMES RONALD, hotel exec.; b. Palouse, Wash., Aug. 31, 1909; s. Charles Allan and Madge (Callahan) C.; Ph.B., U. Chgo., 1931; m. Marie Corrine Franklyn, Aug. 3, 1936 (dec. Apr. 19, 1980); 1 adopted dau., Suzanne Couplin Reese. Gen. mgr. Hotel Waldorf, Toledo, 1934-42, Hotel Chain, Chgo., 1946-60; exec. v.p., dir. Cedar Hotel Co. Inc., 1958-72; partner, mgr. Hotel Douglas, Elgin, Ill., 1960-72, now ret. Fellow Harry S. Truman Library, Independence, Mo., 1974-75. Served from 1st lt. to maj. AUS, 1942-46; ETO. Decorated Bronze Star. Mem. Humane Soc. U.S., U. Chgo. Alumni Assn., Am., Ill. hotel assns., Elgin Assn. Commerce, S.A.R., Nat., N.J. geneal. socs., Conn. Soc. Genealogists (charter), Am. Legion, N.Mex. Mil. Inst. Alumni Assn. (sec.-treas. Chgo. area), Nat. Humane Soc., Soc. Lost Chord, Orange County (N.Y.) Geneal. Soc., Mil. Order World Wars, Phi Kappa Sigma. Republican. Unitarian. Mason (32 deg., Shriner). Contbr. articles to geneal. quars.: Edsall, Winfield, Simpson, Ferris lines. Home: 1170 Dundee Ave Elgin IL 60120 Office: PO Box 345 Elgin IL 60120

COUREY, FRED SAMUEL, former mayor; b. Lennox, S.D.; s. Samuel Thomas and Mabel (Salem) G.; student Lennox public schs. With Courey's Food Mart, Inc., Lennox, 1934—, co-owner, 1946—; city auditor, Lennox, 1948-50, mayor, 1960-80; past mem. Urbanized Devel. Commn., S.Eastern Criminal Justice Commn., S.Eastern Health Planning Council (all of S.E. Council Govts. S.D.); past mem. S.D. State-Local Govt. Study Commn.; mem. S.D. adv. council SBA, 1969—. Gen. chmn. Lennox Diamond Jubilee, 1954; past mem. parish council St. Magdalen Roman Cath. Ch., Lennox; past bd. dirs. Lennox Area Devel. Corp.; project coordinator, program dir. Lennox Area Med. Center, 1975—; mem. adv. council S.D. SBA, 1970—; past bd. dirs. Lennox Area Devel. Corp. Served with AUS, 1941-45; PTO. Decorated Army Commendation medal. Mem. Am. Water Works Assn., Water Pollution Control Fedn., S.D. Water and Wastewater Conf. (past dir.), Am. Fedn. Police, Nat. Police Res. Officers Assn., Am. Law Enforcement Officers Assn., Am. Legion. U.S. C. of C., S.D. Retailers Assn., Am. Mgmt. Assn., Small Towns Inst., Am. Forestry Assn., Smithsonian Instn., Nat. Rifle Assn., Nat. Wildlife Fedn., Early Am. Soc., Am. Mus. Natural History, Nat. Parks and Recreation Assn., Nat. Indsl. Recreation Assn., VFW. Republican. Club: Lennox Comml. (past pres.), Nat. Travel, S.D. Auto. Address: Box 56 Lennox SD 57039

COURTEAU, ELMER JOSEPH, JR., newspaperman, writer; b. Mpls., May 7, 1921; s. Elmer Joseph and Laura (Rivard-Dufresne) C.; B.A., Coll. of St. Thomas, 1947; postgrad. U. Md., 1948, U. Paris (Sorbonne), 1949, U. Wis., 1952; U. Minn., 1961-63; m. Constance Ann Dobmeyer, June 26, 1948; children—Michele, Gregory, Marc, Jeffrey, Jennifer, Gretchen, Kristin. With Duluth News-Tribune and Herald, 1947-48, Hibbing (Minn.) Daily Tribune, 1950-61, St. Paul Pioneer-Press & Dispatch, 1961-66, Mpls. Tribune, 1966—, Cath. Digest, 1969—. Past pres., current bd. dirs., worthy fellow N.W. Ter. French and Can. Heritage Inst. Mem. Am. Hist. Assn., Am. Acad. Polit. Sci., Am. Name Soc., Cath. Hist. Soc. Phila., Minn. Geneal. Soc. (past pres., dir., worthy fellow), La Société Historique de Que. Democrat. Roman Catholic. Co-author: French Canadians of the North-Central States. Home: 201 Liberty Pl South St Paul MN 55075 Office: 425 Portland Ave Minneapolis MN 55415

COURTENAY, VINCENT RAYMOND, writer, communication cons.; b. Eastbourne, Eng., Aug. 2, 1934; came to U.S., 1960; s. Thomas Greer and May Eliza (York) C.; A.B., Wayne State U.; postgrad. U. Windsor (Ont., Can.), U. Ky., N.Y. U., U. Pa.; m. Juanita Elaine DiBattista, Sept. 11, 1981; children by previous marriage—Crispin York, Dawn Renee, Patrick Vincent. Former news editor Mich. Investor; news relations mgr. Henry Ford Mus.; mng. editor The Dearborn Press; Detroit corr. McGraw-Hill World News; spl. corr. Time Mag., Bus. Week; Washington corr. McGraw-Hill; public relations mgr. Campbell-Ewald Advt.; bus. and fin. editor Detroit News; spl. corr., producer Canadian Broadcasting Corp., Windsor; mgr. fin. public relations Am. Natural Resources Co., Detroit, also v.p. Am. Natural Resources Media Co., Detroit, 1967—. Served with Canadian Army, 1951-53; Korea. Named Academician, The Tiberine Acad., Rome, 1966. Mem. Soc. Am. Bus. and Econ. Writers, Public Relations Soc. Am., Mich. Press Assn. Clubs: Detroit Press, Windsor Press. Home: 11806 Valley Blvd Warren MI 48093 Office: 1 Woodward Ave Detroit MI 48226

COURTER, JOHN FORREST, coll. pres.; b. Bennington, Kans., Jan. 1, 1925; s. Forrest and Anna (Tolin) C.; B.A., Kans. Wesleyan U., 1950; M.A., Syracuse U., 1957, Ph.D., 1963; m. Ruth Tice, Aug. 9, 1952; children—Ann Colleen, Cathleen Ruth, Carol Lynn. Admissions counselor Kans. Wesleyan U., Salina, 1950-51, dir. univ. services, 1951-56, dean of students, 1958-64; dean of students Carthage Coll., Kenosha, Wis., 1964-70; acad. dean Westmar Coll., LeMars, Iowa, 1970-79, pres., 1979—. Bd. dirs. LeMars Devel. Commn., Friends of KWIT (Public Radio). Served with inf. U.S. Army, 1943-45. Named Disting. Alumnus, Kans. Wesleyan U., 1979. Mem. Iowa Assn. Ind. Colls. (vice-chmn.), Am. Assn. Higher Edn., Phi Delta Kappa. United Methodist. Club: Lions. Home: 935 4th Ave SE LeMars IA 51031 Office: Westmar College LeMars IA 51031

COURY, ARTHUR JOSEPH, polymer chemist; b. Coaldale, Pa., Dec. 5, 1940; s. Arthur A. and Sophia T. (Korkmas) C.; B.S., U. Del., 1962; Ph.D. (Union Carbide fellow 1964-65), U. Minn., 1965, M.B.A., 1980; m. Audrae R. Stoebner, Apr. 1, 1967; children—Christopher, Timothy. Sr. research chemist II, Gen. Mills Chems., Inc., Mpls., 1965-76; sr. staff scientist, mgr. polymer devel. Medtronic, Inc., Mpls., 1976—; continuing edn. tchr. Hennepin Tech. Center, Mpls.; instr. U. Detroit, 1981, SUNY, New Paltz, 1982. Mem. Am. Chem. Soc. (chmn. awards subcom. Minn. sect. 1978-81), Electrochem. Soc., St. Anthony Park Neighborhood Assn. Author, patentee in field. Home: 2225 Hillside Ave St Paul MN 55108 Office: 6700 Shingle Creek Pkwy Brooklyn Center MN 55430

COURY, JOHN, JR., surgeon; b. Wheeling, W.Va., Oct. 22, 1921; B.S., Washington Jefferson Coll., 1942; M.D., Western Res. U., 1945; postgrad. Wayne State U., 1948-52. Intern, Harper Hosp., Detroit, 1945-46; resident Wayne Med. Center-Children's Hosp., Detroit, 1948-52; practice medicine specializing in surgery, Port Huron, Mich., 1952—; mem. staff Mercy Hosp., 1954—, chief of staff, 1962-64; mem. staff Port Huron Hosp., 1952—, chief of staff, 1974-75; mem. staff Surg. Assos.; cons. to hosps.; instr. and guest lectr. Wayne State U., 1950-52; mem. Mich. Bd. Registration and Licensing in Medicine, 1966-74; mem. Mich. Gov.'s Health Adv. Council, 1972-76; bd. dirs. Mich. Found. for Med. and Health Edn., 1973—; mem. Am. Bar Assn. Commn. on Med. Profl. Liability, 1975—; dir. Mich. Nat. Bank. Bd. dirs. Catholic Social Service, St. Clair County, Mich., 1960-70, St. Clair County United Community Fund, 1960-72; adv. trustee Port Huron Dist. Found., 1962—. Recipient Recognition award St. Clair County, 1974. Diplomate Am. Bd. Surgery. Fellow A.C.S.; mem. AMA (trustee 1976—), Mich. Med. Soc. (pres. 1972-73, Recognition award 1977), Detroit Acad. Surgery. Contbr. articles to med. jours. Office: 1225 10th St Port Huron MI 48060

COUSINO, JOE ANN, sculptress; b. Toledo, Nov. 17, 1925; d. George Carl and Lucille Carolyn (Kocher) Bux; B.A., U. Toledo, 1947; postgrad. U. So. Ill., 1954, U. Mex., 1946, 49, (scholar) Pratt Inst., 1947; children—Paula Rene and Richard Nils (twins). One-woman shows: Toledo Mus. Art, 1949, Newman Town Gallery, Toledo, 1957, Frank Ryan Gallery, Chgo., 1962, Ohio State U. Gallery, 1963, San Giuseppi Gallery Mt. St. Joseph, Cin., 1964, Chiara Gallery, Cleve., 1967, Tadlow Gallery Goldcoast Mich., 1972, Arndt Art Mus., Elmira, N.Y., 1977; numerous invitationals including U.S.A. Dept. Commerce Exposition in Rio de Janerio, Brazil, 1963, Akron Art Inst. Sculptural Internat., 1966, Blossum Center Invitational Kent State U., 1968-70; lectr., instr. in field; mem. Mayor's Com. Arts Toledo, 1974—; instr. art adult dept. YWCA Toledo, 1944-57, YMCA 1945-57; feature artist Univ. workshops, 1966—; dir. Lighting Fixtures, Inc., Toledo, 1958, Cousino Metal Products, 1960-72. Bd. dirs. Friends Univ. Toledo Library, 1977-82; trustee Fedn. Art Soc., 1964—, pres., 1964-66. Recipient numerous art awards including: Ohio State Ceramic Sculpture award, 1955; Jr. League Best in Show, Toledo Mus., 1956; Gold Metal best in show, Religious Art Am., Chgo., 1960; purchase award Toledo Fedn. Lending Collection, Toledo Mus. Art, 1970. Mem. Nat. Craftsmens Council (Ohio del. 1962-65; Ohio Designer Craftsman (trustee 1964-66), Toledo Potters Guild (founder, pres. 1951-53), Am. Archaeology Soc. Episcopalian. Address: 3717 Indian Rd Toledo OH 43606

COUTTS, SHIRLEY SUE WEBB, educator; b. Pensacola, Fla., Jan. 1, 1930; d. Quilla Clifford and Mary Gertrude (McCumber) Webb; B.S., Fla. State U., 1951; M.A., N.E. Mo. State U., 1975; m. Robert L. Coutts, Feb. 19, 1951 (div. Oct. 1973); children—Candila Sue, Robert L., William C., R. Christopher. Elementary classroom tchr., Pensacola. Fla., 1952-53, 58-59, Tallahaassee, Fla., 1959-62, Fairfield, Iowa, 1967-74; elem. curriculum and guidance cons. Arrowhead Area Edn. Agy. 5, Ft. Dodge, Iowa, 1975—. Bd. dirs. Lakota council Girl Scouts U.S.A. Mem. Am., Iowa personnel and guidance assns., Assn. Supervision and Curriculum Devel., Iowa Assn. Supervision and Curriculum Devel., Iowa Sch. Counselors Assn., Phi Delta Kappa (chpt. pres. 1980-82). Home: 607 11th Ave N Fort Dodge IA 50501 Office: 1235 5th Ave S Fort Dodge IA 50501

COUTTS, WARREN HALL, JR., lawyer, rancher; b. El Dorado, Kans., Nov. 6, 1900; s. Warren Hall and Ida Frances (Whitehead) C.; student Kans. State U., 1920-21, U. Kans., 1921-23; J.D., Washburn U., 1924; 1 son, Warren Hall III (dec.). Admitted to Kans. bar, 1924, U.S. Supreme Ct. bar; sr. partner Coutts & Coutts, El Dorado, 1967—; pres. Pan Am. Commerce, Inc.; pres., owner Pine Forest Ranch, Inc., Hall Mar Ranches; breeder registered Herefords. Municipal judge, El Dorado, 1926-30. Founder, Warren Hall Coutts III Meml. Art Gallery, Inc.; mem. forestry com. Conservation Fedn. Mo. Trustee Washburn U. Mem. Am. Hereford Assn., Am. Saddle Horse Breeders Assn., El Dorado, Wichita (soc. fellows art) art assns., Shetland Pony Club Am., Am. Quarterhorse Breeders Assn., Kappa Sigma, Phi Alpha Delta, Theta Nu Epsilon. Episcopalian. Elk. Clubs: Washburn U. W., El Dorado Country. Contbr. to Am. Saddle and Bridle mag., Southwestern Horseman mag. Home: Hall Mar Pl El Dorado KS 67042 Office: 110 N Main El Dorado KS 67042

COUTURE, GWENDOLYN LILLIAN WICKS, educator; b. Bottineau, N.D., Apr. 30, 1918; d. Albert Ace and Lillian (Bittner) Wicks; B.A., Minot (N.D.) State Coll., 1944; M.A., U. N.D., Grand Forks; m. Robert Couture, Sept. 8, 1968 (div.). Office worker, Jamestown, N.D.; tchr. Montpelier (N.D.) High Sch., 1966-68, Springfield (S.D.) Coll., 1970; fin. mgr. Weld Boces, Greeley, Colo., 1970-73; inventory control Montgomery Ward, Greeley, 1973-75; instr. bus. Nebr. Western Coll., Scottsbluff, 1975—; income tax practitioner; leader workshops in time mgmt. Pres. VFW Aux., 1973-75, Am. Legion Aux., 1972-73; jr. v.p. VFW Aux. Recipient Thanks award for scouting. Mem. Nat. Bus. Edn. Assn., NEA, Nebr. Edn. Assn., Carnegians, Inc., Delta Pi Epsilon, Pi Omega Pi. Methodist. Home: 2801 6th Ave Scottsbluff NE 69361 Office: Nebraska Western College Scottsbluff NE 69361

COVER, WILLIAM HENRY, mfg. co. exec.; b. Tunnel Hill, Ill., Aug. 15, 1923; s. David Soloman and Mary Virginia (Thrall) C.; B.S., U. Ill., 1946; m. Jo Richardson, Mar. 9, 1979; children by previous marriage—William D., Janet L., David C. Sales rep. U.S. Agrichem, Sandusky, Ohio, 1947-52, dist. mgr., 1953-60, regional mgr., 1960-64; mgr. site selection, Monsanto Agri Products Co., St. Louis, 1964-65, mgr. training and devel., 1965—; cons. in field. Served with USN, 1943-45. Mem. Nat. Soc. Sales Tng. Execs., Am. Soc. Tng. and Devel. (nat. chmn. sales tng. div. 1974, nat. v.p., bd. dirs. 1975-76, recipient Jim Ball Meml. award, 1975). Contbr. articles to profl. jours. Home: 8526 Eulalie Ave Saint Louis MO 63144 Office: 800 N Lindbergh Blvd Saint Louis MO 63166

COVERDALE, BARBARA LEE BRADLEY, nurse; b. Chgo., Aug. 22, 1933; d. Sterling Hibbard and Francis Evelyn (Bretnall) Bradley; student Baldwin Wallace Coll., 1951-53; R.N. diploma, Cleve. Met. Gen. Hosp., 1956; B.S. in Nursing, Ohio State U., 1959; postgrad. Case Western Res. U., 1961-63; m. William Rodney Coverdale, Jan. 6, 1961; children—Carol Evelyn, Lee Ann, David Bradley, Scott William. Staff nurse Cleve. Met. Gen. Hosp., 1956-61, asst. head nurse, 1957-58, head nurse, 1956-57, 59-61; adminstrv. day supr. Parma (Ohio) Community Hosp., 1961-64, asst. dir. nurses patient care, 1965-69, asst. dir. nurses personnel services and staff devel., 1964-65; asst. dir. staff devel. Fairview Gen. Hosp., Cleve., 1971—; CPR instr. trainer Am. Heart Assn. Parent edn. and substance abuse officer PTA. Mem. Am. Nurses Assn., Ohio Nurses Assn., Greater Cleve. Nurses Assn. (Involved Mem. award 1977), Cleve. Met. Sch. of Nursing Alumni, Am. Heart Assn., Am. Cancer Soc., Alpha Gamma Delta. Home: 6508 Maplecrest Ave Parma Heights OH 44130 Office: Fairview Gen Hosp 18101 Lorain Ave Cleveland OH 44111

COVERT, MAXWELL FREDERICK, coll. pres.; b. Ferndale, Mich., Feb. 19, 1919; s. Maxwell A. and Margaret V. (Miniker) C.; B.S., Wayne State U., Detroit, 1953, M.Ed., 1957; m. M. Joyce Davison, June 22, 1941; children—Judy, Patty, Cindy. Tng. supr. Ford Motor Co., 1938-68; dean, asst. to pres. Macomb County (Mich.) Community Coll., 1968-71; pres. Northwest Tech. Coll., Archbold, Ohio, 1971—; chmn. joint apprenticeship com. Ford Motor Co.; mem. part-time faculty Wayne State U., Bowling Green (Ohio) State U.; cons. in field. Mem. Ferndale Bd. Edn., 1964-68. Recipient Alumni award Wayne State U., 1977. Mem. Ohio Assn. Two-Year Colls. (pres. 1977), Ohio Orgn. Tech. Colls. (pres. 1981), Am. Council Indsl. Arts Edn., Am. Soc. Tng. and Devel., Am. Vocat. Assn., Fluid Power Soc., Henry Ford Trade Sch. Alumni Assn., Am. Tech. Edn. Assn., Am. Assn. Community and Jr. Colls., Ohio Tech. and Community Coll. Assn., Wayne State U. Alumni Assn. Republican. Clubs: Rotary, Shriners. Author: Hydraulic Test Stand, 1965; co-author: Basic Hydraulics for Instructors, 1965. Office: Route 1 Box 246A Archbold OH 43502

COVEY, FRANK MICHAEL, JR., lawyer; b. Chgo., Oct. 24, 1932; s. Frank M. and Marie B. (Lorenz) C.; B.S. with honors, Loyola U., 1954, J.D. cum laude, 1957; S.J.D., U. Wis., 1960; m. Patricia Ann McGill, Oct. 7, 1961; children—Geralyn, Frank M. III, Regis Patrick. Admitted to Ill. bar, 1957, U.S. Supreme Ct. bar, 1965; practiced law, Chgo., 1959—; law clk. Ill. Appellate Ct., 1959; asso. Belnap, Spencer, Hardy & Freeman, 1959-60; asso. McDermott, Will & Emery, 1960-65, partner, 1965—. Instr., Northwestern U. Sch. Law, 1958-59, Loyola U. Coll., 1958-69, 79-80. Research asso. Wis. Gov.'s Com. on Revision of Law of Eminent Domain, 1958; asso. gen. counsel Union League Civic and Arts Found., 1967-69, mng. dir., 1975—, v.p., 1969-72, 73-75, pres., 1972-73; co-dir. Grant Park study team Nat. Commn. on Causes and Prevention of Violence, 1968. Mem. Better Govt. Assn., Chgo. Art Inst.; mem. Chgo. Mus. Natural History, also mem. com. cts. and justice, com. legis. reform; mem. bd. athletics Loyola U., 1970-72, estate planning com., 1969—, mem. com. future law sch., 1975-76, citizen's bd., 1978—, trustee, 1980—. Recipient award Conf. Personal Finance Law, 1955; Founder's Day award Loyola U., 1976, medal of excellence, 1979. Mem. Am., Ill. (Lincoln award 1963), Chgo., 7th Fed. Circuit bar assns., Am. Judicature Soc., Cath. Lawyers Guild, Chgo. Council Lawyers, Internat. Assn. Ins. Counsel, Legal Club Chgo., Law Club Chgo., Chgo. Bldg. Congress (dir. 1978—), Loyola U. Alumni Assn. (pres. 1965-66, bd. govs. 1966-70), North Shore Bd. Realtors (asso.), Law Alumni Assn. (award 1957, v.p. 1968-69, pres. 1969-70, chmn. fund campaign 1967-68, bd. govs. 1972-73), Thomas More Club (chmn. 1973-75), Ill. Hist. Soc., Air Force Assn., Blue Key, Phi Alpha Delta, Alpha Sigma Nu, Pi Gamma Mu, Delta Sigma Rho. Roman Catholic (parish council 1973-75). Clubs: Monroe, Union League (dir. 1977-80, chmn. house com. 1977-80) (Chgo.). Author: Roadside Protection Through Access Control, 1960; also articles, speeches. Contbg. author: Federal Civil Practice in Illinois, 1974, 78, 81; Business Litigation I: Competition and Its Limits, 1978; A Lawyer's Guide to Class Actions, 1979. Home: 1104 W Lonnquist Blvd Mount Prospect IL 60056 Office: 111 W Monroe St Chicago IL 60603

COVEY, GERALD GRANT, constrn. co. exec.; b. Euclid, Ohio, May 1, 1931; s. Gerald Grant and Edith Althea (Tiffany) C.; student Miami U., Oxford, Ohio, 1950-53, Case Inst. Tech., 1953-54, Fenn Coll., 1958-64; m. Gail Ramsdell, Dec. 28, 1963; children—Christopher R., Carrie A., Cathy L., Kellie A. Pres., Gerald G. Covey Co., Rocky River, Ohio, 1957—; v.p. Rossborough Mfg. Co., Cleve., 1973-75, Wescon Inc., Lakewood, Ohio, 1976-80; gen. mgr. Esch Constrn. Co., Cleve., 1975—; owner James Hardware Co., Rocky River, Ohio, 1979—. Served with U.S. Army, 1954-57. Mem. Builders Exchange, Cleve. Growth Assn., C. of C. Republican. Methodist. Clubs: Avon Oaks Country, River Oaks Racquet, Masons. Home: 21040 Lake Rd Rocky River OH 44116 Office: 19030 Lake Rd Rocky River OH 44116

COVEY, ROBERT OTIS, lawyer, savs. and loan exec.; b. Oshkosh, Wis., Jan. 21, 1921; s. David L. and Bessie V. (Otis) C.; B.A., U. Wis., 1942; J.D., Northwestern U., 1948; m. Mary E. Karlen, June 3, 1943; children—Karlen R., Kathleen M., Carol Ann (Mrs. Miles J. Beard), Christopher. Admitted to Ill. bar, 1948, since practiced in Crystal Lake; sr. partner firm Covey, Covey & Waggoner, Crystal Lake, Ill.; pres., chmn. bd. First Fed. Savs. and Loan, Crystal Lake, 1970-79; v.p., regional mgr. 1st Fed. Savs. and Loan Assn. Chgo., 1979—. Pres., Sch. Bd. Dist. 47, 1951-61. Chmn., Citizens for Eisenhower, McHenry County, 1952. Mem. McHenry County (pres. 1962), Chgo., Ill., Am. bar assns. Congregationalist (moderator, chmn. ch. 1970-72). Mason, Lion. Club: Crystal Lake (Ill.) Country. Home: 970 S Shore Dr Crystal Lake IL 60014 Office: 88 Grant St Crystal Lake IL 60014

COVINGTON, CHARLES J., mfg. co. exec.; b. Farmington, Mo., Jan. 8, 1914; s. Mabry J. and Ethel Ann (Covington) C.; student Wichita (Kans.) U.; m. Lois Ellen Combs, Dec. 9, 1939; children—Joe J., Patricia Ann, Jon Scott. With Dowzer Electric div. Sola Basic Industries, Mt. Vernon, Ill., 1938—, pres., 1948—, chmn. bd., 1973—; pres. Electec Apparatus Service, 1956-57, Power Cores, Inc., 1960-72; dir. Security Bank of Mt. Vernon; chmn. bd. King City Fed. Savs. & Loan Assn., Mt. Vernon. Pres. Greater Egypt Planning Commn., 1976-79; chmn. Buffalo Trace council Boy Scouts Am., 1948-53, canoe base, regional chmn., recipient Silver Beaver award 1951, Silver Antelope award, 1960. Chmn. bd. trustees Rend Lake Conservancy Dist. Recipient award Nat. Elec. Mfrs. Assn., Community Service award, 1969. Mem. Nat. Indsl. Service Assn. (pres.), Ill. Mfrs. Assn., Mt. Vernon C. of C. (Best Citizen award 1954, pres.). Lion, Elk, Moose. Clubs: Union League (Chgo.); Missouri Athletic (St. Louis). Home: 1818 Isabella Ave Mount Vernon IL 62864 Office: 117 N 10th St Mount Vernon IL 62864

COVINGTON, JAMES LUTHER, city ofcl., community devel. adminstr.; b. Glendora, Miss., Oct. 4, 1934; s. James L. and Inez (Simes) C.; B.S. in Edn. and Sociology, Tchrs. Coll. N.C., 1953; M.S. in Spl. Edn. St. Louis U., 1962; m. Margaret Thompson, June 30, 1956; children—Kendal, Corey, Kellie. Instr. and adminstrv. asst. jr. high sch. dept. St. Louis Bd. Edn., 1967-68; employment dir. Inner-City YMCA, St. Louis, 1968-69; exec. dir. Page Park YMCA, St. Louis, 1969-71; vocat. counselor sect. vocat. rehab. State Dept. Edn., St. Louis, 1971; group home dir. St. Louis Juvenile Ct., 1971-72; exec. dir. Youth Service System Agy., Mayors Council on Youth, St. Louis, 1972-75; 2d v.p. personnel and ops. Trans Am. Enterprise Ltd., St. Louis, 1975-77; project inst. spl. edn. program State Community Coll., East St. Louis, Ill., 1977; community sch. coordinator Ford Community Sch., St. Louis, 1977-79; community devel. dir. Office of Community Devel., City of Kinloch (Mo.), 1979—; propr., dir. Gateway Profl. Tutors Inc., St. Louis, 1967-68; mem. adult edn. faculty George Washington U., 1955-56. Mem. Citizen Edn. Task Force, St. Louis, 1976-79; bd. dirs. Met. Group Homes of St. Louis, 1970-71. Served with U.S. Army, 1953-55. Recipient Service award YMCA, 1968, Fed. Exec. Bd. Service award, 1974, Dir. Service award U.S. Record Center, 1968, Citizens Edn. Task Force Service award, 1979. Mem. Community Devel. Dirs. Nat. Assn., Am. Corrections Assn. of Group Home Dirs., Omega Psi Phi, Chi Delta Mu. Columnist St. Louis Argus newspaper, 1972-76; editor St. Louis Peoples Guide, 1979-81. Home: 1014 Wylin Ct Ferguson MO Office: City of Kinloch 5990 Monroe St Kinloch MO 63140

COWAN, CHRISTINE, mgmt. cons.; b. Lansing, Mich., Nov. 2, 1952; d. David Avery and Lavonne (Evans) C.; B.S. in Econs., M.I.T., 1975; M.B.A., Harvard U., 1978. Jr. securities analyst Boston Co., 1975-76; corp. asso. Westvaco, N.Y.C., 1978-79, asso. product mgr. chem. div., Charleston, S.C., 1979-81; cons. McKinsey & Co., Cleve., 1981—. Mem. alumnae bd. Laurel Sch., Shaker Heights, Ohio. Mem. Assn. M.B.A. Execs. Republican. Episcopalian. Home: 19406-36 Van Aken Blvd #110 Shaker Heights OH 44122 Office: 100 Erieview Plaza Cleveland OH 44114

COWAN, LAWRENCE, clin. psychologist; b. Detroit, July 23, 1932; s. Benjamin Julian and Dorothy (Eisenstadt) C.; B.A., Mich. State U., 1954; M.A., U. Mo., 1958; Ph.D., Wayne State U., 1967; m. Patricia Ruth Pennington, June 24, 1956; 1 son, David Michael. Sch. psychologist Cherry Hill Sch. Dist., Inkster, Mich., 1958-68; psychol. dir. Midwest Mental Health Clinic, Dearborn, Mich., 1968-69; cons. Center for Forensic Psychiatry, Ann Arbor, Mich., 1969-70; clin. psychologist Southfield, Mich., 1969—; lectr. U. Mich., Dearborn, 1973-74; adj. clin. prof. psychology U. Detroit, 1981; cons. Redford (Mich.) Union Schs., 1971-78; cons. for adminstrv. law hearings Mich. Atty. Gen.'s Office, 1981; pres. Forensic Psychology Inst., 1978—. Served with U.S. Army, 1954-56. Lic. psychologist, marriage counselor, sch. psychologist, Mich.; diplomate Am. Bd. Forensic Psychology. Mem. Mich. Psychol. Assn. (v.p. profl. affairs 1974-76; pres. 1976 named Disting. Psychologist 1981), Am. Assn. Marriage and Family Therapists, Mich. Assn. Marriage Counselors, Am. Psychol. Assn. (council of reps. 1979—), Am. Psychology-Law Soc., Am. Acad. Forensic Psychology, Mich. Soc. Forensic Psychology (founder, pres.). Home: 28262 Greencastle Farmington Hills MI 48018 Office: 24555 Southfield Rd Southfield MI 48075

COWAN, SUE ELLEN, seed co. mgr.; b. Reedsburg, Wis., Jan. 8, 1945; d. Evan L. and Lorna (Lueders) Wheeler; student Wis. State U., Oshkosh, 1964-66; B.S., U. Wis., Madison, 1977; 1 dau., Becky. Clk., Gen. Tel. Co., Reedsburg, Madison, Sun Prairie, Wis., 1966-75; intern Oconomowoc Canning Co., Waunakee, Wis., 1976; intern fertilizer dept. Dane County Farmers Union Coop., Cottage Grove, Wis., 1977; with PAG Seeds/Cargill Inc., 1978—, ter. mgr., Congerville, Ill., 1978—. Mem. PAG Hy Club, DAR (state rec. sec. 1977-80, nat. vice chmn. scholarship com. 1980-83), Am. Soc. Agronomy, Wis. Agrl. and Life Scis. Alumni Assn. (life). Lutheran. Clubs: Bloomington Normal Ag, Order Eastern Star. Address: 50 Village Ct Congerville IL 61729

COWDEN, MARGARET GISONDI, state ofcl.; b. Gloversville, N.Y., Mar. 21, 1929; d. Harvey and Dorothy (Desmond) Gisondi; B.S., Columbia U., 1957; 1 dau., Nina Lucia. Adminstrv. asst. to dean of grad. faculties Columbia U., N.Y.C., 1951-53; tchr. public schs., N.Y.C., 1956-63; sect. supr. Basic Systems, Inc., N.Y.C., 1963-64; writer Holt, Rinehart and Winston, 1964-65; free lance writer, 1966-71; partner Hasty Pudding Catering Service, Macomb, Ill., 1972-74; exec. dir. Ill. Commn. on Status of Women, Springfield, 1974-80; exec. Ill. Dept. Children and Family Services, Springfield, 1980—. Mem. coordinating com. Internat. Women's Yr., 1976-77, Ill. del. nat. conf., 1977; mem. Gov.'s Adv. Com. on Statewide Displaced Homemakers Program, 1979—; mem. adv. bd. Ill. Women's History Week, 1980; mem. Adv. Council Edn. Handicapped Children, 1980-81; mem. health edn. adv. com. Ill. State Bd. Edn., 1981—, early childhood Services Com., 1980—. Mem. Nat. Women's Polit. Caucus, AAUW, Ill. Women's Polit. Caucus (past dir.), Ill. Council Nutrition, Springfield Women's Polit. Caucus. Republican. Unitarian. Office: Ill Dept Children and Family Services One Old State Capitol Plaza Springfield IL 62706

COWGILL, BRUCE HAYDEN, elec. products co. exec.; b. Sewickley, Pa., Jan. 15, 1945; s. Bernard Francis and Lilye (Hayden) C.; B.S. in Ceramic Engring., Alfred U., 1967; m. Patricia Ann Diehl, Aug. 12, 1967; children—Bruce William, Michael Bernard. With Gen. Electric Co., Cleve., 1967—, various positions, 1967-69, project leader photoflash, 1969-70, shop ops. supr., 1970-73, supr. program planning, 1973-75, mfg. adminstr., 1975-79, plant mgr., Jefferson, Ohio, 1979-81, Conneaut, Ohio, 1981—. Library trustee, Jefferson. Mem. Am. Ceramic Soc., Elfun Soc., Delta Sigma Phi. Episcopalian. Clubs: Exchange, Jaycees. Home: 384 Beverly Dr Jefferson OH 44047 Office: 82 W Ashtabula St Jefferson OH 44047

COWLES, WARREN HARDING, research engr.; b. Goodells, Mich., Jan. 27. 1922; s. Artemus William and Blanche Juanita (Pester) C.; B.S. in Aero. Engring., U. Mich., 1945; m. Elizabeth Jane Bannon, Oct. 20, 1973; 1 son. Dennis Michael. Aerodynamicist, McDonnell Aircraft Co., 1945-46; project engr. Chrysler Corp., Highland Park, Mich., 1946-48: dir. tech. programs Holley Carburetor div. Colt Industries Op. Corp., Warren, Mich., 1948—. Mem. Soc. Automotive Engrs. Republican. Roman Catholic. Author: Advanced Fuel Metering Demonstration, 1977. Patentee 31 inventions. Home: 1871 Spring Grove Bloomfield Hills MI 48013 Office: 11955 E Nine Mile Rd Warren MI 48090

COX, ADELINE LORRAINE, hosp. and nursing adminstr.; b. Cadillac, Mich., June 8, 1927; d. Harry C. and Madge E. (Slusser) Briggs; A.A., Graceland Coll., 1947; diploma Independence Sanitarium and Hosp. Sch. Nursing, 1950; B.A., Graceland Coll., 1973; m. Norman E. Cox, Apr. 9, 1950; children—Renee, Candace, Randall. Staff nurse Burge Hosp., Springfield, Mo., 1950-51, Ellis Fischel Cancer Hosp., Columbia, Mo., 1951-52, Sugar Creek (Mo.) Maternity Hosp., 1955-56; staff nurse Independence (Mo.) Sanitarium and Hosp., 1957-60, night supr., 1960-65, dir. nursing, 1968-76, coordinator patient care, 1976-79, asst. hosp. adminstr., 1979—; dir. nursing Jackson County Public Hosp., Kansas City, Mo., 1965-68; mem. adv. bd. Jenny Lund Sch. Practical Nursing, 1970—, Graceland

Coll. Sch. Nursing, 1968. Bd. dirs. Truman Med. Center West, 1978-79, Truman Med. Center East, 1978-79, Harry S Truman Children's Neurol. Center, 1978—, ARC, Independence, Mo., 1974. Mem. Am. Hosp. Assn., Mo. Assn. Nursing Service Adminstrn., Mo. Hosp. Assn., Acad. Health Professions, Reorganized Latter Day Saint Profl. Nurses Assn., Independence Sanitarium and Hosp. Alumni Assn. (v.p. 1968), Am. Coll. Hosp. Adminstrs. Republican. Mem. Reorganized Ch. Latter-day Saints. Author: Nursing Care Plan Guidelines, 1973. Home: 15800 E 45th Place Independence MO 64055 Office: 1509 W Truman Rd Independence MO 64050

COX, CHARLENE, educator; b. Hutchinson, Kans., July 13, 1936; d. Leonard B. and Veleda E. (Smithhisler) Wess; B.Mus., Kans. State U., 1957, M.Mus., 1980; m. Billy Ralph Cox, Aug. 25, 1956; children—Jerry, Julie. Tchr. piano, Manhattan, Kans., 1954-58, 60-61, Denver, 1959, Topeka, 1958, 62—, lectr. pedagogy Kans. State U., 1973—, instr. class piano, 1977—; lectr. Marymount Coll., others, 1973—; choir dir. Most Pure Heart of Mary Roman Catholic Ch., 1972, cantor, 1971-77, organist, 1974-76; organist, choir dir., cantor Christ the King Roman Cath. Ch., 1978—; mem. research com. Standards of Pvt. Educators of Music for Kans., 1976. Bd. dirs., cons. for music edn. Melody Brown Meml., Inc. Alpha Chi Omega Founders fellow, 1973. Mem. Nat. Music Tchrs. Assn. (dir. 1978—, 1st v.p. West Central div.), Kans. Music Tchrs. Assn. (pres. 1976-78, dir. 1979-81), Topeka Music Tchrs. Assn. (pres. 1968-69), Topeka Arts Council (dir. 1977-79), Kans. Alliance Arts in Edn. (dir. sec.), Civic Symphony Soc. (dir. 1979—), Nat. Guild Piano Tchrs. (faculty mem., adjudicator), Dance Arts Topeka (dir. 1981—), Alpha Chi Omega (nat. music com. 1980—), Mu Phi Epsilon, Pi Kappa Lambda. Roman Catholic. Home: 6112 W Smith Pl Topeka KS 66614

COX, DAVID JACKSON, biochemist; b. N.Y.C., Dec. 22, 1934; s. Reavis and Rachel (Dunaway) C.; B.A., Wesleyan U., 1956; Ph.D., U. Pa., 1960; m. Joan M. Narbeth, Sept. 6, 1958; children—Andrew Reavis, Matthew Bruce, Thomas Jackson. Instr. biochemistry U. Wash., 1960-63; asst. prof. chemistry U. Tex., 1963-67, asso. prof., 1967-73; prof., head dept. biochemistry Kans. State U., 1973—; vis. prof. U. Va., 1970-71. NSF Predoctoral fellow, 1956-59; NSF Sr. Postdoctoral fellow, 1970-71. Mem. Am. Soc. Biol. Chemists, Am. Chem. Soc., AAAS, N.Y. Acad. Scis., Phi Beta Kappa, Sigma Xi. Democrat. Presbyterian. Home: 2846 Oregon Ln Manhattan KS 66502 Office: Dept Biochemistry Kans State U Manhattan KS 66506

COX, DONALD BRUCE, real estate exec.; b. Evansville, Ind., July 25, 1928; s. Harry and Elsie Lucille (Roll) C.; ed. U. Evansville; m. Nelda Jean VanMeter, Oct. 21, 1966; children—Jeri Haggard, Dianne Chapman, Denise Cox, Brian Rexing. With real estate and constrn. dept. So. Ind. Gas & Electric Co., 1947-66; propr. Don Cox & Assos., real estate brokerage, Evansville, 1966—; owner, sec. North Park Apts.; pres. Mid-Continent Capitol Corp.; dir. Nat. City Bank, Evansville, Investors Trust Ins. Co.; v.p., treas. Mid-Continent Ins. Agy. Bd. dirs. Welborn Bapt. Hosp., Evansville, Ind. U. Evansville Found.; trustee Evansville-Vanderburgh County Bldg. Authority; chmn. Vanderburgh County Republican Com., 1971-77; Ind. chmn. Pres. Ford Com., 1976, Gov. Robert Orr Com., 1980. Named Ky. Col., 1970, Sagamore of Wabash, 1975, 81, Ambassador of Ind., 1977. Mem. Nat. Assn. Ind. Fee Appraisers (past pres.), Nat. Assn. Real Estate Bds., Nat. Assn. Home Builders, Ind. Real Estate Assn., Evansville Bd. Realtors, Evansville C. of C. (dir. 1981-82). Baptist. Clubs: Evansville Country (pres., dir. 1981), Evansville Kennel. Home: 4029 Fairfax Rd Evansville IN 47710 Office: 1010 Sycamore St Evansville IN 47708

COX, DOROTHY ANNA, educator; b. Farmington, Mich., Mar. 29, 1932; d. Ray J. and Clara Iona (Sheldon) Howard; B.A. in Edn., U. Mich., 1953, M.S., 1972, Ph.D., 1980; m. James M. Cox, June 15, 1951; children—Nancy, Lee, David. Tchr. N.Y.C. Schs., 1953-54, Farmington (Mich.) Schs., 1954-55, Southfield (Mich.) Schs., 1957-58, Clarenceville Public Schs., Livonia, Mich., 1958—; research asst. to prof. Carl Berger, U. Mich., 1979; project asst. NSF, High Scope Ednl. Found., Ypsilanti, Mich., 1980—. Leader Girl Scouts Am., 1962-63; pres. Farmington Area Naturalists, 1972-74; mem. Farmington Hills Parks and Recreation Commn., 1972—, sec., 1978—. Recipient Russell E. Wilson Meml. award Sch. Edn., U. Mich., 1978; Outstanding Jr. High Sci. Tchr. award Mich. Sci. Tchrs. Assn., 1981; named Woman of Distinction, Delta Kappa Gamma, 1981. Mem. NEA, Mich. Edn. Assn., Clarenceville Edn. Assn., Mich. Environ. Edn. Assn. (pres. 1975-77, bd. dirs. 1974-79), Met. Detroit Sci. Tchrs. Assn. (bd. dirs. 1974-76), Mich. Sci. Tchrs. Assn. (bd. dirs. 1975-78), Nat. Sci. Tchrs. Assn., Assn. Supervision and Curriculum Devel., Am. Nature Study Soc. (bd. dirs. 1980—), Nat. Assn. Environ. Edn. (bd. dirs. 1980—, hospitality chmn. 1981 Nat. Conf.). Author: Environmental Encounters for Schools, 1974. Editor: (with W.B. Stapp) Environmental Education Activities Manual, 1974, 79. Home: 32493 Shady Ridge Dr Farmington Hills MI 48018 Office: 20210 Middlebelt Rd Livonia MI 48152

COX, HARDIN CHARLES, state senator; b. Rock Port, Mo., Mar. 4, 1928; B.S. in Bus. Adminstrn., U. Mo., Columbia, 1951; m. Virginia Heifner, Jan. 6, 1952; children—Bryan, Mark. Engaged in ins. and real estate, 1953—; sec.-treas. Farmers Mut. Ins. Co., Rockport; treas. Columbia Mut. Ins. Co., Farmers Mut. Hail Ins. Co., owner Cox and Son Ins. Agy., Rock Port, Hardin Cox Real Estate, Rock Port; mem. Mo. Ho. of Reps., 66-72, 72-74, chmn. legis. research com., 1972, vice chmn. parks and recreation com., 1972; mem. Mo. Senate, 1974—, chmn. banking and fin. instns. com., ways and means com., legis. research com., vice chmn. coms. on ins. and rules, joint rules, resolutions and misc. bills, mem. coms. on agr., conservation, parks and tourism and budget control; founder Fellowship Christian Politicans, 1976. Active local Boy Scouts Am.; chmn., originator God and Man Ann. Services, Lions Eye Bank; chmn. Easter Sunrise Services, Rock Port, 1955; mem. Atchison County Sch. Bd., 1957-64. Served with AUS, 1946-48, 51-53. Recipient Meritorious Service award 4-H Club, 1966; Legis. Conservation award Nat. Wildlife Assn., 1970; Legislator of Decade award Big Lake Improvement Assn., 1972; Appreciation award Mo. Cattlemen's Assn., 1972; named Ark. Traveller, 1973. Mem. Am. Legion, VFW, Rock Port C. of C. Democrat. Lutheran. Home: 602 W Calhoun St Rock Port MO 64482 Office: 300 Main St Rock Port MO 64482

COX, JAMES ANDREW, book rev. editor; b. Los Angeles, Nov. 6, 1942; s. Carl Taylor and Elizabeth (Moore) C.; B.A., Brigham Young U., 1966; M.S.W., U. Wis., 1976; m. Nancy Lorraine Stubbs, Oct. 31, 1969; children—Lee James, Jared James, Micah James, Cannon James, Bethany James. Counselor, Office of Rehab. Services, Salt Lake City, 1966-69; social worker Dane County Dept. Social Services, Madison, Wis., 1969-74; spl. edn. coordinator Brodhead Sch. Dist., Brodhead, Wis., 1974-81; programmer, bd. dirs. WORT-FM, Madison, Wis., 1976-78; sr. editor, dir. The Madison Review of Books, 1976-81; editor, dir. The Midwest Book Rev. Oregon, Wis., 1981—; editor Midwest Bookwatch, Oregon, 1981—; producer/host The Sci. Fiction and Fantasy Hour, WORT-FM/MCAC-TV, Madison, 1976—. Bd. dirs. Madison Community Access Center, 1977-78; producer/dir. WISCON Annual Art Show and Auction, Madison, 1979-81, com. mem., 1976—. Mem. Nat. Fedn. Community Broadcasters, Soc. for Furtherance and Study of Fantasy and Sci. Fiction, Tolkien Soc., Unitarian Soc. Author: The Contributions of Joseph Smith to Plural Marriage, 1964; Jesus the Magician, 1975; The MRB Network, 1979-81; The Midwest Bookwatch, 1981. Address: 278 Orchard Dr Oregon WI 53575

COX, JANET MARIE, phys. therapist; b. Galesburg, Ill., Jan. 7, 1951; d. Robert Henry and Virginia Lois (Clay) C.; B.A. in Biology, Augustana (Ill.) Coll., 1973; cert. in phys. therapy Mayo Found. Sch. Phys. Therapy, Rochester, Minn., 1975; cert. in neurodevel. therapy Georgetown U., 1979. Staff phys. therapist Mayo Clinic, Rochester, 1975-76, Mercy Health Center, Dubuque, 1976-78; phys. therapy cons. Hills & Dales Child Devel. Center, Dubuque, 1977-78, dir. habilitative services, 1978—; phys. therapy cons. Planning and Guidance Center-Devel. Disabilities Council Dist. VIII, Maquoketa, Iowa, 1977-78. Mem. Am. Phys. Therapy Assn., Mayo Clinic Phys. Therapy Alumni Assn. (public relations com. 1976-78), Iowa Phys. Therapy Assn. (dir. 1979-81, chmn. public relations com. 1980—, sec.-treas. N.E. dist. 1980—). Home: 770 Angella St Dubuque IA 52001 Office: 1011 Davis St Dubuque IA 52001

COX, KENNETH R., state senator; b. Ohio, Oct. 8, 1928; s. Dexter L. and Ila B. Cox; ed. U. Akron; married; children—Timothy, Patricia. Mgr. advt. prodn. B.F. Goodrich Co.; mem. Barberton (Ohio) City Council, 1960-66; mayor of Barberton, 1966-73; mem. Ohio Ho. of Reps., from 1973; mem. Ohio Senate, mem. elections com., fin. instns. and ins. com., local govt. and urban affairs com., ways and means com. Active Summit County Mental Health Assn.; trustee Portage Path Community Mental Health Center; mem. adv. bd. Coll. Nursing, trustee U. Akron. Clubs: Elks, Kiwanis. Office: State House 3d Floor Columbus OH 43215

COX, MYRON KEITH, educator; b. Akron, May 6, 1926; s. Carney F. and Nina Castilla (Kenny) C.; B.S., Va. Poly. Inst., 1949; B.S., Pa. State Coll., 1952; M.S., M.I.T., 1957; D.Sc., London Coll., Eng., 1964; m. Emma A. Edwards, July 2, 1950; children—Carney K., Myron D., Eric L., Brett W. Commd. staff sgt. U.S. Air Force, 1950, advanced through grades maj., 1964; radar meteorology staff Hanscom AFB, Mass., 1964-66; electronic countermeasures Wright Patterson AFB, Ohio, 1966-69; ret., 1969; with Wright State U., Dayton, Ohio, 1969—, prof. mgmt. sci., quantitative bus. analysis, 1981—. Bd. govs. Fairborn (Ohio) YMCA, 1972-73. Served with USN, 1944-46. Registered profl. engr., Mass. Mem. Am. Statis. Assn., Assn. Inst. Decision Sci., So. Mktg. Assn., Phi Kappa Phi, Tau Beta Pi, Sigma Xi, Eta Kappa Nu, Beta Gamma Sigma, Alpha Iota Delta. Club: Lions, Masons, Shriners. Patentee surface friction tester; contbr. in field. Home: 2527 Grange Hall Rd Beavercreek OH 45431 Office: Wright State Univ Dayton OH 45435

COX, TAYLOR HOWARD, telephone co. exec.; b. Clarksburg, W.Va., Feb. 28, 1926; s. Wade and Matilda Cox; B.A. cum laude, W.Va. Wesleyan Coll., 1953; M.B.A. (grad. asst. 1954), Ind. U., 1954; m. Betty Leftridge, June 20, 1947 (dec. 1963); children—Taylor Howard, Nancy Cox Willis, Patricia Cox Connor; m. 2d, Edith Burroughs, Dec. 27, 1964; children—Annette Seals Austin, Lamont Seals. Gen. mgr. Home Fed. Savs. & Loan Assn., Detroit, 1954-59; exec. asst. Detroit Coca-Cola Bottling Co., 1959-63; dir. mgmt. div. Motown Records, Detroit, 1964-72; v.p. Invictus Records, Detroit, 1972-74; with Mich. Bell Telephone Co., Detroit, 1974—, urban affairs officer, 1975-78, gen. staff supr. revenue forecasting, 1978—; cons. Inner City Bus. Improvement Forum, Detroit, 1976-78; bd. dirs. Detroit Urban Alliance, 1976-78. Project dir. Clean Detroit com. New Detroit Inc., 1977; mem. crime com. Detroit NAACP, 1976-78; mem. met. area planning com. United Community Services Detroit, 1976-78, mem. youth div., 1977-78. Served with AUS, 1944-46; ETO. Decorated Bronze Star; recipient numerous certs. appreciation. Mem. Detroit Urban League, Am. Bridge Assn. Home: 18403 Northlawn St Detroit MI 48221 Office: 444 Michigan Ave Room 1150 Detroit MI 48226

COX, WILLIAM ANTHONY, surg. pathologist, neuropathologist; b. Clifton, N.J., Mar. 11, 1941; s. James Ebert and Helen (Radice) C.; B.S., Juniata Coll., 1963; M.D., Temple U., 1967; m. Joyce Marie Scharver, Sept. 15, 1973; children—Anthony, Nathaniel, Katrina. Intern, Temple U. Hosp., Phila., 1967-68, resident in pathology, 1968-72; commd. maj. M.C., USAF, 1972, advanced through grades to lt. col., 1976; chief lab. services Westover Regional Hosp., Westover AFB, Mass., 1972-73, Langley Regional Hosp., Langley AFB, Va., 1973-74; resident in forensic pathology Armed Forces Inst. Pathology, Washington, 1974-75, staff, 1976, fellow in neuropathology, after 1976; asst. prof. pathology Uniformed Services U. of the Health Scis., Bethesda, Md., after 1977; surg. pathologist, neuropathologist Cleve. Clinic, 1978-81; now pathologist Deaconess Hosp. of Cleve.; forensic neuropathologist Summit County Coroner's Office. Diplomate Am. Bd. Pathology. Mem. AMA (Physician Recognition award 1973-76), Coll. Am. Pathologists (Physician Recognition award 1976-79), Am. Soc. Clin. Pathology, Internat. Acad. Pathology, Am. Acad. Forensic Sci. Republican. Roman Catholic. Research in immunocytochemistry. Address: 7307 Hayward Rd Hudson OH 44236

COY, FRANCIS ANDREW, mgmt. cons.; b. Cin., Mar. 9, 1914; s. John Andrew and Ellen Nettie C.; student U. Cin., 1933-34, D.C.S. (hon.), 1976; LL.D. (hon.), Wilberforce U., 1971; L.H.D. (hon.), Baldwin Wallace Coll., 1971; m. Virginia Reah Chiles, July 20, 1936; 1 son, Lawrence Andrew. Salesman, buyer Mabley and Carew, Cin., 1936-44; v.p. merchandising O'Neill's Dept. Store, Balt., 1944-51; divisional mdse. mgr. Higbee Co., Cleve., 1951-53; exec. v.p. Cleland-Simpson Co., Scranton, Pa., 1953-56; gen. mgr. May Co. stores, 1956-58; gen. mdse. mgr. May Co., Cleve., 1958-61, pres., 1961-71, chmn. bd., chief exec. officer, 1971-76, v.p. parent co. May Dept. Stores, Inc., 1976; pres. Coy & Assos., Inc., mgmt. cons., Cleve., 1976—; chmn., chief exec. officer, dir. Inarco Corp., Twinsburg, Ohio, 1978—, Internat. Artware Corp. div., Twinsburg, 1978—; dir., mem. adv. com. Nat. City Corp., Nat. City Bank of Cleve.; dir. TransOhio Fin. Corp., Russell, Burdsall & Ward, Inc., Klein Mgmt. Co., Camelback Inn Condo Assn., Grayson Pub. Co. Mem. exec. bd. Greater Cleve. council Boy Scouts Am., 1960—, mem. east central region exec. bd., 1974—, mem. nat. exec. bd., 1975—; life trustee YMCA of Cleve., 1960—; trustee Baldwin Wallace Coll., 1963—, Salvation Army, 1960—, United Torch Services, 1965—; bd. dirs., mem. exec. com. NCCJ, 1961—, Downtown Cleve. Corp., 1975-80, Billy Graham Evangelistic Assn., 1975—, Billy Graham Center, 1975—. Recipient Silver Beaver award Boy Scouts Am., 1963, Silver Antelope award, 1967; Honor award Am. Legion, 1965, Americanism award, 1974; George Washington Honor medal Freedoms Found. at Valley Forge, 1973; Disting. Service award Ohio Council Retail Mchts., 1975. Mem Greater Cleve. Growth Assn. (dir., mem. exec. com. 1966—). Republican. Methodist. Clubs: Pepper Pike Country, Kirtland Country, Canterbury Golf, Walden, Union, Cleve. Athletic, Sky Top, The 50. Home: 13415 Shaker Blvd Cleveland OH 44120 Office: 1999 Enterprise Pkwy Twinsburg OH 44087

COYER, HOWARD FREDRICK, chemist; b. Beaver Dam, Wis., May 22, 1948; s. Howard Clarence and Miriam Ann (Rice) C.; B.S. in Chemistry, U. Wis., Whitewater, 1970; m. Kathleen Susan Mustas, Oct. 1, 1972; children—Sarah, Anna, Jonathan. Prodn. chemist P-L Biochems., Inc., subs. Pabst Brewing Co., Milw., 1970-72, sr. chemist nucleic acid research, 1972—. Research on affinity chromatography, oligodeoxynucleotide and polydeoxynucleotide synthesis, high pressure liquid chromatograph of nucleic acids. Home: 7714 Milwaukee Ave Wauwatosa WI 53213 Office: 1037 W McKinley Ave Milwaukee WI 53205

COYER, WILLIAM FRANK, physician; b. Denver, Apr. 22, 1941; s. Elmer William and Helen Mae (Bacon) C.; B.S., U. N.Mex., 1963; M.D., U. Tenn., 1967. Intern pediatrics U. Tenn. and City of Memphis hosps., 1967-68, resident pediatrics, 1968-69; chief resident pediatrics U. Colo., Denver, 1969-70, perinatal pediatric medicine fellow, 1970-71; teaching cons. Kauikeolani Children's Hosp., Honolulu, 1972-74; clin. asst. prof. pediatrics U. Hawaii, 1973-74; asst. prof. pediatrics Loyola U. Stritch Sch. Medicine, Maywood, Ill., 1974-78, asst. prof. anesthesiology, 1975-78; dir. newborn medicine Foster G. McGaw Hosp., Maywood, 1974-78; dir. perinatal referral center Foster G. McGaw Hosp. and Loyola U. Med. Center, Maywood, 1977-78; asso. prof. pediatrics and obstetrics Wright State U., Dayton, Ohio and dir. newborn medicine Children's Med. Center, Dayton, 1978-81; co-dir. Perinatal Center, dir. continuing med. edn. Central DuPage Hosp., Winfield, Ill., 1981—. Served to maj., M.C., U.S. Army, 1971-74. Diplomate Am. Bd. Pediatrics. Fellow Am. Acad. Pediatrics; mem. AMA, Chgo. Med. Soc., Am. Fedn. Clin. Research. Home: 34 W 111 Country Club Rd Saint Charles IL 60174 Office: Central DuPage Hospital ON 025 Winfield Rd Winfield IL 60190

COYLE, WILLIAM ROBERT, retail exec.; b. Columbus, Ohio, Mar. 16, 1928; s. Avard Robert and Gladies Vella (Marsh) C.; B.Sc., Ohio State U., 1948; m. Marjorie Alden Coyle, June 13, 1956; 1 son, Jeffrey Alan. Tchr. pub. sch., Columbus, 1949-51; founder, pres. Coyle Music Inc., Columbus, 1952—; v.p. Buckeye Music Pub. Inc., 1958—. Named Outstanding Young Man in Music Industry, 1966. Mem. Nat. Assn. Music Mchts. (chmn., past pres.), Nat. Assn. Sch. Music Dealers (past pres.), Am. Music Conf. (dir., sec.), Music Industry Council, Nat. Music Council, Am. Bandmasters Assn., Ohio State U. Alumni Assn. (adv. bd.), Alpha Tau Omega. Republican. Clubs: Presidents Ohio State U., Faculty Ohio State U., Newcomen, Mason, Shriners. Contbr. articles to musical publs. Home: 4944 Sharon Hill Dr Worthington OH 43085 Office: 2864 High St N Columbus OH 43202

COYNE, JOHN THOMAS, marketing and communications exec.; b. St. Paul, Mar. 29, 1934; s. Martin Thomas and Mary Alice (Brodle) C.; B.A., U. Minn., 1957; m. Constance Marie Kowaliw, Aug. 3, 1963; children—Christopher, Eileen, Thomas, Margaret. With Theodore Hamm Brewing Co., St. Paul, 1964-68, mgr. advt. media, 1966-68; with Ellerbe Architects/Engrs./Planners, Bloomington, Minn., 1968-75, dir. mktg. and communications, 1971-73, v.p. mktg. and communications, 1973-75, pres. Coyne-Wilkinson & Assos., Inc., 1975—. Served to lt. AUS, 1957-58. Mem. Nat. Assn. Catholic Alumni Clubs (nat. men's v.p. 1962-63), Mpls. C. of C., Public Relations Soc. Am. (accredited mem., state dir., 1973-74), Sales and Mktg. Execs. (chapter dir. 1975-77), Soc. Mktg. Profl. Services (charter). Home: 1398 Cherry Hill Rd Mendota Heights MN 55118 Office: 5301 Edina Industrial Blvd Minneapolis MN 55435

COYNE, THOMAS JOSEPH, economist, educator; b. Wheeling, W.Va., Dec. 24, 1933; s. Thomas Joseph and Mary Germaine (Fox) C.; B.B.A., Marshall U., 1958; M.B.A., Kent State U., 1961; Ph.D., Case Western Res. U., 1967; postgrad. U. Chgo., 1968, U. Mich., summers 1972, 73; m. Patricia Anne Smith, June 8, 1957; children—Kathleen, Karen, Kevin, Kenneth, Thomas. With B.F. Goodrich Co., Akron, Ohio, 1959-61, Robinson Clay Products Co., Akron, 1961-63, C&O-B&O Ry., Cleve., 1963-65; prof. bus. econs. U. Akron, 1969-81; prof. fin. John Carroll U., 1981—; cons. bds. edn. in state of Ohio; cons. banks, specializing in acquisitions; arbitrator Am. Arbitration Assn., Fed. Mediation and Conciliation Service, 1968—. Vice-pres. research Akron Regional Devel. Bd., 1975-78, chmn. taxation and legis. com., 1975-78. Served with inf. U.S. Army, 1952-54; Korea. Nat. City Bank Cleve. fellow, 1963-65. Mem. Eastern Fin. Assn., Fin. Mgmt. Assn., Midwest Econ. and Midwest Fin. Assn., Nat. Assn. Bus. Economists, So. Fin. Assn., Sigma Phi Epsilon. Roman Catholic. Author: Understanding Managerial Economics, 1975; Readings in Managerial Economics, 3d edit., 1981; also articles and monographs. Home: 535 Haskell Dr Akron OH 44313

CRABB, BARBARA BRANDRIFF, judge; b. Green Bay, Wis., Mar. 17, 1939; d. Charles Edward and Mary (Forrest) Brandriff; A.B., U. Wis., 1960, J.D., 1962; m. Theodore E. Crabb, Jr., Aug. 29, 1959; children—Julia Forrest, Philip Elliott. Admitted to Wis. bar, 1963; asso. firm Roberts, Boardman, Suhr and Curry, Madison, 1962-64; research asst. Law Sch., U. Wis., Madison, 1968-70; research asst. Am. Bar Assn. project on criminal justice standards, Madison, 1970-71; U.S. magistrate, Madison, 1971-79; U.S. dist. judge, 1979—. Membership chmn., v.p. LWV Milw., 1966-68; mem. Gov.'s Task Force on Prison Reform, 1971-73; mem. Jr. League Milw., 1967-68. Mem. Am., Dane County bar assns., State Bar Wis., Nat. Council Fed. Magistrates, Wis. Law Alumni Assn. Office: Box 1724 Madison WI 53701

CRABBÉ, PIERRE O., chemist; b. Brussels, Dec. 29, 1928; s. François and Simone (Doutreligne) C.; Tech. Chem. Engr., Institut Meurice-Chimie, Brussels, 1952; Docteur Chimie, U. Paris, 1954; Docteur es Sci., U. Strasbourg, 1967; m. Lucie de Guchteneere, Apr. 25, 1956; children—Emmanuel, Marie-Noëlle, Véronique. Instr., Inst. Meurice-Chimie, Brussels, 1959-60; dir. chem. research Syntex S.A., Mexico City, 1964-73; prof. U. Iberoamericana, Mexico City, 1962-73; prof. U. Nacional Autonoma Mexico, 1965-74; hon. prof. Inst. Tech. Monterrey, Mex., 1968—; vis. prof. Ga. Inst. Tech., Atlanta, 1968; prof. U. Grenoble (France), 1973-79; prof., chmn. dept. chemistry U. Mo.-Columbia, 1979—; cons. WHO, UNESCO, Internat. Orgn. Chem. Scis. in Devel. Mem. Mexican Acad. Sci., Am. Chem. Soc., Belgian Chem. Soc., Chem. Soc. (London), N.Y. Acad. Sci. Author: (with G. Ourisson, O. Rodig) Tetracyclic Triterpenes, 1964; Optical Rotatory Dispersion and Circular Dichroism, 1965; Introduction to Chiroptical Methods, 1972; Prostaglandin Research, 1977; contbr. articles to profl. jours. Home: 7 E Burnam Rd Columbia MO 65201 Office: Dept Chemistry U Mo Columbia MO 65211

CRABTREE, JOE, financial exec.; b. Tompkinsville, Ky., Mar. 1, 1922; s. Chester and Cecil (Seay) C.; B.S., U. Ill., 1943; m. Carolyn West, May 13, 1972; children—Joel John, Pamela Jean, Wendy Anne. Asst. treas. Pyle Nat. Co., Chgo., 1943-47; cons. Cutler Hammer Inc., Milw., 1947-50; dir. applications Univac div. Sperry Rand Corp., Blue Bell, Pa., 1950-63; controller AIL, Deer Park, N.Y., 1963-69; v.p. Mohawk Data Scis. Corp., Herkimer, N.Y., 1969-71; v.p. finance, treas. Midland Cooperatives, Inc., Mpls., 1971—; dir. Seaway Pipeline Inc.; pres. Claims Recovery, Inc.; v.p., treas. Petroleum Resources Co., Trade Credit Corp., Midland Credit Corp., MCI-E, Inc. Mem. Am. Inst. Accountants, Financial Execs. Inst., Am. Accounting Assn., Assn. Govt. Accountants, Nat. Assn. Accountants, Nat. Soc. Accountants for Coops., Ill., N.Y. socs. C.P.A.'s, North Central Credit Assn., Delta Sigma Pi, Phi Eta Sigma, Beta Gamma Sigma. Episcopalian. Clubs: Mpls. Athletic, Lions. Home: 15140 Woodruff Rd Wayzata MN 55391 Office: 2021 Hennepin Ave E Minneapolis MN 55413

CRADIC, GARY DEAN, clergyman, mfg. co. exec.; b. Hamburg, Iowa, Sept. 17, 1945; s. Harold Dean and Ruth Caroline (Geyer) C.; B.S.L., Midwestern Sch. Evangelism, 1968; m. Sherill Kay Johnson, July 6, 1966; children—Timothy, Kimberly, Kendall, Kendra. Journeyman meatcutter HyVee Food Stores, Fareway Food Stores, Ottumwa and Indianola, Iowa, 1961-76; ordained to ministry Ch. of Christ, 1966; minister chs. Indianola, 1967-71, West Concord, Minn., 1972-74; minister Owatonna (Minn.) Ch. of Christ, 1974—; gen. mgr. Christian Bros. Cabinets, Inc., Owatonna, 1974—. Republican. Home: 1154 E Rose St Owatonna MN 55060 Office: 631 N Cedar St Owatonna MN 55060

CRAFT, ROLF VAUGHN, educator, state ofcl.; b. Waterloo, Iowa, Nov. 1, 1937; s. Vaughn Lafayette and Margaret Louise (Brandhorst) C.; B.S., Iowa State U., 1959, M.S., 1966, Ph.D., 1968; m. Naomi Lee Stadtmueller, Oct. 14, 1961; children—Erik, Andrew. Vice pres. Craft's Inc., Hudson, Iowa, 1960-62; pvt. practice farming, Decorah, Iowa, 1967—; prof. econs. Luther Coll., 1967—; mem. Iowa Senate, 1976—, chmn. ways and means com., 1977—. Served with U.S. Army, 1960. Mem. Am. Agrl. Econs. Assn. Republican. Lutheran. Office: Luther College Decorah IA 52101

CRAGLE, RAYMOND GEORGE, univ. adminstr.; b. Orangeville, Pa., Feb. 28, 1926; s. Ray Ellis and Florence Mae (Decker) C.; B.S., N.C. State U., 1951, M.S., 1954; Ph.D., U. Ill., Urbana, 1957; m. Phyllis Russell, Aug. 5, 1950; children—Donna Lynne, Mark Robert, Matthew Bruce. Prof. U. Tenn., Knoxville, 1957-70; prof., head dept. dairy sci. Va. Poly. Inst. and State U., Blacksburg, 1970-78; asso. dean, dir. Ill. Agrl. Expt. Sta., Coll. Agr., U. Ill., Urbana, 1978—. Served with USAAF, 1944-46, AUS, 1951-52. Active Boy Scouts Am., 1957—. Fellow AAAS; mem. Am. Inst. Nutrition, Am. Dairy Sci. Assn., Am. Soc. Animal Sci. Presbyterian. Contbr. numerous articles, abstracts to profl. jours., popular press. Home: 12 G H Baker Dr Urbana IL 61801 Office: Agrl Expt Sta 211 Mumford Hall U Ill Urbana IL 61801

CRAGUN, JOHN J., educator; b. Kingman County, Kans., July 12, 1926; s. John Layman and Lela Ella (Dutton) C.; B.S., Kans. State U., 1950; M.Ed., Colo. State U., 1961; Ph.D., Mich. State U., 1969; m. Agness Lorraine Richardson, Aug. 12, 1946; 1 son, Donald Wayne. Grad. asst. Kans. State U., 1949-50; tchr. public schs., Kans., 1950-66; mem. faculty div. student teaching and profl. devel. Mich. State U., 1966—, prof., 1979—, dir. tchr. edn. center, 1968—. Bd. dirs. Samaritan Counseling Center, Goodwill Industries. Served with U.S. Army, 1944-45. Decorated Bronze star; recipient meritorious service to edn. award Mich. State U. Coll. Edn. Alumni Assn., 1979. Mem. Mich. Assn. Tchr. Educators, Assn. Tchr. Educators, Assn. Supervision and Curriculum Devel., Confluent Edn. Devel., Council Basic Edn., Phi Delta Kappa, Phi Kappa Phi. Methodist. Office: 253 Erickson Hall Mich State U East Lansing MI 48824

CRAIG, BARBARA JO, nurse; b. Bellefontaine, Ohio, Aug. 24, 1943; d. Theodore and Mary Jo (Woodard) C.; Asso. Sci. in Nursing with honors, St. Clair County Community Coll., 1973; student U. Cin., 1975—. Operating room technician St. Joseph's Hosp., Mt. Clemens, Mich., 1965-66, 67-71; pvt. technician, Southfield, Mich., 1966-67; charge nurse med.-surg. unit Christ Hosp., Cin., 1973-74; operating room staff nurse Providence Hosp., 1974-75, asst. supr., 1975, mgr. dept. surgery, 1975-81, dir. nursing, 1981—; adj. faculty, mem. adv. bd. surg. technologist program Cin. Tech. Coll., also mem. curriculum com. Served with USAF, 1961-65. Mem. Assn. Operating Room Nurses (asso.), Am. Nurses Assn., Cin. Women's Bowling Assn. (pres. city leagues). Roman Catholic. Author papers in field. Office: Providence Hosp 2446 Kipling Ave Cincinnati OH 45239

CRAIG, HAROLD MARVIN, JR., mfg. co. exec.; b. Van Wert, Ohio, Oct. 28, 1933; s. Harold Marvin and Julia Ann (Poe) C.; B.A., Ohio Wesleyan U., 1956; children—David, Douglas, Gary. Dist. mgr. TRW, Inc., Cleve., 1962-64; sales mgr. Lee Motors Products, Cleve., 1965-70; nat. sales mgr. Sorensen Mfg. Co., Gulf & Western Industries, Glasgow, Ky., 1970-81; dir. sales Grote Mfg. Co., Madison, Ind., 1981—. Served to capt. USAF, 1957-61. Named Ky. col.; life mem. Ky. Gov.'s staff; recipient Nat. Top Pick Exec. award Irving Cloud Publs., Chgo., 1981. Mem. Am. Mgmt. Assn., Automotive Service Industry Assn., Motor Equipment Mfrs. Assn., Automotive Warehouse Dist. Assn., Truck Safety Equipment Inst., Truck Body Equipment Assn., Am. Trucking Assn., Council Fleet Specialists, Truck Trailer Mfrs. Assn., Sigma Alpha Epsilon Century. Republican. Methodist. Office: Grote Mfg Co 2600 Lanier Dr Madison IN 47250

CRAIG, ROBERT BRUCE, travel agy. exec.; b. Chgo., Mar. 21, 1930; s. Herbert and Vivian Segrid (Solberg) C.; student Goodman Theatre, Chgo., 1949-50; spl. courses U. Wis., U. Mich., U. Minn.; children—Robert Bruce, Victoria Jean. Salesman, 3M Co., Chgo., 1953-64, tng. mgr., St. Paul, 1964-73; v.p. Varn Products Co., Inc., Addison, Ill., 1973-81; owner, operator travel agy., 1981—; lectr. sales mgmt., chem. safety. Congressional adviser, 1978. Served with U.S. Army, 1951. Mem. Chgo. Club Printing House Craftsmen (pres. 1977-78), Printing Supplyman's Guild. Republican. Clubs: Brookwood Country, Ill. Athletic. Home: 465 W Dominion Dr Wood Dale IL 60191 Office: 905 S Westwood Ave Addison IL 60101

CRAIG, ROBERT CHARLES, educator; b. Sault Sainte Marie, Mich., Mar. 9, 1921; s. Frank Lyle and Sylva Octilla (Crowell) C.; B.S., Mich. State U., 1943, M.A., 1948; Ph.D., Tchrs. Coll. Columbia U., 1952; m. Rosalie Esther Deboer, Sept. 2, 1950; children—Bruce R., Stephen F. (dec.), Jeffrey A., Barbara Anne. Research asso. Tchrs. Coll. Columbia U., 1950-52; asst. prof. State U. Wash., Pullman, 1952-55; research scientist Am. Inst. Research, Pitts., 1955-58; asso. prof. ednl. psychology Marquette U., 1958-62, prof., 1962-66; prof. and chmn. dept. counseling and ednl. psychology Mich. State U., East Lansing, 1967—, dir. Office of Research Consultation, 1966-67, dir. U.S. Office Edn. Grad. Research Tng. program, 1966-72; external evaluator Nat. Council for Accreditation of Tchr. Edn., 1970-75; cons. Am. Inst. Research, 1958—. Served with USNR, 1943-46. Fellow Am. Psychol. Assn., AAAS; mem. Am. Ednl. Research Assn., Nat. Council Measurement in Edn., Sigma Xi, Phi Kappa Phi, Phi Delta Kappa. Author: Transfer Value of Guided Learning, 1953; (with A.M. Dupuis) American Education, Origins and Issues, 1963; Psychology of Learning in the Classroom, 1966; (with H. Clarizio, W. Mehrens) Contemporary Issues in Educational Psychology, 1969, 2d edit., 1981, Contemporary Educational Psychology, 1975; (with V.H. Noll, D.P. Scannell) Introduction to Educational Measurement, 1979. Home: 185 Maplewood St East Lansing MI 48823 Office: 443 Erickson Hall Michigan State University East Lansing MI 48824

CRAIG, ROLLAND EUGENE, accountant, former city ofcl.; b. Danville, Ill., Jan. 6, 1902; s. Wilbur Palmer and Lulu (Johnson) C.; student U. Chgo., 1919-21, Ind. U., 1945-47; C.P.A., U. Ill., 1947; m. Mary A. Yeazel, Feb. 8, 1931. Pvt. practice, C.P.A., Danville, Ill., 1947-65; partner Clifton Gunderson, Coker and DeBruyn, C.P.A.'s, 1965-73; pvt. practice, Danville, 1975—; commr. finance City Danville, 1963-71, mayor, 1971-75. Methodist. Dist. dep. Order Demolay. Mason (33 deg.), Kiwanian. Home: 15 Fletcher Pl Danville IL 61832

CRAIG, SHARON ALANE, labor union ofcl.; b. Noblesville, Ind., Sept. 28, 1947; d. Ralph E. and Virginia K. Craig; student Ind. U., 1970-77. With Ind. Bell Telephone Co., Kokomo, 1968-77; with Communications Workers of Am., AFL-CIO, Indpls., 1977—, staff rep., 1977-81, staff rep., Chgo., 1981—; mem. labor studies adv. com. Ind. U.; mem. Ind. AFL-CIO community services adv. com. NAACP, Indpls. Bd. dirs. City of Hope, Indpls., 1977-80, Howard County Mental Health, 1973-76; mem. planning com. United Way of Howard County, 1976-77; sec. Citizens Action Coalition, 1980—; mem. Ind. Juvenile Justice Task Force; precinct committeeman Democratic Party, Kokomo, 1978. Recipient gold award United Way, 1978. Mem. Coalition of Labor Union Women. Episcopalian. Club: Ind. U. Alumni, Ind. U. of Kokomo Alumni. Home: 1300 E Algonquin Rd Apt 1D Schaumburg IL 60195 Office: Communications Workers Am 790 Busse Rd Elk Grove Village IL 60007

CRAIG, WILLIAM ELLWOOD, children's homes exec.; b. Chester, Pa., June 26, 1915; s. William Ellwood and Josephine Worthington (Willard) C.; B.A., U. Calif. at Berkeley, 1937; B.D., Ch. Div. Sch. of Pacific, 1940; Ph.D., U. Calif. at Los Angeles, 1949; m. Mary Elizabeth Ellis, July 17, 1941 (d. June 1977); children—Mary Catherine (Mrs. Karl A. Selby), Charlotte Elizabeth, Margaret Ellis (Mrs. John D. Graver); m. 2d, Mary-Eliot Miller, Dec. 10, 1977. Ordained priest Episcopalian Ch., 1940; rector, Los Angeles, 1940-48, Grand Island, Nebr., 1948-52, Oklahoma City, 1952-54; dean Christ Cathedral, New Orleans, 1954-56; dir. St. Francis Boys' Homes, Salina, Kans., 1956-80. Mem. nat. council Episcopal Ch., 1949-55, Living Church Found., 1958—. Mem. Nat. Assn. Homes for Boys (exec. sec., 1973-80), Nat. Assn. Tng. Schs., Conf. Tng. Schs. Supts., S.R. (Calif. chaplain 1948). Republican. Elk, Kiwanian. Club: Salina Country. Editor Book of Proc., Nat. Assn. Homes for Boys, 1965—. Home: 901 S Santa Fe Ave Salina KS 67401 Office: Box 1348 Salina KS 67401

CRAIG, WILLIAM LANE, philosopher, educator; b. Peoria, Ill., Aug. 23, 1949; s. Mallory John and Doris Irene (Walker) C.; A.B., Wheaton Coll., 1971; M.A., Trinity Evang. Div. Sch., 1975, M.A., 1976; D.Phil., U. Birmingham (Eng.), 1977; postgrad. (Alexander Von Humboldt Stiftung fellow) U. Munich (W. Ger.), 1978-79; m. Jeanette Laura Coleman, May 13, 1972. Vis prof. Trinity Evang. Div. Sch., Deerfield, Ill., 1980-81, asst. prof., 1981—; lic. minister Missionary Ch. Assn., 1979—. Mem. Am. Philos. Assn., Am. Acad. Religion, Soc. Bibl. Lit., Leibniz Soc. Am., Soc. Christian Philosophers. Author: The Kalam Cosmological Argument, 1979; The Cosmological Argument from Plato to Leibniz, 1980; reviewer Studia Leibnitiana, 1979—. Office: 2065 Half Day Rd Deerfield IL 60015

CRAIGHEAD, RODKEY, banker; b. Pitts., July 24, 1916; s. Ernest S. and Florence L. (Rodkey) C.; B.S., U. Pitts., 1942; postgrad. Grad. Sch. Banking, U. Wis., 1959-61; m. Carol M. Price, June 26, 1943 (dec. June 1978); children—Rodkey, Virginia, Corinne; m. 2d, La Verne Hastings, Mar. 1979. With Mellon Nat. Bank, Pitts., 1936-41; with Detroit Bank & Trust Co., 1946—, v.p., 1961-67, sr. v.p., 1967-69, exec. v.p., 1969-73, dir., 1971—, pres., 1974—, chmn., chief exec. officer, 1977—; pres., dir. Detroitbank Corp., 1974—, chmn., chief exec. officer, 1977-81, ret., 1981; dir. Winkelman Stores, Inc., Detroit, Bd. dirs. Jr. Achievement Mich., Detroit Renaissance, Met. Fund., Detroit Symphony Orch., Detroit Econ. Growth Corp.; chmn. New Detroit Inc. Served to capt. AUS, 1942-46. Mem. Greater Detroit C. of C. (dir.). Presbyterian. Clubs: Detroit Athletic (dir.), Detroit, Economic (dir.) (Detroit); Orchard Lake Country; Bloomfield Hills Country. Home: 3912 Maple Hill E West Bloomfield MI 48033 Office: Fort at Washington Detroit MI 48321

CRAIN, ADA ELIZABETH, ret. librarian; b. Goltry, Okla., Sept. 18, 1904; d. Ernest B. and Maudie H. (Owens) Crain; B.S., Southwest Mo. State U., 1928; postgrad. Nat. U. Mexico, 1937, Mich. State U., 1960; M.Ed., U. Mo., 1940. Prin., Brandsville (Mo.) High Sch., 1928-30, Atlanta (Mich.) High Sch., 1930-42; tchr. Harbor Beach (Mich.) High Sch., 1942-43; prin. Blissfield (Mich.) High Sch., 1943-44; tchr. Big Rapids (Mich.) High Sch., 1944-57; librarian Fowlerville (Mich.) High Sch., 19S7-69, Fowlerville Pub. Library, 1960-65; ret. Recipient award of Appreciation Fowlerville Bd. Edn., 1969; named Fowlerville's Most Outstanding Citizen, VFW, 1976. Mem. Mich. Edn. Assn., NEA, Am. Assn. of Ret. Persons, Mo. Alumni Assn., SW Mo. State U. Alumni Assn. Methodist. Club: Garden. Address: 400 Cedar River Dr Lot 21 Fowlerville MI 48836

CRAIN, LARRY WAYNE, telecommunications co. exec.; b. Poplar Bluff, Mo., June 2, 1949; s. Harry C. and Lola E.C.; B.S. magna cum laude, SE Mo. State U., 1975; M.B.A., U. Mo., 1976. New product planner Hallmark Cards, Kansas City, Mo., 1977-78, bus. planning project mgr., 1978-80; sr. corp. planning analyst United Telecommunications, Inc., Kansas City, Mo., 1980—; bd. dirs. Prime Health, health maintenance orgn., 1980—; instr. mktg. Served with USN, 1968-72. Gregory fellow. Mem. Am. Mktg. Assn., Planning Execs. Inst., Am. Numismatic Assn., Mensa. Club: Kansas City Ski. Author fiction. Home: 1205 W 75th Terr Kansas City MO 64114 Office: United Telecommunications Inc PO Box 11315 Kansas City MO 64112

CRANDALL, JOHN CHAPMAN, mfg. co. exec.; b. Rockford, Ill., Dec. 22, 1929; s. Harold A. and Ruth L. Crandall; B.S. in Mech. Engring., U. Ill., 1958; m. Suzanne Smallwood, Mar. 27, 1954; children—Michael John, Julie Sue. Jr. engr. G. D. Roper Corp., Rockford, 1949-58; sales engr. Barber-Colman Co., Rockford, 1958-60, project engr., 1960-64, mgr. quality and design standards, 1964-74, corp. planning adminstr., 1974—; tchr. applied physics Rock Valley Coll., Rockford, 1972-73. Mem. Rockford-Winnebago County (Ill.) Planning Commn., 1965-79, vice-chmn., 1969, 70, 72, chmn., 1971, 73, 74, 78, 79; adminstrv. bd. chmn. Burritt Community United Meth. Ch., 1968-72; mem. Rock Valley Econ. Devel. Commn., 1980—. Served with U.S. Army, 1951-53. Mem. N. Am. Soc. Corp. Planning, Inc., Am. Soc. Quality Control, Am. Farm Bur. Fedn., Chi Gamma Iota. Republican. Methodist. Clubs: Mensa, U.S. Senatorial. Editor: Quality Audit Program, 1973. Home: 2234 Humboldt Dr Rockford IL 61103 Office: 1300 Rock St Rockford IL 61101

CRANDALL, JOHN LYNN, ins. co. exec.; b. Chgo., Apr. 17, 1927; s. Paul Bertram and Olga (Bliech) C.; B.S. in Fire Protection Engring., Ill. Inst. Tech., 1951; m. Irene Anze Ruenne, Dec. 26, 1973; children by previous marriage—Deborah Crandall Schmude, Jeffrey, Lynne; stepchildren—George Ruenne, Helgi Ruenne Becker. Highly protected risk inspector FIA, Chgo., 1951-53, asst. engring. supr., 1953-56, engring. supr., 1956-59, underwriting supr., special agt., 1959-65; HPR engr., underwriter Kemper Group, Chgo., 1965-67, HPR sales specialist, 1967-71; asst. to dir. underwriting Protection Mutual Ins. Co., Park Ridge, Ill., 1971-73, v.p. underwriting, 1973-78, v.p., dir. underwriting, 1978—. Served with USN, 1945-46. Cert. in Gen. Ins., Ins. Inst. Am., 1969; C.P.C.U., 1972. Mem. Soc. Fire Protection Engrs. (charter), Soc. C.P.C.U.'s (chpt. pres. 1980-81). Republican. Baptist. Home: 320 Forest Ln Schaumburg IL 60193 Office: 300 S Northwest Hwy Park Ridge IL 60068

CRANE, DANIEL B., congressman; b. Chgo., Jan. 10, 1936; A.B., Hillsdale Coll., 1958; D.D.S., Ind. U., 1963; postgrad. U. Mich., 1964-65; m. Judy Van Brunt, 1970; children—Nathan, Joshua, Kimberly, Elizabeth, Emily, Heidi. Pvt. practice dentistry, 1963-67; mem. 96th-97th Congresses from 22d Dist. Ill. Bd. dirs. Danville (Ill.) Family YMCA, Danville C. of C.; past bd. dirs. Vermilion Cancer Soc., Vermilion Humane Soc., Vermilion Rehab.; mem. adv. bd. Am. Conservative Union, Gun Owners Am., Citizens Com. for Right to Keep and Bear Arms, Coalition for Peace Through Strength. Served to capt. U.S. Army, 1967-70. Named One of Outstanding Young Men of Am., 1970. Republican. Methodist. Contbr. articles to profl. publs. Office: 115 Cannon House Office Bldg Washington DC 20515

CRANE, FRANK MELVIN, animal scientist; b. Garden City, Minn., June 10, 1923; s. Lucas Melvin and Marie (Lindquist) C.; B.S., U. Minn., 1948, M.S., 1949, Ph.D., 1954; m. Audrey M. Kraus, June 26, 1948; children—Carolyn Marie, Keith William, Suzanne Blanche, Debora Ann. Instr. animal sci. U. Minn., 1948-51; with Land O'Lakes, Inc., Ft. Dodge, Iowa, 1951—, dir. mktg., 1970-74, v.p. research, 1974—. Chmn., United Way Ft. Dodge, 1977-78; chmn. fin. com. First United Meth. Ch., Ft. Dodge, 1979; bd. dirs. Friendship Haven, Ft. Dodge, 1978—. Served with USNR, 1942-46. Decorated Air medal with 2 gold stars. Mem. Am. Soc. Animal Sci., Am. Feed Mfrs. Assn. (chmn. bd. 1980-81), Am. Dairy Sci. Assn., AAAS, World's Poultry Sci. Assn., Poultry Sci. Soc., Ft. Dodge C. of C. (dir.), Alpha Gamma Rho, Alpha Zeta, Gamma Alpha. Republican. Author papers in field.

CRANE, KATHARINE ELIZABETH, editor, writer; b. Kenton, Ohio; d. George Edward and Kate (Rhodes) Crane; A.B., Smith Coll., 1916; Ph.D., U. Chgo., 1930. Tchr., St. Katherine's Sch., Davenport, Ia., 1916-17, Shippen Sch., Lancaster, Pa., 1920-22, Women's Coll., U. N.C., 1925-26; asst. editor Ency. Social Scis., 1929-30; asst. editor Dictionary Am. Biography, 1930-36, Social Studies and Social Edn., 1936-39; state supr., state guide, Va. Hist. Survey. Library Services, 1940-43; officer Dept. State, 1943-50; historian Mil. Air Transport Service, 1950-60; free-lance writer, 1960—. Author: Status of Countries in Relation to the War, 1944; Blair House, 1946; Mr. Carr of State, 1960. Contbr. articles to profl. jours. Home: 500 North Main St Kenton OH 43326

CRANE, PHILIP MILLER, Congressman; b. Chgo., Nov. 3, 1930; s. George Washington and Cora (Miller) C.; student DePauw U., 1948-50; B.A., Hillsdale Coll., 1952; postgrad. U. Mich., 1952-54, U. Vienna (Austria), 1953, 56; M.A., Ind. U., 1961, Ph.D., 1963; LL.D., Grove City (Pa.) Coll.; Dr. en Ciencias Políticas (hon.), Francisco Marroquín U., 1979; m. Arlene Catherine Johnson, Feb. 14, 1959; children—Catherine Anne, Susanna Marie, Jennifer Elizabeth, Rebekah Caroline, George Washington V, Rachel Ellen, Sarah Emma, Carrie Esther. Advt. mgr. Hopkins Syndicate, Inc., Chgo., 1956-58; teaching asst. Ind. U., Bloomington, 1959-62; asst. prof. history Bradley U., Peoria, Ill., 1963-67; dir. schs. Westminster Acad., Northbrook, Ill., 1967-68; mem. 91st-97th congresses from 12th Ill. Dist., mem. ways and means com. Pub. relations dir. Vigo County (Ind.) Republican Orgn., 1962; dir. research Ill. Goldwater Orgn., 1964; chmn. Ill. Citizens for Reagan Com., 1975; mem. nat. adv. bd. Young Ams. for Freedom, 1965—. Bd. dirs. Intercollegiate Studies Inst.; chmn. Am. Conservative Union, 1977-79; trustee Hillsdale Coll. Served with AUS, 1954-56. Recipient Distinguished Alumnus award Hillsdale Coll., 1968, Independence award, 1974; William McGovern award Chgo. Soc., 1969; Freedoms Found. award, 1973. Mem. Am. Hist. Assn., Orgn. Am. Historians, Acad. Polit. Sci., Am. Acad. Polit. and Social Scis., Phila. Soc., A.S.C.A.P., Phi Alpha Theta, Pi Gamma Mu. Methodist. Author: Democrat's Dilemma, 1964; The Sum of Good Government, 1976; Surrender in Panama, 1977; contbr.: Crisis in Confidence, 1974; Continuity in Crisis: The University at Bay, 1974; Case Against the Reckless Congress, 1976; Can You Afford This House, 1978; View from the Capitol Dome (Looking Right), 1980. Office: Longworth House Office Bldg Washington DC 20515

CRATES, FREDERICK JOE, water mgmt. products mfg. co. exec.; b. Findlay, Ohio, May 3, 1932; s. Don F. and Maxine E. (Deaunee) C.; B.S., Findlay Coll., 1954; postgrad. City Coll. N.Y., 1963; M.S., No. Mich. U., 1968; postgrad. Bowling Green State U., 1967-70; m. Kathleen Louise Child, June 15, 1964; children—James, Krista. Tchr. biology Arcadia (Ohio) High Sch., 1954-57, Findlay (Ohio) High Sch., 1957-70; mgr. quality control Hancor, Inc., Findlay, 1970—, dir. research and devel., corp. dir., 1974—, dir. wastewater mgmt. systems, 1978—; mem. U.S.-USSR Tech. Exchange Com. for Plastic Products for Irrigation and Drainage, 1976-80. NSF grantee, 1963. Mem. Am. Soc. Testing and Materials, Soc. Plastic Engrs., Soc. Quality Control, Nat. Environ. Health Assn., Am. Soc. Agrl. Engrs. Odd Fellow, Rotarian. Home: 13067-T 204 Findlay OH 45840 Office: Box 1047 Findlay OH 45840

CRAVENS, JOE BOB, environ. engr.; b. Guthrie, Okla., May 13, 1952; s. George Vernon and Audrey Blanch (Mustain) C.; B.S. in Aquatic Biology and Chemistry, Okla. State U., 1974, M.S. in Environ. Engring., 1977. Research asso. lipid research clinic Okla. Med. Research Found., 1974-75; grad. research asst. Okla. State U., 1975-77; environ. research engr. Rexnord Corp. Research and Devel., Environ. Research Center, Milw., 1977—. Mem. Am. Water Pollution Control Fedn., Central States Water Pollution Control Fedn., Am. Water Works Assn., Wis. Wastewater Treatment Plant Operators Assn., Nat. Soc. Profl. Engrs., Wis. Soc. Profl. Engrs., U.S. Ski Assn., Milw. Jaycees (external v.p., dir. 1981-82, Spoke of Yr. award 1980-81), Milw. Met. Civic Alliance (dir. 1981-82). Democrat. Baptist. Author papers in field. Office: 5103 W Beloit Rd PO Box 2022 Milwaukee WI 53201

CRAWFORD, DARNELL ALLEN, import and export co. exec.; b. Lockland, Ohio, Apr. 15, 1937; s. Arnell and Minnie (Allen) C.; student public and trade schs., Meridian, Miss., and Forest City, Ark.; m. Florence Coleman, Jan. 1957; children—Derrick, David, Jacqueline, Racheal, Jeffery Darnell, Jr. Pres. Crawfords Import Export, Cin., 1975—. Past pres. Arlington Ridge Corp.; community action chmn. CORE; chmn. local chpt. SCLC; chmn. welfare com. Mid-town Young Democratic Incorp.; bd. dirs. St. Louis Human Devel. Corp., 1966-70, St. Louis Comprehensive Health Center. Served with U.S. Army and USMC Res., 1954-57; Korea. Mem. NAACP, Urban League, Fgn. Policy Assn. (asso.). Office: Crawfords Import-Export 1113 Lincoln St Cincinnati OH 45206

CRAWFORD, DEAN ERNEST, accountant; b. Topeka, Jan. 15, 1940; s. Ernest Percy and Beulah Marie (Jones) C.; student U. Kans., 1959-60; m. Peggy Marie Huffman, Nov. 23, 1966; children—Kelly, Karla, Kevin. Accountant, J.T. Weatherwax, Lawrence, Kans.,

1963-65, Lesh, Bradley, Barrand, Lawrence, 1965-72; pvt. practice accounting, Lawrence, 1972-78; v.p. bus. mgmt. Native Am. Research Assos., Inc. and Native Am. Research Inst., Inc., Lawrence, 1978-79; comptroller Compton Industries, Lawrence, 1979-81; sec.-treas. D & D Tire, Inc., Lawrence, 1981—. Treas. Achievement Place, Inc., 1973-77. C.P.A., Kans. Mem. Am. Inst. C.P.A.'s, Kans. Soc. C.P.A.'s. Club: Optimist. Home: RFD 4 Box 76A Lawrence KS 66044

CRAWFORD, FERRIS NATHAN, educator; b. Frankfort, Mich., Nov. 1, 1912; s. Nathan Jennings and Elizabeth (Lentz) C.; A.B., Central Mich. U., 1935; M.A., U. Mich., 1940; D.Ed., Mich. State U., 1959; m. Eileen Bessie Icheldinger, June 25, 1941; children—Douglas Nathan, Barbara Ann (Mrs. David E. Ellies), Susan Marie (Mrs. William E. Tharr, Jr.), Thomas Alfred. Tchr. high schs., Rose City, Mich., 1935-36, Fairgrove, Mich., 1936-37, Dearborn, Mich., 1939-42; prin. Fairgrove High Sch., 1937-39; adminstr. Ford Airplane Sch., Willow Run, Mich., 1942-45; dir. selective psychol. testing Ford Motor Co., Dearborn, Mich., 1945-46; dir. community sch. service program Mich. Dept. Edn., Lansing, 1946-54, chief higher edn., 1954-58, asst. supt. for gen. edn., 1958-65, asso. supt. for ednl. services, 1966-76; dir. Mid-Am. Cons. Assos., 1977—. Lectr., U. Mich., Mich. State U., 1960-65, U. Tex., 1963; exec. sec. Mich. Commn. on Coll. Accreditation, 1961-66. Recipient Distinguished Pub. Service award Mich. Congress Parents and Tchrs., 1959, Mich. Council Community Coll. Presidents, 1963, Gov.'s Awards Commn. for Distinguished Pub. Employees, 1974, Mich. Council for Exceptional Children, 1975; Distinguished Service awards Mich. Legislature, 1976, Mich. Assn. Sch. Bds., 1976, Mich. Assn. Sch. Adminstrs., 1976, Mich. Community Coll. Assn., 1976; named to Mich. Edn. Hall of Fame, 1979. Mem. Phi Delta Kappa. Author: (with Maurice Seay) The Community School and Community Self-Improvement, 1954. Contbr. numerous articles to profl. jours. Home and office: 2958 Mayfair Dr Lansing MI 48912

CRAWFORD, FRANK PARKER, lawyer, judge, assn. ofcl.; b. Washington, Sept. 25, 1915; s. Frank Joseph and Cecelia Anne (Parker) C.; student Ind. State U., 1933-37; LL.B., Ind. U., 1940; m. Margaret Olivia Green, Oct. 4, 1946; children—Frank Parker, Margaret C., Loretta J., Hugh G. Admitted to Ind. bar, 1940, since practiced in Terre Haute; mem. firm Cooper, Royse, Gambill and Crawford, 1940-46, Gambill, Dudley, Cox and Crawford, 1946-48, Crawford and Crawford, 1948—; atty. City of Terre Haute, 1957-68; judge City Ct., Terre Haute, 1972-80. Instr. Judge Adv. Gen. Dept., Ft. Sheridan, Ill., 1955-64; chmn., legal advisor legal com., region 7, div. on alcoholism, Ind. Dept. Mental Health. Mem. bd. lay advisors St. Anthony Hosp., pres., 1971-73; bd. dirs. Goodwill Industries, Terre Haute, 1970-79; mem. adv. bd. Vis. Nurse Assn., Child Welfare Assn.; founding mem. bd. dirs. Terre Haute Med. Edn. Found., 1969-80, sec., 1969-74; mem. adv. council, counsel Terre Haute Center for Med. Edn., Ind. State U., 1971—. Served to maj. AUS, 1942-46. Mem. Terre Haute (pres. 1957-58), Ind. (bd. mgrs. 1958-59), 6th Dist. (pres. 1958-59) bar assns., Ind. Assn. City and County Attys. (pres. 1964-65), Ind. Assn. City and Mcpl. Judges (pres. 1978-80), Am. Arbitration Assn. (nat. panel arbitration 1973—). Elk, Rotarian (dir. 1971-76). Clubs: Terre Haute Country, Strawberry Hill Cannoneers. Home: 1613 S 6th St Terre Haute IN 47802 Office: 221 Mchts Savings Bldg Terre Haute IN 47807

CRAWFORD, GEORGE LEROY, JR., civil engr.; b. Davenport, Iowa, Mar. 6, 1928; s. George LeRoy and Florence (Gadient) C.; student U. Wyo., 1945-46; B.S., U. Ill., 1950; m. Patricia Ann Schumann, Aug. 15, 1948; children—George LeRoy III, Catherine Ruth, Nancy Jo; m. 2d, Patareka Elfner Korbly, Apr. 6, 1974. Field traffic engr. Ill. Div. Hwys., East St. Louis Dist., 1950-62, dist. traffic engr., 1962-63, sr. field engr. Bur. Traffic, Springfield, 1963-64; prin. G.L. Crawford & Assos., 1964-66; pres. Crawford, Bunte, Roden, Inc., Springfield, 1966-72; v.p. Alan M. Voorhees & Assos., Inc., St. Louis, 1972-73; pres. George L. Crawford & Assos., Inc., Maryland Heights, Mo., 1973—. Served with C.E., AUS, 1945-47. Presbyn. (elder). Mason (Shriner). Home: 11620 Heatherdale Dr Creve Coeur MO 63141 Office: 100 Progress Pkwy Suite 129 Maryland Heights MO 63043

CRAWFORD, JAMES CARROLL, ret. state ofcl.; b. Goldthwaite, Tex., June 15, 1928; s. Dean O. and Doris (Welch) C.; student Macalester Coll., 1948-51, U.S. Army War Coll.; B.A., Minn. Metro State Coll., 1974; student FBI Nat. Acad., 1974; m. Barbara Jean Hall, Dec. 27, 1950; children—James Carroll, Jodie, Jeffrey Garnet. Patrol officer Minn. State Patrol, Forest Lake, 1952-61, sgt. in charge ops. 1961-67, capt. in charge tng., 1967-70, chief, St. Paul, 1973-79; dir. motor vehicles Minn. Dept. Pub. Safety, St. Paul, 1970-73; chmn. curriculum com. Minn. Police Tng. Bd.; adv. Saudi Arabian Hwy. Patrol. Mem. Washington County Adv. Com., 1970—, Forest Lake Police Commn., Stillwater Twp. Joint Planning Commn.; chmn. Forest Lake Planning Commn., 1962; Community Fund chmn. Indianhead council Boy Scouts Am., 1973. Served with USNR, 1946-49, USAF, 1949-50; now brig. gen. U.S. Army Res. Recipient Gov.'s Distinguished Service citation, 1957, Police Service award SAR, Distinguished Service award Minn. Optometric Assn. Mem. Minn. Hwy. Patrol Suprs. Assn. (pres. 1969-70), Minn. Peace and Police Officers Assn., FBI Acad. Assos., Midwest Fleet Safety Suprs. Assn. (hon.), Internat. Assn. Chiefs Police (hwy. traffic safety com., gen. chmn. div. state and provincial 1978-79, treas. 1979-80), Minn. Chiefs Police (legis. com.), Minn. Safety Council, Am. Legion. Mason (Mason of Year 1977). Home: 980 SE 10th Ave Forest Lake MN 55025 Office: PO Box 928 Riyadh Saudi Arabia

CRAWFORD, JAMES WELDON, psychiatrist, educator, adminstr.; b. Napoleon, Ohio, Oct. 27, 1927; s. Homer and Olga (Aderman) C.; A.B., Oberlin Coll., 1950; M.D., U. Chgo., 1954, Ph.D., 1961; m. Susan Young, July 5, 1955; 1 son, Robert James. Intern Wayne County Hosp. and Infirmary, Eloise, Mich., 1954-55; resident Northwestern U., Chgo., 1958-59; practice medicine specializing in psychiatry, Chgo., 1961—; mem. staff Mt. Sinai Hosp., Chgo., Old Orchard Hosp., Skokie, Ill., Ravenswood Hosp., Chgo., Louis A. Weiss Meml. Hosp., Chgo.; clin. asso. prof. dept. psychiatry Abraham Lincoln Sch. Medicine, U. Ill., 1970—; chmn. dept. psychiatry Ravenswood Hosp. Med. Center, 1973-79; chmn. J.W. Crawford Assos., Inc., 1979—. Mem. com. on nat. health ins. Council Community Services Met. Chgo., 1973-75. Bd. dirs. Ravenswood Hosp. Med. Center, 1971-73, Chase House Episcopal Diocese Chgo., 1973-78. Served with M.C., AUS, 1945-46. NIH, Inst. Neurol. Diseases postdoctoral fellow, 1955-59. Fellow Am. Psychiat. Assn.; mem. AMA, AAAS, Assn. Am. Med. Colls., Ill. Psychiat. Soc., Chgo. Med. Soc., AAUP, Sigma Xi. Contbr. articles to profl. jours. Home: 2418 Lincoln St Evanston IL 60201 Office: 840 N Michigan Ave Suite 716 Chicago IL 60611

CRAWFORD, JEAN ANDRE, counselor; b. Chgo., Apr. 12, 1941; d. William Moses and Geneva Mae (Lacy) Jones; student Shimer Coll., 1959-60; B.A., Carthage Coll., 1966; M.Ed., Loyola U., Chgo., 1971; postgrad. Nat. Coll. Edn., Evanston, Ill., 1971-77, Northwestern U., 1976-77; m. John N. Crawford, Jr., June 28, 1969. Med. technologist, Chgo., 1960-61; primary and spl. edn. tchr. Chgo. Pub. Schs., 1966-71, counselor maladjusted children and their families, 1971—; counselor juvenile first-offenders, 1968—. Vol., Sta. WTTW-TV; vol. counselor deaf children and their families. Cert. elem. edn. and spl. edn., pupil personnel services, Ill. Mem. Am., Ill. personnel and guidance assns., Am., Ill. sch. counselors assns., Coordinating Council Handicapped Children, Phi Delta Kappa. Club: Mid-Town Tennis. Home: 601 E 32d St Chicago IL 60616 Office: 2131 W Monroe St Chicago IL 60612

CRAWFORD, JOSEPHINE LACKEY, nurse; b. Ripley, Tenn., Apr. 28, 1921; d. George Henry and Maggie Lue (Richardson) Lackey; R.N., St. Mary's Infirmary, St. Louis, 1944; B.S. in Nursing, St. Louis U., 1972; M.S. in Counselor Edn., So. Ill. U., Edwardsville, 1976; m. Brice Crawford, Sept. 10, 1950 (div.). Nurse, Homer G. Phillips Hosp., St. Louis, 1945-56; nurse Malcolm Bliss Mental Health Center, St. Louis, 1956—, dir. nursing edn., 1971—; cons., speaker in field. Chmn. Valada Barnes-Nina Williams Scholarship Fund, 1978-81; mem. council, recruitment com. Mo. State Dept. Nursing. USPHS trainee, 1966; recipient Community Service award Harmony Grand chpt. Order Eastern Star, 1978; certificate of appreciation Congressman William Clay, 1st Dist. Mo., 1978; service award ARC, 1977, others. Mem. Am., Mo., 3d Dist. nurses assns., N. Am. Assn. Alcohol and Drug Programs, Sigma Gamma Rho (George Washington Carver award 1978), Sigma Theta Tau. Democrat. Baptist. Clubs: Les Femmes, Daus. Isis (imperial dep. Oasis 1977-78, Service award 1978, imperial dep. Mo. 1979-80, dir. edn. project 1980, imperial commandress 1980), Eureka Assembly. Author articles. Address: 4562A Cote Brilliante St Saint Louis MO 63113

CRAWFORD, LESLIE WILLIAM, educator; b. Scobey, Mont., July 29, 1934; student Am. U., Washington, 1952-53; B.S., Eastern Mont. U., Billings, 1956, M.S., 1962; postgrad. Colo. State Coll., Greeley, 1961; Ed.D., U. Calif., Berkeley, 1967. Tchr. pub. schs., Lewistown, Mont., 1955-58, Douglas, Ariz., 1958-59; supr. Eastern Mont. Coll. Campus Sch., 1960-62, vis. lectr. reading and early childhood edn., 1966; curriculum coordinator and supr., lectr. elementary edn. Western Wash. State Coll., 1964-65; research asst. Primary Reading Project, U. Calif., Berkeley, 1966; asst. prof. reading and lang. arts U. Victoria, B.C., 1967-69; asst. prof. Reading Center, Ohio U., 1969-70; vis. asst. prof. U. Wash., 1970; asso. prof., coordinator undergrad. reading and lang. arts Bowling Green State U., 1970-72; asso. prof., dir. elementary edn. Moorhead (Minn.) State U., 1972-74, prof., chairperson dept. edn., 1974-78, spl. asst. to dean edn., 1978-79; cons. Queen of Angels Sch., Duncan, B.C., 1968-69, Athens City Title I Program, 1969-70, Fed.-Hocking Title I Program, 1969-70, Lincoln Internat. Sch., San Jose, Costa Rica, 1973-74, Am. Coop. Sch., Monrovia, Liberia, 1975; asso. dir. Crim Sch. Team Teaching and Individualizing Project, 1971-72; co-chmn. Minn. Conf. on Preparation Program for Elementary Tchrs. in Next Decade, 1976; sec. elem. edn. task force Bd. Teaching, 1977-79. Mem. Internat. Reading Assn. (pres. elect Martha G. Weber chpt. 1971-72, mem. exec. com. Ohio Council), Nat. Council Tchrs. English, Minn. Intercollegiate Faculty Assn., Red River Reading Assn. (v.p.), Phi Delta Kappa. Author: (with Morris Finder) Structural View of English, 1966; (with Donald E. Carline) A Handbook for Teaching Reading in the Content Areas, 1979, rev. edit., 1981; The Answer Book: A Guide to Basic Skills, K-12. Contbr. articles to ednl. jours. Home: 426 Horn Ave Moorhead MN 56560 Office: Edn Dept Moorhead State U Moorhead MN 56560

CRAWFORD, MICHAEL EARL, ednl. adminstr.; b. Cedar Falls, Iowa, Sept. 14, 1938; s. Earl Hebert and Glenola Eileen (Gordon) C.; B.A., U. No. Iowa, 1960, M.A., 1964; m. Virginia Lou James, June 3, 1962; children—Michele, Nicole. High sch. history and govt. tchr., Manchester (Iowa) Public Schs., 1960-63; high sch. distbv. edn. tchr., Cedar Rapids (Iowa) Public Schs., 1964-67; instr. mktg. Kirkwood Community Coll., Cedar Rapids, Iowa, 1967-71, v.p. devel., 1971-75; exec. dir. ACCTion Consortium, Nat. Community Coll. Orgns., Washington, 1975-78; chancellor Eastern Iowa Community Coll. Dist., Davenport, 1978—; mem. Pres.'s nat. adv. council for adult edn.; chmn. Iowa Community Coll. Chief Exec. Officers. Bd. dirs. Area Exec. Council Boy Scouts Am., Downtown Davenport Devel. Corp.; chmn. bldg. fund com. Broadview United Meth. Ch. Recipient Iowa Distbv. Edn. distinguished service award, 1980. Mem. Am. Assn. Community and Jr. Colls. Presidents Acad., Am. Vocat. Assn., C. of C., Phi Delta Kappa. Clubs: Rotary, Masons. Office: 2804 Eastern Ave Davenport IA 52803

CRAWFORD, OLIVE F., educator; b. Ruby, Wis., 1921. B.S. in English, U. Wis., Stevens Point, 1943; M.S. in English Edn., U. Wis., Madison, 1965. Tchr. New London (Wis.) pub. schs., 1946-54; tchr. Wauwatosa (Wis.) Pub. Schs., 1954—, chmn. dept., 1971—; lectr. Carroll Coll., Waukesha, Wis., 1974-78. Mem. Nat., Can., Wis. councils tchrs. English, English Assn. Greater Milw., Nat. Assn. Secondary Sch. Dept. Chmn., NEA, Wis., Wauwatosa edn. assns., Am. Assn. Supervision and Curriculum Devel., Thomas Hardy Soc., Sigma Tau Delta, Delta Kappa Gamma. Certified as tchr., Wis. Office: 7500 Milwaukee Ave Wauwatosa WI 53213

CRAWFORD, PRISCILLA RUTH, human resource and orgnl. devel. specialist; b. Ferndale, Mich., Oct. 13, 1941; d. Ernest H. and Ethel R. (Huth) Thomas; B.A., Butler U., 1962; postgrad. (Fulbright scholar), Goethe U., Germany, 1963; M.A. in Sociology (fellow), Ohio State U., 1965, Ph.D. (NIMH fellow), 1970. Mem. faculty sociology dept. Bklyn. Coll., 1966-67, Ind. U., Indpls., 1967-70; adj. faculty Roosevelt U., Chgo., 1974-77, Ind. U., Purdue U. at Indpls., 1978—; research asso. Gary (Ind.) Income Maintenance Experiment, Ind. U. Northwest, 1970-73; self-employed cons. in human resource and orgn. devel. to numerous social, profl. and bus. orgns., Chgo., 1973-77; dir. workforce devel. State of Ind. Dept. Mental Health, Indpls., 1978—; vol. cons. to numerous women's groups, 1977—; cons. to state agys., also NIMH, 1978—. Bd. dirs. Ind. Conf. on Social Concerns, 1979-81; mem. Gov.'s Spl. Grant Com., Ind. Employment Tng. Council, 1981—; mem. adv. bd. Program in Independent Living, 1980—. Mem. Am. Sociol. Assn., Midwest Sociol. Soc., North Central Sociol. Soc., Am. Mgmt. Assn., Ohio Acad. Sci., Ind. Acad. Social Scis. (dir. 1978-81), AAUP, Phi Kappa Phi, Alpha Lambda Delta.

CRAWFORD, RAYMOND MAXWELL, JR., nuclear engr.; b. Charleston, S.C., July 28, 1933; s. Raymond Maxwell and Mary Elizabeth (Bates) C.; B.S., Wayne State U., 1958, M.S., 1960; Ph.D., U. Calif. at Los Angeles, 1969; m. J. Denise LeDuc, Mar. 10, 1951; children—Denis, Michael, Deborah, Peter, Elizabeth. Instr., Wayne State U., 1960-63; asst. prof. Calif. State U., Northridge, 1963-66; tech. staff Atomics Internat., 1969-71; nuclear engr. Argonne Nat. Lab. (Ill.), 1971-74; asso. and asst. head nuclear safeguards and licensing div. Sargent & Lundy, Chgo., 1974-80; v.p. Science Applications, Inc., Oak Brook, Ill., 1980—; tech. cons. Atomic Power Devel. Assn., 1962-63; summer fellow NASA Lewis Research Center, 1965-66. Scoutmaster and counsellor Boy Scouts Am., 1963-66; active YMCA, 1966-69; active Recs. for Blind, 1964-65. Recipient numerous awards. Mem. Western Soc. Engrs., Am. Nuclear Soc., Am. Inst. Chem. Engrs., Am. Chem. Soc., Nat. Soc. Profl. Engrs., Am. Sci. Affiliation, N.Y. Acad. Scis., AAAS, Sigma Xi, Tau Beta Pi, Phi Lambda Upsilon. Contbr. articles to tech. jours. Home: 1005 E Kennebec Ln Naperville IL 60540 Office: 1211 W 22d St #901 Oak Brook IL 60521

CRAWFORD, WILLIAM BASIL, JR., newspaper reporter; b. Waukegan, Ill., June 22, 1941; s. William Basil and Jane Elinore (Murray) C.; 1 dau., Kirsten Jane; B.A. in History, U. Chgo., 1963. Asst. fiscal officer Chgo. Truck Drivers Union, 1964-68; asst. news editor City News Bur. Chgo., 1968-72; reporter Chgo. Tribune, 1972—; tchr. advanced reporting and basic writing Medill Sch. Journalism, Northwestern U., Evanston, Ill. Mem. Chgo. Reporters Assn., Chgo. Press Club, U. Chgo. Alumni Assn. Recipient Hon. mention Ill. U.P.I., 1974, 2d Place award for investigative reporting, 1975, 78; First Place awards for best investigative story Ill. A.P., 1975, 76, Sweepstakes award for best story in all categories, 1976, 3d Place award for investigative, 1976; Pulitzer prize for Spl. Local Reporting, 1976; Stewart Mott Edn. award, 1977; Jacob Schur award for investigative reporting, 1978. Home: 2159 N Seminary Ave Chicago IL 60614 Office: 435 N Michigan Ave Chicago IL 60610

CRAWSHAW, BARRY SHELDON, ins. exec.; b. Winnipeg, Man., Can., Mar. 26, 1938; s. Serge Benjamin and Bella (Nozick) C.; student Union Coll., Schenectady, N.Y., 1956-57; m. Sonya Adell Hansen, Feb. 19, 1961; children—Victoria Belle, Kenneth Alan. Passenger agt. Chgo. Helicopter Airways, Chgo., 1958-62; asst. mgr. career acctg. div. Continental Assurance Co., Chgo., 1962-64; systems analyst, programmer Continental Assurance Co., 1964-72; systems mgr. CNA Ins. Companies, Chgo., 1972—. Founding chmn. Better Ind. Govt. Assn. Hanover Park, 1971-72, chmn., 1973-74, mem. central com., 1972-73, 74—. Fellow Life Mgmt. Inst. Mem. North Central Systems Devel. Com., Life Office Mgmt. Assn. Republican. Jewish. Club: Lions (pres. 1980-81). Office: CNA Plaza Chicago IL 60685

CRAYCRAFT, ALLIE VERNON, JR., state senator; b. Mount Sterling, Ky., May 30, 1932; s. Allie Vernon and Rose Delle (Blevins) C.; student Muncie (Ind.) Trade Sch.; m. Juanita Frances Vanhoof, June 26, 1955; children—Cheryl, Cindy, Steven, Jeffery, Carol, Gerald, Annette. With Chevrolet, Muncie, Inc., 1950—, now material and production control; now mem. Ind. Senate. Leader Boy Scouts Am., Ind.; trustee Liberty Twp., Ind., 1970-74; mem. Delaware County (Ind.) Welfare Bd., 1970-78; co-chmn. Am. Heart Assn., Ind., 1977, chmn., 1978. Served with USAF, 1952-56. Recipient Heart Assn. award; Freshman Democratic State Senator of the Year, award. Clubs: Liberty Twp. Democratic, Democratic Rooster Booster Men's, Amvets. Office: 1200 W 8th St Muncie IN 47302*

CRAYS, THOMAS COLLISON, banker; b. Danville, Ill., Apr. 26, 1934; s. John Asbury and Lillian Claire (Battershell) C.; B.S., U. Ill., 1958; m. Barbara Ann Huffman, Dec. 9, 1967; children—Anne Elizabeth, Jennifer Courtney, John Forrest. Spl. rep. Fed. Reserve Bank of Chgo., 1958-62; corr. bank rep. Harris Trust & Savs. Bank, Chgo., 1962; exec. v.p. First Nat. Bank of Rossville (Ill.), 1962-66; with Palmer American Nat. Bank, Danville, Ill., 1966—, now pres., chmn. bd. dirs. Chmn., Danville United Way Campaign, 1978, bd. dirs., 1979—; bd. dirs. Center for Children's Service, 1972-79; bd. dirs. Lake View Med. Center, Danville Indsl. Park. Served with U.S. Army, 1954-56. Mem. Ill. State C. of C. (dir.), Ill. Bankers Assn., Am. Bankers Assn. Republican. Clubs: Danville Country, Elks Country, Danville Rotary. Office: 2 W Main St Danville IL 61832

CRAYTON, BILLY GENE, physician; b. Holden, Mo., May 15, 1931; s. John Reuben and Carrie Zona (Head) C.; student Central Mo. State Coll., 1948-49; B.S., Stetson U., 1958; postgrad. U. Kansas City, summer 1955; M.D., U. Mo., 1962. Intern, Mound Park Hosp., St. Petersburg, Fla., 1962-63; practice gen. medicine Latham Hosp., California, Mo., 1963-64, Kelling Clinic and Hosp., Waverly, 1964—, vice chief of staff, 1980—; preceptor in community health and med. practice U. Mo. Sch. Medicine, Waverly, 1968—; sec., dir. Kelling Hosp., Inc., 1969-80; pres. Kelling Clinic, 1971—; pres. Riverview Heights, 1972—. Adviser, Mo. chpt. Am. Assn. Med. Assts., 1973-79. Adviser, Explorer Post Boy Scouts Am., 1968-70. Served with AUS, 1952-54. Mem. Am. Acad. Family Practice, Am., So., Mo. med. assns. Baptist. Home: PO Box 41 Waverly MO 64096 Office: Kelling Clinic and Hosp Waverly MO 64096

CREAL, FLOYD HAROLD, nursing home adminstr.; b. Geneva, Ill., May 18, 1931; s. Floyd Thomas and Naomi Jeanette (Cox) C.; B.B.A., Western Mich. U., 1954; m. Lillian J. Veen, Oct. 13, 1951; children—Mark, Susan, Paul. Attendant, Kalamazoo State Hosp., 1950-52; patrolman Kalamazoo Police Dept., 1952-56; contracts mgr. Nat. Waterlift, Kalamazoo, 1956-60, Westclox, La Salle, Ill., 1960-62, Hercules Powder Co., Salt Lake City, 1962-64, Space Tech. Labs., Redondo Beach, Calif., 1964-65; owner, operator Carriage Inn Convalescent Center, Coldwater, Mich., 1970—, Little People Child Care, Coldwater, 1974—, Bronson (Mich.) Care Center, 1965—; chmn. State of Mich. Nursing Home Adminstrs. Licensure Bd. Chmn. Tri-County Health Service Com., Coldwater. Served with U.S. Army, 1947-48. Fellow Am. Coll. Nursing Home Adminstrs. (pres. Mich. chpt. 1975), Health Care Assn. Mich. (pres. 1971-73, recipient Pres.'s award of excellency 1978), Bronson C. of C. pres. 1968). Republican. Episcopalian. Club: Rotary, Masons, Shriners, Elks. Office: 90 N Michigan Ave Coldwater MI 49036

CREBO, ALAN RICHARD, ophthalmic surgeon; b. Peoria, Ill., Dec. 3, 1940; s. Richard Sherwood and Marguerite Mae C.; B.S., Purdue U., 1963; M.D., U. Fla., Gainesville, 1972; m. Dorothy Jean Westhafer, Dec. 26, 1964; children—Richard Emory, Kathleen Sarah. Intern, U. Ariz. Med. Center, Tucson, 1972-73, resident in ophthalmology, 1974-77; emergency room physician Tucson Med. Center, St. Joseph's Hosp., 1973-74; practice medicine specializing in ophthalmic surgery, Eye Physicians, Inc., Kokomo, Ind., 1977—; chmn. dept. surgery Howard Community Hosp., Kokomo, 1978-79, sec. med. staff, 1978-79, vice chief of staff, 1979-80, chief of staff, 1980—; mem. Ind. Med. Polit. Action Com., 1977—, Physicians Edn. Network, 1978—. Mem. Nat. Com. for Monetary Reform, 1979—; mem. Pres.'s Council, Purdue U. Served to lt. AC, USN, 1963-68. Decorated Silver Star medal, Air medals (14), Purple Heart; diplomate Am. Bd. Ophthalmology. Mem. Am. Acad. Ophthalmology, AMA, Ind. State Med. Assn., Ind. Acad. Ophthalmology and Otolaryngology, Indpls. Acad. Ophthalmology, Howard County Med. Soc., Contact Lens Assn. Ophthalmologists, Am. Intraocular Lens Implant Soc., Am. Assn. Ophthalmology, Aircraft Owners and Pilots Assn., Exptl. Aircraft Assn., Alpha Omega Alpha. Republican. Clubs: Porsche of Am., Internat. Aerobatic, John Purdue Coaches, Purdue Alumni, Purdue U. Gold Coats. Contbr. med. articles to profl. jours. Office: Eye Physicians Inc 3433 S Lafountain St Kokomo IN 46901

CREHORE, CHARLES AARON, lawyer; b. Lorain, Ohio, Sept. 15, 1946; s. Charles Case and Catherine Elizabeth (Kurtz) C.; B.A., Wittenberg U., 1968; postgrad. (Delta Sigma Phi Found. scholar), U. Mich., 1968-69, Cleve. State U., 1972-73; J.D., U. Akron, 1976; m. Kathy Louise Stoecklin, June 28, 1969; 1 son, Charles Case II. Asso. chemist B.F. Goodrich Co., Akron, 1969-70, chemist, 1970-72, patent atty. trainee, 1972-74, sr. patent atty. trainee, 1974-75, patent asso., 1975-76, patent atty., 1976-79; atty. regulatory affairs The Lubrizol Corp., Wickliffe, Ohio, 1979-81, corp. counsel environment, health and safety, 1981—; admitted to Ohio bar, 1976. Kennedy Found. grantee, 1968-69. Mem. Am. Bar Assn., Am. Patent Law Assn., Cleve. Patent Law Assn., Licensing Execs. Soc., Phi Alpha Delta.

Mem. Gen. Ch. New Jerusalem. Home: 18111 Millstone Rd Chagrin Falls OH Office: 29400 Lakeland Blvd Wickliffe OH 44092

CREIGH, DOROTHY WEYER, educator, writer; b. Hastings, Nebr., Dec. 4, 1921; d. Frank E. and Mabelle (Carey) Weyer; A.B., Hastings Coll., 1942; M.S., Columbia U., 1945; m. Thomas Creigh, Jr., July 17, 1948; children—Mary Elizabeth, Thomas, John Weyer, James Carey. Soc. editor Hastings Daily Tribune, 1941-42; tchr. Central City (Nebr.) High Sch., 1942-43; editor weekly newspaper Naval Ammunition Depot, Hastings, 1943-44; news and radio AP, Richmond, Va., 1945-46; with UNRRA, Hankow and Shanghai, China, 1946-48; tchr. Hastings Coll., 1952, 61-68; garden editor Hastings Daily Tribune, 1960; editor Stringing Along music quar., 1967, Adams County Hist. monthly, 1968—. Mem. Nebr. Bd. Edn., 1974—; mem. Nebr. Coordinating Commn. for Post-Secondary Edn., 1978—; dir. Nebr. Arts Council, 1967-80; mem. council Am. Assn. State and Local History, 1978—; bd. dirs. Hastings Civic Symphony, 1950-60, Nebr. Hist. Soc. Found., 1971—. Recipient Marie Sandoz award Nebr. Library Commn., 1981; named Woman of Achievement, Nebr. Bus. and Profl. Women's Clubs, 1979. Mem. Adams County Hist. Soc. (dir.), P.E.O. Presbyterian. Editor Hastings Coll. Alumni Quar., 1949-51; author: (with C. Brock) Journalism for Nebraska High Schools, 1943; (with F.E. Weyer) Hastings College, 75 Years, 1958; Bellevue College, 1962; Tales from the Prairie, Vol. I, 1970, Vol. II, 1973, Vol. III, 1976, Vol. IV, 1979, Vol. V, 1982; Adams County: The People, 1971; Adams County: A Story of the Great Plains (Merit award Am. Assn. for State Local History), 1972; The First Hundred Years (Presbyn. history), 1973; Where in the World Have We Been?, 1973; A Primer for Local Historical Societies, 1976; Nebraska Bicentennial History, 1977; A Handbook for the Great Plains Movies, 1979; Nebraska, Where Dreams Grow, 1980; author, dir. 6 part TV documentary on Gt. Plains, 1978; author cassettes for Exec. Inst., 1973; contbr. articles to mags. and newspapers, chpts. to Rolling Rivers, Worldmark Ency. on Ind. state history. Address: 1950 N Elm St Hastings NE 68901

CREIGH, THOMAS, JR., utility exec.; b. Evanston, Ill., Jan. 3, 1912, s. Thomas and Frances (Connor) C.; grad. Mercersburg (Pa.) Acad., 1929; A.B., Wabash Coll., 1933; m. Dorothy Claire Weyer, July 17, 1948; children—Mary Elizabeth, Thomas III, John, James. With No. Natural Gas Co., 1933-36; with Kan.-Nebr. Natural Gas Co., Inc., 1936—, v.p., 1951-61, pres., 1961-78, chmn. bd., 1978—, also dir.; v.p., dir. Excelsior Oil Corp., 1955-68, pres., 1968—; pres., dir. Western Gas Corp., 1967—; v.p., dir. Helium, Inc., 1960—; sec., dir. Western Plastics Corp., 1953-69; dir. Dunne Gardner Drilling Co., City Nat. Bank, Hastings, Western Alfalfa Corp., Cap-Con Internat Inc., Cape Constrn. Co., Energy Transmission System, Inc., Advanced Fuel Systems, Inc. Trustee Hastings Coll., Inst. Gas Tech. Mem. Am. (dir. 1969-73), Midwest (dir. 1965-68) gas assns., Interstate Natural Gas Assn. (dir. 1967-71, 74—), Slurry Transport Assn. (dir. 1980—), Nebr. Assn. Commerce and Industry (past pres.), Nebr. Council Econ. Edn. (chmn. 1967-70). Presbyterian (trustee). Home: 1950 N Elm St Hastings NE 68901 Office: Kan-Nebr Natural Gas Co Hastings NE 68901

CREIGHTON, MADONNA SUE, telephone co. exec.; b. Warsaw, Ind., Apr. 2, 1944; d. Elery Van and Edna Elizabeth (Pittman) Nellans; cert. profl. sec., Inst. Certifying Secs., 1973; cert. bus. mgmt., Am. Mgmt. Assn., 1980; m. Steven L. Creighton, Dec. 14, 1963; children—Angela Sue, Amy Suzanne. With United Telephone Co. Ind., Warsaw, 1964—, supr. bus. office, 1977-79, dist. mktg. supr., 1979—; pres. United Telephone Employees Fed. Credit Union, 1979-80. Mem. Nat. Secs. Assn. (past chpt. pres.), Warsaw C. of C. Republican. Methodist. Home: Rural Route 9 Southbrook Park Warsaw IN 46580 Office: 122 E Center St Warsaw IN 46580

CREIGHTON, MATTHEW EUGENE, ednl. cons.; b. Chgo., Feb. 8, 1927; s. Matthew Eugene and Mary Cecilia (Cullen) C.; A.B., Loyola U., Chgo., 1949, M.A., 1954; Ph.L., Jesuit Sch. Theology, Chgo., 1951, S.T.L., 1958; Ph.D., Fordham U., 1967. Joined S.J., Roman Catholic Ch., 1944, ordained priest, 1957; tchr. St. Ignatius Prep. Sch., Chgo., 1951-54; instr. Jesuit Sch. Theology, Chgo., 1961-63, asst. prof., 1967-72, asso. prof., 1972-76, prof., 1977-78, chmn. classical studies, 1968-72, asso. dean Grad. Sch., 1970-74; dean Loyola Rome Center, Rome, 1974-76; dir. research services Loyola U., Chgo., 1976-78; pres. Creighton U., Omaha, 1978-81; cons. Assn. Jesuit Colls. and Univs., Washington, 1981—. Bd. dirs. Rockhurst Coll., 1980. HEW grantee, 1968-78. Mem. Am. Classical League, Am. Council on Teaching of Fgn. Langs., Am. Soc. Papyrologists, Chgo. Classical Club, Classical Assn. Middle West and South, Assn. Jesuit Colls. and Univs., Alpha Sigma Nu, Beta Alpha Psi, Beta Gamma Sigma. Clubs: Rotary, K.C. Author: A Summary of the History of Greek and Latin Literature, 1969. Office: Assn Jesuit Colls and Univs 1717 Massachusetts Ave NW Washington DC 20036

CREITZ, LOWELL MILLER, cellist; b. Chgo., Feb. 4, 1931; s. Alford Eugene and Hazel G. (Miller) C.; student Northwestern U., 1949-51, U. Wis., 1956, Princeton U., 1959; pvt. cello studies with Dudley Powers, 1940-50, R. Garbousova, 1951, Mischa Schneider, 1954; m. Joan M. Harrison, Sept. 6, 1953; children—James, Joseph. Solo appearances include: Chgo. Symphony Orch., 1947, CBS Symphony, N.Y.C., 1948, U.S. Marine Band Symphony Orch., 1953-55; cellist Pro Arte Quartet, 1955-78; concert performances in U.S., Can., S.Am., C.Am., Britain and Germany; rec. artist CRI, Lyrichord, TV programs; authority on tenor violin; prof. music U. Wis., Madison, 1955—, asso. dir. Sch. Music, 1981—; guest prof. U. Wyo., 1977. Served with USNR, 1951-53, USMC, 1953-56. Recipient cert. of excellence Central Ednl. Network, 1977, research grants, 1960, 64, 69, 71, 75, 78. Mem. Am. Musical Instrument Soc., Violin Soc. Am., Violon cello Soc., Catgut Acoustical Soc., Am. Fedn. Musicians. Club: Rotary. Research on pedagogy and baroque performance practices. Home: 9238 US Hwy 14 Black Earth WI 53515 Office: 5361 Humanities U Wis Madison WI 53706

CRESS, ALBERT WILLIAM, JR., clergyman, ch. adminstr.; b. Trinidad, Colo., Oct. 9, 1949; s. Albert William and M. Connie (Ortiz) C.; B.A., Central Bible Coll., Springfield, Mo., 1976. Ordained to ministry, Assembly of God Ch., 1979; adminstrv. asst. to state supt. Ill. Dist. Council, Assemblies of God, Carlinville, Ill., 1976—. Served with U.S. Navy, 1969-73. Home: PO Box 225 Carlinville IL 62626 Office: Rural Route 3 Lake Williamson Carlinville IL 62626

CRESS, JOSEPH NICHOLAS, clin. psychologist; b. Adrian, Minn., Feb. 16, 1944; s. Nicholas Arnold and Dorothea Monica (Hartman) C.; A.B., St. Louis U., 1968; M.A., So. Ill. U., 1972, Ph.D. (Univ. Grad. Sch. Dissertation fellow), 1974; m. Elaine Marie Peaslee, July 21, 1974. Co-founder, mem. staff Sophia House, Inc., exptl. high sch., St. Louis, 1966-68; tchr., dir. Oglala Sioux Indian Culture Center, Red Cloud Sch., Pine Ridge, S.D., 1968-70; clin. psychologist Community Mental Health Center, Rock Island, Ill., 1974—; mem. adj. faculty psychology Augustana Coll., Rock Island, St. Ambrose Coll., Davenport, Iowa, U. Iowa, 1975—; psychol. cons. Head Start Programs, various ednl. agys., 1974—. Fellow preparation profl. personnel in edn. of handicapped children, 1970-72. Mem. Am., Upper Mississippi Valley psychol. assns. Contbr. articles to profl. jours. Home: 6296 Dodds Dr Bettendorf IA 52722 Office: 2101 47th St Moline IL 61265

CRESSWELL, JOHN WALTER, business exec.; b. Alton, Ill., Mar. 6, 1952; s. Barnal Walter and Mary Marjorie Johnson (Lynn) C.; A.S., Lewis and Clark Community Coll., Godfrey, Ill., 1973; B.S., So. Ill. U., 1978; children—Kathryn Marie, Kenneth Christopher, Ryan Michael. Mng. officer Staunton Home Assn. (Ill.), 1979—. Christian Scientist. Clubs: Masons, Shriners, Wood River High-Twelve (pres. 1976-77, 80-81), Ainad Temple DeMolay (pres. unit 1977-78). Home: 503 S 12th St Wood River IL 62095 Office: 111 W Main St Staunton IL 62095

CRESWELL, DOROTHY ANNE, computer mfg. co. exec.; b. Burlington, Iowa, Feb. 6, 1943; d. Robert Emerson and Agnes Imogene (Gardner) Mefford; A.A., Burlington Community Coll., 1963; B.A., U. Iowa, 1965; M.S. in Math., Western Ill. U., 1970; m. John Lewis Creswell, Aug. 28, 1965. Bus. computer programmer Mason & Hanger-Silas Mason Co., Inc., Burlington, 1965-70, sci. computer programmer, 1970-74; system programmer Computer Resources div. Contractors Hot Line, Ft. Dodge, Iowa, 1974; dir. data processing Iowa Central Community Coll., 1975-80; systems programming mgr. Norand Corp., Cedar Rapids, Iowa, 1980—. Mem. Data Processing Mgmt. Assn. (sec. Mississippi Valley chpt. 1968-69), Adminstrv. Mgmt. Soc., Assn. Computing Machinery, Iowa Assn. Ednl. Data Systems (pres.). Democrat. Methodist. Home: 363 Hampden Dr NE Cedar Rapids IA 52402 Office: 550 2d St SE Cedar Rapids IA 52401

CRESWELL, ROBERT DELANO, career counselor; b. Akron, Ohio, June 2, 1937; s. Stanley Clayton and Betty Marie (Phillips) C.; B.A., U. Akron, 1970; m. Suzanne Beverly Shaffer, June 23, 1961; 1 son, Mark Douglas. Mgr. customer service and sales B.W. Rogers Co., Akron, 1960-70; counselor Munster, Grom, Owsten & Lantz, Akron, 1970-73, Advance, Personnel, Inc., Canton, Ohio, 1973-74; account exec. Trazman & Assos., Akron, 1974-75; personnel recruiter Ecodyne Corp., Chgo., 1975-76; prin. Compco Communications, Akron, Ohio, 1976—; cons. to advt., public relations industry, workshops and seminars, 1980—. Mem. Am. Polygraph Assn., Am. Soc. Personnel Adminstrn., Am. Mgmt. Assn., Am. Soc. Tng. and Devel., Nat. Small Bus. Assn., Epsilon Delta Chi. Methodist. Author: Clues for Better Interviews, 1980; Things Worth Knowing About Your Job Search, 1980. Office: Suite 1001 Trans-Ohio Bldg Corner Main and Bowery Sts Akron OH 44308

CRETSOS, JAMES MIMIS, sci. info. co. exec., chemist; b. Athens, Greece, Oct. 23, 1929; s. Basil D. and Chrissa B. (Thomaidou) Kretsos; came to U.S., 1946, naturalized, 1955; B.S. in Chemistry, Am. U., 1960, postgrad., 1960-62; m. Barbara Ann Deitz, Mar. 10, 1952; children—Maurice William, Christopher James. Research chemist Melpar, Inc., Falls Church, Va., 1961-63, info. scientist, 1963-64, head tech. info. center, 1964-65, mgr. info. services lab., 1965-67, dir. instructional materials center, Tng. Corp. of Am., Falls Church, 1966-67; dir. info. systems lab. Litton Industries, Bethesda, Md., 1967-69; head sci. info. systems dept. Merrell Dow Pharms., Cin., 1969—; dir. Infoflow, Inc.; cons OEO, Ohio, Ky.-Ind. Regional Library and Info. Council; lectr. U. Cin., 1973-74, U. Ky., 1976-77, 82. Mem. Creative Edn. Found., Buffalo, 1967—. Served with M.C., AUS, 1954-56. Mem. Am. Chem. Soc., Am. Mgmt. Assn., Am. Soc. Info. Sci. (chmn. So. Ohio chpt. 1973-74, chmn. SIG/BC 1973-74, chmn. profl. enhancement com. 1974-75, chmn. 5th mid-year meeting 1976, Watson Davis award 1976, chmn. membership com. 1977, exec. com. 1979, nominations com. 1980, pres. 1979), Am. Fedn. Info. Processing Socs. (dir. 1981-83), Assn. Computing Machinery, IEEE Computer Soc., Drug Info. Assn., Med., Spl. (pres. Cin. chpt. 1974-75, consultation officer 1976-77) libraries assns., Assn. Computational Linguistics, Pharm. Mfrs. Assn., AAAS, Nat. Micrographics Assn. Club: Indoor Tennis. Editor, Health Aspects of Pesticides Abstract Bull., 1967-69; mem. adv. bd. Chem. Abstracts Service, 1981-83. Home: 10701 Adventure Ln Cincinnati OH 45242 Office: 2110 E Galbraith Rd Cincinnati OH 45215

CRIDER, ROBERT AUGUSTINE, internat. fin. co. exec.; b. Washington, Jan. 3, 1935; s. Rana Albert and Terasa Helen (Dampf) C.; student law enforcement U. Md., 1959-63; m. Debbie Ann Lee, Nov. 1960. Police officer Met. Police Dept., Washington, 1957-67; substitute tchr., bldg. trades instr. Maries R-1 Sch., Vienna, Mo., 1968-70; vets. constrn. tng. officer VA Dept. Edn., Mo., 1968-70; constrn. mgr. Tectonics Ltd., Vienna, 1970-79; owner R-A Crider & Assos., St. Louis, 1979—. Served with USAF, 1952-56. Mem. Assn. Ret. Policemen, Internat. Conf. Police, Nat. Police Assn., World Future Soc., Internat. Platform Assn., Nat. Assn. Fin. Consultants, Internat. Soc. Financiers, Am. Legion. Roman Catholic. Clubs: Lions, K.C. (4 deg.). Home: 2644 Roseland Terr Saint Louis MO 63143 Office: R-A Crider & Assos PO Box 3459 Saint Louis MO 63143

CRIM, BOBBY DON, state legislator; b. Kennett, Mo., Dec. 10, 1931; s. Ola Augusta C.; B.A., M.A., U. Mich.; children—Donald, Douglas, David. Tchr., Davison (Mich.) Community Schs., 1959-60, Flint (Mich.) Community Schs., 1961-64; mem. Mich. Ho. of Reps., 1965-66; dir. state and fed. programs Genesee (Mich.) Intermediate Sch. Dist., 1967-68; bd. coordinator Genesee County Bd. Suprs., 1968-69; exec. sec. to speaker of ho. Mich. Ho. of Reps., 1969-72; mem. Mich. Ho. of Reps., 1973—, speaker of ho., 1975—, chmn. select com. to study civil service, 1973-74; legis. liaison Mich. Sch. Fin. Study, 1967. Mem. Davison City Council, 1961-64, 67-68, mayor pro tem, 1963-64, police and fire commr., 1963-64. Served in USN, 1950-54. Named Vol. of Yr. in Mich., Spl. Olympics, 1977; Greater Am. award B'nai B'rith Internat. Found., 1978; Contemporary Challenge award Nat. Conf. on Counseling Minorities, 1980; Adv. award Assn. Retarded Citizens Mich., 1981. Mem. Am. Legion. Democrat. Club: Eagles (Mich. Eagle of Yr. 1977-78). Office: State Capitol Bldg Lansing MI 48909

CRIPPIN, BYRON MILES, JR., lawyer; b. Topeka, Oct. 19, 1928; s. Byron M. and Grace M. (Smith) C.; Asso. Liberal Arts, 1948, B.S. in Law, 1950, J.D., 1952; m. Marie A. Bradbury, Oct. 29, 1955; children—Patricia, David, Linda. Research asst. Calif. law revision project Stanford U., Palo Alto, Calif., 1954-55; admitted to Minn. bar, 1952; law clk. U.S. Dist. Ct., Mpls., 1955-56; corp. atty. law dept. Geo. A. Hormel & Co., Austin, Minn., 1956-68, gen. atty., head law dept., 1968-74, gen. counsel, 1974-81, corp. officer, 1978-81; gen. counsel, dir. devel. Lowell Lundstrom Ministries, Willmar, Minn., 1981—. Past mem. Austin City Charter Commn.; chmn. Mower County Young Republican League, 1956-57; vice chmn. Mower County Rep. Com., 1959-61; chmn. Christian Bus. Men's Com., 1963-64, regional chmn., 1975—; former mem. adv. bd. Salvation Army; chmn. conf. adminstrv. bd. Free Meth. Ch., 1978-80. Served to 1st lt. U.S. Army, 1952-54. Mem. Am. Bar Assn., Minn. Bar Assn., Mower County Bar Assn. (pres. 1961-62), Minn. Corp. Counsel Assn., U. Minn. Alumni Assn., Order of Coif, Scabbard and Blade, Delta Sigma Rho. Home: 303 20th St SW Austin MN 55912 Office: Box 505 Willmar MN 56201-0505

CRIST, WILLIAM GARY, sculptor, educator; b. Pocatello, Idaho, Jan. 17, 1937; s. Norman Benjamin and Margaret Alice Crist; student Olympic Coll., 1955-57; B.A., U. Wash., 1966; M.F.A., Cranbrook Acad. Art, 1971; m. Barbara Alice Mueller, Mar. 18, 1978; 1 dau., Julie Ann. Tchr., Mt. Si High Sch., Snoqualmie, Wash., 1966-69; asst. prof. Wesleyan Coll., Macon, Ga., 1971-72; instr. Cameron U., Lawton, Okla., 1972-74; asso. prof. U. Mo., Kansas City, 1974—; vis. scholar Staatliche Kunstakademie, Düsseldorf, W. Ger., 1981; works in video, laser, computer; exhbns. include: Contemporary Arts Found., Oklahoma City, 1974; Grinstead Gallery, Warrensburg, Mo., 1976; 7E7 Gallery, Lawrence, Kans., 1978; Noho Gallery, N.Y.C., 1979, 80; also numerous juried and invitational shows; propr. Kinetic Concepts, Shawnee Mission, Kans., 1977—; lectr. in field. Served with U.S. Army, 1959-62. U. Mo. Research Council grantee, 1975-81. Mem. Coll. Art Assn., So. Assn. Sculptors. Mem. Christian Ch. (Disciples of Christ). Home: 7516 Juniper Shawnee Mission KS 66208 Office: Art Dept U Mo Kansas City MO 64110

CRISWELL, CHARLES HARRISON, environ. chemist, engr.; b. Springfield, Mo., Jan. 9, 1943; s. John Philip and Elba Anne (Denton) C.; A.B., Drury Coll., Springfield, 1967; postgrad. U. Mo., 1967-68; m. Joyce LaVonne Louth, Apr. 26, 1968; children—Christina Rachel. San. chemist, dir. water pollution control labs. City of Springfield, 1968-72, asso. environ. engr.. chief water pollution control sect., 1972-79; pres., mng. partner Cons. Analytical Services Internat., Inc., Springfield, 1979—; mem. Mo. Joint Hazardous Waste Mgmt. Law Com. and State-Wide Ad Hoc Com. on Hazardous Waste Mgmt. Regulations, Mo. Hazardous Waste Mgmt. Com.; lectr. Springfield Pub. Schs., S.W. Mo. State U. and U. Lab. Sch., Drury Coll. Ruling elder, treas. John Calvin Union Presbytery, 1975—, commr., 1974, 75, 76, mem. Permanent Jud. Commn., 1977—, asst. to stated clk., 1980—; active various coms. 1st and Calvary Presbyn. Ch.; mem. gen. assembly Synod-Presbytery Interjudicatory Consultation on Long-Rang Ch. Fin., 1981. Nominated Outstanding Young Man of Year, Springfield, 1977, 78. Mem. Am. Chem. Soc. (com. environ. analytical methodology 1974—), Am. Inst. Biol. Scis., Mo. Acad. Sci., Springfield Acad. Sci., Mo. Water and Sewerage Conf. (pres. 1974), Mo. Water Pollution Control Assn. (asso. editor newsletter, 1976, chmn. program com. 1977, 82, v.p. 1977-78, pres., chmn. exec. com. 1979-80), Water Pollution Control Fedn. (indsl. waste com. 1975-82, spl. legis. rev. task group 1978—, govt. affairs-indsl. liaison task group 1976—, govt. affairs com. 1977-82, tech. practices com. 1978—, program com. 1980—, chmn. nat. task group on permits and monitoring 1978—, mem. task group on indsl. cost recovery 1978-80, task group on indsl. waste pre-treatment 1980—, chmn. nat. subcom. on changes in indsl. analytical protocols 1980—), Beta Beta Beta (chpt. pres.), Phi Mu Alpha (chpt. sec.). Contbr. articles to profl. jours. Home: 2108 E Montclair St Springfield MO 65804 Office: 2804 E Battlefield Rd Springfield MO 65804

CRITSER, JERRY JOSEPH, govt. ordnance specialist; b. Rensselaer, Ind., Sept. 25, 1932; s. Joseph Merrill and Mabel Berniece (Wallace) C.; student St. Josephs Coll., Collegeville, Ind., 1950-51. Purchasing agt. Miniature Train Co. div. P.A. Sturtevant Co., Rensselaer, 1951-52; equipment specialist ordnance electronics U.S. Army Munitions Command, Joliet, Ill., 1956-73, Ordnance Advanced Armament Systems, Rock Island, Ill., 1973—. Pres., Ventures in Sound Recordings, London and Joliet, Ill., 1952—; producer British theatre pipe organ recs. Served with USAF, 1952-56. Mem. Am. Def. Preparedness Assn., Soc. Logistic Engrs., Chgo. Symphony Soc., Audio Engring. Soc., Ind. Hist. Soc., Am. Theatre Organ Soc., Automatic Mus. Instrument Collectors Assn. Republican. Episcopalian. Mason (Shriner). Curator collection master record library, M. Welte & Sohn, Freiburg, Germany, N.Y., and Kimball-Welte, Chgo. Contbr. to theatre organ publs. Home: 411 Hickory St Joliet IL 60435 Office: US Army Armament Materiel Readiness Command Rock Island IL 61201

CRIVARO, PETE FRANK, mayor Des Moines; b. Des Moines, Aug. 6, 1913; s. John B. and Anita (Perri) C.; student Am. Inst. Bus., Drake U.; m. Louise J. Abruzzese, Apr. 6, 1936; children—John A., Carmella Crivaro Pigneri. Legal sec. City of Des Moines, 1933-36, sec. to mayor, 1936-38, with dept. public works, 1938-56, asst. city mgr., 1956-62, mayor, 1979—; acting city mgr. City of Marion (Iowa), 1963, city mgr., 1964-68; dir. Des Moines Public Housing Authority, 1969-77; community investment dir. Fed. Home Loan Bank Des Moines, 1978-79. Past pres. Des Moines Housing Council, Inc.; former mem. bd. dirs. Home of Oakridge. Served with USN, 1948-50. Mem. Internat. City Mgrs. Assn., U.S. Conf. Mayors, Nat. League Cities, Am. Legion (past post comdr., Humanitarian award). Roman Catholic. Club: Southtown Kiwanis (past pres.). Office: City Hall E 1st and Locust Sts Des Moines IA 50307

CROAK, ANTHONY O'NEIL, JR., mfg. co. exec.; b. St. Louis, Oct. 27, 1932; s. Anthony O'Neil and Virginia Mary (Bergs) O'N.; B.S., John Carroll U., Cleve., 1954; M.S. in Adminstrn., George Washington U., 1970; m. Marjorie Mittong, May 30, 1959; children—Anthony O'Neil, III, Theresa M., Phillip M. Commd. 2d lt. Transp. Corp., U.S. Army, 1954, advanced through grades to lt. col., 1970; service in W. Ger., 1960-63, Vietnam, 1966-67, 70-71; ret., 1975; dir. transp. Owens-Corning Fiberglas Corp., Toledo, 1975—, adv. bd. Center Transp. Policy; dir. ITOFCA, Inc. Chmn. transp. sect. Toledo United Fund, 1977-78. Decorated Legion of Merit, D.F.C., Meritorious Service medal, Air medal (15), Bronze Star, Army Commendation medal. Mem. Nat. Freight Traffic Assn. (dir.), Nat. Indsl. Traffic League, Central Terr. Shippers Adv. Bd., Toledo Transp. Club. Republican. Roman Catholic. Home: 2435 Copland Blvd Toledo OH 43614 Office: Fiberglas Tower Toledo OH 43659

CROCKER, DEAN DEMPSTER, state ofcl.; b. Glendale, Calif., July 19, 1937; s. Arlo Jack and Doris Ruth (Dempster) C.; B.S., Drake U., 1960, M.S., 1969; m. Hazel Kate Harman, June 1, 1957; children—Michael, Steven, Jonathan. Tchr. English and social studies, Des Moines Ind. Sch. Dist., 1960-68, swim coach, 1963-68; coordinator ednl. data processing Polk County (Iowa) Bd. Edn., 1968-69; asst. dir. data processing Iowa Dept. Public Instrn., Des Moines, 1969-70, dir. mgmt. info. div., 1970-78, dir. statewide computer services, 1978—; speaker in field. Adult leader, com. chmn., asst. scoutmaster Mid-Iowa Boy Scouts Am., 1966-81; civil def. shelter mgr.; sec. gov.'s state adv. com. on ednl. data processing, 1972—. Served with USAR, 1957-63. Mem. Internat. Assn. for Ednl. Data Systems (sec. bd. dirs. 1971-74), Iowa Assn. for Ednl. Data Processing Systems (pres. 1970-71, sec.-treas. 1970—). Republican. Lutheran. Author monographs in field; editor AEDS Monitor, 1969-71. Home: 5129 Twana Dr Des Moines IA 50310 Office: Dept Public Instrn Grimes State Office Bldg Des Moines IA 50319

CROCKETT, DAVID MARTIN, record and tape corp. exec.; b. Indpls., Sept. 30, 1948; s. Harold Maxwell and Harriet Elizabeth (Martin) C.; B.S. in Bus. Mgmt., Ind. U., 1970; m. Susan Levindofske, Apr., 1978; 1 dau., Katie Danielle; 1 son by previous marriage, Adam Carr. Mgmt. trainee program Ind. Nat. Bank, Indpls., 1970-72; salesman Smucker Food Co., Indpls., 1972; pres. Father's & Sun's, Inc., Indpls., 1972—, v.p. affiliate corp., Karma Records, Inc., 1972—. Mem. Nat. Assn. Rec. Merchandisers, Black Music Assn. Office: 4100 Industrial Blvd Indianapolis IN 46254

CROCKETT, GEORGE WILLIAM, JR., congressman; b. Jacksonville, Fla., Aug. 10, 1909; A.B., Morehouse Coll., Atlanta, 1931; J.D., U. Mich., 1934; LL.D. (hon.), Morehouse Coll., 1972, Shaw Coll., Detroit, 1973; m. Harriette Clark, 1980; children by previous marriage—Elizabeth Ann Hicks, George W., Ethelene C. Jones. Admitted to Fla. bar, 1934, W.Va. bar, 1935, Mich., 1944; sr.

atty. Dept. Labor, 1939-43; hearings officer Fed. Fair Employment Practices Commn., Washington, 1943; founder, dir. fair employment practices dept. Internat. United Auto Workers, adminstrv. asst., sec.-treas., asso. gen. counsel, 1944-46; sr. mem. firm Goodman, Crockett, Eden & Robb, Detroit, 1946-66; elected judge Recorder's Ct., Detroit, 1966, 72, presiding judge, 1974; vis. judge Mich. Ct. Appeals, 1979; acting corp. counsel City of Detroit, 1980; founder, 1st chmn. Jud. Council, Nat. Bar Assn.; mem. 97th Congresses from Mich. 13th dist. Trustee Morehouse Coll. Mem. Nat. Lawyers Guild, Nat. Bar Assn., NAACP, Kappa Alpha Psi. Baptist. Democrat. Office: US House of Reps Washington DC 20515

CROCKETT, NEWELL PRESTON, accountant; b. Tomahawk, Wis., Jan. 13, 1923; s. Newell Preston and Helen (Knauff) C.; B.S.C., U. Iowa, 1942; m. Marilyn Lee Ames, Aug. 9, 1941; children—Christine Lee, Robert William. With Ernst & Whinney, C.P.A.s, and predecessor, Chgo., 1946—, partner, 1961—. Bd. dirs. Jr. Achievement Chgo. Served to 1st. lt. F.A., AUS, 1943-46. C.P.A., Ill. Mem. Am. Inst. C.P.A.s, Ill. Soc. C.P.A.s, Internat. Trade Club Chgo. Presbyterian. Clubs: Union League, Economic, Mid-Day (Chgo.); Bob O'Link; Westmoreland. Office: 150 S Wacker Dr Chicago IL 60606*

CROFOOT, JOHN WILLIAM, advt. co. exec., bus. exec., state legislator; b. Newton, Kans., Mar. 24, 1927; s. Ray Freeman and Mary Louise (Grimwood) C.; student Kans. State U., 1946-48; m. Marian Lucille Hurst, Feb. 15, 1948; children—David, Pamela, James. Founder, pres. Western Assos., Inc., Cedar Point, 1958—; chmn. bd. Radio Supply Co. Inc., Wichita, Kans., Marion Die & Fixture Co. (Kans.); mem. Kans. Senate, 1970-81. Mem. Republican Precinct Com., Chase County, 1956-70; chmn. Chase County Rep. Party, 1956-58; pres. AAA-Auto Club Kans., 1976-77, bd. dirs., 1978—. Served with USN, 1944-46. Mem. Splty. Advt. Assn. (nat. vice chmn., dir.), Kans. Assn., Commerce and Industry, Am. Legion. Methodist.

CROGHAN, HAROLD HEENAN, lawyer, mfg. co. exec.; b. Sioux City, Iowa, May 20, 1924; s. Edmond Harold and Marie (Heenan) C.; A.B., Lawrence U., Appleton, Wis., 1947; J.D., Cornell U., 1953; m. Mary Gertrude Murphy, Feb. 4, 1948; children—Catherine, John, Loretta, Margaret. Admitted to N.Y. bar, 1953, Mo. bar, 1953, Ohio bar, 1967; asso. firms in Kansas City, 1953-56; corp. counsel Kansas City Gas Service Co., 1956-66; house counsel, then asst. sec.-corp. counsel Philips Industries Inc., Dayton, Ohio, 1966-68, v.p., sec., corp. counsel, treas., 1968-78, exec. v.p. adminstrn., gen. counsel, 1978—, also dir.; dir. Dexter Axle Co., Winbro, Inc., Malta Mfg. Co. Served with USMCR, 1942-46, 50-52. Decorated Navy Cross, Silver Star, Bronze Star, Purple Heart. Mem. Mo. Bar Assn., Ohio Bar Assn., Dayton Bar Assn., Pvt. Carrage Conf. (dir.), Phi Beta Kappa, Phi Delta Theta, Phi Delta Phi. Roman Catholic. Clubs: Dayton City, Dayton Racquet, Chancery, Vanguard, Rockhill, Hollinger Tennis (Dayton). Home: 609 Garden Rd Dayton OH 45419 Office: 4801 Springfield St Dayton OH 45401

CROIS, JOHN HENRY, village govt. ofcl.; b. Chgo., Jan. 13, 1946; s. Henry F. and Dorothy M. (Priebe) C.; B.A., Elmhurst (Ill.) Coll., 1969; M.A., U. Notre Dame, 1972. Asst. to village mgr. Village of Oak Lawn (Ill.), 1975—; coordinator Oak Lawn Swine Flu Immunization Program, 1976. Mem. Internat. City Mgmt. Assn., Am. Soc. Public Adminstrn., Am. Econ. Assn., Ill. City Mgmt. Assn., Ill. Assn. Mcpl. Mgmt. Assts., Metro-Mgrs. Assn. Roman Catholic. Clubs: St. Germaine's Men's, SW Archdiocesan Singles. Home: 10233 S Karlov Ave Oak Lawn IL 60453 Office: 5252 W Dumke Dr Oak Lawn IL 60453

CROLL, ROBERT FREDERICK, educator, economist; b. Evanston, Ill., Feb. 3, 1934; s. Frederick Warville and Florence (Campbell) C.; B.S. in Bus. Adminstrn., Northwestern U., 1954; M.B.A. (Burton A. French scholar) with high distinction, U. Mich., 1956; D.B.A., Ind. U., 1969; D.Litt., John F. Kennedy Coll., 1970; m. Sandra Elizebeth Bell, June 15, 1968; 1 son, Robert Frederick. Instr. Ind. U. Sch. Bus., Bloomington, 1956, researcher in bus. econs., 1960-62; mng. dir. Motor Vehicle Industry Research Assos., Evanston, 1962-63; personal asst. to speaker Ill. Ho. of Reps., 1963-65; asst. prof. bus. adminstrn. Kans. State U., 1965-66; asst. prof. Inst. Indsl. Relations, Loyola U. Chgo., 1966-70; asso. prof. Sch. Bus. Adminstrn., Central Mich. U., 1970-76, prof., 1976—. Mem. platform committee Ind. Republican Com., 1958; Ind. del. Young Rep. Nat. Conv., 1959; nat. chmn. Youth for Goldwater Orgn., 1960-61; chmn. coll. clubs Young Rep. Orgn. Ill., 1960-62; asst. chief page Rep. Nat. Conv., 1964; mem. Mt. Pleasant City Charter Commn., 1973—. Trustee estate of F.W. Croll, Chgo., 1959—. Recipient Grand prize Gov. of Ind., 1958. Accredited personnel diplomate Am. Soc. Personnel Adminstrn. Accreditation Inst. Mem. Soc. Automotive Engrs., A.I.M., Soc. Advancement Mgmt., Am. Econ. Assn., Mt. Pleasant C. of C., Young Ams. for Freedom (founder 1960, vice chmn. 1962-63), Phila. Soc. (founder 1964), Beta Gamma Sigma, Delta Sigma Pi Key, Phi Delta Kappa, Phi Kappa Phi, Pi Sigma Alpha, Delta Mu Delta, Sigma Pi, Alpha Kappa Psi, Sigma Iota Epsilon, Phi Chi Theta. Episcopalian. Clubs: Little Harbor (Harbor Springs, Mich.); Mount Pleasant Country. Author: Fall of an Automotive Empire: A Business History of the Packard Motor Car Company, 1945-1958, others. Contbr. articles to profl. jours. Address: 1224 Glenwood Dr Mount Pleasant MI 48858

CROMLEY, JON LOWELL, lawyer; b. Riverton, Ill., May 23, 1934; s. John Donald and Naomi M. (Mathews) C.; B.S., U. Ill., 1958; J.D., John Marshall Law Sch., 1966. Real estate title examiner Chgo. Title & Trust Co., 1966-70; admitted to Ill. bar, 1966; practiced in Genoa, Ill., 1970—; mem. firm O'Grady & Cromley, Genoa, 1970—. Bd. dirs. Genoa Day Care Center, Inc. Mem. Am. Judicature Soc., Am., Ill., Chgo., DeKalb County bar assns. Home: 130 Homewood Dr Genoa IL 60135 Office: 213 W Main St Genoa IL 60135

CROMWELL, EVALYN TETSU-SEI, librarian; b. Mazon, Ill., Mar. 14, 1915; d. John Sebastian and Ann Marie (Dunlop) C.; diploma Wright Jr. Coll., 1938, library certificate, 1941; student Art Inst., evenings 1945-47; Ph.B., Northwestern U., 1961. With Chgo. Pub. Library, 1941—, jr. library asst. Taft High Sch. Library, 1941-42, Albany Park br. library, 1942-43, children's library asst. Norwood Park sub-br., 1943-54; adult service librarian Hild Library, 1954-75, catalog dept., 1975—. Instr. first aid A.R.C., 1961—, vol. first aid stas., 1961—. Recipient citation A.R.C., 1970. Mem. AAUW (resolutions chmn. bd. dirs. Chgo. br.), Ill. Audubon Soc., ALA, Ill. Library Assn., Sierra Club, Art Inst. Chgo., Field Mus. Natural History (life), Labsum Shedrub Ling, UN Assn. U.S.A., Am. Hiking Soc. Club: Apollo Chorus. Home: PO Box 11074 Chicago IL 60611 Office: 425 N Michigan Ave Chicago IL 60611

CRONCE, ANITA LYNN, occupational therapist; b. Milw., Oct. 1, 1957; d. Llewellyn Walter and Patricia Ann (Zass) C.; B.S. in Occupational Therapy, U. Wis., Milw., 1979. Occupational therapist spl. ednl. needs grant Wee Care Day Care, Milw., 1979-81; occupational therapist, diagnostician DuPage/West Cook Regional Spl. Edn. Assn., 1981—. Registered occuatpional therapist, Wis. Mem. Am. Occupational Therapy Assn., Wis. Occupational Therapy Assn., Ill. Occupational Therapy Assn., Sensory Integration Spl. Interest Group, Pediatric Therapists in Schs., U. Wis. Sch. Allied Health Alumni Assn. (dir. 1980—).

CRONICAN, RICHARD ALAN, computer co. mgr.; b. Yonkers, N.Y., Sept. 5, 1943; s. John G. Sr., and Josephine M. (Ness) C.; student U. Ariz., 1966—; m. Dana S. Yarian, July 3, 1965; children—Kimberly and Kelly (twins), Timothy Alan. Patrolman, police dept. City of Tucson, 1966-69, detective, 1969-70, programmer, analyst dept. fin., 1970-73, sys/prog supr., 1973-74, dir. dept. computer services, 1974-81; exec. dir., regional mgr., prin. cons. Systems & Computer Technology Corp., Malvern, Pa., 1981—; guest lectr. U. Ariz., 1970—, Pima Coll., 1970—; cons. City of Phoenix, S. Tucson. Ordained deacon, Roman Catholic Ch., 1976; bd. dirs. Armory Park Found., 1977—, AMIGOS Bibliog. Council, Dallas, 1979-80; chmn. Diocese of Tucson Pastoral Council, 1977-81, also adult religious instr.; mem. advisory council Pima Coll., Tucson, 1975—. Served with USAF, 1961-65. Mem. Am. Mgmt. Assn., Urban and Regional Info. Systems Assn. (chmn. DP mgmt. spl. interest group), Data Processing Mgmt. Assn. Club: Kiwanis. Home: 6601 Westshore Dr Lincoln NE 68516 Office: 4 Country View Rd Malvern PA 19355

CRONIN, JAMES WATSON, educator, physicist; b. Chgo., Sept. 29, 1931; s. James Farley and Dorothy (Watson) C.; A.B., So. Meth. U., 1951; Ph.D., U. Chgo., m. Annette Martin, Sept. 11, 1954; children—Cathryn, Emily, Daniel Watson. asso. Brookhaven Nat. Lab., 1955-58; mem. faculty Princeton U., 1958-71, prof. physics, 1965-71; prof. physics U. Chgo., 1971—; Loeb lectr. physics Harvard U., 1967. Recipient Research Corp. Am. award, 1967; John Price Wetherill medal Franklin Inst., 1976; E.O. Lawrence award ERDA, 1977; Nobel Prize in Physics, 1980; Sloan fellow, 1964-66; Guggenheim fellow, 1970-71. Mem. Am. Acad. Arts and Scis., Nat. Acad. Sci. Participant early devel. spark chambers; co-discover CP-violation, 1964. Home: 1445 E 56th St Chicago IL 60637

CRONIN, MARTHA PATRICIA, public relations exec.; b. St. Louis, Feb. 22, 1927; d. William Dennis and Bridget Delia (Rogers) C.; student Washington U., St. Louis, 1944-45; B.A., Harris Tchrs. Coll., 1948; M.A., Stanford U., 1958. Tchr., St. Louis public schs., 1948-66; asst. publs. editor St. Louis U., 1966-68; dir. public info. Lindenwood Colls., St. Louis, 1968-73; dir. public relations Mo. Bot. Garden, 1974-76; writer, editor, public relations cons., St. Louis, 1976-80; dir. publs. Humanities Programs for Older Adults, St. Louis Area Agy. on Aging, Mo. Com. on Humanities, 1978-80; dir. public relations Fontbonne Coll., St. Louis, 1980—. Bd. dirs., media cons. St. Louis Area Gray Panthers, 1979—; bd. dirs. Nursing Home Ombudsman Program Greater St. Louis. Capt. USMCR. Recipient regional and nat. awards in publicity and publs. Am. Coll. Public Relations Assn. and Nat. School Public Relations Assn. Fulbright grantee, 1959-60. Mem. Women in Communications, Mo. Press Women, St. Louis Press Club. Roman Catholic.

CRONSTEDT, JANET HAGELMAN, airport exec.; b. Jackson Heights, N.Y., Jan. 18, 1950; d. Harold Raymond and May Eleanor (Stockman) Hagelman; student Gordon Coll., Wenham, Mass., 1968-71; m. Robert Cronstedt, Nov. 27, 1971. Elem. sch. tchr. in N.C., S.C. and Conn., 1971-75; flight attendant TWA, 1975, supr. in-flight services, 1976-78, dir. customer services, 1976, mgr. catering and aircraft provisioning, 1979-80; field mgr. passenger services O'Hare Internat. Airport, Chgo., 1981—. Mem. Nat. Assn. Female Execs.

CROOK, BRIAN MANNING, investment counselor; b. Mpls., Apr. 20, 1935; s. Norris A. and Ethel Albine (Dunn) C.; B.S., U. Minn., 1964; postgrad. U. Mich., 1974-76; m. Kay Noreene Forester, Sept. 25, 1970; 1 son, Bernard Manning. Analyst, U. Minn., Mpls., 1964-66; systems programmer Schlumberger-EMR Computer Div., Mpls., 1966-67; data processing supr. and quality assurance coordinator Com-Share Inc., Chgo. and Ann Arbor, Mich., 1967-68; v.p. Com-Tel Inc., Chgo., 1968-69; v.p. Nat. Computer Franchise Corp., Chgo., 1969-70; software devel. mgr. Computer Operations Inc., Costa Mesa, Calif., 1970; mgr. special systems Com-Share Inc., Ann Arbor, 1971-72; mgr. info. systems Mfg. Data Systems Inc., Ann Arbor, 1972-73; data processing mgr. U.S. Postal Service, Allen Park, Mich., 1973-79; dist. systems mgr. Wang Labs., Inc., Southfield, Mich., 1979— investment mgr. Thomson Investment Services div. Thomson McKinnon Securities, Inc., Northville, Mich., 1980—. Served with U.S. Army, 1957-59. Home: 46133 Nine Mile Rd Northville MI 48167 Office: PO Box 11 Northville MI 48167

CROSBY, FRED MCCLELLAN, retail home and office furnishings co. exec.; b. Cleve., May 17, 1928; s. Fred Douglas and Marion Grace (Naylor) C.; grad. high sch.; m. Phendalyne D. Tazewell, Dec. 23, 1958; children—Fred, James, Llionicia. Vice pres. Seaway Flooring & Paving Co., Cleve., 1959-63; pres. Crosby Furniture Co., Inc., Cleve., 1963-; dir. First Bank Nat. Dir. adv. council Ohio Bd. Workmen's Compensation, 1974—; chmn. Minority Econ. Devel. Corp., 1972-; bd. dirs. Council Smaller Enterprise, Goodwill Industries, Woodruff Hosp., Cleve. Devel. Found., Greater Cleve. Growth Assn.; chmn. bd. dirs. Glenville YMCA, 1973-76; bd. dirs., treas. Urban League Cleve., 1971-78; mem. adv. council Small Bus. Assn.; bd. dirs. Forest City Hosp. Found., Cleve. State U. Found. Served with AUS, 1950-52. Recipient award bus. excellence Dept. Commerce, 1972; Presdl. award YMCA, 1974; Gov. Ohio award community action, 1973; named Family of Yr., Cleve. Urban League, 1971. Mem. Growth Assn. Cleve. (dir.), NAACP (v.p. Cleve. 1969-78), Ohio Council Retail Mchts. (dir.), Ohio Home Furnishing and Appliance Assn. (pres.). Exec. Order Ohio Commodore. Clubs: Mid-Day, Cleve. Play House, Harvard Bus. Sch., Rotary, Clevelander (Cleve.). Home: 2530 Richmond Rd Beachwood OH 44122 Office: 12435 St Clair Ave Cleveland OH 44108

CROSBY, (ZELMA) JEAN, educator; b. Toledo, Dec. 31, 1929; d. Gifford and Zeola Anna (Killan) Lewis; B.M.E., North Central Coll., Naperville, Ill., 1951; postgrad. Wright State U., 1968-69, U. Cin., 1970-75; M.Ed., Xavier U., 1976; m. Burton LeRoy Crosby, Aug. 30, 1947; children—Steven, Michael, Christina. Tchr., pub. schs., Hillside, Ill., 1951-53, Fulton, Ohio, 1955-56, North Baltimore, Ohio, 1956-57, Weston Ohio, 1958-60, Antwerp, Ohio, 1962-65, Celina and St. Henry, Ohio, 1965-66, Rockford, Ohio, 1966-67, Celina, Ohio, 1967-70, Cin., 1970—. Mem. NEA, Ohio Edn. Assn., Ohio Schs. Counselor Assn. Methodist. Home: 2179 Broadhurst Ave Cincinnati OH 45240 Office: 3310 Compton Rd Cincinnati OH 45239

CROSIER, GLEN CARSON, human resources ofcl.; b. Lafayette, Ind., July 28, 1945; s. George S. and Ruth E. (Reece) C.; student in bus. fin. Ind. U., 1963-66; B.A., Ft. Wayne Bible Coll., 1969; M.A. with honors, St. Francis Coll., 1971; m. Sonia Marie McCormick, Mar. 5, 1971; children—Benjamin, Angele. Personnel mgr. Am. Hoist & Derrick Co., Ft. Wayne, Ind., 1970-71; mgr. corp. employment Lord Corp., Erie, Pa., 1971-74; internat. personnel mgr. J.F. Pritchard & Co., Kansas City, Mo., 1974-77; exec. dir. human resources Midwest Research Inst., Kansas City, 1977—. Named Candidate for Civic Leadership, 1981. Mem. Am. Soc. Personnel Adminstrn. (accredited personnel mgr.), Am. Compensation Assn., Am. Productivity Inst., Personnel Mgmt. Assn. Greater Kansas City (pres. 1979, dir. 1980). Republican. Home: 9334 Mullen Rd Lenexa KS 66215 Office: 425 Volker Blvd Kansas City MO 64110

CROSS, GILBERT HALL, state ofcl.; b. Dahlgren, Ill., Aug. 23, 1919; s. Roland Robert and Isabel (Hunter) C.; B.A., Washington U., St. Louis, 1941; student U. Colo., summers 1937, 38, 39; govt. cert. Queens Coll., 1943; m. Grace Caroline Goodwin, July 20, 1946; 1 dau., Clara. Mem. corp. dept. State of Ill., 1949-56; supr. Ill. Narcotic Rehab., 1958-63; personnel dir. City Water, Light and Power Co., Springfield, Ill., 1963-72; EEO tng. coordinator Ill. Dept. Transp., 1972—. Treas. Sangamon County Community Action Com., 1964-66. Chmn. finance bd. Lincoln Library, Springfield, 1964-67. Served with AUS, 1941-45. Decorated Bronze Star. Mem. Internat. Narcotic Officers Enforcement Assn. (charter), Am. Public Power Assn. (mgmt. com. 1965—), Ill. League Mcpl. Employees, Ill. Profl. Employees, ALA, Ill. Hist. Soc. (life), Ill. Assn. Hwy Engrs. (life), DAV, Am. Legion, VFW. Republican. Mem. Christian Ch. (bd. dirs.). Home: 639 W Vine St Springfield IL 62704 Office: Springfield IL 62764

CROSS, HAROLD ZANE, agronomist; b. Portales, N.Mex., Dec. 25, 1941; s. Guy Edner and Hagabelle (Lawson) C.; B.S. with honors (scholar), N.Mex. State U., 1965, M.S., 1967; Ph.D., U. Mo., 1971; m. Glenda Faye Wilhoit, Nov. 24, 1961; children—Carter Dale, Carson Lee, Curtis Don, Cathryn Faye. Rancher, Elida, N.Mex., 1965-67; grad. research asst. N.Mex. State U., Las Cruces, 1965-67; NDEA fellow U. Mo., Columbia, 1967-71; from asst. prof. to asso. prof. agronomy N.D. State U., Fargo, 1971—, mem. Faculty Senate, 1981—; mem. North Central Corn Breeding Research Com., 1971-81, chmn., 1977-78; crops judge N.D. Winter Show, 1972-81. Mem. Am. Soc. Agronomy, Crop Sci. Soc., N.D. Acad. Sci., Am. Genetic Assn., AAAS, Sigma Xi (chpt. treas. 1979-80, pres.-elect 1980-81), Phi Kappa Phi, Alpha Zeta, Gamma Sigma Delta. Contbr. articles to sci. jours. Developer 7 inbred lines of corn. Home: 2102 7th St N Fargo ND 58102 Office: 329 Walster Hall North Dakota State U Fargo ND 58102

CROSS, PEDER JOHN, bank examiner; b. Anoka, Minn., Feb. 8, 1947; s. G.R. and V.M. Cross; B.A., Gustavus Adolphus Coll., 1969; grad. Am. Bankers Assn. seminar Stonier Grad. Sch. Banking, Rutgers U., 1980. With Fed. Deposit Ins. Corp., 1969—, asst. examiner, examiner, field office supr., 1969-78, rev. examiner, 1979—. Home: 15806 W Oaks Minnetonka MN 55343 Office: 730 2d Ave S Suite 266 Minneapolis MN 55402

CROSS, RAYMOND JOSEPH, JR., chem. co. exec., gas co. mgr.; b. Ithaca, N.Y., July 3, 1935; s. Raymond Joseph and Janet (Cleveland) C.; B.S.M.E., Ga. Inst. Tech., Atlanta, 1958; postgrad. U. Tampa, 1961; M.S. in Indsl. Mgmt., Purdue U., Hammond, Ind., 1972; m. Marguerite Adele Ciani, Nov. 17, 1956; children—Raymond Joseph III, John Alexander, Donald James. With Linde div. Union Carbide Corp., Chgo., 1958—, product mgr., N.Y.C., 1972-74, ops. mgr., Chgo., 1974-76, region mgr. Central U.S., Cleve., 1976-77, Midwest regional mgr., Chgo., 1977—; dir. East Chicago Machine Tool Corp. Mem. tax adv. council Lake County, Ind., 1969-70; mem. adv. council businessmen Congressman Adam Benjamin, 1978—; bd. dirs. ARC, 1972; pres. Griffith United Fund, 1967-68; treas. Lake County Young Reps., 1965-66. Served to capt. U.S. Army, 1958-59. Mem. ASME, Ga. Inst. Tech. Alumni Assn., Purdue U. Alumni Assn. Lake County, Purdue U. Lafayette Alumni Assn. Presbyterian. Author: Guided Missile Propellants, 1959. Office: 120 S Riverside Plaza Chicago IL 60606

CROSS, ROBERT WILLIAM, JR., county ofcl.; b. Portsmouth, Ohio, Mar. 25, 1943; s. Robert William and Nola Marie (Lewis) C.; student, Ohio U., 1961-63, 69-71; m. Susanne Williams, Dec. 31, 1964; children—Robin June, Scott James, Angie Marie, Brandy Christine, Molly Suzanne. Asst. bookkeeping dept. Huntington Nat. Bank, Columbus, Ohio, 1963-64; with Detroit Steel Corp., 1964-78; constrn. bricklayer Local 7, Ashland, Ky., 1975-78; commr. Scioto County, Portsmouth, Ohio, 1979—. Central committeeman, mem. exec. bd. Democratic party, 1978—; chmn. bd. trustees United Way, 1981—; vice chmn. trustees Shawnee State Coll. Devel. Fund, 1978-81. Served with USN, 1966-68. Mem. Nat. Assn. Counties, County Commrs. Assn. Ohio, Nat. Assn. Sports Ofcls., Ohio High Sch. Athletic Basketball Ofcls. Assn., Southeastern Ohio Ofcls. Assn., Ohio Assn. Basketball Ofcls. Roman Catholic. Club: Hidden Hills Golf. Home: 1173 N High St Sciotoville OH 45662 Office: Scioto County Court House Room 104 Portsmouth OH 45662

CROSSLAND, WILLIAM EDWARD, safety engr.; b. Detroit, July 13, 1932; s. Ernest Edward and Clara Gertrude (Davis) C.; B.S. in Safety Engring., U. Ala., 1960; postgrad. U. So. Calif.; m. Helen Charlene Thompson, July 23, 1976. Founder, chmn. bd. Internat. Safety Cons., Inc., 1969-81; dir. safety Handy Andy Corp., San Antonio, 1972-73; safety engr. Royal Globe Ins. Co., 1973-74; dir. safety U.S. Air Force, Oklahoma City, 1974-77; safety and health mgr. Dept. of Labor, Kansas City, Mo., 1977—; tchr. safety engring. Okla. State U.; cons. AF Community Coll.; mem. energy com. Fed. Exec. Bd., 1979—. Vol. Kansas City chpt. ARC. Served with USAF, 1951-72. Decorated AF Commendation Medal with 3 oak leaf clusters, AF Meritorious Service Medal with 2 oak leaf clusters; named Top Civilian Safety Dir. in AF, 1974; registered profl. engr., Calif.; cert. safety profl., Ill.; lic. pvt. pilot; cert. police officer, Tex.; 3d degree black belt jud. instr. Mem. Assn. Fed. Safety and Health Profls. (past pres.), Am. Soc. Safety Engrs., Vets. Safety Internat. (past regional v.p.), Nat. Safety Mgmt. Soc., System Safety Soc., Am. Legion, Baptist. Mem. Rosicrucian Order. Contbr. articles to profl. jours.; composer: Never, 1958; Is It the Same, 1978. Trumpeter, guitarist. Office: 911 Walnut St Kansas City MO 64106

CROUCH, HARLAN EVERETT, med. group adminstr.; b. Freeport, Ill., Aug. 16, 1937; s. Harlan E. and Arina Chloe (Asbury) C.; m. Jane Grylls, Nov. 15, 1958; children—John, Van, Susan. Reporter, Dunn & Bradstreet, Des Moines, Iowa, 1955-59; br. mgr. Fed. Discount Corp., Dubuque, Iowa, 1959-65; credit mgr. John W. Thomas Co., Mpls., 1965; mgr. Employers Service, Inc., Mpls., 1966; clinic mgr. U. Minn. Hosps., Mpls., 1966-69; dir. Chgo. hosp. div. Med. Computer Systems, Inc., Chgo., 1969-73; adminstr. Coleman Clinic, Ltd., Canton, Ill., 1973—. Bd. dirs. Community Mental Health Center, Canton; mayor City of Canton, 1977-81; officer Planning and Zoning Commn.; mem. finance com. Wesley Methodist Ch., Canton; mem. steering com., mem. community affairs com. YWCA. Served with USMCR, 1956-58. Fellow Am. Coll. Clinic Mgrs.; mem. Med. Group Mgmt. Assn., Ill. Med. Group Mgmt. Assn. Republican. Clubs: Toastmasters (winner regional speech contest, 1978, 3d place award internat. speech contest 1978); Rotary (Canton). Home: 263 W Chestnut St Canton IL 61520 Office: Coleman Clinic Ltd 175 S Main St Canton IL 61520

CROVISIER, RICHARD CHARLES, mfg. co. exec.; b. Fort Dodge, Iowa, June 29, 1945; s. Milfred Charles and Mabel Francis (Dunkle) C.; student Fort Dodge Community Coll., 1963-65; m. Constance Rae Scott, Aug. 30, 1980; children—Dawn, Delena. Salesman, Oscar Mayer & Co., Davenport, Iowa, 1968-73; property mgr. shopping center Dial Realty, Omaha, 1973-74; with Chief Industries, Grand Island, Nebr., 1974-77, territory sales mgr., 1974-75, regional sales mgr., 1975-76; sales mgr. Caldwell Mfg. Co., Kearney, Nebr., 1977—. Served with U.S. Army, 1966-67. Mem. Iowa Res. Officers Assn., Fed.

Res. Officers Assn. Lutheran. Home: 1212 E 39 St Kearney NE 68847 Office: Kearney Indsl Tract Kearney NE 68847

CROW, GLENN SHATFORD, printing co. exec.; b. Cleve., May 31, 1925; s. Ralph Earl and Fern Lydia (Shatford) C.; B.A., Mt. Union Coll., 1949; m. Anne Marie Deutschmann, Nov. 26, 1955; 1 son, Keith. Salesman, Ohio Mattress Co., Cleve., 1949-54; chief exec. Mercantile Research Co., Cleve., 1955-70, Wishford Co., Cleve., 1962-69; pres. Auburn Industries, Inc., Cleve., 1969—. Sec., treas. B-R Industries, Inc., Cleve., 1973—. Served to 1st lt. AUS, 1943-46. Mem. Phi Kappa Tau. Home: 2919 Warrington Rd Shaker Heights OH 44120 Office: 1260 W 4th St Cleveland OH 44113

CROW, LAWRENCE VERNON, mfg. co. exec.; b. Wichita, Kans., Apr. 18, 1930; s. Chester Harvard and Daisy Violet (Lyda) C.; B.A., U. Okla., 1956; m. Lois Maurine Noyes, Dec. 31, 1971; children—Terri, Steven, David, Kelly; stepchildren—Tanya, Tracy. With IBM Corp., Wichita, 1957—, officer supr., 1960, adminstrv. ops. mgr., Kansas City, Mo., 1963, adminstrn. mgr., Huntington, W.Va., 1965, Wichita, 1970—. Served with USN, 1947-51. Recipient Pres.'s award as Nat. Adminstrn. Mgr. of Yr., Office Products div. IBM Corp., 1972. Mem. Adminstrv. Mgmt. Soc. (chpt. pres. 1978-79), Friends of Nardin (founder, pres. 1977—), Wichita SER/Jobs for Progress (chmn. 1979-80, bd. dirs. 1977—), Amigos de SER (founder Wichita chpt., pres. 1975-76, 76-77). Christian Ch. Home: 1107 N Terrace St Wichita KS 67208 Office: 302 N Rock Rd Wichita KS 67206

CROWDER, BARBARA NELL, educator; b. Danville, Ill., Nov. 8, 1945; d. Earl and M. Maxine (Campbell) C.; B.S., Ind. U., 1967, M.S., 1971; Ed.D., U. Cin., 1980. Tchr. bus. edn. Knox (Ind.) Community Schs., 1967-70; asso. instr., bus. edn. Ind. U., 1970-71; tchr. bus. edn. Merrillville (Ind.) High Sch., 1971-72; supr., instr. secretarial scis. Ind. Vocat. Tech. Coll., Lafayette, 1972-75; exec. sec. Presbytery of Wabash Valley, United Presbyn. Ch. U.S.A., West Lafayette, Ind., 1975-77; grad. asst. vocat. edn. U. Cin., 1977-79; dir. Ind. Curriculum Materials Center, Ind. State U., Terre Haute, 1979-80; coop. edn. coordinator Park County Program Vocat. Area 29, South Vermillion Sch. Corp., Rockville, Ind., 1980-81; asso. prof. bus. Oakland City (Ind.) Coll., 1981—. Cert. as vocat. dir., in bus. edn., Ind.; cert. profl. sec. Inst. Cert. Secs. Life mem. Am. Vocat. Assn., Ind. Vocat. Assn.; mem. Nat. Bus. Edn. Assn., Ind. Bus. Edn. Assn., Council Vocat. Educators, Nat. Fedn. Bus. and Profl. Women, Wabash Valley Bus. and Profl. Women's Club (past treas.), Profl. Secs. Internat., Ind. U. Alumni Assn. (life), Delta Pi Epsilon, Pi Lambda Theta, Phi Delta Kappa, Kappa Kappa Kappa. Democrat. Methodist. Clubs: Order Eastern Star, Ind. U. Varsity. Home: Rural Route 1 Box 31 Attica IN 47918 Office: Oakland City Coll Oakland City IN 47660

CROWDER, HARRY RICHARD, sales mgr.; b. Valley City, N.D., July 24, 1934; s. Harry Richard and Louise Johanna (Leiseth) C.; B.S.E.E., N.D. State U., 1960; postgrad. Iowa State U., 1960-61, U. Minn., 1962-63; children—Craig, Amy Jo. Design engr. Collins Radio, 1960-62; design engr. aerospace and residential div. Honewell Corp., 1962-70; regional sales mgr. Rogers Corp., Mpls., 1970—. Mem. Bd. Appeals, Fridley, Minn., 1972-75; mem. Republican Nat. Com., 1978—. Served with U.S. Army, 1954-56. Registered profl. engr., Minn. Lutheran. Club: Lion. Home: 17 NE 66 1/2 Way Fridley MN 55432 Office: PO Box 32087 Fridley MN 55432

CROWE, CLIFFORD HENRY, JR., retail store exec.; b. Chgo., Mar. 12, 1921; s. Clifford Henry and Norine (Wohlenberg) C.; B.S. in Commerce, State U. Iowa, 1942; M.B.A., Harvard U., 1947; m. Ina Bryson, June 11, 1965; 1 son, Clifford Henry III. Trainee, Gen. Electric Co., 1947-49; with J.C. Penney Co., Inc., 1949—, store mgr., Akron, Ohio, 1957-61, Valley Stream, N.Y., 1961-64, Kokomo, Ind., 1964—. Pres. Grisson AFB Community Council, 1974; mem. Mayor's Community Com. on Drug Abuse, 1974; chmn. adv. bd. Kokomo Center Distbv. Edn. Com.; bd. dirs. Kokomo YMCA, Credit Bur. Kokomo, Ind. Retail Council; bd. dirs. Howard Community Hosp. Found., 1975—, pres., 1978; mem. program adv. com. Ind. U., Kokomo. Served to lt. col USAAF, 1942-45. Decorated Bronze Star; Croix de Guerre (France). Mem. Ind. C. of C., Kokomo Area C. of C. (pres. 1971). Clubs: Elks, Rotary (dir. 1974-76, pres. 1976), Kokomo Country (dir.) (Kokomo). Home: 902 Arundel Ct Kokomo IN 46901 Office: J C Penney Co 1718 E Boulevard Kokomo IN 46901

CROWE, ROBERT LEE, sch. adminstr.; b. Macomb, Ill., Aug. 14, 1937; s. Edward Charles and Helen Francis (Purdy) C.; B.S., Western Ill. U., 1959; M.S., St. Louis U., 1967; Ed.D., Ind. U., 1972; m. Sandra Rae Haring, Aug. 12, 1960; children—Cassandra, Tracy, Robbie, David. Tchr., Macomb Ill., 1959-60, 61-63, Ferguson, Mo., 1960-61; tchr. Parkway Sch. Dist., Chesterfield, Mo., 1963-68, dir. personnel, 1968-72, asst. supt., 1972-75; supt. Jacksonville (Ill.) Sch. Dist., 1975—; lectr. U. Mo., St. Louis, N.E. Mo. U., MacPherson Coll.; cons. in field. Commr. Elks Little League Baseball, Jacksonville; bd. dirs. Jr. Achievement, Jacksonville, Four Rivers Spl. Edn. Dist., West Central Ill., Western Ill. U. Found. Nat. Endowment for Humanities fellow, 1979. Mem. Am. Assn. Sch. Adminstrs., Ill. Assn. Supervision and Curriculum Devel., Ill. Assn. Sch. Adminstrs., Jacksonville C. of C. (dir. 1977-80), Phi Delta Kappa. Clubs: Kiwanis, Elks. Author: The Fastest Trip in the History of Turtle, 1975; Clyde Monster, 1976; Tyler Toad and the Thunder, 1980. Contbr. articles to profl. jours. Home: 4 Sunnydale St Jacksonville IL 62650 Office: 1021 Lincoln St Jacksonville IL 62650

CROWELL, EDWARD PRINCE, assn. exec.; b. Chillicothe, Ohio, Sept. 17, 1926; s. Harrison P. and Jeannette (Sturtevant) C.; student U. Maine, 1946-48; D.O., Kirksville (Mo.) Coll. Osteopathy and Surgery, 1952; m. Elaine Kittelberger, Apr. 14, 1956. Intern Waterville (Maine) Osteo. Hosp., 1952-53; chief resident physician hosps. Phila. Coll. Osteo. Medicine, 1953-56; sr. attending internist Waterville Osteo. Hosp., 1956-63, chmn. dept. medicine, med. dir., 1958-63; asst. exec. dir. Am. Osteo. Assn., Chgo., 1964-66, asso. exec. dir., 1966-68, exec. dir., 1968—, bur. convs., 1968—, chmn. dept. bus. affairs, 1968—. Mem. adv. council Maine Hosp. Constrn. Com., 1959-64. Served with USNR, 1944-46. Diplomate Am. Osteo. Bd. Internal Medicine. Fellow Am. Coll. Osteo. Internists. Home: 3245 Prestwick Ln Northbrook IL 60062 Office: 212 E Ohio St Chicago IL 60611

CROWLEY, FREDERICK ALLISON, ophthalmologist; b. Des Moines, Dec. 16, 1911; s. Daniel F. and Rosemary Catherine (Langdon) C.; B.A., U. Iowa, 1933, M.D., 1937; m. Mildred Kocher, Apr. 5, 1948. Intern, Rochester (N.Y.) Gen. Hosp., 1937-39; resident in surgery Bklyn. Eye and Ear Hosp., 1939-41; surgeon Gailey Eye Clinic, dept. ophthalmology Mennonite Hosp., Bloomington, Ill., 1946-78, surgeon, 1978—. Bd. dirs. Watson Gailey Eye Found., Main Center Corp. Served to maj. U.S. Army, 1942-46. Decorated Bronze Star. Diplomate Am. Bd. Ophthalmology. Fellow A.C.S., Internat. Coll. Surgeons; mem. AMA, Ill. Med. Assn. Home: 117 Bellemont Rd Bloomington IL 61701 Office: Gailey Eye Clinic Bloomington IL 61701

CROWLEY, JOSEPH MICHAEL, elec. engr., educator; b. Phila., Sept. 9, 1940; s. Joseph Edward and Mary Veronica (McCall) C.; B.S., M.I.T., 1962, M.S., 1963, Ph.D., 1965; m. Barbara Ann Sauerwald, June 20, 1963; children—Joseph W., Kevin, James, Michael, Daniel. Vis. scientist Max Planck Inst., Goettingen, W. Ger., 1965-66; asst. prof. elec. engring., U. Ill., Urbana, 1966-69, asso. prof., 1969-78, prof., dir. Applied Electrostats. Research Lab., 1978—; pres. JMC Inc., 1981—; cons. to several corps. Pres., Champaign-Urbana Bd. Cath. Edn., 1978-80. Gen. Motors scholar, 1958-62; AEC fellow, 1962-65; NATO fellow, 1965-66. Mem. IEEE (sr.), Electrostats. Soc. Am., Am. Phys. Soc., Soc. Inf. Display, Mensa. Roman Catholic. Contbr. articles to profl. jours.; patentee ink jet printers. Home: 506 S Elm St Champaign IL 61820 Office: Dept Elec Engring U Ill Urbana IL 61801

CROWLEY, WILLIAM JAMES, pub. utility exec.; b. Joliet, Ill., Oct. 7, 1905; s. William James and Hildegarde (Thompson) C.; B.S.C. cum laude, Northwestern U., 1936, M.B.A., 1946; J.D., DePaul U., 1957; LL.M., John Marshall Law Sch., 1963; m. Claire Frances Gierman, Aug. 30, 1930; children—William James, Susan Claire Crowley Crosby, Rowe Ellen Crowley Moore. With Public Service of No. Ill., 1926-53, Commonwealth Edison Co., 1953-54; comptroller No. Ill. Gas Co., 1954-56, v.p., comptroller, 1956-63, v.p. fin., comptroller, 1963-64, exec. v.p. fin., 1964-68, exec. v.p. fin. and corp. services, 1968-70, also dir.; admitted to Ill. bar, 1957; former chmn. Postal Rate Commn.; dir. Aurora Nat. Bank; dir., chmn., chief exec. officer South Suburban Fed. Savs. & Loan Assn., Harvey, Ill.; lectr. Northwestern U., 1936-51. Mem. Revenue Study Com. State Ill.; bd. dirs. Ill. Com. Constl. Conv., Hosp. Planning Council Met. Chgo.; trustee Ill. Council Econ. Edn., Ingalls Meml. Hosp., Harvey. C.P.A., Ill. Mem. Am., Fed., D.C., Chgo. bar assns., Ill. C. of C. (pres., dir.), Fin. Execs. Inst., Tax Inst. Am., Taxpayers Fedn. Ill., Civic Fedn. Clubs: Mid-Day, Comml., Econ. (Chgo.); Flossmoor Country. Home: 18456 Perth Ave Homewood IL 60430

CROYE, JAMES HOLT, educator; b. Bluefield, W.Va., Jan. 18, 1941; s. Leroy and Pansy Bethel (Holt) C.; B.S., Rio Grande Coll., 1966; postgrad. public health adminstrn. U. Toledo; m. Jeanne Lerouix, Nov. 11, 1975. Tchr., Miami, 1967-68; tchr., dir. activities Stow (Ohio) City Schs., 1968-72; dir. activity therapy inst., Toledo Mental Health Center, 1972-73, program coordinator geriatric center, 1973-74, tng. coordinator geriatric center, 1974-77, dir. human resource devel. dept., 1977-79; dir. med. edn. Flower Hosp., Sylvania, Ohio, 1979—; bd. dirs. Alternate Learning Center, Lucas County Schs., 1978-79, continuing edn. Sylvania Schs., 1979-81. Chmn. alumni fund raising com. Rio Grande Coll., 1979—. Recipient Life Sav. award ARC, 1965. Mem. Assn. Hosp. Med. Edn., Alliance Continuing Med. Edn., Ohio Med. Assn. (site surveyor), Ohio Hosp. Assn., ASTD. Republican. Episcopalian. Home: 3216 Royton Rd Toledo OH 43614 Office: 5200 Harroun Rd Sylvania OH 43560

CRUICKSHANKS, BRYAN, eye surgeon; b. Northumberland, Eng., Oct. 11, 1935; s. William Blackwood and Jessie McLachlan (Brown) C.; M.B., B.S., U. Durham, 1961; m. Mary Watson, May 31, 1962; children—Lindsey Fiona, Giles Fraser. Intern, Royal Victoria Infirmary, Newcastle upon Tyne, Eng., 1961-62; resident Royal Infirmary of Edinburgh (Scotland), 1962-66; sr. registrar Birmingham and Midland Eye Hosp., Eng., 1967-70; tutor ophthalmology U. Birmingham, England, 1967-70; practice medicine specializing in eye surgery, Sarnia, Ont., Can., 1971—; chief eye dept. Sarnia Gen. Hosp.; courtesy staff St. Joseph's Hosp., Sarnia. Served with RAF, 1954-56. Diplomate Am. Bd. Ophthalmology. Fellow A.C.S., Royal Coll. Surgeons (Can.), Royal Coll. Surgeons (Eng.), Royal Coll. Surgeons (Edinburgh), Soc. Eye Surgeons; mem. Internat. Intraocular Implant Club, Am. Intraocular Implant Soc. (founding mem.). Office: 160 Essex Sarnia ON N7T 4R7 Canada

CRUMBAUGH, LEE FORREST, mag. editor; b. Chgo., Dec. 22, 1947; s. John Howard and Edna Elizabeth C.; student Colo. State U., 1965-67; B.S. in Journalism, U. Ill., 1969; M.B.A., U. Chgo., 1971; m. Sherrill Hawthorne Monroe, June 21, 1969; children—Andrew Monroe, Carroll Virginia. Reporter, Hinsdale (Ill.) Doings, 1967; editorial intern Chgo. Daily News, 1968; public relations intern Chgo. Title and Trust Co., 1969; editorial intern U.S. League Savs. Assns., Chgo., 1970; research analyst Savs. and Loan News, 1971-72; mktg. dir., 1972-80, editor, 1980—; instr. journalism George Williams Coll., Downers Grove, Ill. Chmn., Glen Ellyn (Ill.) Fine Arts Festival, 1974, 76; bd. dirs. Housing Alternatives for Glen Ellyn, 1980—; coordinator DuPage County John Anderson Presdl. Primary campaign, 1979-80; bd. dirs. United Way Glen Ellyn, 1978-80, mem. membership services com. United Way Suburban Chgo., 1980—; chmn. Village of Glen Ellyn Environ. Protection Commn., 1979-81. Mem. Am. Mktg. Assn., Sigma Delta Chi. Republican. Mem. United Ch. of Christ. Club: University (Chgo.). Office: 111 E Wacker Dr Chicago IL 60601*

CRUMMETT, WARREN B., chem. co. exec., scientist; b. Moyers, W. Va., Apr. 4, 1922; s. Elmer and Virginia Maude (Smith) C.; B.A., Bridgewater Coll., 1943; Ph.D., Ohio State U., 1951; m. Elizabeth Anne Stathers, Feb. 28, 1948; children—Allan Warren, Daniel David. Chemist, Solvay Process Co., Hopewell, Va., 1943-46; with Dow Chem. Co., Midland, Mich., 1951—, lab. tech. mgr., 1971—; mem. environ. measurements adv. com. EPA, 1976-78. Mem. "Com. of 100" to establish Delta Coll., 1953-56; chmn. curriculum com. Re-look at Midland Schs., 1958; chmn. Race Horse Industry Task Force, Mich. Dept. Agr., 1980; mem. panel Nat. Research Council Can., 1980—. Recipient H.H. Dow Gold medal, 1980. Fellow Am. Inst. Chemists; mem. Am. Chem. Soc. (subcom. on environ. analytical chemistry 1978-80), Research Soc. Am., AAAS, N.Y. Acad. Sci. Republican. Mem. editorial adv. bd. Analytical Chemistry, 1974-76. Home: 808 Crescent Dr Midland MI 48640 Office: 574 Bldg Dow Chem Co Midland MI 48640

CRUTHERS, LARRY RANDALL, parasitologist; b. Kenosha, Wis., Mar. 15, 1945; s. Harold Beale and Irene C.; B.S., Wis. State U., 1967; M.S., Kans. State U., 1971, Ph.D., 1973; m. Susan Margaret Melchert, July 15, 1967; children—Carrie Lyn, Polly Jane. Instr. biology Kans. State U., Manhattan, 1970-73; research investigator E.R. Squibb & Sons, Inc., Three Bridges, N.J., 1974-76, sr. research investigator, 1977-80; sr. parasitologist Diamond Shamrock Corp., Painesville, Ohio, 1980—. Bd. dirs. Hunterdon County (N.J.) Soc. for Prevention of Cruelty to Animals, 1978-80. Mem. Am. Soc. Parasitology, Helminthol. Soc. Washington, Conf. Research Workers in Animal Diseases, N.J. Soc. Parasitology (sec.-treas. 1976-79, pres. 1980), Am. Assn. Vet. Parasitology, Am. Heartworm Soc., Sigma Xi. Club: Kiwanis (dir. 1978). Home: 10268 Cherry Hill Dr Painesville OH 44077 Office: Diamond Shamrock Corp PO Box 348 Painesville OH 44077

CRUZ-PEGUERO, FRANCISCO GASPAR, psychiatrist; b. Bani, Dominican Republic, Jan. 7, 1946; s. Francisco E. and Patria E. (Peguero) Cruz; M.D., U. Mex., 1972; m. Elba E. Santana, Aug. 21, 1971; children—F. Uziel, Isbel E. Intern, Auxilio Mutuo Hosp., San Juan, P.R., 1972-73; resident in psychiatry U. South Fla., 1973-74, Menninger Sch. Psychiatry, 1974-76; staff psychiatrist VA Hosp., Topeka, 1976—, clin. coordinator, bldg. 4, 1979—; mem. faculty Menninger Sch. Psychiatry, Topeka, 1978—, clin. supr., 1978—. Diplomate Am. Bd. Psychiatry and Neurology. Home: 2518 Ashworth Pl Topeka KS 66614

CUBBEDGE, ROBERT ALLEN, mfr.'s agt. co. exec.; b. Toledo, Aug. 4, 1926; s. Robert Allen Kimberley and Marion Alice (Mulholland) C.; B.S. in Indsl. Engring., U. Ala., 1949; m. Marilyn Joan Barker, Nov. 29, 1975; children—Keith, Oticca, Kimberley, Tatjania, Kenneth, Arthur, Donald. Indsl. engr., sales engr. Acklin Stamping div. Tecumseh Products, Toledo, 1949-53; sales engr. Leake Stamping & Engring. Co., Monroe, Mich., 1953-55; sales engr., gen. sales mgr. Kiemle-Hankins Co., Toledo, 1955-71; pres. Cubbedge Controls, Inc., Toledo, 1971—. Chmn. Eagle scout bd. rev. Boy Scouts Am., Toledo, 1966-68; councilman Hope Lutheran Ch., Toledo, 1971-77; chmn. bd. Toledo YMCA Storer Camps, 1975-76. Served with USAF, 1944-45. Mem. Mfrs. Agts. Nat. Assn., IEEE, Instrument Soc. Am., Am. Inst. Indsl. Engrs. (past pres. Toledo chpt.), Toledo C. of C., Nat. Fedn. Ind. Bus., Tech. Soc. Toledo (pres. 1980-81). Clubs: Rotary, Sylvania Country, Toledo Racquet. Home: 4412 Bromley Dr Toledo OH 43623 Office: 5650 W Central Ave Toledo OH 43615

CUCCO, ULISSE P., obstetrician and gynecologist; b. Bklyn., Aug. 19, 1929; s. Charles and Elvira (Garofalo) C.; B.S. cum laude, L.I. U., 1950; M.D., Loyola U., Chgo., 1954; m. Antoinette DeMarco, Aug. 31, 1952; children—Carl, Richard, Antoinette Marie, Michael, Frank, James. Intern, Nassau County Hosp., Hempstead, N.Y., 1954-55; resident in obstetrics and gynecology Lewis Meml. Mercy Hosp., Chgo., 1955-58; practice medicine specializing in obstetrics and gynecology, Mt. Prospect, Ill., 1960—; mem. staff Resurrection Hosp., Chgo., N.W. Community Hosp., Arlington Heights, Ill.; past pres. med. staff, past chmn. dept. obstetrics and gynecology Holy Family Hosp., Des Plaines, Ill.; clin. asst. prof. Stritch Sch. Medicine, Loyola U. Served to capt. M.C., USAF, 1958-60. Diplomate Am. Bd. Obstetrics and Gynecology. Mem. AMA, Am. Coll. Obstetricians and Gynecologists, A.C.S., Am. Fertility Soc., AAAS, Central Assn. Obstetrics and Gynecology, N.Y. Acad. Scis., Ill. Med. Soc., Chgo. Med. Soc., Chgo. Gynecol. Soc., Chgo. Inst. Medicine. Roman Catholic. Club: Sunset Ridge Country. Contbr. med. jours. Office: 221 W Prospect Ave Mt Prospect IL 60056

CULLAN, SAMUEL K., state legislator; b. Hemingford, Nebr., June 20, 1954; s. Harry T. and Lorene C.; grad. Mcht. Marine Acad., 1976; postgrad. Creighton U., 1979. Farmer, engr.; mem. Nebr. Legislature, 1976—. Mem. Soc. Naval Architects and Marine Engrs., Jaycees. Roman Catholic. Club: KC. Home: Hemingford NE *

CULLEN, MAX O'RELL, meat mdsg. cons., author; b. Belle Rive, Ill., Jan. 31, 1903; s. Frank W. and Oma (Smith) C.; student schs., La Grande, Oreg.; m. Margaret Hirons, June 18, 1931; children—Patricia Lucile Cullen Ratcliff, Susan Elizabeth Cullen Cartland. Meat cutter, market mgr., equipment salesman, 1915-28; meat specialist Nat. Live Stock and Meat Bd., 1929-31, dir. dept. meat mdsg., lectr./demonstrator, 1932-53, asst. gen. mgr., 1954-62; cons. meat mdsg., 1963—; pres. Meat Marketing, 1963-65, Mealtime Masterpieces, 1966-73; pres., owner D.B.A. Cullen Enterprises, 1974—; author, collaborator various books, charts, manuals dealing with meat. Served with N.G., 1922-28. Recipient cert. of appreciation Quartermaster Subsistence Research and Devel. Lab., 1946, Am. Meat Sci. award, 1964. Mem. Am. Meat Sci. Assn. (life), Amalgamated Meat Cutters and Butcher Workmen (mem.-at-large). Republican. Methodist. Club: Men's of Plymouth Pl. Retirement Center. Appeared three MGM short features, 1940-41; devel. TV meat programs seen nationally, 1950. Home: 112 Brewster Ln La Grange Park IL 60525 Office: 23 Calendar Ct La Grange IL 60525

CULLEN, TIMOTHY F., state senator; b. Janesville, Wis., Feb. 25, 1944; B.S., U. Wis., Whitewater, 1966; postgrad. No. Ill. U., 1967. Mem. Janesville city council, 1970-71. Formerly Ombudsman staff of Congressman Les Aspin, 1971-74; mem. Wis. Senate, 1974—. Former bd. dirs. Big Bros.; Bd. dirs. YMCA, Fairfield Grange, 1981—. Office: Room 12 South State Capitol Madison WI 53702

CULLEN, WILLIAM JOSEPH, elec. contracting co. exec.; b. Chgo., Nov. 7, 1929; s. Philip Francis and Catherine (Giroux) C.; grad. Washburne Trade Sch.; m. Mary Ann Lucas, Jan. 6, 1951; children—Mary Louise, William Joseph, Margaret, Kathleen, James. Electrician, Calumet Electric Co., Chgo., 1949-52, 1954-55; estimator John W. Breslin Elec. Co., Chgo., 1955-60; pres. Cullen Electric Co., Chgo., 1960—; pres. Arrow Ill. Trucking Co.; dir. East Side Bank & Trust Co.; mem. Chgo. Elec. Commn., 1980—. Active St. Cajetan's Holy Name Soc. Served with USMC, 1952-54; Korea. Recipient Gold Key Award De LaSalle High Sch. Alumni, 1976. Mem. Nat. Elec. Contractors Assn., De LaSalle Alumni Assn. (v.p. 1973-74). Democrat. Roman Catholic. Clubs: K.C., Ridge Country. Home: 2142 W 115th St Chicago IL 60643 Office: 9534 S Torrence Ave Chicago IL 60617

CULLERTON, JOHN JAMES, state legislator; b. Chgo., Oct. 28, 1948; s. John James and Mary Patricia (Tyrrell) C.; B.A., Loyola U., Chgo., 1970, J.D., 1974; m. Pam Wilson, Sept. 8, 1979; 1 dau., Maggie. Admitted to Ill. bar, 1974; atty. Cook County Office Public Defender, 1974-79; mem. Ill. Ho. of Reps. from 12th Dist., 1979—. Del. Democratic Nat. Conv., 1976. Mem. Ill. N.G., 1970-76. Mem. Am. Bar Assn., Ill. Bar Assn., Chgo. Bar Assn. Roman Catholic. Office: 111 W Washington Ave Chicago IL 60602

CULLEY, JOHN BRITT, real estate co. exec.; b. Augusta, Ga., Oct. 29, 1919; s. Fenton Bayard and Emily Britt C.; student Evansville (Ind.) Coll. 1938-39; grad. Lockyear's Bus. Coll., Evansville; m. Mary Parker Nov. 4, 1944; children—John Britt, Mary Gail. Pres., Terminal Warehouse Co. Inc., Evansville, 1980—; gen. mgr. Ingle St. Warehouse Co., Evansville, 1945-76; partner, mgr. M. & J. Co., Evansville, 1958—; owner, mgr. Culley Realty Co., Evansville, 1966—. Vice pres. Community Chest, Evansville; a founder Evansville United Fund; sr. warden St. Pauls Episcopal Ch., Evansville; pres. Evansville Heart Assn; pres. Vanderburgh County Tb Assn. Licensed real estate broker, Ind. Mem. Nat., Ind. assns. realtors, Ind. Warehousemens Assn. (sec.-treas.). Clubs: Kiwanis (past pres.), Evansville Country (past v.p., bd. dirs.), Elks (past exalted ruler), Petroleum. Home: 2334 E Chandler Ave Evansville IN 47714 Office: Suite 100 Executive Park E 101 Plaza Blvd Evansville IN 47715

CULLINAN, PATRICK JOSEPH, greeting card co. exec.; b. Chgo., Mar. 26, 1931; s. Daniel A. and Kathleen S. (Sullivan) C.; B.S., John Carroll U., 1953; m. Mariwin M. Mackey, June 20, 1953; children—Patrick J., Michael J., Daniel C., Elizabeth M., Katherine W. With Hallmark Cards, Kansas City, Mo., 1955—, nat. mgr. dept stores, 1974-76, central div. dept. store mgr., 1976-78, v.p. dept. stores sales, 1978-79, v.p. market devel., 1979-81, v.p. Ambassador cards subs., 1981—. Served with U.S. Army, 1953-55. Mem. Advt. Club Kansas City, Sales and Mktg. Club. Office: Hallmark Cards 25th and McGee Sts Kansas City MO 64108

CULMANN, LOUIS CHARLES, ins. co. exec., real estate broker; b. Indpls., Oct. 13, 1918; s. Louis Jacob and Mamie Katherine (Thomas) C.; B.B.A., In. U., 1941; m. Eulala Joy Miller, Feb. 8, 1943; 1 dau., Pamela Jo. With pension, group, acturial dept. Lincoln Nat. Life, Fort Wayne, Ind., 1946-54; gen. agt. Occidental Life Ins. Co. of Calif., Ft. Wayne, 1955—; partner Loos Ins. Gen. Lines Agy., Ft. Wayne, 1956-78; partner ins. and risk mgmt. Gen. Lines Agy., Ft.

Wayne, 1978—; real estate broker Century 21 Wayne Kruse, Ft. Wayne, 1979—; dir. banking, leasing and real estate mgmt. PAC Fin. Corp. 1973—; dir. Med. & Dental Inc. Mem. Govs. Ins. Com. of Ind., 1958-62; bd. dirs. Lake Luther Camp Inc., Luth. Social Services, Inc.; treas. Allen County Democratic Central Com., 1958-64. Served to maj. U.S. Army, 1941-46, maj. Res. ret. Decorated Bronze Star. Mem. Nat. Assn. Life Underwriters, Internat. Accountants Soc. (life), Ind. U. Alumni Assn. (past pres. Northeast Ind.), Am. Legion, VFW (past comdr.), Res. Officers Assn., Acacia, Alpha Kappa Psi. Lutheran. Clubs: Gideons, Press, Masons. Office: 2118 Inwood Dr Room 114 Fort Wayne IN 46815

CUMMING, JOHN RONALD, library adminstr.; b. Shrewsbury, Mass., Sept. 24, 1915; s. George Hosmer and Isabel Mabel (MacGilvray) C.; B.A., Eastern Mich. U., 1940; M.A., U. Mich., 1945; m. Audrey Marie Severence, Oct. 7, 1939; children—Robert Hugh, John. Tchr., adminstr. Detroit Pub. Schs., 1945-61; dir. Clarke Hist. Library, Central Mich. U., Mt. Pleasant, 1961—; cons. on rare books and manuscripts. Mem. Manuscript Soc., Printing Hist. Soc., Am. Printing Hist. Assn., N. Am. Soc. Sport History, Mich. Hist. Soc. Author: A Guide for the Writing of Local History, 1974; Little Jake of Saginaw, 1978; Runners and Walkers, A Nineteenth Century Sports Chronicle, 1981. Home: 465 Hiawatha Dr Mount Pleasant MI 48858 Office: Clarke Hist Library Central Mich U Mount Pleasant MI 48859

CUMMINGS, JAMES C., JR., polit. orgn. exec.; b. Indpls., Sept. 22, 1929; s. James C. and Lertha Lee (Jarrett) C.; B.S. in Bus. Adminstrn., Ind. Central U.; m. Norma Elaine Lewis, Mar. 30, 1951; children—Cynthia, James C., Cecilia, Ronald, Claudia. Reporter, photographer, then editor Indpls. Recorder, 1948-56; owner newspaper Indpls. Voice, 1957-59; property mgr. Village Mgmt. Co., Indpls., 1960-66; public relations dir. chief Ops. Bd. Fundamental Edn., 1966-70; chmn. Nat. Black Republican Council, 1976—; mem. exec. com. Rep. Nat. Com.; cons. in field. Served with AUS, 1951-53. Recipient various civic and service awards. Mem. Public Relations Soc. Am., Nat. Bus. League, NAACP. Baptist. Office: 150 W Market St Indianapolis IN 46204*

CUMMINGS, LARRY LEE, educator; b. Indpls., Oct. 28, 1937; s. Garland R. and Lillian P. (Smith) C.; A.B. summa cum laude, Wabash Coll., 1959; postgrad. (Woodrow Wilson fellow) U. Calif., Berkeley, 1959-60; M.B.A., Ind. U., 1961, D. Bus. Adminstrn. (Ford Found. fellow, Richard D. Irwin Dissertation fellow), 1964; children—Lee Anne, Glenn Nelson. Asst. prof. Sch. of Bus., Ind. U., Bloomington, 1964-67, asso. prof., 1967; asso. vis. prof. Columbia, N.Y.C., 1967-68; asso. prof. organizational behavior U. Wis., Madison, 1968-70, prof. Grad. Sch. Bus. and Indsl. Relations Inst., 1970-81, Slichter research prof., 1979-81, Romnes fellow, asso. dean Grad. Sch., 1975-81, lectr. dept. of psychology, 1971-81; J.L. Kellogg disting. research prof. Kellogg Grad. Sch. Mgmt., Northwestern U., Evanston, Ill., 1981—; vis. prof. U. B.C., Can., 1971-72; cons. Eli Lilly and Co., Eli Lilly Internat. in London, Bundy Corp., Samsonite Corp., Touché, Ross, Bailey & Smart, Inc., World U., San Juan, P.R.; research proposal reviewer, Can. Council, 1971-74. Bd. dirs. Center for the Study of Organizational Performance, Madison. Recipient McKinsey Found. Mgmt. Research award, 1970. Ford Found. Sr. Research fellow, 1969-70; Richardson Found. Research grantee, 1969. Fellow Acad. of Mgmt. (mem. publs. planning com. 1973-74, v.p. 1978-79), Am. Psychol. Assn. (mem. sci. affiars com. div. 14 1973-76); mem. Midwestern Psychol. Assn., Am. Sociol. Assn., Am. Soc. Personnel Adminstrn. (com. chmn. research com. 1969-70), Soc. Personnel Adminstrn., Indsl. Relations Research Assn., Sigma Xi, Phi Beta Kappa, Beta Gamma Sigma, Sigma Iota Epsilon, Tau Kappa Alpha, Delta Phi Alpha. Author: (with W.E. Scott) Readings in Organizational Behavior and Human Performance, 1969, 2d edit., 1973; (with F.A. Shull and A.L. Delbecq) Organizational Decision Making, 1970; (with D.P. Schwab) Performance in Organizations, 1973; (with R.B. Durham) Introduction to Organizational Behavior, 1980; (with D.L. Harnett) Bargaining Behavior: An International Study, 1980; (with B.M. Staw) Research in Organizational Behavior, Vol. II, 1980, Vol. III, 1981, Vol. IV, 1982; cons. editor Richard D. Irwin Series in Mgmt. and Behavioral Sci., 1972—; editor Acad. Mgmt. Jour., 1975-78; asso. editor Decision Scis., 1972—; mem. editorial bd. Organization and Adminstrv. Scis., 1973-78. Contbr. numerous research articles on organizational psychology and personnel mgmt. to profl. jours. Office: Kellogg Grad Sch Mgmt Northwestern U Evanston IL 60201

CUMMINGS, LARRY LEE, mgmt. specialist, educator; b. Indpls., Oct. 28, 1937; s. Garland R. and Lillian P. (Smith) C.; A.B. summa cum laude, Wabash Coll., 1959; M.B.A. (Woodrow Wilson fellow), Ind. U., 1961, D.B.A. (Ford Found. fellow), 1964; m. Suzanne Jay, June 21, 1959; children—Lee Anne, Glenn Nelson. Asst. prof. Grad. Sch. Bus., Ind. U., Bloomington, 1964-67, asso. prof., 1967; vis. asso. prof. Grad. Sch. Bus., Columbia U., N.Y.C., 1967-68; asso. prof. Grad. Sch. Bus., U. Wis., Madison, 1968-70, prof., 1970-81, lectr. dept. psychology, 1970-81, Donald C. Slichter research prof., 1980-81, H.I. Romnes faculty fellow, 1975-81, asso. dean social scis. Grad. Sch., 1975-78; Ford Found. research fellow Brussels, Belgium, 1969-70; vis. prof. faculty of bus. adminstrn. and commerce U. B.C., Vancouver, Can., 1971-72; vis. prof. Kellogg Grad. Sch. Mgmt., Northwestern U., Evanston, Ill., 1979-80, Kellogg prof. organizational behavior, 1981—; research proposal reviewer Can. Council, 1971-74, NSF, 1977—; cons. Eli Lilly & Co., 1965—, Eli Lilly Internat., London, 1970—, Bundy Corp., 1973—, Moore Bus. Forms, Inc., 1973—, Touche, Ross, Bailey and Smart, N.Y.C., 1968—; external examiner in organizational behavior U. Bradford, Eng., 1977-78; cons. editor Irwin Series in Mgmt. and Behavioral Scis., 1972—; external examiner in organizational theory U. W. Indies, Kingston, Jamaica, 1971-75. Recipient McKinsey Found. Mgmt. Research Design award, 1969; Beta Gamma Sigma Disting. scholar, 1979-80. Fellow Am. Psychol. Assn., Acad. Mgmt. (bd. govs. 1976—, editor 1976-78, pres. 1980-81), Am. Inst. for Decision Scis. (exec. bd. 1976-78, v.p. 1976-78); mem. Soc. Personnel Adminstrn., Am. Sociol. Assn., Midwestern Psychol. Assn., Indsl. Relations Research Assn., Phi Beta Kappa, Sigma Xi, Tau Kappa Alpha, Delta Phi Alpha, Sigma Iota Epsilon. Author: (with F.A. Shull and A.L. Delbecq) Organizational Decision Making, 1970; (with D.P. Schwab) Performance in Organization, 1973; (with D.L. Harnett) Bargaining Behavior: An International Study, 1980; (with R. Dunham) Introduction to Organizational Behavior, 1980; co-editor Ency. of Profl. Mgmt., 1978, Readings in Organizational Behavior and Human Performance, 1969, Research in Organizational Behavior, vols. II, III, 1980, 81; editorial bd. Organization and Adminstrv. Scis., 1974—, Organizational Behavior Teaching Jour., 1977—. Home: 2622 Waunona Way Madison WI 53713 Office: Kellogg Grad Sch Management Northwestern Univ Evanston IL 60201

CUMMINGS, OLIVER WILLIAM, research cons.; b. Cairo, Ill., Sept. 2, 1946; s. William Lawrence and Nellie Marie (Kerr) C.; B.A., So. Ill. U., 1968, M.S., 1969, Ph.D. (fellow), 1972; m. Corenna Craig Dautlick. Intern dept. psychology and research A.L. Bowen Children's Center, Harrisburg, Ill., 1970; instr. So. Ill. U., Carbondale, 1972; test service coordinator Midwest, Houghton Mifflin Co., Geneva, Ill., 1972-76, sr. editor test dept., Iowa City, Iowa, 1976-78; research cons. Grant Wood Area Edn. Agy., 1978-81; sr. evaluation specialist Arthur Andersen & Co., St. Charles, Ill., 1981—. Mem. Am. Personnel and Guidance Assn., Nat. Council Measurement in Edn., Assn. Measurement and Evaluation in Guidance (research award 1981), NEA, Iowa Edn. Assn., Grant Wood Edn. Assn. (pres. 1980-81), Phi Delta Kappa. Baptist. Contbr. articles to profl. jours. Home: PO Box 2022 Iowa City IA 52244 Office: 1405 N 5th Ave Saint Charles IL 60174

CUMMINS, EVELYN FREEMAN, social agy. exec.; b. Beatrice, Nebr., Mar. 24, 1904; d. John Allen and Irene (Townsend) Freeman; student Nebr. Wesleyan, 1920-23; B.A., U. Nebr., 1928; postgrad. U. Chgo., 1934-36, 41; M.S., Columbia, 1946; m. Paul Otto Cummins, Oct. 8, 1927 (dec. Sept. 1943); 1 dau., Beverly Anne (Mrs. Cummins Spangler). Tchr. rural Gage County, Nebr., 1921-22, Wilber, Nebr., 1923-25, Lincoln, Nebr., 1925-27; sch. social worker Lincoln, 1930-36; supr. Fla. Dept. Pub. Welfare, Orlando, 1936-42, dist. dir., 1942-45; dir. Nebr. Gov.'s Com. to Study Services to Blind, Lincoln, 1946-47; field rep. Fla. Dept. Pub. Welfare, Jacksonville, 1948-51, appeals officer, 1950-51; exec. dir. Community Council Oklahoma City Area, 1952-61; exec. dir. spl. projects Chgo. Community Fund, 1962-63; exec. dir. Family Service Assn. La Porte County (Ind.), 1964—; lectr. social problems Purdue North Central; field supr. Valparaiso U., Loyola U., Jane Addams Sch. Social Work, Chgo. Del. Area II Adv. Council on Aging, 1974—; mem. housing com. Mayor of Michigan City (Ind.), 1973; pres. Community Service Council Michigan City, 1966-68; chmn. residential campaign United Way Michigan City, 1966-68. Diplomate Conf. Advancement Pvt. Practice in Social Work. Mem. Nat. Assn. Social Workers, Acad. Certified Social Workers, Council Social Work Edn., Family Service Assns. Ind., Ind. Conf. on Social Concerns, Internat. Platform Assn., LaPorte County Council on Aging (pres. 1978). Democrat. Methodist. Home: 1317 Washington St Michigan City IN 46360 Office: Suite 228 Warren Bldg Michigan City IN 46360

CUMMINS, GEORGE MANNING, JR., physician; b. Davenport, Iowa, May 24, 1914; s. George Manning and Edna Eugenia (Eckstein) C.; B.S., St. Ambrose Coll., 1935; M.D., Rush Med. Sch., 1941; M.S., Northwestern U., 1947; m. Merlene Virginia Anderson, June 11, 1941; children—George Manning III, Gregory M., Gilbert M., Cynthia H., Geoffrey M. Practice medicine, specializing in internal medicine, Chgo., 1946; chief gastrointestinal sect. Chgo. Wesley Meml. Hosp; asst. prof. medicine Northwestern U. Sch. Medicine, 1955—. Served with AUS, 1942-46. Diplomate Am. Bd. Internal Medicine. Fellow A.C.P.; mem. A.M.A., Ill., Chgo. med. socs., Chgo. Inst. Medicine, N.Y. Acad. Scis., Alpha Omega Alpha. Clubs: Mid-Am. (Chgo.); Kenosha (Wis.) Country. Contbr. articles to profl. jours. Home: 6007 7th St Kenosha WI 53142 Office: 251 E Chicago Ave Chicago IL 60611

CUMMINS, JAMES EUGENE, state ofcl.; b. Pioneer, Ohio, Sept. 2, 1943; s. Hubert Henry and Thelma Naomi (Linebrink) C.; B.S. in Agrl. Edn., Ohio State U., 1965, M.S., 1972, Ph.D. in Vocat. Tech. Edn., 1973; m. Suzanne Gay Geyser, Mar. 18, 1973. Tchr. vocat. agr. Indian Lake High Sch., Lewistown, Ohio, 1965-70; intern dir. Penta County Vocat. Sch., Perrysburg, Ohio, 1970-71; supr. adminstrn. and planning Ohio Div. Vocat. Edn., 1973-75, state supr. agrl. edn., 1975—; exec. sec.-treas. Ohio Future Farmers of Am. Camps, Inc., 1975—. Recipient Ohio Vocat. Edn. Leadership award, 1971. Mem. Nat. Assn. Suprs. Agrl. Edn., Am. Vocat. Assn., Nat. Vocat. Agr. Tchrs. Assn., Ohio Vocat. Assn., Ohio Vocat. Agr. Tchrs. Assn., Ohio Edn. Assn., Gamma Sigma Delta, Phi Delta Kappa (chpt. historian 1972-73). Republican. Baptist. Clubs: Sertoma (chpt. chmn. 1972-73), Kiwanis. Home: 11961 Woodbridge Ln Baltimore OH 43105

CUMMINS, MICHAEL DAVID, environ. engr.; b. Dayton, Ohio, Oct. 9, 1948; s. Luverne Elton and Mildred Genevieve (Moore) C.; B.S. in Civil Engring., U. Cin., 1972, M.S. in Civil and Environ. Engring., 1974. Environ. engr. Fed. EPA, Cin., 1974—. Registered profl. engr., Ohio. Mem. Water Pollution Control Fedn. (mem. research com. 1978—), ASCE, Am. Water Works Assn., Sigma Xi, Chi Epsilon, Tau Beta Pi. Home: 3067 Griest Ave Cincinnati OH 45208 Office: 5555 Ridge Cincinnati OH 45268

CUMMISKEY, JEAN CAROL, microbiologist; b. Detroit, July 7, 1932; d. Leo B. and Freida I. (Kleiman) Freshour; B.S., U. Mich., 1953, M.P.H., 1966; Sc.D., Tulane U., 1973; m. Patrick James Cummiskey, Sept. 21, 1954; children—Kevin, Keith, Daniel. Sr. microbiologist Respiratory Care Inc., Arlington Heights, Ill., 1974-76; mgr. quality assurance Lab-Tek div. Miles Labs., Inc., Naperville, Ill., 1976-79, mgr. tech. services, 1979—. Mem. Women in Mgmt., Am. Soc. Microbiology, Tissue Culture Assn., U. Mich. Alumni Assn., Delta Omega, Sigma Xi, Alpha OMicron Pi. Republican. Lutheran. Clubs: Plum Grove, Arlington Tennis. Home: 2 Cedar Glen Rd Rolling Meadows IL 60008 Office: 30W475 N Aurora Rd Naperville IL 60540

CUNNINGHAM, DAVID LEROY, army officer; b. Lakehurst, N.J., July 19, 1944; s. John Marshall and Harriet Ann (Finn) C.; A.Sci., Embry Riddle Aero. U., 1976, B.S., 1976; postgrad. Def. Systems Mgmt. Coll., 1980, Webster (Mo.) Coll., 1981; m. Martha Anne Miller, May 9, 1970; children—Stacy Lorraine, Shannon Angelene. Engr. asst. Boeing Co., Seattle, 1965-67; commd. 1st lt. U.S. Army, 1970, advanced through grades to maj., 1981; comdr. Hdqrs. and Hdqrs. Co., 11th Combat Aviation Group, Vietnam, 1971-72; comdr. Maintenance Platoon, 1st Bn., 17th Air Cav., Ft. Bragg, N.C., 1972-74; comdr. B. Co., 1st Bn., 12th Inf., Fort Hood, Tex., 1976-78; program leader electro-optics-IR countermeasures aircraft survivability equipment Army Research and Devel. Command, St. Louis, 1978—. Mem. Spl. project com. Sorrento Springs Elem. Sch., 1980—. Served with USAF, 1961-65. Decorated Bronze Star medal, Air medal. Mem. Am. Def. Preparedness Assn., Army Aviation Assn., Assn. U.S. Army, 1st Cav. Assn., Embry Riddle Alumni Assn. Home: 328 Bellestri St Ballwin MO 63011 Office: Army Research and Devel Command 4300 Goodfellow Blvd Saint Louis MO 63120

CUNNINGHAM, EDWARD PRESTON, JR., food mfg. co. personnel exec.; b. Hammond, Ind., Sept. 24, 1945; s. Edward Preston and Louise Catherine (Kohler) C.; B.B.A., U. Wis., Madison, 1968, M.B.A., 1969; m. Susan Marie Thompson, Dec. 16, 1967; children—Scott, Jennifer. Personnel supr. Quaker Oats Co., Rockford, Ill., 1972-75, employee relations mgr., 1975-79, employee and community relations mgr., Lawrence, Kans., 1979—. Met. bd. dirs. Nat. Alliance Bus., 1976-78; bd. dirs. U. Kans. Concert Series, 1980—, Friends of Music, Lawrence, 1980—; chmn. commerce and industry unit Lawrence Multiple Sclerosis, 1981—. Served to capt. U.S. Army, 1969-72; Vietnam. Decorated Bronze Star; named Outstanding Young Man Am., U.S. Jaycees, 1981. Mem. Ill. Employment Service, Midwest Indsl. Mgmt. Assn. (instr. 1978-79), Career Edn. in Public Schs. (dir. 1980—), ASTD, Lawrence C. of C. (chmn. edn. com. 1980), Lawrence Personnel Club. Republican. Congregationalist. Club: Cosmopolitan. Home: 2021 Camelback Dr Lawrence KS 66044 Office: 727 Iowa St Lawrence KS 66044

CUNNINGHAM, GLENN SPURGEON, brewery adminstr.; b. Lexington, Va., Feb. 23, 1941; s. Henry Spurgeon and Ethel Grace (McDaniel) C.; B.S. in Bus. Adminstrn., Ferrum Coll., 1963; m. Carol Ross Fitchett, Dec. 21, 1963; children—Sara Dale, John Spurgeon. Sr. safety engr. Newport News (Va.) Shipbldg., 1965-76; safety mgr. Busch Gardens, Anheuser-Busch, Inc., Williamsburg, 1976-78, safety mgr. Williamsburg Brewery, 1978-79, mgr. safety and health St. Louis Brewery, 1979—; mem. adj. faculty Thomas Nelson Community Coll.; mem. St. Louis Area Safety Council, 1980-81. Vol., St. Louis Spl. Olympics Program, 1981; asst. cubmaster Boy Scouts Am. Mem. ASTM, Am. Soc. Safety Engrs., Am. Soc. Amusement Park Security and Safety. Methodist. Club: Manchester (Mo.) Baseball Assn. Office: 721 Pestalozzi St Saint Louis MO 63118

CUNNINGHAM, JOHN EDWARD, cons. elec. engr.; b. Arlington, Mass., Mar. 13, 1923; s. Michael E. and Mary E. C. Engr., Gen. Electric Co., Lynn, Mass., 1947-56; chief spl. project engr. Canoga Electronics Inc., Fort Walton Beach, Fla., 1956-65; project engr. Smith Electronics, Cleve., 1963-67; project mgr. Cleve. Inst. Electronics, Cleve., 1967-76; cons. electronic engr., Avon Lake, Ohio, 1976—. Registered profl. engr., Ohio. Author: Security Electronics, 1970; Building and Installing Electronic Intrusion Alarms, 1972; Understanding and Using the VOM and EVM, 1973; Cable Television, 1976, 80; Broadcast Antennas, 1977; Handbook of Remote Control and Automation Techniques, 1978; Digital Electronics for Broadcasters, 1981; contbr. articles to profl. jours. Mem. cable TV advisory com. FCC; lectr. Case Western Res. U., Lakeland Community Coll., Kent State U., Miami Dade Community Coll. Mem. IEEE (sr.), Cleve. Engring. Soc., Quarter Century Wireless Assn.

CUNNINGHAM, LOUISE STANLEY, social worker; b. Wilmington, Del., Nov. 4, 1943; d. Leonard A. and Anna Margaret (Knighton) S.; B.A., U. Mo., 1965; M.A., Valparaiso U., 1978; m. Rex Cunningham, Oct. 15, 1966; children—Peter Scott, Stephan Mark. Psychiat. social worker Beatty Meml. Hosp., Westville, Ind., 1966-68; field advisor East Lake Porter County Girl Scouts, Gary, Ind., 1968-69; dir. social service Porter Meml. Hosp., Valparaiso, Ind., 1969-73; dir. social service St. Mary Med. Center Hosps., Gary, 1973—; fieldwork instr. Valparaiso U., Ball State U.; instr. community health Coll. St. Francis, Joliet, Ill., 1976. Co-founder Council of Health and Social Services Porter County, 1970-71; mem. Mayor's Task Force on Prevention of Rape, Gary, 1973-74; bd. dirs. Porter County LWV, 1976; v.p. bd. dirs. Gary Community Mental Health Center, 1977-78; mem. Joint Commn. on Accreditation of Hosps., Chgo. Mem. Ind. Soc. Hosp. Social Work Dirs. (pres. 1977-79), Soc. Hosp. Social Work Dirs., Am. Hosp. Assn., Nat. Assn. Social Workers, Ind. Hosp. Assn. Episcopalian. Contbr. article to profl. jour. Office: 540 Tyler St Gary IN 46402

CUNNINGHAM, MARCUS EDDY, engring. exec.; b. Lynn, Mass., Jan. 16, 1907; s. Daniel and Susie (Goad) C.; B.S. Yale, 1928; postgrad. Boston U., 1929; m. Mary Eloise Baird, Feb. 14, 1931 (dec. Nov. 1964); children—Charles Baird, Marcus Eddy; m. 2d, Marilyn Alice Eneix, Oct. 1, 1966. Gen. supt. Daniel Cunningham Constrn. Co., Boston, 1928-32, Austin Co., Cleve., 1932-40; pres., treas., dir. Brady Hill Co., Detroit, 1940—; pres., treas., dir. Cunningham-Limp Co., Detroit, 1948-70, chmn. bd., chief exec. officer, 1970-78; chmn. bd., pres., treas., dir. Cunningham-Limp, Ltd., Toronto, Ont., Can., 1959—; chmn. bd., pres. Cunningham-Limp Internat. S.A., 1963—, Cunningham-Limp Co. de las Americas, S.A., 1966—, Cunningham-Limp de Espana, S.A., 1966—, Cunningham-Limp (France) SARL, 1967-78, Cunningham-Limp Deutschland, Gmbh, 1970-78; chmn. bd., chief exec., pres. Cunningham-Limp Holding Co., 1978—. Dir., v.p. Gulfstream Park Racing Assn., Hallandale, Fla., 1963—. Bd. dirs. Detroit and Nat. council Boy Scouts Am. Mem. Engring. Soc. Detroit, A.I.M. (president's council). Clubs: Yale (Detroit); Bloomfield Hills (Mich.) Country; Oakland Hills Country (Birmingham, Mich.); Indian Creek Country, Jockey (Miami Beach, Fla.); Kenilworth (Bal Harbour, Fla.); Le Mirador Country (Mont Pelerin, Switzerland). Home: 104 Brady Ln Bloomfield Hills MI 48013 (winter) Ocean Blvd Golden Beach FL 33160 Office: 1400 N Woodward Ave Birmingham MI 48011

CUNNINGHAM, PATRICK JOSEPH, JR., alcoholism counselor; b. Chgo., Nov. 29, 1950; s. Patrick Joseph and Sally Mary (Kmiotek) C.; B.S., Western Ill. U., 1975; M.A., Governors State U., 1979. Acad. adv. Triton Coll., 1975-80, biofeedback trainer, 1976-80; acting records evaluator, 1978-79; alcoholism counselor The Abbey, Winfield, Ill., 1981, St. Joseph Hosp., Joliet, Ill., 1981—. Mem. Ill. Personnel and Guidance Assn., Ill. Mental Health Counselors Assn., Biofeedback Soc. Am., Internat. Soc. Gen. Semantics, Ill. Alcoholism Counselors Alliance. Office: 333 N Madison Joliet IL 60435

CUNNINGHAM, SHIRLEY JEAN, ins. co. exec.; b. Eldorado, Ark., Nov. 15, 1943; d. Charles Travis and Gracie Lee (Traylor) Marrable; B.A., DePaul U., 1981; m. Wilbur C. Cunningham, Nov. 23, 1974; children—Tracy Jeannee and Leslie Jeannette (twins). Supr. word processing Blue Cross Assn., Chgo., 1971-73, mgr. word processing, 1974-77; mgr. word processing and telecommunications Blue Cross & Blue Shield Assns., Chgo., 1978-80, sr. mgr. office services, 1981—; mem. citizen adv. com. Thornton Community Coll., 1979—. Mem. adv. bd. United Career Action Now; mem. Vice President's Task Force on Youth Motivation. Recipient cert. of recognition Citizens Adv. Com., 1980. Mem. Internat. Info./Word Processing Assn., Am. Mgmt. Assn., Word Processing Mgmt. Assn., In-Plant Printing Mgmt. Assn., Chgo. Assn. Commerce and Industry (merit employment com.; cert. of merit 1968). Club: Pershing Park Tennis. Home: 2901 Martin Luther King Dr 1802 Chicago IL 60616 Office: 676 N St Clair Chicago IL 60616

CUPKIE, LYNN FREDRICK, coll. dean; b. St. Paul, Sept. 5, 1941; s. Carl G. and Helen E. (Wurm) C.; B.A. in Psychology and History (Minn. Dept. Edn. Scholar), St. Cloud U., 1966, M.S. in Counseling, 1972; Ph.D. in Counseling, U. Mo., Kansas City, 1979; children—Todd Mitchel, Michelle Lynn. Youth social worker Fed. Community Action Program, Cass Lake, Minn., 1966-67; state program dir., field dir. Met. Area Centers-Minn. Assn. for Mental Health, 1967-68; with Nat. Tchr. Corps Program, Mpls. Public Schs., 1968-69; residence hall dir. St. Cloud U., 1969-71, instr., research asst. manpower services project, 1970-71, dir. residence hall programs, 1970-71; counselor learning disabilities program Menorah Med. Center, Kansas City, Mo., 1971-72; counselor Ruth Illmer Assos., Kansas City, Mo., 1972-75; dir. counseling center, coordinator psychology dept. Avila Coll., Kansas City, Mo., 1972-73, dean of students, asso. prof. psychology, 1973—. Post dir. St. Paul Scouts Drum and Bugle Corps, 1964-67; mem. exec. bd. YMCA, 1976-79, coordinator Y-Indian Guides, 1975-77; mem. Greater Kansas City Sports Commn., 1977—; mem. Blue Springs (Mo.) City Planning Commn., 1979—. Served with U.S. N.G., 1964-70. Recipient Outstanding Service award YMCA, 1976, 79. Mem. Assn. Coll. and Univ. Housing Officers, Am. Personnel and Guidance Assn., Mo. Coll. Personnel Assn. (state treas. 1977-78, state sec. 1978-79), Nat. Assn. Student Personnel Adminstrs. (region IV West conf. coordinator 1978—, region IV West v.p. 1980—), Psi Chi. Lutheran. Home: 805 N 37th St Blue Springs MO 64015 Office: Avila Coll 11901 Wornall Rd Kansas City MO 64145

CURLEY, RICHARD DARREL, agronomist; b. Omaha, Oct. 13, 1929; s. Howard Gordon and Edith Orinda (Eriksen) C.; B.S. in Soil Conservation, U. Nebr., 1951, M.S. in Soils, 1956; m. Edith Louise

Valder, Sept. 30, 1951; children—Steven Howard, Christine Anne, Bradley Richard. Fertilizer distbn. analyst TVA, St. Paul, 1957-65, Ithaca, N.Y., 1965-67; supr. market devel. Cominco Am., Spokane, Wash., 1967-68; product mgr. liquids Gulf Oil Corp., Kansas City, Mo., 1968-70; chief agronomist Farmland, Kansas City, 1970-76; fertilizer mgr. Holdrege Seed & Farm Supply, 1977-79; chief agronomist Western U.S., Duval Sales Corp., Topeka, 1979—; pres., gen. mgr., treas., dir. Phos-Tech, Inc. Served as aviator U.S. Army, 1951-54. Recipient Editorial award Crops & Soils Mag., 1959. Mem. Am. Soc. Agronomy, Nat. Fertilizer Solutions Assn., Calif. Fertilizer Assn. (soil improvement com.). Republican. Club: Lions, Masons, Elks. Contbr. articles in field to profl. jours. Home: 6537 SW 28th Terr Topeka KS 66614

CURNOW, JOHN WAYNE, mech. engr.; b. Port Huron, Mich., Mar. 31, 1935; s. Gordon Earl and Lillian Ruth (Burgett) C.; B.S.M.E., U. Mich., 1958; m. Nancy R. Crawford; children—Kevin John, Alan Wayne. Design, devel. engr. indsl. group Sperry Vickers div. Sperry Corp., Troy, Mich., 1965-66, mgr. lab., 1967-70, engring. supr., 1970-72, sect. chief indsl. valve group, 1972-73, chief engr. N.Am. group controls, 1973-75, dir. engring. N.Am. Group Controls, Elect. Products, 1975-80, mgr. engring.-controls N. Am.-Comml. div., 1980—. Bd. govs. Nat. Conf. Fluid Power. Served with U.S. Army, 1958. Mem. Soc. Automotive Engrs. Nat. Fluid Power Assn. Patentee in field. Home: 7000 Gunlock Bay Utica MI 48078 Office: 1401 Crooks Rd Troy MI 48084

CURRAN, CHARLES EDWARD, assn. exec.; b. North Adams, Mass., May 27, 1923; s. George Lally and Claire Elizabeth (Russell) C.; A.B., Harvard U., 1948, M.P.A., 1951, Ph.D., 1960; M.A., U. N.H., 1950; m. Joan Ferris, Feb. 17, 1950; children—Douglas Yale, Jane Withington. Research and budget analyst City of Kansas City, Mo., 1952-55, asst. city mgr., 1955-58; research asso. Inst. for Community Studies, 1958-61; v.p. Kansas City Assn. Trusts and Funds, 1961-73, pres., 1973—. Bd. dirs. Midwest Research Inst., Clearinghouse for Mid-Continent Founds.; trustee Mid-Continent Pub. Library, 1965, 71-74; chmn. bd. govs. Truman Med. Center. Served with C.E., AUS, 1942-46. Mem. Mo. Polit. Sci. Assn., Council on Founds. Democrat. Episcopalian. Club: Lake Quivira Country. Contbr. articles to profl. jours. Home: 1231 W 61st Terr Kansas City MO 64113 Office: 406 Bd of Trade 10th and Wyandotte Kansas City MO 64105

CURRAN, HILDA PATRICIA, social worker; b. Patterson, N.J., Jan. 15, 1938; d. James Patrick and Hilda Lucille (Walsh) Curran; A.B., Hiram Coll., 1959; M.S.W., Ohio State U., 1963; m. Robert Scott Kennon, Nov. 28, 1980. Tchr., Cin. Bd. Edn., 1960; caseworker Franklin County Welfare Dept., Columbus, Ohio, 1960-61; mem. relocation staff Springfield (Mass.) Redevel. Authority, 1963-64; neighborhood organizer Community Council Greater Springfield, 1964-65; mem. program devel. staff United Community Centers, Bklyn., 1965-67; facilities devel. specialist in vocat. rehab. Mich. Dept. Edn., Lansing, 1967-70; program devel. specialist Bur. Community Services, Mich. Dept. Labor, Lansing, 1970-78, dir. Office Women and Work, 1978—. Mem. Ingham County Housing Commn., 1977-79, Ingham County Social Services Bd., 1979—; bd. dirs., officer Big Bros.-Big Sisters Greater Lansing, 1968—; charter mem. bd., officer Big Bros.-Big Sisters Am., 1977—, Big Sisters Internat., 1973-77, pres. 1976-77. Recipient Diana award in govt. YWCA, 1977; ann. award for outstanding achievement Hiram Coll., 1980. Mem. Nat. Assn. Social Workers (mem. del. assembly 1977, 81, pres. Lansing-Jackson chpt. 1978-80, named Lansing-Jackson Social Worker of Yr. 1977), Phi Kappa Phi (life). Clubs: Zonta, Torch (pres. 1979-80) (Lansing). Home: 1505 Osborn St Lansing MI 48915 Office: 309 N Washington St Lansing MI 48909

CURRAN, THOMAS FREDERICK, psychotherapist; b. LaCrosse, Wis., Feb. 6, 1948; s. Lawrence Griggs and Eleanor (Gibson) C.; B.S., U. Wis., 1970; M.S.W., Mich. State U., 1972, Ph.D., 1974; m. Betty Kathryn Larsen, Dec. 21, 1973. Cons., Ingham Med. Center-Community Mental Health Center, Lansing, Mich., 1973-74; asst. prof. Fla. State U., Tallahassee, 1974-77; psychotherapist Genesee Psychiat. Center, Flint, Mich., 1977-81; pres. Northbank Counseling Services, Flint, 1981—; cons. Nat. Council on Alcoholism, 1978—. Mich. State U. Dean's Office fellow, 1972, 73. Mem. Nat. Assn. Social Workers, Am. Psychol. Assn., Council on Social Work Edn. Editorial adv. bd. Jour. of Humanics, 1977—; contbr. articles to profl. jours. Home: 5510 Maple Park Dr Flint MI 48507 Office: Suite 300 Northbank Center 400 N Saginaw Flint MI 48502

CURRIE, ANDREW CARNEGIE, mgmt. cons.; b. Pitts., May 14, 1940; s. Andrew C. and Elizabeth M. (Gasson) C.; B.A., Hiram Coll., 1961; M.S., Purdue U., 1963; Ph.D., Ohio State U., 1968; m. Carol Ann Miller, June 27, 1964; children—Colleen Elizabeth, Caren Marie. Dir. alumni relations and devel. Hiram (Ohio) Coll., 1967-69; dir. devel. and planning Akron (Ohio) Art Inst., 1969-72, dir., 1973; sr. cons. C. W. Shaver & Co., Inc., N.Y.C., 1973-75, regional v.p., 1975-80, exec. v.p., 1980, pres., 1981—, dir., 1976—. Trustee Greater Akron Arts Fedn., 1971-73. Mem. Council on Advancement and Support Edn., Am. Assn. Museums, Am. Symphony Orch. League, Hiram Coll. Alumni Assn. (dir. 1970-73). Clubs: White Bear Yacht; Tower (Mpls.). Home: 7021 W Shadow Lake Dr Lino Lakes MN 55014 Office: 415 Peavey Bldg Minneapolis MN 55402

CURRIE, LAWRENCE EVERETT, psychologist; b. Chgo., Aug. 18, 1945; s. Clarence Clifton and Violante Earlscort (Robertson) C.; B.A., Drake U., 1967; M.A., Iowa, 1969; Ph.D., Syracuse U., 1973; m. June 6, 1970 (div. 1975); children—Jamál Lawrence, Táhirih Louise. Personnel specialist Owens Illinois Corp., Toledo, 1968; staff devel. specialist Hutchings Psychiat. Center, Syracuse, 1972-73; rehab. counselor Iowa Div. Rehab. Edn. and Services, Oakdale, 1969-70; asst. prof. U. Wis. at Stout, Menomonie, 1973-75; asso. exec. dir. research and program devel. Goodwill Rehab. Center, Milw., 1975-77; pvt. practice clin./cons. psychology, Milw., 1977—; staff psychologist Waukesha (Wis.) Meml. Hosp., 1979—. Recipient grants Rehab. Services Adminstrn.; lic. psychologist Nat. Register Health Service Providers in Psychology; cert. rehab. counselor. Mem. Am., Wis. psychol. assns., Am. Soc. Clin. Hypnosis, Soc. for Clin. and Exptl. Hypnosis, Am. Assn. Sex Educators, Counselors and Therapists, Nat., Wis. rehab. assns. Contbr. articles to profl. jours. Home: 9088 N 75th St Milwaukee WI 53223 Office: 9001 N 76th St Suite 303 Milwaukee WI 53223

CURRIER, DENNIS THOMAS, hosp. fin. exec.; b. Detroit, June 10, 1944; s. Vincent James and Jean Enid (Flett) C.; B.S. in Mech. Engring., U. Notre Dame, 1966; M.B.A., U. Mich., 1967; m. Susan Kathryn Toth, Mar. 8, 1975; children—Jean Higgins, Kathryn Connor; children by previous marriage—D. Thomas, Kalin Kathleen. Staff accountant Price Waterhouse & Co., Detroit, 1967-70, cons. mgmt. advisory services, 1970-72, mgr. mgmt. advisory services, 1972-74; v.p. fin., treas. Harper-Grace Hosps., Detroit, 1974—; fin. cons. health care. Precinct del. Mich. Democratic Conv., 1966; chmn. finance com. Roman Catholic parish ch., 1970-71; trustee, mem. exec. com., chmn. fin. com., treas., vice chmn. Family Services, Detroit, C.P.A., Mich. Mem. Am. Inst. C.P.A.'s, Mich. Assn. C.P.A.'s, Engring. Soc. Detroit, Am., Mich. hosp. assns., Tau Beta Pi, Pi Tau Sigma, Beta Alpha Psi. Club: Birmingham Athletic. Home: 565 Wooddale Rd Birmingham MI 48010 Office: 3990 John R St Detroit MI 48201

CURRIER, THOMAS RICHARD, state ofcl., pub. health adminstr.; s. Augustus Bernard and Irene M. (Allen) C.; M.A., Western Mich. U., 1974; m. Frances Gram, Sept. 22, 1973. Ordained to ministry Roman Catholic Ch., 1957; dir. pastoral mission office Diocese of Lansing (Mich.), 1957-70; pres. World Communications, Inc., Lansing, 1971-73; social researcher Mich. Gov.'s Office, Lansing, 1973-74; health adminstr. Mich. Dept. Pub. Health, Lansing, 1974—; mem. faculty social sci. dept. Jackson Community Coll., Jackson, Mich., 1974—; cons. to Health Services Research Inst., U. Tex., San Antonio, 1976—. Recipient Gold Camera award Chgo. Film Festival, 1972. Author: Restructuring the Parish, 1967, Agony and Ecstasy in Building a Christian Community, 1969, The Future Parish, 1970, God As My Other Self, 1972; contbr. articles on pub. health to profl. publs.; producer film programs. Home: 7004 N River Hwy Grand Ledge MI 48837 Office: 3423 N Logan Lansing MI 48906

CURRY, CARLTON EUGENE, automotive mfg. co. exec.; b. Lizton, Ind., Mar. 4, 1935; s. William Daniel Harrison and Minnie Eulalia (Trammel) C.; B.S. in Aero. Engring., Purdue U., 1958; m. Ann Estelle Merritt, July 3, 1957; children—Charles Lynn, Kimberly Sue. Jr. engring. aide Allison div. Gen. Motors Corp., Indpls., 1956, supr. program adminstrn. Detroit Diesel Allison div., Indpls., 1966-73, staff systems analyst, 1973—; gen. engr. U.S. Naval Avionics Facility, Indpls., 1957-66. Mem. Indpls. License Rev. Bd., 1972, Indpls. Bd. Transp., 1973-81; Republican precinct committeeman, 1970, 72, ward chmn., 1972-73, 78-79, area chmn, 1973-77; bd. dirs. Community Action Against Poverty, 1976-81, S.W. Multi-Service Center, Inc., 1977-78; mem. Greater Indpls. Progress Com., 1979. Recipient Citizenship award Am. Legion, 1953; John Bernall Starr scholar, 1953; registered profl. engr., Ind. Mem. Am. Inst. Aeros. and Astronautics, Army Aviation Assn. Mem. Christian Ch. Clubs: Lions (pres. Chapel Hill 1977), Toastmasters Internat. Contbr. analytical articles to profl. jours. Home: 8406 Model Sq Indianapolis IN 46234 Office: PO Box 894 U4 Indianapolis IN 46206

CURRY, GEORGE EDWARD, newspaper reporter; b. Tuscaloosa, Ala., Feb. 23, 1947; s. Homer L. and Martha L. (Harris) C.; student Knoxville Coll., 1970. Reporter, Sports Illus. mag., 1970-72, St. Louis Post-Dispatch, 1972—; instr. journalism St. Louis Community Coll., Forest Park, 1977-78; panelist Weekly Edit., KETC-TV; host Perspective, KSDK-TV; dir. St. Louis Minority Journalism Workshop, 1977—; mem. editorial bd. St. Louis Journalism Rev. Pulitzer Prize nominee, 1977; winner 1st prize (3) Black Excellence in Journalism awards Greater St. Louis Assn. Black Journalists, 1979. Mem. Greater St. Louis Assn. Black Journalists (chmn. exec. bd. 1977-78), Sigma Delta Chi. Author: Jake Gaither: America's Most Famous Black Coach, 1977. Appeared on nat. TV programs including The Today Show. Office: 900 N Tucker Blvd Saint Louis MO 63101

CURRY, JUDITH CAROLYN, nurse; b. West Columbia, S.C., Dec. 6, 1939; d. Charlie Haskell and Carolyn Eunice (Boland) Bickley; B.S. in Nursing, U. S.C., 1962; cert. U. Calif., San Francisco, 1964; M.S. in Nursing, Boston U., 1967, cert. advanced grad. study, 1968; m. John Edward Curry, Jan. 31, 1970. Staff nurse Columbia (S.C.) Hosp., 1962-63; public health nurse Richland County Health Dept., Columbia, 1963-64; clinic nurse Child Evaluation Clinic, S.C. Dept. Health, 1964-66; instr., cons. Shriver Center, Waltham, Mass., 1968-70; asst. prof., chief of nursing Ohio State U. Nisonger Center, Columbus, 1970-74; health liaison specialist Am. Acad. Pediatrics Head Start Consultation Project, Evanston, Ill., 1974-76, Westinghouse Health Systems Head Start Consultation Project, Chgo., 1976—. Registered nurse, S.C., Ill., Ohio, Mass. Fellow Am. Assn. Mental Deficiency (regional nursing chmn. 1972-75), Sigma Theta Tau. Lutheran. Editor: (Kathryn K. Peppe) Mental Retardation: Nursing Approaches to Care, 1978. Home: 30W479 Fairway Dr Naperville IL 60540 Office: Westinghouse Health Systems Head Start Consultation Project 10 S Riverside Plaza Chicago IL 60606

CURTE, LORRAINE VICTORIA KEMPEN, social worker, counselor, gerontologist, nurse; b. Grand Rapids, Mich., Nov. 25, 1924; d. John J. and Mary V. (Klimavicz) Yowaish; student Grand Rapids Jr. Coll., 1942-43; B.S. in Nursing Edn., Loyola U., Chgo., 1947, postgrad., 1948-49; M.A., U. Mich., 1969, postgrad., 1969-76; postgrad. Rutgers U., 1970, DePaul U.; m. John Curte Jr., Dec. 31, 1976; children—Peter Gerard Kempen, Paul Martin Kempen, Mark W. Kempen, Michael Edward Kempen. Nursing instr. various hosps., 1948-60; hosp. supr. Maple Grove Med. Care Facility, Grand Rapids, Mich., 1960-62; instr. nursing edn. Grand Rapids (Mich.) Jr. Coll., 1960-62; instr. Tb nursing and outpatient and personnel health services Kent County (Mich.), Sunshine Hosp., Grand Rapids, 1962-67; nursing educator Blodgett Meml. Hosp. Sch. Nursing, Grand Rapids, 1967-69; gerontologist and nurse Porter Hills Presbyn. Village, Grand Rapids, 1976-81; ct. counselor probation dept. Hall of Justice, 61st Dist. Ct., Grand Rapids, 1968-81; instr. in field various local schs. and colls., Mich., 1970—; cons. area dist. cts. probation depts.; pvt. practice, 1981—. Pres., Kent County Employees Assn., 1966-67, exec. sec., 1967-68; mem. Sr. Citizens Coordinating Com., 1968-71; bd. dirs. Sr. Neighbors, Inc., 1971-78. Cert. social worker, Mich. Mem. Am. Acad. Polit. Sci. and Social Scientists, Mich. League for Human Welfare, Mich. Gerontol. Soc., Gerontol. Soc., Am. Nurses Assn., Grand Rapids Dist. Nurses Assn., Mich. Orgn. for Human Rights (founder Monday night rap group, 1969-79), NOW, U. Mich. Alumni Assn., Loyola U. Alumni Assn., Phi Kappa Phi. Home: 1430 Bradford St NE Grand Rapids MI 49503

CURTIN, KENNETH MICHAEL, state ofcl.; b. N.Y.C., Apr. 7, 1933; s. Michael Joseph and Eunice Marion (Hollerbach) C.; B.A., Evansville Coll., 1955, M.A., 1968; M.S., So. Ill. U., 1980; m. Annetta Esther Folz, Oct. 1, 1955 (dec. June 3, 1978); children—Kathleen Ann, Timothy Michael, Jennifer Lynn. Probation officer Vanderburgh County Juvenile Ct., Evansville, Ind., 1954-56; asst. tng. dir. Indpls. Goodwill, 1956-60; workshop dir. The Rehab. Center, Evansville, 1960-63, Evansville Assn. for the Blind, 1963-70; contracts mgr. Evansville Goodwill, 1972; chief facilities services sect. Ind. Rehab. Services, Indpls., 1972—; lectr. meetings of nat. facilities specialists, 1974, 75, 79. Recipient Spoke award, Evansville Jr. C. of C., 1961, Pres.'s Gold Key award, 1961; Evansville Outstanding Citizen award, 1962. Mem. Am. Inst. Indsl. Engrs., (chpt. pres. 1970), Evansville Musicians Union (dir. 1968, trustee 1970). Republican. Clubs: Masons, Shriners. Patentee in field. Home: 412 Oak Dr Carmel IN 46032 Office: 17 W Market St Box 7070 Indianapolis IN 46207

CURTIS, ALAN S., architect; b. Chgo., Sept. 17, 1950; s. H. Keith and Alice B. C.; A.A., William Rainey Harper Coll., Palatine, Ill., 1971. Designer, HNR & W, Architects and Engrs., Chgo., 1968-71; designer, office mgr. Jessen & Assos., Architect, Park Ridge, Ill., 1971-77; pres. ASC Inc., Architects, Arlington Heights, Ill., 1977—. Mem. AIA. Club: Arlington Heights Kiwanis. Office: 1204 E Central Rd Arlington Heights IL 60005

CURTIS, ALICE READY PARTLOW (MRS. JOHN M. WALMSLEY), writer, former pub. relations exec.; b. Keystone, W.Va.; d. Ira Judson and Andrea B. (Martin) Partlow; A.B., Marshall Coll., 1928; postgrad. King's Coll., U. London (Eng.), 1932, Columbia U., 1933; m. Hal L. Curtis, Apr. 15, 1939 (dec.); m. 2d, John M. Walmsley, Oct. 30, 1975. Writer, Jam Handy Orgn., Detroit, 1941-43; newspaper editor Ft. Wayne Army Post, Detroit, 1943-44; asst. pub. relations dir. Mich. Blue Cross, Detroit, 1944-50; pub. relations dir. YWCA Met. Detroit, 1950-66; pub. relations officer Merrill-Palmer Inst., Detroit, 1966-70; owner Pet Portraits by Alice Curtis, 1966—; owner Alice Curtis Pub. Relations, Grosse Pointe, Mich., 1970-78; pub. relations dir. Cottage Hosp., Grosse Pointe, 1972-78. Recipient citation, journalism dept. Mich. State U., 1950; award Women's Advt. Club Detroit, 1950. Mem. Mich. Hosp. Pub. Relations Assn. (bd. mem. 1971), Pub. Relations Soc. Am. (mem. bd. 1966-68), Mich. Humane Soc., Founders Soc. Detroit Inst. Arts, English-Speaking Union, Friends of Detroit Public Library, Nat. Trust for Historic Preservation. Democrat. Episcopalian. Clubs: Detroit Press, Scarab of Detroit. Author: Is Your Publicity Showing, 1949. Home: 16826 Cranford Ln Grosse Pointe MI 48230 Office: 16826 Cranford Ln Grosse Pointe MI 48230

CURTIS, DAVID E., baking co. ofcl.; b. Dayton, Ohio, Mar. 10, 1937; s. Haskell and Bertie (Wright) C.; B.S. in Bus. Adminstrn., U. Dayton, 1960; m. Nancy L. Edwards, Dec. 24, 1959; children—David Edward, Leigh Anne, Bradley Wayne. Personnel dir. ITT Continental Baking Co., Dayton, 1960-65, Toledo, 1965-80, Columbus, Ohio, 1980—. Past trustee Teamsters Local 365 Health and Welfare Fund. Mem. Toledo Personnel Mgrs. Assn., Toledo Kennel Club (past pres., show chmn. 1976-78), Dachshund Club of Am., Bowling Green (Ohio) Kennel Club (past pres.), Central Ohio Kennel Club (constn. chmn. 1981), Central Ohio Dachshund Club (pres. 1981), Am. Dog Owners Assn., Ohio Dog Owners Assn., New Albany-Plain Twp. Hist. Soc. (pres. 1981). Methodist. Home: 4659 Reynoldburg-New Albany Rd New Albany OH 43054 Office: 697 N Fourth St Columbus OH 43201

CURTIS, DAVID LEONARD, agribusiness exec.; b. Eng., Jan. 26, 1931; came to U.S., 1970; s. Leonard Charles and Alice Mary (Woolard) C.; diploma tropical agr., U. W.I., Trinidad, 1955; postgrad. Cambridge (Eng.) U., 1953-54; Ph.D., Reading (Eng.) U., 1966; m. Dorothy E. Darvill, Aug. 21, 1954; children—Gavin Charles, Tracy Claire. With Brit. Overseas Civil Service, 1955-62; head dept. Agr. Research Inst., Ahmadu Bello U., Nigeria, 1962-67; with DeKalb AgResearch, Inc., 1967—, asst., then mgr. internat. ops., DeKalb, Ill., 1970-77, v.p., 1977—; co. dir., lectr. in field. Mem. Am. Seed Trade Assn., Inst. Biology. Author articles in field. Office: DeKalb AgResearch Inc Sycamore Rd DeKalb IL 60115

CURTIS, GEORGE HARRY, historian, archivist; b. Portland, Oreg., Dec. 2, 1935; s. George and Ruth Aralein (Coates) C.; B.S., Portland State Coll., 1961; M.A., Am. U., 1964; Ph.D., Georgetown U., 1972; m. MarJo Laurelle Docken, Sept. 7, 1963; children—George Harry, Jeffrey Scott. Archivist trainee Office Presdl. Libraries, Nat. Archives, Washington, 1969-71, Center Polar Archives, 1971-72; supervisory archivist Dwight D. Eisenhower Library, Abilene, Kans., 1972-77; asst. dir. Harry S. Truman Library, Independence, Mo., 1977—. Served with USAR, 1958-65. Mem. Soc. Am. Archivists, Am. Hist. Assn., Orgn. Am. Historians, Soc. Historians Am. Fgn. Relations, Am. Mil. Inst. Author articles in field. Home: 409 Victor Dr Blue Springs MO 64015 Office: Harry S Truman Library Independence MO 64050

CURTIS, GEORGE WARREN, JR., lawyer; b. Merrill, Wis., Sept. 24, 1936; s. George Warren and Rose E. (Zimmerman) C.; B.A., U. Minn., 1959; J.D., U. Wis., 1962; m. Mary Kersztyn, Dec. 27, 1973; 1 dau., Emily Jennifer; children by previous marriage—George, Kathy, Eric, Greg, Paul, David. Admitted to Wis. bar, 1962, Fla. bar, 1968; practiced in Merrill, 1962-68, Oshkosh, Wis., 1968—; mem. firms Russell & Curtis, 1962-68, Nolan, Engler, Yakes & Curtis, 1968-74, Curtis, MacKenzie, Haase & Brown, 1974—. Active YMCA. Mem. Delta Sigma Rho. Democrat. Home: 5996 Hwy 21 Omro WI 54963 Office: 429 Algoma Blvd Oshkosh WI 54901

CURTLER, HUGH MERCER, JR., educator; b. Charlottesville, Va., Dec. 31, 1937; s. Hugh Mercer and Nancy Daingerfield (Elsraod) C.; cert. Balt. Poly. Inst., 1955; B.A., St. John's Coll., 1959; M.A., Northwestern U., 1962, Ph.D., 1964; m. Linda Edith Lockwood, June 15, 1962; children—Hugh Mercer III, Rudolph Hirsch. From instr. to asst. prof. U. R.I., Kingston, 1964-66; asst. prof., chmn. dept. humanities Midwestern Coll., Denison, Iowa, 1966-68; prof. philosophy Southwest State U., Marshall, Minn., 1968—, chmn. dept., 1968—. Md. State scholar, 1955-59; Northwestern U. fellow, 1961-64; Young Humanist fellow, 1971-72; vis. fellow Center Study Democratic Instns., 1972. Mem. Am. Philos. Assn., Am. Soc. Value Inquiry, Soc. Philosophy and Public Affairs, Soc. Polit. and Legal Philosophy, Am. Soc. Aesthetics. Author: Prologue to Philosophy, 1977; A Theory of Art, Literature and Tragedy, 1981; Vivas as Critic, 1982; An Annotated Bibliography of the Works of Eliseo Vivas, 1982; What is Art?, 1982. Office: Dept Philosophy Southwest State U Marshall MN 56258

CURZON, ELIZABETH JEANNETTE GORE, pub. accountant; b. Alton, Ill., Oct. 15, 1911; d. Forrest Bird and Annella (Denby) Gore; A.B., U. Ill., 1932, M.S., 1934, postgrad., 1950-54; m. George J. Curzon, Jan. 6, 1930 (div. Apr. 1946); children—Marjorie A., Victoria Curzon Engelhardt, Katherine Curzon Owen. Grad. asst. U. Ill., 1932-34, library research asst. in animal nutrition, 1934-39; office mgr., accountant George J. Curzon, Champaign, Ill., 1940-46; accountant Curzon Parks Bookkeeping Service, Champaign, 1946-55; partner Peer, Hunt & Curzon, C.P.A.'s, Champaign, 1955-78, Clifton Gunderson & Co., 1978—; dir. Clifford Jacobs Forging Co., Clark-Lindsey Inc.; sec. Clark St. Bldg. Corp., Champaign, 1958-72. Treas., Champaign County Community Chest, 1954-55, pres., 1955-56, dir., 1950-56; sec. Com. on Elm Tree Disease, 1954-55; pres. Laymon Convalescent Home, Inc., 1950-63; treas. Champaign County Estate Planning Council, 1969-70, sec., 1970-71, vice chmn., 1971-72, chmn., 1972-73. Bd. dirs. Urban League Champaign County, 1960-66, McKinley YMCA, 1960-66, 68-75. Mem. Ill. Soc. C.P.A.'s (chpt. chmn. 1961-62, chpt. treas. 1960-61, profl. devel. com. 1967-68, state taxation com. 1969-71, com. ann. tax conf. 1972-74), Am. Inst. C.P.A.'s, Am. Forestry Assn., Nat. Audubon Soc., Am. Athletic Assn., Phi Beta Kappa, Phi Upsilon Omicron, Omicron Nu, Alpha Delta Pi. Baptist. Home: 617 W University St Champaign IL 61820 Office: 203 W Clark St Champaign IL 61820

CUSACK, DONALD E., clergyman; b. Chgo., Dec. 6, 1932; s. Thomas F. and Bridget (Murphy) C.; B.A., St. Mary of Lake Sem., 1955, S.T.B., 1957, M.A., 1958, S.T.L., 1959; M.A., Middlebury Coll., 1969. Ordained priest Roman Cath. Ch., 1959; asso. pastor Archdiocese of Chgo., 1959-64, tchr. English high sch., 1964-67; asso. prof. English, Niles Coll., Chgo., 1967-75, treas.-procurator, 1968-74, chairperson dept., 1970-75; rector-prin. Quigley Prep. Sem. North, Chgo., 1975-81; pastor St. Joseph Parish, Wilmette, Ill., 1981—. Mem. adv. bd. Mallinckrodt Coll., Wilmette, 1981—. Mem. Nat. Council Tchrs. English, Assn. Supervision and Curriculum Devel. Home and office: 1747 Lake Ave Wilmette IL 60091

CUSANO, CRISTINO, mech. engr., educator; b. Sepino, Italy, Mar. 22, 1941; s. Crescenzo and Carmela (D'Anello) C.; B.S., Rochester Inst. Tech., 1965; M.S., Cornell U., 1967, Ph.D., 1970; m. Isabella Pera, Aug. 7, 1974. Asst. prof. mech. engring. U. Ill., Urbana, 1970-74, asso. prof., 1974—; cons. Mattison Machine Works, Whirlpool Corp. NSF fellow, 1965-69; recipient Capt. Alfred E. Hunt award. Mem. ASME, Am. Soc. Lubrication Engrs., Am. Soc. Engring. Edn., Sigma Xi, Phi Kappa Phi, Pi Tau Sigma. Roman Catholic. Contbr. articles to profl. jours. Home: 1303 Belmeade Dr Champaign IL 61820 Office: Dept Mech and Indsl Engring 1206 W Green St Univ of Ill Urbana IL 61801

CUSHENBERY, DONALD CLYDE, educator; b. Sharon, Kans., Sept. 24, 1925; s. Jesse Clyde and Lillian May (Schloetzer) C.; B.S., Fort Hays (Kans.) State Coll., 1948; M.S., Kans. Tchrs. Coll. at Emporia, 1954; D.Ed., U. Mo. at Columbia, 1964; m. Elfrieda Berg, Aug. 10, 1951; children—Barbara, Donna, Linda. Tchr., Sharon, Kans., 1944-45, Argonia, 1945-46; prin. coach, Plains, Kans., 1948-53; prin. Lincoln Jr. High, Anthony, Kans., 1953-55; asst. prof. Kans. State Coll., Pittsburg, 1955-64; prof. edn. U. Nebr. Omaha, 1964—, Found. prof., 1971-77, 80-83. Reading workshop dir., tech. cons. Right to Read Program. Recipient Great Tchr. award, 1971. Mem. Nebr. Reading Council (pres.), Phi Delta Kappa. Baptist. Author: Reading Improvement in the Elementary Sch., 1969; Remedial Reading in the Secondary School, 1972; (with Kenneth Gilreath) Effective Reading Instruction for Slow Learners, 1972; (with Helen Howell) Reading and the Gifted Child, 1974; Reading Improvement Through Diagnosis, Remediation and Individualized Instruction, 1977; (with Ronald E. Meyer) Reading Comprehension Mastery Kits, 1980. Home: 919 N 69th St Omaha NE 68132 Office: 60th and Dodge Sts Omaha NE 68182

CUSHINGBERRY, GEORGE, JR., state legislator; b. Detroit, Jan. 6, 1953; s. George and Edna (James) C.; B.A., Wayne State U., 1974; m. Valerie J. Middlebrooks, Dec. 31, 1975 (div.); m. 2d, Maria H. Drew, Aug. 1979; 1 son, George. Mem. Mich. Ho. of Reps. from 4th Dist., 1975—. Exec. vice chmn., interim chmn. Assn. Black Students, Wayne State U., 1972-74; community editor South End Newspaper, Wayne State U., 1973-74; chmn. Nat. Conf. State Legislatures-State Fed. Assembly Urban Devel. Com.; trustee Afro-Am. Mus., Detroit; co-chmn. Concerned Citizens Youth Task Force; bd. dirs. Westside Citizens for Retarded; chmn. bd. dirs. Detroit Action Coop. Recipient Spirit of Detroit award Detroit City Council, 1978; Citizen of Yr. award Mich. Chronicle, 1977; Outstanding Humanitarian Service award Statewide Care Home, 1978; various other awards. Mem. NAACP. Democrat. Baptist. Home: 8625 Marygrove St Detroit MI 48221 Office: State Capitol Bldg Lansing MI 48909

CUSHMAN, JOHN HOWARD, physicist; b. Ames, Iowa, Jan. 19, 1951; s. Howard Robert and Winifred (Wolters) C.; B.S., Iowa State U., 1975, M.S., 1976, Ph.D., 1978; m. Ruth Ann Sulik, Aug. 24, 1974. Asst. prof. soil physics Purdue U., West Lafayette, Ind., 1978—. Mem. Am. Math. Soc., Am. Soc. Agronomy, Soc. Indsl. and Applied Mat., Soil Sci. Soc. Am., Am. Geophys. Union, Sigma Xi. Contbr. articles to profl. jours. Office: Dept Agronomy Purdue U West Lafayette IN 47907

CUSSONS, JAMES MARSAR, city ofcl., state ofcl.; b. Cooperstown, N.D., June 12, 1920; s. James Marsar and Josephine (Schermerhorn) C.; student U. N.D., 1938-40; B.S., Mayville (N.D.) State Coll., 1966; postgrad. U. Nev., 1968, U. Wis., Madison, 1970, N.D. State U., 1974. Asst. mgr. Cussons Seed House, 1946-54; owner Prairie Printers, 1954-64; tchr. Cooperstown Public Schs., 1966-75, prin., 1975-78; planner City of Cooperstown, 1979—; mem. N.D. Senate, 1979—; mgr. Grain Identification Co. Mem. City of Cooperstown Council, 1970-75. Served with U.S. Army, 1941-46. Presbyterian. Clubs: Mason, Am. Legion, VFW, Elks.

CUTHBERT, THOMAS WILLIAM, mfg. co. exec.; b. Cicero, Ill., Jan. 22, 1938; s. Gordon Norman and Eleanor Mae (Johnson) C.; student U. Wis., Oshkosh, 1972-73, Oakland Community Coll., 1974—; m. Judith Ann Lader, Apr. 27, 1963; children—Scott Thomas, Amy Ann. Programmer, Wilson Sporting Goods Co., River Grove, Ill., 1963-65; office mgr., instr. Electronic Machine Accounting Coll., Chgo., 1965-66; programmer analyst Rockwell Internat., Oshkosh, 1966-73, systems analyst, div. hdqrs., Troy, Mich., 1973-74, supr. corp. mgmt. systems devel., 1976-77, project mgr. mfg. systems support, 1977-78, mgr. tech. systems support, 1979—. Served with USN, 1956-60; Taiwan. Mem. Am. Prodn. Inventory Control Soc. (dir. sec. Fox Valley, Wis., chpt. 1971-73). Home: 5067 Timber Ridge Trail Clarkston MI 48016 Office: 2135 W Maple Rd Troy MI 48084

CUTHBERTSON, MRS. GEORGE RAYMOND, club woman; b. Liberty, Mo., Apr. 2, 1911; d. Edgar and Mary Jane (Anderson) Archer; student William Jewell Coll., 1929-31; m. George Raymond Cuthbertson, Sept. 3, 1931. Dist. capt. Mothers' March of Dimes, 1959-60; mem. Bergen County Panhellenic Council 1957-60; mem. woman's com. William Jewell Coll. Mem. Mo. Hist. Soc., Clay County Hist. Soc., DAR, Huguenot Soc. S.C., Clay County Mus. Assn., Alpha Delta Pi. Baptist. Club: Fortnightly. Home: 1921 Clay Dr Liberty MO 64068

CUTICCHIA, MICHAEL ANTHONY, engr.; b. Denver, Dec. 15, 1950; s. John Albert and Annagrace (Hart) C.; B.S. in Physics, Purdue U., 1973; M.S., U. Ill., 1978; m. Linda Joy Vinkemulder, July 2, 1977; 1 dau., Michele Marie. Instr. engring. mechanics U. Ill., Urbana, 1975-78; project engr. Detroit Diesel Allison div. Gen. Motors Corp., Indpls., 1978—. Mem. Am. Phys. Soc., Soc. Exptl. Stress Analysis. Episcopalian. Home: 8012 Trailgate Dr Indianapolis IN 46268 Office: PO Box 894 Speed Code U29A Indianapolis IN 46206

CUTLER, GRANVILLE BERRY, educator; b. Mattoon, Ill., Nov. 22, 1919; s. Granville R. and Margaret A. (Berry) C.; B.S., Western Mich. U., 1942; M.A., U. Mich., 1949; m. Betty J. Erickson, Apr. 21, 1946; 1 dau., Mary Louise. Supr. music Three Oaks (Mich.) Twp. Schs., 1942, 46-52; music instr. Holland (Mich.) pub. schs., 1953-54; instr. brass Hope Coll., 1952-54; asst. supt., secondary prin. Sheridan (Mich.) Rural Agrl. Schs., 1954-57; high sch. prin. Plainwell (Mich.) Pub. Schs., 1957-68; nat. comdr. All Am. Drum and Bugle Corps and Band Assn., 1964—; nat. commr. All Am. Assn. Contest Judges, 1965-68. Served with AUS, 1942-45. Named Hon. Citizen New Orleans, 1965, Jefferson Parrish, La., 1964, Hon. Col. La., 1964. Mem. Mich. (regional pres.), Nat. edn. assns., Am. Fedn. Musicians, Am. Legion (comdr. 1950), V.F.W., Phi Delta Kappa, Alpha Phi Omega, Phi Mu Alpha. Clubs: Lions (pres. chpt. 1964; sec. 1972), Masons (32 deg.). Home: 1627 Lay Blvd Kalamazoo MI 49001

CUTLER, JOHN FREDERICK, engring. exec.; b. Pitts., Aug. 23, 1937; s. John Frederick and Mildred Dorothy (Underwood) C.; B.S.M.E., Purdue U., 1959; m. Diana Sue Larkin, July 7, 1959; children—Michael Alan, Mark Stephen, Michelle Lynne. Design engr. Uniroyal, Indpls., 1959-62; prodn. engr. Richardson Co., Indpls., 1962-63; product engr. Schwitzer Wallace Murray Corp., Indpls., 1963—, v.p. engring. and research, 1979—. Bd. dirs. Internat. Center of Indpls., 1978—; chmn. layout com. Internat. Festival, 1979. Registered profl. engr., Ind. Mem. Soc. Automotive Engrs., Soc. Mfg. Engrs., Castleton Estates Homeowners Assn., Milestone Car Soc. Republican. Presbyterian. Patentee in field. Home: 8309 Castlebrook Dr Indianapolis IN 46256 Office: 1125 Brookside Ave Indianapolis IN 46202

CUTLER, NORMAN BARRY, funeral service exec.; b. Chgo., Mar. 5, 1942; s. Jerome and Hannah (Feinberg) C.; B.S.B.A., Northwestern U., 1964, M.B.A., 1965; m. Gail Weinstein, June 30, 1965; children—Brett, Rebecca. Mgmt. trainee First Nat. Bank of Chgo., 1965-66; with Weinstein Bros., Inc., Wilmette, Ill., 1966—, v.p., 1972—; v.p. Levitt-Weinstein, Inc., North Miami Beach, Fla., 1979—; faculty Worsham Coll., Skokie, Ill., 1981—. Bd. dirs. North Suburban Jewish Community Center, 1975—, also past pres.; gen. co-chmn. Channel 11 Public TV Auction, 1974-75; bd. govs. Congregation Am Shalom, Glencoe, Ill. Mem. Jewish Funeral Dirs. Am. (gov.). Club: B'nai B'rith (v.p.). Office: 111 Skokie Blvd Wilmette IL 60091

CUTLER, ROBERT PORTER, psychiatrist, psychoanalyst; b. Chgo., Nov. 13, 1917; s. Percival Nelson and Mary Asenath (Butler) C.; A.B., Princeton U., 1940; B.M., Northwestern U., 1943, M.D., 1944; certificate Chgo. Inst. Psychoanalysis, 1950; m. Patricia Ann Pickett, Apr. 26, 1950; children—Robert, David, Mary, Elliot. Intern, Cook County Hosp., Chgo., 1944-45, Northwestern U. Preble fellow, 1945-46; resident in psychiatry Ill. Neuropsychiat. Inst., Chgo., 1946-48; fellow Ill. Inst. Juvenile Research, Chgo., 1948-49; practice medicine specializing in psychiatry and psychoanalysis, Kenilworth, Ill., 1949-80, Winnetka, Ill., 1980—; asst. prof. psychiatry Northwestern U., 1950-73; asso. clin. prof. psychiatry U. Ill., 1973—. Pres. Kenilworth Caucus, 1968-69, Kenilworth Hist. Soc., 1968-70. Served with USPHS, 1954-56. Fellow Am. Psychiat. Assn. (life); mem. AMA, Ill., Chgo. med. socs., Ill. Psychiat. Soc., Chgo. Psychoanalytic Assn., Central Neuropsychiat. Assn. Republican. Presbyterian. Clubs: Elm, Triangle (Princeton). Contbr. articles to sci. jours. Home and Office: 459 Provident Ave Winnetka IL 60093

CUTLIP, PAUL WESLEY, bus. exec.; b. Streator, Ill., Nov. 18, 1947; s. William Welrose and Helen Grace (Abbot) C.; B.F.A., Ill. Wesleyan U., 1969; m. Barbara Jean Feurstein, Apr. 23, 1977. Store and display designer FLorsheim Shoe Shops, Chgo., 1969-76; dir. advt., store planning and display Milgram-Kagan Corp., South Holland, Ill., 1976; pres. PC/Lyon Assos., Inc., Chgo., 1976-81; dir. sales promotion and mdse. presentation Florsheim Retail Div., Chgo., 1981—. Mem. Inst. Store Planners, Inst. Bus. Designers (trustee Chgo. chpt., mem. nat. bd. 1981—). Republican. Methodist. Club: Jaycees. Office: 130 S Canal St Chicago IL 60606*

CUTNAW (CUGNEAU), MARY-FRANCES, educator, writer; b. Dickinson, N.D., June 15, 1931; d. Delbert A. and Edith (Calhoun Pritchard) Cutnaw; B.S., U. Wis., 1953, M.S., 1957, postgrad., 1959-60, 67-68. Tchr. Displaced Persons Vocat. Sch., Stevens Point, Wis., 1951-52, Pulaski High Sch., Milw., 1953-55; teaching asst. dept. speech U. Wis.-Madison, 1956-57, spl. asst. Sch. Edn., summer 1957; instr. speech and English, U. Wis.-Stout, Menomonie, 1957-58, dean of women, 1958-59, asst. prof. speech, 1959-64, asso. prof., 1964-74, prof. emeritus, 1974—; hon. scholar, teaching asst. dept. speech U. Wis.-Madison, 1959-60, hon. scholar dept. speech, 1967-68. Organizer, past adviser Young Democratic Orgn., U. Wis.-Stout. Mem. Internat. Platform Assn., U. Wis. Alumni Assn., Assn. U. Wis. Faculties, Wis. Acad. Scis., Arts and Letters, Wis. Women's Network, Am. Quarter Horse Assn., Nat. Soc. Prevention Cruelty to Animals, Nat. Anti-Vivisection Soc., Nat. Ret. Tchrs. Assn., Am. Personnel and Guidance Assn., Smithsonian Asso., Linus Pauling Inst., Center for Study Democratic Instns., ACLU, Common Cause, NOW, Walker Art Center, Phi Beta, Sigma Tau Delta, Pi Lambda Theta, Gamma Phi Beta. Roman Catholic. Clubs: Lake City Yacht; Blaisdell Place (dir.), Calhoun Beach. Contbr. articles to profl. jours. Research in speech proficiency and teaching success, curricular speech for spl. occupational groups, speech as guidance tool. Founder, Edith and Kent P. Cutnaw Scholarship, U. Wis.-Stevens Point. Home: Red Cedar Farm Box 282 Menomonie WI 54751 Winter: Key West FL 33040

CYPERT, SAMUEL ALDEN, acctg. co. exec.; b. Granite, Okla., Aug. 5, 1943; s. Alden E. and Ruth N. (Haynes) C.; B.S. magna cum laude, Southwestern Okla. State U., 1970; m. Merrilee Anderson, May 31, 1975; children—Amelia Lee, Elizabeth Anne; children by previous marriage—Beverly, Clif, Benetta. Editor, pub. Weatherford (Okla.) Advertiser, 1968-70; dir. corp. communications Richardson Co., Des Plaines, Ill., 1970-75; dir. communications Profl. Photographers Am., Des Plaines, 1975-79; dir. communications Peat, Marwick, Mitchell & Co., 1979—; mem. adv. com. on mgmt. and mktg. Ill. State Bd. Edn., 1974-78; editorial cons. Pulse mag., 1978—, Mason's Line, 1978—; public relations cons. Ill. State Vet. Med. Assn., 1979—; instr. fin. writing seminars. Pres., Echo Lake Community Corp., 1981—; Ill. Crusade coordinator Am. Cancer Soc., 1981. Served with USN, 1962-66. Mem. Am. Soc. Assn. Execs. Club: Chgo. Publicity. Contbr. articles to consumer mags. and profl. jours. Home: 23957 N Lakewood Dr Lake Zurich IL 60047 Office: 303 E Wacker Dr Chicago IL 60601

CYR, ARTHUR, assn. exec.; b. Los Angeles, Mar. 1, 1945; s. Irving Arthur and Frances Mary C.; B.A., UCLA, 1966, M.A., 1967, A.M., Harvard U., 1969, Ph.D. (Knox travelling fellow, NDEA Title IV and teaching fellow), 1971; m. Betty Jean Totten; children—David Arthur, Thomas Harold. Teaching fellow Harvard U., 1970-71; program officer internat. and edn. research divs. Ford Found., 1971-74; asst. prof. polit. sci., adminstr. internat. studies UCLA, 1974-76; program dir. Chgo. Council Fgn. Relations, 1976—, v.p., 1981—; lectr. polit. sci. U. Ill., Lake Forest Coll. Served with AUS, 1972. Mem. Japan-Am. Soc. Chgo. (dir.), N.Y. Council Fgn. Relations, Internat. Inst. Strategic Studies, Am. Polit. Sci. Assn., Phi Beta Kappa. Club: Univ. (Chgo.). Author: Liberal Party Politics in Britain, 1977; British Foreign Policy and the Atlantic Area, 1979; contbr. articles profl. jours. Office: 116 S Michigan Ave Chicago IL 60603

CYROL, EDMUND ALEXANDER, mgmt. cons., indsl. engr., labor arbitrator; b. Detroit, Oct. 20, 1915; s. Thomas and Marie Teresa (Bach) C.; B.S. in Mech. Engring., U. Mich., 1939; m. Alyce Tarlo, July 4, 1942. Indsl. engr. Murray Corp. Am., Detroit, 1939-41; tool engr. Packard Motor Car Co., Detroit, 1941-42; pres. E.A. Cyrol & Co., mgmt. cons., Chgo., 1950-80; exec. reservist Bus. and Def. Services Adminstrn., U.S. Dept. Commerce, 1964-74; labor arbitrator Weyenberg Shoe Co., Milw., 1976—, Footwear div. Retail Clks. Internat. Union, 1976—, Fed. Mediation and Conciliation Service, Am. Arbitration Assn.; pres. Computerized Standards, Inc., Chgo., 1972-80; labor arbitrator, 1981—; chmn. Nat. Time & Motion Study and Mgmt. Clinic, 1950-54; tchr. math. shop theory various evening schs., Detroit, 1939-42. Registered profl. engr., Ill. Mem. Soc. Indsl. Engrs., Midwest Indsl. Mgmt. Assn. Club: Ill. Athletic. Author: Standard Data for Turret Lathes and Hand Screw Machines, 1952; contbr. numerous articles on indsl. engring. to profl. and tech. jours. Home: 1444 Sequoia Trail Glenview IL 60025

CZACHORSKI, BARBARA CLAIRE, research co. exec.; b. Grand Rapids, Mich., Sept. 11, 1933; d. Leo Jerome and Claire Marie (Dobkoski) C.; B.A., Mich. State U., 1955; M.A., U. Mich., 1958; Northwestern U. fellow Inst. Advanced Advt. Studies, 1965. Account exec. Leo Burnett Co., Inc., Chgo., 1958-68; mgr. media research J. Walter Thompson Co., Chgo., 1968-70; v.p., mktg. dir. Travel Systems Internat., Oak Brook, Ill., 1970-71; Western div. sales mgr. Arbitron Co., Chgo., 1971—. Mem. Am. Women in Radio and Television. Roman Catholic. Clubs: Broadcast Advt., Chgo. Advt.; Fullerton Tennis, Whitehall. Home: 1115 Plymouth Ct Chicago IL 60605 Office: Arbitron Co 1807 Tribune Tower Chicago IL 60611

CZAPLICKI, ROMAN, chiropractic physician; b. Grudziadz, Poland, Aug. 12, 1931; s. Antoni Konstanty and Dominika (Lojewski) C.; came to U.S., 1945; D.Chiropractic, Nat. Coll. Chiropractic, 1960; Diploma in Acupuncture Medicine, Nat. Chinese Taiee Acupuncture Coll., 1971; asso. degree Chinese medicine, Hon Hing Inst. Chinese Medicine, Hong Kong, 1971; diploma in osteopathy New South Wales Osteo. Coll., Sydney, Australia, 1977; certified chiropractic acupuncturist, Nat. Coll. Chiropractic, Chgo., 1977; Cert. clin. hynotherapist, UCLA, 1980; cert. in electro-acupuncture, Voll method, W. Ger., 1980; m. Marrieta Surowka, Mar. 17, 1969; 1 dau., Tatiana Dominika. Pvt. practice chiropractic, Chgo., 1960-68, Sydney, Australia, 1968-71, Warren, Mich., 1972-78, Villa Park, Ill., 1979—; instr. Chinese medicine Am. Coll. Chiropractic Internists, Detroit, 1972—; mem. Center for Integral Medicine, UCLA. Served with AUS, 1950-52. Fellow Am. Coll. Chiropractic Internists; mem. Am., Mich. (dir. dist. 1, bd. appeals peer review, chmn. com. acupuncture research) chiropractic assns., Am. Assn. Chiropractic Medicine, Fla. State Homeopathic Med. Soc. (charter). Author: Acupuncture—5000 Years of Healing Art, 1975. Office: 207 S Villa Villa Park IL 60181

CZARNECKI, GENEVIEVE ANN, nurse, city ofcl.; b. Detroit, Feb. 20, 1932; d. Edward Francis and Mary Ann (Galazka) Czarnecki; B.S. in Nursing, Wayne State U., 1963, M.S. in Nursing, 1965, postgrad., 1972. Mem. staff, supr. St. Joseph Mercy Hosp., Detroit, 1953-65; instr., lead tchr., asst. dir. for nursing Henry Ford Community Coll., Dearborn, Mich., 1965—; chmn. Region 2 Detroit Bd. Edn., 1970-80, vice chmn. central region Detroit Bd. Edn., 1973—; pres. Detroit Bd. Edn. Sch. Health Council, 1977-80; cons. Henry Ford Hosp., Detroit, 1969-71, Hutzel Hosp., Detroit, 1976-77, Wayne State U., Detroit, 1976-78; adviser Detroit dist. Student Nurse Assn. Trustee New Detroit Inc., 1972-78; senator Mich. Ave. Community Orgn., 1977-79. Recipient Outstanding Service to Polish Community award Polish Am. Congress. Mem. Mich. (instr. 1967, mem. adv. com. on refresher courses for nurses), Detroit (v.p., mem. edn. com.) nurses assns., Nat. League for Nursing, Wayne State U. Alumni Assn., Wayne State U. Coll. Nursing Alumni Assn., Mich. Assn. Sch. Bds., Detroit Women Sch. Adminstrs., Am. Assn. Sch. Adminstrs., Nurses Assn. of Am. Coll. Ob-Gyn., Roman Catholic. Author: (with others) (audio-visual program) Observations of Mother in Labor and Delivery; (modules) Maternal Child Health, Physical Assessment. Home: 8106 Dayton St Detroit MI 48210 Office: 5101 Evergreen St Dearborn MI 48128

CZECH, THOMAS JAMES, investment analyst; b. Hammond, Ind., June 15, 1947; s. Walter James and Ann Marie C.; B.S. in Fin., No. Ill. U., 1969, M.B.A. in Fin., 1971. Investment analyst Blunt Ellis & Loewi, Milw., 1972-77, v.p., sr. investment analyst, 1977-80, chartered fin. analyst, 1980—. Mem. Milw. Investment Analysts Soc., Inst. Chartered Fin. Analysts, Fin. Analysts Fedn. Republican. Roman Catholic. Clubs: Milw. Athletic, Vagabond Ski. Office: 225 E Mason Milwaukee WI 53202

DAANE, ARTHUR RUSSELL, real estate broker; b. Ann Arbor, Mich., May 1, 1950; s. Russell Melville and Hildreth (VanHeitsma) D.; B.S., Ind. U., 1972; m. Pamela Louis Daane, June 21, 1980. Fin. analyst Ford Motor Co., Dearborn, Mich., 1972-74; salesman Price Corp., Holland, Mich., 1975-76; pres. Windcrest Promotions, Inc., mfr. and mktg. golf courses, Holland, 1976—; real estate broker, Holland, 1976—; fin. cons. Republican. Presbyterian. Address: 2054 Lake St Holland MI 49423

DABKOWSKI, JOHN, elec. engr.; b. Chgo., Feb. 15, 1933; s. John and Harriet (Sierakowski) D.; B.S. in Elec. Engring., Ill. Inst. Tech., 1955, M.S., 1960, Ph.D., 1969; m. Cecilia Klonowski, June 26, 1976. Sr. research engr. ITT Research Inst., Chgo., 1957-79; mgr. electromagnetics Sci. Applications, Inc., Schaumburg, Ill., 1979—; lectr. Grad. Sch., Ill. Inst. Tech. Served with AUS, 1955-57. Mem. IEEE, Nat. Assn. Corrosion Engrs., Sigma Xi. Roman Catholic. Author research papers in field. Home: 315 Collen Dr Lombard IL 60148 Office: 1701 E Woodfield Rd Schaumburg IL 60195

DABNEY, JACK LEE, psychologist; b. Dubuque, Iowa, Jan. 27, 1929; s. Claude Orvin and Naomi Helen (Stoker) D.; B.S., U. Nebr., 1951, M.A., 1957; m. Lucille Marie Clarence, June 7, 1952. Psychologist, Douglas County Hosp., Omaha, 1955—, mental health coordinator, 1961-71, supr. Hosp. Annex Alcoholism Treatment Program, 1956-57. Served with AUS, 1953-55. Mem. Am. (asso.), Nebr. (affiliate) psychol. assns. Home: 1879 S 133rd St Omaha NE 68144 Office: 4102 Woolworth Ave Omaha NE 68105

DABY, ELIZABETH J., educator; b. Grafton, N.D., Aug. 11, 1949; d. John W. and Mary Elizabeth (Lewis) Gorder; B.S., N.D. State U., 1971; postgrad. U. Ill., 1973, Ill. State U., 1974, U. N.D., 1979-81; m. Neil W. Daby, Aug. 22, 1971; children—Jon, Brian, Scott. Home econs. tchr. Hillsboro (N.D.) High Sch., 1971-72, East Peoria (Ill.) Community High Sch., 1972-75; dir. vocat. programs for handicapped and disadvantaged Edwardsville (Ill.) Sch. Dist., 1975-78; vocat. resource educator N. Valley Vocat. Center, Grafton, N.D., 1978—. Mem. Am. Vocat. Assn., Nat. Assn. Vocat. Edn. Spl. Needs Personnel, AAUW, N.D. Vocat. Edn. Assn., Phi Upsilon Omicron. Club: P.E.O. Home: 1595 Griggs St Grafton ND 58237 Office: Route 1 Grafton ND 58237

DACHMAN, ROBERT, found. exec.; b. Chgo., Aug. 22. 1926; s. Harry Louis and Rose (Schuffler) D.; student U. Ill.; B.A., Roosevelt U., 1949; m. Jeanne Marie Marantz, Aug. 21, 1961; 1 son, Alan Jay. Staff, Maj. Gen. Julius Klein, 1949-50; area dir. City of Hope, 1950-60; dir. pub. relations and devel. Chgo. Med. Sch., 1960-62; exec. dir. Little City Found., Chgo., 1962—. Trustee Orchard Mental Health Center, Better Boys Found. Served with Armed Forces. Mem. 52 Assn. Club: Variety of Ill. (v.p.), B'nai B'rith. Home: 2305 Greenwood St Northbrook IL 60062 Office: 4801 W Peterson St Chicago IL 60646

DACIO, SOCORRO LARDIZABAL, ret. educator; b. Tagudin, Ilocos Sur, Philippines, Sept. 23, 1907; s. Juan Dacio and Martina Lardizabal; came to U.S., 1966, naturalized, 1972; B.S. Edn., U. Philippines, 1930; M.A., Loyola U., Manila, Philippines, 1958; LL.B., Francisco Law Sch. (Philippines), 1960. Prin., Lubao High Sch., Pampanga, Philippines, 1930-33; tchr. Tagudin St. Augustine's High Sch., Philippines, 1933-46; tchr. Francisco Coll., Manila, 1950-60; instr., head edn. dept. Columban Coll., Olongapo City, Zambales, Philippines, 1960-66; instr. English, world lit., head. English dept. Emmetsburg (Iowa) Community Coll., 1967-70; reading, lang. arts tchr. Donoghue Pub. Sch., Chgo., 1970-78. English Program Devel. Act grantee to Simpson Coll., Indianola, Iowa, 1967, U. Chgo., 1968, Kans. State U., 1969, U. West Fla., 1970. Cert. tchr., Chgo. Mem.

Chgo. Tchrs. Union, AAUW, Community Coll. English Assn., Iowa State Ednl. Assn., Modern Lang. Assn. Author: Rowena (a musical drama), 1938; Nabay-bay-an (play), 1939; The Horrors of the Japanese War in the Philippines (satire), 1946; Is the Noli Me Tangere a Novel?, 1958; Influence Peddling-A Crime Punishable By Law, 1960. Home: 2909 N Sheridan Rd Apt 210 Chicago IL 60657 also Tagudin ILocos Sur Philippines also 17 Cambridge Cubao Quezon City Philippines

DAESCHNER, RICHARD WILBUR, food co. exec., b. Preston, Nebr., July 5, 1917; s. Richard T. and Elma (Beckenhauer) D.; B.S. in Edn., Kans. State Tchrs. Coll., 1937; J.D., Washburn U., 1941; m. Prudence Armstrong, June 6, 1942; children—Richard, Rebecca, Martha. Admitted to Kan. bar, 1941; spl. agt. FBI, Washington, Boston, N.Y.C., Chgo., 1941-48; with employee relations dept. Beatrice Foods Co., Chgo., 1948—, dir. employee relations, 1963-68, dir. personnel and indsl. relations, asst. sec., 1968-73, asst. v.p., 1973-78, v.p., 1978—. Mem. Chgo. Crime Commn. Mem. Chgo. Bar Assn., Grocery Mfrs. Assn., Ill. C. of C., Chgo. Assn. Commerce and Industry, Am. Mgmt. Assn., Chgo. Better Bus. Bur. (dir.), Phi Delta Theta. Republican. Presbyn. (trustee). Clubs: Executive (Chgo.); Inverness Golf. Home: 1700 Appleby Rd Palatine IL 60067 Office: 2 N LaSalle St Chicago IL 60602

DAHL, ANDREW WILBUR, health services exec.; b. N.Y.C., Feb. 19, 1943; s. Wilbur A. and Margret L. Dahl; B.S., Clark U., 1968; M.P.A., Cornell U., 1970; Sc.D., Johns Hopkins U., 1974; m. Janice White, Sept. 4, 1965; children—Kristina, Jennifer, Meredith. Staff asst. Md. Comprehensive Health Planning Agy., Balt., 1970-72; dir. planning St. John Hosp., Detroit, 1972-79; exec. v.p., chief operating officer St. Clair Health Services Corp., Detroit, 1979—; adj. asst. prof. Wayne State U. Med. Sch., 1977—; instr. U. Mich. Bur. Hosp. Adminstrn., 1981. Mem. Mayor's Task Force on Child Abuse and Neglect, Detroit, 1975—; mem. New Detroit Health Com., 1977—; dir. Detroit chpt. ARC, 1977—. Served with USN, 1965-67. Recipient Disting. Service award Mich. Jaycees, 1977, Outstanding Contbns. to Profl. Mgmt. award, Cornell U., 1980. Mem. Am. Coll. Hosp. Adminstrs., Am. Hosp. Assn., Am. Public Health Assn., Mich. Hosp. Assn. Methodist. Club: Grosse Pointe Hunt, Renaissance. Office: 22151 Moross Rd Detroit MI 48236

DAHL, GERALD LUVERN, clin. social worker; b. Osage, Iowa, Nov. 10, 1938; s. Lloyd F. and Leola J. (Painter) D.; B.A., Wheaton Coll., 1960; M.S.W., U. Nebr., 1962; m. Judith Lee Brown, June 24, 1960; children—Peter, Stephen, Leah. Juvenile probation officer Hennepin County Ct. Services, 1962-65; cons. Citizens Council on Delinquency and Crime, Mpls., 1965-67; dir. patient services Mt. Sinai Hosp., Mpls., 1967-69; clin. social worker Mpls. Clinic of Psychiatry, 1969—; asso. prof. social work Bethel Coll., St. Paul, 1964—; spl. instr. sociology Golden Valley Luth. Coll., 1974—. Founder, Family Counseling Service, Minn. Baptist Conf.; bd. dirs. Edgewater Baptist Ch., 1972-75, chmn., 1974-75. Mem. Nat. Assn. Social Workers, AAUP, Minn. Psychol. Soc., Pi Gamma Mu. Author: Why Christian Marriages Are Breaking Up, 1979; Everybody Needs Somebody Sometime, 1980. Office: 4225 Golden Valley Rd Minneapolis MN 55422

DAHL, GREGORY, lawyer, state senator; b. Mpls., Mar. 25, 1952; s. Fred and Lee Dahl; B.A. summa cum laude, St. Olaf Coll., Northfield, Minn., 1974; J.D., Stanford U., 1977. Admitted to Minn. bar, 1977; intern U.S. Congressional Internship Program, 1974; research asst. to U.S. Senator Humphrey, 1976; mem. firm Leonard, Street and Deinard, Mpls., 1977—; mem. Minn. Senate, since 1981—. Mem. White Bear Lake (Minn.) Charter Commn.; pres., mem. council St. Stephen's Luth. Ch. Mem. Minn. Bar Assn., Ramsey County Bar Assn., Hennepin County Bar Assn., Sierra Club, White Bear Lake Hist. Soc. Mem. Democratic Farm Labor Party. Office: Room G-24 State Capitol Saint Paul MN 55155

DAHL, HARRY WALDEMAR, lawyer; b. Des Moines, Aug. 7, 1927; s. Harry Waldemar and Helen Gerda (Anderson) D.; B.A., U. Iowa, 1950; J.D., Drake U., 1955; m. Bonnie Sorensen, June 14, 1952; children—Harry Waldemar, Lisabeth (dec.), Christina. Admitted to Iowa bar, 1955, Fla. bar, 1970; practiced in Des Moines, 1955-59, 70—, Miami, Fla., 1972—; mem. firm Steward & Crouch, Des Moines, 1955-59; Iowa dep. indsl. commr., Des Moines, 1959-62, commr. 1962-71; pres. law firm Harry W. Dohl, P.C., Des Moines, 1970—; mem. firm Underwood, Gillis and Karcher, Miami, 1972-78; adj. prof. law Drake U., 1969—. Exec. dir. Internat. Assn. Indsl. Accident Bds. and Commns., 1972-77; dean Coll. Workmen's Compensation, 1972-76, bd. dirs., 1978—; pres. Workers' Compensation Studies, Inc., 1974—, Workers' Compensation Services, Inc., 1977—, Hewitt, Coleman & Assos. Iowa, Inc., 1975-79; founder, mem. Iowa Workers' Compensation Adv. Com., 1963—. Served with USNR, 1945-46. Recipient Adminstrs. award Internat. Assn. Indsl. Accident Bds. and Commns., 1967. Mem. Assn. Trial Lawyers Am. (chmn. workers compensation sect. 1974-75), Am. (chmn. workers compensation com. 1976—), Iowa bar assns., Fla. Bar, Iowa Assn. Workers' Compensation Lawyers (co-founder, treas. 1978—), Am. Soc. Law and Medicine (council 1975—), Swedish Pioneer Hist. Soc., East High Alumni Assn. (pres. 1975-76), Order of Coif. Lutheran. Mason (Shriner). Clubs: Sertoma (chmn. bd. 1974-75), Des Moines Pioneer. Author: Iowa Law on Workmen's Compensation, 1975; contbr. articles to legal jours. Editor ABC Newsletter, 1964-77. Home: 3005 Sylvania Dr Des Moines IA 50365 Office: 5835 Grand Ave Des Moines IA 50312

DAHL, HENRY LAWRENCE, JR., pharm. co. exec.; b. Topeka, Mar. 5, 1933; s. Henry and Emiline Ruth (Holtz) D.; B.B.A., U. Minn., 1955; m. Gayle Beggs, Oct. 2, 1952; children—Henry Lawrence III, Richard W., Dorothy G., William J., John L., Lorna A. Successively employee relations adminstr. pharm. prodn. div., employee relations adminstr. pharm. research and devel., mgr. corp. employment, mgr. manpower planning Upjohn Co., Kalamazoo, 1957-72, mgr. employee devel. and planning, 1972—; lectr., pub. in field; producer mgmt. devel. motion pictures. Former pres. Immanuel Lutheran Ch.; v.p. Kalamazoo Valley Intermediate Sch. Bd., 1976; sec. Youth Unltd., Inc., 1979; bd. dirs. Kalamazoo YMCA; boys basketball coach; Little League baseball coach; mem. Kalamazoo 2000 Com. Served to 1st lt. USAF, 1955-57. Recipient Upjohn award, 1976. Mem. Kalamazoo Mgmt. Assn. (v.p., 1965), Am. Soc. Personnel Adminstrn. (accredited), Am. Soc. Tng. and Devel., Human Resource Planning Soc., Human Resource Acctg. Assn. Republican. Home: 4109 Canterbury St Kalamazoo MI 49007 Office: 7000 Portage Rd Kalamazoo MI 49001

DAHL, IRWIN ALPHY, coll. adminstr.; b. Mpls., Aug. 13, 1912; s. Ole Ingebretsen and Inga Marie (Svengaard) D.; B.S., U. Minn., 1935, M.A., 1939; grad. Command and Gen. Staff Coll., 1953; postgrad. Stanford U., 1968; m. Marion Catherine Tuttle, June 7, 1939; 1 dau., Mary Katheryn. Instr., U. Minn., 1935-36; tchr. Becker (Minn.) High Sch., 1936-39; prin. Aitkin (Minn.) High Sch., 1939-41; commd. 1st lt. U.S. Army, 1941, advanced through grades to lt. col. 1950; instr. Inf. Sch., Ft. Benning, Ga., 1941-43; officer Inf., ETO, 1943-45; exchange staff officer Canadian Army Sch. Center, Camp Borden, Ont., 1947-49; assigned Q.M. Sch., Ft. Lee, Va., 1949-50; battalion comdr., Korea, 1950; staff officer 8th U.S. Army, Korea, 1951-52; exec. officer U.S. Graves Registration Service, Japan, 1952-53; dir. Office Procurement Policy Office of Q.M. Gen., Washington, 1954-57; student Logistics Mgmt. Inst., 1957; bn. comdr., ETO, 1957-60; asst. comdt. Armed Forces Food and Container Inst., Chgo., 1960-62; logistics officer U.S. Army Support Group, Vietnam, 1962-63; comdg. officer U.S. Army Subsistence Center, Chgo., 1963-65; ret., 1965; dept. mgr. Bank of Am., San Francisco, 1945-47; instr. Thornton Community Coll., 1965-68, dir. instl. resources and devel., 1968-78; ret., 1978. Decorated Bronze Star medal with 2 oak leaf clusters. Mem. U. Minn. "M" Club, Ret. Officers Assn., Alpha Sigma Pi, Phi Delta Kappa. Roman Catholic. Contbr. articles to profl. publs. Home: 418 Springfield St Park Forest IL 60466

DAHL, LEONA MAE, retail store exec.; b. Dawson, Minn., July 18, 1927; d. Edwin L. and Esther E. (Larson) Stratmoen; grad. Minn. Sch. Bus., 1946; m. Frederick A. Dahl, June 19, 1948; children—Rick, Jeffrey, Gregory, Gary. Sec. to v.p. Minn. Fed. Savings and Loan, Mpls., 1946-47, Marsh & McClennan Ins. Co., Mpls., 1947-48; pres. The Dahl House, Northfield, Mankato, Rochester, Owatonna, Winona and Red Wing, Minn., Spencer, Iowa, 1967—. Bd. dirs. Norfield Human Relations Bd., 1976-79. Mem. Minn. Retail Merchants Assn., Nat. Retail Merchants Assn., Minn. Assn. Commerce and Industry, Northfield C. of C. (dir. 1979—). Lutheran. Office: 306 Division St Northfield MN 55057

DAHLAGER, JEROME CHARLES, social worker; b. Montevideo, Minn., July 4, 1940; s. Herman Burnett and Wilma Lillian (Rosvold) D.; B.A., Concordia Coll., Moorhead, Minn., 1962; M.S.W., U. Man. (Can.), 1968; m. Sandra Arlene Hanson, Dec. 27, 1964; children—Michelle Lea, Steven Paul. Social caseworker welfare bd. County of Richland (N.D.), Wahpeton, 1962-66; social worker Area Social Service Center, Jamestown, N.D., 1968-70, social work supr., 1970-71, acting area adminstr., 1971-72; social worker Resocialization Center, VA Med. Center, St. Cloud, Minn., 1972-77, coordinator, 1977-79, social worker Intermediate Med. Service, 1979—. Recipient Superior Performance award VA Med. Center, 1979. Mem. Nat. Assn. Social Workers, Acad. Cert. Social Workers. Lutheran. Home: 907 Brenda Lee Dr Saint Cloud MN 56301 Office: Government Site Saint Cloud MN 56301

DAHLEM, VALENTINE, aerospace engr.; b. Louisville, Sept. 5, 1935; s. Valentine and Ethel Margarette (Elder) D.; B.S. in Aero. Engring., St. Louis U., 1956; M.S., Ohio State U., 1973; m. Shirley Marie Cissell, Oct. 20, 1956; children—Gregory A., Andrew M. Valerie M., Jennifer A. Asso. engr. Marquardt Corp., Van Nuys, Calif., 1956, aeronautical engr., 1959-61; aerospace engr. Flight Dynamics Lab., Wright-Patterson AFB, 1961-65, supervisory aerospace engr., 1965—; mem. U.S.-U.K. Tech. Coordinating Panel. Served with USAF, 1956-59. Recipient Engring. Achievement award Dayton chpt. Research Soc. Am., 1967; Foulois award for outstanding engring. achievement Flight Dynamics Lab., 1973. Mem. AIAA, Sigma Xi. Roman Catholic. Author lab. reports on developments in aerodynamics. Home: 7594 Chambersburg Rd Dayton OH 45424 Office: Flight Dynamics Lab Wright Patterson AFB OH 45433

DAHLEN, LEE ELDON, mfg. co. exec.; b. Milw., Dec. 24, 1939; s. Olfer Julian and Doris Beatrice (Jeske) D.; A. Welding Tech., Milw. Inst. Tech., 1963; m. Barbara Jean Kiefer, Oct. 16, 1965; children—Leann Marie, Lynda Ann, Lee Julian. Technician, Inland Steel Corp., Milw., 1963-68; process engr. West Bend Aluminum Corp. (Wis.), 1968-75; technician A.O. Smith Corp., Milw., 1976-79; sr. mfg. engr. Maysteel Corp., Mayville, Wis., 1979—. Served with U.S. Army, 1957-60. Cert. mfg. engr., Soc. Mfg. Engrs.; cert. welding inspector, Am. Welding Soc. Mem. Am. Welding Soc., Soc. Mfg. Engrs., Nat. Hist. Soc., Sons of Union Vets of the Civil War. Republican. Lutheran. Club: Moose. Home: 1435 Wayne Rd West Bend WI 53095 Office: 800 Horicon St Mayville WI 53050

DAHLIN, MOIRA LINNEA, occupational therapist; b. L.I., N.Y., July 10, 1953; d. William Reinhold and Patricia (Gilmore) D.; student Mich. State U., 1971-74; B.S., Eastern Mich. U., 1975. Staff occupational therapist Macomb Easter Seal Soc., Mt. Clemens, Mich., 1977-79, Detroit Inst. Children, 1979—; fieldwork instr. occupational therapy depts. Wayne State U., 1979—, Eastern Mich. U., 1979—. Mem. Am. Occupational Therapy Assn., Center Study Sensory Integrative Dysfunction. Home: 2200 Crooks Rd Apt 29 Troy MI 48084 Office: 5447 Woodward Ave Detroit MI 48202

DAHLJELM, HARVEY DOUGLAS, air force officer; b. Highland Park, Mich., Feb. 12, 1946; s. Irving LeRoy and Ellen Ann (Mandel) D.; B.S. in Elec. Engring., Mich. State U., 1968; postgrad. No. Mich. U., 1972-75, Mich. Technol. U., 1974-75; M.S. in Elec. Engring., Air Force Inst. Tech., 1976; m. Cathy Anne Caseman, Aug. 11, 1979. Commd. 2d lt. USAF, 1968, advanced through grades to maj., 1979; various assignments including electronic warfare officer 16th spl. ops. squadron Ubon RTAF, Thailand, 1971-72, 644th Bombardment Squadron, Sawyer AFB, Mich., 1972-75; assigned Air Force Inst. Tech., Wright-Patterson AFB, Ohio, 1975-76, SR-71/U-2 devel. engr. aero. systems div. Air Force Systems Command, 1976-80, 524th Bombardment Squadron, Wurtsmith AFB, Mich., 1980—; with Giant Strike Task Force Hdqrs., Marham AFB, Eng., 1973, 43d Strategic Wing Anderson AFB, Guam, 1973, 307th Strategic Wing U-Tapao RTAF, Thailand, 1973; grad. Naval War Coll., 1973, Indsl. Coll. Armed Forces, 1973. Chief cons. Mich. State U. Computer Lab., 1965-68. Asst. dist. commr. Piere Marquette Boy Scouts Am., 1972-75. Decorated D.F.C. (2), Meritorious Service medal, Air medals (12); recipient award Detroit Free Press, 1968. Mem. IEEE (pres. Mich. State U. chpt. 1968, pres. Air Force Inst. Tech. chpt. 1975-76, Outstanding Leadership and Service award 1977), Assn. Computing Machinery (pres. Mich. State U. chpt. 1967), Nat., Mich. socs. profl. engrs., Soc. Am. Mil. Engrs., AAAS, Armed Forces Communication and Electronics Assn., Nat. Eagle Assn., Air Force Inst. Tech. Assn. Grads., Assn. Old Crows (Snow Crows pres. 1972-74, chmn. bd. 1974-75, pres. Gt. Lakes 1981-82), Delta Sigma Phi, Alpha Pi. Club: Mich. State U. Alumni (East Lansing, Mich.). Home: 341 Lexington Ave East Lansing MI 48823 Office: Box 1206 Wurtsmith AFB MI 48753

DAHLSTRAND, JOSEF YNGVE, JR., mfg. co. exec.; b. Wellsville, N.Y., Oct. 16, 1922; s. Josef Yngve and Mildred Anna (Spicer) D.; student Ind. U., 1942-43; B.S.M.E., Purdue U., 1950; m. Marilou Medsker, Oct. 7, 1941; children—Kim, Kurt. Tool designer Chevrolet, Indpls., 1942-43; design engr. Universal Gear Corp., Indpls., 1944; cons. engr., Dahlstrand Engring. Co., Indpls., 1949-50; pres., founder Odin Corp., Indpls., 1950-81, chmn. bd., 1981—; cons. power transmission. Served to staff sgt. U.S. Army, World War II; ETO. Decorated Bronze Star with oak leaf cluster; recipient 3 poetry awards from radio stas., 1977, 78, 79. Mem. ASME, Soc. Automotive Engrs., Soc. Am. Inventors, Purdue Ind. Assn., Purdue Alumni Assn. Democrat. Club: Indpls. Athletic. Contbr. numerous poems to newspapers, mags.; patentee in field. Office: 6736 E 82d St Indianapolis IN 46250

DAHN, CARL JAMES, aero. engr.; b. Chgo., June 22, 1936; s. Carl E. and Genevieve (Bardon) D.; B.S. in Aero. Engring., U. Minn., 1959; m. Rose E. Kucenski, May 25, 1974. Rocket propulsion devel. engr. Aerojet Gen. Corp., Azusa, Calif., 1959-61, propulsion and explosives devel. engr., 1962-63; chief engr. Omega Ordanace Co., Azusa, 1961-62; propulsion and explosives specialist Honeywell, Inc., Mpls., 1963-68; system safety research engr. IIT Research Inst. Systems Hazard Analysis, Chgo., 1968-74; hazards engring. specialist Polytechnic, Inc., Chgo., 1974-77; pres. Safety Cons. Engrs., Inc., Rosemont, Ill., 1977—; instr. explosives, guns and ballistics; cons. in same field. Asst. scout master Mpls. St. Paul council Boy Scouts Am., 1962; area dir. Parents Without Partners, 1973; ward chmn. Republican party, 1964; ward chmn. Democratic party, 1973. Mem. Am. Soc. Safety Engrs., ASTM (com. sec.), System Safety Soc., Soc. Explosives Engrs., Nat. Soc. Profl. Engrs. Democrat. Methodist and Roman Catholic. Club: N.W. Divorced Catholic Group. Researcher, patentee in explosives field. Home: 6118 W Melrose St Chicago IL 60634 Office: 5240 Pearl St Rosemont IL 60018

DAILEY, JAMES ROBERTS, state legislator; b. Riley, Ind., June 22, 1919; s. James Andrew and Ruth Esther (Roberts) D.; B.S., Ind. State U., 1941; m. Anita Louise Arment Walker, 1968; children—Coleen Dailey Dristas, John R., Christopher J. Walker. Partner, Bender Co., Muncie, Ind., 1946-53; pres. Dailey & Co., 1953-80; pres., treas. J. Roberts Dailey & Co., Inc., Tillotson Devel. Corp.; v.p. Muncie Indsl. Devel. Corp.; dir., mem. exec. com. Am. Nat. Bank & Trust Co., Muncie; chmn. bd. Allardt & Dailey, Realtors; mem. Ind. State Ho. of Reps., 1976—, speaker, 1980—. Mem. Ind. Assn. Realtors (pres. 1975-76), Multiple Listing Assn. Muncie. Methodist. Office: Ind Ho of Reps Indianapolis IN 46204

DAILEY, JOSEPH MICHAEL, educator; b. Peoria, Ill., Oct. 26, 1942; s. Joseph Henry and Elenore Mary (Ryan) D.; B.A., St. Norbert Coll., 1964; M.A., Marquette U., 1965; Ph.D. in Communication, U. Ill., 1975; m. Barbara Norman, July 2, 1966; children—Christine Loan, Sean Patrick, Joseph Ryan. Tech. asst. dept. theatre U. Ill., 1968-69; instr. English and speech Danville (Ill.) Jr. Coll., 1969-72; asst. prof. communication, dir. journalism studies Carroll Coll., Waukesha, Wis., 1972—. Chmn. Waukesha Cable TV Commn., 1974-78; pres. Ill. Council on Adoptable Children, 1971-72. Served with U.S. Army, 1966-68. Decorated Bronze star. Mem. Assn. Edn. Journalism, Internat. Communication Assn., Communication Assn. Am. Roman Catholic. Office: Voorhees Hall Carroll Coll Waukesha WI 53186

DAILEY, ROBERT FRANCIS, research engr.; b. Cleve., May 26, 1951; s. Robert Francis and Patricia Jean (Kennedy) D.; B.S. with high honors, U. Notre Dame, 1974; M.S. in Indsl. and Systems Engring., Ohio State U., 1979. Tchr., head math. dept. Hoban High Sch., Akron, Ohio, 1974-77; asst. to dean Coll. Engring. Ohio State U., Columbus, 1977-79; mem. tech. staff Bell Telephone Labs., Naperville, Ill., 1979—; counselor Ill. Benedictine Coll., Lisle, Ill., 1979—. Mem. Ops. Research Soc. Am., Sigma Xi, Phi Kappa Phi, Alpha Pi Mu. Roman Catholic. Home: Brothers of Holy Cross PO Box 460 Notre Dame IN 46556

DAILY, FAY KENOYER, educator; b. Indpls., Feb. 17, 1911; d. Frederick and Camellia Thea (Neal) Kenoyer; A.B., Butler U., 1935, M.S., 1952; m. William Allen Daily, June 24, 1937. Lab. technician Eli Lilly & Co., Indpls., 1935-37, Abbott Labs., North Chicago, Ill., 1939, William S. Merrell & Co., Ohio, 1940-41; lubrication chemist Indpls. Propellor div. Curtiss-Wright Corp., 1945; lectr. botany Butler U., Indpls., 1947-49, instr. immunology and microbiology, 1957-58, lectr. microbiology, 1962-63, mem. herbarium staff, 1949—. Ind. Acad. Sci. research grantee, 1961-62. Mem. Am. Inst. Biol. Sci., Bot. Soc. Am., Phycol. Soc. Am., Internat. Phycol. Soc., Ind. Acad. Sci., Sigma Xi, Phi Kappa Phi, Sigma Delta Epsilon. Republican. Methodist. Contbr. articles to profl. jours. Home: 5884 Compton St Indianapolis IN 46220

DAIZA, FRANK J., mfg. co. exec.; b. Baghdad, Iraq, Aug. 2, 1937; s. Jajjoo S. and Mariam P. (Shammami) D.; came to U.S., 1953, naturalized, 1960; student Baghdad Coll., 1949-53, Highland Park Jr. Coll., 1954; B.S., Great Lakes Coll., 1963; m. Rosetta Scott, Feb. 12, 1960; children—Renee, Kathleen, George, Vanessa. Pres., Hamilton Wholesale, Highland Park, Mich., 1964-67; v.p. Rohr Sales, Detroit, 1967-71; pres. Martin & Snyder Products Sales, Detroit, 1971—, Daiza Inc., Farmington Hills, 1977—. Address: 29818 Deer Run Farmington Hills MI 48018

DAL CANTO, MAURO CARLO, pathologist, educator; b. Soriano, Italy, Jan. 1, 1944; s. Alvaro and Eggi Dal C.; came to U.S., 1969, naturalized, 1976; M.D., U. Pisa (Italy), 1967; m. Mariafiora Neri, Jan. 4, 1968; children—Richard, Albert. Intern, L.I. Coll. Hosp., Bklyn., 1969-70; resident in pathology and neuropathology Albert Einstein Coll. Medicine, Bronx, N.Y., 1970-74; asso. pathology Northwestern U. Med. Sch., Chgo., 1974-75, asst. prof. pathology and neurology, 1975-77, asso. prof., 1977-81, prof. pathology and neurology, 1981—; dir. neuropathology Children's Meml. Hosp., Chgo., 1978-81, Northwestern U. Med. Sch., 1981—; cons. Evanston (Ill.) Hosp. Nat. Multiple Sclerosis Soc. grantee, 1976, 79, NIH grantee, 1976—. Mem. Am. Assn. Neuropathologists, AAAS, Soc. for Neurosci. Roman Catholic. Contbr. articles to profl. jours. Home: 430B W Webster Ave Chicago IL 60614 Office: Northwestern U Medical School Dept Pathology 303 E Chicago Ave Chicago IL 60611

DALE, BARBARA JEAN, retail furniture co. exec.; b. Evanston, Ill., Oct. 21, 1940; d. William James and Celia Josephine (Staerk) Deuerling; student DePaul U., 1960; A.S. in Bus. Adminstrn., Coll. Lake County, Grayslake, Ill., 1980; d. Walter G. Dale, Jr., Oct. 21, 1961; children—Kelley Ann, Linda Marie, Colleen Michele, Erin Renee, Brenda Leigh. Various secretarial and office positions, 1958-62; village clk. Village of Island Lake (Ill.), 1965-69; owner, operator Lake Zurich (Ill.) News Agy., 1970-74; accounts payable mgr. Colby's Home Furnishings, Northbrook, Ill., 1974-81, inventory control mgr., 1981—; treas. United Catholic Credit Union, 1965-80. 4-H Club leader, 1961-81; rhythm guitarist Eight Chair Four sq. dance band, 1979—. Mem. Nat. Assn. Female Execs., Ill. Sq. Dance Callers Assn., Pullman Players Stock Co. Roman Catholic. Clubs: Carousel Cloggers (dir.) (Island Lake, Ill.); Fedn. Lake County Callers.

DALE, JAMES MICHAEL, advt. exec.; b. Highland Park, Mich., Oct. 31, 1948; s. Mark and Evelyn R. Dale; B.A. cum laude, U. Mich., 1970; m. Barbara B. Dale, Dec. 20, 1970; 1 son, Andrew Thomas. Trainee, Campbell Ewald Advt., 1969; copywriter W.B. Doner & Co., 1970, copy chief, 1975, creative dir., 1976—, sr. v.p., 1979—. Recipient Andy awards, Clios, Effies, Caddy awards. Mem. Creative Advt. Club Detroit (pres. 1977), Copy Club N.Y. Democrat. Jewish. Office: 26711 Northwestern St Southfield MI 48034

DALE, JOHN SORENSEN, banker; b. Mpls., Sept. 30, 1945; s. John Sorensen and Ruth Elaine (Bergstrom) D.; B.A., U. Minn., 1968; m. Cheryl Lee Woolley, June 19, 1965; children—John Sorensen, Christopher. With Northwestern Nat. Bank of Mpls., 1968—, sr. analyst, group leader, 1973-74, asst. v.p., 1974-80, sr. investment analyst, 1974—, v.p., 1980—, equity strategist, 1980—. Mem. Fin. Analysts Fedn. (charter fin. analyst), Am. Bankers Assn., Minn. Bankers Assn., Inst. Chartered Fin. Analysts, Twin Cities Soc. Security Analysts, Am. Inst. Banking, Corp. Fiduciaries. Office:

Northwestern Nat Bank of Mpls 7th and Marquette Ave Minneapolis MN 55480

DALE, MARYELLEN, mfg. co. exec.; b. Bedford, Ohio, Nov. 1, 1947; d. Jessie and Luvenia (Kirkland-Rogers) Rogers; student public schs., Bedford, Ohio; children—Celina Louise, Celia Kimberly, Michelle Lynn, Michael Lawrence. Asst. supr. order dept. Williams & Co., Cleve., 1966-68; sales and engring. sec. Interior Steel Equipment Co., Cleve., 1969-71; owner co., Cleve., 1972-74; mgr. advt. adminstrn. CleCon, Inc., Cleve., 1974—; mktg./advt. cons.; proposal writer for fed. funding for community devel. project. Promotion cons. Social Services Dept., County Welfare Foster Child Div., Cleve., 1981—; adv. com. Am. Heart Assn., 1981—. Recipient awards, Cleve. Bus. and Econs. Devel., 1970, Cleve. Advt. Sch., 1976, Splty. Merchandising Corp., 1977. Mem. Internat. Traders, Am. Mgmt. Assn., Black Profl. Assn., Career Guild, Nat. Assn. Female Execs. Baptist. Clubs: Cleve. Advt., Cleve. Communicators. Contbr. articles to profl. jours. Home: 9407 Easton Ave Cleveland OH 44104 Office: 2909 E 79th St Cleveland OH 44104

DALE, RICHARD, polit. scientist; b. Columbus, Ohio, Oct. 22, 1932; s. Edgar and Elizabeth Cullen (Kirchner) D.; m. Doris Mae Cruger, Aug. 18, 1967; A.B., Bowdoin Coll., 1954; postgrad. Columbia U. Coll. Physicians and Surgeons, 1954-55; M.A., Ohio State U., 1957; M.A., Princeton U., 1961, Ph.D., 1962. Instr. govt. U. N.H., 1962-63; asst. prof. polit. sci. No. Ill. U., 1963-66; adj. prof. polit. Sci. So. Ill. U., Carbondale, 1966-67, asst. prof., 1967-71, asso. prof., 1971—; mem. council and exec. com. S.African Inst. Race Relations, 1974-75; mem. adv. bd. Univ. Press Am., 1976-81. Served with U.S. Army, 1957-59. Mem. Am., Midwest polit. sci. assns., Internat. Studies Assn., Inter-Univ. Seminar on Armed Forces and Soc., African Studies Assn., Western Assn. Africanists, Royal United Services Inst. for Def. Studies (London), Botswana Soc., S.W. Africa Sci. Soc., Polit. Sci. Assn. S.Africa, Africa Inst. of S. Africa, S.African Mil. History Soc., Delta Tau Delta. Nat. Def. Fgn. Lang. fellow in Afrikaans, U. Calif., Los Angeles, summer 1964; Am. Philos. Soc. travel grantee, summer 1970, winter 1979-80; Inter-Univ. Seminar travel grantee, winter 1979-80. Author monographs; co-editor, contbr. to Southern Africa in Perspective: Essays in Regional Politics, 1972; mem. editorial adv. bd. Jour. Contemporary African Studies, 1980—. contbr. articles to profl. jours.

DALE, STANLEY IRVIN, JR., lawyer; b. Little Rock, Jan. 2, 1921; s. Stanley Irvin and Kathryn Gladys (Stone) D.; A.A., Mo. Western State Coll., 1940; J.D., U. Mo., 1943; postgrad. U. Hawaii, 1945; m. Glenda Marie Gerard, Feb. 5, 1949; children—Stanley Irvin, Cynthia Susan, Stephen Glenn. Claims atty. St. Joseph Light & Power Co. (Mo.), 1945-46; admitted to Mo. bar, 1943; pvt. practice law, St. Joseph, 1946-48; claims atty. State Farm Ins. Cos., St. Joseph, 1948-50; mayor of St. Joseph, 1950-58; pvt. practice law, sr. mem. firm Dale, Flynn, Mendell & Barnes, St. Joseph, 1958—. Mem. Bd. Police Commrs., City of St. Joseph, 1950-58, mem. charter commn., 1960-61; trustee Mo. Western State Coll.; chmn. Rep. Party of Mo., 1977-78; mem. Rep. Nat. Com., 1977-78. Served with USAAF, 1943-45. Named Most Outstanding Young Man in Mo., Jaycees, 1951. Mem. Am. Bar Assn., Mo. Bar Assn., Am. Legion, V.F.W. Methodist. Clubs: Masons, Shriners. Home: 5114 Stonecrest Terr Saint Joseph MO 64506 Office: Suite 345 Robidoux Center Saint Joseph MO 64501

DALEIDEN, JEROME JOHN, state ofcl.; b. Chgo., Jan. 16, 1944; s. John W. and Helen (Trisilla) D.; B.S. in Civil Engring., U. Ill., Urbana-Champaign, 1967; postgrad. U. Ill., Chgo., 1977—; m. M. Gail McMasters, Oct. 7, 1968. Constrn. engr. Ill. Dept. Transp., Elgin, Ill., 1967-68, designer, Elgin, 1968-70, data processing coordinator, Elgin, 1970-71, dist. 1 data processing mgr., Schaumburg, 1971—. Named Engr. of Yr., Dist. 1 of State of Ill. Dept. Transp., 1981; registered profl. engr., Ill.; certificate in data processing Inst. Cert. Computer Profls. Mem. ASCE. Home: 1204 Highridge Rd Lombard IL 60148

DALEY, ROBERT EMMETT, found. exec.; b. Cleve., Mar. 13, 1933; s. Emmett Wilfred and Anne Gertrude (O'Donnell) D.; B.A. in English, U. Dayton, 1955; M.A. in Polit. Sci., Ohio State U., 1968, M.A. in Public Adminstrn., 1976; m. Mary Berneta Fredericks, June 7, 1958; children—Marianne Fredericks, John Gerard. Part-time copy boy, sports reporter Jour. Herald, Dayton, Ohio, 1953-55, local govt. reporter, Washington corr., fin. editor, 1957-65, public affairs reporter, 1967; staff writer Congressional Quar., Inc., Washington, 1966; traveling press sec. for senatorial candidate John J. Gilligan, Ohio, 1968, for gubernatorial candidate John J. Gilligan, 1970-71, asst. to Gov. Gilligan, 1971-75; public affairs reporter Dayton Daily News, 1969; media relations coordinator Nat. League Cities, Washington, 1976-77; dir. public affairs and communications Charles F. Kettering Found., Dayton, 1977—. Pres. bd. trustees St. Joseph Home for Children. Served with U.S. Army, 1955-57. Mem. Nat. Press Club, Public Relations Soc. Am., Am. Polit. Sci. Assn., Am. Soc. Public Adminstrn., Found. Communications Network (chmn.), Am. Acad. Polit. and Social Sci., Montgomery County Hist. Soc., Sigma Delta Chi (ind. sector public info. and edn. com.). Roman Catholic. Clubs: K.C., Ancient Order Hibernians. Home: 321 Whittington Dr Centerville OH 45429 Office: 5335 Far Hills Ave Dayton OH 45429

DALGAARD, BRUCE RONALD, economist, educator; b. Waukegan, Ill., July 29, 1947; s. Bruce Irving and Lena Alfreda (Pederson) D.; A.B., U. Ill., 1969, M.S. (Earhart Found. fellow), 1974, Ph.D. (Lincoln fellow), 1976; m. Kathleen Marie Albrecht, Aug. 24, 1968. Tchr. social studies Barrington (Ill.) High Sch., 1969-72; lectr. U. Ill., Urbana, 1974-75; asst. prof. econs., dir. Center for Econ. Edn., Lehigh U., Bethlehem, Pa., 1976-80; asst. prof. econ. edn. U. Minn., Mpls., 1980—, dir. Center for Econ. Edn., 1980—; exec. dir. Minn. Council on Econ. Edn., Mpls., 1980—; cons. edn. com. Am. Iron and Steel Inst.; cons. econ. edn. program NSF. Mem. Am. Econ. Assn., Eastern Econ. Assn., So. Econ. Assn., Minn. Econ. Assn., Econ. History Assn., Nat. Assn. Affiliated Econ. Edn. Dirs., Bus. History Conf., History of Econs. Soc., Orgn. Am. Historians, Phi Alpha Theta, Omicron Delta Epsilon. Author: South Africa's Impact on Britain's Return to Gold, 1981; editor: Proc. Steel Industry Economics Seminar, 1977; Variations in Business and Economic History, 1982; contbr. articles to profl. jours. Office: 1169 Mgmt and Econs Bldg U Minn 271 19th Ave S Minneapolis MN 55455

DALIERE, JOHN FRANKLIN, communications co. exec.; b. Cleve., May 23, 1940: s. Mark Hannah and Marie Agnus (Hellriegel) D.; B.A., Colgate U., 1962; diploma in Italian Studies, Syracuse U., 1961; B.S. (Barton Kyle Yount scholar), Am. Grad. Sch. Internat. Mgmt., 1964: diploma in Acctg., Northwestern U., 1963; m. Susan Eleanor Heitmann, Apr. 20, 1964: children—Mark, Eric, Marisa. Mgmt. trainee Continental Bank, 1963; mktg. mgr., br. mgr. Goodyear Internat., Rome, 1964-68; v.p., gen. mgr. Litart-Istituto Internazionale di Arte Liturgica, Rome and Chgo., 1968-71; mgr. internat. ops. Unistrut GTE, Wayne, Mich., 1971-74; v.p., gen. mgr., dir. GTE Unistrut Internat., Inc., Wayne., 1974-81; dir., officer 6 subs., U.K., Mex., South Africa, Can., Holland, Australia, N.Z.; gen. mgr., dir. Adistra Corp., 1981—; lectr. U. Mich., World Trade Inst., N.Y.C., U.S. Dept. Commerce-Internat. Div.; dir. U.S. Dept. Commerce Dist. Export Council, 1978—. Pres. Ann Arbor P.T.O., 1979-80. Served with U.S. Army, 1962. Mem. Manuscript Soc. Roman Catholic. Clubs: Ann Arbor Racquet (dir.), Huron Valley Tennis. Home: 3025 Provincial Dr Ann Arbor MI 48104

DALLAS, DANIEL GEORGE, social worker; b. Chgo., June 8, 1932; s. George C. and Azimena P. (Marines) D.; B.A., Anderson (Ind.) Coll., 1955; B.D., No. Bapt. Theol. Sem., 1958; M.S.W., Mich. State U., 1963; M.Div., No. Bapt. Theol. Sem., 1972, D.Min., 1981; m. G. Aleta Leppien, May 26, 1956; children—Paul, Rhonda. Mem. faculty Mich. Dept. Corrections, Mich. State U., 1963-66; med. social adminstr. Med. Services div. Mich. Dept. Social Services, 1966-68; cons. Outreach Center of DuPage County, 1976—, also dir. social service Meml. Hosp. of DuPage County, Elmhurst, Ill., 1968—; therapist, lectr. Traffic Sch., Elmhurst Coll.; pvt. practice; indsl. cons. Mem. Elmhurst Sr. Citizen Commn., 1976—. Recipient Outstanding Service award Mental Health Assn. Ill., 1978. Mem. Nat. Assn. Social Workers, Soc. Hosp. Social Work Dirs., Am. Hosp. Assn., Nat. Registry of Health Care Providers, Mental Health Assn. Chgo. Club: Rotary. Contbr. articles to profl. jours. Home: 135 S Kenilworth DuPage Med Elmhurst IL 60126

DALLMANN, WILLIAM CHARLES, speech pathologist; b. Detroit, Nov. 16, 1929; s. Bertram and Lillian (Morgan) D.; A.B., San Francisco State U., 1957, M.A., 1963; Ph.D. (NDEA fellow), Purdue U., 1973; m. Constance Joan Covington, June 12, 1960; children—Shane, Alan, Lara. Underwriter, Liberty Mut. Ins. Co., San Francisco, 1957-62; pvt. investigator Kraut & Schneider San Francisco, 1963-64; instr. speech pathology Valparaiso U., 1964-65, asst. prof., 1966-72, asso. prof., 1973-80, prof. communicative disorders, 1981—, dir. speech and lang. clinic, 1964—; pvt. investigator, 1977—; regional mgr., spl. investigator, cons. in forensic hypnosis Wittlinger Agy., 1978—. Served with USN, 1948-49, to 1st lt. U.S. Army, 1951-53; Korea. Mem. Am. Speech, Hearing Assn. (certified in clin. competence in speech pathology), Internat. Soc. Profl. Hypnosis (certified profl. hypnotist), Internat. Soc. Gen. Semantics, Am. Soc. Clin. Hypnosis. Lutheran. Author: Images of God: Excursions into Christian Semantics, 1977. Home: 1905 Rock Castle Park Dr Valparaiso IN 46383 Office: Speech and Lang Clinic Valparaiso U Valparaiso IN 46383

DALLUHN, SALLY MARIE, office supply co. exec.; b. Stillwater, Minn., July 24, 1942; d. Gilbert R. and Eulah M. (Underhill) Schmoeckel; student public schs., Stillwater; m. Dale R. Dalluhn, Apr. 28, 1962; children—Keith R., Timothy A. With Ammerman Co., Stillwater, 1959-62; with Stillwater Book & Stationery Co., Inc., 1967-69, 71—, owner, sec.-treas., 1971—; ind. distbr., 1969-71. Mem. St. Croix Valley Area C. of C. (dir. 1978—, treas. 1981). Club: Stillwater Bus. and Profl. Women's. Office: 114 N Main St Stillwater MN 55082

DALLY, KURT ALAN, mcpl. agy. adminstr.; b. Green Bay, Wis., June 12, 1950; s. Harry Kurt and Opal D.; B.S., U. Wis., Green Bay, 1973; m. Kristen Kay Larson, Feb. 1, 1975; 1 son, Karl Alan. Researcher, Brown County Planning Commn., Green Bay, 1970-72; dir. safety and human resources Green Bay Met. Sewerage Dist., 1973—. Pres., Green Bay Area Safety and Health Com., 1981-82. Cert. wastewater operator, Wis. Mem. ASTD, Am. Soc. Safety Engrs., Nat. Safety Council (exec. com. public employees sect.), Water Pollution Control Fedn., Wis. Wastewater Works Operators Conf. Lutheran. Home: 1207 Raleigh St Green Bay WI 54304 Office: 2231 N Quincy St Green Bay WI 54302

D'ALONZO, RAPHAEL PAUL, chemist; b. Phila., Aug. 24, 1952; s. Gilbert Edward and Pauline May (Townsend) D'A.; B.S. in Chemistry, Phila. Coll. Pharmacy and Sci., 1974; Ph.D. in Analytical Chemistry, U. Mass., 1977. Chemist, Anchem, Inc., Ambler, Pa., 1974; teaching asst. U. Mass., 1974, research asst., 1975-77; analytical chemist Procter & Gamble Co., Cin., 1977—; cons. EPA. Mem. Am. Chem. Soc. (chmn. Cin. sect.; recipient undergrad. award in analytical chemistry 1973), AAAS, Soc. Applied Spectroscopy (chmn. Cin. sect.), Phi Lambda Upsilon. Composer: Initium, 1969. Office: Procter & Gamble Co 11520 Reed Hartman Hwy Cincinnati OH 45241

DALPHIN, JOHN F., univ. adminstr.; b. Bklyn., May 7, 1940; s. Robert Michael and Beatrice (Ashforth) D.; B.Mech.Engr., Clarkson Coll., 1962; M.S., U. N.H., 1964; Ph.D., Clarkson Coll., 1973; m. Lillian Carole Beazley, Mar. 11, 1967; children—Julia C., Edith A., John C., William G., George R. Systems engr. IBM, N.Y.C., 1964-65; asso. prof. computer tech., chmn. dept. Ind. U.-Purdue U. at Indpls., 1967-71; vis. asso. prof. computer sci. Clarkson Coll., 1972-73; dir. computing services, chmn., prof. computer sci. SUNY, Potsdam, 1973-77; dean Sch. of Engring., Tech. and Nursing Ind. U.-Purdue U., Fort Wayne, 1977—. Served to capt. U.S. Army, 1965-66. NSF fellow, 1971-72. Mem. AAAS, Assn. Computing Machinery, Am. Assn. Higher Edn., Am. Soc. Engring. Edn., Math. Assn. Am., Sigma Xi, Tau Alpha Pi, Epsilon Delta Pi, Tau Beta Pi, Pi Tau Sigma, Pi Delta Epsilon. Club: Fort Wayne Engrs. Office: 2101 Coliseum Blvd East Fort Wayne IN 46805

DALTON, HARRY, baseball exec.; b. Springfield, Mass., Aug. 23, 1928; grad. Amherst Coll., 1950. With Balt. Orioles, 1953-71, v.p. and player personnel dir., 1965-71; exec. v.p., gen. mgr. Calif. Angels, 1971-77; exec. v.p., gen. mgr. Milw. Brewers, 1977—. Served to 1st lt., USAF. Decorated Bronze Star. Office: Milw Brewers Milw County Stadium Milwaukee WI 53214*

DALTON, LEROY CALVIN, educator; b. Blue River, Wis., June 13, 1926; s. Edgar LeRoy and Lona Francis (Dyer) D.; B.S., U. Wis., 1950, M.S. in Edn., 1954; M.S in Math., Marquette U., 1964; postgrad. U. Chgo., 1958; m. Evelyn Mae DeJean, Sept. 2, 1950; children—Steven LeRoy, Nanci Jean. Tchr. math. and sci. Spring Green (Wis.) High Sch., 1950-52, McHenry Community High Sch. (Ill.), 1952-53; tchr. math. Wauwatosa (Wis.) High Sch., 1953-61; tchr. math., chmn. math. dept. Wauwatosa West High Sch., 1961—; math. area chmn. Wauwatosa Secondary Schs., 1962-65, 71—. Mem. Wauwatosa Youth Commn., 1971-73; chmn. council on ministries Wauwatosa Ave. Meth. Ch., 1974-76. Named Math. Tchr. of Year, Wis. Soc. Profl. Engrs., 1975; Dist. Tchr. of Yr., 1977; NSF summer fellow Marquette U., 1959-63. Mem. Nat. Council Tchrs. Math. (life, dir. 1977-80, mem. math. curriculum for 1980's com. 1977-80, steering com. priorities in sch. math. project 1977-80, mem. bd. liaison to Math. Tchr. editorial panel 1978-80), NEA (honor award 1970), Math. Assn. Am. (com. on high sch. contests 1965-71), Wis. Math. Council (pres. 1962), Wis., Wauwatosa edn. assns., Milw. Area Math. Council, Phi Delta Kappa, Mu Alpha Theta (nat. pres. 1962-65). Author: (with Laidlaw Bros.) Algebra I, 1967, Algebra 2 and Trigonometry, 1968; Geometry, 1971; Using Algebra, 3d edit., 1981; Using Advanced Algebra, 3d edit., 1981; Using Geometry, 1978; editor Topics for Mathematics Clubs, 1973; editor Clubs sect. Math. Tchr., 1980—. Home: 938 N 115th St Wauwatosa WI 53226 Office: 11400 W Center St Wauwatosa WI 53222

DALTON, RAYMOND ANDREW, univ. adminstr.; b. Chgo., Jan. 15, 1942; s. Chester Mack and Dorothy Laveda (Mitchell) D.; B.S., Ill. State U. at Normal, 1964, M.S., 1966; postgrad. Calif. State U. at Los Angeles, 1967, Otis Art Inst., 1967, U. Ill., 1972-74, U. San Francisco, 1978-79; m. Alfonsa Vicente, Apr. 17, 1979; children—Julio, Carlos, Solange, Gerardo. Tchr. art and English, Antelope Valley High Sch., Lancaster, Calif., 1965-67; tchr. Drew Jr. High Sch., Los Angeles, 1967; asst. dir. registration Office Admissions and Records, U. Ill. at Chgo. Circle, 1968; adminstrv. asst. to chmn. dept. of art, 1969-71, adminstrv. asst. to dean, 1970, asst. dean Coll. Architecture and Art, 1971—, instr. art, 1969-71, asst. prof., 1971—; adminstrv. leave U. P.R., 1977—; adminstrv. cons. U. Lagos (Nigeria), 1981. Cons. Camp Mendenhall, Lake Hughes, Calif., 1966; cons. Park Forest (Ill.) Schs., 1973; drawing tchr. Ill. Inst. Tech., 1973. One-man shows include Zeno Theatre Gallery, Chgo., 1980, UIMC, Chgo., 1981, Inner City Arts Council, Milw., 1981; exhibited in group shows First Nat. Bank of Normal, 1965, Palmdale (Calif.) Art Gallery, 1967, Push Expo, Chgo., 1972, U. Ill. Faculty Exhibit, Chgo., 1972, 74, 79, 80, Joliet West High Sch., 1975. Co-chmn. art com. Push Expo, Chgo., 1972. Mem. Coll. Art Assn., Nat. Conf. Artists, Union Black Arts, Acad. Affairs Adminstrs., Nat. Council Art Adminstrs. Assn. Home: 2722 W Logan Chicago IL 60647

DALTON, TERRENCE BARNEY, health center adminstr.; b. Monroe, Wis., Sept. 7, 1949; s. Robert Joseph and Norine Evelyn (Barney) D.; B.S., U. Wis., Platteville, 1971; M.Ed., Boston U., 1974; m. Sharon Beth Stegner, May 7, 1977. Psychiat. social worker Dodge County Mental Health Center, Juneau, Wis., 1974-76; coordinator alcohol, other drug abuse, Dodge County Human Services Bd., Juneau, 1976-77, program dir. mental health, developmental disabilities, alcohol and other drug abuse, 1977—. Bd. dirs. Dodge County Council Alcohol and Other Drugs, 1976. Served with U.S. Army, 1971-74. Mem. Wis. Assn. Alcoholism, Other Drug Abuse, Am. Personnel and Guidance Assn., Wis. Personnel and Guidance Assn., Alpha Phi Omega (life). Home: 303 S University Ave Beaver Dam WI 53916 Office: 199 Home Rd Juneau WI 53039

DALTON, WALTER WILLIAM, lawyer; b. Nevada, Mo., May 16, 1908; s. Frederick A. and Ida Jane (Poage) D.; student Westminster Coll.; A.B., U. of Mo., 1931, J.D., 1932, A.M., 1933; m. Margaret Clotilda Brown, June 6, 1959 (dec. Apr. 2, 1976). Admitted to Mo. State bar, 1931, practiced in Columbia, 1933-36; gen. atty. St. Louis-San Francisco Ry. Co., 1936-57, gen. solicitor, 1958-73; of counsel Fordyce & Mayne, 1973—; chmn. Mo. R.R. Assn., 1954-68; indsl.-traffic atty. War Dept., Washington, 1941-42. Trustee Mo. Law Sch. Found., v.p., 1979—; trustee State Hist. Soc. Mo., Jefferson Nat. Expansion Meml. Assn., St. Louis. Served to lt. col., USAAF, 1942-46; chief contracts U.S. Air Forces hdqrs. A.A.F., 1945-46; comdr. 9145th Air Res. Group, 1960-61; col. Air Force Res. (JA) Hdqrs. MAC, 1961-68; mem. Air Res. Forces Policy Com., 1961-65; col. USAF (ret.). Fellow Am. Coll. Trial Lawyers; mem. Am., Mo., St. Louis (chmn. trial sect. 1976-77) bar assns., English-Speaking Union (dir. St. Louis), Friends of Mo. Univ. Libraries (past pres.), S.R. (pres. St. Louis chpt. 1977-78), Soc. Colonial Wars (gov. Mo. 1977-79, dep. gov. gen. 1979-81), Phi Delta Phi, Phi Gamma Delta, Blue Key, Mystical Seven. Congregationalist. Clubs: Masons (32 deg.), Mo. Athletic, University (St. Louis); Jefferson. Home: 4 Wakefield Dr Saint Louis MO 63124 Office: Suite 1100 120 S Central Ave Saint Louis MO 63105

DALY, JOEL THOMAS, TV news commentator; b. Great Falls, Mont., Aug. 21, 1934; s. Joseph Earl and Viola (Fenger) D.; B.A. magna cum laude, Yale, 1956; m. Suzon Kay Weis, Aug. 24, 1957; children—Douglas Victor, Scott Thomas, Kelly Kay. Announcer KVNI, Coeur d'Alene, Idaho, 1952, WHBF-TV, Rock Island, Ill., 1954; newscaster WAVZ, New Haven, 1955-56, WGAR, Cleve., 1959, news dir. CFN, Panama, C.Z., 1957-59, WEWS, Cleve., 1960-64; newscaster WJW-TV, Cleve., 1964-67; news commentator WLS-TV, Chgo., 1967—. Foster parent Ill. Children's Home, 1968-71. Chmn., LaGrange (Ill.) Heritage and Archtl. Commn., 1970-72. Served with AUS, 1956-59. Recipient Panama C.Z. Gov.'s award, Best Documentary award Cleve. Press Club, 1964, Outstanding Coverage award Ohio A.P., 1966, Emmy award Chgo. Acad. TV Arts and Scis., 1968, 69, 76, 80, commendation Ill. Police Assn., 1969, Best Editorial award Ill. A.P., 1970, 71, Human Relations award Am. Jewish Congress, 1971, Myrtle Leaf award Hadassah, 1974. Lutheran (youth counselor 1965-67). Home: 211 S LaGrange Rd LaGrange IL 60525 Office: WLS-TV 190 N State St Chicago IL 60601

DALY, PATRICK FRANCIS, architect; b. Chgo., Jan. 25, 1949; s. John F. and Margaret M. (Gleason) D.; B.Arch. in Design with honors and distinction, U. Ill., 1972, B.A. in History of Architecture with honors and distinction, 1972; m. Shirley J. Daly, June 26, 1972; 1 son, Sean. Dir. prodn. Jensen & Jensen Architects, Oak Brook, Ill., 1972-75; v.p. Jack Jacobs & Co., Chgo., 1975-77; partner Court Cons. Ltd., Chgo., 1975-77; prin. Patrick F. Daly Architects & Engrs., Chgo., 1975-77; pres. Patrick F. Daly & Assos. Ltd., Chgo., Oak Brook, 1977—; chmn. bd. Armanco, Inc., Oak Brook, 1977—; pres. Daly Equities Inc., Chgo., 1978—; cons. Gupta Assos., 1977—; pres. Atrium Assn., Inc., 1977—; exec. dir. Systems III, Inc., Chgo., 1972-75. Chmn., archtl. control com. Dutch Hollow Lake (Wis.), 1973-75; bd. dirs. Branigar Corp., Dutch Hollow Lake, LaValle, Wis., 1973-76. Recipient Cert. of Appreciation, Triton Coll., 1977; Chgo. Park Dist. Jr. Citizen of Yr. award, 1967; Alpha Rho Chi medal, 1972; named Youth of Yr., B'nai B'rith, 1967; James scholar, 1967-72; Cardinal Stritch scholar, 1967-72; Serra scholar, 1967; lic. architect, Ariz., Ark., Calif., Colo., Ill., Ind., Iowa, La., Mass., Mich., Minn., Mo., Mont., N.D., N.J., N.Y., Okla., Oreg., Pa., S.D., Tex., Vt., Wash., Wis., Wyo. Mem. Chgo. Council on Fgn. Relations, Internat. Platform Assn., Internat. Biog. Assn., Mus. Contemporary Art, Chgo. Art Inst., Jr. Real Estate Bd. Chgo., AIA, Nat. Council Archtl. Registration Bds., Bldg. Ofcls. and Code Adminstrs. Internat., Internat. Council Shopping Centers, Alpha Rho Chi. Clubs: Carlton, Riverside Golf, Meadow. Contbr. articles to profl. jours. Home: 6 Birch Tree Ct Elmhurst IL 60126 Office: 6160 N Cicero Ave Chicago IL 60646 and 2625 Butterfield Rd Oak Brook IL 60521

DALY, RICHARD PHILIP, elec. engr.; b. White Bear Lake, Minn., June 17, 1924; s. Edward and Rose (Distel) D.; B.E.E., U. Minn., 1949, B.A. in Bus. Adminstrn., 1949, M.B.A., 1950; m. Marguerite Kampmeyer, Dec. 30, 1950; children—Richard, Teresa, Stephen, Mary Michelle. Sr. elec. engr., mgr. fed. govt. sales Univac div. Sperry Rand, St. Paul, 1952-60; founder, successively v.p., pres., chmn. bd. Aries Corp., Mpls., 1960-69; dir. industry mktg./mfg. Control Data Corp., Mpls., 1961-71; pres., treas., dir., chief exec. officer Comserv Corp., Mendota Heights, Minn., 1971—. Served to maj. USAAF, 1943-46, 51-52. Mem. Greater Mpls. C. of C., Am. Mgmt. Assn., U. Minn. Alumni Assn., Pres.'s Assn., Assn. Data Processing Service Orgns. Clubs: Decathlon, K.C. Address: 1385 Mendota Heights Rd Mendota Heights MN 55120

DALY, THOMAS JOSEPH, coatings co. exec.; b. Chgo., Jan. 25, 1929; s. James Thomas and Helen Veronica (Murphy) D.; B.S. in Chem. Engring., Ill. Inst. Tech., 1950, M.S. in Chem. Engring., 1954; m. Catherine Ann Radloff, Oct. 6, 1956; children—Thomas, Kevin, Timothy, Maura, Megan, Mary, Sean. Chemist, Great Lakes Solvents, Inc., Chgo., 1950; chemist Jewel Paint & Varnish Co., Chgo., 1951-62, chief chemist, 1962-68, asst. tech. dir., 1968-73; asst. tech. dir. Gen. Paint & Chem. Co., Cary, Ill., 1973-74, tech. dir., 1974-77, mgr. mfg., 1976-77; dir. mfg. Universal Chems. & Coatings, Inc., 1977—; gen. mgr. chem. metals div. Unichem, 1978—; cons. artist colors, 1966-73, bitumatic coatings, caulks and sealants, 1953-66. Pres. West Glen

Community Assn., Glenview, Ill., 1960-68; v.p. Bel-Air Utility Co., Glenview, 1962-71. Recipient Outstanding Service award Chgo. Soc. Paint Tech., 1972, Service award Fedn. Socs. Coatings Tech., 64, 70. Mem. Chgo. Paint Coatings Assn. (chmn. joint ednl. com. 1966-67), Chgo. Soc. Coatings Tech. (pres. 1971), Chgo. Tech. Socs. Council (gov. 1962-68), Lake Forest (Ill.) Community Music Assn., Lake Forest Hist. Soc. (life). Club: Nifty Niblicks Golf. Contbr. articles to profl. jours.; developer paint products. Home: 943 Longwood Dr Lake Forest IL 60045 Office: Universal Chems & Coatings Inc 1124 Elmhurst Rd Elk Grove Village IL 60007

D'AMATO, BARBARA STEKETEE, writer, lyricist; b. Grand Rapids, Mich., Apr. 10, 1938; d. Harold Arthur and Yvonne Virginia (Watson) Steketee; student Cornell U., 1956-58; B.A., Northwestern U., 1972, M.A., 1973; m. Anthony D'Amato, Sept. 4, 1958; children—Brian Richard D'Amato, Paul Steketee D'Amato. Freelance author, lyricist, 1973—; musical comedies include The Magic Man, Chgo., 1974, London, 1977; The Magic of Young Houdini, Niles, Ill., 1975-77, London, 1976; RSVP Broadway, Chgo., 1980. Author: (novels) The Hands of Healing Murder, 1980, The Eyes on Utopia Murders, 1981. Office: 716 Greenwood Glencoe IL 60022

DAMMANN, KATHLEEN ELLEN, pharmacy dept. bus. mgr.; b. Chgo., June 18, 1954; d. Robert D. and Joanne G. D.; B.Mus.Edn., Northwestern U., 1975. Freelance musician, 1969—; med. sec. to physician, Chgo., 1975-78; bus. mgr. pharmacy dept. Rush-Presbyn.-St. Luke's Med. Center, Chgo., 1978—. Active, Skokie Fine Arts Commn., 1977—, chmn. goals com., 1978—, vice chmn. commn., 1979—; vol. Passavant Meml. Hosp., Chgo. Recipient service award pins, Passavant Meml. Hosp. Mem. Women in Mgmt. (Chgo. Loop chpt.). Lutheran. Home: 7836 Kildare Ave Skokie IL 60076 Office: Pharmacy Dept 1753 W Congress Pkwy Chicago IL 60612

DAMMANN, ROBERT DONALD, ednl. adminstr.; b. Chgo., Mar. 13, 1928; s. Henry William and Adela (Kaufmann) D.; student U. So. Calif., 1947-48; Mus.B., Northwestern U., 1949, B.Mus. Edn., 1950, M.B.A., 1959, M.Mgmt. in Hosp. and Health Services Mgmt., 1978—; m. Joanne Gubbins, Sept. 5, 1953; children—Kathleen Ellen, Donald Alan. Asst. mgr. imports Great Lakes Overseas, Inc., Chgo., 1953-60; researcher marketing Revere Elec. Mfg. Co., Chgo., 1960-64, advt. mgr., 1964-65, mgr. marketing services, 1965-68; mgr. marketing services MSL Steel Co., 1968-69; marketing mgr. Innovex div. Hammond Corp., 1969-70; adminstrv. mgr. dept. anesthesia Northwestern U. Med. Sch., Chgo., 1970-73, dir. adminstrv. services, 1973-78, dir. adminstrv. and fin. services, 1978—, lectr. div. continuing edn., 1978—. Bd. dirs., sec.-treas. Northwestern Found. for Research and Edn., 1980. Served with AUS, 1951-53. Mem. Assn. Am. Med. Colls. (exec. com. bus. affairs group Midwest-Gt. Plains region 1974-75, chmn. bus. affairs group Midwest-Gt. Plains region 1976-77, mem. nat. steering com. 1976—), Phi Mu Alpha. Lutheran. Home: 7836 N Kildare Ave Skokie IL 60076

DAMOTTE, EARL THOMAS, engring. technician; b. Jacksonville, Ill., Oct. 22, 1937; s. Earl Kenneth and Grace Ceclia (Whalen) D.; student Springfield Jr. Coll., 1956-57, U. Ill., 1958-59; m. Mary Jane Gilbert, Oct. 4, 1959; children—Brian Thomas, James Richard, Donald Ray. Draftsman, Allis Chalmers Co., Springfield, Ill., 1963-68; engring. technician Engring. & Planning Cons., Jacksonville, 1968-75; dir. public works City of Virginia (Ill.), 1975-79; draftsman Fiat-Ellis Constrn. Machinery, Inc., Springfield, 1979-80; engring. technician Casler, Houser & Hutchinson Inc., Jacksonville, 1980—. Served with U.S. Army, 1960-63. Mem. Am. Water Works Assn., Am. Soc. Cert. Engring. Technicians. Roman Catholic. Home: Rural Route 1 Box 52 Virginia IL 62691

DANAHY, BARBARA (BARBARA DANAHY CALLAHAN), broadcast journalist; b. N.Y.C.; d. John Joseph and Joan Patricia (Fuller) Danahy; student Manhattanville Coll.; B.A., Wellesley Coll.; m. Daniel Joseph Callahan, Nov. 24, 1979. Producer, KMOX-TV, CBS, St. Louis, 1973-75, exec. news coordinator, 1975-76; exec. producer, anchor, reporter KSD-TV, St. Louis, 1976-79, asst. news dir., anchor, reporter, Sta. KSDK-TV, St. Louis, 1979—; producer, writer documentaries including: Sixteen in Webster Groves. . .Eight Years Later (DuPont-Columbia citation for excellence 1974), Living with Death (local Emmy award for best sta. effort 1976). Mem. AFTRA, Nat. Acad. TV Arts and Scis., Women in Communications, Am. Women in Radio and TV, Radio-TV News Dirs. Assn. (asso.). Home: 57 High Valley Dr Chesterfield MO 63017 Office: KSDK-TV 1111 Olive St Saint Louis MO 63101*

DANBERG, KALE WILLIAM, constrn. co. exec.; b. Mpls., Oct. 20, 1932; s. Lloyd Millford and Violet Gladys (Peterson) D.; student U. Minn., 1952-53; m. Nancy Herberta Broan, Apr. 30, 1954; children—Linda Susan, David William, Jeffrey Kale, Rachel Gretchen. Design-checker Beloit Iron Works (Wis.), 1954-58; design engr. Millerbernd Mfg. Co., Winsted, Minn., 1958-65; gen. mgr. Mattson Bldg. Co., Inc., Cokato, Minn., 1965-74, pres., 1974—. Chmn. bd. trustees, deacon 1st Baptist Ch. of Cokato, 1979; mem. adv. com. Canby Area Vo-Tech, Inver Grove Heights Community Coll.; del. Minn. Small Bus. Conf.; past Cub Scouts master. Served with USMC, 1950-52. Mem. Metal Bldg. Dealers Assn. (past pres. Northland chpt.), Cokato Businessmen's Assn. (past pres.), VFW (past comdr.). Republican. Club: Gideons Internat. Home: 365 5th St W Cokato MN 55321 Office: 575 Cokato St E Cokato MN 55321

DANCER, WILLIAM JENNINGS, JR., retial chain exec.; b. Stockbridge, Mich., Oct. 27, 1914; s. William Gurney and Winnalee Adella (Comstock) D.; B.S., Mich. State U., 1936; m. Betty Jean Terrell, June 29, 1950; children—Melissa Jean, William Terrell. Warehouse mgr. Dancer Co., dept. stores, 1936-45, warehouse and office mgr., 1945-58, treas. corp., 1958-67, pres., 1967—; dir. Stockbridge State Bank. Pres. Community Chest, 1940. Mem. Mich. Retailers Assn., Mich. Bankers Assn. Democrat. Presbyterian. Club: Masons. Home: 700 E Main St Stockbridge MI 49285 Office: 136 S Clinton St Stockbridge MI 49285

D'ANDRIOLE, THEODORE JOHN, advt. exec.; b. Taylor, Pa., Nov. 19, 1943; s. John Joseph and Rose Marie (Lester) d'A.; student U. Tex., Austin, 1962-63; B.A., U. Houston, 1968; m. Mary Anna Chandler, Aug. 18, 1966; children—John Chandler, Charlotte Anna. Reporter, The Houston Chronicle, 1963-69; with Southwestern Bell Telephone Co., 1969—, now div. staff mgr. public relations, corp. hdqrs., St. Louis. Precinct capt. Queeny Twp. Republican party, 1976-80. Mem. Public Relations Soc. Am. (accredited), Internat. Assn. Bus. Communicators, Century Club of Luth. Assn. for Higher Edn. Tau Kappa Epsilon. Republican. Lutheran. Home: 367 Messina Dr Ballwin MO 63011 Office: 1010 Pine St Saint Louis MO 63101

DANFORTH, JOHN CLAGGETT, U.S. Senator; b. St. Louis, Sept. 5, 1936; s. Donald and Dorothy D.; B.A., Princeton U., 1958; B.D., Yale U., 1963, LL.B., 1963, M.A. (hon.); L.H.D. (hon.), Lindenwood Coll.; D.D. (hon.), Lewis and Clark Coll., Portland, Oreg.; LL.D. (hon.), Drury Coll., Maryville Coll., Rockhurst Coll., Westminster Coll., Culver-Stockton Coll.; m. Sally Dobson; children—Eleanor, Mary, D.D., Jody, Thomas. Admitted to N.Y. bar, Mo. bar; asso. firm Davis, Polk, Wardwell, Sunderland & Kiendl, N.Y.C., 1963-66, Bryan, Cave, McPheeters & McRoberts, St. Louis, 1966-68; atty. gen. Mo., 1968-76; mem. U.S. Senate, 1976—, mem. Finance, Commerce and Govtl. Affairs coms.; chmn. Mo. Law Enforcement Assistance Council, 1973-74; ordained to ministry Episcopal Ch.; asst., asso. pastor various chs. in N.Y. and Mo.; hon. canon Christ Ch. Cathedral, St. Louis. Mem. Yale Corp., 1973-79. Recipient Outstanding Young Man award Mo. Jaycees, 1969. Mem. Mo. Acad. Squires, Nat. Jesuit Honor Soc., Alpha Sigma Mu. Office: 460 Russell Senate Office Bldg Washington DC 20510*

DANFORTH, ROBERT CLARKE, physician, educator; b. Flint, Mich., Jan. 17, 1933; s. Herschel Clarke and Margaret Christine (Busby) D.; B.S., U. Wis., 1955, M.D., 1958; m. Phyllis Rae Robertson, June 30, 1956; children—Christine, Douglas. Intern, So. Pacific Gen. Hosp., San Francisco, 1958-59; resident neurology Univ. Hosps., Madison, Wis., 1959-62; practice medicine specializing in neurology, computerized tomography and electroencephalography, Milw., 1964—; mem. staff St. Joseph, Columbia, Milwaukee County, Family, St. Luke's, Milw. Luth., St. Anthony, St. Francis, St. Mary's, St. Michael hosps. (all Milw.); asso. clin. prof. neurology Med. Coll. Wis., 1969—. Pres. Wis. Epilepsy League, 1973-75, mem. adv. bd., 1975—; adv. bd. Myasthenia Gravis Found., mem. med. rev. bd. Wis. Motor Vehicle Dept. Served to lt. comdr. USNR, 1962-64. Cert. Am. Bd. EEG. Diplomate Am. Bd. Psychiatry and Neurology. Fellow Am. Acad. Neurology; mem. Central Assn. Electroencephalography, Am. Electroencephalography Soc., Soc. Computerized Tomography and Neuroimaging, Wis. Neurol. Soc. (pres. 1978-79), AMA, Wis., Milwaukee County med. assns., Milw. Neuropsychiat. Soc., Am. Med. Electroencephalography Soc., Phi Chi, Sigma Alpha Epsilon. Mem. United Ch. Christ (moderator 1979-80). Clubs: Lakeshore (dir. 1978-80), North Shore Racquet. Home: 7450 N Pierron Rd Glendale WI 53209 Office: 3070 N 51st St Milwaukee WI 53210

DANFORTH, WILLIAM HENRY, physician, educator, univ. chancellor; b. St. Louis, Apr. 10, 1926; s. Donald and Dorothy (Claggett) D.; A.B., Princeton, 1947; M.D., Harvard, 1951; hon. degrees: D.Sc., Westminster Coll., 1971, So. Ill. U., 1973, U. Mo., 1981; D.H.L., Culver-Stockton Coll., 1974, Hebrew Union Coll.-Jewish Inst. Religion, 1977; LL.D., Alderson-Broaddus Coll., 1977, Maryville Coll., 1978; H.H.D., Sch. Ozarks, 1980; m. Elizabeth Anne Gray, Sept. 1, 1950; children—Cynthia Danforth Noto, David, Ann, Elizabeth. Intern Barnes Hosp., St. Louis, 1951-52, asst. resident in medicine, 1954-57, resident, 1956-57, mem. staff, 1958—; asst. resident in pediatrics St. Louis Children's Hosp., 1955-56; fellow in cardiology Washington U., St. Louis, 1957-58, instr. medicine, 1957-60, NIH postdoctoral fellow in biochemistry, 1961-63, asst. prof., 1960-65, asso. prof., 1965-67, prof., 1967—, vice chancellor for med. affairs, 1965-71, chancellor, 1971—, chmn. Med. Center Redevel. Corp., 1973—; pres. Washington U. Med. Sch. and Asso. Hosps., 1965-71; chmn. Washington U. Med. Center Redevel. Corp., 1973—; program coordinator Bi-State Regional Med. Program, 1967-69; dir., Ralston Purina Co., Mallinckrodt, Inc., McDonnell Douglas Corp.; mem. nat. adv. heart and lung council NIH, 1970-74; pres. Ind. Colls. and Univs. Mo., 1979—; mem. adv. com. Mo. Coordinating Bd. for Higher Edn., 1976—; mem. adv. bd. St. Louis Area council Boy Scouts Am. Chmn. bd. Danforth Found., 1966—; trustee Am. Youth Found., 1963—, Princeton U., 1970-74; mem. exec. com. St. Louis br. NAACP, 1978—; pres. St. Louis Christmas Carols Assn., 1958-74, chmn., bd. govs., 1975—. Served with USN, 1952-54. Recipient Newton D. Baker award, 1967; Ann. Brotherhood award NCCJ, 1973; Man of Yr. award St. Louis Globe-Democrat, 1978; Exec. of Yr. award Sales and Mktg. Execs. Met. St. Louis, 1980; Human Relations award St. Louis chpt. Am. Jewish Com., 1980. Mem. Am. Soc. Clin. Investigation, Central Soc. for Clin. Research, St. Louis Med. Soc., Nat. Acad. Scis. Inst. Medicine. (council 1977-79). Office: Washington U Saint Louis MO 63130

DANIEL, DONNA MARY, librarian; b. Galion, Ohio, Oct. 19, 1932; d. Ambrose Louis and Gertrude (Daniel) Daniel; B.S., Ohio U., 1956; M.S. in L.S., Western Res. U., 1964. Librarian, Galion Jr. and Sr. High Schs., Galion, 1956-57; tchr. Northridge High Sch., Dayton, 1957-59; librarian Madison High Sch., Mansfield, 1959-66; asst. librarian Mansfield br. Ohio State U., 1966-67; librarian Shelby Jr. High Sch., 1967—. Edn. chmn. St. Joseph's Sch., Galion, 1969-71; sec. council St. Joseph Parish, 1969-71. Mem. N. Central Ohio Tchrs. Assn. Sch. Librarians (sec.-treas. 1962-66), Ohio Assn. Sch. Librarians (regional dir. 1965-67, 74-76), ALA, Ohio Library Assn., NEA, Richland County, Shelby tchrs. assns., Ohio Edn. Assn., Ch. Music Assn. Am., Delta Kappa Gamma. Roman Catholic. Home: 406 Fairview Galion OH 44833

DANIEL, JAMIE L., business cons.; b. Grand Junction, Tenn., Nov. 16, 1921; d. Doctor Newton and Helen Beatrice (Nabers) D.; student U. Miss., 1954-56; m. Paul J. Phyfer, Aug. 1940 (dec. 1954); m. 2d, Donald Lindenberg, June 1956 (div. 1974); children—Paul Jones Phyfer, Daniel Wade Phyfer, Kathryn Anne Phyfer, David Laird Phyfer, Jon Ward Lindenberg, James Frank Lindenberg. Public info. officer Mark VII Corp., Geneva, Ill., 1973-75; v.p. BASIC, Geneva, Ill. and Washington, Va., 1975—; pres. Miscella, Inc., 1976—; real estate broker, 1978—; pres. Dansko, 1980—; vice chmn. bd Hydro-Farms Inc., St. Charles, Ill., 1981—. Vice pres. Ill. LWV, 1967-71; sec. Landmarks Preservation Service, Chgo., 1975-77; bd. dirs. Landmarks Preservation Council Ill., 1975—; chmn. daily procedures No. Ill. Conf., United Meth. Ch., 1972-77. Mem. Chgo. Assn. Commerce and Industry, Mid Am. Arab C. of C. Methodist. Club: Plaza. Contbr. Ill. Voters Handbook for LWV Ill., 1964-71. Home: 41 W 906 Hughes Rd Elburn IL 60119 Office: PO Box 145 Geneva IL 60134

DANIEL, KENNETH LEROY, wholesaling exec.; b. Roosevelt, Utah, Oct. 2, 1945; s. Kenneth Leroy and Lucy May (Sperier) D.; student Okla. State U., 1963-66; B.B.A. in Mktg., Central State Coll., Edmond, Okla., 1970; m. Barbara Joan Schrade, June 29, 1968; 1 dau., Robin Rebecca. Salesman, Burroughs Corp., Oklahoma City, 1966-68; mem. sales and purchasing staff Inland Laminates, Inc., Oklahoma City, 1968-70; owner Midway Sales & Distbg., Topeka, 1970-74, pres., 1975—; pres. Grain States Contracting, Inc., Topeka, 1975-80, Woldan Equipment, Inc., Topeka, 1979—. Bd. dirs. Topeka Halfway House, 1972-74; mem. action auction com. KTWU, 1973-75. Served with Army N.G., 1966-72. Mem. Midwest Roofing Contractors Assn., Nat. Fedn. Ind. Bus., U.S. Jaycees (midwest regional met. chmn. 1974-75), Kans. Jaycees (state chmn. 1973-75), Topeka Jaycees (dir. 1970-74, pres. 1972-73), Topeka Swim Assn. Republican. Clubs: Shawnee Country; Rotary, 20-30 (Topeka). Home: 3254 MacVicar St Topeka KS 66611 Office: PO Box 1002 Topeka KS 66601

DANIELS, CHARLES ANTHONY, polymer phys. chemist; b. Utica, N.Y., Jan. 1, 1943; s. Angele Vincent and Congetta Marie (Bonarrigo) D.; m. Jean Daniels, Sept. 5, 1964; children—Deana, Christopher. B.A., Utica Coll., Syracuse U., 1964; M.S., Case Western Res. U., 1967, Ph.D., 1969, postgrad., 1969. Asso. devel. scientist B.F. Goodrich Chem. Co., Avon Lake, Ohio, 1969, devel. scientist, 1971-77, sr. research and devel. scientist, research and devel. group leader, 1977-78, mgr. polymer characterization, 1978—; adj. prof. chemistry John Carroll U., Cleve., 1972-73. Mgmt. counseller Lorain County (Ohio) Jr. Achievement, 1972-76. Mem. Am. Chem. Soc., Soc. Plastics Engrs. (sub-com. on PVC pipe), Sigma Xi, Phi Kappa Phi. Contbg. author: Physical Aspects of Plastics, Physical and Chemical Structures and Properties, 1977; contbr. chpt. Physical Contents of PVC; articles in field. Home: 242 Sunset Rd Avon Lake OH 44012 Office: BF Goodrich Tech Center PO Box 122 Avon Lake OH 44012

DANIELS, JAMES VINCENT, electronics co. exec.; b. Chgo., May 23, 1909; s. James Patrick and Mary Ellen (Burke) D.; student Northwestern U., 1925-27, Curtis-Wright Flying Service, 1928; m. Marilou Juhnke, Sept. 23, 1939 (dec.); children—Nancy (Mrs. Thomas D. Mahar, Jr.), Barbara, James Vincent, Paul; m. 2d, Rosemary Murnighan Nilson, Nov. 6, 1975. Airplane pilot, instr. Sky Harbor, Northbrook, Ill., 1928-32; sales mgr. Flashtric Neon Signs, Chgo., 1932-36; co-founder Kemlite Labs., Chgo., 1936, pres., dir., 1958—; pres. Electronic Lights, Inc., Chgo., 1965—; dir. 1819 West Grand Bldg. Corp. Mem. Illuminating Engring. Soc., Soc. Photog. Scientists and Engrs., Ill. Mfg. Assn., Chgo. Assn. Commerce and Industry (aviation com.). Patentee in field. Home: 1140 Michigan Ave Wilmette IL 60091 Office: 1819 W Grand Ave Chicago IL 60022

DANIELS, LAMERIAL GARRISON, hosp. exec., nurse; b. Port Gibson, Miss., Oct. 8, 1944; d. George Edward and Thelma Anna (Rowan) Garrison; R.N., Good Samaritan Hosp. Sch. Nursing, 1966; B.S., Central State U., 1978; postgrad. U. Cin.; m. William O. Daniels, Aug. 16, 1969; 1 dau., Leslie M. Public health nurse City of Cleve., 1967-69; health services coordinator Robert Vogel Health Center, Dayton, Ohio, 1971-74; head nurse clinics Good Samaritan Hosp. and Health Center, Dayton, 1974-76, supr. outpatient services, 1976—; cons. Crystal Manor Nursing Homes, 1975—. Mem. Am. Heart Assn. Democrat. Club: Dayton Metropolitan. Home: 3550 Cornell Dr Dayton OH 45406 Office: Good Samaritan Hosp and Health Center 2222 Philadelphia Dr Dayton OH 45406

DANIELS, LARRY JOE, educator; b. Mt. Vernon, Ohio, Dec. 10, 1950; s. Darwin Dewight and Betty Gold (Hays) D.; B.S., Ohio State U., 1972, M.S., 1980; m. Cheryl Ann Eppley, June 16, 1973; children—Dawn, Beth. Tchr. vocat. agr. at high schs. in Delaware and Groveport, Ohio, 1972-76; instr. adult vocat. agr. Wayne County Joint Vocat. Sch., Smithville, Ohio, 1976—; chmn. public affairs council Country Squires Farm Bur., 1977-78. State chmn. Farm Bus. Planning and Analysis Instrs. Mem. bd., treas. Oak Chapel United Methodist Ch., Wooster, Ohio, 1977-81. Mem. Am. Vocat. Assn., Am. Vocat. Agr. Tchrs. Assn., Ohio Vocat. Assn., Ohio Vocat. Agr. Tchrs. Assn., Computing Farmers of Ohio (charter mem.), Gamma Sigma Delta. Republican. Home: 4928 Snoddy Rd Shreve OH 44676 Office: PO Box 378 Smithville OH 44677

DANIELS, RICHARD EVERETT, sem. ofcl.; b. Rockford, Ill., Dec. 6, 1947; s. Marshall E. and Betty E. Daniels; B.A., Trinity Coll., Deerfield, Ill., 1969; M.Ed., Loyola U., Chgo., 1972; M.R.E. cum laude, Trinity Evang. Div. Sch., 1972; M.Div., Bethel Theol. Sem., 1975, D.Min., 1981; m. Nikki L. Weber, Aug. 5, 1972; children—Andrea, Troy Richard. Ordained to ministry Baptist Ch., 1977; asst. dean students Trinity Coll., Chgo., 1972-73, acting dir. alumni, 1973-75; asso. pastor Calvary Bapt. Ch., St. Paul, 1975-77; dean of students Bethel Theol. Sem., St. Paul, 1977—. Mem. Nat. Assn. Student Personnel Adminstrs., Am. Coll. Personnel Assn., Am. Personnel and Guidance Assn., Phi Delta Kappa. Office: Bethel Theol Sem 3949 Bethel Dr Saint Paul MN 55112

DANIELS, ZED REDDISH, mktg. co. exec.; b. St. Louis, Sept. 19, 1925; s. Louis Wesley and Lillian Pearl (Reddish) D.; B.A., Ottawa U., 1949; M.B.A., U. Kans., 1950; m. Elizabeth Louise Love, June 5, 1976; children—Zed Reddish, Nancy, Stephen, Timmothy, Jeffrey, Amy. Dir. mktg. Western Auto Supply Co., Kansas City, Mo., 1950-54; mktg. mgr. Gen. Foods Corp., Battle Creek, Mich., 1954-57; dir. mktg. Crush Internat., Inc., Evanston, Ill., 1957-60; pres. Zed R. Daniels & Assos., Chgo., 1960-62, Don Kemper, Inc., 1962-70; sr. v.p. Tatham Laird & Kudner, 1970-73; chmn., chief exec. officer Mktg. Communications Internat., Inc., 1973—; dir. 41 Royal Palm Corp., SDH Internat., Inc. Served with USNR, 1943-46. Decorated Purple Heart. Mem. Western Advt. Golfers Assn. Republican. Clubs: Bob Olink Golf; Johns Island Golf (Fla.); Bent Pine Country (Fla.). Home: 505 N Lake Shore Dr Chicago IL 60611 Office: Marketing Communications

DANIELSKI, JOHN JULIUS, ophthalmic surgeon; b. Mt. Clemens, Mich., July 10, 1931; s. Julius Sylvester and Helena Lila (Kasprick) D.; B.S. magna cum laude, Wayne State U., 1952, M.D. cum laude, 1955; m. Donna Lou Smith, July 29, 1961; children—Tamara, Ann, John. Intern, Wayne County Gen. Hosp., Eloise, Mich., 1955-56, resident in pathology, 1958-60, in ophthalmology, 1956; pvt. practice medicine, specializing in ophthalmic surgery, Detroit, 1963-65, Garden City, Mich., 1966—; asst. to chief of staff, dir. dept. ophthalmology William Beaumont Hosp., Royal Oak, Mich., 1963-65; staff ophthalmic surgeon Peoples Community Hosp., Wayne, Mich., 1966—, Met. Hosp. West, Westland, Mich., 1972-78; mem. faculty Wayne State U. Coll. Medicine, Detroit, 1964—; FAA med. examiner, 1966-72; founder Surmount, treatment facility for alcoholism. Served with M.C., USAF, 1956-58. Diplomate Am. Bd. Ophthalmology. Mem. Am. Acad. Ophthalmology, AMA, Mich. State, Wayne County med. assns., Mich. Ophthal. Assn., Civil Aviation Med. Assn., Am. Med. Assn. on Alcoholism, Am. Schizophrenia Assn., Nat., Mich. Music Tchrs. Assn., Mich. State U. Alumni Assn., Phi Beta Kappa, Sigma Xi, Alpha Omega Alpha. Democrat. Roman Catholic. Club: Wayne State U. Faculty. Contbr. articles to med. jours. Home: 15988 Westmore Ct Livonia MI 48154 Office: 30900 Ford Rd Garden City MI 48135

DANIELSON, JEANETTE MARILYN, oil co. exec.; b. Windsor Twp., Wis., Oct. 24, 1940; d. Albert Edward and Linda Josephine (Davidson) Moe; student Madison Area Tech. Coll., 1970-80, E.R.T.I. Bus. Sch., 1960; children—Russell Alan, Jeffrey Peter, Eric Lee. Exec. sec. Kerr-McGee Oil Co., Madison, Wis., 1965-70; exec. sec. Atlantic-Richfield Oil Co., Madison, 1970-75; adminstrv. sec. Skelly Oil Co., Madison, 1975-76; adminstrv. asst. Getty Oil Co., Madison, 1976—; mgr., stylist Beeline Fashions, Madison, 1963—. Greater Madison Conv. Bur. hostess, 1980—; chairperson Cerebral Palsy Telethon, 1982. Named March of Dimes Coordinator of Yr., 1976; Woman of Yr., Am. Bus. Women's Assn., 1976, 80; recipient God-Home-Country award, 1960; State of Wis. Key award, 1960. Mem. Am. Bus. Women's Assn. (nat. bd. dirs. 1978-79, pres. Wis. chpt. 1981-82), Four Lakes Secs. Assn. (pres. 1980—). Lutheran. Club: Toastmistress. Home: 918 Moorland Rd Madison WI 53713 Office: Suite 211 2934 Fish Hatchery Rd Madison WI 53713

DANIELSON, RUTH FLORENCE, banker; b. Atwater, Minn., June 1, 1917; d. Louis A. and Kristine Anna (Blohm) Rosenquist; m. Thomas C. Danielson, Aug. 14, 1936; children—Lou Ann, Suzanne; student St. Cloud Tchrs. Coll., 1935-36, 61. With Atwater State Bank, 1936—, v.p., cashier, 1962-74, pres., 1975—, also dir.; agt. Northwest Nat. Ins. Co., 1955-62; propr. Atwater State Agy., 1962—; pres., dir. Ind. State Bank of Minn., 1981—. Sec., treas., Ladies Aid, Immanuel Lutheran Ch., 1940-45, pres., 1949, treas. congregation, 1977—, mem. council, 1976-79; pres. PTA, 1947-48; mem. Kandiyohi County Library Bd., 1964-65; organizer Nutrition for Elderly Program, Atwater, 1977—; trustee Am. Swedish Inst., asst. treas., 1979-80.

Licensed ins. agt. Mem. Am. Ind. Bankers, Minn. Bankers Assn., Eastern Star. Address: Atwater MN 56209

DANILOV, VICTOR JOSEPH, museum adminstr.; b. Farrell, Pa., Dec. 30, 1924; s. Joseph M. and Ella (Tominovich) D.; B.A., Pa. State U., 1945; M.S., Northwestern U., 1946; Ed.D., U. Colo., 1964; m. Toni Dewey, Sept. 6, 1980; children—Thomas J., Duane P., Denise S. Reporter, night city editor Pitts. Sun-Telegraph, 1946-47; reporter, rewriteman Chgo. Daily News, 1947-50; instr. in journalism U. Colo., 1950-51, dir. univ. relations, 1957-60; asst. prof. journalism U. Kans., 1951-53; mgr. public relations Ill. Inst. Tech. and Armour Research Found., 1953-57; pres. Profile Co., 1960-62; exec. editor, pub., exec. v.p. Indsl. Research Inc., Beverly Shores, Ind., 1962-71; v.p., dir. Mus. Sci. and Industry, Chgo., 1971-77, pres., dir., 1978—. Chmn., Chgo. Council Fine Arts, 1976—. Mem. AAAS, Am. Assn. Mus.'s (exec. com. 1975-78), Assn. Sci.-Tech. Centers (dir. 1973—, pres. 1975-76), Internat. Council Mus.'s (vice chmn. internat. com. for mus.'s sci. 1976—), History of Sci. Soc., Soc. Indsl. Archeology, Soc. History of Tech. Clubs: Univ., Tavern (Chgo.). Author: Public Affairs Reporting, 1955; Starting a Science Center, 1977; editor: Applying Emerging Technologies, 1970; Nuclear Power in the South, 1970; The Future of Science and Technology, 1975; Museum Accounting Guidelines, 1976; Traveling Exhibitions, 1978; Towards the Year 2000, 1981. Office: Mus Sci and Industry 57th St and Lake Shore Dr Chicago IL 60637

DANILUK, WILLIAM ALEXANDER, educator; b. Canton, Ohio, May 20, 1944; s. Paul and Helen Daniluk; A.A., Kent State U., B.S. in Edn., 1970, Ed.M., 1972; Ph.D., U. Akron, 1980. Instr. adult basic edn. Sandy Valley Sch. System, Ohio, 1965-71, coach gymnastics, 1970-71; tchr. elem. grades Martin Sch., Canton, 1971-72; guidance counselor elem. schs., Canton, 1972-73; guidance counselor Crenshaw Jr. High Sch., Canton, 1973-78; tchr. elem. grades Belle Stone Sch., Canton, 1978—; guidance rep. Dist. 22, Ohio, 1978—. Mem. adv. com. Stark County Child and Adolescent Service Center, 1976-78; organizer vol. program Stark County Juvenile Attention Center, 1975; bd. dirs. Big Bros. and Sisters, Stark County, 1974-77. Mem. Stark County Guidance Assn. (pres. 1977-78), Ohio Personnel and Guidance Assn. (exec. com. 1977-78), NEA, Ohio Edn. Assn., Canton Profl. Educator's Assn., Ohio Sch. Counselors Assn., East Central Ohio Educators Assn., Phi Delta Kappa. Home: 520 25th NW Canton OH 44709 Office: 800 Market Ave N Canton OH 44702

DANIS, CHARLES WHEATON, bldg. and constrn. co. exec.; b. Dayton, Ohio, Mar. 20, 1915; s. Benjamin George and Grace Esther (Bunce) D.; B.S. in Mech. Engring., Cornell U., 1937; m. Elizabeth Jane Sliter, June 21, 1947; children—Richard Ralph, Charles Wheaton, Amy Louise Danis Sterner, Julie Marie, John Sliter. Engr., Armco Steel Co., Middleton, Ohio, 1937-38; engr. B.G. Danis Co., Dayton 1938-42, v.p., gen. mgr., 1945-66, pres., 1966-71; chmn., chief exec. officer Danis Industries Corp., Dayton, 1971-79, chmn. exec. com., 1979—; chmn., dir. Home Savs. & Loan Assn., Dayton, 1950-81; dir. 1st Nat. Bank, Dayton. Bd. dirs., treas. Dayton YMCA, 1966-73, Jr. Achievement, Dayton, 1970-79; v.p., bd. dirs. Goodwill Industries, Dayton, 1956-64; pres., bd. dirs. Dayton Better Bus. Bur., 1954-60, Engring Found. Dayton, 1966-71; trustee Siena Home for Aged, Dayton, 1967-70, U. Dayton, 1975—, Dayton Found.; trustee, pres. Dayton Catholic Social Services, 1971-72. Served with C.E., AUS, 1942-44. Mem. Dayton C. of C. (dir. 1954-55, 75-77). K.C. Clubs: Dayton Bicycle, Dayton Racquet, Engineers, Moraine Country. Home: 629 Evans Ln Dayton OH 45459 Office: 1801 E 1st St Dayton OH 45403

DANKWERTH, ALAN JAMES, mfg. co. exec.; b. N.Y.C., Aug. 28, 1937; s. Paul and Frieda D.; B.A., N.Y. U., 1958; M.B.A., Pace U., 1969; m. Helen Kleffmann, Jan. 24, 1960; children—Michael, Andrew, Peter. Devel. chemist Inmont Co., Newark, 1959-60; market research analyst Allied Chem. Co., N.Y.C., 1960-63, sales rep., 1963-66; market devel. rep. Sinclair Petro/Chem. Co., N.Y.C., 1966-68; dist. sales mgr., product mgr. Englehard Minerals & Chem. Co., Edison, N.J., 1971-76; dir. mktg. Patco div. C.J. Patterson Co., Kansas City, Mo., 1976-78, dir. designed chems., 1978-80, gen. mgr., v.p., 1980—; also dir.; instr. Rockhurst Coll., Kansas City, 1977—. Mem. mgmt. center com., 1978-79; bd. dirs. Friends In Search of Help, 1964-65; v.p. Troy Hills Civic Assn., Parsippany, N.J., 1963-65; trainer, coach Jr. Achievement; instr. YMCA, 1964-65. Served to capt., Inf., AUS, 1958-59. Mem. Sales and Mktg. Execs. Assn. Kansas City (dir., pres., Fred Klemp award 1978). Club: Kansas City. Home: 9605 W 105th Terr Overland Park KS 66212 Office: 3947 Broadway Kansas City MO 64111

DANKY, JAMES PHILIP, librarian; b. Los Angeles, Oct. 3, 1947; s. Philip Harper and Elizabeth (James) D.; A.B., Ripon Coll., 1970; M.A., U. Wis., Madison, 1973; m. Christine Irene Schelshorn. Welfare clk. Dept. Social Services Los Angeles County, Los Angeles, 1970-71; social worker Jefferson (Wis.) Dept. Social Services, 1971-72; order librarian State Hist. Soc. Wis., Madison, 1973-76, newspapers and periodicals librarian, 1976—; co-dir. Alt. Acquisitions Project, Temple U., Phila., 1978-80; project dir. 1905 Wis. State Census Indexing Project, 1977—. Recipient cert. of Appreciation, Wis. State Geneal. Soc., 1979. Mem. Am. Hist. Assn., ALA, State Hist. Soc. Wis. Office: Newspapers and Periodicals Unit State Hist Soc Wis 816 State St Madison WI 53706

DANLEY, ROBERT BRUCE, radiologist; b. Pitts., Apr. 1, 1948; s. French Charles and Eleanor Louise (Holsinger) D.; B.S., U. Ill., 1970; M.D., Loyola U., 1974; m. Susan Haller, June 24, 1972; children—Katherine, Kristina, Elizabeth. Intern, Foster G. McGaw Hosp., Maywood, Ill., 1974, resident, 1974-78; practice medicine specializing in radiology, Urbana, Ill., 1978—; staff Carle Found. Hosp., Urbana, 1978—; clin. asso. prof. U. Ill. Sch. Medicine, Urbana, 1978—. Diplomate Am. Bd. Radiology. Mem. AMA, Ill. Med. Soc., Champaign County Med. Soc., Ill. Radiol. Soc., Am. Coll. Radiologists. Office: 602 W University Ave Urbana IL 61801

DANNA, SAMMY RICHARD, educator; b. Monroe, La., Mar. 26, 1934; s. Joseph Richard and Lena Margaret (Danna) D.; B.A., N.E. La. U., 1956, M.Ed., 1962; M.A. in Speech, La. State U., Baton Rouge, 1960; Ph.D., U. Mo., 1967; M.Div., Cath. Theol. Union, Chgo., 1972; doctoral study U. Ill., Urbana. Journalism/speech tchr. Neville High Sch., Monroe, 1956-57, pubs. dir. 1959-61; journalism/speech tchr. Southside High Sch., Monroe, 1957-59; mem. faculty Ill. State U., Normal, 1963-64, Quincy (Ill.) Coll., 1967-68; mem. faculty Loyola U. of Chgo., 1969—, prof. communications, 1980—, ops. operations dir. univ. Sta. WLUW-FM, 1978-80, exec. dir., 1980—. Mem. Franciscan Order, deacon Roman Catholic Ch.; sec./historian and charter bd. dirs. Citizens Com. to Save Sta. WEFM, Chgo., 1972—. Grad. asst. U. Ill., 1962-63, U. Mo., 1964-67; Mellon grantee, 1979. Mem. Broadcast Edn. Assn., Nat. Press Photographers Assn., Nat. Assn. Ednl. Broadcasters, Assn. Jesuit Colls. and Univs. (chmn. communications com.), Popular Culture Assn. Democrat. Author monographs, contbr. articles to profl. jours. Office: 820 N Michigan Ave Chicago IL 60611

DANNEWITZ, DEAN VINCENT, cons. employee relations; b. Emmetsburg, Iowa, May 23, 1928; s. John Earl and Edna Irene (Pendlebury) D.; A.A., Worthington Community Coll., 1948; B.B.A., U. Minn., 1956, M.A., 1966; m. Mary Ann Tombers, 1979; children—Debra Lynn, Duane Alan, Brian David. Asst. wage and salary dir. Consumers Power Co., Jackson, Mich., 1956-60; asst. to v.p. indsl. relations Xerox Corp., Rochester, N.Y., 1960-65; mgr. personnel and adminstrn. Control Data Corp., Mpls., 1967-69; v.p. Elmer R. John Assos., Inc., Mpls., 1969-72; pres. Employee Relations Cons., Inc., Mpls., 1972—; exec. dir. Minn. State Adv. Council for Vocat. Edn., 1974-80; lectr. St. Thomas Coll., Augsburg Coll. Mem. long range planning com. Bloomington Bd. Edn., 1976-77. Served with USAF, 1950-54. Mem. Am. Psychol. Assn., Am. Mgmt. Assn., Am. Soc. Personnel Adminstrn., Am. Compensation assn., Assn. Mgmt. Cons.'s, Twin Cities Personnel Assn., U. Minn. Alumni Club. Methodist. Club: Decathlon Athletic. Home and Office: 9637 Little Rd Bloomington MN 55437

D'ANNIBALLE, LEO JOHN, retail co. exec.; b. Steubenville, Ohio, May 1, 1919; s. Alfred Joseph and Elizabeth Maria (Muziani) D'A.; student electronics Montgomery (W.Va.) Inst. Tech., 1941-42, Transylvania U., Lexington, Ky., 1942-43; m. Martha Jane McClelland, May 15, 1953; children—Elizabeth Jane, Leo John. With The Hub, Steubenville, 1937-43, 56-69, mdse. mgr. women's div., 1952-69; div. mdse. mgr. L.S. Good Corp., Wheeling, W.Va., 1969-78, mdse. coordinator in stores, Wheeling, 1979, gen. mgr. Ohio Valley Mall Store, St. Clairsville, Ohio, 1979—. Active local Am. Cancer Soc. Served with AUS, 1943-46. Decorated Legion of Merit. Mem. Steubenville Retail Mcht. Bur. (chmn. 1975), Steubenville C. of C., Am. Fedn. Musicians. Democrat. Roman Catholic. Clubs: K.C., Williams Country (Weirton, W.Va.). Home: 206 Orchard Ln Saint Clairsville OH 43950

DANOFF, MICHAEL, museum adminstr.; b. Chgo., Oct. 22, 1940; s. Maurice and Matilda (Price) D.; B.A. in English, U. Mich., 1962; M.A., N.C. U., 1964; Ph.D., Syracuse U., 1970; m. Frances Evelyn Colker, May 31, 1964; children—Sharon, Brian. Asst. prof. Dickinson (Pa.) Coll., 1970-73; asso. dir., chief curator Milw. Art Mus., 1974-80; dir. Akron (Ohio) Art Mus., 1980—; acquisition dir. HHK Found., Milw., 1977—. Mem. Assn. Art Mus. Dirs., Am. Assn. Mus., Coll. Art Assn. Club: Akron City. Author: From Foreign Shores, 1976; Nancy Eckholm Burkert, 1977; Emergence and Progression, 1979; Image in American Painting and Sculpture, 1950-1980, 1981. Home: 1538 Shanabrook St Akron OH 44313 Office: 70 E Market St Akron OH 44308

DANVILLE, VIRGINIA MAE, dietitian; b. Manistee County, Mich., Feb. 23, 1926; d. Sharon Leroy and Esther Cora (Humes) Grossnickle; B.S., Mich. State Coll., 1949; 1 son, David. Intern, Henry Ford Hosp., Detroit, 1949-50; dir. dietetics Oakwood Hosp., Dearborn, Mich., 1951-55; intern, asst. mgr. Greenfield Mills Restaurant, Detroit, 1957; adminstrv. asst. to dir. deitetics U. Mich. Hosp., Ann Arbor, 1957-58; dir. dietetics Oakwood Hosp., 1958-65, No. Mich. Hosp., Petoskey, 1967—. Mem. Am. Dietetic Assn., Am. Hosp. Food Service Assn., Nutrition Today Soc., Am. Diabetes Assn., Mich. Dietetic Assn. (sec. 1973-75, dist. pres. 1969-71; Outstanding Service award 1981), Zonta Internat., Beta Sigma Phi. Office: 416 Connable St Petoskey MI 49770

DAOUD, GEORGE JAMIL, hotel and motel cons.; b. Beirut, Oct. 20, 1944; came to U.S., 1958, naturalized, 1970; s. Jamil G. and Shafieah E. Daoud; B.S., N.Y. U., 1967; M.P.S., Cornell U., 1969; m. Barbara A. Fisco, Apr. 30, 1972: 3 children. Gen. grm. Holiday Inn, New London and Groton, Conn., 1974-75, Centle Winds Beach Resort, St. Croix, V.I., 1975-78; pres., cons. Motor Inn Mgmt., Inc., Dayton, Ohio, 1978—; v.p. V.I. Hotel and Motel Assn., 1976. Mem. Am. Hotel and Motel Assn. (mem. Ednl. Inst., cert. hotel adminstr.), Ohio Hotel and Motel Assn., Nat. Assn. Rev. Appraisers, Cert. Real Estate Rev. Appraisers. Democrat. Roman Catholic. Club: Masons. Office: PO Box 1417 Dayton OH 45401

DAPKUS, WILLIAM VINCENT, elec. engr.; b. Saginaw, Mich., Mar. 2, 1920; s. Frank and Anna Hursulis (Slogaritus) D.; B.E.E., Bucknell U., 1947; m. Margaret Patricia Paralis, Jan. 29, 1948; children—William, Lynn, Theodore. Engr. aide Tenn. Eastman Co., Oak Ridge, 1944-46; engr. Consumers Power Co., Jackson, Mich., 1948-51; elec. designer Smith Hinchman & Grylls, Detroit, 1953-57; job capt. Cunningham-Limp Co., Birmingham, Mich., 1974— CES Inc, Troy, Mich., 1978-81; cons. engr., 1981—. Activities chmn. local Boy Scouts Am., 1960-65. Served with AUS, 1943-46. Registered profl. engr., Mich. Mem. U.S. Soc. Scientists and Engrs. Democrat. Roman Catholic. Home: 28705 Inkster Rd Farmington Hills MI 48018 Office: SSOE Inc Flint MI

DAPP, THOMAS EDWARD, constrn. co. exec.; b. Milw., Feb. 8, 1941; s. Jean Godfred and Verna Clara (Schumann) D.; B.S. civil engring., U. Wis., 1964, M.B.A., 1965; postgrad., Ind. U., 1971—; m. Susan Daine Ricker, June 24, 1967; children—Nicole Jeanine, Jason Thomas. Project engr. Ryan Inc. of Wis., Milw., 1965-66, systems and prodn. mgr., Janesville, 1966-67, eastern div. and structures mgr., Chgo. and Indpls., 1967-73; pres. Gradex, Inc., Indpls., 1973—; v.p. Midwest Racquetball, Inc., Indpls., 1978—; pres. Dapp, Inc., 1979—; partner Heatherlea Devel., 1979—. Bd. dirs. Ind. Hwys. for Survival. Registered profl. engr., Ind. Mem. ASCE, Nat. Soc. Profl. Engrs., Ind. Constructors Assn., Assn. Gen. Contractors. Am. Road Builders Assn., U. Wis. Alumni Assn., Ind. C. of C., Beta Gamma Sigma, Tau Epsilon. Clubs: Ind. Econ., Sierra, Woodland Country, Carmel Racquet, Brookshire Golf, Kokomo Racquetball, Racquetball Plus, Hoosier Roadrunners, U.S. Golf Assn. Home: 1315 Fairbanks Dr Carmel IN 46032 Office: 6810 N Shadeland Ave Indianapolis IN 46220

DAPPEN, GLEN EUGENE, biologist, educator; b. Lucas, S.D., Mar. 4, 1938; s. Joseph Lester and Rosetta Marie (Smith) D.; B.A. in Chemistry, Sioux Falls (S.D.) Coll., 1960; M.S. in Zoology, U. Nebr., 1965, Ph.D., 1971; m. Barbara Hughes, June 9, 1959; children—Laura Ruth, Patricia Rose. High sch. tchr. Omaha Pub. Schs., 1961-62; lab. asst. U. Nebr. Grad. Sch., 1963-68; research chemist/biologist Nebr. Game Commn., 1967-68; asst. prof. Nebr. Wesleyan U., Lincoln, 1969—; adj. prof. dept. anatomy U. Nebr. Med. Coll.; cons. in parasitology VA Hosp., Lincoln. Chmn. bd. deacons, Christian edn. and mens work Baptist Ch., 1968—. Office Water Resources Research Inst. grantee, 1972-74. Mem. Am. Parasitologists Soc., AAAS, Am. Chem. Soc., Nebr. Acad. Sci., Nebr. Ornithology Soc. Club: Kiwanis Internat. Research in helminthology and pesticide chemistry and comparative immunology. Home: 251 Cottonwood Dr Lincoln NE 68510 Office: Biology Dept Nebr Wesleyan U Lincoln NE 68504

DAPRON, ELMER JOSEPH, JR., advt. exec.; b. Clayton, Mo., Jan. 14, 1925; s. Elmer Joseph and Susanna (Kruse) D. m. Sharon Kay Neuling. Employed in constrn. bus., Fairbanks, Alaska, 1947-48; tech. writer-editor McDonnell-Douglas Corp., St. Louis, 1948-57; free-lance writer, Paris, France, 1957; sr. cons. Kenrick Advt., Inc., St. Louis, 1977—; pres. Cornucopia Communications Inc., 1979—; v.p. Gardner Advt. Co., St. Louis, 1961-76; producer, commentator syndicated TV show Elmer Dapron's Grocery List; commentator Mut. Radio Network, Washington, also Am. Forces Network; communications cons. to govt. and industry. Served with USMCR, 1943-45; PTO; 50-51; Korea. Recipient advt. awards including New Filming Techniques award Internat.-Film Festival, 1969. Hon. fellow Harry Truman Library Inst. Mem. Nat. Agrl. Mktg. Assn. (v.p. 1970—, trustee, Miss. Valley Farm Mktg. Man of Year 1974), Marine Corps League (nat. vice comdt. 1967-69). Clubs: Media, Arena, Four Seasons. Democrat. Contbr. articles to publs. Home: 300 Mansion House Center Saint Louis MO 63102 Office: 319 N 4th St Saint Louis MO 63102

D'AQUILA, THOMAS CARL, lawyer; b. Virginia, Minn., Nov. 4, 1949; s. Carl Mario and Dolores Mae (Casagrande) D'A.; B.B.A. in Acctg., U. Notre Dame, 1972; J.D., U. Denver, 1974; postgrad. U. Exter (Eng.), 1973; Admitted to Colo. bar, 1975, Minn. bar, 1977; interSEC, Denver, 1974-75; with Yegge Hall & Evans, Denver, 1975-76, Henretta, D'Aquila & Cross, Mpls., 1977-81, Popham Haik, Schnobrich, Kaufman & Doty Ltd., 1981—. Mem. Colo. Bar Assn., Hennepin County Bar Assn., Minn. Bar Assn., Am. Bar Assn., Beta Alpha Psi. Office: 4344 IDS Center Minneapolis MN 55402

DARBY, HARRY, former U.S. senator, industrialist, farmer, stockman; b. Kansas City, Kans., Jan. 23, 1895; s. Harry and Florence Isabelle (Smith) D.; B.S. in Mech. Engring., U. Ill., 1917, M.E., 1929; LL.D. (hon.), Kans. State U., Manhattan, St. Benedict's Coll., Atchison, Kans., Westminster Coll., Fulton, Mo., Washburn U., Topeka; D.Comml. Sci., Baker U., Baldwin City, Kans.; m. Edith Marie Cubbison, Dec. 17, 1917 (dec.); children—Harriet (Mrs. Thomas H. Gibson, Jr.), Joan (Mrs. Roy A. Edwards), Edith Marie (Mrs. Ray Evans), Marjorie (Mrs. Eugene D. Alford). With Mo. Boiler Works Co., Kansas City, Mo., 1911-19; with Darby Corp., Kansas City, Kans., 1920—, chmn. bd., owner, 1945—; founder, chmn. bd. dirs. Leavenworth Steel, Inc., Darby Ry. Cars, Inc.; dir. numerous corps. U.S. senator from Kans., 1949-50; mem. Republican Nat. Com. for Kans., 1940-64. Active 4-H Club; chmn. Kans. Hwy. Commn., 1933-37; mem. at large nat. council, mem. regional exec. com. Boy Scouts Am. Trustee Nat. Cowboy Hall Fame; exec. com. Agrl. Hall Fame; chmn. Eisenhower Presdl. Library Commn.; chmn. emeritus Am. Royal Livestock and Horse Show; chmn. bd. Eisenhower Found., Abilene, Kans.; bd. dirs. U. Kans. Research Found., Kan. Heart Assn. Served from 2d lt. to capt., F.A., U.S. Army, 1917-19; AEF. Recipient awards for civic activities. Fellow ASME; mem. Navy League U.S., Kansas City Crime Commn., Kans. Registration Bd. Profl. Engrs., U. Ill. Found., Am. Soc. C.E., Nat., Kans. socs. profl. engrs., Am. Hereford Assn., Am. Nat. Livestock Assn., Kans. Livestock Assn. (exec. com.), Am. Soc. Agrl. Engrs., V.F.W., Am. Legion, 40 and 8, Military Order World Wars. Episcopalian. Mason (32 deg., Shriner, Jester). Clubs: Kansas City, Automobile of Missouri, Saddle and Sirloin, Rotary, River, Terrace, Man of The Month (Kansas City, Kans.); Chicago; Chevy Chase, Capitol Hill (Washington); Cherry Hills (Denver), Burning Tree (Bethesda, Md.). Home: 1220 Hoel Pkwy Kansas City KS 66102 Office: The Darby Corp 1st St and Walker Ave Kansas City KS 66110

D'ARCO, JOHN A., JR., state senator; b. Chgo., Oct. 19, 1944; student U. Miami, 1962-64; grad. Loyola U., 1966; J.D., De Paul U., 1975; m. Michelle D'Arco; children—John III, Mia, Robert. Admitted to Ill. bar, individual practice law, Chgo.; mem. Ill. Ho. of Reps., 1974-76, Ill. Senate, 1976—, chmn. ins. and lic. activities com., 1979. Pres. 12th Dist. Police Dept. Athletic com.; mem. Joint Civic Com. Italian-Ams.; bd. dirs. Near West Side Health Planning Orgn. Democrat. Address: 400 E Randolph St Chicago IL 60601*

DAREHSHORI, NADER FARHANG, sales exec.; b. Shiraz, Iran, Dec. 15, 1936; came to U.S., 1961, naturalized, 1972; s. Zaki F. and Rokhsar (Farsimadan) D.; B.A. in B.A., U. Wis., 1966, postgrad., 1966; m. Anne C. Wagnild, Dec. 14, 1968. Supt. village schs., Shiraz, 1959-61; salesman Houghton Mifflin Co., Geneva, Ill., 1966-75, field sales mgr., 1975-77, sales mgr. of Midwest, 1977—, mem. coll. div. mgmt. com., 1968—. Democrat. Club: Kiwanis. Address: 1900 S Batavia Ave Geneva IL 60134

DARESH, JOHN CHARLES, educator; b. Chgo., Aug. 17, 1948; s. George M. and Anne C. (Sirus) D.; B.A., Loras Coll., 1969; M.A., DePaul U., 1977; Ph.D., U. Wis., Madison, 1978; m. Stephanie M. Probst, June 4, 1977. Tchr., Wahlert High Sch., Dubuque, Iowa, 1969-74, Kenwood High Sch., Chgo., 1975-76; sales mgr. Tri-State Tours, Galena, Ill., 1974-75; project coordinator Wis. Research and Devel. Center for Individualized Schooling, Madison, Wis., 1976-80; asst. prof. ednl. adminstrn. U. Cin., 1981—; cons. to schs.; asst. U. Wis., 1976-78. Active St. Thomas Aquinas Ch., Madison, 1978-80. Mem. Am. Assn. Tchrs. French, Assn. Supervision and Curriculum Devel., Nat. Assn. Secondary Sch. Prins., Phi Delta Kappa, Phi Kappa Phi. Roman Catholic. Author: (with others) The Renewal and Improvement of Secondary Education: Concepts and Practices, 1980; editor: (with J. M. Lipham) Administrative and Staff Relationships in Education, 1979. Home: 6294 Thole Rd Cincinnati OH 45230 Office: Mail Location 2 U Cin Cincinnati OH 45221

DARGAN, DAN W., hosp. adminstr.; b. Madoc, Ont., Can., Mar. 31, 1947; s. Robert E. and Edna B. (Stevenson) D.; B.A., Greenville Coll., 1970; M.H.A., U. Ottawa, Ont., 1972; m. Beth A. Gray, June 8, 1968; children—Andrew Robert, Stephanie DeAnn. Adminstrv. resident St. Clare Hosp., Schenectady, 1971-72; asst. adminstr. St. Mary Hosp., Amsterdam, N.Y., 1972-73, Bethesda Gen. Hosp. and Homes, St. Louis, 1973-76, St. Joseph Hosp., Houston, 1976-78; adminstr. Katherine Shaw Bethea Hosp., Dixon, Ill., 1978—. Bd. dirs. United Fund, Dixon Jr. Achievement. Fellow Am. Coll. Hosp. Adminstrs.; mem. Am. Hosp. Assn., Dixon C. of C. Club: Rotary (dir.). Author: An Overview and Analysis of System Incentive Programs in Hospitals in North America, 1972. Office: Katherine Shaw Bethea Hosp 403 E 1st St Dixon IL 61021

DARGUSCH, CARLTON SPENCER, lawyer; b. Batavia, N.Y., Aug. 19, 1900; s. Julius Herman and Etta (Burnham) D.; student Ind. U., 1921-22, 24, Ohio State U., 1922-25; m. Genevieve Johnston, Nov. 6, 1923; children—Carlton Spencer (dec.), Evelyn Byrd (Mrs. Charles A. Lanphere). Legis. draftsman Ohio Gen. Assembly, 1925; atty. Tax Commn. Ohio, 1925-33; tax commr. Ohio, 1933-37; mem. firm Law Offices Carlton S. Dargusch, Columbus, Ohio; dir. Clark Grave Vault Co. Cons. Helped draft plans for Selective Service, also Universal Mil. Tng.; past asst. dir. for manpower ODM; mem. Am. del. Conf. for Applied Research, Vienna, 1956, India, 1958, USSR, 1960. Trustee Ohio State U., 1938-59, 63-65, chmn. bd., 1944-45, 51-52, 58-59; bd. dirs. Ohio State U. Research Found., 1951-62. Served to brig. gen. U.S. Army, 1940-47. Decorated D.S.M., 1946, Army Commendation medal with cluster; recipient award Ohio State U., 1960. Mem. Am. Assn. Engring. Socs. (dir.), Mil. Order World Wars, Am. Legion, Omicron Kappa Upsilon (hon.), Kappa Sigma, Phi Delta Phi. Mason. Clubs: Army and Navy (Washington); Sphinx (Ohio State U.); Columbus, Columbus Country; Queen City (Cin.); Union (Cleve.); Chemists (N.Y.C.); Chevy Chase (Md.). Author: Estate and Inheritance Taxation (with John Cassidy), 1930, rev. (with Jack H. Bertsch), 1956; Operation of Selective Service in World War II, 1956; also articles. Home: 271 N Columbia Ave Bexley OH 43209 Office: 218 E State St Columbus OH 43215

DARR, ROBERT MARCUS, advt. agy. exec.; b. Cleve., Dec. 2, 1914; s. Marcus M. and Florence (Crosby) D.; student Marquette U., 1946-47. Advt. mgr. Leroi Co., Milw., 1940-48; account exec. Wetzel Bros. Printing Co., Milw., 1948-56; v.p. Franklin-Mautner Advt., Inc.,

Milw., 1956-77; exec. v.p. Owens-Darr Communications Assos., Inc., Milw., 1977—; instr. prins. of advt. Milw. Area Tech. Coll., 1972—. Recipient Communicator of Yr. award Milw. Graphic Arts Assn., 1972. Mem. Assn. Ind. Advertisers (chpt. pres. 1960-61, nat. dir. 1961-62), Am. Advt. Fedn. (gov. 8th dist. 1972-74). Republican. Clubs: Milw. Advt. (pres. 1966-67), Masons Shriners, Tripoli Golf. Home: 3567 W Pelican Ln Brown Deer WI 53209 Office: 312 E Wisconsin Ave Milwaukee WI 53202

DARRAH, RODNEY CARTER, physicist; b. Scottsburg, Ind., Mar. 2, 1947; s. Byron Eugene and Mary ALice (Carter) D.; B.S., Ind. State U., 1969, M.S., 1970; m. Martha Carol Macy, Aug. 26, 1967; 1 son, Jason Rodney. Instr. Ind. State U., Terre Haute, 1970-71; chmn. sci. dept. Aurora (Ind.) High Sch., 1972; vis. scientist electro fluid dynamics Aerospace Research Lab., Wright Patterson AFB, Ohio, 1973, plasma physics lab., 1974; research physicist Universal Energy Systems, Inc., Dayton, Ohio, 1975—, corp. treas., 1980—. Mem. IEEE, Am. Phys. Soc., Am. Inst. Physics, Sigma Pi Sigma. Contbr. articles to profl. jours. Home: 3054 Maginn Dr Beavercreek OH 45385 Office: 3195 Plainfield Rd Dayton OH 45432

DARROW, CLARENCE ALLISON, state legislator; b. Dubuque, Iowa, Mar. 22, 1940; s. Clarence Allison and Joan Kathryn (Reinhart) D.; B.S., Loras Coll., Dubuque, 1962; M.S.W., U. Ill., Champaign, 1966; J.D., Chgo.-Kent Coll. Law, 1971; m. Lili Ruja, Nov. 30, 1963; children—Elizabeth, John, Antoinette, Clarence, Jennifer. Admitted to Ill. bar, 1971; asst. state's atty. Rock Island County (Ill.), 1971-74; mem. Ill. Ho. of Reps., Springfield, 1974—. Bd. dirs. Rock Island County Legal Aid Assn., Quint-Cities Drug Abuse Council, Ill. Law Enforcement Commn., Ill. Pub. Aid Adv. Commn. Named freshman legislator of yr. Ill. Edn. Assn., 1976. Mem. Am., Ill., Rock Island County bar assns. Democrat. Clubs: Elks, Rotary. Office: 1504 Third Ave Rock Island IL 61201

DARST, STEVEN VINCENT, savs. and loan assn. exec.; b. Detroit, Oct. 11, 1939; s. Harry F. and Hannah F. Darst; B.S., Lawrence (Mich.) Inst. Tech., 1961; m. Myrtle E. Williams, June 6, 1981; children—Edward, Mark, Gary, Ginger. With Standard Fed. Savs. & Loan Assn., Troy, Mich., 1961—, v.p., 1974—. Mem. Assn. Systems Mgmt. (internat. pres. 1982—; Disting. Service award 1976). Club: Emerald City Boat (treas. 1981—). Home: 22842 Newberry St Saint Clair Shores MI 48080 Office: 2401 W Big Beaver St Troy MI 48084

DASCHLE, THOMAS ANDREW, congressman; b. Aberdeen, S.D., Dec. 9, 1947; B.A., S.D. State U., 1969; m. Laurie Susan Klinkel; children—Kelley, Nathan, Lindsay. Fin. investment rep.; chief legis. aide, field coordinator Sen. James Abourzek, 1973-77; mem. 96th-97th Congresses from 1st S.D. Dist. Served to 1st lt. USAF, 1969-72. Democrat. Office: Room 439 Cannon House Office Bldg Washington DC 20515

DASHNER, RICHARD FRANCIS, coating co. exec.; b. Oak Park, Ill., Sept. 26, 1931; s. Francis J. and Margaret T. (Tompkins) D.; student Knox Coll., 1949-50; B.S., U. Ill., 1953; m. Alice T. Turner, July 11, 1954; children—Margaret Ruth, John Robert. Indsl. salesman U.S. Gypsum Co., Chgo., 1955-59; indsl. sales engr. Nat. Gypsum Co., Buffalo, 1959-68; constrn. salesman Gen. Electric Silicones, Oak Brook, Ill., 1968-73, constrn. market devel. specialist, 1973-77; pres. A & D Coating Co., Wheaton, Ill., 1977—; dir. Olson Silicone Specialties. Active DuPage council Boy Scouts Am., recipient Scouter's Keys, 1970, 73. Served from 2d lt. to 1st lt. inf. AUS, 1953-55. Mem. Archtl. Aluminum Mfg. Assn. (energy conservation com., sealant com. 1975, reflective insulating glass com.) Constrn. Specifications Inst. (student com. 1970-75, mem. tech. papers com. 1977, dir. 1979), Phi Sigma Kappa. Presbyterian (deacon 1972-75, trustee 1981). Contbr. articles to profl. jours.; patentee structural glazing systems, dry silicone glazing, silicone in thermal breaks. Home: 919 N Washington St Wheaton IL 60187 Office: 208 N West St Wheaton IL 60187

DASKIVICH, RICHARD ANTHONY, elec. engr.; b. Indiana, Pa., Mar. 26, 1941; s. John and Kathryn Daskivich; B.S. in Elec. Engring., Pa. State U., 1963; M.S., Wayne State U., 1967; m. Patricia Ann Medvetz, June 26, 1965. With Gen. Motors Corp., 1963—, sr. engr. computer systems, metrology, electronics, friction, lubrication and wear Research Labs., 1963-80, staff research engr., advanced engine devel. and reliability Detroit Diesel Allison Div., 1980—. Registered profl. engr. Sr. mem. Soc. Mfg. Engrs. Author 40 research reports. Office: 13400 W Outer Dr Detroit MI 48228

DAS VARMA, RANENDRA LAL, physician; b. Bihar, India, Oct. 18, 1935; s. Sachindra Lal and Pari Rani (Mitra) DasV.; came to U.S., 1959, naturalized, 1971; B. Medicine, Prince of Wales Med. Coll. India, 1958, M.D., 1958; m. Janet Wassity Aug. 28, 1965; children—Julie, Jay, Robby. Intern, Perth Amboy (N.J.) Gen. Hosp., 1960; resident Akron (Ohio) City Hosp., 1961-65; mem. staff Permanente Med. Group, Parma, Ohio, 1968-72; dir. div. medicine, dir. coronary care and intensive care units St. Thomas Hosp., Akron, 1972—; clin. asst. prof. medicine Case Western Res. U., 1974—; mem. council chiefs of internal medicine, asso. prof. medicine North East Ohio U., 1975—; vis. physician Cleve. Met. Gen. Hosp. Trustee N.E. Ohio chpt. Am. Heart Assn. Diplomate Am. Bd. Internal Medicine. Fellow Am. Coll. Cardiology, A.C.P., Royal Coll. Physicians and Surgeons Can.; mem. Am., Ohio State med. assns., Am. Soc. Internal Medicine. Hindu. Home: 661 Beaverbrook Dr Akron OH 44313 Office: 661 Beaverbrook Dr Akron OH 44313

DATTA, TAPAN KUMAR, civil engr.; b. Cuttack, India, Sept. 3, 1939; came to U.S., 1967, naturalized, 1980; s. Nihar Ranjan and Indira Dutta; B.C.E., Bengal Engring. Coll., India, 1962, Diploma in Town and Regional Planning, 1965; M.S., Wayne State U., 1968; Ph.D., Mich. State U., 1973; m. Mira Guha, Jan. 30, 1964; children—Rita, Sutapa. Asst. engr. Kuljian Corp., Calcutta, India, 1962-64, project engr., 1964-67; chief transp. engr. Goodell, Grivas, Inc., Southfield, Mich., 1968-72, v.p., 1972—, cons., 1973—; prof., chmn. civil engring. dept. Wayne State U., Detroit, 1978—. Registered profl. engr., Mich., Fla. Mem. Transp. Research Bd., Inst. Transp. Engrs., Am. Public Works Assn., ASCE. Contbr. articles to tech. jours. Home: 1830 Lone Pine Rd Bloomfield Hills MI 48013 Office: Civil Engring Dept Wayne State U 667 Merrick St Detroit MI 48202

D'ATTOMA, JOHN JOSEPH, wholesale wine and spirits co. exec.; b. Bklyn., Sept. 28, 1950; s. John Angelo and Anna Louise (Cantore) D'A.; B.S. in B.A., N.Y. Inst. Tech., 1972; m. Kathryn E. King, Aug. 19, 1972; children—Alyson Marie, Amy Kate, John William. Trade research analyst Joseph E. Seagram & Sons, N.Y.C., 1972-74; with Gen. Wine & Spirits Co., 1974-78, regional mgr., Nebr. and S.D., 1976-77, dist. mgr., Mo. and Kans., 1977-78; mktg. mgr. Gen. Standard, Kansas City, Mo., 1978-79; v.p., dir. sales Jackson Distributing Co., Kansas City, 1979-80, v.p., gen. mgr., 1980—. Active Unico Internat., Kansas City, 1981—, City of Hope, Kansas City, 1981—. Mem. Am. Mgmt. Assn., Wine and Spirits Wholesales Assn. (mem. young execs. council 1981). Home: 606 Lancelot Dr Liberty MO 64068 Office: 8641 NE Underground Dr Kansas City MO 64161

DAUB, HAL, Congressman; b. Fayetteville, N.C., Apr. 23, 1941; s. Harold John and Eleanor M. (Hickman) D.; B.S. in Bus. Adminstrn., Washington U., St. Louis, 1963; J.D., U. Nebr., 1966; m. Cindy S. Shin, Apr. 7, 1968; children—Natalie Ann, John Clifford, Tammy Rene. Admitted to Nebr. bar, 1966; staff intern to U.S. Senator Roman Hruska from Nebr., 1966; asso. firm Fitzgerald, Brown, Leahy & McGill, Omaha, 1968-71; v.p., gen. counsel Standard Chem. Mfg. Co., Omaha, 1971-80; mem. 97th Congress from 2d Dist. Nebr. Jr. pres. Nebr. Founders Day, 1971; treas. Douglas County Republican Com., 1971-74, chmn., 1974-77; mem. Nebr. Rep. Central Com., 1974—; mem. exec. com., bd. dirs. Combined Health Agys. Drive, 1976; pres.-elect Douglas-Sarpy unit Nebr. Heart Assn., 1977. Served to capt. U.S. Army, 1963-68. Decorated Commendation medal (2); named One of 10 Most Outstanding Young Omahan's, Omaha Jaycees, 1976; recipient service award SAC, 1976; Outstanding Vol. of Yr. award Douglas-Sarpy unit Nebr. Heart Assn., 1976. Mem. Omaha Bar Assn., Nat. Assn. Credit Mgmt. (1st v.p. 1977), Delta Theta Phi. Presbyterian. Clubs: Optimists, Masons. Office: 1008 Longworth House Office Bldg Washington DC 20515

DAUBENAS, JEAN DOROTHY TENBRINCK, librarian; b. N.Y.C., Apr. 4, 1940; d. Eduard J.A. and Margaret Dorothy (Schaffner) Tenbrinck; A.B., Barnard Coll., 1962; grad. Am. Acad. Dramatic Arts, 1963; M.A., N.Y. U., 1965; M.L.S., U. Ariz., 1972; postgrad U. Utah, 1975—; m. Joseph Anthony Daubenas, May 29, 1965. Tchr., Beth Jacob Tchrs. Sem. Am., Bronx, 1965-66; caseworker, Dept. Social Services, N.Y.C., 1966-67; actress Boothbay (Maine) Playhouse, others, 1967-70; reference librarian Ariz. State U., Tempe, 1972-75; asst. librarian, asst. prof. library sci. Avila Coll., Kansas City, Mo., 1979—. N.Y. State Regents scholar, 1958-62; U. Ariz. scholar, 1971-72. Mem. ALA, Actors Equity Assn., Beta Phi Mu, Phi Kappa Phi. Roman Catholic. Home: 11525 Baltimore Ave Kansas City MO 64114 Office: 11901 Wornall Rd Kansas City MO 64145

DAUBENDIEK, GENE RUSSELL, utilities co. exec.; b. Cylinder, Iowa, Mar. 12, 1923; s. Carl Henry and Bertha K. (Krecji) D.; B.E.E., Iowa State U., 1944; m. Mary Matilda Phillips, Feb. 18, 1945; children—James Louis, Sarah Ann. Mgr., West Iowa Telephone Co., Osceola, 1943-45; engr. Jefferson (Iowa) Telephone Co., 1943—, sec.-mgr., 1962—; pres. Telephone Constrn., Inc., Jefferson, 1950-64; dir. West Iowa Telephone Co., Remsen, Iowa State Bank, West Bend; trustee W.H. Daubendiek Trust, West Bend. Chmn. Jefferson Airport Commn., 1960-72, Indsl. Bur., 1966; mem. Jefferson City Council, 19S6-58, Jefferson Indsl. Devel. Co., 1960. Mem. Jefferson C. of C., Ind. Telephone Pioneers Assn. (life), Iowa Telephone Assn. (hon. dir.), Orgn. Protection and Advancement Small Telephone Cos. (pres. 1969-71), U.S. Ind. Telephone Assn. (dir.), Theta Xi. Republican. Methodist. Clubs: Green County Golf and Country (past pres.), Elks, Lions (past pres.). Home: PO Box 51 Jefferson IA 50129 Office: PO Box 267 Jefferson IA 50129

DAUBERT, GEORGE A., chem. co. exec.; b. Chgo. Formerly pres., now chmn. bd. Daubert Chem. Co., Oak Brook, Ill., also dir. Address: 1200 Jorie Blvd Oak Brook IL 60521*

DAUBERT, LEROY LINCOLN, engring, co. exec.; b. Lebanon, Pa., Nov. 30, 1911; s. Clarence Elizer and Virginia Ellen (Miller) D.; B.S. in Archtl. Engring., Iowa State U., 1934, B.S. in Mech. Engring., 1936; m. Ruth Thelma Ferce, July 20, 1935; 1 dau., Susan Ann. Engr., Carrier Corp., 1937-41; chief engr. Des Moines Ordnance Plant, 1942-47; engr. Delavan Engring. Co., 1947-52; pres. Deco Engring. Products, Inc., Des Moines, 1952-74, Deco Internat., Inc., Des Moines, 1952—, Daubert Co., Inc., Des Moines, 1974—, Clive Ag Supply, Des Moines, 1974—, D & D Properties, Des Moines, 1974—; chmn. bd. Deco Engring. Products, Inc., 1974—. Chmn. Bd. of Assessment and Review, City of Des Moines, 1958—; pres. Des Moines Sch. Bd., 1961, 66; bd. dirs. Des Moines C. of C., 1969-74, chmn. civic affairs com., 1965-68; chmn. Des Moines Sch. Constrn. Com., 1970—; chmn. capital improvements com. Des Moines Schs.; com. mem. Des Moines Civic Center. Recipient Civic award Des Moines Youth Orgn., 1967; Mayors award Mayors Task Force, 1970. Mem. Internat. Assn. Assessing Officers, Nat. Assn. Assessors, Internat. Producers Council, Am. Soc. Heating and Ventilating Engrs. Presbyterian. Clubs: Des Moines, Embassy, Wakonda Country, Elks, Masons, Shriners. Designed and constructed world's first all brick and tile swimming pool; developed electrostatic spray equipment. Home: 3200 Wauwatosa Dr Des Moines IA 50321 Office: 1904 NW 92d St Ct Des Moines IA 50322

DAUGHERTY, CHARLES HOYL, JR., designer; b. Washington, Feb. 2, 1940; s. Charles Hoyl and Clara (Schorfheide) D.; B.A., So. Ill. U., 1966; m. Cherryl Jean Watts, Aug. 19, 1978; children—Amanda Kay, Karen Kay; stepchildren—Stephnie Peach, Darrin Peach. Student worker, tech. asst. coop. research in design, environ. planning So. Ill. U., Edwardsville, 1961-64, staff asst., asst. to coordinator coop. research in design Center for Study of Crime, Delinquency and Corrections, Univ. Relations and Exhibits, Communications Media Services div., 1965-67, comml. artist II Univ. Exhibits, 1967-68, instructional materials programmer III, 1968-73, asst. coordinator, 1973-74, asst. dir., 1974-75, coordinator for univ. exhibits, 1975-77, coordinator for univ. relations, 1977-79, dir. communications, 1979—, chmn. adminstrv./profl. staff council; design asst. Inst. Bahavioral Research, Washington, 1964-65, project dir. Ill. Dept. Bus. and Econ. Devel., 1975, 76, Ill. Div. Vocat. and Tech. Edn., 1975, 76, Fed. Energy Adminstrn., 1976. Active, So. Ill. U. Bicentennial Commn., 1975-76; bd. dirs. Ill. Coll. Relations Council. Served with USAF, 1958-59, Res., 1959-64. Recipient award of merit Indsl. Designers Soc. Am., 1966; Eagle Scout, Boy Scouts Am., 1950—, Order of Arrow, 1954-58. Mem. Nat. Audio Visual Assn. Republican. Methodist. Clubs: So. Ill. U. Flying Salukis (hon.); Crab Orchard Lake Sailing (harbor master 1976—). Home: 124 N Rod Ln Carbondale IL 62901 Office: Anthony Hall So Ill U Carbondale IL 62901

DAUGHERTY, DAVID BYRNS, assn. exec.; b. Muncie, Ind., May 2, 1949; s. Graden Woodrow and Marion Louis (Walker) D.; B.S., Ball State U., 1975; m. Rhonda Sue Thornburg, Mar. 17, 1982; children—Shelley E., Christina R. Asst. zoning adminstr. City of Indpls., 1975-77; v.p., exec. dir. Downtown Bus. Council, Muncie-Delaware County C. of C., Muncie, 1977-79; downtown devel. dir. Sidney-Shelby County (Ohio) C. of C., 1979—, exec. v.p., 1979—. Served with USN, 1968-72. Mem. Am. C. of C. Execs., Ohio C. of C. Execs. Club: Rotary. Home: 221 A S Ohio Sidney OH 45365 Office: 133 S Ohio Ave Sidney OH 45365

DAUGHERTY, GARY DUANE, civil engr.; b. Lodi, Ohio, May 27, 1950; s. Lavon Luke and Joan Margaret (Sayre) D.; B.S. in C.E., Ohio State U., 1972. With Burbank Grain and Feed Co. (Ohio), 1960-72, Med-Way Chem. Co., Burbank, 1960-72, Nova Grain and Feed Co. (Ohio), 1967-72; asst. head san. engring. dept. Engring. Asso. Ltd., Wooster, Ohio, 1972—; cons. civil engr. in water and wastewater facilities design. Reporting officer Burbank Fire Dept., 1977-80, v.p. firemans assn., 1979—. Registered profl. engr., Ohio. Mem. Nat. Soc. Profl. Engrs., Ohio Soc. Profl. Engrs., ASCE, Ohio Assn. Emergency Med. Services, Nat. Assn. Emergency Med. Technicians, Ohio Emergency Med. Technicians Assn., Nat. Fedn. Amateur Softball Assn. Umpires, Ohio State U. Alumni Assn. Home: 10326 Depot St Burbank OH 44214 Office: 700 Winkler Dr Wooster OH 44691

DAUGHTON, JAMES MICHAEL, mktg. exec.; b. Creston, Iowa, Mar. 19, 1942; s. Francis M. and Margaret E. Daughton; B.S., Drake U., 1964; m. Cherie Cosimini, Sept. 3; children—Pam, Kelley, Susan, Carrie. Communications rep. Northwestern Bell Telephone Co., Grand Island, Nebr., 1964-65, Omaha, 1966, communications supr., 1967, spl. services supr., 1968, sales mgr. large accounts, 1969-70, account mgr. inventory systems, 1971-74, dist. sales mgr., Omaha and inventory systems, 1975, dist. sales mgr. comml. segment for Nebr., 1976, mktg. mgr. comml. segment Nebr., 1977-78, dist. staff mgr. multi-state mktg., 1979-80, dist. staff mgr., 1980—; guest speaker numerous bus. convs., 1971-78. Chmn. nat. firms div. United Community Chest Fund Raising Drive, 1976-78; Douglas County (Nebr.) election insp., 1969-78. Named Man of Yr., Omaha Indsl. Found., 1975. Mem. Omaha Sales and Execs. Assn. (Disting. Sales award 1973), Omaha Jr. C. of C. (award 1974), Minn. Indsl. Devel. Assn. Roman Catholic. Clubs: Elks, Toastmasters (Toastmaster of Yr. award 1970). Home: 10101 S Cedar Lake Rd Minnetonka MN 55343 Office: 75 S 5th St Minneapolis MN 55240

DAUM, HUGH WARNER, frozen food cons.; b. Sioux Falls, S.D., Apr. 7, 1919; s. Henry Frank and Margaret Leona (Callahan) D.; student N.D. State Coll., 1936-37, U. Minn., 1937-38, U. Santa Clara (Cal.), 1941; m. Kathryn Ann Townsend, Dec. 17, 1949; 1 son, Hugh Warner. Dist. sales mgr. Union Sales Corp., Columbus, Ind., 1938-40, Libby, McNeill & Libby, Seattle, 1940-41; pres. Hugh W. Daum Co., Chgo., 1946-48; nat. sales and advt. mgr. John H. Dulany & Son, Fruitland, Md., 1949-50; pres. Hugh W. Daum Co., Crete, Ill., 1950-76; frozen food cons. Louis Hilfer Co., Chgo., 1976—. Commr. Calumet council Boy Scouts Am., 1973—, mem. nat. council, 1972—, recipient Silver Beaver award; active Ill. Assn. for Crippled. Served to maj. AUS, 1941-46. Mem. Midwestern (dir., past v.p., Frozen Gavel, Igloo awards), Nat., Central States (past pres.) frozen foods assns., Merchandising Execs. Club, Nat., Chgo. food brokers assns., Ducks Unlimited, Alpha Tau Omega. Club: K.C. (Crete). Home and office: 585 Aberdeen Dr Crete IL 60417

DAVE, INDRAJIT ACHARATLAL, chemist; b. Anand Gujarat, India, Feb. 17, 1936; came to U.S., 1968, naturalized, 1976; s. Acharatlal Mahashankar and Dahiben Balkrishna (Joshi) D.; B.S. with honors, Sardar Patel U., 1958, M.S., 1960; B.S., Eastern Mich. U., 1968, M.S., 1970; m. Pratima Mohanlal Shukla, May 26, 1966; children—Mona, Margie. Sr. analyst aquatic biology dept. Eastern Mich. U., Ypsilanti, 1968-70; sr. chemist Parke, Davis & Co., Detroit, 1970—. Mem. Assn. Analytical Chemists, Indian Cultural Assn. Democrat. Hindu. Home: 40078 Steel Dr Sterling Heights MI 48078 Office: Parke Davis & Co Lab 870 Parkedale Rd Rochester MI 48063

DAVENPORT, DONALD LYLE, engring. and real estate co. exec.; b. Eau Claire, Wis., Oct. 9, 1930; s. Douglas Benjamin and Leona Margaret (Fairbanks) D.; B.A. in Social Studies, Coll. St. Thomas, St. Paul, 1955; children—Ann, Martin, John, Donna, Jennifer. Adminstrv. asst. to regional mgr. Butler Mfg. Co., Mpls., 1955-58; corp. sec., gen. mgr. Spencer Corp., Eau Claire, 1958-60; sales mgr. Russell Structures Co., Madison, Wis., 1960; former pres. Bldg. Systems, Inc., Middleton, Wis., from 1960; pres. Davenport Assos., engring./real estate firm; bldg. cons. bldg. systems div. J.H. Findorff & Son, Inc., Madison. Former chmn. bd., pres. Jr. Achievement. Served with USAF, 1950-54. Registered profl. engr., Wis.; lic. real estate broker, Wis. Mem. Metal Bldg. Dealer Assn. (pres. 1971), Profl. Engrs. in Constrn., Wis. Soc. Profl. Engrs. (former pres. practice sect.), Johns Manville Dealer Council (chmn.), ARMCO Steel Corp. Dealer Council. Republican. Roman Catholic. Club: Exchange. Home: 7320 Pond View Rd Middleton WI 53562 Office: 302 S Bedford St Madison WI 53703

DAVENPORT, JOHN WESLEY, computer software firm exec.; b. Dallas, Apr. 26, 1941; s. Claude Franklyn and Nancy Jean Davenport; B.A. in Psychology, Tex. Tech. U., 1963; M. Fin. Services, Am. Coll., 1980; m. Alicia Ann Marshaus, July 15, 1978; children—Lea Michelle, Heather Kathleen. Adminstrv. asst. Prudential Ins. Co., Houston, 1968-69; dept. mgr. Tareet Stores, Inc., Houston, 1969-70; salesman Am. Gen. Life Ins. Co., Houston, 1970-71; div. mgr. Prudential Ins. Co., St. Louis, 1971-73; dir. advanced underwriting Gen. Am. Life Ins. Co., St. Louis, 1973-79; dir. mktg. Multiple Funding Corp., N.Y.C., 1979—; guest lectr. St. Louis U.; adj. faculty St. Louis Community Colls. Mem. Nat. Tax Limitation Com., 1978—. Served with U.S. Army, 1963-68. C.L.U. Mem. Am. Soc. C.L.U.'s, Estate Planning Council St. Louis, Nat. Assn. Life Underwriters, Nat. Space Inst., Mensa. Presbyterian. Home: 1 Ozark Ln Arnold MO 63010 Office: 330 W 42d St New York NY 10036

DAVENPORT, PATSY JOANN, ins. co. exec.; b. Shelbyville, Ind., Mar. 15, 1948; d. Ivan E. and Clara L. (Bryan) B.; cert. Central Bus. Coll., 1969; m. William E. Davenport, Sept. 27, 1980. Bookkeeper, Fairland Nat. Bank (Ind.), 1966-67; typist RCA, Indpls., 1967-69; sec. Hayden Corp., Indpls., 1969-70, Archtl. Bldg. Products Co., Indpls., 1970-72; adminstrv. asst. Conn. Mut. Life Ins. Co., Indpls., 1972-80; computer software sales Mchts. Capital Corp., 1980; exec. sec. to dir. Ind. Div. Employment Security, Indpls., 1980-81; exec. sec. to dir. adminstrv. services Ind. Dept. Correction, Indpls.; 1981—. Active, Big Sisters. Cert. profl. sec. Mem. Profl. Secs. Internat., Women in Life Ins. Mem. Christian Ch. Home: 1094 Greenwood Trails West Greenwood IN 46142 Office: 10 N Senate Ave Rm 331 Indianapolis IN 46204

DAVID, DEBRA DONNA, ednl. adminstr.; b. N.Y.C., Feb. 8, 1948; d. Alexander Sandor and Freda Sophie (Hecht) D.; B.A. in Social Sci. (nat. merit scholar), Mich. State U., 1969; M.A. in Sociology, U. Calif., Berkeley, 1970, Ph.D. in Sociology, 1981. Lectr. in sociology U. Mo., Kansas City, 1975-76; research analyst Benjamin Rose Inst., Cleve., 1977-78; dir. gerontology program Elgin (Ill.) Community Coll., 1978—; asso. faculty human services Nat. Coll. Edn., Evanston, Ill., 1981—; mem. NIMH paraprofl. edn. rev. com. NIMH trainee, 1969-72, 74-75; dissertation grantee, Adminstrn. on Aging, 1977-79. Mem. Assn. Gerontology in Higher Edn. (program and publs. coms.), Gerontol. Soc., Am. Sociol. Assn., Am. Personnel and Guidance Assn., Phi Beta Kappa. Condr. research in field; developer model asso. degree program in aging and mental health, 1979. Office: 1700 Spartan Dr Elgin IL 60120

DAVIDSON, GEORGE MORTON (MORT), cons.; b. Indpls., Aug. 3, 1916; s. George William and Mary Elizabeth (Welch) D.; A.B., Ind. U., 1938; m. Jane Suiter, Oct. 6, 1939; children—Karen Lee, Kathy Lynn. Sales rep. T. M. Crutcher Dental Depot, Inc., Indpls., 1938-42, asst. to the pres., 1946-53, sec.-treas. 1953-69, pres., 1969—; chief exec. officer George M. Davidson & Assos., Indpls., 1971—. Mem. Indpls. Com. Fgn. Relations, participant Fgn. Policy Confs., 1950-53; participant in the Joint Civilian Orientation Conference, 1959. Mem. of Indiana House Reps., 1953-58, chmn. mil. and vets. affairs com., 1954-58; mem. Ind. Econ. Council, 1955-57; mem. Com. on Continuity of State Govt., 1956-57. Mem. Marion County Civil Def. Adv. Council, 1957-59; civilian Aid to Secretary of Army, State Ind., 1953-61. Vice chmn. U.S.O., Indpls., 1960—, mem. nat. council, 1961—. Served to 1st lt., AUS, 1942-45; ETO; asst. dir. med. dept.

Indpls. Organized Res. Corp Sch., 1950-51. Decorated Bronze Star, Oak Leaf Cluster, Combat Med. Badge, Meritorious Service Unit Citation, 3 major campaign Battle Stars, Outstanding Civilian Service medal. Mem. Indpls. C. of C. (chmn. nat. def. com. 1951-53), Ind. State C. of C., Indpls. Hosp. Devel. Assn. (asso. bd. dirs. 1955-57), Assn. U.S. Army (Ind. pres. 1962-63, nat. adv. dir. 1958-71), Navy League U.S., 500 Festival Assos. Inc., 75th Div. Vets. Assn., Am. Legion, V.F.W., Ind. U. Alumni Assn., Res. Officers Assn. U.S. (rep. Indpls. chpt. 82d Congress, 1951, past pres., Indpls., chmn. pub. relations com. Ind. dept. 1951), Rep. Vets. Ind. (treas. 1953-57), Mil. Order of World Wars (Indpls. comdr. 1960-62, Ind. State comdr. 1961-62; nat. membership com.), Marion Co. Rep. Vets. World War II, Def. Orientation Conf. Assn., Newcomen Soc. N.Am., Sigma Chi. Presbyterian. Clubs: Columbia; Armed Forces Officers (gov. 1955-57); 300; Indiana Univ. (Indpls.); Indiana State Legislators. Author Ind. Returning Vets. Program; Armed Forces Res. Leave of Absence for Tng. Act. of Ind. Office: 3060 N Meridian St Indianapolis IN 46208

DAVIDSON, HAROLD EUGENE, clergyman; b. West Jefferson, Ohio, Sept. 13, 1927; s. Henry G. and Mable Maurine (Brown) D.; B.A., Otterbein Coll., 1949; B.D., Union Theol. Sem. N.Y.C., 1952; M.Div., Ashland Coll., 1970; D.Min., Meth. Theol. Sch., Ohio, 1974. Asso. editor BoyLand mag., 1945-48; nat. pres. Evang. U.B. Youth, 1947-52; ordained to ministry United Meth. Ch., 1952; asst. pastor Avondale United Meth. Ch., Columbus, Ohio, 1951-52; pastor Como United Meth. Ch., Columbus, 1952-54; chaplain Buckeye Youth Center, Columbus, 1954—. Clin. asso. in pastoral care Meth. Theol. Sem., Delaware, Ohio, 1968—; cons. Buckeye Boy's Ranch, Grove City, Ohio, 1965-74; clin. counselor Hirsch Hall halfway house for boys, Columbus, 1974-77; del. White House Conf. on Children and Youth, 1970; del. to constituting conv. Nat. Council Chs. of Christ in U.S.A., 1950; chmn. youth assembly Internat. Soc. Christian Endeavor, 1951-52. Mem. Nat. Assn. Chaplains for Youth Rehab. (pres. 1962). Author: Adolescence and Juvenile Delinquency, 1960; Understanding Teens, 1965. Home: 2794 Woodstock Rd Columbus OH 43221 Office: 2280 W Broad St Columbus OH 43223

DAVIDSON, HAROLD FRENCH, JR., firearm co. exec.; b. Chgo., July 26, 1920; s. Harold French and Hazel Louise (Ward) D.; student U. Minn., 1946, U. Ill., 1947-48; m. Clara I. Wendling, July 18, 1948 (dec. Apr. 1981); children—Harold French III, Douglas, Roger, Kenneth, William II. Used car salesman, 1939-41; with Brink's Inc., Chgo., 1946-80; owner Harold Firearms Service/Supply Co., Chgo., 1980—; police firearm instr., 1948-81. Served with ordnance corps AUS, 1941-45. Mem. Nat. Sporting Goods Assn., Nat. Shooting Sports Found., Nat. Def. Preparedness Assn., Am. Legion (comdr. 1954-55). Lutheran. Club: Bellwood Moose. Home: 7295 Catherine St Merrillville IN 46410

DAVIDSON, JOHN A., state senator, chiropractor; b. Westpoint, Miss., Aug. 31, 1924; s. Homer F. and Anna (Grosboll) D.; D.C., Nat. Coll. Chiropractic, 1951; m. Shirley Beard, 1953; children—Ann, Jane, John. Chiropractor, Chicago, Ill.; trustee, Found. Chiropractic Edn. and Research, 1967—. Mem. and asst. supr. for Capital Twp., Sangamon County (Ill.) Bd. Suprs., 1959-72, chmn., 1970-72; mem. Ill. State Senate, 1973—. Served in AC, USN, 1943-46; PTO. Decorated Air medal, others. Fellow Internat. Coll. Chiropractic; mem. Ill. Chiropractic Soc. (Chiropractor of Yr. 1962), Am. Chiropractic Assn. (Chiropractor of Yr. 1973), Am. Legion. Methodist. Clubs: Masons, Elks. Office: 718 Myers Bldg Springfield IL 62701

DAVIDSON, JOHN KENNETH, SR., family sociologist, survey researcher educator; b. Augusta, Ga., Oct. 25, 1939; s. Larcie Charles and Betty (Corley) D.; student Augusta Coll., 1956-58; B.S. Ed., U. Ga., 1961, M.A., 1963; Ph.D., U. Fla., 1974; m. Josephine Frazier, Apr. 11, 1964; children—John Kenneth Jr., Stephen Wood. Asst. prof. dept. psychology and sociology Armstrong State Coll., Savannah, 1963-67; asst. prof. dept. sociology Augusta Coll., Augusta, Ga., 1967-74; acting chmn., asst. prof. dept. sociology Ind. U., South Bend, 1974-76; asso. prof. sociology U. Wis.-Eau Claire, 1976-78, prof., 1978—, chmn. dept. sociology, 1976-80; research cons. dept. obstetrics and gynecology Med. Coll. Ga., Augusta, 1969-74, pediatrics, 1972-73, also asso. dir. health care project, 1971-73, research instr., summer 1971, research asso., summer 1972-73, research cons. dept. community dentistry, 1974-79. Program coordinator Community Devel. in Process Phase II and III, Title I Higher Edn. Act of 1965, 1970; mem. sociology and anthropology com. Univ. System Ga., 1970-74, chmn. curriculum sub-com., 1970-72; dir. Sex Edn. The Pub. Schs. and You project Ind. Com. on The Humanities, 1975; mem., chmn. com. on standards and criteria for cert. Nat. Council Family Relations; bd. dirs., pres.-elect Wis. Council on Family Relations; past state chmn. pub. affairs Ind. Assn. Planned Parenthood Affiliates, 1975-76; mem. Eau Claire Coordinating Council. Past bd. dirs. Planned Parenthood North Central Ind., also past chmn. pub. affairs com., 1975-76; former mem. bd. dirs., former 1st v.p. Wis. Family Planning Coordinating Council; bd. dirs., mem. exec. com., chmn. com. on research in social scis., mem. info. and edn. com. Assn. for Vol. Sterilization, Inc. mem. resources allocation com. Planned Parenthood of Wis., Inc.; mem. Eau Claire County Adv. Health Forum; mem. Eau Claire County Task Force on Family Planning. Mem. Am., Wis. sociol. assns., So., Midwest sociol. socs., AAUP, Augusta Coll. Alumni Soc., U. Fla., U. Ga. alumni socs., Groves Conf., Pres.'s Club U. Wis.-Eau Claire, Western Wis. Task Force on Family Planning, Kappa Delta Pi, Phi Kappa Phi, Phi Theta Kappa, Alpha Kappa Delta (pres. Beta chpt. 1971-72, nat. exec. com. 1972—, editor nat. newsletter 1979—). Episcopalian. Asso. editor Jour. Marriage and the Family, 1975—, Jour. Deviant Behavior, 1979—; contbr. articles to profl. jours. Home: 1305 Nixon Ave Eau Claire WI 54701 Office: Dept Sociology Univ Wis Eau Claire WI 54701

DAVIDSON, JOSEPH BRIAN, veterinarian, business exec., author; b. Dumas, Tex., July 7, 1923; s. Robert Barney and Daisy Lelia (Baker) D.; student West Tex. State U., 1941-43; D.V.M., Mich. State U., 1946; m. Lucile Jessie Linton, June 13, 1948; children—Pamela, Deborah, Lucinda. Gen. vet. practice, Brown City, Mich., 1946-59; founder, pres. Hemo-Blend Research, Brown City, 1959—; nutritional field cons. Hill's div. Riviana Foods, Topeka, Custom Blend Feeds, Wheatley, Ont., Can., 1965—; organizer North Plains Land Devel. Corp., Amarillo, Tex., 1971—; organizer, pres. Horse Publs., Canton, Ohio, 1967—, Davidson Pub. Co., Canton, 1970—, Multi-Dent, Inc., Canton, 1971—, Multi-Commerce, Inc., Canton, 1972—, United Cattle Producers, Inc., Canton, 1973—; asso. Vaught Oil Co., Canton, 1966-71; partner Davidson Agri-Bus., Tex., 1972—; co-founder Animal Research Labs., 1974, Profile Mgmt., Inc., 1977, Square Circle Devel. Co., Inc., 1977—, Gasoil Energy, Inc., 1977—, Daisy Mines, Goldfield, Nev., 1978—, Jerl Holdings, Inc., 1978, Flying J Mines, 1979; state veterinarian Mackinac Island, Mich., 1951-57. Mayor of Brown City, 1953-57; county chmn. Citizens for Eisenhower, 1952-53; del. county and state Republican convs., 1951-57. Served with AUS, 1943-44. Recipient numerous plaques, certificates for pub. speaking appearances, service clubs, library assns., others. Mem. Am., Ohio, Mich. vet. med. assns., Ohio Writers, U.S. Trotting Assn., Thoroughbred Racing Protective Bur., Nat. Assn. Watch and Clock Collectors, C. of C. Methodist. Lion, Mason, Elk; mem. Order Eastern Star. Author: Horsemen's Veterinary Adviser, 1967; All Horse Races are Fixed, 1968; Amelia Earhart Returns from Saipan, 1970. Editor Mich. State U. Veterinarian 1946. Home: 2775 Eversholt Circle NW Canton OH 44708 Office: 4450 Belden Village St Canton OH 44718

DAVIES, GRAHAM OVERBY, oral surgeon; b. Chgo., Aug. 9, 1923; s. Clarence Hoover and Lillian (Overby) D.; student Lawrence Coll., 1941-42, U. Chgo., 1948-50; D.D.S., Loyola U., Chgo., 1946; M.S.D., Northwestern U., 1954; m. Suan M. Hartman, Oct. 7, 1957; children—Laura Ann, Julie, Jennifer. Pvt. practice oral surgery, Chgo., 1948—; asso. prof. oral surgery Chgo. Coll. Osteo. Medicine, 1974-77, prof., 1977—; pres. Dagar Products, Inc., 1975; guest lectr. U. Ill., U. Sydney (Australia); spl. cons. Ill. Cancer Detection Program. Bd. dirs. Miss Ind. Scholarship Pageant Corp., 1972-74; trustee Town of Michiana Shores (Ind.), 1960-62; trustee Town of Long Beach (Ind.), 1967-81, pres. bd., 1973, 76; adv. com. Ind. Coastal Zone Mgmt. Program; pres. Long Beach Municipal Water Bd., 1981—; commr. public works Town of Long Beach, 1981—. Served with AUS, 1942-45; capt. USAAF, 1946-48. Mem. Am., Ill., Chgo., Kenwood-Hyde Park (pres. 1958) dental assns., N.W. Ind. Dental Soc., Ill. (charter), Chgo. socs. oral surgeons, Odontographic Soc., Chgo. Inst. Medicine (gov.), Delta Tau Delta, Delta Sigma Delta. Club: Long Beach Country (dir. holding corp. 1972). Author: The Comparative Effects of Various Local Anesthetics on Pulse Wave and Rate, 1954; co-author Phosphate in Lake Michigan, 1974. Home: 2751 Floral Trail Long Beach Michigan City IN 46360 Office: 5200 S Ellis Ave Chicago IL 60615

DAVIES, JACK, state senator; b. Harvey, N.D., Jan. 6, 1932; s. Charles Evan and Marian (Healy) D.; B.A., U. Minn., 1954, J.D., 1960; m. Patricia McAndrews; children—Elizabeth, Ted, John. Admitted to Minn. bar, 1960; practiced in Mpls., 1960-65; mem. Minn. Senate from 60th Dist., 1959—, pres., 1981—; commr. Minn. Uniform Laws, 1966—; prof. law William Mitchell Coll. Law, St. Paul, 1965—. Served with AUS, 1954-56. Mem. Am. Law Inst. Author: Legislative Law and Process in a Nutshell, 1975; (with Lawry) Institutions and Methods of the Law, 1982. Office: 875 Summit Ave Saint Paul MN 55105

DAVIES, JAMES GERALD, coll. adminstr.; b. Johnstown, Pa., Oct. 18, 1947; s. Glyndur James and Maletha Margret (Harker) D.; B.S., Evangel Coll., 1970. Computer operator Univac, Oak Brook, Ill., 1970-71; programmer AT&T, Cleve., 1973-74; systems analyst/programmer Evangel Coll., Springfield, Mo., 1974-75, dir. data processing, 1975—; lectr. in field. Served with U.S. Army, to sgt., 1971-73, with USAR, 1977—. Mem. Data Processing Mgmt. Assn. (dir. 1977-78, pres. Ozark Empire chpt. 1978-79, internat. dir. 1979-81), Nat. NCR Ednl. Users Group (dir. 1980—, pres. 1979-80). Republican. Mem. Assemblies of God. Home: 1406 E Blaine St Springfield MO 65803 Office: 1111 N Glenstone St Springfield MO 65802

DAVIES, JOHN ARTHUR, assn. exec.; b. Cleve., Feb. 29, 1920; s. William Richard and Florence Christina (Koch) D.; B.A., Wesleyan U., 1943; certified profl. mgr. Inst. Profl. Mgrs., Trinity Coll. m. Una Ruth Keeter, Oct. 27, 1951; children—Janet C., Nancy S. Mgr., Flint Ink Corp., Atlanta, 1953-58; materials devel. mgr. Champion Papers Corp., Hamilton, Ohio, 1959-66; exec. v.p. Internat. Assn. Printing House Craftsmen, Inc., Cin., 1966—; dir. edn. council Graphic Arts Tech. Found., Pitts. Cert. watch and clockmaker, Ind. Mem. Nat. Watch and Clock Collectors Assn. Clubs: Elks, Cin. Lions (past pres.). Patentee in field. Home: 5462 Schiering Dr Fairfield OH 45014 Office: 7599 Kenwood Rd Cincinnati OH 45236

DAVIES, JUNE ANNETTE MAY, psychotherapist, life skills educator; b. Highland Park, Mich., Mar. 16, 1940; d. Leonard M. and Lucille Adelle (Seigneur) May; B.A., Wheaton Coll., 1964; M.A., Oakland U., 1977; m. Harold E. Davies; children—James David, Sheryl Lucille, Michael J., Jimmy W. Tchr., Madison Sch. Dist., 1968-74; grad. asst. Oakland U., 1976-77, instr., 1977—; psychotherapist Mt. Clemens (Mich.) Youth and Family Counseling, 1978; pvt. practice psychotherapy, Troy, Mich., 1979—; with Alt. Lifestyles, Inc., Pontiac, Mich., 1981; cons. to govt., edn., industry; spl. services cons. Zion Christian Sch., Clawson, Mich., 1981-82. Mem. Am. Women in Psychology Assn., Am. Personnel and Guidance Assn., Mich. Personnel and Guidance Assn., Mich. Assn. Specialists in Group Work, Am. Coll. Personnel Assn., Assn. for Religious and Value Issues in Counseling, Am. Mental Health Counselors Assn. Methodist. Home: 1855 Washington Rd Rochester MI 48063 Office: 755 W Big Beaver Suite 2112 Troy MI 48084

DAVIES, LYLE KEITH, psychologist; b. Helena, Mont., Oct. 12, 1950; s. Albert Keith and Louise Mary (Wenzler) D.; B.S., Mankato (Minn.) State U., 1972, M.S., 1974; Ed.D., U. S.D., 1980. Photographer, Minn. Soc. Crippled Children and Adults, 1968-72; alcohol services planning coordinator Cascade County, Mont., 1975; dir. Alcoholism Counseling Info. and Referral Center, LeMars, Iowa, 1975-76; asst. prof., field tng. coordinator alcohol and drug abuse studies U. S.D., 1976-80, research asst., 1976-78, judge client counseling competition Law Sch., 1976-78; psychologist Minn. Security Hosp., St. Peter, 1980—; pvt. practice psychology, New Ulm, Minn., 1980—; cons. mgmt. info. systems, 1978—. Served with USAR, 1972-74. Mem. Am. Personnel and Guidance Assn. Author papers in field. Home: 301 S State St New Ulm MN 56073 Office: 118 1/2 N Minnesota St New Ulm MN 56073

DAVIES, TED ALBERT, sales promotion agy. exec.; b. Cleve., Sept. 16, 1926; s. Thomas A. and Esther G. Davies; B.A., Miami U., Ohio, 1949; m. Shirley J. Christner, June 5, 1956; children—Ted Albert, Joyce, Todd. With Brown & Bigelow, Cin. and St. Paul, 1949-70, v.p. sales, 1965-70; pres. Sales Mktg. Inc., Mpls., 1970—. Mem. Basic Mktg. Assn., Savs. Instns. Mktg. Soc. Am. Republican. Presbyterian. Clubs: North Oaks Golf (pres. 1978); Quail Ridge Golf (Boyton Beach, Fla.). Office: Sales Mktg Inc 3329 University Ave SE Minneapolis MN 55414

DAVIS, ALVIN GEORGE, internat. trade cons.; b. Chgo., May 10, 1918; s. Isadore and Mary (Wasserman) D.; m. Rose Lorber, Dec. 14, 1940 (dec. 1980); children—Fred Barry, Glenn Martin. With Sears Roebuck & Co., 1936-40; gen. partner, sales mgr. Ritz Mfg. Co., 1940-41; buyer hobby dept. The Fair, 1941-43; mgr. hobby div. Central Camera Co., wholesalers, 1944; pres., gen. mgr. Nat. Model Distbrs., Inc., 1945-63; pres. Hobbycraft Exports, 1946-62; dir. internat. operations Aurora Plastics Corp., 1951-62, v.p. internat. div., 1962-70; v.p. Aurora Plastics Can., Ltd., 1963-70; mng. dir. Aurora Plastics Nederland N.V., 1964-70, Aurora Plastics Co. U.K. Ltd., Croydon, Eng.; IBM internat. trade and distbn. cons.; now internat. trade cons.; sr. internat. trade specialist U.S. Comml. Service, U.S. Dept. Commerce; lectr. Stuart Sch. Mgmt. and Fin., Ill. Inst. Tech.; dir. Rowe Industries (HK) Ltd., Rowe Industries (Taiwan) (Singapore), Rowe Industries Ltd. Mem., chmn. People to People Com.; scoutmaster, past mem. fin. com. Chgo. council Boy Scouts Am.; info. officer, dep. comdr. CAP. Recipient Berkeley award, 1957, Hobbies award of merit Hobby Industry Assn., 1960, Meritorious award of honor, 1975. Fellow Inst. Dirs. (hon. life) (London); mem. Nat. Rifle Assn. (life), Soaring Soc. Am., Airplane Owners and Pilots Assn., Acad. Model Aeros. (contest dir. 1936-70), Nat. Model R.R. Assn. (life), Model Industry Assn. (dir. 1952-60, sec. 1954-57, pres. 1957-59), Hobby Industry Assn. (hon. life; pres. 1957-59), Chgo. Aeronuts (hon.), PCC Publicity Club. Mason (32 deg., Shriner). Club: Chicago Press. Contbr. articles on internat. merchandising to trade mags. Pub., Cyclopedia of Hobbies, 1946-62; editor Dartnell-Internat. Trade Handbook; contbg. editor Brittanica Jr., 1949.

DAVIS, ANN MARGARET, steel co. exec.; b. Kankakee, Ill., Dec. 9, 1938; d. Maynard Otto and Margaret Mary (Quigley) Weber; B.A. cum laude with honors in English, Miami U., Oxford, Ohio, 1960. Carnegie fellow, coll. placement dir. U. Kans., Lawrence, 1961-62; personnel mgr. Marsh & McLennan, Inc., Chgo., 1964-66; employee benefits adminstr. J.L. Hudson Co., Detroit, 1966-71; staff and union relations mgr. U. Mich., Ann Arbor, 1971-77; v.p. personnel and indsl. relations Ervin Industries, Ann Arbor, 1977—. Mem. Indsl. Relations Assn. Detroit, Phi Beta Kappa. Contbr. to Handbook of Modern Personnel Administration, 1972.

DAVIS, BENNIE W., JR., cosmetologist; b. Lexington, Miss., June 5, 1937; s. Bennie and Annie (Dale) D.; grad. So. Ill. U. Advanced Sch. Cosmetology, Pivot Point Hair Design Sch., Chgo., Fran and Leo's Sch. Beauty Culture, Chgo. Pres., owner Benia De La Coiffures Internat., Inc., Chgo., 1963—; dir., instr. Mr. Maurice's Beauty Coll.; instr. Purdue U., So. Ill. U., Lydia Adams Sch. Cosmetology, Waukesha City Terminal Inst., Pewaukee, Wis., U. S.C., Columbia; Naval Salon training; guest lectr. TV. Recipient numerous awards in cosmetology, including Oscar De Paris award, 1975, Gala award, 1975; named to Chgo. Black Masters Hall of Fame, 1977. Mem. Nat. Hairdressers and Cosmetologists Assn. (ofcl. hair fashion com.), Ill. Hair Fashion Com., Coiffure Designers Salon Owners Assn. (exec. dir.), Clairol Presdl. Haircolorists Council, Jaycees. Baptist. Subject of newspaper articles. Home: 6033 N Sheridan Rd Chicago IL 60660 Office: 17 N State St Chicago IL 60602

DAVIS, BOB J., educator; b. Grand Saline, Tex., June 27, 1927; s. Frank H. and Minerva Catherine (Crocker) D.; B.B.A., U. Houston, 1957, M.B.A., 1961, J.D., 1966; m. Alice Joyce Reagan, Oct. 22, 1948; 1 dau., Paula Lynn. Admitted to Tex. bar, 1966; traffic rep. Texaco, Inc., Houston, 1951-61; traffic mgr. Republic Steel Corp., Cleve., 1961-67; mem. faculty Western Ill. U., Macomb, 1967—, prof. transp., 1973—, dir. exec. devel., 1970—; mem. Macomb Planning Commn., 1971-75, Macomb Municipal Airport Authority, 1980—. Served with USNR, 1944-47. Recipient Sam Harper award Purchasing Agts. Assn. Houston, 1957; named Traffic Man of Year, Transp. Club Houston, 1966, Regional Edn. Man of Year, Delta Nu Alpha, 1980, Coll. Bus. Tchr. of Yr., Western Ill. U., 1981. Mem. Assn. ICC Practitioners (Clyde B. Aitchison award 1966), Am. Soc. Traffic and Transp., Internat. Material Mgmt. Soc. Methodist. Club: Masons. Author bibliographies, reports, articles in field. Home: 1111 E Grant St Macomb IL 61455 Office: 900 W Adams St Macomb IL 61455

DAVIS, BOBBIE ADA, counselor; b. Omaha, May 30, 1936; d. David E. and Ada M. (Redden) Nicholson; B.S., Prairie View (Tex.) A&M U., 1957; M.S., U. Nebr., Omaha, 1974; m. Herbert L. Davis, Sept. 21, 1958; children—Herbert L., Steven C., Terence R. Center dir. YWCA, Omaha, 1960-65; social worker, counselor Omaha Women's Job Corps, Omaha, 1967-69; social worker supr. Parent Child Center, Omaha, 1969-71; counselor, instr. U. Nebr., Omaha, 1971-79; dir. counseling and career devel. Met. Tech. Community Coll., Omaha, 1980—. Sec., Urban League Nebr., 1971-72, bd. dirs., 1970-75; pres. Black Women Unltd., 1976-80; bd. dirs. Girls Club of Omaha, 1974-79, sec., 1976, Dedicated Service award, 1979. Recipient Community Achievement award Coalition of Minority Artists, 1979, award of achievement YWCA, 1977, Change Agt. of Yr. award, 1979. Mem. Am. Personnel and Guidance Assn., Am. Coll. Personnel Assn. (Black Excellence award 1980), Nebr. Assn. Non-White Concerns in Personnel and Guidance, Assn. Non-White Concerns in Personnel and Guidance (Change Agt. of Year 1979), Nebr. Coll. Personnel Assn., Nebr. Personnel and Guidance Assn., Assn. Study of Afro-Am. Life and History. Democrat. Baptist. Club: Eastern Star. Home: 4947 Spaulding St Omaha NE 68104 Office: Met Tech Community Coll 30th and Fort Sts Omaha NE 68111

DAVIS, BRENDA ALICIA, steel co. cons.; b. Chgo., Sept. 6, 1949; d. Charles Edward and Eva Louise D.; B.S.B.A. in Indsl. Mgmt., Roosevelt U., 1977, M.B.A. in Internat. Fin., 1979; postgrad. in bus. policy analysis U. Ill., 1979—. Cons., Gt. Lakes Mgmt. & Cons., Chgo., 1972-73; auditor Cook County (Ill.) States Atty., 1973-79; cons. Inland Steel Co., Chgo., 1979—; cons. UNESCO. Mem. Am. Arbitration Assn. (lic. arbitrator), Better Bus. Bur. Chgo. (lic. arbitrator), Council on Fgn. Relations. Republican. Roman Catholic. Home: 5431 NE River Rd Chicago IL 60656 Office: 30 W Monroe Chicago IL 60605

DAVIS, BRUCE ALLEN, psychologist; b. Monett, Mo., Aug. 13, 1948; s. William Lester and Mable Caroline (Frederickson) D; A.B. in Psychology with honors, Drury Coll., 1970; M.S. in Guidance and Counseling, Southwest Mo. State U., 1974; M.B.A., Drury Coll., 1980. Staff psychologist and marriage counselor Greene County Guidance Clinic, Springfield, Mo., 1974-76, 77-80; asso. psychologist U.S. Fed. Prison Med. Center, Springfield, 1976; indsl. psychologist psychodiagnostician Davis Psychol. Testing Service, Springfield, 1975—; cons. in field. Lic. sch. psychol. examiner, Mo. Mem. Am. Psychol. Assn., Am. Assn. Marriage and Family Therapists, Am. Mgmt. Assns., Mensa, Kappa Alpha Order. Mem. Disciples of Christ Ch. Club: Elks. Office: 1240 S Saratoga Springfield MO 65804

DAVIS, C. R., state senator; B.S., U. Minn., 1968, M.Ed., 1972; m. Collen Maloney; children—Rayford, Marshall, Lance. Farmer; vocat. agrl. instr., Princeton, Minn.; mem. Minn. Senate, 1980—. Mem. Minn. Vocat. Instrs. Assn., MEA Vocat. Educators (past pres.). Mem. Democratic-Farmer-Labor party. Office: 306 State Capitol Saint Paul MN 55155*

DAVIS, CARRIE ELLEN, educator; b. East St. Louis, Ill., Apr. 5, 1930; d. Dewey and Carrie Ellen (Coleman) Thigpen; B.S. in Edn., W.Va. State Coll., 1950; M.S. in Edn., Chgo. State U., 1969; Ed.D., Nova U., 1975; 1 son, Theodore Dimone. Vari-typist Dept. Def., Chgo., 1950-51; supr. IBM procedures Ill. Inst. Tech., Chgo., 1951-55; high sch. bus. edn. tchr., Chgo., 1955-58, 59-60, elem. tchr., 1961-62, 66-69; high sch. tchr., Gary, Ind., 1964-66; asso. prof. secretarial sci. and bus. communication Loop Coll., Chgo., 1969—; mem. faculty Peters Bus. Coll., 1961-64; dir. Reading Center, Mu chpt. Phi Delta Kappa, Inc., 1976-80; sr. lectr. Ahmadu Bello O., Zaria, Nigeria, 1981—. Fellow DuSable Mus.; charter mem. Plano Vision Info. Processing Supporters; mem. NAACP. Recipient service awards Loop Coll., 1972, 73, 74, Kappa Omicron Tau, 1976, 81, DuSable Mus., 1980. Mem. Nat. Bus. Tchrs. Assn., Chgo. Bus. Tchrs. Assn., Am. Bus. Communication Assn., Ill. Bus. Edn. Assn., Am. Vocat. Assn., Assn. for Study of Afro-Am. Life and History, Nat. Council Negro Women, Educators to Africa Assn., Phi Delta Kappa. Author: Learning Theory and Applications, 1978; contbr. writings in field to publs. Home: 3001 S Dr Martin Luther King Jr Dr Apt 818 Chicago IL 60616 Office: Loop College 64 E Lake St Chicago IL 60601

DAVIS, CELIA FAYE, stockbroker; b. Frenchburg, Ky., July 22, 1955; d. Emery C. and Emogene D.; A.A., Ky. Mountain Bible Inst., 1976; B.A., Olivet Nazarene Coll., 1980. Prodn. coordinator Liberty Nat. Pub., Chgo., 1977-78; ops. mgr. The Milw. Co., Chgo., 1980—. Mem. Stockbrokers Assn., Council Career Planning, Am. Entrepreneurs Assn., Soc. Bns. and Profl. Women, Nat. Assn. Female Execs., U.S. Consumer Assn. Republican. Mem. Ch. Nazarene (organist 1981—, exec. v.p. Nazarene Youth Internat. 1981—, adv. mem. worship com. 1981—, mem. music com. 1980—). Home: 1529 Vine Ave Round Lake Beach IL 60073

DAVIS, CHESTER R., JR., lawyer; b. Chgo., Aug. 30, 1930; s. Chester R. and Mead (Scoville) D.; grad. Phillips Exeter Acad., 1947; A.B., Princeton, 1951; LL.B., Harvard, 1958; m. Anne Meserve, Mar. 3, 1962; children—John Chester, Julia Snow, Elizabeth Meserve. Admitted to Ill. bar, 1958; mem. firm Bell, Boyd & Lloyd and predecessor firms, partner, 1968—. Asso. Rush-Presbyn.-St. Luke's Med. Center, Chgo., 1964—, Adlai Stevenson Inst. Internat. Affairs, 1968—, Newberry Library, Chgo., 1974—. Mem. Winnetka (Ill.) Zoning Commn. and Bd. Appeals, 1974-79; mem. Winnetka Plan Commn., 1976—. Sec., bd. dirs. Vascular Disease Research Found.; mem. alumni council Phillips Exeter Acad.; chmn. Winnetka Interch. Council, 1981—. Served to lt. (j.g.) USNR, 1952-56; capt. Res. Mem. Am. (land use and zoning com., urban law sect. 1980—), Ill., Chgo. (chmn. com. civil practice 1969-70, chmn. land use and zoning com. 1981—) bar assns., Am. Soc. Internat. Law, Am. Judicature Soc., Am. Arbitration Assn. (nat. panel arbitrators), Am. Planning Assn., Urban Land Inst., Harvard Law Soc. Ill. (past pres.), Harvard Law Sch. Assn. (nat. v.p. 1970-71). Episcopalian. Clubs: University, Economic, Law, Legal (Chgo.); Princeton (N.Y.C.). Home: 670 Blackthorn Rd Winnetka IL 60093 Office: Three First Nat Plaza Chicago IL 60602

DAVIS, CORNELIA HAVEN CASEY (MRS. FRANK V. DAVIS), club woman, ret. bus. exec.; b. Greenville, Ill., Sept. 17, 1909; d. George Farnum and Cornelia (Ravold) Casey; A.B., Millikin U., 1931; m. Frank V. Davis, May 9, 1936; children—James Casey, Thomas Wait (dec. Apr. 1952), Andrew Waggoner. Bond County statistician Ill. Emergency Relief Commn., 1934-36; sec.-treas. E.H. Paul Co., Hookdale, Ill., 1957-67, Davis & Royer, Inc., Greenville, Ill., 1967-73. Pres. Greenville P.T.A., 1944-45; charter mem. Utlaut Meml. Hosp. Found., 1957; historian Utlaut Meml. Hosp. Aux., 1958-59, pres., 1966-67, rec. sec., 1969-70; pres. Greenville Garden Club, 1954-56; chmn. Bond County chpt. A.R.C., 1962-64, Ill. fund vice chmn., 1966, territorial fund chmn., 1967-68, 69, mem. resolutions com. Bd. dirs. Bond County Tb Assn., 2d v.p., 1965-67, pres., 1969-70; 1st v.p. and fund drive chmn. (Christmas Seals) Heritage Trail Tb and Respiratory Disease Assn., 1970-71; chmn. Greenville and Bond County Bicentennial Commn.; bd. dirs. Greenville Sesquicentennial, 1965. Recipient various citations for service, Good Citizenship medal S.A.R., 1962; Disting. Service award Greenville Jaycees, 1981. Mem. Audubon Soc., Nat. Trust for Historic Preservation, Ill. (life mem.), Bond County (charter, pres., dir.) historic socs., Bond County Fair Assn. (life), DAR (regent Benjamin Mills chpt. 1952-54, 68-70, registrar 1964-66, 1st vice regent 1966-68, dir. 6th Ill. div. 1955-56, Ill. corr. sec. 1956-58, nat. def. com. state chmn. 1963-65), Children Am. Revolution (organizing sr. pres. Hills Ft. Soc. 1955, sr. state pres. 1960-63, nat. life promoter, nat. officers club, hon. sr. state pres.), U.S. Daus. War of 1812 (pres. Kaskaskia chpt. 1963-66, corr. sec. 1966-69, Ill. 2d v.p. 1963-66, 1st v.p. 1966-70, pres. 1970-73, nat. chmn. nat. def. com. 1967-73, hon. state pres.), Ill. Ct. Women Descs. Ancient and Hon. Arty. Co. (Ill. librarian 1963-64, nat. chmn. nat. def. and resolutions com.), Daus. Am. Colonists (chmn. Ill. colonial heritage com.), Col. Daus. 17th Century (charter Ill. chpt., treas.-registrar 1961-66, chpt. pres. 1966-69, corr. secy. gen. 1970-73, nat. chmn. nat. def. and resolutions com. 1967-76, 2d v.p. gen. 1973-76, pres. gen. 1976-79, hon. pres. gen.), Colonial Dames of Am. (rec. sec. chpt. XII 1969-71, 77-81, pres. 1981—), Nat. Soc. Magna Charta Dames, Soc. Descs. Colonial Clergy, Ill. Geneal. Soc., Bond County Art and Cultural Assn. (dir., sec.), Sons and Daus. Pilgrims (chmn. constn. and bylaws com. 1977), Nat. Gavel Soc., Nat. Soc. Daus. Colonial Wars, Order of the Crown in Am., S. Central Ill. Woman's Golf Assn. (chmn. 1953, 66, 71), Delta Delta Delta. Republican. Episcopalian (regional chmn. ch. women Springfield diocese 1966-68). Address: Rural Route 2 Box 49-A Greenville IL 62246

DAVIS, DALE BRAXTON, physician asst.; b. Nevada, Mo., Aug. 16, 1944; s. Charles Braxton and Mary Christina (Dale) D.; student U. Mo., Columbia, 1967-71; Physician Asst. cert. St. Louis U., 1974, B.A., 1976; m. Ruth Ellen Hood, Aug. 5, 1972; 1 son, Christopher Braxton. Emergency room technician U. Mo. Med. Center, Columbia, 1968-69; nursing technician Cloisters of the Valley Convalescence Hosp. and Home, San Diego, 1969; emergency room technician, house orderly Boone County Hosp., Columbia, Mo., 1971; evening supr. Harry S. Truman Meml. VA Med. Center, Columbia, Mo., 1972; physician asst. R. William Burmeister, St. Louis, 1974-75; physician asst., asso. dir. physician asst. program Stephens Coll., 1975-78; adminstr., physician asst. Donald Parkinson, M.D., Springfield, Mo., 1978-79; physician asst. James Sullivan, M.D., Omaha VA Med. Center; clin. asso. U. Nebr. Coll. Medicine, Omaha, 1979—. Served with USNR, 1963-67. Mem. Am. Acad. Physician Assts. (del. 1977-80), Mo. Acad. Physician Assts. (pres. 1979-80), Nebr. Acad. Physician Assts., St. Louis Physician Asst. Soc. (dir. 1973-74). Baptist. Home: 12116 Lamont Omaha NE 68144 Office: Omaha VA Med Center 4101 Woolworth Ave Omaha NE 68105

DAVIS, DANIEL LEIFELD, psychologist; b. Columbus, Ohio, July 18, 1951; s. David W. and Jane L. (Leifeld) D.; B.A., Otterbein Coll., Westerville, Ohio, 1973; M.Ed., Kent (Ohio) State U., 1975; Ph.D., Ohio State U., 1980; m. LeAnn K. Rhoden, July 6, 1974; 1 son, Joshua Leifeld. Dir. Concord Counseling Service, Westerville, 1972-74; juvenile justice planner, adminstrn. justice div. Ohio Dept. Econ. and Community Devel., 1976—; psychologist Columbus Psychol. Services, 1977—, Central Ohio Psychiat. Hosp., 1980; dir. psychology Central Ohio Regional Forensic Hosp., 1981—; vol. counselor Huckleberry House Runaways, Columbus, 1970-72; mem. Westerville Task Force Youth, 1973, North Area Mental Health Assn., 1974; adv. com. Ohio Drug Studies Inst., 1977—; mem. Ohio Drug Treatment Adv. Council, 1977—. Recipient Outstanding Male Sr. award Otterbein Coll., 1973, commendation Ohio Gen. Assembly, 1974. Youth deacon First Community Ch., Columbus, 1970. Author manuals. Home: 1370 Mulford Rd Columbus OH 43212 Office: 24 E Weber Rd Columbus OH 43202

DAVIS, DAVID, psychiatrist, educator; b. Liverpool, Eng., Oct. 5, 1927; s. Solomon A. and Bertha (Finkelstein) D.; came to U.S., naturalized, 1966; M.B., Ch.B., Glasgow (Scotland) U., 1949, M.D., 1974; Diploma in Psychol. Medicine, Conjoint Bd. of Royal Colls. Physicians and Surgeons (Eng.), 1954; m. Phyllis Burman, 1952; children—Jonathan Paul, Jeremy Mark, Timothy Spenser. House officer Stobhill Gen. Hosp., Glasgow, 1949-50; locum gen. practice, London, 1952; registrar in psychiatry St. Crispin Hosp., Northampton and South Ockendon Hosp., Essex, Eng., 1952-55; Fulbright traveling scholar, research fellow in psychiatry Washington U., St. Louis, vis. physician in psychiatry, 1955-57; registrar in psychiatry Bethlem Royal and Maudsley Hosps., U. London Postgrad. Inst. Psychiatry, 1957-59; sr. hosp. med. officer in psychiatry Borocourt Hosp., Henley, Eng. with service at other hosps., 1959-60; asst. prof. psychiatry U. Mo., Columbia, 1960-61, asso. prof., 1961-68, prof., 1968—, dir. inpatient psychiatry service, 1960-68, chief sect. gen. psychiatry, dir. edn. and tng., 1964-68, dir. community cons. program, 1966-72, chmn. dept. psychiatry, 1968-69, asso. chmn. dept. psychiatry, 1971-75, 77—; clin. dir. univ. service Mid-Mo. Mental Health Center, 1967-74, acad. head, 1968-69, asso. acad. head, dir. research and tng., chief sect. gen. psychiatry, 1970-75, chmn. dept. psychiatry, acad. head, 1975-76, chief psychiatry, 1977—; vis. scientist NIMH, 1969-70; vis. prof. U. Edinburgh (Scotland), 1976-77; vis. faculty fellow in community psychiatry Lab. Community Psychiatry, Harvard U. Med. Sch., 1965-67; examiner N.Y. State Dept. Mental Hygiene, 1970—; cons. in field. Pres. Congregation Beth Shalom, Columbia, 1981—. Served as flight lt. RAF, 1950-52. Recipient award for teaching excellence U. Mo. Residents, 1975; Royal Soc. Medicine Wellcome fellow, 1957-59; Am. Fund for Psychiatry teaching fellow, 1961-62; NIMH grantee, 1965-67; lic. in medicine, U.K., Mo. Fellow Am. Psychiat. Assn., AAAS, Royal Soc. Health, Royal Coll. Psychiatrists, Am. Coll. Psychiatrists, Mo. Acad. Psychiatry (pres. 1970); mem. Can. Psychiat. Assn., Mid-Continent Psychiat. Assn., Boone County Assn. Mental Health, Mo. Assn. Mental Health (chmn. adv. com. 1968-74), AAUP, Internat. Assn. Social Psychiatry. Central Mo. Psychiat. Soc. (pres. 1974, chmn. ethics com. 1977—), Mo. Psychiat. Assn. (pres. 1975), AMA, Brit. Med. Dir., Brit. Med. Register, Mo. Acad. Psychiatry (counselor 1975), N. Am. Soc., Royal Coll. Psychiatrists (founding chmn. 1978—), World Psychiat. Assn. (expert com. on clin. psychopathology), Sigma Xi, Phi Beta Pi. Clubs: University, B'nai B'rith (pres. 1965-66). Contbr. articles to med. publs.; cons. editor Jour. Operational Psychiatry. Office: Sch Medicine Dept Psychiatry U Mo 803 Stadium Rd Columbia MO 65201

DAVIS, DONALD DEAN, psychologist; b. Mt. Clemens, Mich., Oct. 31, 1950; s. William James and Dean Angela (Saurini) D.; B.S., Central Mich. U., 1973, M.A., 1977; postgrad. Mich. State U.; student Internat. Inst. Voor Sociale Geschiedenis, Amsterdam, 1971-72, Centre Internat. de Recherches Sur l'Anarchisme, Lausanne, Switzerland, 1971-72. Undergrad. teaching asst. Central Mich. U., 1972-73; bd. dirs. Karate Inst. Mich., 1973-74, chmn. bd. dirs., adv. nat. bd. dirs. Karate Insts. Am., 1974-76; instr. dept. psychology/sociology Mid-Mich. Community Coll., Harrison, 1973-76; econ. and community devel. cons. John Ruggles & Assos., Mount Pleasant, Mich., 1976-77; on-site research dir. Central Mich. U./Pathway-Vanguard Learning Disability Project, Phila., 1977; NIMH trainee Mich. State U., 1977-78, research asst. Center for Evaluation and Assessment, teaching asst. dept. psychology 1978-79, sr. research asst., asst. dir. Center for Evaluation and Assessment, 1979-81, asst. prof. psychology, 1981—. Named Instr. of Year, Karate Insts. Am., 1976; Adminstrn. on Aging, HEW grantee cons., 1978, 79, Mich. Office Services to Aging, Dept. Mgmt. and Budget grantee, 1979, 80, 81. Mem. Am. Psychol. Assn., Am. Sociol. Assn., Midwestern Psychol. Assn., Midwestern Eco-Community Psychology Interest Group. Contbr. articles in field to profl. jours. Home: 4382 Okemos Rd Okemos MI 48864 Office: Dept Psychology Mich State U East Lansing MI 48824

DAVIS, EDITH MARIE, ednl. adminstr.; b. Montgomery, Ala., Apr. 11, 1932; d. Robert Lee and Marietta (Fields) Stringer; B.S. in Secondary Edn., Ala. State U., 1954; M.A. in Reading, Cardinal Stritch Coll., 1977; m. David Lee Davis, June 5, 1954. Tchr. English and music, public schs., Autaugaville, Ala., 1954-62; tchr. social studies and English, Milw. Public Schs., 1963-71, chairperson dept. English, 1967-71, learning coordinator, 1971—. NDEA grantee U. Wis., Milw., summer 1966. Mem. Assn. Supervision and Curriculum Devel., Milw. Tchrs. Edn. Assn., Nat. Council Tchrs. English, NAACP, Ala. State Alumni Assn. (pres. 1978-80), Alpha Kappa Alpha (sec. Milw. chpt. 1965-67), Phi Delta Kappa. Democrat. Baptist. Office: 609 N 8th St Milwaukee WI 53233

DAVIS, EVELYN MARGUERITE B., artist, organist, pianist; b. Springfield, Mo., Oct. 5, 1914; d. Philip Edward and Della Jane (Morris) Bailey; student pub. schs., Springfield; student art Drury Coll.; m. James Harvey Davis, Sept. 22, 1946. Sec., Shea and Morris Monument Co., before 1946; past mem. sextet, soloist Sta. KGBX; past pianist, Sunday sch. tchr., mem. choir East Avenue Bapt. Ch.; tchr. Bible, organist, pianist, vocal soloist and dir. youth choir Bible Bapt. Ch., Maplewood, Mo., 1956-69, also executed 12 by 6 foot mural of Jordan River; pvt. instr. piano and organ, voice, Croma Harp, Affton, Mo., 1960-71, St. Charles, Mo., 1971—; Bible instr. 3d Bapt. Ch., St. Louis, 1948-54; pianist, soloist, tchr. Bible, Temple Bapt. Ch., Kirkwood, Mo., 1969-71; asst. organist-pianist, vocal soloist, tchr. Bible, Bible Ch., Arnold, Mo., 1969; faculty St. Charles Bible Bapt. Christian Sch., 1976-77; ch. organist, pianist, soloist, Bible tchr., dir. youth orch., music arranger Bible Bapt. Ch., St. Charles, 1971-78; organist, vocal soloist, floral arranger, Bible tchr. Faith Missionary Bapt. Ch., St. Charles, 1978—; interior decorator and floral arranger. Fellow Internat. Biog. Assn. (life), Am. Biog. Inst. Research Assn. (life). Mem. Nat. Guild Organists, Nat. Guild Piano Tchr. Auditions, Internat. Platform Assn. Composer: I Will Sing Hallelujah, (cantata) I Am Alpha and Omega, Prelude to Prayer, My Shepherd, O Sing unto The Lord A New Song, O Come Let Us Sing unto The Lord, The King of Glory; The Lord Is My Light and My Salvation; also numerous hymn arrangements for organ and piano. Home: 4 Ranchero Dr Edgewood Acres Saint Charles MO 63301

DAVIS, F(RANCIS) GORDON, public relations exec.; b. Bloomfield, Ind., May 21, 1908; s. Francis Gordon and Grace (Bryan) D.; student Wayne State U., 1925-27, postgrad., 1929-30; B.A., U. Mich., 1929, postgrad., 1930, 42; postgrad. Cleve. Inst. Art, 1936-37, Western Res. U., 1938-39; m. Margaret Aletha Smith, July 13, 1931; children—Margaret Jayne (Mrs. Edward A. Johnson), Marilyn Grace (Mrs. Richard Karl Johnston). Reporter, aviation editor, editorial writer Buffalo Times, 1930-33; feature, editorial, sci. writer Cleve. Press, 1934-42; public relations dir. Mich. Blue Cross-Blue Shield, Detroit, 1942-46; exec. dir. Mich. Health Council, Detroit, 1943-46; owner F. Gordon Davis & Assos., Roscommon, Mich., 1946—. Mem. Public Relations Soc. Am., Am. (chmn. public relations adv. com. 1965, mem. 1968-71, chmn. Conf. Affiliated Soc. Presidents 1969), Ohio hosp. assns., Am. Soc. Hosp. Public Relations Dirs. (pres. 1968-69), Mich. (pres. 1975-76), Southeastern Mich. (pres. 1973-74) hosp. public relations assns. Club: Higgins Lake Boat (dir. 1962-65). Contbr. articles to profl. jours. Home and Office: Route 3 Box 249 Roscommon MI 48653

DAVIS, F(RANCIS) KEITH, civil engr.; b. Bloomington, Wis., Oct. 23, 1928; s. Martin Morris and Anna (Weber) D.; B.S. in Civil Engring., S.D. State U., 1950; m. Roberta Dean Anderson, May 25, 1957; 1 son, Mark Francis. With firm Howard, Needles, Tammen & Bergendoff, Kansas City, Mo., 1950—, asst. chief structural designer, 1960-65, project mgr., sect. chief, 1965-76, dep. chief structural engr., 1976-79, chief engr., 1979—. Bd. advisers N.W. Kans. Area Vocat. Tech. Sch., 1977-80, chmn., 1979-80. Served with AUS, 1951-53. Registered profl. engr., Mo., Iowa. Fellow ASCE; mem. Nat., Mo. socs. profl. engrs., Am. Ry. Engring. Assn. (tech. com. 1981—). Clubs: Homestead Country, Johnson County Outdoor. Home: 5024 Howe Dr Shawnee Mission KS 66205 Office: 1805 Grand Ave Kansas City MO 64108

DAVIS, FORSTER ADAMS, coll. adminstr.; b. Palo Alto, Calif., Apr. 22, 1938; s. Paul Herbert and Helen (Brack) D.; B.A., Mo. Valley Coll., 1968; M.A., U. Oreg., 1970; m. Ina Claire DeGraff, Aug. 27, 1966; children—Heather Lynn, Robert Adams, Evan Paul. Dist. exec. Boy Scouts Am., Fargo, N.D., 1970-76; asso. dir. career planning and placement Moorhead (Minn.) State U., 1976-79; dir. career services St. Olaf Coll., Northfield, Minn., 1979—. Bd. dirs. Community Blood Bank, 1975-79. Served with U.S. Army, 1961-64. Mem. Minn. Tchr. Placement Assn. (pres. 1980—), Twin City Personnel Assn., Meeting Planners Internat., Internat. Assn. Bus. Communicators, Coll. Placement Council, Minn. Govs. Coll. Council, Assn. Minn. Recruiters, Midwest Coll. Placement Assn. Office: St Olaf Coll Northfield MN 55057

DAVIS, FRED E., coll. pres.; b. DeKalb, Mo., July 17, 1925; s. David Emerson and Honor L. (Easter) D.; B.S. in Edn., Northwest Mo. State Coll., 1949, M.S. in Ednl. Adminstrn., 1959; postgrad. Wayne State Univ., Univ. Colo.; m. Margie Ann Ketchem, Aug. 11, 1950; children—Jane Ann, Thomas Guy. Tchr., coach, prin. Fillmore (Mo.) High Sch., 1949-54; tchr. Hillyard Vocat. Sch., St. Joseph, Mo., 1954-55; supt. schs. Andrew County, Savannah, Mo., 1955-59; asst. dir. tchr. edn. and certification Mo. Dept. Edn., Jefferson City, 1959-61, dir. Jr. Coll. Edn., 1961-67; pres. State Fair Community Coll., Sedalia, Mo., 1967—. Bd. dirs. Little League Baseball, 1968, Babe Ruth Baseball, 1974, Ban Johnson Baseball, 1979—, Jr. Achievement, 1980. Served with A.C., U.S. Army, 1943-45. Decorated Air medal with three oak leaf clusters. Recipient Distinguished Alumni award Northwest Mo. State Univ., 1979. Mem. Mo. Assn. Community and Jr. Colls. (pres. 1980), North Central Council Community and Jr. Colls. Presidents (bd. dirs. 1977), Am. Assn. Community and Jr. Colls., Sedalia Area C. of C. (bd. dirs. 1978—, pres. 1981—, outstanding citizenship award 1971). Baptist. Club: Rotary (bd. dirs., pres. 1981—) (Sedalia, Mo.). Office: 1900 Clarendon Rd Sedalia MO 65301

DAVIS, GARY LEE, mfg. co. exec.; b. Winchester, Ind., Feb. 5, 1950; s. Gayland A. and Mable (Bousman) D.; assos. certificate in mech. design Tri State Coll., 1970, B.S. in Mech. Engring., 1973; M.S. in Engring., Purdue U., 1980; m. Kathy S. Roberts, June 12, 1971; 1 dau., Jessica Jean. Product engr. Spicer Axle div. Dana Corp., 1973-81, mgr. advanced engring., 1981—. Registered profl. engr., Ind. Mem. Soc. Automotive Engrs. (sec., treas., chmn. sect. 1979-80), Nat. Soc. Profl. Engrs., Ind. Soc. Profl. Engrs. Roman Catholic. Home: Rt 1 Yoder IN 46798 Office: PO Box 1209 Fort Wayne IN 46801

DAVIS, GLENN ROBERT, assn. exec.; b. Waukegan, Ill., July 20, 1950; s. Arch Eugene and Caroline Dorothy D.; A.A., Kendall Coll., 1970; B.A., U. Ill., 1972. Mgmt. trainee Allstate Ins., Northbrook, Ill., 1972-73; adminstrv. service mgr. Masonite Corp., Chgo., 1973-76; adminstr. asst. Am. Soc. Anesthesiologists, Park Ridge, Ill., 1977-78; exec. dir. Am. Group of C.P.A. Firms, Oak Brook, Ill., 1978—. Registered prin. Nat. Assn. Security Dealers; ednl. grantee Glenview Rotary Club. Mem. Am. Soc. Assn. Execs., Chgo. Soc. Assn. Execs., Am. Soc. Tng. and Devel. Mem. United Ch. of Christ. Office: 1900 Spring Rd Suite 310 Oak Brook IL 60521

DAVIS, JEROME RUSSELL, mktg. and advt. exec.; b. Milw., Apr. 9, 1929; s. George Morton and Emma Alma (Hestler) D.; B.S. in Journalism, U. Wis., 1950, B. Naval Sci., 1950; m. Dorothy Ferne Farmer, Oct. 26, 1951; children—Robert, Diane, Christopher, Andrew. Sales rep. Sperry Rand Univac, 1953-56; market analysis dir. Trayton H. Davis & Assos., 1956-62; gen. sales mgr., v.p. Comfort Printing & Stationery Co., 1962-76; pres. Davis Communications, Inc., St. Louis, 1976—; supr., instr. Dale Carnegie sales course, sales and mktg. sales mgmt. and sales courses. Adult leader Boy Scouts Am., 1960—, Silver Beaver award; former chmn. bd. Webster Hills United Meth. Ch.; del. Mo. East Meth. Ann. Conf. Served to lt. USNR, 1950-53; Korea. Mem. Sales and Mktg. Execs. Internat. (dir.), Sales and Mktg. Execs. Met. St. Louis (past pres.), Advt. Club Greater St. Louis, Press Club Met. St. Louis, St. Louis Regional Commerce and Growth Assn., Scabbard and Blade, Kappa Sigma. Republican. Club: Grand Order Pachyderms. Columnist Polit. Action, 1979-80. Home and office: 440 Selma Ave Saint Louis MO 63119

DAVIS, JIMMIE MARTIN, analytical biochemist; b. Abingdon, Ill., Aug. 26, 1936; s. Howard E. and Portia (Simpson) Davis; B.S., Eureka Coll., 1958; M.S., Western Ill. U., 1969; m. Roberta Cowling, June 30, 1957; children—Ginger Roberta, Jennifer Sue, Martin Dale, Derry Tad. Med. research asso. Galesburg (Ill.) State Research Hosp., 1961-69, research scientist I, 1969-71, research scientist II, 1971-73; lab. supr. Galesburg Cottage Hosp., 1973-77, clin. chemist, 1977—. Mem. John Mosser Library Bd., 1977; asst. dist. commr. Prairie council Boy Scouts Am., 1977. Mem. Am. Physiol. Soc., Soc. Neurosci., Lambda Chi Alpha, Sigma Zeta. Club: Kiwanis (interclub chmn., v.p. 1967-68, pres. 1968-69, trustee 1968—, sec.-treas., lt. gov. div. 19 I-I dist. 1976-77). Contbr. articles to sci. jours., books. Home: 500 W Latimer St Abingdon IL 61410 Office: Cottage Hosp 695 N Kellogg St Galesburg IL 61401

DAVIS, JOHN BYRON, surgeon; b. Omaha, Aug. 8, 1922; s. Herbert H. and Olga (Metz) D.; student Yale, 1941-43, 46-47; M.D., Nebr. Med. Coll., 1951; m. Cornelia Alexander Cowan, July 27, 1946; children—Dana Alexander (Mrs. William Miskell II), John Byron, Cynthia Elise (Mrs. Bruce W. Bringardner). Intern, Presbyn. Hosp. Chgo., 1951-52; resident U. Ill. Research and Ednl. Hosps., Chgo., 1952-56; practice medicine specializing in surgery, Omaha, 1956—; mem. staff Children's Meml., Immanuel, Bishop Clarkson Meml., Meth. hosps., Omaha. Pres. med. staff Immanuel Hosp., 1964; asso. prof. surgery Nebr. Med. Coll., Omaha, 1968—. Served with USNR, 1943-46; ETO, PTO. Fellow A.C.S.; mem. Western Surg. Soc., Am. Thyroid Assn., Am. Geriatrics Soc., N.Y. Acad. Sci., Soc. for Surgery Alimentary Tract. Soc. Head and Neck Surgeons, Pan Am. Med. Assn., Warren H. Cole Surg. Soc., Omaha Mid-West Clin. Soc., Omaha-Douglas County, Nebr. med. socs., Omaha Research Club, Am. Heart Assn., Omaha Clin. Club, Collegium Internationale Chirurgiae Digestivae (titular mem.), Royal Soc. Medicine (affiliate mem.). Contbr. profl. jours. Home: 9937 Devonshire St Omaha NE 68114 Office: West Dodge Med Center Suite 422 8300 Dodge St Omaha NE 68114

DAVIS, JOHN TERRANCE, surgeon; b. Phila., Apr. 11, 1941; s. John Warren and Jean (MacClelland) D.; B.A., Williams Coll., 1963; M.D., U. Pa., 1967; m. Barbara Brewer, July 10, 1965; children—James Melvin, John Gregory. Intern, Hosp. of U. Pa., Phila., 1968, resident in surgery Grad. Hosp., 1968-73, resident in cardiothoracic surgery, 1975; mem. faculty Med. Coll. Ohio, Toledo, 1975—, asso. prof. surgery, chief div. thoracic and cardiovascular surgery, 1979—, also asso. prof. pediatrics. Fellow A.C.S.; mem. Sigma Xi. Author papers in field. Office: CS 10008 Toledo OH 43699

DAVIS, JOSEPH, city ofcl.; b. McKeesport, Pa., Oct. 24, 1942; s. Jesse James and Daisy Lucille (Williams) D.; B.S., U. Cin., 1964; M.A., Oakland U., 1977; div. Tchr. adult edn., Cin., 1964; coach jr. high sch., Cin., 1964-65; asst. registrar U. Cin., 1967-69; admissions advisor Oakland U., Rochester, Mich., 1969-70, asst. dir. admissions and scholarships, 1970-71, asso. dir., 1971-78; investigator Detroit Bd. Police Commrs., 1978—; adv. bd. Raised Aspirations for Youth and Adults, 1974—. Home: PO Box 27313 Detroit MI 48227 Office: 8045 2d Detroit MI 48202

DAVIS, JOSEPH RICHARD, pharmacologist; b. Chgo., May 13, 1936; s. Rubin and Evelyn (Levin) D.; B.S., U. Ill., 1956, M.D., 1958, M.S., 1960; Ph.D., Baylor U., 1961; m. Betty L. Jacobson, June 22, 1958; children—Philip, Eileen, Ann. Prof. pharmacology Loyola U., Chgo. Stritch Sch. Medicine. Recipient Lederle Med. Faculty award, 1965, William B. Peck Sci. Research award Interstate Postgrad. Med. Assn., 1970, Pre-Clin. teaching honors award Stritch Sch. Medicine, 1963, 68, 71, 76. Mem. Am. Assn. Cancer Research, Soc. Pharmacology and Exptl. Therapeutics, Am. Physiol. Soc., Endocrine Soc., Soc. Study Reproduction, Soc. Toxicology, Am. Indsl. Hygiene Assn., Am. Chem. Soc., Am. Soc. Andrology. Jewish. Contbr. articles to profl. jours. Office: Loyola U Chgo Stritch Sch Medicine 2160 S 1st Ave Maywood IL 60153

DAVIS, JOSEPH SAMUEL, dept. store exec.; b. Chgo., Jan. 27, 1930; s. Joseph and Elizabeth (Cowen) D.; student Carleton Coll., 1947-49; B.A., Columbia, 1951; M.B.A., Harvard, 1953; m. Martha Louise Gries, June 18, 1955; children—Elizabeth Louise, Katherine Ann, Mark Bennett, James Lincoln. Mgmt. trainee May D&F, Denver, 1956-57, asst. buyer, 1957-58, buyer, 1958-61; asst. div. mdse. mgr. Kaufmann's, Inc., Pitts., 1961-63, mdse. mgr., 1963-69, gen. mdse. mgr., 1969-72, exec. v.p., 1972-75; pres. G. Fox & Co., Hartford, 1975-79; pres., chief exec. officer O'Neil's, Akron, Ohio, 1979—. Bd. dirs. Akron Action Com., Akron Regional Devel. Bd., Akron Art Mus., Akron Gen. Hosp.; adv. bd. Akron Symphony Orch., Jr. League Akron. Served with USN, 1953-56. Mem. Harvard Bus. Sch. Club of Northeastern Ohio. Home: 155 Hampshire Rd Akron OH 44313 Office: 226 S Main St Akron OH 44308

DAVIS, JUANITA MELBA LAWRENCE, educator; b. Belle Plaine, Kans., May 1, 1936; d. Ulysses Andrew and Carrie Melba (Lawless) Lawrence; student Okla. Christian Coll., 1954-55; B.A. in Speech, Harding Coll., 1960; M.A. in Edn., Kans. State U., 1974; postgrad. Wichita State U.; m. Darrel E. Davis, Aug. 6, 1961 (div. Apr. 1967); children—Brent Thomas, Brian Lane. Sec. Boeing Co., Wichita, Kans., 1957-58; tchr. high sch., Claremore, Okla., 1960-61, Augusta, Kans., 1961-62, 64, Andover, Kans., 1967-69; tchr. jr. high sch., Manhattan, Kans., 1969-74; counselor Carlton Jr. High Sch., Derby, Kans., 1974-79, Derby Jr. High Sch., 1979—; coordinator workshop The Family: Crisis of the 70's, 1978; speaker on one-parent family. Mem. exec. bd. Concerned Citizens for Community Standards. Mem. Kans., South Central Kans. (pres. 1977-79) personnel and guidance assns., NEA, Kans. Edn. Assn., Derby Edn. Assn. Democrat. Mem. Ch. of Christ. Home: 5820 E Skinner St Wichita KS 67218 Office: 715 E Madison Derby KS 67037

DAVIS, KENT DEL MONCE, med. technologist; b. Rice Lake, Wis., Sept. 22, 1940; s. Owen Del Monte and Theresa Naoma (Larson) D.; student Coll. of William and Mary, 1960, York Coll., 1965; m. Beryl Phillips, Aug. 19, 1961; children—Lisa Ann, Kent Del Monce. Supr. animal research Norfolk Gen. Hosp., 1961-62; lab. specialist Mendota State Hosp., Madison, Wis., 1962-64; supr. dept. spl. hematology and coagulation York (Pa.) Hosp., 1964-69; clin. adminstrv. and research technologist, supr. hematology, coagulation, and radioisotopes Harrisburg (Pa.) Hosp., 1969-70; supr. spl. hematology lab. Gundersen Clinic, Ltd., La Crosse, Wis., 1970—; supr. radioimmunoassay Lab., Lutheran Hosp., La Crosse, 1975-76. Served with USN, 1958-61. Mem. Am. Bd. Bioanalysis, AAAS, Internat. Soc. Clin. Lab. Technologists. Baptist. Contbr. articles to profl. jours. Home: Route 3 Box 159C La Crosse WI 54601 Office: 1836 South Ave La Crosse WI 54601

DAVIS, LAURENCE LAIRD, coal co. exec.; b. Cin., June 6, 1915; s. Thomas Jefferson and Jane (Brown) D.; grad. St. Mark's Sch., 1934; A.B., Harvard, 1938; postgrad. London (Eng.) Sch. Econs., 1939; m. Charlotte Rowe Nichols, Oct. 12, 1940 (dec. Sept. 1973); children—Sally Laird (Mrs. Arthur D. Pratt), Laurence Laird, Thomas Jefferson II; m. 2d, Onlee Partin, Nov. 7, 1973; 1 dau., Nancy Matilda Kathleen; stepchildren—Rickey Lee Foland, Stella Logan Turner, Samuel J. Logan, Gregory C. Logan. With First Nat. Bank Cin., 1939-42, 46-70, v.p., 1949-64, vice chmn. bd., 1964-70, also dir.; vice consul, econ. analyst State Dept., 1943-45; financial cons., 1970—; pres., dir. Roberta Coal Co.; pres., dir. Millers Creek Mineral Devel. Co., Burning Springs Land Co. Chmn., English Speaking Union 1965-72; pres. Symphony Orch., 1965-68. Bd. dirs. Christ Hosp. Mem. Greater Cin. C. of C. (pres. 1965-68). Clubs: Commonwealth, Camargo, Queen City (Cin.). Home: 6910 Given Rd Cincinnati OH 45243 Office: 1st Nat Bank Center Cincinnati OH 45202 also Treasure Cay Abaco Bahamas

DAVIS, LAWRENCE, educator; b. Blossburg, Pa., Aug. 17, 1932; s. Harold Irving and Carrie Mae (Rude) D.; B.S., Black Hills State Coll., 1957; M.A., U. S.D., 1958; m. Shirley Leone Blodgett, May 24, 1957; children—Shirleen Deanna (dec.), Darrell Eugene. Speech therapist Sioux City (Iowa) Pub. Schs., 1958-68; asst. prof. speech and hearing sci. Briar Cliff Coll., Sioux City, 1968-74; instr. gen. and related instruction Western Iowa Tech. Community Coll., Sioux City, 1974—. Past pres. Sioux City Lions, 1971, zone chmn., 1977, dep. dist. gov., 1978, dist. gov., 1979-80, mem. Dist. 9X1 Council Govs. Lions of Iowa Dist. 9, host, 1971; mem. Sioux City Human Rights Commn., 1979—. Served with USAF, 1950-54. Mem. Am., Iowa vocat. assns., Council for Exceptional Children (past pres. N.W. Iowa chpt.), Sioux City Schoolmasters Club (past pres.), Iowa Higher Edn. Assn., Am. Legion, Phi Delta Kappa (treas. 1978-79). Methodist (sec. fin. com. 1979, chmn. fin. 1980, trustee 1981—). Home: 3416 Pierce St Sioux City IA 51104 Office: Box 265 Sioux City IA 51106

DAVIS, LESTER WILLIAM, JR., travel exec.; b. Indpls., Dec. 12, 1924; s. Lester W. and Geraldine (Gregory) D.; B.S., Eastern Ill. U., 1947; m. Virginia M. Smith, Feb. 2, 1943; children—Shirley Ann Davis Casey, Debra Diann Davis Babbitt. Radio, TV announcer-news dir. WLBH, Mattoon, Ill., WPRS, Paris, Ill., WFRL, Freeport, Ill., WREX-TV, Rockford, Ill., 1947-57; del. leader dir. coordinator People to People Internat., Winnebago, Ill., Maupintour, Lawrence, Kans., 1957—; trustee, mem. exec. bd. People to People, 1975—. Served with Paratroop Corps, U.S. Army, 1942-45. Mem. VFW. Republican. Presbyterian. Clubs: Lions, Elks, Moose, Masons, Shriners, Germania of Freeport. Home and office: PO Box 32 306 N Elida St Winnebago IL 61088 also 124 S Island Golden Beach FL 33160

DAVIS, LURELL STANLEY, music cons., mail mktg. co. exec.; b. Balt., Apr. 4, 1952; s. William Lurell and Annie Laura (Winston) D.; B.A., Northwestern U., 1975. Founder, mus. dir. Northwestern Community Ensemble, Northwestern U., 1971-74, grad. instr., teaching asst. history of gospel music, 1973; minister music Gresham United Meth. Ch., 1973-74; communications cons. Ill. Bell Telephone Co., Chgo., 1975-76; mgmt. trainee customer services supr. Signature Fin. Mktg., Inc., Chgo., 1977-78, staff asst. to sr. v.p. ops., systems and planning, 1978, tng. mgr., 1978-81; asso. mgr. community orgns. Mayor's Office Spl. Events, Chgo. Internat. Festival, 1981—; tng. specialist CMR, Ltd., Roselle, Ill., 1981—; creator, exec. producer O For a Thousand Tongues to Sing, Grant Park, Chgo., 1980; cons. Chgo. Hist. Soc., 1978-79. Mem. music adv. panel bd. Ill. Arts Council, 1977-81; mus. advisor, cons., asso. dir. Cosmopolitan Community Ch., 1977-80; exec. dir. Gospel Arts Workshop, 1976—; mem. music panel City of Chgo. Council on Fine Arts Artist-in-Residence Program, 1977-81; mem. City of Chgo. Community Arts Devel. Bd., 1981—. Mem. Ill. Tng. and Devel. Assn., Am. Soc. Tng. and Devel. Home: 3916 N Fremont St Chicago IL 60613 Office: Mayor's Office of Spl Events Festival 82 Office 54 W Hubbard St Chicago IL 60610

DAVIS, MARTHA EMILY, pediatric audiologist; b. Phila., Mar. 23, 1944; d. James Bateman and Marjorie Elsie (Friend) D.; B.A., Coll. of Wooster (Ohio), 1966; M.Ed., U. Va., 1968, Ph.D., 1973. Instr. otolaryngology Thomas Jefferson U. Hosp., Phila., 1968-69; instr. pediatrics, pediatric audiologist U. Va., Charlottesville, 1971-79; asst. dir. audiology and speech pathology Cin. Center for Devel. Disorders, asst. prof. audiology U. Cin., 1979—; audiology cons. Central Va. Community Health Center, New Canton, 1974-79. Mem. profl. adv. com. Camp Holiday Trails, Charlottesville, chair, 1977-78. Mem. Internat. Elec. Response Audiometry Study Group, Am. Auditory Soc., Am. Speech and Hearing Assn. (cert. in audiology), Speech and Hearing Assn. Ohio. Home: 24 Edwards Ave Walton KY 41094 Office: Cin Center for Developmental Disorders Pavillon Bldg Elland and Bethesda Aves Cincinnati OH 45229

DAVIS, MICHAEL STEPHEN, counselor; b. Steubenville, Ohio, Feb. 27, 1947; s. Dushan G. and Mary Agnes (Mulrooney) D.; B.A., Kent State U., 1969; M.S. in Edn., U. Dayton, 1975. Tchr., Holy Rosary Central Grade Sch., Steubenville, 1969-72; playground supr., adult leisure edn. dir. City of Steubenville, 1972-73; counselor, chief transitional services Jefferson County Comprehensive Mental Health Center. Steubenville. 1973-77; sr. counselor Family Service Assn., Steubenville, 1977—; cons. social work Jefferson County Headstart Program. Trustee, Jefferson County Young Democrats, 1972. Mem. Am. Personnel and Guidance Assn., Am. Rehab. Counselors, Internat. Assn. Psychosocial Rehab. Democrat. Roman Catholic. Developed psychiat. transitional services program. Home: 216 Opal Blvd Steubenville OH 43952 Office: 725 N 4th St Steubenville OH 43952

DAVIS, MINNIE DELORES, energy co. exec.; b. Laurens, S.C., Oct. 27, 1945; d. John Ed and Minnie Florie (Watts) D.; B.A., No. Ill. U., 1967; M.B.A., U. Chgo., 1973. Tchr., Chgo. Bd. Edn., 1967-72; internal auditor Container Corp. Am., Chgo., 1973-74; sr. corporate auditor NCR Corp., Dayton, Ohio, 1974-76; project specialist, mgmt. J.I. Case Co.-Tenneco, Inc., Racine, Wis., 1976-79, sr. fin. analyst, sales and mktg. fin., 1979-81; dir. strategic planning Peoples Natural Gas Co., Council Bluffs, Iowa, 1981—. Mem. Racine County Foster Care Review Bd., 1979-81; mem. County Comprehensive Employment Tng. Act Consortium Citizens' Task Force, 1979-81; bd. dirs. Racine Area United Way, 1980-81; mem. adv. bd. Fort Valley State Coll. Bus. Program; also vis. prof. for Black Exec. Exchange Program, Nat. Urban League. Mem. NAACP, League Women Voters, Nat. Assn. Accountants, N.Am. Soc. Corp. Planners, Eta Phi Beta, Gamma Eta. Home: 711 N 91st Plaza Omaha NE 68114 Office: Peoples Natural Gas Co 25 Main Pl Council Bluffs IA 51501

DAVIS, O. C., natural gas pipeline co. exec.; b. Roseclare, Ill., May 7, 1920; s. Luther and Elizabeth (St. John) D.; B.S. in Mech. Engring., A. and M. Coll. Tex.; m. Thelma Sherry, Nov. 14, 1942; children—Henry T., Jon F. with Natural Gas Pipeline Co. Am., 1947—, v.p. charge storage, 1963-66, from exec. v.p. to pres., 1966-73; pres., dir. Peoples Energy Corp., 1973-77, chmn. bd., 1977—; also dir.; chmn. bd., dir. Peoples Gas Light & Coke Co., Natural Gas Pipeline Co. Am., North Shore Gas Co., Harper Oil Co., Indsl. Fuels Corp.; dir. Amsted Industries, Harris Bancorp Inc., Harris Trust & Savs. Bank. Served to capt. USAAF, World War II. Mem. Am. Gas Assn., Ind. Natural Gas Assn. Am., Am. Inst. Mining and Metall. Engrs. Clubs: Chgo., Mid-Am., Univ. (Chgo.). Office: Peoples Energy Corp 122 S Michigan Ave Chicago IL 60603

DAVIS, PETER ANTHONY, lawyer; b. Ludington, Mich., Nov. 7, 1936; s. Alexander Wilberforce and Helen Alvina (Peterson) D.; B.A., Miami U., 1960; M.A., U. Kans., 1962; postgrad. Syracuse U., 1962-63; J.D., Northwestern U., 1966; m. Ann Margaret Weber, Nov. 26, 1960. Admitted to Mich. bar, 1966, Calif. bar, 1978, U.S. Supreme Ct. bar, 1980; practiced in Detroit, 1966-70, Ann Arbor, Mich., 1970—; mem. firm Clark, Klein, Winter, Parsons & Prewitt, Detroit, 1966-70; partner firm Hooper, Hathaway, Fichera, Price & Davis, Ann Arbor, 1970-78, firm Davis and Fajen, Ann Arbor, 1978—; instr. polit. sci. U. Kans., 1961-62. Served with AUS, 1956-58. Fellow Grad. Overseas Tng. Program in India, Maxwell Grad. Sch. Citizenship and Pub. Affairs, Syracuse U., 1962-63. Life fellow Am. Trial Lawyers Found.; mem. Am. Arbitration Assn. (nat. panel labor arbitrators 1968—), Def. Research Inst., Am. Judicature Soc., Am., Washtenaw County (chmn. fed. ct. com., chmn. mediation com., mem. judiciary com.), Detroit bar assns., State Bar Mich., State Bar Calif., Am. (labor arbitration and med. malpractice com.), Mich. trial lawyers assns., Pi Sigma Alpha. Author: Discovery Techniques: A Handbook for Michigan Lawyers, 1977; How to Try a Civil Jury Case, 1980; contbr. numerous articles to profl. jours.; also chpts. in books. Home: 2375 Newport Rd Ann Arbor MI 48103 Office: Suite 400 320 N Main St Ann Arbor MI 48104

DAVIS, RANDY LEE, soil scientist; b. Los Angeles, Nov. 23, 1950; s. Willie Vernon and Joyce Catherine (Manes) D.; A.A., Yuba Community Coll., 1972; B.S. in Soils and Plant Nutrition, U. Calif., Berkeley, 1976. U.S. Peace Corps vol. soil scientist Lesotho, So. Africa, 1976-79; soil scientist Hiawatha Nat. Forest, Sault Ste. Marie, Mich., 1979—. Recipient Spl. Achievement award U.S. Forest Service, 1979. Mem. Soil Sci. Soc. Am., Internat. Soc. Soil Sci., Soil Classifiers Assn. Mich., Nat. Geog. Soc. Methodist. Author: My Diary, the early years 1971-73, 1978. Home: 1402 Ashmun St Sault Ste Marie MI 49783

DAVIS, REED ELLSWORTH, real estate broker; b. Humboldt, Nebr., Aug. 29, 1893; s. Adonirum Judson and Elizabeth Jane (Hurley) D.; grad. Chillicothe Bus. Coll., 1916; student Grand Island Coll., 1916-18; m. Myrtle Dorothy Kenworthy, Sept. 1, 1923; 1 son, Reed Ellsworth. Tchr. bus. adminstrn. Grand Island (Nebr.) Acad., 1916-18; motion picture stunt flyer, 1919-20; supr. constrn. of 1st cabin airplane built in U.S., 1921; real estate salesman Burt Fowler Co., Realtors, Omaha, 1922-34; comdr. Civilian Conservation Corps, Cloquet, Minn., 1934-35; real estate salesman Stuht-Bedford Co., Realtors, Omaha, 1936-41; v.p. Hargleroad-Davis Co., Realtors, Omaha, 1949-59; pres. Reed Davis Co., Realtors, Omaha, 1959—. Served with U.S. Army, 1918-19, USAAF, 1941-48, USAF, 1951-52; now col. ret. Mem. NAREB (realtor emeritus), Omaha Bd. Realtors (profl. standards com. 1971-75), Add Sell League Omaha, SAR, Am. Legion (life), Am. Assn. Ret. Persons, Nat. Assn. Uniformed Services (life), Air Force Assn. (charter), Mil. Order World Wars, Res. Officers Assn. (life mem., chpt. sec. 1938-49, state v.p. for air 1953-54), Ret. Officers Assn. (life mem., chpt. pres. 1970-71), Omaha C. of C., Order Daedalians (life), Omega Tau Rho. Mason (Shriner), Nat. Sojourner (mem. in perpetuity), Clubs: Heros of '76 (past comdr.), OX-5 (life mem.), Press, Statesman, Offutt Air Base Officers. Author: The Art and Skill of Real Estate Selling, 1981; From Aviation Section Signal Corps to the U.S. Air Force, in press. Home: 3724 Mason St Omaha NE 68105 Office: 159 N 72d St Omaha NE 68114

DAVIS, RICHARD ALBAN, educator; b. Pasadena, Calif., Apr. 26, 1923; s. Harry Clayton and Harriet Bernadette (O'Connell) D.; A.A., Pasadena Coll., 1946; student U. Calif., Berkeley, 1946-47, Northwestern U., 1947-48; M.A., U. Chgo., 1959; m. Mary Hammel, Feb. 26, 1945; children—James Alban, John Hammel. Editor, Farmers Weekly Rev. of Will County, Ill., 1948-49; chemist, purchasing agt. Bio-Process Co., Joliet, Ill., 1950-53; chief reference librarian John Crerar Library, Chgo., 1956-59; librarian U. Chgo. Labs. for Applied Sci., 1959-60; prof. Grad. Sch. Library Sci., Drexel U., Phila., 1960-68; adj. prof. U. Chgo., 1966-72; prof. Grad. Sch. Library Sci., Rosary Coll., River Forest, Ill., 1971—; cons. U.S. Office of Edn., Washington, 1966-67; cons. Reilly Chem. Co., Indpls., Public Adminstrn. Joint Reference Library, Chgo., Resource Recovery Partners, Glen Ellyn, Ill., Bell Systems Center for Tech. Edn., Lisle, Ill. Bd. dirs. Community of Bala Cymwyd, Pa., 1966-67, Midwest Regional Med. Library, Chgo., 1968-71; Served with USN, 1941-46, 53-54. NSF grantee, 1964-65; U.S. Office of Edn. grantee, 1974-75. Mem. Spl. Libraries Assn., Catholic Library Assn., Assn. Am. Library Schs., Am. Library Assn., U.S. Naval Inst., Phi Beta Kappa, Phi Kappa Phi. Author: Bibliography of Use Studies, 1964; Marysville Public Library, a Case Study, 1976; Thesaurus of Library and Information Science, 2d edit., 1981. Office: 7900 Division St River Forest IL 60305

DAVIS, RICHARD BRADLEY, physician; b. Iowa City, Iowa, Nov. 6, 1926; s. Bradley Nelson and Gladys Mae (Fairbanks) D.; B.S., Yale U., 1949; M.D., State U. Iowa, 1953; Ph.D., U. Minn., 1964; m. Jean Nixeen Anderson, June 22, 1957; children—Janet, Stephen, Catharine. Intern, Mary Fletcher Hosp., Burlington, Vt., 1953-54, resident, 1954-56; instr. U. Minn., Mpls., 1959-64, asst. prof. medicine, 1964-69; vis. investigator Sir William Dunn Sch. Pathology, Oxford, Eng., 1964-65, MRC Blood Coagulation Research Unit, Churchill Hosp., Oxford, 1965; asso. prof. medicine U. Nebr., Omaha, 1969-73, prof. medicine, 1973—, acting dir. div. hematology, 1974-76, prof. pathology, 1976—, dir. hematology div., 1976-79, fellow grad. faculty, mem. exec. grad. council, exec. com. U. Nebr. Hosps., Med. Center. Served with U.S. Army, 1945-46. Borden Undergrad. Med. Research awardee, 1960; USPHS career devel. awardee, 1961-69. Fellow A.C.P.; Central Soc. Clin. Research, Am. Fedn. Clin. Research, Am. Soc. Exptl. Pathology, N.Y. Acad. Scis., Am. Assn. History of Medicine, Soc. Exptl. Biology and Medicine, Am. Soc. Hematology, Royal Micros. Soc., Internat. Soc. Haemostasis and Thrombosis, Omaha Mid-West Clin. Soc., Sigma Xi, Alpha Omega Alpha, Phi Beta Pi, Theta Kappa Psi. Contbr. articles to sci. publs. Home: 3514 S 94th St Omaha NE 68124 Office: 42nd St and Dewey Ave Omaha NE 68105

DAVIS, RICHARD JAMES, typewriter co. exec.; b. Miller, S.D., Nov. 2, 1938; s. Everett Edward and Mildred Louise (Pugsley) D.; A.A., Worthington Jr. Coll., 1958; B.S. in Bus. Adminstrn., U. S.D., 1960; m. Maxine Busch, Feb. 20, 1960; children—Greg, Vicki, Jon, Gary, Jay, Sara, Jerry, Timothy. Asst. stores mgr. S.S. Kresge, Rapid City, S.D., 1960-62, Lincoln, Nebr., 1962-63; founder, Dick Davis Typewriter Co., Mankato, Minn., 1963—, owner, mgr., 1981—. Mem. adv. com. on office equip. repair Fairbault Area Vocat. Sch., 1979-81; bd. dirs. S. Central Minn. Camp Fire, Inc., 1978—, pres., 1979, 80. Recipient Corneia Honors, Jr. C. of C., 1975. Mem. Nat. Office Equip. Dealers Assn., Nat. Fedn. Ind. Bus., Minn. Office Machine Dealers Assn., Mankato Area C. of C., Nat. Office Machine Dealers Assn. Republican. Roman Catholic. Clubs: Sertoma, Bonanza Investment, Hilltop Kiwanis, K.C. Home: 833 Range St N Mankato MN 56001 Office: 525 S Front St Mankato MN 56001

DAVIS, RICHARD JOSEF, aircraft co. exec.; b. N.Y.C., Feb. 9, 1917; s. Emanuel S. and Bettina (Alexander) D.; B.A., U. Wis., 1939; m. Helyne Elizabeth Weber, Dec. 16, 1942; children—Richard Josef, Linda Anne. Washington corr. Newsweek mag., 1940-58; Washington pub. relations rep. Douglas Aircraft Co., Santa Monica, Calif., 1958-60, dir. pub. relations, 1960-65, v.p. pub. relations, 1965-67; corp. v.p. external relations McDonnell Douglas Corp., 1967—. Served with USN, 1942-45. Mem. Nat. Press Club, St. Louis Press Club, Soc. Profl. Journalists, Sigma Delta Chi. Democrat. Home: 738 N Woodlawn Ave Kirkwood MO 63122 Office: PO Box 516 Saint Louis MO 63166

DAVIS, ROBERT EARL, psychologist; b. Cin., June 29, 1940; s. Wilbur Henry and Eleanor A. D.; B.A., Georgetown (Ky.) Coll., 1965; M.Ed., Kent State U., 1968; cert. advanced grad. studies, U. Cin., 1979; m. Jan. 31, 1970 (dec.). Counselor mgr. Ohio Bur. Vocat. Rehab., Cin., 1966-78; pvt. practice family therapy, Cin., 1976—. Lic. psychologist, Ohio; cert. rehab. counselor. Mem. Am. Psychol. Assn., Am. Personnel and Guidance Assn., Am. Assn. Marital and Family Therapists, Nat. Rehab. Assn., Am. Assn. Sex Counselors, Educators and Therapists, Cin. Personnel and Guidance Assn. (dir. 1976-79), Nat. Assn. Social Workers, Ohio Rehab. Counseling Assn. (pres. 1970-72). Presbyterian. Clubs: Cin. Singletons, Masons, Shriners. Home: 12096 Freestone Ct Cincinnati OH 45240 Office: 5900 Boymel Dr Fairfield OH 45014

DAVIS, ROBERT EARL, research pharmacist; b. Jackson, Miss., Mar. 7, 1942; s. F. Earl and Agnes Gloria (Simmons) D.; B.S. in Pharmacy, U. Miss., Ph.D. in Pharmaceutics; m. Patricia Moak, Sept. 14, 1961; children—Diana Lynn, Robert Earl, Karen Leigh. Research pharmacist CIBA Pharm. Corp., Summit, N.J., 1966; chief pharmacist Oxford-Lafayette County Hosp., Oxford, Miss., 1967; instr. pharmacy U. Miss., 1967-68; sr. research asso. pharm. product devel. Mead Johnson & Co., Evansville, Ind., 1968—. Am. Found. Pharm. Edn. fellow, 1965-68. Mem. Am. Pharm. Assn., Acad. Pharm. Scis., Basics and Indsl. Sects. Acad. Pharm. Scis., Omicron Delta Kappa, Rho Chi. Baptist. Contbr. articles to profl. jours. Home: 900 Hartford Ct Evansville IN 47710 Office: 2404 Pennsylvania Ave Evansville IN 47721

DAVIS, ROBERT MADARY, rehab. psychologist; b. Pocomoke, Md., Mar. 6, 1936; s. Clayton Thomas and Sarah Naomi (Madary) D.; B.S., Salisbury State Coll., 1958; M.Ed., Pa. State U., 1962; Ed.D., U. Md., 1968; postgrad. Loyola Coll., 1960, N.Y. U., 1964; m. Barbara A. Smith, Oct. 5, 1965; children—Karen, Kristen. Tchr., Core 8 Balt. County Schs., 1958-60; resident counselor Pa. State U., University Park, 1960-61; counseling intern Pa. Rehab. Center, Johnstown, and Dixon State Hosp., South Mountain, Pa., 1962; vocational rehab. counselor Div. Vocational Rehab., Salisbury, Md., 1962-65; faculty research asst. U. Md., College Park, 1965-66; supr. Title VIA Project, Caroline and Talbot Counties, Md., 1968-69; asst. prof. Pa. State U. and supr. Rehab. Counselor Edn. Unit, Pa. Rehab. Center, 1969-73, asso. prof., coordinator grad. program in rehab. counselor edn., 1973-76; asso. prof., dir. rehab. psychology area of concentration Ind. U./Purdue U., Indpls. 1976-79, prof., dir. rehab. counselor training, 1979-80, prof. psychology, 1980—; guest lectr. Ind. Rehab. Services, 1976-81; lectr. in field; vocat. expert Bur. Hearing and Appeals, Social Security Adminstrn., 1971—. Lic. psychologist, Pa.; certified rehab. counselor. Mem. Am. Psychol. Assn., Pa. Psychol. Assn., Nat. Rehab. Assn.), Vocat. Evaluation and Work Adjustment Assn. (pres. 1980-81), Nat. Rehab. Counseling Assn., Nat. Council on Rehab. Edn., Ind. Rehab. Assn., Ind. Vocat. Evaluation and Work

Adjustment Assn., Ind. Rehab. Counseling Assn., Am. Personnel and Guidance Assn., Nat. Vocat. Guidance Assn., Am. Rehab. Counseling Assn., Iota Alpha Delta. Contbr. articles to profl. jours. Home: 9875 Lakewood Dr E Indianapolis IN 46208 Office: 1201 E 38th St Indianapolis IN 46205

DAVIS, ROBERT PHELPS, surgeon; b. Evanston, Ill., Nov. 9, 1942; s. Carl Braden and Marianne Williams (Hoover) D.; B.A., U. of the South, 1964; M.D., Northwestern U., 1969; Intern, Chgo. Wesley Meml. Hosp., 1969-70; resident in surgery Northwestern U., Chgo., 1970-75; staff surgeon VA Lakeside Hosp., Chgo., 1975—; sr. attending surgeon Columbus Cuneo Med. Center, Chgo., 1975—; asst. prof. clin. surgery Northwestern U. Med. Sch., 1975—. Diplomate Am. Bd. Surgery. Fellow A.C.S.; mem. Soc. Acad. Surgery, Assn. Vets. Surgeons, AMA. Republican. Presbyterian. Clubs: Racquet of Chgo., Saddle and Cycle. Home: 1827 N Orleans St Chicago IL 60614 Office: 467 W Deming Pl Suite 919 Chicago IL 60614

DAVIS, ROBERT W., congressman; b. Marquette, Mich., July 31, 1932; student No. Mich. U., 1950, 52, Hillsdale Coll., 1951-52; B.S., Coll. Mortuary Sci., Wayne State U., 1954; m. Martha Cole, 1976; children—Robert W., Lisa, George. Funeral dir. Davis Funeral Home, St. Ignace, Mich., 1954-66; mem. St. Ignace City Council, 1964-66; mem. Mich. Ho. of Reps., 1966-70; mem. Mich. Senate, 1970-78, majority whip, minority leader; mem. 96th and 97th Congresses from 11th Dist. Mich.; mem. N.E.-Midwest Econ. Advancement Coalition, Congressional Tourism Caucus, Republican Study Club, Conf. Gt. Lakes Congressmen, Environ. Study Conf., Coalition for Peace Through Strength, Congressional Shipyard Coalition, Congressional Steel Caucus. Bd. dirs. Mich. Cystic Fibrosis Assn.; adv. bd. Young Ams. for Freedom. Mem. Mich. Funeral Dirs. Assn., Nat. Rifle Assn. Republican. Clubs: Lions, Eagles, Elks, Masons, Ducks Unlimited. Office: 1224 Longworth House Office Bldg Washington DC 20515

DAVIS, STEPHEN LEE, county ofcl.; b. Kansas City, Mo., Feb. 24, 1947; s. Vernon Elliott and Vera Lucille (Paris) D.; B.A., U. Mo., Kansas City, 1970; m. Susan Alison Heim, Dec. 28, 1971; 1 dau., Jessalyn Brooke. Instr. health, phys. edn. and recreation St. Pius X High Sch., Kansas City, 1970-74; supr. parks and recreation City of Grandview (Mo.), 1974-75, dir. parks and recreation, 1975-78; dir. parks and recreation County of Clay (Mo.), 1978—; partner mgmt. cons. co., Smithville, Mo., 1976—. Mem. Nat. Parks and Recreation Assn., Mo. Parks and Recreation Assn., Nat. Wildlife Fedn., Profl. Grounds Mgmt. Soc., Soc. Friends Missouri Town-1855. Mem. Disciples of Christ. Club: Masons. Contbr. articles to profl. publs. mgmt. by objectives, budgeting principles, personnel mgmt. Research on alcohol as alt. energy source. Home and office: Route 2 Paradise Rd Smithville MO 64089

DAVIS, THOMAS ALAN, univ. adminstr.; b. Marion, Ind., Aug. 5, 1943; s. Robert Johnson and Helen Elizabeth (Spence) D.; B.A., Taylor U., 1968; postgrad. Ind. U., 1968, U. Mich., 1970-71; grad. cert. Multonomah Sch. of the Bible, 1975; M.A., Ball State U., 1975; m. Tara Elyssea Culver, Jan. 3, 1969. Social worker Grant County (Ind.) Opportunity Center, Marion, 1968; sociol. researcher Ranche House Coll., Salisbury, Rhodesia, Africa, 1969; personnel mgr. Bell Fibre Products Corp., Grand Rapids, Mich., 1969-73; missionary coach Overseas Crusade, Rhodesia, 1973-74; dir. career devel./student activities Taylor U., Upland, Ind., 1976-80, dir. career planning and placement, 1981—; cons. Assn. of Christian Sch. Internat., 1980, Anderson Coll., 1979, Huntington Community Schs., 1981. Mem. Grant County Migrant Opportunities Bd., 1968; campaign chmn. United Way, 1969-73; bd. dirs. Grand Rapids Urban League, 1971-72; volunteer YMCA; Salisbury Jr. and Sr. High youth dir., 1967, 68, 70, 71, 72. Served with USN, 1961-64. Mem. Coll. Placement Council, Midwest Coll. Placement Assn. Midwest Coop. Edn. Assn., Council for Advancement Exptl. Learning, Am. Coll. Personnel Assn., Assn. of Christians in Student Devel. Baptist. Clubs: N. Am. Hunting, Appalacian Trail, Greater Horizons. Office: Taylor Univ Upland IN 46989

DAVIS, VIRGINIA SUE, gen. contracting co. exec.; b. Buffalo, Mo., Mar. 2, 1936; d. Argus Dee and Gladys Hazel (Gregg) Neill; B.S. in Edn., Southwest Mo. State U., Springfield, 1958; M.S., Central Mo. State U., Warrensburg, 1973; m. Edward Davis, Aug. 8, 1958; 1 dau., Brenda Kay. Tchr., Lee's Summit (Mo.) Jr. High Sch., 1958-68; tchr. phys. edn. Ed Davis Constrn., Inc., Lee's Summit, 1968—. Mem. Dist. 7 Citizen Adv. Bd. Mem. Mo. State Tchrs. Assn., Phi Kappa Phi. Home: 301 Lincolnwood St Lee's Summit MO 64063 Office: 212 N Main St Lee's Summit MO 64063

DAVIS, WILLIAM DOYLE, JR., real estate appraiser; b. Kansas City, Mo., Sept. 24, 1934; s. Will D. and Lindalou (Turner) D.; B.S. in Agr., U. Mo., 1956, M.S. in Agrl. Econs., 1957. Partner, Appraisal Assos., Kansas City, 1959; pres. Farm Mgmt. Assos., Kansas City, 1959—; instr. Am. Inst. Real Estate Appraisers, Soc. Real Estate Appraisers, Internat. Assn. Assessing Officers. Elder Christian Ch.; chmn., former pres. Agrl. Hall of Fame; former pres. Kansas City Jaycees. Served to 1st lt., AUS, 1957-59. Mem. Appraisal Inst., Am. Inst. Real Estate Appraisers, Soc. Real Estate Appraisers (sr. real estate analyst, past pres.), Am. Soc. Farm Mgrs. and Rural Appraisers, Mo. Soc. Farm Mgrs. (past pres.), Internat. Assn. Assessing Officers. Clubs: Masons, Shriners. Office: Suite 316 1004 Baltimore St Kansas City MO 64105

DAVIS, WILLIAM GRENVILLE, premier of Ont.; b. Brampton, Ont., Can., July 30, 1929; s. Albert Grenville and Vera M. (Hewetson) D.; B.A., U. Toronto, 1951; LL.D., Waterloo Lutheran U., 1963, Western Ont. U., 1965, U. Toronto, 1967, McMaster U., 1968, Queen's U., 1968, Windsor U., 1969; D.U., Ottawa U., 1980; m. Helen MacPhee, 1953 (dec. 1962); children—Neil, Nancy, Catherine, Ian; m. 2d, Kathleen Mackay, 1963; 1 dau., Meg. Called to Ont. bar, 1955; partner firm Davis, Webb and Hollinrake, Brampton, 1955-59; mem. Provincial Parliament Ont. from Peel Riding, 1959, 63, Peel North Riding, 1967, 71; 2d vice chmn. Hydro-Electric Power Commn. of Ont., 1961-62; minister of edn., Ont., 1962-71, also minister of univ. affairs, 1964-71, premier of Ont., 1971—; leader Progressive Conservative Party of Ont., 1971—. Mem. Ont. Bar Assn., Can. Bar Assn. Mem. United Ch. Clubs: Kiwanis, Masons, Albany (Toronto). Author: Education in Ontario, 1965; Building an Educated Society, 1816-1966, 1966; other publs. Address: Office of the Premier of Ont Parliament Bldgs Toronto ON M7A 1A1 Canada

DAVIS, WILMA JEAN, nursing home adminstr.; b. Goodland, Mo., Apr. 24, 1931; d. Sherman L. and Bessie Keith; cert. housing mgmt., Community Sch. Practical Nursing, Columbia U., 1977, cert. activity dir., 1977, med. records cert., 1978; m. Billy Davis, Mar. 15, 1968; children—Jackie, David, Joey, Kelly. Adminstr., Colonial Nursing Home, Bismarck, Mo., 1958—, Lone Pine Congregate Center, Ironton, Mo., 1977—, Belleview (Mo.) Nursing Home, 1956—. Mem. Am. Health Care Assn., Mo. Assn. Lic. Practical Nurses, Mo. Health Care Assn., Activity Dirs. Assn. Mo. Methodist. Club: Order Eastern Star. Address: Box 24 Star Route Belleview MO 63623

DAVISON, BURNS HARRIS, II, lawyer; b. Des Moines, Sept. 15, 1931; s. Burns Harris and Dorothy Margaret (Johnson) D.; B.S., Ind. U., 1953; LL.B., Drake U., 1958; m. Susan Jean Morris, Aug. 28, 1958; children—Burns Harris III, Anna Sue, William M., Robert W. Admitted to Iowa bar, 1958; U.S. Dist. Ct. for Iowa, 1958, U.S. Tax Ct., 1959, U.S. Ct. Appeals bar, 1964, U.S. Supreme Ct. bar, 1978; asso. firm Holliday & Myers, Des Moines, 1958-59; partner firm Jones, Hoffmann & Davison, Des Moines, 1959—. Pres. Hubbell Sch. PTA, Des Moines, 1976-77; vestryman St. Andrew's Episcopal Ch., Des Moines, 1972-75, 76-79, sr. warden, 1979; pres. Des Moines Community Playhouse, 1967. Served to capt. U.S. Army, 1953-55; lt. col. USAR Ret. Decorated Purple Heart. Mem. Am., Iowa State, Polk County bar assns., Res. Officers Assn., Assn. U.S. Army, Am. Law Inst., Info. Council on Fabric Flammability, Am. Judicature Soc., Def. Research Inst., Iowa Def. Counsel Assn., Phi Kappa Psi, Phi Alpha Delta. Republican. Episcopalian. Clubs: Kiwanis (pres. Des Moines chpt. 1970-71), Spirit Lake Yacht. Home: 4812 Algonquin Rd Des Moines IA 50311 Office: 900 Des Moines Bldg Des Moines IA 50309

DAVISON, KENNETH EDWIN, educator; b. East Cleveland, Ohio, May 4, 1924; s. Gordon Edwin and Mildred K. (Smith) D.; A.B., Heidelberg Coll., 1946; A.M., Western Res. U., 1951, Ph.D., 1953; m. Virginia Nell Rentz, June 14, 1959; children—Robert Edwin, Richard Allen. Asst. prof. history, polit. sci. Heidelberg Coll., Tiffin, Ohio, 1952-56, asso. prof. polit. sci., 1956-59, prof., 1959-64, prof. history, dir. Gen. Edn. Program, 1964-67, prof., chmn. Am. studies dept., 1967—; vis. prof. Am. studies Bowling Green State U., 1972, 73, 74, 75; mem. bd. advisers Seneca County Mus., 1976—; cons. Tiffin Hist. Trust, 1976—. Chmn., Heidelberg Community Lecture and Concert Series, 1956-63; mem. Ohio com. for pub. programs in humanities, 1973-80, mem. exec. com., 1977-80; chmn. Tiffin-Seneca Bicentennial Commn., 1974-77. Recipient Ohioana Library Book award, 1973. Am. Philos. Soc. grantee, 1963, 64; Nat. Endowment Humanities summer seminar grantee, 1978, 81; Can. Embassy Faculty Enrichment grantee, 1979, 80, 81. Mem. Orgn. Am. Historians, Western History Assn., Ohio-Ind. Am. Studies Assn. (pres. 1965, 66), Am. Assn. State and Local History, Nat. Trust Historic Preservation, Soc. Ohio Archivists (exec. council 1970-73, v.p. 1972-73), So. Hist. Assn., Ohio Acad. History (editor newsletter 1971-74), Popular Culture Assn. (adv. bd. 1972-75), Am. Studies Assn. (nat. exec. council 1968-78, nat. treas. 1973-78, editor newsletter 1974-75), Ohio Hist. Soc. (research adviser 1968-75), Can. Am. Studies Assn., Assn. Can. Studies in U.S., Center for Study of Presidency (bd. educators 1974—), Victorian Soc. in Am., World Future Soc., Western Res. Hist. Soc., Pi Kappa Delta, Phi Alpha Theta. Presbyterian. Author: Cleveland and the Civil War, 1962; The Presidency of Rutherford B. Hayes, 1972; The American Presidency: A Guide to Bibliographical Sources, 1982; (with others) Ohio Heritage, 1982. Guest editor Ohio History, 1968; editor Hayes Hist. Jour., 1976-82; book rev. editor Presdl. Studies Quar., 1978—. Contbr. to Collier's Ency., 1964, 68, Am. Educator's Ency., 1965, articles and revs. to profl. jours. Home: 125 Hampden Park Tiffin OH 44883

DAVITO, CHARLENE L., nursing adminstr.; b. Westfield, Ill., Sept. 3, 1947; d. Charles W. and Lola M. Goldsmith; grad. St. Joseph Hosp. Sch. Nursing, 1977; postgrad. Lewis U., 1981—; m. Frank L. Davito, July 8, 1967; 1 son, Frank L. Staff nurse Riverside Hosp., Kankakee, Ill., 1977, Morris (Ill.) Hosp., 1977-78; staff nurse Will County Health Dept., Joliet, Ill., 1978-79; dir. nursing Bradley (Ill.) Nursing Centre, 1979; dir. nursing Americana Nursing Center, Joliet, 1980; dir. nursing Briarcliff Manor, Bourbonnais, Ill., 1980-81. Mem. Am. Nurses Assn., Assn. Rehab. Nurses, Ill. Nurses Assn. Roman Catholic. Home: Box 117 Coal City IL 60416 Office: 300 N Madison St Joliet IL

DAVY, MICHAEL FRANCIS, cons. civil engr.; b. Springfield, Mo., Mar. 24, 1946; s. Philip Sheridan and Caecilia Magdalen (Thiemann) D.; B.S. in Civil Engring., U. Wis., 1969; m. Joyce Kaye Young, Aug. 17, 1968; children—Mark Sheridan, Katherine Ann, Jennifer Mary. Engring. aide Wis. Dept. Natural Resources, Madison, 1969; project engr. Davy Engring. Co., La Crosse, Wis., 1969-71, 2d v.p., 1971-74, v.p., 1974—; mgr. Davy Labs., La Crosse, 1975—; mem. civil engr. adv. bd. U. Wis., Platteville, 1973-75. Mem. exec. bd. Gateway Area council Boy Scouts Am., 1973-82; mem. adv. bd. Viterbo Coll., 1978—. Registered profl. engr., Wis., Minn., Ill., Iowa, Mich. Mem. Nat., Wis. (Young Engr. of Year 1976) socs. profl. engrs., Wis. Soc. Land Surveyors, Water Pollution Control Fedn., AAAS, Profl. Engrs. in Pvt. Practice, ASCE (Wis. Young Civil Engr. of Yr. 1980). Home: 615 N 23d St La Crosse WI 54601 Office: 115 S 6th St La Crosse WI 54601

DAVY, PHILIP SHERIDAN, civil engr.; b. Madison, Wis., July 12, 1915; s. Francis Joseph and Mathilda Sarah (Femrite) D.; B.S. in Civil Engring., U. Wis., 1937, M.S. in Civil Engring., 1938; m. Caecilia Magdalen Thiemann, Feb. 8, 1939; children—Katherine Agnes (Mrs. William Bathurst), Patricia Mary (Mrs. Steven Sciborski), Michael Francis, Barbara Jean (Mrs. John Salassa), Thomas Henry, Margaret Theresa (Mrs. Douglas Claeys). Engr., Frank J. Davy & Son, cons. engrs., La Crosse, Wis., 1938-41, Permutit Co., N.Y.C., 1946; v.p. Davy Engring Co., cons. engrs., La Crosse, 1947-56, pres., 1956—; lectr. U. Wis., 1950—, Wis. Dept. Natural Resources, 1970-77; mem. Gov's. Com. on Wis. Water Resources, 1965-66; mem. regional adv. bd. to Dept. Resource Devel., State Wis., 1966-68, chmn., 1968; mem. bd. architects and engrs. region V, GSA, 1979. Campaign chmn. United Fund, LaCrosse, 1961, 72; com. chmn. Gateway area council Boy Scouts Am., 1948-52, bd. mem., 1953-66, 71—, v.p., 1967-70, pres., 1971-73, v.p. Area 1, East Central Region, 1978-80; bd. dirs., pres. United Fund, La Crosse, 1962-65; bd. dirs., chmn. fin. and adminstrn. com. Diocese of LaCrosse, 1969-81; bd. dirs. LaCrosse County Hist. Soc., 1980-81, pres.-elect, 1981-82. Served from 2d lt. to lt. col., C.E., AUS, 1937-46. Decorated Army Commendation medal with cluster, Papal knight comdr. Holy Sepulchre, Diocese of LaCrosse; recipient Silver Beaver, St. George, Silver Antelope and Disting. Eagle awards Boy Scouts Am. Registered profl. engr., Wis., Minn., Iowa, Mich., Ill., Ind.; diplomate Am. Acad. Environ. Engrs. Fellow ASCE (Disting. Service award Wis. sect. 1979); mem. Am. Water Works Assn. (trustee, chmn. Wis. sect. 1957, 60), AAAS, Water Pollution Control Assn., Nat. Soc. Profl. Engrs. (dir. (1967-70), Wis. Soc. Profl. Engrs. (v.p. 1965-67, pres. 1974-75; Engr. of Yr. in Pvt. Practice 1965, Engr. of Yr. 1970), Am. Pub. Works Assn., Greater LaCrosse C. of C. (dir. 1959-62, exec. bd. 1964-67, pres. 1968, Man of Yr. 1973), Internat. Platform Assn., Scabbard and Blade, Tau Beta Pi, Chi Epsilon, Phi Kappa Phi. Clubs: Elks, Serra, La Crosse Country, Rotary. Home: 1230 King St La Crosse WI 54601 Office: 115 S 6th St La Crosse WI 54601

DAWES, WAYNE LEE, pedodontist; b. Wabash, Ind., Apr. 1, 1940; s. Wilbur Calvin and Nada Mary (Shultz) D.; D.D.S. cum laude, Ind. U., 1966; m. Judith Carol Tucker, June 19, 1966; children—Jennifer Lynn, Julia Ann, Janel Nicole, Matthew Edward. Intern, Riley Hosp., Indpls., 1966-67, resident, 1967-68; practice dentistry specializing in pedodontics, Ft. Wayne, Ind., 1968—; mem. staff Luth. Hosp., Ft. Wayne, 1971—, St. Joseph's Hosp., 1969—. Served with AUS, 1958-62. Mem. Am., Ind., Isaac Knapp (treas. 1978-80, pres. 1981-82) dental assns., Ind. Univ. Alumni Assn., Assn. Dentistry for Children, Ind. Fedn. Dentists (v.p. 1978-79), Ind. Pedodontic Soc., Omicron Kappa Upsilon, Delta Sigma Delta (pres. 1964-65, recipient Outstanding Achievement award 1966). Presbyn. Home: 1111 Dodane Rd Fort Wayne IN 46819 Office: 223 E Tillman Road Fort Wayne IN 46816

DAWKINS, MARVA PHYLLIS, psychologist; b. Jacksonville, Fla., Apr. 12, 1948; d. Ralph and Altamese (Padgett) D.; student U. Freiburg (W. Ger.), 1969-70; B.S., Stetson U., 1971; M.S., Fla. State U., 1972, Ph.D., 1975. Research asst. Fla. State U., Tallahassee, 1970-72; clin. intern, psychology dept. Presbyn.-St. Luke's Med. Center and mental health dept. Mile Square Health Center, Chgo., 1973-74; staff psychologist, dir. aftercare treatment program, mental health dept. Mile Square Health Center, Chgo., 1974-75, staff psychologist, coordinator developmental disabilities program, 1976-79; asst. prof. psychology U. North Fla., Jacksonville, 1975-76, Rush U.-Presbyn. St. Luke's Med. Center, Chgo., 1976—; pvt. practice clin. psychology, Oak Park, Ill., 1977—; exec. dir. Inst. for Community Mental Health, 1979—. Registered psychologist, Ill. Mem. Am. Psychol. Assn., Assn. Black Psychologists. Office: 109-1 Harrison St Oak Park IL 60304

DAWLEY, ROBERT MICHAEL, educator; b. Buffalo, June 3, 1948; s. Morris D. and Grace (Carrow) D.; Mus.B., Eastman Sch. Music, 1970; M.A., N.E. Mo. State U., 1972; D.Ed., U. Ill., 1979; postgrad. U. Ariz., Haverford Coll., Temple U.; m. Ofelia Vasquez, June 2, 1973; 1 son, Robert Albert. Dir. Youth Symphony, Corpus Christi, Tex., 1972-74; violinist Corpus Christi Symphony, 1972-74; 1st violinist Tucson Symphony, 1975-76; dir. orch., jazz ensemble Hillsdale Coll. (Mich.), 1978-80; asst. prof. music Purdue U., West Lafayette, Ind., 1980—; 1st viola Lafayette Symphony and Quartet, 1980-81. U. Mich. fellow, 1978; Nat. Endowment Humanities fellow, summer 1980, Purdue Research Found. grantee, 1981. Mem. Coll. Music Soc., Music Educators Nat. Conf., Music Educators Book Soc., Am. String Tchrs. Assn., Nat. Sch. Orch. Assn., Ind. Music Educators Assn., Phi Delta Kappa, Pi Kappa Lambda. Democrat. Composer; Six Bagatelles for String Quartet Demonstration, 1980; contbr. articles to profl. jours. Home: 400 N River Rd #103 West Lafayette IN 47906 Office: Music Div Purdue U West Lafayette IN 47907

DAWSON, GLENN V., state senator; ed. SE Jr. Coll., St. Joseph's Coll., Calumet Coll., Chgo., Marine Nav. Sch. Former mem. Ill. Ho. of Reps.; now mem. Ill. State Senate. Chmn. Calumet Dist. council Boy Scouts Am.; active Thornton Twp. Dem. Orgn. Served with USCG. Recipient Man of Yr. award Kiwanis, 1975, Thornton Twp. Young Democrats, 1977; Exceptional Service award KC, 1980. Mem. Avalon Trails Improvement Assn., E.Side C. of C., United Brotherhood Carpenters, Greater Roseland Orgn., Internat. Marine Lic. Pilots Assn. Clubs: Lions, KC, Kiwanis. Address: 13343 Baltimore Ave Chicago IL 60634*

DAWSON, JAMES RICHARD, fire and safety engr.; b. Fond du Lac, Wis., July 1, 1936; s. Cecil V. and Helen (Greider) D.; A.S., Okla. State U., 1959; m. Martha Bromley, June 10, 1959; children—Heather Joy, Jamie Ruth. With Mut. Fire Inspection Bur. New Eng., Salem, Mass., 1959-61, Home Ins. Co., Milw., 1961-65; safety dir. Amron Corp., a Gulf Western Co., Waukesha, Wis., 1965-69; fire and safety engr. Ind. U., Bloomington, 1969—. Trustee, Bloomington Twp., Ind., 1979—. Cert. safety profl.; cert. master fire fighter. Mem. Waukesha Safety Council (pres. 1969), Am. Soc. Safety Engrs., Nat. Fire Protection Assn., Vets. of Safety, Ind. Twp. Trustees Assn., Ind. Vol. Firemans Assn., Fraternal Order of Police. Republican. United Methodist. Home: 3899 E Bethel Ln Bloomington IN 47401 Office: 625 N Jordan Ave Bloomington IN 47405

DAWSON, JEFFREY OWEN, educator; b. Council Bluffs, Iowa, Aug. 12, 1949; s. Lauren P. and Catherine Elizabeth (Hughes) D.; student Creighton U., 1967-68; B.S., Iowa State U., 1971, M.S., 1973, Ph.D., 1978; m. Norine Elizabeth Nims, June 2, 1974. Park ranger-park planner Eastern Planning and Service Center, U.S. Nat. Park Service, Washington, 1970; civil engring. technician design br. Mo. River div. U.S. Army C.E., Omaha, 1971; research asst. dept. forestry Iowa State U., Ames, 1971-73; nurseryman Iowa Conservation Commn. Nursery, Ames, 1973; forest hand mensuration sect. New Zealand Forest Service, Kaingaroa Forest, via Rotorua, 1973; research asst., research asso. dept. forestry Iowa State U., Ames, 1974-77; asst. prof. forestry U. Ill., Urbana, 1977—. Creighton Prep. Sch. acad. scholar, 1963-67, Creighton U. acad. scholar, 1967-68, U.S. Dept. Agr. Forest Service, N. Central Forest Exptl. Sta. coop. research grantee, 1978-81. Mem. Internat. Soc. Arboriculture, Am. Soc. Plant Physiologists, Soc. Am. Foresters, AAAS, Am. Forestry Assn., N.Y. Acad. Scis., Sigma Xi, Xi Sigma Pi (nat. asso. forester 1978-80), Gamma Sigma Delta. Contbr. articles to profl. jours. Home: 1103 S Orchard St Urbana IL 61801 Office: Dept Forestry 110 Mumford Hall 1301 W Gregory Dr U Ill Urbana IL 61801

DAWSON, JOHN HOWEL, investment dealer; b. Evanston, Ill., Dec. 30, 1944; s. John Albert and Annie Joe (Howel) D.; B.A., Oberlin Coll., 1967. Controller John A. Dawson & Co., Chgo., 1971; v.p. Charles H. Eldredge & Co., Chgo., 1971-72; pres. John Dawson & Assos., Inc., Chgo., 1972—; mem. Midwest Stock Exchange, 1981—. Mem. Chgo. Bicentennial Commn., 1973, Rogers Park Community Council. Served to lt. USN, 1968-71; lt. comdr. Res. Mem. Nat. Assn. Securities Dealers, Inc., Chgo. Assn. Commerce and Industry, U.S. C. of C., Chgo. Hist. Soc., Ill. Soc. Mayflower Descs., Ill. SAR, Soc. Colonial Wars, Naval Res. Assn., U.S. Naval Inst. Baptist. Club: Executives. Home: 7447 N Ashland Ave Chicago IL 60626 Office: 1 N La Salle St Chicago IL 60602

DAWSON, PAUL LAMAR, food products co. exec.; b. Grayville, Ill., Aug. 18, 1905; s. Ludlow William and Sarah Jane (Lamar) D.; student public schs., bus. coll.; m. Dorothy March Dawson, Nov. 25, 1937; adopted children—Phillip L., Christie L. Stores mgr. Kroger Co., 1935-38, dist. mgr., 1938-43, mdse. mgr., 1946-51; pres. Dorothy Dawson Food Products, Inc., Jackson, Mich., 1952-74, chmn. bd., 1974—; mem. Nugget Distbg., Inc., N.Am. Food Service. Active, Shriners Hosp. Crippled Children, Youth Haven Ranch, Compassion Internat., various chs. and children's homes. Served to maj. AUS, 1943-46. Republican. Clubs: Shriners (chmn. Moslem Temple), One Hundred Million Dollar, Masons, Scottish Rite, Hi Twelve, Spring Arbor. Home: PO Box 312 1215 S Brown St Jackson MI 49203 Office: 251-55 W Euclid Ave Jackson MI 49201

DAWSON, THERESA SHEAHEN, speech pathologist; b. Cleve., Sept. 28, 1934; d. Allan Newman and Virginia Lillian (Dougherty) Sheahen; B.A. cum laude, Marygrove Coll., 1958; M.A., Western Reserve U., 1960; m. Robert H. Dawson, Apr. 4, 1959; children—Dawn, Deborah, Angela, Jennifer, Elizabeth. Speech pathologist cleft palate team Mt. Sinai Hosp., Cleve., 1960-62; speech pathologist Fairview Gen. Hosp., Cleve., 1960-62; dir. parent edn. United Cerebral Palsy Assn., Cleve., 1960-73; speech pathologist Lakewood (Ohio) Hosp., 1960—; cons. to nursing homes; speaker in-service meetings at nursing homes and hosps. Treas., St. Raphael Sch. Bd., 1973-76. Certified clin. competence in speech pathology. Mem. Am. Speech-Lang.-Hearing Assn., Marygrove Alumnae Assn. Republican. Roman Catholic. Clubs: St. Raphael Women's Guild, Lakewood Country. Home: 29317 Lincoln Rd Bay Village OH 44140 Office: 14519 Detroit Ave Lakewood OH 44107

DAY, HARRY P., educator; b. Grand Island, Fla., Mar. 12, 1924; s. Harry R. and Roslyn (Pyott) D.; B.A. in Polit. Sci., History, U. Miami (Fla.), 1947; M.A. in Counseling, Psychology, Fla. State U., 1951,

Ed.D. in Ednl. Adminstrn., Tchr. Edn., 1957; m. Dorothy Jane Patton, Aug. 23, 1947; children—Stephen P., Sydney A. Day Fanning. Tchr. history and English, Jackson High Sch., Miami, 1948-51; adminstrv. asst. Am. Council on Edn., 1952-53; teaching asst. Fla. State U., Tallahassee, 1953-57, asst. to bus. mgr., dir. auxs., 1955-57, dir. Lab. Sch., asso. prof. edn., 1958-60, prof., 1959-61, asst. dean of students, 1959-60, asso. dean, 1960-61, dean, 1964-66; sr. staff resident Salzburg (Austria) Seminar in Am. Studies, 1961-64; dir. New Eng. Center for Continuing Edn., Durham, N.H., 1966-76; pres. Spring Hill Center, Wayzata, Minn., 1976-80. Mem. Am. Assn. for Higher Edn., Phi Delta Kappa, Kappa Delta Pi. Contbr. articles to profl. jours.

DAY, JON WESTON, silo co. exec.; b. Lynch, Ky., Sept. 8, 1936; s. Chester Q. and Ethel Lela (Shipley) D.; B.A., Va. Mil. Inst., 1958; postgrad. U. Ky., 1959-61; m. Maria Ann Pagano, Oct. 29, 1960; children—Stacy Ann, Jonathan Woods, Charles Sidney. Indsl. engr. U.S. Steel Corp., Gary, W.Va., Johnstown, Pa., 1959-60; asst. to v.p. Watkins & Assos., Cons. Engrs., Lexington, Ky., 1961-63; sales rep. Columbia Cement div. PPG Industries, 1963-67, sales mgr., 1967-76, regional sales mgr., Pa., W.Va. and Ohio, 1976-79; pres. 1st Colony/Lipp Nat. Co., Marietta, 1979—; dir. WDR Enterprises, Coshocton, Ohio, Smith Concrete, Marietta, Ohio. Active Am. Cancer Soc., United Appeal, others; bd. dirs. Marietta Meml. Hosp., 1969—, Washington County Children's Services, 1978—. Named Citizen of Yr., PPG Industries, 1972. Mem. Asso. Gen. Contractors, W.Va. Builders Supply, Ohio Block Assn., Ohio Ready Mix Assn., C. of C. Roman Catholic. Clubs: Rotary, Elks, Marietta Tennis. Home: 312 Fairview Ln Marietta OH 45750 Office: PO Box 296 Marietta OH 45750

DAY, MARY LOU, educator; b. Missoula, Mont., Jan. 30, 1921; d. George Washington and Ruth Irene (Spangler) D.; student U. Mont., 1938-39; B.S., Wash. State U., 1942; M.S., U. Wash., 1951; Ph.D., Colo. State U., 1971. Research home economist Western Farmers Assn., Seattle, 1944-48; caseworker State Dept. Public Assistance, King County, Seattle, 1952-56; faculty, Seattle U., 1956-61, U. Utah, Salt Lake City, 1963-65, Calif. State Poly. U., San Luis Obispo, 1965-66; sch. lunch cons. State of Oreg., Salem, 1966-67; asst. prof. Central Wash. State Coll., Ellensburg, 1967-68; teaching asst. Colo. State U., Fort Collins, 1968-71; asso. prof. N.Mex. State U., Las Cruces, 1972-78; asso. prof. nutrition U. Mont., Missoula, 1979-81; asso. dir. edn. for dietetics, dept. dietetics and nutrition U. Kans. Med. Center, Kansas City, 1981—. Mem. Am. Dietetic Assn., Am. Public Health Assn., Am. Home Econs. Assn., Soc. for Nutrition Edn., Nutrition Today Soc., Gerontol. Soc., N.Y. Acad. Scis., Sigma Xi, Omicron Nu, Gamma Sigma Delta. Episcopalian. Club: Order of Eastern Star. Home: 13929 W 88th Terr Lenexa KS 66215 Office: Dept Dietetics and Nutrition U Kans Med Center Kansas City KS 66103

DAY, RICHARD LEROY, dentist; b. Gas City, Ind., Mar. 24, 1935; s. Grandville M. and Della (Owen) D.; A.B., Taylor U., 1958; D.D.S., Ind. U., 1962; m. Anne E. Ineson, July 17, 1958; children—Lori Ann, Lisa Ellen. Gen. practice dentistry, Wabash, Ind., 1962—. Mem. Wabash County Bd. Health, 1964—, vice chmn., 1968-70, chmn., 1970-77. Mem. Wabash C. of C., Wabash Valley Dental Soc. (past pres.), Ind. State (dist. del. 1969), Am. dental assns., Grant County Dental Soc., Nat. Rifle Assn. (life), Ind. Sportsmen's Council, Nat. Wildlife Fedn., Wabash Wildlife and Sportsman Assn., Nat. Exchange Club, Xi Psi Phi. Mem. Christian and Missionary Alliance Ch. Contbr. articles in field to profl. jours. Home: 1047 St James Ct Wabash IN 46992 Office: 812 Manchester Ave Wabash IN 46992

DAY, ROLAND BERNARD, state supreme ct. justice; b. Oshkosh, Wis., June 11, 1919; s. Peter Oliver and Joanna King (Wescott) D.; B.A., U. Wis., 1942, J.D., 1947; m. Mary Jane Purcell, Dec. 18, 1948; 1 dau., Sarah Jane. Admitted to Wis. bar, 1947; trainee Office Wis. Atty. Gen., 1947; asso. mem. firm Maloney & Wheeler, Madison, 1947-49; 1st asst. dist. atty. Dane County, 1949-52; partner Day, Goodman, Madison, 1953-57; legal counsel, staff Sen. William Proxmire, Washington, 1957-58; partner Wheeler, Van Sickle, Day & Anderson, Madison, 1959-74; justice Wis. Supreme Ct., 1974—. Mem. Madison Housing Authority, 1960-64, chmn., 1961-63. Regent U. Wis. System, 1972-74. Served with AUS, 1943-46. Mem. Am. Bar Assn., State Bar Wis., Am. Trial Lawyers Assn., Am. Judicature Soc., Ygdrasil Lit. Soc. (pres. 1968). Mem. United Ch. of Christ. Clubs: Madison, Madison Literary. Office: Supreme Ct Chambers 214 E State Capitol Madison WI 53702

DAY, WILLIS FRANKLIN, III, storage co. exec.; b. Toledo, Feb. 4, 1923; s. Willis F. and Ernestine (Kirchmaier) D.; student Northwestern U., 1943; B.S., Miami U., Oxford, Ohio, 1945; m. Rosemary Claypool, Sept. 15, 1944; children—Jane Louise, Deborah Ann, Willis F. IV, John Edward. With Willis Day Storage Co., Toledo, 1939—, pres., 1957—; pres. Willis Day Storage Co., Toledo, 1964—; dir. Ohio Citizens Trust Co., Toledo, Mayflower Warehousemen's Assn., Tecumseh Products Co. Bd. dirs. St. Vincent Hosp., Toledo. Served to lt. (j.g.) USNR, 1943-46. Mem. Am. Legion, Phi Delta Theta. Mason (32 deg.). Clubs: Toledo, Toledo Yacht; Catawba Island (Port Clinton, Ohio); North Cape Yacht (Monroe, Mich.). Home: 3422 Indian Rd Toledo OH 43606 Office: 801 Washington St Toledo OH 43601

DAYON, JOHN DAVID, med. products mgr.; b. Mpls., July 16, 1942; s. Amos Joseph and Isabelle Marie (Striebel) D.; student St. John's U., Minn., 1960-62; B.S. in Bus., Mt. Mercy Coll., 1979; m. Kathleen Dougherty, July 9, 1966; children—Sarah Helen, Amy Margaret, Steven John. Prodn. tester test equipment research and devel. Collins Radio, Cedar Rapids, Iowa, 1967-73; med. customer engr., dist. service mgr. Hewlett-Packard, St. Paul, 1973-77, regional service mgr. med. products, Rolling Meadows, Ill., 1977—. Served with USAR, 1960-61. Mem. Assn. Field Service Mgrs., Am. Mgmt. Assn., Assn. Advancement Med. Instrumentation. Home: 511 Joy Ln Sleepy Hollow IL 60118 Office: 5201 Tollview Dr Rolling Meadows IL 60008

DAYTON, RONALD JAY, sch. prin.; b. Elburn, Ill., Feb. 27, 1949; s. Walter and Eunice (Hoyt) D.; B.A., Aurora Coll., 1971; M.A., No. Ill. U., 1979; m. Alma; children—Rebekah Lee, Angela, Ricky, Andrew. Tchr., Batavia (Ill.) Public Schs., 1971-73, Naperville (Ill.) Public Schs., 1973-79; prin. Maple Park Elem. Sch., Kaneland Sch. Dist. 302, Maple Park, Ill., 1979—; dir. park dist. programs Naperville Public Park Dist., 1973-74; chmn. Kaneland Curriculum council. Mem. Assn. Sch. Curriculum Devel., Nat. Assn. Elem. Sch. Prins., Kane County Elementary Principals Assn. (corr. sec.), Phi Delta Kappa. Presbyterian. Home: 40W757 Route 64 Box 52 Wasco IL Office: Box 128 Maple Park Elem Sch Maple Park IL 60151

DCAMP, CHARLES BARTON, educator, musician; b. Fairfield, Iowa, Feb. 16, 1932; s. Glenn Franklin and Nina Clarice (Larson) DC.; student Bradley U., 1950-51; B.S., U. Ill., 1956, M.S., 1957; Ph.D., U. Iowa, 1980; m. Ruth Joyce MacDonald, June 27, 1953; children—James Charles, Douglas Kevin, David Michael, Richard Manley, Paul Frederick, Jon Barton. Tchr., Watervliet (Mich.) Pub. Sch., 1958-61; tchr. music United Twp. High Sch., East Moline, Ill., 1961-63; band dir. Pleasant Valley (Iowa) Schs., 1963-74; prof. music St. Ambrose Coll., Davenport, Iowa, 1974—, also dir. bands, chmn. div. fine arts and chmn. dept. music; guest dir., adjudicator festivals, music contests Iowa, Ill.; producer Quad-City Music Guild, 1973-77; tchr. woodwinds Bemidji State Coll. Band Camp. Mem. Riverdale Vol. Fire Co., 1966-75, pres., 1971-73. Served with AUS, 1952-55. Mem. Iowa (past pres.), Nat. Cath. bandmasters assns., Coll. Band Dirs. Nat. Assn., Music Educators Nat. Conf., Iowa Music Educators, Am. Fedn. Musicians, Am. Sch. Band Dirs. Assn., Nat. Band Assn., N.E.A. (life), Phi Mu Alpha Sinfonia, Phi Delta Kappa, Tau Kappa Epsilon. Republican. Methodist. Editor, Iowa Music Educator mag., 1979—; contbr. articles to profl. jours. Home: 301 Circle Dr Riverdale Bettendorf IA 52722 Office: St Ambrose Coll Davenport IA 52804

DEAK, CHARLES KAROL, chemist; b. Budapest, Hungary, Sept. 26, 1928; s. Karoly and Ida (Benes) D.; came to U.S., 1955, naturalized, 1961; B.S., Eotvos Coll., Budapest, 1948; student Sorbonne, Paris, 1949; postgrad. Wayne State U., 1957-61; m. Jenny Bocinski, Apr. 9, 1958; children—James, Christine. With Frankel Co., Inc., Detroit, 1957-74, quality control mgr., 1968-71, mgr. tech. services, 1971-74; mgr. Analyatical Assos., Inc., Detroit, 1974-79, pres., 1979—. Cert. profl. chemist. Fellow Am. Inst. Chemists; mem. Am. Chem. Soc., ASTM, Am. Soc. Metals, Assn. Analytical Chemists, Photog. Soc. Am. Roman Catholic. Patentee in chem. firefighting agts. and dense metal separation. Club: Internat. Brotherhood Magicians. Home: 29844 Wagner St Warren MI 48093 Office: 19380 Mount Elliott St Detroit MI 48234

DEAL, DONALD LEWIS, state ofcl.; b. Indpls., May 11, 1936; s. Ralph Lawrence and Helen Elizabeth (Smith) D.; student Valparaiso U., 1957, Ind. U., 1958-61; m. Betty Jane Cox, Dec. 7, 1957; children—Richard, Donna, Cynthia (dec.), Michael. With Grain Dealers Mut. Ins. Co., 1961-71, regional mgr. so. office, 1968-70, multiline underwriting mgr. for Western states, Omaha, 1970-71; supr. property and liability div. Nebr. Dept. Ins., Lincoln, from 1971, now chief property and casualty div.; instr. ins. S.E. Community Coll. Mem. underwriting mgmt. com. Miss. Coastal Pool Plan, 1969-70; chmn. Omaha Ins. Plan, 1971—. Served with AUS, 1954-57. Mem. Chartered Property and Casualty Underwriters Soc. (past pres. Nebr. chpt.). Democrat. Lutheran. Moose. Home: 6320 South St Lincoln NE 68506 Office: State Office Bldg 301 Centennial Mall S Lincoln NE 68509

DEAL, LEO V., educator; b. Parker, Ind., June 16, 1930; s. Fred L. and Mildred L. (Cecil) D.; A.B., DePauw U., 1951; M.A., Ohio State U., 1958; Ph.D., Mich. State U., 1965; m. Nola Jene Arndt, July 5, 1952; children—Eric, Nancy. Tchr., Wellington (Ohio) High Sch., 1955-57, Olmsted Falls (Ohio) High Sch., 1958-59; speech pathologist Lima (Ohio) Hosp., 1959-60; asst. prof. Mich. State U., E. Lansing, 1963-68, asso. prof., 1968-70, prof., 1970—, chmn. dept. audiology and speech scis., 1971—; pres. Lansing Oral Cleft Clinic, 1969-71. Chmn., Lansing Coordinating Com. for Handicapped. 1973-74; bd. dirs. United Ministry of Higher Edn., Mich. State U., 1970-78, chmn. Wesley Found. Bd., 1976-78. Served with USAF, 1951-55. Certified Am. Speech and Hearing Assn. Mem. Am., Mich. speech and hearing assns., Am. Cleft Palate Assn.. Internat. Assn. Logopedics and Phoniatrics, Phi Kappa Phi. Methodist. Contbr. articles to profl. jours, chpts. to books. Home: 1249 Ivanhoe Dr East Lansing MI 48823 Office: Mich State U East Lansing MI 48824

DEAL, MARY HOLMAN, urban planner; b. Evanston, Ill., Feb. 5, 1944; d. George Varnum and Emily L. (Sedlacek) D.; A.B., U. Chgo., 1965, M.A., 1966. Adminstrv. asst. Am. Soc. Planning Ofcls., Chgo., 1966-67; asst. planner Genesee County Met. Planning Commn., Flint, Mich., 1967-70; individual practice as planner and designer, Akron, Ohio, 1970-73; housing planner N.E. Ohio Areawide Coordinating Agy., Cleve., 1973-74; regional planner Miami Valley Regional Planning Commn., Dayton, Ohio, 1974-79; project mgr. nat. competition identifying and promoting urban planning activities and designs for women in urban environments HUD, 1980-81; project mgr. Women and Urban Planning: A Bibliography, HUD and Council Planning Librarians, 1980—. Mem. Am. Inst. Cert. Planners, Ohio Planning Conf., Am. Planning Assn. (nat. task force on planning for women 1979, dir. planning and women div. 1979-81), NOW (treas. Ohio 1975-77), Ohio Women, Inc. (bd. dirs. 1977-78. treas. 1978-79). Contbr. articles to profl. jours. Home: 610 A Dodge Ct Dayton OH 45431

DEALY, ROSS, educator; b. Atlantic, Iowa, Sept. 13, 1933; s. Ray and Gertrude (Sorlien) D.; B.A., So. Methodist U., 1956; M.A., U. Wash., 1962; Ph.D., Ind. U., 1975; M.L.S., U. Oreg., 1978; children—Anette, Nicola, Ian. Buyer, Boeing Co., Seattle, 1958-59; asst. prof. Queens Coll., Charlotte, N.C., 1964-66; lectr. St. Mary-Of-the-Woods Coll., Terre Haute, Ind., 1976; mem. faculty Univ. Wis., Marinette, 1979—, library dir., 1979—. Served with U.S. Army, 1956-58. Recipient Ford Internat. II grants, 1970, 69; Ind. U. grantee, 1970-72; Ford Found. Cross-Cultural fellow, 1973, recipient Grant-in-Aid, 1974. Mem. Am. Hist. Assn., Am. Library Assn., Council Latin Am. History. Democrat. Author: The Politics of an Erasmian Lawyer, 1976. Home: 340 Jefferson St Marinette WI 54143 Office: Univ of Wis Marinette WI 54143

DEAN, EDITH DORIS, sch. counselor; b. Winston-Salem, N.C., Mar. 26, 1929; d. John Sylvester Penn and Lavinia Jewel (McNeely) Penn Hendricks; B.A., Eastern Mich. U., 1951, M.A., 1964; m. Richard E. Sterrett, Feb. 1951 (div. 1958); children—Kay, Richard III, Linda Josephine Myers; m. 2d, Albert C. Dean, Apr. 6, 1959; children—Linda Carol Martin, Charles, Ronald, Mike, Alan. Student aide Eastern Mich. U. Library, 1948-51; camp counselor Detroit Dept. Parks and Recreation, summers 1951-61; tchr. Detroit Bd. Edn., 1951-64, tchr.-counselor, 1966—; employment counselor Mich. Dept. Social Services, Detroit, 1964-65; dir. workshops. Chmn. parish council Presentation-Our Lady of Victory Roman Catholic Ch., Detroit, 1977-79. Named Tchr. of Yr., Wilson Jr. High Sch., 1974. Mem. Am. Personnel and Guidance Assn., Mich. Guidance and Counseling Assn., Detroit Guidance and Counseling Assn., Detroit Fedn. Union (sec. counselors chpt. 1959-79), Cath. Women's Orgn., Detroit Geneal. Soc., Alpha Kappa Alpha. Democrat. Home: 18701 Roselawn St Detroit MI 48221 Office: 11600 E Seven Mile Rd Detroit MI 48205

DEAN, GORDON SPENCER, lab. exec.; b. Dedham, Mass., July 27, 1930; s. Murdoch Henry and Mary (MacLeod) D.; B.S., Mass. Coll. Pharmacy, 1952, M.S., 1954; M.S., U. Mich., 1956, Ph.D., 1958; m. Jean Katheryn MacEwen, Aug. 21, 1954; children—Gordon Kimble, Nancy Elizabeth, Marney Jennifer. Research program adminstr. Smith Kline & French, 1958-62; mem. sales devel. group spl. products dept. Rohm & Haas, Phila., 1962-64, enzyme product mgr., 1964-67, mgr. sales devel. 1967-68; mgr. market devel., indsl. chem. devel., 1968-69; dir. marketing Ott Chem. Co., Muskegon, Mich., 1969-70, v.p. marketing, 1970-72; v.p. marketing Story Chem. Corp., 1972-73; v.p. marketing Lakeway Chems. Inc., Muskegon, 1973-77; founder, pres. Toxicity Research Labs. Ltd., Muskegon, 1977—; instr. U. Mich., 1955-57. Active Cub Scouts. Mem. N.Y. Acad. Sci., Am. Pharm. Assn., Am. Chem. Soc., Am. Found. Pharm. Edn., Sigma Xi, Rho Chi, Kappa Psi, Alpha Chi Sigma. Republican. Roman Catholic. Home: 580 Franklin St North Muskegon MI 49445 Office: 510 W Hackley St Muskegon MI 49447

DEAN, JOHN ROBERT, hosp. exec.; b. Chgo., Nov. 7, 1929; s. Harvey N. and Gertrude N. (Connelly) D.; student Thronton Jr. Coll., 1947-49; B.S. in Pharmacy, Butler U., 1954; M.A., Governors State U., 1975; m. Barbara Ann Carrier, Nov. 17, 1972; children—Jacqueline Ann, William. Pharmacist, Flossmoor (Ill.) Pharmacy, 1956-59; owner pharmacy, Frankfort, Ill., 1959-64; pharmacist Hedges Clinic, Frankfort, 1964-66; dir. pharmacy Tinley Park (Ill.) Mental Health Center, 1966-76; dir. Cermak Meml. Hosp., Chgo., 1976—. Trustee, Village of Frankfort, 1964-72, police commr., 1964-68, chmn. fin., 1968-72. Served with AUS, 1954-56. Mem. Am. Coll. Hosp. Adminstrs., Ill. Hosp. Assn., Ill. Alcoholism and Drug Dependence Assn., Am. Correctional Health Services Assn. Roman Catholic. Club: Moose. Home: 443 E 46th St Chicago IL 60653 Office: Cermak Meml Hosp 2800 S California Ave Chicago IL 60608

DEAN, MARIAN HAZEL THOMSON (MRS. JOSEPH J. DEAN), occupational therapist; b. Ferndale, Mich., May 21, 1931; d. Roderick Fraser and Anne Grace (Cooper) Thomson; student U. Mich., 1949-51; B.S., Eastern Mich. U., 1953; m. Joseph J. Dean, Sept. 29, 1956; children—Jay Fraser, Ellen Louise, Richard Arthur. Staff therapist Detroit Orthopaedic Clinic, 1953-56; sr. staff therapist Ga. Retardation Center, Atlanta, 1970-72; dir. devel. program for multihandicapped child United Cerebral Palsy, Atlanta, 1973; programs dir. United Cerebral Palsy Ind., Indpls., 1973-76; course coordinator, allied health edn. dept. Sister Kenny Inst., Mpls., 1976—; exec. dir. N.E. Learning Center Inc., St. Paul, 1979—; program dir. Phoenix Residence, Inc., St. Paul, 1977-79; mem. adv. com. on phys. handicaps City of Bloomington (Minn.), 1976-79; mem. rehab. and engring. com. Courage Center, 1977-78; chmn. bd. Met. Devel. Achievement Center Council, Inc., 1981—. Den mother Atlanta area Boy Scouts Am., 1972-73; pres. Fontainbleau Swim and Diving Team Booster Club, 1973. Mem. St. Paul Assn. for Retarded Children (legis. com. 1980—), Internat. Platform Assn., N. Suburban C. of C., Gamma Phi Beta. Home: 10316 10th Ave Circle Bloomington MN 55437 Office: 2675 E Hwy 36 North Saint Paul MN 55109

DEAN, MICHAEL LEWIS, educator; b. Stamford, Conn., Feb. 9, 1942; s. Stanley R. and Belle (Katzman) D.; B.A., U. Mich., 1963; M.B.A., Ohio State U., 1965, Ph.D., 1971; m. Carol Lois Hoffman, Mar. 21, 1965; children—Jeffrey Brian, Julie Ellen. Staff asst. food products div. Procter & Gamble, Cin., 1965-66, asst. brand mgr., 1967-68; economist, econ. planning and analysis div. Battelle Meml. Inst., Columbus, Ohio, 1968-70; asst. prof. mktg., mem. grad. faculty Coll. Bus. Adminstrn., U. Cin., 1971-74, asso. prof., mem. univ. grad. faculty, 1974—, coordinator mktg. M.B.A. program, 1975-77; bus. adviser Great Oak Vocat. Sch. Dist., Ohio, 1976-79; pres. Action Data Mktg. Research, Inc., Cin., 1976—. Cons., adviser Lotspeich Schs., Cin., 1975. Recipient nat. award for excellence in pvt. enterprise edn. Freedoms Found., 1978; Outstanding Bus. Coll. Tchr. award U. Cin., 1979, 80. Mem. Assn. Consumer Research, Am. Mktg. Assn., Product Research and Devel. Assn., Beta Gamma Sigma (hon.). Republican. Jewish. Contbr. articles on bus. research and mktg. to profl. jours. Home: 7614 Carriage Ln Cincinnati OH 45242 Office: Mail Location 20 Univ of Cincinnati Cincinnati OH 45221

DEAN, MILDRED PAULINE, interior designer; b. Prestonsburg, Ky., July 20, 1921; d. Dennie D. and Mary Eliza (Baldridge) Conley; student N.Y. Sch. Interior Design, 1975; m. Paul R. Dean, May 3, 1946; 1 son, Alan Richard. Owner, mgr. Interiors by Pauline, Hastings, Mich., 1976—. Mem. adv. bd. Interior Designer mag., 1978. Vice chairperson Barry County Republican Com., 1974-75, treas. 3d dist., 1974-75; chmn. Barry County Cancer Crusade, 1974. Republican. Presbyterian. Clubs: Hastings Women's, Algonquin Lake Assn. Address: Box 68 Hastings MI 49058

DEAN, ROBERT HAL, food co. exec.; b. Mitchell, S.D., June 27, 1916; s. Bernie Bonney and Edna May (Halladay) D.; B.A., Grinnell Coll., 1938; m. Doris Reger, Sept. 28, 1940; children—Donna (Mrs. Tom Doan), David; m. 2d, Gale H. Mullen, May 26, 1979. Mgr., Checkerboard Elevator Co., Buffalo, 1941-43; mgr. Ralston Purina Co., Circleville, O., 1943-45; grain div., St. Louis, 1945-58, pres. internat. div., St. Louis, 1958-61, v.p. of co., asst. to pres., 1958-61, exec. v.p., dir., 1961-64, pres., chief operations officer, 1964-68, pres., 1968-69, chmn. bd., 1968—, chief exec. officer, 1968-81. Office: 1 Mercantile Center Suite 3202 Saint Louis MO 63101

DEAN, TOMMY LEE, coll. dean; b. Trenton, Mo., Sept. 26, 1954; s. Robert Lee Dean; B.S., Culver-Stockton Coll., Canton, Mo., 1977; M.A., N.E. Mo. State U., 1978. Asso. dean students, dean of men Iowa Wesleyan Coll., Mt. Pleasant, 1978—. Mem. Am. Personnel and Guidance Assn., Am. Coll. Personnel Assn., Iowa Student Personnel Assn., Lambda Chi Alpha (charter mem. Kappa Mu Zeta chpt., Wall of Fame award). Mem. Christian Ch. (Disciples of Christ). Club: Masons. Home: McKibbin Hall Dirs Apt Mt Pleasant IA 52641 Office: Iowa Wesleyan Coll Mt Pleasant IA 52641

DEAN, WILLIAM ABBOTT, engr., educator; b. Elizabeth, N.J., Aug. 10, 1942; s. Abbott Bennett and Helen Marie (Grosh) D.; B.Engring., Stevens Inst. Tech., 1964; M.S., So. Meth. U., 1972; m. Betty Gail Goldblatt, Apr. 16, 1977. Commd. 2d lt. USAF, 1964, advanced through grades to capt., 1976; metallurgist USAF Materials Lab., 1964-66; chief photo lab Tan Son Nhut Air Base, Vietnam, 1966-67, test engr. Eglin AFB, Fla., 1967-69, metallurgist Los Angeles Air Force Sta., 1969-71, configuration mgr. Wright-Patterson AFB, Ohio, 1972-76, resigned, 1976; asso. prof. systems mgmt. Air Force Inst. Tech., Wright-Patterson AFB, 1976—; adj. asst. prof. engring. Wright-State U., Fairborn, Ohio, 1974-80. Trustee Forest Ridge Homeowners Assn., 1980—; campaign worker Stevens Alumni Fund, 1973—. Decorated USAF commendation medal with two oak leaf clusters. Recipient Materials Man of the Month award USAF Materials Lab., Wright-Patterson, AFB, 1966. Mem. Air Force Assn., Am. Def. Preparedness Assn. Republican. Methodist. Contbr. articles to profl. publs. Home: 4740 Amberwood Dr Dayton OH 45424 Office: AFIT/LSY Wright-Patterson AFB OH 45433

DEANGELIS, ALDO A., state senator; b. Chicago Heights, Ill., Mar. 25, 1931; grad. Knox Coll., Galesburg, Ill., 1954; postgrad. U. Chgo., Govs. State U.; m. Meredith Roberts; 4 chidlren. Founder, pres. Dial Tube, 1961-65; co-founder, past pres. Vulcan Tube and Metals Co., 1969-78; mem. Ill. State Senate, 1978—; dir. 1st Suburban Bank Olympia fields. Bd. dirs. United Way of Chicago Heights, S. Suburban Surgi-Care Center; former dir. Respond Now; former chmn. Citizens Support Com. Sch. Dist. 161. Served with U.S. Army, 1954-56. Mem. C. of C., Mfrs. Assn. Chgo. (dir.). Republican. Office: State Capitol Springfield IL 62706*

DEARDORFF, DWIGHT LUVERNE, pharmacist; b. Yale, Iowa, Dec. 1, 1907; s. Verne Guy and Nora (Summy) D.; B.S. in Pharmacy, State U. Iowa, 1930, M.S. in Phys. Chemistry, 1935, Ph.D., 1938; m. Mary Bernice Forman, Aug. 29, 1935; children—John Forman, Alan Verne. Pharmacist, McDonald Drug Co., Perry, Iowa, 1930-33; grad. asst. State U. Iowa, Iowa City, 1934-38; research fellow Corn Industries Research Found., Granite City, Ill., 1938-40; prof., head dept. chemistry Iowa Wesleyan Coll., Mt. Pleasant, 1940-42; research fellow fiber tech. Mellon Inst. Indsl. Research, Pitts., 1942-47, sr. research fellow drug standards, 1947-49; asso. prof. pharmacy Coll. Pharmacy, U. Ill., Chgo., 1949-51, prof. mfg. pharmacy, 1951-76, prof. emeritus pharmacy, 1976—; cons. pharm. affairs, 1976—; mgmt. cons. Alcon Labs., Fort Worth, 1956-58; lectr. statis. quality control FDA, Chgo., 1968; lectr. current good mfg. practices Center for Profl. Advancement, Woodbridge, N.J., 1973. Mem. Bd. Edn., Elem. Sch. Dist. 41, Glen Ellyn, Ill., 1957-63, pres., 1962-63; bd. dirs. Jr. Coll. Dist. 502, counties of DuPage, Cook and Will, Ill., 1966-70; mem. citizens task force High Sch. Dist. 87, Glen Ellyn, 1977-78, vice chmn. citizens adv. council, 1965; mem. adv. council DuPage Area Vocat. Edn. Authority, Addison, Ill., 1969—. Mem. Am. Chem. Soc., Am. Pharm. Assn., (pres. Chgo. chpt. 1957-58), Am. Soc. Cons. Pharmacists, Ill. Soc. Hosp. Pharmacists (pres. 1955-56), Am. Assn. Colls. Pharmacy, Am. Coll. Apothecaries, Am. Soc. Hosp. Pharmacists, Am. Inst. History of Pharmacy, Am. Assn. Intra Venous Therapy, Nat. Intravenous Therapy Assn., Acacia, Sigma Xi, Rho Chi, Phi Lambda Upsilon, Phi Delta Chi. United Methodist. Club: Masons. Contbg. author: Remington's Pharmaceutical Sciences, 16th edit., 1980; patentee in field. Address: 238 Crest Rd Glen Ellyn IL 60137

DEASY, DOROTHY BEATRICE, food mfg. co. ofcl.; b. Bronx, N.Y., June 11, 1937; d. Jack and Bianca (Iorio) Federico; student Bklyn. Coll., 1955-56; m. Thomas Deasy, Aug. 11, 1957; children—Theresa, Dorothy. Jr. accountant Peat, Marwick, Mitchell, N.Y.C., 1955-58; supr. A.P. Scafuro, C.P.A., Waldwick, N.J., 1965-73; mgr. adminstrn. Price, Waterhouse & Co., Chgo., 1973-81; mgr. adminstrn. Beatrice Foods, Chgo., 1981—. Mem. Women in Mgmt., Adminstrv. Mgmt. Soc. Home: 211 Lawndale Ave Wilmette IL 60091 Office: Beatrice Foods 2 N La Salle St Chicago IL 60602

DEATER, NED ALAN, ednl. adminstr.; b. Rapid City, Mich., July 28, 1939; s. Harvey O. and Helen N. (Barber) D.; B.B.A., Western Mich. U., 1960; M.A. in Sch. Adminstrn., Mich. State U., 1968; Ed.S. in Sch. Adminstrn., Central Mich. U., 1976; m. Joan E.; children—Shannon, Deanna, Erin. Tchr. Rapid City (Mich.) High Sch., 1962-63, Orchard View High Sch., Muskegon, Mich., 1963-66; supt. Rapid City (Mich.) Pub. Schs., 1966-67; asst. supt. Kalkaska (Mich.) Pub. Schs., 1967—. Chmn., Kalkaska County Commn. on Aging, 1974-75; mem. N.W. Mich. Manpower Consortium. Mem. Am., Mich. assns. for supervision and curriculum devel., Mich. Assn. State and Fed. Program Specialists, Mich. Assn. Sch. Adminstrs., Mich. Assn. Tchr. Educators, Phi Delta Kappa. Club: Rotary (past pres.) (Kalkaska). Home: 431 Aarwood Trail Rapid City MI 49676 Office: Kalkaska Public Schools Cherry St Kalkaska MI 49646

DE ATLEY, JACK HINDS, gen. contractor; b. Champaign, Ill., Nov. 13, 1941; s. Jack Carter and Hilah Maxine (Hinds) DeA.; B.S., So. Ill. U., 1965; m. Judith Ann Reisinger, Aug. 13, 1966; children—Edward Neal, Laura Ann, John Carter, Robert Eugene. Staff acct. Haskins & Sells, C.P.A.'s, St. Louis, 1965-69; v.p. Barber & DeAtley, Inc., Urbana, Ill., 1969—, also dir.; dir. Data Communications Brokers, Inc., Champaign, Ill., Lancer Corp., Ms. America Tennis, L.S.I., Inc. (all Bowie, Md.). C.P.A., Mo., Ill. Mem. Champaign County Contractors Assn., Mo. Soc. C.P.A.s, Champaign C. of C. Republican. Disciples of Christ. Clubs: Champaign Country, Kiwanis, Elks. Home: 1003 Harrington St Champaign IL 61820 Office: 611 N Goodwin St Urbana IL 61801

DE BARONE, ELISSA N., educator, communications cons.; b. Miami, Fla., June 19, 1949; d. Aldo and Elena (Testa) De B.; A.A., Miami-Dade Jr. Coll., 1970; B.A., U. W.Fla., 1972; M.A., U. Ga., 1974; Ph.D., Ohio State U., 1981; m. Steven J. Ring, June 9, 1973. Academic advisor, 1974-77, asst. coordinator developmental edn., Wright State U., Dayton, Ohio, 1975-76, prof. dept. communication, 1977—, dir. forensics, 1978-79, dir. cable TV, 1980-81; advisor The Daily Guardian; cons. Sta. WDTN-TV. Mem. Speech Communication Assn., AAUW, Am. Personnel and Guidance Assn., ACLU, Phi Beta Kappa, Phi Kappa Phi. Democrat. Roman Catholic. Contbr. articles to profl. jours. Office: Dept Communications Wright State U Dayton OH 45435

DE BLAISE, ANTHONY WALTER, pub. works co. exec.; b. Racine, Wisc., Apr. 28, 1928; s. Anthony and Ella Julia (Lockhart) DeB.; B.C.E., U. Wis., Madison, 1952; student Marquette U., 1954; m. Laura Stasieluk, Apr. 19, 1952; children—Loni (Mrs. Ronald Klassen), Renee (Mrs. Richard Dietz). Amy. Staff engr. Kenosha (Wis.), 1952-55, asst. city engr., 1955-59, dir. pub. works, 1959-64; dir. pub. works and utilities Flint (Mich.), 1964—; surveyor, engr. DC Surveying Co., 1953-59. Chmn. Mass Transp. Authority; mem. Flint Tech. Adv. Com., Genesee Metro Planning Com., Flint Planning Com., Harbor Com. Kenosha. Recipient Outstanding Service award Flint Planning Com., 1974; Engr. of Year award Mich. Soc. Profl. Engrs. (Flint chpt.), 1975; award of merit Mich. Mcpl. League, 1977. Mem. Wis. Soc. Profl. Engrs. (v.p. 1964), Am. Pub. Works Assn. (pres. Inst. Municipal Engring. 1977-78), Am. Road Builders Assn. (bd. airport div. 1973), Profl. Engrs. Wis. Club: Kiwanis (pres.). Home: 1602 Linwood Ave Flint MI 48503 Office: Dir Pub Works and Utilities 1101 S Saginaw Flint MI 48502

DEBLASIS, JAMES MICHAEL, opera assn. adminstr.; b. N.Y.C., Apr. 12, 1931; s. James and Sarah (De Felice) deB.; B.F.A., Carnegie Mellon U., 1959, M.F.A., 1960; m. Ruth Hofreuter, Aug. 25, 1957; 1 dau., Blythe. Mem. drama faculty Carnegie Mellon U., 1960-62; head dept. drama Onondaga Community Coll., Syracuse, N.Y., 1963-72; head Opera Workshop, Syracuse, N.Y., 1969-70; advisor opera Corbett Found., Cin., 1971-76; gen. dir. Cin. Opera Assn., 1973—; artistic advisor Pitts. Orch., 1979—; free lance internat. stage dir. of operas. Served with U.S. Army, 1951-53. Mem. Actors Equity, Am. Guild Mus. Artists, Beta Theta Pi. Republican. Episcopalian. Clubs: Carnegie Mellon Drama Alumni. Office: 1241 Elm St Cincinnati OH 45210

DE BLOOM, CARL GEORGE, JR., newspaper editor; b. Columbus, Ohio, Jan. 25, 1918; s. Carl George and Elizabeth (Jones) DeB.; ed. public schs.; m. Betty Jane Ayres, Jan. 25, 1940; 1 son, Gary G. Mem. staff Columbus Dispatch, E.W. Scripps Co., 1936—, chief Washington bur., 1960-66, mng. editor, 1966-68, exec. mng. editor, 1968-69, exec. editor, from 1969, now editor-in-chief; on leave as press sec. to Vice Pres. Agnew, 1970; v.p. O Mag., Inc., 1979—; dir. Dispatch Printing Co. Chmn. exec. com. Columbus Zool. Park Assn., 1978—; bd. dirs. United Way, 1978; trustee, v.p. Dispatch Charities; trustee St. Anthony Hosp., 1976—, Columbus Automobile Club, 1976—. Served to 2d lt. inf. AUS, 1943-45. Mem. Sigma Delta Chi. Methodist. Club: Nat. Press, Ohio Press. Home: 7836 Riverside Dr Dublin OH 43017 Office: Columbus Dispatch 34 S 3d St Columbus OH 43216*

DE BOER, RONALD PETER, psychologist; b. Grand Rapids, Mich., Nov. 12, 1937; s. Peter and Eleanor (Van Oostendorp) DeB.; B.A., Mich. State U., 1960, M.A., 1962; Ph.D., Walden U., 1981; children—Laurel Lynne, Ronald Scott, Michael Jon, Michele Ann. Sch. psychologist Harper Creek and Springfield Pub. Schs., Battle Creek, Mich., 1962-66; counseling psychologist, dept. psychology State Tech. Inst. and Rehab. Center, Plainwell, Mich., 1966-78; program dir. Out-patient Chronic Pain and Stress Mgmt. Clinic, Marshall, Mich., 1979—; pvt. practice clin. psychology, Battle Creek, 1970—. Pres., Local Council for Exceptional Children, 1965-66, dir., 1964-65; pres. Shrion, Inc., Battle Creek, 1967-70, treas.. 1967-70. HEW grantee, 1960-62. Mem. S.W. Mich. Sch. Psychologist Council (past treas.), Mich. Assn. Profl. Psychologists, Am. Personnel and Guidance Assn. Presbyterian (elder). Home: 510 Sherman Dr Marshall MI 49068 Office: 15209 W Michigan Ave Marshall MI 49068

DE BRUIN, JACK PETER, photographer; b. The Hague, Netherlands, May 8, 1923; s. Franciscus Laurentius and Lucy (Pronk) de B.; came to U.S., 1957, naturalized, 1964; B.S., Coll. Chem. Tech., Netherlands, 1941; A.A., Netherlands Art Inst., 1948; diplomas Dutch Sch. Profl. Photography, 1948, U. Cambridge, 1955, McCrone Research Inst., Chgo., 1972; m. Rosamund Hamre-Mertes, Nov. 26, 1977. Owner portrait studio, The Hague, 1948-50; head sect. photography Central Bur. Stats., The Hague, 1950-53; dir. photography Med. Biol. Lab., Nat. Def. Research Council, Netherlands, 1953-57; asst. photographer U. Ill. Med. Center, Chgo., 1957; dir. dept. med. illustration Presbyn.-St. Luke's Hosp., Chgo., 1957-64, dir. dept. photography Mt. Sinai Hosp., Chgo., 1964-68; bio-med. photographer U. Health Scis./Chgo. Med. Sch., 1968-79, instr. med. photography, 1973—, instr. med. communications, 1974-76, asst. prof. med. communications, 1976—, asst. prof. dept. med. edn., 1979—, dir. dept. biomed. photography, 1979—; instr. U. Ill. at Chgo., 1961-65, adj. prof., 1970; photog. cons. Chgo. Med. Sch. Quar., 1971. Served with Dutch Resistance, 1940-45, Netherlands Army, 1944-45. Recipient 1st prize in research photography, Netherlands, 1954, 1st prize in gen. photography, 1954-56; cups in research photography, 1955, 56; gold medal for motion picture, 1964. Mem. Biol. Photographers Assn. (registered biol. photographer 1966, Evelyn Palmer award 1961, mem. nat. ho. of dels.), Sci. Research Soc. N.Am., Nat. Audio-Visual Assn. (asso.), Internat. Visual Literacy Assn. (life), State Micros. Soc., Ill. (life), Midstates Indsl. Photographers Assn., Univ. Photographers Assn. Am., Nat. Photo Instrs. Assn., Soc. Tchrs. Profl. Photography, Photog. Soc. Am., Internat. Photographers Soc., Sigma Xi (asso.). Clubs: Shriners, Masons, K.T. Office: 3333 Green Bay Rd North Chicago IL 60064

DE BRULER, ROGER O., justice Ind. Supreme Ct.; b. 1934; A.B., LL.B., Ind. U. Admitted to bar, 1960; now justice Supreme Ct. of Ind., has also served as chief justice. Office: Supreme Court of Indiana 321 State House Indianapolis IN 46204

DE CABOOTER, PHILIP HAROLD, civil engr.; b. Waukesha, Wis., Oct. 10, 1941; s. Adolph Fredrick Charles and Ruth Johnette Eleanora, DeC.; B.S. cum laude, Marquette U., 1967, M.S., 1971; m. Patricia Elizabeth Sauer, June 8, 1968; children—Steven, Daniel, Kevin. With Wis. Dept. Transp., 1961—, civil engr., Madison, 1967-73, contracts engr., 1973—; instr. civil engring. Marquette U., 1970, 72, U. Wis., 1971; cons. Limnetics, Inc., Milw., 1972. Recipient Fred Burggraf award Hwy. Research Bd. of Nat. Acad. Scis., 1973. Mem. ASCE, Nat., Wis. socs. profl. engrs., Sigma Xi, Tau Beta Pi, Chi Epsilon. Contbr. articles to profl. jours. Home: 944 Derby Dr Sun Prairie WI 53590 Office: 4802 Sheboygan Ave Madison WI 53702

DE CAMBALIZA, NOEL RICHARD, sch. social worker; b. Mpls., Dec. 11, 1934; s. Harold Gerard and Lois Antrim (Abram) DeC.; B.A., Hamiline U., St. Paul, 1960; M.S.W., U. Nebr., 1965; m. Nordis Mae Hoover; children—Brenda, Dana, Blaine, Cheryl. Part-time pvt. practice social work, 1965—; probation officer Hennepin County (Minn.) Ct. Services, 1965; sch. social worker Learning Centers and Remedial Instrn. Dist. 281, Robbinsdale, Minn., 1968-71, Dist. 1, Mpls. Summer Sch. Program, 1971-72, Robbinsdale Sch. Social Worker Dist. 281, New Hope, Minn., 1966—; cons. in field, 1971—. Mem. adv. bd. Asbury Methodist Hosp., St. Louis Park, Minn., 1977-80; councilman City of Hanover (Minn.), 1974-80, mayor, 1981—; bd. dirs. N.W. League Municipalities, 1974—. Grantee NIMH, 1965; recipient Service award N.W. Human Services Council, 1977, 78. Mem. Nat. Assn. Social Workers, Acad. Cert. Social Workers, Minn. Corrections Assn., Minn. Welfare Assn., Midwest Social Workers Conf., Minn. Sch. Social Workers Assn. (past pres.), Minn. Assn. Children with Learning Disabilities. Methodist. Club: Hanover Lions (dir. 1977—. Home: 11625 Riverview Rd NE Hanover MN 55341 Office: 4148 Winnetka Ave N New Hope MN 55427

DE CAMP, JOHN WILLIAM, lawyer, state senator; b. Neligh, Nebr., July 6, 1941; s. Hewitt and Blanche DeC.; B.A., U. Nebr., LL.D.; m. Ma Thi Nga, Oct. 16, 1978; 1 dau., Jennifer. Mem. Nebr. Legislature, Lincoln, 1971—; owner apt. complexes in Nebr. Served to capt. U.S. Army, 1968-70. Decorated Bronze Star. Mem. Nebr. Bar Assn. Republican. Roman Catholic. Office: State Capitol Lincoln NE 68509

DE CARBONNEL, FRANÇOIS ERIC, mgmt. cons.; b. Paris, Dec. 7, 1946; came to U.S., 1979; s. Charles Eric and Elizabeth (Chevreux) De C.; diploma Ecole Centrale, Lyon, France, 1970; M.S. in Indsl. Adminstrn. (Smith award), Carnegie-Mellon U., 1972; m. L. Vercambre, Feb. 16, 1968; children—Geoffroy, Antoine, Thomas, Matthieu. With Boston Cons. Group, 1972-81, v.p., dir., Chgo., 1979-81; chief operating officer, exec. v.p. Strategic Planning Assos., Inc., Washington, 1981—. Mellon fellow 1971. Club: Met. (Chgo.). Author: Les Mecanismes Fondamenteaux de la Competitivite, 1980. Home: 7118 Arrowood Rd Bethesda MD 20034 Office: Watergate 600 Washington DC 20037

DE CARLO, MICHAEL JOSEPH, podiatrist; b. Cleve., Dec. 2, 1926; s. Michael and Anna Theresa (Novario) De C.; student Ohio U., 1944, Western Res. U., 1948; B.S., Baldwin-Wallace Coll., 1950; D.P.M., Ohio Coll. Podiatric Medicine, 1954; diploma Acad. Health Scis., U.S. Army, 1975; m. Mary Ann Geiger, July 12, 1958; children—Dawn, Alicia, Karen, Heather, Michael. Pvt. practice podiatry, Elyria, Ohio, 1954—; instr. Ohio Coll. Podiatric Medicine, 1954-69; clin. instr. Cleve. Foot Clinic, 1954-69. Served with U.S. Army, 1944-46, USAR, 1963-79; lt. Col. Res. ret. Recipient Recognition award ADA and Fedn. Dentaire Internationale, 1964. Mem. Am. Podiatry Assn., Ohio Podiatry Assn., Northeast Ohio Acad. Podiatry, Am. Public Health Assn., Assn. Mil. Surgeons U.S., Ohio Coll. Podiatric Medicine, Am. Legion, Alpha Gamma Kappa. Clubs: Kiwanis, K.C. Home: 152 Hillcrest Ln Elyria OH 44035 Office: 436 E River St Elyria OH 44035

DE CARLUCCI, DONALD CLINTON, capital resource devel. co. exec.; b. Pitts., June 6, 1941; s. Donald Asto and Evelyn Louvaine (Dunn) DeC.; B.A., U. Pitts., 1976; m. Jean Marie Markl, Apr. 26, 1977; children—Allyson Lynne, Lori Marie. Owner, DCA Assos. Co., Washington also Pitts., 1964-69; asst. exec. dir. OIC, Pitts., also Chgo., 1970-78; pres. DeCarlucci Industries, Chgo., 1978—. Chmn. bd. Kids Are Special People Too, Inc., Chgo., 1977—; ward chmn. Washington Republican Com., 1967-69, mem. advance team Nixon-Agnew Presdl. Campaign, 1967-68; co-founder, bd. dirs. Help Your Police Fight Crime, Inc., Washington, 1965; mem. Pa. Commn. for Human Rights, 1976; adv. Western Pa. council Boy Scouts Am., 1975-76; mem. Human Relations Commn., Matteson, Ill. Served with USAF, 1960-64. Republican. Presbyterian. Office: 846 University Ave Matteson IL 60443

DECATUR, IRVING CHASE, III, bus. exec.; b. Melrose, Mass., Apr. 28, 1950; s. Irving Chase, Jr. and Nellie Ible (Bishop) D.; B.A., Johns Hopkins U., 1972; M.S., U. Chgo., 1974, M.B.A., 1977; m. Cecile Marie DeRouin, Sept. 25, 1975. Teaching asst. U. Chgo., 1973-74; mgr. planning and fin. Am. Assn. Ins. Services, Chgo., 1974-77; mgr. banking and fin. industry group Arthur Anderson & Co. mgmt. cons. div., Chgo., 1977-80; exec. v.p. Newcomb Securities Co., Chgo. and N.Y.C., 1980-81; pres. Commonwealth Energy, Inc., Detroit, 1981—; dir. Energistics, Inc., Simply Elegant Creations (both Detroit). Mem. Am. Mgmt. Assn. Mem. United Ch. of Christ. Office: 21301 Telegraph Rd Southfield MI 48034

DECK, ROBERT ANDREW, accountant cons.; b. Massillon, Ohio, Jan. 2, 1910; s. Andrew Auth and Mary Ann (Kennedy) D.; student Kent State U., 1932-33; m. Dorothy Mary Harvey, Oct. 27, 1931; children—Robert Edward, Joseph Charles. Accountant, Milcor Steel Co., Canton and Milw., Wis., 1932-40; with Am. Electric Switch & Goods Roads Machinery, Minerva, Ohio, 1941-66, controller, sr. adminstr., 1957-66; pvt. practice cons. accountant, Minerva, Ohio, 1966—. Pub. accountant, Ohio. Mem. Nat. Soc. Accountants, Nat. Soc. Bus. Budgeting, Internat. Platform Assn. Clubs: Rotary, K.C. Home and Office: 323 East Line St Minerva OH 44657

DECKER, BETH FRANCIS, nursing adminstr.; b. Croswell, Mich., Sept. 14, 1923; d. Frank William and Delta Ferne (Francis) Gray; diploma St. Joseph Hosp. Sch. Nursing, 1946; m. K. Ward Decker, Sept. 3, 1949; 1 son, Rex A. Staff nurse Good Samaritan Hosp., Cin., 1946, St. Joseph's Hosp., Mt. Clements, Mich., 1946-47; office nurse, Deckerville, Mich., 1947-50; staff nurse Deckerville Hosp., 1950-70; office nurse, Bad Axe, Mich., 1971-73; inservice dir. Huron Meml. Hosp., Bad Axe, 1973-77, dir. nursing service, 1977—; instr. emergency med. technicians, 1973—. Bd. dirs. East Central Mich. Emergency Med. Services, 1976—; pres., 1976—; bd. dirs. Health Systems Agy., 1977—, v.p., 1977-78. Served with Cadet Nurses Corps, 1943-46. Mem. Am., Mich., Sanilac Dist. (pres. 1972-73), ARC nurses assns., Natural Childbirth Assn., Mich. Ambulance Assn., Mich. Hosp. Pub. Relations Assn., Emergency Dept. Nurses Assn., East Central Mich. Dist. Nursing Adminstrs. (1st v.p. 1981—), Am. Legion Aux. (pres., sec. local unit 1955-65). Republican. Methodist. Home: 2672 Black River St Deckerville MI 48427 Office: 110 S Van Dyke Bad Axe MI 48413

DECKER, CRAIG DAVID, mfg. co. exec.; b. Port Chester, N.Y., June 27, 1945; s. Frederic Charles and Elizabeth Lorraine (Lutsch) D.; B.A., Allegheny Coll., 1967. With Procter and Gamble Co., Cin. and Mexico City, 1967—, orgn. cons., Cin., 1977-79, sr. cons. orgn. planning U.S. and internat., 1979—; cons. HUD, 1980, 81. Vice chmn. campaigns, City Council, 1977, 79, 81; bd. dirs. Resident Home for Mentally Retarded, Hamilton County (Ohio), 1973-75. Mem. European Tng. and Orgn. Devel. Network, Power and Systems Internship Program, Nat. Soc. Performance and Instrn., Orgn. Devel. Network, ASTD, World Future Soc.

DECKER, LEONARD LLEWELLYN, heavy equipment mfg. co. exec.; b. Lansing, Mich., May 2, 1941; s. Llewellyn Irvin and Alma (Schultz) D.; B.S. in Commerce and Marketing (J.W. Knapp Co. retailing scholar, 1966-67, achievement scholar, 1967), Ferris State Coll., 1967; M.B.A., Eastern Ill. U., 1972; m. Joanne Marie Damon, Aug. 1, 1964. Salesman, Fed. Dept. Stores, Lansing, 1959-63; insp. Oldsmobile div. Gen. Motors Corp., Lansing, Mich., 1963-65; salesman Burton Bootery, Big Rapids, Mich., 1965-67; market analyst Blaw-Knox Constrn. Equipment, Inc. div. White Consol. Industries, Mattoon, Ill., 1967-73, mgr. marketing research, 1973-75, internat. sales mgr., 1975-81, dir. internat. ops., 1980—. Mem. Am. Marketing Assn. (chpt. sec. 1973, talk-in chmn.). Lutheran (bd. dirs.). Club: Internat. Trade (Chgo.). Home: 2236 Seneca Dr Charleston IL 61920 Office: East Route 16 Mattoon IL 61938

DECKER, PETER W., Bible coll. ofcl., former chem. co. exec.; b. Grand Rapids, Mich., Mar. 20, 1919; s. Charles B. and Ruth E. (Thorndill) D.; B.S., Wheaton Coll., 1941; postgrad. Northwestern U., 1942-43, U. Mich., 1958-60; D.Sc. (hon.), London Inst. Applied Research, 1973, LL.D., 1975; m. Margaret I. Stainthorpe, June 10, 1944; children—Peter, Marilyn, Christine, Charles. Advt. dept. Hotels Windermere, Chgo., 1942, Princess Pat Cosmetics, Chgo., 1943; market research investigator A.C. Nielson Co., Chgo., 1944-48; pres. Peter Decker Constrn. Co., Detroit, 1948-60; sales mgr. Century Chem. Products Co., Detroit, 1961-62, v.p., 1962-63, pres., 1963-75; sr. partner G & D Advt. Assos., 1967-78; v.p., treas., exec. dir. Christian Edn. Advancement, Inc., 1975-77, exec. dir., 1978—; registrar, instr. N.T. Greek and Theology Birmingham (Mich.) Bible Inst., 1973—. Neighborhood commr. Boy Scouts Am., 1961-66, merit badge counselor; emeritus, 1979—; mem. Bd. Rev., Beverly Hills, Mich., 1957-63; chmn. bd. review Southfield Twp., Mich., 1964-67; bd. dirs., past pres. Beverly Hills Civic Assn.; bd. dirs. Mich. Epilepsy Center and Assn., 1957-71, exec. com., 1962-67. Mem. Detroit Soc. Model Engrs. (pres. 1958, 62, dir. 1955-71), Chem. Splty. Mfg. Assn., AAAS, Nat. Geog. Soc., Internat. Platform Assn., ASTM, Smithsonian Instn. Assos., Archaeol. Inst. Am., Bibl. Archaeol. Soc., Bible-Sci. Assn., Creation Research Soc. Republican (sustaining mem. Oakland County, Mich.). Baptist (trustee, instr. Bible Inst.). Author: Getting To Know New Testament Greek. Home: 33210 Rosevear Dr Beverly Hills Birmingham MI 48009 Office: 280 E Lincoln Birmingham MI 48009

DECOOK, RICHARD CYRIL, business exec.; b. Detroit, May 24, 1942; s. Cyril B. and Naomi C. DeCook; B.B.A., U. Mich., 1965; m. Mary E. Schwalm, Oct. 10, 1964; children—Elizabeth Anne, Susan Marie, Jennifer Lynn. With Ernst & Whinney, C.P.A.'s, Jackson, Mich., 1965-77, audit mgr., 1972-77; treas. Aeroquip Corp., Jackson, 1977-80; treas. Libbey-Owens-Ford Co., Toledo, 1981—. Bd. dirs. Mich. Space Center, 1979-81; mem. Land of Lakes council Boy Scouts Am., 1976-79; active United Way. C.P.A., Mich. Mem. Am. Inst. C.P.A.'s, Mich. Assn. C.P.A.'s, Tax Execs. Inst., Fin. Execs. Inst., Greater Jackson C. of C. (dir. 1980). Republican. Roman Catholic. Home: 3851 Brookside Toledo OH 43606 Office: 811 Madison Ave Toledo OH 43695

DE COSTER, MILES MCCALL, artist, publisher; b. California, Mo., Mar. 13, 1950; s. Richard Joseph and Jane Delores (Herst) DeC.; B.F.A., Washington U., 1972; M.F.A., Sch. Art Inst. Chgo., 1979. Editor, printer Sch. Art Inst. Publs. Office, Chgo., 1977-79; editor Argot mag., Chgo., 1979—; artist-in-residence Chgo. Council Fine Arts, 1979-80; asst. dir. Word City: Chgo. Print Center, 1980—; pres. Art Equity Inc., 1980—; vis. faculty U. Ill., Chgo. Circle, 1980-81, Art Inst. Chgo., 1981; co-founder Permanent Press, Chgo., 1978—. Author: Scotoma, 1978; Photoaccuracy, 1978; Coloracy, 1979; The Cereal Wars, 1979; Sleight of Hand, 1980.

DE CRAENE, JANET KAY, spl. educator; b. River Falls, Wis., Nov. 12, 1944; d. Gordon Dale and D. Virginia (Biller) Griffey; B.S., U. Wis., 1966; postgrad. Coll. of Racine, 1972-74; m. Dale Phillip De Craene, Aug. 21, 1976. Phys. edn. helping tchr. United Sch. Dist. 1, Racine, Wis., 1967-70; phys. edn. specialist Jerstad-Agerholm Elem. Sch., Racine, 1970-73, tchr., 1973-76; project dir. YWCA, St. Paul, 1977; dir. Adult Day Activities Center, St. Croix Health Center, New Richmond, Wis., 1977-81; tchr. gifted and talented River Falls (Wis.) Public Schs., 1981—; Title III phys. edn. specialist; elem. phys. edn. techniques instr. Coll. of Racine, 1972; coop. phys. edn. tchr. Carthage Coll., 1967-73; spl. olympics coach. Vol. organizer inner-city youth activities, Racine, Wis., 1967-70; del. Wis. Edn. Council, 1968, 76; active St. Croix/Pierce counties Humane Soc., 1976—; vol. tchr., 1976-77; vol. spl. coach and chaperone Spl. Olympics, 1978-81; v.p. Indianhead Area Spl. Olympics, 1980; mem. adv. com. Wis. Indianhead Tech. Inst., 1979-81. Mem. Racine Women Tchrs. Assn. (pres. 1975-76), NEA, Wis. Edn. Assn., Racine Edn. Assn., Wis. Assn. Phys. Edn., Health and Recreation, AAHPER, St. Croix County Assn. Retarded Citizens, Wis. Epilepsy Assn., Kinnickinnic Hist. Soc. Lutheran. Home: Route 3 PO Box 89 Plainview Dr River Falls WI 54022 Office: Route 2 PO Box 16A New Richmond WI 54017

DE DECKERE, DORIS C., pub. relations exec.; b. Grosse Pointe, Mich., Aug. 21, 1926; d. George Joseph and Lillian Anna (Pipper) Clutterbuck; ed. Wayne State U.; student U. Mich. Extension, Detroit Inst. Musical Arts; m. Robert O. DeDeckere, Sept. 9, 1950; children—Robert, David, James, Adrienne. Exec. sec. Recorder's Court, Detroit, from 1968; vice chmn. Mayor's Narcotics Com., Detroit; chmn. Pub. Health Commn.. Detroit, 1970-73; asso. dir. Mayor's Com. Human Resources Devel., 1973-74; dir. pub. relations Metro Detroit March of Dimes, 1974-77, 78—, Detroit Inst. of Tech., 1977-78; coordinator Ethnic Classroom Project at Wayne State U.; pub. relations cons. to community theatre groups, colls. and businesses; free lance writer, 1965—. Chmn. Housing Poor Peoples March for Eastside of Detroit, 1967; chmn. Christian Services St. Matthews Ch., 1969-72; pres. bd. trustees Detroit Community Music Sch.; trustee Project Headline. Recipient Spirit of Detroit medal, 1973. Mem. Women in Communication, Pub. Relations Soc. Am., Univ. Cultural Center Assn., Detroit Press Club, Econ. Club of Detroit, Friends of Detroit Library, Women's Economic Club, Friends of Natural History Mus. Roman Catholic. Club: Breakfast of Detroit (pres.). Contbr. poetry to various mags. and articles to community publs. Home: 4842 Audubon Detroit MI 48224 Office: 20100 Greenfield Detroit MI 48235

DEDEKE, GARY RUSSELL, architect; b. St. Louis, Mar. 1, 1952; s. Russell Albert and Loraine Marie (Roberts) D.; Asso. Archtl. Tech., with honors, Meramec Community Coll., 1972; B. Tech. in Architecture, with honors, Washington U., St. Louis, 1978; m. Janet Sue Arnold, May 27, 1978; 1 son, Robert David. Archtl. draftsman Burks & Landberg Architects Inc., St. Louis, 1972-78; architect, project mgr., asso., sec. corp. Kurt Landberg Architect, Inc., St. Louis, 1978—. Adv. com. Meramec Community Coll., 1972-78. Cert., Nat. Council Archtl. Registration Bds. Mem. AIA (asso. drafting award St. Louis chpt. 1972), Mo. Council Architects. Mem. United Ch. Christ. Home: 8606 Larry Del Saint Louis MO 63123 Office: Kurt Landberg Architect 915 Olive St Room 1010 Saint Louis MO 63101

DEDRICK, WARREN FREDERICK, info. systems auditor; b. Bklyn., Apr. 23, 1934; s. Floyd F. and Martha W. (Warren) D.; A.B. in History, Dickinson Coll., 1956; B.S. cum laude, Lake Erie Coll., 1975; m. Carol Ann Hammer, May 18, 1963; children—Leslie, Christine, Karen, Stacey. Computer analyst Republic Steel, Cleve., 1963-65; sr. systems analyst Eaton Corp., Cleve., 1965-80, supr. info. systems audits, 1980—; prin. BCD & Assos., Inc.; instr. Lake Erie Coll. Chmn. air pollution adv. com. Lake County Health Dept. Served to capt. U.S. Army, 1956-63. Mem. Nat. Assn. Accts. (v.p. membership Cleve.-East chpt.), Assn. Computing Machinery, EDP Auditors Assn. Methodist. Club: Jaycees (pres. Ohio JCI senate). Home: 95 Bryn Mawr Dr Painesville OH 44077 Office: PO Box 6688 Cleveland OH 44101

DEER, E. DOROTHY, adminstr., occupational therapist, rehab. counselor; b. Pitts., Apr. 1, 1920; d. Lewis Hutchinson and Martha (Caughey) Deer; certificate in occupational therapy Richmond Profl. Inst., 1945; B.S., San Jose State Coll., 1964, M.S., 1966. Dir. music and recreation N.H. State Hosp., Concord, 1946-47; asst. to exec. dir. Am. Occupational Therapy Assn., N.Y.C., 1947-48; asst. dir. occupational therapy Eastern State Hosp., Williamsburg, Va., 1948-50; therapist VA Hosp., Vancouver, Wash., 1950-54; dir. occupational therapy U. Okla. Med. Center, Oklahoma City, 1954-57; dir. occupational therapy Central State Hosp., Norman, Okla., 1957-59; indsl. therapist Agnews State Hosp., San Jose, Calif., 1964-67; counselor Santa Clara County Welfare Dept., San Jose, 1967-68, Clay County Health Dept., Liberty, Mo., 1968-70; vocat. rehab. counselor Kansas City (Kans.) Dist. Office, 1970-72; work evaluator Indsl. Rehab. Center, Merriam, Kans., 1972-74; supr. evaluation Jewish Vocat. Services, Kansas City, Mo., 1974-78; rehab. facilities specialist Kans. Div. Vocat. Rehab., Topeka, 1978—; cons. Juvenile Ct., Clay County, 1968-70, Clay County Rural Schs., 1968-70. Mem. exec. bd. Clay-Platte Health and Welfare Council, Clay County, 1968-71, Mental Health Services Corp., Clay County, 1968-72. Mem. AAUW, Nat. Rehab. Assn., Am. Occupational Therapy Assn. (del. ho. of dels. 1955-58, sec. 1957-58), Mo. Occupational Therapy Assn., Nat. Assn. Rehab. Counselors, Nat. Vocat. Evaluation and Work Adjustment Assn. (dir.), Vocat. Evaluation and Work Adjustment Assn. (bd. Mo. chpt.), N.E. Kans. Rehab. Assn., Kans. Rehab. Assn. (membership sec. 1971-72). Office: Biddle Bldg 2700 W 6th St Topeka KS

DEERE, CYRIL THOMAS, computer co. exec.; b. Rockville, Conn., Apr. 28, 1924; s. Albert Bertram and Belle Murdie (King) D.; B.S., Yale, 1949; m. Shirley Ann Scheiner, June 2, 1945; children—Sandra Deere Leinz, Kathryn Deere Bailey. With Lee Paper Co., Vicksburg, Mich., 1949-50, Addressograph-Multigraph Corp., Hartford, Conn., 1950-55, Cleve., 1955-69; with Data Card Corp., Mpls., 1969—, v.p. mktg., 1969-75, sr. v.p., 1975-77, exec. v.p., 1977-80, pres., 1980—, dir., 1977—, dir. Plastics div., 1974—; pres., dir. Canadian Data Card Ltd., Toronto, Ont., 1974—; chmn. bd. Data Card Internat., 1977-78; dir. Data Card Japan Ltd. Served with USMC, 1943-44. Decorated Purple Heart. Mem. Am. Nat. Standards Inst. (1st chmn. credit card standards com. 1968-73), Input/Output Systems Assn. (pres. 1975). Clubs: Interlachen Country; Yale of N.W.; Normandale Tennis. Home: 5646 Interlachen Circle Edina MN 55436 Office: 11111 Bren Rd W Minnetonka MN 55343

DEERY, HUGH GUNNER, ins. and real estate exec.; b. Calamine, Wis., Aug. 18, 1920; s. John Hugh and Minna (Gunner) D.; B.S., U. Wis., Platteville, 1947; m. Jody Mabel Hirsbrunner, Oct. 9, 1948; children—Gunner, Ted, Jack, Tom, Sue, Brad, Chuck, David. Owner, operator Hugh Deery Agy., ins., Rockford, Ill., 1957—, Rockford Speedway, 1959—, Forest Hills Lodge, Rent-A-Sign Co., Checker Flag Room, Inc., Uncle Jack's, Inc., HuJo Inc. (all Rockford); leader seminars in auto race organizing. Alderman, City of Rockford, 1961-69. Served with USNR, 1943-46. Recipient various sales and racing awards; named Auto Race Promoter of Year, 1977. Mem. Assn. Motor Sports Ill. (past v.p.), Ins. Agts. Assn. Ill. (past dir.), Profl. Ins. Agts. Assn. Ill., Nat. Assn. Mut. Agts., U. Wis. Alumni Assn., Lyran Singing Soc. Republican. Roman Catholic. Club: K.C. (4 deg.). Home: 1030 N 2d St Rockford IL 61107 Office: 2401 W Main St Rockford IL 61103

DEFOSSET, DONALD, wholesale paper sales co. exec.; b. Cin., Nov. 12, 1921; s. Joseph Gustav and Alice (Sandman) DeF.; student U. Cin., 1945-46; m. Marilyn Herzog, Aug. 24, 1946; children—Donald, Daniel. Salesman Phillips Glass Co., Cin., 1945-46; dist. mgr. Ft. Howard Paper Co., St. Louis, 1947-67; exec. v.p. Royal Papers, Inc., St. Louis, 1967—. Active P.T.A., Boy Scouts Am. Served with AUS, 1941-45. Presbyn. (deacon). Home: 10228 Thornwood Dr Ladue MO 63124 Office: 1218 S Vandeventer St Saint Louis MO 63102

DEGERSTROM, JAMES MARVIN, health service orgn. exec.; b. Owosso, Mich., Aug. 9, 1933; s. John Marcellus and Emma Judith (Folkedahl) D.; B.S. in M.E., Mich. State U., 1955; M.B.A., DePaul U., 1966; m. Ann Blandford, July 3, 1964. Adminstrv. asst. Sunbeam Corp., Chgo., 1955-61; mfg. supt. Internat. Register Co., Inc., Chgo., 1961-65; sr. engr. Kitchens of Sara Lee, Inc., Deerfield, Ill., 1965-71; pres. Edmanson Bock Caterers, Chgo., 1972; mgr. bldg. ops. Jewel Cos., Inc., Barrington, Ill., 1972-81; dir. plant ops. Copley Meml. Hosp., Aurora, Ill., 1981—; bd. dirs., treas. Credit Union, Kitchens of Sara Lee, 1966-70. Served with USAF, 1957-65. Recipient cert. of recognition, Am. Inst. Plant Engrs. Nat. Conf., 1977. lfem. Am. Inst. Indsl. Engrs., Am. Inst. Plant Engrs. (sec. 1977-79). Home: 8650 N Elmore St Niles IL 60648 Office: Lincoln and Western Aves Aurora IL 60507

DE GIROLAMO, DALE ALLEN, sch. adminstr.; b. Cleve., Sept. 13, 1946; s. Michael Peter and Betty Jeanne (Holland) DeG.; B.S. in Edn., Kent State U., 1969, M.A., 1972; m. Elaine Marie Burke, Apr. 14, 1973; children—Amy Marie, Thomas Allen. Speech lang. pathologist Elyria (Ohio) City Schs., 1969-74, Lorain County Health Dept., Elyria, 1969-74; coordinator speech, language and hearing therapy services Lorain County Bd. Edn., Elyria, 1974-79; dir. No. Ohio Spl. Edn. Regional Resource Center, Oberlin, 1979—; instr. speech language pathology Baldwin-Wallace Coll., Berea, Ohio, 1974—. Mem. Am. Speech and Hearing Assn. (certificate of clin. competence), No. Ohio Language Speech and Hearing Assn., Ohio Speech and Hearing Assn. (pres. 1978-79), Council for Exceptional Children, Council Adminstrs. Spl. Edn., Buckeye Assn. Sch. Adminstrs., Ohio Bd. Speech Pathology and Audiology, Phi Delta Kappa. Editor: Journal of the Association for Precision Speech Therapy and Communications Technology, 1976-78. Home: 311 Crestview Dr Elyria OH 44035 Office: RD 1 15233 Route 58 S Oberlin OH 44074

DEGLER, WILLIAM HENRY, investment adv.; b. Ft. Wayne, Ind., Oct. 7, 1946; s. Harold Edward and Mary Ellen (Frushour) D.; B.S. (Central Soya Merit scholar), Mich. State U., 1969; NIH fellow Northwestern U., Evanston, Ill., 1969-70; m. Sandra Kay DeMuth, Oct. 12, 1968; children—Victoria Lynn, Elizabeth Ann. Dir. fin. systems Nat. Computer Network of Chgo., Inc., 1970-80; pres. Chronometrics Inc., commodity advisement and analysis, Chgo., 1981—. Pres. Elk Grove Festival Chorus, 1975-76, mem., 1973—. Mem. Mensa, Triple Nine Soc. Home: 7902 Kingsbury Dr Hanover Park IL 60103 Office: 327 S LaSalle St Chicago IL 60604

DEGOOD, DOUGLAS KENT, mayor; b. Tiffin, Ohio, May 4, 1947; s. Kenneth and Freda (Ohler) DeG.; B.A., U. Toledo, 1968, M.A., 1973; m. Karen Chapman, 1975; children—Alexander, Kevin. Former tchr. Toledo public schs.; Toledo C. of C., (mgr. Urban Affairs, cons. adminstrv., council for bus.); mem. Toledo City Council, 1974-77, mayor, 1977—; mem. Lucas County Youth Service Coordinating Council; trustee Lucas County Improvement Corp. Served with Ohio Air N.G., 1969-75. Mem. U.S. Conf. Mayors, Nat. Assn. Regional Counties. Unitarian. Address: 525 N Erie St Safety Bldg Room 310 Toledo OH 43624

DE GRADO, BETTY LOU, real estate broker; b. Burbank, Calif., Apr. 21, 1934; d. Harvey Orville and Isabel Marion (Melville) Angermeir; student pub. schs., Burbank; children—James Harvey, William Frank. Sales asso. Rich Port Realtors, Oak Brook, Ill., 1971-76, sales mgr., 1976-78, v.p., 1978—; exec. v.p. Am. Growth Real Estate Corp., Oak Brook, 1979—; exec. v.p. Midwest Club Co., Oak Brook, 1980—. Mem. Nat. Assn. Realtors, Realtors Nat. Mktg. Inst. Grad. Realtors Inst., DuPage Bd. Realtors, Oak Brook Assn. Commerce and Industry, U.S. Power Squadron Womens Aux. Republican. Home: 101 Lake Hinsdale Clarendon Hills IL 60514

DE GRAFFENRIED, VELDA MAE CAMP (MRS. THOMAS P. DE GRAFFENRIED), clin. lab. exec.; b. Kirwin, Kans.; d. George Robert and Laura (Woodward) Camp; student No. Ill. U., 1959-60; m. Thomas P. de Graffenried, May 23, 1942; children—Donna Rae (Mrs. Kenneth George Pigott), Albert Lawrence II, Nicholas Thomas. With De Graffenried & Fisher Clin. Labs., DeKalb, Ill., 1957—, office mgr., 1957-64, exec. sec., 1964—, also dir. pub. affairs. Vice-pres. Haish Sch. PTA, DeKalb, 1958-59; den mother cub scouts Chief Shabbona council Boy Scouts Am., 1957-60; supr. Teen Age Club, Louisville, 1949-50; county crusade chmn. Am. Cancer Soc., 1965, exec. bd. DeKalb County, 1964—, chairwomen, 1970—, co-bd. chmn. DeKalb County unit, 1973-79, chmn. bd., 1979-80, also chmn. ann. Radiothon for Cancer, 1973-80; sec. DeKalb County Soc., 1969-70, chmn., 1970-72. Recipient commendation Am. Cancer Soc., 1965, 75, spl. award, 1974; commendation Boy Scouts Am., 1955. Mem. DeKalb County Med. Soc. Women's Aux. (pres. 1973) DeKalb Hosp. Aux. Methodist. Home: 1208 Sunnymeade Trail DeKalb IL 60115

DEGRAVELLES, WILLIAM DECATUR, JR., physician; b. Jennings, La., Feb. 20, 1928; s. William Decatur and Ara May (Zenor) deG.; B.S., S.W. La. Inst., 1949; M.D., Tulane U., 1952. Intern Charity Hosp. La., New Orleans, 1952-53; splty. tng. in phys. medicine, rehab. N.Y. U., Bellevue Med. Center, N.Y.C., 1953-56; practice medicine, specializing in phys. medicine and rehab.; dir. rehab. service Duke Med. Center, Durham, N.C., 1956-58; chief phys. medicine and rehab. Iowa Meth. Hosp., Des Moines, 1958—; chief phys. medicine and rehab. Younker Meml. Rehab. Center, Des Moines, 1958—, med. dir., 1958—. Med. cons. Easter Seal's Camp Sunnyside, Des Moines; chmn. med. adv. com. Polk County (Iowa) Nat. Found., 1958-65; mem. Gov.'s Com. on Employment Handicapped, 1964. Bd. dirs. Goodwill Industries, Inc., Des Moines, Iowa Easter Seal Soc. Named Physician of Yr., Gov.'s Com. on Employment of Handicapped, 1968, President's Com. on Employment of Handicapped, 1978; recipient Cotton award Iowa chpt. Arthritis and Rheumatism Assn., 1965; award Iowa Parks and Recreation Assn., 1974; Public Citizen of Yr. award Nat. Assn. Social Workers, 1977, Iowa Public Citizen of Yr. award, 1977; Disting. Service award Iowa Gov.'s Com. on Employment of Handicapped, 1976; citation Nat. Therapeutic Recreation Soc., 1977; Gallantry award Nat. Easter Seal Soc. and Iowa Easter Seal Soc., 1978; diplomate Am. Bd. Phys. Medicine and Rehab. Mem. A.M.A., Iowa, Polk County med. socs., Muscular Dystrophy Assn. Am. (med. adviser Polk County chpt.), Nat. Multiple Sclerosis Soc. (chmn. med. adv. com. central Iowa chpt., 1958-66), Iowa Rehab. Assn. (bd. dirs., past pres.), Internat. Assn. Rehab. Facilities (dir. 1973-76). Home: 6024 Ronwood Dr Des Moines IA 50312 Office: 1200 Pleasant St Des Moines IA 50308

DEGRIJS, LEO CHARLES, banker; b. Batavia, Java, 1926; grad. Vrijzinnig Christelijk Lyceum, The Hague, Netherlands, 1943; married. With Netherlands Post Tel. & Tel. Co., 1943-45, Netherlands-Indies Civil Adminstrn., 1945-49; insp. of police in various countries, 1947-63; with Continental Ill. Nat. Bank and Trust Co., Chgo., 1963—, assigned internat. banking dept., second v.p. and head Tokyo and Osaka, 1964, v.p. 1967, head Far East Group, 1968, head Asial Pacific & Africal/Middle East groups, 1973, sr. v.p., 1974, head internat. banking dept., 1976, banking sers., 1980, exec. v.p. 1981; dir. Continental Bank SA, NV Brussels, Continental Ill. Leasing Corp., Continental Bank Internat., Continental Internat. Fin. Corp., Continental Ill. Ltd., London, Continental Ill. Bank (Canada). Address: care Regina Wells 200/24 231 S LaSalle St Chicago IL 60693

DEGROW, ALVIN JAMES, state legislator; b. Bad Axe, Mich., June 1, 1926; s. Russel James and Vera Mae (Harneck) DeG.; student public schs., Mich.; m. Judith A. Haist, Aug. 25, 1946; children—David, Michael, Jane. Owner, operator Ben Franklin Store, variety store, Pigeon, Mich., 1951—; mem. Mich. Senate, 1968—. Served with USN, 1944-46. Republican. Methodist. Club: Rotary (club pres. 1962, dist. gov. 1964-65). Office: State Capitol Lansing MI 48909

DEGRUSON, EUGENE HENRY, librarian; b. Girard, Kans., Oct. 10, 1932; s. Henry Dieudonne and Clemence (Merciez) DeG.; B.S.Ed., Pittsburg State U., 1954, M.S., 1958; postgrad. U. Iowa, 1958-60. Tchr. speech and theatre Highland Park High Sch., Topeka, 1954-58; grad. asst. in communications U. Iowa, 1958-60; instr. in lang. and lit. Kans. State Coll., Pittsburg, 1960-63, asst. prof. English, 1962-68; asso. prof. library sci. Pittsburg State U., 1968—, spl. collections librarian, 1968—. Mem. Kans. Library Assn., NEA, Bibliographical Soc. Am. Democrat. Author: Kansas Authors of Best Sellers, 1970; That Printer of Udell's: A Dramatization of Harold Bell Wright's Novel, 1975; contbg. author First Printings of American Authors, 1978—; Bibliography of American Literature, 1973—; editor Library Bull., 1968-74; poetry editor Little Balkans Rev., 1980—. Office: Pittsburg State U Pittsburg KS 66762

DEGRYSE, CHARLES WILLIAM, bus. exec.; b. Chgo., Mar. 3, 1905; s. Charles Henry and Martha (Doyle) DeG.; student St. Cyril Coll., 1921-23; LL.B., Loyola U., 1927, LL.M., 1932; m. Sara Marie O'Malley, May 1, 1937 (dec. 1972); children—Charles William, Sara Ann, Martha Jane, Mary Ellen, John Paul, Philip Martin; m. 2d, Virginia Gorman, 1975. Admitted to Ill. bar, 1930; practice in Chgo., 1932-36, N.Y.C., 1936-38; gen. ins. broker Rockwood Co., Chgo., 1938-41; dist. mgr. Research Inst. Am., Cleve., 1942-43, div. mgr., Milw., 1943-44, Chgo., 1944-45; atty. Quarrie Corp., Chgo., 1945-46; spl. agt. Northwestern Mut. Life Ins. Co. of Milw., Chgo., 1946—; pres. 1500 Hinman Corp. Lay chmn. archdiocesan com. on scouting area Evanston Council; mem. citizens bd. Loyola U., Chgo.; dir. North Shore unit Am. Cancer Soc. Recipient Sidenburg award Loyola U., 1980. Mem. Chgo. Bar Assn., Ill. Bar Assn., Chgo. Assn. Life Underwriters, Chgo. C. of C., Chgo. Life Ins. and Trust Council, Loyla U. Alumni Assn. (past pres.), Delta Theta Phi. Clubs: Union League (Chgo.); University (Evanston); Michigan Shores (Wilmette, Ill.). Home: 1500 Hinman Ave Evanston IL 60201

DEGUZMAN, RICARDO DOMINGO, endocrinologist; b. Gapan, Philippines, Feb. 22, 1930; s. Victorino Garcia DeGuzman and Pascuala Domingo; M.D., U. Philippines, 1955; m. Dolores Dimaguila, Mar. 19, 1958; children—Robert, Raul. Intern, Philippines Gen. Hosp., Manila, 1954-55; resident in internal medicine Lakewood Hosp., Cleve., 1958-61; asst. prof. Med. Coll., U. of the East, Philippines, 1963-66; chief sect. endocrinology VA Med. Center, Dayton, Ohio, 1969—; asst. clin. prof. Wright State U. Med. Sch., Dayton, 1976—. Diplomate Am. Bd. Internal Medicine. Mem. Montgomery County Med. Soc., Ohio Med. Assn., A.C.P. Republican. Roman Catholic. Home: 5017 James Hill Rd Kettering OH 45429 Office: 4100 W 3d St Dayton OH 45428

DEINZER, GEORGE WILLIAM, coll. exec.; b. Tiffin, Ohio, Nov. 1, 1934; s. Harvey Charles and Edna Louise (Harpley) D.; A.B., Heidelberg Coll., 1956; postgrad. Washington U., 1956-57. Asst. to dir. phys. plant Heidelberg Coll., 1957-58, admissions counselor, 1958-60, dir. admissions, 1960-71, dir. fin. aids, asso. dir. admissions, 1971-80; exec. dir. Tiffin-Seneca United Way, 1980—. Voting rep. Coll. Entrance Examination Bd., 1963—; fin. aid cons. Nat. Collegiate Athletic Assn.; cons. Ohio Scholarship Funds, 1960-61. Pres., chmn. allocations com., bd. dirs. United Way; pres. lay bd. Mercy Hosp.; treas., bd. dirs. N.W. Ohio Health Planning Assn. Mem. Nat., Ohio (regional coordinator, treas., state trainer, chmn. needs analysis com.) assns. student fin. aid adminstrs., Ohio Athletic Conf. Fin. Dirs. (past chmn.), Internat. Platform Assn., Am. Personnel and Guidance Assn., Am. Coll. Personnel Assn., U.S. Naval Inst., Buckeye Sheriffs Assn., Beta Beta Beta. Republican. Club: Rotary (dir., pres. 1982-83). Contbr. articles to profl. jours. Home: 197 Jefferson St Tiffin OH 44883

DEISS, MARY LINDA, ins. co. exec.; b. Joliet, Ill., Oct. 14, 1947; s. Paul Michael and Georgia Frances (Perry) D.; B.S. magna cum laude, Coll. St. Francis, Joliet, Ill., 1969; M.S., U. Ill., 1970; postgrad. Lewis U., 1979—. With Ill. R B Jones, Inc., Chgo., 1970—, underwriter, 1971—, dept. mgr., 1973—, asst. v.p., 1977—. Asst. treas. Women's Auxiliary St. Joseph Hosp., Joliet, Roman Catholic. Clubs: St. Ray's Bridge, St. Paul's Women's. Home: 2000 Black Rd Joliet IL 60435 Office: 175 W Jackson St Chicago IL 60604

DE JARNETTE, SHIRLEY SHEA, corp. fin. ofcl.; b. Bradford, Pa., Feb. 21, 1943; d. James Harold and Jean Lorrain (Dennis) Shea; A.A., Stephens Coll., 1963; B.S. in Bus. Adminstrn., U. Mo., 1966; m. Jaquelin Harrison DeJarnette, Mar. 21, 1978; 1 dau., Shea Ann. Trust officer Boatmen's Nat. Bank, St. Louis, 1966-74; mgr. investor relations and pension funds Kraft, Inc., Glenview, Ill., 1974-77; dir. investment research Cummins Engine Co., Columbus, Ind., 1977-78; asst. treas., dir. pension fund investments Mead Corp., Dayton, Ohio, 1978-79; founder So. Ohio Pension Group; asst. treas. DeJarnette Investment Advisor; bd. advisors Sentinel Pension Inst. Bd. dirs., fin. com., investment com. U. Dayton. Chartered fin. analyst. Mem. Inst. Chartered Fin. Analysts, Fin. Analysts Fedn., Investment Analysts Soc. Chgo., Cin. Soc. Fin. Analysts, Phi Chi Theta. Episcopalian. Clubs: Country of Va.; Wintergreen Country; Dayton Racquet. Office: Courthouse Plaza NE Dayton OH 45463

DE JONG, JAMES ALLAN, educator; b. Paterson, N.J., July 10, 1941; s. Peter Ymen and Joanne Henrietta (Heyns) De J.; A.B., Calvin Coll., 1963; B.D., Calvin Theol. Sem., 1966; Th.D., Free U. Amsterdam, 1970; m. Lois De Kock, June 14, 1963; children—Kurtis, Kristin, Kyle. Ordained to ministry, Christian Reformed Ch., 1970; asst. prof. theology Trinity Christian Coll., 1970-74; asso. prof. theology Dordt Coll., 1974—. Bd. dirs. Crossroads Services. Recipient Christian Reformed Ch. Centennial Missions scholarship, 1966; Netherlands Orgn. for Pure Sci. Research grantee, 1968, 70; Nat. Endowment Humanities grantee, 1977. Mem. Am. Soc. Ch. History, Conf. on Faith and History, Evang. Theol. Soc. Author: As the Waters Cover the Sea, 1970; Soundings, 1976; co-author Landmarks, 1977; contbr. The New International Dictionary of the Christian Church, 1974; Eerdmans Handbook of the History of Christianity, 1977; editor: Renewal; Jubilee: Dordt College Hymnal, 1981; co-editor: Building the House, 1981; cons. editor The Banner. Office: Theology Dept Dordt Coll Sioux Center IA 51250

DEKEMA, KYLE JAMES, distbg. co. exec., computer software co. exec.; b. Kalamazoo, Apr. 15, 1951; s. James and Henrietta (Klein) D.; B.A. in Acctg., Western Mich. U., 1973; m. Jan M. Myers, Sept. 16, 1978. Auditor, Seidman & Seidman C.P.A.'s, Kalamazoo, 1973-74; corp. controller Anderson & Son, Inc., Kalamazoo, 1974—; v.p., treas. Source One Distbr. Mgmt., Inc., Kalamazoo, 1975—, also dir. Home: 507 Montrose Ave Kalamazoo MI 49008 Office: 1480 S 11th St Kalamazoo MI 49009

DEKOSTER, LUCAS JAMES, state senator; b. Hull, Iowa, June 18, 1918; s. John and Sarah K. (Poppen) DeK.; student Kan. State Coll., 1935-36; B.S. in Mech. Engring., Iowa State Coll., 1939; J.D. cum laude, Cleve.-Marshall Law Sch., 1949; m. Dorothea L. Hymans, Dec. 30, 1942; children—Sarah Kay, Jacqueline Anne, John Gordon, Claire Ellen, Mary Denise. Aero. research scientist NACA, 1940-48; admitted to Ohio bar 1949, Iowa bar, 1952; asso. J. Darrell Douglass, patent atty., Cleve., 1948-52; pvt. practice law, Hull, 1952—; mem. Iowa Senate, 1964—. Pres. Hull Bldg. & Loan Assn. (Iowa); pres. Mut. Fire and Automobile Ins. Co., Cedar Rapids. Mem. Am., Iowa, Sioux County bar assns., Hull Bus. and Profl. Men's Club (past pres.). Office: 1106 Main St Hull IA 51239

DEKREY, DONALD HENRY, clin. psychologist; b. Pettibone, N.D., Sept. 29, 1927; s. John and Hannah Fredricka (Begeman) DeK.; B.A., U. N.D., 1951, M.A., 1953, Ph.D., 1962; m. Ione Louise Anderson, June 20, 1951; children—Nancy Lynn, Steven John, Daniel Peter, Elizabeth Ann. Psychology intern Central State Hosp., Indpls., 1956-57; staff psychologist State Hosp., Jamestown, N.D., 1957-58; asst. prof. psychology Bemidji State U., 1958-61; chief psychologist Upper Mississippi Mental Health Center, Bemidji, Minn., 1961—; psychologist Diamond Head Day Hosp., Honolulu, 1967-68; child treatment dir. Gateway Mental Health Center, Pocatello, Idaho, 1972. Mem. Am. Psychol. Assn. Lutheran. Office: Box 646 15th Delton Sts Bemidji MN 56601

DELAHANTY, EDWARD LAWRENCE, mgmt. cons.; b. South Bend, Ind., Feb. 17, 1942; s. Edward Lawrence and Rosemary Margaret (DeVreese) D.; B.S. in Math., U. Notre Dame, 1963; m. Rebecca A. Paczesny, June 22, 1963; children—David Edward, Debra Ann. Asst. actuary Aetna Life & Casualty Co., Hartford, Conn., 1963-70; mng. partner Hewitt Assos., Mpls., 1971—, mem. exec. com., 1981—; dir. Brandt Barringmann Inc. Enrolled actuary. Fellow Soc. Actuaries mem. Am. Acad. Actuaries, Am. Soc. Personnel Adminstrs., Twin Cities Actuarial Club, Twin Cities Personnel Assn., Midwest Pension Conf. Clubs: Wayzata Country (dir. 1978—), Mpls. Athletic. Home: 511 N Ferndale Rd Wayzata MN 55391 Office: 1115 1st National Bank Bldg Minneapolis MN 55402

DE LANCEY, WILLIAM JOHN, steel co. exec.; b. Chgo., June 2, 1916; s. John Richmond and Louise Ella (Hart) DeL.; B.A., U. Mich., 1938, J.D., 1940; m. Sally Ann Roe, July 10, 1940; children—Ann Louise, Mark Roe. Admitted to N.Y. bar, 1941; asso. firm Cravath, De Gersdorff, Swaine & Wood, N.Y.C., 1940-52; with Republic Steel Corp., Cleve., 1952—, v.p., gen. counsel, 1961-71, exec. v.p., 1971-73, pres., 1973—, chief exec. officer, 1974—, chmn., 1979—; dir. Ameritrust Corp., Ohio Bell Telephone Co., Sherwin Williams Co., Standard Oil Co. (Ohio), Beatrice Pocahontas Co., Met. Life Ins. Co., Republic Supply Co., Res. Mining Co. Trustee, chmn. Ednl. TV Assn. Met. Cleve.; vice chmn. bd. dirs. Univ. Hosps.; active Mus. Arts Assn., Case Western Res. U. Served with USNR, 1943-45. Decorated Commendation medal. Mem. Internat. Iron and Steel Insts., Am. Iron and Steel Inst. (chmn.). Editor: Mich. Law Rev., 1939-40. Office: 1707 Republic Bldg Cleveland OH 44101

DELAUER, CHARLES PAUL, mfg. co. exec.; b. Charles Peter and Margaret Mary (Tibaldi) DeL.; student John Carrol U., 1969-71; m. Leona Mary Simens, Aug. 21, 1971; children—Michelle Lee, Christine Noelle. Sr. systems analyst Addressograph Multigraph Corp., Cleve., 1972-76; mgr. info. systems Mayfran Inc., Cleve., 1976-77; v.p. Micro-Base Corp., Dayton, 1977-79; regional sales mgr. Visual Tech. Inc., Andover, Mass., 1979—. Republican. Roman Catholic. Office: 2042 Washington Creek Ln Centerville OH 45459

DELAY, ROBERT PAUL, savs. and loan exec.; b. Cedar Rapids, Iowa, Mar. 24, 1934; s. William Earl and Marie Frances (Mulherin) DeL.; B.A. in Acctg., Loras Coll., 1956; m. Marjorie Rita Hurley, June 11, 1960; children—Michael R., Diane M., Matthew J., Mark T. Bank examiner FDIC, Washington, 1958-63; cashier, dir. Fairbank State Bank (Iowa), 1964; with Cedar Falls Savs. and Loan Assn. (Iowa), 1965—, now pres. Trustee, Cedar Falls Utilities; bd. dirs. Sta. KUNI-KHKE Public Radio; trustee Clay Endowment Fund Cedar Falls Hist. Soc. Served with U.S. Army, 1956-57. Mem. U.S. Savs. and Loan League, Iowa Savs. and Loan League. Republican. Roman Catholic. Clubs: Beaver Hills Country, Rotary (Cedar Falls). Home: 1600 Picturesque Dr Cedar Falls IA 50613 Office: 301 Washington St Cedar Falls IA 50613

DEL CASTILLO, JULIO CESAR, neurosurgeon; b. Havana, Cuba, Jan. 21, 1930; s. Julio Cesar and Violeta (Diaz de Villegas) Del C.; came to U.S., 1961, naturalized, 1968; B.S., Columbus Sch., Havana, 1948; M.D., U. Havana, 1955; m. Rosario Freire, Sept. 18, 1955; children—Julio Cesar, Juan Claudio, Rosemarie. Intern, Michael Reese Hosp., Chgo., 1955-56; resident Cook County Hosp., Chgo., 1957, Lahey Clinic, Boston, 1957-58, U. Pa. Grad. Hosp., 1958-60; research asst. dept. gen. surgery Jackson Meml. Hosp., Miami, Fla., 1962-64; practice medicine, specializing in neurosurgery, Havana, 1960-61, Quincy, Ill., 1965—; mem. staff Blessing Hosp., Quincy, pres. staff, 1972-74; mem. staff St. Mary's Hosp., Quincy. Bd. dirs. Western Ill. Found. for Med. Care, 1970—; trustee Blessing Hosp., 1972-74. Mem. Am. Acad. Model Aeros., Congress Neurol. Surgeons, AMA, A.C.S., Adams County Med. Soc. (sec., treas. 1966-75, pres.), Ill. Med. Soc., Exptl. Aircraft Assn. Rotarian (dir. 1970-72, pres. 1976-77). Home: 14 Curved Creek Quincy IL 62301 Office: 1124 Broadway Quincy IL 62301

DE LERNO, MANUEL JOSEPH, elec. engr.; b. New Orleans, Jan. 8, 1922; s. Joseph Salvador and Elizabeth Mabry (Jordan) De L.; B.E. in Elec. Engring., Tulane U., 1941; M.E.E., Rensselaer Poly. Inst., 1943; m. Margery Ellen Eaton, Nov. 30, 1946 (div. Oct. 1978); children—Diane, Douglas. Devel. engr. indsl. control dept. Gen. Electric Co., Schenectady, 1941-44; design engr. Lexington Electric Products Co., Newark, 1946-47; asst. prof. elec. engring. Newark Coll. Engring., 1948-49; test engr. Maschinenfabrik Oerlikon, Zurich, Switzerland, 1947-48; application engr. Henry J. Kaufman Co., Chgo., 1949-55; pres. Del Equipment Co., Chgo., 1955-60; v.p. Del-Ray Co., Chgo., 1960-67; pres. S-P-D Services Inc., Forest Park, Ill., 1967-81, S-P-D Industries, Inc., Berwyn, Ill., 1981—; mem. standards making coms. Nat. Fire Protection Assn. Internat. Served as lt. (j.g.) USNR, 1944-45, to lt. comdr., 1950-52. Registered profl. engr., Ill. Mem. IEEE (sr.), Ill. Soc. Profl. Engrs., Soc. Fire Protection Engrs., Am. Water Works Assn. Home: 67 Warwick Rd Winnetka IL 60093 Office: 3105 S Ridgeland Ave Berwyn IL 60402 also PO Box 96 Kenilworth IL 60043

DELGADO, JOSEPH RAMON, business exec.; b. Chgo., Mar. 4, 1932; s. Joseph Ramon and Florence (Nelson) D.; B.A. in English, U. Ill., 1958. With Campbell-Mithun Advt., Chgo., 1960-68, purchasing agt., dir. office services, 1964-68; purchasing agt., asst. to pres., asst. to treas. Maxant Button & Supply Co., Chgo., 1968-70; asst. purchasing agt., administrv. asst. Soiltest, Inc., Evanston, Ill., 1970—. Mem. Lyric Opera Subscription Com., 1957. Observer, Joint Civic Com. on Elections, 1965; election judge primary and gen. elections, 1968, 70. Served with AUS, 1952-54. Mem. Purchasing Agts. Assn. Chgo. (co-chmn. publicity and pub. relations com. 1963-64), U. Ill. Alumni, Illiniweks, Chgo. Symphony Soc. (charter). Lutheran. Republican. Clubs: Whitehall, Barclay, Ltd., International (Chgo.). Dance choreographer for various groups and individuals. Home: 900 Lakeshore Dr Chicago IL 60611 Office: 2205 Lee St Evanston IL 60202

DEL GIUDICE, JOSEPH, psychiatrist; b. N.Y.C., Apr. 25, 1926; s. Joseph and Frances (Bruder) Del G.; A.B. in Bacteriology, U. Calif. at Los Angeles, 1954; M.D., Calif. Coll. Medicine, U. Calif. at Irvine, 1958; m. Eileen Finbar Coleman, Oct. 5, 1973; children—Kira Dominique, Guy Joseph, Michael Joseph. Intern, Normandy Hosp., St. Louis, 1958-59; practice gen. medicine, Anaheim, Calif., 1959-64; resident Sepulveda (Calif.) VA Hosp.-UCLA, 1964-67; research asso. in psychiatry Sepulveda VA Hosp., 1967-69; practice medicine specializing in psychiatry, Los Angeles, 1969—; clin. instr. psychiatry U. Calif. Center for the Health Scis., Los Angeles, 1967-69, asst. clin. prof. in psychiatry, 1969—, lectr. in psychopharmacology, 1969-76; staff psychiatrist and police liaison cons. Los Angeles County Dept. of Mental Health, Santa Monica, Calif., 1969-70; clin. cons. psychopharmacology Sepulveda VA Hosp., 1970—; dir. clin. services Los Angeles, 1970-74, regional dir., 1975-78; med. dir. So. Hills Mental Health Center, Jasper, Ind., 1979—; vis. cons. and lectr. psychopharmacology Camarillo (Calif.) State Hosp., 1973-76. Fellow Royal Soc. Health; mem. AAAS, N.Y. Acad. Sci., Internat. Directory of Investigators in Psychopharmacology, Nat. Hist. Soc. Editor (with W.G. Clark) Principles of Psychopharmacology 1970. Contbr. articles on alcoholism and psychopharmacology to profl. jours. Home: RFD 2 Jasper IN 47546 Office: 939 Memorial Dr Jasper IN 47546

DELHAUER, ROBERT ALLAN, merchandising exec.; b. Chgo., July 23, 1926; s. William H. and Elfrieda (Hill) D.; student Ill. Inst. Tech., 1947-48; B.A., Midwestern Conservatory, 1951; postgrad. N.Y. U., 1969—; m. Sarah Elizabeth Horton, Oct. 1, 1949; children—Mark Stuart, Paul Quinn, Rebecca Joyce. Mem. staff food mktg. div. Libby McNeil & Libby, Chgo., 1948; dept. mgr. consumer goods, buyer Biddle Purchasing Co., Chgo., 1949-54, mdse. mgr., 1957-64, asst. v.p. merchandising, N.Y.C., 1964-67, v.p. div. mgr., 1967-74, sr. v.p. sales and merchandising, 1974-76, sr. v.p., gen. mgr. Midwest, 1976—, chief exec. officer, 1978—, dir., 1968—; exec. v.p., dir. Harben Co. subsidiary, 1972-79, pres., 1979—; chmn., mng. dir. Biddle Purchasing Co., Ltd., 1971—; pres. Harben Import Co., 1979—; dir. Centennial Industries, Inc.; cons. Nat. Am. Wholesale Grocers Assn., 1969—. Served to 1st lt. AUS, World War II; ETO. Republican. Presbyn. Mem. Chgo. Housewares Club. Club: Execs. (Chgo.). Home: 5 Pembrook Dr Indian Head Park IL 60525 Office: 78 S LaSalle St Aurora IL 60507

DELIFORD, MYLAH EAGAN, educator; b. Chgo., Nov. 7, 1948; d. Charles Leopold George and Shirley Rita (Bennett) Eagan; B.S., Chgo. State U., 1969; M.A., Northeastern U., 1977; m. Albert Deliford, Jr., Nov. 27, 1971. Classroom tchr. Chgo. Bd. Edn., 1969—. Mem. Nat. Council Tchrs. Math., Assn. Tchr. Educators, Chgo. Tchrs. Union. Democrat. Roman Catholic. Club: Woman's Internat. Bowling Congress. Home: 12151 S Wentworth St Chicago IL 60628 Office: 5250 S Rockwell St Chicago IL 60632

DELLA CROCE, CHARLES ROBERT, personnel exec.; b. Boston, Aug. 31, 1938; s. Albert and M. Louise (Cataldo) D.; B.S.B.A., Boston Coll., 1960; M.B.A., Boston U., 1971; m. Carol A. Cook, May 7, 1966; children—Christina, Charles, Matthew, Andrew. Corporate mgr. employment and affirmative action Gillette Co., Boston, 1971-74, corporate mgr. tng. and devel., 1974-76, div. mgr. indsl. relations, Andover, Mass., 1976-78, dir. employee relations, St. Paul, 1978—; instr. Boston State Coll., 1976-78, U. Minn., 1978—; mem. adv. bd. employer edn. service U. Minn., 1979—; mem. adv. bd. Women's Edn. Center, Lexington, Mass., 1975-77. Served to 1st lt. U.S. Army, 1961-63. Recipient Certificate of Achievement, Jr. Achievement, 1970, Certificate of Recognition Young Women's Leadership Devel. Program, 1969. Mem. ASTD, Am. Soc. Personnel Adminstrn., Am. Soc. Productivity Improvement, Twin Cities Personnel Assn. Roman Catholic. Office: 5th and Broadway St Paul MN 55101

DELONG, BARBARA JANE, educator; b. Evansville, Ind., May 2, 1934; d. John Vickery and Virginia Marie (Polk) DeL.; B.S., Ind. State U., 1956, M.S., 1960; Ph.D., U. Iowa, 1967. Tchr., Mooresville (Ind.) Public Schs., 1956-57; instr. YWCA, Indpls., 1957-59; mem. faculty Ind. State U., Terre Haute, 1960-70, asst. prof., 1967-70; mem. faculty dept. phys. edn. So. Ill. U., Edwardsville, 1970—, prof., 1981—, chmn. phys. edn. div., 1972—. Mem. NEA, AAUP, AAPHER, Nat. Assn. Phys. Edn. in Higher Edn., Nat. Assn. Sport and Phys. Edn. Home: 160 Arlington Dr Granite City IL 62040 Office: Box 67A Southern Ill U Edwardsville IL 62026

DE LONG, DWIGHT MOORE, entomologist; b. Corning, Ohio, Apr. 6, 1892; s. George Washington and Addie (Moore) DeL.; B.S., Ohio Wesleyan U., 1914, D.Sc., 1941; M.S., Ohio State U., 1916, Ph.D., 1922, D.Sc. (hon.), 1977; D.Sc. (hon.), Bowling Green State U., 1971; m. Fanny Merchant, Dec. 22, 1917 (dec. June 1974); m. Aileen Selman, Apr. 1975; children—Joan Elizabeth (Mrs. Robert L. Snouffer), Eleanor Jane (Mrs. David A. Wiedie), George Wesley. Grad. asst., asst. zoology, entomology Ohio State U., 1914-17, instr., 1918, asst. prof., 1921-23, prof., 1923-62, prof. emeritus, 1962—, dir. Franz Theodore Stone Lab., 1936-37; entomologist Pa. Dept. Agr., 1918-21; sci. expdns. to Mexico, 1939, 41, 45, 54; entomologist NSF, Europe, 1960, Alaska, 1964, Panama, 1967. Recipient Disting. Tchg. award Ohio State U., 1962. Mem. AAAS, Ohio Acad. Sci. (v.p., 1930, 32, pres. 1959), Entomol. Soc. Am. (chmn. North Central br. 1960, Founder's Meml. award 1964), Washington Entomol. Soc., Soc. Systematic Zoology, Sigma Xi. Author: (with D. J. Borror) An Introduction to the Study of Insects, 1958, 5th edit. (with Borror and C.A. Triplehorn), 1981. Contbr. numerous articles to sci. jours. Formulation, publs. recommended controls for several field and household economic insect pests; described several genera and several hundred species of leafhoppers new to sci. Home: 1967 Collingswood Rd Columbus OH 43221 Office: 1735 Neil Ave Columbus OH 43210

DELOUGHERY, GRACE, nursing home adminstr.; b. Allison, Iowa, Jan. 17, 1933; d. Ed F. and Alma K. (Kampman) Meinen; B.S., U. Minn., 1955, M.P.H., 1960; Ph.D., Claremont Grad. Sch., 1966; m. Henry O. Deloughery, Nov. 30, 1962; children—Paul Edward, Michael, Kathleen. Staff nurse Mpls. Dept. Pub. Health, 1955-59; research fellow U. Minn. Sch. Pub. Health, 1960-63; sch. nurse Val Verde Sch. Dist., Perris, Calif., part-time 1963-66; community coordinator, nurse in Title I pilot project in San Jacinto, Riverside (Calif.) County Schs., 1966, cons. Title I, 1966-67; asso. prof. U. N.C. Coll. Nursing, 1967-68; asst. prof. U. Calif. Sch. Nursing, Los Angeles, 1968-72; dean Center Nursing Edn., Spokane, 1972-74; prof., head dept. nursing Winona (Minn.) State U., 1975-77; adminstr. Deloughery Home Sr. Adults, 1977—; participant seminars, condr. workshops, cons. in field. Recipient award for research Calif. Edn. Research and Guidance Assn., 1967. Fellow Am. Pub. Health Assn., Am. Assn. Social Psychiatry (treas. 1974-78); mem. Am. Nurses Assn., Nat. League Nursing, Am. Sch. Health Assn., Internat. Mental Health Fedn., Wash. Pub. Health Assn., Acad. Polit. and Social Sci., Acad. Polit. Sci., Pi Lambda Theta. Lutheran. Club: Winona Country. Contbr. to profl. jours. Home: Pleasant Valley Terr Winona MN 55987 Office: Deloughery Home Sr Adults Lewiston MN 55952

DEL RIO, FERNANDO JOSE, physician; b. Havana, Cuba, Aug. 24, 1928; came to U.S., 1956, naturalized, 1962; s. Jose and Carmela (Bernal) Del R.; B.S., LaSalle Sch. and Havana Inst., 1946; M.D., Havana Med. Sch., 1953; m. Fanny Sigarroa, Sept. 12, 1953; children—Fanny Maria, Carola, Fernando Jose. Intern, Columbus Hosp., 1956-57; resident, Cook County Hosp., Chgo., 1958-59, 65-66, Columbus Hosp., Chgo., 1964-65; sr. attending physician and med. cons. Belmont Community Hosp., Chgo., 1961, Columbus Hosp., 1966, Norwegian Am. Hosp., Chgo., 1970, attending physician, cons., Grant Hosp., 1976—; practice medicine specializing in internal medicine, Chgo., 1966—. Cook County Hosp. gastroenterology fellow, 1965; diplomate Am. Bd. Internal Medicine. Mem. AMA, Chgo. Med. Soc., Ill. Med. Soc., ACP. Roman Catholic. Home: 6146 N Knox St Chicago IL 60646 Office: 2815 N Kimball St Chicago IL 60618

DE LUCA, ARNOLD ARTHUR, newspaper exec.; b. Chgo., Jan. 11, 1939; s. Arthur Giatino and Ida E. (Bottigiliero) De L.; B.S., No. Ill. U., 1965; M.B.A., U. Chgo., 1975; m. Judith Elaine Heise; children—Arthur Dominic, Adrianne Marie. Regional sales rep. Diebold, Inc., Canton, Ohio, 1960-62; display advt. sales rep. Calumet Pub. Co., Lansing, Ill., 1961-63; regional sales mgr. Olympic Home Food Service, Chgo., 1963-65; display advt. mgr. Daily Jour., Dear Publs., Washington, 1965-67, advt. dir., 1967-71, gen. mgr., 1971; promotion mgr. Copley Newspapers, Elgin div., Wheaton, Ill., 1972-74, dir. sales, 1974—; asso. pub. Journals & Topics Newspapers, Des Plaines, Ill., 1980—; instr. Coll. of DuPage, 1973—; instr. to newspaper industry, sales seminars and workshops. Chmn., Wheaton Sister City Commn., 1970—; founder Bicentennial Freedom Forest, 1976, Operation Help, 1970, Operation Helping Hand, 1972, Operation Friendship, 1973; bd. dirs. Wheaton United Fund, Jr. Achievement, DuPage County council Boy Scouts Am., 1978—. Mem. Ill., No. Ill., Inland daily press assns., Nat. Newspaper Assn., Internat. Newspaper Advt. Execs., Chgo. Press Club, Glen Ellyn, Wheaton (pres., dir.) chambers commerce, No. Ill. U. Alumni Assn. (dir., mem. exec. bd.), Theta Chi, Lions Club, Glen Oak Country Club, DuPage County Exec. Club, U. Chgo. Exec. Club. Recipient numerous awards from profl. assns., also Outstanding Young Am. award Jaycees, 1974. Author: The Idea Machine, 1973; Newspaper Advt. Sales Tng. Program, 1976; contbr. articles to trade pubs. Home: PO Box 173 Wheaton IL 60187 Office: 362 S Schmale Rd Wheaton IL 60187

DELUCA, RICKY ALAN, meat packing co. exec.; b. Martins Ferry, Ohio, Jan. 18, 1952; s. Lawrence P. and Mildred (Plinta) DeL.; student Ohio U., 1970-72, Jefferson County Tech. Inst., 1973-75; m. Robin Lee Conaway, June 28, 1975; 1 son, Bradley Michael. Sports writer Times-Leader, Martins Ferry, 1969-80, news reporter, writer, 1977-79; editor Company A Newsletter, Bellaire, Ohio, 1977—; with DeLuca Packing Co., Inc., Rayland, Ohio, 1970—, sec.-treas., dir., 1974—; free-lance writer, 1975-78. Pres. Warren Twp. Boys Baseball Assn., 1973-74; founder Warren Twp. Colt League, 1974. Recipient citation Yorkville (Ohio) City Council, USAR, 1979, 80, 81. Mem. Am. Assn. Meat Processors, Ohio Meat Industries, Am. Meat Industry, Ohio Prep Sports Writers Assn. (award 1977, 80, 81). Clubs: Indian (Tiltonsville, Ohio); Upper Ohio Valley Dapper Dan. Home: RD 1 Larges Hill Rayland OH 43943 Office: RD 3 Box 28 Rayland OH 43943

DELUHERY, PATRICK JOHN, state senator; b. Birmingham, Ala., Jan. 31, 1942; s. Frank B. and Lucille (Donovan) D.; B.A. with honors, U. Notre Dame, 1964; B.Sc. (Econ.) with honors, London Sch. Econs., 1967; m. Margaret Morris, 1973; children—Allison, Norah, Rose. Legis. asst. U.S. Senator Harold Hughes and U.S. Senator John Culver, Washington, 1969-75; asst. prof. econs. and bus. adminstrn. St. Ambrose Coll., Davenport, Iowa, 1975—; mem. Iowa State Senate, 1979—. Democrat. Roman Catholic. Home: 129 E Rusholme St Davenport IA 52803 Office: Iowa Senate Statehouse Des Moines IA 50319

DEL VALLE, HELEN CYNTHIA, artist; b. Chgo., Sept. 22, 1933; d. Andrew Jack and Mary Texanna (Cohen) DelValle; student Pa. Acad. Fine Arts, 1952; B.J., Northwestern U., 1960. Tchr. art, math., history, Fla., 1952-54; artist, designer, Chgo., 1954-59; free-lance artist, 1959—; group exhbns. include: Mcpl. Art League of Chgo., U. State Mus., Mid Am. Art Assn., Am. Soc. of Artists, Northshore Art Guild; one woman shows include: Balzekas Mus., Chgo., 1973, Chgo. Public Library, 1972, 73, 75, Combined Ins. Co. Am., Chgo., 1970, 71, 72, 74, 75, Am. Soc. Artists, Chgo., 1971, 1977, also others. Recipient Portraiture award, 1961; internat. award for landscape painting, Switzerland, 1975; 27 merits of honor from U.S. and Europe. Mem. Am. Soc. Artists (membership chmn. 1970—, also dir., v.p.), Nat. League Am. Pen Women (Dingle award Chgo. chpt. 1971, traditional in oil award 1971, landscape in watercolor award 1973, 1st award in painting 1979, 3d place award Chgo. br. 1980, award for watercolor state art show), Mcpl. Art League Chgo. (hon. mention 1973), Nat. Soc. Artists, Internat. Poetry Soc., Ill. Poetry Soc., Poets and Patrons. Author poems. Address: PO Box 958 Chicago IL 60690

DEMANN, MICHAEL MARCUS, psychologist; b. Mpls., June 1, 1932; s. George S. and Mary Hazel (Short) DeM.; B.A., U. Minn., 1955, M.A., 1958, Ph.D., 1960; m. Carol L. Knutson, Feb. 10, 1961; children—James G., Susan M., John P. Mem. staff VA Hosp., Mpls., 1960-61; with Rohrer, Hibler & Replogle, 1961-65; pvt. practice psychology, St. Paul, 1965—; cons. Social Security Adminstrn., Mpls., 1966-67. Dir. Internat. Graphics Corp., Mpls. Bd. dirs. Opportunity Workshop, Mpls., 1962-69; bd. govs. St. Mary's Jr. Coll., Mpls. Served with Med. Service Corps, AUS, 1950-52. Mem. Am., Minn. (exec. council 1971-73) psychol. assns., Am. Legion. Episcopalian (sr. warden). Home: 6513 Stauder Circle Edina MN 55436 Office: 6750 France Ave S Minneapolis MN 55435

DEMAREST, DONALD DEGRAY, editor, writer; b. New Orleans, Mar. 1, 1919; s. Donald DeGray and Ruth Bouligny (Wood) D.; student Pembroke Coll., Cambridge (Eng.) U., 1938-40; B.A. magna cum laude, Mexico City Coll., 1955; m. Elizabeth Curry, May 12, 1945; children—Dana Michele, Ruth, Marie-Noel, John Charles, Jose. Asst. editor Penguin Books, N.Y.C., 1945-46; asso. editor New

American Library, N.Y.C., 1947-50; exec. editor Pellegrini & Co., N.Y.C., 1950-51; asst. editor Mexico This Month, Mexico City, 1952-58; book page editor Mexico City Daily News, 1953-58; Mexico City corr. Texas Observer, 1956-58; asso. dir. Centro Mexicano De Escritores, Mexico City, 1951-58; exec. editor Acad. Guild Press, Fresno, Calif., 1958-65; editorial dir. Catechetical Guild, St. Paul, 1965-70; project editor Ednl. Materials Corp., St. Paul, 1970-71; editor The Eastsider, 1971-72; freelance writer, columnist, St. Paul, 1971-74; mem. faculty Metropolitan State Univ., St. Paul, 1971—; curriculum editor Minn. Dept. Edn., St. Paul, 1974—; mgr. Christopher Awards for Lit., N.Y.C., 1950; dir. 1st Twin Cities Writers Workshop, St. Paul, 1971. Mem. Gov.'s Task Force Cable TV, St. Paul, 1970-72. Served with USNR, 1941-45. Recipient Award for Artistic Criticism, Cath. Press Assn., 1970; Rockefeller fellow in creative writing, Mexico, 1953. Mem. Assn. Curriculum Devel., Nat. Assn. Govt. Communicators. Democrat. Roman Catholic. Club: St. Paul Indoor Tennis. Author: Fabulous Ancestor, 1954; The Dark Virgin, 1956; The First Californian, 1963; Marriage Encounter: A Guide to Sharing, 1977; contbr. articles to various publs.; mem. bd. contbrs. Mpls. Star, 1981—. Home: 420 Clinton St Saint Paul MN 55107 Office: Room 652 Capitol Square Bldg 550 Cedar St Saint Paul MN 55101

DEMARTE, MARK ANTHONY, advt. exec.; b. Chgo., Jan. 21, 1952; s. Michael and Caroline Rita (Colangelo) DeM.; B.A., DePaul U., 1973, M.B.A., 1976. Sales promotion specialist Volvo of Am. Corp., Rockleigh, N.J., 1976-79; supr. advt./sales promotion Continental Grain Co., Chgo., 1979—; communications cons. Josephinum High Sch., 1979-81. Adminstrv. cons. local sr. citizens action club, Chgo., 1979—. Recipient Flair award Advt. Fedn. of St. Louis, 1980; Nat. Agri-Mktg. Assn. awards for advt., 1979, 80. Mem. Nat. Agri-Mktg. Assn., Bus./Profl. Advt. Assn. Roman Catholic. Club: Chgo. Advt. Home: 5029 S Lawler St Chicago IL 60638 Office: 10 S Riverside Plaza Chicago IL 60606

DEMAS, JEAN V., real estate co. exec.; b. Oak Park, Ill., Dec. 30, 1940; d. Charles William and Helen Alice (Kyriakopulos) Demas; B.A., Northwestern U., 1962; postgrad. DePaul U. Coll. of Law, 1979—; m. Harry T. Dallianis, Dec. 8, 1962 (div. 1979); children—Irene Lorraine, Thomas Harry. Tchr., Von Steuben High Sch., Chgo., 1962-65; sec.-treas. Ideal Real Estate & Ins. Brokerage, Inc., Chgo., 1965-72, v.p., exec. dir., 1972-79, dir. corporate relocation, 1975-81; dir. Ideal Realty Co. Mem. Lincolnwood (Ill.) Community Council, 1972—; treas. Lincolnwood Homeowners Assn., 1974-75. Precinct capt. Lincolnwood Citizens Action Party, 1977; mem. Lincolnwood Bicentennial Com., Lincolnwood Friends of Library, Lincolnwood Library Steering Com., 1978—; coordinator Ill. 15th dist. Equal Rights Amendment, 1977-78; dir. Sts. Peter and Paul Greek Orthodox Ch. Sch. Bd., 1977-79; mem. Lincolnwood PTA; den leader Cub Scout troop Boy Scouts Am., 1978-79. Cert. sr. rev. appraiser Nat. Assn. Rev. Appraisers. Mem. Nat. Assn. Realtors, Realtors Nat. Mktg. Inst., Ill. Assn. Realtors, Chgo. Real Estate Bd. (chairperson sales council 1980—), North Side Real Estate Bd., Nat. Assn. Ind. Fee Appraisers, North Suburban Chicagoland Real Estate Bd. (pres. 1976-77, dir. 1978-80), RELO/Inter-City Relocation Service (Chgo. met. area chairperson 1975-76), LWV, Zeta Tau Alpha. Contbr. articles to profl. jours. Office: 3459 W Foster Ave Chicago IL 60625 Mailing address: 6842 N Kostner Lincolnwood IL 60646

DEMASO, HARRY AUGUSTINE, state senator; b. Battle Creek, Mich., Feb. 24, 1921; grad. Argubright Coll. Bus., Battle Creek, 1942; student Mich. State U., 1943; m. Mary Jayne Hocott, June 7, 1947; children—David Ray, Thomas Eugene. Supr., Battle Creek Twp., 1952-65, Calhoun County Bd. Suprs., 1962-65; mem. Mich. Ho. of Reps. from 45th Dist., 1957-66, Mich. Senate from 20th Dist., 1966—; past dir. Battle Creek Twp. Civil Def.; past pres., sec.-treas. Calhoun County chpt. Mich. Twp. Assn.; past bd. dirs. Battle Creek Area Devel. Corp.; past chmn., exec. dir. Calhoun County Safety Com.; past chmn. Calhoun County Planning Com.; past gen. chmn. com. constl. conv. Mich. Assn. Suprs.; mem. tech. com. Mich. Crime and Delinquency Council, 1960—; past chmn. Battle Creek Area Govt. Council. Past v.p., trustee Argubright Coll. Bus.; ch. sch. tchr. Birchwood Methodist Ch. Served with USAAF, 1943-45. Recipient numerous service awards, certificates of appreciation. Mem. Am. Legion, VFW. Republican. Clubs: Riverside Country, Masons. Address: 40 S Lavista Blvd Battle Creek MI 49015

DEMAY, MARY DORYCE, mfg. co. exec.; b. Douglasville, Ga., Mar. 17, 1935; d. Adrian Hugh and Emma Pearl (Layton) Smallwood; student Bluefield State Coll., 1953-54, Macomb County Community Coll., 1963-68; m. Edward Gordon DeMay, Apr. 16, 1955 (div.); children—Dana, Renee, Karen. With Mich. Bell Telephone Co., Detroit, 1957-58, ITE Circuit Breaker Co., Detroit, 1960-65; legal sec. Sol Stein, Southfield, Mich., 1965-70; clerical office mgr. Macomb County Planning Commn., Mt. Clemens, Mich., 1970-79; supr. records and reprogramming The Cross Co., Fraser, Mich., 1979—. Mem. Nat. Micrographics Assn., Am. Mgmt. Assn., Engring. Micrographics Soc. Office: 17801 Fourteen Mile Rd Fraser MI 48026

DE MERITT, DAVID FRANKLIN, fed. correctional officer; b. Jamaica, Queens, N.Y., Feb. 1, 1944; s. Franklin and Lorraine Francis (Steiner) De M.; student U. Ariz., 1962-64, 69-70; m. Karen Jo Mesich, June 29, 1973; children—Scott Franklin, Heidi Lorraine. Booking officer, computer specialist, prisoner mgmt. Pima County Sheriff's Office, Tucson, 1971-78; sr. correctional officer U.S. Dept. Justice, Fed. Prison System, Sandstone, Minn., 1978—. Vice-pres. Young Americans for Freedom, 1970-71. Served with AUS, 1966-69. Mem. Fraternal Order of Police, Am. Security Council, Am. Def. Preparedness Assn., Nat. Rifle Assn. Republican. Presbyn.

DEMETRAL, DAVID GEORGE, psychologist; b. Evergreen Park, Ill., Dec. 4, 1953; s. George D. and Shirley W. D.; B.A. cum laude, Wabash Coll., 1976; M.A., U. of Pacific, 1978; M.S.W., U. Mich., 1981. Psychologist, Stockton (Calif.) State Hosp., 1976-78; behavior analyst Valley Mountain Regional Center, Stockton, 1978-79, co-ordinator behavioral services, 1979-80; coordinator parent and child tng. Inst. for Study Mental Retardation and Related Disabilities, Ann Arbor, Mich., 1980—; cons. Human Services Project, Inc. Recipient citation of Excellence in Psychology, 1974. Mem. Assn. Behavior Analysts, Am. Psychol. Assn., No. Calif. Behavior Therapy Assn., Assn. Advancement Behavior Therapy, Am. Assn. Sex Educators, Counselors and Therapists, Psi Chi. Author: Community Living Skills Scale, 1977; Sex Education Family Planning Course for People, 1977; Different Shades of Grey, 1981; also articles. Home: 1255 S Maple Apt 202 Ann Arbor MI 48103 Office: Inst for Study Mental Retardation and Related Disabilities 130 S 1st St Ann Arbor MI 48103

DEMETRAL, GEORGE DAVID, telephone co. ofcl.; b. Chgo., Mar. 23, 1927; s. William James and Emma Katherine (Hoeffling) D.; ed. high sch.; m. Shirley Wright, Mar. 17, 1949; children—David George, Ann Marie, Dawn Katherine, Dale Sharon. Apprentice cable splicer Ill. Bell Telephone Co., 1948-52, cable splicer, 1952-55, electronic technician, mobile radio and microwave, 1955-67, foreman installation repair, 1967-68, coordinator spl. projects Kincaid, Eastern Airlines, Willowcrest Cut-over (Schaumburg-Hoffman Estates), 1968-71, mgr. constrn. LaGrange, Wheaton, Hinsdale and Westmont dists., 1971-80, Villa Park dist., 1980—. First lt. Worth (Ill.) Vol. Fire Dept., 1956-69; treas. Worth Salvation Army, 1958-64; instr. 1st. aid ARC, 1959-69; active Little League, Boy Scouts Am. Served with USNR, 1945-48, 49-51; ATO, POT, Korea. Mem. Telephone Pioneers Am. (council v.p.), Ill. Firemen's Assn. Roman Catholic. Clubs: Moose, Lions. Home: 12122 Spring Dr Palos Park IL 60464 Office: 900 N Villa Villa Park IL 60181

DEMETRION, JAMES THOMAS, mus. adminstr.; b. Middletown, Ohio, July 10, 1930; s. Tom and Susie (Tsifiklis) D.; B.S. in Edn., Miami U., 1952; postgrad. San Jose State Coll., 1954-55, UCLA, 1958-62, (Fulbright grantee) U. Vienna, 1962-63; m. Barbara Louise Parrish, Aug. 20, 1954; 1 dau., Elaine Louise. Tchr., Yuba City (Calif.) Union High Sch., 1955-58; instr. art history Pomona (Calif.) Coll., 1963-64; curator Tamarind Lithography Workshop, Los Angeles, 1961-62; curator Pasadena (Calif.) Art Mus., 1964-66, dir., 1966-69; dir. Des Moines Art Center, 1969—; chmn. mus. adv. panel Nat. Endowment for the Arts, 1974-76. Served with U.S. Army, 1952-54. Mem. Assn. Art Mus. Dirs. (pres. 1979-80, v.p. 1978-79, treas. 1976-77), Am. Assn. Museums, Am. Fedn. Arts. Author mus. catalog essays. Office: Des Moines Art Center Greenwood Park Des Moines IA 50312

DEMHARTER, DOROTHY ELIZABETH CROW, hosp. adminstr.; b. Akron, Ohio, Jan. 28, 1927; d. Edmond Daniel and Dorothy Josephine (Starner) Crow; grad. City Hosp. of Akron Sch. Nursing, 1948; m. William Charles Demharter, Feb. 14, 1948; children—William Michael, Sharon Lee, Cynthia Louise. Pvt. duty nurse, 1951-53; staff nurse Massillon Ohio State Hosp., 1959-60, supr., 1961-68, Medicaid/Medicare coordinator, geriatric program, 1968-72, adminstrv. asst. to supt., 1972-76, acting supt., 1975-76, asst. supt., 1976—. Asst. leader, then leader 4-H Clubs, 1969-74. Mem. Am. Nurses Assn., Stark County Mental Health Profls. Office: Massillon State Hosp 3000 Erie St SW Box 540 Massillon OH 44646

DE MICHAEL, THOMAS PATRICK, univ. adminstr.; b. Cleve., Mar. 13, 1942; s. Benjamin Patrick and Florence Ann (Morato) DeM.; B.S. in Bus. Adminstrn., Kent State U., 1969; m. Barbara Schikowski, Aug. 31, 1968; 1 son, Christopher. Mgr. food service Kent State U., 1968-69, mgr. food service Kent Student Center, 1969-72, asst. dir. food service, 1972-75, dir. food service, 1975-80, adminstrv. asst. bus. services, 1980-81, asst. to dir. bus. services, 1981—. Mem. Ohio State Restaurant Assn., Ohio State Tavern Assn. Roman Catholic. Home: 506 Silver Meadows Blvd Kent OH 44240 Office: Univ Supply Center Kent State University Kent OH 44242

DEMONTMOLLIN, PHIL, newspaper exec.; b. Jacksonville, Fla., May 11, 1940; s. Philip and Ruth (King) deM.; student U. Miami, 1959-60; m. Dolores Bennett, Aug. 10, 1968; children—Philip III, David. Sales promotion mgr. Miami (Fla.) Herald, 1959-70; v.p. sales Macon (Ga.) Telegraph and News, 1971-77; asst. to v.p. Knight-Ridder Newspapers, Inc., Miami, 1978; pres., gen. mgr. Lexington (Ky.) Herald-Leader Co., 1979-80; pres., chief exec. officer Ft. Wayne (Ind.) Newspapers, Inc., 1980—. Pres., Middle Ga. council Girl Scouts U.S.A., 1971-76, Central Ga. Mental Health Assn., 1977; trustee United Way Middle Ga., 1973-76. Named Outstanding Young Man of Macon, City of Macon, 1974, 1 of 5 Outstanding Young Men in Ga., Ga. Jaycees, 1975; recipient Thanks Badge, Girl Scouts U.S.A., 1976. Mem. Am. Newspaper Pubs. Assn., So. Newspaper Pubs. Assn., Internat. Newspaper Advt. Execs. Assn. (v.p. 1976-77). Republican. Episcopalian. Club: Fort Wayne Country. Home: 5903 N Bridge Rd Fort Wayne IN 46804 Office: 600 W Main St Fort Wayne IN 46802

DE MOSS, FLORA PAULINE, carpet and antique store exec.; b. Martinsville, Mo., June 20, 1911; d. William Daniel and Margaret Ann (Mock) Young; student Central Bus. Coll., 1929-31, Carpet and Vinyl Installation Sch., 1975-77; m. Lewis Redmon Reynolds, Feb. 16, 1939 (dec.); m. 2d, Azriah Clark DeMoss, June 21, 1956 (dec.). Sec. to atty., Bethany, Mo., 1929-31; cashier, hostess Y-Barbeque, St. Joseph, Mo., 1932-39; with Venner Plant, Marshfield, Oreg., 1939-40; partner Reynolds Chrysler & Cadillac Service, St. Joseph, 1941-51, 1st Mercury Outboard Motor & Speed Liner Boats, St. Joseh, 1946-56; boat racer, 1949-55; founder, owner Clarks Carpets & Antiques, St. Joseph, 1956—; owner restaurant, beauty shop, St. Joseph, 1956-80; real estate exec., 1956-78; salesman Royal Neighbors Am., Davenport, Iowa, 1956-79, dist. dep., 1956-79. Charity vol., 1951—. Mem. St. Joseph C. of C. (Women's div.), Am. Legion Aux., Exec. Female. Methodist. Clubs: Automobile of Am., Moose, Eagles, Order Eastern Star. Home: 415 N 12th St Saint Joseph MO 64501 Office: 1206 Frederick Ave Saint Joseph MO 64501

DEMPSEY, BARBARA LEE, journalist; b. Elkhart, Ind., Mar. 19, 1942; d. Robert James Fackelman and Mary Maxine (Oaks) Fackelman Lindley; A.B. in Music, Central Mich. U., 1965; m. James Howard Dempsey, Oct. 16, 1965; children—Julie Bronwen, Jocelyn Lee. Soc. and arts reporter Elkhart Truth, 1965-66, edn. writer, 1973-77; pub. information officer Ind. Dept. Public Instrn., 1977-80; music-drama writer, court reporter Bloomington (Ind.) Daily Herald Telephone, 1966-69; writer public relations Juhl Advt. Agency, Elkhart, 1971-73. Bd. dirs. Montessori Sch., Elkhart, 1974-76, v.p., spring 1976. Recipient 1st place Community Service-Public Affairs reporting Ind. Asso. Press 1974, Sch. Bell award Ind. State Tchrs. Assn. 1975, 2d Pl. Best Series, Hoosier State Press Assn., 1969. Mem. Edn. Writers Assn. Methodist. Home: 71138 Meadow Dr Edwardsburg MI 49112

DEMPSEY, JERRY EDWARD, mfg. co. exec.; b. Landrum, S.C., Oct. 1, 1932; s. Adolphus Gerald and Willie Ceyattie (Lee) D.; B.S. in Mech. Engring., Clemson U., 1954; M.B.A., Ga. State Coll., 1968; m. Harriet Coan Calvert; children—Jerrie E., Harriet R., Margaret. Southeastern regional mgr. York div. Borg-Warner Corp., Atlanta, 1962-69; gen. mgr. York-Can. subs. Borg-Warner Corp., Rexdale, Ont., Can., 1969-72; exec. v.p. York div. Borg-Warner Corp., York, Pa., 1972-77, corp. v.p., Chgo., 1977-79, pres., 1979-80, pres., chief exec. officer, 1980—, also dir.; dir. Nalco Chem. Co. Mem. bus. adv. bd. Krannert Sch. Mgmt., Purdue U.; bd. dirs. Adler Planetarium; bd. visitors U. Pitts. Served to 1st lt. Ordnance Corps, U.S. Army, 1954-56. Registered profl. engr., Ga., Ont. Mem. NAM (dir.), ASHRAE, Soc. Automotive Engrs. Clubs: Univ. (Chgo.); Butterfield Country, Econ.; York (Pa.) Country. Office: Borg-Warner Corp 200 S Michigan Ave Chicago IL 60604

DEMPSEY, JOHN REXFORD, ins. broker; b. Corry, Pa., Dec. 25, 1935; s. Rexford and Lilah (Hinman) D.; B.S., Cornell U., 1957; C.L.U., 1962; m. Barbara Bentley, Aug. 13, 1960; children—Kimberly, Michael, John. Engaged in ins. bus., 1957—; pres. Jack Dempsey Assos., Inc., Ann Arbor, 1968—; speaker in field. Chmn. devel. council Hospice of Washtenaw. Mem. Am. C.L.U.'s, Million Dollar Round Table (div. v.p.), Seven Million Dollar Forum, Life Ins. Counselors Mich., Estate Planning and Life Underwriters Assn. Washtenaw County (past pres.), Ann Arbor C. of C. (past pres.). Republican. Presbyterian. Club: Barton Hills Country (past pres.). Home: 2171 S 7th St Ann Arbor MI 48103 Office: 1925 Pauline Plaza Ann Arbor MI 48106

DEMPSTER, ALAN RICHARD, architect; b. Sioux Falls, S.D., June 20, 1947; s. Adrian Robert and Hazel Marie (Stegen) D.; student Technische Hochschule Darmstadt, W. Ger., 1970; B.Arch., Iowa State U., 1971; m. Susan Floyd, Oct. 3, 1975; 1 dau., Catherine Marie. Draftsman, Spitznagel Partners, Sioux Falls, 1971-72; designer Bennie Gonzales, Phoenix, 1972-74; project architect Spitznagel Partners, Sioux Falls, 1974-75; project architect Van De Walle & Assos., Sioux Falls, 1975-76; architect, founder Architecture, Inc., Sioux Falls, 1976—, also sec.-treas. bd. Vice-pres. bd. dirs. Historic S.D. Found., 1978—; bd. dirs. Children's Inn; pres. Forum, Sioux Falls, 1975. Mem. AIA (v.p./pres.-elect S.D. soc.), Nat. Trust Hist. Preservation, Assn. Preservation Technology, Iowa State U. Alumni Assn. Republican. Congregationalist. Architect: Credit Union Center, Sioux Falls, 1977, Soo Square, renovation of Phillips Block, Sioux Falls, 1980. Home: 1716 S West Ave Sioux Falls SD 57105 Office: 335 N Main Ave Sioux Falls SD 57102

DEMUZIO, VINCENT THOMAS, state senator; b. Gillespie, Ill., May 7, 1941; s. Vincent T. and Catherine (Murphy) D.; student So. Ill. U.; m. Deanna Clemonds, June 23, 1962; children—Bradley, Stephanie. Exec. dir. Ill. Valley Econ. Devel. Corp.; mem. Ill. Senate, 1974—, chmn. Senate Fin. and Credit Regulations Com., mem. Agr., Conservation and Energy Com., mem. Senate Local Govt. Com., mem. Higher Edn. Com., mem. Senate Democratic Study Group, mem. Joint House-Senate Child Care Com. Mem. State Comprehensive Health Planning Commn., Adv. Council on Aging, Electronic Funds Transfer System Commn. Recipient Outstanding Legislator award Fedn. of Ind. Ill. Colls. and Univs., 1977, Legislator of the Yr. award Ill. Edn. Assn., 1976. Roman Catholic. Clubs: Moose, Elks, K.C. (Carlinville). Home: 4 Valley Ln Carlinville IL 62626 Office: Room 119 State Capitol Springfield IL 62706

DEN BESTEN, RONALD WAYNE, mfg. corp. exec.; b. Harvey, Ill., Jan. 23, 1948; s. Alfred and Sylvia Den B.; B.S. in Indsl. Engring., U. Mich., 1970; m. Nancy Sue Tinholt, July 5, 1969; children—Sara, Eric. Various engring. positions, mfg. mgmt. program Gen. Electric Co., 1970-72; asst. plant mgr. Drives, Inc., Fulton, Ill., 1970-72, office mgr., 1973, v.p., 1973-77, pres., 1977—. Treas., v.p. pres. Fulton Community Fund, 1973-76; treas. Bethel Christian Reformed Ch., 1974-76; treas. Fulton Community Christian Sch. Bd., 1977-80; mem. Fulton Scholarship Loan Fund, 1979-80; bd. dirs. Clinton Area Devel. Corp. Served with Army N.G., 1970-76. Mem. Am. Chain Assn., Am. Soc. Agrl. Engrs., Am. soc. Indsl. Engrs., Internat. Mgmt. Council, Farm and Indsl. Equipment Inst., Farm Equipment Mfrs. Assn., Nat. Assn. Mfrs., Nat. Fedn. Ind. Businessmen, Ill. Mfrs. Assn., U.S. C. of C., Fulton C. of C. (v.p., pres., 1975-79), Alpha Pi Mu. Republican. Home: 3 Rose Ln Fulton IL 61252 Office: 1009 First St Fulton IL 61252

DENEVAN, WILLIAM M., geographer; b. San Diego, Oct. 16, 1931; s. Lester W. and Wilda M. Denevan; Ph.D., U. Calif., Berkeley, 1963; m. Patricia Sue French, June 21, 1958; children—Curtis, Victoria. Mem. faculty dept. geography U. Wis., Madison, 1963—, prof., 1972—, chmn. dept., 1980—. Served with U.S. Navy, 1953-55. Fulbright grantee, 1957; NRC grantee, 1961-62; Ford Found. grantee, 1965-66; NSF grantee, 1972-73; Guggenheim fellow, 1977-78. Mem. Assn. Am. Geographers, Am. Geog. Soc., AAAS, Am. Anthrop. Assn. Author: The Upland Pine Forests of Nicaragua, 1961; The Aboriginal Cultural Geography of the Llanos de Mojos of Bolivia, 1966; The Native Population of the Americas in 1492, 1976; contbr. articles to profl. jours. Office: Dept Geography Univ of Wis Madision WI 53706

DENGLER, PEGGY ELLEN, occupational therapist; b. New Castle, Ind., Nov. 14, 1950; d. Grant E. and Mary Alice (Clutter) Stewart; B.S., Ind. U., 1973, M.S., 1977; m. Robert A. Dengler, Nov. 1, 1975. Supr. occupational therapy Parkview Meml. Hosp., Fort Wayne, Ind., 1973-76; asst. head dept. occupational therapy, asst. prof. U. Ill., Champaign, 1977-81; asst. prof. U. Ill. Med. Center, Chgo., 1981—. Mem. Am. Occupational Therapy Assn., Ill. Occupational Therapy Assn. (treas. 1979—). Clubs: Sweet Adelines, Order of Eastern Star. Contbr. articles to profl. jours. Home: 21 Kyle Ct Willowbrook IL 60514 Office: U Ill 1919 W Taylor St Chicago IL 60612

DENGLER, ROBERT ANTHONY, human resources exec.; b. Upper Darby, Pa., Aug. 23, 1947; s. Anthony William and Harriett Josephine (Schneider) D.; B.S. in Bus. Adminstrn., Drexel U., 1970, M.B.A. in Orgn. Behavior and Devel. (Blue Cross Assn. Pa. fellow), 1972; m. Peggy Ellen Stewart, Nov. 1, 1975. Instr. behavioral scis., mgmt. devel. lab. Drexel U., Phila., 1972; cons. orgnl. devel., Phila., 1972-73; dir. edn. Parkview Meml. Hosp., Ft. Wayne, Ind., 1973-76; dir. human resources Mgmt. Americana Healthcare Corp., Monticello, Ill., 1976-81. Served with Adj. Gen. Corps, U.S. Army, 1972-81. Mem. Am. Soc. for Tng. and Devel., Am. Soc. for Health Manpower Edn. and Tng. Club: Shriners. Home: 21 Kyle Ct Willowbrook IL 60514

DE NINNO, JOHN LOUIS, mfg. co. exec.; b. Pitts., July 6, 1933; s. Louis Peter and Suzanne P. (Maurice) DeN.; B.S., U. Pitts., 1956; M.S., Case Western Res. U., 1973; m. Patricia Ann Gaughan, June 6, 1959; children—Karen L., Lynn S., Lisa A., Gregory J. Sr. indsl. engr. Jones & Laughlin Steel Corp., Pitts., 1956-61; mgr. indsl. engring. Cyclops Corp., Pitts., 1961-65; plant mgr. The Stanley Works, Conn., 1965-70; dir. mfg. engring. Warner & Swasey Co., Cleve., 1970-72; pres. Reliable Products Co., Cleve., 1972-76, Crystaloid Elctronics Co., Stow, Ohio, 1976-76, Investors Growth Corp. and subs., Hudson, Ohio, 1976—; lectr. Sch. Bus., Cuyahoga Community Coll., Stark Tech. Coll. Chmn. Library Bd., Scott Twp., 1963. Served to capt. USAF, 1957-60. Mem. Am. Inst. Indsl. Engrs. Roman Catholic. Clubs: Country (Hudson); Cleveland Athletic; Univ. (Pitts.). Home: 2259 Danbury Ln Hudson OH 44236 Office: PO Box 671 Hudson OH 44236

DENMAN, NICHOLAS WERNER, ins. co. exec.; b. Rottenberg, Germany, Jan. 27, 1946; s. Charles Newton and Hilda Metilda D.; B.A., Kent State U., 1974; diploma in risk mgmt.; diploma in claims; m. Barbara Jean Schiltz, Oct. 12, 1968; children—Stephen, Lara, Shaun. Supr., Sugardale Foods, Canton, Ohio, 1967-69; police officer Canton Police Dept., 1969-73, Kent State Police Dept., North Canton, Ohio, 1969-74; claims adjuster gen. casualty Nationwide Ins. Co., Canton, 1974-77, claims coordinator, 1977-80, dist. claims mgr., Cleve., 1980—; mem. adv. com. on security and loss control Walsh Coll., 1981—. Mem. Mayor's Commn. to Hire Vietnam Vets., Canton, Ohio, 1970-71. Served with U.S. Army, 1964-67. Decorated Silver Star, Bronze Star. Mem. Am. Legion (2d vice comdr. 1969-70), Internat. Soc. C.P.C.U., Assn. Arson Investigators, Canton Claims Man Assn. Democrat. Roman Catholic. Club: Masons. Home: 193 Randal Circle North Canton OH 44720 Office: 5626 Broadview Rd Cleveland OH 44646

DENNIS, JOHN, state senator; b. Patton, Mo., July 31, 1917; ed. public schs.; m. Myrtle Pratt, Dec. 2, 1939; 3 children. Pres., Bank of Chaffee; mem. Mo. Senate, 1976—. Served with AUS, World War II; PTO. Mem. Nat. Sheriffs Assn., Mil. Police, Nat. Rifle Assn., Am. Legion, VFW. Democrat. Methodist. Clubs: Masons, Scottish Rite, Shriners, Elks. Office: State Capitol Jefferson City MO 65101*

DENNIS, LUCILLE, artist; b. Terre Haute, Ind., Feb. 10, 1910; d. Max and Anna (Shatsky) Shower; Ph.B., U. Chgo., 1931; diploma Chgo. Acad. Fine Arts, 1932; m. Albert Dennis, Feb. 17, 1946; 1 dau., Martha Lynn. Designer, Edson Novelty Co., Chgo., 1933-40; exhibited in one-person shows Rose-Hulman Inst., Terre Haute, Ind., 1971, Ind. State U., Terre Haute, 1966; group shows Hoosier Salon, Indpls., Ind. Artists Club, Inc., Indpls., 1981, Ind. Realists, Swope Art Gallery, Terre Haute, 1980, Evansville Tri-State, Sheldon Swope Art Gallery, many others, 1945-81; represented in permanent collections including Psi Iota Sorority, Ind. U., Bloomington, numerous pvt. collections; work in Artists U.S.A., 1976-78. Bd. dirs. Y-Teen Activities, YWCA, 1966-67. Recipient E. Kirk McKinney merit award Hoosier Salon, Indpls., 1967, Psi Iota Purchase award, 1971. Mem. Ind. Artists Club, Nat. League Am. Pen Women, Ind. Realists Artists, Ind. Heritage Arts, Nat. Lit. Soc., Fedn. Jewish Women, Vigo County Mental Health Assn., Hoosier Salon Patrons Assn., U. Chgo. Alumni Assn. (life). Home: 710 S 8th St Terre Haute IN 47807

DENNISON, KUMPOL, surgeon; b. Pattani, Thailand, Feb. 20, 1939; s. Kamol and Payom (Poonsombat) Dhanasene; came to U.S., 1966, naturalized, 1976; M.D., U. Med. Sci., Bangkok, Thailand, 1963; m. Lourdes G. Madayag, Feb. 16, 1967; children—Paul, Marissa, Gary. Intern, Grace Hosp., Detroit, 1966-67, resident in gen. surgery, 1967-71; fellow in cardiovascular surgery William Beaumont Hosp., Royal Oak, Mich., 1971-72; practice medicine specializing in surgery, Merrillville, Ind., 1972—. Fellow A.C.S.; mem. Ind. State, Lake County med. socs. Buddhist. Clubs: Youche Country, Gary Country. Home: 12603 Van Buren St Crown Point IN 46307 Office: 8695 Connecticut St Suite D Merrillville IN 46410

DENNY, FREDERICK GAIL, stone co. exec.; b. Harrisburg, Ill., Mar. 22, 1940; s. James Gail and Nell M (Nagle) D.; student So. Ill. U., 1957; m. Sherra Lynn Geltosky, Dec. 12, 1959; children—Jeffery Gail, Frederick Brett. Operator Fred Denny Trucking Co., Harrisburg, 1958-68; partner Denny & Church Excavating Co., 1967-75; sec.-treas. Gail Denny Trucking Co., Inc., Harrisburg, 1970—, Denny & Simpson Stone Co., Inc., 1960—; partner Colonial Devel. Co., 1971-76, Saline River Devel. Co., 1978—, Worldwide Constrn. Co., Harrisburg, 1978—, Rosann Mining Corp., Manila, Philippines, 1981—; chmn. bd. Colonial Recreation and Mobil Home Sales, Inc., Harrisburg, 1972-76; pres. D and S Coal Co. Inc., Madisonville, Ky., 1976-80, Tri-Lakes Investment, Inc., 1973—, Equality Mining Co., Harrisburg, 1977—, Gail Denny Trucking of Ky., Madisonville, 1980—; co-owner Gray Plaza Motel, Harrisburg, Ill., 1978—; v.p. Horses Unltd. mag., 1973-74; sec. Bob Barnett Redi-Mix, Harrisburg, 1976—, Big Ridge Coal Co., Harrisburg, 1977—; treas. Am. Mining Installations, 1977-80; dir. Hardin County Materials, Inc., 1973—. Pres. Egyptian Truck Owners Assn., 1970. Elk. Home: 10 Dogwood Pl Harrisburg IL 62946 Office: Rural Route 2 Harrisburg IL 62946

DENONN, CHARLES EDWARD, air force officer; b. Hempstead, N.Y., June 2, 1942; s. Charles Lester and Viola Jeanette (Stiner) D.; B.Th. with highest honors, Bapt. Bible Sem., Johnson City, N.Y., 1965; B.A. in Linguistics, SUNY, Binghamton, 1967; M.S. in Econs., S.D. State U., 1973; postgrad. in history Black Hills State Coll., 1974-76; m. Ruth Ellen Andrews, Aug. 15, 1964. Commd. 2d. lt. U.S. Air Force, 1967, advanced through grades to maj., 1979; served Ground Electronics Engring. Installation Agy., McClellan AFB, Calif., 1968-69, Viet Nam, 1969-70; missile combat crew comdr., instr. Ellsworth AFB, S.D., 1970-73, alt. positive control code custodian, 1973-75, codes div. sr. instr., 1975-76; asst. prof. aerospace studies Air Force ROTC, Ill. Inst. Tech., Chgo., 1976—. Exec. dir. Chgo. USO Mil. Social Recreation Council, 1976—. Decorated Republic of Viet Nam Galantry Cross with palm, Civic Action medal, Campaign medal, Meritorious Service medal, USAF Commendation medal with oak leaf cluster; named Air Force ROTC recruiter of yr., Ohio Valley, 1977, Ill., 1977. Mem. Nat. Hon. Soc., Air Force Assn., Res. Officers Assn., Alpha Gamma Epsilon. Baptist. Club: Oak Park Ski. Guest Black Viewpoint Talk Show sta. WBMX, 1977. Office: AFROTC Detachment 195 Illinois Institute of Technology Chicago IL 60616

DENOYER, ARSENE J., former community relations exec.; b. Limestone Twp., Kankakee County, Ill., Dec. 21, 1904; s. Arsene and Julia (Clark) D.; student parochial schs. of Kankakee and Bourbonnais, Ill. Field dir. Am. Nat. Red Cross, 1943-48; sales United Educators, Inc., 1932-42, community relations, 1948-63, asst. treas., community relations director, 1963-81; asst. treas. Book House for Children, 1963-81. Bd. dirs. NCCJ; past pres. Chgo. Civitan Club; chmn. Lake County chpt. ARC, Lake County Adv. Bd. for Spl. Edn.; mem. Ill. Gov.'s Adv. Bd. for Devel. Disabilities, Commn. for Interstate Edn. Served as 1st sgt. USAAF, 1942-43. Mem. Am. C. of C. Execs., Chairs of Pvt. Enterprise, D.A.V. (life), Ill. Assn. C. of C. Execs., Chgo. Assn. Commerce and Industry (govtl. affairs com., mass transp. com.), Waukegan-Lake County C. of C. Club: Swedish Glee (Waukegan). Home: 805 Baldwin Ave Waukegan IL 60085

DENTON, ALTA PATRICIA, univ. personnel ofcl.; b. St. Joseph, Mo., Jan. 4, 1936; d. Don Virgle and Gladys (Dutton) Denton; B.S., Oklahoma City U., 1958; postgrad. U. Chgo., 1958-59. Interviewer, counselor pub. co. Reuben H. Donnelley Corp., Chgo., 1961-62; employment mgr. U. Ill. at Chicago Circle and Med. Center, 1965-68, asso. dir. orgn. devel., 1980—; employment mgr. U. Ill. Med. Center, Chgo., 1962-65, 68-72, asso. dir. personnel services, 1972-80, mgr. human resource devel., 1979-80. Mem. bus. adv. council Jones Comml. High Sch., 1967-79, mem. ednl. council, 1970-71; mem. Gamma Phi Beta Endowment Loan Bd., 1972—. Mem. Coll. and U. Personnel Assn. (dir. 1971-73, chmn. 1970-71, communications adv. com. 1972-75; mem. EEO council), Soc. Personnel Adminstrs. (treas. 1972), Internat. Assn. Personnel Women (conf. chmn. 1974), Women in Personnel (pres. Chgo. affiliate 1970-71), Chgo. Hosp. Personnel Mgmt. Assn. (sec. 1967-68), Gamma Phi Beta (Lindsey Barbee nat. fellow 1958, treas. Glen Ellyn, Ill. alumnae 1981-82). Presbyterian. Home: 747 Willis St Glen Ellyn IL 60137 Office: 808 S Wood St Chicago IL 60612

DENTON, EUGENE HAROLD, city ofcl.; b. St. Joseph, Mo., Nov. 13, 1933; s. Albert Walter and Bertha Lenore (Dittemore) D.; B.A., U. Mo., 1955; M.Pub.Adminstrn., U. Kans., 1965; postgrad. (Fulbright scholar), U. Cologne (Germany), 1959-60; married; children—Regena, Walter. Newswriter, St. Joseph Gazette, 1951-52, Sta. KFEQ-AM-TV, St. Joseph, 1955-56; with research and budget dept. City of Ft. Worth, 1960-63; asst. to city mgr., 1963-68; asst. city mgr. City of Dallas, 1968-76; city mgr. City of Wichita (Kans.), 1976—. Served as officer U.S. Army, 1956-57. Mem. Am. Soc. Public Adminstrn., Internat. City Mgmt. Assn., Phi Beta Kappa, Pi Sigma Alpha. Office: Office of City Mgr City Hall 455 N Main St Wichita KS 67202

DENTON, LIONEL ARTHUR, electronics co. exec.; b. Columbus, Ohio, Dec. 1, 1922; s. Arthur Samuel and Florence Nathalia (Harrington) D.; B.S., Ohio State U., 1948; m. Frances Louise Vaughan, Apr. 7, 1943. Sec.-treas. Ohio Semicondrs., Inc., Columbus, 1956-62; pres. Halmar Electronics, Inc., Columbus, 1962—; dir. Ohio Semitronics, Inc., Columbus; trustee Blue Cross Central Ohio. Vice chmn. United Way Franklin County, 1973; mem. exec. bd. Central Ohio council Boy Scouts Am.; trustee, treas. Mercy Hosp., Columbus; adv. council Columbus dist. SBA. Served with USAF, 1943-45. Mem. NAM, Ohio Mfrs. Assn., Newcomen Soc. N. Am., Columbus Indsl. Assn. (pres. 1973-74), Columbus C. of C., Ohio State U. Assn., Delta Sigma Pi. Presbyn. Rotarian. Home: 952 Amberly Pl Columbus OH 43220 Office: 900 N Hague Ave Columbus OH 43204

DENTON, RAY DOUGLAS, ins. co. exec.; b. Lake City, Ark., May 16, 1937; s. Ray Dudney and Edna Lorraine (Roe) D.; B.A., U. Mich., 1964, postgrad., 1969-70; J.D., Wayne State U., 1969, postgrad., 1964-65; m. Cheryl Emma Borchardt, Mar. 9, 1964; children—Ray D., Derek St. Clair, Carter Lee. Claims rep. Hartford Ins. Co., Crum & Forster, Detroit, and Am. Claims, Chgo., 1962-73; partner Chgo. Metro Claims, Oak Park, Ill., 1974-75; founder, pres. Ray D. Denton & Assos., Hinsdale, Ill., 1975—. Mem. Pi Kappa Alpha, Phi Alpha Delta. Home: 25 N Stone LaGrange IL 60525 Office: 120 E Ogden St Hinsdale IL 60521

DEORE, JAMES HART, assn. exec.; b. Connellsville, Pa., Feb. 9, 1944; s. James F. and Rita H. (Hart) DeO.; B.A. in Psychology, St. Vincent Coll., Latrobe, Pa., 1965; postgrad. in Clin. Psychology, W.Va. U., 1966; M.S. in Rehab. Services Adminstrn., DePaul U., 1969; m. June Williams, May 24, 1969; children—Jeanine, James, Jeffrey. Workshop supr. Jewish Vocat. Service, Chgo., 1966-68; program dir. Countryside Center for the Handicapped, Barrington, Ill., 1968-73; exec. dir. Ray Graham Assn. for the Handicapped, Elmhurst, Ill., 1973—, Found. for the Handicapped, Elmhurst, 1975—; mem. Gov.'s Com. for the Handicapped; grad. faculty DePaul U., Chgo., leader workshops in field. Mem. Roselle (Ill.) Bd. Edn., 1980—. Recipient P.J. Trevethan award Ray Graham Assn./DePaul U. Dept. Rehab. Adminstrn., 1980. Mem. Nat. Rehab. Assn. (adminstrv. and supervision div.), Ill. Rehab. Assn., Ill. Assn. Rehab. Facilities (treas. bd. dirs., 1977), Ill. Assn. Retarded Citizens (exec. dir.'s com.). Roman Catholic. Contbr. writings in field to profl. publs. Home: 155 E Granville Roselle IL 60172 Office: 970 N Oaklawn Elmhurst IL 60126

DEPEW, EDDIE GERALD, chem. co. exec.; b. East Bernstadt, Ky., Aug. 13, 1940; s. Charles Hughes and Nannie Kathleen (Hibbard) D.; B. Indsl. Engring., Gen. Motors Inst., 1963; M.B.A., Miami U., Oxford, Ohio, 1967; m. Carolyn Lee Stoppiello, May 16, 1964; children—Dawn Annette, Deena Marie. Process engr., methods engr. Delco Moraine div. Gen. Motors Corp., Dayton, Ohio, 1958-67; indsl. engr. Monsanto Research Corp., Miamisburg, Ohio, 1967-71, data processing sr. systems analyst, 1971-75, applications devel. mgr., 1975-78, mgr. data processing devel., 1979—; mgr. industries profl. group, applications systems div. Guide Internat. Corp., Chgo., 1977-78, sub-div. mgr. Industry Applications-Systems Devel. div., 1979—. Mem. Am. Prodn. Inventory Control Soc., Soc. Mfg. Engrs., Assn. Computing Machinery. Republican. Home: 1302 McGuire St E Miamisburg OH 45342 Office: PO Box 32 Miamisburg OH 45342

DERJANECZ, JANOS JOHN, surgeon; b. Peterhida, Hungry, Dec. 11, 1927; s. Derjanecz and Gerdelus (Margit) D.; came to Can., 1960, naturalized, 1966; M.D. (hon.) U. Pecs; m. Brenda Bellamy, Feb. 1st. 1963; children—Anna, Catherine Suzanne. Intern, St. George Hosp., 1953-54; resident, Eng. and Can., 1959-63; practice gen. surgery; mem. staff Stvenson Meml. Hosp. Alliston, Ont., Can., 1966—; demonstrator Inst. Physiology U. Pecs, 1950-54. Fellow Internat. Coll. Surgeons. Diplomate Internat. Bd. Proctology. Mem. Can., Ont. med. assns. Roman Catholic. Author numerous publs. in field. Home: 142 Victoria St W Alliston ON Canada Office: 146 Victoria St W Alliston ON Canada

DERNER, CAROL ANN NIEDHAMMER (MRS. GEORGE B. DERNER), librarian; b. Evansville, Ind., May 12, 1934; d. Jacob Christopher and Catherine Loretta (Grant) Niedhammer; B.A. in Am. Lit., Ind. U., 1956, M.A. in Library Sci., 1958; m. George B. Derner, May 4, 1957. Bookmobile librarian Gary (Ind.) Pub. Library, 1956-57, young adult librarian, head popular library, head extension dept., 1963-67; children's librarian Bloomington (Ind.) Pub. Library, 1958-59, Pub. Libraries Lake County, Ind., 1959-60; high sch. librarian Valparaiso (Ind.), 1960-63, then librarian Gary Pub. Library; head librarian Elmwood Park (Ill.) Pub. Library, 1968-76; asst. dir. Lake County Pub. Library, Merrillville, Ind., 1976—. Pres., YWCA, Gary, 1966-67; bd. dirs. League Women Voters, Elmwood Park, 1970-76. Mem. Am., Ill. (sec. pub. library sect. 1973-74), Ind. library assns., Ind. U. Grad. Library Sch. Alumni Assn. (bd. dirs. 1978-80), Northwest Ind. Women's Network, Library Adminstrs. Conf. No. Ill. (sec. 1971-72). Club: Altrusa of No. Cook (dir. 1975-76). Home: 1749 W 56th Ave Merrillville IN 46410 Office: 1919 W Lincoln Hwy Merrillville IN 46410

DE ROSA, ANTHONY SALVATORE, food broker, cons.; b. Chgo., Jan. 1, 1928; s. Salvatore and Margherita (Sanmarco) DeR.; grad. high sch.; children—Salvatore, Anthony, Ross. Asst. supt. Globe Auto Glass, 1951-53; sales mgr. Bunge Bros. Fuel Co., 1955-59; supr. Amfood Industries, Inc. (formerly Henry's Drive-In, Inc.), 1959-60, v.p., 1960-68, exec. v.p., 1968—, pres., 1970, chmn bd., 1972-81; owner Sigrid Sales & Mktg. Inc., sales reps., brokers, cons. to food service industry, 1981—. Served with USNR, 1945-46. Recipient Civic Leadership award Am. Jewish Co., 1979. Mem. Nat. Assn. Rev. Appraisers, Am. Assn. Cert. Appraisers, Appraisers Info. Center. Inventor ventilating system. Home: 2617 Knob Hill Rd McHenry IL 60050

DERR, JOHN FREDERICK, health care products co. exec.; b. Chgo., Aug. 23, 1936; s. Annette Bahlow D.; student Purdue U., 1954-58, Ind. U., 1970-71, Columbia U., 1972; m. Polly Laughlin Pease, Sept. 7, 1963; children—Deborah L., Jennifer B. Projects mgr., hosp. group product mgr., dir. hosp. market planning, dir. products and systems devel. E.R. Squibb & Sons, Princeton, N.J., 1966-74; v.p. mktg. Searle Diagnostics, Des Plaines, Ill., 1974-76, v.p. imaging mktg. products group, gen. mgr. sales/service div., 1977-79, dir. sales and service, 1979; v.p. med. systems div., mgr. nuclear and ultrasound div. Siemens Co., Iselin, N.J., 1980; sr. v.p. internat. mktg. Nat. Med. Enterprise, Los Angeles, 1981—. Mem. exec. bd. Ind. Grad. Sch. Bus., 1970—. Served with USNR, 1959-63; capt. Res. Mem. Am. Mktg. Assn., Naval Res. Assn., Soc. Nuclear Medicine, U.S.-Arab C. of C. Republican. Presbyterian. Home: 213 Knoxboro Ln Barrington IL 60010 Office: 2901 28th St Santa Monica CA 90405

DERRINGER, GEORGE CARL, statistician; b. Pitts., June 1, 1940; s. George Joseph and Catherine (Lederer) D.; student Carnegie Mellon U., 1958-61; B.S., U. Akron, 1966, M.S. in Polymer Chemistry, 1970, M.S. in Stats., 1975; children—Sean, Timothy, Regan. Chemist, Am. Hard Rubber Co, Akron, Ohio, 1962-65; research chemist, statistician PPG Industries, Inc., Barberton, Ohio, 1965-75; sr. statistician Union Carbide Corp., South Charleston, W.Va., 1976; prin. research scientist Battelle Meml. Inst., Columbus, 1976—. Mem. Am. Chem. Soc., Am. Statis. Assn., AAAS, N.Y. Acad. Scis. Contbr. articles to profl. jours. Home: 4511 Loos Circle East Columbus OH 43214 Office: Battelle Memorial Institute 505 King Ave Columbus OH 43201

DERRY, CHARLES DALE, TV exec.; b. Detroit, Dec. 13, 1941; s. Charles Louis and Samuella Stanley (Dale) D.; B.A., U. Detroit, 1965; postgrad. Wayne State U., 1966-67; m. Patricia Ann Sitek, Aug. 8, 1969. Chief photographer, producer, dir. U. Detroit TV Centre, 1961-65; engr. sta. WXYZ-TV, Detroit, 1964, stage mgr., 1968—; asso. dir. audio visual communication U. Detroit Sch. Dentistry, 1965-66; engr. sta. WKBD-TV, Detroit, 1966-68. Freelance dir., producer, photographer; TV cons., instr. Madonna Coll., 1970—. Mem. Dirs. Guild Am., Friends of Photography, Indsl. Photographers Mich., Associated Photographers Internat., Soc. Motion Picture and TV Engrs., Detroit Puppeteers Guild, Dexter Hist. Soc., Alpha Epsilon Rho. Roman Catholic. Bd. advs. Photographers Forum nat. mag. Home: 8660 Merkel Rd Dexter MI 48130 Office: 20777 W Ten Mile Rd Southfield MI 48075

DERWINSKI, DENNIS ANTHONY, dentist; b. Chgo., Oct. 18, 1941; s. Anthony Joseph and Julia Donata (Pochron) D.; D.D.S., Marquette U., 1965; m. Mary Pamela Butler, Feb. 11, 1964 (div. Dec. 8, 1975); children—Julie Elizabeth, Nancy Carol, John Christopher, Amy Stuart, Mollie Maureen, Courtney Marie; m. 2d, Gayle Marie Sondelski, Oct. 8, 1977; 1 son, Anthony Edward. Resident, Cook County Hosp., Chgo., 1967-68; practice dentistry, Wausau, Wis., 1968—. Pres., chmn. bd. Riverview Dental Assos. Service Corp., 1968—, Riverview Dental Bldg. Ltd., 1968—; dir. Davison Communications Inc.; cons. hosp. com. Wis. Dental Soc., 1972-75. Mem. com. Samoset Council Boy Scouts Am., 1971-75. Bd. dirs. Montessori Sch. Wausau, 1971-75, pres. 1976-77; mem. St. Frances Cabrini Bd. Edn., 1978—. Served with USAF, 1965-67. Mem. Am. Dental Assn., Wis. Dental Soc., North Central Acad. Dental Group Practice, Central Wis. Dental Soc. Roman Catholic. Home: 1209 E Crocker St Wausau WI 54401 Office: 630 1st St Wausau WI 54401

DERWINSKI, EDWARD JOSEPH, congressman; b. Chgo., Sept. 15, 1926; s. Casimir Ignatius and Sophia (Zmijewski) D.; B.Sc. in History, Loyola U., 1951; m. Patricia Van der Giessen. Rep. 24th Dist., Ill. Gen. Assembly, 1957-58; mem. 86th-97th Congresses. from 4th Dist. Ill., mem. fgn. affairs com., P.O. and civil service com. Served with inf. U.S. Army, 1945-46. Mem. Polish Highlanders Alliance Am. (past nat. dir.), Cath. War Vets., Polish Alma Mater, Am. Legion, Polish Legion Am. Vets. (past state vice comdr.), VFW, Polish Nat. Alliance, Alpha Delta Gamma. Republican. Roman Catholic. Moose, K.C. Kiwanian. Office: 1401 Longworth House Office Bldg Washington DC 20515

DERZON, GORDON M., hosp. adminstr.; b. Milw., Dec. 28, 1934; B.S., Dartmouth Coll., 1957; M.H.A., U. Mich., 1961; married. Adminstrv. resident Bklyn. Hosp., 1960-61, adminstrv. asst., 1961-63, asst. exec. dir., 1963-65, exec. dir., 1966-67; exec. dir. State U. Hosp., Bklyn., 1967-68, Kings County Hosp. Center, Bklyn., 1968-74; supt. U. Wis. Hosps. and Clinics, Madison, 1974—; asso. prof. State U. N.Y., 1967-74; asso. clin. prof. U. Wis., Madison. Mem. Am. Hosp. Assn. (del.-at-large), Am. Coll. Hosp. Adminstrs. Contbr. articles to profl. jours. Home: 3421 Circle Close Madison WI 53705 Office: 600 Highland Ave Madison WI 53792

DESBERG, DANIEL, urologist; b. Cleve., Aug. 23, 1925; s. Barney W. and Ethel S. (Siegel) D.; B.S., John Carroll U., 1950; M.D., Ohio State U., 1954; m. Edith Katz, Sept. 14, 1952; children—Diane, Gail, Gary. Intern, Cleve. Met. Gen. Hosp., 1954-55, resident in surgery, 1955-56, resident in urology, 1956-59, Am. Cancer Soc. fellow, 1958-59; practice medicine specializing in urology, Cleve., 1959—. Served with U.S. Army, 1944-46. Mem. AMA, A.C.S., Am. Urol. Assn., Cleve. Urol. Soc., Ohio Med. Assn., Cleve. Acad. Medicine, Phi Delta Epsilon. Jewish. Office: 6801 Mayfield Mayfield Heights OH 44124

DESCHNER, REINHART PHILLIP, engr.; b. Bebe, Tex., May 4, 1927; s. Henry and Hannah (Seipman) D.; B.S., Southwestern U., 1949; m. Rebecca Ann Tittle, Dec. 17, 1949; children—William, Robert, Monte, Rose Ann, Mary Janette. Shift chemist Stanolind Oil & Gas Co., Brownsville, Tex., 1951-57; tech. service rep. Amoco Chem. Corp., Chgo., 1957-59, tech. asst. to plant supt., Seymour, Ind., 1959-66, asst. project chem. engr., 1966-67, project chem. engr., 1967-71, devel. engr., 1971-72, project engr., 1972-76; environ. engr. Humko Products div. Kraftco Corp., Champaign, Ill., 1976-77, engring. mgr., 1976—; cons. Northrup Ventura, Philippines, 1967, Saudi Arabia, 1969, Seymour Chem. Recycling, Seymour, Ind., 1971-76; owner, mgr. Renshed Tech. Cons., Seymour, 1971—. Precinct committeeman Republican party, 1960-76; active Boy Scouts Am., 1949-76; starter for state meets, judge Jr. Olympics, pres. Seymour Swim Club; chmn. edn. com. Seymour C. of C., 1969-74. Served with USNR, 1945-47. Certified wastewater operator; recipient Dist. Statuette, Boy Scouts Am., 1966; Good Samaritan award, City of Seymour, 1971. Mem. Am. Chem. Soc., Am. Rocket Soc., Am. Inst. Aeros. and Astronautics, Water Pollution Control Fedn. Republican. Methodist. Contbr. research for patents held by Amoco Chem. Corp. Home: Rural Route 1 Monticello IL 61856 Office: 710 N Mattis St Champaign IL 61820

DES COMBES, GARY NORMAN, mfg. co. exec.; b. Springfield, Ohio, Aug. 23, 1951; s. Norman Lewis and Mary Catherine (Ferguson) Des C.; student Wright State U., 1970-72, Clark Tech. Coll., 1972; m. Annita Dawn Vannorsdall, Feb. 24, 1973; children—Cheryl Dawn, Angela Michell. Vice pres. Plasticlad Co., Springfield, Ohio, 1970—. Mem. hosp. corp. fund Community Hosp. Springfield and Clark County. Mem. Nat. Mgmt. Assn. (dir. 1980—), Springfield Area C. of C. (mfrs. council), Springfield Mgmt. Assn. (v.p. 1978-79, pres. 1979-80, chmn. bd. 1980-81). Republican. Methodist. Home: 4460 E Route 54 Urbana OH 43078 Office: PO Box 775 Springfield OH 45501

DESHETLER, KENNETH EDWARD, ins. co. exec.; b. Toledo, Aug. 17, 1928; s. Leo J. and Elsie M. DeS.; B.A., Toledo U., 1957; J.D., Ohio State U., 1958; m. Elizabeth A. Brinton, Aug. 15, 1953; children—Laura J., Dana M. Individual practice law, 1958-65; asst. city law dir., Toledo, 1961-62; prosecutor City of Toledo, 1963-64; chief pros. atty., Toledo, 1964-65; municipal judge, Toledo, 1965-71; dir. Ohio Dept. Ins., 1971-75; of counsel firm Lane, Alton and Horst, Columbus, Ohio, 1975-76; v.p. Nationwide Ins. Cos., Columbus, Ohio, 1976—. Served with USAF, 1950-53. Mem. Am. Bar Assn., Ohio Bar Assn., Columbus Bar Assn., National Assn. Ins. Commrs. (past pres.), Columbus Area C. of C. Presbyterian. Office: Nationwide Ins Cos One Nationwide Plaza Columbus OH 43216

DE SHIELDS, ROBERT W., dentist; b. Cleve., May 29, 1935; s. William Henry and Leila Pearl (Hanna) DeS.; D.D.S., Ohio State U., 1959, M.S., 1964; children by previous marriage—Dana Lynn, William Douglas, Richard Walter. Practice dentistry specializing in clin. orthodontics, Cleve., 1964—; dental missionary to Guatamala, Allied Dental Med. Missions Youngstown, Ohio, 1975-78, to Nicaragua, 1976. Served with USAF, 1959-62. Mem. Am., Ohio, Cleve. dental assns., Cleve. Soc. Orthodontists, Ohio Assn. Orthodontists, Am. Assn. Orthodontists, Am. Cleft Palate Assn. Club: Vermilion Boat. Contbr. articles to profl. jours. Home: 22617 Creek Bend Ct Strongsville OH 44136 Office: 7155 Pearl Rd Cleveland OH

DESLAURIERS, JOHN ANDRE, constrn. co. exec.; b. Mpls., Aug. 1, 1928; s. Earl Andre and Lorraine Margaret (Sinclair) DesL.; student John's U., 1948; B.S., U. Minn., 1952; m. Mary Louise Schrantz, May 21, 1955; children—Mark Daniel, Mary Barbara, James Vincent, Jacquline Jean, John Joseph. Design and chief sewer engr. St. Paul Public Works Dept., 1954-68; sr. engring. specialist Camp, Dresser & McKee, Boston, 1968-69; v.p. Watermation, Inc., St. Paul, 1970; chief engr., v.p. Lametti & Sons, Inc., St. Paul, 1970-76; mgr. Fullfacer div. N.Am. Atlas Copco, Inc., St. Paul, 1976-80; pres. Continental Tunneling Corp., 1980—. Served with U.S. Army, 1952-54. Registered profl. engr., Minn., Mass. Roman Catholic. Home: 1765 Upper Afton Rd St Paul MN 55106 Office: Continental Tunneling Corp 1349 S Robert St West St Paul MN 55118

DESMITH, JULIAN WAYNE, health care adminstr.; b. Lansing, Mich., Jan. 21, 1934; s. Oscar Francis and Alpha Winnifred (Chaffee) DeS.; cert. advanced mgmt. St. Lawrence Sch. of X-Ray, 1952, A.A. in Bus. Mgmt., 1977, B.B.A., 1980; m. Marie Altha Lonier, Feb. 11, 1956 (dec. Aug. 14, 1969); m. 2d Judith Marina Thelen, June 13, 1970; children—Catherine J., Christopher J., Collette M., Gregory S., Paul F., Monique R., Brad J. Chief radiol. tech. Eaton Rapids Community Area Hosp., Mich., 1957-62; adminstrv. dir. radiology Ingham Med. Center, Lansing, Mich., 1962-76; adminstrv. asst. health and safety mgmt. systems and risk mgmt., 1976—; cons. in field. Chmn. Capitol Area United Way, Ingham Med. Center, 1978-81. Recipient Key Man award Eaton Rapids Jaycees, 1950; Technologist of Yr. award Mich. Soc. Radiol. Technologists, 1969. Mem. Am. Hosp. Assn., Soc. Hosp. Risk Mgrs., Mich. Soc. Hosp. Risk Mgrs., Am. Soc. Safety Engrs., Am. Soc. Radiol. Technologists, Mich. Soc. Radiol. Technologists (life). Republican. Roman Catholic. Home: 5490 W Clark Rd Lansing MI 48906 Office: 401 W Greenlawn St Lansing MI 48909

DESPRES, LEO ARTHUR, anthropologist; b. Lebanon, N.H., Mar. 29, 1932; s. Leo Arthur and Madeline (Bedford) D.; B.A., U. Notre Dame, 1954, M.A., 1956; Ph.D., Ohio State U., 1960; m. Loretta LaBarre, Aug. 19, 1953; children—Christine, Michelle, Denise, Mary Louise, Renee. Asst. prof. Ohio Wesleyan U., Delaware, 1961-63; from asso. prof. to prof. anthropology Case Western Res. U., Cleve., 1963-74, also chmn. dept.; prof., chmn. dept. sociology and anthropology U. Notre Dame (Ind.), 1974-80, prof. anthropology, 1980—. Social Sci. Research Council fellow, Guyana, 1960-61; Fulbright fellow, 1970-71. Fellow AAAS; mem. Am. Anthrop. Assn., Central State Anthrop. Soc., Am. Ethnological Soc., Soc. Applied Anthropology. Roman Catholic. Author: Cultural Pluralism and Nationalist Politics in British Guiana, 1967; editor and contributor: Ethnicity and Resource Competition in Plural Societies. Office: Dept Sociology and Anthropology Univ of Notre Dame Notre Dame IN 46556

DESPREZ, NORMA ZANK, mfg. co. exec.; b. Eau Claire County, Wis., May 20, 1920; d. Herman J. and Johanna (Kuehn) Zank; B.A. magna cum laude, Wis. State U., Eau Claire; m. Louis W. Desprez, Jan. 28, 1944; children—Louis Paul, Joel. With War Dept., Washington, 1941-46, Wis. Dept. Taxation, Eau Claire, Wis., 1946-51, Davis A. Donnelly, state senator, 1959-65; v.p. Dadco Diversified, Inc., Eau Claire, 1965—. Dir. St. John's Lutheran Jr. Choir, Eau Claire, 1964-75; incorporator Women's Community Center, Eau Claire, 1976; mem. coms. Democratic Party, 1968—. Mem. NOW, LWV. Office: Dadco Diversified Inc 2543 Clairemont Pkwy Eau Claire WI 54701

DES ROCHES, BERNARD JOSEPH, employment counselor; b. Rolla, N.D., Aug. 11, 1927; s. Amedee Joseph and Marie (Lammers) DesR.; B.S. in Econs., N.D. State U., Fargo, 1954; M.S. in Counseling, Bemidji State U., 1970; m. Madonna Marie Hince, Oct. 1, 1960; children—James, Richard, Michael, Kathleen, David. Adminstrv. asst. Bulova Watch Co., Rolla, 1953-54; dist. mgr. Job Service N.D., Devils Lake, 1954-58, counseling supr., Fargo, 1972—; social worker Diocese of Crookston, Red Lake Falls, Minn., 1958-72. Sec., mem. council Red Lake Falls Housing and Redevel. Authority, 1969-72; pres. Reile's Acres Home Owner's Assn., 1974-75. Served with U.S. Army, 1946-47. Mem. Am. Personnel and Guidance Assn., Internat. Assn. Personnel in Employment Security, N.D. Personnel and Guidance Assn., Fargo-Moorhead Personnel Assn. Roman Catholic. Home: Rural Route 2 Fargo ND 58102 Office: Box 168 Fargo ND 58102

DESSALET, SAMUEL ROBERT, acctg. exec.; b. York, Pa., Apr. 14, 1932; s. Jack Rose and Ethel (Werner) D.; B.S. in Commerce, Rider Coll., 1957; m. Nancy Lee Ashmore, Jan. 29, 1953; children—Deborah Lee, Sharon Lynne, Theresa Louise, Samuel Robert. Staff acct. Price Waterhouse & Co., Newark, 1957-61; mem. controller's staff Remington Rand Systems Div., N.Y.C., 1961; sr. bus. analyst, asst. sect. head Bayonne & Bayway Refineries, Humble Oil & Refining Co., Bayonne and Linden, N.J., 1961-65; chief acct., tax mgr. Bro Dart Industries, Newark, 1965-67; dir. corp. acctg. No. Natural Gas Co., Omaha, 1967-68; controller, systems mgr. Nat. Poly Products div. No. Petrochem. Co., Mankato, Minn., 1968—. Loaned exec. Mankato Area United Way, 1978; trustee Centenary United Methodist Ch., Mankato, 1972-81, treas., 1977—; bd. dirs. Multi-Ch. Found., Inc., 1974-81, chmn. bd., 1978-81. Served with AUS, 1952-54. C.P.A., N.J., Nebr. Mem. Am Inst. C.P.A.'s, N.J. Soc. C.P.A.'s, Nebr. Soc. C.P.A.'s, Nat. Assn. Accts. (pres. S. Central Minn. chpt. 1976-77, nat. dir. 1978-80, del. Minn. Council). Republican. Club: Mankato Exchange (1st v.p. 1973). Home: 10 N Hill Ct Rt 5 Mankato MN 56001 Office: 2111 3d Ave PO Box 1180 Mankato MN 56001

DE STASIO, MICHAEL BARTHOLOMEW, mktg. exec.; b. Phila., Aug. 9, 1946; s. Bartholomew Thomas and Josephine Dolores (Orlando) De S.; B.S., Aero-Space Inst., 1972; m. Lois Welker, Nov. 29, 1975. Cons. elec. draftsman A & T Engring., Chgo., 1970-72; computer programmer No. Trust Bank, Chgo., 1973; product mktg. mgr. Telemed div. Becton-Dickenson and Co., Hoffman Estates Ill., 1973-80; regional mktg. mgr. System Devel. Corp., 1980-81; mktg. and sales mgr. Interad Systems, Inc., Schaumburg, Ill., 1981—. Served with U.S. Army, 1966-69. Decorated Purple Heart, Bronze Star, Air medal. Home: 1813 N Raleigh Ln Hoffman Estates IL 60195 Office: 1100 Remington Rd Schaumburg IL 60195

DE STEPHEN, ALBERT MICHAEL, mech. engr.; b. Canton, Ohio, Feb. 17, 1920; s. Anthony and Jennie (DeGiacomo) DeS.; B.M.E., Internat. Corr. Schs., 1960; m. Helen Marie Skivolocke, Sept. 19, 1943; 1 dau., Norma Jean. With research and devel. div. Babcock and Wilcox Co., Alliance, Ohio, 1950-52, 54—, asst. supt. welding mills div. tubular products, 1965-73, supt. welding mills div. tubular products, 1973—. Served with USAAF, 1942-46. Mem. ASME (sec. Canton Alliance Massilon sect. 1961—), Assn. Iron, Steel Engrs. Republican. Roman Catholic. Patentee non-destructive testing welded steel tubing. Home: 1774 Federal St Alliance OH 44601 Office: 640 Keystone St Alliance OH 44601

DETERING, EDMUND LOUIS, hosp. adminstr.; b. St. Louis, June 28, 1913; s. Edmund L. and Ida Louise (Buerkle) D.; A.B., Washington U., St. Louis, 1941, M.A. in Edn., 1948, Ph.D., 1955; m. Betty Maxine Dunahugh, Aug. 23, 1941; children—Sandra Joyce,

Susan Jane. Tchr. pub. schs., University City, Mo., 1937-40; asst. in math. Washington U., St. Louis, 1941-42; tchr., prin. Avery Sch., Webster Groves, Mo., 1947-56; mem. relations dir. Asso. Credit Burs. Am., St. Louis, 1956-62; dir. community relations St. Luke's Hosps., St. Louis and Chesterfield, Mo., 1962—. Bd. dirs. Episcopal-Presbyterian Found. for Aging, 1976—; moderator Elijah Parish Lovejoy Presbytery, Presbyn. Ch., St. Louis, 1976; chmn. bd. mgr. Thompson Retreat and Conf. Center, 1976-81; bd. dirs. Webster Groves Civic Symphony, 1975-81, v.p., 1976-78. Served as lt. USCGR, 1942-46. Mem. Am. Hosp. Assn., Am. Soc. Hosp. Pub. Relations, Phi Delta Kappa (life), Kappa Delta Pi (pres. Beta Iota chpt. 1957-58). Clubs: Masons (master 1974-75, dist. dep. grand master 1979-80), Order of Eastern Star, Rotary (pres. Webster Groves 1960, gov. dist. 605 1964-65, 68-69, internat. dir., mem. exec. com. 1977-79). Home: 442 Saddlespur Rd Webster Groves MO 63119 Office: St Lukes Hosp 5535 Delmar Blvd Saint Louis MO 63112 also St Lukes Hosp 232 S Woods Mill Rd Chesterfield MO 63017

DETERS, DAVID HAROLD, educator; b. Caledonia, Minn., July 22, 1947; s. Harold Frank and Carol Lorraine (Burton) D.; B.A. in Spanish U. Iowa, 1969, M.A. in Spanish, 1975, M.A. in Community Coll. Counseling, 1977; M.Div., Dubuque Theol. Sem., 1973; m. Charlene Marie Clay, June 9, 1973. Counselor for dormitory community, teaching asst. in Greek, Dubuque (Iowa) Theol. Sem., 1970-71; tchr., counselor for bilingual diagnostic learning center John Hyson Mission Sch., Chimayo, N.Mex., 1971-72; community youth counselor Truchas Mission, Truchas, N.Mex., 1971-72; teaching asst. in Spanish, U. Iowa, Iowa City, 1973-75; bilingual career counselor Muscatine (Iowa) Community Coll., 1976-77, bilingual adult basic edn. instr., counselor, 1977—. Mem. Labor Council on Latin Am. Affairs. Community coll. counseling and teaching certs., Iowa; cert. TESL, Iowa. Mem. Iowa Assn. Lifelong Learners, Adult Edn. Assn. Mem. United Ch. of Christ. Club: Elks (Muscatine). Author: El Libro Colorante del Alfabeto ABC, 1971; editor Azteca, 1978. Office: Muscatine Community Coll 152 Colorado St Muscatine IA 52761

DETWEILER, JOHN ADAM, physician; b. Pine Grove, Pa., Apr. 16, 1924; s. John A. and Bessie (Philips) D.; B.S., Lebanon Valley Coll., 1948; M.D., Tufts U., 1952; m. Elaine Wedemeyer, Sept. 6, 1946; children—Judith, Joan, Jeanne. Intern, St. Francis Hosp., 1952-53; med. resident Hines VA Hosp., Hines, Ill., 1953-56; internist, Arlington Heights, Ill., 1956—; chief of staff N.W. Community Hosp., Arlington Heights, 1965; clin. asso. prof. medicine. U. Ill. Coll. Medicine, 1963—. Chmn. Bd. Health, Village Arlington Heights. Served with AUS, 1946-48. Diplomate Am. Bd. Internal Medicine. Fellow A.C.P., Am. Coll. Chest Physicians; mem. Phi Rho Sigma. Home: 1201 Sunset Terr Arlington Heights IL 60005 Office: 1430 N Arlington Heights Rd Arlington Heights IL 60004

DETWEILER, PAUL BUTLER, indsl. physician: b. Peoria, Ill., Feb. 16, 1926; s. Howard Butler and Edith Frances (Planck) D.; A.B., Tex. Christian U., 1949; M.D., U. Ill., 1954; m. Doris Lee Danni, Aug. 19, 1950; 1 son, Mark P. Intern, Methodist Hosp. Central Ill., Peoria, 1954-55; missionary United Christian Missionary Soc., also operator hosp., India, 1958-63; partner Hanna Clinic, Peoria, 1963-69; staff physician Caterpillar Tractor Co., East Peoria, Ill., 1969-75, plant med. dir. Basic Engine Plant, Mossville, Ill., 1975-79, med. dir. Tech. Center, Mossville, 1979—. Served with USNR, 1943-46. Fellow Royal Soc. Health; mem. Am., Central States occupational med. assns., AMA, Ill., Peoria County med. assns. Mem. Disciples of Christ. Clubs: Peoria Harbor Mariners Yacht, Ill. Valley Power Squadron (comdr.). Home: 4324 N Nelson Dr Peoria IL 61614 Office: Tech Center Caterpillar Tractor Co Mossville IL 61552

DEUBNER, SCOTT DUANE, mfg. co. exec.; b. Columbus, Ohio, Mar. 26, 1948; s. Russell Leigh and Irene Christine (Schuetter) D.; B.A., Ohio State U., 1970; m. Donna Chris Coachman, June 10, 1972; 1 son, Scott Christopher. With Scientific Columbus unit Esterline Corp., 1970—, now v.p. mfg. Mem. Am. Mgmt. Assn. Clubs: Rotary (sec. Capital City W. chpt.), Brookside Golf and Country, Pres.'s of Ohio State U. Home: 7114 Stone Ct Worthington OH 43085 Office: 1900 Arlingate Ln Columbus OH 43228

DEUSTER, DONALD EUGENE, state legislator; b. Milw., Sept. 26, 1929; s. Sarto Louis and Dorothy Marguerite (Sanders) D.; B.A., Ripon (Wis.) Coll., 1952; LL.B., UCLA, 1957; m. Katharine B. Brink, June 20, 1953; children—Mary, Ruth, Jane, Anne. Admitted to Ill. bar, 1957; asst. counsel Kemper Ins. Group, Chgo., 1957-62; congl. asst., 1962-69; congl. relations officer Dept. Transp., Washington, 1969-71; mem. Ill. Ho. of Reps. from 32d Dist., 1973—; instr. Congl. procedure Library of Congress, 1963-69. Republican precinct committeeman Libertyville (Ill.) Twp., 1960, 62; chmn. edn. com. Lake County Central Rep. Com., 1961-62. Served as officer USAR, 1961-62; Korea. Recipient Disting. Service award Chgo. Jaycees, 1960. Mem. Ill. Bar Assn., Calif. Bar Assn., Lake County Bar Assn. Presbyterian. Club: Mundelein (Ill.) Rotary. Office: 26 W Maple St Hwy 176 Mundelein IL 60060

DEUTSCH, OWEN CHARLES, mag. pub. exec.; b. Chgo., Jan. 9, 1936; s. Conrad Alexander and Betty (Liebermann) D.; student U. Mich., 1956-57; B.A., Roosevelt U., 1960, postgrad., 1960-61; postgrad. Loyola U. Sch. Law, 1961-62. Advt. rep. Commerce mag., Chgo., 1962-70; advt. dir. Chicago mag., Chgo., 1970—; lectr. pub. confs.; cons. in field. Mem. Chgo. Advt. Club, Sales and Marketing Execs. Assn. Chgo. (Disting. Sales award 1968), City and Regional Mag. Assn. Club: U. Chgo. Track. Home: 1700 E 56th St Apt 1205 Chicago IL 60637 Office: 500 N Michigan Ave Chicago IL 60611

DEVANNY, MILDRED ELIZABETH SMITH, genealogist, club woman; b. Carrollton, Ill., Nov. 11, 1901; d. Robert Eugene and Mary Elizabeth (Scorggins) Smith; student Lincoln Bus. Coll., 1920; m. John Stormont Devanny, Aug. 5, 1924; 1 dau., Jacquelen Jeanne Devanny Vance. Owner, tchr. Devanny Dancing Sch., Lincoln, Ill., 1942-47; dir. ARC Camp Revues, 1944-45; condr. geneal. seminars throughout Ill., DAR and various geneal. socs., 1970—; library asst., genealogy Lincoln and Springfield libraries, 1970—; state chmn. Ill. Geneal. Seminars, 1970—. Recipient award for short story Fedn. Women's Clubs, 1960. Mem. Ill. Geneal. Soc. (dir. 1970-73), Decatur Geneal. Soc., Logan County Geneal. Soc., DAR (Ill. officer 1964-66, 68-70, regent 1978-79), Colonial Daus. 17th Century (Ill. pres. 1976-79), Huguenot Soc. (charter), Magna Charta Barons, Am. Assn. Ret. Persons. Episcopalian. Club: Lincoln Woman's (pres. 1960). Author: Sarah Margaret Lurton, Her Ancestors and Descendants, 1959; The Genealogy of Lora Mae Hannum, 1975; Revolutionary Soldiers Buried in Illinois, 1975; Revolutionary Soldiers Buried in Logan County Illinois, 1975; Campbell and Allied Families, 1976; Annotated List of Genealogical and Local History Sources in Lincoln County Pub. Library, 1977; Robert Monroe Smith, The Cumberland Presbyterian Minister, 1977.

DEVERMAN, DARRELL LEE, retail fertilizer co. exec.; b. Lincoln, Ill., June 8, 1940; s. Walter A. and Lydia (Last) D.; student public schs., Lincoln; m. Betty A. French, Nov. 2, 1958; children—Diane Lynne, David Wayne. Mgr., W. R. Grace & Co., Lincoln, 1964-66, Arco Farm Center, Covell, Ill., 1970-72, Am. Cyanamid Co., Auburn and Illiopolis, Ill., 1970-72; pres. Atlanta Ag Center, Inc. (Ill.), 1973—. Mem. Planning Commn., City of Atlanta, 1978—; bd. dirs.,

chmn. long range planning com. Atlanta Indsl. Devel. Corp., 1978-79; mem. Logan County Community Resource Devel. Council, 1980—. Mem. Nat. Fertilizer Solutions Assn., Fertilizer Inst., Ill. Fertilizer and Chem. Assn. Republican. Lutheran. Clubs: Rotary (past pres) (Atlanta); Elks (Lincoln); Bloomington-Normal Ag; Beason Sportsman's. Home: Karen Ct Atlanta IL 61723 Office: PO Box 425 Atlanta IL 61723

DEVIENCE, ALEXANDER, JR., lawyer; b. Chgo., Nov. 18, 1938; s. Alexander and Charlotte D.; B.A., U. Md., 1964; J.D., Loyola U., Chgo., 1967. Admitted to Ill. bar, 1968; asso. firm John H. McCollom, Chgo., 1967-70; individual practice law, Chgo., 1970—, also prof. bus. law and bus. adminstrn. DePaul U., Chgo., 1971—. Sec., Regional Recidivist Alcoholism Programs. Served with USN, 1956-64. Mem. Am. Bar Assn., Ill. Bar Assn., Chgo. Bar Assn., Am. Bus. Law Profs. Assn. Lutheran. Home: 630 Sylviawood St Park Ridge IL 60068 Office: 69 W Washington St Chicago IL 60602

DEVINE, JAMES EDWARD, clin. psychologist; b. Balt., Jan. 19, 1950; s. Harry John and Marjorie Marie (McKeon) D.; student Spring Hill Coll., 1968-70; B.S. in Psychology, La. State U., 1972; M.A. in Psychology, U. Miss., 1974, Ph.D. in Clin. Psychology, 1979; m. Frances Marian Parker, Dec. 30, 1972; 1 son, James Edward, Behavior mgr. Eufaula (Ala.) Adjustment Center, 1972; Manpower Devel. Tng. Act asst. U. Miss., University, 1972-74, USPHS fellow, 1974-75, asst., summer 1974; bd. dirs. Rapline, 1975-76; intern. Chgo.-Read Mental Health Center, Cook County Hosp., 1976-77; dir. behavior therapy Levensen Center for Mentally Handicapped, Chgo., 1977; psychologist pediatric and internal medicine residency tng. program Ill. Masonic Hosp., Chgo., 1978; research cons. pain treatment center Marianjoy Rehab. Hosp., Wheaton, Ill., 1978; pvt. practice clin. psychology, Libertyville, Ill.; adj. clin. asso. U. Ill., Chgo.; cons. Lake Forest (Ill.) Hosp. Pain Treatment Center, Sch. Assn. for Spl. Edn. Du Page County, 1978—, Lake County Juvenile Probation, Waukegan, Ill.; outpatient therapist Tupelo (Miss.) Mental Health Complex, 1974; coordinator personal adjustment center, Region II Mental Health and Mental Retardation Center, Oxford, Miss., 1975-76. Registered psychologist, Ill. Mem. Am. Psychol. Assn., Internat. Assn. for Study of Pain, Midwest Soc. for Study of Pain, Psi Chi. Roman Catholic. Condr. research in biofeedback, behavior therapy, hypnosis; writer grants; contbr. papers to profl. confs. U.S., Can. Home: 24 N 6th Des Plaines IL 60016 Office: 1641 N Milwaukee #10 Libertyville IL 60048

DE VINE, JOHN BERNARD, lawyer; b. Ann Arbor, Mich., Feb. 5, 1920; s. Frank Bernard and Elizabeth Catherine (Doherty) DeV.; A.B., U. Mich., 1941; J.D., Harvard U., 1948; m. Margaret Louise Burke, Apr. 23, 1949; children—Margaret Louise DeVine Mumby, Ann Elizabeth DeVine Hawkins, Kathleen Kennedy, Susan Joan, John Kennedy. Admitted to Mich. bar, 1948; partner firm DeVine, DeVine & Serr, Ann Arbor, 1948—; asst. pros. atty. County of Washtenaw, Mich., 1948-52; dir. Nat. Bank & Trust Co. of Ann Arbor, Nat. Ann Arbor Corp.; mem. Detroit adv. bd. Mich. Consol. Gas Co. Founder NCCJ, Ann Arbor; chmn. Catholic Social Services, Washtenaw County, 1960-64; bd. dirs. Ann Arbor Devel. Council, Nat. Inst. for Burn Medicine. Served to lt. U.S. Navy, 1942-46. Mem. Am. Bar Assn., Mich. Bar Assn. (dir.), Washtenaw County Bar Assn., Am. Soc. Hosp. Attys. (pres.), Mich. Soc. Hosp. Attys. (past pres.), Mich. Hosp. Assn. Roman Catholic. Club: Barton Hills Country. Home: 2121 Wallingford Rd Ann Arbor MI 48104 Office: 300 National Bank & Trust Bldg Ann Arbor MI 48104

DEVINE, JOHN PATRICK, fire chief Chgo.; b. Phila., June 9, 1931; student Prince Georges Community Coll., 1969-70; m. Loretta Jean Van Wie, Apr. 12, 1958; children—John, Kathleen, Michael, Jane. With D.C. Fire Dept., Washington, 1954-81, tng. officer, 1963-65, 68-70, capt., 1970, bn. fire chief, 1971-74, dep. fire chief, 1974-76, asst. fire chief, 1976-81; fire chief City of Chgo., 1981—. Served with USMCR, 1951-54. Mem. Internat. Assn. Fire Service Instrs. Office: City Hall 121 N LaSalle St Chicago IL 60602*

DE VINE, LAWRENCE, theater critic; b. N.Y.C., Sept. 21, 1935; s. John Justin and Hazel (Tippit) DeV.; student Georgetown U., 1953-54; B.S. in Journalism, Medill Sch. Journalism, Northwestern U., 1957; postgrad. (Nat. Endowment for Humanities profl. journalism fellow) U. Mich., 1975-76; m. Jane Christian, 1959 (div. Apr. 1968); children—John Justin, II, Ellen Morse; m. 2d Lucy Memory Williamson, July 26, 1968. Theater critic Miami (Fla.) Herald, 1962-67, Los Angeles Herald-Examiner, 1967-68, Detroit Free Press, 1968—; Critic fellow Eugene O'Neill Theater Center, Waterford, Conn., 1971, asso. dir. Nat. Critics Inst., 1973—; critic-in-residence Am. Coll. Theater Festival, 1978-80, mem. nat. playwrighting jury, 1979; mem. Pulitzer Prize jury for drama, 1981—; lectr. in theater criticism U. Detroit, 1974. Served with CIC, U.S. Army, 1958-62. Mem. Am. Theatre Critics Assn. (chmn. exec. com.), Beta Theta Pi. Roman Catholic. Contbr. articles to Yale Drama Rev., N.Y. Mag., Los Angeles Times, and Knight-Ridder news wire syndication. Office: Detroit Free Press Detroit MI 48231

DEVINE, PATRICK JAMES, mfg. co. exec.; b. Fornfelt, Mo., May 5, 1914; s. Patrick James and Nancy Pauline (McGaugh) D.; student public schs., St. Louis; m. Gertrude Edna Kaveney, Dec. 29, 1940; 1 dau., Gertrude Pauline. With Potter Electric Signal Co., 1935-38, 49-80, pres., dir., St. Louis, 1974-80; with Gen. Alarm Corp., Boston, 1939-49; v.p., dir. Potter Electric Signal and Mfg. Co., Toronto, Ont., Can., 1970-80. Served with USNR, 1941-45. Mem. Security Equipment Industry Assn. (dir. 1976-80), Nat. Burglar and Fire Alarm Assn. (regional v.p. 1970-71, Man of Yr. award 1979), Central Sta. Elec. Protection Assn. (dir. 1977-80), Nat. Fire Protection Assn. Roman Catholic. Clubs: Mo. Athletic, Horwood Hills Country, Ocean Reef, Rotary. Patentee in field. Home: 4920 Kennewick Dr Florissant MO 63033 Office: 2081 Craig Rd Saint Louis MO 63141

DEVINEY, MARVIN LEE, JR., chem. co. exec.; b. Kingsville, Tex., Dec. 5, 1929; s. Marvin Lee and Esther Lee (Gambrell) D.; B.S. in Chemistry and Math., S.W. Tex. State U., San Marcos, 1949; M.A. in Phys. Chemistry, U. Tex. at Austin, 1952, Ph.D. in Phys. Chemistry, 1956; m. Marie Carole Massey, June 7, 1975; children—Marvin Lee III, John H., Ann-Marie K. Devel. chemist Celanese Chem. Co., Bishop, Tex., 1956-58; research chemist Shell Chem. Co., Deer Park, Tex., 1958-66; sr. scientist, head group phys. and radio-chemistry Ashland Chem. Co., Houston, 1966-68, mgr. sect. phys. and analytical chemistry, 1968-71, mgr. sect. phys. chemistry div. research and devel., Columbus, Ohio, 1971—. Mem. sci. adv. bd. Am. Petroleum Inst. Research Project 60, 1968-74. Mem. ednl. adv. com. Columbus Tech. Inst., 1974—, Central Ohio Tech. Coll., 1975—. Served to lt. col., USAR. Humble Oil Research fellow, 1954. Fellow Am. Inst. Chemists (pres. Ohio Inst. 1978-79); mem. N.Y., Tex. acads. scis., Am. Def. Preparedness Assn., Am. Carbon Soc., Am. Assn. Textile Chemists, Colorists, Am. Chem. Soc. (chmn. chpt. exec. bd. 1969, Best Paper award rubber div. 1967, 70. Honorable Mention awards 1968, 69, 73; symposium co-chmn., book editor 1975), Engr.'s Council Houston (sr. councilor 1970-71), Sigma Xi, Phi Lambda Upsilon, Alpha Chi, Sigma Pi Sigma. Contbr. articles to profl. jours. Home: 6810 Hayhurst Worthington OH 43085 Office: Box 2219 Columbus OH 43216

DEVISE, PIERRE ROMALN, educator, city planner; b. Brussels, Belgium, July 27, 1924; s. Victor Pierre and Madeleine (Cupers) deV.; B.A., U. Chgo., 1945, M.A., 1958; m. Margaret Ahern, Nov. 16, 1978; children—Peter Charles, Daniel Romain. Came to U.S., 1935, naturalized, 1958. Chancellor, Belgian Consul, Chgo., 1945-47, comml. attache, 1947-56, Belgian Consulate Gen., Chgo.; planning dir. Hyde Park-Kenwood Conf., 1956-57; research planner Northeastern Ill. Planning Commn., 1958-60; sr. planner Chgo. City Planning Dept., 1961-63; asst. dir. Hosp. Planning Council for Met. Chgo., 1964-70; asst. dir. Ill. Regional Med. Program, 1971-73; prof. urban scis. U. Ill., 1972—. Lectr., De Paul U., 1962—; vis. lectr. U. Mich., 1966, U. Hawaii, 1968, U. Ill., 1969, 70, U. Ia., 1971, U. Chgo., 1972; prin. investigator Chgo. Regional Hosp. Study, 1966—; exec. dir. Chgo. Commn. to Study Conv. Week Disorders, 1968-70; cons. Chgo. Commn. on Human Relations, 1966—, Chgo. Model Cities Program, 1968—, Cook County Council of Govts., 1968—, Comprehensive Health Planning, Inc., 1971—; Census Bur., 1973—, U.S. Senate Health Subcom., 1974, HEW, 1975—, House Ways and Means Com., 1975—, Senate Banking Com., 1976—. Bd. dirs. Old Town Boys Club. Mem. Am. Statist. Assn., Chgo. Assn. Commerce and Industry, Am. Pub. Health Assn., Planned Parenthood Assn. Chgo., Assn. Am. Geographers. Club: City (Chgo.). Author monographs including Suburban Factbook, 1960; Social Geography of Metropolitan Chicago, 1960; Chicago's People, Jobs and Homes, 1963; Chicago's Widening Color Gap, 1967; Chicago's Apartheid Hospital System 1968; Chicago: 1971, Ready for Another Fire, 1971; Misused and Misplaced Hospitals and Doctors, 1973; Chicago's Future, 1976; Chicago: Transformations of an Urban System, 1976; Chicago in the Year 2000, 1978. Office: U Ill Box 4348 Chicago IL 60680

DEVITT, EDWARD JAMES, judge; b. St. Paul, May 5, 1911; s. Thomas Phillip and Catherine Ethel (McGuire) D.; LL.B., U. N.D., 1935, B.S., 1936; m. Marcelle M. LaRose, Apr. 22, 1939; children—Marcelle Terese, Timothy Patrick. Admitted to D.C., Minn., Ill., N.D. bars; practiced law, E. Grand Forks, Minn., 1935-39; municipal judge, 1935-39; asst. atty. gen. Minn., 1939-42; instr. law U. N.D., 1935-39, St. Paul Coll. Law, from 1945; practice law, St. Paul, 1946—; mem. 80th Congress from 4th Minn. Dist.; probate judge Ramsey County (Minn.), St. Paul, 1950-54; U.S. dist. judge Dist. Minn., 1954—, now chief dist. judge. Served as intelligence officer USN, 1942-46. Decorated Purple Heart. Mem. Am., Minn., Ramsey County bar assns., Am. Legion, VFW, DAV, St. John's U. Alumni Assn. (pres.), Order of Coif, Phi Delta Phi, Beta Gamma Sigma, Delta Sigma Rho, Blue Key. Republican. Roman Catholic. Clubs: K.C., St. Paul Athletic. Office: 734 Federal Bldg 316 N Robert St Saint Paul MN 55101*

DEVITT, TIMOTHY WARREN, environ. cons.; b. Cambridge, Mass., Aug. 2, 1944; s. Edward John and Doris Rita (Berthiaume) D.; B.S. in Chem. Engring., U. Calif., Berkeley, 1967; postgrad. U. Calif., Berkeley, 1966-67, U. Cin., 1968-70; m. Linda Ann Kirk, May 20, 1971. Chem. process engr. Stauffer Chem. Co., Richmond, Calif., 1966-67; research engr. U.S. EPA, Cin., 1967-69, project officer, 1969-70; chem. engr. PEDCo. Environ., Inc., Cin., 1970-72, project mgr., 1972-75, v.p. corp. devel., 1975—, dir., 1980—; v.p. Bioassay Systems, Cambridge, 1978-81, chief exec. officer, 1981—, also dir.; dir. PCS, 1979—, PCM, 1979—. Served with USPHS, 1967-70. Recipient Outstanding Achievement award, Ohio Soc. Profl. Engrs.; registered profl. engr., Ohio, Mass.; diplomate Am. Acad. Environ. Engrs. Mem. Air Pollution Control Assn., Am. Inst. Chem. Engrs., Soc. Profl. Engrs. Club: Sandusky Sailing. Contbr. articles in field to profl. jours. Home: 3427 Paxton Ave Cincinnati OH 45208 Office: 11499 Chester Rd Cincinnati OH 45246

DE VOE, HELEN POINDEXTER, civic worker; b. Henry County, Ind., Sept. 16, 1921; d. Archie R. and Inez (Houdeshell) Poindexter; B.S., Ball State U., 1959; m. Paul Volney De Voe, Jan. 9, 1943; children—James Frederick, Judith Ann DeVoe Stafford. Bd. dirs. United Cerebral Palsy, Muncie, Ind., 1960-61, Hostess House, Marion, Ind., 1962-65, Grant County Soc. for Crippled Children, 1962-63; bd. dirs. Grant County Community Concert Assn., 1963-72, treas., 1966-71; bd. dirs. Art Gallery, 1962-65, docent, 1961-65; docent Grant County Hist. Mus., 1969-74; trustee United Presbyn. Ch., Marion, 1975-77, bd. ruling elders, 1970-73, bd. deacons, 1963-66; registrar Gen. Francis Marion chpt. Nat. Soc. DAR, 1968-70, treas., 1965-66, regent, 1966-68; pres. Pioneer Benjamin Mendenhall chpt., 1965-67; 3d v.p. Ind. State soc. Nat. Soc. Colonial Dames XVII Century, 1967-69, 1st v.p., 1969-71, state pres., hon. state pres., 1971-75, chaplain gen. nat. soc., 1979—, organizing sec. gen. nat. soc., 1977-79, nat. chmn. scholarships, 1981—. Mem. AAUW, P.E.O., Nat. Soc. Daus. Colonial Wars (state chaplain 1980—), Nat. Soc. Daus. Founders and Patriots Am. (state parliamentarian 1976-79), Nat. Soc. of Dames of Ct. of Honor, Nat. Huguenot Soc., Nat. Soc. Daus. Am. Colonists (2d vice regent Mississinewa chpt. 1979—), Nat. Soc. Magna Charta Dames, Soc. Friends of St. George, Descs. of Knights of Garter, Order of Washington, Nat. Soc. U.S. Daus. 1812 (2d v.p. Ind. 1981—), Ind. Hist. Soc., Historic Landmarks Found. Ind., Nat. Trust for Hist. Preservation, Ind. State Mus. Soc., Smithsonian Instn. (asso.), Nat. Archives (asso), Phoenix Art Mus., Ariz. Costume Inst., Delta Phi Delta, Kappa Delta Pi, Psi Iota Xi. Republican. Club: Meshingomesia Country (Marion).

DEVOE, JAMES KENT, electronics co. exec.; b. Lima, Ohio, Feb. 18, 1937; s. Robert James and Dora Pauline DeV.; B.S., Ohio State U., 1960, M.Sc., 1961; m. Loretta Downing, Mar. 20, 1959 (dec. 1980); children—Mark Alan, Michele Annette, Melissa Anne, Michael Andrew. Vice pres., sr. asso. research dir. Batten Barton Durstine & Osborn, N.Y.C., 1962-66; sr. v.p., gen. mgr. Cargill, Wilson & Acree, Richmond, Va., 1966-70; pres. Dusenberry Advt., N.Y.C., 1970-72; sr. v.p., mgmt. supr. N.W. Ayer, N.Y.C., 1972-77; v.p. consumer communications RCA Sales Corp., Indpls., 1977—; adj. asst. prof. mktg. N.Y. U. Bus. Sch., 1965-66. Trustee Huguenot Presbyn. Ch., Pelham, N.Y.; elder 1st Presbyn. Ch., Noblesville, Ind. Mem. Ohio Soc. Profl. Engrs. Republican. Office: 600 N Sherman Dr Indianapolis IN 46201

DEVORE, KIMBERLY K., health care adminstr.; b. Louisville., June 19, 1947; d. Wendell O. and Shirley F. DeV.; student (Florence Allen Scholar), Xavier U., 1972-76; A.A., Coll. Mt. St. Joseph, 1979. Patient registration supr. St. Francis Hosp., Cin., 1974-76; cons., bus. mgr. Family Health Care Found., Cin., 1976-77; exec. dir. Hospice of Cin., Inc., 1977-80; pres. Micro Med, 1979—; v.p. Sycamore Profl. Assn., 1979—; partner Enchanted House, 1979—, sec., 1979-80, treas., 1980-81. Mem. service and rehab. com. Hamilton County unit Am. Cancer Soc., 1977-78. Mem. Nat. (treas., sec.; chmn. longterm planning com.), Ohio (co-founder, pres., state chmn.) hospice orgns., Better Housing League, Nat., Ohio, fedns. bus. and profl. women's clubs, Cin. Bus. and Profl. Women's Club (pres. 1973-75). Club: Cin. Woman's.

DE VOTO, DONALD EDWIN, mgmt. cons.; b. Marshall, Ind., Feb. 27, 1918; s. William Michael and Grace (Tague) DeV.; A.B., Wabash Coll., 1939; postgrad. Purdue U., 1939, McGill U., 1940; m. Madonna Warner, Sept. 26, 1942; children—Eric, Craig. Instr. Romance langs., English, Wabash Coll., 1939-41; with R.R. Donnelley & Sons Co., Chgo., 1941-57; sr. cons. Booz, Allen & Hamilton, Chgo., 1957-58; pres. DeVoto & Berry Partners, Ltd. (and predecessor firms), Chgo., 1959—. Pres., bd. dirs. Am. Internat. Hosp. Mem. Assn. Exec. Recruitive Cons. (pres. 1971-72, dir.), Chgo. C. of C., Phi Beta Kappa. Presbyn. (elder). Clubs: University (Chgo.), Ruth Lake Country (Hinsdale, Ill.). Home: 100 Ann St Clarendon Hills IL 60514 Office: 120 S Riverside Plaza Chicago IL 60606

DEVRIES, HARVEY G., coll. pres.; b. Toledo, Iowa, Feb. 8, 1929; s. Charles and Jennie DeV.; A.A., N.W. Jr. Coll., Orange City, Iowa, 1948; B.A., Bethel Coll., 1950; B.D., Bethel Theol. Sem., 1955; M.A., No. Baptist Theol. Sem., 1967; m. Geraldine Daley, July 25, 1952; children—Timothy, Jana. Ordained to ministry, Baptist Ch., 1957; pastor chs., Glen Flora, Wis., 1954-56, Benson, Minn., 1956-63, Benson, Minn., 1959-61, Hillside, Ill., 1963-64; regional dir. devel. Bethel Coll. and Sem., St. Paul, 1964-66, v.p. public affairs, 1965-79, acting pres., 1975-76, pres., chief exec. officer Bethel Coll. and Sem. Found., 1979—. Dir., St. Paul ARC. Mem. Council for Advancement Small Colls., Council for Advancement and Support of Edn. Club: Mpls. Athletic. Office: 3900 Bethel Dr St Paul MN 55112

DEVRIES, MARVIN FRANK, mech. engr., educator; b. Grand Rapids, Mich., Oct. 31, 1937; s. Ralph B. and Grace (Buurma) DeV.; B.S., Calvin Coll., 1960; B.S., U. Mich., 1960, M.S., 1961; Ph.D., U. Wis., 1966; m. Martha Lou Kannegieter, Aug. 29, 1959; children—Mark Alan, Michael John, Matthew Dale. Instr., U. Wis.-Madison, 1962-66, asst. prof. mech. engring., 1966-70, asso. prof., 1970-77, prof., 1977—; cons. Metcut Research Assos., Inc.; Fulbright-Hays vis. prof. Cranfield (Eng.) Inst. Tech., 1979-80. Mem. Soc. Mfg. Engrs. (sec.-treas.), ASME, Numerical Control Soc., Internat. Instn. for Prodn. Research, Calvin Coll. Alumni Assn. (past pres. Wis. chpt.). Mem. Christian Ref. Ch. Author 1 book in field of mfg. processes and computer aided mfg.; contbr. numerous articles to profl. jours. Office: 1513 University Ave Madison WI 53706

DEW, DANIEL CHING-YEE, surgeon; b. Hong Kong, Apr. 10, 1940; s. Arthur Boon-Seng and Rosalind (Lui) D.; came to U.S., 1960; A.B., Taylor U., Ind., 1964; M.D., U. Ind., 1968; m. Cynthia Yuet-Man, June 15, 1968; children—Nathaniel, Timothy. Intern, Grace Hosp., Detroit, 1968-69, resident in gen. surgery, 1969-73; practice medicine specializing in surgery, Elkhart, Ind., 1973—; gen. surgeon, active staff Elkhart Gen. Hosp., 1973—, chief surgery, 1979. Diplomate Am. Bd. Surgery. Fellow A.C.S.; mem. AMA, Ind. Med. Assn., Christian, Elkhart County med. socs. Office: Elkhart Clinic 303 S Nappanee St Elkhart IN 46514

DEWALD, RONALD L., physician, educator; b. Aurora, Ill., Oct. 4, 1934; s. Lee H. and Elsie (Kellen) DeW.; B.S., U. Ill., 1955, M.D., 1959; m. Mary Lee Johnstone, July 21, 1956; children—Ann Elise, Lee Fraser, Christopher James, Ronald Lee. Intern, Presbyn. St. Lukes Hosp., Chgo., 1959-60; resident U. Ill. Hosp., Chgo., 1960-62, 64-65; asst. prof. orthopaedic surgery, 1965-67, asso. prof., 1967-71; prof., chmn. dept., Stritch Sch. Medicine Loyola at Chgo., 1972-73; prof. Rush Med. Coll., Chgo., 1973—. Cons. surgeon Ill. Div. Services for Crippled Children, 1967—, Ill. Childrens Hosp. Sch., Chgo., 1968—, Holy Family Hosp., Des Plaines, 1972—, Hines (Ill.) VA Hosp., 1972—; asso. surgeon Shriners Hosp. for Crippled Children, Chgo., 1972—. Served to capt. M.C., AUS, 1962-64. Diplomate Am. Bd. Orthopaedic Surgery (bd. examiners 1973—). Fellow A.C.S.; mem. A.M.A. (Hektoen Silver medal 1971), Chgo., Ill. med. socs., Chgo., Clin. orthopaedic socs., Scoliosis Research Soc. (founding, dir.), Am. Acad. Orthopaedic Surgeons (regional admissions chmn. 1975—), Ill. Orthopaedic Assn., Am. Orthopaedic Assn. Contbr. articles to profl. jours. Office: 1725 Harrison St W Chicago IL 60612

DE WALT, ARTHUR RALPH, architect; b. Cleve., Jan. 13, 1938; s. Augustus Ralph and Augusta Mae (Rishel) DeW.; student Rensselaer Poly. Inst., 1955-58; B. Arch., Western Res. U., 1963. Partner William B. Morris, Architect, Shaker Heights, Ohio, 1963-65; partner Morris and DeWalt, Architects, Shaker Heights, 1965-68; partner Morris, DeWalt, Cullen, Whitley & Whitley, Architects and Planners, Shaker Heights, 1968-70; individual practice architecture, Cleve., 1970—; cons. architect The H.L. Vokes Co., Cleve. and Detroit, Simon & Co., Cleve. Instr. Cuyahoga Community Coll., 1967-71. Chmn. Archtl. Bd. of Review, Eastlake, Ohio, 1973—, city architect, 1980—; chmn. Archtl. Bd. of Review, Mayfield Heights, Ohio, 1974—, city architect, 1977—. Scoutmaster Greater Cleve. council Boy Scouts Am., 1971. Registered architect, Ohio, Ill., N.J., Pa., Mich. Mem. A.I.A. (corporate mem.), Architects Soc. Ohio (recipient design honor award, 1965, 66, 67, 68), Soc. Archtl. Historians, Nat. Council Archtl. Registration Bds., Delta Kappa Epsilon. Presbyn. Clubs: Hermit, University (Cleve.). Office: 35555 Curtis Blvd Eastlake OH 44094

DEWANE, JOHN RICHARD, mfg. co. exec.; b. Cooperstown, Wis., Mar. 4, 1934; s. Clarence John and Arvilla Anne (Gannon) D.; B.S.M.E., U. Wis., 1957; M.B.A., U. Minn., 1973; m. Judith Anne Arnold, Mar. 17, 1974; 1 dau., Kelly Susanne. Dir. mktg. planning Honeywell, Inc., Washington, 1974-76, dir. mktg., Mpls., 1976-78, v.p. service engring., 1979-81, v.p. bus. devel., 1981—. Vice chmn. Community Long-Range Improvement Com., Maple Grove, Minn., 1980-81; mem. Polit. Action com., Honeywell, 1979-81. Served with USN, 1957-60. Navy scholar, 1952-57. Mem. Assn. Unmanned Vehicles, U.S. Navy League, Air Force Assn., Assn. U.S. Army, Am. Def. Preparedness Assn., Mpls. C. of C. (aviation com. 1980-81). Office: 2600 Ridgeway Pkwy Minneapolis MN 55440

DEWAR, ROBERT EARL, chain store exec.; b. Traverse City, Mich., Nov. 20, 1922; s. Floyd C. and Irlene (Nash) D.; student Alma Coll., 1940-42; LL.B., Wayne State U., 1948; student U. Mich. Grad. Sch. Bus Adminstrn., 1963; m. Nancy Jane Miller, Sept. 26, 1944; children—Robert Earl, Jane Elizabeth, John. Admitted to Mich. bar, 1948; gen. practice law, Detroit, 1948-49; with S.S. Kresge Co. (now K-Mart Corp.), 1949—, asst. v.p. finance, 1963-65, v.p. finance, 1965-66, adminstrv. v.p., 1966-68, exec. v.p. adminstrn. and finance, 1968-70, pres., chief adminstrv. officer, 1970-72, chmn. bd., chief exec. officer, 1972-80, chmn. exec. and fin. coms., 1980—. Served as pilot USNR, 1942-45. Decorated Air medal (2). Presbyterian. Office: 3100 W Big Beaver Troy MI 48084*

DEWEESE, MARY LOUISE, polit. worker; b. Oakland City, Ind., Aug. 8, 1921; d. Alta Roy and Dolly Gertrude (Davis) Bruner; m. Elwood Jesse DeWeese, Sept. 25, 1937; children—Deanna, Beverly Sue, Elwood Wesley, Alan Roy. Salesman, Stuart McGuire Co. Inc. Telephoner, Common Cause, 1979—; mem. Nat. Wildlife Fedn., 1979—; mem. Democratic Nat. Com., 1974—. Mem. Nat. Small Bus. Assn., Am. Legion Aux., Blue Star Mothers, Eagles. Home: 410 W Hamilton Ave Flint MI 48503

DE WINDT, EDWARD MANDELL, mfg. co. exec.; b. Great Barrington, Mass., Mar. 31, 1921; s. Delano and Ruth (Church) deW.; student Williams Coll., 1939-41; m. Betsy Bope, June 21, 1941; children—Pamela, Delano II, Dana, Elizabeth, Edward Mandell. With Eaton Corp., Cleve., 1941—, gen. mgr. stamping div., 1954-59, v.p. sales, 1959-61, group v.p. internat., 1961-66, pres., 1967-69, chmn. bd., chief exec. officer, 1969—, also dir.; mem. exec. com., dir. Ohio Bell Telephone Co.; dir. Kraft, Inc., AmeriTrust Corp., AmeriTrust, UAL, Inc., United Airlines, Inc. Trustee Cleve. Ednl. Television Assn., Cleve. Clinic; bd. dirs. United Way Am., Univ. Sch., NCCJ; adv. council Big Bros.-Big Sisters Am. Decorated comdr. Order Brit. Empire; commendatore Italian Republic. Mem. Soc. Automotive Engrs., Soc. Cin., Am. Soc. Corporate Execs., Bus. Council. Clubs: Union, Tavern, Pepper Pike Country, Kirtland (Cleve.); Bloomfield Hills (Mich.) Country; Augusta (Ga.) Nat.; Blind Brook (N.Y.); Laurel Valley, (Ligonier, Pa.); Links (N.Y.C.); Seminole, Jupiter Island (Fla.). Office: 100 Erieview Plaza Cleveland OH 44114

DEWIRE, NORMAN EDWARD, religious ofcl.; b. Cin., Mar. 5, 1936; s. Ormsby and Lucille (Binder) D.; B.S. in Edn., Ohio U., 1958; S.T.M., Boston U., 1962; D.D., Adrian (Mich.) Coll., 1976; D.Min., McCormick Theol. Sem., 1979; m. Shirley Woodman, June 16, 1957; children—Cathy Lynn, Deborah Kay. Ordained to ministry Methodist Ch., 1959; pastor, Jacksonville, Ohio, 1957-58, Charlton City (Mass.) Meth. Ch., 1958-62, Central Meth. Ch., Detroit, 1962-67; exec. sec. Detroit Conf. Bd. Missions and Ch. Extension, United Meth. Ch., 1967-69, exec. dir. Joint Strategy and Action Com., N.Y.C., 1969-75, gen. sec. Gen. Council on Ministries, United Meth. Ch., Dayton, Ohio, 1975—; del. 5th Assembly World Council Chs., Nairobi; governing bd. Nat. Council Chs. of Christ in U.S.A., del. to consultation on ch. union; v.p. Ch. World Service. Former pres., founding bd. Offenders Aid Restoration of U.S.; trustee, mem. exec. com. United Theol. Sem.; bd. dirs. Otterbein Home, Nat. Rural Housing Coalition, Grafton Hills Assn.; mem. exec. com. West Ohio Bd. Ordained Ministry; chmn. social and internat. affairs com. World Meth. Council. Recipient award for pub. service Dept. Justice and U.S. Atty. Gen., 1974. Mem. N.Am. Acad. Ecumenists, Asso. Ch. Press, Am. Mgmt. Assn., Kappa Delta Pi. Club: Dayton Racquet. Author: (with others) Discovering God's Mission in Our Community, 1968; contbr.: New Occasions, 1975; The Church and the Rural Poor, 1975. Home: 34 W Dixon Ave Dayton OH 45419 Office: 601 W Riverview Ave Dayton OH 45406

DEWITT, JOAN MARIE, chemist; b. St. Louis, June 16, 1935; d. Daniel Harry and Adele Mary (Kottenstette) DeW.; B.S., St. Louis U., 1959. Lab technician LaFrance Mfg. Co., St. Louis, 1956-59, chemist, 1959-79; chemist Carboline Co., St. Louis, 1979—. Mem. evangelization com. Archdiocese St. Louis, 1977—; nat. treas. Christian Life Communities, 1967-71. Recipient award Nat. Fedn. Christian Life Communities, 1971, John XXIII Christian Life Community Leadership award, 1971. Mem. Soc. Die Casting Engrs. (nat. dir., Service award 1971), Am. Chem. Soc., AAAS, Am. Soc. Metals. Roman Catholic. Home: 9 Godfrey Ln Ferguson MO 63135 Office: 350 Hanley Industrial Ct Saint Louis MO 63144

DEWITT, WILLIAM ORVILLE, baseball exec.; b. St. Louis, Aug. 3, 1902; s. William Joseph and Lulu May (Sowash) D.; student St. Louis U., 1925-27, Law Sch., 1928-31, Washington U., St. Louis, 1927-28; m. Margaret Holekamp, Mar. 21, 1936; children—Joan, Donna Dorothy, William O. Office boy for St. Louis Browns, 1916; stenographer St. Louis Cardinals, 1917-25, treas., 1926-35, v.p., 1936; v.p., gen. mgr. St. Louis Browns, 1936-48, pres., 1949-51, v.p., 1952-53; asst. gen. mgr. N.Y. Yankees, 1954-56; baseball coordinator, 1957-59; pres. Detroit Baseball Co., 1959-60; v.p., gen. mgr. Cin. Baseball Club Company, 1960-61, pres., gen. mgr., owner, 1961-66; baseball cons., 1967-72; pres. William O. DeWitt & Assos.; chmn. bd. Chgo. White Sox, 1975-80; admitted to Mo. bar, 1931, Fed. bar, 1958, U.S. Supreme Ct. bar, 1972. Mem. Major League Exec. Council, 1948-50, 77-79; mem. com. to select vet. players to Baseball Hall of Fame, 1972—; mem. adv. bd. Salvation Army, Boys Club of Cin. Named Major league exec. of year, 1944. Mem. Mo. Bar Assn., Bar Assn. St. Louis, Delta Theta Phi, Alpha Sigma Nu. Presbyterian. Clubs: Masons (33 deg., DeMolay legion of honor), Shriners; University (St. Louis); Queen City, One Hundred, Cincinnati Country, Recess, Commonwealth (Cin.); Little (Gulfstream, Fla.); Ocean, Yacht (DelRay Beach, Fla.). Home: 2444 Madison Rd Cincinnati OH 45208 also 1465 Lands End Rd Point Manalapan FL 33462

DEWOLF, ALIDOR JOSEPH, machine tool co. exec.; b. Chgo., Mar. 19, 1916; s. Louis Joseph and Gabrella (LaGrou) DeW.; student DePaul U., 1935-36; B.S., Loyola U., 1936-38; m. Geraldine Ann Dreis, Aug. 21, 1944; children—Debra, Richard, Linda, Peggy. With Dreis and Krump Mfg. Co., Chgo., 1945—, controller, 1945-50, sec., also gen. sales mgr., 1950-55, pres., 1955-76, chmn., 1976—. Served to lt. (j.g.), USNR, 1941-45. Mem. Nat. Machine Tool Builders Assn. (dir. 1961-66, pres. 1966-67). Clubs: Beverly Country (pres. 1968-69, dir. 1952-55, 58-59) (Chgo.); Country of Florida, Ocean of Florida (DelRay Beach); Butterfield Country (Hinsdale, Ill.). Home: 4 Oak Brook Club Dr G107 Oak Brook IL 60521 Office: 7400 S Loomis Blvd Chicago IL 60636

DE WOLFE, JOHN CHAUNCEY, III, lawyer; b. Oak Park, Ill., July 24, 1944; s. John Chauncey Jr. and Dorothy Sinclair (Fulton) De W.; A.B., Brown U., 1965; J.D., Cornell U., 1968; div.; children—Geoffrey, Warren, Lucinda. Admitted to Ill. bar, 1968; since practiced in Chgo.; mem. firm De Wolfe, Mills & Markley and predecessor firms, 1968—, partner, 1970—; dir. Oak Hill Farms, Chgo., 1st DuPage Corp., Hinsdale, Ill., Mem. ednl. evaluation commn. Sch. Dist. 208, Cook County (Ill.), 1968-70. Mem. DuPage County (Ill.) Rep. Orgn., 1973—, committeeman, 1973-76; vice chmn. Lawyers for Reagan Com., 1980. Trustee St. Leonard House, Episcopal Diocese of Chgo., 1974—, pres., 1975-79; trustee Pop Warner Little Scholars, 1975—. Served as midshipman USNR, 1961-65. Recipient Cornelius W. Wickersham award Fed. Bar Council, 1968. Mem. Am. (com. chmn. 1979—), Ill. State, Chgo., Du Page County bar assns., Chgo. Estate Planning Council, Legal Club of Chgo., Chgo. Hist. Soc., Art Inst. Chgo., Phi Alpha Delta. Republican. Episcopalian (vestryman). Clubs: Union League (Chgo.); Prarie (Harbert, Mich.). Home: 5513 Lakeside Dr Lisle IL 60532 Office: 135 S La Salle St Chicago IL 60603

DEXTER, DONALD HARVEY, surgeon; b. Maywood, Ill., Apr. 8, 1928; s. Harry Malcolm and Theodora Jane (Trelawny) D.; B.S., Tulana U., 1948; M.D., Northwestern U., 1950; m. Esther Ruth Reeve, May 16, 1953; children—Donald H., Jr., Scott Reeve, Bryce Malcolm, Margaret Helen. Intern, Cook County Hosp., Chgo., 1950-51; resident in surgery Ill. Central Hosp., Chgo., 1951-52, Cook County Hosp., Chgo., 1955-58; practice medicine specializing in surgery, Macomb, Ill., 1958—, sr. mem. Macomb Clinic; prof. dept. health scis. Western Ill. U., 1975—, team physician; coroner McDonough County, Ill., 1964-76. Mem. Western Ill. U. Found. Served with USN, 1953-54. Named Outstanding Citizen of Macomb, Jaycees, 1972, Macomb Area C. of C., 1973; recipient award of recognition Devel. Center at Western Ill. U. and Macomb Area C. of C., 1977; diplomate Am. Bd. Surgery. Fellow A.C.S. (pres. Ill. chpt. 1972); mem. AMA, Ill. State Med. Soc., Ill. Surg. Soc., MW Surg. Assn., Internat. Assn. Coroners and Med. Examiners, Phi Beta Kappa. Republican. Episcopalian. Club: Rotary. Home: Tower Rd Rural Route #1 Macomb IL 61455 Office: Macomb Clinic 505 E Grant St Macomb IL 61455

DEYOUNG, LILLIAN JEANETTE, coll. dean; b. Ogden, Utah, July 26, 1926; d. Peter and Gertrude DeY.; B.S., U. Utah, 1950, M.S., 1955, Ph.D., 1975. Dir. Sch. Nursing St. Luke's Hosp., Denver,

1955-72; asso. prof., curriculum coordinator Intercollegiate Center for Nursing Edn., Spokane, Wash., 1972-73; asst. dir. nursing service U. Utah, Salt Lake City, 1973-75; dean Coll. Nursing, prof. nursing U. Akron (Ohio), 1975—; mem. program adv. com. Northeastern Ohio Univs. Colls. Medicine, 1978—. Bd. trustees, bd. dirs. Akron Gen. Med. Center. Mem. Am. Assn. Higher Edn., Am. Nurses Assn., Nat. League Nursing, ARC, State Bd. Nurse Registration and Nursing Edn., Ohio League Nursing, Ohio Nurses Assn. Author: Foundations of Nursing, 1966, 2d edit., 1972, 3d edit., 1976; Dynamics of Nursing, 4th edit., 1981. Home: 711 Lafayette Dr Akron OH 44303 Office: Coll Nursing U Akron Akron OH 44325

DE YOUNG, LYNDEN EVANS, music educator; b. Chgo., Mar. 6, 1923; s. John Vanderbilt and Effie Irene DeY.; Mus.M., Roosevelt U., Chgo., 1951; Mus.D., Northwestern U., 1966; m. June Hope Shabago, Sept. 24, 1950; children—Anne Elizabeth, Paul Nicholas. Jazz trombonist and arranger, 1938-46; instr. music theory Roosevelt U., Chgo., 1951-53, instr. evening div., 1953-59; tchr. music Ill. public schs., 1953-66; asst. prof. music theory and composition Sch. Music, Northwestern U., Evanston, 1966-71, asso. prof., 1972—, chmn. dept. music theory, 1967-75; guest lectr. on jazz Chgo. area colls., 1976-78; composer-in-residence North Shore area public schs., 1977; judge Lake Forest Symphony Solo Competition, 1977-78; leader marching band Lake Bluff (Ill.) 4th of July Parade, 1962—. Served with U.S. Army, 1943-46. Recipient Avis award, 1966, Thor Johnson Brass Ensemble Composition award, 1951; cert. tchr., Ill. Mem. Am. Soc. U. Composers, Nat. Assn. Composers, Am. Musicol. Soc., Nat. Assn. Jazz Educators, Midwest Theory Soc., Am. Fedn. Musicians, AAUP, Coll. Music Soc., Pi Kappa Lambda (pres. Alpha chpt. 1969-70). Methodist. Contbr. articles on music theory to scholarly jours.; composer: Two Brass Quintets, 1951, Divertissement for brass choir, 1953, Homage to Dixieland (percussion ensemble), 1974, Chamber Music for alto saxophone, oboe, bassoon, piano and vibraphone, 1975; Praise the Lord (chorus, chamber orch. and organ), 1976; Voices of Brass (brass septet), 1981. Home: 664 Pine Ct Lake Bluff IL 60044 Office: School of Music Northwestern Univ Evanston IL 60201

DHARMAPURI, VIDYASAGAR, pediatrician; b. India, Aug. 16, 1939; came to U.S., 1963, naturalized, 1979; s. Chakradhara Swamy and Venkatamma Dharmapuri; M.B.B.S., Osmania Med. Coll., Hyderabad, 1961; M.Sc. in Physiology, U. Man. (Can.), 1971; m. Nagamani R. Beligere, June 6, 1968; children—Sahana, Sadhana, Sanjay. Intern Vassar Hosp., Poughkeepsie, N.Y., 1963-64; resident in pediatrics Grassland Hosp., Valhalla, N.Y. and Albany Med. Center, 1964-65, Pitts. Children's Hosp., 1965-66; fellow in neonetology Pa. Hosp. and Phila. Children's Hosp., 1965-68; teaching fellow U. Man. (Can.), 1971; asso. dir. nurseries Cook County Hosp., Chgo., 1971-74; dir. newborn nurseries U. Ill. Med. Center, Chgo., 1974—, prof. pediatrics, 1977—, dir. neonatology, 1974—. Pres. Hindu Temple Greater Chgo.; mem. adv. bd. India Abroad Found. Diplomate Am. Bd. Pediatrics. Fellow Royal Coll. Phys. and Surg. Can.; mem. Am. Pediatric Soc., Am. Thoracic Soc., Royal Soc. Medicine, Soc. Critical Care Medicine (council), Internat. Coll. Pediatrics, Soc. Pediatric Research, Perinatal Research Soc., Chgo. Lung Assn., Midwest Soc. Pediatric Research, Chgo. Pediatric Soc., Chgo. Heart Assn. Editorial bd. Jour. Critical Care Medicine, Perinatology/Neonatology Jour., Indian Jour. Pediatrics. Home: 804 Wildwood Ct Oak Brook IL 60521 Office: 840 S Wood St Chicago IL 60612

DIAMOND, KENNETH JOSEPH, state ofcl.; b. Phila., Aug. 6, 1946; s. Sidney Louis and Beatrice Bella (Carlin) D.; B.S., Coll. Emporia, 1968; M.S., Emporia State U., 1972; Ph.D., U. Nebr., 1976; 1 dau., Shayna Joanne. Asst. dir. Comprehensive Health Planning, Nebr. Dept. Health, Lincoln, 1974-76; asst. prof. sociology U. Nebr., 1976—; dir. div. health systems planning and implementation, Nebr. Dept. Health, Lincoln, 1976-77; dir. Nebr. State Health Planning and Devel. Agy., Lincoln, 1977—; cons. in field. Chmn. Health Task Force for the Medically Underserved in Western Nebr., 1974-75; mem. adv. bd. Nebr. Annual Social Indicator Survey, 1975—; mem. Nebr. State Citizens Mental Health Adv. Council, 1976—; mem. adv. council Nat. Service Health Corps, 1979—. Served with U.S. Army, 1968-70. NIMH fellow, 1973-74. Mem. AAAS, Am. Health Planning Assn. (dir.), Am. Public Health Assn., Royal Soc. Health, Am. Sociol. Assn., Midwest Sociol. Assn., Nebr. Public Health Assn. Home: 4611 Grassridge Rd PO Box 94651 Lincoln NE 68509 Office: 301 Centennial Mall S Lincoln NE 68509

DIAMOND, RUTH LOIS, civic worker; b. Albany, N.Y., Oct. 4, 1930; d. William H. and Bess (Sadosky) Abramson; student Met. Jr. Coll., Kansas City, Mo., 1948-49; B.J., U. Mo., 1952, postgrad., 1978—; m. Myron S. Diamond, June 27, 1954; 1 son, Michael Wayne. Advt. copywriter Kansas City Star, 1952, Mid-Continent Jeweler, Kansas City, 1952-54; sec.-treas. Myron S. Diamond, Co., Inc., Kansas City, Mo., 1960—; pres. Young Matron's Group, Hadassah, Kansas City, 1958-59, v.p. fund-raising Kansas City chpt., 1977; pres. Beth Horon chpt. B'nai B'rith Women, 1970-72, cons. Dist. 2, 1975-77, pres. Greater Kansas City (Mo.) Council, 1977-78, mem. regional bd., 1978—, editor Gateway Regional newsletter; pres. sisterhood Ohev Sholom synagogue, Prairie Village, Kans., 1974-76, religious sch. tchr., 1970—, bd. dirs., mem. exec. com., 1976—; tchr. United Religious Sch., 1976—; editor organizational newspapers. Mem. Ohev Sholom Centennial Com.; public relations specialist Gateway region B'nai B'rith Women, 1981-82; mem. steering com. Mo. Humanities Com., 1978; free lance writer; communications cons. Recipient Honor award State of Israel Bonds, 1977, Dist. awards for community service and newspaper editing B'nai B'rith Women. Mem. Women in Communications, U. Mo. Alumni Assn., Phi Sigma, Alpha Epsilon Rho. Home: 8217 Briar St Prairie Village KS 66208

DIANA, JOSEPH ANTHONY, found. exec.; b. New Castle, Pa., June 26, 1924; s. Joseph Anthony and Emma (Eardly) D.; B.A., U. Mich., 1946, postgrad, 1950-51; m. Kathryn June Matthews, June 26, 1946; children—Mark Stephen, Chris Joseph, Todd Francis, Paul Jeffrey. Asst. bus. mgr. Inst. Sci. and Tech., 1954-59, bus. mgr., 1959-60; asst. controller U. Mich., Ann Arbor, 1969-70; v.p. fin. and mgmt. SUNY, Stony Brook, 1970-75; asso. v.p. bus. affairs, vice chancellor adminstrv. affairs U. Ill., Urbana, 1975-79; v.p. adminstrn., treas. John D. and Catherine T. MacArthur Found., Chgo., 1979—; interim pub. Harper's Mag., 1980—. Republican. Roman Catholic. Home: 2011 Silver Ct W Urbana IL 61801 Office: 140 S Dearborn St Chicago IL 60603

DIANO, JACQUES YENNI, elec. co. exec.; b. New Orleans, Sept. 30, 1938; s. Albert Laurence and Marie Kinta (Yenni) D.; B.A., Southeastern La. U., 1962; M.B.A., Loyola U., 1968; m. Judy Rae Jones, Jan. 2, 1963; children—Jacques Yenni, Justin, Jane, Julie. With Ford Motor Co., various locations, 1965-72; mgr. distbn. sales Am. Bosch Electric Products div. Ambac Industries Inc., Columbus, Miss., 1972-76; mgr. indsl. sales chem.-plastics div. Gen. Tire & Rubber Co., Ionia, Mich., 1976; sales mgr. Koontz-Wagner Electric Co., South Bend, Ind., 1976-81; gen. sales mgr. Flanders Electric Co., Evansville, Ind., 1981—. Served with USNR, 1962-65. Mem. Can. Automotive Electric Assn. (dir. 1975-76). Republican. Roman Catholic. Clubs: Point O'Woods Golf and Country, Kiwanis of South Bend. Home: 53344 Bonvale Dr South Bend IN 46635 Office: Flanders Electric Co Evansville IN

DIAS, JERRY RAY, chemist, engr., educator; b. Oakland, Calif., Oct. 26, 1940; s. Francis Frederick and Margurette Ruth (Bass) D.; B.S. with honors in Chemistry, San Jose State Coll., 1965; Ph.D. (NIH predoctoral fellow, 1968-70), Ariz. State U., 1970; m. Barbara Jean Turner, July 13, 1958; children—Rene Barbara, Harvey William, Jennifer Jean. Process engr. Fairchild Corp., Mountain View, Calif., 1966; grad. teaching asst. Ariz. State U., Tempe, 1965-68; night instr. Chabot Coll., Hayward, Calif., 1970-72; postdoctoral fellow Stanford (Calif.) U., 1970-72; asst. prof. U. Mo., Kansas City, 1972-78, asso. prof., 1978—; chemist Mobay Chem. Corp., Kansas City, summer 1978; chemist EPA, Region VII, summers 1979, 80; advt. and bus. mgr. Kansas City Chemist; indsl. cons. Fulbright scholar, Yugoslavia, 1981. Mem. Am. Chem. Soc. (chmn. Kansas City sect., 1978), Nat. Soc. Profl. Engrs. (Mo. Western chpt.), Am. Electroplaters Soc. (mem. nat. tech. edn. bd. 1978-81), Electrochem. Soc., ASTM (various coms.), Am. Inst. Chem. Engrs., Phi Lambda Upsilon, Phi Kappa Phi. Republican. Roman Catholic. Research on synthetic-mechanistic organic chemistry, environ. chemistry and mass spectrometry; contbr. numerous articles to sci. publs. Home: 10001 W 93d St Overland Park KS 66212 Office: Dept Chemistry University of Missouri Kansas City MO 64110

DIAZ, ARTHUR, pub. co. exec.; b. Mount Carmel, Pa., July 1, 1926; s. John and Josephine D.; B.A., Albright Coll., 1950; M.A., Pa. State U., 1952; m. Ramona Latorre, Apr. 25, 1952; children—James, Ramon, Bonita, Jeffrey, Saundra. With Centre Daily Times, State College, Pa., 1950-55; v.p. circulation Easton (Pa.) Express, 1955-63; dir. Pulitzer Broadcasting, St. Louis, 1968-76; circulation dir. St. Louis Post Dispatch, 1964-76; v.p., gen. mgr. Paddock Pubs., Arlington Heights, Ill., 1977—; pres. Family TV of Elgin (Ill.), 1980-81; chmn. Pinellas Broadcasters, Largo, Fla., 1980-81; dir. Pulitzer Pub. Co. Served with USAAC, 1944-46. Mem. Internat. Newspaper Advt. and Mktg. Execs. Assn., Internat. Circulation Mgrs. Assn., Internat. Newspaper Promotion Assn., Am. Mgmt. Assn., Am. Newspaper Pubs. Assn., Inland Daily Press Assn. Clubs: Meadow (Chgo.), Media (St. Louis). Home: 833 Partridge Dr Palatine IL 60067 Office: PO Box 280 Arlington Heights IL 60006

DIAZ, GREGORIO, computer scientist; b. Sao Paulo, Brazil, June 24, 1947; s. Fernando E. and Martha C. (Fernandez) D.; came to U.S., 1969; student Universidad Central de Venezuela, 1968-69; B.A., U. Kans., 1972, M.S., 1974; m. Paula L. Oldehoeft, Sept. 10, 1980. Computer systems analyst Bur. of Child Research, U. Kans., Lawrence, 1972-74, coordinator for computer applications, 1974-78, dir. computer applications, 1978—, lectr. dept. computer sci., 1977—; cons. Centro de Rehab., Santo Domingo, Dominican Republic, 1978—, Instituto Panameño de Rehabilitacion Especial, Panama City, Panama, 1978, Greenbriar Center, Lewisburg, W. Va., summer 1980. Mem. Assn. for Computing, Digital Equipment Users Soc. Contbr. papers in field to profl. meetings and jours. Home: 2814 University Dr Lawrence KS 66044 Office: Bureau Child Research Univ Kansas Lawrence KS 66045

DIAZ, LOUIS ALBERT, mech. engr., researcher, educator; b. St. Croix, V.I., Oct. 31, 1950; s. Louis Albert and Agneta Magdalen (Hansen) D.; B.S. in M.E., Mich. Tech. U., 1972, M.S. in M.E., 1978; postgrad. Purdue U., 1968-82; m. Paulette Thompson, Dec. 28, 1974. Mech. engr. Jacksonville (Fla.) Naval Air Sta., 1973-76; heat transfer instr. Purdue U., 1979—. Mem. ASME, Sigma Xi, Tau Beta Pi. Republican. Roman Catholic. Club: Purdue Camera. Home: 116 Woodland Terr West Lafayette IN 47906 Office: Heat Transfer Lab Purdue U West Lafayette IN 47907

DIAZ GRANADOS, FREDERICK ANTONIO, supt. schs.; b. Santa Marta, Colombia, June 13, 1933; came to U.S., 1933, naturalized, 1955; s. Humberto Federico and Beatrice Irene (Steinmetz) D.; B.A., Lehigh U., 1954; M.N.S. Ariz. State U., 1962; postgrad. St. Lawrence U., 1964, U. Redlands, 1965-67, Azusa Pacific Coll., 1972-74, Calif. State U., Los Angeles, 1975, U. Calif., Irvine, 1975; Ph.D., Faith Evangelistic Christian Sch., 1981; m. Loretta Minnie Wimmer, Nov. 20, 1954; children—Ricky Carlos, Cathy Jean. Instr., Keystone Jr. Coll., La Plume, Pa., 1955-56; head dept. math. Perkiomen Sch., Pennsburg, Pa., 1956-59; head math. and sci. dept. Flintridge Prep. Sch., Pasadena, Calif., 1959-69; headmaster Ojai (Calif.) Valley Lower Sch., 1969-71, The Bidwell Sch., Lodi, Calif., 1971-72, Orange (Calif.) Christian Sch., 1972-74, Santa Ana (Calif.) Christian Sch., 1974-76; pres. Faith Christian Sch., Williamsville, N.Y., 1976-77; supt. Sunshine Bible Acad., Miller, S.D. 1977—; NSF cons., Uruguay, 1966. Bd. dirs. Ojai Trails Assn., 1970-71. Mem. Am. Assn. Sch. Adminstrs., Nat. Sci. Tchrs. Assn., Am. Assn. Physics Tchrs., Nat. Council Tchrs. Math. Republican. Home and office: Star Route 5 Box 2900 Miller SD 57362

DICK, CHARLES T., educator; b. Cleve., Mar. 5, 1947; s. Charles A. and Mary Kay (Bub) D.; B.S. in Bus. Adminstrn., Xavier U., Cin., 1969, M.B.A. in Data Processing, 1974; M.Ed. in Bus. Edn., U. Cin., 1971, postgrad., 1974—; m. Anne M. Gardner, Aug. 10, 1974; 1 son, Charles R. Tchr. Cin. Bd. Edn., 1969-72, bus. edn. supr.-intern, 1972-73, asso., 1973-79, asst. treas., 1979—; part-time instr. U. Cin., 1975—; cons. govt. and pvt. groups. Data processing adv. com. J. Russell Lee Vocat. Center, 1981. Cert. data processing, Data Processing Mgmt. Assn., 1978; supt. cert., Ohio. Mem. Am. Vocat. Assn., Ohio Vocat. Assn., Assn. Sch. Bus. Ofcls., Ohio Assn. Sch. Bus. Ofcls., Am. Assn. Sch. Adminstrs., Nat. Bus. Edn. Assn., Ohio Bus. Tchrs. Assn., Phi Delta Kappa, Delta Pi Epsilon. Office: 230 E 9th St Cincinnati OH 45202

DICK, HERMAN FRANK, ednl. cons.; b. Detroit, Sept. 22, 1930; s. Herman and Hildegard D.; B.S., Eastern Mich. U., 1963; M.A., U. Mich., 1966; Ed.D., Wayne State U., 1973; m. Marietta J. Service, July 16, 1950; children—Herman Eric, Heidi Sue. Farmer, 1948-60; tchr. handicapped children Willow Run Sch.-Ypsilanti (Mich.) Jr. High Sch., 1963-65; asst. prof. Eastern Mich. U., Ypsilanti, 1965-67; cons. handicapped students Oakland Schs., Pontiac, Mich., 1967—, dir. curriculum mgmt. spl. edn.; adj. prof. Wayne State U., Detroit; guest instr. Ind. State U., Terre Haute, Central Mo. State U. Driver Edn. for Handicapped. Fellow Am. Assn. on Mental Deficiency; mem. Mich. Assn. on Mental Deficiency, Council for Exceptional Children. Contbr. articles in field to profl. jours. Home: 2766 Costa Mosa Pontiac MI 48055 Office: 2100 Pontiac Lake Rd Pontiac MI 48054

DICK, JOHN HOWARD, venture capital co. exec.; b. Chgo., Dec. 29, 1946; s. Albert Blake, III, and Elisabeth (York) D.; B.A., Nasson Coll.; M.S., Lake Forest Coll.; m. Brenda Johnson, Oct. 3, 1970; children—Elisabeth G., Phoebe A. With A.B. Dick Co., Chgo., 1969—, mktg. mgr., 1978-80, pres. Dicksfield Properties, 1980—, Pocket Docket Co., 1980—, J. Dick & Co., 1981—. Treas., Dick Family Found.; bd. dirs. Lake Forest Open Lands Assn. Clubs: Exec., Economic, Chgo., Racquet, Onwentsia (bd. govs.). Home: 900 Woodbine Ln Lake Forest IL 60045 Office: 135 S LaSalle St Chicago IL 60603

DICK, MARVIN EDGAR, dentist; b. LaHarpe, Kans., Jan. 25, 1918; m. Arthur Clarence and Altie (Wardell) D.; student Madison Coll., 1940; D.D.S., Emory U., 1943; m. Emma Laura Canfield, Dec. 23, 1940; children—Doyle M., Milton L., Helen Elaine. Practice dentistry, Wichita, Kans., 1944-54, 56—; lectr. in field; established dental clinic, Philippines, 1967; mem. splty. adv. com. Kans. Diabetes Research Center. Sponsor CAP. Served to maj. Dental Corps, USAF, 1954-56. Mem. ADA, Kans., Wichita Dist. dental assns., Flying Dentists Assn. (charter mem.), Acad. Gen. Dentistry, Acad. Dentistry for Children (charter mem. Kans. chpt.), Aircraft Owners and Pilots Assn. Republican. Seventh Day Adventist (elder). Home: Rte 2 111 Douglass KS 67039 Office: 536 S Bluff St Wichita KS 67218

DICKEN, DONALD RAY, glass mfg. co. exec.; b. New Orleans, Oct. 27, 1942; s. John Raymond and Kathryn Marquart Dicken; B.S. in Mech. Engring., Kans. State U., 1965; m. Betty Anne Randall, June 12, 1965; children—Scott Randall, Kirby Kathryn. Mfg. mgmt. trainee Gen. Electric Co., Cin., 1965-66; vol. Peace Corps, Afghanistan, 1966-68; with Corning Glass Works, Corning, N.Y., 1970-76, gen. supr. forming and maintenance, 1975-76, plant mfg. engr., State College, Pa., 1977-78, plant prodn. supr., 1978-81, project dir., Greenville, Ohio, 1981—. Vice pres. Lemont/Houserville Sch. PTA, State College, 1979-80; local pack cubmaster Cub Scouts, 1978-81. Served with USAR, 1968-70. Mem. ASME. Republican. Club: Elks. Home: 1058 Buckeye Dr Greenville OH 45313 Office: Corning Glass Works Greenville OH 45331

DICKEN, WILLIAM HOWARD, JR., mfg. co. exec.; b. Columbiana, Ohio, Aug. 17, 1931; s. William Howard and Helene Lois (Crist) D.; grad. Sch. of aviational Trades, N.Y.C., 1949; m. Myrtle Irene Capen, May 21, 1955; stepchildren—John Murrell, Robert Murrell. Supr., Nat. Can Corp., various locations, 1965-73; shift supr. Ball Metal Container Group, Findlay, Ohio, 1973-74; head dept. Owens-Ill. Metal Container, Perrysburg, Ohio, 1974-77, mfg. specialist, 1977-80, lithography specialist, Constantine, Mich., 1980—. Mem. council St. Joseph-Branch County pvt. initiative sector CETA and PISP Consortium, 1981—. Recipient Service award, Jr. Achievement, 1977-79. Mem. Nat. Mgmt. Assn. (dir Toledo chpt. 1977-80; recipient Meritous award 1979), Nat. Metal Decorators Assn., Am. Soc. Tng. Dirs. (dir. Michiana chpt.). Republican. Baptist. Clubs: Masons, Shriners. Home: 61243 Timberland Dr Jones MI 49061 Office: PO Box 218 Constantine MI 49064

DICKENS, HAL GEORGE, advt. exec.; b. Chgo., Mar. 1, 1932; s. Harry and Betty (Ziv) D.; student Sorbonne, Paris, 1946; B.A.E., Art Inst. Chgo., DePaul U., 1950; m. Laima Jakutis, June 17, 1974; children by previous marriage—Kim, Craig, Hal G. Vice pres. E.H. Weiss, 1954-59, McCann Erickson, 1959-61, Grant Advt. Agy., 1961-63, North Advt. Agy., 1965-66; dir. mktg. Coca-Cola Bottling Co. of Chgo., 1963-64; pres. Dickens Advt., Inc., Park Ridge, Ill., 1966-76; exec. dir. Community Currency Exchange Assn. Ill., Inc., 1976-79; pres. Hal Dickens Advt., Chgo., 1979—; dir. North Community State Bank (Chgo.). Served with AUS 1952-53. Republican. Roman Catholic. Clubs: Merchandising, Marketing Execs. Contbr. articles to trade publs. Home: 109 Burnside Ct Vernon Hills IL 60061 Office: 456 W Frontage Rd Northfield IL 60093

DICKERSON, DONALD ROBERT, organic chemist; b. Champaign, Ill., Jan. 21, 1925; s. Lee Alexander and Mildred Alice (Lindsey) D.; B.S., U. Ill., 1950, M.S., 1958, Ph.D. (Gen. Foods Co. fellow 1961-62), 1962; m. Eileen Ann O'Donnell, Feb. 3, 1951; children—Kathleen Ann, Stephen Philip. Chief chemist Clark Microchem. Lab., Urbana, 1951-53; with Ill. Geol. Survey, Champaign, 1953—, chemist, 1962-72, organic chemist, 1972—. Served with M.C., AUS, 1944-46. Mem. Am. Chem. Soc., Ill. Acad. Sci. (council 1973—, pres. 1979-80), Sigma Xi, Chi Gamma Iota, Gamma Sigma Delta. Roman Catholic. Club: Kiwanis. Home: 703 S Pine St Champaign IL 61820 Office: 615 E Peabody Dr Champaign IL 61820

DICKERSON, FREDERICK REED, lawyer, educator; b. Chgo., Nov. 11, 1909; s. Fred George and Rena (Reed) D.; grad. Lake Forest Acad., 1927; A.B., Williams Coll., 1931; LL.B., Harvard, 1934; LL.M. (Univ. fellow 1938-39), Columbia U., 1939, J.S.D., 1950; m. Jane Morrison, June 14, 1939; children—Elizabeth Ann (Mrs. David D. Brown), John Scott, Martha Reed. Admitted to Mass. bar, 1934, Ill. bar, 1936, U.S. Supreme Ct. bar, 1943; asso. firm Goodwin, Procter & Hoar, Boston, 1934-35, McNab, Holmes & Long, Chgo., 1936-38; asst. prof. law Washington U., St. Louis, 1939-40, U. Pitts., 1940-42; atty. OPA, 1942-47; asst. legis. counsel U.S. Ho. of Reps., 1947-49; Joint Army-Air Force Statutory Revision Group; chmn. com. on codification, dep. asst. gen. counsel U.S. Dept. Def., 1949-58; prof. law Ind. U., 1958—, asso. dean, 1971-75; distinguished vis. prof. law So. Ill. U., 1975. Pres., F.G. Dickerson Co., Chgo., 1948—; chmn. commn. on uniform laws State of Ind., 1969-81; mem. Ind. Statute Revision Commn., 1969-70; cons. Dept. Def., 1958-59, 66, FAA, 1960-65, Dept. Transp., 1967-69, Pres.'s Com. on Consumer Interests, 1967-68, Commn. on Govt. Procurement, 1971-72, Gen. Accounting Office, 1973-76; lectr. Northwestern U., 1938, Am. U., 1956, 58, Practising Law Inst., 1961, 79, U.K. Govt. Legal Officers' Course, 1972, U.S. CSC, 1971-76, Center for Adminstrv. Justice, 1975-79. Recipient Distinguished Civilian Service award Dept. Def., 1957; Ford Found. law faculty fellow Harvard, 1961-62. Mem. Am. Law Inst., Am. (chmn. standing com. law and tech. 1968-69, chmn. standing com. legis. drafting 1969-73), Ind. bar assns., Order Coif, Phi Alpha Delta, Phi Gamma Delta. Methodist. Author: Products Liability and the Food Consumer, 1951; Legislative Drafting, 1954; Fundamentals of Legal Drafting, 1965; Interpretation and Application of Statutes, 1975. Editor: Legal Problems Affecting Private Swimming Pools, 1961; Product Safety in Household Goods, 1968; Professionalizing Legislative Drafting—The Federal Experience, 1973; Proc. International Seminar and Workshop on the Teaching of Legal Drafting, 1977; Cases and Materials on Legislation, 1978; Materials on Legal Drafting, 1981; mem. adv. bd. Jurimetrics Jour., 1962—, Jour. Legislation, 1971—; contbr. articles to Harper's Mag., Esquire, Ency. Americana.

DICKEY, JULIA EDWARDS, mgmt. and promotional cons.; b. Sioux Falls, S.D., Mar. 6, 1940; d. John Keith and Henrietta Barbara (Zerell) Edwards; student DePauw U., 1958-59; A.B., Ind. U., 1962, M.L.S., 1967, postgrad., 1967—; m. Joseph E. Dickey, June 18, 1959; children—Joseph E., John Edwards. Asst. acquisitions librarian Ind. U. Regional Campus Libraries, 1965-67; head tech. services Bartholomew County Library, Columbus, Ind., 1967-74; reference coordinator Southeastern Ind. Area Library Service Authority, Columbus, 1974-78, dir., 1978-80; pres. Jedco Enterprises, 1981—; legis. strategy chmn. Ind. Library Coop. Devel., 1975. Mem. Columbus exec. bd. Mayor's Task Force on Status of Women, 1973—; del. Ind. Sch. Nominating Assembly, 1973-75, 75-77; sec. bd. dirs. Human Services Inc. (Bartholomew, Brown and Jackson Counties community action program), 1975, pres., 1976, 78; mem. adv. council Ind./Nat. Network Study, 1977-78; bd. dirs. Columbus Women's Center; precinct coordinator Vols. For Bayh, 1974; sheriff Columbus 1st precinct, 1975, clk., 1976-77, insp., 1978, judge, 1980; treas. Hayes for State Rep., 1978. Mem. ALA, Ind. Library Assn. (dist. chmn. 1972-73, chmn. library edn. div. 1980-81), Library Assts. and Technicians Round Table (chmn. 1968-69), Tech. Services Round Table (chmn. 1971-72, sec. library planning com. 1969-72), AAUW (pres. 1973-75), Bartholomew County Library Staff Assn. (pres. 1975-76), Psi Iota Xi. Club: Zonta. Home and office: 511 Terrace Lake Rd Columbus IN 47201

DICKEY, NORMA JEAN ANN, computer software cons.; b. Cleve., Aug. 9, 1952; d. John and Norma Frances (Rysek) D.; B.S., Wheeling (Ill.) Coll., 1974. Tchr. math. Nazareth Acad., Parma Heights, Ohio, 1974-79; adviser students traveling through Europe, Am. Inst. Fgn. Studies, summers 1979-80; tchr. math. and computer sci. St. Joseph Acad., Cleve., 1980-81; software specialist Retail Info. Systems, 1981—; negotiator tchrs. assns. Mem. Cleve. Diocesan Math. Tchrs. Assn. (dir.). Home: 7714 Lucerne Dr Apt R2 Cleveland OH 44130 Office: 7550 Lucerne Dr Cleveland OH 44130

DICKIE, RUTH STRATHEARN, dietitian; b. N. Freedom, Wis., Feb. 19, 1913; d. Robert Bruce and Anna (Adams) D.; B.S., U. Wis., 1934, M.S., 1947. Dietetic intern Cook County Hosp., Chgo., 1935-36; dietitian River Pines Sanatorium, Stevens Point, Wis., 1937-40; chief dietitian Wis. State Sanatorium, Wales, 1940-42; dir. food and nutrition services U. Wis. Center Health Scis., Madison, 1942-69, dir. univ. dietetic internships, 1952-67, dir. instl. food and nutrition telephone confs. univ. extension and center health scis., 1969—; dir. Bank of N. Freedom, 1950-70. Mem. AAAS, Am. Dietetic Assn. (del. 1950-59, sec. ho. dels. 1956-57), Am. Home Econs. Assn., AAUP, Internat. Assn. Home Economists, Am. Soc. Tng. and Devel. (sec. S. Central Wis. chpt. 1974-75), Wis. Dietetic Assn. (pres. 1951-52), Madison Dietetic Assn. (pres. 1944-45), Am. Public Health Assn., Wis. Public Health Assn., Assn. U. Wis. Faculty Women, Wis. Home Econs. Assn. (historian 1980-81), Internat. Assn. Milk and Food Technologists, Nutrition Today Soc., Soc. Internat. Devel. (sec. Madison chpt. 1976—), Inst. Food Technologists, Soc. Nutrition Edn., U. Wis. Home Econs. Alumni Assn. (pres. 1948-49), Wis. Nutrition Council (pres. 1980-81), Wis. Coalition for Public Health, Madison Rose Soc. (pres. 1954-55), Wis. Women's Network, Wis. Women's Polit. Caucus, Sigma Delta Epsilon (chpt. pres. 1975-76, nat. pres. 1977-79), Phi Upsilon Omicron. Club: Madison Zonta (pres. 1956-57). Author: Diet in Health and Diseases: Rational and Practice, 1974; History of Women in Cooperative University Extension, 1980; co-author: Univ. Wis.-Univ. Hosps. Dietetic Manual, 1954; contbr. profl. publs. Home: 501 Clifden Dr Madison WI 53711 Office: 610 Walnut St Madison WI 53706

DICKINSON, DANIEL J., steel co. mgr.; b. Amboy, Ill., Oct. 17, 1950; s. Oliver Paul and Eileen (Cotter) D.; student Western Ill. U., 1968-69, U. Ill., 1970-71; m. Diane Levan, Sept. 4, 1971; children—Traci Lynn, Sarah Elizabeth. Advt. asst. Northwestern Steel & Wire Co., Sterling, Ill., 1973, supr. advt., 1974, advt. mgr., 1978—. Bd. dirs. Sterling-Rock Falls Family YMCA, 1979-81, pres., 1980; mem. chmn. citizens adv. council Unit Sch. Dist. 5, 1980-81. Mem. Nat. Agri-Mktg. Assn., C. of C. Republican. Club: Ambassador. Home: Rural Route 1 Sterling IL 61081 Office: 121 Wallace St Sterling IL 61081

DICKINSON, RUTH CURD, univ. ofcl.; b. Wilmore, Ky., Apr. 27, 1933; d. Robert Franklin and Ruth Dale (Peckinpaugh) Curd; A.B., U. Chgo., 1952; M.P.A., U. Kans., 1976; divorced; children—Jacob John Louis, Sara, Ann. Researcher, Topeka Inst. Urban Affairs, 1967; research asso., asst. to dir. community devel. services League Kans. Municipalities, Topeka, 1969; asst. to exec. sec. gov. Kans. com. White House Conf. Children and Youth, 1969-71; asst. to dir. staff devel. and tng. Topeka State Psychiat. Hosp., 1970-71; dir. public info. and vol. services Topeka State Hosp., 1971-76; policy analyst Kans. State Planning and Research, Topeka, 1976-79; asso. dir. devel. U. Chgo., 1979—; guest lectr. Washburn U., Topeka, 1967-77. Chmn. human resources study and fund drive Topeka LWV, 1961-72, bd. dirs., 1964-65, 69; chmn. capitol complex adv. com. U. Kans., 1978-79. Mem. Am. Soc. Public Adminstrn. (v.p. Kans. chpt.), Women in Communications, Jr. League Chgo., Pi Sigma Alpha. Episcopalian. Club: Quadrangle. Office: Univ Chicago 5733 S University Chicago IL 60637

DICKINSON, WILLIAM REYNOLDS, lawyer; b. Chgo., May 8, 1913; s. William Reynolds and Anna (Wilson) D.; A.B., magna cum laude, Yale, 1934, LL.B., 1937; m. Anne L. Knowles, July 22, 1945; children—Amy T., Anna W. (Mrs. Richard B. Platt), William Reynolds III. Admitted to Ill. bar, 1938; with Wilson & McIlvaine, Chgo., 1937—, partner, 1952—. Pres., dir. Chgo. Summer Resort Co., State Safety Co.; dir. KEY Television, Inc., Walker-Neer Mfg. Inc. Trustee Chgo. Zool. Soc.; sec., bd. dirs. Schweppe Found., Chgo.; bd. dirs. Field Mus. Natural History, Children's Meml. Hosp., John Crerar Library. Served to lt. USCGR, 1942-46. Mem. Am., Ill., Chgo. bar assns., Phi Beta Kappa, Zeta Psi. Clubs: Legal, Law, Attic, Casino, Metropolitan, Commercial (Chgo.); Old Elm (Ft. Sheridan, Ill.); Onwentsia (Lake Forest, Ill.); Valley of Montecito, Santa Barbara, Birnam Wood (Santa Barbara, Calif.); Belvedere Golf (Charlevoix, Mich.). Home: 770 W Westleigh Rd Lake Forest IL 60045 Office: 135 S LaSalle St Chicago IL 60603

DICKLICH, RONALD ROBERT, state senator; b. Hibbing, Minn., June 14, 1951; s. Bogdun Robert and Mildred (Kelsey) D.; B.S. cum laude in History and Polit. Sci., U. Minn., Duluth, 1974; m. Joanne Hamre, July 20, 1973; children—Julie, Rhonda, Thomas. With Sellars Constrn. Co., Hibbing, 1972-74; research historian State of Minn., Chisholm, 1974-77; commr. St. Louis County, Minn., 1977-81; mem. Minn. Senate, 1981—. Mem. Democratic-Farmer-Labor Party. Mem. Serbian Orthodox Ch. Office: 306 State Capitol Saint Paul MN 55155

DICKMANN, LEONORE WADE, educator; b. Rawlins, Wyo., Aug. 30; d. Rolland Irene (Popper) Wade; Ph.D., U. Wis., 1967; m. Lloyd H. Dickmann, Aug. 24, 1957. Tchr., Milw. Public Schs., also vice prin., supr., 1945-67; prof. curriculum U. Wis., Oshkosh, 1967—. Recipient Disting. Teaching award, 1971; Danforth Found. award, 1974. Mem. Assn. Supervision and Curriculum Devel., Creative Edn. Found., World Future Soc., Phi Delta Kappa, Delta Kappa Gamma. Office: U Wis Algoma Blvd Oshkosh WI 54901

DICKOW, JAMES FRED, distbn. exec.; b. Chgo., Mar. 27, 1943; s. Fred Henry and Margaret Isabelle (Arnold) D.; B.S.M.E., Purdue U., 1965, M.S.M.E., 1967; m. Yvonne Alberta Zabilka, Aug. 20, 1966. Mech. engr. CPC Internat., Argo, Ill., 1965-66; engr. McDonnell Douglas Corp., St. Louis, 1967-70; project engr. Delco Electronics div. Gen. Motors Corp., Milw., 1970; mgmt. cons. Drake Sheahan/Stewart Dougall, Chgo., 1971-72; dir. distbn. planning and services Will Ross div. G.D. Searle Corp., Milw., 1972-80; mgr. phys. distbn. Gentec Health Care, Milw., 1980—. Mem. ASME, Nat. Council Phys. Distbn. Mgmt., Internat. Materials Mgmt. Soc., Soc. Logistics Engrs., Phi Kappa Theta, Pi Tau Sigma, Phi Eta Sigma. Home: 7029 N Fairchild Circle Milwaukee WI 53217 Office: 1647 S 101st St Milwaukee WI 53212

DIEDERICHS, JANET WOOD, pub. relations exec.; b. Libertyville, Ill.; d. J. Howard and Ruth (Hendrickson) Wood; B.A., Wellesley Coll., 1950; m. John Kuensting Diederichs, 1953. Sales agt. Pan Am. Airways, Chgo., 1951-52; regional mgr. pub. relations Braniff Internat., Chgo., 1953-69; pres. Janet Diederichs & Assos., Inc., pub. relations cons., Chgo., 1970—. Mem. pub. affairs com. Nat. Trust for Historic Preservation, 1973-80; mem. regional com. on Marshall scholars for Brit. govt., 1975-78; bd. dirs. Chgo. Conv. and Tourism Bur., Internat. House, U. Chgo.; mem. long-range public relations planning com. Art Inst. Chgo. Mem. Nat. Acad. TV Arts and Scis., Soc. Am. Travel Writers, Chgo. Assn. Commerce and Industry, Pub. Relations Soc. Am., Publicity Club Chgo., Chgo. Network, Chgo. Press Club. Clubs: Econ. (com.), Mid-Am. (dir. 1977-79), Woman's Athletic (Chgo.). Home: 229 E Lake Shore Dr Chicago IL 60611 Office: 333 N Michigan Ave Chicago IL 60601

DIEDERICHS, JOHN KUENSTING, appliance mfg. co. exec.; b. Chgo., July 16, 1921; s. John Peter and Clara Henrietta (Kuensting) D.; A.B., U. Chgo., 1943, postgrad., 1946-47; postgrad. Northwestern U., 1952-53; m. Janet Barbara Wood, Sept. 26, 1953. With sales adminstrn. Pan Am. and Pan Am. Grace Airways, 1946-52; profl. staff cons. Booz Allen & Hamilton, 1952-56; chmn. engring. econs. research dept. Armour Research Found., 1956-62; v.p. research and devel. Chgo. Mill & Lumber Co., 1962-64; v.p. corp. planning and devel. Sunbeam Corp., Oak Brook, Ill., 1965—; dir. Ill. Water Treatment Co., Oster Corp., Mich. Ave. Bldg. Corp. Bd. dir. Sta. WFMT-FM, Chgo.; trustee Sta. WTTW-TV, PBS, Chgo. Served with USN, 1943-46. Mem. Internat. Econometric Soc., Nat. Assn. Bus. Economists, Tech. Assn. of the Graphic Arts, Screen Printers Assn., Soc. Photog. Engrs. and Scientists, Mensa. Republican. Presbyterian. Clubs: Chicago, Tavern, Casino, Internat., Mid-America, Economic. Editorial reviewer Jour. Techno-economics. Office: 2001 S York Rd Oak Brook IL 60521

DIEDRICH, RICHARD JOHN, ins. co. exec.; b. St. Paul, June 5, 1936; s. Carl Anthony and Alice V. (May) D.; student Macalester Coll., 1953-54; B.S., U. Minn., 1959; m. Judith Parish, Aug. 12, 1961; children—Pamela H., Stuart B., John C. With St. Paul Fire and Marine Ins. Co., 1959—, gen. mgr., Cleve., 1973-77, v.p. fidelity and surety bond dept., St. Paul, 1977-80, divisional v.p. property underwriting, 1980—; dir. Custom Thermoform, Inc. Trustee, Salem Found., 1979—; mem. exec. bd., exploring chmn. Hiawatha council Boy Scouts Am., Syracuse, N.Y., 1967-72, vice chmn. exploring, mem. exec. bd. Greater Cleve. council, 1973-77, mem. exec. bd. Indianhead council, St. Paul, 1977—; mem. exec. bd. Sci. Mus. Minn., 1980—; mem. exec. bd. Big Bros. Greater Cleve., 1975-76, Minn. Opera Co., 1978-80; trustee Oakland Cemetery Assn., 1979—. Served with USAF, 1954-58. Recipient William E. Spurgeon award Greater Cleve. council Boy Scouts Am. Mem. Surety Assn. Am. (exec. bd.). Republican. Roman Catholic. Clubs: Minn. (St. Paul); Somerset Country, Pool and Yacht, Lilydale Tennis. Home: 680 Arcadia Dr Saint Paul MN 55118 Office: St Paul Fire and Marine Ins Co 385 Washington St Saint Paul MN 55102

DIEHL, PAUL EUGENE, optometrist; b. Belleville, Ill., Sept. 23, 1936; s. Carl and Lucille (Bell) D.; A.A., Belleville Area Coll., 1954-56; O.D. (fellow), Ill. Coll. Optometry, 1959; m. Sharon Lee Busekrus, Apr. 8, 1961; children—Deborah Paulette, David Paul, Jonathan Brian. Individual practice optometry, St. Louis, 1959, Belleville and Cahokia, Ill., 1962—; sec.-treas. DEMI Corp., 1981—. Pub. speaker numerous civic orgns. and parent-tchr. groups. Served with USAF, 1959-62. Recipient John Marsh music award Belleville Area Coll., 1955. Mem. Am., Ill., Southwestern optometric assns., Optometric Extension Program, Tomb and Key, Phi Theta Kappa. Mem. First Assembly of God Ch. (deacon bd. 1970-72, fin. chmn. 1978—). Club: Rotary (dir. 1977—). Research on soft contact lenses. Home: 21 Andora Dr Belleville IL 62220 Office: 2801 W Main St Belleville IL 62220 also 1020 Camp Jackson Rd Cahokia IL 62206

DIEHL, WILMA J. MANNING, educator; b. Ianark, Ill., May 16, 1932; d. Harold H. and Helen (Schrock) Manning; B.S., U. Ill., 1954; reading specialist So. Ill. U., 1980; m. Glenn A. Diehl, June 7, 1957; children—Melvin, Karen, Kahla, Kathy. Home adv. Ill. Extension Service, Whiteside County, 1954-56; home economist Kellogg Co., Battle Creek, Mich., 1956-57; tchr. elem. sch., Jerseyville, Ill., 1969-75; remedial reading tchr. Public Schs. Carrollton (Ill.), 1975—. Mem. Ill. Reading Assn., Internat. Reading Assn., Assn. Supervision and Curriculum Devel., Am. Fedn. Tchrs., Delta Kappa Gamma, PEO. Methodist. Club: Eastern Star. Home: Rural Route 1 Carrollton IL 62016 Office: 4th St Carrollton IL 62016

DIELEMAN, WILLIAM WILBUR, state legislator; b. Oskaloosa, Iowa, Jan. 19, 1931; s. Garret Jan and Jozena (DeGeus) D.; B.A., Calvin Coll., Grand Rapids, Mich., 1959; M.A., State U. Iowa, Iowa City, 1966; m. Emily June Langstraat, Aug. 30, 1951; children—Wendell E., Cynthia E. Dieleman DeYoung, Kristen E. Tchr. social studies Pella (Iowa) Christian High Sch., 1959-74; agt. Bankers Life Ins. Co. Nebr., 1974—; mem. Pella City Council, 1970-75; mem. Iowa Ho. of Reps. from 70th Dist., 1974—. Mem. Iowa Capital Planning Commn.; del. local and state Democratic Convs., 1963—. Served with U.S. Army, 1953-55. Asian Affairs Inst. grantee, 1972. Mem. Central Iowa Regional Assn. Local Govt. (vice chmn. 1974), Am. Legion, Iowa Assn. Life Underwriters, Nat. Assn. Life Underwriters, Nat. Conf. State Legislators, Farm Bur. Democrat. Mem. Christian Reformed Ch. (elder 1978-80). Home: 518 Woodlawn Dr Pella IA 50219 Office: PO Box 139 317 High Ave E Oskaloosa IA 52577

DIEMAND, EUGENE AUGUST, printing co. exec.; b. York, Pa., Feb. 23, 1925; s. Eugene Paul and Alice (Hauser) D.; student Western Res. U., 1943-44; diploma Charles Morris Price Sch. Advt., Phila., 1954; Grad. Indsl. Coll. Armed Forces, 1972, Air Command and Staff Coll., Air U., 1972, Air War Coll., 1975; m. Ruth Jane Maute, Sept. 1, 1951; children—Kim, Steven, Jeffrey, Christopher. Apprentice chef John Wanamaker, Phila., 1942; supr. prodn. Gen. Accident F & L Co., Phila., 1946-56; advt.-sales promotion mgr. Am. Casualty Co., Reading, Pa., 1956-65; mgr. advt. Marsh & McLennan, Inc., ins. brokers, Chgo., 1965-73; pres. Diemand Printing Co., Chgo., 1973—. Mem. Palmyra (N.J.) City Council, 1962-65. Served with USAAF, 1943-46; PTO; and USAF, 1951-53; Korea; lt. col. Res. ret. Mem. Ins. Advt. Conf. (dir.). Mason. Home: 625 S Wheaton Ave Wheaton IL 60187 Office: 323 S Franklin St Chicago IL 60606

DIERCKS, RICHARD ALLEN, TV exec.; b. Austin, Minn., Dec. 31, 1941; s. Richard Allen and Louis (Braun) D.; B.S. in B.A., U. Minn., 1965; m. Shirley Jean Venard, Oct. 10, 1966 (div. 1976); children—Adrienne, Erika, Kate. Account supr. Campbell-Mithun Advt., Inc., Mpls., 1965-71; v.p. Knox-Reeves Advt., Inc., Mpls., 1971-74; pres., chief exec. officer Emcom, Inc., Mpls., 1975—; exec. producer Better Homes and Gardens TV Show, 1971-72; dir. Riverview Tower Corp., 1979-81. Bd. dirs. Lowry Hill Assn., 1969-73. Mem. Minn. Civil Liberties Union (dir. 1965-68), Minn. Advt. Fedn. Producer, feature film "It Ain't Easy", 1972. Office: 4000 W 76th St Minneapolis MN 55435

DIERKS, CARL GAYER, city ofcl.; b. Hudson, S.D., Jan. 11, 1940; s. Herman and Martha J. (Gayer) D.; student S.D. State U., 1957-61; m. Sandra M. Davis, June 30, 1961; children—Lori, Greg, Lisa, Jeff. Surveyor, DeWild Grant Reckert & Assos., Rock Rapids, Iowa, 1960-68; project engr. Brady Cons., Spearfish, S.D., 1968-73; city engr. Chadron (Nebr.), 1973-79, city mgr., 1979—; pvt. cons. engr., Chadron, 1975-78. Vice-pres. Nebr. Planning and Zoning Assn., 1980-81; bd. mem. N.W. Nebr. Community Action, 1979—. Served with U.S. Army, 1958-62. Registered profl. engr., Nebr., S.D. Mem. Internat. City Mgmt. Assn., Nebr. City Mgmt. Assn. (pres.), League Nebr. Municipalities (legis. com.), Public Risk Mgmt. Assn., Internat. Personnel Mgmt. Assn., Nat. Soc. Profl. Engrs. Republican. Roman Catholic. Clubs: Ridgeview Country, Elks. Home: 802 W 6th St Chadron NE 69337 Office: 234 Main St Chadron NE 69337

DIERKSEN, CAROL ANN, educator; b. Hull, Iowa, Mar. 5, 1943; d. Edward Gustav and Frances Jeanette (Becker) Stange; B.A. in Elementary Edn. and Deaf Edn. magna cum laude, Augustana Coll., Sioux Falls, S.D., 1965; postgrad U. Minn., 1966, 75; M.A. in Speech Pathology, Northwestern U., 1968; postgrad. U. N.Mex., 1971, Mankato State U., 1972, U. Wis., 1974, Transformational Generative Grammar for Deaf Students Inst., U. Ill., 1978; m. Eugene Alvin Dierksen, Nov. 21, 1970. Spl. tchr. Minn. Sch. for the Deaf, Faribault, 1965-67, speech therapist, 1968-71, curriculum coordinator, 1971-72, coordinator Title I, 1972-74, supr. middle sch., 1974-77, supr. lower and middle sch., 1977-80, prin. elem. sch., 1980—; lectr. in field. Certified elementary tchr., hearing impaired tchr., speech pathology, supr. speech, supr. hearing impaired, Minn. Mem. Am. Speech-Lang.-Hearing Assn. (cert. of clin. competence in speech pathology), Minn. Found. for Better Hearing and Speech, Educator Network, NEA, Minn. Edn. Assn., Minn. Sch. Deaf Edn. Assn. (sec. 1966-67, pres. 1974), Conf. Am. Instrs. of the Deaf, AAUW (chairperson world affairs study group 1972-78). Lutheran. Home: 209 N Elm St Owatonna MN 55060 Office: Minnesota School for the Deaf Box 308 Faribault MN 55021

DIETERICH, NEIL, state senator; b. Lincoln, Nebr., Mar. 28, 1943; student Wharton Sch. Fin. U. Pa.; B.S., J.D., U. Minn.; m. Janet; 1 son, Nathan. Admitted to Minn. bar; practice law; referee conciliation ct.; mem. Minn. Ho. of Reps., 1972-76, Minn. Senate, 1976—. Mem. Minn. Bar Assn. (family law com.), Citizens League, St. Anthony Park Assn., Ramsey County Bar Assn. Mem. Democratic-Farmer-Labor party. Office: 326 State Capitol Saint Paul MN 55155*

DIETERLE, DAVID ANTHONY, educator; b. Dayton, Ohio, May 11, 1949; s. Wilburn John Marianne (Zink) D.; B.A., Central Mich. U., 1971, M.A., 1974, M.A., 1975; Robert V. Horton-Goldman Sachs Econ. Edn. scholar Purdue U., 1981-82; m. Aug. 6, 1971 (dec.); children—Branda Marie, Laura Leigh. Tchr. elem. sch., Remus, Mich., 1971, Mt. Plesant, Mich., 1972—; asso. dir., elem. econ. edn. specialist Center for Econ. Edn., Central Mich. U., 1979—. Fundraiser, Mich. Spl. Olympics. Mem. Nat. Council Social Studies, Econ. Edn. Spl. Interest Group, Assn. Supervision and Curriculum Devel., Assn. Tchr. Edn., Found. Econ. Edn., Phi Delta Kappa. Roman Catholic. Club: K.C. Office: Center Econ Edn Central Mich U Mount Pleasant MI 48858

DIETRICH, GEORGE CHARLES, chem. co. exec.; b. Detroit, Feb. 5, 1927; s. George Sylvester and Catherine Elizabeth (Cable) D.; B.S., U. Detroit; m. Dorothy Ann Flanigan, Aug. 21, 1955; children—Linda Marie, Elizabeth Ann, George Charles. Field sales mgr. Allied Chem. Co., Chgo., 1960-64; dir. sales Aerosol Research Co., North Riverside, Ill., 1964—; pres. Aeropres Corp., Chgo., 1964-65, Diversified Chems. & Propellants Co., Westmont, Ill., 1965—, also dir.; chmn. bd. ChemSpec Ins. Ltd., 1st Bank Corp., Naperville, Ill.; dir. 1st Bank of Naperville, Am. Nat. Bank, De Kalb, Ill., Diversified CPC Internat., Anaheim, Calif. Served with USNR, 1945-46. Mem. Chem. Splty. Mfrs. Assn. (gov., chmn. bd.), Chgo. Drug and Chem. Assn., Chgo. Perfumery Soap and Extract Assn., Nat. Paint and Coatings Assn., Econs. Club Chgo., Execs. Club Chgo. Roman Catholic. Clubs: Butler Nat. Golf, Olympia Fields Country, Boca Raton Hotel and Club, Butterfield Country. Home: 1 Charleston Rd Hinsdale IL 60521 Office: 350 E Ogden Ave PO Box 447 Westmont IL 60559

DIETRICH, SUZANNE CLAIRE, instructional designer; b. Granite City, Ill., Apr. 9, 1937; d. Charles Daniel and Evelyn Blanche (Waters) D.; B.S. in Speech, Northwestern U., 1958; M.S. in Pub. Communication, Boston U., 1967; postgrad. So. Ill. U., 1973—. Intern, prodn. staff Sta. WGBH-TV, Boston, 1958-59, asst. dir., 1962-64, asst. dir. program Invitation to Art, 1958; cons. producer dir. dept. instructional TV radio Ill. Office Supt. Pub. Instruction, Springfield, 1969-70; dir. program prodn. and distbn., 1970-72; instr. faculty call staff, speech dept. Sch. Fine Arts So. Ill. U., Edwardsville, 1972—, grad. asst. for doctoral program office of dean Sch. Edn., 1975-78; research asst. Ill. public telecommunications study for Ill. Public Broadcasting Council, 1979-80; cons. and research in communications, 1980—; exec. producer, dir. TV programs Con-Con Countdown, 1970, The Flag Speaks, 1971. Roman Catholic. Home: 1011 Minnesota Ave Edwardsville IL 62025

DIETRICH, WILLIAM CARL, food co. exec.; b. Le Sueur, Minn., Mar. 16, 1932; s. William Frederick and Dolores Geraldine (Moran) D.; grad. Mercersburg (Pa.) Acad., 1950; B.S. in Biochemistry, U. Minn., 1955; m. Corinne Jean Borchert, Oct. 3, 1964; children—Mary Elizabeth, Dolores Jean. With Green Giant Co., Le Sueur, 1955—, v.p. prodn., 1970-75, v.p. ops., mem. mgmt. com., 1975-77, sr. v.p., 1977-80; v.p. consumer group ops., mem. mgmt. com. Pillsbury Co. (merged with Green Giant Co. 1980), 1980—; dir. First State Bank Apple Valley (Minn.), Community Investment Enterprises, Mpls.; mem. Minn. Economic Devel. Commn.; adv. com. U. Minn. Inst. Agr., Forestry and Econs.; chmn., Dodge County Heart Fund. Bd. dirs. KIDS, Inc., Dolores G. Dietrich Meml. Found. Mem. Nat. Food Processors Assn. (dir.), Minn. Canners and Freezers Assn. (pres., dir. 1968-69), Phoenix, Gray Friars, Phi Gamma Delta. Roman Cath. Club: Le Sueur Country (pres. 1971). Home: 548 S Main St Le Sueur MN 56058 Office: 1100 N 4th St Le Sueur MN 56058

DIETRICH, WILLIAM THOMAS, mgmt. devel. cons.; b. St. Louis, Mar. 29, 1944; s. William and Margaret Irene (Von Dach) D.; B.S., Millikin U., 1967; M.B.A., Case Western Res. U., 1972; Ph.D., Southeastern U., 1978; m. Mary J. Brennan, June 5, 1965; children—Adam T., Bren W. Engring. draftsman Caterpillar Tractor Co., Decatur, Ill., 1965-67, mgmt. trainee, East Peoria, Ill., 1967-68, assembly foreman, Cleve., 1968-69, quality assurance gen. supr., 1969-72, job analysis supr., Mentor, 1972-74, mgr. program devel., 1974-78, mgmt. devel. cons., Peoria, Ill., 1978—; instr. Ill. Central Coll., East Peoria, 1976—. Blackstone Engring. scholar, Millikin U., 1962-66; Caterpillar Ednl. Assistance Plan scholar, Case Western Res. U., 1968-72. Mem. Am. Soc. Tng. and Devel., Am. Mgmt. Assn. Republican. Presbyterian. Home: 64 Tonti Ct Sparland IL 61565 Office: 100 NE Adams St Peoria IL 61629

DIETSCH, CORA MARIE (CORKY), consumer products co. exec.; b. Cin., May 18, 1949; d. John George and Melba Leola (Houck) Ehrnschwender; B.S. in Bus. Adminstrn., Findlay Coll., 1975; 1 dau., Tina Marie. Collection mgr. Sears, Roebuck and Co., Findlay, Ohio, 1967-68; employee services asst. Cooper Tire & Rubber Co., Findlay, 1968-78; personnel mgr. Libby, McNeill & Libby, Inc., Leipsic, Ohio, 1978-80; mgr. personnel services The Nestle Co., Burlington, Wis., 1980; mgr. indsl. relations Armour-Dial Co., Montgomery, Ill., 1980-81; mgr. labor relations, 1981—. Adviser, Jr. Achievement, 1968-73; past mem. Lima Area Safety Council; 1st aid instr./trainer. Mem. Nat. Alliance Bus., Am. Soc. Personnel Adminstrs., Personnel Indsl. Relations Assn., Valley Indsl. Personnel Assn. Republican. Methodist. Home: 54 Sonora Dr Montgomery IL 60538 Office: 2000 Aucutt Rd Montgomery IL 60538

DIETZ, NORBERT WILLIAM, ins. co. exec., ret. army officer; b. Botkins, Ohio, May 9, 1921; s. Frank George and Mary Kathryn (Wesbecher) D.; m. Jeanie Belle Reedy, Apr. 19, 1947; children—Norbert, Joyce, Wayne. Served as pvt. U.S. Army, 1944-52, commd. 2nd lt., 1952, advanced through grades to maj., 1962; ret., 1964; with SAFECO Ins. Co. Am., Cin., 1964—, supt. services dept., 1975—. Pres. Mom and Dads Club, St. Rita Sch. for Deaf, 1966-72, pres. Festival, 1972-75, 79—, chmn., 1973—, mem. fin. com., 1975—, mem. gov. bd., 1977—; mem. fin. bd. St. Matthias Parish, Cin., 1973—. Decorated Bronze Star medal, Army Commendation medal. Named Man of Year Tri-County Sertoma Club, Cin., 1975. Home: 11526 Ivyrock Ct Cincinnati OH 45240 Office: 5901 E Galbraith Rd Cincinnati OH 45236

DI FULIO, RONALD ANTHONY, drug stores chain exec.; b. Syracuse, N.Y., Oct. 15, 1937; s. Anthony and Anna (Mengal) DiF.; student pub. schs., North Syracuse, N.Y.; m. Shirley Neimeier, Jan. 12, 1957; children—Kevin James, Rickie Scott, Lori Ann. Patrolman, detective North Syracuse (N.Y.) Police Dept., 1969-74; regional security supr. White Dept. Stores, Syracuse, N.Y., 1972-74; regional dir. loss prevention Gray Drug Stores, Inc., Ft. Lauderdale, Fla., 1974-76, corporate dir. loss prevention, Cleve., 1976—; instr. Ohio Peace Officers Tng. Council. Mem., sgt. Onondaga County CD, Syracuse, 1967-69; cubmaster, pack chmn. Boy Scouts Am., 1970-71; sec.-treas. North Syracuse Police Benevolent Assn., 1971-74. Cert. profl. examiner Fla. Polygraph Assn.; cert. psychol. stress examiner Fla. Polygraph and Stress Evaluators Assn. Mem. Nat. Assn. Chain Drug Stores, Nat. Retail Mchts. Assn., Internat. Soc. Stress Analysts, Fla. Polygraph and Stress Evaluators, Greater Cleve. Fraud Investigators Assn., Ohio Retail Mchts. Assn. Office: Gray Drug Stores Inc 666 Euclid Ave Cleveland OH 44114

DILENSCHNEIDER, ROBERT LOUIS, public relations co. exec.; b. N.Y.C., Oct. 21, 1943; B.A. in Communications Arts, U. Notre Dame, 1965; M.A. in Public Relations, Ohio State U., 1967; m. Janet Hennessy, Sept. 6, 1969. Account supr. Hill and Knowlton, Inc., N.Y.C., 1967-70, v.p., 1970-73, sr. v.p., 1973-78, mng. dir. Midwest region, sr. v.p., Chgo., 1978-80, exec. v.p., 1980—, also dir. Bd. dirs. N.Y.C. Council of Chs., 1976-78, United Charities Chgo. Recipient Big Apple award Jaycees, 1978. Mem. Public Relations Soc. Am., Nat. Acad. TV Arts and Scis., Sigma Delta Chi. Clubs: Economic, Executives, Chicago, Headline, Tavern, (Chgo.). Home: 915 Shabona Ln Wilmette IL 60091 Office: 111 E Wacker Dr Chicago IL 60601

DILLAHUNTY, BOBBIE ALENE, ednl. adminstr.; b. Texarkana, Ark., June 8, 1939; d. John Dennis and Mattie Lee (Dansby) Williams; student Kans. State Coll., 1959-61; B.S., U. Wis., Milw., 1970, M.A., 1977; children—Gregory Bernard, Cleophus, Darryl, David Jon. Tchr., Milw. Public Schs., 1970-76, supervising tchr., 1977—. Recipient Community Service award Milw. Head Start Program, 1979. Mem. Nat. Council Tchrs. Math., Adminstrs. Supervising Council, Black Adminstrs. Suprs. Council (sec.), Wis. Math. Council (elem. v.p.), Milw. Adminstrs. and Suprs. Council, Milw. League Urban Educators, Delta Kappa Gamma (chpt. treas.), Alpha Kappa Alpha. Roman Catholic. Home: 4555 N 37th St Milwaukee WI 53209 Office: 5225 W Vliet St Milwaukee WI 53205

DILLE, ELDON RAY, chem. engr., cons.; b. DeWitt, Mo., Aug. 16, 1937; s. Raymond Ellis and Charlotte Elaine (Shepard) D.; B.S., U. Mo., Rolla., 1961. With Cook Paint and Varnish Co., Kansas City, Mo., 1964-68. Western Electric Co., Lee's Summit, Mo., 1968-69; sr. devel. engr. Chemagro Corp., Kansas City, Mo., 1969-70; chem. engring. cons. Burns & McDonnell Engring. Co., Kansas City, Mo., 1977—. Served with C.E., AUS, 1961-63. Registered profl. engr., Mo. Mem. ASME (chmn. performance test code com. 40), Am. Inst. Chem. Engrs., ASTM, Nat. Assn. Corrosion Engrs., Alpha Chi Sigma. Republican. Baptist. Home: Box 652 Kansas City MO 64141 Office: Box 173 Kansas City MO 64141

DILLER, JAMES GORDON, plastic surgeon; b. Allen County, Ohio, May 23, 1929; s. Clarence D. and Ruth M. (Claudon) D.; student Wheaton (Ill.) Coll., 1947-51; M.D., Ohio State U., 1955; m. Jean Miller, June 21, 1952; children—Collette, Janelle, Christopher, Jeanine, Nicole. Intern, Blodgett Meml. Hosp., Grand Rapids, Mich., 1955-56; med. missionary, Belgian Congo, 1957-60; resident in gen. surgery Cleve. Clinic, 1960-64, resident in plastic surgery, 1964-66; practice medicine specializing in plastic surgery Toledo Clinic, 1966—, mem. exec. com. Toledo Clinic, Inc., 1969-70, pres. Toledo Clinic Corp., 1970; chief plastic surgery dept. Flower Hosp., chief staff, 1979—. Founding mem. Christian Counseling Center Toledo, 1974-76, Midwest Med. Mission, 1981—. Recipient Service to Man award Toledo Sertoma Club, 1981. Diplomate Inst. Tropical Medicine, Antwerp, Nat. Bd. Med. Examiners, Am. Bd. Surgery, Am. Bd. Plastic Surgery. Fellow Am. Coll. Surgeons; mem. AMA, Ohio State Med. Assn., Lucas County Med. Soc., A.C.S., Toledo Surg. Soc., Toledo Plastic Surgeons, Ohio Valley Plastic Surg. Soc., Am. Soc. Plastic Reconstructive Surgery. Contbr. articles in field to profl. jours. Office: 4235 Secor Rd Toledo OH 43623

DILLER, MARY ANN, univ. adminstr.; b. Kansas City, Mo., Sept. 13, 1924; d. Edward and Willa Vaughn (Gates) Diller; A.B., MacMurray Coll., 1945; A.M., U. Ill., 1948; Ph.D., Mich. State U., 1973. Tchr. history Roxana High Sch., 1945-46; asst. in rhetoric and history U. Ill., 1946-48; tchr. history and English, Belleville (Ill.) Twp. High Sch. and Jr. Coll., 1948-49; tchr. social scis. Danville (Ill.) Jr. Coll., 1949-66, head social sci. dept., 1958-66, dean adult edn., 1966-75; regional program dir. for continuing edn. and pub. service U. Ill., 1975—. Vice pres. Vermilion County Citizens for Community Action, 1964-66; mem. bd. Children's Home of Vermilion County, 1969-75; mem. faculty adv. com. Ill. Bd. Higher Edn., 1968-70. Mem. Nat., Ill., Danville (pres. 1959-60, 63-64) edn. assns., Ill. Adult Edn. Assn. (mem. exec. bd. 1965-70, 71-79, pres. 1973), Ill. Adult and Continuing Educators Assn., Nat. Assn. Public Continuing and Adult Edn. (publ. com. 1975-77, higher edn. com. 1975-76), Adult Edn. Assn. U.S.A. (chmn. bylaws com. 1979—), Nat. Univ. Continuing Edn. Assn., AAUW (Danville pres. 1969-70, Ill. bd. mem. 1967-73), Sigma Phi Gamma (pres. 1961-62), Pi Alpha Theta, Delta Kappa Gamma, Kappa Delta Pi, Phi Kappa Phi, Phi Delta Kappa. Presbyn. Author: (with Violet Malone) The Guidance Function and Counseling Roles in an Adult Education Program, 1978. Home: 1426 Mayfair Rd Champaign IL 61820

DILLEY, ROBERT SYDNEY, educator; b. Edmonton, Eng., June 21, 1942; came to Can., 1969; s. Sydney James and Elsie Florence (Mirams) D.; B.A., U. Cambridge, 1964, M.A., 1968, M.Litt., 1973; m. Clementina Maria Anna Ribeirinho Pinto Coelho Afonso, June 2, 1979; 1 dau., Elise Clementina Ribeirinho. Lectr. geography U. Pitts., 1967-69; lectr. Lakehead U., Thunder Bay, Ont., 1969-74, asst. prof., 1974-77, asso. prof., 1977—, chmn. dept., 1974-77. Mem. historic sites adv. bd. Lakehead Region Conservation Authority, 1973-75; trustee Can. Assn. Univ. Tchrs. Def. Fund, 1980—. Mem. Assn. Am. Geographers, Canadian Assn. Geographers, Inst. Brit. Geographers, Brit. Agrl. History Soc. Club: Thunder Bay Cricket (pres. 1979—). Contbr. articles to profl. jours. Home: Rural Route 13 Thunder Bay ON P7B 5E4 Canada Office: Dept Geography Lakehead Univ Thunder Bay ON P7B 5E1 Canada

DILLING, KIRKPATRICK WALLWICK, lawyer; b. Evanston, Ill., Apr. 11, 1920; s. Albert W. and Elizabeth (Kirkpatrick) D.; engring. student Cornell U., 1939-40; B.S. in Law, Northwestern U., 1942; student DePaul U., 1946-47, L'Ecole Vaubier, Montreux, Switzerland; Degré Normal, Sorbonne U., Paris, France; m. Betty Ellen Bronson, June 18, 1942 (div. July, 1944); m. 2d, Elizabeth Ely Tilden, Dec. 11, 1948; children—Diana Jean, Eloise Tilden, Victoria Ely, Albert Kirkpatrick. Def. work Am. Steel Foundries, East Chicago, Ind., 1942-43; admitted to Ill. Bar, 1947; mem. firm Dilling, Dilling & Gronek, 1948—; gen. counsel Nat. Health Fedn., Am. Massage and Therapy Assn.; pres. P.E.P. Industries, Ltd.; v.p. Midwest Medic-Aide, Inc.; dir. Ry. Devel. Corp., Chgo. Truck Leasing Corp., Harbil, Inc. Bd. dirs. Nat. Health Fedn., Nat. Safety Council. Served to 1st lt. AUS, 1943-46. Mem. Am., Ill., Chgo. bar assns., Am. Trial Lawyers Assn., Cornell Soc. Engrs., Am. Legion, Air Force Assn., Pharm. Advt. Club, Navy League, Delta Upsilon. Republican. Episcopalian. Clubs: Lake Michigan Yachting Assn.; Cornell U. Club Chicago. Lectr. and author on public health law. Home: 1120 Lee Rd Northbrook IL 60062 also Casa Dorado Indian Wells CA Office: 188 W Randolph St Chicago IL 60601

DILLING, RICHARD ALLEN, educator; b. Everett, Pa., July 30, 1940; s. John Ealor and Janet Joanne (Clapper) D.; B.S., Shippensburg State U., 1962; M.S., Purdue U., 1968, Ph.D., 1975; m. Linda Marlene Edmiston, Aug. 17, 1968; children—Dawn Denise, John Marvin, Richard Allen. Tchr. physics, chemistry, math. Central High Sch., Martinsburg, Pa., 1964-65, E. Side High Sch., Butler, Ind., 1965-66; faculty Grace Coll., Winona Lake, Ind., 1966—, prof. sci. edn.; lectr. in field. Chmn., United Way, Winona Lake, 1978-79; pres. Parent-Tchr. Fedn. of Warsaw Christian Sch., 1976-77, 81-82; active Winona Lake Grace Brethren Ch. Recipient Alva McClain award for excellence in teaching, Grace Coll., 1978-79. Mem. Am. Assn. Physics Tchrs., Nat. Sci. Tchrs. Assn., Nat. Assn. for Research in Sci. Teaching, Assn. for Edn. of Tchrs. in Sci. Republican. Nat. Fellowship of Grace Brethren. Contbr. articles to profl. jours. Home: 5 W Baker St Warsaw IN 46580 Office: Grace Coll Winona Lake IN 46590

DILLMAN, WILLIAM DAVID, packing co. ofcl.; b. Evanston, Ill., Feb. 10, 1933; s. David D. and Josephine H. (Cox) D.; student U. Denver, 1952-53, Northwestern U., 1955, U. Ill., 1955-56; m. Jean Bennett, Nov. 24, 1957; children—Donna, Ann, Kathryn, Thomas. Reporter, City News Bur. Chgo., 1956-58, Chgo. Tribune, 1958-60, Chgo. Sun Times, 1960-65; asst. to pres., mgr. public relations Consol. Foods Corp., Chgo., 1965-69; bur. chief Jour. Commerce, N.Y.C., 1969-70; asst. dir. public relations Esmark, Inc., Chgo., 1970-80; mgr. public relations Swift Ind. Packing Co., Chgo., 1980—. Served with U.S. Army, 1953-55. Mem. Chgo. Newspaper Reporters Assn., Public Relations Clinic Chgo., Chgo. Press Vets., Chgo. Headline Club, Chgo. Press Club, Sigma Delta Chi. Home: 1210 Michigan St Evanston IL 60202 Office: 115 W Jackson Blvd Chicago IL 60604

DILLON, JOAN KENT, civic worker; b. Lafayette, Ind., Apr. 30, 1925; d. Richard and Gladys (Schroeder) Kent; B.A., Smith Coll., 1947; M.A., U. Mo., 1969; m. George Chaffee Dillon, Sept. 11, 1948; children—Kent Chaffee, Courtney, Emily Lorillard. Chmn. sales and rental gallery Nelson Art Gallery, Kansas City, Mo., 1956-63; tchr. history Sunset Hill Sch., Kansas City, Mo., 1958-69; pres. Performing Arts Found., Folly Theatre Restoration, Kansas City, 1978-81; dir. Kansas City Trusts and Found., 1976-81; pres. Kansas City Arts Council, 1980; dir. Historic Kansas City, 1972-81; mem. Mo. Adv. Council for Historic Preservation, 1978-81; trustee Nat. Trust for Historic Preservation, 1978-81; dir. League Historic Am. Theaters, 1975-81; mem. Kansas City Mcpl. Art Commn., 1970-80; mem. Nat. Assn. Schs. of Dance and Theater Accreditation Commn., 1979-81; mem. Nat. Assn. Schs. Arts Accreditation Commn., 1981. Mem. Women in Founds., Soc. Archtl. Historians, Mo. Heritage Trust. Congregationalist. Clubs: Kansas City Country, Central Exchange Women's, River. Office: Folly Theater 300 W 12th St Kansas City MO 64105

DILLON, JOSEPH GERALD, Realtor, real estate developer; b. Chgo., Sept. 1, 1934; s. Joseph Gerald and Anne (Dwyer) D.; student John Carroll U., 1952-54; B.A., Loyola U., Chgo., 1956; m. Beverly Tanty, Jan. 2, 1960; children—Joseph, Kathleen, David, Daniel. Mem. real estate staff Material Service div. Gen. Dynamics Corp., Chgo., 1959-60; v.p. Monticello Realty div. Henry Crown & Co., Chgo., 1960-67; partner Harrington, Tideman & O'Leary, Chgo., 1967-75; v.p., dir. Arthur Rubloff & Co., Chgo., 1975-79; pres., dir. Joseph Dillon & Co., indsl. and comml. real estate, Chgo., 1980—. Served to capt. AUS, 1956-57. Mem. Nat. Assn. Indsl. and Office Parks (pres. Chgo. chpt. 1978), Soc. Indsl. Realtors (dir. 1975-77), Assn. Indsl. Real Estate Brokers Chgo. (pres. 1974), Urban Land Inst., Indsl. Devel. and Research Council, Chgo. Real Estate Bd. Clubs: Chgo. Athletic Assn.; Skokie Country (Glencoe, Ill.). Home: 551 Monroe St Glencoe IL 60022 Office: 631 Busse Rd Bensenville IL 60106

DILLON, MABEL MARGARET, security service corp. ofcl.; b. Kenosha, Wis., Dec. 19, 1905; d. Andrew Bernard and Minnie Augusta (Ferch) Schmitz; student acctg. Seth Boyden Sch., 1927; m. Thomas Francis Dillon, Feb. 9, 1933 (dec. 1971). Sec. to pres. Indsl. Food Crafts, Inc., Elizabeth, N.J., 1949-53; pvt. sec. Simmons Co., Kenosha, Wis., 1953-60; sec. Kenosha City Hall, 1961-64; pvt. sec. corp. counsel Kenosha County, 1964-71; exec. lt. adminstrv. services Schmitt Investigation & Security Service, Kenosha. Pres. St. Catherine's Hosp. Aux., 1975-77, Kenosha Woman's Club, 1978-80; active Cath. Women's Club, Hist. Mus., United Way; bd. dirs. Mental Health Assn. Kenosha County, 1979—, Kenosha Symphony Assn., 1981—. Mem. Bus. and Profl. Women's Club Kenosha (pres. 1960-61, state Woman of Yr. 1968, local 1975, pres. Dist. 9 1966-68), Legal Secs. Orgn. Racine and Kenosha (recording sec., 1968), Fedn. Women's Clubs Wis. (rec. sec. 1st div. 1980). Democrat. Roman Catholic. Clubs: Ladies Aux. of the Eagles, Schubert (pres. 1981—) (Kenosha). Organized 3 new clubs for Bus. and Profl. Women. Home: 7319 3d Ave Kenosha WI 53140

DILLON, PHILLIP MICHAEL, constrn. co. exec.; b. Ypsilanti, Mich., July 15, 1944; s. Robert Timothy and Maxine Helen (Elliott) D.; student Mich. State U., 1962-66; m. Phyllis Louise Brooks, Jan. 21, 1978; children—Richard, Debora, Michael, Robert, Karen. Store mgr. Morse Shoe, Inc., Detroit, 1964-68, asst. dir. store planning and constrn., Canton, Mass., 1968-72; dir. store planning and constrn. Stride Rite Corp., Boston, 1972-74; sr. v.p. Capitol Cos., Inc., Arlington Heights, Ill., 1974—, chmn. exec. council Capitol Constrn. Mem. Inst. Store Planners. Roman Catholic. Club: Green Acres Sportsman. Office: 304 E Rand Rd Arlington Heights IL 60004

DILLON, RICHARD WAYNE, supermarket exec.; b. Hutchinson, Kans., Sept. 8, 1927; s. Ray E. and Stella A. (Schmitt) D.; student Kans. U., 1949-51; m. Carolyn A. Critser, May 3, 1952; children—Bradley D., William R., Steven R. Meat supr. Dillon Food Stores, 1953-57, v.p., 1957-65; exec. v.p. Dillon Co., Inc., Hutchinson, 1965-79, pres., 1979—; dir. Salt City Fed. Savs. & Loan Assn. Trustee Kans. 4-H Found.; former pres., mem. Hutchinson Sch. Bd. Served with USAAF, 1945-46. Home: Rural Route 5 Box 106A Hutchinson KS 67501 Office: 700 E 30th St Hutchinson KS 67501

DILLON, SALLY IRENE, forensic scientist; b. Joliet, Ill., Mar. 21, 1947; s. Thomas Eugene and Irene Louise (Castelli) D.; B.S., Coll. St. Francis, 1968. Crime lab. analyst Bur. Sci. Services, Ill. Dept. Law Enforcement, Joliet, 1969-71, criminalist, 1971-72, supervising criminalist, 1972-77, asst. lab. supr., 1977-78, dir. Maywood (Ill.) Lab., 1978—. Recipient Achievement award Ill. Dept. Law Enforcement, 1977. Fellow Am. Acad. Forensic Scis.; mem. Midwestern Assn. Forensic Scientists (charter, pres. 1982), Forensic Sci. Soc. Gt. Britain, Am. Soc. Crime Lab. Dirs. (sec. 1982), Am. Mgmt. Assn. Roman Catholic. Office: 1401 S Maybrook Dr Maywood IL 60153

DILSAVER, DONNA BOLTON, utility exec.; b. Oatville, Kans., July 19, 1932; d. Raymond H. and Juanita J. (Craig) Bolton; B.A. in Sociology, Friends U., Wichita, Kans., 1954; workshops Kans. U., Kans. State U.; m. R.L. Ryan (dec. 1953); 1 son, Ron; m. 2d, Dick Dilsaver, June 17, 1961. Sports writer Wichita Eagle, 1948-52; office mgr. John Coultis Interiors, Wichita, 1953-55; public relations adv. Wichita Area Girl Scout Council, 1955-66; mem. public relations staff Kans. Gas and Electric Co., Wichita, 1967—, communications specialist, 1975—; condr. journalism workshops. Mem. Wichita Conv. Tourism Adv. Bd., 1977-81; public relations cons. Wichita United Way, 1956-70, 81; bus. cons. Wichita Jr. Achievement, 1976-79; mem. selections com. Girl Scouts, 1970; mem. Wichita Bicentennial Com., 1976. Recipient various service awards. Mem. Nuclear Energy Women, Women in Energy (founder), Nat. Fedn. Press Women (awards), Kans. Press Women (awards), Am. Women in Radio and TV, Energy Advocacy Conf. Mem. Christian Ch. (Disciples of Christ). Office: 120 E 1st St Wichita KS 67202

DILTS, JUDITH ANN, educator; b. Louisville, July 24, 1946; d. Walter Emmett and Betty Jane (Prinz) D.; A.B., Ind. U., 1968, M.A., 1975, Ph.D., 1976. Research asst. Ind. U., Bloomington, 1968-71, research asso., 1971-72; instr. in biology William Jewell Coll., Liberty, Mo., 1975-76, asst. prof. biology, 1976-81, asso. prof., 1981—; vis. prof. U. S.D., summer 1980; microbiol. cons. Antigen Lab., Liberty, 1976-78; research cons., bd. dirs. Internat. Med. Scis., Inc., Kansas City, Mo., 1978—. USPHS tng. grantee in genetics, 1972-76. Mem. AAAS, Am. Soc. Microbiology, Mo. Acad. Scis., Sigma Xi. Episcopalian. Contbr. writings in field to profl. publs. Office: Dept Biology William Jewell College Liberty MO 64068

DI MARTINO, DAVID ROSS, educator; b. Rochester, N.Y., Feb. 28, 1947; s. Salvatore Joseph and Rose Mary (Bilotti) DiM.; B.A., State U. N.Y., Albany, 1969; M.A., State U. N.Y., Binghamton, 1970; Ph.D., Syracuse U., 1975; m. Lorraine A. Seidel, Aug. 26, 1967; 1 son, Kris David. Instr., Ohio State U., Marion, 1971-74, asst. prof., 1975-78; sr. research asso. U. Nebr., Omaha, 1978—; cons. Urban Systems Research, Engring., Inc., OEO project, 1973. Mem. Citizen's Adv. Com. to Ohio EPA, Scioto River basin, 1976—; mem. Commn. on Nat. Settlement Systems, Internat. Geog. Union, 1976—. Dell Plain fellow Syracuse U., 1970-71; Nat. Acad. Sci./NRC grantee, 1976, Midwestern Univs. Consortium for Internat. Activities grantee, 1976, Ohio State Faculty research grantee, 1975-76; Fulbright-Hays research grantee, 1980. Mem. Internat. Geog. Union, Assn. Am. Geographers, Am. Geog. Soc., Conf. Latin Americanist Geographers, Nat. Council Geog. Edn., Socially and Ecologically Responsible Geographers, Soc. N.Am. Cultural Survey, Am. Planning Assn. Contbr. articles to profl. jours. Home: 10813 Prairie Village Dr Omaha NE 68144 Office: Univ Nebraska 60th and Dodge Sts Omaha NE 68182

DI MENZA, SALVATORE, psychologist; b. Chgo., May 2, 1938; s. Salvatore and Bartalomea (Gallina) diM.; A.B., DePaul U., 1960, M.A., 1964; postgrad. Loyola U., 1961-64, Ill. Inst. Tech., 1964, 72; m. Greta Van der Meer, Aug. 4, 1973 (div. 1980). Dir. research Ill. Drug Abuse Program, Chgo., 1972-73; dir. mgmt. systems Ill. Drug Abuse Program, 1973; dir. drug abuse div. Joint Commn. Accreditation of Hosps., Chgo., 1973-76, asso. program dir. for planning and devel., 1976-78; mng. partner Health Resources Mgmt. Systems, Chgo., 1978-80, AGI, Rolling Meadows, Ill., 1981—; v.p. J.W. Crawford Assos., Inc., Chgo., 1979—; cons. bus. formation and mgmt.; developer nat. standards for providing mental health treatment services, also large scale employee assistance programs and mental health services for industry. Recipient Superior Achievement award State of Ill., 1972. Fellow Royal Soc. Health; mem. Am. (asso.), Ill. psychol. assns., Am. Pub. Health Assn., Alcohol and Drug Problems Assn., Am. Health Planning Assn., Assn. Mental Health Adminstrs. Contbr. articles to profl. jours. Home: 2837 S Princeton Ave Chicago IL 60616 Office: 3831-D Industrial Ave Rolling Meadows IL 60008

DIMMERLING, HAROLD J., bishop; b. Braddock, Pa., Sept. 23, 1914; ed. St. Fidelis Prep. Sem., Herman, Pa., St. Charles Sem., Columbus, Ohio, St. Francis Sem., Loretto, Pa. Ordained priest Roman Catholic Ch., 1940; consecrated bishop, 1969; bishop Diocese of Rapid City (S.D.), 1969—. Office: 606 Cathedral Dr PO Box 679 Rapid City SD 57701*

DIMMICK, WILLIAM ARTHUR, bishop; b. Paducah, Ky., Oct. 7, 1919; s. James Oscar and Annis Amanda (Crouch) D.; B.A., Berea Coll., 1946; M.Div., Yale U., 1949, D.D., Berkeley Divinity Sch., 1975; M.A., George Peabody Coll., 1955. Ordained priest Episcopal Ch., 1955; rector St. Philips Ch., Nashville, 1955-60; dean St. Marys Cathedral, Memphis, 1960-73; rector Trinity Ch., Southport, Conn., 1973-75; bishop Episcopal Diocese No. Mich., Marquette, 1975—. Pres., Memphis and Shelby County Health and Welfare Planning Council, 1970-73. Mem. Standing Liturgical Commn., Episcopal Ch. Asso. Parishes. Office: 131 E Ridge St Marquette MI 49855

DIMOND, DAVID LAURENCE, educator; b. St. Louis County, Mo., Dec. 11, 1935; s. Joseph Earl and Dorothy Lee D.; B.S., Central Methodist Coll., 1957; M.S., So. Ill. U., 1966; Ed.D., U. Mo., 1973; 1 son, Michael Laurence. Prodn. planner McDonnell Douglas Aircraft, St. Louis, 1958-60; field rep. McKesson Robbins Chem. Co., 1960-61; elem. tchr. Hazelwood (Mo.) Sch. Dist., 1961-63,

Pattonville (Mo.) Sch. Dist., 1963-66; dean men Central Meth. Coll., 1966-68, asso. prof. edn., 1968—; cons. Mo. Dept. Elem. and Secondary Edn.; sponsor, adv. Alpha Phi Omega. Chmn. troop com. Gt. Rivers council Boy Scouts Am., 1975—; chmn. City of Fayette (Mo.) Parks and Recreation Bd., 1978-79; mcpl. judge City of Fayette, 1980—; mem. adminstrv. bd. Linn Meml. United Methodist Ch., Fayette; deacon First Presbyterian Ch., Ferguson, Mo. Mem. Mo. State Tchrs. Assn., Assn. Supervision and Curriculum Devel., Colls. Tchr. Edn., Phi Delta Kappa. Clubs: Lions (pres. 1981) (Fayette); Masons (dist. dep. grand master), Shriners (pres. 1975). Home: 305 Corprew Fayette MO 65248 Office: Central Meth Coll Fayette MO 65248

DINELLO, GILBERT JOHN, state senator, real estate broker; b. Detroit, Feb. 28, 1935; s. Carl A. and Carla (Paiano) DiN.; B.S. in Bus. Adminstrn., U. Detroit, 1959. With Mich. Nat. Bank Detroit, 1969-72; real estate broker, East Detroit, Mich., 1972—; mem. Mich. Ho. of Reps., 1973-78, Mich. State Senate, 1979—. Served with Mich. Army NG, 1959-62. Roman Catholic. Office: Mich State Senate State Capitol Lansing MI 48909*

DING, GAR DAV, architect, educator; b. Canton, China, Nov. 14, 1929; s. Chew Cheung and Ngan She (Ho) D.; came to U.S., 1966; B.Arch., U. Auckland (N.Z.), 1953; B.Engring., U. Canterbury (N.Z.), 1959; M.Engring. Sci., U. New S. Wales, 1961; m. Maisie Young, Aug. 24, 1954; children—David, Judy, Derek, Walter. Lectr., then sr. lectr. archtl. sci. U. Sydney (Australia), 1959-66; prof., chmn. environ. systems studies Va. Poly. Inst. and State U., Blacksburg, 1966-72; prof., dir. grad. studies in architecture Miami U., Oxford, Ohio, also U. Cin., 1972-73; prof. architecture, head dept. U. Ill., Urbana, 1973-80, research prof. architecture, 1980—; mem. bldg. research adv. bd. Nat. Acad. Sci., 1976—; housing com. New River Dist. Valley Planning Commn., 1970-72; mem. public adv. panel region 5 GSA, 1978; cons. in field. Humes Industries scholar, 1956; C.S. McCully scholar, 1957; recipient Research award Royal Inst. Brit. Architects, 1966; research grantee Dept. Army, 1968, NSF, 1976, 81. Fellow N.Z., Royal Australian insts. archietects; mem. ASCE, Instn. Engrs. Australia, Assn. Collegiate Schs. Architecture (bd. dirs. 1979—). Co-author: Models in Archiyecture, 1968; contbg. author: Metropolitan Transportation Planning, 1975. Home: 10 Forest View St Mahomet IL 61853 Office:

DINGELL, JOHN DAVID, congressman; b. Colorado Springs, Colo. July 8, 1926; s. John D. and Grace (Bigler) D.; B.S. in Chemistry, Georgetown U., 1949. J.D., 1952. Admitted to D.C. bar, 1952, Mich. bar, 1953; asst. pros. atty., Wayne County (Mich.), 1953-55: mem. 84th to 88th Congresses from 15th Dist. Mich., 89th-97th Congresses from 16th Dist. Mich., chmn. subcom. on energy and power Interstate and Fgn. Commerce Com., mem. Small Bus. Com., Mcht. Marine and Fisheries Com., mem. Office Tech. Assessment. Served as 2d lt. inf. AUS. 1945-46. Mem. Delta Theta Phi. Office: 2221 Rayburn House Office Bldg Washington DC 20515*

DINGER, MARVIN L., lawyer, state senator; b. Ironton, Mo., Sept. 30, 1921; s. Edward and Bertha (Zude) D.; J.D., Washington U., St. Louis, 1955; children—Paula Kay, Mary Katharyn. Admitted to Mo. bar, 1955; asso. Charles E. Gray Law Firm, St. Louis, 1955-59; individual practice law, Ironton, 1959—; pros. atty. Iron County, 1963-64; mem. Mo. Ho. of Reps., 1964-74, Mo. Senate, 1974—. Served in USAC, 1943-46, USAF, 1947-52. Mem. Mo. Bar, 42d Jud. Bar Assn., Am. Judicature Soc., VFW. Democrat. Lutheran. Clubs: Lions, Elks. Office: 202 S Shepherd St Ironton MO 63650

DINGMAN, MAURICE J., bishop; St. Paul, Iowa, Jan. 20, 1914; s. Theodore and Angela (Cohitte) D.; ed. St. Ambrose Acad., Davenport, Iowa, 1936, N. Am. Coll. and Gregorian U., Rome, Catholic U. Am. Ordained priest Roman Cath. Ch., 1939; instr. St. Ambrose Acad., 1940-43; vice chancellor Diocese of Davenport (Iowa), 1942-45; prin. Hayes High Sch., Muscatine, Iowa, 1953-58; domestic prelate, 1956; appointed bishop Diocese of Des Moines, 1968—. Office: PO Box 1816 180 37th St Des Moines IA 50312

DINGMAN, RITA, nursing cons.; b. Lee County, Iowa, Apr. 22, 1919; d. Henry G. and Ellen (Hellman) Dingman; diploma St. John's Hosp., St. Louis, 1945; B.S., St. Louis U., 1948; M.P.H., Yale, 1959. Dental asst., Ft. Madison, Iowa, 1936-37; sec. credit dept. W. A. Sheaffer Pen Co., 1937-42; pub. health staff nurse Catholic Charities, Alton, Ill., 1947-49, Alaska Dept. Health, Valdez, 1949-51; rehab. cons. liberty Mut. Ins. Co., Dallas, 1952-58; supr. Vis. Nurse Assn., Houston, 1959-61; nursing cons. Colo. Dept. Pub. Health, Denver, 1962-76; clin. instr. pub. health nursing Iowa Wesleyan Coll., Mt. Pleasant, 1978-81; asst. prof. Sch. Pub. Health, U. Minn., Mpls., 1978-81. Bd. dirs. emeritus Colo. Heart Assn., 1978—; pres. bd. trustees Cattermole Meml. Library, Ft. Madison, 1981—; adv. bd. Lee County Public Health Nursing, 1980—. Recipient Pfizer award U.S. CD Council, 1970; Gold Heart award Colo. Heart Assn.; Distinguished Service award Colo. Pub. Health Assn., 1977; Rita Dingman lectureship established U. Minn. Sch. Public Health, 1981. Fellow Am. Public Health Assn.; mem. Colo. Heart Assn. (pres. 1976-77). Roman Catholic. Home: 1518 Ave H Fort Madison IA 52627

DINKEL, JOSEPH WILLARD, elec. engr.; b. Galion, Ohio, Aug. 19, 1918; s. LeRoy Frederick and Jessie Edna (Barr) D.; B.S. in Elec. Engring., Case Inst. Tech., 1949; B.A. in Math, Wittenberg U., 1943; m. Eleanor Jane Dickson, Sept. 7, 1947; children—Barbara Jane, Betty Ann. Drug clk., Seemann's Drug Store, Galion, 1936-39; research engr. Jack & Heintz, Bedford, Ohio, 1949; elec. engr. Taylor Elevator Co., Inc., Cleve., 1949-58, v.p., chief engr., 1958—. Mem. adv. bd. Trade Sch. Served with USN, 1943-46, 50-52. Mem. IEEE (sr.), Am. Def. Preparedness Assn., Cleve. Engring. Soc. Republican. Lutheran. Home: 22269 Berry Dr Rocky River OH 44116 Office: 2011 St Clair Ave Cleveland OH 44114

DINKINS, THOMAS ALLEN, III, tractor co. ofcl.; b. St. Louis, Dec. 29, 1946; s. Thomas Allen and Catherine (Fabick) D.; student St. Louis U., Christian Bros. Coll., 1964; m. Donna Berra, Apr. 29, 1967; 1 son, Thomas Allen IV. Field engr. Honeywell Info. Systems, St. Louis, 1970-74; parts clk. John Fabick Tractor Co., St. Louis, 1962-66, systems analyst, 1974-78, asst. service mgr., 1978-81, product support ops. mgr., 1981—. Served to sgt. USAF, 1966-70. Mem. Nat. Model R.R. Assn. Home: 9123 Hatton Dr Saint Louis MO 63126 Office: 1 Fabick Dr Fenton MO 63026

DINSMOORE, LEO FRANK, mfg. co. exec.; b. Wayne, Mich., Oct. 8, 1947; s. William Joseph and Catherine Suzzanne (Sheridan) D.; student Mich. State U., 1965-68; m. Janet Claire Szatkowski, Dec. 13, 1968; 1 son, Christopher Lee. Traffic mgr. Leo Burnett & Co., Detroit, 1968-69; advt. coordinator Brooks & Perkins, Inc., Southfield, Mich., 1969-70, advt. mgr., 1970-75, dir. advt. and public relations, 1975—, v.p., gen. mgr. BP Mktg. Services subs., Southfield, 1974—. Mem. Bus. and Profl. Advt. Assn. (dir. Detroit chpt. 1977-79) (third v.p. 1981-82), Detroit Bus. Publs. Audit of Circulation, Inc., Psi Upsilon. Republican. Roman Catholic. Club: Polish Yacht. Home: 1443 Harvard Rd Grosse Pointe MI 48230 Office: 750 Honeywell Center Southfield MI 48075

DIOMEDE, MATTHEW, univ. adminstr., poet; b. Yonkers, N.Y.; s. Frank and Josephine D.; B.A., Fordham U., 1962, M.S., 1965; M.A., L.I. U., 1975; m. Barbara Ruth Rogers, June 29, 1968. Adj. asso. prof. SUNY, Farmingdale, 1973-79, English and writing specialist, 1977-79; coordinator communications unit U. Mo., St. Louis, 1979—; chair evaluation com. Nat. Assn. Remedial Devel. Postsecondary Edn. Conf., 1980; contbr. poetry to numerous publs. and anthologies; poetry readings. Recipient cert. of merit Disting. Contbrs. to Poetry, 1970-76, cert. of merit J. Mark Press, 1970; recipient Bronze medal of honor Centro Studi e Scambi Internazionali, 2d prize State of Maine Writers Conf.; speaker L.I. Writers Conf.; recipient L.I. U. Alumni Poetry award, 1978, Grad. poetry award, 1975; award finalist Va. Commonwealth U. Contemporary Poetry Series, 1975. Mem. Nat. Council Tchrs. of English, Conf. Coll. Composition and Communication, N.Y. English Council, Poetry Soc. N.H., Writing Program Adminstrn. Club: Fordham U. Spiked Shoe (v.p., chmn. bd.). Home: 1434 Glenpeak Dr Maryland Heights MO 63043 Office: U Mo 8001 Natural Bridge Rd Saint Louis MO 63121

DI PONIO, CONCETTA CELIA, mfg. co. systems security coordinator; b. Detroit, June 2, 1921; d. Antonio and Mary (Franciosi) Di P.; B.B.A. magna cum laude, U. Detroit, 1973, M.A., 1974, M.B.A., 1975; A.C. cum laude, Henry Ford Community Coll., 1969. Various clerical positions F.W. Woolworth Co., Detroit, 1940-41; office mgr., instr. Design and Engring. Inst., Detroit, 1947-52; propr., mgr. TRI-D Constrn. Co., Detroit, 1955-68; instr. bus. Detroit Coll. Bus., Dearborn, Mich., 1975—; mgmt. tchr. Henry Ford Community Coll., Dearborn, 1979—; with Ford Motor Co., Dearborn, 1942—, div. prodn. surplus liaison, 1952-55, statis. analytical coordinator, 1955-66, parts program coordinator, 1966-74, mgmt. info. system programmer analyst, 1974-81, systems security coordinator, parts and service div., 1981—. Italian translator of letters, corr. and blue prints, 1960—; chmn. M.B.A. confs., 1973-76. Founder 9 collegiate councils U. Detroit, 1977—, pres. univ. bd. dirs., 1978—. Recipient Lawrence Canjar Woman of Yr. award U. Detroit, 1974-75; Divisional Community Services award Ford Motor Co., 1973, Nat. Citizen of Yr. award, 1973, Nat. Town Crier award, 1973; Top Ten Working Woman award Detroit C. of C., 1969; M.B.A. award, 1974-76; Centennial Alumni award, 1976. Mem. Am. Mgmt. Assn., Am. Bus. Women's Assn., Nat. Assn. for Female Execs., Nat. Bus. Edn. Assn., Women's Econ. Club: Ford Motor Employee Recreation Assn., U. Detroit Nat. Alumni Assn. (pres. 1978—), Sparks Wheelchair Basketball Assn., Alpha Sigma Nu (pres. 1973—), Beta Gamma Sigma, Phi Gamma Nu (pres. 1971-72), Phi Gamma Nu Alumnae (pres. 1973-77), Alpha Sigma Lambda, Alpha Kappa Psi. Clubs: Old Timers, Quarter Century, Ford Motor Girls (pres. 1965-69). Home: 22204 W Seven Mile Rd Detroit MI 48219 Office: Ford Motor Co The American Rd FMCC Bldg Rm 1957 Dearborn MI 48121

DIRCK, EDWIN L., state senator; b. St. Louis, July 7, 1928; grad. Bailey Tech. Sch.; m. Helen Dougherty, Aug. 1946; children—Linda Dirck Hennessy, Edwin, Sheila. Locomotive engr. Terminal R.R., St. Louis, 1948—; mem. Mo. Ho. of Reps., 1972-77, Mo. Senate, 1977—. Del. Democratic Nat. Party Conf., 1978; active local Dem. groups. Mem. Locomotive Firemen and Engineermen (trustee local, vice chmn. grievance com.), Brotherhood Locomotive Engrs. Roman Catholic. Clubs: Lions, St. Kevin's Athletic Assn. Office: State Capitol Jefferson City MO 65101*

DIRCZ, THEODORE FRANCIS, data processing cons.; b. Tacoma, Apr. 29, 1949; s. Martin Peter and Joan Marie (Moody) D.; student U.S. Air Force Acad., 1967-69, U. Wis., Madison, 1969-70; B.Computer Sci., U. Minn., Mpls., 1977; m. Donna Idabel May, Aug. 28, 1971; children—Jeffry, Lora. Computer operator First Computer Corp., St. Paul, 1970-72, computer programmer, 1972-75; computer programmer U.S. Postal Service, St. Paul, 1975-77; computer cons., Mpls., 1975-77; project mgr. Internat. Graphics Co., Mpls., 1977-78; owner, operator Dircz & Assos., computer cons., St. Paul, 1978—; pres. MiniMax, Inc., St. Paul, 1979—; v.p. ops. Coastal Info. Systems Inc., 1980—. Vocat. sch. teaching cert., Minn.; cert. in data processing Inst. for Cert. of Computer Profls., 1979. Mem. Ind. Computer Cons. Assn., Assn. Systems Mgmt., Data Processing Mgmt. Assn., Minn. Regional Users Group Hewlett Packard Computers (membership dir.), St. Paul C. of C. Home: 317 Burlington Rd Saint Paul MN 55119 Office: Dircz & Assos 1865 Old Hudson Rd Saint Paul MN 55119

DIRKES, MARGARET ANN, educator; b. Detroit, July 16, 1929; d. Vincent Matthias and Alma Ann (Yott) D.; B.S., Siena Heights Coll., 1955; M.A., U. Detroit, 1962; Ed.D., Wayne State U., 1974. Elem. and secondary sch. tchr., Mich. and Ohio, 1950-69; secondary sch. prin., Mich., 1969-71; research asst., instr. edn. and career opportunity program Wayne State U., Detroit, 1972-74; prof. math. edn., edn. for gifted Ind. U.-Purdue U., Ft. Wayne, 1974—. NSF grantee, 1965. Mem. Nat. Assn. Gifted Children, Council Exceptional Children, Nat. Assn. Gifted, Nat. Council Tchrs. Math., Sch. Sci. and Math., Am. Ednl. Research Assn., Creative Edn. Found., Phi Delta Kappa. Author: Learning to Think — To Learn, 1981; contbr. articles to profl. jours. Office: 2101 Coliseum Blvd E Fort Wayne IN 46805

DIRKS, HAZEL MARIE, nurse; b. Ellis County, Kans., Nov. 21, 1925; d. Frederick William and Florence Elma (Carter) Mickelson; diploma Halstead Hosp. Sch. Nursing, 1948; m. Fred Dirks Jr., Dec. 5, 1948; children—Jerald Frederick, Duane Daryl. Staff nurse, charge nurse Halstead (Kans.) Hosp., 1966-69, coronary care charge nurse, 1969-72, night house supr., 1972—; staff nurse, relief house supr. Axtell Christian Hosp., Newton, Kans., 1957-66. Methodist. Home: 333 Weaver Ave S Hesston KS 67062 Office: 328 Poplar St Halstead KS 67056

DISBERGER, JAY MARION, motel exec.; b. Council Grove, Kans., Apr. 11, 1934; s. Marion H. and Glendean (Dunkel) D.; B.S., Kans. State U., 1958, M.S., 1965; postgrad. Columbia U., Kans. State U., Emporia (Kans.) State Tchrs. Coll.; m. Vina E. Plunkett, Aug. 18, 1956; children—Colleen, Dennis, Patrick, Michael, Carol, Connie, Russell, David, Robert. Mgr., IHC Agy., Syracuse, Kans., 1958-59; mgmt. trainee Farmland Industries, 1959-60; mgr. Farmers Coop, Ft. Scott, Kans., 1960-61; tchr. Los Angeles City Schs., 1963-64, Simi (Calif.) Unified Schs., 1964-65; prin. Pomona (Kans.) High Sch., 1965-68, Haven (Kans.) High Sch., 1968-70; prof. Hutchinson Community Coll., 1970-80; mgr., owner Best Western Crown & Chief Motels, Colby, Kans., 1980—. Judge, Nat. Future Farmers Am. Floriculture Contest, 1980, 81, supt., 1975-79. Served with USAF, 1953-55. Mem. NEA, Am. Vocat. Assn., Colby C. of C., Soil Conservation Soc., Holy Name Soc., Phi Delta Kappa. Republican. Roman Catholic. Club: K.C. Address: Route 1 Box 12M Colby KS 67701

DISBROW, CORLYSS MORREL, mktg. exec.; b. Macomb, Okla., July 17, 1928; s. Peyton Lafayette and Jane Elinor Morrel; B.S., So. Ill. U., Edwardsville, 1966; M.S.C., St. Louis U., 1971; children by previous marriage—Nicholas (dec.), Michael Ran. Research analyst Ill. Dept. Bus. and Econ. Devel., Springfield, 1969-76; partner, owner D/C Mktg. Co., Springfield, 1977—, also speech writer, dir. mktg. Mem. Am. Mktg. Assn. Republican. Roman Catholic. Contbr. series of articles to XX Chromosome mag., 1978. Office: 625 S 5th St Springfield IL 62703

DISENHOUSE, HARVEY ALAN, psychologist; b. N.Y.C., Nov. 10, 1945; s. Irving and Ruth (Wilner) D.; B.A., Kans. State U., 1968; M.S., Emporia State U., 1969; Ph.D., U. Iowa, 1972; m. Patricia Ann Woeppel, May 31, 1970; children—Rebecca, Daniel, Joshua. Research asst., psychometrist Emporia (Kans.) Unified Schs., 1968-69; instr. dept. spl. edn. U. Iowa, Iowa City, 1969-71; psychotherapist Mental Health Inst., Independence, Iowa, 1971; psychologist Davis County Schs., Bloomfield, Iowa, 1971-75; sch. psychologist Area Ednl. Agy. 15, Ottumwa, Iowa, 1975-77, supr. psychologists, phys. therapists and occupational therapists, 1977—; cons. Rathbun Area Mental Health Center, Centerville, Iowa, 1981—; psychologist Specialized Child Health Clinic, Ottumwa, 1978—; pediatric psychologist Ottumwa Pediatrics, P.C., 1981—. Bd. dirs. Binai Jacob Synagogue, Ottumwa, 1979—. Mem. Am. Psychol. Assn., Iowa Psychol. Assn. Democrat. Club: B'nai B'rith. Home: 1340 Bladensburg Rd Ottumwa IA 52501 Office: Route 5 Box 55 Ottumwa IA 52501

DISHOP, RICHARD THOMAS, automotive dealer; b. Wauseon, Ohio, Aug. 24, 1942; s. Albert Henry and Amelia A. D.; student U. Automotive Mgmt., New Orleans, 1980; m. Janice Elain Longstreet, July 5, 1973; children—Teresa, Anthony, Jodi. Barber, 1961-64; gen. mgr. Turnpike Travelers, Bowling Green, Ohio, 1967-71; owner, operator Dishop Datsun-Internat. Trucks, Bowling Green, 1972—; owner, operator RTD & Assos., collection agy., 1972-75; mem. Mid Am. Bank Adv. Bd., 1971-80, pres., 1972. Named to Outstanding Young Men Am., U.S. Jaycees, 1973; recipient Quality Dealer award Datsun, 1975, 80. Mem. Am. Imported Automobile Dealers Assn., Nat. Auto Dealers Assn., Bowling Green Auto Dealers (sec.-treas. 1978-81), Ohio Auto Dealers Assn. Republican. Lutheran. Clubs: Falcon, Elks, Bowling Green State U. Pres.'s. Home: 14251 Gorrill Rd Bowling Green OH 43402 Office: Dishop Datsun-Internat Trucks Route 25 Bowling Green OH 43402

DISKERUD, CLAYTON L., social scientist; b. Mpls., Mar. 23, 1937; s. David L. and Helma P. (Nelson) D.; B.S., Carthage Coll., 1955; M.A., U. Minn., 1963; postgrad. Reed Coll., 1964, U. Minn., 1973-74; m. Shirley L. Eller, Aug. 22, 1959; children—William David, Debra Jean. Research asst. U. Minn., 1959-61, instr. social sci., 1964-65; tchr., Anoka, Minn., 1960-62; instr. Carthage Coll., Kenosha, Wis., 1962-64, asst. prof., 1965-67, dir. spl. schs., 1967-74, chmn. social sci. program, 1974—; adj. prof. Pepperdine U., Los Angeles, 1975—. Supr., Protestant Youth council, 1962-63; specialist Kenosha County Schs., 1962-63; cons. Racine Pub. Schs., 1966. Partner, Diskerud Resort Annandale, Minn., 1969—. Precinct chmn. Democratic party, 1960-62; campaign cons., 1966-72; delegate Dem. Farm Labor Conv., 1962. Asia Soc. fellow; Martin Luther Faculty fellow; Ill. Synod Scholar, grantee Luth. Bd. Coll. Edn. Mem. Annandale Resort Owners Assn., Nat., S.E. Wis. (chmn. 1965-69) councils social studies, Adult Edn. Assn. Wis., Nat. Assn. Summer Sessions, Alumni Council Carthage Coll. (chmn. continuing edn. 1966-69), Phi Alpha Theta, Phi Delta Kappa, Tau Sigma Chi. Lutheran. Contbr. numerous articles to profl. publs. Home: 2136 24th Ave Kenosha WI 53140

DI SPIGNO, GUY JOSEPH, psychologist; b. Bklyn., Mar. 6, 1948; s. Joseph Vincent and Jeanne Nina (Renna) DiS.; B.S., Carroll Coll., 1969; M.A. (fellow), No. Ill. U., 1972; M.Ed., Loyola U., 1974; Ph.D., Northwestern U., 1977; m. Gisela Riba, May 23, 1979; children—Michael Paul, Abie Francis. Instr., No. Ill. U., DeKalb, 1969-70; chmn. humanities dept. Quincy (Ill.) Boys' High Sch., 1970-71; dir. religious edn. St. Mary's Ch., DeKalb, 1971-72; dir. edn. Immaculate Conception Parish, Highland Park, Ill., 1972-77; dir. human resources Am. Valuation Cons., Des Plaines, Ill., 1977-79; psychologist Hay Assos., Chgo., 1979-80; v.p. psychol. services Exec. Assets Corp., Chgo., 1980—. Mem. Highland Park Human Relations Commn., 1975-77, Home Owners and Businessmen's Assn., Highland Park, 1976-77; mem. legis. com. Vernon Hills (Ill.) Sch. Bd. Clifford B. Scott scholar, 1967. Mem. Community Religious Edn. Dirs. (nat. vice chmn. 1971-73), Am. Psychol. Assn., Ill. Psychol. Assn., Nat. Registry Health Service Providers in Psychology, Am. Personnel and Guidance Assn., Carroll Coll. Alumni Assn., Phi Alpha Theta, Sigma Phi Epsilon. Mem. United Ch. of Christ (deacon). Contbr. articles to profl. jours. Home: 1023 Chatham Pl Vernon Hills IL 60061 Office: 1E Wacker Dr Chicago IL 60601

DISTELDORF, DONALD NICHOLAS, accountant; b. Chgo., Sept. 26, 1927; s. Nicholas J. and Lillian (Doether) D.; B.S. in Accounting, DePaul U., 1951; m. Therese Boettger, June 17, 1950; children—Joan, Susan, Janet, Donald J. Jr. accountant Marshall Berman & Co., Chgo., 1950-51; sr. accountant P. L. Crawford & Co., Chgo., 1952-56; pvt. practice accounting, Oak Lawn, Ill., 1956—. Treas. Evergreen Park (Ill.) Swimming Pool Orgn., 1956-58, pres., 1960-61. Served with U.S. Army, 1945-46. C.P.A., Ill. Club: Elks. Home: 3157 W 101st St Evergreen Park IL 60642 Office: 5017 W 95th St Oak Lawn IL 60453

DITTMANN, JOHN FRED, engring. mgr.; b. Frontenac, Kans., Nov. 8, 1920; s. Gus and Veronica (Fecho) D.; B.S., Dickinson Coll., 1943; M.Sc., U. Kans., 1949; m. Iris Glee Tyler, Aug. 3, 1942; children—Dr. J. Paul, Jay T. Chemistry instr., football coach Southwestern Coll., 1946-48; mgr. lead-acid battery labs. Eagle-Picher Industries, Inc., Joplin, Mo., 1952-61, mem. engring. staff, dir. battery research and devel., 1962-65, mgr. reliability Apollo Program, 1966-68, mgr. engring., 1969—. Served to capt., USAAF, 1944-46; ETO. Mem. Electrochem. Soc., AAAS, Am. Ordnance Assn., Am. Soc. Quality Control, Am. Chem. Soc., Spiva Art Center, Omicron Delta Kappa, Sigma Alpha Epsilon. Republican. Methodist. Contbr. articles on batteries to profl. jours. Patentee in field. Home: 531 Park Ave Joplin MO 64801 Office: PO Box 130 Seneca MO 64865

DITTMANN, REIDAR, educator; b. Tonsberg, Norway, Jan. 15, 1922; came to U.S., 1945, naturalized, 1950; s. Gustav Adolf and Solveig (Tovsen) D.; student Oslo Conservatory, Oslo U., 1941-43; B.Mus., St. Olaf Coll., 1947, B.A., 1949; M.A., U. Wash., 1954, Ph.D., 1975; m. Chrisma J. Skoien, Dec. 18, 1947; children—Reidar, Solveig, Rolf, Kristin, Lisa. Mem. faculty St. Olaf Coll., Northfield, Minn., 1947—, dir. internat. studies, 1964-75, prof. art and Norwegian, dir. galleries, 1975—; cons. Mpls. Inst. Arts. Chmn., Rice County Democratic-Farmer-Labor Party, 1961-62. Served with Norwegian Resistance, 1941-43; Norwegian Army Intelligence interned in Buchenwald Camp, 1943-45. Recipient award for inter-religious service Jewish Community Council, 1968; decorated St. Olav medal (Norway). Mem. Norwegian-Am. Hist. Assn., Soc. Advancement Scandinavian Studies, Coll. Art Assn. Author: The Educational System of Norway, 1969; Edvard Munch and Henrik Ibsen, 1977; translator, editor: Edvard Munch: Close-up of a Genius, 1968; picture editor Franklin Library Ibsen edit., 1981; composer. Home: 908 W 1st St Northfield MN 55057 Office: Saint Olaf College Northfield MN 55057

DIVITA, JAMES JOHN, historian, educator; b. Chgo., Jan. 20, 1938; s. Charles Vincent and Theresa Irene (Rohde) D.; B.A., DePaul U., 1959; A.M., U. Chgo., 1960, Ph.D., 1972; m. Mary Frances Beckmeyer, Aug. 22, 1964; children—Lawrence Charles, Mary Theresa, Michael Paul and Anne Catherine (twins). Instr. history, Marian Coll., Indpls., 1961-64, asst. prof., 1964-70, asso. prof.,

1970-76, prof., 1976—. Mem. Am. Hist. Assn., Am. Cath. Hist. Assn., Ind. Hist. Soc., Soc. Italian Hist. Studies. Roman Catholic. Contbr. articles to profl. jours. Home: 3208 Acacia Dr Indianapolis IN 46224 Office: History Dept Marian College Indianapolis IN 46222

DIVNEY, HERBERT PHILLIPS, clin. psychologist; b. Columbus, Ohio, Apr. 3, 1923; s. James and Narelle (Phillips) D.; B.A., Kent State U., 1948; M.A., Cath. U. Am.; m. Dorothy Smith; children—Ann, James, Malcolm, Marc. Clin. psychology tng. program intern Perry Point VA Hosp. (Md.), 1950-51; mem. staff Apple Creek State Hosp., Apple Creek, Ohio, 1952-66, chief psychologist, 1959-66, dir. psychol. service, 1974-77; psychologist Hampshire Country Sch., Rindge, N.H., 1955-56; cons. psychologist Boys Village, Smithville, Ohio, 1955-66; cons., therapist Ashland (Ohio) Family Services, 1966-68; psychologist, therapist Dr. Abdon Villalba, Cuyahoga Falls, Ohio, 1967-68; dir. Alcohol Edn. and Tng. Program, Fallsview Mental Health Center, Cuyahoga Falls, 1966-68; psychologist, adminstr. S.E. Colo. Family Guidance Center, LaJunta, 1968-73; dir. psychol. services Tiffin (Ohio) Mental Retardation Center; cons. Tuscarawas Comprehensive Community Health Center, Dover, Ohio, 1976-77, Crossroads Counseling Center, 1981—; mem. Ohio Statuatory Com. on Behavior Modification. Mem. exec. bd. So. Colo. region Boy Scouts Am., 1971-72. Mem. Am., Ohio psychol. assns., Ohio State Assn. Psychologists and Psychol. Assts. (treas. 1976-77). Home and Office: 600 N River Rd Tiffin OH 44883

DIX, RALPH EUGENE, office supply co. exec.; b. Leavenworth, Kans., July 16, 1926; s. Grover Webster and Mary Alice Dix; student public schs., Leavenworth; m. Mary Margaret DeCoursey, Dec. 2, 1944; children—Ralph Eugene, Carey Ann. Grocery store clk., 1947-48; owner Ralph's Grocery, 1948-60; in material control Gen. Motors Corp., 1949-59; salesman Sears Roebuck & Co., Leavenworth, 1959-68; owner Dix & Son Office Supply, Leavenworth, 1968—; sr. partner Platte Office Supply, Parkville, Mo., 1978—; partner Discount Carpet Warehouse, Leavenworth, 1978—. Mem. Leavenworth Urban Renewal Bd., 1969—; bd. dirs. Leavenworth Downtown Assn., 1974-75; Guatemalan consul Midwest region. Served with U.S. Army, 1944-46. Mem. Leavenworth C. of C. (dir. 1970-72), V.F.W., Am. Legion. Republican. Club: Eagles. Home: 2608 S 14th St Leavenworth KS 66048 Office: 419 Delaware St Leavenworth KS 66048

DIX, RAYMOND EUGENE, publishing co. exec.; b. Wooster, Ohio, Aug. 5, 1908; s. Emmett C. and Edna Marian (Voorhees) D.; student Ohio Wesleyan U., 1926-28; B.J., U. Mo., 1930; H.H.D., Coll. Wooster, 1966; L.H.D., Defiance Coll., 1968; m. Carolyn Victoria Gustafson, Oct. 15, 1932; children—R. Victor, Edna C. (Mrs. David Crocker), Ellen Dix Dungan. Editor Ravenna (Ohio) Record, 1930-31; advt. mgr. Daily Record, Wooster, 1931-40, mng. editor, 1940-53, pub., 1953—; pres. Ashland Pub. Co., Wooster, 1966—; dir. Wayne County Bank. Trustee Methodist Theol. Inst., Del. Mem. Ohio Newspaper Assn. (past pres.), Inter-Am. Press Assn. (dir. treas. 1968-73, pres. 1976), Wooster C. of C. (pres. 1942-43). Rotarian (pres. 1945-46). Home: 647 Northwestern St Wooster OH 44691 Office: E Liberty St Wooster OH 44691

DIXIT, SUNIT SURESH, chemist; b. Delhi, India, Dec. 8, 1944; s. Suresh Chaturlal and Narendraben Savailal (Yajnik) D.; came to U.S., 1970, naturalized, 1978; B.Sc. with honors, U. Bombay, 1966, Ph.D., 1970; m. Remedios C. Cabatu, June 23, 1973; children—Nimish S.C., Rajesh. Research asso. Queen's U. of Belfast (No. Ireland), 1971-72; research scientist Gaylord Research Inst., Whippany, N.J., 1972-73; sr. research chemist Am. Hoeschst Corp., Murray Hill, N.J., 1973-79; research supr. Richardson Graphics Co., 1979-80, mgr. plant and tech. services, Orland Park, Ill., 1980—. Fellow Royal Chem. Soc. (U.K.); mem. Am. Chem. Soc. Hindu. Contbr. articles on polymer chemistry to nat. and internat. sci. jours. Home: 1604 Indian Trail Naperville IL 60565 Office: 9797 W 151st St Orland Park IL 60462

DIXON, ALAN JOHN, U.S. senator; b. Belleville, Ill., July 7, 1927; s. William G. and Elsa (Tebbenhoff) D.; B.S., U. Ill., 1949; LL.B., Wash. U., 1949; m. Joan Louise Fox, Jan. 17, 1954; children—Stephanie Jo, Yearian, Jeffrey Alan Dixon, Elizabeth Jane Dixon. Admitted to Illinois bar, 1950, since practiced in Belleville; police magistrate, Belleville, 1949; asst. atty. St. Clair County, 1950; mem. Ill. Ho. Reps., 1951-63; mem. Ill. Senate, 1963-71, minority whip senate; chmn. Jud. Adv. Council; treas. State of Ill., 1971-77, sec. of state, 1977-81; mem. U.S. Senate from Ill., 1981—. Mem. C. of C., Am. Legion. Club: Nat. Democratic, St. Clair County, Columbia Country. Office: United States Senate Washington DC 20510

DIXON, FREDERICK WILLIAM, physician; b. Columbus, Ohio, Mar. 18, 1912; s. Charles Roy and Louise (Beck) D.; B.A., Ohio State U., 1933, M.D., 1936; m. Ruth Fern Hankins, July 14, 1936; 1 dau., Barbara Ruth (Mrs. Gale James Eastwood). Intern, Harper Hosp., 1936-37; gen. practice medicine, Dearborn, Mich., 1938—; indsl. physician Murray Corp., Detroit, 1937-42, 46-48; mem. staff Oakwood Hosp. Troop committeeman Detroit Area council Boy Scouts Am., 1948—; mem. adv. com. League Women Voters, 1950-54; contbg. mem. Detroit Symphony Orch. Served to maj. M.C., AUS, USAAF, 1942-46; col. Res., staff specialist SSS; comdg. officer Detroit Moblzn. Unit, 1961-72. Ret. from Army Res. as Col., M.C., 1972. Meritorious Service award Selective Service System. Mem. A.M.A., Mich., Wayne County, Dearborn (past pres.) med. socs., Assn. Mil. Surgeons U.S., Res. Officers Assn., Air Force Assn. (charter mem.), Mich. Assn. Professions (organizer, charter mem.), Am. Acad. Gen. Practice, Alpha Kappa Kappa, Alpha Sigma Phi. Republican. Mason (32 deg., Shriner). Club: Dearborn Country. Home: 245 S Martha St Dearborn MI 48124 Office: 530 N Telegraph Rd Dearborn MI 48128

DIXON, GEORGE HALL, bank exec.; b. Rochester, N.Y., Oct. 7, 1920; s. George Hall and Frances (Wheeler) D.; B.S., U. Pa., 1942; M.B.A., Harvard U., 1947; LL.D. (hon.), Carroll Coll., Helena, Mont.; m. Marjorie Freeman, Apr. 3, 1948; children—George E., Andrew T., Candis H. Pres. First Nat. Bank Mpls., 1968-76, chmn., 1972-76, also dir.; dep. sec. treasury Dept. of Treasury, Washington, 1976-77; pres. First Bank System, Inc., Mpls., 1977—, also dir.; dir. First Nat. Bank St. Paul, First Trust Co. St. Paul, First Nat. Bank Mpls., Donaldson Co., Inc., Bloomington, Minn., Northwestern Nat. Life Ins. Co., Mpls., Soo Line R.R. Co., Mpls., Internat. Multifoods Corp., Mpls., Minn. Orchestral Assn., Mpls.; dir., past pres. United Way Mpls.; trustee Carleton Coll., Northfield, Minn., Sci. Mus. Minn. Served to capt. U.S. Army. Mem. Atlantic Inst. (gov. Paris), Am. Gas Assn. (mem. banking adv. council). Republican. Presbyterian. Clubs: Links (N.Y.); Mpls., Minn. Office: PO Box 522 Minneapolis MN 55480

DIXON, KENT DARKLEY, advt. agy. exec.; b. Duluth, Minn., Sept. 27, 1926; s. Robert and Florence (Darke) D.; B.A., U. Minn., 1950; m. Marilyn L. Blair, Oct. 1, 1953. Various sales, advt. positions Internat. Milling Co., 1950-53; copy writer, account exec. Ruthrauff & Ryan Agy., Inc., 1953-55; marketing mgr. Rap-In-Wax Paper Co., Mpls., 1955-57; founder Kent Dixon Advt. Agy., Mpls., 1957, owner 1957—. Lectr. advt., pub. relations Mgmt. Center, Coll. St. Thomas, St. Paul, 1960—; lect. advt. U. Minn.; speaker numerous food merchandising convs. Founder Ernie Swift Meml. Conservation Com., 1969. Founding dir. Northern Environmental Council, Duluth, Minn., 1970. Served with AUS, World War II. Mem. Mpls. Advt. Club, Aircraft Owners and Pilots Assn., Young Men of Minn. Club: Minn. Press. Home: 4709 Meadow Rd Minneapolis MN 55424 Office: 711 W Lake St Minneapolis MN 55408

DIXON, MARGUERITE ANDERSON, nurse, educator; b. Pitts., May 18, 1930; d. William Orlando and Ida Mary (Taylor) A.; B.A., Andrews U., 1952; B.S. in Nursing, U. Ill., 1959, M.S. in Nursing, 1972, postgrad., 1978—; m. Relyea M. Dixon, June 15, 1952; children—M. Elise, R. Paul. Research asst. Michael Reese Pediatric Inst., Chgo., 1952-53, Coll. Dentistry, U. Ill., 1953-57; student asst. U. Ill. Hosp., Chgo., 1957-59, staff nurse, 1959-60, asst. head nurse, 1960, head nurse, 1960-61, supr., 1961-70, asst. dir. nursing, 1971-75; asst. prof. Coll. Nursing, U. Ill., Chgo., 1975-78. Bd. dirs. Campus Green Townhouse Assn., 1975. Am. Nurses Assn. clin. fellow, 1978—. Mem. Am. Nurses Assn., Ill. Nurses Assn., Nat. League for Nursing, Sigma Theta Tau. Home: 812 S Laflin St Chicago IL 60607 Office: care U Ill Coll Nursing 845 S Damen Ave Chicago IL 60612

DIXON, MICHAEL A., architect; b. Chgo., Sept. 14, 1948; s. Fulton A. and Patricia K. (Broderick) D.; B.Arch., U. Ill., 1971; m. Sally Ann Linsky, Aug. 11, 1973; children—Thomas, Jennifer. Prin., Dixon Assos., Architects, St. Charles; adj. faculty Triton Coll. Bd. dirs. Restorations of Kane County, Inc. Mem. AIA (dir. chpt.), Evans Scholars Alumni Assn. Roman Catholic. Home: 1413 S 7th St Saint Charles IL 60174 Office: 37W222 Route 64 Saint Charles IL 60174

DIXON, RUTH DOROTHY, newspaper tng. exec.; b. Richland Center, Wis., Sept. 19, 1949; d. Walter Roland and Dorothy Ida (Wegner) Buhl; B.A. in Theatre-Speech, Macalester Coll., 1971. Personnel staffing specialist Fed. Govt., St. Paul and Mpls., 1971-73; publicity dir. Cricket Theatre, Mpls., 1973-74; asso. producer, researcher writer Minn. Public TV Network, St. Paul, 1974-76; project coordinator Minn. Bicentennial Comm., St. Paul, 1976; promotion dir. Minn. Public Radio Network, St. Paul, 1976-77; promotion copy coordinator Mpls. Star and Tribune Newspapers, Mpls., 1977-79, circulation tng. mgr., 1979—. Chairperson Merriam Park Dist. Planning Com., St. Paul, 1975-77; mem. Merriam Park Community Council, St. Paul, 1976-77; pres. Assn. St. Paul Communities, 1976-78. Recipient Merit award Minn. Edn. Assn., 1975, 76, Sch. Bell award, 1976; cert. recognition Minn. Bicentennial Commn., 1976. Mem. Am. Soc. Tng. and Devel., Minn. Assn. Continuing Adult Edn., Assn. Ednl. Data Systems, Am. Mgmt. Assn., Central States Circulation Mgrs. Assn. Home: 3120 Colfax Ave S Minneapolis MN 55408 Office: 425 Portland Ave Minneapolis MN 55488

DIXON, SAMUEL HEIL, automobile agy. exec.; b. Celina, Ohio, Feb. 15, 1928; s. Samuel D. and Lillian K. (Heil) D.; student Gen. Motors Inst., 1946-48; m. Judy Dixon; children—Samuel K., Teresa A., Randolph G. With Sam Dixon Motor Sales Inc., Celina, 1946—, v.p., 1956—. Served with U.S. Army, 1950-52; Korea. Mem. Nat. Automobile Dealers Assn., Ohio Automobile Dealers Assn. (trustee 1973-79), Auglaize-Mercer County Automobile Dealers Assn. (sec.-treas. 1971—), VFW, Am. Legion. Republican. Clubs: Masons, Shriners, Elks (past exalted ruler), Moose, Eagles. Home: 119 Johnson Ave Celina OH 45822 Office: Sam Dixon Motor Sales Inc Walnut at Warren St Celina OH 45822

DIXSON, J. B., state public relations exec.; b. Norwich, N.Y., Oct. 19, 1941; d. William Joseph and Ann Wanda (Teale) Barrett; B.S., Syracuse U., 1963; postgrad. in bus. adminstrn. Wayne State U., 1979—; M.A., Central Mich. U., 1982. Public relations editorial asst. Am. Mus. Natural History, N.Y.C., 1963-64; writer/producer Norman, Navan, Moore & Baird Advt., Grand Rapids, Mich., 1964-67; prin. J.B. Dixson Communications Cons., Detroit, 1967-74; dir. Public Info. Services div. Mich. Employment Security Commn., Detroit, 1974—; lectr., speaker in field at colls., univs., community orgns. Mem. Detroit Mayor's Transition Com. of 100, 1972; mem. bd. mgmt. Detroit YWCA, 1974; chmn. Detroit Women's Equality Day Com., 1975; bd. dirs., founding mem. Feminist Fed. Credit Union, Detroit, 1976; founding mem. Mich. Women's Campaign Fund, 1980; mem. Mich. Task Force on Sexual Harassment in Workplace. Named Outstanding Sr. Woman in Radio and TV, Syracuse U., 1963; recipient Five Watch award Am. Women in Radio and TV, Mich., 1969, cert. of recognition Detroit City Council, 1976. Design in Mich. award Mich. Council of Arts/Gov. William G. Milliken, 1977, Achievement award Dept. Labor, 1979, Spirit of Detroit award Detroit City Council, 1980; subject of Mich. Senate Resolution 412, 1979. Mem. Public Relations Soc. Am. (accredited), Nat. Assn. Govt. Communicators (Blue Pencil award 1977, Gold Screen award 1980), Econ. Club Detroit, Internat. Assn. Personnel in Employment Security. Clubs: Thames Yacht, Maple Grove Gun, Detroit Press. Author: Guidelines for Non-Sexist Verbal and Written Communication, 1976; Sexual Harassment on The Job, 1979. Office: 7310 Woodward Detroit MI 48202

DIZZONNE, MICHAEL FRANK, psychometrist; b. Chgo., Feb. 28, 1941; s. Frank and Angeline Catherine (Pisano) D.; B.A., Roosevelt U., 1965; M.Ed., Loyola U. At Chgo., 1975. Psychometrist, VA Hosp., North Chicago, Ill., 1968—; pvt. practice as psychometrist, 1977—. Mem. Am., Ill., Midwest psychol. assns., Nat. Psychiat. Assn., Am. Council Counselors, Therapists and Educators, Nat. Acad. Neuropsychology. Roman Catholic. Home: 2321 W Washington St Waukegan IL 60085 Office: VA Hospital North Chicago IL 60064

DLABAL, JOHN JEROME, JR., educator; b. Wilson, Kans., Aug. 14, 1930; s. John Jerome and Philomena (Pospisil) D.; B.S., Fort Hays State U., 1957; M.S., Kans. State U., 1960; Ed.D., Kans. U., 1966; m. Martha Myers, Aug. 8, 1953; children—Anita, Theresa, John, Edward, Cecilia, Daniel, David. Tchr. elem. schs., Kans., 1948-54, Manhattan, Kans., 1957-60, elem. prin., 1960-64; mem. faculty No. Ill. U., DeKalb, 1965-70, asst. dir. extension, 1971-75, prof. edn., 1975—; trading adv. Heinold Commodities, 1980—. Served with AUS, 1954-56. Mem. Assn. Continuing Edn. Profs. (exec. v.p.), Assn. Supervision and Curriculum Devel., Phi Delta Kappa. Republican. Roman Catholic. Author: Reading Book, 1968; contbr. articles to profl. jours. Home: 1208 Stafford St DeKalb IL 60115 Office: Sch Edn No Ill U DeKalb IL 60115

DLOUHY, JOHN ANTON, mfg. co. exec.; b. Oak Park, Ill., Aug. 10, 1930; s. Clarence O. and Ruth M. D.; B.S. in Metall. Engring., Mich. Tech. U., 1954; M.B.A., U. Chgo., 1976; m. Mary Jane Clark, June 18, 1955; children—Faye M., Mary B., Kathleen A., John C. With Emil J. Paidar Co., Chgo., 1954-73; plant mgr. to pres. Hirsch Co., Skokie, Ill., 1973-77; v.p. mfg. Bloomfield Industries div. Beatrice Foods, Inc., Chgo., 1977-78; v.p. mktg. Benton Harbor Engring. div. Koehring Co., Benton Harbor, Mich., 1979-80; v.p. ops. to pres. MPS Internat., dir., 1965—; v.p. Prodn. Tool Corp., Chgo., 1980—, also dir.; sr. partner EMPACO. Essential worker Argonne (Ill.) Nat. Lab., 1948-52; bd. dirs. ARC, Oak Park, Ill., 1963. Mem. Am. Soc. Metals, Am. Iron and Steel Engrs., Am. Prodn. and Inventory Control Soc., Chgo. C. of C. and Industry. Club: Ill. Athletic. Patentee in field. Home: 1123 Ashland Ave River Forest IL 60305 Office: 1229 E 74th St Chicago IL 60619

DOBBS, DONALD EDWIN ALBERT, elec. products co. exec.; b. Ft. Wayne, Ind., Oct. 8, 1931; s. Edmund F. and Agnes (Stempnick) D.; B.S., Marquette U., 1953; m. Beatrice A. Spieker, July 27, 1957; children—Margaret L. Howard, Christopher E.J., Laura C. Prebe. Reporter, Cath. Chronicle, Toledo, 1953; indsl. editor, pub. relations Nat. Supply Co., Toledo 1955-59; employee communications exec. Prestolite Co., an Eltra Co., Toledo, 1959-61, public relations dir., 1961-80, dir. communications, 1980—. Past chmn. Maumee Valley Hosp. Sch. Nursing Com.; pres. Internat. Inst., Toledo, 1970-73; past chmn. Child Nutrition Center, Toledo; past mem. Ohio Adv. Council Vocat. Edn.; vice chmn. Mayor's Citizen Devel. Forum; chmn. bd. dirs. Mercy Hosp.; bd. dirs. Frederick Douglass Community Assn.; pres. bd. dirs. Crosby Gardens; pres. Ohio Friends of Library; past chmn. Salvation Army; past pres. Toledo Council of World Affairs, Toledo Hearing and Speech Center, Friends of Toledo/Lucas County Library; past pres. bd. dirs. Internat. Park; pres. bd. dirs. Toledo Life Care. Served with AUS, 1953-55. Mem. Marquette U. Alumni Assn. N.W. Ohio (past pres., area dir.), Soc. Profl. Journalists, Public Relations Soc. Am. (pres.-elect N.W. Ohio), Automotive Public Relations Council (pres.), Cath. Interracial Council (past pres.). Democrat (past nat. com. Wis. Young Dems.). Roman Catholic. Kiwanian (past pres. Toledo, Mid-City Athletic League, Kiwanis Youth Found.; lt. gov. 1974-75). Clubs: Toledo Press, Toledo Mud Hens Diamond (charter). Home: 2433 Meadowwood Dr Toledo OH 43606 Office: 511 Hamilton St Toledo OH 43694

DOBOGAI, JOHN EDWARD, JR., tax analyst, lectr.; b. Milw., Oct. 14, 1941; s. John Edward and Betty Jean (Holzman) D.; B.S. in Bus. Adminstrn., U. Va., 1968; m. Suzanne Lee Rouse, Mar. 25, 1970; children—Deborah Lee, John Edward, III, Michael Edward, Sarah Lee, Jessica Lee. Tax mgr. Clifton-Gunderson C.P.A. Firm, Macomb, Ill.; dir. numerous corps. U.S. tax expert liaison to Can., 1968. Chmn. United Givers Fund Medford, 1974-76; del. U.S. Bicentennial Com., 1975. Scoutmaster, Boy Scouts Am. Trustee Boys to the Woods Found. Served with USAF, 1960-64. Mem. Am. Legion, Medford Jaycees, Va. Life Underwriters Assn. Republican. Mormon. Kiwanian. Home: 808 E Washington Macomb IL 61455 Office: 444 N Lafayette Macomb IL 61455

DOBRICK, JO-ANNE SHAYE, art gallery exec.; b. Detroit, Sept. 19, 1945; d. Nathan and Lillian (Davis) Shaye; student Ohio State U., 1963-65, Art Inst. Chgo., 1970-71; B.A., Roosevelt U., 1972; m. Howard Dobrick, Dec. 9, 1968; 1 dau., Rebecca Ellen. With United Air Lines, 1966-67, retail advt. dept. Chgo. Tribune, 1968-70; tchr. Evanston (Ill.) Dist. 65, 1970-72; dir. Dobrick Gallery, Chgo., 1974—, pres. Dobrick Gallery Ltd., 1974—; lectr. to charitable, interest groups. Participant, Art in Pub. Places, 1975; chmn. art com. Channel 11 Pub. Broadcasting, 1975—. Sec. for Park Art div. Friends of the Park; bd. dirs. for Near North Affiliates to Mus. Contemporary Art. Mem. Chgo. Art Dealers Assn. Office: 216 E Ontario St Chicago IL 60611

DOBSON, JOHN JOSEPH, JR., pub. accountant; b. Kansas City, Mo., Oct. 23, 1914; s. John J. and Mattie (McPherson) D.; A.B., U. Mo., 1938, M.A., 1939; m. Phyllis Marie Land, Nov. 20, 1940; children—Bette Gae, John Joseph III. Partner, Arthur Young & Co., Kansas City, Mo., 1939-52, John Dobson & Co., South Bend, Ind., 1953—; dir. 1st Fed. Savs. & Loan Assn., South Bend. Mem. City Plan Commn., Kansas City, Mo., 1947-53. Pres. Michiana Watershed, South Bend. Served with AUS, 1942-43. C.P.A., Mo., Kan., Ind., Mich., Ill. Mem. Am. Inst. C.P.A.'s, Ind., Mich. assns. C.P.A.'s, Nat. Assn. Accountants, South Bend Estate Planning Council, South Bend C. of C. Am. Legion, D.A.V., Alpha Chi Sigma, Delta Sigma Pi, Kappa Sigma. Presbyn. Clubs: Summit, Indiana (South Bend). Home: 1628 Hoover Ave South Bend IN 46615 Office: 224 W Jefferson Blvd South Bend IN 46601

DOBSON, JOHN MCCULLOUGH, historian; b. Las Cruces, N.Mex., July 20, 1940; s. Donald Duane and Carolyn Margaret (Van Anda) D.; B.S., Mass. Inst. Tech., 1962; M.S., U. Wis., 1964, Ph.D., 1966; m. Cynthia Davis, Aug. 29, 1963; children—David, Daniel. Asst. prof. history Calif. State U., Chico, 1966-67; fgn. service officer U.S. Dept. State, Washington, 1967-68; asst. prof., asso. prof., now prof. history Iowa State U., Ames, 1968—; vis. asso. prof. history U. Md., summer 1972, spring 1976; Fulbright lectr. Univ. Coll., Dublin, 1979-80. U.S. Internat. Trade Commn. grantee, 1976. Mem. Am. Hist. Assn., Orgn. Am. Historians, Soc. Historians of Am. Fgn. Relations, AAUP. Author: Politics in the Gilded Age: A New Perspective on Reform, 1972; Two Centuries of Tariffs: The Background and Origins of the U.S. International Trade Commn., 1977; America's Ascent, 1978. Home: 2019 Kildee St Ames IA 50010 Office: Dept History Iowa State U Ames IA 50011

DOCKEMEYER, JOSEPH ROBERT, SR., hosp. ofcl.; b. Chagrin Falls, Ohio, Jan. 17, 1930; s. Bernard Joseph and Mary Lillian (Beavins) D.; B.S. in Bus. Adminstrn., Brescia Coll., Owensboro, Ky., 1964; m. Mildred B. Byrne, Jan. 12, 1952; children—Joseph Robert, Alan Lee, Roger Earl, Sheila Rose, Blaine Eric, Neil Craig, Glenn Bernard, Valerie Ann. Cook, Hotel McCurdy, Evansville, Ind., 1955-57, cook Gen. Electric Co., Owensboro, 1957-58, cafeteria mgr., Tell City, Ind., 1958-64; dir. food service Deaconess Hosp., Evansville, 1964-67; dir. food service St. Joseph Meml. Hosp., Kokomo, Ind., 1967—, pres. mgmt. council, 1972; bd. dirs. Meals on Wheels Howard County, 1971-79; mem. program com. Tri State Hosp. Assembly Ednl. Conf. Food Service Mgmt., 1979. Served with USAF, 1951-55. Named Outstanding Coop. Edn. Employer, Kokomo Area Vocat. Sch., 1973. Fellow Health Care Food Service Adminstrs.; mem. Am. Soc. Hosp. Food Service Adminstrs. (pres. Hoosier chpt. 1975, 78, nat. com. vol. effort and cost containment 1979—). Democrat. Roman Catholic. Home: 2333 Westdale Ct Kokomo IN 46901 Office: 1907 W Sycamore St Kokomo IN 46901

DOCKHORN, ROBERT JOHN, physician; b. Goodland, Kans., Oct. 9, 1934; s. Charles George and Dortha Mae (Horton) D.; B.A., U. Kans., 1956, M.D., 1960; m. Beverly Ann Wilke, June 15, 1957; children—David, Douglas, Deborah. Intern, Naval Hosp., San Diego, 1960-61, resident in pediatrics, Oakland, Calif., 1963-65; resident in pediatric allergy and immunology U. Kans., 1967-69; resident in pediatric allergy and immunology Children's Mercy Hosp., Kansas City, Mo., 1967-69, chief allergy-immunology div., 1969—; practice medicine specializing in allergy and immunology, Prairie Village, Kans., 1969—; clin. prof. pediatrics and medicine U. Mo. Sch. Medicine, Kansas City. Diplomate Am. Bd. Pediatrics, Am. Bd. Allergy and Immunology. Fellow Am. Acad. Pediatrics, Am. Coll. Allergists (pres. 1981—), Am. Acad. Allergy; mem. AMA, Kans., Johnson County med. socs., Kans. (pres. 1976-77), Mo. (sec. 1975-76) allergy socs., Joint Council of Allergy and Immunology (pres. 1979). Contbr. articles to med. jours. Home: 8510 Delmar Ln Prairie Village KS 66208 Office: 5300 W 94th Terr Prairie Village KS 66207

DOCKINS, GLENN, JR., librarian; b. Scopus, Mo., Dec. 29, 1925; s. Glen and Stella Lee (Teeters) D.; student U. Nebr., 1965; B.S. in Edn., S.E. Mo. State Coll., 1951; M.L.S., George Peabody Library Sch., 1964; m. Cleta Mae Rolf, July 26, 1958; children—Maria Antonia, Tammy Leigh, Rebekah Kaye. Librarian, Flat River (Mo.) Jr. High Sch., 1961-65; library dir. Mexico (Mo.)-Audrain County Library, 1965-67; exec. library dir. Cumberland Trail Library System, Flora, Ill., 1967—; cons. library bldgs. Served with USNR, 1944-46. Mem. ALA, Ill. Library Assn., Mo. Tchrs. Assn., Alpha Beta Alpha.

Methodist. Clubs: Masons, Elks. Contbr. articles to profl. jours. Office: Cumberland Trail Library System 12th and McCawley Flora IL 62839

DOCTORIAN, DAVID, state senator; b. Beirut, Lebanon, Nov. 9, 1934; A.B., B.S. in Edn.; M.A. in Am. History; M.A. in Polit Sci.; m. Phyllis Ann Traylor, Aug. 12, 1959; 4 children. Prof. govt. and French, chmn. div. social sci. Moberly (Mo.) Jr. Coll.; ordained to ministry Christian Ch.; minister, Plevna Christian Ch.; mem. Mo. Senate, 1977—. Mem. Mo. Polit. Sci. Assn., Am. Council Tchrs. Fgn. Langs., Mo. State Tchrs. Assn., Macon County Gun Owners Assn., Mo. Citizens for Life. Republican. Office: State Capitol Jefferson City MO 65101*

DODD, EDWIN D(ILLON), mfg. exec.; b. Point Pleasant, W.Va., Jan. 26, 1919; s. David Rollin and Mary Grace (Dillon) D.; B.S. in Bus. Adminstrn., Ohio State U., 1941; Indsl. Adminstrn., Harvard, 1943; LL.D. (hon.), U. Toledo, 1970, Washington and Jefferson Coll., 1972; m. Marie Marshall, Apr. 18, 1942; 1 dau., Marjorie Lee (Mrs. Jay Wannamaker). Engr. airplane div. Curtiss-Wright Corp., 1941-42; pub. relations rep. Owens-Ill. Glass Co., 1946-49, pub. relations dir., 1949-54, prodn. mgr. Libbey Glass div. Owens-Ill., 1954-56, factories mgr. Libbey Glass div., 1956-58; v.p., asst. gen. mgr. Owens-Ill. Paper Products div. (formerly Nat. Container Corp.), 1958; v.p. Owens-Ill. Glass Co. (name changed to Owens-Ill., Inc. 1965), 1959-64, gen. mgr. paper products div., 1959-61, gen. mgr. forest products div., 1961-68, exec. v.p. corp., 1964-68, pres., chief operating officer, 1968—, chief exec. officer, 1972—, chmn., 1976—, also dir.; dir. Valdosta So. R.R. Co., 1966-68; pres. Forest Products Corp., 1959-68; pres., dir. Valdosta So. R.R. Co., Marinette, Tomahawk and Western R.R., 1961-68; pres. Bahamas Agrl. Industries Ltd., 1962-66, chmn. bd., 1966—; dir. Ohio Bell Telephone, Nat. Petro Chem., Toledo Trust Co., Goodyear Tire & Rubber Co., Toledo Trust corp., Inc.; pres., dir. Sabine River & No. R.R. Co., 1966-68; pres., chmn. bd. Owens-Ill. Timber Corp., 1962-68, Angelina Plywood, 1966-68. Mem. Pres.'s Nat. Indsl. Pollution Council, 1970; mem. Lucas County Republican Finance Com., 1970; trustee Toledo Hosp., Toledo Mus. Art, pres. Maumee Valley Country Day Sch., 1965-67, trustee, 1962-68; chmn. bd. dirs. Ohio State U. Devel. Fund, 1978-79, Am. Forest Inst., Am. Paper Inst., 1966-68; trustee Nat. Center for Resource Recovery; bd. dirs. Fourdrinier Kraft Board Inst., 1964-68, chmn., 1967-68; bd. govs. Nat. Council of Paper Industry for Air and Stream Improvement, 1964-68; past pres. Toledo Bd. Edn.; bd. dirs. Toledo-Lucas County Port Authority, 1962—; mem. Toledo Commn. for Community Devel., 1963—; chmn. bd. visitors Berry Coll., 1978-80; mem. council Nat. Municipal League, 1953-55, 57-59, 61-63, 65-67, regional v.p., 1967—; mem. bd. devel. council Med. Coll. Ohio; 1st chmn. bd. trustees Greater Toledo Corp. Served from pvt. to maj. AUS, 1943-46; PTO. Decorated Legion of Merit, 1946, Mil. Merit medal Chief of Staff, Philippine Army, 1946; recipient Distinguished Service award Toledo Jr. C. of C., 1955, Ohio Jr. C. of C., 1955; Distinguished Citizen's award Nat. Municipal League, 1959. Mem. Fibre Box Assn. (dir. 1960-68, pres. 1964-65), Toledo C. of C. (trustee 1973-74, now chmn.), Nat. Paperboard Assn. (dir. 1964-65, exec. com. 1964-68), Am. Soc. Corporate Execs., Nat. Indsl. Conf. Bd., Internat. Corrugated Case Assn. (dir. 1967—, pres. 1967-68), Cum Laude Soc., Confrerie des Chevaliers, Harvard Bus. Sch. Assn. (pres. exec. council 1972-73, vis. com. 1974—), Phi Gamma Delta. Presbyn. (trustee 1966-67, elder 1970—). Clubs: Mid-Am. (Chgo.); Toledo, Harvard Business School, Belmont Country, Toledo Country, Inverness Country (Toledo); Lyford Cay (Nassau, Bahamas); Links, Economic (N.Y.C.); Blind Brook (Purchase, N.Y.); Augusta (Ga.) Nat. Golf; Muirfield Village Golf (Dublin, Ohio); Rockwell Springs Trout. Home: 5029 Corey Rd Toledo OH 43623 Office: Owens-Ill Inc One SeaGate Toledo OH 43666

DODD, JAMES ARTHUR, library dir.; b. N.Y.C., Feb. 17, 1925; s. Charles Allen and Florence (Warner) D.; B.A. cum laude, Northland Coll., Ashland, 1950; M.S. in L.S., U. Wis., 1951; postgrad. Wayne State U., 1958; m. Nancy Ann Hoecker, Oct. 20, 1951; children—Elizabeth, Paul Henry. Youth librarian, adult asst. Detroit Pub. Library, 1951-56, br. library 1st asst., 1956-59; br. librarian Grosse Pointe (Mich.) Pub. Library, 1959-64; library dir. Adrian (Mich.) Coll., 1964—; cons. Siena Heights Coll., Adrian, 1975-78. Bd. dirs. Lenawee County United Fund, pres., 1973; bd. dirs., exec. bd., sec. Goodwill Industries, pres., 1980-82; trustee Mich. Library Consortium, also mem. personnel com.; hon. chmn. United Way Lenawee County. Mem. ALA, Mich. Acad. Sci., Arts and Letters, Mich. Library Assn. (exec. bd. acad. div. 1973, sec.-treas. acad. div., mem. public relations com. 1978-80), Mich. Archives Assn., U. Wis. Library Sch. Alumni Assn. (pres. 1972-73), AAUP (past sec., treas. local chpt.). Methodist (past pres. men's club, sec. council on ministries, pastor parish com.). Kiwanian. Club: Lenawee Country (past treas., dir.). Contbr. articles to profl. jours. Home: 4771 Devonshire Dr Adrian MI 49221

DODDERIDGE, RICHARD WILLIAM, advt. co. exec.; b. Council Grove, Kans., Oct. 3, 1926; s. Russell Reubin and Rachel Augusta (Jacobs) D.; B.S., Kansas State U., 1947; student Harvard Grad. Sch. Bus. Advanced Marketing Seminar, 1968; m. Cornelia Ann Thornberry, Oct. 25, 1952; children—Richard William, John Russell, Daniel James. Sports dir. KFBI, Wichita, Kans., 1947; account exec. Bruce B. Brewer Co., Inc., Kansas City, Mo., 1947-67, exec. v.p., 1967-72, pres., 1972-74; pres. Brewer Advt. Inc. div. Young & Rubican Inc., 1974-81, dir., 1981—. Vice chmn. Better Bus. Bur., Kansas City, 1964-66; vice-chmn. Citizens Assn., Kansas City, Mo., 1959-60; mem. Camp Gravois com. YMCA, Kansas City, 1963-68; mem. Starlight Theatre Assn., 1964—; mem. Kansas City (Mo.) Motion Picture Bd. Appeals, 1951; pres. Mission Woods Homes Assn., 1966-67, City council, Mission Woods, Kans., 1969-75; mem. journalism adv. council Kans. State U. Trustee, Kansas City Mus., Kans. State U. Found., 1979—; bd. dirs. Kansas Art Center Found., Pub. TV 19, 1973—; bd. govs. Kansas City Art Inst., 1977—. Served with USAAF, 1944-45. Named man of the year Am. Advt. Fedn., 9th Dist., 1967; recipient Silver medal award Am. Advt. Fedn. Printers' Ink, 1967; named Mem. of the Year, Advt. and Sales Execs. Club., 1959. Mem. Advt. and Sales Execs. Club (bd. govs. 1961-73, pres. 1969-70, trustee 1973-76), Am. Advt. Fedn. (dist. gov., 1961-62; nat. dir. 1968-72, 79—, chmn. pub. affairs com. 1972-73), Am. Assn. Advt. Agys. (com. govt. and pub. relations 1967-74, chmn. Mo. council 1975-76), Kansas City C. of C. (prime time steering com. 1973-75). Republican. Episcopalian (vestryman 1969-74). Rotarian. Clubs: Kansas City Press, Kansas City, Carriage (dir. 1972-75, v.p. 1974-75), Midnighters. Home: 5333 Mission Woods Rd Shawnee Mission KS 66205 Office: 3 Crown Center 2440 Pershing Rd Kansas City MO 64108

DODDS, DOROTHYMAE, educator; b. Mankato, Minn., Nov. 4, 1927; d. William McKinley and Frances Mathilda (Leslie) Grimes; B.S., Moorhead (Minn.) State U., 1948, M.S., 1979; m. Robert Warren Dodds, Aug. 21, 1948; children—Laura Leslie, Michael Robert. Elem. instr. Mpls. Public Schs., 1948-53; sec.-treas. Dodds Drug, Inc., Red Lake Falls, Minn., 1954—; instr. sales, mktg. and mgmt., program head Thief River Falls (Minn.) Area Vocat. Tech. Inst., 1979—. Com. chmn. Grand Forks (N.D.) council Girl Scouts U.S.A., 1963-70, neighborhood chmn., 1960, v.p., 1970-75, Thanks badge, 1972; com. chmn. Civic and Commerce Assn. of Red Lake Falls, 1971-74; mem. Region I Minn. Arts Adv. com., 1976-80; bd. trustees Citizens for the Arts, St. Paul, 1978—. Recipient awards for painting. Mem. Minn. Edn. Assn., Am. Vocat. Assn., Distributive Edn. Clubs Am. (cert. of appreciation Minn., nat. plaque of appreciation). Republican. Presbyterian. Home: 107 7th St NE Red Lake Falls MN 56750 Office: Hwy 1 E Thief River Falls MN 56701

DODGE, OLIVIA IRVINE, nature center exec.; b. St. Paul, Oct. 7, 1918; d. Horace Hills and Clotilde (McCullough) Irvine; student Rasmussen Bus. Sch., 1938-39; m. Arthur Murray Dodge, July 3, 1958; 1 son, Thomas Irvine. Librarian VA Hosp., Mpls., 1954-57; pres., founder Thomas Irvine Dodge Nature Center, West St. Paul, Minn., 1967—. Bd. dirs. Nat. Council for Youth Found., Children's Hosp. St. Paul, Minn. Zool. Soc.; trustee Natural Sci. for Youth Found, Oakland Cemetery, St. Paul; v.p. prodn. dept., St. Paul ARC World War II. Recipient Woman of Year award St. Paul Booster's News, 1968, Dist. 197 West St. Paul award, 1973, Urban Space award Minn. Environ. Concerns Inc., 1974, Founders Fund award Natural Sci. for Youth Found., 1975, cert. of appreciation Dakota County Area Vocat. Tech. Inst., 1976, citizen of month cert. St. Paul Dispatch and Pioneer Press, 1977, conservation achievement award Garden Club Am., 1978, hon. citizen achievement award City of Mpls., 1978, Spurgeon's award, 1980. Mem. Sierra Club, Izaak Walton League, Am. Forestry Assn., Save the Redwoods League, Nat. Audubon Soc., Nat. Wildlife Fedn., Nature Conservancy. Episcopalian. Clubs: St. Paul Garden (publicity chmn. 1974-76), Elephant, Somerset, White Bear Yacht, Minnesota, Pool and Yacht. Home and Office: 1668 Delaware Ave St Paul MN 55118

DODSON, IRMA MARY, educator; b. Danville, Ill., Oct. 23, 1913; d. Jesse Robert and Naomi Mott (Browning) D.; B.S. in Edn., Ind. State U., 1952, M.A., 1964. Tchr., Tillotson Sch., Potomac, Ill., 1933-37, Diamond Sch., Danville, Ill., 1937-46, Catlin (Ill.) Consol. Schs., 1946-58, Crichfield Sch., LaPorte, Ind., 1958-68; prof. Cedarville (Ohio) Coll., 1968-78, prof. emerita, 1978—, part-time supr. student tchrs., 1978—; condr. seminars. Recipient award and plaque Cedarville Coll., 1978. Mem. Assn. Childhood Edn. Internat. (v.p. LaPorte chpt. 1964-65, pres. 1965-66), Ill. Edn. Assn. (sec. East Central div. 1948-49, pres. div. 1949-50), Internat. Reading Assn., AAUW, Ohio Assn. Tchr. Edn., Children's Lit. Assn., Nat. Council Tchrs. of English, Nat. Educators Fellowship, Delta Kappa Gamma (pres. chpt. 1976-78). Baptist. Contbr. articles to religious jours. Office: Box 601 Cedarville OH 45314

DODSON, JOHN ROBERT, burial services adminstr.; b. Cheyenne, Wyo., Mar. 2, 1949; s. Donald R. and Dorothy Jean (Downey) D.; grad. Worsham Coll., 1973-74, m. Pamela Sue Bertels, Nov. 30, 1974. Intern, Abts Mortuary, Pekin, Ill., 1974-75; asso. with Marks Funeral Home, Edwardsville, Ill., 1975-76; propr., dir. Stumpf Funeral Home, Pana, Ill., 1976—; pres. Pana Indsl. Devel. Corp., 1981—. Served with U.S. Army, 1969-71; Vietnam. Decorated Bonze star. Mem. Ill. Funeral Dirs. Assn., Nat. Funeral Dirs. Assn., Internat. Order of Golden Rule, Pana Jaycees (pres. 1977-78), Pana C. of C. (dir. 1976—, pres. 1981-82), Am. Legion, VFW. Lutheran. Clubs: Rotary, Lions. Address 112 Kitchell Ave Pana IL 62557

DODSON, OSCAR HENRY, museum dir., numis. cons.; b. Houston, Jan. 3, 1905; s. Dennis Seth and Maggie (Sisk) D.; B.S., U.S. Naval Acad., 1927, postgrad., 1936; M.A., U. Ill., 1953; m. Pauline Wellbrock, Dec. 17, 1932; 1 son, John Dennis. Commd. ensign USN, 1927, advanced through grades to rear adm., 1957, ret. 1957; asst. prof. history U. Ill., 1957-59; dir. Money Museum, Nat. Bank of Detroit, 1959-65, World Heritage Mus., U. Ill., Urbana, 1966-73; acting dir. Champaign County Hist. Mus., 1980; mem. Ann. Assay Commn., 1948. Decorated Silver Star. Fellow Am. Numis. Soc., Royal Numis. Soc. London, Explorers Club; mem. Am. Mil. Inst., Am. Archaeol. Inst., Am. Numis. Assn. (pres. 1957-61; Farren Zerbe award 1968), Internat. Banknote Soc. London (hon.), U.S. Naval Acad. Alumni Assn. (life), U.S. Naval Acad. Found., U. Ill. Found., U. Ill. Alumni Assn. (life mem., Loyalty award 1966, president's council). Clubs: Torch, Rotary (pres. Champaign, Ill. 1972-73); Army-Navy (Washington); New York Yacht (N.Y.C.); Champaign Country; Circumnavigators. Author: Money Tells the Story, 1962. Contbr. articles to profl., numismatic jours. Office: 484 Lincoln Hall Urbana IL 61801

DOELLE, MICHAEL BUELL, lawyer; b. Detroit, June 23, 1934; s. Buell Arnold and Marie Patrice (Horrigan) D.; A.B., U. Mich., 1957, LL.B., 1961; m. Kathleen Clare Denton, Sept. 1, 1973; children—Susan Sage, William Arnold, Martha Martin, Sarah Buell. Admitted to Mich. bar; law clk. to judge U.S. Ct. of Appeals for 6th Circuit, Cin., 1961-62; asso. firm Vandeveer, Haggerty, Doelle, Garzia, Tonkin & Kerr, Detroit, 1962-66; asso. firm McClintock, Fulton, Donovan & Waterman, Detroit, 1966-69; v.p. legal affairs, asso. gen. counsel Blue Cross and Blue Shield of Mich., Detroit, 1969—. Mem. Am. Bar Assn., Mich. Bar Assn., Detroit Bar Assn., Am. Judicature Soc., Nat. Health Lawyers Assn., Am. Hosp. Lawyers Assn., Mich. Hosp. Lawyers Assn. Democrat. Roman Catholic. Club: Carrigan Creek Yacht. Home: 4556 Lakeshore St Port Huron MI 48060 Office: 600 Lafayette St Detroit MI 48226

DOEMENY, LAURENCE JAMES, adminstrv. chemist; b. San Diego, Aug. 11, 1942; s. E. Paul and Dorothy Irene (Burke) D.; A.B., San Diego State U., 1965, M.S., 1968; Ph.D. (Am.-Chem. Soc. petroleum research fund fellow), Calif., Santa Barbara, 1970; m. Jane Susan Rankine, Aug. 9, 1969; children—Emmerich John, Erika Jane. Research asso., chemistry dept. U. Minn., Mpls., 1970-71, instr. Sch. Pub. Health, 1971-73; aerosol physicist Nat. Inst. Occupat. Safety Health USPHS, Cin., 1973-74, chief, measurements systems sect., 1974-80, chief monitoring and control research br., 1980—; adj. asst. prof. environ. health U. Cin., 1979—; convenor Internat. Standards Orgn. group on respirable dust, 1979—. Recipient Commendation medal USPHS, 1980. Mem. Am. Chem. Soc. (chmn. div. chem. health and safety 1980-81), Am. Phys. Soc., AAAS. Contbr. articles to sci. jours.

DOEREN, STEPHEN EARL, criminologist, educator; b. Oskkosh, Wis., July 14, 1950; s. Earl B. and Lola G. (La Fortune) D.; B.A. summa cum laude, Ottawa U., 1972; M.A. (teaching asst.), U. N.Mex., 1974; Ph.D., La. State U., 1978; m. Sara Lynn Thiele, Jan. 5, 1974; 1 son, David Earl. Teaching asst. dept. sociology La. State U., 1974-76, research asso. dept. rural sociology, summer 1975; penologist La. Dept. Corrections, Baton Rouge, 1976, corrections treatment adminstr., 1976; dir. Victim/Witness Assistance Bur., Office of Dist. Atty., East Baton Rouge Parish, 1976-77; asst. prof. dept. adminstrn. justice Wichita (Kans.) State U., 1977—, undergrad. coordinator dept. adminstrn. justice, 1977-78. 81-82; cons. Sedgwick County (Kans.) Dist. Atty.'s Office, 1977; book reviewer McGraw-Hill Pub. Co., Harper & Row Pub. Co., MacMillan Pub. Co. Vol. coach St. Pius X High Sch. Am. Legion Baseball Team, Albuquerque, summer, 1971; vol. tutor children's ward Bernalillo County Hosp., Albuquerque, 1972; vol. St. Luke's Childhood Learning Center, Baton Rouge, 1975-77; mem. adv. bd. Larned (Kans.) State Hosp., 1978—; judge behavioral scis. div. La. State Sci. Fair, Baton Rouge, 1975; bd. dirs. Halfway House for Adults, Inc., Wichita, 1979—, August Eleven Council, Wichita, 1977—, v.p., 1979-80, pres., 1980—, mem. exec. bd., 1979—; co-chmn. Inter-Faith Ministries Jail and Prison Task Force, Wichita, 1981; project evaluator Wichita-Sedgwick County Met. Area Planning Dept., Wichita, 1977—. Nat. Assn. Intercollegiate Athletics scholar-athlete, 1970-71. Mem. Acad. Criminal Justice Scis., Am. Soc. Criminology, Am. Correctional Assn., Kans. Criminal Justice Educators Assn. (program com. 1979), Correctional Edn. Assn., Am. Sociol. Assn., Midwestern Assn. Criminal Justice Educators, Nat. Correctional Recreation Assn. (program com. 1980), Kans. Acad. Sci., Am. Quarter Horse Assn., Okla. Quarter Horse Assn., Kans. Quarter Horse Assn., Phi Kappa Phi, Gamma Sigma Delta, Sigma Alpha. Roman Catholic. Contbg. author: Introduction to Criminal Justice: Theory and Practice, 1979; co-author: Community Corrections, 1982; contbr. articles on crime prevention, correctional institutions and criminal justice to profl. jours. Home: Route 1 Box 168AA Augusta KS 67010 Office: Dept Adminstrn Justice Wichita State Univ Box 95 Wichita KS 67208

DOERMANN, PAUL EDMUND, surgeon; b. Kodaikanal, India, Aug. 3, 1926 (parents Am. citizens); s. Carl M. and Cora (Knupke) D.; student Ohio State U., 1944; B.S., Capital U., 1947; M.D., U. Mich., 1951; m. W. Ernestine McPherson, May 3, 1953; children—William McPherson, Marcia, Paula Michelle, Diana, Charles. Intern, Louisville Gen. Hosp., 1951-52, resident in surgery, 1952-53; resident in surgery Milw. County Hosp., 1955-58; med. missionary Luth. Mission Hosp., Madang, New Guinea, 1958-59; surgeon Linvill Clinic, Columbia City, Ind., 1960-61; practice medicine specializing in surgery, Huntington, Ind.; pres. med. staff, chief surg. service Huntington Meml. Hosp.; pres. Huntington Surg. Corp. Served from 1st lt. to capt., AUS, 1953-55. Luth. Acad. scholar. Diplomate Am. Bd. Surgery. Fellow A.C.S.; mem. Huntington County, Christian med. socs., Am. Assn. Physicians and Surgeons, Pvt. Doctors Am., Huntington C. of C. Lutheran. Rotarian. Home: Rural Route 8 Box 325 Grimm Rd Huntington IN 46750 Office: 1751 N Jefferson Huntington IN 46750

DOERR, JOHN JOSEPH, univ. adminstr., educator; b. Freeport, Ill., Dec. 21, 1936; s. Joseph and Irma (Mercier) D.; B.A., No. Ill. U., 1958; M.Ed., Kent State U., 1960; Ed.D., U. Mo., Columbia, 1967; m. Gail Louise Johnson, Dec. 27, 1958; children—Michael Joseph, Anna Louise, Leslie Rae. Tchr. math. Arlington Heights (Ill.) High Sch., 1958-59; counselor Blue Island (Ill.) High Sch., 1960-63; dir. guidance Univ. High Sch., Ill. State U., Normal, 1964-66; asst. prof. edn. U. Mo., Kansas City, 1967-69, asso. prof., 1969-73, prof. counselor edn., 1973—, asst. dean edn., 1970-73, dean, 1973-79, vice-chancellor adminstrv. affairs, 1979—; cons. U.S. Dept. Labor, 1970-74. Club: Kiwanis. Office: 5100 Rockhill Rd Kansas City MO 64110

DOETSCH, GUNTER HUGO KARL WILHELM, film co. exec.; b. Frankfurt/Main, West Germany, Mar. 4, 1926; s. Hugo Karl Wilhelm and Wilhelmine Margarete (Barth) D.; grad. Real Gymnasium of Frankfurt, 1945; LL.M., U. Frankfurt, 1951; m. Joyce M. Utz, Dec. 20, 1975; children—Hugo IV, Günter Alexander II, Catherine Morin-Barth. Came to U.S., 1956, naturalized, 1959. Legal cons. copyright and patent law Dr. Wolff & Tritschler Studio, Frankfurt/Main, Germany, 1952-55, asst. to pres., 1955-56, photo-journalist, Algiers, Italy, Switzerland, France, Eng., 1956-57; with foto-doetsch films, Chgo., 1957-63; pres., chief exec. officer LaRue Communications, Inc., Chgo., 1963—, pres., chief exec. officer Scientificom div., 1969—, Artcom div., 1971—, H.B. Assos. div., 1976—. Instr. advanced motion picture techniques Sch. of Art Inst. Chgo., 1968—. Chmn. design com. Biol. Photog. Assn. Congress Biocommunications 72, Chgo. Recent films include: Continuous Monitoring in the Critically Ill Patient (Am. Film Festival award 1973), Calcium Metabolism: The Consequences of Dietary Deficiency (U.S. Indsl. Film Festival award 1974), Serious Burn Management in the Office, 1974, Cyclic AMP and Drug Interaction in Vascular Smooth Muscle, 1974, Fire in the Patient Care Facility: Rehearsal for Survival, 1975, Apexcardiography: A Consideration for Early Detection, 1975, SST for All-in-One Blood Collection and Analysis, 1975, Horizons: Oral Surgery (Chgo. Internat. Film Festival award), 1975, TMO: Travenol Membrane Oxygenator, 1976, The Photrax System, 1976, Milestones in Veterinary Medicine, 1976, Techniques in Blood Culturing, 1976, Modern Methods of Venous Blood Collection, 1976, The Drug Selection Illusion, 1977, Emergency Management of Cervical-Spine Injuries, 1977, Emergency Management of Major Thermal Burns, 1977, Intravenous Therapy—Physical and Psychological Care of the Patient, 1978, Fundamentals of Intravenous Therapy, 1978, Total Parenteral Nutrition, 1978, Emergency Management of Accidental Hypothermia, 1978, Emergency Management of Major Thermal Burns sound/slide program, 1978, Emergency Management of Accidental Hyperthermia, 1979, Minor Burns: Evaluation and Treatment, 1979, Mothers in Conflict—Children in Need (Am. Film Festival award), 1979, Angina Pectoris: Clinical Presentation and Its Treatment with Nitroglycerine Ointment, 1980, Disaster: Prehospital Management of Mass Casualties, 1980, Injection Technique: An Important Nursing Skill, 1980, Build Your Own City-Build Your Own Walls: The Person with Epilepsy, 1980, Suffer the Children-Silence No More, 1980, Innovating for Life, 1981, Contributions to Intravenous Therapy, 1981, Contributions to Blood Therapy, 1981, Contributions to Dialysis, 1981, Contributions to Medical Care, 1981. Office: 708 N Dearborn St Chicago IL 60610

DOGANGÜN, BURHAN CAHIT (DOUG), data processor, govt. ofcl.; b. Diyarbakir, Turkey, Apr. 25, 1923; came to U.S., 1956, naturalized, 1964; s. Numan Sabit and Naciye D.; B.S. in Engring., Mil. Engring. Sch., Ankara, Turkey, 1944; M.B.A., Ohio State U., 1963; m. Nejla Cetinerler, Dec. 1, 1949; children—Numan G., Serpil N. Commd. officer Turkish Army, 1942, advanced through grades to capt., 1949, served C.E., chief of stock control, 1949-53, ret., 1953; mgr. orgn. and tng. Makina & Kimya Endustrisi, Turkey, 1954-56; time and methods engr. Jeffrey Mfg. Co., U.S.A., 1956-57; indsl. engr. Bell Sound, 1958-59; project engr. U.S. Army Mobility Support Center, 1960-64; mgr. data processing Steel Products Engring. Co., 1964-66; mgr. computer programming State of Ohio, Columbus, 1966-68, sr. systems analyst Fairchild/Hiller, 1967-68, Swan Rubber Co., 1970-73; research asso. Ohio Dept. Mental Health and Retardation, 1968-69, mgr. mgmt. systems, 1973—. Pres. Turkish-Am. Assn., Columbus, 1971-73; treas. UN Festival Com., 1970-76; v.p. Ethnic Assns. Mid-Ohio, 1978. Recipient cert. of recognition for devel. forms mgmt. program, Dept. Mental Health, 1980. Moslem. Developer automated parts manual system U.S. Army,

1962-64. Home: 2698 Mt Holyoke Rd Columbus OH 43221 Office: 30 E Broad St Columbus OH 43215

DOGGETT, JOHN NELSON, JR., ch. adminstr.; b. Phila., Apr. 3, 1918; s. John Nelson and Winola (Ballard) D.; B.A., Lincoln U., 1942; M.Div., Union Theol. Sem., N.Y.C., 1945; D.D., Bethany Sch. Religion (Calif.), 1948; M.Ed., St. Louis U., 1969, Ph.D., 1971; m. Juanita Toley, Aug. 2, 1973; children by previous marriage—Lorraine, John, William, Kenneth. Ordained to ministry United Methodist Ch., 1943; civilian chaplain S. Gate Community Ch., San Francisco, 1945-47; organizing pastor Downs Meml. Meth. Ch., Oakland, Calif., 1947-49; pastor Scott Meml. Meth. Ch., Pasadena, Calif., 1950-53, Hamilton Meml. Meth. Ch., Los Angeles, 1953-64, Union Meml. United Meth. Ch., St. Louis, 1964-76; dist. supt. United Meth. Ch., St. Louis, 1976—; staff Pastoral Counseling Inst., St. Louis, 1968—; instr. foundations of edn. Harris Tchrs. Coll., St. Louis, 1971-75; asso. prof. practical theology Met. Coll., St. Louis, 1976-77; commr. Nat. Council Chs. of Christ, 1981. Pres. bd. dirs. St. Louis Christian Med. Center, Central Med. Center Hosps., St. Louis, 1973—; pres. St. Louis NAACP, 1973-81; bd. dirs. United Way St. Louis, 1974—; mem. Commn. on Alternatives to Prison, 1981, Citizens Com. Mo. Dept. Corrections, 1974-80, Mayor's Task Force on Hunger, 1981. Named Minister of Year, St. Louis Argus Newspaper, 1971; recipient Outstanding Alumni award St. Louis U., 1981. Mem. Am. Assn. Pastoral Counselors, Am. Personnel and Guidance Assn., Mo. Council Chs., Met. Ministerial Alliance, St. Louis Police-Clergy Assn., Human Devel. Corp. (Met. Bicentennial award 1976), Phi Delta Kappa, Alpha Phi Alpha. Democrat. Mason, Shriner. Home: 126 Glen Cove Dr Chesterfield MO 63017 Office: 4625 Lindell Blvd Suite 416 Saint Louis MO 63108

DOHENY, DONALD ALOYSIUS, lawyer, business exec.; b. Milw., Apr. 20, 1924; s. John Anthony and Adelaide (Koller) D.; student U. Notre Dame, 1942-43; B.Mech. Engring., Marquette U., 1947; J.D., Harvard, 1949; postgrad. indsl. engring. and bus. adminstrn. Washington U., 1950-56; m. Catherine Elizabeth Lee, Oct. 25, 1952; children—Donald Aloysius, Celeste Hazel, John Vincent, Ellen Adelaide, Edward Lawrence II, William Francis, Madonna Lee. Asst. to civil engr. Shipbuilding div. Froemming Bros., Inc., Milw., 1942-43; draftsman, designer The Heil Co., Milw., 1944-46; admitted to Wis. bar, 1949, Mo. bar, 1949; mem. firm Igoe, Carroll & Keefe, St. Louis, 1949-51; asst. to v.p. and gen. mgr., chief prodn. engr., gen. adminstr., dir. adminstrn. Granco Steel Products subsidiary Granite City Steel, Granite City, Ill., 1951-57; asst. to pres. Vestal Labs., Inc., St. Louis, 1957-63; exec. v.p., dir. Moehlenpah Engring., Inc., Hydro-Air Engring., Inc., 1963-67; pres. dir. Foamtex Industries, Inc., St. Louis, 1967-75; exec. v.p., dir. Seasonal Industries, Inc., Portsmouth, Va., 1973-75; mem. law firm Donald A. Doheny, St. Louis, 1967—; mem. firm Doheny & Assos., Mgmt. Counsel, St. Louis, 1967—; pres., dir. Mktg. & Sales Counsel, Inc., St. Louis, 1975—; pres., dir. Mid-USA Sales Co., St. Louis, 1976—; lectr. bus. orgn. and adminstrn. Washington U., 1950-74. Served as pvt. AUS, 1943-44; 1st lt. Res., 1948-52. Registered profl. engr., Mo. Mem. Am. Judicature Soc., Am. Marketing Assn. (nat. membership chmn. 1959), Am., Mo., Wis., Milw. bar assns., Bar Assn. St. Louis (gen. chmn. pub. relations 1955-56, vice chmn., sec.-treas. jr. sect. 1950, 51), Marquette Engring. Assn. (pres. 1946-47), Engring. Knights, Am. Legion, Tau Beta Pi, Pi Tau Sigma. Clubs: K.C., Notre Dame (pres. 1955, 56), Marquette (pres. 1961) (St. Louis); Stadium, Engineers, Mo. Athletic, Arena. Office: 2284 Weldon Pkwy Saint Louis County MO 63141 also 408 Olive St Suite 400 Saint Louis MO 63102

DOHLMAN, DENNIS RAYE, oil co. exec.; b. Iowa Falls, Iowa, Mar. 16, 1946; s. Lowell L. and Harmena (Ploeger) D.; B.S., Iowa State U., 1968; m. Mary Ilene Ontjes, Sept. 2, 1966; children—John Bradley, Rebecca Ralene. Process engr. No. Petrochem. Co., Morris, Ill., 1968-70, maintenance engr., 1970-72, asst. utility area supt., 1972-74, utility area supt., 1974-76; plant supt. Aminoil USA, Inc., Tioga, N.D., 1977—. Mem. Am. Inst. Chem. Engrs., Gideons. Home: 322 Hanson St Tioga ND 58852 Office: Box 457 Tioga ND 58852

DOHMEN, FREDERICK HOEGER, wholesale drug co. exec.; b. Milw., May 12, 1917; s. Fred William and Viola (Gutsch) D.; B.A. in Commerce, U. Wis., 1939; m. Gladys Elizabeth Dite, Dec. 23, 1939 (dec. 1963); children—William Francis, Robert Charles; m. 2d, Mary Alexander Holgate, June 27, 1964. With F. Dohmen Co., Milw., 1939—, successively warehouse employee, sec., v.p., 1944-52, pres., 1952—; dir. The F. Dohmen Co., 1947—, chmn. bd., 1952—. Bd. dirs. St. Luke's Hosp. Ednl. Found., Milw., pres., 1969-72, chmn. bd., 1972-73; bd. dirs. U. Wis.-Milw. Found., 1976-79, bd. visitors, 1978—; asso. chmn. Nat. Bible Week, Laymen's Nat. Bible Com., N.Y.C., 1968—. Mem. Nat. Wholesale Druggists Assn. (chmn. mfr. relations com. 1962, resolutions com. 1963, mem. of bd. control 1963-66), Nat. Assn. Wholesalers (trustee 1966-75), Druggists Service Council (dir. 1967-71), Wis. Pharm. Assn., Miss. Valley Drug Club, Beta Gamma Sigma, Phi Eta Sigma, Delta Kappa Epsilon. Presbyn. Clubs: University, Town (Milw.). Home: 3903 W Mequon Rd 112 N Mequon WI 53092 Office: W 194 N 11381 McCormick Dr Germantown WI 53022

DOHNAL, WILLIAM EDWARD, steel co. exec.; b. Cleve., May 25, 1912; s. Frank and Anna (Florian) D.; grad. Cleve. Coll. Western Res. U., 1940; m. Alta Louella Bingham, June 1, 1933; children—David, Dennis. Auditor, Lybrand, Ross Bros. and Montgomery, 1942-45; acting auditor Cleveland-Cliffs Iron Co., Cleve., 1946-47, auditor, 1947-53, asst. treas., 1953-58, comptroller, 1958-63, v.p., comptroller, 1963-64, v.p. internat., 1964-73, sr. v.p., 1973—; pres., mng. dir. Cliffs Western Australia Mining Co. Pty Ltd. C.P.A., Ohio. Mem. Am. Soc. C.P.A.'s, Ohio Soc. C.P.A.'s, Cleve. Council World Affairs. Clubs: Clevelander, Cleve. Athletic; Weld (Perth, Australia). Home: 5241 Chickadee Ln Lyndhurst OH 44124 and 1 Wingfield Ave Crawley Western Australia 6009 Australia Office: Union Commerce Bldg Cleveland OH 44115

DOHRING, GRACE HELEN, chiropractor, med. supply co. exec.; b. Detroit, May 6, 1921; d. Fred Henry and Martha Helen (Thiel) Johnson; acupuncture cert. Hong Kong Med. Coll.; D. Chiropractic, Detroit Coll. Chiropractic, 1942; D. Naturopathy, Am. Coll. Naturopathy, 1944; Dr., Am. Sch. Neuropathy, 1944; postgrad. Nat. Coll. Chiropractic, 1949, Am. Coll. Chiropractic Internists, 1973-75, Palmer Chiropractic Coll., 1977, Ryodoraku Automatic Nervous System Soc. Japan, 1973; m. Albert A. Dohring, June 30, 1951; children—Charles, Deborah, Joan. Gen. practice chiropractic medicine, Detroit, 1942-60, Dearborn, Mich., 1960—; pres. Doctor's Supply Internat., Dearborn, 1972—, pres. research protocol project; mem. faculty Nat. Chiropractic Coll., 1975, Quebec (Can.) Osteopathic Coll., 1975; tchr. seminars, Boston, Chgo., Kalamazoo, Toronto, Ont., Can., 1975; ordained minister, 1979; cons. in field; dir. Doctors' Supply Research Soc.; acupuncture lectr., seminar tchr., 1973—. Cert. in basic sci., Minn., Mich.; cert. drugless practitioner, Can. Fellow Am. Coll. Neuropathy; mem. Kyoto Pain Control Inst., Fla. Homeopathic Soc., Internat. Acupuncture Soc., Soc. Chinese Acupuncture and Cautery, Acupuncture and Research Soc., Soc. Chinese Medicine, Am. Center Chinese Medicine (life), Acupuncture Ryodoraku Assn. (charter), Am. (charter), Mich. State chiropractic assns., Nat. Small Bus. Assn., Nat. Assn. Female Execs., Acupuncture Center for Chinese Medicine (life), German Acad. Auricular Medicine, Nat. Fedn. Health (life). Club: Eastern Star (pastmatron). Author: Acupuncture-Electric, 1972; Ear Acupuncture Wall Chart, 1974. Patentee acupuncture devices. Office: 24028 Union St Dearborn MI 48124

DOHRMAN, GARY LEE, publishing co. exec.; b. Columbus, Ohio, Aug. 19, 1940; s. Lee Winifred and Mary Maria (Norton) D.; B.R.E., Piedmont Bible Coll., Winston-Salem, N.C., 1962; postgrad. Northwestern U., Chgo., 1964-65; m. Barbara Blake, June 30, 1961; children—Allison, Rebecca, Melanie. With customer service div. Sears, Roebuck & Co., Winston-Salem, 1958-62; C.L.U., Am. Nat. Ins. Co., Winston-Salem, 1962-63; mgr. mail order div. Moody Bible Inst., Chgo., 1963-66; mgr. Piedmont Gospel Bookstore, Winston-Salem, 1967-70; dist. mgr., catalog cons. Zondervan Corp. of Nashville, Grand Rapids, Mich., 1970-78, mgr. Retail Mktg. Services div., 1978-81, regional sales mgr., 1981—; radio announcer Sta. WMBI, Chgo., 1964-65; minister of music 1st Bapt. Ch., Whiting, Ind., 1963-64, Oak Park Ave. Bapt. Ch., Oak Park, Ill., 1964-66, Cedar Forest Bapt. Ch., Winston-Salem, 1967-70. Mem. Am. Mktg. Assn., Direct Mail Mktg. Assn., Internat., Nat. wildlife assns., Gideons Internat. Office: 1415 Lake Dr SE Grand Rapids MI 49506

DOHRMANN, RICHARD JOHN, mech. engr.; b. St. Louis, May 13, 1932; s. Peter Paul and Olinda Barbara (Keim) D.; B.S., U. Iowa, 1956, M.S., 1958; m. Joyce Warzeniak, Dec. 19, 1954; children—David Alan, Katherine Elizabeth, Clark Richard. Analytical engr. Babcock & Wilcox Co., 1957-62, sr. analytical engr., 1962-63, chief applied mechanics, 1963-72, mgr. planning, 1972-74, mgr. planning and exploratory research, 1974-77, mgr. planning Contract Research div., 1977-80, mem. staff Research & Devel. div., 1980—. Bd. dirs. Alliance (Ohio) YMCA, 1963-65; exec. bd Boy Scouts Am., 1970—, mem. nat. council, 1978-79. Served with C.E., U.S. Army, 1952-54. Mem. ASME, Sigma Xi. Mem. United Ch. of Christ. Clubs: Alliance Country, Masons. Contbr. articles to profl. jours. Home: 1335 Parkway Blvd Alliance OH 44601 Office: 1562 Beeson St Alliance OH 44601

DOHRMANN, RUSSELL WILLIAM, chems. co. exec.; b. Clinton, Iowa, June 29, 1942; s. Russell Wilbert and Anita Doris Miller D.; B.S., Upper Iowa U., 1965; M.B.A., Drake U., 1971; m. M. Jean Stapleton; children—Angela, Michelle, Sarah, Kellie. Jr. accountant Chamberlain Mfg. Corp., Clinton, 1965, sr. accountant, 1966, plant controller, Derry, Pa., 1967-68; cost and procedures mgr., fin. cost analyst, mgr. acctg. Frye Copysystems Inc. div. Wheelabrator-Frye Inc., Des Moines, 1968-71, group controller Internat. div., N.Y.C., 1972-73, v.p., controller Frye Copysystems Inc., Des Moines, 1974-78, v.p., group controller chems. and coatings group, 1979-80, exec. v.p., gen. mgr., 1980-81, pres., 1981—. Mem. Des Moines C. of C., Nat. Assn. Accountants, Nat. Audubon Soc. Home: 1810 78th St Windsor Heights IA 50322 Office: Frye Copysystems 7445 University Des Moines IA 50311

DOISY, EDWARD ADELBERT, biochemist; b. Hume, Ill., Nov. 13, 1893; s. Edward Perez and Ada (Alley) D.; A.B., U. Ill., 1914, M.S., 1916; Ph.D., Harvard U., 1920; D.Sc., Washington U., 1940, Yale U., 1940, U. Chgo., 1941, Central Coll. 1942, U. Ill., 1960, Gustavus Adolphus Coll., 1963; LL.D., St. Louis U., 1955; Docteur honoris causa, U. Paris, 1945; m. Alice Ackert, July 20, 1918 (dec. 1964); children—Edward Adelbert, Robert Ackert, Philip Perez, Richard Joseph; m. 2d, Margaret McCormick, Apr. 19, 1965. Asst. in biochemistry Harvard Med. Sch., 1915-17; instr., asso. and asso. prof. biochemistry Washington U. Sch. Medicine, St. Louis, 1919-23; prof. biochemistry, dir. dept. St. Louis U. Sch. Medicine, 1923-65, Distinguished Service prof. biochemistry, emeritus, also dir. emeritus Edward A. Doisy dept. biochemistry, 1965—, adminstrv. bd.; dir. dept. biochemistry, biochemist St. Mary's Hosp., St. Louis, 1924—. Served to 2d lt. U.S. Army, 1917-19. Several named lectures at various univs. and soc. meetings. Recipient Gold medal St. Louis Med. Soc., 1935; Philip A. Conne medal Chemists Club N.Y., 1935; St. Louis award, 1939; Willard Gibbs medal, 1941; Am. Pharm. Mfg. Assn. award, 1942; Squibb award, 1944; Barren Found. medal, 1972; shared Nobel Prize in Physiology and Medicine with Dr. Henrik Dam, 1943. Mem. League of Nations com. for standardization sex hormones, London, 1932, 35. Mem. Am. Soc. Biol. Chemists (council 1926-27, 34-37, 40-45, pres. 1943-45), Am. Chem. Soc., Nat. Acad. Scis., Am. Philos. Soc., Pontifical Acad. Scis., Am. Acad. Arts and Scis., Phi Beta Kappa, Sigma Xi, Phi Kappa Phi, Alpha Omega Alpha. Author: Sex and Internal Secretions (with Edgar Allen and Charles H. Danforth), 1939. Contbr. articles on blood buffers, sex hormones, vitamin K. and antibiotic compounds to profl. jours. Home: 4B Colonial Village Ct Webster Groves MO 63119 Office: 1402 S Grand Blvd Saint Louis MO 63104

DOLAN, JAY PATRICK, educator; b. Bridgeport, Conn., Mar. 17, 1936; s. Joseph Thomas and Margaret (Reardon) D.; A.B., St. John's Sem., 1958; S.T.L., Gregorian U., Rome, 1962; Ph.D., U. Chgo., 1970; m. Patricia McNeal, May 26, 1973; children—Patrick Joseph, Mark McNeal. Asst. prof. U. San Francisco, 1970-71; asso. prof. dept. history U. Notre Dame, 1971—, also dir. Cushwa Center for Study Am. Catholicism, 1977—; cons. Nat. Endowment Humanities, 1976—, Elkhart (Ind.) Bicentennial Commn., 1975-76. Fellow Rockefeller Found., 1969-70, Shelby Cullom Davis Center Hist. Studies, Princton U., 1973-74; Am. Council Learned Socs. fellow, 1978-79. Mem. Am. Cath. Hist. Assn. (John Gilmary Shea award 1975), Am. Soc. Ch. History (exec. council 1977-80), Orgn. Am. Historians. Author: The Immigrant Church: New York's Irish and German Catholics 1815-1865, 1975; Heritage of '76, 1976; Catholic Revivalism, 1977. Editorial bd. Jour. Am. Ethnic History. Home: 16130 Brockton Ct Granger IN 46530 Office: Dept History Univ Notre Dame Notre Dame IN 46556

DOLAN, RICHARD CLARENCE, mgmt. cons.; b. River Grove, Ill., Feb. 24, 1932; s. Clarence and Gladys (Montgomery) D.; B.A. in Econs., DePaul U., 1954; postgrad. Mich. State U., 1962-63, Northwestern U., 1958—; m. Elaine P. Maechtle, June 8, 1957; children—Kathleen, Kevin, Peggy, Kelly. Asso., A.T. Kearney, Inc., Chgo., 1964-68, Lamson Griffiths, Inc., Chgo., 1968-69; exec. v.p. Witt & Dolan, Inc., Oak Brook, Ill., 1970-80; pres. Career Decision, Inc., Itasca, Ill., 1981—; guest lectr. various univs. Bd. dirs. DuPage County Girl Scouts U.S.A., 1968-74; semi-pro mgr. Amateur Baseball, 1958-79. Served with U.S. Army, 1954-56. Mem. Am. Soc. Tng. and Devel. (sec.-treas. 1961-63), Hosp. Fin. Mgmt. Assn. Roman Catholic. Contbr. articles to profl. jours. Home: 530 Birch St Itasca IL 60143 Office: 500 Park Blvd Suite 515 Hamilton Lakes Itasca IL 60143

DOLAND, GREGORY BERNARD, ednl. adminstr.; b. Lafayette, Ind., July 27, 1947; s. Emerson Bernard and Ruth Maxine (Pearson) D.; B.S., Ind. State U., 1970, M.S., 1975, Ed.S., 1981. Tchr., teaching prin. North Vermillion Schs., Perrysville, Ind., 1970-77; prin. North Newton Schs., Morocco, Ind., 1977-79; tchr., coordinator spl. edn. Seeger High Sch., West Lebanon, Ind., 1980—. Mem. Assn. Supervision and Curriculum Devel., Assn. Retarded Citizens, U.S. Inst. Theatrical Tech., Nat. Council Tchrs. Math., Phi Delta Kappa. Club: Lions. Home: PO Box 405 West Lebanon IN 47991

DOLCH, DOUGLAS G., info. systems ofcl.; b. Cleve., Oct. 16, 1940; s. George H. and Ruth D. D.; A.A., Valparaiso U., 1961; attended Nat. Cash Register and IBM Edn. Centers, 1961-80. With George Worthington Co., Cleve., 1961—, mgr. info. systems, 1976—, mem. corp. data processing com. Served with USAR, 1965-67. Mgmt. certificate Republic Indsl. Edn. Inst., 1971, systems generalist certificate, Profl. Systems Course, 1973. Mem. Found. for Adminstrv. Research in Systems, Valparaiso U. Alumni Assn. Home: 6950 Woodwalk Dr Brecksville OH 44141 Office: 802 St Clair Ave NW Cleveland OH 44113

DOLE, ROBERT J., U.S. senator; b. Russell, Kans., July 22, 1923; s. Doran R. and Bina Dole; student U. Kans., U. Ariz.; A.B., Washburn Municipal U., Topeka, LL.B. Admitted to Kans. bar; mem. Kans. Ho. of Reps., 1951; pvt. practice law, Russell, 1953-61; Russell County atty., 1953-61; mem. 87th Congress 6th Dist. of Kans., mem. 88th-90th congresses, 1st Dist. Kans.; now mem. U.S. Senate from Kans. Chmn., Republican Nat. Com., 1971-73; Rep. candidate for v.p., 1976. Served with 10th Mountain Div., 75th Inf. Div., AUS, World War II. Decorated Bronze Star with cluster. Mem. Am. Legion, V.F.W., 4-H Fair Assn., Kappa Sigma. Methodist. Mason (Shriner), Elk, Kiwanian. Home: Russell KS 67665 Office: New Senate Office Bldg Washington DC 20510

DOLEZAL, DALE FRANCIS, truck mfg. co. exec.; b. Ronan, Mont., Apr. 9, 1936; s. Henry Lewis and Regina Marie Dolezal; B.S. in Indsl. Engring., Mont. State U., 1961; student Program for Mgmt. Devel., Bus. Sch., Harvard U., 1974; m. Patricia Louise Johnson, Aug. 27, 1960; children—Craig, Kelly, Kathleen, Kari. Indsl. and methods engr. Westinghouse Electric Corp., Sunnyvale, Calif., 1961-63; chief indsl. engr. Clarke Equipment Corp., Spokane, Wash., 1963-65; mgr. materials Freightliner Corp., Portland, Oreg., 1965-67; with Internat. Harvester Co., 1967—, dir. purchasing and inventory mgmt., Chgo., 1977-80, dir. materials and ops. planning, 1980—; dir. Real Am. Corp.; mem. bd. bus. and indsl. advisers U. Wis., Madison; bd. dirs. Ops. Tng. Inst. Mem. parents adv. bd. Naperville (Ill.) Central High Sch., 1977—; mem. adv. bd. Sch. Dist. 203, Naperville, 1978—. Served with USMC, 1954-57. Registered profl. engr., Oreg. Mem. Am. Inst. Indsl. Engrs., Am. Prodn. and Inventory Control. Soc. Republican. Roman Catholic. Clubs: Rotary, K.C., Harvard (Chgo.). Contbr. articles to trade jours. 401 N Michigan Ave Chicago IL 60611

DOLIBOIS, JOHN ERNEST, ambassador; b. Luxembourg, Dec. 4, 1918; s. Charles Nicholas and Maria M. (Winter) D.; came to U.S., 1931, naturalized, 1941; A.B., Miami U., Oxford, O., 1942; m. Winifred Englehart, Jan. 17, 1942; children—John Michael, Robert Joseph, Brian Charles. Indsl. engr. Procter and Gamble Co., Cin., 1942, 46-47; mem. faculty Miami U., Oxford O., 1947-66, v.p., 1966-81; U.S. ambassador to Luxembourg, 1981—. Mem. Bd. Fgn. Scholarships, 1969-77. Mem. Tallawanda Sch. Dist. Citizens Com., 1960-65; mem. Community Improvement Corp. Oxford, 1966-71. Bd. dirs. Oxford Community Chest; trustee, bd. dirs. Miami Found. Served to capt. AUS, 1942-46. Decorated officer Grand Ducal Order Crown Oakleaves, comdr. Order of Merit (Luxembourg); recipient Silver Beaver award Boy Scouts Am., 1957; Benjamin Harrison medal Miami U.; hon. consul of Luxembourg for Ohio, 1977-81. Named Man of Yr., Oxford, 1963. Mem. Newcomen Soc., Am. Alumni Council, Phi Beta Kappa, Beta Theta Pi, Omicron Delta Kappa, Phi Eta Sigma, Psi Chi. Home: 118 Hilltop Rd Oxford OH 45056

DOLKOWSKI, MARJORIE J., dental asst.; b. Cin., Jan. 30, 1923; d. Raymond and Pauline E. (Spicer) King; grad. summa cum laude, U. Cin., 1974; m. Joseph H. Dolkowski, Sept. 17, 1944; 1 dau., Marcia J. Dental asst. various dental offices; tchr. dental assisting Patterson Coop. High Sch., Dayton, Ohio, 1968—, coordinator, 1971—; curriculum developer in dental assisting Ohio Dept. Vocat. Edn. Recipient Outstanding Tchr. award for health occupations State of Ohio, 1974. Mem. Ohio Dental Assts. Assn. (sec., scholarship named in her honor 1980), Ohio Commn. Dental Assts. Testing, NEA, Ohio Edn. Assn., Dayton Edn. Assn., Nat. Assn. Parliamentarians, Ohio Vocat. Assn. Republican. Home: 3517 Shroyer Rd Kettering OH 45429 Office: Patterson Cooperative High School 118 E 1st St Dayton OH 45402

DOLNEY, DENNIS DEAN, veterinarian; b. St. Paul, Sept. 8, 1946; s. Jerome and Sylvia Marie (Block) D.; student S.D. State U., 1964-66; D.V.M., Iowa State U., 1970; m. Betty Lee Dargatz, Aug. 19, 1967; children—Andrea Michele, Christine Evalyn. Veterinarian, Howard (S.D.) Veterinary Clinic, 1970-71, Groton (S.D.) Veterinary Clinic, 1971-73; veterinary animal health and meat insp. Animal and Plant Health Inspection Service, Sioux Falls, S.D., 1973; partner Milbank (S.D.) Veterinary Clinic, 1973-78; pvt. practice vet. medicine, Waubay, S.D., 1978—. Health officer, Milbank, 1974-76. Mem. Northeast S.D. Veterinary Assn. (pres.), S.D., Minn. veterinary med. assns., AVMA. Roman Catholic. Home and office: Rural Route 1 Box 96 Waubay SD 57273

DOLSON, VIVIAN ANTOINETTE, office furniture mfg. co. exec.; b. Chgo., July 17, 1925; d. Werner Henry and Lillian Rose (Ghilardi) Steger; student DePaul U., 1943-46; m. Sept. 10, 1948 (div.); children—Bill, David. Asst. registrar DePaul U., 1952-55, exec. sec., 1955-58; asst. personnel dir. Stat. Tabulating Co., Chgo., 1958-61; owner, operator Dolson Market Research, Chgo., 1961-75; dist. sales mgr. for Ill. and Wis., Borroughs/Lear Siegler Co., Chgo., 1975-78, asst. nat. sales mgr., Kalamazoo, 1978-81; nat. sales mgr. Marvel Metals Products, Chgo., 1981—; career cons. Triton Jr. Coll. Mem. Am. Market Research Assn., Nat. Office Products Assn. Am. Mgmt. Assn. Home: Apt 318 17 W 724 Butterfield Rd Oakbrook Terrace IL 60181 Office: 3843 W 43d St Chicago IL 60632

DOMINICAK, ROBERT HARRY, civil engr.; b. Pukwana, S.D., Feb. 26, 1941; s. Harry Michael and Virginia June (Mesnard) D.; B.S. in Civil Engring., S.D. Sch. Mines and Tech., 1968; m. Sharon Faye Faller, Nov. 26, 1960; children—Bradley Robert, Curtis Leigh. Vice pres., engr. Thomas & Lockwood, cons. engrs., Rapid City, S.D., 1968-76; v.p. Thomas, Erickson, Dominicak & Crow Cons. Engrs. Inc., Rapid City, 1976-80; partner Crow Dominicak Assos., cons. engrs., Rapid City, 1980-81; sr. project engr. KKBNA, Glenwood Springs, Colo., 1981—. Mem. adminstrve. bd., past chmn. finance com. Methodist Ch.; active Boy Scouts Am., 1970-74, mem. unit com. Penjahame Dist. Com., 1975-77, dist. chmn., council exec. bd., 1971-81, v.p. adminstrn. Black Hills Area council, 1977-80, council commr., 1980-81, recipient Dist. Merit award, 1973. Registered profl. engr., S.D., Mont., Colo., Wyo.; registered land surveyor, S.D. Mem. Am. Concrete Inst., ASCE (past br. pres., pres. S.D. sect.), S.D. Engring. Soc., Nat. Soc. Profl. Engrs., Am. Congress on Surveying and Mapping. Republican. Methodist. Clubs: Optimist, Elks. Home: 222 Stanley Ct Rapid City SD 57701

DOMMEL, JAMES HOMER, mfg. co. exec.; b. Dana, Iowa, Sept. 14, 1936; s. Homer K. and Marian P. Dommel; B.A., U. No. Iowa, 1958, M.A., 1964; M.E.P., U. Minn., 1971; m. Darlene Hurst, Oct. 15,

1961; children—Diann, Christine, David. Tchr. public schs., Grinnell, Iowa, 1958-60; adminstr. Orono (Minn.) Sch. Dist., 1961-69; adminstrv. v.p. Nat. Car Rental, Mpls., 1969-74; risk mgr. Internat. Multifoods, Mpls., 1974-79; risk mgr. H.B. Fuller Co., St. Paul, 1979—. Active United Fund, YMCA. Served with U.S. Army, 1960-61. Mem. Risk and Ins. Mgmt. Soc., Am. Mgmt. Assn., Phi Delta Kappa. Lutheran. Home: 510 Westwood Dr N Golden Valley MN 55422 Office: 2400 Kasota St Saint Paul MN 55108

DOMPKE, NORBERT FRANK, photography studio exec.; b. Chgo., Oct. 16, 1920; s. Frank and Mary (Manley) D.; grad. Wright Jr. Coll., 1939-40; student Northwestern U., 1946-49; m. Marjorie Gies, Dec. 12, 1964; children—Scott, Pamela. Cost comptroller, budget dir. Scott Radio Corp., 1947; pres. TV Forecast, Inc., 1948-52, editor Chgo. edit. TV Guide, 1953, mgr. Wis. edit., 1954; pres. Root Photographers, Inc., Chgo., 1955—. Served with USAAC, 1943-47. C.P.A., Ill. Mem. United Photographers Orgn. (pres. 1970-71), Profl. Photographers Am., Profl. Sch. Photographers Am. (v.p. 1966-67, sec.-treas. 1967-69, pres. 1969-70, dir. 1971-78), Ill. Small Bus. Men's Assn. (dir. 1970), Ill. Assn. Profl. Photographers, Ill. Profl. Sch. Photographers Assn., Chgo. Assn. Commerce and Industry (edn. com. 1966—), NEA, Nat. Sch. Press Assn., Ill. High Sch. Press Assn., Nat. Collegiate Sch. Press Assn., Ill. C. of C. Co-founder T. Guide, 1947. Clubs: Carlton; Whitehall; International; Tonquish Creek Yacht, Chgo. Press. Home: 990 N Lake Shore Dr Chicago IL 60611 Office: 1131 W Sheridan Rd Chicago IL 60660

DOMPKE, RICHARD KENNETH, mgmt. cons.; b. Chgo., May 13, 1929; s. Bernard Stephen and Margaret Dorothy (Granner) D.; student in Architecture, Ill. Inst. Tech., 1947-49; B.S. in Indsl. Engring., Northwestern U., 1955; m. Gayle Mary Kenney, Jan. 18, 1956. Indst. engr. Reynolds Metals Co., Phoenix, 1956-59, plant indsl. engr., McCook, Ill., 1959-67; partner/dir. Deloitte Haskins & Sells, Chgo., 1967—. Republican committeeman, 1960-61; mem. Lake Forest (Ill.) Bldg. Rev. Bd., 1981—. Certified mgmt. cons.; registered profl. indsl. engr. Mem. Am. Inst. Indsl. Engrs. (dir. Chgo. chpt.), Inst. of Mgmt. Consultants, Am. Production and Inventory Control Soc., Am. Compensation Assn., Tau Beta Pi. Clubs: University Club of Chgo., Northwestern Alumni Club of Chgo., Alpha Delta Phi. Contbr. articles to profl. publs. Home: Lake Forest IL Office: 200 E Randolph Dr Chicago IL 60601

DON, DANIEL ARTHUR, lawyer; b. Chgo., Feb. 2, 1932; s. Edward and Irene (Kinzelberg) D.; B.A. cum laude, Yale U., 1953, LL.B., 1958. Admitted to Ill. bar, 1958, since practiced in Chgo.; atty. Arvey, Hodrs & Martynband, 1958-71; partner firm Kallen, Don & Simon, Chgo., 1972-78; lectr., author Ill. Inst. Continuing Legal Edn., 1965-71. Bd. dirs. young peoples div. Jewish Fedn. Chgo., 1962-66, Bur. Jewish Employment Problems, 1966—, Park View Home for Aged, 1968—. Served to 1st lt. AUS, 1953-55. Mem. Chgo. (mem. comml. law com.), Ill. (chmn. uniform comml. code com. 1969), Am. (mem. com. consumer class actions) bar assns., Phi Beta Kappa. Club: Standard (Chgo.). Office: 990 Lake Shore Dr Chicago IL 60611

DON, NORMAN S., psychologist, educator; b. Oct. 2, 1934; B.S. in Chemistry and Chem. Engring., U. Mich., 1956; M.S. in Physical Chemistry and Physics, U. Chgo., 1960; Ph.D. in Clin. Exptl. Psychology, Union Grad. Sch., 1974. Researcher, Research Insts., U. Chgo., 1961-64, researcher dept. psychiatry, then research asso., 1974-75; instr., then internal cons. City Colls. Chgo., 1965-68; v.p. research CODA, Inc., Chgo., 1968-69; pres. Computer Forecasters, Inc., 1969-71; cons. Manteno (Ill.) State Hosp., 1972-75; pvt. practice psychology, 1975—. Cons. U. Ill., U.S. CSC, OEO, Ill. Regional Med. Program, HEW, Welfare Council Met. Chgo., Region 5 Nat. Tng. Center on Drug Abuse, Safer Found., also industry, Blue Cross/Blue Shield; adj. faculty adviser Univ. Without Walls, Chgo.; lectr. Calif. Sch. Profl. Psychology, Los Angeles, numerous other univs. and groups. Mem. AAAS, Biofeedback Soc. Am., Biofeedback Soc. Ill. (dir.), Am. Psychol. Assn. Contbr. articles, books to profl. lit. Address: 180 N Michigan Ave Chicago IL 60601

DONAHEY, GERTRUDE WALTON, state treas. Ohio; b. Goshen, Ohio, Aug. 4, 1908; d. George Sebastian and Mary Ann (Thomas) Walton; grad. bus. coll.; D.Public Service (Hon.), Rio Grande U.; m. John W. Donahey, Apr. 12, 1930 (dec.); 1 son, John William. Pvt. sec., to 1930; treas., sec., State of Ohio, 1971—; mem. exec. com., bd. dirs. Ohio Mental Health Assn.; chmn. ops. support Ohio Democratic Com., 1963—, mem.-at-large platform com., 1964, 68; field aide in Central and South Ohio for U.S. Senator Young, 1963-69, later staff asst.; del. Dem. Nat. Conv., 1964, del.-at-large, mem. platform and resolutions com., 1968; trustee Better Bus. Bur. Central Ohio. Mem. Mcpl. Fin. Officers Assn. (past pres.), Nat. Assn. Auditors, Comptrollers and Treas. (treas. 1975—), Delta Kappa Gamma. Episcopalian. Office: 1 State Office Tower 30 E Broad St Columbus OH 43215

DONAHUGH, ROBERT HAYDEN, library adminstr.; b. St. Paul, May 20, 1930; s. Robert Emmett and Elmyra Elanore (Hayden) D.; B.A., Coll. St. Thomas, 1952; M.A., U. Minn., 1953. Instr. English, speech Robert Coll., Istanbul, Turkey, 1956-57; head tech. services Canton (Ohio) Public Library, 1957-62; asst. dir. Public Library of Youngstown and Mahoning County (Ohio), 1962-79, dir., 1979—. Served with Mil. Police Corps, U.S. Army, 1954-56. Mem. ALA, Ohio Library Assn. (editor assn. bull. 1968-72, pres. 1975), Midwest Fedn. Library Assns. (pres. 1979-83). Clubs: Elks, Rotary. Author: Evaluation of Reference Resources in 8 Public Libraries in 4 Ohio Counties, 1970; contbr. book revs. to Library Jour., 1958—; host Books Etc. program Sta. WYSU-FM, public radio, 1975—. Home: 509 Ferndale Youngstown OH 44511 Office: 305 Wick Youngstown OH 44503

DONALD, WILLIAM CLYDE, II, clergyman; b. Battle Creek, Mich., Nov. 28, 1918; s. William Clyde and Louella (Shattuck) D.; A.B., Albion Col, 1940; B.D., Garrett Bibl. Inst., 1943; D.D., Northwestern U., 1947; m. Carolyn Marie Fosberg, July 28, 1943; 1 dau., Pamela Marie (Mrs. John Gislason). Chaplain Deaconess Hosp., Milw., 1948-56; pastor Bethel Evangelical and Reformed Ch., Milw., 1949-57, Bethel Evangelical and Reformed Ch., Detroit, 1957-70, Peoples Ch. Chgo., 1970-73; sr. minister 1st Congl. Ch., Benton Harbor, Mich., 1973-77; interim pastor specialist Plymouth Congl. Ch., Mpls., 1977-79; part-time faculty Wayne State U., 1950-70. Chmn. bd. Third Securities Corp., Rockford, Ill., 1965-77. Mem. Am. Protestant Hosp. Assn. (fellow coll. chaplains), Nat. Assn. Congl. Christian Chs. (commn. on ministry 1978—), Tau Kappa Epsilon. Mem. B'nai B'rith (hon.). Home: 1116 Lakeside Dr Mackinaw City MI 49701

DONALDSON, MARCELINE MALICA, fin. and mktg. cons., b. New Orleans, Oct. 25, 1937; d. Maurice and Doris Gaynelle (Taylor) Donaldson; grad. N.Y. U.; student Program for Mgmt. Devel., Harvard, 1971; children—Elise Karen Leon, Malica Aronowitz, Michelle, Jacqueline Aronowitz. Owner, Ma-Li-Kai, Inc., Mpls., 1965-69; stock broker Dain, Kalman & Quail, Inc., Mpls., 1969-71; sales and mktg. with Pillsbury Co., Mpls., 1972-73; owner, pres. Donaldson & Assos., Inc., Wayzata, Minn., 1973-77; sales/mktg. Gen. Systems div. IBM, Cin., 1977—. Precinct chmn. Republican Party, 1974—; mem. nat. fund raising com. Black Women's Community Devel. Found.; nat. bd. NOW, 1973-75; fund raiser legal def. fund NAACP. Mem. Acad. Mgmt., Needlework Guild Minn., Ripon Soc. (dir.), Minn. Center Arts and Edn. Clubs: Minn. (v.p.); Harvard Bus. Sch. (Cin.). Republican. Episcopalian. Home: 2324 Madison Rd Cincinnati OH 45208 Office: 580 Walnut St Cincinnati OH 45202

DONALSON, JAMES RYAN, real estate broker; b. Kansas City, Mo., Jan. 7, 1945; s. Joseph Elmer and Betty Lee (Cousins) D.; B.S. (Mo. Real Estate Assn. scholar), U. Mo., 1967; m. Sandra Lynn Yockey, Dec. 26, 1964; children—Kimberly Kay, Debra Lynn, Jennifer Lee. Loan officer City Wide Mortgage Co., Kansas City, 1967; interviewer personnel Panhandle Eastern Pipe Line Co., Kansas City, 1968; partner Donalson Realtors, Kansas City, 1969—; pres. Classic Homes, Kansas City, 1973—, Donalson Devel. Co., 1980—, Diversified Investments (formerly Donalson & Assos. Realtors), 1980—; bd. dirs. Multiple Listing Service Greater Kansas City, 1971-75, treas., 1972-73. Bd. dirs. Platte County unit Am. Cancer Soc., 1973-75. Mem. Nat. Assn. Real Estate Bds., Mo. Assn. Realtors (dir. 1974-75), Real Estate Bd. Kansas City (dir. 1978-80), Platte County Bus. and Profl. Men's Assn., U. Mo. Alumni Assn., Homebuilders Assn. Greater Kansas City. Baptist. Lion (dir. 1974-76). Office: 7526 NW Prairie View Rd Kansas City MO 64151

DONATI, ROBERT MARIO, physician, educator; b. Richmond Heights, Mo., Feb. 28, 1934; s. Leo S. and Rose Marie D.; B.S. in Biology, St. Louis U., 1955, M.D., 1959. Intern St. Louis City Hosp., 1959-60; asst. resident John Cochran Hosp., St. Louis, 1960-62; fellow nuclear medicine St. Louis U., 1962-63; practice medicine specializing in nuclear medicine, St. Louis, 1963—; mem. staff John Cochran Hosp., also St. Louis U., 1963—, mem. faculty Sch. Medicine, 1963—, asst. prof. internal medicine, 1965-68, asso. prof., 1968-74, prof., 1974—, prof. radiology, 1979—, dir. div. nuclear medicine, 1968—; adj. prof. internal medicine Washington U., St. Louis; chief nuclear medicine services St. Louis VA Med. Center, 1968-79, chief staff, 1979—; mem. interagy. radiation task force HEW, 1978-79. Co-chmn. St. Louis Italian Am. Bicentennial Commn., 1976; mem. St. Louis Citizens Edn. Task Force, 1976-78; mem. desegregation monitoring and adv. com. U.S. Dist. Ct., 1981—. Served to capt. AUS, 1966-68. Recipient Army Commendation medal. Diplomate Am. Bd. Nuclear Medicine (dir. 1980—). Mem. AMA (nuclear medicine residency rev. com. 1978-80), St. Louis Med. Soc., Am. Fedn. Clin. Research (counciler 1967-70), Central Soc. Clin. Research, A.A.U.P., N.Y. Acad. Scis., Soc. Exptl. Biology and Medicine, Soc. Nuclear Medicine (acad. council 1970—, trustee 1977-80, publs. com. 1978-81, vice chmn. edn. 1978), Am. Coll. Nuclear Physicians, Am., Internat. socs. hematology, Soc. Med. Consultants to Armed Forces, Sigma Xi. Roman Catholic. Club: Cosmos (Washington). Editor: (with W.T. Newton) Radioassay in Clinical Medicine, 1974. Contbr. articles to profl. jours. Research in clin. investigative nuclear medicine and control of cellular proliferation. Home: 5335 Botanical Ave Saint Louis MO 63110 Office: St Louis VA Med Center 11JC Saint Louis MO 63125

DONCHIN, EMANUEL, psychologist; b. Tel Aviv, Apr. 3, 1935; came to U.S., 1961; s. Michael and Guta D.; B.A., Hebrew U., 1961, M.A., 1963; Ph.D., UCLA, 1964; m. Rina Greenfarb, June 3, 1955; children—Gill, Opher, Ayala. Teaching and research asst. psychology Hebrew U., 1958-61; research asst. psychology UCLA, 1961-63, research psychologist, 1964-65; research asso. neurology Stanford U., 1965-66, neurobiology br. NASA Ames Research Center, Moffett Field, Calif., 1966-68; asso. prof. psychology U. Ill., 1968-72, prof. psychology and physiology, 1972—, head dept. psychology, 1980—. Served with Israeli Army and Kibbutz Eyal, 1952-57. Recipient numerous research grants. Fellow AAAS, Am. Psychol. Assn.; mem. Am. EEE Soc., Psychonomic Soc., Soc. Neuroscis., Soc. Psychophysiol. Research (pres. 1980). Editor: (with Donald B. Lindsley) Average Evoked Potentials, NASA, 1969; contbr. sci. articles to profl. jours., chpts. in books. Home: 305 W Indiana St Urbana IL 61801 Office: Dept Psychology 603 E Daniel St Champaign IL 61820

DONELAN, PATRICK MICHAEL, investment co. exec.; b. St. Louis, Jan. 10, 1940; s. Patrick J. and Kathleen Theresa (Connolly) D.; B.A., U. Mo., 1962; m. Carol Francis Luke, Sept. 21, 1963; children—Sean Michael, Elizabeth Luke, Ellen Lacey, Catherine Cunliff. Account exec. Newhard, Cook & Co., 1966-68; co-founder Donelan Phelps & Co., Inc., St. Louis, 1968, exec. v.p., sec., 1968—; chmn., chief exec. officer Kieffer Paper Mills, Inc., Brownstown, Ind.; vice chmn. bd. Brentwood Bancshares Corp., St. Louis, 1978—; dir., mem. exec. com. Am. Investment Co., 1977-80, Kieffer Paper Mills Inc., Brentwood Bank, Intercapco West, Inc.; participant Fin. Analysts Fedn., Harvard Grad. Sch. Bus., 1973. Mem. St. Louis County Historic Bldgs. Commn.; bd. dirs. Catholic Cemeteries Archdiocese St. Louis; trustee Newman Found., Washington U., St. Louis; vice-chmn. Midland dist. Boy Scouts Am.; bd. dirs. U. Mo. Devel. Fund, 1980—, exec. com., 1981—. Served as officer USAF, 1962-66. Decorated Commendation medal with oak leaf cluster. Mem. Young Pres.'s Orgn., St. Louis Soc. Fin. Analysts. Clubs: Racquet, Noonday, Univ., St. Louis, Old Warson. Home: 52 Huntleigh Woods Village of Huntleigh MO 63131 Office: 7800 Bonhomme St Saint Louis MO 63105

DONER, FREDERICK NATHAN, advt. agy. exec.; b. Detroit, Nov. 6, 1943; s. Wilfred B. and Ruth Weiss D.; B.A., U. Mich., 1965, M.A. in English Lit., 1966; m. Michele Oka, Aug. 15, 1966; children—Jordan Wilfred, Jeremy Kenneth. Teaching fellow dept. English U. Mich., 1966-68; copywriter W.B. Doner & Co., Detroit, 1968-72, account exec., 1972-73, -73, v.p., 1974-76, account supr., 1977, mgmt. supr., sr. v.p., 1978—, dir., 1979—. Bd. dirs. Friends of Modern Art, Detroit Inst. Arts, 1972—, Meadow Brook Art Gallery, Oakland U., Rochester, Mich., 1970-77, Save Orch. Hall, Inc., Detroit, 1979—; pres. Concerned Citizens of Franklin (Mich.), 1973-79. Recipient nat. awards for advt. field including Clio gold award, 1974; One Show Gold award, 1974. Club: Adcraft (Detroit). Featured in book The One Show, 1974; dir., writer film Barbara and Yetta; writer, producer You've Gotta Have Art, 1975; writer comic strip Business as Usual, Detroit Free Press, 1981. Office: 26711 Northwestern Hwy Detroit MI 48075

DONESA, ANTONIO BRAGANZA, neurosurgeon; b. Manila, Philippines, July 27, 1935; s. Alfonso Pinson and Flora (Braganza) D.; B.S., U. Philippines (Manila), 1956, M.D., 1959; m. Barbara Louise Quinn, Nov. 30, 1962; children—Carmen, Christopher. Came to U.S., 1959, naturalized, 1969. Intern St. Mary's Hosp., Waterbury, Conn., 1959-60; resident U. Ala. Med. Center, Birmingham, 1961-65; practice medicine specializing in neurosurgery, Ft. Wayne, Ind., 1966—; pres. Neurosurgery, Inc., Ft. Wayne, 1971—, also dir.; mem. staff Parkview, St. Joseph's, Lutheran hosps. (all Ft. Wayne); cons. Marion (Ind.) Gen. Hosp., VA Hosp., Ft. Wayne. Recipient Certificate Leadership award March Dimes, 1972, Certificate Appreciation award Heart Fund, 1971. Mem. AMA, Assn. Philippine Practicing Physicians in Am., Ft. Wayne Acad. Medicine and Surgery, Ind. Philippine Med. Assn. (past pres.), Am. Coll. Internat. Physicians (founder, exec. dir.), Ind., Allen County med. socs., Congress Neurol. Surgeons, Soc. Philippine Neurol. Surgeons in Am. (past pres.). Clubs: Masons (32 deg.), Shriners, Summit (Ft. Wayne). Home: 8215 Tranquilla Pl Fort Wayne IN 46815 Office: 3030 Lake Ave Fort Wayne IN 46805

DONEWALD, MARIAN, speech and hearing clinician, educator; b. St. Louis, July 1911; d. Harry William and Daisy Elizabeth (Eissler) Donewald; student U. Colo., 1937-38; A.B., U. Evansville, 1948; M.S., Purdue U., 1950. Tchr. Wheeler Sch., Evansville, Ind., 1935-48; speech and hearing clinician Evansville-Vanderburgh Sch. Corp., 1948—; lectr. speech Purdue U., Lafayette, Ind., 1952-64, dir. summer workshops, 1952-64; lectr. speech Community Coll., U. Evansville, 1955-76, ret., 1976; cons., pvt. therapist, 1976—. Mem. Christian edn. com. 1st Presbyterian Ch., Evansville, 1965-68, altar com., 1969—; Democratic precinct committeeman, mem. adv. bd. Evansville Knight Twp., 1975-79; trustee Campground Cemetery, Evansville, 1966—, sec. bd., 1970—; historian Old Court House, 1976—. Mem. Am. (state del. 1966-68), Central States, Ind. speech and hearing assns., Internat. Council for Exceptional Children, NEA, Ind. State, Evansville tchrs. assns., Speech Communication Assn., Cleft Palate Assn., Internat. Platform Assn., Assn. Tchr. Educators, Kappa Kappa Iota. Clubs: Flower Growers Garden, Rotary. Author: See and Say Book, 1961. Home: 2900 Bellemeade Ave Evansville IN 47714

DONLEY, GRAHAM VAUGHN, audiovisual co. exec.; b. Chgo., July 15, 1945; s. David Charles and Louise Marcella (Jung) D.; B.S., Bradley U., 1970. Tchr., Chgo. Bd. Edn., 1971-72; technician Audio Visual Techniques, Inc., Elk Grove, Ill., 1972-79; pres. AB Prodns., Chgo., 1979-80, Media Control, Inc., Chgo., 1980—. Mem. Nat. Audio Visual Assn., Assn. Multi Image, Chgo., Unltd. Office: 110 N River Rd Des Plaines IL 60016

DONNELLEY, GAYLORD, printing co. exec.; b. Chgo., May 19, 1910; s. Thomas E. and Laura L. (Gaylord) D.; A.B., Yale U., 1931; postgrad. Cambridge U., 1931-32; LL.D. (hon.), Wabash Coll., 1965, Yale U., 1974, U. Chgo., 1976, U. S.C., Spartanburg, 1979; m. Dorothy Williams Ranney, May 4, 1935; children—Elliott R., Strachan, Laura Donnelley Wheeler. With R.R. Donnelley & Sons Co., Chgo., 1932—, comptroller, office mgr., 1940-42, sec., 1945-47, exec. v.p., 1947-52, pres., 1952-64, chmn. bd., 1964-75, chmn. exec. com., 1975—; past dir. Borg-Warner Corp., Dun & Bradstreet Corp., Reuben H. Donnelley Corp., First Nat. Bank of Chgo., First Chgo. Corp., Lakeside Bank; dir. Lantana Boatyard, Inc. Vice chmn. exec. com. Chgo. Community Trust, 1968-79; mem. bus. adv. council Chgo. Urban League, 1969—; adv. bd. Ill. Dept. Conservation, 1978—; mem. Ill. Bd. Higher Edn., 1979—; adv. council Jr. Achievement, 1955—; mem. policy com. South Side Planning Bd., Chgo., 1966—; adv. bd. YMCA Met. Chgo., 1963—; pres. Community Fund Chgo., 1969-71, bd. dirs., 1964-73; mem. Ill. Nature Preserves Commn., 1968-74; trustee Savs. & Profit Sharing Fund of Sears Employees, 1976-81, Lincoln Acad. of Ill., 1978-79; trustee Newberry Library, 1953-72, life trustee, 1972—, first v.p. of bd., 1970; mem. governing com. Orchestral Assn., 1971; bd. advisors Council for Fin. Aid to Edn., 1971—; trustee Sarah Lawrence Coll., 1965-73, hon. trustee, 1973—; mem. Com. for Corp. Support of Pvt. Univs., 1977-80; chmn. Am. Friends of Cambridge U., 1977—, dir., 1969—; bd. dirs. Nat. Wildlife Found., 1981—; trustee U. Chgo., 1947-80, life trustee, 1980—, chmn. bd. trustees, 1970-76; mem. devel. bd. Yale U., 1964-71; mem. council Children's Meml. Hosp., 1977—; hon. bd. advisers Mercy Hosp., 1971—, lay bd. trustees, 1965-71; chmn. bd. Beverly Farm Found., 1962-64; elder First Presbyn. Ch., Libertyville; hon. governing mem. Art Inst. Chgo., 1980—; dir. Protestant Found. of Greater Chgo., 1970-79; trustee United Presbyn. Found., 1963-75, 1st v.p., 1972-73; trustee N. Am. Wildlife Found., 1980—, Ducks Unltd. Found., 1978—, Nat. Recreation Found., 1969—; mem. nat. com. Ams. for Coast, 1980—; mem. nat. adv. bd. Center for Book in Library of Congress, 1980—. Recipient Yale medal, 1972; The Lambs Good Shepherd award, 1978; Citations to Disting. Citizens award Protestant Found. Greater Chgo., 1977; Oak Leaf award The Nature Conservancy, 1976; Conservation Merit award Ill. Dept. Conservation, 1981; Lewis Meml. award Printing Industries Am., 1976; Philanthropist award Nat. Soc. Fundraising Execs., 1980; Charles H. Wacker award United Charities, 1980; numerous others. Fellow Royal Soc. for Encouragement Arts, Mfg. and Commerce; mem. Smithsonian Assos. (dir.), Ducks Unltd. (pres. 1975-77, trustee 1962-80, trustee emeritus 1980—; chmn. exec. com. 1978-80, vice chmn. bd. 1977-78), Ducks Unltd. (Can.) (trustee 1968-80, hon. dir. 1980—), Ducks Unltd. de Mexico (trustee 1976-79), Nat. Recreation and Parks Assn. (life trustee, Spl. Recognition award 1975). Clubs: Carolina Plantation Soc. (pres.) (Charleston, S.C.); Coleman Lake (Goodman, Wis.); Old Elm (Highland Park, Ill.); Onwentsia (Lake Forest, Ill.); Shoreacres Golf (Lake Bluff, Ill.); Links, Grolier (N.Y.C.); Casino, Caxton, Chgo., Chgo. Commonwealth, Comml., Econ., Execs., Quadrangle, Racquet, Univ., Wayfarers (Chgo.). Author: To Be A Good Printer, 1977. Office: 2223 Martin Luther King Dr Chicago IL 60616

DONNELLY, ANNE MARIE, catering cons.; b. Chgo., Nov. 28, 1938; d. William L. and Anne E. (Gribbon) Earth; student De Paul U., 1956-59; m. Maurice L. Donnelly, Jan. 11, 1964 (dec. 1973); children—Patricia Anne, Michael Jude. With South Shore View Hotel, Chgo., 1953-66, asst. catering mgr., 1960-66; owner Annette's Catering, Chgo., 1966-73; sr. cons. D'Masti Custom Caterers, Blue Island, Ill., 1976—. Den mother cub scouts Chgo. Area council Boy Scouts Am., 1975-78; mgr. Mt. Greenwood Girls Softball Team, 1976-78, coach, 1979—; officer Band Boosters, 1975-79; active Chgo. Policemen's Annuity Fund, Mt. Assisi Parents Assn., St. Christina Home Sch. Guild, choir, Altar and Rosary Soc.; vol. St. Christina Sch., 1973-78. Mem. Nat. Bus. and Profl. Women. (Beverly br.), Nat. Assn. Female Execs., Nat. Restaurant Assn., No. Ill. Food Execs. Assn., Ret. Policemen's Assn., Nat. Hist. Soc. Office: 11915 S Western Ave Blue Island IL 60406

DONNELLY, PHYLLIS BESWICK, reading cons.; b. Elk Point, Alta., Can., Nov. 19, 1939; naturalized, 1966; d. Colin Alfred John and Ruby Ellen (Gudwer) Beswick; student U. Alta., 1957-58, Northwestern U., 1961-62, Ind. U., 1962-63, M.S. in Edn., 1967 B.S. in Edn., Bethel Coll., Mishawaka, Ind., 1964; m. John Vincent Donnelly, Nov. 28, 1975; children—Deirdre, Sean, Patrick. Elem. tchr. Strathearn Elem. Sch., Edmonton, Alta., Can., 1958-61, Harris Sch., Chgo., 1961-62, Culver (Ind.) Community Schs., 1964-66; reading cons., curriculum writer Cleveland Hts.-University Hts. Bd. of Edn., Cleveland Heights, Ohio, 1967—, program dir. Right-to-Read, 1974—. Pres. Judson Park Evening Aux. Vols. Mem. Internat. Reading Assn., Mary C. Austin Reading Council, Am. Fedn. Tchrs., Ohio Fedn. Tchrs., Cleveland Hts.-University Hts. Fedn. Tchrs., AAUW (elected to Ohio Roster of Women 1977). Democrat. Author: Reading Evaluation, 1974, Primary Reading Writing and Listening Skills, 1977; co-author: Developmental Reading Guides, vols. 1, 2, 1975, vol. 3, 1976. Home: 10494 Lake Shore Blvd Cleveland OH 44108 Office: 2155 Miramar Blvd Cleveland Heights OH 44118

DONNELLY, RICHARD MORRILL, advt. co. exec.; b. St. Louis, Nov. 10, 1926; s. Richard Morrill and Helen (Schreiber) D.; student U. Wyo., 1944, Yale, 1945; B.S. in Bus. and Pub. Adminstrn., Washington U., St. Louis, 1950; m. Gail S. children from previous marriage—Lisa Anne, Jeffrey Scott, Jana Lynne. Account supr. Gardner Advt., 1954-64; pres. Donnelly & Toben, St. Louis, 1964-65, Donnelly & Dolen, advt., 1965-66, Ridgway Advt. Agy., 1966-67,

Rutledge Advt., 1967-68, Donnelly & Weston Advt., Inc., 1968-70, Donnelly & Stanton Advt., 1970-74, Donnelly Advt. Co., 1975—; dir. Burlen Industries, Inc., Jack and Jill Products, Inc., Hatter Pub. Co., The Garrett, John Simmons & Assos. Alumni bd. govs. Washington U. Served with AUS, 1944-46. Mem. Beta Theta Pi (dir. 1968-71), Delta Sigma Pi. Clubs: Washington University (bd. govs. 1969-70, pres. 1970-71), Racquet (dir. 1975—), Media (St. Louis); Strathalbyn Farms (dir. 1976—). Home: 9373 Ladue Rd Saint Louis MO 63124 Office: 9326 Olive Street Rd Saint Louis MO 63132

DONNELLY, ROBERT TRUE, chief justice Mo. Supreme Ct.; b. Lebanon, Mo., Aug. 31, 1924; s. Thomas and Sybil (True) D.; student U. Tulsa, 1942-43, Ohio State U., 1943; J.D., U. Mo., Columbia, 1949; m. Wanda Sue Oates, Nov. 16, 1946; children—Thomas Page, Brian True. Admitted to Mo. bar, 1949; practiced law, Greenfield, Springfield and Lebanon, Mo., 1949-65; justice Supreme Ct. Mo., 1965—, chief justice, 1973-75, 81—; city atty. City of Lebanon, 1954-55; asst. atty. gen. State of Mo., 1957-61; mem. bar com. 26th Jud. Circuit, 1956-65. Mem. Lebanon Bd. Edn., 1959-65. Served with inf. U.S. Army, World War II; ETO. Decorated Purple Heart. Mem. Am. Judicature Soc., Mo. Bar (bd. govs. 1956-63), Order of Coif, Order of Barristers. Presbyterian. Office: Supreme Ct Bldg Jefferson City MO 65101

DONNEM, SARAH LUND, civic worker; b. St. Louis, Apr. 10, 1936; d. Joel Y. and Erle Hall (Harsh) Lund; B.A., Vassar Coll., 1958; m. Roland W. Donnem, Feb. 18, 1961; children—Elizabeth Prince, Sarah Madison. Tech. aide Bell Labs., Whippany, N.J., 1959-60; chmn. placement vol. opportunities N.Y. Jr. League, 1972-73, asst. treas. 1974-75, chmn. urban problems relating to mental health, 1967-69, mem. project research com., 1967-71, chmn., mem. bd. mgrs. 1973-74; chmn. community research D.C. Jr. League, 1970-71, mem. bd. mgrs., 1970-71; mem. Stratford Hall (N.Y.) Com., 1970—; bd. dirs. East Side Settlement House, Bronx, N.Y., 1972—, v.p., 1975-76, chmn. Nat. Horse Show Benefit, 1976; bd. dirs. Stanley M. Isaacs Neighborhood Center, N.Y.C., 1973-76, v.p., 1975-76; bd. dirs. Presbyn. Home for Aged Women, N.Y.C., 1974-76, v.p., 1976; mem. exec. bd. N.Y. Aux. of Blue Ridge Sch., 1971-75, sec., 1965-67, pres., 1973-75; budget and benevolence com. Brick Presbyn. Ch., N.Y.C., 1973-76, mem. social service com., 1973-74, chmn. fgn. students com., 1963-64. Bd. dirs. Search and Care, N.Y.C., 1973-76, Project LEARN, Cleve., 1978—; mem. Fedn. Community Planning, Cleve., Council on Older Persons, 1978—, mem. Future Planning Task Force, 1980-81, Commn. on Social Concerns, 1982; trustee Golden Age Centers Greater Cleve., 1979—, women's council, 1978—, 1st v.p., 1980-81, pres., 1981—; chmn. Western Res. Antiques Show, 1979, 80; mem. women's com. Cleve. Orch., 1979—; bd. dirs. Cleve. Ballet, 1980—, exec. com., 1981, chmn. legis. advocacy com., 1981—. Named Vol. of the Year, N.Y. Jr. League, 1975. Mem. Nat. Inst. Social Scis. (mem. memberships com. 1972—), Nat. Soc. of Colonial Dames, Western Res. Hist. Soc. (mem. women's advisory council 1977; corr. sec. 1978). Republican. Presbyterian. Clubs: Colony (N.Y.C.); Chevy Chase (Washington); Kirtland (Cleve.). Address: 2945 Fontenay Rd Shaker Heights OH 44120

DONNEWALD, JAMES HENRY, state senator; b. Carlyle, Ill., Jan. 29, 1925; s. John Henry and Cecelia Louise (Luepke) D.; student St. Louis U., 1942-44; LL.B., Lincoln Coll. Law, Springfield, Ill., 1949; m. Ruth Evelyn Holtgrave, June 24, 1953; children—Eric, Craig, Jill. Admitted to Ill. bar, 1951; practiced in Breese; mem. Ill. Senate, 1964—, asst. majority leader 77th, 79th gen. assemblies, chmn. Assignment Bills Com., vice chmn. Reapportionment Com., 1971-73, asst. minority leader 78th Gen. Assembly, mem. Assignment Appropriation Com., Exec. and Senate Ops. Com., 1973—, chmn. Com. Assignment Bills. Precinct committeeman Democratic party, Carlyle, 1948-50; supr. Carlyle Twp., 1949-51; mem. Ill. Ho. of Reps. for 51st (now 55th) Dist., 1960-64. Served with Armed Forces, Korea. Mem. Am. Legion. Roman Catholic. Lion, Elk, Moose, K.C. Office: 550 N 2d St Breese IL 62230

D'ONOFRIO, PETER JOSEPH, paramedic; b. Bronx, N.Y., Sept. 20, 1947; s. Elia Danato and Concetta Chella (Diorio) D'O.; Asso. Applied Sci. in Mktg., Sinclair Community Coll., 1973; B.S. in Bus., U. Dayton, 1974, M.B.A., 1975, B.S. in Edn., 1975. Coordinator software documentation and distbn., internat. div. N.C.R. Corp., Dayton, Ohio, 1971; program dir. young adult dept. YMCA, Dayton, 1972-74; adminstrv. asst. Kettering (Ohio) Fire Div., 1974-76; instr. bus. tech. div. Sinclair Community Coll., 1976—; instr. Miami Twp. Police Acad., 1981—; paramedic, firefighter Wayne Twp. Fire Dept., Dayton, 1976-78; emergency room paramedic technician Kettering (Ohio) Med. Center, 1978; asst. mgr. Friendly Family Restaurant, Kettering, 1978-79; mobile intensive care paramedic, 1979—; fire insp., arson investigator Miami Twp. Fire Dept., Montgomery County, Ohio, 1980—. Vice pres., treas. Cath. Youth Orgn., 1961-65; pres. young adult council YMCA, 1970-71, chmn. young adult program com., 1971-72. Served in USAF, 1967-71. Certified cardiopulmonary instr. ARC, advanced cardiac life support provider. Mem. Internat. Assn. Arson Investigators, Am. Mktg. Assn., AAUP, Hamilton Civil War Round Table, 35th Ohio Vol. Inf. Civil War Reenactment Group, Phi Theta Kappa. Home: 2512 Santa Rosa Dr Kettering OH 45440 Office: 2700 Lyons Rd Miamisburg OH 45342

DONOHO, LORA HIATT, educator, athletic dir.; b. Opdyke, Ill., May 22, 1931; d. James Arthur and Josie Thomas (Holdman) Hiatt; A.B., Olivet Nazarene Coll., 1953; M.S. in Edn., So. Ill. U., 1962; Ph.D., U. Ill., 1970; m. John Donoho, June 20, 1959. Tchr. phys. edn., biology public schs., Ill., 1953-60; prof. phys. edn. Trevecca Coll., Nashville, 1970-72; asst. acad. dean Olivet Nazarene Coll., Kankakee, Ill., 1972-75; athletic dir., prof. phys. edn. Mt. Vernon (Ohio) Nazarene Coll., 1975—. Twp. auditor, Bourbonnais, Ill., 1964-72. Mem. Am. Coll. Sports Medicine, AAHPER. Office: Mt Vernon Nazarene Coll Martinsburg Rd Mt Vernon OH 43050

DONOHO, SHELBA JEAN, nursing home adminstr.; b. Westphalia, Kans., Dec. 9, 1946; d. Kenneth Charles and Esther Marguerite (Hammond) Volland; B.S. in Edn., Emporia (Kans.) State U., 1968; m. Terry Lee Donoho, Dec. 21, 1968; children—LeShelle Kae, Stephanie Ann. Tchr., La Cygne (Kans.) High Sch., 1968-69; nutritionist Wabash Meml. Hosp., Decatur, Ill., 1970-72, Lincoln Manor, Decatur, 1972-75; nursing home adminstr. Lincoln Manor North, Decatur, 1975—. Bd. dirs. Family Service of Decatur. Recipient outstanding work in home econs. award Proctor and Gamble, 1968. Mem. Am. Bus. Women Assn. (sec., hospitality chmn. Decatur chpt., Woman of Yr. 1980), Ill. Nursing Home Adminstrs. Assn., Ill. Health Care Assn. (dir., mem. edn. com., peer rev. com., membership com., pres. Decatur chpt.); United Presbyn. Women's Assn. Presbyterian. Home: 3280 Vining Dr Decatur IL 62521 Office: 2650 N Monroe St Decatur IL 62526

DONOHUE, CARROLL JOHN, lawyer; b. St. Louis, June 24, 1917; s. Thomas M. and Florence (Klefisch) D.; A.B., Washington U., St. Louis, 1939, LL.B. magna cum laude, 1939; m. Juanita Maire, Jan. 4, 1943 (div. 1973); children—Patricia Carol Stevens, Crhistine Ann Smith, Deborah Lee; m. 2d, Barbara Lounsbury, Dec. 29, 1978. Admitted to Mo. bar, 1939; asso. law firm Hay and Flanagan, St. Louis, 1939-42, firm Salkey and Cornfeld, St. Louis, 1946-49; partner firm Husch, Eppenberger, Donohue, Elson and Jones, St. Louis, 1949—. Mayor, Olivette, Mo., 1953-56. Campaign chmn. ARC, St. Louis County, Mo., 1950; mem. adv. com. Child Welfare, St. Louis, 1952-55, exec. com. Slum Clearance, 1949, bond issue com., 1955, St. Louis County Bond Issue screening and supervisory coms., 1955-61, county citizen's com. for better law enforcement, 1953-56; chmn. com. on immigration policy, 1954-56. Chmn. County Bd. Election Commrs., St. Louis County, Mo., 1960-65; vice-chmn. bd. Regional Commerce and Growth Assn., 1981. Served from apprentice seaman to lt. USNR, 1942-45. Decorated Bronze Star, Navy and M.C. medal. Mem. Mo. Bar (mem. bd. govs., 1948-50, 52, 54, 56; chmn. ann. meeting), St. Louis Bar Assn., (pres. 1954-55, v.p. 1948-49, treas. 1951-54), Order of Coif, Omicron Delta Kappa, Sigma Phi Epsilon, Delta Theta Phi. Club: Missouri Athletic. Office: 100 N Broadway Saint Louis MO 63101

DONOHUE, DANIEL WILLIAM, ins. agt.; b. Chgo., Mar. 18, 1946; s. William John and Mildred Francis (Kabat) D.; diploma Chgo. City Jr. Coll., 1971; m. Shirley I. Beintum, Feb. 2, 1973. Import-export trainee J.E. Bernard, 1970; sales clk. Clark Equipment, 1970-71, purchasing agt., 1971-73; ins. agent Prudential Ins. Co., Matteson, Ill., 1973—; instr. Joliet Jr. Coll. Deacon, Calvary Reformed Ch., Orland Park, Ill., 1978-81, ch. treas., 1980. Recipient Rookie of Year award River Oaks Prudential Office, 1974, William E. Brownfield award Jaycees, 1977. Mem. Nat. Assn. Life Underwriters, Jaycees (v.p. 1976-77). Address: 360 Thorndale Dr Frankfort IL 60423

DONOHUE, WILLIAM FRANCIS, health care adminstr.; b. Rome, N.Y., June 3, 1935; s. William Francis, Jr., and Selina (Bowen) D.; cert. inhalation therapy Yale Med. Center, 1962; B.A., Antioch Coll., 1973; cert. health care adminstrn. Trinity U., 1978. Chief inhalation therapist Lancaster (Pa.) Gen. Hosp., 1962-63, Western Pa. Hosp., Pitts., 1963-65; tech. dir. respiratory care Edgwater Hosp., Chgo., 1965-69; dean allied health scis. Central YMCA Community Coll., Chgo., 1969-75; asst. adminstr. Louise Burg Hosp., Chgo., 1975-77; dir. material mgmt. and quality assurance Provident Hosp., Chgo., 1977—; health scis. adv. com. dept. human relations City of Chgo., 1969-76; health occupations adv. com. Chgo. City Colls., 1974—. Recipient 2d prize for sci. exhibits Pa. Med. Soc., 1965. Mem. Am. Coll. Hosp. Adminstrs., Am. Hosp. Assn., Chgo. Hosp. Council, Risk Mgmt. Assn., Am. Public Health Assn., Royal Soc. Health. Asso. editor Inhalation Therapy, 1964-69; contbr. numerous articles profl. jours. Home: 1030 N State St Chicago IL 60610 Office: 426 E 51st St Chicago IL 60615

DONOVAN, FRANK WILLIAM, lawyer; b. Washington, Sept. 12, 1905; s. Frank Dennis and Catherine (Connor) D.; A.B., Notre Dame U., 1926; LL.B., Harvard U., 1929; m. Helen Turner, June 25, 1938 (div. May 1947); children—Frank William, Julia Donovan O'Meara, Russell Hodges; m. 2d, Elizabeth Chetwoode Hodges, June 19, 1947 (dec. Nov. 1967); m. 3d, Ana Maria Fuentes-Munizaga, Dec. 8, 1969. Admitted to Mich. bar, 1930; partner firm Yerkes, Goddard & McClintock, Detroit, 1932-38; individual practice, Detroit, 1938-41; partner firm Fulton & Donovan, Detroit, 1941-50, firm McClintock, Fulton, Donovan & Waterman, 1950-73, McClintock, Donovan, Carson & Roach, 1973-80, Donovan, Hammond, Carson, Ziegelman, Roach & Sotiroff, 1980—. Dir. Bob-Lo Co., Detroit, Chase Newark Corp., Hartford, Conn., D.T. Chase Co., Hartford, W.H. Edgar & Son, Detroit, Zenith Labs, Inc., Northvale, N.J., Ryerson & Haynes, Inc., Jackson, Chase Devel. Corp., Hartford. Chmn. Italian Flood Relief Com., Detroit, 1966. Chmn. bd. Detroit Grand Opera Assn., Detroit Symphony Orch., Etruscan Found., David T. Chase Found., mem. senate Stratford Shakespearean Festival Found. (Can.); mem. Met. Opera Assn. N.Y.; trustee Inst. Advanced Pastoral Studies, Bloomfield Hills, Mich., Shakespearean Drama Festival Found., Inc., N.Y.C.; bd. govs. Am. Mental Health Found. Recipient Award Merit, Am. C. of C. for Italy, 1967, Citation Appreciation, Greater Mich. Found., 1963; Frank W. Donovan Dayproclaimed in recognition of cultural contributions, City Detroit, 1963. Clubs: Detroit, Country of Detroit, Renaissance (Detroit); Grosse Pointe (Mich.); La Coquille (Palm Beach, Fla.). Home: 17160 E Jefferson Grosse Pointe MI 48230 Office: 400 Renaissance Center Suite 1100 Detroit MI 48243

DONOVAN, JOHN ANTHONY, bishop; b. Chatham, Ont., Can., Aug. 5, 1911; s. John J. and Mary C. (O'Rourke) D.; B.A., Sacred Heart Sem., 1932; student N.A. Coll., Rome (Italy), 1936; J.C.L., Pontificial Athenaeum of Lateran, Rome, 1947; LL.D., U. Detroit, 1952 Ordained priest Roman Cath. Ch., 1935, domestic prelate, 1949; pastor St. Aloysius' Ch., Detroit, also chancellor Archdiocese Detroit, 1951-58, St. Veronica's Ch., East Detroit, 1958-67; titular bishop of Rhasus and aux. bishop of Detroit, 1954-67; vicar gen. Archdiocese Detroit, 1959-67; bishop of Toledo, 1967-81; ret., 1981.

DONOVAN, MARGARET HENDERLITE, pianist, educator; b. Baird, Tex., May 6, 1925; d. Peter Baxter and Jessie (Newton) Henderlite; A.A., Tarleton State U., 1943; B.Mus. cum laude (T scholar), Am. Conservatory of Music, 1945, M.Mus. cum laude, 1953, postgrad., 1953; m. Russell J. Donovan, Sept. 4, 1949; children—Russell John, Peter Henderlite, Rachel Lynn, Margaret Newton, Tammy Jayne. Duo pianist with Charles W. Froh, Tex. State U., Stephenville, 1939-43; pianist, accompanist New Trier High Sch., Winnetka, Ill., 1945-47, Am. Conservatory of Music, Chgo., 1943-53, mem. faculty, 1954—; mem. piano faculty Park Forest Conservatory of Music, Park Forest, Ill., 1958—; pvt. piano instr., 1954—; adjudicator Nat. Guild of Piano Playing Auditions, 1960—, Soc. of Am. Musicians, 1962, Ill. Fedn. Music Clubs and Auditions, Chgo., 1962—. Recipient Hattstaedt Gold medal Piano award, 1945. Mem. Lakeview Mus. Soc., Cordon Club, Nat. Soc. Lit. and Arts, Am. Coll. Musicians, Soc. Am. Music, Music Tchrs. Nat. Assn., Internat. Platform Assn., Sigma Alpha Iota. Presbyn. Home: 1872 Reichert Ave Sauk Village IL 60411

DONOVAN, PAUL V., bishop; b. Bernard, Iowa, Sept. 1, 1924; s. John J. and Loretta (Carew) D.; student St. Joseph Sem., Grand Rapids, Mich.; B.A., St. Gregory Sem., Cin., 1946; postgrad. Mt. St. Mary Sem. of West, Cin.; J.C.L., Pontifical Lateran U., Rome, 1957. Ordained priest Roman Catholic Ch., 1950; asst. pastor St. Mary Ch., Jackson, Mich., 1950-51; sec. to bishop of Lansing (Mich.) and asst. pastor St. Peter Ch., Eaton Rapids, Mich., 1951-55; sec. to bishop, 1957-59; pastor Our Lady of Fatima Ch., Michigan Center, Mich. and St. Rita Mission, Clark Lake, Mich., 1959-68; pastor St. Agnes Ch., Flint, Mich., 1968-71; bishop of Kalamazoo, 1971—; mem. liturgical commn. Diocese of Lansing, chmn., 1963, mem. Cath. Bd. Edn. Jackson and Hillsdale counties; mem. bishop's personnel com., priests' senate. Bd. dirs. Family Services and Mich. Children's Aid. Office: 215 N Westnedge Ave Kalamazoo MI 49006*

DONOVAN, SANDRA STERANKA, businesswoman, scientist; b. Cleve., Sept. 20, 1942; d. William and Clare Marie (Foresta) Steranka; m. Paul C. Donovan, July 16, 1966; 1 son, Todd Christopher. B.A. magna cum laude, Case Western Res. U., 1964, M.S., 1966, Ph.D., 1969. Research chemist Hercules, Inc., Wilmington, Del., 1969-70; sr. research asso. Horizons, Inc., Cleve., 1971-73, research and devel. group leader, 1973-76, mgr. research and mktg., 1976-78; mgr. comml. devel. projects Sohio, Cleve., 1978—. Mem. bd. overseers Case Western Res. U., 1972-78, mem. vis. com to sch. mgmt., 1973-79. Recipient Lubrizol award, 1962; Olin Freedman Towers prize, 1967; Jr. Achievement Service award, 1979; YWCA Woman of Achievement award, 1981. Mem. Flora Stone Mather Coll. Alumnae Assn. (dir. 1973-79), Western Res. Coll. Alumni Assn. (dir. 1975-79), Phi Beta Kappa, Sigma Xi, Iota Sigma Pi. Contbr. articles to profl. jours. Home: 246 Hawthorne Dr Chagrin Falls OH 44022 Office: Midland Bldg Cleveland OH 44115

DOODY, JAMES RAYMOND, ednl. adminstr.; b. Murphysboro, Ill., Mar. 28, 1937; s. Ashton Raymond and Vera Naoma (Schumacher) D.; student So. Ill. U., 1955-61; m. Mary Kay Squires, Aug. 20, 1960; children—Michael Raymond, Jane Ann. Substitute tchr., Madison County, Ill., 1961; asst. dir. pub. relations and advt. Boatmen's Nat. Bank, St. Louis, 1962-65; asst. mgr. advt. and sales promotion Presstite div. Interchem. Corp., St. Louis, 1965-67; dir. pub. info. Monticello Coll., Godfrey, Ill., 1967-69; dir. pub. relations North Central Coll., Naperville, Ill., 1969—; pres. Ill. Coll. Relations Conf., 1977. Bd. dirs. Naperville Community Fund, 1972-79, v.p., 1976-79; founder Naperville-North Central Coll. Community Concert Assn., 1974, v.p., 1974-77, pres., 1977—; mem. Naperville Bicentennial Commn., 1974-76, Naperville Sesquicentennial Commn., 1979—. Served with U.S. Army, 1959-60. Recipient Disting. Community Service award, Naperville, 1981. Mem. Pub. Relations Soc. Am. (accredited), Council for Advancement and Support of Edn. (2 pub. leadership awards), Naperville C. of C. (dir. 1973-75), Publicity Club of Chgo. Methodist. Home: 80 Waxwing Ave Naperville IL 60540 Office: 30 N Brainard St Naperville IL 60540

DOOLEY, DALE ALLEN, electronic banking co. exec.; b. Hartington, Nebr., May 8, 1941; s. Ted Raymond and Jessie Adel (Bobenmeyer) D.; student Wayne State Tchrs. Coll., 1958-59; m. Margie May Short, Sept. 21, 1963; children—Kelly Alan, Terry Dean, Todd Michael. Programmer, Dial Financial, Des Moines, 1968-70, systems analyst, 1970-72, mgr. systems and programming, 1972-75, sr. mktg. rep. mktg. research and devel., 1975-76; exec. dir. Iowa Transfer System, Inc., Des Moines, 1976—, now pres. Mem. Iowa Automated Clearing House Assn. (adminstr. 1978—, sec. corp. 1979—), Iowa Bankers Assn. (v.p. 1979), Nat. Automated Clearing House Assn. (dir. 1980). Office: Iowa Transfer System Inc 430 Liberty Bldg Des Moines IA 50308

DOOLEY, GERALD FRANCIS, telephone switching co. exec.; b. Troy, N.Y., June 14, 1937; s. Peter Joseph and Katherine Rita (McMorrow) D.; B.S.E.E., Rensselaer Poly. Inst., 1959; M.E.E., N.Y. U., 1961; m. Colleen Bernadette Heron, June 16, 1962; children—Erin Marie, Kevin, Patrick, Brian, Brendan. Mem. tech. staff Bell Telephone Labs., Murray Hill, Holmdel, N.J., 1959-64; mem. staff staff Computer Scis. Corp., Falls Church, Va., 1964-67; with No. Electric Co., Galion, Delaware, Ohio, 1967-78, v.p. product devel., 1976-77; v.p., tech. dir. telecommunications switching div. ITT North, Delaware, Ohio, 1978—. Bd. dirs. Jr. Achievement, 1970-72, pres., 1972. Mem. IEEE, Armed Forces Communications and Electronics Assn., Nat. Mgmt. Assn., Am. Mgmt. Assn., Tau Beta Pi, Eta Kappa Nu. Roman Catholic. Club: K.C. Patentee in field. Contbr. articles to profl. jours. Office: PO Box 20345 Columbus OH 43220

DOOLEY, J. GORDON, food scientist; b. Nevada, Mo., Nov. 15, 1935; s. Howard Eugene and Wilma June (Vanderford) D.; B.S. with honors in Biology, Drury Coll., Springfield, Mo., 1958; postgrad. (NSF grantee) U. Mo., Rolla, 1961, (NSF grantee) Kirksville (Mo.) State Coll., 1959; M.S. in Biology (NSF grantee), Brown U., 1966; postgrad. bus. mgmt. Alexander Hamilton Inst., 1973-75, No. Ill. U., 1964. Tchr. sci. Morton West High Sch., Berwyn, Ill., 1963-64; dairy technologist Borden Co., Elgin, Ill., 1964-65; project leader Cheese Products Lab., Kraft Corp., Glenview, Ill., 1965-73; sr. food scientist Wallerstein Co. div. Travenol Labs., Inc., Morton Grove, Ill., 1973-77; mgr. food sci. GB Fermentation Industries, Inc., Des Plaines, Ill., 1977-79, mgr. product devel., 1979—; sci. lectr. seminars, Mexico, 1975; asso. mem. Ad Hoc Enzyme Tech. Com., 1978—. Recipient Spoke award Nevada (Mo.) Jr. C. of C., 1960. Mem. Am. Dairy Sci. Assn., Inst. Food Technologists, Am. Chem. Soc., Cousteau Soc., Am. Inst. Biol. Scis., Nat. Sci. Tchrs. Assn., Whey Products Inst., Beta Beta Beta, Phi Eta Sigma. Republican. Presbyterian. Clubs: Toastmasters Internat. (pres. Baxter Labs. club 1976-77); Brown U. (Chgo.). Patentee in food and enzyme tech. field; contbr. sci. articles to profl. jours. Home: 990 Browning Ln Lake Zurich IL 60047 Office: 1 N Broadway Des Plaines IL 60016

DOOLEY, JO ANN CATHERINE, accountant; b. Cin., Nov. 24, 1930; d. Joseph Frank and Margaret Mary (Flynn) D.; student U. Cin., 1965-67. Asst. accountant Gardner Publs., Inc., Cin., 1953-67, controller, sec. employees profit sharing trust, 1967—, now also sec./treas.; advt. mgr. Woman CPA mag., 1977—. Mem. Am. Soc. Women Accountants, Am. Mgmt. Assn., Nat. Assn. Female Execs., Cincinnati Women's Forum, St. Francis-St. George Hosp. Aux. Office: 600 Main St Cincinnati OH 45202

DOOLEY, ROBERT DANIEL, radiologist; b. Alameda, Calif., Aug. 6, 1923; s. Daniel Raymond and Anna Nora (Shannon) D.; student Loyola U., Chgo., 1941-43; B.S., U. Ill., 1944, M.D., 1946; m. Dorothy Jane Klink, June 8, 1946; children—Michael, Karen, Dorian, Joyce. Intern, U.S. Marine Hosp., S.I., N.Y., 1946-47, resident in radiology, Balt., 1947-50; radiologist U.S. Marine Hosp., Chgo., 1950-52; asst. radiologist Little Co. of Mary Hosp., Evergreen Park, Ill., 1952-53; radiologist Garfield Park Hosp., Chgo., 1953-55, 57-62; radiologist Community Meml. Gen. Hosp., La Grange, Ill., 1955—, chief of staff, 1979-81; asst. prof. radiology Rush Med. Sch., Chgo., 1971—. Trustee La Grange Village Library, 1968-74. Served with USPHS, 1946-52. Diplomate Am. Bd. Radiology. Fellow Internat. Coll. Surgeons, Am. Coll. Radiology (councilor); mem. AMA, Ill. State, DuPage County (pres. 1974-75) med. socs., Ill. (pres. 1976-78), Chgo. (trustee 1971-81) radiol. socs. Club: Les Gourmets (Chgo.). Home: 6 Oak Brook Club Dr J-108 Oak Brook IL 60521 Office: 40 S Clay St Hinsdale IL 60521

DOOLITTLE, JOHN ELDON, obstetrician, gynecologist; b. Mulliken, Mich., June 14, 1930; s. Frank E. and Ruth (Collins) D.; student U. Mich., 1948-51; M.D., 1955; m. Marilyn Yvonne Snyder, July 12, 1952; children—Frank Jeffrey, Nancy Lynn, Jean Michelle, James Eric. Intern, J.D. Munson Hosp., Traverse City, Mich., 1955-56; resident Miami Valley Hosp., Dayton, Ohio, 1959-63; pvt. practice medicine specializing in obstetrics and gynecology Niles, Mich., 1963—; chief surgery Pawating Hosp., Niles; dir. Clinique des Femmes. Trustee March of Dimes of Berrien County. Served with USAF, 1956-58. Diplomate Am. Bd. Obstetrics and Gynecology. Fellow A.C.S., Am. Coll. Obstetrics and Gynecology; mem. S.W. Mich. Perinatal Assn. (past pres.), Undersea Med. Soc. Republican. Unitarian. Club: Summit (South Bend, Ind.). Home: 1601 Echo Valley Niles MI 49120 Office: 9 S St Joseph Ave Niles MI 49120

DOOLITTLE, MEG ELIZABETH, nurse; b. Phila., May 5, 1947; d. John Stanley and Zelda Elizabeth (Day) Burvainis; diploma Bryan Meml. Hosp., Lincoln, Nebr., 1968; M.B.A., U. Nebr., 1979. Staff nurse, then head nurse Creighton Meml. St. Joseph's Hosp., Omaha, 1969-74; adminstr. nursing staff Lutheran Gen. Hosp., Omaha, 1974-78; v.p. Luth. Med. Center, Omaha, 1978-80; pvt. med. cons., 1980—. Mem. Am. Soc. Health, Manpower, Edn. and Tng., Am. Hosp. Assn., Nebr. Nurses Assn. (spl. recognition 1976, outstanding recognition continuing edn. 1978, 80), Nebr. League Nursing, Nebr. Hosp. Assn. Author papers, studies in field. Office: 10407 Devonshire Circle Suite 100 Omaha NE 68114

DOOLITTLE, RICHARD IRVING, ednl. adminstr.; b. Oceanside, N.Y., Feb. 4, 1933; s. Irving Warren and Helen Landon (Clampit) D.; B.S., Syracuse U., 1954; M.B.A., N.Y. U., 1964; m. Lorraine Ann Francois, June 29, 1958; children—Donna Claire and Caren Marie (twins). Asso. sec. N.Y. chpt. banking sch. Am. Inst. Banking, 1956-65; dir. ops. Am. Inst. Banking ednl. div. Am. Bankers Assn., Washington, 1965-74; asso. dir. Stonier Grad. Sch. Banking, Rutgers U., 1965-74; exec. v.p. Grad. Sch. Banking, U. Wis.-Madison, 1974—; asso. dir. Internat. Banking Summer Sch., Brown U., 1972. Mem. Dane County Public Affairs Council, Served with AUS, 1954-56. Mem. Am. Mgmt. Assn., Am. Soc. Assn. Execs., Am. Inst. Banking (dist. council 1977-79), Am. Council Edn. (program adv. com. 1982—), Kappa Sigma, Omega Gamma Delta; hon. mem. N.Y. chpt. Am. Inst. Banking Alumni Assn. Episcopalian. Clubs: Madison, Rotary. Home: 3014 Pelham Rd Madison WI 53713 Office: 122 W Washington Ave Madison WI 53703

DOORENBOS, NORMAN JOHN, ednl. adminstr.; b. Flint, Mich., May 13, 1928; s. Garrett Jake and Victoria (Manery) D.; B.S. in Chemistry, U. Mich., 1950, M.S. in Pharm. Chemistry, 1951, Ph.D. in Pharm. Chemistry, 1953; m. Rosa Lee Smith LeTourneau, Feb. 2, 1979; children—Beverly, Phyllis, David LeTourneau, Donna, Alice, Robin LeTourneau, Gail, David, Yvette LeTourneau, Robert LeTourneau, Martha. Research chemist Ansco, Binghamton, N.Y., 1953-56; asst. prof., asso. prof., prof. U. Md., Balt., 1956-65; prof. medicinal chemistry U. Miss., Oxford, 1965-77, prof., chmn. pharmacognosy, 1967-77; dean Doll. of Sci., prof. physiology So. Ill. U., Carbondale, 1977—; dir. Marine Field Sta., Cayman Islands, 1970-74; dir. Bitter End Field Sta., 1974—; cons. on drugs and toxins various ednl., profl., govt., indsl. groups. Research grantee Mallinckrodt Chem. Works, Smith, Kline and French Lab., Merck, Sharp & Dohm, Sterling Winthrop Research Inst., Nat. Drug Co., Walker Labs., Penick Co., USDA, FDA, Nat. Marine Fisheries, Sea Grant Program, Century Am. Corp., Hokin Found., Fabik Found. Mem. Soc. for Econ. Botany, Am. Soc. Pharmacognosy, AAAS, Am. Pharm. Assn., Acad. Pharm. Scis., Am. Chem. Soc., Ill. Acad. Scis., Miss. Acad. Scis., Md. Acad. Scis., Assn. Island Marine Labs. of the Caribbean, Smithsonian Inst., Sigma Xi, Phi Lambda Upsilon, Rho Chi. Baptist. Contbr. papers to profl. publs.; patentee. Office: College of Science Southern Illinois Univ Carbondale IL 62901

DORAN, JAMES GOLDEN, ednl. camp exec.; b. Madison, Wis., Apr. 12, 1919; s. John Harry and Nora (McCooey) D.; Ph.B., Marquette U., 1947; postgrad. Loyola U. at Chgo., 1954, U. Ill. at Urbana, 1965; m. Joyce Gail Cole, Feb. 8, 1954; children—Charles Cole, Mary Noreen, Sean Patrick. Tchr., Pub. Sch. Dist. 15, McHenry, Ill., 1952-68; reading specialist, 1968—; dir. Arrowhead Reading Camp for Boys, Minocqua, Wis., 1967-74; owner, dir. Algonquin Reading Camp for Boys, Rhinelander, Wis., 1975—. Bd. dirs. The Little Sch., Crystal Lake, Ill., 1970-74, YMCA, Crystal Lake, 1967-68. Served with USAAF, 1941-45. Mem. N.E.A., Assn., Am. Camping Assn., Midwest Assn. Pvt. Camps., Wis. Tennis Assn., Cath. Order Foresters (youth dir. 1955-68, award 1973), Phi Delta Kappa. Address: Route 3 Rhinelander WI 54501

DORATHY, ROBERT G., mfg. co. exec.; b. Prophetstown, Ill., July 16, 1918; s. John L. and F. Leona (Given) D.; B.A., Grinnell Coll., 1940; m. Emma Lou Cushing, Apr. 26, 1947; children—Steven R., Julia R. Prodn. mgr. Eclipse Lawn Mower Co., Prophetstown, 1941-54, controller, 1954-59; controller Penberthy div. Houdaille Industries, Inc., Prophetstown, 1959—; dir. Rock River Lumber & Grain Co., Inc., Prophetstown, 1971-76, chmn. bd. dirs., 1976—. Sec., elementary bd. edn. Prophetstown, 1959-65, community high sch. bd. edn., 1966-69. Served with AUS, 1943-46; ETO. Mem. Am. Legion (comdr. 1951-52, chmn. exec. bd. 1948-68). Republican. Home: 414 Johnson Ave Prophetstown IL 61277 Office: PO Box 112 Prophetstown IL 61277

DORFMAN, ISAIAH S., lawyer; b. Kiev, Russia, Mar. 17, 1907; s. Samuel and Ella (Kite) D.; brought to U.S., 1913, naturalized, 1931; Ph.B., U. Chgo., 1927, J.D., 1931; m. Lillian Schley, Oct. 6, 1934; children—Paul, Tom, John. Admitted to Ill. bar, 1931; regional atty. Region 13, NLRB, Chgo., 1937-42, chief spl. litigation unit, Washington, 1942-43; chief analyst Office Strategic Services, U.S. Govt., London, Eng., 1943-44; attache U.S. embassy, Stockholm, Sweden, 1944-45; sr. partner firm Dorfman, Cohen, Laner & Muchin, Ltd., Chgo., 1945—. Instr. labor law Law Sch., Nat. Univ., Washington, 1942-43. Mem. Am. Bar Assn., Chgo. Bar Assn. (chmn. com. unauthorized practice law 1966-67), Ill. Bar Assn. Jewish religion. Mem. B'nai B'rith. Club: Standard (Chgo.). Home: 260 E Chestnut St Chicago IL 60611 Office: 1 IBM Plaza Chicago IL 60611

DORFMAN, MARK S(TANLEY), economist; b. Chgo., Apr. 14, 1945; s. Daniel B. and Mildred (Trilling) D.; B.S., Northwestern U., 1966; M.S., U. Ill., 1967, Ph.D., 1970; m. Marcia Tuckey, June 8, 1968; 1 son, Matthew James. Asst. prof. fin. Miami U., Oxford, Ohio, 1970-73, asso. prof., 1973-79, prof., 1979—; cons. U.S. Senate Subcom. on Judiciary and Life Ins. Industry. Bd. dirs. Stochos Asset Mgmt., 1980, Andrus Found. grantee, 1980-81. Christian Scientist. Author: Introduction to Insurance, 1978, 2d edit., 1982; contbr. numerous articles to profl. jours. Office: 209 Laws Hall Miami U Oxford OH 45056

DORGAN, BYRON L., congressman; b. Dickinson, N.D., May 14, 1942; B.S., U. N.D., 1964; M.B.A., U. Denver, 1966; children—Scott M., Shelley L. Tax commr. State of N.D., 1969—; mem. 97th Congress from N.D. (rep.-at-large). Chmn. Multistate Tax Commn., 1972-74, Gov. N.D. Commn. Air Transp.; mem. nat. adv. bd. Tax Action Campaign; mem. Gov. N.D. Energy Council, Gov. N.D. Econ. Devel. Task Force, N.D. Bd. Equalization; exec. com. Nat. Assn. Tax Adminstrs., 1972-75; mem. exec. com. N.D. Democratic Party. Address: 427 Cannon House Office Bldg Washington DC 20515*

DORGAN, CHARLES EDWARD, mech. engr., educator; b. Cullison, Kans., Apr. 21, 1937; s. John Henry and Mary Margaret (Probst) D.; B.S. in Agrl. Engring., Kans. State U., 1959; M.S. in Mech. Engring., U. Pitts., 1965; Ph.D., U. Wis., 1976; m. Joan Marie Roth, Aug. 10, 1963; children—Marie, Jason, Chad. Engr., John Deere Co., Waterloo, Iowa, 1959-60; commd. 2d lt. USAF, 1960, advanced through grades to maj., 1971; various engring. positions, Wyo., Alaska, Vietnam; course dir. Air Force Inst. Tech., Wright-Patterson AFB, Ohio, 1969-71; ret., 1971; course dir., prof. engring. U. Wis.-Extension, Madison, 1971-77, dir. Energy Tech. Center, 1977—. Decorated Bronze Star, Air Force Commendation medal. Recipient Energy award Dept. Energy, 1980. Mem. ASHRAE, Assn. Energy Engrs. (nat. v.p. 1978-79, Energy award 1979), Am. Soc. Agrl. Engrs., ASME, Nat. Soc. Profl. Engrs., Wis. Soc. Profl. Engrs., Am. Conf. Govt. Indsl. Hygienists, Sigma Xi, Sigma Tau. Republican. Roman Catholic. Home: 305 Valley View St Verona WI 53593 Office: 432 N Lake St Madison WI 53706

DORGAN, ROBERT THOMAS, agrl. tractor mfg. exec.; b. Chgo., Apr. 22, 1925; s. Walter H. and Juanita M. (Corbett) D.; student Sch. Profl. Supr. U. Chgo., 1958-60; B.A., Roosevelt U., 1976; m. Shirley M. Schomer, May 10, 1947; children—Robert Thomas, Linda Lee. With Internat. Harvester Co., 1946—, machine operator, 1946-48, mgmt. trainee, 1948-49, mgr. various positions, Chgo. and Louisville, 1949-73, mgr. mfg. ops. Farmall Plant, Rock Island, Ill., 1973—. Jr. Achievement advisor, Chgo., 1953-55; active Big Bro. program, Chgo., 1958-59; dir. Holy Name Soc., Chgo., 1959-63; mem. adv. bd. Salvation Army, Rock Island, Ill., 1976—; bd. dirs. Upper Rock Island YMCA, 1979—; trustee Franciscan Hosp., Rock Island, 1980—. Served with U.S. Army, 1943-46. Named Man of Year for youth work St. Turibius Cath. Ch., Chgo., 1961; named Father of Year Chgo. Tribune, 1962. Mem. Am. Soc. Quality Control (sr.), Soc. Automotive Engrs., Soc. Mfg. Engrs. (cert. mfg. engr.), Am. Def. Preparedness Assn. (bd. dirs. Iowa-Ill chpt. 1977—). Roman Catholic. Home: 3507 21st St Rock Island IL 61201 Office: 500 42d St Rock Island IL 61201

DORIWALA, BAQARALI AHMADALI, engr.; b. Bhadsura, India, Apr. 10, 1950; s. Ahmadali Safderali and Bhuribai Ahmadali (Hasanali) D.; came to U.S., 1971, naturalized, 1975; B.M.E. cum laude (Open Merit scholar), Villanova U., 1973; M.M.E., Ill. Inst. Tech., 1977; M.B.A., Baldwin Wallace Coll., 1978; m. Jophin Khokawala, Mar. 11, 1976; children—Moiz B., Mansoor B., Lubaina B. Salesman Sherwin-Williams Co., Phila., 1971-73, project engr., Chgo., 1973-76, Cleve., 1976-79; div. engring. rep. SCM Corp., Cleve., 1979-81, mgr. project engring., Joliet, Ill., 1981—. Registered profl. engr., Ohio, Calif. NSF research fellow, 1972. Mem. Tau Beta Pi, Pi Tau Sigma. Moslem. Contbr. articles to profl. jours. Home: 712 Timber Trail Naperville IL Office: PO Box 796 Joliet IL 60464

DORMAN, JAMES LEE, business exec.; b. Jerome, Idaho, Dec. 10, 1932; s. James E. and Ilena (Johnson) D.; B.B.S., Idaho State U., 1955; M.B.A., U. Denver, 1960; m. Beverly Charlotte Owen, Dec. 19, 1953;children—Dee Ann Lynn, James Lee, Michelle Jean. Comml. audit mgr. Arthur Andersen & Co., Chgo., 1960-66; corporate controller Foote, Cone & Belding, Inc., Chgo., 1966-68; controller UIP Corp., Milw., 1968—, exec. v.p., 1969-71, pres., 1971-74; v.p. dir. Super Steel Products Corp., Milw., 1974-76, now dir.; pres., Marquette Capital Co., Milw., 1974-76; pres., chief exec. officer Kempsmith Machine Co., Milw., Zerand Corp., New Berlin, Wis.; chmn. bd. Hough Mfg. Corp., Janesville, Wis.; dir. Automatic Fire Protection Corp. Wis., Inc., Buckstaff Co., Oshkosh, Wis. Bd. dirs. Lakeland Coll., Sheboygan, Wis. to 1977. Served to lt. AUS, 1955-59. Recipient Armed Forces Chem. Assn. award, 1953. Mem. Ill., Wis. socs. C.P.A.'s, Am. Inst. C.P.A.'s, Wis. Mfrs. Assn., Young Pres.'s Orgn. Clubs: Western Racquet (Elm Grove, Wis.), Univ. Home: 2140 Elm Tree Rd Elm Grove WI 53122

DORN, ALVA LOUIS, newspaper editor; b. N.Y.C., Nov. 16, 1911; s. George Alva and Janet (Schmidt) D.; student U. Mo., 1929-31; m. Edna May Lucas, July 11, 1936; 1 dau., Maryrose (Mrs. Roger E. Hopkins). City editor Schenectady Union-Star, 1940-43, news editor, 1943-46; mng. editor Monroe (Mich.) Evening News, 1946-48; picture editor Kalamazoo Gazette, 1948-77, photo columnist, 1959—; photography columnist Saginaw (Mich.) News, Toledo Blade, Owensboro (Ky.) Messenger-Inquirer, Muskegon (Mich.) Chronicle; condr. weekly photog. program Sta. WUHQ-TV, Battle Creek-Kalamazoo, radio AM-93, Battle Creek; instr. photography Kalamazoo Community Sch. for Adults, 1952-74, Kalamazoo Valley Community Coll., 1974—; photog. writer, lectr., exhibitor, judge. Bd. dirs. Kalamazoo Home for Aged, 1954-60, Kalamazoo Inst. Arts, 1960-64. Winner black and white print competition U.S. Camera mag., 1960; recipient Outstanding Journalism award Kalamazoo Woman's Club, 1978. Fellow Photog. Soc. Am. (editor Camera Club Bull. 1959-61, chmn. Western Mich. chpt. 1962-63), New Pictorialist Soc.; mem. Photo Guild Kalamazoo (pres., founder), Mich. Press Assn. (pres. editorial div. 1949-50), Kalamazoo Camera Hobbyists (pres., founder 1952), Nat. Press Photographers Assn. (life mem.; Bert Williams award 1976), Pi Kappa Alpha. Episcopalian. Clubs: Torch, Masons. Author: One-Minute Photo Lessons, 1980. Home: 3823 Dale St Kalamazoo MI 49001

DORN, GARY RAYMOND, printing co. exec.; b. Chgo., Apr. 8, 1933; s. Fred H. and Freida H. (Wagner) D.; student Western Res. U., 1961-62; m. Elsie Marie Walledom, June 5, 1953; children—Lynn, Karen, Bradley, Robert, Paul. Salesman, Redson-Rice Corp., Chgo., 1952-56; v.p., sales mgr. D.F. Keller Co., Chgo., 1956-64; pres., dir. Bradley Printing Co., Elmhurst, Ill., 1964—; v.p. Interpac Corp., Wheeling, Ill.; dir. 1st Nat. Bank of Lake Zurich (Ill.). Bd. dirs. Summit Sch., Dundee, Ill., 1972-78. Served with USAF, 1950-52. Mem. Printing Industry of Ill. Club: Inverness Country. Home: 1931 Camphill Circle Dr Inverness IL 60067 Office: 730 Oak Lawn Elmhurst IL 60126

DORN, GORDON HERMAN, lab. exec.; b. Mt. Calvary, Wis., Mar. 4, 1935; s. Herman John and Louise (Schaefer) D.; grad. public schs.; m. Mary Claire Pilon, Nov. 26, 1956; children—Ann, Sheila, Mike, Vicki, Pat, Lisa. With Ozite Corp., Milw., 1957; with Albert Trostel & Son, Milw., 1957-69, hide buyer, 1969; dir. purchasing Chris Hansens Lab. Inc., Milw., 1969—; cons. by-products meat industry. Trustee, dir. Catholic Knights Ins. Served with AUS, 1953-55. Mem. Soc. Packaging and Handling Engrs., Am. Purchasing Soc., Pvt. Truckers Soc. Republican. Roman Catholic. Home: W 142 N 6769 Washington Menomonee Falls WI 53051 Office: 9015 W Maple St Milwaukee WI 53214

DORN, RALPH EARL, educator; b. Appleton, Wis., Jan. 31, 1945; s. Ralph Joseph and Ethel Theresa (Kloes) D.; B.S., U. Wis., Oshkosh, 1971; M.S., U. Wis., Milw., 1973, postgrad., 1975; Ed.D., Nova U., Ft. Lauderdale, 1979. Regular substitute tchr. Milw. Pub. Schs., 1973-74; reading specialist Unified Sch. Dist. 1, Fredonia, Wis., 1974-79; reading specialist, speed reading instr. Milw. Area Tech. Coll., 1975-79; supr. adult basic edn. and goal-oriented adult learning (GOAL) Moraine Park Tech. Inst., 1979—, speed-reading instr., 1980—. Active, Big Bros. Am. Recipient Youth of Month award Appleton Optimist Club, 1963. Mem. Wis. Reading Assn. (exec. bd. 1977-78), Washington-Ozaukee Reading Council (sec. 1976-78), Wis. Assn. Adult and Continuing Edn., Phi Delta Kappa. Contbr. articles to profl. jours. Home: 862 Kings Ct Fond du Lac WI 54935 Office: Moraine Park Tech Inst 235 N National Ave Fond du Lac WI 54935

DORNBROCK, WILLIAM LEE, mech. engr.; b. Detroit, Feb. 25, 1942; s. William C. and Margaret A. (Ettle) D.; B.M.E., Lawrence Inst. Tech., 1966; M.B.A., Wayne State U., 1977. Project engr. Pioneer Engring. Co., 1959-64; owner, pres. Maranco Co., Sterling, Mich., 1964-66; sr. design engr. Fisher Body div. Gen. Motors Corp., Warren, Mich., 1966-69; sales application engr. Eaton Corp., Southfield, Mich., 1969-72; engring. mgr. Chrysler Corp., Detroit, 1972-81; owner, pres. Maranco Inc., Sterling, Mich., 1981—. Bd. commrs. Lennox County, Mich., 1970-74. Mem. Soc. Automotive Engrs., Am. Soc. Body Engrs., Am. Soc. Plastics Engrs. Club: North Channel Yacht. Home: 11825 Seaton St Sterling Heights MI 48077 Office: 11825 Seaton St Sterling Heights MI 48077

DORNER, HELEN MARGARET, hosp. exec., nurse; b. N.Y.C., Mar. 9, 1932; d. Joseph Matthew and Margaret (Maga) D.; R.N., Meth. Hosp. Sch. Nursing, 1953; B.S. in Personnel Mgmt., Chgo. State U., 1975. Staff nurse Meth. Hosp., Bklyn., 1953-59; nurse spring tng., summer camp Bklyn. Dodgers, 1955-57; staff nurse Wesley Pavilion, Northwestern Meml. Hosp., Chgo., 1957-59, head nurse, 1959-61, supr., 1961-75, dir. central service, 1975—; v.p., treas. mgmt. M.J. Bollock & Assos., Inc., Mgmt. Cons., Oakbrook Terrace, Ill., 1978—. Mem. Am. Hosp. Assn., Luth. Med. Mission Assn. (pres. Chgo. chpt. 1974—), Chgo. Assn. of Hosp. Central Service Personnel. Republican. Lutheran. Home: 1 S 95 Spring Rd Oakbrook Terr Elmhurst IL 60126 Office: Northwestern Meml Hosp Fairbanks and Superior Sts Chicago IL 60611

DORNER, JOSEPH LAWRENCE, vet. clin. pathologist, educator; b. Dover, Del., Mar. 2, 1936; s. Joseph Matthew and Margaret (Maga) D.; A.A.S., State U. N.Y., 1954; B.S., U. Ill., 1962, M.S., 1965, D.V.M., 1964, Ph.D., 1968; m. Marianne Nachum, Aug. 30, 1958; children—Joseph Philip, Kurt Matthew. Clinician, Small Animal Medicine, U. Ill. Coll. Veterinary Medicine, 1968, clin. pathologist, 1969—. Recipient Distinguished Teaching award, 1972, Alumni Merit award, 1973. Mem. Am., Ill. State, Eastern Ill. vet. med. assns., Am. Soc. Vet. Clin. Pathologists (chmn. consultation com. 1970-71), Am. Assn. Vet. Clinicians, Omega Tau Sigma, Phi Zeta (pres. 1971), Gamma Sigma Delta, Sigma Xi. Contbr. articles to sci. jours. Office: Sch Veterinary Medicine U Ill Urbana IL 61801

DORNSEIF, ALLAN WALTER, ednl. adminstr.; b. Chgo., Apr. 14, 1931; s. Arlie Christian and Anna Elvira (Holmgreen) D.; B.A., DePaul U., 1956, M.Ed., 1967; Ed.D., No. Ill. U., 1975; m. Georgia Jean Trojahn, Mar. 24, 1956; children—Elise, Keith, Scott, Ursula, Christiann. Tchr., The Day Sch., Chgo., 1956-58, Chgo. Public Schs., 1958-60; tchr. Calumet Sch. Dist. 132, Calumet Park, Ill., 1960-65, prin., 1965-67; curriculum dir. Matteson (Ill.) Sch. Dist. 162, 1967-69, asst. supt., 1969—; adj. prof. Nat. Coll. Edn., Evanston, Ill., 1980—. Mem. Bd. Edn. Summit Hill Dist. 161, Will County, 1966-70; liaison to Park Forest (Ill.) Human Relations Commn., 1974—. Served with U.S. Army, 1951-53. Mem. Assn. Supervision and Curriculum Devel. (dir. 1978-82), Ill. Assn. Supervision and Curriculum Devel. (pres. 1980-81), S. Suburban Curriculum Assn., Am. Ednl. Research Assn., Council Exceptional Children, Assn. Gifted. Author: Relationship of Achievement and Self-Concept to Open Education, 1975; contbr. articles to profl. jours. Home: 445 Homan St Park Forest IL 60466 Office: 21244 Illinois St Matteson IL 60443

DOROSCHAK, JOHN Z., dentist; b. Solochiw, Ukraine, Feb. 11, 1928; s. William and Anna (Stroczan) D.; came to U.S., 1950, naturalized, 1954; student U. Minn., 1955-57, B.S., 1959, D.D.S., 1961; m. Nadia Zahorodny, June 30, 1962; children—Andrew, Michael, Natalie, Maria. Pvt. practice dentistry, Mpls., 1961—. Cons., St. Joseph's Home for Aged, Mpls., 1974-77, Holy Family Residence, St. Paul, 1977—. Mem. steering com. St. Anthony West Neighborhood, Mpls., 1971-72; chmn. Mpls. dentists com. Little Sisters of the Poor Devel. Program, 1975; Webelos leader troop 50, Boy Scouts Am., 1975-76; pres. N.E. Regional Sch. Assn. Parents and Tchrs., 1978-79; bd. dirs. East Side Neighborhood Service, 1972; treas. Plast Inc., Ukrainian youth orgn., Mpls., 1979—; mem. Sr. Citizen Centers Health Adv. Com., Mpls., 1979—. Served with AUS, 1953-55. Mem. Am. Dental Assn., Minn. Dental Assn. (com. on dental care access 1980—), Minn. Soc. Preventive Dentistry (dir. 1977—, treas. 1979-81), Am. Soc. Dentistry for Children, Mpls. Dist. Dental Soc. (nursing home subcom. 1974—, chmn. 1979), Minn. chpt. Ukrainian Med. Assn. (sec. treas. 1971-75), Ukrainian Profl. Club, Psi Omega. Mem. Ukrainian Catholic Ch. (campaign chmn. 1966-80, mem. ch. com. 1965—). Club: University Minnesota Alumni (charter mem.). Home: 919 Main St NE Minneapolis MN 55413 Office: Broadway and University Profl Bldg 230 NE Broadway Minneapolis MN 55413

DOROTHY, LOU ANN, lawyer; b. Mt. Vernon, Ill., July 19, 1925; d. Obe A. and B. Eva (Milburn) Grant; B.S. in Law, U. Ill., 1947; m. Morton F. Dorothy, Jr., Dec. 7, 1946 (dec. May 1963); children—Morton F. III, Syren Jo (Mrs. Claude R. McElvain), John J., Sarah F. (Mrs. John E. Lee). Admitted to Ill. bar, 1949; mem. firm Dorothy & Dorothy, Mt. Vernon, 1949-67, Lou Ann Dorothy, Mt. Vernon, 1971-76; asst. dir. Womble Mountain Legal Aid, Harrisburg, Ill., 1967-68; info. rep. to dir. personnel State of Ill., 1968; staff atty. Peoria (Ill.) Legal Aid, 1968-69; asst. and acting dir. Legal Aid Jackson and Williamson County (Ill.), 1969-71; exec. dir. Jefferson County Housing Authority, 1975-78; individual practice law, 1978—; various positions in fields law, bus., journalism and investigation; certified housing dir. Bd. dirs. Jefferson County Found. for Vision and Learning Disorders. Mem. Ill., Jefferson County bar assns., Ill. Sheriffs Assn., Internat. Platform Assn., Am. Legion Aux. (pres. 1950), DAV Aux., Bus. and Profl. Women's Club (sec. Peoria luncheon group 1969), U. Ill. Alumni Assn. (life), Smithsonian Instn., Am. Contract Bridge League, Alpha Xi Delta. Presbyterian. Club: Order Amaranth (historian). Home and Office: Route 1 Texico IL 62889

DORRANCE, WILLIAM HENRY, engr., corp. exec.; b. Highland Park, Mich., Dec. 3, 1921; s. William Henry and Bernice (Updike) D.; B.S.E., U. Mich., 1947, M.S.E., 1948; Sc.D., Occidental U., St. Louis, 1978; m. Janet Rogers, Aug. 30, 1946; children—Cynthia Ann, Rebecca Hall, William Henry, Jay Bolton. Chief, aerodynamics Aero. Research Center, U. Mich., Ann Arbor, 1947-51, Convair Div. Gen. Dynamics Corp., San Diego, 1951-55; sr. staff scientist Convair Gen. Offices, San Diego, 1955-61; group dir. Aerospace Corp., Los Angeles, 1961-64; v.p. Conductron Corp. Ann Arbor, 1964-69, dir., 1965-69; chmn., chief operating officer Interface Systems Corp., 1967-70; pres. Orgn. Control Services Corp., Ann Arbor, 1970—. Div. leader United Fund Drive, Northridge, Calif., Ann Arbor, 1964-65. Vice pres. San Diego Young Republicans, 1952-53. Mem. vestry St. Dustan's Ch., 1952-55. Served with USAF, 1943-45. Decorated air medal, 5 oak leaf clusters, presdl. unit citation. Recipient citation Am. Rocket Soc. San Diego sect., 1958. Mem. Ann Arbor C. of C. (dir.), Nat. Fedn. Ind. Bus's, Sigma Xi, Phi Kappa Phi, Theta Chi. Episcopalian. Club: Barton Hills Country (dir., treas. 1976-78, pres. 1978-79). Author: Viscous Hypersonic Flow, 1962. Contbr. numerous articles to profl. jours. Patentee in field. Home: 11 Heatheridge St Ann Arbor MI 48104 Office: OCS Inc 1925 Pauline Blvd Ann Arbor MI 48103

DORSCH, ROBERT EUGENE, mech. engr.; b. South Bend, Ind., June 30, 1931; s. Francis J. and Ethel H. (Horvath) D.; A.S., Acme Inst. Tech., 1955; B.S.M.E., Pacific Internat. Colls. Arts and Scis., 1961, M.S.M.E., 1968; B.S. in Math., Cooks Inst. Electronics Engring., 1971; postgrad. U. Wis., 1977; m. Joann Ruth Rawles, July 2, 1955; children—Candis, Julie, Robby. Designer automation machinery Rockwell Corp., 1959-61; project engr. Uniroyal, Inc., Mishawaka, Ind., 1961-70, sr. engr. stress analysis and design, 1970-79, chief engr. marine products design, 1979—. Served with USMC, 1950-53. Registered profl. engr., Ind. Mem. Nat. Soc. Profl. Engrs., Ind. Soc. Profl. Engrs. Republican. Episcopalian. Patentee in field. Office: 312 N Hill St Mishawaka IN 46544

DORSKY, WILLIAM, architect; b. Cleve., Apr. 18, 1932; s. Jack and Mae (Levine) D.; B.Arch., Western Res. U., 1956; children—Sharon, Steven, Robert, Jodi. Architect with Garfield, Harris, Robinson and

Shafer, Cleve., 1956-59; founder, pres. William Dorsky Associates, Inc., Cleve., 1959—, Miami, Fla., 1970—, Los Angeles, 1980—; major archtl. works include: Bonaventure Community, Broward County, Fla., 1973, R.H. Myers Apts., Cleve., 1978, Plaza Venetia, apt., club and hotel, Miami, Fla., 1979, Developers Diversified corp. hdqrs., Cleve., 1979, Villa Regina condominium apts., Miami, 1980. Del. to White House Conf. on Aging, 1981; mem. Miami (Fla.) Jewish Fedn. Com., 1980-81; bd. dirs. Fairmount Temple, Cleve., 1963-66. Recipient Bldg. Design award Ohio Prestressed Concrete Assn., 1966; registered profl. architect, 28 states. Mem. AIA (Bldg. Design award 1976, Award of Excellence 1978, 80), Soc. Am. Registered Architects (Award of Excellence 1978, 80), Am. Assn. Homes for Aging, Western Gerontol. Soc., Nat. Council on Aging, Zeta Beta Tau (chpt. pres. 1953-54). Clubs: Beechmont Country, Millcreek Racquet, Jockey. Office: 23200 Chagrin Blvd Cleveland OH 44122

DORSTE, THOMAS CHARLES, architect; b. Anderson, Ind., Feb. 12, 1923; s. Louis Thomas and Mary Samantha (Haughton) D.; student Ball State U., 1939; B.Arch., Mass. Inst. Tech., 1947; m. Eleanor Claire Edwardson, Apr. 8, 1944; children—Robert Edwardson, Sarah Haughton, Craig Thomas; m. 2d, Sandra Lucas Smith, 1979. Designer, draftsman Anderson & Beckwith, Boston, 1947-50; chief draftsman Burns & Burns Indpls., 1950-53; partner Dorste & Pantazi, Indpls., 1953-59; owner Thomas C. Dorste, Indpls., 1959-61; v.p., treas. James Assos., Indpls., 1961—; pres. James & Berger, architects, engrs., economists, Indpls., 1967— (dir. both firms); dir. James Assos., Vincennes, Lafayette and Fort Wayne, Ind. Mem. econ. devel. com. City Indpls., 1972-75, adv. com. Indpls. Dept. Devel., 1960-65, policy com. City Market, 1974. Mem. ednl. council Mass. Inst. Tech., 1965—, Nat. Trust for Historic Preservation, 1974—, Indpls. Mus. Soc., 1971—, Indpls. Symphony Soc., 1971—. Pres., bd. dirs. Indpls. Leadership Com., 1970-73. Served with C.E., AUS, 1942-46. Mem. A.I.A., Ind. Soc. Architects, Mass. Inst. Tech. Club Ind., Amateur Fencers League Am. Club: Indpls. Fencing. Architect: Ind. U. Univ. Schs., 1963; Greenwood Shopping Center, 1966; Indpls. Regional Postal Facility, 1971; Indpls. Conv. Center, 1972; Ind. U. Retirement Community, 1981; others. Home: 765 W Hawthorne Zionsville IN 46077 Office: 2828 E 45th St Indianapolis IN 46205

DORTCH, RICHARD NEIL, educator; b. Stewart County, Tenn., Feb. 6, 1940; s. Carl and Elizabeth (Cook) D.; B.S., Austin Peay State U., Clarksville, Tenn., 1960; M.S., No. Ill. U., DeKalb, 1967; Ph.D., U. Wis., 1976; m. June 2, 1962; children—Ami Desiree, Geoffrey Lee. Tchr., Dickson (Tenn.) High Sch., 1959-66; faculty No. Ill. U., 1966-68; prof. Coll. Bus. and Econs., U. Wis., Whitewater, 1968—; cons. John Deere Corp., Mercy Hosp. Mem. Nat. Bus. Tchrs. Assn., Wis. Bus. Tchrs. Assn., Milw. Bus. Tchrs. Assn., Delta Pi Epsilon, Gamma Theta Upsilon, Pi Sigma Epsilon. Republican. Methodist. Club: Masons (32 deg.). Editor: Adult Basic Education: The School, Community Clientele, 1968; contbr. articles to profl. jours. Home: 151 S Elizabeth St Whitewater WI 53190 Office: Coll Bus and Econ U Wis Whitewater WI 53190

DORUS, ELIZABETH, psychologist, geneticist; b. Parsons, Kans., Dec. 6, 1940; d. Ronald Oscar and Ethel (Lane) Bankson; B.A., Valparaiso U., 1962; Ph.D., U. Chgo., 1971; M.A., U. Pa., 1975; m. Walter Dorus, Jr., June 30, 1968; children—Stephen. Intern clin. psychology Duke U. Med. Center, 1964-65; consulting psychology Mental Health div. Chgo. Bd. Health, 1967-71; instr. psychology U. Pa., 1972-73, research fellow Found. Fund for Research in Psychiatry, 1972-73; research fellow Ill. State Psychiatric Inst., Chgo., 1974-75; research fellow Nat. Inst. Health dept. medicine U. Chgo., 1975-76, research asso., asst. prof. dept. psychiatry, 1977—. NIMH Research Scientist Devel. award, 1977—. Mem. Am. Psychol. Assn., Am. Soc. Human Genetics, Behavioral Genetics Assn., Soc. Social Biology. Contbr. articles to Archives of Gen. Psychiatry, British Journal of Psychiatry, Science, and others. Office: Dept Psychiatry U Chgo 950 E 59th St Chicago IL 60637

DORWARD, DAVID WILLIAM, mycologist; b. Columbus, Ohio, June 5, 1956; s. Donald Lyle and Helen (Birkett) D.; B.S. in Botany, Miami U., Oxford, Ohio, 1979, M.S. in Botany, 1981. Grad. teaching asst. in botany Miami U., 1979-80; plant pathologist R and T Landscaping Inc., Cin., 1981—. Sigma Xi research grantee, 1980. Mem. Sigma Xi (asso.), Phi Sigma Club: Order of DeMolay. Contbr. articles to profl. jours. Home: 321 1/2 W High St Oxford OH 45056

DORWEILER, PAUL LAWRENCE, electronic engr.; b. Mpls., Jan. 11, 1934; s. Peter Paul and Dora (Peterson) D.; student U. Minn., 1957-58, Mankato State Coll., 1963-64; B.S., Northwestern Electronics, 1959; m. Jean C. Dorweiler, June 6, 1959; children—Kevin, Pamela, Lisa, Kimberly. Fed. electric radician Fed. Elec. Co., Dewline, Alaska, 1959; mgr. Minn. Airmotive Radio-Flying Cloud Fld., Hopkins, Minn., 1960-63; supr. tech. publs. E.F. Johnson Co., Waseca, Minn., 1966-67; mgr. Ben's Aircraft Radio, Waterloo, Iowa, 1967; editor Ojibway Press, Duluth, Minn., 1967-70; free lance writer, 1967—; owner Paul Lawrence & Assos., 1972—; mgr. publs. Telex Corp., Mpls., 1972-76; prodn. engr. S.C. Electronics, Inc., Mpls., 1976-77; mgr. publs. Microcomponent Technology, 1977-80, FMC/NOD, Coon Rapids, Minn., 1981—. Served with USNR, 1954-56. Mem. IEEE, Internat. Platform Assn., Soc. Tech. Communication (certificate of achievement 1975), VFW, Am. Legion, Pilots Internat., Writer's Workshop. Clubs: Minn. Press, Elks, K.C. Home and Office: 10319 Wintergreen St Coon Rapids MN 55433

DOSADO, ELPIDIO ARANAS, microbiologist; b. Sogod, Cebu, Philippines, Feb. 6, 1939; came to U.S., 1951, naturalized, 1973; s. Elpidio Bacayo and Aurelia (Aranas) D.; B.A., Ind. U., 1966; M.S., Miami U. (Ohio), 1968, Ph.D., 1975; m. Jennifer Joan Mucha, June 6, 1967; children—Laura Lisa, Daniel. Predoctoral fellow dept. microbiology Miami U., Oxford, Ohio, 1972-75; postdoctoral investigator biol. chemistry Oak Ridge Asso. Univs., 1975-77; cons., investigator Oak Ridge Nat. Lab., 1975-77; tech. supr. Lab. Research Co. (Labreco), Lansing, Ill., 1977—. Served with USAF, 1957-61. USPHS fellow, 1975-77; Presdl., teaching and doctoral dissertation fellow Miami U., 1972-75; recipient Orton K. Stark award Miami U., 1968. Mem. AAAS, Am. Soc. Microbiology, Sigma Xi. Roman Catholic. Contbr. articles to profl. jours. Home: 6543 Ohio Ave Hammond IN 46323 Office: 800 MacArthur Suite 19 Munster IN 46321

DOSSETT, DENNIS LEE, educator/indsl. psychologist; b. Pensacola, Fla., Feb. 1, 1946; s. Myron George and Lucille Faye (Haskins) D.; B.S. in Edn., U. Idaho, 1969, B.S. in Psychology, 1969; M.S., U. Wash., 1971, Ph.D., 1978; m. Karen Ann Cushing, Mar. 23, 1969; children—Michelle Leigh, Lisa Marie. Behavioral scientist U.S. Air Force, Keesler AFB, Miss., 1971-74; staff psychologist Weyerhaeuser Co., Tacoma, 1976-78; asst. prof. psychology U. Nebr., Omaha, 1978—; cons.; dir. Center Applied Psychol. Services, U. Nebr., Omaha, 1981—. Served with USAF, 1971-74. Decorated Air Force Commendation medal. Mem. Am. Psychol. Assn., Midwest Psychol. Assn., Acad. Mgmt., Midwest Acad. Mgmt. Mem. Christian Ch. of Universal Philosophy. Contbr. articles to profl. jours. Home: 1868 N 150th Ct Omaha NE 68154 Office: Dept Psychology U Nebr Omaha NE 68182

DOSSETT, JON LOREN, heat treating co. exec.; b. Terre Haute, Ind., Jan. 28, 1940; s. Ota Lewis and Grace Ann (Tatlock) D.; B.S. in Metall. Engring., Purdue U., 1965; m. Gwendolyn Jane Brown, Jan. 28, 1961; children—Melissa Jane, Jon Loren, Jennifer. Asst. chief metallurgist Link Belt div. FMC Corp., Indpls., 1965-69; metallurgy mgr. Warner Gear div. Borg Warner Co., Muncie, Ind., 1970-74; supr. metall process control Internat. Harvester Corp., Hinsdale, Ill., 1974-76; div. mgr. Lindberg Heat Treating Co., Melrose Park, Ill., 1977—. Registered profl. engr., Ind., Ill. Mem. Am. Soc. Metals (advisory tech. awareness council 1975—, chmn. div. heat treating 1976—, tech. divs. bd. 1976—), Soc. Automotive Engrs., Am. Foundryman's Soc. Republican. Methodist. Contbr. articles to profl. jours.; chmn. editorial bd. Jour. Heat Treating, 1977—. Home: 941 Valley View Rd Downers Grove IL 60515 Office: 1975 N Ruby St Melrose Park IL 60160

DOTSON, JAMES HUGH, mfg. co. exec.; b. Blount County, Tenn., June 5, 1940; s. James Luther and Leathie Mae (Jones) D.; B.A. (scholar), Morehead State Coll., 1960; M.S.I.E., U. Tenn., 1968; postgrad. Milw. Sch. Engring., 1973-74, U. Ala., Birmingham, 1977-78; m. Hildegard T.M. Denzer, Aug. 18, 1962; children—David H., Lori L. With Eaton, Yale & Towne, Lenior City, Tenn., 1963-68, Procter & Gamble, Albany, Ga., 1968-72, St. Regis Paper Co., Jacksonville, Fla., 1972-77; project engr. Rust Engring. Co., Portland, Oreg., 1977-80; mgr. C.E. Bauer, Springfield, Ohio, 1980—; dir. Project Mgmt.-World Wide. Coordinator, area chmn. Pop Warner Football, Portland. Served with AUS, 1960-63. Levi-Strauss fellow, 1963-68. Mem. TAPPI, ASME, Can. Pulp and Paper Assn. Republican. Episcopalian. Home: 2255 Ballentine Pike Springfield OH 45502 Office: PO Box 968 Springfield OH 45501

DOTTERER, LEWIS LEROY, sch. psychometrist; b. Kokomo, Ind., Apr. 8, 1952; s. Lewis Jacob and Marjorie Pauline (Henry) D.; B.S., Ball State U., Muncie, Ind., 1974, M.A., 1976; postgrad. counseling psychology Mich. State U., 1977—; m. Phoebe Beth Shotton, Nov. 24, 1974. Orderly, Logansport (Ind.) State Hosp., 1971; grad. asst. ednl. psychology Ball State U., 1974-75, grad. asst. counseling center, 1975-76; intern in sch. psychometry, Anderson and Muncie, Ind., also police screening, Muncie, psychometric tester physically handicapped children Isanogel Rehab. Center, 1975-76; sch. psychometrist Whitley County Schs., Columbia City, Ind., 1976-77; cons. Whitley County Assn. Mentally Retarded; teaching asst. Mich. State U., 1977-78, asst. coordinator undergrad. edn. course, 1978-79, doctoral intern Counseling Center, 1979-81; prevention specialist Region 13 Substance Abuse Prevention Edn. Program, Lansing, Mich., 1979-80; asst. tchr. coll. Edn., Mich. State U., 1980-82; instr. Lansing Community Coll., 1981—. researcher adult adjustment patterns. Sunday sch. tchr. Pennway Ch. of God, Lansing, also mem. bd. Family Life Center. Mem. Am. Psychol. Assn., Am. Personnel and Guidance Assn., Mich. Personnel and Guidance Assn., Assn. Counselor Edn. and Supervision, Phi Delta Kappa. Mem. Ch. of God-Anderson, Ind. Home: 1624 C Spartan Village East Lansing MI 48823 Office: 301 Erickson Hall Mich State Univ East Lansing MI 48823

DOTY, STEWART WALTER, graphic designer; b. Wausau, Wis., Feb. 1, 1949; s. Spencer Whitney and Barbara Anne (McClure) D.; B.F.A., Mpls. Coll. Art and Design, 1972; m. Johanna Jonas, Oct. 7, 1972. Staff photographer Becker Studios, Wausau, 1972-74; photographer Maracomm Advt., Wausau, 1974-75; info. officer A. Ward Ford Meml. Inst., Wausau, 1975-76; art dir. Marathon Press Co., Inc., Wausau, 1976-81; art dir. Creative Dimensions Advt., Appleton, Wis., 1981—. Served with USAR, 1972-78. Mem. Minn. Graphic Designers Assn. (dir., 2d v.p. 1980), Soc. Typographic Arts, Nat. Motorsports Press Assn. Sr. editor Stock Car Racing mag., 1975—. Home: 725 D Starboard Ct W Oshkosh WI 54901

DOTZENROD, JAMES ALLEN, farmer, state legislator; b. Breckinridge, Minn., Dec. 14, 1946; s. Ralph Clarence and Erma Martha (Feistner) D.; A.S., N.D. State Sch. Sci., 1966; B.S.E.E., N.D. State U., 1968; student Squadron Officers Sch., 1971. Owner, operator farm, Wyndmere, N.D., 1972—; mem. N.D. Senate, 1978—. Chmn., Wyndmere Airport Authority, 1976—; past pres. Wyndmere Community Club, 1979; mem. council Wyndmere Lutheran Ch. Served to capt. USAF, 1968-72, with Air N.G., 1973. Mem. Aircraft Owners and Pilots Assn., Am. Legion. Democrat. Club: Elks (Fargo, N.D.).

DOUBLE, PAUL BERNARD, warehousing and transp. services co. exec., sporting goods mfg. co. exec.; b. Stratford, Ont., Can., Oct. 9, 1941; came to U.S., 1952, naturalized, 1962; s. Bernard Theodore and Eleanor Marie (Nelson) D.: student St. Clair County Community Coll., 1965-68, San Diego City Coll., 1961-65; m. Norma Matar, May 11, 1968; children—John Paul, Eric Nelson, Matthew Matar. Area sales mgr. Diamond Crystal Salt Co., Winona, Minn., 1965-73; pres. Canamer Corp., Winona, 1973-75; pres., chmn. Internat Canamer Inc., Winona, 1974—; pres. Cover America, Inc., Winona, 1979—; chmn. bd. Cover America, Inc. Chmn. Winona Twp. Bd. Suprs., 1970-81; treas. Winona Area Ambulance Service Bd., 1975-80. Bd. dirs. Winona Public Schs., 1981—. Served with USN, 1959-62. Mem. Indsl. Fabrics Assn. Internat., Nat. Assn. Sporting Goods Mfrs. Republican. Episcopalian. Patentee in field. Home: Two Glen Mary Rd Winona MN 55987 Office: Airport Office Plaza PO Box 38 Winona MN 55987

DOUBLEDAY, STEPHEN JAMES, plastics co. exec.; b. Kansas City, Mo., Apr. 5, 1948; s. Floyd E. and Janet E. (Strain) D.; B.S. in Bus. Adminstrn., Rockhurst Coll., 1971; m. Michele L. Lowe, Apr. 19, 1975; children—Allison Michele, Adam Taylor. Sr. auditor Arthur Andersen & Co., Kansas City, Mo., 1970-74; asst. controller Conchemco Inc., Lenexa, Kans., 1974-77; controller Plastic Sales & Mfg. Co. Inc., Kansas City, Mo., 1977-81, v.p. fin., chief fin. officer, 1981—; dir. Popplewell & Co., Kansas City, Mo. Mem. Internat. Mgmt., Processing, and Reporting System Users Group (pres.), Beta Sigma Tau. Republican. Baptist. Home: 7000 Rene Shawnee KS 66216

DOUGAN, ALBERTA MACKE, educator; b. Cape Girardeau, Mo., Nov. 5, 1945; d. Albert Henry and Dorothy E. (Probst) M.; B.S.Ed., S.E. Mo. State U., 1967; M.A. in Modern European History, U. Mo., Columbia, 1971; postgrad. in social studies edn. (Alpha Xi Delta Alumni scholar) Ind. U., Bloomington, 1979—; m. R. Neil Dougan, July 17, 1971. Tchr. social studies Jackson (Mo.) High Sch., 1967-69, Hickman High Sch., Columbia, 1970-71, Cape Girardeau Central High Sch., spring 1972; asst. prof. edn. assigned as tchr., supr. social studies Univ. High Sch., S.E. Mo. State U., 1972—; sec.-treas. Alpha Xi Delta Bldg. Corp. Recipient Francis T. Kuechenmeister award Alpha Xi Delta, 1968, Outstanding Young Educator award Cape Girardeau Jaycees, 1978. Mem. S.E. Mo. Council Social Studies (pres. 1977-78, chairperson dist. social studies fair 1978-79), Mo. Council Social Studies, Nat. Council Social Studies, Assn. Supervision and Curriculum Devel., Nat. Assn. Lab. Schs., Mo. State Tchrs. Assn., S.E. Mo. State U. Community Tchrs. Assn. (sec.-treas. 1981-82), Kappa Delta Pi, Alpha Delta Kappa, Phi Alpha Theta. Methodist. Home: 505 N High St Jackson MO 63755 Office: Univ High Sch SE Mo State U Cape Girardeau MO 63701

DOUGHERTY, CHARLES RICHARD, ceramics co. exec.; b. Cairo, Ill., Sept. 19, 1931; s. Charles Russell and Ellis Etta (Cullum) D.; B.S. E.E., U. Ill., 1957; postgrad. Syracuse U., 1958, Harvard U., 1962; m. Betty L. Phillips, July 21, 1951; children—Carol Lynn Dougherty Moffitt, Christi Rae Dougherty Daugherty, Carla Ann, Caren Lea. Engr. ballast dept. Gen. Electric, Danville, Ill., 1957-62, application engr., product planner Gen. Electric Miniature Lamp Div., Cleve., 1962-69; dir. sales, Gen. Instruments/Signalite Div. for lamps, Neptune, N.J., 1969-73; div. gen. mgr. Hadley (Pa.) Components Div. GTI Corp., 1973-76; v.p., gen. mgr. Diamonite Products Div., Spartek, Inc., Shreve, Ohio, 1976—; pvt. practice mktg. and engring. cons., 1974-76; dir. Savs. and Loan Assn. Dir. Credit Union; scoutmaster Piankeshaw Council Boy Scouts Am., 1959-62; bd. dirs. United Way; trustee NE Ohio Emergency Service. Served with USMC and USMCR, 1951-57. Registered profl. engr., Ill. Mem. IEEE, Ceramics Assn., C. of C. Republican. Methodist. Club: Rotary. Author, co-editor Glow Lamp Manual, 1962, 63; editor Solid State Lamp Manual, 1968; patentee. Home: 1540 Saunders Wooster OH 44691 Office: 453 McConkey St Shreve OH 44676

DOUGHERTY, DANIEL JOSEPH, banker; b. Pitts., Aug. 28, 1931; s. Robert Joseph and Margaret Claire (McMahon) D.; B.A., Duquesne U., 1954; m. Rose Marie Boyle, May 30, 1954; children—Dennis, Colleen, Mary, Daniel. Advt. asst. Rockwell Mfg. Co., Pitts., 1957; asst. advt. mgr. Calgon Co., Pitts., 1958-62; account exec. Marsteller Inc., Pitts., 1962-64; v.p. mktg. Pitts. Nat. Bank, 1964-74; v.p. mktg. Union Commerce Corp., Cleve., 1974—; sr. v.p. mktg. and retail banking Union Commerce Bank, Cleve. 1975—. Bd. dirs. Playhouse Sq. Assn., Downtown Bus. Council, Real Property Inventory Assn.; co-chmn. Cleve. Research Council. Served with USAF, 1954-57. Mem. Am. Mktg. Assn., Am. Banking Assn., Sales and Mktg. Execs. Assn., Bank Mktg. Assn., Bank Adminstrn. Inst. Clubs: Cleve. Athletic, Walden Golf, Communicators. Office: Union Commerce Bank Union Commerce Bldg Cleveland OH 44115

DOUGHMAN, JAMES CLAYTON, public affairs exec.; b. Cleve., Sept. 8, 1927; s. Harold C. and Ruth (Burgess) D.; student Ohio U., 1946-50; m. Jane Adair Willis, Apr. 11, 1953; children—James Clayton, Thomas Willis. Various indsl. sales and mgmt. positions Gen. Motors, Cleve., 1950, Ford Motor Co., Cleve., 1950, Kaiser Aluminum Co., Cleve., 1954-65; dir. public affairs Nordson Corp., Amherst, Ohio, 1966—. Active in fund raising drives for United Way, Jr. Achievement, Salvation Army and other community orgns., 1970—; v.p. Firelands area council Boy Scouts Am., 1970—; mem. Cityview Building Adv. Com., Lorain, 1970-77; bd. dirs. Elyria Salvation Army, 1974-79, Ohio Citizens Council for Health and Welfare, 1973—. Served with USN, 1944-46. Named Man of Year, Amherst Women's League, 1977. Mem. Ohio C. of C., U.S. C. of C., Amherst C. of C., Elyria C. of C. (dir. 1979), Nat. Alliance Businessmen Lorain County (met. dir. 1970-71). Republican. Home: 736 Wagar Rd Rocky River OH 44116 Office: Nordson Corp 555 Jackson St PO Box 151 Amherst OH 44001

DOUGLAS, GEORGE HALSEY, educator; b. East Orange, N.J., Jan. 9, 1934; s. Halsey M. and Harriet Elizabeth (Goldbach) D.; A.B. with honors in Philosophy, Lafayette Coll., 1956; M.A., Columbia U., 1966; Ph.D., U. Ill., 1968; m. Rosalind Braun, June 19, 1961; 1 son, Philip. Tech. editor Bell Telephone Labs., Whippany, N.J., 1958-59; editor Agrl. Expt. Sta., U. Ill., Urbana, 1961-66, instr. Dept. English, 1966-68, asst. prof. English, 1968-77, asso. prof. English, 1977—. Mem. Am. Studies Assn., MLA, Am. Bus. Communication Assn. Author: H.L. Mencken Critic of American Life, 1978; The Teaching of Business Communication, 1978; Rail City: Chicago and Its Railroads, 1981; editor Jour. Bus. Communication, 1968—; contbr. articles to profl. jours. Home: 1514 Grandview Dr Champaign IL 61820 Office: Dept English English Bldg U Ill Urbana IL 61801

DOUGLAS, LEONARD, ednl. adminstr.; b. Detroit, Aug. 8, 1931; s. Andrew and Zoda Mae (Sutton) D.; B.S., Ala. State U., 1954; M.Ed., Wayne State U., 1964; Ph.D., U. Mich., 1969; m. Julia Lee Peters, Nov. 17, 1956; children—Dwayne Elden, Andrea Denise, Daryl Edwin. Tchr., Barbour Sch., Detroit Public Schs., 1957-62, counselor, 1962-66, regional coordinator basic adult edn., 1965-67, coordinator youth work-tng. programs, 1966-68, asst. prin., 1968-70, secondary prin., 1970-71, 72—; prof. dept. edn.-psychology Ky. State Coll., Frankfort, 1971-72. Bd. dirs. Maintenance Central for Seniors, 1980—, Lula Belle Stewart Single Parent Center, 1974-76; active Afro-Am. Mus. Detroit. Served with U.S. Army, 1954-56. Mott Community Edn. fellow U. Mich., 1967-68. Mem. Nat. Community Sch. Edn. Assn., AAUP, Detroit Assn. Sch. Adminstrs. and Suprs., Met. Detroit Soc. Black Edn. Adminstrs., Detroit Jr. High and Middle Sch. Prins. Assn., Met. Detroit Schoolmen's Club, Phi Delta Kappa, Omega Psi Phi. Clubs: Kiwanis, Lafayette Park (Detroit). Contbr. articles to profl. jours. Home: 20015 Prest St Detroit MI 48235 Office: 2322 Dubois St Detroit MI 48207

DOUGLAS, MARK EDWARD, air force officer; b. Tampa, Fla., Aug. 2, 1950; s. Jack Hilton and Mary Elizabeth (Brogan) D.; B.S., Colo. State U., 1975; M.B.A., So. Ill. U., 1979; m. Carol Ann Zuleger, Sept. 26, 1968; children—Celeste Angela, Patrick Edward. Enlisted U.S. Air Force, 1969, advanced through grades to capt., 1979; aircraft maintenance control officer, Altus AFB, Okla., 1976-79; aircraft maintenance spl. projects officer Hdqrs. SAC, Offutt AFB, Nebr., 1979-80, chief Aircraft Data Br. Hdqrs., 1981—. Mem. Air Force Assn., Beta Gamma Sigma. Baptist. Home: 3420 Duane Ave Omaha NE 68123

DOUGLAS, PAUL LOUIS, state ofcl.; b. Sioux Falls, S.D., Sept. 19, 1927; s. Louis Paul and Victoria (Karavaselis) D.; B.S., U. Nebr., 1951, J.D., 1953. Admitted to Nebr. bar, 1953; individual practice law, Lincoln, 1953-56; with County Atty.'s Office, Lancaster County, Lincoln, 1956-74, chief dep. county atty., 1959-60, county atty., 1960-74; atty. gen. Nebr., Lincoln, 1975—. Served with USMC, 1945-47. Mem. Nebr., Lincoln bar assns., Nat. Assn. Attys. Gen., Midwest Attys. Gen. (chmn.), Am. Legion, Lincoln C. of C. Republican. Greek Orthodox. Clubs: Masons (32 deg.), Shriners, Order Eastern Star, Elks. Office: Office of Atty Gen Dept of Justice State House Lincoln NE 68509*

DOUGLASS, CLYDE MILTON, JR., elec. engr.; b. Salem, Mo., Mar. 23, 1945; s. Clyde Milton and Olive Mae (Preston) D.; B.S. in Elec. Engring., U. Mo., Rolla, 1968; m. Wilma Elaine Parrish, July 26, 1969; 1 dau., Deborah Ann. Staff, U. Mo., 1968-70; gen. mgr. Am. Tuner Service, Columbia, Mo., 1970-73; chief engr. Ramada Inn., Columbia, 1974-77; asso. dir. plant facilities Iowa Meth. Med. Center, Des Moines, from 1977; now dir. plant ops. St. Luke's Meth. Hosp., Cedar Rapids, Iowa. Registered profl. engr., Mo., Iowa. Mem. Nat. Soc. Profl. Engrs., IEEE, ASHRAE, Nat. Fire Protection Assn., Am. Soc. Hosp. Engring. Mem. Ch. of God. Home: PO Box 2355 Cedar Rapids IA 52406

DOUGLASS, JEAN HALL, Realtor; b. St. Louis, Oct. 23, 1946; s. Jean Hall and Helen Regina (Walsh) D.; A.B., St. Louis U., 1968; grad. Realtors Inst.; m. Mary Constance Dulle, Dec. 28, 1968; children—Michael Christopher, Elizabeth Anne, Gregory John, Kathleen Mary. Tchr. Am. Govt., McCluer High Sch., St. Louis, 1968-69; asso. Ira E. Berry, Inc., St. Louis, 1969-74, v.p., 1972-74;

founder J.H. Douglass, Realtor, St. Louis, 1974-80, Wolk/Douglass, Inc., Realtors, St. Louis, 1980-81; dir. tax shelter investments Stifal, Nicolaus & Co., Inc., St. Louis, 1981—; instr. real estate licensing courses Real Estate Bd. Met. St. Louis Pre-License Sch., 1975—, dean faculty, dir. edn., 1977-79; partner Wolk/Douglass Real Estate Courses, 1976—. Mem. Nat. Assn. Realtors, Mo. Assn. Realtors (dir.), Real Estate Bd. Met. St. Louis (dir. 1977-79), Farm and Land Inst. (accredited mem.), Real Estate Securities and Syndication Inst. (pres. 1981). Home: 730 Crab Thicket Ln Des Peres Saint Louis MO 63131

DOURLAIN, ROBERT JOSEPH, cosmetic co. exec.; b. Oak Park, Ill., May 12, 1948; s. Lionel James and Mary (Divita) D.; B.S., Ind. State U., 1974; postgrad. in chem. engring. M.W. Coll. Engring., 1976—; m. Debra Louise Nelson, Sept. 21, 1974; 1 son, Michael Andrew. Chem. compunder supr. Jovan Inc., Bensenville, Ill., 1974-76, compounding supt., 1976-78, mgr. dept. compounding, 1978-80, maintenance mgr., 1980—. Mem. caucus for conservative congress Nat. Tax Limitation Com. Served with USN, 1966-70. Decorated Purple Heart (U.S.); Cross of Gallantry (Vietnam). Roman Catholic. Home: 43 N Glenview St Lombard IL 60148 Office: 600 Eagle Dr Bensenville IL 60106

DOUTHETT, ROGER LYNN, computer software cons.; b. Wichita, Kans., June 22, 1947; s. William B. and Daisy Gertrude (Mott) D.; B.S., Kans. State U., 1969; M.B.A., Wichita State U., 1975; m. Shelley Diane Becker, Dec. 18, 1976; 1 dau., Tiffany Diane. Pres., R.L. Douthett & Assos., Inc., Wichita, 1974—, Douthett Enterprises, Inc., 1978—, DMW Equipment Corp., 1981—; mng. partner D-K Properties; tchr. computer sci. Wichita State U., 1974-79; career cons. computer sci. Wichita State U.; pres. bd. Camerata Musica, Inc. Mem. Assn. Computing Machinery, Am. Prodn. and Inventory Control Soc. Home: 315 S Crestway St Wichita KS 67218 Office: 906 N Main St Wichita KS 67203

DOUTY, RICHARD THOMAS, civil engr.; b. Williamsport, Pa., July 12, 1930; s. Richard Otis and Helen Anna (Sauter) D.; B.C.E., Lehigh U., 1956; M.S., Ga. Tech. Inst., 1957; Ph.D., Cornell U., 1964; m. Patricia Marie Hopkins, June 27, 1959; children—Richard Keith, Eric Thomas, Ellen Marie, Christopher Brandon. Mgmt. trainee fabricated steel div. Bethlehem Steel Co. (Pa.), 1957-58; asst. prof. civil engring. U. Mo., Columbia, 1962, prof. civil engring., 1970—; sabbatical leave sr. research fellow U. Pa., Phila., 1969-70; cons. in field. Mem. NRC Selection Bd. Research Associateship. Served with USN, 1950-54. NSF research grantee. Mem. ASCE (com. electronic computation). Contbr. numerous articles to profl. jours. Home: 1412 Ridgemont Ct Columbia MO 65201 Office: Dept Civil Engring U Mo Columbia MO 65201

DOVERSBERGER, RICHARD ARTHUR, indsl. engr.; b. Warren, Ind., July 19, 1926; s. Jacob Ezra and Orpha Nadean (Bardsley) D.; B.S., Ball State U., 1947, M.A., 1965; m. Jacqueline Anne Stroup, July 22, 1950 (div. Jan. 1973); children—Debra Anne, Cynthia Kay; m. 2d, Connie Jo Ford Davidson, May 28, 1976 (div. Dec. 1976). Tchr., coach Richland Twp. High Sch., Larwill, Ind., 1947-48; cost estimator Beaver Machine Corp., Warren, 1948-50; with Caswell-Runyon Corp., Huntington, Ind., 1950-53; with RCA Corp., Marion, Ind., 1953-72, econ. analyst, 1963-72, facilities planner, plant layout, 1965-72; indsl. engr. Gatke Corp., Warsaw, Ind., 1972; with Square D Corp., Huntington, 1972-73; with Wofac Co., cons. engring., Ft. Wayne, Ind., 1973-75; indsl. engr., Wabash Magnetics, Huntington, 1975—. Mem. Huntington County Draft Bd., 1970—; vol. ARC, 1973. Bd. dirs., treas. Salamonie Summer Festival, Warren, 1971, 72. Served with AUS, 1948-49, 50-51. Inducted into Huntington County (Ind.) Sports Hall of Fame, 1976. Mem. Am. Inst. Indsl. Engrs., Am. Econ. Assn., Nat. Hist. Soc., Am. Wildlife Fedn., Am. Legion (2d vice comdr. Post 98, Columbia City, Ind. 1980, comdr. 1981-82), Phi Delta Kappa (pres. 1972, 73, 76), Alpha Phi Gamma. Mason (past master, sec.), Kiwanian (dir. 1972, 73). Home: Rural Route 8 Crampton Ave Columbia City IN 46725 Office: Wabash Inc 806 N Cass St Wabash IN 46992

DOW, JOHN, JR., ednl. adminstr.; b. Dec. 20, 1940; s. John and Lynell (Brown) D.; B.S., Ind. State U., 1963, M.S., 1968; Ph.D., Mich. State U., 1971; m. Gloria; children—Anthony, Kelli, Jaime. With Grand Rapids (Mich.) Public Schs., 1963—, asst. prin. middle sch., 1968-69, dir. Title IV, 1969-70, asst. dir. secondary edn., 1970-71, asst. supt., 1971-73, dep. supt., 1973-78, supt. schs., 1978—; cons. Chmn. bd. Grand Rapids Student Coll. Fund; bd. dirs. Grand Rapids Urban League, Grand Rapids YMCA, United Fund and Community Services, Urban League Housing; mem. Mayor's Com. on Central Area Housing. Recipient Disting. Alumni award Ind. State U., 1979. Mem. Am. Assn. Sch. Adminstrs., Assn. Supervision and Curriculum Devel., Mich. Alliance Black Educators, Mich. Assn. Sch. Adminstrs., Mich. Assn. Sch. Bds., Mich. Assn. Supervision and Curriculum Devel., Nat. Alliance Black Sch. Educators, Mid-Am. Assn. Supts., Horace Mann League U.S. Clubs: Peninsular, Rotary. Office: 143 Bostwick NE Grand Rapids MI 49503*

DOWD, GERI ANDREA HACKER, author, editor; b. Chgo., Feb. 6, 1902; d. Frederick William and Selma (Petersohn) Hacker; student Northwestern U., 1935-36, 46, Chgo. Tchr's. Coll., 1958-59; A.A., Wright Jr. Coll., 1958; B.A., Roosevelt U., 1961, postgrad. Sch. Sociology, 1968—; m. Lawrence Bernard Dowd, Apr. 14, 1934. Author: Circus Parade, 1950, Bonny and Barry, Busy Scientists, 1951, Discussion on the Etiology and Chemotherapy of Cancer and Other Virus Diseases, 1952, Suzy Sewzy, 1953, Lunar Glass: A Possible Key to a New Selenology, 1969; author play: The First Easter, 1962; contbr. stories, articles, revs. to newspapers, popular mags., profl. jours., 1914—; credit mgr., legal counsel to firms, 1928-39; columnist, founder woman's page Elm Leaves, Oak Park, Ill., 1941-44; pub., editor World Arts & Sci. Pub. Co., Elmwood Park, Ill., 1945—; playwright, producer, dir. local theatre groups. First chief of staff Elmwood Park Emergency Feeding and Housing, 1942-66; founder, librarian tchr. Westwood Evang. Luth. Ch. Library, Elmwood Park, 1961-66; active ARC. Recipient German Scholar of Year award Wright Jr. Coll., 1958; certified tchr. kindergarten through 12th grade, Ill. Fellow Menninger Found. (charter); mem. Chgo. Assn. Credit Men, Children's Reading Profl. Round Table, Women's Nat. Book Assn., Am. Acad. Arts and Scis., Robert Maynard Hutchins Center Study Democratic Instns., Nat. Space Inst., Planetary Soc., Bibl. Archeol. Soc., Am. Judicature Soc., Am. Acad. Polit. and Social Sci., Psychotherapy, Social Sci. Rev., Forum of Contemporary History, World Future Soc., Ill. State Acad. Sci., AAAS, Astron. Soc. Pacific, Fedn. Am. Scientists, Union Concerned Scientists, Am. Inst. Physics, Roosevelt U. Alumni Assn., Elmwood Park Women's Club (pres. emeritus 1941-43, hon.), Ill. Fedn. Women's Clubs (dist. Past Pres's. Club 1944—), Phi Beta Kappa, Phi Theta Kappa. Home and Office: 7922 Oakleaf Ave Elmwood Park IL 60635

DOWELL, JESSE MURRAY, JR., banker; b. Chgo., July 25, 1926; s. Jesse Murray and Lydia (Lacey) D.; B.S., with highest honors, U. Ill., 1949, M.S. in Agrl. Econs., 1969; m. Dorothy Carr, May 6, 1951; children—Ellen, Murray. Farmer, Mahomet, Ill., 1949-51; profl. farm mgr. Dowell Agrl. Service, Champaign, 1952-71; mgr. farm dept. Bank of Ill., Champaign, 1971-79; 2d v.p. in charge land acquisition East half U.S., Continental Bank, Chgo., 1979—; instr. part-time farm mgmt. U. Ill., 1970-71; bd. dirs. U. Ill. Coll. of Agr. Alumni, Urbana. Bd. dirs. Maynard Lake Sub-div., Champaign. Served with USN, 1944-46. Mem. Ill. Soc. Farm Mgrs. and Rural Appraisers (chmn. legis. com. 1973, pres. 1968), Am. Soc. Farm Mgrs. and Rural Appraisers (mem. legis. com. 1976—, vice chmn. 1979, chmn. 1980, 1st v.p. 1981), U.S.C. of C. (food and agr. com. 1979—), Jr. C. of C. (pres. Champaign 1958), Am. Legion. Methodist. Clubs: Lincolnshire Fields Country, Masons. Editor: Jour. Am. Soc. Farm Mgrs. & Rural Appraisers, 1965, 66; creator idea Fed. Grains Ins. Corp., 1973. Home: 1814 Maynard St Champaign IL 61820 Office: Continental Bank 30 N LaSalle St Chicago IL 60693

DOWELL, MICHAEL BRENDAN, chemist; b. N.Y.C., Nov. 18, 1942; s. William Henry and Anne Susan (Cannon) D.; B.S., Fordham U., 1963; Ph.D., Pa. State U., 1967; m. Gail Elizabeth Renton, Mar. 16, 1968; children—Rebecca, Margaret. Physicist, U.S. Army Frankford Arsenal, Phila., 1967-69; research scientist Parma (Ohio) Tech. Center, Union Carbide Corp., 1969-74, devel. mgr. carbon fiber applications, 1974-76, group leader metals and ceramics research, 1976-80, sr. group leader process research, 1980—. Chmn. 14th Congressional Dist. steering com. Common Cause, 1974-76; officer, trustee Hudson Montessori Assn., 1974-79. Served to capt. ordnance, AUS, 1967-69. Mem. Am. Chem. Soc., Am. Phys. Soc., Am. Carbon Soc., Phi Lambda Upsilon. Roman Catholic. Contbr. articles to profl. jours. Home: 368 N Main St Hudson OH 44236 Office: PO Box 6087 Cleveland OH 44101

DOWELL, WILLIAM EDGAR, coll. pres., clergyman; b. Red Bank, Tex., July 8, 1914; s. Albin McClain and Elizabeth (Andrus) D.; D.Div., Bob Jones U., 1967; D.Th., Bible Bapt. Sem., 1949; m. Nola Mae Calahan, Sept. 2, 1934; children—Janet Rodgers, William E., Clyde Paul. Ordained to ministry, Bapt. Ch., 1934; pastor Northside Bapt. Ch., Merkel, Tex., 1934-35, First Bapt. Ch., Corcorcan, Calif., 1935-36, La Habra, Calif., 1937-41, High St. Bapt. Ch., Springfield, Mo., 1941-63, Jacksonville (Fla.) Bapt. Temple, 1963-68; exec. v.p. Bible Bapt. Coll., Springfield, 1968-75, pres., 1975—; pastor Bapt. Temple, Springfield, 1974—. Recipient Pioneer award, North Springfield Betterment Assn., 1976; Outstanding Achievement award, Commerce Bank, 1974; KYTV Appreciation citation, 1961. Mem. Bapt. Bible Fellowship Internat. (pres. 1950-54, 63-67). Republican. Author: The Birth Pangs of Baptist Bible Fellowship, 1977; The Church, Its Ministry, Its Method, and Its Message, 1980. Home: 3244 N Pickwick St Springfield MO 65803 Office: 628 E Kearney St Springfield MO 65802

DOWER, EDWARD LOUIS, educator; b. Takoma Park, Md., Jan. 4, 1945; s. Clancy Melvin and Verna May (Thompson) D.; B.A., Pacific Union Coll., 1967; M.Div., Andrews U., 1969, Ed.D., 1980; m. Donna Fern Piner, Sept. 4, 1966; children—Christine, Carla, Erik. Ordained to ministry Seventh-day Adventist Ch., 1974; pastor Ill. Conf. Seventh-day Adventists, 1969-73; religion tchr. Spring Valley Acad., Centerville, Ohio, 1973-77, Andrews Acad., Berrien Springs, Mich., 1977—; supervising instr. edn. Andrews U., 1977—. Mem. Religious Edn. Assn., Assn. Supervision and Curriculum Devel., Phi Delta Kappa. Home: 601 Meadowlark Ln Berrien Springs MI 49103 Office: Andrews Acad Berrien Springs MI 49103

DOWLING, EDWARD JOSEPH, plant breeder; b. Chgo., May 2, 1951; s. Edward Joseph and Mary Jane (Simmons) D.; B.S. in Agrl. Bus., Iowa State U., 1973, B.S. in Agronomy, 1974; postgrad. in plant breeding So. Ill. U., 1980; m. Marcia R. Tweed, June 16, 1973; children—Jennifer K., Julie C. Corn breeder Clyde Black and Son Seed Co., Ames, Iowa, 1975-77; research sta. mgr. Jacques Seed Co., Lincoln, Ill., 1977—; cons. Simillas Tuniche (Chilean seed corn co.), 1980. Mem. Am. Seed Trade Assn., Am. Agronomy Soc., Am. Crop Sci. Soc., Am. Soil Sci. Soc., Com. for Advancement Sci. and Tech. Roman Catholic. Club: K.C. Home: 709 Grand St Lincoln IL 62656 Office: Box 370 Lincoln IL 62656

DOWLING, PAUL THOMAS, corp. exec.; b. St. Louis, Aug. 3, 1919; s. Thomas John and Cora Amanda (Wilson) D.; B.S. in Metallurgy, Mo. Sch. Mines, 1940; D.Engring. (hon.), U. Mo., Rolla, 1976; m. Eleanor Irene Heimberger, Sept. 20, 1941. With Inland Steel Co., 1939-40, Jones and Laughlin Steel, 1940-41, Granite City Steel, 1941; with St. Louis Ordnance Dist., 1941-44; with Nooter Corp., St. Louis, 1946—, exec. v.p., 1964-68, pres., dir., 1968-71, chief exec. officer, 1971-76, chmn. bd., chief exec. officer, 1976—; dir. Mercantile Bank Corp. Bd. dirs. Jr. Achievement, United Way, Boy Scouts Am.; trustee William Woods Coll.; trustee Freedoms Found., Valley Forge; chmn. Chancellor's Devel. Council, U. Mo., Rolla. Served with USNR, 1944-46. Recipient Spoehrer award Jr. Achievement, 1979. Mem. Mo. Soc. Profl. Engrs., Nat. Soc. Profl. Engrs., Steel Plate Fabricators Assn. (past pres.), Tubular Exchanger Mfrs. Assn. (past pres.), Nat. Assn. Constrn. Boilermaker Employers (dir.), Nat. Constrn. Employers Council (dir.), St. Louis Regional Commerce and Growth Assn. (dir.), Am. Inst. Mining, Metall. and Petroleum Engrs., Am. Petroleum Inst., Am. Soc. Metals. Presbyterian. Clubs: Mo. Athletic, Old Warson Country (St. Louis); Petroleum (Houston); Carlton (Chgo.). Office: Nooter Corp PO Box 451 Saint Louis MO 63166

DOWN, (WILLIAM) JACK, ednl. adminstr.; b. Lansing, Mich., July 22, 1924; s. Eldon Eugene and Frankie (Kuhlman) D.; B.A., Mich. State U., 1946, M.A., 1954, Ph.D., 1974; m. Marilyn Elaine Burley, Aug. 31, 1946; children—Elaine Lenore Down Angstman, Eugene Thomas, Evan Jack. Tchr. pub. schs., Holt, Mich., 1949-51, Lansing, Mich., 1954-55; dir. Vocat. Sch., Am. Samoa, 1951-53; prin. K-12, Webberville, Mich., 1955-56; guidance dir. East Lansing, Mich., 1956-66; dir. Am. Coop. Sch., Santa Cruz, Bolivia, 1965-66; ednl. adviser Dept. State U.S., Vietnam, 1966-68; asst. guidance dir., pub. schs. St. Johns, Mich., 1968-70; coordinator vocational tests State Prison So. Mich., Jackson, 1972-74; dir. guidance Colegio Nueva Granada (Bogota), 1974-75; prin. Am. Coop. Sch., Monrovia, Liberia, 1976-79; partner, v.p. SNARB Realty Co., 1965—. Bd. dirs. Lansing Child Guidance Clinic, 1957-61; internat. adv. Coop. Housing Found., 1980—. Recipient Social Service medal Premier Vietnam, 1968, Ford Found. grantee, 1970; So. Ill. U. grantee, 1970-71; Dissemination of Knowledge Found. grantee 1970. Mem. Am. Personnel and Guidance Assn., Am. Psychol. Assn., Assn. Emotion Disturbed, Nat. Edn. Assn. Research on fatalism among religious groups, especially Buddhist and Christian, France, Vietnam and U.S.; contbr. articles to edn. and travel jours. Home: 2510 Haslett Rd East Lansing MI 48823

DOWNEN, MADELINE ELIZABETH MORGAN, hosp. librarian; b. Pontiac, Mich., Aug. 17, 1930; d. Albert Oran and Hazel Marie (Fisk) Morgan; student Ind. U., 1948-50; B.S. in Edn., Calumet Coll., 1978; cert. hosp. librarianship Am. Hosp. Assn. Inst., 1964; certificate media mgmt. Med. Library Assn., 1972; m. Evan Ray Downen, Dec. 3, 1949 (div. 1968); children—Charles Albert, Linda Carol (Mrs. Dennis Smith), Gregory Lyn. Apprentice med. librarian St. Catherine Hosp., East Chicago, Ind., 1947-50, med. librarian, 1962-65, supr. McGuire Meml. Library, 1965—. Med. library cons. Our Lady of Mercy Hosp., Dyer, Ind., 1969-70; mem. state med. library cons. com. Ind. U. Sch. Medicine, 1973; coordinator Midwest Health Sci. Library Network Consortia, N.W. Ind. Health Sci. Library Consortium, 1975—; chmn. N.W. Ind. Health Sci. Library Consortium, 1975—. Pres. East Chicago Mothers Club, 1966-67. Mem. Med. Library Assn., Regional Med. Library Council (by-laws com. representing hosp. library 1971), Ind. Health Sci. Librarians Assn. (pres. 1981—). Mem. Christian Ch. Home: 6730 Alexander Ave Hammond IN 46320 Office: 4321 Fir St East Chicago IN 46312

DOWNEND, PAUL EUGENE, accountant; b. Toledo, Aug. 16, 1907; s. William Joseph and Della M. (Keller) D.; student pub. schs.; m. Mary B. Butler, Nov. 27, 1952. Supr., Ernst & Ernst, Toledo, 1930-42; v.p., sec., controller, dir. Ohio Locomotive Crane Co., Bucyrus, 1942; pres., dir. Superior Equipment Co., Bucyrus, 1943; pres., dir. Channel Grove Land Improvement Co.; mgr. Mar-Nol Co.; sec. Peneagle Corp.; v.p., dir. Second Nat. Bank, Bucyrus, Ohio, Oakwood Cemetery Assn. Chmn. Bucyrus City Planning Commn.; chmn. Crawford County Republican Exec. Com.; mem. Crawford County Bd. Electors. Pres., bd. dirs. Bucyrus Community Hosp.; chmn. bd. dirs. Crawford County Soc. Crippled Children. C.P.A., Ohio. Mem. Am. Inst. Accountants, Ohio Soc. C.P.A.'s, Am. Ordnance Assn. (life), Assn. Ohio Commodores. Clubs: Masons, Shriners, Jesters, Rotary (past pres.), Elks (past trustee), Columbus Athletic, Catawba Cliffs Beach, Crawford Country Auto (v.p., dir.). Home: 325 Joan Dr Bucyrus OH 44820 Office: Hopley Ave Bucyrus OH 44820

DOWNER, ROBERT NELSON, lawyer; b. Newton, Iowa, July 15, 1939; s. Lowell William and Mabel (Hannon) D.; B.A., U. Iowa, 1961, J.D., 1963; m. Jane Alice Glafka, May 29, 1971; children—Elise Michelle, Andrew Nelson. Admitted to Iowa bar, 1963; asso. mem. firm Meardon, Sueppel, Downer & Hayes and predecessor firms, Iowa City, 1963-68, partner, 1969—. Trustee Christian Retirement Services, Inc., Iowa City, 1967—; spl. adviser Iowa Crime Commn., 1967-68; vice chmn. Citizens Better Iowa City, 1968-69, chmn., 1969-70; mem. Alumni Council U. Iowa, 1971—. Pres. bd. trustees Iowa City Public Library, 1973-74; mem. central com. Johnson County Republican Com., 1972-74, chmn. finance, 1974-77; mem. Iowa Supreme Ct. Continuing Legal Edn. Com., 1975—. Named Outstanding Young Religious Leader Iowa Jr. C. of C., 1970. Mem. Iowa City C. of C. (pres. 1979), Johnson County (pres. 1976), Iowa (chmn. com. continuing legal edn. 1976-77, mem. com. on taxation 1978-79), Am. bar assns., Johnson County Farm Bur., Phi Delta Phi, Omicron Delta Kappa, Phi Kappa Sigma, U. Iowa Alumni Assn. (life mem.). Methodist. Clubs: University Athletic (Iowa City); Des Moines; Rotary. Home: 2029 Rochester Ct Iowa City IA 52240 Office: 122 S Linn St Iowa City IA 52240

DOWNER, THOMAS SANDERS, buyer; b. LaCrosse, Wis., Aug. 8, 1949; s. Sanders Curtis and Elaine Frances (Curran) D.; B.S., U. Wis., 1975, postgrad., 1978—; m. Linda Louise Wehrs, Mar. 6, 1976; 1 son, Jonathan Sanders. Journalist/reporter La Crosse (Wis.) Radio (WLCX), 1976-77; vets. job counselor State of Wis. Job Service, La Crosse, 1977-78, planning analyst, Div. Manpower Services, 1978-79; buyer/system devel.-procedures analyst UOP Norplex Div., La Crosse, 1979—; v.p. Curran Elevator Corp., Bangor, Wis., 1975—. Served with USAF, 1969-73. Mem. Assn. for Systems Mgmt. (profl.). Democrat. Lutheran. Home: 1112 Oak Ave N Onalaska WI 54650 Office: 1300 Norplex Dr La Crosse WI 54601

DOWNES, JEAN FRITCHLEY, educator; b. Canton, Ohio, Nov. 23, 1929; B.S., Kent State U., 1951, M.S., 1977. Tchr. home econs. Dennison (Ohio) Exempted Village, 1951-52; tchr. home econs. Sandy Valley High Sch., Magnolia, Ohio, 1960-67; vocat. home econs. job tng. tchr. Canton (Ohio) South High Sch., 1967-77, tchr. vocat. food service, 1977—; cons. Ohio Dept. Edn. Mem. Ohio Vocat. Edn. Assn. (Disting. Service award 1978), Am. Water Ski Assn. (mem. Midwest regional council 1980-81), Ohio Water Ski Assn. (Ohio council 1980-81; dir. 1975-80, Disting. Service award 1981), Ohio Vocat. Assn. (sec. treas. home econs. sect 1975-77), NEA, Nat. Assn. Vocat. Home Econs. Tchrs., Ohio Edn. Assn., Stark County Home Econs. Assn., Canton Local Edn. Assn., Am. Water Ski Ednl. Found., Am. Fgn. Student Assn. Lutheran. Clubs: Lake Mohawk Water Ski, Rebekahs. Home: 78 Oneida Trail Malvern OH 44644

DOWNEY, JOHN WILHAM, composer, educator; b. Chgo., Oct. 5, 1927; s. James Bernard and Augustina (Haas) D.; Docteur es Lettres (Ph.D.), U. Paris-Sorbonne, 1956; Prix de Composition (scholar), Paris Conservatory, 1956; m. Irusha Czuszak; children—Lydia, Marc. Chmn. humanities dept., Mayfair Br., Chgo. City Coll., 1958-64; prof. theory and composition U. Wis., Milw., 1964—; instr. music theory, De Paul U., 1960-64, Roosevelt U., 1961; resident artist MacDowell Colony, summers 1971, 75-77, fall 1978; composer numerous works including Cello Sonata, recorded CRI label, 1968; Agort, Woodwind quintet, recorded Orion label, 1973; Adagio Lyrico for two pianos, Octet for Winds, What If?, for mixed choir, solo tympany and brass octet, A Dolphin, voice and chamber ensemble, recorded Orion label, 1977, String Quartet No. 2, recorded Gasparo label, 1980, The Edge of Space (fantasy for bassoon and orch.), 1981. Bd. dirs., Rondel Arts Studio, Milw. 20th Century Ensemble; mem. Wis. Arts Bd. Fulbright Scholar to France, 1952-54, 1979; scholar, French Govt., 1954-55, teaching fellow, 1955-56; teaching fellow, German Govt., 1956-57; Copley Found. grantee, 1957-58, 58-59; decorated Chevalier de l'Ordre des Arts et Lettres (France); recipient awards U. Wis., 1971, 73, 75, 77, 79, Ford Found., 1976, Nat. Endowment for the Arts, 1977; Disting. Alumni award De Paul U., 1969; Disting. Citizen in Music award Civic Music Assn. Milw., 1980. Mem. Am. Soc. Univ. Composers, Am. Music Center, ASCAP (awards, 1974-78), Am. Fedn. Musicians, Wis. Contemporary Music Forum (founder, chmn., 1970—), Center Twentieth Century Studies, Phi Kappa Phi, Delta Omicron (nat. patron). Author: La Musique populaire dans l'Oeuvre de Bela Bartok, also several articles. Office: Univ of Wisconsin School of Fine Arts - Music Milwaukee WI 53201

DOWNING, JOAN FORMAN, editor; b. Mpls., Nov. 16, 1934; d. W. Chandler and Marie A. (Forster) Forman; B.A., U. Wis., 1956; children—Timothy Alan, Julie Marie, Christopher Alan. Editorial asst. Sci. Research Assos., Chgo., 1960-61, asst. editor, 1961-63; asst. editor Children's Press div. Regensteiner Pub. Enterprises, Inc., Chgo., 1963-66, asso. editor, 1966-68, mng. editor, 1968-78, editor-in-chief, 1978-81, sr. editor, 1981—; dir. Chgo. Book Clinic, 1973-75, publicity chmn., 1973-74. Election judge Cook County (Ill.), 1974—. Mem. Alpha Phi. Democrat. Author: (with Eugene Baker) Workers Long Ago, 1968; Junior CB Picture Dictionary, 1978; Baseball is our Game, 1982; project editor: 15 vol. Young People's Story of Our Heritage (Graphic Arts Council of Chgo. award), 1966; 20 vol. People of Destiny (Chgo. Book Clinic award), 1967-68; 20 vol. Enchantment of South and Central America, 1968-70; 36 vol. Open Door Books, 1968; 42 vol. Enchantment of Africa, 1972-78; multi-vol. World at War, 1980—. Home: 2414 Brown Ave Evanston IL 60201 Office: 1224 W Van Buren St Chicago IL 60607

DOWNS, DALE DEAN, educator; b. Platt County, Ill., June 16, 1934; s. Paul Maurice and Thelma Katherine (Greve) D.; B.E., Eastern Ill. U., 1956; M.Ed., U. Ill., 1961, Advanced Cert., 1963; Ed.D., Ind. U., 1971; m. Lois Ann Winkler, June 3, 1956; children—Alan Dale, Daniel Dean. Tchr., Community Unit Dist. #2 Public Schs., Mattoon, Ill., 1956-57, 59-63; asst. prof. Eastern Ill. U., Charleston, 1963-71, asso. prof., 1971-78, prof., 1978—. Served with AUS, 1957-59. Mem. NEA, Individually-Guided Edn. Assn.,

Internat. Reading Assn., Ill. Reading Council (v.p.-elect 1981-82), Nat. Council Social Studies, Assn. Supervision and Curriculum Devel., Ill. Assn. Supervision and Curriculum Devel., Phi Delta Kappa, Kappa Delta Pi. Methodist. Clubs: Masons, Elks, Kiwanis, Jaycee. Home: 506 Warren St Charleston IL 61920 Office: Dept Elem Edn Eastern Ill Univ Charleston IL 61920

DOWNS, GARY EUGENE, educator; b. Schuyler County, Ill., Aug. 15, 1938; s. Clifford and Beulah Margarette (Chipman) D.; B.S., Western Ill. U., 1964, M.S., 1969; Ed.D., U. No. Colo., 1972; m. Norma Jean Rebman, July 7, 1956; children—Kevin Eugene, Kraig Alan. Tchr., Avon (Ill.) High Sch., 1963-65, Rich Twp. High Sch., Olympia Fields, Ill., 1965-71; instr. U. No. Colo., 1971-72; state sci. cons. Iowa Dept. Pub. Instrn., 1972-75; asso. prof. elem. edn. Iowa State U., Ames, 1975—; cons. Ginn & Co. Mem. NEA, Nat. Sci. Suprs. Assn. (pres. 1981-82), Nat. Sci. Tchrs. Assn., Iowa Edn. Assn., Am. Assn. Physics Tchrs., Iowa Council Sci. Suprs. (pres. 1972-75), Council of State Sci. Suprs. Assn., Sch. Sci. and Math. Assn., Iowa Acad. Sci., Nat. Assn. for Research in Sci. Teaching, Lambda Sigma Tau, Sigma Pi Sigma, Phi Delta Kappa, Sigma Zeta. Republican. Methodist. Contbr. articles to profl. jours. Home: 3809 Toronto St Ames IA 50010 Office: Iowa State U N126 Quadrangle Ames IA 50011

DOWNS, RUBYE P. BLACKBURN, ednl. adminstr.; b. Malden, Mo., Apr. 2, 1921; d. Joseph Henry and Mahala Jane (Warner) B.; student S.E. Mo. State Tchrs. Coll., 1939-43; A.B., Marymount Coll., 1959; M.A., Central Mich. U., 1965; m. Robert T. Downs, Mar. 2, 1945 (dec.); children—Janet Alice Downs Fezatte, Thomas Warren. Asst. instr. films, orgn. materials and others Mil. Sch., Malden (Mo.) AFB, 1943-45; tchr. rural sch., New Madrid, Mo., 1940-43; tchr., mem. curriculum team Hermiston (Oreg.) Public Schs., 1958-59; tchr. Salina (Kans.) Public Schs., 1959-62; tchr.'s supr. student teaching and adult edn., public schs., Oscoda, Mich., 1962-66; dir. media services Unified Sch. Dist. 305, Salina, 1966—; mem. media faculty Emporia State U., summers, 1969-70; cons. library media. Deaconess, First Christian Ch., Salina, 19—. Mem. ALA, Am. Assn. Sch. Librarians, Assn. Supervision and Curriculum Devel., United Sch. Adminstrs. Kans., Kans. Sch. Library Media Dirs. (chmn. 1968-69), Kans. Assn. Sch. Librarians (pres. 1970-72), Kans. Assn. Edn. Communication and Tech., Kans. Assn. Supervision and Curriculum Devel. (sec.-treas. 1974-75), Internat. Reading Assn., Assn. Childhood Edn. Internat., Assn. Ednl. Communications and Tech., Delta Kappa Gamma. Club: Order Eastern Star. Author Salina Public Schs. Non-Print Media Catalog. Home: 2370 Mayfair Salina KS 67401 Office: 119 E Mulberry Salina KS 67401

DOYLE, DAVID CHARLES, cons. co. exec.; b. Cheboygan, Mich., Sept. 28, 1952; s. Orlando and Jeanne (St. Amand) D.; A.S. in Data Processing, Ferris State Coll., 1973; B.S. in Data Processing, Ferris State Coll./Mich. State U., 1974. Computer programmer, analyst State of Mich., Lansing, 1973-75, sr. programmer, analyst, 1975-76, asst. programming supr., 1976, programming supr., 1977—; owner, operator Doyle Systems Consultants, Detroit, 1978— cons. in field.; instr. Lansing Community Coll. Mem. Assn. Systems Mgmt., Am. Mgmt. Assn. Home: 2692 Coral Dr Troy MI 48098 Office: 6934 W Fort St Detroit MI

DOYLE, DONALD VINCENT, state senator; b. Sioux City, Iowa, Jan. 13, 1925; s. William E. and Nelsine E. (Sparby) D.; B.S., Morningside Coll., Sioux City, 1951; J.D., U. S.D., 1953; m. Janet E. Holtz, Aug. 9, 1963; 1 dau., Dawn Renee. Admitted to S.D., Iowa bars, 1953; pvt. practice, Sioux City, 1953—; mem. Iowa Ho. of Reps. from Woodbury County, 1956-80, Iowa Senate, 1981—. Served with USAAF, 1943-46. Recipient award Woodbury County Peace Officers, 1974, Restoration Club Sioux City, 1964, Outstanding Elected Ofcl. award Iowa Corrections Assn., 1979. Mem. Iowa, Woodbury County bar assns., CBI Vets. Assn. (past nat. judge adv.), Am. Legion, VFW, DAV. Democrat. Office: PO Box 941 Sioux City IA 51102

DOYLE, JAMES EDWARD, judge; b. Oshkosh, Wis., July 6, 1915; s. James Edward and Agnes Catherine (McCarthy) D.; A.B., U. Wis., 1937; LL.B., Columbia, 1940. m. Ruth Bachhuber, Aug. 10, 1940; children—Mary, James Edward, Catherine, Anne. Admitted to Wis. bar, 1940; asso. firm LaFollette, Sinykin & Doyle, Madison, 1948-65; U.S. dist. judge Western Dist. Wis., 1965—. Mem. Am., Wis., Dane County bar assns., Am. Law Inst. Home: 1114 Mohican Pass Madison WI 53711 Office: Fed Bldg Monona Ave PO Box 591 Madison WI 53701

DOYLE, JAMES THOMAS, advt. firm exec.; b. Detroit, July 14, 1933; s. Edmund Thomas and Mamie Irene (Wepplo) D.; B.S., Wayne State U., 1956; m. Patricia Jean Godon, Nov. 29, 1958; children—Greg, Kerry and Kevin (twins). Account exec. J. Walter Thompson Co., Detroit, 1956-64; account dir. McCann-Erickson Co., Detroit, 1964-66; advt.-mktg. mgr. Ford Motor Co., Dearborn, Mich., 1966-70; sr. v.p., mgmt. supr. Grey Advt., Detroit, 1970-75; pres. D'Arcy, MacManus & Masius, Inc., Bloomfield Hills, Mich., 1975—. City councilman, mayor pro-tem, Dearborn Heights, Mich., 1965-73. Named an Outstanding Young Man, City of Dearborn Heights, 1966; recipient Civic Service awards Ford Motor Co., 1966, 67. Mem. Detroit Advt. Assn. Methodist. Clubs: Adcraft of Detroit, Renaissance (Detroit); Bloomfield Hills Country; Dearborn Country, Dearborn Racquet. Home: 26216 Sims Dr Dearborn Heights MI 48127 Office: D'Arcy MacManus & Masius Inc 10 W Long Lake Rd Bloomfield Hills MI 48013

DOYLE, JERRY JAMES, ednl. cons.; b. Arvilla, N.D., June 24, 1939; s. Raymond Dewey and Eva Henrietta (Sellin) D.; B.A., U. Minn., 1964, M.A., 1967; Ph.D. (NSF fellow 1972-73), U. Iowa, 1977; m. Phyllis Marie Harms, June 17, 1969; children—Brenda, Marcia. Tchr. sci. Wheeling (Ill.) High Sch., 1965-74; instr. edn. U. Iowa, 1974-77; ednl. cons. Area Edn. Agy. 16, Ft. Madison, Iowa, 1977—. Shell Merit fellow, 1971. Mem. Nat. Sci. Tchrs. Assn., Nat. Sci. Suprs. Assn., Assn. Supervision and Curriculum Devel., Nat. Assn. Research Sci. Teaching, Phi Delta Kappa. Methodist. Author papers in field. Home: 816 Avenue C Fort Madison IA 52627 Office: 305 Avenue F Fort Madison IA 52626

DOYLE, JOHN STUART, advt. agy. and real estate exec.; b. Chgo., Oct. 20, 1915; s. Patrick Francis and Kathryn E. (Kelleher) D.; Ph.B., De Paul U., 1938, J.D., 1982; M.Ed., Chgo. Tchrs. Coll., 1940; postgrad. Ill. Inst. Tech., 1942, 47-49; fellow Northwestern U., 1938-39; postgrad. Loyola U. Bus. Sch., 1950-51; m. Marie Josephine Haug, Feb. 21, 1944; children—John Stuart, Geoffrey, Donald, Susan, Charles, Deborah, Michael, Paul. Dir. religious printing div. Cuneo Press, 1941-42; commd. ensign U.S. Navy, 1944, advanced through grades to lt. comdr., 1952; ret., 1961; gen. mgr. Morgan Mfg. Corp., 1951-52; advt. mgr. Velsicol Chem. Corp., 1952-53; account exec. Foote, Cone & Belding, Chgo., 1953-59; v.p., account supr. Compton Advt., Chgo., 1959-66, also Edward H. Weiss & Co., Advt. Agy., 1966-68; pres. MMI Corp.; sec. Brand Group; founder, pres. Juris Doctor Assos., 1980—; dir. Rockwood & Co., Gt. Am. Industries, Superior Seal Corp., Emlin Cosmetics, others; tchr. Kelvyn Park and Wendell Phillips high schs., 1940-42, Northwestern U. Bus. and Journalism Schs., 1954-66. Vice chmn. Chgo. City Coll. Bd., 1966-70; founder, exec. sec. Council of Community Coll. Bds., 1968-71; vice chmn. Citizens Com. for Gun Control Legis.; exec. dir. Chgo. com. Ill. Sesquicentennial, 1967-68; dir. alumni relations De Paul U., 1969-71. Recipient Putnam 1st place award for most successful indsl. advt., 1955, two 1st place Toppers awards, 1954, 55, 1st place Asso. Bus. Publs. award, 1954, 55. Mem. Am. Bar Assn., Phi Alpha Delta. Roman Catholic. Club: Evergreen Bath and Tennis. (Chgo.). Pub., DePage mag., 1969-72. Author: Christmas Interlude, 1942. Contbr. articles to mags. Home: 2031 W Hunt Ave Chicago IL 60620 Office: 910 S Michigan Ave Chicago IL 60605

DOYLE, JOSEPH FRANCIS, II, hosp. adminstr.; b. Cin., Jan. 14, 1948; s. Joseph Francis and Doris (Caldwell) D.; A.S. in Credit Mgmt., U. Cin., 1969, B.B.A. in Mgmt., 1971; M.Ed. in Guidance, Xavier U., 1974, M.B.A. in Mgmt., 1979; m. Marta Waldorf Doyle, May 26, 1979. Patient accounts analyst Bethesda, Hosp., Cin., 1971-72; unit mgr. Jewish Hosp., Cin., 1972-79; asst. adminstr. Children's Psychiat. Center of Jewish Hosp., Cin., 1979—; dir. Jewish Hosp. Employees Fed. Credit Union, treas., 1976. Career advisor Career Resource Center of U. Cin. Mem. Am. Hosp. Assn., Assn. M.B.A. Execs., Tri-State Health Adminstrs. Forum, U. Cin. Alumni Assn., Am. Diabetes Assn. Roman Catholic. Home: 5834 Pandora Ave Cincinnati OH 45213 Office: 3140 Harvey Ave Cincinnati OH 45229

DOYLE, KENNETH OWEN, JR., psychologist; b. Menominee, Mich., Mar. 2, 1943; s. Kenneth Owen and Loretta (Mayer) D.; student Mt. St. Paul's Coll., 1962-64, Pontificia U. Gregoriana, Rome, 1964-65; A.B., Marquette U., 1966; Ph.D., U. Minn., 1972; m. Lynn Richardson, May 15, 1971; 1 dau., MacKenzie Richardson. Instr., research fellow dept. psychology U. Minn., Mpls., 1968-72, acting dir., research asso. Measurement Services Center, 1972—. Mem. Am. Psychol. Assn., Am. Ednl. Research Assn., Nat. Council Measurement in Edn. Author: Interaction, 1973; Student Evaluation of Instruction, 1975; Education/Psychology Journals: Scholar's Guide, 1975. Home: 3332 22d Ave S Minneapolis MN 55407 Office: U Minn Measurement Service Center 9 Clarence Ave SE Minneapolis MN 55414

DOYLE, WILLIAM JAY, II, bus. cons.; b. Cin., Nov. 7, 1928; s. William Jay and Blanche (Gross) D.; B.S., Miami U., Oxford, Ohio, 1949; postgrad. U. Cin., 1950-51, Xavier U., 1953-54, Case Western Res. U., 1959-60; m. Joan Lucas, July 23, 1949; children—David L., William Jay, III, Daniel L. Sales rep. Diebold, Inc., Cin., 1949-52, asst. br. mgr., 1953-57, asst. regional mgr., Cin., 1957-62, regional mgr., Cin., 1962-74; founder, chief exec. officer Central Bus. Systems & Security Concepts Co. div. Central Bus. Equipment Co., Inc., Cin., 1974—, dir. parent co. and divs.; dir. Perry Broadcasting Co., Beautiful Island Broadcasting Co., Sports Broadcasting Packagers Co.; speaker on bus systems, security concepts. Mem. music and auditing coms. Ch. of the Savior, Methodist ch., Montgomery, Ohio. Mem. Bus. Systems and Security Mktg. Assn. (nat. dir. nat. pres. 1980-81), Nat. Assn. Accts. Republican. Clubs: Masons, Shriners. Contbr. articles to co. and trade publs.; developer new concepts in tng., cash and securities handling, other areas of bus. Home: 202 Shakerdale Rd Cincinnati OH 45242 Office: 10839 Indeco Dr Cincinnati OH 45241

DOYLE, WILLIAM OWENS, ins. co. exec.; b. Manhasset, L.I., N.Y., June 17, 1944; s. Thomas Joseph and Anne (Sellman) D.; A.F.A., Silvermine Coll. Art, New Canaan, Conn., 1965; diploma Sch. Dayton Art Inst., 1968; B.F.A., U. Dayton, 1970, B.S., 1974; grad. Life Underwriters Tng. Council, 1978; m. Sandra Klatt, Mar. 25, 1972. Indsl. designer Fiberglass of Ohio, Dayton, 1967-69; tchr. Springfield (Ohio) Catholic Central High Sch., 1970-71, Alter High Sch., Dayton, 1971-75; sales rep. Met. Life Ins. Co., Dayton, 1975-76, sales, mgr., 1976—. Mem. Dayton Assn. Life Underwriters, Oakwood Community Jaycees (bd. dirs.). Home: 1350 S Heincke Rd Miamisburg OH 45342 Office: 7051 Corporate Way Centerville OH 45459

DRACH, DUDLEY, Realtor, lawyer; b. Cleve., Dec. 14, 1900; s. Jacob W. and Ellen (O'Brien) D.; B.A., Baldwin Coll., 1922; LL.D., Cleve.-Marshall Law Sch., 1922, Dr. Law, 1968. Admitted to Ohio bar, 1922; practiced in Lakewood, 1930—; pres., co-owner West Side Realty Co., 1931—; fee appraiser govt. agys., 1935—. Pres. Cleve. Real Estate Bd., 1944; chmn. Bd. Valuation, 1957, 63, 67. Served with U.S. Army, 1917-18. Recipient Real Estate Dean Valuation awards, 1966. Mem. Am. Soc. Appraisers, Nat., Ohio, Cleve. real estate bds., Soc. Real Estate Appraisers, Am. Legion, Am. Turners. Elk. Club: Westwood Country (Rocky River, Ohio). Home: 2089 Wooster Rd Rocky River OH 44116 Office: 15600 Madison Ave Lakewood OH 44107

DRAGE, FLORENCE, social worker; b. Cleve., Sept. 10, 1923; d. Oliver and Rose Kraus; A.A. summa cum laude, Lakeland Community Coll., 1975; B.S. magna cum laude, Cleve. State U., 1976; M.S.S.A., Case Western Reserve U., 1979; m. John E. Drage, Jr., Nov. 10, 1941; children—John E., Rosemary Hale. Coordinator social services Sr. Citizens Council Lake County, Eastlake, Ohio, 1975-76; psychotherapist Lake County Mental Health Center, Mentor, Ohio, 1978; dir. aging program Catholic Service Bur. Lake County, Painesville, Ohio, 1979—; cons. sr. citizens area council community orgn., Lake County Area, 1978—. Mem. Nat. Assn. Social Workers, Acad. Cert. Social Workers, Am. Orthopsychiat. Assn., Case Western Res. U. Alumnae Assn., Cleve. State U. Alumnae Assn. Roman Catholic. Home: 2090 Country Club Dr Wickliffe OH 44092 Office: 455 Ameritrust Bldg 8 N State St Painesville OH 44077

DRAGOZETICH, WILLIAM JOHN, army officer; b. Chgo., July 12, 1940; s. George John and Estelle Frances (Staszak) D.; B.S. in Mgmt., U. Ill., 1962; M.B.A., James Madison U., 1973; grad. U.S. Army Command and Gen. Staff Coll., 1974. Commd. 2d lt., U.S. Army, 1962, advanced through grades to lt. col., 1978; platoon leader, Germany, 1962-63; tactical dir. 94th Air Def. Arty. Group, Germany, 1963-65; battery exec. officer, Germany, 1965-66; bn. adj., Ft. Lewis, Wash. and Vietnam, 1966-67; battery comdr., Ft. Bliss, 1968-69; adv. mil. mission to Saudi Arabia, 1969-70; prof. mil. sci. Washington and Lee U., 1970-73; brigade adjutant Homestead AFB, 1974-75, bn. exec. officer 1975-76; brigade tactical ops., plans and ops., Korea, 1977; liaison officer MILPERCEN, Alexandria, Va., 1978-80; prof. mil. sci. U. Ill. Chgo. Circle, 1980—. Decorated Bronze Star, Meritorious Service medal, Air medal, Joint Services Commendation medal, Army Commendation medal. Mem. Assn. U.S. Army, Assn. M.B.A. Execs., 4th Inf. Div. Assn., Am. Mgmt. Assn., U. Ill. Alumni Assn. Home: 6133 W 81st Pl Burbank IL 60459 Office: University of Illinois Box 4348 Chicago IL 60689

DRAGSETH, KENNETH ALLEN, ednl. adminstr.; b. Madison, S.D., Sept. 10, 1945; s. Ingvald Arthur and Gamanda Levina (Reinertson) D.; A.A., Waldorf Coll., 1965; B.A., Gustavus Adolphus Coll., 1967; M.A., U. Minn., 1972, Ph.D., 1980; m. Mari Lynne Carlson, Aug. 24, 1968; children—David, Dana. Asst. to campus prin. for instrn. Edina (Minn.) Public Schs., 1979-81, dean students, 1977-79, tchr. math., 1967-69, 71-79, coordinator secondary curriculum and instrn., 1981—. Mem Big Bros., 1969-72, Kinsman Program, 1974-75; coach, community programs, 1979-81; pres. Edina Community Lutheran Ch., 1979-80; del. precinct and county convs., 1972, 74, 76, 78. Served with USN, 1969-71. NSF grantee, 1969-72. Mem. Minn. Assn. Secondary Sch. Prins., Nat. Assn. Secondary Sch. Prins., Assn. Supervision and Curriculum Devel., Nat. Tchrs. Math., Lake Conf. Prins. Assn., Hennepin County Prins. Assn. Club: Calhoun Beach. Home: 6904 Antrim Rd Edina MN 55435 Office: 6754 Valley View Rd Edina MN 55435

DRAKE, CARL BIGELOW, JR., financial services co. exec.; b. St. Paul, July 15, 1919; s. Carl Bigelow and Louise Delano (Hadley) D.; B.A., Yale U., 1941; m. Charlotte Hannaford Day, Mar. 12, 1977; children by previous marriage—Carl Bigelow, Eleanor Drake McLear, Trevor R. Various field and underwriting positions St. Paul Fire & Marine Ins. Co., 1941-63, asst. to pres., 1963-66, v.p., asst. to pres., 1966-68, exec. v.p., 1968-69, pres., 1969-73; pres., chief exec. officer of parent co. The St. Paul Cos., Inc., 1973-78, chmn. bd., chief exec. officer, 1977—; dir. Honeywell, Inc. Chmn. St. Paul United Way, 1974; trustee Macalester Coll. Served to lt. comdr. USNR, 1942-45. Mem. Am. Ins. Assn. Republican. Presbyterian. Clubs: Minn., St. Paul Athletic, Minneapolis, Somerset Country; Yale (N.Y.C.). Home: 1695 Delaware Ave Saint Paul MN 55118 Office: 385 Washington St Saint Paul MN 55102

DRAKE, DONALD ANSON, II, orthodontist; b. Mitchell, S.D., Mar. 13, 1948; s. Don A. and Barbara (Maurice) D.; B.A., U. of South Dakota, 1970; D.D.S., Loyola U., Maywood, Ill., 1974; M.S.D., St. Louis U., 1976; m. Cecelia E. Hearne, Apr. 15, 1968; children—Donald A. Drake, III, Courtland Michael Drake. Resident in orthodontics St. Louis U. Med. Center, (Mo.), 1974-76; gen. practice dentistry, Sioux Valley Hosp., (S.D.), 1976-77, McKennan Hosp., 1976-77. Advisory bd. Clift Palate, S.D., 1977; coach Little League, Sioux Falls, 1977, grade sch. basketball team, 1978-79. Recipient ROTC award, 1967. Mem. Am. Dental Assn., Am. Orthodontic Assn., Midwestern Soc. of Orthodontists, South Eastern S.D. Dental Soc., Orthodontic Research Found., Tweed Found., Polit. Sci. Club (sec., v.p.), Hippocatis (v.p.), Sioux Falls Jaycees, Blue Key, Delta Tau Delta, Xi Psi Phi (sec.), Omicron Kappa Upsilon. Episcopalian. Clubs: Elks, Rotary, Masons. Contbr. articles in field. Home: 4404 S Duluth St Sioux Falls SD 57105 Office: 3307 S Lincoln St Sioux Falls SD 57105

DRAKE, JUSTIN RIGGS, metall. engr., corporate materials research dir.; b. Sullivan, Ind., Nov. 14, 1921; s. Roy Calvin and Hazel (Riggs) D.; m. Helen Benedict, June 19, 1942; children—Justin, Philip Roy. B.S., in Metall. Engring., Purdue U., 1950. Foundry tech. Harrison Steel Casting Co., Attica, Ind., 1940-42; research metall. engr., metall. lab. Caterpillar Tractor Co., Peoria, Ill., 1950-55, research supr., 1955-60, project leader, 1961-65; mgr. metall. research Cummins Engine Co., Columbus, Ind., 1966-72, dir. materials research, 1973—. Pres. P.T.A., Morton, Ill., 1963-64; trustee Methodist ch., Morton, 1963-65; mem. adminstrv. bd. Asbury Meth. Ch., Columbus, 1978-81; Republican precinct committeeman, 1973-77; scoutmaster Boy Scouts Am., 1953-54. Mem. Am. Soc. Metals (Indpls. exec. com. 1975-77, chmn. Indpls. chpt. 1979-80). Author tech. papers in field.

DRAKE, RICHARD FRANCIS, state senator; b. Muscatine, Iowa, Sept. 28, 1927; s. Frank and Fladys (Young) D.; student Iowa State U.; B.S., U.S. Naval Acad., 1950; m. Shirley Jean Henke; children—Cheryll Dee, Ricky Lee. Commd. ensign U.S. Navy, advanced through grades to lt. comdr., 1954; capt. minesweeper U.S.S. Crow; farmer, mgr., 1954—; mem. Iowa Senate. Chmn., Young Republican Orgn. Iowa, 1954-56; adminstrv. asst. Muscatine County Rep. Com., 1956-57, chmn., 1958-66; 1st dist. chmn. Rep. party, 1966—; chmn. Nat. Task Force Rail Line Abandonment and Curtailment; chmn. states and rail problems Midwestern Council State Govts., 1978-79. Mem. Farm Bur. Lutheran. Clubs: Masons, Elks, Order Eastern Star. Office: State Enate Des Moines IA 50319*

DRALLE, CARL WILLIAM, metals co. exec.; b. Milw., June 28, 1926; s. Carl William and Alma Lydia (Giesecke) D.; B.S., U. Wis., 1950; m. Virginia Helen Dobbs, Aug. 4, 1951; children—William George, Richard Louis, Douglas Charles. With Ampco Metal, Inc., Milw., 1950—, market devel. mgr. process industries, 1970-77, mgr. market devel., 1977—. Committeeman, North Bergen (N.J.) council, Boy Scouts Am., 1965-70, chmn., 1967-70. Served with AUS, 1943-46. Mem. Nat. Assn. Corrosion Engring., Am. Water Works Assn., Marine Tech. Soc., Am. Welding Soc., Am. Powder Metallurgy Inst. Lutheran. Mason. Clubs: Copper, Highlander Racquet. Home: 17975 Continental Dr Brookfield WI 53005 Office: 1745 S 38th St Milwaukee WI 53215

DRANCHAK, RONALD JOSEPH, human resources exec.; b. Scranton, Pa., Mar. 2, 1939; s. Joseph and Jean (Sienkievicz) D.; B.S., Widner Coll., 1961; postgrad. Rensselaer Poly. Inst., 1966-67; m. Patricia L. Condon, June 18, 1960; children—Kimberley, Damon, Kevin. Mgr. indsl. relations Armco Steel Co., Marion, Ohio, 1970-72; mgr. personnel and indsl. relations ITT Grinnell, Columbia, Pa., 1972-75; v.p. personnel and indsl. relations AMF-Harley-Davidson, Milw., 1975-78; exec. v.p. Jonas & Assos., Milw., 1978-79; v.p. human resources Douwe Egberts Superior Co., Chgo., 1979—. Chmn. cub scout program Boy Scouts Am. Served to 1st lt. U.S. Army, 1961-64. Mem. Am. Soc. for Personnel Adminstrn. (accredited exec. in personnel), Am. Compensation Assn., C. of C., Jr. C. of C. (v.p.). Clubs: Lions, Indsl. Mgmt. Home: 278 Pebble Creek Dr Barrington IL 60010 Office: 990 Supreme Dr Bensenville IL 60106

DRAVES, CHARLES EDWARD, advt., mktg. and public relations co. ofcl.; b. Gary, Ind., Jan. 15, 1937; s. Kenneth Fred and Constance D.; B.A. in Creative Writing, Purdue U., 1962; m. Rebecca Timmons, June 22, 1963; children—Ken, John, Elizabeth, Carolyn. Writer, editor Prudential Co., Jacksonville, Fla., 1967-70; public relations account exec. Fahlgren & Assos., Parkersburg, W.Va., 1970-71; mktg. cons. N.W. Ayer ABH, Indpls., 1971, supervising cons., Chgo., 1973-76; advt. mgr. TRW/Ross Gear Div., Lafayette, Ind., 1977-81; mktg. mgr. Concept Mktg. inc., Lafayette, 1982—. Served with USN, 1956-59. Recipient Effie award Am. Mktg. Assn., 1979. Mem. Public Relations Soc. Am., Mktg. Communications Execs. Internat. Contbr. articles to profl. pubs. Home: 818 Barlow St West Lafayette IN 47906 Office: 412 Main St PO Box 1218 Lafayette IN 47902

DRAZGA, LINDA MARIE, mfg. co. exec.; b. Chgo., Mar. 30, 1952; d. Stanley James and Ann Theresa (Novak) D.; With Kraft Inc., Chgo., 1976—, application analyst data processing ops., 1981—. Mem. Am. Mgmt. Assn., Nat. Assn. Female Execs. Roman Catholic. Home: 8009 Edgewater Rd North Riverside IL 60546 Office: 1 Kraft Ct Glenview IL 60025

DRAZIC, MILIMIR, coll. learning resource adminstr.; b. Kikinda, Yugoslavia, Apr. 22, 1926; came to U.S., 1956, naturalized, 1961; s. Aleksandar and Danica (Sedmakov) D.; diploma U. Belgrade, 1950; cert. grad. studies U. Copenhagen, 1954; M.S.L.S., U. Ky., 1958; m. Milana Preradov, Sept. 18, 1948; 1 son, George Alexander. Head librarian Glencoe (Ill.) Public Library 1961-66; dir. library services Manchester (Conn.) Community Coll., 1966-74; dir. library Learning Resource Center Castleton State Coll., 1974-77; dir. Learning Resource Center, McCook Community Coll., 1978—, prof. European langs., 1950—; del. Nebr. Pre-White House Conf. on Libraries and Info. Services, Lincoln, 1979. Served with U.S. Army, 1944-45. U.

Chgo. fellow, 1959-62. Mem. ALA (life). Contbr. numerous articles and revs. to profl. jours. Home: Apt 4 611 Norris Ave McCook NE 69001 Office: 1205 E 3d St McCook NE 69001

DREESZEN, ELVIE LUVERNE, state senator, farmer; b. Douglas Twp., Ida County, Iowa, Aug. 7, 1920; s. Rudolph John and Louise Wilhelmina (Bruene) D.; student public schs., Cushing, Iowa; m. Norma Lucille Crane, June 2, 1946; children—Roger Lee, Lanyce Kay, Randall James, Carolyn Louise. Farm hand, 1937-42; farmer, Cushing, 1946—; agrl. aide to Congressman Wiley Mayne of Iowa, 1972-75; mem. Iowa Senate, 1981—; gen. supr. Select Pork Inc., 1978—, Maple Valley Pork Inc., 1980—; editorial writer Ida County Courier, weekly, 1975-80. Mem. platform com. Iowa Republican Party; mem. Iowa Water Pollution Control Commn., 1969-72; dir. Holstein (Iowa) Community Sch. Dist.; mem. Ida County Bd. Rev., 1960-65. Served with U.S. Army, 1942-45. Recipient numerous soil conservation awards; Iowa Master Farmer award; leadership awards Fed. Land Bank System, Ida County 4-H. Mem. Farm Bur., Am. Soybean Assn., Soil Conservation Soc. Am., Pork Producers, Beef Producers, Am. Legion. Lutheran. Club: Kiwanis.

DREFS, JEROLENE AMELIA, electric machinery mfg. co. exec.; b. Phila., Oct. 4, 1935; d. James Vincent and Mary Anna (Haury) Bizzaro; B.B.A. in Acctg., Cleve. State U., 1970, M.B.A., 1973; grad. Advanced Mgmt. Program, Harvard, 1979; m. Alfred David Drefs, Apr. 4, 1954; 1 son, Mark Allan. With Sherwin-Williams Co., 1971-76, asst. controller, 1973-76; controller, then v.p. Turbodyne Corp. subs. Studebaker-Worthington, Inc., 1976-78, v.p. fin., treas. Electric Machinery Co. subs., Mpls., 1979; with Newsweek mag., N.Y.C., 1979—; mem. acctg. adv. com. U. Minn.; tchr. control and audit aspects of computer systems Cleve. State U., part-time 1974-75; tchr. managerial acctg. Grad. Sch., Coll. St. Thomas, St. Paul, part-time 1978-79. C.P.A., Ohio. Mem. Am. Inst. C.P.A.'s, Fin. Execs. Inst., Am. Soc. Women Accountants, Inst. Internal Auditors, Ohio Soc. C.P.A.'s. Club: Mpls. Athletic. Author papers in field.

DREHER, AMY JO, ednl. cons.; b. Wooster, Ohio, Apr. 3, 1953; d. Oscar Willis and JoAnn (Lahmers) Patterson; student Ashland Coll., 1971-72; B.S. in Edn. with honors, Kent State U., 1975, M.Ed., 1977; m. Bernard Harry Dreher, May 5, 1973; 1 son, Aaron Dale. Program aide Tuscarawas County Bd. Mental Retardation, New Philadelphia, Ohio, 1972-75, tchr., 1975-77; instr. Walsh Coll. br. Dayton U., Canton, Ohio, 1980—; program cons. Ohio Dept. Mental Retardation and Developmental Disabilities, Columbus, 1977—; mem. Tuscarawas County Developmental Disabilities Speakers Bur., 1980—. Trainer foster parent edn. program Child Welfare League Am.; mem. Region 6 Human Rights for Handicapped Com. United Comml. Travelers Am. grantee, 1972-76; cert. elem. edn., spl. edn. tchr., spl. edn. supr., Ohio. Mem. Assn. for Severely Handicapped, Assn. Supervision and Curriculum Devel., Profl. Assn. for Retarded, Kappa Delta Pi. Home: 1302 Kingwood Dr Bolivar OH 44012 Office: PO Box 1180 Cambridge OH 43725

DREISBACH, DAVID WALTER, EDP systems analyst; b. Findlay, Ohio, Jan. 4, 1939; s. Ralph F. and Mildred M. Dreisbach; student (Honor scholar) Ohio No. U., 1957-58; B.S. in Edn., Bowling Green (Ohio) State U., 1964; M.A. (NSF grantee), U. Mo., Kansas City, 1968, postgrad., 1968-75; m. Brenda Lee Dreisbach, Sept. 12, 1959; children—David Walter II, Daniel Ralph. Tchr. electronics Hilo (Hawaii) High Sch., 1964-65; tchr. math. and physics Rosedale High Sch., Kansas City, Kans., 1965-73; computer programmer/analyst Hallmark Cards, Kansas City, Mo., 1973-75; sr. EDP systems analyst Mich. Consol. Gas Co., Detroit, 1976—; instr. math. Wayne State U., Detroit, 1978—. Mem. father's com. Boy Scouts Am., 1974—, sec., 1976-77, chmn., 1977—. Mem. Assn. Computing Machinery. Nazarene. Home: 26124 San Rosa Dr Saint Clair Shores MI 48081 Office: Mich Consol Gas Co One Woodward Ave Detroit MI 48226

DRESCHHOFF, GISELA AUGUSTE MARIE, physicist, educator; b. Moenchengladbach, Germany, Sept. 13, 1938; came to U.S., 1967, naturalized, 1976; d. Gustav Julius and Hildegard Friederieke (Krug) D.; Ph.D., Tech. U. Braunschweig (Germany), 1972; Staff scientist Fed. Inst. Physics and Tech. Germany, 1965-67; research asso. Kans. Geol. Survey, Lawrence, 1971-72; vis. asst. prof. physics U. Kans., 1972-74, dep. dir. radiation physics lab. Space Tech. Center, 1972-78, asso. dir. radiation physics lab., 1979—, adj. asst. prof. physics, 1974; asso. program mgr. NSF, Washington, 1978-79. Named to U. Kans. Women's Hall of Fame, 1978; recipient Antarctic Service medal U.S.A., 1979. Mem. Am. Phys. Soc., Am. Geophys. Union, AAAS, Am. Polar Soc., Antarctican Soc., Sigma Xi. Patentee identification markings for gemstones. Home: 2908 W 19th Lawrence KS 66044 Office: Space Tech Center 2291 Irving Hill Dr Lawrence KS 66045

DREVS, ROBERT ANTHONY, bus. info. systems co. ofcl.; b. Oak Park, Ill., Jan. 6, 1945; s. Walter Gregory and Rosemary Rita (LaValle) D.; B.B.A., U. Notre Dame, 1966; M.B.A., Northwestern U., 1967; postgrad. Ohio State U., 1970-73; m. Margaret Ann Martin, June 21, 1969; children—Kathryn Elaine, John Martin. Instr. So. Ill. U., Carbondale, 1973-75; asst. prof. mktg. U. Notre Dame, (Ind.), 1975-80; dir. mgmt. edn. NCR Corp., Dayton, 1980—; owner, prin. strategic mktg. cons. firm, Granger, Ind., 1975—. Served to lt. USNR, 1967-70; Vietnam. Mem. Am. Mktg. Assn., Am. Soc. Tng. and Devel., Sales and Advt. Execs., Beta Gamma Sigma. Roman Catholic. Office: 101 W Schantz St Dayton OH 45479

DREWS, HERBERT RICHARD, retail co. exec.; b. Mpls., May 3, 1924; s. Herbert H. and Zola (Howard) D.; B.S., U. Minn., 1948, J.D., 1950; m. Marlys Corinne Olson, Apr. 10, 1952; children—Pamela Kay, Richard Earl. Admitted to Minn. bar, 1950; spl. agt. FBI, N.Y.C., 1950-52; atty., Walgreens, Chgo., 1952-56, asst. dir. employee relations, 1956-59, dir. employee relations, 1959-69, v.p. human resources, 1969-78, sr. v.p. human resources, 1978—. Mem. adv. com. Coll. Commerce and Bus. Adminstrn., U. Ill. at Urbana, 1973—. Served with USAAF, 1943-46. Mem. Am. Mgmt. Assn. (human resources council), Am. Retail Fedn. (employee relations com.), Ill. C. of C., Fed. Bar Assn., Nat. Restaurant Assn., Phi Delta Theta, Phi Delta Phi. Republican. Lutheran. Clubs: Rotary, Execs., Economic (Chgo.). Home: 62 Fox Trail Lincolnshire IL 60015 Office: 200 Wilmot Rd Deerfield IL 60015

DREWS, WILLIAM EDWARD GEORGE, mfg. co. exec.; b. Cleve., Oct. 23, 1936; s. William Edward and Matilda Barbra D.; student U. Dayton, 1954-75; m. Donna Lee Benyi, June 15, 1968; 1 dau., Dawn. Applications engr. Cleve. Inst., 1957-68; product mgr. Micro Metrical Co., Ann Arbor, 1968-70; sales tng. mgr. Bendix Indsl. Metrology, Ann Arbor, 1970-71; product mgr. A&M div. Bendix Co., Dayton, Ohio, 1971-75; group sales mgr. Rank Precision Industries, Des Plaines, Ill., 1975—. Mem. Soc. Mfg. Engrs. (awardee, chmn. gaging div. rep. to Dept. Def. inspection and test subcom.), Am. Nat. Standards Inst. (mem. B89 and B46 coms.). Contbr. articles to profl. jours. Office: 411 E Jarvis St Des Plaines IL 60018

DREYER, E. JAMES, ins. exec.; b. Alexandria, Minn., Oct. 17, 1935; s. Ernest John and Amelia Emma (Kahle) D.; A.A., Luther Coll., 1955; grad. Worsham Coll. Mortuary Sci., 1956; cert. Am. Coll. Life Underwriters, 1972; m. Louise Barbara Buchner, May 11, 1957; children—Lori Louise, Ernest James, John Michael. Mortician, Furth & Co., Chgo., 1956; dist. rep. Aid Assn. for Lutherans, Chgo., 1956-63, asst. supt. agys., Appleton, Wis., 1963-72, regional dir. agys., 1972-73, asst. v.p. sales devel., 1973-74, 2nd. v.p. adv. and sales devel., 1974-79, 2nd. v.p. communications, 1979-80, v.p. corp. relations and communications, 1980—. Chmn., mem. exec. com. United Way Budget Panel, Appleton, 1975—; elder Good Shepherd Ch., Appleton, 1974-76, pres. 1969-73, 77-79, mem. bd. evangelism, 1964-68, tchr. high sch. Bible class, 1976-81; pres. bd. dirs. Jr. Achievement; chmn. NCCJ. Mem. Nat. Assn. of Life Underwriters, Life Advertisers Assn., Am. Advt. Fedn., Luth. Life Ins. Soc. of Can. (dir. 1973-80), Vis. Nurses Assn. (dir. 1974-80), Fraternal Ins. Counselors Assn., Wis. Ins. Club. Lutheran. Home: 225 E McArthur St Appleton WI 54911 Office: 4321 N Ballard Rd Appleton WI 54919

DREYFUS, LEE SHERMAN, gov. of Wis.; b. Milw., June 20, 1926; s. Woods Orlo and Clare (Bluett) D.; B.A., U. Wis., 1949, M.A., 1952, Ph.D., 1957; m. Joyce Mae Unke, Apr. 5, 1947; children—Susan Lynn, Lee Sherman. Radio actor sta. WISN, Milw., 1933-49; instr. U. Wis., 1949-52; gen. mgr. radio sta. WDET, Detroit, 1952-56; asst. prof. speech Wayne State U., 1956-60, asso. prof. speech, asso. dir. mass communications, 1960-62; gen. mgr. sta. WHA-TV, Madison, Wis., 1962-65; dir. instructional resources U. Wis., 1965-67, prof. speech, chmn. radio-TV and films, 1962-67; pres., chancellor U. Wis., Stevens Point, 1967-79; gov. State of Wis., Madison, 1979—; cons. in field. Chmn. Army adv. panel on R.O.T.C. affairs, 1969-73; chmn. Gov.'s Blue Ribbon Commn. on cable TV, 1971; ednl. cons. to sec. defense and sec. Army; chief mission under Vietnam contract for Higher Edn., U. Wis., Stevens Point Found. Inc.; dir. Sentry Broadcasting Corp. Bd. dirs. Am. Assn. State Colls. and Univs., del. to Poland, 1973, Peoples Republic China, 1975, Taiwan, 1976. Bd. dirs. Wis. Ballet Co., Birmingham (Mich.) Young People's Theatre, St. Michael's Hosp., Stevens Point, Sentry Found. Served with USNR, 1944-46. Recipient citation for mental health Gov. Mich.; Pres.'s medallions Assn. U.S. Army, 1973, 74. Mem. Nat. Gov.'s Assn. (vice chmn. internat. trade and fgn. relations), Nat. Assn. Ednl. Broadcasters (dir.), Speech Assn. Am. (chmn. radio-TV film com.), Broadcast Pioneers Am., DeMolay (Legion of Honor), com. on State-Local Relations, com. Nat. Resources and environ. mgmt.; vice-chmn. Midwest Gov.'s Conf.; Nat. co-chmn. Am. Energy Week, 1981; Phi Beta Kappa, Phi Eta Sigma, Phi Kappa Phi, Kappa Sigma, Phi Tau Phi. Republican. Episcopalian. Clubs: Masons, Am. Legion, VFW. Author: Televised Instruction, 1962; World's First Intercontinental Video Classroom Connection via Earlybird Satellite, 1965. Office: Office of Governor State Capitol Madison WI 53702*

DREZDZON, WILLIAM LAWRENCE, educator; b. Milw., Feb. 19, 1934; s. Edward Kenneth and Mildred Mary (Schneider) D.; B.S. in Math., St. Mary's U., 1957; M.S. in Math. (Esso Oil Co. fellow), Ill. Inst. Tech., 1964; children—Gregory Francis, Andrea Louise. Tchr. math., chemistry, St. Michael's High Sch., Chgo., 1957-59, Lane Tech. High Sch., Chgo., 1959-66; software design engr. A.C. Electronics div. Gen. Motors, Oak Creek, Wis., 1966-67; prof. math., chmn. dept. Kennedy-King Coll., Chgo., 1967-71; prof. math. and learning lab. coordinator Oakton Community Coll., Morton Grove, Ill., 1971—; cons. nat. calculus survey, 1975. NSF grantee, 1961-65; Chgo. Bd. Edn. grantee, summer 1964; NSF coop. program, 1971, 72; Chautauqua Course grantee, 1975—. Mem. Math. Assn. Am. (chmn. jr. coll. com. Ill. sect., 1971-74), No. Ill. Math. Assn. Community Colls. (founding pres., 1971, 72), Am. Math. Assn. Two-Yr. Colls. (chmn., 1975, pres. 1979), Nat., Ill. councils tchrs. math., Ill. Assn. Community Colls. (pres. 1979), Met. Mathematics Club of Gtr. Chgo., Adler Planetarium Soc., Ill. Assn. Personalized Learning Programs, Analytic Psychology Club of Chgo., Delta Epsilon Sigma. Regional editor Math. Assns. of Two-Year Colleges Jour., 1970—; author: Curriculum Guide of Transfer Courses for the Ill. Community College Board, 1974; Math. Research and Teaching Techniques, 1973, 76; contbr. articles td jours. Office: Oakton Community Coll 1600 E Golf Rd Des Plaines IL 60016

DRIEVER, STEVEN LEIBY, geographer; b. Nyack, N.Y., Apr. 27, 1947; s. Lawrence S. and Frances A. Driever; B.A. with distinction, U. Va., 1969; M.S., Northwestern U., 1970; Ph.D., U. Ga., 1977; m. Patricia A. Nielsen, June 14, 1969 (div.); 1 son, Steven N. Asst. prof. geography U. Mo., Kansas City, 1977—, dir. urban affairs program, 1979—. Served to capt. USMCR, 1970-76. Mem. Assn. Am. Geographers, Conf. Latin Am. Geographers, Mo. Acad. Sci. (chmn. geography sect.), Mo. Council Geog. Edn. (pres.), Sigma Xi, Phi Kappa Phi, Delta Upsilon. Republican. Presbyterian. Home: 5106 W 49th St Roeland Park KS 66205 Office: Dept Geoscis Univ Mo Kansas City MO 64110

DRISCOLL, DANIEL DELANO, photographer; b. Williamsburg, Iowa, Mar. 19, 1946; s. Vincent Edmund and Hilda Gertrude (Schmidt) D.; student U. Iowa, 1964-66; B.A., Loras Coll., 1969; student Winona Sch. Profl. Photography, summers 1969-71: m. Constance Elizabeth Kelleher, Feb. 28, 1970; children—Duree Danielle, Darren Daniel. With Hilda's Photography, Williamsburg, Ia., 1969-72; owner Driscoll Gallery, Williamsburg, 1973—, Kent Studio, Iowa City, 1975-76. Named Iowa Photographer of Year, 1975, 76, 77; Iowa fellow of photography, 1975; named Heart of Am. Photographer, 1976, 77; recipient Frank W. Medlar Meml. trophy for best portrait, 1975, 76, 77. Mem. Minn. (sweepstakes winner 1973, 74), Neb. (photographer of year 1974), Pa. (top out of state photographer 1974), Va., Am. (Master of Photography degree 1977) profl. photographers assns. Contbr. articles to profl. jours. Home: 302 W State St Williamsburg IA 52361 Office: 521 Court St Williamsburg IA 52361

DRISCOLL, GLEN ROBERT, univ. pres.; b. Sligo, Ohio, Apr. 29, 1920; s. William Arthur and Jennie Mabel (Smith) D.; student DePauw U., 1938-41; B.A., U. Louisville, 1947, LL.D., 1973; M.A., U. Minn., 1949, Ph.D., 1952; m. Dorothy June Little, Nov. 9, 1941; children—David Arthur, Robert Earl, Nancy Lee (Mrs. Russell Husted); m. Emma Jean Bolt, June 18, 1978; stepchildren—Todd Allen Seeley, Brian Christopher Bolt. Instr. history U. S.D., Vermillion, 1949-52, asst. prof., 1952-56, prof., 1956-64; prof. history, chmn. div. social scis. U. Mo., St. Louis, 1964-65, dean Coll. Arts and Scis., 1965-68, dean faculties, 1968-69, chancellor, 1969-72; pres. U. Toledo, 1972—; NSF lectr. U. Nebr., U. Tex.; dir. WGTE-TV, Toledo, N.W. Ohio Blue Cross-Blue Shield, First Nat. Bank, Toledo. Mem. Woodrow Wilson Found. Regional Bd., 1969-72; bd. dirs. Toledo Symphony Orch. Assn.; trustee Boys Club Toledo. Served with USAAF, 1942-46. Mem. Am. Council Edn., Am. Assn. State Colls. and Univs. (com. grad. studies, resolutions com.), Ohio Acad. Scis., Société d'Histoire Moderne, Soc. French Hist. Studies, Am. Assn. Higher Edn., Toledo Area C. of C., Phi Alpha Theta, Delta Chi. Methodist. Clubs: Toledo Press, Belmont Country, Toledo. Home: 3425 W Bancroft St Toledo OH 43606

DRISCOLL, JUSTIN ALBERT, bishop; b. Bernard, Iowa, Sept. 30, 1920; s. William Joseph and Agnes Mary (Healey) D.; B.A., Loras Coll., Dubuque, Iowa, 1942; postgrad. Cath. U. Am., Washington, 1942-45, Ph.D., 1952. Ordained priest Roman Catholic Ch., 1945, bishop, 1970; instr. high sch., 1945-48; sec. to Archbishops of Dubuque, 1949-51; supt. Cath. Schs., Dubuque, 1953-67; dir. Confraternity of Christian Doctrine, 1953-67; chaplain Mt. St. Francis Convent, Dubuque, 1954-67; pres. Loras Coll., 1967-70; bishop Diocese of Fargo, N.D., 1970—; instr. Briar Cliff Coll., Sioux City, Iowa. Active Red River Valley council Boy Scouts Am. Mem. Nat. Council Cath. Bishops, Red River Valley Hist. Soc., Iowa, N.D. hist. socs. Clubs: Elks, K.C. Author: The Pastor and the School, 1964; With Faith and Vision: History of Catholic Schools, 1965; Necrology of Priests of Dubuque, Iowa, 1967. Office: 1310 Broadway Fargo ND 58107

DRISKELL, CLAUDE EVANS, dentist; b. Chgo., Jan. 13, 1926; s. James Ernest and Helen Elizabeth (Perry) D., Sr.; B.S., Roosevelt U., 1950; B.S. in Dentistry, U. Ill., 1952, D.D.S., 1954; m. Naomi Roberts, Sept. 30, 1953; 1 dau., Yvette Michele; stepchildren—Isaiah, Ruth, Reginald, Elaine. Practice dentistry, Chgo., 1954—. Adj. prof. Chgo. State U., 1971—; dean's aide, adviser black students Coll. Dentistry U. Ill., 1972—; dental cons., supervising dentist, dental hygienists supportive health services Bd. Edn., Chgo., 1974. Vice pres. bd. dirs. Jackson Park Highlands Assn., 1971-73. Served with AUS, 1944-46; ETO. Fellow Internat. Biog. Assn., Royal Soc. Health (Gt. Britain), Acad. Gen. Dentistry; mem. Lincoln (editor), Chgo. dental socs., Am., Nat. (editor pres.'s newsletter; dir. pub. relations, publicity; recipient pres.'s spl. achievement award 1969) dental assns., Am. Assn. Dental Editors, Acad. Gen. Dentistry, Soc. Med. Writers, Soc. Advancement Anesthesia in Dentistry, Omega Psi Phi. Author: The Influence of the Halogen Elements upon the Hydrocarbon, and their Effect on General Anesthesia, 1962. Asst. editor Nat. Dental Assn. Quar. Jour., 1977—. Contbr. articles to profl. jours. Home: 6727 S Bennett Ave Chicago IL 60649 Office: 11139 S Halsted St Chicago IL 60628

DROEGEMUELLER, ARTHUR CLARENCE, pub. accountant; b. Chgo., June 6, 1904; s. William A. and Ida W. (Lannefeld) D.; Ph.B., U. Chgo., 1925; C.P.A., U. Ill., 1930; m. Katherine H. Meyer, Nov. 19, 1927 (div.), children—Joan Louise (Mrs. Richard J. Wilke), Katherine Ellen (Mrs. R. Thomas Saether); m. 2d, Marjorie Adams Aldrich, 1954; 1 stepson, Frederick B. Aldrich. Pub. accountant, 1923—; with Frazer and Torbet, C.P.A.'s, 1930-54, partner, 1941-54; sr. partner Droegemueller, Brady & Nelson, C.P.A.'s, 1955-56; partner Main & Co., C.P.A.'s 1956-63, Main Lafrentz & Co., C.P.A.'s, 1963-65; individual practice, 1965—. Treas. Chgo. Luth. Theol. Sem., 1939-60; mem. bd. mgmt. Onward Neighborhood House (pres. 1950-51). C.P.A., Ill., Tex., Wis. Mem. Am. Inst. C.P.A.'s, Ill. Soc. C.P.A.'s (sec.-treas. 1946-48), Phi Pi Phi (nat. treas. 1933-39), Alpha Sigma Phi. Lutheran. Club: Union League. Home and Office: 309 Tanglewood Ln Naperville IL 60540

DROTNING, PHILLIP THOMAS, oil co. exec.; b. Deerfield, Wis., July 4, 1920; s. Edward Clarence and Martha (Skaar) D.; student U. Wis., 1937-41; m. Loretta Jayne Taylor, Nov. 3, 1964; children—Meredith Anne, Maria Kristina, Misya Kerri. Reporter, Wis. State Jour., Madison, 1943-44; editorial page writer Milw. Jour., 1944-45; freelance author, 1945-47; exec. sec. to gov., Wis., 1948-55; v.p. Northwest Airlines, Inc., 1956-61; spl. asst. to adminstr. NASA, Washington, 1961-65; exec. communications cons. Standard Oil Co. (Ind.), 1965-66; mgr. communications Am. Oil Co., Chgo., 1967-68; dir. urban affairs Standard Oil Co. of Ind., Chgo., 1968-72, dir. pub. affairs ops., 1973, dir. corp. social policy, 1973—. Dir. Highland Community Bank, Chgo., 1973-79. Bd. dirs., first v.p. Child Care Assn. Ill., 1973-76, pres., 1976-78; bd. dirs. T.R.U.S.T., Inc., 1976-79, pres., 1979—. Served with USMCR, 1941-43. Mem. Pub. Relations Soc. Am., Nat. Assn. Mfrs. (chmn. urban affairs com. 1969-71), Nat. Minority Purchasing Council (pres. 1972-77). Clubs: National Press, International, Federal City (Washington); Lake Forest (Ill.); Plaza (Chgo.). Author: A Guide to Negro History in America, 1968; Black Heroes in our Nation's History, 1969; A Job with a Future in the Petroleum Industry, 1969; Up from the Ghetto, 1970; New Hope for Problem Drinkers, 1977; Taking Stock: A Woman's Guide to Corporate Success, 1977; Putting the Fun in Fundraising, 1979; How To Get Your Creditors off Your Back without Losing Your Shirt, 1979; editorial advisory bd. The Chicago Reporter, 1971—; contbr. numerous articles to pubs. Home: 400 N Washington Rd Lake Forest IL 60045 Office: 200 E Randolph Dr Chicago IL 60601

DRUMMOND, JAY RENARD, advt. agy. exec.; b. Oakland, Calif., Nov. 22, 1944; s. John William and Doris Irene (Beton) D.; grad. Alexander Hamilton Inst., 1973; children—Jay Renard, DeAnna Darlene. With Spartan Industries, 1962-64; retail merchandiser Mattel, Inc., 1964-67; store mgr. Gateway Co., Kansas City, Mo., 1967-69; mktg. dir. Metcalf South Shopping Center, Overland Park, Kans., 1969-70; promotion dir., mktg./advt. mgr., dir. J.C. Nichols Co., Kansas City, Mo., 1970-79; account exec. N.W. Ayer Inc., Detroit, 1979—; mktg./advt. cons., 1969-79. Active Head Start Program, 1969-75, Progressive Alert for Parents, Kansas City, Mo., 1969-79, Leukemia Soc. Am., 1978-79, Jr. Achievement, 1969-79; advisor United Way, 1970-79; bd. dirs. Greenway Fields Homes Assn., 1978-79. Recipient awards U.S. Army, 1974, 79, U.S. Army Res., 1973, Civil Def., 1970, Greater Kansas City Mchts. Assn., 1970-79, Radio and TV Council, 1970's. Mem. Detroit C. of C., Assn. U.S. Army, Friends Greenfield Village and Henry Ford Mus., Smithsonian Assos., Nat. Fedn. Ind. Bus., Nat. Geog. Soc. Club: Adcraft (Detroit). Office: NW Ayer Inc 428 Clinton St Detroit MI 48226

DRUMMY, WILLIAM WALLACE, JR., physician; b. Omaha, Jan. 3, 1923; B.S., Villanova Coll.; M.D., Harvard U., 1948. Intern, then resident in internal medicine Boston City Hosp., 1948-49, 51-52; research fellow in endocrinology New Eng. Med. Center Hosp.-Ziskind Meml. Lab., Boston, 1952-53; practice medicine specializing in internal medicine, Terre Haute, Ind., 1972—; mem. staff Union, Terre Haute Regional hosps.; asso. prof. Ind. U. Med. Sch., 1972-76, mem. adj. faculty Terre Haute Center of Med. Edn., 1981—. Served as officer M.C., USAF, 1950-56. Diplomate Am. Bd. Internal Medicine. Office: 1024 S 6th St Terre Haute IN 47807

DRURY, JOHN, TV journalist. Formerly reporter, newscaster WBBM-TV, WLS-TV, Chgo.; now newscaster WGN-TV and Radio, Chgo. Bd. dirs. Summit Sch., East Dundee, Ill. Recipient award for best enterprise reporting A.P., 1971; Best Documentary award U.P.I., 1973; Med. Journalism award State Med. Soc., 1973. Mem. Sigma Delta Chi (bd. dirs.). Club: Headline of Chgo. Office: WGN-TV and Radio 2501 W Bradley Pl Chicago IL 60618

DRYDEN, RAYMOND EDWARD, mktg. exec.; b. Omaha, June 20, 1946; s. Ray J. and Cecilia A. Dryden; B.A., (Thomas L. Yates scholar), Tex. Christian U., 1968; M.S. (J.W. Young fellow), U. Ill., 1969; m. Mary Teresa Caparas, Jan. 16, 1971; children—Marissa J., Christopher E. In account mgmt. positions Compton Advt. Inc., N.Y.C. and overseas, 1970-73, William Esty Advt. Inc., N.Y.C., 1973-75; v.p. mktg., consumer products div. Swift & Co., Chgo., 1975-80, Abbott Labs., 1980—. Named Outstanding Advt. Grad., Tex. Christian U., 1968. Mem. Kappa Tau Alpha. Club: K.C. Office: North Chicago IL 60064

DUBANIEWICZ, PETER PAUL, artist, educator; b. Cleve., Nov. 17, 1913; s. Joseph and Elizabeth (Boboryk) D.; grad. Cleve. Inst. Art, 1935; postgrad. Boston Mus. Sch. Fine Arts, 1935-38; m. Frances C. Kriss, May 20, 1946; children—Dennis, Amy, Paula. Instr. Cleve. Inst. Art, 1945-79, Western Res. U., Cleve., 1977—. One man-shows of paintings include: Ursuline Coll., Pepper Pike, Ohio, 1975, U. Dayton (Ohio), 1979; numerous group shows including: Met. Mus. N.Y.C., 1941, 56, Corcoran Mus., Cleve. Inst. Art, Beck Centre, Lakewood, Ohio; represented in numerous permanent collections including: Cleve. Mus. Art, Butler Art Inst., various public bldgs. and pvt. collections. Served with C.E., U.S. Army, 1941-44. Recipient numerous awards including: Iroquois award Polish Am. Nat. Show, 1950; First Prize award Water Color Soc., 1951; Gov.'s award Ohio State Fair, 1957; Buffalo Art award, 1963. Mem. Cleve. Soc. Artists (pres. 1949-51), Polonaise Arts of Cleve. (pres. 1949-50), Am. Water Color Soc. Home: 3289 Fairmount Blvd Cleveland Heights OH 44118 Office: Cleveland Inst Art 11141 E Blvd Cleveland OH 44106

DUBAY, LIONEL A., wire products co. exec.; b. Old Town, Maine, Sept. 16, 1948; s. Ernest A. and Coral G. Dubay; B.S., U. Maine, 1972; m. Gwendolyn A. Johnson, June 5, 1971; children—Ty Brandon, Tara Lee. Nat. consumer products mgr. Cornish Wire Co., Williamstown, Mass., 1973-77; Eastern regional sales mgr. Woods Wire Co., Carmel, Ind., 1977-79, nat. sales mgr., 1979-81, v.p. sales, Hardware div., 1981, v.p. mktg., 1981—. Asst. baseball and soccer coach; Coach Boone County Basketball League, 1981. Methodist. Home: 200 Governors Ln Zionsville IN 46077 Office: Woods Wire Co 510 3d Ave SW Carmel IN 46032

DUBES, GEORGE RICHARD, geneticist; b. Sioux City, Iowa, Oct. 12, 1926; s. George Wesley and Regina Eleanor (Kelleher) D.; B.S., Iowa State U., Ames, 1949; Ph.D., Calif. Inst. Tech., Pasadena, 1953; m. Margaret Joanne Tumberger, July 25, 1964; children—George Richard, David Frank, Deanna Marie, Kenneth Wesley, Deborah Joanne, Keith Timothy. Research asso. McCollum-Pratt Inst. for Research in Micronutrient Elements, Johns Hopkins U., 1953-54; research asso. sect. virus research dept. pediatrics U. Kans. Sch. Medicine, Kansas City, Kans., 1954-56, asst. prof., 1956-60, asso. prof., 1960-64; head viral genetics Eppley Cancer Inst., U. Nebr. Med. Center, Omaha, 1964-68, asso. prof. dept. med. microbiology, 1964-81, prof., 1981—; vis. lectr. U. Baghdad (Iraq), U. Mosul (Iraq), 1977. Co-pres., Adams Sch. PTA, Omaha, 1976-77; mem. Omaha Public Schs. Citizens Adv. Com., 1977-80. Served with AUS, 1945-46. AEC fellow, 1951-52; Caltech McCallum fellow, 1951-52; Nat. Inst. Allergy and Infectious Diseases grantee, 1966-69; NIH Gen. Research Support grantee, 1964-72. Mem. Am. Assn. Cancer Research, AAAS, Am. Genetic Assn., Am. Inst. Biol. Scis., Am. Soc. Microbiology, Biometric Soc., Genetics Soc. Am., Nebr. Acad. Scis., N.Y. Acad. Scis., Sigma Xi. Author: Methods for Transfecting Cells with Nucleic Acids of Animal Viruses: A Review, 1971. Contbr. numerous articles to sci. jours. Home: 7515 Lawndale St Omaha NE 68134 Office: Dept Med Microbiology U Nebr Coll Medicine 42d and Dewey Ave Omaha NE 68105

DUBETZ, MICHAEL, educator; b. Hazel Creek, Pa., Nov. 11, 1909; s. Thomas and Mary (Nesterak) D.; B.S., Kent State U., 1941; postgrad. U. Pitts., 1940-46; M.Ed., U. So. Calif., 1953; postgrad. Ohio State U., summers 1949-56; m. Shirley A. Robb, June 11, 1955; children—Nancy, Paul, Michael, Dianne, Mary. Grade sch. prin., Jefferson County, Ohio, 1937-41, tchr. English and speech Jefferson County Jr. High Sch., 1935-41, High Sch., 1940-41; supt. Springfield Twp. Sch. Dist., Bergholz, Ohio, 1946; tchr. speech and dramatics Gibsonburg (Ohio) High Sch., 1945, Circleville (Ohio) High Sch., 1946-47; asso. prof. speech Kent (Ohio) State U., 1948-81, emeritus prof. speech, 1981—, dir. student speakers bur., 1954-68, chmn. Buckeye Tournament Student Timekeepers, 1958-67, dir. play prodns., Kent-Canton, 1948-50. Adviser, Eastern Orthodox Fellowship, 1960-62. Served with U.S. Army, 1942-45. Mem. Speech Assn. Am., Speech Communication Assn. Ohio, Central States Speech Assn., Ohio Assn. Coll. Tchrs. Speech, AAUP (membership com., 1950-58), Phi Delta Kappa, Alpha Psi Omega, Alpha Phi Omega, Phi Sigma Kappa. Contbr. article to profl. publ. Home: 3464 Sandy Lake Rd Ravenna OH 44266 Office: Dept Speech Kent State University Kent OH 44242

DUBIN, HOWARD VICTOR, dermatologist; b. N.Y.C., Mar. 28, 1938; s. Meyer and Blanche D.; A.B., Columbia U., 1958, M.D., 1962; m. Patricia Sue Tucker, June 10, 1962; children—Douglas Scott, Kathryn Sue, David Andrew, Michael Stonier. Intern, U. Mich., 1962-63, resident in internal medicine, 1963-64, resident in dermatology, 1968-70, asst. prof., 1970-72, asso. prof., 1972-75, clin. asso. prof., 1975-77, clin. prof., 1977—; resident in internal medicine Columbia-Presbyterian Med. Center, N.Y.C., 1966-68; practice medicine specializing in dermatology, Ann Arbor, Mich., 1970—. Trustee, Greenhills Sch., Ann Arbor, 1979—, pres. bd. trustees, 1981-82. Served with U.S. Army, 1964-66. Diplomate Am. Bd. Dermatology, Am. Bd. Internal Medicine. Fellow A.C.P.; mem. Am. Acad. Dermatology, Soc. Investigative Dermatology, Dermatology Found., Mich. Dermatol. Soc., AMA, Mich. Med. Soc., Washtenaw County Med. Soc., Sigma Xi. Club: Rotary. Contbr. articles to profl. jours. Office: 3250 Plymouth Rd Ann Arbor MI 48105

DUBNOW, BEATRICE, educator. Tchr., Chgo. public schs., 1954-64, reading clinician Bur. Child Study, 1964-67; asso. prof. Roosevelt U., Chgo., 1967-76, prof., 1976—, dean's grant fellow Coll. Edn., 1979-80. Bd. dirs. Citizens' Schs. Com., Chgo., 1974—; pres. Women's Scholarship Assn. Roosevelt U., 1975-78; bd. dirs. Roosevelt U. Women's Scholarship Assn., 1978—. Mem. Internat., Chgo. Area reading assns., Children's Lit. Assn., Nat. Council Tchrs. English (participant profl. assemblies), Assn. Childhood Edn. Internat., Nat. Soc. Study Edn., Internat. Council Edn. for Teaching, Nat. Council Children with Learning Disabilities, Ill. Reading Council, Am. Ednl. Research Assn., Franklin Honor Soc. Recipient Kate Maremont Dedicated Tchr. award, 1968; contbr. articles to profl. jours.; co-developed The Self-Report Reading Scale. Office: Coll Edn 430 S Michigan Ave Chicago IL 60605

DUBUS, ANNA MADEAN, ednl. adminstr.; b. Bay, Ark., May 5, 1937; d. James A. and Laura Abgill (Mitchell) Blalock; B.S.E., Ark. State U., 1960; M.S. in Vocat. Bus. and Office Edn., U. Mo., Columbia, 1974; m. James Wilton DuBus, Dec. 19, 1959; children—James Kendall, Lyle Wilton. Acctg. clk. Southwestern Bell Telephone and Telegraph, Memphis, 1956-58; tchr. Cash (Ark.) Public Schs., 1959-60, Risco (Mo.) Public Schs., 1961-64, Mexico (Mo.) Public Schs., 1964-68; tchr., coordinator Mexico Area Vocat. Sch., 1968-79, job placement specialist, 1979—. Mem. Am. Vocat. Assn., Mo. State Tchrs. Assn., Mo. Vocat. Assn., Mexico Community Tchrs. Assn., Delta Kappa Gamma. Home: 1505 Webster Dr Mexico MO 65265 Office: 905 N Wade Mexico MO 65265

DUCHARME, ROBERT GEORGE, urban planning cons. co. exec.; b. Mapleville, R.I., Sept. 8, 1925; s. Homer George and Fabiola Florestine (Rock) D.; A.B., Goddard Coll., 1951; M.A. in Econs., Syracuse U., 1952, Ph.D. in Econs., 1964; m. Myra Edelman Swanson, July 26, 1970; children—Robyn, Peter, Donna; stepdaus.—Dawne, Gail Swanson. Research asst. Planning Commn., City of Syracuse, 1952-56; chief planning analyst Dept. Planning, City of Milw., 1956-60, planning coordinator Mayor's Office, 1960-62; dep. dir. Northeastern Ill. Planning Commn., Chgo., 1962-79; prin. Robert G. Ducharme Inc., Deerfield, Ill., 1979—; lectr. econs. and stats. U. Wis., Milw. Mem. Deerfield Village Planning Commn., 1972-75; chmn. Deerfield Sch. Consolidation Study Com., 1973. Served with USAAF, 1943-45. Decorated Air medal with 4 clusters. Mem. Met. Housing and Planning Council, Chgo. Assn. Commerce and Industry, Am. Econ. Assn., Am. Inst. Cert. Planners, Am. Planning Assn., Lambda Alpha. Contbr. articles in field. Home and Office: 1300 Charing Cross Rd Deerfield IL 60015

DUCHESNEAU, PAUL MCLEAN, physician; b. Auburn, Mass., June 9, 1923; s. A. P. and Gladys (McLean) D.; B.S., U. R.I., 1948; M.D., Boston U., 1952; m. Renate Elizabeth Halley, May 23, 1953; 1 son, David. Intern, Percy Jones Army Hosp., Battle Creek, Mich., 1952-53; resident in radiology Roosevelt Hosp., N.Y.C., 1954-57; adj. radiotherapist Hosp. for Spl. Surgery, N.Y.C., 1957-58; staff radiologist Meml. Hosp., N.Y.C., 1958-60; staff radiologist Cleve. Clinic, 1960—, head neuroradiology, 1965—. Scoutmaster Boy Scouts Am., 1967-72. Served to capt. USAF, 1943-46, 52-54. Mem. Am. Soc. Neuroradiology, Radiologic Soc. N.Am., Am. Coll. Radiology, Ohio State Med. Assn., AMA. Clubs: Mentor Harbor Yachting, Cleve. Ski. Home: 2977 Fontenay Rd Shaker Heights OH 44120 Office: 2020 E 93d St Cleveland OH 44106

DUCHOSSOIS, RICHARD L., corp. exec.; b. Chgo., 1921; student Morgan Park Mil. Acad.; student Washington and Lee U., Lexington, Va. Pres., chief exec. officer, dir. Duchossois-Thrall Group, Inc., Chicago Heights, Ill.; chmn. Thrall Car Mfg. Co., Transportation Corp. of Am., Chamberlain Mfg. Corp.; pres., dir. Arthur Equipment Co.; dir. Olympia State Bank, Chgo. Short Line R.R., LaSalle Nat. Bank, Chgo., Western Stoneware Co., Am. High Speed Rail Corp. Office: PO Box 218 Chicago Heights IL 60411

DUCKRO, PAUL NICHOLAS, clin. psychologist; b. Dayton, Ohio, Aug. 23, 1947; s. Robert Joseph and Isabella (Spadavecchia) D.; Ph.D., Tex. Tech. U., 1977; 1 dau., Amy. Psychologist, Malcolm Bliss Mental Health Center, St. Louis, 1977—; asst. prof. dept. psychiatry Washington U., St. Louis, 1977-82; asst. prof. dept. psychiatry St. Louis U., 1982—, dir. biofeedback services, 1982—. Mem. Am. Psychol. Assn., Mo. Psychol. Assn.

DUDEK, BERNARD JOSEPH, computer specialist; b. Chgo., Dec. 30, 1941; s. Barney Joseph and Essie Pauline (Carter) D.; B.S. in Math., U. Ill., 1972; M.B.A., DePaul U., 1976; m. Jane Pierce Rood, May 6, 1967; 1 son, Bernard Joseph. Computer operator Argonne (Ill.) Nat. Lab., 1966; mgr. data processing U. Ill., Chgo., 1966-74, Bell and Howell Corp., Chgo., 1974-76, Morton Norwich Corp., Chgo., 1976—; instr. bus. adminstrn. Elmhurst (Ill.) Coll., 1973—; cons. in field. Served with U.S. Army, 1964-66. Mem. Assn. Computing Machinery, Soc. Certified Data Processors, Data Processing Mgmt. Assn. (certified data processor 1973). Home: 786 S Swain St Elmhurst IL 60126 Office: 110 N Wacker Dr Chicago IL 60606

DUDEWICZ, EDWARD JOHN, educator; b. Jamaica, N.Y., Apr. 24, 1942; s. Edward George and Adele (Drula) D.; S.B., Mass. Inst. Tech., 1963; M.S., Cornell U., 1966, Ph.D., 1969; m. Patricia Anne Scott, July 6, 1963; children—Douglas, Robert, Carolyn. Asst. engr. AVCO Corp., Wilmington, Mass., 1963; asst. prof. statistics U. Rochester, 1967-72, asst. prof. biostatistics, 1971-72; asso. prof. statistics Ohio State U., 1972-77, prof., 1977—, chmn. grad. com. statistics and biostatistics, 1973-75, 78-80; vis. scholar, vis. asso. prof. Stanford U., 1976; vis. prof. U. Louvain (Belgium), 1979; cons. in field. Office Naval Research grantee, 1967-72, 79—; U.S. Army grantee, 1972-74; NSF fellow, 1966-67; NATO grantee, 1978—; Nat. Cancer Inst. grantee, 1979—. Fellow N.Y. Acad. Scis., Inst. Math. Stats., Am. Statis. Assn.; mem. Math. Assn. Am., AAUP, Japan Statis. Soc., Am. Soc. Quality Control (Jack Youden prize 1981), Sigma Xi (research award Ohio State U. chpt. 1977), Phi Kappa Phi. Author: Introduction to Statistics and Probability, 1976; Solutions in Statistics and Probability, 1980; The Handbook of Random Number Generation and Testing, 1981; The Complete Categorized Guide to Statistical Selection and Ranking Procedures, 1981; editor: Statis. Theory and Method Abstracts, 1975—, Am. Jour. Math. and Mgmt. Scis., 1979—; contbr. articles to profl. jours. Home: 2524 Dorset Rd Upper Arlington OH 43221 Office: Dept Statistics Ohio State U Columbus OH 43210

DUDLEY, DAVID BARKER, food co. exec.; b. Columbus, Ohio, Apr. 6, 1930; s. Robert Lewis and Virginia (Barker) D.; B.S., Ohio State U., 1952; m. Susan Heath, Aug. 23, 1953; children—Karen Sue Nevergall, Ann Louise. With M&R Dietetic Labs., Inc., Columbus, 1954-64, dir. sales spl. products div., 1960-64; with L.K. Baker & Co., Columbus, 1964—, sec.-treas., 1964-68, exec. v.p., 1968—. Mem. city council City of Grandview Heights, Ohio, 1972—, pres., 1980—. Served to lt. Q.M.C., AUS, 1952-54. Mem. U.S. Power Squadrons, Nat. Food Processors Assn. (dir. 1971-72, 74-76), Ohio Food Processors Assn. (dir. 1968-75, 78-79, pres. 1972), Ohio Automatic Merchandising Assn. (dir. 1970—), Inst. Food Technologists, Charity Newsies, Columbus C. of C., Columbus Maennerchor, Delta Tau Delta. Clubs: The Crew's Nest (Put-in-Bay, Ohio); Nor'Easter (Catawba Island, Ohio). Home: 1117 Wyandotte Rd Columbus OH 43212 Office: 1215 W Mound St Columbus OH 43223

DUDLEY, DURAND STOWELL, librarian; b. Cleve., Feb. 28, 1926; s. George Stowell and Corinne Elizabeth (Durand) D.; B.A., Oberlin Coll., 1948; M.L.S., Case Western Res. U., 1950; m. Dorothy Woolworth, July 3, 1954; children—Jane Elizabeth, Deborah Anne. Librarian, Marietta (O.) Coll. Library, 1953-55, Akron (O.) Pub. Library, 1955-60; librarian Marathon Oil Co., Findlay, O., 1960—, sr. law librarian, 1974—. Mem. Spl. Libraries Assn., Am. Assn. Law Libraries. Presbyterian (deacon). Home: 865 Maple Ave Findlay OH 45840 Office: Marathon Oil Co 539 S Main St Findlay OH 45840

DUDLEY, HORACE CHESTER, scientist, educator; b. St. Louis, June 28, 1909; s. Horace Chester and Rhoda Olivette (McAdoo) D.; A.B., Mo. State Coll., 1931; Ph.D. in Chemistry, Georgetown U., 1941; postgrad. U. Calif., 1948, USN courses, 1948-49, Oak Ridge Inst. Nuclear Studies, 1949, U.S. Army Tng. Center, 1949, N.Y. U., 1957; m. Thelma Avis Scott, June 13, 1935 (dec.); children—Jeanette, David; m. 2d, Joan Marie Kallenback, Nov. 6, 1954; children—Robert, Susan. Lab. asst. U.S. Bur. Standards, Washington, 1931-32; jr. chemist bur. chemistry Dept. Agr., Washington, 1933-34; asst. chemist div. med. research Chem. Warfare Service, Edgewood Arsenal, Md., 1934-36; biochemist USPHS, Bethesda, Md., 1936-42; commd. lt. USN, 1942, advanced through grades to capt., 1955; explosives specialist, comdg. officer USN units, PTO, 1942-47; head div. biochemistry USN Med. Research Inst., Bethesda, 1947-52; head sect. allied sci. Med. Service Corps, Washington, 1949-52; head radioisotope lab. dept. radiology U.S. Naval Hosp., St. Albans, N.Y., 1952-62; ret., 1962; prof. physics, chmn. dept. physics U. So. Miss., 1962-69; prof. radiation physics U. Ill. Med. Center, Chgo., 1969-77; ret., 1977; dir. RadSafety Assos.; mem. coop. clin. research program, med. library Hines (Ill.) VA Med. Center, 1980—; cons. in field, 1947—. Decorated Bronze Star, Sec. Navy medal; recipient Am. Chem. Soc. prize, 1929; AEC grantee, 1963-64; NSF grantee, 1963, 65; U. So. Miss. grantee, 1965, 66, 67; U. Ill. grantee, 1970, 72. Fellow AAAS; mem. Am. Phys. Soc., Health Physics Soc., Am. Assn. Physics Tchrs., Am. Assn. Physicists in Medicine, Am. Bd. Health Physics (certified), Sigma Xi. Club: Masons. Author: New Principles in Quantum Mechanics, 1959; Morality of Nuclear Planning, 1976; contbr. articles to profl. jours.; patentee in field. Home: 405 W 8th Pl Hinsdale IL 60521

DUDLEY, JOHN HENRY, floriculture-horticulture co. exec.; b. Detroit, Nov. 17, 1912; s. Henry Augustus and Margaret Helen (Bigelow) D.; grad. Detroit U. Sch. 1932; B.A., Mich. State U., 1937; student Am. Mgmt. Assn. seminars; m. Elizabeth Baird Dean, June 21, 1940; children—John Henry, Thomas Dean. With John Henry Co., 1937—, gen. mgr., 1939-62, pres., 1939-72, chmn. bd., 1972-78, hon. chmn. bd., 1978; mem. fin. staff of U.S. Senator Robert P. Griffin, 1978; judge Bicentennial Rose Parade, Pasadena, Calif., 1976; speaker to florist meetings. Former v.p., chmn., bd. dirs. Mich. United Fund; past pres., campaign chmn. United Community Chest Greater Lansing Area; past area chmn. Project Hope; past chmn. Ingham County Rehab. Centers; past mem. Mich. Gov.'s Com. Traffic Safety; past mem. state bd. Am. Cancer Soc., past campaign chmn., past pres. Ingham County unit; past chmn. United Negro Coll. Fund, YMCA; chmn. spl. study and adv. com. YMCA-YWCA; mem. Pres.'s Commn. White House Fellowships, 1976—; mem. Los Angeles Olympic Organizing Com., 1984; bd. dirs. Student Loan Mktg. Assn., 1975-78. Served from lt. (j.g.) to lt. comdr., USNR, 1942-45. Decorated Navy Marine medal, Bronze Star; named to Floriculture Hall of Fame, 1966, Fla. Florists Hall of Fame, 1978. Mem. Soc. Am. Florists (past pres., past chmn. nat. advt. council, nat. edn. com., gold medal 1979), Florists Telegraph Delivery Assn. (dir. 1950, nat. award), All Florist Industry Congress (founder, co-chmn.), Mich. Florists Assn. (past pres., dir., chmn. prizes, awards com., mem. com., publs. com., Outstanding Service award, nat. award), Wholesale Florists and Florist Suppliers Am. (past treas., dir., Lee Kintzele award 1973), Florists Transworld Delivery Assn. (past dir.), Soc. Am. Florists Endowment (charter, founder, trustee, v.p., treas., chmn.), Am. Inst. Floral Designers (hon.). Rotarian. Clubs: Lansing City (pres. 1959), Lansing Automobile, Lansing Country (past pres., bd. govs.); Detroit, Detroit Economic; Los Angeles Country; Capitol Hill, Metropolitan (Washington); New York Metropolitan. Home: 610 W Ottawa St Lansing MI 48933 also 875 Comstock Ave Apt 17-F Los Angeles CA 90024

DUDLEY, PAUL V., bishop; b. Northfield, Minn., 1926; s. Edward Austin and Margaret Ann (Nolan) D.; student Nazareth Coll., St. Paul Sem. Ordained priest Roman Cath. Ch., 1951; titular bishop of Ursona, aux. bishop of St. Paul-Mpls., 1977-78; bishop of Sioux Falls, S.D., 1978—. Office: Chancery Office 423 N Duluth Ave Sioux Falls SD 57104*

DUERBUSCH, TOM HENRY, sr. sci. systems analyst; b. St. Louis, Aug. 30, 1954; s. John Paul and Emily D.; B.S., U. Mo., St. Louis, 1976. Cons., Marketeam Assos., St. Louis, 1974-77; programmer Fin. Automation, Inc., St. Louis, 1977, Nationwide Fin. Services, St. Louis, 1978—; sr. sci./systems analyst Modern Urban Systems Tech., 1979—; cons. Modern Urban Systems Tech., Inc., St. Louis, 1978—; sci. programmer analyst U. Mo., St. Louis, 1974-79. Mem. St. Louis Area Computer Club, U.S. Robotics Soc. Home: 1532 Marbella Apt 9 Saint Louis MO 63138 Office: 8420 Delmal Saint Louis MO 63124

DUERRE, JOHN ARDEN, microbial physiologist, biochemist; b. Webster, S.D., Aug. 21, 1930; s. Dewey H. and Stella M. (Barber) D.; B.S., S.D. State U., 1952, M.S. (Lederle fellow), 1956; Ph.D., U. Minn., 1960; m. Benna Bee Harris, June 16, 1957; children—Gail, Dawn, Arden. Research asso., AEC fellow Argonne (Ill.) Nat. Lab., 1960-61; research bacteriologist NIH Rocky Mountain Lab., Hamilton, Mont., 1961-63; asst. prof. microbiology U. N.D. Med. Sch., 1963-65, asso. prof., 1965-71, prof. microbiology, 1971—; vis. scientist neuropsychiat. research unit Research Council Lab., Carchalton, Surrey, Eng., 1969-70. Chmn. Grand Forks County (N.D.) Wildlife Fedn., 1965-67, 77-78, Grand Forks chpt. Ducks Unltd., 1970, 77-78; dist. dir. N.D. Wildlife Fedn., 1976-77. Served with U.S. Army, 1953-55. Recipient Career Devel. award NIH, 1965-75; NIH grantee, 1966, 71-81; NSF grantee, 1963-71. Mem. N.Y., N.D. acads. scis., Am. Soc. Microbiologists, Fedn. Am. Soc. Exptl. Biology, Henrici Soc., Sigma Xi (Outstanding Research award 1977). Democrat. Clubs: Grand Forks Curling, Grand Forks Gun, Elks. Contbr. numerous articles to profl. publs. Home: 918 N 26th St Grand Forks ND 58201 Office: U ND Med Sch Grand Forks ND 58201

DUESENBERG, RICHARD WILLIAM, lawyer, business exec.; b. St. Louis, Dec. 10, 1930; s. (John August) Hugo and Edna Marie (Warmann) D.; B.A., Valparaiso U., 1951, J.D., 1953; LL.M., Yale, 1956; m. Phyllis Evelyn Buehner, Aug. 7, 1955; children—Karen, Daryl, Mark, David. Admitted to Mo. bar, 1953; prof. law N.Y. U. Sch. Law, 1956-62, dir. Law Center Publs., 1960-62; sr. atty. Monsanto Co., St. Louis, 1963-70, asst. gen. counsel, asst. sec., 1975-77, v.p., sec., gen. counsel, 1977—; dir. law Monsanto Textiles Co., St. Louis, 1971-75; corp. sec. Fisher Controls Co., Marshalltown, Iowa, 1969-71; corp. sec. Olympia Industries, Inc., Spartanburg, S.C., 1974-75; vis. prof. law U. Mo. Sch. Law, 1970-71; faculty Banking Sch. of South La. State U., 1967—; mem. legal adv. com. Chem. Mfrs. Assn., Washington; dir. Fisher Controls Co. of Del., St. Louis, 1979-80. Bd. dirs. Luth. Med. Center, St. Louis, 1973—, vice chmn., 1975-80; bd. dirs. Valparaiso U., 1977—, chmn. bd. visitors Law Sch., 1966—; bd. dirs. Bach Soc. of St. Louis, 1965—, pres., 1973-77; mem. adv. bd. Southwestern Legal Found., Dallas, 1977—; mem. lawyers adv. council NAM, Washington, 1980—; mem. com. on interag. coordination Adminstrv. Conf. of U.S., 1980—. Served with AUS, 1953-55. Recipient Distinguished Alumnus award Valparaiso U., 1976. Mem. Am. Law Inst., Assn. Gen. Counsel, Luth. Acad. for Scholarship, Am. Arbitration Assn. (mem. nat. panel arbitrators 1960), Am. (chmn. subcom. on sales, bulk transfers and title documents 1970-76, com. on uniform comml. code 1976-79, mem. council sect. on corps., banking and bus. law 1979—), Mo., St. Louis, Internat. bar assns., Am. Judicature Soc., Order of Coif. Lutheran. Author (with L. King) Sales and Bulk Transfers Under the Uniform Commercial Code, 2 vols., 1966, rev. edits., 1977, 80; New York Law of Contracts, 3 vols., 1964; Missouri Forms and Practice Under the Uniform Commercial Code, 2 vols., 1966. Editor: Ann. Survey of Am. Law, N.Y. U., 1961-62; bd. contbg. editors, adv. Corp. Law Rev., 1977—; contbr. articles to law revs., jours. Home: 9124 Glencrest Dr Saint Louis MO 63126 Office: 800 N Lindbergh Blvd Saint Louis MO 63166

DUESENBERG, ROBERT HENRY, lawyer; b. St. Louis, Dec. 10, 1930; s. Hugo John August and Edna (Warmann) D.; B.A., Valparaiso U., 1951, LL.B., 1953; LL.M., Harvard, 1956; m. Lorraine F. Hall; children—Lynda Renee, Kirsten Lynn, John Robert. Admitted to Mo. bar, 1953; practiced in St. Louis, 1956-58; became counsel Wabash R.R. Co., St. Louis, 1958 (merged into N. & W. Ry. 1964), gen. atty., until 1965; counsel, then asst. gen. counsel Pet., Inc., 1965-77, v.p., gen. counsel, 1977—; dir. Gerber-Barthel Truck & Tractor Corp., Inc., Gerber-Barthel, Inc., Pipe Systems, Inc. Sec., treas., legal adviser Am. Kantorei. Bd. dirs. Luth. Publicity Orgn. Chmn., Young Republican Club, Porter County, Ind., 1948. Mem. adv. bd. Southwestern Legal Found.; mem. Mo. Coordinating Bd. for Higher Edn., chmn., 1978-81; mem. Pres.'s Council, Valparaiso U., 1979—. Served with Judge Adv. Gen. Corps., AUS, 1953-55. Mem. Am. (mem. membership com.), Mo., St. Louis (chmn. antitrust com. 1971-73, v.p. bus. law sect. 1972-73, chmn. sect. 1973-74) bar assns., Am. Judicature Soc., Nat.

C. of C. (antitrust policies com.), Am. Frozen Foods Inst. (legal com.), Nat. Assn. Mfrs. (legal com.), Grocery Mfrs. Am. Inc. (legal com., legal exec. com.), St. Louis Council on World Affairs, Valparaiso U. Alumni Assn. (dir.), Pi Gamma Mu, Pi Sigma Alpha. Lutheran. Club: Harvard (St. Louis). Contbr. articles to legal publs. Home: 9026 Whitehaven St St Louis County St Louis MO 63123 Office: 400 S 4th St Louis MO 63166

DUFEK, RONALD DWANE, service sta. owner; b. Geddes, S.D., Oct. 20, 1939; s. Ernest and Rose (Sejnoha) D.; student So. State Coll., 1965; m. Maureen Neihus, Nov. 22, 1969; children—Ernest, Terry, Mike, Tammy, Stacey, Ryan, Jodi. Owner, operator Dufs Standard Sta., Geddes, S.D., 1966—. Pres. Geddes (S.D.) Devel. Corp., 1969—; sec. Geddes Hist. Soc., 1970—; state dir. Geddes Jaycees, 1973; mem. Geddes City Council, 1979—. Served with U.S. Army, 1959-62. Mem. Common Cause, Nat. Small Bus. Assn., Nat. Fedn. Ind. Bus. Methodist. Clubs: Geddes Commercial (pres. 1970, 71), Geddes Baseball (bd. dirs. 1966—). Home and office: Box 297 Geddes SD 57342

DUFF, DONALD LEE, ins. co. exec.; b. Middletown, Ohio, Sept. 27, 1934; s. Glenn Edward and Lennie (Spencer) D.; B.S. in Bus. Adminstrn., Olivet Coll., 1958; postgrad. Ind. U., 1968, Fort Wayne Art Sch., 1972; m. Donna M. Lanman, July 20, 1957. With Mut. Security Life Ins. Co., Fort Wayne, 1958-62, asst. field supr., 1962-64, asst. supt. agys., 1964-67, dir. group and pension sales, 1968-77, asst. v.p., dir. mktg., 1968-70, v.p. mktg. services, 1977-81; pres. Gt. Fidelity Life Ins. Co., Fort Wayne, 1981—; instr. Am. Coll., 1971-72. Fund solicitor United Arts Fund dr., Fort Wayne, 1977; trustee Huntington Coll., 1972—, mem. exec. com., 1974—, vice-chmn., 1974—, pres., 1974—; ambassador Associated Colls. Ind., 1976-77; chmn. fin. com., mem. bd. adminstrn., exec. com. Nat. Assn. Evangelicals; deacon, chmn. bd. Emmanuel Community United Bretheran Ch., Fort Wayne. Served with USAF, 1961-63. C.L.U. Mem. Life Ins. Mkgt. Research Assn. (vice chmn. mktg. services officers com.), Am. Soc. C.L.U.s (pres. Fort Wayne 1969-70). Republican. Mem. United Brethern in Christ. Home: 1824 Old Lantern Trail Fort Wayne IN 46825 Office: 3511 Hobson Rd PO Box 2272 Fort Wayne IN 46801

DUFF, THOMAS B., educator; b. Hampton, Minn., Feb. 18, 1938; s. Bruce L. and Winnifred B. Duff; B.S., Winona (Minn.) State Coll., 1963; M.A., U. Minn., 1968, Ph.D., 1976; m. Mary K. Daleiden, July 2, 1966; children—Gerald A., Robert B. Tchr., head bus. edn. dept. Chosen Valley High Sch., Chatfield, Minn., 1963-66; tchr. bus. edn. Richfield (Minn.) Sr. High Sch., 1967-75, area leader, 1972-74; asst. prof. bus. and office edn. U. Minn., Duluth, 1975-79, asso. prof., head dept., 1979—. Mem. selection com., bd. dirs. Am. Field Service, Richfield, 1970-75; coach, sec. Eastern Little League, Duluth, 1975-81; mem. central agy. relations com. and panel United Way Greater Duluth, 1978-81. Served with U.S. Army, 1956-59. Recipient Robert E. Slaughter Research award Gregg div. McGraw-Hill Book Co., 1977. Mem. Am. Bus. Communications Assn., Am. Council Consumer Interests, Am. Vocat. Assn., Adminstrv. Mgmt. Soc., Assn. Retarded Citizens Duluth, Minn. Bus. Educators, Nat. Bus. Edn. Assn. (exec. bd.), North Central Bus. Edn. Assn. (adminstrv. bd.), Phi Delta Kappa, Delta Pi Epsilon. Author: General Business in Our Modern Society, 1979. Office: Bus and Office Edn Dept U Minn Social Sci 116 2400 Oakland Ave Duluth MN 55812

DUFFY, EDWARD WILLIAM, mfg. co. exec.; b. LaSalle, Ill., Sept. 25, 1919; s. Edward J. and Margaret (Brunick) D.; grad. LaSalle-Peru Jr. Coll., 1938; student Loyola U., Chgo., also exec. devel. program, Cornell U.; m. Rosemary G. Dee, June 28, 1941; 1 dau., Jill Anne. Research chemist, 1941-45; engaged in sales, mdsg. and sales mgr., 1945—; v.p. U.S. Gypsum Co., 1963-69, exec. v.p., 1969-71, pres., 1971—, vice chmn., 1981—; dir. Am. Nat. Bank & Trust Co. Chgo., UNR Corp., W.W. Grainger Corp., Harnischfeger Corp., Walter E. Heller Corp. Home: 1815 W Ridgewood Ln Glenview IL 60025 Office: 101 S Wacker Dr Chicago IL 60606

DUFFY, GEORGE CHRISTOPHER, JR., television sta. exec.; b. Cleve., Aug. 15, 1936; s. George Christopher and Dorothy Cecelia (Rooney) D.; m. Roberta Hahn, Sept. 22, 1962; children—Maureen, Karen, Susan, Christopher; student U. Miami (Fla.), 1954-55, Ohio State U., 1955-58, U. So. Calif. Sch. of Cinema, summer 1957. Promotion rep. TV Guide mag., Cleve., 1959-62; asst. promotion dir. WJW-TV, Cleve., 1962-64; promotion dir. WCPO-TV, Cin., 1964-65; dir. advt. and promotion KYW-TV, Phila., 1965-66; dir. advt., promotion and press info. WLS-TV, Chgo., 1966-71, dir. programming, 1973-75; dir. broadcasting KMOX-TV, St. Louis, 1971-73; v.p., gen. mgr. WTHR, Indpls., 1975—. Bd. dirs. Greater Indpls. Progress Com., Jr. Achievement, Crossroads Rehab. Center, Kidney Found. Ind., Cathedral High Sch.; trustee St. Mary of the Woods Coll. Mem. Nat. Assn. Broadcasters, Nat. Assn. Television Program Execs., Ind. Broadcasters Assn., USMC Combat Corrs. Assn., Marine Corps Res. Officers Assn. Recipient Clio award, 1970, Chgo. Film Festival award, 1969-70, Broadcast Promotion Assn. award, 1969-70; named USMC Reservist of Year, 1974. Office: WTHR 1401 N Meridian St Indianapolis IN 46220

DUFFY, NORBERT EARL, educator; b. Fairbank, Iowa, Oct. 11, 1922; s. Earl Peter and Ethel (Kobbe) D.; student Upper Iowa U., 1947-50; B.S., Iowa State U., 1952; m. Oct. 14, 1950; children—Norbert Earl, Helen, Gregory, Karen, Daniel, Thomas. Tchr. vocat. agr., Blairsburg, Iowa, 1952-56; owner Duffy's Farm Service, Charles City, Iowa, 1957-63; tchr. vocat. agr. high sch. Waukon, Iowa, 1963—; adv. N.E. sect. Future Farmers Am. Served with AUS, 1943-46; ETO. Mem. Iowa Edn. Assn., Allamakee County Edn. Assn., NEA, Nat. Voct. Agr. Tchrs. Assn., Iowa Vocat. Agr. Tchrs. Assn., Iowa Vocat. Assn., VFW, Am. Legion. Democrat. Roman Catholic. Club: K.C. Home: 11 11th St NW Waukon IA 52172 Office: High Sch 3d Ave NW Waukon IA 52172

DUFFY, RICHARD EDWARD, railroad corp. exec.; b. Boston, Dec. 2, 1928; s. Leo L. and Margaret R. D.; A.A., Gen. Coll. of Boston U., 1950; student Sorbonne, 1954; U. Md. Overseas Extension, Frankfurt, W. Ger., 1952; m. Elizabeth Sara Gifford, Aug. 4, 1951; children—Gifford R., Elizabeth J. News writer, public info. div. U.S. Army, Europe, 1951-53; columnist, reporter, Am. Daily, Frankfurt, W. Ger., 1953-54; editor, columnist, reporter European edition N.Y. Herald-Tribune, Paris, France, 1954-55; reporter New Bedford (Mass.) Standard-Times, 1955-56, Boston Post, 1956; account exec., staff writer Carl Byoir & Assos., N.Y.C., 1957-66, account exec., 1969-78, v.p., 1972-76, sr. v.p., 1976-78; dir. alumni affairs Boston U., 1966-69; v.p. public relations Burlington No. Inc., St. Paul, 1978—. Served with U.S. Army, 1946-48, 50-51. Mem. Public Relations Soc. Am. (Silver Anvil awards, 1958, 65, 66, 71), R.R. Public Relations Assn. Roman Catholic. Clubs: Minnesota, North Oaks, Minn. Press. Office: 176 E Fifth St Saint Paul MN 55101

DUFFY, WILLIAM EDWARD, JR., educator; b. Fostoria, Ohio, Aug. 30, 1931; s. William Edward and Margaret Louise (Drew) D.; B.S., Wayne State U., 1958, M.Ed., 1960; Ph.D., Northwestern U., 1967; m. Sally King Wolfe, Nov. 21, 1958 (div. 1978). Tchr., Detroit pub. schs., 1957-61; instr. social studies Northwestern U., Evanston, Ill., 1961-65; asst. prof. edn. U. Iowa, Iowa City, 1965-70, asso. prof., 1970—, coordinator Soc. Found. Edn. program, 1978—, chmn. div. founds., postsecondary edn., 1981—; lectr. in field. Served with USAF, 1951-54. Fellow Philosophy of Edn. Soc. Editorial bd. Ednl. Philosophy Theory, 1969-71; contbr. book revs. and articles to profl. publs. Home: 376 Samoa Pl Iowa City IA 52240 Office: N 438 LC U Iowa Iowa City IA 52242

DUFOUR, GERALD LOUIS, constrn. co. exec.; b. Escanaba, Mich., Mar. 12, 1931; s. Louis D. and Priscilla M. (Lafave) D.; B.S. in Civil Engring., Mich. Technol. U., 1953; m. Mary Susan Way, Nov. 28, 1953; children—Jeffrey, David, Michael, Thomas, Timothy, Kelly, Tracy, Kris. Gen. mgr. Drobac Constrn. Corp., 1958-63; pres. Ma-Con Constrn. Corp., Germantown, Wis., 1963—; pres. Gencon Corp., 1979—. Bd. dirs. Highland Bluff Ednl. Center. Served with C.E. U.S. Army, 1953-55. Mem. Mason Contractors Am. (region v.p.), Masonry Inst. Wis. (dir.). Republican. Roman Catholic. Clubs: West Bend Country, Kettle Moraine Tennis. Home: 5290 Boettcher Dr West Bend WI 53095 Office: N115 W19000 Edison Dr Germantown WI 53022

DUGAN, PAUL V., lt. gov. Kans.; b. 1939; B.S., Regis Coll.; LL.B., Washburn U. Admitted to Kans. bar, 1964; lt. gov. Kans., 1979—. Democrat. Office: Office of Lt Gov State House Topeka KS 66612*

DUGDALE, SHARON LAVONNE, educator; b. Louisville, Mar. 17, 1946; d. Harry Benjamin and Dorothea Catherine (Eubanks) Saxton; B.A., Mich. State U., 1967; postgrad. Ind. U., 1966, Coll. DuPage, 1969-70; M.A. (teaching asst.), U. Ill., 1973. Tchr. math., Williamston, Mich., 1967-69; elem. sch. tchr., Lisle, Ill., 1970; specialist, then sr. specialist automated edn. Computer Based Edn. Research Lab., U. Ill., Urbana, 1972-81, dir. Plato Math. project, 1978—; cons. NSF grantee, 1980-81. Mem. Nat. Council Tchrs. Math., Assn. Supervision and Curriculum Devel., Assn. Ednl. Data Systems, Assn. Devel. Computer-Based Instrn. Systems. Author: (with David Kibbey) Computer-Based Instruction: The Plato Fractions Curriculum, 1972-76; Computer-Based Instruction: Prototype Courseware for Teaching High School Algebra, 1980-81. Home: 713 S Maple St Urbana IL 61801 Office: 103 S Mathews St Urbana IL 61801

DUGGAN, JEROME TIMOTHY, ret. pub. utility exec., lawyer; b. Kansas City, Mo., Oct. 30, 1914; s. Jerry F. and Claire (Aaron) D.; A.B., U. Mo., 1936, LL.B., 1938; m. Dorothy Blanche Castle, May 4, 1940; children—Jerome Castle, Dorothy Lucinda. Admitted to Mo. bar, 1938; in gen. law practice, Kansas City, Mo., 1938-40; asso. Hook & Thomas, 1938-40; asst. city counselor, Kansas City, Mo., 1940-42; regional rationing atty. OPA, 1942-43; in gen. law practice, also mem. Gage, Hillix & Phelps, 1946-50; gen. counsel The Gas Service Co., 1950-56, v.p., gen. counsel, 1956-63, exec. v.p., gen. counsel, 1963-68, pres., 1968-78, chmn. bd., 1978-79, also dir. Chmn. Kansas City (Mo.) Housing Authority, 1947-50; dir. Indsl. Council Kansas City (Mo.), 1951-55; mem. Municipal Services Commn., 1955-56; bd. dirs. Citizens Regional Planning Council, Greater Kansas City Area Safety Council; gov. Am. Royal Assn., 1960—; mem. Bus. and Indsl. Devel. Commn. Kansas City; vice chmn. Kansas City Tourist Commn.; mem. exec. com. Asso. Industries Mo., 1962—; trustee Mo. Pub. Expenditure Survey, 1962—; pres. Asso. Industries Mo., 1970-72. Pres. bd. trustees Research Hosp. and Med. Center, 1970-71; trustee Midwest Research Inst., Jacob Loose Found.; regent Rockhurst Coll.; bd. dirs. Downtown, Inc. Served as lt. USN, 1943-46. Mem. Mo. Bar Assn., Am. Gas Assn. (dir.), Greater Kansas City C. of C. (dir.), Kans. Assn. Commerce and Industry (dir.), Sigma Nu, Phi Delta Phi. Clubs: Kansas City (pres. 1976-77), Mission Hills Country. Home: 11215 Holly Kansas City MO 64114

DUGGAN, RICHARD THOMAS, educator; b. Mpls., Sept. 18, 1940; s. Francis Victor and Dorothy Helen D.; A.A., U. Minn., 1964; diploma in farrier sci. Anoka Tech. Coll., 1970; B.S., U. St. Cloud, 1980; m. Nancy Elizabeth Eastman, Oct. 10, 1970; children—Hedda Terese, Robert Eastman, Danner Carter. Pvt. practice horseshoeing, 1970-72; instr. farrier sci. Anoka (Minn.) Vocat. Trade Inst., 1972-76; founder, establisher, instr. Minn. Sch. Horseshoeing & Blacksmithing, Anoka, 1976—; pres. Minn. Horse Exposition, Inc., 1981—; owner, operator R.T. Duggan Co., Anoka, 1973—. Served with U.S. Army, 1959-62. Mem. Am. Vocat. Assn., Minn. Farrier's Assn. (founder, pres. 1971, editor newsletter 1971—, dir. 1976—), Minn. Horse Council (dir.), Am. Farriers Assn., U. Minn. Alumni Assn., St. Cloud State U. Alumni Assn. Contbr. articles to profl. jours. Office: Minnesota School of Horseshoeing and Blacksmithing 6260 Hwy 10 NW Anoka MN 55303

DUHME, CAROL MCCARTHY, civic worker; b. St. Louis, Apr. 13, 1917; d. Eugene Ross and Louise (Roblee) McCarthy; A.B., Vassar Coll., 1939; m. Sheldon Ware, June 12, 1941 (dec. 1944); 1 son, David; m. 2d, H. Richard Duhme, Jr., Apr. 9, 1947; children—Benton (dec.), Ann, Warren. Tchr. elementary sch., 1939-41, 42-44; dir. Christian edn. 1st Congregational Ch., St. Louis, 1960-62, trustee, 1964-66, mem. ch. council, 1974-75, deaconess, 1978—; former bd. dirs. Community Music Schs., St. Louis, Community Sch., Ch. Women United, John Burroughs Sch., St. Louis Bicentennial Women's Com., St. Louis Jr. League; pres. St. Louis Vassar Club; pres. bd. dirs. YWCA, St. Louis, 1973-76; bd. dirs. Chautauqua (N.Y.) Instn., 1971-78, Mo. Bapt. Hosp., 1973—, North Side Team Ministry, 1968—, Eden Theol. Sem., 1979—; v.p. bd. dirs. UN Assn., St. Louis, 1976—; pres. bd. dirs. Family and Childrens Service Greater St. Louis, 1977—; chmn. Benton Roblee Duhme Scholarship Fund; trustee Joseph H. and Florence A. Roblee Found., St. Louis; mem. corp. assembly Blue Cross Hosp. Service of Mo., 1978—; mem. Chancellor's long-range planning com. Washington U., St. Louis, 1980—. Recipient Mary Alice Messerley award for volunteerism Health and Welfare Council St. Louis, 1971, Vol. of Yr. award, YWCA, 1976; Woman of Achievement in Community Leadership award St. Louis Globe Democrat, 1980. Home: 8 Edgewood Rd St Louis MO 63124

DUHME, H. RICHARD, JR., sculptor, educator; b. St. Louis, May 31, 1914; s. Herman Richard and Ruth Frances (Leggat) D.; student Pa. Acad. Fine Arts, 1932-38, U. Pa., 1934, Am. Sch. Classical Studies, Athens, Greece, 1941; B.F.A., Washington U., 1953; m. Carol Louise McCarthy, Apr. 9, 1947; children—David W., Benton Roblee, Ann Duhme Welker, Warren L. Prof. sculpture Washington U., St. Louis, 1947—; head sculpture dept. Chautauqua Instn. Summer Sch., 1953—; head sculpture dept. Syracuse U. Chautauqua Center, 1953-69. Served with USAAF, 1942-46. Decorated Bronze stars. Fellow Nat. Sculpture Soc.; mem. Allied Artists Am. Clubs: St. Louis Country, Univ. Office: Washington Univ Saint Louis MO 63130

DUICK, GREGORY FRANCIS, cardiologist; b. Evanston, Ill., Feb. 6, 1946; s. Emory Lawrence and Rosily Margaret Duick; A.B. in Chemistry, Knox Coll., Galesburg, Ill., 1968; M.D., Loyola U., Chgo., 1972; m. Peggy Ann Cyrier, Sept. 25, 1971; children—Michael, Carrie. Intern, Los Angeles County-U. So. Calif. Med. Center, 1972-73, resident in internal medicine, 1973-75, fellow in cardiology, 1975-77; fellow in nuclear medicine Vanderbilt U., Nashville, 1980; practice medicine specializing in cardiology, Wichita, Kans., 1977—; dir. Cardiac Catheterization and Non-Invasive Heart Labs., also co-dir. nuclear cardiology dept. St. Francis Hosp., Wichita; med. dir. Midwest Cardionics Inc., Wichita, North Central Echo Labs., St. Paul; cardiovascular dir. Kans. Emergency Med. Services; asso. clin. prof. medicine Wichita div. U. Kans.; mem. Wichita Cardiology Assos. Diplomate Am. Bd. Internal Medicine, Sub-bd. Cardiovascular Medicine. Fellow Am. Coll. Cardiology; mem. A.C.P., Am. Heart Assn., Kans. Heart Assn., Kans. Med. Soc., Sedgwick County Heart Assn., Knox Coll. Alumni Assn., Loyola-Stritch Alumni Assn. Roman Catholic. Office: 1035 N Emporia St Suite 130 Wichita KS 67203

DUKE, PHYLLIS MAE, TV producer and writer; b. La Crosse, Wis., May 8, 1927; d. Sidney Parkman and Myrtle Bernice (Hoyard) Murat; student Northwestern U., 1946-48; B.A. cum laude, Marquette U., 1966; M.S. (fellow), U. Wis., Milw., 1967; children—Kirby Kim, Karen Kay. Continuity writer Sta. WTMJ, WTMJ-TV, Milw., 1950-57; TV producer and writer Sid Stone Advt. Agy., Milw., 1960-66; tchr. pub. schs. Menomonee Falls, Wis., 1967-70; TV producer and coordinator Sch. Nursing, U. Wis., Milw., 1970—. Vol. Cream City Neighborhood Health Center Center, Milw., 1971-73, Guadalupe Center, Milw., 1973—, Casa Maria, 1974—, Amigos de las Americas, 1974—. Recipient numerous awards for TV programs. Mem. Health Sci. Communications Assn. (dir. 1973—, exec. com. 1976—, assn. mgr. 1979—, Golden Raster award). Author: Media Guide on Death and Dying, 1978. Contbg. editor Med. Media Directory, 1976, 77, 78, 79, 80; editorial adv. bd. Biomed. Communications mag., 1977—. Home: 2343 N 115th St Wauwatosa WI 53226 Office: Sch Nursing U Wisconsin Milwaukee WI 53211

DUKE, WILLIAM THOMAS, JR., rubber co. exec.; b. Akron, Ohio, Apr. 24, 1933; s. William Thomas and Grace (Mosely) D.; B.S. in Journalism, Kent State U., 1955; postgrad. Ohio State U., 1974-75; m. Ann Barrett; children—Andrew, Benjamin, Heather, Terrill. Advt. and publicity copywriter Ohio Edison Co., Akron, 1955-57, editor Ohio Edisonian, 1957-59; mgr. employee communication Cooper Industries, Mt. Vernon, Ohio, 1959-61; mgr. community relations and employee communication, 1961-66; community and public affairs mgr. BF Goodrich Co., Akron, Ohio, 1966-71, mgr. public relations tire div., 1971-73, corp. mgr. community relations, 1973-75, dir. community relations, 1975—; mem. Ohio Ednl. Broadcasting Commn., 1976-81. Vice-pres. civic affairs Akron Regional Devel. Bd., 1979-80, v.p. assos., 1981—; bd. dirs. Kent State U. Found.; chmn. Pvt. Industry Council. Named Disting. Alumnus, Kent State U. Sch. Journalism, 1979; chmn. Met. Human Services Commn. Mem. Public Relations Soc. Am. (accredited), Nat. Alliance Bus. (metro chmn. 1978-79), Press Club Akron, Kent State U. Alumni Assn. (pres. 1978-79). Clubs: Akron City, Rotary. Home: 1285 DeWitt Dr Akron OH 44313 Office: 500 S Main St Akron OH 44318

DUKES, JACK RICHARD, educator; b. Indpls., Jan. 21, 1941; s. Richard Eugene and Kathleen (Cox) D.; B.A., Beloit Coll., 1963; M.A., No. Ill. U., 1965; Ph.D., U. Ill., 1970; m. Joanne Petty, June 15, 1963; children—Gregory Scott, Richard Aaron. Asst. prof. Macalester Coll., St. Paul, 1969-70; asso. prof. Carroll Coll., Waukesha, Wis., 1970-75, asso. prof., 1975—, chmn. dept. history, 1972—, dir. Russian Area Studies program, 1972-75; vis. asso. prof. U. Calif., Santa Barbara, 1980-81; Scholar-Diplomat Program participant U.S. Dept. State. Nat. Endowment for Humanities fellow, 1974; U. Ill. asso. in Russian history, 1977; fellow in residence, U. Calif., Santa Barbara, 1977-78. Mem. Am. Hist. Assn., Am. Assn. for Advancement Slavic Studies, Conf. Group Study Central European History, Soc. History Am. Fgn. Relations. Contbr. articles to profl. jours. Home: 114 W Laflin St Waukesha WI 53186

DUKEWITS, WALTER CARL, educator; b. Newton, Kans., Aug. 12, 1904; s. John W. and Clara (Boerger) D.; B.A., Concordia Sem., St. Louis, 1929; M.A., U. Nebr., 1930; Ed.D., Columbia, 1949. Missionary in South India, 1930-56; prin. Concordia High Sch., Vadakangulam, Tin.Dt. South India, 1938-56; prof., dean students St. John's Coll., Winfield, Kans., 1956-60, prof. religion, alumni affairs, 1960-80. Mem. AAAS, St. John's Coll. Alumni Assn. (treas., dir. Ednl. Found.), Phi Delta Kappa. Home: 509 College St Winfield KS 67156

DULANY, DONELSON EDWIN, educator; b. Shreveport, La., Dec. 9, 1928; s. Donelson Edwin and LaVera (Jackson) D.; A.B., U. Tenn., 1948; Ph.D., U. Mich., 1955; m. Elizabeth Gjelsness, Mar. 19, 1955; 1 son, Christopher Daniel. Instr. psychology U. Mich., 1952-54; research fellow Harvard U., 1958; asst. prof. U. Ill., 1956-59, asso. prof., 1959-64, prof., 1964—. Served with U.S. Army, 1954-56. NSF grantee, NIH grantee. Mem. Am. Psychol. Assn., Psychonomic Soc., Soc. Philosophy and Psychology. Author: (with John Street) Teaching of English to Spanish Speaking Soldiers, 1956; (with Paul Henle, Charles Stevenson, Roger Brown) Language, Thought and Culture, 1958; editor: (with R. DeValois, D. Beardslee, M. Winterbottom) Contributions to Modern Psychology, 1958. Home: 73 Greencroft St Champaign IL 61820 Office: Dept Psychology U Ill 603 E Daniel Champaign IL 61820

DULL, LLOYD WILLIAM, ednl. cons.; b. Berne, Ind., Oct. 23, 1917; s. Verne Ezra and Anna Viola (Hisey) D.; B.S., Bowling Green State U., 1941; M.A., Ohio State U., 1946, Ph.D., 1960; m. Marjorie Waneta Boyer, June 9, 1946; 1 son, Mark Randall Boyer. Tchr. elem. and secondary schs., Rockford, Ohio, 1937-42; tchr. high sch., Celina, Ohio, 1946-48; tchr. high sch., dean boys, Findlay, Ohio, 1948-50, 52-56; coordinator secondary schs., Hancock County, Ohio, 1956-60; asst. supt. curriculum Canton (Ohio) Public Schs., 1960-66, Akron (Ohio) Public Schs., 1966-76; ednl. cons., Columbus, Ohio and Akron, 1976—. Served with U.S. Army, 1942-45, 50-52; PTO; Korea. Recipient award for excellence as educator Ohio Senate, 1976. Mem. Nat. Assn. Supervision and Curriculum Devel. (dir. 1966-74), Ohio Assn. Supervision and Curriculum Devel. (pres. 1968-69), NEA, Ohio Edn. Assn. (Disting. Service award 1968), Nat. Assn. Secondary Sch. Prins., Phi Delta Kappa (life, Leadership in Edn. award 1977). Methodist. Club: Masons. Author: Supervision: School Leadership Handbook, 1981; editor: Heart of Instruction Series, 1977; Improving Supervision in Vocational Education, 1978; Leadership Practices for Directors of Vocational Education, 1979. Home and office: 1129 Walton Dr Akron OH 44313

DULL, PAUL PHELLIS, ret. judge; b. Celina, Ohio, May 30, 1907; s. Edgar M. and May (Phellis) D.; A.B., Ohio Wesleyan U., 1929; A.M., Columbia, 1931; J.D., Ohio State U., 1937; m. Dorothy E. Anderson, Dec. 23, 1933 (dec.); children—Peter Phellis, Jill; m. 2d, Alberta B. Buerkle, Apr. 7, 1966. Instr. polit. sci. U. Ky., 1931-32; publicity and student promotion Kan. Wesleyan U., 1933; pvt. law practice, Celina, 1937-44, 46-47; judge Common Pleas Ct., Mercer County, Ohio, 1947-74, ret., 1974. Bd. dirs. Mercer County chpt. A.R.C., Soc. Crippled Children. Served with USAAF, 1944-45. Mem. Am., Ohio, Mercer County bar assns., Am. Legion, Am. Judicature Soc., Acad. Polit. Sci., Am. Acad. Polit. and Social Sci., Ohio Hist. Soc., Sigma Alpha Epsilon, Phi Delta Phi, Omicron Delta Kappa, Pi Sigma Alpha, Kappa Delta Pi, Pi Delta Epsilon. Mason, Moose, Eagle, Woodman of the World. Author (books of verse): Sprouts From A Small Potato, 1940; Salt To Taste, 1948; Letting Out the Seams, 1954; Unmarked Intersections, 1966; Back Track, 1976; also jud. opinions and legal articles. Home: 659 N Walnut St Celina OH 45822 Office: Court House Celina OH 45822

DUMETT, RAYMOND EPHRAIM, educator, historian; b. Seattle, Jan. 4, 1931; s. Ray E. and Evelyn (Ross) D.; B.S., U. Wash., 1954, M.A., 1957; Ph.D., U. London, 1966; m. Ardis Jean Ivarson, Sept. 1960; children—Susan Clark, Ann-Marie. Instr. history Ohio State U., 1964-68; asst. prof. Purdue U., 1968-74, asso. prof., 1974—, chmn. univ. sen. com. on internat. programs, 1976-79; vis. prof. U. Brit. Columbia, Can., 1978. Precinct committeeman Democratic Party, 1969-71; bd. dirs. Internat. Center, West Lafayette, 1977—. Served with USAF, 1955-58, to capt. with USAFR, 1959-65. Research grantee U. London, 1961-63, Hoover Inst., Stanford U., 1967, Rockefeller Family Fund, 1969, Ford Found., 1971, African Studies Assn., 1971. Mem. Am. Forum for Internat. Study of Cleve. (nat. dir.), Ind. Consortium for Internat. Programs (dir.), AAUP (v.p. Purdue U. chpt.), Royal African Soc. London, African Studies Assn. U.S., Am. Hist. Assn., Social Sci. History Assn., African-Am. Inst. Contbr. numerous articles on African and econ. history to profl. jours.; co-author: Problems of Rural Development: Case Studies and Multidisciplinary Perspectives, 1975; West African Cultural Dynamics, 1980. Home: 1540 Marilyn Ave West Lafayette IN 47906 Office: Dept History Purdue U West Lafayette IN 47907

DUMKE, MELVIN PHILIP, dentist; b. Sleepy Eye, Minn., Jan. 23, 1920; s. Herman Gustav and Elsie Ida (Battig) D.; D.D.S., U. Minn., 1943; m. Phyllis Lorraine Steuck, June 25, 1950; children—Pamela, Bruce, Shari. Practice dentistry, Sleepy Eye, 1946-50, Morgan, Minn., 1950-66, Mankato, Minn., 1966—. Lectr. dental assts. Mankato State Coll., 1967-69. Mem. Town Council, Morgan, 1960-65. Bd. control Martin Luther Acad., New Ulm, Minn., 1965-79; bd. dirs. The Lutheran Home, Belle Plaine, Minn., 1981—. Served to capt., Dental Corps, AUS, 1943-46. Fellow Royal Soc. Health, Internat. Coll. Dentists; mem. ADA (ho. of dels. 1977—), Minn. Dental Assn. (chmn. peer rev. com. 1973-79, mem. ho. of dels. 1978—, v.p. 1981), So. Dist. Dental Soc. (exec. council), South Central Dental Study Club (pres. 1970), Fedn. Dentaire Internationale, Pierre Fouchard Acad., Mankato C. of C., U. Minn. Alumni Assn., V.F.W. (recipient Distinguished Service award 1966, comdr. 1965), Am. Legion, Psi Omega. Lutheran (pres. congregation 1970). Lion (pres. 1965, 74, zone chmn. 1975). Clubs: Mankato Golf, U. Minn. Sch. Dentistry Century. Home: 364 Carol Ct Mankato MN 56001 Office: 430 S Broad St Mankato MN 56001

DUNBAR, JAMES T., corp. exec.; b. Columbus, Ohio, June 28, 1948; s. Earl T. and Olive Jean D.; B.S. in Fin., Ohio State U., 1970; M.B.A., Central Mich. U., 1974; m. Carolyn Lee, Aug. 16, 1969; children—Brian James, Melissa Jean. Detroit zone mgr. Ford Motor Co., 1974-76, Phila. zone mgr., 1976-78; product mgr. Onan Corp., Mpls., 1978-80; v.p. planning and research Midland Coops., Inc., Mpls., 1981—. Chmn. parent adv. com. Winnetka Sch.; bd. mgmt. YMCA. Served with U.S. Army, 1971-74. Lutheran. Home: 11730 51st Ave N Plymouth MN 55442 Office: 800 53rd Ave NE Minneapolis MN 55440

DUNBAR, ROBERT ALEXANDER, cons. soil and found. engr.; b. Eveleth, Minn., Sept. 30, 1928; s. Robert George and Ethel Irene (Saari) D.; B.C.E., Cornell U., 1954, M.C.E., 1958; m. Wanda F. Kerr, May 2, 1959; 1 son, Douglas R. Project engr. Photog. Survey Corp., Toronto, Ont., Can., 1955-56; project civil engr. Canadian Colombo Plan (Ceylon), 1956-57; chief geol. engr. Photronix, Inc., Columbus, Ohio, 1958-60; owner, prin. engr. Dunbar Geotech. Engrs., Columbus, 1960—; lectr. air photo interpretation dept. geodetic sci. Ohio State U., 1960-64. Served with U.S. Army, 1946-48; Japan. Recipient Bausch & Lomb Photogrammetric award, 1955. Registered profl. engr. Ohio, W.Va., Ky., Ind., Pa., Ont. Mem. ASCE, Am. Cons. Engrs. Council, Nat. Soc. Profl. Engrs., ASTM, Geol. Soc. Am., Am. Concrete Inst., Am. Soc. Photogrammetry, Am. Arbitration Assn. (panel arbitrators). Clubs: Masons, Scioto Boat, Nat. Flyers Assn. (Columbus), Internat. Aerobatics. Office: 1286 W Lane Ave Columbus OH 43221

DUNBAR, WANDA KERR (MRS. ROBERT A. DUNBAR), advt. agy. exec.; b. Mansfield, Ohio, Oct. 9, 1931; d. Martin Wayne and Blanche B. (Parker) Kerr; student Capital U., 1949-50; B.S. in Journalism, Ohio State U., 1953, postgrad., 1956, 61; student Columbus Sch. Arts and Design, 1957-58; m. Robert A. Dunbar, May 2, 1959; 1 son, Douglas. Pub. relations dir. Columbus Goodwill Industries (Ohio), 1952, Dayton Goodwill Industries Rehab. Center (Ohio), 1953-55; community relations officer, heading promotion of bond issue Slum Clearance Dept. City Columbus, 1955-57; editor internal mag., co. photographer Ross Labs., Columbus, 1957-60; pres., dir. Wanda Kerr Dunbar, Inc., advt. agy., Columbus, 1961—; pub., editor, advt. mgr. Ohio Contractor, Ohio Contractors Assn., 1962-79. Sec., Wing 41, Nightingale Cottage Convalescent Home for Children, 1965, pres., 1966; public relations adv. bd. Learning Connection. Recipient Mag. award 1st place Asso. Contractors Am., 1965; 1st pl. Dayton Community Chest contest in pub. relations, 1953. Mem. Women in Constrn. (charter), Women in Communications, Ohio Contractors Assn., Nat. Fedn. Ind. Bus., Columbus Area C. of C., Columbus Advt. Fedn., Builders Exchange of Central Ohio, Ohio State U. Alumni Assn., Upper Arlington Civic Assn. Republican. Mem. First Community Ch. Club: Scioto Boat (Columbus). Home: 2474 Buckley Rd Columbus OH 43220 Office: 4645 Executive Dr Columbus OH 43220

DUNBAR, WILLIAM CHARLES, state senator; b. Terre Haute, Ind., July 10, 1942; s. James H. and Gertrude Irene (Schott) D.; student Ind. State U.; m. Martha Joy Dunbar, 1962; children—Jeff, Jay, Julie. Sales rep. Stuart-Carey, 1958-62; with Anaconda Aluminum Co., 1962-65; gen. mgr. Dorsett Auto Sales, 1965-75; real estate agt., Terre Haute, 1975—; mem. Ind. State Senate, 1975—, chmn. corrections subcom.; cons. Bland Trucking Co. Bd. dirs. Light House Mission. Named Mission Man of Yr., 1979; recipient Defender of Freedom award, 1979. Mem. Terre Haute C. of C. Clubs: Gideons, Masons, Pachyderm (Terre Haute); Morgan (Washington); Indpls. Press, Columbia. Office: Ind State Senate State House Indianapolis IN 46204*

DUNCAN, DANIEL MERRITT, orgn. sci. cons.; b. LaPorte, Ind., Nov. 9, 1938; s. Daniel Fayette and Emma Lauretta (Myers) D.; B.S., Ohio State U., 1961; M.A., Mich. State U., 1967; children—Stephanie Lyn, Eric Douglas, Hillary Jennifer. Asst. dir. personnel R.R. Donnelley & Sons Co., Old Saybrook, Conn., 1961-63; supr. mgmt. and orgn. devel. Gen. Motors Inst., Flint, Mich., 1963-71; faculty, asst. dean U. Wis., Milw., 1971-77; mgr. human resources cons. services Arthur Young & Co., Milw., 1977-80; v.p. Schwarzkopf Cons., Inc., Elm Grove, Wis., 1980—; vis. prof. Alverno Coll., Roosevelt U.; dir. Family Health Plan, Inc. Mem. Mequon-Thiensville Sch. Dist. Bd. Edn., 1979—; exec. v.p. Milw. Kickers Soccer League, 1976-79. Mem. Soc. Gen. Systems Research (officer), Am. Soc. Personnel Adminstrn., ASTD, Inst. Study of Systems Renewal, Human Resource Planning Soc., Phi Gamma Delta. Contbr. articles to profl. jours. Office: 15285 Watertown Plank Rd Elm Grove WI 53122

DUNCAN, DAVID FRANK, community health specialist, educator; b. Kansas City, Mo., June 26, 1947; s. Chester Frank and Maxine (Irwin) D.; B.A., U. Mo., Kansas City, 1970; postgrad. Sam Houston State U., 1971; Dr.P.H., U. Tex., 1976; 1 foster son, Kevin Rheinboldt. Research asst. U. Kans. Bur. Child Research, 1967-68; supr. Johnson County Juvenile Hall, Olathe, Kans., 1968-70; asst. to warden Draper Correctional Center, Elmore, Ala., summer 1970; supr. Harris County Juvenile Hall, Houston, 1970-71; project dir. Who Cares, Inc. Drug Abuse Treatment Center, Houston, 1971-73; exec. dir. Reality Island Halfway House, Houston, 1974-75; research asso. Tex. Gov.'s Office, Austin, summer 1975; research asso. Inst. Clin. Toxicology, clin. toxicologist Ben Taub Gen. Hosp., Houston, 1975-76; asst. prof. health sci. SUNY, Brockport, 1976-78, asso. prof., 1978, acting chmn. dept. health sci., summer 1978; prof. health edn., coordinator community health program So. Ill. U., Carbondale, 1978—; chmn. So. Ill. Health Edn. Task Force, 1979—; bd. dirs. Ill. Public Health Continuing Edn. Council; cons. to numerous health, edn. instns. Mem. Am. Public Health Assn. (chmn. sect. mental health), Ill. Public Health Assn. (exec. council), Soc. Epidemiologic Research, AAAS, Ill. Acad. Sci., N.Y. Acad. Sci. Democrat. Methodist. Author: Drugs and the Whole Person, 1982; contbr. articles to profl. jours.; editorial bd. Health Values, 1980—, Jour. Drug Edn., 1981—, Internat. Jour. Mental Health, 1982—. Home: 21 Cypress Dr W Rural Route 2 Carbondale IL 62901 Office: Dept Health Edn So Ill U Carbondale IL 62901

DUNCAN, DOUGLAS JON, opera co. adminstr.; b. Osage, Iowa, Aug. 2, 1950; s. Wendell A. and Karen M. D.; B.M., Simpson Coll., 1972; M.Music, Phila. Musical Acad., 1974; m. Maria DiPalma, May 22, 1976. Asst. prof. music Simpson Coll., Indianola, Iowa, 1975-80; mng. dir. Des Moines Metro. Opera, 1974—. Office: Des Moines Metro Opera Inc 600 N Buxton St Indianola IA 50125

DUNCAN, JAMES H., JR., advt. exec.; b. Kalamazoo, Aug. 23, 1947; s. James H. and Colleen Patricia (Cloney) D.; B.A., Western Mich. U., 1974; m. Janet D. Gallihugh, July 3, 1970; children—Erica, Rebecca. Account mgr., research dir. Fairfield Broadcasting Co., Kalamazoo, 1974-76; account mgr., then media dir. Gilmore Advt., Kalamazoo, 1976-78, v.p., media dir., 1978—; lectr. Mich. State U., Western Mich. U.; cons. in field. Bd. dirs. S.W. Mich. Girl Scouts, 1976-77, New Vic Theatre, 1980—. Served with AUS, 1968-71; Vietnam. Decorated Army Commendation medal; named Advt. Person of Yr., Kalamazoo Advt. Club, 1978. Mem. Nat. Assn. Broadcasters, Kalamazoo Advt. Club (pres. 1978), Grand Rapids (Mich.) Advt. Club. Club: Park. Author: Am. Radio. Home: 2913 Brandywine Rd Kalamazoo MI 49001 Office: 200 Michigan Bldg Kalamazoo MI 49007

DUNCAN, LELAND RAY, religious denomination exec.; b. Bee Branch, Ark., Nov. 9, 1929; s. Enoch R. and Julia C. (Lane) D.; B.A., Oakland City Coll., 1962, D.D., 1974; m. Ruth Tindall, May 28, 1952; children—Wally, Greg. Owner, operator Twin City Radio & TV Repair Service, 1955-59; ordained to ministry Baptist Ch., 1960; pastor Gen. Bapt. Ch., Spurgeon, Ind., 1960-62, 1st Gen. Bapt. Ch., Heber Springs, Ark., 1962-65, Owensboro, Ky., 1965-69, Poplar Bluff, Mo., 1969-71; exec. dir. Gen. Bapt. Home Mission Bd., Inc., Poplar Bluff, 1972—; pres. Gen. Bapt. Investment Fund, Inc., Poplar Bluff, 1974—; mem. Gen. Bapt. Survey Com., 1963-68, pres., 1965-68; mem. Gen. Bapt. Home Mission Bd., 1968-71; tchr. various seminars, 1962—. Served with U.S. Army, 1951-53. Mem. North Am. Bapt. Fellowship. Contbr. articles to Gen. Bapt. Messenger. Office: 100 Stinson Dr Poplar Bluff MO 63901

DUNDURS, JOHN, civil engr., educator; b. Riga, Latvia, Sept. 13, 1922; s. Janis and Auguste (Reichmanis) D.; B.S.M.E., Northwestern U., 1951, M.S., 1955, Ph.D. (Royal E. Cabell fellow), 1958; m. Valda Gaiss, Apr. 26, 1952; children—Nora, Renate, Ilse. Instr., Northwestern U., Evanston, Ill., 1955-58, asst. prof. civil engring., 1958-61, asso. prof., 1961-66, prof., 1966—, chmn. council on theoretical and applied mechanics, 1969-73. Fellow ASME, Am. Acad. Mechanics; mem. ASCE (past chmn. engring. mechanics div.), Sigma Xi, Tau Beta Pi, Pi Tau Sigma. Contbr. articles in field to profl. pubs. Home: 9449 Lawndale Ave Evanston IL 60203 Office: Northwestern U Evanston IL 60201

DUNEA, GEORGE, physician; b. Craiova, Rumania, June 1, 1933; s. Charles L. and Gerda (Low) D.; came to U.S., 1964; M.D., U. Sydney (Australia), 1957; m. Mary Mills Barr, 1969; stepchildren—Mary Louise, John (Barr); 1 dau., Melanie. Intern, Royal N. Shore Hosp., Sydney, 1958-59; resident in internal medicine, Australia and Eng., 1959-63; nephrology fellow Cleve. Clinic, Presbyn.-St. Luke's Hosp., Chgo., 1964-66; practice internal medicine specializing in nephrology, Chgo., 1972—; attending physician Cook County Hosp., 1966—, dir. dept. nephrology-hypertension, 1969—; prof. medicine U. Health Scis.-Chgo. Med. Sch.; vis. prof. medicine Rush Med. Coll. Active various civic coms. Diplomate Am. Bds. Internal Medicine, Nephrology. Fellow A.C.P., Royal Coll. Physicians (London, Edinburgh); mem. AMA, Am. Soc. Nephrology, Brit. Med. Assn., Soc. Med. History. Author monthly letter Brit. Med. Jour.; contbr. chpts. to books, articles to profl. jours. Home: 222 E Chestnut St Chicago IL 60611 Office: 1835 W Harrison St Chicago IL 60612

DUNETZ, ANNELIESE ANTONIE, photographer; b. Dortmund-Hörde, Westfalen, W. Ger., Feb. 13, 1929; d. August and Erna Anna (Wiemer) Brensing; came to U.S., 1955, naturalized, 1958; student photography Rochester (N.Y.) Inst. Tech., 1967-69; children—Rondald, Roger, Rodney. Owner, photographer Photog. Art by Ann, C.P.P., Kenton, Ohio, 1955—. Cert. profl. photographer, Ohio. Mem. Profl. Photographers Assn. Am. (accorded nat. cert. 1980), Profl. Photographers Assn. Ohio (medal of honor 1978). Democrat. Home and Office: 214 N Detroit St Kenton OH 43326

DUNHAM, AUDIAN D., retail exec.; b. Albuquerque, May 15, 1941; s. William Dale and Evelyn Elaine (Ward) D.; B.A. in Bus. and Psychology, Rollins Coll., Winter Park, Fla., 1967; postgrad. Fla. Inst. Tech., Melbourne; m. Jane Phyllis Mercer, June 15, 1963; 1 son, Jerin Joseph. With Boeing Co., Seattle, 1962-64, 66-69, Xerox Corp., Rochester, N.Y., 1969-77; prin. Harbridge House, Inc., mgmt. cons., Boston, 1977-79; dir. mgmt. edn. and tng. Rockwell Internat. Co., Pitts., 1979-80; v.p. orgn. and mgmt. devel. Federated Dept. Stores, Cin., 1980—; pres. Dunham Enterprises, 1979; dir. Assessment Designs, Inc., Winter Park, Fla.; cons. in field. Mem. Am. Soc. Tng. and Devel., Am. Soc. Personnel Adminstrn., Exec. Study Conf. Group, Human Resources Planning Soc., Midwest Human Resources Planning Group. Editorial bd. Shelby Directories, 1979-80. Office: 7 W 7th St Cincinnati OH 45202

DUNHAM, DELLA MAE, librarian; b. Chgo., June 27, 1923; d. William James and Bessie Lee (Twety) Collier; B.S. in Edn., Chgo. State U., 1971, M.S., 1973; M.A. in Urban Studies, Loyola U., Chgo., 1979; m. George Dunham, Feb. 25, 1950; children—Kirk L., Eric Powell. Civilian, 5th U.S. Army HDqrs., Chgo., 1956-66; mem. library staff Chgo. State U., 1966—, instr., reference librarian, 1975-76, coordinator public services Douglas Library, 1976—, asst. prof., 1979—. Mem. ALA, Ill. Library Assn., Ill. Assn. Media Edn., Am. Fedn. Tchrs. (Merit award 1978). Roman Catholic. Home: 9144 S Aberdeen St Chicago IL 60620 Office: Chgo State Univ 95th St and King Dr Chicago IL 60628

DUNK, JOHN RUSSEL, ret. supt. schs.; b. Lafayette, Ind., Feb. 20, 1920; s. Russel E. and Maude A. (Bolyard) D.; student Central Normal Coll., 1940-41; B.S., Ind. State Tchrs. Coll., 1947, M.S., 1951; supt.'s license Ind. U., 1957; m. Laura Ellen Day, Dec. 24, 1944; children—Janice Dianne, Jeffrey John, Jeannine Lynnette. Indsl. arts tchr., athletic coach Wanatah (Ind.) High Sch., 1947-51; prin. Mill Creek (Ind.) High Sch., 1952-57; prin. Rolling Prairie (Ind.) High Sch., 1957-62; supt. Clinton Hanna Noble (Ind.) Consol. Sch. dist., 1962-80. Pres. Laporte County Govs. Youth Council Ind.; chmn. LaPorte County chpt. ARC, LaPorte County Crippled Children and Adults; troop com. chmn. Boy Scouts Am.; mem. LaPorte County Fair Bd. and Scholarship Com.; mem. study commn. Purdue U., 1957-62; mem. study council Ind. U., 1962—; mem. Ind. Sch. Bus. Commn., 1979-80. Served as cpl., inf., AUS, 1941-45, ETO, Africa. Decorated Purple Heart, Bronze Star; recipient outstanding tchr. award indsl. arts State of Ind., 1949. Mem. Ind. Assn. Pub. Sch. Supts., Am. Assn. Sch. Adminstrs., Ind., Nat. sch. bds. assns., P.T.A., Phi Delta Kappa, Epsilon Pi Tau. Methodist mem. financial bd., chmn. com. all-ch. employment. Mason, Elk; mem. Order Eastern Star. Home: 80 Keston Elm Dr LaPorte IN 46350

DUNKAS, NICHOLAS, psychiatrist; b. Athens, Greece, Dec. 19, 1926; s. John N. and Frosin (Harides) D.; M.D., U. Athens, 1953; m. Catherine Kannis, Sept. 13, 1955; children—Grace Alice, John Alexander, Stella Marie. Intern, Meth. Hosp., Peoria, Ill., 1955-56; resident in psychiatry Ill. State Psychiat. Inst., Chgo., 1957-62; practice medicine specializing in psychiatry, Chgo., 1962—; asst. prof. clin. psychiatry Northwestern U. Med. Sch.; founding mem. Northwestern Inst. Psychiatry; mem. staff Northwestern Meml. Hosp.; sr. attending physician Ill. Masonic Med. Center, Henrotin Hosp.; cons. psychiatrist Forkosh Hosp., Martha Washington Hosp., Chgo.; pres. Transcultural Center for Human Relations, Inc., Chgo.; asso. Athenian Inst. Anthropos, Athens, Greece. Diplomate Am. Bd. Psychiatry and Neurology. Fellow Am. Psychiat. Assn.; mem. Am. Geriatric Soc., AMA, Chgo. Med. Soc., Ill. Psychiat. Soc., Am. Assn. Group Psychotherapy, Am. Assn. Social Psychiatry, Hellenic Med. Soc. (past pres.), Greek Orthodox. Contbr. articles to profl. jours.; research in transcultural psychiatry. Home: 1210 Sheridan Rd Evanston IL 60202 Office: 168 N Michigan Ave Suite 800 Chicago IL 60601

DUNKELBERGER, DENNIS ALAN, advt. agy. exec.; b. Dayton, Ohio, Dec. 17, 1946; s. Jack Edward and Evelyn Mae (Steiner) D.; B.F.A., Miami U., Ohio, 1969; m. Nancy Jo Nassif, Apr. 15, 1972; 1 son, Jeffery Alan. Artist, Standard Register Co., Dayton, 1969; designer E.F. MacDonald Incentive Co., Dayton, 1969-72; designer, illustrator Penny-Ohlmann-Neiman, Dayton, 1972-73, art dir., 1973-74, creative dir., 1974-75; pres., creative dir. Dennis Dunkelberger Advt., Dayton, 1975—. Bd. dirs. Dayton Sertoma Club, 1977, Bldg. Bridges Inc. div. Montgomery County Juvenile Ct.; campaign planner Dayton Sch. Bd., 1970. Recipient many advt. awards including Best of Show, Dayton Advt. Club, 1975, 76, Champion Paper award, 1975, Chrysler-Plymouth Spl. award, 1971; logos pub. in Carter's Trademarks/5, Gilbert 100 Best Letterheads, Mead Paper award, 1977, 78. Mem. Dayton Advt. Club, Am. Mktg. Assn., Dayton Bus. Forum (pres. 1978), Dayton C. of C., 304 for Big Brothers Dayton. Democrat. Lutheran. Clubs: Dayton Racquet, Miami Valley Country, Dayton Court House, Phi Kappa Tau. Office: 515 Belmonte Park N Dayton OH 45405

DUNKLE, LISA MARIE, pediatrician; b. Ann Arbor, Mich., Oct. 31, 1946; d. Robert Henry and Dorothy Rose (Heagstedt) Dunkle; A.B., Wellesley Coll., 1968; M.D. (Scholar 1972), Johns Hopkins U., 1972; m. Richard James Scheffler, Dec. 28, 1972; children—Richard James, Margaret Dorothy. Intern, St. Louis Children's Hosp., 1972-73, resident in pediatrics, 1973-74, fellow in pediatric infectious diseases, 1974-76; practice medicine specializing in pediatrics, St. Louis, 1976—; asst. in pediatrics Washington U. Med. Sch., St. Louis, 1972-74, fellow in pediatric infectious diseases, 1974-76; asst. prof. pediatrics, instr. microbiology St. Louis U. Med. Sch., 1976-79, asso. prof. pediatrics, asst. prof. microbiology, 1979—, dir. div. pediatric infectious diseases; chmn. infection control com. Cardinal Glennon Meml. Hosp. for Children, St. Louis, 1976—, mem. child abuse mgmt. com., 1976-79, chmn. library com., 1977-79; mem. ednl. policy com. St. Louis U. Sch. of Medicine, 1977—, dir. student teaching, dept. pediatrics, 1980—; vis. faculty Washington U. Med. Center, St. Louis, 1978, Meml. Med. Center, Savannah, Ga., 1981. Diplomate Am. Bd. Pediatrics, Nat. Bd. Med. Examiners; registered physician, Mo. Fellow Am. Acad. Pediatrics; mem. Am. Soc. Microbiology, Infectious Disease Soc. Am., Midwest Soc. Pediatric Research (council mem. 1978—), Johns Hopkins Med. and Surg. Soc., N.Y. Acad. Scis., Sigma Xi. Republican. Presbyterian. Club: Wellesley. Contbr. articles in field to profl. jours. Office: 1465 S Grand Blvd Saint Louis MO 63104

DUNLEAVY, RAYMOND AUGUSTINE, III, paper products mfg. co. exec.; b. Cin., Aug. 22, 1950; s. Raymond Augustine and Helen Elizabeth (Moore) D.; B.Chem. Engring., Ga. Inst. Tech., 1973; m. Vickie Lynn Clark, June 11, 1971; children—Sean Patrick, Timothy Ryan, Lauren Colleen. Product devel. engr. Procter & Gamble, Cin., 1973-78; sr. research engr. Am. Can Co., Neenah, Wis., 1978-79, supr. new product devel., 1979-81, mgr. product devel., 1981—. Republican. Mormon. Home: 8 Adams Ln New Milford CT 06776 Office: American Ln Greenwich CT 06830

DUNMIRE, RAYMOND VERYL, librarian; b. Vandergrift, Pa., Dec. 17, 1925; s. Robert Braden and Fay (Stubrick) D.; B.A., Thiel Coll., 1950; M.A., Fla. State U., 1957; m. Ruth March, Apr. 4, 1953; children—Perry Carl, Cary Allan, Barry Ivan. Prof., head librarian Thiel Coll., Greenville, Pa., 1953-65; dir. libraries Southeastern Community Coll., Whiteville, N.C., 1965-69; dir. libraries, asso. prof. Augustana Coll., Sioux Falls, S.D., 1969—; inter-library loan librarian U. Fla. at Gainesville, 1960-61, instr. Sch. Edn., 1961-62. Cons., evaluator So. Assn. Secondary Schs. and Colls., various locations, 1968—. Mem. com. Cub Scouts Am., Sioux Falls. Bd. dirs. Center Western Studies, Sioux Falls. Served with USAAF, 1943-46. Mem. ALA (life), Southeastern, S.D. library assns., N.C. Lit. and Hist. Soc., Assn. Ednl. Communications and Tech., AAUP, Beta Phi Mu, Phi Alpha Theta, Delta Sigma Phi. Lutheran (mem. ch. council). Contbr. articles to profl. jours. Office: Mikkelsen Library Augustana Coll Sioux Falls SD 57102

DUNN, CAROL KEATTS, musician, educator; b. Chgo., July 17, 1930; d. William Wayne and Ferol (Davis) Keatts; student Ill. Wesleyan U., 1948-52; m. Robert J. Dunn, May 5, 1961; children—Holly Dunn Di Domenico, Joy Dunn Williams. Tchr. piano and organ, 1950—; dir. numerous ch. choirs; dir. county women's chorus asso. with Purdue U. Music-in-Extension, 1959—; cellist with string ensemble; performing counselor Sounds of Hope concert tour of Europe, 1979, 81; cons. Internat. Piano Teaching Found. Mem. Delta Omicron. Methodist. Arranger, composer music for chorus, choir and piano teaching. Home: 129 N Ironwood Dr South Bend IN 46615

DUNN, ELAINE SMUCKLER LIEBMAN, speech-lang. pathologist; b. Milw., Apr. 12, 1924; d. Robert Henry and Celia (Berliand) Smuckler; B.S., U. Wis., 1945; M.A., Northwestern U.,

1962, Ph.D., 1964; m. Albert Liebman, Dec. 17, 1944 (div. 1959); children—Jeffrey, Vance; m. 2d, Arthur Seymour Dunn, Nov. 11, 1965; stepchildren—Fredrick, Daniel, Charlotte, Nancy. Speech correction tchr. Madison (Wis.) pub. schs., 1944-46; grad. asst. speech correction dept. U. Wis., Madison, summer 1945; tchr. Central Inst. for Deaf, St. Louis, 1949-50; grad. asst. Northwestern U. Sch. Speech, Evanston, Ill., 1960-61, asst. prof., 1964-66; pvt. practice speech and lang. pathology, Evanston, 1966—; speech-lang. pathologist St. Francis Hosp., Evanston, 1966—; pres., dir. Elaine S. Dunn, Ph.D. Ltd., Evanston, 1971—. Active PTA, Boy Scouts Am. Northwestern U. fellow, 1961. Mem. Am. Speech, Lang. and Hearing Assn. (mem. profl. services bd. 1979-81), Chgo. Speech and Hearing Assn. (pres. 1977-79), Ill. Speech and Hearing Assn., Am. Acad. Pvt. Practice in Speech Pathology and Audiology (exec. bd. 1981—), Council Exceptional Children, Alexander Graham Bell Assn. for Deaf, Am. Cleft Palate Assn., Am. Auditory Soc., LWV, Phi Beta Kappa, Phi Kappa Phi, Pi Lambda Theta. Jewish. Home: 720 Oakton St Apt 5H Evanston IL 60202 Office: 636 Church St Evanston IL 60201

DUNN, FRANCIS GILL, state justice; b. Scenic, S.D., Nov. 12, 1913; s. Thomas Bernard and Mary (Gill) D.; student Dakota State Coll., 1931-34; LL.B., U. S.D., 1937; LL.M., George Washington U., 1948; m. Eldred Elizabeth Wagner, 1942; children—David, Rebecca Dunn Smith, Thomas, Carol Dunn Norbeck. Individual practice law, Madison, S.D., 1937-41, Sioux Falls, S.D., 1954-56; sec. to U.S. Senator W. J. Bulow, 1941-42; trial atty. U.S. Dept. Justice, Washington, 1946-50; asst. U.S. atty. for S.D., 1950-54; municipal judge, Sioux Falls, 1956-59, circuit judge, 1959-73; justice S.D. Supreme Ct., Pierre, 1973—, chief justice, 1974-79. Served to lt. USN, 1942-46. Mem. Am., S.D. bar assns., VFW, Delta Theta Phi. Roman Catholic. Club: Elks. Office: Supreme Ct Capitol Bldg Pierre SD 57501*

DUNN, HORTON, JR., chem. research co. information scientist; b. Coleman, Tex., Sept. 3, 1929; s. Horton and Lora Dean (Bryant) D.; B.A. summa cum laude, Hardin-Simmons U., 1951; M.S., Ph.D., Case Western Res. U. Research chemist Lubrizol Corp., Cleve., 1953-70, dir. tech. info. center, 1970-79, supr. info. services, 1980—; chmn. bd., bus. mgr. Isotopics, Cleve., 1964-67, editor, 1961-63. Mem. Am. Chem. Soc. (chpt. treas. 1968-70), Am. Soc. for Info. Sci. (chpt. pres. 1973-74), A.A.A.S., Beta Phi Mu, Alpha Chi. Contbr. articles to profl. jours. Patentee in field. Home: 530 Sycamore Dr Cleveland OH 44132 Office: 29400 Lakeland Blvd Wickliffe OH 44092

DUNN, JAMES B(ERNARD), mining co. exec., state senator; b. Lead, S.D., June 27, 1927; s. William B. and Lucy M. (Mullen) D.; B.S. in Bus. Adminstrn. and Econs., Blackhills State Coll., 1962; m. Elizabeth A. Lanham, Sept. 5, 1955; children—Susan, Tom, Mary Elizabeth, Kathleen. With Homestake Mining Co., Lead, 1947—, asst. dir. public affairs, 1962-78, dir. dept. public affairs, 1978—; mem. S.D. Ho. of Reps., 1971-72, S.D. Senate, 1973—; chmn. exec. bd. S.D. Legis. Research Council; mem. exec. bd. Nat. Conf. State Legislatures. Served with U.S. Army, 1945-47. Mem. AIME, Am. Mining Congress. Republican. Roman Catholic. Author co. centennial book, 1976. Office: PO Box 887 Lead SD 57754

DUNN, JIM, congressman; b. Detroit, July 21, 1943; s. James Whitney and Pauline Dunn; B.A., Mich. State U., 1967; m. Gayle Lynn Yerkey, 1967; children—Jeffrey, Julie, Kate. Pres. Dunn & Fairmont, builders and developers, East Lansing, Mich.; mem. 97th Congress from 6th Mich. Dist.; mem. Small Bus. Adv. Council. Mem. Lansing Council Arts. Mem. Nat. Bd. Realtors, Nat. Home Builders Assn., Mich. Home Builders Assn., Aircraft Owners and Pilots Assn., Lansing C. of C. Republican. Address: 1630 Longworth House Office Bldg Washington DC 20515*

DUNN, LEE JOSEPH, JR., lawyer; b. Boston, Sept. 16, 1943; s. Lee Joseph and Irene Elizabeth D.; A.B., Columbia U., 1966; J.D., Case Western Res. U., 1970; LL.M., Harvard U., 1971. Admitted to Kans. bar, 1973, Ill. bar, 1979; instr. Boston U. Law Sch., 1972; spl. asst. atty. gen. State of Kans., 1973-77; legal counsel U. Kans. Med. Center, 1973-77, asst. prof. med. jurisprudence, 1973-77; gen. counsel Northwestern Meml. Hosp., Chgo., 1977—; mem. adv. bd. Law and Medicine Center, Odessey Inst., Inc. Mem. Am. Acad. Forensic Scis., Am. Coll. Legal Medicine (Pres.'s award), Am. Soc. Law and Medicine (sec.), Am. Bar Assn., Ill. Bar Assn., Kans. Bar Assn., Am. Soc. Hosp. Attys., Ill. Assn. Hosp. Attys. (v.p.), Chgo. Bar Assn., Wyandotte County Bar Assn., Boston Latin Sch. Assn. (trustee 1971-74). Clubs: Columbia U. (Chgo.); Harvard (Chgo., N.Y.C.). Editor Boston Latin Sch. (Alumni) Bull., 1972-79; bd. editors Am. Jour. Law and Medicine. Office: Northwestern Meml Hosp Superior St and Fairbanks Ct Chicago IL 60611

DUNN, LEHMANN MAYNARD, cons. civil engr., land surveyor; b. Port Huron, Mich., Mar. 1, 1914; s. Maynard E. and Hazel E. (Lehmann) D.; B.S. in Civil Engring., Mich. Technol. U., 1935; m. Annetta Jane Broeckaert, Aug. 17, 1940; children—David B., Daniel L., Deryl D. Commd. 2d lt. C.E., U.S. Army, 1935, advanced through grades to lt. col. Res., ret.; surveyor Detroit Dist., U.S. C.E., 1935-36, 2d lt. 6th Engrs., Ft. Lawton, Wash., 1936-37; constrn. insp. U.S. Bur. of Reclamation, Coulee Dam, Wash., 1937-38; mining engr. P.I.M. Co., Vulcan, Mich., 1938-41; with C.E., U.S. Army, Erie Proving Ground, Ohio, 1941-42; partner Blue Water Concrete and Constrn. Co., Port Huron, 1947-48; pres. Dunn Constrn. Engring., Inc., Port Huron, 1948-80. Dir. Indsl. Devel. Corp., Port Huron, 1950-52. Mem. City of Port Huron Code Rev. Com., 1951-53, City of Port Huron Bldg. Code Bd. of Appeals, 1955-57; mem. Mich. Housing Code Commn., 1956-57. Active Blue Water council Boy Scouts Am., 1948—, pres., 1960-63, 65-67; mem. Port Huron Found., 1951—, Port Huron Mus. of Arts and History, 1963—, Mich. Tb and Respiratory Disease Assn., 1952—, Mich. United Conservation Club, 1960—. Served to 1st lt. C.E., U.S. Army, 1942-45; PTO; lt. col. Res. (ret.). Registered profl. engr. and land surveyor, Mich. Recipient Silver Beaver award, Boy Scouts Am., 1964. Mem. Nat. Soc. Profl. Engrs. (life, dir. 1956-60), Mich. Soc. Profl. Engrs. (dir.-at-large 1951-54, pres. 1954-56), Profl. Engrs. in Pvt. Practice, Profl. Engrs. in Constrn. (chmn. planning and ethics), Mich. Soc. Registered Land Surveyors, Mich. Assn. Professions (dir. 1970—), Port Huron C. of C. (dir. 1970-72, v.p. 1972-73), Metal Bldg. Dealers Assn. (chmn. ethics com. 1970-72, dir. 1970-74, pres. 1972-73), Gt. Lakes Metal Bldg. Erectors Assn. (pres. 1978-80, 1st hon. mem. 1981). Presbyterian. Clubs: Masons (life), Mich. Technol. U., Varsity, Alumni, Huskies, Rotary (pres. Port Huron 1959-60, gov. Dist. 633, 1976-77); Skippers Booster (St. Clair County Community Coll.). Home: 5690 Lakeshore Rd Port Huron MI 48060 Office: Port Huron MI 48060

DUNN, RICHARD LLOYD, mag. editor; b. Pitts., July 18, 1943; s. John Howard and Norma Ellen (Price) D.; B.S., Iowa State U., 1966; m. Patricia Jo Miller, June 17, 1966; children—Russell, Lee Ellen, Ryan. With Tech. Pub. Co., Barrington, Ill., 1969—, mng. editor Plant Engring. mag., 1974-79, editor Purchasing World mag., 1979—. Served to lt. U.S. Navy, 1966-69. Recipient Jesse H. Neal award Am. Bus. Press. Mem. Am. Soc. Bus. Press Editors, Soc. Profl. Journalists, Nat. Assn. Purchasing Mgmt., Am. Prodn. and Inventory Control Soc., Purchasing Mgmt. Assn. Chgo., Am. Trucking Assn. Methodist. Office: 1301 S Grove Ave Barrington IL 60010

DUNN, ROBERT GEARHART, state ofcl.; b. Mpls., Jan. 25, 1923; s. George Robert and Marguerite Morrow (Gearhart) D.; B.A., Amherst Coll., 1948; m. Mary Louise Caley, June 23, 1951 (dec. 1969); children—Ruth Caley, Susan Lydia, George Robert, Elizabeth Ann, William Campbell; m. 2d, Bette Lee Hedenstrom, Nov. 11, 1972; stepchildren—Robert Paul Hedenstrom, Mary Lee Hedenstrom Leirmo. Vice pres., gen. mgr. Inland Lumber Co., Princeton, Minn., 1953-66, pres., 1967—; mem. Minn. Ho. of Reps., 1965-72; mem. Minn. senate, 1973-80, asst. minority leader; chmn. Minn. Waste Mgmt. Bd., 1980—. Chmn., Mille Lacs County chpt. ARC, 1959; trustee 1st Congl. Ch., Princeton, 1957; mem. Minn. Council State Parks, St. Paul-Mpls. Com. on Fgn. Relations. Served with USMCR, 1942-46, 50-52. Republican. Mem. Northwestern Lumbermens Assn. (dir. Mpls. 1967-70), Princeton C. of C. (pres. 1958). Home: 708 Fourth St S Princeton MN 55371 Office: Waste Mgmt Bd 123 Thorson Bldg 7323 58th Ave N Crystal MN 55428

DUNN, ROSEMARIE THERESA, hosp. adminstr.; b. Bklyn., Oct. 2, 1952; d. Daniel and Myrtle Mae (Georgi) Benedetto; B.S. summa cum laude, St. Louis U., 1974, M.B.A., 1979; m. Raymond J. Dunn, Aug. 11, 1973. Dir. med. records Barnes Hosp., St. Louis, 1974-79, asst. adminstr., 1979-80, asso. adminstr., 1980—; mem. faculty St. Louis U., 1974—, Belleville Community Coll., 1974—, Ill. State U., 1975—. Recipient award Monticello Found., 1975. Mem. Am. Med. Records Assn., Assn. M.B.A. Execs., Mo. Med. Records Assn. (pres.), Eastern Mo. Med. Records Assn. (pres.). Home: 4214 St Linus Dr Saint Ann MO 63074 Office: 4949 Barnes Pl Saint Louis MO 63110

DUNN, SHARON KLUNK, psychologist; b. Carrollton, Ill., Aug. 8, 1950; d. Peter Michael and Lillian Ann (Gress) Klunk; A.B., U. Mo., 1972, M.Ed., 1973; m. David Andrew Dunn, Nov. 24, 1972; 1 dau., Heather Anne. Employment counselor Deck & Decker Employment Service, Columbia, Mo., 1973; placement coordinator, rehab. counselor Saginaw Valley Rehab. Center, Saginaw, Mich., 1974-75; staff psychologist Caro (Mich.) Regional Mental Health Center, 1975—; faculty psychology Delta Coll., 1976-77. Licensed psychologist, Mich. Mem. AAUW (pres. Cass City, Mich. chpt., chmn. various coms.), Am. Assn. on Mental Deficiency. Roman Catholic. Home: 6794 Third St Cass City MI 48726 Office: Lock Box A Caro MI 48723

DUNN, WINIFRED WIESE, occupational therapist; b. St. Louis, Mar. 26, 1950; d. Ignatius Joseph and Mary Louise (Marxer) W.; B.S. in Occupational Therapy, U. Mo., 1972, M.S. in Edn. and Spl. Edn., 1973; postgrad. U. Kans.; m. Robert G. Dunn, Aug. 17, 1973; children—James Daniel, Jessica Morgan. Staff, Liberty (Mo.) Public Schs., 1973-80; instr. psychology of exceptional child, William Jewell Coll., 1974-80; instr. exceptional child in classroom, Webster Coll., 1979-80; facilitator of pediatric services St. Luke's Hosp., Kansas City, Mo., 1980—; cons. in field. Mem. Am. Occupational Therapy Assn., Assn. Children with Learning Disabilities, Council Exceptional Children, Kans. Occupational Therapy Assn., Mo. Assn. Children with Learning Disabilities, Pi Lambda Theta. Roman Catholic. Home: 904 NE 60th Terr Kansas City MO 64118 Office: Saint Luke's Hospital Preschool ETD Bldg 44th St and Wornall St Kansas City MO 64111

DUNNE, GEORGE W., govt. ofcl.; b. Chgo.; ed. Northwestern U., Evanston, Ill.; 3 children. Asst. supt. Chgo. Park Dist., to 1955; mem. Ill. Ho. of Reps., 1955-61, majority leader, 1961; mem. Cook County Bd. Commrs., Chgo., 1961—, pres., 1969—; chmn. Cook County Dem. Party, 1976—. Served with U.S. Army, World War II, Korea. Democrat. Office: 150 E Huron St Chicago IL 60611*

DUNNE, MAURICE F., JR., ednl. adminstr.; b. Chgo., Nov. 30, 1926; s. Maurice F. and Janette M. (Pyott) D.; B.S., Northwestern U., 1949, A.B., 1975, M.A., 1980; M.B.A., Harvard U., 1952; m. Eleanor Isham, Sept. 14, 1957; children—Ralph, Maurice F., Tara. Asst. mgr. Pyott Foundry and Machine, Chgo., 1948-53; account exec. Grant Advt. and MacFarland, Aveyard and Co., Chgo., 1954-58; treas. Michael Kirby Skating Schs., River Forest, Ill., 1958-63; exec. v.p. Daily News Tribune, LaSalle, Ill., 1963-65; pres., dean Lake Forest (Ill.) Sch. Mgmt., 1965—; chief exec. officer, dir. Earldun Broadcasting Inc.; chief exec. officer Recreation Mgmt. Corp.; dir. Gen. Alloys; cons. Tulane Bus. Sch.; acad. adv. council Walden U. Trustee, Lake Forest Acad. and Ferry Hall, 1967-78, Lake Forest Coll., 1976—; mem. Chgo. Crime Commn., 1980—; active Lake Forest/Lake Bluff Crusade of Mercy, 1981, Lake Forest Police Commn. Mem. Am. Soc. Tng. and Devel., Acad. of Mgmt., President's Assn. (Chgo. chpt.). Roman Catholic. Clubs: Onwentsia (Lake Forest), Shoreacres (Lake Bluff), Little Harbor (Harbor Springs, Mich.). Patentee method of making flat belt pulleys. Office: Lake Forest College Lake Forest IL 60045

DUNNE, PHILIP ROEMER, communications cons.; b. Utica, N.Y., Aug. 29, 1932; s. Philip LeRoy and Avis Roemer (Gardiner) D.; B.S., Lafayette Coll., 1957; m. Jane Rush Thornbury, Oct. 5, 1957; children—Ryan Williams, Peter Roemer. Dir. public relations Am. Newspaper Publs. Assn. Research Inst., 1957-59; v.p. Cenco Inc., Chgo., 1960-72; pres. Pet Group, Inc., Geneva, Ill., 1972-75, also Vapor Control Inc., Geneva; partner RVI Corp., Chgo., 1975-79; mng. partner Dunne & Partners, Chgo., 1979—; dir. Synerdata Systems, Inc. Bd. dirs. Mid America Wine and Food Council. Served as cpl. AUS, 1953-55. Mem. Soc. Typographic Arts, Am. Mktg. Assn., Am. Soc. Wine Educators, Delta Kappa Epsilon. Republican. Episcopalian. Clubs: Brotherhood Knights of the Vine (Ill. comdr., master knight), Conferis des Vignerons de Saint Vincent Macon, Skyline, Cliff Dwellers, Saddle and Cycle, Racquet of Chgo. (past pres., gov.); Yale of N.Y.C. Food and wine editor Chicagoland Mag., 1978-79. Home: 1209 Astor St Chicago IL 60610 Office: 233 E Ontario St Chicago IL 60611

DUNNETTE, MARVIN DALE, psychologist; b. Austin, Minn., Sept. 30, 1926; s. Rodney Arthur and Mildred Geneva (Notestine) D.; B.Ch.E., U. Minn., 1948, M.A., 1951, Ph.D., 1954; m. Leaetta Marie Hough, Feb. 2, 1980; children by previous marriage—Nancy Dawn, Peggy Jo, Sheryl Jean. Research fellow dept. metallurgy U. Minn., 1948-49, research fellow, asst. prof. psychology, 1951-55; adviser employee relations research Minn. Mining and Mfg. Co., St. Paul, 1955-59; vis. asso. prof. U. Calif., Berkeley, 1962; chmn. bd. Decision Systems, Inc., Mpls., 1963-65; pres. Personnel Decisions, Inc., Mpls., 1966-75, chmn. bd., 1975—; pres. Personnel Decisions Research Inst., Mpls., 1975—; prof. psychology U. Minn., Mpls., 1961—; mem. research and devel. adv. group Army Research Inst. Social and Behavioral Scis., 1972-76, chmn. sci. adv. panel, ad hoc com. on personnel research and tng., 1975; mem. personnel research adv. group Bur. Naval Research, 1970-75. Served with USMC, 1944-46. Ford Found. fellow, 1964-65; recipient James A. Hamilton Outstanding Book award Am. Coll. Hosp. Adminstrs., 1972. Mem. Am. Psychol. Assn. (pres. div. 14, 1966-67, bd. sci. affairs 1975-77, James McKeen Cattell award 1965), AAAS. Author: (with W.K. Kirchner) Psychology Applied to Industry, 1965; Personnel Selection and Placement, 1966; (with J.P. Campbell and E.E. Lawler, K.E. Weick) Managerial Behavior, Performance and Effectiveness, 1970; editor: Work and Non Work in the Year 2001, 1973; Handbook of Industrial and Organizational Psychology, 1976; cons. editor Jour. Applied Psychology, 1950-75; contbr. articles to profl. jours. Home: 370 Summit Ave St Paul MN 55102 Office: 2415 Foshay Tower Minneapolis MN 55402

DUNNING, LESLIE LEON, aero. engr.; b. Francisco, Ind., Oct. 31, 1922; s. David and Ruth Ellen (McEllhiney) D.; B.S. in Aero. Engring., Purdue U., 1950; M.B.A. in Engring. Adminstrn., Air Force Inst. Tech., 1959; m. Elaine Margie Loomis, Jan. 3, 1944; children—Daniel Duane, Deborah Dayl. Commd. 2d. lt. USAF, 1944, advanced through grades to col., 1968, project officer, Wright-Patterson AFB, Ohio, 1957-63, systems program dir., specialized aircraft, 1974-75, asst. dep. for systems, 1976, dep. for remotely piloted vehicles and air launched strategic missiles, 1976-77; system project officer, Hdqrs. Air Force Systems Command, 1963-66; asst. for F/FB-111 DCS systems, 1970-71; dir. tactical units ops. center, Nakhon Phanom, Thailand, 1966-67; systems project officer, dir. aero. systems, Hdqrs. USAF, 1967-69, program element monitor, 1969, dir. prodn. DCASR, Phila., 1971-74. Served with USAAF, 1942-46. Decorated Air medal with six oak leaf clusters, Bronze Star, Meritorious Service medal, Legion of Merit; recipient certificates of achievement, 1972, outstanding achievement plaques, 1971, 73. Dayton; named Outstanding Alumni, Francisco High Sch., 1978. Asso. fellow, Am. Inst. Aeros. and Astronautics; mem. Aviation Hall of Fame Assn., Am. Def. Preparedness Assn., Nat. Assn. Unmanned Vehicle Systems, Air Force Assn. Presbyterian. Club: Wright-Patterson Officers'. Home: 3340 Beaumonde Ln Kettering OH 45409

DUNUNG, PRAFULLA VASANTRAO, architect, cartoonist; b. Kolhapur, India, June 16, 1938; came to U.S., 1972, naturalized, 1972; s. Vasantrao B. and Kusum A. (Bagi) D.; B.Arch., Bombay (India) U., 1962; M. Arch., Liverpool U., 1969; m. Vaijayanti M. Shah, May 30, 1962; 1 dau., Sanjyot. Lectr. architecture Liverpool (Eng.) Sch. Architecture, 1969-71; sr. architect Unit Constrn. Co., Liverpool, U.K., 1965-72; architect-designer Austin Co., Des Plaines, Ill., 1972—. Mem. Indian Inst. Architects, AIA (asso.). Jain. Office: Austin Co 2001 Rand Rd Des Plaines IL 60016

DUPIES, DONALD ALBERT, civil engr.; b. Waukegan, Ill., Apr. 17, 1934; s. Renie Bernard and Catharine Marie (Dowe) D.; B.C.E., Marquette U., 1957; m. Margaret T. McKibbin, Sept. 29, 1962; children—Mark, Patrick, Peggy, Colleen. With Howard, Needles, Tammen & Bergendoff, Milw., 1959—, office engr., 1969-71, engr. in charge, 1971-74, asso., 1974-79, partner, 1980—. Bd. dirs. Centurions of St. Joseph Hosp., Milw., 1971-76; cubmaster Milwaukee County council Boy Scouts Am., 1973-75. Served with C.E., U.S. Army, 1957-59. Registered profl. engr., Wis., Ill. Mem. ASCE, Wis. Assn. Mfr. and Commerce, Wis. Council for Transp. Info., Engrs. and Scientists of Milw., Inst. Transp. Engrs., Am. Mgmt. Assn., Internat. Bridge, Tunnel and Turnpike Assn., Bicentennial Engring., Sci. and Tech. Exposition and Conf. Council, Am. Pub. Works Assn., Water Pollution Control Fedn., Transp. Research Bd., Assn. Wis. Planners, Marquette U. Engring. Alumni Assn. (dir. Milw. 1976—), Tau Beta Pi, Chi Epsilon. Roman Catholic. Home 4733 N Cumberland Blvd Whitefish Bay WI 53211 Office: 6815 W Capital Dr Milwaukee WI 53216

DUPUIS, WAYNE JOSEPH, ins. co. exec.; b. Detroit, Nov. 1, 1929; s. Arthur Joseph and Helen Marie (Buckley) D.; student Eastern Mich. U., 1947-50, U. Mich. Extension Sch., 1952-53; m. Josephine Ghidoli, July 3, 1952 (dec. July 1979); children—Lynda Dupuis, Mark. Vice pres. James T. Barnes & Co., mortgage banking, 1956-62; pres. Gold Star Agy. Inc., Detroit, 1962—, Nat. Fin. Planning, Inc., Detroit, Various Markets Inc.; sec. Ajax Corp., P.R., 1965—; dir. Old Pioneer Life Ins. Co., 1967—. Mem. Detroit Assn. Ins. Agts., Builders and Trades Detroit, Greater Detroit Bd. Commerce. Clubs: Detroit Yacht (commodore), Detroit Athletic. Home: 789 Briarcliff St Grosse Pointe Woods MI 48236 Office: 300 First National Bldg Detroit MI 48226

DU PUY, ELBERT NEWTON, obstetrician and gynecologist; b. Parral, W.Va., Oct. 19, 1904; s. Elbert Stephenson and Lillian (Dixon) DuP.; B.S., U. W.Va., 1930; M.D., Duke U., 1932; m. Ruth Christine Griffenhagen, May 7, 1938; children—James Newton, Karl Frederick Griffenhagen, William Edwin Stuart. Intern, Ch. Home and Infirmary, Balt., 1933; resident in obstetrics Univ. Hosp., Balt., 1934-36; fellow Rotunda Hosp., Dublin, Ireland, 1931; practice medicine specializing in obstetrics and gynecology, Beckley, W.Va., 1936-42, Quincy, Ill., 1946—; mem. staff Blessing Hosp., 1946—, pres. staff, 1974-76, chief obstetrics and gynecology, 1973-75; mem. staff St. Mary Hosp., 1946—, chief obstetrics and gynecology, 1975-77; asso. clin. prof. ob-gyn So. Ill. U., Springfield. Mem. nat. council Boy Scouts Am., 1968—; trustee Robert Morris Coll., Carthage, Ill., 1964-69, Kiwanis Internat. Spastic Paralysis Research Found., 1956—; mem. Quincy Bd. Edn., 1958-63, pres., 1962-63. Served with MC, U.S. Army, 1942-46; MTO. Decorated Silver Star, Bronze Star; recipient Silver Beaver award Boy Scouts Am., 1972. Diplomate Am. Bd. Obstetrics and Gynecology. Fellow Am. Coll. Obstetrics and Gynecology (founder), A.C.S., Royal Soc. Medicine (Eng.), Am. Acad. Geriatrics, Am. Acad. Psychosomatic Medicine, Royal Soc. Health (Eng.), Edn. and Sci. Found. of Ill. Med. Soc. (founder); mem. AMA (Physicians' Recognition award), World, So. med. assns., Central Assn. Obstetricians and Gynecologists, Assn. Mil. Surgeons, Ill. (past pres., past chmn. bd. trustees), Adams County (past pres.) med. socs. Congregationalist. Clubs: Univ. (Chgo.); Quincy (Ill.) Country; Masons, Shriners, Jesters. Home: 18 Country Club Dr Quincy IL 62301 Office: 1101 Maine St Quincy IL 62301

DUPUY, JANICE MARIE, gas co. ofcl.; b. San Angelo, Tex., Aug. 13, 1945; d. Loranzia and Alice Josephine (Jones) Outin; student U. Alaska, 1963; B.S., Angelo State U., 1967; M.S., U. Nebr., 1972; m. Wardell Raymond Dupuy, Dec. 17, 1965. Instr., Kadena (Okinawa) Edn. Center, 1967; teen club coordinator Kadena Youth Center, 1969; counselor Omaha Opportunities Industrialization Center, 1970; tchr. Omaha Pub. Schs., 1971, counselor, 1975-77; asst. dir. Family Adv. Center, Taiwan, 1972-75; home-sch. liaison Bellevue (Nebr.) Pub. Schs., 1977-79; tng. specialist No. Natural Gas Co., Omaha, 1979-80; cons. Internorth, Inc., 1980-81; mgr. employee relations Peoples's Natural Gas, Council Bluffs, Iowa, 1981—. Regional rep. Children's Mental Health Adv. Com., 1976-79; Mem. Nebr., Am. personnel and guidance assns., Am. Soc. Tng. and Devel., Nat. Organizational Devel. Network. Methodist. Club: Altrusa. Home: 515 Laurel Circle Bellevue NE 68005 Office: People's Natural Gas Co Council Bluffs IA

DURAN, ROBERT JACKSON, hand surgeon; b. McAlester, Okla., June 1, 1923; s. Samuel Montgomery and Fanny (Plunkett) D.; student Westminster Coll., 1941-42, Northeastern State U., 1942-43, Emory U., 1943; M.D., U. Okla., 1947; m. Joanne Kreisle, July 3, 1948; children—Martha Jane (Mrs. Richard E. Hennessey), William David, Samuel Montgomery. Intern, Meth. Hosp., Indpls., 1947-48; resident surg. pathology St. Elizabeth Hosp., Lafayette, Ind., 1948-49; resident gen. surgery Scott and White Clinic, Temple, Tex., 1949-50; resident gen. and plastic surgery Mayo Clinic, Rochester, Minn., 1953-56; practice medicine specializing in plastic, reconstructive and hand surgery, Columbus, Ohio, 1956—; mem. staffs Univ. Hosp., Children's Hosp., St. Anthony Hosp., Mount Carmel Hosp.; faculty Ohio State U., Columbus, 1957—, clin. prof., co-dir. hand service, 1968—. Served to capt. USAF, 1950-52. Diplomate Am. Bd. Plastic

Surgery. Fellow A.C.S.; mem. A.M.A., Am. Soc. for Surgery of the Hand, Am. Soc. Plastic and Reconstructive Surgery, Am. Assn. Plastic Surgeons, Ohio Med. Assn., Ohio Valley Plastic Surgery Soc., Columbus Surg. Soc. (pres. 1968), Columbus Acad. Medicine, Ohio Acad. Sci., Phi Chi. Republican. Methodist. Clubs: Faculty; Scioto Country, Rotary. Contbr. articles to profl. jours. Office: 1275 Olentangy River Rd Columbus OH 43212

DURANT, PAUL DILLINGHAM, II, ins. co. exec.; b. Ann Arbor, Mich., Feb. 20, 1931; s. Wentworth Tenney and Katherine (Henning) D.; B.B.A., North Tex. State U., 1958; m. Carolyn Peterson, June 2, 1967; 1 son, Jon Paul. Staff accountant Peat, Marwick, Mitchell & Co., Dallas, 1958-59; comptroller Steere Tank Lines, Inc., Dallas, 1959-64; accountant Paul D. Durant, C.P.A., Dallas, 1964-65; v.p., controller, asst. treas. Gt. Commonwealth Life Ins. Co., Dallas, 1965-68; pres., dir. Investers Found. Life Ins. Co., Dallas, 1969; cons. Fin. and Acquisitions, Dallas, 1968-69; exec. v.p., treas., dir., co-founder Am. Bus. & Commd. Life Ins., Co., Dallas, 1969-73; treas., v.p. Southland Life Ins. Co., 1973-77; v.p. fin. services, treas. Sentry Life Ins. Co. Served with Signal Corps. U.S. Army, 1951-53. Mem. Am. Inst. C.P.A.'s, Am. Accounting Assn., Tex. Soc. C.P.A.'s, Wis. Inst. C.P.A.'s, Fin. Execs. Inst. Methodist. Home: 155 N Maple Bluff Rd Stevens Point WI 54481 Office: 1800 North Point Dr Stevens Point WI 54481

DURBNEY, CLYDROW JOHN, clergyman; b. St. Louis, Sept. 27, 1916; s. Eearl Elmer and Conetta Mae D.; A.B., Gordon Coll. Theology and Missions, 1950; B.D., Eden Theol. Sem., 1953; S.T.M., Concordia Theol. Sem., 1954, postgrad. 1954-59; postgrad Eden Sem., 1973-75; D.D., Am. Bible Inst., 1980; m. Mattie Lee Neal, Oct. 27, 1968. Clk., U.S. Post Office, St. Louis, 1941-54; instr. Western Bapt. Bible Coll., St. Louis, 1954-67; asst. pastor Central Bapt. Ch., St. Louis, 1954; ordained to ministry Nat. Bapt. Ch., 1952; ghetto evangelist Ch. on Wheels, 1952—. Served with AUS, 1942-46; ETO. Decorated Bronze Star. Recipient Disting. World Service award Central Bapt. Ch. Prayer Aux., 1974. Mem. Internat. Platform Assn., Inst. Research Assn., Gordon Alumni Assn., Anglo Am. Acad., Assn. Clin. Pastoral Edn., Nat. Geog. Soc., Smithsonian Instn. Republican. Author: With Him in Glory, 1955; Adventures in Soul Winning, 1966; contbr. to New Voices in Am. Poetry, 1972—. Home: 8244 Addington Dr Berkeley MO 63134 Office: 2843 Washington Blvd Saint Louis MO 63103

DURBROW, BRIAN RICHARD, mgmt. cons.; b. Milw., Apr. 26, 1940; s. Robert James and Marianne Winifred (Pengelly) D.; A.A., U. Fla., 1961; B.B.A., U. Iowa, 1962; M.S., No. Ill. U., 1968; Ph.D., Ohio State U., 1971; diploma, Indsl. Coll. Armed Forces, 1972; m. Barbara Helen Mustine; children—Robert E., William D. Jr. accountant Buick-Oldsmobile-Pontiac div. Gen. Motors Corp., South Gate, Calif., 1962-64, sr. accountant Chevrolet div., Janesville, Wis., 1964-66; payroll supr. No. Ill. U., 1966-68; financial analyst Ohio State U., 1968-70; pres. B.R. Durbrow and Assos., Cin., 1969-72; asst. prof. mgmt. Wright State U., Dayton, 1970-71; prof. financial mgmt. Air Force Inst. Tech., 1972-73; pres. Barbrisons Mgmt. Systems, Inc., Cin., Tampa, Fla., 1972—; v.p. PMC Assos., Cin., 1976-78, Selindex, Inc., Tulsa, 1977—, Effectiveness, Inc., Tampa, 1978-80; vis. prof. mgmt. U. Ala., 1975; asso. prof. mgmt. Xavier U., Cin., 1975-77; speaker Nat. Mgmt. Assn. Active Young Republicans, Calif., Wis., Ill.; vice chmn. Young Reps., Janesville, Wis., 1964, chmn., 1965-66, county treas., 1964, vice chmn., 1965, chmn., 1966, 1st dist. vice chmn., 1965-66, mem. city, county, dist. and state exec. bd., 1965-66, conv. del., 1965; pres. Mgmt. Research and Devel. Inst., Cin., 1976-80, merged with Barbrisons Mgmt. Systems, Inc., 1980, pres., 1980—. Mem. Acad. Mgmt., Nat. Mgmt. Assn., Soc. Advancement Mgmt., Am. Soc. Tng. and Devel., Internat. Council for Small Bus. Mgmt. Devel., Nat. Small Bus. Assn., Assn. Mgmt. Consultants, Fla. Council of 100, Commerce Execs. Soc., Sigma Iota Epsilon, Beta Gamma Sigma, Delta Tau Delta, Delta Sigma Pi. Author: Inter-Firm Executive Mobility, 1971; Management Dynamics, 1974; editor various reference works. Contbr. articles to profl. jours. Office: 2957 Annwood St Cincinnati OH 45206

DURENBERGER, DAVID FERDINAND, U.S. senator; b. St. Cloud, Minn., Aug. 19, 1934; s. George G. and Isabelle M. (Cebulla) D.; B.A. cum laude in Polit. Sci., St. Johns U., 1955; J.D., U. Minn., 1959; m. Gilda Beth Baran, Sept. 4, 1971; children by previous marriage—Charles, David, Michael, Daniel. Admitted to Minn. bar, 1959; mem. firm LeVander Gillen Miller & Durenberger, South St. Paul, 1959-66; exec. sec. to Gov. Harold LeVander, 1967-71; counsel for legal and community affairs, corp. sec. H.B. Fuller Co., St. Paul, 1971-78; U.S. senator from Minn., 1979—, mem. fin. com., govtl. affairs com., select com. on intelligence, select com. on aging, chmn. intergovtl. relations subcom., health subcom.; mem. presdl. adv. com. on federalism, adv. commn. on intergovtl. relations, 1981—. Co-chmn. NAIA Football Bowl Playoff, 1963; div. chmn. United Fund of South St. Paul, 1965; chmn. citizens sect. Minn. Recreation and Park Assn., 1971-72; mem. South St. Paul Parks and Recreation Commn., 1971-72; chmn. Metro Council Open Space Adv. Bd., 1972-74; commr. Murphy-Hanrehan Park Bd., 1973-75; chmn. Save Open Space Now, 1974, Close-Up Found. Minn., 1975-76, Social Investment Task Force, Project Responsibility, 1974-76, Spl. Ser. div. St. Paul Area United Way, 1973-76; chmn. bd. commrs. Hennepin County Park Res. Dist.; vice chmn. Met. Parks and Open Space Bd.; exec. vice chmn. Gov.'s Commn. on Arts; exec. dir. Minn. Constl. Study Commn., Supreme Ct. Adv. Com. on Jud. Responsibility; pres. Burroughs Sch. PTA, Mpls.; chmn. Dakota County Young Republican League, 1963-64; dir. legal council Minn. Young Rep. League, 1964-65; co-chmn. State Young Rep. League Conv., 1965; del. State Rep. Conv., 1966, 68, 70, 72; 1st vice chmn. 13th Ward Mpls. Rep. Party, 1973-74; bd. dirs. Met. Parks Found., Public Service Options, Inc., St. Louis Park AAU Swim Club, Minn. Landmarks, 1971-73, Public Affairs Leadership and Mgmt. Tng., Inc., 1973-75, U. Minn. YMCA, 1973-75, Community Planning Orgn., Inc., St. Paul, 1973-76, Project Environ. Found., 1974-75, Urban Lab., Inc., 1975, Nat. Recreation and Park Assn., Within the System, Inc., 1976—; trustee Children's Health Center and Hosp., Inc., Mpls.; mem. exec. com. Nat. Center for Vol. Action, Minn. Charities Rev. Council. Served as 2d lt. U.S. Army, 1955-56, as capt. Res., 1957-63. Named Outstanding Young Man in South St. Paul, 1964, One of Ten Outstanding Young Men in Minn., 1965. Mem. Am. Bar Assn., Minn. Bar Assn., Corp. Council Assn., St. Johns U. Alumni Assn. (pres. Twin Cities chpt. 1963-65, nat. pres. 1971-73), Mpls., C. of C., St. Paul Area C. of C., Gamma Eta Gamma (chancellor 1958-59, v.p. Alumni Assn. 1965-75). Roman Catholic. Club: K.C. Office: 353 Russell Senate Office Bldg Washington DC 20510

DURIC, MIODRAG, elec. engr.; b. Zagreb, Yugoslavia, Feb. 27, 1940; s. Aleksandar and Stevanka (Smud) D.; came to Can., 1968, naturalized, 1976; B.S., U. Zagreb, 1964; postgrad U. Windsor (Ont., Can.), 1975—; m. Vjekoslava Majer, Nov. 1, 1958; 1 son, Robert. Project engr., Rade Koncar electrification of railways, Zagreb, 1964-68; design engr. Detroit Edison Co., 1968-70; co-founder, engring. supr. elec. dept. CDA Engring., Detroit, 1970—. Registered profl. engr., Ont., Mich. Mem. Assn. Profl. Engrs. Ont. Author: (with Velimir Babic) Electric Traction, 1967; contbr. articles to profl. jours. Home: 440 Laporte Ave Windsor ON N8S 3R2 Canada Office: 220 Bagley Suite 800 Detroit MI 48226

DURKIN, JOHN CUTHBERT (JACK), mfg. co. exec.; b. Sewickley, Pa., Aug. 6, 1934; s. John William and Mary Catherine (Dempsey) D.; B.S., John Carroll U., 1961; M.B.A., Kent State U., 1980; m. Margaret Mary Murtagh, July 21, 1962; children—Sean Thomas, Patrick Joseph, Mary Catherine. Mgmt. trainee, IBM Corp., Cleve., 1961-64; supr. personnel services White Motor Corp., Cleve., 1964-67; mgr. human resources Parker Hannifin Corp., Cleve., 1967-73; dir. employee relations Addressograph-Multigraph Corp., Cleve., 1973-76, Ohio-Sealy Mattress Co., 1976-77; dir. employee relations Stouffer Foods Corp. Cleve., 1977—; adj. prof. bus. Notre Dame Coll. of Ohio, South Euclid, 1981—. Mem. adv. bd. Sr. Citizens Employment Com.; co. chmn. United Way. Served with USN, 1953-57. Mem. Stouffer Polit. Action Com., Am. Soc. Personnel Adminstrn., Alumni Assn. John Carroll, Kent State U Alumni Assn. Republican. Roman Catholic. Home: 1044 Homestead Rd South Euclid OH 44121 Office: 5750 Harper Rd Solon OH 44139

DURKIN, JOHN S., data processing co. exec.; b. Monticello, N.Y., Oct. 16, 1945; s. John A. and Marion (Cross) D.; B.A., Mich. State U., 1967; m. L. Joan Ruof, June 29, 1968; children—John, Janeen. Auditor, Touche Ross & Co., Cleve., 1967-68; auditor Arthur Andersen & Co., Cin., 1970-71; v.p. Kanter Corp., Cin., 1971-75; pres. Econ. Data Inc., Cin., 1975—, also dir. Financial adviser, Cin. Assn. Children with Learning Disabilities, 1977. Served with AUS, 1968-70. C.P.A., Ohio. Mem. Ohio Soc. C.P.A.'s. Republican. Episcopalian. Clubs: Cin. Athletic, Bankers. Home: 5880 Winton Ridge Cincinnati OH 45232 Office: One E 4th St Suite 1606 Cincinnati OH 45202

DURLAK, JOSEPH ALLEN, clin. psychologist, educator; b. Chgo., Aug. 27, 1945; s. Joseph F. and Frances Mary (Czarny) D.; B.S. with honors, Loyola U. Chgo., 1967; M.S., Vanderbilt U., 1968, Ph.D., 1971; m. Christine Marie Polk, June 7, 1969. Clin. psychologist Dwight David Eisenhower Med. Center, Augusta, Ga., 1975-76; asst. prof. So. Ill. U., Carbondale, 1976-79, asso. prof., 1979-80; asso. prof. psychology Loyola U., Chgo., 1980—; faculty U. Md. Overseas Div., 1972-75, Boston U., 1974, Augusta Coll., 1975-76. Served with U.S. Army, 1969-76. NDEA fellow Vanderbilt U., 1967-71. Mem. Am. Psychol. Assn. Editorial bd. Am. Jour. Community Psychology, 1981—; contbr. articles to profl. jours. Home: 2401 Ridgeway St Evanston IL 60201 Office: Loyola U Dept Psychology 820 N Michigan Ave Chicago IL 60611

DUROCHER, CHARLES OLIVER, assn. exec.; b. Detroit, July 7, 1920; s. Otto Oliver and Louise Madeline (Van Coillie) D.; B.A., Mich. State U., 1963, M.A., 1964; m. Alba Estrella Sanchez, May 22, 1943; children—Dianne, Charles Oliver, Yvette, Dennis, Michael, Lorraine, Andrew, Gerard. Enlisted in U.S. Navy, 1941, commd. ensign, 1942, advanced through grades to comdr., 1956; ret., 1962; legis. analyst Mich. State Senate, Lansing, 1965-66; systems analyst Mich. Dept. State, Lansing, 1967-72; exec. asst. State of Mich. Office of Gov., Lansing, 1973-75; regional dir. Am. Assn. Motor Vehicle Adminstrs., Okemos, Mich., 1976—. Decorated Air medals (4). Mem. Navy League, Pi Gamma Mu. Author: This is Sauffley, 1959. Address: 3608 W Arbutus St Okemos MI 48864

DURRETT, JOSEPH PARK, food co. exec.; b. Charleston, S.C., Aug. 9, 1945; s. Van Dawson and Eloise (Barwick) D.; B.Econs., Duke U., 1967; M.B.A., U. Pa., 1969; m. Cathy Abdun-nur, Jan. 3, 1981; children by previous marriage—Scott Fairfield, Christopher Park. Asso. advt. mgr. Procter & Gamble, Cin., 1969-80; v.p., dir. grocery products Kraft, Inc., Glenview, Ill., 1980—. Recipient United Appeal award of merit, 1979. Clubs: Univ. (Cin.); Execs. (Chgo.). Office: Kraft Ct Glenview IL 60025

DUS, KARL MARIA, biochemist; b. Vienna, Austria, Jan. 2, 1932; s. Karl Arthur and Johanna (Novak) D.; came to U.S., 1958; Ph.D. in Chemistry, U. Vienna, 1958; m. Martha Mahler, June 5, 1971; children—Johanna, Melinda May. Research fellow in medicine Mass. Gen. Hosp., Harvard Med. Sch., Cambridge, 1958-60; research asso. biochemistry Brandeis U., Waltham, Mass., 1960-61; asst. research chemist U. Calif., San Diego, 1961-65, asso., 1965-68; asst. prof. biochemistry U. Ill., Urbana, 1968-73; asso. prof. St. Louis U. Med. Sch., 1974—; vis. maître de recherches in genetics and physiology Centre National de la Recherche Scientifique, Gif-sur-Yvette, France, 1965-66. NIH, NSF grantee, 1969—. Mem. Am. Chem. Soc., Am. Soc. Biol. Chemists, Am. Inst. Chemists, AAAS, N.Y. Acad. Sci., Am. Soc. Photobiology. Roman Catholic. Patentee on instrument design. Contbr. articles in field to profl. jours. Home: 411 S Holmes St Kirkwood MO 63122 Office: 1402 S Grand Blvd Saint Louis MO 63104

DUSTHIMER, THOMAS LEE, banker; b. Danville, Ill., Dec. 27, 1934; s. William V. and Elizabeth D.; B.S.A., Ind. U., 1957, M.B.A., 1958; postgrad. Wis. Sch. Banking, 1963-65; m. Lois V. Young, Apr. 29, 1961; children—Lynn, Diane, Jill. With corr. bank div. Am. Fletcher Nat. Bank & Trust Co., Indpls., 1958-65, asst. cashier, 1961-63, asst. v.p., 1963-65, v.p. in charge nat. div., 1965-68, asst. to pres., 1968-69, sr. v.p. in charge corp. div., 1969; pres., dir. Mark Twain Bancshares, Inc., St. Louis, 1969-70; pres., chief exec. officer, dir. Miami Beach First Nat. Bank (Fla.), 1970-72; pres., chief exec. officer, dir. Coral Gables First Nat. Bank (Fla.), 1972-73; pres., chief exec. officer, dir. First Nat. Bank, Elkhart, Ind., 1973—, chmn. bd., 1981—. Bd. dirs., chmn. Century Fund dr. Jr. Achievement, 1973—; bd. dirs. Aux Chandelles, 1974—; dist. chmn. U.S. Savs. Bonds, 1974—; mem. Downtown Redevel. Com., 1974—; bd. dirs. Elkhart Gen. Hosp., 1975—; mem. Pres. Adv. Council Goshen Coll., 1975—; bd. dirs. Wells Cargo, 1976—; trustee YMCA Endowment Trust Co., 1976—; mem. exec. com. Elkhart Gen. Hosp., 1978—, chmn. fin. com., 1979—; mem. Joint YW/YMCA Community Project Found. Com., 1979—; chmn. Elkhart County Maternal and Child Health Bldg. Fund, 1979—; mem. Elkhart Mayor's Econ. Adv. Council 1981—; chmn. Ind. Enterprize Zone Commn., 1981—. active League Econ. Devel., Fin. Assos. 14. Served to 1st lt. U.S. Army, 1958-59. Recipient award United Fund, 1976, Others award Salvation Army, 1978, Outstanding Service award Urban League, 1979. Mem. Am. Bankers Assn. (banking advisor 1980—), Ind. Bankers Assn. (dir. 1981), Indiana Soc. Chgo. Club: Columbia (Indpls.). Office: First Nat Bank PO Box 460 Elkhart IN 46515

DUTT, JAMES L., food co. exec.; b. Topeka, Kans., Feb. 11, 1925; B.S., Washburn U., Topeka, 1950; M.B.A., U. Dayton (Ohio), 1966. With Beatrice Foods Co., 1947—, exec. v.p. charge dairy and soft drink divs., 1974, dir. internat. dairy ops., 1974-75, pres. internat. food ops., 1975, corp. exec. v.p., 1975-77, pres., chief operating officer, 1977—, chmn. bd., chief exec. officer, 1979—; dir. GATX Corp. Bd. dirs. Nat. 4-H Council, Chgo. Council Fgn. Relations, Art Inst. Chgo., Lyric Opera Chgo., Orchestral Assn. Chgo. Mem. Grocery Mfrs. Am. (dir.), Conf. Bd. (dir.), Chgo. Assn. Commerce and Industry (dir.). Address: Beatrice Foods Co 120 S LaSalle St Chicago IL 60602

DUTY, ALLENE BEAUMONT (MRS. SPENCER CUMMER DUTY), author; b. Cleve., Jan. 29, 1912; d. John Erwin and Grace Forbes (Allen) Beaumont; B.S., Western Res. U., 1935; diploma Cleve. Sch. Art, 1935; m. Spencer Cummer Duty, Dec. 29, 1936 (dec. June 1973); children—Nancy Allen (Mrs. James Douglas Campbell, Jr.), Spencer Beaumont. Former pres. women's adv. council Western Res. Hist. Soc.; former v.p. jr. council Cleve. Mus. Art; past mem. sr. bd. Amasa Stone House. Author: The Kreider Family, 1953; The Duty Family, 1972; The Forbes Family, 1972; The Taylor Family, 1972; Addenda to Cummer Memoranda, 1972; The Allen Family, 1973; The Ancestors and Descendants of Ephraim Simmons, 1977; The Ancestors and Descendants of The Honorable Calvin Pease and Laura Grant Risley Pease, His Wife of Suffield, Conn., Rutland, Vt. and Warren, Ohio; The Beaumont Family, 1980. Clubs: Kirtland Country, Intown (Cleve.). Home: 3450 Green Rd Cleveland OH 44122

DUVICK, DONALD NELSON, plant breeder; b. Sandwich, Ill., Dec. 18, 1924; s. Nelson Daniel and Florence Henrietta (Appel) D.; B.S., U. Ill., 1948; Ph.D., Washington U., St. Louis, 1951; m. Selma Elizabeth Nelson, Sept. 10, 1950; children—Daniel, Jonathan, Randa. With Pioneer Hi-Bred Internat., Inc., Johnston, Iowa, 1951—, corn breeding coordinator Eastern and So. div., 1965-71, dir. corn breeding dept., 1971-75, dir. plant breeding div., 1975—; lectr. in field. Pres., Johnston Consol. Sch. Bd., 1965-67. Served with AUS, 1943-46. Pioneer Hi-Bred fellow U. London, 1968. Fellow Crop Sci. Soc. Am.; mem. Bot. Soc. Am., Genetics Soc. Am., Am. Soc. Plant Physiologists, N.Y. Acad. Scis., AAAS, Am. Soc. Agronomy, Am. Seed Trade Assn., Council Agrl. Sci. and Tech. Republican. Mem. United Ch. Christ. Author articles on genetics and plant breeding, developmental anatomy and cytology, cytoplasmic inheritance, quantititive genetics. Asso. editor Plant Physiology, 1977-78. Home: 6837 NW Beaver Dr Johnston IA 50131 Office: 7301 NW 62d Ave Johnston IA 50131

DUZEY, JAROSLAW M., mfg. corp. exec.; b. Peremyszl, Ukraine, Nov. 26, 1923; came to U.S., 1949, naturalized, 1955; s. Ivan and Anastazja (Hrycyk) Duzyj; student Veterinarian Coll. Lviv, Ukraine, 1942-44; m. Olya Lash, July 12, 1952; children—Andrey I., Olya M., Yuriy H. Draftsman, Creative Industries, Detroit, 1950-52; inspector G & W Tool & Mfg. Co., Detroit, 1952-54; supr. G & W Automation, Detroit, 1954-55; v.p., pres. Cylectron Corp., Warren, Mich., 1956—; v.p., pres. Step, Inc., Warren, 1968—; pres. Inton Investment Co., Ltd., Toronto, Ont., Can., 1971-78. Sch. bd. Immaculate Conception High Sch., 1967—, mem. scholarship bd., 1967-79, PTA pres., Hamtramck, Mich., 1968-72; pres. Ukrainian Nat. Assn., Br. 20, Warren, 1970—; pres. Am. Ukrainian Rep. Assn., Warren, 1972—; Rep. precinct del., Warren, 1970-80; Ronald Reagan del. Mich. State Rep. Conv., 1976; pres. Senator R. Griffin Club, Warren, 1972-76; bd. Mich. Nationalities Council, Detroit, 1975-79; mem. Ukrainian Studies Com. Harvard U., 1975—; v.p., then pres. St. Josaphat Ukrainian Cath. Ch. com., Warren, 1972—; pres. Am.-Ukrainian Econ. Council, 1978—; mem. Ordinance Assn. U.S.A.; mem. Ukrainian Studies Com. U. Mich., Ann Arbor, 1980—; chmn., pres. Ukrainian Cultural Center, Warren, 1980—; mem. Trembita Choir, Detroit, 1966-79. Recipient certificate of appreciation, City of Warren, 1980, spl. award Ukrainian Cath. High Sch., Hamtramck, 1975, leadership award Mich. Chpt. Nationalities Council, 1978, various sports awards and trophies. Home: 26657 Haverhill Warren MI 48091 Office: 24027 Ryan Rd Warren MI 48091

DUZY, ALBERT FRANK, cons. mech. engr.; b. Ambridge, Pa., Jan. 3, 1921; s. Frank Joseph and Julia (Koteles) D.; B.S. in Mech. Engring., Carnegie-Mellon U., 1955; m. Margaret Kathryn Meyer, Jan. 17, 1946; children—Adrienne M. Gill, Julianne M. Greenbank, Albert Frank. Fuels specialist Eastern Gas & Fuel Assos., Pitts., 1947-56, Babcock & Wilcox Co., Barberton, Ohio, 1957-71; v.p. Paul Weir Co., Chgo., 1971—. Chmn. Barberton United Fund, 1966. Served with USN, 1939-46; PTO, ETO, NATOUSA. Registered profl. engr., Ohio, Pa. Mem. ASME (Best Paper award 1967-68, certificate of appreciation jointly with IEEE and ASCE 1971-72, communications policy bd., power dept. policy bd., permanent rep. to Am. Power Conf., also coms., exec. com. Chgo. sect., Percy Nicholls award in field solid fuels 1978), Nat. Soc. Profl. Engrs. Republican. Club: Tower (Chgo.). Contbr. numerous articles to profl. pubis. Home: 1615 E Central Rd Apt 310B Arlington Heights IL 60005 Office: 20 N Wacker Dr Chicago IL 60606

DWIGHT, DONALD RATHBUN, newspaper publisher; b. Holyoke, Mass., Mar. 26, 1931; s. William and Dorothy Elizabeth (Rathbun) D.; A.B., Princeton U., 1953; D.Sc. (hon.), U. Lowell (Mass.), 1974; m. Susan Newton Russell, Aug. 9, 1952; children—Dorothy Campbell, Laura Newton, Eleanor Addison, Arthur Ryan, Stuart Russell. Reporter, asst. to pub. Holyoke (Mass.) Transcript-Telegram, 1955-63, asso. pub., 1966-69; asso. commr. Mass. Dept. Public Works, 1963-66, commr. adminstrn. Commonwealth of Mass., 1969-70, lt. gov., 1971-75; asso. pub., v.p. Mpls. Star and Tribune, 1975-76, pub., sr. v.p., 1976-81, exec. v.p., dir., 1981—, pres., pub. Star & Tribune Newspapers, 1981—; dir. Newspapers of New Eng. Inc., Greenfield (Mass.) Recorder, Pillsbury Co. Bd. dirs. Guthrie Theater Found., 1976—, chmn., 1979-82; mem. Town Meeting South Hadley (Mass.), 1957-69; mem. Mpls. Soc. Fine Arts, 1976—; trustee Twin Cities Public TV, 1976—; bd. dirs. Downtown Council Mpls., 1977—. Served to lt. USMCR, 1953-55. Mem. Am. Newspaper Pubs. Assn., Sigma Delta Chi. Republican. Episcopalian. Clubs: Princeton (N.Y.C.); Chatham (Mass.) Beach and Tennis. Home: 1625 W 26th St Minneapolis MN 55405 Office: 425 Portland Ave Minneapolis MN 55488

DWORAK, DONALD N., state legislator; b. David City, Nebr., Dec. 3, 1934; B.S., U. Nebr.; m. Judy Kosch, Sept. 28, 1963; children—Donald Paul, Anthony John. Pres., Nebraskaland Allied Agy.; mem. Nebr. Legislature, 1974—. Del. Republican Nat. Conv., 1976, 80; mem. indsl. adv. com. Nebr. Dept. Correction Services; chmn. transp. task force Midwestern Conf. Council State Govts.; area adv. ARC, United Fund. Mem. Platte Valley Assn. Life Underwriters (past pres.), Am. Coll. Life Underwriters, Nebr. Ind. Agts. Assn., Nebr. Mut. Agts. Assn., Fellowship Christian Athletes, Farm Bur., Nebr. Wildlife Fedn., U. Nebr. Alumni Assn., Izaak Walton League, Ducks Unltd. Office: 1363 26th Ave Columbus NE 68601*

DWORKIN, HOWARD JERRY, nuclear physician, educator; b. Bklyn., Oct. 29, 1932; s. Joseph Henry and Molly M. (Hodas) D.; B.S. in Chem. Engring., Worcester Poly. Inst., 1955; M.D., Albany Med. Coll., 1959; M.S. in Radiation Biology, U. Mich., 1965; m. Carole Joan Meyer, July 5, 1955; children—Rhonda Fran, Steven Irving, Paul J. Intern, Albany (N.Y.) Hosp., 1959-60; resident Rochester (N.Y.) Gen. Hosp., 1960-62; resident U. Mich. Hosps., 1962-64, asst. coordinator nuclear medicine unit, 1963-66, instr., 1965-66; asst. prof. medicine U. Toronto (Ont., Can.), 1966, asso. prof., 1967; head dept. nuclear medicine Princess Margaret Hosp., Toronto, 1967; head nuclear medicine sect., radiology Nat. Naval Med. Center, Bethesda, Md., 1967-69; dir. sch. nuclear medicine tech. William Beaumont Hosp., Royal Oak, Mich., 1969—, chief dept. nuclear medicine, 1969—, dir. nuclear medicine resident tng. program, 1970—; clin. asst. prof. dept. medicine Wayne State U. Med. Sch., Detroit, 1970—; asst. clin. prof. dept. radiology Mich. State U., East Lansing, 1976—; clin. prof. med. physics Center for Health Scis., Oakland U., Rochester, Mich., 1977—. Served with USN, 1967-69. Diplomate Am. Bd. Internal Medicine. Fellow A.C.P., Am. Bd. Nuclear Medicine; mem. Soc. Nuclear Medicine (trustee 1973-81, v.p. 1982-83), Am. Fedn. Clin. Research, Am. Thyroid Assn., Endocrine Soc., AMA Am. Coll. Nuclear Physicians (sec. 1974-77, pres. 1978-79). Patentee radioactive labeled protein material process and apparatus; Author: (with N. Aspin, R.G. Baker) Clinical Use of

Isotopes in the Physics of Radiology, 1969; Part Two, Clinical Procedures in Radioisotope Laboratory Procedures, 1969; contbr. articles and chapters to med. jours. and texts. Home: 5540 Northcote Ln West Bloomfield MI 48033 Office: Dept Nuclear Medicine William Beaumont Hosp Royal Oak MI 48072

DWORKIN, SIDNEY, bus. exec.; b. Detroit, 1921; B.A., Wayne State U., 1942; married. Partner, Dworkin, Boone & Gross, C.P.A.'s, 1950-66; indsl. acct., 1966; pres., chief exec. officer, dir. Revco D S Inc., Twinsburg, Ohio, 1966—; dir. Neutrogena Corp., Eclipse Industries, Inc., No. Instruments Co., Nat. City Bank Corp., Fabric Centers Corp. Mem. Nat. Assn. Chain Drug Stores (vice chmn., dir.). Served in U.S. Army, 1943-45. Office: Revco D S Inc 1925 Enterprise Pkwy Twinsburg OH 44087*

DWYER, DAVID WAYNE, mfg. co. exec.; b. Anchorage, Alaska, Sept. 9, 1953; s. Marvin Harold and Elsie Elaine (Myatt) Westfall; B.A. in Acctg., Loyola U., 1975; m. Sharon Lee Wojcicki, May 8, 1976; 1 son, David Douglas. Cost accountant U.S. Gypsum Co., Franklin Park, Ill., 1975-77, auditor corp. hdqrs., 1977-78, analyst, 1978-79, steel buyer, 1979—. C.P.A., Ill. Mem. Am. Inst. C.P.A.'s. Office: 9595 W Grand Ave Franklin Park IL 60131

DWYER, MARIE RITA ROZELLE (MRS. JOHN D. DWYER), educator; b. N.Y.C., Sept. 4, 1915; d. Charles W. and Agnes (Coyle) Rozelle; student L'Assomption, Paris, France, 1932-33; B.A., Notre Dame Coll., 1936; M.A., Fordham U., 1938; postgrad. St. Louis U.; student Sorbonne, Paris, summers 1933-37, 52; m. John D. Dwyer, Sept. 8, 1942; children—John Duncan, Joseph Charles, James Gerard, Jerome Valentine. Tchr. French, Sch. of Edn., Fordham U., N.Y.C., 1938-42, Notre Dame Coll., N.Y.C., 1939-40, Coll. of St. Rose, Albany, N.Y., 1949-53, Washington U., St. Louis, 1959-60; faculty French dept. Webster Coll., 1966-74; dir. community services Internat. Students Program, St. Louis U., 1974—; faculty Meramec Community Coll., St. Louis, 1968-70. Active community fund drives, including Greater St. Louis Fund for Arts and Edn.; bd. dirs. St. Louis Christmas Carols Assn., 1962-64, Parish Council, 1966-67; adult adviser cultural program for young adults Archdiocesan Council Cath. Youth, 1961-67; mem. Archdiocesan Council Laity Charities. Mem. Am. Assn. Tchrs. French (pres. St. Louis chpt. 1955-56), Mo. Acad. Sci. (life mem., editorial staff transactions 1969-72, chmn. linguistics sect. 1970-76, past mem. exec. bd.), Alliance Française, Société Française (past sec.), KC Aux. (past pres.), AAAS (rep. Mo. Acad. Sci. at conv. in Mexico City 1973), Notre Dame Coll. Alumnae Assn. (past pres.), Internat. Fedn. Cath. Alumnae (past pres. Albany), Jesuit Mothers Guild (pres. 1963-65), Cath. Women's League (pres. 1964-66), Archdiocesan Council Cath. Women (mem. coms. family life teen-age code, corr. sec. 1963-64, pres. 1964-66 South Central dist.), Nat. French Honor Soc., AAUP, MLA, Mo. MLA (v.p. 1961-63), Central States Conf. on Teaching Fgn. Langs., Société International de la Linguistique, Linguistic Soc. Am., Fgn. Lang. Assn. Mo. (past v.p., sec. 4-Coll. Consortium (Webster, Fontbonne, Maryville and Lindenwood) 1972-73), Centro Studie Scambi Internazionali (mem. internat. com.), Smithsonian Instn. Nat. Assos., Internat. Platform Assn., Pi Delta Phi, Alpha Sigma Nu,. Club: St. Louis University Faculty Women's (pres. 1956-58, dir. 1959—). Extensive travel for ednl. and linguistic research. Home: 526 Oakwood Ave Webster Groves MO 63119 Office: St Louis U 20 N Grand Blvd St Louis MO 63103

DWYER, MARTIN CHARLES, indsl. exposition co. exec.; b. Cleve., Jan. 6, 1921; s. Martin Charles and Adelaide (Moran) D.; B.A., John Carroll U., 1942; postgrad. Ia., 1942-43, Columbia, 1943, Cleve. Coll., 1945-46; m. Gail Alberta Martin, June 15, 1946; children—Martin Charles III, Linda Gail, Patricia Anne. Editor sales promotion pieces lamp dept. Gen. Electric Co., 1946-48; mgr. Cleve. Conv. Bur., 1948-55; exhibit mgr. Nat. Retail Lumber Dealers, Washington, 1955-60; pres. Martin C. Dwyer, Inc., Chgo., 1960—, gen. mgr. NEFTA-GAZ EXPO 1973, U.S. petroleum equipment exposition, Moscow, USSR, 1973. Gen. chmn. March of Dimes, Chgo., 1965. Served to lt. AC, USNR, 1942-46. Recipient Excellence award Exhibitors Adv. Council, 1959, Constrn. Man of Year award Engrng. & News Record, 1966. Mem. Am. Soc. Assn. Execs., Nat. Assn. Exhibit Mgrs. Rotarian. Clubs: North Shore Country (Glenview, Ill.); Tulsa; Kenwood Country (Bethesda, Md.). Home: 2946 Indian Wood Rd Wilmette IL 60091 Office: 400 N Michigan Ave Chicago IL 60611

DWYER, PAUL SUMNER, educator; b. Chester, Pa., Dec. 8, 1901; s. Edmund Benison and Anna Belle (Tracy) D.; A.B., Allegheny Coll., 1921; M.A., Pa. State U., 1923; Ph.D., U. Mich., 1936; Sc.D., U. Windsor (Ont., Can.), 1971; m. Florence Bayliss Brown, June 29, 1932; children—John Michael, David James. Instr., Pa. State U., 1921-26; asst. prof. math., Antioch U., 1926-29, asso. prof., 1929-33, prof., 1933-36; research asso. in ednl. investigations U. Mich., 1936-43, asst. prof. math. and stats., 1937-42, asso. prof. 1942-46, prof., 1946-71, prof. emeritus stats., 1971—, cons., asso. dir. Statis. Research Lab., 1944-46, dir., 1966-71; cons. fire control project Princeton U., 1942; cons. personnel research br. Dept. Army, 1949-52. Fellow Inst. Math. Stats., Am. Statis. Assn., AAAS; mem. Psychometric Soc., Biometric Soc., Econometric Soc., Am. Math. Soc., Math. Assn. Am., Internat. Statis. Inst., Phi Beta Kappa, Phi Kappa Phi, Sigma Xi, Sigma Pi Sigma, Alpha Chi Rho. Home: Box 767 Mackinaw City MI 49701 Office: 1325 Lilac Ave East Lansing MI 48823

DYCHE, DAVID ANDREW, dredge and dock co. exec.; b. Cleve., Dec. 7, 1926; s. David and Olive D.; student Ohio State U., 1946. Pres., owner Dyche Dredge & Dock Co., Cleve., N.Y.C., W. Indies and Miami, Fla., 1946—; chief exec. officer 12 other corps. Active Boy Scouts Am., ARC. Mem. U.S. Olympic Com. Served to capt. USN, 1945; PTO. Mem. Nat. Maritime Hist. Soc., Smithsonian Instn., Lloyds of London, Nat. Geog. Soc., Whale Protection Soc., Internat. S.S. Masters Assn. Clubs: Cleve. Yacht, Univ., Cleve. Athletic; Nassau Harbor; Bahamian Crown Colony, Cat Cay. World class long distance internat. swimming champion, 1949. Home: 12700 Lake Ave Cleveland OH 44107 Office: PO Box 2619 Cleveland OH 44107

DYCK, GEORGE, med. educator; b. Hague, Sask., Can., July 25, 1937; s. John and Mary (Janzen) D.; came to U.S., 1965; student U. Sask., 1955-56; B.Christian Edn., Canadian Mennonite Bible Coll., 1959; M.D., U. Man., 1964; postgrad. Menninger Sch. Psychiatry, 1965-68; m. Edna Margaret Krueger, June 27, 1959; children—Brian Edward, Janine Louise, Stanley George, Jonathan Jay. Fellow community psychiatry Prairie View Mental Health Center, Newton, Kans., 1968-70, clin. dir. tri-county services, 1970-73, med. dir., 1980—; prof. dept. psychiatry U. Kans. Sch. Medicine, Wichita, 1973—, chmn. dept., 1973-80. Bd. dirs. Mennonite Mut. Aid, Goshen, Ind., 1973—, Mid-Kans. Community Action Program, 1970-73, Wichita Council on Drug Abuse, 1974-76. Diplomate Bd. Psychiatry and Neurology, Royal Coll. Physicians and Surgeons (Can.) in Psychiatry. Fellow Am. Psychiat. Assn. (sec. Kans. dist. br. 1976-78, pres.-elect 1980-82); mem. AMA, Kans. Med. Soc. Mennonite. Office: 1901 E 1st St Newton KS 67114

DYE, CALVIN CECIL, accountant; b. Marietta, Ohio, Nov. 10, 1926; s. Cecil Congleton and Leona Gladys (Roth) D.; student Ohio U., 1944, Stanford, 1945; A.B., Marietta Coll., 1949; m. Phyllis Maxine Dobbins, Apr. 24, 1949; children—Gary Lee, Joyce Elaine, Janet Maxine, Nancy Jayne. Staff accountant Cecil C. Dye, pub. accountant Marietta, 1946-58; partner Dye & Dye, Marietta, 1958—, Caroal Realty Co., Marietta, 1970—; sec. Marietta Royalty Co., F.J. Peavy Investment Inc., 1960—, Constn. Stone Co., Marietta, 1962-72; treas. Hub Freight Systems, Inc., Marietta, Valley Apts., Inc., 1974-78; dir. Rejer Transport Inc., R.O. Wetz Inc., Marietta. Spl. agt. for ministerial land rental collection Ohio State Auditor, 1967—; clk. Marietta Twp., 1965-67; city auditor Marietta, 1972-78; merit badge counselor Katooga council Boy Scouts Am., 1962—. Mem. Republican Central Com., 1974—; mem. exec. com. Washington County Republicans, 1972—. Served with AUS, 1944-45, USAAF, 1945-46. Mem. Pub. Accountants Soc. Ohio (pres. Marietta chpt. 1963-67, treas., 1967—), Nat. Soc. Pub. Accountants (Accreditation Council for Accountancy 1974—), Ohio Hist. Soc., Fraternal Order Police Assos. Methodist. Club: Marietta Bowling Assn. (treas. 1961—). Home: 611 3d St Marietta OH 45750 Office: 225 Putnam St Marietta OH 45750

DYE, LLOYD ARTHUR, III, finance co. exec.; b. Nowata, Okla., Feb. 1, 1935; s. Lloyd Arthur and Lily Florence (Whitson) D.; student pub. schs. Nowata; m. Karen Lovelle Price, July 2, 1965; children—Melissa Noelle, Elizabeth Michelle. Adminstrv. asst. Coop. Refinery Assn., Wellington, Kans., 1953-62; mgmt. liaison Petroleum, Inc., Wichita, Kans., 1962-66; owner, mgr. Lloyd A. Dye & Assos., oil industry cons., Wichita, 1966-70; pres., owner Liberty Capital Corp., Wichita, 1970—; part-owner, sec.-treas. Wiki Wiki Corp. Democrat. Home: 6223 Peach Tree Ln Wichita KS 67218 Office: PO Box 18206 Wichita KS 67218

DYE, RICHARD OMAR, chem. co. exec.; b. Detroit, Feb. 5, 1932; s. Fred O. and Beatrice L. (Stone) D.; student Wayne State U., 1950-52, U. Detroit, 1956-58; m. Norma E. Johnson, Oct. 7, 1954; children—Jennifer S., Jeffrey R., Gregory D. Exec. v.p. Pressure Vessel Service, Inc., Detroit, 1958-69; pres. Dy-Chem Products Co., Inc., Warren, Mich., 1969—. Precinct capt. Republican Party, Royal Oak, Mich., 1958-62. Served with U.S. Navy, 1952-56. Mem. Econ. Club Detroit, Chem. and Allied Industries Assn. of Mich. Presbyterian. Club: Forest Lake Country. Home: 2204 Park Ridge Dr Bloomfield Hills MI 48013 Office: 21704 Hoover Rd Warren MI 48089

DYE, RICHARD WAYNE, ins. co. exec.; b. Birmingham, Ala., Jan. 31, 1937; s. Arlie and Flora (Donaldson) D.; Asso. in Bus., Flint Jr. Coll., 1958; B.S., Eastern Mich. U., 1961; M.A., Central Mich. U., 1964, ednl. specialist, 1968; m. Sylvia Kathleen McKinsey, June 30, 1962; children—Lora Ann, Amy Elizabeth. Bus. tchr., coach Millington (Mich.) Public Schs., 1962-63; bus. tchr., coach, counselor Blanchard (Mich.) Public Schs., 1963-64, prin., 1964-66; bus. mgr. Essexville (Mich.) Public Schs., 1966-67; supt. Rapid River (Mich.) Public Schs., 1967-69; agent State Farm Ins. Co., Escanaba, Mich., 1969-71, owner, mgr., agt. 1971—. Chmn. ch. council Calvary Luth. Ch., 1969-81; chmn. Delta County Zoning Bd. Appeals, 1976-80; mem. Delta Planning Commn., 1980—; mem. Ensign Fire Dept., 1978-81, fire chief, 1978. Served with N.G., 1959-65. Mem. Central Upper Penninsula Life Underwriters Assn., Nat. Rifle Assn., Nat. Def. Preparedness Assn. Club: Masons. Home: Rural Route 3 Rapid River MI 49878 Office: State Farm Ins Co 1005 Ludington St Escanaba MI 49829

DYER, TIMOTHY JAMES, sch. supt.; b. Ypsilanti, Mich., Dec. 29, 1937; s. John F. and Genevive (Lynn) D.; B.A. in Polit. Sci., Eastern Mich. U., 1961, M.A. in Ednl. Adminstrn., 1965; Ed.D. in Curriculum Devel., Wayne State U., 1974; postgrad. (East-West fellow scholar), U. Hawaii, 1971. Tchr. Wayne (Mich.) Meml. High Sch., 1961-66, asst. prin., 1966-68; asst. prin. Wayne Meml. High Sch., 1966-68; prin. Adlai E. Stevenson Jr. High Sch., Westland, Mich., 1968-73; supt. Wayne-Westland Community Sch. Dist., 1973—; cons. U. Mich. Sch. Edn., 1974—. Regent, Eastern Mich. U., Ypsilanti, 1973—. Pres. Nat. Newman Student Fedn., 1963-64, U.S. Youth Council, 1964-65, Nat. Council of Catholic Youth, 1966-67; mem. YMCA, western Wayne County, 1973—. Councilman, City of Ypsilanti, 1965-70, mayor pro tem, 1967-68, mayor, 1969-70; dir. Washtenaw County (Mich.) Bd. of Pub. Works, 1968-70, Washtenaw County Bd. of Canvassers, 1970-72. Trustee Peoples Community Hosp. Authority, 1966-72. Named Outstanding Young Man in Ypsilanti, 1967; named Outstanding Young Man in Mich., 1968; named One of the Ten Outstanding Young Men in Washtenaw County, 1970. Mem. Nat., Mich. assns. sch. adminstrs., Am. Acad. Sch. Adminstrs., Mich. Assn. Sch. Bds., Assn. Pub. Sch. Systems, Assn. Sch. Bus. Ofcls., Mich. Assn. Suprs. and Curriculum Devel., Wayne, Westland chambers commerce, Assn. Governing Bds. for Colls. and Univs., Phi Kappa Delta. Rotarian (Community Achievement Recognition award 1974). Club: First Friday Club of Wayne. Home: 38344 Carolon Blvd Westland MI 48185 Office: 3712 Williams St Wayne MI 48184

DYER, WILLIAM ALLAN, JR., newspaper exec.; b. Providence, Oct. 23, 1902; s. William Allan and Clara (Spink) D.; grad. Lawrenceville Sch., 1920; B.Ph., Brown U., 1924; LL.D., Ind. U., 1977; m. Marian Elizabeth Blumer, Aug. 9, 1934; children—Allan H., William E. Reporter, Syracuse (N.Y.) Jour., 1923; various advt. positions Syracuse (N.Y.) Post-Standard, 1925-41; v.p., gen. mgr. Star Pub. Co., Indpls., 1944-49; v.p. Indpls. Newspapers, Inc., 1949-75, gen. mgr., 1949-74, pres., 1975—; pres. Muncie Newspapers, Inc., 1975—; dir. Standard Life Ins. Co. Ind.; dir. Central Newspapers, Inc., Indpls., 1949—, exec. v.p. 1964-73; N.Y.C. dir. Met. Sunday Newspapers, 1951-75, pres., 1969-75; dir. Am. Newspaper Pub. Assn. bur. advt., 1963-69, Research Inst., 1955-62, pres., 1963-64; pres. Central Newspapers Found. Indpls. Mem. exec. com. United Fund Indpls., 1954-70, pres. 1970; v.p. Comm. Service Council, Indpls. 1967-68; v.p., bd. dirs. Ind. State Symphony Soc.; pres. Goodwill Industries Found. of Central Ind., 1980—. Trustee, Brown U., 1952-59; pres. Indpls. Community Hosp. Found., 1976—. Served to lt. comdr., USNR, 1941-44. Recipient Advt. Club Torch of Truth award, 1975; Am. Advt. Fedn. silver medal, 1971. Mem. Better Bus. Bur. Indpls. (dir. 1950-65, pres. 1958, 65), Nat. Better Bus. Bur. (dir. 1950-70), Council Better Bus. Burs. (dir. 1970, 79—), Indpls. C. of C. (dir. 1967—, v.p. 1970-71), Am. Newspaper Publishers Assn. (labor relations com. 1953-63), Indpls. Advt. Club (dir. 1952-54, pres. 1952-53), Indpls. Comm. Hosp. Assn. (dir. 1952-54, 66-69, v.p. 1954). Club: Brown U. Ind. (Brown Bear award, 1968, sec. 1946-52, pres. 1952-54). Home: 401 Buckingham Dr Indianapolis IN 46208 Office: 307 N Pennsylvania St Indianapolis IN 46204

DYER-BENNET, JOHN, emeritus educator; b. Leicester, Eng., Apr. 17, 1915; s. Richard Stewart and Miriam (Clapp) Dyer-B.; came to U.S., 1925, naturalized, 1942; A.B., U. Calif., Berkeley, 1936, A.M., 1937; M.A., Harvard, 1939, Ph.D., 1940; m. Mary Abby Randall, June 14, 1951; children—David, Barbara. Instr. math. Vanderbilt U., 1940-41, 45-46; from instr. to asso. prof. Purdue U., 1946-51, 52-60; faculty Carleton Coll., Northfield, Minn., 1960—, prof. math., 1965-80, emeritus, 1980—, chmn. dept. math. and astronomy, 1964-66, tennis coach, 1961-80, soccer coach, 1963—; T.C. Wollan Meml. Distinguished lectr. math. Concordia Coll., Moorhead, Minn., 1972. Served to 1st lt. AUS, 1941-45, as capt., 1951-52. NSF sci. faculty fellow, 1958-59. Mem. Am. Math. Soc., Math Assn. Am., AAUP (nat. council 1967-70), ACLU, Phi Beta Kappa, Sigma Xi. Democrat. Home: 907 Winona St Northfield MN 55057

DYKES, ARCHIE REECE, ins. exec.; b. Rogersville, Tenn., Jan. 20, 1931; B.S. cum laude, East Tenn. State U., 1952, M.A., 1956; Ed.D. (Ford Found. fellow), U. Tenn., 1959. Tchr., Church Hill (Tenn.) High Sch., 1952-55, prin., 1955-58; supt. Greenville (Tenn.) Schs., 1959-62; prof., dir. Center Advanced Grad. Studies in Edn., U. Tenn.-Memphis State U., 1962-66; Am. Council Edn. fellow U. Ill., 1966-67; chancellor U. Tenn. at Martin, 1967-71, U. Tenn. at Knoxville, 1971-73; chancellor U. Kans., Lawrence, 1973-80; pres., dir. Security Benefit Life Ins. Co., Topeka, 1980—; mem. Edn. Commn. States, 1973-76, Nat. Advisory Council Edn. Professions Devel., 1975-76; vice-chmn. Com. Operation U.S. Senate, 1975-76; mem. adv. com. U.S. Army Command and Gen. Staff Coll., Ft. Leavenworth, Kans., chmn., 1978—; dir. Fleming Cos., Inc., Esmark, 1st Nat. Bank, Kansas City, Russell Stover Co. Trustee U. Mid-Am., 1973—, chmn., 1978-79; trustee Nelson Gallery, Kansas City, 1973—, Harry S. Truman Library Inst., 1973—; mem. consultative bd. regents U. Qatar, 1979—. Mem. Am. Council Edn., Nat. Assn. State Univs. and Land Grant Colls. (council of presidents, dir. 1975-78), Kans. Assn. Commerce and Industry, Am. Assn. Higher Edn., Phi Kappa Phi. Author: School Board and Superintendent, 1965; (with others) Philosophic Theory and Practice in Educational administration, 1966; Faculty Participation in Academic Decision Making, 1968; Presidential Leadership in Academe, 1967; Faculty Participation in Governance, 1968. Office: Security Benefit Life Ins Co 700 Harrison Topeka KS 66636

DYKMAN, HAROLD ALBERT, osteopathic physician; b. Grand Rapids, Mich., Oct. 8, 1914; s. Albert and Jennie (Datema) D.; A.B., Calvin Coll., 1938; D.O., Kirksville Coll. Osteopathy and Surgery, 1941; M.D., Kansas City U. Physicians and Surgeons, 1942, Dr.P.H., 1942; Ph.D., Trinity Coll. and Sem., 1960, Th.D., 1962, D.D., 1963, LL.D., 1966; grad. Hong Kong Coll. Chinese Acupuncture, 1971; postgrad. tng., Japanese Acupuncture, Tokyo, 1971; m. Lucille V. Hawkins, Aug. 31, 1937; children—Dwight A., Charlene A. Intern, Saginaw Osteo. Hosp., 1942, chief staff, 1966, later mem. staff; practice osteopathic med., specializing in internal med., Saginaw, 1942-74; sr. staff officer VA Hosp., Battle Creek, Mich., 1974—. Surgeon, staff officer U.S. Merchant Marine. Diplomate Am. Bd. Psychiatry. Fellow Am., Internat. colls. angiology; mem. Am., Mich. osteo. assns., Saginaw Valley Assn. Physicians and Surgeons, Am. Coll. Gen. Practitioners, Am. Inst. Hypnosis, Am. Med. Soc. Vienna, Am. Ministerial Assn., Psi Sigma Alpha, Kappa Phi Epsilon. Congregationalist. Mason (32 deg., K.T., Shriner), Elk, Germania. Home: 108 Christopher Ln Battle Creek MI 49015 also VA Hosp 115 Battle Creek MI 49016

DYKSTRA, RICHARD ALLEN, electronics engr.; b. Cedar Grove, Wis., June 12, 1948; s. Henry and Elsie Mae (Janisse) D.; B.S., Milw. Sch. Engring., 1971; m. Linda Anzia, Aug. 31, 1968; children—Stacy, Christopher, Sally, Erin. Elec. engr. Engine Devel. Lab., Kohler Co. (Wis.), 1971-73, electronics project engr., 1973-79, electronics engring. supr., 1979—. Alumni counselor Milw. Sch. Engring., 1971—, indsl. adv. com., 1975—; mem. indsl. adv. com. Lakeshore Tech. Inst., 1977—; mem. Cedar Grove-Belgium Area Schs. Needs Assessment Com., 1975-76, mem. citizens adv. com., 1976—. Recipient award for outstanding achievement Milw. Sch. Engring. Alumni Assn., 1969. Mem. IEEE, Inst. Noise Control Engring., Engine Mfrs. Assn., Tau Omega Mu. Contbr. articles to profl. jours. Home: 169 Ramaker Ave Cedar Grove WI 53013 Office: Kohler Co Engine Devel Lab 44 High St Kohler WI 53044

DYKSTRA, RONALD JAY, radio sta. exec.; b. Grand Rapids, Mich., Sept. 16, 1941; s. Peter J. and Ruth Kathryn (Sandel) D.; student Grand Rapids Jr. Coll., 1960; m. Carole J. Duimstra, Oct. 8, 1965; children—Michelle Lynn, Nicole Marie, Ryan Jason. Sales rep. Sta. WZZM-TV, 1965-70; sta. mgr. Sta. WZZM-FM, 1970-74; sales rep. Sta. WOTV-TV, 1974-76; gen. mgr. Sta. WCUZ-AM-FM, Grand Rapids, 1976—. Pres., Grand Rapids Jr. Achievement, 1981-82; v.p. United Way of Kent County, 1981-82; bd. dirs. Downtown, Inc.; elder Fellowship Christian Ref. Ch. Recipient Bronze Achievement award Grand Rapids Jr. Achievement. Mem. Nat. Assn. Broadcasters, Mich. Assn. Broadcasters, Press Club Grand Rapids (dir.), Humane Soc. Kent County (past pres.), Grand Rapids Jaycees (v.p. 1974, Disting. Service award). Republican. Club: Downtown Grand Rapids Rotary. Office: 1 McKay Tower Grand Rapids MI 49803

DYLAG, HELEN MARIE, psychiat. clin. nurse specialist; b. Cleve., Oct. 14, 1950; d. Stanley John and Helen Agnes (Jarkiewicz) D.; B.S. in Nursing summa cum laude, St. John Coll. of Cleve., 1971; M.S. in Nursing (NIMH trainee), Ohio State U., 1973. Registered nurse drug dependency unit VA Hosp., Brecksville, Ohio, 1971-72; psychiat. clin. nurse specialist consultation and edn. dept. Marymount Hosp. Mental Health Center, Garfield Heights, Ohio, 1973-78, dir. consultation and edn. dept., 1978—; faculty continuing edn. in nursing Cleve. State U. Mem. Am. Nurses Assn and Council of Advanced Practitioners in Psychiat.-Mental Health Nursing, Sigma Theta Tau. Contbr. chpts. to books, articles to profl. jours. Home: 5709 Onaway Oval Parma OH 44130 Office: 12300 McCracken Rd Garfield Heights OH 44125

DYSERT, FREDA M., ednl. cons.; b. Greenwood, Ind., Feb. 21, 1917; d. John and Dora Jane (Surface) Mullinix; B.S., Ind. State U., 1951, M.S., 1955, ednl. specialist cert., 1963, postgrad., 1964-65; m. Milford Robert Dysert, July 31, 1943; 1 son, Stephen. Tchr. elem. public schs., Ind., 1936-64; elem. supr. Met. Sch. Dist. of Pike Twp., Marion County, 1964-68; reading specialist, Richmond, Ind., 1973-74; ednl. cons. Ginn and Co. ednl. group Xerox Corp., Lexington, Mass., 1968-79. Mem. NEA, Nat. Ret. Tchrs. Assn., Ind. Ret. Tchrs. Assn. Republican. Home and Office: 5110 Kessler Blvd N Dr Indianapolis IN 46208

EADIE, GEORGE ROBERT, engr.; b. Eldorado, Ill., Sept. 24, 1923; s. Joseph Powell and Myrtle Olive (Bacon) E.; B.S., U. Ill., 1949, M.S., 1956; E.M., 1957; m. Ruth V. Butler, June 17, 1943; children—Carolyn Madge, Rosalyn Kay. Engring. and mgmt. positions in coal industry, Pa., Okla., Ill., 1949-54; asso. prof. mining engring. U. Ill., Urbana, 1954-62, prof. gen. engring., 1968-76; engring. and mgmt. positions, Freeman Coal Corp., W. Frankfort, Ill., 1962-65; asso. editor Coal Mining and Processing mag., Chgo., 1965-68; adminstr. Ill. State Geol. Survey, 1968-76; prof. mining engring. tech., Ind. State U., Evansville, 1976—. Served to lt. col., USAFR, 1942-69. Decorated D.F.C., Air Medal with two oak leaf clusters, Purple Heart. Mem. Soc. Mining Engrs., Am. Inst. Mining Engrs., Ill. Mining Inst., Ind. Mining and Tech. Soc., Am. Soc. Engring. Edn. Contbr. tech. articles on mine safety, ventilation and edn. to publs. Home: 1500 Roosevelt Ave Eldorado IL 62930 Office: Indiana State University Evansville 8600 W University Blvd Evansville IN 47712

EADIE, ROBERT DAVID, engr.; b. Youngstown, Ohio, June 1, 1929; s. Robert and Jean R. (Meek) E.; cert. Internat. Corr. Sch., Scranton, Pa., 1954; m. Jayne Wallace, Apr. 17, 1947; children—David M., J.R., Susan E. Marquard. Sr. div. plant engr. axle div. Eaton Corp., Cleve., 1977—. Mem. ASHRAE, Cleve. Engring. Soc., Am. Inst. Plant Engrs., Cleve. Elec. League (bd. dirs.). Club: Masons. Home: 1595 Wrenford Rd South Euclid OH 44121 Office: 739 E 140th St Cleveland OH 44110

EAGLE, NELSON WESLEY, ednl. adminstr.; b. Kankakee, Ill., Jan. 22, 1949; s. Glenn Wilbur and Rosalyn Eagle (Wade) E.; B.S., Trevecca Nazarene Coll., 1978; M.S. in Edn., Ind. U., 1981; m.

Beverly Jean Welsh, June 9, 1973. Dir., Kiddie Prep Sch., Ft. Wayne, Ind., 1978-80; dir. Aboite Childcare Center, Ft. Wayne, 1980—, Pine Hills Kiddie Garden, Ft. Wayne, 1980—; cons. program coordinator Child Care Corner, Ft. Wayne, 1979-80; pres. Eagle Ednl. Co.; cons. for devel. new child care centers; mem. day care services com. City of Ft. Wayne, 1980. Served with USN, 1968-75. Mem. Assn. Supervision and Curriculum Devel., Nazarene Assn. Pre-Schs. Republican. Home: 4257 Reed Rd Fort Wayne IN 46815 Office: 7222 W Jefferson Fort Wayne IN 46804

EAGLETON, THOMAS FRANCIS, U.S. senator, lawyer; b. St. Louis, Sept. 4, 1929; s. Mark David and Zitta Louise (Swanson) E.; B.A. cum laude, Amherst Coll., 1950; LL.B. cum laude, Harvard U., 1953; m. Barbara Ann Smith, Jan. 20, 1956; children—Terence, Christin. Admitted to Mo. bar, 1953; practiced in St. Louis, 1953—; past mem. firm Eagleton & Eagleton; circuit atty., St. Louis, 1957-60; became atty. gen., State of Mo., 1960; lt. gov. of Mo., 1964-68; U.S. senator from Mo., 1968—. Served with USNR, 1948-49. Office: 1209 Dirksen Senate Office Bldg Washington DC 20510

EAGLIN, RUSSELL LEROY, union ofcl., electronic technician; b. Indpls., May 11, 1947; s. Charles A. and Patricia G. (Williams) E.; student labor studies and elec. engring. tech. Ind.-Purdue U., Indpls., 1970—; m. Gail Lynn Snellings, Sept. 5, 1970; children—Julie, David, Kari. Electronic technician Naval Avionics Center, Indpls., 1970—; pres. Am. Fedn. Govt. Employees, AFL-CIO Local 1744, 1977—; chmn. edn. com. Central Labor Council, Marion County AFL-CIO. Chmn. Fed. Health and Safety Council of Ind., 1979—; del. Pres.'s Com. on Employment of Handicapped, 1978-80; mem. agy. relations adv. com. United Way Greater Indpls., 1980—; bd. dirs. Citizens' Action Coalition Ind., 1980—. Served with USMC, 1966-70; Viet Nam. Recipient Certificate of Appreciation, United Way of Greater Indpls., 1978-80. Mem. Nat. Rifle Assn. Democrat. Home: 7601 E Ruskin Pl Indianapolis IN 46226 Office: 6000 E 21st St Code 442 Indianapolis IN 46218

EAGON, BURDETTE WILMONT, univ. dean; b. Oshkosh, Wis., Dec. 22, 1919; s. Joseph Arthur and Belle (Stutzman) E.; B.S. in Elem. Edn., Oshkosh State Tchrs. Coll., 1947; M.S., U. Wis., Madison, 1951; Ed.D. in Ednl. Supervision and Adminstrn., George Peabody Coll. Tchrs., 1955; m. Sarah Jane Richards, June 19, 1947; children—Brian Richard, John Stevens, Sally Jo, James Burdette, Thomas Barrow, Mary Ann, Jean Annette. Tchr. elem. schs., Beloit, Stevens Point and Madison, Wis., 1948-50; mem. faculty Wis. State U., Stevens Point (now U. Wis.), 1950—, dean Coll. Edn., 1960-70, asso. vice chancellor acad. affairs, also dean ednl. services and innovative programs, 1970-80, dean acad. support programs, 1980—; chief party, cons. Higher Edn. Survey Team, Vietnam, 1967-74; chmn. visitation teams Nat. Com. Accrediatation Tchr. Edn., 1966-73; coordinator, cons. tchr. edn. N. Central Assn., 1968-70; tchr., adminstrs. Semester in Taiwan, spring 1978; cons. Srinakharinwot U. Prasarnmit, Bangkok, Thailand, 1980. Coordinator, Vietamese Refugee Settlement Program in Central Wis., 1975—; bd. dirs. Suzuki Found., 1976—. Served with USN, 1944-46. Recipient various certs. of recognition, citations. Mem. Am. Assn. Colls. Tchr. Edn., Council U. Wis. Libraries, Wis. Assn. Suprs. for Curriculum Devel., Wis. Assn. Acad. Librarians, Council Library and Network Devel., Council Advancement Exptl. Learning, U. Wis. System Undergrad. Teaching Improvement Council, Phi Delta Kappa. Author articles in field. Editor ednl. reports. Office: 201 Learning Resources Center U Wis Stevens Point WI 54481

EAKIN, THOMAS CAPPER, sports promotion exec.; b. New Castle, Pa., Dec. 16, 1933; s. Frederick William and Beatrice (Capper) E.; B.A. in History, Denison U., 1956; m. Brenda Lee Andrews, Oct. 21, 1961; children—Thomas Andrews, Scott Frederick. Life ins. cons. Northwestern Mut. Life Ins. Co., Cleve., 1959-67; regional dir. sales Empire Life Ins. Co. Ohio, 1967-68; dist. mgr. Putman Pub. Co., Cleve., 1968-69; regional bus. mgr. Chilton Pub. Co., Cleve., 1969-70; dist. mgr. Hitchcock Pub. Co., Cleve., 1970-72; pres. TCE Enterprises, Shaker Heights, Ohio, 1973—; trustee Newcomerstown (Ohio) Sports Corp., 1975-80. Founder, nat. chmn. Cy Young Centennial, 1967, Cy Young Golf Invitational, 1967-79; mem. adv. bd. Cleve. Indian Old Timers Com., 1966-67; founder, pres. Golf Internat. 100 Club, Shaker Heights, 1970—, founder, pres. Ohio Baseball Hall of Fame, 1976—, Ohio Baseball Hall of Fame Celebration, 1977-79; Ohio Baseball Hall of Fame and Mus., 1980—; founder, chmn. Ohio Baseball Hall of Fame Golf Invitational, 1980—; hon. dir. Tuscarawas County (Ohio) Old Timers Baseball Assn., 1972—, commendation award, 1970; Ohio exec. sponsor chmn. World Golf Hall of Fame, Pinehurst, N.C., 1979—; fund rep. Boy Scouts Am., Cleve., 1959-60, United Appeal, 1959-63, Heart Fund, 1963-64; mem. Cleve. Council Corrections, 1971-73; chmn. Class of 1952 money raising and reunion coms. Univ. Sch. Alumni Fund, 1966; mem. adv. bd. Cuyahoga Hills Boys Sch., Warrensville Heights, Ohio, 1971—, Camp Hope, Warrenville Twp., 1973; founder, dir. TRY (Target/Reach Youth), 1971—, Interact Club Shaker Heights, 1971—; founder, pres., dir. Cy Young Mus., 1970-80; mem. exec. com. Tuscarawas County Am. Revolution Bicentennial Commn., 1974-76; bd. mem. Shaker Heights Youth Center, Inc., 1975; adv. bd. Fitness Evaluation Services, Inc., 1977-79; bd. dirs. Tuscarawas Valley Tourist Assn., 1979-81, Buckeye Tourist Assn., 1979-80. Served with AUS, 1956-58. Recipient commendation awards Cy Young Centennial Com., 1967, Tuscarawas County C. of C., 1967, Sporting News, 1968, Gov. James A. Rhodes Ohio, 1968, 75, Gov. John J. Gilligan Ohio, 1972, 74, Newcomerstown C. of C., 1967; Outstanding Contbn. to Baseball award baseball commr. William Eckert, 1967; Sport Service award Sport mag., 1969; Civic Service award Cuyahoga Hills Boys Sch., 1970; citation of merit La. Stadium and Expn. Dist., 1972; Presdl. commendation Richard M. Nixon, 1973, Gerald R. Ford, 1977; Distinguished Service award Camp Hope, 1974; Founder's award Interact Club Shaker Heights, 1974; Proclamation award-Thomas C. Eakin Day, City of Cleve., 1974; Gov.'s award for community action State of Ohio, 1974; award of achievement Ohio Assn. Hist. Socs., 1975; Chief Newawatowes award Newcomerstown C. of C., 1975; commendation Ohio Senate, 1976, 79, Ohio Ho. of Reps., 1978, Ohio Am. Revolution Bicentennial Adv. Commn., 1976; certificate of merit Tuscarawas County Am. Revolution Bicentennial Commn., 1976, appreciation award, 1977; cert. of merit State of La., 1978, Ohio Gov.'s award, 1978, Founder's award TRY Target/Reach Youth, 1979; named hon. citizen City of New Orleans, 1978. Mem. Denison U. Cleve. Men's Club (v.p. 1964-65), Tuscarawas County Hist. Soc. (trustee 1978—), Internat. Platform Assn., Shaker Hist. Soc. (trustee 1980-82), Phi Delta Theta (pres. Cleve. alumni club 1970, Appreciation award 1971, dir. 1971-75, exec. com. nat. Lou Gehrig award com. 1975—, Outstanding Alumnus award 1975, trustee Ohio Iota chpt. 1979-82). Baptist (mem. bd. 1966-69). Clubs: Rotary (Outstanding young Rotarian award, 1962, pres. Shaker Heights 1970-71, founder and chmn. club's Internat. student exchange program U.S. and Can. 1965-70, trustee V. Blakeman Qua Scholarship Fund 1972-73, founder, chmn. Henry G. Duchscherer Meml. award 1971—); Wahoo (dir. 1975-77); Executive (Woodmere, Ohio). Address: 2729 Shelley Rd Shaker Heights OH 44122

EARLE, BETTY L., librarian; b. Appleton, Wis., Aug. 13, 1919; d. Fred T. and Emma M. (Trost) Stilp; B.A., Lawrence Coll., 1941; B.L.S., U. Wis., Madison, 1945; m. June 18, 1949 (div.); children—Mary Elizabeth, Michael F., Patrick T., Carol M., Robert B. Librarian, Oak Park (Ill.) Public Library, 1945-50, St. Francis Library, Appleton, Wis., 1960-67, Fox Valley Tech. Inst., Appleton, 1968—. Sec. parish corp., Roman Cath. Ch., mem. parish council; mem. bd. edn. Xavier High Sch. Mem. NEA, Wis. Edn. Assn. Council, Wis. Library Assn., AAUW, Am. Vocat. Assn., Wis. Assn. Vocat. and Adult Edn., Alpha Chi Omega. Home: 1528 N Appleton Appleton WI 54911 Office: PO Box 2277 Appleton WI 54913

EARLE, DOUGLAS ROGER, govt. ofcl.; b. Plainwell, Mich., Dec. 13, 1942; s. William J. and Cora Johnson; B.A. with high honors, Mich. State U., 1965; J.D. with honors (trustee scholar), George Washington U., 1968; m. Ellisa Dawn Mills, Sept. 7, 1963; children—Eric Douglas, Loren Dawn. Admitted to Va. bar, 1968, D.C. bar, 1975, Mich. bar, 1976; asst. counsel Legis. and Spl. Counsel div. Labor Dept., Washington, 1968-70; asso. counsel Senate Labor Subcom., 1971; atty. advisor Office of Solicitor, Labor Dept., Washington, 1972; on loan Mich. Dept. Labor, Lansing, 1974-76, dir. Hearings Office, 1976-79, dir. Bur. Safety and Regulation, 1979—; lectr. Mich. State U. Sch. Indsl. Relations also Practicing Law Inst. Mem. Declining Enrollment Council, Lansing (Mich.) Sch. Dist., 1979-80. Mem. Practicing Law Inst., Am. Bar Assn., Fed. Bar Assn., Va. State Bar Assn., Mich. Bar Assn., D.C. Bar Assn., Phi Alpha Delta, Tau Sigma, Pi Gamma Mu, Phi Kappa Phi. Democrat. Home: 3113 Boston Blvd Lansing MI 48910 Office: 7150 Harris Dr PO Box 30015 Lansing MI 48909

EARLE, ELINOR SOUTHGATE, librarian; b. Union City, Ind., Mar. 24, 1921; d. Thomas Evans and Elinor (Southgate) Earle; A.B., U. Ky., 1942; M.A., Ohio State U., 1946; B.S. in L.S., U. Ill., 1947. Tchr. English, McDowell County, W.Va., 1942-43; asst. reference librarian Lincoln Library, Springfield, Ill., 1947-48; asst. in reference Akron (Ohio) Pub. Library, 1948-51, head gen. reference, 1951-57, asst. librarian West Hill br., 1959-60, librarian, Kenmore br., 1961-81; base librarian AFB, Phalsbourg, France, 1957-59. Chmn. research com. Summit County Com. for Peace, 1969-71. Corr. sec. Ohio Family Historians, 1967-73. Served with WAVES, 1944-45. Mem. ALA, Ohio Library Assn., Akron Assn. U. Women, Daus. Am. Colonists (vice regent 1964-68, regent 1968-70, sec. 1970-72, registrar 1976—), D.A.R., United Daus. Confederacy (state chmn. So. lit. 1974—), Ohio Soc. Dames Ct. Honor (registrar 1967—), Ohio Soc. Huguenots (librarian 1966-72, cons. genealogist 1972—). Home: 77 Fir Hill Akron OH 44304

EARLY, BERT HYLTON, lawyer, mgmt. cons.; b. Kimball, W.Va., July 17, 1922; s. Robert Terry and Sue Keister (Hylton) E.; student Marshall U., 1940-42; A.B., Duke U., 1946; J.D., Harvard U., 1949; m. Elizabeth Louise Henry, June 24, 1950; children—Bert Hylton, Robert Christian, Mark Randolph, Philip Henry, Peter St. Clair. Admitted to W.Va. bar, 1949, Ill. bar, 1963, Fla. bar, 1981; asso. firm Fitzpatrick, Marshall, Huddleston & Bolen, Huntington, W.Va., 1949-57; instr. Marshall U., 1950-53; asst. counsel Island Creek Coal Co., 1957-60, asso. gen. counsel, 1960-62; dep. exec. dir. Am. Bar Assn., 1962-64, exec. dir., 1964-81; v.p. Wells Search Assos., Chgo., 1981—; mem. W.Va. Jud. Council, 1960-62; vice chmn. Conf. Nat. Orgns., 1971-73; mem. Task Force on Govtl. Regulation and Press Freedom, Twentieth Century Fund, 1971. Mem. Huntington City Council, 1961-62; bd. dirs. Huntington Public Library, 1951-60, Morris Meml. Hosp. Crippled Children, 1953-60, Huntington Galleries, 1961-62, W.Va. Tax Inst., 1961-62, Robert Crown Center for Health Edn., 1970-76, United Charities Chgo., 1972-80, Community Renewal Soc., 1965-76; trustee Davis and Elkins Coll., 1960-63; mem. vis. com. U. Chgo. Law Sch., 1975-78. Served to 1st lt., pilot, USAAC, 1943-45. Fellow Am. Bar Found. (life); mem. Am. Law Inst. (life), Am. (ho. of dels. 1958-59, nat. chmn. Jr. Bar Conf. 1958), Internat. (asst. sec.-gen. 1967—), Inter-Am., W.Va., Chgo. bar assns., W.Va. State Bar (chmn. jr. sect. 1951), Fla. Bar, Am. Judicature Soc., Nat. Legal Aid and Defender Assn. Democrat. Presbyterian. Clubs: Economic (Chgo.); Univ. (Washington and Chgo.); Hinsdale (Ill.) Golf. Home: 136 S Oak St Hinsdale IL 60521 Office: 444 N Michigan Ave Chicago IL 60611

EARLY, DAVID ORA, JR., publishing co. exec.; b. Columbus, Ohio, Aug. 21, 1947; s. David Ora and Helen Louise (Pearcy) E.; B.S., U. Wis., Oshkosh, 1969; m. Sandra Kuckuk, Dec. 22, 1973; children—Ryan, Jennifer. Adminstr., Crivitz Youth Center, 1973-76; circulation mgr., sales rep. Shawano Shoppers Guide (Wis.), 1976-80, sales mgr., 1980—, treas., 1977—. Div. chmn. Shawano Area United Way, 1979, campaign chmn., 1980. Served with USAR, 1969-71. Mem. Nat. Assn. Advt. Pubs., Wis. Assn. Advt. Pubs., Shawano Area C. of C. Republican. Presbyterian. Club: Shawano Optimist (pres. 1979; Optimist of Year award 1980). Office: PO Box 469 Shawano WI 54166

EASH, MAURICE J., univ. adminstr.; b. Fulton County, Ind., Dec. 20, 1928; s. Edward A. and Gertrude Ethel (Barkman) E.; B.Sc., Manchester Coll., 1950; M.A., Ohio State U., 1955; Ed.D., Columbia U., 1959. Mem. faculty Ball State U., 1959-65, Hunter Coll., U. City N.Y., 1965-69; mem. faculty U. Ill., Chgo., 1969—, now dean Coll. Edn. Served with U.S. Army, 1950-52. Mem. AAAS, N.Y. Acad. Sci., Phi Delta Kappa. Contbr. articles to profl. publs. Office: Coll Edn U Ill Chgo Circle Box 4348 Chicago IL 60680

EASLEY, MICHAEL WAYNE, dentist; b. Bryan, Ohio, Aug. 25, 1947; s. Warren Harding and Jeanne Ruth (Sargeant) E.; student Mich. State U., 1965-66; D.D.S., Ohio State U., 1974; postgrad. U. West Fla., 1974-76; M.P.H., U. Mich., 1979; B.S., SUNY, 1980; m. Carol R. McCabe, Jan. 23, 1976; 1 son, Alec. Commd. ensign Dental Corps, U.S. Navy, 1971, advanced through grades to lt. (s.g.), 1974; commd. lt. comdr. USPHS, 1976; dental surgeon Med. Center for Fed. Prisoners, Springfield, Mo., 1976-78; chief dental officer Milan Fed. Correctional Inst., Milan Mich., 1978-79; dir. Div. Dental Health, Ohio Dept. Health, Columbus, 1980—; clin. instr. dept. community dentistry U. Mich., Ann Arbor, 1978-79; adj. asst. prof. dept. community dentistry Ohio State Univ., Columbus, 1980—; clin. instr. dept. community dentistry Case-Western Res. U., Cleve., 1981—. Dental cons. USPHS, Region V, 1979—; cons. Jour. Pub. Health Dentistry, 1981—. Dist. service dir. Explorer Scouts, Columbus, 1980—. Mem. Columbus Dental Soc., Ohio Dental Assn., Am. Dental Assn., Am. Public Health Assn., Ohio Public Health Assn., Ohio Rural Health Assn., Am. Assn. Public Health Dentists, Assn. State and Territorial Dental Dirs., Assn. Mil. Surgeons U.S., Am. Correctional Health Services Assn., Med. Amateur Radio Council. Author: (with Richard Lichtenstein) Dental Health Programs for Correctional Institutions, 1979; contbr. articles to profl. jours. Home: PO Box 15606 Columbus OH 43215 Office: Div of Dental Health Ohio Dept of Health PO Box 118 Columbus OH 43216

EASTBURN, RICHARD A., service co. exec.; b. West Chester, Pa., Jan. 16, 1934; s. Louis W. and Alma S. (Shellin) E.; B.A., Shelton Coll., 1956; M.S.T., N.Y. Theol. Sem., 1959; M.Ed., Temple U., 1970; M.B.A., Columbia U., 1979; m. Heidi Fritz, June 15, 1963; children—Karin J., R. Marc. Ordained to ministry Am. Baptist Conv., 1959; minister, Laurelton, N.J., 1959-61; dir adult programs Central YMCA, Phila., 1961-65; dir. Opportunities Industrialization Center, Phila., 1965-67; mgr. tng. and devel. Missile & Surface Radar div. RCA, Moorestown, N.J., 1967-68, mgr. mgmt. tng. govt. and comml. systems group, dir. mgmt. devel., 1969-71; group mgr. personnel for internat. field ops. Digital Equipment, Maynard, Mass., 1971-75; corp. dir. orgn. and mgmt. devel. Am. Standard, Inc., N.Y.C., 1975-79; corp. dir. mgmt. devel. TRW, Inc., Cleve., 1979—; pres. Retirement Community Concepts, 1981—; producer, moderator Ask the Clergy, Sta. WIP, Phila., 1965-67. Bd. dirs. exec. program adv. bd. U. Ind.; bd. dirs. Burlington County Community Com., 1967-69. Recipient Disting. Community Service award Shelton Coll. Alumni, 1956; Dedicated Service award Phila. March of Progress, 1967. Mem. Am. Soc. Tng. and Devel. (dir., 1979-80), Orgn. Devel. Network. Mem. United Ch. Christ. Clubs: Chagrin Valley Athletic, A & A Sportsman. Home: 213 Monticello Dr Chagrin Falls OH 44022 Office: TRW Inc 23555 Euclid Ave Cleveland OH 44117

EASTERDAY, MICHAEL JOSEPH, accountant; b. Salina, Kans., Apr. 14, 1941; s. Joseph Francis and Florence I. (Sandstrom) E.; B.S. cum laude, St. Benedict's Coll., 1963; M.S., U. Kans., 1964; m. Mary Alice Shea, Aug. 11, 1962; children—Mary Theresa, Anne Christine, Joseph Michael, Catherine Elizabeth. With Peat, Marwick, Mitchell & Co., 1964—, mgr., 1970-74, partner, 1973—, mng. partner, Wichita, Kans., 1974-79, mng. partner, Omaha, 1979—. Active various community drives; mem. pastoral council Diocese of Kansas City-St. Joseph, 1970-74, pres. pastoral council, 1971-73; vice chmn. exec. com. bd. trustees KPTS Sunflower Ednl. TV, 1978—; pres. Wichita Econ. Edn. Found., 1978—; treas., bd. dirs. Wichita Symphony Soc., 1979; mem. exec. com. Council Cath. Laity, Kansas City-St. Joseph, 1970-73; mem. U.S. Cath. Bishop Nat. Adv. Council, 1973-74. Bd. dirs. Catholic Family and Community Services, 1972-74, Wichita Area Devel., Kans. Ind. Coll. Fund; bd. dirs. Benedictine Coll., Athison, Kans., 1971—, chmn. bd. govs., 1973-75; bd. dirs. United Way of Midlands, Holy Sepulchre Cemetery Assn., Jr. Achievement Omaha, Inc., Met. Area Arts Council, Nebr. Goodwill Industries, Inc.; NCCJ, Wichita Festivals, bd. advisers U. Kans. Sch. Bus., 1976—; mem. nat. finance com. Nat. Conf. Catholic Charities, 1977—; mem. archbishop's com. for edn. devel. Archdiocese of Omaha; mem. exec. bd. Mid-Am. council Boy Scouts Am.; mem. endowment com. Christ the King Parish; mem. adv. bd. Douglas County Republican Com.; bd. dirs., mem. fin. com. Duchesne Acad.; chmn. chancellor's adv. bd. U. Nebr., Omaha; chmn. Econ. Edn. Task Force. Recipient Outstanding Alumni award Benedictine Coll., 1979; C.P.A., Mo., Kans., Nebr. Mem. Am. Inst. C.P.A.'s, Mo., Kans. socs. C.P.A.'s, Nat. Assn. Accountants (Kansas City chpt. sec. 1970-71, v.p. 1971-73, pres. 1973-74), Hosp. Financial Mgmt. Assn., St. Benedict's Coll. Alumni (Kansas City pres. 1968-70), Wichita C. of C. (bd. dirs. 1979), Greater Omaha C. of C. (legis. com.), Beta Gamma Sigma. Clubs: Omaha Downtown Rotary, Omaha Country, Plaza. Home: 9707 Fieldcrest Dr Omaha NE 68114 Office: 600 Kiewit Plaza Omaha NE 68131

EASTERLING, DOUGLAS NELSON, ednl. adminstr.; b. Eufaula, Ala., Feb. 24, 1948; s. Carlton Nelson and Georgia (Redwine) E.; student Emory U., 1966-67; B.A., U. Tex., 1970; M.Public Adminstrn., U. Mass., 1973; postgrad., U. Minn., 1979—; m. Roberta Rae Parker, Aug. 23, 1969; children—Thea Catherine, Camden Charlotte. Public assistance caseworker San Antonio Dept. Welfare, 1970-71; instr. Massasoit Community Coll., Brockton, Mass., 1973-74; exec. dir. Maine Adv. Council on Vocat. Edn., Augusta, 1974-78; coordinator Southwest and West Central Consortium, Marshall, Minn., 1978—; dean of Continuing Edn., Inver Hills Community Coll., Inver Grove Heights Minn. Mem. Am. Vocat. Assn., Am. Soc. Public Adminstrn., Am. Assn. Higher Edn., Minn. Vocat. Equity Council, Adult Edn. Assn. USA, Minn. Assn. Adult Continuing Edn., Missouri Valley Adult Edn. Assn. Democrat. Office: Inver Hills Community Coll Inver Grove Heights MN

EASTLUND, MARVIN EUGENE, physician; b. Breman, Ind., Apr. 25, 1944; s. Allen Edward and Ruth Mae (Barden) E.; A.B., Manchester Coll., 1966; M.D., Ind. U., 1970; m. Phyllis Diane Brower, June 4, 1966; children—Shelly Lynn, Kimberly Diane, Darcy Kay (adopted), John Bradley (adopted). Intern, St. Vincent Hosp., Indpls., 1970-71, resident in ob-gyn., 1971-74; practice medicine specializing in ob-gyn., Ft. Wayne, Ind., 1976—; mem. staff Ft. Wayne Ob-Gyn. Inc., 1976—, pres., 1979-80; mem. staff Parkview Meml. Hosp., Ft. Wayne; Mem. bd., sec. Blackhawk Christian Sch.; bd. dirs. Ft. Wayne Area Youth for Christ. Served with M.C., USN, 1974-76. Named to Outstanding Young Men of Am., U.S. Jaycees, 1978; diplomate Am. Bd. Obstetrics-Gynecology. Fellow Am. Coll. Obstetricians and Gynecologists; mem. AMA, Ind. Med. Assn., Ft. Wayne Med. Soc., Ft. Wayne Acad. Medicine and Surgery, Ft. Wayne Ob-Gyn. Soc., Ind. Ob-Gyn. Soc., Am. Assn. Gynecologic Laparoscopists. Baptist. Home: 5431 Vance Ave Fort Wayne IN 46815 Office: 3124 E State Blvd Fort Wayne IN 46805

EASTMAN, ADALINE JONES, educator; b. Phila., Apr. 9, 1924; d. Harry Elmer and Mary Elizabeth (Saul) Seitz; B.S., Shippensburg (Pa.) State Coll., 1945; M.A., Ohio State U., 1957, Ph.D., 1964; m. Herschel F. Eastman, Mar. 1, 1975; children by previous marriage—William R. Jones; 1 son, Michael H. Sec. to pres. Shippensburg State Coll., 1943-45; head bus. edn. dept. Blacklick Twp. High Sch., Twin Rocks, Pa., 1945-52; sec. to mgr. dept. engring. econs. Battelle Meml. Inst., Columbus, Ohio, 1952-53; tchr. bus. and English, Reynoldsburg, Ohio, 1953-56; chmn. dept. bus. edn. Capital U., Columbus, 1956-64; prof., coordinator vocat. tchr. edn. program Ball State U., Muncie, Ind., 1964—. State chmn. Ind. chpt. Future Bus. Leaders Am., 1965-72; pres. Blacklick Twp. PTA, 1950-51. Recipient Jessie S. Heiges Disting. Alumnus award Shippensburg State Coll., 1978. Mem. Nat. Bus. Edn. Assn. (Coll. Tchr. of Yr. 1980), North Central Bus. Edn. Assn. (Disting. Service award 1972, pres. 1979-80), Am. Vocat. Assn. (award of merit 1979), Nat. Assn. Distributive Edn. Tchrs., Council Distributive Tchr. Edn., Ind. Bus. Edn. Assn. (service award 1977), Ind. Distributive Edn. Assn., Ind. Vocat. Assn. (award of merit 1970, Outstanding service award 1976), Ind. Council Vocat. Adminstrs., Ind. Bus. Educators Club (pres. 1968-69), Delta Pi Epsilon, Pi Lambda Theta, Delta Kappa Gamma. Lutheran. Clubs: Elks, Toastmistress (treas. Muncie 1975-76). Home: 401 Winthrop Rd Muncie IN 47304 Office: Box 76 Whitinger Coll Bus Bldg Ball State U Muncie IN 47306

EASTMAN, KERMIT LEROY, ednl. adminstr.; b. Thief River Falls, Minn., Mar. 21, 1927; married 2 children. B.S. in Elemenary Edn., Moorhead (Minn.) State U., 1953; M.S. in Curriculum, Adminstrn., U. N.D., Grand Forks, 1958. With St. Cloud (Minn.) Sch. Dist. 742, 1959—, asst. supt., 1966-69, supt., 1969—. Mem. Am., Minn., Central Minn. assns. sch. adminstrs., Assn. Tchr. Educators, Phi Delta Kappa. Home: 1621 14th Avenue S St Cloud MN 56201 Office: 628 Roosevelt Rd Saint Cloud MN 56301

EASTMAN, ROGER WILLIAM, civil engr., steel mfg. co. exec.; b. Inwood, Iowa, Aug. 10, 1942; s. Harley Francis and Goldie Evelyn (Iseminger) E.; M.S. in Civil Engring., S.D. State U., 1970; m. Patricia Elaine Mize, June 21, 1968; children—Tricia Elaine, Judson William. Engring. trainee Pittsburgh-Des Moines Steel Co., Des Moines, 1970-72, project engr. for bridge in N.Y.C., 1972, resident field engr., constrn. depts., various locations, 1972, field project engr., N.Y.C., 1973-74, dir. quality assurance mgr. central div., 1974—; cons. steel constrn. Ch.-sch. supt. Westover Bapt. Ch., 1972-78. Served with U.S. Army, 1962-65. Am. Inst. of Steel Constrn. grantee, 1969; registered profl. engr. Mem. ASCE, Am. Welding Soc., Am. Soc. Non-destructive Testing. Republican. Home: 409 NE Crestmoore St Ankeny IA 50021 Office: 1015 Tuttle St Des Moines IA 50308

EASTO, PATRICK CLIFFORD, educator; b. Detroit, July 19, 1940; s. Howard Grover and Mary Veronica (Russell) E.; B.S., Eastern

Mich. U., 1966; M.A., Wayne State U., 1968; Ph.D., Syracuse U., 1973. Asst. prof. sociology Eastern Mich. U., Ypsilanti, 1970-75, asso. prof., 1975—; research asso. Inst. Labor and Indsl. Relations, U. Mich., 1974; court sociologist 3d Jud. Circuit Ct. Detroit, 1975-80; cons. Mich. Supreme Ct., 1980—. Campaign adv. to Senate race, Calif., 1978. Served with USN, 1959-63. Mem. Am., Mich. sociol. assns., So. Sociol. Soc., Internat. Platform Assn. Contbr. articles to profl. jours. Home: 13167 Lake Point Blvd Belleville MI 48111 Office: Dept Sociology Eastern Mich Univ Ypsilanti MI 48197

EASTON, PAUL, automobile co. exec.; b. Youngstown, Ohio, Apr. 10, 1931; s. Hugh Emmett and Naomi Elizabeth (Shook) E.; student Youngstown State U., 1956, Hiram (Ohio) Coll., 1977—; m. Elva Wright, Apr. 30, 1960; children—Celeste Marie, Rebecca Mae. Clk.-typist Fruehauf Trailer Co., Youngstown, 1949; acctg. clk. Republic Steel Corp., Youngstown, 1949-52; clk.-steno Erie Lackawanna R.R., Youngstown, 1954-59, sec., gen. chmn. Brotherhood of R.R. Trainmen, Youngstown, 1959-64; with Gen. Motors Corp., 1964—, supr. salaried personnel, 1969-76, gen. supr. personnel adminstrn., 1976-79, human resources coordinator, Warren, Ohio, 1976—. Cons., Vocation Agy., United Presbyn. Ch., U.S.A., N.Y.C., 1977—; elder Westminster United Presbyn. Ch., 1980—; mem. exec. com. Community Corp., 1980—; mem. Choffin Career Center adv. com. Youngstown City Schs., 1979; lectr. to civic groups on handwriting analysis and identification of questioned documents and signatures. Served with U.S. Army, 1952-54; Korea. Decorated Army Commendation medal. Named Protestant Man of Yr., 1977. Cert. graphoanalyst, 1973, questioned document examiner, 1979; accredited personnel mgr., 1976. Mem. Internat. Graphoanalysis Soc. (editor Ohio chpt. 1975-77), World Assn. Document Examiners, Am. Soc. Personnel Adminstrn., Am. Mgmt. Assn., Mahoning Valley Indsl. Mgmt. Assn., Internat. Platform Assn., NAACP. Republican. Home: 193 Green Bay Dr Youngstown OH 44512 Office: PO Box 1406 Warren OH 44482

EASTWOOD, ROBERT PARKER, former educator; b. DuBois, Nebr., Oct. 24, 1899; s. Robert Arthur and Mary Margaret (Mahood) E.; B.Sc., U. Nebr., 1922, M.A., 1923; Ph.D., Columbia U., 1940; m. Marcia Octavia Staton, June 24, 1925; 1 dau., Grace Ellen. Instr., U. Nebr., 1923-24; lab. supr. Columbia U., 1924-26, statis. asst., 1926-29, instr., 1929-41, asst. prof. econs. and bus., 1941-45, asso. prof., 1945-52, prof. bus. stats., 1952-68, prof. emeritus, 1968—; asst. dean Sch. Bus., 1950-54; vis. prof. Smith Coll., summer 1942, Robert Coll., Istanbul, Turkey, spring 1965, winter, 1966; mem. N.Y. State Milk Mktg. Com. on Pricing, 1949-51. Served with Students Army Tng. Corps, 1918. Mem. Am. Statis. Assn. Author: Quantitative Methods of Sales Control, 1941. Home: 6625 Bethany Park Dr Lincoln NE 68505

EATMON, MARY BETH, counselor, educator, ednl. adminstr.; b. Paragould, Ark., Jan. 11, 1922; d. Riley Hall and Mary Agnes (Spaini) Johnson; B.S., Bradley U., 1966, M.A., 1971; m. Press Eatmon, Sept. 14, 1941; children—Carolyn, Pressie, Diane, Deborah, Cynthia. Tchr., Paragould Pub. Schs., 1941-48, Homewood Heights Schs., Creve Coeur, Ill., 1961-72; tchr., asst. prin. La Salle Sch., Creve Coeur, 1972—; guidance counselor Dist. 76, Creve Coeur, 1978—; supervising tchr. U. Ill., 1973-75. Tchr. young married McArthur Drive Ch., North Pekin, Ill., 1979-80. Mem. Nat., Ill., Creve Coeur, edn. assns., Am. Personnel and Guidance Assn., Am. Sch. Counselor Assn., Ill. Personnel and Guidance Assn., Ill. Sch. Counselor Assn., Internat. Platform Assn., PTA (life), Pi Lambda Theta. Democrat. Baptist. Home: 200 W Summit St Washington IL 61571 Office: 800 Groveland Ave Creve Coeur IL 61611

EATON, DONNA LEE, educator; b. Lancaster, Ohio, July 22, 1944; d. Devon William and Esther Marie (Graf) Tipple; student Ohio U., 1962-64; B.S. in Edn., Miami U., Ohio, 1966; m. Roland Edmound Eaton, Aug. 2, 1964; children—Trent Edward, Todd William. Tchr. home econs. Lancaster (Ohio) City Schs., 1966-67; job training tchr. Penta County Joint Vocat. Sch., Perrysburg, Ohio, 1969-72; home econs. tchr., chmn. dept. Genoa (Ohio) Area Schs., 1973—; cooperating tchr. office of student tchrs. Bowling Green (Ohio) State U., 1970—. High sch. rep. Bicentennial Com. Genoa, 1976. Recipient Ray Thompson Outstanding Tchr. award Genoa Area High Sch., 1979; named Ohio Home Econs. Tchr. of Yr., 1980. Mem. Ohio Vocat. Assn., Am. Vocat. Assn., NEA, Ohio Edn. Assn., Am. Home Econs. Assn., Ohio Home Econs. Assn., Phi Upsilon Omicron. Methodist. Club: Perrysburg Elem. Schs. Mothers. Home: 26954 Heatherford Dr Perrysburg OH 43551 Office: 2980 N Genoa Clay Center Rd Genoa OH 43430

EATON, JAMES ALLEN, JR., med. research analyst; b. El Dorado, Kans., Jan. 15, 1946; s. James Allen and Mary E. (Lehr) E.; B.S., Kans. State U., 1969, M.S., 1976; 1 son, James Allen, III. Adminstrv. asst. Larned (Kans.) State Hosp., 1970-71; lab. technician Hardin County Hosp., Elizabethtown, Ky., 1972-73; instr. dept. anatomy and physiology Coll. Vet. Medicine, Kans. State U., 1973-76; med. research analyst law firm Shook, Hardy & Bacon, Kansas City, Mo., 1976—. Served with U.S. Army, 1971-73. Decorated Army Commendation medal; recipient Grad. Research Excellence award Internat. Poultry Assn., 1975. Mem. Sigma Xi (Grad. research and Thesis Excellence award 1976). Author papers in field. Home: 3525 NE 72d Terr Kansas City MO 64119 Office: 1101 Walnut St 20th Floor Kansas City MO 64106

EATON, JAMES WOODFORD, assn. exec.; b. Indpls., Apr. 19, 1942; s. James Woodford and Genevee (Oliver) E.; B.A., Butler U., 1964; M.A., Kent State U., 1967, Ph.D., 1973; m. Linda McKinney, Aug. 27, 1966; 1 dau., Victoria Lynn. Grad. asst. in history Kent (Ohio) State U., 1964-66, teaching fellow in history, 1966-68, instr. history Tuscarawas campus, 1968-72; staff Dover-New Philadelphia (Ohio) Times-Reporter, 1972-79. bus. editor, 1973-79; public info. specialist Ohio Mid-Eastern Govts. Assn., Cambridge, 1979-81; staff mem. Tuscarawas County C. of C., New Philadelphia, Ohio, 1981—. Mem. Ohio Devel. Assn. (treas.), Dover Hist. Soc. Mem. Christian Ch. Home: 221 E 10th St Dover OH 44622 Office: 1323 4th St NW New Philadelphia OH 44663

EATON, KENNETH JAY, mgmt. engr.; b. San Francisco, Apr. 24, 1924; s. William Jay and Cecile (Rubens) E.; student Chgo. Wright Coll., 1940-42; B.A., Ill. Inst. Tech., 1947; B.S., U. Wyo., 1944, M.S., 1950; m. Betty I. Goodman, June 20, 1949; children—Richard Neal, Carole Anne. Lectr. U. Wis., 1947-48; instr. Ill. Inst. Tech., 1950-51; mgmt. engr. Container Corp. of Am., 1946-47; engring. dir. Asso. Bus. Cons., 1947—; group v.p., dir. Arvey Corp., 1955-70; dir. Dynascan Corp.; pres. Small Bus. Mgmt. Investors of Ill., Central Adminstrn. Corp., Eaton Bros. Realty Investment Co.; dir. United Travel, Inc. Active Boy Scouts, Chgo. Boys Club. Served with AUS, 1942-45. Registered profl. engr., Ill.; cert. mgmt. cons. Mem. Am. Arbitration Assn., Soc. for Advancement of Mgmt., Pilots' Assn., Sigma Iota Epsilon. Home: 3044 Grant St Evanston IL 60201 Office: 17 E Chestnut St Chicago IL 60611

EATON, MERRILL THOMAS, psychiatrist; b. Howard County, Ind., June 25, 1920; s. Merrill Thomas; A.B., Ind. U., 1941, M.D., 1944; m. Louise Foster, Dec. 23, 1942; children—Deirdre Ann, Thomas Anthony, David Foster. Intern, St. Elizabeth Hosp., Washington, 1944-45; resident in psychiatry Colo. State Hosp., Pueblo, 1947-48, Sheppard and Enoch Pratt Hosp., Towson, Md., 1948-49; mem. faculty Kans. U. Med. Sch., 1949-60, asso. prof. psychiatry, 1954-60; mem. faculty U. Nebr. Med. Sch., Omaha, 1960—, prof. psychiatry, 1963—, chmn. dept., 1968—; dir. Nebr. Psychiat. Inst., 1968—. Served to capt. M.C., AUS, 1945-47. Diplomate Am. Bd. Psychiatry. Fellow A.C.P., Am. Psychiat. Assn.; mem. Am. Assn. Chmn. Depts. Psychiatry, Assn. Am. Med. Colls., Group Advancement Psychiatry (chmn. com. mental health services 1970-73, chmn. publs. bd. 1976—), Nebr. Med. Assn., Nebr. Psychiat. Soc. (pres. 1973-75). Author: Psychiatry, 4th edit., 1981; co-author: Treating Sexual Problems in Medical Practice, 1979. Office: 602 S 45th St Omaha NE 68106

EATON, RICHARD ROE, educator, counselor; b. Festus, Mo., Jan. 22, 1939; s. Leo Glenman and Ruth Elizabeth (Sago) E.; B.S. in Edn., S.E. Mo. State U., 1962; M.Ed., U. Mo., Columbia, 1965; Ph.D. in Counselor Edn., St. Louis U., 1977. Tchr., Arcadia Valley Schs., Ironton, Mo., 1958-61; jr. high sch. tchr. Hazelwood Sch. Dist., St. Louis, 1962-67; high sch. counselor Ladue Sch. Dist., St. Louis, 1967—; adj. instr. St. Louis U., 1977; instr. psychology Am. Inst. Banking; cons. in field. Cert. rational emotive psychotherapist Inst. Advanced Study in Rational Emotive Psychotherapy; lic. psychologist, Mo. Mem. Am., St. Louis personnel and guidance assns., Mo. Guidance Assn., Nat. Assn. Humanist Educators, Ladue Community Tchrs. Assn., NEA, Mo. Nat. Ednl. Assn., Mo. Assn. for Humanistic Edn. and Devel. (charter), S.E. Mo., U. Mo.-Columbia, St. Louis U. alumni assns. Methodist. Home: 1180 Moorlands Dr Saint Louis MO 63117 Office: 1201 S Warson Rd Saint Louis MO 63124

EATON, ZELWIN B., univ. adminstr.; b. Mexico, Mo., June 23, 1943; s. Zetho E. and Mildred I. (Lindahl) E.; B.S. Edn. in Geography with honors, N.E. Mo. State U., Kirksville, 1967, M.A., 1969; m. Jacquelyn Sykes, Dec. 26, 1969. Asst. prin. Kirksville RIII Sch. Dist., 1967-70; asst. dir. housing N.E. Mo. State U., 1970-72, investigator safety and security, 1972-77, asst. to dean students, 1977—. Mem. Kirksville Planning and Zoning Commn., 1974—. Mem. Internat. Assn. Arson Investigators, Internat. Narcotic Enforcement Officers Assn., Nat. Exec. Housekeepers Assn., Mo. Coll. Personnel Assn., Blue Key, Kappa Delta Pi, Phi Delta Kappa (past pres.), Alpha Phi Sigma. Mem. Christian Ch. (Disciples of Christ). Clubs: Kiwanis, Shriners. Home: 904 E Wall St Kirksville MO 63501 Office: 103 A/H Bldg NE Mo State Univ Kirksville MO 63501

EBANN, CHARLES KEITH, chem. co. exec.; b. Chgo., Feb. 14, 1947; s. Robert Benno and Louise Margaret (Fricke) E.; B.S., Iowa State U., 1969; m. Mary Ellen Spencer, Aug. 4, 1973. Process supr. Morton Chem. Co., Ringwood, Ill., 1969-72, process engr., Chgo., 1972-73, purchasing agt., 1973-79, dir. purchases, 1979—. Pres., Bright Oaks Homeowners Assn., 1975-77, bd. dirs., 1973-77. Mem. Am. Inst. Chem. Engrs., Nat. Assn. Purchasing Mgmt. Clubs: Anvil, Tower, Masons. Home: 860 Broadway St Crystal Lake IL 60014 Office: Morton Chem Co 2 N Riverside Plaza Chicago IL 60606

EBBING, BERNARD WILLIAM, agr. cons.; b. Eagle Grove, Iowa, Dec. 19, 1920; s. William Bernard and Margaret (Sweeney) E.; B.S., Iowa State U., 1943; m. Virginia M. Buckwalter, June 19, 1943; children—Mary Ann (Mrs. Peter Reiter), Jane Ann (Mrs. Kreg Leymaster). Vocat. agrl. instr. West Union, Iowa, 1946-51; with The Rath Packing Co., Waterloo, Iowa, 1951-78, dir. hog procurement and agrl. relations, 1963-78; agrl. cons., Waterloo, Iowa, 1978—; dir. Livestock Conservation Inst., South St. Paul, Minn., 1962—; nat. swine judge, swine cons. Vice-pres., dir. Nat. Cattle Congress. Served with USMCR, 1943-46. Decorated Purple Heart medal. Mem. Nat. Mgmt. Assn., Waterloo C. of C. (mem. agrl. com. 1952—), Am. Legion. Republican. Roman Catholic. Club: Waterloo Elks. Address: 1126 Bourland St Waterloo IA 50702

EBELING, KENNETH ARNOLD, indsl. engr.; b. Bemidji, Minn., June 3, 1942; s. Erhardt Harold and Leona Gertrude (Hieserich) E.; B.S. in Indsl. Engring., N.D. State U., 1965, M.S. in Indsl. Engring., 1967; Ph.D. in Indsl. Engring., Kans. State U., 1974; m. Adah Christine Enzi, Sept. 5, 1964; children—Timothy Allen, Thomas Arnold. Facilities engr., devel. lab. IBM, 1965; mem. project staff N.D. State U., 1966-68; instr. dept. indsl. engring., Kans. State U., Manhattan, 1971-74; asso. prof. indsl. engring. N.D. State U., Fargo, 1965—. NSF fellow, 1970-72; registered profl. engr., N.D. Mem. Nat. Soc. Profl. Engrs., N.D. Soc. Profl. Engrs. (pres. chpt. 4 1981), Tau Beta Pi, Phi Kappa Phi. Roman Catholic. Home: 3010 9th St N Fargo ND 58102 Office: Dept Indsl Engring ND State U Fargo ND 58105

EBERHARDT, BETTY MAE EHRHART, economist; b. New Orleans, Oct. 31, 1928; d. Ernest Spengler and Alice Agnes (Furlong) Ehrhart; B.S., Nicholls State U., 1967; M.A., (Found. for Econ. Edn. fellow; Tulane fellow), Tulane U., 1974; children—Elizabeth Eberhardt Wigginton, Richard W., Jr., Patrick D., William D. Economist, planning div. U.S. Army Corps Engrs., New Orleans, 1970-77, chief, gen. water resources devel. sect., 1976-77, economist, planning div., Lower Mississippi Valley Div., Vicksburg, 1977-79, div. economist Ohio River Div., Cin., 1979—. Recipient Outstanding and Sustained Superior Performance award U.S. Army, 1972. Mem. Am. Econ. Assn., So. Econ. Assn., Soc. Govt. Economists, Soc. Am. Mil. Engrs. Home: 3228 Pebblebrook Ln Cincinnati OH 45239 Office: PO Box 1159 Cincinnati OH 45201

EBERIUS, KLAUS OTTO, machine tool import co. exec.; b. Koethen, Germany, Feb. 13, 1940; s. Otto and Gertrud (Marx) E.; came to U.S., 1972; engring. degree Akademie of Engring., Cologne, Germany, 1967; m. Amei Brauns, Apr. 17, 1964; children—Edda, Susanne. Asst. plant mgr. Anton Piller Kg., Osterode, Germany, 1967-68; mgr. tng. center VDF Corp., Hannover, Germany, 1968-72; tech. services mgr. Upton, Bradeen & James, Sterling Heights, Mich., 1972-73, mgr. metal cutting div., 1973-76; v.p., gen. mgr. Unitec Nat. Co., Broadview, Ill., 1976-79; pres., dir. Uni-Sig Corp., 1979—; instr. programming night sch., Hannover. Mem. U.S. Senatorial Adv. Bd. Recipient award NC-Research, 1969. Mem. Numerical Control Soc., Soc. Mfg. Engrs., Am. Mgmt. Assn., German Am. C. of C. Home: 3802 Richard Dr Elgin IL 60120 Office: 2805 S 19th Ave Broadview IL 60153

EBERSOLE, JO ANN, dietitian; b. Corpus Christi, Tex., Feb. 13, 1945; d. Ronald A. and Ruth A. (White) E.; B.S. in Dietetics, Mich. State U., 1967. Dietitian, St. Lawrence Hosp., Lansing, Mich., 1968-69; asst. chief dietitian Children's Meml. Hosp., Chgo., 1969-72; dir. food services Walther Meml. Hosp., Chgo., 1972-78, Forkosh Meml. Hosp., Chgo., 1979—; instr. workshops 1975—. Mem. Am. Dietetic Assn., Am. Soc. Hosp. Food Service Adminstrs., Ill. Dietetic Assn., Chgo. Dietetic Assn. (treas., chmn. peer rev. 1978-80). Roman Catholic.

EBERT, CARROL E., retail exec.; b. 1924; B.B.A., U. Wis., 1949; With Touche, Ross & Co., Chgo., 1960-66; v.p. fin. and ops. T. A. Chapman Co., 1966-67; v.p., treas., dir. Wieboldt Stores, Chgo., 1968-72; v.p. Carson Pirie Scott & Co., Chgo., 1972-74, v.p. fin. and treas., 1974-78, exec. v.p. fin. and adminstrn., 1978-81, chmn. bd., pres., 1981—, also dir.; dir. Carson Internat. Inc. Office: Carson Pirie Scott & Co 1 S State St Chicago IL 60603*

EBERT, IAN OLERIA, elec. engr., educator; b. Mingo, Iowa, Mar. 13, 1920; s. Albert Jerome and Grace Mabel (Adkins) E.; B.S. in Elec. Engring., Iowa State U., 1942; M.S. in Elec. Engring., U. Ill., 1947; m. Doris Elizabeth Fuller, Oct. 18, 1945; children—James Ian, Barbara Elizabeth. Research scientist Naval Research Lab., Washington, 1943-48; asst. prof., asso. prof. elec. engring. Mich. State U., East Lansing, 1948-62; advisor, prof. telecommunications Engring. Coll., Poona, India, 1962-63; asso. prof. elec. engring. Mich. State U., 1963—; electronics cons. Mich. Industries, 1950—; con. on elec. and electronics safety for law firms and ins. cos. Mem. East Lansing Elec. Bd., 1970—. Served with USN, 1943-45. Mem. AAAS, Am. Soc. for Engring. Edn. Home: 1842 Linden St East Lansing MI 48823 Office: Elec Engring Dept Mich State Univ East Lansing MI 48824

EBERT, PHYLLIS KAY, educator; b. Gary, Ind., Sept. 13, 1944; d. L.M. and Verna I. (Gunther) E.; B.A. (Inland Steel scholar), Purdue U., 1966, M.A., 1967; M.B.A., So. Ill. U., 1975, postgrad., 1976—. Yard dept. stenographer Inland Steel Co., East Chgo., Ind., 1962-66; tchr. public schs., Tinley Park, Ill., 1967-68, Hicksville, N.Y., 1967-70; merchandiser Goldblatts Dept. Store, Markham, Ill., 1967-68, Gimbels Dept. Store, Garden City, N.Y., 1968-69; instr. English dept. So. Ill. U., Carbondale, 1970-74; asst. mgr. Wall Street Quadrangles, Carbondale, 1971-75; instr. adminstrv. scis. dept. So. Ill. U., Carbondale, 1974-75; asst. prof. acctg. and fin. Richland Community Coll., Decatur, Ill., 1976-79; asst. prof. bus. adminstrn. Millikin U., Decatur, Ill., 1975—, dir. profl. devel. programs, 1980—; cons. communications and mgmt. Choir dir., Sunday sch. supt., mem. bd. edn., mem. organ com. St. Paul's Lutheran Ch., 1976—; speaker to numerous orgn. on women in mgmt., women in society, coping with male politics. Permanent master tchr. cert., N.Y. State. Mem. AAUW (Millikin Corp. rep. 1977—), Am. Bus. Communications Assn., Am. Soc. for Tng. and Devel. (pres. Central Ill. chpt. 1978-79), Faculty Woman to Woman (coordinator), Am. Mgmt. Assn., Midwest Case Writers Assn., Midwest Bus. Adminstrn. Assn., Am. Bus. Women's Assn., NOW, Mensa, Alpha Kappa Psi. Republican. Author: (with R.R. Knudson) Sports Poetry, 1970. Office: Millikin U Decatur IL 62522

EBERT, ROGER JOSEPH, film critic; b. Urbana, Ill., June 18, 1942; s. Walter H. and Annabel (Stumm) E.; B.S., U. Ill., 1964; postgrad. U. Cape Town (South Africa), 1965, U. Chgo., 1966-67. Staff writer Champaign-Urbana News Gazette, 1958-66; film critic Chgo. Sun-Times, 1967—; co-host Sneak Previews, PBS, 1977—; film critic Sta. WMAQ-TV, Chgo., 1980—; instr. Chgo. City Coll., 1967-68; lectr. fine arts U. Chgo. extension, 1969—; lectr. film Columbia Coll., Chgo., 1972-73, 76-77. Recipient award Chgo. Headline Club, 1963, Overseas Press Club award, 1963; Chgo. Newspaper Guild award, 1973; Pulitzer prize for disting. criticism, 1975; Chgo. Emmy award, 1979. Rotary fellow, 1965. Mem. Am. Newspaper Guild, Nat. Soc. Film Critics, U. Ill. Alumni Assn. (dir. 1975—), Phi Delta Theta. Clubs: Arts, Cliff Dwellers (Chgo.). Author: An Illini Century, 1967; (screen play) Beyond the Valley of the Dolls, 1970; Beyond Narrative: The Future of the Feature Film, 1978. Office: 401 N Wabash Ave Chicago IL 60611

EBERT, TRUDY MARY, civic worker; b. St. Paul, Feb. 15, 1925; d. Edward M. and Gertrude C. (Connell) O'Leary; student U. Minn., 1948-49, St. Catherines Coll., 1967-68; m. Robert A. Ebert, Feb. 8, 1947; children—Kathryn Ebert-Hilger, Richard Friess. Disaster driver unit Ramsey County (Minn.) chpt. ARC, 1947-58; active PTA, Nativity, Derham Hall, St. Thomas Mil. Acad., St. Paul, 1957-71; nat. bd. dirs., pres. St. Croix Valley council Camp Fire Girls Am., 1956-67; chairperson Community Chest, St. Paul, 1958; pres., bd. dirs. Ramsey County Bar Assn. Aux., 1961—; bd. dirs., pres. Inter Club Council, St. Paul, 1966-80; treas. Lawyers Wives Minn., 1968-70; pres. Women's Orgn. of Decathalon Athletic Club, Bloomington, Minn., 1969; pres. Nat. Lawyers Wives aux. Am. Bar Assn., 1974; mem. Minn. Gov.'s Vol. Task Force, 1975-79; pres. Minn. Hist. Soc. Women's Orgn., 1977-80; organizer Children and Law, Minn., 1968, nat., 1970; chairperson Republican Precinct, St. Paul. Recipient Outstanding Community Service award St. Paul Community Chest, 1959, Ernest Thomas Seton award Nat. Camp Fire Girls, 1966, Vol. Service award Minn. Gov., 1979, and other service awards. Mem. Minn. Hist. Soc., Ramsey County Hist. Soc., Good Old Girls Minn. Roman Catholic. Clubs: Univ. of St. Paul, St. Paul Athletic (aux. pres. 1970), St. Paul Women's, St. Paul Pool and Yacht. Home: 534 S Mississippi River Blvd Saint Paul MN 55116

EBERTS, JAMES LEE, acct.; b. Hamden, Ohio, Dec. 1, 1950; s. James Robert and Nellie Louise (Wiseman) E.; B.B.A., Ohio U., 1973; m. Diana S. McClelland, June 10, 1973; 1 dau., Jamie Lee. Staff acct. Brown, Armstrong & Jackson, C.P.A.'s, Athens, Ohio, 1973-76; comptroller Security Bank of Athens, 1976; prin. James L. Eberts, C.P.A., Wellston, Ohio, 1976—; treas., bd. dirs. James R. Eberts Constrn. Corp., Eberts Coal Co., Inc.; instr. Hocking Tech. Coll., Rio Grande Community Coll., 1976. Mem. Am. Inst. C.P.A.'s, Ohio Soc. C.P.A.'s. Republican. Methodist. Club: Vinton County Jaycees (treas.), Eagles. Office: 5 S Ohio Ave Wellston OH 45692 also 12 1/2 N Court St Athens OH 45701

EBLING, RICHARD CHARLES, restaurant exec.; b. St. Louis, Jan. 10, 1940; s. Arthur Blaine and Katherine (McDonald) E.; B.Ed., U. Mo., 1962, M.Ed., 1966; m. Kathryn Marie Schopp, Dec. 26, 1964; children—Susan Elizabeth, Kathryn Konrad. Tchr. Ritenoir Sch. Dist., St. Louis, 1963-64; sales mgr. Ralston Purina Co., St. Louis, 1966-75; pres. Ebling Enterprises, Inc., Osaga Beach, Mo., 1975—. Dir. Camp Wah-Kon-Dah, Rocky Mt., Mo., 1965. Mem. Osaga Beach C. of C., Lake of the Ozarks Assn., Mo. Restaurant Assn., Sigma Chi (Xi-Xi chpt., life loyal Sig). Republican Clubs: Ducks Unlimited, Elks, M-Men's. Home and Office: Route 2 Box 48 Osaga Beach MO 65065

EBNER, JUDITH MARILYN, ednl. adminstr.; b. Grove City, Pa., Nov. 19, 1939; d. Emil Emanuel and Gladys Mary (Morton) E.; B.M., U. Mich., 1962, M.M., 1964; postgrad. Columbia U., 1963-72. Tchr. vocal music Frewsburg (N.Y.) Central Sch., 1964-65, East Williston (N.Y.) Public Schs., 1965-74; stock broker First Investors Corp., N.Y.C., 1973-75; tchr. vocal music Beecher Community Schs., Flint, Mich., 1975-79; staff asso. Flint Community Schs., 1979—. Mem. Greater Flint Fine Arts Council; mem. U. Mich. Regents-Alumni Scholarship Interview Com.; mem. Dailey Community Ednl. Council, Flint; past bd. dirs. East Williston Community Concert Assn. Recipient Outstanding Tchr. award Beecher Community Schs., 1977. Mem. Am. Assn. Sch. Adminstrs., Assn. Supervision and Curriculum Devel., Council Basic Edn., Council Ednl. Facility Planners, Internat. Soc. Study Edn., Music Educators Nat. Conf., Mich. Music Educators Assn. (dir.), Mich. Council Women in Ednl. Adminstrn. (state treas.), Phi Delta Kappa, Delta Kappa Gamma, Mu Phi Epsilon. Clubs: Zonta Internat., U. Mich. Alumni. Co-author music curriculum guides. Home: 3601 Balfour Ct Apt 15 Flint MI 48507 Office: 924 E 6th St Flint MI 48503

EBY, LAWRENCE THORNTON, bldg. materials co. exec.; b. South Bend, Ind., May 3, 1916; s. Ralph C. and Edna May (Thornton) E.; B.S. in Chem. Engring., U. Notre Dame, 1938, M.S., 1939, Ph.D., 1941; m. Claudine Isabelle Hart, June 8, 1941; children—Jane Sue Eby Korner, Claudia Ann. Research chemist Esso Research & Engring. Co., Linden, N.J., 1941-57; asst. mgr. market devel. Enjay Chem. Co., Elizabeth, N.J., 1957-64; pres. Protective Treatments, Aeroplast Corp., Dellrose Industries, Dayton, O., 1964-65; dir. devel. Chrysler Corp., Trenton, Mich., 1965-67; mgr. polymer div. U.S. Gypsum Co., Des Plaines, Ill., 1967-73, asso. dir. research, 1973—. Lectr., 1st Symposium on Polymers Nat. Council Sci. and Tech.,

Mexico, 1972. Chmn. Mental Health Fund, Linden, N.J., 1954-55. Recipient Honor award U. Notre Dame, 1965. Mem. Am. Chem. Soc., Am. Inst. Chemists (Honor scroll 1961), Soc. Plastics Engrs., Comml. Devel. Assn., Chem. Market Research Assn., AAAS, Am. Assn. Textile Chemists and Colorists, TAPPI, Akron Rubber Group, Assn. Iron and Steel Engrs., Am. Indsl. Hygiene Assn., Alpha Chi Sigma. Presbyn. (elder 1946—, pres. bd. trustees 1961, 79). Contbr. articles to profl. jours. Patentee in field. Home: 102 S Kennicott Ave Arlington Heights IL 60005 Office: 1000 E Northwest Hwy Des Plaines IL 60016

ECHELBARGER, DENNIS MICHAEL, accountant; b. Muskegon, Mich., May 1, 1941; s. Charles Theron and Dorothy Marguerite (Kelly) E.; B.A., Aquinas Coll., 1964; m. Diane Jean Vink, June 20, 1964; children—Dennis E., David G., Deanna L., Daniel B., Deborah R. Accountant, Bayle & Norman, Grand Rapids, Mich., 1964-69; partner Bayle, Norman & Echelbarger, Grand Rapids, 1969-75; v.p., sec., mgr. F & A Cheese Corp., Grand Rapids, 1975-77; prin. Dennis M. Echelbarger, C.P.A., Grand Rapids, 1977-78; partner Echelbarger & Langenfeld, C.P.A.'s, Grand Rapids, 1978-80, Echelbarger & Himebaugh, C.P.A.'s, Grand Rapids, 1980—; part-time tchr. Davenport Sch. Bus., Grand Rapids, 1979. Bd. dirs. Grand Valley Co-op Credit Union, 1974—, pres., 1977—; sec. Kentwood Community Econ. Devel. Commn., 1975-78; bd. dirs., treas. Princeton Estates Homeowners Assn., Grand Rapids, 1975-78; mem. St. Mary Magdalen Bd. Edn., Grand Rapids, 1975-78, St. Mary Magdalen Fin. Commn., 1978—; sec., treas. Ravines Estates Assn., 1978—; mem. evaluations com. Diocesan Devel. Fund, 1978-79. C.P.A., Mich. Mem. Am. Inst. C.P.A.'s, Mich. Assn. C.P.A.'s (state small practitioners com. 1979—), Western Mich. Assn. C.P.A.'s (steering com. for continuing edn. 1980—), Aquinas Coll. Alumni Assn. Clubs: Grand Rapids Econ., Caledonia Lions. Home: 9600 Ravine Ridge Dr Caledonia MI 49316 Office: 700 36th St SE Grand Rapids MI 49508

ECHOLS, M. EVELYN, travel cons.; b. LaSalle, Ill., Apr. 5, 1914; d. Francis Ira and Mary Irene (Coleman) Bassett; grad. Josephinum Acad., Chgo., 1931; m. David H. Echols, Aug. 31, 1951; children—Susan Echols O'Donnell, William. Pres., founder Internat. Travel Tng. Courses, Inc., Chgo., Los Angeles, San Francisco, Washington, 1962—; partner Internat. Travel Industry Cons. Bd. dirs. Mental Health Soc. Greater Chgo., U. Ill. Sch. Bus., Alliance Francaise; bd. dirs., v.p. United Cerebral Palsy; bd. dirs., chmn. tourist com. Chgo. Conv. and Tourism Bur.; vice chmn. adv. bd. Northwestern Psychiat. Hosp. Mem. Chgo. Execs. Club, English Speaking Union, Acad. TV Arts and Scis., Am. Soc. Travel Agts. Home: 200 E Delaware St Chicago IL 60611 Office: Time-Life Bldg 303 E Ohio St Chicago IL 60611

ECHOLS, RAYMOND PAUL, univ. dean; b. Portsmouth, Va., Sept. 6, 1922; s. William Thomas and Winona Eulia (Mills) E.; A.B., Marion Coll., 1943; B.D., Garrett Theol. Sem., 1947; M.S., Ind. U., 1970, Ed.D., 1976; m. Shirley Thomson, Mar. 30, 1968; children—Elaine, Paulette, Jay. Ordained to ministry Methodist Ch., 1947; pastor, Goldsmith, Ind., 1944-47, Carmel, Ind., 1947-51, Kendallville, Ind., 1951-56, Logansport, Ind., 1956-62, Bloomington, Ind., 1962-65, Indpls., 1965-67; dean student services Ind. U., Kokomo, 1967—. Chmn. blood program ARC, 1957-60; bd. dirs. United Way Campaign, Logansport, Bloomington, Kokomo, Ind.; vice-chmn. Council Social Agys., Bloomington pres. Creative Arts Council, Kokomo; active Boy Scouts Am. Mem. Am. Assn. Collegiate Registrars and Admissions Officers, Nat. Assn. Student Personnel Adminstrs., Phi Delta Kappa. Methodist. Clubs: Elks, Lions, Kiwanis (bd. dirs.). Home: 415 N Western Ave Kokomo IN 46901 Office: 2300 S Washington St Kokomo IN 46901

ECKARDT, ROBERT EDWARD, health gerontologist; b. N.Y.C., June 29, 1951; s. Robert Edward and Mary Lenore (Harvey) E.; B.A. with honors, Grinnell (Iowa) Coll., 1973; Thomas J. Watson fellow, Spain and Denmark, 1973-75; M.P.H. (Klare Meml. fellow 1976-77), U. Mich., 1977, cert. aging, 1977. Research asst. Mich. Dept. Public Health, 1976-77; planning asso. Fedn. Community Planning, Cleve., 1977—; coordinator Long Term Care Gerontology Center, Cleve., 1979—; lectr. Case Western Res. U. Mem. Am. Public Health Assn., Gerontol. Soc. Am., Ohio Public Health Assn., Phi Beta Kappa. Author monograph in field. Home: 2753 Euclid Heights Blvd Cleveland Heights OH 44106 Office: 1001 Huron Rd Cleveland OH 44115

ECKART, DENNIS EDWARD, congressman; b. Cleve., Apr. 6, 1950; s. Edward Joseph and Mary Delores (Luzar) E.; B.A., Xavier U., Cin., 1971; J.D., Cleve. Marshall Law Sch., 1974; m. Sandra J. Pestotnik, Jan. 24, 1975; 1 son, Edward John. Admitted to Ohio bar, 1974; asst. county prosecutor Lake County, 1974; mem. Ohio Ho. of Reps. from 18th Dist., 1975-81, chmn. Cuyahoga County del., 1979-81; mem. 97th Congress from 22d Ohio Dist. First v.p. Slovene Nat. Benefit Soc., Chgo. Democrat. Roman Catholic. Office: 1222 Longworth House Office Bldg Washington DC 20515

ECKBERG, ROBERT HANSEN, co-owner machine shop; b. Grand Rapids, Mich., Aug. 10, 1914; s. Oscar and Clara Peterine (Hansen) E.; student Grand Rapids Jr. Coll., 1931-33; m. Irene G. Swart, Dec. 20, 1941; children—William Robert, Donald Ralph. Partner, Eckberg Motor Rebuilding Co., Grand Rapids, 1941—, gen. mgr., 1965—. Served with U.S. Army, 1941-45. Mem. Nat. Assn. Engine Rebuilders, Better Bus. Bur., C. of C. Republican. Lutheran. Home: 1636 Lotus St SE Grand Rapids MI 49506 Office: 347 LaGrave St Grand Rapids MI 49503

ECKENHOFF, EDWARD ALVIN, health care exec.; b. Durham, N.C., Mar. 4, 1943; s. James Edward and Bonnie Lee E.; B.A., Transylvania U., 1966; M.A., U. Ky., 1968; M.H.A., Washington U., 1974; m. Judi G. Vicich, May 17, 1978. Vice pres., adminstr. Rehab. Inst. Chgo., 1976—; instr. Med. Sch., Northwestern U., preceptor Grad. Sch. Bus.; mem. Ill. Commn. on Health Assistance Programs; mem. Ill. adv. com., chmn. exec. com. Internat. Yr. of Disabled; surveyor Commn. Accreditation of Rehab. Facilities, bd. dirs., 1980—; mem. com. accreditation and edn. Am. Phys. Therapy Assn. Bd. dirs. Operation ABLE, Chgo., Access Living of Met. Chgo., Chgo. Area council Boy Scouts Am., Am. Chamber Symphony, Chgo. Fellow Inst. Medicine Chgo.; mem. Am. Coll. Hosp. Adminstrs., Am. Hosp. Assn. (governing council), Am. Congress Rehab. Medicine, Chgo. Hosp. Council (chmn. com. rehab. 1978—). Episcopalian. Home: 900 N Lake Shore Dr Chicago IL 60611 Office: 345 E Superior St Chicago IL 60611

ECKERT, JOHN SAMUEL, cons. chem. engr.; b. Delta, Ohio, June 29, 1910; s. Gottleib Lee and Margaret (Schug) E.; B.Chem. Engring., Ohio State U., 1933; m. Vera K. Mills Ream, Feb. 14, 1981. Jr. compounder, jr. engr. Goodyear Tire & Rubber Co., Akron, Ohio, 1934-37; dept. supt. E.I. du Pont de Nemours & Co., Inc., Cleve., 1937-42; constrn. engr. area supt. B. F. Goodrich Co., Borger, Tex., 1942-44; dir. engring. Chem. Process Products div. The Norton Co., Akron, 1944-75; ret., 1976; cons. mass transfer ops. field, 1975—; lectr. chem. engring. Ohio State U., 1961—, adj. asso. prof., 1969-75; lectr. mass transfer various univs. Fellow Am. Inst. Chem. Engrs.; mem. Air Pollution Control Assn., Nat. Assn. Corrosion Engrs., Am. Soc. Metals. Mason. Contbr. articles on mass transfer to profl. jours. Patentee in field. Address: 216 Hollywood Ave Akron OH 44313

ECKERT, LAWRENCE RUSSELL, civil engr.; b. Youngstown, Ohio, Dec. 3, 1949; s. Louis Russell and Agnes Boyd Eckert; B.S., Youngstown State U., 1973; m. Mary Catherine John, Mar. 21, 1970; children—Jilie, Amy. Salesman, Comml. Shearing, Inc., Youngstown, 1970-73, engr., 1973-78, chief engr., 1978—; mem. transp. research bd. NRC. Mem. ASCE, Am. Underground Assn. Republican. Home: 3505 Darbyshire St Canfield OH 44406 Office: 1775 Logan Ave Youngstown OH 44501

ECKERT, RALPH JOHN, ins. co. exec.; b. Milw., Mar. 12, 1929; s. John C. and Vlasta (Stauber) E.; B.S., U. Wis., 1951; m. Greta M. Allen, July 11, 1953; children—Maura Eckert Benseler, Peter, Thomas, Karen, Edward. With Benefit Trust Life Ins. Co., Chgo., 1954—, pres., chief exec. officer, 1971-72, pres., chmn. bd., 1972—, also dir.; mem. bd. Ill. Life Ins. Council, pres., 1978-79. Bd. govs. Augustana Center. Served with AUS, 1951-53. Fellow Soc. Actuaries; mem. Am. Acad. Actuaries, Chgo. Actuarial Club (pres. 1965), Health Ins. Assn. Am. (dir. 1980—), Ill. Life and Health Ins. Guaranty Assn. (chmn. 1980). Lutheran. Mason. Clubs: Michigan Shores (Wilmette, Ill.); Cedar Lake Yacht (Slinger, Wis.). Office: 1771 W Howard St Chicago IL 60626

ECKHARDT, WILLIAM EDWARD, psychologist, educator; b. Phila., Sept. 21, 1918; s. William Joseph and Mary Josephine (Powers) E.; B.A., Swarthmore Coll., 1953; M.A., Richmond Profl. Inst., 1954; Ph.D., U. Ky., 1960; m. Margaret Ellen Abbott, Aug. 8, 1942; children—William, Edward, Christopher, Steven. Chief psychologist, state hosps of N.C., 1954-58; asst. prof. psychology Western Ky. State Coll., 1960-61; chief psychologist Mental Health Inst., Clarida, Iowa, 1961-62, Broadlwans Hosp., Des Moines, 1962-65; faculty Coll. Osteo. Medicine and Surgery, Des Moines, 1965-67; asst. prof., chief psychologist Can. Peace Research Inst., Oakville, Ont., 1967-79; dir. Peace Research Lab., St. Louis, 1980—. Served with USAAF, 1944-46; ETO. Mem. Am. Psychol. Assn., Can. Peace Research and Edn. Assn., Internat. Peace Research Assn., Consortium on Peace Research Edn. and Devel. Author: Compassion - Toward a Science of Value, 1972, Governments Under Fire - Civil Conflict and Imperialism, 1977, Compassion Manual, 1976, 79, 80. Editor Jour. Human Relations, 1973, Peace Research Jour., 1978—. Home: 800 Kingsland St Saint Louis MO 63130 Office: Peace Research Lab 6251 San Bonita St Saint Louis MO 63105

ECKHOFF, GILBERT BRUCE, food co. exec.; b. Momence, Ill., Aug. 1, 1938; s. Gilbert Robert and Dorothy Lee E.; B.S., Olivet Coll., 1962; m. Marilyn June, Aug. 27, 1960; children—Christine Lynn, Joy Lynn. With Gen. Foods Corp., 1959-71, mgr. commodity procurement, White Plains, N.Y., 1967-71; v.p. purchasing Henningsen Foods, Inc., Omaha, 1971-74, v.p. ops., 1974—, also dir. Named Man of Yr., Nebr. Poultry Industries, 1979. Mem. Nebr. Poultry Industries (pres. 1978-79, dir.), Nebr. Egg Promotion Bd. (chmn. bd.), Am. Egg Bd. (dir.), Indsl. Mgmt. Assn. (v.p.), Nebr. Poultry Bd. (dir. 1978-79). Republican. Methodist. Clubs: Omaha Press, Happy Hollow Country, Omaha Field, Concord. Office: 14334 Industrial Rd Omaha NE 68144

ECKLOFF, MAURINE CHRISTINE NELSON, educator; b. Upland, Nebr., Apr. 18, 1928; d. Henry Victor and Christine (Raun) Nelson; student Hastings Coll., 1945-47; B.A., U. Denver, 1948; M.S., Kearney State Coll., 1961; Ph.D., U. Nebr., 1974; m. Warren Nathaniel Eckloff, Sept. 3, 1954; children—Nathan, Ann, Ward. Script writer Sta. KNX-CBS, Los Angeles, 1949; tchr. speech and English, Public Schs. Broken Bow (Nebr.), 1949-50; program mgr., broadcaster Sta. WGET, Gettysburg, Pa., 1951-52; traffic mgr. Sta. KBTV, Denver, 1953-54; telecaster Woman's Voice program Sta. KHOL-TV, Kearney, Nebr., 1954-61; prof. speech Kearney State Coll., 1962—, chmn. dept., 1978—, mem. senate, 1977-80. Mem. Bd. Edn. Minden (Nebr.) Public Schs., 1972-77, pres., 1976-77. Kearney State Coll. research grantee, 1972, 73. Mem. Am. Women in Radio and TV (pres. Nebr. chpt. 1958), AAUW (first v.p. Nebr. div. 1962-64), Kearney State Coll. Edn. Assn. (pres. 1966-67), Nebr. Speech Communication Assn. (1st v.p. 1971-73, chmn. research 1976-78), Speech Communication Assn. Am., Internat. Communication Assn., Nebr. State Edn. Assn., Inst. Gen. Semantics, Kearney State Coll. Faculty Women (pres. 1977-78), Delta Kappa Gamma (v.p. 1978-80), Sigma Tau Delta, Gamma Phi Beta. Methodist (sec. TV, Radio and Film Commn., Nebr. conf. 1960-62). Contbr. articles to profl. jours. Home: Rural Route 1 Minden NE 68959 Office: Kearney State College Kearney NE 68847

ECKRICH, DONALD P., food products co. exec.; b. 1925; B.S., U. Mich., 1948; married. With Peter Eckrich & Sons Inc. (acquired by Beatrice Foods Co. 1974), 1948-74, chmn. bd., pres., chief exec. officer, to 1974; pres. meat div. Beatrice Foods Co., Chgo., 1974-75, exec. v.p. splty. meats and wholesale div., 1975-77, vice-chmn. bd. and pres. domestic food ops., 1977-79, pres., chief operating officer, 1977—, also dir. Office: Beatrice Foods Co 2 N La Salle St Chicago IL 60602*

ECKRICH, DONALD WALTER, educator; b. Rochester, N.Y., Oct. 17, 1947; s. Norman James Edward and Elizabeth Magdeline E.; B.A., Alfred U., 1969; M.B.A., C.W. Post Coll. L.I. U., 1971; D.B.A., U. Ky., 1975; m. Georgetta Ann Riege, Aug. 22, 1970; children—Michael James Edward, Sara Beth. Asst. prof. bus. adminstrn. So. Ill. U., Carbondale, 1975-77; asso. prof. mktg. Ill. State U., Normal, 1977—, coordinator grad. programs and student services Coll. Bus., 1979-80; dir. grad. program and research, 1980—; pres. Marfax Research mktg. cons., 1980—; instr. hunter safety Ill. Conservation Dept., 1977—. Served with inf. AUS, 1971. Mem. Am. Mktg. Assn., So. Mktg. Assn., Midwest Bus. Assn. Home: 202 Edwards Dr Normal IL 61761 Office: Grad Programs Coll Bus Ill State U Normal IL 61761

ECKSTEIN, GREGORY THOMAS, physician; b. Chgo., July 7, 1937; s. George Charles and Grace (Blank) E.; student Loyola U., Chgo., 1955-58, M.D., 1962; m. Sandra Swinbanks, Oct. 20, 1962; children—Gregory Thomas, Michael Patrick. Intern, Milw. County Gen. Hosp., 1962-63; resident in internal medicine Henry Ford Hosp., Detroit, 1965-68; practice medicine specializing in internal medicine, McHenry, Ill., 1968—; mem. staff McHenry Hosp., chmn. dept. internal medicine, 1980—; clin. asst. Stritch Sch. Medicine, Loyola U., 1970-74; med. dir. McHenry-Lake County Emergency Med. Services Program, 1974-75. Pres. Montini Sch. Bd., 1972-74; pres. parish council St. Patrick's Roman Cath. Ch., 1976-78. Served to capt. M.C., AUS, 1963-65. Decorated Army Commendation medal. Diplomate Nat. Bd. Med. Examiners, Am. Bd. Internal Medicine. Mem. AMA, Ill., No. Ill., McHenry County med. socs. Home: 6214 Katmai Trail McHenry IL 60050 Office: 4306-A Crystal Lake Rd McHenry IL 60050

ECORD, CHARLES ALLEN, mfg. co. exec.; b. Topeka, Jan. 31, 1950; s. Elwood Morris and Patricia Jean (Miller) E.; B.B.A., Wichita State U., 1972; m. Carol Anne Sims, May 22, 1971; children—Kristin Kay, Clinton S. With Cessna Aircraft Co., Wichita, 1973-81, buyer supr. Pawnee div., 1976-77, procurement mgr. supply div., 1977-81; procurement mgr. Boeing Mil. Aircraft Co., 1981—. Chpt. Dad, Order Demolay, 1971-72; active Big Brothers Wichita, 1976—. Cert. purchasing mgr. Mem. Nat. Assn. Purchasing Mgrs. Methodist. Club: Masons. Home: 3826 E Funston St Wichita KS 67218 Office: 901 George Washington Blvd Wichita KS 67218

EDDY, WILLIAM BAHRET, educator; s. Luther M. and Margaret (Womer) E.; B.S., Kans. State U., 1955, M.S., 1957; Ph.D. in Indsl. Psychology, Mich. State U., 1963. Research asso. Kansas City (Mo.) Mental Health Found. and Inst. for Community Studies, 1962-65; dir. Center for Mgmt. Devel., U. Mo., Kansas City, 1966-70, dir. public adminstrn., 1972-77, Kemper prof. adminstrn. Sch. Adminstrn., 1973—; asso. dir. Fed. Exec. Inst., Charlottesville, Va., 1971-72. Accredited group trainer and orgn. devel. specialist Internat. Assn. Applied Social Scientists; lic. organizational psychologist. Mem. Am. Psychol. Assn., Am. Soc. Public Adminstrn., Nat. Tng. Labs. Inst. Applied Behavioral Sci. Author: (with others) Work Inhibition and Rehabilitation, 1968; (with J.V. Spotts) Behavioral Science Approaches to Employee Relations, 1970; editor: (with R.T. Golembiewski) Organization Development in Public Administration: Public Sector Applications of OD Technology, 1978, Organization Development in Public Administration: Organization Properties and Public Sector Features, 1978; (with W. Burke) Behavioral Science and the Manager's Role, 1980; co-editor, mng. editor jour. Adminstrn. and Soc., 1976-80; editorial bd. Public Administration and Policy Series; contbr. numerous articles on behavioral sci. to profl. jours. Office: Sch Adminstrn U Mo Kansas City MO 64110

EDELSBERG, CHARLES MARC, ednl. adminstr.; b. Cleve., Jan. 21, 1950; s. Julius and Helen (Goldstein) E.; B.A. summa cum laude with honors, Ohio State U., 1972, Ph.D., 1980; M.A.T., Brown U., 1975; m. Leslie F. Grand, Mar. 31, 1974. Humanities tchr., curriculum developer St. Xavier Acad., Providence, 1975-77; cons. R.I. U. Curriculum Research and Devel. Center, Providence, 1976-77; grad. fellow, teaching asst. Ohio State U., Columbus, 1977-80; project dir. Franklin County Dept. Edn., Basic Skills Improvement Program, Columbus, 1980—; cons. Advance man for U.S. Senator Howard M. Metzenbaum of Ohio, 1974. Flesher fellow, 1979. Mem. Nat. Council Tchrs. English, Assn. Supervision and Curriculum Devel., Conf. Lang. Attitudes and Composition, Am. Ednl. Studies Assn., Central Ohio Assn. for Gifted Children, Phi Beta Kappa, Phi Kappa Phi. Home: 372 E Tulane St Columbus OH 43202 Office: 80 E Fulton St Columbus OH 43215

EDELSON, DAVID, state ofcl.; b. N.Y.C., Jan. 28, 1919; s. Max and Freida (Epstein) E.; B.A., N.Y. U., 1948; M.S.W., Columbia U., 1950; M.H.A., Northwestern U., 1958; m. Miriam Osnovitz, Apr. 3, 1943; children—Richard, Jeffrey. Dir., Nat. Travelers Aid Assn., Belleville, Ill., 1952-54; dir. social service Evansville (Ind.) State Hosp., 1954-56; psychiat. social work supr. Dixon (Ill.) State Sch., 1956-57; asst. supt., adminstr. East Moline (Ill.) State Hosp., 1958-62; supt. Dixon Developmental Center, 1962-78; program policy adv. Ill. Dept. Mental Health and Developmental Disabilities, 1978—; mem. Gov.'s Adv. Council on Mental Retardation, 1963. Licensed nursing home adminstr., Ill. Fellow Am. Assn. Mental Deficiency; mem. Nat. Assn. Pub. Residential Facilities, Nat. Assn. Supts. Pub. Residential Facilities for Mental Retardation (dir. 1976—), Ill. Council for Exceptional Children, Lee County Mental Health Assn., Dixon C. of C., Ill. Assn. for Mentally Retarded (Leadership award 1968). Office: Rural Route 1 Dixon IL 61021

EDELSTEIN, WARREN STANLEY, educator; b. Balt., June 11, 1937; s. Solomon and Cecile (Klaw) E.; B.A., Lehigh U., 1958; postgrad. Johns Hopkins U., 1958-59; M.A., Duke U., 1961; Ph.D., Brown U., 1964; m. Rosalie Toby Kuperman, June 27, 1965; 1 dau., Francesca. Asst. prof. math Ill. Inst. Tech., 1965-71, asso. prof., 1971-80, prof., 1980—. Postdoctoral fellow Johns Hopkins U., 1964-65; grantee Office Naval Research, NSF, Argonne Nat. Lab. Mem. Soc. Indsl. and Applied Math., Soc. Engring. Sci., Am. Acad. Mechanics. Contbr. articles to profl. jours. Home: 6218 N Campbell St Chicago IL 60659 Office: Dept Math Ill Inst Technology Chicago IL 60616

EDGAR, IRVING I., psychiatrist; b. Roswadow, Poland, July 4, 1902; s. Asher Laser and Bella Gitel (Schlussel) Itzkowitz; brought to U.S., 1910, naturalized, 1916; B.A., Wayne State U., 1925, B.M., 1926, M.D., 1927, M.A., 1933; m. Gertrude Forman, Nov. 6, 1971; children—David L., Richard S., Joyce Vronsky. Intern Grace Hosp., Detroit, 1926-27; practice medicine specializing in psychiatry, Detroit, 1927—; med. dir. Island View Adolescent Center, Detroit, 1971-74; cons. Grace, Sinai, Jennings Meml., Crittenton hosps. (all Detroit). Diplomate Am. Bd. Psychiatry and Neurology. Fellow A.C.P., Am. Psychiat. Assn.; mem. Jewish Hist. Soc. Mich. (pres. 1964-73), Am. Jewish Hist. Soc. (exec. council 1975—). Author: Shakespeare, Medicine and Psychiatry, 1970; Essays in English Literature and History, 1971; Origins of the Healing Art, 1978; Meditations in an Anatomy Laboratory and Other Poems, 1979. Editor Mich. Jewish History mag., 1973-79. Home: 29233 Wellington Ct Apt 61 Southfield MI 48076 Office: 1036 David Whitney Bldg Detroit MI 48226

EDGAR, JAMES ROBERT, sec. state Ill.; b. Vinita, Okla., July 22, 1946; s. Cecil E. and Elizabeth M. (Moore) E.; B.S., Eastern Ill. U., 1968; postgrad. U. Ill., 1968-69; m. Brenda M. Smith, 1967; children—James Bradley, Elizabeth Ann. Legis. intern with pres. pro tem Ill. Senate, 1968; key asst. to speaker Ill. Ho. of Reps., 1972-74; aide to pres. Ill. Senate, 1974; aide to Ill. Ho. Majority, 1976, mem. Ho., 1976-79; aide to gov. Ill., 1979-80; sec. of state Ill., 1980—. Republican precinct committeeman; treas. Coles County Rep. Com., 1974; mem. Ill. Ho. Rep. Campaign Com.; pres. Coles County Hist. Soc., 1976-79; dir. state services Nat. Conf. State Legislatures, 1975-76. Baptist. Office: State Capitol Room 213 Springfield IL 62706

EDGAR, NEAL LOWNDES, librarian; b. N.Y.C., June 21, 1927; s. William John Brown and Margaret Baker (Thomas) E.; A.B. (Converse scholar 1947-48), Trinity Coll., Hartford, Conn., 1950; M.A., SUNY, Albany, 1958, M.S. in L.S., 1958; A.M.L.S. (Carnegie scholar 1963-64), U. Mich., 1964, Ph.D., 1965; m. Susanna Jane Capper, May 7, 1966. Acquisitions librarian SUNY, Albany, 1958-61; residence halls librarian U. Mich., Ann Arbor, 1961-65; serials cataloger Library of Congress, 1965-66; acquisitions librarian Kent (Ohio) State U. Library, 1967, serials librarian, 1968-77, research librarian, 1977-79, asso. curator spl. collections, 1979—, also mem. part-time faculty Sch. Library Sci. Grantee Kent State U., 1975—. Mem. AAUP, ALA, No. Ohio Tech. Services Librarians. Author: A History and Bibliography of American Periodicals, 1810-1820, 1975; editorial bd. The Serials Librarian, Title Varies; contbr. articles and revs. in profl. jours. Home: 1378 Athena Dr Kent OH 44240 Office: Kent State Univ Libraries Kent OH 44242

EDGELL, GEORGE PAUL, lawyer; b. Dallas, Mar. 9, 1937; s. George Paul and Sarah Elizabeth (McDonald) E.; B.S. in Aero. Engring., U. Ill., 1960; J.D., Georgetown U., 1967; m. Karin Jane Williams; 1 son, Scott Rickard. Admitted to Va. bar, 1967, D.C. bar, 1968, Ill. bar, 1980; patent examiner U.S. Patent Office, Washington, 1963-65; partner firm Schuyler, Birch, McKie & Beckett, Washington, 1969-80, asso., 1965-69; group patent counsel Gould Inc., Rolling Meadows, Ill., 1980—. Vol. tutor Hopkins Ho., 1968-69; officer St. Stephen's Dads' Club, 1975-77. Served with USMC, 1960-63. Mem. Am., D.C., Ill., Va. bar assns., Am. Patent Law Assn., Licensing Execs. Soc. Republican. Presbyterian. Clubs: Army Navy Country, Meadow. Home: 5403 Chateau Dr Rolling Meadows IL 60008 Office: 10 Gould Center Rolling Meadows IL 60008

EDGERLEY, EDWARD, JR., cons. engr.; b. Lancaster, Pa., Mar. 8, 1931; s. Edward and Mary (McNeal) E.; student Franklin and Marshall Coll., 1949; B.S., Pa. State U., 1952; S.M., Mass. Inst. Tech., 1954; Ph.D., U. Calif. at Berkeley, 1968; m. Mary Replogle, Nov. 6, 1954; children—Mark Edward, Dale Lee, Craig Alan, Darla Jean.

Teaching asst. Mass. Inst. Tech., 1952-54; mem. faculty Washington U., St. Louis, 1957-73, asso. prof. civil and environmental engring., 1962-73, asso. dean engring., 1968-69, program chmn. environmental engring., 1969-73. Exec. v.p. Ryckman Edgerley Tomlinson & Assos., cons. engrs., St. Louis, 1957-75, pres., 1975-78; pres. Environ. and Energy Cons. Inc., St. Louis, 1979—; dir. Group Health Plan of Greater of St. Louis, 1979—. Chmn. pack com. Cub Scouts Am., 1968-69, 75-79; troop chmn. Boy Scouts Am., 1969-74. Bd. dirs. St. Louis Alliance for Regional Community Health, 1970-74. Served as officer USAF, 1954-57. Recipient Publ. award, Resources div. Am. Water Works Assn., 1962. Mem. Am. Soc. C.E., Greater St. Louis Air Pollution Assn. (pres. 1969), Am. Chem. Soc. Rotarian. Club: Mass. Inst. Tech. (pres. 1968-69) (St. Louis). Presbyn. (elder). Contbr. sci. articles to jours. Home: 582 Brookhaven Ct Kirkwood MO 63122 Office: 2350 7th Blvd Saint Louis MO 63104

EDGERTON, F(REDRICK) VAN, coll. ofcl.; b. Allegan, Mich., Nov. 27, 1947; s. Fredrick G. and Gertrude (VandeBunte) E.; B.A., Alma Coll., 1974; postgrad. Central Mich. U., 1978—; m. Patricia Louise Dehne, Sept. 8, 1973. Asst dir. placement Alma (Mich.) Coll., 1975, coordinator practicums, 1975—, dir. placement, 1977—. Bd. dirs. Alma Highland Festival and Games, 1979—, pres., 1981-82; v.p. bd. dirs. Mid-Mich. Community Action Council, 1980—. Served with AUS, 1969-72. Decorated Bronze Star. Mem. Mich. Coll. and Univ. Placement Assn. (pres. 1980-81), Midwest Coll. Placement Assn., Mich. Acad. Sci., Arts and Letters. Presbyterian. Club: Kiwanis (1st v.p., dir.). Home: 229 Purdy Dr Alma MI 48801 Office: Alma Coll Alma MI 48801

EDGERTON, WILLIAM BENBOW, educator; b. Winston-Salem, N.C., Mar. 11, 1914; s. Paul Clifton and Annie Maud (Benbow) E.; B.A., Guilford Coll., 1934; M.A., Haverford Coll., 1935; Ph.D., Columbia U., 1954; m. Jewell Mock Conrad, June 6, 1935; children—Susan, David. Tchr. French, German, Spanish, English, secondary schs. in U.S. and France, 1935-39; faculty French and Spanish, Guilford Coll., 1939-47; faculty Russian lit. Pa. State U., University Park, 1950-56, U. Mich., Ann Arbor, 1954-55, Columbia U., N.Y.C., 1956-58; prof. Slavic langs. and lits. Ind. U., Bloomington, 1958—, chmn. Slavic dept., 1958-65, 69-73, acting dir. Russian and East European Inst., 1981—; cons. Ford Found., 1952-61; mem. joint com. on Slavic studies Am. Council Learned Socs., 1951-62, chmn., 1958-61. Bd. dirs. Am. Friends Service Com., 1956-59; trustee Guilford Coll., 1969—; mem. vis. com. for Slavic studies Harvard U., 1967-77; mem. adv. com. Nat. Humanities Center, 1978—. Recipient Josef Dobrovsky medal, Czechoslovak Acad. Sci., 1968; Am. Council Learned Socs. fellow, 1948-50; Guggenheim fellow, 1963-64. Mem. MLA (exec. council 1962-65, Am. Assn. for Advancement Slavic Studies (pres. 1961), Internat. Comparative Lit. Assn. Democrat. Quaker. Gen. editor: Columbia Dictionary of Modern European Literature, 1980; translator, editor: Satirical Stories of Nikolai Leskov, 1969; editor Ind. Slavic Studies, III, 1963, IV, 1967; editor: Am. Contributions to the Fifth Internat. Congress of Slavists, 1963; contbr. articles to profl. jours. Home: 1801 E Maxwell Ln Bloomington IN 47401 Office: Ballantine 502 Ind U Bloomington IN 47405

EDGERTON, WINFIELD DOW, gynecologist; b. Caruthersville, Mo., Nov. 8, 1924; s. Winfield Dow and Anna Kathryn (Hale) E.; student Central Coll., Fayette, Mo., 1942-44; M.D., Washington U., St. Louis, 1947; m. Rose Marie Cahill, June 24, 1945; 1 son, Winfield Dow. Intern, St. Luke's Hosp., St. Louis, 1947-48; resident Chgo. Lying-In Hosp., 1948-49, Free Hosp. for Women, Brookline, Mass., 1951, U.S. Naval Hosp., Chelsea, Mass., 1951-53; practice medicine specializing in obstetrics and gynecology, Davenport, Iowa, 1955—; mem. staff St. Luke's Hosp., also dir. obstetrics and gynecology; clin. asst. prof. obstetrics and gynecology U. Iowa Coll. Medicine, 1971-78, clin. asso. prof., 1979—. Served to lt., M.C., USN, 1949-55. Fellow Am. Coll. Obstetricians and Gynecologists (past chmn. Iowa sect.), Royal Soc. Medicine; mem. Central Assn. Obstetricians and Gynecologists, Am. Fertility Soc., Am. Assn. Gynecologic Laparoscopists (past trustee), Gynecologic Laser Soc., AMA, Iowa, Scott County (past pres.) med. socs. Republican. Congregationalist. Club: Davenport. Contbr. articles to med. jours. and texts. Home: 4 Lombard Ct Davenport IA 52803 Office: 121 W Locust St Davenport IA 52803

EDISON, ROBERT GAY, chem. products co. exec.; b. Chgo., June 14, 1928; s. Sylvan M. and Anita Gay (Gore) E.; B.S., Northwestern U., 1949; m. Joyce Lerner, Nov. 27, 1953; children—Pamela, Marcey, Steven. Vice pres. S.M. Edison Chem. Co., Chgo., 1949-52, exec. v.p., 1954-60; founder, pres. The Hosiery Mate Co., Chgo., 1960—, also dir.; dir. Kleen Chem. Mfg. Co., Hosiery Mate Co. Can. Ltd. Served with USN, 1952-54. Mem. Soc. Cosmetic Chemists. Home: 3032 University Ave Highland Park IL 60035 Office: 2501 N Sheffield Ave Chicago IL 60614

EDKINS, FRANK ROBERT, mfg. co. exec.; b. London, May 18, 1924; came to U.S., 1953, naturalized, 1958; m. Robert Alfred and Louisa Emily (Watson) E.; student Brit. Inst. Engring. Tech., 1946-48; m. Gertrue Ellen Newman, July 24, 1948; children—Robert, David, Timothy. Gen. mgr. Robert A. Main & Sons, Chgo., 1967-70; plant supr. Bison Gear and Engring., Downers Grove, Ill., 1970-74; with Nat. Electronics, La Fox, Ill., 1974—, now mfg. and production control mgr. Served with RAF, 1943-47. Mem. Ch. of Eng. Club: Mason. Home: 20 E Larkspur Ln Bristol IL 60512

EDMINSTER, RALPH RAY, pathologist; b. Muncie, Ind., Nov. 8, 1935; s. Leonard Ralph and Ruby Irene (Drumm) E.; B.A., DePauw U., 1958; M.D., Washington U., St. Louis, 1962; m. Nancy Susan Jameson, June 12, 1960; children—Susan Beth, Jean Marie, Ann Louise. Intern, Butterworth Hosp., Grand Rapids, Mich., 1962-63, resident in pathology, 1963-67; asso. pathologist, dermatopathologist E.W. Sparrow Hosp., Lansing, Mich., 1967—; asso. clin. prof. pathology Mich. State U. Coll. Human Medicine. Diplomate Am. Bd. Dermatology, Am. Bd. Pathology. Fellow Coll. Am. Pathologists, Am. Soc. Clin. Pathologists; mem. AMA, Phi Beta Kappa. Republican. Office: Sparrow Hosp Box 30480 Lansing MI 48909

EDMOND, MARY ANN, educator; b. Newport, Tenn., June 14, 1937; d. Percival Wade and Nannie Mae (Miller) Dykes; B.S., Knoxville Coll., 1958; M.A., Western Mich. U., 1971; postgrad. Wayne State U., 1979-81; m. Leroy Roscoe Edmond; children—Chana' Yvette, Deidra Rachell, Ivan Alexander Edmond. Vocal tchr. Newport, 1956-57; Rosedale, Miss., 1958-59, 60-61, Rogersville, Tenn., 1959-60; tchr., Public Schs., Grand Rapids, Mich., 1961-70, asst. prin., 1970-73, dir. mulicultural edn., 1973-80, supr. social studies, multicultural edn., 1980-81. Trustee, St. Luke Ch., 1978-81, minister music, 1962—, recipient Black Achievement award, 1979; vol. United Way, 1969-80. Mem. Negro Bus. and Profl. Women (woman of yr. 1969), Mich. Assn. Supervision and Curriculum Devel., Assn. Supervision and Curriculum Devel., Mich. Council Social Studies, Mich. Black Hist. Sites Ass., Grand Rapids Hist. Soc., NAACP, Alpha Kappa Alpha. Producer, scriptor, host Underground Railroad in Michigan, 8 part cable TV and video tape series, 1980. Home: 1360 Forrester St SE Grand Rapids MI 49508 Office: 143 Bostwick St NE Grand Rapids MI 49502

EDMONDSON, KEITH HENRY, pharm.-chem. co. exec.; b. Wheaton, Ill., May 16, 1924; s. Edwin Ray and Mildred Lorraine (Henry) E.; B.S. in Chem. Engring., Purdue U., 1948, M.S. in Chem. Engring., 1949; m. Peggy Eleanor Wood, Sept. 22, 1945; children—Robert Earl, Kris E., John David, Keith Clark. With Upjohn Co., Kalamazoo, 1949-62, 67—, dir. chem. prodn., 1962, v.p., gen. mgr. chem. div., 1967—; v.p., then exec. v.p. Upjohn Internat., Kalamazoo, 1962-67. Trustee Kalamazoo Bd. Edn., from 1958, also v.p., then pres., until 1962; mem. adminstrv. bd. First United Methodist Ch., Kalamazoo. Served to 1st lt. USAAF, 1942-45. Decorated D.F.C. with oak leaf cluster, Air medal with 6 oak leaf clusters. Mem. Am. Inst. Chem. Engrs., Am. Chem. Soc., Kalamazoo Mgmt. Assn. (pres. 1957), Kalamazoo C. of C. (dir. 1971-74), Sigma Xi, Tau Beta Pi, Phi Lambda Upsilon. Republican. Office: 7000 Portage Rd Kalamazoo MI 49001

EDMUNDS, PALMER DANIEL, lawyer, educator; b. Terre Haute, Ill., Oct. 29, 1890; s. Amos and Mary Ann (Campbell) E.; A.B., Knox Coll., 1912, LL.D., 1945; LL.B., Harvard U., 1915; LL.D., John Marshall Law Sch., 1973, Piedmont Coll., 1975; m. Margaret Burton, June 29, 1932 (dec. 1964); m. 2d, Sarah Shepard Brown, 1970. Admitted to Ill. bar, 1915, since practiced in Chgo.; dir., counsel Ill. Service Recognition Bd., 1922-25; mem. firm Dodd, Matheny & Edmunds, 1925-29; commr. Supreme Ct. Ill., 1929-32; mem. firm Dodd & Edmunds, Chgo., 1932-58; lectr. conflict of laws and Ill. practice John Marshall Law Sch., Chgo., 1926-58, prof. law, 1958—, lectr. fed. practice, 1938-58, dir. Lawyers Inst.; vis. prof. law Knox Coll., 1944-57; compliance commr. WPB and Civilian Prodn. Adminstrn., 1944-47; hearing commr. NPA, 1951-53. Charter mem. World Peace Through Law Center. Trustee John Marshall Law Sch. First lt. A.E.F., 1917-19; capt. O.R.C. Past comdr. Black Hawk Post, Am. Legion, Chgo., past historian Dept. of Ill. Mem. Am. Polit. Sci. Assn., Am. Acad. Polit. and Social Sci., Fgn. Policy Assn., Am., Ill., Chgo., Internat. bar assns., India Soc., Internat. Law, Ill. Hist. Soc., S.A.R., Nat. Sojourners, Am. Bantam Assn., Sebright Club Am., 40 and 8, Soc. of 28th Div., Com. for Continuation Congl. Christian Chs. U.S., Phi Gamma Delta, Delta Sigma Rho. Democrat. Conglist. Mason, Elk. Club: Harvard (Chgo.). Author: (with W. F. Dodd) Illinois Appellate Procedure, 1929; Edmunds Common Law Forms, 1931; Illinois Civil Practice Forms, 1923; Edmunds Federal Rules of Civil Procedure, 1938; Cyclopedia of Federal Procedure Forms, 1939; Law and Civilization, 1959; co-author Encyclopedia of Federal Procedure, 2d edit., 1944; Edmunds Conflict of Laws, 1948. Editor, compiler: Jones Illinois Statutes Annotated, vols. 18-22, 24. Home and Office: Gilman IL 60938

EDWARDS, EDGAR EVERETT, JR., ins. co. exec.; b. Norfolk, Va., June 2, 1937; s. Edgar Everett and Ernestine Amanda (King) E.; B.B.A. in Mgmt. and Econs., William and Mary Coll., 1959; m. Patricia Lee Moore, June 7, 1958; children—Steve, Scott, Stacey. Regional v.p. Conn. Gen. Life Ins. Co., Hartford, 1959-79; sr. v.p. marketing Blue Cross & Blue Shield United Wis., Milw., 1979—; gen. mgr. Health Ins. Corp., 1979—. Served with Army Nat. Guard, 1956-64. Mem. Am. Marketing Assn., Sales and Marketing Execs. Clubs: Milwaukee Athletic; Kiwanis. Home: N 7 W 29595 Thames Ct Waukesha WI 53186 Office: 401 W Michigan St Milwaukee WI 53201

EDWARDS, EUGENE O'BRIEN, electronics mfg. co. exec.; b. Bentonville, Ark., Apr. 21, 1925; s. Oscar and Elsie Marie (Pierce) E.; student Draughons Sch. Bus., 1946, Syracuse U., 1966-67; m. Perneiche Alice Hobbs, Apr. 18, 1946; children—William O., Richard L., Jerry O., Stephen L. Chief engr. KBIX and KBIX-FM Radio, Muskogee, Okla., 1947-54; engring. supr. Tulsa Broadcasting Co., Muskogee, 1954-57; with Gates div. Harris Intertype Corp., Quincy, Ill., 1957—, v.p. sales, 1971-77, v.p. mktg., 1977—. Served with USMCR, 1942-45. Mem. Nat. Assn. Broadcasters (asso.), Nat. Assn. Ednl. Broadcasters (asso.), Nat. Assn. FM Broadcasters (asso.), Sales and Mktg. Execs. Club Quincy (pres. 1966), Sales and Mktg. Execs. Internat., Armed Forces Communications and Electronics Assn., Am. Mgmt. Assn., Internat. Christian Broadcasters. Republican. Baptist. Clubs: Quincy Country, Bella Vista Country, Sheridan Swim, Quincy Rotary. Home: 2310 N Willmar St Quincy IL 62301 Office: 30th and Wisman Ln Quincy IL 62301

EDWARDS, GEORGE, judge; b. Dallas, Aug. 6, 1914; s. George Clifton and Octavia (Nichols) E.; B.A., So. Meth., U., 1933; M.A., Harvard, 1934; J.D., Detroit Coll. Law, 1949; m. Margaret McConnell, Apr. 10, 1939; children—George Clifton III, James McConnell. Coll. sec. League Indsl. Democracy, 1934-35; prodn. worker Kelsey Hayes Wheel Co., 1936; rep. UAW-CIO, 1937, dir. welfare dept., 1938-39; dir., sec. Detroit Housing Commn., 1940-41; mem. Detroit Common Council, 1941-49, pres., 1945-49; admitted to Mich. bar, 1944; with firm Edwards & Bohn, Detroit, 1946-50, Rothe, Marston, Edwards and Bohn, 1950-51; probate judge charge Wayne County Juvenile Ct., 1951-54; judge 3d Jud. Circuit, Wayne County, 1954-56; justice Supreme Ct. Mich., 1956-62; commr. of police City Detroit, 1962-63; judge U.S. Ct. Appeals, 6th circuit, 1963—, chief judge, 1979—. Chmn. com. adminstrn. criminal laws Jud. Conf. U.S., 1966-70; mem. Nat. Com. Reform of Fed. Criminal Laws, 1967-71. Chmn. S.E. Mich. Cancer Crusade, 1950-51; chmn. 13th Congressional Dist. Democratic party Wayne County, 1950-51. Served from pvt. to lt., inf. AUS, 1943-46. Recipient award for community work for social progress Workmen's Circle, 1949; award for community work for civil rights St. Cyprian's Episcopal Ch., 1950; Americanism award Jewish War Vets., 1953; award for outstanding achievement juvenile rehab. VFW, 1953; St. Peter's medal for outstanding service to youth St. Peter's Episcopal Ch., Detroit, 1956; August Vollmer award Am. Soc. Criminology, 1966; Judiciary award Assn. Fed. Investigators, 1971. Mem. VFW, Am. Legion, Am., Mich., Detroit bar assns., Nat. Council Judges, Nat. Council on Crime and Delinquency, Inst. Jud. Adminstrn., Phi Beta Kappa, Kappa Sigma. Democrat. Episcopalian. Mason. Author: The Police on the Urban Frontier, 1968; (with others) The Law of Criminal Correction, 1963; Pioneer-at-Law, 1974; also articles on crime and delinquency. Home: 4057 Egbert Cincinnati OH 45220 Office: US Courthouse Cincinnati OH 45202

EDWARDS, GERALD FREDRICK, ednl. adminstr.; b. Pardeeville, Wis., Dec. 26, 1928; s. Fred Eugene and Mae Estelle (Wilson) E.; B.S., U. Wis., LaCrosse, 1955, M.S., Madison, 1957; Ed.S., U. Iowa, 1976; m. Carol S. Judd, July 14, 1956; children—John Douglas, Elizabeth Jean, David Judd. Tchr., Public Schs. Melrose (Wis.), 1950-52, St. Paul, 1955-56, Marshfield (Wis.), 1957-59; asst. prof. edn., dir. sch. camping Antioch Coll., Yellow Springs, Ohio, 1959-65; elem. supr. Public Schs. Edenton (Wis.), 1965-68; curriculum dir., asst. supt. Public Schs. Marion (Iowa), 1968-77; dist. adminstr. Public Schs. Marion (Wis.), 1977—; cons. outdoor edn. Dist. chmn., adviser scoutmaster, post adv. Boy Scouts Am., 1945—; dir. Little League Baseball, 1970-75. Served with AUS, 1946-47. Mem. Assn. Supervision and Curriculum Devel., Am. Assn. Sch. Adminstrs., Nat. Soc. Study Edn., Wis. Assn. Sch. Dist. Adminstrs. Methodist. Clubs: Rotary, Masons. Author: Teacher's Guide to School Camping, 1960; The Environment of Man, 1972; Brain Teasers, 1974. Home: 506 Sherman St Marion WI 54950 Office: 1001 N Main St Marion WI 54950

EDWARDS, HENRY A., JR., accountant; b. Aurora, Mo., June 4, 1941; s. Henry A. and Patsy H. (Hudson) E.; B.S. in B.A., U. Mo., 1973; m. Joyce R. Reed, Apr. 4, 1964; children—Bryan Christopher, Bradley Clinton. Field auditor Philco Ford, Louisville, 1965-67; field auditor Borg Warner, St. Louis, 1967; salesman Penn Mut., St. Louis, 1967-71; customer service mgr. Beneficial Mgmt. Corp., St. Louis, 1971-73; systems accountant Farmers Home Adminstrn., St. Louis, 1974-75, supervisory accountant, Quality Control br., 1975-79, Gen. Ledger br., 1979, dep. dir. Ops. div., 1980—. Vol. cons. on cash flow, acctg., audit requirements, United Ch. of Christ, St. Louis, 1978-81; baseball coach, mgr. Y-Winner Program, St. Charles Jr. Baseball Assn., 1979-81. Served with U.S. Army, 1963-65. Recipient Cert. of Merit, Farmers Home Adminstrn., 1976. Mem. Assn. Govtl. Accountants. Home: 2904 Park Ave Saint Charles MO 63301 Office: 1520 Market St Saint Louis MO 63103

EDWARDS, HOMER FLOYD, JR., educator; b. Forsyth, Ga., June 25, 1918; s. Homer Floyd and Mary Beulah (Jay) E.; B.A., Emory U., 1947, M.A., 1948, Ph.D., 1964; m. Marjorie H. Duncan, Apr. 29, 1967; one son, Christopher B. Instr. classics Emory U., Atlanta, 1954-55, instr. French and German, Emory-at-Oxford, 1955-57; asst. prof. humanities Morehouse Coll., Atlanta, 1959-63, Wayne State U., Detroit, 1963-65; faculty, head dept. theoretical studies Cranbrook Acad. Art, Bloomfield Hills, Mich., 1967-75; asso. prof. humanities Wayne State U., 1965—, chmn. dept. humanities, 1964-75; adj. prof. history U. Windsor (Ont., Can.), 1977-79; music critic Detroit Monitor, 1968—; dir. Passau-Augsburg program Mich. Consortium Medieval and Early Modern Studies, Detroit, 1977—; asso. fellow U. Mich., 1978—. Served with AUS, 1943-45. Univ. fellow Emory U., 1958-59. Mem. AAUP, Am. Musicol. Soc., Am., Brit. socs. aesthetics, Assn. Gen. Studies, Coll. Art Assn., Mind Assn. (Eng.), Modern Lang. Assn., Am. Hist. Assn., Hist. Assn. (Eng.), Mich. Acad., Nat. Assn. Humanities Edn. Episcopalian. Clubs: Scarab; Faculty of Wayne State U. Home: 201 E Kirby St Apt 1204 Detroit MI 48202

EDWARDS, IAN KEITH, obstetrician, gynecologist, clin. dir.; b. Spartanburg, S.C., Mar. 2, 1926; s. James Smiley and Georgina (Waters) E.; A.B., Duke U., 1949, M.D., 1953; m. Glenda Melissa Joselyn, Dec. 27, 1968; children—Darien, Jennifer, Carol, Terry. Spl. study pediatrics St. Bartholomew's Hosp., London, 1952; resident in obstetrics and gynecology Grady Meml. Hosp., Atlanta, 1955-58; chief obstetrics and gynecology Valley Forge (Pa.) Army Hosp., 1958-61; practice medicine specializing in ob-gyn, Olney, Ill., 1969—; partner Trover Clinic, Madisonville, Ky., 1961-68, Weber Med. Clinic, Olney, 1969—, dir. dept. ob-gyn, 1970-74, 78—, mem. exec. steering com., 1969-72, 78—; chief of staff Hopkins County (Ky.) Hosp., 1967-68, Richland Meml. Hosp., Olney, 1974-76; clin. instr. ob-gyn U. Ky. Med. Center, Lexington, 1965-68; cons. Childbirth Edn. League. Mem. Found. com. Olney Central Coll. Served to capt. M.C., U.S. Army, 1954-55; Korea. Diplomate Am. Bd. Ob-Gyn. Fellow Am. Coll. Obstetricians and Gynecologists; mem. Phila. Obstet. Soc., Am. Legion, VFW, AMA, Ill., Hopkins County (pres. 1968), Richland (pres. 1974-76) med. socs., Ill. Soc. Ob-Gyn. Democrat. Methodist. Contbr. articles to med. jours. Clubs: Lions, Kiwanis. Office: Weber Med Clinic 1200 N East St Olney IL 62450

EDWARDS, JAMES LYNN, educator; b. Yates Center, Kans., Jan. 1, 1952; s. Raymond P. and Evelyn I. (Patterson) E.; A.S., Butler County Community Coll., 1971; B.S.E., Emporia State U., 1973, M.S., 1979; m. Nioma R. Lemke, Aug. 4, 1973; 1 dau., Jessica Ann. Tchr. distributive edn. Shawnee Mission (Kans.) West High Sch., 1973-74, Wichita Heights (Kans.) High Sch., 1976-78; asst. mgr. S.S. Kresge, Joplin, Mo., 1974-75, K-Mart South County, St. Louis, 1975-76; instr. mktg. and distributive edn. Butler County Community Coll., El Dorado, Kans., 1978—; salesman Am. Amicable Life Ins. Co., 1980—. Mem. Am. Vocat. Assn., NEA, Distributive Edn. Clubs Am., Kans. Bus. Occupations Assn. (pres. 1981-82), Kans. Vocat. Assn., El Dorado Jaycees, Delta Pi Epsilon. Mem. Christian Ch. (Disciples of Christ). Home: 304 N Washington St El Dorado KS 67042 Office: Butler County Community College Haverhil and Towanda Ave El Dorado KS 67042

EDWARDS, JOHN REES, psychologist; b. Youngstown, Ohio, June 13, 1942; s. Donald Rees and Mary Marcella (Newman) E.; B.A., Athenaeum of Ohio, Cin., 1964, M.A., 1967; Ph.D., Kent State U., 1976. Ordained priest Roman Catholic Ch., 1968; asso. pastor St. John's Roman Catholic Ch., Canton, Ohio, 1968-72; dir. counseling Rio Grande (Ohio) Coll., 1976-77; instr. U. S.C., Beaufort, 1977-78; sch. psychologist Beaufort County (S.C.) Schs., 1977-78; mental health counselor Child and Adult Mental Health Center, Youngstown, 1978—; bd. govs. Pastoral Counseling Service of the Canton Council Chs., 1970-72. Bd. dirs. Canton Jaycees, 1971-72; mem. Fair Employment Practices Commn., Canton, 1970-72. Recipient cert. of merit Am. Cancer Soc., 1980, 81. Mem. Am. Psychol. Assn., Am. Personnel and Guidance Assn., Assn. Religious and Value Issues in Counseling. Home: 4689 Woodhurst Dr Apt 8 Youngstown OH 44515 Office: 1001 Covington St Youngstown OH 44510

EDWARDS, MARGENE MAE, univ. records mgr.; b. Highland, Ill., June 3, 1931; d. Freemon H. and Cornelia (Schoeck) Schmidt; student So. Ill. U., 1968-70; m. Robert Miles Edwards, Jan. 22, 1949; children—Robert Miles, Debra, Thomas, Demaris. Office mgr. Madison Service Co., Marine and Edwardsville, Ill., 1961-72; records mgr., micrographics So. Ill. U., Edwardsville, 1972—; cons. area records and micrographic services. Mem. Assn. Records Mgrs. and Adminstrs., Nat. Micrographics Assn. (treas. St. Louis chpt.). Home: Route 1 Box 192 Marine IL 62061 Office: So Ill U Box 11 Edwardsville IL 62026

EDWARDS, OTIS CARL, JR., sem. dean; b. Bienville, La., June 15, 1928; s. Otis Carl and Margaret Lee (Hutchinson) E.; B.A., Centenary Coll., 1949; S.T.B., Gen. Theol. Sem., 1952; postgrad. Westcott House, Cambridge, Eng., 1952-53; S.T.M., So. Meth. U., 1962; M.A. (Univ. fellow), U. Chgo., 1963, Ph.D., 1971; D.D., Nashotah House, 1976; m. Jane Hanna Trufant, Feb. 19, 1957; children—Carl Lee, Samuel Adams Trufant, Louise Reynes. Ordained priest Episcopal Ch., 1954; curate Episcopal ch., Baton Rouge, 1953-54, vicar, Abbeville, La., 1954-57, Waxachachie, Tex., 1960-61, rector, Morgan City, La., 1957-60, priest in charge, Chgo., 1961-63; instr. Wabash Coll., 1963-64; asst. prof. Nashotah (Wis.) House, 1964-69, asso. prof., 1969-72, prof., 1972-74, sub-dean, 1973-74, acting dean, 1973-74; dean Seabury-Western Theol. Sem., Evanston, Ill., 1974—. Chmn. Council for Devel. of Ministry, Episcopal Ch.; chmn. Council Sem. Deans; mem. Bd. for Theol. Edn.; mem. Gen. Bd. Examining Chaplains; chmn. campus affairs com., trustee Kendall Coll. Recipient Spl. award Mystery Writers Am., 1965. Mem. Soc. Bibl. Lit., Cath. Bibl. Assn., Am. Acad. Religion, Chgo. Soc. Bibl. Research. Democrat. Author: How It All Began, 1973; The Living and Active Word, 1975; (with Robert Bennett) The Bible for Today's Church, 1979. Book rev. editor Anglican Theol. Rev., 1971-76, v.p. of corp., 1975—. Contbr. articles and book revs. to various jours. and mags. Home: 625 Garrett Pl Evanston IL 60201 Office: 2122 Sheridan Rd Evanston IL 60201

EDWARDS, RICHARD PIERRE, metallurgist; b. Muncie, Ind., July 17, 1928; s. Johnson Pierre and Gladys Ellen (Keever) E.; B.S. in Metall. Engring. Purdue U., 1950; m. Margaret Jean McClung, Mar. 9, 1952; children—Kenneth R., Jean A. Mgr. quality assurance Warner Gear, Muncie, 1971-73; mgr. mfg. services TEGA div. Borg Warner, Troy, Mich., 1973-77, mgr. metallurgy Warner Gear div., Muncie and Auburn, Ind., 1977—. Served to 1st lt. AUS, 1951-52; Korea. Registered profl. engr., Ind. Mem. Am. Soc. Metals, Soc. Automotive Engrs. Presbyterian. Clubs: Masons, Purdue. Home: 2604 W Queensberry Dr Muncie IN 47302 Office: PO Box 2688 Muncie IN 47302

EDWARDS, ROBERT ALBERT, city ofcl.; b. Hillsboro, Ill., Sept. 15, 1932; s. Albert N. and Pauline R. E.; B.A., Millikin U., 1954; M.G.A., U. Pa., 1955; m. Mary A. Brand, Dec. 27, 1953; children—Karen, Sheryl, Robert, Eric. Adminstrv. asst. City of Evanston (Ill.), 1955-58; city mgr., Savanna, Ill., 1958-62, College Park, Md., 1962-71; chief adminstrv. officer Prince George's County (Md.), 1971-75; city mgr., Cleveland Heights, Ohio, 1975-78; dir. public service City of Akron, Ohio, 1978-80, dep. Mayor for econ. devel., 1980—. Bd. dirs. United Cerebral Palsy Prince George's County. Mem. Internat. Platform Assn., Internat. City Mgrs. Assn., Md. Mcpl. League (mem. bd.). Presbyterian. Contbr. articles to profl. jours. Home: 550 Garnette St Akron OH 44313 Office: 166 S High St Akron OH 44308

EDWARDS, ROBERT HAZARD, coll. pres.; b. London, May 26, 1935; s. Arthur Robinson and Marjorie Hazard (Mayes) E.; A.B., Princeton U., 1957; B.A., Cambridge (Eng.) U., 1959, M.A. (hon.), 1977; LL.B., Harvard U., 1961; m. Ellen Ramsey Turnbull, Sept. 10, 1966; children—Elizabeth, Daphne, Nicholas. Admitted to Fed. bar, D.C., 1961; Ford Found. fellow in Africa, 1961-63; with UN polit. affairs Dept. State, 1963-65; with Ford Found., 1965-77, rep. for Pakistan, 1968-72, head Middle East and Africa, 1973-77; pres. Carleton Coll., Northfield, Minn., 1977—; dir. Great No. Ins. Co., First Nat. Bank of Mpls. Trustee African-Am. Inst., Deerfield Acad., Sci. Mus of Minn.; bd. dirs. Gen. Service Found.; overseer U. Minn. Sch. Mgmt. Mem. Council on Fgn. Relations. Office: Carleton College Northfield MN 55057

EDWARDS, ROY ANDERSON, III, banker; b. New London, Conn., Nov. 23, 1945; s. Roy A. and Joan C. (Darby) E.; B.S. in Bus. Adminstrn., U. Kans., 1968, M.B.A., 1973; m. Terry Kistler Beach, Sept. 5, 1970; children—Ross Darby, Roy Beach, Carrie Kistler. Mem. audit staff Arthur Young & Co., Kansas City, Kans., 1973-75; fin. cons., v.p. Clay Blair Services Corp., Kansas City, 1974-75; v.p. in gen. mgmt. Douglas County State Bank, Lawrence, Kans., after 1975, pres., chief exec. officer, dir., to 1981; pres., chief exec. officer First Nat. Bank, Hutchinson, Kans., 1981—; propr. Mitchell-Hill Seed Co., St. Joseph, Mo., 1971—; dir. Cottonwood Inc. Fin. chmn. Douglas County Republican Com., Kans., 1976-77; chmn. Kans. U. Affairs Com., 1977-78, Kans. Spl. Olympics Com., 1977— bd. dirs. Lawrence (Kans.) Art Center, 1976, The Lawrence Villages, 1976. Served to lt. USN, 1968-71. Mem. Young Bank Officers Kans., Lawrence C. of C. (dir.), Lawrence Humane Soc. (chmn. 1975-77), Am. Bankers Assn. (mgmt. and tng. com. bank personnel div.), Kans. Bankers Assn., U. Kans. Alumni Assn., Phi Delta Theta, Alpha Kappa Psi. Republican. Episcopalian. Clubs: Lawrence Country, Rotary (dir.) (Lawrence). Contbr. articles on fin. to profl. jours. Home: 110 W 29 St Hutchinson KS 67501 Office: First Nat Bank Sherman and Main Sts Hutchinson KS 67501

EDWARDS, VANCE DAVID, non-profit housing co. exec.; b. Flint, Mich., Aug. 2, 1953; s. Herbert Edgar and Delores Ann (Hudock) E.; student Mich. Tech. U., 1971-72; AA. in Community Edn. with honors, Mott Community Coll., 1974; B.S., Central Mich. U., 1975, also postgrad.; 1 dau., Barbie Kay Edwards Herzog. Asst. community sch. dir., Flint (Mich.) area, 1975-77, spl. edn. instr., 1977, res. juvenile officer, 1977—; exec. dir. Group Living Facilities, Flint, 1978—. Mem. Mich. Assn. Non-Profit Resdl. Facilities, Adult Foster Care Providers Genesee County, State-Wide Care Home Assn., Genesee County Assn. Retarded Citizens, Fraternal Order Police, Sons Am. Legion, Nat. Assn. Pvt. Facilities for Mentally Retarded, Nat. Assn. Developmental Disabilities Mgrs., Genesee County Juvenile Assn. Home: 11430 Wing Dr Clio MI 48420 Office: G-5095 Van Slyke Rd Flint MI 48507

EDWARDS, WILLIAM DELBERT, real estate agt., farm mgr.; b. Audubon, Iowa, July 4, 1922; s. Roy William and Gretta Wanita (Yager) E.; B.S., Iowa State U., 1952; postgrad U. Nebr., Omaha, 1957; m. Barbara Ann Caldwell, Nov. 28, 1941; children—Ellen Ann, Paul William, Chester Roy. Tchr. vocat. agr. Iowa Falls and Shelby, Iowa, 1952-57; owner Farm Supply Co., Shelby, 1953-65; regional facilities mgr. Gulf Oil Corp., Kansas City, Mo., 1965-71; owner, mgr. Edwards Real Estate Inc., Clarion, Iowa, 1976—; owner, mgr. Edwards Farms. Mem. Shelby County Sch. Bd.; chmn. Wright County Republican Com. also dist. committeeman. Served with USAAF, 1943-46. Mem. Fertilizer and Chem. Assn. (state dir. 1958-67), Nat. Real Estate Assn., Iowa Real Estate Assn., Wright County Bd. Realtors, Am. Soc. Farm Mgrs. and Rural Appraisers, Am. Farm Bur., Am. Legion. Clubs: Rotary (past dist. gov.), Shriners, Masons. Home: 311 11th St NE Clarion IA 50525

EELLS, WILLIAM HASTINGS, automobile co. exec.; b. Princeton, N.J., Mar. 30, 1924; s. Hastings and Amy (Titus) E.; B.A., Ohio Wesleyan U., 1946; M.A., Ohio State U., 1950. Asst. to dir. Inst. Practical Politics, Ohio Wesleyan U., 1948-50, asst. dir., 1952-53, dir., 1953-57; instr. dept. polit. sci., 1952-59; instr. polit. sci. Mt. Union Coll., 1950-51; coordinator Atomic Devel. Activities, State of Ohio, 1957-59; Midwest regional mgr. civic and govtl. affairs Ford Motor Co., Columbus, 1959—. Mem. Ohio Gov.'s Cabinet, 1957-59; chmn. bd. Blue Cross, 1967-72, Blossom Music Center, Cleve., 1967-75; chmn. Gov.'s Council on Rehab., 1966-68; mem. exec. com. Met. Opera's Nat. Council, 1967—; pres. Nat. Council High Blood Pressure Research, 1974-79; v.p. Lake Erie Watershed Conservation Found., 1970-79; chmn. Ohio Adv. Council Coll. Prep. Edn., 1981—; mem. Nat. Council on Arts, Nat. Endowment for Arts, 1976—; bd. dirs. Am. Heart Assn., 1974-79, award for disting. service, 1979; trustee Cleve. Orch., 1964—, Ednl. TV, Cleve., 1965-75, Cleve. Playhouse, 1965—, Cleve. Ballet, Cleve. Zoo, Columbus Symphony, Columbus Assn. Performing Arts, 1980—, Cleve. Luth. Hosp. Recipient awards including USCG Distinguished award, 1965, Silver medal Royal Life Saving Soc., Ohio State U. Devel. award, 1967, Silver medal Japanese Red Cross Soc., award Ohio Arts Council, 1979, Ohio Theatre Alliance, 1981. Mem. SAR, Ohio C. of C. (v.p.), Ohio Mfrs. Assn. (trustee), Ohio Public Expenditure Council (pres. 1981—), Pi Sigma Alpha, Pi Gamma Mu, Omicron Delta Kappa, Delta Tau Delta. Republican. Presbyn. Clubs: Princeton (N.Y.); U. Columbus; Union (Cleve.); F Street (Washington). Author: Your Ohio Government, 1953, 6th edit., 1967. Contbr. articles to profl. publs. Home: 54 Elmwood Dr Delaware OH 43015 Office: 37 W Broad St Columbus OH 43215

EFFINGER, THOMAS JOSEPH, city ofcl., educator; b. Winamac, Ind., June 17, 1943; s. Carl J. and Hilda R. (Reutebuch) E.; B.S., St. Joseph Coll., Rensselaer, Ind., 1965; M.S., Ind. U., Bloomington, 1972; postgrad. Ind. State U., Terre Haute, 1978—; m. Carolanne Williams, July 9, 1966; children—Joseph, Julie, Jennifer. Tchr., Rensselaer Central Sch. Corp., 1966—; supt. dept. park and recreation City of Rensselaer, 1967—. Chmn., Jasper County (Ind.) chpt. ARC. Mem. Rensselaer Central Tchrs. Assn. (v.p.), Ind. Park and Recreation Assn., Nat. Park and Recreation Assn., Ind. State Tchrs. Assn., NEA, Ind. U. Alumni Assn. Democrat. Roman Catholic. Club: K.C. Home: 623 Dean Pl Rensselaer IN 47978 Office: Rensselaer Parks and Recreation PO Box 304 Rensselaer IN 47978

EGAN, ROBERT JOSEPH, lawyer, state senator; b. Elmhurst, Ill., Nov. 11, 1931; s. Mathias and Elizabeth (Quill) E.; B.A., St. Norbert Coll., 1953; J.D., Loyola U., 1959; m. Marie Terese Gillespie, 1958; children—Elizabeth, Margaret, Sarah, Robert, Frank. Admitted to Ill. bar; practice law, Chgo.; mem. Ill. State Senate, 1971—. Served to 1st lt. U.S. Army, 1954-56. Mem. Ill. Bar Assn., Chgo. Bar Assn., Phi Alpha Delta. Roman Catholic. Office: One N LaSalle St Chicago IL 60602*

EGEL, LAWRENCE, psychologist, educator; b. Chgo., June 11, 1940; s. Milton and Dorothy Lillian (Levin) E.; B.A. in Psychology, Roosevelt U., 1965; M.S. in Psychology, Ill. Inst. Tech., 1971, Ph.D. in Psychology, 1975; m. Maria Gutsmiedl, Jan. 12, 1968; children—Barbara, Lisa. Research asso. Chgo.-Read Mental Health Center, Chgo., 1968-70, night clin. officer on duty, 1970-71, asst. unit chief, 1971-72, research supr., sr. clinician anti-recidivism program, 1972; crisis worker Ravenswood Hosp., Chgo., 1972; instr. exptl. psychology and physiol. psychology Coll. of St. Francis, Joliet, 1974-76; chief psychologist Will County Mental Health Clinic, Joliet, Ill., 1973-78; community prof. human realtions Governors State U., Park Forest South, Ill., 1978-79, lectr. psychology, counseling, 1980—; pvt. practice forensic, psychodiagnostic, neuropsychodiagnostic and theraputic psychology, Joliet, 1976—; mem. adv. bd., cons. Will County Crisis Line; chmn. bd., v.p. HEM, Inc., Joliet. Diplomate in clin. psychology Am. Bd. Profl. Psychology; registered clin. psychologist; cert. sch. psychologist, Ill. Mem. Am. Psychol. Assn., Midwest Psychol. Assn., Ill. Psychol. Assn., Internat. Neuropsychology Soc., AAAS, Assn. Symbolic Logic, Nat. Acad. Neuropsychology, Neurosci. Soc., Psychology-Law Soc., Nat. Assn. Sch. Psychologists, Ill. Assn. Sch. Psychologists. Jewish. Office: 310 Hammes St Joliet IL 60435

EGELAND, BYRON RICKER, educator; b. Roland, Iowa, Nov. 2, 1938; s. Ernie A. and Eleanor M. (Ricker) E.; B.A., Drake U., 1961; M.A., U. Iowa, 1963, Ph.D., 1966; m. Janet Burns, Aug. 20, 1966. With Syracuse U., 1966-72; faculty U. Minn., Mpls., 1972—, prof. psychology, 1973—. Served with U.S. Army, 1956. Grantee in field. Fellow Am. Psychol. Assn.; mem. Soc. Research Child Devel., Am. Ednl. Research Assn., Council Exceptional Children. Editorial bd. Developmental Psychology, 1980—, Am. Jour. Mental Deficiency, 1981—, Contemporary Ednl. Psychology, 1976-79, Jour. Sch. Psychology, 1977-80; contbr. chpts. to books, articles to profl. jours. Home: 237 Woodlawn Ave Saint Paul MN 55105 Office: N4548 Elliott Hall U Minn Minneapolis MN 55455

EGERMAN, JEANETTE FRANCES, educator; b. St. Cloud, Minn., Mar. 4, 1927; d. John and Frances (Sand) Goedker; A.A., St. Cloud U., 1964, B.S., 1970, M.S., 1978; m. Robert Egerman, July 31, 1948; children—Susan, Mary, Jean, Ben, Joann, Margaret. Acct., St. Peter (Minn.) State Hosp., 1966-68, Gillette State Hosp., St. Paul, 1968-70; spl. edn. tchr. Brainerd (Minn.) State Hosp., 1970-73; tng. coordinator Glacial Ridge Training Center, Willmar (Minn.) State Hosp., Willmar, 1973—; lectr. in field; conductor workshops. Mem. Am. Assn. on Mental Deficiency, Minn. Edn. Assn., State Residential Schs. Edn. Assn., NEA, Nat. Assn. Retarded Citizens, Library of Spl. Edn. Author: Communications Instructor's Manual, 1979; Confrontation Avoidance Management, 1980. Home: Skyline Estates 301 Spicer MN 56288 Office: Glacier Ridge Tng Center Willmar State Hosp Willmar MN 56201

EGGEN, JERALD DWAIN, ednl. adminstr.; b. Watertown, S.D., Dec. 30, 1935; married, 3 children. B.S. in Bus. Adminstrn., S.D. State U., Brookings, 1957. Bus. mgr. Watertown Ind. Sch. Dist. #1, 1959—. Pres., Crusade chmn. Cod. County chpt. Am. Cancer Soc., 1968-70; bd. dirs., treas. Jenkins Methodist Nursing Home, 1978—, Mellette House Meml. Assn., 1978—; sr. warden Trinity Episcopal Ch., 1980—; mem. diocesan council Episc. Diocese S.D.; mem. Watertown City Planning Commn., 1978—; mem. mayor's steering com. for Watertown Centennial Celebration, 1978—. Mem. Assn. Sch. bus. Ofcls. U.S. and Can., S.D. Assn. Sch. Bus. Ofcls. (pres. 1969). Club: Rotary (Watertown). Home: 612 2nd St NE Watertown SD 57201 Office: 200 9th St NE Watertown SD 57201

EGINTON, CHARLES THEODORE, ofcl. VA; b. Staples, Minn., 1914; M.B. with distinction, U. Minn., 1938, M.D., 1939, M.S. in Surgery, 1942; m. Sally Eginton; children—William C., Julie Ann, Mark Theodore. Intern Ancker Hosp., St. Paul, 1938-39; fellow in surgery Mayo Found., Rochester, Minn., 1939-42; asst. in surgery Mayo Clinic, 1941-42; chief surg. ser. VA Hosp., Fargo, N.D., 1967-71, chief of staff, 1971-78, chief surg. services, 1978—; clin. prof. surgery U. N.D., 1970—; adj. prof. pharmacy N.D. State U., 1970—. Served to maj. M.C., AUS, 1942-46. Diplomate Am. Bd. Surgery. Fellow A.C.S., Internat. Coll. Surgeons; mem. AMA, Phi Beta Kappa, Alpha Omega Alpha. Home: 509 N Shore Dr Detroit Lakes MN 56501 Office: VA Center Fargo ND 58102

EGTS, WILLIAM DELMAR, mfg. co. exec.; b. Findlay, Ohio, Oct. 31, 1937; s. Enorval Delmar and Eliza Mae (Dorman) E.; student public schs.; m. Ella Sue Wainscott, June 10, 1961; children—Stephanie Suzanne, William Delmar. Enlisted in U.S. Navy, 1955, advanced through ranks to E-7, 1974; service in China and Vietnam; ret., 1974; with Budd Co., 1974—, maintenance foreman, N. Baltimore, Ohio, 1975—. Home: 1821 Brookside Dr Findlay OH 45840 Office: 100 S Poe Rd North Baltimore OH 45872

EHINGER, ANTHONY LEIGH, plastics co. exec.; b. West Branch, Mich., Nov. 13, 1942; s. Roy A. and Grace O. E.; B.S. in Bus. Adminstrn., Central Mich. U., 1971, M.B.A., 1972; m. Martha Ann Buchanan, Mar. 6, 1971. Dir. purchasing-accounts payable Robinson Industries, Inc., Beaverton, Mich., 1972-75; controller Franklin Forge & Mfg., Inc., West Branch, 1975-80, Gilreath Mfg. Inc., Howell, Mich., 1981—. Served with U.S. Army, 1966-70. Mem. Assn. M.B.A. Execs., Sigma Iota Epsilon. Home: 1031 Tracilee Dr Howell MI 48843 Office: 3240 W Grand River St Howell MI 48843

EHLERT, DENNIS, educator; b. East St. Louis, Ill., Aug. 2, 1944; s. Walter and Helen (Meni) E.; B.A., Harris Tchrs. Coll., 1969; M.A., Washington U., St. Louis, 1972; Ph.D., St. Louis U., 1980; cert. adminstrn. So. Ill. U., Edwardsville, 1978; m. Marilyn A. Hemmen, Apr. 3, 1971; 1 dau., Denise Brooke. Tchr., Bryan Hill Elem. Sch., St. Louis Bd. Edn., 1969-70; tchr. Mesnier and Heege Sch., Affton, Mo., 1973-76; unit chmn. Jefferson Sch., St. Louis, 1976-79; prin. South Iron R-1 Elem. Sch., Annapolis, Mo., 1979—. Served with AUS, 1963-66. Mem. Assn. Supervision and Curriculum Devel., Nat. Assn. Elem. Sch. Prins., NRA. Club: Lions (pres.). Home: Box 56 Annapolis MO 63620 Office: South Iron R-1 Elementary Sch Annapolis MO 63620

EHLERT, JOHN AMBROSE, publisher; b. Albany, Minn., July 20, 1945; s. Melvin George and Helen Mary (Borgerding) E.; B.A., St. Mary's Coll., 1967; m. Katherine Myers, Nov. 23, 1969; children—Adam, Zachary. Editor, Snow Sports Pubs., Inc., Mpls., 1970-75; pres., pub. JAE Communications, Inc., Wayzata, Minn., 1976-80; pres., pub. Winter Sports Pub., Inc., Milw., 1980—; lectr. in field. Mem. City Council, City of Minnetonka Beach (Minn.), 1976-78, mayor, 1978-79. Served with USMC, 1967-69. Recipient Internat. Snowmobile Industry Assn. Journalism awards, 1975, 76, 77, 79. Mem. Minn. Press Club. Republican. Clubs: Lafayette. Founder, Midwest Snowmobiler Mag., 1976; founder, pub. Snowmobile Mag., 1980; pub. Archery World Mag., 1981. Office: 225 E Michigan St Milwaukee WI 53202

EHRAMJIAN, VARTKES HAGOP, fin. exec.; b. Syria, Nov. 2, 1932; came to U.S., 1959, naturalized, 1966; s. Hagop and Naomi E.; B.A., Eastern Mich U., 1962; M.B.A., Ind. U., 1963; m. Laura L. Schmoker, June 7, 1962; children—James C., Tamar M., Alyce M., Ricardo L., Kathleen Marie. Sr. fin. analyst Ford Motor Co., 1963-68; internat. financing mgr. Cummins Engine, 1968-70, regional mgr., So. Latin Am., 1970-71, pres. Cummins S.A. Brazil, 1971-72, dir. internat. bus. devel., 1972-75, asst. treas. internat., 1975-79; asst. treas. The Bendix Corp., Southfield, Mich., 1979—; lectr. Ind. U. Served with inf. Syrian Army, 1955-56. Mem. Am. Mgmt. Assn., U.S. C. of C. (export policy task force). Republican. Armenian Orthodox. Club: Harrison Lake Country. Home: 30850 Cheviot Hills Dr Franklin MI 48025 Office: Executive Offices Bendix Center Southfield MI 48037

EHRKE, WALTER LOUIS, wholesale drug co. exec.; b. West Allis, Wis., Sept. 24, 1911; s. Gustav Paul and Mathilda Caroline (Pawelk) E.; student U. Wis., 1929-31; m. Helen Margaret Luettgen, Mar. 30, 1940; children—Lance, Lauren Ehrke Lauritch, Muriel Ehrke Stanton, Eric. Supt. Yahr-Lange Drug Co., Inc., Milw., 1942-46, Milw., Rockford, Ill., and LaCrosse, Wis., 1946-53, gen. ops. mgr., 1953-64, dir., Milw., 1962—, v.p., 1964-72, sr. v.p., 1972—; operation mgr. Crandon Drug Co., Miami, Fla., 1953-62, v.p., 1962-72, pres., 1972—, also dir.; designer, gen. ops. mgr. Crandon Drug Co., Fort Lauderdale, Fla., 1962-70; designer, pres. Crandon Drug Co., Lakeland, Fla., 1976—. Mem. Nat. Wholesale Drug Assn. (mem. systems com. 1973-74, chmn. 1974-75), Travellers of Wis. Roman Catholic. Kiwanian. Home: 2645 Willow Springs Dr Brookfield WI 53005 Office: 800 Wall St Elm Grove WI 53122 also 500 NE 191st St Miami FL 33162

EHRLE, ELWOOD BERNHARD, univ. adminstr.; b. Paterson, N.J., Nov. 13, 1933; s. Elwood F. and Katherine S. (Ploch) E.; B.S., Rutgers U., 1954; M.A., Columbia U., 1955; Ph.D., Pa. State U., 1958; m. Nancy Decker, Aug. 4, 1956; children—Erik, Bernhard, Royce. Prof. biology SUNY, Geneseo, 1958-68; asso. dir., office of biol. edn. Am. Inst. Biol. Scis., Washington, 1968-71; dean Sch. Arts and Sci., Mankato (Minn.) State U., 1971-76; v.p. acad. affairs Ind. State U., Terre Haute, 1976-80, Western Mich. U., Kalamazoo, 1980—. Past lay leader Geneseo Methodist Ch.; tng. instr. Honey Creek Vol. Fire Dept., Vigo County, Ind. Recipient various profl. awards and grants. Mem. AAAS, Nat. Assn. Biology Tchrs., Am. Inst. Biol. Scis., Am. Assn. for Higher Edn., Sigma Xi. Club: Rotary (charter mem.) (Terre Haute). Contbr. articles in field to profl. jours. Office: Western Mich Univ Kalamazoo MI 49008

EHRLICH, AVA, writer; b. St. Louis, Aug. 14, 1950; d. Norman and Lillian (Gellman) Ehrlich; B.S.J., Northwestern U., 1972, M.S.J., 1973; M.A., Occidental Coll., 1976; m. Barry Freedman. Broadcast writer EPA, Chgo., 1973-74; reporter, asst. mng. editor Lerner Newspapers, Chgo., 1974-76; news editor, reporter, documentary writer CBS Radio, KMOX, St. Louis, 1976-79; producer news and documentaries Sta. WXYZ-TV, ABC, Detroit, 1979—; instr. Florissant Valley Community Coll., St. Louis, 1978-79; freelance writer, 1970—; guest editor Mademoiselle Mag., 1971; documentaries include: When Life Is Measured in Minutes 1977; The High Cost of Sanity, 1978. Trustee Coro Found., 1976-77; v.p. Coro Assos. of Midwest, 1977—; supporting mem. Hope and Home Family Services, Chgo., 1974-77. Recipient citation for community service Norridge (Ill.) Sch. Dist. 234, 1975; 1st place investigate reporting Mo. Broadcasters Assn., 1978; Media award Mo. Mental Health Assn., 1978; Media award Nat. Mental Health Assn., 1978, 79; Coro Found. fellow in pub. affairs, 1975-76; Danforth Found. mgt. leadership fellow, 1978-79; 1st pl. award Mich. AP, 1980. Mem. Women in Communications, AFTRA (chpt. dir. 1980-81), Soc. Profl. Journalists (bd. dirs.), Mo. Press Women, NOW, Kappa Tau Alpha. Democrat. Jewish. Home: 23741 Walden Ct Southfield MI 48034 Office: 20777 W 10 Mile Rd Southfield MI 48075

EHRLICH, ROY MELVEN, state senator; b. Hoisington, Kans., Dec. 6, 1928; s. Geroge and Katherin (Bitter) E.; student U. Corpus Christi, 1946-47, Barton County Jr. Coll., 1971-72; m. Lita Jean Ochs, 1950; children—Jolene Ehrlich Morgenstern, Karla, Lonney, Rox Ann. Farmer-rancher, Hoisington; former mem. Kans. Ho. of Reps.; mem. Kans. Senate. Mem. twp. bd., Barton County, 1961-66, co-commr., 1967-70; mem. Kans. State Republican com. Served with U.S. Army, 1962-63. Clubs: Eagles, Masons, Shriners. Contbr. local newspapers. Office: Route 1 Box 92 Hoisington KS 67544*

EHRLICHER, EDWARD JOHN, personnel ofcl.; b. Chgo., Nov. 24, 1943; s. Frederick Erasmus and Rose Rita (Meyer) E.; A.A., Kennedy-King Jr. Coll., 1968; B.A., Roosevelt U., Chgo., 1972. Clk., supr., mgr. check processing div., personnel specialist LaSalle Nat. Bank, Chgo., 1967-74; personnel asst. Nystrom div. Carnation Co., Chgo., 1974-77, asst. personnel mgr., 1977—. Mem. Jane Addams Center Bd., Hull House Assn. Served with AUS, 1962-65. Mem. Am. Soc. Personnel Adminstrn. (accredited), Soc. Personnel Adminstr. Greater Chgo., N.W. Personnel Assn. Chgo. Home: 1405 W Edgewater Ave Apt 2 Chicago IL 60660 Office: 3333 N Elston Ave Chicago IL 60618

EHRNSCHWENDER, ARTHUR ROBERT, gas and electric utility co. exec.; b. Cin., Oct. 3, 1922; s. Arthur M. and Lydia C. (Widmer) E.; M.E., U. Cin., 1948, B.S. in Commerce, 1959; M.B.A., Xavier U., 1959; Dr. Tech. Letters, Cin. Tech. Coll., 1980; m. Grace S. Popplewell, Oct. 1950; children—Barry N., Scott A. Field engr. SKF Bearing Co., Cin., 1948-49; Chevrolet field rep. Gen. Motors Corp., Cin., 1949-50; sr. v.p. adminstrv. services Cin. Gas & Electric Co., 1952—; trustee Thrift Savs. and Loan, Cin., 1959—, chmn. bd., 1981; dir. Jetcom, Inc., Cin., O.K.I. Supply Co., Cin., Hwy. Rental Co. Trustee, Deaconess Hosp., 1970—, pres. bd. trustees, 1978—; trustee Goodwill Industries, 1961—, pres., 1966-71; trustee Cin. Assn. for Blind, 1965—, Hamilton County YMCA, 1974—. Served with U.S. Army, 1943-46, 1950-52. Decorated Bronze Star; recipient Disting. Alumni award U. Cin., 1974, MBA Exec. Achievement award, Xavier Univ., 1979. Registered profl. engr., Ohio, Ky. Mem. Soc. Automotive Engrs., Engring. Soc. Cin., Greater Cin. Indsl. Relations Assn., Edison Electric Inst., Am. Gas Assn. Presbyn. Clubs: Queen City; Cin. Country; Errol Estate Golf and Country; Mason (Shriner). Home: 5161 Salemhills Ln Cincinnati OH 45230 Office: PO Box 960 Cincinnati OH 45201

EIBERT, PAUL DONALD, mfg. co. exec.; b. St. Paul, Apr. 30, 1920; s. Lawrence J. and Helen M. (Bauer) E.; B.A., Coll. St. Thomas, St. Paul, 1942; m. Dorothea F. Stubbs, Jan. 15, 1972; children—Bruce, Arthur, Catherine, Vicki, Mark, John, Sally. Vice pres. Eibert Coffee Co., St. Paul, 1946-52, pres., 1952-66; v.p. corp. devel. CFS Continental, Inc., Chgo., 1966—. Bd. dirs. Mounds Park Hosp., St. Paul, 1960-66; bd. dirs. St. Paul Winter Carnival, pres., 1963. Served to capt. USAAF, 1942-46. Decorated Air medal, D.F.C. Club: Union League (Chgo.). Office: CFS Continental Inc 100 S Wacker Dr Chicago IL 60606

EICHER, GLEN, urban planner; b. Vandalia, Ill., June 23, 1936; s. L. Eugene and L. Cleo (Harper) E.; student Belleville Jr. Coll., 1956; B.F.A. in Landscape Architecture, U. Ill., 1959; m. Jacque Mullane, Aug. 16, 1958; children—Kent A., Jeffrey T., Karen K. Planner, Ill. Dept. Local Govt. Affairs; cons. Gen. Planning and Resource Cons., St. Louis; subdiv. planner St. Louis County (Mo.); planner Wichita-Desgwich County Met. Area Planning Commn.; exec. dir. Vermilion County (Ill.) Regional Planning Commn., Vermilion CETA. Active troop Boy Scouts Am.; mem. subarea bd. E. Central Ill. Health Systems. Mem. Vermilion County Mus. Soc., Am. Planning Assn., Am. Inst. Cert. Planners. Methodist. Club: Rotary. Office: Rural Route 1 Box 261 Oakwood IL 61858*

EICHNER, EDUARD, obstetrician, gynecologist; b. Cleve., Nov. 11., 1905; s. Nathan Jacob and Dora (Guren) E.; A.B., Case Western Res. U., 1925, M.D., 1929; m. Helen Augusta Short, Sept. 11, 1931; children—William Eduard, Judith Eichner Henderson. Intern, St. Alexis Hosp., Cleve., 1929-30; resident obstetrics St. Ann Hosp., Cleve., 1930-31; proctor-tng., intervals obstetrics and gynecology Mt. Sinai Hosp., Cleve., 1932-36; gen. practice medicine, Cleve., 1931-37; practice medicine specializing in obstetrics and gynecology, Cleve., 1938—; obstetrician, gynecologist, dir. family planning clinic Mt. Sinai Hosp., Cleve., 1954-72, asso. vis. physician, dir. family planning, 1972-78, cons., 1978—; asso. clin. prof. obstetrics and gynecology Case Western Res. U. Sch. Medicine, Cleve., 1973—; med. dir. preterm, 1974-77, cons., 1977—; mem. med. adv. bd. Met. Health Planning Com., Cleve. Dist., 1974—; clin. adv. bd. Cuyahoga County Bd. Mental Retardation, Cleve., 1969—; mem. Am. Com. on Maternal Welfare, Chgo., 1947-60. Trustee Circle Workshop, Cleve., Parents Vol. Assn., Cleve., 1972—. Served with USNR, 1942-46. Recipient Disting. Achievement and Service award Mt. Sinai Hosp., 1979; awards for original investigation Am. Coll. Obstetricians and Gynecologists, 1954, 63, Ohio Med. Assn., 1955, 63, A.C.S., 1955, Modern Medicine, 1956; diplomate Am. Bd. Ob-Gyn. Fellow A.C.S., Am. Coll. Obstetrics and Gynecology, Internat. Coll. Surgeons (v.p. sect. obstetrics-gynecology 1979, chmn. 1966); mem. A.M.A., Central Assn. Obstetricians and Gynecologists, Endocrine Soc., Soc. for Exptl. Biology and Medicine, Am. Fertility Soc., Am. Inst. Biologic Sci., Internat. Soc. for Research in Reproduction, Pan-Pacific Surg. Assn., Pan-Am. Med. Soc., N.Y. Acad. Sci., Med. Alumni Assn. Case Western Res. U. (pres. 1967), Cleve. Soc. Obstetricians and Gynecologists (pres. 1960), N.E. Ohio Gynecologic Cancer Group (chmn. edn. 1978-81), Cleve. City Club, Sigma Xi, Kappa Nu, Phi Lambda Kappa. Contbr. numerous articles to profl. jours. Home: 3333 Daleford Rd Shaker Heights OH 44120 Office: 5 Severance Circle Dr Cleveland OH 44118

EIFERT, OTTO RICHARD, bassoonist; b. N.J., Oct. 24, 1927; s. Otto and Margaret E.; grad. artist diploma Curtis Inst. Music, 1952; m. Patricia Schofield, 1952. Bassoonist, Cleve. Orch., 1952-53, New Orleans Symphony, 1953-61; prin. bassoonist Cin. Symphony, 1961—; prof. bassoon U. Cin. Coll. Conservatory of Music, 1962—. Served in U.S. Army, 1946-47. Mem. Internat. Double Reed Soc. Episcopalian. Contbg. editor Instrumentalist mag., 1972—; editor Kozeluch Bassoon Concerto, 1975. Office: 1241 Elm St Cincinnati OH 45201

EIFRIG, JAMES EDWARD, advt. agy. exec.; b. Chgo., Jan. 11, 1949; s. E. E. and Mary P. (Diehl) E.; B.A., Denison U., 1971. Account exec. Weber Cohn Riley, Chgo., 1972-75; account supr. Don Tennant Co., 1975-77; account supr. Kloppenburg, Switzer & Teich, Milw., 1977—; instr. advt. U. Wis., 1980—. Trustee, Village of Oconomowoc Lake Bd. Dirs., 1979—; mem. fund raising com. Milwaukee County Performing Arts Fund, 1979. Mem. Milw. Advt. Club (awards com. 1980, Speaker's Bur. 1980-81), Am. Mktg. Assn., Am. Assn. Advt. Agys. Clubs: Ducks Unltd. (publicity chmn. 1981), Milw. Athletic; Oconomowoc Lake. Office: 1201 N Prospect St Milwaukee WI 53202

EIGEL, THOMAS JOHN, former air force officer, electronics corp. exec.; b. St. Louis, Aug. 30, 1934; s. Edwin George and Katherine (Rohan) E.; B.S.I.E., St. Louis U., 1956; M.S., San Diego State U., 1972; m. Gail Victoria Keenan, Nov. 29, 1958; children—Thomas Jr., Kathleen, Victoria, Andrea, Christina. Commd. 2d lt. U.S. Air Force, 1956, advanced through grades to lt. col., 1972; aircraft comdr. of tankers, forward air controller, Vietnam, 1968; dep. dir., configuration mgr. armament systems div., Wright Patterson AFB, Ohio, 1973-79; mgr. configuration and data mgmt. Northrop Def. Systems, Rolling Meadows, Ill., 1979—; lectr. in field. Decorated DFC, Meritorious Service medal. Mem. Am. Def. Preparedness Assn., Air Force Assn., Soc. of Logistics Engrs., Sigma Iota Epsilon, Beta Gamma Sigma. Republican. Roman Catholic. Club: K.C. Home: 772 Harvard Ct Palatine IL 60067 Office: Northrop Corp Defense Systems Div 600 Hicks Rd Rolling Meadows IL 60008

EIGHMEY, DOUGLAS JOSEPH, JR., hosp. ofcl.; b. Cambridge, N.Y., Dec. 19, 1946; s. Douglas Joseph and Theresa E. (McGuire) E.; B.S. in Biology, SUNY, Cortland, 1968; M.P.H., U. Tenn., 1971; m. Karen S. Rife, Apr. 27, 1973; 1 dau., Sarah Elizabeth. Public health cons. Ohio Dept. Health, Columbus, 1971-76, supr. cert. of need program Ohio Dept. Health, 1976-78; v.p. Central Ohio River Valley Assn., Cin., 1978-79, St. Francis-St. George Hosp., Inc., Cin., 1979—. Recipient award USPHS, 1970. Mem. Am. Hosp. Assn., Ohio Hosp. Assn., Am. Coll. Hosp. Adminstrs., Ohio Hosp. Planning Assn. (dir.-at-large 1980—), Am. Soc. Hosp. Planning, Am. Soc. Law and Medicine, Ohio Public Health Assn., Nat. Assn. Clock and Watch Collectors, St. Vincent DePaul Soc. Roman Catholic. Clubs: Rotary (Cin.); Elks. Office: 3098 Queen City Ave Cincinnati OH 45238

EILAU, LEMBIT, adminstrv. elec. engr.; b. Tartu, Estonia, Dec. 25, 1921; came to U.S., 1949, naturalized, 1956; s. Peeter and Mathilde (Porgassaar) E.; B.S. in Elec. Engring., Tech. Sch. Dorpat (Estonia), 1944; M.B.A., Loyola U. Chgo., 1972; m. Luule Paid, Feb. 23, 1952; 1 dau., Ann Marie. Designer, Pioneer Service & Engring. Co., Chgo., 1951-57; group leader V.E. Alden Engrs., Chgo., 1957-59; elec. engr. R.E. Hattis Engrs., Skokie, Ill., 1959-60; head elec. br. Harza Engring Co., Chgo., 1960—, asso., 1970-78, sr. asso., 1978—, v.p., 1981—. Registered profl. engr., Ill., Calif., Colo., Fla., other states. Mem. Internat. Conf. Large High Tension Electric Systems, IEEE (internat. practices subcom.). Office: Harza Engineering Co 150 S Wacker Dr Chicago IL 60606

EILER, LARRY TRACY, computer services co. exec.; b. Syracuse, N.Y., May 31, 1939; s. George Rogers and Helen Louise (Tracy) E.; B.A., Syracuse U., 1964, M.A., 1966; m. Sandra Louise Mercier, Jan. 23, 1965; children—Tracy, Jennifer, Derek, Lauren, Jerrett, Sean. Sr. v.p. Hutchins/Darcy, Inc., Rochester, N.Y., 1970-76; account exec. Carl Byoir & Assos., Honeywell Corp., Mpls., 1976-78; dir. communications Honeywell Aero-Def. Group, Mpls., 1978-80; dir. corp. relations Comshare, Inc., Ann Arbor, Mich., 1980—; lectr. U. Minn., 1977-79, Syracuse U., 1965-68. Bd. dirs. Boy Scouts Am., Rochester, 1974-75, Mpls., 1977-80, Ann Arbor, 1980—, v.p., Mpls., 1978-79; bd. dirs. United Way, Mpls., 1978-79. Served with U.S. Army Res., 1964-70. Mem. Nat. Investor Relations Inst., Public Relations Soc. Am. (nat. accreditation bd. 1979). Republican. Roman Catholic. Clubs: Minn. Press, Detroit Press, Nat. Press, Economic of Detroit. Home: 4712 Breezewood Ct Ann Arbor MI 48103 Office: Comshare Inc 3001 S State St Ann Arbor MI 48104

EILRICH, GARY LEE, agrl. chem. co. mgr.; b. Ellsworth County, Kans., Oct. 14, 1940; s. Martin Wilhelm Fredrich and Edna Lois (Keys) E.; B.S. magna cum laude in Agrl. Edn., Kans. State U., 1962, M.S. in Agronomy, 1964; Ph.D. in Plant Physiology and Biochemistry (Univ. fellow 1964-67), U. Ill., 1968; m. Mary Sue Scheidenhelm, June 19, 1965; children—Dale Brian, Douglas John. Research asst. dept. agronomy Kans. State U., 1962-64; research fellow dept. agronomy U. Ill., 1964-68; sr. research biologist Monsanto Co., St. Louis, 1968-74, sr. research specialist, 1974-75; mgr. program planning Agrl. Chems. div. Diamond Shamrock Corp., Cleve., 1976-78, mgr. comml. devel., 1978-81, tech. dir., 1981—; adv. on use of fungicides on soybeans and wheat, various firms and univs. Brazil, 1978. Judge, St. Louis Post-Dispatch Sci. Fair, 1972-74; mem. Christian Edn. Commn., Presbyn. Ch., 1972-74, chmn., 1975, elder, 1975; trustee Meth. Ch., 1978-81, chmn., 1980-81; active YMCA Indian Guides, 1976-78, 79-81. Mem. Am. Soc. Plant Physiologists, Am. Soc. Agronomy, Crop Sci. Soc. Am., Weed Sci. Soc. Am., Am. Phytopath. Soc., Plant Growth Regulator Working Group, Council for Agrl. Sci. and Tech., N.E. Weed Sci. Soc., So. Weed Sci. Soc., FarmHouse, Sigma Xi, Phi Eta Sigma, Kappa Delta Pi, Alpha Zeta, Gamma Sigma Delta, Phi Kappa Phi. Republican. Contbr. articles to profl. publs. Home: 5291 Hickory Dr Lyndhurst OH 44124 Office: 1100 Superior Ave Cleveland OH 44114

EINHORN, STEPHEN EDWARD, merger and acquisition cons.; b. Bklyn., June 25, 1943; s. Benjamin and Rosalind (Nuss) E.; B.A., Cornell U., 1964; postgrad. Wharton Sch. U. Pa., 1965-66; M. Chem. Engring., Bklyn. Poly. Tech. Inst., 1966; m. Nancy Lore, May 22, 1965; children—David, Daniel. With Adelphi Industries, Carlstadt, N.J., 1964-75, gen. v.p., 1974-80; partner Mertz, Einhorn & Assos., mergers and acquisitions consultants, Milw., 1980—; specializing in fgn. investments in U.S. and Mid-Western mfg. concerns, also chem. cos. Lic. real estate broker, Wis. Mem. Nat. Assn. Merger and Acquisition Consultants, Inst. Bus. Appraisers. Patentee on handling latex paint. Home: 8049 N Links Way Milwaukee WI 53217 Office: Mertz Einhorn & Assos 2401 N Mayfair Rd Milwaukee WI 53226

EINODER, CAMILLE ELIZABETH, educator; b. Chgo., June 15, 1937; d. Isadore and Elizabeth T. (Czerwinski) Popowski; student Fox Bus. Coll., 1954; B.Ed. in Biology, Chgo. Tchrs. Coll., 1964; M.A. in Analytical Chemistry, Gov.'s State U., 1977; m. Joseph X. Einoder, Aug. 5, 1978; children—Carl Frank, Mark Frank, Vivian Einoder, Joe Einoder, Tim Einoder, Sheila Einoder, Secretarial positions, Chgo., 1955-64; tchr. biology Chgo. Bd. Edn., 1964—, tchr. biology and agr., 1975-81, tchr. biology, agr. and chemistry, 1981—; human relations coordinator Morgan Park High Sch., 1980—; career devel. cons. for agr. related curriculum. Bds. dirs., founding mem., author constn. Community Council, 1970; bd. dirs., edn. cons. Neighborhood Council, 1974; rep. Chgo. Tchrs. Union, 1969. Hme: 10637 S Claremont St Chicago IL 60643 Office: 1744 W Pryor St Chicago IL 60643

EIS, LORYANN MALVINA, educator; b. Muscatine, Iowa, Apr. 3, 1938; d. Chester N. and Anna M. (Lenz) E.; A.B., Augustana Coll., 1960; M.Ed., U. Ill., 1963; postgrad. Montclair State Coll., 1965-67, Indiana U. of Pa., 1968, U. Iowa, 1970, Western Ill. U., 1978-80. Circuit analysis engr. Automatic Electric Co., Northlake, Ill., 1960-61; math. tchr. Orion (Ill.) Community Sch. Dist., 1961-63; math. tchr., dept. chmn. United Twp. High Sch., East Moline, Ill., 1963—. Bd. sec. Citizens to Preserve Black Hawk Park Found., 1977—; mem. Moline YWCA. Mem. NEA, Ill. Edn. Assn., Nat. Council Tchrs. of Math., Ill. Council Tchrs. of Math., Classroom Tchrs. Assn., Assn. Supervision and Curriculum Devel., Rock Island Scott Counties Sci. and Math. Tchrs. Assn., Women in Ednl. Adminstrn., AAUW (state pres.; grantee 1975-76), Delta Kappa Gamma (state corr. sec.), Am. Philatelic Soc., TransMiss. Philatelic Soc., Quad City Stamp Club. Republican. Lutheran. Cons. General Mathematics Textbook, 1978-79. Home: 2037 15th St Moline IL 61265 Office: 42nd Ave and Archer Dr East Moline IL 61244

EISEMAN, ROBERT HARRY, coll. ofcl.; b. Eureka, S.D., Mar. 1, 1934; s. Jacob and Rose (Junker) E.; B.S. in Secondary Edn., No. State Coll., 1961; postgrad. Mankato State Coll., 1979—; m. Elfrieda Magdalena Lindemann, June 22, 1958; children—Dana, Roberta, Robin. Coach football, track and wrestling Eureka Public Schs., 1965-69; athletic dir., dir. upkeep properties, Pillsbury Coll., 1969—, registrar, 1970-80; pres. Twin River Collegiate Athletic Conf.; treas. No. Intercoll. Christian Athletic Conf. Del., Steele County (Minn.) Republican Com., 1980. Served with U.S. Army, 1953-55, USAR, 1973—. NSF grantee, 1969. Mem. Minn. Coaches Assn., Minn. Athletic Dirs. Assn., Am. Legion. Baptist. Home: 1024 E Vine St Owatonna MN 55060 Office: 315 S Grove Owatonna MN 55060

EISENBERG, ELIZABETH GERTRUDE STRICK, occupational therapist; b. Chgo., July 23, 1954; d. Henry and Florence (Zeltner) Strick; B.S. in Occupational Therapy, Kans. U., 1979, now postgrad.; postgrad. Central Mo. State U.; m. Roger Eisenberg, Nov. 22, 1977; 1 son, Chaim. Youth center coordinator Jewish Community Center Assn.; 1969-72, bd. dirs., 1971-72; occupational therapist Vis. Nurse Assn., Kansas City, Mo., 1979-81, Shawnee Mission Hosp., 1981—; occupational therapy cons. med. lodges, Leavenworth, Kans., 1981—. Mem. Kans. Occupational Therapy Assn., Am. Occupational Therapy Assn., World Fedn. Occupational Therapy. Jewish. Clubs: Aviv, Sisterhood of Young Israel. Office: 527 W 39th St Kansas City MO 64111

EISENBERG, HENRY WILLIAM, surgeon; b. Worcester, Mass., Apr. 19, 1942; s. Harold M. and Miriam G. E.; A.B., Brown U., 1964; M.D., Columbia U., 1968; m. Ellen Gans, Nov. 15, 1969; children—Betsy, Julie. Intern, Univ. Hosps., Cleve., 1969-70, resident in surgery, 1970-72, 73-74; spl. fellow Cleve. Clinic, 1972-73; practice medicine specializing in colon and rectal surgery, Cleve., 1974—; mem. surg. staff Mt. Sinai, St. Luke's, Surburban hosps.; asst. clin. prof. surgery Case Western Res. U.; prof. surgery Ohio Coll. Podiatric Medicine; cons. proctologist Diamond Shamrock Corp.; cons. Eli Lilly Co. Served as maj. USAR, 1971-77. Diplomate Am. Bd. Surgery, Am. Bd. Colon and Rectal Surgery. Fellow A.C.S.; mem. Am. Soc. Colon and Rectal Surgeons, AMA, Royal Soc. London, Med. Arts Club Cleve. Club: Oakwood. Office: Parkway Med Center 3619 Park E Cleveland OH 44122

EISENBRAUN, DAL (IKE), ins. co. exec.; b. Tripp, S.D., June 29, 1935; s. Alvin H. and Bertha P. (Goldhammer) E.; B.S., S.D. State U., 1957, M.S., 1958; m. Carol Van Ness, Apr. 1, 1956; children—Pamela K., Michael D. Tchr., coach Brookings (S.D.) High Sch., 1959-63; agt. State Farm Ins., Brookings, 1963-66, agy. tng. dir., Santa Ana, Calif., 1966-69, agy. mgr., San Bernadino, Calif., 1969-70, agy. dir., Costa Mesa, Calif., 1970-76, exec. asst. agy., Bloomington, Ill., 1976-79, dep. regional v.p., Marshall, Mich., 1979—. Served with U.S. Army, 1958-59. Mem. Nat. Assn. Life Underwriters, Gen. Agts. and Mgrs. Assn., Soc. C.L.U.'s, Nat. Mgmt. Assn. (adv. bd.). Republican. Lutheran. Home: 131 Whisperwood Ln Battle Creek MI 49015 Office: 410 East Dr Marshall MI 49069

EISENMANN, HAZEL PUTA, ednl. adminstr.; b. Mishicot, Wis., May 14, 1924; d. Edward and Josephine Puta; B.S., U. Wis., Oshkosh, 1953; M.Ed., U. Wis., Milw., 1958; postgrad. U. Minn., 1959, Silver Lake Coll., 1959-68, U. Calif., Berkeley, 1960; m. Frederick C. Eisenmann, June 1, 1946. Tchr., Superivising tchr. Manitowoc County (Wis.) Schs., 1953-56; instr. Manitowoc County Tchrs. Coll., 1956-61; elem. coordinator, prin. Mishicot (Wis.) Community Schs., 1961—; instr. Silver Lake Coll., 1965-68. NSF scholar, 1960. Mem. Assn. Supervision and Curriculum Devel., Ceramic Guild Am., Assn. Wis. Sch. Adminstrs. Lutheran (Wis. Synod). Home: 878 Randolph St Mishicot WI 54228 Office: 510 Woodlawn St Mishicot WI 54228

EISLER, JOEL ROBERT, rental co. exec.; b. Cin., Oct. 14, 1947; s. Bernard Louis and Meigh (Schatz) E.; student U. Mass., 1965; B.A., Lynchburg Coll., 1969, postgrad., 1970; postgrad. George Washington U., 1971, Bowie State Coll., 1978; m. Fredericka Schellenberg Boehm, Feb. 17, 1980. Accountant, Lynchburg (Va.) Gen. Hosp., 1967-70; asst. dir. fin. Hosp. Sick Children, Washington, 1970-72; asst. dir. housekeeping div. Macke Co., Cheverly, Md., 1972-73; accounting mgr., fuel oil burner service Amerada Hess Corp., Landover, Md., 1973-75; controller, dir. adminstrn. Cort Furniture Rental Corp. subs. Mohasco Corp., Amsterdam, N.Y., 1975-78, supervising dist. mgr. Cort Furniture Rental, Mpls., 1978-81; controller, chief fin. officer M.R. Enterprises Ltd. holding co. for MR Rents and Revzen Bus. Interiors. Campaign worker city elections, Bowie, Md., 1970-76; bd. dirs. Minn. Multihousing Assn.; mem. transp. bd. City of Bloomington. Mem. Nat. Assn. Accountants, Bloomington C. of C. Democrat. Jewish. Club: Jaycees (past pres. Bowie, past state v.p.). Home: 7500 W 100th St Bloomington MN 55438 Office: 222 W Hubbard St Chicago IL 60610

EISNER, JEROME ALLAN, sales trainer; b. Sheboygan, Wis., July 6, 1945; s. Harold Frederick and Frieda (Diener) E.; B.S., U. Wis., 1968; Edn. Cert., Alverno Coll., 1971; m. Eileen Ann Dixon, Aug. 17, 1968; children—Elizabeth Ann, Kimberly Jinmee. Tchr., St. Mary's Sch., South Milw., 1968-69, Pius XI High Sch., Milw., 1969-71; salesman R. L. Polk & Co., Madison, Wis., 1971-72; audio-visual editor 3M Co., St. Paul, Minn., 1972-73, tech. writer, trainer, 1973-76, sales adminstrn., salesman, 1976-78; sales tng. program developer Golle & Holmes Corp., Mpls., 1978—. Bd. dirs. Project Concern Minn., 1980—, Minn. Jr. C. of C. Found., 1980—; mem. Hennepin County A-V Technicians Adv. Com., 1973-74; dir. S.E. Minn. Adoptive Parents Group, 1977—; pres. Washington County Adoptive Parents Assn., 1977—; mem. Cottage Grove Hazardous Waste Citizens Com., 1978; parliamentarian Cottage Grove Jr. C. of C., 1975, v.p., chaplain, 1976-77; Midwest region coordinator U.S. Jr. C. of C., 1977-78. Recipient Clayton Frost Meml. award, U.S. Jr. C. of C., 1981. Mem. Am. Soc. Tng. and Devel., Personal Dynamics Assn., Advanced Learning Network. Lutheran. Home: 6948 Innsdale Ave South Cottage Grove MN 55016 Office: 5720 Green Circle Dr Minnetonka MN 55343

EISTERHOLD, ROSALYN MARY, govt. ofcl.; b. Jefferson City, Mo., June 5, 1954; d. Michael Sebastian and Marie Barbara (Boes) E.; student public schs., Westphalia, Mo. Sec., Public Sch. Retirement System Mo., Jefferson City, 1971-76; adminstrv. aide Office Public Counsel, Jefferson City, 1976-81. Roman Catholic.

EKBLAD, ARTHUR, state legislator N.D.; b. Ryder, N.D., Feb. 28, 1930; s. Axel H. and Gladys M. Ekblad; B.A., Valley City (N.D.) State Coll., 1952; m. Gladys L. Emery, Mar. 30, 1951; children—Warren E., Laurine R., Eric E. With Standard Oil Co., 1952-56; with Blue Cross/Blue Shield N.D., 1956—, dist. mgr. mktg., 1960—; mem. N.D. Ho. of Reps. from 5th Dist., 1974—. Republican precinct committeeman, 1966—. Mem. Greater Minot (N.D.) Assn. (chmn. 1969-71), Minot C. of C. (chmn. public affairs com.), Minot Amateur Radio Assn. (past pres.). Methodist. Clubs: Elks, Toastmasters (past dist. gov.). Home: 1210 7th St SW Minot ND 58701 Office: Box 759 Minot ND 58701

EKHOLM, JAMES ARLYN, bus. machines mfg. co. mktg. exec.; b. Sioux Falls, S.D., Oct. 3, 1942; s. Evert Richard and Elizabeth Margaret (Griffith) E.; B.S. in Bus. Adminstrn., Augustana Coll., Sioux Falls, 1966; m. Judie Lynn Slama, Sept. 24, 1966; children—Christopher James, Janna Lee. Gen. salesman Dakota Turf Supply, Sioux Falls, 1958-66, with Burroughs Corp., Sioux City, Iowa, 1966-74, zone mgr., Des Moines, 1974-78, govt. coordinator, Detroit, 1978-80, market mgr., office automation, 1980-81, mgr. market planning, 1981—. Served with Army N.G., 1964. Republican. Mem. Assemblies of God Ch. Home: 29584 Pipers Ln Farmington Hills MI 48018 Office: 1 Burroughs Pl Detroit MI 48232

EKISS, JOHN PATTON, sales exec.; b. Akron, Ohio, Mar. 7, 1929; s. John Keith and Beatrice Lillian (Beldon) E.; student Baylor U., 1948-51; m. Muriel Jean Bondurant; children by previous marriage—Karen, Patton, Christopher. Zone mgr., Dr Pepper Co., Dallas, 1960-64; dist. franchise mgr., Frostie Co., Camden, N.J., 1964-67, Nesbitt Food Products, Los Angeles, 1967-69; area sales mgr. Chattanooga Glass Co., 1969-76; pres. E & E Sales Co., Grandview, Mo., 1976—. Recipient Manhood award VFW, 1944. Clubs: Advt. and Sales Execs., Toastmasters. Home: 6325 E 127th St Grandview MO 64030 Office: PO Box 409 Grandview MO 64030

EKKEBUS, DANIEL ELOY, mgmt. cons.; b. Chgo., June 24, 1943; s. Eloy Daniel and Catherine Marie (Fuhrmann) E.; B.B.A., U. Notre Dame, 1965; m. Barbara Vandivier, Aug. 12, 1967 (div.). Vice pres. sales Laird, Inc., 1967-73; v.p. sales G.H. Walker, Laird, Inc., Chgo., 1973-76; v.p. Rambert & Co., Lake Bluff, Ill., 1976-77; chmn. bd. Bardan Group, Inc., Lake Bluff, 1977—; pres. Kishwaukee Plastics Co., Garden Prairie, Ill., Kishwaukee Plug Co., Garden Prairie. Home: 840 Deerpath Rd Lake Forest IL 60045

EKLEBERRY, LEVI NEAL, camp adminstr.; b. Sycamore, Ohio, Nov. 2, 1919; s. Orely and Bernice Leona (Shedenhelm) E.; student Northeastern U., 1968; m. Olive Gertrude Larick, May 21, 1943; children—Patricia Jo (Mrs. Gene Manson), Carol Sue (Mrs. Dale Flockerzie). Mill operator Swan Rubber Co., Carey, Ohio, 1945-47; forest ranger Mohican Forest, Perrysville, Ohio, 1947-65; camp adminstr. Wooster Forest, Perrysville, 1965—; security guard Prichart Security Inc., Akron, Ohio, 1973—. Served with AUS, 1942-43, USAAF, 1943-45. Recipient Conservation award Richland County, 1969; named Outstanding Ranger, Sohio mag., 1963. Mem. Am. Camping Assn., Am. Forestry Assn., Assn. Camp Adminstrs. U.S.A., Ohio State Patrol Aux., Am. Legion, Aircraft and Pilots Assn., Nat. Rifle Assn. Republican. Presbyn. (elder, commr. to synod). Rotarian (chmn. program com. 1968), Lion, Mason. Home: RFD 2 Perrysville OH 44864 Office: Wooster Outdoor Center Perrysville OH 44864

EKLUND, KENT EMMET, state ofcl.; b. Jamestown, N.Y., Apr. 17, 1946; s. Emmet E. and Marion E. (Corimer) E.; B.A., Augustana Coll., 1968; Ph.D., U. Pa., 1973; m. Katherine Anderson, Jan. 27, 1968; children—Andrew Kent, Nathan Dale. Instr. to asso. prof. St. Olaf Coll., Northfield, Minn., 1972-79; successively asst. commr., dep. commr., commr. Minn. Dept. Econ. Devel., 1979-81; commr. Minn. Dept. Energy, Planning and Devel., St. Paul, 1981—. Mem. Rice County Planning Commn., 1975-77, chair, 1977; mayor City of Northfield, 1978-79. Lutheran. Office: 550 Cedar St Saint Paul MN 55101*

EKLUND, WAYNE OSCAR, publishing co. exec.; b. Brockton, Mass., May 20, 1929; s. Roy Forest and Virginia Anna (Rosequist) E.; A.A.S., Rochester Inst. Tech., 1958, B.S., 1959; m. Eleanor Lois Baker, Aug. 4, 1956; children—Shawn Joanne, Mark Jonathan, Alane Ruth, Bryan Timothy. Graphic arts buyer Scripture Press Publications, Wheaton, Ill., 1959-62, v.p., 1970—; v.p. Acme Press, Chgo., 1962-70; mem. council Scripture Press. Found. (U.K.) Ltd., London, 1974—; sec. bd. Urban Ministries, Inc., Chgo., 1980—. Served with USN, 1950-54. Mem. Printing Industry Am., Evangelical Christian Pubs. Assn., Printing Industry Ill. Republican. Club: Lions (pres.) (Wheaton, Ill.). Home: 829 N Stoddard St Wheaton IL 60187 Office: 1825 College Ave Wheaton IL 60187

EKVALL, BERNT, dentist; b. Nora, Sweden, June 25, 1915; s. Johan Alexis and Elin Karolina (Persson) E.; L.D.S., U. Stockholm, 1944; D.D.S., U. Mich., 1951; m. Margit Andersson, June 23, 1940 (separated 1978); 1 dau., Lucie Margita. Came to U.S., 1949, naturalized, 1954. With Swedish Govt. Dental Services, 1943-45; pvt. practice dentistry Sweden, 1945-49, Clinton, Mich., 1951-52, Dearborn, 1951-55, 57-58, Detroit, 1958—; mem. staff Alexander Blain Meml. Hosp. Vice pres. Scandinavian Am. Republican Club, 1960-68, pres., 1968-72; treas. Rep. State Nationalities Council, 1971-73; Bd. dirs. Scandinavian Symphony Soc., 1961-72; bd. mgrs. Hannan br. YMCA, 1962—, chmn. Eastside br., 1976. Served to capt. AUS, 1955-57. Fellow Royal Soc. Health, Internat. Acad. Dentistry, Acad. Gen. Dentistry, Internat. Coll. Dentists; mem. Am., Mich. dental assns., Detroit Dist. Dental Soc., Detroit Dental Clinic Club (membership sec. 1972-73, sec. 1973-74, pres. 1975-76), Bunting Periodontal Study Club, Mich. Acad. Gen. Dentistry (sec. 1975-76, v.p. 1976-78, pres. 1978-80). Clubs: Economic, Renaissance (Detroit); Grosse Pointe Hunt. Home: 1063 Woodbridge E Saint Clair Shores MI 48080 Office: 2141 E Jefferson Ave Detroit MI 48207

ELAM, DANIEL FRANK, clin. social worker; b. Cedar Rapids, Iowa, Nov. 15, 1945; s. Max B. and Alice Rose (Brown) E.; B.A., So. Ill. U., 1968; M.S.W., U. Ill., 1976; m. 2d, Janice Mae Buff, July 3, 1973; children—Bruce Alan, David Frank. Caseworker, Ill. Dept. Public Aid, Harvey, Ill., 1968-74; intern Little Company of Mary Hosp., Evergreen Park, Ill., 1974-75, Sch. Dist. 158, Lansing, Ill., 1975-76; sch. social worker Dist. 157, Calumet City, Ill., 1976-80; dir. social services Trade Winds Rehab. Center, Gary, Ind., 1980—. Mem. Nat. Assn. Social Workers, N. Am. Soc. Adlerian Psychology, Am. Orthopsychiat. Assn., Acad. Cert. Social Workers, Oak Park Coin (pres. 1979, dir. 1980), Am. Numis. Assn. (life), Token and Medal Soc. (life), Civil War Token Soc. (life), Nat. Scrip Collectors Assn., Merchant Token Collectors Assn., Am. Vectorist Assn., Ind.-Ky.-Ohio Token and Medal Soc. Office: 5901 W 7th Ave Gary IN 46406

ELASARIAN, ANNA, public housing authority exec.; b. Waukegan, Ill., Sept. 18, 1940; d. Ohan and Siranoush (Garabedian) Elasarian; student Carthage Coll., 1964, Coll. Lake County, Grayslake, Ill., 1974-76. Stenographer, Fansteel Metall. Corp., North Chgo., 1958-60; legal sec. Dixon and Seidenfeld, Waukegan, Ill., 1961-62; sec., accountant Waukegan Housing Authority, 1962-67, asst. exec. dir. to part-time dir., 1962-67, exec. dir., 1977—. Mem. task force com. United Way; mem. bd. Lake County Community Action Project, 1977—, sec., 1979—; bd. dirs., mem. Cardiac Charities Lake County, 1977-80. Mem. NAACP, Lake County Urban League, Nat. Assn. Housing and Redevel. Ofcls. (cert. public housing mgr.), Public Housing Authorities Dirs. Assn., Ill. Assn. Redevelopment Authorities, Am. Soc. Profl. and Exec. Women, Nat. Assn. Female Execs., Chgo. Council Fgn. Relations, Smithsonian Assos., Am. Film Inst., Cousteau Soc., Phi Theta Kappa. Episcopalian. Club: Altrusa Internat. Office: 200 S Utica St Waukegan IL 60085

ELBERT, JOHN ALLAN, orthodontist; b. Rice Lake, Wis., Mar. 13, 1924; s. John Walter and Hattie (Pollatz) E.; student St. Olaf Coll., 1941-43; D.D.S., U. Marquette, 1946; postgrad. U. Minn., 1959-61; m. Mary Treat Stebbins, Aug. 10, 1946; children—John Arthur, Stephen Thomas, Bruce William, James Edward. Individual practice gen. dentistry, Rice Lake, 1948-59, practice orthodontics, 1961—. Chmn. Barron County (Wis.) Republican party, 1961-62. Served with Dental Corps, AUS, 1946-48. Mem. ADA, Wis. Dental Assn., Wis. Orthodontic Soc., Am. Assn. Orthodontists, Ducks Unltd. (chpt. chmn.), Delta Sigma Delta. Episcopalian (sr. warden 1964-65). Elk, Kiwanian. Home: Route 1 Box 242A Rice Lake WI 54868 Office: 515 N Main St Rice Lake WI 54868

ELDEN, JOHN DEMARLEY, ins. co. exec.; b. Duluth, Minn., Jan. 2, 1931; s. William Elden and Amelia Josephine (Sather) E.; A.A., U. Minn., 1950; m. Joan Phyliss Tweten, Aug. 16, 1958; children—Gregory William, Julie Marie, Diana Lynn. Agt., Mut. Benefit Life Ins. Co., 1954-58, supr., 1958-63, asst. gen. agt., 1963-67; regional sales mgr. Am. States Life Ins. Co., Indpls., 1967-72; dir. marketing Wis. Life Ins. Co., Madison, 1972-76; agency dir. Fin. Security Life Ins. Co., Moline, Ill., 1976-77, agency v.p., 1977—. Served with U.S. Army, 1950-52; Korea. C.L.U. Mem. Am. Soc. C.L.U., Nat. Assn. Life Underwriters, Moline Rock Island Life Underwriter Assn. Lutheran. Clubs: Optimists, Quad City Sales Execs., Moose, Elks. Home: 48 Geneseo Hills Geneseo IL 61254 Office: 716 17th St Moline IL 61265

ELDER, JEAN KATHERINE, educator; b. Virginia, Minn., May 30, 1941; d. Clarence Adrian and Katherine C. (Miltich) Samuelson; B.S., U. Mich., 1963, A.M., 1966, Ph.D., 1969. Tchr. 5th grade Ypsilanti (Mich.) pub. schs., 1963-64; tchr. educable mentally retarded Quantico (Va.) Marine Corps Dependent Sch., 1964-65; dir. remedial reading program Iron Mountain (Mich.) pub. schs., 1966; research asst. U. Mich., 1966-69; asst. prof. spl. edn. Ind. U., Bloomington, 1969-70, cons. lab. ednl. devel., 1970-71; research asso. Center Ednl. Research and Devel. Mental Retardation, Bloomington, 1969-71; dir. delinquency modification through edn. project Marquette (Mich.)-Alger Intermediate Sch. Dist.-Marquette County Probate Ct., 1971-72; asst. prof. edn. No. Mich. U., Marquette, 1972-76, asso. prof., 1977-78, coordinator Title IX, 1975-76; project dir., asso. scientist Specialist Office Three, Wis. Research and Devel. Center Cognitive Learning, U. Wis., Madison, 1976-77; assoc. prof. med. edn. Coll. Human Medicine, Mich. State U., 1978—; cons. in field. Bd. dirs. Child and Family Service Upper Peninsula Mich.; mem. Pres.'s Com. on Mental Retardation, 1976—; mem. Mich. Public Health Adv. Council; adv. Council Bur. Rehab. U.S. Office Edn. fellow, 1966-69. Mem. Am. Assn. Mental Deficiency, Am. Assn. Edn. Severely/Profoundly Handicapped, Nat., Mich. (dir.) assns. retarded citizens, Council Exceptional Children, AAUW (del. Mich.), Assn. Am. Med. Colls., Soc. Tchrs. Family Medicine, Mich. Assn. Educators Learning Disabled, Pi Lambda Theta, Phi Delta Kappa, Delta Kappa Gamma. Lutheran. Club: Zonta. Author: (with others) Planning Individualized Education Program in Special Education, 1977. Contbr. articles to profl. jours. Home: 1400 Gray St Marquette MI 49855 Office: Coll Human Medicine Mich State U 540 W Kaye Ave Marquette MI 49855

ELDER, KAREN HANSEN, office automation cons.; b. Grosse Pointe, Mich., Nov. 14, 1942; d. Raymond Arthur and Beatrice F. (Kiernan) Hansen; student Macomb County Community Coll., 1962-63, Oakland Community Coll., 1974-76; 1 dau., Kristen Hansen. Cons., partner Central Word Processing Systems, Birmingham, Mich., 1979—. Recipient Certificate of Appreciation, Am. Word Processing Assn., 1980. Mem. Am. Word Processing Assn. (chpt. pres. 1980-81), Internat. Entrepreneur's Assn., Internat. Info. Word Processing Assn., Nat. Assn. Women Bus. Owners, Nat. Assn. Female Execs. Republican. Presbyterian. Author: Office Automation Simplified, 1980. Home: 5311 Breeze Hill Pl Troy MI 48098 Office: 700 E Maple St Birmingham MI 48011

ELDER, LOWELL LEVON, mech. engr.; b. Mark Center, Ohio, Feb. 8, 1926; s. Levon A. and Gladys L. (Worthington) E.; B.S. in Mech. Engring., Ohio State U., 1949; m. Margy Ann Boone, Aug. 22, 1948; children—Debbie Kay, Nancy Ann. Jr. corrosion engr. Atlantic Seaboard Corp., Elkins, W.Va., 1949-50; corrosion engr. Columbia Gas System Service Corp., Columbus, Ohio, 1950-53, asst. sr. transmission engr., 1953-55, sr. transmission engr., 1955-60, supervisory engr., 1960-65, sr. research engr., 1965-74, mgr. research adminstrn., 1974—; vice chmn. petroleum and natural gas sector Am. Nat. Metric Council. Served with USAAF, 1944-46; PTO. Registered profl. engr., Ohio. Mem. ASME (chmn. gas piping standards com. 1970—, vice chmn. code for pressure piping, mem. council codes and standards, research, profl. and public affairs, mem. nat. nominating com., safety codes and standards com. 1974—, also mem. council public affairs), Am. Gas Assn. (metrication task com.). Republican. Methodist. Clubs: Shriners, Masons, Sports Car Am. Home: 2187 Glenmere Rd Columbus OH 43220 Office: 1600 Dublin Rd Columbus OH 43215

ELDER, NATHAN R., educator; b. Atlanta, Dec. 18, 1921; s. Paul and Annie (Ryals) E.; B.S., N.C. A.&T. State U., 1950; M.S., Chgo. State U., 1977, M.A., 1980; m. Helen Muckle, June 12, 1944; children—Marilyn Ann, Nathan R., Linda Susan. Biochemist, VA Hosps., Albany, N.Y., 1955-57, Chgo., 1957-59, Downey, Ill., 1959-60; chemist US Food and Container Inst., Chgo., 1960-63; tchr. physics, gen. sci. Lakeview High Sch., Chgo., 1973—. Bd. dirs. Physics Inst. Ill. Inst. Tech., 1972-74. Served with AUS, 1942-45; ETO. Decorated Combat Infantryman's Badge. Mem. AAAS, Am. Chem. Soc., Am. Inst. Chemists, Alpha Phi Alpha, Phi Delta Kappa. Home: 5141 S Drexel Ave Chicago IL 60615 Office: 4015 N Ashland Ave Chicago IL 60613

ELDREDGE, JANE MACDOUGAL, state senator; b. Norwalk, Conn., Feb. 8, 1944; d. William Wallace, Jr. and Janann (Moeller) MacDougal; B.A., Smith Coll., 1965; J.D., U. Kans., 1977; m. Charles Child Eldredge, III, June 11, 1966; children—Henry Gifford, Janann Bateson. Systems analyst A.I.C. Co., Mpls., 1969-70, U. Kans., 1971-74; admitted to Kans. bar, 1977, since practiced in Lawrence; mem. Kans. Senate from 2d Dist., 1981—. Bd. dirs. Lawrence chpt. LWV, 1971-73, Achievement Place for Boys, Lawrence, 1977-80, Trinity Foster Home, Lawrence, 1979-80, Pinckney Neighborhood Assn., Lawrence, 1970-76. Mem. Am. Bar Assn., Kans. Bar Assn., Douglas County Bar Assn., Downtown Lawrence, Assn., Lawrence C. of C. Republican. Episcopalian. Club: Alvamar Racquet and Swim Country. Home: 511 Ohio St Lawrence KS 66044 Office: 839 1/2 Massachusetts St Lawrence KS 66044

ELDRIDGE, MABEL ELIZABETH, educator; b. Franklin, Ohio, Feb. 7, 1900; d. William Bevan and Winifred (Earhart) E.; B.E., Miami U., Oxford, Ohio, 1922, postgrad., 1944-45, 54, 56, 59; M.Ed., U. Cin., 1943; student McGill U., Montreal, Can., 1926, U. Chgo., 1930, U. Sorbonne, Paris, 1950. Tchr. English and French, Lemon Twp. High Sch., Monroe, Ohio, 1922-23, Middletown (Ohio) High Sch., 1923-55, dean of girls, 1930-62; tchr. creative writing and world lit., 1955-62; lectr. English, tchr. children's lit. Miami U., Middletown (Ohio) Br., 1967-72, staff Internat. Children's Lit. Workshop, European Study Center, Luxembourg, 1974; dealer in out-of-print books Hillside Book Cellar, Franklin, 1975-76; instr. English, Middletown Bus. Coll., Franklin, 1977-78; lectr. childrens lit. and local history. Mem. adv. bd. Y-Teens, Middletown, 1930-62; bd. dirs. Middletown Civic Assn., 1936-39, Middletown Girls' Club, 1936-62, Ohio Dist. YWCA, 1941-47; trustee Franklin Pub. Library, 1967-71, v.p., 1970-71; resource cons. in local history Franklin Community Resources Workshop, 1971. Recipient Bishop medal for Meritorious Pub. Service, Miami U., 1955; certificate of appreciation Middletown Sch. Bd., 1962; named Woman of Year, Middletown Bus. and Profl. Women's Club, 1969; many others. Mem. Franklin Area Hist. Soc. (pres. 1974-75), Ohio Assn. Women Deans, Adminstr. and Counselors, Nat., Ohio, Ret. tchrs. assns., Nat. Writers Club, Delta Kappa Gamma, Kappa Delta Pi. Republican. Baptist. Clubs: Ten O'Clock Scholrs, O.M.T. Contbr. articles and book revs. to jours. and newspapers. Home: 215 E 2d St Franklin OH 45005

ELDRIDGE, PAMELA ANN, tractor co. ofcl.; b. Glen Ellyn, Ill., Apr. 8, 1957; d. Kenneth L. and Nancy V. (Vahey) E.; B.S. in Journalism and Advt., U. Kans., 1979. Intern, Foote, Cone & Belding, Chgo., 1978; advt. and promotion mgr. Martin Tractor Co., Topeka, 1979—. Office: 1737 SW 42d St Topeka KS 66601

ELEVELD, ROBERT JAY, lawyer; b. Grand Rapids, Mich., Aug. 3, 1936; s. John H. and Dena (Klooster) E.; A.B., Dartmouth Coll., 1958; LL.B., U. Mich., 1961; m. Marilyn Wolf, Dec. 27, 1980; children by previous marriage—Robert Jay, Karen Lynn. Admitted to Mich. bar, 1961; mem. firm Varnum, Riddering, Wierengo & Christenson, Grand Rapids, 1961—, partner, 1968—. Mem. East Grand Rapids City Commn., 1971-73; chmn. Kent County Republican Party, 1972-74, 5th Dist. chmn., 1974-76; mem. Mich. State Bd. Ethics, 1978—, chmn., 1981—. Served with Mich. Air N.G., 1961-67. Mem. Am. Bar Assn., Mich. Bar Assn., Grand Rapids Bar Assn. (pres. 1982—), Internat. Assn. Ins. Counsel. Home: 1120 Plymouth St SE Grand Rapids MI 49506 Office: 800 Mutual Home Bldg Grand Rapids MI 49503

ELIAS, JAMES PAUL, computer communications specialist; b. Windber, Pa., Oct. 7, 1946; s. John Paul and Margaret Ann (Kaplan) E.; B.A. in History, St. Vincent Coll., Latrobe, Pa., 1968; postgrad. Cleve. State U., 1971-72; m. Carol Lee Oleksia, Nov. 9, 1968. Mktg. trainee IBM, Cleve., 1968-69; systems engr. Erie Lackawanna Ry., Cleve., 1969-72; systems engr. Memorex, Cleve., 1972-73; computer systems cons. Systemation, Cleve., 1973; sr. computer communications specialist McDonnell Douglas Automation Co., St. Louis, 1974—; mem. bd. dirs. COMTEN Users Exchange, Inc., 1978—. Active Explorer Scouts. Mem. McDonnell Douglas Mgmt. Club. Home: 3012 Westminster Dr Saint Charles MO 63301 Office: PO Box 516 Saint Louis MO 63166

ELICAÑO, RENE VENZON, mgmt. cons., indsl. exec., educator; b. Manila, Philippines, Jan. 16, 1938; s. Tranquilino E. and Quintina (Venzon) E.; B.A. in Gen. Engring., Ateneo U., 1956; M.S. in Indsl. Engring., Stanford, 1957; M.B.A., Marquette U., 1959; Ph.D. in Bus. Adminstrn., Mich. State U., 1967; m. Anita Hansen, May 10, 1969. Mgr. ops. research Allis-Chalmers Mfg. Co., Milw., 1957-62; mgr. Prodn. Control div. and dir. mgmt. systems. Lear Siegler, Inc., Grand Rapids, Mich., 1962-69; dir. corporate planning and systems Kaiser Jeep Corp., Toledo, 1969-70; owner, pres. Sanford Rose Assos., Toledo, 1970-80; prof. U. Toledo, 1976—, dir. Mgmt. Center and chmn. computer systems and prodn. mgmt. dept., 1976—; mgmt. cons., developer tng. programs for industry and govt. Named Outstanding Young Man of Philippines, Mem. Am. Inst. Indsl. Engrs. (dir. 1956—), Ops. Research Soc. Am., Toledo C. of C. Contbr. articles to profl. and trade jours. Home: 4037 Overlook Blvd Toledo OH 43607

ELIEFF, LEWIS STEVEN, stockbroker; b. Sofia, Bulgaria, Aug. 2, 1929; s. Steven and Vera (Svetcoff) E.; B.B.A., U. Mich., 1953, M.B.A., 1954; m. Evanka Brown, May 25, 1958; children—Nancy Ann, Robert and Richard (twins). Statistician, tax accountant Gen. Motors Corp., Flint, Mich., 1954-60; stockbroker William C. Roney & Co., Flint, 1960-73, ltd. partner, 1973-79, gen. partner, 1979—; weekly stock market columnist Grand Blanc (Mich.) News, Tri-County News, Fenton, Mich.; tchr. stock market curriculum Flint Pub. Schs., 1960-68, Genesee County Community Coll., 1968-73, U. Mich. Extension and Grad. Study Center, Flint Campus. Mem. Grand Blanc Twp. Econ. Devel. Commn.; mem. regents-alumni scholarship com. U. Mich., 1977—. Served with AUS, 1954-56. Mem. U. Mich. Alumni Club and Assn. Clubs: Rotary, University (Flint). Home: 6612 Kings Pointe Grand Blanc MI 48439 Office: Bristol Place G-4488 W Bristol Rd Flint MI 48507

ELIOPOULOS, ANDREW JAMES, elec. engr.; b. Akron, Ohio, Sept. 8, 1928; s. James Andrew and Demetra E.; B.E.E., U. Akron, 1953; m. Sylvia Pachares, Aug. 19, 1951; children—James, Tom, Gus, Louis. Leader tech. staff RCA Moorestown Balistic Early Warning System, Moorestown, N.J., 1959-64, Burlington Apollo Rendezvous Radar and Transponder, Burlington, Mass., 1964-71; ops. mgr. Digital Security Systems, Natick, Mass., 1971-74; v.p. constrn. programs Whittaker Community Devel. Corp., Knoxville, Tenn., 1974-75; dir. maintenance Deaconess Hosp., Cleve., 1976-78, constrn. mgr., 1977-81; dir. plant ops. St. Thomas Hosp. Med. Center, Akron, Ohio, 1981—; tchr. evening classes U. Dayton, 1956-58. Pres., St. Nicholas Greek Orthodox Ch. Council, Lexington, Mass., 1973; bd. dirs. Holy Trinity Ch., Canton, Ohio, 1978—. Served to lt. USAF, 1954-59. Recipient Tech. Excellence award RCA-Lunar Excursion Module Radar, 1969. Registered profl. engr., Ohio, Mass., N.J. Mem. IEEE, Aircraft Owners and Pilots Assn. Greek Orthodox. Club: Holy Trinity Men's. Home: 2564 58th St NE Canton OH 44721 Office: 444 N Main St Akron OH 44310

ELIOT, ROBERT SALIM, cardiologist; b. Oak Park, Ill., Mar. 8, 1929; s. Salim and Ruth (Buffington) Elia; B.S., U. N.Mex., 1952; M.D., U. Colo., 1955; m. Phyllis Allman, June 15, 1957; children—William Robert, Susan Elaine. Intern, Evanston Hosp., 1955-56; resident in medicine U. Colo., 1956-58, fellow in cardiology, 1958-60; trainee cardiovascular pathology U. Minn., Charles T. Miller Hosp., St. Paul-Mpls., 1962-63; practice medicine specializing in cardiology; instr. U. Minn., 1963-65, asst. prof., 1965-67; mem. faculty U. Fla., Gainesville, 1967-72, prof. medicine, 1969-72; chief div. cardiology VA Hosp., Gainesville, Fla., 1970-72; prof. medicine U. Nebr. Med. Center, Omaha, 1972—, dir. div. cardiology, 1972-80, dir. Cardiovascular Center, 1972—, chmn. dept. preventive and stress medicine, 1981—; med. dir. Internat. Stress Found., 1977—; cardiology cons. Cape Kennedy, 1971-77; cons. Kellogg Found., 1978; tchr., lectr. Nebr. Outreach program; pres. Alachua County Heart div. 1969-70; chmn. Nat. Goals and Objectives for Stress Mgmt. for surgeon gen. U.S.A., 1980—; nat. and internat. lectr. in field; pres.-elect Interstate Postgrad. Med. Assembly, 1981; chmn. com. on prevention coronary disease in occupational setting Bethesda Conf., 1980-81; cons., report contbr. on role central nervous system and sudden death Nat. Acad. Scis., 1980-81; cons., lectr. on stress mgmt., health promotion and disease prevention in occupational setting to numerous corps., public and profl. orgns. Served to capt. AUS, 1960-62. USPHS, VA, Fla. Heart Assn. grantee. Fellow A.C.P., Clin. Council Am. Heart Assn., Am. Coll. Cardiology (continuing edn. com. mountain states coordinator for continuing edn., long range planning com., exec. com., gov. for Nebr., vice chmn. bd. govs., 1976-77, chmn. bd. govs., 1977-78, trustee, 1978—, chmn. liaison com. Am. Coll. Cardiology-Am. Acad. Family Physicians), N.Y. Acad. Scis.; mem. AMA, Nebr. Med. Assn., Central Soc. Clin. Investigation, Biophys. Soc., Acad. Behavioral Medicine Research (charter), Soc. Behavioral Medicine (charter), Am. Inst. Stress (dir. 1980—), Alpha Omega Alpha, Phi Sigma, Phi Rho Sigma. Author: Stress and the Major Cardiovascular Disorders; editor: The Acute Cardiac Emergency, Stress and the Heart, Practical Mmgt. of Hypertension, Cardiac Emergencies; mem. editorial bd. Heart & Lung, 1972—; contbr. numerous articles to profl. jours. creator edn. TV series Heartline to Health. Home: 405 Ridgewood Dr Bellevue NE 68005 Office: Univ Nebr Med Center 42d and Dewey Sts Omaha NE 68105

ELISEO, THOMAS STEPHAN, psychologist; b. Bklyn., Apr. 9, 1932; s. Frank and Leonarda (Caruso) E.; B.A., Queens Coll., 1953; M.S., Purdue U., 1959, Ph.D., 1960. Clin. psychologist VA Hosp., Lebanon, Pa., 1960-63, Psychiat. Services, Knoxville, Tenn., 1963-64; pvt. practice clin. psychology, Rockford, Ill., 1964—; adj. prof. Rockford Coll., 1965-77; cons. Swedish Am. Hosp., Rockford, 1965—. Served with AUS, 1953-55. Diplomate Am. Bd. Profl. Psychology. Mem. Am. Psychol. Assn., AAAS, Soc. Clin. and Exptl. Hypnosis. Democrat. Contbr. articles to profl. jours.

ELIZALDE, PATRICIA ELAINE ALLEN, sch. counselor; b. Flint, Mich., Sept. 5, 1954; d. Valgene and Cecile Lorene (Bell) A.; B.A. in Psychology, U. Mich., 1977; M.A. in Ednl. Adminstrn., Central Mich. U., 1978; m. Francisco Xavier Elizalde, Jr., Jan. 1, 1980. Probation officer Vol. Services of Genesee County, Flint, 1976-77; caseworker/inter Youth Service Bur. Genesee County, Flint, 1976-77; caseworker CERCA Center, Flint, 1977; coordinator center for student orgns. Central Mich. U., Mt. Pleasant, 1977-78, intern, office of admissions, 1978; counselor youth employment and tng. program Flint Bd. Edn., 1978—. Recipient cert. of appreciation Genesee County Probate Ct., 1976; cert. of achievement La Raza Adv. com. to Mich. Bd. Edn., 1978; cert. of recognition Student Assn. Central Mich. U., 1978. Mem. Am. Coll. Personnel Assn., Assn. Chicanos for Coll. Admissions, U. Mich. Alumnae Assn., Central Mich. U. Alumnae Assn. Democrat. Baptist. Home: 3207 Dearborn Ave Flint MI 48507 Office: Flint Bd Edn 923 E Kearsley St Flint MI 48502

ELKIND, MORTIMER MURRAY, biophysicist; b. Bklyn., Oct. 25, 1922; s. Samuel and Yetta (Lubarsky) E.; B.M.E., Cooper Union Sch. Engring., 1943; M.M.E., Poly. Inst. Bklyn., 1949; M.S. in Elec. Engring., M.I.T., 1951, Ph.D. in Physics, 1953; m. Karla Annikki Holst, Jan. 27, 1960; children—Sean Thomas, Samuel Scott, Jonathan Harald. Asst. project engr. Wyssmont Co., N.Y.C., 1943; project engr.

Safe Flight Instrument Corp., White Plains, N.Y., 1946-47; head instrumentation sect. Sloan Kettering Inst. Cancer Research, 1947-49; physicist Nat. Cancer Inst., M.I.T., 1949-53, Donner Lab., U. Calif., Berkeley, 1953-54; physicist Lab. Physiology, Nat. Cancer Inst., Bethesda, Md., 1954-67, sr. research physicist, 1967-69; sr. biophysicist biology dept. Brookhaven Nat. Lab., Upton, L.I., N.Y., 1969-73; guest scientist MRC exptl. radiopathology unit Hammersmith Hosp., London, 1971-73; sr. biophysicist div. biology and med. research Argonne (Ill.) Nat. Lab., 1973-81, head mammalian cell biology group, 1973-81, asst. dir. research tng., 1976-78; prof. radiology U. Chgo., 1973-81; chmn. dept. radiology and radiation biology Colo. State U., 1981—. Served with USNR, 1944-46. Recipient E. O. Lawrence award AEC, 1967, Superior Service award HEW, 1969, L. H. Gray medal Internat. Com. Radiation Units and Measurements, 1977, E. W. Bertner award M. D. Anderson Hosp. and Tumor Inst., 1979, Arthur W. Erskine award Radiol. Soc. N.Am., 1980; U.S. Nat. Cancer Inst. spl. fellow, 1972-74. Mem. Radiation Research Soc. (pres. 1981—), Biophys. Soc., Tissue Culture Assn., Am. Assn. Cancer Research, AAAS, Am. Soc. Therapeutic Radiologists, Author: (with G. F. Whitmore) The Radiobiology of Cultured Mammalian Cells, 1967. Home: 1521 Linden Lake Rd Fort Collins CO 80524 Office: Dept Radiology and Radiation Biology Colo State U Fort Collins CO 80523

ELKINS, JAMES PAUL, physician; b. Lincoln, Nebr., Mar. 20, 1924; s. James Hill and Antonia (Wohler) E.; M.D., U. Va., 1947; m. May Hollingsworth Reynolds, June 15, 1946; children—Patricia May Elkins Riggs, Paulette Frances Elkins Phillips, James Barrington. Intern, DePaul Hosp., Norfolk, Va., 1947-48; resident in ob-gyn Alexandria (Va.) Hosp., 1948-49, Franklin Sq. Hosp., Balt., 1949-50, St. Rita's Hosp., Lima, Ohio, 1950, Tripler Army Hosp., Honolulu, 1953-54; practice medicine specializing in ob-gyn, Indpls., 1954-73; chief ob-gyn St. Francis Hosp., Beech Grove, Ind., 1965-66; mem. teaching staff Gen. Hosp., Indpls., 1954-73; dep. coroner Marion County, 1965-74; med. cons. disability determination div. Ind. Rehab. Services; med. dir. Phys. Exams. Inc.; ringside physician Ind. State Athletic Commn., Indpls. Pal Club. Service chmn. Beech Grove unit Am. Cancer Soc. Served with AUS, 1949-54. Mem. Am. Coll. Ob-Gyn, AMA, Ind. Obstet. and Gynecol. Soc., Ind. State Med. Assn., Marion County Med. Soc., Indpls. Press Club, Police League Ind., Fraternal Order Police, Nat. Sojourners, 500 Festival Assos., U.S. Auto Club (life), Phi Chi. Clubs: Scottish Rite, Masons, Shriners (life). Home: 2045 Lick Creek Dr Indianapolis IN 46203 Office: 9th Floor Illinois Bldg 17 N Market St PO Box 7069 Indianapolis IN 46207

ELKOURI, ED RICHARD, podiatrist; b. Wichita, Kans., Nov. 15, 1950; s. George E. and Elva S. (Shadid) E.; B.S., Friends U., 1973; D.P.M., Ill. Coll. Podiatric Medicine, 1978. Pvt. practice podiatry, Wichita, 1978—; mem. public relations com. Health Fair. Mem. Am. Podiatry Assn., Kans. Podiatry Assn., Alpha Gamma Kappa. Club: Jogging. Contbr. articles on keloids to profl. jours. Office: 1301 N West St Wichita KS 67203

ELLEGOOD, RICHARD THOMAS, optician; b. St. Louis, June 13, 1952; s. Albert Lawrence and Ellamae Thelma (Slade) E.; student United Electronics Inst., Meramec Community Coll.; m. Cynthia G. Tretter, Apr. 25, 1975; children—Andrew James, Anne Marie. Store mgr. Drs. Optical Service, St. Louis, 1971-74; gen. mgr. County Optical Service, St. Louis, 1974-75; gen. sales mgr. Erker Bros. Optical Co., St. Louis, 1975-80; pres. OPTEK, Inc. Family Vision Centers, St. Louis, 1980—. Mem. Opticians Assn. Mo. (co-chmn. Eastern chpt.), St. Louis Soc. for Blind, South Kingshwy. Businessman's Assn. Served with Air N.G., 1970-76. Baptist. Clubs: Kiwanis, Masons (32 deg.). Home: 804 Alleghany St Saint Louis MO 63125 Office: 4251 S Kingshighway Saint Louis MO 63109

ELLENBECKER, JAMES WALTER, state ofcl.; b. Sioux Falls, S.D., June 19, 1946; s. Walter Albert and Catherine (Ivory) E.; B.A. in Bus. Adminstrn., No. State Coll., 1968; m. Kathleen Jean Gustaf, June 1, 1968; children—Bradley James, Ryon Walter. Manpower planner S.D. State Planning Agy., 1970-73; CETA adminstr. S.D. Dept. Labor, 1973-78, acting sec. of labor, 1978-79; sec. social services S.D. Dept. Social Services, Pierre, 1979—. Served with AUS, 1968-70. Mem. High Plains Wildlife Assn. Roman Catholic. Club: Howacota Archery. Office: Kneip Bldg Pierre SD 57501

ELLENS, JAY HAROLD, theologian, educator; b. McBain, Mich., July 16, 1932; s. John S. and Grace (Kortmann) E.; A.B., Calvin Coll., 1953, B.D., Calvin Sem., 1956; Th.M., Princeton Sem., 1965; Ph.D., Wayne State U., 1970; m. Mary Jo Lewis, Sept. 7, 1954; children—Debra, Jackie, Dan, Beckie, Rocky, Brenda. Ordained to ministry, Christian Reformed Ch., 1956; pastor Newton (N.J.) Christian Reformed Ch., 1961-65; pastor North Hills Ch., Troy, Mich., 1965-68; pastor Univ. Hills Ch., Farmington Hills, Mich., 1968-79; prof. communication psychology Calvin Sem., 1967-70, Oakland Community Coll., 1970-74, Oakland U., 1974-79; pvt. practice psychotherapy, Farmington Hills, Mich., 1967—; religious broadcaster TV, weekly, 1970-74, and periodically to date; lectr. humanities classics Wayne State U., John Wesley Coll., 1970—; vis. lectr. Princeton U., 1978—. Served to col. AUS, 1956-61. Created knight by Queen Juliana, 1974. Mem. Christian Assn. Psychol. Studies (exec. sec. 1974—), AAUP, Am. Psychol. Assn., Soc. Bibl. Lit. and Exegesis, Speech Communication Assn., Mil. Chaplain Assn., Reserve Officers Assn., Archaeol. Inst. Am., Am. Personnel and Guidance Assn., Mil. Order World Wars, Am. Sci. Assn., World Assn. Christian Communicators. Republican. Presbyterian. Author: History of TV Format Development, 1970; Models of Religious Broadcasting, 1974; Chaplain (Major General) Gerhart W. Hyatt: An Oral History, 1977; editor: Ethical Reflections, 1977; Eternal Vigilance, 1980; God's Grace and Human Health, 1982; contbr. articles to profl. jours. Home: 26705 Farmington Rd Farmington Hills MI 48018

ELLENSON, GERALD MARTIN, psychiat. social worker; b. Monticello, Minn., Jan. 13, 1918; s. Sever Edward and Gladys (Hoblit) E.; B.A., Hamline U., 1946; M.S.W., U. Minn., 1959; m. Phyllis Harriet Storch, Sept. 5, 1958; children—(by previous marriage)—Gerald Seward, Steven Martin, Gordon Eugene; stepchildren—Karen Cecilia (Mrs. John Thomas), James Richard, Linda Louise. With Koochiching County Welfare Dept., International Falls, Minn., 1946-49; field rep. Minn. Dept. Pub. Welfare, 1949-55, caseworker, 1959-60; dir. Cass County Welfare Dept., Walker, Minn., 1955-57; clin. social worker psychiatry Hennepin County Gen. Hosp., Mpls., 1960-63; clin. social worker Hennepin County Mental Health Center, Day Hosp., Mpls., 1963-67, sr. psychiat. social worker, 1967-69, acting dir., 1968, dir., 1969-70, prin. psychiat. social worker, 1969-70; pvt. practice marriage and family counseling, Mpls., 1963—; clin. field instr. U. Minn. Grad. Sch. Social Work, 1964—; pvt. practice Met. Psychiat. Clinic, 1970-71; cons. Met. Mental Health Center, 1970-71; sr. psychiat. social worker Crisis Intervention Center, Hennepin County Med. Center, 1971—, asst. dir., 1976—. Served with USAAF, 1943-45. Decorated Air medal with five oak leaf clusters. Mem. Nat. Assn. Social Workers (chpt. chmn. mental health council 1966). Acad. Certified Social Workers, Minn. Welfare Assn., Minn. Soc. for Clin. Social Work. Methodist. Home: 3410 Pleasant Ave S Minneapolis MN 55408 Office: Hennepin County Med Center 7th St and Park Ave Minneapolis MN 55404

ELLERY, JOHN BLAISE, educator, author; b. N.Y.C., Feb. 3, 1920; s. William Hoyt and Thea (Kavanagh) E.; A.B., Hamilton Coll., 1948; M.A., U. Colo., 1950; Ph.D., U. Wis., 1954; m. Ellen Jane Savacool, Sept. 21, 1946; children—Thea Jane, Martha Ann, Sarah Savacool, John Blaise, Jessica Joyce. Instr., U. Colo., 1948-50; asst. prof. U. Iowa, 1952-56; asso. prof. Wayne State U., 1957-61; prof., chmn. dept. English, East Tenn. State U., Johnson City, 1961-66; on leave, sr. lectr. Njala U. Coll., West Africa, 1966-68; asst. to chancellor U. Wis.-Stevens Point, 1968-74, vice chancellor, 1974-80, acting chancellor, 1978-79, dean Coll. Natural Resources, 1970-72. Mem. Wis. Gov.'s Commn. on Edn., 1969; pres. Central Wis.-Managua com. Partners of Ams., 1976-78, exec. com., bd. dirs. Wis.-Nicaragua, 1978—, pres., 1981—. Served to ensign USNR, 1937-41; with inf. AUS, 1941-45; to col. Army N.G. Decorated Conspicuous Service Cross, Silver Star, Bronze Star with oak leaf cluster, Purple Heart with oak leaf cluster (U.S.); Croix de Guerre, médaille Militaire Fourragère; recipient Patriotic Civilian Service award U.S. Army. Mem. Ret. Officers Assn., Assn. U.S. Army, Res. Officers Assn. Contbg. author: Introduction to Graduate Study in Speech and Drama, 1961; Essays on Language and Literature, 1969; author: John Stuart Mill, 1964; Linguistic Impedance and Dialect Interference Among Certain African Tribes, 1970, also short stories, articles. Home: 4217 Janick Circle N Stevens Point WI 54481

ELLIE, YVONNE KISSINGER, ednl. adminstr.; b. Wisconsin Rapids, Wis., Mar. 21, 1936; d. Alfred J. and Louise J. (Brockman) Kissinger; B.S., Coll. St. Teresa, 1958; M.S., U. Wis., Stevens Point, 1978; postgrad. U. Wis., Madison; 1979; m. Gene C. Ellie, June 28, 1958; children—Gregory, Jean Marie, Katherine, Daniel, David, Brian. Tchr., Mpls. Public Schs., 1958, Lowell Sch., Moses Lake, Wash., 1958-59, Vesper Elem. Sch., Wisconsin Rapids, 1967-78, Mead, Howe, Woodside Schs., Wisconsin Rapids, 1978-79; adminstrv. intern Grove and Pitsch Elem. Sch., Wisconsin Rapids, 1979-80, prin., 1980—; mem. Wood County Environ. Edn. Com. Chmn. unified bargaining com. Central Wis. Uniserve Council, 1976-79. Mem. Wisconsin Rapids Tchrs. Assn. (pres. 1978-79), LWV, NEA, Wis. Edn. Assn. (council), Wisconsin Rapids Edn. Assn., Internat. Reading Assn., Wis. Reading Assn., Central Wis. Reading Assn., Nat. Assn. Elementary Prins., Assn. Wis. Sch. Adminstrs., Assn. Supervision and Curriculum Devel., Phi Delta Kappa (mastery learning pilot study 1980—). Home: 5885A Elm Lake Rd Wisconsin Rapids WI 54494 Office: 2750 Lincoln St Wisconsin Rapids WI 54494

ELLINGER, JOHN MICHAEL, univ. adminstr.; b. Columbus, Ohio, Oct. 19, 1948; s. Harley Andrew and Florence Louise (Karn) E.; B.S., Ohio State U., 1970; M.S., 1972; m. Clair Elizabeth Wuichet, June 20, 1970; children—Eve, Daniel, Justin. Coordinator, Farm Bus. Planning and Analysis, Athens, Ohio, 1972-73, Wayne County, Ohio, 1973-76; supr. agr. and home econs. program South Wayne County, Ohio, 1976-79; asso. dir. Ohio unions Ohio State U., 1979—. Chmn., Sch. Day Tour for 5th Graders County of Wayne, 1976-79, chmn. profl. in-service day, 1977-79. Served with USAF, 1970-72. Mem. Ohio State U. Alumni Assn., Am. Vocat. Assn., Ohio Vocat. Assn., Nat. Vocat. Agr. Tchrs. Assn., Ohio Vocat. Agr. Tchrs. Assn., Assn. Coll. Unions Internat. Republican. Methodist. Clubs: Kiwanis, Ohio State U. Alumni, Masons, YMCA Indian Princess. Home: 1659 Essex Rd Columbus OH 43221 Office: 1739 N High St Columbus OH 43210

ELLIOTT, EVANGELINE WILSON, hosp. ofcl.; b. Chgo., June 26, 1941; d. Jackie and Lillian Evelyn (Lowry) Wilson; L.P.N., Cabrini Sch. Practical Nursing, 1964-65; m. John Wallace Elliott, June 30, 1973; children—Louis, Chiquita. Nurse, Cook County Sch. of Nursing, Chgo., 1965-66, Med. Staffing for Nurses, Chgo., 1968-70, Alice Toch Registry for Nurses, Chgo., 1970-71; asst. supr. central service Columbus Hosp., Chgo., 1974-80; supr. central service Hosp. of Englewood, Chgo., 1980—. Mem. Am. Soc. for Central Service Personnel, Chgo. Assn. Hosp. Central Service Personnel. Roman Catholic. Home: 3950 N Lake Shore Dr Chicago IL 60613 Office: Hosp of Englewood 6001 S Green St Chicago IL 60621

ELLIOTT, JOHN ANDREW, hotel exec.; b. Bklyn., Nov. 24, 1900; s. Henry Michael and Josephine (Grundy) E.; Ph.B., U. Notre Dame, 1925; m. Virginia Baker, Aug. 24, 1927 (dec. June 1951); m. 2d, Marian Reichert Geyer, Jan. 27, 1959; 1 dau., Alexandra Geyer Elliott (Marston). Asst. mgr. Nelson Hotel, Rockford, Ill., 1925-27; asst. mgr. Hotel Stoddard, LaCrosse, Wis., 1927-28, gen. mgr., pres., 1928-72; pres. No. Hotel Co., LaCrosse, 1951—; owner, mgr. Cass Realty Co., LaCrosse, 1952—. Mem. bd. Gateway area Boy Scouts Am., 1976—. Decorated knight of Malta, knight comdr. Holy Sepulchre (Vatican). Mem. Am. Hotel and Motel Assn. (dir. 1960-70), Wis. Innkeepers Assn. (pres. 1959-60, chmn. bd. 1960-61, dir. 1971-73), LaCrosse C. of C. (dir. 1969-71), Notre Dame Alumni Assn. Roman Catholic. Clubs: K.C., Rotary (pres. 1967-68), LaCrosse Country; Surf (Surfside, Fla.). Home: Elliott Arms Apts LaCrosse WI 54601

ELLIOTT, LELAND BRUCE, mfg. co. exec.; b. Superior, Nebr., Sept. 15, 1951; s. Cecil Leland and Lloyda Jean (Cook) E.; B.A., Kearney State Coll., 1973; M.S., Fort Hays State U., 1976; postgrad. Va. Poly. Inst. and State U., 1979; m. Marie Louise Hrnicek, June 10, 1972; 1 son, Daniel Lee. Mgmt. trainee J.C. Penney Co., Miami, Okla., 1973-75; resident mgr. H.B. Reed Adult Adjustment Center, Hays, Kans., 1975-76; assessment center adminstr. Psychol. Cons., Inc., Richmond, Va., 1979; indsl. psychologist US. Geol. Survey Dept. Interior, Reston, Va., 1979; dir. indsl. cons. KE Assos., Muscatine, Iowa, 1980—; personnel dir. Ring King Visibles, Inc., Muscatine, 1980—; adj. instr. Muscatine Community Coll., 1981, Iowa Wesleyan U., Mt. Pleasant, 1981—. Mem. Personnel Dirs. Assn., Muscatine C. of C., Am. Soc. Personnel Adminstrs., Am. Soc. Tng. and Devel., Psi Chi, Phi Theta Kappa, Mu Alpha Theta, Psi Chi, Phi Theta Kappa, Mu Alpha Theta. Republican. Roman Catholic. Home: 2206 1/2 Lucas St Muscatine IA 52761 Office: 215 W 2d St Muscatine IA 52761

ELLIOTT, ROBERT BETZEL, physician; b. Ada, Ohio, Dec. 8, 1926; s. Floyd Milton and Rose Marguerite (Betzel) E.; B.A., Ohio No. U., 1949; M.D., U. Cin., 1953; m. Margaret Mary Robichaux, Aug. 26, 1954; children—Howard A., Michael D., Robert Bruce, Douglas J., John C., Joan O. Intern, Charity Hosp., New Orleans, 1953-54; resident pathology Baptist Meml. Hosp., Memphis, 1958-59; practice medicine, specializing in family practice, Ada, 1954—; staff Ohio No. U. Health Service, 1960-70. Mem. Ada Exempted Village Sch. Bd., 1960—, pres., 1966-69, 72—, v.p., 1971—. Coroner Hardin County, 1973—. Served with AUS, 1945-46; PTO. Diplomate Am. Bd. Family Practice. Mem. AMA, Ohio State Med. Assn., Hardin County Med. Soc. (pres. 1964), Am., Ohio, Lima acads. family physicians, Am. Coll. Health Assn. Democrat. Presbyn. Mason (Shriner, 32 degree), Elk. Home: 4429 State Route 235 Ada OH 45810 Office: 302 N Main St Ada OH 45810

ELLIOTT, THOMAS ALBERT, physician; b. Elkhart, Ind., Dec. 31, 1920; s. Lloyd Albert and Cora Mae (Keyser) E.; B.S., Northwestern U., M.D., 1946; m. Mary Noble, June 15, 1942; children—Kathryn Alice, David Lloyd, Thomas Noble, Douglas William, Elizabeth Keyser, Cora Juliette. Intern, Cook County Hosp., Chgo., 1946; fellow in internal medicine Oschner Clinic, New Orleans, 1949-51, mem. staff, 1951; practice medicine specializing in internal medicine, Elkhart, Ind., 1952—; mem. staff Elkhart Gen. Hosp., 1952—, chief of staff, 1964—, cons. internal medicine, 1952—, dir. coronary care unit, 1964—; organizer mem. internal med. staff Elkhart Clinic, 1954—; cons. internal medicine Goshen (Ind.) Gen. Hosp.; a founder, pres. FIDE Corp., 1954—; dir. St. Joseph Valley Bank, Elkhart. Mem. community adv. council South Bend br. Ind. U. Sch. Medicine; founder, pres. United Health Found., 1961—; founder, v.p., pres., bd. dirs. Elliott Found. for Med. Edn. and Research, 1960—; founder, 1st pres., bd. dirs. Adult and Child Guidance Clinic; past pres., past bd. dirs. Mental Health Assn.; v.p., bd. dirs. N. Central Ind. Med. Edn. Found.; bd. dir. Elkhart Gen. Hosp. Assn., 1963-67, trustee, bd. dirs. hosp. found.; bd. dirs. South Bend Med. Found., Inc., 1965-70, No. Ind. Health Services Agy.; past bd. dirs. ARC, Retarded Children's Soc. Served to capt. M.C., U.S. Army, 1943-48. Diplomate Nat. Bd. Med. Examiners, Am. Bd. Internal Medicine. Fellow A.C.P. (life); mem. AMA, Internat., Am. Socs. internal medicine, Am., Ind. thoracic socs., Pan Am. Med. Assn., Am., Ind. (dir. 1974—) heart assns., Ind. Med. Assn. (pres. 13th dist. 1960), Elkhart County Med. Soc. (pres. 1976), Am. Legion, Mensa, Beta Theta Pi, Nu Sigma Nu. Unitarian. Clubs: Elks, Elcona Country. Contbr. articles in field to profl. jours. Home: 5 Kim Ct Elkhart IN 46514 Office: 303 S Nappanee St Elkhart IN 46514

ELLIS, DWIGHT BENJAMIN, former resort assn. exec.; b. Columbus, Ohio, May 28, 1918; s. Benjamin Franklin and Edna Forest (Wanless) E.; B.C.S., Benjamin Franklin U., 1941; m. Ruth Elizabeth Lawrence, July 18, 1937; children—Lawrence Dwight, Nancy Lynn (Mrs. Bruce M. Draudt). IBM operator B.F. Goodrich, Akron, Ohio, 1936-38; spl. agt. FBI, U.S. Dept. Justice, Washington, 1938-42, Indpls., 1942-43, Pitts., 1943-44, Phila., 1944-46, Cleve., 1946-49, 63-68, Akron, 1949-63; exec. dir. Lakeside (Ohio) Assn., religious family resort, 1968-81, mgr. Lakeside Summer Symphony, 1968-81. Methodist. Kiwanian. Home: 1202 Prairie St Lakeside OH 43440

ELLIS, GEORGE MICHAEL, business exec.; b. Zanesville, Ohio, Dec. 5, 1954; s. George Joseph and Adele Clare (Hatem) E.; student Ohio U., 1972-74. Electrician, Ellis TV and Appliance, New Lexington, Ohio, 1969-74; lineman Perry Cablevision, Inc., New Lexington, 1974-76, installer, 1974-75, technician, 1975-76; electro-mech. repair technician Nicofibers, Inc., Shawnee, Ohio, 1976-80; owner Ellis Photographics, New Lexington, 1974—, D & E Electric, New Lexington, 1977—; owner, dir. ops. Crazy Mamas, Columbus, Ohio, 1979—. Bd. dirs. Campus Discotheques Am., Inc., Columbus, 1979-81. Mem. Refrigeration Service Engrs. Soc. Internat. Roman Catholic. Clubs: K.C., Elks. Office: PO Box 1116 Columbus OH 43216

ELLIS, GILBERT R., finance co. exec.; b. Mo., 1915. With Household Finance Corp. (now Household Internat.), 1935—, v.p., 1956-65, sr. v.p., 1965-66, exec. v.p., 1966-72, pres., 1972-77, chief exec. officer, 1973—, chmn. bd., 1974—, also chmn. exec. com. Office: Household Internat 2700 Sanders Rd Prospect Heights IL 60070

ELLIS, HELENE RITA WEISMAN, social worker; b. St. Paul, Sept. 20, 1935; d. Moe and Cele (Sidletsky) Weisman; B.S. with high distinction, Coll. of Edn., U. Minn., 1956; postgrad. Northwestern U., 1959-60; M.S.W., Loyola U., Chgo., 1974; postgrad. Alfred Adler Inst., Chgo., 1969-77; m. Bernard Maurice Ellis, Sept. 30, 1956; children—Miriam Tamara, Arienne Ida, Elia M., Eve Minna. Tchr., Roosevelt High Sch., Mpls., 1957-58, Barrington (Ill.) Consol. High Sch., 1958-59, Congregation Solel, Highland Park, Ill., 1960-70; sch. social worker Dist. 39 Schs., Wilmette, Ill., 1974—. Bd. dirs. Sager Solomon Schechter Day Sch., Northbrook, Ill., 1976-78. Certified social worker, Ill.; teaching certificate, Minn., Ill. Mem. Nat. Assn. Social Workers, Acad. Certified Social Workers, NEA, Ill. Assn. Sch. Social Workers (dir.), Ill., Wilmette edn. assns., N.Am. Soc. Adlerian Psychology, Pioneer Women, Phi Beta Kappa, Pi Lambda Theta, Alpha Sigma Nu. Home: 145 Euclid Ave Glencoe IL 60022 Office: 615 Locust Rd Wilmette IL 60091

ELLIS, JACK GRAVES, univ. ofcl.; b. Frankfort, Ky., May 14, 1934; s. Earl Graves and Sally Mae (True) E.; student Miami U., Oxford, Ohio, 1952-54; B.S., Ohio U., 1957; m. Dewana Sue Mathis, Jan. 16, 1960; children—Sallie Renee, Rebecca Suzanne, Patricia Leah, Joel Mathew. Credit analyst Atlantic Richfield Co., Los Angeles, 1957-58; systems analyst Remington Rand Corp., Los Angeles, 1958-59; dist. mgr. Speery Rand Corp., Pomona, Calif., 1959-60; mfg. rep. Pacific Bus. Interiors, Los Angeles, 1961-67; exec. dir. Ohio U. Alumni Assn., Athens, 1967-70, dir. devel., 1970—, exec. dir. Ohio Univ. Fund, Inc., 1973—. Bd. dirs. Athens Concerned Citizens Against Drug Abuse, 1980—. Mem. Council Advancement and Support Edn., Ohio Assn. Devel. Officers, Athens C. of C. Republican. Home: 17 Mulligan Rd Athens OH 45701 Office: Ohio Univ 305 McGuffey Hall Athens OH 45701

ELLIS, JAMES EDWARD, educator; b. Cin., Aug. 5, 1936; s. Hillman Edward and Lillian Jewel (Taylor) E.; B.S., Xavier U., Cin., 1957; M.A. in Langs., N. Am. Coll., Rome, 1960; m. Fran Ellis, Dec. 19, 1980; children—Rod, Rich, Russ, Rand, Michael. Pres., J.E. Designs Inc., Erlanger, 1973-78; engaged in real estate; councilman of Erlanger, 1968-73, mayor, 1973-78. Pres. No. Ky. Area Planning Commn., 1976—; mem. Ky. Crime Commn., 1976—; pres. No. Ky. League Govts., 1976—. Served with USAF, 1961. Fulbright scholar, 1957. Mem. Nat. Assn. Realtors. Home and office: 43 Creekwood Cincinnati OH 45246

ELLIS, JAMES H., ednl. adminstr.; b. Danville, Ill., Aug. 25, 1932; s. Harold John and Mildred Louise (Crawford) E.; B.S., U. Ill., 1963, M.S., 1965; Ed.D., Walden U., 1971; m. Josephine Ann Flannery, Jan. 29, 1952; children—Tony, Rodney. Tchr., Public Schs. Oakwood (Ill.), 1960-64, supt. Oakwood Grade Sch., 1964-67; adminstrv. asst. Danville Public Schs., 1966-67; supt. Oakwood Schs., 1967-70; supt. ednl. service region Vermilion County, Danville, 1970—. Mem. Internat. Reading Assn., Ill. Assn. Sch. Adminstrs., Am. Assn. Sch. Adminstrs., Ill. Twp. Ofcls. Assn., Vermilion County Prins. Assn., Ill. Supt. Ednl. Service Regions Assn., NEA, Assn. Sch. Bus. Ofcls., Ill. Assn. Supervision and Curriculum Devel., Nat. Assn. Secondary Sch. Prins., Nat. Assn. Elem. Prins., Phi Delta Kappa, Phi Rho Pi. Clubs: Elks, Moose, Lions. Home: 135 Mauck Ln Danville IL 61832 Office: 307 Courthouse Danville IL 61832

ELLIS, JAMES VERNON, metal processing co. exec.; b. Detroit, Feb. 15, 1953; s. James Marvin and Beverly (Lyons) E.; B.A., Western Mich. U., 1976; postgrad. Wayne State U., 1979—; m. Jane I. Parker, Aug. 2, 1978. Owner, Jay Steel Trucking Co., Farmington Hills, Mich., 1971-74; mgmt. trainee Edgcomb Metals, Greenville, S.C., 1976-78; supr. Meier Metal Service Center div. Kuhlman Corp., Hazel Park, Mich., 1978—. Active YMCA, 1974—; vol. counseling leader Juvenile Offender Program, 1977-78; area coordinator Young Republicans, 1977-78. Mem. Am. Mgmt. Assn., Employment Counsellors Assn., Mich. High Sch. Athletic Assn. (sports ofcl.). Methodist. Clubs: DeMolay, Elks. Author: Meier Metal Multi-Media Training Course, 1979, Meier Metal Safety Manual, 1979. Home: 1580 Connecticut Walled Lake MI 48088 Office: Meier Metal Service Center div Kuhlman Corp 1471 E Nine Mile Rd Hazel Park MI 48030

ELLIS, JOSEPH GILBERT, cardiologist; b. Chgo., Feb. 20, 1935; s. Joseph Gilbert and Ruth Cora (Arenson) E.; student U. Chgo., 1950-53; B.A., U. Calif., 1956; M.D., Stanford, 1962; m. Janet Lynn Connor, Apr. 14, 1976. Intern, U. Ill. Hosp., Chgo., 1962-63; resident in medicine Stanford (Calif.) Hosp., 1963-64; Nat. Heart Inst. trainee in cardiology Scripps Clinic, La Jolla, Calif., 1964-66; mem. med. staff Scripps Clinic, La Jolla, Calif., 1966-67; practice medicine specializing in cardiology, Danville, Ill., 1968-74, Urbana, Ill., 1974—; mem. staff, dir. cardiac catherization and angiography lab. Carle Hosp., 1974—; clin. asso. U. Ill. Basic Scis. Med. Sch.; cons. VA Hosp., Danville; Tb control officer Vermilion and Champaign counties, Ill. Served with USNR, 1956-57. Tex Heart Inst. fellow in cardiology, 1970. Fellow Am. Coll. Physicians, Am. Coll. Angiology; mem. AMA. Developer hemodialysis unit for E. Central Ill., cardiac lab. for Central Ill. Home: 1904 S Vine Urbana IL 61801 Office: 602 W University Ave Urbana IL 61801

ELLIS, ROBERT GRISWOLD, engring. co. exec.; b. Kokomo, Ind., Dec. 28, 1908; s. Ernest Eli and Ethel (Griswold) E.; A.B., Ind. U., 1934; m. Florence S. Fisher, June 28, 1966. Mem. staff Ind. U., Bloomington, 1930-34; researcher Blackett-Sample-Hummert Inc., Chgo., 1934, asst. mgr. merchandising, 1935-36; prodn. mgr. Harvey & Howe, Inc., Chgo., 1936-37; dist. mgr. L.F. Grammes & Sons, Inc., Allentown, Pa., serving Chgo. and Midwest, 1937-45; with Ellis & Co., Chgo. and Park Ridge, Ill., 1945—, pres., chief engr., 1948—, mng. dir., chief engr. Ellis Internat. Co., Chgo. and Park Ridge, Ill., 1965—, chief engr. Ellis Engring. Co., Park Ridge, 1969—. Chmn. Citizens Com. for Cleaner and More Beautiful Park Ridge, 1957-60; trustee, treas. bd. dirs. 1st United Methodist Ch., Park Ridge, 1974-77. Recipient Civic Achievement award City of Park Ridge, 1959. Mem. Soc. Automotive Engrs., Armed Forces Communications and Electronics Assn. (life), Ind. U. Alumni Assn. (life), Quartermaster Assn. (pres. Chgo. chpt. 1957-58), Ind. Acad. Sci., Am. Powder Metallurgy Inst., Ill. Acad. Sci., Mfrs. Agts. Assn. Gt. Britain and Ireland, Internat. Union Comml. Agts. and Brokers, Am. Logistics Assn., Am. Soc. Metals, Indiana Soc. of Chgo. Republican. Clubs: Internat. Trade, Union League, Varsity (pres. Chgo. 1957), Ind. U. Alumni (pres. Chgo. 1956-57). Home: 643 Parkwood St Park Ridge IL 60068 Office: Box 344 306 Busse Hwy Park Ridge IL 60068

ELLIS, ROBERT PEELE, III, real estate broker; b. Wilson, N.C., June 19, 1938; s. Robert Peele, II, and Ruth (Hawkins) E.; student pub. schs., Wilson, N.C.; m. Loris Ann Yelineck, Oct. 1, 1960; children—John H., Robert D., Marjorie E., Edwin B. Broker, Routh Robbins Real Estate Corp., Alexandria, Va., 1962-65, Lucey Realty Service, Madison, Wis., 1966-71; broker, McKy Ellis Realty Inc., Madison, 1972—,also v.p., sec.; dir. Bank of Shorewood Hills; mem. Wis. Real Estate Examining Bd., 1975—, chmn., 1975-78; pres. Wis. Real Estate Rev. Inc. Mem. Wis. Vets. Bd., 1974-76; vice chmn. Dane County (Wis.) Cancer Assn., 1976. Served with USAF, 1956-60. Mem. Nat. Assn. Realtors, Madison Bd. Realtors, Mendota Assn. Wis. Realtors Assn. Democrat. Roman Catholic. Office: 14 N Carroll St Madison WI 53703

ELLIS, WILLA, educator; b. England, Ark., Dec. 5, 1930; d. Willie Lee and Lucinda (Johnson) Palmore; B.S., So. Ill. U., 1962, M.S., 1970; Ph.D., St. Louis U., 1980; m. Clarence Ellis, Jan. 27, 1949; children—Kelvin LeMont, Clarence, Monte Leon, Edgar T. Elem. tchr. East St. Louis (Ill.) Sch. Dist. 189, Monroe Sch., 1963—, tchr. 4th grade, 1979—. Dir. children's div. New Salem Dist. Congress Christian Edn., East St. Louis, 1979—; dir. Christian edn. St. Mark Baptist Ch., East St. Louis, 1979. Recipient cert. recognition Women of Essence Daus. of Essence, 1981. Mem. Am. Fedn. Tchrs., NAACP (cert. merit 1973), Assn. Supervision and Curriculum Devel., Internat. Reading Assn. Democrat. Clubs: Sponsorettes Boys' Club East St. Louis, Inc., Metro-East Women of Achievement (treas.). Research on reading achievement of pupils from fatherless and father-present homes, 1975; condr. expt. in creative writing for elem. pupils, 1977. Home: 613 N 13th St East Saint Louis IL 62205 Office: 1620 M L King Dr East Saint Louis IL 62205

ELLIS, WILLIAM DONOHUE, author; b. Concord, Mass., Sept. 23, 1918; s. William Otterbein and Maude (Donohue) E.; B.A., Wesleyan U. Conn., 1941; m. Dorothy Ann Naiden, June 13, 1942; children—William Naiden, Sarah Elizabeth. Writer, Storycraft, Inc., Cleve., 1947-52; writer, pres. Edit. Services, Inc., Cleve., 1952—; mem. staff Writers Conf., U. N.H., 1958; novels include: The Bounty Lands, 1952; Jonathan Blair, Bounty Lands Lawyer, 1954; The Brooks Legend, 1958; (non-fiction) How to Win the Conference, 1955; The Cuyahoga, 1966; Clarke of St. Vith, 1974; Land of the Inland Seas, 1974; Early Settlers, 1976; Angoff's Army, 1980; On the Oil Lands, 1981. Served with AUS, 1941-46. Decorated Bronze Star, Purple Heart; recipient Ohioana Fiction award, 1952; Western Res. Hist. Soc. award, 1952; Top Fiction of Year award Saturday Rev., 1954; Cleve. Arts Council Lit. award, 1967; nominated for Pulitzer prize, 1954. Mem. Authors Guild. Home: 1060 Richmar Dr Westlake OH 44145 Office: Dover Bay Junction Tower Dover Rd Bay Village OH 44140

ELLIS, WINIFRED LEA, nurse, educator; b. Steinauer, Nebr., June 15, 1936; d. Theodore and Esther Ruby (Wolff) Bartels; R.N., Lincoln Gen. Hosp., 1959; B.S., Midland Luth. Coll., 1956; m. Charles K. Ellis, Apr. 28, 1962; children—Christine Kay, Elizabeth Marie. Counselor, Services for Visually Impaired, 1959-62; nursing instr. Lincoln Gen. Sch. Nursing, 1962-67; inservice instr. Beatrice (Nebr.) State Devel. Center, 1974-78; nursing instr. S.E. Community Coll., Beatrice, 1979—; lectr. Vol., ARC; mem. Beatrice Jr. High Parents Council. Mem. Nat. League Nursing, Nat. Vocat. Assn. (del.), Nebr. Vocat. Assn., S.E. Community Coll. Faculty Assn., AAUW. Lutheran. Club: 3-Cs Saddle. Home: 1608 N 17th St Beatrice NE 68310 Office: Southeast Community College Beatrice NE 68310

ELLISON, NANCY MAY KNIGHT, hosp. ofcl.; b. Daytona Beach, Fla., May 12, 1936; d. Harry Cyril and Alyce Rebecca Knight; A.B., U. Mich., 1958; m. Richard Duane Ellison, Sept. 1, 1956; 1 dau., Lorry Rebecca. Reporter, Ypsilanti (Mich.) Daily Press, 1957; librarian journalism dept. U. Mich., 1957-59; copywriter Sta. WPAG, Ann Arbor, Mich., 1964-66; dir. public relations Ann Arbor United Fund, 1966-69; office supr. Edwards Bros. Book Mfg. Co., Ann Arbor, 1970-72; scheduler advt. Midwestern Broadcasting Co., Traverse City, Mich., 1973-74; dir. public relations Munson Med. Center, Traverse City, 1974—. Mem. Torch Lake Twp. Zoning Bd., 1974-76. U. Mich. Regents Alumni scholar, 1954-58. Mem. Internat. Assn. Bus. Communicators, Am. Soc. Hosp. Public Relations, Mich. Hosp. Public Relations Assn. (mem. bd., dist. chmn., treas. 1976—), Traverse City Ad Club (dir.), Theta Sigma Phi. Presbyterian. Author articles in field. Home: Box 565 Golden Beach Dr Kewadin MI 49648 Office: Munson Med Center 6th and Madison Sts Traverse City MI 49684

ELLOR, JAMES WILLIAM, med. social worker, clergyman; b. Abington, Pa., Apr. 23, 1951; s. John Barkley and Marjory Jean (Hooper) E.; B.A., Kent (Ohio) State U., 1973; M.A. in Social Work, U. Chgo., 1976; M.Div., McCormick Theol. Sem., Chgo., 1978. Founder, dir. Housing Rehab., Inc., McElworth, Ohio, 1970-73; exec. dir. North Shore Interfaith Housing Council, Wilmette, Ill., 1973-74; asst. coordinator seniors health program Augustana Hosp., Chgo., 1976-78; spl. project coordinator Johnston R. Bowmen Center, Rush-Presbyn.-St. Luke's Hosp., Chgo., 1978-80; chaplain Methodist Home, Chgo., 1978-80; mem. staff Sch. Social Service Adminstrn., U. Chgo., 1980—; instr. Kendall Coll., 1981—; vis. lectr. McCormick Theol. Sem., 1976—; field work supr. Loyola U., Chgo., McCormick Theol. Sem.; adj. faculty Nat. Coll. Edn., 1979—; cons. Prime Time Day Center, Presbyn. Retirement Home; cons. oncology dept. Thorak Hosp. Cert. social worker, Ill. Mem. Gerontol. Soc., Nat. Assn. Social Workers, Acad. Cert. Social Workers, Nat. Interfaith Coalition Aging, Activity Therapist Assn., Ill. Assn. Utilization Rev. Coordinators. Author papers in field. Home: 5303 W 23d St Cicero IL 60650 Office: 969 E 60th St Chicago IL 60637

ELLSWORTH, JOHN CHARLES, furniture mfg. co. exec.; b. Willoughby, Ohio, Aug. 9, 1935; s. Ralph Henry and Edythe Lucretia (Noon) E.; B.A., Mt. Union Coll., 1957; postgrad. Western Res. U., 1957-59; m. Catherine Ann Segar, Nov. 21, 1939. With Ellsworth Cabinet, Inc., Willoughby, 1963—, pres., 1975—; dir. Prentke-Romich Co., Shreve, Ohio; mem. adv. council SBA; bd. dirs. Small Bus. Found. Am., 1981—. Bd. dirs. West End YMCA. Served to lt. U.S. Navy, 1959-64. Mem. Council Smaller Enterprises (chmn. 1981), Greater Cleve. Growth Assn. (vice chmn. 1981). Office: 4610 Hamann Pkwy Willoughby OH 44094

ELLSWORTH, STEPHEN RANDALL, mayor, ins. co. exec.; b. Fayette County, Ill., Feb. 3, 1943; s. Ralph Randall and Twila Mae (Cunningham) E.; student St. Louis Christian Coll., 1961-62; m. Rae Marie Yehling, Feb. 22, 1964; children—Kris, Kurt. Owner, operator Texaco Service Sta., Edwardsville, Ill., 1965-67; agt. State Farm Ins. Cos., Edwardsville, 1967—; mayor City of Edwardsville, 1977—. Exec. bd. Boy Scouts Am., 1973-77; bd. dirs. United Fund, 1976-77, YMCA, 1975-77; chmn. nominating com. Adv. Council, Edwardsville Sch. Bd., 1975. Recipient Keyman award, Jr. C. of C., 1971, Disting. Service award, 1973, others; Millionaire Club award, 1974; Legion of Honor award, 1977-78; named one of 10 outstanding young persons Ill., 1979. Mem. Lewis and Clark Underwriters Assn., Edwardsville C. of C., Southwestern Ill. Council of Mayors. Christian Ch. Clubs: Career Achievement, Millionaire, Moose. Home: 827 Amherst Pl Edwardsville IL 62025 Office: 1403 Troy Rd Edwardsville IL 62025

ELMORE, KATHLEEN ANN MARIE, food co. exec.; b. Indpls., Sept. 9, 1952; d. Martin Alfred and Florence Cecilia (Miara) E.; B.S., Purdue U., 1974; M.B.A., Central State U., Okla., 1978. Regional merchandiser Castle & Cooke Foods, Inc., Indpls., 1975, divisional merchandiser, New Orleans, 1975-76, asst. dist. sales mgr., Dallas, 1976, dist. sales mgr., Oklahoma City, 1976-77; mgr. field mktg. projects Pizza Hut div. PepsiCo., Inc., Wichita, Kans., mgr. market research, 1979-81; mgr. sales planning Stokely-Van Camp Inc., Indpls., 1981—. Recipient Panhellenic Outstanding Sr. award, Purdue U., 1974; Ind. State scholar, 1970-74, Am. Bus. Women's Assn. scholar, 1971-73; Purdue U. Centennial grantee, 1974. Mem. Assn. M.B.A. Execs.

ELMORE, WALTER LUCIEN, educator; b. Hodgenville, Ky., Dec. 20, 1918; s. Lucien L. and Grace E. E.; B.A., Georgetown (Ky.) Coll., 1942; M.A., U. Ky., 1948; postgrad. U. Ill., 1949; m. Jane E. Derrick, Oct. 28, 1943; children—Walter Ronald, Steven Wayne. Tchr., coach Georgetown (Ky.) High Sch., 1946-48, Eastern State High Sch., Charleston, Ill., 1948-54; asso. prof. edn. and phys. edn., coordinator student tchrs. Eastern Ill. U., Charleston, 1954—; head starter Ill. High Sch. state track meet. Trustee First Bapt. Ch., Charleston. Served to lt. USN, 1942-45. Mem. AAHPER, Ill. Assn. Health, Phys. Edn. and Recreation (state legis. minuteman, Quarter Century Club award 1972), Ill. Assn. Tchr. Edn., Ill. Assn. Tchr. Educators, Ill. High Sch. Assn. Clubs: Eastern Ill. U. Edn. (adv. 1975-76), Eastern Vets. Assn., Elks. Author: Physical Fitness Monagraph, 1951; Preparation for Student Teaching and Beginning Teaching, 1965; First Year Physical Education Teacher, 1964. Home: 303 Chamberlin Dr Charleston IL 61920 Office: Eastern Illinois University Charleston IL 61920

ELROD, ROBERT GRANT, lawyer; b. Indpls., Feb. 24, 1940; s. French McElroy and B. Burrlene (Holland) E.; B.A. with honors, DePauw U., 1962; J.D. cum laude, Harvard, 1965; m. Beverly Anne Wahl, Aug. 23, 1964; children—Franklin Matthew, Benjamin Grant, Jeremiah French, Jonathan Robert. Admitted to Ind. bar, 1965; since practiced in Indpls.; asso. firm Elrod, Taylor & Williams, 1965-66; partner firm Elrod & Elrod, Indpls., 1967-69, Elrod, Elrod & Mascher, Indpls., 1980—; asst. county atty., Indpls., Marion County, Ind., 1967-68, county atty., 1969, asst. atty., city-county legal div., 1970-71, gen. counsel, city-county council, 1972—; dir. Bel-Mar Products Corp. Treas., Young Republicans Marion County, 1968-69, sr. v.p., 1969-71, pres., 1971-73; 11th dist. chmn. Ind. Young Rep. Fedn., 1971-74, nat. committeeman, 1975-77; del. Rep. State Conv., 1968, 70, 72, 74, 76, 78; precinct committeeman Rep. party, 1970-78, ward chmn., 1977-80. Recipient Outstanding Male Young Rep. award Ind. Young Rep. Fedn., 1972, Marion County, 1974. Mem. Am., Ind. State, Johnson County, Indpls. bar assns., Am. Judicature Soc., Comml. Law League Am., Indpls. Bar Found., Am. Soc. Hosp. Attys. Methodist. Mason. Clubs: Columbia (Indpls.); Valle Vista (Greenwood, Ind.). Home: 6730 S Arlington Ave Indianapolis IN 46227 Office: 803 First Fed Bldg Indianapolis IN 46204 also 310 Nat Bank of Greenwood Greenwood IN 46142

EL SAFFAR, RUTH SNODGRASS, educator; b. N.Y.C., June 12, 1941; d. John Tabb and Ruth (Wheelwright) Snodgrass; B.A., Colo. Coll., 1962; Ph.D., Johns Hopkins U., 1966; m. Zuhair M. El Saffar, Apr. 11, 1965; children—Ali, Dena, Amir. Instr. Spanish, Johns Hopkins U., 1963-65; instr. English, Univ. Coll. Baghdad, 1966-67; asst. prof. Spanish, U. Md., Balt. County, 1967-68; asst. prof. U. Ill., Chgo. Circle, 1968-73, asso. prof., 1973-78, prof., 1978—; Nat. Endowment for Humanities summer seminar dir., 1979. Woodrow Wilson fellow, 1962; Nat. Endowment for Humanities fellow, 1970-71; Guggenheim fellow, 1975-76; Am. Council Learned Socs. grantee, 1978. Mem. Modern Lang. Assn. (exec. council 1974-78), Am. Assn. Tchrs. Spanish and Portuguese, Midwest Modern Lang. Assn. Author: Novel to Romance: A Study of Cervantes' Novelas Ejemplares, 1974; Distance and Control in Don Quixote, 1975; Cervantes' Casamiento engañoso and Coloquio de los perros, 1976. Home: 7811 Greenfield River Forest IL 60305 Office: Dept Spanish U Ill Chicago Circle Chicago IL 60680

ELSASSER, EDWARD ORR, historian; b. Oak Park, Ill., Feb. 16, 1918; s. William Everett and Bertha Gertrude (Orr) Kenyon; student U. Mich., 1936-37; B.A., Bethany Coll., 1942; M.A., Clark U., 1948; Ph.D., U. Chgo., 1954; m. Leila Marie Mitchell, Feb. 8, 1975; children—Brian Jensen, Eric Orr. Lectr. history Roosevelt U., Chgo., 1954-55; asst. prof. Western Mich. U., Kalamazoo, 1955-59, asso. prof., 1959-64, prof., 1964—. Mem. Kalamazoo Housing Bd. Appeals, 1971-75, chmn. 1973-75; bd. dirs. Kalamazoo Council on Human Relations, 1959-62; mem. Kalamazoo Hist. Commn., 1978-79. Served with AUS, 1942-44. Decorated Bronze Star. Fulbright grantee, Argentina, 1963. Mem. AAUP (pres. Western Mich. U. chpt. 1965-66), InterAm. Assn. Democracy and Freedom, Am. Hist. Assn., Latin Am. Studies Assn., Conf. Latin Am. History, Midwest Assn. Latin Am. Studies, Soc. History of Edn. Republican. Episcopalian. Contbr. articles to profl. jours. Home: 3124 Winchell St Kalamazoo MI 49008 Office: Western Mich Univ Kalamazoo MI 49008

ELSE, WILLIS IRL, banker; b. Fairbury, Nebr., Dec. 24, 1931; s. Irl Roy and Helen Gertrude (Lynch) E.; B.S., Northwestern U., 1953; M.S., U. Ill., 1958; student U. Chgo., 1959-63; m. Marion Essie Eggers, Dec. 23, 1961; children—Sharon Lee, John Frazer, Robert Irl. Asst. cashier First Nat. Bank of Chgo., 1962-67, asst. v.p., 1967-69; vice-pres. Citibank, N.A., N.Y.C., 1969-76; pres., chief exec. officer Akron (Ohio) Nat. Bank, 1977-79, also dir.; pres. No. group BancOhio Nat. Bank, Akron, 1979-81, exec. v.p. BancOhio Nat. Bank, Columbus, 1981—, also dir.; pres., dir. Akron Small Bus. Devel. Corp., Geneal. Systems Inc.; sec., dir. Fairbury Ins. Agy., Inc.; dir. Else Investment Co., Fairbury. Bd. dirs. Akron Regional Devel. Bd., 1977—; trustee Western Res. Acad., Hudson, Ohio, Akron City Hosp., Akron City Hosp. Found. Served with AUS, 1953-56. Mem. Am. Bankers Assn., Am. Statis. Assn., Robert Morris Assos., Soc. Genealogists, Nat. Geneal. Soc. Republican. Lutheran. Club: Portage Country, (Akron). Author: A Handbook of Legal and Ethical Restrictions on Financial Advertising, 1964. Office: 155 E Broad St Columbus OH 43265

ELSENER, JAMES EDWARD, trade assn. exec.; b. Oak Park, Ill., Oct. 29, 1943; s. George Elmer and Helen Dorothy (Johnson) E.; student Albion Coll., 1961-62; B.A., Western Mich. U., 1970; postgrad. (Bagehot fellow), Columbia U., 1975-76; m. Patricia Anne Stemper, Oct. 5, 1974; children—Alyce Elizabeth, Samuel James. Reporter, asst. city editor City News Bur. Chgo., 1970-72, Chgo. Tribune, 1972-77; exec. dir. Suburban Newspapers of Am., Inc., Chgo., 1977—; account exec. Smith, Bucklin & Assos., Chgo., 1977. Served with USMC, 1962-66. Mem. Newspaper Assn. Mgrs., Inc. Home: 523 Belleforte Ave Oak Park IL 60302 Office: 111 E Wacker Dr Chicago IL 60611

ELSTON, RUTH MARIE, counselor; b. Mendota, Ill., June 10, 1949; d. Gerald Francis and Dorothy Helen (Spanier) E.; B.Mus. in Edn., Ill. State U., Normal, 1971; M.A. in Human Devel. Counseling, Sangamon State U., Springfield, Ill., 1979. Music tchr. Springfield public schs., 1971-74; crisis counselor, victim advocate, mem. exec. bd. Rape Info. and Counseling Service, Springfield, 1976—; alcoholism and rehab. counselor McFarland Mental Health Center, Springfield, 1978-79; grad. asst. instructional services Sangamon State U., 1977-79; vol. counselor Springfield Area Parents Anonymous, 1977—; VISTA mem. St. Louis Abused Women Support Project, St. Louis, resident service coordinator, 1979-80; counselor Life Skills Found. for Retarded, St. Louis, 1980—. Active Ill. ERA, 1976—; mem. council Coll. Fine Arts, Ill. State U., 1970-71. Mem. Am. Personnel and Guidance Assn., Am. Mental Health Assn., Assn. Humanistic Edn. and Devel., Am. Rehab. Counselors Assn. Roman Catholic. Office: 2709 Locust Suite 8 Saint Louis MO 63103

ELSTON, WAYNE LEROY, mcpl. ofcl.; b. Regent, N.D., May 11, 1916; s. Fred Roy and Ellen Elizabeth (Olson) E.; student public schs.; m. Irene Delores Richardson, Oct. 24, 1939; children—Del Roy, Damaras, Danny, Dana. With Civilian Conservation Corps, 1934-39; farm laborer, 1949-54; pipefitter foreman Utah Constrn. Co. at Angostura Dam, Hot Springs, S.D., 1946-49; foreman mcpl. water-wastewater Brookings (S.D.) Mcpl. Utilities, 1954-79, supr. waste-wastewater dept., 1979—, dir. Credit Union, 1976—. Active youth baseball programs, 1960—. Served with inf. AUS, 1945-46. Mem. Am. Fedn. Police, S.D. Water and Wastewater Conf. (Price-Reese award 1975), Smithsonian Inst. Assos., Am. Legion (past comdr.). Baptist. Home: 402 5th Ave S Brookings SD 57006 Office: Brookings Mcpl Utilities 525 Western Ave Brookings SD 57006

ELTINGE, LAMONT, mfg. co. exec.; b. Chgo., May 9, 1926; s. Orville Lamont and Lillian (Steininger) E.; B.S.M.E., Purdue U., 1947; M.S.M.E., Ill. Inst. Tech., 1956, Ph.D., 1965; m. Ethel Jackman, June 13, 1953; children—Barbara Ruth, John Lamont. Trainee, foreman electromotive div. Gen. Motors Corp., Chgo., 1947-51; automotive engr., sect. leader Am. Oil, Whiting, Ind., 1951-62; research asst. Inst. Gas Tech., Chgo., 1963-64; dir. automotive research Ethyl Corp., Detroit, 1964-68; v.p. research and tech. Cummins Engine Co., Inc., Columbus, Ind., 1968-73; dir. research Eaton Corp., Southfield, Mich., 1973—; mem. adv. panel Office of Tech. Assessment, 1976-77. Mem. adv. com. Bradley U., U. Va.; elder 1st Presbyterian Ch., Northville, Mich., 1979—. Served with USNR, 1944-46. Mem. Soc. Automotive Engrs. (bd. dirs.), ASME, Am. Petroleum Inst., Combustion Inst., Sigma Xi. Patentee in field. Home: PO Box 251 Northville MI 48167 Office: PO Box 766 Southfield MI 48037

ELVING, PHILIP JULIBER, chemist, educator; b. Bklyn., Mar. 14, 1913; s. Bernard David and Rose (Juliber) E.; A.B., Princeton U., 1934, A.M., 1935, Ph.D., 1937; m. Beulah Londow Round, June 20, 1937; children—Elizabeth Elving Bass, Louise Elving Carr. Instr. chemistry Pa. State U., 1937-39, prof., 1949-52; instr. chemistry Purdue U., 1939-41, asst. prof., 1941-43, asso. prof., 1947-49; head analytical, phys. chemistry div. research lab. Publicker Industries, Inc., 1943-45, asst. dir. chem. research, 1945-47; vis. prof. chemistry Harvard U., 1951-52, Hebrew U., 1966, 73, 81; prof. chemistry U. Mich., Ann Arbor, 1952—; mem. Internat. Com. for Electrochem. Thermodynamics and Kinetics, 1960-69, NRC Com. Analytical Chemistry, 1958-61. Recipient Anachem award Detroit sect. Am. Chem. Soc., 1958, Fisher award analytical chemistry Am. Chem. Soc., 1960. Mem. Am. Chem. Soc. (div. chmn.), Electrochem. Soc. (dir., div. chmn.), Brit. Chem. Soc., Phi Beta Kappa, Sigma Xi, Phi Lambda Upsilon. Jewish. Editor: (with I.M. Kolthoff) Treatise on Analytical Chemistry 1959—; (with J.D. Winefordner) Chemical Analysis Series, 1957—; contbr. articles to profl. jours., chpts. to books. Home: 2309 Devonshire Rd Ann Arbor MI 48104 Office: Dept Chemistry U Mich Ann Arbor MI 48109

ELWELL, KENNETH RAY, ret. dentist, educator emeritus; b. East Liverpool, Ohio, Jan. 23, 1912; s. Harry Elmer and Grace Emma (Thomas) E.; student Ohio U., 1929-31; B.S.D., Northwestern U., 1937, D.D.S., 1937; M.P.H., U. Mich., 1957; m. Argie Cappelli, Dec. 25, 1933; children—Carole Elwell Parjari, Katherine Elwell Gardner, James T. Resident dentist State Soldiers Home, Sandusky, Ohio, 1937-40; commd. 1st lt., Dental Corps, U.S. Army, 1940, advanced through grades to col. USAF, 1956; asst. dental surgeon, Carlisle Barracks, Pa., 1940; staff dental surgeon 66th Inf. Div., 1943-45; chief dentist 235th Gen. Hosp., France, 1945-46, 113th Evacuation Hosp. and 388th Sta. Hosp., Germany, 1946-48; base dental surgeon, Grenier AFB, 1948, Offutt AFB, 1948-52; command dental surgeon SAC, 1948-52; chief preventive dentistry and research div. Office Asst. Surg. Gen. for Dental Services, 1952-56; chief dentist PACAF Base Command, 1957-60; dir. dental services USAF Med. Service Sch., 1960-65; command dental surgeon Air Force Systems Command, 1965-67, ret., 1967; asso. prof. public health dentistry, 1967-72, chmn. dept. community dentistry Case Western Res. U., Cleve., 1967-77, prof. dept. community dentistry, 1972-80, emeritus prof., 1980—, cons. dept. community dentistry, 1980—; mem. dental study sect., div. research grants NIH, USPHS, com. on dentistry, div. med. scis. NRC, Nat. Acad. Scis.; tech. adviser Air Force dental tng. films on preventive dentistry and practice mgmt.; program dir. USPHS grant Tng. a Community-Minded Dentist; program coordinator USPHS and Am. Coll. Dentists 7-11 Ann. Insts. for Advanced Edn. in Dental Research; mem. adv. com. Met. Health Planning Corp., Cleve.; mem. Cleve. Dental Health Task Force, 1968-70; chmn.

search com. for dental dir. Met. Hosp., Cleve. trustee, exec. council, adv. com. on alcoholism Cleve. Neighborhood Health Services, Inc.; mem. adv. com. Health Consumer Affairs; mem. adv. group Youngstown Area Health Edn. Network, 1970-80. Diplomate Am. Bd. Dental Public Health. Fellow Am. Public Health Assn. (vice chmn., acting chmn. dental health sect. 1962-63), Am. Coll. Dentists; mem. Am. Acad. Periodontology, ADA (life mem., chmn. pub. health sect. 1970), Ohio Dental Assn. (life), Cleve. Dental Soc. (life), Am. Assn. Dental Schs., Internat. Assn. Dental Research, Am. Assn. Public Health Dentists (life mem., exec. council 1970-79, sec.-treas. 1973-76, pres.-elect 1976-77, pres. 1977-78), Omega Beta Pi, Alpha Chi, Omicron Kappa Upsilon (pres. Upsilon chpt. 1976-77). Clubs: Masons (32 deg.), Shriners, Commd. Officers of Cleve. Decorated Legion of Merit, Bronze Star medal with oak leaf cluster, Air Force Commendation medal with oak leaf cluster, U.S. Army Commendation medal, Medaille de la Reconnaissance Française (French). Author: (with Kenneth A. Easlick) Classification and Appraisal of Objections to Fluoridation, 1960; Statistical Methods for Oral Research, 1969; Biostatistics for Dental Students, 1968. Contbr. articles to profl. jours. Home: 4661 W Farnhurst Rd South Euclid OH 44121

ELWOOD, DAVID LEQUE, psychologist; b. New Castle, Ind., Feb. 14, 1930; s. Marion Lee and Mollie Novella (Boone) Ellwood; m. Ella Mae Anderson, June 23, 1956; children—Michael David, Mark Stephen, John Andrew. B.A. cum laude, Olivet Nazarene Coll., 1955; M.A., So. Ill. U., 1958; Ph.D., Purdue U., 1963. Certified psychologist, Ind. Intern, Anna (Ill.) State Hosp., 1957-58; staff psychologist LaRue D. Carter Memorial Hosp., Indpls., 1958-60; staff psychologist Quinco Consulting Center, Columbus, Ind., 1962-73, prin. investigator research projects NIMH, 1967-76, chief of research, 1973-76, mgr. admission and automated services, 1976-78; cons. psychologist Madison (Ind.) State Hosp., 1964-67; pvt. practice psychology, Columbus, 1978—; adj. asso. prof. psychology U. Louisville, 1972-75. Bd. dirs. Opportunity Center, Inc., Columbus, 1965-73, pres. 1971; v.p., bd. dirs. Region Ten Mental Retardation, Inc., Columbus, 1970-71; trustee, sec. Ch. of the Nazarene, Columbus, 1973-77; dir. Inst. Continuing Edn. in Psychology, 1973-76. Mem. Am., Ind. (pres. 1977—) psychol. assns., Internat. Assn. Applied Psychology, Am. Soc. Clin. Hypnosis, Phi Delta Lambda. Contbr. articles in field to profl. jours. Home: 3422 Grove Pl Columbus IN 47201 Office: 2530 Sandcrest Blvd Columbus IN 47201

ELY, ROBERT LEROY, criminalist; b. Lancaster, Ohio, Sept. 9, 1934; s. Paul Raymond and Marjorie (Davis) E.; student Ohio State U., 1967-69, Ohio U., 1967, Ind. U., 1968, Ohio State Hwy. Patrol Tng. Acad., 1956; m. Lois Ellen Ward, July 20, 1956; children—Sharon, David, Elizabeth, JoAnn, Paula. Patrolman, Ohio State Hwy. Patrol, Mansfield, 1956-59, Circleville, 1959-67, cpl. investigation and identification sect. Cambridge Dist. Hdqrs., 1967-69, mem. sci. staff Crime Lab., Gen. Hdqrs., Columbus, 1967-69, sgt., crime lab. dir., 1969—. Mem. Ohio Assn. Criminalists (chmn. 1975-76), Pickaway County Hist. Soc. (pres. 1976-77), Ohio State Hist. Soc., Nat. Muzzle Loading Rifle Assn. Home: 1117 McGraw Rd Circleville OH 43113 Office: 660 E Main St Columbus OH 43205

ELY, WAYNE HARRISON, broadcast engr.; b. Alliance, Ohio, Aug. 31, 1933; s. Dwight Harrison and Mable Evellen (Jones) E.; student Mount Union Coll., 1955-56, Ohio U., 1956-62; m. Roslyn Rose Ambrose, June 14, 1964; children—Eric, Kevin, Gayle, Mitchell. Transmitter engr. Sta. WOUB-AM-FM, Ohio U., Athens, 1958-62; studio field engr. ABC, N.Y.C., 1962-66, 67-72; studio engr. CBS, N.Y.C., 1966-67; transmitter supr. Sta. WOUC-TV, Ohio U., Quaker City, 1972—; tchr. radio tech. Ohio U., Zanesville. Served with C.E., U.S. Army, 1952-54. Mem. Soc. Broadcast Engrs. (sr. broadcast engrs. cert.). Home: Box 283 Cambridge OH 43725 Office: WOUC-TV Route 3 Quaker City OH 43773

EMERSON, WILLIAM, Congressman; b. St. Louis, Jan. 1, 1938; s. Norvell Preston and Marie (Reinemer) E.; B.A., Westminster Coll., Fulton, Mo., 1959; LL.B., U. Balt., 1964; m. Jo Ann Hermann, June 21, 1975; children—Victoria Marie; children by previous marriage—Elizabeth, Abigail. Spl. asst. to U.S. Rep. Robert F. Ellworth, 1961-65; adminstrv. asst. to U.S. Rep./Senator Charles McC. Mathias, Jr., 1965-70; dir. govt. relations Fairchild Industries, Germantown, Md., 1970-74; dir. public affairs Interstate Natural Gas Assn., 1974-75; exec. asst. to chmn. Fed. Election Commn., Washington, 1975; dir. fed. relations TRW Inc., Washington, 1975-79; pres. William Emerson & Assos., govt. relations cons., De Soto, Mo., 1980; mem. 97th Congress from 10th Mo. dist. Capt. USAF Res. Republican. Presbyterian. Office: 418 Cannon Office Bldg Washington DC 20515

EMERY, MARIE THERESE, assn. exec.; b. St. Louis, Sept. 27, 1933; M.A., U. Detroit, 1955; M.A., Mich. State U., 1965, Ph.D., 1969. Leader, Siena Heights Coll. Adrian council Girl Scouts U.S., 1955-59; prin. St. Antoninius Sch., Cin., 1956-60; coordinator practice teaching programs Mich. State U., East Lansing, 1960-73; dept. head Gabriel High Sch., Lansing, Mich., 1960-73; dir. Mich. Fleet Safety Program, Mich. Dept. Budget and Mgmt., Lansing, 1974; cons. Motorcycle Safety Found., Washington, 1975; dir. Rose A. Clark Sch. at Lansing Ice Arena, 1975-78; exec. dir. Mich. Women For Hwy. Safety, East Lansing, 1973; active in traffic safety, including coordinator task forces to solve traffic safety problems, organizer citizen's support for legis. in hwy. traffic safety; Mich. rep. Hwy Safety Leaders, 1973—. First aid instr. ARC. Recipient Profl. of Yr. award Mich. Safety Conf., 1979; award for Excellence, Exxon Corp., 1979, 80; citation for vol. services VFW, 1979; Disting. Achievement award Mich. Driver and Traffic Safety Edn. Assn., 1981, grantee, 1973; Mich. Office Hwy. Safety Planning grantee, 1976, 79. Mem. NEA, 99's, Airplane Owners and Pilots Assn., Mich. Safety Conf., Adrian Dominican Community, Mich. Farm Bur., Mich. Women for Hwy. Safety. Republican. Roman Catholic. Clubs: Zonta, Gruman Airplane. Author: Pedestrian Safety Guide, 1980; Mich. Women for Hwy. Safety Bull., 1973-82. Home: 3142 Lake Lansing Rd East Lansing MI 48823 Office: Room 66 Kellogg Center Hwy Traffic Safety Center Mich State U East Lansing MI 48824

EMISON, JAMES WADE, petroleum mktg. co. exec.; b. Indpls., Sept. 21, 1930; s. John Rabb and Catherine (Stanbro) E.; B.A., DePauw U., 1952; children—Catherine Elizabeth Emison-Stoick, Elizabeth Ann, Thomas Weston, William Ash. Sales mgr. Oskey Bros. Petroleum Co., St. Paul, 1960-66; v.p. mktg. Newfoundland Refining Co., Ltd., N.Y.C., 1966-69; v.p. Oskey Gasoline and Oil Co., Mpls., 1969-77; pres. Western Petroleum Co., Mpls., 1976—; mem. Nat. Petroleum Council, 1970—; founder, dir. Suburban Nat. Bank, Eden Prairie, Minn. Trustee, DePauw U. Served with USMC, 1952-56. Mem. Marine Corps Assn. (bd. govs.), DePauw U. Alumni Assn. (past pres., dir.). Home: 18702 Heathcote Dr Wayzata MN 55391 Office: Cabriole Center 9531 W 78th St Eden Prairie MN 55344

EMMERICH, JAMES CHARLES, athletic trainer, coach; b. New Ulm, Minn., Mar. 18, 1911; s. Charles and Bertha (Keckeisen) E.; B.S., S.D. State Coll., 1940. Asso. prof. phys. edn., coach of track and field, also cross country, trainer S.D. State Coll. Brookings, 1940-60; phys. therapist Drs. Dooley Clinic, Pomona, Calif., 1962; vis. lectr. Eastern Mich. U., Ypsilanti, 1966, Calif. Western U., San Diego, 1968. Am. Specialist U.S.A. State Dept., 1961. Coach track and field; trainer, adminstrv. asst. Amateur Athletic Union of U.S.A., U.S. Olympic com., 1956—; state leader Pres.'s Council Phys. Fitness. Served with AUS, 1942-46. Named S.D. Coll. Coach of Year, 1954; elected to Helms Hall Track and Field Coaches Hall Fame, N. Central Collegiate Athletic Hall Fame, S.D. State U. Athletic Hall Fame, S.D. Sports Hall Fame, S.D. Cowboy and Western Heritage Hall of Fame; recipient Disting. Service award S.D. State U. Jackrabbit Club, 1977. Mem. Nat. Athletic Trainers Assn., Internat., U.S. track coaches assns., Assn. U.S. Army, Am. Legion, DAV, Am. Assn. Ret. Persons, S.D. State U. Alumni Assn., S.D. Ret. Tchrs. Assn., U.S. Olympic Soc., Brookings C. of C. (Community Service award 1981), Am. Turners, Blue Key, Phi Kappa Phi, Alpha Zeta, Pi Gamma Mu. Conglist. Clubs: Elks (Elk of Yr. award 1977), Lions. Address: General Delivery Brookings SD 57006

EMMERT, ROBERT EDWARD, tractor co. ofcl.; b. Ferris, Ill., Nov. 15, 1930; s. Richard Lowell and Lola Ellen (Deitrich) E.; B.S. in Mech. Engring., Bradley U., 1960; m. Joyce Marilyn Glay, Sept. 9, 1953; 1 dau., Kristen Lian. Jr. service engr. Caterpillar Tractor Co., Peoria, Ill., 1960-61, service tng. instr., 1961-63, asst. staff service engr., 1963-65, staff service engr., 1965-81, asst. div. mgr., 1981—. Served with USAF, 1950-56; mem. Res., 1956-75. Mem. Soc. Automotive Engrs., Res. Officers Assn., Air Force Assn. Republican. Clubs: Masons, Shriners. Home: 365 S Mississippi Ave Morton IL 61550 Office: 100 NE Adams St Peoria IL 61629

EMMONS, JOHN HOWARD, educator; b. Ashland, Ohio, Apr. 17, 1942; s. Howard A. and Dorothy (Glenn) E.; married. B.S. in Indsl. Arts Edn., Ohio State U., Columbus, 1964; M.A. in Edn., Kent State U., Ohio, 1972; m. Marcella Grossy; children—Maria Marcella Virginia, John Marcel Anthony. Tchr. indsl. arts, Canton (Ohio) City Sch. Dist., 1964—, curriculum asst. indsl. arts, 1973—. Mem. NEA, Ohio Edn. Assn., Ohio Indsl. Arts Assn., E. Central Ohio Edn. Assn., E. Central Ohio Indsl. Arts Assn., Canton Profl. Educators Assn., Am. Indsl. Arts Assn., Epsilon Pi Tau. Home: 3751 Fulton Dr NW Canton OH 44718 Office: 800 Market Ave North Canton OH 44703

EMRICK, DONALD DAY, chemist; b. Waynesfield, Ohio, Apr. 3, 1929; s. Ernest Harold and Nellie (Day) E.; B.S. cum laude, Miami U., Oxford, Ohio, 1951; M.S., Purdue U., 1954, Ph.D., 1956 Grad. teaching asst. Purdue U., Lafayette, Ind., 1951-55; with chem. and phys. research div. Standard Oil Co. Ohio, 1955-64, research asso., 1961-64; cons., sr. research chemist research dept. Nat. Cash Register Co., Dayton, Ohio, 1965-72, chem. cons., 1972—. Mem. AAAS, Am. Chem. Soc., Phi Beta Kappa, Sigma Xi. Patentee in Field. Contbr. articles to profl. jours. Home: 4240 Lesher Dr Kettering OH 45429

EMRICK, RAYMOND TERRY, educator; b. Paris, Ill., Aug. 9, 1915; s. Terry Clifford and Maude Pearl (Hickman) E.; B.S., Ind. State U., 1953, M.S., 1954; postgrad. U. Ill., 1958, Inst. Coll. Armed Forces, Washington, 1969-72; Ph.D., Walden U., 1972. Acct., Houston Acctg. Firm, Paris, Ill., 1937-38; unit buying control supr. Sears, Roebuck & Co., Terre Haute, Ind., 1938-41; tchr. East Peoria (Ill.) High Sch., 1955-56, public schs. Western suburbs Chgo., 1957-65; teaching fellow in edn. and psychology Ind. State U., 1962-63; research asso. Ind. State U., Terre Haute, 1967; mem. faculty Olney (Ill.) Central Coll., 1967—, instr. psychology, human growth and devel., 1967—, mem. president's adv. com., 1973-79; psychologist, Olney, 1968-81; pres. Student Tchrs. Council, Ind. State U., 1953-54. Served with USAF, 1942-45, 51-52. Mem. Internat. Platform Assn., Ret. Officers Assn., Res. Officers Assn., Mil. Order World Wars, Soc. Commd. Officers, Am. Legion, VFW, Community Concert Assn., Ind. State U. Alumni Assn., Phi Delta Kappa. Club: Elk. Home: 108 Dogwood Dr Olney IL 62450 Office: 305 N West St Olney IL 62450

ENCKELL, THOMAS RALPH, ballet dancer, choreographer, performing arts adminstr.; b. Helsinki, Finland, Oct. 14, 1942; s. Carl Frederick Ralph Alexandre and Marie-Christine (Soderhjelm) E.; student of Boris Kniaseff, Nicholas Zvereff, Nicholas Oboukhov, Pierre Vladimirov, Alfredo Corvino, Margaret Craske, and others; m. Katharyn Horne, Oct. 25, 1965; 1 dau., Kirsi Margaret; 1 stepchild, Collie MacCardell. Mem. Gloria Contreras Dance Group, 1960-62, Met. Opera Ballet, 1962-65; soloist Finnish Nat. Ballet, 1965-66; prin. Manhattan Festival Ballet, 1966-69, Malmo Stadsteater, Sweden, 1969-75; numerous appearances Finnish and Swedish TV; appeared in Prince Igor, N.Y.C. Opera, 1969; guest artist Gothenburg Ballet, Sweden, summer, 1971, Cramer Ballet, E. German tour, summer, 1973, Festival Ballet of San Antonio, Tex., summer, 1974, 75, Des Moines (Iowa) Ballet, Kalamazoo (Mich.) Ballet, and others; appeared in Swan Lake, Giselle, Nutcracker Suite. Tchr., Riita Vainio's Sch. of Dance, Helsinki, Finland, 1965-66, Helsingborg Stadsteater, Sweden, 1970-72, Cramer Ballet, Sweden, 1973, Sarah Quinn Jones Sch. of Ballet, Lake Charles, La., 1975, 76, 77, Omaha Ballet Co., 1975—; dir. Omaha Ballet Center, 1977—; mem. faculty U. Nebr., Omaha; adv. on dance Nebr. Arts Council; choreographer for various ballet companies including: La. Concert Ballet, Jewish Community Center. Mem. Mayor's Task Force on the Arts. Mem. Mid-States Regional Ballet Assn. (dir. 1978—, exec. v.p. 1975-78). *

ENGEL, JUAN JACOBO, gastroenterologist; b. Bogota, Colombia, Dec. 25, 1940; s. Paul and Josefina (Monath) E.; came to U.S., 1967, naturalized, 1976; B. Degree, Am. Sch. Quito (Ecuador), 1958; M.D., U. Central Ecuador, 1966; m. Ruth M. Schumann, Dec. 26, 1965; children—Miriam, Jessica. Intern, Mt. Sinai Hosp., Chgo., 1967-68; resident in medicine Boston VA Hosp., 1968-70, resident in gastroenterology, 1970-72; research fellow in gastroenterology U. Ill. Hosp., Chgo., 1972-73, attending physician, 1973-74; asso. attending physician Michael Reese Hosp., Chgo., 1974-77; asso. attending physician, dir. gastroenterology sect. Luth. Gen. Hosp., Park Ridge, Ill., 1978—; cons. in gastroenterology West Suburban Hosp., Oak Park, Ill., 1976—; teaching cons. West Side VA Hosp., Chgo., 1980—; teaching fellow Boston U., 1969-72; instr. medicine Abraham Lincoln Sch. Medicine, U. Ill., Chgo., 1972-74, asst. prof. medicine, 1978—; asst. prof. medicine Pritzker Sch. Medicine U. Chgo., 1974-77. USIS traveling fellow 1963. Diplomate Am. Bd. Internal Medicine, with subsplty. in gastroenterology. Researcher prostaglandins and gastric secretion. Home: 723 William St River Forest IL 60305

ENGEL, RONALD L., energy co. exec., lawyer; b. Gary, Ind., Jan. 16, 1938; s. Aaron M. and Anna E.; B.S. in Chem. Engring. with honors, U. Ill., 1959; J.D. with honors, U. Chgo., 1962; m. Alix L. Schwartz, Dec. 23, 1962 (separated 1980); children—Alison Gayle, Carilyn Joan, Lauren Stacey. Admitted to Ill. bar, 1962, practiced in Chgo., to 1981; partner firm Kirkland & Ellis, 1962-81; chmn. JMB Energy Co., Chgo., 1981—. Mem. Order of Coif, Tau Beta Pi, Phi Lambda Upsilon, Phi Delta Phi. Clubs: Mid-Am., Standard, Saddle and Cycle. Home: 260 E Chestnut Pl Chicago IL 60611 Office: 875 N Michigan Ave Suite 3900 Chicago IL 60611

ENGELBERG, MARVIN WOOLF, audiologist, speech pathologist; b. Dallas, Sept. 28, 1930; s. Ben and Felice (Wolf) E.; B.S., Tex. A&M U., 1952; M.A. in Audiology and Speech Pathology, U. Ill., 1954; Ph.D. in Audiology and Speech Pathology, U. Mich., 1958; m. Irene Dorothy Silverman, May 15, 1960; children—Suzanne, David. Audiologist, Portland (Oreg.) Hearing and Speech Center, 1958-61, also speech pathologist; chief audiology and speech pathology service VA Med. Center, Cleve., 1961—; adj. prof. U. Akron (Ohio), 1976—; chief cons. in audiology HCI, Inc., Rockford, Ill., 1967—; lectr. audiology Case Western Res. U., Cleve., 1967—; chmn. audiology and speech pathology VA Med. Dist. 13, 1973-80. Pres. B'nai Israel Congregation, Mayfield Hts., Ohio, 1970-71; trustee Akiva Hebrew High Sch., Beachwood, Ohio, 1977—; trustee Mayfield Hillcrest Synagogue, 1971—. Recipient Superior Performance award VA, 1966, 69, 71, 79, Fed. Career Service award, 1974; Nat. Comdr. award DAV, 1978; cert. of appreciation Jewish Theol. Sem. Am., 1979. Mem. Am., Ohio speech and hearing assns., Ohio Council Audiology. Author: Audiological Evaluation for Exaggerated Hearing Level, 1970; contbr. articles to profl. jours. Home: 3906 Meadowbrook Blvd University Heights OH 44118 Office: 10701 East Blvd Cleveland OH 44106

ENGELHARDT, PATRICIA ELAINE, interior designer; b. Omaha, Nov. 19, 1929; d. William H. and Louise Emily (Harvey) Casey; B.S., Creighton U., 1961, postgrad. (grantee) U. Nebr., Omaha, summer 1966, 67; m. William A. Engelhardt, June 16, 1966; children—Linda, Jacqueline, Christine, Michael, Rebecca, Wesley, Julie. Tchr. Omaha public schs., 1961-68; interior designer Byrds Interiors, Omaha, 1974, Drina's Interiors, Bellevue, Nebr., 1975, Patrician Touch, Omaha, 1975—; instr. Creighton U. Vol., Children's Mus. Workshop; active Joslyn Woman's Assn., Joslyn Meml., Arthritis Found.; vol. reader Jr. Theatre, Duchesne Acad. Daisy Parade of Homes; worker several congr. campaigns. Mem. Florence Hist. Soc., Florence Arts and Humanities, Small Bus. Council Omaha., Smithsonian. Democrat. Roman Catholic. Home and Office: 3630 State St Omaha NE 68112

ENGERAN, WHITNEY JOHN, JR., painter, educator, critic; b. New Orleans, Feb. 1, 1934; s. Whitney John and Nora Marie (Boudreaux) E.; B.A., Spring Hill Coll., Mobile, Ala., 1956, M.A., 1958; S.T.L., St. Louis U., 1966; children—Whitney John, Alyce Renee. One man shows: Orleans Gallery, New Orleans, 1967, Shircliff Gallery, Vincennes, Ind., 1974, Barnwell Art Center, Shreveport, La., 1975, St. Mary of the Woods Gallery, Terre Haute, Ind., 1977; group shows include: Topeka Art Guild Gallery, 1962, Sheldon Swope Art Gallery, Terre Haute, 1972, 78, Mo. State Council on Arts, St. Louis, 1972, Barnhart Loft Gallery, Terre Haute, 1979, Turman Art Gallery, Terre Haute, 1981; represented in permanent collections: Ind. State U., Terre Haute, Harold E. Simon Collection, Birmingham, Ala.; chmn. dept. visual arts Loyola U., New Orleans, 1966-68; asso. prof. Stephens Coll., Columbia, Mo., 1968-71; chmn. dept. art Ind. State U., 1971-78, prof. art theory and criticism, art and human body, art appreciation, 1971—, dir. Turman Gallery, curator permanent collection, 1971-75; lectr. in field. Eli Lilly grantee, 1973. Mem. Nat. Assn. Art Adminstrs., Coll. Art Assn. Democrat. Roman Catholic. Contbr. articles to Choice mag., Arts mag. Home: 1509 S Center St Terre Haute IN 47802 Office: Art Dept Ind State U Terre Haute IN 47809

ENGLANDER, ANN, hosp. adminstr., editor, writer; b. Cin., July 13, 1932; d. Henry Stanley and Adele (Covy) E.; student U. Mich., 1950-52; B.S., Northwestern U., 1954, M.A., 1956, Ph.D., 1966. Asst. editor lang. arts dept. Sci. Research Assos., Chgo., 1966-69; sr. editor lit. and arts Britannica Jr. Ency., 1969-72; asso. editor lit. and arts Ency. Britannica, 1972-73; vis. lectr. Medill Sch. Journalism, Northwestern U., 1974; adminstrv. coordinator alcoholism treatment program Inst. Psychiatry, Northwestern Meml. Hosp., Chgo., 1975-80, adminstrv. coordinator chem. dependence program, 1980—; instr. clin. psychiatry Northwestern U. Med. Sch., Chgo., 1975-80; freelance editor, 1966—. Mem. MLA. Office: 320 E Huron St Chicago IL 60611

ENGLE, ARTHUR WILLIAM, assn. exec.; b. Elyria, Ohio Mar. 23, 1935; s. Arthur W. and Mary E. (Ebersole) E.; B.B.A., Northwestern U., 1971; m. Dagny M. Nylen, Aug. 25, 1956; children—Scott, Jeff, Mark. Dir. adminstrv. services Hosp. Financial Mgmt. Assn., Chgo., 1967-71; gen. mgr. Am. Judicature Soc., Chgo., 1971-74; pres. Mgmt. Cons. Assos., also Assn. Mgmt. Center, Communications Mktg. Supply Center, A.M.C. Pub. divs. Engle Corp., Evanston, Ill., 1974—; exec. v.p. Assn. Rehab. Nurses, Chgo., 1974-77; exec. dir. Chgo. Assn. Fed. Employees, 1976-79, Internat. Assn. Enterostomal Therapists, 1976-80, Nat. Assn. Dome Home Mfrs., 1978—, Ill. Mfrs. Reps. Assn., 1978-80, Community Assn. Inst. Ill., 1978—, Nat. Inst. Steel Detailing, 1979—, Worthington Indsl. Pump Distbrs. Assn., 1980—. Named Outstanding Young Man of Year, Lorain, Ohio, 1961, Outstanding Local Pres. Ohio, Jaycees, 1961. Mem. Am., Chgo. socs. assn. execs., Inst. Assn. Mgmt. Cos., Adminstrv. Mgmt. Soc., Acad. Certified Adminstrv. Mgrs., Am. Soc. Assn. Execs., Profl. Conv. Mgmt. Assn. Kiwanian (dir. Chgo.). Editor Jour. Nat. Assn. Ct. Adminstn., 1972-74. Office: 2506 Gross Point Rd Evanston IL 60201

ENGLE, JOHN DAVID, JR., educator, writer; b. Yocum, Ky., Sept. 29, 1922; s. John David and Mary Angeline (Combs) E.; B.A., U. Ky., 1950, M.A., 1953; m. Anita Marie Jacobs, Aug. 20, 1948 (div. Nov. 1972); m. Gretchen Gray Dieffenbach, June 13, 1978; children—Mariamne A., Brent Elwin, Derrick R. Tchr. English and creative writing in high schs., Belfry, Ky., 1950, Jenkins, Ky., 1950-51, Athens, Ky., 1951-53, Lafayette High Sch., Lexington, Ky., 1953-56, Princeton High Sch., Cin., 1956-78; asso. editor Writer's Digest, 1967—; mem. Ohio Arts Council Poets-in-the-Schs. Program; poet-in-residence various Ohio schs.; lectr.; lit. adviser Ohio Arts Council, 1973-75; poetry books include: Modern Odyssey, 1971; Laugh Lightly, 1974; Sea Songs, 1977; Spiritually Speaking, 1979; Cycle of Beauty, 1980; poetry represented in Anthology of Modern Verse, 1980, also two Japanese coll. anthologies; dramas include: The Opening Door, 1957; The Charm, 1958. Served with USAAF, 1942-45. Recipient poetry awards Ind. U. Writers Conf., Nat. Fedn. State Poetry Socs., Ky. Poetry Soc., Ohio Poetry Day and spl. service to poetry awards. Mem. Poetry Soc. Am., Nat. Fedn. State Poetry Socs., Verse Writers Guild Ohio. Home: 988 Bowen Rd Route 1 Canal Winchester OH 43110

ENGLE, PATRICIA ANN PENDLETON, constrn. co. exec.; b. Raytown, Mo., July 30, 1931; s. Frederick Alexander and Hildred Viola (Brown) P.; student pub. schs., Raytown and Kansas City, Mo.; m. George I. Engle, Oct. 9, 1963; children—James D., Stanley M., Michelle, Rene, Garry, Catherine. With Eaton Metal Products Co., Billings, Mont., 1949, AEC, Los Alamos, N.Mex., 1949-51, Safety Drivers Ins. Co., Kansas City, Mo., 1951-52; with Mid-Western Constrn. Co. of Mo., Raytown, 1960—, co-owner, sec.-treas., 1970—; pres. GP&M Constrn. Co. Served with USNR, 1948-52. Mem. Nat. Exec. Secs. Assn., Am. Bus. and Profl. Women in Constrn., Constrn. Women's Assn. (pres. 1980—), Am. Bus. Women's Assn. Home: 1701 E R D Mize Rd Blue Springs MO 64015 Office: 9814 E 53d St Raytown MO 64133

ENGLEHART, THEODORE MCNUTT, mfg. co. exec.; b. Brazil, Ind., May 9, 1920; s. Ira Holland and Virginia (McNutt) E.; student DePauw U., 1938-40; B.A., Butler U., 1947; m. Nancy Campbell, Apr. 22, 1944; children—Nancy Anne, Theodore M. (dec.). With Ind. Gear Works (Buehler Corp. since 1966), Indpls., 1940-66, exec. v.p., 1960-66, sr. v.p., 1966-70, also dir.; with Circle Leasing Corp., Indpls., 1970-72; exec. v.p. J.C. Wilson Engring. Corp., Indpls., 1972—; pres. Lab. Equipment Corp., Mooresville, Ind., 1973—, T.M. Englehart Corp., 1978—; dir. J.C. Wilson Engring. Corp., Circle Leasing Corp.,

Wellman Dynamics Corp.; sec., dir. State Gear Co., Inc. Pres. bd. trustees Winona Meml. Hosp. Served to 1st lt. USAF, WW II. C.P.A.; recipient cert. Winona Meml. Hosp., 1968. Mem. Am. Gear Mfrs. Assn. (pres. 1968, cert. 1968), Soc. Automotive Engrs., Am. Legion. Republican. Methodist. Club: Meridian Hills Country. Patentee in marine propulsion (3). Home: 7771 Spring Mill Rd Indianapolis IN 46260 Office: 156 E Harrison St Mooresville IN 46158

ENGLER, FREDERICK ERNST, printing co. exec.; b. Cin., Apr. 2, 1928; s. Frederick Karl and Magdalen Elizabeth (Seibert) E.; student U. Ky., 1948-50; B.S. cum laude, Xavier U., 1956; m. Lois M. Hughes, June 11, 1955; children—Marian, Frederick, Theresa, Michael, Gregory. Chief fin. officer Greenwald Jewelers, Cin., 1951-56; controller Elder Johnston Dept. Store, Dayton, Ohio, 1956-59; asst. controller Top Value Stamps, Dayton, 1959-66; div. controller, resident mgr. St. Regis Paper Co., Troy, Ohio and Attleboro, Mass., 1966-72; controller/treas., dir. DAP Products and DAP Duratite Can. subs. Schering Plough, Inc., Dayton, 1972-79; sr. v.p. fin., dir. United Color Press, Dayton, 1979—. Active Dayton Amateur Baseball Commn., 1968—, pres., 1974-75; dir. Miami Valley Football Assn., 1968-76; bd. govs. Xavier U., 1960, recipient Outstanding Alumnus award, 1960; commr. Cath. Youth Orgn., 1966—; athletic dir., coach St. Albert the Great, 1964—. Served to sgt. USMC, 1946-48, 50-51. Quiz kid, 1941-43. Mem. Dayton Area C. of C., Alpha Sigma Phi. Roman Catholic. Home: 3601 Delaine Ave Kettering OH 45429 Office: United Color Press 240 W 5th St Dayton OH 45402

ENGLER, JOHN MATHIAS, state senator Mich.; b. Mt. Pleasant, Mich., Oct. 12, 1948; s. Mathias John and Agnes Marie (Neyer) E.; B.S. in Agrl. Econs., Mich. State U., 1971; m. Colleen House, Apr. 5, 1975. Mem. Mich. Ho. of Reps., 1970-78, Mich. senate, 1979—. Bd. dirs. Mich. State U. Agr. and Natural Resources Alumna; del. White House Conf. on Youth, 1972. Recipient Disting. Service to Agr. award Mich. Agr. Conf., 1974. Mem. Nat. Conf. State Legislators. Republican. Roman Catholic. Club: Detroit Economic. Office: Box 30036 State Capitol Lansing MI 48909

ENGLER, STEVE, state senator; b. Randolph, Minn., Nov. 6, 1949; B.A., Mankato State U., 1971. Farmer; mem. Minn. Senate, 1976—. Republican. Office: 116 State Office Bldg Saint Paul MN 55155*

ENGLISH, EVA UBER, vol. arts council exec.; b. Neumarkt, Silesia, Apr. 20, 1925; came to U.S., 1954, naturalized, 1957; d. Konrad and Margarete (Reimann) Uber; Lab. Asst. Dipl., Fachschule for Chemistry and Physics, 1943; m. Charles B. English, Oct. 3, 1954; children—Gwendolyn, Carolyn (dec.). Lab. asst. Bosch GmbH., Reichenbach, Silesia, 1944; cons. edn. br. Am. Consulate, Frankfurt, W. Ger., 1947-54; pres. Champaign County Mental Health Assn., Urbana, Ohio, 1967-69; mem. Logan-Champaign County 648 Bd. Mental Health and Retardation, 1970-77, v.p., 1970-72; bd. dirs. Springfield (Ohio) Symphony Orchestra Assn., 1968-80; founder, pres. vol. exec. dir. Champaign County Arts Council, 1974-79, also trustee, chmn. arts-in-schs. program, 1974—. Home: 5185 Waldenbergland Rural Route Cable OH 43009 Office: PO Box 271 Urbana OH 43078

ENGLISH, MARK GREGORY, lawyer, public utility exec.; b. Mpls., Oct. 14, 1951; s. Earl Mark and Georgia Corrine (LaStrange) E.; B.E.E. with high distinction, U. Minn., 1973, J.D. magna cum laude, 1976; m. Renee Ann Thielen, Aug. 31, 1979; children—Janelle, Brandon. Admitted to Minn. bar, 1976, Mo. bar, 1981; asso. Arvesen Law Firm, Fergus Falls, Minn., 1976-77; partner firm Arvesen, Donoho, Lundeen, Hoff, Svingen & English, Fergus Falls, 1978-80; atty. Kansas City Power & Light Co. (Mo.), 1981—. Fellow Brit. Royal Soc. for Encouragement of Arts, Mfrs. and Commerce (silver medal, outstanding baccalaureate grad. U. Minn., 1973); mem. Am. Bar Assn., Minn. Bar Assn. (tax com. council, 1978-80), Otter Tail County Bar Assn. (pres., 1980), Mo. Bar Assn., Minn. Jaycees (state gen. counsel, 1979-80, 1st place population div. individual devel. chpt. v.p., 1979). Home: 10924 W 65th St Shawnee KS 66203 Office: KCPL Legal Dept 1330 Baltimore Kansas City MO 64105

ENGLISH, RICHARD ALLYN, sociologist, social work educator; b. Winter Park, Fla., Aug. 29, 1936; s. Wentworth and Mary English; A.B., Talladega Coll., 1958; M.A. (Woodrow Wilson fellow), U. Mich., 1959, M.S.W., 1964, Ph.D., 1970; m. Ireita Geraldine Williams, June 29, 1978. Dir. vocat. and youth services Flint (Mich.) Urban League, 1959-61, acting exec. dir., 1961-62; social group worker Neighborhood Service Orgn., Detroit, 1963-65; mem. faculty (part-time) Sch. Social Work, Wayne State U., 1965-67; lectr. U. Mich., Ann Arbor, 1967-70, asst. prof. social work, 1970-72, asso. prof., 1972-74, prof., 1974—, asso. v.p. acad. affairs, 1974-81; vis. scholar Paul Baerwald Sch. Social Work, Hebrew U., Jerusalem, Israel, 1975; vis. prof. Howard U., fall 1981; Am. Psychol. Assn.-Nat. Inst. Edn. fellow, 1981; cons. to various schs. social work, public sch. dists. and pvt. founds., 1969—; pres. Council on Social Work Edn., 1981—. Bd. dirs. Internat. Assn. Schs. Social Work. Mem. Nat. Assn. Social Workers, Nat. Council Family Relations, Am. Sociol. Assn., Internat. Council Social Welfare. Contbr. articles to profl. publs.; editor: A Book of Readings: Human Service Organizations, 1974. Home: 1334 Orkney Dr Ann Arbor MI 48103

ENGLISH, RICHARD FRANKLIN, ins. co. exec.; b. Maumee, Ohio, Oct. 1, 1926; s. Walter John and Mary J. (Bowman) E.; student Am. Coll.; m. Joyce Arlene Neifer, Mar. 31, 1946; 1 dau., Rosemary. Field underwriter Mut. of N.Y., 1956-58, asst. mgr., 1958-62; mgr.-trainee, 1962-64, agy. supr., Toledo, 1964-78, asso. mgr. Toledo agy., 1978—. Served with USNR, 1944-46. C.L.U. Mem. Nat. Assn. Life Underwriters, Ohio Assn. Life Underwriters, Toledo Assn. Life Underwriters, Am. Assn. C.L.U.'s, C.L.U.'s Assn., Aircraft Owners and Pilots Assn., U.S. Seaplane Pilots Assn., Exptl. Aircraft Assn. Republican. Methodist. Club: Masons. Home: 164 S Nancy Dr Port Clinton OH 43452 Office: Mut of NY 5810 Southwyck Blvd Toledo OH 43614

ENGLISH, ROBERT JACKSON, broadcasting exec.; b. Travis AFB, Calif., July 26, 1951; s. Paul Jackson and Olga Ouida (Ward) E.; B.S. in Journalism, U. Tex., Austin, 1973; m. Debra Annette Duncan, Jan. 12, 1974; children—Travis Jackson, Lacey Anne. With sta. KBUY, Ft. Worth, 1973, sta. KCUB, Tucson, 1973-77; with sta. WUBE AM/FM, Cin., 1977—, gen. mgr., 1979-80, v.p., 1981—; v.p., gen. mgr. sta. WMLX, 1981—; agenda chmn. Country Radio Seminar, 1981-82. Mem. Ohio Assn. Broadcasters, Advt. Golfers Assn., Greater Cin. Radio Broadcasters Assn. (v.p. 1981—), Cin. Ad Club. Club: Cin. Rotary. Office: 225 E 6th St Cincinnati OH 45201

ENGLISH, STEPHANIE ANN, advt. agy. exec.; b. York, Pa., Nov. 7, 1948; d. Richard Bolles and Rae Jean (Leach) E.; student Carroll Coll., Waukesha, Wis., Northwestern U. Evening Sch. Media buyer Ed H. Weiss & Co., Chgo., 1967-68; with Leo Burnett U.S.A., Chgo., 1968—, asso. media dir., 1977-79, v.p., asso. media dir., 1979—. Benefit chmn. Met. Bd. Youth Guidance, 1981-82. Mem. Chgo. Advt. Club (dir.), Women's Advt. Club Chgo. (membership chmn. 1979-81). Club: Downtown Court. Office: Leo Burnett Prudential Plaza Chicago IL 60601

ENGLISH, WALLACE DAVIS, physician; b. Paris, Mo., Feb. 12, 1908; s. Joseph Shelby and Georgia E. (Davis) E.; A.B., U. Mo., 1929; M.D., Washington U., 1933; m. Frances Sue Hodge, Mar. 10, 1930; children—Frank, Merrill, Ronald, Alan; m. 2d, Frieda M. Lomax, Mar. 9, 1944; children—Joe Shelby, Timothy. Intern, St. Louis City Hosp., 1933-34; practice medicine, specializing in surgery, Cardwell, Mo., 1933—; mem. staff Dunklin County Meml. Hosp., Kennett, Mo., chief of staff, 1953-54, vice chief staff, 1951; surgeon Cotton Belt R.R., St. Louis Southwestern R.R., 1950—. Mem. voting bd. Mo. Blue Shield Ins. Co., 1961—; trustee St. Louis Blue Shield, 1968-77. Mem. finance com. Buffalo Twp. Boy Scouts Am., 1949-51. Served to capt. M.C., AUS, 1942. Recipient resolutions and plagues on Dr. English Day, Town of Cardwell and surrounding community, 1978. Fellow Am. Soc. Abdominal Surgeons, Am. Acad. Family Physicians; mem. A.M.A., Am. Heart Assn., Mo. Med. Assn. (mem. council 1961-78), Dunklin County, Miss. Valley med. socs., Am. Acad. Gen. Practice, Future Farmers Am. (hon. mem. Cardwell chpt.), Alpha Kappa Alpha. Baptist. Rotarian (past sec., pres.), Mason; mem. Order Eastern Star. Club: Weimaraner (Cardwell). Contbr. articles to profl. jours. Address: PO Box 107 Cardwell MO 63829

ENGUS, EARL NORMAN, chemist, cons.; b. Chgo., Feb. 18, 1938; s. Earl F. and Bette E. (Norman) E.; student U. Chgo., 1959-61; B.S., Ill. Inst. Tech., 1967, M.S., 1968; m. Lorraine Marion Hoernel, Dec. 29, 1962; children—Elsbeth Ann, Erik Cary. Chemist, Best Foods Co., Chgo., 1963-68, prodn. foreman, 1966-67, plant supt., 1967-68; mktg. mgr. MGD Graphic Systems, div. N. Am. Rockwell, Cicero, Ill., 1968-70; prodn. planning and control mgr. Hamilton Industries, div. U.S. Industries, 1970-72; materials mgr. Dodge Trophies div. Leisure Group, Crystal Lake, Ill., 1972-73; dir. mfg. Rembrandt Lamps, div. Scott & Fetzer, Chgo., 1973-74, v.p. mfg., 1974-76; v.p. ops. Mogen David Wine Corp., div. Coca Cola Bottling Co. of N.Y., Chgo., 1976-80; pres., chief exec. officer, chief operating officer Am. Bus. Ops. Corp., Woodridge, Ill., 1980—. Served with U.S. Army, 1961-63. Mem. Assn. of M.B.A. Execs., Chgo. C. of C., Pacific Rocket Soc., Am. Mgmt. Assn., Am. Soc. Enologists, Sigma Iota Upsilon, Delta Upsilon. Republican. Methodist. Club: Masons. Asst. editor Iowa State Scientist Mag., 1957. Home: 7912 Westview Ln Woodridge IL 60515

ENNEKING, CLARENCE BERNARD, electronic service co. exec.; b. Melrose, Minn., Aug. 20, 1931; s. Henry John and Rose (Theilen) E.; student DeForest Coll., 1949-51, N.W. Electronics Coll., 1954-55; m. Eugenia Ann Sand, Nov. 9, 1957; children—Timothy, Todd, Sandra, Bradley, Jill. Printed circuit supr. Univac Co., St. Paul, 1955-57; plant mgr. Fabri-Tek, Amery, Wis., 1957-62, Eau Clair, Wis., 1962-65, St. Cloud, Minn., 1965-66, Hong Kong, 1966-74, circuits gen. mgr., Baldwin, Minn., 1974-76; pres. D M A Inc., Amery, 1976—; also dir.; cons. new printed circuit plants. Chmn. for fin. and spiritual com. St. Joseph's Catholic Ch., Amery. Served with USMC, 1951-54. Mem. Smithsonian Assos., Marriage Encounter Community. Club: Amery Community (pres. 1970). Home: 332 South St Amery WI 54001 Office: 119 W Birch St Amery WI 54001

ENNIS, THOMAS MICHAEL, community mental health adminstr.; b. Morgantown, W.Va., Mar. 7, 1931; s. Thomas Edson and Violet Ruth (Nugent) E.; student W.Va. U., 1949-52; A.B., George Washington U., 1954; J.D., Georgetown U., 1960; m. Julia Marie Dorety, June 30, 1956; children—Thomas John, Robert Griswold (dec.). Subrogation-arbitration examiner Govt. Employees Ins. Co., Washington, 1956-59; asst., legis. analyst to v.p. pub. affairs Air Transport Assn. Am., Washington, 1959-60; dir. ann. support program George Washington U., 1960-63; nat. dir. devel. Project HOPE, People to People Health Found., Inc., Washington, 1963-66; nat. exec. dir. Epilepsy Found. Am., Washington, 1966-74; exec. dir. Clinton, Eaton, Ingham Community Mental Health Bd., 1974—; clin. instr. dept. community medicine and internat. health Georgetown U. Sch. Medicine, 1967-74; adj. asso. prof. dept. psychiatry Coll. Medicine, Mich. State U., 1975—; cons. health and med. founds., related orgns.; cons. Am. Health Found., 1967-69, Reston, Va.-Georgetown U. Health Planning Project, 1967-69; mem. adv. bd. Nat. Center for Law and Handicapped; advisor Nat. Reye's Syndrome Found.; mem. Pres.'s Com. on Employment Handicapped, Internat. Bur. Epilepsy, Nat. Com. for Research in Neurol. Disorders; mem. nat. adv. bd. Developmental Disabilities/Tech. Assistance System, U. N.C. Nat. del. trustee, v.p. Nat. Capitol Area chpt., bd. dirs., exec. com. Nat. Kidney Found., 1969—, pres., 1972—; bd. dirs. Nat. Assn. Pvt. Residential Facilities for Mentally Retarded, Epilepsy Found. Am.; bd. dirs., v.p. Epilepsy Center Mich.; bd. dirs., pres. Mich. Mid-South Health Systems Agy. World Rehab. Fund fellow, Norway, 1980. Mem. Nat. Rehab. Assn., Am. Public Health Assn., Nat. Epilepsy League (dir.), Mich. Assn. Community Mental Health Bd. Dirs. (pres.), AAAS, Phi Alpha Theta, Phi Kappa Psi. Contbr. articles on epilepsy to profl. jours. Home: 4361 Wausau Okemos MI 48864 Office: 300 Washington Sq Lansing MI 48933

ENOCH, ROBERT LOUIS, ednl. adminstr.; b. Lima, Ohio, Sept. 14, 1927; s. Louis Leroy and Mary Margaret (Draa) E.; student Bluffton Coll., 1947-48, Ohio No. U., 1948-51, San Miguel Art Inst., 1951-53; LL.B., Salmon P. Chase Coll. of Law, 1957, J.D., 1968; postgrad. U. Cin., 1966-71, U. Md., 1973-75; m. Jayne Chilton Parks, Aug. 14, 1964. Asso. phys. dir. YMCA, Lima, 1945-50; law clk. with Benjamin Schwartz, Cin., 1953-57; probation officer, referee Hamilton County (Ohio) Juvenile Ct., 1957-60; with broadcast industry, 1960-65; tchr., dept. head Clermont Northeastern High Sch., Clermont County, 1965-73; guidance dir. comprehensive and vocat. edn. Great Oaks Joint Vocat. Sch. Dist. 73, Cin., 1968-79, supr. (dean) student affairs, 1979—; pres. Robert L. Enoch & Assos., Inc., Cin., 1977—; cons. candidate, Ohio Ho. of Reps., 1960. Pres., S.W. Ohio Assn. for Developmentally Disabled, 1978-80; presenter Hamilton County Juvenile Ct., 1976—; trustee Bob Hope House, 1978-80. Served with USCG, 1945. Martha Jenning Inst. fellow, 1967-68. Mem. Ohio Vocat. Assn., Am. Vocat. Assn., Phi Alpha Delta, Phi Delta Kappa. Republican. Episcopalian. Club: Masons, Shriners. Contbr. articles to profl. jours. Home: 7301 Kingswood Dr West Chester OH 45069 Office: 3254 E Kemper Rd Cincinnati OH 45241

EPHRAIM, DONALD MORLEY, lawyer; b. Chgo., Jan. 14, 1932; s. Jacob H. and Belle (Freundlich) E.; B.S.C., DePaul U., 1952; postgrad. Northwestern U.; C.P.A., U. Ill., 1953; J.D., U. Chgo., 1955; m. Sylvia Zupnik, Aug. 13, 1964 (div. Aug. 1981); children—David Marc, Eliot Scott, Eric Alan. Admitted to Ill. bar, 1955; atty. Ross, McGowan & O'Keefe, Chgo., 1955; C.P.A., Arthur Andersen & Co., Chgo., 1957-60; atty. Pennish, Steel & Rockler, Chgo., 1960-63, Schradzke, Gould & Ratner, Chgo., 1963-65, practice law Chgo., 1965—; pres., dir. Presdl. Properties, Ltd., 1970—, Donald M. Ephraim, Ltd., 1976—, Franklin Nat. Marine Corp., 1977; v.p., dir. Continental Marine Corp., 1976—, Kurtis Prodns., Ltd., 1977—; trustee various pension and profit sharing trusts. Served with AUS, 1956-57. C.P.A., Ill. Mem. Am., Ill., Chgo. bar assns., Am. Assn. Atty.-C.P.A.'s, Am. Inst. C.P.A.'s, Ill. Soc. C.P.A.'s, Chgo. Estate Planning Council, Nat. Acad. TV Arts and Scis. (gov. Chgo. chpt.), Phi Sigma Delta, Pi Gamma Mu. Jewish. Home: 1560 N Sandburg Terrace Chicago IL 60606 Office: 172 N Franklin St Chicago IL 60606

EPP, LEONARD GEORGE, educator; b. Neptune, N.J., Aug. 14, 1944; s. Leonard George and Grace (Jaqui) E.; B.A., Gettysburg Coll., 1966; M.S., Pa. State U., 1968, Ph.D., 1970; m. Gretchen Lynn Field, June 14, 1969. Vis. scientist Ill. Inst. Tech., Chgo., 1971-75, Ind. U., Bloomington, 1977, 80, Ohio State U., Columbus, 1979, Zoologische Institut, U. Zurich, Switzerland, 1977, 78, 79; faculty Mt. Union Coll., Alliance, Ohio, 1970—; mem. seminar on Socio-Econ. Devel. in India, New Delhi, 1976, in Egypt, Cairo, 1981. Recipient Great Tchr. award Mt. Union Coll., 1977. Mem. AAAS, Am. Soc. Zoologists, Soc. for Devel. Biology, Sigma Xi. Clubs: YMCA, Elks. Contbr. articles in field to profl. jours. Address: Mount Union Coll Alliance OH 44601

EPPSTEIN, RICHARD TUTEUR, consumer orgn. exec.; b. Toledo, Aug. 20, 1947; s. Richard Curtiss and Marilyn (Tuteur) E.; B.A. in Edn., U. Toledo, 1969; grad. Better Bus. Bur. Inst. Exec. Devel., Washington, 1976; m. Grace Yuk-Chun, Dec. 8, 1973; 1 son, Andrew Curtiss. With consumer edn. div. Better Bus. Bur. Toledo, 1972-73, mgr. div., 1973-75, v.p., 1975-77; pres. Better Bus. Bur. Stark County, Canton, Ohio, 1977-79; pres. Ohio Better Bus. Bur., 1978-80, sec. Dist. II, 1978-80, Better Bus. Bur. N.W. Ohio and Southeastern Mich., Toledo, 1979—. Served with USAR, 1969-71; Vietnam. Decorated Bronze Star, Army Commendation medal; recipient Consumer Info. Achievement award Council Better Bus. Burs., 1976. Mem. Toledo Ad Club, Toledo Scott Alumni Assn. (dir.). Clubs: Rotary, Press (Toledo). Office: 405 N Huron St Toledo OH 43604

EPSTEIN, EDNA SELAN, lawyer; b. Yugoslavia, July 26, 1938; d. Carl and Lotte (Eisner) Selan; came to U.S., 1944, naturalized, 1951; A.B. cum laude, Barnard Coll., 1960; M.A. (AAUW fellow), Johns Hopkins U., 1961; Ph.D., Harvard U., 1967; J.D. cum laude (Law Rev.), U. Chgo., 1973; m. Wolfgang Epstein, June 12, 1961; children—Matthew, Ezra, Tanya. Asst. prof. French, U. Ill., Chgo. Circle, 1967-70; admitted to Ill. bar, 1973; with Cook County State's Atty., 1973-75; mem. firm Sidley & Austin, Chgo., 1976—; mem. faculty Mich. Inst. Continuing Legal Edn., 1977, Nat. Inst. Trial Advocacy, 1979-81, Ill. Inst. Continuing Legal Edn., 1981; vis. lectr. U. Chgo. Sch. Law, 1980, 81. Bd. govs. Hyde Park-Kenwood Community Conf., 1974-77; bd. dirs. Friends of Parks, 1978—, Music of the Baroque, 1981—; mem. Citizens Com. for Victim Assistance, 1976-78; mem. Mayor Byrne's Transition Task Force, 1979; mem. profl. adv. com. Cook County State's Atty., 1981-1982; del. Dem. Nat. Conv., 1980, also mem. rules com. Mem. Am. (chmn. trial evidence com. 1977-81), Chgo. bar assns., Chgo. Council Lawyers (bd. govs. 1975-77), Phi Beta Kappa, Order of Coif. Contbr. articles to profl. jours. Office: Suite 4800 One First Nat Plaza Chicago IL 60603

EPSTEIN, IRWIN JOSEPH, internist; b. Bronx, N.Y., Apr. 20, 1947; s. Morris L. and Sadelle (Posner) E.; B.A., SUNY, Buffalo, 1967, M.A. (USPHS research fellow), 1970; M.D., McMaster U., 1973; m. Harriet Hoffman, May 22, 1967; children—Joshua, Seth, Dustin. Intern, McMaster U., 1973; resident; chief resident and fellow in internal medicine McMaster U., 1973-76; physician Med. Arts Clinic, P.C., Minot, N.D., 1976—, also dir.; attending staff Trinity Hosp.; staff, dir. ICU, St. Joseph's Hosp.; asst. prof. medicine U. N.D. Fellow A.C.P.; mem. AMA, Am. Soc. Internal Medicine, Am. Soc. Clin. Oncology, Ducks Unltd. Clubs: Minot Country, Elks. Office: Medical Arts Clinic 6th St and 17th Ave SE Minot ND 58701

ERB, RANDALL JAY, pharmacist, tech. co. exec.; b. Elkhart, Ind., Sept. 19, 1946; s. Edwin Franklin and Jean Katherine (Garver) E.; B.S., Purdue U., 1969, M.S., 1971, Ph.D., 1977; m. Connie Mae Lyons, Aug. 17, 1968. Instr. pharmacy Purdue U., West Lafayette, Ind., 1970-71; pres. Pharmadynamics Research Inc., West Lafayette, 1977—, chmn. bd., 1978—; lectr. in field. Served with U.S. Army, 1971-74. Mem. Acad. Pharm. Scis., Am. Pharm. Assn., Sigma Xi, Rho Chi, Kappa Psi, Phi Eta Sigma, Phi Lambda Upsilon. Home: 109 Tamiami Ct West Lafayette IN 47906 Office: 500 Sagamore Pkwy W West Lafayette IN 47906

ERDAHL, ARLEN INGOLF, congressman; b. Blue Earth, Minn., Feb. 27, 1931; s. Christian A. and Inga (Fosness) E.; B.A., St. Olaf Coll., 1953; M.P.A., Harvard U., 1966; m. Ellen Marie Syrdal, 1958; children—Rolf C., Eric A., John F., Lars P., Laura M., Kari E. Mem. Minn. Ho. of Reps., 1963-70; sec. of state State of Minn., 1970-74; mem. Minn. Public Service Commn., 1975-78; mem. 96th-97th Congresses from 1st Minn. Dist. Active Boy Scouts Am., Farm Bur., ARC. Served with U.S. Army, 1954-56. Recipient Freedoms Found. award, 1955; Disting. Alumnus award St. Olaf Coll., 1972; Disting. Service award Jaycees, 1965, others. Mem. Am. Legion. Republican. Lutheran. Office: 1518 Longworth House Office Bldg Washington DC 20515

ERDMAN, DARYL ALLAN, supermarket exec.; b. Rochester, Minn., June 29, 1939; s. Earl G. and Leone B. (Mertz) E.; B.A. in Math. and Bus. Adminstrn., Luther Coll., 1961; M.B.A., Mich. State U., 1962; m. Audrey N. Pederson, June 18, 1961; children—Scott Allan, Denae Diane, Laura Louise. Co-founder Erdman Supermarkets, Inc., operators 5 supermarkets, Rochester, 1962—, v.p., 1965—; v.p., past owner Minnewawa Lodge Resort, Nisswa, Minn., 1976—; part owner Aldeen's Men's Wear, Rochester, 1974—; pres. Rotab Inc., Rochester, 1976—; pres., owner Tie Rack, Rochester, 1970-76; instr. food mktg. Rochester Community Coll., 1977; del. White House Conf. on Small Bus., 1980; mem. Midwest adv. com. SBA, mem. Minn. Coalition on Small Bus. Mem. adv. com. Minn. Vocat.-Tech. Schs., mem. advisory com. distributive edn., 1974—; chmn. bldg. com. Holy Cross Luth. Ch., 1969-72; mem. advisory com. mktg. Rochester Community Coll., 1976—; mem. Olmstead County Adv. Com. on Disaster Preparedness; mem. admissions adv. council Luther Coll., 1972-76; chmn. council Bethlehem Luth. Ch. Recipient Disting. Service award Luther Coll., 1976. Mem. Rochester Area C. of C. (v.p., dir.), Phi Kappa Phi, Beta Gamma Sigma. Club: Sertoma. Home: 901 17th St NE Rochester MN 55901 Office: 1652 Hwy 52 N Rochester MN 55901

ERDMANN, MARVIN ELMER, wholesale food co. exec.; b. Milw., July 1, 1930; s. Walter and Lenora E.; student public schs., Milw., m. Lois Jean Yellick, Apr. 14, 1951; children—Mark Karter, Scott Kevin, Kim Robin. With A&P Tea Co., Milw., 1944-60, dept. mgr., 1949-51, store mgr., 1953-60; store mgr. Paulus Foods, Cedarburg, Wis., 1960-63; with Super Valu Stores, Inc., 1963—, field supr., 1964-69, sales mgr., Mpls., 1969-74, retail ops. mgr., Mpls., 1974-77, pres. Bismarck (N.D.) div., 1977—; lectr. bus. adminstrn. at high schs., colls. Chmn. property mgmt. Good Shepherd Ch. Served with U.S. Army, 1951-53. Decorated Bronze Star, Am. Spirit medal. Mem. N.D. Food Retailers Assn. (legis. cons.), Greater N.D. Assn. (speaker), Bismarck C. of C. (dir., mem. exec. com., mem. indsl. com.). Republican. Lutheran. Clubs: Apple Creek Country, Supreme Ct. Racquetball. Home: 1217 Crestview Ln Bismarck ND 58501 Office: 707 Airport Rd Bismarck ND 58502

EREL, SHARON LEE PERKINS, internist; b. Toledo, July 14, 1935; d. Ernest and Mae (Henry) Perkins; B.S., U. Toledo, 1957; M.D., U. Istanbul, 1968; m. Sahabettin Erel, Jan. 18, 1957; children—Robert Huseyin, Murad Richard. Intern, Toledo Hosp., 1969-70, asst. dir. med. edn., 1973-74; resident Med. Coll. Ohio at Toledo, 1970-73, active staff, clin. instr. internal medicine, 1973—,

Am. Cancer Soc. grantee, 1972-73; practice medicine specializing in internal medicine, Sylvania, Ohio, 1973—; mem. staffs Flower, Toledo, Med. Coll. hosps. Mem. exec. com. of med. adv. bd. Kidney Found.; mem. med. adv. bd. Planned Parenthood, Vis. Nurse Service; med. dir. N.W. Ohio Hospice Assn. Mem. AMA, Ohio Med. Assn., Assn. Practitioners of Infection Control, Toledo Acad. Medicine. Club: Zonta. Office: 6465 Monroe St Sylvania OH 43560

ERICKSON, DONALD B., agrl. economist; b. Laramie, Wyo., June 9, 1934; s. Bror A. and Sarah Loraine (Bartholomew) E.; B.S., U. Wyo., 1955, M.S., 1960; Ph.D., Purdue U., 1964; m. Phyllis L. Hanson, Aug. 23, 1964; children—Sara Rose, Sonja Lucille. Asst. prof. S.D. State U., 1963-66; asso. prof., state leader CRD extension program Kans. State U., 1966-72, prof. agrl. econs., 1972-78, asst. dept. head charge extension programs, 1978—; cons. Mem. Lutheran Ch. Council. Internat. Farm Youth Exchange del. to Argentina, 1955-56; Fulbright scholar New South Wales U., Australia, 1958-59. Mem. Am. Agrl. Econs. Assn., Community Devel. Soc. (sec.-treas.), Western Agrl. Econs. Assn. Republican. Club: Solar Kiwanis (sec.). Author expt. sta publs.; contbr. articles to profl. jours., periodicals. Home: 2841 Nevada St Manhattan KS 66502 Office: Dept of Economics Kansas State University Manhattan KS 66506

ERICKSON, ELLSWORTH BURCH, educator; b. Wisconsin Dells, Wis., Feb. 14, 1924; s. Julius T. and Isabelle M. (Burch) E.; cert. Arts and Lang., U. Florence (Italy), 1945; B.S. in Art. Edn. and Journalism, U. Minn., Mpls., 1949, M.Ed. in Art Edn., and Curriculum and Instruction, 1951; m. H. Dian; children—Sheryl, Kent, Valerie, Kurt, Cynthia (dec.), Laura, Beret, Erik. Chmn. art lab. sch. U. Minn., Mpls., 1950-54; coordinator art, co-coordinator arts courses and presentation opportunity community mems., Mounds View Public Schs., St. Paul, 1954—; founder Studio 621, art research center and gallery, St. Paul; author test questions art, art edn. and humanities Am. Guidance Service, St. Paul, 1971-72; specialist art edn. Hamlin U., St. Paul, 1972—. Bd. deacons, mem. choir St. Mark's Lutheran Ch. Mem. Art Educators Minn. (co-founder), Minn. Alliance Arts in Edn. (dir. 1975-80), NEA, Nat. Art Educators Assn., Minn. Ednl. Assn., Am. Legion, DAV, VFW. Author: Artist in Residence, Organic Architecture-Frank Lloyd Wright of Taliesin West, Creativity and Self Expression Through Publications; (with others) Who Am I?, (with others) Humanities. Author Nat. Public Radio art edn. program Art As Core. Home: 2338 E 15th Ave North Saint Paul MN 55109 Office: 1900 W County Rd F Saint Paul MN 55112

ERICKSON, HILMER EHRENBERG, vocat. guidance counselor; b. Mpls., June 9, 1932; s. Hilmer Alvin and Stella Johanna Augusta (Ehrenberg) E.; student U. Fla., 1953-55, U. Miami, 1955-62; Asso. Sci., Miami Dade Coll., 1964; B.A., Fla. Atlantic U., 1965, M.Ed., 1970; m. Gloria Ann Olesen, Oct. 18, 1975. Patrolman, Dade County Public Safety Dept., Miami, Fla., 1956-60, detective sgt., 1960-66, criminal intelligence, 1966-69; pres. Fla. Atlantic U. Alumni Assn., Boca Raton, 1969-72; sr. counselor vocat. guidance Minn. Dept. Econ. Security, St. Paul, 1972—; dir. M.H. Graham Corp., Biloxi, Miss. Sustaining mem. Rep. Nat. Com., 1974-77; commr. Golden Valley Human Rights Commn. Served with USNR, 1951-53; mem. Res. Mem. Res. Officers Assn. (life), Naval Res. Assn. (life), U.S. Naval Inst., Navy League, Am. Def. Preparedness Assn., Nat. Rifle Assn. (life), Am. Legion (post comdr. 1959-60), 40 and 8, Am. Swedish Inst., Sons of Norway. Lutheran. Clubs: Ft. Snelling Officers, Masons, Shriners. Home: 4022 Wayzata Blvd Golden Valley MN 55416 Office: Minn Dept Econ Security 390 N Robert St Saint Paul MN 55101

ERICKSON, LEROY, state senator, farmer; b. DeLamere, N.D., May 15, 1926; s. Ed and Agnes (Martinson) E.; grad. high sch.; m. Lila Moxness, Nov. 10, 1946; children—Marsha Susag, Kim Mund. Rep. N.D. Legislature, 1967-68, 73-80, N.D. Senate, 1981—; grain farmer, DeLamere. Del., N.D. Constnl. Conv., 1972; twp. supr., 1952-54; mem. County Sch. Reorgn. Bd., County Spl. Edn. Bd.; dir. S.E. Mental Health; active PTA, Farm Bur. Task Forces. Recipient Sparkplug award for communication for agr., 1981. Mem. Farm Bur., Internat. Flying Farmers, N.D. Stockmen's Assn. (legis. rep.), Aircraft Owners and Pilots Assn. Republican. Lutheran. Club: Milnor Satellite. Home and Office: Rural Route DeLamere ND 58022

ERICKSON, LUCERNE REDD, ednl. adminstr.; b. Buffalo, Feb. 12, 1923; d. Ernest Clarence and Arvilla Marian (Terwilliger) Redd; B.S., Ohio No. U., 1961; M.S., Ind. U., 1965, Ed.D., 1973; m. Omar Isadore Erickson, June 9, 1941; children—Omar Stephen, Karen Kjarista, Karl Dennis. Coordinator curriculum Allen County, Lima, Ohio, 1966-69; instr. Ohio State U., Lima, 1969-70; county curriculum coordinator Van Wert County, (Ohio), 1971-73; coordinator Auglaize County curriculum, Wapakoneta, Ohio, 1973—; mem. adv. bd. Area XI Back to Basics. Ednl. chmn. Shawnee United Meth. Ch., 1978, adminstrv. bd., 1978-80. Margaret Webb Blanton scholar Delta Kappa Gamma, 1970-71; Ind. U. grantee, 1970-71. Mem. AAUW (pres. Lima br. 1981—), Ohio Sch. Suprs. Assn. (state pres. 1981), Ohio Assn. Sch. and Curriculum Developers, West Central Ohio Sch. Suprs. Republican. Club: Eastern Star. Home: 3140 Juliette St Lima OH 45805 Office: Court House Wapakoneta OH 45895

ERICKSON, MARILYN MAE, lumber co. adminstr.; b. Mpls., June 13, 1937; student schs. Mpls.; m. Thomas Earl Erickson, Mar. 16, 1960; children—Jeanine, Daniel, Johnna, Heather, Stephanie. With Osborne McMillen Elevator Co., Mpls., 1955-59, sta. WCCO-TV, Mpls., 1959-61, Peat, Marwick, Mitchell & Co., Mpls., 1966-79; adminstrv. support services supr. Fullerton Lumber Co., Mpls., 1979—. Mem. In-Plant Printing Mgmt. Assn. Democrat. Roman Catholic. Home: 2624 118th Ave NW Coon Rapids MN 55433 Office: 1200 Roanke Bldg PO Box 430 Minneapolis MN 55440

ERICKSON, ROY FREDERICK, JR., hosp. adminstr.; b. Chgo., Aug. 16, 1928; s. Roy Frederick and Irene Elsa E.; B.S. in Bus. Adminstrn., Northwestern U., 1950, M.S. in Hosp. Adminstrn., 1956; m. Julia Ellen Raffington, Oct. 18, 1958; children—Elizabeth, Peter, Stephen. Asst. adminstr. Decatur (Ill.) Meml. Hosp., 1956-60; adminstr. Passavant Meml. Area Hosp., Jacksonville, Ill., 1960-64; adminstr. Blessing Hosp., Quincy, Ill., 1964-72; pres. Ball Meml. Hosp., Muncie, Ind., 1972—; adj. prof. physiology and health sci. Ball State U., 1979-81; mem. asso. faculty Muncie Center for Med. Edn.; mem. Central Ind. Health Systems Agy.-Area II Council; bd. dirs. Bi State Regional Med., 1969-72. Served with USAF, 1950-54. Mem. Am. Hosp. Assn., Ind. Hosp. Assn. (dir. 1976—), Am. Coll. Hosp. Adminstrs., Am. Mgmt. Assn. Methodist. Club: Rotary. Home: 4201 University Ave Muncie IN 47304 Office: 2401 University Ave Muncie IN 47303

ERICKSON, SALLY WISHEK LOVELL, lumber co. exec.; b. Aberdeen, S.D., Sept. 30, 1928; d. Max A. and Viola L. (Hezel) Wishek; B.A., U. Ariz., 1950; M.S. in Guidance and Edn., No. State Coll., Aberdeen, 1970; m. Orrin B. Lovell, June 30, 1951 (div. 1970); children—James, Faith, Kent, Christopher, Gregory; m. 2d, Donavan L. Erickson, May 27, 1973. Elementary tchr., Riverdale, N.D., 1950-51; addiction counselor Jamestown (N.D.) State Hosp., 1971-72; elementary sch. counselor, Belcourt, N.D., 1973-75; sec.-treas. Kash Is King Home Center, Mobridge, S.D., 1980—; v.p., dir. Wishek Investment Co., Inc., Ashley; v.p. Union Elevator Co., Ashley, dir. McIntosh County Bank, Ashley, N.D. Mem. Am. Personnel and Guidance Assn., Am. Legion Aux., Alpha Phi. Address: Ashley ND 58413

ERICKSON, SCOTT WILLIAM, cons. firm exec.; b. Brodhead, Wis., Jan. 21, 1948; s. Orville Arnold and Eleanor Mary (Johnson) E.; B.A., U. Minn., Morris, 1970; M.A., U. Minn., Mpls., 1973, Ph.D., 1978. Instr. edn. U. Minn., Mpls., 1973-77; pres., cons. Future Systems, Ins., Mpls., 1977—; adj. asst. prof. edn. U. Minn., Mpls., 1979—. Recipient Provost's award U. Minn., Morris, 1970. Mem. World Future Soc., Minn. Futurists Assn. (v.p. academics 1976-78, pres. 1978-80, dir. 1976—). Author articles on the future of edn., also exploration and industrialization of space; editor Futurics, Quar. Jour. Futures Research, 1977-80, bd. editors, 1980—. Office: 1422 W Lake St Suite 207 Minneapolis MN 55408

ERICKSTAD, RALPH JOHN, state chief justice; b. Starkweather, N.D., Aug. 15, 1922; s. John T. and Anna L. Erickstad; student U. N.D., 1940-43; B.S. in Law, U. Minn., 1947, LL.B., 1949; m. Lois Katherine Jacobson, July 30, 1949; children—John Albert, Mark Anders. Admitted to N.D. bar, 1949; mem. firm Teigen & Erickstad, Devils Lake, N.D., 1950-54; police magistrate, Devils Lake, 1951-53; states atty., Ramsey County, 1953-57; mem. firm Erickstad & Foughty, 1954-62; asso. justice Supreme Ct. of N.D., Bismarck, 1963-73, chief justice, 1973—. Mem. Gov.'s Spl. Com. on Labor, 1960; past commr. Missouri Valley council Boy Scouts Am.; mem. N.D. Senate, 1957-62, asst. majority floor leader; chmn. bd. trustees Missouri Valley Family YMCA, 1966-77; mem. Task Force on Public Image of Cts., Williamsburg Conf. Recipient Silver Beaver award Boy Scouts Am., 1967, Sioux award U. N.D., 1973; 1st Disting. Service award Missouri Valley YMCA, 1978. Mem. Am., N.D., Burleigh County bar assns., Am. Judicature Soc., Am. Law Inst., Nat. Conf. Chief Justices (exec. council 1977—). Republican. Lutheran. Club: Kiwanis. Office: Supreme Ct ND Capitol Bldg Bismarck ND 58505

ERICSON, ELMER WALTER, investor, businessman; b. West Hoboken, N.J., Feb. 4, 1905; s. William Albert and Hedvig Sophia (Lindblom) E.; student Northwestern U., 1923-25; m. Marie Harlacher, Dec. 26, 1929 (dec. 1968); m. 2d, Gloria Canavera, 1973 (dec. 1979). Copywriter, R.R. Donnelley & Sons, Co., Chgo., 1925-27; sales mgr., dir. Barrett Bindery Co., Chgo., 1927-47; founder, pres. Sales Tools, Inc., Des Plaines, Ill., 1947-60; investor, Sturgeon Bay, Wis., 1960—. Treas., Door County Natural Beauty Council, 1973—. Mem. Sales Execs. Club. Patentee loose leaf binders, sales presentation aids. Address: Rt 8 4401 County M Rd Sturgeon Bay WI 54235

ERIE, ELROY EDMUND, health agy. exec.; b. Saint Cloud, Minn., Sept. 3, 1940; s. Elroy McKinley and Mildred Catherine (Nohner) E.; B.A. with honors in Geography, St. Cloud State U., 1970; M.P.A. with highest distinction, Ind. U., 1974; m. Jane McIntosh, Oct. 13, 1964; children—Marina K., Jane C., Sheena K., Ann M. Research dir., asst. to mayor City of St. Cloud, 1968-69; research asso. St. John's Univ., Collegeville, Minn., 1969-72; dir. sustaining program St. Mary's Coll., Notre Dame, Ind., 1972-74; adminstrv. cons. City of Mpls., 1975-77; research cons. Minn. Found., St. Paul, 1977-78; exec. dir. Minn. Soc. for Prevention of Blindness, St. Paul, 1978—. Served with USMC, 1959-67. Mem. Nat. Assn. Fund Raising Execs. (sec.), Minn. Assn. Health Agy. Execs. Club: Rotary. Home: 3882 Ballawtrae Rd Apt 6 Eagan MN 55122 Office: 550 Ewdicott Bldg St Paul MN 55101

ERIKSON, STANLEY, polit. scientist; b. Chgo., Aug. 17, 1906; s. Charles Frederick and Selma Charlotte (Dahlstrom) E.; B.A., U. Wis., 1929; J.D., Northwestern U., 1933, Ph.D., 1939; m. Lila L. Ellstrom, June 12, 1937; children—Robert Stanley, Allen F. (dec.). Research asst. Ill. Legis. Council, 1939-42; dir. war records and research Ill. War Council, 1942-44; asst. prof. polit. sci. Rockford Coll., 1944-48; prof. Augustana Coll., Rock Island, Ill., 1948-74; works include: (with Bellows and Winter) Political Science: Introductory Essays and Readings, 1971, People and Politics, an Introduction to Political Science, 1977, rev. edit., 1980. Mem. Rock Island City Council, 1957-61. Mem. AAUP, Am. Polit. Sci. Assn., Midwest Polit. Sci. Assn. Episcopalian. Home: 3932 8th Ave Rock Island IL 61201

ERLENBORN, JOHN NEAL, congressman; b. Chgo., Feb. 8, 1927; s. John H. and Veronica M. (Moran) E.; student U. Notre Dame, 1944, U. Ill., 1945-46; J.D., Loyola U. (Chgo.), 1949; m. Dorothy C. Fisher, May 10, 1952; children—Debra Lynn, Paul Nelson, David John. Admitted to Ill. bar, 1949; practiced in Wheaton, Ill., 1949-50, mem. firm Erlenborn and Bauer, 1952-63, Erlenborn, Bauer, and Hotte, 1963-71; mem. 89th-97th Congresses 14 dist. Ill. Mem. Ill. Ho. of Reps., 1956-64; assistant States Atty., DuPage County, Ill., 1950-52. Served with USNR, 1944-46. Mem. Am. Legion, C. of C. Republican. Club: Lions (Elmhurst, Ill.). Office Rayburn House Office Bldg Room 2206 Washington DC 20515

ERNEST, PAUL HENRY, ophthalmologist; b. Toledo, Ohio, Dec. 21, 1947; s. Robert Paul and Eleanor Ann (Nowak) E.; student Henry Ford Community Coll., 1965-66, Northwestern U., 1966-69; M.D., Wayne State U., 1973; married; children—Alicia Ann, Hookki, Michi, Kimberly Gail. Intern, Grace Hosp., Detroit, 1973-74; resident in ophthalmology Wayne State U., Detroit, 1974-77, fellow Kresge Eye Inst., 1977-78; practice medicine, specializing in ophthalmology, Jackson, Mich., 1978—; mem. staff W.A. Foote Hosp., Jackson. Diplomate Am. Bd. Ophthalmology. Mem. Mich. Med. Soc., AMA, Am. Intraocular Implant Soc., Am. Assn. Ophthalmology. Presbyterian. Club: Jackson Country. Office: 306 W Washington St Suite 101 Jackson MI 49201

ERNEST, ROBERT C., corp. exec.; b. 1924; ed. U. Wis., M.I.T. With Kimberly-Clark Corp., 1952—, v.p. paper products, 1971, group v.p. fine paper and spltys. group, 1971, dir., 1971, exec. v.p., 1972, pres., 1978—. Office: Kimberly Clark Corp N Lake St Neenah WI 54956

ERNEY, RICHARD ALTON, hist. soc. exec.; b. Stryker, Ohio, Dec. 15, 1924; s. Arthur Frank and Opal Marie (Bowman) E.; B.A., Denison U., 1948; M.A., Tchrs. Coll., Columbia U., 1950, Ph.D., 1957; m. Alice Estelle Craig, Dec. 27, 1950. Field rep. State Hist. Soc. Wis., Madison, 1957-60, state archivist, 1960-63, asso. dir., 1963-77, dir., 1977—; mem. Archives Adv. Council U.S., 1968-74, Nat. Hist. Publs. and Records Commn., 1975—. Served with USAAF, 1943-46. Recipient alumni citation Denison U., 1978. Fellow Soc. Am. Archivists; mem. Am. Assn. for State and Local History (treas. 1972-78, v.p. 1980—), Nat. Trust for Historic Preservation, Wis. Acad. Scis., Arts and Letters. Congregationalist. Club: Madison. Author: The Public Life of Henry Dearborn, 1979; contbr. articles and book revs. to profl. jours. Office: 816 State St Madison WI 53706

ERNST, RONALD LEROY, mgmt. cons.; b. Toledo, Ohio, Mar. 15, 1949; s. Richard Harry and Audrey Jayne (Sprengel) E.; B.S., Ind. U., 1971; M.B.A., Ohio State U., 1972; m. Virginia Walters, June 17, 1972. Research and cons. asso. Mgmt. Horizons, Inc., Worthington, Ohio, 1971-75, sr. cons. asso., Columbus, 1976-79; v.p. Mgmt. Horizons, 1979-81, sr. v.p., 1981—; dir., 1981—; project mgr. mktg. research Federated Dept. Stores, Cin., 1975-76; lectr. in bus. adminstrn. Franklin U., 1972-73. Mem. Am. Mktg. Assn., Am. Mgmt. Assn., Assn. M.B.A. Execs. Lutheran. Contbr. articles to profl. jours. Home: 1099 Kirk Ave Worthington OH 43085 Office: 450 W Wilson Bridge Rd Worthington OH 43085

ERON, LEONARD DAVID, psychologist; b. Newark, Apr. 22, 1920; s. Joseph and Sarah (Hilfman) E.; B.S., CCNY, 1941; M.A., Columbia U., 1946; Ph.D., U. Wis., 1949; m. Madeline Marcus, May 21, 1950; children—Joan Eron Hobson, Don M., Barbara F. Asst. prof. psychology Yale U., 1948-55; research dir. Rip Van Winkle Found., 1955-62; prof. psychology U. Iowa, 1962-69; prof. psychology, research prof. social scis. U. Ill., Chgo., 1969—; Fulbright lectr. Free U. Amsterdam, 1967-68. Served to 1st lt., AUS, 1942-45. Recipient Fulbright sr. scholar award Queensland U., Australia, 1977; diplomate Am. Bd. Profl. Psychology. Fellow AAAS, Am. Psychol. Assn. (award for disting. profl. contbn. to knowledge 1980), Am. Orthopsychiat. Assn. Author: Experimental Approach to Projective Techniques, 1965; Classification of Behavior Disorders, 1967; Relation of Theory to Practice in Psychotherapy, 1969; Learning of Aggression in Children, 1971; Growing Up to Be Violent, 1977; Abnormality: Experimental and Clinical Approaches, 1977; editor: Jour. Abnormal Psychology, 1973-80. Home: 1616 Sheridan Rd Wilmette IL 60091 Office: Dept of Psychology Box 4348 Chicago IL 60680

ERSKINE, ADDINE GRADWOHL (MRS. LUCIAN ERSKINE), scientist, educator, author; b. Omaha; d. Harry C. and Jennie (Ettman) Gradwohl; grad. Harris Tchrs. Coll. (now Harris-Stowe Coll.), St. Louis; student McGill U., 1932; D.Sc. (hon.), Tech. Coll. Sussex, 1970; D.Litt. (hon.), Internat. Free Protestant Episcopal U., 1968; m. Lucian Erskine, Mar. 26, 1932 (dec. Feb. 1962); step-children—Lucian Jr., Frank S. (dec. 1974). Formerly tchr. St. Louis pub. sch. system; med. technologist Gradwohl Lab., St. Louis County Hosp., St. Louis; asst. dir., later asso. dir., prin. Gradwohl Sch. Lab. Technique, St. Louis; former asst. editor The Lab. Digest, later asso. editor; former vis. prof. biol. Scis. Lane Coll., Jackson, Tenn. Spl. cons. to med. div. U.S. Dept. State, 1967-68. Pres. bd. dirs. Gradwohl Sch. Lab. Technique. Recipient award Clara Maass Soc. of N.J. Hosp. Assn., 1963; Honor Key award Alumni Assn. of Gradwohl Sch., 1962; Eloy Alfaro Grand Cross and Certificate, Republic of Panama, 1965; Scroll of Appreciation, U.S. Sec. of State, 1968; spl. award for contbns. to sci. edn. Lane Coll., 1969; hon. fellow Harry S. Truman Library Inst., 1978. Fellow Royal Soc. Tropical Medicine and Hygiene (London), AAAS, Royal Micros. Soc. (London), Philos. Soc. Eng. (hon. life); mem. Mo. State Tchrs. Assn., Internat. Coll. Tropical Medicine, N.J. Acad. Sci., St. Louis Acad. Sci., N.Y. Acad. Sci., Nat. Wildlife Preservation Soc., Am. Guild Organists, Internat. Soc. for Clin. Lab. Tech. (award for excellence in editorial work 1968, hon. life mem.; cons. to credentialing commn.), Am. Soc. Microbiology (editor Mo. br. Newsletter, award for contbns. Mo. br. 1979), Castro County Hist. Mus. (Dimmitt, Tex.) (charter mem.). Author: Principles and Practice of Blood Grouping, 1973, (with W.W. Socha) 2d edit., 1978; contbg. author: Clinical Laboratory Methods and Diagnosis; co-author: Laboratory Technique, 1932; Questions in Laboratory Methods, 1967; Blood Types, Transfusions, Rh, and Heredity, 1970. Home: 3721 Clifton Ave Saint Louis MO 63109 Office: 3514 Lucas Saint Louis MO 63103

ERTEL, PAUL ANTHONY, rubber products co. exec.; b. Cleve., Sept. 1, 1952; s. Elmer Anthony and Helen Jean (Ketchum) E.; B.B.A., U. Dayton, 1975. Inventory control analyst Bearings, Inc., Cleve., 1972-75; gen. mgr. equipment div. Luntz Corp., Cleve., 1975-80; gen. mgr. Ohio Grand Tire Co. div. Stein Inc., Cleve., 1980—. Chmn., Parties-in-the-Park, 1978-79; mem. Cleve. Citizens League. Mem. Cleve. UpDowntown Inc., Cleve. Engring. Soc., Playhouse Sq. Assn., Alpha Kappa Psi. Roman Catholic. Clubs: Cleve. City, Jaycees (Cleve.). Home: 4181 Silsby Rd Cleveland OH 44118 Office: PO Box 7756 Cleveland OH 44131

ERWIN, CHESLEY PARA, JR., utility co. exec.; b. Milw., Apr. 6, 1953; s. Chesley Para and Constance June (Raab) E.; student Occidental Coll., 1971-72; A.B., Stanford U., 1974; M.A. in Public Policy and Adminstrn., U. Wis., Madison, 1976, M.S. in Bus., 1976; m. Karen Jane Leonard, Dec. 27, 1974. Intern, Bur. Fiscal Policy Planning and Analysis, Wis. Dept. Revenue, 1976; energy researcher energy systems and policy research group Inst. Environ. Studies, U. Wis., Madison, 1974-76; health planning analyst Wis. Dept. Health and Social Services, Madison, 1976-77; energy analyst Office State Planning and Energy, Wis. Dept. Adminstrn., Madison, 1977-78; govt. relations specialist Wis. Power & Light Co., Madison, 1978-81; regulatory affairs advisor, 1981—. Mem. New Republican Conf. Wis., 1976—; coordinator Anderson for Pres., Dane County, Wis., 1979-80; alt. del. Rep. Nat. Conv., 1980. Mem. Am. Econs. Assn., Am. Soc. Public Adminstrn., Oconomowoc Jaycees. Republican. Home: 820 Old Tower Rd Oconomowoc WI 53066 Office: PO Box 192 222 W Washington Ave Madison WI 53701

ESCALERA, SAUL JOAQUIN, metallurgist; b. Cochabamba, Bolivia, May 31, 1939; came to U.S., 1977, permanent resident; s. Juan Cancio and Arminda Maria (Vasquez) E.; Mining Engr., Universidad Técnica de Oruro, Bolivia, 1962; M.S., N.Mex. Inst. Mining & Tech., 1966, Ph.D., 1971; m. Kathleen Kay Woynowskie, Sept. 5, 1969; children—Diego Joaquín, Katia Giselle. Prof., Dept. Metallurgy, Universidad Tecnica de Oruro, Bolivia, 1971-74; project coordinator Mineral Tech. Div., Centro Tecnologico de Minas Gerais, Belo Horizonte, Brazil, 1974-76; group leader Mining Chems. Research, Sherex Chem. Co., Dublin, Ohio, 1977—; prof. grad. sch. metallurgy Universidad Federal de Minas Gerais Belo Horizonte, Brazil, part-time, 1974-76. Fulbright scholar, 1964-66; N.M. Bur. Mines Research scholar, 1967-70. Mem. Soc. Mining Engrs. of AIME, Canadian Inst. Mining and Metallurgy, Am. Chem. Soc. Club: Sawmill Athletic. Contbr. articles to profl. jours.; author: Thesis Manual for Science and Technology, 1975; Hydrometallurgy - Theory and Practice, 1981; inventor in field. Home: 3153 Saybrook Ct Dublin OH 43017 Office: 5777 Frantz Rd Dublin OH 43017

ESCHBACH, JESSE ERNEST, fed. judge; b. Warsaw, Ind., Oct. 26, 1920; s. Jesse Ernest and Mary W. (Stout) E.; B.S., Ind. U., 1943, J.D. with distinction (Hastings scholar), 1949; m. Sara Ann Walker, Mar. 15, 1947; children—Jesse Ernest III, Virginia. Admitted to Ind. bar, 1949; partner firm Graham, Rasor, Eschbach & Harris, Warsaw, 1949-62; city atty., Warsaw, 1952-53; dep. pros. atty. 54th Jud. Circuit Ct. Ind., 1952-54; judge U.S. Dist. Ct. No. Dist. Ind., 1962-74, chief judge, 1974—. Pres. Endicott Church Furniture, Inc., 1960-62; sec., gen. counsel Dalton Foundries, Inc., 1957-62. Trustee, Ind. U., 1965-70. Served with USNR, 1943-46. Recipient U.S. Law Week award, 1949. Mem. U.S. (labor relations com. 1960-62), Warsaw (pres. 1955-56) chambers commerce, Nat. Assn. Furniture Mfrs. (dir. 1962), Ind. Mfrs. Assn. (dir. 1962), Am., Ind. (bd. mgrs. 1953-54, ho. dels. 1950-60, 7th Circuit Fed. bar assns., Am. Judicature Soc., Order of Coif. Presbyterian. Rotarian (pres. Warsaw 1956-57). Editorial staff Ind. Law Jour., 1947-49. Office: Fed Bldg 1300 S Harrison Room 243 Fort Wayne IN 46802

ESCHBACHER, KENNETH HENRY, retail co. exec.; b. Cleve., Jan. 29, 1947; s. Frank Edward and Irma Freida (Mueller) E.; B.Adminstrv. Sci., Ohio State U., 1969; m. Judith Jo Donda, June 21, 1969; children—Timothy Joseph, Amanda Christina. Mgr. trainee

J.C. Penney's, Mansfield, Ohio, 1970; asst. mgr., sportswear buyer Schwartz's Apparel, Dover, Ohio, 1971; store mgr., gen. merchandiser Kline Co. Inc., Dover, 1971-74; exec. v.p. Schwartz-Klines, New Philadelphia, Ohio, 1974-78, pres., 1978—, pres. subs., Wilson's Dept. Stores, Inc., Daniel's Women's Wear, Inc.; instr. retailing Kent State U., 1979. Chmn. comml. div. Tuscarawas County United Way Campaign, 1981-82. Mem. Nat. Retail Mchts. Assn., Men's Retailers Am., Dover Retail Mchts. (pres. 1972-73), Monroe Mall Mchts. Assn. (pres. 1974-75), Tuscarawas C. of C. (trustee), Aircraft Owners and Pilots Assn. Office: 1260 Monroe St New Philadelphia OH 44663

ESCOTT, JOHN JOSEPH, physician; b. Toledo, Sept. 28, 1948; s. Robert Milton and Jeanne Ellen (Fournier) E.; B.S. in Biology, U. Toledo, 1970; M.D., Wayne State U., 1974; m. Elaine Rita Dwyer, Nov. 29, 1975; children—Amy Marie, Sarah Margaret. Intern, Oakwood Hosp., Dearborn, Mich., 1974-75, resident in family practice, 1975-77; practice medicine specializing in family medicine, Iron River, Mich., 1977—; asso. dir. family practice residency William Beaumont Hosp., Troy, Mich.; asso. clin. prof. Wayne State U., Detroit, 1982—; mem. staffs Iron County Gen. Hosp., Crystal Falls Community Hosp. Recipient Physician's Recognition award AMA, 1977; diplomate Am. Bd. Family Physicians. Mem. Mich. Med. Soc., Iron-Dickinson County Med. Soc. Club: Iron County Engrs. Home: 7 4th St Iron River MI 49935 Office: 1500 W Ice Lake Rd Iron River MI 49935

ESKEW, CAROLYN ELIZABETH, personnel adminstr.; b. Campbell, Mo., Nov. 4, 1942; d. Rudolph and Helen L. (Carrell) Preslar; B.Music Edn., DePauw U., 1964; M.Music Edn., Murray State U., 1969; m. Ralph Eskew, Dec. 11, 1976. Band dir. public schs., Effingham, Ill., 1964-67, Calloway County, Murray, Ky., 1967-69; personnel dir. Carondelet Foundry Co., St. Louis, 1970—. Mem. Am. Soc. Personnel Adminstrn., Internat. Assn. Personnel Women, Mu Phi Epsilon. Methodist. Office: 2101 S Kingshighway Saint Louis MO 63110

ESLER, HAROLD DEAN, psychoanalyst; b. Detroit, Oct. 7, 1930; s. Daniel B. and Mary G. (Esler) E.; B.S., Wayne State U., 1957, M.A., 1959; Ph.D., Mich. State U., 1964; m. Nancy L. Valentine, Aug. 12, 1955; children—Pamela M., Laura V., Diana L. Staff psychologist Northville State Hosp., 1959-61; sch. psychologist Lansing Schs., 1961-62; chief psychologist, clin. dir. W.J. Maxey's Boy's Tng. Sch., 1962-64; out-patient child psychologist Plymouth State Home, 1964-66; chief psychologist intense treatment unit Northville State Hosp., 1966-70; pvt. practice psychoanalysis, 1959—; cons. psychoanalyst Mexico Inst. Psychoanalysis. Served with USMC, 1951-53. Mem. Am., Mich. psychol. assns., Mich. Cons. Psychologists Assn., S.W. Assn. Psychoanalysis (v.p.), Nat. Assn. Psychoanalysis (dir.), Internat. Psychoalaytic Fedn. (dir.), Midwest Psychoanalytic Inst. (pres.). Democrat. Roman Catholic. Home: 1075 Suffield St Birmingham MI 48009 Office: 625 Purdy St Birmingham MI 48009

ESLING, HARRY ROBERT, JR., steel products mfg. co.; b. Detroit, June 13, 1932; s. Harry Robert and Helen Frances (Moore) E.; B.S., Mich. State U., 1955, M.B.A., 1977; m. Kathryn Louise Brownyer, Aug. 4, 1962; children—Lynne, Karen, Lisa. Buyer, Ford Motor Co., 1956-58; sales mgr. Hurd Lock & Mfg. Co., Detroit, 1958-65; sales rep. Rockwell Internat. Co., 1965-68; account mgr. Dura Corp., 1968-69; sales mgr. Midland Frame div. Midland Ross Corp., Southfield, Mich., 1969-76; v.p. sales Midland Steel Products Co., Southfield, 1976-79, pres., Cleve., 1979—, also dir. Served with USAF, 1950-52. Mem. Soc. Automotive Engrs., Automotive Orgn. Team, Automotive Original Equirment Mfrs. Assn., Mensa. Republican. Episcopalian. Clubs: Detroit Athletic, Avon Oaks Country, Myrtle Beach Nat. Golf. Office: 10 615 Madison Ave Cleveland OH 44102

ESLINGER, KENNETH NELSON, JR., educator; b. Hennepin, Ill., Mar. 2, 1941; s. Kenneth Nelson and Pearl Mae (Bolte) E.; B.S., Ind. State U., 1963; M.A., Ohio State U., 1968, Ph.D., 1971; m. Denise M. Juba, July 22, 1979. Vis. asst. prof. sociology Ohio State U., Lima, 1972, asst. prof., sociology 1972-73; asst. prof. sociology Cleve. State U., 1973—, dir. M.A. Program in Sociology, 1979-80; vis. asst. prof. sociology John Carroll U., Cleve., 1980—. Mem. Am. Sociol. Assn., Nat. Council on Family Relations, Soc. for Study of Social Problems, Alpha Kappa Delta. Contbr. articles in field to profl. jours. Home: 17927 Whitney Rd Strongsville OH 44136 Office: Dept Sociology John Carroll U Cleveland OH 44118

ESPARZA, ALAN DALE, architect; b. Great Falls, Mont., June 20, 1950; s. Michael T. and Betty Lucile (Kjellgren) E.; B.Arch., N.D. State U., 1973; m. Deborah Ann Orth, May 27, 1973. Designer, Van Buren & Firestone, Architects, Columbus, Ohio, 1973-77; designer Wolfgang Doerschlag, Architects, Columbus, 1977-79; prin., pres. Alan D. Esparza, Architect, Inc., Columbus, 1980—; prin., v.p. Esparza-Eversole, Inc., design and bldg. cons., Columbus, 1981—. Cert. architect Nat. Council Archtl. Registration Bds. Mem. Constrn. Specifications Inst. Lutheran. Office: 3040 Riverside Dr Suite 213 Columbus OH 43221

ESPINOSA, GUSTAVO ADOLFO, radiologist, educator; b. Colombia, June 8, 1944; came to U.S., 1969, naturalized, 1976; s. Hector Octavius and Olga I. (Milanes) E.; B.S., St. Joseph Coll., Colombia, 1960; M.D. magna cum laude, U. Xaveriana, Colombia, 1968; m. Cecilia Troncoso, June 4, 1968; children—Gustavo Adolfo, David A., Susan M. Intern, Providence Hosp., Washington, 1969-70; resident in radiology Cook County Hosp., Chgo., 1971-75, attending radiologist, 1976—; attending radiologist West Side VA Hosp., Chgo., 1977—, chmn. dept., 1977—; attending U. Ill. Hosp., 1977—; asso. prof. U. Ill. Med. Sch.; med. dir. Sch. X-ray Tech., Malcolm X Coll., Chgo. Diplomate Am. Bd. Radiology. Mem. Radiol. Soc. N.Am., AMA, Am. Coll. Radiology, Am. Inst. Ultrasound in Medicine, Ill. Med. Soc., Ill. Radiol. Soc., Chgo. Med. Soc., Chgo. Roentgen Soc., Chgo. Ultrasound Soc. Office: 820 S Damen Ave Chicago IL 60680

ESPOSITO, MARGUERITE ANNE, food co. exec.; b. Chgo., Feb. 4, 1954; d. Alfred F. and Anne Esposito; B.S., Ind. U., 1976. With Quaker Oats Co., Chgo., 1975—, account mgr., 1978-79, field sales tng. supr. food service div., 1979-81, mgr. sales tng., 1981—. Mem. Am. Mktg. Assn. Club: Restaurant Women's of Chgo. Office: Quaker Oats Co Merchandise Mart Plaza Chicago IL 60654

ESSEKS, JOHN DIXON, polit. scientist; b. N.Y.C., Dec. 24, 1938; s. Samuel S. and Mary Wilma (Dixon) E.; A.B., Oberlin Coll., 1960; A.M. (Woodrow Wilson fellow), Harvard U., 1963, Ph.D. (Fng. Area Tng. fellow), 1967; m. Mary Jean Radcliff, May 17, 1963; children—Elizabeth, Rosemary. Asst. prof. polit. sci. U. Wis., Oshkosh, 1966-68; asst. prof. No. Ill. U., DeKalb, 1968-72, asso. prof., 1972—; cons. Nat. Agrl. Lands Study, 1979-81, DeKalb County, 1979-80. Social Sci. Research Council grantee, 1970. Mem. Am. Soc. Public Adminstrn., Am. Planning Assn., Policy Studies Orgn., Phi Beta Kappa. Episcopalian. Edit. bd. African Studies Rev., 1974-78; contbg. editor l'Afrique de l'Independance Politique a l'Independance Economique, 1975; contbr. articles to profl. jours. Home: 108 Manor Dr DeKalb IL 60115 Office: Dept Polit Sci No Ill U DeKalb IL 60115

ESSER, DONALD JOSEPH, engring. co. exec.; b. Madison, Wis., Apr. 25, 1924; s. Raymond Frank and Emma Frances (Gugel) E.; B.S.M.E., U. Wis., Madison, 1949; postgrad. U. Wis., Milw., 1957-71; m. Virginia Ann Irgens, Aug. 28, 1954; children—Peter, Susan. Engr., Gen. Electric Co., Lynn, Mass., 1949-53; project engr. Allis-Chalmers Corp., Milw., 1953-57; sales engr. George H. Fredricks & Co., Inc., Milw., 1957-62, v.p., 1962-71, prs., 1971—, dir., 1961—; instr. mech. engring. U. Wis.-Madison, 1948-49. Active Boy Scouts Am., 1967-70; ski instr. Chgo. Tribune Free Ski Sch., 1968-72, Blizzard Ski Sch., 1967-76. Served in USAAC, 1943-46; ETO. Registered profl. engr., Wis. Mem. ASME (sec. Milw. sect. 1957, sect. treas. 1958, dir. 1957—), Instrument Soc. Am., Milw. Council Engr. and Sci. Socs. (ASME del. 1978—, treas. 1979—, dir. 1979—). Wis. Alumni Assn. (life), U.S. Tennis Assn., Phi Gamma Delta. Club: Western Racquet (charter, dir. 1979—, sec. 1981) (Elm Grove, Wis.). Home: 2037 Sunset Ct Wauwatosa WI 53226 Office: PO Box 10340 4524 W Burleigh St Milwaukee WI 53210

ESSERMAN, LOIS BENDES, ednl. diagnostician, therapist; b. Mpls., Sept. 22, 1926; d. Jacob Harry and Pauline Pearl (Berman) Bendes; B.A., U. Mich., 1948; M.A., Northwestern U., 1969; m. Howard James Lurie, May 20, 1951; children—James Harrison, Frederick Allan, Kottie Suzanne; m. 2d, Norman S. Esserman, July 27, 1979. Speech therapist Rockford (Ill.) Coll., 1948, Wyandotte (Mich.) Pub. Schs., 1948-50, Michael Reese Hosp., Chgo., 1950-53; diagnostician learning disabilities, tchr. Highland Park (Ill.) Sch. Dist. 107, 1969—; tchr. edn. program Inst. Psychoanalysis, 1975-79; coop. supr., student tchrs. in learning disabilities Northwestern U., Evanston, Ill., clin. lectr. dept. communications, 1978—; mem. working com. Ill. Guide Lines Learning Disabilities, 1977; speaker conf. on learning disabilities Chgo. Fedn. Union Am. Hebrew Congregations, 1973, speaker nat. conf., 1977—. Bd. dirs. Congregation Solel, Highland Park. Mem. Phi Delta Kappa (sec. 1978—). Home: 911 Rollingwood Dr Highland Park IL 60035 Office: 2075 Saint Johns Ave Highland Park IL 60035

ESSEX, WANDA ELIZABETH, speech pathologist; b. Benham, Ky., Jan. 25, 1925; d. Nathaniel Otto and Elizabeth Marie (Ausmus) Irwin; student Cath. U., Washington, 1945-47; B.S., U. Nebr. at Lincoln, 1969, M.A., 1973; m. Earl Woodrow Essex, Nov. 28, 1947; children—Michael, Elane, Christopher. Classifier fingerprints FBI, Washington, 1943-45; sec. Library of Congress, Washington, 1948-49; speech pathologist Edn. Service Unit 6, Milford, Nebr., 1969, Fremont (Nebr.) Pub. Schs., 1969—; pvt. practice speech pathology Meml. Hosp. Dodge County, Fremont, 1975—. Mem. Am. (cert. clin. competence), Nebr. speech and hearing assns., Council Exceptional Children (pres. Mideast Nebr. chpt. 1976-77), NEA, Fremont Edn. Assn., Nebr. Edn. Assn., AAUW, Bus. and Profl. Women, Delta Kappa Gamma, Phi Delta Kappa, Beta Sigma Phi. Home: 2481 N Nye Ave Apt 318 Fremont NE 68025 Office: 957 N Pierce St Fremont NE 68025

ESSIG, RICHARD NORMAN, mfg. co. exec.; b. Sanborn, Minn., May 28, 1933; s. Joseph J. and Marie D. (Pabst) E.; student Ariz. State U., 1960-64, U. Mass., 1972-74; m. Corinne J. Skjervold, Dec. 27, 1951 (div. Dec. 31, 1979); children—Linda J., Michael R.; m. 2d, Mary D. Morelli, Jan. 5, 1980. Journeyman maintenance man Interstate Power Co., 1952-60; powerline constrn. Ariz. Pub. Service Co., 1960-67; S.E. regional sales engr. Malleable Iron Products, Birmingham, Ala., 1967-69, N.E. regional sales mgr., Greenfield, Mass., 1969-70; nat. sales and mktg. mgr. Injection Molded Plastics Products, Greenfield, 1970-75; tech. mgr. Reliable Electric Co., Franklin Park, Ill., 1975-78; v.p. sales, mktg. and engring., Plastigage Corp., Jackson, Mich., 1978—; cons., 1967—. Mem. IEEE, Vt. Elec. Assn., Electric Council New Eng., Nat. Soc. Profl. Engrs., Internat. Assn. Elec. Engrs., Am. Nat. Standards Inst., Am. Mgmt. Assn., Am. Mktg. Assn., ASTM, Nat. Elec. Mfrs. Assn. Republican. Club: Odd Fellows. Home: 3836 E Walmont Ave Jackson MI 49203 Office: PO Box 1167 Jackson MI 49204 also Plastigage Corp 2917 Wildwood Ave Jackson MI 49204

ESSMAN, JOHN FREDRICK, screw machine product co. exec.; b. St. Louis, June 22, 1943; s. Orvell Woodrow and Florence Edna (Thornhill) E.; student U. Mo., 1961-69; m. Joyce F. Kassel, May 31, 1969; children—Stephanie, Coleen. Screw machine operator Measuregraph Co., St. Louis, 1963-74, sales engr., 1972-74; plant mgr. Chase Brass & Copper Screw Machine Shop, Pioneer, Ohio, 1974-76; owner, pres. Essman Screw Products Inc., 1976—. Mem. Nat. Screw Machine Products Assn., Soc. Mfg. Engrs., Am. Soc. Metals, Jaycees. Republican. Club: Rotary. Home: Route 5 Bryan OH 43506 Office: 705 S Union Bryan OH 43506

ESTABROOK, WESLEY ADRIAN, JR., relay mfg. exec.; b. Pochatoula, La., Mar. 23, 1925; s. Wesley Adrian and Mary Louise (Davies) E.; student Cornell U., 1942; B.S., B.E., Yale U., 1947; m. Beverly Seiler Nemeyer, July 5, 1950; children—Shelley, Wesley, Dale. With Gen. Electric Co., Utica and Syracuse, N.Y., 1949-59, gen. mgr., Portsmouth, Va., 1959-69; pres. Audio Devices, Stamford, Conn., 1969-72, C.P. Clare & Co., Chgo., 1972-79. Speaker, N.Y. State Small Bus. Forums. Area chmn. Savs. Bonds, Portsmouth, 1967-68; chmn. Skenandoah dist. Boy Scouts Am., 1963-64. Bd. dirs. Portsmouth Gen. Hosp., 1967-69. Served to ensign USNR, World War II. Mem. Nat. Assn. Relay Mfrs., Am. Legion. Methodist. Republican. Club: Execs. (Chgo.). Home: 400 Sheridan Rd Wilmette IL 60091

ESTER, MARY ELLEN, cosmetologist, esthetician; b. Carey, Ohio, Apr. 26, 1926; d. John Cleveland and Flora Effie Ellen (Snider) Leasure; lic. Cleve. Acad. Cosmetology, 1945; grad. Realtors Inst., U. Mich., 1975; cert. Newspaper Inst. Am., 1980; m. Henry Ester, Aug. 25, 1946; 1 dau., Barbara Rosanne Ester Christensen. Tchr. cosmetology Am. Beauty Sch., Cleve., 1969-70; owner, mgr. Fair Lady Beauty Salon, Fairview Park, Ohio, 1960-70; staff Martin, Ketchum & Martin Inc., Realtors, Livonia, Mich., 1972-76; esthetician, rep. Adrien Arpel Skin Care and Cosmetics, Halles-Westgate Beauty Salon, Fairview Park, 1977—; tchr. adult edn., cons. adult classes Lakewood High Sch. Campaign mgr. local polit. elections, 1959, 63, 71. Mem. Women's Council Realtors, Bus. and Profl. Women, Nat. Hairdressers and Cosmetologists Assn. Home: 18849 Timber Ln Fairview Park OH 44126 Office: Halles-Westgate Beauty Salon Fairview Park OH 41126

ESTES, DAN L., mktg. exec.; b. Anderson, Ind., Feb. 3, 1945; s. Robert W. and Orvilla (Eutsler) E.; B.A., Ind. U., 1967; M.A., Purdue U., 1969; m. Peggy A. Nordeen, May 25, 1980; children—Danny, Jefferson. Project dir. Richardson-Smith, Inc., Columbus, Ohio, 1969-70; promotion dir. Playboy Enterprises, Chgo., 1970-75; v.p., creative dir. Sperry-Boom, Inc., Chgo., 1975-78; prin., v.p. Starmark, Inc., Chgo., 1978—; prin., v.p. Datafacts Internat., also Downhome, Inc., Chgo., mem. faculty Ohio State U., 1969-70. Mem. Am. Mktg. Assn., Am. Mgmt. Assn., Advt. Club Chgo. Author: The No-Nonsense Guide to Starting Your Own Business, 1980. Office: 706 N Dearborn Pkwy Chicago IL 60610

ESTES, NAOMI E., mgmt. info. systems ofcl.; b. San Diego, Jan. 25, 1949; d. Joseph Winston and Mary June (Lothberg) E.; B.S. in Mgmt. Info. Systems and Mgmt., Univ. Without Walls, U. Minn., 1982. With Mgmt. Info. Systems Research Center, U. Minn., Mpls., 1969-81, asst. dir., 1979-81, founding staff, mng. editor MIS Quar., 1976-81, mem. editorial policy com., 1982—, mem. adv. council Univ. Without Walls, 1979-80; mgr. ISD advanced tng. and adminstrn. Investors Diversified Services, Inc., Mpls., 1981—; research and bus. practices cons. Regents scholar U. Minn., 1978-81. Mem. Soc. for Mgmt. Info. Systems (sec., mem. founding bd. dirs. Upper Midwest Chpt., 1979-80, mem. nat. exec. council, 1980-82, program chmn. nat. conf., 1979. Home: 4820 W 39th St Apt 122 Saint Louis Park MN 55416 Office: IDS Tower Minnesota Minneapolis MN 55402

ETEROVICH, ALICE MARIE TROYAN, educator; b. Pleasant City, Ohio, Aug. 5, 1923; d. Steve and Marie (Slifko) Troyan; B.S. in Edn., Kent State U., 1945; postgrad. U. Wis., 1947; M.A., Western Res. U., 1960; m. Anthony W. Eterovich, June 22, 1950; 1 dau., Karen Ann. Tchr., Tremont Jr. High Sch., Cleve., 1945-47; tchr. phys. edn. and modern dance Lincoln Jr. High Sch., Cleve. and Lincoln Sr. High Sch., 1947-53; tchr. phys. edn. and modern dance James Ford Rhodes High Sch., Cleve., 1953-56, head dept., 1953-56; instr. modern dance Oberlin (Ohio) Coll., 1949-50; guidance counselor, vocat. dir. West Tech. High Sch. and Lincoln Jr. High Sch., Cleve., 1962-67; guidance and ednl. counselor John Marshall High Sch., Cleve., 1967-79; supr. counselors non-public aux. services Cleve. Public Schs., 1979—. Hostess, USO, 1943-46; phys. therapist asst. Crile Mil. Hosp., 1945; instr. Cleve. adult recreation YWCA, 1945-53; supr. Cleve. Summer Recreation, 1948, 49; coach girls basketball Cath. Youth Orgn., 1948, 49. Mem. AAUW (charter mem. Parma br.), Am., Northeastern Ohio personnel and guidance assns., Am. Sch. Counselor Assn., Ohio Counselor Assn., Ohio Assn. Gifted Children, Northeastern Ohio Women Deans, Adminstrs. and Counselors Assn. (sec. 1963-64). Byzantine Catholic. Contbr. to publs. in field. Home: 3223 Somia Dr Parma OH 44134

ETHEREDGE, FOREST DEROYCE, state legislator; b. Dallas, Oct. 21, 1929; s. Gilbert W. and Theta E. (Tate) E.; B.S., Va. Poly. Inst. and State U., 1951; M.S., U. Ill., 1953; postgrad. Northwestern U., 1953-55; Ph.D., Loyola U., Chgo., 1968; m. Joan Mary Horan, Apr. 30, 1955; children—Forest William, John Bede, Mary Faith, Brian Thomas, Regina Ann. Mem. faculty City Colls. of Chgo., 1955-65, chmn. dept. phys. sci., 1963-65; dean of instruction Rock Valley Coll., Rockford, Ill., 1965-67, v.p., 1966-67; pres. McHenry County Coll., Crystal Lake, Ill., 1967-70, Waubonsee Community Coll., Sugar Grove, Ill., 1970-81; mem. Ill. Senate, 1981—; dir., sec. No. Ill. Public Telecommunication Corp., 1977-81. Bd. dirs. Mercy Center for Health Care Services, 1972—, Aurora Community Concert Assn., 1974-80, Suburban Community Coll. TV Consortium, 1978-81; pres. Aurora (Ill.) United Way, 1979-81. Mem. Ill. Council Public Community Coll. Presidents (chmn. 1967—), Greater Aurora C. of C. (bd. dirs. 1978—), Chgo. Met. Higher Edn. Council (dir. 1978-79), Sigma Xi, Phi Delta Kappa, Sigma Gamma Epsilon. Club: Rotary. Home: 68 S LeGrande Blvd Aurora IL 60506 Office: 52 W Downer Pl Aurora IL 60507

ETHERIDGE, ROBERT FILES, univ. adminstr.; b. Fairfield, Ill., May 13, 1925; s. William H. and Nellie J. (Files) E.; B.A., B.S., So. Ill. U., 1948, M.S., 1949; Ed.D., Mich. State U., 1958; m. Veda Marie Hallem, Dec. 25, 1947; children—Robert H., Michael S. Asst. dean men So. Ill. U., 1949-58; asst. dir. mens div., student affairs Mich. State U., 1958-59; dean men Miami U., Oxford, Ohio, 1959-60, dean students, 1960-66, exec. dean student affairs, 1966-68, v.p. student affairs, 1969—; mem. com. on univ. relations Nat. Interfrat. Council, 1980-81; chmn. Inter-Univ. Council Student Affairs Adminstrs. of Ohio, 1978—. Served with USNR, 1943-45. Recipient Outstanding Alumnus award So. Ill. U., 1970; A.K. Morris Alumni award Miami U., 1975. Mem. Nat. Assn. Student Personnel Adminstrs. (v.p. 1964-65, regional v.p. 1966-68), Am. Personnel and Guidance Assn., Nat. ROTC Colls. and Univs. (pres. 1976—), Nat. Assn. State Univs. and Land Grant Colls. (chmn. council on student affairs 1977-78), Nat. Vice Presidents for Student Affairs Group, Ohio Assn. Student Personnel Adminstrs. (pres. 1965-66), Navy League. Methodist. Clubs: Kiwanis; Torch. Contbg. author: Trends and Issues in Higher Education, 1972. Home: 1 Iveswood Dr Oxford OH 45056 Office: 101 Roudebush Hall Miami U Oxford OH 45056

ETHINGTON, IVAN CLAIRE, ry. exec.; b. Alden, Iowa, Jan. 20, 1922; s. Harold J. and Helen G. (Clute) E.; B.S. in Civil Engring., Iowa State U., 1948; postgrad. exec. mgmt. program Northwestern U., 1961, advanced mgmt. program Harvard, 1967; m. Lois Jean Garner, Oct. 10, 1942; children—Pamela (Mrs. Jay Galligan), Jay, Claire, Steven. With C., B. & Q. R.R. and Burlington No., Inc., 1948—, v.p. operations, Chgo., 1965-70, regional v.p., 1970-71, v.p. ops., St. Paul, 1971-75, sr. v.p. mktg., 1976-80, exec. v.p., 1981—; pres. Western Fruit Express; dir. Trailer Train Co., Duluth Union Depot & Transfer, Burlington Truck Lines, BN Air Freight, Inc. Served to 1st lt. AUS, 1942-45. Mem. Am. Ry. Engring. Assn., Phi Delta Theta. Presbyn. Clubs: Union League (Chgo.), St. Paul Athletic, North Oaks Golf (St. Paul). Home: 4 Meadow Ln North Oaks St Paul MN 55110 Office: 176 E 5th St St Paul MN 55101

ETHRIDGE, DAVID ALLAN, mental health adminstr.; b. Canton, Ill., Oct. 12, 1933; s. Joseph Wesley and Freida Marie (Wright) E.; student U. Ill., 1951-53; B.S., Western Mich. U., 1956; M.A., Wayne State U., 1966; Ph.D., Mich. State U., 1974; m. JoAnn Lee Lawhead, May 19, 1956; children—Barry, Deborah, Todd. With Mich. Dept. Mental Health, Lansing, 1956-70, chief Bur. Operational Planning, 1970-74; supt. Riverside Center, Ionia, Mich., 1974-76; facility dir. Oakdale Regional Center for Devel. Disabilities, Lapeer, Mich., 1976—; lectr. U. Mich., Ann Arbor, 1973—; adj. prof. psychology dept. Western Mich. U., 1974—; cons. Comprehensive Community Mental Health Center, Staffing Grants, Region V, NIMH, Chgo., 1971—; cons. in field. Served to 1st lt., USAF, 1956-58. Recipient Mich. Minuteman award, 1969. Fellow Am. Occupational Therapy Assn.; mem. Mich. Occupational Therapy Assn. (presdl. award 1972), Nat. Assn. State Activity Therapy and Rehab. Dirs., Mich. Rehab. Assn., Mich. Rehab. Counseling Assn., Nat. Rehab. Assn., Nat. Assn. Supts. Residential Facilities for Mentally Retarded, Am. Assn. on Mental Deficiency. Club: Rotary. Contbr. articles to profl. jours. Home: 2775 W Genesee St Lapeer MI 48446 Office: W Genesee St Lapeer MI 48446

ETTER, IRVIN BOYD, assn. exec.; b. Coalinga, Calif., Apr. 12, 1928; s. Bertram Willis and Jeniveve Bell (Williams) E.; B.A. in Indsl. Relations, Bethany Coll. of W.Va., 1954; m. Joyce Elaine Rasic, Sept. 11, 1971; children—Cynthia Kay, Mark Irvin, Leslie Leigh. Supr. safety U.S. Steel Corp., Cleve., 1954-58, supr. labor relations and safety, Waukegan, Ill., 1958-65; dir. corp. safety and gen. mgr. corp. personnel and safety Wheeling Pitts. Steel Corp., 1965-78; mgr. indsl. dept. Nat. Safety Council, Chgo., 1978-80, dir. occupational safety and loss control cons., 1980—. Pres., W.Va. Safety Council, 1972; asso. chmn. Upper Ohio Valley United Way, 1977-78. Served with USAF, 1946-48. Cert. safety profl. Mem. Am. Soc. Safety Engrs. Republican. Lutheran. Clubs: Waukegan City, Glen Flora Country. Home: 2608 Vercoe St Waukegan IL 60085 Office: 444 N Michigan Ave Chicago IL 60611

ETTINGER, JOSEPH ALAN, lawyer, educator; b. N.Y.C., July 21, 1931; s. Max and Frances E.; B.A., Tulane U., 1954, J.D. with honors, 1956; children—Amy Beth, Ellen Jane. Admitted to La. bar, 1956, Ill. bar, 1959; asst. corp. counsel City of Chgo., 1959-62; practiced in Chgo., 1962-73, 76—; sr. partner firm Ettinger & Schoenfield, Chgo., 1980—; asso. prof. law Chgo.-Kent Coll., 1973-76; chmn. Village of Olympia Fields (Ill.) Zoning Bd. Appeals, 1969-76; chmn. panel on corrections Welfare Council Met. Chgo., 1969-76. Served to capt., Judge Adv. Gen. Corps, U.S. Army, 1956-59. Recipient Service award Village of Olympia Fields, 1976. Mem. Chgo. Bar Assn., Assn. Criminal Def. Lawyers (gov. 1970-72). Clubs: Ravisloe Country, Carlton Club, Contbr. articles to profl. publs. Office: 180 N La Salle St Chicago IL 60601

EUCHNER, EVERETT BRUCE, chem. co. exec.; b. Chgo., Jan. 9, 1924; s. Charles Andrew and Joan (Dienert) E.; B.S. in Chem. Engring., Purdue U., 1948; M.S. in Organic Chemistry, Case-Western Res. U., 1952; m. Patricia Enz, Aug. 21, 1948; children—Renee, Jenee, Elaine, Eric. With Glidden Coating and Resin, Cleve., 1948—, dir. polymer research, 1961-64, mgr. regional labs., 1964-65, dir. research center, 1965-75, v.p., dir. research and devel., 1976—. Bd. dirs. Community Chest, 1962-64; mem. Zoning Bd. Appeals, Avon Lake, Ohio, 1962-68; mem. Bldg. Code Bd. Appeals, Avon Lake, 1962-68. Served with USAAF, 1942-45. Decorated D.F.C. Mem. Am. Chem. Soc., Cleve. Engring. Soc., Soc. Plastics Industry, Fedn. Socs. Paint Tech., Indsl. Research Inst., Sigma Xi. Office: 16651 Sprague Rd Strongsville OH 44136

EULER, WILLIAM DALE, smelting co. exec.; b. St. Louis, July 14, 1929; s. Fred Christ and Francis P. (Wood) E.; B.S., Univ. Coll., 1958; M.B.A., Pacific Western U., 1981; m. Lora Eaton, Dec. 16, 1950. Mgr. edn. and tng. Wagner Electric Corp., St. Louis, 1952-68; with St. Joe Minerals Corp., Herculaneum, Mo., 1968—, indsl. relations mgr., 1980—. Served with U.S. Army, 1950-51. Mem. Am. Soc. Personnel Adminstrs., Tng. Dirs. Assn., Am. Legion. Mem. Christian Ch. Clubs: Shriners, Elks. Home: 502 Briar Ridge Frontenac MO 63131 Office: St Joe Minerals Corp 881 Main St Herculaneum MO 63048

EVANS, BARRY CRAIG, fin. cons.; b. Cin., Dec. 12, 1944; s. Tracy Warren and Dorothy (Burton) E.; B.S. in Bus., Miami U., Oxford, Ohio, 1967. Partner, Evans & Co., bus. ins. and estate rev. cons., Cin., 1971-80; pres., chief exec. officer Cin. Fin. Cons., Inc., 1980—; dir. advanced underwriting and agt. devel. Mass. Mut. Life Ins. Co., Cin., 1978-79; guest lectr. U. Cin., Miami U., Oxford, estate planning councils, civic groups. VIP chmn. East Seal Soc., Cin.; mem. Republican Nat. Com.; founder, benefactor Barry C. Evans Ins. Advancement Award and Fund, Miami U. Served to capt. USAF, 1967-71; Vietnam. Decorated Bronze Star, Air Force Commendation medal; recipient Silver medal as outstanding Air Force ROTC Cadet, Chgo. Tribune, 1964; Nat. Quality award Nat. Assn. Life Underwriters, 1972—; named to Leaders' Club Inner Circle, Mass. Mut. Life Ins. Co., 1974, 76, 78, 79, Pres.'s. Club, 1972—. C.L.U. Mem. Am. Soc. C.L.U.'s (trustee Cin. chpt., pres.), Million Dollar Round Table (life mem., Nat. Sales Achievement award 1977-80), Internat. Assn. Fin. Planners, Nat. Assn. Life Underwriters, Cin., No. Ky. (dir. 1977-81) estate planning councils, Cin. C. of C. Presbyterian. Clubs: Bankers (gov., chmn. membership); Queen City Assn., The One Hundred (Cin.); Miami U. Pres.'s, Miami Alumni, Miami Men's, Towers. Pub. The Evans Letter. Home: 8561 Arborcrest Dr Amberley Village OH 45236 Office: 4400 Carew Tower 441 Vine St Cincinnati OH 45202

EVANS, CHARLES HOWARD, JR., surgeon; b. Syracuse, N.Y., Oct. 1912; s. Charles Howard and May Charlotte (MacKinnon) E.; student Duke U., 1930-33; M.D., C.M., McGill U., 1937; m. Mary Jane Richholt, Sept. 20, 1942; children—Charles Howard III, Madelyn J. Rotating intern Royal Victoria Hosp., Montreal, Que., Can., 1936-37; intern pathology Inst. Pathology, Univ. Lakeside Hosps., Cleve., 1937-38; intern medicine U. Chgo. Clinics, 1938-39; intern surgery Barnes Hosp., Shriners' Hosp. for Crippled Children, Children's Hosp., Barnard Skin and Cancer Hosp., St. Louis, 1938-39; fellow surgery, asst. in orthopedics and surgery, asst. surgeon Mayo Found. and Mayo Clinic, Rochester, Minn., 1940-44; surgeon Blanchard Valley Hosp., Findlay, Ohio, 1944—, Findlay Clinic, 1950—; instr. pathology Western Res. U., Cleve., 1937-38. chief surgeon Northwestern Ohio CD Corps, col., corps surgeon Ohio NG, 1955-61. Recipient Silver Beaver award Boy Scouts Am., 1966, Ohio Commendation Medal Ohio NG O.D.C., 1977. Diplomate Am. Bd. Surgery, Am. Bd. Abdominal Surgery. Mem. Internat. Coll. Surgeons, Am. Soc. Abdominal Surgeons, AMA, AAAS, Northwestern Ohio Med. Assn. (past pres.). Republican. Presbyterian. Club: Kiwanis. Home: 140 W Hobart Ave Findlay OH 45840 Office: 1900 S Main St Findlay OH 45840

EVANS, CHARLES SAMUEL, psychologist; b. Rochester, Minn., Feb. 8, 1949; s. D.P. and Lois (Baskin) E.; B.A. in Psychology, Drake U., 1971, M.A. in Gen. Exptl. Psychology, 1975; m. Judith Ann Hobson, May 26, 1973. Charge animal lab. Drake U. Psychology Labs., 1971, statistician, research analyst Met. Criminal Justice Center, 1971-73; psychologist Rochester State Hosp., 1974-81, dir. Diagnosis, Evaluation and Treatment Center, 1977-81; psychologis Harley and Nelson Clinic, Mpls., 1981—. Lic. psychologist, Minn. Mem. Am. Assn. Mental Deficiency, Minn. Assn. Behavior Analysts, Assn. Behavior Analysts, Mayo Clinic Neurosci. Club, Biofeedback Soc. Minn. Specialist in behavior modification, biofeedback, mental retardation, self-injurious behavior, communication with non-verbal individuals. Address: Harley and Nelson Clinic LL04 Met Med Office Bldg 825 S 8th St Minneapolis MN 55404

EVANS, CHARLES SAMUEL, educator; b. Chillicothe, Mo., Oct. 5, 1947; s. Everett Samuel and Velma Lucille (Mantzey) E.; B.S., Central Mo. State Coll., 1969, M.S., 1972; postgrad. S.E. Mo. State U., 1975, 77, Harvard U., 1979; Ph.D., U. Mo., 1980; m. Mary Amelia Motley Evans, Aug. 6, 1977. Tchr. social studies high sch., Caruthersville, Mo., 1972-78; part-time supr. social studies Caruthersville Sch. Dist. 1975-78; asst. dir. Office Ednl. Field Experiences, U. Mo., Columbia, 1979-80; coordinator secondary edn. William Woods Coll., Fulton, Mo., 1980—. Served with U.S. Army, 1970-72. Mamie J. McCormick fellow, 1979—. Mem. Nat. Council for Social Studies, Mo. Council for Social Studies, Assn. for Supervision and Curriculum Devel., Assn. Tchr. Educators, Phi Delta Kappa, Phi Alpha Theta, Kappa Delta Pi, Phi Sigma Pi. Presbyterian. Home: 1215 El Chaparral Ave Columbia MO 65201 Office: William Woods Coll Fulton MO 65251

EVANS, (THOMAS) COOPER, congressman, farmer; b. Cedar Rapids, Iowa, May 26, 1924; s. Thomas and Ora E.; B.S. in Mech. Engring., Iowa State U., 1949, M.S. in Civil Engring., 1955; m. Jean Ruppelt, 1948; children—James, Charles. Commd. officer C.E., U.S. Army; with AEC, 1956-58; mem. staff U.S. Army Gen. Staff, Pentagon, Washington, 1962-63; dir. advanced manned lunar mission NASA, 1963-65; ret., 1965; former mem. Iowa Ho. Reps.; farmer, 1965—; mem. 97th Congress from Iowa. Fin. chmn. Iowa Republican Party. Methodist. Office: 317 Cannon House Office Bldg Washington DC 20515*

EVANS, DANIEL LEE, telephone co. exec.; b. Omaha, Nov. 14, 1947; s. Curtis L. and Minnie E. (Thornton) E.; B.A., U. Nebr., 1970; m. Darlene J. Eggleston, June 28, 1968; children—Denise, Don. Underwriter, systems analyst Mut. of Omaha, 1970-74; systems supr. Lozier Corp., Omaha, 1974; programmer-analyst State of Nebr., Lincoln, 1975-76; computer analyst, staff supr. budgets Northwestern Bell Co., Omaha, 1976—. Chmn. program com. Omaha Unemployment Task Force, 1977. Served with Army NG, 1970-76. Recipient Northwestern Bell V.I.P. award, 1979, 80, 81. Mem. Omaha Jaycees (v.p., dir. 1976-77, pres. subgroups 1977-78, recipient Silver Key award 1977, Brownfield award 1977, Gold Key award 1978, named an outstanding young man Am. 1977), Northwestern Bell Jaycees (pres. 1977-78, outstanding Jaycee 1978). Presbyterian. Clubs: Toastmasters (pres. 1979, dist. gov. 1980, Outstanding Div. Gov. 1981), Masons. Office: 1314 Douglas St Omaha NE 68102

EVANS, DAVID LYNN, farm equipment mfg. co. ofcl.; b. Red Oak, Iowa, June 26, 1941; s. John Louis and Margaret Alice (Young) E.; B.S., Iowa State U., 1964; M.B.A., U. Pa., 1966; m. Mary Susan Ricke, Aug. 4, 1963; children—John Louis, Mary Lynn, Sarah Leigh, Michael Ricke. With Deere and Co., Moline, Ill., 1964—, various positions fin. div., indsl. equipment div., corp. staff depts., 1966-77, mgr. mktg. assets, 1977—; dir., cmn. audit com. Mut. Selection Fund, Inc. Dir. World Federalists Assn., 1980-82, v.p. Midwest Region, 1977-82; dir. Campaign for UN Reform, 1979-82, sec., 1980-81, treas., 1982—; trustee John Deere Dealer Group Ins. Trust, 1981—; elder Presbyn. Ch. Mem. Quad Cities World Affairs Council, Am. Econ. Assn., UN Assn., Iowa Mfrs. Assn. (chmn. econ. edn. com., 1979-81). Republican. Clubs: Constitution, Elks. Contbr. article to jour. Home: 33 Oakbrook Dr Bettendorf IA 52722 Office: John Deere Rd Moline IL 61265

EVANS, DAVID WALTER, Congressman; b. Lafayette, Ind., Aug. 17, 1946; s. Isaac Walter and Margaret Laurine (Reppert) E.; B.A. in Polit. Sci., Ind. U., 1967; postgrad. Ind. U. and Butler U., 1967-72; m. Darlene Marie Ginder, Feb. 20, 1975; 1 dau., Jennifer Marie. Tchr., asst. prin. St. Ann's Sch., Indpls., 1968-72, St. Andrew's Sch., Indpls., 1972-74; mem. 95th-97th Congresses from 6th Ind. Dist. Bd. dirs. Ind. Soc. of Washington. Recipient Democrat of Year award 19th Dist. Dem. Club, 1974; named Outstanding Young Hoosier, Ind. Jaycees, 1977. Mem. Franklin Jaycees. Club: Kiwanis. Office: 438 Cannon House Office Bldg Washington DC 20515

EVANS, ETHEL GRACE, dietitian; b. Salem, Ind., May 13, 1926; d. Roy M. and Martha Ellen (Temple) Evans; B.S., Purdue U., 1948; postgrad. Iowa State Coll., 1955. Prodn. mgr. Lucina Dining Service, Ball State Tchrs. Coll., Muncie, Ind., 1948-50, asst. dir., 1950-56, adminstrv. dietitian, mgr. Woodworth Halls Dining Service, 1956-67, unit mgr. LaFollette Dining Service, 1967—. Mem. campus campaign com. for Ball Found. and campus devel. Ball State U., 1979-81; mem. Affirmative Action Grievance Appeals Bd., 1979-81. Recipient 1st award Institutions Mag. 1956. Mem. Nat. Assn. Coll. Univ. Food Service, Asso. Coll. and Univ. Housing Officers, Nat., Ind. restaurant assns., Purdue Alumni Assn. (dir. Muncie chpt. 1970-79), AAUW. Democrat. Baptist. Clubs: Soroptimists Internat. Ball State U. Pres.'s Century (Muncie). Home: 206 W 10th St Muncie IN 47302 Office: LaFollette Dining Service Ball State University Muncie IN 47306

EVANS, GREGORY THOMAS, Canadian justice; b. McAdam, N.B., Can., June 13, 1913; s. Thomas Vincent and Mary Ellen (McDade) E.; B.A., St. Joseph's U., N.B., 1934; LL.B., Osgoode Hall Law Sch., Toronto, 1939; LL.D. (hon.), St. Thomas U., Fredericton, N.B., 1963; Ph.D., U. Moncton (N.B.), 1964; m. Zita Callon, Oct. 1, 1941; children—Thomas, John, Gregory, Rory, Mary, Kerry, Brendan, Catherine, Erin. Called to bar, 1939, created queen's counsel, 1953; sr. partner firm Evans, Evans, Bragagnolo, Perras & Sullivan, Timmins, Ont., 1938-63; justice Supreme Ct. Ont., 1963-65, Ct. Appeal Ont., 1965-76; chief justice High Ct., Supreme Ct. Ont., 1976—; bd. dirs. Can. Scholarship Trust Found. Pres. Ont. English Catholic Edn. Assn., 1961; Vice chmn. Can. Jud. Council, 1981—; v.p. Can. Inst. for Advanced Legal Studies, 1978—. Decorated knight comdr. Order St. Gregory Gt., 1980. Mem. Can. Bar Assn. (v.p. Ont. 1962), Law Soc. Upper Can. (bencher 1961), Ont. Legal Aid Com., Medico Legal Soc. Roman Catholic. Clubs: University (Toronto); Lions (internat. counsellor). Address: Osgoode Hall 130 Queen St W Toronto ON M5H 2N5 Canada

EVANS, HELEN WITTEN, state ofcl.; b. Tazewell, Va., Aug. 5, 1905; d. Joseph and Sallie (Witten) Witten; student Ohio State U., 1940; m. John C. Evans, Dec. 1927; 1 son, John R. Tchr., Tazewell Public Schs., 1924-27; case reviewer div. aged Ohio Dept. Public Welfare, 1939-51; asst. cashier, public relations Treas. State of Ohio, 1952-58; welfare auditor Auditor State of Ohio, 1958-62; dep. dir. Ohio Dept. Indsl. Relations, Columbus, 1962-70, dir., 1975—; staff mem. Ohio Republican Council, 1970-74, founder, exec. sec., 1952—. Alt.-at-large Rep. Nat. Conv., 1972; del.-at-large Rep. Nat. Conv., 1976; nat. del. White House Commn. on Aging, 1981. Recipient Gov.'s award for excellence, 1980, Carnegie Roundtable award for meritorious service, 1981. Mem. Internat. Assn. Govt. Labor Ofcls., Ohio Commodores. Methodist. Office: 2323 W 5th Ave Columbus OH 43216*

EVANS, JAMES DAVID, educator; b. Warren, Ohio, Oct. 15, 1946; s. LeRoy Eugene and Charlotte Geraldine (Brooks) E.; B.S., Geneva Coll., 1968; M.S. (research asst.), Iowa State U., 1969, Ph.D., 1974; m. Lois Ann Palyash, Dec. 23, 1967; 1 dau., Laura Lynn. Instr. psychology Geneva Coll., Beaver Falls, Pa., 1969-72; instr. psychology part time Iowa State U., Ames, Iowa, 1972-74; asso. prof. psychology The Lindenwood Colls., St. Charles, Mo., 1974—, chmn. dept., 1978—; cons. in field. NSF fellow. Mem. Am., Midwestern, Mo. psychol. assns., Psychonomic Soc. Methodist. Author numerous publs. in field. Home: 3 Norwell Ct Saint Charles MO 63301 Office: Watson & Kings Hwy Saint Charles MO 63301

EVANS, JAMES WILLIAM, mfg. co. exec.; b. Cin., Oct. 8, 1925; s. James Frank and Mary Elizabeth (VanWinkle) E.; B.S., U. Cin., 1951; m. Mary Louise Rempe, Dec. 21, 1946; children—Michael William, Sherry Lynn. Project engr. Cin. Milacron Co., 1947-58; sr. design engr. King Machine Tool Co., Cin., 1958-61; chief engr. Karl Kiefer Machine Co., Cin., 1961-62; with Cherry Burrell Corp., Cedar Rapids, Iowa, 1962—, v.p. engring., 1974—. Mem. tech. adv. com. Kirkwood Community Coll., Cedar Rapids, Iowa, 1974—; pres. N. Coralville Lake Manor Improvement Assn., 1976—. Served with USNR, 1944-46. Mem. Tau Beta Pi, Pi Tau Sigma. Republican. Presbyterian. Home: 130 Thompson Dr SE Cedar Rapids IA 52403 Office: 2400 6th St Cedar Rapids IA 52405

EVANS, JERRY JOE, pediatrician; b. Hammond, Ind., July 23, 1937; s. George Thomas and Marion Ruth (Gruen) E.; B.A., DePauw U., 1959; M.D., Northwestern U., 1963; m. Linda Ann Simmance, Sept. 1, 1962; children—Jeffery Charles, Gregory Gruen, Jennifer Jo. Commd. lt. U.S. Navy, 1963, advanced through grades to lt. comdr., 1968; intern U.S. Naval Hosp., Chelsea, Mass., 1963-64, resident in pediatrics, 1967-69; med. officer U.S.S. Tallahatchie County, 1964-66, U.S. Naval Hosp., Naples, Italy, 1966-67; resident in pediatrics Tufts New Eng. Med. Center, Boston, 1969; chief pediatrics U.S. Naval Hosp., Pensacola, Fla., 1970-71; ret., 1971; pvt. practice pediatrics, Saginaw, Mich., 1971—; mem. staffs St. Luke's Hosp., St. Mary's Hosp., Saginaw Gen. Hosp., Saginaw Osteo. Hosp., St. Joseph Hosp., Tawas, Mich.; pres. bd. dirs. Saginaw County Child Devel. Centers, Inc., 1973-75; trustee East Central Mich. Comprehensive Health Planning Council, Inc., 1974-78. Diplomate Am. Bd. Pediatrics. Mem. Am. Acad. Pediatrics, Perinatal Assn. Mich. (trustee), Northeastern Pediatric Soc. (treas. 1976-77), Saginaw County, Mich. State med. socs. Methodist. Home: 1430 Avon St Saginaw MI 48602 Office: 4855 Berl Dr Saginaw MI 48604

EVANS, JOHN HARVEY, ins. rep.; b. Storm Lake, Iowa, Oct. 7, 1945; s. Glenn William and Viola Marie (Madsen) E.; grad. Dale Carnegie, 1973; m. Rosalie Mae Johnsn, June 29, 1969; 1 son, Nicholas John. Supermarket mgr., 1966-68; meatcutter, 1968-72; dist. rep. Aid Assn. for Lutherans, Storm Lake, 1972—, mem. pres.'s cabinet, 1976-80; course moderator Life Underwriter Tng. Council, 1975, 77, 79. Served with U.S. Army, 1963-66. Named to Million Dollar Round Table, 1976-80; recipient Nat. Sales Achievement and Health Ins. Quality awards Nat. Assn. Life Underwriters, 1973-80. Mem. N.W. Central Life Underwriters Assn. (pres. 1978-79). Republican. Lutheran. Office: 800 Onieda St Suite B PO Box 1213 Storm Lake IA 50588

EVANS, MALINDA MURPHEY, librarian; b. Bloomington, Ill., Sept. 11, 1935; d. Earl C. and Imogene (Swigart) Murphey; B.S. in L.S., Ill. State U., Normal, 1973; m. Donald Lee Evans, Apr. 25, 1976; children by previous marriage—Melanie, Laurie, Patrick. Librarian, Vespasian Warner Pub. Library, Clinton, Ill., 1973—; author weekly column Bookmarks, Clinton Daily Jour.; pub. sec. Jr. Mens Round Table, 1977. Mem. Am., Ill. (dir.-at-large jr. mems. round table), Am. Bus. Women's Assn. (sec. 1976, pres. 1977, Woman of Yr. 1977). Methodist. Home: 40 Park Ln Clinton IL 61727 Office: 120 W Johnson St Clinton IL 61727

EVANS, MARK IRA, obstetrician-gynecologist; b. Bklyn., May 14, 1952; s. Robert Bernard and Sonia Beatrice (Silverstein) E.; B.S. magna cum laude, Tufts U., 1973; M.D. with distinction in research, SUNY, Bklyn., 1978; m. Wendy JoAnne Greenwood, Sept. 5, 1981. Research asso. Nassau County Med. Center, East Meadow, N.Y., 1973, Rebecca Sieff Med. Center, Safad, Israel, 1974; rotating intern dept. ob-gyn., U. Chgo., 1978-79, resident, 1979-82; fellow Interinst. Genetics Program, NIH, Bethesda, Md. and dept. ob-gyn George Washington U., Washington, 1982—; spl. adv. to dir. Nat. Center Health Care Tech., Office Health Resources, Stats. and Tech., Dept. Health and Human Services, 1980-81. Mem. Am. Coll. Obstetricians and Gynecologists (jr. fellow, chmn. Ill. sect. Jr. Fellow div. 1981-82), Am. Fedn. for Clin. Research, AMA, Sigma Xi, Psi Chi. Contbr. articles to profl. jours. Home: 5020 S Lake Shore Dr Apt 3317 Chicago IL 60615 Office: 5841 S Maryland Ave Chicago IL 60637

EVANS, MARTHA MACCHESNEY, educator; b. Chgo., Nov. 2, 1941; d. Luther Johnson and Harriet (MacChesney) E.; A.A., Kendall Jr. Coll., 1961; B.A., Roosevelt U., 1964; M.A., Northeastern Ill. U., 1974; cert. advanced study Nat. Coll. Edn., 1981. Tchr. lang. arts East Maine Jr. High Sch., Des Plaines, Ill., 1965-66; caseworker Cook County Dept. Public Aid, Chgo., 1966-67; tchr. English coordinated basic English program Farragut High Sch., Chgo., 1968-73, reading lab. dir., 1973-74, reading clinician Wells High Sch., Chgo., 1974—; mem. reading clinic adv. bd. Chgo. Bd. Edn., 1976-78. Chmn. membership com. 2d Unitarian Ch. Chgo., 1978-79, pres. Womans Group, 1979-80. Mem. Internat. Reading Assn., Chgo. Area Reading Assn., Assn. Curriculum Devel., Assn. Children with Learning Disabilities. Home: 1940 Sherman St Evanston IL 60201 Office: Wells High School 936 Ashland Ave Chicago IL 60622

EVANS, MILTON DURRELL, univ. adminstr.; b. Glenfield, N.D., July 12, 1917; s. Nathan Durrell and Mattie Blanche (Simmons) E.; B.A., Wayne State U., 1940; M.A., U. Nebr., 1947, Ph.D., 1954; m. Leola A. Husemoller, Nov. 24, 1938; children—Milton Douglas, Sheila Kathleen. Tchr. Dunbar (Nebr.) pub. schs., 1937-39; tchr., coach Riverton (Iowa) Consol. Schs., 1939-41, prin., 1941-43; supt. Elk Creek (Nebr.) pub. schs., 1945-47, Am. Dependents Sch., Heidelberg, Germany, 1947-48; regional supt. Am. Dependents Sch., Heidelberg, 1948-51; instr. secondary edn. U. Nebr., Lincoln, 1951-54; dean men Nebr. Wesleyan U., Lincoln, 1954-57, chmn. Dept. Edn., 1954-62, dean of students, 1962-72, dean summer sch., 1972-78, v.p. for student affairs, 1972—. Active Boy Scouts Am., Lincoln, 1954-64, Girl Scouts U.S.A., Lincoln, 1970-76; mem. PTA Citizen's Adv. Council to Lincoln Sch. Bd., 1962-69; bd. govs. Bryan Meml. Hosp., 1966-72; bd. dirs. Brownville Village Theatre, 1974—; mem. Mayor's Com. for Handicapped, Lincoln, 1974-76; bd. govs. UN, 1970-75; trustee Univ. Place Art Center, 1977—; mem. gov. com. on manpower Nebr. Health Project, 1972-76; pres. Univ. Pl. Devel. Corp., 1978-79, pres., 1978-80; mem. Univ. Pl. Community Orgn., 1972—, pres., 1981-82. Served with USAAF, 1943-45. Mem. Nebr. Personnel and Guidance Assn. (pres. 1960-61), Nebr. Coll. Personnel Assn. (pres. 1959-60), Nebr. Council for Tchr. Edn. (pres. 1964-66), Nebr. Instl. Placement Assn. (pres. 1960-61), Capitol City Edn. Assn. (pres. 1959), Nat. Assn. Student Personnel Adminstrs., Nebr. Commn. on Secondary Sch./Coll. Relations (pres. 1964), Kappa Delta Pi, Phi Delta Kappa, Phi Kappa Phi, Pi Gamma Mu. Clubs: Univ., Candlelight, Racquet, Nebr. Sch. Master's. Address: Nebr Wesleyan Univ Lincoln NE 68504

EVANS, ROBERT LEONARD, physiologist; b. Duluth, Minn., May 30, 1917; s. John Leonard and Amy (Magnusson) E.; student Duluth Jr. Coll., 1934-36; B.Chemistry, U. Minn., 1938, M.S., 1939, Ph.D., 1951; m. Frances J. Bentley, Dec. 21, 1941 (dec.); children—Amy Elizabeth, Thomas Randall, Julia May; m. 2d, Elsie F. Hardy, Jan. 11, 1957. Asso. metallurgist U.S. Bur. Mines, Salt Lake City, 1940-44; research asso. Allegany Ballistics Lab., Cumberland, Md., 1944-45; instr. math. and mechanics U. Minn., Mpls., 1945-54, asst. prof. physiology, 1954-63, asso. prof. biometry and math. biology, 1963-70, lectr. physiology, 1970—. Rockefeller Found. grantee, 1954-59; USPHS grantee, 1958-68, 1966-69. Mem. AAAS, Am. Chem. Soc., Minn. Acad. Sci. (pres.), Wilderness Soc., Nature Conservancy, Sigma Xi. Unitarian. Author: The Fall and Rise of Man, If..., 1973; contbr. articles on chemistry, math. and biomed. research to profl. jours. Patentee in hydrometallurgy. Home: 2500 St Anthony Blvd Minneapolis MN 55418 Office: Dept Physiology U Minn Minneapolis MN 55455

EVANS, ROBERT LIONEL, distbg. co. exec.; b. Omaha, Nov. 10, 1922; s. Kenneth A. and Elsie B. (Sharp) E.; student Drake U., 1940-41; B.A., U. Iowa, 1947; m. Mary Ellen Murphy, Sept. 3, 1947; children—Thomas L., Sally Ann Evans Schulz, Mary Beth Evans Hughes, James S., Patricia Sue. Farmer, Emerson, Iowa, 1946-56; salesman Adams & Kelly Co., Omaha, 1956-57; salesman Dewey Portland Cement Co., Davenport, Iowa, 1958-61; mgr. Hooker Glass & Paint Co., Davenport, 1961-65; salesman Eastin Phelan Corp., Davenport, 1965-66, sales mgr., 1966-70; v.p. sales Eastin Phelan Distbg. Corp., Davenport, 1970-77, pres., 1977-79, owner, pres., 1979—; chmn. Regency Fin. Group; v.p., fin. sec. Life Group, Inc. Pres., Assumption High Sch. Bd., Davenport, 1974-75. Served with USNR, 1943-46; PTO. Mem. Am. Legion. Republican. Episcopalian. Clubs: Masons (master Emerson 1957), Shriners, Elks (exalted ruler Red Oak, Iowa 1952), Rotary, Lake Davenport Sailing (commodore 1969). Home: 2503 Fulton Ave Davenport IA 52803 Office: 1235 W 5th St Davenport IA 52808

EVANS, WILLIAM G., pub. relations and advertising exec.; b. Mounds, Ill., Aug. 25, 1921; s. William Grant and Isabella Margareta (Frick) E.; student Mo. U., 1940-42; B.S., St. Louis U., 1952; m. Norma Frieda Mueller, Dec. 14, 1946; children—William Grant, Norman Henry, Rebecca Susanne. Tchr., prin. Lutheran Schs., St. Louis area, 1948-60; holder various positions community edn., organization and development with pub. and pvt. agencies, St. Louis area, 1960-67; cons. pub. relations and advt., St. Louis, 1967-68; dir. pub. relations, advt. Blue Cross Hosp. Service, Inc., St. Louis, 1968—; lectr. in pub. relations and communications. Bd. dirs. Heart Assn., St. Louis, 1977—, Lutheran Mission Assn., St. Louis, 1976—, Humane Soc. of St. Louis, 1974-77, vice chmn., 1974; panel mem. United Way Fund Dr., St. Louis, 1969-74. Served with USMC 1942-45. Mem. Press Club of Greater St. Louis, Internat. Assn. Bus. Communicators, Advt. Club of Greater St. Louis, Media Club. Lutheran. Contbr. numerous articles in fields to various publications. Home: 1760 Parker Rd Florissant MO 63033 Office: 4444 Forest Park Saint Louis MO 63108

EVARTS, GEORGE WILLIAM, investment banker; b. Newburgh, N.Y., July 18, 1936; s. Morley Kellogg and Jennie Hall (Stone) E.; student Cornell U., Ithaca, N.Y., 1954-57; B.S. in Indsl. Mgmt., Carnegie-Mellon U., Pitts., 1959; m. Marylyn L. Sayle, Apr. 10, 1965; children—Daniel W., L. Paisley, Michael S. Plant location engr. The Austin Co., 1961-62; asso. Case & Co., Inc. Mgmt. Cons.'s, 1962-66; dir. corporate growth Youngstown Steel Door Co., Cleve., 1966-68; v.p. corporate fin. Disbro & Co., Inc., Cleve., 1968-71, Baker & Co., Inc., Cleve., 1971-74; pres. Evarts Capital, Inc., Beachwood, Ohio, 1975—; sec. Dickinson Co. Trustee, pres. Orange Community Athletic Assn.; mem. Cleve. Orch. Chorus; mem. alumni council Phillips Exeter Acad. Served to 1st lt., C.E., AUS, 1960-61. Republican. Methodist. Office: Suite 640 Three Commerce Park Sq 23200 Chagrin Blvd Beachwood OH 44122

EVENS, RONALD GENE, physician; b. St. Louis, Sept. 24, 1939; s. Robert and Dorothy (Lupkey) E.; B.A., Washington U., 1960, M.D., 1964, postgrad. bus. and edn., 1970-71; m. Hanna Blunk, Sept. 3, 1960; children—Ronald Gene, Christine, Amanda. Intern, Barnes Hosp., St. Louis, 1964-65; resident Mallinckrodt Inst. Radiology, 1965-66, 68-70; research asso. Nat. Heart Inst., 1966-68; asst. prof. radiology, v.p. Washington U. Med. Sch., 1970-71, prof., head dept. radiology, dir. Mallinckrodt Inst. Radiology, 1971-72, Elizabeth Mallinckrodt prof., head radiology dept., dir. Mallinckrodt Inst., 1972—, mem. bd. Washington U. Med. Center, 1980—; radiologist in chief Barnes and Childrens Hosp., St. Louis, 1971—; mem. adv. com. on specialty and geog. distbn. of physicians Inst. Medicine, Nat. Acad. Scis., 1974-76; dir. City Bank St. Louis; chmn. bd. Med. Care Group St. Louis, 1980—. Lodge adviser, Order of Arrow, Boy Scouts Am., 1975—; elder Glendale Presbyterian Ch., 1971-74; bd. dirs. St. Louis Comprehensive Neighborhood Health Center, OEO, 1970-74. Served with USPHS, 1966-68. James Picker Found. advanced acad. fellow, 1970; Hickey lectr., 1976; recipient Distinguished Service award St. Louis C. of C. 1972; Fellow Am. Coll. Radiology; mem. Mo. Radiol. Soc. (pres. 1977-78), Soc. Nuclear Medicine (trustee 1971-75), AMA, St. Louis Med. Soc., Mo. State Med. Assn., Soc. Chmn. Acad. Radiology Depts. (pres. 1979), Radiol. Soc. N.Am., Assn. Univ. Radiologists, Am. Roentgen Ray Soc. (exec. com. of exec. council 1980—), Phi Beta Kappa, Alpha Omega Alpha (Sheard-Sanford award). Contbr. over 100 articles to profl. jours. Office: 510 S Kingshighway Saint Louis MO 63110

EVENSON, DAVID A., comml. laundry co. exec.; b. St. Paul, Feb. 11, 1935; s. Clifford A. and Thora (Flekke) E.; B.A., U. Minn., 1957; m. Carmen Buckner, Mar. 25, 1966; 1 son, Eric A. Vice-pres. River Falls Launderers & Cleaners (Wis.), 1958-64; mgr. Tumpane Laundry, Ankara, Turkey, 1966-67; pres. Johnson Mankato Laundry, Mankato, Minn., 1968; cons., dir. 3-F Co., Madison, Wis., 1968-70; partner, sec.-treas. Red Wing Laundry, Inc. (Minn.), 1964-65, 70-74, 75-76, 77—; gen. mgr. Combines Services, Inc., Miami, Fla., 1974; mng. dir. Jet Wascherei G.M.B.H., Wurzburg, Fed Republic Germany, 1976-77. Scoutmaster Boy Scouts Am., 1959-64. Mem. Internat. Fabricare Inst., U. Minn. Alumni Club. Republican. Lutheran. Home: Rural Route 4 Red Wing MN 55066 Office: 315 Plum St Red Wing MN 55066

EVERETT, JAMES ALBERT, advt. and pub. relations co. exec.; b. Alton, Ill., Mar. 20, 1928; s. Jesse James and Lucy Pearl (Eggen) E.; A.A., Graceland Coll., 1948; B.S., Brigham Young U., 1950; M.A., U. Chgo., 1959; m. Marolyn Ardis Briggs, Aug. 17, 1952; children—Mary Lynne, Randi Susan. Mng. dir. Frazar Internat. (Scandinavia), Stockholm, 1960-63; v.p. Robert R. Mullen & Co., Stockholm, 1963-67, Amsterdam, 1968-72, Washington, 1972-74; pres. Everett, Brandt & Bernauer, Inc., Independence, Mo., 1974—; mng. dir. The Brussels Times, 1970-71; bd. govs. Internat. Sch. Amsterdam; mem. Randstad Com. Bd. dirs. Friends of Kansas City Aquarium, Com-Unity, Inc.; pres. Boy's Club Independence. Recipient certificate of appreciation People-to-People, 1966. Mem. Public Relations Soc. Am. (pres. Kansas City chpt.), John Whitmer Hist. Assn., Independence, Greater Kansas City (Mo.), Blue Springs (Mo.) chambers commerce, Friends of Truman Campus. Republican. Mem. Reorganized Ch. Jesus Christ of Latter-Day Saints. Clubs: Rotary (v.p., dir.) (Independence); Pachyderm (Kansas City). Home: 3913 Ponderosa St Lee's Summit MO 64063 Office: 314 W 24 Hwy Independence MO 64050

EVERETT, RONALD EMERSON, govt. adminstr.; b. Columbus, Ohio, Jan. 4, 1937; s. John Carmen and Hermione Alicia (Lensner) E.; B.A., Ohio U., 1959; postgrad. Baldwin-Wallace Coll., 1962-63; attended U.S. Army Command and Gen. Staff Coll., 1975-78, U.S. Army War Coll., 1981—; m. Nancy Helen Leibersberger, Aug. 10, 1963; children—Darryl William, Darlene Anne, John Lee. Reporter, Dun & Bradstreet, Cleve., 1960-66; program analyst Lewis Research Center, NASA, Cleve., 1967-70, contract price analyst and negotiator, 1970—. Served with inf. U.S. Army, 1960. Decorated Meritorious Service medal, Army Commendation medal; recipient NASA Group Achievement awards, Sustained Superior Performance award, 1974, 80. Mem. Assn. Govt. Accts., Res. Officers Assn., Am. Def. Preparedness Assn., Am. Security Council, Republican. Mem. Reformed Ch. in Am. Home: 27904 Blossom Blvd North Olmsted OH 44070 Office: 21000 Brookpark Rd Cleveland OH 44135

EVERETT, THELMA FAYE, educator; b. Pilot Point, Tex., Oct. 6, 1929; s. Jimmie Porter and Era Mae (Holley) Huntley; B.S., Wiley Coll., 1951; postgrad. Wayne State U., 1958-60, U. Mich., 1964, Oakland U., 1974; M.A., U. Detroit, 1976; 1 child, Denoris. Tchr., Detroit Public Schs., 1957-59, Pontiac (Mich.) Public Schs., 1961-66, Highland Park (Mich.) Public Schs., 1966—. Precinct rep. Democratic Com., 1973-75. Recipient Disting. Service award Highland Park Fedn. Tchrs., 1977. Mem. Am. Fedn. Tchrs. Address: 1957 Hyde Park Rd Detroit MI 48207

EVERINGHAM, LYLE J., grocery chain exec.; b. Flint, Mich., May 5, 1926; s. Kenneth L. and Christine (Everingham) E.; student U. Toledo, 1956-63; m. Rlene Lajiness, Mar. 31, 1929; children—Nancy, Mark, Christine. With Kroger Co., 1946—, v.p. Dayton div. (Ohio), 1963-64, v.p. produce merchandising, Cin., 1964-65, successively v.p., from 1966, sr. v.p., now pres., chmn., chief exec. officer; pres. Wesco Foods. Active Mt. Lookout Civic Club; mem. adv. bd. Nat. and Cin. Salvation Army, co-chmn. Cin. Served with cav. AUS, 1943-46. Roman Catholic. Clubs: Cin. Country, Queen City, Comml. (Cin.). Office: Kroger Co 1014 Vine St Cincinnati OH 45201

EVERS, CHARLES HUBERT, drug treatment adminstr.; b. Harvey, Ill., Aug. 28, 1923; s. Hubert H. and Frances E.H. (Kortz) E.; B.S., U. Ill., 1947; m. Dolores Frances Martozie, Dec. 14, 1963; children—Marian Ruth, Cynthia Jean. Bldg. trade contractor pvt. practice Chgo., 1947—; salesman real estate McKey & Poague, Chgo., 1964-70. Baird & Warner Inc., Chgo., 1970-75; founder, dir. Project Reconciliation, Chgo., 1963—. Mem. Ill. com. Nat. Council Crime and Delinquency, 1970—; developer correctional programs for drug abusers, addict-felons; established instnl. drug abuse therapy program Ill. Dept. Corrections, 1976; founder, supr. drug abuse prevention unit Salvation Army Community Corrections Program, Chgo., 1979. Served with USAF, 1943-45. Mem. Am. Soc. Criminology, Am. Correctional Assn., Correctional Edn. Assn., Am. Acad. Polit. and Social Scis. Presbyterian. Home: PO Box 43 Blue Island IL 60406

EVERT, EDWARD PAUL, JR., r.r. exec.; b. Michigan City, Ind., Apr. 19, 1939; s. Edward Paul and Alice Therese (Sheehan) E.; B.S. in Econs., U. Detroit, 1963, M.A. in Econs., 1964; m. Colleen Finnerty, Apr. 20, 1963; children—Kathleen Marie, Jennifer Erin. Fin. analyst Chrysler Corp., 1963-64; spl. rep. to G.S.T., Milw. Rd., 1964-67; asst. supt. car service Chgo. & North Western Transp. Co., Chgo., 1967-68, mgr. on line ops., 1968, dir. data communications, 1969-71, dir. telecommunication and data entry, 1971-75, dir. computer ops., 1975-79, dir. planning, 1979—. Mem. fin. com. St. Ignatius Coll. Prep. Sch., Chgo. Mem. Assn. Am. R.R.'s, Western Ry. Club, Nat. Trust for Hist. Preservation, Smithsonian Assos., Planning Execs. Inst. (chmn. evening spl. program), Midwest Planning Assn., Nat. Hist. Soc., Field Mus. Natural History, Nat. Geog. Soc., N.Y. Central System Hist. Soc., Mens Found. of Community Hosp., St. Francis Club Alumni Found. Republican. Roman Catholic. Home: 945 Sunset Rd Geneva IL 60134 Office: One Northwestern Center Chicago IL 60606

EVERTS, CARL HENRY, educator; b. Grafton, Nebr., Nov. 25, 1930; s. John Peter and Anna (Wietzke) E.; B.S., Concordia Coll., Seward, Nebr., 1953; M.A., U. Mich., 1958; Ed.D., U. Tex., 1968; m. Helen Boernsen, June 2, 1953; children—Marcia, Karla, Michael, Jennine. Tchr., St. Paul Luth. Sch., Flint, Mich., 1953-58; prin. St. John Luth. Sch., Paullina, Iowa, 1958-59; athletic dir. Concordia Coll., Austin, Tex., 1959-69; chmn. div. health, phys. edn. and recreation Concordia Coll., Seward, 1969—. Chmn., United Fund Drive, Flint, 1956; chmn. Hope Luth. Bd. Edn., Austin. Mem. AAHPER, Am. Sch. Health Assn., Nat. Assn. Phys. Edn. in Higher Edn. Lutheran. Club: Kiwanis (dir.). Contbr. articles to profl. jours. Office: Concordia Coll Seward NE 68434

EVILSIZER, BRADLEY NEAL, state ofcl.; b. Nashville, Ill., Jan. 17, 1938; s. Edward A. and Freida G. (Taylor) E.; student So. Ill. U. Vocat. Tng. Inst., 1958-59; m. Mary Ann Crain, Nov. 26, 1960; children—Brian, Melody. With E & E Mine Service, 1956-64, Freeman Coal Mining Corp., 1965-74, U.S. Bur. Mines, Benton, Ill., 1974; dept. chmn. mining tech. program Rend Lake Coll., Ina, Ill., 1974-77; dir. Ill. Dept. Mines and Minerals, Springfield, 1977—; del. Interstate Coal Compact Commn. Mem. AIME, Ind. Mining Inst., Ill. Mining Inst. (dir.), Mine Insps. Inst. Am. (exec. bd.), Nat. Assn. State Mining Adminstrs. (chmn. coal), Mine Elec. Group. Republican. Clubs: Christopher Saddle, Elks. Home: 1105 S Emma St Christopher IL 62822 Office: Room 704 William Stratton Bldg Springfield IL 62706

EVNEN, EVERETT ARNOLD, poultry and egg co. exec.; b. Lincoln, Nebr., Dec. 8, 1927; s. Eli Meyer and Dorothy (Lettween) E.; B.S., U. Nebr., 1950; m. Elaine Rae Sherman, June 24, 1951; children—Robert Barnett, Richard Lewis, Jane Ellen, Judith Ann. Sec., Tri-State Produce Co., Sioux City, Iowa, 1951-56; poultry distbr. Nat. Poultry Market, Lincoln, 1956-57; pres., owner Lincoln Poultry and Egg Co., 1957—; v.p. Capitol Broadcasting Co., 1966-75; sec. Eggs, Inc., 1965-77; pres. EPF Enterprises, 1967—, Lincoln Irrigation Co.; v.p. Brody's Internat. Inc.; dir. Vicorp, Inc., Darcom, Gateway Bank of Lincoln; mem. Lloyds of London. Trustee, treas. Madonna Home; trustee Nebr. Wesleyan U.; pres. Tifereta Israel Synagogue Found. Served with AUS, 1946-47. Mem. Exec. Club (pres. 1970), Nat. Ind. Poultry and Food Distbrs. Assn. (pres. 1970-73, Man of Year award 1973), Nebr. Alumni Assn., Am. Legion, Zeta Beta Tau Alumni Assn. (pres. 1968-69). Republican. Mason (Shriner), Elk; mem. B'nai B'rith. Jewish (treas. synagogue 1969-73). Home: 3020 O'Reilly Dr Lincoln NE 68502 Office: 20th and M Sts Lincoln NE 68510

EWALD, ROBERT FREDERICK, ins. co. exec.; b. Newark, May 5, 1924; s. Frederick J. and Florence (Reiley) E.; B.S., Rutgers U., 1948; m. Jeanine Martinez, Jan. 3, 1976; children—Steven A., Robert T., George E., John C., William F. Asst. corp. auditor Prudential Ins. Co., Newark, 1948-62; audit mgr. N.Y. Life Ins. Co., N.Y.C., 1962-65; treas., controller Mass. Gen. Life, Boston, 1965-69; adminstrv. v.p. Res. Life Ins. Co., Dallas, 1969-71; pres. Nat. Ben Franklin Life Ins. Co., Chgo., 1971-77; mgmt. cons., 1978; pres. Blue Cross Plan of Rockford (Ill.), 1979—; pres. Life Ins. Assos., Inc., Rockford, 1980—, also dir. Trustee, Ill. Hosp. and Health Services Inc., Life Ins. Assos., Inc., North Communities Health Plan, Inc., Communities Health Plan, Inc. Served with U.S. Army, 1943-46. Fellow Life Mgmt. Inst.; mem. Life Office Mgmt. Assn., Adminstrv. Mgmt. Soc., Fin. Execs. Inst., Am. Arbitration Assn., Mensa, Am. Mgmt. Assn. Home: 12 Wisner St Park Ridge IL 60068 Office: 227 N Wyman St Rockford IL 61101

EWALD, ROGER ADOLPH, ophthalmologist; b. LaSalle, Ill., Oct. 1, 1934; s. Edward Francis and Josephine Loretta (Bartoli) E.; student U. Notre Dame, 1952-54; M.D., St. Louis U. 1960; Lancaster Course, Colby Coll., 1965; m. Edith Selena Reinsch, Dec. 22, 1956; children—Edward II, Kurt, Richard II, Stephen, Vincent. Intern Walter Reed Gen. Hosp., Washington, 1960-61, resident pathology, 1961-62, resident ophthalmology, 1964-67, research staff Inst. Research, 1962-64; commd. 1st lt. U.S. Army, 1960, advanced through grades to lt. col., 1969; chief eye, ear, nose throat service U.S. Army Hosp., Ford Ord, Calif., 1967-69; asst. chief ophthalmology service Letterman Gen. Hosp., San Francisco, 1969-70; ret., 1970; practice ophthalmology Carle Clinic Assn., Urbana, Ill., 1970—, bd. govs., 1977-81; mem. staff Carle Found Hosp., Urbana, head dept. ophthalmology, 1973-77, 81—; cons. staff McKinley Hosp., 1971—; clin. asso. ophthalmology Sch. Basic Med. Scis. U. Ill., Urbana-Champaign, 1971-79, clin. asst. prof. ophthalmology Sch. Clin. Medicine, 1979—; dir. 1st State Bank of Monticello (Ill.), 1977—. Recipient Beaumont Research prize, 1960; Lederle Research fellow, 1958. Diplomate Am. Bd. Ophthalmology, Nat. Bd. Med. Examiners. Fellow A.C.S., Am. Acad. Ophthalmology and Otolaryngology, Pan-Pacific Surg. Assn., Soc. Mil. Ophthalmologists; mem. Am., Ill. (dir. 1976-81) assns. ophthalmology, Ill. Soc. Ophthalmology and Otolaryngology, Am. Intra-Ocular Implant Soc., Chgo. Ophthalmologic Soc., A.M.A., Ill. Med. Soc., Champaign County Med. Soc., Alpha Kappa Kappa, Alpha Omega Alpha. Republican. Roman Catholic. Clubs: Decatur (Ill.); Monticello Country. Contbr. articles to profl. jours. and books. Home: 24 Foothill Rd Monticello IL 61856 Office: 602 W University Ave Urbana IL 61801

EWICK, CHARLES RAY, librarian; b. Shelbyville, Ind., Sept. 13, 1937; s. Laurel R. and Loraine Pearl (Tufts) E.; B.A., Wabash Coll., 1962; M.A., Ind. U., 1966; m. Joann Hotchkiss, June 14, 1958; children—David Lee, Jeffrey Allen. Cons., Ind. State Library, Indpls., 1966-68, asst. dir., 1968-72, dir., 1978—; dir. Rolling Prairie Libraries, Decatur, Ill., 1972-78. Mem. ALA, Ind. Library Assn., Phi Beta Mu. Presbyterian. Office: Ind State Library 140 N Senate Ave Indianapolis IN 46204

EWING, RAYMOND PEYTON, ins. co. exec., pub. relations dir.; b. Hannibal, Mo., July 31, 1925; s. Larama Angelo and Winona Fern (Adams) E.; A.A., Hannibal La-Grange Coll., 1948; B.A., William Jewell Coll., 1949; M.A. in Humanities, U. Chgo., 1950; m. Audrey Jane Schulze, May 7, 1949; 1 dau., Jane Ann. Marketing mgmt. trainee Montgomery-Wards, Chgo., 1951-52; sr. editor Commerce Clearing House, Chgo., 1952-60; corp. communications dir. Allstate Ins. Cos. & Allstate Enterprises, Northbrook, Ill., 1960—, issues mgmt. dir., 1979—; pub. relations dir. Chicago Mag., 1966-67, book columnist, 1968-70; staff Book News Commentator, Sta. WRSV, Skokie, Ill., 1962-70; lectr. pub. relations. Mem. Winnetka (Ill.) Library Bd., 1969-70; pres. Skokie Valley United Crusade, 1964-65. Bd. dirs. Suburban Community Chest Council, Onward Neighborhood House, Chgo., Kenilworth Inst. Served with AUS, 1943-46; ETO. Mem. Pub. Relations Soc. of Am. (accredited; Silver Anvil awards for pub. service, 1970, 72, for fin. relations 1970, for bus. spl. events 1976), Publicity Club of Chgo. (v.p. 1967, bd. dirs. 1966-68; Golden Trumpet award for pub. affairs, 1969, 70, 72, 79, for fin. relations 1970), Insurers Public Relations Council (pres. 1980-81), Mensa, World Future Soc., U.S. Assn. for Club of Rome, Chgo. Press Club, Chgo. Poets and Writers Found. (pub. relations dir. 1966-67). Author: Mark Twain's Steamboat Years, 1981; editor: Publicity Club of Chgo. Jour., 1971—; contbr. articles to mags. Home: 316 Richmond Rd Kenilworth IL 60043 Office: Allstate Plaza Northbrook IL 60062

EWING, ROBERT PAUL, ins. co. exec.; b. Kirksville, Mo., Feb. 8, 1925; s. Leo M. and Eva (Dodson) E.; B.S., N.E. Mo. State Coll., 1948; children—Robert I., Michael J., Patricia; m. 2d, Nancy Best, 1972. With Bankers Life & Casualty Co., Chgo., 1948—, exec. v.p., 1965-74, pres., 1974—, chmn. bd., 1978—; chmn. Bankers Life of N.Y., 1978—, Union Bankers Ins. Co., 1978—; exec. v.p. Bankers Multiple Line Ins. Co., Des Moines, 1970—; dir. Constn. Life Ins. Co., Chgo., Union Bankers Ins. Co. Dallas. Bd. dirs. Evanston Hosp. Served with USAAF, 1943-45. Mem. Internat. Assn. Health Underwriters, Nat. Assn. Life Underwriters. Club: Glen View Country. Office: 4444 Lawrence Ave Chicago IL 60630

EWOLDSEN, HAROLD EUGENE, agrl. chem. co. exec.; b. Woodburn, Iowa, Sept.23, 1923; s. Andrew Marion and Agnes Veda (Perdue) E.; B.S. in Agronomy, Iowa State Coll., 1948; m. Zelma Rosalee Craft, Dec. 19, 1943; children—Philip, James, Richard, Mark, David. Tchr. public schs., Osceola, Iowa, 1948-52; salesman Swift & Co., 1952-61; pres., chief exec. officer So. Minn. Agrl. Chem. Co., Waldorf, Minn., 1961-64; retail sales mgr. Agrl. Chem. div. Gulf Oil Co., Redwood Falls, Minn., 1964-72; state sales mgr. Roadrunner Realty, Phoenix, 1972-75; plant mgr. Terra Western Chem. Co., Marshall, Minn. and Carroll, Iowa, 1975-80; dir. retail tng. Terra Chem. Internat., Inc., Sioux City, Iowa, 1980—. Dist. edn. commr. Boy Scouts Am.; county and state del. Minn. Republican Com., 1971-72, 75-76. Served with USAF, 1942-45, U.S. Army, 1945-46, 50-51. Mem. Am. Soc. for Trainer and Dirs., Nat. Fertilizer Solutions Assn. Mem. Disciples of Christ Ch. Home: 2408 S Royce St Sioux City IA 51106 Office: Box 1828 Sioux City IA 51102

EXLEY, CHARLES ERROL, JR., office equipment mfg. co. exec.; b. Detroit, Dec. 14, 1929; s. Charles Errol and Helen Margaret (Greenizen) E.; B.A., Wesleyan U., Middletown, Conn., 1952; M.B.A., Columbia U., 1954; m. Sara Elizabeth Yates, Feb. 1, 1952; children—Sarah Helen, Evelyn Victoria, Thomas Yates. With Burroughs Corp., Detroit, 1954-76, v.p. fin., 1971-73, exec. v.p. fin., 1973-76, also dir.; pres., mem. exec. com. NCR Corp., Dayton, Ohio, 1976—, also dir. Trustee Wesleyan U.; chmn. pacesetter com. United Way, 1972, chmn. 1982 campaign. Mem. Fin. Execs. Inst. Clubs: Grosse Pointe (Mich.); Dayton Racquet, Moraine Country (Dayton). Office: 1700 S Patterson Blvd Dayton OH 45479

EXON, J(OHN) JAMES, U.S. Senator; b. Geddes, S.D., Aug. 9, 1921; s. John James and Luella (Johns) E.; student U. Omaha, 1939-41; m. Patricia Ann Pros, Sept. 18, 1943; children—Stephen James, Pamela Ann, Candace Lee. Mgr., Universal Finance Corp., Nebr., 1946-53; pres. Exon's, Inc., Lincoln, Nebr., 1954-71; gov. State of Nebr., 1971-79; U.S. Senator from Nebr., 1979—. Mem. exec. com. Nat. Govs. Conf., 1971, Democratic Govs. Conf., 1971, 74; vice chmn. Midwest Govs. Conf., 1973, chmn., 1974; co-chmn. Old West Reg. Commn., 1974-75. Active state, local, nat. Dem. coms., 1952—; del. Dem. Nat. Conv., 1964, 68, 72, 76; Dem. nat. committeeman, 1968-71, 81—. Served with Signal Corps, AUS, 1942-45. Mem. Lincoln C. of C., Nat. Office Products Dealers, Am. Legion. Mason (32 deg., Shriner), Clubs: Elks, Optimists Internat. (past lt. gov. Nebr. dist.). Office: 3313 Dirksen Senate Office Bldg Washington DC 20510

EXSTROM, SHEILA MARIE, nurse; b. Holdrege, Nebr., Dec. 15, 1942; d. Walter Eugene and Merinda Mathilda (Danielson) E.; R.N., Immanuel Hosp. Sch. Nursing, 1964; B.S. in Nursing, U. Nebr.,

Omaha, 1968; M.A., Ariz. State U., 1973. Staff nurse Immanuel Med. Center, Omaha, 1964-65, nursing supr., inservice instr., 1966-68, asst. dir. inservice edn., 1968-69, dir. inservice edn., 1969-74, dir. nursing service, 1974-80; asst. adminstr. Lincoln (Nebr.) Gen. Hosp., 1980—; staff nurse Midway Hosp., St. Paul, 1965-66; cons. Freizen Internat. Active Nebr. Heart Assn., Omaha Community Playhouse. Named Nurse of Yr. for profl. achievement, 1973; recipient Disting. Service award Nebr. Nurses Assn., 1980; Leadership in Nursing award Nebr. Hosp. Assn., 1981. Mem. Am. Nurses Assn. (vice chmn. conf. group on inservice edn., dist. pres., state dir., state sec., state pres., chmn. task forces, nat. del.), Nat. League for Nursing, Comprehensive Health Planning Assn., Sigma Theta Tau. Democrat. Lutheran. Clubs: Order Eastern Star, Altrusa, Toastmasters, Ak-Sar-ben. Contbr. articles to Nebr. Nurse. Home: 4424 S 58th St Lincoln NE 68516 Office: 2300 S 16th St Lincoln NE 68502

EYERLY, JOYCE ANN KRUER, biomed. engr.; b. New Albany, Ind., May 30, 1954; d. Raymond John and Catherine Magdalen (Miller) K.; B.S.E., Purdue U., 1976; postgrad. St. Francis Coll., Fort Wayne, Ind., 1977-78, Coll. of St. Thomas, Mpls., 1981—; m. R. Michael Eyerly, Oct. 6, 1979. Devel. mgr. research and devel. Zimmer-USA, Warsaw, Ind., 1976-77, sr. devel. mgr., 1977-80; sr. design engr. Medtronic Inc., Mpls., 1980—. Coach, player community softball teams. Mem. ASTM (chmn. task force on elec. stimulation of tissue), Assn. Advancement Med. Instrumentation, Tau Beta Pi. Roman Catholic. Co-inventor elec. bone growth stimulator. Office: 6972 Central Ave NE Minneapolis MN 55432

EYERMAN, THOMAS JUDE, architect; b. Columbus, Ohio, June 11, 1939; s. Raymond Jacob and Lucille (Garno) E.; B.Arch., Ohio State U., 1963; M.B.A., Harvard U., 1965; m. Mary Kay Evans, Nov. 3, 1962; children—Matthew, David, Nicole. With Skidmore, Owings & Merrill, Chgo., 1966—, asso. partner, 1971-73, gen. partner, 1973—. Co-chmn. Com. on Fgn. and Domestic Policy; trustee, mem. research and policy com. Com. for Econ. Devel.; trustee Chgo. Orch. Assn.; bd. dirs. Harvard Bus. Sch. of Chgo., mem. dean's fund; mem. com. for tomorrow Ohio State U.; sustaining fellow, mem. governing bd. Art Inst. Chgo. Recipient Texnikoi award as outstanding alumnus Ohio State U. Coll. Engring., 1974. Fellow A.I.A. (Chgo. treas. 1972, dir. Chgo. chpt., chmn. office practices com. 1974); mem. Harvard Bus. Sch. Assn., Phi Delta Theta. Clubs: Harvard, Arts, Met., Monroe, Pres.'s of U. Chgo., Execs., (Chgo.). Author: Financial Management Concepts and Techniques for the Architect, 1973. Home: 1046 N Grove Ave Oak Park IL 60302 Office: 33 W Monroe St Chicago IL 60603

EYRE, IVAN, artist, educator; b. Tulleymet, Sask., Can., Apr. 15, 1935; s. Thomas and Kay Eyre; m. Brenda Fenske, June 14, 1957; children—Keven, Tyrone. Mem. faculty U. N.D., 1958-59; mem. faculty U. Man., Winnipeg, (Can.), 1959—, prof. drawing and painting, 1975—, head drawing dept., 1974—; one man shows include Montreal Mus. Fine Arts, 1964, Winnipeg Art Gallery, 1964, 66, 74, 82, Fleet Galleries, Winnipeg, 1965, 69, 71, Albert White Galleries, Toronto, 1965, Atelier Vincitore Gallery, Brighton, Eng., 1967, Jerrold Morris Gallery, Toronto, 1969, 71, 73, Frankfurter Kunst Kabinett, Frankfurt, Ger., 1973, Burnaby Art Gallery, 1973, Siemens Werk, Erlangen, Germany, 1974, New Brunswick Mus., St. John, 1976, Equinox Gallery, Vancouver, 1978, 81, Mira Godard Gallery, Toronto, 1978, 80, Mira Goddard Gallery, Calgary, 1979, Robert McLaughlin Gallery, Oshawa, 1980; group shows include London Art Gallery, 1963, Agnes Lefort Gallery, Montreal, 1964, Nat. Gallery, Ottawa, 1965, 67, 74, Toronto Gallery, 1968, Montreal Mus. Fine Arts, 1970, 76, Art Gallery Ont., 1970, 76, Winnipeg Art Gallery, 1976, Glenbow-Alta. Inst., Calgary, 1976, Vancouver Art Gallery, 1977, Saskatoon Art Gallery, 1977, Harbourfront Art Gallery, Toronto, 1977, Fine Arts Gallery, U. B.C., 1977, Mendel Art Gallery, Saskatoon, 1979, The Gallery Stratford (Ont.), 1979, Art Gallery of Peterborough, 1979, Equinox Gallery, 1980, Bishop's U., Que., 1980, Edmonton Art Gallery, 1981; represented in permanent collection at Winnipeg Art Gallery, Nat. Gallery, Ottawa, Vancouver Art Gallery, Montreal Mus. Fine Arts. Can. Council sr. fellow, 1966. Mem. Royal Acad. Arts. Subject of book Ivan Eyre (George Woodcock), 1981. Home: 1098 Trappistes St Norbert MB R3V 1B8 Canada Office: Sch Art U Manitoba Winnipeg MB Canada

FABER, CHARLES PHILIP, investment adv. co. exec.; b. Sheboygan, Wis., Aug. 1, 1941; s. Charles W. and Bernetta P. (Metscher) F.; B.B.A. (Dow-Corning scholar), U. Wis., 1966, M.B.A. (Research fellow), 1967; m. Jane E. Schneider, Dec. 22, 1962; children—Charles R., David R. Field rep. Caterpillar Tractor Co., Peoria, Ill., 1967-68; mktg. mgr. Apache Corp., Mpls., 1969-72, sales rep., 1973-74; gen. mgr. Apache Programs, Inc., Mpls., 1974-76, br. mgr., Milw., 1976-77; exec. v.p., dir. Investment Search, Inc., Annapolis, Md., 1978—; dir. WFK Leasing Co., Gloucester Prodn. Co. Served with U.S. Army, 1961-63. Mem. Internat. Assn. Fin. Planners, Assn. for Continuing Edn. in Bus., Nat. Assn. Securities Dealers (licensed prin.), Beta Gamma Sigma. Club: Moose Lake Yacht. Home: W 332 N 6556 N Moose Ln Nashotah WI 53058

FABIAN, LEONARD WILLIAM, anesthesiologist, educator; b. Little Rock, Nov. 12, 1923; s. Leonard Edward and Susan Ellen (Chitwood) F.; B.S., U. Ark., 1950, M.D., 1951; m. Elizabeth Mardelle Bishop, Jan. 8, 1947; children—Beverly, Susan, Leonard William, Edward, Ronald. Intern, U. Ark. Hosp., 1951-52, resident in anesthesiology, 1952-54; fellow Phila. Children's Hosp., 1954; instr. in anesthesiology U. Ark., 1954-55; asst. prof. anesthesiology Duke, 1955-58; prof., chmn. dept. anesthesiology U. Miss. Med. Center, 1958-71; prof. Washington U., St. Louis, 1971—; mem. staffs Barnes and Associated Hosps., St. Louis, St. Louis Children's Hosp.; nat. cons. emeritus in anesthesiology Surgeon Gen. USAF. Served with USN, 1942-46; PTO. Diplomate Am. Bd. Anesthesiology. Fellow Am. Coll. Anesthesiologists (chmn. bd. govs. 1964-65); mem. Am. Soc. Anesthesiologists, Internat. Anesthesia Research Soc., AMA, St. Louis, Mo. State med. socs., Mo., St. Louis socs. anesthesiologists, Assn. Univ. Anesthetists, Am. Fedn. Clin. Research, Assn. Physician Faculty of Nurse Anesthesia Schs., Mo., St. Louis (chmn. com. on cardiopulmonary resuscitation, comr.) heart assns. Contbr. numerous articles to profl. publs.; editor: Anesthesia and the Circulation, 1964; Clinical Anesthesia: A Decade of Clinical Progress, 1971. asso. editor Clin. Anesthesia, 1965—, Survey Anesthesiology, 1965—. Home: 1570 Foxleigh Ct St Louis MO 63131 Office: 660 S Euclid Ave St Louis MO 63131

FABINO, ROBERT ALLEN, counselor; b. Chgo., Apr. 1, 1936; s. Ambrose and Myrtle Lillian (Brenn) F.; B.A., Roosevelt U., 1962, M.A., 1972; cert. psychotherapy Chgo. Med. Sch., 1974; Ph.D., Walden U., 1981; 1 son by previous marriage, Kevin. Vocat. counselor Cook County Dept. Public Aid, 1962-63; career counselor, 1962-72; pvt. practice alcoholism and drug dependency counseling, Chgo. and Glen Ellyn, Ill., 1972—; instr. Triton Coll., River Grove, Ill., 1968-73; adj. instr. dept. psychiatry Chgo. Med. Sch., 1974-77; lectr. drug and alcohol abuse, radio, TV; cons. Pullman-Standard Inc.; cons. Alcoholism and Drug Dependence Council DuPage County, 1972-75. Pres., Friends of Library, Villa Park; chmn. float com. N.W. Homeowners Assn., Villa Park. Mem. Villa Park Jaycees (dir.), Am. Personnel and Guidance Assn., Ill. Group Psychotherapy Assn., Ill. Alcoholism and Drug Dependence Assn., Alcohol and Drug Problems Assn. N.Am., Franklin Players, Schaumburg Players, Act IV. Office: 664 N Michigan Ave Chicago IL 60611

FABITO, DANIEL CERVANTES, surgeon; b. Philippines, Jan. 28, 1942; came to U.S., 1965; s. Rufo M. and Rosario C. (Cervantes) F.; M.D., Far Eastern U., Manila, Philippines, 1964; m. Melinda Ayala, July 1, 1967; children—Melissa, D. Marc, D. Everett. Rotating intern Deaconess Hosp., Milw., 1965, resident in surgery, 1966; resident in surgery Mo. Baptist Hosp., St. Louis, 1967-71, now staff; practice medicine specializing in gen. and vascular surgery, St. Louis, 1971—; mem. staff Luth. Med. Center, St. Louis, chmn. dept. surgery, 1980—; mem. staff Depaul Hosp., St. Louis. Diplomate Am. Bd. Surgery. Philippine Bd. Surgery. Fellow A.C.S., Soc. Philippine Surgeons Am. (gov. 1979—), Philippine Coll. Surgeons; mem. St. Louis County Med. Soc. (councilor 1976-77), Mo. Med. Assn. (del. 1976-78), Assn. Philippine Practicing Physicians in Am. (v.p. 1977-78, pres. 1980-81), Philippine Med. Assn. Greater St. Louis (pres. 1974). Home: 882 Amersham Dr Saint Louis MO 63141 Office: 120 Progress Pkwy Saint Louis MO 63043

FACENTE, GARY, publisher; b. Teaneck, N.J., Aug. 3, 1944; s. Alfred A. and Pauline F.; B.A., MacMurray Coll., 1966; m. Jane Carlin, June 22, 1968; children—Blake Carlin, Brooke Lynn. Tchr., N.Y.C. Schs., 1966-67; research fellow U. Denver, 1967-68; asst. to mayor, N.Y.C., 1968-71; mktg. exec. McGraw-Hill Book Co., N.Y.C., 1971-75; gen. mgr. Follett Pub. Co., Chgo., 1975-80, v.p., editor-in-chief, 1980—; adj. asst. prof. edn. Chgo. State U., 1976-77. Mem. Assn. Am. Pubs., Chgo. Press Club. Contbr. to Chgo. Sun Times. Home: 2818 Harrison St Evanston IL 60201 Office: 1010 W Washington Blvd Chicago IL 60607

FACHES, WILLIAM GEORGE, lawyer; b. Cedar Rapids, Iowa, Feb. 15, 1928; s. George Vlasios and Androniki (Panagopoulos) F.; student Coe Coll., 1947-48; B.A., U. Iowa, 1951, J.D., 1955; m. Mary Matzanias, Dec. 6, 1959; children—Andrea Lynn, Allison Lynn. Admitted to Supreme Ct. Iowa, 1955, U.S. Supreme Ct., 1971, U.S. Dist. Ct. No. Dist. Iowa, 1955, U.S. Dist. Ct. So. Dist. Iowa, 1970; mem. firm Reilly & Faches, Cedar Rapids, 1955-67; 1st asst. county atty., Linn County, 1965-67, county atty., 1967-74; sr. mem. firm Faches, Gloe & Quint (and predecessor firms), Cedar Rapids, 1967—. Mem. Mayors Ad Hoc Com. on Alcholism, 1967-68, Linn County Crime Commn., 1971-73; bd. dirs. Sixth Jud. Dist. Iowa Community Corrections, 1978—, chmn. bd., 1978—; chmn. inheritance tax appraisal Linn County, 1980—. Pres., Young Democrats, 1960; mem. central com. Linn County Dem. Com., 1956-58, 60-68. Bd. dirs. Linn County Assn. Mentally Retarded, 1968-72, Cedar Rapids Teen Club, 1968-76. Served with Air Corps, AUS, 1946-47. Recipient Civil Libertarian award Iowa Civil Liberties Union, 1974; Man of Yr. award Iowa Corrections Assn., 1980. Mem. Linn County, Iowa bar assns., Iowa County Attys. Assn., Nat. Dist. Atty.'s Assn., Am. Judicature Soc., Phi Alpha Delta. Greek Orthodox. Home: 1901 5th Ave SE Cedar Rapids IA 52403 Office: 318 Paramount Bldg Cedar Rapids IA 52401

FADA, CHARLES VERNON, elec. engr.; b. Montgomery County, Iowa, Oct. 27, 1932; s. Alexander Charles and Ruth R. (Kneedy) F.; B.S.E.E., State U. Iowa, 1956; M.S.E.E., Air Force Inst. Tech., 1968; m. Norma Jean Peterson, June 22, 1957; children—David, Robert, Lori. Commd. 2d lt. USAF, 1956, advanced through grades to lt. col., 1976, ret., 1978; program mgr. Electronic Warfare Center, Systems Research Labs., Inc., Dayton, Ohio, 1978—. Decorated Air medal with 7 oak leaf clusters, DSM. Named Most Outstanding Chief Engr. of the Yr., Aeronautical Systems Div., Air Force Systems Command, 1975. Mem. Am. Def. Preparedness Assn. Clubs: Assn. Old Crows, Lions (pres. 1981—), Optimist (charter mem.). Home: 1817 Southlawn Dr Fairborn OH 45324 Office: 2800 Indian Ripple Rd Dayton OH 45440

FADDEN, NEALE RAYMOND, mathematician; b. Sterling, Ill., Nov. 12, 1937; s. E. Wayne and Edna (Hardy) F.; student U. Ill., 1955-57; B.S., Ill. State U., 1959, M.S., 1963; m. Elizabeth Shively, Dec. 18, 1966; 1 dau., Michelle; stepchildren—Gerald, Lisa, Steven. Tchr. math Henry (Ill.) High Sch., 1959-63; instr. math Belleville (Ill.) Area Coll., 1963—. Pres., Belleville Area Community Concert Assn., 1977—, bd. dirs., 1971—; bd. dirs. Trailblazers Inc., 1971-74, Ill. Childrens Home and Aid Soc., 1978—. Fulbright Hayes teaching fellow, Cornwall Tech. Coll., Eng., 1969-70. Mem. Ill. Council Tchrs. Math (dir. 1981—), Nat. Council Tchrs. Math, Math Assn. Am., AAUP, Ill. Math. Assn. Community Colls. Mem. Union United Meth. Ch., Belleville. Home: 125 N Douglas St Belleville IL 62221 Office: 2500 Carlyle Rd Belleville IL 62220

FADNESS, PETER ANDREW, employment counselor; b. Portage, Wis., July 30, 1932; s. Andrew C. and Elva F.; B.S., U. Wis., Eau Claire, 1958; M.Ed., U. Mo., 1967; m. Karen LaVon Bowen, Aug. 11, 1973; children—William, Angela, Benjamin A. Elec. contractor, Rio, Wis., 1951-53; salesman Group Health Mut. Ins. Co., St. Paul, 1958-60; employment counselor Wis. Job Service, Eau Claire, 1960—; cons. in field. Served with USN, 1953-54. Licensed electrician. Mem. Wis. Personnel and Guidance Assn., Wis. Employment Counselors Assn. (pres. 1970), Am. Guild Organists (dean Chippewa Valley chpt. 1966, 67, 70). Congregationalist. Clubs: Masons (exec. com. Eau Claire Consistory, Scottish Rite, 32 deg., Meritorious Service award 1981), Shriners. Home: 3516 Brian St Eau Claire WI 54701

FAESSLER, EDWIN JOSEPH, mgmt. cons.; b. Cin., Nov. 27, 1944; s. Edwin C. and Rosemarie (Schlie) F.; B.A. in Psychology, U. Cin., 1967; M.S.W., Ohio State U., 1969; m. Deborah Braun, Nov. 25, 1978; children by previous marriage Joseph Michael, Robert James. Clin. instr. psychiat. social work U. Cin., 1971-72; dir. therapeutic foster home project Children's Home of Cin., 1972-75; asst. prof. Edgecliff Coll., Cin., 1974-78, program dir. social work, 1975—; pres. Interpersonal Communication Assos., Inc., Cin., 1977-79; adj. asst. prof. dept. social work U. Cin., 1978-79; dir. social service Jewish Hosp. Cin., 1977—; cons. to various schs., ch. groups and hosps., Cin. area, 1974—; panel speaker weekly program Sta. WVXU, 1977—. Mem. human resources com. Gt. Rivers council Girl Scouts U.S., 1977—; pres. Norwood Bd. Health, 1977—; bd. dirs. Norwood Service League, Parents Exploring Adventure of Childbirth Experience, chmn., 1978-79; mem. Bd. Mental Health Services of N. Central Hamilton County, 1981—. Mem. Council on Social Work Edn., Cin. Assn. Home Care Agys. (mem. adv. com. 1978-79), Soc. for Hosp. Social Work Dirs., AAUP. Home: 5228 Parmalee Pl Cincinnati OH 45212 Office: 5258 Montgomery Rd Cincinnati OH 45212

FAESTEL, DAVID JOEL, investment and oil exploration and drilling co. exec.; b. Waukesha, Wis., July 2, 1944; s. Gerald Henry and Harriet (Kubal) F.; B.A., Marquette U., 1968; M.B.A., U. Wis., 1970; m. Catherine Delores McCormick, June 19, 1971; children—Joel, Paul, Todd. Regional mgr. Multicon Properties, Inc., Columbus, Ohio, 1970-72; fin. analyst IC Industries, Chgo., 1972-73; pres. Faestel Investments, Inc., Crystal Lake, Ill., 1973—; pres. Petren Resources Corp.; pres., dir. Petren Drilling Corp., 1980—; dir. Trachte Metal Bldgs. Lic. real estate broker, Ill. Mem. Am. Petroleum Inst., Ind. Petroleum Assn. Am., Self Service Storage Assn., C. of C., Am. Simmnetal Assn. Roman Catholic. Club: Kiwanis (past pres.). Office: 200 Corporate Corner 101 Virginia St Crystal Lake IL 60014

FAGERBERG, ROGER RICHARD, lawyer; b. Chgo., Dec. 11, 1935; s. Richard Emil and Evelyn (Thor); B.S. in Bus. Adminstrn., Washington U., St. Louis, 1958, J.D., 1961, postgrad. 1961-62; m. Virginia Fuller Vaughan, June 20, 1959; children—Steven Roger, Susan Vaughan, James Thor, Laura Craft. Grad. teaching asst. Washington U., St. Louis, 1961-62; admitted to Mo. bar, 1961, since practiced in St. Louis; asso. firm Rassieur, Long & Yawitz, 1962-64; partner firm Rassieur, Long, Yawitz & Schneider and predecessor firms, 1965—. Mem. exec. com. citizens' adv. council Pkwy. Sch. Dist., 1974—, pres.-elect, 1976-77, pres., 1977-78; bd. dirs. Parkway Residents Orgn., 1969—, v.p., 1970-73, pres., 1973—. Mem. Am., St. Louis bar assns., Mo. Bar, Christian Bus. Men's Com. (dir. 1975-78), Full Gospel Bus. Men's Fellowship, Order of Coif, Omicron Delta Kappa, Beta Gamma Sigma, Pi Sigma Alpha, Phi Eta Sigma, Phi Delta Phi, Kappa Sigma. Republican. Presbyterian (elder, congregation pres. 1968-70, 77-78). Clubs: Kiwanis (dir. 1972-74, 76-79, v.p. 1978-79), Masons, Shriners. Home: 13812 Clayton Rd Manchester MO 63011 Office: 700 Boatmen's Tower Saint Louis MO 63102

FAHNER, TYRONE CLARENCE, state atty. gen.; b. Detroit, Nov. 18, 1942; s. Warren George and Alma Fahner; B.A., U. Mich., 1965; J.D., Wayne State U., 1965; LL.M., Northwestern U., 1971; m. Anne Beauchamp, July 2, 1966; children—Margaret, Daniel, Molly. Admitted to Mich. bar, 1968, Ill. bar, 1969; mem. criminal def. litigation unit Northwestern U., 1969-71; asst. U.S. atty. for No. Dist. Ill., Chgo., 1971-75, dep. chief consumer fraud and civil rights, 1973-74, chief ofcl. corruption, 1974-75; mem. firm Freeman, Rothe, Freeman & Salzman, Chgo., 1975-77; dir. Ill. Dept. Law Enforcement, 1977-79; partner firm Mayer, Brown & Platt, Chgo., 1979-80; atty. gen. State of Ill., Springfield, 1980—; instr. John Marshall Law Sch., 1973-76. Ford Found. fellow, 1969-71. Mem. Am. Bar Assn., Ill. Bar Assn., Mich. Bar Assn., Chgo. Bar Assn., Am. Judicature Soc., Nat. Assn. Attys. Gen. Republican. Lutheran. Office: 500 2d St Springfield IL 62706 and 160 N LaSalle Chicago IL 60601

FAHY, EDWARD JOSEPH, lawyer; b. Toluca, Ill., Mar. 26, 1911; s. Michael and Josephine (Luppens) F.; A.B., Georgetown U., 1933, J.D., 1937; m. Helen C. Simmons, Nov. 6, 1937; children—Michael Joseph, Mary Katherine (Mrs. C.W. Norwood), Jean Marie Hanley. Admitted to U.S. Dist. Ct. and Ct. of Appeals, 1936, Ill. bar, 1937, U.S. Ct. Appeals, 1949, Supreme Ct. U.S., 1956; practiced in Rockford, Ill., 1939—; pres. Fahy & Cheney, Ltd., Rockford, Ill., 1980—. Mem. Am., Ill. State (chmn. labor law sect. 1951-53), Winnebago County bar assns., Rockford C. of C. (dir. 1963-66), Pi Gamma Mu. K.C. Contbr. articles to profl. jours. Home: 1821 Harlem Blvd Rockford IL 61103 Office: Suite 202 303 N Main St Rockford IL 61101

FAILE, JAMES KENNETH, banker; b. Cleve., Feb. 14, 1932; s. Fred Guthrie and Elizabeth Jane (Hay) F.; B.A., Ohio Wesleyan U., 1954; m. Dorothy Ann Pleasance, Aug. 22, 1953; children—James David, John Frederick, Karen Jo. With Leonard Electric Mfg. Co., Cleve., 1954-62, sales rep., 19 -62; with Cleve. Trust Co. (named changed to Ameritrust Co. 1979), 1962—, mgr. systems, 1966-69, mgr. application devel., 1969-74, v.p. computer services, 1974-78, v.p. regional processing for statewide network, 1978—. Mem. Bank Adminstrn. Inst., Assn. Systems Mgmt. (v.p. 1972-73). Republican. Presbyterian. Club: Ohio Wesleyan Odevene (pres. Cleve. chpt. 1974-75). Office: Ameritrust Co 900 Euclid Ave Cleveland OH 44101

FAIR, JOSEPH JAMES, chem. engr.; b. Dover, Ohio, Mar. 14, 1948; s. James Emerson and Eva Mae (Wagner) F.; student Otterbein Coll., 1966-68; B.S. in Chem. Engring., Ohio State U., 1971, M.S., 1971. Dairy mgr. Big Bear, New Philadelphia, Ohio, 1964-66, summer, 1967; asst. operator Dover Chem. Co. (Ohio), summer 1969; devel. engr. Inland div. Gen. Motors Corp., Dayton, Ohio, 1971—. Registered profl. engr., Ohio. Mem. Soc. Automotive Engrs., Am. Inst. Chem. Engrs., So. Ohio Rubber Group div. Am. Chem. Soc., Order of Engrs. Methodist. Home: 11960 Steck Rd Rural Route 1 Brookville OH 45309 Office: 2701 Home Ave Dayton OH 45417

FAIR, WILLIAM ROBERT, physician; b. Norristown, Pa., Mar. 29, 1935; B.S., Phila. Coll. Pharmacy, 1956; M.D., Jefferson Med. Coll., 1960; m. Mary Ann Collins, Sept. 9, 1961; 1 son, William. Intern, Womack Army Hosp., Fort Bragg, N.C., 1960-61; resident in gen. surgery Martin Army Hosp., Fort Benning, Ga., 1963-64; resident in urology Stanford (Calif.) U. Med. Center, 1964-68, asst. prof. surgery, 1968-72, asso. prof., 1972-75; prof. surgery, chmn. div. urology Wash. U., St. Louis, 1975—, acting head dept. surgery, 1978—. Served with M.C., U.S. Army, 1960-64. Diplomate Am. Bd. Urology. Mem. Internat. Soc. Nephrology, Nat. Kidney Found. (trustee), Nat. Urol. Forum, AAAS, Am. Soc. Nephrology, A.C.S., Am. Urol. Assn., Am. Fedn. for Clin. Research, Soc. Univ. Surgeons, Assn. for Acad. Surgery, Pan Pacific Surg. Assn., Soc. Univ. Urologists, Am. Assn. Genitourinary Surgeons. Mem. internat. editorial bd. Jour. Internat. Med. Research, 1972—; mem. editorial bd. Urology Digest, 1971, Investigative Urology, 1973—; asst. editor Jour. Urology, 1974—; contbr. articles to profl. jours. Home: 13253 Takara Dr Saint Louis MO 63131 Office: Washington U Sch Medicine 660 S Euclid Saint Louis MO 63110

FAIRAND, BARRY PHILIP, physicist; b. Watertown, N.Y., May 20. 1934; s. Charles Francis and Dorothy Marie (Piche) F.; B.S., Le Moyne Coll., 1955; M.S., Detroit U., 1957; Ph.D., Ohio State U., 1969; m. Jeanine Fontana, June 13, 1959; children—Mary, Joan, John, Amy, Ann. Sr. scientist Battelle Meml. Inst., Columbus (Ohio) Labs., 1957-80; pres. Laser Tech. Inc., 1980—. Mem. Am. Phys. Soc., Photo-optical Instrumentation Engrs. Soc., N.Y. Acad. Scis., Sigma Xi, Sigma Pi Sigma. Contbr. articles to profl. jours. Patentee laser shock processing of materials, laser atomization of metals, laser generated x-rays, applying radiation. Home: 1169 Regency Dr Columbus OH 43220 Office: 368 W Park Ave Columbus OH 43223

FAIRBANKS, DAVID PAUL, motor co. exec.; b.Odell, Nebr., Dec. 25, 1942; s. Donald Paul and Rema Jewel (David) F.; A.A., Fairbury Jr. Coll., 1962; B.S. in Mech. Engring., Kans. State U., 1965; m. Twila Bohlmeyer, July 14, 1963; children—Tamara Sue, Daniel Paul. Design engr. Schaffer, Shirmer & Eflin, Architect-Engrs., Wichita, Kans., 1968-69; project engr. constrn. Skelly Oil Refinery, Eldorado, Kans., 1969-71; project engr. Ownes Corning Fiberglas, Kansas City, Kans., 1971-74; plant engring. mgr. Kawasaki Motor Corp. U.S.A., Lincoln, Nebr., 1974—; cons. designer corrosive chem. ventilation systems. Registered profl. engr., Kans. Mem. Am. Inst. Plant Engrs. (pres. chpt. 1979-80), Profl. Engring. Industry (chmn. 1979-81), Nat. Soc. Profl. Engrs. Lutheran. Home: Route 1 Roca NE 68430 Office: 6600 NW 27th St Lincoln NE 68524

FAIRBANKS, VIRGIL FOX, hematologist; b. Ann Arbor, Mich., June 7, 1930; s. Avard Tennyson and Beatrice Maude (Fox) F.; B.A., U. Utah, 1951; M.D., U. Mich., 1954; m. Sheary Jill Eggertsen, Nov. 25, 1955; children—Eric, Julie, Caroline. Intern, Bellevue Hosp., N.Y.C., 1954-55; resident in internal medicine Salt Lake County Hosp., VA Hosp., Salt Lake City, 1957-59; fellow Scripps Clinic, LaJolla, Calif., 1959-60; hematologist City of Hope Med. Center,

Duarte, Calif., 1960-63, Los Angeles County Hosp., 1960-63, Permanente Med. Group, Portland, Oreg., 1964-65; cons. in hematology Mayo Clinic and Found., Rochester, Minn., 1965—; mem. faculty U. Calif. Coll. Medicine, Los Angeles, 1963-64, U. Oreg. Med. Sch., 1964-65; asso. prof. medicine Mayo Grad. Sch. Medicine, Rochester, 1974—; prof. lab. medicine and internal medicine Mayo Sch. Medicine, 1978—. Served with USN, 1955-57. Fellow Internat. Soc. Hematology. Mem. Am. Fedn. Clin. Research, Am. Soc. Hematology, Am. Coll. Physicians, Am. Soc. Human Genetics, Academic Clin. Lab. Physics and Scientists, Central Soc. Clin. Research, Zumbro Valley Med. Soc. Democrat. Author: (with E. Beutler and J.L. Fahey) Clinical Disorders of Iron Metabolism, 1963, 1971; Hemoglobinopathics and Thalassemias, 1980; Current Hematology, Vol. 1, 1981; contbr. articles to med. jours. and textbooks. Home: 620 Colombia Ct NE Rochester MN 55901 Office: Mayo Clinic 200 1st St SW Rochester MN 55901

FAIRCHILD, ROBERT CHARLES, pediatrician; b. Kansas City, Mo., Dec. 22, 1921; s. Charles Clement and Ada Mae (Baker) F.; postgrad. Kansas City Jr. Coll., 1938-40; B.A., U. Kans., 1942, M.D., 1950; m. Patricia Louise Russell, May 28, 1964; children—Robert, Nancy, Rex Hartman, Dan Hartman. Intern, Kansas City Gen. Hosp., 1950-51; resident in pediatrics Univ. Kans. Med. Center, 1951-53; practice medicine specializing in pediatrics, Mission Kans., 1953-70; dir. area clinics Children's Mercy Hosp., Kansas City, Mo., 1970-74, dir. outpatient services, 1974—; prof. pediatrics Univ. Mo.-Kansas City Sch. Medicine, Univ. Kans. Sch. Medicine. Mem. advisory com. Asso. Degree Nursing Program, Johnson County Community Coll., Vis. Nurses Assn. Served to major U.S. Army, 1942-46. Decorated Bronze Star. Recipient Porter Scholarship award, Univ. Kans. Sch. Medicine, 1950, Physician's Recognition award, AMA, 1978. Diplomate Am. Bd. Pediatrics. Mem. AMA, Mo. State Med. Assn., Jackson County Med. Soc. (pres.), Kansas City SW Pediatric Soc., Kansas City SW Clin. Soc., Am. Acad. Pediatrics, Alpha Omega Alpha, Nu Sigma Nu, Sigma Nu. Presbyterian. Contbr. articles in field to med. jours. Lectr. in field. Home: 8425 Reinhardt Ln Leawood KS 66206 Office: 24th & Gillham Rd Kansas City MO 64108

FAIRCHILD, THOMAS E., fed. judge; b. Milw., Dec. 25, 1912; s. Edward Thomas and Helen (Edwards) F.; student Princeton U., 1931-33; A.B., Cornell U., 1934; LL.B., U. Wis., 1938; m. Eleanor E. Dahl, July 24, 1937; children—Edward, Susan, Jennifer, Andrew. Admitted to Wis. bar, 1938; practiced in Portage, Wis., 1938-41, Milw., 1945-48, 53-56; atty. OPA, Chgo., Milw., 1941-45, hearing commr. Chgo. region, 1945; atty. gen. Wis., 1948-51; U.S. atty. Western Dist. Wis., 1951-52; asso. justice Supreme Ct. Wis., 1957-66; judge U.S. Ct. Appeals 7th Circuit, Chgo., 1966—, chief judge, 1975-81. Democratic candidate for senator from Wis., 1950, 52. Mem. Am. Law Inst. (council), Am., Wis., Milw. bar assns., Phi Delta Phi. Democrat. Presbyterian. Club: KP. Office: 219 S Dearborn St Chicago IL 60604

FAIRES, C(ARL) DICKSON, JR., lawyer; b. Edwardsville, Ill., Dec. 3, 1936; s. Carl Dickson and Lela (Christy) F.; student Trinity Sch., N.Y.C., 1952-54, U. Okla., 1954-57; B.S., Ind. U., 1960, LL.B., 1964; m. Lynda Shytle, Mar. 30, 1968 (div. 1977); children—Kimberly Lynne, Carl Dickson III. Admitted to Ind. bar, 1964; dep. atty. gen. Ind., 1964-65; partner firm White, Raub, Reis & Wick, Indpls., 1965-73; partner firm Buckley, Frost & Faires, Indpls., 1973-74, Frost & Faires, Indpls., 1974—. Mem. Indpls. Mus. Art, 1968—; v.p. Happy Hollow Children's Camp. Served with AUS, 1960-61. Mem. Am., Ind., Indpls. bar assns., Ind. Def. Lawyers Assn. (pres. 1980-81), Nat. Rifle Assn., Nature Conservancy, Newcomen Soc. N.Am., Ducks Unltd. (central Ind. chmn.). Republican. Clubs: Lambs, Racquet, University (Indpls). Author: Courts and Code. Home: 7621 Somerset Bay Apt B Indianapolis IN 46240 Office: 3665 N Washington Blvd Indianapolis IN 46205

FAIT, GARY LYNN, publisher, editor; b. Mt. Pleasant, Pa., May 18, 1948; s. Clark Alfred and Dolly Gertrude (Hendricks) F.; B.A., Milligan Coll., 1970; m. Linda Louise Davis, June 12, 1971; children—Amber Elizabeth, Emily Kathryn. News editor Farmer's Advance, Camden, Mich., 1971-72; editor Times Rev., Flint, Mich., 1972-73; co-owner, co-pub., editor Suburban News, Flint, 1973—; v.p. Eastland Press Inc., Flint, 1973—. Sec., Genesee Twp. (Mich.) Econ. Devel. Corp., 1977-78, chmn. 1979—; mem. community adv. bd. Sta.-WFUM-TV, U. Mich.-Flint, 1980—; chmn. charter rev. com. City Davison (Mich.), 1980—. Recipient Internat. award Internat. Assn. Fire Fighters AFL-CIO-CLC, 1975. Mem. Mich. Press Assn. (3d Pl. award for best local column 1978), Nat. Newspaper Assn. Mem. Ch. of Christ. Office: 4461 Richfield Rd Flint MI 48506

FAIT, LAWRENCE EDWARD, optometrist; b. Morse, Wis., June 20, 1923; s. Edward C. and Sophia M. (Swetz) F.; student U. Wis., 1941-43, Carleton Coll., 1943-44; B.S., Dr. Optometry cum laude, Ill. Coll. Optometry, 1947; m. Marie R. Richter, Apr. 15, 1944; children—Robert L., James C., Thomas G., William J. (dec.), Gary P., Kathleen M., Joanne M. Pvt. practice optometry, Burlington, Wis., 1947—; instr. Ill. Coll. Optometry, 1946-47; cons. Internat. Corr. Soc. Optometry. Served with USAAF, 1942-44. Mem. South Eastern Wis. Optometric Soc., Burlington Hist. Soc., Accademia di S. Marciano (Italy), U. Wis. Alumni Assn., N.Am. Indian Relic Collectors Assn., Am. Optometric Assn. (Recognition award 1980), Am. Legion, Circus Hist. Soc., Arms and Armour Soc. (Eng.), Wis., Balkan and E. European geneal. socs., Augustan Soc., Wis. Hist. Soc., Wis. Optometric Assn., Wis. Geneal. Soc., Internat. Wildlife Fedn., Mzuri Safari Found., Fishing Hall Fame, Tomb and Kev (pres. 1946-47), Internat. Game Fish Assn., Oriental Inst. U. Chgo., Smithsonian Instn., Am. Mus. Natural History, Nat. Audubon Soc., Alpha Kappa Lambda, Omega Delta. K.C. (4 deg.). Clubs: U.S. Broadbill, Safari Internat. Home: 117 Midwood Dr Burlington WI 53105 Office: 309 McHenry St Burlington WI 53105

FAITHORN, WALTER ERNEST, JR., mfg. co. exec.; b. Chgo., Nov. 1, 1915; s. Walter Ernest and Elsie (Dixon) F.; grad. Phillips Acad., Andover, Mass., 1934; A.B., Harvard U., 1938; m. Eleanor Rand, Feb. 22, 1941 (div.); children—Eleanor Perry, Elizabeth Dixon; m. 2d, Mary Valentine Scott, July 28, 1958; 1 son, Charles Wallace. Able seaman Donnaldson Line, Glasgow, Scotland, 1938; chief factory cost accountant Dorr Pump Co., Whitewater, Wis., 1938-39; machine tool operator to sales engr. Alemite and Instrument div. Stewart-Warner Corp., Chgo., 1939-42; asst. to vice chmn. WPB, Washington, also asst. sec. Combined Brit.-Canadian Am. Prodn. and Resources Bd., Office Pres. U.S., 1942-43; rep. Stewart-Warner Corp., Washington, 1946-53, asst. sec., govt. mgr., 1953-67, export mgr., Chgo., 1967-70, mgr. internat. ops., 1971-76, dir. internat. mktg., asst. gen. mgr. Internat. div., 1976—; v.p. Indsl. Alemex, S.A., Mexico; dir. Stewart Warner Ltd. Eng., Stewart Warner Alemite GmbH, Germany. Dist. dir. Adlai Stevenson for Pres. Campaign, 1952. Bd. govs., chmn. finance com. Key Sch., Annapolis, Md., until 1968; trustee, chmn. fin. com., mem. exec. com., treas., Latin Sch. of Chgo., 1972-74; trustee, mem. exec. com. Roycemore Sch., Evanston, Ill., 1976-79. Served to lt. USCGR, 1943-46. Mem. Am. Ordnance Assn. (chmn. fuze sect. 1963-68), Revel Athletic Assn. (past dir.). Democrat. Unitarian. Clubs: Univ., Arts (Chgo.); Metropolitan (Washington); Severn Sailing Assn. (Annapolis, Md.); Oconomowoc (Wis.) Lake; Directors (London). Home: 2518 Orrington Ave Evanston IL 60201 also Whitehall Rd St Margarets Annapolis MD 21401 Office: 1826 Diversey Pkwy Chicago IL 60614

FAITZ, EVERETT KARL, JR., city ofcl.; b. Chgo., Aug. 16, 1932; s. Everett Karl and Harriet (Stanton) F.; student Wilson Jr. Coll., 1950-51, U. Ill., 1952-54; B.B.A. with Distinction, Northwestern U., 1972; m. Susanne Ewing, July 14, 1956 (div. Feb. 1971). News rep. F.W. Dodge Corp., 1955-60; bldg. insp. Village of Oak Lawn (Ill.), 1960-63, bldg. commr., 1963-81, also dir. bldg. and zoning, 1963-81. Mem. faculty U. Ill. Acad. for Code Adminstrn. and Enforcement, 1969—, U. Wis. Extension Div., 1973—; zoning cons., adviser to Oak Lawn Planning and Devel. Commn., 1963—; co-adviser Ill. Contractor License Legislation, 1967—; zoning cons. Village of McCook (Ill.), City of Hickory Hills (Ill.); mem. Ill. Bldg. Code Adv. Commn., 1969—; bd. dirs. Council Am. Bldg. Ofcls., 1978; mem. cert. policy bd. Nat. Acad. Code Adminstrn. Chmn. Community Chest, Oak Lawn, 1968, co-chmn., divisional leader, 1965-71 active Boy Scouts Am., Salvation Army; leader YMCA, 1957, 63. Recipient Distinguished Service award Evergreen Park-Oak Lawn Jr. C. of C., 1965. Named one of Outstanding Young Men of Am., Outstanding Young Ams., Inc., 1967. Mem. S. Suburban Bldg. Ofcls. Assn. (pres. 1964-66, exec. bd. 1966—), Suburban Bldg. Ofcls. Conf. (mem. exec. bd. 1966—, chmn. code change com. 1966—, pres. 1971-72), Bldg. Ofcls. and Code Adminstrs. Internat. (exec. bd. 1978), Am. Soc. Testing Materials, Nat. Fire Prevention Assn., Western Soc. Engrs., Pershing Rifles, Order Arrow, Delta Mu Delta, Alpha Phi Omega. Clubs: Nomads Ski; Oak Lawn Racquet, Chicago Double JJ. Contbr. articles to Boca News, Bldg. Ofcl. mags., Nat. Acad. Code Adminstrn. Folio. Home: 4124 W 98th St Oak Lawn IL 60453

FALBO, RONALD JAMES, electric co. exec.; b. Joliet, Ill., Jan. 6, 1942; s. James Dominic and Harriet (Nurczyk) F.; student Joliet (Ill.) Jr. Coll., 1961-62. Mgr., Lee's Super Mart, Joliet, Ill., 1959-64; with Commonwealth Edison Co., 1968—, now office supr. Dresden Nuclear Power Sta., Morris, Ill. Served with U.S. Army, 1964-66. Home: Rural Route 4 Box 121 Cottage Rd Wilmington IL 60481 Office: Rural Route 1 Dresden Rd Morris IL 60450

FALCONE, ROBERT EDWARD, surgeon; b. Sulmona, Italy, Apr. 12, 1950; came to U.S., 1952, naturalized, 1968; s. Joseph and Sophie Falcone; B.A. in Chemistry cum laude, Kent (Ohio) State U., 1973; M.D. cum laude, Ohio State U., Columbus, 1976. Intern and resident in surgery Riverside Meth. Hosp., Columbus, 1976-81, now mem. staff; practice medicine specializing in gen. surgery, Columbus, 1981—; mem. staff Grant Hosp., St. Anne's Hosp.; clin. instr. surgery Ohio State U. Med. Sch. Mem. Am. Coll. Emergency Room Physicians, Sigma Xi, Alpha Omega Alpha. Author numerous papers in field. Home: 177 E Kossuth St Columbus OH 43206 Office: 3545 Olentangey River Rd Columbus OH 43214

FALES, WILLIAM HAROLD, vet. microbiologist, educator; b. Redding, Calif., Dec. 29, 1940; s. William Harold and Elizabeth Irene (MacKay) F.; A.A. in Med. Tech., Shasta Coll., 1961; B.A. in Microbiology, Calif. State U., San Jose, 1964; M.S. in Bacteriology, U. Idaho, Moscow, 1971, Ph.D., 1974; m. Susan J. Tucker, Dec. 28, 1963; children—Amanda Jean, Rebecca Sue. Grad. research asst. dept. bacteriology and biochemistry, Coll. Agr., U. Idaho, Moscow, 1969-74; research asso. dept. vet. microbiology, Coll. Vet. Medicine, U. Mo., Columbia, 1974-75, asso. prof., dept. vet. microbiology, clin. microbiologist Vet. Med. Diagnostic Lab. and Teaching Hosp., Coll. Vet. Medicine, 1975—, mem. U. Mo. grad. faculty, 1979, doctoral faculty, 1981; invited cons. nat. coms. Contagious Equine Metritis, U.S. Animal Health Assn., 1979; condr. research in field. Served to capt. Med. Services Corps, U.S. Army, 1966-69. Mem. AAAS, Am. Assn. Vet. Lab. Diagnosticians, Am. Soc. Microbiology, Conf. Research Workers in Animal Diseases, Am. Assn. Lab. Animal Sci., Am. Soc. Microbiology, Mo. West Central Vet. Med. Assn., Am. Acad. Microbiology, N.Y. Acad. Scis., U.S. Animal Health Assn., Sigma Xi (research award U. Idaho, 1973), Phi Zeta (hon.). Contbr. writings to profl. publs.; presenter profl. papers to confs. U.S., Switzerland; reviewer Am. Jour. Vet. Research, American Jour. Vet. Med. Assn. Office: Vet Med Diagnostic Lab Univ Mo Columbia MO 65211

FALK, MARSHALL ALLEN, physician; b. Chgo., May 23, 1929; s. Ben and Frances (Kamins) F.; B.S., Bradley U., 1950; M.S., U. Ill., 1952; M.D., Chgo. Med. Sch., 1956; m. Marilyn Levoff, June 15, 1952; children—Gayle Debra, Ben Scott. Intern, Cook County Hosp., Chgo., 1956-57; gen. practice medicine, Chgo., 1959-64, specializing in psychiatry, 1964—; mem. staff Edgewater Hosp., Chgo., St. Mary's of Nazareth Hosp.; prof., dep. chmn. psychiatry Chgo. Med. Sch.; dean Chgo. Med. Sch. U. Health Scis., 1974—, v.p., 1981—; mem. Ill. Hosp. Licensing Bd., 1981—; v.p. Ill. Council of Deans, 1979-81, pres., 1981—. Mem. adv. com. to Commr. of Health, City of Chgo. Served to capt. AUS, 1957-59. Recipient Alumnus of Year award Chgo. Med. Sch., 1976. Diplomate Am. Bd. Psychiatry, 1969. Fellow Chgo. Inst. Medicine, Am. Psychiat. Assn., Am. Coll. Psychiatrists; mem. AMA, Chgo., Ill. (contbn. to edn. Silver Award 1968, chmn. council mental health 1971-74) med. socs., Ill. Psychiat. Soc. Author articles on med. econs., research and psychiat. drugs. Home: 226 Kilpatrick St Wilmette IL 60091 Office: 3333 Greenbay Rd North Chicago IL 60064

FALLAH, ABRAHAM, physician; b. Kashan, Iran, Oct. 23, 1942; s. Ali Fard and Aliah Fallah; M.D., Tehran U. Med. Sch., Iran, 1967; m. Fatima Gilack, Sept. 12, 1966; children—Marc Alireza, Melissa Mariam. Intern, Nat. Iranian Oil Co. Hosp., Tehran, 1966, Tehran U. Hosp., 1966-67, Iranian Army Family Health Center, 1967-69, Northern Westchester Hosp., Mt. Kisco, N.Y., 1969-70; resident in internal medicine Grasslands Hosp., Westchester Med. Sch., 1970-71, Bklyn. Cumberland Med. Center, 1971-73, chief resident in internal medicine, 1972-73; fellow in gastroenterology Henry Ford Hosp., Detroit, 1973-75; cons. gastroenterology Ingalls Meml. Hosp., Harvey, Ill., 1975-81; staff internal medicine and gastroenterology St. Francis Hosp., Blue Island, Ill., 1975-81. Diplomate Am. Bd. Internal Medicine. Mem. AMA, Ill. State, Chgo. med. socs., Am. Coll. Physicians, Am. Soc. Gastroenter-intestinal Endoscopy. Home: 1704 Cambridge Flossmoor IL 60422 Office: 71 W 156th St Suite 203 Harvey IL 60426

FALLER, DOROTHY ANDERSON, social worker; b. Chgo., July 6, 1939; d. Albert T. and Lillian G. (Chalbeck) Anderson; student Ill. Wesleyan U., 1956-59; A.B., U. Ill., 1959-60; M.S.S.A., Case Western Res. U., 1975; m. Adolph Faller, Sept. 5, 1959; children—Carl, Kurt. Child welfare worker Klamath County Public Welfare Commn., Klamath Falls, Oreg., 1960-67; social services cons. Ind. State Dept. Public Welfare, 1968-72; adminstrv. asst. United Meth. Children's Home, Berea, Ohio, 1974; research asst. Case Western Res. U., Sch. Applied Social Scis., 1975; social services supr. Ohio Dept. Public Welfare, Cleve., 1975-81; exec. dir. Cleve. Internat. Program, 1981—; cons. to Cleve. Found., Am. Sickle Cell Anemia Found., John A. Yankey & Assos.; field instr. Case Western Res. U., 1976-77, lectr., 1981. Bd. dirs. West Shore Unitarian Ch., 1978-81. Mem. Am. Public Welfare Assn., Nat. Assn. Social Workers, Ohio Assn. for Gifted Children, Nat. Foster Parents Assn., Child Welfare League Am., Ohio Assn. Child Caring Agys., Case Western Res. U. Sch. Applied Social Scis. Alumni Assn. (v.p. Cleve. unit); Sigma Kappa (pres. 1959), Alpha Lambda Delta (pres. 1956). Unitarian. Editor, contbr. Ohio Children's Budget Project: A Public Policy Study, 1975. Home: 17703 Woodbury Ave Cleveland OH 44135 Office: 1001 Huron Rd Room 306 Cleveland OH 44115

FALLERIUS, HENRY ROWLAND, tech. coll. pres.; b. Mamaroneck, N.Y., Jan. 17, 1923; s. B.S., Ill. Inst. Tech., 1950; postgrad. Ohio State U., U. Minn., U. Mich.; LL.D. (hon.), Ashland (Ohio) Coll., 1979; m. Jane Caldwell, July 26, 1952. Indsl. engr. Ford Motor Co., Chgo., 1950-56; supr. indsl. engring., then mgr. quality control Mansfield Tire & Rubber Co. (Ohio), 1956-65; instr. indsl. engring. Mansfield Sch. Tech., 1965-68, dir., 1968-69; pres. North Central Tech. Coll., Mansfield, 1969—; mem. com. members Ohio Bd. Regents, 1969—. Chmn. adv. com. Mansfield Reformatory, 1972-73; chmn. Johnny Appleseed council White Eagle dist. Boy Scouts Am., 1976; sr. warden Grace Episcopal Ch., Mansfield, 1972; bd. dirs. Miss Mansfield Beauty Pagent, 1959. Served with AUS, 1942-45; ETO. Decorated Purple Heart. Mem. North Central Assn. Colls. and Schs., Ohio Orgn. Tech. Colls. (pres. 1975; Outstanding Pres. award 1975), Ohio Tech. and Community Coll. Assn., Ohio Vocat. Assn., Mansfield C. of C. Clubs: Rotary, Elks. Office: 2441 Kenwood Circle PO Box 698 Mansfield OH 44901

FALLEY, MARGARET DICKSON (MRS. GEORGE FREDERICK FALLEY), author, genealogist; b. Mpls., Nov. 8, 1898; d. George E. and Edith (Baker) Dickson; B.S., Northwestern U., 1920; m. George Frederick Falley, Mar. 10, 1921 (dec. 1962); children—Katharine (Mrs. Edward H. Bennett, Jr.), Margaret Jane (Mrs. Raymond M. Galt), Carol (Mrs. Warner G. Baird, Jr.), Priscilla (Mrs. Henry W. Apfelbach). Ann. lectr. to Am. Inst. Genealogy at Nat. Archives, Washington, 1955-60, Geneal. Inst. Samford U., Birmingham, Ala., 1967; participant Inst. Humanistic Studies, Aspen, Colo., 1967; geneal. lectr. state, tchr. hist. socs., clubs, orgns. Mem. exec. bd. library council Northwestern U., 1979—. Recipient Merit award Nat. Geneal. Soc., 1963; cert. of merit Nat. Library Ireland and Public Record Offices Dublin and Belfast, 1979. Fellow Am. Soc. Genealogists (v.p. 1962-63); mem. Harleian Soc. (London) (Am. rep. council), New Eng. Historic Geneal. Soc. (colonial mem.), mem. Northwestern U. Alumni Assn. (v.p. 1935-36), Northwestern U. Settlement Sr. Bd. (pres. 1945-46), Colonial Dames Am., DAR, Nat. Soc. Descs. Lords of Md. Manors, Daus. of Barons of Runnymeade, Kappa Kappa Gamma (Outstanding Alumnae award 1970). Methodist. Clubs: Union League (Chgo.); Glen View (Golf, Ill.); John Evans (founding mem.) (Northwestern U.). Author: Richard Falley and Some of His Descendants Including Grover Cleveland, 1952; Palmer Genealogy, Part I (English and Irish Ancestry of George Palmer), 1957; Irish and Scotch-Irish Ancestral Research, 2 vols., 1962; Baird-Green and Allied Families, Part II, 1976; contbr. articles to geneal. jours. Address: 1500 Sheridan Rd Wilmette IL 60091

FALLON, GERALD EDWARD, mfg. co. exec.; b. Cleve., July 30, 1944; s. Edward P. and Jean Y. Fallon; B.S. in Engring., U. Notre Dame, 1966; M.B.A., Case Western Res. U., 1972. Engr., NASA, Cleve., 1966-72; pres. Rujon, Cleve., 1972-73; gen. mgr. Taylor Freezor, Toronto, Ont., Can., 1973-74; mng. partner FKR Co., Cleve., 1974—; pres. Urban Industries, Galion, Ohio, 1976—; lectr. in field. Bd. dirs. Ohio Mobile Home Assn., 1977-78. Mem. Am. Orgn. Pilots Assn., ASME, AIAA. Roman Catholic. Clubs: LCYC Yacht, NASA Flying, Cleveland. Home: 12900 Lake Rd Lakewood OH 44107 Office: 19706 Center Ridge Rd Rocky River OH 44116

FALLON, MICHAEL PATRICK, elec. research and devel. found. exec.; b. Balt., Aug. 19, 1940; s. Eugene Lee and Cecily M. (Hill) F.; B.S., U. Md., 1968; M.S. in Mgmt. and Fin., DePaul U., 1972; M.B.A., U. Chgo., 1978; diploma engring. and applied sci. U. Wis., 1979; postgrad. Ill. Inst. Tech. Law Sch., 1980-81; m. Alvera Nastase, Oct. 3, 1958; children—Kevin, Tanya, Tara. Bus. research analyst Square D, 1968-72; cons. Turbine Engine div. Ford Motor Co., Dearborn, Mich., 1972-73; mgr. mktg. and planning Powers Regulator Co., Skokie, Ill., 1973-76; exec. dir. Elec. Industry Study Bd., Chgo., 1977—; dir. Consol. Industries. Commr. Park Ridge (Ill.) Mayor's Youth Council; pres. Park Ridge (Ill.) Sports Inc., 1970-74; pres., commr. Park Ridge Recreation and Park Dist., 1980-81. Cert. real estate appraiser and broker. Mem. Am. Mgmt. Assn., Assn. Energy Engrs., Am. Soc. Assn. Execs., Nat. Assn. Profl. Engrs., IEEE. Clubs: Plaza, International, Park Ridge Country. Contbr. articles to profl. jours. Home: 300 Talcott Pl Park Ridge IL 60068 Office: 1 E Wacker Dr Chicago IL 60601

FALLS, OSWALD BENJAMIN, JR., cons. engr.; b. Denison, Tex., Apr. 28, 1913; s. Oswald Benjamin and Glennie (Parker) F.; B.S., U. Richmond, 1934; B.S., MIT, 1936, M.S., 1937; LL.D., Spring Arbor Coll., 1976; m. Mary Elizabeth Laird, Dec. 19, 1936; children—Harriet Elizabeth (Mrs. W.H. Burnett), Margaret Parker (Mrs. R.J. DiBianco), Susan Laird (Mrs. Venard Fegley). Test engr. to mktg. mgr. Gen. Elec. Co., 1935-63; pres. Commonwealth Assos., Inc., Jackson, Mich., v.p., dir. Commonwealth Services, Inc., Jackson, v.p. Commonwealth Services Internat., Inc., 1963-70; v.p. Ralph M. Parsons Co., N.Y.C., 1970-71; with IAEA, Vienna, Austria, 1972-73; dir. Arabian Devel. Assos., 1963-70, Nat. Bank of Jackson. Pres., dir. Boy Scouts Am.; bd. dirs. Goodwill Industries, 1st Baptist Ch. of Jackson; v.p., bd. dirs. Mich. Bapt. Homes, Inc.; mayor city of Jackson, 1979-81. Recipient Engr. of Year award Mich. Soc. Profl. Engrs., 1976. Mem. IEEE, Am. Nuclear Soc., Sigma Pi Sigma, Omicron Delta Kappa, Sigma Alpha Epsilon, Tau Beta Pi. Republican. Clubs: Country, Town (Jackson). Contbr. articles to profl. jours. Home: 2107 Dale Rd Jackson MI 49203 Office: 728 W Michigan Ave Jackson MI 49201

FALVEY, EDWARD DANIEL, JR., hosp. system exec.; b. Detroit, Dec. 27, 1939; s. Edward Daniel and Marie Elizabeth (Taubitz) F.; B.A., U. Detroit, 1963; postgrad. U. Mich., 1964-69, Eastern Mich. U., 1964-65; M.H.A., U. Minn., 1981; m. Carolyn Elizabeth McKernan, Aug. 8, 1964; children—Michele, Jennifer, Daniel. Various positions Univ. Hosp., Ann Arbor, Mich., 1963-69; dir. personnel Pontiac (Mich.) Gen. Hosp., 1970-73, dir. patient care, 1974-76, asst. v.p. adminstrn., 1976-78; dir. personnel U. Colo., Denver, 1973-74; corp. dir. human resources Sisters of Mercy Health Corp., Farmington, Mich., 1978—; seminar leader U. Mich. Bur. Indls. Relations, 1967-70; adv. com. program in health services adminstrn. Mercy Coll. Detroit, 1978—. Served with N.G., 1963. HEW mid-career tng. prin. researcher grantee, 1980-81. Mem. Greater Detroit Area Hosp. Personnel Adminstrs. Assn. (pres. 1973-74). Roman Catholic. Club: Rochester Hills Racquet. Office: Sisters of Mercy Health Corp 28550 W Eleven Mile Rd Farmington Hills MI 48018

FAN, SEN, educator; b. Kiangsu, China, Aug. 17, 1927; s. Chin-Mon Fan and Fong Shih Fan; came to U.S., 1960, naturalized, 1970; B.S., Taiwan Normal U., 1954; M.S., U. Ill., 1961; postgrad. Brown U., 1965-66, U. Calif., Santa Barbara, 1968-71; m. Hsu Ying, Jan. 5, 1958; children—Paul, Grace, Robert. Instr. math. Chia-Kao High Sch., Taiwan, 1953-54, Cheng Kung U., Taiwan, 1954-58, Nanyang U., Singapore, 1958-60; asso. prof. math. Morningside Coll., Sioux City, Iowa, 1966-68; instr. math. U. Minn., Morris, 1961-64, asst. prof., 1964-66, 68-71, asso. prof., 1971—; coordinator, 1975—. NSF fellow, 1965-66, NSF grantee, U. Minn. grantee. Mem. Math. Assn. Am., W.

Central Council Tchrs. Math., Kappa Mu Epsilon, Pi Mu Epsilon. Office: U Minn Morris MN 56267

FANKHAUSER, LOUIS JAY, banker, ins. agt.; b. Humboldt, Nebr., Oct. 24, 1931; s. Daniel Arthur and Loretta Grace (Chandler) F.; B.M.E., U. Kans., 1958; M.S., Kans. State U., 1965; m. Janice Bee Meyer, Aug. 21, 1955; children—Gregory Lynn, Jamie Scott, Lisa Jann. Dir. music Onaga (Kans) High Sch., 1958-61, Humboldt (Nebr.) High Sch., 1961-66, Alma (Nebr.) High Sch., 1963-64, Bern (Kans.) High Sch., 1968-70, 71-72; cashier State Bank of Bern, 1966—; partner Fankhauser and Sheik, ins. agy., Bern, 1966—; chmn. bd. Bern Extrusion Inc., 1975—. Mem. Planning Commn. City of Bern, 1978—; mem. Republican com. Washington Twp., Nemaha County, Kans., 1968—. Served with USNR, 1951-55; Korea. Mem. Nemaha County Bankers Assn. (pres. 1967-68), Kans. Bankers Assn. (key banker Nemaha County 1977—), Profl. Ins. Agts. Kans., Kans. Real Estate Assn., Nebr. Real Estate Assn., Kans. Alumni Assn., Phi Delta Kappa. Methodist. Clubs: Lions (pres. charter club Bern 1972, permanent rec. sec. 1972—), Am. Legion, Masons, Shriners, K.T., Elks. Home: PO Box 36 Bern KS 66408 Office: PO Box 123 Bern KS 66408

FANNING, RONALD HEATH, architect, engr.; b. Evanston, Ill., Oct. 5, 1935; s. Ralph Richard and Leone Agatha (Heath) F.; B.Arch., Miami U., Oxford, Ohio, 1959; m. Jenine Vivian Schnelle, Jan. 9, 1960; children—Anthony Lee, Traycee Anne. Pres., Fanning/Howey Assos., Inc., Celina, Ohio, 1959—; partner Manning Partnership, Celina, 1978—; pres. Fanning Group, Inc., Celina, 1979—; sec.-treas. V.S.P. Securities, Inc., Mineral Endowment, Inc. County chmn. Young Republicans, 1969-71. Served with USMC, 1960-68. Registered architect, Ohio, Ind., Mich., Ky., N.Y., Fla., Ill., Ala., Nev., Mo., La.; cert. Nat. Council Archtl. Registration Bds.; registered profl. engr., Ohio, Ind. Mem. Architects Soc. Ohio, AIA, Ohio Soc. Profl. Engrs., Nat. Soc. Profl. Engrs., Soc. Mktg. Profl. Services. Republican. Methodist. Club: Elks. Home: 422 Magnolia St Celina OH 45822 Office: 540 E Market St Celina OH 45822

FANTZ, RAINETTE EDEN, clin. psychologist; b. Cleve., Dec. 13, 1922; d. Dimitri Dimiter and Anna (Asher) Dobreff; student Cleve. Inst. Art, 1941-43, Flora Stone Mather Coll., 1941-43; B.S. magna cum laude, Western Res. U., 1951, Ph.D., 1962; m. Robert L. Fantz, Nov. 2, 1960; 1 dau., Lorian. Comml. artist Bailey's, Cleve., 1943-48; free-lance artist, 1943-48; actress leading roles Repertory Theatre, Washington, 1952-53; cons. Cleve. Diabetes Assn., 1955; asst. psychologist Fairview Park (Ohio) Public Schs., 1956-57; asst. psychologist Highland View Hosp., Cleve., 1957-62; psychologist James R. Hodge, M.D., Akron, Ohio, 1958-63; pvt. practice clin. psychology, Cleve., 1962—; mem. faculty Gestalt Inst. of Cleve., 1968—, chmn. intensive postgrad. program, 1973—. Mem. Am. Psychol. Assn., Ohio Psychol. Assn., Cleve. Psychol. Assn., Am. Acad. Psychotherapists, Cleve. Acad. Cons. Psychologists (past pres.), Assn. for Advancement of Psychology, Cleve. Inst. Music, Cleve. Inst. Art, Cleve. Mus. Art, Supporters of Cleve. Orchestra, ACLU, Common Cause, Phi Beta Kappa. Contbr. chpts. to books; editor publs. in field. Home: 11 Mornington Ln Cleveland Heights OH 44106 Office: 1588 Hazel Dr Cleveland OH 44106

FARABAUGH, MARLYCE MARIE BIELAK, utility co. exec.; b. Gary, Ind., Oct. 21, 1953; d. John and Charlotte Claire (Petersen) Bielak; student Ind. U., 1971-73; certificate system design programming IBM, Chgo., 1973; m. Mitchell L. Farabaugh, Sept. 25, 1976; 1 son, Kevin Jonathan. Mgr. data processing Gary-Hobart Water Corp., Gary, Ind., 1973—. Vol. Lake Area United Way. Recipient Marian award Roman Cath. Ch., 1967. Mem. Am. Mgmt. Assn., System/3 Forum, Smithsonian Assos., N.W. Ind. Urban League (dir. 1979—), Nat./Internat. Wildlife Fedn. (asso.). Roman Catholic. Office: 650 Madison St Gary IN 46402

FARAH, CAESAR ELIE, educator; b. Portland, Oreg., Mar. 13, 1929; s. Sam Khalil and Lawrice F.; student Internat. Coll. Beirut, 1941-45; B.A., Stanford U., 1952; M.A., Princeton U., 1955, Ph.D., 1957; m. Marsha B. McDonald, June 5, 1977; children by previous marriage—Ronald, Christopher, Ramsey, Laurence, Raymond, Alexandra. Public affairs asst., cultural affairs officer ednl. exchanges USIS, New Delhi, 1957-58, Karachi, Pakistan, 1958; asst. to chief Bur. Cultural Affairs, Washington, 1959; asst. prof. history and Semitic Langs. Portland (Oreg.) State U. 1959-63; asst. prof. history Calif. State U., Los Angeles, 1963-64; asso. prof. Near Eastern studies Ind. U., Bloomington, 1964-69; prof. Middle Eastern and Islamic studies U. Minn., Mpls., 1969—; cons. U.S. Army, 1962-63; vis. prof. Harvard U., summers 1964, 65; guest lectr. Fgn. Ministry Spain, Iraq, Lebanon, Ministry Higher Edn., Saudi Arabia, Syrian Acad. Scis. resource person on Middle East, media and service groups Minn., 1977—. Mem. Oreg. Republican Com., 1960-64. Recipient cert. of merit Syrian Ministry Higher Edn.; Fulbright Hayes scholar, 1966-68; Am. Philos. Soc. fellow, 1970-71. Mem. Stanford U Alumni Assn. (leadership recognition award), Stanford Club Minn. (dir., pres. 1979), Am. Oriental Soc., Royal Asiatic Soc. Gt. Britain, Am. Hist. Assn., Middle East Studies Assn. N.Am., Am. Assn. Tchrs. Arabic (exec. bd.), Pi Sigma Alpha. Greek Orthodox. Club: Princeton. Author: The Addendum in Medieval Arabic Historiography, 1968; Islam: Beliefs and Observances, 2d ed., 1981; Eternal Message of Muhammad, 1965; Ta'rikh Baghdad li-Ibn al-Najjar, 2 vols., 1980; contbr. articles to profl. jours. Home: 3847 York Ave S Minneapolis MN 55410 Office: 160 Klaeber Ct U Minn Minneapolis MN 55455

FARGO, PAUL GENNARO, lawyer; b. Boston, July 20, 1927; s. Anthony Allen and Mary (Zajac) F.; B.S. in Bus. Adminstrn., Boston U., 1950, J.D., 1951; LL.M. in Labor Law, N.Y.U., 1952; LL.M. in Taxation, Northeastern U., 1953; m. Karen Peterson; children—Paul, Carolyn. Admitted to Mass. bar, 1952, Mo. bar, 1955, Ill. bar, 1956, Minn. bar, 1969, U.S. Supreme Ct. bar, 1979; asso. firm Avery, Dooley, Post & Avery, Boston, 1953-54, firm Reeder, Gisler, Griffin & Dvsart, Kansas City, Mo., 1954-55; atty. law dept. Montgomery Ward & Co., Chgo., 1955-56; atty. legal dept. Gen. Finance Corp., Evanston, Ill., 1956-58; asst. gen. counsel Central Standard Indemnity Co., Chgo., 1958-60; legis. atty. Alliance of Am. Insurers, 1960-65; practiced in Chgo., 1956-65; asst. dir. (staff) Am. Bar Assn., 1965-68; sec.-gen. counsel John Alden Life Ins. Co., Chgo., 1968-70; sr. atty., asst. sec. Nat. Homes Corp., Lafayette, Ind., 1970-73; asso. counsel, asst. sec. No. Am. Cos., 1975-80; pvt. practice law, 1973—. Recipient full tuition scholarships, Parshard Holding Corp., Cambridge, Mass., 1945-53. Mem. Mo. Integrated Bar Assn., Am. Ill., Chgo., Boston bar assns., Assn. Trial Lawyers Am., Boston U. Nat. Alumni Council. Methodist. Asso. editor The Forum. Home: 2740 Orchard Ln Wilmette IL 60091

FARHA, WILLIAM FARAH, food co. exec.; b. Lebanon, Nov. 27, 1908; s. Farah Farris and Nahima (Salamy) F.; grad. Indsl. Coll. Armed Forces, 1948, Brookings Inst., 1968; m. Victoria Barkett, Apr. 15, 1934; 1 son, William George. With F & E Wholesale Grocery Co., 1929-64; pres. River Bend Shopping Center, Wichita, William F. Farha & Son Enterprises. Chmn. Wichita Leadership Prayer Breakfast; invited to attend Presdl. Prayer Breakfast in Eisenhower, Kennedy, Johnson, Nixon and Ford adminstrns.; field adviser nat. bd. SBA, 14 years; former chmn. Wichita Police and Firemen Pension Plan. Past trustee Wichita Symphony Soc.; former mem. nat. bd. Inst. Logopedicts; mem. U.S. Congressional Adv. Bd.; former mem. bd. St. Joseph Research Hosp. Center; mem. bd. advisers Salvation Army; bd. dirs. NCCJ, Kans. Found. for Blind; trustee met. bd. YMCA, Antiochian Greek Orthodox Archdiocese of All N.Am.; mem. internat. bd. YMCA World Service; nat. bd. Am. Security Council; past mem. bd. govs. St. Jude Research Hosp., Memphis; mem. Rep. Nat. Com. Hon. col. State of Okla.; named to Wisdom Hall Fame, 1970; recipient Gold Medallion Antiochian Patriarch of Damascus, 1952; Antonian Gold medal of merit Antiochian Orthodox Christian Archdiocese N.Y. and all N.Am., 1972; Brotherhood award Kans. NCCJ, 1979. Mem. Wichita Ind. Bus. Men's Assn. (adv. bd.), Nat. Security Council (adv. bd.), Wichita C. of C. (past dir.). Rotarian. Club: Rolling Hills Country. Home: 8630 Shannon Way Wichita KS 67206 Office: 2220 Somerset Wichita KS 67204

FARION, DMYTRO, physician; b. Bohatkivci, Ukraine, Oct. 30, 1921; s. Stephen and Anna (Stochanska) F.; M.D., U. Munich, 1950; m. Maria Irena Cybyk, Apr. 24, 1949; children—George Zenon, Roma Maria, Anna Maria, Irene Maria, Marko Oleh. Came to U.S., 1951, naturalized, 1956. Intern St. Peter's Hosp., Bklyn., 1951-53; resident North Community Hosp., Glen Cove, N.Y., 1953-55; practice medicine specializing in gen. practice, Cleve., 1955—; mem. staff Deaconess Hosp., Cleve. Dir. Parma Savs. Co., 1964-67. Mem. St. Josaphat Sch. Bd., Parma 1971—. Mem. A.M.A., Ohio State Med. Soc., Cleve. Acad. Medicine, Cleve. Health Mus., Cleve. Mus. Natural History, Cleve. Med. Library Assn., Ukrainian Med. Assn. N. Am. Republican. Home: 6305 S Park Blvd Parma OH 44134 Office: 5604 Memphis Ave Cleveland OH 44144

FARIS, DON W., educator; b. Vinton, Iowa, Jan. 10, 1933; s. Donald A. and Nell J.F.; B.S., Iowa State U., 1957; postgrad. Carleton Coll., 1959, U. Mo., 1960-61; M.Ed., U. N.C., 1962; m. Kay Callyear Austin, Nov. 12, 1981; children—Terylle Leigh, Caroline, Aaron, Donald, Mary, Ann, John, David. Tchr., Hansell Consol. Sch., 1957, Northwood-Kensett High Sch., Northwood, Iowa, 1958-61; instr. East Carolina Coll., Greenville, N.C., 1962-64; sr. instr. sci. edn. Miami U., Middletown, Ohio, 1966—, coordinator edn. and fine arts, 1972—; tennis coach, 1976—. Bd. dirs. Middletown Area YMCA, 1975-77. Served with U.S. Army, 1958. Mem. Nat. Sci. Tchrs. Assn., Ohio Council Elem. Sch. Sci., Sch. Sci. and Math. Assn., Soc. Coll. Sci. Tchrs. Clubs: Wildwood Country, Middletown Tennis. Mem. editorial bd. Miami U. Sch. Edn. Rev. Home: 818 Clearfield Ln Cincinnati OH 45240 Office: 4200 E University Blvd Middletown OH 45042

FARKAS-CONN, IRENE SEKELY, cons.; b. Budapest, Hungary, 1928; came to U.S., 1947; d. George Sekely and Sidonia (Weiss) Schalk; A.B., Barnard Coll., Columbia U., 1947-48; M.A., Bryn Mawr Coll., 1949; M.A., U. Chgo., 1967; m. Arthur L. Conn, June 10, 1972; children by previous marriage—Andrew Martin Farkas, Elizabeth Pirie Farkas. Research asso. biochem. research Rockefeller U., N.Y.C., 1949-52, Case Western Res. U., Cleve., 1954-58, coordinator, project mgr. computerized med. info. retrieval projects, 1959-64; cons. info. resource mgmt., tech. transfer, office automation, 1964-78; coordinator planning/devel. Chgo. State U., 1970-75; v.p. Arthur L. Conn & Assos., Ltd., Chgo., 1978—; lectr. U.S. and abroad. Mem. U.S. Nat. Com., Internat. Fedn. Documentation, 1980—; U.S. rep. Info. for Industry Com., 1981—; mem. U.S. Nat. Com. for UNESCO Gen. Info. Programme and its Bur., 1980—. Mem. Am. Soc. Info. Sci. (bd. dirs. 1972-75, Watson Davis award 1977), Am. Inst. Chem. Engrs. (dir. mgmt. div. 1979-81). Contbr. articles to profl. jours. Address: 1469 E Park Pl Chicago IL 60637

FARLEY, DOROTHY BIEBER, art gallery dir.; b. St. Louis, May 27, 1927; d. Ralph Paul and Ida (Parker) Bieber; B.F.A. in Art Edn., U. Ill., 1949; m. Donald Gene Farley, June 16, 1951; children—Dale Ellen, Ronald Wesley. Secondary sch. art tchr., Ferguson, Mo., 1949-51; secondary art tchr. Normandy, Mo., 1955-57; art gallery dir. Craft Alliance, St. Louis, 1970—; exhbn. juror, lectr., cons., 1977—; treas. Craft Alliance, 1967-68; pres. Craft Alliance, 1968; enamel artist, 1955—. Community chmn. March of Dimes, Creve Coeur, Mo., 1963; mem. University City Loop Spl. Bus. Dist. Adv. Commn., 1981—; city clk. City of Crystal Lake Park (Mo.). Mem. Am. Crafts Council (sec. n. central region, 1973—), World Crafts Council, Advocates for the Arts, Craft Alliance Gallery (exhibiting mem.), Soc. N. Am. Goldsmiths, Surface Design Assn., Glass Art Soc., Enamel Guild West, Area Coordinating Council for Arts. Home: 2332 Putter Ln St Louis MO 63131 Office: 6640 Delmar Blvd University City MO 63130

FARLEY, FRANKLYN HOOVER, psychologist; b. Edmonton, Alta., Can.; B.A., U. Sask. (Can.), Saskatoon, 1960, M.A., 1963; Ph.D., U. London, 1966; m. Sonja, Sept. 21, 1963. Research asst. U. London, 1964-66; asst. prof. ednl. psychology U. Wis., Madison, 1966-69, asso. prof., 1969-73, prof., 1973—. Bd. dirs. Madison Urban League, 1976—; vice chmn. Madison Affirmative Action Commn., 1978-80. Fellow AAAS, Am. Psychol. Assn. (pres. div. ednl. psychology 1978-79), Brit. Psychol. Soc., Can. Psychol. Assn., Soc. Personality Assessment; mem. Am. Ednl. Research Assn. (pres. 1980-81), Wis. Ednl. Research Assn. (pres. 1977-79), Midwestern Ednl. Research Assn. (v.p. and pres.-elect 1980-81), Fedn. Behavioral Psychol. and Cognitive Scis. (sec.-treas. 1981-84). Contbr. numerous articles to profl. jours.; editor: (with N.J. Gordon) Psychology and Education—The State of the Union, 1981; (with J. Strelau and A. Gale) Biological Bases of Personality and Individual Differences, 1982; editor Ednl. Psychologist, 1972-78. Home: 4222 Yuma Dr Madison WI 53711 Office: U Wis 1025 W Johnson St Madison WI 53706

FARLEY, HELEN MARY, recreation park exec.; b. Chorlton, Nottinghamshire, Eng., lMay 11, 1927; came to U.S., 1949, naturalized, 1955; d. Peter James and Alison A. (Dean) Leighton; student Birmingham (Eng.) Children's Hosp., 1947-49; m. Don J. Farley, Apr. 12, 1977; children by previous marriage—Allison Nisbet, Matthew Nisbet, Margaret Nisbet, Elizabeth Nisbet. Nurse, Pasadena (Calif.) City Hosp., 1949-50; feature writer, columnist DeKalb (Ill.) Chronicle, 1967-69; free-lance artist, 1972-74; with Royal Realty, DeKalb, 1974-76; mgr. farm, Earlville, Ill., 1974-77; developer, founder Stone House Park Inc., Earlville, 1977, exec. dir., pres., 1977—. Mem. DeKalb County Bd. Family Service, 1956-67. Mem. DeKalb Real Estate Bd., PTA. Republican. Home and Office: RFD 3 Earlville IL 60518

FARLEY, LLOYD EDWARD, educator; b. Nebr. Sand Hills nr. Broken Bow, Nebr., June 20, 1915; s. Arthur L. and Effie (Tyson) F.; A.B., Kearney State Coll., 1945; M.A., Stanford, 1947, Ed.D., 1950; postgrad. U. Hawaii, U. Oreg., Princeton U. Tchr. elementary and secondary schs., also adminstr., 1937-41, 47-51; ednl. specialist U.S. Govt., Washington, Anchorage, Edwards, Calif., 1952-60; prof. edn. U. Alaska, Anchorage, 1960-64; Louis D. Beaumont Distinguished prof. edn., head div. social sci., Marshall faculty William Woods Coll., Fulton, Mo.; chmn. dept. edn. Westminster and William Woods Colls., Fulton, 1964-80, prof. edn. emeritus, 1980—; vis. prof. St. Cloud State U., summers 1968-72. Served to maj. AUS, 1941-46. Named Hon. Tchr. Korea; recipient Centennial medal William Woods Coll. Mem. Mo. Tchrs. Assn., Nat. Assn. Tchr. Educators, Internat. Council on Edn. for Teaching, Phi Delta Kappa, Kappa Delta Pi (hon. mem., named Outstanding Educator). Methodist. Kiwanian. Address: 12 Tucker Ln Fulton MO 65251

FARLEY, WILLIAM FRANCIS, corp. exec.; b. Pawtucket, R.I., Oct. 10, 1942; s. John F. and Barbara (McGarrity) F.; A.B., Bowdoin Coll., 1964; J.D., Boston Coll., 1969; postgrad. N.Y. U., 1969-72; m. Jacqueline Merrill, Sept. 30, 1978; children—Natalie, Ned. Sales mgr. Crowell Collier & MacMillan, 1966-69; admitted to Mass. bar, 1969; regional mgr., dir. mergers and acquisitions NL Industries, N.Y.C., 1969-73; head corp. fin. dept. Lehman Bros., Inc., Chgo., 1973-78; chmn. bd. Farley Industries, Chgo., 1977—. Bd. dirs. Goodman Theatre; bd. overseers Bowdoin Coll. Mem. Am. Bar Assn., Mass. Bar Assn. Clubs: Chgo., Saddle and Cycle, Met., Chgo. Bowdoin, Kennebunk River, Ill. Athletic. Office: 233 S Wacker Dr Chicago IL 60606

FARMAKIS, GEORGE LEONARD, educator; b. Clarksburg, W.Va., June 30, 1925; s. Michael and Pipitsa (Roussopoulos) F.; B.A., Wayne State U., Detroit, 1949, M.S.Ed., 1950, M.A., 1966, Ph.D., 1971; M.A., U. Mich., 1978; postgrad. Columbia U., Yale U., Queens Coll. Tchr., audio-visual aids dir. Roseville (Mich.) Public Schs., 1957-61; tchr. Highland Park (Mich.) Public Schs., 1961-70, resource specialist, 1971—; instr. Highland Park Community Coll., 1966-68, Wayne County Community Coll., 1969-70; founder Ford Sch. Math. High Intensity Tutoring Program, 1971; chairperson Highland Park Sch. Dist. Curriculum Council and Profl. Staff Devel. Governing Bd., 1979—; participant ESEA Title I/Nat. Diffusion Network. Served to cpl., USNG, 1948-51. Recipient spl. commendation Office of Edn., 1978. Mem. Mich. Assn. Supervision and Curriculum Devel., Am. Hist. Assn., Nat. Council Social Studies, Acad. Polit. Sci., Am. Philol. Assn., Assn. Supervision and Curriculum Devel., Internat. Reading Assn., U. Mich. Alumni Assn., Wayne State U. Alumni Assn., Internat. Platform Assn., Modern Greek Studies Assn., Nat. Assn. Adminstrs. State and Fed. Edn. Programs, Mich. Assn. Adminstrs. State and Fed. Edn. Programs Specialists, Mich. Reading Assn., Mich. Tchrs. Math., Phi Delta Kappa. Greek Orthodox. Contbr. to New Voices in American Poetry, 8th and 9th eds. Home: 752 Trombley Rd Grosse Pointe Park MI 48230 Office: 20 Bartlett St Highland Park MI 48230

FARMANN, KATHLEEN ELIZABETH, law librarian; b. Addison, N.Y., Aug. 21, 1920; d. Michael Francis and Elizabeth Lee (McClintock) Godfrey; A.B., Trinity Coll., Washington, 1941; J.D., Cath. U., 1945; M.L.L., U. Wash., Seattle, 1957; m. Stanley L. Farmann, June 14, 1958. Admitted to D.C. bar, 1945; asso. firm Covington & Burling, 1945-53; asst. law librarian Ohio State U., 1957-61, asst. dir. research services, 1962-66; law librarian Hawaii Supreme Ct., 1961-62; law librarian U. Notre Dame, 1966—, asst. to dean Law Sch., 1975-77. Exchange student Dept. of State, 1942. Mem. Bar Assn. D.C., Ohio Regional Assn. Law Libraries (past pres.), Am. Assn. Law Libraries. Democrat. Roman Catholic. Home: 19053 Summers Dr South Bend IN 46637 Office: Box 535 Notre Dame IN 46556

FARMER, DAVID JAMES, ops. research analyst; b. Denver, Oct. 2, 1936; s. James Lenard and Clara Agnes (Wellman) F.; B.S. in Physics, Colo. State U., 1960; postgrad. U. Ala., 1966-70; m. Patty Lou Lightsey, Dec. 25, 1960; children—David Stanley, Matthew Jay, Ruth Renee. Physicist, operations research analyst U.S. Army Missile Command, Huntsville, Ala., 1963-72; supervisory operations research analyst U.S. Army Combined Arms Study and Analysis Agy., Ft. Leavenworth, Kans., 1972—. Served with AUS, 1960-63. Decorated Army Commendation Medal. Mem. Am. Phys. Soc., Assn. U.S. Army, Colo. State U. Alumni Found., Full Gospel Bus. Men's Assn. Internat. Republican. Mem. Disciples of Christ Ch. Home: Route 4 Box 358 Leavenworth KS 66048 Office: CACDA ATCA CAT Fort Leavenworth KS 66027

FARNER, ROBERT LEWIS, physician; b. Streator, Ill., Feb. 4, 1930; s. Lewis Frederick and Marie (Vallazza) F.; student Wartburg Coll., 1948-51; M.D., U. Ill., 1955; m. Kathleen A. Murray, Apr. 6, 1958; children—Robert M., David L., Charles B. Intern Ill. Central Hosp., Chgo., 1955-56; practice medicine, specializing in family medicine, Toluca, Ill., 1958—; mem. staff St. Mary's Hosp., Streator, Ill. Served with USAAF, 1956-58. Fellow Am. Acad. Family Physicians (charter); mem. A.M.A., Ill. Med. Soc., Engle Lane Theatre, Smithsonian Instn., Nat. Hist. Soc., Alpha Kappa Kappa. Lutheran. Home: 403 W Santa Fe Ave Toluca IL 61369 Office: 204 E Santa Fe Ave Toluca IL 61369

FARNHAM, HARRY JUD, lawyer; b. Lincoln, Nebr., Sept. 20, 1925; s. Harry C. and Grace M. (Binfield) F.; LL.D., U. Colo., 1949; m. Sally Link, June 10, 1946; children—Jeff, Dan, Amy. Admitted to Nebr. bar, 1949, since practiced in Omaha and Elkhorn, Nebr. Mem. Nebr. State Racing Commn., 1961—, chmn., 1963—; pres. Nat. Assn. State Racing Commrs., 1969. Mem. legacy com. Morris Animal Found. Served with USMCR, 1943-45. Recipient Racing Man of Year award Jockeys' Guild, 1970; Distinguished Service award Am. Horse Council, 1972; Man of Year award Horseman's Benevolent Protective Assn., 1970; named to Nebr. Racing Hall of Fame, 1971, Gt. Plains Amateur Boxing Assn. Hall of Fame, 1975. Fellow Am. Acad. Matrimonial Lawyers; mem. Am., Nebr., Omaha bar assns. Democrat. Mason (33 deg.). Home: Rural Route 2 Elkhorn NE 68022 Office: 105 Hillrise Center Elkhorn NE 68022

FARQUHAR, ROBERT NICHOLS, lawyer; b. Dayton, Ohio, Apr. 23, 1936; s. Robert Lawrence and Mary Frances (Nichols) F.; A.B., Kenyon Coll., 1958; J.D., Cornell, 1961; m. Elizabeth Lynn Bryan, Aug. 29, 1959 (div. 1971); children—Robert Nichols, Laura Ann; m. 2d, Carol A. Smith, Dec. 27, 1975. Admitted to Ohio bar, 1961, U.S. Dist. Ct., 1962, U.S. Ct. Appeals, 1966, U.S. Supreme Ct. bar, 1978; asso. Altick & McDaniel, Dayton, 1961-69; partner firm Gould, Bailey & Farquhar, and predecessor firms, Dayton, 1969-78, Brumbaugh, Corwin & Gould, Dayton, 1978-80, Altick & Corwin, 1981—; dir. ACB Am., Inc., Dayton. City atty., Centerville, Ohio, 1969—. Mem. Montgomery County Rep. Central Com., 1965-69, Exec. Com., 1968-69. Bd. dirs. Centerville Hist. Soc., 1971-75, pres., 1973-74; trustee Montgomery County Legal Aid Soc., 1972-76; trustee Dayton Law Library Assn., 1972—, sec., 1975—; mem. congressional screening com. U.S. Naval Acad., 1979—. Mem. Am., Ohio, Dayton (sec., exec. com. 1975-76) bar assns., Delta Phi, Phi Delta Phi. Episcopalian. Clubs: Dayton Bicycle, Dayton Lawyers. Home: 32 Williamsburg Ln Centerville OH 45459 Office: 1300 Talbott Tower Dayton OH 45402

FARRAGHER, WILLIAM EDGAR, marketing cons.; b. Youngstown, Ohio, July 22, 1922; s. William Edgar and Jessie Alice (Selby) F.; A.B., Ohio Wesleyan U., 1949; postgrad. Kenyon Coll., U. Wis.; m. Arden Louise Smith, Dec. 29, 1951; children—Kelly Ann Paros, Allison Selby Gray, Mark Douglas, Kate Louise (dec.); 1 foster son, Robert Schellenbarger. Copywriter, Arthur Towell Advt. Agy., Madison, Wis., 1950-51; asst. advt. mgr. Magnecord, Inc., Chgo., 1951-52; copywriter Howard Swink Advt. Agy., Marion, Ohio, 1952-53; plant mgr. Instantwhip, Inc., Columbus, Ohio, 1953-54; account exec. Robert Joyce Advt. Agy., Youngstown, 1954-55; pres. Tower Asso., advt. agy., Youngstown, 1955-57; dir. advt. Youngstown Sheet & Tube Co. div. Lykes Corp., 1957-69; exec. v.p.

Thomas/Farragher Asso., advt. agy., Youngstown, 1969-71; pres. Farragher Mktg. Services, Canfield, Ohio, 1971—; mng. dir. Bradford Inst., Canfield, 1973—; ltd. duty instr. Youngstown State U., 1956—; chmn. bd. trustees Center for Mktg. Communications, Princeton, N.J., 1968-69. Lic. lay reader Episcopal Ch., Ohio Diocese; mem. vestry St. John's Episc. Ch., Youngstown; mem. bishop's council Ohio Diocese, 1970-71. Served with M.C., U.S. Army, 1942-46. Cert. bus. communicator. Mem. Public Relations Soc. Am. (accredited), Am. Mktg. Assn., Bus.-Profl. Advt. Assn., Ohio Wesleyan U. Alumni Assn. (pres. 1980-81, dir. 1975—). Home: 275 Bradford Dr Canfield OH 44406 Office: PO Box 39 Old Courthouse Bldg 7 Court St Canfield OH 44406

FARRAN, DON WILSON, author; b. Rowan, Iowa, Mar. 24, 1902; s. John Simon and Charlotte (Duncan) F.; student U. Iowa, 1922-1923, Dartmouth Coll., 1942-43. Editor, Fed. Writers Project, Des Moines, 1937; state dir. Fed. Hist. Survey, Des Moines, 1937-38; regional dir. Fed. Theatre Service Bur., Chgo., 1938-39; nat. editor Fed. Am. Imprints Inventory, Chgo. and Washington, 1940-41, nat. dir., 1941-42; asst. nat. dir. Hist. Records Survey, 1941-42; commd. lt. U.S. Navy, 1942, advanced through grades to comdr., 1953; writer/dir./producer films U.S. Navy, head worldwide motion picture prodn. Coast Guard, 1958-64; ret., 1964; author books: (with MaMurtrie) Wings for Words, 1940; Ballad of the Silver Ring, 1935; author plays: (with others) Off The Record, 1939; Broadway D., 1940; Pie in the Sky, 1939, Dirt; biographer of actor Richard Bennett, 1936; screenwriter 140 motion pictures for USN, USCG, State Dept., White House, 1942-64; writer screenplay The Seventh Fleet, 1956; contbr. numerous short stories, articles, poems to nat. mags.; cons. Iowa Bicentennial, 1976. Decorated Gen. Alfaro gold medal (Ecuador); recipient awards, including: First prize Liberty Mag. Short Story Contest, 1933, award Edinburgh Film Festival, 1959, Am. Film Festival, 1959, 1960, 1961, 1962, 1963, 1964. Fellow Internat. Soc. Biographers, Internat. Acad. Poets (Eng.); mem. Gypsey Lore Soc. Gt. Britain, Calif. Writers Club, Iowa Authors Club (pres. 1933, 1934), Screenwriters Guild Am., Am. Poetry Soc. (v.p. 1928-29). Home: Rowan IA 50470

FARREHI, CYRUS, cardiologist; b. Malayer, Iran, Jan. 26, 1935; s. Mansoor and Nikzad (Agah) F.; M.D., U. Tehran, 1958; m. Z. Jane Christensen, June 6, 1964; children—Peter M., Paul C., Lisa N., Mary M. Rotating intern Wayne County Gen. Hosp., Eloise, Mich., 1959-60, med. resident, 1960-62; cardiology fellow U. Oreg. Med. Sch., Portland, 1962-64; teaching fellow dept. medicine U. Alta. Med. Sch., 1964-66; asst. prof. medicine U. Oreg. Med. Sch. also dir. cardiac catheterization lab. VA Hosp., Portland, 1966-69; cons. in cardiovascular diseases, Flint, Mich., 1969—; chmn. dept. medicine McLaren Gen. Hosp., Flint, 1971-73, dir. cardiovascular diagnostic service, 1973—; sec., dir. Ind. Practice Assos., Flint, 1979—; clin. asso. prof. medicine Mich. State U., 1973-78, clin. prof., 1978—; adj. prof. health care and human services U. Mich., Flint, 1981. Diplomate Am. Bd. Internal Medicine, Am. Bd. Cardiovascular Diseases. Fellow A.C.P., Royal Coll. Physicians and Surgeons Can., Am. Coll. Cardiology, Clin. Council Am. Heart Assn.; mem. Detroit Heart Club, Genesee County Med. Soc. (dir. 1980—). Roman Catholic. Contbr. articles to med. jours. Home: 8398 Old Plank Rd Grand Blanc MI 48439 Office: 1071 N Ballenger Hwy Flint MI 48504

FARRELL, DAVID C., retail exec.; b. 1933; grad. Antioch Coll., 1956. Pres., Kaufmann's, 1966-75; pres., chief operating officer May Dept. Stores, St. Louis, 1975-79, pres., chief exec. officer, 1979—, also dir. Office: May Dept Stores 611 Olive St Saint Louis MO 63101*

FARRELL, EDWARD WAGNER, dentist, dental educator; b. Youngstown, Ohio, Jan. 12, 1921; s. John Edward and Florence Mary (Wagner) F.; B.S., Muskingum Coll., 1943; D.D.S., Western Res. U., 1946; M.S., U. Mich., 1952; M.P.H., U. N.C., 1964; m. Marilyn Mae Quailey, June 7, 1947; children—Sandra Lynn, Scott Lee, Susan Jane, Sherry Lee. Dentist, VA Ohio, 1948-50; pvt. practice dentistry, Youngstown, Ohio, 1952-62; dental cons. Ohio Dept. Health, Cuyahoga Falls and Bowling Green, 1962-65; dental dir. Ariz. Dept. Health, Phoenix, 1965-69, Fla. Dept. Health, Jacksonville, 1969-75; dir. dental aux. edn. Ind. U. Sch. Dentistry, N.W. Campus, Gary, 1975—. Served with U.S. Army, 1943-45, USN, 1946-48. Mem. Am. Dental Assn., Am. Assn. Public Health Dentists, Am. Public Health Assn., Am. Assn. Dental Schs., Ind. Dental Assn., N.W. Ind. Dental Soc., Chgo. Dental Soc., Delta Sigma Delta, Southlake Dental Study Club. Republican. Club: Rotary (Gary, Ind.). Author: Dental Materials Lecture/Study Guide, 1981; Oral Pathology Lecture/Study Guide, 1981; contbr. articles in field to profl. jours. Home: 907 Seneca Dr Crown Point IN 46307 Office: 3223 Broadway Gary IN 46409

FARRELL, ESTON CHRISTIS, JR., biochemist; b. Washington, July 18, 1938; s. Eston Christis and Gertrude (Smith) F.; B.A., Eastern Nazarene Coll., 1961; M.S., Ohio State U., 1968, Ph.D., 1971; m. Judith Kinsey, Sept. 2, 1961; children—Kathryn, Andrew, Sarah, Margaret. Dir. labs. Ethel Lucas Hosp., Acornhoek, East Transvaal, S. Africa, 1971-72; dir. toxicology and endocrinology analysis Clin-Chem. Labs., Boston, 1972-74; biochemist Ohio Valley Hosp., Steubenville, Ohio, 1974—. Bd. dirs. Christian Family Life, Akron Dist. Assembly, Ch. of Nazarene. NIH trainee clin. chemistry, 1968-71. Mem. Am. Assn. Clin. Chemistry (chmn. continuing edn. Ohio Valley sect. 1976—), Am. Assn. for Solar Energy, Energy Conservation Found. Republican. Author: Histochemistry of Creatine Phosphokinase, Vol. 3 of Electron Microscopy of Enzymes, 1974. Home: 16901 McIntosh Rd Wellsville OH 43968 Office: Ohio Valley Hosp 380 Summit Ave Steubenville OH 43952

FARRELL, JAMES SANFORD, cons., mfrs. rep.; b. Chgo., July 4, 1915; s. Francis John and Julia (Mayer) F.; grad. Campion Prep. Sch., 1932-35; student U. Cin., 1935-36, Xavier U., 1936-37; m. Eileen Joan Stuhlreyer, June 7, 1938; children—Eileen Joan, Patricia Ann, James Sanford, Frances Marie. With Internat. Harvester Co., Milw., 1937-40; sales, marketing, store mgmt. S.D. Warren Co., Boston, 1940-41, asst. sales mgr. Diem & Wing Paper Co., Cin., 1941-46; asst. sales mgr. Pioneer Pub. Co., Chgo., 1946-49; v.p. sales and mktg. Western Pub. Co., Racine, Wis., 1949-66; v.p., dir. Artists & Writers Press Inc., 1954-66, Guild Press Inc., 1954-66 (both N.Y.C.); pres., dir. RCS Press, Chgo., 1966-68; pres. Sanford Assos. Inc., Lake Forest, Ill., 1970—; pres., dir. Dean Hicks Co., Grand Rapids, Mich. Served to lt. USNR, 1942-45. Mem. Ohio Soc. of N.Y. Clubs: Knollwood (Lake Forest, Ill.); Cornell (N.Y.C.); Mchts. and Mfrs. (Chgo.); Pinehurst (N.C.) Country. Home: 771 McKinley Ave Lake Forest IL 60045 also 816 Lake Forest Dr Pinehurst NC 23874 Office: 222 Wisconsin Ave Lake Forest IL 60045

FARRELL, LAWRENCE MICHAEL, actuarial cons. co. exec.; b. St. Louis, Aug. 25, 1944; s. Lawrence Michael and Catherine Isabelle (Hughes) F.; B.A., St. Louis U., 1965, postgrad. Law Sch., 1965-67; m. Jane M. Bronson, Nov. 19, 1966; children—Lawrence M., Maura E., Andrew B. Actuarial student Gen. Am. Life Ins. Co., St. Louis, 1966-68, underwriter, 1968-69, regional pension supr., 1969-71; v.p. pension div. Pension & Group Services, Inc., Kalamazoo, 1971-77, exec. v.p., 1977—. Active various fund raising activities. Mem. Am. Acad. Actuaries, Am. Soc. Pension Actuaries. Democrat. Roman Catholic. Clubs: K.C., Kalamazoo Country. Home: 5037 Stonehenge St Portage MI 49081 Office: 308 Michigan Bldg Kalamazoo MI 49007

FARRER, CLAIRE ANNE RAFFERTY, anthropologist, educator; b. N.Y.C., Dec. 26, 1936; d. Francis Michael and Clara Anna (Guerra) Rafferty; B.A. in Anthropology, U. Calif., Berkeley, 1970; M.A. in Anthropology, U. Tex., Austin, 1974, Ph.D. in Anthropology, 1977; 1 dau., Suzanne Claire. Various positions, 1953-73; fellow Whitney M. Young, Jr. Meml. Found., N.Y.C., 1974-75; arts specialist, grant adminstr. Nat. Endowment for Arts, Washington, 1976-77; Weatherhead resident fellow Sch. Am. Research, Santa Fe, 1977-78; asst. prof. anthropology U. Ill., Urbana, 1978—; cons. in field, 1974—; mem. film and video adv. panel Ill. Arts Council; mem. Ill. Humanities Council, 1980—. Active various civic orgns. Recipient 8 awards, fellowships and grants. Fellow Am. Anthrop. Assn., Soc. for Applied Anthropology, Assn. for Anthrop. Study of Play; mem. Am. Ethnol. Soc., Am. Folklore Soc., Am. Soc. for Ethnohistory. Quaker. Co-founder, co-editor Folklore Women's Communication, 1972—; editor spl. issue Jour. Am. Folklore, 1975; editor: Women and Folklore, 1976; co-editor: Forms of Play of Native North Americans, 1979. Office: 109 Davenport Hall 607 S Mathews U Ill Urbana IL 61801

FARRIS, JAMES RUSSELL, geologist; b. Ft. Worth, Tex., Apr. 23, 1937; s. Maldon Floyd and Mary Helen (Anderson) F.; student Baylor U., 1955-57, M.A., 1965; student Am. Inst. Banking, Los Angeles, 1957, Hardin Simmons U., B.A., 1963; postgrad. Mesa Coll., 1973-75, Ohio U., 1976-79; m. Mava Janeece Johnston, Aug. 3, 1962; children—Gwendolyn Camille, Elizabeth Renee, Allison Nicole. Chief geologist First Worth Corp., Denton, Tex., 1965-69; sr. petrologist, mgr. mineralogy petrology lab. Lucius Pitkin Inc., Grand Junction, Colo., 1969-73; pres. Ventucross Corp., Grand Junction, 1973-74, also dir.; regional staff geologist Coastal States Energy Corp., Houston, 1974-75; chief geologist, mgr. logging div. Mineral Service Co., Grand Junction, 1975-76; sr. geologist Am. Electric Power Corp., Lancaster, Ohio, 1976-79; pres., chmn. bd., dir. Ventio Co., 1979—; dir. Crystal Minerals Corp., 1979—. Active Boy Scouts Am., Abilene, Tex., 1960-63, Waco, Tex., 1963-64, Grand Junction, Colo., 1970-72; advisor 4H, Athens, Ohio, 1978-80. Recipient Abilene Geol. Soc. award, Most Outstanding Geology Student, 1961-62, 62-63. Mem. Am. Mgmt. Assn., Internat. Platford Assn., Am. Geol. Inst., Soc. Petrol. Engrs. and Soc. Mining Engrs. of Am. Inst. Mining Engrs., Soc. Advancement Mgmt., The Clay Minerals Soc., ASTM, Mineral. Soc. Am., N. Am. Thermal Analysis Soc., The Coblentz Soc., Colo. Mining Assn., Houston Geol. Soc., Ariz. Small Mine Operators Assn., AAUP, Internat. Assn. Study of Clays Geol. Soc. of Am., Soc. Eco Paleo & Min. Baptist. Club: Mason. Home: Route 6 Box 45 Athens OH 45701 Office: PO Box 2817 Abilene TX 79604

FARSTAD, ELMER KARLEIF, real estate cons., appraiser; b. Trondheim, Norway; Nov. 22, 1921; s. Johan Magnus and Anne Elise (Pedersen) F.; came to Can., 1925, naturalized, 1937; diploma Dominion Bus. Coll., 1940; m. Muriel Kathleen Dracass, Nov. 6, 1948; children—Corinne Savoie, Brenda Hillman, Karla. Mem. staff Farstad Cabinet Shop, Winnipeg, Man., 1946-47; Aronovitch & Leipsic Ltd., Winnipeg, 1947-49, Oldfield Kirby & Gardner Ltd., Winnipeg, 1950-55, L.A. MacDonald Ltd. Winnipeg, 1956, Royal Trust Co., Winnipeg, 1957-62; prin. E. Karl Farstad & Assos. Ltd., Winnipeg, 1962—; lectr. in field. Served with Royal Norwegian Air Force, 1942-45. Mem. Winnipeg Real Estate Bd., Appraisal Inst. Can., Am. Inst. Real Estate Appraisers, Winnipeg C. of C., Viking Club Winnipeg (pres. 1972-73). Mason. Club: Niakwa Country. Home: 98 Duluth Bay Winnipeg MB R2J 1W5 Canada Office: 506 211 Portage Ave Winnipeg MB R3B 2A2 Canada

FARY, JOHN G., Congressman; b. Chgo., Apr. 11, 1911; student Real Estate Sch. Ill., Loyola U., Midwest Inst.; m. Lillian Makowski, 1934; children—James, Mary Ann. Mem. Ill. Gen. Assembly, 1955-75; mem. 94th-97th congresses from 5th Ill. Dist. Mem. Polish Nat. Alliance, Polish Roman Catholic Union, Chgo. C. of C. Clubs: Moose, Eagles, Kiwanis, Lions, K.C. Office: Room 1121 Longworth House Office Bldg Washington DC 20515

FASCIA, REMO MARIO, aero. engr.; b. Buenos Aires, Argentina, Oct. 5, 1922; came to U.S., 1956, naturalized, 1963; s. Remo Raul and Maria Juana (Dematteis) F.; B.S. in Elec. Engring., Otto Krause Indsl. Sch., Argentina, 1941, M.S. in Aero. Engring., U. La Plata (Argentina), 1948; m. Olive G. Parsons, July 24, 1960. Quality control engr. Defense Dept., Argentina, 1942-48, flight test engr. Argentina Air Force, 1949-54; prof. aerodynamics and aircraft structures Air Force Inst., Buenos Aires, 1950-53; chief procurement testing engr. Techint-Dalmine, Argentina, 1955-56; sr. design engr. Convair, San Diego, 1956-60; asst. project engr. Ford Motor Co., Buenos Aires, 1960; structural engr. Lockheed Aircraft Corp., Burbank, Calif., 1960; sr. structural engr. Norair Aircraft div. Northrop Co., Hawthorne, Calif., 1961-62, sect. chief engr., 1966-70; sr. design engr. N.Am. Aviation, Downey, Calif., 1962-63; scientist specialist Douglas Aircraft Corp., Long Beach, Calif., 1963-66; configuration synthesis engr. specialist McDonnell Douglas Co., St. Louis, 1970—; dir. Fascia Aero Consultants, 1965—; mgr. S.Am. Mktg. Consultants, 1970—; partner Profl. Profile, Leadership and Creativity Evaluation Services, 1975—; guest lectr. assessment of profl. creativity versus graphoanalysis, 1975-80. Hon. rep. of mayor City of St. Louis, 1975—; treas. Mo. McCarthy for Pres. Campaign, 1976. Mem. AIAA, Internat. Graphoanalysis Soc., Soc. Aero. Weight Engrs., St. Louis Council of World Affairs. Roman Catholic. Clubs: St. Louis Ambassadors, Gaslight, Marriot Swim and Tennis. Address: One Alden Ln Creve Coeur MO 63141

FASONE, SALVATORE ANTHONY, agri-business co. exec.; b. Kansas City, Mo., Jan. 16, 1940; s. Anthony Frank and Mary Ann (Tumino) F.; B.M.E., Mo. Sch. Mines and Metallurgy, 1961; m. Josephine Lucille Sallee, Feb. 11, 1961; children—Anthony, Jean Marie, Mary Beth. Instrumentation engr. Boeing Co., Aerospace div., Seattle, 1961, machine design engr., Wichita, Kans., 1962; process engr. Remington Arms Co., Lake City Arsenal, Mo., 1962-63, ballistics engr., 1963-64; mech. engr. engine testing Farmland Industries, North Kansas City, Mo., 1964-65, mgr. petroleum testing lab., 1966-72, mgr. fuels and lubricants research, 1972—, dir. petroleum research, 1978—. Mem. Coordinating Research Council, 1966—. Mem. Soc. Automotive Engrs. (chmn. Kansas City sect. 1975, regional adviser 1977-78), ASTM, Am. Petroleum Inst. Roman Catholic. Clubs: Am. Sons of Columbus, Civic Italian-Am. Orgn. Home: 404 N Gladstone Blvd Kansas City MO 64123 Office: Farmland Industries Research Center 103 W 26th Ave North Kansas City MO 64116

FASSINGER, CHARLES RICHARD, mgmt. cons.; b. Cleve., Aug. 4, 1930; s. Charles Rudolph and Elfaieda (Winkler) F.; diploma indsl. electronics Fenn Coll. Tech. Inst., 1954; m. Janet Marie Duffett, Dec. 22, 1951; children—Susan Marie, Jill Carol, Glen Edward. Vice pres., plant mgr. Universal Welder Co., Cleve., 1948-57; asst. chief engr. Avto Arc Weld Mfg. Co., 1957-60; v.p. Scott Tarrell Inc., Cleve., 1960-71; mgr. systems div., 1971-72; mktg. mgr. Cecil Equipment Co., Medina, Ohio, 1972-74; mgmt. cons., Cleve., 1974-75; pres. Techniweld Inc., Cleve., 1975—. Bd. dirs., pres. YMCA, 1972—; trustee, pres. North Hills Water Dist., 1974—; trustee, pres. Willow Lake Homeowners Corp., 1975-78. Served with AUS, 1951-54. Decorated Bronze Star. Mem. Am. Welding Soc. (dir., chmn. 1964-72), Aircraft Owners and Pilots Assn., Assn. U.S. Army. Club: Rotary. Home: 8402 Edge Lake Oval Sagamore Hills OH 44067 Office: 6001 Breakwater Ave Cleveland OH 44102

FASSLER, CRYSTAL G., advt. agy. exec.; b. Marion, Ohio, Mar. 15, 1942; d. Lloyd C. and Iola M. (Runkle) Mahaffey; student public schs., Prospect, Ohio; m. Donald D. Fassler, May 6, 1960; 1 son, Curtis A. Media buyer H. Swink Advt., Marion, 1968-73; media buyer and planner Tracey Locke Advt., Columbus, Ohio, 1973-74, Lord, Sullivan & Yoder Advt., Marion, 1974—. Home: 1846 Smeltzer Rd Marion OH 43302 Office: 196 S Main St Marion OH 43302

FAST, LARRY EDWARD, wire and cable co. exec.; b. Winchester, Ind., June 9, 1947; s. Clarence Edward and Marjorie Ruth (Alexander) F.; B.S., Ind. U., 1969; m. Cathy Lou Skinner, Aug. 29, 1971; children—Jennifer Kay, Scott Edward. With Belden Corp., Richmond, Ind., 1972—, asst. prodn. control mgr., 1975-77, prodn. control and warehousing mgr., 1977-79, mfg. mgr., 1979-80, plant mgr., 1980—. Bd. dirs., mem. exec. com. Jr. Achievement, 1981. Served with USAF, 1969-72. Mem. Electronic Industries Assn., Wire Assn., Richmond Area C. of C. Republican. Club: Toastmasters Internat. (ednl. v.p. 1977, pres. 1978). Office: Box 1327 Richmond IN 47374

FATH, MICHAEL ALBERT, chem. co. exec.; b. Cleve., Sept. 30, 1939; s. Michael A. and Bertha (Krehlik) F.; B.S., Kent State U., 1961, M.S., 1964; m. Joan M. Schromen, Apr. 11, 1964; children—Michael, Brian. Analyt. chemist, polymer technologist B.F. Goodrich Co., Akron, Ohio, 1964-68; research chemist rubber tech. Goodyear Tire & Rubber Co., Akron, 1968-73; tech. service mgr. Burton Rubber Co. (Ohio), 1973-74; project mgr. Rubber Chems. div. Monsanto Co., Akron, 1974—; lectr. rubber tech. Akron U., 1979-80, also over 100 tech. lectrs. on rubber tech. throughout world. Mem. Wadsworth (Ohio) Community Band, 1975—; mem. Wadsworth Hosp. Assn. Fund Raising Project, 1977-78. Mem. Am. Chem. Soc., Akron Rubber Group, Detroit Rubber Group, N.E. Ohio Rubber Group, Akron Polymer Lectr. Group, Archaeol. Soc. Ohio. Contbr. articles to tech. jours.; patentee vulcanization systems for rubber, thermoplastic compositions. Home: 271 Knollwood Dr Wadsworth OH 44281 Office: 260 Springside Dr Akron OH 44313

FAUBER, BERNARD M., retail co. exec.; b. 1922; married. With K Mart Corp., 1942—, asst. mgr. So. region, 1961-65, exec. asst. to pres., 1965-66, Western regional mgr., 1966-77, v.p., 1968-77, sr. exec. v.p., chief adminstrv. officer, 1977-80, chmn., chief exec. officer, 1980—, also dir. Served with USN, 1941-45. Office: K Mart Corp 3100 W Big Beaver Troy MI 48084

FAULK, DAVID LEE, internist; b. Rochelle, Ill., Feb. 2, 1947; s. Elliott and Helen Jean (Van Meter) F.; B.A. in Gen. Sci., U. Iowa, 1969, M.D., 1973; m. Martha Louise Svendsen, June 26, 1976. Intern, Presbyn.-St. Luke's Hosp., Chgo., 1973-74, resident in medicine, 1974-76; fellow in gastroenterology U. Iowa Hosps., Iowa City, 1976-78; staff physician Glen Ellyn (Ill.) Clinic, 1978—; attending staff Central DuPage Hosp., Winfield, Ill., Edward Hosp., Naperville, Ill., Glendale Heights (Ill.) Community Hosp.; cons. staff Delnor Hosp., St. Charles, Ill., Community Hosp., Geneva, Ill. Diplomate Am. Bd. Internal Medicine, Am. Bd. Gastroenterology. Fellow A.C.P.; mem. Am. Gastroenterol. Assn., Am. Soc. Gastrointestinal Endoscopy, AMA, Chgo. Soc. Gastroenterology, Omicron Delta Kappa. Research on intestinal pseudo-obstruction and intestinal motility. Home: 871 Crescent Blvd Glen Ellyn IL 60137 Office: 454 Pennsylvania Ave Glen Ellyn IL 60137

FAULKNER, CHARLES BRIXEY, govt. ofcl., lawyer; b. Springfield, Mo., Feb. 11, 1934; s. Charles Franklin and Josephine Frances (Brixey) F.; B.S., U. Ark., 1956; LL.B., U. Mo., 1960; m. Noralee Phariss, Dec. 29, 1956; children—Charlesa, Charles Byron. Admitted to Mo. bar, 1960, Fed. bar, 1962; partner Ratican & Faulkner, Aurora, Mo., 1960-71; legal adviser U.S. Bur. Prisons, U.S. Med. Center, Springfield, Mo., 1972; regional atty U.S. Bur. Prisons, Kansas City, Mo., 1974—; pros. and county atty., Lawrence County, Mo., 1961-70; city atty. Aurora, 1970-72, Marionville, Mo., 1961-72. Chmn. bd. dirs. A.R.C., Lawrence County, 1963-65. Served with 1st div., 26th Inf., AUS, 1956-57. Recipient Kansas City Trust award in estate planning, 1960. Mem. 39th Jud. Circuit Bar Assn. (v.p. 1966-70), Scabbard and Blade, Beta Gamma Sigma. Rotarian (dir. 1961-72). Editorial bd. Mo. Law Rev., 1958-60. Home: 312 S Elliott St Aurora MO 65605 Office: KCI Bank Bldg 8800 NW 112th St Kansas City MO 64153

FAULKNER, EDWIN JEROME, ins. co. exec.; b. Lincoln, Nebr., July 5, 1911; s. Edwin Jerome and Leah (Meyer) F.; B.A., U. Nebr., 1932; M.B.A., U. Pa., 1934; m. Jean Rathburn, Sept. 27, 1933. With Woodmen Accident & Life Co., Lincoln, 1934—, successively claim auditor, v.p., 1934-38, pres., 1938-77, dir., 1938—, chmn. bd., chief exec. officer, 1977—; pres., dir. Comml. Mut. Surety Co., 1938—; dir. First Nat. Bank, Lincoln Tel. & Tel. Co., Universal Surety Co., Inland Ins. Co. Chmn. Health Ins. Council 1959-60. Chmn. Lincoln-Lancaster County Plan Commn., 1948-68; mem. medicare adv. com. Dept. Def., 1957-71; chmn., trustee Bryan Meml. Hosp.; trustee Doane Coll., Cooper Found., Lincoln Found., Nebraskans for Pub. TV, Nebr. Hist. Soc.; chmn. U. Nebr. Found. Served from 2d lt. to lt. col. USAAF, 1942-45. Decorated Legion of Merit, recipient Distinguished Service award U. Nebr., 1957, Nebr. Builders award, 1979; Harold R. Gordon Meml. award Internat. Assn. Health Ins. Underwriters, 1955, Ins. Man of Year award Ins. Field, 1958, Exec. of Year award Am. Coll. Hosp. Adminstrs., 1971. Mem. Am. Coll. Life Underwriters (trustee), Health Ins. Assn. Am. (1st pres. 1956), Am. Legion, Am. Life Conv. (exec. com. 1961—, pres. 1966-67), Phi Beta Kappa, Phi Kappa Psi, Alpha Kappa Psi (hon.). Republican. Presbyn. Clubs: Masons, Elks. Author: Accident and Health Insurance, 1940; Health Insurance, 1960; editor: Man's Quest for Security, 1966. Home: 4100 South St Lincoln NE 68506 Office: 1526 K St Lincoln NE 68508

FAULKNER, FREDERICK LEWIS, JR., computer co. exec.; b. Chgo., June 23, 1925; s. Frederick Lewis and Violet Beatrice (Cooksey) F.; B.S., Ill. Inst. Tech., 1949; m. Helen Anne Enzenberger, Feb. 1, 1947 (dec. Oct. 1978); children—Anne, Frederick Lewis, Kristin; m. Elizabeth Royce, 1981. Gen. mgr. Chief Printing Co., Chgo., 1949-62; mem. sales staff Stewart & Fryer Printing Co., Chgo., 1962-64; exec. v.p., gen. mgr. Edward Keogh, Printing Co., Chgo., 1964-68; founder, pres. Graphic Arts Data Service, Chgo., 1966—; co-pub. Index to U.S. Govt. Periodicals. Mem. Cook County Dist. 106 Bd. Edn., 1959-64; trustee Village of Western Springs, 1963-67. Served with Signal Corps, AUS, 1943-46. Mem. Printing Industry Am., Lithographers Club Chgo., Chgo. Club Printing House Craftsmen, Alpha Sigma Phi. Club: Univ. Chgo. Home: 27 Highridge Rd Clarendon Hills IL 60514 Office: 200 W Monroe St Chicago IL 60606

FAUSAK, WILLIAM ARTHUR, writing instrument mfg. co. exec.; b. Jersey City, Oct. 31, 1938; s. William Otto and Eleanore Louise (Carnie) F.; B.S., U. Pa., 1961; m. Carol Jean Davis, Sept. 16, 1967; 1 son, Erik Davis. Auditor, Uniroyal, Inc., N.Y.C., 1963-66; sr. internal auditor GAF Corp., N.Y.C., 1966-68; fin. controls supr. Random House, Inc., N.Y.C., 1968-70; sr. auditor The Singer Co.,

N.Y.C., 1970-77, supr. audits, mgr. audits, 1970-75, dir. trade relations, Eastern Europe and USSR, 1975-77; dir. corporate internal auditing The Parker Pen Co., Janesville, Wis., 1977—. Served with USNR, 1961-63. Cert. internal auditor, 1973. Mem. Inst. Internal Auditors. Clubs: Janesville Country, Blackhawk Curling. Home: 3207 Crystal Springs Rd Janesville WI 53545 Office: One Parker Pl Janesville WI 53545

FAUST, WILLIAM PAUL, state senator; b. Bucyrus, Ohio, Mar. 29, 1929; s. Paul Joseph and Teresa Gertrude (Johnson) F.; A.B., U. Mich., 1952; student Ind. U., 1948-50; postgrad. Eastern Mich. U., 1956-57, No. Mich. U., 1981; LL.D., Schoolcraft Coll., 1979. Editor, Wayne (Mich.) Dispatch, 1952-59; mng. editor Asso. Newspapers, Wayne, 1960-62; supr. Nankin Twp., Mich., 1963-65; mem. Mich. State Senate, Lansing, 1967—, majority leader, 1977—. Mem. exec. com. Nat. Conf. State Legislatures, 1981—. Democrat. Roman Catholic. Office: Mich State Senate Lansing MI 48909

FAVA, JOE (GIUSEPPE MARIA), musician, educator; b. Detroit, May 28, 1911; s. Stephen (Stefano) and Rose (Maria Rosaria) F.; ed. Northeastern High Sch., Detroit, 1923-27; m. Mary Crupi, Jan. 20, 1945; children—Stephen Joseph, Rosemary, Carmela Marie. Staff guitarist Sta. WJR, Detroit, 1934-52; freelance staff Stas. WWJ and WXYZ, Detroit, 1932-52; guitarist Detroit Symphony Orch., 1935-60; appeared on Ford Summer Hour, Detroit, Stroh Radio Program, Detroit; tchr. Teal Music Sch., Detroit, 1935-52; owner, operator Fava Music Co., Detroit, 1954—; faculty Wayne State U., Detroit, 1967—, dir. guitar studies, 1967—, prof. music, 1974—. Mem. Classic Guitar Soc. Mich. (founder, pres. 1955), Guitar Found. Am. div. Am. String Tchrs. Assn., Coll. Music Soc., Detroit Fedn. Musicians. Roman Catholic. Author: Joe Fava Comprehensive Guitar Method, 3 vols., 1962; Folk Guitar Book, 1964; Mancini Magic for Guitar, 1966; Youmans, 1958; Gershwin, 1959. Office: Fava Music Studio 720 Forest Ave Birmingham MI 48008 also 312 Music Wayne State U 5980 Cass Ave Detroit MI 48202

FAVOR, FREDERICK, former newspaper editor; b. Chgo., Dec. 22, 1910; s. Frederick Zebulon and Mary Inez (Stahl) F.; B.S., Northwestern U., 1932; m. Florence Alice Theodora Vail, Dec. 27, 1943 (dec.); children—Frederick Vail, Mary Alice (Mrs. S.L. Mecker), Margaret Ann. Editor Haliday Pubs., Winnetka, Ill., 1933-35; reporter Evanston (Ill.) News-Index, 1935-36; editorial staff mem. Hollister Pubs., Wilmette, Ill., 1936-57, editor, 1957-64; editorial staff mem. Citizen Pubs., LaGrange, 1964-75, editor, 1965-75, ret., 1975. Bd. dirs. New Trier Twp. Citizens' League, 1961-65. Served with USNR, 1940-46, 51-53. Home: 11 6th Av La Grange IL 60525

FAW, MELVIN LEE, physician; b. Kansas City, Mo., Dec. 4, 1925; s. Floyd Butler and Ivalee Muriel (Harvey) F.; student U. Kans., 1943-44, Baylor U., 1945; B.S., Washburn U., 1948; M.D., Washington U., St. Louis, 1951; m. Anna Margaret Rose, July 17, 1948; children—Linda, Gary, David, Nancy. Intern, Washington U. Service St. Louis City Hosp., 1951-52, resident in internal medicine 1952-54; resident in internal medicine U. Kans. Hosp., Kansas City, 1954-55; practice medicine specializing in internal medicine and cardiology Welborn Clinic, Evansville, Ind., 1955—, mng. partner, 1965-78; pres. med. staff Welborn Hosp., 1980, chief medicine, 1958-64, dir. cardiovascular services, 1981—; mem. So. Ind. Health Service Agy., 1976—. Served with inf. AUS, 1944-45. Decorated Bronze Star medal with oak leaf cluster, Purple Heart, Combat Infantryman Badge; recipient Disting. Service award U. Evansville, 1980. Fellow Am. Coll. Chest Physicians; mem. A.C.P., Am. Soc. Internal Medicine, AMA, Ind. Med. Assn., Vanderburgh County Med. Soc., Phi Kappa Phi. Methodist. Home: 2400 E Chandler St Evansville IN 47714 Office: Welborn Clinic 421 Chestnut St Evansville IN 47713

FAWCETT, JAMES DAVIDSON, herpetologist, educator; b. New Plymouth, N.Z., Jan. 10, 1933; s. James and Edna Lola (Catterick) F.; B.Sc., U. N.Z., 1960; M.Sc., U. Auckland (N.Z.), 1964; Ph.D., U. Colo., 1975; m. Georgene Ellen Tyler, Dec. 21, 1968. Head dept. biology Kings Coll., Auckland, 1960; grad. demonstrator dept. zoology U. Auckland, 1961-62, sr. demonstrator, 1963-64; grad. asst. U. Colo., 1969-72; instr. biology U. Nebr., Omaha, 1972-75, asst. prof., 1975-81, asso. prof., 1981—. Recipient Great Tchr. award U. Nebr., 1981. Mem. Royal Soc. N.Z., N.Z. Assn. Scientists, Am. Soc. Zoologists, Soc. Systematic Zoology, Herpetologists League, Brit. Soc. Herpetologists, AAAS, Nebr. Herpetological Soc. (pres. 1979-80), Sigma Xi (pres. Omaha chpt. 1980-81), Phi Sigma. Contbr. articles to profl. jours. Home: 7305 Grant Omaha NE 68134 Office: Biology Dept U Nebr Omaha NE 68182

FAXON, JACK, state senator Mich.; b. Detroit, June 9, 1936; s. Morris and Pauline (Krimsky) F.; B.S. in Edn., Wayne State U., 1956, M.S. in Edn., 1958; M.A. in History (fellow), U. Mich., 1962. High sch. tchr., Detroit, 1956-64; mem. Mich. Ho. of Reps., 1965-71, mem. appropriation, edn., mental health, colls. and univs. coms.; mem. Mich. Senate, 1971—, pres. pro tempore, chmn. edn. com., vice-chmn. commerce com., mem. labor and retirement com., chmn. joint legis. com. on the arts; headmaster Lycee Internat., 1968—. Precinct del. City of Detroit, 1960; del. Mich. Constl. Conv., Lansing, 1961-62; bd. advisors Sch. Theology of Diocese of Mich., 1969—; active Right to Read Adv. Council, Council on Elementary and Secondary Edn., Anti-Defamation League, ACLU. Eagleton fellow Rutgers U., 1967. Mem. Edn. Commn. of the States (commr.) Nat. Conf. State Legislatures, Edn. Task Force. Democrat. Home: 15343 Warwick St Detroit MI 48223 Office: State Capitol Lansing MI 48909

FAY, LEONARD EDWARD, chiropractor, ednl. adminstr.; b. Chgo., Aug. 23, 1925; s. Leonard Theodore and Marie (Barbian) F.; B. Gen. Edn., Morton Coll., 1945; D. Chiropractic, Nat. Coll. Chiropractic, 1949; m. Angela Mary Marrese, Sept. 9, 1950; children—Marilen (Mrs. Richard F. Reimer), John, Catherine (Mrs. David C. Frost), Richard, Anne, Marianne. Mem. faculty Nat. Coll. of Chiropractic, Lombard, Ill., 1949-51, asst. to pres., 1962-64, v.p., 1964-67, exec. v.p., 1967—; pvt. practice chiropractic medicine, Chgo., 1950-75. Cons. Medicare, Ill. Med. Services, 1973—, CNA Ins. Co., 1973—, Travelers Ins. Co., 1975—; mem. adv. com. Ill. Dept. Pub. Aid. Fellow Internat. Coll. Chiropractors; mem. Am., Ill., Chgo. chiropractic assns., Council on Chiropractic Edn. (v.p. 1972-74, pres. 1974-76), Nat. Chiropractic Assn. (Ill. del. 1961-62), Council on Chiropractic Roentgenology, Council on Chiropractic Neurology (pres. 1971-72), Am. Assn. for Higher Edn., Am. Pub. Health Assn., Am. Assn. Univ. Adminstrs., N.Y. Acad. Scis., Sigma Phi Kappa, Eta Nu, Pi Kappa Alpha (pres. and trustee 1972-74). Roman Catholic. Lion. Home: 22 WO 64 Stratford Pl Glen Ellyn IL 60137 Office: 200 E Roosevelt Rd Lombard IL 60148

FAY, ROGER JOSEPH, mfg. co. exec.; b. Dubuque, Iowa, Aug. 22, 1923; s. Rollo Joseph and Dorcas Mary (Flin) F.; B.S., Bradley U., 1948; m. Lillian Virginia Allen, Aug. 30, 1947; children—Deborah Ann, Stephen Roger. Supr. parts contact div. Caterpillar Tractor Co., 1948-50, product support mktg. rep. U.S., 1950-51, product support mktg. rep. for Mexico, Central and South Am., 1952-55, product support mktg. mgr. Latin Am. div., 1955-64, Canadian div., Peoria, Ill., 1964-81, S. Am. div., 1981—, also mem. parts distbn. task force; cons. Banff Sch. Mgmt., U. Alta. Mem. parish council Holy Family Ch., 1966-67; coach Little League baseball, 1965-67, also basketball; solicitor St. Francis Bldg. Fund, 1968. Served with USMC, 1942-46. Mem. Am. Hist. Assn., Civil War Hist. Soc. Republican. Roman Catholic. Golden Gloves champion, 1942-46. Home: 1015 Hiawatha Dr Dunlap IL 61625

FAYED, MUHAMMED EL-SAWI, chem. engr.; b. Sal-Haghar, Egypt, Jan. 18, 1943; s. Al-Sawi Ibrahim and Fathiya Mohamad (Hitata) F.; came to U.S., 1975; B.Sc. with honors, Cairo U., 1964, M.Sc., 1968; Ph.D., U. Waterloo (Ont., Can.), 1972; m. Salwa H. Abou-Omar, Apr. 1, 1971; children—Marwan Muhammad, Nora. Plant chem. engr. Abou-Zaabal Fertilizer and Chem. Co., Cairo, 1964-67; NRC of Can. grantee, research asso., process engr. U. Waterloo and Spring Chem. Ltd., Toronto, Ont., 1972-74; process mgr. Peabody Engring. Can., Mississauga, Ont., 1974-75; process and research engr. Pullman Kellog Co., Houston, 1975-77; prof. chem. engring. Inst. Gas Tech., Chgo., 1977-78; specialist, cons. chem. engr., Milton, Ont., 1980—. Govt. Can. youth grantee, 1971. Mem. Am. Inst. Chem. Engrs. (mem. nat. com., chmn. area 2H of nat. com.), Canadian Soc. Chem. Engrs. (exec. com. Toronto), Assn. Profl. Engrs. Ont., Egyptian Assn. Profl. Engrs. Contbr. articles to profl. jours. Address: 790 Syer Dr Milton ON L9T 4E3 Canada

FAZIO, ANTHONY LEE, investment co. exec.; b. Wheeling, W.Va., Jan. 27, 1937; s. Frank G. and Julia Louise (DeFillipo) F.; B.S. in Elec. Engring., W.Va. U., 1959; m. Faye Elizabeth Kelly, Sept. 3, 1964; children—Tracey Lee, Kelly Ann. With computer div. RCA, 1964-72, mgr. product mktg., 1970-71, mgr. systems planning, 1971-72; dir. bus. and product planning Univac, 1972-73, dir. product mktg. and bus./product planning N.Am., 1973-75, regional mgr., 1975-77; v.p. sales Sycor Inc., Ann Arbor, Mich., 1977—, v.p. sales No. Telecom Systems Corp., 1978-79, v.p. mktg., 1979-80; pres. Gibbs Irwin Investments Co., 1981—. Served with Signal Corps, U.S. Army, 1959-61. Mem. Data Processing Mgmt. Assn. (cert. in data processing), Tau Beta Pi, Eta Kappa Nu. Republican. Methodist. Home: 2730 Oldewood Ct Wayzata MN 55391 Office: PO Box 1222 Minneapolis MN 55440

FAZIO, CARL, food co. exec. Chmn. bd. Fisher Foods, Inc.; dir. Midwest Bank & Trust Co. Mem. nat. bd. Am. Com. on Italian Migration; bd. dirs. Greater Cleve. Growth Assn., Nat. Center Resource Recovery; trustee John Carroll U., Cleve. Mem. Food Mktg. Inst. (dir.). Club: K.C. (4 deg.). Address: Fisher Foods Inc 5300 Richmond Rd Bedford Heights OH 44146

FAZIO, VICTOR WARREN, surgeon; b. Sydney, Australia, Feb. 2, 1940; s. Victor Warren and Kathleen Eleanor (Hills) F.; came to U.S., 1972; M.B., B.S., U. Sydney, 1964; m. Carolyn Sawyer, Dec. 2, 1960; children—Victor Warren III, Jane, David. Resident in surgery St. Vincents Hosp., Sydney, 1969-72, sr. registrar, 1971-72; lectr. anatomy U. New South Wales, 1967-68; chief resident gen. surgery Lahey Clinic, Boston, 1972-73; spl. fellow colon and rectal surgery Cleve. Clinic, 1973-74, chmn. dept. colon and rectal surgery, 1975—, program dir., 1975—; practice medicine specializing in surgery, Cleve.; chmn. dept. colon and rectal surgery Cleve. Clin. Found. Diplomate Am. Bd. Colon and Rectal Surgery. Fellow A.C.S., Royal Australian Coll. Surgeons; mem. AMA, Am. Soc. Colon and Rectal Surgeons, Soc. Surgery of Alimentary Tract, Central Surg. Assn. Roman Catholic. Home: 17414 Woodland St Shaker Heights OH 44120 Office: Cleveland Clinic 9500 Euclid Ave Cleveland OH 44106

FEAGLES, GERALD FRANKLIN, account exec.; b. Kansas City, Kans., Dec. 8, 1934; s. George Joseph and Florence Ada (Johnson) F.; student Kansas City Jr. Coll., 1953-55; m. Eleanor Jean Holder, Aug. 31, 1957; 1 son, Gerald Franklin. Various mktg. positions Sears Roebuck & Co., Kansas City, Mo., 1963-70; sales engr. E.F. Hauserman, Lenexa, Kans., 1970-74, br. mgr. Tex., 1974-75, account mgr., 1977-78, account exec., 1978—; cons., analyst in field. Active Boy Scouts Am. Mem. Constrn. Specifications Inst., Producers Council, Asso. Gen. Contractors Assn. Baptist. Home: Route 1 Box 36K Basehor KS 66007 Office: 8900 Indian Creek Pkwy Overland Park KS 66210

FEARNEHOUGH, GEORGE SAMUEL, microbiologist; b. Failsworth, Eng., July 14, 1922; s. John and Ida Jane (Buckthought) F.; came to U.S., 1961, naturalized, 1969; grad. Coll. of Tech., Manchester U. (Eng.), 1950; m. Mary Elizabeth Wright, July 25, 1969; stepchildren—David Michael, Robert Alan; 1 dau., Mary Kathleen. Chief technologist N.W. Regional Lab., Pub. Health Lab. Service, Manchester, 1948-57; sr. technologist Provincial Dept. of Health, Ont., Can., 1957-61; instr. microbiology Med. Sch., U. Mich., Ann Arbor, 1961-69; chief microbiologist Peoples Community Hosp. Authority, Wayne, Mich., 1969—. Lectr. bacteriology Inst. of Med. Lab. Tech., Eng., 1954-57; lectr. in microbiology Ont. Dept. of Health, 1957-61; examiner Can. Soc. Lab. Tech., 1958-61; lectr. Eastern Mich. U., 1970; instr. microbiology Washtenaw Community Coll., 1964-69. Pres. Citizens Adv. Council to Washtenaw County Drain Commr., 1973-75. Ordained elder United Presbyn. Ch. of Am., 1973; interim minister First Congl. Ch., Ann Arbor, 1963-64; lay preacher Meth. Ch. of Britain, Manchester, 1941-57. Fellow Royal Microscopical Soc.; mem. Am. Soc. for Microbiology, Am. Pub. Health Assn., Mich. Soc. for Infection Control (editor 1974-80, pres. 1980-82), Assn. Practitioners of Infection Control. Author: Elementary Medical Microbiology Manual, 1966; contbr. articles on microbiology and infection control to profl. publs. Home: 35 Revere Ct Ann Arbor MI 48104 Office: People's Community Hosp Authority Annapolis Ave Wayne MI 48184

FEARS, GARY R., mgmt. co. exec.; b. Granite City, Ill., June 8, 1946; s. Floyd Ray and Edna Pauline (Brawley) F.; student Western Ill. U., 1964-65; B.A., So. Ill. U., 1971; div.; 1 son, Victor. Nat. mktg. mgr. Sears Tax Service, Chgo., 1970-72; pres. Estar Corp., Colo. Springs, Colo., 1972-73; tng. cons. Ill. Dept. Local Govt. Affairs, Springfield, 1973, chief adminstrv. officer community services, 1973-74; spl. asst. to sec. Ill. Dept. Transp., Springfield, 1974-76; pres. South Western Mgmt. Inc., Granite City, Ill., 1976—. Co-chmn. Madison County Citizens for McCarthy, 1968; state chmn. McCarthy Students for Humphrey, 1968; organizer Dan Walker for Gov., 1972; So. Ill. campaign coordinator Carter for Pres., 1976, 80; mem. exec. com. Democratic Nat. Finance Council. Mem. ACLU, Acad. Polit. Sci., Council State Community Affairs Agys. Democrat. Address: 6 Barbara St Granite City IL 62040

FEATHERSTONAUGH, HENRY GORDON, psychologist; b. San Diego, Nov. 11, 1917; s. Henry Stuart and Evelyn (Borrow) F.; B.S., U. Calif., Berkeley, 1939; M.S., Lehigh U., 1974; Ph.D., U. Mo., 1978; m. Nancy Ellen Couper, July 28, 1945; children—Wendy, Rusby. Chemist, H.J. Heinz Co., Berkeley, Calif., 1938-40; dist. mgr. Union Carbide Corp., N.Y.C., 1945-73; geriatric services coordinator The Center for Mental Health, Anderson, Ind., 1979—; lectr. in field. Exec. bd. Madison County Council on Aging, 1979—. Served with U.S. Army, 1941-43, USAAF, 1943-45; ATO. Decorated Air medal with oak leaf cluster, D.F.C.; Lehigh U. teaching asst. and tuition grantee, 1972-73; U. Mo. research grantee, 1974-78. Mem. Am. Psychol. Assn., Internat. Assn. Applied Psychology, Am. Assn. Sex Educators, Counselors and Therapists, Am. Chem. Soc., Internat. Platform Assn., Psi Chi, Phi Kappa Phi. Contbr. articles to profl. jours. Home: 2115 Meridian St Anderson IN 46014 Office: PO Box 1258 Anderson IN 46015

FEAZELL, ROBERT RAY, accountant; b. Portsmouth, Ohio, Aug. 31, 1940; s. William Franklin and Clara Lee (Hasler) F.; student U. Cin.; m. Glenda Ruth Cantrel, Feb. 27, 1960; children—Kevin, Michael, William, Todd. Clk., Merry Mfg. Co., Cin., 1957-60; bookkeeper Dallas Trucking Co., Cin., 1960-62; controller Mees Distbg. Inc., Cin., 1962-66, Four Seasons Co., Cin., 1966-68; owner, exec. partner Robert R. Feazell & Co., Cin., 1960—; dir. F & N Motor Inc., No. Hills Oil Inc. Adviser, Jr. Achievement, 1960-65; mem. nat. adv. council Nat. Fedn. Ind. Bus., 1972-77; adv. bd. Vocat. Sch., Diamond Oaks, 1976-77. Mem. Nat. Soc. Pub. Accountants (dir. 1972-76, bd. govs. 1977—), Pub. Accountants Soc. Ohio (pres. 1972, chmn. bd. 1973), Mt. Healthy Bus. Assn. (pres. 1977). Republican. Methodist. Clubs: Clovernook Country, Bankers, Masons, Shriners. Home: 1072 Galbraith Rd Cincinnati OH 45231 Office: 9284 Compton Sq Cincinnati OH 45231

FEDELLE, ESTELLE, artist; b. Chgo.; d. John and Julia (Porebski) Szymanski; student Am. Acad., 1944-47, Northwestern U., 1949-51, Inst. Design, Art Inst. Chgo.; also pvt. study. Exhibited in 47 one-man shows including Wheaton (Ill.) Pub. Library, Libertyville (Ill.) Art League; exhibited in group shows Visual Arts Center, Chgo., Chgo. Pub. Library, Ill. State Fair, Baron Galleries of Chgo. and Las Vegas, Grand Central Gallery, N.Y.C., numerous others; painted portraits; pvt. art tchr., 1950—; dir. Fedelle Sch. Art, Chgo. Recipient 70 awards for painting including Margaret R. Dingle award, 1953; certificate of Merit Distinguished Service in Art, 1967. Mem. Royal Soc. Art London (hon.), Artists Guild Chgo., Austin-Oak Park-River Forest Art League, Nat. League Am. Pen Women, Park Ridge, Municipal Regent art leagues, Laurel Art League, Author: How To Begin Painting for Fun, 1964; contbg. author: Fun Book on Painting, How to Paint from your Color Slides; columnist Art and You, Leader Newspapers. Home: 1500 S Cumberland St Park Ridge IL 60068 Office: Fedelle Studio 6733 N Olmsted Chicago IL 60631

FEDOR, GEORGE EDWARD, lawyer; b. Slovakia, Mar. 28, 1909; s. George and Mary (Talas) F.; came to U.S., 1913, naturalized, 1921; B.A., Western Res. U., 1931; LL.B. magna cum laude, Cleve. Law Sch., 1939; m. Helen R. Evansick, Apr. 24, 1934; children—Bruce G., Dennis G., Donna M. Fedor Wimbiscus, Thomas J., Mark Q., Louise A. Fedor Ortiz, Renee M. Fedor Bauchmoyer, Christopher A. Salesman, Standard Oil Co., Cleve., 1930-46, bus. devel. specialist, 1945-46; admitted to Ohio bar, 1940, since practiced in Cleve.; asso. firm Fedor & Fedor; dir. Law City of Lakewood, 1956-59. Pres., Lakewood Slovak Civic Club, 1941-42; mem. Lakewood Planning Commn., 1955-57; mem. adv. bd. St. Andrew's Abbey, Cleve., 1967—; mem. Ohio Ho. of Reps., 1949-52; chmn. speaker's bur. Cuyahoga County Democratic Com., 1947-48; trustee Citizens League, Cleve., 1955-61, St. Augustine Manor, Cleve., 1971-78. Recipient Outstanding Alumni award Cleve. Marshall Law Sch., 1964. Mem. Am. Judicature Soc., Am., Cleve., Cuyahoga County, Ohio bar assns., 1st Catholic Slovak Union, 1st Catholic Slovak Ladies Assn., Nat. Slovak Soc., Catholic Slovak Sokol. Democrat. Roman Catholic. Home: 18603 W Valley Ln Fairview Park OH 44126 Office: 600 Terminal Tower Cleveland OH 44113

FEE, DOROTHEA LILLIAN, nursing adminstr.; b. Wheeling, W.Va., Aug. 17, 1929; d. Harvey Gorrell and Elva (Borck) F.; R.N., Wheeling Hosp. Sch. of Nursing, 1950; B.S. in Nursing Edn., U. Steubenville, 1954; M.A., U. Pitts., 1961. Staff nurse Wheeling Hosp., 1950-51; head nurse Ohio Valley Gen. Hosp., Wheeling, 1951-56, asst. dir. nursing, 1956-63; dir. nursing Charleston (W.Va.) Meml. Hosp., 1963-71; dir. nursing Wesley Meml. Hosp., Chgo., 1971-73; asst. v.p. nursing Children's Meml. Hosp., Chgo., 1973-75; v.p. patient care The Jewish Hosp., Cin., 1975-81. Col., U.S. Army Res. Mem. Am. Nurses Assn., Am. Soc. Nursing Service Adminstrs., Ohio Soc. Hosp. Nursing Service Adminstrs., Res. Officers Assn., Sigma Theta Tau.

FEELY, WILLIAM PETER, III, mfg. co. exec.; b. Oak Park, Ill., July 4, 1933; s. William Peter and Ruth F.; B.S. magna cum laude, St. Joseph's Coll., 1955; M.B.A., U. Chgo., 1974; m. Shirley AnnVokac, June 25, 1955; children—Dawn Denise, William Peter IV. With Zenith Radio Corp., Chgo., 1959-77, gen. mgr. transp., 1977, dir. transp. Quasar Electronics, 1977-78, dir. purchasing and transp. Matsushita Indsl. Co., 1979-80, asst. to pres., 1981—. Bd. dirs. St. Joseph's Coll. Ind., 1976-80, Coll. DuPage, Glen Ellyn, Ill., 1978-80. Served to lt. USNR, 1955-59. Mem. Assn. Systems Mgmt., Am. Prodn. and Inventory Control Soc. Republican. Roman Catholic. Home: 945 S Grant Ave Villa Park IL 60181 Office: 9401 W Grand Ave Franklin Park IL 60131

FEENEY, DONALD PETER, physician; b. Bklyn., Aug. 30, 1930; s. Edward A. and Madeline J. (Cusack) F.; B.S., Holy Cross Coll., 1952; M.D., Cornell U., 1956; m. Frances M. Clegg, Apr. 26, 1958; children—Carol, Laura, Douglas, Gregory. Intern in surgery Yale Med. Coll., 1956-57; resident in gynecology N.Y. Hosp. Cornell U., N.Y.C., 1957-58; resident in urology Mayo Clinic, Rochester, Minn., 1960-63; practice medicine specializing in urology, Rockford, Ill., 1964—; clin. asst. prof. urology U. Ill. Med. Coll., 1973—. Served with M.C., USAF, 1958-60. Mem. A.C.S., Am., N. Central urol. assns., Chgo., Urol. Soc. Roman Catholic. Office: 2300 N Rockton Ave Rockford IL 61101

FEGERT, CHARLES DONALD, newspaper exec.; b. Chgo., Nov. 8, 1930; s. Charles Donald and Virginia Louise (Henault) F.; A.A., Morgan Park Jr. Coll., 1950; B.B.A., Loyola U., 1952; m. Barbara Jean Huffman, Sept. 3, 1977; children—Michael, Lisa, Charles Donald. With Chgo. Sun-Times, 1955—, retail supr., 1962-64, retail mgr., 1964-69, advt. mgr., 1969-72, v.p. advt. and mktg., 1972-79, exec. v.p. advt./circulation, 1979—. Bd. dirs. Better Bus. Bur. Met. Chgo., Chgo. Conv. and Tourism Bur., NCCJ, Children's Inst. for Devel. Disabilities, Little City; trustee Brain Research Found., U. Chgo., Nat. Jewish Hosp./Nat. Asthma Center; v.p. Spl. Children's Charities; mem. adv. bd. St. Mary of Nazareth Hosp.; mem. exec. bd. Chgo. Area council Boy Scouts Am. Served with USCG, 1953-55. Recipient Chgo. Conf. for Brotherhood award, 1975, Spirit of Life award City of Hope, 1978, Humanitarian award Am. Jewish Com., 1978. Mem. Internat. Newspaper Advt. Execs. (mem. plans com. 1973—), Chgo. Advt. Club (dir.). Clubs: Evanston Golf, Mid-Am., Tavern, Metropolitan, Whitehall, Economic of Chgo. (com. econ. devel. 1965—), International, Carlton; East Bank, Center. Office: 401 N Wabash Ave Chicago IL 60611

FEHRLE, CARL CHRISTIAN, educator; b. Kent, Iowa, June 11, 1923; s. Fred and Margaretha (Eberle) F.; B.S. in Edn., Drake U., 1955, M.S. in Edn., 1959; Ph.D., State U. Iowa, 1964; m. Norma Pauline Schaffer, Nov. 27, 1950; children—Kimberly Lynn, Margaret Joleen. Elem. tchr. Union County (Iowa) rural public schs., 1942-43; jr. high tchr. Griswold (Iowa) Public Sch., 1943-44; elem. prin. Corning (Iowa) Public Sch., 1944-49; elem. tchr. Des Moines public schs., 1950-52, asst. to prin., 1952-59, elem. prin., 1959-63; asst. prof. elem. edn. Drake U., Des Moines, 1966-68; asso. prof. and edn. specialist continuing profl. edn. U. Mo., Columbia, 1968-72, prof. edn., 1972—, project dir. law focused edn., 1973—. Served with C.E., U.S. Army, 1950-51. Decorated Bronze Star. Mem. NEA, Assn. for Supervision and Curriculum Devel., Nat. Prins. Assn., Phi Delta Kappa, Epsilon Sigma Phi. Republican. Methodist. Contbr. articles on edn. to profl. jours. Home: 3000 Arlington St Columbia MO 65201 Office: 309 Edn Bldg Univ Mo Columbia MO 65211

FEIBEL, FREDERICK ARTHUR, ins. agt.; b. Chgo., Oct. 27, 1942; s. Fred and Emma F.; B.S.E.E., Purdue U., 1964; M.B.A., Northwestern U., 1970; m. Marlene Ruth Edwards, Aug. 7, 1965; 1 son, Frederick Curtis. Project engr. Johnson Controls Corp., Milw., 1964-69; sr. mgmt. cons. Arthur Andersen & Co., Chgo., 1970-76; rep. pension fund evaluation A.G. Becker Securities Co., Chgo. 1976-77; spl. agt. Northwestern Mut. Life Ins. Co., Milw., 1977—. Chmn., Village of Northbrook (Ill.) Bicentennial Commn., 1975-76; v.p., Northbrook Civic Found., 1977, pres., 1978, also bd. dirs.; pres. Northbrook Hist. Soc., 1977, also bd. dirs.; deacon Northfield Community Ch. Recipient disting. service award State of Ill., 1976, Northbrook Rotary Man of Yr. award, 1978-79; C.L.U. Mem. Nat. Assn. Life Underwriters, Million Dollar Round Table, Eta Kappa Nu, Tau Beta Pi. Office: Collins & Assos 208 S LaSalle St Suite 2010 Chicago IL 60604

FEIBEL, ROBERT MARKS, ophthalmologist; b. Cin., June 30, 1943; s. Adolph H. and Ruth Claire (Marks) F.; A.B., Johns Hopkins U., 1965; M.D. magna cum laude, Harvard U., 1969; m. Jane Adele Miskoe, July 16, 1967; children—Juliet Ann, Carolyn Jane. Intern, Beth Israel Hosp., Boston, 1969-70; resident in ophthalmology Barnes Hosp., St. Louis, 1970-73; instr. in ophthalmology Washington U., St. Louis, 1973-74, asst. prof. clin. ophthalmology, 1974—; practice medicine specializing in ophthalmology, St. Louis, 1974—; mem. staff Barnes, Jewish, Children's hosps. Bd. dirs. St. Louis chpt. Am. Jewish Com., Opera Theater St. Louis. Mem. AMA, Am. Acad. Ophthalmology, Am. Intra-Ocular Implant Soc., Phi Beta Kappa, Alpha Omega Alpha, Omicron Delta Kappa. Contbr. articles to profl. jours. Home: 42 Pointer Ln Saint Louis MO 63124 Office: 1034 S Brentwood Blvd Saint Louis MO 63117

FEIGHNY, LEO GLYNN, mktg. research co. exec.; b. Kansas City, Mo., Oct. 26, 1949; s. Robert Eugene and Helen Louise (Glynn) F.; B.S. in Bus. Adminstrn. and Econs., Marymount Coll., Salina, Kans., 1971; M.B.A., Wichita State U., 1976; m. Karen Marlene Pfeifer, Aug. 22, 1970. Bus. mgr. Larson Chevrolet, Ellsworth, Kans., 1972; office mgr. Tindall Pontiac, San Antonio, 1973-75; research analyst MarketAide Co., Salina, 1977, dir. research, 1977—. Mem. devel. com. of bd. dirs. Marymount Coll., 1977—. Mem. Am. Mktg. Assn., Nat. Agrl. Mktg. Assn., Omicron Delta Epsilon. Republican. Roman Catholic. Club: Rotary. Home: 2131 Applewood Ln Salina KS 67401 Office: MarketAide Co PO Box 1645 Salina KS 67401

FEIKENS, JOHN, judge; b. Clifton, N.J., Dec. 3, 1917; s. Sipke and Corine (Wisse) F.; A.B., Calvin Coll., Grand Rapids, Mich., 1939; J.D., U. Mich., 1941; LL.D., U. Detroit, 1979, Detroit Coll. of Law, 1981; m. Henriette Dorothy Schulthouse, Nov. 4, 1939; children—Jon, Susan Corine, Barbara Edith, Julie Anne, Robert H. Admitted to Mich. bar, 1942; gen. practice law, Detroit; dist. judge Eastern Dist. Mich., 1960-61, 70—. Past co-chmn. Mich. Civil Rights Commn.; past chmn. Rep. State Central Com.; past mem. Rep. Nat. Com. Past bd. trustees Calvin Coll. Fellow Am. Coll. Trial Lawyers; mem. Am., Detroit (dir. 1962, past pres.) bar assns., State Bar Mich. (commr. 1965-71). Club: University of Michigan. Home: 10750 Koebbe Rd Manchester MI 48158 Office: Fed Bldg Detroit MI 48226

FEILER, STUART IRWIN, historian; b. Newark, July 5, 41; s. Morris E. and Annette R. (Bleyfeder) F.; A.A., Sper Coll. Judaica and Oakton Community Coll., 1975; B.A., Northeastern Ill. U., 1975, M.A., 1977; m. Arlene Marilyn Dusick Dec. 25, 1959; children—David Dean, Brett Alan. Various te hing positions Jewish history and mysticism High Sch. Jewish Studies, Chgo. Jewish Youth Council Free High Sch., various temples, 1971—; guest lectr. Jewish history Chg. Theol. Sem. 1974, Am. social history Northeastern Ill. U., Chgo., 1976-77; tchr. High Sch. Jewish Studies, Skokie, Ill., 1973—; theatre and film critic Lerner Newspapers, Chgo.; lectr. in field. Youth dir. Niles Twp. Jewish Congregation, 1972; area chmn. Maine Twp. Republican party, 1969—. Served with USAF, 1958-60. Gen. Assembly Ill. scholar, 1974—. Mem. Am. Hist. Assn., Orgn. Am. Historians, Nat. Trust Historic Preservation, Assn. Nat. Archives, Jewish Geneal. Soc. Ill. (pres.), Phi Alpha Theta. Home: 7773 Nordica Ave Niles IL 60648

FEINKNOPF, MARK GOODMAN, architect; b. Columbus, Ohio, Oct. 15, 1936; s. Mark D. and Katherine (Goodman) F.; B.S., Yale U., 1958; M.Arch., Harvard U., 1963; m. Sheila Levison, June 18, 1961; children—Mark Bradley, Kimberly Sue. Planner, Planning Service Group, Boston, 1962-63; mem. faculty dept. architecture Ohio State U., 1963-69; designer Mark Feinknopf Co., Columbus, 1963-67; partner Mark Feinknopf & Assos., Columbus, 1966-70, Feinknopf, Feinknopf, Macioce & Schappa, Columbus, 1971-77, Feinknopf, Macioce and Schappa, 1977—; sec. Star-Nelson Furniture Stores, 1971—. Mem. Ohio Environ. Task Force for Developmentally Disadvantaged, 1970-74; mem. Devel. Com. Greater Columbus, 1971—, mem. steering com., 1975—, chmn., 1980-81; mem. Citizen's Adv. Council to Mid-Ohio Regional Planning Commn., 1968—, pres., 1972-73; mem. mayors Econ. Council, 1981—; trustee Vision Center, 1973-79, Columbus Acad., 1973-78, 81—, Columbus Indsl. Devel. Corp., 1968-69, Center for Public Edn., 1981—, Archtl. Found. Central Ohio, 1980—. Served with U.S. Army, 1958-59. Recipient Young Leadership award Temple Israel, 1975; Mayor's award for community service, 1980; AIA Sch. award, 1963. Mem. AIA (chpt. exec. com. 1973-80, pres. 1978-79), Columbus C. of C. (trustee 1974-78, Downtown action com. 1969—, pres. 1974-78). Jewish. Major works include: Huntington Nat. Bank Univ. Br. (AIA honor award), 1978; Huntington Nat. Bank Nationwide Br. (AIA award of Merit), 1978; Glenwood Recreation Center (AIA Honor award), 1976; Fairwood Recreation Center (AIA award of Merit), 1977; Rochester (Minn.) Downtown Devel. Plan, 1978; renovation Columbus Mus. Art, 1979; redevel. plan High St. and State Capitol, Columbus, 1979; redevel. Harding Hosp. (7 bldgs.), 1981; redevel. Columbus Acad. (3 bldgs.), 1980. Home: 136 N Roosevelt Ave Columbus OH 43209 Office: 14 E Gay St Columbus OH 43209

FEIRICH, JOHN COTTRILL, lawyer; b. Chgo., Jan. 2, 1933; s. John Kenneth and Mary (Roy) F.; student Northwestern U., 1951-53; J.D., U. Ill., 1956; children—John Charles, Elizabeth Suzanne. Admitted to Ill. bar, 1956, U.S. Supreme Ct. bar, 1962; practiced in Carbondale, 1956—; partner firm Feirich, Schoen, Mager, Green & Assos., 1977—; spl. asst. atty. gen. State of Ill., 1958-62. Founder, pres. Air Ill., Carbondale, 1970—; pres. So. Ill. Sailing Sch., Carbondale, 1968—. Mem. com. pattern jury instrn. Ill. Supreme Ct., 1966-79. Chmn. Carbondale Pub. Bldg. Commn., 1965-67; mem. com. on sch. problems Carbondale Grade Sch., 1968; mem. Carbondale Community High Sch. Bd. Edn., 1969-75. Chmn. bd. dirs. YMCA, Carbondale, 1958-62; bd. dirs. Carbondale chpt. United Fund, 1959-67. Mem. Am. (nat. dir. 1962-63, exec. council 1979), Ill. (pres. 1982-83) bar assns., Am. Judicature Soc. (dir.), Am. Coll. Trial Lawyers, U.S. Yacht Racing Union. Elk, Lion. Club: Chgo. Yacht. Home and office: 2001 W Main St Carbondale IL 62901

FEIST, MARIAN JEAN, dietitian; b. Johnstown, Pa., Mar. 23, 1921; d. Harlan Oscar and Bridget Matilda (Hagen) Mock; B.S. in Foods and Nutrition, Seton Hill Coll., Greensburgh, Pa., 1942; postgrad. U. Cin., 1973-74; m. Arthur William Feist, Sept. 5, 1953. Dietetic intern Good Samaritan Hosp., Cin., 1942-43; dietitian Allegheny Gen. Hosp., Pitts., 1943-48; adminstrv. dietitian Conemaugh Valley Meml. Hosp., Johnstown, 1948; mem. staff Good Samaritan Hosp., 1948—, dir. nutrition, 1969—; lectr. in field. Mem. Am. Dietetic Assn. (life mem.; registered), Ohio Dietetic Assn. (registered; chmn. ann. conv. 1965), Cin. Dietetic Assn. (pres. 1971-72), Cin. Restaurant Assn., Am. Hosp. Soc. Food Service Adminstrs., Nutrition Today Soc., Ohio Restaurant Assn., Nat. Restaurant Assn., Am. Diabetic Assn. Roman Catholic. Office: 3217 Clifton Ave Cincinnati OH 45220

FEIST, RICHARD FRANK, mfg. co. exec.; b. Karlsruhe, N.D., Apr. 3, 1934; s. Frank A. and Catherine (Senger) F.; student pub. schs., Karlsruhe; m. Irene Gefroh, Aug. 19, 1953; children—Michael, Marylin, Myron, Mark, Marlene, Maynard, Marvin, Mary. Constrn. supt. Feist Constrn. Co., Minot, N.D., 1951-61, now dir.; mgr. Minot Sash & Door Inc., 1961-64, pres., engr. mgr., 1964—; dir. Feist Co., Feist Cupboards Co., Magic City Lumber Co., Sawyer Beef Center, Terrace Heights Devel. Co. (all Minot). Mem. governing bd. St. Joseph's Hosp., Minot, 1977—; bd. regents Bishop Ryan High Sch., Minot, 1979—; v.p. Community Shared Services-Ambulance Health Care, Minot. Mem. Asso. Gen. Contractors, Archtl. Woodworkers Inst. Roman Catholic. Clubs: K.C., Elks, Eagles. Address: PO Box 479 Hwy 2 E Minot ND 58701

FEIT, JEROME ANTHONY, chemist; b. Chgo., Aug. 4, 1922; s. Aloysius J. and Barbara (Piper) F.; Student Northwestern U., 1942, Purdue U., 1943; B.S., Northwestern U., 1949; m. Genevieve Trella, June 14, 1947; children—Jerome Jeffrey, Antonia Camille (Mrs. Carl Paul Adducci), Lawrence Anthony. Cons. chemist, 1950: founded Jerome & Co., cosmetics co., 1959-65, pres., chmn. bd. Jerome Labs., Inc., Chgo., 1965—. Served with USAAF, 1942-46; ETO. Fellow Am. Inst. Chemists, Am. Chem. Soc., ASTM, Smithsonian Instn., Audubon Soc.; mem. Chgo. Perfumery, Soap and Extract Assn. (dir.), Soc. Cosmetic Chemists (treas.), Ill. Mfrs. Assn., Chgo. Drug and Chem. Assn. Club: Variety of Ill. Patentee in field; musical composer. Office: 95 E Bradrock Dr Des Plaines IL 60018

FEJER, PAUL HARALYI, design engr.; b. Gyoma, Hungary, Feb. 27, 1921; s. Lajos Haralyi Fejer and Laura (Varasdi) Persaits F.; B.S., Ludovica Academia, Budapest, Hungary, 1944; m. Maria Wasylchenko, Nov. 16, 1946; children—Paul Haralyi, Alexandra Martha, Douglas Kay. Came to U.S., 1949, naturalized, 1955. Sr. product analyst Chrysler Corp., Highland Park, Mich., 1962-68; sr. design engr. Ford Motor Co., Mt. Clemens, Mich., 1968—. Served to 2d lt. Hungarian Army, 1944-45. Mem. Macomb Electronics Assn. (treas. 1958), Indsl. Math. Soc. (treas. 1970-73), Soc. Automotive Engrs., Soc. Plastic Engrs., Soc. Mfg. Engrs., Soc. Exptl. Stress Analysis. Author: The Measuring Numbers System, 1975; Fundamentals of Dynamic Geometry: The Fejer Vector System, 1980. Originator measuring numbers system for measuring continuous magnitudes, dynamic geometry. Home: 23 Lodewyck St Mount Clemens MI 48043 Office: 151 Lafayette St Mount Clemens MI 48043

FELD, THOMAS ROBERT, coll. pres.; b. Carroll, Iowa, Sept. 30, 1944; s. Edward Martin and Elaine Josephine (Wirtz) F.; B.A., Loras Coll., 1966; M.A., No. Ill. U., 1969; Ph.D., Purdue U., 1972; m. Donna Jean Jorstad, June 1, 1968; children—Jacqueline Joan, William Jay. Instr., asst. prof. Loras Coll., Dubuque, Iowa, 1966-70; v.p. devel. Lea Coll., Albert Lea, Minn., 1972-73, Central Meth. Coll., Fayette, Mo., 1973-76; acting pres., 1976-77; pres. Mount Mercy Coll., Cedar Rapids, Iowa, 1977—. Bd. dirs. Linn County Assn. Retarded Citizens, Cedar Rapids Symphony, Iowa Coll. Found. Mem. CMC Colls. Asso. (bd. dirs.), Iowa Assn. Ind. Colls. and Univs. (bd. dirs.). Roman Catholic. Club: Rotary. Home: 7009 Kent Dr NE Cedar Rapids IA 52402 Office: 1330 Elmhurst Dr NE Cedar Rapids IA 52402

FELDER, BRUCE BENJAMIN, title ins. co. exec.; b. Cleve., Sept. 27, 1937; s. Emanual H. and Theresa C. (Benjamin) F.; student John Carroll U., 19S5, Cleve. Marshall Law Sch., 1959; m. Linda G. Steinsapir, June 23, 1963; children—Teri, Traci, Todd. Dep. clk. Ct. of Common Pleas, Cuyahoga County, Ohio, 1958, clk., 1959; founder Legal Messenger Service, Inc., (co. name changed to Record Data, Inc. 1972), Cleve., 1959, pres., chief exec. officer, treas., 1959—, also pres., treas., chief exec. officer subs. Record Title Agy., Inc., 1972—, subs. Record Data Appraisal Service, Inc., 1974—; speaker to numerous consumer fin. and lending orgns. Trustee, Mt. Sinai Med. Center, Cleve., 1978—; chmn. communications com. Jewish Community Fedn. Cleve.; mem. Leadership Cleve. project Cleve. Growth Assn., 1981; former mem. Metzenbaum for Senate Exec. Com.; former co-chmn. fin. com. Ohio Congressman Dennis Eckart. Mem. Nat. Second Mortgage Lenders Assn. (dir., exec. com.), Am. Land Title Assn., Ohio Land Title Assn. Democrat. Jewish. Mason. Home: Winding Creek 3200 Som Center Pepper Pike OH 44124 Office: 725 St Clair Ave NW Cleveland OH 44113

FELDHUSEN, JOHN FREDERICK, psychologist, educator, author; b. Waukesha, Wis., May 5, 1926; s. John C. and Luella Elsie (Gruetzmacher) F.; B.A., U. Wis., 1949, M.S., 1955, Ph.D., 1958; m. Hazel J. Artz, Dec. 20, 1954; children—Jeanne, Anne. Counselor, Wis. Sch. for Boys, 1949-51; tchr. Northwestern Acad., Lake Geneva, Wis., 1951-54; instr. (part-time) Madison (Wis.) Bus. Coll., 1955-58; instr. U. Wis. Eau Claire, 1958-59, asst. prof., 1959-61, asso. prof., 1961-62; asso. prof. ednl. psychology Purdue U., West Lafayette, Ind., 1962-65 prof., 1965—, dir. Gifted Edn. Resource Inst., 1978—. Pres., PTA West Lafayette, 1969. Served with U.S. Army, 1944-45. U.S. Office Edn. grantee, 1967-71. Fellow Am. Psychol. Assn.; mem. Am. Ednl. Research Assn., Nat. Assn. Gifted Children (pres.-elect 1981), Council Exceptional Children, Nat. Council Measurement in Edn., Phi Delta Kappa. Author: (with W. Krypsin) Writing Behavioral Objectives: A Guide for Planning Instruction, 1974, Analyzing Classroom Dialogue, 1974, Developing Classroom Tests, 1974; (with S.J. Moore, D.J. Treffinger) Global and Componential Evaluation of Creativity Instructional Materials, 1970; (with D.J. Treffinger, P. Pine and others) Teaching Children How to Think, 1975; (with Treffinger) Creative Thinking and Problem Solving in Gifted Education, 1980; The Three Stage Model of Course Design, 1980; contbr. over 125 articles on ednl. psychology and teaching methods to profl. jours.; editorial bd. Gifted Child Quar., 1976—; editor The Ednl. Psychologist, 1966-69, Ednl. Psychology Series, 1976—; cons. editor Burgess Pub. Co., 1967-76. Home: 2187 Tecumseh Park Ln W Lafayette IN 47906 Office: Educational Psychology Purdue Univ W Lafayette IN 47906

FELDMAN, ARTHUR MITCHELL, mus. adminstr.; b. Phila., Dec. 22, 1942; s. Joseph and Cecilia F.; B.S., Villanova U., 1964; M.A. in Art History and Archaeology, U. Mo., 1970; m. Laurel Bucky, June 22, 1969; children—Aaron Nathan, Jordon Ariel. Vis. curator Nelson Gallery Atkins Mus., Kansas City, Mo., 1970, Victoria and Albert Mus., London, 1971; asso. curator, asst. adminstr. Renwick Gallery Smithsonian Instn., Washington, 1971-72; dir. Spertus Mus. of Judaica, Chgo., 1972—. Mem. Am. Assn. Mus. Contbr. articles to profl. jours. Office: 618 S Michigan Ave Chicago IL 60605

FELDMAN, BURTON GORDON, advt. exec.; b. Chgo., Dec. 19, 1915; s. Maurice J. and Goldye (Gordon) F.; B.S., Northwestern U., 1933; m. Dorothy Straus, Dec. 28, 1942 (d. 1969); children—Roger, Susan; m. 2d Judith Levinson Miller, 1970. Group copy chief Foote, Cone & Belding, Chgo., 1942-46; v.p. charge Chgo. office Buchanan & Co., 1946-48; exec. v.p. Post, Keyes, Gardner, 1948-59; pres. Burton G. Feldman, Inc., 1959-68; chmn. bd. Feldman & Assos. Advt., Inc., Chgo., 1968-74; pres. Instant Printing Corp., Chgo., 1972—; pres. Phoenix Electric Co., Chgo., 1963-68, chmn. bd., 1968—, dir., 1963—; v.p. mktg., dir. Cummins Tool Corp., 1977-80. Pres., James Gordon Found., 1962—; v.p. bd. fellows Brandeis U., 1981—. Mem. Pi Lambda Phi, Sigma Delta Chi. Club: Brandeis U. (pres. 1980—) (Chgo.). Home: 175 E Delaware Chicago IL 60611 Office: 222 N LaSalle St Chicago IL 60601

FELDMAN, EDGAR ALLAN, surgeon; b. Chgo., Apr. 16, 1936; s. Irving and Beatrice (Berg) F.; B.S., U. Ill., 1956, M.D., 1960; m. Ina Y. Scheckman, June 21, 1959; children—Robert A., Steven I., Susan L., Laura B. Resident in gen. surgery Brooke Gen. Hosp., Ft. Sam Houston, Tex., 1960-65, chief resident, 1964-65; chief of surgery Dewitt Army Hosp., Ft. Belvoir, Va., 1965-66; chief surgeon, army hosp., Ft. Carson Colo., 1966-68; surgeon 5th Inf. Div., Ft. Carson, Colo., 1968-69; attending surgeon Sherman Hosp., and St. Joseph Hosp., Elgin, Ill., 1969—, Suburban Med. Center, Hoffman Estates, Ill., Good Shepherd Hosp., Barrington, Ill.; cons. surgeon Geneva (Ill.) Community Hosp. Pres., Dist. Bd. Edn. Schaumburg (Ill.), 1974—; trustee Suburban Med. Center; bd. dirs. Crescent Counties Found. for Med. Care. Served with M.C., U.S. Army, 1960-69. Diplomate Am. Bd. Surgery. Fellow A.C.S., mem. Kane County (Ill.) Med. Soc. (dir. 1975—). Contbr. articles to surg. jours. Office: 1795 Grandstand Pl Elgin IL 60120

FELDMAN, EGAL, historian, educator; b. N.Y.C., Apr. 9, 1925; s. Morris and Chaya Feldman; B.A., Bklyn. Coll., 1950; M.A., N.Y.U., 1954; Ph.D., U. Pa., 1959; m. Mary Kalman, June 28, 1959; children—Tyla, Auora, Naomi. Asst. prof. history U. Tex. at Arlington, 1960-66; asso. prof. history U. Wis.-Superior, 1966-68, prof., 1968—, chmn. dept. history and philosophy, 1973—, dean Coll. Letters and Scis., 1977-81. Named Tchr. of Year, U. Wis., 1969, recipient Inst. Jewish Research award, 1954, Max Levine award, 1975. Jewish. Author: Fit for Men: History of New York's Clothing Trade, 1960; The Daeyfus Affair and the American Conscience, 1981. Contbg. author books, contbr. articles to profl. publs. Home: 2019 Weeks Ave Superior WI 54880 Office: Sundquist Hall Superior WI 54881

FELDMAN, HARRIS JOSEPH, radiologist, educator; b. Balt., Mar. 4, 1942; s. Charles William and Ruth (Emanuel) F.; A.B., Western Md. Coll., 1963; M.D., U. Md., 1967. Intern, Mercy Hosp., Balt., 1967-68; resident in radiology George Washington U. Hosp., Washington, 1968-71; staff radiologist U. Ill. Hosp., Chgo., 1973-77, Bethany Meth. Hosp., Chgo., 1977—, Walther Meml. Hosp., Chgo., 1977—; cons. radiologist Langley AFB Hosp., 1972-73; asst. prof. Abraham Lincoln Sch. Medicine, U. Ill., Chgo., 1974-77, clin. asst. prof., 1977—. Served with M.C., USN, 1971-73. Diplomate Am. Bd. Radiology. Mem. AMA, Ill., Chgo. med. socs., Am. Coll. Radiology, Ill., Chgo. radiol. socs., Radiol. Soc. N.Am. Home: 1339 N Dearborn St Chicago IL 60610 Office: 6450 N California Ave Chicago IL 60645

FELDMAN, JAMES DENNIS, sales promotion exec.; b. Cambridge, Mass., June 18, 1945; s. Walter Sidney and Eve Minnie (Cohen) F.; student U. Ill., 1962-63, Kans. State U., 1963-66, Washburn Law Sch., 1966-67, Emporia U., 1967-69; M.B.A., U. Ill., 1977. Pres., Photographs Unlimited, Topeka, Kans. and Champaign, Ill., 1966—; pres., dir. Consol. Camera Centres, Champaign, 1974-79, Freelance ADS, Inc., Champaign, 1975-79, Advanced Bus. Electronics, Inc., Champaign, 1977-80; pres. Advt. & Design Services, Inc., 1976—; dir. Asset Mgmt. Corp., Homewood, Ill., 1975—; instr. Parkland Coll.; lectr. U. Ill., Am. Mktg. Assn., Notre Dame U. Active United Way. Recipient Outstanding Probation Officer award Shawnee County Juvenile Ct., 1967. Cert. photo counselor. Mem. Photo Mktg. Assn., Nat. Assn. Real Estate Brokers, Aircraft Owners and Pilots Assn., Nat. Assn. Ind. Camera Stores, Nat. Assn. Audio-Visual Dealers, Profl. Photographers Assn., Nat. Premium Sales Execs. Inc. (asso. dir.), Premium Industry Club (seminar dir.), Am. Mgmt. Assn., Promotion Mktg. Assn. Am., Nat. Assn. Bus. Execs., Campus Mchts. Assn. (dir.), Ill. Pilots Assn. (dir.). Jewish. Office: Box 8334 Chicago IL 60680

FELDMAN, SCOTT HEYWOOD, TV newsman; b. St. Louis, July 8, 1949; s. Marvin and Bernadine (Silverman) F.; B.A. in Radio-TV-Film, U. Denver, 1971; m. Janet Jeffries, July 27, 1975. Newswriter, KOA-AM-TV, Denver, 1969; newsman WOHO-AM, Toledo, Ohio, 1972-73, WERE-AM, Cleve., 1973; reporter/anchor WAKR-AM-TV, Akron, Ohio, 1973-74; reporter/anchor KSTP-TV, Mpls./St. Paul, 1974-76, KTAR-TV, Phoenix, 1976-78, KMBC-TV, Kansas City, Mo., 1978—. Host Cerebral Palsy Telethon, Kansas City, 1978. Served with U.S. Army N.G. Res., 1970-76. Recipient Humanitarian award Public Relations Soc. Am., 1978. Mem. Am. Fedn. Radio-TV Artists. Office: 1049 Central Ave Kansas City MO 64105

FELDMAN, SIDNEY LOWENROSEN, editor and pub.; b. Chgo., Sept. 10, 1909; s. Joseph and Millie (Lowenrosen) F.; student Wilson Jr. Coll., 1948, Roosevelt Coll., 1948-50; m. Ann McPhillips, Aug. 17, 1941; children—Joseph S., Ellen C. Feldman Ryan. Editor, pub. Bridgeport News, Chgo., 1948—. Bd. mgrs. Chgo. Valentine Boys Club. Served with USAAF, 1941-42. Club: Moose. Office: 3506 S Halsted St Chicago IL 60609

FELDMAR, GARY IRWIN, printing co. exec.; b. Chgo., May 16, 1939; s. Milton and Dorothy (Zaritzky) F.; B.A., U. Ill., 1961; m. Barbara Pitts, Mar. 20, 1976; children—Brad, Jill. Sales rep., then v.p. Excello Press, Inc., Chgo., 1961-75, pres., 1976—; pres. Byer Intermark, Inc., Chgo., 1971-76; dir. United Equitable Ins. Corp. Mem. Direct Mail Mktg. Assn., Chgo. Assn. Direct Mail, Printing Inst. Ill. Clubs: Standard (Chgo.); Green Acres Country. Address: 6625 W Diversey Ave Chicago IL 60635*

FELDSTEIN, ALAN, apparel co. exec.; b. Los Angeles, June 14, 1936; s. Sol and Betty (Goussak) F.; B.S. in Bus., U. So. Calif., 1958; children—Beth, Ross. Salesman, Aileen Knitwear, 1960-63, Jonathan Logan Inc., 1963-75; pres. Saltzman-Feldstein Assos., Inc., sales agt., Chgo., 1975-79; pres. Seles Agy. for Center Stage, 1979—, Gailord

Classics, 1979—. Served with AUS, 1958-59. Club: B'nith B'rith. Address: 1143 Apparel Center Chicago IL 60654

FELDSTEIN, CHARLES ROBERT, fund raising counsel; b. Chgo., Nov. 9, 1922; s. Herman and Fannie (Frank) F.; student Northwestern U., 1940-42; A.M., U. Chgo., 1944; postgrad. Harvard, 1945-46; m. Janice Ruth Josephson, Sept. 6, 1948; children—James Frank, Frances Emily, Thomas Mark. Asst. dir. Hillel Founds., Harvard, Radcliffe, Mass. Inst. Tech., 1944-45, dir. Tufts and Simmons Colls., 1945-46; dir. advt. Field's Stores, Inc., N.J., 1946-48; exec. asst. to v.p. U. Chgo., 1948-51, dir. devel., 1951-1953; pres. Charles R. Feldstein & Co., Inc., 1953—; dir. Charles Frank & Co. Mem. vis. com. to Sch. Social Service Adminstrn., U. Chgo. Bd. dirs. Center Psychosocial Studies; trustee Inst. Psychoanalysis, Chgo. Mem. Am. Assn. Fund-Raising Counsel, Pub. Relations Soc. Publicity Club. Jewish (bd. dirs. congregation). Clubs: Standard, Attic, Quadrangle, Cliff Dwellers, Harvard of N.Y. Home: 70 E Cedar St Chicago IL 60611 Office: 135 S LaSalle St Chicago IL 60603

FELDSTEIN, IDELL, writing cons.; b. Chgo., May 27, 1927; d. Hyman and Celia (Wolfe) Lovitz; Ph.B. (Scholar 1945), U. Chgo., 1946, B.A. in English, 1964, M.A., 1969; postgrad. Northwestern U., 1970; m. Harold Feldstein, Jan. 18, 1948; children—Hyland, Fanchon. English tchr. Thorntown Twp. High Sch., Harvey, Ill., 1965-67; instr. bus. English, Moraine Valley Community Coll., Palos Hills, Ill., 1970; instr. lit. St. Xavier Coll., Chgo., 1970; head English and speech, div. gen. and tech. studies Ind. U., Gary, 1970-77; writing cons. for bus., industry, sci. Vol. tchr. English to Russian immigrants, Mem. Nat. Council Tchrs. of English, Conf. on Coll. Composition and Communication (guest speaker nat. convs., 1971, 72), Soc. Tech. Communicators, Am. Tchrs. Tech. Writing, Am. Bus. Communication Assn. Home and Office: 7141 N Kedzie Chicago IL 60645

FELT, MICHAEL GENE, communications exec.; b. Phila., Apr. 17, 1947; s. Cornelius Eugene and Marjorie Elaine (Brener) F.; B.A. in Broadcasting, Marquette U., Milw., 1969, M.A. in Communications, 1971; m. Anne Irene Toedt, June 6, 1971. With Internat. Harvester Co., 1973-79, supr. videotape prodn., Sheridan, Ill., 1974-79; mgr. audio/visual services First Nat. Bank of Chgo., 1979—; media cons. Served to 1st lt. AUS, 1971-73. Mem. Internat. Indsl. TV Assn., Am. Soc. Tng. and Devel. Home: 417 Mooseheart Rd Morris IL 60450 Office: First Nat Bank of Chgo 2 First Nat Plaza Chicago IL 60670

FELTENSTEIN, HARRY DOUGLAS, JR., public utility co. exec.; b. Springfield, Ill., Feb. 9, 1920; s. Harry Douglas and Alice N. (Fenney) F.; student Tex. A&M U., Bradley U.; m. Mary Ruppel, June 15, 1946; children—Paul, Kathy, Mark. With Central Ill. Light Co., Peoria, successively salesman, mgmt., staff, v.p., exec. v.p., pres.; TP&W R.R., Comml. Nat. Bank of Peoria, Edison Electric Inst. Bd. dirs. Proctor Hosp., Everett McKinley Dirksen Center, Bradley U., Urban Land Inst.; mem. Peoria Downtown Devel. Council. Served with USAF, 1941-45. Mem. Peoria C. of C. (dir.). Episcopalian. Club: Rotary. Office: 300 Liberty St Peoria IL 61602

FELTES, JOHN, machinery co. exec.; b. Bitburg, Germany, Oct. 21, 1936; s. Matthias and Katharina (Hettinger) F.; student Bus. Coll., Handels Sch., Bitburg, 1950-52; B.B.A., Industrie and Handelskammer, 1955; m. Barbara Lambrecht, Sept. 19, 1964; children—Eric, Robert. Came to U.S., 1958, naturalized, 1966. With banks, Irrel, Germany, 1953-57, Trier, Germany, 1957-58; with Seiwert, Chgo., 1958-59; asst. office mgr., 1961-65; office mgr. Weiler Engrings., Inc., Elk Grove, Ill., 1966-68, asst. sec., treas., 1968—; sec., treas. A.L.P., Inc., Elk Grove, 1968—. Served with AUS, 1959-61. Home: 731 Tarbat Ct Inverness Barrington PO IL 60010 Office: 2445 E Oakton St Elk Grove IL 60005

FELTMANN, JOHN MEINRAD, former advt. and radio exec.; b. St. Louis, Jan. 30, 1910; s. Henry Conrad and Catherine (Lake) F.; certificate in commerce and finance St. Louis U., 1938; m. Adeline A. Fiedler, Nov. 25, 1944; children—John Thomas, Mary Anne Kenney, Robert Joseph, James Anthony (dec.). Clk., Nat. Telephone Directory Co., St. Louis, 1924-36, auditor, 1936-60; sec., dir. Von Hoffmann Corp., Union, N.J., 1947-60, treas., dir., 1960-67, v.p., treas., dir., 1967-69; dir. Von Hoffmann Press, Inc., St. Louis, 1947-69, treas., dir., 1960-69; treas. dir. Publishers Lithographers, Inc., St. Louis, 1959-69; sec., treas. von Hoffmann Realty and Mortgage Corp., 1954-59; v.p., treas., dir. Victory Broadcasting Corp., Jacksonville, Fla., 1968-78, ret., 1978; v.p. treas. Nat. Telephone Directory Corp., Union, N.J., 1968-72, dir., 1968—, exec. v.p., 1972-78, also cons.; dir. Mid-State Printing Co., Jefferson City, Mo., 1947-54. Sec., treas. George Von Hoffmann Found., 1954-59. Mem. Delta Sigma Pi, Roman Catholic. Club: Mo. Athletic. Home: 7250 Christopher Dr Saint Louis MO 63129

FELTNER, PAULA JO, educator; b. Rock Springs, Wyo., Nov. 29, 1946; d. Joseph and Joanne Frances (Marinoff) F.; B.A. in Polit. Sci., U. Wyo., 1969, M.A. (fellow), 1970; postgrad. U. Ky., 1971-75; m. Michael K. Eberle, Sept. 30, 1975. Teaching asst. U. Wyo., Laramie, 1969-70; asst. U. Ky., Lexington, 1970-74; prof. polit. sci. Luther Coll., Decorah, Iowa, 1975—; now dir. House Republican Caucus, Iowa Gen. Assembly, Des Moines; pub. relations cons. firm Michael Goldstein Co., N.Y.C., summers 1968, 69, 73. Mem. Iowa Women's Polit. Caucus, Iowa Women's Polit. Task Force, LWV, NOW, AAUP, AAUW, Sierra Club, ACLU, Am., Midwest, So. polit. sci. assns., Iowa Fedn. Rep. Women, Pi Sigma Alpha. Republican. Home: 1212 64th St Des Moines IA 50320 Office: House Rep Caucus Iowa Gen Assembly State Capitol Bldg Des Moines IA 50320

FELVER, CARL EUGENE, nurse; b. Willard, Ohio, June 3, 1941; s. Paul Robert and Gertrude Ann Frankart; B.S., Kans. State U., 1968, M.S., 1971; R.N., Stormont Vail Sch. Nursing, 1976; m. Ella Rae Briggs, May 27, 1977; children from previous marriage—Sharon K., James J.; stepchildren—Kenny S. Havenstein, Michael S. Havenstein. Tchr., Highland Park High Sch., Topeka, 1968-69, Manhattan (Kans.) Jr. High Sch., 1969-72, Mulvane (Kans.) High Sch., 1972-73; nursing tech., nursing asst., R.N., Stormont-Vail Hosp., Topeka, 1973-76; R.N. Emergency Dept., St. Francis Hosp. and Med. Center, Topeka, 1976-78; instr. Stormont Vail Regional Med. Center Sch. Nursing, Topeka, 1978-80; dir. nursing services Willard Area Hosp., Inc., 1980—. Served with USN, 1960-64. Mem. Nat. League Nursing. Home: 705 Dale St Willard OH 44890 Office: 110 E Howard St Willard OH 44890

FENDRICH, CHARLES WELLES, III, real estate firm exec.; b. Glen Cove, N.Y., Dec. 30, 1952; s. Charles Welles and Roberta Knope F.; B.A. in Biology, Dartmouth Coll., 1975; postgrad. Rutgers U., 1975-76; M.B.A. in Mktg., George Washington U., 1979; m. Ann Rowe Krieger, June 17, 1978. Asst. to pres. Railwest, Inc., Washington, 1977; v.p. Fendrich Assos., Inc., Princeton, N.J., 1978-81; pres. 2-Way Communications, Inc., Washington, 1979-81; gen. mgr. Am. Control, Inc., Washington, 1979-81; asst. property mgr. La Salle Partners Inc., comml. real estate firm, Chgo., 1981—. Mem. Beta Gamma Sigma. Home: 9312 N Lord Ave Skokie IL 60077 Office: 208 S LaSalle St Suite 500 Chicago IL 60604

FENG, TSE-YUN, engr., educator; b. Hangchow, China, Feb. 6, 1928; s. Shih-ching and Lin Shao; B.S., Nat. Taiwan U., 1950; M.S., Okla. State U., 1957; Ph.D., U. Mich., 1967. m. Elaine Hu, June 12, 1965; children—Wu-chun, Wu-chi, Wu-che, Wu-chang. Asst. engr. Tawian Power Co., 1950-56; sr. designer Ebasco Services, N.Y.C., 1957-60; teaching fellow U. Mich., 1962-65, research asst., 1965-66, asst. research engr., 1966, research asso., 1967; asst. prof. elec. and computer engring. Syracuse U., 1967-71, asso. prof., 1971-75; prof. elec. and computer engring. Wayne State U., 1975-79; prof., chmn. computer sci. Wright State U., Dayton, Ohio, 1979-80; prof. computer and info. sci. Ohio State U., Columbus, 1980—; cons. Transidyne Gen., Syracuse U., Pattern Analysis and Recognition Corp.; chmn. Internat. Conf. on Parallel Processing, 1975—; dir. N.E. Consortium for Engring. Edn., 1976—; cons. USAF. Mem. IEEE (mem. del. Chinese Electronics Soc. PRC 1978, leader del. 1980, del. to Popov Soc. Congress, USSR 1978), IEEE Computer Soc. (pres. 1979-80, presiding officer governing bd. 1979-80, mem. governing bd. 1977-78, 81—, chmn. exec. com. 1979-80, Honor Roll award 1978, Disting. Visitor 1973-78, Spl. award 1981, chmn. nominations com. 1981—, chmn. membership com. 1981—, chmn. standards com. 1974-78), Assn. Computing Machinery, Am. Nat. Standards Inst. (info. systems standards mgmt. bd. 1974-78), Am. Fedn. Info. Processing Socs. (dir. 1979-80, nominations com. 1979-80), Sagamore Computer Conf. (chmn., editor proc. 1972-75), Hon. Order of Ky. Cols., Phi Kappa Phi, Tau Beta Pi, Eta Kappa Nu, Sigma Xi, Phi Tau Phi. Contbr. articles to profl. jours. Editor-in-chief IEEE Transactions on Computers, 1982—. Patentee in field. Home: 1604 Stormy Ct Xenia OH 45385 Office: Dept Computer and Info Sci Ohio State U Dayton OH 43210

FENGER, GEORGE, state legislator; b. Omaha, Nov. 15, 1925; student U. Nebr., Lincoln; m. Jean Bennett, Feb. 14, 1950; children—Carolyn Baker, Caryn Demaree, George A. Owner, operator service sta.; mem. Nebr. Legislature, 1980—. Mem. Republican State Central Com., 1978-80. Mem. Alpha Sigma Phi. Office: 1501 Fort Crook Rd S Bellevue NE 68005*

FENIMORE, TERRENCE LEE, pharm. co. exec.; b. West Palm Beach, Fla., Aug. 28, 1943; s. Gerald E. and Lila E. (Finney) F.; B.S. in Chem. Engring., Rose Hulman Inst. Tech., 1965; M.S., No. Ill. U., 1970; m. Rose Ann Park; children—Angela Jean, Robert David. Process engr. Amoco Chem. Corp., Joliet, Ill., 1965-70; biochem. engr. Eli Lilly & Co., Indpls., 1970-73, ops. coordinator fermentation pilot plant, 1973-75, dept. head antibiotic fermentation and initial purification, 1975-79, dept. head insulin purification, 1979-80, dept. head recombinant DNA insulin purification, 1980—. Founder, chmn. Orme Park Community Assn., 1972, 73; chmn. Smith Valley Community Center, 1977—. Named Jaycee of Year, 1978, recipient Key Man award, 1974, 76. Mem. Am. Inst. Chem. Engrs., White River Twp. Jaycees (pres. 1975), Mensa. Home: 5265 Comet Dr Greenwood IN 46142 Office: Dept IC-229 Indianapolis IN 46285

FENNELLY, WILLIAM AUGUSTINE, pharm. co. exec.; b. N.Y.C., Nov. 13, 1936; s. William A. and Helen S. Fennelly; A.B. with honors, Holy Cross Coll., 1958; M.B.A., U. Pa., 1960; m. Mary Anna McNamara, Sept. 11, 1965; children—Julie, Beth Ann. With Johnson & Johnson, New Brunswick, N.J., 1961-66, dept. mgr., until 1966; with Pfizer, Inc., N.Y.C., 1966-76, ops. planning mgr., until 1976; v.p. domestic mfg. Baxter-Travenol, Deerfield, Ill., 1976—. Mem. Pharm. Mfrs. Assn., Parenteral Drug Assn. Republican. Roman Catholic. Club: Lake Forest, Chgo. Curling. Office: 1 Baxter Pkwy Deerfield IL 60045

FENNEMA, OWEN RICHARD, food chemist; b. Hinsdale, Ill., Jan. 23, 1929; s. Nick and Fern Alma (First) F.; B.S., Kans. State U., 1950; M.S., U. Wis., 1951, Ph.D., 1960; m. Ann Elizabeth Hammer, Aug. 22, 1948; children—Linda Gail, Karen Elizabeth, Peter Scott. With Pillsbury Co., 1953-57; mem. faculty U. Wis., Madison, 1960—, prof. food chemistry, 1969—, chmn. dept., 1977-81. Served with AUS, 1951-53. Recipient Excellence in Teaching award U. Wis. Coll. Agr., 1977. Fellow Inst. Food Technologists (pres. 1982—; nat. sci. lectr. 1967, 73-76, Cruess award 1978); mem. Am. Chem. Soc., Soc. Cryobiology, Am. Dairy Sci. Assn., Am. Inst. Nutrition, Council Agrl. Sci. and Tech., Gamma Sigma Delta, Phi Tau Sigma. Co-author: Low-Temperature Preservation of Foods and Living Matter, 1973. Editor: Principles of Food Science, parts I and II, 1975-76; Proteins at Low Temperatures, 1979. Home: 5010 Lake Mendota Dr Madison WI 53705 Office: Dept Food Sci U Wis Madison WI 53706

FENNER, HARWOOD HUSS, roofing and sheet metal co. exec.; b. Rochester, N.Y., Oct. 10, 1933; s. Harwood Clyde and Dorthea Mae (Huss) F.; student Mich. State U., 1952-54; m. Claudette Jean Ballard, Jan. 23, 1960; children—Debra Lynn, Susan Gail, Michael Wayne, Pamela Jean. Accountant, Fabricated Steel Co., South Bend, Ind., 1958-61; mgr. Gen. Roofing & Insulation Co., South Bend, 1961-68; pres., owner Fenner Roofing and Sheet Metal Inc., Sodus, Mich., 1968—. Served with AUS, 1954-57. Mem. South Bend Joint Apprenticeship Roofing Com. (pres.), Associated Roofing Contractors Western Mich. (sec.-treas.), Nat., Mich. (past pres.) roofing contractors assns., Midwest (dir.), Mich. roofing assns., Sheet Metal Assn. Mich. Congregationalist. Club: Rotary. Home: 3030 Dozer Dr Saint Joseph MI 49085 Office: 3834 Pipestone Rd Sodus MI 49126

FENNESY, THOMAS VINCENT, engr.; b. Kansas City, Mo., Aug. 10, 1931; s. John J. and Charlotte (Maloney) F.; B.S., U. Kans., 1959; m. Marilyn T. (Carrigan) F., Aug. 24, 1957; children—Vincent, Gerard, Jack, Nancy. Data process engr. McDonnell Aircraft Co., 1959-60; elec. design engr. Lutz & May, Kansas City, Mo., 1960-62; design engr. Lutz, Daily & Brain, Overland Park, Kans., 1962-65, elec. engr., 1965-67, mgr. dept. elec. engring., 1967—. Registered profl. engr. Mo., Kans., Tex., Nebr., Colo., Mich., Iowa, Minn. Mem. IEEE, Mo. Soc. Profl. Engrs. Club: Victory Hills Country. Home: 909 Tam-o-Shanter St Kansas City MO 64145 Office: 6400 Glenwood St Shawnee Mission KS 66202

FENNO, JAMES ROBERT, pharmacist; b. Milw., Aug. 10, 1943; s. Robert Ray and Loraine Emma Hazel (Hardtke) F.; B.S. in Pharmacy, U. Wis., 1961-66, postgrad., 1974-76; m. Jane Helen Stenerson, Oct. 15, 1966; children—James Andrew, Lauri Jane. Asst. dir. pharmacy Appleton (Wis.) Meml. Hosp., 1968-73; clin. cons. pharm. services, Appleton, 1973-74, 76-77; clin. pharmacy specialist U. Wis. Med. Center, Madison, 1974-76; dir. pharmacy and clin. pharmacy services St. Joseph's Hosp., Chippewa Falls, Wis., 1977—; tchr. and cons. at various hosps. Cons. mem. bd. dirs. Chippewa United Way; bd. dirs. Chippewa unit Am. Cancer Soc.; past bd. dirs. Outagamie unit Am. Cancer Soc., Citizens Police Res., Outagamie County Heart Watch Program, Outagamie County Health Resources; past cons. mem. Drug Council, Inc. Mem. Am. Pharm. Assn., Acad. Gen. Practice (charter), Am. Soc. Hosp. Pharmacists, Am. Inst. History of Pharmacy, Outagamie County Pharm. Assn., Wis. Pharm. Assn. (dir.), Chippewa Valley Pharm. Assn. (pres.), Wis. Soc. Hosp. Pharmacists. Home: 815 Dwight St Chippewa Falls WI 54729 Office: St Joseph's Hosp 2661 Country Trunk I Chippewa Falls WI 54729

FENSKE, TIMOTHY JOSEPH, clergyman; b. Conneaut, Ohio, Oct. 11, 1947; s. Raymond Henry and Isabelle Agatha (Reinhard) F.; B.Sociology, Quincy Coll., 1971; M.Div., Cath. Theol. Union, 1975; M.Ed., John Carroll U., 1979. Ordained priest Roman Catholic Ch., 1975; tchr., counselor, chaplain Padua (Ohio) High Sch., 1975-78; asst. prin., tchr., chaplain Trinity High Sch., Garfield Heights, Ohio, 1978-79; tchr., coach, counselor, chaplain Cardinal Mooney High Sch., Youngstown, Ohio, 1979-81; tchr., chaplain, adminstr. St. Thomas Aquinas High Sch., Louisville, Ohio, 1981—; tchr. adult edn. St. Mathias Parish, Youngstown, 1980. Recipient award Cath. Fedn. Community Services, 1978. Mem. Nat. Cath. Edn. Assn., Assn. Supervision and Curriculum Devel., Theta Alpha Kappa. Roman Catholic.

FENSTERSTOCK, LYLE SUMNER, fin. cons. co. exec.; b. N.Y.C., Mar. 24, 1948; s. Nathaniel and Gertrude F.; B.A. cum laude, Brandeis U., 1969; M.B.A., (Lamont fellow), Harvard U., 1971; m. Linda Painter, Nov. 18, 1972. Vice pres. Warburg, Paribas, Becker, Chgo., 1971-75; investment banker Salomon Bros., Chgo., 1976; dir. bus. devel. Quaker Oats, Chgo., 1976-78; pres. Fensterstock & Co., Chgo., 1978—. Mem. Assn. Corp. Growth, Assn. Accts. for Coops. Club: Carlton. Home: 200 E Delaware Pl 34C Chicago IL 60611 Office: 401 N Michigan Ave Suite 215 Chicago IL 60611

FENTON, JEAN GILTNER, architect; b. Welch, W.Va., Nov. 19, 1921; d. James Bristow and Marian Orna Eloise V. (Bornemann) Giltner; student Wheaton Coll., Norton, Mass., 1940, Boston U., 1941-43; Wyndham Coll., Boston, 1944; B.Arch., Western Res. U., 1949; m. D.G. Fenton, 1943 (dec. 1944); m. 2d, Warren Edward Finkel, Jan. 25, 1954 (div. 1974). Estimator, Roediger Constrn. Co., Cleve., 1947-49; architect Outcalt-Guenther Architects, Cleve., 1949-50, 54; estimator F.E. Young Constrn. Co., San Diego, 1950-51; designer, job coordinator George A. Fuller, San Diego, 1951-52; architect San Diego Unified Sch. Dist., 1952-53; partner Finkel & Finkel, Architects, Lorain, Ohio, 1954-74; prin. Jean Giltner Fenton, Lorain, 1974—; faculty, Lorain County Community Coll., 1975—; mem. adv. bd. WUAB-TV. Schweinfurth scholar, 1949. Mem. AIA, Architects Soc. Ohio. Important works include Lorain Community Hosp., Murray Ridge Sch., Lorain City Hall; (with others) Lorain County Community Coll., addition to Bettcher Industries, Birmingham, Ohio, 1976, Golden Acres-Lorain County Home, addition to YMCA, residences and additions to residences, Nord Mental Health Center, Lorain County Met. Park Complex, County Mental Retardation Group Homes, Floro Med. Office Bldg. Office: 2316 Harborview Blvd Lorain OH 44052

FENTON, RUSSELL SANBERG, mfrs. rep.; b. Pitts., June 18, 1917; s. Patrick Henry and Mary Wilhelmina (Yokee) F.; grad. high sch.; m. Eleanor Hope Forbes, Sept. 15, 1941; children—Judith Lynn (Mrs. George Micklos Gomory), Karen Hope, Priscilla Beth (Mrs. James John Siwek). Molder, Universal Steel Co., 1935-37; owner, operator Fenton Radio Co., Bridgeville, Pa., 1937-41; parts mgr. Motor-Radio Distbg. Co., Pitts., 1941-42; quality control mgr. Gen. Electric Co., Bridgeport, Conn., 1942-45, product mgr., sales mgr. component parts div., Syracuse, N.Y., 1945-50, v.p., gen. mgr., dir. Permoflux Corp., Chgo., 1950-56; partner Gianaras Sales Co., Chgo., 1956-80; v.p. Transformer Mfrs., Inc., Chgo., 1956-80; founder, pres. Fenton Products Co., Northfield, Ill., 1976—, Fenton Sales Co., Northfield, 1980—; dir. Superior Valve & Fitting Co., Pitts. Chmn. Northfield Community League, 1953-56; mem. Northfield Safety Commn., 1959-60, Northfield Adv. Commn., 1965-68, Human Relations Commn., 1966-70; sr. warden St. James The Less, Northfield, Ill., 1972. Mem. Electronic Industries Assn. (chmn. speaker div., mem. exec. bd. parts div.), Radio Old Timers (life). Mason (Shriner). Club: Glenbrook Shrine (dir., past pres.) (Glenview). Patentee in field. Home: 308 Eaton St Northfield IL 60093 Office: 7051 W Wilson St Chicago IL 60656

FENWICK, DONALD DEAN, psychologist, educator; b. Grant, Nebr., Apr. 4, 1938; s. Earl William and Fanchon Phyllis (Sexson) F.; B.A., Nebr. State Coll., 1962; M.A., U. Nebr., 1965, Ed.D., 1967; m. Carol Sue Roberts, June 30, 1973. Sch. psychologist Dept. of Def. Overseas Dependents Schs., Pacific Area, Japan, 1967-69; learning disabilities cons., sch. psychologist Dept. Def., European Area, Eng. and Germany, 1969-73; sch. psychologist, coordinator pupil personnel services Mediterranean dist. U.S. Dependents Ednl. System, European Area, Athens, Greece, 1973-75, Naples, Italy, 1975-76; psychologist Dist. 1, Dept. Def. Overseas Dependent Schs., 1976-81, coordinator spl. edn. Pacific Area Regional Office, 1981—. Coordinator child study groups and family counseling services Dept. Def., Heidelberg, Germany, 1971-73. Home: 628 Washington Ave Grant NE 69140 Office: Dept Def Dependent Schs Pacific Area Regional Office PSC 1 Box 26927 APO San Francisco CA 96230

FENYES, IMRE, pathologist, lab. adminstr., educator; b. Budapest, Hungary, Nov. 21, 1926; s. Lajos and Julia (Englerth) F.; came to U.S., 1957, naturalized, 1962; M.D., U. Budapest, 1951; m. Jacqueline M. Walko, Aug. 19, 1962; 1 son, Richard M. Staff pathologist Michael Reese Hosp., Chgo., 1965-67; asso. dir. labs. and pathology dept. Edgewater Hosp., Chgo., 1968—; asst. prof. pathology Chgo. Med. Sch., 1976—. Fellow Coll. Am. Pathologists; mem. AMA (Continuing Med. Edn. award 1976), Chgo. Path. Soc. Roman Catholic. Contbr. articles on pathology to med. jours. Home: 2025 Sherman Ave Evanston IL 60201

FERCH, DAVID LUVERNE, library adminstr.; b. Waterloo, Iowa, Sept. 28, 1948; s. Dale Ernest and Francys Evelyn (Nikolas) F.; B.A. (Newberry Library Student fellow), Coe Coll., 1972; M.A. (DuPont Research fellow in history), Coll. William and Mary, 1978; M.L.S., Rutgers U., 1976; Ph.D., U. Iowa, 1979—; m. Julia Anna Kohl, Sept. 21, 1969. Head reference services Mount Mercy Coll., Cedar Rapids, Iowa, 1976-79, dir. library services, 1979—; mem. library services adv. bd. Kirkwood Community Coll., Cedar Rapids, Iowa, 1980—. Mem. AAUP, Am. Hist. Assn., Assn. Bibliography History, Iowa Hist. Materials Preservation Soc., Iowa Library Assn., Orgn. Am. Historians, Phi Beta Kappa, Phi Kappa Phi. Home: 7311 Idledale Rd NE Cedar Rapids IA 52402 Office: 1330 Elmhurst Dr NE Cedar Rapids IA 52402

FERDERBER, CHARLES JOSEPH, hosp. ofcl.; b. Madrid, Iowa, Sept. 21, 1915; s. Izidore and Matilda E. (Eskra) F.; diploma Moline (Ill.) Bus. Coll., 1937; m. Elizabeth Mary Gallagher, Sept. 24, 1949; children—Charles Joseph, Scott Kevin, Mary Jane. Artist-illustrator, Rock Island (Ill.) Arsenal, 1941-43; commd. 2d lt. Med. Service Corps, U.S. Army, 1943, advanced through grades to col., 1968; service in Europe and Far East; ret., 1968; dir. mgmt. services Deaconess Hosp., Evansville, Ind., 1968—; lectr. in field, also condr. seminars. Past chmn. bd. Goodwill, Inc., Evansville. Decorated Army Commendation medal (2). Mem. Am. Mgmt. Assn., Am. Hosp. Assn., Am. Inst. Indsl. Engrs. (sr.), Hosp. Mgmt. Systems Soc., Hosp. Fin. Mgmt. Assn., Am. Inst. Suggesters Systems (past pres.), Kennel Club. Democrat. Roman Catholic. Club: K.C. (3 deg.). Author: Hospital Work Simplification, 1977; also articles. Home: Route 5 Box 304 Baseline Rd Evansville IN 47711 Office: 600 Mary St Evansville IN 47710

FERGUSON, ARDALE WESLEY, indsl. supply exec.; b. Cedar Springs, Mich., Aug. 6, 1908; s. George Ardale and Alice Lucina (Andrus) F.; student pub. schs.; m. Hazel Frances Lokker, Oct. 28, 1931; children—Constance Ann (Mrs. Donald F. Klaasen), Mary Alice (Mrs. Robert A. Ritsema), Judy Kaye (Mrs. Charles Ruffino); m. 2d., G. Dolores Laker, Aug. 1976. Sales exec. John Deere Plow Co., Lansing, Mich., 1935-50; exec.-treas., mgr. Ferguson Welding Supply Co., Benton Harbor, Mich., 1950-76; sec.,-treas. Lape Steel Stores, Inc., Benton Harbor, 1976—; dir. Modern Light Metals, Inc. Mem. Benton Twp. Bd. Rev., 1963, Mich. Econ. Advancement Council, 1963-64; chmn. Mich. Hwy. Commn., 1964-68; pres. Twin Cities Community Chest, 1956. Treas. Mich. Republican Central Com., 1957-61; del. to Rep. Nat. Conv., 1960. Recipient award of spl. merit, Twin Cities Community Chest, 1956. Methodist. Clubs: St. Joseph-Benton Harbor Rotary (pres. 1960), Berrien Hills Country, Mountain Shadows Country, Peninsular. Home: 2609 Golfview Dr Apt 105 Troy MI 48084 Office: PO Box 964 Benton Harbor MI 49022

FERGUSON, DAVID, steel co. exec.; b. Bklyn., May 9, 1921; s. David and Marion M. (Fitch) F.; B.A., Yale U., 1943; postgrad. Harvard U., 1966; m. Barbara Hopkins, June 5, 1948; children—Sandra E. Ferguson McPhee, Nancy H. Ferguson Ferguson. With, U.S. Steel Co., 1946—, area dir. public affairs, Chgo., 1975-81, gen. mgr. public affairs, 1981—. Trustee, Roosevelt U.; chmn. bus. adv. com. Chgo. State U., 1976—. Served with USAAF, 1943-46. Mem. Public Relations Soc. Am. (mem. nat. bd. 1981—). Episcopalian. Clubs: Union League, Glen View Golf, Met.; Congressional (Washington). Office: US Steel Corp 208 S LaSalle St Chicago IL 60604

FERGUSON, DENNIS EARL, mech. engr.; b. Wabasha, Minn., July 14, 1945; s. Irvie Ashal and Mary Alice (Erickson) F.; B.M.E. with distinction, U. Minn., 1972, M.S., 1978; m. Anita Lynn Robertson, June 23, 1967; children—Tamara Lynn, Jeffrey Earl. Engring. records clk. IBM, Rochester, Minn., 1967-69; mech. engr. 3M Co., St. Paul, 1972—, sr. project engr., 1978—; cons. in field. Scoutmaster, Boy Scouts Am., Haskins, Nebr., 1966-67. Served with U.S. Army, 1963-66. Recipient Proctor & Gamble Award of Merit, 1975; registered profl. engr., Minn. Mem. ASME (session vice chmn. 1978), U. Minn. Alumni Assn., Nat. Model R.R. Assn. Republican. Evangelical Ch. Contbr. articles to profl. jours. Home: 3018 Furness Ct Maplewood MN 55109 Office: 900 Bush Ave Bldg 42 6W 05 Saint Paul MN 55144

FERGUSON, ELIZABETH (LIBBY) SHANLEY, publisher; b. St. Louis, June 11, 1926; d. Connor Bernard and Marie Doris (Maull) Shanley; B.A., Duke U., 1947; m. Thomas B. Ferguson, Jan. 31, 1948; children—Linda Ferguson Benoist, Thomas B., Scott Shanley. Writer, St. Louis Mag., 1970-72, advt. mgr., mag. mgr., 1972-74, pub., 1974—. Mem. Audit Bur. Circulation, Standard Rate and Data, St. Louis Regional Commerce and Growth Assn., Better Bus. Bur. St. Louis, City Regional and Mag. Assn. Episcopalian. Clubs: Bellerive Country, Creve Coeur Racquet. Office: 7110 Oakland Ave Saint Louis MO 63117

FERGUSON, EVA DREIKURS, psychologist, scientist, educator; b. Vienna, Austria, Aug. 28, 1929; d. Rudolf and Sadie (Ellis) Dreikurs; B.A. with honors, U. Ill., 1950; M.A. with honors, Melbourne (Australia) U., 1953; Ph.D., Northwestern U., 1956; m. John A. Ferguson, Jan. 28, 1950 (div. 1969); children—Rodney, Beth, Bruce, Linda. Sociologist, Lady Gowrie Child Center, Melbourne, 1951-52; intern in psychology Ill. Neuropsychiat. Hosp., Chgo., 1954-55; postdoctoral fellow Western Psychiat. Inst., Pitts., 1956-58; psychologist Craig House for Children, Pitts., 1959-62; asst. prof. psychology Melbourne U., 1962-65; asso. prof. psychology So. Ill. U., Edwardsville, 1965-69, prof., 1969—. Recipient award in sociology Chi Omega, 1950. Mem. AAAS, (life), Am. Psychol. Assn., Sigma Xi. Author: Motivation: An Experimental Approach, 1976; cons. editor: Psychology of Women Quar., Jour. Individual Psychology; contbr. articles to profl. jours. Office: Dept Psychology So Illinois Univ Edwardsville IL 62025

FERGUSON, FRANCIS EUGENE, ins. co. exec.; b. Batavia, N.Y., Feb. 4, 1921; s. Harold M. and Florence F. (Munger) F.; B.S. in Agrl. Econs., Mich. State U., 1947, LL.D. (hon.), 1972; D.C.L. (hon.), Ripon Coll., 1978; m. Patricia J. Reddy, Aug. 11, 1945; children—Susan L., Patricia A. Asst. sec.-treas. Nat. Farm Loan Assn., Lansing, Mich., 1947-48; appraiser Fed. Land Bank, St. Paul, 1948; extension specialist Mich. State U., 1951; with Northwestern Mut. Life Ins. Co., Milw., 1951—, v.p. mortgages, 1963-67, pres., 1967-80, chmn. bd., chief exec. officer, 1980—, also dir.; dir. Allen-Bradley Co., Milw., Djinnii Industries, Inc., Dayton, Ohio, Green Bay Packaging, Inc. (Wis.), Ralston Purina Co., St. Louis, Rexnord, Inc., Milw., Singer Co., Stamford, Conn., WICOR and Wis. Gas Co., Milw. Served to capt. USAAF, World War II; Germany. Mem. Alpha Zeta. Republican. Clubs: Milw., Univ. Milw., Milw. Country. Office: 720 E Wisconsin Ave Milwaukee WI 53202

FERGUSON, GARY LOREN, health and mgmt. cons.; b. Sioux City, Iowa, Aug. 13, 1937; s. Donovan Hugh and Izetta Marie (Blades) F.; B.A. (scholar), U. Iowa, 1963; Ph.D., Ariz. State U., 1967, M.H.S.A., 1975; m. Mary Anne Perino Lehnen, Sept. 9, 1979. Research asst. U. Iowa Med. Sch., 1963; grad. asst. chemistry Ariz. State U., 1963-67; research chemist duPont Co., 1967-70; exec. analyst George S. May Internat. Co., San Francisco, 1972-74; sr. mgmt. analyst and preceptor VA Med. Center, Columbia, Mo., 1977—; mem. adj. faculty Va. Commonwealth U., Richmond, 1969-70, U. Mo., Columbia, 1978-81. Treas., Bethany Homeowners Assn., 1973-75; blood drive coordinator Boone County (Mo.) chpt. ARC, 1977-79. Served with U.S. Army, 1958-61. Recipient Merit award, scholarship Iowa State U., 1955-57. Mem. Hosp. Mgmt. Systems Soc., Sigma Xi, Alpha Chi Sigma, Beta Gamma Sigma. Home: 1016A College Park Dr Columbia MO 65201 Office: 800 Stadium Rd Columbia MO 65201

FERGUSON, HARRY, engring. scientist; b. Dayton, Ohio, May 1, 1914; s. Robert and Isabella (Gamble) F.; B.S., Boston U., 1939; A.M., Harvard U., 1949; Ph.D., U. Pitts., 1958; m. Helen B. Baker, July 7, 1941. Mem. faculty Ohio U., Northeastern U., Tufts U., 1939-50; applied mathematician Wright-Patterson AFB, 1950-56, aero. research engr., 1956-59; asso. prof. math. U. Cin., 1959-66, prof. engring. scis., 1966—; v.p., owner Ferguson Sales, Inc., Alpha, Ohio. Mem. Am. Math. Soc., Math. Assn. Am., Soc. Indsl. and Applied Math., Soc. Natural Philosophy, Am. Soc. Engring. Edn., Alpha Tau Omega. Methodist. Clubs: Harvard (Dayton), Masons, Shriners. Home: 5105 Weston Circle Dr Dayton OH 45429 Office: Dept of Engineering Science U Cincinnati Cincinnati OH 45221

FERGUSON, JOHN BOWIE, profl. hockey team exec.; b. Vancouver, B.C., Can., Sept. 5, 1938; s. John Bowie and Mary Stuart (Howie) F.; student public schs.; m. Joan Elizabeth Bate, Sept. 5, 1959; children—Christina, Catherine, John, Joanne. Profl. hockey player Montreal Canadiens, 1963-71; pres. now also v.p., gen. mgr. Winnipeg Jets, Nat. Hockey League. Address: Winnipeg Jets 15-1430 Maroons Rd Winnipeg MN R3G 0L5 Canada

FERGUSON, JOHN RICHARD, publishing co. exec.; b. Columbus, Ohio, Oct. 23, 1937; s. Charles A. and A. Mildred (Weate) F.; A.A., Graceland Coll., 1957, B.L.S., 1973; student Harbor Coll., 1957, Calif. State Coll., 1965, Rockhurst Coll., 1970-71; children—Steven Paul, Connie Marie. Mgr. retail depts. Sears Roebuck and Co., Riverside, Calif., 1959-63, personnel mgr., 1964-66; ordained to ministry Reorganized Ch. of Jesus Christ of Latter-day Saints, 1955; minister Long Beach (Calif.) Ch., 1963-64; dist. pres. Reorganized Ch. of Jesus Christ of Latter Day Saints, Los Angeles, 1966-68; asst. mgr. Herald Pub. House, Independence, Mo., 1968-69, mgr., 1969—; pres. Silver Fox Ltd., realty, Ferguson Realty; dir. Sta. KMOS-TV, Sta. KCMW-TV, Standard State Bank. Pres. Independence Bd. Edn., 1970-76; v.p. Independence Neighborhood Councils; bd. dirs. Health Missions Internat., Buckhorn Camp., Met. Kansas City chpt. Leukemia Soc., Independence YMCA; dir. citizen's adv. council N.W. Mo. Div. Probation and Parole; pres., dir. Kansas City Area Drug Abuse Program; bd. dirs. N.E. Jackson County Mental Health Center. Mem. Protestant Church-Owned Publs. Assn. (dir. 1970—), Independence C. of C. (dir. 1977-79, pres. 1978-79, Citizen of Yr. 1979). Clubs: Lions (charter pres. Independence 1970), Independence Rotary. Contbr. articles to religious publs. Home: 527 S Crysler Apt B Independence MO 64052 Mailing address: 3225 S Noland Rd PO Drawer HH Independence MO 64055

FERGUSON, MARY ROSALIE SCHMIDT, telephone co. exec.; b. Indpls., Jan. 1, 1939; d. Francis John and Catherine Marie (Osterman) Schmidt; student Butler U., 1957—; div.; 1 dau., Kimberlie Marie. With Ind. Bell Telephone Co., Indpls., 1957—, office supr., 1965-71, staff asst., 1971-72, staff supr., 1972-73, account mgr., 1973-79, specialist, 1979—; workshop and seminar leader on mgmt. technique and growth opportunities for women. Mem. Indpls. Mus. Art Speaker's Bur., 1973-74, v.p., bd. dirs. bus. unit group, 1973-74; mem. resdl. exec. com. Am. Cancer Soc. Mem. Am. Bus. Women's Assn. (chpt. pres. 1972-73, 74-75, Nat. Bus. Women of Year 1972-73), Ind. State Symphony Soc. (women's com.), Fine Arts Soc. Indpls., Network of Women in Bus. (chmn. profl. devel. com., exec. bd. 1982-85), Ind. Bell Bus. Club (pres. 1979-80), Bell Mgmt. Club (dir. 1973—), LWV, Nat. Assn. Female Execs. Roman Catholic. Club: Ind. Bell Women's (pres. 1972-73) (Indpls.). Home: 7831 Somerset Bay Indianapolis IN 46240 Office: 240 N Meridian St Indianapolis IN 46204

FERIS, DOROTHY AMELIA, aircraft corp. exec.; b. Downers Grove, Ill., Sept. 21, 1922; d. Joseph and Frances (Dvorak) Slanec; student public schs., Downers Grove, Ill.; children—Herbert Charles, Timothy Lee. Sec., Joseph T. Ryerson & Sons, Chgo., 1940-44; sec.-treas. Taylorcraft Aviation Corp., Alliance, Ohio, 1968-76, pres., 1976—. Mem. Alliance C. of C., Aircraft Owner's and Pilot's Assn., Taylorcraft Owner's Club, Exptl. Aircraft Assn. Home: 32 S Wilmette St Westmont IL 60559 Office: PO Box 243 14600 Commerce St NE Alliance OH 44601

FERLIN, FRANK, JR., labor ofcl.; b. Olphant Furnace, Pa., Nov. 24, 1935; s. Frank J. and Ann D. (Bandzuch) F.; student State Tchrs. Coll., California, Pa., 1959, John Carroll U., 1960; m. Margaret T. Patchan, Feb. 13, 1960; children—Mark E., Marilyn A. With Pa. Dept. Hwys., 1957; with Nickel Plate R.R., Cleve., 1957-70, resident engr., 1965-70; v.p., vice gen. chmn. Nickel Plate Lodge 563-5 of Am. Ry. and Airway Suprs. Assn., 1964-68, pres., gen. chmn. lodge, 1968-70; v.p., field rep., dir. Am. Ry. and Airway Suprs. Assn., Chgo., 1970-72, fin. sec.-treas., 1972-74, pres., chmn. bd. dirs., 1974—. Served with USMC, 1954-57. Mem. Ry. Labor Execs. Assn. (exec. bd.), Nat. R.R. Adjustment Bd., AFL-CIO (mem. edn. com.), Am. R.R. Editors. Democrat. Roman Catholic. Club: K.C. Office: 4250 W Montrose Ave Chicago IL 60641

FERMOILE, JAMES L.S., printing co. exec.; b. Niagara Falls, N.Y.; student U. Buffalo; B.G.S., Wayne State U.; m. Ann Marie Cusick, Aug., 1968. With Moore Bus. Forms, Inc., N.Y. State and Detroit, 1954-70, nat. account sales mgr., 1965-70; v.p., sales mgr. Mid West Graphic Inc., Livonia, Mich., 1970-73; chmn. bd. M.W.G. Corp., Detroit, 1973—; pres. Ferm Assts.; treas., dir. Casa Balcona. Mem. Mich. del. Pres.'s Com. on Small Bus.; bd. dirs. Polit. Action Com., Detroit. Mem. Nat. Bus. Forms Assn., Data Processing Mgmt. Assn., Wayne State U. Alumni Assn., Detroit C. of C., Alpha Delta Tau (hon.), Gamma Delta Psi. Clubs: Detroit Yacht; President's.

FERNANDEZ, RALPH G., indsl. controls co. exec.; b. Havana, Cuba, Oct. 24, 1945; s. Joseph Fernandez and Ena F.; came to U.S., 1962; B.S. in Engring. Physics, St. Ambrose Coll., 1970; m. Cynthia Jane Nelson, June 20, 1970; children—Anthony Michael, Kara Jane. With Eagle Signal Co., Davenport, Iowa, 1970—, sr. system sales engr., 1974, system sales supr., 1974—, field sales mgr., 1979—. Republican. Roman Catholic. Home: 3239 E 18th Pl Davenport IA 52803 Office: 736 Federal St Davenport IA 52803

FERRARI, JOYCE MARIE, bus. exec., educator; b. Crosby, Minn., Mar. 11, 1936; d. Walter E. and Alice P. (Midthun) Heineman; student Minn. Sch. Lab. Techniques, 1955; A.A., Brainerd Jr. Coll., 1968; B.S., U. Minn., Duluth, 1970, M.A., 1981; B.A. in Nursing, St. Scholastica, Duluth, 1981; m. John Raymond Ferrari, Apr. 21, 1956; children—Ricky, Deanna Marie. Med. technician Good Samaritan Hosp., Williston, N.D., 1955-56, Cuyuna Range Clinic, Crosby, 1956, Aitkin (Minn.) Community Hosp., 1957-58, St. Joseph Hosp., Brainerd, Minn., 1959-67; tchr. 2d grade Aitkin Sch. Dist. #1, 1970—; owner, operator dee j's, clothing store and beauty shop, Crosby, 1976—. Recipient foster parent cert., Minn., cert. learning disabilities tchr., Minn. Mem. Minn. Edn. Assn., Assn. Supervision and Curriculum Devel. Republican. Lutheran. Clubs: Order Eastern Star, Royal Neighbors. Address: 20 2d St SE Crosby MN 56441

FERRARO, LANCELLOTTO ANGELO, photographer, microfilm services co. exec.; b. Kalamazoo, Aug. 12, 1921; s. Marion and Giovanna (Philippi) F.; student Western Mich. U., 1958; degree Winona Sch. Photography, 1960; m. Charlotte Anne Grant, June 22, 1949; children—Lancelotte Joffre, Sharon Rose, Laura Ann, Katherine Louise, Gina Maria, Marc Eric. Owner, operator Lance Ferraro Photography Studio, Kalamazoo, 1967—, Lance Ferraro Cinema Service, 1971—; pres. Micro-Cine-Systems, Inc., Kalamazoo, 1971—; writer, photographer Detroit Free Press, Grand Rapids (Mich.) Press, 1962-67; chmn. Mich. cert. Commn. for Profl. Photographers, 1976-79. Bd. dirs. Kalamazoo Youth Theatre; chmn. Vine Neighborhood Bus. Devel. Assn., 1979. Cert. photographer, Mich. Mem. Profl. Photographers Am. (nat. award 1978), Profl. Photographers Mich. (past pres., chmn.), Kalamazoo Profl. Photographers (past pres.), Mich. Live Steam Assn. (past pres.), Nat. Microfilm Assn., Nat. Records Mgmt. Assn., Am. Records Mgmt. Assn. Author: One Hour in Our History, 1965. Office: 1309 S Westnedge Ave Kalamazoo MI 49008

FERREL, LOWELL ORA, clin. psychologist; b. Imperial, Nebr., July 27, 1944; s. Lowell Orlan and Donnabeth (Ferebee) F.; B.A. magna cum laude, William Jewell Coll., 1969; M.A., U. Ark., 1972, Ph.D., 1975; m. Jennalea Ann Smith, July 2, 1966; 1 son, Thomas Robert. Pvt. practice clin. psychology, Kansas City, Mo., 1975—; part-time adj. prof. pastoral care Midwest Bapt. Theol. Sem., 1975-80. Mem. Am. Psychol. Assn., Mo. Psychol. Assn. (ethics com. 1981, public relations com. 1980-81), Am. Assn. Family Therapists, Am. Soc. Clin. Hypnosis, Am. Acad. Neuropsychologists, Am. Assn. Pastoral Counselors (profl. affiliate). Republican. Baptist. Home: 1608 NE 68th Terr Kansas City MO 64118 Office: 3100 Broadway Suite 1220 Kansas City MO 64111

FERRELL, ROBERT LEE, surgeon; b. West Union, W.Va., Sept. 8, 1939; s. John Bruce and Hester Isabelle (Hogue) F.; B.S., Fairmont (W.Va.) State Coll., 1961; M.D., W.Va. U., 1965; m. Janet Sue Cusick, Nov. 5, 1965; children—Carolyn Sue, Cynthia Lou, James Bruce, Daniel Tyler. Resident gen. surgery Creighton U., Omaha, 1968-69, resident in otorhinolaryngology U. Nebr., 1969-72; practice medicine specializing in otorhinolaryngology and facial plastic surgery, Rapid City, S.D., 1973—; attending staff Rapid City Regional Hosp., chief of surgery, 1980—; cons. staff Ft. Meade VA Hosp.; asso. staff Nebr. Meth. Hosp., Omaha, Children's Meml. Hosp., Omaha; fellow ENT br. Armed Forces Inst. Pathology, 1971; former program dir. U. Nebr.-Pine Ridge Oglala Sioux Otitis Media Program, 1971-76; asst. prof. U. Nebr. Coll. Medicine, 1972; asso. clin. prof. U. S.D. Coll. Medicine, 1975; guest faculty S.D. Acad. Family Practice, 1981. Served with M.C., USAF, 1966-68. Decorated Bronze Star, Air medal with oak leaf cluster; medal of Honor (Viet Nam). Fellow Am. Acad. Otolaryngology, A.C.S., Am. Acad. Facial Plastic and Reconstructive Surgery; mem. S.D. Acad. Otolaryngology (sec. 1975-76), Nebr. Acad. Otolaryngology, AMA, S.D. State Med. Assn. (dist. councilor 1979—), Rapid City Med. Soc. (pres. 1978-81), Ducks Unlimited (sponsor chmn.), Rushmore Retriever Club. Home: 511 Berry Pine Rd Rapid City SD 57701 Office: 629 Quincy St Rapid City SD 57701

FERRIER, DALE OTIS, wire die co. exec.; b. Ft. Wayne, Ind., Oct. 14, 1936; s. Otis George and Violet Lee (Campbell) F.; B.S., Ft. Wayne Bible Coll., 1968; M.S. in Bus. Adminstrn., Ind. U., 1973; postgrad., Walden U., 1979—; m. Patty Jane Bewley, June 14, 1958; children—Jeffrey Eugene, Edward Dale, Ruth Elaine. With Ind. Wire Die Co., Ft. Wayne, 1954—, gen. mgr., 1959—, pres., 1966—; instr. Dale Carnegie courses, 1966—; dir. Brotherhood Mut. Ins. Co. Mem. fin. com. Dan Coats for Congress; chmn. bd. Harvester Ave. Missionary Ch.; chmn. gov. bd. Ft. Wayne Bible Coll.; public speaker. Mem. Am. Mgmt. Assn., Am. Diamond Die Mfg. Assn. (sec.), Christian Businessmen's Com., YMCA. Club: Rotary. Contbr. articles to mags. Office: Ind Wire Die Co 314 E Wallace St Fort Wayne IN 46803

FERRINGTON, LEONARD CHARLES, JR., aquatic entomologist; b. Wilkinsburg, Pa., July 28, 1948; s. Leonard Charles and Martina Agnes F.; student Community Coll. Allegheny County, 1970-71; B.S. in Biol. Scis. cum laude, U. Pitts., 1975, Ph.D. in Biol. Scis. (teaching fellow), 1980; m. Deborah Ann Stinner, Sept. 8, 1978. Heavy equipment operator and laborer Ferroslag div. Spang & Co., Butler, Pa., 1969-70; asst. scientist Kans. Biol. Survey, Lawrence, 1980—; courtesy asst. prof. entomology U. Kans.; cons. aquatic assessment. Served with USMC, 1966-68; Vietnam. Decorated Purple Heart (2), Navy Achievement medal with Combat V; recipient Stanton C. Crawford award for excellence in teaching U. Pitts., 1977, Liesure K. Darbaker bot. prize Pymatuning Lab. of Ecology, 1980. Mem. DAV, YMCA, N.Am. Benthological Soc., Pa. Entomol. Soc., Wildlife Soc., Sigma Xi. Contbr. articles on aquatic ecology and entomology to profl. jours. Home: 1645 Rhode Island St Lawrence KS 66044 Office: 2045 Ave A Lawrence KS 66045

FERRIS, RICHARD J., airline exec.; b. Sacramento, 1936; B.S., Cornell U., 1962; postgrad. U. Wash. Grad. Sch. Bus. Staff analyst and restaurant mgr. Olympic Hotel, to 1971; gen. mgr. Savoy Plaza, Anchorage Westward Hotel, Continental Plaza Hotel, Carlton Hotel; project officer-new constrn. Western Internat. Hotels, to 1971; pres. carrier's food services div. United Air Lines, Chgo., 1971-75, sr. v.p. mktg., 1975-76, pres., 1976-79, chmn., chief exec. officer, dir., 1979—; dir. UAL, Inc., Western Internat. Hotels. Office: PO Box 66100 Chicago IL 60666*

FESCO, EDWARD JOHN, surgeon; b. Tarrytown, N.Y., July 10, 1930; s. John and Mary (Lantosh) F.; B.S., Villanova (Pa.) U., 1952; M.D., Northwestern U., 1956, M.S., 1955; m. Anne Elizabeth Condron, June 1956; children—Eileen, Mary, John, Nora, Carol, Beth. Intern, Presbyn.-St. Luke's Hosp., Chgo., 1956-57; resident in surgery VA Hosp., Hines, Ill., 1957-61; practice medicine specializing in gen. surgery, La Salle, Ill., 1963—; pres. med. staff Ill. Valley Hosp., La Salle; trustee Mid-State Found. for Med. Care, 1978-81, sec., 1982—. Served with M.C., USAF, 1961-63. Diplomate Am. Bd. Surgery. Fellow A.C.S.; mem. AMA, La Salle County Med. Soc. (pres. 1976). Roman Catholic. Home: 709 3d St La Salle IL 61301 Office: 206 Marquette St La Salle IL 61301

FESEMYER, ARTHUR JOHN, ednl. adminstr.; b. Donora, Pa., Dec. 28, 1925; s. Arthur H. and Jessie Catherine (Gates) F.; B.S., Kent State U., 1951, M.C.D., 1955; M.A. (NDEA scholar), U. Pitts., 1967; m. Jane S. Innes, May 6, 1946; children—Elizabeth, Susan, Becky, Carol, Amy, David, Thomas. Tchr., Ravenna (Ohio) Public Schs., 1951-54, prin., 1967-69, coordinator secondary edn., 1970—; tchr. Akron (Ohio) Schs., 1954-60; counselor Aurora (Ohio) Schs., 1959-67. Served with U.S. Army, World War II. Recipient Doer's award Ohio Edn. Assn., 1970. Mem. Assn. Supervision and Curriculum Devel., Ohio Assn. Supervision and Curriculum Devel., N.E. Ohio Assn. Supervision and Curriculum Devel. (treas./sec. 1975-80). Roman Catholic. Clubs: Kiwanis, Elks. Office: 507 E Main St Ravenna OH 44266

FESS, MARILYNN ELAINE (MRS. STEPHEN W. FESS), occupational therapist; b. Casper, Wyo., June 20, 1944; d. Frederick Eugene and Norma Pence (Jarrett) Ewing; B.S., Ind. U., 1967, M.S., 1977; m. Stephen W. Fess, Nov. 26, 1966. Staff occupational therapist Marion County Gen. Hosp., Indpls., 1966-70; supr. phys. dysfunction unit, 1970-72; supr. adult occupational therapy Ind. U. Med. Center, Indpls., 1972-74, instr. occupational therapy curriculum, 1974-76; hand therapist Strickland & Steichen, M.D.'s, Inc., 1974-79; designer, developer, dir. hand therapy Hand Rehab. Center Ind., 1976-79; cons. hand rehab. and hand research, 1979—; cons. to hand surgeons various hosps. and nursing homes. Mem. exec. bd. Ind. Cerebral Vascular Accident Com., 1973-76. Mem. Am. Occupational Therapy Assn., Am. Soc. Hand Therapists (founding, mem. at large exec. bd. 1978-79), Orgn. Affiliate Pres.'s (sec. 1976-78), Ind. Occupational Therapy Assn. (sec. 1969-71, v.p. 1972-73, pres. 1974-76, hand therapy liaison to exec. bd. 1978—). Author: (with others) Hand Splinting Principles and Methods, 1980; also articles. Patentee externally powered hand orthosis. Office: 635 Eagle Creek Ct Zionsville IN 46077

FESSLER, WILLIAM GARY, food processing equipment co. exec.; b. Piqua, Ohio, Oct. 15, 1946; s. Charles William and Kathryn Louise (Miller) F.; B.S. in Applied Sci. in Systems Analysis, Miami U., Oxford, Ohio, 1968; m. Nancy Jo Gump, Nov. 22, 1978; 1 son, Michael William; children by previous marriage—Tiffany Ilene, Farrah D'Ann. Programmer analyst Champion Papers, Inc., Hamilton, Ohio, 1966-69; sr. systems analyst McCall Computer Services Co., Dayton, Ohio, 1969-76; mgr. systems and programming Ponderosa System, Inc., Dayton, 1976-79; mgr. devel. services Hobart Corp., Troy, Ohio, 1979—; data processing cons. Mem. Assn. for

Systems Mgmt., Assn. Computing Machinery. Democrat. Methodist. Club: Elk. Home: 108 W Vanlake Dr Vandalia OH 45377 Office: Hobart Corp World Headquarters Dr Troy OH 45374

FETHERHUFF, ARDEN J., retail exec.; b. Aberdeen, S.D., June 30, 1942; s. Ravone Archabold and Alta Mary (Riesdorph) F.; E.E., S.D. Sch. Mines and Tech., 1963; B.S. in Bus. Adminstrn., No. State Coll., 1965; m. Sharon Joyce Schlepp, Apr. 18, 1965; children—Steve, Dana. Systems mgr. Control Data, Mpls., 1966-69; mgr. fin. systems Target Stores, Mpls., 1969-70; systems mgr. Electronic Data Systems Co., Mpls., 1970-77; asst. v.p., dir. mgmt. info. services Am. Nat. Bank, St. Paul, 1977-79; ind. data processing cons., 1979-80; dir. adminstrn. and mgmt. info. services Coast to Coast Stores, Minnetonka, Minn., 1980—. Mem. Am. Soc. Performance Improvement, Assn. Systems Mgmt., Soc. Mgmt. Info. Services. Home: 13516 Nicollet Ln Burnsville MN 55337 Office: 10801 Red Circle Dr Minnetonka MN 55343

FETRIDGE, BONNIE-JEAN CLARK (MRS. WILLIAM HARRISON FETRIDGE), civic worker; b. Chgo., Feb. 3, 1915; d. Sheldon and Bonnie (Carrington) Clark; student Girls Latin Sch., Chgo., The Masters Sch., Dobbs Ferry, N.Y., Finch Coll., N.Y.C.; m. William Harrison Fetridge, June 27, 1941; children—Blakely (Mrs. Harvey H. Bundy III), Clark Worthington. Bd. dirs. region VII com. Girl Scouts U.S.A., 1939-43, mem. nat. program com., 1966-69, mem. nat. adv. council, 1972—, mem. internat. commr.'s adv. panel, 1973-76, mem. Nat. Juliette Low Birthplace Com., 1966-69, region IV selections com., 1968-70; bd. dirs. Girl Scouts Chgo., 1936-51, 59-69, sec., 1936-38, v.p., 1946-49, 61-65, chmn. Juliette Low world friendship com., 1959-67, 71-72; mem. Friends of Our Cabana Com. World Assn. Girl Guides and Girl Scouts, 1969—, mem. membership com., 1975—; asst. sec. The Dartnell Corp., bus. pubs., Chgo., 1981—; bd. dirs. Jr. League of Chgo., 1937-40, Vis. Nurse Assn. of Chgo., 1951-58, 61-63, asst. treas., 1962-63; women's bd. dirs. Children's Meml. Hosp., 1946-50. Staff aide, ARC and Motor Corps, World War II. Vice pres. Latin Sch. Parents Council, 1952-54; bd. dirs. Latin Sch. Alumni Assn. 1964-69, Fidelitas Soc., 1979; women's bd. U.S.O., 1965-75, treas., 1969-71, v.p., 1971-73; women's service bd. Chgo. Area council Boy Scouts Am., 1964-70, mem.-at-large Nat. council, 1973-76, mem. nat. Exploring com., 1973-76; governing mem. Anti-Cruelty Soc.; asso. Nat. Archives. Recipient Citation of Merit for community contbns. in field of human relations Sta. WAIT, Chgo., 1971. Mem. Nat. Soc. Colonial Dames Am. (Ill. bd. mgrs. 1962-65, 69-76, 78—, v.p. 1970-72, corr. sec. 1978-80, 1st v.p. 1980—, state chmn. geneal. info. services com. 1972-76, hist. activities com. 1979—, mus. house com. 1980—, room and flag com. 1981—), Youth for Understanding (couriers bicentennial project), English-Speaking Union, Chgo. Dobbs Alumnae Assn. (past pres.), Nat. Soc. DAR, Chgo. Geneal. Soc., Conn. Soc. Genealogists, New Eng. Historic Geneal. Soc., N.Y. Geneal. and Biog. Soc., Newberry Library Assos., Chgo. Hist. Soc. Guild. Republican. Episcopalian. Clubs: Casino, Saddle and Cycle, Woman's Athletic. Home: 2430 Lakeview Ave Chicago IL 60614

FETRIDGE, CLARK WORTHINGTON, pub.; b. Chgo., Nov. 6, 1947; s. William Harrison and Bonnie Jean (Clark) F.; B.A., Lake Forest Coll., 1969; M.B.A., Boston Coll., 1971; m. Jean Hamilton Huebner, Apr. 19, 1980. Money market specialist Continental Ill. Nat. Bank, Chgo., 1971-73; asst. to pres. Dartnell Corp., Chgo., 1973, sec., 1974, v.p., 1976-77, sr. v.p., 1977-78, pres., 1978—. Trustee, Lake Forest Coll.; treas. Latin Sch. Chgo. Alumni Assn.; asst. treas. U.S. Found. for Internat. Scouting; vice-chmn. Nat. Eagle Scout Assn.; chmn. 1200 Club Ill.; mem. Internat. Com., Boy Scouts Am.; bd. govs. United Republican Fund of Ill.; del. Republican Nat. Conv., 1976; Republican candidate for Congress, 1972. Mem. Tau Kappa Epsilon. Episcopalian. Clubs: Saddle and Cycle, Chgo., Casino, Racquet, Chgo. Yacht, Stevensville Yacht. Office: 4660 N Ravenswood Ave Chicago IL 60640

FETRIDGE, WILLIAM HARRISON, publisher; b. Chgo.; s. Matthew and Clara (Hall) F.; B.S., Northwestern U., 1929; LL.D., Central Mich. U., 1954; m. Bonnie Jean Clark, June 27, 1941; children—Blakely Fetridge Bundy, Clark Worthington. Asst. to dean Northwestern U., 1929-30; editor Trade Periodical Co., 1930-31, Chgo. Tribune, 1931-34, H. W. Kastor & Son, 1934-35, Roche, Williams & Cleary, Inc., 1935-42; mng. editor Republican Mag., 1939-42; asst. to pres. Popular Mechanics mag., 1945-46, v.p., 1946; exec. v.p., 1953-59; v.p. Diamond T Motor Truck Co., Chgo., 1959-61; exec. v.p. Diamond T div. White Motor Co., 1961-65; pres. Dartnell Corp., Chgo., 1965-78, chmn. bd., chief exec. officer, 1978—; dir. Bank of Ravenswood. Pres., United Republican Fund Ill., 1967-73, 79-80, hon. pres., 1973-79; Rep. state finance chmn., 1967-74; alt. del.-at-large Rep. Nat. Conv., 1956, del.-at-large, 1968; campaign mgr. Merriam for Mayor of Chgo., 1955; chmn. Midwest Vols. for Nixon, 1960; chmn. Nixon Recount Com., 1960, Rep. Forum, 1958-60; mem. Rep. Nat. Finance Com., 1968-73; trustee Lake Forest Coll., 1969-77, Am. Humanics Found., Jacques Holinger Meml. Assn.; pres. U.S. Found. Internat. Scouting, 1971-79, hon. chmn., 1979; vice chmn. World Scout Found., Geneva, 1978—; del. World Scout confs., Rhodes, Greece, 1963, Helsinki, Finland, 1969, Tokyo, 1971, Nairobi, Kenya, 1973, Denmark, 1975, Montreal, 1977; past pres. bd. trustees Latin Sch. Chgo.; nat. v.p. Boy Scouts Am., 1958-76. Served as lt. comdr. USNR, 1942-45. Recipient Silver Buffalo, Silver Beaver and Silver Antelope awards Boy Scouts Am., also Distinguished Eagle Scout award; Bronze Wolf, World Scout Bur., Nairobi, Kenya, 1973; Disting. Citizen's award St. Andrew Soc., 1980; Abraham Lincoln award United Republican Fund, 1980. Mem. Navy League U.S. (past regional pres.; trustee Chgo. council), Soc. Midland Authors, Grand Priory Malta (chevalier), Sovereign Order St. John of Jerusalem, Beta Theta Pi. Clubs: Chgo., Union League, Saddle and Cycle, Casino (Chgo.); Chikaming Country; Rotary/One. Author: With Warm Regards, 1976; editor: The Navy Reader, 1943; The Second Navy Reader, 1944; American Political Almanac, 1950; The Republican Precinct Workers Manual, 1968. Home: 2430 Lakeview Ave Chicago IL 60614 Office: Dartnell Corp 4660 N Ravenswood Ave Chicago IL 60640

FETZER, JOHN EARL, bus., baseball, broadcasting exec.; b. Decatur, Ind., Mar. 25, 1901; s. John Adam and Della Frances (Winger) F.; student Purdue U., 1921; A.B., Andrews U., 1927, LL.D. (hon.), 1980; student U. Mich., 1929; LL.D. (hon.), Western Mich. U., 1958, Kalamazoo Coll., 1972, Andrews U., 1980; Litt.D. (hon.), Elizabethtown Coll., 1972; D.Eng. (hon.), Lawrence Inst. Tech., 1979; m. Rhea Maude Yeager, July 19, 1926. Owner, chmn. bd. Fetzer Broadcasting Co., 1930—, Fetzer TV Corp., Kalamazoo-Grand Rapids, Mich., 1970—, Cornhusker TV Corp., Lincoln, Nebr., 1953—; chmn., owner Detroit Tigers, Am. League Baseball Club, 1956—, Fetzer Music Corp., Fetzer TV, Inc., Cadillac, Mich., 1958-79, John E. Fetzer, Inc., 1968—; chmn. Wolverine Cablevision, Inc., 1967—; dir. emeritus Am. Nat. Bank & Trust Co., Kalamazoo. Chmn., Maj. League TV Com., 1963-71. U.S. Censor of radio, 1944-45; reporting to Gen. Eisenhower, engaged in ETO radio studies in Eng., France, Russia, Germany, Italy and other European countries, 1945; fgn. corr. radio-TV-newspaper mission Europe and Middle East, 1952; mem. mission Radio Free Europe, Munich, Germany, and Austrian-Hungarian border, 1956; Broadcasters Mission to Latin-Am., Dept. State, 1962, Detroit Tiger Baseball tour of Japan, Okinawa, Korea, under auspices Dept. State, 1962; mem. A.P. tour Europe, 1966; Dept. State del. Japanese-U.S. TV Treaty, 1972; mem. adv. bd. N.Am. Service, Radio Diffusion Française, Paris, 1946-47. Trustee Kalamazoo Coll., 1954—. Recipient Broadcast Pioneers award, 1968; Disting. Service award Nat. Assn. Broadcasters, 1969; Mich. Frontiersman award, 1969; Fourth Estate award Am. Legion, 1972; citation Mich. Legislature, 1972; C. of C. Detroit Tiger 75th Anniversary award, 1976; Mich. Legis. citation, 1976; Nebr. Pub. TV citation, 1976; Summit award Detroit C. of C., 1977; Abe Lincoln Railsplitter award So. Bapt. Radio and TV Commn., 1979. Fellow Royal Soc. Arts London; mem. Nat. Assn. Broadcasters (chmn. TV bd. 1952), C. of C. (past pres.), Nat. Geneal. Soc., Acad. Polit. Sci., Am. Soc. Mil. Engrs., IEEE (life mem.), Internat. Radio and TV Execs. Soc., Broadcast Pioneers (19th Mike award to Sta. WKZO 1981), Alpha Kappa Psi. Presbyn. Mason (33 deg., Shriner), Elk. Clubs: Park, Kalamazoo Country (Kalamazoo); Economic, Detroit Athletic, Press, Detroit (Detroit); Tucson Country. Author: One Man's Family, 1964; The Men from Wengen and America's Agony, 1972. Contbr. Radio and Television Project, Columbia, 1953. Home: 2714 Clovelly Rd Kalamazoo MI 49008 Office: Kalamazoo MI 49008 also Tiger Stadium Detroit MI 48216

FEVURLY, JAMES ROBERT, educator; b. Easton, Kans., Jan. 28, 1926; s. Edgar Earl and Nellie Esther (Murray) F.; B.A., U. Kans., 1950; M.A., 1954, Ed.D., 1977; m. Meredith Ann Reynolds, May 22, 1973; children—Keith, Chris, Deborah, Marcella, Carol, Anna, Karen. Dir. biol. control lab. Jensen-Salsbery Labs., Kansas City, Mo., 1954-60; dir. biol. prodn. Haver-Lockhart Labs., Shawnee, Kans., 1960-69; tchr. chemistry, biology United Sch. Dist. 453, Leavenworth, Kans., 1970—; lectr. in field. Sec. Leavenworth County Mental Health Assn., 1965-66. Served with USAAF, 1944-46. U.S. Navy Microbiol. Research grantee, 1951-54. Mem. N.Y. Acad. Scis., AAAS, Am. Ednl. Research Assn., Sigma Xi, Phi Sigma, Phi Delta Kappa. Republican. Presbyterian. Club: Elks. Contbr. articles to profl. jours. Home: 206 Arch St Leavenworth KS 66048 Office: 10th Ave and Halderman St Leavenworth KS 66048

FEWELL, BOBBY LEE, civil engr.; b. North Vernon, Ind., Dec. 22, 1927; s. J. Frank and Jessie Mae (Dilk) F.; student Purdue U., 1951-54; m. Helen Mae Bannister, Aug. 10, 1949; 1 son, Lee Scott. Asst. project engr. Ind. Hwy. Commn., Seymour, Ind., 1955-58; cons. engr. C.E. Williams & Assos., Indpls., 1958-61; project engr. Ind. Hwy. Comm., 1961-71; pres. B.L. Fewell & Assos., Inc., North Vernon, Ind., 1971—; pres. Fewell and Elsner Inc., doing bus. as Jennings Industries, 1979—; dir. Lee's Inns of Am., 1975—. Charter mem. Jennings County Area Planning Commn., 1966-69. Served as sgt. USAF, 1945-48. Mem. Nat. Ind. socs. profl. engrs. Methodist. Mason (Shriner). Home: Box 41 North Vernon IN 47265 Office: Box 41 138 E Walnut St North Vernon IN 47265

FIANDACA, JAMES PATRICK, telephone co. mgr.; b. Sioux City, Iowa, Mar. 20, 1944; s. Pasquale C. and Helen F. (Conway) F.; student No. Ill. U., DeKalb, 1962-63, Elgin (Ill.) Community Coll., 1963-65, U. Ill., 1965-66; m. Judith Gail Fleishman, June 25, 1966; 1 dau., Teresa Lynn. With Ill. Bell Telephone Co., 1967—, asst. staff supr., 1974-75, market mgr. transp., Chgo., 1975—, mgr. trucking industry, 1980—. Mem. Ill. Trucking Assn. Office: 1 Crossroads of Commerce Rolling Meadows IL 60008

FICHT, MARY ANNETTE, indsl. hygienist, public health ofcl.; b. Chgo., Nov. 20, 1946; d. Edwin Francis and Genevieve Marie (Filwett) F.; B.A., St. Dominic Coll., 1968; M.A., Western Mich. U., 1969; M.A., Northeastern Ill. U., 1975; M.P.H., U. Ill., 1980. Dir. internat. health Am. Med. Student Assn., Chantilly, Va., 1971-75, cons., 1976, 77; cons. Ill. Family Planning Council, Inc., Chgo., 1976-77, Am. Coll. Ob-Gyn, Chgo., 1977—, McHenry County Dept. Public Health, Woodstock, Ill., 1979—; environ. health cons. Sch. Public Health, U. Ill. Med. Center, Chgo., 1981; indsl. hygienist No. Petrochem. Co., Morris, Ill., 1981—; cons. to various orgns. and agys. Recipient Leadership award U. Ill. Med. Center Alumni Assn., 1979; USPHS trainee, 1978-80. Mem. Am. Conf. Govt. Indsl. Hygienists, Am. Indsl. Hygiene Assn., Am. Public Health Assn., Ill. Public Health Assn., Assn. Am. Med. Colls., Am. Personnel and Guidance Assn., Ill. Guidance and Personnel Assn. Author, editor Internat. Health Quar. News, 1972-75; editor: International Medical Programs Available to American Medical Students, 1972.

FICKEL, VIOLA RUTH, ednl. adminstr.; b. Columbus, Ohio, Mar. 26, 1926; d. Frederick Charles and Ruth Ann (Tope) Daniel; student Ohio State U., 1941-42; m. C. Ramon Fickel, May 12, 1951; children—Randall Lee, Terrence Lynn, Tami Rae. Exec. sec. State Auto Ins., Columbus, 1942-50; office mgr. United Hobby, Columbus, 1951-53; sales mgr. Acorn Realty, Worthington, Ohio, 1969-75, adminstrv. sec., 1975-78; benefits and records specialist Columbus Tech. Inst., 1978—. Publicity chmn. Sharon Community Council, 1979-81; pres. Sharon PTA, 1975. Mem. Ohio Coll. Assn. (mem. steering com. 1979—), Columbus Bd. Realtors, Ohio Bd. Realtors. Democrat. Methodist. Home: 346 E Lincoln Ave Columbus OH 43214 Office: 550 E Spring St Columbus OH 43215

FICKLE, WILLIAM DICK, lawyer; b. Kansas City, Mo., Oct. 29, 1943; s. William and Elvarea (Dick) F.; B.A., Westminster Coll., Fulton, Mo., 1965; J.D., U. Mo., Columbia, 1969; m. Jane Thompson Jones, Nov. 29, 1969; children—Tara Elizabeth, William Dick. Admitted to Mo. bar, 1968; asso. firm James, McFarland, Trimble, Austin, North Kansas City, Mo., 1971-72; pros. atty. Platte County (Mo.), 1973-74; partner firm Fickle & Hull, Platte City, Mo., 1973-74, firm Clevenger, Fickle & McGinness, Platte City, 1975—. Mem. Mo. Ho. Reps., 1974-79; bd. dirs. Eyebank of Kansas City, Mo., Home Health Services Clay-Platte and Jackson Counties. Served with U.S. Army, 1969-70. Decorated Legion of Honor. Mem. Mo. Bar, Platte County Bar Assn. (v.p.). Democrat. Episcopalian. Clubs: Masons, Shriners, Jesters. Home: 7708 NW Mastern Kansas City MO 64152 Office: 204 Marshall Rd Platte City MO 64079

FIDDICK, PAUL WILLIAM, broadcasting co. exec.; b. St. Joseph, Mo., Nov. 20, 1949; s. Lowell Duane and Betty Jean (Manring) F.; B.J., U. Mo., Columbia, 1971; m. Peggy Patricia Anderson, Nov. 18, 1972; Acct. exec. Sta. KCMO, Kansas City, Mo., 1971-72; acct. exec. Sta. WEZW, Milw., 1972-74, sales and mktg. dir., 1974-76, v.p., gen. mgr., 1976—; sr. v.p. Multimedia Broadcasting Co., 1981—; mem. faculty U. Wis., 1978—; mem. adv. com. Sta. WUWM-FM. Mem. Milw. Area Radio Stas. (chmn. 1979-81), Milw. Advt. Club (dir. 1977-80). Co-authored and produced radio sales film. Office: 735 W Wisconsin Ave Milwaukee WI 53233

FIECHTER, RAY ALLEN, distbg. co. exec.; b. Decatur, Ind., Nov. 20, 1945; s. Homer H. and Clara M. (Schladenhauffen) F.; B.M.E., Purdue U., 1970; m. Carol Payne, July 18, 1965; children—Shantelle Rae, Shurell Alane. Process engr. Corning Glass Co., Bluffton, Ind., 1964-66; research and devel. engr. Detroit Diesel Allison div. Gen. Motors Corp., Indpls., 1970-71; applications engr. Schwitzer div. Wallace Murray Co., Indpls., 1971-72, sales mgr., 1972-78; divisional mgr. Davidson, Inc., Indpls., 1978—. Bd. dirs. Ind. chpt. Arthritis Found. Mem. ASME, Soc. Profl. Engrs., Nat. Fluid Power Soc. Home: 226 Mill Farm Rd Noblesville IN 46060 Office: 5610 Dividend Dr Indianapolis IN 46241

FIELD, MARSHALL, V, communications and real estate exec.; b. Charlottesville, Va., May 13, 1941; s. Marshall IV and Joanne (Bass) F.; B.A., Harvard U., 1963; m. Joan Best Connelly, Sept. 5, 1964 (div. 1969); 1 son, Marshall; m. 2d, Jamee Beckwith Jacobs, Aug. 19, 1972; children—Jamee, Stephanie Caroline, Abigail Beckwith. With N.Y. Herald-Tribune, 1964-65; dir. Field Enterprises Inc., Chgo., 1965—, mem. exec. com., 1966—, chmn. bd., 1972—, mem. exec. com. Chgo. Sun-Times, 1965—, pub., 1969-80; dir. 1st Nat. Bank Chgo., 1st Chgo. Corp. Mem. adv. bd. Chgo. area council Boy Scouts Am.; mem. Chgo. com. Chgo. Council on Fgn. Relations; mem. profl. journalism adv. com. Stanford U.; mem. adv. bd. Brookfield Zoo, Broader Urban Involvement and Leadership Devel., Inc., Presdl. Classroom Young Ams.; trustee, vice-chmn. Art Inst. Chgo.; trustee Field Mus. Natural History, Rush-Presbyn.-St. Luke's Med. Center, Mus. Sci. and Industry; governing mem. Orchestral Assn., Chgo.; hon. bd. dirs. Corp. for Open Lands (Corlands); bd. dirs. Chgo. Boys' Clubs, Internat. Atlantic Salmon Found., McGraw Wildlife Found., Nat. Book Com., Field Found. of Ill., Lincoln Park Zool. Soc., Restoration Atlantic Salmon in Am. Inc.; bd. overseers Harvard Coll.; hon. bd. dirs. Nat. Commn. Prevention of Child Abuse; adv. bd. Dialogue with the Blind. Mem. Nature Conservancy, Chgo. Zool. Soc. Clubs: Casino, Chgo., Comml., Harvard, Hundred of Cook County, Mchts. & Mfrs., Mid-Am., Tavern, Racquet (Chgo.); River (N.Y.C.); Somerset (Boston); Jupiter Island (Hobe Sound, Fla.); Owentsia (Lake Forest, Ill.); McGraw Wildlife (Dundee, Ill.). Office: 401 N Wabash Ave Chicago IL 60611

FIELD, MAXWELL JOHN, real estate investment co. exec.; b. London, Eng., June 1, 1934; s. Frederick John and Amelia Glasspool Dean (Allford) F.; student Coll. of Estate Mgmt., London, 1952-56; m. June Edith Madeline Martin, Feb. 2, 1957; children—Guy William, Gillian Rosemary, Duncan Maxwell. Came to Can., 1957. Articled pupil Messrs. Howell & Brooks, Chartered Surveyors, London, 1951-55; profl. asst. Messrs. Gerald Eve & Co., Chartered Surveyors, London, 1955-57, Messrs. W.H. Bosley & Co. Ltd., Toronto, Ont., Can., 1957-62; property mgr. MEPC Canadian Properties Ltd., Toronto, 1963-65; devel. mgr. Monarch Investments Ltd., Toronto, 1965-70; dir., mem. exec. com. Marathon Realty Co. Ltd., Toronto, 1970—; chmn., chief exec. officer, dir. Marathon U.S. Holdings, Inc., Marathon U.S. Realties, Inc., Marathon Devel. Calif., Inc., Marathon Devel. Oreg., Inc., Marathon Devel. Ga., Inc.; dir. Marathon Aviation Terminals Ltd. Fellow Royal Instn. Chartered Surveyors; mem. Ont. Land Economists. Clubs: Cambridge, Granite (Toronto); Whitlock Golf and Country (Montreal). Home: Apt 4612 175 E Delaware Chicago IL 60611 Office: Suite 2550 One First Nat Plaza Chicago IL

FIELDING, IVOR RENÉ, chemist; b. Jefferson, Iowa, July 3, 1942; s. Leslie Wayne and Roberta (Oakes) F.; B.A., Simpson Coll., 1964; postgrad. U. Colo., 1964, Kans. State U., 1964-66; M.S., Creighton U., 1970; Ph.D., U. Pitts., 1970; M.S., Midwest Coll. Engring., 1977; m. Anna Theresa Damas, Aug. 10, 1968; children—Maria Ona, Krista Terese. Teaching asst. Kans. State U., Manhattan, 1964-66, Creighton U., Omaha, 1966-68; teaching, research asst. U. Pitts., 1968-70; research chemist Amoco Chems. Corp. div. Standard Oil Ind., Naperville, Ill., 1970-77, sr. research chemist, 1977—. Class agt. Simpson Coll. Alumni Annual Fund, 1972-73, class coordinator, 1974-75. Simpson Coll. grantee, 1960-64; NSF grantee, 1968-70. Mem. Am. Chem. Soc., Am. Inst. Chemists, Sigma Xi, Sigma Tau Delta, Phi Lambda Upsilon. Patentee in field. Home: 115 N Brainard St Naperville IL 60540 Office: PO Box 400 Naperville IL 60566

FIELDS, CLYDE DOUGLAS, hosp. adminstr.; b. Owen County, Ind., June 6, 1932; s. Arthur LaVerne and Mary Elizabeth (Smith) F.; B.S. cum laude in Bus. Adminstrn., Ind. Central U., 1963; M.B.A., Butler U., 1968; m. Barbara Marie Ott, Aug. 25, 1956; children—Gayla Jean Fields (dec.), Douglas Jay, Angela Kay. With Crosley div. Avco Mfg. Co., Richmond, Ind., 1950-51; with Allison div. of Gen. Motors Corp., Indpls., 1951-64; with Linde and Materials Systems divs. Union Carbide Corp., Indpls., 1964-69; dir. fin. affairs Bartholomew County (Ind.) Hosp., Columbus, 1969-71, asst. exec. dir., 1972; v.p. fin. and asst. treas. Meth. Hosp. of Indiana, Inc., Indpls., 1973-77, v.p. adminstrn., asst. treas., 1978-80, sr. v.p., asst. treas., 1981—, bd. dirs., asst. treas. Meth. Hosp. Found., 1973—; faculty, staff leadership confs AMA, 1979; lectr. grad. program in health care adminstrn. Ind. U. Sch. Medicine, 1980—. Chmn. adminstrv. bd. Center United Meth. Ch., Indpls., 1976-77, chmn. staff parish relations com., 1978, lay del. ann. conf., 1976—, cert. lay speaker, 1979—; bd. dirs. Ecumenical Assembly of Bartholomew County Churches, Inc., 1970-72, treas., 1971; chmn. adminstrv. bd. and Council on Ministries, Asbury United Meth. Ch., 1970-72; bd. dirs. Ch. Fedn. Greater Indpls., 1978-81, chmn. fin. com., 1978-79; bd. dirs. Perry Sr. Citizens Service, 1977-80; bd. dirs. Bartholomew County chpt. Ind. Assn. for Retarded Children, 1971-72, treas., 1971; bd. dirs., chmn. Econ. Devel. Com. of Community Action Program, Bartholomew, Brown and Jackson Counties (Ind.), 1972; trustee Ind. Central U., 1981—. Served with USN, 1952-56. Mem. Hosp. Fin. Mgmt. Assn. (William G. Follmer Merit award 1974, advanced mem. dir. 1974, mem. edn. council 1976-77), Assn. for Systems Mgmt. (Gold Achievement award Ind. chpt. 1969, chpt. pres. 1971-72 Internat. Merit award 1975), Ind. Hosp. Assn. (council on fin. 1973-79, public relations adv. com. 1977—, council on govt. relations 1980—), Ind. Central U. Bus. Assn., Ind. Central U. Alumni Assn. (bd. dir. 1975—, pres. 1979-80), Midwest Pension Conf. (Ind. chpt.). Republican. Club: Kiwanis (sec. 1973-74, v.p. 1974-76, pres. 1976-77, named Disting. Club pres. 1977). Home: 540 Ho Hum Ct Greenwood IN 46142 Office: Methodist Hosp of Indiana 1604 N Capitol Ave Indianapolis IN 46202

FIELDS, CURTIS GREY, telephone co. exec.; b. Goldsboro, N.C., Oct. 23, 1923; s. C.F. and Ethel B. Fields; B.S. in Math. and Physics, East Carolina U., 1955; m. Jean L., Apr. 5, 1953; children—Curtis G., Dwayne L. With Carolina Tel. & Tel., 1955-72, gen. director mgr., div. comml. mgr., until 1972, gen. comml. supr., 1971-72; gen. comml. mgr. United Telephone Co. of Ohio, Mansfield, 1972-74, v.p. adminstrn., 1974-79, pres., 1979—, also dir.; dir. 1st Bucke Bank. Bd. dirs. United Community Services. Mem. Ohio Telephone Assn. (dir.), Mansfield C. of C. (dir.). Episcopalian. Clubs: Westbrook Country, Lakewood Racquet. Office: 665 Lexington Ave Mansfield OH 44907

FIELDS, DONALD LEE, pediatrician; b. Muncie, Ind., May 3, 1928; s. Ellis Loree and Sarah Isabelle (Moomaw) F.; A.B., Ball State U., 1950; M.D., Ind. U., 1955; m. Elizabeth Ann Jarrett, Aug. 23, 1952; children—Richard, Ann, Barbara, Donald Scott. Intern, Riverside (Calif.) Gen. Hosp., 1955-56; resident in pediatrics Ind. U. Med. Center, 1958-60, asst. in pediatrics, 1977—; practice medicine specializing in pediatrics, Kokomo, Ind., 1960—; mem. staffs Howard Community Hosp., St. Joseph Hosp; cons. Grissom AFB, Ind. Served with USAF, 1956-58. Diplomate Am. Bd. Pediatrics. Fellow Am. Acad. Pediatrics (exec. com. Ind. chpt.); mem. AMA, Ind. State Med. Assn., Howard County Med. Soc. Republican. Methodist. Club: Rotary. Home: 3304 Tallyho Dr Kokomo IN 46901 Office: 3804 Southland Ave Kokomo IN 46901

FIELDS, LADONNA COURTNEY, social worker, tng. adminstr.; b. Mayfield, Ky., Nov. 16, 1953; d. Eugene and Frances Estelle (Riley) Courtney; A.A. in Sociology, Belleville Area Coll., 1974; B.S. in

...ology, Ill. State U., 1976; postgrad. Sangamon State U.; m. Jerome ...ancis Fields, June 12, 1976. Home trainer, caseworker McLean County Assn. for Retarded Citizens, Bloomington, Ill., 1976-78; social worker Aid to Retarded Citizens, Inc., Springfield, Ill., 1978-79; tng. adminstr. Ill. Assn. of Rehab. Facilities, Springfield, 1979—. Recipient cert. of appreciation Springfield Area Parents Anonymous, 1979; Staff award Ill. Assn. Rehab. Facilities, 1980; registered social worker Ill. Dept. Registration and Edn. Mem. Am. Assn. Mental Deficiency, Am. Soc. Tng. and Devel. Home: Springfield IL 62703 Office: 206 S 6th Suite 300 Springfield IL 62701

FIELDS, THEODORE, cons. med. physicist; b. Chgo., Jan. 23, 1922; s. Samuel and Jean (Golber) F.; B.S., U. Chgo., 1942; M.S., 1953, DePaul U.; m. Audrey Helena Engerman, June 24, 1945; children—Brad, Scott, Gary. Pres., Isotope Measurements Lab., Northbrook, Ill., 1969—, Health Physics Assos., Northbrook, 1961—, Fields, Griffith, Hubbard & Assos., Glencoe, Ill., 1974—; lectr. radiology U. Chgo., 1980—. Served with USAAF, 1945-46. Fellow Am. Coll. Radiology, Am. Pub. Health Soc.; mem. IEEE, Radiol. Soc., N. Am., Radiation Research Soc., Am. Phys. Soc., Health Physics Soc., Am. Assn. Physicists in Medicine, Sigma Xi. Author: Clinical Use of Radioisotopes, 1957, 61; Treatment of Toxic Goiter with Radioactive Iodine, 1953; contbr. articles to profl. jours. Patentee in field. Home: 1141 Hohlfelder Rd Glencoe IL 60022 Office: 3304 Commercial Rd Northbrook IL 60062

FIELEKE, CATHARINE NICHOLSON (MRS. LESSLY C.A. FIELEKE), author, reader, lectr., columnist; b. Ash Grove, Mo., Sept. 27, 1909; d. John Warren and Mattie (Duncan) Nicholson; student Drury Coll., Olivet Coll., U. Chgo.; m. Lessly C.A. Fieleke, Dec. 24, 1929; children—Norman, Sharon Fieleke Cohly, Cathy Fieleke Butterfield, Lessly, Laurel Fieleke Shoshani, Curtis, Teresa Fieleke Brooks. Pres., Fieleke Implement Co., 1965-67. Recipient awards Woman's Club, Am. Pen Women, others. Mem. World Soc. Poets Intercontinental, Pen Women (pres. Chgo. br. 1974-76, chmn. Nat. Mid.-Adminstrn. Congress 1977), Nat. Writers Club, Internat. Platform Assn., Internat., Ill. (v.p.) poetry socs., Am. Acad. Poets, Internat. Biog. Assn., Friends Am. Writers, Children's Reading Round Table, Chgo. Poets and Patrons, Kankakee Area Writers Group. Baptist. Club: Women's. Author: (poetry) Run-off from Northern Springs; Summer Solstices; Aspects of Autumn; The White Fields of Winter; author, prodn. asst. American Poetry Series, 1965; scripts for ednl. tapes Imperial Internat. Learning, Kankakee, Ill.; lectures, poetry editor Pen Woman mag.; contbr. articles and poems to newspapers and mags., column to area newspapers. Home: 312 Ohio St Momence IL 60954

FIELY, DOUGLAS RAYMOND, printmaker, educator; b. Celina, Ohio, June 2, 1950; s. Raymond J. and Katherine A. (Blair) F.; B.A., Bowling Green U., 1972, M.A., 1976, postgrad., 1978—; m. Julia Jane Uribes, Nov. 21, 1980; 1 dau. by previous marriage, Georgia Rae; 2 stepsons—Alex, Aaron. Art tchr. and dir. Community Action Commn., Celina, 1969-70; instr. art Stryker (Ohio) High Sch., 1972—; one-man shows of prints include: Wright State U., Celina, 1975, Defiance (Ohio) Coll., 1976, 78; group shows include: Ohio State Fair Fine Arts Exhbn., Columbus, 1976, 77, Toledo (Ohio) Mus. Art, 1977-78, Purdue U., Lafayette, Ind., 1977; 16th Bradley Nat. Print and Drawing Exhbn., Peoria, Ill., 1977, Newport, R.I., 1977. Recipient Profl. award Ohio State Fair, 1976. Mem. Ohio Edn. Assn., NEA, Stryker Edn. Assn., Stryker Tchrs. Assn. (pres. 1976-78), Internat. Soc. Artists, U.S. Jaycees. Roman Catholic. Illustrator: Seizure Mag., 1975; Clouds Blowing Away, 1976. Address: RFD 2 PO Box 78 Stryker OH 43557

FIETSAM, ROBERT CHARLES, accountant; b. Belleville, Ill., Oct. 18, 1927; s. Celsus J. and Viola (Ehret) F.; B.S., U. Ill., 1955; m. Miriam Runkwitz, Apr. 12, 1952; children—Robert C., Guy P., Nancy A., Lisa R. Claims adjuster Ely & Walker Dry Goods, St. Louis, 1947-48; jr. accountant Price Waterhouse & Co., 1949-54; staff accountant J.W. Boyle & Co., East St. Louis, 1955-59; owner R.C. Fietsam, C.P.A., Belleville, Ill., 1959-68, mng. partner R.C. Fietsam & Co. C.P.A.'s, 1969—. Past pres. Signal Hill Improvement Assn.; mem. Bell-Scott Com., 1979—; bd. dirs., pres. Belleville Center, Inc. Served with USAF, 1951-53. Recipient Optimist of Year award Optimist Club, Belleville, 1977. C.P.A., Mo., Ill. Mem. Ill. Soc. C.P.A.'s (past pres. So. chpt., Mr. So. Chpt. award 1976, state dir. 1979-81), Mo. Soc. C.P.A.'s, Am. Inst. C.P.A.'s (council 1981—), U. Ill. Alumni Assn. (life), U. Ill. Greater Belleville Illini Club (past pres.), Belleville C. of C. (past pres.), Belleville Jr. C. of C. (life, Key Man award 1959-60, Outstanding Citizen award 1976), Lambda Chi Alpha Alumnae Assn. Mem. United Ch. of Christ (past pres.). Elk, Moose. Clubs: St. Clair Country, Optimist (pres. 1979-80, Disting. Pres. award Internat. orgn. 1979-80, Optimist of Yr. award Ill. Dist. 1980) (Belleville). Home: 9 Gerold Ln Belleville IL 62223 Office: 325 W Main Belleville IL 62220

FIFE, ROBERT LEE, mfg. co. exec.; b. Oil City, Pa., Apr. 21, 1933; s. Samuel R. and Rachel (Miller) F.; B.A., Pa. State U., 1955; B. Fgn. Trade, Am. Grad. Sch. Internat. Mgmt., 1959; postgrad. Stanford U., 1974; m. Nancy Ann Newton, Aug. 29, 1959; children—Eric R., Robyn L. Office mgr. Crucible div. Colt Industries, Inc., Nassau, Bahamas, 1960-62, sales mgr., Paris, 1962-64, N. European sales dir. Copenhagen, Denmark, 1964-67; product sales mgr. Howmet Corp., Lancaster, Pa., 1967-72, dir. mktg., Greenwich, Conn., 1972-76; gen. mgr. specialty products group Gen. Portland, Inc., Dallas, 1976-77; v.p. mktg. G&W Energy Products Group, Gulf & Western Mfg. Co., Oak Brook, Ill., 1977-78; v.p., gen. mgr. Taylor-Bonney div. G&W, Southfield, Mich., 1978-80; pres. G&W Taylor-Bonney Internat., Southfield, 1980—. Served with U.S. Army, 1956-58. Home: 26025 Woodlore Dr Franklin MI 48025 Office: G&W Mfg Co PO Box 999 Southfield MI 48037

FIGGE, FREDERICK H., JR., pub. co. exec.; b. Chgo., Apr. 8, 1934; s. Frederick H. and Theodora M. (Hosto) F.; B.S., U. Ill., 1956; m. Beverly J. Menz, June 20, 1956; children—Dora, Ann, Jane, Fred C. With Arthur Young & Co., 1958-64; with Ency. Britannica, Inc., Chgo., 1964—, v.p., treas., 1974—. Bd. dirs. Coll. of Commerce, U. Ill. Served with U.S. Navy, 1956-58. Mem. Am. Inst. C.P.A.'s, Ill. Soc. C.P.A.'s, Beta Theta Pi, Beta Gamma Sigma. Democrat. Congregationalist. Club: LaGrange Country. Office: 425 N Michigan Chicago IL 60611

FIGHTMASTER, WALTER JOHN, coll. ofcl.; b. Barberton, Ohio, Dec. 14, 1930; s. Verderman Cantrill and Amanda (Stone) F.; B.S., U. Louisville, 1952, M.A., 1954; m. Sue N. Tabler, June 8, 1958. Cons. psychologist Kemper & Assos., Louisville, 1952-54; research psychologist George Washington U., Washington, 1957-58; sr. indsl. psychologist Martin Marietta Corp., Balt., 1958-59, Westinghouse Electric Corp., Balt., 1959-60; staff psychologist Bendix Corp., Ann Arbor, Mich., 1960-63; chief staff psychologist Ling-Temco-Vought, Inc., Warren, Mich., 1963-65; dir. community services Oakland Community Coll., Bloomfield Hills, Mich., 1965-68, exec. dir. of community services, 1968-71, provost Southeast campus, 1971—. Chartered com. mem. Oakland County Police Acad. Served to capt. USAF, 1954-57. Commd. col. Hon. Order Ky. Cols., 1966. Licensed psychologist, D.C.; licensed psychologist, Mich. Mem. Am. Assn. Jr. Coll., A.A.A.S., Am., Midwestern, D.C., Eastern, Mich. Ky. psychol. assns., U.S.A., Mich. adult edn. assns., Nat., Mich. assns. for pub. sch. adult edn., N.E.A., Mich Soc. for Instrnl. Tech. (past pres.), Am. Assn. Community and Jr. Colls. (past dir.), Nat. Council on Community Services (past sec. and pres.), Psi Chi. Home: 5400 Sunnycrest Rd West Bloomfield MI 48033 Office: Oakland Community Coll Southeast Campus 22322 Rutland Dr Southfield MI 48034

FILEMYR, EDWARD JOSEPH, III, real estate broker, trainer, farmer; b. Phila., Oct. 24, 1932; s. Edward J. and Evelyn (Matlack) F.; B.S. in Bus., Temple U., 1954; student Wis. Sch. Real Estate, Waukesha Tech. Inst.; m. Sara A. Walker; children—Edward Joseph IV, Richard G., Ann Evelyn, Kathryn L., Janet Lynn. Agt., Colonial Life Ins. Co., 1956-57; field sales and service, area sales rep., product supr., product mgr. Electric Storage Battery Co., 1957-70; indsl. market mgr. Globe Union Battery Div., 1970-73; broker, owner Country Place Realty, 1973-80; real estate adv. bd., instr. Lakeshore Tech. Inst., 1975—, Wis. Sch. Real Estate, 1973-80; sales trainer, real estate sch. adminstr. ERA of Wis., 1980—. Bd. dirs. Sheboygan County Arts Council; mem. Town of Sherman Plan Commn., Sheboygan County Housing Commn., Random Lake Art Support; former clk. Milw. Meeting Soc. of Friends; fin. chmn., mem. adminstrv. bd. Zion United Meth. Ch. Served to 1st lt., AUS, 1954-56. Cert. resdl. specialist Nat. Assn. Realtors, Grad. Realtors Inst.; assessor Wis. Dept. Revenue. Mem. Sheboygan County Bd. Realtors, Wis. Realtors Assn. (dir.), Internat. Materials Mgmt. Soc. Clubs: Lions (past pres., dist. cabinet sec.-treas. 1981-82), Masons. Home: Route 1 County A Adell WI 53001

FILING, DAVID PETER, audio-visual technician; b. Medway, Maine, Apr. 12, 1949; s. Peter and Fern (Heilman) F.; A.A. in Indsl. Tech., Akron U., 1972; m. Laura Mae Achberger, Nov. 12, 1976. High Pressure boiler fireman aux. tender Ohio Edison Gorge Power Plant, Akron, 1970-72; banbury operator Goodyear Tire Co., Akron, 1972-76; audio-visual technician Cuyahoga Falls (Ohio) pub. schs., 1976—; auditorium mgr. Cuyahoga Falls High Sch.; v.p., bd. chmn. F-M Prodns., Inc., Cuyahoga Falls, 1975—; lectr., workshop dir. on audio-visual equipment. Club: Lions. Home: 2029 10th St Cuyahoga Falls OH 44221 Office: 431 Stow Ave Cuyahoga Falls OH 44221

FILKINS, JAMES HEASOM, educator; b. Coffeyville, Kans., Dec. 18, 1925; s. James Frederick and Wilma Blanche (Heasom) F.; B.S., Hardin-Simmons U., 1949; M.B.A., U. Dallas, 1968-70; Ph.D., N. Tex. State U., 1973; m. Lois Jean Popp, July 28, 1950; children—Timber Lee, Terence James, Tamara Jean. Chem. engr. Pure Oil Co., 1949-52; tech. service dir. Comml. Testing & Engring. Co., 1952-53; regional mgr. Indsl. Filter Mfg. Co., 1953-55; dist. mgr. Waukesha Sales & Service, 1955-58; ind. mgr. Sun Oil Co., 1958-69; v.p., dir. mktg. Freguson Industries, 1969-70; asst. prof., controller, asso. dean U. Dallas, 1970-73; v.p., dir. Mgmt. Labs. Am., 1971-73; asso. prof., chmn. dept. bus. adminstrn., dir. M.B.A. programs Coll. of Racine (Wis.), 1973-74; asso. prof. bus. adminstrn. St. Marys Coll., Notre Dame, Ind., 1974-76; prof., dir. grad. mgmt. programs Aquinas Coll., Grand Rapids, Mich., 1976-77; prof. Coll. of St. Thomas, St. Paul, 1977—; cons. Tex. Instruments, Inc., Campbell Taggart, State of Minn., others. Trustee, chmn. Ursuline Endowment Fund, Dallas, 1967-73. Served with USMCR, 1943-45. Mem. Am. Mktg. Assn. Internat. Materials Mgmt. Soc., Fin. Execs. Inst., Planning Execs. Inst., Sigma Iota Epsilon, Beta Gamma Sigma. Author: (with Donald L. Caruth) Lexicon of American Business Terms, 1973. Home: 10600 Aquila Ave S Bloomington MN 55438 Office: College of St Thomas St Paul MN 55105

FILLMORE, WILLIAM JAMES, IV, social orgn. cons.; b. Cape Town, South Africa, Nov. 12, 1940; came to U.S., 1962, naturalized, 1972; s. William J. and Daphne W. (Lang) F.; student U. Cape Town, 1960-62; B.A., Andrews U., 1965; M.A., U. Chgo., 1969; postgrad. Gestalt Inst. Chgo., 1975, U. Ill., 1977; m. Kathleen Elaine Dehnicke, Oct. 17, 1976; children—William James V, Anita Kathleen. Child care counselor Luth. Welfare Services of Ill., Park Ridge, 1965-68; psychiat. social worker Inst. for Psychiat. and Psychosomatic Research, Chgo., 1970-71; group therapist Michael Reese Hosp., Chgo., 1970-71, caseworker Wexler Outpatient Clinic, 1970-71; personnel supr. Ill. Bell Telephone Co., Chgo., 1971-72; pvt. practice psychotherapy, Chgo., 1972—; organizational cons. Organizational Consultants, Inc., Chgo., 1973-76, pres., 1976—; lectr. Aurora Acad. Mgmt., 1980-81. Bd. dirs. St. James Cathedral Counselling Center, 1979-81. Recipient Outstanding New Citizen citation, 1972. Mem. Internat. Assn. Applied Social Scientist, Internat. Registry of Orgn. Devel. Profls., Chgo. Orgn. Devel. Assn., Chgo. Hist. Soc., Chgo. Assn. of Commerce and Industry. Author: (poetry) Hum Drum Things, 1975; co-author: Group Work with Geriatric Patients. Home: 1129 N Rossell Oak Park IL 60302 Office: Organizational Consultants Inc 16 E Erie St Chicago IL 60611

FINCH, DONALD GEORGE, poet; b. Peoria, Ill., June 30, 1937; s. Lloyd Lindo and Jean Alberta Harsy; student Bradley U., 1955—. Works include: On Strawberry Eve, 1972; She Waits for Me, 1972; A Dandelion is Not a Rose, 1973; Georgia, 1976; We Are All the Children of God Through Jesus, 1977. With Peoria Post Office. Served with USAF, 1957-60. Mem. Peoria Poetry Club (v.p.), United Amateur Press, Am. Biog. Inst., Intercontinental Biog. Assn., DAV. Methodist. Home: 331 NE Perry Apt 2 Peoria IL 61603

FINCH, EUGENE CLIFFORD, wholesale trade exec.; b. Fosston, Minn., Sept. 11, 1915; s. Henry Kirk and Louise Minnie (Routmann) F.; student pub. schs.; m. Joyce Dorothea Goodchild, Sept. 18, 1947; children—Jeanne, Eugene Clifford, Suzanne, Caroline, Kirk. Vice-pres., gen. mgr. Keegan Farm Equipment Co., Mpls., 1954-59; pres. Finch Distbg. Co., Mpls., 1959-65; pres. Select-O-Rax, Inc., Burnsville, Minn., 1965—, chmn. bd., 1978—, also dir. Served with AUS, World War II. Mem. Babbitt (Minn.) Youth Clubs (hon.), Nat. Assn. Rec. Merchandisers, Nat. Assn. Ind. Record Distbrs., Nat. Assn. Truck Stop Operators, Am. Zool. Soc., Am. Legion, Internat. Platform Assn., Internat. Clergy Assn., Nat. Writers Club, Smithsonian Assos., Cousteau Soc., DAV (life). Club: Racquet (Palm Springs, Calif.). Home: 6930 Rosemary Rd Eden Prairie MN 55343

FINCH, F. SINCLAIR, physician; b. Armada, Mich., Aug. 24, 1914; s. Floyd S. and Rosetta May (Sinclair) F.; A.B., Wayne State U., 1936, M.B., 1940, M.D., 1941; m. Marseline A. Metz, Jan. 13, 1942; children—Robert S., Patricia A. Intern Grace Hosp., Detroit, 1940-41; resident Saratoga Gen. Hosp., Detroit, 1941-42, 46-48, mem. staff, 1948—, chief staff, 1963-64; pvt. practice medicine and surgery, East Detroit, 1948-81; nat. chief med. officer Unlimited Power Boat Assn. Served to maj. M.C., AUS, 1942-46. Mem. Spirit of Detroit Assn., Phi Rho Sigma. Club: Detroit Yacht (fleet surgeon 1964, 68). Home: 894 N Renaud St Grosse Pointe Woods MI 48236 Office: 21325 Gratiot St East Detroit MI 48021

FINCH, JOHN ROBERT, computing services co. exec.; b. Hoschton, Ga., July 17, 1937; s. Charles Steven and Fannie Lou (Slaton) F.; student Franklin U., 1955-57; B.S., Allied Inst. Tech., 1962; postgrad. Roosevelt U., 1964-65, DePaul U., 1975-76; m. Dean Ware, Apr. 27, 1968; children—Miguel, Rodney, Jody. Bus driver Chgo. Transit Authority, 1957-65; draftsman GTE Corp., Northlake, Ill., 1966-67; programmer Sargent & Lundy, Engrs., Chgo., 1968-72; sr. programmer Cook County Hosp., Chgo., 1972; lead program analyst Blue Cross/Blue Shield, Chgo., 1972-76; sr. technician Montgomery Ward, Chgo., 1976-77; project mgr. Cook County Hosp., 1977-79; pres. FCS Computing Services, Chgo., 1979—. Served with U.S. Army, 1953-55. Office: FCS Computing Services 189 W Madison Ave Chicago IL 60602

FINCH, JOSEPH WARREN, civil engr., surveyor; b. Youngstown, Ohio, Aug. 7, 1923; s. John P. and Mable A. (Poorman) F.; B.C.E., Cornell U., 1947; m. Norinne A. Lyden, July 25, 1944; children—Madonna, Cathy, Michael. Project engr. Joseph Bucheit Co., 1947-48; chief engr. Edward J. De Bartolo Corp., 1948-52; mgr. sales Webrib div., Copperweld Steel Co., 1952-53; gen. supt. constrn. E.J. DeBartolo Corp., 1953-57, mgr. constrn., 1962-70; pres. J.W. Finch Constrn. Co., 1957-62; v.p., project mgr. Park City Shopping Center, 1970-71; project mgr. Hannon Co., 1971-72; v.p. constrn. Stratford Enterprises, Youngstown, Ohio, 1972—; owner J.W. Finch & Son, contractors and engrs., Youngstown, 1972-75, pres. J.W. Finch & Son, Inc., 1975—. Mem. Mahoning County Planning Commn., 1963-65; mem. Bd. Bldg. Standards State Ohio, 1972-76; mem. Bd. Zoning Appeals, Boardman Twp., 1979—. Served to capt. AUS, World War II; ETO. Decorated Bronze Star medal. Fellow ASCE; mem. Am. Legion, Sigma Phi Epsilon. Elk. Clubs: Chesterton, Cornell (Youngstown). Address: 7427 Westview Dr Youngstown OH 44512

FINDLEY, PAUL, congressman; b. Jacksonville, Ill., June 23, 1921; s. Joseph S. and Florence Mary (Nichols) F.; A.B., Ill. Coll., 1943, LL.D. (hon.), 1973; L.H.D. (hon.), Lindenwood Coll., 1969; m. Lucille Gemme, Jan. 8, 1946; children—Craig Jon, Diane Lillian. Pres., pub. Pike Press, Inc., Pittsfield, Ill., 1947—; mem. 87th-97th Congresses from 20th Dist. Ill.; mem. ho. fgn. affairs com., ho. com. on agr. Del. to NATO Parliamentarians Confs., 1965, 66, 67; del. North Atlantic Assembly, 1968-70, 72-73, 76-77, 78-79. Bd. dirs. Fed. Union, Inc., Washington, Abraham Lincoln Assn., Springfield, Ill., Lincoln Group of Washington. Trustee Ill. Coll. Served to lt. (j.g.) USNR, World War II. Recipient Outstanding Service award So. Ill. U. Sch. Agr., 1970; Hon. State Farmer degree Ill. Future Farmers Am., 1971; Logan Hay medal Abraham Lincoln Assn., spl. medal SAR; Estes Kefauver Union of the Free award Fed. Union, 1976; Outstanding Achievement award Future Farmers Am. Alumni, 1978. Mem. Ill. Press Assn. (past dir.), Am. Legion, V.F.W., Amvets, Am. Soc. Internat. Law, Am. Acad. Polit. and Social Sci., Internat. Movement for Atlantic Union (sec.), Nat. Future Farmers Am. Alumni Assn. Phi Beta Kappa. Republican. Conglist. Lion. Author: Federal Farm Fable, 1968; Abraham Lincoln: The Crucible of Congress, 1979. Home: 115 W Jefferson St Pittsfield IL 62363 Office: House Office Bldg Washington DC 20515

FINDORFF, JOHN REEVE, constrn. co. exec.; b. Madison, Wis., Aug. 7, 1918; s. Milton Bremer and Leona Lovina (Reeve) F.; student U. Wis., 1936-38; B.S., Lehigh U., 1941; m. Carol Flora Kay, June 13, 1945; children—Alicia (Mrs. Orvin Nordness, Jr.), Tecla (Mrs. Kenneth Rowin, Jr.), Claire (Mrs. Franklyn Halverson). Gen. contractor, J.H. Findorff & Son, Inc., Madison, Wis., 1941—, now chmn. bd., chief exec. officer. Served to lt. (j.g.) USCGR, 1942-46. Bd. dirs. Vilas Park Zool. Soc., 1964—, pres., 1974. Mem. Asso. Gen. Contractors (state pres. 1974, dir. 1971—). Clubs: Madison, Maple Bluff Country, (Madison). Home: 25 Cambridge Ct Madison WI 53704 also Valhalla Townhouse 5 Cable WI 54821 Office: 601 W Wilson St Madison WI 53701

FINER, NORMAN SIDNEY, hosp. adminstr. researcher; b. Utica, N.Y., Dec. 14, 1920; s. Allen and Bessie (Blackstone) F.; student Tchrs. Coll. Albany, N.Y., 1941-43; B.A., Syracuse U., 1947; M.A., 1949; M.S., Columbia U., 1953; m. Doris Fay, Nov. 25, 1953; children—Atalie, John, Allen, Richard. Resident in hosp. adminstrn. Beth Israel Hosp., Boston, 1952-53, adminstrv. asst., 1953-54; adminstrv. dir. Jewish Hosp., Cin., 1954-77, cons., 1978; research asso. hosp. adminstrn. Xavier U., Cin., 1979—; real estate asso. Theodore Mayer & Brother, Cin., 1979—. Trustee, Home Aid Service, Cin., 1971-79; v.p., 1976-77; trustee Assn. Home Care Agencies, Cin., 1976—; pres. Roselawn Community Council, Cin., 1979-81, bd. dirs., 1977—. Fellow Am. Public Health Assn.; mem. Am. Hosp. Assn., Am. Coll. Hosp. Adminstrs., Ohio Hosp. Assn., Ohio Public Health Assn., Cin. Bd. Realtors, Ohio Assn. Realtors, Nat. Assn. Realtors. Democrat. Jewish. Club: Yachdav. Home: 7310 Parkdale Ave Cincinnati OH 45237 Office: 36 E 4th St Cincinnati OH 45202

FINESMITH, STEPHEN HARRIS, scientist, psychologist; b. N.Y.C., Nov. 7, 1934; s. Murray and Cele (Lerner) F.; B.B.A., Coll. City N.Y., 1955; postgrad. State U. N.Y. at Buffalo, 1955-59, 71-74, U. Wis., 1976-77, Wis. Sch. Profl. Psychology; m. Barbara Kaden, Aug. 28, 1955 (div. June 1977); children—Terri, Robin; m. 2d, Cher Halliday, Aug. 3, 1979 (div. Sept. 1979). Asso. scientist Systems Devel. Corp., Santa Monica, Cal., 1959-60; asst. prof. Rutgers U., New Brunswick, N.J., 1960-62; systems analyst Internat. Tel. & Tel. Co., Paramus, N.J., 1962-63; prin. systems design engr., head new techniques and systems group Univac div. Sperry Rand Corp., St. Paul, 1963-67; asso. prof. U. So. Miss., Hattiesburg, 1967-68; asso. prof. Mankato (Minn.) State Coll., 1968-71; prof. Governors State U., Park Forest South, Ill., 1971-72; pres., Serendipity Systems, Inc., Janesville, Wis., 1973-75, now chmn. bd.; prof., chmn. psychology dept. Milton (Wis.) Coll., 1972-76; asst. dir. Bur. Systems and Data Processing, Wis. Dept. Revenue, Madison, 1976-79; psychotherapist, communications therapist. Cons. In Mental Health, Janesville, 1973-74. Research scientist, human relations lab. cons., 1960—. Mem. Am. Psychol. Assn. (asso.), AAAS, Assn. Humanistic Psychology, Assn. for Computing Machinery. Club: Country (Lake Windsor, Wis.). Inventor bionic evolutionary adaptive stock trading system, 1964. Home: 6669 Fairway Circle Windsor WI 53598

FINK, DENNIS LEE, educator; b. Chicago Heights, Ill., Feb. 26, 1942; s. Reinhardt Henry and Mabel (Emde) F.; B.S. with honors in Edn., Ill. State U., 1965, M.S., 1967; m. Patsy Ann Wilhelmsen, Aug. 29, 1964; children—Melissa Lynn, Greg Robert. Tchr. history Homewood-Flossmoor (Ill.) High Sch., 1966—; supr. student tchrs. No. Ill. U., DeKalb, 1970—, instr. grad. edn., 1974—. Home: 1245 Thomas St Homewood IL 60430 Office: 999 Kedzie St Flossmoor IL 60422

FINKEL, WARREN EDWARD, architect; b. Elyria, Ohio, Nov. 2, 1920; s. Edward Raymond and Hazel (Allen) F.; ed. Western Res. U. (now Case Western Res. U.), 1950; m. Doris Croyle, Nov. 4, 1977. With Dalton-Dalton, Cleve., 1950, R.G. Wheeler, San Diego, 1951-52, Weinberg & Teare, Cleve., 1953-54; partner Jean Fenton Finkel-Warren Edward Finkel, Lorain, Ohio, 1955—; pres. Finkel & Finkel, Inc.; treas. Lorain Community Broadcasting Co.; dir. Central Security Nat. Bank. Mem. Lorain Community Devel. Com.; mem. capital improvement com. Lorain United Appeal; mem. Urban Renewal-Community Devel. Com. Served with USN, 1938-45. Registered architect, Ohio, Mich., Fla., N.C., Nat. Council Archtl. Registration Bds. Mem. AIA (corp.), Architects Soc. Ohio, Lorain C. of C. (pres. 1967). Rotarian. Prin. works include: Oak Hills Country Club, Lorain, 1960, 1st Ch. of Christ, Scientist, Lorain, 1960, Lorain Community Hosp., 1962, Firelands Retirement Center, Lorain-Oberlin, 1963, Lorain Nat. Bank, 1964, Lorain County

Community Coll., 1965, Lorain County Red Cross Hdqrs, 1966, Lorain County Sch. for Retarded Children, 1967, Lorain Family YMCA, 1968, Lorain Community Hosp., 1969, Lorain County Community Coll., 1970, Lorain City Hall, 1971, Learning Resource Center, 1974, Elyria Savs. and Trust Bank, 1976, Fine Arts Center, 1977, Stark Tech. Coll., 1979, St. Joseph Hosp., 1981, Harshaw Chem. Co. offices and plant, 1981. Office: PO Box 382 Lorain OH 44052

FINKES, WILLIAM HOWARD, banker; b. Columbus, Ohio, May 17, 1947; s. Howard William and Mary Alice F.; B.B.A. in Fin. cum laude, Ohio U., Athens, 1969; m. Barbara Louise Norris, June 28, 1969. Maintenance man Seal of Ohio Girl Scout Council, summers 1967-68; mgmt. trainee Banc Ohio/Ohio Nat. Bank, Columbus, 1969-70, cash position analyst cashier's dept., 1970-73, customer securities bookkeeping mgr., asst. cashier, 1973, asst. v.p., mgr. cash asset control, money transfer sect. Active Banc Ohio Corp. Govt. Awareness Assn. Mem. Am. Inst. Banking. Office: 155 E Broad St Columbus OH 43265

FINKL, WILLIAM FREDERICK, steel co. exec.; b. Chgo., 1896; grad. Armour Tech. Inst., Chgo., 1918. Formerly vice chmn., treas., now chmn. bd. A. Finkl & Sons, Chgo. Trustee (Life) IIT. Mem. Am. Soc. Metals. Address: 2011 N Southport Ave Chicago IL 60614

FINKS, JAMES EDWARD, profl. football club exec.; b. St. Louis, Aug. 31, 1927; s. William T. and Margaret (Hays) F. B.A., Tulsa U., 1949; m. Maxine Anne Stemmons, Sept. 24, 1951; children—James Edward, Danny, David, Tommy. Quarterback, Pitts. Steelers Profl. Football Club, 1949-55; asst. coach U. Notre Dame, 1956-57; gen. mgr. Calgary (Can.) Can. Football League, 1957-64; gen. mgr. Minn. Vikings Profl. Football Club, 1964-74, v.p., 1969-73, exec. v.p., 1973-74; v.p., gen. mgr., chief ops. officer Chgo. Bears Profl. Football Club, 1974—. Office: Chicago Bears 55 East Jackson Suite 1200 Chicago IL 60604*

FINLEY, JOSEPH ROBERT, orgn. exec.; b. Morgantown, W.Va., Apr. 11, 1953; s. Cecil Clay and Lucy Louise (King) F.; A.A., Parkersburg Community Coll., 1973; B.A., Ohio State U., 1975; M.Ed., Ohio U., 1978; m. Debra Lynn Minerd, Apr. 10, 1976. Owner, operator Joseph Finley Painting, Belpre, Ohio, 1971-76; counselor Washington County Open Door Home, Marietta, Ohio, 1977-78, dir., 1980—; dist. exec. Boy Scouts Am. Inc., Parkersburg, W.Va., 1978-80. Bd. dirs. Parkersburg Big Bros., 1975-76; cons. St. Joseph's Hosp., Parkersburg; mem. Washington County Youth Services Coordinating Council. Mem. Am. Personnel and Guidance Assn., Am. Mental Health Counselors Assn., Pub. Offenders Counselors Assn., Ohio State U., Ohio U., Parkersburg Community Coll. alumni assns. Methodist. Club: Lions. Home: 5 Sue Dr Apt 2 Athens OH 45701

FINN, BARBARA JO, counselor; b. St. Louis, Apr. 10, 1942; d. Edward Taylor and Evelyn (Conniff) Eaton; B.A., Washington U., St. Louis, 1964, M.A. in Edn., 1974; postgrad. St. Louis U., 1974-76; Ed.D., Clayton U., 1977; m. Kenneth Wayne Finn, Oct. 9, 1964. Tchr., Mehlville Sch. Dist., St. Louis, 1964-73, sch. counselor, 1973-74, 77-81, dir. parent edn., 1974-81; mem. managerial communications program Printing Industries St. Louis, 1976-77; cons. in field, 1974—. Mem. foster parent group St. Louis County Juvenile Ct., 1974-76; mem. parenting task force com. Mo. Gov.'s Conf. Edn., 1976-79. Mem. Nat. Council on Family Relations, Am. Personnel and Guidance Assn., Mo., St. Louis guidance assns., Gamma Phi Beta, Phi Beta Kappa, Kappa Delta Pi. Contbr. articles to profl. jours. Home: 12120 Bridle Trail Ln Saint Louis MO 63128 Office: 3120 Lemay Ferry Rd Saint Louis MO 63125

FINN, JULIA ELIZABETH, counselor; b. St. Louis, Aug. 10, 1926; d. Carl Jacobs and Pauline Frances (Young) F.; A.B., Washington U., St. Louis, 1947, M.A. in Edn., 1963. Research technician Washington U. Sch. Medicine, St. Louis, 1947-52; tchr. Clopton High Sch., Clarksville, Mo., 1953-54, Hancock High Sch., Lemay, Mo., 1954-60; counselor Sumner High Sch., St. Louis, 1963-65, St. Charles (Mo.) Sr. High Sch., 1965—. Alderman, Portage des Sioux, Mo., 1974-80. Mem. Am. Personnel and Guidance Assn., Nat. Vocat. Guidance Assn., Am. Sch. Counselors Assn., Mo. State Tchrs. Assn., AAUW, Kappa Delta Pi. Contbr. articles to med. research jours. Home: 1850 Main St Portage des Sioux MO 63373 Office: St Charles Sr High Sch Kingshwy and Waverly St Saint Charles MO 63301

FINN, MARY MURPHY, orch. adminstr.; b. Phila., June 27, 1939; d. Albert Vincent and Mary Catherine (Martin) Murphy; B.A. in Art, Duchesne Coll., 1961; B.A. in Music, St. Mary's Coll., Omaha, 1962; children by previous marriage—Thomas Jerard, Mary Catherine. Tchr. instrumental music Council Bluffs (Iowa) Public Schs., 1961-63; asst. mgr. Omaha Symphony Orch., 1969-75; mgr. Nebr. Chamber Orch., Lincoln, 1975-77; exec. dir. Omaha Pops Orch., 1977—; free-lance comml. artist, 1957—; cons. computer programming, 1977—; bd. dirs. Voices of Omaha; music contractor for Labor Unions' Septemberfest. Recipient Service award Omaha Musicians Assn., 1977, 78; numerous scholarships. Mem. Am. Fedn. Musicians, Am. Symphony Orch. League, Chamber Music Players Am. Democrat. Roman Catholic. Contbr. articles to various publs. Home and Office: 5167 Jackson St Omaha NE 68106

FINNARN, THEODORE ORA, lawyer; b. Greenville, Ohio, Aug. 20, 1949; s. Theodore Lincoln and Jeannie (Kelman) F.; B.Ed., Miami U., 1972; J.D. cum laude, U. Toledo, 1976; m. Holly C. Bankson, Sept. 15, 1973; children—Shawn April, Theodore O. Acting dir. Preble County Community Action Com., 1973, program developer, 1972-73; chief agrl. engr. Finnarn Farms, Greenville, Ohio, 1976—; admitted to Ohio bar, 1976, U.S. Dist. Ct. So. Ohio bar, 1978; individual practice law, Greenville, 1976—; sec.-treas. Finnarn Devel. Corp., 1977—. Bd. dirs. Darke County Center for Arts; active Greenville Friends of the Library, 1977—; sec.-treas. Greenville Boys Clubs, Inc., 1977—. Mem. Assn. Trial Lawyers Am., Ohio Acad. Trial Lawyers, Am., Ohio, Darke County bar assns., Ohio Farmers Union, Darke County Farmers Union (sec.-treas.), Scribes, Phi Alpha Delta. Democrat. Presbyterian. Editor articles in legal jours. Home: 3060 US Rt 127S Greenville OH 45331 Office: 127 W 5th St Greenville OH 45331

FINNEGAN, THOMAS JOSEPH, lawyer; b. Chgo., Aug. 18, 1900; s. Thomas Harrison and Marie (Flanagan) F.; J.D., Chgo. Kent Coll. of Law, 1923; m. Hildreth Millslagel, July 1, 1933 (dec. Mar. 1977). Admitted to Ill. bar, 1923, and since practiced in Chicago; mem. firm Fithian, Spengler & Finnegan, 1935-51; mem. firm Korshak, Oppenheim & Finnegan, 1951—. Mem. Am., Fed., Ill., Chgo. bar assns., Chgo. Law Inst., Phi Alpha Delta. Home: 5630 Sheridan Rd Chicago IL 60660 Office: 69 W Washington St Chicago IL 60602

FINNEY, FLORENCE ARLENE, ednl. adminstr.; b. Beaver, Wis., July 11, 1916; d. Barney Ellsworth and Esther (Johnson) Nelson; student (4H scholar) U. Wis., Madison, 1933-34, Marinette (Wis.) Tchrs. Coll., 1934-35; B.A., Wis. State U., Oshkosh, 1960, postgrad., 1960-70; M.A., No. Mich. U., Marquette, 1970, reading specialist, 1971; postgrad. Wis. State U., Superior, 1970-73, No. Mich. U., 1979-80; m. Glenn Ellsworth Finney, May 30, 1946; children—Sherry Lee, Michael Nelson, Susan Kay, Mark Allen. Tchr. elementary schs., Pound, Wis., 1935-36, 41-42, Beaver, Wis., 1936-40, Loomis, Wis., 1940-41; typist Allis-Chalmers, Milw., 1942; instr. radio-radar War Dept., Boca Raton, Fla. and Air Force, Truax Field, Madison, Wis., 1942-46; tchr. elem. Crivitz, Wis., 1953-70, prin., 1970-79, curriculum coordinator and reading supr., 1979—. Leader 4-H Clubs, 1935-41, 46-48, 58-72; dir. ch. chorus, 1958-62; a founder Crivitz Library, 1977, mem. program com., 1977—; bd. dirs. LacBaie council Girl Scouts U.S.A., 1979—. Mem. PTA, AAUW, Wis. Reading Assn., Internat. Reading Assn., Assn. for Supervision and Curriculum Devel., Wis. Assn. Sch. Adminstrs., Nat. Assn. Elem. Sch. Prins., Delta Kappa Gamma. Club: Crivitz Woman's (founder, pres. 1975-76, 77-78, named Woman of Yr. 1979). Home: PO Box 56 Crivitz WI 54114 Office: Crivitz Sch Crivitz WI 54114

FINNEY, JOAN MARIE MCINROY, state treas. Kans.; b. Topeka, Feb. 11, 1925; d. Leonard L. and Mary M. (Sands) McInroy; B.A., Washburn U.; m. Spencer W. Finney, Jr., July 24, 1957; children—Sally, Dick, Mary. Sec. Washington and Topeka offices U.S. Senator Frank Carlson, 1953-69; commr. elections Shawnee County, Kans., 1970-72; adminstrv. asst. to mayor of Topeka, 1973-74; treas. State of Kans., Topeka, 1974—. Pres., Girls' Club Topeka, 1981. Mem. Kans. Women's Polit. Caucus, Am. Legion Aux., Bus. and Profl. Women's Club (Woman of Yr. 1980), Sigma Alpha Iota. Roman Catholic (bd. dirs. mem. fin. com.). Home: 4600 W 19th St Topeka KS 66604 Office: Office of State Treasurer 535 Kansas PO Box 737 Topeka KS 66603

FINNICUM, WILLIAM LEAS, III, architect; b. Bellvue, Pa., Aug. 3, 1946; s. William Leas and Priscilla Thompson (Burkhart) F.; B.Arch., Ohio U., 1969; m. W. Mariah Holleman, May 29, 1970; children—Justin Leas, Elyse Adrian. Designer, Campbell Green Cunzolo, Sewickley, Pa., 1969-70, Carl G. Baker and Assos., Beaver, Pa., 1971-72; partner Anthony J. Stillson and Assos., Pitts., 1973-74; propr. William L. Finnicum Architect, Birmingham, Mich., 1974—. Appointee, Franklin Village Hist. Commn.; apptd. bldg. ofcl. Village of Franklin. Methodist. Home: 27245 Scenic Hwy Franklin MI 48025

FINO, TIMOTHY A., mgmt. cons.; b. Warren, Pa., Aug. 12, 1948; s. Alex F. and Marie K. F.; B.E.E., U. Detroit. 1971; M.S., Mich. State U., 1973; m. Joanne Huseman, July 17, 1971; children—Brian, Steven, Mark. Logical design engr. Tex. Instruments Co., Dallas, 1973-77; cons. Touche Ross & Co., Detroit, 1977-80; pres. Mini/Micro Computer Applications, Inc., Bloomfield Hills, Mich., 1980—. Alumni bd. dirs. Mich. State U. Registered profl. engr., Mich., Tex. Mem. IEEE, Assn. Computing Machinery. Home: 1949 Devonshire St Bloomfield Hills MI 48013 Office: 1411 N Woodward Suite 8 Bloomfield Hills MI 48013

FINSTAD, MARTIN M., ret. educator; b. Winger, Minn., Feb. 11, 1900; s. Martin and Martha (Lutness) F.; B.A., St. Olaf Coll., 1920; postgrad U. Minn., 1921-22; B.D., Chgo. Luth. Theol. Sem., 1934; M.A. in Edn., Northwestern U., 1936, M.A. in History and Social Studies, 1939, postgrad. 1944-45; M. Divinity, Luth. Sch. Theology, Chgo., 1972; m. Gertrude Gilbert, May 29, 1930 (dec.); m. 2d, Olga Olive Dicke, Sept. 9, 1978. Prin. Nelson (Minn.) Consol. Sch., 1920-21; supt. Montrose (Minn.) Pub. Schs., 1922-24; tchr. history Stillwater (Minn.) High Sch., 1924-31; instr. social studies Proviso Twp. High Sch., Maywood, Ill., 1934-65, instr. psychology, evening sch., 1944-55. Pres. Maywood Pub Library Bd., 1955-69; village clk., Maywood, 1961-69; active other civic affairs. Bd. dirs. Chgo. Luth. Theol. Sem., 1954-63. Served with U.S. Army, 1918. Recipient Churchman of Yr. award Ch. Fedn. Greater Chgo., 1958. Mem. Nat. Council for Social Studies, Adult Edn. Assn., A.L.A., Internat. Inst. Municipal Clks., N.E.A., Am. Legion (vice comdr. Ill. 1950-51), Ill. Tchrs. Assn. (dir. 1958-61), Phi Delta Kappa. Republican. Lutheran. Mason (K.T., 32 deg., Shriner). Contbr. articles to profl. jours. Home: 350 W Schaumburg Rd A352 Schaumburg IL 60194

FIONDO, JOHN PHILLIP, sch. adminstr.; b. Detroit, Apr. 6, 1929; s. Phillip and Rose (Marandola) F.; B.S., Wayne State U., 1958, M.S., 1962, Ph.D., 1967; m. Silvia Gudy Netto, Nov. 30, 1957; children—Stephen, Andrea. Elementary sch. tchr. Detroit Pub. Schs., 1957-62, psychologist, 1962-69, adminstrv. psychologist, 1969—. Adj. prof. U. Mich., Ann Arbor, 1971—, Mercy Coll. Detroit, 1973—, Wayne State U., Detroit, 1968—; cons. psychologist pvt. practice, Grosse Pointe Woods, Mich., 1969—; cons. Mich. Office Vocat. Rehab., 1968—. Mem. Am. Psychol. Assn., Am. Assn. Mental Deficiency, Phi Delta Kappa. Home: 23324 Colonial Ct S St Clair Shores MI 48080 Office: 20323 Mack Grosse Pointe Woods MI 48236

FIORE, NICHOLAS FRANCIS, metall. engr.; b. Pitts., Sept. 24, 1939; s. William Henry and Margaret Angeline (Scinto) F.; B.S., Carnegie Mellon U., 1960, M.S., 1963, Ph.D., 1964; m. Sylvia Marie Chinque, Aug. 13, 1960; children—Maria, Nicholas, Kristin, Anthony. Project engr. Carnegie Inst. Tech., 1963; asst. prof. dept. metall. engring. and materials sci. U. Notre Dame (Ind.), 1966-69, asso. prof., 1969-71, prof., 1971—, chmn. dept., 1969—; corp. dir. tech. Cabot Corp., Boston, 1982—; vis. scientist Argonne Nat. Lab., 1975; cons. Ford Motor Co., DuPont Co., Argonne Nat. Lab., Miles Labs., Union Carbide Co., Corning Glass, U.S. Army, NSF. Tech. cons., City of South Bend, 1978-81; chmn. bd. Primary Day Sch., Inc., 1975—. Served with U.S. Army, 1964-66. Recipient Adams Teaching award Am. Welding Soc., 1971. Mem. AAUP, Am. Soc. Metals, Am. Inst. Mining, Metall. and Petroleum Engrs., Nat. Metall. Engring. Depts. Chmn. Assn. (nat. chmn.), Alpha Sigma Mu (internat. pres.). Roman Catholic. Contbr. articles to profl. jours. Home: Box E Notre Dame IN 46556 Office: 125 High St Boston MA 02110

FIORELLA, JOHN ANTHONY, ednl. cons., psychologist; b. Kansas City, Mo., Nov. 2, 1941; s. John Jacob and Sarafina Mary (Diesi) F.; student Conception Sem. Coll., 1958-61, St. Thomas Sem. Coll., 1961-62; B.A., Rockhurst Coll., 1964; M.A., U. Mo., Kansas City, 1967. Tchr., Bishop Miege High Sch., Shawnee Mission, Kans., 1964-67; dir. guidance Bishop Hogan High Sch., Kansas City, Mo., 1967-68, Barstow Sch., Kansas City, 1968-79; sch. psychologist St. Paul's Episcopal Day Sch., Kansas City, 1978—; v.p. Robertson & Fiorella, Inc., Kansas City, 1981—. Adviser, Am. Field Service, Kansas City, 1970-76; sch. coordinator United Way, Kansas City, 1978. Life cert. K-12 counselor and K-12 psychol. examiner, Mo.; lic. psychologist, Mo. Mem. Am. Personnel and Guidance Assn., Mo. Psychol. Assn. Republican. Roman Catholic. Club: K.C. Office: Robertson & Fiorella Inc 4400 Broadway Kansas City MO 64111

FIRESTONE, GARY LEE, ins. agy. exec.; b. Warsaw, Ind., July 12, 1934; s. Burdette H. and Helen B. F.; B.A., DePauw U., 1956; m. Patricia Pranter, Oct. 15, 1971; children—Kathryn, Kurt, Kaye, Kristin. Agt., Coll. Life Ins. Co., 1960-67, mgr., 1967-72, regional dir. agys. 1972-76; prin. Firestone/Yott & Assos., Indpls., 1976—. Served with USAF, 1957-60. C.L.U. Mem. Million Dollar Round Table (life), Nat. Assn. Life Underwriters, Indpls. Assn. Life Underwriters, Gen. Agts. and Mgrs. Assn., Estate Planning Council. Presbyterian. Club: Kiwanis. Home: 3016 Woodshore Ct Carmel IN 46032 Office: Firestone/Yott & Assos 3500 W DePauw Blvd Indianapolis IN 46268

FIRL, DONALD HAROLD, educator; b. Red Wing, Minn., June 28, 1926; s. Max Richard and Henrietta Louise (Diercks) F.; married, 6 children. B.A. in Math. and English Edn., Gustavus Adolphus Coll., St. Peter, Minn., 1950; M.S. in Modern Algebra Stats., Kans. State U., Manhattan, 1952; specialist in math. and curriculum U. No. Iowa, Cedar Falls, 1963; m. Veryl Emma Bowen; children—Cara Firl Leeper, Heidi Firl Hilton, Jared, Christopher, Thomas, Jennifer. Instr. math. and English, St. Peter (Minn.) High Sch., 1952-57; instr. math. John Marshall High Sch., Rochester, Minn., 1957-62; cons. math. Rochester Ind. Sch. Dist. 535, 1963—. Elder, Ch. Jesus Christ of Latter-day Saints. Author: Random House Mathematics Series, A.J. Nystrom Primary Mathematics Charts. Editor: The Mathematics Student. Contbr. articles in field to profl. jours. Home: 2104 5th Ave NE Rochester MN 55901 Office: Coffman Bldg 203 Rochester MN 55901

FISCH, ROBERT OTTO, med. educator; b. Budapest, Hungary, June 12, 1925; s. Zoltan and Irene (Manheim) F.; came to U.S., 1957, naturalized, 1965; med. diploma U. Budapest, 1951; study art Acad. Fine Arts, Budapest, 1943, Walker Art Center, Mpls., 1968-69, U. Minn., 1969-70, Mpls. Coll. Arts and Design, 1970-76; m. Joyce D.E. Gulasch, May 30, 1969; 1 dau., Rebecca A. Gen. practice medicine, Hungary, 1951-55, pub. health officer, 1955; pediatrician Hosp. for Premature Children, Budapest, 1956; intern Christ Hosp., Jersey City, 1957-58; intern pediatrics U. Minn. Hosps., 1958-59, resident, 1959-60, research fellow, 1961; instr. U. Minn. Sch. Medicine, 1961-63, asst. prof., 1963-72, asso. prof., 1972-79, prof., 1979—, dir. phonylketonuria clinic, 1961—, dir. child care clinic, 1972—; Minn. dir. child devel. study, collaborative study of 14 med. univs. of U.S., 1963-75. Mem. Am. Acad. Pediatrics, Assn. Ambulatory Pediatric Services. Contbr. to publs. in field. Exhibited art works in various one-man and group shows. Home: 2298 Folwell St Saint Paul MN 55108 Office: Box 384 Mayo Hosp U Minn Minneapolis MN 55455

FISCHBACH, JULIUS, clergyman; b. Huntington, W.Va., Apr. 25, 1894; s. Julius and Mary (Woody) F.; A.B., U. Mich., 1917; Th.M., So. Bapt. Theol. Sem., 1920; D.D., Hillsdale Coll., 1943; m. Mary Mildred Bibb, June 17, 1925; children—David Bibb, Mary Ellen (Mrs. William H. Heater). Ordained to ministry Bapt. Ch., 1918; pastor Mo. Hope Ch., W.Va., 1920-25, Morgantown, W.Va., 1925-28, 1928-36; pastor First Ch., Lansing, Mich., 1936-61, pastor emeritus, 1961—; interim minister Bapt. chs., Mich., 1962, Madison, Wis., 1963, Providence, R.I. and Clearfield, Utah, 1964, Mpls., Yakima, Wash., 1965 San Bernardino, Calif., 1966, Mich., 1967-71; asso. minister Peoples Ch., East Lansing, Mich., 1972-80, emeritus, 1980—; guest minister to chs. in Scotland and Eng., 1951; around the world tour of mission fields, preaching in Philippines, Burma, Assam, India and Eng., 1955. Chmn. Nat. Adv. Com. Juvenile Protection, 1954-56; mem. Nat. Ch. Extension Com., 1952-55, pastoral relations com. Bapt. Ministers Council, 1948-50, gen. council of Am. Bapt. Conv., 1947-53 (mem. exec. com. 1952, 53), mem. commn. on ministry, 1951, dir. Green Lake Assembly, 1952, 53, chmn. com. Children and Church, 1940-44, council on finance and promotion, 1936-39, on Christian Edn., 1942-46, mem. Convocation team, 1942, leader Christian Life Crusade team, 1945. Dir. Lansing YMCA, 1939-54; pres. W.Va. Bapt. Assembly, 1933-36; mem. W.Va. Bapt. Exec. Bd., 1930-36; sec. W.Va. Bapt. Edn. Soc., 1930-36. Trustee Hillsdale Coll., 1945-54, Alderson-Broaddus Coll., 1932-36. Mem. Mich. Bapt. Conv. (exec. com. 1939-59, pres. 1955-58), Mich. Council Chs. (commn. internat. relations), Radio Com. for Chs. (chmn.), Civil Rights Com. Clubs: Kiwanis (pres. 1961; Legion of Honor 1971), Inter-City Wranglers, Friendly Hour, The Club. Author: Squaring Up, 1941; Story Sermons for Boys and Girls, 1947; Sermonettes for Boys and Girls, 1949; Children's Sermons in Stories, 1955; The Juvenile Protection Story, 1955; Talks for Children on Christian Ideals, 1959; The Children's Moment, 1966; Tell Us A Story, 1978; also articles. Contbr. to book: A Treasury of Story Sermons for Children, 1957. Daily radio program, Thought For the Day, 1950-63. Home: 1122 N Genesee Dr Lansing MI 48915

FISCHER, ELMER CARL, JR., architect; b. Springfield, Ill., Apr. 19, 1939; s. Elmer Carl and Frances Louise (Ball) F.; B.Arch., Washington U., 1963; m. Glynda Kay Robley, May 16, 1975; children—Michelle Irene, Karen Marie, Susan Nicole. Project architect Ferry & Henderson Architects, Springfield, 1966-70; partner Graham, O'Shea & Wisnosky, Architects, Springfield, 1970-73; partner Collaborative Design, Springfield, 1973-76; pres., chmn. bd. Carl Fischer Assos., Inc., Springfield, Ill., 1976—. Recipient gift and decorative accessories nat. design award, 1976; cert. Nat. Council Archtl. Registration Bds. Mem. Ill. Historic Sites Commn., 1979—; bd. dirs. Family Service Center of Sangamon County, 1976-80; mem. Springfield Arts Commn., 1977-80; profl. adv. Land of Lincoln council Girl Scouts U.S.A. Served with USNR, 1962-66. Mem. AIA (mem. nat. com. regional planning and natural resources), Nat. Trust Historic Preservation. Roman Catholic. Club: Sangamo, Island Bay Yacht. Dir., Inland Architect, 1979—. Home: 502 S Walnut St Springfield IL 62704 Office: 100 N 1st St Suite 1 South Springfield IL 62701

FISCHER, HENRY FRED, savs. and loan exec.; b. Fair Haven, Minn., Nov. 9, 1938; s. Fred Henry and Ann Evelyn (Steenlage) F.; student U. Minn., 1956-57; m. Janet M. Torgerson, Aug. 11, 1963; children—Jennifer, Christopher. Exec. dir. Minn. D.F.L. party, 1968-70; dir. orgn. Wendell Anderson for Gov. Com., 1970; spl. asst. to U.S. Sen. Walter F. Mondale, 1970-72; chmn. Minn. Democratic Party, 1972-75; prin. JMF, Inc., Mpls., 1975-80; v.p. public and urban affairs Twin City Fed. Savs. and Loan Assn., 1981—. Bd. dirs. Twin Cities Indsl. Opportunities Center; v.p. Dem. State Chairmen's Assn., 1973-77; sec. Midwest Dem. Conf., 1973-76; mem. Dem. Nat. Com., 1972-76. Mem. Savs. League Minn., Campaign Planners Assn. Lutheran. Author polit. monographs. Home: 7643 W 85th St Bloomington MN 55438

FISCHER, KURT RONALD, mfg. co. exec.; b. Syracuse, N.Y., Dec. 23, 1954; s. Henry John and Helen Ann (Viel) F.; B.A., Elmira Coll., 1976; m. Sarah Elizabeth Keyser, Sept. 9, 1978. With Corning Glass works, various locations, 1976—, recruiting specialist, Corning, N.Y., 1978-79, supr. personnel, Danville, Ky., 1979-81, Greenville, Ohio, 1981—. Bd. dirs. Jr. Achievement, 1979-80. Mem. Central Ky. Personnel Assn., Am. Soc. Personnel Adminstrs. Presbyterian. Club: Rotary. Home: 103 Wellsley Ct Greenville OH 45331 Office: Corning Glass Works Martin St Greenville OH 45331

FISCHER, ROBERT ELWOOD, elec. engr.; b. Hagerstown, Md., Mar. 8, 1944; s. Perry E. and Mary Louise (Downs) F.; B.S.E.E. (Nat. Merit scholar), Yale U., 1966; M.S.E.E., Poly. Inst. Bklyn., 1970; m. Margaret Ann Rallo, Aug. 13, 1966. Communications systems engr. Space div. Gen. Electric Co., Valley Forge, Pa., 1966-77; dir. systems engring. Telecommunications and Electronic Warfare div. Magnavox Electronic Systems Co., Ft. Wayne, Ind., 1977—. Mem. IEEE, Am. Mgmt. Assn., Nat. Mgmt. Assn., Tau Beta Pi. Roman Catholic. Clubs: Ft. Wayne Racquet, Elks. Home: 1005 Pencross Dr Fort Wayne IN 46825 Office: 1313 Production Rd Fort Wayne IN 46808

FISCUS, RICHARD EUGENE, legal adminstr.; b. Lawrenceville, Ill., June 11, 1930; s. Clifford Leo and Leona Thelma (Holsen) F.; student Eastern Ill. U., 1948-50; B.S., U. Ill., 1966; m. Barbara June Wilkes, Feb. 19, 1951; children—Susan Diane, David Michael.

d. 2d lt. U.S. Air Force, 1953, advanced through grades to lt. 1969; ret., 1972; legal adminstr. Ice, Miller, Donadio & Ryan, pls., 1972—. Decorated Air medal. Mem. Assn. Legal Adminstrs. (Midwest regional v.p. 1973-76), Ind. Legal Adminstrs. Assn. (pres. 1975). Home: 12804 Andover Dr Carmel IN 46032 Office: 111 Monument Circle Indianapolis IN 46204

FISH, DAVID FREDERICK, counselor; b. Harlingen, Tex., May 1, 1944; s. David Charles and Marjorie Grace (Baker) F.; B.A., U. Iowa, 1966; M.Ed., U. No. Iowa, 1968; m. Mary Helen O'Brien, 1979. Residence hall dir. Ball State U., Muncie, Ind., 1968-72; counselor Hawkeye Inst. Tech., Waterloo, Iowa, 1972-79; admissions officer, 1979—. Mem. Assn. Collegiate Registrars and Admissions Officers. Democrat. Home: 4117 Hillside Dr Cedar Falls IA 50613 Office: PO Box 8015 Waterloo IA 50704

FISHER, BARBARA ANN, county ofcl.; b. South Bend, Ind., Mar. 30, 1952; d. Verner Jasper and Janet Stowell (Smith) Fisher; B.A., Western Mich. U., 1973, M.A., 1976; m. George A. Short; children—David James, Michael Fisher-Short. Veterans coordinator Kalamazoo Valley Community Coll., 1974; sec. Western Mich. U., Kalamazoo, 1974-75, student supr., 1975-77; child guidance worker Kalamazoo County Juvenile Home, 1975; case mgr., community placement program Kalamazoo County Dept. Mental Health, 1977—; coordinator adult foster care tng. program Mich. Dept. Social Services 1981, curriculum developer programs for mentally ill, 1981—; part-time instr. Kalamazoo Valley Community Coll., 1978—. Vol., Kalamazoo County Juvenile Ct., 1975—; past mem. Sheriffs Dept. Mounted Div. Aux. Sec.-treas., Service Employees Internat. Union, 1980-82. Western Mich. U. bd. trustees scholar, 1973; lic. social worker, Mich. Home: 5473 West E Ave Kalamazoo MI 49009 Office: Community Placement Program 230 N Burdick St Kalamazoo MI 49006

FISHER, CHARLES RAY, microbiologist; b. Carrollton, Mo., July 30, 1940; s. Vestel M. and Virginia Lucille (Moore) F.; B.A., Central Meth. Coll., 1961; M.S., Purdue U., 1963, Ph.D., Ill. State U., 1968; m. Ella Maria Mercado, Aug. 13, 1979; children—Charles R., Leigh Ann, Sean Paul. Asso. prof. Radford (Va.) U., 1976-79; sr. Fulbright prof. Ege U., Izmir, Turkey, 1979-80; prof. chemistry and biology Central Meth. U., Fayette, Mo., 1980-81; prof. microbiology U. Dominica Med. Sch., Dominica, 1981—. Mem. Am. Soc. Microbiology, AAAS, Soc. Indsl. Microbiology, Am. Inst. Biological Sci. Methodist. Contbr. articles to profl. jours. Home: 505 N Linn Fayette MO 65248 Office: U Dominica Sch Med PO Box 266 Roseau Dominica Windward Islands

FISHER, CHARLES THOMAS, III, banker; b. Detroit, Nov. 22, 1929; s. Charles Thomas, Jr. and Elizabeth Jane (Briggs) F.; A.B. in Econs., Georgetown U., 1951; M.B.A., Harvard, 1953; m. Margaret Elizabeth Keegin, June 18, 1952; children—Margaret Elizabeth (Mrs. F. Macy Jones), Charles Thomas IV, Curtis William, Lawrence Peter II, Mary Florence. With Touche, Ross, Bailey & Smart, C.P.A.'s, Detroit, 1953-58; asst. v.p. Nat. Bank Detroit, 1958-61, v.p., 1961-66, sr. v.p., 1966-69, exec. v.p., 1969-72, pres., chief adminstrv. officer, 1972—, also dir.; pres., dir. NBD Bancorp, Inc., 1973—; dir. Internat. Bank of Detroit, Detroit Edison Co., Hiram Walker-Resources, Ltd., Gen. Motors Corp., Am. Airlines. Mem. Mackinac Bridge Authority. Bd. dirs. Greater Detroit Area Hosp. Council; trustee Mt. Elliott Cemetery, Detroit. Named Detroit Young Man of Year, Detroit Jr. Bd. Commerce, 1961. C.P.A., Mich. Mem. Assn. Res. City Bankers, Am. Inst. C.P.A.'s, Mich. Assn. C.P.A.'s. Republican. Roman Catholic. Clubs: Bloomfield Hills (Mich.) Country; Country of Detroit (Grosse Pointe); Detroit Athletic, Detroit, Recess, Yondotega (Detroit); Links (N.Y.C.). Office: National Bank Detroit Detroit MI 48232

FISHER, ERMAN CALDWELL, city ofcl.; b. Mt. Sterling, Ky., Oct. 10, 1923; s. Cato and Mattalean W. (Tyler) F.; cert. Highland Park Jr. Coll., 1947, Wayne State U., 1965, B.E. in Archtl. Engring., Detroit Inst. Tech., 1954; m. Ruby Nelson, June 28, 1947; children—Paul Cato, Nancy Carol. With Aero. Products, Inc., Detroit, 1943, Great Lakes Mut. Life Ins. Co., Detroit, 1946-48; prin. constrn. insp. City of Detroit Water Dept., 1948-68, mgr. plant, bldg. and mech. maintenance, 1968-77; dep. dir. Detroit Water and Sewage Dept., 1977-80, asst. dir. tech. support, 1980-81; dir. phys. plant Wayne State U., Detroit, 1980—. Bd. dirs. Shaw Coll., 1970-73; del. state conv. Republican party, 1954-55; now mem. Democratic State Central Com. Served with U.S. Army, 1943-46. Recipient Edward Dunbar Rich Service award, 1974. Mem. Am. Pub. Works Assn. (past pres. Inst. Bldgs. and Grounds 1977—, v.p. Detroit Met. br.), Assn. Phys. Plant Adminstrs. Univs. and Colls., Phylon Soc. Wayne State U., NAACP (life), Am. Water Works Assn., Water Pollution Control Fedn., Engring. Soc. Detroit, Soc. Municipal Engrs., DAV (life), Alpha Phi Alpha. Club: Lions. Home: 16614 Princeton St Detroit MI 48221 Office: 5454 Cass Ave Detroit MI 48202

FISHER, GARY ALLEN, banker; b. Van Wert, Ohio, Feb. 27, 1950; s. Marvin Dale and Billie Joan (Roth) F.; student Ohio No. U., 1968-72, Kent State U., 1975, Ball State U., 1978; diploma in Bank Mgmt., Am. Inst. Banking. Mgmt. trainee Van Wert (Ohio) Nat. Bank, 1968-72, installment loan officer, 1973-77, asst. v.p., br. mgr., 1978-80, asst. v.p. in charge bus. devel. and mktg., 1980—; bd. dirs. Am. Inst. Banking; tchr. money mgmt. area high schs. Bd. dirs. Van Wert County Heart Fund, 1975—; county co-chmn. United Way, 1978; adv. Jr. Achievement, 1976; county chmn. March of Dimes, 1975; active YMCA. Served with U.S. Army, 1968. Named Jr. Rotarian, 1968. Mem. Am. Mgmt. Assn., Am. Banker Inst., Bank Adminstrn. Inst. Republican. Clubs: Van Wert Sertoma, Am. Bowling Congress, Moose, Am. Legion. Home: 816 W Main St Van Wert OH 45891 Office: 102 E Main St Van Wert OH 45891

FISHER, GILBERT, III, state ofcl.; b. Memphis, Mar. 7, 1937; s. Gilbert and Ruby Nell (Thomas) F.; B.S. in Polit. Sci., Tenn. State U., 1959, M.S. in History, 1960; M.B.A. in Mgmt., Wayne State U., 1969; Ph.D. in Gen. Edn. Adminstrn., U. Mich., 1972; Ford Motor Co. Fund postdoctoral fellow U. Manchester (Eng.) and Inst. Internat. Edn., 1973; m. Patricia Elaine Pyrant, July 25, 1964; 1 son, Mark David. Child care counselor Jewish Family Service Fedn. Met. Chgo., 1960-61; tchr. social studies Clintondale High Sch., Mt. Clemens, Mich., 1961-64, Most Holy Trinity Cath. Sch., Detroit, 1964-65; mgmt. trainee Mich. Blue Cross Blue Shield, Detroit, 1965-66; div. coordinator, mgmt. devel. indsl. relations div. staff, Gen. Parts div. Ford Motor Co., Rawsonville, Mich., 1966-68; adminstr. corp. employment and placement, corp. personnel staff Chrysler Corp., Highland Park, Mich., 1968-70; asst. prof. mgmt. and personnel Coll. Bus. and Adminstrn., U. Detroit, 1970-71; dir. New Thrust Program, Detroit Urban League, 1970-72; adminstrv. intern Detroit Public Schs., 1972-73; dir. personnel devel. Cyphernetics Corp., Ann Arbor, Mich., 1973-74; labor relations and hourly personnel rep., Casting div. Ford Motor Co., Dearborn, Mich., 1974; community sch. dir. Pontiac (Mich.) Bd. Edn., 1974-79; dir. office mgmt. and staff devel. Mich. Dept. Social Services, Lansing, 1979—; mem. train-the-trainer task force Dept. Health and Human Services, 1980-81; mem. steering com. Region V Child Welfare Tng. Center. Mem. exec. planning bd. Child Welfare League Am., 1982. Mem. Am. Soc. Tng. and Devel., Internat. Personnel Mgmt. Assn., Cranbrook Inst. Sci., Am. Mgmt. Assn., Mich. State Council Tng. Dirs., Alpha Phi Alpha, Phi Delta Kappa. Roman Catholic. Home: 5594 W Outer Dr Detroit MI 48235

FISHER, GLORIA KATHERINE, public relations exec.; b. Rock Island, Ill., July 4, 1924; d. William and Katherine Barbara (Traenkenschuh) Breisacher; student public schs., Peoria, Ill. Writer, photographer Peoria Jour. Star, 1942-47; advt. asst. Am. Distilling Co., Pekin, Ill., 1947-52; writer Davenport (Iowa) Daily Times, 1952-55; dir. public relations WBIR-TV, Knoxville, Tenn., 1955-57; dir. public relations-advt. Davenport Petersen Harned Von Maur, 1959-73; dir. pub. relations Davenport Osteo. Hosp., 1976—. Bd. dirs. Good Samaritan Nursing Home, Heart Assn., 1977-79, Am. Cancer Soc., 1979—. Mem. Am. Hosp. Soc. Public Relations, Am. Osteo. Hosp. Public Relations, Iowa-Ill. Public Relations Assn., Iowa Hosp. Public Relations Assn., Quill Scroll, C. of C. Lutheran. Club: Quota. Office: 1111 W Kimberly St Davenport IA 52806

FISHER, HARRIET RUTH, dietitian; b. Detroit, Aug. 23, 1922; d. Oliver Herman and Olive Nellie (Smith) Grunow; B.S., Mich. State U., 1944; m. Clarence Jacob Fisher, Jan. 9, 1954 (div.). Intern, Peter Brigham Hosp., Boston, 1944-45; clin. dietitian Evanston (Ill.) Hosp., 1946, Vets. Hosp., Downey, Ill., 1946-47, Scripps Clinic, LaJolla, Calif., 1947-51, San Diego County Hosp., 1951-53; dietitian Oakwood Hosp., Dearborn, Mich., 1960-62, acting chief dietitian, 1962-63, adminstrv. dietitian, 1963-66, dir. dietetics, 1966—; clin. asso. Eastern Mich. U. Mem. adv. com. Henry Ford Community Coll. Mem. Am. Dietetic Assn., Am. Soc. Hosp. Food Service Adminstrs. (Am. S.E. Mich. chap.). Episcopalian. Home: 2060 Corlette St Brighton MI 48116 Office: 18101 Oakwood St Dearborn MI 48124

FISHER, HERBERT HIRSH, lawyer; b. Rome, N.Y., Mar. 24, 1927; s. Kalman Nathan and Libby (May) F.; student U. Minn., Yale U.; B.A., U. Wis., 1949, LL.B., 1952; m. Ida Curtis; 1 son, Martin. Admitted to Wis. bar, 1952, Ill. bar, 1953; practiced in Milw., 1952; mem. firm Landon L. Chapman, Chgo., 1953-56; partner Robinson & Fisher, 1956-60; individual practice of law, Chgo., 1960-64, 68—; mem. firm Stradford, Lafontant, Fisher & Malkin, Chgo., 1964-68. Bd. dirs. Nat. Assn. Housing Coops., 1975—, sec., 1980—; exec. v.p., pres. Chatham Avalon Park Community Council, 1963-66; bd. dirs., officer Chatham Park Village Coop., 1962-69. Served with U.S. Army, 1944-47. Home: 2130 Lincoln Park W Chicago IL 60649 Office: 69 W Washington St Chicago IL 60602

FISHER, JAMES LEE, lawyer; b. Akron, Ohio, Apr. 10, 1944; s. James Lee and Maxine (Sumner) F.; student M.I.T., 1962-63; B.S. in Civil Engring., U. Akron, 1968, J.D., 1971; m. Nancy Lorenz, Dec. 20, 1980. Admitted to Ohio bar, 1971; city planner City of Akron, 1968-73, community renewal atty., 1973; v.p. Brunswick Management Co., Akron, 1973-77; pvt. practice law James L. Fisher Co., L.P.A., Akron, 1977—. Pres., Copley Homeowners Assn., 1978-80; mem. Summit County Planning Commn., 1979—. Registered profl. engr., Ohio. Mem. Akron Bar Assn., Ohio Bar Assn., Am. Bar Assn., Ohio Planning Conf., Akron Assn. Realtors, Ohio Assn. Realtors, Nat. Assn. Realtors. Republican. Mem. United Ch. Christ. Club: Copley Lions. Home: 205 Mackinaw Rd Akron OH 44313 Office: 159 S Main St Akron OH 44308

FISHER, JOHN ALEXANDER, JR., banker; b. Detroit, July 4, 1942; s. John Alexander and Jeanette Catherine (Simm) F.; B.S. in Commerce, U. Detroit, 1965; M.B.A., Wayne State U., 1967; m. Mary Ann Ceckowski, Sept. 9, 1966; children—Stacey Ann, Melissa Lynn. Advt. and sales promotion specialist Detroit Diesel Engine div. Gen. Motors, 1965-67; asst. prof. Coll. Bus., Eastern Mich. Univ., Ypsilanti, Mich., 1967-71; mgr. advt. Nat. Bank Detroit, 1971-75; v.p., dir. mktg. Central Nat. Bank, Chgo., 1975-81, v.p. personal banking, 1981—. Mem. Bank Marketing Assn., No. Ill. Bank Marketing Assn. (pres. 1981-82), Sales/Mktg. Assn. Chgo., Blue Key. Republican. Roman Catholic. Club: Knights of Columbus. Office: Central National Bank 120 S LaSalle St Chicago IL 60603

FISHER, JOHN EDWIN, ins. co. exec. b. Portsmouth, Ohio, Oct. 26, 1929; s. Charles Hall and Bess (Swearingin) F.; student U. Colo., 1947-48, Ohio U., 1948-49, Franklin U., Columbus, Ohio, 1950-51; m. Eloise Lyon, Apr. 25, 1949. With Nationwide Mut. Ins. Co., Columbus, 1951—, v.p., office gen. chmn., 1970-72, pres., gen. mgr., dir., 1972-81; gen. chmn., chief exec. officer, 1981—; dir. Nationwide Mut. Fire Ins. Co., Nationwide Life Ins. Co., Nationwide Gen. Ins. Co.; chmn. Neckura-Neckermann Versicherungs A.G., Oberursel, Germany, 1976—; dir. Battelle Commons Corp. Pres. Nationwide Found., 1972—; bd. dirs. Otterbein Coll., Children's Hosp. Mem. Chartered Property and Casualty Underwriters Assn., Chartered Life Underwriters Soc., Assn. Ohio Life Ins. Cos. (past pres.), Ohio Ins. Inst. (pres. 1975-77), Nat. Assn. Ind. Insurers, Am. Risk and Ins. Assn., Griffith Ins. Found. (pres. 1978-80), Property-Casualty Ins. Council (chmn. 1981), Ohio Assn. Life Underwriters (pres. 1972-75), Columbus C. of C. Office: One Nationwide Plaza Columbus OH 43216

FISHER, LAWRENCE EDMOND, cement mfg. co. exec.; b. Long Beach, Calif., Aug. 10, 1949; s. Louis Everard and Blanche Elaine (Dvorak) F.; B.S. in Engring., U. Calif., Los Angeles, 1972; M.B.A., U. So. Calif., 1976; m. Sherrie Jean Nobles, May 5, 1979; children—Andrea Jean, Michael Lawrence, Patrick Thomas. Engr., Conrad Assos., Van Nuys, Calif., 1973-74; project mgr. Los Angeles World Trade Center, 1974-76; bus. analyst Vetco Inc., Ventura, Calif., 1976; mgr. mfg. planning Vetco Offshore Group, Ventura, 1977-79; exec. v.p. Chem Tech Services, 1979—; instr. Ventura Coll., 1977. Mem. Am. Petroleum Inst., Am. Concrete Inst., Am. Prodn. and Inventory Control Soc., U. So. Calif. M.B.A., U. Calif. Los Angeles Engring., UCLA alumni assns. Republican. Home: 378 Hawthorn Ln Winnetka IL 60093 Office: PO Box 190 Kenilworth IL 60043

FISHER, LESTER EMIL, zoo dir.; b. Chgo., Feb. 24, 1921; s. Louis and Elsie (Vodicka) F.; D.V.M., Iowa State U., 1943; m. Wendy Astley-Bell, Jan. 23, 1981; children—Jane Serrita, Katherine Clark. Mem. faculty Animal Care sect. Northwestern Med. Sch., Chgo., 1946-47; dir. Berwyn (Ill.) Animal Hosp., 1947-62; dir. Lincoln Park Zoo, Chgo., 1962—. Served with U.S. Army, 1943-46. Mem. Am. Assn. Zool. Parks and Aquariums (pres. 1971-72), Internat. Union Dirs. Zool. Gardens (v.p. 1978—). Home: 3180 N Lake Shore Dr Chicago IL 60657 Office: 2200 N Cannon Dr Chicago IL 60614

FISHER, MARJORIE HELEN, librarian; b. Losantville, Ind., Nov. 27, 1924; d. James Cleo and Isie May (Sutton) Hardwick; student Olivet Nazarene Coll., 1943-45; A.B., Ball State U., 1947; postgrad Ariz. State Tchrs. Coll., 1949, Ind. U., 1955, Ind. State U., 1957, Butler U., 1958; m. Delmar Fisher, Sept. 29, 1950; children—Deljon Ray, Madge Denise Fisher Gaines. Tchr., Superior (Ariz.) Elem. Schs., 1947-48, Yuma (Ariz.) schs., 1949-51; tchr. English, librarian Hamlet (Ind.) High Sch., 1952-56; dir. library services Plymouth (Ind.) Community Sch. Corp., 1957—; organizer Divine Heart Sem. Library, Donaldson, Ind., 1960. Mem. AAUW (sec. 1979-80), NEA, Ind. State Tchrs. Assn., Assn. Ind. Media Educators. Home: 917 N Walnut St Plymouth IN 46563 Office: 810 N Randolph Plymouth IN 46563

FISHER, NED LAWRENCE, lawyer; b. Waukegan, Ill., Dec. 28, 1947; s. Henry D. and Florence C. (Cook) F.; B.A., Cornell U., 1970; J.D., U. Mich., 1973. Congressional intern for Congressman Robert McClory, summers 1970, 71, 72; admitted to Ill. bar, 1973; partner firm Hall, Meyer, Fisher, Holmberg and Snook, Waukegan, 1973—; spl. asst. atty. gen. Ill. depts. Transp. and Conservation, 1975—. Chmn. profl. peer group div. United Way Lake County (Ill.), 1978-80; pres. Waukegan Twp. Young Republicans, 1976-78, treas., 1978-80; bd. dirs. Jacob Blumberg Meml. Blood Bank, Waukegan, 1976—, v.p., 1978, pres., 1979—; bd. dirs. Lake County Rep. Fedn., 1975—, v.p., 1977—. Served from 2d lt. to capt. USAR, 1970-78. Recipient Disting. Service award Waukegan-North Chicago Jaycees, 1978. Mem. Am. Bar Assn., Ill. State Bar Assn. (council, young lawyers sect. 1975—, sec. 1981—), Lake County Bar Assn. (public relations chmn. 1974-76, fin. chmn. 1978, treas. 1979-81), Chgo. Bar Assn., Waukegan-Lake County C. of C. (chmn. nat. legis. affairs com. 1975-78, dir. 1979—, exec. com. 1980—, chmn. site acquisition com. 1981). Jewish. Club: Moose. Home: 2313 N Jackson St Waukegan IL 60087 Office: 25 N County St Waukegan IL 60085

FISHER, PAUL VICTOR, refrigerated warehouse exec.; b. Hardin County, Iowa, July 17, 1923; s. Julius and Elizabeth (Roelfs) F.; ed. pub. schs.; spl. classes Wichita State U.; m. Ruth Jean Bear, June 9, 1943; children—Julie Ann, Norman Paul, Jean Elizabeth. Farmer nr. Ackley, Iowa, 1943-49; mcht. Fisher Hardware, Boone, Iowa, 1949-56; officer, mgr. Kans. Ice & Cold Storage Inc., Hutchinson and Wichita, Kans., 1956-57; pres. United Refrigerated Services, Inc., Wichita, 1978—, United of Kans., 1980—, United of Del., 1980—. Mem. Internat. Assn. Refrigerated Warehouses (past chmn. Mo. Valley chpt., dir.), Sales and Mktg. Execs., Wichita C. of C., Allied Food Club. Republican. Presbyterian. Club: Masons. Home: 1441 N Rock Rd #1202 Wichita KS 67206 Office: 2707 N Mead St Wichita KS 67219

FISHER, PIERRE JAMES, JR., physician; b. Chgo., Oct. 29, 1931; s. Pierre James and Evelyn (Trevithick) F.; student Ball State U., 1951-52, Taylor U., 1949-51; M.D., Ind. U., 1956; m. Carol Ann Walton, Mar. 16, 1950; children—James Walton, David Alan, Steven Edward, Teresa Ann. Intern, U.S. Naval Hosp., San Diego, 1956-57, resident in surgery, 1957-61; practice medicine specializing in surgery Surgeons Inc., Marion, Ind., 1965—. pres., 1977—; mem. staff Marion Gen. Hosp., also chief staff, 1970. Served with USN, 1956-65. Recipient Physicians Recognition award AMA, 1974, 77, 80. Diplomate Am. Bd. Surgery. Fellow ACS; mem. AMA, Grant County Med. Soc. (pres. 1980), Marion Area C. of C. (v.p. 1979-81). Methodist. Club: Rotary. Home: 911 Overlook Rd Marion IN 46952 Office: 500 Wabash Ave Surgeons Inc Marion IN 46952

FISHER, RANDY ALAN, social worker; b. Miami, Okla., Aug. 18, 1946; s. Arch U. and Helen Louise (Carrithers) F.; B.S., George Williams Coll., 1968; M.S.W., U. Ill., 1973; m. Deborah Lee Mattil, Aug. 25, 1967; children—Wendy Christine, Paul Andrew, Jonathan David. Sch. social worker Mannheim Dist. 83, Melrose Park, Ill., 1973—; Ill. rep. Midwest Sch. Social Work Council, 1978, pres., 1981—. Served with U.S. Army, 1968-71. Decorated Bronze Star. Mem. Nat. Assn. Social Workers, Ill. Assn. Sch. Social Workers (treas. 1977-79), Internat. Assn. Pupil Personnel Workers, Acad. Certified Social Workers. Methodist. Editor Sch. Social Work Jour., 1979—; author: School Social Work in the Literature: A Bibliography, 1979. Home: 9955 W 144th St Orland Park IL 60462 Office: PO Box 2072 Northlake IL 60164

FISHER, RAY GEORGE, elec. engr.; b. Cuyahoga Falls, Ohio, Dec. 20, 1927; s. Willard Lloyd and Bernice Sarra (Alleman) F.; student profl. courses; m. Wanda Marie Jane Jacobsen, Apr. 30, 1955; children—Susan M., Sarra J. Supt. service dept. U.S. Trading Co., Liberia, 1958-60; elec. constrn. foreman and control writing foreman Dixie Elec. Co., Ft. Lauderdale, Fla., 1969-72; elec. constrn. supr. Clark Elec. Co., Orlando, Fla., 1972-75, Brown Root Co., Waynesboro, Va., 1975-77; elec. engr., then supr. elec. dept. Continental Can Co., Mt. Vernon, Ohio, from 1977; now service engr. Reliance Elec. Co., Cleve.; tchr. in field. Tchr. CPR and first aid ARC, Utica, Ohio. Mem. Utica Med. Service, Internat. Mgmt. Council. Republican. Baptist. Clubs: Masons, Shriners. Designer prodn. machines, 1970-71. Home: 112 N Main St Utica OH 43080 Office: 4950 E 49th St Cleveland OH 44125

FISHER, ROBERT BAKER, assn. exec.; b. Boone, Iowa, Feb. 10, 1943; s. John Albert and Ruth Ann (Baker) F.; B.A., Jamestown (N.D.) Coll., 1965; postgrad. Drake U., 1965-66; grad. Inst. Orgn. Mgmt., 1977; m. Carol Ann Jackson, Nov. 5, 1966; children—Rebecca B., Christopher Aaron. Tchr., Sigourney (Iowa) Community Schs., 1966-67, Queen Bee Schs., Glendale Heights, Ill., 1967-69; bus. devel. officer Gary-Wheaton Bank, Wheaton, Ill., 1970-71; exec. v.p. Kewanee (Ill.) C. of C., 1971-74; pres., Greater Aurora (Ill.) C. of C., 1974—. Regent, Inst. Orgn. Mgmt., 1978—. Recipient Disting. Service award Aurora Jaycees, 1978. Mem. Assn. Am. C. of C. Execs., Ill. Assn. C. of C. Execs. Roman Catholic. Clubs: Union League (sec. chpt. 1979—), Moose, K.C. Home: 637 N Edgelawn Dr Aurora IL 60506 Office: 40 W Downer Pl Aurora IL 60507

FISHER, ROBERT ERWIN, automotive engr.; b. Lansing, Mich., Aug. 16, 1926; s. Marcus Cecil and Alice Etta (Whelan) F.; B.S., Purdue U., 1953; m. Mary Helen Donaldson, June 24, 1950; children—Bruce Alan, Katharine Sue, Dianne Marie. With Oldsmobile div. Gen. Motors Corp., Lansing, Mich., 1950—, project engr., 1956, sr. project engr., 1959—. Scoutmaster, Boy Scouts Am., Lansing, 1961-74. Served with USAAF, 1945. Mem. Soc. Automotive Engrs. Home: 3319 Sunnylane Lansing MI 48906 Office: 1014 Townsend St Lansing MI 48933

FISHER, WILL STRATTON, engr.; b. Nashville, June 27, 1922; s. Will Stratton and Estelle (Carr) F.; B.S.E.E., Vanderbilt U., 1947; m. Patricia A. Fesco, Nov. 10, 1945; children—Patricia Jo, Will Stratton, Robert J. With Lighting Bus. Group, Gen. Elec. Co., Cleve., 1947—, mgr. advanced application engring., 1971—. Served to 1st lt. C.E., AUS, 1943-46. Fellow Illuminating Engring. Soc. N.Am. (pres. 1978-79, Disting. Service award 1980); mem. Internat. Commn. Illumination (U.S. expert on tech. com. 3.3), ASHRAE, IEEE. Methodist. Contbr. articles profl. jours. Patentee Parabolic wedge louver; developer concepts for utilizing heat from lighting systems to heat bldgs.; designer calorimeter; developer procedure for calculating contbn. of lighting to heating of bldgs. Home: 120 Meadowhill Ln Moreland Hills OH 44022 Office: General Electric Co Nela Park Cleveland OH 44112

FISHER-CONLEY, MYRA ANN, real estate broker; b. Ft. Wayne, Ind., Jan. 23, 1939; d. Elvin Edwin and Etheldra Marie (Schultz) Rehklau; B.S., Purdue U., 1973; student Christian Coll., Columbia, Mo., 1957-58, St. Francis Coll., 1969, Ind. U. Purdue U., Ft. Wayne, 1969-72; children—Scott David Gilliom, Steven Lee Gilliom. Corp. sec. Reliable Stores, Inc., Reliable Oil, Inc., and Rehklau Realty, Inc., Ft. Wayne, 1963-78; pvt. practice speech pathology, Ft. Wayne, 1975—; broker asso. Rousseau Realtors, Ft. Wayne, 1979-81; broker asso. Roth Wehrly Realtors, Ft. Wayne, 1981—. Vol., Allen County Cancer Soc., 1974-77. Mem. Ft. Wayne Bd. Realtors, Nat. Assn.

Realtors, Ind. Assn. Realtors, Ind. Speech and Hearing Assn., N.E. Ind. Speech Pathologists, Council Exceptional Children, Ft. Wayne Art Mus. Alliance. Clubs: Ft. Wayne Amateur Radio, Fort Wayne Womens, Order Eastern Star. Home: 3319 Montana Dr Fort Wayne IN 46815 Office: 6605 E State Blvd Fort Wayne IN 46815

FISHETTI, JOHN, cartoonist; b. Brooklyn, N.Y., Sept. 27, 1916; s. Peitro and Emanuela (Navarra) F.; student Pratt Inst., 1947-40; D.F.A. (hon.) Colby Coll., 1969; m. Karen Mortenson, Oct. 25, 1948; children—Peter, Michael. Worked on animated films for Walt Disney; drew his 1st editorial cartoons for Chgo. Sun (now Sun-Times); did illustrations for Coronet, Esquire, Sat. Evening Post, Collier's N.Y. Times; became syndicated cartoonist Newspaper Enterprise Assn., 1950; staff cartoonist N.Y. Herald Tribune, 1962; later cartoonist Publishers' Newspaper Syndicate (now subsidiary Field Enterprises Inc.): now chief editorial cartoonist Chgo. Daily News; with Pub.'s Hall syndicate. Served with Signal Corps., AUS. Recipient Pulitzer Prize, 1969; named Best Editorial Cartoonist, Nat. Cartoonist Soc., 4 times, Sigma Delta Chi award, 1954, 56. Am. Civil Liberties award, 1972, N.Y. Newspaper Guild Front-page award, 1962. Office: 401 N Wabash Ave Chicago IL 60611*

FISHLEIGH, CLARENCE TURNER, cons. engr.; b. Chgo., July 31, 1895; s. John A. and Henrietta P. (Turner) F.; B.S.E.E., U. Mich., 1917; J.D., Detroit Coll. Law, 1939; m. Thea Holste, May 16, 1923; children—Elayne (Mrs. M. Russell Bramwell), Marilyn (Mrs. Pierce). Mech. prodn. Ford Motor Co., 1919-22; exptl. motor testing, asst. prodn. mgr. Am. Car and Foundry Co., Chgo., also Rich Tool Co., Detroit, 1923-24; mgr. Clarence T. Fishleigh Co., 1924-30; asso. engr., cons. engr. Walter T. Fishleigh, 1930-47; cons. engr., Detroit, 1947-51, Chgo., 1951—. Splty. automotive engr., patent experting. Served as 2d lt., USAAC, 1917-19. Decorated Croix de Guerre. Registered profl. engr., Ill., Mich., N.Y., Ohio, Fla., Tex. Mem. Soc. Automotive Engrs., Am. Soc. M.E., Western Soc. Engrs., Engring. Soc. Detroit, Am., Mich. patent law assns., Patent Law Assn. of Chgo., Am., Ill., Mich., Chgo. bar assns., Sigma Nu Phi, Kappa Sigma. Club: Union League (Chgo.). Address: 920 Kenton Rd Deerfield IL 60015

FISHMAN, ARNOLD LAWRENCE, direct mktg. co. exec.; b. Bklyn., Apr. 17, 1926; s. Harry and Dora (Rechter) F.; B.A., Queens Coll., 1947; M.A., Columbia U., 1949; M.B.A., N.Y. U., 1966; m. Grace Reifberg, Dec. 25, 1960; children—George, Hilary. Mgr. applications services IBM, N.Y.C., 1961-66; dir. mgmt. scis. Miles Labs., Elkhart, Ind., 1967-69; dir. market planning Paramount Pictures, N.Y.C., 1969-70, Franklin Mint, Franklin Center, Pa., 1970-74, Citibank, N.Y.C., 1974-78; pres. cons. group Maxwell Sroge Co., Inc., Chgo., 1978-81; pres. Mktg. Logistics, Deerfield, Ill., 1981—. Campaign mgr. Truman for Pres., 1948; campaign mgr. Robert Kennedy for Pres., Elkhart, 1968. Served with U.S. Army, 1944-46. Recipient Theodore Roosevelt Assn. Achievement medal, 1934. Mem. Am. Mktg. Assn., Am. Statis. Assn., Am. Mgmt. Assn., Ops. Research Soc. Am. Club: Elks. Editor-in-chief Pulse Intercollegiate Lit. Mag., 1946-47. Home: 1460 Cloverdale St Highland Park IL 60035 Office: 108 Wilmot Rd Deerfield IL 60015

FISK, ROBERT CLARK, lawyer; b. Curlew, Iowa, Apr. 6, 1917; s. Orville B. and Grace (Foster) F.; student Ft. Dodge Jr. Coll., 1933-35; B.A., U. Iowa, 1938, J.D., 1941; m. Ruth A. Gordon, July 20, 1957. Admitted to Nebr. bar, 1941, Ia. bar; practice in Omaha, 1941—; mem. firm Finlayson, McKie & Fisk, 1965—; dir. Central States Health & Life Co., Omaha, Bank of Millard, Omaha. Lectr., Creighton U. Law Sch., Omaha, 1952-77. Served to maj. M.I., AUS, 1942-46. Mem. Am., Iowa, Nebr., Omaha bar assns., Omaha C. of C., Ak-Sar-Ben, Am. Legion, Res. Officers Assn. Republican. Methodist. Mason (32 degree), Kiwanian. Home: 2608 N 51st Ave Omaha NE 68104 Office: 1375 One First Nat Center Omaha NE 68102

FISSINGER, EDWIN RUSSELL, music educator; b. Chgo., June 15, 1920; s. Paul Cleveland and Isabel (Sweney) F.; B.Mus., Am. Conservatory of Music, 1947, M.Mus., 1951; D.Mus.Arts, U. Ill., 1962; m. Cecile Patricia Monette, Feb. 27, 1943; children—Edwin Monette, Laura. Instr. music Am. Conservatory of Music, Chgo., 1947-54; instr. music U. Ill., Urbana, 1954-57, chmn. dept. music Chgo. Circle campus, 1957-67; prof., chmn. dept. music N.D. State U., Fargo, 1967—, dir. concert choir, 1967—; cons. in field. Served with USAAF, 1942-44. Decorated Purple Heart; recipient Kimball award for composition, 1950. Mem. Am. Choral Dirs. Assn., Music Educators Nat. Conf. Composer numerous compositions including To Everything There is a Season, 1976; Babylon, 1976. Home: 57 15th Ave N Fargo ND 58102 Office: Music Dept ND State U Fargo ND 58105

FITCH, EDWARD HUBBARD, rubber co. exec.; b. Phila., Aug. 9, 1906; s. Edward Hubbard and Bessie (McFarlin) F.; B.A., Williams Coll., 1929, M.B.A., Harvard, 1931; m. Jane Farrell, Oct. 16, 1943; children—Farrell, Edward Hubbard, Jonathan Winchester. With B.F. Goodrich Co., Akron, Ohio, 1931-71, dir. gen. mktg. services, 1968-71; dir. Robin Hill Inc., Hudson, Ohio. Founding pres. Hudson Heritage Assn., 1962-64, pres., 1974-75; campaign vice chmn. United Fund-Red Cross, Summit County, 1970, gen. campaign chmn., 1971; chmn. Akron met. area Nat. Alliance Businessmen, 1972-73; mem. Akron Manpower Area Planning Council, 1972-73; mem. adv. bd. Met. Akron Jobs Council, 1974—. Trustee United Found. Summit County, 1972-76, United Community Council Summit County, 1972-76, Hudson Bicentennial Commn. Mem. Aviation Distbrs. and Mfrs. Assn. (pres. 1961), Episcopalian (sr. warden 1957). Rotarian. Clubs: Wings (N.Y.C.); Metropolitan (Washington). Home: 2727 Hudson-Aurora Rd Hudson OH 44236 Office: Robin Hill Inc Box 637 Hudson OH 44236

FITHIAN, FLOYD, congressman; b. Vesta, Nebr., Nov. 3, 1928; s. James Creston and Eva May (Ballard) F.; B.A., Peru (Nebr.) State Coll., 1951; M.A. in History, U. Nebr., 1955, Ph.D. in Am. history, 1964; m. Marjorie Heim, Nov. 1, 1952; children—Cindy, Judy, John. Former tchr. history and govt. high schs.; formerly asso. prof. Am. history Purdue U., West Lafayette, Ind.; mem. 94th to 97th Congresses from 2d Ind. dist., mem. coms. on agr. and govt. ops., mem. rural caucus. Active Democratic campaigns, Tippecanoe County, Ind.; Served with USN, 1951-54. Mem. Am. Legion, Am. Hist. Assn., Orgn. Am. Historians, Tippecanoe County Hist. Soc., Ind. State Council Social Studies (past pres.). Methodist (tchr., lay speaker). Contbr. articles to profl. jours. Office: 1210 Longworth House Office Bldg Washington DC 20515 also 3707 Pleasant Ridge Rd Annandale VA 22003

FITZGERALD, JAMES FRANCIS, cable TV exec.; b. Janesville, Wis., Mar. 27, 1926; s. Michael Henry and Chloris lHelen (Beiter) F.; B.S., Notre Dame U., 1947; m. Marilyn Field Cullen, Aug. 1, 1950; children—Michael Dennis, Brian Nicholas, Marcia O'Loughlin, James Francis, Carolyn Dewitz, Ellen Putnam. With Standard Oil Co. (Ind.), Milw., 1947-48; pres., chmn. bd. F.W. Oil Co., Janesville, 1950-73; v.p. Creston Park Corp., 1957—; pres. Sunnyside, Inc., 1958—, Total TV, Inc., cable TV systems, Wis. and Fla., 1965—, Janesville Indsl. Devel. Corp., 1966—; dir. 1st Nat. Bank, Koss Corp.; chmn. bd. Milw. Profl. Sports and Services (Milw. Bucks). Bd. govs. NBA, also chmn. TV com. Served to lt. (j.g.) USNR, 1944-45, 51-52. Recipient Janesville Man of Year award Jr. C. of C. Mem. Chief Execs. Forum, World Bus. Council, Wis. Petroleum Assn. (pres. 1961-62). Roman Catholic. Clubs: Janesville Country (past pres.), Milw. Athletic. Office: 839 Harding St Janesville WI 53545

FITZGERALD, JOHN WARNER, judge; b. Grand Ledge, Mich., Nov. 14, 1924; s. Frank D. and Queena (Warner) F.; B.S., Mich. State U., 1947; J.D., U. Mich., 1954; m. Lorabeth Moore, June 6, 1953; children—Frank Moore, Eric Stiles, Adam Warner. Mem. pub. relations staff Mich. State U., 1947-52; admitted to Mich. bar, 1954, practiced in Grand Ledge; mem. firm Fitzgerald & Wirbel; legal counsel Mich. Senate, 1955-58; state senator 15th Mich. Dist., 1958-65, chmn. senate bus. com., 1961-65; judge Mich. Ct. Appeals, Lansing, 1965-74, chief judge pro tem, 1965-74; justice Mich. Supreme Ct., 1974—, dep. chief justice, 1976—. Bd. dirs. Thomas M. Cooley Law Sch., 1975—. Served U.S. Army, 1942-44. Mem. Inst. Jud. Adminstrn., Am., Mich., Eaton County (pres. 1963) bar assns., Hist. Soc. Mich. Home: Grand Ledge MI 48837 Office: Law Bldg Lansing MI 48901

FITZ-GERALD, ROGER MILLER, lawyer; b. N.Y.C., July 13, 1935; s. Gerald Hartpence and Rovenia Francis (Miller) F-G; B.S. with honors, U. Ill., 1957, J.D. with honors, 1961; m. Martha Ann Odell, Oct. 28, 1967; children—Kathleen Odell, Maureen Roxanne, Arthur Thomas. Admitted to Ill. bar, 1961, U.S. Dist. Ct. bar, 1961, bar U.S. Patent and Trademark Office, 1965, Ct. Customs and Patent Appeals, 1978; asso. firm Kirkland, Ellis, Hodson, Chaffetz & Masters, Chgo., 1961-64, Fitch, Even, Tabin & Luedeka, specializing in fgn. patent law, Chgo., 1964-72; patent atty. Bell & Howell Co., Chgo., 1972-74, sr. patent atty., 1974-75, group patent atty., 1975-76, group patent counsel, 1976—. Constl. revision chmn. Ill. Young Republican Orgn., 1968-70. Served with AUS, 1957. Mem. Am., Ill. State, Chgo. bar assns., Patent Law Assn. Chgo., Am. Patent Law Assn., Order of Coif, Phi Beta Kappa, Phi Eta Sigma, Phi Delta Phi, Delta Upsilon (province gov. 1969-75). Republican. Author: (with Ferdinand J. Zeni) Precinct Captain's Guide, 1968; contbg. author: Materials on Legislation (Read, MacDonald, Fordham and Pierce), 1973. Office: 7100 McCormick Rd Chicago IL 60645

FITZGERALD, THOMAS, state legislator; b. Omaha, Feb. 29, 1920; grad. high sch.; m. Lorraine Fitzgerald, Sept. 25, 1948; children—Linda Fitzgerald Kass, Thomas III, Gayle Fitzgerald Sturm. Mem. Nebr. Legislature, 1978—. Mem. Am. Assn. Ret. Persons, Arts and Humanities Council Florence, Am. Legion, VFW, DAV, Florence Hist. Found. Clubs: Eagles, Kiwanis, Little Vikes, North Omaha Comml., Optimists. Home: 8104 N Ridge Dr Omaha NE 68112*

FITZ GERALD, THOMAS JOE, psychologist; b. Wichita, Kans., July 8, 1941; s. Thomas Michael and Pauline Gladys (Zink) F.; B.A., San Francisco State Coll., 1965; M.A., U. Utah, 1969, Ph.D., 1971. Dir. behavioral services programs VA Hosp., Topeka, 1971-73; pvt. practice as psychologist, Topeka, 1973-74, Prairie Village, Kans., 1974—; clin. instr. Menninger Sch. Psychiatry, Topeka, 1972-74; sec.-treas. Kans. Bd. Psychologist Examiners, 1976-79, 79-80, chmn., 1980—; pres. Psychol. Services Corp., Prairie Village, 1974—. Mem. Gov.'s Commn. on Criminal Adminstrn., 1974-76; vice-chmn. Gov.'s Com. on Med. Assistance, 1978-80; mem. Mid-Am. Health Systems Agy., 1979—. Served with USMCR, 1958-60. Mem. Am., Kans. (pres. 1980-81), Mo., Calif. psychol. assns., Kans. Assn. Profl. Psychologists (pres. 1981-82, Outstanding Psychologist award 1979, 80), Greater Kansas City Soc. Clin. Hypnosis (pres. 1978-81). Office: 2108 W 75th St Suite 400 Prairie Village KS 66208

FITZGERALD, THOMAS ROLLINS, univ. adminstr.; b. Washington, Feb. 23, 1922; s. Thomas Rollins and Bessie (Sheehy) F.; B.A., Woodstock (Md.) Coll., 1945, M.A., 1948; S.T.L., Facultes St. Albert de Louvain (Belgium), 1953; Ph.D., U. Chgo., 1957. Joined Soc. of Jesus, 1939, ordained priest Roman Catholic Ch., 1952; instr. classics Novitiate St. Isaac Jogues, Wernersville, Pa., 1957-58, dean studies, asst. prof. classics, 1958-64; dean Coll. Arts and Scis., Georgetown U., 1964-66, acad. v.p., 1966-73; pres. Fairfield (Conn.) U., 1973-79, St. Louis U., 1979—; pres. Conn. Conf. Ind. Colls., 1975-77; mem. New Eng. Bd. Higher Edn., from 1977. Trustee, Gonzaga High Sch., Washington, 1969-74; chmn. bd. trustees St. Peter's Coll., Jersey City, 1969-75; trustee U. Scranton (Pa.), 1974-77, Boston Coll. High Sch., 1976-79; bd. dirs. Nat. Assn. Ind. Colls. and Univs., 1977-79. Democrat. Address: St Louis University Saint Louis MO 63103*

FITZ GIBBONS, JAMES PATRICK, obstetrician, gynecologist; b. Chgo., Mar. 16, 1908; s. James Joseph and Ellen (O'Brien) FitzG.; B.S.M., Loyola U., Chgo., 1934, M.D., 1936; m. Rita Ann Fisher, Aug. 8, 1950; children—Margaret Ellen, Michael James, Ann, Thomas Patrick, James Jospeh, Robert Emmett. Practice medicine specializing in obstetrics and gynecology, Chgo., sr. attending physician Grant Hosp., Chgo., Swedish Covenant Hosp., Chgo.; clin. asso. prof. dept. obstetrics and gynecology Abraham Lincoln Sch. Medicine U. Ill., Chgo. Served as capt. M.C., U.S. Army, 1941-46. Fellow A.C.S., Am. Coll. Obstetrics and Gynecology; mem. Ill., Chgo. med. socs., AMA. Home: 2944 Grant St Evanston IL 60201 Office: 2073 N Lincoln Ave Chicago IL 60614

FITZPATRICK, CHRISTINE MORRIS, TV exec.; b. Steubenville, Ohio, June 10, 1920; d. Roy Elwood and Ruby Lorena (Mason) Morris; student U. Chgo., 1943-44; B.A., Roosevelt U., 1947; postgrad. Trinity Coll., Hartford, Conn., 1970; m. T. Mallary Fitzpatrick, Jr., Dec. 19, 1942; 1 son, Thomas Mallary III. Asso. dir. Joint Human Relations Project, City of Chgo., 1965-66; tchr. English, Austin Sch. for Girls, Hartford, 1966-70; promotion coordinator Conn. Pub. TV, Hartford, 1971-72, dir. community relations, 1972-73, v.p., 1973-77; pub. relations/pub. affairs cons. Commonwealth Edison Co., Chgo., 1977-79; dir. spl. events Chgo. Public TV, 1979—; pres. New Eng. chpt. Am. Women in Radio and TV, 1976-77; v.p. Public Relations Clinic Chgo., 1980-81. Pres., Chgo. chpt. LWV, 1962-64, v.p. Hartford chpt., 1971-73; bd. advisers Greater Hartford Mag., 1975-77; bd. dirs. World Affairs Center, Hartford, 1975-77; mem. adv. council Am. Revolution Bicentennial Commn. Conn., 1975-77. Mem. Pub. Relations Soc. Am. (dir. Conn. Valley chpt. 1976-77), Nat. Assn. Ednl. Broadcasters, Chgo. Council Fgn. Relations, Chgo. Architecture Found., Art Inst. Chgo. Mem. United Ch. Christ. Clubs: Arts, Chgo. Press (Chgo.). Home: 2500 N Talman Ave Chicago IL 60647 Office: WTTW Channel 11 5400 N St Louis Ave Chicago IL 60625

FITZPATRICK, JAMES A., ins. co. exec.; b. Dayton, Ohio, Mar. 10, 1940; s. James A. and Ruby J. Fitzpatrick; children—Debby, James A. Agt., then state mgr. Res. Life Ins. Co., Columbus, Ohio, 1964-70; trainer, then asst. agy. dir. Universal Guarantee Life Ins. Co., Columbus, 1970-74; state mgr. Columbia Ins. Co., Indpls., 1974-76; v.p. Greenfield Assos., Inc., Indpls., 1976-81, pres., 1981—; founder, 1977, since pres. Greenfield Fin. Corp., Indpls.; chmn. bd. Greenfield Life Ins. Co., 1980—; dir. Med. Investors, Inc. Served with USMC, 1959-63. Registered health underwriter. Mem. Nat. Assn. Health Underwriters (regional v.p. 1979-80), Life Underwriters Assn., Indpls. C. of C. (dir.), Greenfield C. of C. (v.p.). Clubs: Elks, Masons, Sertoma. Office: 2 W Main St Greenfield IN 46140

FITZPATRICK, JAMES BROCK, automotive co. exec.; b. Washington, Mar. 7, 1932; s. James T. and Marian F.; B.B.A., 1954; m. Janet M. Blair, Dec. 26, 1970; children—Mark J., Kevin S., David B., Kathleen K. Trainee Gen. Motors Corp., 1954, supr. ops. analysis, 1963-67, asst. dir. ops. analysis, 1967, gen. dir. ops. analysis Chevrolet Motor div., 1967-68, asst. div. controller, 1968-72, asst. corp. controller, 1972-76, dir. corp. product planning, Detroit, 1976-78, divisional comptroller Pontiac Motor Div. (Mich.), 1978—. Served to lt., j.g., USN, 1954-58. Club: Recess. Office: One Pontiac Plaza Pontiac MI 48053

FITZSIMMONS, LOWELL (COTTON), profl. basketball coach; b. Hannibal, Mo., Oct. 7, 1931; s. Clancy and Zelda Curry (Gibbs) F.; B.S., Midwestern U., Wichita Falls, Tex., 1956, M.A., 1957; m. JoAnn D'Andrea, Feb. 2, 1978; 1 son, Gary. Tchr., coach Moberly Jr. Coll., 1957-67; tchr., coach Kans. State U., 1967-70; profl. coach Nat. Basketball Assn., 1970—; now coach Kansas City Kings. Named Coach of Yr. Nat. Basketball Assn., 1979, Sporting News, 1979, Sportcasters, 1981. Office: 1800 Genessee Kansas City MO 64102

FIUZAT, YAHYA, agrl. edn. manpower planning and devel. cons.; b. Tabriz, Iran, Mar. 12, 1925; came to U.S., 1971; s. Abolgasem and Monireh (Emad) F.; M.S., Iowa State U., 1952, Ph.D., U. Mo., 1973; m. Fatemeh Paknia, Aug. 13, 1951; children—Homa, Homayoon, Hadi. Supr., supt. Mamazan Agr. Edn. and Varamin Agr. Devel., Iran, 1949-62; dir. planning and devel. Ahwaz Agr. Coll., Iran, 1962-68; pres. Edn. Corps Tchrs. Coll., Iran, 1968-71; asso. prof. Birooni Rural U., Iran, 1971-78, dir. instnl. research, 1975-76, v.p. research, 1976-77; pvt. practice agr. edn. manpower planning and devel. cons., Columbia, Mo., 1978—. Fulbright fellow, 1951-52; Brit. Council fellow, 1959; Eisenhower exchange fellow, 1966; Iran Ministry Higher Edn. fellow, 1971-74. Mem. Am. Vocat. Assn., Phi Delta Kappa. Contbr. in field. Home: 1256 S Pecos St Columbia MO 65201

FIVEK, MINA EVELYN CLANCY, youth advocate, tax cons.; b. Hebron, Ill., July 26, 1907; d. Joseph and Nita Helen (Giddings) Clancy; B.A., Elmhurst (Ill.) Coll., 1976; m. Emanuel Fivek, Sept. 15, 1928; children—Nita Naomi, Gloria Cecile, Karl Webster. With M&M/Mars, Chgo., 1947-72; acct. Hartranft Inc., Chgo., 1972-73; tax cons. H&R Block, Bensenville, Ill., 1975—; cons. Ill. Commn. on Delinquency Prevention, Ill. Status Offender Services, 1973—; youth advocate Status Offender Service, Ill. Dept. Children and Family Services, 1973; lectr. juvenile delinquency. Mem. John Ericsson Republican Club of DuPage County, 1971—, sec., 1981-82; founder Bensenville Rep. Women's Club, 1973; mem. Addison Twp. Rep. Precinct Com., 1973-78, York Twp. Rep. Precinct Com., 1978-81, Elmhurst Precinct Com., 1981-82; life mem. Rep. Nat. Com., 1979—; treas., bd. dirs. Highland Lakes Condominium Assn.; mem. Youth Commn. Lombard (Ill.), 1978-79. Cert. tutor Laubach Literacy Internat. Mem. Am. Soc. Notaries, Nat. Assn. Female Execs. Inc., AAUW, Am. Security Council, LWV, Women of Moose, Beta Sigma Phi (life). Clubs: Order of Eastern Star (grand lectr. 1963-65, worthy matron 1962, cert. of achievement, longevity service award Bensenville chpt. 1972), Gaslight; Capitol Hill (life) (Washington); United Airlines Red Carpet.

FIZZELL, ROBERT LESTER, assn. exec., educator; b. Chgo., Apr. 29, 1939; s. James Albert and Gladys Muriel (Blankley) F.; B.A., Beloit Coll., 1961; M.A.T., Northwestern U., 1966, Ph.D., 1975; m. Marjorie Ann Moss, June 11, 1960; children—Richard Allan, James Tobias, Ronald Lester. Tchr. social studies, track coach Niles Twp. High Sch., West Div., Skokie, Ill., 1966-73; program coordinator Niles Twp. Action Learning Center, Skokie, 1973-77; asso. prof. ednl. founds. dept. Western Ill. U., 1977—; exec. dir. Ill. Community Edn. Assn., Macomb, 1980—; cons. ednl. program devel. and evaluation. Pres., Planning Consortium for Children's Services in Ill., 1979-81. Served with U.S. Army, 1961-64. Mem. Ill. Alternative Edn. Assn. (pres., founder 1979—), Am. Fedn. Tchrs., Nat. Community Edn. Assn., Ill. Community Edn. Assn., Assn. Supervision and Curriculum Devel., World Future Soc., Phi Delta Kappa. Author: The Schooling Style Inventory, 1978; The Truants Alternative Program: An Evaluation, 1978. Home: 1706 Riverview Dr Macomb IL 61455 Office: 456 Stipes Hall Western Ill U Macomb IL 61455

FLAGLER, ROBERT LOOMIS, mfg. co. exec.; b. Chgo., Feb. 17, 1940; s. Holland J. and Francis Eugenia (Loomis) F.; B.A., U. Miss., 1964; children—Ann Holland, Robert Stephen. Asst. to v.p., gen. mgr. Sta. WSNS-TV, Chgo., 1967-70; v.p., gen. mgr. Telemation Prodns., Inc., Glenview, Ill., 1970-79, also dir., v.p. adminstrv. officer, 1979; pres., chief operating officer Ocenco, Inc., Northbrook, Ill., 1979—, also dir.; dir. Video Support Co., Inc., Wis. Edn. Industries. Mem. Video Tape Producers Assn., U. Miss. Alumni Assn., Am. Mining Congress, Indsl. TV Soc., Nat. Assn. Sales and Mktg. Execs. Republican. Episcopalian. Club: Lions. Home: 134 Green Bay Rd Winnetka IL 60093 Office: 400 Academy Dr Northbrook IL 60062

FLAHERTY, JOHN JOSEPH, quality assurance co. exec.; b. Chgo., July 24, 1932; s. Patrick J. and Mary B. F.; B.E.E., U. Ill., 1959; m. Norrine Grow, Nov. 20, 1932; children—John, Bridgette, George, Eileen, Daniel, Mary, Michael, Amy. Design engr. Admiral Corp., Chgo., 1959-60; project engr. Magnaflux Corp., Chgo., 1960-79, v.p., mgr. research and engring., 1979—. Served with AUS, 1951-53. Mem. Am. Soc. Non-Destructive Testing, I.E.E.E., Am. Soc. Quality Control. Roman Catholic. Numerous patents on nondestructive testing, including med. ultrasonic; laser scanning. Home: 671 Grosvener Ln Elk Grove Village IL 60007 Office: 7300 W Lawrence Ave Chicago IL 60656

FLAHIFF, GEORGE BERNARD, archbishop; b. Paris, Ont., Can., Oct. 26, 1905; s. John James and Eleanor Rose (Fleming) F.; B.A., St. Michael's Coll., U. Toronto, 1926; student U. Strasbourg (France), 1930-31; Dipl. Archiviste-Paleographe, Ecole Nat. des Chartes, Paris, France, 1935; hon. degree in law U. Seattle, 1965, U. Notre Dame, 1969, U. Man., 1969, U. Windsor, 1970, U. Winnipeg, 1972, U. Toronto, 1972; S.T.D., Université Laval, Quebec, 1974, St. Bonaventure U., 1975, U. St. Thomas, Houston, 1977. Ordained priest Roman Catholic Ch., 1930; prof. medieval history Pontifical Inst. Medieval Studies and U. Toronto, 1935-54, sec. Inst., 1943-51; superior-gen. Basilian Fathers, 1954-61; archbishop of Winnipeg, Can., 1961—; named to Coll. Cardinals, 1969; mem. Sacred Congregation for Religious, Sacred Congregation for Edn. Decorated companion Order Can., 1974. Home: 39 Bishop's Ln Winnipeg MB R3R 0A8 Canada Office: 50 Stafford St Winnipeg MB R3M 2V7 Canada

FLANAGAN, EDWARD JOSEPH, chiropractor; b. Cleve., Feb. 13, 1931; s. Edward Joseph and Esther Mary (White) F.; student Kent State U., 1950-52; D. Chiropractic, Great Lake Coll. Chiropractic, 1961; postgrad. roentgenology Lincoln Chiropractic Coll., 1968-70; m. Betty Sue Boone, Apr. 24, 1954; children—Linda, Susan, June, Collette, Lori, Mary Lou, Eddie. Pvt. chiropractic practice, North Olmsted, Ohio, 1961—; lectr.; cons. x-ray specialist Assos. Diagnostic Center, Akron, Ohio; owner Lorain Chiropractic Center, Memphis Chiropractic Center. Served with USNR, 1952-54. Licensed mechanotherapist, Ohio. Diplomate Am. Bd. Chiropractic Roentgenology. Mem. Am., Ohio, Northeastern Ohio chiropractic

Contbr. articles to profl. jours. Home: 31686 Lake Rd Avon Lake OH 44012 Office: 27712 Lorain Ave North Olmsted OH 44070

FLANAGAN, GEORGE CLEMENT, physician; b. Chgo., Aug. 24, 1928; s. Charles Larkin and Helen Marie (Sullivan) F.; M.D., U. Chgo., 1953; children—George Hunter, Elizabeth Hanford. Intern, U. Chgo. Clinics, 1953-54; resident Presbyn.-St. Luke's Hosp., Chgo., 1957-60; asso. prof. medicine U. Ill. Med. Schs., Chgo., 1967-69; asso. prof. medicine Rush Med. Coll., Chgo., 1971—, asso. dean, 1974—. Served with USNR, 1954-56. Mem. ACP, AMA, Assn. Am. Med. Colls. Roman Catholic. Home: 8144 W 26 St North Riverside IL 60546 Office: 600 S Paulina St Chicago IL 60612

FLANAGAN, JAMES BRIERTON, JR., mgmt. cons.; b. Chgo., Mar. 25, 1948; s. James Brierton and Lela Agnes (Wester) F.; B.S., U. Ill., Chgo., 1969; m. Rochelle F. Parente, Aug. 31, 1968; children—Angela, James Brierton III. Systems project mgr. MacNeal Hosp., Berwyn, Ill., 1970-72; mgr. systems devel. U. Chgo. Hosps., 1972-74; mgr. adminstrv. services Arthur Andersen & Co., Chgo., 1974—. Mem. fin. com. Red Cross Blood Program. C.P.A., Ill. Mem. Am. Inst. C.P.A.'s, Ill. C.P.A. Soc., Hosp. Mgmt. Systems Soc., Hosp. Fin. Mgmt. Assn. Roman Catholic. Home: 9745 S Leavitt St Chicago IL 60643

FLANAGAN, PAUL KING, owner ins. agy.; b. Huron, S.D., Dec. 30, 1932; s. Earl F. and Ruby T. (Dinkins) F.; B.F.A. cum laude, U. S.D., 1954; m. Laura M. Wickham, Nov. 22, 1951; children—Jeanne, Valerie, Dan, Kathleen, Lisa. Gen. mgr. U. S.D. Book & Supply Inc., 1954-59; exec. dir. U. S.D. Student Union, 1954-59; owner, mgr. Flanagan Agy., ins., Huron, S.D., 1959—. City commr. City of Huron, 1973-80, mayor, 1980—. Recipient Huron Distinguished Service award Huron Jaycees, 1970. C.L.U. Mem. Am. Ind. Agts. Assn., Am. Soc. C.L.U. (pres. Eastern S.D. chpts.), Nat., S.D. (pres, nat. committeeman 1972-78, Agt. of Yr. award 1978), assns. life underwriters, Huron Life Underwriters Assn. (pres. 1960), Huron C. of C. (pres. 1968), Jaycees (pres. Vermillion 1958, Huron 1962), Izaak Walton League Am. Democrat. Roman Catholic. Club: Elks (pres. 1969). Home: 1478 Utah Ave SE Huron SD 57350 Office: 50 3d St SW Huron SD 57350

FLANDERS, DWIGHT PRESCOTT, economist, ret. educator; b. Rockford, Ill., Mar. 14, 1909; s. Daniel Bailey and Lulu Iona (Nichol) F.; B.A., U. Ill., 1931, M.A., 1937; postgrad. Beloit Coll., 1933-34; Ph.D., Yale, 1939; m. Mildred Margaret Hutchison, Aug. 27, 1939; children—James Prescott, Thomas Addison. Instr. coll. algebra Burr Sch., Beloit (Wis.) Coll., 1933-34; instr. U.S. history secondary schs., Rockford, 1934-36; asst. prof. econs. and statistics Syracuse U., 1939-42; prof. econs. U. Ill., Urbana-Champaign, 1946-77, prof. emeritus, 1977—, chmn. masters research seminar, 1947-74. grad. adviser, 1949-75, prof. emeritus dept. family and consumer econs. Coll. of Agr., 1980—; cons. in field. Del., Hazen Nat. Conf. Religion and Edn., 1948. Pres. Three Lakes (Wis.) Waterfront Homeowners Assn., 1969-71, mem. ofcl. bd., 1971—. Served with AUS, 1930, 42-46. Recipient Best Grad. Tchr. award Coll. Commerce, U. Ill., 1977. Mem. Am. Econ. Assn., Econometric Soc., Royal Econ. Soc., Phi Beta Kappa, Phi Kappa Phi, Alpha Kappa Psi, Beta Gamma Sigma (pres. U. Ill. chpt. 1959-60, historian 1960-77), Chi Beta, Chi Psi. Club: Yale (Chgo.). Asso. editor Current Econ. Comment, 1946-54. Author monographs, books; contbr. articles to profl. publs. Home: 719 S Foley Ave Champaign IL 61820 Office: Dept Econs U Ill Urbana IL 61801

FLANERY, DENNIS HAROLD, county ofcl.; b. Kansas City, Mo., Oct. 28, 1949; s. Wendell Harold and Ila Rea (Williams) F.; diploma Water and Wastewater Tech. Sch., Neosho, Mo., 1972; spl. course U. So. Calif., 1977; m. Sharon L. Ozbolt, Aug. 23, 1969; children—Sharrese Lynn, Brent Michael. Mem. staff Jackson County Public Water Supply Dist. 1, Grandview, Mo., 1969—, supt., 1973-76, asst. mgr., 1976-79, mgr., 1979—; chmn. adv. com. Mo. Safe Drinking Water Adv. Council, 1978—; vice chmn. Mo. Citizens Com. for Safe Water, 1980; chmn. bd. dirs. Cass County Public Water Supply Dist. 3, 1978—; dir. Commerce Bank of Grandview. Mem. Am. Water Works Assn. (sectional seminar leader, trustee Mo. sect. 1980), Mo. Water and Sewage Conf., Mo. Rural Water Assn. (dir. 1980), Grandview C. of C. (dir. 1981). Baptist. Club: Masons. Compiler manual. Home: 1409 Farview Rd Raymore MO 64083 Office: 13015 15th St Grandview MO 64030

FLAVIN, GLENNON P., bishop; b. St. Louis, Mar. 2, 1916; grad. St. Louis Prep. Sem., Kendrick Sem. Ordained priest Roman Catholic Ch., 1941; sec. to archbishop St. Louis, 1949-57; consecrated bishop, 1957; ordained titular bishop of Joannina and aux. bishop St. Louis, 1957-67; bishop Diocese of Lincoln (Nebr.), 1967—. Office: 3400 Sheridan Blvd PO Box 80328 Lincoln NE 68501*

FLEE, KENNETH CURTIS, JR., graphic arts service exec.; b. Madison, Wis., Feb. 6, 1943; s. Kenneth Curtis and Helen Elizabeth (Koon) F.; student U. Wis., 1961-66; m. Lois Kay Lythjohan, Sept. 19, 1964; children—Laurie Lynn, Christine Karen. Free lance artist Fleetwood Art Studio, Madison, 1961-68, pres., 1974—; publs. editor Dept. Natural Resources, State of Wis., Madison, 1968-74; cons. small computer software. Mem. Nat. Model Railroad Assn. (dir. S. Central Wis. div.). Home: 2508 Valley Forge Dr Madison WI 53719 Office: 6333 Odana Rd Madison WI 53719

FLEENER, DOROTHY MAY, appliance mfg. exec.; b. Cedar Hill, Tenn., Nov. 15, 1924; d. James Turner and Maude Mae (Lawrence) Perry; grad. Lockyears Coll. Bus., 1949; m. Jesse W. Fleener, Mar. 22, 1953. Credit mgr. Glidden Co., Evansville, Ind., 1950-60; sec. to pres. Craddock Furniture Corp., Evansville, 1963-75; adminstrv. asst. installation and service Engring. div. Gen. Electric Co., Evansville, 1973—. Pres., Southwestern Ind. Status of Women Assn., 1976—. Mem. Am. Bus. Women's Assn., Nat. Secs. Assn. (pres. Evansville chpt. 1970-71), Evansville Bus. and Profl. Women's Club (treas. 1971-72, sec. 1972-73, 2d v.p. 1973-74, 1st v.p. 1974-75, pres. 1975-76). Republican. United Methodist. Mem. Order Eastern Star, Altrusa. Home: 301 Logwood Dr Evansville IN 47710 Office: 2709 Washington Ave Evansville IN 47714

FLEISCHER, JACK, mfg. co. exec.; b. Port Chester, N.Y., Apr. 19, 1919; s. Isaac and Ella (Baruch) F.; student St. Petersburg Jr. Coll., 1936-39; B.S., U. Fla., 1940; postgrad U. N.C., 1951-52; M.S., N.C. State U., 1953; m. Bess Wiener, Dec. 7, 1947; children—Marjorie Fleischer Simon, Nancy Fleischer Hoffman. Asst. prof. N.C. State U., Raleigh, 1953-60; sr. statistician B.F. Goodrich Co., Akron, Ohio, 1960-64, mgr. mktg. research, 1964-70, dir. mktg. research, 1970—; cons. Research Triangle Inst., 1956-60. Chmn. econ. subcom. United Way, Akron, 1960-69; mem. Blueprint for the 70's com. Akron Bd. Edn., 1968-69. Served with AUS, 1943-47. Mem. Am. Statis. Assn., Am. Mktg. Assn., Sigma Xi. Club: Rosemont Country. Home: 71 Pembroke Rd Akron OH 44313 Office: 500 S Main St Akron OH 44318

FLEISCHER, JOHN GERHART, mfg. co. exec.; b. Oberndorf, Austria, Sept. 22, 1951; came to U.S., 1954, naturalized, 1964; s. John and Hedy (Breitfuss) F.; A.S. in Electronics Engring., Ohio Inst. Tech., 1971, B.S. in Electronics Engring., 1972; m. Nancy Jean Bush, Apr. 2, 1976; children—Debbie Sue, Troy. Sr. electronic technician Reliance Electric/Toledo Scales, Westerville, Ohio, 1972-75; design and field engr. H. C. Price Co., Grove City, Ohio, 1975-77; with Briscoe Mfg. Co., Columbus, Ohio, 1977—, mgr. engring. and product devel., 1982—. Treas. Holy Cross Luth. Ch. of the Deaf, Columbus, 1980—; basketball and softball coach Westerville Recreation Dept., 1976-80; co-chmn. ways and means com. A.G. Bell Sch. for Hearing Impaired, Columbus, 1978. Mem. IEEE, Nat. Elec. Mfrs. Assn. (chmn. tech. com. of electric heating element industry), Nat. Assn. Non-Destructive Testing. Home: 3995 Tri Corner Ct Gahanna OH 43230 Office: 1055 Gibbard Columbus OH 43230

FLEMING, BRUCE THOMAS, realtor; b. Watseka, Ill., Apr. 11, 1920; s. Blythe and Mabel (Kirkpatrick) F.; B.S. in Agrl. Econs., Purdue U., 1942; m. Betty Jean Gordon, June 12, 1943; children—Philip J., Anthony P., Thomas J. Loan supr. U.S. Dept. Agr., Crown Point, Ind., 1942-46; owner, operator Fleming Realty Co., Crown Point, Ind., 1946—, v.p., treas. Fleming, Corbin & Bates Ins. Inc.; sec., part-owner Turnkey Builders Inc.; treas., part-owner All Seasons Home Inc.; v.p., dir. Manor Homes Corp.; pres. S. Suburban Multiple Listing Service, 1973-74; past pres. S. Lake County Bd. Realtors, 1960. Past pres. Civic Club, 1955; mem. tech. adv. com. N.W. Ind. Regional Planning Commn., past fin. chmn. Methodist Ch., Crown Point. Named realtor of year, 1974. Mem. Am., Ind., Crown Point real estate assns., Am., No. Ind. assns. home builders, Am. Soc. Farm Mgrs. and Rural Appraisers, Soc. Residential Appraisers, Jaycees (past pres. Crown Point 1950), Indiana Soc. Chgo. Clubs: Youche Country, Lakes of Four Seasons Country, Crown Point Bridge League; Masons, Shriners. Home: 4110 Hermits Ln Crown Point IN 46307 Office: 216 E Joliet St Crown Point IN 46307

FLEMING, DAVID DIEHL, hosp. ofcl.; b. Galesburg, Ill., Oct. 12, 1923; s. Herbert Mark and Ruth (Diehl) F.; B.A., Monmouth (Ill.) Coll., 1946; m. Mary Huntoon, June 7, 1947; children—Michael, David, Joel. Mem. staff Monmouth Coll., 1946-72, asst. to pres., 1966-72; v.p. devel. Galesburg (Ill.) Cottage Hosp., 1972—; dir. Nat. Bank Monmouth, 1966—. Vice pres., trustee E.A. Mellinger Ednl. Found. Served with AUS, 1942-45, 51-53. Mem. Nat. Assn. Hosp. Devel., Am. Soc. Hosp. Public Relations. Republican. Presbyterian. Clubs: Galesburg Rotary; Monmouth Country. Home: 1115 E Detroit Ave Monmouth IL 61462 Office: 695 N Kellogg St Galesburg IL 61401

FLEMING, DOUGLAS G., feed co. exec.; b. Harvey, Ill., Apr. 28, 1930; s. Harold L. and Genevieve (Hodges) F.; B.S., Mich. State U., 1954; m. Sara L. Waters, May 25, 1952; children—Christine J., James C. With Central Soya Co., 1954—, asst. mgr. field ops., Ft. Wayne, Ind., 1963-65, v.p., dir. mktg., 1965-70, exec. v.p., 1970-76, pres., 1976-79, chmn., pres., chief exec. officer, 1980—, also dir.; chmn. O's Gold Seed Co., Parkersburg, Iowa; dir. Ft. Wayne Nat. Bank, Tokheim Corp., Midwestern United Life Ins. Co., Arvin Industries. Bd. dirs. United Way Allen County. Served to 2d lt. AUS, 1951-53. Mem. Am. Feed Mfrs. Assn. Clubs: Ft. Wayne Country, Summit (Ft. Wayne). Home: 16817 Tonkel Rd Leo IN 46765 Office: 1300 Fort Wayne Nat Bank Bldg Box 1400 Fort Wayne IN 46801-1400

FLEMING, GEORGE ROBERT, psychologist; b. New Haven, Conn., July 24, 1947; s. George Robert and Susie Mae F.; B.A., Hillsdale Coll., 1969; M.A., Mich. State U., 1972, Ph.D., 1975; m. Micheline Alys Beam, May 20, 1978. Dir., East N.Y. Mental Health Clinic Adult Day Treatment Program, N.Y.C., 1973-77; chmn. psychology dept. Malcolm-King Harlem Coll. Extension, N.Y.C., 1979, adj. prof., 1977-79; staff psychologist Bedford-Stuyvesant Community Mental Health Center, N.Y.C., 1977-79; cons. Detroit Public Schs., 1981—, Centrax Diversified Services, 1977—, City of Detroit Comprehensive Youth Services Program, 1980—; dir. Central City br. Children's Center, Detroit, 1979—. NIMH fellow, 1974-75. Mem. Nat. Black Child Devel. Inst. (mem. steering com. met. Detroit 1981), Nat. Register Health Service Providers in Psychology, Am. Psychol. Assn., Assn. Black Psychologists, Am. Orthopsychiat. Assn., Internat. Neuropsychol. Soc., Mich. Soc. Licensed Psychologists, Mich. Assn. Black Psychologists (chmn. 1981-82), Omicron Delta Kappa. Home and Office: 1301 Orleans Detroit MI 48207

FLEMING, MILO JOSEPH, lawyer; b. Roscoe, Ill., Jan. 4, 1911; s. John E. and Elizabeth (Shafer) F.; A.B., U. of Ill., 1933, LL.B., 1936; m. Dorothea H. Kunze, Aug. 15, 1942 (dec. 1944); m. 2d, Lucy Anna Russell, June 30, 1948; step-children—Michael Russell, Jo Ann Russell (Mrs. Clemens); 1 dau., Elizabeth. Pvt. practice law, 1936-42, 58-59; mem. firm Pallissard and Fleming, Watseka, Ill., 1942-46, Pallissard, Fleming & Oram, 1946-58, Fleming & McGrew, 1960-76, Fleming, McGrew and Boyer, 1977, Fleming & Boyer, 1977-79, Fleming, Boyer & Strough, 1980—; master in chancery, Iroquois County, Ill., 1943-44. City atty., Watseka, Ill., 1949-57, 61—, Gilman, Ill., 1966-69; village atty. Milford, Ill., 1942-70, Wellington, 1962-72, Woodland, 1958-79, Danforth, 1961-78, Crescent City, Martinton, Sheldon, 1946-79, Onarga, Cissna Park, Beaverville, Papineau; atty. Lake Iroquois Lot Owners Assn. and Central San. Dist.; asst. atty. gen. Iroquois County, 1964-69; pres. Iroquois County Devel. Corp., 1961-68; bd. dirs. Belmont Water Co., 1963-81; farmer. Chmn., Iroquois County Universities Bond Issues Campaign, 1960; mem. State Employees Group Ins. Adv. Commn., Ill., 1975-78; trustee Welles Sch. Fund, Watseka, 1978—. Candidate, state rep., Apr. 1940; life mem. U. Ill. President's Council, 1979—. Mem. Am. (vice chmn. com. ordnances and adminstrv. regulations 1968-69, 73-75, chmn. 1969-72, 75-78, mem. council local govt. sect. 1976-79, mem. council sect. urban, state and local govt. law 1979-80), Ill., Iroquois County (pres. 1966-67) bar assns., Def. Research Inst., Internat. Platform Assn., Smithsonian Instn., Phi Eta Sigma, Sigma Delta Kappa. Democrat. Methodist. Mason (Shriner, 32 deg.), Odd Fellow (mem. jud. and appeals com. Ill. 1960-62, grand warden Ill. 1962, dep. grand master 1963, grand master 1964; grand rep. 1966; trustee Old Folks Home, Mattoon, Ill., 1966-71, sec. bd. 1966-68, vice chmn. bd. 1970—, atty. 1966—, 2d v.p. No. Assn. in Ill. Odd Fellows and Rebekahs 1981; recipient Meritorious Service Jewel, Grand Encampment of Ill. 1980). Author: One Hundred Twenty-five Years of Odd Fellowship at Watseka, Illinois. Prepared Municipal Code for City of Watseka, 1953, 80, Milford, 1957, Martinton, 1960, Crescent City, 1960, Woodland, 1961, Cissna Park, 1961, Papineau, 1978. Home: 120 W Jefferson Ave Watseka IL 60970 Office: Fleming Boyer & Strough Odd Fellows Bldg 216 E Walnut St Watseka IL 60970

FLEMING, PAUL DANIEL, JR., state ofcl.; b. Nashport, Ohio, Oct. 21, 1915; s. Paul Daniel and Nina Rose (Cartnal) F.; student Ohio Wesleyan U., 1936; m. Margie E. Bowman, Jan. 31, 1942; children—Paul Daniel, III, William B., Patricia M. Sports editor Times Recorder, Zanesville, Ohio, 1937-41; state editor Dayton (Ohio) Jour., 1944; Sunday sports editor Columbus (Ohio) Citizen, 1945-49; editor Hoof Beats mag., 1950-55; adminstrv. asst. to auditor State of Ohio, 1955-63; exec. sec. Ohio Racing Commn., 1963—. Served with AUS, 1941-44. Mem. Nat. Assn. State Racing Commrs., U.S. Harness Writers Assn., Thoroughbred Club Am., Sigma Chi. Republican. Methodist. Club: Shriners. Office: 30 E Broad St Columbus OH 43215

FLEMING, PAUL MICHAEL, physician; b. Milw., Dec. 14, 1940; s. Edward P. and Jean E. (Fons) F.; B.S. in Biology, Marquette U., 1962, M.D., 1966; m. Carol Ann Jones, June 11, 1966; children—Edward Paul Kathryn Elizabeth, Ryan Michael. Intern, San Diego County U. Hosp., 1966-67; resident in neurosurgery Good Samaritan Hosp. and Med. Center, Portland, Oreg., 1967-70; resident otolaryngology U. Chgo., 1972-75; practice medicine specializing in otolaryngology, Sheboygan, Wis., 1975—; mem. staff Providence Hosp., Portland, 1970, St. Nicholas Hosp., Sheboygan, 1975—, mem. outpatient services com., 1976—, sec.-treas. of staff, 1981—; mem. staff Sheboygan Meml. Hosp., 1975—, med cons., 1975—; mem. staff Sheboygan Clinic, 1975—; mem. faculty (part-time) Med. Coll. Wis., 1976—. Served with M.C., USN, 1970-72. Diplomate Am. Bd. Otolaryngology. Mem. A.C.S., Am. Acad. Otolaryngology, Am. Council Otolaryngology, Wis. Otolaryngol. Soc., Sheboygan County Med. Soc. (continuing med. edn. com. 1978—), Wis. State Med. Soc., Milw. Soc. Head and Neck Medicine and Surgery. Republican. Roman Catholic. Club: Elks. Contbr. articles to med. jours. Home: 1708 Plainwood Dr Sheboygan WI 53081 Office: 1011 N 8th St Sheboygan WI 53081

FLEMING, RICHARD LELAND, exec. search cons.; b. Jackson, Mich., Apr. 25, 1929; s. Leland Addis and Mary Thompson F.; B.S. in Mktg., Ind. U., 1950, M.B.A., 1951; m. Anne Rowland, Aug. 20, 1950; children—Kathy, Jim, Julie. Personnel services dir. Armstrong Cork Co., Pitts., 1951-53; personnel dir. Vernco Corp., Columbus, Ind., 1953-55; dir. internat. personnel Cummins Engine Co., Columbus, 1957-66, corp. personnel dir., 1966-68; pres. Fleming Assos., Columbus, 1968—; mem. adv. council Ind. U. Exec. Devel., 1976-81; mem. Ind. State Personnel Bd., 1971-81; mem. exec. council Ind. U. Sch. Bus., 1963-66. Mem. Columbus City Council, 1964-72. Served as lt. USNR, 1955-57. Mem. Am. Soc. Personnel Adminstrn., Beta Gamma Sigma. Republican. Methodist. Club: Harrison Lake Country. Home: 9527 W Mirror Rd Columbus IN 47201 Office: PO Box 604 1428 Franklin St Columbus IN 47201

FLEMING, THOMAS CRAWLEY, physician, editor; b. Chgo., June 16, 1921; s. Frederic Sydney and Margaret (Moore) F.; student Calif. Inst. Tech., 1940-42; M.D., Columbia U., 1945; m. Katherine Slaughter, Oct. 14, 1949; children—Sandra, Wendy, Margot, Frederic. Med. intern St. Luke's Hosp., N.Y.C., 1945-46; instr. physiology Coll. Physicians and Surgeons, Columbia U., N.Y.C., 1948-50; dept. clin. research Hoffmann-LaRoche, Nutley, N.J., 1950-55, dir. med. info., 1955-56, product devel. mgr., 1956-57; dir. clin. research Mead Johnson & Co., Evansville, Ind., 1957-58, product devel. mgr., 1958-59; med. dir. Warner-Chilcott Labs., Morris Plains, N.J., 1959-60; exec. v.p., med. dir. Robert E. Wilson, Inc., N.Y.C., 1960-62; dir. med. edn., chief chronic medicine Bergen Pines County Hosp., Paramus, N.J., 1962-64; med. dir. Sudler & Hennessey, Inc., N.Y.C., 1964-73; med. dir. Little Hill-Alina Lodge, Blairstown, N.J., 1974-79; editor-in-chief Postgrad. Medicine, Mpls., 1979—. Served to capt. M.C., U.S. Army, 1946-48. Mem. Am. Med. Soc. on Alcoholism. Contbr. articles to profl. jours.

FLEMING, WILLIAM JOSEPH, chem. engr.; b. Lima, Ohio, May 10, 1950; s. Joseph Edward and Mary Roesetta (Perrin) F.; B.S. in Chem. Engring., U. Cin., 1973; m. Georgia Jo Battista, Aug. 9, 1975; children—Josephine Margaret, Christine Marie. Process engr. Diamond Shamrock Corp., Ashtabula, Ohio, 1973, Houston, 1973-74, Painesville, Ohio, 1974-76, staff engr., Chgo., 1977-78, prodn. supt., 1978—, mgr. silicates engring. Soda Products Div., 1981—. Research on hot lime-soda-phosphate external treatment facilities, energy mgmt. and power engring. Home: Beckett Ridge 8131 Timberjack Way West Chester OH 45069 Office: 4701 Paddock Rd Cincinnati OH 45229

FLESHER, EVERETT CECIL, soil scientist; b. McKendree, W.Va., Dec. 2, 1926; s. Everett Cecil and Grace D. (Huffman) F.; B.S. in Agriculture, W.Va. U., 1950, postgrad., 1953-55; m. Virginia Sue Darby, June 21, 1953; children—Rita, Allen, Lora, Nora. Instr. vocat. agr. Bruceton Mills (W.Va.), High Sch., 1952-53, Chuckery-Darby High Sch., Unionville Center, Ohio, 1955-56; with U.S. Soil Conservation Service, 1956—, soil scientist, Columbus, Ohio, 1956-63, party leader Henry County soil survey, 1963-67, party leader Williams County Soil Survey, Bryan, Ohio, 1967-70, staff soil scientist, Defiance, Ohio, 1970-80, party leader, Defiance County Soil Survey, 1974-81, area soil scientist, Area Office, Defiance, 1981—. Cubmaster, Boy Scouts Am., 1964-66, 1968, troop com. chmn., 1971-74. Served with U.S. Navy, 1945-46, U.S. Army, 1950-52. Mem. Am. Soc. Agronomy, Soil Sci. Soc. Am., Soil Conservation Soc. Am., Internat. Soc. Soil Sci., Ohio Assn. Pedologists, Orgn. Profl. Employees U.S. Dept. Agr., Am. Registry Cert. Profls. in Agronomy, Crops and Soils Ltd., Am. Legion (post comdr. 1970-72, post adj. 1972-81, post service officer 1977—). Republican. Methodist. Clubs: Lions, Methodist Men's, Moose (Bryan, Ohio). Home: 414 Rosemont Ave Bryan OH 43506 Office: US Soil Conservation Service Box 15 Rural Route 2 State Route 66N Defiance OH 43512

FLETCHER, DONALD JOSEPH, city-county govt. aviation adminstr.; b. Piqua, Ohio, Dec. 9, 1944; s. Joseph Nevin and Florence Helen (Darr) F.; B.B.A., U. Toledo, 1970, M.A. in Polit. Sci., 1972; m. Juanita Mary Kroll, Oct. 7, 1977; 1 son, David Jonathan. With Toledo-Lucas County Port Authority, 1971—, airport mgr., 1974-75, dir. aviation, 1975—; mem. U. Toledo M.P.A. Adv. Com.; mem. Bowling Green State U. Aviation Mgmt. Program Adv. Com. Served with USAF, 1963-67. Mem. Am. Soc. Public Adminstrn. (pres. 1978-79), Am. Assn. Airport Execs. (Ohio del. 1978-79), Ohio Airport Mgrs. Assn. (sec.-treas. 1979-81), Am. Legion. Roman Catholic. Club: K.C. (grand knight 1975-76). Office: 241 Superior St Toledo OH 43604

FLETCHER, FLOYD MILTON, JR., real estate broker; b. Salem, Ind., Oct. 21, 1917; s. Floyd Milton and Hazel (Goodpasture) F.; diploma Cunningham's Horology Sch., 1949; student Reppert Sch. Auctioneering, 1964; m. Frances Elizabeth Trueblood, June 6, 1937; children—Sandra Lee Fletcher Clark, Marilyn Elizabeth Fletcher Brown. With Smith Cabinet Co., Salem, 1935-37, Links Handle Factory, Salem, 1937-38, Kroger Co., St. Louis, 1938-39; mgr. Jay C Store, Ind., 1939-58; watchmaker, Salem, 1948-60; real estate broker, Salem, 1960—; pres. Fletcher Estates, Inc., Salem, 1963—; owner Fletcher Real Estate Agy. and Auction Service, Salem, 1960—; auctioneer, 1964—. Served with U.S. Army, 1943-45. Mem. Ind. Assn. Realtors, Nat. Assn. Realtors, Nat. Assn. Rev. Appraisers, Profl. Real Estate Brokers Assn., Am. Coll. Real Estate Cons., Realtors Nat. Mktg. Inst., Am. Legion (past comdr.), D.A.V. (comdr. 1979-80), Farm and Land Inst., Am. Assn. Cert. Appraisers, Inst. Bus. Appraisers, Nat. Appraisers Inst., Ind. Auctioneers Assn., Nat. Auctioneers Assn., Cert. Auctioneers Inst., Ky. Bd. Auctioneers. Club: K.P. Home: Rural Route 3 Salem IN 47167 Office: 202 W Market St Salem IN 47167

FLETCHER, GENEVA, state ofcl.; b. Unionville, Ind., Mar. 18, 1940; d. James Ivan and Ruby Alice (Sluss) F.; B.S., Ind. U., 1963, M.S., 1965; postgrad. Ind. U., 1974-76, Ind. State U., 1973-74, Purdue U., 1974-76. Tchr. vocat. home econs. Tunnelton (Ind.) High Sch., 1963-70; state cons. Ind. Dept. Public Instrn., Indpls., 1970-72; asst. dir. vocat. edn. Ind. State Bd. Vocat. and Tech. Edn., 1972-75, dep.

state dir. vocat. edn., 1975—. Mem. Ind. Vocat. Assn. (recipient Outstanding Service award 1974, Appreciation award 1974), Ind. Council Vocat. Adminstrs., Am. Vocat. Assn., Am. Tech. Edn. Assn., Nat. Assn. State Dirs. Vocat. Edn., Ind. Postsecondary Vocat. Edn. Assn. (charter), Nat. Assn. Vocat. Tech. Edn. Communicators (charter). Contbr. articles to profl. jours. Home: 5851 Squirrels Run Apt D Indianapolis IN 46254 Office: 17 W Market St Suite 401 Indianapolis IN 46204

FLICK, PAUL JOHN, artist; b. Rock Island, Ill., Feb. 5, 1943; s. P. J. and Cora Agnus (Burney) F.; B.A., U. Minn., 1970, M.F.A., 1972. One-man shows include: U. Minn. Studio Gallery, Mpls., 1972; C.S.B. St. Louis Park, 1975-76; Northland Gallery, St. Louis Park, 1976; group shows include: U. Minn. Studio Gallery, 1970, 71, 72; Minn. Mus. Art, St. Paul, 1976, Waggoner Gallery, Chgo., Randolph St. Gallery, Chgo.; represented in permanent collections including: U. Minn., U. Tenn.; also numerous pvt. collections, U.S., Japan; pvt. tchr. art; cons. CSB Gallery, De Novo Mag. Served with USMC, 1962-66. Mem. Artists Equity Assn. Minn. (pres. 1976-77, dir. 1977-78), Twin City Metro Art Alliance, Artists Rights Today, Minn. Artists Assn., Theta Minn. Home: 4032 Lyndale Ave S Minneapolis MN 55409

FLIEGLER, DOROTHY SCHERR (MRS. LOUIS A. FLIEGLER), occupational therapist; b. N.Y.C., June 19, 1921; d. Morris and Rose E. (Marcus) Scherr; B.A., Hunter Coll., 1942; B.A., Columbia, 1945; m. Louis A. Fliegler, June 29, 1945; children—Gail, Susan. Govt. ordnance insp. N.Y. Ordnance Dept., N.Y.C., 1943-45; occupational therapist Army Hosp., Tilton Gen. Hosp., 1945, N.Y.C. Hosp., Welfare Island, N.Y.C., 1945, VA Hosp., Brentwood Gen. Hosp., Letterman Gen. Hosp., Bronx VA Hosp., 1945-47; tchr. physically handicapped, Syracuse, N.Y., 1956-60; tchr. mentally retarded, Denver, 1960-66; tchr. learning disabled, Akron, Ohio, 1966—. Instr. ceramics U. Wyo., Sheridan, 1953. Bd. dirs. sheltered workshop United Cerebral Palsy Center, Denver, 1954. Mem. B'nai B'rith Women, NEA, Am. Occupational Therapy Assn., Ohio, Akron edn. assns., ORT. Home: 1827 Kingsley Ave Akron OH 44313 Office: 55 S Portage Path Akron OH

FLIESSER, ELAINE RUTH, social worker; b. Danville, Ill., Aug. 4, 1942; d. Werner and Ilse Johanna (Jacob) F.; B.S., U. Ill., 1964, M.S.W., 1967. Social worker Operation Headstart, Steubenville, Ohio, 1966, Children's Clin. Services, Springfield, Ill., 1966-67, Public Schs. Dist. U-46, Elgin, Ill., 1967-80; sch. social work supr. 4 Rivers Spl. Edn. Dist., Jacksonville, Ill., 1980-81; sch. social worker Kendall County Spl. Edn. Coop., Plano, Ill., 1981—; mem. Pupil Personnel Services Adv. Bd., Ill. Bd. Edn., 1977-78, Pupil Personnel Services Consortium, 1977-80 adv. com. Sch. Social Work, U. Ill. Mem. Ill. Assn. Sch. Social Workers (pres., dir.), Nat. Assn. Social Workers (nat. sch. social work conf. planning task force), Acad. Cert. Social Workers. Council Exceptional Children. Jewish. Home: 1248 California Ave Aurora IL 60506 Office: Kendall County Spl Edn Coop Plano IL 60545

FLINDT, CONSTANZE DITZ, plastics mfg. corp. exec.; b. Brux, Czechoslovakia, Oct. 13, 1927; d. Franz Ditz and Louise Ditz-Dostal; came to U.S., 1963; M.S., U. Munich, 1950; diploma U. Geneva, 1953, Cambridge (Eng.) U., 1954. m. Herbert Flindt, July 3, 1956 (dec.); 1 dau., Allegra. Pres., Battenfeld Corp. Am., Skokie, Ill., 1963—. Mem. Soc. Plastics Industry (dir. 1979—), Soc. Plastic Engrs. (awards com.), Plastics Inst. Am. (trustee, treas., mem. coms.), Skokie C. of C. (v.p. 1978-80). Roman Catholic. Home: 2544 Marian Ln Wilmette IL 60091 Office: Battenfeld Corp Am 7301 N Monticello Ave Skokie IL 60076

FLINK, JANE DUNCAN, newspaper editor; b. Atlanta, Feb. 17, 1929; d. James Archibald and Frances (Watkins) Duncan; student Carleton Coll., 1948-49, U. Mo., 1967, Columbia (Mo.) Coll., 1974-75; m. Richard Albert Flink, Nov. 20, 1954; children—Jennifer, Elizabeth, Caroline, Charles Albert, James Duncan. Reporter, Greendale Village Life and Tri-Town News, Greendale, Wis., 1958-61; reporter, photographer, feature writer, editor Central Mo. Rural and Farm Life Mag., Centralia (Mo.) Fireside Guard, 1973-78; briefly editor Bus. Briefs, MFA Oil Co., Columbia, Mo., 1977; editor Events, Bus., Kingdom Daily News, Fulton, Mo., 1978—. Republican committeewoman Ward I, Centralia, 1972, 74, 76; mem. exec. bd. Friends of Churchill Meml., Fulton; mem. Boone County Commn. on Child Abuse. Recipient numerous editorial awards. Mem. Nat. Fedn. Press Women, Mo. Press Women (dist. v.p. 1978-79; chmn. honors, awards 1979—), Mo. Press Assn., Sigma Delta Chi, Centralia Hist. Soc. Clubs: Centralia Country, Centralia Women's. Home: The Clearing Route 4 Centralia MO 65240 Office: Kingdom Daily News 307 Court St Fulton MO 65251

FLINN, CHARLOTTE S., human resources cons.; b. N.Y.C., Dec. 13, 1933; d. Oscar Abraham and Sophie (Leff) Stiglitz; B.A., Queens Coll., City U. N.Y., 1963; postgrad. Nat. Coll. of Edn.; m. Robert D. Flinn, Sept. 7, 1975; 1 dau., Thea Lisa. Tchr. academically talented Morris Twp., N.J., 1963-65; tchr. behavioral and learning disabled Starling Jr. High Sch., Columbus, Ohio, 1965-66; fgn. policy leader, local, state, and nat. LWV, Columbus, 1966-72; tchr. accelerated and devel. reading Shepard Jr. High Sch., Deerfield, Ill., 1972-73; group leader, trainer Effectiveness Tng. Assos., Pasadena, Calif., 1972-76; tchr., tchr. staff trainer LASS modular and affective edn. Fairview South Jr. High Sch., Skokie, Ill., 1974-76; v.p., prin. Flinn Consultants, Inc., Highland Park, Ill., 1976—; prin., dir. client services Job/Search Network, Lake Forest, Ill., 1981; cons. employment counselor for NOW, Chgo.; speaker in field of careers for women; founder Moving Up career devel. seminars. Candidate for County Bd. Suprs., Lake County, Ill., 1972; co-chmn. polit. campaign Lake County, 1974; planner, chmn. LWV confs. on Mil. Spending and Nat. Security, 1969; LWV del. to internat. econ. devel. aid conf., 1970, del. to first convocation of Nat. Com. on U.S. China Relations, 1969; active NOW, Nat. Women's Polit. Caucus, ACLU, Unitarian-Universalist Service Com.; vice chmn. adminstrn. North Shore Unitarian Ch., Deerfield, Ill. Mem. Internat. Orgn. Women Execs., Nat. Assn. Female Execs., Women in Mgmt., Women in Communications, Mensa, United Chpts. of Phi Beta Kappa. Researcher, designer, author curricula: Academically Talented Learners, Morristown, 1965; Behavioral and Learning Disabled, Columbus, 1966; Language Arts and Social Studies Modules, Skokie, 1974-76, Affective Education Program, Skokie, 1974-76.

FLINN-WAGNER, SHARON ROSE, occupational therapist, med. service co. exec.; b. Lafayette, Ind., June 3, 1952; d. John Edward and Lea Rose (Songderath) Flinn; B.S. in Occupational Therapy, Ind. U., 1974; student Cleve. State U., 1976—; m. James C. Wagner, Oct. 5, 1979. Occupational therapist Cleve. Clinic Found., 1974-78; prin. Occupational Therapy Circuit Inc., Cleve., 1978—; therapeutic sales rep. Ohio Med. Equipment Distbr., Cleve., 1979—; dir. dept. occupational therapy St. Vincent Charity Hosp., Cleve., 1980—; cons. home health, industry, hand rehab.; condr. profl. workshops. Recipient Recognition award Occupational Therapy Assn. of Ohio, 1980. Mem. Am. Occupational Therapy Assn., Ohio Occupational Therapy Assn. (program chairperson state conf. 1981), Cleve. Occupational Therapy Assn. (chairperson public relations 1975-77, treas. 1976, pres. 1977-79), Arthritis Found., Am. Soc. Hand Therapists (active founding mem.). Roman Catholic. Research on facilitating reduction of hand edema, chronic hand pain, joint replacements of hand. Office: 2351 E 22d St Cleveland OH 44115

FLINT, LOWELL TRUMAN, marriage and family counselor; b. Wolcottville, Ind., July 13, 1935; s. Truman Sutton and Birdena Clare (Healey) F.; A.B., Marion (Ind.) Coll., 1959; M.Ed., U. N.C., Greensboro, 1971; Ed.D., Duke U., 1973; m. Doris Mitchell, Aug. 17, 1956; children—Karen, Kathy, Lisa. Ordained elder Ch. of Nazarene, 1960; pastor Chs. in N.C. and S.C., 1959-73; tchr. Marlboro County public schs., Bennettsville, S.C., 1959-63; instr. Bible and theology John Wesley Coll., Greensboro, 1965-67; prof. psychology Olivet Nazarene Coll., Kankakee, Ill., 1973—, also dir. coll. counseling center; propr. College Plaza Counseling Center, Bourbonnais, Ill., 1978—. Bd. dirs., treas. Kankakeeland Community Action Program, 1974-77. Mem. Am. Personnel and Guidance Assn., Assn. Religious and Value Issues in Counseling, Ill. Personnel and Guidance Assn., Kappa Delta Pi. Home: 19 Arrowhead Dr Bourbonnais IL 60914 Office: Box 75 Olivet Nazarene Coll Kankakee IL 60901

FLINT, ROBERT NORTON, health care cons.; b. Detroit, Feb. 6, 1929; s. Robert Norton and Irene Adele (Jones) F.; B.S., Cornell U., 1958; M.E.A., George Washington U., 1969; m. Joann Marie Janick, Mar., 1975; children—Michael B., Sandra S., Brian N., Duane T., Darren R., Ryan R. With Westinghouse Electric, Pitts., 1958-60, Koppers Co., Pitts., 1960-62; dir. personnel research dept. Booz Allen & Hamilton, Washington, Chgo., 1962-70; dir. staff selection Norton Assos., Inc., N.Y.C., 1970-72; dir. physician recruitment Marion (Ohio) Gen. Hosp., 1976-80; pres., dir. physician recruitment Robert Flint Assos., Inc., Columbus, Ohio, 1978—; dir. physician recruitment and indsl. medicine programs Indsl. Health Care Assos., Chgo., 1980—. Served with USAF, 1950-54. Mem. Am. Hosp. Assn. (faculty med. services div.), Am. Soc. Health Manpower, Edn. and Tng., Am. Soc. Hosp. Planning, Fedn. Am. Hosps. Office: 4400 N High St Columbus OH 43214

FLITCRAFT, RICHARD KIRBY, II, chem. co. exec.; b. Woodstown, N.J., Sept. 5, 1920; s. H. Milton and Edna (Crispin) F.; m. Bertha LeSturgeon Hitchner, Nov. 14, 1942; children—Alyce, Anne, Elizabeth, Richard. B.S., Rutgers U., 1942; M.S., Washington U., St. Louis, 1948. With Monsanto Co., St. Louis, 1942—, dir. inorganic research, 1960-65, dir. mgmt. info. and systems dept., 1965-67, asst. to pres., 1967-68, group mgr. Electronics Enterprises, 1968-69, gen. mgr. Electronic Products Div., 1969-71, v.p., dir. Monsanto Research Corp., 1971—, v.p. ops., 1975-76, pres., 1976—. Mem. AAAS, Am. Chem. Soc., Am. Inst. Chem. Engrs., Am. Inst. Chemists, Am. Mgmt. Assn., N.Y. Acad. Scis., Research Soc. Am., Soc. Chem. Industry. Sigma Xi. Home: 6051 Kimway Dr Dayton OH 45459 Office: 1515 Nicholas Rd Dayton OH 45407

FLOOD, PAUL EDWARD, chem. engr.; b. Chgo., May 7, 1926; s. Walter Henry and Marguerite Theresa (Clinnin) F.; B.S. in Chem. Engring., Ill. Inst. Tech., 1946; m. Jacquie M. Humecke, Nov. 18, 1950; children—Nancy L. Flood Gangler, Kathi S., Paul Edward, Patrick J., Robert A. Engring. technician Walter H. Flood & Co., Inc., Hillside, Ill., 1946-48, pres., treas., 1973—; mgr. research Precision Sci. Co., Chgo., 1948-56; dir. Drexel Nat. Bank, Chgo., 1979—. Vice chmn. Lyons Twp. High sch. Caucus, 1970-71; dir. Chgo. Engring. and Sci. Center, 1962-73; trustee Ill. Inst. Tech., 1980-85. Served to lt. (j.g.), USNR, 1944-46. Registered structural engr., Ill.; registered profl. engr., Ill., Ind., Mich., Wis. Mem. Ill. Soc. Profl. Engrs. (pres. 1975-76), Cons. Engrs. Council of Ill. (v.p. 1979—), Ill. Inst. Tech. Alumni Assn. (pres. 1978-79). Roman Catholic. Home: 531 W Harding St LaGrange IL 60525 Office: 4421 Harrison St Hillside IL 60162

FLORA, JAIRUS DALE, JR., educator; b. Northfield, Minn., Mar. 27, 1944; s. Jairus Dale and Betty Ruth (Garvin) F.; B.S. magna cum laude, Midland Luth. Coll., 1965; postgrad. Tech. U. Karlsruhe (W. Ger.), 1965-66; M.S., Fla. State U., 1968, Ph.D., 1971; m. Sharyl Ann Hughes, Aug. 18, 1967; 1 son, Edward Hughes. Asst. prof. biostats. Sch. Public Health, U. Mich., Ann Arbor, 1971-73, asst. prof. and asst. research scientist Hwy. Safety Research Inst., 1973-76, asso. prof. biostats. and asso. research scientist, 1976-79, asso. prof. biostats. Sch. Public Health, 1979-81, prof. biostats., 1981—; cons. statistician Nat. Burn Info. Exchange, 1971-76. German Acad. Exchange Service fellow, 1965-66; NASA traineeship, 1966-69; NIH traineeship, 1969-71; Nat. Hwy. Traffic Safety Adminstrn. research grantee, 1974-81. Mem. Am. Statis. Assn., Biometric Soc., Inst. Math. Stats., Internat. Soc. Burn Injuries, N.Y. Acad. Sci., AAAS, Blue Key, Sigma Xi. Republican. Methodist. Club: Masons. Contbr. articles to profl. jours.; editoral collaborator Annals of Thoracic Surgery, Mathematical Biosciences, Biometrics, 1979—. Home: 2894 Ticknor Ct Ann Arbor MI 48104 Office: Dept Biostats M4011 Sch of Public Health Univ of Mich 109 S Observatory St Ann Arbor MI 48109

FLORES, ANTHONY ROBERT, grocery mfg. exec.; b. Guanaja, Honduras, Nov. 23, 1941; came to U.S., 1948, naturalized, 1967; s. Paul H. and Ellen (Dale) F.; B.B.A., Pierce Coll., 1964; postgrad. Youngstown State U., 1968, 69; m. Kathleen E. Kent, Aug. 31, 1963; children—Anthony Robert (dec.), Andrew, Timothy, Amy Rebecca, Kimberly. Asst. store mgr. Foods Co. Markets, Los Angeles, 1964-66; account sales rep. Lever Bros. Co., Youngstown, Ohio and Cleve., 1966-69, dist. field sales analyst, 1970, unit mgr., 1971-74, field operation analyst, N.Y.C., 1974-75, market sales mgr. foods div., Rocky River, Ohio, 1976-79, market sales mgr. personal products div. Cleve. and Pitts. dists., 1979—. Mem. Brunswick (Ohio) City Council, 1978—, chmn. congressional liaison com., 1978-79, chmn. utilities and environment coms.; bd. dirs. Miss Medina County Pageant. Served to capt. USMCR, 1961-64. Recipient Ohio Jaycee Recruitment award, 1972; named Jaycee of Yr., 1971, 72, 73. Mem. Associated Grocery Mfrs. Reps. of Cleve. (asst. sec.), Eagle Oaks Property Owners Assn. (pres. 1975-77), VFW. Lutheran. Club: Franklin Philatelic. Home: 874 Crabapple Dr Brunswick OH 44212 Office: Lever Bros Co 21010 Center Ridge Rd Rocky River OH 44116

FLORES, LUIS GILBERTO, educator; b. Lima, Peru, Oct. 29, 1943; came to U.S., 1978; s. Enrique Bartolome and Maria Delfina (Arciniega) F.; Agr. Engr., Agrarian U. Peru, 1967; M.B.A., Grad. Bus. Sch., Lima, Peru, 1971; D.B.A., Tex. Tech. U., 1976; m. Maria Teresa Espejo, Oct. 11, 1973; children—Luis Fernando, Jose Antonio, Claudia Maria. Asst. mgr. Inmobiliaria Urbanizadora San Fernando, Lima, 1965; gen. mgr. Corp. Agricola E Indsl. Santa Teresa, Satipo, Peru, 1967-70; project advisor Motor Columbus Cons. Co., Lima, 1971-72; instr. mgmt. Grad. Sch. Bus. Adminstrn., Lima, 1971-72, asso. prof., 1976-78, dir. grad. programs, 1976-78, vis. prof., 1980—; research asst. Tex. Tech. U., 1972-76, instr., 1974-76, vis. prof., 1977, 79; project advisor Cepur Cons. Co., Lima, 1976; advisor, project mgr. Novoa-Stiglich Cons. Co., Lima, 1976-77; asso. prof. mgmt. U. North Ala., 1978-80; asso. prof. No. Ill. U., 1980—; cons. in field. Ford Found. fellow, 1972-76; AID fellow, 1972-76; Fulbright fellow, 1972-76. Mem. Acad. Mgmt., Midwest Acad. Mgmt., Acad. Internat. Bus., Latin Am. Studies Assn., Midwest Latin Am. Studies Assn., Asociacion de Grads. of ESAN. Home: 1709 Cedarbrook St Sycamore IL 60178 Office: Northern Illinois University College of Business DeKalb IL 60115

FLORESTANO, DANA JOSEPH, architect; b. Indpls., May 2, 1945; s. Herbert Joseph and Myrtle Mae (Futch) F.; B. Arch., U. Notre Dame, 1968; m. Peggy Joy Larsen, June 6, 1969. Designer, draftsman Kennedy, Brown & Trueblood, architects, Indpls., 1965-69, Evans Woolen Assn., architects, Indpls., 1966; designer, project capt. James Assos., architects and engrs., Indpls., 1969-71; architect, v.p. comml. projects Multi-Planners Inc., architects and engrs., 1972-73; pvt. practice architecture, Indpls., 1973—; pres. Florestano Corp., constrn. mgmt., Indpls., 1973—; co-founder, pres. Solargenics Natural Energy Corp., Indpls., 1975—; prof. archtl. and constrn. tech. Ind. U.-Purdue U. at Indpls.; instr. in field. Tech. adviser hist. architecture Indpls. Model Cities program, 1969-70; mem. Hist. Landmarks Found. Ind., 1970-72; chmn. Com. to Save Union Sta., 1970-71, founder, pres. Union Sta. Found. Inc., Indpls., 1971—. Recipient 2d design award Marble Inst. Am., 1967, 1st design award 19th Ann. Progressive Architecture Design awards, 1972; Design award for excellence in devel. Marriott Inn, Indpls., Met. Devel. Commn.-Office of Mayor, 1977; 1st place award design competition for Visitor's Info. Center, Cave Run, Lake, Ky., 1978; 2d design award 1st Ann. Qualified Remodeler, Nat. Competition for Best Rehab. Existing Structures in Am., 1979. Mem. U. Notre Dame Alumni Assn., Notre Dame Club Indpls., A.I.A. (nat. com. historic resources 1974—, commn. on community services, Speakers Bur. Indpls. chpt. 1976—), Ind. Soc. Architects (chmn. historic architecture com. 1970—), Constrn. Specifications Inst., Constrn. Mgrs. Assn. Ind. (incorporator, dir. 1976—). Home: 5697 N Broadway St Indianapolis IN 46220 Office: 6214 N Carrollton Ave Indianapolis IN 46220

FLORIAN, MARIANNA BOLOGNESI, civic worker; b. Chgo.; d. Giulio and Rose (Garibaldi) Bolognesi; B.A. cum laude, Barat Coll., 1940; postgrad. Moser Bus. Sch., 1941-42; m. Paul A. Florian III, June 4, 1949; children—Paul, Marina, Peter, Mark. Asst. credit mgr. Stella Cheese Co., Chgo., 1942-45; With ARC ETO Clubmobile Unit, 1945-47; mgr. Passavant Hosp. Gift Shop, 1947-49; pres., Jr. League Chgo., Inc., 1957-59; pres. woman's bd. Passavant Hosp., 1966-68; bd. dirs. Northwestern Meml. Hosp., 1974—, mem. exec. com., 1974-79; pres. Women's Assn., Chgo. Symphony Orch., 1974-77; chmn. Guild Chgo. Hist. Soc., 1981—; v.p., exec. com. Orchestral Assn., 1978—; mem. women's bd. Northwestern U.; mem. vis. com. dept. music U. Chgo., 1980—; trustee Chgo. Hist. Soc., 1981—. Recipient Citizen Fellowship, Inst. Medicine Chgo., 1975. Clubs: Friday (pres. 1972-74), Contemporary; Winnetka Garden.

FLORIAN, SONIA ATZEFF, radio sta. exec.; b. Oak Park, Ill., Sept. 22, 1935; d. Nicola and Olga (Laftery) A.; B.A., Roosevelt U., 1960; m. William C. Florian, June 22, 1967. Program dir. WNIB, Chgo., 1958-76, mgr., 1976—. Bd. dirs. Chgo. Audubon Soc., 1970—. Home: 3100 N Sheridan Rd Chicago IL 60657 Office: 12 E Delaware St Chicago IL 60611

FLORY, CLYDE REUBEN, JR., physician; b. Sellersville, Pa., Oct. 2, 1933; s. Clyde Reuben and Miriam Wagner (Hummel) F.; B.A., Lehigh U., 1955; M.D., Johns Hopkins U., 1959; m. Karen Colleen McComb, Mar. 9, 1963; children—William Brian, Robert Scott, Timothy Allen. Intern, resident in internal medicine and allergy Henry Ford Hosp., Detroit, 1959-64; pvt. practice medicine, specializing in allergy-immunology, Lansing, Mich., 1964—; faculty Mich. State U. Coll. Human Medicine, East Lansing, 1973—, asso. clin. prof. medicine, 1976—; chief, allergy sub-div. Ingham Med. Hosp., Lansing, 1975—; teaching staff E.W. Sparrow Hosp. Pres. ch. council St. Paul Luth. Ch., East Lansing, 1973. Diplomate Am. Bd. Allergy and Immunology. Fellow Am. Acad. Allergy and Immunology, Am. Coll. Allergists, Am. Assn. Clin. Immunology and Allergy, Am. Coll. Chest Physicians (asso.); mem. AMA, Mich., Ingham County med. socs., Mich. Allergy Soc. (sec.), Mich. Lung Assn. (bd. dirs. Central region 1973—), Mich. Thoracic Soc. Phi Beta Kappa. Club: Masons. Home: 1022 Whitman Dr East Lansing MI 48823 Office: 201 W Hillsdale St Lansing MI 48933

FLORY, WILLIAM NELSON, banker; b. Pawnee City, Nebr., June 28, 1927; s. Harry Davis and Florence Elizabeth (Nye) F.; B.A., U. Chgo., 1948; postgrad. Sch. Bank Mktg., Northwestern U., 1954; m. Greta Wiley, Dec. 31, 1970; 1 dau., Valerie B. With Harris Trust and Savs. Bank, Chgo., 1948—, asst. v.p., 1960-66, v.p., 1966—, div. adminstr. mktg. services, 1967—. Dir., v.p. United Cerebral Palsy Assn. Greater Chgo., 1964—, mem. exec. com.; trustee Chgo. Pops Orch. Assn.; group founder Nat. Repertory Theatre Found., Chgo.; treas., gov. Sarah Siddons Soc.; charter meme. Mus. Contemporary Art; dir. Public Service Communications Council of Met. Chgo. Served with U.S. Army, 1945-46. Mem. Am. Inst. Banking, Assn. for Modern Banking in Ill. (public info. com.), Bank Mktg. Assn. (past pres.), Chgo. Fin. Advertisers (past pres.), Ill. Bankers Assn. (past pres.), Bank Wire (public relations and mktg. advt. com.), Chgo. Advt. Club, Chgo. Assn. Commerce and Industry, Ill. C. of C., Chgo. Symphony Soc., Lyric Opera Guild, U. Chgo. Alumni Assn. (v.p., life mem. nat. alumni fund bd., mem. citizens bd.), Phi Delta Theta (past pres., trustee house fund). Republican. Presbyterian. Clubs: Publicity, Bankers, Chgo. Press, University, Barclay. Office: Harris Trust and Savs Bank 111 W Monroe St Chicago IL 60690

FLOURNOY, KAY BARBARA, interior designer; b. Detroit, Sept. 16, 1940; s. Dale K. and Gertrude Janet (Findlay) Boyles; B.S., Mich. State U., 1962; m. Peter Farrar Flournoy, Mar. 31, 1967; children—William Peter, Catherine Isabel. Sr. residential interior designer J.L. Hudson Co., Detroit, 1962—, sr. designer, Pontiac, Mich., 1970—. Vice pres. Carl Sandburg Community Sch. Assn., 1977-78, pres. PTA, 1978-79; mem. Waterford Schs. Legis. Com., 1979. Recipient Mother of Year award J.L. Hudson Co. Pontiac, 1974. Republican. Presbyterian. Office: 269 N Telegraph St J L Hudson Co Pontiac MI 48054

FLOWERS, JAMES ROBERT, printing co. exec.; b. Effingham, Ill., Jan. 21, 1944; s. John William and Violet Eta (Bell) F.; ed. public schs.; m. Virginia Karen Rexroad, Mar. 1, 1969; children—James Robert, John William. Apprentice book binder World Color Press Inc., Effingham, 1970-72, supr., 1972-74, mem. tng. dept., 1974-75, dir. tng., 1976—, video producer, 1979—; founder Media-Memories, 1980—; cons. schs., civic orgns., small businesses. Served with U.S. Army, 1961-65. Mem. Am. Soc. Tng. and Devel. Producer, cons. audio visual programs. Home: 300 S Race St Teutopolis IL 62467 Office: South Route 45 Effingham IL 62401

FLUEGEL, NEAL LALON, musician, assn. exec., educator; b. Freeport, Ill., Mar. 21, 1937; s. Nelson Otto and Elnora (Beine) F.; B.A. in Edn., Ariz. State U., 1960; M.M., So. Ill. U., 1963; postgrad. U. Wis., 1965-66; m. Diane Francis Hanson, Dec. 27, 1957; children—Taunia Suzanne, Kyra Michaelle. Tchr. pub. schs. Ill., 1960-62; instr. music Ariz. State U., Tempe, 1964-65; teaching fellow U. Wis., 1965-66; asso. prof. music Ind. State U., Terre Haute, 1966—, also chmn. Annual Contemporary Music Fest., 1971—. Prin. percussionist Phoenix Symphony Orch., 1964-65, Madison (Wis.) Symphony Orch., 1965-66; now timpanist Terre Haute Symphony Orch.; chmn. Indpls. Symphony-Ind. State U. Contemporary Music Festival; regular appearances About Music TV series, Channel 2, Terre Haute, 1971-72. Mem. Percussive Arts Soc. (internat. exec. sec.; editor Percussionst jour.), Music Tchrs. Nat. Assn. (chmn. brass, woodwind and percussion div. 1973-77, state pres., 1st v.p. East region, mem. nat. public relations com.), Mid-East ...nental Music Conf. (chmn. percussion activities), Music ...ators Nat. Conf. (percussion program chmn. 1968), Nat. Assn. ...l. Wind and Percussion Instrs., Am. Musicol. Soc., Am. Bell Assn., ...appa Kappa Psi, Phi Mu Alpha (mem. Sinfonia). Optimist (pres.). Home: 130 Carol Dr Terre Haute IN 47805

FLYNN, DALLAS EDWARD, mfg. co. exec.; b. Starbuck, Minn., Nov. 9, 1942; s. Emerson Edward and Francis (Brosh) F.; B.S. in Indsl. Edn., Mankato State U., 1967, M.S. in Spl. Edn., 1968; postgrad. U. Minn.; m. Devona Ann Anderson, Apr. 11, 1964; children—Lisa Marie, Michael Edward, Leslie Ann. Program supr. in vocat. edn. Anoka (Minn.) Vocat. Tech. Inst., 1968-73; vocat. dir. Career Edn. Center, Audubon, Minn., 1974-76; owner, operator Colonial Paint and Decorating, Detroit Lakes, Minn., 1977-79; v.p. Mid-Am. Builders Supplies, Detroit Lakes, 1978-79; pres. Mid-Am. Industries, Detroit Lakes, 1979—. Served with U.S. Army, 1960-63; Vietnam. Roman Catholic. Mem. DAV, K.C. (dir. and recorder local club 1977—), Rotary (dir. local club 1974-79, v.p. club 1978-79). Home: Box 30B Rural Route 4 Detroit Lakes MN 56501 Office: 811 8th St SE Detroit Lakes MN 56501

FLYNN, JAMES T., lawyer, state ofcl.; b. Chgo., Sept. 25, 1944; s. Thomas Edward and Ann (Davoli) F.; B.A. Econs., Marquette U., 1970; J.D., 1973; m. Mary C. Basso, Dec. 27, 1969; children—Kathleen, Joseph. Tchr. sci. and social studies St. Rose Elementary Sch., Milw., 1968-70; law clk. firm Goldberg, Previant and Uelman, Milw., partner firm Piaskoski & Flynn, Milw., 1973—; mem. Wis. Senate, 1972—. Coordinator United Way, 1973. Mem. Wis. Bar Assn., Milw. Bar Assn., Milw. Jr. Bar Assn., Am. Bar Assn., West Allis Bar Assn. Democrat. Roman Catholic. Club: Holy Name Soc. Office: 4818 S 76th St Greenfield WI 53220

FLYNN, MICHAEL FRANCIS, priest, psychologist; b. Chgo., Dec. 2, 1935; s. Michael Joseph and Mary Ellen (Lydon) F.; B.A. in Philosophy, St. Bonaventure U., 1958, B.S. in Math., 1960; theology certificate Whitefriars Hall, 1962; M.A., DePaul U., 1966; Ph.D., Loyola U., Chgo., 1974. Ordained priest Roman Catholic Ch., 1961; tchr., counselor DeSales High Sch., Louisville, 1962-63; asst. prin., tchr., counselor Carmel High Sch. for Boys, Mundelein, Ill., 1963-68; dir. Carmelite Inst. Renewal, Mundelein, 1968-70; psychology clk. West Side VA Hosp., Chgo., 1970-71, dir. tng., clin., psychologist, 1974—; clin. intern psychology Ill. Psychiat. Inst., Chgo., 1971-72, research intern psychology, 1972-73; HEW research fellow Ill. Mental Health Insts., Chgo., 1973-74; asst. prof. psychiatry U. Ill., Chgo., 1974—; asst. prof. Ill. Sch. Profl. Psychology, 1977-78; psychology cons. Marriage Tribunal, Catholic Archdiocese of Chgo., 1974; diagnostic cons. Chgo. Police Dept., 1977—; pastoral counselor, marital therapist Nativity of Our Lord Parish, Chgo., 1971—; asst. prof. Chgo. Sch. Profl. Psychology, 1979—. Mem. Am., Ill. psychol. assns., Ill. Group Psychotherapy Soc., Assn. Psychology Internship Centers. Democrat. Home: 653 W 37th St Chicago IL 60609 Office: Psychology Dept 116B PO Box 8195 Chicago IL 60680

FLYNN, ROBERT JAMES, veterinarian; b. Chgo., Jan. 8, 1923; s. James Robert and Rose (Kunz) F.; student Kennedy-King Coll., 1940-41; D.V.M., Mich. State U., 1944; m. Doris Jean Ashe, Dec. 19, 1942; children—Robert J., Jean B. (Mrs. Joseph Palumbo), Susan J., Nancy J. (Mrs. James Masters), James R., Betty J. With Argonne Nat. Lab. (Ill.), 1948-81, successively supr. animal quarters, 1948-55, asso. veterinarian, 1948-66, sr. veterinarian, 1966-81, research on care and diseases of lab. animals, 1948-76, asst. dir. for animal facilities, 1962-76, research on biology of aging, 1971-74, on viral carcinogenesis, 1976-77, on environ. impacts, 1977-81; vet. insp. state of Ill., 1944-57; veterinarian, Lake County, Ill., 1957-76, rabies insp., 1970-73, animal control adminstr., 1973—; veterinarian Lake County Health Dept., 1976—; mem. NRC, 1967-70, mem. com. vet. med. research and edn., 1968-72. Served with AUS, 1943-44. Diplomate Am. Coll. Lab. Animal Medicine (dir. 1956-64, 73-75, sec.-treas. 1956-62, pres. 1963). Mem. Am. Assn. Lab. Animal Sci. (dir. 1949-65, sec.-treas. 1953-62, pres. 1963-64, Griffin award 1968, R.J. Flynn award 1969). Editor numerous texts, including: Laboratory Animal Science: a review of the literature, 1966; (with W.F. Riley, Jr. and K.W. Smith) The Year Book of Veterinary Medicine, vols. 1, 2 and 3; Parasites of Laboratory Animals, 1973; Laboratory Animal Science, 1976-78. Contbr. numerous articles to profl. jours. Organizer, participant in nat. and internat. symposia. Home: 421 E Westleigh Rd Lake Forest IL 60045 Office: 2400 Belvidere St Waukegan IL 60085

FOERSTER, BERND, educator; b. Danzig, Dec. 5, 1923; s. Joseph and Martha (Brumm) F.; came to U.S., 1947, naturalized, 1954; student Columbia U., 1948-49; B.S. in Architecture, U. Cin., 1954; M.Arch., Rensselaer Poly. Inst., 1957; m. Enell Dowling, May 13, 1950; children—Kent, Mark (dec.). With Govt. of Netherlands, 1945-47; with various architects and engrs. offices, 1950-59; instr. U. Cin., 1954; instr. Rensselaer Poly. Inst., Troy, N.Y., 1954-56, asst. prof., 1956-62, asso. prof., 1962-65, prof., 1965-71; prof., dean Coll. Architecture and Design, Kans. State U., Manhattan, 1971—; cons. in field; chmn. Gov.'s Adv. Com. on Hist. Preservation in N.Y. State, 1968-71; chmn. Manhattan Downtown Redevel. Adv. Bd., 1979—; mem. Kans. Bldg. Commn., 1980—. Pres., Manhattan Arts Council, 1976-77; pres. trustees Riley County Mus., 1977. Mem. AIA (com. on hist. resources 1977—), Kans. soc. AIA (sec. 1975, pres. 1979, exec. com. 1975-80, state preservation coordinator 1979—), Soc. Archtl. Historians, Nat. Trust Hist. Preservation (adv. 1979-81, trustee 1981—), Nat. Council Preservation Edn. (dir. 1980—, vice-chmn. 1981—), Kans. Preservation Alliance (dir. 1979—), The Land Inst. (dir. 1976—), Nature Conservancy. Club: Rotary. Author: Man and Masonry, 1960; Pattern and Texture, 1961; Architecture Worth Saving in Rensselaer County, New York, 1965; (with others) Independence, Missouri, 1978; films: Man and Masonry, 1961; What Do You Tear Down Next?, 1964; Earth and Fire, 1964; Assault on the Wynantskill, 1967. Home: 1123 Pioneer Ln Manhattan KS 66502 Office: Kans State U Manhattan KS 66506

FOGERTY, ROBERT PAUL, historian; b. Elwood, Ind., Sept. 12, 1905; s. Michael Joseph and Antoinette Genevieve (Hueper) F.; A.B., U. Notre Dame, 1928; LL.B., St. Thomas Law Sch., 1933; M.A., U. Minn., 1936, Ph.D., 1942; m. Ralpha Chamberlain James, June 22, 1943; children—James Edward, Mary Curran. Admitted to Minn. bar, 1934; instr., Coll. St. Thomas, 1928-36, asst. prof., 1936-42, prof. history, 1946-75, prof. emeritus, 1975—, dir. Div. Social Scis., 1957-75, chmn. dept. history, 1970-75; vis. prof. U. Minn., 1950, Macalester Coll., 1969; mem. Minn. State Rev. Bd. Nat. Register of Historic Places, 1970—, chmn., 1974-75; reviewer Div. Research Grants, NEH, 1976—. Mem. Gov.'s Commn. on Constl. Revision, Minn., 1950-51. Served to maj. USAAF, 1942-46. Mem. Am. Assn. Colls. for Tchr. Edn. (instl. rep. 1960-72), Am. Hist. Assn., Orgn. Am. Historians, Minn. Hist. Soc., Nat. Trust for Historic Preservation, Upper Midwest History Conf. (chmn. 1953-54, 62-63, sec. 1960-61), Coll. St. Thomas Alumni Assn., Notre Dame Alumni Assn. Roman Catholic. Author: An Institutional Study of the Territorial Courts in the Old Northwest, 1788-1848, 1942. Home: 1780 Hampshire Ave Saint Paul MN 55116 Office: Box 4158 Coll St Thomas Saint Paul MN 55105

FOGERTY, ROBERT PAUL, historian; b. Elwood, Ind., Sept. 12, 1905; s. Michael Joseph and Antoinette Genevieve (Hueper) F.; A.B., U. Notre Dame, 1928; LL.B., St. Thomas Law Sch., 1933; M.A., U. Minn., 1936, Ph.D., 1942; m. Ralpha Chamberlain James, June 22, 1943; children—James Edward, Mary Curran. Instr., Coll. St. Thomas, 1928-36, asst. prof., 1936-42, prof. history, 1946-75, prof. emeritus, 1975—, dir. div. social scis., 1957-75, chmn. dept. history, 1970-75; admitted to Minn. bar, 1934; vis. prof. U. Minn., 1950, Macalester Coll., 1969; mem. Minn. state rev. bd. Nat. Register of Historic Places, 1970—, chmn., 1974-75; reviewer div. research grants Nat. Endowment for Humanities, 1976—. Mem. Minn. Gov.'s Commn. on Constnl. Revision, 1950-51. Served to maj. USAAF, 1942-46. Mem. Am. Assn. Colls. for Tchr. Edn. (instnl. rep. 1960-72), Am. Hist. Assn., Orgn. Am. Historians, Minn. Hist. Soc., Nat. Trust for Historic Preservation, Upper Midwest History Conf. (chmn. 1953-54, 62-63, sec. 1960-61), Coll. St. Thomas Alumni Assn., Notre Dame Alumni Assn. Roman Catholic. Author: An Institutional Study of the Territorial Courts in the Old Northwest, 1788-1848, 1942. Home: 1780 Hampshire Ave Saint Paul MN 55116 Office: Box 4158 Coll St Thomas Saint Paul MN 55105

FOGO, WILLIAM ROLLIN, chemist; b. Richland County, Wis., Mar. 29, 1938; s. Rollin Franklin and Thelma Lorraine (Stayton) F.; B.S., Wis. State U., Platteville, 1960; m. Marguerite Ohrt, June 2, 1978. Lab. technician Endocrine Labs., Inc., Madison, Wis., 1961-63; supervising technician, 1963-67; lab. supr. FS Services, Inc., Mendota, Ill., 1967-76, area feed quality supr., Tiffin, Iowa, 1976—. Treas., Mendota council Campfire Girls Am., 1968-71; bd. dirs. Triumph Youth League, Mendota, 1972-76; mem. adminstrv. bd. United Methodist Ch., West Branch, Iowa. Served with U.S. Army, 1956-60. Mem. Am. Assn. Feed Microscopists (dir.). Home: PO Box 329 West Branch IA 52358 Office: PO Box 8 Tiffin IA 52340

FOK, THOMAS DSO YUN, civil engr., educator; b. Canton, China, July 1, 1921; s. D.H. and C. (Tse) F.; came to U.S., 1947, naturalized, 1956; B.Eng., Nat. Tung-Chi U., Szechuan, China, 1945; M.S., U. Ill., 1948; M.B.A. (Dr. Nadler Money Markteen scholar), N.Y. U., 1950; Ph.D., Carnegie-Mellon U., 1956; m. Maria M.L. Liang, Sept. 18, 1949. Structural designer Lummus Co., N.Y.C., 1951-53; design engr. Richardson, Gordon & Asso., cons. engrs., Pitts., 1956-58; asso. prof. engring. Youngstown (Ohio) U., 1958-68, dir. Computing Center, 1963-67; partner Cernica, Fok & Assos., cons. engrs., Youngstown, 1958-64; prin. Thomas Fok & Assos., cons. engrs., Youngstown, 1964-65; partner Mosure-Fok & Syrakis Co., Ltd., cons. engrs., Youngstown, 1965-76; cons. engr. Mahoning County Engr., Ohio, 1960-65, engr., 1960—; pres. Computing-Systems & Tech., Youngstown, 1967-72; chmn. Thomas Fok and Assos., Ltd., cons. engrs., Youngstown, 1977—. Trustee Pub. Library of Youngstown and Mahoning County, 1973—, Youngstown Ednl. Found., 1975—; trustee Youngstown State U., 1975—, chmn., 1981—. Recipient Walter E. and Caroline H. Watson Found. Disting. Prof.'s award Youngstown U., 1966. Registered profl. engr. N.Y., Pa., Ohio, Ill., Ky. W.Va., Ind., Md. Fellow ASCE; mem. Am. Concrete Inst., Internat. Assn. for Bridge and Structural Engring., Am. Soc. Engring. Edn., Nat. Soc. Profl. Engrs., A.A.A.S., Soc. Am. Mil. Engrs., Ohio, N.Y. acads. scis., Sigma Xi, Beta Gamma Sigma, Sigma Tau, Delta Pi Sigma. Rotarian. Contbr. articles to profl. jours. Home: 325 S Canfield-Niles Rd Youngstown OH 44515 Office: 3896 Mahoning Ave Youngstown OH 44515

FOLDA, RICHARD GERALD, lawyer; b. Schuyler, Nebr., Oct. 9, 1923; s. Kajetan J. and Tillie L. (Pakes) F.; LL.B., U. Nebr., 1949; m. Marianne Srb, July 19, 1949; children—Kathryn J., Gail Ellen. Admitted to Nebr. bar, 1949; pvt. practice, Schuyler, 1950—; partner Folda & Co., 1950—; dir. Security Fed. Savs. and Loan Assn.; dir., sec.-treas., mng. officer, 1958-64, pres., dir., mng. officer, 1964—; Nebr. dir. Fed. Home Loan Bank of Topeka, 1976-78; pres. Midwest Savs. Conf., 1963-64; city atty. Schuyler, 1950-58. Pres., Schuyler Bd. Edn., 1950-58, pres., 1963-78. Served from pvt. to lt. USAAF, 1943-45. Mem. Am., Nebr., Colfax County (pres. 1958) bar assns., Sixth Jud. Dist. Bar (sec. 1957), C. of C., Nebr. State Sch. Bds. Assn. (dir. 1966—, pres. 1970-71), Nebr. League Savs. and Loan Assn. (pres.), U.S. Savs. and Loan League (Nebr. dir. 1970-74), Sigma Phi Epsilon, Phi Delta Phi, Innocents Soc., Am. Legion, 40 and 8. Republican. Roman Catholic. Clubs: Rotary (past pres.), Lions (past pres.), Schuyler Country (past pres.), Kosmet. Home: 1500 Indian Heights Schuyler NE 68661 Office: 1103 B St Schuyler NE 68661

FOLEY, ANNA BERNICE WILLIAMS (MRS. WARREN MASSEY FOLEY), exec., librarian, author; b. Wigginsville, Ohio, Nov. 20, 1902; d. Karl Howland and Bertye (Young) Williams; student U. Cin., 1920-24, Columbia, 1931, Nanking (China) Lang. Coll., 1926; Grad. Sch. cert. Jesus Coll., Oxford U., 1969; m. Warren Massey Foley, Feb. 25, 1924; children—Williams Massey, Karlanne (Mrs. William Scully Hauer). Radio commentator WKRC, Cin., 1934, WSAI, Cin., 1938; commentator WCPO-TV, Cin., 1939-44; lectr. fashions U. Cin. Evening Coll., 1941-44; spl. events coordinator Mabley & Carew Dept. Store, 1951-66; model McCall Patterns-Singer Sewing Machine Co., Moscow, USSR, 1957; dir. The Martha Kinney Cooper Ohioana Library Assn., Columbus, Ohio, 1966-77, also editor Quar. Mag., Yearbook, 1966-77. Lectr. creative writing; book reviewer Sunday Columbus Dispatch, 1967-77, The Asia Mail, 1976-77. Mem. lit. panel Ohio Arts Council, 1966-70; bd. dirs. Ohio Poetry Day, 1968-77. Recipient Valley Forge honor cert. Freedoms Found.; cert. Columbus Art League, 1976. Mem. English Speaking Union (br. pres. 1966-69), World Assn. Women Journalists and Writers, Ohio Press Women, Women in Communications (pres. 1973-74), Overseas Press Club of Am., MacDowell Soc., DAR, Sigma Delta Chi, Kappa Kappa Gamma (Achievement award 1974). Author: (juvenile books) Star Stories (also in Chinese), Spaceships of the Ancients; Korean Legends, 1979; Thunder God, 1980; Why the Cock Crows Three Times, 1980; The Gazelle and the Hunter, 1980; author weekly column Columbus Scene, in Forest Hills Jour., 1971-77. Home: 10224 Linden Ln Overland Park KS 66207

FOLEY, EDWARD MINTER, primary metals producing co. exec.; b. Bassett, Va., Dec. 15, 1929; s. Ansley Tinsley and Mildred (Minter) F.; B.S., U. Tenn., 1960; m. Evelyn Jo Cooter, Apr. 28, 1951; children—Mildred Kathleen, Edward Minter. Research physicist nuclear div. Union Carbide Corp., Oak Ridge, 1955-66; sr. research physicist Union Carbide Corp., Greenville, S.C. and Kokomo, Ind., 1966-69; sr. research engr. stellite div. Cabot Corp., Kokomo, 1970-72, mgr. powder metals parts mfg. stellite div., 1972-74, product mgr. stellite div., 1974-78, market devel. and sales mgr., powder products, stellite div., 1978-80, Eastern Region mgr. Wear Tech. Div., 1980—; dir. Powder Metallurgy Industries Fedn., 1975-78. Served with U.S. Army, 1953-55. Recipient IR-100 award Indsl. Research Mag., 1974. Mem. Metal Powder Industries Fedn. (Part of Year award of distinction 1974, mem. pub. relations council 1975—), Powder Metallurgy Industries Assn. (pres. 1978-80), Metal Powder Producers Assn. (dir. 1978-80), Am. Welding Soc., Am. Powder Metallurgy Inst., Am. Soc. Metals, Nat. Rifle Assn. (life), Nat. Geog. Soc., Smithsonian Assos. Methodist. Clubs: Masons, Order Eastern Star, Shriners, Elks. Patentee in field. Home: RR 2 Box 142 Russiaville IN 46979 Office: 1020 W Park Ave Kokomo IN 46901

FOLEY, J. PATRICK, hotel exec.; b. Kelso, Wash., Feb. 12, 1932; s. James and Verna Foley; grad. Wash. State U., 1955; m. Paula Green, June 7, 1969; children—Sean, Erin. With Western Internat. Hotels Co., 1958-61; with Hyatt Hotels Corp., Rosemont, Ill., 1961—, exec. v.p., 1972-77, pres., 1977—. Served to 1st lt. AUS, 1955-56. Mem. Am. Hotel and Motel Assn. Address: 9701 W Higgins Rd Rosemont IL 60018*

FOLEY, KEVIN MICHAEL, scientist, lawyer; b. Cin., Nov. 22, 1942; s. Matthew Joseph and Mary Alice (Keller) F.; m. Jeanne Ann Westrick, Aug. 21, 1965; children—Tony, Keith, Brian; B.S., Xavier U., 1964; Ph.D., Purdue U., 1970; J.D., Capital U., 1974. Admitted to Ohio bar, 1975, U.S. Supreme Ct. bar, 1979; teaching asst. Purdue U., 1964-65, instr., 1965-66; sr. scientist Owens-Corning Fiberglas Corp., Granville, Ohio, 1970-75; sr. research and devel. scientist The Andersons, Maumee, Ohio, 1975—. Chmn. Lucas County Med. Malpractice Arbitration Panel, 1976, 78, 80. Mem. Am. Assn. Cereal Chemists, Inst. Food Techs., Am. Oil Chemists Soc., Inst. for Briquetting and Agglomeration, Am. Chem. Soc., Am. Assn. Lab. Animal Sci., Ohio, Lucas County, Toledo bar assns., Toledo Patent Law Assn. Recipient Order of the Curia, 1975; Stauffer Chem. Co. fellow, 1967; Phillips Petroleum Co. fellow, 1968; Petroleum Research Fund fellow, 1969. Contbr. articles to profl. jours.; holder numerous patents. Home: 540 Dussel Dr Maumee OH 43537 Office: PO Box 119 Maumee OH 43537

FOLKERTS, BYRON LEE, mfg. co. exec.; b. Great Bend, Kans., Dec. 6, 1953; s. Doyle Dean and Ina Lea (Minson) F.; student Barton County Community Coll., 1972-73; m. Gia M. Stalcup, May 2, 1981. With Great Bend Mfg. Co. (Kans.), 1973—, purchasing agt., 1979-80, dir. purchasing, 1980—. Home: 2800 17th St Great Bend KS 67530 Office: 705 Harrison St Great Bend KS 67530

FOLKMAN, JEROME DANIEL, clergyman; b. Cleve., Sept. 25, 1907; s. Ben and Rose (Tronstein) F.; A.B., U. Cin., 1928; B.H.L., Hebrew Union Coll., 1928, rabbi, 1931, D.D., 1957; student U. Mich., 1934-36; Ph.D., Ohio State U., 1953; m. Bessie Schomer, Dec. 14, 1930 children—Moses Judah, David Hillel, Joy Folkman Moss. Rabbi, Temple Beth Israel, Jackson, Mich., 1931-36, Temple Emanuel, Grand Rapids, Mich., 1937-47; rabbi Temple Israel, Columbus, Ohio, 1947-73, rabbi emeritus, 1973—; adj. prof. sociology Ohio State U., 1963—; Englander Meml. lectr. Hebrew Union Coll., 1957; McKinley vis. scholar Walsh, Malone and Mt. Union colls., 1976; Benjamin Tintner Meml. lectr. N.Y. Assn. Reform Rabbis, 1976; vis. prof. Otterbein Coll., Westerville, Ohio, 1977-79; lectr. religion Pontifical Coll. Josephinum, Worthington, Ohio, 1979; vis. lectr. religion Capital U., Columbus, 1980—. Founder, 1st pres. Kent County (Mich.) Council Social Agys., 1939-42; dir. Family and Children's Service Bur. of Franklin County, 1948-56, chmn. case com., 1950-51; mem. penal study com. Ohio State Post-War Commn., 1948-49; mem. Mayor's Adv. Com. on Pub. Relations, 1952-53, Columbus Commn. on Pub. Relations, 1953-56; pres. Ohio Conf. on Family Relations, 1955-57; mem. Ohio State Mental Health Survey, 1955-57; bd. govs. Hebrew Union Coll., Jewish Inst. Religion, 1952-56; bd. dirs. Community Chest Columbus and Franklin County, 1955-56, Grant Hosp., 1960—, Am. Cancer Soc., Franklin County unit, 1966-73, Ministers Life and Casualty Union, 1966-71, Ohio Citizens Council Health and Welfare, 1966-69, Franklin U., Columbus, 1979—; trustee Columbus Hosp. Fedn., 1956-71, Union of Am. Hebrew Congregations, 1960-64; mem. Columbus Adv. Council on Naval Affairs, 1958-73; bd. dirs. Franklin County chpt. Nat. Found., 1958-59, Franklin County Heart Assn., 1959-73; mem.-at-large, exec. com. Nat. Council Family Relations, 1961-63; mem. adminstrv. com., v.p. United Community Council; bd. dirs. Columbus Urban League, 1962-65, Better Bus. Bur. Central Ohio, 1977—; cons. religious resources to President's spl. asst. for mental retardation, 1963-65; mem. Ohio Comprehensive Mental Health Planning Project, 1963-65, Ohio Commn. on Nursing, 1973-75; alumni bd. overseers Hebrew Union Coll., Jewish Inst. Religion, 1966-70. Recipient Forney W. Clement Meml. award Mich. Dist. Kiwanis, 1944; Gold Key as Outstanding Citizen under 35 yrs. of age Grand Rapids Jaycees, 1939; named one of ten outstanding citizens of Columbus, Columbus Citizen, 1954; B'nai B'rith Sanford Lakin award, 1961; Citizen of Year award Frontiers Internat., 1967; Gov. Ohio's award, 1968; Disting. Contbn. to Edn. award Central Ohio chpt. Pi Lambda Theta, 1965; Outstanding Citizenship award Central Ohio chpt. Pub. Relations Soc. Am., 1974; Excellence in Teaching citation Student Council Coll. Arts and Scis., Ohio State U., 1976; Disting. Service award Ohio State U. Alumni Assn., 1979. Fellow Am. Sociol. Assn.; mem. Soc. Sci. Study Religion, Synagogue Council Am. (commn. family life), Family Service Assn. Am. (dir. 1965-68), Jewish Family Service Assn. Columbus (v.p. 1966-68), Columbus Bd. Rabbis (chmn. 1967, 72-73), Central Conf. Am. Rabbis (chmn. com. marriage, home and family 1950-58, exec. bd. 1957-59, chmn. com. Judaism and medicine 1963-65, chmn. com. retirement 1975—, fin. sec. 1969-71), Internat. Council Christians and Jews (gov. body 1948-50), Soc. Study Social Problems, U.S. Navy League (co-chaplain 1980—), Alpha Kappa Delta. Clubs: B'nai B'rith; Kiwanis; Torch (pres. 1976-77), Faculty (Ohio State Univ.). Author: The Cup of Life, 1955; Design for Jewish Living, 1955; (with Nancy M. Clatworthy) Marriage Has Many Faces, 1970. Mem. editorial adv. bd. Highlights for Children, 1953—. Home: 2538 Maryland Ave Columbus OH 43209

FOLLANSBEE, DOROTHY L. (DOROTHY L. LELAND), publisher; b. St. Louis, Mar. 24, 1911; d. Robert Leathan and Minnie Cowden (Yowell) Lund; grad. Sarah Lawrence Coll., 1931; m. Austin Porter Leland, Apr. 24, 1935 (dec. 1975); children—Mary Talbot Leland MacCarthy, Austin Porter Jr. (dec.), Irene Austin Leland Barzantny; m. 2d, Robert Kerr Follansbee, Oct. 20, 1979. Pres., Station List Publ. Co., St. Louis, 1975—; dir. Downtown St. Louis Inc. Hon. chmn. Old Post Office Landmark Com., 1975—; bd. dirs. Services Bur. St. Louis, 1943, pres., 1951; bd. dirs. Robert E. Lee Meml. Assn.; mem. St. Louis County Parks and Recreation Dept., 1969; bd. dirs. Stratford Hall, Va., 1953—, pres., 1967-70, treas., 1970—; bd. dirs. Historic Bldgs. Commn. St. Louis County, 1959—, Mo. Hist. Soc., 1960—, Mo. Mansion Preservation Com., 1975—, Chatillon DeMenil House, 1977-79. Recipient Landmarks award Landmarks Assn. St. Louis, 1974; Pub. Service award GSA, 1978; Crownenshield award Nat. Trust for Hist Preservation, 1979. Mem. Colonial Dames Am., Episcopalian. Clubs: St. Louis Country, Princeton of N.Y., St. Louis Jr. League. Home: 35 Pointer Ln St Louis MO 63124 also 1001 River Oaks Dr Pittsburgh PA 15215 Office: 818 Olive St St Louis MO 63101

FOLLETT, MARY VIERLING, artist, art conservator; b. Chgo., Feb. 9, 1917; d. Arthur Garfield and Grace May (Cummings) Vierling; student U. Southern Calif., 1932-34, grad. Acad. Profl. Art Conservators, 1975, Masters, 1978; m. Garth Benepe Follett, Feb. 16, 1945; 1 dau., Dawn Goshorn; 3 stepchildren. Exhibited in group shows Palette and Chisel Acad. Fine Arts, 1975, 76, 77, 78, Municipal Art League, 1972-78, others; represented in permanent collection Fla., Calif., Italy, others; owner, mgr. Paintin' Place, gallery, Oak Park, Ill., 1973—; dir. Palette and Chisel Acad. Fine Arts, Chgo. Vice pres. Oak Park LWV, 1952-54, welfare chmn., 1956-58; treas. Oak Park Council Internat. Affairs, 1962-74. Recipient Gold medal Palette and Chisel Acad. Fine Arts, 1976-77, 1st award Civics and Art Found.

Union League Chgo., 1977. Mem. Oak Park River Forest Art League (v.p.), Internat. Acad. Fine Arts, Pen Women Am., Municipal Art League Chgo., Am. Soc. Artists, Art Inst. Assos. Oak Park and River Forest (women's bd. 1967—), Oak Park River Forest Hist. Soc. Club: 19th Century Women's. Home: 1440 Park Ave River Forest IL 60305 Office: 820 North Blvd Oak Park IL 60301

FOLLIS, THOMAS BURTON, veterinarian; b. Bowling Green, Ky., Mar. 26, 1927; s. William Blackburn and Grace Neel (Russell) F.; B.S., Western Ky. State Coll., 1950; D.V.M., Ohio State U., 1954; Ph.D., Utah State U., 1972; m. Nancy Louise Sisson, June 12, 1954; children—Karen Wright, David Sisson. Diagnostician, Reynoldsburg (Ohio) Diagnostic Lab., 1954-55; practice veterinary medicine, Taylorsville, Ky., 1954-69; head veterinary medicine and research World Wildlife Safari, Winston, Oreg., 1972-73; mgr. veterinary services Ralston Purina Co., St. Louis, 1973-76, asst. dir. corp. regulatory compliance, 1976-79; pres. Regulatory Adv. Group, Inc., St. Louis, 1979—, TONA 2S, Inc., 1979—. Mem. Sch. Bd. Spencer County, Ky., 1969; mem. Library Bd., Spencer County; chmn. Infantile Paralysis Found., Spencer County. Served with USAC, 1945-47. Utah Dept. Natural Resources fellow, 1969-72. Mem. F-2 Wildlife Assos. (co-founder), AVMA, Am. Animal Hosp. Assn., Nat. Wildlife Found., Ky. Vet. Med. Assn., Fine Arts Assn. Lindenwood Coll., Assn. St. Louis Art Museum, Nat. Assn. Realtors. Methodist. Club: Masons. Editor: The Morphology of Canine and Feline Blood Cells (R.R. Rich), 1974; Allergic Inhalant Dermatitis (Anderson), 1975; Management and Nutrition of Dogs and Cats, 1976. Contbr. articles to profl. jours. Home: 1312 S 10th St Saint Louis MO 63104 Office: Regulatory Adv Group 4679 S Grand Blvd Saint Louis MO 63111

FOLLMAR, JEROME ALBERT, dentist; b. Hammond, Ind., Dec. 19, 1929; s. John Joseph and Marie Bertha (Retzloff) F.; student Butler U., 1960-61; D.D.S., Ind. U., 1966; m. Jacqueline Frances Wyld, Dec. 11, 1971; children—Frederick Johnones, Nancy Sue, Allison Leigh, Jerome Albert II, Amy Lynn, Jack David, Joseph Allen, James Arthur. Gen. practice dentistry, Indpls., Anderson, Ind.; chief dental service Central State Hosp., Indpls., 1967-73, chief med. staff, 1972-73. Asst. clin. instr. James W. Riley Children Hosp. Dental Clinic, 1968-73. Cons., Head Start; mem. council St. Mary's Parrish; mem. Ind. State Nutritional Council, 1979—; mem. state-wide adv. com. Ind. Nutrition Edn. and Tng. Program. Served with AUS, 1952-54. Mem. Am. Soc. Dentistry for Children (mem. exec. com. Ind. unit 1968-73, sec.-treas. 1973-75, v.p. 1975-77, pres. 1977-78), Am. Soc. Forensic Odontology, Am., Ind. dental assns., Madison County Dental Soc. (pres. 1978-79), East Central Dental Soc. (pres. 1979-80), Ind. Pub. Health Dentists Orgn. (pres. 1970), Indpls. Dist. Dental Soc., Westside Dental Group (pres. 1968). Home: 2316 Wildwood Dr Anderson IN 46011 Office: 123 W 12th St Anderson IN 46016

FOLLMER, ROBERT FRANCIS, mfg. co. exec.; b. The Dalles, Oreg., Feb. 4, 1944; s. Francis Edwin and Irene Emily (Drock) F.; B.S., UCLA, 1965; m. Deanna Kathern Brown, Nov. 15, 1980. Western regional mgr. Nat. Student Mktg. Group, Los Angeles, 1968-70; sales rep. dental div. Penwalt Corp., San Francisco, 1970-73, dental div. Chematron Corp., San Francisco, 1973-77, Philips Med. Systems Co., San Francisco, 1977-78; dir. mktg. and sales X-Ray div. Den-Tal-Ez Mfg. Co., Des Moines, 1978—. Served with USMCR, 1965. Recipient awards appreciation. Mem. Am. Acad. Dental Radiology (asso.), Bay Area Diagnostic Ultra Sound Soc. Republican. Episcopalian. Club: Echo Valley Golf and Country (Des Moines). Home: 1625 Cambourne Ln Schaumburg IL 60194

FOLTZ, THOMAS JAMES, computer co. exec.; b. Indpls., May 18, 1946; s. James Gerald and Barbara Alice (Dickey) F.; B.S., Rose Hulman Inst. Tech., 1968, M.S., 1971; m. Evelyn Rebecca Wilkinson, Dec. 22, 1979. With NASA, Cape Canaveral, Fla., 1968; numerical analyst Gen. Motors, Indpls., 1969-70; sr. systems analyst Ind. Blue-Cross-Blue Shield, Indpls., 1970-77; sr. ops. cons. Ind. Bell Telephone, Indpls., 1977-79; pres., chief exec. officer Total Systems, Inc., Indpls., 1979—, dir. Robotics div., 1979—. Exec. dir. United Conservatives of Ind., 1977—; exec. bd. Christian Freedom Council, 1974-77; deacon E. 91st St. Christian Ch., Indpls., 1977—; campaign coordinator various candidates U.S. Senate and state office. Named Hon. Sec. of State, Ind., 1980. Mem. Assn. for Computing Machinery, Creation Research Soc. Republican. Contbr. articles to profl. jours. Office: 8900 Keystone Crossing Suite 680 Indianapolis IN 46240

FONDA, JOHN REAGAN, engr., mfg. co. exec.; b. Knoxville, Tenn., Aug. 25, 1917; s. Howard E. and Mabel (Reagan) F.; student Wayne State U., Mich. State U.; m. Joyce May Rupprecht, Feb. 21, 1949. With Dihydrol Co., 1946—, sec.-treas., 1950-60, pres., Highland Park, Mich., 1960—. Registered profl. engr., Mich. Mem. Nat. Assn. Corrosion Engrs., Am. Water Works Assn., Am. Soc. San. Engrs. (pres.). Baptist. Mason (32 deg., Shriner). Research in water chemistry. Patentee on equipment for chem. treatment water. Home: 30815 Billington Ct Birmingham MI 48010 Office: 150 Victor Ave Detroit MI 48203

FONDER, AELRED CHARLES, dentist; b. Sisseton, S.D., Nov. 11, 1916; s. John Joseph and Albertina (Nigg) F.; student Huron Coll., 1936, St. Henry's Coll., 1938-39, St. Paul Sem., 1940; B.A. in Philosophy and Chemistry, St. John's U., 1943; postgrad. Sch. Dentistry, No. Pacific Coll., 1943-44; D.D.S., Northwestern U., 1946; postgrad. U. Ill., 1946; m. Jane Marie Schoenberg, May 13, 1944; children—Nancy (Mrs. Randolph Wayne Osborn), Thomas, Robert, John, James. Practice dentistry, Hubbard Woods, Ill., 1946-49, Winnetka, Ill., 1949-53; founder Rehab. Inst. Chgo., 1952, Am. Acad. Maxillofacial Prosthetics, 1953; established maxillofacial prosthetics program U.S. Army and Air Force, Brooke Army Hosp., Tex., 1955; practice dentistry specializing in medico-dental research and temporo mandibular joint problems, Rock Falls, Ill., 1955—; staff U. Ill. Coll. Dentistry, 1946-47, now asst. prof.; staff Northwestern U. Dental Sch., 1947-49; dir. Dental Research Found., Rock Falls. Research Maxillofacial prosthetics U. Chgo., 1964-65; lectr. Michael Reese Hosp., Chgo., 1967-68; developer Sterling Profl. Bldg. (Ill.), 1967-68. Co-Founder Self-Help Enterprises, Sterling-Rock Falls, Ill., 1959. Bd. dirs. Found. Internat. Coop. Served with USNR, 1943-45, to capt. AUS, 1953-55. Fellow Ill. Dental Soc., Royal Soc. Health (Eng.); mem. Am. Acad. Maxillofacial Prosthetics (founder), Internat., Am., Ill. dental socs., Am. Acad. Physiol. Dentistry, Am. Acad. Functional Prosthodontics, Am. Assn. for Advancement Tension Control, Internat. Assn. Preventive Medicine, Psi Omega. Roman Catholic. Author: The Dental Physician; Goodbye Headaches; Physiopathology of Stressful Disorders; others. Editor: Basal Facts. Contbr. articles to profl. jours. Inventor functional artificial hand for amputees, 1952, artificial skin-like materials, 1953. Home: 1512 1st Ave Sterling IL 61081 Office: 303 W 2d St Rock Falls IL 61071

FONDILLER, SHIRLEY HOPE ALPERIN (MRS. HARVEY V. FONDILLER), nurse, journalist, educator; b. Holyoke, Mass.; d. Samuel and Rose (Sobiloff) Alperin; grad. Beth Israel Hosp. Sch. Nursing, Boston; B.S., Tchrs. Coll. Columbia U., 1962, M.A., 1963, M.Ed., 1971, Ed.D., 1979; m. Harvey V. Fondiller, Dec. 27, 1957; 1 son, David Stewart. Staff asst. Am. Nurses Assn., N.Y.C., 1963-64, dir. ednl. adminstrs., cons. and tchrs. sect., 1964-66, coordinator Am. Nurses Assn.-Nat. League for Nursing careers program, 1967-70; coordinator clin. sessions Am. Nurses Assn., 1971-72, editor Am. Nurse, Kansas City, Mo., 1975-78; asso. prof., asst. to dean for spl. projects Rush-Presbyn.-St. Luke's Med. Center, 1979—; cons. N.Y. State Asso. Degree Nursing Project, 1964. Mem. Kappa Delta pi, Sigma Theta Tau. Writer, columnist Nursing World, 1955-60; film reviewer Am. Jour. Nursing, 1963-64, Film News, 1963-66; writer, dir. The Open Door, radio documentary, 1960; contbg. editor Am. Jour. Nursing, 1971-75; also books and articles. Home: 1550 N Lake Shore Dr Chicago IL 60610 Office: 1753 W Congress Pkwy Chicago IL 60612

FOOTE, JOEL LINDSLEY, biochemist; b. Cleve., Jan. 11, 1928; s. Joel Lindsley and Beth Eliza (Brainard) F.; B.S. in Edn., Miami U., 1952; postgrad. Ohio State U., 1955; Ph.D., Case Inst. Tech., 1960; m. Alice Lydia Tanner, June 16, 1951; children—Robert Lindsley, Karen Ann. Tchr. sci., Wilminton (Ohio) pub. schs., 1952-53; tchr. sci. and mathematics, Springfield (Ohio) pub. schs., 1953-56; NSF postdoctoral fellow, U. Mich., Ann Arbor, 1960-62, instr. and asst. research biochemist, 1962-65; successively asst. prof., asso. prof., prof. Western Mich. U., Kalamazoo, 1965—. Originator, founding chmn. City of Kalamazoo Environ. Concerns Com., 1970-72; Kalamazoo County Democratic exec. com., 1968—; candidate for county commr., 1968, 70. Served with USN, 1946-48. NIH research grantee, 1966-70. Mem. Am. Soc. Biol. Chemists, Am. Chem. Soc., AAAS, AAUP, Phi Beta Kappa, Sigma Xi. Unitarian. Contbr. articles in field to sci. publs. Home: 3623 Lancaster Dr Kalamazoo MI 49007 Office: Dept Chemistry Western Mich Univ Kalamazoo MI 49008

FOOTE, PAUL SHELDON, educator; b. Lansing, Mich., May 22, 1946; s. Harlon Sheldon and Frances Norene (Rotter) F.; B.B.A., U. Mich., 1967; M.B.A. (Loomis-Sayles fellow), Harvard U., 1971; advanced profl. cert. N.Y. U., 1975; postgrad. doctoral program Mich. State U., 1975—; m. Badri Seddigheh Hosseinian, Oct. 25, 1968; children—David, Sheila. Br. mgr., divisional mgr. Citibank, N.Y.C., Bombay, India and Beirut, Lebanon, 1972-74; mgr. planning and devel. Singer Co., Africa/Middle East, 1974-75; instr. U. Mich., Flint, 1978-79; lectr. acctg. Mich. State U., East Lansing, 1977; asst. prof. U. Windsor (Ont., Can.), 1979-81; asso. prof. Saginaw Valley State Coll., University Center, Mich., 1981—; pres. The Computer Coop., Inc., 1981—. Served to lt. AUS, 1968-69. Haskins and Sells Doctoral Consortium fellow, 1977. Mem. Am. Accounting Assn., Nat. Assn. Accountants, Club: Circumnavigators. Home: 2795 Southwood East Lansing MI 48823 Office: Saginaw Valley State College University Center MI 48710

FOOTE, RITA MCDONALD, ednl. adminstr.; b. Dearborn, Mich., 1929; d. Martin E. and Elizabeth McDonald; B.S.Ed. in English, U. Detroit, 1950; M.Ed. in Guidance and Counseling, Wayne State U., 1961; m. Cecil R. Foote; children—Michael Cheryl. Chmn. dept. English Southfield (Mich.) High Sch., Southfield Pub. Schs., 1954-64, counselor, 1962-64, asst. prin., 1964-65, curriculum supr. pub. schs., 1965—. Mem. Am. Assn. Supervision and Curriculum Devel., Mich. Assn. Supervision and Curriculum Devel. (bd. dirs., sec. 1978-79, pres. 1980—), Oakland County (Mich.) Curriculum Council (pres. 1974-75), Am. Sch. Counselors Assn., Oakland Area Counselors Assn., Am., Mich. personnel and guidance assns., Nat., Mich. assns. secondary sch. prins., NEA (life), Mich. Edn. Assn. (life). Office: 18330 George Washington St Southfield MI 48075

FOOTLIK, IRVING MELVIN, cons. engr.; b. Chgo., Feb. 7, 1918; s. Louis and Rose (Elman) F.; B.S., Ill. Inst. Tech., 1939; m. Sylvia Gollay, Mar. 10, 1940 children—Janice B., Robert B. Jr. engr. U.S. Air Corps, Dayton, O., 1939-41; chief perishable tool sect. U.S. Army Ordnance, Chgo., 1941-45; asst. to v.p. Ekco Products Co., Chgo., 1946-48; gen. plant mgr. Galter Products, 1948-50; cons. engr. Footlik and Assos., Evanston, Ill., 1950—, pres., 1950—; dir. Met. Bank; lectr. Mem. Skokie Traffic Safety Commn., 1971-74; mem. citizens adv. group Winnetka Plan Commn., 1977; pres. Mayer Kaplan Jewish Community Center. Recipient Am. Material Handling Soc. honors award, U.S. Army Ordnance Civilian meritorious service award, Internat. Materials Mgmt. Soc. Ten Year Presdl. award. Mem. Assn. Profl. Material Handling Cons. (sec.), ASME, Internat. Material Mgmt. Soc., Ill. C. of C., Ill. Soc. Profl. Engrs., Am.-Israel Chamber Commerce and Industry (v.p.). Material handling editor: Supply House Times mag. Contbr. to publs. in field. Address: 1548 Tower Rd Sylvia Ln Winnetka IL 60093 Office: 2521 Gross Point Rd Evanston IL 60201

FOOTLIK, ROBERT BARRY, engr.; b. Chgo., Oct. 29, 1946; s. Irving M. and Sylvia (Gollay) F.; B.S.I.E., Ill. Inst. Tech., 1968; m. Beth Ann Iglitzen, Dec. 16, 1969; children—Jennifer, Ari Seth. Exec. v.p. Footlik and Assos., Evanston, Ill., 1971—; mem. adv. bd. Met. Bank & Trust Co., Addison, Ill.; lectr., cons. in field. Bd. dirs. North Shore Assn. for Retarded. Lic. profl. engr., Ill., 1972. Mem. Nat., Ill. (Young Engr. of Year 1972) socs. profl. engrs., Internat. Materials Mgmt. Soc. (pres. Chgo. chpt. 1976-77, v.p. 1979, sec. 1980), Assn. Profl. Material Handling Cons., Midwest Indsl. Mgmt. Assn. Contbr. articles to profl. jours. Home: 940 Sheridan Rd Glencoe IL 60022 Office: 2521 Gross Point Rd Evanston IL 60201

FORAKER, ROBERT ALLEN, banker; b. Canton, Ohio, Dec. 1, 1944; s. Robert E. and Ester (Freudeman) F.; student Akron U., 1968-69, Fla. Tech. Coll., 1976; grad. Exec. Devel. Sch., U. Wash.; m. Mary F. Mucci, Sept. 10, 1966; children—Robert Anthony, Robynn Marie. With Central Trust, Canton, 1962-69, sr. programmer, 1965-69, sales rep., 1967-69; with Citizens Savs. of Canton, 1969—, officer, asst. treas., 1971—, asst. v.p., 1979-80, v.p., 1980—, service mgr., 1973-77, sales and service mgr., 1975-77; owner, dir. Ohio Microfilm, Inc., 1975-76; part owner Pure Water Unltd., 1981—, Nat. Clean Water Soc. Ohio, 1981—. Served with Ohio N.G., 1965-71. Mem. Savs. and Loan Inst., Savs. Assn. Ohio (public affairs com.), Sales and Mktg. Execs. Democrat. Roman Catholic. Patentee 24 hour home bank. Home: 3600 21st St NW Canton OH 44708 Office: 100 Central Plaza S Canton OH 44708

FORBES, DAVID MORSE, plastics mfg. co. personnel exec.; b. Bloomington, Ind., Oct. 2, 1942; s. Melvin Floyd and Evelyn Noamia F.; student Ind. U., 1960, Eastern Ariz. Jr. Coll., 1963-64; B.S., Ind. State U., 1968; m. Betty Lou Rader, Sept. 3, 1965; children—Scott, Diana Lynn. Engr., asst. plant mgr. H. W. Gossard, Ishpeming, Mich., 1968-69; foreman J. L. Case Co., Winneconne, Wis., 1969-70; foreman Gilson Bros. Co., Plymouth, Wis., 1970-72, fabrication foreman, 1972-74, also safety dir.; safety dir. Alma Pastics Co., Edinburgh, Ind., 1974-78, personnel supr., 1978-81, supr. employee relations, 1981—; cons. in field; partner Forbes Enterprises. Mem. Driftwood Valley Arts Council. Mem. Am. Soc. Safety Engrs. Baptist. Home: Rural Route 2 Box 132 Hope IN 47246 Office: 600 S Kyle Edinburgh IN 46124

FORBES, EDWARD CARTER, food mktg. exec.; b. Niagara Falls, Ont., Can., July 25, 1939; came to U.S., 1942, naturalized, 1968; s. Edward Colin and Marjorie Isabel (Carter) F.; B.B.A., U. Mich., 1961, M.B.A., 1962; m. Roxann Rhinerson, Aug. 11, 1962; children—Edward Scott, Elizabeth Datin, Katherine Carter. Various mktg. positions Gen. Mills, Inc., Mpls., 1962-70; partner Gull Lake Conf., 1970-72; chief operating officer D'Amores, Inc., 1972-74; dir. mktg. Pillsbury Co., 1974-78; pres. Forbes/Wetherall, 1978—; pres., chmn. John Baker & Son, 1978—. Episcopalian. Club: Mpls. Athletic. Home: 1414 Holdridge Circle Wayzata MN 55391 Office: Forbes/Wetherall 601 Peavey Bldg 730 2nd Ave S Minneapolis MN 55412

FORBES, FRANKLIN SIM, educator, lawyer; b. Kingsport, Tenn., Sept. 21, 1936; s. Harvey Sim and Virginia Smith (Pooler) F.; B.A., U. Hawaii, 1955; J.D., U. Iowa, 1963; m. Suzanne Marie Willard, June 30, 1962; children—Franklin Sim, Anne Marie. Admitted to Hawaii bar, 1963, Nebr. bar, 1964; law clk. to chief justice Hawaii Supreme Ct., 1963; mem. faculty U. Nebr. Coll. Bus. Adminstrn., Omaha, 1965—, prof. law, 1965—, chmn. dept. law and soc., 1970—; pvt. practice, Omaha, 1964—. Mem. integration com. Omaha Sch. Bd., 1974; mem. St. James Bd. Edn., Omaha, 1974; pres. parish council St. James Roman Catholic Ch., 1975. Recipient Real Dean award U. Hawaii, 1959; Gt. Tchr. award U. Nebr. Law Sch., 1978, 81, Chancellor's medal, 1977; Rotary Found. grantee, Australia, 1972. Mem. Am. Bar Assn., Am. Judicature Soc., Midwest Bus. Adminstrs. Assn., Midwest Bus. Law Assn. (pres. 1975), Omaha Bar Assn. (del. Conf. Future of Law 1979), Alpha Phi Omega, Phi Alpha Delta, Beta Gamma Sigma, Phi Theta Chi. Democrat. Club: Rotary. Contbr. articles and revs. to legal publs. Office: Univ Nebr Omaha NE 68182

FORBES, FRED WILLIAM, architect, engr.; b. East Liverpool, Ohio, Aug. 21, 1936; s. Kenneth S. and Phylis C. F.; B.S. in Architecture, U. Cin., 1960, postgrad. in Civil Engring.; m. Carolyn Lee Eleyet, Dec. 27, 1969; children—Tallerie Bliss, Kendall Robert. Material research engr. U.S. Air Force Materials Lab., 1960-61, structural research engr. Flight Accessories Lab., 1961-63, tech. area mgr. Aero Propulsion Lab., 1964-67; prin. Fred W. Forbes, Architect, Xenia, Ohio, 1966-68; br. chief U.S. Air Force Aero Propulsion Lab., Wright Patterson AFB, Ohio, 1967-72, pres. Forbes and Huie, Xenia, 1968-73; pres. Forbes, Huie & Assos., Inc., Xenia, 1973-76; pres. Fred W. Forbes & Assos., Inc., Xenia, 1976—; instr. U. Dayton, 1963-64. Past pres. Xenia Area Living Arts Council. Recipient Exceptional Civilian Service award U.S. Air Force, 1966; Archtl. Award of Excellence for Moraine Civic Center, Masonry Inst., 1976, Archtl. Award of Merit for Xenia br. of 3d Nat. Bank, 1980; Dayton City Beautiful award for Martin Electric Co., 1977. Fellow Brit. Interplanetary Soc.; mem. Greene County Profl. Engrs. Soc. (past pres.), Am. Astron. Soc. (past nat. dir.), AIA, Ohio Soc. Profl. Engrs. (Young Engrs. award 1970), Nat. Soc. Profl. Engrs. (top 5 Outstanding Young Engr. award 1972), Xenia Area C. of C. (dir., past v.p. treas. sec.), Theta Chi. Republican. Methodist. Contbr. 24 articles to profl. jours.; patentee in field. Home: 465 Lamplighter Pl Xenia OH 45385 Office: 158 E Main St Xenia OH 45385

FORBES, MAGGIE LOUISE, dietitian; b. Jackson, Miss., July 24, 1940; d. William Aaron and Juanita Louise (McGee) F.; B.S. in Foods, Nutrition and Instl. Mgmt., Wayne State U., 1962. Staff dietitian Fordham Hosp., City of N.Y. Hosp., 1964-66, head dietitian, 1966; asst. chief dietitian, V.I. Govt.-Charles Harwood Meml. Hosp., St. Croix, 1966-68; theraputic dietician Annapolis Hosp., Wayne, Mich., 1969-71, adminstrv. dietitian, 1971-75, dir. dietetics, 1975—; cons., preceptor for dietetic asst. and dietetic technician programs at various colls.; cons. comml. foods program Milton Middle Sch. Mem. Am. Dietetic Assn., Am. Soc. Hosp. Food Service Adminstrs., Mich. Dietetic Assn. Roman Catholic. Office: 33155 Annapolis Rd Wayne MI 48184

FORBES, RAYMOND HORACE, educator, counselor; b. Omaha, Oct. 9, 1923; s. Conrad Raymond and Lillian (Bilder) F.; B.A., Pomona Coll., 1946; postgrad. U. Ala., 1946-47, Middlebury Coll., 1946, 47; M.A., U. Ill., 1948; postgrad. U. Minn., certificate Ph.D., 1956; certificate Bestätigung für Germanisten, Goethe Inst. (Munich, Germany), 1958; m. Ethel Asserina Nelson, Aug. 26, 1955; children—Jennifer, Jane, Heather, Cynthia, Pamela, Geoffrey and Catherine (twins). Instr. German, U. Ala., 1946-47; asst. prof. dept. German, W.Va. U., Morgantown, 1950-51, U. of South, Sewanee, Tenn., 1951-52; asst. prof. German and English, Jamestown (N.D.) Coll., 1952-53; instr. Pensacola (Fla.) Jr. Coll., 1956-62; asst. prof. German Ripon (Wis.) Coll., 1962-63; asst. prof. German St. Cloud (Minn.) State Coll., 1963-70, chmn. fgn. lang. dept., 1964-65; prin. Holy Innocents High Sch., St. Cloud, 1971-72; dir. Metaphys. Research Inst., 1972—; counselor Minn. Dept. Econ. Security, 1975—; painter in oils. Served with AAC, 1942-43. Fulbright fellow, 1958. Mem. MLA, Ind. Order Foresters, Internat. Platform Assn., Smithsonian Instn., Am. Metaphys. Assn., Internat. New Thought Alliance, Am. Legion, Delta Phi Alpha, Epsilon Delta Chi. Republican. Lutheran. Home: 801 34th Ave N Saint Cloud MN 56301 Office: PO Box 981 Saint Cloud MN 56301

FORD, ARTHUR GOLD, radio sta. exec.; b. St. Louis, July 23, 1922; s. Louis and Florence (Landsbaum) F.; B.J., U. Mo., 1947; m. Naomi Baskin, Dec. 25, 1943; children—Dennis J., Marc D., Bruce H. Reporter, Evansville (Ind.) Courier, 1947-48; owner food store, St. Louis, 1949-53; radio sta. sales mgr. Radio Sta. KSTL, St. Louis, 1953-68, v.p., gen. mgr., 1968—. Pres., Creve Coeur (Mo.) Twp. Republican Orgn., 1962-76. Served with U.S. Army, 1943-47. Decorated Order of St. George (Italy). Mem. St. Louis Radio Broadcasters Assn. (pres. 1981-82), Kappa Tau Alpha, Phi Eta Sigma, Phi Sigma Iota. Republican. Jewish. Home: 613 A Broadmoor Dr Chesterfield MO 63017 Office: 814 N 3d St Saint Louis MO 63102

FORD, BERNARD ROBERT, communications co. exec.; b. Bklyn., Sept. 25, 1943; s. Bernard and Agnes Mary (Snead) F.; B.S. (scholar), N.Y. U., 1965; M.B.A., U. Wis., 1972; m. Ruby Ann Smith, Apr. 14, 1974. Facilities analyst corporate planning Am. Airlines, N.Y.C., 1970; mktg. analyst Minn. Mining & Mfg. Co., St. Paul, 1971; ops. staff asst. ITT, N.Y.C., 1972-74, ops. staff project leader, 1974-75, ops. staff exec., 1975, asst. product line mgr. natural resources, 1977-78; dir. mkt. devel. O.M. Scott, Marysville, Ohio, 1978-79, dir. export and market services, 1979—; vis. prof. Black Execs. Exchange Program. Served to capt. USAF, 1965-70. Recipient Black Achievers award ITT, 1980. Mem. Am. Mktg. Assn., Kappa Phi Kappa. Democrat. Congregationalist. Home: 1114 Woodman Dr Worthington OH 43085 Office: 333 N Maple St Marysville OH 43040

FORD, DIANE LEE, accountant; b. Green Bay, Wis., Oct. 20, 1953; d. Robert Claire and Marlene Joyce (Von Holten) Dockry; B.A. in Bus. Adminstrn. cum laude (scholar), U. Wis., Green Bay, 1975; M.B.A., U. Wis., Oshkosh, 1981; m. Patrick Ford, Aug. 12, 1977. Corp. fin. accountant Wis. Public Service Corp., Green Bay, 1975—. Bd. dirs. Christian Outreach, Grace Luth. Ch., Green Bay, 1978—. Mem. Nat. Assn. Accountants (dir. membership acquisition No. Wis. chpt.), AAUW. Home: 2347 Libal St Green Bay WI 54301 Office: 700 N Adams St Green Bay WI 54305

FORD, GARY HOLLOWAY, mfg. co. exec.; b. Balt., May 15, 1945; s. Carroll Frederick and Virginia (Johnson) F.; B.S. in Chem. Engring., Pa. State U., 1967; postgrad. Wayne State U., 1968-70; M.B.A., Mich. State U., 1972; m. Adelaide Andrews, Sept. 16, 1967; children—Carolyn Ford, Joanna Ford. Supr. mfg. ops. Parke-Davis & Co., Detroit, 1967-69, mfg. rep., 1969-70, mgr. mfg. ops., 1970-73, product planning mgr., 1973-74, materials mgr., 1974-78; corp. materials mgmt. and systems mgr. Shedd's div. Beatrice Foods,

978-79; dir. materials mgmt. Cadillac Gage div. Ex-Cell-O Warren, Mich., 1979—. Mem. Am. Prodn. and Inventory l Soc., Advanced Mgmt. Club Detroit, Econ. Club Detroit. ublican. Episcopalian. Home: 844 Pilgrim Birmingham MI 48009 ice: 25760 Groesbeck Hwy Warren MI 48089

FORD, GARY ROY, ednl. adminstr.; b. Detroit, Dec. 27, 1940; s. Eugene R. and Edna E. (Matero) F.; married, 4 children. Ph.B. in Modern European History, U. Detroit, 1963; M.A. in Reading, Eastern Mich. U., Ypsilanti, 1968; Ph.D. in Ednl. Adminstrn., U. Mich., 1975; m. Patricia A. Abraham; children—Shawn, Tamara, Lisa, Christopher. Tchr., Livonia (Mich.) Pub. Schs., 1963-65; reading cons. Taylor (Mich.) Schs., 1965-75, dir. community edn., 1975—. Chmn., Taylor Library Commn. Mem. NEA, Mich. Edn. Assn., Mich., assn. supervision and curriculum devel., Nat. Community Edn. Assn., Phi Delta Kappa. Certified as tchr., Mich. Home: 8105 W Parkway St Detroit MI 48239 Office: 9551 Westlake Taylor MI 48180

FORD, JOHN BATTICE, III, import-export co. exec.; b. Detroit, July 3, 1924; s. John Battice and Katharine (Tanner) F.; B.S., Yale, 1949; m. Peggy Powers, July 12, 1980; 1 son, John Battice IV. Adminstrv. asst. Nat. Bank of Detroit, 1950-53; asst. treas. Huron Portland Cement Co., Detroit, 1953-58, treas., 1958-59; owner, pres. TRADCO/DETROIT, Inc., 1960-69; pres. H.M. Robins Co., 1961-67; pres. Gentrex, Inc., 1969—. Bd. dirs. U.S. Com. for Refugees, Leader Dogs, United Found., Detroit chpt. ARC, Meals for Millions/Freedom From Hunger Found.; pres. Detroit Grand Opera Assn. Mem. Founders Soc. Detroit Inst. Arts. Episcopalian. Clubs: Detroit, Country of Detroit; Grosse Pointe (Mich.); Yale (N.Y.C.); Anglers (Key Largo, Fla.); Bath and Tennis (Delray, Fla.). Home: 39 Waverly Ln Grosse Pointe Farms MI 48236 Office: Gentrex Inc 22725 Greater Mack Ave Saint Clair Shores MI 48080

FORD, JON ALLAN, psychologist; b. Iowa Falls, Iowa, July 17, 1943; s. Verner Allen and Edna Marie (Huse) F.; B.A. in Math., U. No. Iowa, 1966, M.A. in Psychology, 1968; doctoral candidate Ind. U.; m. Carolyn Kay Stewart; children—Jon, Sara, Christine. Tchr. math. and sci., Iowa, 1967-69; teaching asst. U. No. Iowa, 1969-70; psychol. intern Area Edn. Agy. 7, Cedar Falls, Iowa, 1970-71; psychologist Joint County Sch. Dist., Cedar Falls, 1971-72; asso. instr. Ind. U., 1972-73, psychotherapist univ. developmental tng. center, 1972-73; treatment supr. severe emotional disabilities program Area Edn. Agy. 7, Cedar Falls, 1973—; pvt. practice, 1972—; adj. asst. prof. U. No. Iowa, 1975; cons., workshop leader in field. Mem. Am., Iowa psychol. assns., Nat., Iowa edn. assns., Iowa Sch. Psychologists Assn., Internat. Neuropsychol. Soc., Contbr. articles to profl. publs. Home: 1805 Rainbow Dr Cedar Falls IA 50613 Office: 3712 Cedar Heights Dr Cedar Falls IA 50613

FORD, LEE ELLEN, scientist, educator, lawyer; b. Auburn, Ind., June 16, 1917; d. Arthur W. and Geneva (Muhn) Ford; B.A., Wittenberg Coll., 1947; M.S., U. Minn., 1949; Ph.D., Iowa State Coll., 1952; J.D., U. Notre Dame, 1972. CPA auditing, 1934-44; asso. prof. biology Gustavus Adolphus Coll., 1950-51, Anderson (Ind.) Coll., 1952-55; vis. prof. biology U. Alta. (Can.), Calgary, 1955-56; asso. prof. biology Pacific Luth. U., Parkland, Wash., 1956-62; prof. biology and cytogenetics Miss. State Coll. for Women, 1962-64; chief cytogeneticist Pacific N.W. Research Found., Seattle, 1964-65; dir. Canine Genetics Cons. Service, Parkland, 1963-69. Sponsor Companion Collies for the Adult, Jr. Blind, 1955-65; dir. Genetics Research Lab., Butler, Ind., 1955-75, cons. cytogenetics, 1969-75; legis. cons., 1970-79; dir. chromosome lab. Inst. Basic Research in Mental Retardation, S.I., 1968-69; exec. dir. Legis. Bur. U. Notre Dame Law Sch., also editor New Dimensions in Legislation, 1969; bd. dirs. Ind. Interreligious Com. on Human Equality; exec. asst. to Gov. Otis R. Bowen, Ind., 1973-75; dir. Ind. Commn. on Status Women, 1973-74; bd. dirs. Ind. Council Chs.; editor Ford Assos. Inc., pubs., 1972-78; mem. Pres.'s Adv. Council on Drug Abuse, 1976-77. Admitted to Ind. bar, 1972. Adult counselor Girl Scouts; bd. dirs. Ind. Task Force Women's Health; mem. exec. bd., bd. dirs. Ind.-Ky. Synod Lutheran Ch. Am. Mem. or ex-mem. AAUW, AAAS, Genetics Soc. Am., Am. Human Genetics Soc., Am. Genetic Assn., Am. Inst. Biol. Scis., Am. Soc. Zoologists, La., Miss., Ind., Iowa acads. sci., Bot. Soc. Am., Ecol. Soc. Am., Am. (dir.), Ind. (dir.), DeKalb County (dir.) bar assns., Humane Soc. U.S. (dir.), DeKalb County Humane Soc. (dir.), Ind. Fedn. Humane Socs. (dir. 1978—), Nat. Assn. Women Lawyers (dir.), Bus. and Profl. Women's Club, Nat. Assn. Republican Women (dir.), Women's Equity Action League (dir.), Assn. So. Biologists, Phi Kappa Phi. Club: Altrusa. Editor: Breeder's Jour., 1958-63; numerous vols. on dog genetics and breeding, guide dogs for the blind. Contbr. articles on cytogenetics, dog breeding and legal topics to profl. jours. and popular publs.; active contbr. Am. Kennel Club Gazette, others. Researcher in field. Home and Office: 824 E 7th St Auburn IN 46706

FORD, LUCILLE GARBER, economist, educator; b. Ashland, Ohio, Dec. 31, 1921; d. Ora Myers and Edna Lucille (Armstrong) Garber; A.A., Stephens Coll., 1942; B.S. in Commerce, Northwestern U., 1944, M.B.A., 1945; Ph.D., in Econs., Case Western Res. U., 1967; m. Laurence Wesley Ford, Sept. 1, 1946; children—Karen Elizabeth, JoAnn Christine. Instr., Allegheny Coll., Meadville, Pa., 1945-46, U. Ala., Tuscaloosa, 1946-47; personnel dir., asst. sec. A.L. Garber Co., Ashland, 1947-67; prof., chmn. dept. econs. Ashland Coll., 1970-75, dir. Gill Center for Econ. Edn., 1975—, v.p., dean Sch. Bus. Adminstrn. and Econs., 1980—; dir. Ohio Edison, Nat. City Corp., Shelby Mut. Ins. Co.; lectr. in field. Candidate for Lt. Gov. of Ohio, 1978; trustee Stephens Coll., 1977-80; elder Presbyn. Ch.; active ARC. Recipient Outstanding Alumni award Stephens Coll., 1977; Outstanding Prof. award Ashland Coll., 1971, 75. Mem. Am. Econs. Assn., Nat. Indsl. Research Assn., Am. Arbitration Assn. (profl. arbitrator), Omicron Delta Epsilon, Alpha Delta Kappa. Republican. Presbyterian. Author: University Economics—Guide for Education Majors, 1979; Economics: Learning and Instruction, 1981; contbr. articles to profl. jours. Home: 1717 Upland Dr Ashland OH 44805 Office: Ashland College Ashland OH 44805

FORD, WILLIAM CLARK, civil engr.; b. Gainesville, Fla., May 4, 1942; s. William Adam and Avis Opal (Clark) F.; B.S. in Civil Engring., U. Mo., Rolla, 1966, M.S. in Civil Engring., 1972; m. Sara Elizabeth Baker, June 11, 1966; children—Susan Elizabeth, Kristin Kimberly, Melissa Katherine. Environ. engr. Ill. Dept. Public Health, Springfield, 1966-67; engr. William A. Ford and Assos., Cons. Engrs., Kirkwood, Mo., 1971-72; chief engr. Public Drinking Water program Mo. Dept. Natural Resources, Jefferson City, 1973—, program dir., 1981—. Asst. coach Girl's Summer Softball, 1977, 78; trustee Bethel Ch., 1980—. Office of Water Programs EPA grantee, 1970-71; registered profl. engr., Mo. Served to capt., Med. Service Corps, U.S. Army, 1967-70. Recipient Army Commendation medal. Mem. Nat. Soc. Profl. Engrs., Mo. Soc. Profl. Engrs., Am. Water Works Assn. (chmn. Mo. sect. 1978), Fulton Jaycees (v.p. 1976), Chi Epsilon. Office: PO Box 1368 Jefferson City MO 65102

FORD, WILLIAM CLAY, automotive mfg. exec., profl. football team exec.; b. Detroit, Mar. 14, 1925; s. Edsel Bryant and Eleanor (Clay) F.; B.S., Yale, 1949; m. Martha Firestone, June 21, 1947; children—Martha, Sheila, William Clay, Elizabeth. Sales and advt. staff Ford Motor Co., 1949, indsl. relations, labor negotiations with U.A.W., 1949, quality control mgr. gas turbine engines Lincoln-Mercury div., Dearborn, Mich., 1951, mgr. spl. product operations, 1952, v.p., 1953, gen. mgr. Continental div., 1954, group v.p. Lincoln and Continental divs., 1955, v.p. product design, 1956-80, vice chmn. bd., 1980—, also chmn. exec. com., dir. Pres., owner Det. Lions Profl. Football Club; chmn. Edison Inst., Edsel B. Ford Inst. for Med. Research; trustee Eisenhower Med. Center, Thomas A. Edison Found.; sec.-treas. Henry Ford Hosp.; bd. dirs. Nat. Tennis Hall of Fame, Boys Clubs Am. Mem. Soc. Automotive Engrs. (asso.), Automobile Old Timers, Econ. Club Detroit (dir.), Phelps Assn., Psi Upsilon. Club: Masons (K.T.), (Detroit). Office: Ford Motor Co Dearborn MI 48121 also care Detroit Lions 1200 Featherstone Rd Box 4200 Pontiac MI 48057

FORD, WILLIAM DAVID, Congressman; b. Detroit, Aug. 6, 1927; s. Robert H. and Jean B. Ford; student Wayne State U.; B.S., J.D., U. Denver; hon. doctorate Central Mich. U., Eastern Mich. U., Mich. State U., No. Mich. U., Grand Valley State Coll., U. Detroit, Wayne State U., Westfield (Mass.) State Coll.; children—William D., Margaret Helene, John Phillip. Practice law, 1952—; justice of peace, Taylor Twp., Mich., 1955-57; city atty. Melvindale (Mich.), 1957-59; twp. atty. Taylor, 1957-64; Mich. senator, 1963-64; mem. 89th-97th congresses from 15th Mich. Dist., mem. edn. and labor com., chmn. post office and civil service com., 1981—; Nat. Democratic whip-at-large, 1975—; house rep. to White House Library Conf.; mem. Dem. Policy and Steering Com.; del. Mich. Constl. Conv., 1961-62. Served with USNR, 1944-46, USAF, 1950-57. Named Outstanding Young Man of Taylor, 1962. Mem. Downriver (pres. 1961-62), Mich., Am. bar assns., Taylor Jr. C. of C. (charter), Phi Delta Phi. Mem. United Ch. of Christ. Mason (33 deg., Shriner), Moose, Eagle, Rotarian. Home: Taylor MI 48180 Office: Cannon House Office Bldg Washington DC 20515

FORD, WILLIAM ELLIS, psychologist; b. Sewickley, Pa., July 6, 1945; s. Robert William and Theresa Louise (Weber) F.; B.S., U. Pitts., 1967; M.S., U. Mass., 1970, Ph.D., 1973; m. Maria Jane Fradel, July 29, 1967. Trainee, VA Hosp., Northampton, Mass., 1967-71; intern Norfolk (Nebr.) Regional Center, 1971-72, staff psychologist, 1973; dir. data systems div. Nebr. Dept. Public Instns., Lincoln, 1973-75; dir. Nebr. Div. on Alcoholism, Lincoln, 1975-79; dep. dir. Nebr. Dept. Public Instns., 1979—; clin. asso. prof. U. Nebr., Lincoln, 1976—; instr. med. psychology Nebr. Psychiat. Inst., Omaha, 1976—; chmn. adv. council Midwestern Area Alcohol Edn. and Tng. Program; cons. Nat. Inst. on Alcohol Abuse and Alcoholism. Mem. Am. Psychol. Assn., Nebr. Psychol. Assn., Nat. Assn. State Alcohol and Drug Abuse Dirs., Phi Beta Kappa, Phi Eta Sigma, Psi Chi. Home: 7544 South St Lincoln NE 68506 Office: Box 94728 Lincoln NE 68509

FOREMAN, JAMES LOUIS, judge; b. Metropolis, Ill., May 12, 1927; s. James C. and Anna Elizabeth (Henne) F.; B.S., U. Ill., 1950, J.D., 1952; m. Mabel Inez Dunn, June 16, 1948; children—Beth Foreman Banks, Rhonda Foreman Riepe, Nanette. Admitted to Ill. bar; individual practice law, Metropolis, Ill.; partner firm Chase and Foreman, Metropolis, until 1972; Ill. state's atty., Massac County; asst. atty. gen., State of Ill.; chief judge So. Dist. of Ill., East St. Louis, 1972—. Pres. Bd. of Edn., Metropolis. Served with USNR, 1945-46. Mem. Am. Bar Assn., Ill. State Bar Assn., Metropolis C. of C. (past pres.). Republican. Home: PO Box 866 Metropolis IL 62960 Office: PO Box 186 East St Louis IL 62202

FOREMAN, NORMAN RAY, energy co. exec.; b. Grand Island, Nebr., Aug. 7, 1937; s. John Charles and Caecelia (Bogus) F.; student St. Benedicts Coll., 1955-56; B.S. in Bus. Orgn. and Adminstrn., U. Nebr., 1964; m. Ursula Giessel, Nov. 24, 1961; children—John Charles, Douglas Allen. Prodn. supr. Delco-Remy div. Gen. Motors Corp., Anderson, Ind., 1964-65; with No. Natural Gas Co., 1965-75, zone mgr., Dubuque, Iowa, 1970-72, div. mgr., Council Bluffs, Iowa, 1972-75; mgr. supply and mktg. UPG, Inc., subs. No. Natural Gas, Omaha, 1975-76, v.p., gen. mgr. 1976—; sr. v.p. No. Propane Gas Co., 1980—; bd. dirs., treas. Dubuque Indsl. Bur., 1971-72. Bd. dirs. Dubuque United Fund, 1971-72, Council Bluffs (Iowa) United Fund, 1974-75. Served with USAF, 1956-60. Mem. Gas Processors Assn., Nat. Liquid Petroleum Gas Assn. (dir. 1981-82), Council Bluffs C. of C. (pres. 1975). Republican. Roman Catholic. Office: 2223 Dodge St Omaha NE 68102

FORIEST, JOSEPH LENARD, city ofcl.; b. New Orleans, Dec. 10, 1946; s. J.L. and Nat Lee Foriest; B.A. in World History and Philosophy, Chgo. State U., 1971; postgrad. in philosophy (grad. asst.), Oxford (Eng.) U., 1977; m. JoAnn Monier; 1 son, Jamil Josef. Program adv., off campus contact agt. Chgo. City Colls., 1968-70, fin. aid coordinator, dir. fed. work study program, 1975-76; counselor Chgo. State U., 1970-71, lectr., 1977—; loan officer Talman Fed. Savs. & Loan Assn., Chgo., 1972-74; accounts mgr. Alpha Marvis Enterprises, Chgo. and Atlanta, 1976-77; fin. processing officer Chgo. Dept. Planning, 1977-79, Chgo. Dept. Housing, 1980—. Mem. Am. Theosophical Soc., Ancient Order of Anacalypsis, Chgo. State U. Alumni Assn., Afro-Am. History Club, Newberry Library. Democrat. Home: 1404 W Harrison St 60607 Mailing Address: PO Box 3780 Mdse Mart Chicago IL 60654

FORLINI, FRANK JOHN, JR., cardiologist; b. Newark, Mar. 30, 1941; s. Frank and Rose Theresa (Parussini) F.; B.S. in Biology, Villanova (Pa.) U., 1963; M.D., George Washington U., 1967; m. Joanne Marie Horch, July 19, 1969; children—Anne Marie, Victoria, Frank, Anthony. Intern, Bklyn.-Cumberland Med. Center, Bklyn., 1967-68, resident, 1968-70; fellow Cardiology Inst. Med. Sci., Pacific Med. Center, San Francisco, 1970-72; sr. partner The Forlini Med. Specialty Clinic, Rock Island, Ill., 1974—; adj. prof. pharmacy Long Island U., Bklyn., 1970. Chmn. D.C. Young Republicans, 1965-66; exec. com. mem. Rep. Central Com., Washington, 1965-66. Served to maj. USAF, 1972-74. Nat. Inst. Heart Disease NIH-USPHS grantee, 1964-66. Fellow Am. Coll. Cardiology. Roman Catholic. Contbr. articles in field to profl. jours. Office: 2701 17th St Rock Island IL 61201

FORMANEK, LUELLA HELEN, govt. staff mem., civic worker; b. Mpls., Aug. 11, 1924; d. Peter Paul and Mary Ann (Stepanek) Formanek; student U. Minn., 1957. Model, N.Y.C., 1946-55; traffic expert Ill. Central R.R. Co., Mpls., 1957-64; govt. employee, clk. XIV Army Corps, Vets. Ins., U.S. Post Office. Vol. Semper Fidelis, 1943, USO, 1943, Community Chest, 1945-46; chmn. Merry-Go-Round Gold Ring Club for Aged, Greenwich, Conn., 1950-53; vol. Greenwich Hosp., 1952-54; mem. aux. St. Mary's Hosp., Mpls., 1963; active Nat. Council Cath. Women, 1950—, Women in Service to Edn. Orgn., 1974—, Kidney Found. Upper Midwest, 1978—, Epilepsy Found., 1978—, City of Hope, 1978—, Trust, 1975—, March of Dimes, 1974—, Am. Heart Assn., 1974—, Cath. Jr. League, 1964—; also numerous other health programs. Home: 4452 Portland Ave S Minneapolis MN 55407

FORNATTO, ELIO JOSEPH, physician; b. Turin, Italy, July 2, 1928; s. Mario G. and Julia (Stabio) F.; M.D., U. Turin, 1952; m. Mary Elizabeth Pearson, Dec. 17, 1960; children—Susan, Robert, Daniel. Came to U.S., 1953, naturalized, 1962. Intern Edgewater Hosp., Chicago, 1956-57; resident U. Illinois, 1953-56; practice medicine, specializing in otolaryngology, Elmhurst, Ill., 1958—; mem. staff Chgo. Eye, Ear, Nose and Throat Hosp., Meml. Hosp. DuPage County; clin. asst. prof. otolaryngology Stritch Sch. Medicine, Loyola U., 1967—; med. dir. Chgo. Eye, Ear, Nose and Throat Hosp., 1966-69; dir. laryngectomee program DuPage County chpt. Am. Cancer Soc., 1977—. Founding mem. Deafness Research Found. Diplomate Am. Bd. Otolaryngology. Mem. A.M.A., Ill. Med. Soc., Pan Am. Med. Assn., Am. Soc. Ophthalmologic and Otolaryngologic Allergy, Am. Acad. Otolaryngology and Head and Neck Surgery. Home: 200 W Jackson St Elmhurst IL 60126 Office: 172 Schiller St Elmhurst IL 60126

FORNELLI, JOE PETE, ret. civil engr.; b. Roseland, Kans., Dec. 8, 1915; s. Michele and Margherita (Marietta) F.; B.S. in Civil Engring., U. Kans., 1939; m. Mary Kathryn Watson, June 30, 1961; 1 son, Mike Amos. Insp. U.S. Engrs., St. Joseph, Mo., 1939-40; civil engr. Carter Oil Co., St. Elmo, Ill., 1939, 40; insp. Navy Dept., Parris Island, S.C., 1940-41; instrument man Consoer, Townsend & Quinlan, Parsons, Kans., 1941-42; party chief William S. Lozier, Inc., DeSoto, Kans., 1942-43; airways engr. CAA, 1943-45, 46-47; resident engr. Wilson Engrs., Salina, Kans., 1948; owner Fornelli Constrn. Co., Atwood, Kans., 1949-56; area supt. Girdler Co., Lawrence, Kans., 1953-54; civil engr. CAA, Kansas City, Mo., 1956-58, FAA, Kansas City, Mo. and Des Plaines, Ill., 1959-80. Served with AUS, 1945-46. Mem. ASCE, Am. Legion, Sigma Tau. Home: 16601 E 31st St Independence MO 64055

FORNEY, CRAIG BRUCE, fin. planning co. exec.; b. Sioux City, Iowa, Oct. 29, 1949; s. Donald W. and Betty L. (Johnson) F.; B.S., U. Nebr., 1972; m. Kathleen Chandler, Sept. 6, 1975; children—Marissa, Nichole. Registered rep. Pa. Securities Co., Omaha, 1972-73, Bell Funding Corp., Omaha, 1973-76; gen. agent Western Res. Life Ins., Omaha, 1976—, pres. Fin. Planning Corp. of Am., Omaha, 1975—; gen. agt. Old Line Life, 1979—; gen. partner Design, Ltd., investment club; regional dir. Tax Shelter Digest; registered rep. Cardell & Assos., Inc.; dir. The Paragon, Abaris Republic Corp.; instr. Coll. Fin. Planning. Served with USAF, 1969-75. Cert. fin. planner. Mem. Internat. Assn. Fin. PLanners, Internat. Platform Assn., Inst. Cert. Fin. Planners. Home and Office: 9218 Leavenworth St Omaha NE 68114

FORNSHELL, DAVE LEE, ednl. broadcasting exec.; b. Bluffton, July 9, 1937; s. Harold Christman and Mary Ann Elizabeth (Fox) F.; B.A., Ohio State U., 1959; m. Elizabeth Slagle Clinger, Nov. 11, 1978; 1 son, John David. Continuity dir. WTVN-TV, Columbus, Ohio, 1959-61; traffic dir., asst. program mgr. WOSU-TV, Columbus, 1961-69; ops. mgr. Md. Center for Pub. Broadcasting, Balt., 1969-70; exec. dir. Ohio Ednl. TV Network Commn., Columbus, 1970—; dir., mem. exec. com. Central Ednl. Network; exec. com. CEN Post-Secondary Edn. Council, Ohio Post-Secondary Telecommunications Council; pres. Ohio Radio Reading Services. Pres. Landings Residents Assn., 1973; active March of Dimes, 4-H. Served with USAF, 1961-62. Recipient award Dayton Fedn. Women's Clubs, 1974. Mem. N.G. Assn., Ohio State U. Alumni Assn., Nat. Acad. TV Arts and Scis. (2d v.p. Columbus 1968-69, gov. 1970—), Nat. Assn. TV Program Execs., Am. Assn. Higher Edn., Nat. Assn. Ednl. Broadcasters (chmn. state adminstrs. council), Health Scis. Communications Assn., Alpha Epsilon Rho, Alpha Delta Sigma, Sigma Delta Chi. Clubs: Univ., Kiwanis. Home: 240 Larrimer Ave Worthington OH 43085 Office: 2470 N Star Rd Columbus OH 43221

FORREST, GEORGE JOSEPH, fin. exec.; b. Detroit, Nov. 15, 1928; s. Charles H. and Lillian (Reiss) F.; B.S., U. Detroit, 1955; A.M.P., Harvard Bus. Sch., 1975; m. Kathryn Jean Dilworth, Aug. 13, 1960; children—George Joseph, Ann, Michael. Acct., Ralph Genter & Co., C.P.A.'s, Detroit, 1955-60; partner Barnowski, Hart & Forrest, C.P.A.'s, Berkley, Mich., 1960-64; controller for seven corps. with common ownership, Detroit, now Guardian Industries, 1964-68; sr. v.p. Sandy Corp., Southfield, Mich., 1968—, dir., 1971—; dir. Bill Sandy Orgn. Ltd.; mng. partner Communications Center. Bd. dirs. Villa Marie, Sr. Citizen Living Complex, Livonia, 1976—; com. mem., counselor Boy Scouts Am., Detroit, 1975—. Served with U.S. Army, 1951-53. C.P.A., Mich. Mem. Mich. Assn. C.P.A.'s, Am. Inst. C.P.A.'s, Nat. Assn. Accts. Republican. Roman Catholic. Clubs: Detroit Athletic, K.C., Elks. Home: 15351 Susanna Circle Livonia MI 48154 Office: 16025 Northland Dr Southfield MI 48075

FORREST, KAY FRANCES, communications and curriculum cons.; b. Balt., Apr. 5, 1934; d. Wilbur Coleman and Edna Earle (Johnson) F.; B.A., Goucher Coll., 1956; M.A., Northwestern U., 1979. Tchr., Glencoe (Ill.) Public Schs., 1963—; communications cons. Bell & Howell Corp., A.B. Dick Co., Internat. Minerals Corp., McDougal Littel Co.; editorial cons. Follet Publ. Co.; freelance writer Unfinished Furniture mag.; mem. Ill. Commn. on Status of Women, 1979. Mem. Nat. Council Social Studies, NEA, Am. Assn. Supervision and Curriculum Devel., Nat. Assn. Tchrs. English. Recipient Career Edn. award Ill. Dept. Edn./Ill. Commn. Status of Women, 1979. Home: 1700 F Northfield Sq Northfield IL 60093 Office: 620 Greenwood Ave Glencoe IL 60022

FORSLUND, ROBERT LEE, food mfg. co. exec.; b. Harcourt, Iowa, Apr. 9, 1938; s. Monrad William and Elsie Maye (Swanlund) F.; student Drake U., 1960; m. Mary Kay Wingert, June 2, 1962; children—Robert Lee, Kristen Kay. With George A. Hormel & Co., Austin, Minn., 1961—, mktg. mgr. internat. div., 1979—; dir. Stefanutti/Hormel, Santo Domingo, Dominican Republic, Vista Internat. Packaging, Kenosha, Wis. Served with U.S. Army, 1960-62. Republican. Presbyterian. Club: Austin Country. Home: 101 22d St NW Austin MN 55912 Office: 501 16th Ave NE Austin MN 55912

FORSMAN, SHIRLEY JEAN, nurse; b. Phila., Feb. 6, 1930; d. Hartley F. and Ellen T. (Carroll) Ness; A.A. in Nursing, Sacramento City Coll., 1966; B.S.N., Sacramento State Coll., 1971; M.A., Calif. State U., 1973; m. Willard John Forsman, June 18, 1949 (dec.); children—Daniel (dec.), John, Katie, Nancy. Staff nurse Kaiser Permanente Hosp., Sacramento, 1963-66; supervising head nurse psychiatry Eskaton Am. River Hosp., Carmichael, Calif., 1966-70, hosp. supr., 1970-71; dir. nursing edn. Golden Key Coll., Sacramento, 1971-74; dir. nursing services Douglas County Hosp., Alexandria, Minn., 1974-75; dir. public health Kandiyohi County Community Health Dept., Willmar, Minn., 1975-77; dir. nursing services Rice Meml. Hosp., Willmar, 1977-79; master staffing coordinator Roseville (Calif.) Community Hosp., 1980-81; instr. Am. River Coll., Sacramento, 1980-81; cons. Central Minn. Area Health Edn. Consortium, 1975—; mem. adv. com. to Lic. Practice Nurse Program, Minn.-Dakotas, 1974—; mem. Child Abuse Team, U. Minn. Continuing Edn. for R.N.s, 1978—; faculty/lectr. various schs., colls., instns., 1968—. HEW grantee, 1971. Mem. Am. Nurses Assn., Minn. Nurses Assn., Nat. Council Nursing Service Facilitators, Minn. State Council Nursing Service Adminstrs., Minn. Hosp. Assn. Area Nursing Service Adminstrs., AAUW, Am. Legion Aux. Clubs: Bus. and Profl. Women, Eagles Aux. Home: 1500 SE 10th St Willmar MN 56201

FORSYTHE, JAMES LEE, historian, univ. dean; b. Bransford, Tex., Dec. 18, 1934; s. Roy Theodore and Irma May (Smith) F.; B.S., N. Tex. State U., 1960, M.A., 1962; Ph.D. (fellow), U. N.Mex., 1971; m. Sherrill Kay Zartman, Aug. 10, 1956; children—James Lee, Garen David, Dana Sean. Transp. agt. Delta Air Lines, Dallas, 1952-62; asst.

prof. history Ft. Hays (Kans.) State Coll. (now Ft. Hays State U.), 1963-68, asso. prof. history, 1968-71, prof., 1971—, chmn. dept. history, 1975-81, dean of grad. sch., 1981—; mem. Kans. Hist. Records Adv. Bd., 1976—; mem. Kans. State Historic Sites Bd. of Rev., 1980—; dir. Kans. Oral History Project, 1969—. Treas., Ellis County Young Democrats, 1966-70; precinct committeeman, 1974—. Served with Air N.G., 1953-55; U.S. Army, 1955-57. Recipient Distinguished Alumni award Grapevine (Tex.) High Sch., 1970; Harry S. Truman Library Inst. Nat. and Internat. Affairs grantee, 1967, 72. Mem. Rocky Mountain Social Sci. Assn. (exec. council), Western Social Sci. Assn. (pres. 1976-77), AAUP (pres. Kans. 1972-73), Kans. State Hist. Soc. (dir. 1977—), Kans. Com. for Humanities (exec. com. 1975-81, chmn. 1981—), Agrl. History Assn., Orgn. Am. Historians, So., N.Mex., Kans. (v.p. 1980-81), Western hist. assns., Phi Alpha Theta, Pi Sigma Alpha, Phi Kappa Phi, Phi Delta Kappa. Baptist. Author: The First 75 Years: A History of Fort Hays State University, 1909-1977, 1977; contbr. articles in field to profl. jours. Home: 2927 Walnut St Hays KS 67601 Office: Grad Sch Fort Hays State U 600 Park St Hays KS 67601-4099

FORT, W. HOWARD, lawyer; b. Tuscumbia, Ala., July 18, 1915; student U. Kans.; B.S., Ohio State U., 1940; postgrad. U. Wash.; J.D., Ohio State U., 1946; m. Ruth Wilson; children—Gailmarie, William H. Admitted to Ohio bar, 1947; partner firm Schwab, Grosenbaugh, Fort & Seamon Co., L.P.A., Akron, Ohio, 1978—; dir. 1st Nat. Bank of Akron, Goodyear Tire and Rubber Co., Ohio Bell Telephone Co. Pres., Akron Community Service Center and Urban League, 1953-56; bd. dirs. Akron Child Guidance Center, 1961-63; chmn. bd. U. Akron, 1974-77; mem. exec. bd. Akron Regional Devel. Bd.; bd. dirs. Akron Gen. Med. Center; mem. exec. com. Goals for Greater Akron; mem. exec. bd. North Central Assn. Colls. and Schs.; bd. dirs. Great Trail Council Boy Scouts Am.; chmn. Summit County chpt. ARC, 1979—; bd. dirs. U. Akron Found.; chmn. Akron City Planning Commn., 1967, 70; mem. Summit County Children's Services Com. Recipient Silver Beaver award Boy Scouts Am., 1971; service award U. Akron Alumni Assn., 1977; Absalom Jones Service award, 1978; named Citizen Extraordinaire, Akron Urban League, 1978. Mem. Akron Bar Assn., Akron Barrister's Club, Am. Bar Assn., Am. Judicature Soc., Ohio Bar Assn., NAACP (life). Office: 40 E Mill St Akron OH 44308

FORTE, EUGENE ANDREW, co. exec.; b. Cin., July 21, 1949; s. Anthony and Mary Dolores (Sparks) F.; B.S., U. Cin., 1975, M.B.A., 1979; m. Phyllis Chandler, Dec. 11, 1976; children—Andrew Ray, Gina Marie. With P/E Devel. Co., Cin., 1968-74; dist. mgr. E. W. Buschman Co., Cin., 1974-79, sales mgr., 1979-80; pres. Forte Indsl. Equipment Systems, Cin., 1980—. Served with USMC, 1969-71. Mem. Assn. MBA Execs. Home: 1426 Hunter Rd Fairfield OH 45014 Office: 11499 Chester Rd Cincinnati OH 45246

FORTNER, LARRY LLOYD, ednl. adminstr.; b. Detroit, July 20, 1942; s. Larry Wesley and Mabel Laurine (Johnson) F.; B.A., Wayne State U., 1963, M.A. (fellow), 1964; edn. specialist Eastern Mich. U., 1975; postgrad. U. Mich., 1982; m. Suzanne Marie Krawec, June 4, 1976. Teaching fellow Wayne State U., 1963-64; sci. tchr. Redford Union Schs., 1964-72, Farmington (Mich.) Schs., 1972-76; asst. prin., Paw Paw, Mich., 1976-77; high sch. prin. St. Agatha High Sch., Redford, Mich., 1977—; community edn. intern Livonia (Mich.) Public Sch., 1975, dir. driver edn., 1976-77; mem. Cert. High Sch. Prins. Bd., 1979-82. Recipient Service award Mich. Assn. Secondary Prins., 1979. Mem. Cath. Assn. Secondary Adminstrs. (pres. 1980-82). Roman Catholic. Clubs: Rotary (Redford). Invented ring swing outfit for adults and children, 1964. Home: 28573 Newport St Farmington Hills MI 48018 Office: 25707 Pembroke St Redford MI 48240

FORTUNE, MICHAEL JOSEPH, educator; b. N.Y.C., Aug. 28, 1922; s. Sean and May (Vaughan) F.; B.S., U. Wis., Madison, 1949, Ph.D. (doctoral fellow), 1965; M.A., U. Minn., 1952; m. Genevieve Hintz, May 27, 1944; children—Michael, Patrick, Richard, Ronald, Susan, Sandra, Sharon, Laura. Tchr., Three Lakes, Wis., 1955, U. Wis., Stevens Point, 1956-66; chmn. dept. English, Mundelein Coll., Chgo., 1967-72, prof. English and religion, 1974—; chmn. dept. comparative lit. and fgn. langs. U. Wis., Stevens Point, 1972-74. Served with USAAF, 1943-46. Decorated Air medal; recipient Excellence in Teaching award U. Wis., Stevens Point, 1965. Mem. MLA. Author: The Dramaturgy of the Beaumont and Fletcher Canon, 1965; The Creative Philosopher: An Unpublished Letter of Albert Camus, 1966. Home: 1848 Balsam Rd Highland Park IL 60035 Office: 6363 Sheridan Rd Chicago IL 60660

FORTY, ROBERT JOHN, air conditioning and heating co. exec.; b. Chgo., May 5, 1940; s. Robert A. and Gwendolyn (Kretsinger) F.; B.S., Kans. State Coll., Emporia, 1965; m. Sandra Lea Leino, Aug. 21, 1965; children—Eric, Tara. West Central dist. mgr. Century Creations, Venice, Calif., 1969-72; sales mgr. Comfortlease, Inc., Glen Ellyn, Ill., 1972-74; pres. Calcorp Inc., North Aurora, Ill., 1974-76; owner, pres. Energy Services Air Conditioning and Heating Co., Naperville, Ill., 1976—, also dir. Adv. bd. Coll. of DuPage Air Conditioning and Heating Sch. Mem. Naperville C. of C., Refrigeration Service Engrs. Soc. DuPage County. Republican. Club: Kiwanis. Home: 1536 North Columbia St Naperville IL 60540 Office: 508 W Fifth Ave Naperville IL 60540

FOSDICK, LEE BEACH, chem. engr.; b. Cin., July 29, 1922; s. Cedric Earl and Isabella Greer (Morrow) F.; B.Chem. Engring., Ohio State U., 1948; S.M., Harvard U., 1955; m. Florence Moore Urmston, Sept. 18, 1948; children—Laura Lee Fosdick Murray, Howard Morrow. With Ohio Dept. Health, 1948-57, prin. indsl. hygiene engr., 1955-57; indsl. hygiene engr. Standard Oil Co. Calif., San Francisco, 1957-59; with Argonne (Ill.) Nat. Lab., 1959—, exec. asst. to lab. dir., 1971-80, staff exec. Office of Dir., 1980—. Served with AUS, 1942-46. Registered profl. engr., Ohio; cert. Am. Acad. Indsl. Hygiene. Fellow Am. Public Health Assn.; mem. Am. Indsl. Hygiene Assn. (pres. Chgo. sect. 1964-65, nat. chmn. tech. publs. 1963-69, nat. chmn. banquets 1966-67), Health Physics Soc. (chmn. comml. exhibits nat. conf. 1962), Air Pollution Control Assn., Am. Standards Assn., Sigma Xi, Tau Beta Pi, Delta Omega. Author papers in field. Home: 680 Grand Ave Glen Ellyn IL 60137 Office: 9700 S Cass Ave Argonne IL 60439

FOSHEIM, JON, justice S.D. Supreme Ct.; b. Howard, S.D., Jan. 25, 1923; s. Oscar A. and Margaret A.; student Gen. Beadle Coll., Madison, S.D., 1941-42; LL.B., U. S.D., 1946; m. Mary Lou Olson, Dec. 28, 1948; children—Patricia, Jon, Douglas, Peggy, Todd. Admitted to S.D. bar, 1946; practiced law, Huron, S.D., 1946-59; states atty. Beadle County (S.D.), 1951-55, dep. states atty., 1955-57; judge Circuit Ct., 1959-79, presiding judge, 1975-79; justice S.D. Supreme Ct., 1979—. Served with U.S. Army, 1942-43. Mem. Izaak Walton League, Am. Legion. Democrat. Roman Catholic. Office: Supreme Ct State Capitol Pierre SD 57501

FOSHER, MONTE EUGENE, agrl. distbg. co. exec.; b. Lusk, Wyo., Oct. 2, 1952; s. Raime Vern and Marian Jane F.; B.S., U. Wyo., 1971-76; m. Gail Annette Heckens, Feb. 15, 1975. With Fed. Land Bank of Omaha, 1976-77; sales mgr. Am. Colloid Co., Scottsbluff, Nebr., 1977-81, ops. supt., 1981—. Trustee, Eastside Ch. of Christ, Scottsbluff, also supt. Sunday Sch. Mem. Wyo. Grain Feed and Seed Dealers Assn. (dir. 1978—, pres. 1980-81). Republican. Club: Denver Feed and Grain. Office: Am Colloid Co 1702 E Overland St Scottsbluff NE 69361

FOSS, HOWARD SAMUEL, JR., def. mfg. co. exec.; b. Pitts., May 30, 1938; s. Howard Samuel and Lois Eurilda (Mutimer) F.; B.B.A., Thiel Coll., 1960; postgrad. Cleve. State U., 1977—; m. Marie Elizabeth Muskey, Sept. 24, 1976; children—Daryl Edward, Bradley Howard; stepchildren—Paul Joseph Werner, Mary Ellen Werner Brougher, Jean Marie Werner, Jo Ann Werner, Patricia Ann Werner. Div. indsl. engr. Automatic Sprinkler div. ATO, Inc., Cleve., 1969-71; mfg. supt. Phil Mar div. Thomas Industries, Euclid, Ohio, 1971-74; asst. plant mgr. Cleve. Steel Container Corp., 1974-75; plant mgr. Air Tech. Industries, Mentor, Ohio, 1975-77; mgr. ops. support and cost estimating Gould, Inc., Ocean Systems Div., Cleve., 1977—; instr. bus. adminstrn. Lakeland Community Coll. External program dir. North Olmsted chpt. Ohio Jaycees, 1973-74; packmaster Boy Scouts Am., 1972-76. Mem. Soc. Logistics Engrs., Am. Mgmt. Assn., Alpha Chi Rho. Republican. Lutheran. Club: Edgewater Yacht (Cleve.). Home: 7296 Button Rd Mentor OH 44060 Office: 18901 Euclid Ave Cleveland OH 44117

FOSS, KARL ROBERT, income tax auditor; b. Madison, Wis., Aug. 26, 1938; s. Robert Henry and Ethel Caroline (Huston) F.; student U. Wis., 1956-59, 62; B.S., Madison Bus. Coll., 1961. Auditor income tax Wis. Dept. Revenue, Madison, 1962—; owner, mgr. LIST, Middleton, Wis., 1968-76. Bd. dirs. Middleton Hist. Soc., 1976-81, v.p., 1980; legis. adv. Old Car Hobby, 1971-81. Co-recipient Spl. Interest Autos Appreciation award, 1971. Mem. Wis. Automobile Clubs in Assn. Inc. (co-founder 1971, pres. 1972-74, 77, 78, 80, v.p. 1975-76, 79), Oldsmobile Club Am. (nat. dir. 1973—, treas. 1981—), Accounting and Mgmt. Assn. (treas. 1981), Contemporary Hist. Vehicle Assn., Studebaker Drivers Club, Nash Car Club Am., Crosley Car Club, Antique Automobile Club Am., Model T Ford Am. Publisher: Suppliers List, 1968, Suppliers List Directory, 1969. Home: 1619 Middleton St Middleton WI 53562

FOSS, LUKAS, composer, condr., musician; b. Berlin, Germany, Aug. 15, 1922; s. Martin and Hilde (Schindler) F.; student Paris Lycee Pasteur, 1932-37; grad. Curtis Inst. Music, 1940; spl. study Yale U., 1940-41; pupil of Paul Hindemith, Julius Herford, Serge Koussevitzky, Fritz Reiner, Isabelle Vengerova, Randal Thompson, Rosario Scalero, Felix Wolfes; 3 hon. doctorates; m.; 2 children. Came to U.S., 1937, naturalized, 1942. Former prof. UCLA in charge orch. and advanced composition; former condr., music dir. Buffalo Philharmonic; faculty Harvard U., 1970-71; prin. condr., mus. dir. Bklyn. Philharmonia, from 1971; now music dir., condr. Milw. Symphony Orch.; composer, condr., pianist; orchestral compositions performed by many orchs.; best known works include (opera) The Jumping Frog; The Prairie; 3 string quartets; Song of Songs; Parable of Death, Griffelkin (opera in 3 acts); Psalms; Baroque Variations; Paradigm; Geod; Orpheus Time-Cycle, Percussion Concerto, Echoi; American Cantata; piano pieces, ballets; works commd. by Kulas Found., League of Composers, Nat. Endowment for Arts, N.Y. Arts Council, NBS opera on TV, others. Founder, Center Creative and Performing Arts, Buffalo U. Guggenheim fellow, 1945; recipient N.Y. Critic Circle citation for Prairie, 1944, Soc. for Pub. Am. Music award for String Quarter in G, 1948; Rome prize, 1950; Horblit award for Piano concerto No. 2, 1951, Naumberg Rec. award for Song of Songs, 1957; Creative Music grant Inst. Arts and Letters, 1957; N.Y. Music Critics Circle award for Time-Cycle orch. songs, 1961, for Echoi, 1963; Ditson award for condr. who has done the most for Am. music, 1973; N.Y.C. award for spl. contbn. to arts, 1976; ASCAP award for adventurous programming, 1979. Mem. Nat. Inst. Arts and Letters. Address: care Milwaukee Symphony Orch 929 N Water St Milwaukee WI 53208 also Bklyn Philharmonic 30 Lafayette Ave Brooklyn NY 11217

FOSS, RICHARD W., banker; b. Burlington, Vt., June 17, 1926; s. Cleo Justus and Vera (Fullington) F.; student U. Vt., 1946-48; LL.B., Boston U., 1951; postgrad. Northwestern U., 1957, 58-59, Advanced Mgmt. Program Harvard U., 1972; m. Marilyn Sias Campbell, Oct. 20, 1951; children—Deane C., Kimberly. Admitted to Vt. bar; asso. firm Lathan, Hill & Peisch, Burlington, 1951-56; with trust div. Howard Nat. Bank & Trust Co., Burlington, 1956-62; v.p. Marine Midland Bank-Western, 1962-67; sr. v.p. Marine Midland Bank Central, 1967-69; sr. v.p. Marine Midland Banks Inc. and Marine Midland Bank-N.Y., 1969-75, exec. v.p. parent co., 1975-80; sr. v.p. trust investment services div. Continental Ill. Nat. Bank and Trust Co., Chgo., 1980—; chmn. bd. Continental Ill. Internat. Adv. Corp., Geneva, 1981—. Bd. dirs. Charles A. Lindbergh Meml. Fund, N.Y.C. Served with USMC, 1944-46. Mem. Am. Bankers Assn., N.Y. Soc. Security Analysts, Fin. Analysts Fedn., Am., Vt. bar assns., Alpha Tau Omega. Club: Met.; Glenview. Office: 231 S LaSalle St Chicago IL 60693*

FOSSATI, CHARLES GLEN, inventor; b. Buenos Aires, Argentina, Mar. 6, 1926; s. Carlos Luis and Glenys Jane (Gould) F.; came to U.S., 1928; naturalized, 1946; B.A., U. Mich., 1949, M.A., 1952; m. Rosamonde Davis, June 11, 1949; children—Linda, Carlos, Lee, Catherine. Instr. in Romance langs. U. Mich., Ann Arbor, 1951-52; founder Service Tectonics, Inc., Adrian, Mich., 1962; founder, pres. Maskote Corp., Detroit, 1972. Served in USN, 1943-46. Patentee in indsl. processes, machinery, vacuum metalizing. Mem. Soc. Plastic Engrs., Cousteau Soc., Econ. Club Detroit. Clubs: Masons, Windsor Yacht, Grosse Pointe Sail, Great Lakes Cruising, Grosse Pointe Boat. Home: 39 Lakecrest Ln Grosse Pointe Farms MI 48236 Office: 19850 Harper Ave Harper Woods MI 48225

FOSTER, ADON MARVIN, concertmaster; b. Cortland, N.Y., Nov. 10, 1919; s. Leo J. and Edna M. (Wadsworth) F.; B.Mus., Eastman Sch. Music, Rochester, N.Y., 1947, M.Mus., 1948; m. Audrey Eileen Hands, Mar. 2, 1944 (dec. Apr. 1981); children—Deborah Ann, Diane Victoria. Head string dept. Western Ky. State Coll., Bowling Green, 1948-53; mem. faculty Miami U., Oxford, Ohio, 1953—; concertmaster Dayton (Ohio) Philharm. Orch., 1958-70, 72—. Served with AUS, 1942-45. Mem. Am. String Tchrs. Assn., Am. Fedn. Musicians. Episcopalian. Home: 201 Oakhill Dr Oxford OH 45046

FOSTER, ALAN G., educator; b. Girard, Ill., Mar. 31, 1933; s. Ralph and Mildred Mae (Hays) F.; B.S., Ill. State U., 1955; M.A., U. Ill., 1962; m. Winifred Drinhaus, Aug. 12, 1961; 1 dau., Kathryn Ann. Tchr., public schs., Plano, Ill., 1956-57, Hopedale, Ill., 1957-58; tchr. math., head dept. Community High Sch., Villa Park, Ill., 1958—. Mem. Nat. Council Tchrs. Math., Ill. Council Tchrs. Math. (pres. 1976-77), Am. Fedn. Tchrs., NEA, Sch. Sci. and Math. Assn. Lutheran. Author: Algebra I and Algebra II, 1978; Geometry, 1980. Office: 213 N Lombard Rd Addison IL 60101

FOSTER, BETTY LOUISE, educator; b. Lincoln, Nebr., Nov. 12, 1943; d. Burt Willis and Elizabeth Julia Hunt; B.S. in Elem. Edn., U. Nebr., 1965, postgrad. in Elem. Edn. Reading; postgrad. in Elem. Edn. and Reading, Kearney State Coll., endorsement in teaching reading; m. Gary A. Foster; children—Ann Louise, Geofrey Algot. Tchr. reading departmentalized grades 5-6 South Sioux City (Nebr.) Schs., 1967-69, supplemental reading tchr. Title I, 1970-71; supplemental reading tchr. Title I Grand Island (Nebr.) Schs., 1971—. Organizer, tchr. Head Start in South Sioux City Community Center and Chs., 1968-69; active Girl Scouts U.S.A., 1970—; v.p. Neighborhood Taskforce, Inc., 1980-82; pres. S. Locust/Barr Neighborhood Assn., 1980-81; mem. Mayor's Taskforce for Tornado Recovery, 1980-81. Mem. Nat., Nebr., Grand Island edn. assns., Internat. (sec. Central Council 1974—), Nebr., State reading assns., PTA of Children with Learning Disabilities, AAUW (pres. Grand Island br., br. pres. 1979-80, state v.p. 1981-82, state topic chmn. 1980-81), Nebr. Coalition of Women, Alpha Delta Kappa. Developed self correcting games. Certified in elementary edn., kindergarten-6th grade, Neb., Iowa; specialist in diagnosis and remediation of reading problems with learning disabilities problems, gifted children. Home: 1311 S Lincoln St Grand Island NE 68801 Office: 1314 W 7th St Grand Island NE 68801

FOSTER, DONNA FITZPATRICK, educator; b. Tuscola, Ill., Jan. 13, 1949; d. Vincent Norman and Marian Louise (Mumbower) Fitzpatrick; student U. Kans., 1968-70; B.A., Sangamon State U., 1971, M.A., 1974; m. William Schell Foster, Aug. 5, 1972; 1 child, Shannon. Tchr., Springfield (Ill.) S.E. High Sch., 1971-74; public info. officer Ill. Dept. Transp., Springfield, 1974-75; exec. asst. to dir. Ill. Dept. Conservation, Springfield, 1975-76; adminstrv. asst. to chmn. dept. surgery So. Ill. U. Sch. Medicine, Springfield, 1976-80; instr. communications Lincoln Land Community Coll., Springfield, part-time, 1976-77, instr. English, 1980—. Recipient Conservation Merit award Ill. Dept. Conservation, 1976. Mem. Nat. Council Tchrs. of English, Springfield Art Assn., Delta Gamma Alumnae Assn. Baptist. Home: 2910 Victoria Dr Springfield IL 62704 Office: Shepherd Rd Springfield IL 62707

FOSTER, EDWARD TERENCE, JR., bldg. design and constrn. co. exec.; b. Omaha, Mar. 11, 1941; s. Edward Terence and Mary Marcia (Hibbard) F.; B.S. in Civil Engring., M.I.T., 1963, M.S. in Nuclear Engring., 1964; Ph.D. in Engring., U. Calif., Berkeley, 1967; m. Mary Laura Ramsey, Aug. 28, 1965; children—Hilary, Sydney. Sr. research engr. Caltech/NASA Jet Propulsion Lab., Pasadena, Calif., 1967-68; v.p. HDR Systems, Omaha, 1970-75; pres. Systems Cons.'s, Omaha, 1975-76; v.p. Foster Western, Inc., Omaha, 1976—, also dir.; pres. Nicholas Industries, Omaha, 1977—, also dir.; dir. First West Side Bank; dir. Western Heritage Museum; Fulbright-Hays vis. prof., Skopje, Yugoslavia, 1971. Mem. Omaha Com., Council on Fgn. Relations, 1972—; mem. Omaha Symphony Council, 1974-80. Served as capt. AUS, 1968-70. Registered profl. engr., Nebr., Alaska, Calif., Colo., Fla., Iowa, N.Y., S.D.; Wyo. cert. Nat. Council Engring. Examiners. Mem. Nat. Soc. Profl. Engrs., Soc. Cert. Data Processors, ASCE, Omaha Engrs. Club, Assn. Computing Machinery, Hobie Catamaran Class Assn., Train Collectors Assn., Sigma Xi, Tau Beta Pi, Chi Epsilon. Episcopalian. Author: Civil Engineering in Alaska, 1973. Office: Nicholas Industries 4360 Nicholas St Omaha NE 68131

FOSTER, F BLANCHE, librarian; b. Centerville, Tenn., Jan. 6, 1919; d. George and F. Blanche (Nunnelly) Foster; B.S., Tenn. State U., 1940; B.L.S., Atlanta U., 1947; A.M. in Library Sci., U. Mich., 1953. Librarian, prof. Sam Houston Coll., Austin, Tex., 1947-50; librarian, lectr. Detroit Pub. Schs., 1951-70; lectr. U. Ibadan (Nigeria), 1971-73; librarian South Vigo High Sch., Terre Haute, Ind., 1974-80. Chmn., Martin Luther King Jr. Day, Terre Haute, 1975—. Mem. ALA, Am. Fedn. Tchrs., YWCA, NAACP. Author: Kenya, 1969; Dahomey, 1971; The West Indies, 1976; East Central Africa, 1981. Home: 2239 Spruce St Terre Haute IN 47807

FOSTER, GEORGE RAINEY, hydraulic engr.; b. Fayetteville, Tenn., July 4, 1943; s. Kenneth Grady and Odelle (Rainey) F.; B.S. in Agrl. Engring., U. Tenn., 1966; M.S., Purdue U., 1968, Ph.D., 1975; m. Melanie Joyce Pierce, July 12, 1969; children—Aaron Trent, Yvette Marie. Hydraulic engr. Agrl. Research Service, Dept. Agr., Lafayette, Ind., 1968—; cons. in field. Recipient Superior Service award Dept. Agr., 1981. Mem. Am. Soc. Agrl. Engrs., Soil Conservation Soc. Am., Am. Geophys. Union, Sigma Xi, Gamma Sigma Delta, Alpha Epsilon. Mem. Ch. of Christ. Author articles in field. Devel. computer programs to model soil erosion process. Home: 5133 W State Rd 26 West Lafayette IN 47906 Office: Nat Soil Erosion Lab Purdue U West Lafayette IN 47907

FOSTER, GERALD ALVIN, psychologist; b. Colby, Wis., Aug. 31, 1928; B.S., U. Wis., Stevens Point, 1955; M.A., U. Mich., 1960; Ed.D., Ariz. State U., 1963. Tchr. social studies, athletic coach Oconto (Wis.) Bd. Edn., 1955-59; asso. prof. psychology and edn. Ind. State U., Terre Haute, 1962-65; mgr. guidance, counseling and psychol. services Job Corps Center, Westinghouse Mgmt. Services, Inc., Edinburg, Ind., 1965-66; program dir. for adult basic edn. U.S. Office Edn., Nat. U. Extension Assn., Washington, 1966-68; asso. dir., div. edn. and tng. activities Avco Econ. Systems Corp., Washington, 1968-69; psychol. cons. to mgmt. Rohrer, Hibler & Reploge, Boston, 1969-70; psychologist, personnel dir. E.E.O. officer C.N. Flagg & Co., Inc., Meriden, Conn., 1970-76; pvt. practice psychology, East Hampton, Conn., 1976-78; pres., treas. U.P. Sales and Pan-Quest Inc., 1978—; chmn. transactional analysis seminar Am. Mgmt. Assn., N.Y.C., 1973. Served with U.S. Army, 1946-48, 50-51; Korea. Author, dir.: A Census and Industrial Survey of Oconto, Wis., 1958; Schizophrenia: A Progressive Teleologic Regression, 1961; An Analysis of the Effects of Counseling with Academically Talented Male University Freshmen, 1962; The Drop-Outs of a County School System, 1964; Negative Aspects of Standardized Testing, 1964; Evaluation of Adult Basic Education Teacher Training Program, 1968; Identification Program for Talented Nationals, 1970. Address: 1504 Garfield Ave Marquette MI 49855

FOSTER, JOHN WILLARD, optometrist; b. Black River Falls, Wis., Sept. 5, 1925; s. Leo W. and Martha (Dietsche) F.; student U. Minn., 1943-48; B.S., Pacific U., 1951, O.D., 1953; m. Dolores Schlaeger, Sept. 3, 1949; children—John, Jeffrey, Gregory, Gary, Mark. Practice optometry, Thorp, Wis., 1953—, Owen, Wis., 1957—, also Neillsville, Wis. Mem. Am. Optometric Found., Optometric Extension program. Mem. Am., Wis. optometric assns., Illuminating Engring. Soc. (asso.), Minn. Fedn. Engring. Socs., Blue Key, Omega Delta, Beta Sigma Kappa, K.C., Lion (pres., dir., chmn. visually handicapped children com.). Address: Box 31 Neillsville WI 54456

FOSTER, JOYCE ANN, tech. writer; b. Louisiana, Mo., Dec. 8, 1942; d. Ralph Pendleton and Sybil Bernice (Creech) Norton; cert.

... Internat. Corr. Schs., 1976; postgrad. U. Mo., 1976, ...on U., St. Louis, 1979; divorced; children—Tina Louise, ...Lee. Sec., Sverdrup Corp., Engrs., Architects, Planners, and ...rn. Mgmt., St. Louis, 1960-68, project asst., document ...rdinator 1971—; writer Delta Junction (Alaska) Midnight Sun, ...969-71; writer, research asst. Bibl. Research Center, Delta Junction, 1969-71. Mem. Nat. Assn. Female Execs., Am. Mgmt. Assn., Am. Legion Aux. (past pres., sec., v.p.). Republican. Methodist. Home: 12462 Horizon Village Dr Apt C St Louis MO 63138 Office: 801 N 11th Blvd St Louis MO 63101

FOSTER, KENNETH ROBERT, mfg. co. exec.; b. Hillsboro, Ohio, Sept. 11, 1929; s. M.R. and O.M. (Pendell) F.; B.S. in Bus. Adminstrn., Ohio State U., 1956; m. Christine Nelson, Nov. 15, 1980; children by previous marriage—Marcus R., Gretchen L. With Cummins Engine Co., 1957-64, McConway Torley Co., 1964-66, Teledyne Continental, 1966-70; with Internat. Harvester, Schaumburg, Ill., 1970—, v.p., dir. investments, 1980—. Served with USN, 1951-55. Mem. Soc. Automotive Engrs. (dir. minter, dir. maquimex). Republican. Club: Elgin Country. Office: 300 Paseo de la Reforma 17th Floor Mexico City DF 6 Mexico

FOSTER, L(EIGH) CURTIS, electronics mfg. co. exec.; b. Montreal, Que., Can., Aug. 24, 1925; came to U.S., 1943; s. John Stuart and Flora Marion (Curtis) F.; B.Sc. (scholar), McGill U., Montreal, 1950, Ph.D. (scholarship), 1956; m. Anne Elizabeth Stark, Jan. 23, 1948; children—Karen Anne, John Curtis. With Zenith Research Radio Corp., Menlo Park, Calif., 1956-72, exec. v.p., gen. mgr., 1956-72; v.p., gen. mgr. Applied Tech. Co., Sunnyvale, Calif., 1972-74; v.p. engring. Motorola Inc., Schaumburg, Ill., 1974—; dir. Tegal Corp.; cons. to industry. Recipient devel. award Bur. Ordnance, 1946. Mem. IEEE, Am. Phys. Soc. (sr.). Club: St. Francis Yacht. Patentee in field. Address: Motorola Inc 1303 E Algonquin Rd Schaumburg IL 60196

FOSTER, LAWRENCE WITCHER, mgmt. specialist; b. Oklahoma City, Feb. 20, 1944; s. Lawrence W. and Pauline N. (Hardin) F.; B.A., U. Okla., 1966; M.B.A., Harvard U., 1968; Ph.D., U. Tex., Austin, 1973; m. Helen Currie, Sept. 2, 1967; children—Jane Sydney, Andrew Lawrence. Partner Van Es Assos., Washington, 1971; asst. prof. mgmt. Mich. State U., East Lansing, 1973-75, asso. prof., 1975—; cons. to mgmt. Served with U.S. Army, 1968-70. Decorated Army Commendation medal, Bronze Star with oak leaf cluster; Recipient Tchr.-Scholar award Mich. State U., 1976; NSF grantee, 1975-76. Mem. Am. Psychol. Assn., Acad. Mgmt. (outstanding article award 1975), Am. Inst. Decision Scis. Presbyterian. Author: Organizations: Structure, Process, Behavior, 1976; Managing Organizations, 1981; contbr. articles to profl. jours. Home: 345 University Dr East Lansing MI 48823 Office: Grad Sch Bus Mich State U East Lansing MI 48824

FOSTER, LOWELL WALTER, elec. co. exec.; b. Mpls., Oct. 22, 1919; s. Walter James and Ferne Constance (Edmunds) F.; grad. USCG Acad., 1944; student U. Minn., 1950, Mpls. Inst. Arts, 1953; m. Marion Jane Bjorklund, Feb. 5, 1944; children—Michael Lowell, Janette Marie, John Edward. With Honeywell, Inc., Mpls., 1946-77, successively tool designer, lead tool designer, asst. supr. tool design, lead standardization engr., sr. standardization engr., prin. standardization engr., project adminstr., sr. project adminstr., dir. corporate standardization services, dir. corp. standardization, 1974-77, dir. industry standards, 1977; pres. Lowell W. Foster Assos., Inc., 1977—; adviser drafting curriculum Mpls. Pub. Schs., 1973—; engring. cons.; tech. adviser Ferris State Coll., Big Rapids, Mich., 1970—. Active Viking council Boy Scouts Am., 1956-59, 73-77; v.p. John Ericsson Sch. P.T.A., 1971—. Bd. dirs. Am. Nat. Standards Inst. Served with USCG, 1941-46; PTO. Registered profl. engr. Fellow Standards Engrs. Soc. (Leo B. Moore award 1973, Distinguished Service award Minn. sect. 1970); mem. Internat. Standards Orgn., Soc. Mfg. Engrs., Air Conditioning and Refrigeration Inst., Soc. for Advancement Mgmt., Honeywell Engrs. Club (past pres.), Am. Legion, Author 19 books, numerous articles. Home: 3120 E 45th St Minneapolis MN 55406 Office: Lowell W Foster Assos Inc Minneapolis MN 55406

FOSTER, RICHARD JOHN, photographer; b. London, July 7, 1948; came to U.S., 1950, naturalized, 1980; s. Frederick Edward Richard and Patricia Marguerite Monica (Greenwood) F.; student Brown U., 1966-67, New Coll., 1967-69; m. Deborah Jean McMasters, Sept. 14, 1974. Disc jockey Sta. WBRU-AM-FM, Providence, 1966-67; with Sta. WYND, Sarasota, Fla., 1968; computer programming systems analyst Nat. Bus. Lists, Chgo., 1969-71; asst. photographer Alfa Studios, Chgo., 1971-73; asso. photographer Shigeta Wright, Chgo., 1973-74; head photographer Jack O'Grady Studios, Chgo., 1974-75; pres. Richard Foster Photography, Ltd., Chgo., 1975—; exhibited Chgo., 1981, Focus Galleries, San Francisco, 1981. Active NW Community Orgn., 1972-75. Recipient numerous arts and advt. awards for photographs, art direction and creativity. Mem. Christian Ch. Home: 1479 Tower Rd Winnetka IL Office: 501 N Rush St Chicago IL 60611

FOSTER, SARA ANN ZINK, social worker, educator; b. Greencastle, Ind., Feb. 19, 1927; d. Harold and Anne (Kemp) Zink; student DePauw U., 1944-46; B.A., U. N.Mex., 1948; postgrad. Cambridge (Eng.) U., 1948-49; M.A.S.A., Ohio State U., 1952; postgrad. U. Wis., 1972-74; m. Charles Foster; 1 dau., Anne Claire; m. 2d, John Ferguson, May 20, 1974. Research analyst High Commn. for Germany, 1950-51; psychiat. social worker Ohio Div. Mental Hygiene, 1952-53, research analyst, 1954-55; caseworker, researcher Northside Day Nursery, also casework researcher Westside Day Nursery, Columbus, Ohio, 1955-56; caseworker Franklin County Children's Services, Columbus, 1956-63, supr., 1959-63; instr. Ohio Wesleyan U., 1963-68; asst. prof. social policy Coll. Social Work, Ohio State U., 1963—. NIMH fellow, 1972-74. Mem. Nat. Assn. Social Workers (del. state bd. 1976-77), Council Social Work Edn. (ho. dels. 1976-79), Ohio Social Service Educators, AAUP, Ohio Women Inc. (dir.). Democrat. Methodist. Author numerous articles on women's issues in social work practice. Home: 5812 Olentangy Blvd Worthington OH 43085 Office: 200 F Stillman Hall 1947 N College Rd Columbus OH 43210

FOSU, AUGUSTIN KWASI, economist, educator; b. Ghana, Aug. 3, 1951; s. Kofi and Akua (Donkor) Ayirebi; B.A. cum laude, Lawrence U., 1973; M.A. (fellow), Northwestern U., 1975, Ph.D., 1979. Instr., asst. prof. econs. Kalamazoo Coll., 1977-79; asst. prof. econs. Oakland U., Rochester, Mich., 1979—. Oakland U. summer fellow, 1980. Mem. Econ. Soc. Mich., AAUP, Am. Econs. Assn., Phi Beta Kappa. Editor: Pan Africanist, 1976-77. Office: Sch Econs and Mgmt Oakland U Rochester MI 48063

FOUDREE, CHARLES M., electronics co. exec.; b. Macon County, Mo., June 29, 1944; s. L. Winifred and Lois H. (Malone) F.; B.S. in Acctg., N.E. Mo. State U., Kirksville, 1966; m. Colleen Patton, Aug. 9, 1964; children—Mark, Melanie. Accountant, Peat, Marwick, Mitchell, Kansas City, Mo., 1966-72; v.p. fin., treas., sec. dir. SAB Harmon Industries, Inc., Grain Valley, Mo., 1972—. Bd. dirs., v.p. Independence YMCA, 1979—, chmn. bd., 1981-82; bd. dirs. Greater Kansas City YMCA; mem. Independence Tourism Adv. Bd.; senator Jaycees Internat., 1976; C.P.A., Mo., Kans. Mem. Nat. Assn. Accts., Am. Inst. C.P.A.'s, Mo. Soc. C.P.A.'s, Mo. Jr. C. of C. (dist. dir. 1974-75), Independence Jr. C. of C. (pres. 1973-74, dir. 1980—), Independence C. of C. (dir. 1980-82). Methodist. Club: Rotary (Independence). Home: 16309 E 38th St Terr Independence MO 64055 Office: SAB Harmon Industries Inc Grain Valley MO 64029

FOUFAS, PLATO CHRIS, lawyer, real estate developer, investor; b. Chgo., Sept. 24, 1932; s. Chris and Urania F.; B.S., Northwestern U., 1954, J.D., 1960; m. Teddy Mouzakeotis, Sept. 10, 1965; children—Christopher, Timothy. Admitted to Ill. bar, 1960; owner, operator Plato Foufas & Co., Chgo., 1960—, Plato Foufas Investments, Inc., Chgo., 1975—, The Bayshore Co., Chgo., 1973—, also pres., chmn. bd.; developer 120 Madison Bldg., 1963, Plaza del Lago, Westerfield Sq., 1500 Sheridan Rd., 1625 Sheridan Rd., 1965-69. Trustee, treas. Roycemore Sch., Evanston, Ill., 1979-81. Served to lt. USAF, 1957-58. Mem. Chgo. Bar Assn., Chgo. Realty Bd., Beta Theta Pi, Delta Sigma Rho. Clubs: Tavern, Saddle and Cycle (Chgo.). Office: 1 E Wacker Dr Chicago IL 60601

FOULKE, RICHARD BRADLEY, banker; b. Wayne County, Ind., May 18, 1935; s. Paul Raymond and Dorthey (Thomas) F.; grad. Ind. Bus. Coll., 1964; m. Barbara Ann Harter, Dec. 26, 1954; children—David Bradley, Andrea Lynn. Office mgr. Henry County Farm Bur., 1960, Ramsey Auto Sales, 1965; with 2d Nat. Bank, Richmond, Ind., 1966-81, automated service officer, 1974-79, purchasing officer, 1979-81; auditor Citizens State Bank, New Castle, Ind., 1981—. Served with USAF, 1954-57. Mem. Assn. for Systems Mgmt., Purchasing Mgmt. Assn., Bank Adminstrn. Inst. Methodist. Club: Toastmasters. Home: PO Box 226 Hagerstown IN 47346

FOUNTAIN, RONALD GLENN, corp. exec.; b. Mason City, Wash., Feb. 12, 1939; s. Aldine Shirah and Ella Maude (Fordham) F.; B.S., Valdosta State Coll., 1963; student Ga. Southwestern Coll., 1957-59; m. Joan Hightower, Aug. 22, 1968; children—John Hightower, Dana Leigh. With Citizens and So. Nat. Bank, Valdosta, Atlanta, 1963-68; v.p. Barnett Banks of Fla., Pensacola, from 1968; v.p. 1st Western Bank, Birmingham, 1970-73; v.p. Central Bancshares of the South, Birmingham, 1973-74; treas. White Consol. Industries, Inc., Cleve., 1974—. Mem. Nat. Investor Relations Inst., Fin. Execs. Inst. Club: Cleve. Athletic. Home: 20933 Lake Rd Rocky River OH 44116 Office: 11770 Berea Rd Cleveland OH 44111

FOUST, MARGARET JANE, dietitian; b. Youngstown, Ohio, July 28, 1922; d. Lester L. and Elizabeth F.; B.S., Kent State U., 1953. Intern, Harper Hosp., Detroit, 1953-54; clin. dietitian Cleve. Clinic Hosp., 1954-58, asst. dir. dietetics, 1959-63, dir. dietetics, 1964-72; dir. dietetics St. Vincent Hosp. and Med. Center, Gladieux Food Mgmt., Toledo, 1972-75; dir. dietetics Youngstown Hosp. Assn., South Unit, 1975-78, dir. dietetics Service Direction, Inc., 1978-79; dir. dietetics Ashtabula County Nursing Home, Kingsville, Ohio, 1979; dir. Ashtabula Gen. Hosp., 1979—. Mem. Am. Dietetic Assn., Am. Hosp. Assn. of Food Service Adminstrs., North Eastern Assn. Hosp. Food Service Adminstrs., Ohio Dietetic Assn. (chmn.), Mahoning Valley Dietetic Assn. (dir.), Cleve. Dietetic Assn. (past pres.). Methodist. Contbr. chpt. to Gastroenterology, 1970; contbr. articles to profl. jours. Home: 1011 Carriage Hill Ashtabula OH 44004 Office: Ashtabula Gen Hosp Ashtabula OH 44004

FOUTS, FRANK RICHARD, farmer; b. Oak Park, Ill., June 25, 1947; s. Willard Lincoln and Helen Florence (Koerper) F.; B.S., No. Ill. U., 1969; m. Martha Jean Beetz, July 6, 1968; children—Garvin Keith, Matthew Jason, Benjamin Cody. Staff, Am. Home Foods Co., Des Plaines, Ill., 1969; field rep. Fouts & Co., Downers Grove, Ill., 1971-72; farm employee, Mendota, Ill., 1972-74, owner/operator, 1975—; investment cons., 1971—; cons. in field. Chmn., LaSalle County (Ill.) Christian Rural Overseas Program (CROP), 1974-77, walk chmn., 1978. Served with USAF, 1970-71. Mem. Profl. Farmers Am., Am. Farm Bur. Methodist. Home and Office: 4019 E 050 Rd Route 2 Mendota IL 61342

FOUTS, KEITH EDWIN, ret. graphic arts co. exec.; b. Ellisville, Ill., Jan. 28, 1920; s. Arthur Lee and Eva Rae F.; student Ind. U., 1946-47, LeTourneau Tech. Inst., 1949-50, U. Ill., Urbana, 1954-55, U. Mich., 1966, Rochester Inst. Tech., 1968; m. Carol Le Tourneau, Aug. 24, 1941; children—Ronald Keith, Carolyn Jeanne, Nancy Lee. Repairman, Peoria Typewriter Co. (Ill.), 1935-36; apprentice toolmaker LeTourneau Co., Peoria, 1936, lithographer apprentice, 1937; lithographer Ins. Research and Rev. Service, Indpls., 1939, 41; freelance lithographer, Indpls., 1946-48; mgr. printing plant Longview, Tex., 1949-51; mgr. offset printing Univ. Press, U. Ill., Urbana, 1951-59; lithog. printing supply, equipment sales Roberts & Porter Co., Chgo., 1959-77, sales mgr., Des Plaines, Ill., 1977-80; lectr. in field. Served with USAAF, 1942-45. Mem. Illiana Printing Craftsman's Club. Republican. Home: 5110 N Sheridan Rd Peoria IL 61614

FOWLER, DONN NORMAN, dentist; b. Denver, June 7, 1922; s. Roy Eugene and Vera Louise (Alderson) F.; B.S., Northwestern U., 1945, D.D.S., 1953; m. Charlotte Jean Goff, Mar. 18, 1944; children—Donna Jean (Mrs. Donald J. McLoughlin), Linda (Mrs. Malcolm Cardy), Charles R., Peter N., Paul R. Gen. practice dentistry, Glenview, Ill., 1953—; instr. Coll. Dentistry, Northwestern U., Chgo., 1953-55. Trustee, Kendall Coll., Evanston, Ill. Served to lt. (j.g.) USNR, 1943-46; PTO. Mem. Pierre Fauchard Acad., Acad. Gen. Dentistry, Am. Dental Assn., Chgo. Dental Soc., North Suburban Acad. Dental Research (past pres.), Glenview C. of C., Pi Kappa Alpha. Methodist (lay del. to ann. conf.). Kiwanian. Home: 1548 Maple Ave Northbrook IL 60062 Office: 1761 River Dr Glenview IL 60025

FOWLER, JACK EDWARD, counselor; b. Columbus, Ind., Jan. 5, 1947; s. Lawrence Alfred and Norma Jean (Prall) F.; B.S., Purdue U., 1971, M.S., 1973; postgrad. Ind. State U., 1975—; m. Anna Mae Rains, June 6, 1970; children—Elizabeth Anne, Eric Wesley. Dir. Clark Residence Hall, Vincennes (Ind.) U., 1973-74, dir. housing, dir. Clark Hall, 1974-77, dir. Clark Residence Hall, 1977-78; counselor youth program, adult basic edn., 1978-79; command adminstrv. officer U.S. Army N.G., Terre Haute, Ind., 1980—. Served to capt. Army N.G., 1966—. Alumni scholar Purdue Alumni Assn., 1965; Ind. State U. grad. fellow, 1978, 79. Mem. Am. Personnel and Guidance Assn., Am. Coll. Personnel Assn., Assn. Coll. and Univ. Housing Officers (state rep. 1976-77), Assn. Supervision and Curriculum Devel., N.G. Assn. U.S., N.G. Assn. Ind., Assn. Purdue U. Counseling and Guidance Students, 38th Supply and Transport Bn. Officers Assn., Phi Delta Kappa. Democrat. Methodist. Home: Rural Route 2 Box 268 Vincennes IN 47591 Office: HQ 38th Supply and Transport Bn 3614 Maple Ave Terre Haute IN 47804

FOWLER, JAMES DANIEL, JR., financial co. exec.; b. Washington, Apr. 24, 1944; s. James Daniel and Romay (Lucas) F.; student Howard U., 1962-63; B.S., U.S. Mil. Acad., 1967; M.B.A., Rochester Inst. Tech., 1975; m. Linda Marie Raiford, May 25, 1968; children—Kimberly, Scott. With Xerox Corp., Rochester, N.Y., 1971-75, mgr. personnel adminstrn., 1974-75; sr. cons. D.P. Parker & Assos., Inc., Wellesley, Mass., 1975-76; mgr. staffing ITT World Hdqrs., N.Y.C., 1976-78; v.p., dir. adminstrn. ITT Aetna, Englewood, Colo., 1978, ITT Consumer Fin. Corp., Mpls., 1978—. Trustee, nominating com. U.S. Mil. Acad. Served to capt. U.S. Army, 1967-71. Decorated Bronze Star (2), Army Commendation medal with 2 oak leaf clusters; recipient Black Achiever award ITT, 1979. Mem. Am. Soc. Personnel Adminstrn., Twin Cities Personnel Assn., Assn. M.B.A. Execs., Am. Mgmt. Assn., Nat. Consumer Fin. Assn. Office: 300 S County Rd 18 Suite 700 Minneapolis MN 55426

FOWLER, JOSEPH DAVID, mfrs. rep.; b. Valley Falls, S.C., June 15, 1920; s. Boyce Lee and Queen Victoria F.; B.S. in Agr., Clemson U., 1942; children—Joseph David, Catherine Alice, Susan Annette. Various sales and sales mgmt. positions Ralston Purina Co., 1946-58, Stickell's, 1958-61, Hales and Hunter, 1961-63; mfrs. rep. Del and Pro Chem. Spltys., 1967—, Republic Powdered Metals, 1977-79; ind. rep. J A J Assos., mfrs. rep., Iowa City, 1963—. Served to capt. Signal Corps, 1942-46. Mem. Iowa Assn. Sch. Bds., Iowa Assn. Pupil Transp., Animal Protection League. Republican. Lutheran. Clubs: Masons, Shriners. Office: J A J Assos 504 Kenwood Dr Iowa City IA 52240

FOWLER, LUCY BARR (MRS. CHARLES WORTHINGTON FOWLER II), occupational therapist; b. Allentown, Pa., Feb. 19, 1932; d. William Bryce and Lucy Agnes (Chaundy) Barr; B.S. in Phys. Edn., Pa. State U., 1953; certificate occupational therapy U. Pa., 1956; m. Charles Worthington Fowler II, July 21, 1956; children—Charles Worthington III, Ellen Bryce, Timothy Neville. Staff occupational therapist, recreation dir. Palo Verde Psychiat. Hosp., Tucson, 1967-68; staff occupational therapist Nebr. Psychiat. Inst.-U. Nebr. Med. Center, Omaha, 1970-72; dir. occupational therapy Island of Hope Alcoholic Rehab. and Research Center, Omaha, 1973-76, Douglas County (Nebr.) Community Mental Health Center, Omaha, 1977-80, Jenny Edmundson Meml. Hosp., Council Bluffs, Iowa, 1980—; mental retardation and nursing home cons. Costume chmn., designer Omaha Ballet Soc., 1971-75; costumer Creighton U. Dance Co., 1975-77; bd. dirs. Voices of Omaha, Nebr. Choral Arts Soc., Omaha Symphonic Chorus, Omaha Assistance League (charter mem.). Certified profl. alcoholism counselor, Nebr. Mem. Am., Nebr. (treas., finance chmn. 1972-74, editor newsletter 1978-80) occupational therapy assns., World Fedn. Occupational Therapists, Nat. Assn. Alcoholism Counselors, Nebr. Assn. Alcoholism Counselors, Handweavers Guild Am., Omaha Spinners and Weavers Guild, DAR, St. Andrews Scottish Soc., Audubon Soc. (rec. sec.), Pa. State U. Alumni of Nebr. (dir.), Chi Omega (alumnae v.p. 1973-74). Republican. Episcopalian. Clubs: Regency Lake and Tennis (Omaha); Gavin's Point Yacht (Yankton, S.D.). Home: 1329 S 93d St Omaha NE 68124 Office: 933 E Pierce St Council Bluffs IA 51501

FOWLER, MARILYN HAISLUP, human resources devel. exec.; b. Indpls., Oct. 28, 1934; d. Emmett Rex and Beatrice Frances (Berry) Haislup; A.A., William Woods Coll., 1951; B.A., U. Mo., 1953, M.P.A., 1975; m. Lee Montgomery, Sept. 5 1954 (div.); children—Lee Montgomery, Thomas Scott, Christopher Brosing. Dir. community devel. and edn. Kansas City (Mo.) Urban League Family Planning Project, 1972-74; research asst. Sch. Adminstrn., U. Mo., Kansas City, 1974-75; dir. Family Planning Tng., Region VII, Kansas City, 1975-77, dir., 1977—; pres. Devel. Systems, Inc., Kansas City, 1979—; instr. Avila Coll., 1981. Chmn. nat. bd. info. and edn. com. Planned Parenthood, Fedn. Am., 1973-75; chmn. Kansas City Metro. Commn. on Status of Women, 1979-81. Mem. Women in Mgmt., Nat. Family Planning and Reproductive Health Assn., Am. Public Health Assn., Am. Soc. for Public Adminstrn., Nat. Women's Health Network, Internat. Relations Council. Democrat. Episcopalian. Office: 3706 Broadway Suite 301 Kansas City MO 64111

FOWLER, STEVE, state legislator; b. Lincoln, Nebr., Aug. 8, 1950; student U. Nebr.; m. Vickie Horton, Sept. 6, 1980. Mem. Nebr. Legislature, 1972—, chmn. Rules com., 1979-80, Neb. Retirement Systems com., 1980. Mem. Nat. Conf. State Legislatures (energy policy com. arts task force). Address: 1044 H St Lincoln NE 68508*

FOX, ALAN HUGO, woodwind instruments mfr.; b. Chgo., Apr. 1, 1934; s. Hugo E. and Mary M. (Richter) F.; B.S. in Chem. Engring., Purdue U., 1955; m. Pamela Michue, June 13, 1964; 1 dau., Karen Ann. Sales coordinator Procon, Inc., Des Plaines, Ill., 1957-60; v.p., gen. mgr. Fox Products Corp., designer profl. bassoons and contrabassoons, South Whitley, Ind., 1960-69, pres., 1970—. Served to 1st lt. AUS, 1955-57. Mem. Internat. Double Reed Soc. (co-founder). Club: Wawasee Sailing (commodore 1972) (Lake Wawasee, Ind.). Home: Rural Route 1 South Whitley IN 46787 Office: Fox Products Corp South Whitley IN 46787

FOX, CHARLES D'ARCY, investment co. exec.; b. St. Louis, July 29, 1936; s. Charles Smith and Helen (D'Arcy) F.; student Brown U., 1954-59; m. Juanita Eden, Dec. 20, 1975; children—Amber, Carmen, Amanda, Samuel. With A.G. Edward & Sons, Inc., St. Louis, 1960—, mgr. Western region bond dept., 1962-65, research asso., 1965-66, corp. v.p., asst. sec., dir. tng. and registration, 1966—. Pres., fin. dir. Adult Edn. Council of Greater St. Louis, 1975—. Served with U.S. Army, 1959-60. Mem. Am. Soc. Training and Devel., Internat. Assn. Fin. Planners. Club: Racquet. Home: 16138 Chesterfield Lake Dr Chesterfield MO 63017 Office: 1 N Jefferson St Louis MO 63103

FOX, GERALD EDWIN, surgeon; b. Watseka, Ill., Jan. 22, 1941; s. Willis Orville and Hazel Amelia (Bowen) F.; B.S., Bradley U., 1964; M.D., U. Ill., 1966; m. Julie Carol Duis, Sept. 6, 1964; children—Charlene Deanne, Bryan Joseph, Cynthia Marie. Intern, St. Francis Hosp., Peoria, Ill., 1966-67; resident in gen. surgery William Beaumont Hosp., Royal Oak, Mich., 1969-73, chief surg. resident, 1972-73; attending surgeon Good Samaritain Hosp., So. Ill. Clinic, Mt. Vernon, Ill., 1973—. Served with USAF, 1967-69. Mem. AMA, A.C.S., Am. Trauma Soc., Am. Soc. Abdominal Surgeons. Lutheran. Office: 1 Doctors Park Rd Mt Vernon IL 62864

FOX, H. RONALD, librarian; b. Valentine, Nebr., Apr. 12, 1938; s. U. Wesley and Margaret Z. (Manifold) F.; B.A., Nebr. Wesleyan U., 1962; postgrad. Kearney State Coll., 1965-67; M.L.S., U. Okla., 1967-68. Reference librarian Wayne (Nebr.) State Coll., 1968-71; chief librarian VA Med. Center, Grand Island, Nebr., 1971—. Mem. Am., Nebr. Med., library assns., Midcontinental Regional Med. Library Group, Employees Assn. VA Hosp., YMCA. Republican. United Methodist. Mason (Shriner); mem. Order Eastern Star. Club: Kiwanis (dir.). Home: 112 W 16th St Grand Island NE 68801 Office: Library VA Hosp Grand Island NE 68801

FOX, HARRY JAMES, real estate exec.; b. New Orleans, Nov. 27, 1943; s. Harry James and Isabel (Peters) F.; B.A., Knox Coll., 1965; J.D., U. Ill., 1968; m. Mary Alexis Pocotte, Dec. 20, 1969; children—Robert Pocotte, Alexis Kincade, Caroline Walker. Admitted to Ill. bar, 1968; staff atty. Legal Aid Bur., Chgo., 1968-70; supervisory atty. E. Garfield Neighborhood Legal Services, Chgo., 1970-72; v.p. SPA/REDCO, Inc., Chgo., 1972-75; v.p., gen. counsel, sec. Dovenmuehle, Inc., Chgo., 1975-80, dir., officer eleven operating subs.; pres. Manhattan Realty Devel., Inc., Arlington Heights, Ill., 1980—. Bd. dirs., pres. Chgo. Mural Project/Community Mural Group, 1970—; bd. dirs., v.p.-program Corlands, Inc.; adv. recreation and open space com. Northeastern Ill. Planning Commn., 1974—.

Mem. Am. Bar Assn., Chgo. Bar Assn. Club: Univ. (Chgo.). Home: 2237 N Seminary St Chicago IL 60614 Office: 85 W Algonquin Rd Arlington Heights IL 60005

FOX, JOHN H., real estate devel. co. exec.; b. Lancaster, Ohio, Feb. 12, 1945; s. Herbert A. and Norma Neal (Moody) F.; B.S., Northwestern U., 1968; m. Jeanne Louise Brady, Apr. 6, 1968; children—Sarah Ellen, John Brady. Comml. loan officer Merc. Bank Kansas City, 1968-72; comml. mortgage banker Jones & Co., Kansas City, Mo., 1972-76; real estate devel. J.C. Nichols Co., Kansas City, 1976—. Mem. C. of C. Kansas City, Real Estate Bd. Kansas City, Mortgage Bankers Assn. Republican. Presbyterian. Clubs: Mission Hills Country, Plaza. Home: 5612 Tahoe Ln Fairway KS 66205 Office: 310 Ward Pkwy Kansas City MO 64112

FOX, JOHN JAY, JR., architect, engr.; b. Chgo., June 21, 1919; s. John Jay and Ellen Sarah (McCotter) F.; B.S. in Architecture, Armour Inst. Tech., 1940; m. Lorraine Whalen, Feb. 5, 1949; children—John Jay, Michael, James, Marguerite, Colleen, Daniel. Partner firm Fox and Fox, Chgo., 1946—; mem. com. on standards and tests, City of Chgo., 1964—; del. Ill. Architecture/Engring. Council, 1979—, Ill. Architects Polit. Action Com., 1980—. Trustee Bros. of the Good Shepherd, Inc., 1971—; mem. alumni bd. Ill. Inst. Tech., 1973-75; mem. bd. dirs. (hon.) Cardinal Stritch Found., 1967—. Registered architect, Ill., Wis., Ind., N.Y., Minn.; profl. engr., Ill. Mem. Ill. Soc. Architects (dir. 1972-75, 80—, v.p., 1976-79), Delta Tau Delta. Clubs: Beverly Country, Grand Beach, K.C. Recipient award of Merit, Triton Coll., 1969. Home: 9900 S Longwood Dr Chicago IL 60643 Office: 11 S LaSalle St Chicago IL 60603

FOX, JOHN PHILIP, accountant; b. Chgo., Sept. 8, 1940; s. John Henry and Alice E. (Sturm) F.; B.S. in Commerce, De Paul U., 1964, M.B.A., 1967; m. Susan I. Holden, Aug. 1, 1959; children—Bridget Renee, John S. Mgr., Harris Kerr Forster & Co., Chgo., 1963-70; treas. Anvan Cos., Glen Ellyn, Ill., 1970-72; owner John P. Fox & Co., Villa Park, Ill., 1972—; fin. cons.; dir. various corps. Mem. Villa Park Traffic and Safety Comm., 1973—. C.P.A., Ill. Mem. Am. Inst. C.P.A.'s, Ill. Soc. C.P.A.'s, Villa Park C. of C., Am. Mgmt. Assn., Pi Gamma Mu. Clubs: Lions, Moose. Home: 1101 Rand Rd Villa Park IL 60181

FOX, LAWRENCE MARTIN, veterinarian; b. Chgo., Feb. 26, 1946; s. Alexander Louis and Annette (Singer) F.; B.S., U. Ill., 1966, D.V.M., 1968; m. Carlina Mary Renzy, Mar. 18, 1967; children—Kevin Lawrence, Brandon Douglas, Robin Christopher. Practice vet. medicine, Chgo., 1970-72, River Grove, Ill., 1972—; dir. Elmwood-Grove Animal Hosp., Ltd., River Grove, 1972—; cons. on animal control Leyden Twp., Elmwood Park and Franklin Park, Ill., 1974—; treas., dir. Oak Park (Ill.) Village Humane Soc., 1974-76. Sec., Willard Sch. PTA, River Forest, Ill., 1978-79, v.p., 1979-80, pres., 1980-81; picture parent River Forest Schs., 1980-81; bd. mgrs. River Forest Schs., 1980; cubmaster Boy Scouts Am., River Forest, 1979-81, also Webelos leader, 1979-81. Served as capt. Vet. Corps, U.S. Army, 1968-70. Diplomate Am. Bd. Vet. Practitioners. Mem. Am., Ill. State, Chgo. (edn. com. 1981) vet. med. assns., Am. Animal Hosp. Assn., Vet. Inst. for Practicioners, Chgo. Zool. Soc., Mensa. Club: River Grove Lions (lion tamer, tail twister, dir. 1972—). Contbr. articles to profl. jours., 1968—. Home: 1200 Franklin Ave River Forest IL 60305 Office: 8035 Grand Ave River Grove IL 60171

FOX, NOEL PETER, fed. judge; b. Kalamazoo, Aug. 30, 1910; s. Charles K. and Caroline C. (Kokx) F.; Ph.B., Marquette U., 1933, J.D., 1935; m. Dorothy Ann McCormick, Aug. 1, 1934; children—Maureen, Noel Joseph, Virginia Lynn. Admitted to Wis. bar, 1935, Mich. bar, 1935, also U.S. Supreme Ct.; asso. firm Bunker Rogoski & Dunn, 1935-39, Fox & Beers, 1945-49; pvt. practice, 1935-44, 46-51; asst. pros. atty., Muskegon County, 1937-39; circuit judge 14th Jud. Circuit of Mich., 1951-62; U.S. dist. judge Western Dist. Mich., 1962—, chief U.S. dist. judge, 1971—. Mem. faculty Fed. Jud. Center for Seminars for Newly Apptd. Dist. Judges, 1970-72. Served with USNR, World War II. Mem. Mich. Judges Assn. (past pres.), Dist. Judges Assn. (pres. 1976), State Bar Mich. (past chmn. ct. adminstrn. com.), Nat. Jesuit Scholastic and Hon. Soc., Fed., Am., Muskegon, Grand Rapids bar assns., Jud. Conf. Com. Trial Practice and Techniques, Am. Judicature Soc. Office: 416 Federal Bldg 110 Michigan St NW Grand Rapids MI 49503

FOX, PAUL FABIAN, surgeon; b. Chilton, Wis., Jan. 28, 1911; s. Leo Patrick and Pauline Adelaide (Hanert) F.; B.S., U. Notre Dame, 1931; M.D., Loyola U., Chgo., 1934; m. Mardie Elizabeth Stevens, Nov. 28, 1936; children—Elizabeth, Paul, Alice Fox McMahon, James Sheila Fox McLaughlin, Lawrence. Intern, Cook County Hosp., Chgo., 1934-36; resident surgery Children's Meml. Hosp., Chgo., 1951-52; practice medicine, specializing in surgery, Chgo., 1937—; attending staff Cook County Hosp., Chgo., Loyola Med. Center, Chgo., 1937—; mem. staff St. Anne's Children's Meml. Hosp.; clin. prof. surgery Loyola U. Med. Sch., Chgo., 1969—, acting chmn. dept. surgery, 1969-70. Bd. dirs. Suburban Cook County Tb Dist., 1965-68. Recipient Stritch medal Loyola U., 1978. Diplomate Am. Bd. Surgery. Fellow A.C.S.; mem. Chgo. (pres. Aux Plaines br. 1952), Ill. med. socs., Chgo. (pres. 1966), Ill., surg. socs., AMA, Central, Western surg. assns., Inst. Medicine Chgo., Soc. Surgery Gastrointestinal Tract, Alpha Omega Alpha. Roman Catholic. Contbr. articles profl. pubs. Home: 1046 Monroe Ave River Forest IL 60305 Office: 7234 W North Ave Elmwood Park IL 60635

FOX, RONALD ERNEST, clin. psychologist; b. Conover, N.C., May 11, 1936; s. Fred Yount and Carolyn Victoria (Weeks) F.; A.B., U. N.C., 1958, M.A., 1961, Ph.D., 1962; m. Margaret Elizabeth Smith, Dec. 27, 1956; children—Kelley Victoria, Brett Anthony, Jonathan Eric. Asst. prof. dept. psychiatry and psychology U. N.C., 1963-68; asso. prof. dept. psychiatry and psychology Ohio State U., 1968-74, prof., 1974—, coordinator edn. and tng. dept. psychiatry, 1968—, dir. Family Therapy Clinic, Ohio State U. Med. Sch., 1970—; dean Sch. Profl. Psychology, Wright State U., 1977—; cons. Midwest Career Devel. Center, Columbus. Diplomate Am. Bd. Profl. Psychology. Fellow Am. Psychol. Assn.; mem. Ohio Psychol. Assn., Am. Acad. Psychotherapists, Am. Soc. Psychologists in Pvt. Practice, Assn. Psychology Internship Centers. Club: Worthington Community Theater. Author: (with others) Patients View Their Psychotherapy, 1968; (with others) Abnormal Psychology, 1972; contbr. articles to sci., profl. jours. Home: 415 Kramer Rd Dayton OH 45419 Office: Wright State U Dayton OH 45435

FOX, THEODORE ALBERT, orthopaedic surgeon; b. Chgo., Feb. 16, 1913; s. Albert and Jennie (Friedman) F.; B.S., U. Chgo., 1933, M.D., 1937; m. Marcella Schaeffer, June 14, 1936; children—Susan, Nancy. Intern, Cook County Hosp., 1937-39, fellow in pathology, 1939, resident in fractures, 1939-40; resident in gen. surgery Mt. Sinai Hosp., N.Y.C., 1940-41; resident in orthopaedic surgery U. Ill., 1945-47; practice medicine specializing in orthopaedic surgery, 1947—; asso. prof. orthopaedic surgery U. Ill., 1950—; attending orthopaedic surgeon Ill. Masonic Med. Center, 1949—, chmn. orthopaedic sect., 1970—; med. dir. Center for Sports Medicine, 1975—; orthopaedic surgeon Chgo. Bears Football Club, 1947-78; chmn. subcom. on athletic injuries Chgo. Com. on Trauma, A.C.S., 1970-75. Served as comdr. USNR, 1941-46. Fellow A.C.S., Am. Acad. Orthopaedic Surgeons; mem AMA, Chgo. Med. Soc., AAAS, Assn. Am. Med. Colls., Clin. Orthopaedic Soc., Am. Med. Writers Assn., Latin Am. Soc. Orthopaedic and Traumatology, Interstate Orthopaedic Soc., Midwest Orthopaedic Soc., Am. Geriatric Soc., Pan Am. Med. Assn., Ill. Soc. Med. Research. Club: Briarwood Country (Deerfield, Ill.). Contbr. articles, chpts. to med. jours. and texts. Home: 1170 Oak St Winnetka IL 60093 Office: 836 Wellington Chicago IL 60657

FOX, THURMAN ORVILLE, mus. adminstr.; b. Oshkosh, Wis., Aug. 7, 1922; s. Orville W. and Frances L. (Smith) F.; B.S., U. Wis., 1947, M.S., 1949; m. Betty Lou Patch, June 17, 1950; children—James T., Beth L. Tchr., Beaver Dam Jr. High Sch., 1947-48, Madison W. Jr. High Sch., 1949-56; chief Office of Sch. Services State Hist. Soc. Wis., Madison, 1956-64, dir. mus., 1964—; cons. Am. Assn. State and Local History. Served with AC, U.S. Army, 1943-46. Ford Found. grantee, 1952-53. Mem. Am. Assn. State and Local History, Am. Assn. Mus., Nat. Trust Hist. Preservation. Club: Rotary. Office: 816 State St Madison WI 53706

FOX, WILLIAM GORDON, printing co. exec.; b. Evanston, Ill., Apr. 20, 1930; s. Stuart K. and Ruth (Bartels) F.; B.A. in Econs., Cornell U., 1952; m. Constance E.; children—James, Mary, Gwynne. Salesman, Wallace Press div. Wallace Bus. Forms, Chgo., 1954-61, sales mgr., 1961-67, gen. mgr., 1968—, v.p., 1969-76; exec. v.p. Johnson & Quin, Chgo., 1976-78, pres., 1978—. Served to 1st lt. F.A., AUS, 1952-54. Mem. Chgo. Execs. Club, Delta Tau Delta. Club: Cornell (Chgo.). Home: 525 Lee Rd Northbrook IL 60062 Office: 5544 W Armstrong Ave Chicago IL 60646

FOXEN, GENE LOUIS, ins. exec.; b. Chgo., Mar. 28, 1936; adopted son Henry and Mary Foxen; student public schs.; children—Dan, Kathleen, Michael, Patricia, James, Karen. With New Eng. Life Ins. Co., 1957—, asso. gen. agt., 1970-73, gen. agt., Chgo., 1973—. Cubmaster DuPage council Boy Scouts Am., 1963; Midwest regional dir. Adoptees Liberty Movement Assn. Served with USMC, 1954-57. Recipient life membership award Gen. Agents and Mgrs. Conf.; named to Hall of Fame, New Eng. Life Ins. Co., 1972, to Million Dollar Round Table, 1973-80; C.L.U. Mem. Nat. Assn. Life Underwriters, Execs. Club Chgo., Gen. Agents and Mgrs. Assn., Am. Soc. C.L.U.'s (pres. Chgo. chpt. 1977-78, v.p. Midwest region 1981-82), Chgo. Estate Planning Council (pres.), Am. Soc. Life Underwriters. Republican. Roman Catholic. Club: Metropolitan. Home: 1549 Mirror Lake Dr Naperville IL 60540 Office: 120 S Riverside Plaza Chicago IL 60606

FRADE, PETER DANIEL, chemist; b. Highland Park, Mich., Sept. 3, 1946; s. Peter Nunes and Dorathea Grace (Gehrke) F.; B.S. in Chemistry, Wayne State U., 1968, M.S., 1971, Ph.D., 1978. Chemist, Henry Ford Hosp., Detroit, 1968-75, analytical chemist, toxicologist, dept. pathology, div. pharmacology and toxicology, 1975—; research asso. in chemistry Wayne State U., Detroit, 1978-79; vis. scholar U. Mich., Ann Arbor, 1980-82. Recipient David F. Boltz Meml. award Wayne State U., 1977. Fellow Am. Inst. Chemists; mem. Fedn. Am. Scientists, Am. Chem. Soc., AAAS, IntraSci. Research Found., Soc. Applied Spectroscopy, Am. Assn. Clin. Chemistry, Assn. Analytical Chemists, N.Y. Acad. Scis., Am. Pharm. Assn., Acad. Pharm. Scis., Am. Coll. Toxicology, Royal Soc. Chemistry (London), Titanic Hist. Soc., Bibl. Archaeology Soc., Virgil Fox Soc., Founders Soc. Detroit Inst. Arts, Sigma Xi, Phi Lambda Upsilon, Alpha Chi Sigma. Lutheran. Contbr. sci. articles to profl. jours. Office: Henry Ford Hosp 2799 W Grand Blvd Detroit MI 48202

FRAEDRICH, ROYAL LOUIS, mag. editor; b. Weyauwega, Wis., Apr. 23, 1931; s. Clarence Otto and Libbie Clara (Trojan) F.; B.S., U. Wis., 1955; m. Phyllis Bohren, June 26, 1955; children—Lynn, Craig, Ann, Sarah, Paul. With Doane Agrl. Service, St. Louis, 1955-57; info. specialist Mich. State U., East Lansing, 1957-59; mng. editor Agrl. Pubs., Inc., Milw., 1959-64; editor Big Farmer mag., Milw., 1964-69, Frankfort, Ill., 1969-73, Farm Futures mag., pub. Communications Top Farmers Am. Assn., Milw., 1973—; v.p., dir. Big Farmer Inc., 1969-73; v.p. Market Communications Inc., Milw., 1973—. Vice pres. Grace Lutheran Ch., Menomonee Falls, Wis., 1963, mem. stewardship com., 1965-67, sec. bd. elders, 1974-77. Mem. Am. Agrl. Editors Assn., Agrl. Relations Council. Office: 225 E Michigan St Milwaukee WI 53202*

FRAHM, CHARLES HAROLD, mfg. co. exec.; b. Racine, Wis., Apr. 1, 1937; s. Harold Albert and Betty T. F.; cert. U. Wis., 1957; spl. courses U. Wis. Extension, Am. Mgmt. Assn.; m. Alice E. Hein, Feb. 24, 1962; children—Jeff, Joel. Advt. sales rep. Racine Jour. Times, 1957-60; asst. advt. mgr. In-Sink-Erator Co., Racine, 1960-64, advt. mgr., 1964-66, advt. and sales promotion mgr., 1966-72, mktg. and advt. mgr., 1972-73, v.p. mktg. services, 1973—; v.p. mktg. Gold Medal, Inc., Racine, 1981—; dir. Lewisan Products, Gardewick Industries; mem. public relations com. Plumbing-Heating Cooling Info. Bur. Served with Air Force N.G., 1954-62. Mem. Sales and Mktg. Execs. Club (v.p.), Advt. Club Racine (past pres., Advt.-Mktg. Man of Yr. 1971), Am. Advt. Fedn. (past gov. 8th dist.). Assn. Home Appliance Mfrs., Mktg. Mgmt. Council Racine (past pres.). Lutheran. Home: 3330 Taurus Dr Racine WI 53406 Office: 4700 21st St Racine WI 53406

FRALEY, ROBERT DOUGLAS, real estate devel. co. exec.; b. Lexington, Ky., Oct. 6, 1940; s. Robert Gray and Mildred Ruth (Brown) F.; B.S., Morehead (Ky.) State U., 1962; M.B.A., Ind. U., 1964; m. Leonie Jeanne Fossoul, Nov. 25, 1970; children—Anne, Robert, Elizabeth, Cathy, Michele. Mgr., Peat, Marwick, Mitchell & Co., Houston, 1964-68, 71-72, Brussels, 1969-71; sec., treas., controller Gulf Republic Fin. Corp., Houston, 1972-74; controller Federated Stores Realty, Inc., Cin., 1974—. C.P.A., Tex. Mem. Am. Inst. C.P.A.'s, Tex. Soc. C.P.A.'s, Nat. Assn. Accts., Phi Kappa Phi, Beta Alpha Psi. Office: 7 W 7th St Cincinnati OH 45202

FRANCE, RICHARD XAVIER, playwright, educator; b. Boston, May 5, 1938; spl. playwriting fellow Yale U., 1964-65; M.F.A. in Playwriting, Carnegie-Mellon U., 1970, Ph.D. in Theatre History, 1973; married; 2 children. Instr. English, Allegheny Community Coll., Pitts., 1970-72; asst. prof. theatre arts R.I. Coll., 1972-73; vis. asst. prof. playwriting SUNY, Geneseo, 1973-74; asst. prof. theatre and drama Lawrence U., Appleton, Wis., 1974-76, chmn. dept., 1976—; film and drama critic Sta. WQED-TV, Pitts., 1969-72, producer, writer, narrator sta. prodn. The Market Sq. Revival, 1971; writer, narrator U.S. Army Pictorial Center, N.Y.C., 1966-67; resident playwright U. Pitts., 1965-66, Music and Art Inst. San Francisco, 1961-63; playwright, observer Am. Conservatory Theatre, 1965-66, Actors Workshop, San Francisco, 1960-62. Grantee Ford Found., 1979, Rockefeller Found., 1970, Lawrence U., 1975, 76, Wis. Council Arts, 1976; fellow NDEA, 1969-71, Nat. Endowment Arts, 1973, 79-80; summer stipendee Nat. Endowment Humanities, 1977, ind. fellow, 1979; recipient Sam S. Schubert Playwriting Fellowship award, 1965, John Golden Playwriting Fellowship award, 1965. Mem. Authors League, Dramatists Guild Am. (grantee 1967), Am. Theatre Assn. (chmn. playwrights program 1975-77), Office Advanced Drama Research, Nat. Acad. TV Arts and Scis. Author: The Theatre of Orson Welles, 1977; (plays) The Magic Shop, 1972, Fathers and Sons, 1972, The Adventure of the Dying Detective, 1974, The First Word and the Last, 1974, One Day in the Life of Ivan Denisovich, 1974, The Image of Elmo Doyle, 1976, Feathertop, 1979; Station J, 1979; also articles. Office: Dept Theatre and Drama Lawrence Univ Appleton WI 54911

FRANCHIK, CAROL ANN, mfg. co. exec.; b. Chgo., Jan. 5, 1939; d. Florian J. and Mildred E. (Backofen) Ostrowski; student Morton Coll., 1964; m. Bill D. Franchik, Jan. 19, 1957; 1 son, Mark William. Legal sec. Hajek & Hucek, Cicero, Ill., 1956-58, Kirkland & Ellis, Chgo., 1958-59, 63-67; exec. sec. DeSoto Chem. Coatings, Chgo., 1961-63; adminstrv. mgr. Wildman, Harrold, Allen & Dixon, Chgo., 1967-79; v.p., controller Duff & Phelps, Inc., Chgo., 1979—; pres. Law Officers Mgrs. Assn., Chgo., 1976. Mem. adv. bd. Prairie State Coll., 1978-79; exec. bd. Fullersburg Homeowners Assn., 1980-81. Mem. Assn. Legal Adminstrs. Nat. Fedn. Bus. and Profl. Women's Clubs, Inc. Home: 526 Bonnie Brae Hinsdale IL 60521 Office: 55 E Monroe St Chicago IL 60603

FRANCIS, EMILE PERCY, profl. hockey team exec.; b. N. Battleford, Sask., Can., Sept. 13, 1926. Player, Chgo. Black Hawks, NHL, 1946-48, N.Y. Rangers, 1946-52, other NHL teams, 1953-60; coach Guelph farm team Ont. (Can.) Hockey League, 1961-63; asst. gen. mgr., then gen. mgr. N.Y. Rangers, 1963-74, coach, 1965-76; gen. mgr. St. Louis Blues, 1976—, coach, 1982—. Address: St Louis Blues 5700 Oakland Ave St Louis MO 63110*

FRANCIS, ERLE WILLIAM, lawyer; b. Westmoreland, Kans., Aug. 31, 1909; s. Erle Seth and Margaret (Hesse) F.; J.D., Washburn U., 1933; m. Marie Margaret Price, Sept. 2, 1939; children—Sarah (Mrs. Charles N. Henson), Mary Louise (Mrs. Gerald L. Counter), Michael Erle. Admitted to Kans. bar, 1933; atty. Kan. Vehicle Dept., 1938; asso. firm Crane & Crane, 1933-37; partner firm Francis & Francis, 1937-57; practice law, Topeka, 1957—; asst. atty. gen. for Kans. Bd. Edn., 1969-75, atty., 1976—. Bd. dirs., past pres. Kans. Children's Service League. Served with USNR, 1943-47. Mem. Kans., Topeka (pres. 1971) bar assns., Native Sons Kans. (pres. 1939), SAR (pres. Kans. 1965), Kappa Sigma. Republican. Congregationalist. Clubs: Masons (grand high priest Kans. 1977), Elks, Topeka High Twelve (pres. 1950), Topeka Knife and Fork (pres. 1964-65), Shawnee Country (pres. 1963) (Topeka). Home: 1608 High St Topeka KS 66604 Office: 700 Kansas Ave Topeka KS 66603

FRANCIS, JAMES THOMAS, architect; b. Canton, Ohio, Dec. 29, 1924; s. James Charles and Maxine Margret (Firestone) F.; B.S. in Architecture, U. Cin., 1950; m. Beverly Jane Elizabeth Aho, Feb. 1, 1945; children—James Stuart, Thomas John. Draftsman, Alfred J. Martina, Architect, Cin., 1948-50; draftsman Richard Hawley Cutting, Architect, Cleve., 1951; asso. architect Green, Smith & Assos., Architects, Painesville, Ohio, 1952-59; partner Green, Smith & Francis, Architects, Painesville, 1960-64, Smith & Francis, 1964-72; pvt. practice architecture, Madison, Ohio, 1972—; fallout shelter analyst Dept. Def. Chmn., lMadison Civic Assn., 1961-62. Served with USAF, 1942-45. Mem. Nat. Council Archtl. Registration Bds. Presbyterian. Clubs: Elks; Painesville Exchange; Madison Country. Patentee in field. Office: 1899 Hubbard Rd Madison OH 44057

FRANCIS, JOSEPH SNELSON, cons. engr.; b. Canton, N.C., Jan. 13, 1914; s. William Lee and Iva (Snelson) F; student Berea (Ky.) Coll. and Ia. State Coll.; B.S. in Mech. Engring., U. N.C., 1938; m. Gertrude R. Cherry Withers; children—Joseph Gregory, Roger. Successively design engr. for J.V. Deloi Engring. Co., Durham, N.C.; Mojonnier Bros. Co., Chgo., Consol. Aircraft Corp., San Diego, Internat. Harvester Co., Chgo.; pres. Francis Co., 1940—; owner Western Research & Engring. Co. Registered profl. engr. Ill., Okla., Ga., Tex., Colo. Mem. Soc. Automotive Engrs., Am. Soc. M.E., Army Ordnance Assn. Mason (32 deg., Shriner). Office: 3200 E 87th St Chicago IL 60617

FRANCIS, LEROY ANDREW, lawyer; b. Terre Haute, Ind., June 14, 1910; s. Nathan I. and Flora I. (Campbell) F.; B.S., Ind. U., 1948, J.D., 1949; m. Mary Kathryn Reveal, Oct. 4, 1935; children—Richard L., Mary Kay, William Jay, Sharon Rose. Admitted to Ind. bar, 1949; since practiced in Terre Haute; mem. firms Hilleary, Shafer & Francis, 1949-73, Francis, Brames & Cook, 1973-79, Francis, Cook & Rider, 1979—. Pres., Sunset Harbor, Inc., 1965-73; judge Superior Ct., Vigo County, Ind., 1958. Served to lt. col. AUS, 1941-45. Decorated Bronze Star medal. Mem. Am., Ind., Terre Haute bar assns., C. of C., Ind. U. Alumni Assn., Delta Tau Delta, Sigma Delta Kappa, Delta Sigma Pi. Mason (33 deg., Shriner), Elk. Club: Terre Haute Country. Home: 2220 N 10th St Terre Haute IN 47804 Office: 101 Sycamore Bldg Terre Haute IN 47807

FRANCIS, SYBIL ELDRIDGE, state ofcl.; b. Los Angeles, Aug. 14, 1947; d. Thomas William and Frances Pauline (Graves) Eldridge; B.A. cum laude, North Central Coll., 1974; M.A., Northwestern U., 1977, Ph.D., 1979; m. Paul R. Francis (dec.); 1 dau., Elizabeth Anne. Lectr., Northwestern U., 1977-78; dir. research and planning Ill. State Scholarship Commn., Deerfield, 1978-79, dir. agy. services and organizational devel., 1979—; dir. Ill. State Student Fin. Aid Tng. Program; dir. Ill. Edn. Info. Centers; cons. in field. Mem. Ill. Assn. Fin. Aid Adminstrs., Am. Mgmt. Assn., Am. Mktg. Assn., Am. Soc. Tng. and Devel., Phi Delta Kappa. Home: 1906 Greendale Ave Park Ridge IL 60068 Office: 102 Wilmot Rd Deerfield IL 60015

FRANCISCO, BARBARA JEAN WHITEAKER, mfg. co. exec.; b. Benham, Ky., Aug. 1, 1943; d. Charles Edward and Mildred Louise (Highfield) Whiteaker; student Berea Coll., 1961. Operator, Am. Tel. & Tel., Louisville, 1963; insp. Union Carbide Corp., E. Chgo., Ind., 1964-69; with Nat. Can Corp., Chgo., 1970—, regional mgr. quality control, 1979—. Mem. Am. Soc. Profl. and Exec. Women, Nat. Metal Decorators Assn. Democrat. Club: Order of Eastern Star. Office: 8101 W Higgins Rd Chicago IL 60631

FRANCISCO, JAMES LEE, state senator; b. Lamar, Colo., Oct. 10, 1937; s. James Rufus and Wilma G. (White) F.; student Wichita State U., Friends U.; m. Sharon Lynn Maddas, 1958; children—James D., Brenda L., Debra M., Jerald L. Mem. Kans. Senate, 1973—. Committeeman, Kans. Democratic party; del. Dem. Nat. Conv., 1968. Served with USMC, 1958-60. Mem. Am. Legion, Internat. Assn. Machinists, Kans. State Fedn. Labor, Kans. State Council Machinists. Methodist. Club: Lions. Address: Mulvane KS *

FRANCISCO, WILLIAM ROSS, entertainment co. exec.; b. Kingsport, Tenn., Nov. 13, 1946; s. Ross and Margaret Elizabeth (Jackson) F.; A.B., Fla. So. Coll., 1969; m. Ginger Louise Casity, Aug. 11, 1967; children—William Casity, Suzanne Lynn. Reporter, Lakeland (Fla.) Ledger, 1967, Wonn Radio, Lakeland, 1968-69; mgr. public relations Lakeland Area C. of C., 1969-71; advt. and sales mgr. Walt Disney World, Fla., 1971-74; mgr. mktg. Busch Gardens, Williamsburg, Va., 1974-77; dir. corp. mgmt. Busch Entertainment Corp., St. Louis, 1977—; travel mktg. cons. Mem. alumni endowment public relations com. William and Mary U., 1976-80; bd. dirs. Boys Clubs Am., Lakeland, 1970. Served with USAF, 1969. Recipient Discover Am. Travel award, 1977, 78, 80, Addy Advt. awards, 1977, 78, 79. Mem. Travel Industry Am., Internat. Assn. Amusement Parks and Attractions, Va. Travel Council. Methodist. Office: 500 Community Federal Center Des Peres MO 63131

RDATH AMOND, ednl. adminstr.; b. Wehrum, Pa., 5; d. Arthur and Helen Lucille (Sharp) Amond; B.S. in t State U., 1947, M.A., 1948; Ph.D., Western Res. U., 1956; Mack Franck, Mar. 18, 1945; children—Sheldon Mack, ace Lucille. Instr., U. Akron, 1947-50; sch. psychologist Summit nty (Ohio) Schs., 1950-60; dir. Akron (Ohio) Speech and Reading enter, 1950—; coordinator spl. academic class, Wadsworth; cons. pre-Sch. program Richfield United Ch. Christ; dir. Barnhill's West, Inc. Founder, current dir. 4-U Twirling Unltd. Baton Twirling Assn. Mem. Am. Speech and Hearing Assn. (clin. certification), Internat. Reading Assn., Ohio Edn. Assn., Mensa. Club: Soroptimist. Author: Your Child Learns, 1974; weekly ednl. column Wodsworth News Banner, 1970-76. Home: 631 Ghent Rd Akron OH 44313 Office: 700 Ghent Rd Akron OH 44313

FRANCK, FRED WILLIAM, social worker; b. Osceola, Iowa, Nov. 6, 1948; s. Charles Fred and Doris Lucille (Beaman) F.; B.A. in Psychology, U. No. Iowa, 1971; M.S.W., U. Iowa, 1973; m. Rebecca Kay Johnson, Aug. 22, 1969; 1 dau., Amanda Renee. Social worker Dept. Social Services State of Iowa, Muscatine, 1971-72, casework supr., Forest City, 1974-75; dir. Family and Children's Service, Muscatine, 1975-80; pvt. practice partner Tri-County Counseling Service, Wilton, Iowa, 1980—; adj. practicum instr. U. Iowa, Marycrest Coll. Mem. adminstrv. bd. Big Bros./Big Sister, Muscatine, 1976-77; mem. adv. bd. Adult Edn. Center Muscatine Community Coll., 1978-79. Recipient Am. Citizenship award, 1966; cert. social worker, U.K. Mem. Nat. Assn. Social Workers, Acad. Cert. Social Workers, Alpha Phi Omega. Democrat. Home: 1104 7th St Durant IA 52747 Office: 208 1/2 W 4th St PO Box 947 Wilton IA 52778

FRANCK, MICHAEL, lawyer, assn. exec.; b. Berlin, Germany, Oct. 6, 1932; s. Wolf and Marga (Oppenheimer) F.; came to U.S., 1941, naturalized, 1950; B.A., Columbia Coll., 1954; J.D., Columbia U., 1958; m. Carol E. Eichert, May 29, 1965; children—Michele, Lauren, Rebecca, Jennifer. Admitted to N.Y. State bar, 1958, Mich. bar, 1970; trial counsel Liberty Mut. Ins. Co., Bklyn., 1958-60; chief litigator, com. on grievances Assn. Bar City of N.Y., 1960-70; reporter spl. com. on evaluation disciplinary enforcement Am. Bar Assn., 1968-70; cons. spl. com. on disciplinary procedures, bd. governance Pa. Supreme Ct., 1969-72; spl. counsel Phila. Ct. of Common Pleas, 1970-73; exec. dir. State Bar of Mich., Lansing, 1970—. Mem. Commn. on Uniform State Laws, 1975—, Mich. Malpractice Arbitration Adv. Com., 1975—. Served with U.S. Army, 1954-56. Mem. Am. Bar Assn. (chmn. com. on evaluation of fee dispute procedures 1972-73, standing com. profl. discipline 1973—, chmn. 1979—, long-range planning council 1979—, chmn. sect. bar activities 1975-76, del. 1976-78), State Bar Mich., N.Y. State Bar Assn., Ingham County Bar Assn. Contbr. articles to bar jours. Office: 306 Townsend St Lansing MI 48933

FRANCONA, NICHOLAS TORRESSO, JR., dentist; b. Chgo., June 15, 1949; s. Nicholas Torresso and Jessie J. (Paulson) F.; B.S., Loyola U., Chgo., 1971, postgrad. in biology, 1972, D.D.S., 1976. Faculty, Loyola U., Chgo., 1972; pvt. practice dentistry, Lincolnshire, Ill. 1977—. Mem. ADA, Ill. Dental Soc., Chgo. Dental Soc., Lincolnshire C. of C. (sec., dir. 1978-79). Home: 428 W Russell Barrington IL 60010 Office: 430 N Milwaukee Ave Lincolnshire IL 60069

FRANK, DAVID SCOTT, psychologist, educator; b. Chambersburg, Pa., Mar. 2, 1930; s. George A. and Elizabeth A. (Feldman) Trail; B.S., Shippensburg State Coll., 1954; M.Ed., Western Md. Coll., 1958; postgrad. U. Mo., Temple U.; Ed.D., W.Va. U., 1972; m. Doris Jean Witmer, Sept. 12, 1954 (div.); children—Kimberley Michelle, David Scott III; m. 2d, Luz Maria Latoni, June 24, 1968; stepchildren—James Brian, Edward Scott, Karen Irene. Tchr. area schs., Carlisle, Pa., 1954-58; guidance counselor, sch. psychologist No. Joint Schs., Dillsburg, Pa., 1958-64; pvt. practice as psychologist and counselor, 1958-68; asso. prof. Shippensburg (Pa.) State Coll., 1965-67; asst. prof. edn. Purdue U., Westville, Ind., 1967-72; pres. David S. Frank Psychol. Services Inc., Michigan City, Ind., 1972—. Cons. Pa. Dept. Vocational Rehab., 1958-68; vocational expert Social Security Adminstrn., Bur. Hearings and Appeals, HEW, 1964—; psychologist LaPorte County Superior and Circuit Cts., 1970-75; psychologist drug abuse treatment program Ind. State Prison, 1975-78, clin. dir. therapeutic community tomorrows aspirations, 1976-78. Active LaPorte County Youth Service Bur., 1972-75, Meals on Wheels, 1973-77; mem. admission com. United Fund, 1972-78; bd. dirs. Family and Children's Service, Michigan City, Ind., 1968-77, No. Ind. Council Children with Learning Disabilities; bd. dirs. Michigan City Scholarship Found., 1975—, pres., 1979. Served with USMC, 1949-52. Mem. Am. Personnel and Guidance Assn., Nat. Vocat. Guidance Assn. (profl. mem.), Nat. Rehab. Assn., Nat. Rehab. Counseling Assn. (profl. mem.), Ind. Corrections Assn. (certificate of merit 1971), A.A.U.P. (pres. local chpt. 1969-71), Pa. Sch. Counselors Assn., Internat. Bd. on Counseling Services, Internat. Transactional Analysis Assn., Assn. Counselor Educators and Suprs., Wrestling Referees Assn. (pres. 1964-65), Phi Delta Kappa. Presbyn. (deacon). Contbg. author: New Developments In Educating the Able, 1966. Home: 3207 Cleveland Ave Michigan City IN 46320 Office: David S Frank Psychol Services Inc 1101 E Coolspring Ave Michigan City IN 46320

FRANK, DON, state senator; ed. U. Minn. Mem. Minn. Senate, 1980—. Councilman, Spring Lake Park, Minn.; mem. Spring Lake Park Liquor Commn., 1972-73, Variance Com.; mem. council St. Timothy's Ch.; pres. Park Terrace PTA, Spring Lake Park Planning and Zoning Commn., Anoka County Mass Transit Adv. Com.; mem. central com. Democratic-Farmer-Labor party; vice chmn. Anoka County Joint Law Enforcement Com., Anoka County Task Force Battered Women. Club: Moose. Office: 23D State Capitol Saint Paul MN 55155*

FRANK, KURT A., state senator; b. Milw., Mar. 20, 1945; B.S., U. Wis., Milw., 1967; J.D., Marquette U., 1971. Admitted to Wis. bar; practice law, Milw.; mem. Wis. Senate, 1970—, majority caucus sec. Mem. nat. hon. adv. com. Voices in Vital Am. Served with Army NG, 1968-71. Mem. Isaac Walton League, Wis. Consumers League, Wis. Allied Co. Sr. Citizens. Democrat. Office: Room 8 South State Capitol Madison WI 53702*

FRANK, LARRY ROBERT, mil. aviator; b. Duluth, Minn., Sept. 14, 1954; s. Robert William and Maralyn Elizabeth (Reponen) F.; B.S. cum laude in Physics, U. Minn., Duluth, 1977; m. Lizabeth Louise Seiberlich, June 2, 1979. Commd. 2d lt. U.S. Air Force, 1977, advanced through grades to capt., 1981; instr., helicopter pilot, ops. officer Ellsworth AFB, S.D., 1980—, instr., trainer CPR, 1979—. CPR instr. ARC, 1979—; sustaining mem. Republican Nat. Com., 1979—; mem. nat. adv. bd. Am. Security Council, 1979—. Mem. Air Force Assn., Am. Def. Preparedness Assn., Order of Daedallions. Roman Catholic. Home: 1872 Frank Rd Cloquet MN 55720 Office: Det 2 37 ARRS (MAC) DO Ellsworth SD 57706

FRANK, ROBERT EDWIN, hosp. adminstr.; b. St. Louis, Nov. 30, 1926; s. Edwin J. and Genevieve Ernestine (Graeff) F.; m. Mary Catherine Porter, Sept. 10, 1949; children—Michael, Nancy Frank Vahldieck; B.S., St. Louis U., 1950; M.H.A., Washington U., 1962. Asst. personnel dir. Gen. Cable Co., 1950-53; personnel dir. DePaul Hosp., St. Louis, 1953-61; intern hosp. adminstrn. Barnes Hosp., St. Louis, 1961, asst. dir., 1961-64, asso. dir., 1964-65, acting dir., 1965-66, dir., 1966—, pres., 1973—; asst. prof. program in health care adminstrn. Washington U. Sch. Medicine. Mem. Am. Coll. Hosp. Adminstrs., Am. Hosp. Assn. (council on fin.), Mo. Hosp. Assn. (chmn. 1981), Hosp. Assn. Met. St. Louis. Clubs: Forest Hills, Round Table. Home: 1525 Hampton Hall Dr Chesterfield MO 63017 Office: Barnes Hosp Plaza Saint Louis MO 63110

FRANK, ROBERT GEORGE, clin. psychologist; b. Paris, Mar. 25, 1952; s. Fred James and Dorothea Vernice (Plaut) F.; B.S., U. N.Mex., 1974, M.A., 1977, Ph.D., 1979; m. Carol Ann Cross, Aug. 17, 1974. Teaching asst. dept. psychology U. N.Mex., 1974-77, NIMH trainee, 1977-78; clin. psychology intern dept. psychiatry and behavioral scis. U. Wash., Seattle, 1978-79; asst. prof. med. psychology dept. phys. medicine and rehab. U. Mo. Sch. Medicine, Columbia, 1979—, asst. prof. dept. psychiatry and dept. psychology U. Mo., 1979—. Mem. Am. Psychol. Assn., Soc. Behavioral Medicine, Am. Soc. Clin. Hypnosis, Assn. for Advancement of Psychology. Roman Catholic. Home: 4508 Georgetown Dr Columbia MO 65201 Office: Rusk Rehab Center U Mo Health Scis Center Columbia MO 65212

FRANK, ROSEMARY LEE, educator; b. Mattoon, Ill., July 20, 1949; s. Paul Lee and Pauline (Bailey) Allen; B.S. in Edn./History, Eastern Ill. U., Charleston, 1971, B.S. in Spl. Edn., 1973; m. John P. Frank; 1 dau., Paula Lee. Spl. edn. tchr. VIT Community Unit 2, Table Grove, Ill., 1973—. Mem. Council for Exceptional Children, NEA, Ill. Edn. Assn., Assn. for Learning Disabilities, VFW Aux. Cert. in learning disabilities, educable mentally retarded, trainable mentally retarded, Ill. Home: 520 Cole St Bushnell IL 61422 Office: Table Grove IL

FRANK, RUBY MERINDA, employment agy. exec.; b. McClusky, N.D., June 28, 1920; d. John J. and Olise (Stromme) Hanson; student coll., Mankato, Minn., also Aurora (Ill.) Coll.; m. Robert G. Frank, Jan. 14, 1944 (dec. 1973); children—Gary Frank, Craig. Exec. sec., office mgr. Nat. Container Corp., Chgo., 1943-50; owner, operator Frank's Office & Employment Service, St. Charles, Ill., 1957—; dir. St. Charles Savings & Loan Assn. Sec. bd. trustees Delnor Hosp., St. Charles, 1959—, also life mem. Women's aux.; vice chairwoman Kane County (Ill.) Republican Com., 1968-77; pres. Women's Rep. Club, 1969-77; adv. council Dellora A. Norris Cultural Arts Center. Mem. St. Charles C. of C. (pres., dir. 1976—), Kane-DuPage Personnel Assn. (v.p. 1971—), Nat., Ill. employment assns., Ill. Assn. Personnel Cons. (dir.). Lutheran. Clubs: St. Charles Country; Execs. of Chgo. Contbr. weekly broadcast Sta. WGSB. Home: 534 Longmeadow Circle Saint Charles IL 60174 Office: Arcada Theater Bldg 12 S 1st Ave Saint Charles IL 60174

FRANK, ZOLLIE SYDNEY, automobile dealer; b. Dayton, Ohio, Jan. 1, 1907; s. Charles and Lena (Kessler) F.; student Ohio State U.; m. Elaine Spiesberger, Jan. 1, 1938; children—Laurie Frank Liebermann, James, Nancy Lee Frank Kaplan, Charles. Pres., Z Frank, Inc., Chgo., 1936—, Four Wheels, Inc., Chgo., 1939—, Laurie James, Inc., Chgo., 1944—, Five Wheels, Inc., 1950—, Globe Auto Leasing, Chgo., 1953—, Wheels, Inc., Chgo., 1953—; chmn. C. James, Inc., Chgo., 1952—; mem. Presdl. Adv. Com. Small Bus. Affairs, Presdl. Adv. Com. on Gen. Motors Corp.; pres. Chgo. Area Chevrolet Dealers Advt. Council. Bd. dirs. Michael Reese Hosp., Chgo., Lyric Opera, Chgo.; trustee Loyola U., Chgo. Recipient Regional Quality Dealer award Time mag., 1976. Mem. Am. Automobile Assn., Chevrolet Dealers Assn., Chgo. Automobile Trade Assn., Chgo. Assn. Commerce, Ill. C. of C., N. Town C. of C. Jewish. Address: 6200 N Western Ave Chicago IL 60659*

FRANKEL, PENINA, counseling psychologist; b. Jersey City, N.J., June 3, 1933; d. Harry and Masha (Resnik) Ducoff; student Bklyn. Coll., 1950-53; B.A. summa cum laude, Wayne State U., Detroit, 1959; M.S., State U. N.Y., Albany, 1969; Ph.D., Northwestern U., 1979; m. Reuven Frankel, Aug. 31, 1953; children—Hillel, Aaron, Noam. Employment advisor Oakland U., Rochester, Mich., 1969-70; ednl. and vocational counselor Jewish Vocational Service, Chgo, 1971-76, also coordinator, dir. Career Devel. Workshops Women, Chgo., 1971-77; counseling psychologist Roosevelt U., Chgo., 1976-78, dir. Project Attain, 1978-79; family life educator Jewish Family and Community Service, Chgo., 1979—. Certified counselor Inst. for Psychoanalysis, Chgo., 1975. Mem. Am. Personnel and Guidance Assn. (certified rehab. counselor), Am. Psychol. Assn., Ams. for Mental Health in Israel. Jewish. Author: Working Women: a Study of Education and Promotability, 1979; author multi-media cantatas: (with Reuven Frankel) Jerusalem, Echo of Eternity; From Minsk to Manhattan, 1975. Home: 700 Wilmot Deerfield IL 60015 Office: Jewish Family Service 2710 W Devon Chicago IL 60659

FRANKEN, EDMUND ANTHONY, JR., pediatric radiologist, educator; b. Springfield, Mo., Oct. 28, 1936; s. Edmund Anthony and Eloise (Appleby) F.; student St. Louis U., 1954-57; M.D., U. Okla., 1961; m. Penelope Ann Vanderhook, Nov. 25, 1960; children—Kenneth, Katherine (dec.), Michael, Jennifer. Intern, St. Johns Hosp., Tulsa, 1961-62; resident in radiology Ind. U. Med. Center, Indpls., 1964-67, asst. prof. radiology, 1967-71, asso. prof., 1971-75, prof., 1975-79; fellow in neuroradiology Mallinckrodt Inst. Radiology, St. Louis, 1967; dir. radiology James Whitcomb Riley Hosp. for Children, 1967-79; prof. and head dept. radiology U. Iowa Coll. Medicine, 1979—; academic practice medicine specializing in pediatric radiology; dir. radiology U. Iowa Hosps. and Clinics. Served with USPHS, 1962-64. Fellow Am. Coll. Radiology; mem. Marion County (Ind.) Med. Soc., Ind. State, Am. med. assns., Ind. (pres.), Am. Roentgen ray socs., Radiol. Soc. N.Am., Assn. Univ. Radiologists, Soc. Pediatric Radiology, European Soc. Pediatric Radiology (asso.). Roman Catholic. Author: Gastrointestinal Radiology in Pediatrics, 1975; contbr. articles to med. jours. Home: 13 Lakeview Dr Iowa City IA 52240 Office: U Iowa Hosps Iowa City IA 52242

FRANKENBERG, JULIAN MYRON, assn. exec.; b. Chgo., Jan. 18, 1938; s. Lester and Bess (Adler) F.; B.S., U. Ill., 1961; M.S., U. Minn., 1963; Ph.D., U. Ill., 1968; m. Natalie Kushner, Aug. 25, 1962; 1 dau., Lisa Lauren. Asst. dean U. Ill. Coll. Liberal Arts and Sci., 1967-72, dir. Health Professions Info. Office, 1972—; exec. dir. Nat. Assn. Advisers for Health Professions, 1980—; cons. in field. Pres. Rolling Acres Homeowners Assn., 1972-78. Fellow Com. Instl. Coop., 1967-68. Mem. Assn. Am. Med. Colls., Nat. Assn. Advisers Health Professions, Central Assn. Advisors Health Professions (pres. 1981—), Am. Rifle Assn., Bot. Soc. Am., Ducks Unlimited, Sigma Xi. Jewish. Author articles in field. Office: 610 E John St 2SSB HPIO U Ill Champaign IL 61820

FRANKENFELD, DONALD L., state senator; b. Feb. 13, 1948; A.B. cum laude, Yale U., 1970; M.B.A., Harvard U., 1975; m. Jean Kingsbury, Aug. 23, 1969; 2 children. Stockbroker, Rapid City, S.D.; mem. S.D. Senate, 1976—. Bd. govs. St. Martin's Acad.; mem. Rapid City (S.D.) Community Blood Bd. Republican. Address: State Capitol Pierre SD 57501*

FRANKLE, ALLAN HENRY, psychologist; b. Des Moines, Nov. 5, 1921; s. Harry Raymond and Ruth (Cohen) F.; student U. Chgo., 1939, Ph.D., 1953; student U. Minn., 1943; m. Esther Alpern, June 22, 1947; children—Katherine, Jonathan. Dir. Des Moines Child Guidance Center, 1947-52; pvt. practice clin. psychology, Des Moines, 1952—; Univ. fellow Drake U., 1970—; vis. clin. asso. prof. psychology U. Iowa, 1969-70; cons. clin. psychology Broadlawns Polk County Hosp., 1967—; cons. VA Hosp., Knoxville, Iowa, 1976-81; supervising psychologist N.Am. Mensa, 1966-78. Served with U.S. Army, 1943-45. Decorated Bronze Star. Diplomate Am. Bd. Profl. Psychology. Fellow Am. Orthopsychiat. Assn.; mem. Am., Iowa (pres. 1960-61, Disting. Service award 1973) psychol. assns., Am. Acad. Psychotherapists, Internat. Neuropsychology Soc., Brit. Psychol. Soc. (fgn. mem.), Sigma Xi, Psi Chi, Mensa. Democrat. Jewish. Contbr. articles to profl. jours. Home: 717 54th St Des Moines IA 50312 Office: 550 39th St Des Moines IA 50312

FRANKLIN, CARTHEL FLOYD, realty exec.; b. Rittman, Ohio, Aug. 26, 1920; s. William Frederick and Queen Rebecca (Dickerson) F.; student Purdue U., 1939-40; m. Mary Beth Franklin; 1 dau., Catherine F. Real estate broker, Chgo., 1946-54; gen. sales mgr. Swift Homes, Inc., Pitts., 1954-62; v.p. sales Gen. Homes subsidiary Koppers Co., Ft. Wayne, Ind., 1962-64; pres. C.F. Franklin & Co., Inc., Ft. Wayne, 1964—. Pres., Allied Real Estate Bd., Chgo., 1954. Served with USCGR, 1942-45. Mem. Ft. Wayne Bd. Realtors, Nat. Assn. Flight Instrs., Am. Legion, Soaring Soc. Am., Quiet Birdmen, Aircraft Owners and Pilots Assn. Mason (Shriner, K.T.), Elk, Kiwanian. Address: 9622 Aboite Center Rd Fort Wayne IN 46802

FRANKLIN, FREDERICK RUSSELL, assn. exec.; b. Berlin, Germany, Mar. 20, 1929; s. Ernest James and Frances (Price) F.; A.B., Ind. U., 1951, J.D. with high distinction, 1956; m. Barbara Ann Donovan, Jan. 26, 1952; children—Katherine Elizabeth, Frederick Russell. Admitted to Ind. bar, 1956; trial atty. criminal div. and ct. of claims sect., civil div. U.S. Dept. Justice, Washington, 1956-60; gen. counsel Ind. State Bar Assn., Indpls., 1960-67; dir. continuing legal edn. for Ind., adj. prof. law Ind. U., Indpls., 1965-68; staff dir. profl. standards Am. Bar Assn., Chgo., 1968-70; exec. v.p. Nat. Attys. Title Assurance Fund, Inc., Indpls., 1970-72; staff dir. legal edn. and admissions to the bar Am. Bar Assn., Chgo., 1972—. Trustee, Olympia Fields (Ill.) United Methodist Ch. Served to capt. USAF, 1951-53. Mem. Am., Ind., Ill. bar assns., Fed. Bar Assn. (officer, found. bd. dirs. 1974—, historian 1979—, nat. council 1965—, nat. v.p. 1967-69, pres. 1965-66, chmn. admission to practice and recert. com. 1980—), Nat. Orgn. Bar Counsel (pres. 1967), Order of Coif, Phi Delta Phi. Kiwanian, Elk. Home: 3617 Parthenon Way Olympia Fields IL 60461 Office: 1155 E 60th St Chicago IL 60637

FRANKLIN, MARGARET LAVONA BARNUM (MRS. C. BENJAMIN FRANKLIN), civic leader; b. Caldwell, Kans., June 19, 1905; d. LeGrand Husted and Elva (Biddinger) Barnum; B.A., Washburn U., 1952; student Iowa State Tchrs. Coll., 1923-25, U. Iowa, 1937-38; m. C. Benjamin Franklin, Jan. 20, 1940; children—Margaret Lee (Mrs. Michael J. Felso), Benjamin Barnum. Tchr. pub. schs., Union, Iowa, 1925-27, Kearney, Nebr., 1927-28, Marshalltown, Iowa, 1928-40; advance rep. Chautauqua, summers 1926-30. Mem. Citizens Adv. Com., 1965-69; mem. Topeka Hosp. Aux. Recipient Waldo B. Heywood award Topeka Civic Theatre, 1967; named Outstanding Alpha Delta Pi Mother of Kans., 1971; Topeka Public Library award, 1977. Mem. DAR (state chmn. Museum 1968-71), AAUW, Topeka Art Guild, Topeka Civic Symphony Soc. (dir. 1952-57, Service Honor citation 1960), Doll Collectors Am., Marshalltown Community Theatre (pres. 1938-40), Topeka Pub. Library Bd. (trustee 1961-70, treas., 1962-65, chmn. 1965-67), Shawnee County Hist. Soc. (dir. 1963-75, sec. 1964-66), Nat. Multiple Sclerosis Soc. (dir. Kans. chpt. 1963-66), Stevengraph Collectors Assn., Friends of Topeka Public Library (dir. 1970-79, Disting. Service award 1980), P.E.O., Topeka Stamp Club, Alpha Beta Gamma, Nonoso. Republican. Mem. Christian Ch. Clubs: Western Sorosis (pres. 1960-61), Minerva, Woman's (1st v.p. 1952-54).

FRANKLIN, TOM, advt. agy. exec.; b. New Rockford, N.D., Nov. 6, 1948; s. Lawrence Seymour and Myrtle Pauline (Grina) Anderson; student pub. schs., New Rockford; m. Betty Anne Cole, June 20, 1970; children—Nicole Rae, Amy Jean, Ryan Glenn. Announcer, KRSD Radio, Rapid City, S.D., 1970, KCCR Radio, Pierre, S.D., 1970; announcer, music dir. KOVC Radio, Valley City, N.D., 1970-72, KKLS Radio, Rapid City, 1972-79; owner, creative dir. Tom Franklin & Assos., Advt., Rapid City, 1979—. Vice pres. PTO, Rapid City, 1979-80; mem. Rapid City Conv. Visitors Bur. adv. com., 1981, chmn. tourism 81 com., 1981—. Served with USAF, 1966-70. Recipient Dale Carnegie Human Relations award, 1979; awards for creative excellence, S.D. Advt. Fedn., 1973-81, 8th Dist. Advt. Fedn., 1975, 78, 80, Ingstad Broadcasting, 1975, others. Mem. Black Hills Advt. Fedn. (co-founder, 1st pres.), Rapid City C. of C. Republican. Lutheran. Clubs: Black Hills Advt., Rapid City Noon Optimists (bd. dirs. 1980-82). Voice talent, producer audio portion Dragons are too Seldom fairytale puppet packets, 1979—. Home: 4018 Helen Ct Rapid City SD 57701 Office: 1101 E Philadelphia St Rapid City SD 57701

FRANKS, ALLEN PAUL, research inst. exec.; b. Cleve., Nov. 12, 1936; s. Stanley Arthur and Helen Dorothy (Kulwicki) F.; student U. Miami, 1955-56; B.S., Case Western Res. U., 1959, LL.B., 1963, J.D., 1968; m. Cary Bajko, Feb. 2, 1963; children—Mathew, Sara. Patent atty. B.F. Goodrich Co., Akron, Ohio, 1963-65; chemist, mgr. paint testing lab. P.P.G. Industries, Barberton, Ohio, 1965-66; tech. dir., lab. mgr. Reichhold Chems., Ind., Cuyahoga Falls, Ohio, 1966-76; faculty Inst. Astral Studies, Inc., Akron, 1974—, dir., 1975—, pres., 1977—; mgr. tech. sales Sovereign Chem. Co., Cuyahoga Falls, 1980—; lectr. astrology, biorhythms Akron U., 1974—, Kent (Ohio) State U., 1973—. Bd. dirs. Persephone Found., Bath, Ohio, 1974—, chmn., 1981—. Served with USCGR, 1954-62. Fellow Am. Inst. Chemists; mem. N.Y. Acad. Scis., AAAS, Ohio Inst. Chemists (treas. 1976—), Am. Chem. Soc., Akron Rubber Group, Northeast Ohio Rubber Group, Phi Delta Phi, Mensa, Intertel. Club: University (Akron). Author: Astrobiological Birth Control, 1978. Contbr. articles to profl. jours. Home: 340 Hollywood Ave Akron OH 44313

FRANSWAY, ROBERT LEROI, psychiatrist; b. Green Bay, Wis., July 2, 1922; s. Oliver Francis and Otilia (McCloskey) F.; B.S. cum laude, U. Wis., 1948, M.D., 1951; M.S. in Psychiatry, U. Mich., 1968; m. Claire Sandra Giancola, May 19, 1947; children—Paul R., Renee T. (Mrs. Lowell R. Spotts), Lynn M., Anthony F. Intern, Mercy Hosp., Des Moines, 1951-52; resident psychiatry Northville (Mich.) State Hosp., 1964-67; resident pathology St. Joseph Hosp., Milw., 1956-57; asst. med. dir. Continental Assurance Co., Chgo., 1952-53; gen. practice Fond du Lac, 1953-56; plant physician Ford Motor Co., Wayne, Mich., 1957-59; clin. investigator, coordinator Parke Davis & Co., Ann Arbor, Mich., 1959-64, 67-69; practice medicine specializing in psychiatry, Ann Arbor, 1967—. Cons. psychiatry Washtenaw Community Coll., Ann Arbor, 1968-69; cons. alcoholism therapy St. Joseph Mercy Hosp., Ann Arbor, 1972-76; chief of staff Mercywood Hosp., Ann Arbor, 1975. Served to 1st. lt. USAAF, 1942-44, AUS, 1944-46. Diplomate Am. Bd. Psychiatry. Mem. AMA, Am. Psychiat. Assn., AAAS, N.Y. Acad. Sci., Mich. Med. Soc. Roman Catholic. K.C. Research drugs for cardiovascular, renal, allergy treatment, 1959-64, psychiat. and neurol. applications,

1967-69. Home: 2785 Park Ridge Dr Ann Arbor MI 48103 Office: 3001 S State Rd Ann Arbor MI 48104

FRANTA, WILLIAM ROY, educator; b. St. Paul, May 21, 1942; s. Roy Andrew and Helen Aleta (Nicholson) F.; B.S., U. Minn., 1964, M.S., 1966, Ph.D., 1970. Asst. prof. computer sci. U. Minn., Mpls., 1970-76, asso. prof., 1976-81, prof., 1981—, asso. dir. Univ. Computer Center, 1976—, co-dir. Microelectronic and Info. Scis. Center, 1980-81, asso. dir., 1981—; mem. computer adv. com. Sci. Mus. Minn., 1981—; mem. tech. adv. com. 1st Midwest Capital Corp., 1981. NSF grantee, 1979-81. Mem. IEEE, Inst. Mgmt. Scis., Assn. Computing Machinery. Author: The Process View of Simulation, 1977; (with I. Chlamtac) Local Networks: Motivation, Technology, Performance, 1981; (with others) Formal Methods of Program Verification and Specification, 1981. Office: 143 Shepherd Lab 100 Union St Minneapolis MN 55455

FRANTEL, EDWARD WILLIAM, beverage co. exec.; b. Wauwatosa, Wis., Mar. 18, 1925; s. Edward S. Frantl and Myrtle E. (Fischer) Hollmann Frantl; B.S. in Bus. Adminstrn., Marquette U., 1948; m. Charlotte Lieg, Aug. 24, 1946; 1 son, Scott. Field sales supr. H.J. Heinz Co., 1948-53; with Miller Brewing Co., Milw., 1953-79, field sales mgr., 1968-72, dir. sales, 1972-74, v.p. sales, 1974-79; pres., chief exec. officer Seven-Up Co., Clayton, Mo., 1979—; v.p. Philip Morris Inc.; officer, dir. Seven-Up U.S.A., Inc.; dir. Mission Viejo, Cheer Up Co., Marbert, Inc., Seven-Up Bottling of Phoenix, Inc., Seven-Up Bottling Co. of Norfolk, Inc., Seven-Up Can. Ltd., Ventura Coastal Corp., Warner-Jenkinson Co., Inc., Warner-Jenkinson Co. of Calif., Warner-Jenkinson East, Inc., Golden Crown Citrus Corp.; officer, dir. Dixi Cola, Inc. Served with U.S. Army, World War II. Decorated Bronze Star with oak leaf cluster, Purple Heart with oak leaf cluster; recipient Philip Morris Gold Ring award, 1979. Mem. Sales and Mktg. Execs. Milw., Bus. Adminstrn. Alumni Assn. Marquette U. (Man of Yr. 1978), Confrerie de la Chaine des Rotisseurs. Clubs: St. Louis, Milw. Athletic. Office: Seven-Up Co 121 S Meramec Ave Clayton MO 63105

FRANTZ, DEAN LESLIE, analyst; b. Beatrice, Nebr., Mar. 27, 1919; s. Oscar Calvin and Flora Mae (Gish) F.; B.A., Manchester Coll., 1942; M.Div., Bethany Theol. Sem., 1945; diploma in analytical psychology C.G. Jung Inst., Zurich, Switzerland, 1977; m. C. Marie Flory, Aug. 31, 1940; children—Marilyn, Shirley, Paul. Ordained to ministry Ch. of Brethren, 1940; pastor, Pleasant Hill, Ohio, 1945-51, Mt. Morris, Ill., 1951-57; faculty Bethany Theol. Sem., Oak Brook, Ill., 1957-64; dir. ch. relations Manchester Coll., North Manchester, Ind., 1964-72; pvt. practice Jungian analyst, Ft. Wayne, Ind., 1977—. Mem. Internat. Assn. Analytical Psychology. Home: 1633 Goldspur Dr Fort Wayne IN 46804 Office: 6017 Stoney Creek Dr Fort Wayne IN 46825

FRANTZ, STEVEN HAROLD, career devel. specialist; b. Belleville, Ill., Feb. 21, 1950; s. Harold F. and Doris M. (Reed) F.; B.A., Augsburg Coll., Mpls., 1972; M.A., U. Minn., 1980; m. Darla Lovaas, July 22, 1972. Tchr., Robbinsdale (Minn.) Sch. Dist. Evening Sch., 1973-74; mgr. career resource center Minn. Environ. Scis. Found., 1972-74; counselor, dir. career resource center S. Washington County (Minn.) Schs., Cottage Grove, 1974-78; self-employed cons., 1973-78; career devel. specialist Minn. Dept. Edn., St. Paul, 1978—. Mem. Am. Personnel and Guidance Assn., Nat. Vocat. Guidance Assn., Am. Sch. Counselors Assn., Minn. Personnel and Guidance Assn., Minn. Vocat. Guidance Assn. (pres.), Minn. Sch. Counselors Assn., Am. Vocat. Assn., Minn. Vocat. Assn. Co-author: Career Development: The Family-Home-Community Project, vols. 2 and 3, 1973, 74; Planning Together, 1979; Partners: CETA, Education, Youth, 1978; Secondary School Dropouts, 1981. Home: 109 Windsor Ct New Brighton MN 55112 Office: 733 Capitol Sq 550 Cedar St Saint Paul MN 55101

FRANTZ, WILLIAM BRUCE, data processing exec.; b. Butler, Pa., Feb. 22, 1924; s. Gerald Bruce and Pearl Mary (Cousins) F.; student U. Mo., 1943-44. Asst. to pres. Graham Aviation, Butler, Pa., 1940-51, dir. aircraft maintenance, Marianna, Fla., 1951-61; self-employed cons., Akron, Ohio, 1961-62; dir. adminstrn. Graham Engring., Houston, 1963-71; pres., treas. Systems Data, Inc., Akron, 1971—, chmn. bd., 1969—. Served to 2d lt. USAAF, 1943-45. Home: 4230 Hunsicker Dr Akron OH 44319 Office: 2830 Copley Rd Akron OH 44321

FRANZ, EUGENE JOSEPH, cons. co. exec.; b. Chgo., Aug. 28, 1944; s. John Peter and Helen (Zygmont) F.; diploma Divine Heart Sem., Donaldson, Ind., 1962; m. Frances Smith, Apr. 4, 1964; children—Darlene, Kathryn. Bookkeeper, Continental Bank, Chgo., 1962-63; research technician Ill. Central R.R., Chgo., 1963-65; system analyst/project leader AMA, Chgo., 1965-72; with Consumer Systems, 1972—, regional dir., Minnetonka, Minn., 1979-81, regional v.p., 1981—. Chmn. council St. Joseph's Ch., Hopkins, Minn., 1980—. Mem. Soc. Mgmt. Info. Systems. Roman Catholic. Author: (with C.N. Theodore) Reclassification of Physicians, 1968. Office: 10601 Wayzata Blvd Minnetonka MN 55343

FRANZ, LYDIA MILLICENT TRUC (MRS. ROBERT FRANZ), real estate exec.; b. Chgo., Jan. 11, 1924; d. Walter and Lydia (Kralovec) Truc; Mus.B., Ill. Wesleyan U., 1944; Mus.M., Northwestern U., 1949; m. Robert Franz, Aug. 27, 1952. Tchr. music pub. schs., Muskegon, Mich., 1947-48; mktg. research analyst Grant Advt. Agy., Chgo., 1949; asst. to dir. mktg. research Sherman Marquette Advt. Co., Chgo., 1952; asst. to pres., dir. media and research Andover Advt. Agy., 1952-55; salesman Boehmer & Hedlund, realty, Barrington, Ill., 1960-63; pres. Century-21-Country Squire, Inc., Barrington, 1963—. Mem. real estate adv. com. William Rainey Harper Coll., Palatine, Ill., 1971—; mem. adv. com. Office of Real Estate Research, U. Ill., 1981—. Served with WAC, 1944-46. Mem. Women in Real Estate (pres. 1966-67), Barrington Bd. Realtors (pres. 1968-69), Ill. Assn. Realtors (bd. dirs. Real Estate Edn. Found., dir. 1972-75, treas. 1982, gov. Realtor's Inst. of Ill. 1972-78), Nat. Assn. Realtors (dir. 1982), Realtors Nat. Mktg. Inst. (gov. 1979-80), Century 21 Brokers Council No. Ill. (pres.), Barrington C. of C. (v.p. 1968-71, pres. 1974, dir. 1972-75), Am. Cryptogram Soc., Am. Contract Bridge League, Barrington Bus. and Profl. Women's Club, Mensa, Sigma Alpha Iota. Republican. Home: Timberlake 76 Lake View Pkwy Barrington IL 60010 Office: 209 Park Ave Barrington IL 60010

FRANZ, ROBERT JOHN, JR., educator; b. Columbus, Ohio, Aug. 15, 1937; s. Robert John and Mary Barbara (Martin) F.; B.A., St. Charles Coll., Columbus, Ohio, 1961; NSF grantee Ball State U., Muncie, Ind., 1970; M.A.T. (NSF grantee), Mich. State U., 1973; m. Roberta Jane Baum, Apr. 20, 1963; children—Robert III, C. Gregory, Brian, Douglas. Instr. Biology DeSales High Sch., Columbus, Ohio, 1962-70, chmn. Biology dept., 1967-72; asst. prof. secondary edn. Ohio Dominican Coll., Columbus, 1972—, advisor secondary students, 1972—, sec. edn. adv. bd., 1980—, faculty mem. student affairs com., 1981-82. Chmn. United Way, 1980, 81; adv. Kiwanis Key Club, 1968-72; exec. com. Columbus Diocesan Elem. Sch. Bd., 1979-82; faculty rep. Campus Ministry, 1981—; mem. speakers' bur. Ohio Dominicans, 1979—. Mem. Am. Assn. Coll. Tchrs. in Edn., Ohio Assn. Coll. Tchrs. in Edn., Assn. Supervisors and Curriculum Devel. Democrat. Roman Catholic. Home: 2049 Brittany Rd Columbus OH 43229 Office: 4212 Sunbury Rd Columbus OH 43219

FRARY, RICHARD SPENCER, office machines co. exec.; b. Greybull, Wyo., Jan. 29, 1924; s. Frederick Spencer and Margaret Lee Ellen (Chalfant) F.; B.S., in E.E., U. Colo., 1949; postgrad. N.Mex. A&M U., 1954-55, U. Pa., 1955-56, So. Meth. U., 1956-57; m. Eros Hunsaker, July 19, 1946; children—Richard, Jr., Lorraine, John, James. Engring. mgr. RCA, Cherry Hill, N.J., 1952-62; v.p. Ultronic Systems Corp., Pennsauken, N.J., 1962-67; v.p. govt. systems Sperry Univac, various locations, 1967-80; v.p. research and engring. A.B. Dick Co., Niles, Ill., 1980—. Served with USMC, 1943-45, 1950-51. Mem. IEEE, Assn. for Computing Machinery. Republican. Mormon. Office: 5700 W Touhy Ave Niles IL 60648

FRASER, DONALD MACKAY, mayor, former congressman; b. Mpls., Feb. 20, 1924; s. Everett and Lois (MacKay) F.; B.A. cum laude, U. Minn., 1944, LL.B., 1948; m. Arvonne Skelton, June 30, 1950; children—Thomas Skelton, Mary MacKay, John DuFrene, Lois MacKay, Anna Tallman (dec.), Jean S. Admitted to Minn. bar, 1948; practice in Mpls., 1948-62; partner firm Lindquist, Fraser & Magnuson, and predecessors, 1950-62; mem. Minn. Senate, 1954-62, sec. Senate Liberal Caucus, 1955-62; mem. 88th-95th Congresses from 5th Dist. Minn., mem. internat. relations com., budget com., sec., whip, chmn. Dem. study group; mayor City of Mpls., 1980—; mem. study and rev. com. Dem. Caucus; congl. adviser U.S. del. to Law of Sea Conf., 1972-78, to UN Conf. on Disarmament, 1968-73, to UN Commn. on Human Rights, 1974; U.S. del. to 30th session UN Gen. Assembly, 1975, organizer regional presdl. candidate forums, 1975; mem. Commn. on Role and Future of Presdl. Primaries, 1976-77. Vice chmn., mem. bd. Mpls. Citizens Com. on Pub. Edn., 1950-54. Sec. Minn. del. Democratic Nat. Conv., 1960, mem. rules com., 1972, 76; chmn. Minn. Citizens for Kennedy, 1960; mem. platform com. Dem. Nat. Conv., 1964; chmn. commn. on party structure and del. selection Nat. Dem. Com., 1971-72, chmn. subcom. on internat. orgns.; nat. chmn. Dem. Conf., from 1976. Served as lt. (j.g.) USNR, 1944-46. Mem. Mpls. Fgn. Policy Assn. (pres. 1952-53), Citizens League Greater Mpls. (sec. 1951-54), Minn., Hennepin County bar assns., U. Minn. Law Alumni Assn. (dir. 1958-61, 79—), Ams. for Dem. Action (nat. pres. 1973-75), Univ. Dist. Improvement Assn. (pres.). Office: Office of the Mayor City Hall Minneapolis MN 55415*

FRASER, JAMES EARL, mfrs. rep.; b. Mpls., July 28, 1917; s. Clyde Elwood and Pearle (Dunklee) F.; student U. Wis., 1935, 36, U. Idaho, 1936, 37; m. Alma Sophia Bleicher, Nov. 29, 1941; children—James Earl, Joanne Alma Fraser Dennis, Mary Elizabeth Fraser Weathers. Chmn., J. Earl Fraser Co., Inc., Detroit, 1969—; pres. Jefair Co. of Detroit, 1975—; dir. Dorrie Process Co., Inc., Norwalk, Conn., Monroe City Diecasting Co., Kuhlman Diecasting Co., Diemakers, Inc., Monroe City, Mo. Mem. Soc. Automotive Engrs., Soc. Auto Body Engrs. Republican. Methodist. Clubs: Grosse Pointe Yacht (commodore 1963); Country of Detroit, Detroit Golf, Renaissance, Detroit Athletic (Detroit); Bermuda Dunes Country (Calif.); Jupiter Hills (Fla.) Country; Recess, Otsego Ski. Home: 80 S Deeplands Rd Grosse Pointe Shores MI 48236 Office: 21115 Mack Ave Grosse Pointe Woods MI 48236

FRASER, LEILA, city ofcl.; b. Chgo., May 26, 1942; d. Paul and Emily (Dzierzyck) Hucko; A.B. in Polit. Sci. with high distinction, U. Ill., 1964, M.A., 1966, Ph.D., 1971; m. Meredith W. Watts, Sept. 20, 1979; children—Alec Fraser, Christopher Watts. Teaching asst. Carleton U., Ottawa, Can., 1967-68; lectr. polit. sci. U. Ky., Lexington, 1970, asst. dir. Office for Internat. Programs, 1970-72, acting dir., 1972; staff asso. to vice chancellor U. Wis., Milw., 1972-73, asst. to vice chancellor, 1973-76, asst. vice chancellor, 1976-77, asst. to the chancellor, 1977; fin. and econ. researcher money market dept. Harris Trust & Savs. Bank, Chgo., 1974; chief adminstr. to mayor, Milw., 1977—; U.S. rep. to 20th Gen. Conf. of UNESCO, Paris, France, 1978. Mem. nominations com. Planning and Allocation Council, United Way of Greater Milw., 1977—; bd. dirs., 1st v.p. Milw. Council on ALcoholism, 1976—; mem. pres.'s council Concordia Coll., 1979—; adv. com. on women and minorities Commr. Securities, State of Wis., 1976-80; bd. dirs. Community Pride Expo, 1980—, Milw. Exposition, Conv. Center and Arena, 1978—, Milw. Symphony Orch., 1979—, Ind. Milw. Performing Arts Cos., 1979—; mem. Am. council on edn. Nat. Commn. Higher Edn. Issues, 1981—. Am. Council on Edn. fellow, 1976-77. Mem. Am. Soc. for Public Adminstrn., Am. Polit. Sci. Assn., Midwest Polit. Sci. Assn., Women's Caucus for Polit. Sci., Phi Beta Kappa, Phi Delta Kappa. Home: 3459 N Frederick Ave Milwaukee WI 53211 Office: Mayor's Office 200 E Wells St Milwaukee WI 53202

FRASS, MELVIN RAYMOND, ednl. adminstr.; b. Toledo, June 15, 1930; s. Joseph Edward and Benigna Anastasia (Palicki) F.; B.A., U. Toledo, 1974, M.A., 1977; m. Beverly Eileen, Sept. 28, 1951; children—Terry, Tim, Tana, Tracey, Todd. Owner, operator Automatic Appliance Service, Toledo, 1953-65; vocat. tchr. Toledo Macomber Vocat. High Sch., 1965-76; trade and industry supr. Sylvania (Ohio) City Schs., 1976-77; vocat. dir. Tri-Rivers Jr. Vocat. Sch., Marion, Ohio, 1977—; supt. Delaware (Ohio) City-County Joint Vocat. Sch., 1981; cons. Instructional Materials Lab., Ohio State U., Served with U.S. Army, 1948-49. Mem. Am. Vocat. Assn., Ohio Vocat. Dirs. Assn., Iota Lambda Sigma. Republican. Roman Catholic. Clubs: Lions. Exchange (Marion). Home: 2339 Newmans Cardington Rd W Prospect OH 43342 Office: 2222 Marion Mt Gilead Rd Marion OH 43302

FRAZEE, P.C., lawyer; b. Mt. Hope, Kans., Sept. 10, 1905; s. Charles and Lula (Martin) F.; LL.B., U. Kans., 1931; m. Catherine McAdam, Jan. 13, 1936. Admitted to Kans. bar 1931, since practiced in Syracuse; also abstracter real estate. Mem. Am., Kans., S.W. Kans. bar assns., Kans. Abstract Assn., V.F.W. Am. Legion, C. of C., Sigma Nu. Presbyn. Elk, Rotarian. Home: 701 Sumner St Syracuse KS 67878 Office: 301 N Main St Syracuse KS 67878

FRAZHO, JOYCE (MARTY) KATHERINE, clin. psychiat. social worker; b. North Boston, N.Y., Apr. 11, 1936; d. William August and Bernice Dorothy (Monckton) Schindler; A.S. summa cum laude, Oakland Community Coll., 1976-78; B.S.W., Wayne State U., 1980, M.S.W., 1981; m. Howard J. Frazho, Aug. 20, 1967. Dir. Outpatient Clinic, Salvation Army Harbor Light, Detroit, 1974-77; therapist didactics and coordinator Central Diagnostic and Referral Center, Robinwood Clinic, Detroit, 1977; therapist, didactics Psychol. Resources, Inc., Bloomfield Hills, Mich., 1977-80; dir. substance abuse program The Behavior Center, Birmingham, Mich., 1980—. Midwest Inst. Alcohol Studies scholar, 1975; Alcohol Therapist Tng. Program scholar, 1975-76; Merit scholar, 1978-80; Grad. Profl. scholar, 1980-81; cert. alcohol and drug counselor. Mem. Mich. Assn. Alcohol and Drug Counselors, Mich. Alcohol and Addiction Assn., Nat. Assn. Social Workers, Mich. Soc. Clin. Social Work, Wayne State U. Alumni Assn. Democrat. Research on equality between female and male in social work profession, didactic substance abuse prevention programs. Home: 1514 Washington Blvd Apt 609 Detroit MI 48226 Office: 111 S Woodward Ave Suite 250 Birmingham MI 48011

FRAZIER, GLENN GREVE, architect; b. Centralia, Ill., Oct. 23, 1925; s. Roy Estee and Mildred Mary (Greve) F.; B.S., U. Ill., 1948. With H. Samuel Kruse, Architect, 1942-43; partner S.A. Clausen & Assos., 1948-52; owner Glenn G. Frazier & Assos., Urbana, Ill., 1952—, br. office, Leesburg, Fla., 1956-61; dist. dir. Central Nat. Life Ins. Co., Jacksonville, Ill., 1962-65, dir., 1966-70; dir. Am. Comml. Investment Corp., 1965-78; vis. prof. U. Ill., 1972-73; mem. Gov.'s Rev. Bd. for Architecture Exams., 1960. Pres., United Community Council, 1964-65; bd. dirs. Family Service, 1958-64, pres., 1961; bd. dirs. United Fund, 1964-65; mem. adv. com. Lake Land Coll., 1971—. Fellow Constrn. Specifications Inst. (chpt. pres. 1968, 69, 71-73, region dir., mem. nat. bd. dirs. 1975-78), Gargoyle Soc., Nat. Council Archtl. Registration Bds., Alpha Delta Phi. Methodist. Clubs: Mo. Athletic, Masons, Shriners, Elks. Designer: So. Hills bldgs. So. Ill. U., 1959, Burnsides Research Lab., U. Ill., 1962, Nat. hdqrs. Nat. Council Tchrs. English, 1969, Rolla (Mo.) Nursing Home, 1978, Lincoln Land Downs Race Track, Sherman, Ill., 1979. Home: 120 S Race St Urbana IL 61801 Office: 122 S Race St Urbana IL 61801

FRAZIER, JIMMY LEON, physician; b. Beaumont, Tex., Aug. 29, 1939; s. Leon and Thelma (Cooper) F.; B.S., Tex. So. U., 1960; M.D., Meharry Med. Coll., 1967; m. Shirley Jolley, June 26, 1971; children—Keith, David, Andrea Nichole. Tchr. math. Beaumont (Tex.) Sch. Dist., 1960-63; aerospace engr. NASA, Houston, summer 1964; intern, Good Samaritan Hosp., Dayton, Ohio, 1967-68, resident in internal medicine, 1971-72; practice medicine specializing in family practice, Park DuValle Health Center, Louisville, 1968-69, Dayton, Ohio, 1972—; mem. staff Good Samaritan Hosp., St. Elizabeth Hosp., 1972—; mem. admission com. Wright State U. Med. Sch., Dayton, 1978-80. Served to maj. U.S. Army, 1969-71. Diplomate Am. Bd. Family Practice. Fellow Am. Acad. Family Physicians; mem. Gem City Med. Soc. (pres. 1976-78), AMA, Ohio Med. Soc., Nat. Med. Assn., Montgomery County Med. Assn., Alpha Phi Alpha. Methodist. Clubs: Dayton Selectmen, Dayton Racquet, Masons (Shriner). Home: 543 Valewood Ln Dayton OH 45406 Office: 1401 Salem Ave Dayton OH 45406

FRAZIER, JOHN HOWIE, JR., steel co. exec.; b. Pitts., Mar. 5, 1921; s. John H. and Bertha (Allison) F.; student Coll. of Wooster, 1939-40; B.A., U. Mich., 1942; m. Virginia Lindenmuth, Jan. 25, 1944; children—Dianne (Mrs. Robert Lytle), Jeffrey, Deborah. Office mgr. Sennett Steel Corp., Detroit, 1946-52; partner Tartan Steel Co., Detroit, 1952-57; v.p. Mich. Metal Processing Corp., Detroit, 1957-69, pres., 1969—; pres. M&F Cartage Co., Detroit, 1959—. Exec. adv. bd. Fla. Atlantic U. Served to 1st lt. USAAF, 1942-45. Decorated Air medal, Purple Heart. Mem. USCG Aux. Presbyn. Clubs: Kiwanis, Detroit Yacht; Mackinac Island (Mich.) Yacht. Home: 144 Claremont Dr Dearborn MI 48124 also 2871 N Ocean Blvd Boca Raton FL 33432 also 8281 Clinton-Macon Rd Clinton MI 49236 Office: 6650 Mt Elliott Ave Detroit MI 48211

FRAZIER, JOHN HUGH, JR., grain co. exec.; b. Toledo, Sept. 27, 1917; s. John Hugh and Minnie Alice (Smith) F.; B.S., U. Pa., 1939; m. Dolores Thornhill, June 14, 1941; children—John Hugh III, Richard Thornhill. Warehouse examiner U.S. Dept. Agr., Indpls., 1940-42; v.p. P.R. Markley, Inc., Phila., 1946-52, pres., 1952—; pres. Tarheel Grain Co., Inc., Morehead City, N.C., 1952-62, Beam & Co., 1964—, Am. Mining & Exploration Co., 1965—; partner Hennessy & Assos., 1969-76; v.p. Bunge Corp., Phila., 1962-69; v.p. Tiger Tails Farms, Inc., Dyersburg, Tenn.; dir. Frazier-Parrott div. Heinold Commodities Inc.; dir. Comml. Exchange of Phila., 1953-56, v.p., 1956-68. Mem. Comml. Exchange Phila., 1953-56, v.p., 1956-58; mem. Chgo. Bd. Trade, 1968—, dir., 1974-76, vice chmn., chmn. fin. com., 1977—; mem. agrl. adv. com. Fed. Energy Office, 1974-76; chmn. Feed Grain Contract Com., 1976-77. Sec. Troop Com., Troop 19, Boy Scouts Am., Bryn Mawr, 1961-64. Trustee P.W. Markley Trust, Nat. Grain and Feed Found. Served to 1st lt., USNR, 1943-46. Mem. Nat. Assn. Grain and Feed Assn. (dir., mem. exec. com. 1960-64, pres. 1971-74, chmn. exec. com. 1974-76), Internat. Platform Assn. Presbyn. (deacon, elder, trustee). Mason. Clubs: Union League, Downtown (Phila.); Overbrook Golf (Radnor, Pa.); Capitol Hill (Washington); Monroe (Chgo.). Home: 400 E Outer Dr Apt 2719 Chicago IL 60601 also 2800 S Ocean Blvd Boca Raton FL 33432 Office: Bd Trade Chicago IL 60604

FRECKA, JOHN ALLISON, steel co. exec., lawyer; b. Ironton, Ohio, Jan. 12, 1929; s. James Harold and Margaret Helene (Fowler) F.; B.S., Marshall U., 1950; J.D., Wayne State U., 1967; m. Lois Joann Williams, Sept. 23, 1950; children—Deborah, David, John, Mary Anne. Personnel mgr. Detroit Strip div. Cyclops Corp., Detroit, 1951-64, turn supt., 1964-68, gen. supt., 1969-73, gen. mgr., 1974-76; admitted to Mich. bar, 1967; v.p. Empire-Detroit Steel div. Cyclops Corp., Mansfield, Ohio, 1976-78, pres., 1979—. Mem. Mich. Bar Assn. Home: 2065 Matthes Dr Mansfield OH 44906 Office: 913 Bowman St Mansfield OH 44901

FREDELAKE, DIANA MARIE, advt. agy. exec.; b. Dodge City, Kans., Oct. 24, 1945; d. Anthony Joseph and Genevieve Beatrice (Kerschen) Arensdorf; student Dodge City Community Coll.; children—Dawn Renee, Michelle Marie. Telephone operator Southwestern Bell, Dodge City, 1963-65; exec. sec. Dodge City Med. Center, 1965-66; with Lane & Leslie Advt. Agy., Inc., Wichita, Kans., 1973—, media dir. 1975—. Mem. Wichita Advt. Club. Democrat. Roman Catholic. Home: 2702 Maxwell St Wichita KS 67217 Office: Lane & Leslie Advt Agency Inc 221 S Broadway Wichita KS 67201

FREDERICK, CLARA MAY, educator; b. Douglas County, Ill.; d. William Leslie and Cora Mabel (Hall) Queen; A.B., Defiance Coll., 1946; M.S., Ohio State U., 1964, Ph.D., 1967; m. Victor Ray Frederick, June 27, 1936; children—Barbara Ann, Rosemary, Victor Ray. High sch. tchr. history and biology, Clark County, Ohio, 1945-46, 55-56, 66; asst. prof. biology Urbana (Ohio) Coll., 1967-70, asso. prof., 1970-77, prof., 1977—. Elder, 1st Presbyn. Ch., 1975—. Mem. Am. Hort. Soc., Am. Fern Soc., Bot. Soc. Am., Ohio Acad. Sci., Ohio Biol. Soc., Am. Rose Soc. Republican. Home: 145 Tanglewood Dr Urbana OH 43078 Office: Urbana College College Way Urbana OH 43078

FREDERICK, MELVIN LYLE, state senator; b. West Concord, Minn., Nov. 24, 1929; s. Elmer and Martha E. (Pagel) F.; grad. high sch.; m. Donna M. Christopherson, 1956; children—Mitchell Scott, Debra Leigh, Michael Alan. Registered rep. Dain, Bosworth, Inc., Rochester, Minn., 1973—; mem. Minn. Senate, 1970—. Republican precinct chmn., West Concord, 1961-67; vice chmn. Dodge County Rep. Com., 1965-67, chmn., 1967-69; vice chmn. First Dist. Rep. Com., 1969-72. Served with Army NG, 1948-52; Korea. Mem. Minn. Food Retailers Assn., West Concord Businessmen's Assn. Republican. Methodist. Clubs: Lions, Masons. Office: 122A State Office Bldg Saint Paul MN 55155

FREDERICK, VIRGINIA FIESTER, state legislature; b. Rock Island, Ill., Dec. 24, 1916; d. John Henry and Myrtle (Montgomery) Heise; B.A., U. Iowa, 1938; postgrad. Lake Forest (Ill.) Coll., 1942-43; m. Charles Donnan Fiester, Sept. 1, 1937 (dec. 1975); children—Sheryl Fiester Mestemaker, Alan Richard, James Donnan; m. 2d, Kenneth Jacob Frederick, Nov. 9, 1978. Freelance fashion designer, Lake Forest, 1952-78; pres. Mid Am. China Exchange,

Ill. Ho. of Reps. from 31st Dist., 1979—. Bd. dirs. UN —; alderman, City of Lake Forest, 1974-78. Recipient man of Achievement award, 1978, Lottie Holman 1st Term or award, 1980. Mem. LWV (past chpt. pres.), AAUW (past pres.). Republican. Methodist.

REDERICKS, HENRY JACOB, lawyer, counselor; b. St. Louis, Dec. 1, 1925; s. Henry Jacob III and Mary Elizabeth (Pieron) F.; J.D., St. Louis U., 1950, postgrad. Sch. Commerce and Finance, 1945-47; m. Marjorie Helen Kiely, 1951 (div. 1962); children—Joseph Henry, James Andrew, Elizabeth Ann; m. Susan Kay Brennecke, 1971; 1 son, William Michael. Admitted to Mo. bar, 1950; practice law, St. Louis County, 1950—; with firm Mark D. Eagleton, 1960, Goldenhersh, Fredericks & Newman, 1961-69, Friedman and Fredericks, 1969-81; chief trial atty. for circuit atty. St. Louis, 1955; 1st asst. to circuit atty., 1957; spl. asst. to circuit attys., 1960-81; asst. U.S. atty. Eastern Dist. Mo.; lectr. in field. Mem. Mo. Athletic Commn. 1974-76; boxing chmn. Mo. Athletic Commn. and Ozark AAU, 1977. Served with USAAF, 1943-46; ETO. Decorated Air medal with 4 battle stars. Mem. Am., Mo., St. Louis County bar assns., Am. Trial Lawyers Assn., Internat. Platform Assn., Delta Theta Phi. Home: 2243 Whitby Rd Clarkson Valley MO 63017 Office: US Ct and Custom House Office of US Atty Saint Louis MO 63101

FREDERICKS, MARSHALL MAYNARD, sculptor; b. Rock Island, Ill., Jan. 31, 1908; s. Frank A. and Frances Margaret (Bragg) F.; student John Huntington Poly. Inst., Cleve.; grad. Cleve. Sch. Art, 1930; student Heimann Schule, Schwegerle Schule, Munich, Germany, Academie Scandinav, Paris, France, pvt. studios Rome and London, Carl Milles' Studio, Stockholm, Sweden, Cranbrook Acad. Art Bloomfield Hills, Mich.; recipient 3 hon. doctorates in fine arts; m. Rosalind Bell Cooke, Sept. 9, 1943; children—Carl Marshall and Christopher Matzen (twins), Frances Karen Bell, Rosalind Cooke, Suzanne Pelletreau. Faculty Cleve. Sch. Art, 1931, Cranbrook Acad. Art, Kingswood Sch., Cranbrook, 1932-42; Royal Danish consul Mich.; local, nat., internat. exhbns. art since 1928 include: Carnegie Inst., Cleve. Mus., Pa. Acad., Chgo. Art Inst., Whitney Mus., Detroit Art Inst., Denver Mus., Phila. Internat. Invitational, N.Y. World's Fair Am. Art Exhbn., Modern Sculpture Internat. Exhbn. Detroit, Internat. Sculpture Show Cranbrook Mus., A.I.A., Nat. Sculpture Soc., Architectural League of N.Y., Mich. Acad., Brussels, others; commns. include: N.Y. World's Fair Baboon Fountain, Levi Barbour Meml. Fountain, Rackham Meml. Bldg., Fort Street Sta., Vets. Meml. Bldg., Detroit; adminstrn. bldg., war meml. U. Mich., Louisville Courier-Jour. Bldg., Jefferson Sch., Wyandotte, Mich., Holy Ghost Sem., Ann Arbor, Mich., union bldg. Ohio State U., Ford Rotunda, Marc Joslyn Meml., Alvan Macauley Meml. City-County Bldg., Ford Auditorium, Detroit Zoological Garden, also the Indian River Shrine, State Dept. Fountain, Washington; Cleve. War Meml. Fountain, Milw. Pub. Mus. Sculpture, N.Y. World's Fair permanent sculpture, Fed. Bldg. sculpture, Cin., Community Nat. Bank, Pontiac, Mich., Sir Winston Churchill Meml., Freeport, Bahamas, Two Sister fountain, Cranbrook, Michigan, Dallas Library sculpture, Henry Ford Meml., Dearborn, Mich., fountain Oakland U., Rochester, Mich., Midland (Mich.) Center Arts, Crittenton Hosp., Rochester, Mich., Fgn. Ministry, Copenhagen, many others; portrait commns. include: Senator Arthur Vandenburg, Willard Dow, Midland, Mich., George G. Booth Meml., Cranbrook, Mrs. Horace Rackham Meml., Yoshita, Pres. John F. Kennedy, others; works included numerous museums, pvt., civic collections. Co-founder, dir. DIADEM Program for Internat. Exchange of Handicapped; trustee Am. Scandinavian Found., People-to-People Program. Served with C.E., AUS, 1942-44, lt. col. 20th bomber command; 8th Air Force, Okinawa, 1944-45. Decorated knight Order of Dannebrog, 1963, officer, 1971, comdr.'s cross, 1978; knight 1st class order St. Olav (Norway), 1972; recipient of 1st prize Cleve. Mus. Art, 1931, Anna Scripps Whitcomb prize Detroit Inst. Arts, 1938; 1st prize internat. exhbn. Dance Internat., Rockefeller Center, N.Y.C., 1st prize Barbour Meml. nat. competition, medal Mich. Inst. Architects, fine arts gold medal A.I.A., 1952, gold medal honor Mich. Acad. Arts, Letters, Sci., 1953; Achtl. League of New York; Golden Plate award Am. Acad. Achievement; citation Am. Inst. Decorators, Nat. Soc. Crippled Children and Adults, State of Mich., U. Detroit, others; Henry Hering medal Nat. Sculpture Soc., 1972. Fellow Internat. Inst. Arts and Letters: mem. Mich. Soc. Architects, AIA, St. Dunstans Dramatic Guild, Mich. Acad. Sci., Arts and Letters, C. of C., Nat. Acad. Design, Am. Inst. Decorators, Nat. Soc. Interior Designers, Beta Sigma Phi, Alpha Beta Delta. Clubs: Royal Swedish Yacht; Orchard Lake Country; Architectural League N.Y. (N.Y.C.) Prismatic (Detroit); Royal Norwegian Yacht; Royal Danish Yacht. Home: 440 Lake Park Dr Birmingham MI 48009 Studio: 4113 N Woodward Ave Royal Oak MI 48072 also East Long Lake Rd Bloomfield Hills MI 48072

FREDERICKSON, DENNIS RUSSEL, state senator, farmer; b. Brookville Twp., Minn., July 27, 1939; s. Louis B. and Mary Johana (Kragh) F.; B.S., U. Minn., 1961; m. Marjorie Dianne Davidson, July 15, 1961; children—Kari, Karl, Disa. Farmer, Morgan, Minn.; dir. Redwood Electric Coop.; mem. Minn. State Senate, 1980—. Commr. Redwood County, 1972-80. Served with USNR, 1962-67. Mem. Am. Soc. Agrl. Econs., Am. Soc. Animal Sci., SW Farm Mgmt. Assn., Council Agrl. Scis. and Tech. Republican. Presbyterian. Office: Room 133 State Office Bldg Saint Paul MN 55155

FREDERICKSON, KEITH ALVIN, advt. agy. exec.; b. Wakefield, Nebr., June 11, 1925; s. Alvin Frederick and Evelyn Edith (Gunning) F.; B.Sc. in Agrl. Journalism, U. Nebr., 1950; postgrad. Iowa State U., 1952-54; m. Grace Adair McConnell, Sept. 14, 1956; children—Jon Paul, Kelley Adair. Copywriter, Western Advt. Agy., Chgo., 1954-55, Sta. WDSU-TV, New Orleans, 1955-56; prodn. mgr. Ayres/Swanson, Lincoln, Nebr., 1957-59; creative coordinator Savage-Dow Assos., Omaha, 1959-66; founder, pres. Frederickson/Hounshell Advt., Omaha, 1966—. Mem. Douglas County Election Bd., 1961—, supr., 1975—. Served with USN, 1943-46, 50-52; PTO. Mem. Nat. Agrl. Mktg. Assn. (past pres.), Omaha Agri-Bus. Club (past pres.), Omaha Ad Club. Republican. Presbyterian (trustee). Clubs: Omaha Optimist (past pres.), Masons. Address: Frederickson/Hounshell Assos 809 S 75th St Omaha NE 68114

FREDLUND, PHYLLIS JEAN, educator; b. Dawson, Minn., June 23, 1928; d. Walter Nelton and Emma Annette (Anderson) Swenson; student Luther Coll., Decorah, Iowa, 1946-47; A.A., Clifton (Tex.) Coll., 1948; B.S., Mankato (Minn.) State U., 1966, postgrad., 1969-81; m. Wilford Fredlund, June 26, 1948. Elem. tchr. Yellow Medicine County Rural Sch., Canby, Minn., 1950-57, Clarkfield (Minn.) Public Sch., 1957—; chmn. instrn. and profl. devel. council S.W. UniServ, Marshall, Minn., 1971-81; mem. Minn. Bd. Teaching, St. Paul, 1979-83; chmn. S.W. and West Central ednl. coop. service unit Tchr. Center Policy Bd., 1977-81. Caucus del. to county and dist. Republican Conv., 1978-80; deacon Granite Falls Lutheran Ch., 1982—. Recipient Outstanding Elem. Tchr. of Am. award, 1972. Mem. Minn. Edn. Assn. (instrn. profl. devel. council 1971-81), Clarkfield Tchrs. Assn., Minn. Edn. Assn., NEA, Nat. Council Tchrs. Math., Assn. Supervision and Curriculum Devel., AAUW, Delta Kappa Gamma. Republican. Contbr. articles to profl. publs. Home: 104 Skyline Dr Granite Falls MN 56241 Office: Clarkfield Public Sch Clarkfield MN 56223

FREDRICKS, EDGAR JOHN, state senator; b. Holland, Mich., June 27, 1942; s. Russel John and Audrey Kathryn (Beckman) F.; A.B., Calvin Coll., 1964; M.A., Western Mich. U., 1967, M.A., 1968. Mem. staff U.S. Congressman Guy VanderJagt, 1967; exec. dir. Mich. Citizens for Nixon, 1968; with Fgn. Service Inst., Dept. State, Washington, 1969; vice consul Am. embassy, Seoul, Korea, 1970-72; fgn. service res. officer Dept. State, polit. officer Bur. Internat. Orgn. Affairs, Washington, 1972-74; mem. Mich. Ho. of Reps. from 54th Dist., 1975-78; mem. Mich. Senate, 1978—. Mem. U.S. del. UN Trusteeship Council, N.Y.C., 1972, 73; vice chmn. Mich. Conservative Union, 1977-79, chmn., 1979—; bd. dirs. Am. Legis. Exchange Council. Recipient award Mayor of Seoul, Korea, 1972. Mem. Christian Reformed Ch. Author: MacArthur: His Mission and Meaning, 1968. Home: 844 Millbridge PV Holland MI 49423 Office: State Senate State Capitol Lansing MI 48909

FREDRICKSON, MARY FRANCES LONG (MRS. EDWARD FREDRICKSON), ret. assn. exec., journalist; b. Burlington, Ia., Mar. 13, 1915; d. John Edgar and Crystal (Henry) Long; grad. high sch.; student Dale Carnegie, 1967-68; m. Edward E. Fredrickson, Nov. 26, 1935; children—James Edward, Thomas Henry, Lawrence Francis, Dennis Paul. Women's editor Lead (S.D.) Daily Call and Deadwood Pioneer-Times, 1958-64, 66-73; exec. sec. Lead C. of C., 1973-80, ret., 1980; part-time reporter Whitewood (S.D.) Centennial, 1980—. Active U.S.O. Community Concert Assn., A.R.C., Heart Fund; v.p. St. Patrick's P.T.A., 1951-53; mem. exec. com. Deadwood-Lead Centennial, Inc.; publicity chmn. Lawrence County unit Am. Cancer Soc.; del. S.D. Pledge 55 Conf.; past pres. Republican Women; lector, parish council sec. Roman Cath. Ch. Recipient Jane McLean award for best piece writing in Lead Woman's Club creative writing contest, 1954; 1st prize for critic's rev. S.D. Press Women, 1971, 72. Mem. Nat. League Am. Pen Women (v.p. Black Hills br. 1964-66, pres. 1966-68, pres. S.D. 1968-70), Black Hills Art Assn. (publicity com. 1963-64), S.D. Press Women, Lead-Deadwood Bus. and Profl. Women, DAR (Black Hills chpt.). Republican. Home: 504 Grand Ave Lead SD 57754 Office: 100 E Main St Lead SD 57754

FREE, DOYLE HENDERSON, poultry orgn. exec.; b. Blue Springs, Nebr., Sept. 1, 1920; s. Harry Walker and Minnie Mae (McPheron) F.; B.S., U. Nebr., 1943, postgrad., 1949-51; m. Edna Louise Gill, Dec. 27, 1942; children—James Doyle, Russel Kenan, Bette Louise, Wayne Henderson. Prof. mil. sci. Colo. State U., Ft. Collins, 1948-49; exec. sec. Nebr. Poultry Improvement Assn., 1950-69; gen. mgr. Nebr. Poultry Industries, Inc., 1969—; chief div. poultry and egg devel. utilization and mktg. Nebr. Dept. Agr., 1976—. Bd. dirs. Nebr. Agrl. Council, 1971—, pres., 1974, chmn. legis. com., 1975—; Nebr. state coordinator Nat. Poultry Improvement Plan, 1953—; mem., gen. conf. com., nat. poultry improvement plan U.S. Dept. Agr., 1954-56; legis. rep. Nat. Turkey Fedn., 1973; bd. dirs. Midwest Poultry Fedn., 1974—, mem. pullorum com., north central states disease conf., 1966-70; pres. Nat. Good Egg Club, 1956-58. Mem. com., troop 50 Boy Scouts Am., 1954—. Served to capt. AUS, 1943-49. Recipient Blue Rooster award Poultry and Egg Nat. Bd., 1959, Scouting award Troop 50, Boy Scouts Am., 1958; named Nebr. Poultryman of Yr., Nebr. Poultry Industries, Inc., 1975. Mem. Poultry Sci. Assn., Am. Soc. Assn. Execs., Res. Officers Assn. U.S., Am. Legion, Sigma Xi, Gamma Sigma Delta (award of merit Nebr. chpt. 1976). Republican. Methodist (chmn. ofcl. bd. 1973-76). Club: Kiwanis. Home: 4146 Y St Lincoln NE 68503 Office: Mussehl Hall U Nebr Lincoln NE 68503

FREEBAIRN, ALONZO GEORGE, educator; b. Pitts., Jan. 9, 1922; s. Thomas and Margret (Montooth) F.; B.A., Earlham Coll., 1943; M.A., Concordia Tchrs. Coll., 1971; m. Bettie Ruth Hargrave, Apr. 1, 1944; children—Judith Lynn, Donald Scott, Bruce Douglas. Sec., YMCA, Detroit, 1945-50, Chgo., 1950-60; social worker Cook County Office Equal Opportunity Settlement Houses, Chgo., 1960-69; tchr. Dist. 25 Schs., Arlington Heights, Ill., 1970—. Served with AUS, 1943-45. Certified social worker; certified YMCA sec. Mem. Am. Personnel and Guidance Assn., Nat. Vocat. and Guidance Assn., NEA, Am. Legion (post comdr. 1979-80). Presbyterian. Clubs: Moose, Lions (sec. 1964-67). Home: 730 E 164th St South Holland IL 60473

FREED, CATHERINE CAROL MOORE (MRS. DEBOW FREED), educator; b. Omaha, Dec. 27, 1925; d. Prentice Lauri and Henryetta (Banker) Moore; B.A., B.F.A., U. Tex., 1948; M.A., U. Kans., 1961; m. DeBow Freed, Sept. 10, 1949; 1 son, DeBow II. Mem. faculty St. Mary's Coll., Xavier, Kans., 1958-59, U. Kans., Lawrence, 1959-61, U. N.Mex., Albuquerque, 1961-65, Huntingdon Coll., Montgomery, Ala., 1965-67, Ladycliff Coll., Highland Falls, N.Y., 1967-69. Adviser, Albuquerque Sch. System on Gifted Child Edn., 1962-64; writer, producer film on purposes and objectives of PTA, 1964; elder United Presbyterian Ch. U.S.A., commr. 189th Gen. Assembly; moderator Gt. Rivers Presbytery, 1979; pres. Alliance Community Concert Assn., 1970-74. Mem. Speech Assn. Am., Nat. Council Tchrs. English, Daus. of U.S. Army (pres. chpt. Ft. Benning, Ga. 1954-55), Internat. Platform Assn., P.E.O., Mortar Bd., Phi Beta Kappa, Kappa Phi, Delta Sigma Rho, Pi Kappa Delta, Alpha Psi Omega, Alpha Delta Pi. Home: 115 W Lima Ave Ada OH 45810 Office: Ohio Northern U Ada OH 45810

FREED, DEBOW, coll. pres.; b. Hendersonville, Tenn., Aug. 26, 1925; s. John Walter and Ella Lee (DeBow) F.; B.S., U.S. Mil. Acad., 1946; grad. U.S. Army Command and Gen. Staff Coll., 1959; M.S., U. Kans., 1961; Ph.D., U. N.Mex., 1966; grad. U.S. Air War Coll., 1966; m. Catherine Carol Moore, Sept. 10, 1949; 1 son, DeBow, II. Commd. lt. U.S. Army, 1946, advanced through grades to col., 1967; instr. The Inf. Sch., 1953-56; comdr. 32d Inf., 1956-57; instr. Command and Gen. Staff Coll., 1957-58; chief nuclear br. U.S. Atomic Energy Agy., 1961-65; instr. physics dept. U.S. Mil. Acad., 1967-69, ret., 1969; dean Mt. Union Coll., 1969-74; pres. Monmouth Coll., 1974-79; pres. Ohio No. U., Ada, 1979—; officer Consortia of Colls. and Univs. Vice pres., dir. Buckeye council Boy Scouts Am., 1972-74, dir. Prairie council, 1974-78. Decorated Bronze Star, Legion of Merit, 1967, 69; Legion of Honor (Iran), 1953; recipient various civic and service awards. Associated Western Univs. fellow, 1963-65; AEC fellow, 1963-65; Fgn. Policy Research Inst. fellow, 1966. Author: Using Nuclear Capabilities, 1959; Pulsed Neutron Techniques, 1965; contbr. articles, revs. to profl. publs.; editor: Atomic Development Report, 1962-64. Office: Office of Pres Ohio No U Ada OH 45810

FREED, JACOB BRESSLER, mfg. co. exec.; b. York, Pa., Mar. 7, 1921; s. Claude Raymond and Laura Virginia (McNamee) F.; B.S.M.E., N.C. State U., 1947; m. Norma Ailene Carder, July 31, 1948; children—Kenneth C., James E., Lori A. Engr., Duriron Co., Dayton, Ohio, 1947-59, dir. engring., 1959-63; v.p. engring. Union Pump Co., Battle Creek, Mich., 1963-65, v.p. mfg. and engring., 1965-70, pres., chief exec. officer, 1970—; dir. Fed. Home Life Ins. Co., PHF Life Ins. Co., Riverside Ins. Co., Wolverine Ins. Co., Mich. Nat. Bank. Chmn. mfg. div. Battle Creek United Fund Campaign, 1973; dir. United Arts Council, Battle Creek, 1973; dir. Family and Childrens Services Agy. Calhoun County, 1971; city commr. Battle Creek, 1968; dir. Community Hosp., Olivet Coll. Served with USN. Fellow ASME; mem. Hydraulics Inst. (pres. 1976), Detroit Engring. Soc., Am. Petroleum Inst. Congregationalist. Clubs: Lions, Rotary, Masons. Patentee in field. Office: 87 Capital Ave SW Battle Greek MI 49016

FREEDMAN, DAVID NOEL, clergyman, educator; b. N.Y.C., May 12, 1922; s. David and Beatrice (Goodman) F.; student CCNY, 1935-38, UCLA, 1938-39; Th.B., Princeton Theol. Sem., 1944; Ph.D. (William S. Rayner fellow) in Semitic Langs. and Lit., Johns Hopkins U., 1948; D.Litt. (hon.), U. of the Pacific, 1973; D.Sc. (hon.), Davis and Elkins Coll., 1974; m. Cornelia Anne Pryor, May 16, 1944; children—Meredith Ann, Nadezhda, David Micaiah, Jonathan Pryor. Ordained to ministry Presbyn. Ch., 1944; pastor Presbyn. Chs. in Deming, Wash., 1944-45; asst. instr. Johns Hopkins U., Balt., 1947-48; asst. prof. O.T., Western Theol. Sem., Pitts., 1948-51, prof. Hebrew and O.T., 1951-60; prof. Hebrew and O.T., Pitts. Theol. Sem. (successor to Western Theol. Sem.), 1960-61, James A. Kelso prof., 1961-64; prof. O.T., San Francisco Theol. Sem., 1964-70, dean of faculty, 1966-70, Gray prof. O.T. exegesis, 1970-71; prof. O.T., Grad. Theol. Union, Berkeley, Calif., 1964-71; prof. Bibl. studies U. Mich., Ann Arbor, 1971—, dir. program on studies in religion, 1971—; Danforth vis. prof. Internat. Christian U., Tokyo, 1967; vis. prof. Hebrew U., Jerusalem, 1976-77, Macquarie U., North Ryde, New South Wales, Australia, 1980, Brigham Young U., Provo, Utah, 1981, 82, U. Queensland, St. Lucia, Brisbane, Australia; cons. to Reader's Digest, Atlas of the Bible, 1979—, Funk & Wagnall Pub. Co., New Ency., 1979—; tech. cons. to Milberg Productions, 1961—; ann. dir. Albright Inst. Archaeological Reserach, Jerusalem, 1969-70, 76-77; editorial cons. Macmillan Co., 1961-66; mem. task force on bibl. authority and interpretation United Presbyn. Ch. in U.S., 1979—; vis. lectr. various colls. and sems., 1948—. Recipient Laymen's Nat. Bible Com. Ann. award, 1978; Guggenheim fellow, 1958-59. Mem. Am. Acad. Religion, Soc. Bibl. Lit. (pres. midwest br. 1964), Am. Schs. Oriental Research (editor Bull. 1974-78), Soc. for Sci. Study Religion, Am. Oriental Soc., World Council of Chs., Am. Assn. Colls. (mem. commn. on religion in higher edn. 1974—), Am. Archeol. Inst., U. Mich. Research Club, Bibl. Colloquium (sec. treas. 1958—), Explorers Club. Author books on Bible and Christianity, 1949—, including: William Foxwell Albright: Twentieth Century Genius, 1975; (with B. Mazar and G. Cornfeld) The Mountain of the Lord, 1975; (with W. Phillips) An Explorer's Life of Jesus, 1975; Pottery, Poetry, Prophecy, 1980; co-author: Commentary on Hosea, 1980; contbr. numerous articles and Bibl. studies to scholarly jours.; editor-in-chief Anchor Bible Series, 1971—; co-editor Computer Bible Series, 1975—. Home: 1520 Broadway Ann Arbor MI 48105 Office: Studies in Religion 468 Lorch Hall U Mich Ann Arbor MI 48109

FREEDMAN, SAMUEL, chief justice Man.; b. Russia, Apr. 16, 1908; s. Nathan and Ada (Foxman) F.; B.A., U. Man., 1929, LL.B., 1933; LL.D. (hon.), U. Windsor, 1960, Hebrew U., 1964, N.D. State U., 1965, U. Toronto, 1965, U. Man., 1968, Brock U., 1968, McGill U., 1968, Queen's U., 1969, Dalhousie U., 1971, York U., 1971, Trent U., 1972, William Mitchell Coll. Law, St. Paul, 1973; D.Canon Law, St. John's Coll., 1967; D.C.L., U. Western Ont., 1973; m. Claris Brownie Udow, June 29, 1934; children—Martin H., Susan R., Phyllis C. Called to bar, Man., 1933; mem. firm Steinkopf, Lawrence & Freedman, 1933-45, Freedman and Golden, 1946-52; judge Ct. of Queen's Bench of Man., 1952-60; judge Ct. of Appeal for Man., 1960-71, chief justice of Man., 1971—; chancellor, U. Man., 1959-68. Bd. govs. Hebrew U., Jerusalem, 1955—; chmn. Rhodes Scholarship Selection Com. for Man., 1956-66; mem. adv. bd. Centre of Criminology, U. Toronto; bd. dirs. Confederation Centre of Arts, Charlottetown, P.E.I.; pres. Man. Law Sch. Found., 1965-75. Mem. Man. Bar Assn. (pres. 1951-52), Med.-Legal Soc. Man. (pres. 1954-55), Can. Bar Assn. Jewish. Club: B'nai B'rith (past pres. Winnipeg lodge), Glendale Country. Home: 425 Cordova St Winnipeg MB R3N 1A5 Canada Office: Law Courts Broadway Ave Winnipeg MB R3C 0V8 Canada

FREEHAFER, ALVIN ARTHUR, physician, educator; b. Phila., Dec. 12, 1924; s. Fred K. and Mary (Arthur) F.; B.S., Wooster Coll., 1947; M.D., Hahnemann Med. Coll., 1951; m. Margaret Irene Gulban, June 28, 1952; children—Nancy Jean, Carol Ann, Sally Lynn, John Richard. Intern, Abington (Pa.) Meml. Hosp., 1951-52; resident Univ. Hosps., Cleve., 1957-60; practice medicine, Hatboro, Pa., 1952-54, specializing in orthopedic surgery, Cleve., 1960—; asso. prof. orthopaedic surgery Case Western Res. U., Cleve., 1965-79, prof., 1979—; dir. orthopaedics Cuyahoga County Hosp., 1971—, also chief spinal cord injury service. Served with USAF, 1954-56. Fellow A.C.S.; mem. Am. Acad. Orthopaedic Surgeons, A.M.A., Internat. Med. Soc. Paraplegia, Clin. Orthopaedic Soc., Am. Congress Rehab. Medicine, Am. Orthopaedic Assn., Am. Soc. Surgery of Hand. Contbr. articles to profl. jours. Home: 195 Sterncrest Dr Moreland Hills OH 44022 Office: 3395 Scranton Rd Cleveland OH 44109

FREEL, ETHEL LENORE, rehab. counseling supr.; b. Soda Springs, Idaho, June 7, 1914; d. John Harrison and Mona (Elrod) Turnbull; student Ill. Inst. Tech., 1936-37; M.A. in Social Scis., U. Chgo., 1952; m. Robert M. Freel, Feb. 15, 1946 (dec. Feb. 1966); 1 dau., Betty Joanne. Job interviewer Ill. Employment Service, Chgo., 1939-42, labor utilization technician, 1943-46; youth counselor Ind. Employment Service, Gary, 1964-65; counselor div. vocat. rehab. Ind. Rehab. Service, East Chicago, 1965-76, area supr., 1976—; bd. dirs. Tri-City Comprehensive Mental Health Center, 1974-76. Served to lt. (j.g.) USN, 1944-46. Mem. Nat. Rehab. Assn., Nat. Rehab. Counseling Assn. (pres. Ind. 1971, regional certifying officer 1971), AAAS, AAUW, Chgo. Art Inst., Mental Health Assn. Lake County (dir. 1968—, sec. 1974-80), Epilepsy League Northwest Ind. (dir. 1974-80). Home: 2117 Tupelo Ln Chesterton IN 46304 Office: 57 S Michigan St Valparaiso IN 46383

FREEMAN, BARBARA JOSEPH, psychologist; b. Trenton, N.J., Jan. 5, 1945; d. Gerhard H. and Miriam (Selden) Joseph; B.A./B.Sc., Ohio State U., 1966; M.A., U. Cin., 1968; m. Marc Alan Freeman, June 26, 1966; children—Lee Aaron, Michael Elliot. Staff psychologist Marion County Child Guidance Clinic, Indpls., 1968—; lectr. Butler U., Indpls., 1971—; cons. Hebrew Acad. Indpls., 1971—. Group treas. Hadassah-Hasachar, 1971-73. Mem. Am., Ind. psychol. assns., AAUP. Home: 100 W 54th St Indianapolis IN 46208 Office: 1949 E 11th St Indianapolis IN 46201

FREEMAN, PATRICK EUGENE, securities account exec.; b. St. Louis, Mar. 25, 1952; s. Robert Francis and Jayne F.; B.S. in Fin., St. Louis U., 1975; m. Kathleen Koors, Aug. 19, 1972; children—Catherine, Sean, Christopher. Account exec. R.Rowland & Co., St. Louis, 1975-77; communications cons. Southwestern Bell, St. Louis, 1977-79, account exec. securities, from 1979; now mem. A.G. Edwards nat. account team Am. Tel. & Telegraph Long Lines Div. Served with Air N.G., 1970-76. Registered rep. N.Y. Stock Exchange. Mem. Kans. Grain and Feed Dealers Assn. Republican. Roman Catholic. Club: Mo. Athletic (St. Louis). Office: 1034 S Brentwood St Saint Louis MO 63117

FREEMAN, RAYMOND SAVAGEAU, pediatrician, hosp. adminstr.; b. Denver, Nov. 17, 1920; s. William Bradly and Gertrude Eda (Savageau) F.; B.A., Yale, 1943; M.D., U. Colo., 1950; m. Babette Hartzell Stiefel, Apr. 20, 1961; children—William B., Gary Stiefel, Raymond S., Scott Dana, Peter Alexis. Practice medicine specializing in pediatrics, Denver, 1953-59; pediatrician Mowery Clinic, Salina, Kans., 1959—; pres. med. staff Asbury Hosp., Salina, 1968—; health officer, Saline County, Kans., 1965-70. Diplomate Am. Bd. Pediatrics. Fellow Am. Acad. Pediatrics; mem. Saline County Med. Soc. (pres.

1976). Republican. Episcopalian. Office: 737 E Crawford Ave Salina KS 67401

FREEMAN, RICHARD MYRON, physician; b. Merced, Calif., Aug. 19, 1933; s. Myron Jay and Louise Irene (Devaurs) F.; B.S., U. Redlands (Calif.), 1955; M.D., Stanford U., 1959; m. Barbara Griffith, Aug. 31, 1957; children—Richard Griffith, Amy, Catherine, Ann. Resident in internal medicine Stanford U. Med. Center, 1959-62; fellow in nephrology N.C. Meml. Hosp., Chapel Hill, 1962-63; asst. dir., staff physician, hemodialysis unit VA Hosp., Iowa City, Iowa, 1966-68; asst. prof. medicine and urology, dir. clin. nephrology Vanderbilt U., Nashville, 1968-69; prof. medicine, dir. hemodialysis, asso. chmn. ednl. programs dept. internal medicine U. Iowa, Iowa City, 1969—; mem. Iowa Renal Disease Adv. Com., Des Moines, 1972-76. Served to capt., M.C., U.S. Army, 1964-66. Recipient C.V. Mosby honor award, 1959; Nat. Found. fellow, 1962. Fellow A.C.P. (dir.), Am. Coll. Nutrition; mem. Nat. Kidney Found. (chmn. nat. med. adv. bd. 1977-78, v.p. 1978-80, pres. 1980—). Contbr. articles to med. jours. Home: 248 Hutchinson St Iowa City IA 52240

FREEMAN, RUBY JEWEL, educator; b. Dermott, Ark., Nov. 12, 1946; d. Ernest Vernon and Julia Ann Freeman; B.S. in Instl. Dietetics, AM&N Coll., Pine Bluff, 1967; M.A., Governors State U., Park Forest, Ill., 1978; 1 son, Lazeric Fridell. Dietitian, St. Francis Hosp., Evanston, Ill., 1967-68, St. Bernard's Hosp., Chgo., 1968-69; tchr.-coordinator summer youth program Washington Park YMCA, Chgo., 1978—; tchr., reading coordinator grades 3-8 Chgo. Bd. Edn., 1969—. Recipient High Acad. Achievement award Pine Bluff (Ark.) AM&N Coll., 1967. Mem. Assn. Supervision and Curriculum Devel. (chmn. program devel. 1974-76), Am. Fedn. Tchrs., Ill. Assn. Supervision and Curriculum Devel. Address: 425 E 41st St Chicago IL 60653

FREEMAN, WILLIAM MURIEL, clin. psychologist; b. Franch Lick, Ind., Oct. 13, 1932; s. William Stanford and Amanda Victoria (Fentress) F.; student U. Innsbruck (Austria), 1954-58; Ph.D. in Clin. Psychology, U. Louisville, 1972; m. Mary Colleen Welch, Dec. 27, 1968; children—Mary Michelle, Steven William. Clin. dir. Ky. Dept. Child Welfare Reception Center, Louisville, 1972-74, River Region Community Mental Health Center, 1974-76, Seven Counties Community Mental Health Center, 1976-78; pvt. practice clin. psychology Asso. Psychol. Services, Louisville, 1978—; cons. child protection bd. Floyd County Welfare, Ind. Mem. Am. Psychol. Assn., Ky. Psychol. Assn., Ind. Psychol. Assn., Assn. for Advancement of Psychology, Am. Soc. Clin. Hypnosis, Psychosomatic Med. Soc. Republican. Roman Catholic. Contbr. articles to profl. publs. Office: Suite 1138 Medical Arts 1169 Eastern Pkwy Louisville KY 40217

FREHE, DONALD JOSEPH, broadcasting co. exec.; b. Chgo., Jan. 31, 1945; s. Daniel Joseph and Mary Alice (Tammone) F.; student Wright Jr. Coll.; m. Barbara Jean Ianello, Sept. 18, 1965; 1 son, Joseph James. Accountant, Sahara Coal Co., Chgo., 1964-67; Zenith Radio-Rauland Div., Melrose Park, Ill., 1967-68; v.p., treas. Bing Crosby Productions, Chgo., 1968-71; pres. Vipro Program Services, Chgo., 1971—. Mem. River Grove and Elmwood Park (Ill.) Youth Commns., 1971—. Mem. Nat. Acad. TV Arts and Scis., Nat. Assn. TV Program Execs. Roman Catholic. Office: Vipro Program Services 645 N Michigan Ave Chicago IL 60611

FREILINGER, JOHN JOSEPH, speech and lang. pathology cons.; b. Denver, Apr. 21, 1933; s. Joseph Peter and Ann Isabel (Harnby) F.; B.A., U. No. Colo., 1955, M.A., 1960; postgrad. U. No. Colo., 1961, Pa. State U., 1963; Ph.D., U. Kans., 1973. Head speech and hearing clinician Weld County (Colo.) Crippled Children and Adults Speech and Hearing Clinic, Greeley, 1959-60; speech clinician Scott County (Iowa) Bd. Edn., 1960-62, hearing clinician, 1962-65; cons. clin. speech and lang. services Iowa Dept. Pub. Instrn., Des Moines, 1965-68, 72—; supr. speech and hearing clinic, instr. U. Kans., 1968-69; mem. council on speech, hearing and lang. disorder Iowa Dept. Health. Mem. West Des Moines Vol. Fire Dept. Served with USAF, 1955-59. Pa. Bur. Vocat. Rehab. fellow, Pa. State U., 1964; U.S. Bur. Edn. for Handicapped fellow, 1969-72. U.S. Rehab. Service Adminstrn. traineeship, 1971-72. Fellow Am. Speech and Hearing Assn.; mem. Am., Iowa speech and hearing assns., Council Exceptional Children, Council for Langs, Speech and Hearing Cons. in State Edn. Agys. (pres.). Author: (with R.E. Shine) Practical Methods of Speech Correction for the Classroom Teacher, 1962. Asso. editor Asha, 1967-71. Home: 8924 Buena Vista Ct Des Moines IA 50322 Office: Grimes State Office Bldg Des Moines IA 50319

FREIRE, GLORIA MEDONIS, social worker; b. Pitts., Apr. 19, 1929; d. Vincent X. and Anastasia T. (Puida) Medonis; B.A. in Polit. Sci. and Econs., Carlow Coll., 1950; M.S.S.A., Case-Western Res. U., 1955; m. Luis Francis Freire, Aug. 30, 1958; children—Michael, Charles. Teen-age dir. Merrick House, Cleve., 1955-62; group psychotherapist Cleve. Psychiat. Inst., 1966-73; lectr. Sch. Applied Social Scis., Case-Western Res. U., Cleve., 1973-75; cluster dir. Golden Age Centers, Cleve., 1975-76; specialist Community Guidance and Human Services, Cleve., 1976—, staff tng. and devel. coordinator, 1977, dir. consultation and edn., 1978—. Chmn. steering com. East Community Task Force on Desegregation; chmn. Consultation and Edn. Council Cleve.; coordinator Christian Formation Community of St. Malachi, 1975-77, coordinator liturgy commn., 1978-80; mem. Urban League Edn. Adv. and Task Force on Minimum Competency, 1978—. Mem. Nat. Assn. Social Workers (task force on desegregation 1974—, coordinator polit. action com. 1977, dir. Cleve. chpt. 1975-77, sec.-treas. Ohio council of chpts. 1975-76; co-chmn.), Acad. Cert. Social Workers, Am. Group Psychotherapy Assn., Tri-State Group Psychotherapy Soc. Democrat. Roman Catholic. Editor: SASS mag., Case-Western Res. U. Alumni, 1973-79. Home: 5001 Tuxedo Ave Cleveland OH 44134 Office: 3740 Euclid Ave Cleveland OH 44115

FREISER, LEONARD H., librarian, publisher, coll. pres.; b. N.Y.C., Feb. 9, 1925; s. Abraham and Henrietta (Graubard) F.; Mus. B., Manhattan Sch. Music, 1948; M.A., Columbia, 1948, M.L.S., 1955; m. Helen Hammer, Dec. 13, 1950; children—Leslie, Erik. Instr. music U. Sask., Can., 1948, Hunter Coll., N.Y.C., 1949, Evansville (Ind.) Coll., 1950; asst. prof. music San Jose (Calif.) State Coll., 1951; trainee, br. librarian Bklyn. Pub. Library, 1954-57; chief librarian Glens Falls (N.Y.) City Library, 1957-60; vis. asso. prof. library sci. State U. N.Y., Albany, 1959-60; chief librarian Toronto (Ont., Can.) Bd. Edn., 1960-68; exec. dir. L.I. Library Resources Council, 1968-70; dep. chief librarian Chgo. Pub. Library, 1970-72; dir. Wilmette (Ill.) Pub. Library, 1972-73; with Nat. Coll. Edn., Evanston, Ill., 1972—, dir. libraries, 1973-78, dir. grad. program in library sci. and media, 1975-78, dir. performing arts, 1976-78; pub. Am. Families Pub., 1978—; pres. Chgo. Conservatory Coll., 1979—; exec. dir. Urban Libraries Council, 1970-72; cons. Fed. City Coll., Washington, U.S. Office Edn., Calgary (Alta.) Sch. Bd., Montreal Protestant Sch. Bd., Toronto Pub. Library, U. Pres.'s of Ontario, Centre for Culture and Tech. Pres., World Affairs Council, Glens Falls, 1959-60; co-chmn. Evanston Cable TV Com., 1973-75. Trustee Glens Falls Bd. Adult Edn. Pres.'s scholar Columbia U., 1949. Mem. ALA (councillor 1963-68, chmn. nat. conf. children and TV 1976, chmn. spl. resolutions 1978), Ont. Library Assn. (pres. 1965-66). Contbr. articles to mags. and newspapers. Home: 530 Washington Ave Wilmette IL 60091 Office: 410 S Michigan Ave Chicago IL 60605

FREKING, FREDERICK WILLIAM, bishop; b. Heron Lake, Minn., Aug. 11, 1913; s. August and Rosa (Oberbroeckling) F.; A.B., St. Mary's Coll., 1934, LL.D., 1958; student North Am. Coll., Rome, 1934-39; S.T.B., Gregorian U., 1937; J.C.D., Cath. U. Am., 1948. Ordained priest Roman Cath. Ch., 1938; asst. pastor St. John's Ch., Rochester, Minn., 1940-43; supt. Lourdes High Sch., Rochester, 1941-43, pastor St. John's Ch., Winona, Minn., 1943-45; 1st editor Winonan edit. Our Sunday Visitor, 1943-45; sec. to Bishop Leo Binz, Winona, 1948-50; mem. Civil Corp., Diocese of Winona, 1943-53. sec. corp., 1950-53; sec. Diocesan Matrimonial Tribunal, Diocese of Winona, 1948-50; defender of marriage bond, 1950-53; vice chancellor Diocese of Winona, 1950-51, chancellor, 1951-53, diocesan dir. cemeteries, 1950-53; pastor Holy Cross Ch., Dakota, Minn., 1950-51, also with mission at Precious Blood Ch., LaMoille, Minn.; pastor St. Mary's Ch., Minnieska, Minn., 1951-53, also with mission, St. Paul's Ch., Minnesota City; spiritual dir. North Am. Coll., Rome, 1953-57; named papal chamberlain by Pope Pius XII, 1949, domestic prelate, 1954, Bishop of Salina, Kans., 1958-65, bishop of La Crosse (Wis.) diocese, 1965—. Adv. bd. Boy Scouts Am., 1958—, Marymount Coll., Salina, 1958—. Decorated Knight Comdr. Holy Sepulchre, 1958. Mem. Nat. Cath. Rural Life Conf. (pres.). Phi Kappa Theta. K.C. (4). Address: 4238 Mormon Coulee Rd PO Box 982 LaCrosse WI 54601

FRELS, LOIS MARIAN PARNELL (MRS. CALVIN EDWIN FRELS), educator; b. Geneseo, Ill., Nov. 20, 1929; d. Floyd Vinton and Mary Jane (Davis) Parnell; R.N., Moline (Ill.) Pub. Hosp., 1950; student Pub. Health, U. Minn., Loyola U., Chgo., 1951-54; B.S., Augustana Coll., Rock Island, Ill., 1959; M.A., U. Iowa, 1964; diploma for testing, Marianne Frostic Center Ednl. Therapy, Los Angeles, 1969; Ph.D., U. Minn., 1977; m. Calvin Edwin Frels, Oct. 28, 1950; children—Mark Edwin, Arlan James. Sch. nurse East Moline Elementary Schs., 1951-54; pub. health work East Moline Vis. Nurses Assn., 1955-57; sch. nurse, project dir., nurse cons. United Twp. High Sch., East Moline, 1957-67; instr. psychology Blackhawk Jr. Coll., Moline, part time 1966-68; tchr., dir. gifted program Silvis (Ill.) Elementary Schs., 1968; counselor Pleasant Valley (Iowa) High Sch., 1969-70; asst. prof. Marycrest Coll., Davenport, Iowa, 1970-73; chmn. div. nursing Iowa Wesleyan Coll., Mt. Pleasant, 1973-76; dir. div. nursing Bradley U., Peoria, Ill., 1976—. Sec., East Moline Community Resource Council, 1965-67; mem. Riverdale Unit 100 Bd. Edn., Port Byron, Ill., 1964-67, 68-74; chmn. Rock Island County Fact Finding Com. White House Conf. Children and Youth, 1970, del. to conf., 1970; organizer Little White House Conf. Children and Youth, Rock Island County, 1969; 2d v.p. Rock Island County Welfare Council, 1968-70; mem. ednl. task force Rock Island Model Cities Project, 1969-70. Bd. dirs. Opportunity Mentally Handicapped. Ill. Dept. Pub. Instrn. grantee Western Ill. U., 1968; grantee div. nursing U. Minn., 1972-73. Fellow Am. Sch. Health Assn. (chmn. sch. nurse study com. 1973-77, Disting. Service award 1978); mem. Am., Ill. nurses assns., Am. Pub. Health Assn., Am. Edn. Research Assn., NEA, Iowa League for Nursing (pres. 1976, 77), Ill. League for Nursing (v.p. 1979), Nat. League for Nursing (sec. Midland assembly 1979), Royal Soc. Health (London), Pi Lambda Theta, Phi Kappa Phi, Sigma Theta Tau. Home: 25329-1 Ave N Hillsdale IL 61257 Office: Bradley Univ Peoria IL 61625

FRELS, MARK EDWIN, farm bur. exec.; b. Moline, Ill., Nov. 12, 1954; s. Calvin Edwin and Lois Marian (Parnell) F.; student U. Madrid, 1968, 70; B.A., Iowa Wesleyan Coll., 1976. Farmer, Rock Island County, Ill., to 1977; technician U.S. Dept. Agr., Soil Conservation Service, Rock Island County, 1976-77; semi-profl. photographer, Galesburg, Ill., 1972—; mgr. Knox County Farm Bur., Galesburg, Ill., 1977—. Leader, 4-H Club, 1974-77; mem. Ill. Council Youth, 1970-71; dir. farm drive Knox County United Way, 1978; del. White House Conf. on Youth, 1970; baseball coach Little League, 1971-75; mem. youth council Rock Island County Coop. Extension Service, 1975-77, mem. exec. council, 1975-77. Recipient Citizenship award Ill. 4-H, 1971, state photography award 4-H Club Congress, 1973. Mem. Galesburg Jr. C. of C., Blue Key. Methodist. Home: 2762 No 10 Springer Rd Galesburg IL 61401 Office: 180 S Soangetaha Rd Galesburg IL 61401

FRENCH, MARCUS EMMETT, mfg. co. exec.; b. Worcester, Mass., Jan. 21, 1929; s. Emmett A. and Marion A. (Brady) F.; B.S. in Chemistry, Holy Cross Coll., 1952, M.S. in chemistry, 1953; postgrad. exec. devel. program Dartmouth Coll.; m. Mary M. Nugent, Sept. 25, 1954; children—Carol E., Margaret A., Marci M. Sect. leader Allied Chem. Corp., Buffalo, 1953-59; devel. chemist Hewitt Robbins Corp., Franklin, N.J., 1959-60; v.p. Gen. Foam div. Tenneco Chems., Inc., Hazleton, Pa., 1960-70; pres. Janesville Products unit AMCA Internat. Corp., Norwalk, Ohio, 1970—; dir. TWU Realty Co. Trustee, Textile Workers Pension Plan; mem. St. Pauls Sch. Bd., Norwalk; bd. dirs. Alcohol Center Huron County. Served with U.S. Army, 1946-48. Mem. ASTM, Soc. Automotive Engrs., Soc. Plastics Engrs., Detroit Engring. Soc., Norwalk C. of C. (dir.). Clubs: K.C., Plumbrook Country; Renaissance (Detroit); Colesium (Cleve.). Patentee on methods of urethane foam in U.S. and fgn. countries. Home: 6 Hillcrest Ct Milan OH 44846 Office: PO Box 349 Norwalk OH 44857

FRENCH, ROBERT LEE, mgmt. cons.; b. Middletown, Mo., Dec. 18, 1929; s. Lee and Pearl Marie F.; B.S., U. Mo., 1951, M.S. in Bus. Adminstrn., 1951; m. Barbara Gail Burks, Sept. 17, 1950; children—Carol Jean, Cynthia Ann, James Robert, John Richard. Sr. indsl. engr. Chrysler Corp., Detroit, 1951-60; chief mng. engr. Boats div. Brunswick Corp., Warsaw, Ind., 1960-63; chief indsl. engr. Arnold Engring. div. Allegheny-Ludlum, Marengo, Ill., 1963-66; v.p., dir. Mfg. Household div. Hamilton-Cosco Inc., Columbus, Ind., 1966-70; v.p., gen. mgr. Buckeye Plastics div. Buckeye Internat., Columbus, Ohio, 1970-72; v.p., gen. mgr. Buckeye Ware Inc., Regal Ware Inc., Wooster, Ohio, 1972-74; pres. R.L. French & Co., Inc., South Bend, Ind., 1974—; chmn., chief exec. officer On-Line Data Inc., Mishawaka, Ind.; pres. Computerized Mfg. Mgmt. Corp., Medina, Ohio. Pres. Bartholomew County (Ind.) chpt. ARC, 1969. Found. for Youth, Wooster, Ohio, 1973. Served with USAF, 1950-51. Mem. Assn. Mgmt. Cons., Soc. Profl. Mgmt. Cons. Republican. Mem. Christian Ch. (Disciples of Christ). Home and Office: 1240 E Irvington St South Bend IN 46614

FRENKEL, JACOB AHARON, economist, educator; b. Tel-Aviv, Israel, Feb. 8, 1943; came to U.S., 1967; s. Kalman H. and Lea (Zwibaum) F.; B.A., Hebrew U., 1966, M.A., 1967; Ph.D. in Econs., U. Chgo., 1970; m. Niza Yair, Sept. 3, 1968; children—Orli-Miriam, Tahl-Ida. Teaching asst. dept. econs. Hebrew U., Jerusalem, 1966- adj. sr. lectr. econs., 1972-73; instr. money and banking Ind. U., Ga 1968-69; asst. prof. internat. econs. and fin. Grad. Sch. Bus., U. Chgo 1970-71, asst. prof. dept. econs., 1973-74, asso. prof., 1974-78, prof., 1979—, vis. asst. prof. Grad. Sch. Bus., summer, 1972; sr. lectr. econs. Tel-Aviv U., 1971-73, vis. prof. dept. econs., 1980; guest participant Securities Groups Internat. Monetary Adv. Bd., 1980; adv. in econs. to Harvard U. Press, 1980—; research asso. (hon.) dept. econs. Harvard U., Cambridge, Mass., 1978; research asso. Nat. Bur. Econ. Research, 1978—; research fellow Lehrman Inst., 1981-82; mem. econs. adv. panel NSF, 1980—. Ford Found. grantee, 1975-76; NSF grantee, 1978-81. Mem. Am. Econ. Assn. Author: (with others) The Economics of the Sector Owned by Organized Labor, 1964; Macroeconomics: Lecture Notes, 1965; (with H.G. Johnson) The Monetary Approach to the Balance of Payments, 1976; The Economics of Exchange Rates, 1978; (with R. Dornbusch) International Economic Policy: Theory and Evidence, 1979; contbr. numerous articles to econs. jours.; editor Jour. Polit. Economy, 1975—; adv. council Carnegie-Rochester conf. series on Public Policy, 1977—; editorial bd. Jour. Monetary Econs., 1978—; adv. editor Econs. Letters, 1980—. Office: 1126 E 59th St Chicago IL 60637

FRENKEL, MARVIN ALLEN, glove co. exec.; b. Detroit, May 3, 1926; J.D., U. Miami, 1950; postgrad. Ind. U., Mich. State U., Wayne State U., 1966, 74-76. Pres., Advance Glove Mfg. Co., Detroit; mem. indsl. sector adv. com. on leather and leather products Nat. Def. Exec. Res. Trustee, Mich. Cancer Found.; trustee, mem. exec. com. Detroit Inst. Tech.; mem. exec. com. Detroit Round Table; bd. dirs., mem. exec. com. NCCJ, Inc.; mem. adv. bd. Music Hall Center for Performing Arts. Mem. Am. Def. Preparedness Assn. (past pres. Mich. chpt.), Am. Logistics Assn. (dir., pres. 1971-72 Mich. chpt.), U. Miami Nat. Corps. and Founds. Com., Detroit Com. on Fgn. Relations, Econ. Club Detroit, Engring. Soc. Detroit. Clubs: Detroit Rotary, One Hundred, Standard, Franklin Hills Country. Author: Slave Trade-U.S.A. and the Looting of America Including Your Food, Wages and Savings, 1973; The Abridging of our Freedom of the Press-Without Really Trying. Patentee in varied fields. Office: 901 W Lafayette Blvd Detroit MI 48226

FRENZEL, BILL, Congressman; b. St. Paul, July 31, 1928; s. Paul William and Paula (Schlegel) F.; B.A., Dartmouth Coll., 1950, M.B.A., 1951; m. Ruth Purdy, June 9, 1951; children—Deborah Anne, Pamela Ruth, Melissa Lee. With Mpls. Terminal Warehouse Co., 1954-69, mgr., 1957-60, pres., dir., 1960-69; mem. Minn. Legislature, 1962-70; mem. 92d-97th congresses from 3d Minn. Dist. Former mem. adv. council Minn. Dept. Employment Security. Served with USNR, 1951-54; Korea. Mem. Am. Legion, C. of C., Citizens League. Home: Golden Valley MN Office: 1026 Longworth House Office Bldg Washington DC 20515

FRENZEL, OTTO NICHOLAS, JR., banker; b. Indpls., May 6, 1899; s. Otto Nicholas and Caloline G. (Goepper) F.; student Cornell U., 1921; LL.D., Ind. Central U., 1965; D.Arts, Butler U., 1978; m. May 8, 1924; children—Eleanor Frenzel Bookwalter, Otto Nicholas. With Mchts. Nat. Bank & Trust Co., Indpls., 1917—, pres., 1945-66, chmn. bd., 1966-69, chmn. exec. com., 1970—; chmn. bd. Mchts. Nat. Corp., Indpls., 1972-79; pres. Ind. Trust Co., Indpls., 1936-45; dir. Am. States Ins. Co., Am. States Life Ins. Co., Am. Economy Ins. Co.; past dir. Pa. R.R., Pa. Central Co., Lykes-Youngstown Co., Stokely-Van Camp Co., Am. United Life Ins. Co. Trustee, Butler U., YMCA, Indpls.; bd. dirs. United Way of Indpls., Community Hosp. of Indpls. Found. Served with USN, World War II. Mem. Indpls. C. of C. (dir., life), Ind. State C. of C. (dir., life). Clubs: Columbia, Indpls. Athletic, Meridian Hills, Woodstock, Traders Point Hunt, Walloon Lake Country, Dramatic. Office: 1 Merchants Plaza Indianapolis IN 46204

FRERICKS, DONALD JOHN, educator; b. Minster, Ohio, Jan. 10, 1935; s. Leo Henry and Loretta Pauline (Busse) F.; B.S., U. Dayton, 1956; M.A., Miami U., 1958; Ph.D., Ohio State U., 1970; m. Patricia Lou Ross, Aug. 30, 1958; children—Donald, Margaret, Catherine, Theresa, Joseph, Amy. Tchr., coach Chaminade High Sch., Dayton, Ohio, 1956-60, dir. athletics, counselor, 1961-65; asst. cashier Minster State Bank (Ohio), 1960-61; teaching asso. Miami U., Oxford, Ohio, 1965-66; supr., asst. dir. tchr. cert. Ohio Dept. Edn., Columbus, 1966-78; asso. prof. ednl. adminstrn. U. Dayton, 1978—. Recipient Disting. Alumni award Miami U. 1974. Mem. Am. Assn. Sch. Adminstrs., Nat. Orgn. Legal Problems Edn., Ohio Assn. Secondary Sch. Adminstrs., Ohio Assn. Sch. Personnel Adminstrs. (Disting. Service award 1978), Nat. Cath. Edn. Assn., Phi Delta Kappa. Republican. Roman Catholic. Home: 5399 Brainard Dr Kettering OH 45440 Office: 300 College Park Dayton OH 45469

FRETLAND, DONALD JOHN, biochemist; b. Chgo., Dec. 8, 1943; s. Jefferson Donald and Dorthea Carlene (Carr) F.; B.S. in Chemistry, North Park Coll., 1967; M.S. in Biochemistry (USPHS fellow), Ill. Inst. Tech., 1970; m. Janet L. Van Arsdale, Mar. 30, 1974. Research biochemist Searle Labs. div. G.D. Searle & Co., Skokie, Ill., 1967—. Mem. Am. Chem. Soc., N.Y. Acad. Scis., Egypt Exploration Soc. Author: (novels) Morning of the Tiger, 1968, The Persimmion Sequence, 1970, Winds of Heliopolis, 1972. Office: 4901 Searle Pkwy Skokie IL 60077

FREY, DEWAYNE L., coll. dean; b. Keokuk, Iowa, Nov. 25, 1938; s. Walter E. and Marie F.; student Western Ill. U., 1959; B.S., Iowa Wesleyan U., 1963; M.Ed., U. Ill., 1968; Ed.D., Nova U., 1978; m. Barbara A. Short, Aug. 19, 1961; children—Jack, Mike, Cindy. Tchr. math, sci., coach Parkersburg (Iowa) High Sch., 1963-64; tchr. math, coach Warsaw (Ill.) High Sch., 1964-67; instr. math Black Hawk Coll., Moline, Ill., 1968-73; dir. indsl. tech., 1973-78, dean careers, 1978—. Mem. Pvt. Industry Council Quad Cities, 1979-81; mem. adv. St. Marys Bd. Edn., 1969. Served with AUS, 1956-59. NSF grantee, summers 1964, 67, 1968. Mem. Am. Vocat. Assn., Nat. Council Local Adminstrs., Ill. Vocat. Assn., Ill. Council Local Adminstrs., Am. Tech. Assn., Phi Delta Kappa. Home: 5317 28th Ave Moline IL 61265 Office: 6600 34th Ave Moline IL 61265

FREY, DONALD NELSON, mfg. co. exec., engr.; b. St. Louis, Mar. 13, 1923; s. Muir Luken and Margaret Bryden (Nelson) F.; student Mich. State Coll., 1940-42; B.S., U. Mich., 1947, Ph.D., 1950, D.Sc. (hon.), 1965; D.Sc. (hon.), U. Mo., Rolla, 1966; children by previous marriage, Donald Nelson, Judith Kingsley, Margaret Bente, Catherine, Christopher, Elizabeth; m. 2d, Mary Elizabeth Cameron, June 30, 1971. Instr. metall. engring. U. Mich., 1949-50, asst. prof. chem. and metall. engring., 1950-51; research engr. Babcock & Wilcox Tube Co., Beaver Falls, Pa., 1951; various research positions Ford Motor Co., 1951-57, various engring. positions Ford div., 1958-61, product planning mgr., 1961-62, asst. gen. mgr. Ford div., 1962-65, gen. mgr., 1965-68, co. v.p., 1965-67, v.p. for product devel., 1967-68; pres. Gen. Cable Corp., N.Y.C., 1968-71; chmn. bd. Bell & Howell Co., Chgo., 1971—, pres., 1973—, also chief exec. officer; dir. Babcock

...lacron Inc., Spring Mills, Inc. Mem. devel. ...3—; trustee Carnegie Found. for Advancement ... Childrens Meml. Hosp., Chgo., Lyric Opera, ...abetes Assn. Served with AUS, 1943-46. Named ...of Yr., Engring. Soc. Detroit, 1953; recipient Russell ...ard Soc. Automotive Engrs., 1956; named Outstanding ...Coll. Engring., U. Mich., 1957; Outstanding Young Man of ...etroit Jr. Bd. Commerce, 1958. Mem. AIME (chmn. Detroit ...; chmn., editor Nat Symposium on Sheet Steels 1956), Am. Soc. ...etals, Nat. Acad. Engring. (mem. council 1972), ASME, Soc. Automotive Engrs. (vice chmn. Detroit 1958), Detroit Engring. Soc. (dir. 1962—), Elec. Mfrs. Club, N.Y. Council on Fgn. Relations, Sigma Xi, Phi Kappa Phi, Tau Beta Pi, Phi Delta Theta. Clubs: Chicago, Saddle and Cycle, Tavern (Chgo.). Home: 1500 N Lake Shore Dr Chicago IL 60610 Office: 7100 McCormick Rd Chicago IL 60645*

FREY, H. GARRETT, stock broker; b. Cin., Dec. 2, 1938; s. John H. and Mary G. (Grever) F.; student U. Detroit, 1956-57, U. Cin., 1957-59, U. Miami, 1960-61; m. Mary Knollman, July 23, 1960; children—John, Robert, Meg, Amy, Brad, Julie. Salesman, Verkamp Corp., Cin., 1958-60, Formica Corp., Cin., Miami, Fla., and Hartford, Conn., 1960-62; stockbroker Westheimer & Hayden Stone, Cin., 1962-64; stockbroker Harrison & Co., 1964-66, gen. partner, 1966-73, mng. partner, 1972-77; v.p. Bache Halsey Stuart Shields Inc., Cin., 1977-79; chmn. bd. Queen City Securities Corp., Cin., 1979—; dir. Broadcast Mgmt. Corp. Mem. investment com. Sisters of Charity, Cin., 1970; trustee, treas. St. Joseph Cemetery, Cin.; pres. Springer Ednl. Found.; v.p. Cath. Social Services of SW Ohio. Served with AUS, 1959. Named Big Brother of the Year, 1968. Mem. Cin. (v.p. 1970-72, trustee 1979—), N.Y., Am. stock exchanges, Purcell High Sch. Alumni (pres. 1972-73), Chgo. Bd. Options Exchange, Cath. Big Bros. Cin. (pres. 1966-67). Roman Catholic (council pres. 1971-72). Clubs: Cincinnati Stock and Bond (pres. 1969), Buckeye (pres. 1968-69). Home: 3660 Kroger Ave Cincinnati OH 45226 Office: 300 Formica Bldg Cincinnati OH 45226

FREY, JAMES GOTTFRIED, profl. baseball mgr.; b. Cleve., May 26, 1931; s. John B. and Rose S. (Schaffer) F.; student Ohio State U.; m. Joan Miller, Mar. 15, 1952; children—James Michael, Cindy Sue, Mary Elizabeth, Jennifer Lynn. Former profl. baseball player with Boston Braves, Phila. Phillies, St. Louis Cardinals, minor league mgr., scout Balt. Orioles, 1964-70, coach, Balt., 1970-79; mgr. Kansas City (Mo.) Royals, 1980—. Office: PO Box 1969 Royals Stadium Kansas City MO 64141

FRICK, WILLIAM RAY, mus. curator; b. Manitowoc, Wis., Mar. 13, 1941; s. Ray J. and Dorothy M. (Les Monde) F.; B.S., U. Wis., 1964; pvt. study with Rajko Lozar (Yugoslav art historian), 1964-68; pvt. study oil painting Dorothy Frick, 1962-68; 1 son, Marc Andre. Curator of exhibits Rahr Civic Center, Manitowoc, Wis., 1965-67, asst. to dir., 1967-68; dir. Huntington Hist. Soc., L.I., 1969-71; advisor Victorian decorative arts to pvt. collectors, 1971-73; curator exhibits N.C. Dept. Cultural Resources and Historic Sites System, Raleigh, 1973-76; curator collections Milw. Hist. Soc., 1976—; advisor to pvt. collectors, 1976—; lectr. in field. Pres., Little Gallery Inc., N.E. Wis. Art Orgn., 1970-72. Recipient U. Wis. Delta Sigma Rho Radio award, 1962. Mem. U.S. Commn. Mil. History, Internat. Commn. Mil. History, Am. Assn. Museums. Roman Catholic. Contbr. articles to profl. jours. Home: 815 E Knapp St Milwaukee WI 53202 Office: 910 N 3rd St Milwaukee WI 53201

FRICKE, CHARLES ROBERT, elec. engring. mgr.; b. Buffalo, Mar. 26, 1948; s. Donald Stuart and Rosella Nemes (Radics) F.; B.S. in Elec. Engring., Mich. Tech. U., 1970, B.S. in Engring. Adminstrn., 1970; M.B.A., Bradley U., 1980; 1 dau., Dawn Marie. With Ill. Power Co., 1970-71, 74—, engr. service area, Galesburg, 1977-79, area engring. supr., 1979-80, supr. distbn. design, 1980-81, gen. mgr. dept. public utilities, Virginia, Minn., 1981—; mem. faculty Bradley U., 1980, Richland Coll., 1981, Masabi Coll., 1982. Chmn. 1st aid Knox County chpt. ARC, 1977-79, dir., 1978-79, fund drive chmn., 1979, bd. dirs. Macon County chpt., 1980, mem. council Heart of Ill. Div., 1980, Midwestern field officer, 1980; bd. dirs. Knox County United Way, 1975-77; bd. dirs. Knox County BB-BS, Inc., 1975, 77-79, pres., 1976; v.p. Knox County Audubon Soc., 1975-79. Served with USAR, 1971-74. Registered profl. engr., Ill. Mem. Galesburg Jaycees (v.p. 1976; Dir. of Yr. award 1975, Presdl. Achievement award 1976, President's trophy 1976), Galesburg Humane Soc. (dir. 1978-79), Beta Gamma Sigma, Phi Kappa Phi. Republican. Roman Catholic. Home: 2330 9th St S Virginia VA 55792 Office: 620 S 2d St Virginia MN 55792

FRICKE, GORDON HUGH, chemist; b. Buffalo, Apr. 18, 1937; s. John Carl and Mildred Joanne (Hughes) F.; A.B., Goshen Coll., 1964; M.A., State U. N.Y. at Binghamton, 1966; Ph.D., Clarkson Coll. Tech., 1971; m. Sharon Lee Roesch, July 2, 1960; children—Gretchen Anne, Jason Scott. Teaching, research asso. State U. N.Y. at Buffalo, 1970-71, summer 1971; postdoctoral research fellow Wright State U., 1971-72; asst. prof. chemistry Ind. U.-Purdue U., Indpls., 1972-75, asso. prof., 1975—, acting asst. dean acad. affairs, 1978-79; on leave to Dow Chem. Co., Indpls., 1980-81. AEC-Health and Safety Lab. fellow, 1966-70; Ind. U. Found. grantee 1973, 75, 77; Eli Lilly & Co., grantee, 1973; Purdue U. X-L grantee, 1977; recipient L.T. Jones award for outstanding sci. tchr. Ind. U.-Purdue U., 1977; Lola Loshe award for service to students Ind. U.-Purdue U., 1978. Mem. Am. Chem. Soc. (sec. Ind. sect. 1977, chmn. Ind. sect. 1979), Sigma Xi (program com. 1977-78, research com. 1978-79, sec. 1979-81). Baptist. Home: 1925 N Mitthoefer Rd Indianapolis IN 46229 Office: Dept Chemistry 1201 E 38th St Indianapolis IN 46205

FRICKE, LOUIS HENRY, JR., elec. engr.; b. St. Louis, Dec. 22, 1928; s. Louis Henry and Violet Loretta (Fightmaster) F.; B.S.E.E., St. Louis U., 1951, M.S.(R), 1957. With Monsanto Co., St. Louis and St. Peters, Mo., 1957—, sr. research specialist, St. Peters, 1971-75, prin. engr., St. Louis, 1975-81, engring. group cons., 1981—. Mem. IEEE, Instrument Soc. Am., Am. Inst. Chem. Engrs., Horseless Carriage Club Am./Mo., Kaiser-Frazer Owners, Reo of Am., Sigma Xi. Democrat. Episcopalian. Patentee in process dynamics identification process control instrumentation and silicon process automation. Home: 7421 Zephyr Pl Maplewood MO 63143 Office: 800 N Lindbergh Blvd Saint Louis MO 63166

FRICS, LASZLO, veterinarian; b. Hungary, Apr. 27, 1909; came to U.S., 1951, naturalized, 1956; s. Gyula and Ida (Honeczy) F.; D.V.M., Royal Hungarian U. Sci. and Agr., Budapest, 1932; Ph.D. cum laude in Physiology, Technicum and Oeconomicum Jozsef Nádor U. Budapest, 1939; m. Margit Maria Harto Szokolay, May 19, 1940; children—Laszlo Agoston, Kornelia Frics Smith, Agoston Zsigmond. Asst. instr. Sci. and Agr. U. Budapest, 1930-32; practice race horse vet. medicine, Hungary, 1934-39; govt. dist. veterinarian, 1939-45; veterinarian, W. Ger., 1945-51, Cleve. and Akron, Ohio, 1951-54, Emery, S.D., 1954—. Served to capt. Hussar Regt. Life mem. S.D. Vet. Med. Assn. Roman Catholic. Club: K.C. Research on blood, nutrition in animals. Address: Emery SD 57332

FRIDLEY, RUSSELL WILLIAM, historian; b. Oelwein, Iowa, Mar. 21, 1928; s. Lloyd and Laura (Tift) F.; B.A., Grinnell Coll., 1950; M.A., Columbia, 1953; Litt.D., Concordia Coll., Moorhead, Minn., 1980; m. Metta Holtkamp, Feb. 26, 1954; children—Scott, Nancy, Jane, Susan, Elizabeth, Jennifer. Asst. dir. Minn. Hist. Soc., St. Paul, 1953-54, dir., 1954—; v.p. Grinnell (Iowa) Coll., 1966; vice chmn. Nat. Advisory Council on Hist. Preservation, 1967-70; mem. Nat. Mus. Act Adv. Council, 1976—; dir. div. edn. and pub. program Nat. Endowment for Humanities, 1968-69; chmn. Minn. Humanities Com., 1970—. Bd. dirs. Hubert H. Humphrey Inst. Public Affairs, 1979—, James J. Hill Reference Library, 1980—; trustee Charles A. Lindbergh Fund, 1981—. Served with U.S. Army, 1946-48; PTO. Mem. Am. Assn. Mus. (dir. 1969-73), Am. Assn. State and Local History (pres. 1966-68), Nat. Conf. State Hist. Preservation Officers (v.p. 1977—). Author: Minnesota: A Students Guide to Localized History; The Uses of State and Local History; Historic Sites of North Dakota; Minnesota: A State That Works. Home: 740 Amber Dr Saint Paul MN 55112 Office: 690 Cedar St Saint Paul MN 55101

FRIEBEN, WILLIAM ROBERT, microbiologist; b. Johnstown, Pa., Jan. 25, 1946; s. William Robert and Margaret (Kulback) F.; B.S., U. Pitts., 1967; Ph.D. (NDEA fellow, NIH fellow), U. Ky., 1971; m. Linda Lee Mangus, Aug. 19, 1967; children—Brian David, Kerry Jason. Research asso. U. Wis. Food Research Inst., Madison, 1972-74; microbiology sect. leader McGaw Labs., Milledgeville, Ga., 1974-77; project leader Upjohn Co., Kalamazoo, 1977—; co-chmn. Parenteral Drug Asso. Task Force on Dry Heat Sterilization, 1979-80, sec. research com., 1980-81, program com., 1980-81. Mem. Am. Soc. Microbiology, Inst. Food Technologists, Parenteral Drug Assn., Sigma Xi. Democrat. Club: Am. Motorcycle Assn. Contbr. articles to profl. jours.; referee Jour. of Parenteral Drug Assn., 1979-80. Office: 7171 Portage Rd Kalamazoo MI 49001

FRIEDBERG, STANTON A., physician; b. Chgo., Mar. 15, 1908; A.B., Dartmouth Coll., 1929; M.D., Rush Med. Coll. U. Chgo., 1934; m. Martha Asher; 4 children. Rotating intern Presbyn. Hosp., Chgo., 1933-34, asst. resident in pathology, 1934-35, combined grad. tutor, fellow, 1935-36; resident Mcpl. Contagious Disease Hosp., Chgo., 1935; resident in otolaryngology Cook County Hosp., Chgo., 1936-38, asso. attending otolaryngologist, 1936-42; attending otolaryngologist Presbyn-St. Luke's Hosp., 1958—, chmn. dept., 1958-74; attending physician VA Hosp., Hines, Ill., 1946-54; cons. in field; clin. asst. otolaryngology Rush Med. Coll., 1938-40, clin. instr., 1940-42, prof., 1970—, chmn. dept., 1970-74; clin. asso. U. Ill. Coll. Medicine, 1942-46, clin. asst. prof., 1947-52, clin. asso. prof., 1952-63, clin. prof., 1963-70. Bd. dirs. Hyde Park-Kenwood Community Cong., 1950-52; bd. dirs. S. Park Improvement Assn., 1954-64, pres., 1961-64. Diplomate Am. Bd. Otolaryngology. Mem. Inst. Medicine Chgo., ACS. Chgo. Laryngol. and Otol. Soc. (pres. 1957-58), Am. Physicians Art Assn., Am. Acad. Ophthalmology and Otolaryngology, Am. Broncho-Esophagological Assn. (pres. 1963-64), Am. Rhinological, Otol. and Laryngol. Soc., Am. Laryngol. Assn., Soc. Med. History Chgo. (council), Soc. Univ. Otolaryngologists, Assn. Am. Med. Colls., AAAS, Phi Beta Kappa, Alpha Omega Alpha. Editorial bd. Annals of Otology, Rhinology and Laryngology, Pediatrics Digest; contbr. numerous articles to profl. jours. Address: 5730 S Kenwood Chicago IL 60637

FRIEDEL, JANICE NAHRA, coll. ofcl.; b. Davenport, Iowa, Aug. 19, 1950; d. Joseph Anthony and Jeanette Amelita (Otto) Nahra; student (Alumnae scholar) Marycrest Coll., 1968-70; B.A., U. Iowa, 1972, M.A., 1976, Ph.D., 1980; postgrad. Western Ill. U., 1976, U. Scranton (Pa.), 1977; fellow Stanford U., 1978-79; m. Michael Gerald Friedel, June 2, 1973. Secondary tchr. Davenport (Iowa) Public Schs., 1972-78; instr. history St. Ambrose Coll., Davenport, 1978; coordinator secondary curriculum Lakeland Area Edn. Agy., Cylinder, Iowa, 1978-80; research asst. U. Iowa, Iowa City, 1979-80; coordinator dist. support services Loess Hills Area Edn. Agy. 13, Council Bluffs, Iowa, 1980-81; asst. to pres. for community edn. Scott Community Coll., Eastern Iowa Community Coll. Dist., Bettendorf, 1981—; asst. adj. prof. U. Iowa; cons. N.W. Ednl. Coop., Arlington Heights, Ill.; non-sexist edn. cons. U. No. Iowa. Mem. Women's Edn. Coalition, Davenport, 1974-76; minimal competencies citizens adv. com. Davenport Bd. Edn., 1977-78; mem. Iowa State Research Com. on Talented and Gifted Edn., 1978-80, nat. adv. com. sexism and social justice Nat. Council Social Studies. Recipient Paul C. Packer award U. Iowa Coll. Edn., 1976; Delta Delta Delta inservice scholar, 1971; Freedom Found. fellow, 1977; Found. Econ. Edn., 1976; ESEA Title III grantee, 1974; Title IV grantee, 1978. Mem. Iowa Edn. Assn., NEA, Nat. Assn. Secondary Sch. Prins., Assn. Supervision and Curriculum Devel., Am. Ednl. Research and Evaluation Assn., U. Iowa Alumni Assn., Iowa Assn. Supervision and Curriculum Devel., Am. Hist. Assn., Nat. Hist. Assn., Soc. Hist. Edn., Orgn. Am. Historians, Nat. Women's Studies Assn., Nat. Council Social Studies, Phi Delta Kappa, Pi Lambda Theta. Author: An Administrative Guide: Implementing a Plan for a Multicultural, Nonsexist Educational Program, 1980; Changes in Knowledge and Attitudes of Secondary Education Students After a Module in Special Education, 1980; book rev. editor Iowa Curriculum Bull., 1980—; contbr. to Notable American Women, 1980, The Palimpsest, 1981, others. Home: 2930 Windsor Dr Bettendorf IA 52722 Office: Scott Community College Eastern Iowa Community College Dist Belmont Rd Bettendorf IA 52722

FRIEDLAND, JOHN E., state senator; b. Elgin, Ill., Sept. 25, 1937; grad. Elgin Community Coll., Aurora Coll.; m. Marlene Diedrick; children—Linda, Renee, Susan. Former mem. Ill. Ho. of Reps.; now mem. Ill. Senate. Vice chmn. Elgin Twp. Republican Central Com. Served with USN. Clubs: Masons, Shriners, Elks, Eagles. Address: State Office Bldg Room 2032 Springfield IL 62706*

FRIEDLAND, RUTH VOLID, art gallery exec.; b. Chgo.; ed. Art Inst. Chgo., 1942, U. Chgo., 1964. Copy chief, creative dir., Chgo., 1939-45; fashion designer, co-founder Paradise-Volid, 1945-48; art tchr., 1955-57; creative dir. King Korn Stamp Co., Chgo., 1962-70; public relations exec. The Merchandising Group, Chgo., 1968-72; art cons. Collector's Showroom, Inc., Chgo., 1970—, also pres., cons. to designers, architects, corps. to place fine art in corp. and residential environments; speaker in field; guest speaker U. Ill., Columbia Coll. Affiliate bd. Mus. Contemporary Art, Chgo. Subject of article, picture Chgo. Sun Times, Oct., 1977. Mem. Chgo. Assn. Commerce and Industry, French-Am. C. of C., Industry Found. of Am. Soc. Interior Designers, AIA Found., Art Inst. Chgo. (life mem.), Archives of Am. Art. Clubs: Pres.'s, Arts (Chgo.). Contbr. to profl. publs. Home: 225 W Illinois St Chicago IL 60610 Office: Collector's Showroom Inc and R Volid Friedland Galleries 325 N Wells St Chicago IL 60610

FRIEDLANDER, DANIEL SIMON, communications co. exec.; b. Chgo., Apr. 11, 1933; s. Leo and Ann (Simon) F.; B.J., U. Colo., 1955; m. Shirley Tishcoff, Sept. 6, 1959; children—Janet, Alan, Robert. Asst. editor City News Bur. Chgo., 1955-57; editor AP, Chgo., 1958; editor Chgo. Am., 1959-61; pub. Warren-Newport News, Gurnee, Ill., 1960-63; co-founder, regional editor Metalworking News, Chgo. and N.Y.C., 1961-69; pres. Universal Communications, Chgo., 1969—, Simon & Friedlander Ltd., Chgo., 1976, Wenzel Trucking Co., Chgo., 1974—, Friedlander Communications, Ltd., Chgo., 1977—; dir. Tra Mor Corp. Chmn. Waukegan Twp. (Ill.) Democrats, 1967-68; chmn. numerous presidential, senatorial, gubernatorial and congl. campaigns; bd. dirs. Citizens Com. for Children and Parents Under Stress, Chgo.; treas., v.p., adv. bd. No. Ill. region B'nai B'rith Youth Orgn.; bd. dirs. Lakeview council Girl Scouts USA. Mem. Assn. Corp. Growth (v.p.), Soc. Profl. Journalists, Greater Lincolnshire C. of C. (pres. 1979-81). Jewish. Clubs: Chgo. Press (editor newspaper 1970-78), Chgo. Headline (dir., editor newspaper 1975-76, treas. 1982), Execs. of Chgo., Rotary, B'nai B'rith. Home: 2014 N Jackson St Waukegan IL 60085 Office: 2203 Lakeside Dr Bannockburn IL 60015

FRIEDMAN, CHARLES STUART, chem. co. exec.; b. Cleve., May 12, 1943; s. Armin Sam and Miriam F.; B.S., John Carroll U., 1965; M.S., Xavier U., 1969; m. Gail Rene Horwitz, July 23, 1967; 1 son, David. With Monsanto Research Corp., Miamisburg, Ohio, 1967-80, research group leader environ. analysis, Dayton, Ohio, 1980—. Mem. Am. Chem. Soc. (chmn. public relations com. Dayton), DECUS ComputerSoc. Office: 1515 Nicholas Rd Dayton OH 45418

FRIEDMAN, DEAN ALAN, advt. agy. exec.; b. Newark, Apr. 7, 1951; s. Daniel Alan and Rolla Joanne (Jacob) F.; B.G.S., U. Mich., 1973; student Lafayette Coll., 1971; m. Aviva Beth Sallen, Aug. 14, 1978; 1 son, Ari Daniel. Media buyer W. B. Doner & Co., Detroit, 1973-74, asst. account exec., Balt., 1974-75, account exec., Detroit, 1975-76, account mgr., 1976-78, account supr., 1979-81, v.p., account supr., 1981—; partner Oil Assos. Investment Co., Southfield, Mich., 1973—, Proudfoot Farms, Birmingham, Mich., 1979—. Clubs: Adcraft of Detroit; Franklin Hills Country. Office: PO Box 422-A Detroit MI 48232

FRIEDMAN, FRANK H., ednl. psychologist; b. Phila., Apr. 11, 1953; s. Charles and Hope (Julius) F.; B.A., Muhlenberg Coll., 1973; M.S., Purdue U., 1975, Ph.D., 1977; m. Susan Bell, July 31, 1976. Grad. research asst. Purdue U., West Lafayette, Ind., 1973-75, grad. teaching asst., 1975-77; asst. prof. psychology Vincennes (Ind.) U., 1977-80, dir. instl. research, 1980—, Title III grant coordinator, 1981—; presenter papers at profl. convs., condr. workshops; speaker numerous civic orgns. Active Big Bros. Am., Vincennes, 1977—. David Ross fellow, 1973-75; Purdue Research Found. fellow, 1977-78; named Outstanding Young Man Am., U.S. Jaycees, 1978; Vincennes U. minigrantee, 1978-80. Mem. Am. Psychol. Assn., Am. Ednl. Research Assn., AAUP, ACLU, Assn. Instl. Research, Phi Beta Kappa. Contbr. articles to profl. jours. Home: 1202 E Sycamore St Vincennes IN 47591 Office: Vincennes Univ Vincennes IN 47591

FRIEDMAN, GLENN R., rehab. psychologist; b. Cleve., Apr. 9, 1948; s. Glenn Emmerson and Emma Rae (Morehart) F.; M.A. in Clin. Psychology magna cum laude, Cleve. State U., 1974, B.A., 1970; m. Catherine Morrison; Intern vocat. development center, Cleve., 1973-74; substitute tchr. spl. edn. Cleve. Bd. Edn., 1971-72; tchr. Learning Community Free Sch., Cleveland Heights, Ohio, 1971-72; asst. psychologist I, Vocat. Devel. Center, Ohio, 1974, asst. psychologist, supr. work adjustment services, 1975-76, psychologist, 1976—; vocat. rehab. specialist Warrensville (Ohio) Center, 1976-79; rehab. coordinator United Cerebral Workshop Cleve., 1981—. Mem. ACLU, Am. Psychol. Assn., Nat. Rehab. Assn., Nat. Rehab. Counselors Assn., Vocat. Evaluation and Work Adjustment Assn., Cousteau Soc., Western Pa. Conservancy. Recipient Self Realization fellowship; cert. rehab. counselor, Ohio, 1975, emergency med. technician, Ohio, 1977. Developer evaluation, meditation, vocat. rehab. programs; establishment pre-vocat. workshop and Evaluation and Adjustment Program, Warrensville Center, 1976. Home: 14601 Glencliffe Rd Cleveland OH 44111 Office: 3222 Carnegie Ave Cleveland OH 44115

FRIEDMAN, JEROME JAY, lawyer; b. Cory, Pa., Apr. 5, 1906; s. Simon Friedman and Bertha (Brodsy) F.; A.B., U. Mich., 1927, L.L.B., J.D., 1929; m. Margaret Byfield, Oct. 17, 1942; children—Mary Lee, James Alexander. Admitted to Ill. bar, 1930, and since practiced in Chgo. Chmn. law and order com., city commn. on Human Relations, 1949-57; mem. Mayor's Commn. on Human Relations, 1948-69, temp. acting chmn., 1968, hon. appointee spl. housing and pub. accomodation matters; chmn. exec. com. Joint Def. Appeal of Chgo., 1952-53; chmn. Bishop Shiel Youth of Year award, Chgo., 1951; pres. Chgo. B'nai B'rith Council, 1939; mem. Civil Rights Com., Chgo., also chmn.; mem. exec. com. Chgo. Fedn. U.A.H.C., 1960-63; chmn. lawyers div. Jewish Fedn. Met. Chgo., 1965. Pres. Sinai Temple, Chgo. Served as capt. USAAF, 1942-46. Recipient citations for civic contbns. Mem. Am., Ill., Chgo. bar assns., Anti Defamation League (chmn. Chgo. exec. com. 1949-51, mem. nat. commn. 1954-55). Jewish. Clubs: Standard, Lake Shore Country, Executives. Home: 1000 Lake Shore Plaza Chicago IL 60611 Office: 33 N LaSalle St Chicago IL 60602

FRIEDMAN, LISA GAIL, mfg. co. exec.; b. Chgo., Aug. 17, 1955; d. Ronald and Sally Edith (Gold) F.; B.S., U. Ill., Champaign, 1977. Product mktg. rep. Moore Bus. Forms, Glenview, Ill., 1977-78, product planning specialist, 1978, computer support specialist, 1978-79, advt. and promotion specialist, 1979-81, merchandising/promotion mgr., 1981—. Mem. Direct Mktg. Assn., Women in Info. Processing, Chgo. Advt. Club, Direct Mktg. Assn. Chgo. Office: 2215 Sanders St Northbrook IL 60025

FRIEDMAN, MARTIN, mus. adminstr.; b. Pitts., Sept. 23, 1925; s. Israel and Etta (Louik) F.; student U. Pa., 1943-45; B.A., U. Wash., 1947; M.A., UCLA, 1949; postgrad. Columbia U., 1956-57, U. Minn., 1958-60; m. Mildred Shenberg, Sept. 3, 1949; children—Lise, Ceil, Zoe. Instr. art, curriculum cons. Los Angeles City Schs., 1949-56; instr. art UCLA, 1950-51; curator Walker Art Center, Mpls., 1958-60, dir., 1961—; commr. Am. Exhbn., Sao Paulo Bienal, 1963; mem. Nat. Council on Arts, 1978—. Served with USNR, 1943-46. Bklyn. Mus. fellow, 1956-57; Belgian-Am. Ednl. Found. grantee, Brussels, 1957-58. Mem. Assn. Art Mus. Dirs. (pres. 1978-79, trustee), Am. Fedn. Arts (trustee 1972-81), Coll. Art Assn. Am. (dir. 1973), Internat. Exhbns. Com., Nat. Collection of Fine Arts Commn., Nat. Endowment for Arts (co-chmn. mus. panel 1977-78). Clubs: Century Assn., Mpls. Contbr. articles to profl. jours. author book, catalogue essays. Office: Walker Art Center Vineland Pl Minneapolis MN 55403

FRIEDMAN, MICHAEL, physician; b. Munich, Germany, Oct. 21, 1948; came to U.S., 1949, naturalized, 1953; s. Aron and Irene (Heisler) F.; B.A., Yeshiva U., 1968; M.D., U. Ill., 1972; children—Marc Benjamin, Susan, Amy Elana, Brian Stewart. Intern, Ill. Masonic Hosp., Chgo., 1972-73; resident in gen. surgery U. Ill., 1973-74, in otolaryngology, 1974-77; practice medicine specializing in head and neck surgery, Chgo., 1977—; head neck and head surgery Ill., Masonic Hosp., Chgo., 1977—, head of head and neck rehab. center, 1977—; asst. prof. U. Ill. Med. Sch., Chgo., 1977—; lectr. in field. Diplomate Am. Bd. Otolaryngology. Mem. Ill. Med. Soc., Am. Acad. Otolaryngology, Am. Assn. Jewish Scientists (chmn. med. div. 1979—). Jewish. Contbr. articles in field to med. jours. Office: 30 N Michigan Ave Suite 1107 Chicago IL 60602

FRIEDMAN, MIRIAM ZAVELSON, social worker; b. Cleve.; d. Abraham Philip and Sophie (Miller) Z.; B.A., Flora Stone Mather Coll., Western Res. U.; m. Harry Martin Friedman (dec.); 1 son, Richard Everett. Welding insp. Republic Steel, Cleve., 1942-45; occupational therapist aide Cleve. Met. Gen. Hosp., Brecksville VA Hosp., Mt. Sinai Hosp., Cleve., 1946-47; founder, exec. dir. Red Wing Day Camp, Inc., Hinckley, Ohio, 1947-74; ct. liaison officer/intake social worker Cuyahoga County (Ohio) Youth Devel. Center, Hudson, 1975—. Trustee Salzedo Sch. of Harp. Fellow Cleve. Mus. Art (life); mem. Am. Camping Assn. (pres. Lake Erie sect. 1958-59, chmn. Region 3, mem. nat. bd. 1961-69, past v.p., sec., gen. chmn. central regions conv. 1971), Mt. Sinai Hosp. Aux. (life), Flora Stone Mather Coll. Alumni Assn. (life), Lake Forest Country Club Women's Assn. (bd. mem. 1952-53), United Order True Sisters, Women's City Club Cleve., Nat. Conf. Social Welfare, Met. Mus. Art. Home: 738-3 Claridge Ln Aurora OH 44202 Office: 996 Hines Hill Rd Hudson OH 44236

FRIEDMAN, PAUL GERALD, educator; b. N.Y.C., Sept. 18, 1941; s. David and Martha F.; B.A., Queens Coll., CUNY, 1962, M.S., 1965; Ph.D., Pa. State U., 1971; m. Reva Jenkins, July 17, 1981. 1 son, Jeremy. Tchr. secondary schs. N.Y.C., 1962-64; instr. speech Pa. State U., 1964-67; cons. Alameda County (Calif.) Schs., 1967-68; lectr. speech Queens Coll., 1968-71; asso. prof. communication studies U. Kans., Lawrence, 1971—; cons., tng. human relations processes. Danforth asso., 1978. Mem. Internat. Communication Assn. (dir. instructional communications 1976-78), Speech Communication Assn., Mortar Bd. (outstanding educator 1976). Author: Interpersonal Communication: Innovations in Instruction, 1978; Listening Processes: Attention, Understanding, Evaluation, 1978; Shyness and Reticence in Children, 1979; Communication in Conferences: Parents-Teachers-Students, 1980; Teaching the Gifted in Speech Communication and Leadership, 1981; Training: A Handbook, 1982. Home: 2415 Harvard Rd Lawrence KS 66044 Office: U Kans 3090 Wescoe St Lawrence KS 66045

FRIEDMAN, ROBERT LLOYD, radiologist; b. Bklyn., Sept. 20, 1913; s. Samuel and Sadie (Reich) F.; B.S., N.Y. U., 1934; M.D., Royal Colls. Edinburgh, 1940; m. Elsie Korzenik, Jan. 11, 1942 (dec. 1977); 1 son, Michael Jon; m. 2d, Norma Barnebey, Dec. 2, 1978. Intern, Newark Beth Israel Hosp., Newark, 1941-42; resident Bklyn. Jewish Hosp., 1947-50; asst. chief dept. radiology VA Hosp., Richmond, Va., 1950-53; asst. clin. prof. radiology Coll. Medicine, Richmond, 1950-53; staff dept. radiology Grant Hosp., Columbus, Ohio, 1953-66, chief dept., 1966—; asst. clin. prof. radiology Sch. Medicine Ohio State U., 1953-78, asso. clin. prof., 1978—. Trustee, Temple Tifereth Israel, 1966-68, Columbus Jewish Fedn., 1970-72. Served with M.C., U.S. Army, 1942-46. Decorated Purple Heart. Fellow Am. Coll. Radiology; mem. AMA, Am. Coll. Radiology, Radiol. Soc. N.Am., Roentgen Ray Soc., Acad. Medicine Franklin County, Central Ohio Radiol. Soc. (pres. 1962-63), Ohio State Radiol. Soc. (exec. com.). Jewish. Clubs: Winding Hollow Country, B'nai B'rith, Am. Jewish Congress. Contbr. articles to radiol. jours. Home: 102 Bishop Sq Bexley OH 43209 Office: 3341 E Livingston Ave Columbus OH 43227

FRIEDMAN, SEYMOUR, coll. ofcl.; b. Chgo., Sept. 8, 1923; s. Mayer and Esther F.; spl. cert. Northwestern U., 1940; B.S., U. Ill., 1947; m. Ruth Lee Spiegel, Mar. 18, 1951; children—Marc Alan, Sharon Diane, Michael Neil. Overnight news mgr. Internat. News Service, Chgo., 1947-58; asst. editor World Book Ency., 1958-59; public relations account exec. Harshe-Rotman, Inc., Chgo., 1959-60; asst. to dir. public relations U. Chgo., 1960-67; dir. public info. City Colls. Chgo., 1967—; cons. Conf. on Origins of Man, Chgo., 1965, George Williams Coll., YMCA, South Shore Commn., S.E. Chgo. Commn. Mem. public relations adv. com. Mus. Contemporary Art, Chgo., 1975. Served with U.S. Army, 1943-45; ETO. Mem. Public Relations Soc. Am. (Silver Anvil award 1967), Council Advancement and Support of Edn. (regional treas. 1976-78, chmn. site selection com. 1980), Sigma Delta Chi, Chgo. Headline Club (chmn. publicity 1965-70), Chgo. Publicity Club. Clubs: Chgo. Press, Quadrangle (Chgo.). Editor: Price Theory, 1966, 70; Dr. Charles B. Huggins and the Nobel Prize, 1967; Directory of Black Studies in Metropolitan Chicago, 1968; Directory of Black Studies in Illinois, 1969. Office: 180 N Michigan Ave Chicago IL 60601

FRIEDMAN, SONYA, psychologist; b. Bklyn., Mar. 27, 1936; d. Joseph B. Kiel and Frieda (Beekman) Goldman; B.A., Bklyn. Coll., 1956; M.Ed., Wayne State U., 1963, Ph.D., 1967; m. Stephen Friedman, Aug. 5, 1956; children—Sharon, Scott. Speech and hearing therapist Des Moines Public Schs., 1956-59; speech therapist Pontiac (Mich.) Public Schs., 1959-62; cons. psychologist Rochester (Mich.) Community Schs., 1963-76, Bloomfield Hills (Mich.) Schs., 1977—; pvt. practice The Behavior Center, Birmingham, Mich., 1967—; daily radio program Sta. WXYZ, 1978—; daily talk show Sta. WDIV-TV, 1981—. Bd. dirs. Nat. Orgn. to Insure Support Enforcement, Nat. Orgn. Non-Parents. Cert. sex therapist; named one of Top 10 Women Detroit, 1979. Mem. Am., Mich. psychol. assns., Am. Assn. Marriage Counselors, World Future Soc., Am. Orthopsychiat. assn. Recipient Headliner award Wayne State U. Alumnae Assn., 1974; certified cons. psychologist; certified marriage counselor; certified sex therapist. Columnist, Birmingham (Mich.) Eccentric, 1970-74. Author: I've Had It, You've Had It, 1974. Resident psychologist AM-Am., AM-N.Y., AM-Detroit, Morning Exchange, Cleve.; syndicated TV series: For A Better Life; spl. correspondent ABC-TV News, 1976—; daily live 3-hour radio program Sta. WXYZ. Home: 2960 Middlebelt Rd Orchard Lake MI 48033 Office: The Behavior Center 111 S Woodward Ave Birmingham MI 48011

FRIEDMAN, STEVEN HERBERT, hosp. adminstr.; b. Chgo., Sept. 11, 1942; s. Ben and Mary Friedman; B.S. in Indsl. Engring., U. Ill., 1964; M.B.A., Loyola U., Chgo., 1970; Ph.D. in Health Services Adminstrn., Pacific U., 1979; m. Lorrie Madia; children—Scott, Lisa. Corp. engr. staff Surg. Supply Co., New Brunswick, N.J., 1964-67; staff mgr. Chgo. Hosp. Council, 1967-70; staff asso. Am. Hosp. Assn., Chgo., 1970-73; pres. Associated Health Mgmt., Mt. Prospect, Ill., 1973-76; adminstr. Ill. Central Community Hosp., Chgo., 1977—, chief exec. officer, 1978—; lectr. hosp. mgmt. U. Saskatoon, Sask., Can., 1972, U. P.R., San Juan, 1972; instr. (part-time) indsl. engring. Ill. Inst. Tech., Chgo., 1969-70, Saulk Valley Jr. Coll., 1975. Program counselor jr.'s div. Chgo. Jewish Community Center, 1960-62; mem. devel. com. YMCA, 1977-78. Recipient award Ill. Central Community Hosp., 1978, award U.S. Racquetball Assn., 1978. Mem. Am. Hosp. Assn. (editorial bd. 1970-71), Hosp. Mgmt. Systems Soc. (sec. 1970-72), Am. Inst. Indsl. Engrs., Am. Coll. Hosp. Adminstrs. Contbr. articles on hosp. mgmt. to profl. publs. Home: 8939 Parkside Ave Morton Grove IL 60053 Office: Ill Central Community Hosp 5800 Stony Island Ave Chicago IL 60637

FRIEDRICH, CHARLES WILLIAM, indsl. relations exec.; b. Elgin, Ill., Aug. 30, 1943; s. Charles Kenneth and Veronica Elizabeth (Sharpe) F.; B.A., Parsons Coll., 1967; student Loras Coll., 1961-63; m. Janet Lee West, June 20, 1970; children—Joan Elizabeth, Charles Kenneth II. Salesman Bendix Corp., South Bend, Ind., 1967; safety dir., asst. personnel mgr. Nat. Castings div. Midland Ross, Cicero, Ill., 1968-69; personnel mgr. Continental Tube Co. div. Hofmann Industries, Bellwood, Ill., 1969, asst. indsl. relations mgr., 1970, Midwest dir. indsl. relations Hofmann Industries, 1971-73; dir. indsl. relations, gen. mgr. Lemont Shipbuilding and Repair Co. (Ill.), 1973-75; indsl. relations exec. Modern Mgmt. Methods, Inc., Deerfield, Ill., 1975-77; pres. Standard Cons. Services Co., Inc., Hinsdale, Ill., 1977—. Pres., Burr Ridge (Ill.) Park Dist. Bd.; treas. Palisades Sch. Dist. Mem. Packard Automobile Classics Club, Alpha Phi Omega. Club: K.C. (rec. sec. Mayslake council). Home: 10S431 Glenn Dr Hinsdale IL 60521 Office: 19 W Chicago Ave Hinsdale IL 60521

FRIEDRICH, GUSTAV WILLIAM, educator; b. Hastings, Nebr., Mar. 2, 1941; s. Edwin August and Ellen Marie Margaret (Meyer) F.; A.A., Concordia Coll., 1961; B.A. summa cum laude, U. Minn., 1964; M.A., U. Kans., 1967, Ph.D. with honors, 1968; m. Erena Rae Bakeberg, Aug. 4, 1961; 1 son, Bruce Gregory. 7th grade tchr., Young America, Minn., 1961-62; instr. U. Kans., 1964-68; asst. prof. to asso. prof. Purdue U., 1968-77; prof., chmn. dept. speech U. Nebr., Lincoln, 1977-81; prof., chmn. dept. communications U. Okla., Norman, 1982—. Recipient Outstanding Young Tchr. award, 1968. Mem. Am. Assn. Advancement Humanities, AAAS, AAUP, Am. Ednl. Research Assn., Am. Forensics Assn., Am. Psychol. Assn., Central States Speech Assn. (pres., service award 1978), Internat. Soc. History of Rhetoric, Internat. Communication Assn., Nat. Council Measurement in Edn., Speech Communication Assn., Delta Sigma Rho. Democrat. Author: Teaching Speech Communication in the Secondary School, 1973; Public Communication, 1975; Classroom Communication, 1976; Education in the '80's, 1981; editor: Communication Edn., 1979-81; contbr. articles to profl. jours. Home: 1007 Thistlewood Dr Norman OK 73069 Office: 331 Kaufman Hall U Okla Norman OK 73019

FRIEDRICH, PAUL WILLIAM, anthropologist, linguist, educator, poet; b. Cambridge, Mass., Oct. 22, 1927; s. Carl Joachim and Lenore Louise (Pelham) F.; B.A., Harvard U., 1950, M.A., 1951; Ph.D., Yale U., 1957; m. Deborah Joanna Gordon, Aug. 9, 1975; children—Maria Elizabeth, Susan Guadalupe, Peter Roland, Katherine Ann. Research asso. Russian Research Center, Harvard U., 1949-51; research asso. Yale U., 1952-54; mem. faculty U. Conn., 1956-57, Harvard U., 1957-58, Deccan Coll., Poona, India, 1958-59, U. Pa., 1959-62; mem. faculty U. Chgo., 1962—, prof. anthropology and linguistics, 1967—. Served with AUS, 1946-47. Wenner-Gren Found. grantee, 1955; Sterling fellow, 1956-57; Social Sci. Research Council fellow, 1966-67. Mem. Linguistic Soc. Am. (chmn. program com. 1972, chmn. nominating com. 1975). Author: Agrarian Revolt in a Mexican Village, 1977; Proto-Indo-European Trees, 1970; The Tarascan Suffixes of Locative Space, 1971; The Meaning of Aphrodite, 1978; Bastard Moons, 1979; Language, Context and the Imagination, 1979. Home: 5550 S Dorchester Ave Apt 609 Chicago IL 60637 Office: Haskell Hall Chicago IL 60637

FRIEDRICHS, NIELS GEORG, bus. exec.; b. Luebeck, West Germany, Dec. 22, 1929; s. Peter H. and Gertrud (Hahn) F.; came to U.S., 1958; ed. Katharineum, Luebeck, 1949; m. Ilona Grund, Dec. 18, 1957; children—Kirsten, Dirk. Printer, Flint, Mich., 1959-61; salesman Lufthansa Airlines, Chgo., 1961-63; mng. dir. German Am. C. of C., Chgo., 1963—; lectr. in field. Bd. govs. Internat. House, U. Chgo.; vice chmn. Fgn. Trade Commrs. Group, Chgo. Recipient Order of Merit (Fed. Republic Germany), 1978. Mem. Internat. Trade Club (Chgo.), Chgo. Assn. Commerce and Industry, Assn. German Fgn. Chamber Mgrs. (Bonn, Germany). Lutheran. Clubs: Ill. Athletic, Execs., Lake Point Tower (Chgo.). Home: 515 Linden Ave Wilmette IL 60091 Office: 77 E Monroe St Suite 604 Chicago IL 60603

FRIEDT, GLENN HARNER, JR., fin. cons.; b. Detroit, Nov. 23, 1923; s. Glenn H. and Lucy (Lawrence) F.; student Duke, 1941-42, Northwestern U., 1942-44; B.A. in Econs., U. Mich., 1947; J.D., Wayne State U., 1950. Admitted to Mich. bar, 1951; asst. to pres. United Platers, Inc., Detroit, 1950-53, v.p., 1953-59, pres., gen. mgr., 1959-63, chmn., 1963-65; v.p., dir. Metal Finishers, Inc., Cleve., 1959-68; asst. to chmn. Gulf & Western Industries, Inc., N.Y.C., 1965-66; dir. Am. Pres.'s Life Ins. Co., 1965-69, exec. v.p., 1966, pres., treas., 1966-68, chmn. bd., 1968-69; pres., dir. Friedt Assos. Corp., 1969—; chmn. Invest, Inc.; treas., dir. Automotive Accessories, Inc.; v.p. So. United Industries, Inc.; chmn., dir. Flowtrans Ltd. (Can.), Lauderdale Yacht Basin, Inc., Tom Smith, Inc., United Flowers-By-Wire Can. Ltd., Pacific Alliance Corp. Mem. Am., Mich., Detroit bar assns., World Bus. Council, Am. Electroplaters Soc. (exec. bd. Detroit 1959-66), Detroit C. of C. (past com. mem.), Am. Legion, Theta Delta Chi. Clubs: Coral Beach and Tennis, Detroit Athletic, Indian Village Tennis, Marina Bay, N.Y. Athletic, Palm Bay, One Hundred of Detroit, Otsego Ski, Tower, University (Detroit); Le Club (N.Y.) (Ft. Lauderdale); Masons, Shriners. Office: Penthouse 350 Bay St Toronto ON M5H 3N9 Canada

FRIEND, DAVID WESLEY, advt. exec.; b. Olney, Ill., Oct. 29, 1946; s. Clifford Wesley and Mary Jane (Smith) F.; B.S., Ind. U., 1970; children—Jenny, Jason. Advt. mgr. Ransburg Corp., Indpls., 1970-72; v.p. The Jaqua Co., Grand Rapids, Mich., 1972-81, pres., 1981—, also dir.; Mem. Indsl. Marketers West Mich. Club: Grand Rapids Breakfast. Home: 502 Storrs St SE Grand Rapids MI 49507 Office: 101 Garden St SE Grand Rapids MI 49507

FRIEND, JAMES, educator; b. Chgo., July 21, 1932; s. Oscar Falker and Sylvia (Porges) F.; B.A. cum laude, U. Ill., 1954; M.A. in English, U. Conn., 1956; m. Beverly Oberfeld, Mar. 15, 1959; children—Tracy Dee, Marla Rose, Instr. in English, U. Conn., Storrs, 1954-56, Ill. Inst. Tech., Chgo., 1957, U. Ill. at Navy Pier, Chgo., 1957-62; asso. prof. English, Chgo. State U., 1962—. Mem. Bd. Edn. Dist. 74, Lincolnwood, Ill., 1975-78, pres., 1976-77. Recipient Johnson Found. Disting. Teaching award, 1968, Nobel Prize for Lit. nominating com. hon. degree, Phi Eta Sigma, 1961; named Critic of Year, Duke U., 1968. Mem. AAUP, MLA, Midwest MLA, Nat. Council Coll. Publ. Advisers, Chgo. Press Vets. Assn., Chgo. Friends of Lit. (v.p. 1967—), Nat. Council Sch. Bds., Sigma Alpha Mu. Jewish. Author: An English Literary History, 1969; author musical adaptation For Whom the Bell Tolls, (Hemingway), 1962; composer and lyricist: Christmastime Waltz; critic, reviewer publs. including Chgo. Daily News, Chgo. Sun-Times, Newsday, Intermission Mag., Saturday Review. Home: 3415 W Pratt Lincolnwood IL 60645 Office: Chicago State University 95th Street at King Drive Chicago IL 60628

FRIEND, JEWELL ANNE, univ. dean; b. N.Y.C., Feb. 15, 1926; d. David Jerome and Estelle Evelyn (Coleman) Ryan; A.B., U. Miami (Fla.), 1959; A.M., Tulane U., 1960; Ph.D., So. Ill. U., 1970; m. Joseph Harold Friend, Aug. 19, 1967 (dec.). Mem. lit. faculty Stephens Coll., Columbia, Mo., 1961-67; mem. faculty So. Ill. U., Carbondale, 1967—, asso. prof. English as 2d lang., 1974—, dean gen. acad. programs, 1979—, prof. English, 1982—; cons. in field, manuscript reviewer, 1972—. Pres. Hill House, Inc., drug rehab., Carbondale, 1980—. Served with USCGR, 1942-46. Postdoctoral fellow U. Mich., 1973; grantee Nat. Endowment Arts, So. Ill. U. Mem. Nat. Council Tchrs. English, Assn. Supervision and Curriculum Devel., MLA, Wat. Women's Studies Assn., Nat. Assn. Women Deans, Assn. Deans Gen. and Liberal Studies, So. Ill. Assn. Tchrs. English, Ill. Assn. Tchr. Educators, Ill. Assn. Dangerous Drug Abuse, Phi Kappa Phi. Democrat. Author curriculum materials, articles, reports. Office: Dean Gen Acad Programs So Ill U Carbondale IL 62901

FRIEND, MARYANNE BERNICE, advt. agy. exec.; b. Milw., J 13, 1947; d. Robert E. and Bernice K. (Leigh) F.; B.A., Marquette 1967; postgrad. Northwestern U., 1971-72. Successively med planner, market researcher, project dir., supr., research account exec account exec. Young & Rubicam Advt., Inc., 1969-75; successively account exec., group account mgr., sr. v.p. and mgmt. rep. Stern Walters/Earle Ludgin, Inc., Chgo., 1975—; dir. Performance Achievement Group. Mem. Chgo. Ad Club, Am. Mktg. Assn. Clubs: Metropolitan, Internat. Home: 3810 N Kenmore St Chicago IL 60612 Office: 150 E Huron St Chicago IL 60611

FRIEND, MILTON, govt. lab. adminstr.; b. Malden, Mass., Dec. 11, 1935; s. Leo and Fannie (Gventer) F.; B.S., U. Maine, Orono, 1958; M.S., U. Mass., 1965; Ph.D., U. Wis., Madison, 1971; m. Jacqueline Elsa Siegel, Sept. 13, 1964; children—Lisa Jennifer, Scott David. Asst. waterfowl biologist Vt. Dept. Fish and Game, Milton, 1956; conservation helper Mass. Dept. Fish and Game, Westborough, 1958; upland game bird biologist N.Y. State Conservation Dept., Delmar, 1960-61; sect. chief for wildlife pathology and physiology, 1961-66; pesticide research biologist Denver Wildlife Research Center, 1971-72, chief sect. pesticide-wildlife ecology, 1973-75; dir. Nat. Wildlife Health Lab., U.S. Fish and Wildlife Service, Madison, Wis., 1975—; adj. asst. prof. U. Wis., Madison; keynote speaker 3d Internat. Wildlife Disease Conf., Munich, W. Ger., 1975, Wildlife Disease Assn. Meeting, 1980. Speaker for civic groups. Served with U.S. Army, 1958-60. NSF grantee, 1973-75. Mem. Wildlife Soc. (cert. wildlife biologist), Wildlife Disease Assn. (sec. 1971-73, pres. 1973-74), Am. Assn. Vet. Lab. Diagnosticians, U.S. Animal Health Assn., AAAS, Sigma Xi. Contbr. numerous chpts., articles to profl. publs. Office: 6006 Schroeder Rd Madison WI 53711

FRIEND, ROBERT NATHAN, fin. counselor, economist; b. Chgo., Feb. 2, 1930; s. Karl D. and Marion (Wollenberger) F.; A.B., Grinnell Coll., 1951; M.S., Ill. Inst. Tech., 1953; m. Lee Baer, Aug. 12, 1979; children—Karen, Alan. With K. Friend & Co., Chgo., 1953—, v.p., early 1960's, 1st v.p., 1964—, dir. merger activities with Standard Oil Co. (Ind.), trustee employees' benefit trust, 1958—; active R. Friend Investments, registered investment counselors. Admissions cons. Grinnell Coll., Ill. Inst. Tech., 1968-70; alumni career counselor Ill. Inst. Tech. Bd. dirs. Travel Light Theatre. Fellow Econ. Edn. and Research Forum; mem. Greater Chgo. Gasoline Marketers Assn. (v.p., dir.), Am. Finance Assn., So. Finance Assn., Execs. Club Chgo., Am. Acad. Polit. and Social Sci., Am. Assn. Individual Investors (dir., co-editor jour.), Am. Assn. Commodity Traders, Vintage Soc., Renaissance Soc., Sarah Siddons Soc., Chgo. Hist. Soc., Art Inst. Chgo. (life), Mus. Contemporary Art, Newcomen Soc. N. Am., Chgo. Council Fgn. Relations, Am. Econ. Assn., Acad. Polit. Sci., Found. for Study of Cycles, Econ. Time Found. Club: Carlton. Home: 1209 N Astor St Chicago IL 60610 Office: 222 W Adams St Chicago IL 60606

FRIESENHENGST, ALFRED RUDOLF, retail store exec.; b. Lorain, Ohio, Aug. 27, 1910; s. Rudolf Karl and Wilhelmina Marie (Duldner) F.; A.B. (Ohio scholar), Western Reserve U., 1932; m. Helen Marie Horrall, June 6, 1937; children—Mary Jeanette Friesenhengst Rhoads, Nancy Marie Friesenhengst Briggs. Mgr., F.W. Woolworth Co., Washington, Ind., 1934-41, Libertyville, Ill., 1940-41; owner, operator A.R. Friesenhengst Variety and Clothing Stores, Shoals, Ind., 1941-62, Loogootee, Ind., 1944-62, Crane, Ind., 1946-58, Mitchell, Ind., 1956-58, French Lick, Ind., 1958-62, Huntingburg, Ind., 1948-51; owner, operator Alco Dime Stores, Shoals, Loogootee, French Lick, 1962—, Shoals Discount Mart, 1958—, A.R. Friesenhengst Wholesale Co., Shoals, 1948—; pres., chmn. bd. A.R. Friesenhengst, Inc., Shoals, 1962—; advisory com. John Wesley Ins. Co., Ind., 1974—; advisory bd. Vincennes (Ind.) U., 1975—. Chmn., Martin County Sch. Reorganization Com., 1958-62, Martin County Overall Economic Devel. Com., 1962-63, Tri-County Anti-Poverty Program, 1962-63. Mem. Ind. Retail Assn., C. of C., Nat. Ind. Bus. Methodist. Clubs: Lions, Kiwanis, Masons, Shriners, Alpha Nu Zeta, Lambda Chi Alpha. Home: Rural Route 2 Hwy 50 Shoals IN 47581 Office: Box 10 623 Main St Shoals IN 47581

FRISBIE, RICHARD PATRICK, communications cons., author; b. Chgo., Nov. 27, 1926; s. Chauncey Osborn and Pearl Genevieve (Harrison) F.; student U. Chgo., 1944; B.A., U. Ariz., 1948; m. Margery Rowbottom, June 3, 1950; children—Felicity, Anne Celeste, Thomas, Ellen, Paul, Patrick, Teresa, Margaret. Writer, editor Chgo. Daily News, 1948-55; with Cunningham & Walsh, Inc., 1958-61, Hill, Rogers, Mason & Scott, Inc., 1961-63; creative dir. Campbell-Ewald Co., Chgo., 1964-66; editor-in-chief Chgo. mag., 1971-73; owner, operator Richard Frisbie Communications Co., Chgo., 1966—. Bd. dirs. Arlington Heights (Ill.) Meml. Library, 1967—, treas., 1971-73, pres., 1973-79; bd. dirs. North Suburban Library System, 1976, 77, treas., 1978, pres., 1979-81. Served with USN, 1945. Mem. Soc. Midland Authors (treas. 1980-81), Authors Guild, Chgo. Press Vets., ALA, Ill. Library Assn. Roman Catholic. Club: Chgo. Press. Author: (with Margery Frisbie) The Do-It-Yourself Parent, 1963; How To Peel a Sour Grape, 1965; Family Fun and Recreation, 1964; Who Put the Bomb in Father Murphy's Chowder?, 1968; It's A Wise Woodsman Who Knows What's Biting Him, 1969; Basic Boat Building, 1975; contbr. articles to various mags. Home: 631 N Dunton Ave Arlington Heights IL 60004 Office: Richard Frisbie Communications Co 333 N Michigan Ave Chicago IL 60601

FRISCHENMEYER, EDWIN F., real estate broker; b. Piqua, Kans., Mar. 23, 1926; s. Henry Charles and Mary Mildred (Fleiss) F.; student Iola (Kans.) Jr. Coll., 1949-50, Ottawa (Kans.) U., 1952; children—Michael Leo, Suzanne. Real estate sales agt., loan officer Regional Investment Co., Kansas City, Mo., 1957-64; owner, broker Woods & Co., Kansas City, Mo., 1967—. Sec.-treas. S. br. Real Estate Bd. Kansas City, 1971, vice-chmn., 1972, chmn., 1973. Served with USNR, 1944-46; PTO. Mem. V.F.W., Mo. Real Estate Assn., Nat. Assn. Realtors. Home: 4110 E 107th Terr Kansas City MO 64137 Office: 8800 Blue Ridge St Kansas City MO 64138

FRISTOE, MACALYNE (WATKINS), speech pathologist, educator; b. Nashville, Tenn., Mar. 14, 1931; d. George Miller and Brownie Mitchell (Appleton) Watkins: B.A., Vanderbilt U., 1953, M.S., 1960, Ph.D., 1972; children by previous marriage—James Houston Fristoe, Andrew McLean Fristoe. Instr. speech pathology Vanderbilt U., 1964-67, instr. psychology, 1971-72, asst. prof. psychology, 1972-74; asst. prof. U. Ala., Birmingham, 1974-76, dir. lang. intervention study project, 1974-76; asso. prof. audiology and speech scis. Purdue U., W. Lafayette, Ind., 1976—, dir. Speech Clinic, 1976-79; cons. to various schs., fed. and health orgns., 1976—. Mem. exec. bd. Nat. Council on Communicative Disorders, 1979—. Lic. speech pathologist, Ind.; NDEA fellow, 1969. Mem. Am. Psychol. Assn., Am. Speech-Lang.-Hearing Assn. (cert. speech pathologist; chairperson conv. subcom. lang. devel., lang. disorders 1977-78), Tenn. Speech and Hearing Assn. (editor jours. 1960-61), Ind. Speech and Hearing Assn., Council for Exceptional Children (pres. div. children with communication disorders 1978-79, asso. editor Jour. Childhood Communication Disorders 1975-79), Am. Assn. on Mental Deficiency, Assn. for Women in Psychology, Phi Beta Kappa, Sigma Xi. Unitarian. Co-author: Goldman-Fristoe Test of Articulation, 1969; Goldman-Fristoe-Woodcock Test of Auditory Discrimination, 1970; Goldman-Fristoe-Woodcock Auditory Skills Test Battery, 1975; contbr. chpts. to books, articles to profl. jours.

[illegible]yette IN 47905 Office: Dept Audiology and [illegible]iv W Lafayette IN 47907

[illegible]HN ORVILLE, mfg. exec.; b. Milw., May 6, 1930; [illegible] and Loretta May (Fleming) F.; A.B., Ripon (Wis.) [illegible] Rosemary Jene Goulet, Aug. 9, 1952 (dec. July 1978); [illegible] Craig John, Lynn Mary, Todd Michael, Eric Matthew, [illegible]n. Sales mgr. duplicating products internat. 3M Co., St. Paul, [illegible]63, mgr. internat. mktg., 1965-68, dir. internat. mktg. graphic [illegible]ems group, 1968-72, v.p., gen. mgr. 3M Bus. Products Sales, Inc., [illegible]972-80, v.p. bus. communication products div., 1980-81, v.p. copying products div., 1981—. Vice chmn. United Fund Drive, 1962-63. Served with inf. AUS, 1954-56. Mem. Computer and Bus. Equipment Mfrs. Assn. Roman Catholic. Clubs: Edina (Minn.) Country; Decathlon Athletic, Normandale Racquet. Home: 6612 Gleason Rd Edina MN 55435 Office: 3M Center Bldg 220 9W Saint Paul MN 55101

FRITZ, AXEL MARVIN, biomed. instruments mfg. co. exec.; b. Mpls., Sept. 15, 1925; s. Axel Marvin and Beatrice Lily (Canfield) F.; B.A., U. Minn., 1954; M.A., U. Mich., 1955; postgrad. Yale U., 1956; m. Jo-Ann Hermann, Apr. 21, 1976; children—Eeris S. Fritz Johnson, Caara Fritz, Scott Nye, Julie Nye. Am. consulate gen., Hamburg, Germany, 1956-59; market mgr. Honeywell, Mpls., 1959; with Geophys. Spltys., Mpls., 1960-62; mfr.'s rep. AMF Assos., Mpls., 1963-66; pres. Bison Instruments, Inc., Mpls., 1966-78, Britt Corp., Mpls., 1979; pres., chmn. Sciencare Corp., Biomed. Instrumentation, Mpls., 1980—; dir. Custom Design, Wright Closers, others. Served to 2d lt. USAAF, 1943-46, with CIC, U.S. Army, 1949-52. Decorated Bronze Star. Mem. Am. Geophys. Union, Am. Geol. Inst., AAAS, Geol. Soc. Am., Soc. Exploration Geophysicists, European Assn. Exploration Geophysicists, Internat. Fedn. Med. and Biol. Engring., U.S. Naval Inst., Single-Handed Sailing Soc., Nat. Aviation Club. Clubs: Robert Gordon Sproul Assos., Masons. Developer seismic signal enhancement averaging instruments; author numerous articles in applied earth scis. Home: 6960 Ticonderoga Trail Eden Prairie MN 55344 Address: PO Box 175 Chanhassen MN 55317 Office: Eden 100 Bldg Mail Sta 202 5100 Eden Ave Minneapolis MN 55436

FRITZ, DONALD WAYNE, educator; b. Monroe, Wis., June 11, 1933; s. Clifford M. and Helen May (Kubly) F.; B.A., Miami U., Oxford, Ohio, 1956, M.A., 1959; Ph.D., Stanford U., 1968; postgrad. (Leverhulme fellow) U. London, 1966-67. Mem. faculty So. Methodist U., 1959-63, Stanford U., 1967-68; mem. faculty Miami U., 1968—, prof. Brit. lit., 1978—, grad. adv., 1971-74, dir. grad. study, 1974—, dir., trustee, pres. Jungian studies, 1976-79. Mem. exec. com. Butler County Democratic Party, 1978—. Served with U.S. Army, 1956-58. Summer research fellow Miami U., 1972, 76, 81, grantee, 1978. Mem. MLA, Midwest Modern Lang. Assn., Southeastern Medieval Assn., New Chaucer Soc., Jungian Studies Conf. (dir.). Contbr. articles to profl. jours. Home: 4 Ives Wood Dr Oxford OH 45056 Office: 356 Bachelor Dept English Miami Univ Oxford OH 45056

FRITZ, MARK SHEVILLE, hosp. adminstr.; b. Winamac, Ind., Nov. 1, 1948; s. Ralph Waldo and Marilyn Capper (Heinsen) F.; B.S. in Bus. Adminstrn., Ind. U., 1971; M.B.A. in Finance, U. Detroit, 1975; m. Connie Woolson, Feb. 5, 1972; children—Robin, Kimberley, Tiffany, Nicholas. Audit examiner, asst. audit mgr. Detroit Bank & Trust Co., 1971-73; acct., fin. analyst William Beaumont Hosp., Royal Oak, Mich., 1973-74; successively internal auditor, dir. acctg. services, dir. material services, asst. adminstr., v.p. Bloomington (Ind.) Hosp., 1974—. Pres. bd. dirs. Planned Parenthood of S. Central Ind. Served with Army NG, 1970-76. Mem. Am. Soc. Purchasing and Materials Mgrs., Am. Coll. Hosp. Adminstrs., Ind. Hosp. Purchasing Mgmt. Assn., Delta Sigma Pi. Democrat. Methodist. Clubs: Elks; Bloomington North Rotary (sec.). Home: 5821 E St Rd 46 Bloomington IN 47401 Office: PO Box 1149 Bloomington IN 47402

FRITZ, RALPH DANIEL, JR., educator; b. Valparaiso, Ind., May 31, 1950; s. Ralph Daniel and Patricia Ann (Filer) F.; A.S., Vincennes U., 1970; B.S., Manchester Coll., 1973; m. Sarah Jane McCasland, Sept. 13, 1980. Tchr., Pioneer Regional Sch. Corp., Royal Center, Ind., 1974-76; substitute tchr., Porter County (Ind.) Schs., 1976-79, Portage Twp. (Ind.) Schs., 1980-81; instr. Porter County Assn. for Retarded Citizens, 1981—; pre-sch. tchr. YMCA Nursery Sch., Valparaiso, Ind., 1978-80. Sec., Royal Center Jaycees, 1975; 1st v.p. Valparaiso Community Theatre Guild, 1980-81. Contbr. articles to Tchr. mag., 1977, 79. Home: 372 Millport Valparaiso IN 46383

FRITZELL, STELLA HOUGE, state senator N.D.; b. Bucyrus, N.D., Oct. 3, 1909; d. Gunder and Carrie (Engen) Houge; B.S. cum laude, U. Minn., 1931; m. Kenneth E. Fritzell, June 24, 1933 (dec. Feb. 1957); children—Peter, Sara (Mrs. Ugur Hanhan), Erik, Anne. Dietic intern U. Minn. Hosps., 1931-32; research technician and nutritionist U. Minn. Hosps. and Mpls. Welfare Dept., 1932-40; stock broker, Grand Forks, N.D., 1959-71; mem. N.D. Senate 1971—, now from 43d Dist. Mem. Grand Forks Park Bd., 1960-72 (pres. 1972-74); mem. N.D. Dist. Park Commrs., Grand Forks Planning and Zoning Commn.; legis. com. N.D. Recreation and Park Assn., Grand Forks Bd. Budget Rev.; del. Constl. Conv., 1970-71. Mem. Pine to Prairie Girl Scouts Trust Com.; active local bldg. coms. YM-YWCA; mem. United Hosp. Corp. Recipient Pub. Ser. award U. N.D. students, 1970, Legis. Conservationist of Yr. award N.D. Wildlife Fedn. (state trapshooting champion 1969); named Outstanding Woman Legislator, 1975. Mem. Bus. and Profl. Women's Club, Audubon Soc., Natural Sci. Soc. N.D., Wildlife Fedn. Republican. Home: 3720 Cherry St L-45 Grand Forks ND 58201

FRITZLEN, DAVID GLENN, advt. agy. exec.; b. Louisville, July 6, 1944; s. Glenn A. and Mary Jane (Higgins) F.; B.A., Loyola U., Los Angeles, 1967; children—Carin Elizabeth, Christopher David. Mgmt. trainee Goodyear Tire and Rubber Co., Los Angeles, 1967; dealer sales rep. Union Oil Co. of Calif., Los Angeles, 1967-69, automotive spl. events rep., Palatine, Ill., 1969-73; spl. events coordinator Castrol Oils, Inc., Hackensack, N.J., 1973-74; account exec. D'Arcy-MacManus & Masius, Inc., Chgo., 1975-76, account supr., 1976-80, v.p., account supr., 1980—. Mem. Am. Auto Racing Writers and Broadcasters Assn., U.S. Auto Club, Championship Auto Race Teams. Office: 200 E Randolph Chicago IL 60601

FRITZSCHE, JOSEPH LEE, bank exec.; b. Camden, N.J., Oct. 15, 1947; s. Alan Norman and Anna Margaret (Bretvik) F.; B.A., Taylor U., 1969; M.A., Ball State U., 1970; m. Marcia Kay Schilling, Aug. 8, 1970; children—Kristina Lyn, Erik Josef. Dir. fin. aid Taylor U., Upland, Ind., 1970-75, dir. career devel., 1973-75; asst. to v.p. adminstrn. Mut. Security Life Ins. Co., Ft. Wayne, Ind., 1975-77, dir. human resources, 1977-80; v.p. human resources Lincoln Nat. Bank & Trust Co., Ft. Wayne, 1980—; lectr. bus. and econs. Manchester (Ind.) Coll., 1977-78, 79-80. Mem. Am. Mgmt. Assn., Am. Compensation Assn., Am. Soc. Personnel Adminstrn., NE Ind. Personnel Assn. (pres. 1979-80, 80-81), Ft. Wayne Christian Businessmen's Assn. (program chmn.), Ft. Wayne chpt. Taylor U. Alumni Assn. (pres.). Republican. Baptist. Home: 4106 Gallmeyer Ct Fort Wayne IN 46815 Office: 116 E Berry St Fort Wayne IN 46802

FROBASE, CAROLYN ANN, coll. adminstr.; b. Tiffin, Ohio, Oct. 28, 1938; d. Sidney Earl and Beatrice Idona (Brillhart) McNeal; B.A., Hiram Coll., 1960; M.Ed., Bowling Green State U., 1977; children—Debra Lynne, Julie Kay. Tchr., Park Jr. High Sch., Chardon, Ohio, 1959-61, Scipio Republic (Ohio), 1962-63; adminstrv. asst. Office Admissions, Heidelberg Coll., Tiffin, Ohio, 1974-76, asst. dir. admissions, 1976-77; counselor, adv. U. Toledo, 1978-79; dir. alumni relations Hiram (Ohio) Coll., 1979—. Mem. Nat. Assn. Women Deans, Adminstrs. and Counselors, Council Advancement and Support of Edn., Ohio Ind. Coll. Advancement Assn. (sec.). Mem. United Ch. of Christ. Office: Hiram Coll Hiram OH 44234

FROEHLICH, ADELE, editor; b. Chgo., July 8, 1918; d. A.I. and Frances Elizabeth (Welch) F. Vocal instr. McHenry (Ill.) Community High Sch., 1944-68; with McHenry Plaindealer, 1941—, mng. editor, 1947—; voice tchr., McHenry, 1951-75. Founder, dir. McHenry Choral Club, 1940—; dir. St. Patrick's Ch. Choir, 1960—, McHenry County Vocal Festival, 1972. Recipient Service award C. of C., 1972; Woman of Year award Bus. and Profl. Women's Club, 1976; 1st place editorial award Ill. Agrl. Assn., 1954; hon. mention Ill. Press Assn., 1973, 74, 1st place editorial award, 1973. Republican. Roman Catholic. Club: McHenry County Tennis (past v.p., Women's Tennis Title holder). Office: 3812 W Elm St McHenry IL 60050

FROELICH, WOLFGANG ANDREAS, neurologist; b. Berlin, Apr. 8, 1927; s. Andreas Ferdinand and Ilsa Gertraud Schultz (Engelhard) F.; came to U.S., 1955, naturalized, 1960; M.D., Free U., Berlin, 1955; m. Jean Small, Nov. 28, 1959; children—Morna, Leslie, Mark, Stefan, Andrew. Intern, Huron Rd. Hosp., Cleve., 1955-56, resident in surgery, 1956-57; asst. resident in neurology Barnes Hosp., St. Louis, 1957-58, resident in neurology, 1958-59, chief resident, instr. neurology, 1959-60; resident in psychiatry Cleve. Psychiat. Inst., 1960-61; practice medicine specializing in neurology, psychiatry and encephalography, 1961—; instr. neurology Washington U., St. Louis, 1959-60; chief div. neurology Huron Rd. Hosp., Cleve., 1967—; pres. med. staff Windsor Hosp., Cleve., 1971-73; mem. active staff St. Luke's, Windsor hosps.; cons. staff Geauga Community, Marymount, Shaker Med. Center hosps. Served with German Army, 1944-45. Diplomate Am. Bd. Psychiatry and Neurology, Pan. Am. Med. Assn. Fellow Am. Acad. Neurology; mem. Cleve. Acad. Medicine, Cleve. Soc. Neurology and Psychiatry, Ohio State Med. Assn., Am. Electroencephalographic Soc., Am., Ohio psychiat. assns., No. Ohio Neurol. Soc., Epilespy Found. Am. Club: Cleve. Racquet. Contbr. articles to med. jours. Home: 14807 Shaker Blvd Shaker Heights OH 44120 Office: 3609 Park E #304-N Beachwood OH 44122

FROEMSDORF, DONALD HOPE, coll. dean; b. Cape Girardeau, Mo., Mar. 4, 1934; s. Rudolph Fred and Marie (Mammon) F.; B.S., S.E. Mo. State U., Cape Girardeau, 1955; Ph.D., Iowa State U., 1959; m. Joy Lou Kasten, May 29, 1954; 1 dau., Dawn Elaine. Asst. project chemist Standard Oil Co. (Ind.), Whiting, 1959-60; asso. prof. chemistry S.E. Mo. State U., 1960-66, prof. chemistry, 1966—, chmn. div. scis., 1970-76, dean Coll. Scis., 1976—. DuPont Research fellow, 1958; Petroleum Research Fund grantee, 1962-72; NSF grantee, 1964-71, 75-76. Mem. Am. Chem. Soc., AAAS, Mo. Acad. Sci. Club: Lions Internat. Contbr. articles to sci. jours. Office: Coll Scis Southeast Mo State U Cape Girardeau MO 63701

FROHMADER, MARY ELLIN, assn. exec.; b. Chgo., May 9, 1917; d. John VanEman and Ellinor (Lewis) Berger; B.A., Carroll Coll., 1938; M.A., U. Wis., 1939; m. Stanley Harrison Frohmader, June 20, 1941; children—John Lawrence, Margaret Jane, Richard Lewis, Elizabeth Ellin. Tchr., Wayland Acad., Beaver Dam, Wis., 1939-41; mem. staff Presbyn. Student Center, U. Wis., 1941-43; 2d v.p. Phi Beta Fraternity, 1959-65, nat. pres., 1965-74; nat. pres. Profl. Panhellic Assn., 1973-77; nat. pres. Profl. Frat. Assn., 1977-78; treas. Interfrat. Research and Adv. Council, 1979—. Elder, Presbyn. Ch., 1975-81; active John Knox Presbytery, Civic Music Assn., Civic Opera Guild; bd. dirs. Presbyn. Student Found., Nat. Interfrat. Found., YWCA. Mem. AAUW, Phi Beta. Home: 514 LeRoy Rd Madison WI 53704

FROHOCK, JOAN (WALTON), indsl. supply co. exec.; b. Des Moines, Aug. 6, 1939; d. John Martin and Dorothy (McCauley) Walton; A.A., Stephens Coll., Columbia, Mo., 1958; B.A., U. Wis., 1961; J.D., Drake U., 1964; m. Richard Wyman Frohock, June 27, 1964; children—Kent Martin, Trent Warren. With Standard Bearings Co. of Des Moines, 1956—, v.p., 1962-74, pres., 1974—, pres. Standard Bearing Co. of Mason City (Iowa), 1978—; pres. ICOM Systems, Inc., 1979—; pres. Standard Bearing Co. of Davenport, Inc., Standard Bearings Co. of Sioux City, Inc. Mem. Iowa State Bar Assn., Greater Des Moines C. of C. Republican. Episcopalian. Office: 2350 Hubbell Ave PO Box 823 Des Moines IA 50304

FROHRIB, DARRELL ALBERT, educator; b. Oshkosh, Wis., June 25, 1930; s. Albert August and Caroline Irene (Yorty) F.; B.S., Mass. Inst. Tech., 1952, M.S., 1953; Ph.D., U. Minn., 1966; m. Betty Jane Eserhut, Sept. 12, 1955; children—Ellen Marie, Sandra Jean, Paul Darrell. Engr., Sperry Gyroscope Co., Great Neck, N.Y., 1953-59; lectr. in mech. engring. U. Minn., Mpls., 1959-66, asst. prof., 1966-68, asso. prof., 1968-74, prof., dir. design center in mech. engring., 1974—, grad. faculty in bio-engring., 1968—, dir. grad. program in biomed. engring., 1978-81. Mem. Gov.'s Commn. on Handicapped, State of Minn., 1974-75; mem. adv. com. Courage Center, Golden Valley, Minn.; v.p. Pilgrim Luth. Ch., St. Paul, 1975. Fulbright fellow, 1970; NIH grantee, 1973-77. Mem. ASME, Sigma Xi, Tau Beta Pi, Pi Tau Sigma. Lutheran. Patentee in field; contbr. articles to profl. jours. Home: 2144 Princeton Ave Saint Paul MN 55105 Office: Room 325 The Design Center Mech Engring Dept U of Minn Minneapolis MN 55455

FROILAND, SVEN GORDON, biologist; b. Astoria, S.D., May 4, 1922; B.S., S.D. State U., 1943; M.A., U. Colo., 1951, Ph.D., 1957; D.Hum. Luther Coll., 1978; married; 6 children. Mem. faculty Augustana Coll., Sioux Falls, S.D., 1946—, prof. biology, 1957—, chmn. dept., 1953-70, chmn. div. natural sci., 1959-76, dir. Center Western Studies, 1976—; dir. Black Hills Natural Sci. Field Sta., 1970-79; vis. scholar U. Ariz., 1970-71. Mem. AAAS, Ecol. Soc. Am., Am. Inst. Biol. Scis., Nat. Assn. Biology Tchrs., Soc. Study Evolution, Western History Assn. Address: Center Western Studies Augustana Coll 29th and S Summit Sioux Falls SD 57197

FROMM, MARTIN, trade assn. exec.; b. Wuerzburg, Germany, Dec. 1, 1914; s. Henry and Bertha (Landauer) F.; m. Dorothy Lindauer, Dec. 15, 1941; children—William M., Barbara Fromm Fogel. Chmn. bd., pres. Martin Fromm & Assos., Kansas City, Mo., 1945—. Pres., Temple B'nai Jehudah, Kansas City, 1962-65; v.p. bd. Jewish Geriatric and Convalescent Center, 1975-79; trustee Menorah Med. Center, 1962—; mem. Kansas City Area council Boy Scouts Am., 1958-63. Served with Ordnance Dept., U.S. Army, 1941-45. Mem. Am. Soc. Assn. Execs. Clubs: Masons, Scottish Rite. Office: 9140 Ward Pkwy Kansas City MO 64114

FROMME, ALEX M., justice Kans. Supreme Ct.; b. Hoxie, Kans., Mar. 11, 1915; s. Joseph H. and Frances (Morgan) F.; A.B., LL.B., Washburn U.; m. Ruth Marie Kesler, Sept. 16, 1939. Admitted to Kans. bar, 1939, since practiced in Hoxie; individual practice, 1939-48; partner firm Fromme & Fromme, 1949-66; county atty. Sheridan County, 1941-48; justice Kans. Supreme Ct., 1966—; partner Fromme Ins. Agy., Hoxie; dir. First Nat. Bank Hoxie. Instl. rep. local council Boy Scouts Am., 1948-49; home service chmn. Sheridan County chpt. ARC, 1941-47; pres. Sheridan County Community Fund, 1964-65. Mem. Am., Kans. (pres. 1961-62), N.W. Kans. (past mem. council) bar assns., Nat. Conf. Bar Presidents. Club: Rotary (local pres. 1947-48). Contbr. articles to legal jours. Home: 5108 Shunga Dr Topeka KS 66614 Office: Kansas Judicial Bldg 301 W 10th St Topeka KS 66612

FROMMERT, BEVERLEY JEAN, veterinarian; b. Detroit, June 15, 1938; d. Arthur Emil John and Vera Vivian (Helzerman) F.; B.S., Mich. State U., 1962, D.V.M., 1964; m. Henry Abraham Kallet, July 22, 1967. Asso. veterinarian Allen Park (Mich.) Veterinary Hosp., 1964-67; owner Brookeside Veterinary Hosp., Ann Arbor, 1972—; mem. Mich. Bd. Vet. Examiners, 1978—. Bd. dirs. Mich. Vet-Pac, 1978—. Mem. AVMA, Am. Animal Hosp. Assn., Mich. Veterinary Med. Assn., Washtenaw Acad. Veterinary Medicine. Home: 3324 Bluett Dr Ann Arbor MI 48105 Office: 3010 Warren Rd Ann Arbor MI 48105

FRONTIER, JAMES LEONARD, sch. adminstr.; b. Chgo., Dec. 26, 1950; s. Dominic and Adeline (Gentile) F.; B.A. in Edn., Western Ill. U., 1973; M.S. in Guidance and Counseling, Northeastern Ill. U., Chgo., 1978; m. Katherine A. Tidd, Dec. 17, 1978. Tchr., Lodge Grass, Mont., 1973, Cicero (Ill.) Public Schs., 1974-78; dir. Title IV Part C Project, Bellwood (Ill.) Sch. Dist., 1978—; cons. Nystrom Co., Dist. 122. Mem. Assn. Supervision and Curriculum Devel., Ill. Assn. Supervision and Curriculum Devel. Roman Catholic. Home: 5601 W Bernice St Chicago IL 60634 Office: 640 Eastern Ave Bellwood IL 60104

FROOM, ROBERT ELDEN, ins. agy. exec.; b. Youngstown, Ohio, Sept. 28, 1920; s. Earl Watson and Emily Josephine (Roop) F.; student Ohio State U., 1942; m. Aug. 10, 1947; children—Heidi Linn, Bonnie, Holly. Agt., New Eng. Mut. Life Ins. Co., Youngstown, 1945-56, agy. mgr., 1964-68, gen. agt. for 11 countries, 1968—; dist. mgr. Cleveland-Weber Agy., Youngstown, 1956-64; pres. Robert E. Froom & Assos., Inc., fringe benefit mktg. co., Youngstown, 1960—; v.p., treas. Lenfro, Inc.; dir. various cos. Pres., Boardman (Ohio) Civic Assn., 1960; sec. Mahoning County (Ohio) Airport Authority, 1971-72. Served with cav. USAAF, as pilot, 1942-45. Decorated D.F.C., Air medal; recipient Nat. Quality award Nat. Assn. Life Underwriters, 1949. Mem. Nat. Assn. Pension Cons. and Adminstrs., Million Dollar Round Table (life), Youngstown C. of C., Youngstown Assn. Life Underwriters (pres. 1955-56), Gen. Agts. and Mgrs. Assn. (pres. chpt. 1970-71), Am. Coll. Life Underwriters (C.L.U. 1951, pres. Youngstown chpt. 1956-57), Hump Pilots Assn., Global Ministries United Methodist Ch. Clubs: Youngstown, Boardman Tennis and Swim, Masons, Shriners. Author: Money Making Axioms, 1948; Five Activities in the Sale of Pension Plans, 1969. Home: 434 Rockland Dr Youngstown OH 44512 Office: 5700 Market St Youngstown OH 44512

FROST, DONALD RICHARD, ednl. adminstr.; b. Arthur, N.D., Nov. 21, 1928; s. Bernard Leo and Elizabeth Ann (Bahl) F.; B.S., State Tchrs. Coll., Valley City, N.D., 1950; M.A., U. No. Colo., 1957, Ed.D., 1964; m. Joanne Rosonke, June 1, 1957; children—Joseph, Patrick, Michael. Tchr., coach Consol. Sch., Arthur, 1950-51, Ind. Dist., Elma, Iowa, 1954-57; high sch. prin. Community Dist., Buffalo Center, Iowa, 1957-59; ednl. cons. Bremer County (Iowa) Supt.'s Office, 1959-64; curriculum dir. Leyden High Schs., Franklin Park and Northlake, Ill., 1964-78; asst. supt. for adminstrn. Community High Schs. Dist. 99, Downers Grove, Ill., 1978—; mem. faculty Triton Community Coll., 1968-69; co-dir. Inst. on Grad. Competencies, Vail, Colo., 1978; mem. adv. bd. Nat. Coll. Edn., Lombard (Ill.) Campus, 1979-82; mem. bd. control DuPage Area Vocat. Edn. Authority, 1979—; mem. Nat. Conf. Adv. Com. Children and TV: Implications for Edn., Ohio U.; speaker in field. Bd. dirs. Addison (Ill.) Community Chest, 1969—; v.p. St. Joseph Parish Council, Addison, Ill., 1969-73; pres. St. Joseph Sch. Bd., 1969-75, cons., 1975—; chmn. Parochial Sch. Bd., St. Joseph Parish; cubmaster pack 416 Addison council Boy Scouts Am., 1980-81. Served with U.S. Army, 1952-54. Mem. Assn. Supervision and Curriculum Devel. (dir. 1974-80, exec. council 1975-80, pres. 1978-79, chmn. bd. trustees Found. 1981—), Ill. Assn. Supervision and Curriculum Devel. (treas. 1968-70, pres. 1973-74, Spl. Recognition award 1980), NEA (life), West Suburban Curriculum Assn., Assn. Sch. Adminstrs., World Council for Curriculum and Instrn., Phi Delta Kappa. Club: K.C. Contbr. forewards, chpts. to profl. publs.; mem. editorial adv. bd. Edn. Digest, 1978-81. Home: 454 Pioneer Dr Addison IL 60101 Office: 1860 63d St Downers Grove IL 60516

FRUHAUF, ANTHONY BRAMLEY, ednl. adminstr.; b. Detroit, Feb. 2, 1942; s. M. H. and A. B. (Bramley) F.; B.A., Brown U., 1963; postgrad. U. Nuevo Leon (Mex.), 1963-64, U. Los Andes, Colombia, 1967-68; M.B.A., Harvard U., 1971; m. Hannecristl Kuiperi, Sept. 4, 1965; children—Gianna, Christopher. Dir. fin. affairs U. Liggett Sch., Grosse Pointe, Mich., 1973-78; pres., headmaster The Prairie Sch., Racine, Wis., 1978—. Mem. exec. bd. Racine Symphony Orch.; bd. dirs. Jr. Achievement, Racine. Fullbright scholar, 1963-64. Mem. Nat. Assn. Ind. Schs., Ind. Schs. Assn. Central States, Cum Laude Soc. Republican. Episcopalian. Club: Rotary. Office: 4050 Lighthouse Dr Racine WI 53402

FRUIT, CHARLES BARCO, brewery exec.; b. Edwardsville, Ill., Dec. 25, 1946; s. Roy H. and Marie B. (Baird) F. B.A., Williams Coll., 1969; m. Sharon L. Nemnich, Aug. 15, 1970. Vice pres. media Gardner Advt. Co., St. Louis, 1970-76; corp. media dir. Anheuser-Busch, Inc., St. Louis, 1976—. Bd. dirs. Kidney Found. of Eastern Mo. and Metro East, 1980—. Mem. Assn. Nat. Advertisers, St. Louis Advt. Club. Home: 1231 Randle St Edwardsville IL 62025 Office: 721 Pestalozzi St Saint Louis MO 63118

FRY, CHARLES GEORGE, theologian, educator; b. Piqua, Ohio, Aug. 15, 1936; s. Sylvan Jack and Lena Freda (Ehle) F.; B.A., Capital U., 1958; M.A., Ohio State U., 1961, Ph.D., 1965; B.D., Evang. Lutheran Theol. Sem., 1962, M.Div., 1977; D.Min., Winebrenner Theol. Sem., 1978. Ordained to ministry Lutheran Ch. U.S.A, 1963; pastor St. Mark's Luth. Ch. and Martin Luther Luth. Ch. (both Columbus, Ohio), 1961-62, 63-66; theologian-in-residence North Community Luth. Ch., Columbus, 1971-73; instr. Wittenberg U., 1962-63; instr. Capital U., 1963-75, asst. prof. history and religion, 1966-69, asso. prof., 1969-75; asso. prof. hist. theology, dir. missions edn. Concordia Theol. Sem., Ft. Wayne, Ind., 1975—; vis. prof. Damavand Coll., Tehran, Iran, 1973-74, bd. dirs., 1976—; vis. prof. Reformed Bible Coll., 1975-79, Concordia Luth. Sem. at Brock U., summer 1977, St. Francis Coll., 1980—; bd. dirs. Zwemer Inst., 1978—; mem. Luth.-Baptist Dialogue team Luth. Ch. U.S.A.-World Bapt. Alliance, 1978-81; vis. theologian Luth. Ch. Venezuela, 1981, Nat. Presbyterian Ch. Mexico, 1977, 79, First Community Ch., Columbus, 1971-73; mem. N.Am. Laussane Com., 1977-78. Recipient Praestantia award Capital U., 1970, Concordia Hist. Inst. citation, 1977; Regional Council for Internat. Edn. research grantee, 1969. Mem. Am. Hist. Assn., Am. Acad. Religion, Middle East Studies Assn., Middle East Inst., Brit. Interplanetary Soc., Phi Alpha Theta. Democrat. Author books, including: Age of Lutheran

Orthodoxy, 1979; Lutheranism in America, 1979; Islam, 1980, 2d edit., 1982. Home: 158 W Union St Circleville OH 43113 Office: Concordia Theol Sem 6600 N Clinton St Fort Wayne IN 46825

FRY, CHARLES GEORGE, clergyman, educator; b. Piqua, Ohio, Aug. 15, 1936; s. Sylvan Harmon and Lena Freda Marie (Ehle) F.; B.A., Capital U., 1958; M.A., Ohio State U., 1961, Ph.D., 1965; B.D., Evang. Luth. Theol. Sem., 1962, M.Div., 1977; D.Min., Winebrenner Theol. Sem., 1978; m. Christel Heischmann, Nov. 24, 1971 (div. 1980). From instr. to asso. prof. Capital U., Columbus, Ohio, 1963-75; asso. prof., dir. missions edn. Concordia Theol. Sem., Ft. Wayne, Ind., 1975—; adj. prof. Ref. Bible Coll., Grand Rapids, Mich., 1975-79, St. Francis Coll., Ft. Wayne, 1979—; vis. prof. Wittenberg U., 1971, 62-63, Damavand Coll., Tehran, Iran, 1973-74, Concordia Sem., Brock U., St. Catharines, Ont., Can., 1977; pastor Martin Luther Luth. Ch., Columbus, 1963-66; vicar St. Mark's Luth. Ch., Columbus, 1961-62; theologian-in-residence North Community Luth., Columbus, 1971-73; vis. theologian Nat. Presbyn. Ch. of Mex., 1977, 79, Luth. Ch. Venezuela, 1981. Bd. dirs. Damavand Coll., 1976—, Samuel Zwemer Inst., 1978—, Luth.-Jewish Dialogue, 1974-75, Luth. Bapt. Dialogue, 1978-81, Fellowship of Faith, 1969-79. Recipient Praestanita award Capital U., 1970; Commendation, Concordia Hist. Inst. of St. Louis, 1977; Am. Luth. Ch. grantee, 1962. Mem. Am. Hist. Assn., Am. Acad. Religion, Conf. on Faith and History, Middle East Studies Assn., Middle East Inst. Democrat. Author: The Way, the Truth, the Life, 1982; Islam, 1980; The Middle East: Crossroads of Civilization, 1973; Lutheranism in America, 1979; Age of Lutheran Orthodoxy, 1979; An Anthology of Middle Eastern Literature, 1975; Europe in Transition, 1970; The Past in Perspective, 1970; Middle East in Transition, 1970, others; contbr. articles to profl. jours. Home: 158 W Union St Circleville OH 43113 Office: 6600 N Clinton St Fort Wayne IN 46825

FRY, J(OHAN) TRILBY, educator; b. Quincy, Mass., Apr. 27, 1937; d. Paul A. Gifford and Mary Gifford Blunt; A.A., Westbrook Coll., 1957; B.S. in Edn., Tufts U., 1960; M.A., Western Mich. U., 1971; children—Eluned, Erik, Kari. Staff occupational therapist hosps. in Mass. and Minn., 1961-63; tchr. applied arts and home mgmt. Skills Mpls. Soc. for Blind, 1964-68; supr. Minn. Services for Blind, St. Paul, 1968; tutor Kalamazoo Central High Sch., 1969; rehab. tchr. VA Hosp., West Haven, Conn., 1969; occupational therapist, ward supr. Gaylord Hosp., Wallingford, Conn., 1970-72; asst. prof. occupational therapy, clin. coordinator Quinnipiac Coll., 1972-79; asst. prof. occupational therapy U. N.D., Grand Forks, 1979—; sec. ann. meeting New Eng. Occupational Therapy Edn. Council, 1977, chmn. steering com., 1977, sec. steering com. 1978. Mem. N.D. Occupational Therapy Assn. (asst. editor newsletter 1979-80, chmn. com. on practice 1979-81, program chmn. 1980-82, pres. 1982-84), Am. Occupational Therapy Assn. (rep. U. N.D. Commn. on Edn. 1980, rep. Commn. on Practice from N.D. 1980-81), World Fedn. Occupational Therapy Established formal techniques of daily living program for blinded vets. in VA system, 1969. Home: 1019 15th Ave S Grand Forks ND 58201 Office: Dept Occupational Therapy U ND Univ Sta Grand Forks ND 58202

FRY, JOHN ALFRED, cons. engr.; b. Cleve., July 26, 1901; s. Harry McCook and Minerva Arvella (Hoak) F.; A.B., Ohio Wesleyan U., 1924; postgrad. in Engring., Case Inst. Tech., 1925, Grad. Sch., Case Western Res. U., 1932-34; student Engring. Sch., Ft. Belvoir, Va., 1939, Command and Gen. Staff Coll., Ft. Leavenworth, Kans., 1942; m. Helen M. Geib, Dec. 15, 1951. Commd. 2d. lt, U.S. Army, 1925, advanced through grades to lt. col., 1953, served C.E., ret., 1961; design specialist Goodyear Aerospace, Akron, Ohio, 1961-66; profl. engr. Ohio Dept. Hwys., Ashland, 1966-73; engring. cons., Wadsworth, Ohio, 1973—. Founding master councilor Order of DeMolay, Cleve., 1921. Registered profl. engr., Ohio, Pa., Ind. Mem. ASME, Am. Soc. Metals, Nat. Aero. Soc., Soc. Am. Mil. Engrs., Am. Ordnance Soc., Ohio Wesleyan Alumni Assn. (pres. Cleve. chpt. 1934), Case Alumni Assn. (pres. Akron chpt. 1961), Alpha Tau Omega. Republican. Episcopalian. Clubs: Chgo. Athletic Assn., S. Shore Country (Chgo.); Masons (Delaware, Ohio); K.T., Scottish Rite, Shriners (Columbus). Home: 8150 River Styx Rd Wadsworth OH 44281

FRY, WILLIS FRANCIS, hosp. adminstr.; b. Dixon, Ill., Sept. 12, 1941; s. Paul J. and Lauretta M. (Brady) F.; B.A., U. Notre Dame, 1963; M.S., Trinity U., 1969; student Loyola U., Chgo., 1964-65; m. Bonita Sue DeSplinter, May 22, 1965; children—Willis Francis, Dennis Michael, Amy Marie, Megan Anne. Various mgmt. positions Rush-Presbyn. St. Luke's Hosp., Chgo., 1963-66; research asst. Tex. Hosp. Assn., San Antonio, 1967; adminstrv. resident Emanuel Hosp., Portland, Oreg., 1967-68, adminstrv. asst., 1968-69; v.p. Mercy Hosp. and Med. Center, Chgo., 1970-75; pres. St. Francis Hosp., Waterloo, Iowa, 1975—; instr. The Loop Coll., City Colls. Chgo., 1972-74; prof. Govs. State U., Park Forest South, Ill., 1974-75. Chmn. hosp. div. United Way of Black Hawk County, Iowa, 1977-79, chmn. planning and allocation com., 1981—, bd. dirs., 1980—; bd. dirs. Black Hawk County Area Med. Edn. Found., 1977—, Iowa Conf. Cath. Hosps., 1977—; asst. dist. chmn. Winnebago council Boy Scouts Am., Waterloo, Iowa, 1978-80. Mem. Waterloo C. of C. (dir. 1978-81), Am. Coll. Hosp. Adminstrs., Am. Hosp. Assn., Cath. Health Assn., Iowa Hosp. Assn. (chmn. council on health services 1977—). Roman Catholic. Contbr. articles to profl. publs. Home: 373 Derbyshire Rd Waterloo IA 50701 Office: 3421 W 9th St Waterloo IA 50702

FRYDENLUND, ARTHUR JORGEN, motel exec.; b. nr. Buffalo, S.D., Aug. 16, 1907; s. Olaf and Ella (Halvorson) F.; student pub. schs.; m. Elaine A. Eyler, June 25, 1934; children—Gerald, John, Karen (Mrs. Gerald Bouzek), Jane (Mrs. Elliott Moore), Eric. Barber, Prairie du Chien, Wis., 1932-51; owner Motel Brisbois, Prairie du Chien, 1951—, Moto-Miter Co., Prairie du Chien, 1959—. City chmn. Heart Fund, Prairie du Chien, 1962; mem. adv. bd. Campion Jesuit High Sch., 1970—; mem. Father Marquette Tercentenary Com., 1972—; pres. Blackhawk Com., 1974—. Mem. County Bd. Suprs., chmn. health com., 1974—, mem. social services com. Bd. dirs. Indsl. Devel., 1952-63, pres., 1963—; trustee Meml. Hosp., 1957—; mem. transit com. Milw. R.R.; dir. 9 county tourist promotion Hidden Valley, 1979. Mem. Wis. Innkeepers (v.p. 1974—), Prairie du Chien C. of C. (pres. 1959, dir. 1952—, named Man of Yr. 1978), Gt. Fire Engine Race Am. (dir. 1972—). Methodist. Patentee in field. Home: 533 N Marquette Rd Prairie du Chien WI 53821

FRYDMAN, MORRIS, data processing co. exec.; b. Aalan, Germany, May 2, 1948; came to U.S., 1958, naturalized, 1966; s. Abe and Rachel (Alperowitz) F.; B.S., U. Cin., 1970; M.B.A., U. Chgo., 1976; m. June Back, Mar. 31, 1973; children—Jason, Alexandra. Asso. indsl. engr. Armco Steel, 1967-69; staff cons. Citibank, 1969-70; self-employed data processing cons., N.Y.C., 1970-74; sr. data processing cons. McDonnell Douglas Corp., Chgo., 1974-76; dir. mktg. Itel Corp., San Francisco, 1976-79; exec. v.p. Charter Data Products, Bannockburn, Ill., 1979—, also dir. Mem. Optical Character Recognition Users Assn. Office: 2275 Half Day Rd Bannockburn IL 60015

FRYE, MARIANNE ELIZABETH, educator; b. Oak Park, Ill., Jan. 9, 1929; d. Bernhard Paul and Elizabeth Catherine (Wanderer) Reinsch; B.S., Fla. So. Coll., 1950; Ph.D., U. N.D., 1972; m. Gustav W. Frye, July 3, 1970; children—Ellen Marie Wallace, Teresa Ann Schuh, Roger Allen Icenogle. Instr., Childersburg (Ala.) Elem. Sch., 1954-56, Johnston City (Ill.) High Sch., 1958-62, So. Ill. U., Extension, Carbondale, 1960-62; chmn. bus. dept. Moreno Valley High Sch., Sunnymead, Calif., 1962-66; instr. adult edn. Yacaipa (Calif.) High Sch., 1962-64; chmn. bus. dept. Mt. San Jacinto Coll., Gilman Hot Springs, Calif., 1966-68; instr. St. Croix Sch. Dist., Solon Springs, Wis., 1969-72; instr. bus. edn. Wis. Indianhead Dist., Superior, 1972-74; asst. prof. U. Minn., Duluth, 1974-77; asst. prof. U. Wis., Superior, 1977-79, asso. prof., 1979—; cons. in bus. edn. to various secondary schs., colls. and sch. dists., 1965—. NSF grantee, 1962-63; Vocat. Tchr. Educator Self-Improvement grantee, 1976; named Outstanding Sci. Tchr. of Morena Valley area, 1963-65, 77. Mem. Am. Fedn. Tchrs. (rec. sec. 1973-74), Nat. Secs. Assn., Classroom Educators in Bus. and Office Edn. Episcopalian. Club: Campus (dir. 1975-77). Author: (handbooks) Typewriting Techniques and Production Typewriting I, 1977, Introduction to Accounting, 1977, Introduction to Data Processing, 1977, Occupational Model, Medical Secretary, 1978, Operating the Word Processing Typewriter Using the CPT Cassetype System, 1978, Occupational Model, Correspondence Secretary, 1980; contbr. articles on bus. edn. to profl. publs. Home: Box 73B Wascott WI Office: Sch Bus and Econs Wis Superior WI 54880

FRYE, MYRON E., automotive co. exec.; b. Spencer, Ind., Dec. 20, 1939; s. Harley M. and Pearl H. (Dowdell) F.; student Purdue U., 1958-60; B.S. with highest distinction summa cum laude, Ind. U., 1962; postgrad. Ind. Univ. Grad. Sch., 1962-63, Harvard Grad. Bus. Sch., 1977; m. Janet S. Meadows, June 5, 1960; children—Kimberly Ann, Scott Edward. Mgmt. trainee purchasing dept. Ford Motor Co., Dearborn, Mich., 1963-66; sr. buyer, purchasing Am. Motors Corp., Detroit, 1966-70; corp. materials mgr. Philips Industries, Dayton, Ohio, 1970-74; dir. materials White Farm Equipment Co., White Motor Corp., Oak Brook, Ill., 1974-75; v.p. purchasing and adminstrn. Maremont Corp., Chgo., 1975—; adj. faculty Ind. U., Richmond, 1972-74, Gary, 1976-78, Earlham Coll., Richmond, 1972-74, Purdue U., Lafayette, Ind., 1972-74; condr. seminars and symposiums various univs. and colls., 1976—; cons. to various cos., 1976—. Mem. Nat. Assn. Purchasing Mgmt., Am. Purchasing Soc. Mem. Christian. Ch. Contbr. articles to various publs. Office: Maremont Corp 200 E Randolph Dr Chicago IL 60601

FRYER, EDWARD ROY, automotive engr.; b. Detroit, May 16, 1923; s. Edward Roy and Jewel (Steensma) F.; student Gen. Motors Inst., 1941-43; B.M.E., Mass. Inst. Tech., 1945; commd. U.S. Naval Res. Midshipman's Sch. Columbia U., 1945; m. Audrey Marie Osmon, July 5, 1945; children—Jeffrey, Susanne, Debra-Ellen, Kevin, Tammy. Jr. engr. Nat. Acme Co., Cleve., 1946-47; with Euclid Rd. Machinery Co. (became Terex div. Gen. Motors Co. 1969), 1947-81, product engr., Euclid, Ohio, 1953-69, asst. chief engr., Hudson, Ohio, 1969-81, div. metric coordinator, 1973-81; design cons. Regco Inc., Euclid, 1981—. Served with USNR, 1943-46. Mem. Soc. Automotive Engrs. Contbr. numerous articles to profl. jours.; patentee in field. Home: 966 Oakview Dr Highland Heights OH 44143 Office: 5405 Darrow Rd Hudson OH 44236

FRYKBERG, W. RANDOLPH, govt. service agy. exec.; b. Hackensack, N.J., Mar. 19, 1947; s. William Samual and Virginia Ann (Walker) F.; A.A., U. Fla., 1967; B.A., Western Mich. U., 1968, M.A., 1973, Sp.A., 1974, Ph.D., 1976; M.S., U. Mich., Ann Arbor, 1972; m. Diane Kay Rollins, June 21, 1970; 1 son, Andrew Timothy. Research biologist Parke-Davis & Co., Ann Arbor, 1969-71; instr. intern Grand Valley State Coll. and Western Mich. U., 1972-73; project dir. EPA and Muskegon County (Mich.) Dept. Public Works, Muskegon County Wastewater Mgmt. System, 1974-76; asst. dir., environ. programs mgr. N.E. Mich. Council Govts., Gaylord, 1976-79, exec. dir., 1979—; mem. Public Involvement Work Group; mem. Great Lakes Basin Commn., 1977-80; tech. advisor to Dept. Energy; commr. Mich. Air Pollution Control Commn., 1982—. Tng. advisor for No. Mich, Nat. Ski Patrol System, Inc., 1970-80. HEW Higher Edn. grad. fellow, 1972-74; EPA grantee, 1974-76; recipient commendation Resource Conservation and Devel. Program, 1979. Mem. Water Pollution Control Fedn., Mich. Water Pollution Control Fedn., Am. Water Resources Assn., N. Am. Benthological Soc., N. Am. Lake Mgmt. Soc., Mich. Soc. Planning Ofcls., Micro-Computers in Planning. Clubs: Charlevoix (Mich.) Yacht; Walloon Lake (Mich.) Yacht; Eagles. Home: PO Box 298 Walloon Lake MI 49796 Office: PO Box 457 114 N Court St Gaylord MI 49735

FRYKENBERG, ROBERT ERIC, historian; b. India, June 8, 1930; s. Carl Eric and Doris Marie (Skoglund) F.; B.A., Bethel Coll., 1951; M.A., U. Minn., 1953; M.Div., Bethel Theol. Sem., 1955; postgrad. U. Calif., Berkeley, 1954-58; Ph.D., U. London, 1961; m. Carol Enid Addington, July 1, 1952; children—Ann Denise, Brian Robert, Craig Michael. Research asst. U. Calif., Berkeley, 1955-57; instr. Oakland (Calif.) Jr. Coll., 1957-58; Rockefeller fellow in Indian history London U., 1958-61; research, teaching fellow U. Chgo., 1961-62; asst. prof. history U. Wis.-Madison, 1962-67, asso. prof., 1967-71, prof., 1971—, dept. chmn., center dir. South Asian studies, 1970-73; vis. prof. U. Hawaii, 1968. Guggenheim Found. fellow; 1968-69; Fulbright-Hays fellow, 1965-66; Nat. Endowment for Humanities sr. fellow, 1975-76. Fellow Royal Asiatic Soc., Royal Hist. Soc.; mem. Soc. South Indian Studies (pres. 1968-70), Am. Inst. Indian Studies (trustee), Assn. Asian Studies, Inst. Hist. Studies, Inst. Asian Studies (India), Inst. Advanced Christian Studies (dir.). Author: Guntur District, 1788-1848: A History of Local Influence and Central Authority in South India, 1965; Land Control and Social Structure in Indian History, 1969; Land Tenure and Peasant in South Asia: An Anthology of Recent Research, 1977. Office: Dept History U Wis Madison WI 53706

FU, PAUL SHAN, law librarian; b. Shen-Young, China, Sept. 7, 1932; s. Moon S. and Shih Wei (Chang) F.; came to U.S., 1961, naturalized, 1973; LL.B., Soochow U., 1960; M.C.L. (Grad. fellow), Coll. Law, U. Ill., 1962; M.S. in L.S., Villanova U., 1968. Asst. law librarian, lectr. in law Detroit Coll. Law, 1968-69; law librarian, asso. prof. law Ohio No. U. Coll. Law, Ada, 1969-72; law librarian Supreme Ct. Ohio Law Library, Columbus, 1972—; cons. Hancock County Law Library Assn., Findlay, Ohio, 1973, Clinton County Law Library Assn., Wilmington, Ohio, 1975. Mem. Am. (cert.; chmn. state, court, county law libraries sect.), Ohio regional assns. law libraries, ALA, Am. Soc. Internat. Law, Am. Trial Lawyers Assn. Club: Kiwanis (Ada). Author: Law Library Handbook of the Supreme Court of Ohio, 1975; contbr. articles to legal library jours. Home: 940 Evening St Worthington OH 43085 Office: 30 E Broad St Columbus OH 43215

FUHRER, LARRY, investment banker; b. Ft. Wayne, Ind., Sept. 23, 1939; s. Henry Roland and Wilhelmine Ellen (Kopp) F.; A.B., Taylor U., 1961; postgrad. No. Ill. U., 1965—; m. Linda Larsen, Dec. 31, 1962; 1 son, Lance. Exec. club dir. Youth for Christ, Miami, Fla., 1961; publs. mgr. Campus Life mag. Wheaton, Ill., 1962-65; asst. to pres. Youth for Christ Internat., Wheaton, 1965-66; asso. dir. devel. Ill. Inst. Tech., 1966-68; exec. asst. to pres. The Robert Johnston Corp., Los Angeles, Chgo., N.Y.C., 1968-69; pres. Compro, Inc., Glen Ellyn, Ill., 1966-72, The Centre Capital Group Inc., Wheaton; pres. Killian Assos. Inc., Wheaton, 1973-75; chmn. Equibanque Ltd., 1973-79, Q. Media Group Inc., Rockford, Ill.; dir. Fin. Services Group Ltd., Equity Realty Group Inc., Presdl. Services Inc., Int Telemedia Ltd.; ednl. mgmt. cons. numerous pvt. colls. and sems. dirs. Chicagoland Youth for Christ. Mem. Am. Mgmt. Assn., A Inst. Mgmt. Cons.'s, DuPage Bd. Realtors, Nat., Ill. assns. realto Am. Mktg. Assn., Mortgage Bankers Assn. Presbyterian. Club: Unio League (Chgo.). Home: 125 W Seminary St Wheaton IL 60187 Office. 226 E Roosevelt Rd Wheaton IL 60187

FUHRER, WILHELMINE ELLEN, accountant; b. Defiance, Ohio, Jan. 12, 1914; d. Herman C. and Rose Amelia (Wandt) Kopp; ed bus. coll.; m. Henry R. Fuhrer, June 25, 1936; children—Larry Rolland, Eugene Leo, Beverly Wilhelmine. Circulation mgr. Nat. Stock Dog mag., Butler, Ind., 1960—; individual practice tax computation and accounting, Auburn, Ind., 1940—. Mem. Nat., Ind. socs. pub. accountants, Am. Bus. Women's Assn., Am. Forestry Assn., Arbor Assn. Author, Bus. Report, now pub. in The New Entrepreneurs (Terri Tepper); subject of N.Y. Times article, 1981. Home: Rural Route 2 Rd 35 Auburn IN 46706

FUJIMURA, THOMAS MINORU, counselor, educator; b. Haleiwa, Hawaii, Apr. 28, 1943; s. Jitsuo and Hachime (Shibao) F.; B.E., U. Hawaii, 1965; M.S., Ind. State U., 1966; M.S., Ind. U., South Bend, 1979; Ed.S., Ind. U., Bloomington, 1981; m. Sherrill Louise Edgington, Aug. 16, 1969; children—Troy Thomas, Ty Matthew. Tchr., Hilo (Hawaii) High Sch., 1966-67, South Broward High Sch., Hollywood, Fla., 1969-70; tchr. Waialua High and Intermediate Sch., Waialua, Hawaii, 1970-72, registrar, counselor, 1973-75; recruiting and placement officer Ind. Vocat. Tech. Coll., South Bend, 1975-78; dir. admissions and community services Ancilla Coll., Donaldson, Ind., 1978-79; sch. guidance counselor Culver (Ind.) Community Schs., 1979—; mem. profl. devel. com. Mid-West Coll. Placement Assn. Mem. Gov.'s Com. on Children and Youth, 1974-75. Served with U.S. Army, 1967-69. Recipient Recognition award Women's Aux. Culver VFW, 1978; appreciation cert. Plymouth Kiwanis Club, 1978, Elkhart Optimist Club, 1978, Plymouth Optimist Club, 1979; Ind. Bd. Vocat. Tech. Edn. grantee, 1976-78; cert. emergency med. technician, Ind. Mem. NEA, Nat. Bus. Edn. Assn., Am. Personnel and Guidance Assn., Am. Coll. Personnel Assn., Ind. Assn. Coll. Admission Counselors, Ind. State Tchrs. Assn. (minority affairs com.), Ind. Assn. Coll. Registrars and Admission Officers. Roman Catholic. Clubs: Masons, Shriners, Scottish Rite, Order of Eastern Star, Odd Fellows. Home: Rural Route 1 Box 118 Culver IN 46511 Office: Culver Community Schs Culver IN 46511

FUJISHIRO, SHIRO, metallurgist; b. Kakogawa, Hyogo Prefecture, Japan, Oct. 18, 1930; s. Manji and Shizue (Yumoto) F.; came to U.S., 1956, naturalized, 1972; B.S. in Phys. Chemistry, Tohoku U., Japan, 1953; grad. Sch. Metall. Engring., U. Pa., 1960; Ph.D. in Phys. Chemistry, Kyoto U., Japan, 1962; postgrad. in metallurgy Cambridge (Eng.) U., 1968-69; m. Tomoko Takahashi, Oct. 28, 1959; children—Felix, Charlotte. Research chemist Inst. Indsl. Sci., Kyoto (Japan) U., 1953-57; research asst. U. Pa., Phila., 1957-60; chief heat treatment br. Research Lab., Nippon Steel Co., Sagamihara, Japan, 1960-63; research metallurgist USAF Materials Lab., Wright Patterson AFB, Dayton, Ohio, 1963—; vis. scholar Cambridge (Eng.) U., 1968-69. Named Materials Man of Month USAF Materials Lab, 1966; recipient Sci. Achievement award Air Force System Command, 1970. Mem. Am. Inst. Metall. Engrs., Electron Microscope Soc. Am., Phys. Soc. Japan, Sci. Research Soc. Am. Contbr. articles to profl. jours.; patentee in field. Home: 1640 Spillan Rd Yellow Springs OH 45387 Office: AFML/LLS Wright Patterson AFB Dayton OH 45433

FUKUSHIMA, MASAYA, computer services exec.; b. Wakayama, Japan, May 25, 1939 (parents Am. citizens); s. Shozo Frank and Miyoko June (Kuwahara) F.; B.A. in Math. and Zoology, U. Calif., 1963; m. Donna Jo McKinsey, Sept. 20, 1963; children—Karen Mika, Melissa Miya. Product mgr. clin. data systems Control Data Corp., La Jolla, Calif., 1963-71; adminstr. Medlab Computer Services, Inc. div. Control Data Corp., Salt Lake City, 1971-73; mgr. health care systems Xerox Corp., El Segundo, Calif., 1973-75; sr. mgr. Internat. Devel. Comshare, Inc., Ann Arbor, Mich., 1975-79; v.p. Mfg. Data Systems Inc. Internat., 1979—; bd. dirs. Miroku-Comshare, Inc., Tokyo. Republican. Shinto. Designer on-line data acquisition and large data base mgmt. systems for clin. labs. and hosps., computer-aided design and computer-aided mfg. systems. Home: 8614 Meadowland Saline MI 48176 Office: 4251 Plymouth Rd Ann Arbor MI 48105

FULL, RAY HENRY, food products co. exec.; b. Vermilion, Ohio, Mar. 11, 1918; s. Otto Fred and Gertrude (Nau) F.; grad. St. Petersburgh Jr. Coll., 1939; student Fenn Coll., 1950-51, Baldwin Wallace Coll., 1951-52; m. Dawn N. Malson, Nov. 28, 1947; foster children—Carol Skiles, Barbara Ivey. Dir., Kishman Fish Co., Vermilion, Ohio, 1951—, pres., 1960—; pres. So. Lake Erie Inc., 1956-66, R & D Enterprises, 1963—, Conneaut Fisheries, 1972—, Shoreline Fisheries, 1977—; dir. Erie County Bank, 1972—, Lorain (Ohio) Community Hosp., 1976—; adviser Great Lakes Fisheries Commn., 1963—, Great Lakes Commn., 1963-70; mem. Am. Fisheries Advisory Com., 1959-67, 1970-71, Marine Fisheries Advisory Com., 1971-75. Chmn. Festival of the Fish, 1967, 68, 69; sec. Vermilion Planning Commn., 1951-60, Vermilion, Ohio; chmn. Flood Control Com., Vermilion, 1970—, Vermilion United Fund, 1971-74, Vermilion Port Authority, 1975-76, Lorain County (Ohio) Home Town Careers, 1968—; mem. Gov. Gilligan Conservation Task Force, 1973-74; mem. Erie County Republican Central Com., 1968—, chmn., 1978—; bd. dirs. Lorain County United Community Services, 1971-76, Lorain County United Health Found., 1972-76; trustee Wilbur Meml. Fund, 1961—; mem. exec. com. Lorain Community Hosp., 1978—. Recipient Disting. Service award City of Vermilion, 1966. Mem. Lake Erie Resources Council (pres. 1964-65), Am. Fisheries Soc., Internat. Oceanographic Found., Animal Protection League, Vermilion C. of C. (trustee 1965-75, pres. 1968), Ohio Comml. Fisherman's Assn. (pres. 1958-66, sec. 1970-74), Gt. Salis Hist. Soc. (treas., exec. com.). Clubs: South Shore Cruising (hon. mem.), Vermilion Boat (dir. 19—, commodore 1951), Rotary (dir. 19—, pres. 1954—). Mem. United Ch. of Christ. Home: 5419 Willow Ln Vermilion OH 44089 Office: Dept Natural Resources Shoreline Mgmt Commn PO Box 22 Vermilion OH 44089

FULLER, BENJAMIN FRANKLIN, physician; b. St. Paul, Aug. 7, 1922; s. Benjamin Franklin and Luella Amelia (Pfaff) F.; B.A., U. Minn., 1942, B.S., 1943, M.D., 1946, M.S. in Internal Medicine, 1950; m. Carol Marie Myre, Sept. 24, 1945; children—Constance J., Benjamin F., Geraldine A., Lynn M. Intern, U. Minn. Hosp., Mpls., 1945-46, resident in medicine; fellow in internal medicine Mayo Found., 1947-50; practice medicine specializing in internal medicine, St. Paul, 1951-66; prof. head dept. family practice and community health U. Minn., Mpls., 1968-71, prof. dept. internal medicine, head sect. primary care, 1972—; chief of staff elect United Hosps., St. Paul. Served with USAF, 1946-47, 53. Fellow A.C.P., Am. Coll. Angiology; mem. Ramsey County Med. Soc., Minn. Med. Assn., AMA, Assn. Minn. Internists (pres.), Minn. Acad. Medicine, St. Paul Soc. Internal Medicine (pres.), Sigma Xi, Alpha Omega Alpha. Methodist. Author: Physician or Magician?, 1978. Home: 2641 S Shore Blvd White Bear Lake MN 55110 Office: 3615 Grand Ave White Bear Lake MN 55110

...LEY, utility co. exec.; b. Glasco, Kans., ... Newell and Cora A. (Forkner) F.; B.S. in ..., 1950; M.S. in Engring. Mgmt., Mo. U., 1974; ...app, July 21, 1946; children—Christine Anne, ...avid Gilbert. Elec. design engr. Black & Veatch ...ansas City, Mo., 1950-52; plant engr. and constrn. ...Empire Dist. Electric Co., Joplin, Mo., 1952-56, chief ...-63, plant supt., 1963-67, constrn. elec. cons., 1967-74, ...n. adminstrn., 1974-78, supt. environ. engring. and liaison, ... Mem. Joplin Bd. of Realtors. Served with USNR, 1943-46; ... Registered profl. engr., Kans. Mem. IEEE, Central Engring. ...c., Christian Bus. Mens Com., Power Engring. Soc. Republican. Presbyterian. Clubs: Masons, Shriners, Optimists. Home: 3007 Silver Creek Dr Joplin MO 64801 Office: 602 Joplin St Joplin MO 64801

FULLER, JACK ALLEN, univ. ofcl.; b. Cedar Rapids, Iowa, June 26, 1945; s. Joshua Jason and Mary Etta (Higgins) F.; B.S. in E.E., Iowa State U., 1967; M.A. in Bus. Adminstrn., U. Iowa, 1971; Ph.D. in Bus. Adminstrn., U. Ark., 1972; m. Connie Ann Patterson, Mar. 6, 1966; children—Christine Ann, Jonathan Jason. Asst. prof. mgmt. Coll. Bus. Adminstrn., U. Okla., Norman, 1972-78; asso. prof., coordinator grad. programs Sch. Bus., U. No. Iowa, Cedar Falls, 1978-79, chmn. mgmt. div., 1979-80, asso. dean, coordinator grad. programs, 1980—; mgmt. cons. Equitable Life Assurance Soc. U.S., 1979—. Bd. dirs. 1st United Meth. Ch., Cedar Falls, 1980—. Mem. Acad. Mgmt., Am. Inst. for Decision Scis., Am. Prodn. and Inventory Control Soc., Mensa, Delta Sigma Pi, Phi Delta Theta, Tau Beta Pi, Eta Kappa Nu, Omicron Delta Epsilon, Sigma Iota Epsilon, Beta Gamma Sigma, Sigma Iota Delta. Club: Rotary (Cedar Falls). Contbr. writings to profl. publs. in field. Office: School of Business Univ Northern Iowa Cedar Falls IA 50614

FULLER, JERRY KEITH, civil engr.; b. Kansas City, Mo., Oct. 30, 1947; s. Charles Alfred and Martha Jane (Richardson) F.; B.S. in Civil Engring., U. Mo., Rolla, 1969; M.S. in Civil Engring., U. Mo., Columbia, 1973; M.B.A. (Exec. fellow), Rockhurst Coll., 1982; m. Nancy Ann Becker, Mar. 31, 1978; children—Christopher Todd, Jami Elizabeth. Engr. Armco Inc., Kansas City, Mo., 1969-80, sr. civil engr., 1980—. Sec., North Kansas City Park Bd., 1974-76; trustee North Kansas City Meml. Hosp., 1976—, chmn. bd. trustees, 1978—; pres. Norclay Sch. PTA, 1979-81. Named outstanding civic leader So. Clay County Jaycees, 1981; registered profl. engr., Mo. Mem. ASCE, Nat. Soc. Profl. Engrs., Chi Epsilon, Theta Tau. Home: 1441 E 21st Ave North Kansas City MO 64116 Office: Armco 7000 Roberts Rd Kansas City MO 64125

FULLER, LAWRENCE BELL, agrl. chem. co. exec.; b. Stafford, Ariz., Oct. 10, 1943; s. LaVaun O. and Marie (Bell) F.; B.S., U. Ariz., 1966; M.A., Ariz. State U., 1969; M.B.A., Ariz. State U., 1971; m. Ann Carolyn Payne, Mar. 1, 1972. Product mgr. W.R. Grace & Co., 1972-74; mgr. supply and distbn., purchasing Beker Industries, Conda, Idaho, 1974-79; mgr. nat. sales and purchasing Estech Gen. Chem. Corp., St. Louis, 1979—; chemistry instr. Ariz. State U., 1968-69. Am. Plant Food Assn. grantee, 1964-65. Mem. Soil Sci. Soc. Am.

FULLER, RAYMOND EUGENE, educator; b. Gary, Ind.; s. Richard Baxter and Sarah (Wilson) F.; student Ind. State U.; B.A., Ky. State U., 1965; M.S., Ind. U., 1973; adminstrv. lic. DePaul U., 1977. Caseworker, Lake County Dept. Public Welfare, Gary, 1965-66; asst. dist. mgr. circulation dept. Post Tribune, Gary, 1979-80; tchr. elem. math. Gary Community Sch. Corp., 1966—. Served with U.S. Army, 1959-61. Mem. Gary Tchrs. Union, Assn. for Supervision and Curriculum Devel. Democrat. Baptist. Home: 5806 Kennedy Terr Gary IN 46403

FULLER, RAYMOND EVERETT, physician; b. Dennison, Ohio, Nov. 3, 1927; s. Otis Everett and Irene (Zimmerman) F.; B.S., Capitol U., 1949; M.D., Ohio State U., 1954; m. Lillian Louise Martin, Mar. 19, 1951; children—Steven, Timothy, James, Sharon, Charles. Intern, Blodgett Meml. Hosp., Grand Rapids, Mich., 1954-55, resident, 1955-56; resident in internal medicine Henry Ford Hosp., Detroit, 1958-60; practice medicine specializing in internal medicine, Grand Rapids, 1961—; dir. cardiovascular lab. Blodgett Meml. Med. Center, Grand Rapids, 1961—, also cons; cons. Butterworth Hosp., St. Mary's Hosp., Grand Rapids; asso. clin. prof. Mich. State U., 1973—. Served with M.C., U.S. Army, 1956-58. Mich. Heart Assn. grantee, 1963-64, 74-75. Diplomate Am. Bd. Internal Medicine. Fellow A.C.P.; mem. Am. Soc. Internal Medicine, AMA, Mich. State, Kent County med. socs., Am., Mich. (pres. 1974) heart assns. Republican. Contbr. articles to profl. jours. Home: 2249 Shawnee SE Grand Rapids MI 49506 Office: 1900 Wealthy St Grand Rapids MI 49506

FULLER, RAYMOND HAROLD, civil engr.; b. New Plymouth, Ohio, Jan. 12, 1910; s. Charles C. and Chloie Ellen (Meyers) F.; B.S., Ohio U., 1932; m. Rhoda M. Hewitt, Dec. 17, 1938; children—Robert, Mary Ellen (Mrs. Joseph Van Buskirk), Ronald. State and county hwy. engr., Ohio, 1933-35; asso. engr. Burgess & Niple, cons. engr., Columbus, Ohio, 1935-42; chief sna. facilities sect. 5th Service Command Hdqrs. Army Service Forces, Columbus, Ohio, 1942-45; mem. Burgess & Niple, Ltd., cons. engr., specializing in waterworks, wastewater control design and mgmt., Columbus, 1946-81, exec. dir., 1960-72, chmn. bd., 1976-79; dir. Gammatronix Corp., Columbus. Commr. Ohio River Valley Sanitation Commn., 1966-72, chmn., 1971-72; mem. Ohio River Basin Planning Commn., 1970-72. Recipient Meritorious Service award Dept. Army, 1946, Fuller award Am. Water Works Assn., 1958, Distinguished Cons. award Cons. Engrs. Ohio, 1975. Registered profl. engr., Ohio. Mem. ASCE, Am. Water Works Assn., Nat., Ohio socs. profl. engrs., Water Mgmt. Assn. Ohio (trustee 1972-78, treas. 1977). Methodist. Mason. Clubs: Columbus Engineers, University (Columbus). Contbr. articles to profl. and tech. jours. Home: 4321 Olentangy Blvd Columbus OH 43214 Office: 5085 Reed Rd Columbus OH 43220

FULLER, WILLIAM SAMUEL, state ofcl. Nebr.; b. Rockford, Ill., June 2, 1926; s. William Arthur and Loyda Mae (Wylam) F.; Mus.B., Westminster Choir Coll., 1950; M. Mus. Edn., N. Tex. State Coll., 1951; Ed.D., Ind. U., 1960; m. Marjory LaVerne Thomas, June 11, 1950; children—Heidi, Grant, Thomas, Dirck. Supr. pub. sch. and choral music, El Dorado, Ark., 1951-54; teaching asst. Sch. Music, Ind. U., 1954-55, critic instr. math. Univ. Sch., 1954-56, univ. research asso. adminstrv. studies and instl. relations, 1956-58, dir. bur. phys. facilities studies, 1961-64; specialist coll. and univ. facilities U.S. Office Edn., Washington, 1958-61; dir. office planning higher edn. N.Y. State Dept. Edn., Albany, 1964-71, asst. commr. higher edn., 1973-76; exec. dir. Nebr. Coordinating Commn. for Postsecondary Edn., Lincoln, 1976—; dir. N.Y.C. Regents Adv. Com., 1971-73. Active local Boy Scouts Am. Trustee Westminster Choir Coll. Served with USNR, 1944-46. Recipient Alumni Merit award Westminster Choir Coll., 1970. Mem. Assn. Instl. Research, Assn. State Higher Edn. Exec. Officers (exec. com.), Soc. Coll. and Univ. Planning. Methodist. Office: State Office Bldg Lincoln NE 68509

FULTON, LOUANNA BAHR, registered nurse; b. Murray, Utah, Oct. 14, 1948; d. Hubert Arthur and Eleanor May (Stewart) Bahr; A.A., U. S.D., 19—, B.A., 1971; m. Kenneth Alan Fulton, Jan. 7, 1977. Staff nurse, U. Minn. Hosp., Mpls., 1970, Dakota Hosp., Vermillion, S.D., 1970-71, Bennett Clarkson Hosp., Rapid City, S.D., 1971, St. Mary's Hosp., Tucson, 1971, Tucson Med. Center, 1971-76; health nurse Lincoln (Nebr.) Lancaster County Health Dept., 1976-77; staff nurse St. John Hosp., Leavenworth, Kans., 1977; staff nurse, evening supr. OB, Atchison (Kans.) Hosp., 1977—. Mem. Kans. Health Occupations Edn. Assn. (sec. treas. 1979-82), Emergency Dept. Nurses Assn., Kans. Vocat. Assn., Am. Vocat. Assn., N.E. Kans. Area Vocat. Tech. Sch. Assn., U. S.D. Alumni Assn., Kans. Health Occupations Edn. Assn., Am. Acad. Trauma Specialists, Pi Beta Phi. Democrat. Mem. United Ch. of Christ. Office: 1501 Riley St Atchison KS 66002

FULTZ, NORMA JOYCE, librarian, educator; b. Bloomington, Ind., Jan. 23, 1932; d. Ray Levi and Helen Mildred (Myers) F.; B.S. in Edn., Ind. U., 1952, M.A. in L.S., 1957, M.S. in Instrnl. Systems Tech., 1970; postgrad. Creighton U., 1963, Purdue U., 1967; M.A. in English, Ball State U., 1980. Sch. librarian, New Castle (Ind.) Elem. Schs., 1952-56, Beery Jr. High Sch., Columbus, Ohio, 1957-59, Arsenal Tech. High Sch., Indpls., 1959-60, Acad. Immaculate Conception, Ferdinand, Ind., 1962-65; sch. librarian, media specialist Mater Dei High Sch., Evansville, Ind., 1965-70; asst. edn. and psychology librarian, asst. prof. So. Ill. U., Carbondale, 1970-72; ednl. resources librarian for multi-media, asst. prof. library service Ball State U., Muncie, Ind., 1972—; mem. adv. bd. Inst. for Study Bibliotherapy, Inc., Ft. Wayne, Ind. NDEA Media Inst. grantee Purdue U., 1967. Mem. Assn. Ednl. Communications and Tech., Assn. Supervision and Curriculum Devel., Assn. Ind. Media Educators. Contbr. articles to profl. jours. Home: 3015 Bethel Ave Apt 28 Muncie IN 47304 Office: Ednl Resources Room 5 Bracken Library Ball State U Muncie IN 47306

FUNK, ALBERT PETER, rubber co. exec.; b. LaCrosse, Wis., Aug. 6, 1919; s. Albert Peter and Dorothy R. (Rendell) F.; B.A., U. Notre Dame, 1940; J.D., U. Wis., 1946; m. Mary P. Maloney, Jan. 3, 1942; children—Terrell Ann Funk Gagermeier, Mary Ellin Funk Osmond, Gretchen R. Funk Geary, Katherine J. Funk Lynch, Albert Peter III. Admitted to Wis. bar, 1946; asso. firm Lees and Bunge, LaCrosse, Wis., 1946-51; sec., counsel LaCrosse Rubber Mills Co. (Wis.), 1947-54, pres., chief exec. officer, 1954-78, chmn. bd., chief exec. officer, 1978—; dir. First Bank N.A., Milw.-LaCrosse, LaCrosse Cooler Holding Co. Bd. dirs., chmn. bd. St. Francis Hosp., La Crosse, 1964-76; trustee LaCrosse Public Library; bd. dirs. LaCrosse Found. Served with U.S. Army, 1942-45; ETO. Decorated Purple Heart, Bronze Star. Mem. Am. Bar Assn., State of Wis. Bar Assn., La Crosse County Bar Assn. Roman Catholic. Clubs: LaCrosse, LaCrosse Country. Office: LaCrosse Rubber Mills Co 1407 St Andrew St LaCrosse WI 54601

FUNK, ARVILLE LYNN, lawyer; b. Corydon, Ind., Dec. 11, 1929; s. Herman E. and Elsie (McMonigle) F.; B.A. in History, Ind. Central Coll., 1955; M.S. in Edn., Butler U.; LL.B., Ind. U., 1963, J.D., 1967; ; m. Rosemary E. Springer, Aug. 25, 1956; children—Cynthia Lynn, Mark Andrew (dec.). Head history dept. Perry Central Jr. High Sch., 1955-61, Perry E. Jr. High Sch., Indpls., 1961-65; admitted to Ind. bar, 1963; partner law firm Hays, O'Bannon & Funk, Corydon, Ind., 1965—; atty. Crawford County, City of Corydon; gen. counsel Ind. Toll Bridge Commn., 1969—. Instr. history Purdue U. extension. Hist. advisor Ind. Dept. Conservation, 1961—; publs. chmn. Marion County Civil War Centennial Commn., 1961-65; chmn. Harrison County Bicentennial Commn. Del., Ind. Republican State Conv., 1966, 68, 70, 72, 74. Pres., dir. North Am. Indian Found., 1966-67. Served to capt. AUS, 1947-48, 50-52. Recipient Nat. Classroom Tchrs. medal Freedom Found., 1962. Mem. Am., Ind., Harrison County (pres.) bar assns., Ind., Harrison County (dir.) hist. socs., C. of C. (dir.), Ind. Central Coll. Alumni (dir.), Phi Delta Phi. Methodist (pres. bd. trustees). Rotarian (dir.). Author: Tales of Our Hoosier Heritage, 1965; 1966; Harrison County In Sesquicentennials Year, Indiana's Birthplace, 1966; Our Historic Corydon, 1967; Pioneers of Harrison County, 1967; Hoosiers in the Civil War, 1968; A Sketchbook of Indiana History, 1969; The Morgan Raid in Indiana and Ohio, 1971; Squire Boone in Indiana, 1973; Historical Almanac of Harrison County, 1974; Revolutionary War Era in Indiana, 1975; Revolutionary War Soldiers in Harrison County, 1975; A Hoosier Regiment in Dixie, 1978; The Battle of Corydon, 1976; The Hoosier Scrapbook, 1981; contbr. articles to profl. jours.; editor Teaching Ind. History, 1962-64. Home: 780 Country Club Rd PO Box 66 Corydon IN 47112 Office: 303 N Capitol Ave Corydon IN 47112

FUNK, JAMES WILLIAM, JR., ins. agy. adminstr.; b. Vincennes, Ind., May 31, 1947; s. James William and Elizabeth (Bauer) F.; B.A., Butler U., Indpls., 1969; m. Janis Burrell, Aug. 11, 1973; children—Christopher James, Kelly Elizabeth. Mem. campaign staff U.S. Senator Birch Bayh, Indpls., 1968; bus. cons. Dun & Bradstreet, Inc., Indpls., 1969-71; dir. ops. Terry Properties Inc., Springfield, Ill., 1971-72; personnel mgr. Am. Underwriters, Inc., Indpls., 1972-73, adminstrv. asst. to pres., 1973-75, asst. sec., 1975-78, v.p. public relations, 1978-79; adminstrv. mgr. Affiliated Agys., Inc., Indpls., 1979—. Sec., treas. Central N. Civic Assn., Indpls., 1976, pres., 1977-78. Mem. Ind. Soc. Chgo., Independent Ins. Agts. Ind. (legis com., agy. co. relations com.), Profl. Ins. Agts. Ind. (co-chmn. legis. com., treas. polit. action com.), Indpls. Personnel Assn. Roman Catholic. Clubs: Preussian Benefit Soc., Heimaths Benefit Soc., K.C. Home: 5832 Winthrop Ave Indianapolis IN 46220 Office: 2506 Willowbrook Pkwy Indianapolis IN 46205

FUNK, WILLIAM JOSEPH, engring. co. exec.; b. Waterloo, Iowa, Dec. 4, 1919; s. Joseph Oliver and Maude Mabel (Stover) F.; B.S., Iowa State U., 1948; m. Margaret Laughlin, Sept. 28, 1941; children—Karen Miller, Katherine Sipos, Margaret Jane. With McKee Corp. (name later changed to Davy Inc.), Cleve., 1949—, chief estimator, 1954-57, proposal coordinator, 1957-59, asst. sales mgr., 1960, mgr. fgn. projects, 1960-61, dist. sales mgr., 1961-69, div. v.p., asst. div. mgr. P & C, 1969-72, div. v.p. mktg., 1972-74, staff v.p., asst. to pres., 1974-76, sr. v.p., asst. to pres., 1976-79, sr. v.p. adminstr., Davy Inc., 1979—, also dir. Div. mgr. United Way Services of Cleve., 1977-79. Served with AUS, 1942-47. Mem. Am. Petroleum Inst., Cleve. Engring. Soc., Am. Assn. Cost Engrs., Soc. Advanced Mgmt., Sales and Mktg. Execs. of Cleve., Greater Cleve. Growth Assn., K.C. Republican. Roman Catholic. Clubs: Chagrin Valley Country (trustee 1979-81), Rotary. Home: 229 Ben Shaw Rd Aurora OH 44202 Office: 6200 Oak Tree Blvd Cleveland OH 44131

FURCON, JOHN EDWARD, indsl. and organizational psychologist; b. Chgo., Mar. 17, 1942; s. John F. and Lottie (Janik) F.; B.A., DePaul U., 1963, M.A., 1965; M.B.A., U. Chgo., 1970; m. Carolyn Ann Warden, Aug. 15, 1964; children—Juliana, Annalisa, Diana. With Human Resources Center (name formerly Indsl. Relations Center), U. Chgo., 1963-81, project dir., 1966-81, research psychologist, div. dir., 1970-81; with Mng. Change div. Harbridge House, Inc., Northbrook, Ill., 1981—; mem. faculty Traffic Inst., Northwestern U., 1969—, DePaul U. Sch. for New Learning, 1974—; cons. U.S. Justice Dept., bus., ednl. and govt. orgns. Served to lt. AUS, 1963-65. Mem. Am., Ill. psychol. assns., Indsl. Psychology Assn. Chgo. (chmn. 1973-75), Internat. Assn. Chiefs of Police, Ill. Assn. Chiefs of Police. Contbr. articles on employee selection and performance appraisal to profl. jours. Office: Mng Change Div Harbridge House Inc 2875 Milwaukee Ave Northbrook IL 60062

FURGASON, JENNINGS RALPH, mfg. co. exec.; b. Walcott, Wyo., Dec. 1, 1931; s. Ora Lee and Opal Catherine (Alter) F.; B.S. in M.E., U. Wyo., 1958; M.B.A., Calif. State U., 1968; m. Marlene Ruth Bush, June 14, 1953; children—Lori Kathryn, Jay Randall. Mfr. mfg. Interstate Electronics Corp., Anaheim, Calif., 1962-69; mgr. mfg. Dalmo Victor Co., Belmont, Calif., 1969-74; v.p., gen. mgr. Mobility Systems Inc., Green, N.Y., 1974-77; v.p. sales Raymond Corp., Greene, N.Y., 1977-78; pres., chief exec. officer Lift-A-Loft Corp., Muncie, Ind., 1978—; dir. Lift A Loft Corp. Served with USN, 1950-54; Korea. Mem. Am. Mgmt. Assn., Material Handling Equipment Dealers Assn., Delaware County C. of C. Baptist. Clubs: Shriners, Delaware Country. Home: 3509 W University Ave Muncie IN 47304 Office: 201 E Jackson St Muncie IN 47305

FURGISON, CLIFFORD FREDRIC, psychotherapist; b. Chgo., Dec. 4, 1948; s. Jack Warren and Vernie Florence (Snyder) F.; B.A., Eastern Mich. U., 1971, M.A., 1975; m. Carolyn Stephanie Albrecht, June 27, 1970; 1 dau., Tracie Michelle. Tchr. Manchester (Mich.) Pub. Schs., 1971-73, staff therapist, dept. substance abuse Providence Hosp., Southfield, Mich., 1975-76, dir. dept. substance abuse, 1976—; guest lectr. Wayne State U., 1976-77, U. Detroit, 1976; cons. in field. Certified alcoholism counselor; certified social worker, Mich. Mem. Am. Personnel and Guidance Assn., Mich. Assn. Alcoholism Counselors, Mich. Alcohol and Addiction Assn., Alcohol and Drug Problem Assn. N. Am. Contbr. articles to profl. jours. Home: 5754 Kilbrennan Birmingham MI 48010 Office: 16001 W 9 Mile Rd Southfield MI 48075

FURLAN, FRANK JACK, civil engr.; b. Waukegan, Ill., Oct. 13, 1929; s. Frank Matt and Antoinette Marie (Brence) F.; B.S.C.E., Chgo. Tech. Coll., 1953; m. Ione Carolyn Walenter, Oct. 18, 1952; children—Karen Marie, Diane Louise. Rodman, Gt. Lakes Naval Tng. Center, 1948-50; engr.-in-tng. William T. Hooper Engrs., Waukegan, 1952-53; surveyor, engr., jr. partner No. Ill. Survey Co., Waukegan, 1953-58, owner, operator, 1958—; city engr. City of North Chicago (Ill.), 1960—; village engr. Lindenhurst (Ill.), 1968—, Round Lake Park (Ill.), 1974—; interim city engr. City of Waukegan, 1977—; dir. Bank Waukegan. Supr., Lake County (Ill.) Bd., 1969-73. Served with USN, 1950-52. Mem. Nat. Soc. Profl. Engrs., Ill. Soc. Profl. Engrs., Am. Water Works Assn., ASTM, Ill. Profl. Engrs. Found. (founder mem.), Central States Water Pollution Control Assn., Soc. Am. Mil. Engrs., ASTM, Cons. Engrs. Council Ill., Council for Promotion of Profl. Employment Practices. Democrat. Roman Catholic. Clubs: Waukegan Yacht, Swedish Glee, Gaslight, Elks, Eagles. Home: 2632 E Bonnie Brook Ln Waukegan IL 60085 Office: 3233 W Grand Ave Suite A Waukegan IL 60085

FURLONG, NADINE MARY, nursing adminstr.; b. Detroit, Mar. 7, 1945; d. William Garfield and Violet Melinda (Herford) F.; R.N., Henry Ford Hosp., Detroit, 1966; B.S. in Nursing magna cum laude, U. Mich., 1976, M.S. in Psychiat. Nursing, 1978; m. Jan Frederick Miller, Oct. 1980. Staff nurse William Beaumont Hosp., Royal Oak, Mich., 1966; spl. edn. nurse teaching asst. Hawthorn Children's Psychiat. Center, Northville, Mich., 1966-70; head nurse inpatient unit York Woods Children's Psychiat. Center, Ypsilanti, 1970-73; dir. Ann Arbor program Browndale Group Home, 1973; instr. inservice nursing edn., then nursing edn. dir. Center Forensic Psychiatry, Ann Arbor, 1974-78; dir. nursing Met. Regional Psychiat. Hosp., Eloise, Mich., 1978-79; exec. dir. Mich. Nurses Assn., 1979—; treas. Washtenaw County Staff Devel. Com. in Nursing, 1977-78, chmn., 1978-79. cons. mental health tech. program Washtenaw Community Coll., 1976-77; adj. asst. prof. U. Mich. Sch. Nursing, 1979-80. Bd. dirs. ARC, 1976—, exec. bd., 1977—, 1st v.p., 1979-80, pres., 1981-82; instr., trainer CPR. James B. Angel scholar, 1976; recipient A.J. Brown Public Health Nursing award, 1976. Mem. Am. Nurses Assn. (adv. council), Mich. Nurses Assn., Sigma Theta Tau. Home: 2934 Northlawn Ypsilanti MI 48197 Office: 120 Spartan Ave East Lansing MI 48823

FURLONG, PATRICK DAVID, counselor; b. Cleve., Sept. 27, 1948; s. Harold Joseph and Jean Ann (Blair) F.; B.A. magna cum laude, Lake Erie Coll., Painesville, Ohio, 1975. Staff psychometrist VA Med. Center, North Chicago, Ill., 1975-78; chief psychometrist Northwestern U. Med. Sch., Chgo., 1978-80; counselor/coordinator vets. affairs Columbia Coll., Chgo., 1980-81; asst. coordinator internat. edn. Roosevelt U., Chgo., 1981—. Served with USN, 1967-71; Vietnam. Decorated Navy Achievement medal with combat V. Mem. N.Y. Acad. Scis., Am. Personnel and Guidance Assn., Am. Coll. Personnel Assn., Ill. Psychol. Assn., Psi Chi. Office: 430 S Michigan Ave Chicago IL 60605

FURMAN, JAMES MERLE, state ednl. agy. exec.; b. Kansas City, Mo., Apr. 3, 1932; s. James Merle and Andrey Eldena (Phillips) F.; B.A., Ohio State U., 1954; LL.D. (hon.), Ill. Coll., 1976; L.H.D. (hon.), Nat. Coll. Edn., 1978; m. Carol Ann McGhee, June 10, 1977; children—Mark Carter, Douglas Walter. Research asso. Ohio Legis. Service Commn., Columbus, 1955-61; dir. Community Research, Inc., Dayton, Ohio, 1962-64; exec. officer Ohio Bd. Regents, Columbus, 1964-70; dir., exec. coordinator Wash. State Council on Higher Edn., Olympia, 1970-74; exec. dir. Ill. Bd. Higher Edn., Springfield, 1975—; mem. exec. com. State Higher Edn. Planning Commns., U.S. Office Edn.; bd. advisors Fund for Improvement of Postsecondary Edn.; mem. student fin. assistance study group HEW. Mem. Edn. Commn. of States, Western Interstate Commn. on Higher Edn., State Higher Edn. Exec. Officers (pres. 1979-80), Nat. Center for Higher Edn. Mgmt. Systems (dir.). Office: 500 Reisch Bldg Springfield IL 62701*

FURMAN, LEOLA EMERALD, educator; b. Thief River Falls, Minn., Apr. 3, 1939; d. Chester Arnald and Helga (Ose) Dyrud; B.A., Augsburg Coll., 1961; M.S.W., U. Chgo., 1965; m. Philip John Furman, Aug. 25, 1963; children—Erik Ose, Jon Dyrud. Social worker Child and Family Services, Mpls., 1961-62; psychiat. social worker Rochester (Minn.) State Hosp., 1963-64, 66-67; marriage and family counselor Child and Family Services, Norfolk, Va., 1965-66; sch. social worker, Rochester, 1967-69; marriage and family counselor Child and Family Services, Springfield, Ill., 1970-72; asst. prof. social work dept. U. N.D., Grand Forks, 1974—. Mem. Nat. Assn. Social Workers, Council Social Work Edn., Nat. Council Family Relations, AAUP, Nat. Assn. Higher Edn., AAUW. Republican. Lutheran. Home: 625 Belmont Rd Grand Forks ND 58201 Office: U ND 308 Sayre Hall Grand Forks ND 58201

FURMAN, ROBERT HOWARD, pharm. co. exec.; b. Schenectady, Oct. 23, 1918; s. Howard Blackall and Jane Blessing (MacChesney) F.; A.B. (Allison prize 1939), Union Coll., Schenectady, 1940; M.D., Yale U., 1943; m. Mary Frances Kilpatrick, Feb. 10, 1945; children—Carol K. Furman Friedman, Jane C. Furman Dougherty, Robert Howard, Hugh Patrick. Intern, then asst. resident in medicine New Haven Hosp., 1944-45; asst. in medicine Yale U. Med. Sch., 1944-45; asst. resident physician, then resident physician Vanderbilt U. Hosp., 1948-50; from research asst. in medicine to asst. prof. Vanderbilt U. Med. Sch., 1946-52; asso. prof., then prof. research medicine U. Okla. Med. Sch., 1952-70; prof. medicine Ind. U. Med. Sch., 1970—; head cardiovascular sect. Okla. Med. Research Found. and Hosp., 1952-70, asso. dir. found., 1957-70; exec. dir. clin. research Eli Lilly and Co., Indpls., 1970-73, v.p. corp. med. affairs, 1976—; v.p. Lilly Research Labs., 1973-76; mem. vis. staff Wishard Meml. Hosp., Indpls., 1971; pres. Okla. Heart Assn., 1967-68; mem. cardiovascular study sect. Nat. Heart Inst., NIH, 1960-63, heart spl. projects com., 1963-66; bd. mgrs., sci. adv. com. Wistar Inst., 1972-78; sci. adv. com. Hormel Inst., Austin, Minn., 1973—. Mem. council Inst. Adminstrn. and Mgmt., trustee, bd. advs. Union Coll.; asso. trustee U. Pa.; mem. clin. scis. panel Nat. Research Council. Served to comar. M.C., USNR, 1945-46, 55-57. Diplomate Am. Bd. Internal Medicine. Fellow Am. Coll. Cardiology, A.C.P., N.Y. Acad. Scis., Royal Soc. Medicine; mem. Am. Assn. World Health (dir. 1974—), AAAS, Am. Clin. and Climatol. Assn., Am. Fedn. Clin. Research, Am. (fellow council arteriosclerosis; nat. bd. dirs., exec. and central coms.; chmn.

research com. 1964-65), Ind. (dir.), Marion County heart assns., Am. Physiol. Soc., Am. Soc. Clin. Pharmacology and Therapeutics, Am. Soc. Internal Medicine, Assn. Yale in Medicine, Central Soc. Clin. Research (council 1963-66), Endocrine Soc., Ind., Marion County med. assns., Soc. Exptl. Biology and Medicine, So. Soc. Clin. Research, Southwestern Soc. Naturalists, Wilson Ornithol. Soc., Nat. Audubon Soc., Sigma Xi, Alpha Omega Alpha, Delta Upsilon. Clubs: Cosmos, Capitol Hill (Washington); Confrerie des Chevaliers du Tastevin; Internat. (Chgo.). Contbr. to med. jours.; mem. editorial bds. jours. Office: 307 E McCarty St Indianapolis IN 46285

FURNEY, THOMAS ALBERT, info. systems exec.; b. Ft. Wayne, Ind., June 23, 1940; s. Kenneth Albert and Beda E.; B.S. in Indsl. Mgmt., Purdue U., 1964; m. Sally Joann Beaver, Nov. 20, 1965; children—Christopher George, Jeffrey John. Systems mgr. Gen. Tire and Rubber Co., Wabash, Ind., 1965-69; systems analyst Univac div. Sperry Rand Co., Ft. Wayne, 1969-70; data center mgr. Compumatics, Inc., Ft. Wayne, 1970-74, dir. info. systems, 1974-78, pres., 1978—. Vice-pres. Westlawn Civic Assn.; pres. Anthony Wayne Ch. of God. Mem. Data Processing Mgmt. Assn. Home: 611 Nordale Dr Fort Wayne IN 46804 Office: 1619 Magnavox Way Fort Wayne IN 46804

FURNISH, DOROTHY JEAN, educator; b. Plano, Ill., Aug. 25, 1921; d. Reuben M. and Mildred Lorraine (Feller) Furnish; B.A., Cornell Coll., Mt. Vernon, Iowa, 1943, M.A., Garrett-Theol. Sem., Northwestern U., 1945, Ph.D., 1968. Dir. Christian edn. Trinity United Meth. Ch., Hutchinson, Kans., 1945-52, 1st United Meth. Ch., Lincoln, Nebr., 1952-65; prof. Christian edn. Garrett-Evang. Theol. Sem., Evanston, Ill., 1968—. Mem. AAUP, Assn. Profs. and Researchers in Religious Edn., United Meth. Assn. Profs. of Christian Edn. Author: Exploring the Bible with Children, 1975; DRE/DCE: History of a Profession, 1976; Living the Bible with Children, 1979. Office: 2121 Sheridan Rd Evanston IL 60201

FURRER, JOHN RUDOLF, bus. exec.; b. Milw., Dec. 2, 1927; s. Rudolph and Leona (Peters) F.; B.A., Harvard U., 1949; m. Annie Louise Waldo, Apr. 24, 1954; children—Blake Waldo, Kimberly Louise. Spl. rep. ACF Industries, Madrid, Spain, 1949-51; asst. supr. Thermonuclear Devel. & Test-Los Alamos, Eniwetok Atoll, 1952-53; mgr. Talgo project ACF Industries, 1954-56; dir. product devel. dept. Am. Car & Foundry Div., N.Y.C., 1956-59; dir. machinery/systems group FMC Corp., San Jose, Calif., 1959-67, gen. mgr. Engineered Systems div., 1967-69, v.p. in charge planning dept. Central Engring. Labs. and Engineered Systems div., Chgo., 1970, group v.p. in charge Material Handling, Mining and Environ. Equipment, 1971-77, v.p. corp. devel., 1977—. Pres., bd. dirs. Santa Clara County Vol. Bur.; v.p., bd. dirs. Children's Home Soc. Calif.; bd. dirs. Ming Quong Children's Center; bd. govs. San Francisco Bay Area Council. Served with USNR, 1945-46. Mem. ASME. Clubs: Harvard (N.Y.C. and Chgo.); Glen View Country (Golf, Ill.); Economic, Mid-Am. (Chgo.). Patentee in field. Home: 62 Woodley Rd Winnetka IL 60093 Office: 200 E Randolph Dr Chicago IL 60601

FURSTE, WESLEY LEONARD, II, surgeon; b. Cin., Apr. 19, 1915; s. Wesley Leonard and Alma (Deckebach) F.; A.B. cum laude, Harvard U., 1937, M.D., 1941; m. Leone James, Mar. 28, 1942; children—Nancy Dianne, Susan Deanne, Wesley Leonard III. Intern, Ohio State U. Hosp., Columbus, 1941-42; fellow surgery U. Cin., 1945-46; asst. surg. resident Cin. Gen. Hosp., 1946-49; sr. asst. surg. resident Ohio State U. Hosps., 1949-50, chief surg. resident, 1950-51; practice medicine specializing in surgery, Columbus, 1951—; instr. Ohio State U., 1951-54, clin. asst. prof. surgery, 1954-66, clin. asso. prof., 1969-74, clin. prof. surgery, 1974—; mem. surg. staffs Mt. Carmel, Children's, Grant, Univ., St. Anthony, Riverside, Meth. hosps. (all Columbus); surg. cons. Dayton (Ohio) VA Hosp., Columbus State Sch., Ohio State Penitentiary, Mercy Hosp., Columbus; regional adv. com. nat. blood program ARC, 1951-68, chmn., 1958-68; invited participant 2d Internat. Conf. on Tetanus, WHO, Bern, Switzerland, 1966, 3d Internat. Conf., Sao Paulo, Brazil, 1970, 5th Internat. Conf., Ronneby Brunn, Sweden, 1978, invited rapporteur 4th Internat. Conf., Dakar, Senegal, 1975; mem. med. adv. com. Medic Alert Found. Internat., 1971-73, 76—, bd. dirs. 1973-76; founder Digestive Disease Found. Mem. Ohio Motor Vehicle Med. Rev. Bd., 1965-67; bd. dirs. Am. Cancer Soc. Franklin County, pres., 1964-66. Served to maj., M.C., AUS, 1942-46; CBI. Diplomate Am. Bd. Surgery. Mem. Central Surg. Assn., Soc. Surgery of Alimentary Tract, AAAS, ACS (chmn. Ohio com. trauma; nat. subcom. prophylaxis against tetanus in wound mgmt., chmn. com. for selection Ohio Disting. Service award; Ohio adv. com.), Am. Assn. Surgery of Trauma, Ohio, Columbus surg. assns., AMA, Am. Trauma Soc. (founding mem., dir.), Ohio Med. Assn., Acad. Medicine Columbus and Franklin County, Acad. Medicine Cin., Am. Public Health Assn., Am. Med. Writers Assn., Robert M. Zollinger Club, Mont Reid Grad. Surg. Soc., Am. Geriatrics Soc., N.Y. Acad. Scis., Assn. Physicians State of Ohio, Collegium Internationale Chirurgiae Digestivae, Assn. Am. Med. Colls., Internat. Brotherhood Magicians, Soc. Am. Magicians. Presbyterian. Clubs: Scioto Country, Ohio State Univ. Golf, Ohio State Faculty (Columbus); Univ. (Cin.); Harvard (Boston). Prime author: Tetanos; contbg. author: Advances in Military Medicine, 1948; Management of the Injured Patient; contbr. articles to profl. jours. Home: 3125 Bembridge Rd Columbus OH 43221 Office: 3545 Olentangy River Rd Columbus OH 43214

FUSARO, JANIECE ELAINE BARRE, librarian; b. Detroit, Feb. 7, 1925; d. William and Augusta Rose (Siebenbrunner) Barre; adopted d. Elizabeth Marie (Siebenbrunner) Moses; B.A., U. Minn., 1946, M.A., 1949, B.S. in L.S., 1953, Ph.D., 1968; postgrad. Middlebury Coll., 1949, Stephens Coll., 1968; m. Ramon M. Fusaro, Aug. 4, 1951; children—Lisa Ann, Toni Ann. Teaching asst. German dept. U. Minn., Mpls., 1947-50, acquisitions librarian U. Minn. Library, 1951-53; prof. German, Coll. St. Catherine, St. Paul, 1964-65; librarian Anoka-Ramsey Community Coll., Coon Rapids, Minn., 1965-69, 70-71; program dir. Minn. Higher Edn. Coordinating Commn., St. Paul, 1969-70; mem. community faculty Met. State U., St. Paul, 1971-79; asso. prof. Metro State U., St. Paul, 1979—; library cons. Golden Valley Luth. Coll., Minn., 1968, writers conf. U. Wis.-River Falls, 1976. Dir. statewide library survey Minn. Higher Edn. Coordinating Commn., 1970; mem. Minn. Planning Com. on Library Automation, 1971, Minn. Adv. Com. on Inter-library Cooperation, 1971. Bd. dirs. Riverside Center, Mpls., 1970-74. Named Minn. Librarian of Year, Minn. Library Assn., 1969; Teaching Excellence award Met. State U., 1977, 80. Mem. Minn. Library Assn. (life), ALA (life), Minn. Assn. Adult and Continuing Edn. (dir. library sect. 1979-80), Alpha Lambda Psi. Contbr. articles to profl. jours. Home: 3108 36th Ave NE Minneapolis MN 55418 Office: Metro State U 7th and Robert St St Paul MN 55101

FUSON, DONNA BELLE CARTER, ednl. adminstr.; b. Canton, Ill., Dec. 22, 1935; d. Paul Clayton and Elnora Ellen (Kramer) Carter; B.S., Ill. State U., 1957; M.S., No. Ill. U., 1968; m. William Jean Fuson, Aug. 6, 1960; children—Kathryn Suzanne, David William. Primary tchr. Dennis Sch., Decatur, Ill., 1957-59; stewardess, United Air Lines, Chgo., 1959-60; primary tchr. Ogden Ave. Sch., Dist. 102, LaGrange, Ill., 1960-63; elementary sch. counselor Sch. Dist. 103, Lyons, Ill., 1968-69; coordinator Project EVE, Northwest Ednl. Coop., Arlington Heights, Ill., 1972-75; dir. Career Edn. Service Center, Arlington Heights, 1975—; cons. edn. div. Nat. Dairy Council. Mem. Christian edn. commn., Sunday sch. tchr., tchr. trainer First Presbyterian Ch., Western Springs, Ill.; bd. dirs., pres. Western Springs, PTA; mem. Western Springs Sch. Bd.; mem. caucus com. Cook County High Sch. Dist. 204. Mem. Am., Ill. (v.p. for elementary) sch. counselor assns., Am. Personnel and Guidance Assn., Ill. Guidance and Personnel Assn. (govt. relations chmn.). Home: 4234 Franklin Ave Western Springs IL 60558

GAAR, NORMAN EDWARD, lawyer, state senator; b. Kansas City, Mo., Sept. 29, 1929; s. William Edward and Lola Eugene (McKain) G.; student Baker U., 1947-49; A.B., U. Mich., 1955, J.D., 1956; m. Joanne M. Rupert, Aug. 1, 1953; children—Anne, James, William, John. Admitted to Mo. bar, 1957, Kans. bar, 1962, U.S. Supreme Ct. bar, 1969; asso. firm Stinson, Mag, Thomson, McEvers & Fizzell, Kansas City, 1956-59; partner firm Stinson, Mag & Fizzell, Kansas City, 1959-79; partner Gaar & Bell, Kansas City, Mo., Overland Park, Kans., and Wichita, Kans., 1979—; mem. Kans. Senate, 1965—, majority leader, 1976-80; dir., gen. counsel J.A. Tobin Constrn. Co., Kansas City, Kans.; mem. faculty N.Y. Practising Law Inst., 1969-74; adv. dir. Panel Pubs., Inc., N.Y.C. Mcpl. judge City of Westwood, Kans., 1959-63, mayor, 1963-65. Served with U.S. Navy, 1949-53. Decorated Air medal (2); named State of Kans. Disting. Citizen, 1962. Mem. Am. Bar Assn., Am. Judicature Assn., Nat. Conf. State Legislatures, Am. Radio Relay League, Antique Airplane Assn., Exptl. Aircraft Assn. Republican. Presbyterian. Clubs: Woodside Racquet, Brookridge Country. Office: 14 Corporate Woods 640 8717 W 110th St Overland Park KS

GAASEDELEN, NEWELL ORVILLE, investment assn. exec.; b. Mpls., Sept. 5, 1915; s. Nels O. and Isabel (Naeseth) G.; B.B.A., U. Minn., 1938; Indsl. Adminstr., Harvard U., 1943, M.B.A., 1946; m. Jane Ann Lobstein, Nov. 22, 1950; children—James Robert, Barbara Lynn, Jon Richard. Lectr. econs. U. Minn., Mpls., 1946-56; securities analyst Mpls. Tchrs. Retirement Fund Assn., 1950-67, exec. sec., 1967—; pres. Kans Okla. Cons. Oil Co., Mpls., 1951—, also dir.; pres. Search Investments Corp. Mpls., 1960-63, also dir.; chmn. bd. Waters Instruments Inc., Rochester, Minn., 1959—, dir. 1965-67; incorporator Edina (Minn.) State Bank, also dir.; pres. Berkshire Investment Co., Mpls.; Employers Overload Co., Served to comdr. Supply Corps, USNR, 1943-46, 50-52. Mem. Fin. Analysts Fedn., Naval Res. Assn., Harvard Bus. Alumni Assn., Twin City Soc. Security Analysts, Torske Klubben, Sons Norway, Nordsmans Forbundet, Aircraft Owners and Pilots Assn., Am. Legion, Beta Gamma Sigma. Lutheran. Clubs: Six O'Clock, Edina Country, Mpls. Athletic. Subject of feature articles and radio interviews on innovative investing. Home: 4818 Golf Terr Edina MN 55424 Office: 951 NW Bank Bldg Minneapolis MN 55402

GABBARD, AVERY DALE, ret. ednl. adminstr.; b. Jasonville, Ind., Jan. 24, 1912; s. Cleve H. and Pansy Fay (Beckwith) G.; B.S. in Elementary Edn., Ind. State U., 1941, B.S. in Secondary Edn., 1942, M.S., 1952; m. Juanita Weaver, Apr. 29, 1933; 1 son, L. Joe. Adminstr., basketball coach, tchr., Greene County, Ind., 1933-40; tchr., coach, Vigo County, Ind., 1940-42; asst. prin. high sch. Greene County, 1942-50; prin. West Washington Elementary Sch., Campbellsburg, Ind., 1964-75; tchr. psychology and social studies All Saints Episcopal Pvt. High Sch., Vicksburg, Miss., 1976-77. Mem. Ind. Tchrs. Assn. (chmn. legis. com. 1952-64), N.E.A., Ind. (exec. bd. 1974-75), Nat. elementary prins. assns., Campbellsburg Tchrs. Assn. (pres.). Scoutmaster, Boy Scouts Am., 1952-55. Mem. Pi Gamma Mu, Phi Delta Kappa. Democrat. Baptist (licensed minister, deacon). Mason, Lion, Fraternal Order Police (asso.). Home: 170 Laura Ln Bloomfield IN 47424

GABBERT, ROY ELLIS, lawyer; b. Portsmouth, Ohio, Apr. 4, 1925; s. George Gilbert and Lena (Rider) G.; B.A., Ohio State U., 1949, LL.B., 1951, J.D., 1967; m. Virginia Faye King, Apr. 28, 1946; children—Robin, Terri; m. 2d, Betty Miller, Dec. 29, 1962; children—Gay, Roy Ellis. Admitted to Ohio bar, 1952, since practiced in West Union; gen. counsel World's Plowing Matches, 1957; asst. atty. gen. Ohio, 1959-63; pres. Reggo Builders. Dir. Credit Bur. Adams County, Inc.; sec. Adams County Devel. Corp. Chmn. Adams County chpt. A.R.C. Mayor West Union, 1953; dep. dir. Adams County Civil Def. Served with AUS, 1943-46: PTO. Decorated Bronze Star. Mem. Ohio, Adams County (sec. 1953-69, 71—, pres. 1970) bar assns., 741st Vets. Assn. (pres.). Home: RFD 1 West Union OH 45693 Office: 301 N Market St West Union OH 45693

GABEL, DUANE ROBERT, constrn. co. exec.; b. Fremont, Wis., May 17, 1928; s. Edward John and Luella Gladys (Thomas) G.; Heating, Ventilating and Air Conditioning Technician, Milw. Sch. Engring., 1946; m. Corinne Joyce Black, Jan. 29, 1949; children—Steven D., Barbara D., Brian D. Sales engr. Trane Co., LaCrosse, Wis., 1947-48, Appleton, Wis., 1948-52; project engr. August Winter & Sons Inc., Appleton, 1952—, sec., 1953-67, v.p., 1967-70, pres., 1970-80, chmn. bd., 1980—; dir. Valley No. Bank. Mem. Appleton Bd. Heating Examiners, 1970-81. Registered profl. engr., Wis., Mich., Minn. Mem. Fox Cities Chamber Commerce and Industry (formerly Appleton Area C. of C.) (pres. 1976), Wis., Nat. socs. profl. engrs., ASHRAE, Nat. Assn. Power Engrs. Republican. Methodist. Club: Riverview Country. Home: 2900 E Crestview Dr Appleton WI 54911 Office: 2323 N Roemer Rd Appleton WI 54911

GABER, MARTIN, electronics co. exec.; b. Chgo., Sept. 24, 1917; s. Jacob Leon and Bertha (Berman) G.; S.B., Northwestern U., 1939; m. Lita Leance, Apr. 20, 1941; children—Richard, Susan Gaber Lazar, Pamela, Debra. Project engr. Bell and Howell Co., Lincolnwood, Ill., 1942-45; pres. Continental Corp., Chgo., 1945-54; chmn. bd., pres. Chgo. Switch, Inc., 1954-80; fin. and investment cons., 1980—; broker electronics and carbon industries. Chmn. Am. Assn. for UN of the North Shore, 1953. Mem. Electronics Industries Assn., Chgo. Symphony Orchestral Assn., Newberry Library Assn., Northwestern U. Library Assn., Chgo. Commons Assn., Common Cause, Bus. and Profl. People for Pub. Interest, Chgo. Lit. Club. Club: Cliffdwellers. Patentee self mailers, elec. switch structures. Home: 2301 Greenwood Ave Wilmette IL 60091 Office: 1714 N Damen Ave Chicago IL 60647

GADBERRY, JOSEPH LAFAYETTE, educator; b. Fargo, N.D., June 8, 1940; s. Joseph Lafayette and Helen Adeline (Ydstie) G.; B.A., Concordia Coll., 1962; M.S., N.D. State U., 1966; Ph.D., U. Nebr., 1975; m. Betty Helen Eisenbeis, Nov. 25, 1966; 1 son, Brett Jason. Instr. biology Wis. State U., River Falls, 1966-67; instr. bacteriology S.D. State U., Brookings, 1967-70; asst. instr. Dept. Med. Microbiology U. Nebr., Omaha, 1970-76; asst. prof. Dept. Microbiology, Miami U., Oxford, Ohio, 1977-80; asst. prof. Dept. Microbiology, U. Health Sci., Kansas City, Mo., 1980—. Volunteer in counseling, rehab. Nebr. Penal Complex, 1976; mem.-at-large, exec. com. Christian Coop. Nursery Sch., Oxford, 1977-78. Miami U. Ohio grantee, 1977-79; Analytical Products grantee, 1979-80, U. Health Scis. grantee, 1981; Remel Labs. Inc. of Lenexa, Kan. grantee, 1981. Registered microbiologist Am. Bd. Med. Microbiologists. Mem. Am. Soc. Microbiology, Assn. of Practitioners in Infection Control, Soc. Hosp. Epidemiologists Am., Sigma Xi, Beta Beta Beta, Phi Sigma Upsilon. Republican. Lutheran. Club: Lions (pres.). Contbr. articles to profl. jours. Office: 2105 Independence Blvd Kansas City MO 64124

GADD, LINDA G., ednl. adminstr.; b. Pitts., Dec. 17, 1947; d. Henry E. and Grace C. (Duncan) Schwarzbach; B.A., U. Pitts., 1968; certificate in edn. Miami U., 1971; M.Ed., Xavier U., 1975; grad. Dale Carnegie Course, 1979; m. Ebbie L. Gadd, Dec. 19, 1970; Tchr. english, Wayne Local Schs., Waynesville, Ohio, 1969-70, Dayton (Ky.) City Schs., 1971-73, Lakota Local Schs., West Chester, Ohio, 1973-77, counselor/career counselor, 1977-80; summer s specialist Gen. Electric Co., Evendale, Ohio, 1978-79; sch. prob officer Butler County Juvenile Ct., Hamilton, Ohio, 1979-80; ca edn. dir. Butler County, Ohio, 1980—; cons. in field; lectr. in fie trainer Ohio Reading Grant, 1977-78; initiator Career Devel. Gran 1979-81, Sex Equity Grant, 1981. Ordained elder, Presbyn. Ch 1977-80, deacon, 1973-76, mem. adult Christian edn. com., 1978-81, chmn. Christian edn., 1978-79. Mem. Career Edn. Assn., Am. Vocat. Assn., Ohio Vocat. Assn., Ohio Sch. Counselors Assn., Right to Read Dir. Republican. Editor, chief writer Butler County Lang. Arts Curriculum Guide, 1976. Home: 31 Bab Ln Hamilton OH 45013 Office: 3603 Hamilton Middletown Rd Hamilton OH 45011

GADJEV, IVAN ILIEV, veterinarian; b. Bulgaria, Dec. 23, 1937; came to U.S., 1968, naturalized, 1975; s. Ilia Todorov and Katerina (Ivanov) G.; vet. technician Higher Vet. Med. Inst., Sofia, Bulgaria, 1961, D.V.M., 1968; m. Florence Christoff, Jan. 28, 1973; children—Katerina, Ilia, Theodore, Christopher. Practice vet. medicine specializing in large animals, Nevrokop, Bulgaria, 1967-68; small animal practice, Detroit Owen Animal Hosp., 1970-74; owner, dir. Northland Vet. Hosp., Inc., 1974—. Mem. AVMA, Mich. Vet. Medicine Assn., Southeastern Mich. Vet. Med. Assn. Bulgarian Eastern Orthodox. Home: 25043 Lyncastle Farmington Hills MI 48018 Office: 18531 W 8 Mile Rd Detroit MI 48219

GAENG, PAUL AMI, educator; b. Budapest, Hungary, Aug. 17, 1924; s. Hans Peter and Therese (Brule) G.; came to U.S., 1948, naturalized, 1955; grad. U. Geneva, 1948; M.A., Columbia U., 1950, Ph.D. (Woodbridge hon. fellow), 1965; m. Joan Elisabeth Gallagher, Apr. 6, 1967. Fgn. editorial asst. McGraw-Hill Book Co., N.Y.C., 1951-54; translator-interpreter Guaranty Trust, N.Y.C., 1954-56; fgn. lang. tchr. Montclair (N.J.) Acad., 1957-63; asst., asso. then full prof., dept. chmn. fgn. langs. Montclair State Coll., Upper Montclair, N.J., 1964-69; asso. prof. Romance philology U. Va., Charlottesville, 1969-72; head dept. Romance lang. and lit. U. Cin., 1972-76; head dept. French, U. Ill., Urbana-Champaign, 1976—; vis. lectr. Hofstra Coll., Hempstead, N.Y., 1963, Queens Coll., N.Y.C., 1966, Columbia, 1967-69; asso. Center Advanced Studies, U. Ill., Urbana, 1982. Decorated chevalier dans l'ordre des Palmes Academiques. Mem. AAUP, MLA, Société de linguistique romane, Am. Soc. Geolinguistics (treas. 1965-68). Author: An Inquiry into Local Variations in Vulgar Latin, 1968; Introduction to the Principles of Language, 1971; Studies in Honor of Mario Pei, 1972; A Study of Nominal Inflection in Latin Inscriptions, 1977; (with Mario Pei) The Story of Latin and the Romance Languages, 1976. Contbr. articles on lang. teaching and philology to various jours. Home: 2009 Peach St Champaign IL 61820

GAETH, MATTHEW BEN, state senator; b. Oak Harbor, Ohio, June 1, 1921; s. Charles J. and Sophena (Millinger) G.; B.S. in Bus. Adminstrn., Bowling Green (Ohio) State U., 1943; m. Thelma D. John, Oct. 29, 1943; children—John, William, Gretchen. Service sta. operator, 1946-48; with vending bus., 1948-65; safety dir. City of Defiance (Ohio), 1962-65, mayor, 1965-74; mem. Ohio State Senate, 1975—. Republican fin. chmn. Defiance County, 1972-73; former pres. Defiance United Way. Served with USNR, 1943-45. Decorated Purple Heart; named Conservation Legislator of Yr., 1982. Mem. Ohio Mcpl. League (past pres.), Mayors Assn. Ohio (past pres.), Defiance Area C. of C., Am. Legion, VFW. Presbyterian. Clubs: Defiance Rotary, Elks, Eagles, Masons. Office: State house Columbus OH 43216*

GAFFNEY, JOHN LEONARD, assn. exec.; b. Manistique, Mich., Mar. 21, 1926; s. Bernard Farrell and Lora (Leonard) G.; B.S., No. Mich. U., 1948; M.A., U. Mich., 1952; Ed.S., Mich. State U., 1962; LL.D., Nazareth Coll., 1974, Northwood Inst., 1975, Madonna Coll., 1978; Ph.D., Lawrence Inst. Tech., 1975; Ph.D., Cleary Coll., 1979; m. Helen Marie Miller, June 21, 1949; children—David, Kathleen, James. Coach, tchr., Portage Twp. pub. schs., Houghton, Mich., 1949-61; dir. guidance Haslett (Mich.) Pub. Schs., 1961-63; dir. Job Tng. Center, Lansing, 1963-65; dir. edn. Mich. Cath. Conf., Lansing, 1965-71; pres. Assn. Ind. Colls. and Univs. Mich., Lansing, 1971—. Vice pres. Diocesan Bd. Edn. Lansing, 1971-75. Cons. Mich. Adv. Council on Post-Secondary Edn., 1971—. Served with USNR, 1944-46. Named Mich. Upper Peninsula Basketball Coach of Year, 1955. Mem. Exec. Dirs. State Assns. Ind. Colls. (exec. com., chmn. 1974-76), Nat. Assn. Ind. Colls. and Univs. (dir. 1976-77, 80-82), Nat. Assn. Bds. Edn. (exec. com. 1972-75), Am. Soc. Assn. Execs. Roman Catholic. Home: 824 Locher Rd DeWitt MI 48820 Office: 830 Michigan National Tower Lansing MI 48901

GAGE, CALVIN WILLIAM, advt. agy. exec.; b. Mpls., Feb. 14, 1929; s. Robert Percy and Rachel (Green) G.; A.B., Cornell U., 1951; M.A., U. Minn., 1953; m. Margaret Borchmann, Sept. 6, 1958; children—Andrew, Carolyn. Food-drug field auditor A.C. Nielsen Co., Chgo., 1954-55; with Leo Burnett Co., Inc., Chgo., 1955—, group research dir., 1977-79, sr. v.p., dr. research, 1979—. Mem. Am. Mktg. Assn., Mktg. Sci. Inst., Advt. Research Found. Clubs: University, Plaza (Chgo.). Office: Leo Burnett Co Inc Prudential Plaza Chicago IL 60601

GAGESCH, HILDA GERDA, health care adminstr.; b. Chgo., Oct. 3, 1926; s. Thomas L. and Sofia (Eckardt) G.; B.A., Case Western Res./Ursuline Coll., 1979. X-ray technician Univ. Hosps. of Cleve., 1952-57, supr. div. coordinator program, 1965-67; asst. chief x-ray technician Childrens Hosp., Cin., 1957-59; chief x-ray technician Forest City Hosp., Cleve., 1958-65; dir. unit mgmt. Hillcrest Hosp., Cleve., 1967-77, dir. systems and ops., 1978-80, dir. div. profl. services, 1980—. Adviser explorer post Boy Scouts Am.; trustee Schnurmann House. Mem. N.E. Ohio Public Relations Assn. Club: Cleve. Hiking. Home: 6809 Mayfield Rd Apt 1466 Mayfield Heights OH 44124 Office: 6780 Mayfield Rd Mayfield Heights OH 44124

GAGNE, FRANCIS ROLAND, JR., safety engr.; b. Dover, N.H., Dec. 29, 1950; s. Francis Roland and Velma Pricella (Sturgeon) G.; student Sch. of Ozarks, 1969, Wichita State U., 1974—; m. Kristi L. Davis, Jan. 30, 1981; 1 son by previous marriage, Francis Roland. Indsl. nurse Gates Learjet, Wichita, Kans., 1974, indsl. hygiene health/safety specialist, 1975, supr. health services, safety, workers compensation and indsl. hygiene, 1977, mgr. health safety, workers compensation tng. and communications, 1978-81, dir. employee relations, 1981—; cons. in field; lectr. in field. Chmn. aerospace sect. Nat. Safety Council. Served with USN, 1969-74. Mem. Am. Soc. Tng. and Devel., Am. Soc. Safety Engrs., Am. Soc. for Personnel Adminstrn. Contbr. articles to profl. jours. Office: 8220 W Harry St Wichita KS 67277

GAGNON, CHARLES EUGENE, sculptor; b. Mpls., Feb. 24, 1935; s. Eugene Walter and Inez (Wood) G.; A.A., U. Minn., 1956, B.S., 1958, M.Ed., 1960; postgrad., Florence, Italy, 1963-65, Assisi, Italy, 1968, Paris, 1970; m. Arlyn Lois Wind, Nov. 21, 1964. Group exhbns. include Nat. Acad. Galleries, N.Y.C., 1962, Nat. Arts Club, N.Y.C., 1962, Walker Art Center Biennial, Mpls., 1962, Madison Ave. Gallery (Two Man Show award, Purchase prize), N.Y.C., 1962, Ahda Artz Gallery, N.Y.C., 1963, Village Art Center, N.Y.C., 1963, Mpls. Inst. Arts, 1963, Internat. Art Galleries, Chgo., 1964-65, Defiance (Ohio) Coll., 1972; sculpture included in public and pvt. collections in U.S., U.K., Europe; prin. works include Processional Cross, St. John's Ch., Darwin, Minn., 1966, Dancer Stretching, Mayo Clinic, Rochester, Minn., 1969, Renaissance Man and Woman, Kenyon Coll., Gambier, Ohio, 1973, Creation, Temple Jeremiah, Chgo., 1975,

...on, 1973, St. Francis and the Birds, St. ...1969, bronze portrait Hubert H. Humphrey, ...on (Minn.), 1979, Mother and Child, Baldwin ... Medicine, Rochester, others; lectr., vis. artist ...so cons. to chs. Roman Catholic.

...**ARY JO,** hosp. exec. housekeeper; b. Duluth, Minn., ...; d. Walter and Agnes Lorraine (Benson) Horn; student ...Duluth, 1974, Coll. of St. Scholastics, 1977-78; m. Dennis ... Gagnon, Jan. 21, 1961; children—Keith Dennis, William ...d. Mgr. Horn's Restaurant, Scanlon, Minn., 1959-60; ...usekeeping supr. St. Luke's Hosp., Duluth, 1967-74, dir. housekeeping and laundry, 1974—, ad hoc com. for jr. exec. housekeepers; instr. seminars in linen control and housekeeping. Mem. Nat. Exec. Housekeepers Assn., Adminstrv. Mgmt. Soc. Clubs: Soroptimist Internat., Women's Internat. Bowling Assn. Home: 1828 E 7th St Duluth MN 55812 Office: 915 E 1st St Duluth MN 55805

GAGNON, RICHARD JOHN, TV exec.; b. Detroit, Dec. 9, 1935; s. John Baptist and Laura (Fitzpatrick) G.; B.A., Mich. State U., 1959; m. Carol Susan Hennecke, June 5, 1965; children—Richard John, Laura Fitzpatrick, Andrea Therrien. Public relations central staff Ford Motor Co., Dearborn, Mich., 1959-60; sr. producer Campbell Ewald Advt., Detroit and N.Y.C., 1961-65; exec. producer J. Walter Thompson Co., N.Y.C., 1966-68; pres. Gen. TV Arts, Bloomfield Hills, Mich., 1969—; mktg. advisor Scherer Thompson, Inc., Auburn Heights, Mich. Sustaining mem. Republican Nat. Com., 1981. Recipient several Clio awards, 1964—, Internat. Broadcast awards, Los Angeles, N.Y. Internat. Film Festival awards. Mem. Assn. Ind. Comml. Producers, Detroit Artists Market. Clubs: Grosse Pointe (Mich.); Renaissance (Detroit). Home: 69 Touraine Rd Grosse Pointe Farms MI 48236 Office: 70 E Long Lake Rd Bloomfield Hills MI 48013

GAHALA, ESTELLA MARIE, educator; b. Alva, Okla., Mar. 28, 1929; d. Ivan G. and Margaret E. (Beck) Crouse; B.A. magna cum laude, Wichita (Kans.) State U., 1953; M.A., Middlebury (Vt.) Coll., 1963; Ph.D., Northwestern (Ill.) U., 1980; m. John W. Gahala, Nov. 24, 1964. Tchr. public high schs., Wichita, Kans., Harper, Kans., Topeka, Amarillo, Tex., Northbrook, Ill., 1953-64; French tchr., chmn. fgn. langs. Evanston (Ill.) Twp. High Sch., 1964-73; chmn. fgn. langs. Lyons Twp. High Sch., La Grange, Ill., 1973-81, dir. curriculum and instruction, 1980—; editorial cons. Scott Foresman, Glenview, Ill., 1975—. Recipient Chevalier de l Ordre des Palmes Academiques (France); French Govt. Services Culturels grantee, 1972. Mem. Am. Assn. Tchrs. French (exec. council 1976-81), Am. Council on Teaching Fgn. Langs., Ill. Fgn. Lang. Tchrs. Assn., Assn. Supervision and Curriculum Devel., Ill. Assn. Supervision and Curriculum Devel., N.W. Ill. Assn. Supervision and Curriculum Devel., Ill. Edn. Assn., NEA, Les Rosettes et Rubens de France, Phi Delta Kappa. Co-author: Son et Sens, 1981; contbr. articles to profl. publs. Home: 1103 S Hamlin St Park Ridge IL 60068 Office: 100 S Brainard St La Grange IL 60525

GAIHA, VISHNU DAS, cardiologist; b. New Delhi, India, May 2, 1945; s. P.D. and Bhagwati Devi (Johri) G.; came to U.S., 1969; M.B., B.S., All India Inst. Med. Scis., 1969; m. Purnima Saxena, Nov. 11, 1973. Intern Albert Einstein Med. Center, Phila., 1969-70; resident in internal medicine Northwestern U. Hosp., Chgo., 1970-72; fellow in cardiology U. Mich. Hosp., Ann Arbor, 1972-74; practice medicine specializing in internal medicine and cardiology, Evanston, Ill., 1974—; mem. staff St. Francis, Forkosh, Swedish Covenant hosps.; clin. asst. prof. Loyola U. Med. Sch. Diplomate Am. Bd. Internal Medicine, Am. Bd. Cardiovascular Disease. Fellow Am. Coll. Internat. Physicians, Am. Coll. Chest Physicians, Am. Coll. Cardiology; mem. ACP, Am. Heart Assn., Heart Assn. N. Cook County (v.p.). Home: 2940 Moonhill Dr Northbrook IL 60062 Office: 800 Austin St Suite 605A Evanston IL 60202

GAINES, ROBERT ALAN, public relations cons.; b. Chgo., Sept. 24, 1949; s. Harry B. and Rolinda Johnson (Joseph) G.; B.S., U. Ill., 1972. Producer, Sta. WGN-TV, Chgo., 1971; dir., producer WFLD-TV, Chgo., 1969; mem. public relations staff office products div. IBM, Chgo., 1972; spl. asst. to Gov., Springfield, Ill., 1973; mem. nat. staff Democratic Presidential campaign com., Atlanta, 1976; dep. dir. Inaugural Parade Com., Washington, 1976; personnel specialist White House, Washington, 1977; pres. Profls. Ltd., Public Relations Cons., Chgo., 1977—. Cons. media relations Kennedy for Pres., 1979—. Mem. Chgo. Council on Fgn. Relations. Jewish. Clubs: Chgo. Press, Publicity. Office: Suite 1300 520 N Michigan Ave Chicago IL 60611

GAINEY, HARVEY NUETON, trucking co. exec.; b. Nicholls, Ga., Nov. 20, 1942; s. Lloyd F. and Rita Mae (Tanner) G.; student pub. schs., Nicholls, Ga.; m. Annie E. Carter, Nov. 9, 1962; children—Angela Marie, Harvey N. Rate analyst Ryder Truck Lines, Inc., Jacksonville, Fla., 1962-68, rate audit mgr., 1968-71, traffic mgr., 1970-71; dir. traffic Helms Express, Irwin, Pa., 1971-76, v.p. sales, 1976-80; v.p. mktg. Interstate System Inc., Grand Rapids, Mich., 1980-81, exec. v.p., 1981, pres., 1981—. Mem. Am. Trucking Assn. (dir.), Sales and Mktg. Council, Am. Soc. Traffic and Transp., Eastern Shipper-Metor Carrier Council, Delta Nu Alpha. Democrat. Home: 1221 Troon Ct SE Grand Rapids MI 49506 Office: 110 Ionia Ave NW Grand Rapids MI 49501

GAIO, RAYMOND LEE, architect; b. Springfield, Ill., May 3, 1938; s. Americo and Edith E. (Bloom) G.; student Millikin U., summer 1960; profl. architecture degree U. Notre Dame, 1961. Designer, draftsman Spangler, Beall, Salogga & Bradley, Decatur, Ill., 1961-62; designer, planner, draftsman, client relations Leo A. Daly Co., Omaha, 1962-63; schematic design draftsman Perkins & Will, Washington, 1963-64; dir. Dept. of State, chpt. and student affairs A.I.A., Washington, 1964-69; mgr. client relations Vincent G. Kling & Assos., Phila., 1969-70; pres., chief exec. officer, treas. Gaio Assos., Ltd., Washington, also Los Angeles, other prin. Am. cities and London, Eng., 1970—; pres. B.I.D.S., Inc., Washington, Springfield, Ill., also Los Angeles, C.G. Evergreene Cos. Inc., Springfield; dir. corporate devel. Gruen Assos., Los Angeles, N.Y.C., Washington, Vienna, Teheran, 1970. Lectr. various univs.; archtl. orgn. mgmt. cons. to U.S. and internat. firms. Adviser, Jr. Achievement, Omaha, 1962-63; mem. Royal Ct. of Ak-Sar-Ben, 1962-63; adviser, lectr. Heights Study House, Washington, 1965; mem. joint engring. council Notre Dame U., 1958-59, 606-1. Licensed architect, U.S.V.I. Mem. ASC-AIA (nat. pres. 1960-61), AIA (corporate mem.; co-chmn. nat. task force in student action programs), Notre Dame Alumni Assn. Republican. Roman Catholic. Author: A.I.A. Organizational Guidelines Manual; A.I.A. Student Chapter Handbook; The State Organization; Chapter Organization. Contbr. articles to profl. jours. Office: BIDS Ops Center PO Box 3344 Springfield IL 62708 also Washington DC also Los Angeles CA 90005 also London EC4Y 1HA England

GAISSER, HARRY WILLIAM, JR., architect; b. Nashville, Ark., June 21, 1945; s. Harry William and Agnes Minona (Hipp) G.; B.S., U. Cin., 1969. Architect charged with Provinces of Safi and Ouarzazate, Marrakech Regional office of Morrocan Ministry Housing and Urban Devel., 1969-73; architect Fosse & Assos., Inc., Evansville, Ind., 1973—, chief design architect, corp. officer, 1978—. Mem. history adv. com. Evansville Mus. Arts and Sci., 1977—; bd. dirs. Friends Willard Library, Evansville, 1978—; mem. Ind. Gov.'s Original Evansville Preservation Commn., 1979—; sec. Reitz Home Preservation Soc., 1979—. Registered architect, Ind. Mem. AIA, Ind. Soc. Architects, U. Cin. Alumni Assn., Victorian Soc. Am., Middle East Inst. Baptist. Club: Kiwanis. Founder sch. drafting, design Marrakech, 1971, developer master plan for Island of Essaouira, Morocco, 1971, Taroudant, Morocco, 1972; renovation Evansville Mus. Arts and Sci., 1977, 79. Home: 219 Oak St Evansville IN 47713 Office: Fosse & Assos Architects Inc Suite 202 Union Fed Bldg 501 Main St Evansville IN 47708

GAITHER, JOHN FRANCIS, accountant; b. Louisville, Oct. 26, 1918; s. Thomas R. and Marice F. Gaither; B.C.S., U. Notre Dame, 1941; postgrad. U. Louisville; m. Marjilee Schaeffer, Nov. 26, 1942; children—John Francis, James M. Controller, Evansville (Ind.) div. Whirlpool Corp., 1946-54; asso. prof. fin. U. Evansville, part-time 1946-56; sr. partner Gaither, Koewler, Rohlfer & Luckett, C.P.A.'s, 1954—; city controller, dep. mayor City of Evansville, 1972-76. Past pres. Buffalo Trace council Boy Scouts Am.; past co-chmn. Summa Fund drive U. Notre Dame; adv. com. Ind. Vocat. Rehab.; fin. com. Roman Cath. Diocese Evansville; past trustee Brescia Coll., Owensboro, Ky.; mem. regional community adv. council Ind. U. Med. Sch.; v.p. community adv. council Evansville Center Med. Edn.; chmn. Gov. Ind. Select Com. Ednl. Fin., Gov. Ind. Commn. Energy and Utility Regulation Adv. Com.; mem. Ind. Transp. Coordinating Bd.; treas. Vand County Rep. Central Com.; Gov.'s rep. Ind. Hosp. Rate Rev. Commn.; active local YMCA, Cancer Soc., Serra Club. Served as officer USNR, 1941-46. Recipient various awards Boy Scouts Am.; C.P.A., Ind. Mem. Am. Inst. C.P.A.'s, Evansville, Ind., Ill., Ky. assns. C.P.A.'s, Nat. Assn. Accountants (past pres. Evansville), Ind. Assn. Cities and Towns Controllers Assn. (past pres.), Ind. Soc. Chgo. (v.p. 1979-81), SAR, Evansville C. of C. Republican. Clubs: Evansville Country (past pres.), Kennel, Petroleum, Press (Evansville); Columbia (Indpls.). Contbr. articles to profl. jours. Home: 730 Colony Rd Evansville IN 47714 Office: 111 Main St Evansville IN 47708

GAJL-PECZALSKA, KAZIMIERA JANINA, pathologist; b. Warsaw, Poland, Nov. 15, 1931, came to U.S., 1970, naturalized, 1977; d. Kazimierz Emil and Anna (Gervais) Gajl; M.D., U. Warsaw, 1955, Ph.D. in Immunopathology, 1964; m. 1949 (div. 1969); children—Kazimierz, Andrzei. Intern, U. Warsaw Hosps., 1953-55, resident in pathology, 1955-58; asst. pediatrician Warsaw Children's Hosp., 1955-58, head dept. pediatric pathology, 1958-65; adj. prof. dept. pathology Postgrad. Med. Sch., Warsaw, 1965-70; resident in pathology U. Minn., 1970-72, asst. prof., 1972-75, asso. prof., 1975-79, prof., 1979—. NIH postdoctoral fellow in immunopathology, Mpls., 1968-69; WHO fellow in immunofluorescence, Paris, 1967, WHO fellow in pediatric pathology, London, 1962; NIH research grantee 1975—. Diplomate Am. Bd. Pathology, Polish Bd. Pediatrics, Polish Bd. Pathology. Mem. Am. Soc. Exptl. Pathology, Am. Soc. Cytology, Brit. Soc. Pediatric Pathology, Minn. Soc. Pathologists, Polish Soc. Pediatrics, Polish Soc. Pathology. Contbr. articles, papers to profl. jours, meetings. Home: 1700 W 90th St Minneapolis MN 55431 Office: 446 Jackson Hall U Minn Minneapolis MN 55455

GALAN, GREGORY JOHN, lawyer; b. Cleve., July 15, 1949; s. John and Anne (Hotz) G.; A.B., Case Western Res. U., 1971; M.A., U. Conn., 1973; J.D., Cleveland Marshall Coll. Law, 1975; B.S. in Acctg., Cleve. State U., 1976; m. Aug. 3, 1974. With Ebenger & Assoc., Cleve., 1972-73, Cleve. Regional Sewer Dist., 1973, Ben Lewitt Co., Cleve., 1975; partner Milburn, Cannon, Stern & Aveni, Painesville, Ohio, 1975-79, Galan, Ziccarelli & Deeb, Painesville, 1979—; chmn. bd. dirs. Ohio Convenient Food Mart, Inc., 1976—; instr. real estate law and tax Lakeland Community Coll., 1975-79; admitted to Ohio bar, 1975. Mem. Am. Bar Assn., Ohio Bar Assn., Lake County Bar Assn., Mentor C. of C., Painesville Jr. C. of C. Eastern Orthodox Ch. Club: Rotary (editor 1977). Home: 7509 Belvedere Dr Mentor OH 44060 Office: 8 N State St Suite 370 Painesville OH 44077

GALBRAITH, JOHN DRUMMOND, JR., health care exec. and constrn. co. exec.; b. Evanston, Ill., Nov. 2, 1919; s. John Drummond and Louise Ruggles (Lane) G.; B.S. in Chem. Engring., Yale U., 1943; m. Angeline Lorene Johnson, May 4, 1945; children—Angeline (Mrs. Charles F. Brown III), John Drummond III. Chem. research engr. Pureoil Co., Chgo., 1943-46; ter. mgr., sales engr. Mobile Co., South Bend, Ind. and No. Ill., 1946-54; v.p. G.A. Johnson & Sons, Chgo., 1954-60, pres., 1960-79, chmn. bd., 1975—; pres. Brentwood North Nursing and Convalescent Home, River Woods, Ill.; gen. partner Riverwoods Assos. Mem. adv. bd. Peacock Camp for Crippled Children, Lake Villa, Ill., 1953—, pres., 1959-66; mem. caucus com. Village of Winnetka (Ill.). Mem. Am. Soc. Chem. Engrs., Soc. Colonial Wars in State of Ill., Alpha Delta Phi. Episcopalian. Clubs: Glen View (Golf, Ill.); Indian Hill (Winnetka); Racquet, Yale (Chgo.); Ponte Vedra Country (Ponte Vedra Beach, Fla.); Lake Geneva (Wis.) Country. Office: 828 Foster St Evanston IL 60201

GALBRAITH, VICTORIA BRAUCKMAN, advt. agy. exec.; b. Phila., Sept. 1, 1952; d. George William and Marian Rose (Falco) Brauckman; B.A., New Eng. Coll., 1974; m. John Drummond Galbraith III, May 17, 1975; 1 dau., Jessica Leigh. Prodn. coordinator Post-Keyes & Gardner Advt., Chgo., 1974; account supr. Jack E. Schlegel, Advt., Chgo., 1974—. Active Jr. League of Chgo., 1977—, reporter Topics; public relations chmn. Landmarks Preservation Fund of Ill., 1978—. Mem. Women in Communications. Republican. Clubs: Glen View (Ill.); Lake Geneva (Wis.) Country. Home: 580 Hawthorn Ln Winnetka IL 60093 Office: Jack E Schlegel Advt 221 N LaSalle St Suite 1154 Chicago IL 60601

GALBRETH, RAYMOND DOUGLAS, assn. exec.; b. St. Louis, Sept. 25, 1946; s. Albert Henry and Opal Alfretta (McDaniel) G.; B.S.B.A., U. Mo., 1969, M.B.A., 1971; postgrad. St. Louis U., 1974-79; m. Janet Lee Davis, June 24, 1978. Asst. prof. mgmt. S.E. Mo. State U., Cape Girardeau, 1971-79; exec. dir., editor Delta Chi Fraternity, Iowa City, Iowa, 1979—. Served with Mo. N.G., 1970-77. Mem. Am. Soc. Assn. Execs., Fraternity Execs. Assn., Collegiate Fraternity Editors Assn., Delta Chi, Delta Sigma Pi. Editor, Delta Chi Quar., 1979—. Home: 2027 10th St Ct Coralville IA 52241 Office: 314 Church St Iowa City IA 52240

GALE, JOHN CARVER, JR., computer scientist; b. Boston, June 3, 1945; s. John Carver and Sarah Eleanor (Colley) G.; B.S. in Elec. Engring., Purdue U., 1968; M.B.A., No. Ill. U., 1975. With Arnold Engring. Co., 1968-69, 71-75, supr. process engring., 1973-75; from account mgr. to dist. mgr., mgr. data base services ADP Network Services, Ann Arbor, Mich., 1975-79; systems devel. mgr. Internat. Harvester Co., Hinsdale, Ill., 1980-81, mgr. group tech. implementation and adminstrn., 1981—. Served with U.S. Army, 1969-71. Mem. Am. Mgmt. Assn., Am. Mktg. Assn., Assn. Computing Machinery, IEEE, Chgo. Council Fgn. Relations, Chgo. Met. Ski Council (regional v.p. 1977-78). Republican. Episcopalian. Speaker Nat. Info. Conf., 1979, Info. Mgmt. Conf. for Mfg., 1982. Home: 312 Lawndale St Elmhurst IL 60126 Office: 16 W 260 83d St Hinsdale IL 60521

GALE, LARRY RICHARD, state govt. ofc.; b. Newport, Ohio, Feb. 28, 1921; s. Larry Richard and Alice Elizabeth (Neptune) G.; A.B., Ohio U., Athens, 1942, M.S., 1947; m. Norma Schultheis, Apr. 24, 1942; children—Maureen Gale Hayes, Larry Richard, III. Biologist, then wildlife extension agt. Ohio Conservation Dept., 1942-47; biologist, then game dir. Ky. Dept. Fish and Wildlife Resources, 1947-56; with Mo. Dept. Conservation, 1957—, dep. dir., 1974-78, dir., 1979—; past chmn. Miss. Flyway Council, Nat. Waterfowl Council; pres. S.E. Assn. Fish and Wildlife Agys. 1971, Internat. Assn. Fish and Wildlife Agys., 1980-81. Bd. govs. Meml. Hosp., Jefferson City, Mo., 1968-81; chmn. Mo. State Govt. div. United Way, 1980. Served with USMCR, 1942-45. Decorated Silver Star. Mem. Wildlife Soc., Am. Fisheries Soc., Am. Forestry Assn., Nat. Wildlife Fedn., Izaak Walton League, Am. Legion, VFW, Conservation Fedn. Mo., Mo. Sheriff's Assn., Ducks Unlimited, Nat. Audubon Soc., Nat. Rifle Assn., 4th Marine Div. Assn. Democrat. Episcopalian. Office: PO Box 180 Jefferson City MO 65102

GALE, ROBERT IVAN, aviation planning exec.; b. Pontiac, Mich., Mar. 14, 1921; s. Alfred W. and Lena Irene (Bartlett) G.; B.S., Mich. State U., 1940; postgrad. Wayne State U., 1941; m. Bonnie Abbott, July 2, 1976; children—R. Bradley, William A., Paula E., Robert I. Corp. pilot, 1940; aero. engr. N.Am. Aviation, Detroit, 1940; airline pilot United Airlines, 1941; air traffic controller FAA, Washington, Cleve., Chgo., 1942-48, air traffic br. chief, Chgo. and Kansas City, 1949-55, chief planning br., Washington, 1955-57, chief regulations and procedures div., Washington 1957-61, regional dir. Pacific region, 1961-65, area mgr., Kansas City, 1965-70, chief air traffic div. Central region, 1970-79; pres. Robert I. Gale & Assos., Inc., aviation cons. firm, Kansas City, 1979—; partner Cudney, Fowler, Smith & Gale, investors. Pres., Falls Church PTA, 1942; mem. Falls Church Sch. Bd., 1942; active Boy Scouts Am., 1950-71, Lutheran Ch.; chmn. United Fund, Hawaii. Air transport rated pilot conventional and jet. Mem. Air Traffic Control Assn. (dir. 1959-60), Air Force Assn., Nat. Assn. Ret. Fed. Employees, Mo. Pilots Assn. (dir.), Aircraft Owners and Pilots Assn., World Aerospace Edn. Orgn., Am. Legion, VFW. Clubs: Pontiac-Oakland Internat.; Brookridge Golf and Country; Golden Falcon Air; Lions; Toastmasters. Office: 409 W 116th St Kansas City MO 64114

GALENS, GILBERT J., rheumatologist; b. Detroit, Mar. 7, 1933; s. Harry and Grace (Sweet) G.; B.S. with high distinction, Wayne State U., Detroit, 1954, M.D., 1957; m. Jane Odell Herriman, Aug. 12, 1962; children—David Matthew, Stephen Andrew, Judith Ellen, Daniel Keith. Intern, Mt. Zion Hosp., San Francisco, 1957-58; asst. resident, then resident in medicine U. Mich. Hosp., 1960-62, jr. clin. instr., 1962-63, fellow rheumatology Rackham Arthritis Research Unit, also teaching asso., 1963-64; practice medicine specializing in rheumatology, Birmingham, Mich., 1964—; mem. attending staff, chief div. rheumatology St. Joseph Mercy Hosp., Pontiac, Mich., William Beaumont Hosp., Royal Oak, Mich.; asso. staff Sinai Hosp., Detroit; clin. asst. prof. Wayne State U. Med. Sch. Bd. dirs. Wing Lake Farms Assn., 1972. Served to lt. M.C., USNR, 1958-60. Diplomate Am. Bd. Internal Medicine. Mem. AMA, Mich., Oakland County med. assns., Am. Rheumatism Assn., Mich. Rheumatism Soc. (pres. 1972), Phi Beta Kappa. Jewish. Club: Men's Health of Jewish Community Center. Contbr. articles to profl. jours. Home: 6765 Orinoco Circle Birmingham MI 48010 Office: 31815 Southfield Rd Birmingham MI 48009

GALIETTA, PETER JAMES, diversified bus. exec.; b. N.Y.C., May 20, 1942; s. Alfred J. and Dorothy (Daley) G.; B.S., Bradley U., 1965; m. Judith Ann Becker, Sept. 6, 1964; children—Peter, Dana Lyn, Christian R. Comptroller, sec.-treas. Deluxe Mobile Home Sales, Inc., Peoria, Ill., 1965—, Deluxe Mobile Home Park, Inc., Peoria, 1965-79, Peoria Acceptance Corp., 1975—; sec.-treas. Bon-Aire Manor, Inc., Peoria, 1972—; owner, gen. mgr. Rehab. Equipment & Supply, Peoria, 1970—, also dir. Bon Aire Manor, Inc.; dir. Entice. Treas., dir. Crippled Children Center, Inc., 1977—. Mem. Nat. Trust Hist. Preservation, Am. Surg. Trade Assn., Delta Upsilon. Republican. Roman Catholic. Clubs: St. Mark's Men's, Moss Beadley Civic Assn. Home: 1823 W Moss Ave Peoria IL 61606 Office: 2800 W Farmington Rd Peoria IL 61604

GALINIS, NORBERT MICHAEL, ednl. adminstr.; b. Detroit, Sept. 9, 1944; s. Charles Joseph and Marie Rita (Wojtczak) G.; B.S., Western Mich. U., 1967; postgrad. U. Mich. Tchr. history Willow Run Community Schs., Ypsilanti, Mich., 1969-73, tchr. indsl. arts, 1973-80, ednl. asst. House B, Edmonson Middle Sch., 1980—. Field sports dir. Boy Scouts Am., 1968-70, camp dir., 1971-74. Mem. NEA, Mich. Edn. Assn., Nat. Hist. Soc., Assn. Supervision and Curriculum Devel., Mich. Assn. Middle Sch. Educators, Pi Kappa Alpha (dist. pres. 1971-73 Disting. Service award 1972). Office: 1800 E Forest St Ypsilanti MI 48197

GALLAGHER, BERNARD JOHN, valve and fitting co. exec.; b. Washington, Sept. 24, 1937; s. Howard Edward and Mary Antoinette (Doyle) G.; B.M.E., Case Inst. Tech., 1959; student Kent State U., 1969; m. Margaret Rose McNally; children—Mary Michelle, Brigid Ann. Design engr. Nupro Co., Willoughby Hills, Ohio, 1957-59, machining, project and design engr., 1959-60, chief engr., 1961-62, plant mgr., 1962-64, gen. mgr., 1964-68, exec. v.p., 1968—; v.p. Whitey Co., 1970—; pres. Ekohwerks Co., 1974—; dir. internat. ops. Solon Export Co., 1975—. Mem. ASME, Soc. Mfg. Engrs. Roman Catholic. Club: Cleveland Athletic. Patentee valve and filter tech. Home: 6465 Gates Mills Blvd Gates Mills OH 44040 Office: Nupro Co 4800 E 345th St Willoughby Hills OH 44094

GALLAGHER, DENNIS HUGH, TV, film and multi-media writer/producer; b. Chgo., May 2, 1936; s. Frederick Hugh and Mildred Agnes (Buescher) G.; student Wright Coll., 1954-56, Ill. Inst. Tech., 1956-57; B.Sc. in Physics, U. Ariz., 1966. Dir., Noble Planetarium and Obs., Ft. Worth Mus. Sci. and History, 1960-64; planetarium dir. Man. Mus. Man and Nature, Winnipeg, Can., 1966-70; pres. Omnitheatre Ltd., Winnipeg, 1970-72; pres. Gallagher & Assos., Chgo., 1972-78, Internat. Travel Theatres, Chgo., 1978—; mem. faculty in astronomy and civil engring. U. Man., 1967-68; cons. edn., theater, 1967—. Served with USAR, 1959-65. Mem. Planetarium Assn. Can. (founding pres. 1968-69), Internat. Council Planetarium Execs., Am. Astron. Soc., Nat. Acad. TV Arts and Scis., Am. Soc. Tng. and Devel., Internat. TV Assn., Assn. Multi-Image, Chgo. Film Council. Author: North American Planetariums, 1966; Planetariums of the World, 1969; contbr. articles to profl. jours.; writer, producer, dir. multi-media road show: The Beginning & End of the World, 1972. Office: PO Box 511-C Prospect Heights IL 60070

GALLAGHER, IDELLA JANE SMITH (MRS. DONALD A. GALLAGHER), found. ofcl., author; b. Union City, N.J., Jan. 1, 1917; d. Fred J. and Louise (Stewart) S.; Ph.B., Marquette U., 1941, M.A., 1943, Ph.D., 1963; postgrad. U. Louvain, Belgium, U. Paris; m. Donald A. Gallagher, June 29, 1938; children—Paul B., Maria Noel. Lectr. philosophy Marquette U., 1943-52, 54-56; instr. philosophy Alverno Coll., Milw., 1956-58; asst. prof. philosophy Villanova U., 1958-62; asst. prof. philosophy Boston Coll., 1962-68, asso. prof., 1968-69; asso. prof. philosophy U. Ottawa, 1969-71, prof., 1971-73; projects adminstr. DeRance Found., Milw., 1973-80, v.p., 1981—; vis. prof. philosophy Niagara U., 1976-81. Mem. Sudbury (Mass.) Com. for Human Rights, 1963-69; trustee Mt. Senario Coll., Ladysmith, Wis., 1976—. Recipient Sword and Shield award St. Louis U., Baguio City, Philippines, 1975. Mem. Metaphys. Soc. Am., Am. Cath. Philos. Assn. (exec. council 1967-69), Am. Soc. Aesthetics, Assn. Realistic Philosophy, AAUP, Brit. Soc. Aesthetics, Canadian Philos. Assn., Canadian Assn. U. Tchrs., Phi Alpha Theta, Phi Delta Gamma. Author: (with D. A. Gallagher) The Achievement of Jacques and Raissa Maritain, 1962; The Education of Man, 1962; (with D. A. Gallagher) A Maritain Reader, 1966; (with D.A. Gallagher) St. Augustine—The Catholic and Maniehaean Ways of Life, 1966. Morality in Evolution: The Moral Philosophy of Henri Bergson, 1970.

Gen. editor: Christian Culture and Philosophy Series, Bruce Pub. Co., 1965-68. Contbr. to New Cath. Ency., also articles to profl. jours. Home: 7714 W Wisconsin Ave Wauwatosa WI 53213 Office: DeRance Found 7700 W Bluemound Rd Milwaukee WI 53213

GALLAGHER, JAMES MILLER, govt. ofcl.; b. Ft. Wayne, Ind., June 22, 1935; s. Edward Francis and Helen Lambert (Miller) G.; B.S., U.S. Naval Acad., 1957; M.Pub. Adminstrn., U. Dayton, 1969; m. Nancy Jo Kuhbander, June 8, 1957; children—Timothy Michael, Mary Jean. Regional rep. Autonetics div. Rockwell Internat., Dayton, 1960-61; with Aero. Systems div. Wright-Patterson AFB, Ohio, 1961-80, asst. program dir. F-4 program, 1973-75, asst. dep. airlift/tanker aircraft, 1975-76, asst. program dir., dep. for F-16, 1976-80; dep. asst. to comdr. for internat. logistics Hdqrs. Air Force Logistics Command, 1980—; mem. U.S. Govt. Sr. Exec. Service, 1980—. Mem. Ohio 3d Congl. dist. Naval Acad. Screening Com., 1965—, chmn., 1974—; mem. Centerville (Ohio) Bd. Archtl. Rev., 1974-78, chmn., 1975-78. Served with USAF, 1957-60. Named Greater Dayton Area Supr. Year, 1972, Supr. Year Miami Valley chpt. Federally Employed Women, 1975; recipient Exceptional Civil Service award USAF, 1977. Mem. Am. Def. Preparedness Assn., U.S. Naval Acad. Alumni Assn. Roman Catholic. Home: 294 Cherry Dr Centerville OH 45459 Office: Dep Asst Internat Logistics (AFLC/MI) Wright-Patterson AFB OH 45433

GALLAGHER, JAMES VINCENT, state senator; b. Carroll, Iowa, Feb. 18, 1933; s. Vincent and Benita F.; student State Coll. Iowa, 1959-62, Grand View Coll., 1979-80, U. No. Iowa, 1980-81; m. Corlene Spaen, 1955; children—Michael, Daniel, John Steven, Thomas, Kathleen (dec.). Toll terminal technician Bell Telephone Co., Waterloo, Iowa, 1982—; mem. Iowa Ho. of Reps., 1964-68, Iowa Senate, 1972—. Served with U.S. Army; Korea. Named Ky. Col.; Iowa Legis. Conservationist, 1965. Mem. Iowa Wildlife Fedn. Roman Catholic. Democrat. Office: State Senate Des Moines IA 50319*

GALLAGHER, NANCY LORETTO, dietitian; b. Denver, Dec. 6, 1943; d. Edward Lewis and Celia Naomi (Jackson) G.; B.S., Colo. State U., 1965; M.A., Central Mich. U., 1978. Dietetic intern Cook County Hosp., Chgo., 1966-67, therapeutic dietitian, 1967-68; therapeutic dietitian Passavant Hosp., Chgo., 1968; coordinator clin. dietetics Northwestern Meml. Hosp., Chgo., 1968—. Mem. Am. Mgmt. Assn., Am. Dietetic Assn., Am. Diabetes Assn., Ill. Dietetic Assn., Chgo. Dietetic Assn., Chgo. Nutrition Assn., Chgo. Area Runners Assn., Chgo. Council on Fgn. Relations. Roman Catholic. Home: 2115 N Sedgwick Ave Apt 2E Chicago IL 60614 Office: Northwestern Memorial Hospital Passavant Pavilion Room 272B Superior and Fairbanks Ct Chicago IL 60610

GALLAGHER, PATRICK JOHN, agronomist; b. Kansas City, Kans., Jan. 31, 1947; s. Michael Edward and Barbara Jean (Griffiths) G.; B.S., Kans. State U., 1969; M.S. in Agronomy, 1971, Ph.D. in Soil Fertility, 1976; m. Patricia A. Martincich, Aug. 24, 1968; children—Peter Michael, Pamela Ann. Research asst. Kans. State U., 1969-76, research asso., 1976-77; research agronomist Tribune (Kans.) Experiment Sta., 1977—; cons. in field. Served with USNG, 1969-76. Sears Roebuck scholar, 1965; recipient Kans. Fertilizer and Chem. Inst. Outsanding Sr. award, 1968. Mem. Am. Soc. Agronomy, Soil Sci. Soc. Am., Sigma Xi, Gamma Sigma Delta. Contbr. articles in field to profl. jours. Home and Office: Tribune Experiment Sta Tribune KS 67879

GALLAGHER, RAYMOND JOSEPH, bishop; b. Cleve., Nov. 19, 1912; s. Hugh and Ella (Reedy) G.; B.A. John Carroll U., Cleve., 1934; student St. Mary's Sem., Cleve., 1939; M.S.W., Loyola U., Chgo., 1948. Ordained priest Roman Catholic Ch., 1939; asst. pastor St. Colman Ch., Cleve., 1939-44; dir. Cath. Youth Service Bur., Cleve., 1948-55; dir. St. Anthony's Home For Boys, Cleve., 1949-61; sec. Nat. Conf. Cath. Charities, Washington, 1961-65; bishop of Lafayette (Ind.), 1965—. Founder Cath. Big Brothers, Cleve., 1951, Cath. Child Guidance Clinic, Cleve., 1953, Don Bosco Sch. For Boys, Cleve., 1957; vice chmn. White House Conf. Children and Youth, 1960; mem. exec. planning com. White House Conf. Aging, 1961; vice chmn., mem. nat. exec. com. Citizens Crusade Against Poverty. Bd. dirs. Nat. Council Aging, United Community Funds and Councils Am., Nat. Social Welfare Assembly, Nat. Housing Conf.; trustee Nat. Council Crime and Delinquency. Served to lt. USNR, 1944-46. Recipient Alumni award Loyola U., Chgo., 1960. Mem. Nat. Cath. Edn. Assn. (pres.-gen. 1968, chmn. bd. 1969—), Alpha Sigma Nu. Address: 610 Lingle Ave Lafayette IN 47902

GALLAGHER, RICHARD ELLIS, analytical chemist; b. Janesville, Wis., Feb. 3, 1940; s. Lloyd William and Rose Alta (Glaser) G.; student Beloit (Wis.) Coll., 1958-60; B.S. in Chemistry, Iowa State U., 1963; M.B.A., Ball State U., 1977; m. Patty Ann Pearson, Nov. 30, 1963; children—Deborah, Rebecca, Susan, Michael. Student engr. Rep. Steel Corp., Chgo., 1963-65; sr. exptl. chemist Delco-Remy div. Gen. Motors Corp., Anderson, Ind., 1965—. Mem. phys. com. Anderson YMCA, 1978-80, vol. award; chair Gymnastics Parents Booster Club, 1978-80; bd. deacons 1st Presbyterian Ch., Anderson, 1968-71. Mem. Am. Chem. Soc., Sigma Nu. Co-developer zinc-nickel-oxide battery for use in elec. vehicle. Home: 908 Fremont Dr Anderson IN 46012 Office: 2401 Columbus Ave Anderson IN 46018

GALLAGHER HAUGH, JOYCE EILEEN, educator; b. Ironton, Ohio, Sept. 3, 1937; d. Lawrence James and Frances Irene (Wilson) G.; B.S. in Elementary Edn., Coll. St. Teresa, Winona, Minn., 1967; M.Ed. in Guidance Counseling in Elementary Sch., Ohio U., Athens, 1970; Ph.D., Loyola U., Chgo., 1975; m. Charles R. Haugh, July 29, 1978. Elementary sch. tchr., then jr. high sch. tchr., Ill., Ohio and Minn., 1958-68; instr. psychology Coll. St. Teresa, 1969-72, v.p. student affairs, dean students, 1975-76; dir. instl. research St. Mary's Coll., Winona, 1976-77, asso. prof. psychology, 1977—, asst. dean academic advising, 1977-80, dir. grad. program in counseling and psychol. services, 1979—. NDEA fellow, 1968-69. Mem. Am., Minn. personnel and guidance assns., Nat. Assn. Women Deans, Adminstrs. and Counselors, Am. Psychol. Assn., Phi Delta Kappa, Psi Chi. Roman Catholic. Home: 74 Hillsdale Ct Winona MN 55987 Office: St Mary's Coll Winona MN 55987

GALLAHER, STUART WILLIAM, architect; b. Appleton, Wis., Apr. 11, 1931; s. William U. and Winefred S.(Stuart) G.; student Lawrence U., 1949-50; B.Arch., U. Ill., 1955; m. Emmy Bunks, June 9, 1956; children—Stacia Leigh, William Stuart. Staff, Shattuck & Siewert Assos. Neenah, Wis., 1957-60; architect John J. Flad & Assos., Madison, 1960-64, Fritz & Rosenthal & Assos., Madison, 1964-65; pres. Stuart William Gallaher, Architect, Inc., Madison, 1965—. Mem. City of Madison Bldg. Bd. Examiners and Appeals, 1978—. Served to 1st. lt., C.E., U.S. Army, 1955-57. Allerton Travelling fellow, 1954. Mem. AIA. Conglist. Designer: Garner Park Pavilion, Madison, 1975; Hilton Inn, Lake Geneva, Wis., 1976; Olbrich Bot. Center Complex, Madison, 1977; Office-Store-Factory Avanti Foods Co., Walnut, Ill., 1978; entrance bldg. Swiss Hist. Village, New Glarus, Wis., 1979; Chalet Landhaus Hotel, New Glarus, 1980; Islamic Student Center Complex, Madison, 1981. Home: 5150 Door Dr Madison WI 53705 Office: Stuart William Gallaher Architect Inc 702 N Blackhawk Ave Madison WI 53705

GALLANIS, THOMAS CONSTANTINE, obstetrician and gynecologist; b. Chgo., Mar. 6, 1927; s. Constantine A. and Kathryn (Koclanes) G.; student U. Ill., 1945-48; B.S., Northwestern U., 1949, M.D., 1952; m. Jeanette Andria Nassos, Apr. 2, 1979; children—Kathryn Ann, Craig. Intern, Passavant Meml. Hosp., Chgo., 1952-53, resident in obstetrics and gynecology, 1953-56; practice medicine specializing in obstetrics and gynecology, Evanston, Ill., 1956—; mem. staff Evanston Hosp., Glenbrook Hosp.; faculty dept. obstetrics and gynecology Northwestern U. Med. Sch., 1956—. Diplomate Am. Bd. Obstetrics and Gynecology. Fellow Am. Coll. Obstetricians and Gynecologists; mem. AMA, Ill., Chgo. med. socs., Chgo. Gynecologic Soc., Phi Rho Sigma. Greek Orthodox. Home: 1346 Somerset Dr Glenview IL 60025 Office: 2500 Ridge Ave Evanston IL 60201

GALLAUGHER, JAMES RANKIN, engr.; b. East Moline, Ill., July 27, 1935; s. Elbert Roy and Myrtis (Dykes) G.; B.S. in Gen. Engring., U. Ill., 1957; student Nat. Def. U., Ft. McNair, Washington, 1980; m. Joan Ellen Getty, Sept. 1, 1957; children—Kathryn, Jeffrey, Cynthia, Joel. Small arms project engr. Army Weapons Command, Rock Island, Ill., 1962-65, chief, tech. mgmt. div., project mgr. rifles, 1965-71, project engr. cannon launched guided projectile, project mgr. arty., 1971-73, army small arms program coordinator Army Armament Command, 1972-74, dir. indsl. base engring. activity, Rock Island, 1974—; pres. Gallaugher, Inc., 1962—. Mem. adv. council Coll. Engring., Iowa State U., 1981—. Served with USN, 1957-62; served to capt. C.E., USNR, 1962—. Recipient various Performance awards U.S. Army, 1962—, Outstanding Res. Seabee Detachment award USN, 1970. Mem. Nat. Rifle Assn., Am. Def. Preparedness Assn. (pres. Iowa-Ill. chpt. 1980—), Naval Res. Assn. (chpt. pres. 1978), Delta Phi (pres. 1956-57). Clubs: Masons (32 deg.). Home: 2375 5th St East Moline IL 61244 Office: US Army Indsl Base Engring Activity Rock Island IL 61299

GALLE, OSWIN KARMIE, JR., chemist; b. Valley Center, Kans., Feb. 11, 1932; s. Oswin K. and Sarah (Schmidt) G.; B.S., Bethel Coll., 1957; postgrad. U. Kans., 1958-65; m. Edna Marie Thieszen, June 1, 1957; children—Michael Lee, Suzanne Marie. Analytical chemist Kans. Geol. Survey, Lawrence, 1957—, chief chemist geochemistry sect., 1968-72, research asso., 1975—, chief chemist, 1972—. Chmn. credit com. Kans. U. Fed. Credit Union, 1970—. Mem. Assn. Ofcl. Analytical Chemists, ASTM, Soc. Applied Spectroscopy (program chmn. Kansas City sect. 1973-74, chmn. 1976, chmn. publs. com. 1973-74, chmn. Meggars award com. 1975, chmn. hon. membership com. 1979, chmn. publicity com. 1981), Sigma Xi. Contbr. articles in analytical chemistry to profl. jours.; editorial bd. Applied Spectroscopy, 1976. Home: Rural Route 4 PO Box 69 Lawrence KS 66044 Office: Kans Geol Survey 1930 Ave A Campus West Lawrence KS 66044

GALLES, GLEN FRANK, mgmt. cons.; b. Mpls., Apr. 1, 1916; s. Frank Anthony and Bessie (Anderson) G.; B.B.A., U. Minn., 1941; m. Dorothy A. Miller, Dec. 16, 1942; children—Bruce, Allen, Patricia. Salesman, Burroughs Adding Machine Co., Mpls., 1941-42; corp. dir. personnel ops. Honeywell, Inc., Mpls., 1946-67; corp. dir. organizational planning The Pillsbury Co., Mpls., 1968-72; mgmt. cons. The Galles Resource, Apple Valley, Minn., 1972—; instr. indsl. relations dept. U. Minn., 1975-79. Chmn., Mpls. CSC, 1957-64, Mpls. Citizens Task Force-Police, 1967; dir. Citizens League of Twin Cities, 1965-67. Served to capt. USAAF, 1942-46. Cert. mgmt. cons. Mem. Am. Soc. Personnel Adminstrn. (accredited), Assn. Mgmt. Cons.'s, Twin Cities Personnel Assn., U. Minn. Sch. Bus. Alumni Assn. (pres.), U.S. C. of C., Apple Valley C. of C. (pres. 1980-81), Delta Sigma Pi. Clubs: Decathelon Athletic, Order DeMolay, The Grafil. Home: 309 Cimarron Rd Apple Valley MN 55124 Office: 7373 W 147th St Apple Valley MN 55124

GALLI, MICHAEL ANGELO, physicist, electronics engr.; b. Nanticoke, Pa., Dec. 27, 1934; s. Angelo John and Viola Dianne (Medoski) G.; B.S. in Physics (Electronics), U. Scranton, 1956; student U. Ala., 1957-60, U. Md., 1961-64; m. Ann Manley, June 30, 1967; 1 son, Paul Michael. Engr., RCA, Camden, N.J., 1956-57, Philco Corp., Lansdale, Pa., 1961; physicist David Taylor Model Basin, Carderock, Md., 1961, Diamond Ordnance Fuze Labs, Washington, 1961-62, NASA, Goddard Space Flight Center, Greenbelt, Md., 1962-73; disability retiree from Fed. Govt., 1973. Served to 1st lt., Ordnance Corps, U.S. Army, 1957-60. Recipient several letters of appreciation, NASA, other groups. Mem. Am. Phys. Soc., IEEE. Address: 2486 Winding Hills Dr Columbus OH 43224

GALLIGAN, FRANK DANIEL, automotive parts co. exec.; b. Bronx, N.Y., Apr. 15, 1938; s. Frank A. and Mary G. (Moran) G.; B.S., U. Scranton, 1960; grad. exec. devel. program U. Ill., 1975; m. M. Elizabeth Jordan, Oct. 14, 1961; children—Michael F., Eileen M., Paul F. Vice pres. mktg. Toledo Tools Co., 1971-74; nat. sales mgr. AP Parts Co., Toledo, 1974-77; gen. sales mgr. McQuay-Norris, Inc., St. Louis, 1977—. Pres., Brightwaters Acres Civic Assn., 1965-66; mem. bus. adv. com. Lucas County Port Authority, 1976-77. Mem. Automotive Parts and Accessories Assn., Automotive Service Industries Assn. (mem. young exec. nat. bd. dirs. 1977-78). Republican. Roman Catholic. Club: Glen Echo Country (St. Louis). Office: 2320 Marconi Ave Saint Louis MO 63110

GALLIVAN, LAURA LYN, assn. exec.; b. Piggott, Ark., Oct. 30, 1949; d. Richard Lynn and Edith Mae (Bain) Gower; student Rock Valley Coll., 1968, So. Ill. U., 1969; m. Patrick John Gallivan, Apr. 8, 1980. Stewardess, N.W. Orient Airlines, Mpls.-St. Paul, 1970-72; employment cons. Exec. Staffing, Inc., Washington, 1972-73; cosmetologist Lord & Taylor, Washington, 1973-74; rep. NASCO Inc., Springfield, Tenn., 1974-76; promotion dir. Signal Hills Shopping Center, West St. Paul, Minn., 1976-79; with Downtown Council, St. Paul Area C. of C., 1979-81, dir., 1979—; part-time instr. Inver Hills Community Coll., Inver Grove Heights, Minn., 1978—, mem. adv. com. small bus. mgmt. program, 1979—; bd. dirs. Downtown Community Devel. Council, St. Paul, 1980—. Mem. Am. C. of C. Execs., Tchrs. Retirement Assn., Delta Zeta. Clubs: North Oaks Golf, St. Paul Athletic. Home: 595 Mercury Circle Shoreview MN 55112 Office: 701 NCLT 445 Minnesota St Saint Paul MN 55101

GALLIVAN, PATRICK THOMAS, agrl. co. exec.; b. Macon County, Ill., July 23, 1932; s. William Francis and Catherine Agnes (Cantwell) G.; B.S., U. Ill., 1954; m. Patricia C. Flynn, June 16, 1956; children—Kitty, Carolyn, Mary. Tchr. vocat. agr. public schs., Forrest, Ill., 1954-59; mgr. fertilizer plant Zorn, Inc., Forrest, 1959-60; ter. sales mgr. Cargill, Inc., Effingham, Ill., 1960-72, dist. sales mgr. Seed div., Pontiac, Ill., 1972—. Mem. Ill. Seed Dealer Assn., Ind. Seed Trade Assn. Democrat. Roman Catholic. Clubs: K.C., Moose. Home: 5 Edgewood Dr Pontiac IL 61764 Office: Cargill Inc PO Box 557 Pontiac IL 61764

GALLO, MICHAEL SAM, mfg. co. exec.; b. Kenosha, Wis., Jan. 29, 1917; s. Joseph and Sofie (Bonidio) G.; student public schs., Racine, Wis.; m. Feb. 5, 1940; children—Judith Gallo Simpson, Saralee Gallo Mayew, Mary Gallo Sollman. Pres., Gallo Mfg. Co. Inc., Racine, 1949—, Gen. Packaging Co., Racine, 1965—. Mem. adv. bd. Breakthru Community Center, Racine, 1976—; supr. Racine County Bd., 1980—. Roman Catholic. Clubs: Italian Am., Roma Lodge. Inventor various products, including sprayers, hobby kits, games. Office: 1312 N Memorial Dr Racine WI 53404

GALLOWAY, EDWARD JAMES, health care admin Wilmington, Del., Sept. 20, 1932; s. Edward J. and Cecilia M. G.; student Towson Tchrs. Coll., 1950-51, U. Md. in Japan, 19 student U. Wittenberg, 1955-56, U. Dayton, 1960-61, 74-75, W State U., 1970-71, Antioch Coll., 1979—; m. Karen D. Munn, 19, 1977; children—Timothy James, J. Matthew Thompson, M Allen Thompson, Tamara Joan, Pamela Jean. Enlisted U.S. Air For 1952, advanced through grades to tech. sgt., 1972; med. technicia 8th USAF Hosp., Johnson AFB, Japan, assigned to Korea, 1952-54; dir. admissions USAF Hosp., Wright-Patterson, Dayton, Ohio, 1954-61; Air Force liaison Fort Wainwright, Fairbanks, Alaska, 1961-62; dir. med. records USAF Hosp., Wright-Patterson AFB, 1962-65; dir. med. services 6044th USAF Dispensary, Seoul, Korea, 1965-66; dir. admissions and outpatient records USAF Hosp., Westover AFB, Springfield, Mass., 1967-68; recruiter USAF Recruiting Service, Indpls., 1968-69; health resources mgr. USAF Med. Center, Wright-Patterson AFB, Dayton, Ohio, 1969-72, ret., 1972; dir. ambulatory services Good Samaritan Hosp. and Health Center, Dayton, Ohio, 1972-76, asst. v.p. ops., 1976—. Chmn. disaster plan rev. task force Western Ohio Emergency Med. Services Council, 1974-76. Recipient Achievement award Dayton Safety Council, 1979. Mem. Am. Acad. Med. Adminstrs. (dir. Ohio 1978—), Am. Hosp. Assn., Am. Acad. Health Adminstrs., Ohio Hosp. Assn. (mem. environ. services com. 1978—), Dayton C. of C. (mem. energy task force 1979—), Nat. Alliance for Energy Contingency Planning for Health Resources. Democrat. Roman Catholic.

GALLUN, ROBERT LOUIS, research entomologist; b. Milw., Feb. 21, 1924; s. George O. and Viola C. (Paul) G.; B.S., Mich. State U., 1948, M.S., 1950; Ph.D., Purdue U., 1960; m. Geraldyne Marie Dexter, June 25, 1949; children—Christine Marie, Robert Craig. Entomologist, U.S. Dept. Agr., Minot, N.D., 1950-52; mem. faculty Purdue U., West Lafayette, Ind., 1952—, entomologist, 1952-62, research entomologist, 1962-64, project leader, 1964-69, research entomologist, research leader, 1970—; tchr., cons. Served with inf. U.S. Army, 1943-45. Decorated Bronze Star. Fulbright scholar, 1980. Mem. Entomol. Soc. Am., Crops Sci. Soc., Am. Soc. Agronomy, Am. Genetic Assn., Am. Registry Prof. Entomologists, Sigma Xi. Club: Optimist. Contbr. articles to various publs. Office: Room 3 Agr Adminstrn Bldg Purdue Univ West Lafayette IN 47907

GALMICHE, JOHN EDWARD, III, profl. hockey club exec.; b. St. Louis, Feb. 3, 1948; s. John Edward and Gladys Marie (Farasy) G.; B.S., St. Louis U., 1970; m. Rosemary Ann Failoni, Dec. 27, 1969; children—Christina, Jennifer, Abigail. Asst. mgr. Home Life of N.Y., St. Louis, 1970-72; gen. mgr. St. Louis Stars Soccer Club, 1972-77; pres. Total Mktg. Assos., St. Louis, 1977-78; dir. mktg. St. Louis Blues Hockey Club, 1978—; partner, dir. West County Travel Agy., 1978—. Bd. dirs. Stuttgart Sister City, 1974—. Mem. Sales and Mktg. Execs. of St. Louis, St. Louis Conv. and Tourist Bur. Clubs: Advt. of St. Louis, Am. Bus. Clubs, Direct Mktg. of St. Louis, Norwood Hills Country, Castle Oak Country, Chesterfield Optimist, Rotary of St. Louis, Assn. Internationale des SKAL Clubs. Home: 1536 Woodroyal East Chesterfield MO 63017 Office: St Louis Blues Hockey Club 5700 Oakland Ave Saint Louis MO 63110

GALT, RAYMOND MASSON, physician; b. Evanston, Ill., May 28, 1914; s. Arthur Thomas and Ida May (Cook) G.; B.A., Williams Coll., 1936; M.D., Northwestern U., 1940; m. Jane Falley, May 1, 1943; 1 dau., Katharine Hughes. Intern Evanston Hosp., 1939-40; resident in pathology Passavant Hosp., Chgo., 1940-41; resident in internal medicine Cook County Hosp., Chgo., 1942, attending physician, 1947-72; practice medicine specializing in internal medicine, Chgo., 1943—; mem. staff Rush Presbyn.-St. Luke's, Augustana hosps.; asst. prof. medicine U. Ill. Med. Sch., Chgo., 1949—. Trustee, Village of Golf (Ill.), 1952-56. Served to capt. M.C., AUS, 1943-46. Decorated Bronze Star, Silver Star; Croix de Guerre with étoile d'argent (France). Fellow A.C.P.; mem. AMA, Ill., Chgo. med. socs. Republican. Mem. Winnetka (Ill.) Bible Ch. Club: Glen View. Home: 56 Overlook Dr Golf IL 60029 Office: 2155 N Cleveland St Chicago IL 60614

GALVIN, JOSEPH JERRY (JJ), telephone co. mgr.; b. Chgo., Nov. 4, 1950; s. Jerry J. and Mary Jeanne (Didion) G.; B.S. in Geology and Math., U. Ill., Chgo. Circle, 1972; m. Michelle Dorn, July 23, 1972; 1 dau., Cheryl. Systems analyst Sargent & Lundy Engrs., Chgo., 1973-75, Marshall Field & Co., Chgo., 1975-76; sr. analyst Mgmt. Systems Tech. Co., Chgo., 1976-78; sr. analyst internat. systems div. First Nat. Bank Chgo., 1978-80; asst. mgr. network staff Ill. Bell Telephone, 1980—; owner Unicorn Computer Services, Ltd., Chgo. Chmn., Bolingbrook (Ill.) Zoning Bd. Appeals, 1978—; trustee Fountaindale Library Dist., Will and Dupage Counties, Ill., 1978—; Republican precinct committeeman Will County, 1978-79, DuPage County, 1980—. Mem. Servas Internat., DuPage Apple Users Group. Home: 673 Banbury Way Bolingbrook IL 60439 Office: Ill Bell Box 176 Chicago IL 60690

GALVIN, ROBERT W., radio mfg. exec.; b. Marshfield, Wis., Oct. 9, 1922; student U. Notre Dame, U. Chgo.; LL.D. (hon.), Quincy Coll., St. Ambrose Coll., DePaul U., Ala. State U. With Motorola, Inc., Chgo., 1940—, chmn. bd., chief exec. officer, 1964—, also dir. Bd. dirs. Jr. Achievement of Chgo.; trustee Ill. Inst. Tech.; former mem. Pres.'s Commn. Internat. Trade and Investment; mem. 12 Fellows U. Notre Dame. Served with Signal Corps, AUS, World War II. Named Decision Maker of Yr., Chgo. Assn. Commerce and Industry-Am. Statis. Assn., 1973. Mem. Electronics Industries Assn. (pres. 1966, medal of Honor 1970, dir.). Office: Motorola Inc 1303 Algonquin Rd Schaumburg IL 60196*

GALYARDT, CYNTHIA CARSWELL, state ofcl.; b. Emporia, Kans., Jan. 1, 1934; d. Jay Horton and Lena (Anderson) Carswell; B.S., Kans. State U., 1955; m. Milton Andrew Galyardt, Feb. 12, 1955; children—Susan Irene, Thomas Milton, Mark Andrew. Editor, Kans. Bus. Rev., Lawrence, 1966-71; research asst. Kans. Geol. Survey, Lawrence, 1971-72; dir. public info. Kans. Lung Assn., Topeka, 1972-74; communications coordinator Kans. Commn. on Alcoholism, Topeka, 75; prevention cons. SRS Alcohol and Drug Abuse Services, 1975—. Recipient Contest awards Kans. Press Women, 1968, 70, 73. Mem. Women in Communications (pres. Lawrence chpt. 1966-68, Kans. Assn. for Sch. Health, Nat. Assn. Prevention Profls., Nat. Policy Council, Public Health Assn., DAR, Kappa Kappa Gamma. Club: Soroptimist International (Lawrence). Home: 325 Homestead Dr Lawrence KS 66044 Office: 2700 W 6th St Topeka KS

GAMBILL, BETHANY LUELLA, tel. co. exec.; b. Painesville, Ohio, Oct. 12, 1953; s. Garfield and Shirley Mae (Jones) Johns; A.S. in Computer Programming, Inst. Computer Mgmt., Cleve., 1973; student Cuyahoga Community Coll., 1974; m. Stephen Carl Gambill, May 21, 1977. Bookkeeper, asst. to art dir. Revere Chem. Corp./Monroe Co., Solon, Ohio, 1973-75; with Mid Continent Tel. Corp., Hudson, Ohio, 1975—, transmission coordinator, 1976, toll coordinator, 1977—. Mem. Nat. Fedn. Bus. and Profl. Women. Home: 2201 Schubert St Cuyahoga Falls OH 44221 Office: 100 Executive Pky Hudson OH 44236

STEVENS, dietitian, hosp. exec.; b. ... Glenn Harrison and Sylvia Alice ... Mich. State U., 1948; M.A., Wayne State ... Gambill, June 16, 1956 (dec.); 1 son, Blair ... U. Kans. Hosp., 1949; dir. dietetics Highland ...49-56, Deaconess Hosp., Cleve., 1957-69; food ... Med. Center, Chgo., 1969-72; dir. dietetics Central ...sp. Clinic, Chgo., 1973-74; dir. food services Riverside ... Kankakee, Ill., 1974—. Mem. Am. Dietetic Assn., Am. ... Food Service Adminstrs., Home Econs. Assn. (pres. Cleve. ...), Beta Sigma Phi. Methodist. Clubs: Bus. and Profl. Women ... pres.), Cleve., Zonta Internat. (chmn. public affairs com. ...kakee club 1978-79, mem. wayfarers com. 1978-79), Order ...astern Star (worthy matron 1981), White Shrine, Pythian Sisters. Home: Route 2 Box 336 Kankakee IL 60901 Office: Hosp of Englewood 6001 S Green St Chicago IL 60621

GAMBLE, MICHAEL LEE, civil engr., county ofcl.; b. Elkhart, Kans., Mar. 15, 1943; s. Leo E. and Mary A. (Brewer) G.; A.A., Dodge City Community Coll., 1963; B.S.C.E., Kans. State U., 1966; m. Cherry P. Smith, July 8, 1972; children—Andrew Lee, Elizabeth Marie. Rotational trainee Kans. Hwy. Commn., Topeka, 1966-67, project engr., Meade, 1967-69, Liberal, 1969-75; county engr. County of Meade (Kans.), 1975—, coordinator emergency preparedness, 1975—. Active Boy Scouts Am. Mem. ASCE, Nat. Assn. County Engrs., Am. Rd. and Transp. Builders Assn., Kans. Emergency Preparedness Assn. (Area 6 v.p.), Kans. State U. Alumni Assn. Methodist. Club: Kiwanis (dir. Meade 1977—, v.p. 1980-81). Home: RFD Meade KS 67864 Office: Courthouse Meade KS 67864

GAMBLE, RANELLE ALEASE, lawyer; b. N.Y.C., June 2, 1941; d. Albert Reginald and Everlee (Holman) G.; B.A., N.Y. U., 1966; J.D. cum laude, Cleve. State U., 1972. Caseworker N.Y.C. Dept. Social Services, 1966-68; admitted to Ohio bar, 1972; atty. FTC, Cleve., 1972-74; atty. Cleve. Electric Illuminating Co., 1974—, sr. corp. atty., 1980—. Bd. dirs. Project Friendship, Cleve., 1980-82; bd. dirs. Council Human Relations, 1980, sec. bd. trustees, 1981-82; bd. dirs. Cleve. Heights Cable TV Adv. Commn., 1979-82; trustee Legal Aid Soc. Cleve., 1981—; chmn. Democratic task force Cuyahoga Women's Polit. Caucus, 1980. Recipient YWCA/SOHIO Career Woman of Achievement award, 1979; Greater Cleve. PanHellenic Council Outstanding Service award, 1976. Mem. Cleve. Women Lawyers Assn. (pres. 1978-80), Cleve.-Marshall Law Alumni Assn. (pres. 1981-82), Cuyahoga County Bar Assn. (sec., trustee), Greater Cleve. Bar Assn., Ohio Bar Assn., Nat. Assn. Women Lawyers, Black Women Lawyers Assn., Nat. Assn. Negro Bus. and Profl. Women, Cuyahoga Women's Polit. Caucus, Delta Sigma Theta (pres. chpt. 1977-81). Roman Catholic. Club: Women's City. Contbr. articles to profl. jours. Home: 1040 Helmsdale Rd Cleveland Heights OH 44112 Office: PO Box 5000 55 Public Sq Cleveland OH 44113

GAMBLE, THOMAS ELLSWORTH, univ. ofcl., health professions educator; b. Chgo., Nov. 14, 1941; s. Slade leBlount and Anna Marie (VanDuzer) G.; B.A., Northwestern U., 1964; Ed.M., U. Ill., 1970, Ph.D., 1973; m. Donna Kay Dersch, Nov. 3, 1973; children—Brendan, Oscar, Shari, Rebecca. Asst. to dean Office Student Personnel, U. Ill., Urbana, 1968-71, Sch. Basic Med. Scis., Urbana, Coll. Medicine, Urbana, 1971-72, asst. dean, 1972-76, asst. prof. higher edn. Coll. Edn., 1972-77, asst. prof. health professions edn. Center for Ednl. Devel., 1972-78, asso. prof., 1978—, asst. to chancellor U. Ill. Med. Center, Chgo., 1976-78, asst. chancellor, 1978—; tech. cons. Mus. Sci. and Industry, Chgo., 1977—. Served with U.S. Navy, 1964-68; Vietnam; comdr. Res. Mem. Am. Assn. Community and Jr. Colls., Am. Assn. Higher Edn., Assn. Am. Med. Colls., Assn. for Study Higher Edn., Am. Edn. Research Assn., Am. Council on Edn. (instl. del. 1977—), Phi Delta Kappa, Beta Beta Beta, Phi Kappa Phi, Kappa Delta Pi, Chi Gamma Iota. Presbyterian (deacon). Contbr. articles on health edn. to profl. publs. Home: 1203 W Cleven Mt Prospect IL 60056 Office: Office of the Chancellor 1737 W Polk St Chicago IL 60612

GAMBLIN, RODGER LOTIS, research co. exec.; b. St. Louis, Sept. 18, 1932; s. Granville Lotis and Opal Ora (Taylor) G.; B.S., Princeton U., 1954, M.A., 1963, Ph.D., 1965; M.B.A., Wright State U., 1981; children—Anne W., Rodgers W.B., Lawrence R., Sarah A., Amanda T. Foreman, Phelps Dodge Co., Fort Wayne, Ind., 1954-55; research staff Princeton (N.J.) U., 1955-59; area mgr. IBM, Boulder, Colo., 1959-76; v.p. research and devel. Mead Corp., Dayton, Ohio, 1976-80, pres. Dayton Tinker Corp., 1980—; dir. Yellow Springs Instrument Co. Mem. Am. Phys. Soc., AAAS, Mensa, Sigma Xi. Republican. Presbyterian. Patentee in field; contbr. articles to profl. jours. Home: 1506 Shroyer Rd Dayton OH 45419 Office: Dayton Tinker Corp 143 Westpark Rd Dayton OH 45459

GAMBOA, LUCITO GAMBOA, pathologist; b. Pampanga, Philippines, Jan. 7, 1929; s. Serapion Maniago and Jacinta (Lapuz) G.; came to U.S., 1952, naturalized, 1959; M.D., U. Santo Tomas, Philippines, 1952; M.S., U. Colo., 1955; m. Sylvia Roque, Sept. 18, 1953; children—Richard R., Virginia L., Debra Lynn. Intern, Mercy Hosp., Denver, 1952-53; resident in pathology Gen. Rose Meml. Hosp., Denver, 1953-58; chmn. dept. pathology, dir. Labs. Edgewater Hosp., Chgo., 1958-68, dir. pathology and clin. labs., 1979—; pathologist, dir. blood bank Little Co. of Mary Hosp., Evergreen Park, Ill., 1969-79; instr. Med. Sch. Northwestern U., Chgo., 1958-60. Recipient Distinguished Physician award Philippine Med. Assn. Chgo., 1966. Mem. Coll. Am. Pathologists, AMA, Internat. Acad. Pathology, Am. Assn. Blood Banks, Am. Soc. Cytology, Am. Soc. Clin. Pathologists, Soc. Nuclear Medicine, Assn. Philippine Practicing Physicians Am. (pres. 1972-74). Roman Catholic. Home: 35 Bradford Ln Oak Brook IL 60521

GAMMON, JUANITA LAVERNE, artist, educator; b. McLeansboro, Ill.; d. Lloyd W. and Grace F. (Munsell) G.; B.F.A., M.F.A., U. Ill. Exhibited at NAD, N.Y.C., U. Ill., Parkland Coll., others; represented in numerous collections; head communications career program (art, advt., journalism, broadcasting) Parkland Coll., Champaign, Ill., 1967—, also editor coll. mag. Intercom; free lance illustrator, copywriter, guest lectr., art show judge, condr. workshops; former dir. Corn Country Graphics; supr. Champaign County Art Show, 1973—; bd. dirs. East Central Ill. Cultural Affairs Consortium, 1973; mem. art acquisition com. Parkland Found. Mem. NEA, Ill. Art Edn. Assn., Assn. Jr. Colls., Ill. Hist. Soc., U. Ill. Alumni Assn., Art Alumni Assn., Parkland Art Assn. (sponsor), Champaign-Urbana Advt.-Art Club (past treas., dir.). Home: 711 W Healey St Champaign IL 61820

GAMMUTO, JOHN JOSEPH, SR., utility co. exec.; b. Chgo., Jan. 7, 1925; s. Philip D. and Mary (Elia) G.; B.S. in Elementary Edn., 1974, M.A. in Curriculum and Adminstrn., 1976; postgrad. U. Chgo., 1977; Ph.D., Loyola U.; m. Catherine H. Maher, Dec. 22, 1945; children—John Joseph, Catherine, James, Andrew. With Commonwealth Edison Co., 1955—, staff asst. gen. office, Chgo., 1970-76, gen. supr. tng. generating stas., prodn. dept., 1977—. Commr., counselor W. Suburban council Boy Scouts Am., 1965-77. Served with USN, 1943-46, 50-51; PTO; Korea. Certified tchr., ednl. adminstr., Ill. Mem. Coll. DuPage, DePaul U., Loyola U. alumni assns., Am. Nuclear Soc., ASME, Adult Edn. Assn., Ill. Tng. Dirs. Assn., Am. Soc. Tng. and Devel., Assn. Study Higher Edn., DePaul Geog. Soc., VFW, Kappa Delta Pi, Phi Delta Kappa. Roman Catholic. Home: 4804 Oakwood Ave Downers Grove IL 60515 Office: 1910 S Briggs St Joliet IL 60436

GAMON, ADAM EDWARD, II, internist, chem. co. exec.; b. Hillside, N.J., Sept. 6, 1918; s. Adam Edward and Mary (Yanick) G.; B.S., Alfred U., 1939; M.D., Temple U., 1943; m. Lottie Irene Snyder, Sept. 8, 1939; children—Judith Diane, Robert Edward. Intern, N.Y.C. Hosp., 1944, resident in pathology, 1946, asst. med. resident, 1947-48, chief med. resident, 1948-49; resident internal medicine Saginaw (Mich.) Gen. Hosp., 1946-47; pvt. practice internal medicine, Englewood, N.J., 1949-50; practice medicine specializing in internal medicine, Saginaw, 1950-69; with Mich. State Disability Determination Service, Lansing, 1969-71; med. dir. Malleable Iron div. Gen. Motors Corp., Saginaw, 1971-73; med. dir. Dow Corning Corp., Midland, Mich., 1973—; chief of medicine St. Luke's Hosp., Saginaw, 1953-67; cons. St. Mary's Hosp., Gen. Hosp., St. Luke's Hosp., Saginaw, Midland Hosp.; dep. coroner Saginaw County (Mich.), 1973—; cons. physician Social Security Adminstrn., HEW, Saginaw, 1973-77. Served to capt., M.C., U.S. Army, 1944-46. Diplomate Am. Bd. Internal Medicine. Fellow A.C.P. (life), Am. Coll. Angiology; mem. Am. Soc. Internal Medicine, Mich., Midland County med. socs., AMA, Mich. Soc. Internal Medicine, Indsl. Med. Assn., Pan Am. Med. Assn., Am. Radio Relay League. Inventor Disposable tracheotomy set, portable bed chair. Home: 15317 W Brant Rd PO Box 57 Brant MI 48614 Office: Dow Corning Corp S Saginaw Rd Midland MI 48640

GAMSKY, NEAL RICHARD, univ. adminstr.; b. Menasha, Wis., Feb. 17, 1931; s. Andrew and Lillian Gamsky; B.S., U. Wis., 1954, M.S., 1959, Ph.D., 1965; m. Irene Janet Jimos, Aug. 16, 1956; children—Elizabeth, Patricia. Counselor, Appleton (Wis.) Pub. Schs., 1959-62; dir. edn. Wis. Diagnostic Center, Madison, 1962-67; dir. research and pupil services Coop. Edn. Service Agy., Waupun, Wis., 1967-70; dir. student counseling center Ill. State U., Normal, 1970-73, v.p., dean student affairs, 1973—; ednl. and counseling cons. Wis. Div. Mental Hygiene, 1967. Served with AUS, 1954-56; ETO. Profl. Rehab. fellow, 1968. Mem. Am. Psychol. Assn., Am. Personnnel and Guidance Assn., Nat. Assn. Student Personnel Adminstrs., Am. Assn. Higher Edn., Am. Council Edn. Author: (with others) The Counselor's Handbook, 1974; also articles, monograph. Home: 114 Cheltenham Dr Normal IL 61761 Office: 506 DeGarmo Hall Ill State U Normal IL 61761

GANDRUD, EBENHARD STEWART (GANDY), mfg. co. exec.; b. Detroit Lakes, Minn., Oct. 19, 1902; s. Albert E. and Kari (Dahlen) G.; B.S., U. Minn., 1934; m. Edith M. Christensen, July 16, 1935; children—Linda (Mrs. H.L. Stoddard), Dale E. Agrl. extension agt., Pipestone Minn., 1934-37; founder, pres. Gandy Co., Owatonna, Minn., 1936—. Mem. exec. bd. Gamehaven council Boy Scouts Am., 1945-75; pres. Gandrud Found., 1940—. Served with War Manpower Commn., World War II. Recipient award for outstanding contbn. to Am. Agr. Congress of U.S., 1967; Silver Beaver award Boy Scouts Am., 1971; Outstanding Achievement award U. Minn., 1980. Mem. Am. Soc. Agrl. Engrs., N.A.M., Minn. C. of C. (past dir.), Sons of Norway. Lutheran. Elk, Rotarian. Club: Mpls. Athletic. Patentee in field. Home: 517 E School St Owatonna MN 55060 Office: Box 528 Owatonna MN 55060

GANDY, JOYCE ANN, assn. exec.; b. Picher, Okla., Feb. 5, 1937; d. Sheppard Levi and Naydeen Maxine (Phillips) G.; A.A., Parsons Jr. Coll., 1957; student dance, Thalia Mara, Gertrude Edwards Jory, Robert Joffrey, Luigi, Frank Wagner. Owner, instr. Joyce's Dance Studio, Parsons, Kans., 1953-66; gen. sec. Nat. Acad. Ballet & Theater Arts, N.Y.C., 1966-72; sec., adminstrv. asst. to office/convs. mgr. Am. Inst. Steel Constrn., N.Y.C., 1973-79, office mgr., Chgo., 1979-80, personnel adminstr., 1980—. Cert. in Cecchetti dance method. Office: 400 N Michigan Ave Chicago IL 60611

GANG, STUART WORTHINGTON, advt. agy. exec.; b. N.Y.C., Oct. 18, 1928; s. James and Sylvia Susan (Weitz) G.; B.A., U. Minn., 1951; m. Marjorie Paul, Aug. 14, 1979. Newsman, Sta. KSTP-TV, Mpls., 1951-55, Sta. WTCN-TV, Mpls., 1955-56, Sta. WCCO-TV, Mpls., 1956-57; edn. TV coordinator Minn. Pvt. Coll. Council, 1957-59; advt. and public relations dir. Minn. Florists Assn., 1959-67; pres. Gang & Assos., St. Paul, 1967-72; v.p. Gang & Withy, Inc., St. Paul, 1972-79; pres. Stu Gang & Assos., Inc., St. Paul, 1979—; v.p. Stuart Research and Devel. Corp. Pres., Lakeshore Players, 1964-66; 3d v.p. Humane Soc. Ramsey County. Mem. Advt. Agy. Council N.W., Public Relations Soc. Am., St. Paul Winter Carnival Assn. Clubs: St. Paul Athletic (chmn. publs. com., dir.), St. Paul Rotary (past dir.). Home: 1355 Colonial Dr Roseville MN 55113 Office: 350 Robert St Saint Paul MN 55101

GANGWARE, EDGAR BRAND, JR., educator; b. Sandusky, Ohio, May 17, 1922; s. Edgar Brand and Louise Wilhelmina (Schoeneman) G.; B.S., Wittenberg U., 1943, Mus.B., 1947; Mus.M., Northwestern U., 1948, Ph.D., 1959; m. Dorcas Euana Biniores, Sept. 3, 1949; children—Edgar Brand III, Frank Roy, Robert William. Asst. band dir. Northwestern U., Evanston, 1947-49; dir. bands, instr. theory Boston U., 1949-50; dir. bands, dir. summer music clinic Bemidji (Minn.) State U., 1952-66; prof. music N.E. Ill. U., Chgo., 1966—; clinician, condr. Chmn., Civic Music Assn. Bemidji, 1964-66; mem. Northbrook Caucus, 1973-74. Mem. Civil Youth Bd., Northbrook, 1970-72. Served to 1st lt. AUS, 1942-46; PTO. Mem. Am. Bandmasters Assn. (dir. 1973-75), Coll. Band Dirs. Nat. Assn., Music Educators Nat. Conf., Ill. Music Edn. Assn., A.A.U.P. Lion. Compositions for concert band, brass choir, others. Editor, The Sch. Musician Dir./Tchr., 1979—. Home: 1225 Candlewood Hill Rd Northbrook IL 60062 Office: 5500 N St Louis St Chicago IL 60625

GANNON, CLIFFORD W., state senator; ed. public schs.; m. Kathleen Long, May 29, 1948; 4 children. Real estate developer; dir. Charterbank of DeSoto; mem. Mo. Ho. of Reps., 1972-74, Mo. Senate, 1974—. Served with Mo. N.G. Mem. DeSoto C. of C. (past pres.). Baptist. Clubs: Lions, Rotary. Office: State Capitol Jefferson City MO 65101*

GANNON, PAUL GABRIEL, surgeon; b. Jersey City, June 2, 1928; s. James J. and Mary (Hurley) G.; B.A. cum laude, Holy Cross Coll., 1950; M.D., Marquette U., 1954; M.S., U. Minn., 1961, Ph.D., 1973; m. Rozalija Mavric, June 14, 1954; children—Barbara, Paul, James, Mary Ann. Intern, Madigan Army Hosp., Tacoma; fellow gen. surgery Mayo Clinic, Rochester, Minn., 1957-61; practice medicine specializing in gen. surgery, San Diego, 1961-63; resident cardiovascular and thoracic surgery U. Minn., Mpls., 1963-67, clin. prof. surgery, 1978—; practice medicine specializing in thoracic and cardiovascular surgery, Mpls., 1967—. Served to capt. USAF, 1955-57. Mem. A.C.S., AMA, Soc. Thoracic Surgeons, Minn. State Med. Assn. (Best Sci. award 1974), Minn. Surg. Soc., Mpls. Surg. Soc., Minn. Thoracic Soc., Twin City Thoracic and Cardiovascular Surg. Soc., Hennepin County Med. Soc., Mayo Clinic Med. Found. Alumni. Editorial bd. Minn. Medicine, 1971—. Home: 508 Westwood Dr S Minneapolis MN 55416 Office: 2545 Chicago Ave Suite 111 Minneapolis MN 55404

GANNON, RICHARD GALEN, state senator; b. Goodland, Kans., July 29, 1950; s. Bill E. and Geraldine F. Gannon; B.S. in Edn., Kans. U., 1973, postgrad., 1975; m. Martha Ellen Wall, Nov. 26, 1981; 1 dau., Jessica Michelle. Vice pres. Rocking Chair Farms, Inc., Goodland, 1973—; mem. Kans. Senate from 40th Dist., 1976—. Chmn. Sherman County Democratic Central Com., 1975-76. Mem. Kans. U. Alumni Assn., Acacia, Acacia Alumni (pres. adv. bd. 1981—). Roman Catholic. Clubs: Elks, K.C. (3 deg.). Office: 402S State Capitol Topeka KS 66612

GANS, ERNA IRENE, printing co. exec.; b. Bielsko, Poland; d. Adolf and Rosa (Pelzman) Reicher; came to U.S., 1948, naturalized, 1953; B.A., Roosevelt U., 1971; M.A., Loyola U., Chgo., 1974; m. Henry Gans, Apr. 16, 1947; children—Alan, Howard. Asst. prof. dept. sociology Loyola U., Chgo., 1976; pres. Internat. Label & Printing Co., Bensenville, Ill., 1972—. Chmn., Skokie (Ill.) Youth Commn., 1968—; bd. govs. Israel Bond Orgn.; founder, chmn. Holocaust Meml. Found. Ill. Mem. Am. Sociol. Assn., Nat. Fedn. Ind. Bus., Am. Acad. Polit. and Social Sci. Democrat. Jewish. Clubs: B'nai B'rith (pres. 1976—). Home: 2812 Woodland Dr Northbrook IL 60062 Office: 810 Maple Lane Bensenville IL 60106

GANT, GEORGE ARLINGTON LEE, chemist; b. Wilson, N.C., Dec. 5, 1941; s. George William and Georgia Eugenia (Cooke) G.; B.S., N.C. Agrl. and Tech. State U., 1962, M.S., 1965; M.B.A., Central Mich. U., 1973; P.M.D., Harvard U., 1980; m. Ruth Jacqueline Jeffers, Dec. 5, 1964 (div.); children—Jon Patrick, Jeannine Patricia. Chemist, Dow Corning Corp., Midland, Mich., 1965-66, research chemist, 1966-72, research group leader, 1972-75, sr. supr. tech. service and devel., 1975-77, sect. mgr. tech. service and devel., 1977-79, mgr. elastomers tech. service and devel., 1979—; instr., lectr. in field. Mem. Mich. Multiple Sclerosis Soc., 1974—; v.p., 1977-78, pres., 1978-81; mem. adv. bd. Lake Huron Area Council Boy Scouts Am., 1970-73, Salvation Army, 1973-77. Mem. Am. Chem. Soc., Wire Assn., Sigma Xi, Sigma Iota Epsilon (past pres. Central Mich. U. chpt.), Alpha Phi Alpha. Mem. Ch. of God. Clubs: Kiwanis, KiWassee Midland (pres., lt. gov. 1979-80). Contbr. articles to profl. jours.; patentee in field. Home: 1604 W Sugnet St Midland MI 48640 Office: Dow Corning Corp S Saginaw Midland MI 48640

GARBER, JOSEPH MAX, fin. co. exec.; b. Dayton, Ohio, May 22, 1920; s. Harry and Ida G.; B.S. in Bus. Adminstrn. summa cum laude, Ohio State U., 1949; student U. Cin., 1940-42; m. Carole Schneider, May 17, 1942; 1 son, Richard. Communications specialist Air Force Nat. Airport, Washington, 1947-48; mgmt. trainee Credit Bur. of Cin., Inc., 1949-50, dept. mgr., 1950-59, treas., 1959-69, v.p., 1969-76, exec. v.p., 1976-77, pres., 1977—, also dir.; dir., nat. chmn. Asso. Credit Bureaus, 1980—; instr. in mgmt. Bus. Insts. at Kansas U., 1968-70, Ind. U., 1972-73, U. N.C., 1971. Bd. dirs. ARC, Pub. Dental Service Soc., 1973—. Served with USAF, 1942-47; ETO; lt. col. Res. Recipient Paul Bunyan award, 1975-76, Internat. Leadership award, 1973. Mem. Am. Mgmt. Assn., Am. Soc. Assn. Execs., Am. Collectors Assn., Associated Credit Burs., Cin. C. of C., Air Force Assn., Am. Meteorol. Assn. Clubs: Harpers, Cin., Bankers. Contbr. numerous articles on industry and fin. to profl. publs.; instrumental in developing fed. debt collection legislation. Home: 5657 Kugler Mill Rd Cincinnati OH 45236 Office: PO Box 1239 Cincinnati OH 45201

GARBER, SHELDON, hosp. exec.; b. Mpls., July 21, 1920; s. Mitchell and Esther (Amdur) G.; B.A., U. Minn., 1942; postgrad. U. Chgo., 1952-53; m. Elizabeth Sargent Mason, May 16, 1949; children—Robert Michael, Daniel Mason, Sarah Sargent. Reporter, editor U.P.I., Mpls., Chgo., Springfield, Ill., 1938-58; dir. media services U. Chgo., 1958-64; asso. dir. communication Blue Cross Assn., Chgo., 1964-69; exec. v.p. Charles R. Feldstein & Co., 1969-73; v.p. philanthropy and communication Rush-Presbyn.-St. Luke's Med. Center, Chgo., 1973—, sec. bd. trustees, 1976—; cons. Commn. on Drug Safety, Great Books Found., Am. Assn. U. Programs in Hosp. Adminstrn., Am. Nurses Found., Sigma Theta Tau; mem. faculty Inst. on Indsl. and Tech. Communications, Colo. State U., Fort Collins, 1970. Adv. bd. Internat. Inst. Edn.; trustee Citizens Information Service; mem. bd. Nat. Soc. Fund Raisers, 1974-77; bd. dirs. Urban Gateways. Served to 1st lt. C.E., AUS, 1942-46, 50-52. Fellow Royal Soc. Health (London); mem. Public Relations Soc. Am., Publicity Club Chgo., Am. Soc. Hosp. Public Relations Dirs., Am. Public Health Assn., AAAS, Nat. Assn. Sci. Writers, Am. Med. Writers Assn., Inst. Medicine Chgo., Sigma Delta Chi. Clubs: Quadrangle, Cliff Dwellers (Chgo.). Office: 600 S Paulina St Chicago IL 60612

GARCIA, CASIMIRO CRISOSTOMO, JR., obstetrician, gynecologist; b. Manila, Feb. 5, 1940; s. Casimiro Almonte and Nelly Cosme (Crisostomo) G.; came to U.S., 1964, naturalized, 1973; B.S., U. Philippines, 1960, M.D., 1964; m. Theresa Ann Jenks, Sept. 24, 1966; children—Kristine Marie, Anthony Casimir. Rotating intern St Vincent's Hosp. and Med. Center, Toledo, 1964-65; resident in obstetrics and gynecology Michael Reese Hosp. and Med. Center, Chgo., 1966-69; clin. fellow gynecol. oncology U. Miss., Jackson, also clin. instr., 1969-70; individual practice medicine, specializing in obstetrics, gynecology, Belleville, Ill., 1971—. Diplomate Am. Bd. Obstetrics and Gynecology. Fellow Am. Coll. Obstetricians and Gynecologists, A.C.S., Internat. Coll. Surgeons, Am. Soc. Abdominal Surgeons; mem. Am. Fertility Soc., St. Louis Gynecol. Soc., AMA, Ill., St. Clair County med. socs., Am. Assn. Gynecol. Laparoscopists, Am. Assn. Pro-Life Obstetricians and Gynecologists, So. Med. Assn. Roman Catholic. Home: 18 Gerold Ln Belleville IL 62223 Office: 6400 W Main St Belleville IL 62223

GARCIA, JUAN CARLOS, physician; b. Asuncion, Paraguay, Feb. 6, 1945; s. Francisco and Alice Clotilde (Florentin) G.; came to U.S., 1971; B.S. and Letters, Goethe's Coll., Asuncion, 1962; M.D. summa cum laude, Nat. U., Asuncion, 1968; m. Maria N. Macchi, Sept. 30, 1969; children—Johnny, Ronald, Patricia. Resident in medicine, instr. Nat. U. Med. Hosp., Asuncion, 1969-70; rotating intern, Berwyn, Ill., 1971-72; resident in medicine Michael Reese Hosp., Chgo., 1972-74, fellow in hematology, 1974-75; fellow in hematology Michael Reese Hosp.-U. Ill. Med. Sch., Chgo., 1975-76; practice medicine specializing in hematology and oncology, South Bend, Ind., 1976—; attending physician St. Joseph, Meml. hosps., South Bend; dir. oncology unit, chmn. oncology com. St. Joseph Med. Center. Diplomate Am. Bd. Internal Medicine, Am. Bd. Hematology. Roman Catholic. Contbr. articles to profl. publs. Home: 5311 Kingsmill St South Bend IN 46614 Office: 912 E LaSalle St South Bend IN 46617

GARCIA, LUIS ARTURO, otolaryngologist; b. Fajardo, P.R., Dec. 30, 1944; s. Federico L. and Juanita (Martinez) G.; B.S., U. Dayton, 1965; M.D., Marquette U., 1969; m. Patricia Ellen Carroll, Aug. 13, 1966; children—Anne, David, Matthew, Patrick. Intern, Stamford (Conn.) Hosp., 1969-70; resident in otolaryngology Tulane Med. Sch., New Orleans, 1974-77; practice medicine specializing in otolaryngology, Mason City, Iowa, 1977—; with Surg. Assos. of North Iowa. Served with U.S. Army, 1971-74. Recipient Appreciation cert. Pres. Nixon, 1974. Mem. AMA, Iowa Med. Soc., Am. Council Otolaryngology, Am. Acad. Otolaryngology. Roman Catholic. Diplomate Am. Bd. Otolaryngology. Home: 3 Boulder Rd Mason City IA 50401 Office: 910 N Eisenhower St Mason City IA 50401

GARDNER, CHARLES GARY, comml. and indsl. developer; b. Pratt, Kans., Feb. 27, 1931; grad. U. Ala., 1957; postgrad. U. Ariz., U. Okla. Engaged in comml. and indsl. devel., 1974—; pres. Greater State St. Council, Chgo., 1978—; pres., owner Community Dynamics Corp., Chgo., 1981—; mem. faculty, thesis cons. Econ. Devel. Inst., U. Okla.; lectr. workshops and seminars; bd. dirs. Am. Econ. Devel. Council; mem. Gt. Lakes Area Devel. Council, Ill. Devel. Council, State St. Mall Commn. Mem. Internat. Downtown Execs. Assn., Ill. Downtown Devel. Assn., Ill. Retail Mchts. Assn., Chgo. Assn. Commerce and Industry. Address: Greater State St Council 36 S State St Chicago IL 60603

GARDNER, DOUGLAS BAXTER, mfg. co. exec.; b. Shanghai, China, July 23, 1927; s. Cecil Banks and Vivian (Baxter) G.; B.S. in Engring., UCLA, 1950; m. Leonor Wenona Bailly, Apr. 24, 1954 (dec. Dec. 1970); children—David, Cynthia, Howard; m. 2d, Inara Helga Svarups, Dec. 7, 1974. Stress engr. Lockheed Aircraft Corp., 1950-52; project engr., project mgr., engring. mgr.-sci. and process instrument div. Beckman Instruments, Fullerton, Calif., 1952-67; v.p., gen. mgr. Instrument div. Fisher Sci. Corp., Pittsburg, Pa., 1967-70; gen. mgr. Varian Aerograph Co., Walnut Creek, Calif., 1970-72; mng. dir. Varian Techtron Pty Ltd., Melbourne, Australia, 1972-76; v.p., gen. mgr. Vitek Systems Inc. subs. McDonnell Douglas, Hazelwood, Mo., 1976-81; exec. v.p. Travel Designs, Inc., St. Louis, 1981—. Served with USN, 1945-46. Mem. Am. Soc. Microbiology, Health Industries Mfrs. Assn. Home: 1871 Woodmark St Saint Louis MO 63131 Office: 333 Northwest Plaza Saint Louis MO 63074

GARDNER, FRANCES SHAW, ednl. adminstr.; b. Dyersburg, Tenn., Feb. 15, 1932; d. James Henry and Mary (Menzies) Shaw; B.S., Tenn. State U., 1953, M.S., 1959; Ed.D., Wayne State U., 1979; m. William Ernest Gardner, June 10, 1957; children—William, Ernest. Tchr., Nashville City Schs., 1954-60, Detroit Public Schs., 1960-70, reading specialist, 1970-73; asst. prin. in charge Mary McLeod Bethune Primary Sch., Detroit, 1973—. Ruling elder Hope Presbyn. Ch., 1979-81; mem. planning com. Mini White House Conf. on Black Aged, Nat. Center/Caucus on Black Aged, 1980; nat. del. White House Conf. on Aging, 1981. Mem. Coalition Black Greek Women, Nat. Council Negro Women, Detroit Womens Econ. Club, Internat. Reading Assn., Assn. Supervision and Curriculum Devel., Met. Detroit Reading Council, Mich. Reading Assn., Met. Detroit Assn. Black Sch. Educators, Alpha Kappa Alpha (pres. Detroit chpt.). Office: 13001 Fenkell St Detroit MI 48227

GARDNER, GEORGE HERBERT, JR., acct.; b. Ravenna, Ohio, Sept. 27, 1947; s. George H. and Esther A. (Korb) G.; B.B.A., Kent State U., 1973; m. Robin Chandler, Sept. 27, 1975. Staff acct. Gen. Tire & Rubber Co., Akron, Ohio, 1973-74, cost acct., Mogadore, Ohio, 1974-77, acctg. dept. supr., Akron, 1977-78, chief acct., Bryan, Ohio, 1978-81, controller, 1981—; dir. Essman Screw Products, Inc. Advisor, Jr. Achievement, 1973-74; sec.-treas. Hearing Impaired Philanthropy, 1970-78; mayor Oak Meadows Subdivision, Bryan, 1980-81; vol. Am. Cancer Soc., 1980. Served with U.S. Army, 1966-69. Decorated Army Commendation medal, Bronze Star medals (2). Profl. acct., Ohio. Mem. Public Accts. Soc. Ohio, Nat. Assn. Accts., Aircraft Owners and Pilots Assn. Clubs: Rotary, Moose, Orchard Hills Country. Home: Oak Meadows Bryan OH 43506 Office: 927 S Union St Bryan OH 43506

GARDNER, HOWARD GARRY, pediatrician; b. Gary, Ind., Oct. 5, 1943; s. Oscar and Anita (Arenson) G.; B.A., Ind. U., 1965; M.D., 1968. Intern, then resident in pediatrics Cardinal Glennon Hosp., St. Louis, 1968-73; practice medicine specializing in pediatrics, Hinsdale, Ill., 1973—; mem. attending staff Hinsdale Sanitarium and Hosp.; courtesy staff Loyola McGaw Hosp., Maywood, Ill.; clin. asso. prof. Loyola U. Med. Sch.; med. adv. bd. Parent and Childbirth Edn. Soc.; co-chmn. med. adv. bd. Easter Seal Soc., Villa Park, Ill. Served with USNR, 1969-71; Vietnam. Diplomate Am. Bd. Pediatrics. Recipient Outstanding Clin. Prof. award Loyola U., 1978; Tchr. of Yr. award Hinsdale Hosp. Family Practice Residency, 1981. Mem. Am. Acad. Pediatrics, Chgo. Pediatric Soc., Loyola-Hinsdale Pediatric Affiliation (dir.). Contbr. articles to profl. jours. Home: 103 W 65th Lake Dr Westmont IL 60559 Office: 805 Plainfield Rd Darien IL 60559

GARDNER, JOYCE ALENE, realtor, builder; b. Evansville, Ind., Aug. 15, 1928; d. John J. and Ruth Noyes (Thompson) Becker; student Ind. U., 1955-56; m. William F. Gardner, 1952; 1 dau. from previous marriage, Patricia Ruth Markel Frazier. Model, Patricia Stevens Co., 1955-57; with Suno Oil Co., Evansville, 1946-48, Aurora Gasoline Co., 1951-53; sec. treas. South Lake Homes, Inc., Crown Point, Ind., 1968—; salesman Ennis Realty, Hammond, Ind., 1970-72, Biggs Realty, Crown Point, 1972-75, Smith Realty, Merrillville, Ind., 1975-78, Crown Point, 1978—. Republican. Mem. United Ch. of Christ. Home: 326 Sea Anchor Dr Osprey FL 33559 Office: PO Box 202 Crown Point IN 46307

GARDNER, JUNIUS RAYMOND, engring. firm cons.; b. Winnebago, Ill., Mar. 12, 1900; s. Junius Slyter and Ella (Phelps) G.; B.C.E., U. Ill., 1923; m. Norene Mary Moore, Aug. 20, 1927 (dec. May 1972); children—Mary Ann, Margaret June (Mrs. Roy Oth). With Warren & Van Praag Inc., Decatur, Ill., 1937-42, 46—, mng. agt., 1946-70, cons., 1970-76; cons. Bainbridge, Gee, Milanski & Assos., Decatur, 1976—. Served with USNR, 1918-21, to capt. San. Corps, AUS, 1943-45; ETO. Registered profl. engr., Ill. Fellow ASCE (pres. Central Ill. chpt. 1957-58); mem. Cons. Engrs. Council Ill. (pres. 1959-60), Ill. (past chmn.), Nat. socs. profl. engrs., Am. Water Works Assn., Nat. Water Well Assn. Clubs: Masons, K.T., Shriners. Contbr. profl. jours. Home: 145 N Taylor Ave Decatur IL 62522 Office: 1999 W Grand Ave Decatur IL 62522

GARDNER, ROBERT HARRY, public relations exec.; b. Chgo., May 21, 1913; s. Harry Montgomery and Virginia (Jones) G.; B.A., Amherst Coll., 1936; postgrad. U. Chgo., 1949-51; m. Jean Seymour, Dec. 2, 1950; children—Todd R. (dec.), George S., Elizabeth M. With traffic dept. Ill. Central system Western Electric Co., Chgo., 1936-38; radio writer Sta. WLS, Chgo., 1938; radio writing and prodn. staff Ruthrauff & Ryan Advt., Chgo., 1938-42; account exec. Mitchell McKeown Orgn., Chgo., 1942-47; chmn., treas. Gardner, Jones & Co., Inc., Chgo., 1947-78; sr. cons. Hill and Knowlton, Inc., Chgo., 1979—; pres. Spl. Assignment Public Relations, Inc., Chgo., 1981—; lectr. Roosevelt U., 1951-53. Pres., Assn. House Chgo., 1969-71. Bd. dirs. Cook County Sch. Nursing, 1968-70. Served with U.S. Army, 1943-46. Mem. Public Relations Soc. Am., Publicity Club Chgo., Delta Tau Delta. Clubs: Rotary, Amherst, Tavern, University (Chgo.). Author: Financial Public Relations, 1970. Home: 935 N Grove Ave Oak Park IL 60302 Office: 111 E Wacker Dr Chicago IL 60601

GARDNER, RONALD GENE, coll. dean; b. Ottumwa, Iowa, Apr. 23, 1937; s. Merritt William and Jewel (Ballew) G.; B.A., B.S., N.E. Mo. State U., 1959; M.S., Winona State U., 1969; Ph.D., Iowa State U., 1974; m. Mary Ann Bloss, Aug. 30, 1958; children—Lana Sue, Lisa Ann, Lance William. Instr. bus. adminstrn. Indian Hills Community Coll., Ottumwa, 1964-67, dean instnl. services, 1976—; asst. supt. adult edn. N.E. Iowa Tech. Inst., Calmar-Dubuque, 1967-76; mem. Iowa Task Force Non-Traditional Degree Programs, 1973-74, Iowa Adv. Com. on Community Colls., 1971-72, Statewide Community Coll. Athletic Com., 1967; pres. State Exec. Council Community Coll. Athletics, 1977-79; chmn. Ottumwa Community Schs. Credit Union, 1979—. Bd. dirs. YMCA, 1977-81. Mem. Ottuma Ambassadors Chamber, Ottumwa C. of C., Iowa Assn. Area Community Colls. and Vocat. Tech. Insts. (pres. 1971-72), Iowa Area Community Coll. Adult Dirs. Assn. (chmn. 1970-71), Iowa Assn. Lifelong Learning (dir. 1974-76), Phi Delta Kappa, Phi Kappa Phi. Clubs: Rotary (dir.), Ottumwa Country (dir.). Home: 17 Woodshire St Ottumwa IA 52501 Office: Indian Hills Community Coll Ottumwa IA 52501

GARDNER, WILLIAM EARL, univ. adminstr.; b. Hopkins, Minn., Oct. 11, 1928; s. William Henry and Ida (Swenson) G.; B.S., U. Minn., 1950, M.A., 1959, Ph.D., 1961; m. Marcia Frances Anderson, Nov. 4, 1950; children—Mary Gardner Fenwick, Bret, Anne, Eric. Tchr. pub. schs. Balaton, Rockford, New Ulm, Minn., 1950-54; instr. Univ. High Sch., U. Minn., Mpls., 1954-61; prof. edn. U. Minn., 1961—, asso. dean Coll. Edn., 1970-77, dean, 1977—, dir. Minn. Curriculum Lab., 1965-67; vis. prof. U. York (Eng.), 1967-68. Mem. Bd. Edn., St. Louis Park, Minn., 1972-77; mem. Bd. Teaching, 1973-79. Mem. Nat. Council Social Studies, Am. Edni. Research Assn., Assn. Supervision and Curriculum Devel., Luth. Human Relations Assn., Phi Delta Kappa. Lutheran. Author: (with others) Education and Social Crisis, 1967; Social Studies in Secondary Schools, 1970; Selected Case Studies in Am. History, 1971. Home: 2631 Burd Pl St Louis Park MN 55426 Office: 104 Burton Hall U Minn Minneapolis MN 55455

GAREE, WAYNE ALAN, ins. co. mgr.; b. Cin., Sept. 15, 1945; s. Lionel Leonard and Mary Jean (Weimeyer) G.; B.A., Morehead State U., 1967; postgrad. U. Oreg., 1967-68; m. Peggy, Sept. 4, 1965; children—Jane Ann, Paula Kay, Susan Elaine. Group trainee Travelers Ins. Co., Hartford, Conn., 1968-69, field rep., Seattle, 1969-71, account exec., Portland, Oreg., 1971-74, sr. account exec., Cin., 1974-75; sales rep. State Mut. Life, Cin., 1975-76, dist. group mgr., Cin., 1976-81, regional group mgr., 1981—. Youth dir. Bapt. Ch., youth choir dir.; pres. Bowling League; coach volleyball and softball teams. Republican. Home: 4734 Cabin Ridge Dr Batavia OH 45103 Office: State Mutual Life 621 Mehring Way Suite 418 Cincinnati OH 45202

GARFIELD, JUANITA WILMOTH, educator; b. Bellepoint, W.Va., July 20, 1930; d. Clayton and Margaret (Weaver) Weeks; A.B., Marshall U., 1954, M.A., 1958; Ed.D., U. Mo., 1968; postgrad. Wayne State U., 1964-65, Eastern Mich. U., 1980-81; m. James M. Garfield, Nov. 23, 1973; children—Jonathan Noel Wilmoth, Penny Lynn Wilmoth; stepchildren—Robert, Mary Jean, Nancy Ruth. Tchr., Deckerville Community Schs., 1956-58; tchr., asst. prin. Farmington Public Schs., 1958-66; instr. U. Mo., Columbia, 1966-68; prof. tchr. edn. Eastern Mich. U., Ypsilanti, 1968—, coordinator Career Edn. Center, 1973-76, coordinator sch. assistance, 1979-81; vis. lectr. Auburn (Ala.) U., 1971-72. Vol., Girl Scouts U.S.A., 1979, Heritage Festival, Ypsilanti, 1980. Career Edn. Consortium annual grantee, 1973-76; Mich. Dept. Edn. career edn. media grantee, 1976. Mem. Am. Assn. Supervision and Curriculum Devel., Assn. Edn. Young Children, Mich. Reading Assn., Pi Lambda Theta, Phi Delta Kappa. Baptist. Club: Washtenaw Country. Contbr. articles to profl. jours. Home: 885 Cliffs Dr 303 Ypsilanti MI 48197 Office: 305 Pierce Hall Eastern Mich U Ypsilanti MI 48197

GARFINKEL, JOSEPH, mdse. and mgmt. exec.; b. N.Y.C., Aug. 27, 1915; s. Hyman and Jennie (Levin) G.; B.S., U. Pa., 1942; postgrad. U. Cin., 1961; m. Ruth Helen Mauer, Dec. 29, 1946; children—Barbara Louise, Robert Michael. Exec. trainee, jr. exec. merchandising L. Bamberger & Co. div. R. H. Macy Co., Newark, 1946-57; buyer L. Bamberger and Co., 1952-57; mdse. mgr. Federated Dept. Stores, Cin., 1957-63; mgmt. cons., Springfield, Mass., 1963-64; gen. mgr. Rayco Div., B.F. Goodrich Co., Paramus, N.J., 1964-70, mdse. mgr., Akron, 1970-72, dir. mktg., 1972-73, gen. mdse. mgr., 1973-80; v.p. B-Dry System, Inc., 1980—. Served to capt. AUS, 1942-46. Mem. Springfield C. of C., Nat. Indsl. Conf. Bd., Internat. Franchise Assn., Am. Mktg. Assn. Club: B'nai B'rith. Home: 2520 Brice Rd Akron OH 44313 Office: 1341 Copley Rd Akron OH 44320

GARFINKLE, RONALD GEORGE, accountant; b. Chgo., June 14, 1938; s. Philip G. and Pearl (Wasserman) G.; B.S., Washington U., St. Louis, 1960, M.B.A., 1961; m. Jill Komiss, June 26, 1960; children—Robert, Richard, Judith, Lauren. Pvt. practice accounting, Chgo., 1966—. Served with USNR, 1962-65. C.P.A., Ill. Mem. Am. Inst. C.P.A.'s, Ill. Soc. C.P.A.'s. Club: Brairwood Country. Home: 2376 Sheridan Rd Highland Park IL 60035 Office: 1737 W Howard St Chicago IL 60626

GARG, VIJAY KUMAR, assn. exec., civil engr.; b. Jagangirabad, Uttar Pradesh, India, July 7, 1938; s. Reoti Saran and Prem (Vati) G.; came to U.S., 1965, naturalized, 1976; B.Sc., Banaras U., 1960; M.S., U. Calif., Berkeley, 1965; Ph.D., Ill. Inst. Tech., 1973; m. Pushpa Bansal, May 11, 1961; children—Neena, Meena, Ravi. Asst. prof. structural engring. U. Jodhpur, India. 1960-65; structural engr. Chgo. Bridge & Iron Co., Oakbrook, Ill., 1967-69; project engr., devel. engr. Electro-Motive div. Gen. Motors Corp., LaGrange, Ill., 1969-76; mgr. dynamics research Assn. Am. R.R.'s, Chgo., 1976—; adj. asso. prof. Ill. Inst. Tech., Chgo., 1976-78; chmn. civil engring. Midwest Coll. Engring., Lombard, Ill., 1977—. Registered profl. engr., structural engr., Ill. Fellow ASCE; mem. ASME, Am. Ry. Engrs. Assn. Hindu. Author: (with S. Divakaran) Structural Analysis, 1962, Strength of Materials, 1967; contbr. articles to profl. jours.; patentee locomotive truck design. Home: 146 Somerset St Willowbrook IL 60521 Office: 3140 S Federal St Chicago IL 60616

GARIN-VARGAS, PURA GEMARINO, anesthesiologist; b. Guimbal, Philippines; d. Ricardo and Purification (Gemarino) G.; A.A., U. San Agustin, Philippines, 1952; M.D., U. Santo Tomas, Manila, Philippines, 1957; m. Andres I. Vargas, Mar. 15, 1960; children—Andrew, Albert, Arthur. Intern, Lynn (Mass.) Gen. Hosp., 1958-59, resident in pathology, 1959-60; resident in Ob-Gyn, Balt. City Hosp., 1960-61, Sinai Hosp., Balt., 1961-62; resident in anesthesiology Montefiore Hosp. and Med. Center, Bronx, N.Y., 1962-65, chief resident, 1964-65; house physician Suburban Hosp., Cleve., 1969; jr. attending anesthesiologist St. Vincent Charity Hosp., Cleve., 1970; chief anesthesiologist Fisher Titus Hosp., Norwalk, Ohio, 1970—, chief of med. staff, 1979. Bd. dirs. South Shore Lung Assn., 1976—, treas., 1978—; bd. dirs. Huron County chpt. Am. Cancer Soc., 1977—. Diplomate Am. Bd. Anesthesiology. Fellow Am. Coll. Anesthesiology; mem. Huron County Med. Assn., Ohio State Med. Assn., AMA, Am. Soc. Anesthesiologists, Am. Soc. Regional Anesthesia, Ohio Anesthesiologists Assn., Am. Med. Women's Assn., Profl. Womens Assn. Roman Catholic. Office: 257 Benedict Ave Norwalk OH 44857

GARLAND, DONALD MERRILL, physician; b. St. Paul, Oct. 7, 1935; s. Donald Field and Anne Clara (Merrill) G.; B.A., U. Minn., 1957; M.D., U. Rochester (N.Y.), 1961; M.P.H., U. Mich., 1964; m. Patricia Mary Olsson, June 16, 1981; children by previous marriage—Lorraine Anne, Tracy Marie, Karen Elizabeth. Intern, Highland Hosp., Rochester, 1961-62, resident, 1962-63; resident U. Mich. Hosp., Ann Arbor, 1963-65; asso. med. dir. Pontiac Motor div. Gen. Motors Corp., Pontiac, Mich., 1965-74; med. dir. Mpls. area Honeywell Inc., Mpls., 1974—. Diplomate Am. Bd. Preventive Medicine. Mem. AMA, Minn. State, Hennepin County med Am. Acad. Occupational Medicine, Am., North Central occup med. assns. Office: Honeywell Inc Honeywell Plaza Minneapolis 55408

GARMEZY, NORMAN, psychologist; b. N.Y.C., June 18, 1918; Isadore and Laura (Weiss) G.; B.B.A. in Econs., Coll. City N.Y., 193 M.A. in Guidance and Counseling, Columbia U., 1940; Ph.D. in Clin Psychology, State U. Iowa, 1950; m. Edith Linick, Aug. 8, 1945; children—Kathy, Andrew, Lawrence. USPHS fellow in clin. psychology Worcester (Mass.) State Hosp., 1947-48; asst. prof. to prof. psychology Duke U., Durham, N.C., 1950-61, dir. undergrad. studies, 1951-56, dir. clin. psychology tng. program, 1957-60; tng. specialist in psychology NIMH, Bethesda, Md., 1956-57; sr. research psychologist Worcester State Hosp.; prof. U. Minn., Mpls., 1961—, dir. Center for Personality Research, 1962-67; clin. prof. psychiatry dept. U. Rochester (N.Y.) Sch. Medicine, 1969-79; vis. prof. U. Copenhagen, 1965-66, U. P.R., 1969, Cornell U., 1969-70, Stanford U., 1979-80; fellow Center for Advanced Study in Behavioral Scis., 1979-80; vis. colleague Inst. Psychiatry, Maudsley Hosp., London, 1975-76; Lasker lectr. Michael Reese Hosp. & Med. Center, Chgo., 1971; Phillips lectr. Haverford (Pa.) Coll., 1973; mem. com. on research in schizophrenia Scottish Rite, Boston, 1968-82; cons. NIMH, past mem. grants coms.; spl. rev. cons. Nat. Inst. Drug Abuse, 1974—; mem. task force on research Presdl. Commn. on Mental Health, 1977-78; dir. Founds. Fund for Research in Psychiatry, 1976—. Served with U.S. Army, 1943-45. Recipient Lifetime Research Career award NIMH, 1962—; co-recipient Stanley Dean award for basic behavioral research in schizophrenia, 1967. Fellow Am. Psychol. Assn. (Distinguished Scientist award sect. 3, 1974, Master lectr. 1975, pres. div. clin. psychology 1977-78), Am. Psychopath. Assn.; mem. AAUP, AAAS, Psychonomic Soc., Soc. Research in Child Devel., Assn. Child Psychology and Psychiatry, Assn. Advancement Psychology (chmn. bd. trustees 1976-78), Sigma Xi. Club: Cosmos (Washington). Contbr. numerous articles in field to books and profl. jours.; author (with G. Kimble and E. Zigler) Principles of General Psychology, 5th edit., 1980; mem. internat. adv. editorial bd. Schizophrenia Bull., 1974—, Psychol. Medicine, 1976—; corr. editor Jour. Child Psychology and Psychiatry, 1975—. Home: 5115 Lake Ridge Rd Edina MN 55436 Office: N419 Elliott Hall U Minn Minneapolis MN 55455

GARN, PAUL DONALD, educator; b. Fremont, Ohio, July 7, 1920; s. Charles Verner and Margaret Jeannette (Horn) G.; B.S., Ohio State U., 1948, M.S., 1949, Ph.D., 1952; m. Betty Jane Reid, July 14, 1979; children by previous marriage—Michael Charles, David Allen, Kathy Anne. With Bell Telephone Labs., Murray Hill, N.J., 1952-63; faculty U. Akron (Ohio), 1963—, now prof. chemistry; with U.S. Nat. Bur. Standards, Washington, 1972-75; guest prof. U. Cologne (Germany), 1973-74; cons. Glass Containers Corp. Served with U.S. Army, 1939-41, 42-46. Recipient DuPont-ICTA award, 1977; Humboldt fellow, 1973-74; various research grants. Fellow N.Am. Thermal Analysis Soc. (pres. 1969); mem. Am. Chem. Soc., Internat. Confedn. for Thermal Analysis (council 1974—), Am. Inst. Chemists (fellow), Sigma Xi, Phi Lambda Upsilon. Presbyterian. Author: Thermoanalytical Methods of Investigation, 1965. Editorial bd. Jour. Thermal Analysis, 1969—, NATAS Notes, 1980—. Home: 2241 Massillon Rd Akron OH 44312 Office: 302 E Buchtel Ave Akron OH 44325

GARNER, COLUMBUS GREENE, forest products co. exec.; b. Sparta, Ga., Nov. 3, 1920; s. William S. and Mary L. (Boyer) G.; B.B.A. in Acctg., U. Ga., 1948; A.M.P., Harvard U., 1964; m. Marie Hilton, Aug. 16, 1952; children—Tracie Marie, Hilton Greene. With Atlanta Paper Co., 1949-53; mem. Mead Packaging div. The Mead Corp., Dayton, Ohio, 1953-69, group v.p., 1969-78, sr. group v.p., 1978-80, pres., chief operating officer, 1980-81, chief exec. officer, 1981—, also dir.; dir. 1st Nat. Bank of Atlanta. Served with USAAF, 1942-44. Club: Dayton Rotary. Office: Courthouse Plaza NE Dayton OH 45463

GARNER, LARRY LEN, splty. chems. mfg. co. exec.; b. Eli, Nebr., June 11, 1934; s. Len M. and Ruth (Galloway) G.; B.S., Chadron State Tchrs. Coll., 1959; m. Edna J. Espetveidt, Aug. 25, 1965; children—Laird, Lori. Phys. edn. tchr., coach public schs., Cherry County, Nebr., 1954-55, 58-60, Cold Lake, Alta., Can., 1960-63, Sylvan Lake, Alta., 1963-67; phys. edn. cons. public schs., Topeka, 1967-68; pres. Garner Enterprises, Topeka, 1968-71, Manhattan Foam Co. (Kans.), 1975-78, Garnite Systems, Inc., Chapman, Kans., 1978—. Served with U.S. Army, 1955-58. Mem. Nat. Fedn. Ind. Bus., Kans. Assn. Commerce and Industry. Club: Lions. Home: 108 W 8th St Chapman KS 67431 Office: Garnite Systems Inc PO Box 502 Chapman KS 67431

GARNER, SUELLYN, ednl. adminstr.; b. Olney, Ill., Dec. 7, 1942; d. Charles H. Lindsey and Lucile (Wiles) Cooley; M.A., Eastern Ill. U., 1964, principalship cert., 1981; m. Donald P. Garner, June 12, 1966; children—Josh Adam, Dirk Andrew. Accompanist, East Leyden High Sch., Franklin Park, Ill., 1964-65, asst. choral dir., 1965-66; tchr. music Jefferson Jr. High Sch., Charleston, Ill., 1966-67, Charleston Jr. High Sch., 1974-76; instr. music Lakeland Coll., Mattoon, Ill., 1968-74, Eastern Ill. U., 1978-79; dir. project arts in basic edn. Community Unit Dist. No. 1, Charleston, 1980—; pvt. piano tchr., 1960-80. Mem. arts adv. bd. Ill. State Bd. Edn. Mem. Music Educators Nat. Conf., Nat. Art Edn. Assn., Assn. Supervision and Curriculum Devel., Ill. Alliance for Arts Edn. (membership chmn.), Phi Delta Kappa, Sigma Alpha Iota. Home: 770 12th St Charleston IL 61920

GARNETT, ROBERT FREDERICK, univ. adminstr.; b. Evansville, Ind., Oct. 23, 1933; s. James Rudy and Mary Lucile (Raley) G.; B.A., U. Evansville, 1956; M.S., Purdue U., 1962, Ph.D., 1966; m. Dianne K. Wampler, July 24, 1976; children—Robert, Jane, Anne. Teller, Citizens Bank, Evansville, 1958-59; tchr. Evansville-Vanderburgh County Schs., 1959-61; asst. dir. Univ. Evening Coll., U. Evansville, 1962-63, dir. counseling center, 1963-67, coordinator grad. studies in counseling, guidance counselor, 1967-74, prof. edn., 1972-74, dean Sch. Edn., 1974-78, v.p. univ. planning, 1978—; cons.; chairperson tchr. accreditation teams State of Ind., 1957-80; mem. Ind. Career Edn. Adv. Com., 1974-75, Ind. Adv. Com. for Pupil Personnel Service, 1973-76. Bd. dirs. Family and Children's Services, 1972-75, Vanderburgh County Assn. Mental Health, 1963-73. Served to 1st lt. USMC, 1956-58. NDEA fellow, 1962-63; Gen. Electric fellow, 1960; recipient awards. Mem. Assn. Colls. Tchr. Edn., Assn. Devel. Computer-Based Instrn. Systems, Nat. CVIS Consortium, Am. Personnel and Guidance Assn., Phi Delta Kappa, Phi Kappa Phi. Republican. Mem. Christian Ch. Co-editor Hoosier Guidelines, 1969-72; co-author: A Survey of Adult Education in the State of Indiana, 1971; project dir. televised career edn. series, 1975-76. Home: 1635 Brookside Dr Evansville IN 47714 Office: PO Box 329 Evansville IN 47702

GARREN, MORTON ALAN, electronics co. exec.; b. Mpls., Nov. 3, 1930; s. Nathan Oscar and Jennie (Schusterman) Gurewitz; student U. Minn., 1954-55, Am. Inst. of the Air, 1955-56; m. Marilyn Anita Blinder, June 7, 1953; children—Howard Mark, Steven Richard. Announcer, TV weatherman KMSP TV, Mpls., 1960-66; liquor

Co., Mpls., 1966-73; sales mgr. Dial 4; exec. v.p., gen. mgr. Audio-Sine, mktg., also corporate dir.; gen. mgr. s, Inc., 1979—. Hon. guardian City of AF, 1951-54. Mem. Assn. Multi Image, ator, researcher, producer UFO Fact or Fiction series, 1972-75. Home: 1644 Texas Ave S 55426 Office: 510 Halsey Ln Minneapolis MN

T, CHARLES WESLEY, therapist and counselor; b. ville, Tex., Apr. 17, 1923; s. Charles Ballard and Opal (Shaver) .A., So. Meth. U., 1943, B.D., 1946, M.A., 1948; Ph.D., N.Y. U., 53; m. Avis Devon Bedford, Sept. 24, 1979; children—Susanna Wesley, Charles Davidson, Alice Frances, Thomas Ruston. Pvt. practice therapy, Prairie Village, Kans., 1970—; cons. Johnson County Dist. Cts., 1970—. Mem. Am. Psychol. Assn., Kans. Psychol. Assn. Research in geriatrics.

GARRETT, JOHN PATRICK, ednl. adminstr.; b. Aurora, Ill., May 5, 1942; s. John George and Twila Louise (Oswald) G.; B.S., So. Ill. U., 1965; M.S., 1974, Ph.D., 1981; m. Ann Michele Rosson, Dec. 28, 1966; children—Joseph Charles, Matthew Alexander, Katherine Valerie. Tchr. sci. Mt. Vernon (Ill.) Twp. High Sch., 1966-67, 70-75, adminstrv. asst., 1975-79, asst. prin., 1979—. Chmn. library services com. Mt. Vernon Public Library Bd. Trustees, 1980—. Served with USN, 1966-70; Vietnam. Mem. Assn. Supervision and Curriculum Devel., Nat. Assn. Secondary Sch. Prins., Ill. Library Assn. Home: 721 Magnolia St Mount Vernon IL 62864 Office: Mt Vernon Twp High Sch Mount Vernon IL 62864

GARRETT, ROBERT ARTHUR, radio sta. exec.; b. Kansas City, Kans., Nov. 21, 1948; s. Gerald Arthur and Icel Dorene (Platter) G.; B.S. in Journalism, U. Kans., 1970; m. Janice Hess, July 31, 1971; 1 son, Benjamin Arthur. Account exec. Stas. KBEA-KBEY, Kansas City, Kans., 1971-72, Sta. KUDL, Kansas City, 1972-75; account exec. Sta. KYYS, Kansas City, 1975-76, sales mgr., 1976-77, sta. mgr., 1978-79; gen. mgr. Sta. KYYS, Kansas City, 1979—. Mem. Advt. Sales and Exec. Club, Sigma Delta Chi. Composer numerous songs. Office: 3030 Summit St Kansas City MO 64108

GARRETT, ROBERT DEAN, ins. co. exec.; b. Fairfield, Ill., Apr. 13, 1933; s. Roy Smith and Halene (Pickett) G.; student public schs., Carmi, Ill.; m. Peggy Jean Spence, Dec. 8, 1955; children—Evelyn, Brenda, Ronald. With U.S. Post Office, Chgo., 1954-60, Gen. Telephone Co., So. Ill., 1960-67; agt. MFA Ins. Co., Mt. Carmel, Ill., 1967-70; with Fed. Kemper Ins. Co., Decatur, Ill., 1970—, v.p. adminstrn., 1977—. Bd. dirs. Jr. Achievement, Decatur, 1978—, Decatur Boys Club, 1979—, Council of Community Services, Decatur, 1978—. Served with USAF, 1950-54. Recipient Cert. in Gen. Ins., Ins. Inst. Am., 1975. Mem. Nat. Assn. Ind. Insurers (mem. personnel com.), C. of C., Decatur Personnel Relations Assn. Methodist. Home: 2241 W Packard St Decatur IL 62526 Office: 2001 E Mound Rd Decatur IL 62526

GARRISON, MORROW BROWN, mfg. co. exec.; b. Danville, Ala., Mar. 21, 1930; s. Leldon D. and Grace Loraine (Sharp) G.; B.S., Northeastern U., 1957; m. Gertrude Bouzan, June 13, 1953; 1 dau., Brenda Gail. Mem. audit staff Arthur Anderson & Co., Chgo., 1957-59; internal auditor Avildsen Tools & Machines, Chgo., 1959-64; controller, v.p., Am. Machine & Sci., Inc., Elgin, Ill., 1964-79, dir., pres., 1979—; pres., dir. Metetelic Corp., Elgin, LeWa Co., Elgin, Bldg. Mgmt. Corp., Elgin, Ill. Property Mgmt. Corp., Elgin; pres. Mfrs. Acceptance Corp., Elgin; sec., treas., dir. Chgo. Capital Corp.; pres. Park Safe Deposit Co., Elgin; sec., dir. Master Machine Tools, Inc., Hutchinson, Kans.; pres., dir. Quasar Contemporaries, Inc., Mt. Prospect, Ill.; pres., dir. Chelco Corp., Elgin, GSC, Inc., Elgin; dir. Gaertner Sci. Co., Chgo.; sec., treas., dir. Newco, Inc., Waukegan, Ill. Served with USN, 1948-52. Clubs: Union League, Northeastern U. Alumni. Office: 530 Slade Ave Elgin IL 60120

GARRISON, RAY HARLAN, lawyer; b. Allen County, Ky., Aug. 6, 1922; s. Emmett Washington and Ollie Irene (Keen) G.; B.A., Western Ky. U., 1942; M.A. (fellow), U. Ky., 1944; postgrad. Northwestern U., 1945-46; J.D., U. Chgo., 1949; m. Eunice Anne Bolz, Oct. 7, 1961. Tax accountant Ky. Dept. Revenue, Frankfort, 1943, supr. escheats, 1944-45, fiscal analyst, 1945; research asst. Bur. Bus. Research, U. Ky., Lexington, 1943-44; admitted to Ky. bar, 1951, Ill. bar, 1962, U.S. Ct. Appeals bar, 1962, Tax Ct. U.S. bar, 1962, U.S. Ct. Internat. Trade bar, 1968, U.S. Supreme Ct. bar, 1980; research asso. Fedn. Tax Adminstrs., Chgo., 1946-52; spl. atty. U.S. Treasury Dept., St. Louis, 1952-57, spl. asst., 1957-59, asst. regional counsel, 1959-61; sr. counsel Internat. Harvester Co., Chgo., 1961—. Lectr. Loyola U., Chgo., 1949-51. Del. Ill. Constnl. Conv., 1969-70. Mem. Ill. Racing Bd., 1975—; mem. adv. bd. Ill. Thoroughbred Breeders Fund, 1976—. Mem. N.A.M. (mem. taxation com. 1969—), Ill. Mfrs. Assn. (mem. taxation com. 1969—), Motor Vehicle Mfrs. Assn. (mem. taxation com. 1963—), Nat. Tax Assn., Am., Ill., Ky., Chgo. bar assns., Nat. Assn. State Racing Commrs., Chgo. Tax Club, Beta Gamma Sigma, Ill. Hist. Soc., South Suburban Geneal. and Hist. Soc. (dir. 1973-77), Ky. Hist. Soc., Mecklenburg Hist. Assn. Club: Filson. Contbr. articles to various publs. Home: 2625-F Hawthorne Ln Flossmoor IL 60422 Office: 401 N Michigan Ave Chicago IL 60611

GARRISON, WILLIAM LLOYD, social worker; b. Ridgway, Pa., Dec. 26, 1939; s. Lloyd and Mary Rebecca (Morrow) G.; B.A. in Psychology, Ohio Wesleyan U., 1962; postgrad Garrett Theol. Sem., 1962-63; M.S.W., Fla. State U., 1967; M.S. in Mgmt., Case Western Res. U., 1976; m. Mary Jo Florio, May 30, 1964; children—David, Mark. Caseworker, Mcpl. Ct. Chgo., 1963-64, United Cerebral Palsy Assn., Phila., 1964-65; psychiat. social worker Bellefaire, Shaker Heights, Ohio, 1967-74; dir. personnel and tng. Center for Human Services, Cleve., 1974-81, dir. resource devel., 1981—; adj. instr. Sch. Applied Social Sci., Case Western Res. U., 1974-80; v.p. E.A. Mabry Inc., Akron, Ohio, 1970—. Dist. Cub Scout chmn. Boy Scouts Am., 1978-81, dist. chmn., 1981—; mem. Big Bros. Cleve., 1968-73; pres. Mayfield Heights Homeowners Assn., 1974—; mem. bd. Garfield Meml. United Meth. Ch., 1979—; bd. dirs. Reach Out, 1977—. Recipient Award of Merit, Boy Scouts Am., 1980. Fellow Menninger Found.; mem. Acad. Cert. Social Workers, Nat. Assn. Social Workers, Am. Soc. Personnel Adminstrs., Personnel Accreditation Inst. (accredited), Nat. Eagle Scout Assn., Phi Mu Alpha. Office: 1001 Huron Rd Cleveland OH 44115

GARSON, WILLIAM J., banker, writer; b. Hammond, Ind., May 1, 1917; s. John Soterus and Helen Glenn (McKennan) G.; B.A., Milton Coll., 1939; postgrad. Grad. Sch. Bank Mktg., Northwestern U., 1968; m. Florence Rebecca Penstone, Sept. 21, 1974; children (by previous marriage)—Geneva (Mrs. Robert LaMay), Gary William. Mng. editor, reporter, columnist Rockford (Ill.) Register-Republic, 1939-55; pub. relations dir. Sundstrand Corp., Rockford, 1956-65; community info. officer Rockford C. of C., 1965-66; dir. spl. services City Nat. Bank & Trust Co. Rockford, 1966—; pub. relations cons. imagination plus, Rockford, 1955-66. Bd. dirs. Tb Assn., Heart Assn., A.R.C., 1952-54; Recipient George Washington Honor awards Freedoms Found., 1965-66. Mem. Am. Interprofl. Inst., Rockford C. of C. (Community Service award 1952), Am. Inst. Banking, Bank Mktg. Assn., Internat. Assn. Bus. Communicators, Internat. Word Processing Assn., Rockford Hist. Soc. (pres.). Methodist. Author: Daddy Wore An Apron, 1974; Brother Earth, 1975; The Knight on Broadway, 1978; also numerous short stories and articles; co-author: Political Primer, 1960; We The People..., 1976. Home: 3516 Meadow Ln Rockford IL 61107 Office: Box 3126 Rockford IL 61106

GARTNER, MICHAEL GAY, newspaper exec.; b. Des Moines, Oct. 25, 1938; s. Carl David and Mary Marguerite (Gay) G.; B.A., Carleton Coll., 1960; J.D., N.Y. U., 1969; m. Barbara Jeanne McCoy, May 25, 1968; children—Melissa, Christopher, Michael. Admitted to N.Y. bar, 1970, Iowa bar, 1979; with Wall St. Jour., N.Y.C., 1960-74, page one editor, 1970-74; exec. editor Des Moines Register and Tribune, 1974-76, editor, 1976—, v.p., 1975-76, exec. v.p., 1977, pres., 1978—, also dir.; dir. Comml. Printing, Inc. Bd. dirs. Living History Farms, Des Moines, trustee Simpson Coll. Mem. Am. Soc. Newspaper Editors (dir. 1979—), Assn. Bar City N.Y., Am. Bar Assn., Am. Press Inst. (dir. 1980—). Clubs: Embassy, Des Moines, Wakonda (Des Moines); Garden of the Gods (Colorado Springs). Author syndicated column. Office: 715 Locust St Des Moines IA 50304

GARTNER, W. JOSEPH, business exec.; b. Chgo., Apr. 8, 1928; s. Andrew W. and Edith M. (Frame) G.; B.A., Knox Coll., 1950; postgrad. Northwestern U., 1954-60; m. Lois Ellen McQueen, Aug. 7, 1954; children—Lisa Dianne, Bryan Wright, Andrew Scott. Creative writer Montgomery Ward & Co., Chgo., 1953-58; planning and research mgr. Lions Internat., 1958-62; creative account supr. E.F. McDonald Co., 1962-63; dir. response advt. mgr. Encyclopaedia Britannica, 1964-68; creative dir. V.J. Giesler Co., 1968-74; pres. Gartner & Assos., Inc., 1974—. Served with inf. U.S. Army, 1951-53. Mem. Nat. Soc. Fund Raising Execs. (dir. 1979-81), Assn. for Children with Learning Disabilities (nat. pres. 1971-72), Ill. Assn. for Children with Learning Disabilities (pres. 1968-70), Direct Mail Mktg. Assn., Direct Mktg. Creative Guild, Chgo. Assn. Direct Mktg. Congregationalist. Clubs: Cliff Dwellers, Lions (Glen Ellyn, Ill.). Home: 406 Hill Ave Glen Ellyn IL 60137 Office: Gartner & Assos 2 N Riverside Plaza Suite 2400 Chicago IL 60606

GARTON, ROBERT DEAN, state senator; b. Chariton, Iowa, Aug. 18, 1933; s. Jesse Glenn and Ruth Irene (Wright) G.; B.S., Iowa State U., 1955; M.S., Cornell U., 1959; m. Barbara Hicks, June 17, 1955; children—Bradford, Brenda. Personnel rep. Cummins Engine Co., Columbus, Ind., 1959-61; owner Garton Assos., exec. search, Columbus, 1961—, Careers Center Employment Agy., 1973—; mem. Ind. Senate, 1970—, minority caucus chmn., 1976—, 79, majority caucus chmn., 1979-81, pres. pro tempore, 1981—. Pres. Ind. Pub. Health Found., 1976—; chmn. Ind. Civil Rights Commn., 1969-70; mem. exec. com. Nat. Fedn. Young Republicans, 1966; mem. adv. bd. Ind. Assn. Indsl. Nurses, 1972—; bd. dirs. Rural Water System, Columbus, 1969—, Ind. Wilderness Challenge, Inc.; v.p. Ind. Rural Water Assn., 1979—; hon. bd. mem. Five-County Big Bros. and Sisters, Inc. Served with USMCR, 1955-57. Named Hon. Citizen Iowa, 1962; winner internat. speech contest Toastmasters, 1962; recipient Distinguished Service award Jr. C. of C. Columbus, 1968, One of 5 Outstanding Young Men in Ind., 1968. Mem. Beta Theta Pi. Rotarian. Home: Rural Route 14 Box 103 Wood Lake Columbus IN 47201 Office: 606 Franklin St Columbus IN 47201

GARTRELL, RICHARD BLAIR, travel mktg. exec.; b. Oakland, Calif., Dec. 7, 1940; s. Thorold Ivan Lance and Phyllis May Gartrell; B.A. in Speech, San Francisco State U., 1963, M.A. in Speech Communication, 1969; postgrad. U. Nebr., 1970-80; m. Joan Frances White, Aug. 5, 1967; children—Diane Lillian, Lance Richard. Grad. asst. dept. speech communications San Francisco State U., 1968-69; asst. prof. speech communications and dir. forensics Doane Coll., Crete, Nebr., 1969-76; dir. div. of travel and tourism Nebr. Dept. of Econ. Devel., Lincoln, 1976-80; dir. Ann Arbor (Mich.) Conf. and Visitors Bur., 1980—; resource cons. to U. Nebr. Agrl. Communication Employment Seminar, 1977, 78; communication cons. Dorsey Labs., Lincoln, 1973; mem. tourism and recreation adv. com. Old West Regional Commn., 1979-80. Mem. Citizens Com. for Nebr. Studies, 1979-80; chmn. socials concerns com. St. Paul Meth. Ch., Lincoln, 1971-73; deacon Presbyn. Ch., 1980—; bd. dirs. Old West Trail Found., 1979-80. Served to lt. USN, 1964-68; Vietnam. Named Outstanding Young Coll. Speech Tchr. of Nebr., 1972; recipient Outstanding Service award Nebr. Speech Communication Assn., 1978. Mem. Am. Soc. Assn. Execs., Nat. Tour Brokers Assn., Assn. of Travel Mktg. Execs., Mich. Assn. of Conv. and Visitors Bureaus (dir. 1981—), Internat. Assn. Conv. and Visitors Bureaus, Am. Bus Assn., Navy League, U.S. Naval Inst., Pi Kappa Delta (province historian 1970-73). Republican. Presbyterian. Contbr. articles on speech communications to profl. publs. Office: Ann Arbor Conference and Visitors Bureau 207 E Washington Ann Arbor MI 48104

GARVELINK, ROGER HERMAN, supt. schs.; b. Holland, Mich., Apr. 12, 1936; s. Louis and Georgianna (Speet) G.; A.B., Hope Coll., 1958; M.A., U. Mich., 1961, Ph.D., 1970; m. Carol Nieuwsma, Aug. 7, 1959; children—Todd, Bradford, Wendell. Math. and sci. tchr., Mount Clemens, Mich., 1958-59; math. tchr., Zeeland, Mich., 1959-62; jr. high sch. prin., Grosse Ile, Mich., 1963-66; high sch. prin., West Bloomfield, Mich., 1966-72; asst. supt., West Bloomfield, 1972-75; supt. Monroe-Woodbury, N.Y., 1975-78; supt., Birmingham, Mich., 1978—; adj. prof. Eastern Mich. U., 1972—, Oakland U., 1980-81. Trustee, Tuxedo Park Hosp.; adv. Channel 13, N.Y.C.; chmn. United Found. Mem. Am. Assn. Sch. Adminstrs., Assn. Supervision and Curriculum Devel., Mich. Assn. Sch. Bds., Mich. Assn. Supervision and Curriculum Devel. Club: Rotary. Home: 31349 Sleepy Hollow Birmingham MI 48010 Office: 550 W Merrill St Birmingham MI 48012

GARVIN, THOMAS MICHAEL, cookie/cracker mfg. co. exec.; b. Chgo., Dec. 31, 1935; s. Thomas Martin and Mary I. (Egan) G.; B.S., Loyola U., Chgo., 1957, M.B.A., 1969; m. Mary K. Hayes, Oct. 18, 1958; children—Thomas M., Martin J., Kevin P., Michael J., Kathleen M. Auditor, Coopers & Lybrand, Chgo., 1958-61; asst. to controller EKCO Products Co., Chgo., 1961-65; group controller housewares, 1965-69; corp. controller Keebler Co., Elmhurst, Ill., 1969-71, fin. v.p. and treas., 1971-74, exec. v.p. ops., 1974-76, pres., chief operating officer, 1976-78, pres., chief exec. officer, 1978—; dir. U.B. (Holdings) US Ltd. Bd. dirs. Keebler Found.; mem. lay bd. Benet Acad.; adv. bd. Loyola U. Served with M.I.. U.S. Army, 1958. C.P.A., Ill. Mem. Biscuit and Cracker Mfrs. Assn. (chmn. 1980-82), Ill. Soc. C.P.A.s. Clubs: Executives, Chgo. Golf (Chgo.); Metropolitan (N.Y.C.). Office: One Hollow Tree Ln Elmhurst IL 60126

GARY, DOUGLAS EDMOND, advt. agy. exec.; b. Salina, Kans., July 19, 1922; s. Charles Hamilton and Eloda Claire (Smalley) G.; diploma in lang. studies Johns Hopkins U., 1944; B.S., Kans. State U., 1947; m. Elizabeth Jane Fickel, Aug. 10, 1944; children—Sarah Elizabeth, Leslie Ann. With, Sta. KBUC, Montrose, Colo., 1947-48, Sta. WRBL, Columbus, Ga., 1948-50, Sta. KVGB, Great Bend, Kans., 1950-63, Stas. KZIX and KCOL, Fort Collins, Colo., 1963-65; public relations dir. Drury Coll., Springfield, Mo., 1965-73; v.p. Uhlis Advt. Agy., Springfield, 1973-78; founder, pres. Gary Advt. & Public Relations, Ltd., Springfield, Mo., 1978—. Served with U.S. Army, 1942-46; ETO. Mem. Am. Advt. Fedn., Profl. Journalism Soc., Sigma Delta Chi, Sigma Phi Epsilon, Phi Mu Alpha. Presbyterian. Club: Springfield Ad (dir. 1980—). Home: 2205 Ridgewood Dr Springfield MO 65804 Office: Gary Advertising & Public Relations Ltd 1835 S Stewart St Springfield MO 65804

GARZIA, RICARDO FRANCISCO, computer co. exec.; b. Buenos Aires, Argentina, Sept. 19, 1926; s. Mario Francisco and Zulema Maria (Alvarez) G.; came to U.S., 1967, naturalized, 1975; B.S. in Elec. Engring., Otto Krause Sch., 1945; M.S. in Elec. Engring., La Plata U., 1950; m. Julia Elisa Berrud, Oct. 2, 1948; children—Liliana Julia, Silvia Cristina, Mario Ricardo, Fernando Marcelo. Prof. Nat. Indsl. Sch., Buenos Aires, 1951-53; prof., Nat. Tech. U., Buenos Aires, 1954-67, chmn. elec. dept., 1964-67, dir. computer center, 1964-67; prin. engr. Gen. Dynamics/Electronics, Rochester, N.Y., 1967-69; computer scientist Computer Scis. Corp., Huntsville, Ala., 1969-71; mgr. tech. applications The Babcock & Wilcox Co., Barberton, Ohio, 1971—. Consejo Nacional de Investigacions Cientificas y Tecnicas grantee Mass. Inst. Tech., 1960-61. Mem. IEEE, Instrument Soc. Am., Ops. Research Soc. Am. Author: Transformada Z, 1966; Introduccion a la Computation Digital, 1968; contbg. author: Large-Scale Dynamical Systems, 1976, Rational Fault Analysis, 1977. Home: 509 Vosello Ave Akron OH 44313 Office: 20 S Van Buren St Barberton OH 44203

GARZONETTI, JEFFREY ROCCO, probation officer; b. Chgo., June 25, 1953: s. Angelo Rocco and Emily Mary (Schmidt) G.; A.S. in Police Adminstrn., Triton Coll., 1974: student U. Ill., Chgo., 1975; B.A. in Polit. Sci., DePaul U., 1976, M.A. in Public Adminstrn./Mgmt. Scis., 1982. Desk officer Triton Coll. Police Dept., 1972-74; ramp service Flying Tiger Cargo Line, Chgo., 1974-75; clk., messenger Kirkland & Ellis, Chgo., 1975-76; bus operator Chgo. Transit Authority, summers 1975-76: adult probation officer Cook County, Chgo., 1977—; personal probation officer for Judge Barbaro, Criminal Div. Chmn. social com. young adult div. Joint Civic Com. of Italian Americans, 1977-78, pres., 1978—; precinct capt. 36th Ward Regular Democratic Orgn., 1974—. Served to 2d lt. CAP/USAF Aux. Mem. DePaul U. Alumni Assn. Roman Catholic (mem. Holy Cross Council). Club: KC.

GASS, MARCELLE BURDETTE, educator; b. Jewell County, Kans., Apr. 23, 1919; d. Dyrel L. and Emma L. (Kuiken) Burdette; B.S., U. Kans., 1949; M.S., Wichita State U., 1966: Ph.D., Kans. State U., 1975; m. Carney Brooks Gass, July 3, 1942; children—John Carney, Julie Ann Gass Hedrick. Civil Service payroll clk., 1942-46; with Wichita (Kans.) State U., 1964—, asst. prof. bus. edn. Coll. Bus. Adminstrn., 1966—. Mem. Internat. Word Processing Assn., Nat. Bus. Edn. Assn., Mountain-Plains Regional Bus. Edn. Assn., Kans. Bus. Edn. Assn., Council Univ. Women, Beta Gamma Sigma. Methodist. Home: 1152 Chipper Ln Wichita KS 67212 Office: 116 Business Edn Coll Bus Adminstrn Wichita State U Wichita KS 67208

GASSERT, EDWARD FREDERICK, city ofcl.; b. Cin., Apr. 26, 1934; s. George P. and Lila J. (Brinkman) G.; student Ohio Coll. Applied Sci., 1957-58, U. Cin., 1976—; m. Marjorie Rose Jones, Oct. 13, 1956; children—Michelle Elaine, Yvonne Marie, Lawrence Edward. Electrician and telephone repairman apprentice, mem. plant fire brigade, fire brigade instr. Cin. Milling Machine Co., 1956-59; firefighter Evendale (Ohio) Fire Dept., 1959-63, engr., 1959-61, aerial truck operator, 1962, drillmaster, 1962-63, fire lt., 1963-66, instr. fire safety, 1960—, asst. fire chief, 1966-67, fire chief, 1967—; Ohio State fire instr., 1960—; fire service adv. to dir. Hamilton County CD, 1970—; mem. Ohio State Fire Commn., 1979-80; instr. fire adminstrn. Internat. City Mgrs. Assn., 1972—; hon. prof. fire sci. program U. No. Ky., 1974-78. Active Dan Beard council Boy Scouts Am., 1970—; pres. Hamilton County Disaster Coordinating and Planning Council, 1979-80. Served with USN, 1952-56; PTO. Recipient numerous awards including: letter of commendation Pres. Richard Nixon, 1973, Community Action award Gov. of Ohio, 1973, cert. of honor Greater Cin. C. of C., 1975, Silver Beaver award Boy Scouts Am., 1976, cert. of appreciation ARC, 1980. Mem. Internat. Assn. of Fire Chiefs (cert. of appreciation 1976), Hamilton County Fire Chiefs Assn. (award 1972, pres. 1971-72), Nat. Fire Protection Assn., U.S. CD Council, Internat. Assn. Arson Investigators (cert. of appreciation 1970), Cin. Fire and Arson Investigators, S.W. Ohio Indsl. Fire Protection Assn., Tri-State Emergency Assn., S.W. Ohio Fire Chief's Assn., Millcreek Valley Fire Assn. (Outstanding Contbn. award 1979), Ohio Fire Chief's Assn., Fellowship Christian Firefighters, Antique Fire Apparatus Assn., Soc. for Preservation and Appreciation Antique Motor Fire Apparatus, U.S. Figure Skating Assn., Bldg. Ofcls. and Code Adminstrs., Hamilton County CD, Iota Lambda Sigma. Mem. Christian Ch. Clubs: Masons, Shriners. Author Fire Safety Tchrs. Guide, 1970; contbr. articles on fire safety and fire sci. to profl. publs.; developed automatic alarm system used in Hamilton County. Home: 3703 Moorhill Dr Evendale OH 45241 Office: Evendale Fire Dept 10500 Reading Rd Evendale OH 45241

GASSMAN, MAX PAUL, mech. engr.; b. Bonesteel, S.D., Sept. 1, 1930; s. Walter Ernest and Elizabeth (Schibli) G.; B.S. in Mech. Engring., S.D. Sch. Mines and Tech., 1956; M. Mech. Engring., Iowa State U., 1963; m. Gail Elizabeth Evans, Aug. 5, 1955; children—Paul Michael, Philip Walter. With John Deere Co., Waterloo, Iowa, 1956—, sr. design engr., 1965-68, sr. design analyst, 1968-79, diagnostic coordinator, 1979—; v.p. John C. Rider & Assos., Inc. Cubmaster, Winnebago Council Boy Scouts Am., 1967-70, scoutmaster, 1970-74. Pres. bd. dirs. Splash Inc., 1970; pres. Lord of Life Luth. Ch., Waterloo. Served with USAF, 1948-52. Registered profl. engr., Iowa. Mem. Nat. Soc. Profl. Engrs. (chmn. Iowa sect. profl. engrs. in industry group), Iowa Engring. Soc. (pres. bd. dirs. N.E. Iowa 1971-72, Anson Marston award 1972), ASME (dir. 1971-72), Waterloo Tech. Soc. (chmn. tech. student activity com. 1970-71), Am. Soc. Agrl. Engrs. (chmn. T-5 computer com. 1975-76), Soc. Automotive Engrs. Club: John Deere Supervisors (Waterloo). Patentee in field. Home: 551 Alpine St Waterloo IA 50702 Office: Product Engring Center Waterloo IA 50704

GAST, HARRY T., JR., state senator; b. St. Joseph, Mich., Sept. 20, 1920; s. Harry T. and Fern (Shearer) G.; student Mich. State U., 1939-41; m. Vera Jean Warren, 1944; children—Barbara Gast Moray, Linda, Dennis. Treas., Lincoln Twp. (Mich.), 1946-64, supr., 1965-70; co-supr. Berrien County (Mich.), 1965-69; mem. Berrien County Bd. Public Works and Bd. Health, 1965-70; former mem. Mich. Ho. of Reps.; now mem. Mich. Senate. Mem. Farm Bur., Mich. United Conservation Clubs. Baptist. Club: Lions. Office: PO Box 43 Capitol Bldg Lansing MI 48901*

GASTON, BARRY E., radio sta. exec.; b. Kansas City, Mo., Aug. 18, 1942; s. V. L. and Betty Eleanor (Corliss) G.; B.S., Wichita State U., 1964; postgrad. Harvard U., 1968-69; m. Constance Deloris Myers, Feb. 24, 1968; children—Jack Barry, Brian Allen, William Robert. Announcer, Sta. KFBI, Wichita, 1957-59; announcer, promotion mgr., program dir., ops. mgr. Sta. KFH, Wichita, 1960-68; with Susquehanna Broadcasting Corp., 1968-78, gen. mgr., corp. v.p. Sta. WLQA, Cin., 1973-78; exec. v.p., gen. mgr., gen. operating partner Sta. KFH/KBRA, Wichita, 1978—; instr. broadcasting sales U. Cin.; mem. adv. bd. dirs. Audio Reader. Mem. Advt. Club Wichita, C. of

C. Republican. Presbyterian. Club: Rotary. Office: 104 S Emporia St Wichita KS 67202

GASTON, DWIGHT MOORE, real estate broker; b. Woodward, Okla., Feb. 13, 1932; s. Virgil Albert and Rosa Emma (Savage) G.; student Washburn U., Topeka, 1951-52; grad. Realtors Inst., 1977; m. Norma Lenninger, Oct. 31, 1953; children—Jane Ann, Julie Lea. With Halliburton Oil Well Cementing Co., 1954-57, Skelly Oil Co., 1957-69; real estate broker, auctioneer, Mission, Kans., 1975—. Served with AUS, 1952-54. Cert. residential specialist. Mem. Nat. Assn. Realtors, Realtors Nat. Mktg. Inst., Nat. Auctioneering Assn., Kans. Assn. Realtors, Kans. Auctioneering Assn., Am. Legion. Baptist. Clubs: Elks, Eagles, Masons. Home: 5513 W 53d St Mission KS 66202 Office: Allied Auction Center 5943 Merriam Ln Merriam KS 66203

GASTON, HUGH PHILIP, marriage counselor, educator; b. St. Paul, Sept. 12, 1910; s. Hugh Philander and Gertrude (Heine) G.; B.A., U. Mich., 1937, M.A., 1941; postgrad. summers Northwestern U., 1938, Yale U., 1959; m. Charlotte E. Clarke, Oct. 1, 1945 (dec. 1960); children—Gertrude E. Gaston Crippen, George Hugh. Counselor, U. Mich., Ann Arbor, 1936; tchr., counselor W. K. Kellogg Found., Battle Creek, Mich., 1937-41; tchr. spl. edn., Detroit, 1941; instr. airplane wing constrn. Briggs Mfrs. Co., Detroit, 1942; psychologist VA, 1946-51; sr. staff asso. Sci. Research Assos., Chgo., 1951-55; marriage counselor Circuit Ct., Ann Arbor, 1955-60; pvt. practice marriage counseling, Ann Arbor, 1955—; former chief Guidance Center, U. Mich. and Mich. State U.; lectr., Eastern Mich. U., Ypsilanti, 1964-67, asst. prof., 1967-81. Acting postmaster, Ann Arbor, 1960-61. Chmn. Wolverine Boys State, Am. Legion, 1957-82; chmn. com. on Christian marriage Presbytery So. Mich., 1962-69; mem. exec. com., legis. agt., chmn. legis. com. Mich. Council Family Relations, 1972-74; bd. dirs. Internat. Parents Without Partners, 1968-69, 1st pres. Mich. chpt., 1961. Served with U.S. Army, 1943-46. Decorated Purple Heart (2), Bronze Star; Medallion of Nice (France); named Citizen of Year, Am. Legion, 1968, Single Parent of Yr., 1978. Mem. Am. Assn. Marriage Counselors, Am. Personnel and Guidance Assn., Nat. Vocat. Guidance Assn., D.A.V. (past comdr.), Am. Soc. Tng. Dirs., Mich. Indsl. Tng. Council (charter), SAR (past pres.), U. Mich. Band Alumni Assn. (pres. 1957-58), Mil. Order Purple Heart (nat. exec. com. 1977-82), Phi Delta Kappa (past pres. U. Mich.). Clubs: Rotary, Econ. of Detroit. Address: 1404 Cambridge Rd Ann Arbor MI 48104

GASTON, JACK WARREN, educator; b. Detroit, Nov. 2, 1923; s. James Russell and Emma Edna (Ruff) G.; B.S., S.W. Mo. State U., 1948; M.S., U. Tenn., 1950; postgrad. U. Ark., 1950-51, U. Ill., 1954-58; m. Lela Kruse, June 6, 1947; children—Stephen Douglas, Judith Lela. Instr., William Chrisman High Sch., Independence, Mo., 1948-49, U. Ark., Fayetteville, 1950; mdse. mgr. Ozark Frozen Foods, Springfield, 1950-51; instr. S.W. Mo. State U., Springfield, 1951-52; prof., chmn. dept. mktg., Millikin U., Decatur, Ill., 1952—, dir. Small Bus. Devel. Center, 1974—; pres. Bus. Research Assos., Decatur, 1980—. Mem. Macon County bd., 1965—, vice chmn., 1980—, chmn. personnel com., 1968—, chief labor negotiator, 1969—; bd. dirs. Small Bus. Council, 1978; mem. regional plan commn., Macon County, 1978; bd. dirs. Mental Health Bd., 1970-78. Served with USN, 1942-46. Mem. Am. Mktg. Assn., Ill. State and County Ofcls. Assn., Small Bus. Inst. Dirs. Assn., Midwest Econ. Assn., Acad. Mgmt., Phi Kappa Phi. Republican. Lutheran. Contbr. articles to profl. jours. Home: 5 Lincoln Pl Decatur IL 62522 Office: 1184 W Main St Decatur IL 62522

GASTON, OTIS TELL, broadcast exec.; b. Downs, Kans., Sept. 28, 1918; s. Otis Tell and Agnes Amanda (Chapman) G.; B.A., Bethany Coll., Lindsborg, Kans., 1940; spl. student Northwestern U., 1946; m. Harriet S. Evans, Dec. 23, 1946; children—Jane Ashley, Laurel Evans. Tchr., Marquette Sch., 1940-42; announcer Sta. KSAL, Salina, Kans., 1946; news editor Sta. WKZO, 1947-50; v.p. radio, dir. Fetzer Broadcasting Co., Kalamazoo, also sta. mgr. WKZO Radio, 1950—. Bd. dirs. Goodwill Industries, 1971—. Served with USNR, 1942-45; PTO. Mem. Mich. Assn. Broadcasters (pres. 1976), Nat. Assn. Broadcasters, Broadcast Pioneers, Kalamazoo C. of C. (dir. 1959-62). Presbyterian. Clubs: Optimist (pres. 1958-59), Masons. Home: 604 Norton Dr Kalamazoo MI 49001 Office: 590 W Maple St Kalamazoo MI 49008

GATES, ALLEN BENSON, aerospace and communications co. exec.; b. Westwood, Calif., Feb. 6, 1940; s. St. Clair and Dora Lavaun (Morey) G.; B.S.M.E., U. Nev., 1961, M.S.M.E., 1963; S.M. in Mgmt., M.I.T., 1977; Ph.D. in Systems Engring., Case Western Res. U., 1971; m. Elizabeth Ankers, July 4, 1960; children—Allison, Tod, Jeffrey. Controls engr., missile systems analysis Naval Weapons Center, China Lake, Calif., 1962-78; long range planning mgr. Ford Aerospace & Communications Corp., Newport Beach, Calif., 1978-79, thermal imaging program mgr., Detroit, 1979-80, v.p. tech. affairs, 1980—. Served in U.S. Army, 1963-66. Recipient Naval Weapons Center Tech. Dirs. award, 1973; Naval Weapons Center fellow, 1966-69; Sloan fellow, 1976-77. Mem. Assn. U.S. Army, AIAA, Nat. Security Industry Assn. Republican. Club: Rotary. Home: 336 Greenwood Birmingham MI 48009 Office: PO Box 43342 Detroit MI 48232

GATES, C. W., mortgage banker, city ofcl.; b. Pine Bluff, Ark., Aug. 13, 1923; s. Lance and Mattie (Berry) G.; student Stowe Tchrs. Coll., Washington U., St. Louis; m. Harriet Cecilia Craddock, June 14, 1947; children—Mark D., Lisa B. With C.W. Gates Realty Co., Inc., St. Louis, 1959—, pres., 1959—; pres. Gateway Nat. Bank, St. Louis, 1964—, radio sta. 1310, St. Louis, 1966—, Nat. Assurance Co., St. Louis, 1966—; vice chmn. Vbic Way Broadcasting Co., St. Louis, 1969—; v.p. Mid-Central Mortgage Co., St. Louis, 1964—. Police commr., St. Louis, 1966—. Bd dirs. Jr. Achievement, St. Louis, Boy Scouts Am., St. Louis, Cath. Charities, St. Louis, United Fund, St. Louis, Health and Welfare Council, St. Louis, Urban League, St. Louis, N.A.A.C.P.; trustee YWCA, St. Louis. Served with AUS, 1942-45; ETO. Clubs: St. Louis Press, Advertising Greater St. Louis, Media. Home: 5249 Lindell Blvd St Louis MO 63108 Office: 2921 Union Blvd St Louis MO 63115

GATES, RICHARD DANIEL, plastic and rubber co. exec.; b. Trenton, Mo., Mar. 27, 1942; s. Daniel G. and Effie Wright (Johnson) G.; B.S., U. Mo., 1964; M.C.S., Rollins Coll., 1968; P.M.D., Harvard Bus. Sch., 1976; m. Jean P. Gates, Jan. 26, 1966; 1 son, Daniel Wright. Mgmt. asso. Western Electric Co., N.Y.C., 1964-66; bus. mgmt. adminstr. Martin Marietta Aerospace Co., Orlando, Fla., 1966-68, chief indsl. engring., 1968-69; fin. analyst Martin Marietta Hdqrs., N.Y.C., 1969-70, sr. acct., 1970-71; controller Dragon Cement Co. div. Martin Marietta Co., 1971-72; controller Martin Marietta Aggregates N.E. Div., 1972-73; asst. controller Rubbermaid Inc., Wooster, Ohio, 1973-77, asst. treas., 1977-79, treas., 1979-80, v.p. and treas., 1980—. Mem. Wooster City Fin. Task Force; active Cub Scouts. Mem. Beta Gamma Sigma, Omicron Delta Kappa. Clubs: Harvard Bus. Sch., Wooster Country. Office: Rubbermaid Inc 1147 Akron Rd Wooster OH 44691

GATLIN, ELISSA LYNN, educator, univ. ofcl.; b. Gary, Ind., Aug. 10, 1948; d. George Arthur and Elsie Whitford G.; B.S., Western Mich. U., 1970; M.A., Mich. State U., 1971, Ph.D., 1976. Speech and lang. therapist Mich. Sch. for Blind, Lansing, 1971-73; para-profl. counselor ACCESS Center Provincial Hosp. and Surgi-Clinic, East Lansing, Mich., 1973-76; asst. prof., coordinator speech and lang. clinic Northeastern State U., Tahlequah, Okla., 1976-80; asst. dir. admissions Coll. Osteopathic Medicine, Mich. State U., East Lansing, 1980—; cons. Cookson Hills Head Start, Salvation Army Services to Children; mem. adv. bd. Tulsa Urban League Housing, Info. Counseling Bur. Mem. Okla. Edn. Assn., NEA, Council Exceptional Children, Am. Speech and Hearing Assn., Nat. Black Assn. Speech Lang. and Hearing, AAUW, Phi Delta Kappa, Delta Kappa Gamma. Democrat. Baptist. Office: Office Admissions Coll Osteopathic Medicine Mich State U East Lansing MI 48824

GATTO, DOMINICK DAN, electro plating co. exec.; b. Chgo., Oct. 27, 1920; s. George and Emily (Manuzzi) G.; student Herzl Jr. Coll., Chgo., 1940-42, LaSalle Extension, Chgo., 1949, Walton Sch. Commerce, Chgo., 1968; m. Norma Delia Gentile, Sept. 12, 1943; children—George, Robert, Patricia, Dominick, Jeannine, Vince. Asst. comptroller Truck Rail Terminals, Inc., Chgo., 1942-60; asst. comptroller Lasham Cartage Co., Inc., Chgo., 1960-70; controller Arrow Motor Transit Co., Cicero, Ill., 1971-73; pres., treas. Wesko Plating Inc., Chgo., 1974—. Commr. minor league Villa Park (Ill.) Baseball League; exec. v.p. Villa Park Youth Football, 1976, treas., 1977-80. Mem. Nat. Assn. Metal Finishers, Am. Electroplaters Soc., Chgo. Electroplaters Inst., Ill. Mfrs. Assn., Nat. C. of C., Ill. State C. of C., Chgo. Assn. Commerce and Industry. Republican. Office: 423 N Spaulding Ave Chicago IL 60624

GATTO, LOUIS CONSTANTINE, coll. pres.; b. Chgo., July 4, 1927; s. Louis S. and Marie (Bacigalupo) G.; student Amherst Coll., 1945-46; B.A., St. Mary's Coll., Minn., 1950; postgrad U. Minn., 1950-51; M.A., DePaul U., 1956; Ph.D., Loyola U., Chgo., 1965; m. Kathleen M. Paquette, July 7, 1951; children—Christine Gatto Swickard, Beth, Mark, Gregory, Janine Gatto Bass, Sandra. Speech asst. St. Mary's Coll., 1949-50; staff artist TV Times, Mpls., 1950-51; chmn. dept. English Zion (Ill.)-Benton High Sch., 1951-56; tchr. New Trier High Sch., Winnetka, Ill., 1956-57; instr. English, St. Josephs Coll., Rensselaer, Ind., 1957-58, asst. prof., 1958-63, asso. prof. Medieval and Renaissance lit., 1963-66, prof., 1966-71, asst. acad. dean, dir. summer session, 1967, acad. dean, 1968, v.p. acad. affairs, 1969-71; pres., prof. English, Marian Coll., Indpls., 1971—. Mem. Ind. Northwest Consortium Pvt. and Pub. Instns., 1968-71, selection com. Ind. Fulbright Found., 1968-70; mem. community adv. council Indpls. Pub. Schs., 1976-77; mem. policy adv. council parent/child devel. project Bank Street Coll. Edn.; mem. Hist. Landmarks Found. Ind., 1973—; mem. adv. com. Alcohol Safety Action Project, 1972-75; mem. exec. com., adv. bd. Center for Econ. Edn., Ind. U.-Purdue U., Indpls.; mem. exec. com. Ind. Conf. on Higher Edn., 1973-75, 78—, pres., 1979-80; chmn. council of presidents Consortium for Urban Edn., 1974-75, pres., 1975—. Bd. dirs. Greater Indpls. Progress Com., Catholic Social Services, sec., 1978-80; bd. dirs. WYFI-TV; bd. dirs. Ind. Health Careers, Inc., vice-chmn., 1979-81, chmn.-elect, 1981—; bd. dirs. Asso. Colls. Ind., treas., 1976-78; bd. dirs. Hosp. Audiences, Indpls., 1974-76; bd. dirs. Independent Colls. and Univs. Ind., chmn. 1979-80. Served with AUS, 1945-46. Mem. Am., Ind., confs. on higher edn., Nat. Cath. Edn. Assn., MLA, Renaissance Soc. Am., Medieval Acad. Am., Ind. Coll. English Assn. (bus. mgr. Associator 1965-66), Indpls. C. of C., Indpls. Mus. Art, Alpha Phi Omega. Clubs: Indpls. Athletic, Kiwanis. Contbr. articles to profl. jours. Home: 3024 Cold Spring Rd Indianapolis IN 46222

GATTOZZI, ANGELO LUCIANO, engr.; b. Matrice, Campobasso, Italy, Dec. 12, 1947; s. Domenico Germano and Angiolina (Appugliese) G.; B.S., Case Western Res. U., 1971, M.S., 1975, Ph.D., 1978; accounting certificate John Carroll U., 1976. Grad. asst. Case Western Res. U., 1971-74; engr. Reliance Electric Co., Cleve., 1974-77, project mgr., 1977-80; pres. Tyler Power Systems, Inc., Mentor, Ohio, 1980—. C.P.A., Ohio. Mem. IEEE, Am. Inst. C.P.A.'s, Am. Mgmt. Assn., ASTM. Author: IEEE Industry Applications; IEEE Magnetics. Home: 2110 Apple Dr Euclid OH 44143 Office: 8648 Tyler Blvd Mentor OH 44060

GAU, MILDRED JOSEPHINE, educator, coll. dean; b. Conover, Wis., Mar. 28, 1921; d. George Carl and Anna Linnea (Sandbeck) Dobbs; B.Ed., U. Wis., Whitewater, 1942, M.S., 1973; m. Donald Robert Gau, July 31, 1943; children—Robert Alan, Judith Ann Gau Hart. Tchr., Jefferson (Wis.) High Sch., 1942-44; clk.-stenographer U.S. Civil Service, Miami, Fla., 1945-46; sec. Meyers Equipment Co., Milw., 1946-47; tchr. Spencerian Bus. Coll., Milw., 1947-48; tchr. Milw. Area Tech. Coll., 1955-80, secretarial sci. dept. chmn., 1971-75, supr. bus. and gen. edn. West Campus, West Allis, 1980-81, dean bus. div., 1981—. Pres., S. 55th St. Sch. PTA, 1959. Mem. Word Processing Soc. (pres. 1979-80), Am. Vocat. Assn., Wis. Assn. Vocat. and Adult Edn., Classroom Educators in Bus. and Office Edn., Nat. Bus. Edn. Assn., Wis. Bus. Edn. Assn. (pres. 1973), Wis. Vocat. Bus. Edn. Assn. (pres. 1970), Milw. Area Bus. Edn. Assn., Internat. Info./Word Processing Assn., Adminstrv. Mgmt. Soc., Data Processing Mgmt. Assn., U. Wis.-Whitewater Nat. Alumni Assn., Delta Pi Epsilon, Sigma Sigma Sigma. Lutheran. Clubs: Luther Manor Aux., Order Eastern Star. Columnist, The Word mag., 1979, 80; contbr. articles in field to profl. jours. Home: 6100 W Stonehedge Dr Milwaukee WI 53220 Office: 1015 N 6th St Milwaukee WI 53203

GAUL, WILLIAM MARTIN, architect; b. Belleville, Ill., Aug. 23, 1933; s. William Henry and Catherine Mary (Lang) G.; B.Arch., U. Ill., 1957; m. Mary Patricia Murphy, Dec. 28, 1963; children—William Louis, Lisa Marie. Draftsman Weisenstein, Rogers & Hausmann Architects, Belleville, 1960-62; project architect Childs & Smith, Inc., architects, Chgo., 1962-64; with Hague-Richards Assos. Ltd., Chgo., 1964-76, sr. v.p., 1974-76; organizer Gaul-Tater Assos., Chgo., 1976-79; prin. Gaul & Assos., AIA, Chgo., 1979—. Served to lt. comdr. USNR, 1957-60; comdg. officer Res. Engring. Co. 9-1, 1969-72, comdr., 1975—. Mem. A.I.A., Nat. Council Archtl. Registration Bds., Naval Res. Assn., Res. Officers Assn., Alpha Rho Chi. Clubs: University, Economic (Chgo.). Home: 2111 Lincolnwood St Evanston IL 60201 Office: 415 N Dearborn St Chicago IL 60610

GAULT, LON ANDREW, educator; b. Clinton, Iowa, Feb. 10, 1924; s. Andrew Corbet and Lydia Frieda (Wurster) G.; B.A., Ind. U., 1948; M.A., U. Iowa, 1950; Ed.D., Stanford U., 1970; m. Kathryn R. Nichols, July 14, 1945; children—Rebecca, Beverly, Lonne Kathryn, Gretchen, Annette, Elizabeth. History tchr. Clinton (Iowa) Public Schs., 1951-57; history instr., asst. dir. evening sch. Lyons Twp. Jr. Coll., La Grange, Ill., 1957-65, asst. dir., 1965-67; instr. history Coll. of DuPage, Glen Ellyn, Ill., 1967—, dean of instruction, 1975-79; Big Band Ballroom host Sta. WDCB, 1977—. Active Common Cause. Served with U.S. Army, 1943-45; ETO. Recipient William M. Locke history award, 1948; Japan Soc.-Asia Found. fellow, 1957; William Robertson Coe fellow, 1961; Jr. Coll. Kellogg fellow, 1964-65. Mem. NEA, American West, Big Bands, Phi Delta Kappa, Ill. Faculty Assn. (adv. council). Methodist. Authority on Big Bands and history of ballrooms. Home: 1622 Wadham Ct Wheaton IL 60187 Office: College of DuPage 22 and Lambert Sts Glen Ellyn IL 60137

GAULT, ROGER CLYDE, ednl. counselor, clergyman; b. Detroit, Feb. 1, 1933; s. Noble Clyde and Gertrude Lee (Rogers) G.; A.A., Graceland Coll., 1953; B.S., Eastern Mich. U., 1959, MA., 1961; postgrad. theology Sch. of Restoration, 1967-68; Ed.D., Wayne State U., 1979; m. Georgia Lee Harris, Sept. 12, 1953; children—Bradley Clyde, Murray Allen. Guidance counselor Wayne (Mich.) Meml. High Sch., 1959-62, Pioneer High Sch., Ann Arbor, Mich., 1962-66, Power Jr. High Sch., Farmington, Mich., 1969—; pvt. practice guidance counseling, 1969—; counseling chmn. Farmington Schs., 1970—; Oakland County counseling dir., 1976-78; ordained to ministry Reorganized Ch. Jesus Christ of Latter Day Saints, 1952; pastor, Wayne, 1962-63, Plymouth, Mich., 1964-65, Sandusky, Mich., 1966, Sacramento, 1967-68, Detroit, 1969-78; dir. pastors, Detroit-Windsor Met. Areas, dir. camps and retreats, 1970-78; dir. ministerial edn., 1974-78. Leader, Boy Scouts Am., 1970-75, active youth assistance, 1976-77. Served with inf. U.S. Army, 1973-75. Mem. Am. Personnel and Guidance Assn., Mich. Personnel and Guidance Assn., Mich. Secondary Counselors Assn., Phi Delta Kappa. Home: 31411 Gable St Livonia MI 48152 Office: Power Jr High Sch 34740 Rhonswood St Farmington MI 48024

GAUNAURD, HENRY, real estate exec.; b. Havana, Cuba, Sept. 9, 1946; came to U.S., 1961; B.S. in Psychology and History, Loyola U. Chgo. With Draper and Kramer, Inc., Chgo., 1971—, now v.p. and sr. appraiser. Cert. property mgr.; sr. real property appraiser. Mem. Chgo. Real Estate Bd., Nat. Assn. Realtors, Ill. Assn. Realtors, Inst. Real Estate Mgmt., Soc. Real Estate Appraisers, Appraisal Com. of Ill. Mortgage Bankers Assn. Office: Draper and Kramer Inc 33 W Monroe St Chicago IL 60603

GAUSELMAN, JAMES RICHARD, mktg. rep.; b. Cin., Mar. 30, 1951; s. Robert Charles and Margaret Sarah (Rickard) G.; student Ohio Coll. Applied Sci., 1969-71; B.A., Xavier U., 1977, postgrad., 1980—; 1 dau., Kristina Lyn. Audio visual specialist Bethesda Hosps., Cin., 1972-77; mgr. Tandy Corp./Radio Shack, Cin., 1977-79; photographer Scripps-Howard Broadcasting/WCPO TV, Cin., 1979; promotion dir. Buford TV, Inc., WBTI-TV, Cin., 1979-82; ind. mktg. rep., Cin., 1982—. Media com. mem./cons. Juvenile Diabetes Found.; mem. public service com. AD II. Mem. Broadcasters Promotion Assn., Inc.

GAUTHIER, CLARENCE JOSEPH, utility exec.; b. Houghton, Mich., Mar. 16, 1922; s. Clarence A. and Muriel V. (Beesley) G.; B.S.M.E., U. Ill., 1943; M.B.A., U. Chgo., 1960; m. Grayce N. Wicall, July 25, 1941; children—Joseph H., Nancy M. With Pub. Service Co. No. Ill., 1945-54; with No. Ill. Gas. Co., 1954—, v.p. fin., 1960-62, v.p. ops., 1962-64, exec. v.p., 1965-69, pres., 1969-76, chmn., 1971—, chief exec. officer, 1971-81, dir., 1965—; chmn., pres., chief exec. officer, dir. NICOR Inc., 1976—; chmn., chief exec. officer, dir. all NICOR subs.; dir. GATX Corp., GDC, Inc., Naperville Nat. Bank and Trust Co. (Ill.), AEGIS Ltd. (vice chmn. 1978—), Chgo. and North Western Transp. Co., Nalco Chem. Co., Sun Electric Corp. Mem. pres.'s council U. Ill., 1978—; mem. Northwestern U. Assos., 1977—; bd. sponsors Evang. Hosp. Assn., Oak Brook, Ill., 1977—; chmn. devel. campaign Good Samaritan Hosp., Downers Grove, Ill., 1974-77; bd. dirs. Gas Research Inst., 1977—. Trustee George Williams Coll., Downers Grove, 1968-77, Ill. Inst. Tech., 1976—, Ill. Inst. Tech. Research Inst., 1976-80, Council Energy Studies, 1977—; trustee Inst. Gas Tech., 1964-78, chmn. bd. trustees, 1976-78; bd. dirs. Mid-Am. chpt. ARC, 1962-78; trustee Met. Crusade of Mercy, Chgo., 1965-77; citizens bd. U. Chgo., 1972—; bd. govs. Soc. Environ. Awareness, George Williams Coll., 1973—. Served to capt., C.E., U.S. Army World War II; PTO. Decorated Silver Star, Bronze Star with V; recipient Distinguished Alumnus award Coll. Engring., U. Ill., 1971, Alumni Honor award, 1974; Loyalty award U. Ill. Alumni Assn., 1977; registered profl. engr., Ill. Mem. Am. (dir. 1970-76, chmn. bd. 1974-75, Distinguished Service award 1976), Midwest (dir. 1964-67), So. (dir. 1966-69) gas assns., Ind. Natural Gas Assn. Am. (dir. 1972-73), Chgo. Assn. Commerce and Industry (dir. 1966-71, 73-79), Ill. C. of C. (Ill. savs. bond com. 1975—), Internat. Gas Union (council 1970-75, chmn. com. on gas utilization), AAAS, Am. Fin. Assn., Am. Mgmt. Assn., Pres.'s Assn., U. Chgo. Grad. Sch. Bus. Alumni Assn. (pres. 1964-65), U. Ill. Found. (U. Ill. adv. council 1981—), ME-IE Alumni Assn. (dir. 1973—, pres. 1976-77), Sigma Pi, Beta Gamma Sigma, Tau Nu Tau, Tau Beta Pi, Pi Tau Sigma (Eminent Engr. hon. status). Clubs: Econ., Chgo., Comml., Mid-Am. (Chgo.); Butler Nat. Golf. Contbr. articles to profl. jours. Office: PO Box 200 Naperville IL 60566

GAUTHIER, T(HEOPHILE) EMIL, med. equipment co. exec.; b. Warroad, Minn., Dec. 11, 1910; s. Odilon and Mathilda (Gauthier) G.; grad. Coyne Coll., 1932; student Rochester Community Coll., 1942, U. Minn., 1943; m. Dorothy Ranney, Sept. 11, 1941; children—Janice (Mrs. Arthur Ley), Thomas, Lawrence. Gen. service worker Mayo Clinic, Rochester, Minn., 1934-37; service mgr. Sears Roebuck & Co., Rochester, 1937-40; asst. prodn. mgr. Waters-Conley Co., Rochester, 1940-46, Kepp Co., Rochester, 1946-47; organizer Rochester Products Co., 1947, mgr., 1947-66; organizer, mgr. Rochester Med. Equipment Co., 1966-72; organizer Gauthier Industries, Inc., sec.-treas., dir., 1974—; dir. Am-Pro, Inc., Rochester, Ability Bldg. Center, Rochester. Mem. Rochester Utility Bd., 1956-66, pres., 1956-65; chmn. com. on urban environment City of Rochester, 1974; active Boy Scouts Am., 1924-65; pres. St. Francis P.T.A., 1953; mem. Service Corps of Ret. Execs., 1976—. Recipient Pres.'s award Soc. Mfg. Engrs., 1966, 71, 73. Registered mfg. engr. Mem. Soc. Mfg. Engrs., Am. Mgmt. Assn., Rochester C. of C. (chmn. indsl. com. 1953-58), Coast Guard Aux. (flotilla vice-comdr. 1971-72). Roman Catholic. K.C., Elk. Developed plastic needle for prolonged intravenous therapy, artificial kidney machine for home patients. Home: 1210 4th St NW Rochester MN 55901 Office: Gauthier Industries Inc 300 1st St NE Rochester MN 55901

GAUVREAU, PAUL RICHARD, diversified mfg. exec.; b. Chgo., Nov. 24, 1939; s. Paul O. and Pheme Gauvreau; B.S.C., Loyola U., Chgo., 1961; M.B.A., U. Chgo., 1976; m. Helen Holman, Apr. 28, 1962; children—Caren, Paul Stephen, Paul Andrew, Julie Ann, Paul David. With Price Waterhouse & Co., C.P.A.'s, Chgo., 1961-66; chief accountant, then asst. treas. Pittway Corp., Northbrook, Ill., 1966-72, treas., 1972—, fin. v.p., 1979—; v.p., treas., dir. Penton/IPC, Inc.; v.p. Pittway Corp. Can., Ltd., Pittway Real Estate Inc., Clearwater, Fla., C & A Investments, Inc., Clearwater, Saddlebrook Resorts, Inc., Wesley Chapel, Fla.; v.p., treas. Pittway Corp. Found. Treas., City of Prospect Heights (Ill.), 1978—. Mem. Fin. Execs. Inst. Address: Pittway Corp PO Box 602 Northbrook IL 60062

GAVLOCK, EUGENE HARLAN, retail drinking water equipment co. exec.; b. Rockford, Ill., Mar. 28, 1925; s. Paul G. and Melvina C. (Smith) G.; master barber degree Cedar Rapids Barber Coll., 1955; m. Margaret Berneice Andersen, Feb. 15, 1952; children—Gregory Douglas, Sheryl Lynn, Carol Jean, Sharon Kay, Peggy Ann, Karla Raye, Kary Kaye. Drummer, bandleader various nat. bands, Gene Harlan Orch., 1942-54; barber, Waterloo, Iowa, 1954-60; owner, mgr. Violet Ray Coin Laundry, Waterloo, 1960-65; pres. Locktow Products, Inc., Waterloo, 1965-70; auto. salesman Simpson Dodge, Waterloo, 1967-70; pres. Pure Water Assos., Waterloo, 1974-79, Pure Water Assos., Internat., Inc., Waterloo, 1979—; pres., founder Distillerland Discount Centers, Inc., Cedar Falls, Iowa, 1979—.

Named Outstanding Sales Individual for Yr., Pure Water, Inc., 1979. Mem. C. of C., Family Motor Coach Assn. Home: 2714 Alameda St Cedar Falls IA 50613 Office: 2915 McClain Dr Cedar Falls IA 50613

GAWTHROP, LOUIS C., educator; b. Balt., Oct. 27, 1930; s. Louis and Claudia (Smith) G.; A.B., Franklin and Marshall Coll., 1958; M.A., Johns Hopkins U., 1960, Ph.D., 1962; m. Virginia L. Bonelli, May 31, 1958; children—Tracy Marshall, Nicholas Andrew, Anne Elizabeth. Legis. asst. Legis. Council Md., 1959, 60; jr. instr. polit. sci. Johns Hopkins U., Balt., 1958-62; instr. polit. sci. U. Pa., Phila., 1962-63, asst. prof. polit. sci., 1963-67; asso. prof. polit. sci. SUNY, Binghamton, 1967-72, prof. polit. sci., 1972-77, acting chmn. dept. polit. sci., 1976-77; research cons. dept. internal affairs Commonwealth of Pa., summer 1963; prof. public and environ. affairs Ind. U., Bloomington, 1978—, vis. prof. Maxwell Sch., Syracuse (N.Y.) U., 1973, 1975; vis. fellow Netherlands Inst. for Advanced Study in Humanities and Social Scis., 1973-74. Served with USAF, 1951-54. Mem. Am. Polit. Sci. Assn., Am. Soc. Public Adminstrn. Democrat. Author: Bureaucratic Behavior in the Executive Branch: An Analysis of Organizational Change, 1969; The Administrative Process and Democratic Theory, 1970; Administrative Politics and Social Change, 1971. Editor-in-chief Public Adminstrn. Rev., 1977—.

GAY, ALFONSO YOUNG, surgeon; b. Negros Occ., Philippines, Aug. 17, 1935; s. Antonio G. and Mary (Young) G.; M.D. cum laude, U. Santo Tomas, 1960; m. Lilia Gomez, May 13, 1961; children—Shirley Ann, Alfonso Young, Catherine, Christine. Surg. resident Negros Occ. Provincial Hosp., Philippines, 1961-65; intern Drs. Hosp., Seattle, 1966-67, resident in surg. pathology, 1967; resident in gen. surgery Good Samaritan Hosp., Cin., 1967-71, fellow in peripheral vascular disease, 1971-73; chief of surgery Hocking Valley Community Hosp., Logan, Ohio, 1973—; pres. Gay and Labrador M.D.'s, Inc., Logan. Diplomate Am. Bd. Surgery. Fellow A.C.S.; mem. AMA, Ohio State Med. Assn. Contbr. research article to med. publ. Home: 728 Glenwood Dr Logan OH 43138 Office: 751 State Route 664 N Logan OH 43138

GAYDOS, FRANCIS ANTHONY, coll. pres.; b. St. Louis, Sept. 14, 1921; s. George William and Kathryn (Budenholzer) G.; B.A., St. Mary's Sem., 1943; M.A., St. Louis U., 1953; S.T.D., St. Thomas U., 1956. Joined Congregation of the Mission, 1939, ordained priest Roman Catholic Ch., 1947; acad. dean St. Thomas Sem., Denver, 1956-65; pres. Cardinal Glennon Coll., St. Louis, 1965-69, 1975—, DeAndreis Inst. Theology, Lemont, Ill., 1969-75. Home and office: 5200 Glennon Dr St Louis MO 63119

GAYLORD, SANFORD FRED, physician; b. Cleve. May 18, 1923; s. Samuel Goldberg and Eva Neidus; student John Carroll U., 1945-47; M.D., Chgo. Sch. Medicine, 1951, M.B., 1951; m. Sarah Leslie Hoffman, Jan. 1, 1944; children—Scott, Randy, Gregg, Shelley, Wendy, Judd, Brett, Glenn; m. 2d, Sondra Hill, Mar. 29, 1980. Intern, Ill. Central Hosp., Chgo., 1951-52; resident Dearborn VA Hosp., 1952-53, Mt. Sinai Hosp., Cleve., 1953-54; practice medicine specializing in internal medicine, gastroenterology, Youngstown, Ohio, 1954—; chief of medicine, chief gastroenterology St. Elizabeth Med. Center, Youngstown; cons. gastroenterology Northeastern Ohio Coll. Medicine, 1976—; asst. prof. medicine Northeastern Ohio U. Coll. Medicine. Vice pres. Youngstown Symphony Soc., 1965-70. Served with USAAF, 1942-45; ETO. Decorated D.F.C. with 3 oak leaf clusters. Diplomate Am. Bd. Internal Medicine. Fellow A.C.P., Am. Coll. Gastroenterology; mem. AMA, Am. Soc. Internal Medicine, Am. Soc. Gastrointestinal Endoscopy, Ohio State, Mahoning County med. socs., Ohio Soc. Internal Medicine, Flying Physicians Assn., Aircraft Owners and Pilots Assn. Jewish. Clubs: local swim and tennis, B'nai B'rith Mahoning Lodge. Former piano student of Boris Goldovsky, 1st place winner piano Nat. Solo Contest, 1939, 1940, 1941; Vitamin B12 therapy in multiple sclerosis, tetracycline flourescence in stomach cancers. Home: 5670 Lamplighter Dr Girard OH 44420 Office: 1005 Belmont Ave Youngstown OH 44504

GEAKE, CAROL LYNNE, veterinarian; b. Grand Rapids, Mich., Feb. 19, 1941; d. John Edward and Alice Geraldine (Bussler) Rens; B.S. in Zoology, U. Mich., 1961, M.S. in Parasitology, 1963; D.V.M., Mich. State U., 1968; m. R. Robert Geake, June 9, 1962; children—Roger Rens, Tamara Lynne, William Rens. Research asst. Mollusk div. Museum of Zoology, U. Mich., Ann Arbor, 1960-63, research asst., dept. indsl. toxicology Sch. Pub. Health, U. Mich., 1963-66; asso. veterinarian Plymouth (Mich.) Veterinary Hosp., 1969-70; pvt. practice, Northville, Mich., 1971—; cons. in field. Project leader Wayne County 4-H Veterinary Sci., 1968-72; trustee St. Mary Hosp., Livonia, Mich., 1980—. Mem. Am., Mich., Southeastern Mich., Women's veterinary med. assns., Am. Assn. Equine Practitioners, Northville Bus. and Profl. Women's Club, Phi Sigma, Phi Zeta. Contbr. articles to profl. jours. Home and Office: 48525 W Eight Mile Rd Northville MI 48167

GEAKE, RAYMOND ROBERT, state senator; b. Detroit, Oct. 26, 1936; s. Harry Nevill and Phyllis Rae (Fox) G.; B.S. in Spl. Edn., U. Mich., 1958, M.A. in Guidance and Counseling, 1959, Ph.D. in Edn. and Psychology, 1963; m. Carol Lynne Rens, June 9, 1962; children—Roger Rens, Tamara Lynne, William Rens. Coordinator child devel. research Edison Inst., Dearborn, Mich., 1962-66; dir. psychology dept. Plymouth (Mich.) State Home and Tng. Sch., Mich. Dept. Mental Health, 1966-69; pvt. practice ednl. psychology, Northville, Mich., 1969-72; mem. Mich. Ho. of Reps., 1973-76, Mich. Senate, 1977—. Trustee-at-large Schoolcraft Community Coll., 1969-72, chmn. bd. trustees, 1971-72; vice chmn. nat. adv. com. on mental health and illness of elderly HEW, 1976-77. Mem. N.E.A. (life), Mich. Soc. Geneal. Research. Republican. Rotarian. Co-author: Visual Tracking, a Self-instruction Workbook for Perceptual Skills in Reading, 1962. Office: Capitol Bldg Lansing MI 48901

GEARHART, OTTO ARNOLD, JR., tire co. exec.; b. Akron, Ohio, Sept. 16, 1947; s. Otto Arnold and Gladys N. (Massey) G.; B.S.M.E., U. Akron, 1970, M.B.A., 1976; m. Rita Ann Vargo, Aug. 8, 1970; children—Stephannie Suzanne, Emilie Jane. With B.F. Goodrich, Akron, 1968—, asst. product mgr. radial truck tire, 1974-75, asst. product mgr. non-radial passenger tires, 1975-76, product mgr. radial passenger tires, 1976-77, product mgr. passenger tires, 1977-79, group product mgr., passenger tires and performance light truck tires, 1979; group product mgr. truck and bus tires Firestone Tire & Rubber Co., Akron, 1979-80, dir. product planning, 1980-81, v.p. product planning, 1981—. Mem. Am. Mktg. Assn. Mem. United Ch. of Christ. Home: 6760 Hammock Ave NW Canal Fulton OH 44614 Office: 1200 Firestone Pkwy Akron OH 44317

GEARTY, EDWARD JOSEPH, former state senator Minn.; b. Mpls., Mar. 17, 1923; s. John Edward and Elletta Winnifred (Newton) G.; B.A., St. Thomas Coll., 1952; LL.B., Georgetown U., 1955; m. Lorraine M. Breher, Aug. 7, 1965; 1 dau., Ann Therese. Commr., Mpls. Park Bd., 1959-62; mem. Minn. Ho. of Reps., 1963-70, Minn. Senate, 1971-80, pres., 1977-80. Served with USN, 1942-48. Home: 3810 Xerxes Ave N Minneapolis MN 55412 Office: 1102 W Broadway Minneapolis MN 55411

GEARY, D(ONALD) BRUCE, fin. exec.; b. Centralia, Ill., Sept. 2, 1952; s. Donald G. and Arline R. (Heyduck) G.; A.A., Kaskaskia Coll., 1972; B.S. in Acctg., Ill. State U., 1973; m. Janice Jane Arnold, Oct. 20, 1979; 1 son, Christopher Floyd. Self-employed acct., Centralia, 1970—; asst. mgr. Western Gardens Mobile Homes, Centralia, 1970-72; real estate salesman, Centralia, 1974; v.p., dir. Geary-Boyll, Inc., Centralia, 1975—; sr. v.p., sec.-treas., dir. Affordable Inns, Inc., Mt. Vernon, Ill., 1976—; dir. Union House Furnishing Co., Inc., Centralia, Home Fed. Savs. & Loan Assn.; cons. in field. Bd. dirs. Centralia Care Center, Centralia Cultural Soc., S. Central Ill. Community Concert Assn., Centralia Redevel. Commn., Centralia City schs.; former treas., dir. Centralia Improvement Corp.; former chmn. public relations council St. Mary's Hosp. Recipient Community-wide Disting. Service award, 1979; cert. hotel adminstr. Am. Hotel/Motel Assn. Mem. Nat. Assn. Realtors, Real Estate Securities and Syndication Inst., Centralia Jaycees (past treas.; Keyman of Year award 1976-77). Club: Centralia Optimist. Office: PO Drawer D 1501 E 2d St Centralia IL 62801

GECHT, JOEL ROBERT, psychologist; b. Bronx, N.Y., Aug. 31, 1951; s. Max and Ceil Harriet (Reinstein) G.; B.A., City U. N.Y., 1973, M.S., 1974; Ph.D., Fla. State U., 1978; m. Phyllis Friedman, Aug. 31, 1975. Intern, Fla. State U. Community Counseling Clinic, 1975-78, Fla. Dept. Health and Rehab. Services, 1976-77; Tchr., adminstr. spl. edn. Paul Klapper Sch., Flushing, N.Y., 1974-75; counselor academic advisor Fla. State U., Tallahassee, 1976-78; staff clin. psychologist N.W. Community Mental Health Center, Inc., Lima, Ohio, 1978-80; clin. and adminstrv. coordinator, counseling div. Pradco Psychol. Cons. Firm, Cleve., 1980—; instr. psychology Northwestern Coll., Lima, 1980; cons. psychologist. Mem. Am. Psychol. Assn., Ohio Psychol. Assn., Cleve. Psychol. Assn., Acad. Psychologists in Marital, Sex and Family Therapy, Am. Assn. Marriage and Family Therapy (dir. mem.), Ohio Assn. Marriage and Family Therapy, Am. Soc. Tng. and Devel. Office: 29225 Chagrin Blvd Pepper Pike Cleveland OH 44122

GEDGAUDAS, EUGENE, radiologist; b. Lithuania, Oct. 7, 1924; came to U.S., 1963, naturalized, 1968; M.D., U.Munich, 1948; married; children—Kristina, Nora, Sandra. Intern, St. Boniface Hosp., Winnipeg, Man., Can.; resident in radiology St. Boniface Hosp., Winnipeg, U. Minn., Hosp., Mpls.; chmn. cardiac unit, asso. radiologist St. Boniface Gen. Hosp., Winnipeg, 1958-63, also dir. dept. radiology Mericordia Gen. Hosp., Winnipeg; asst. prof. radiology U. Minn., Mpls., 1963-67, asso. prof., 1967-69, prof., 1969—, head radiology, 1969—, chmn. council clin. scis. Med. Sch., 1975—. Diplomate Am. Bd. Radiology. Fellow Royal Coll. Physicians and Surgeons Can., Am. Coll. Radiology, Internat. Coll. Surgery; mem. AMA, Radiol. Soc. N.Am., Am. Roentgen Ray Soc., Minn. Radiology Soc., Minn. Acad. Medicine, Assn. Univ. Radiologists, Soc. Chmn. Acad. Radiology Dept. Contbr. articles to profl. jours. Home: 26 Evergreen Rd North Oaks St Paul MN 55110 Office: Box 292 Radiology 420 Delaware St SE Minneapolis MN 55455

GEER, EMILY APT, historian; b. West Unity, Ohio, July 28, 1912; d. Norman J. and Pearl W. (Bayes) Apt; B.S., Bowling Green U., 1936, M.A., 1952; Ph.D., Case Western Res. U., 1962; m. Stanley L. Fisher, Mar. 17, 1934 (dec. 1945); children—Constance (dec.), Norman; m. 2d, Ralph H. Geer, Nov. 1, 1947. Tchr. elementary pub. schs., West Unity, 1932-35; staff asst. R.H. Macy & Co., N.Y.C., 1937-42; propr., mgr. Fisher-Smith Archery Co., Bryan, Ohio, 1945-48; instr. history Bowling Green Ohio State U., 1952-62; mem. faculty Findlay (Ohio) Coll., 1964-77, prof. history, 1968-77, chmn. div. social scis., 1966-77, prof. emeritus, 1977—. Pres. N.Y.C. Archers, 1941-42. Mem. Am. Hist. Assn., Orgn. Am. Historians, Ohio Acad. History (exec. council 1971-74, chmn. com. status of women historians 1974-76), AAUW (br. chmn. of coms. 1962-64), Am. Studies Assn., Phi Delta Kappa, Phi Alpha Theta, Pi Kappa Delta, Chi Omega. Methodist. Editorial bd. Hayes Hist. Jour., 1976-. Contbr. articles to hist. jours. Home: 4 Parkwood Dr Bowling Green OH 43402

GEHRING, FREDERICK WILLIAM, mathematician, educator; b. Ann Arbor, Mich., Aug. 7, 1925; s. Carl E. and Hester McNeal (Reed) G.; B.S.E. in Math., U. Mich., 1946, M.A. in Math., 1949; Ph.D. (Fulbright fellow) in Math., Cambridge U., Eng., 1952, Sc.D., 1976; Ph.D. (hon.) U. Helsinki (Finland), 1977; m. Lois Caroline Bigger, Aug. 29, 1953; children—Kalle Burgess, Peter Motz, Benjamin Peirce. Instr., Harvard U., 1952-55; instr. math. U. Mich., Ann Arbor, 1955-56, asst. prof., 1956-59, asso. prof., 1959-62, prof., 1962—, chmn. dept. math., 1973-75, 77—; vis. prof. Harvard U., 1964-65, Stanford U., 1964, U. Minn., 1971, Inst. Mittag-Leffler, Sweden, 1972. Served with USNR, 1943-46. Fulbright fellow, 1958-59; NSF fellow, 1959-60; Guggenheim fellow, 1958-59; Sci. Research Council sr. fellow Imperial Coll., Cambridge U., 1981; Humboldt fellow Tech. U., Berlin, 1981. Mem. Math. Assn. Am., Am. (council 1980—), Swiss, Finnish, London math. socs., Assn. Women in Math., Finnish Acad. Sci. Editor Duke Math. Jour., 1963-80, D. Van Nostrand Pub. Co., 1963-69, North Holland Pub. Co., 1970—, Springer-Verlag, 1974—; editorial bd. Procs. Am. Math. Soc., 1962-65, Ind. U. Math. Jour., 1967-75, Math. Revs., 1969-75, Bull. Am. Math. Soc., 1979—; contbr. articles on research in pure math. to sci. jours. Home: 2139 Melrose Ave Ann Arbor MI 48104

GEHRING, LAWRENCE, JR., supt. schs.; b. Elgin, Iowa, Apr. 20, 1926; s. Lawrence and Edna Sarah (Brackin) G.; B.A., U. No. Iowa, 1953, M.A., 1956; Ph.D., U. Iowa, 1975; m. Shirley Irene Boyle, Nov. 27, 1947; children—Mary, Russell, Joan, Mark. Tchr. public schs., Iowa, 1953-66; prin. Horace Mann High Sch., Gary, Ind., 1966-72, Central High Sch., Davenport, Iowa, 1972-78; supt. Ottawa Twp. High Sch. Dist., Ottawa, Ill., 1978—. Served with USN, 1945-47, 50-51. Recipient Perry Eugene McClenahan award, U. Iowa, 1976. Mem. Ottawa Area C. of C. (dir. 1981), Nat. Assn. Secondary Sch. Prins. Am. Assn. Sch. Adminstrs., Ill. Assn. Sch. Adminstrs., Phi Delta Kappa. Roman Catholic. Club: Rotary. Home: 317 Heritage Ln Ottawa IL 61350 Office: 211 E Main St Ottawa IL 61350

GEHRING, MARY EVELYN, dietitian; b. Brinkley, Ark., Dec. 24, 1929; d. Paul and Mary Grace (Porter) G.; B.S., Miss. Women's U., 1951. Dietetic intern Charity Hosp., New Orleans, 1951-52; asst. therapeutic dietitian Meth. Hosp. of Ind., Indpls., 1952-53, head therapeutic dietitian, 1953-56, dir. nutrition and dietetics, 1956—. Named Woman of Year, Indpls. C. of C., 1970. Mem. Am. Dietetic Assn., Am. Soc. Hosp. Food Service Adminstrs., Central Dist. Dietetic Assn. Republican. Methodist. Home: 8124 N Campbell St Indianapolis IN 46250 Office: Meth Hosp of Ind 1604 N Capitol St Indianapolis IN 46202

GEHRKE, CHARLES WILLIAM, biochemist; b. N.Y.C., July 18, 1917; s. Henry Edward and Louise (Mader) G.; B.A. in Biochemistry, Ohio State U., 1939, B.S. in Edn., 1941, M.S. in Biochemistry and Bacteriology, 1941; Ph.D. in Agrl. Biochemistry, Ohio State U., 1947; m. Virginia Dorothy Horcher, Dec. 25, 1941; children—Charles William, Jon Craig, Susan Gay. Prof., head dept. chemistry Missouri Valley Coll., Marshall, Mo., 1942-49; instr. agrl. chemistry Ohio State U., Columbus, 1945-46; asso. prof. agrl. chemistry U. Mo., Columbia, 1949-54, prof. biochemistry, 1954—, also mgr. Expt. Sta. Chem. Labs., 1954—, Honors lectr., 1978-79; co-investigator lunar samples NASA, 1969-75; speaker on molecular biology, numerous univs.; participant profl. Symposium, Freiburg, W. Ger., 1981. Recipient Faculty Alumni Gold Medal award U. Mo., 1975; Chromatography medal award Acad. Scis. USSR, 1980. Fellow Am. Inst. Chemists, Assn. Ofcl. Analytical Chemists (Harvey W. Wiley award 1971, chmn. Magruder standard sample subcom. 1958-79, dir. 1980, editorial com. 1980); mem. Am. Soc. Biol. Chemists, Am. Chem. Soc. (pres. Mo. sect. 1958-59, 78-79; Spencer award 1979), Am. Dairy Sci. Assn. (chmn. com. on protein nomenclature 1961-62), Fedn. Am. Socs. Exptl. Biology, AAAS, Internat. Soc. Study of Origin of Life, N.Y. Acad. Sci., Sigma Xi (Research award 1980). Clubs: Cosmopolitan Luncheon, Univ. (pres. 1981). Contbr. 200 articles on analytical chemistry, chromatography, and instrumental methods to sci. jours.; editorial bd. Jour. Chromatography, 1971—, AutoAnalysis, 1976-77, Jour. Chromatographic Sci., 1978—; author: 75 Years of Chromatography-A Historical Dialogue. Home: 708 Edgewood Ave Columbia MO 65201 Office: Agr Bldg Room 4 U MO Columbia MO 65211

GEHRKEN, LUDWIG WOELTJE, newspaper editor; b. Bremen, Ger., Jan. 23, 1940; came to U.S., 1965; s. Ludwig Heinrich and Irmgard Ilse (Meissner) G.; student in journalism, law and sociology, univs. Freiburg, Berlin, Hamburg and Munich, 1961-65; divorced; children—Goetz Ludwig, Antje-Irmgard, Solveig-Lara. Journalist, broadcaster in W. Ger., 1962-63; program dir., disc jockey Radio Internat., Chgo., 1965; freelance journalist for W. German newspapers, press services and radio stas., 1965; editor Abendpost Co., daily, Chgo., 1967—. Served with German Army, 1960-61. Mem. Internat. Assn. German Journalists Outside Ger., Schwaben Internat., Verein der Auslandsdeutschen, German-Am. Hist. Soc. (pres.), Sigma Delta Chi. Home: 5543 N Campbell Ave Chicago IL 60625 Office: 223 W Washington St Chicago IL 60606

GEHRT, EARL BENJAMIN, physician; b. Manhattan, Kans., July 12, 1932; s. John Henry and Helen (Wahl) G.; B.S., Kans. State U., 1954, M.D., 1962; m. Joanne Ruby Robbins, Dec. 22, 1957; children—Stanley Dean, Susan Kay, Julie Lynn, Dian Marie. Intern, Broadlawn Polk County Hosp., Des Moines, 1962-63; practice medicine specializing in family practice, Chanute, Kans., 1963—; affiliate Ashley Clinic; partner, staff Neosho Meml. Hosp.; asst. prof. Kans. U. Med. Center. Mem. Unified Dist. 413 Sch. Bd., 1969-78, pres., 1975, 76, 77. Served as pilot SAC, 1955-57. Diplomate Am. Bd. Family Practice. Mem. Am. Acad. Family Practice, S.E. Kans. Med. Soc. (past pres.), Kans. Med. Soc., AMA, Chanute C. of C. (named Progress Partner of Year 1976). Republican. Lutheran (past pres. congregation). Home: 1101 S Larson St Chanute KS 66720 Office: 505 S Plummer St Chanute KS 66720

GEIB, CHRISTOPHER WILLIAM, air force officer; b. Berea, Ohio, Sept. 29, 1951; s. William David and Edith Ella (Berg) G.; B.S. in Chemistry, Ohio No. U., 1973; m. Elizabeth Jean Roddy, Aug. 19, 1972; children—Jonathan Holiday, Matthew Christopher. Polymer research and devel. chemist Glidden-Durkee Co., Strongsville, Ohio, 1973-76; regional sales mgr. Vita-Mix Corp., Cleve., 1976-77; dist. sales rep. VWR Sci., Inc., Columbus, Ohio, 1977-78; commd. 2d lt. USAF, 1978, advanced to 1st lt., 1980; subcontract program mgr. USAF, Wright Patterson AFB, Ohio, 1978-80, data link devel. mgr., 1980-81; assigned to 351st Strategic Missile Wing, Whiteman AFB, Mo., 1981—. Vice pres. bd. mgrs. Westview Homeowners Assn., 1973-77; scoutmaster, unit commr. Cleve. council Boy Scouts Am., 1975-77, scoutmaster, dist. commr. Miami Valley council, 1979-81. Lic. pvt. pilot. Mem. Am. Water Works Assn., Air Force Assn., Am. Chem. Soc., Aircraft Owners and Pilots Assn., Nat. Rifle Assn. Home: 727 McConnell Ln Whiteman AFB MO 65305 Office: 351st Strategic Missile Wing/509th Strategic Missile Squadron Whiteman AFB MO 65305

GEIGER, DAVID SCOTT, mathematician; b. N.Y.C., Jan. 3, 1928; s. Earl Russel and Margaret Rose (Scott) G.; student U. So. Calif., 1948-51; B.S., U. Ill., 1954, Ph.D., 1961. Computer programmer U. Ill., Urbana, 1960-64; engaged in math. research. Served with U.S. Army, 1946-47. Mem. Am. Math. Soc., Friends of Animals.

GEIGER, HANS FREDERICH, engr., mfg. co. exec.; b. Indpls., Apr. 12, 1900; s. John George and Lena Barbara (Schmidt) G.; B.S. in Civil Engring., Purdue U., 1923; m. Florence T. Donovan, Nov. 2, 1929. Supr. constrn. Conder & Culdbertson Co., Indpls., 1923-25; supt., constrn. Colven Constn. Co., Indpls., 1925-26; chief engr. Geiger & Peters Inc., Indpls., 1926-30, self employed constrn. engr., 1930-47; salesmgr. Geilo Products, Indpls., 1950—. Served with N.G., 1940-45. Mem. Profl. Engrs. Assn., Purdue U. Alumni Assn., U.S. Power Squadron. Republican. Clubs: Mercator (past pres.), North Side Optimist (past pres.), Masons. Shriners, Elks. Patentee comml. slope gauge, direct reading course plotter, tri-roll dispenser, drafting slope gauge, furnace economizer means. Home and Office: 5845 N New Jersey St Indianapolis IN 46220

GEIGER, NANCY KAY, educator; b. Canton, Ohio, Dec. 26, 1954; d. Walter W. and Janice M. Geiger; B.A. cum laude, Mt. Union Coll., 1977; postgrad. U. Akron, 1978—. Presch. instr. Carroll Hills Tng. Center, Carrollton, Ohio, 1977-79, primary instr., 1979—, ednl. coordinator, 1979-80. Mem. Carroll County Council for Retarded Citizens; pianist Salem Reform Ch., 1978—, sec. Sunday Sch. Willing Workers, 1978-80. Mem. Profl. Assn. for Retardation. Office: 3011 Waynesburg Rd NW Carrollton OH 44615

GEIGLE, ROBERT RAYMOND, govt. ofcl.; b. Eureka, S.D., Dec. 23, 1947; s. Oscar and Minnie Irene (Ankerson) G.; B.S., Augustana Coll., 1969, M.A.T., 1973; adminstrv. cert. No. State Coll., 1978. Elem. tchr. Herreid (S.D.) Public Schs., 1969-74, rural sch. Winner (S.D.) Public Schs., 1974-76; tchr. Pollock (S.D.) Public Schs., 1976-79, elem. prin., 1976-79; program specialist, sect. for spl. edn., gifted and talented programs S.D. Edn. Dept., Pierre, 1979—; mem. Nat. Council Accreditation Tchr. Edn., 1976—. Organist, Pollock (S.D.) Lutheran Ch. and Peace Luth. Ch., Herreid, S.D., 1969-79; dir. Community Choir, Herreid, 1976-79. Mem. Council Exceptional Children, Nat. Assn. State Dirs. Spl. Edn., Sioux Falls Symphony Assn., Pierre Community Concert Assn., NEA, S.D. Edn. Assn., Assn. Supervision and Curriculum Devel., S.D. Assn. Supervision and Curriculum Devel., Nat. Assn. Gifted Children, Nat. Council State Dirs. Programs for Gifted, Augustana Alumni Assn. Republican. Clubs: Fellows Augustana Coll.; Pierre Players Asso. Producers. Author: Information and Resource Guide: Gifted Programs in South Dakota, 1981. Home: 417 S Tyler Pierre SD 57501 Office: RF Kneip Bldg Pierre SD 57501

GEIS, MILTON ARTHUR, artist, TV sta. exec.; b. Milw., Jan. 31, 1926; s. Edgar Jacob and Olga Luise (Jennrich) G.; student U. Florence, Italy, 1946, Columbia U., 1946; diploma Layton Sch. Art, Milw., 1951; m. Donna Ellen Holtz, Aug. 21, 1954; children—Joseph, Kalen. One man shows: St. Louis U., 1974, Ralston Purina Center, 1975, Frame Guild Gallery, 1976, Hardy Meml. Gallery, 1977, William Engel Gallery, 1979; group shows include: Butler Inst. Am. Art, Am. Watercolor Soc., Allied Artists Am., Audubon Artists Am., Nat. Arts Club, Salmagundi Club, Nat. Soc. Painters in Casein and Acrylic, Knickerbocker Artists Am., Rocky Mountain Nat.; represented in permanent collections: Meadows Mus., Centenary Coll., Tex. Tech. U. Mus., Milw. Art Inst., U. Wis., also pvt.

collections; art dir. Sta. WBAY-TV, Green Bay, Wis., 1952-56, Sta. WXIX-TV, Milw., 1956-60; dir. design Sta. KMOX-TV, St. Louis, 1960—, Served with U.S. Army, 1944-46. Recipient numerous art dir. and design awards, local Emmy award; Milw. Art Inst. Purchase award, 1956, Jean Despujols award, 1976, Meadows Mus. Purchase award, 1976, Arthur Stockstrom award St. Louis Artists Guild, 1976, Sarah Longmire award, 1979, M.C. Schworm award, 1980, Elizabeth Carson award, 1981; Grumbacher award Nat. Art Club, 1980. Mem. Ala. Nat. Watercolor Soc., Midwest Watercolor Soc., Nat. Soc. Painters in Casein and Acrylic, St. Louis Artists Guild, Peninsula Arts Assn., Broadcast Designers Assn., Audubon Artists of Am. Lutheran. Home: 8978 Lindenhurst Dr Saint Louis MO 63126 Office: 1 Memorial Dr Saint Louis MO 63102

GEISBERGER, GEORGE BAHR, educator; b. Freeport, Ill., Jan. 21, 1935; s. August and Rose Anna (Bahr) G.; B.A., Rockford Coll., 1956, M.A., 1962; postgrad. U. Wis. Tchr., Harlem Jr. High Sch., Rockford, Ill., 1956, Union (Ill.) Sch., 1957-62; head tchr. Argyle Sch., Rockford, 1962-64; chmn. sociology dept., dir. field work placement program Milton (Wis.) Coll., 1964-70; program coordinator U. Wis. Extension, Madison, 1972-77; dir. Dept. Edn., Beloit (Wis.) Meml. Hosp., 1977—; title search/cons. recreational devels., 1970-76. Sec.-treas. chpt. Muscular Dystrophy Assns. Am. Mem. AAUP, Am. Judicature Soc., Wis. Soc. for Health Manpower Edn. and Tng., Phi Delta Kappa. Home: PO Box 704 Rockford IL 61105 Office: 1969 W Hart Rd Beloit WI 53511

GEISENDORFER, JAMES VERNON, author; b. Brewster, Minn., Apr. 22, 1929; s. Victor H. and Anne B. (Johnson) G.; student Augustana Coll., 1950-51, Augsburg Coll., 1951-54, Orthodox Luth. Sem., 1954-55; B.A., U. Minn., 1960; LL.D., Burton Coll. and Sem., 1961; m. Esther Lillian Walker, Sept. 23, 1949; children—Jane, Karen, Lois. Grain buyer Pillsbury Mills, Inc., Worthington, Minn., 1947-48; hatchery acct., Worthington, 1949-50; night supr. Strutwear, Inc., Mpls., 1951-52; dispatcher Chgo. and North Western Ry., 1953-54; office mgr. Froedtert Malt Corp., Mpls., 1955-56, Nat. Automotive Parts Assn., 1957-60; sr. creative writer Brown & Bigelow, St. Paul, 1960-72; religious researcher, writer, 1972—; research cons. Inst. for the Study of Am. Religion; mem. panel of reference Chelston Bible Coll., New Milton, Eng. Recipient Amicus Poloniae medal Polish Ministry of Culture and Edn., 1969. Mem. Am. Acad. Religion, Can. Soc. for the Study of Religion, Aristotelian Soc. Lutheran. Author: (with J. Gordon Melton) A Directory of Religious Bodies in the United States, 1977; contbr. articles to books and periodicals; cons. editor Directory of Religious Organizations in the United States, 1977. Address: 1001 Shawano Ave Green Bay WI 54303

GEISLER, NATHAN DAVID, stockbroker; b. Kokand, Russia, Jan. 22, 1946; s. Leon and Esther (Korn) G.; B.A., Ohio State U., 1968; J.D., U. Toledo, 1970. Sr. account exec. Merrill Lynch Pierce Fenner & Smith, Toledo, 1973—. Served to capt. USAF, 1971-73. Mem. Am. Mgmt. Assn., Internat. Platform Assn., Air Force Assn., Ohio Air N.G. Assn., Ohio State Alumni Assn., U. Toledo Alumni Assn., Phi Alpha Delta. Home: 5906 Cresthaven Ln Apt C-2 Toledo OH 43614 Office: 300 Madison Ave Toledo OH 43604

GEISS, DOROTHY ELIZABETH, retail trade exec.; b. Youngstown, Ohio, Nov. 18, 1918; d. Jacob D. and Elizabeth (Wilson) Geiss; student pub. schs. Sec. Gen. Fireproofing Co., Youngstown, 1937-45; traffic clk. Strouss, Youngstown, 1945-47, traffic mgr., 1947-75, dir. transp., 1975—. Mem. bus. tech. adv. com. Ohio Bd. Regents, 1973-80; mem. transp. adv. bd. Youngstown State U., 1977-80. Mem. Nat. Retail Merchants Assn. (chmn. traffic group 1977-80, dir. 1956-80, silver plaque 1980), C. of C. Traffic Group, Delta Nu Alpha (Transp. Person of Yr. 1978). Author: A Mini Traffic Course, 1969. Home: 650 Niles-Cortland Rd NE Warren OH 44484 Office: 20 W Federal St Youngstown OH 44503

GEIST, CHRISANN SCHIRO, rehab. counselor; b. Chgo., Dec. 31, 1946; d. Joseph Frank and Ethel (Fortunato) Schiro; B.S., Loyola U., Chgo., 1967, M.Ed., 1970; Ph.D. (research grantee), Northwestern U., 1974; m. Glen O. Geist, Aug. 10, 1978; children—Jennifer, Daniel, Lori, Steven. Sci. tchr. Northbrook (Ill.) Jr. High Sch., 1967-70; dir. career counseling and placement Mundelein Coll., Chgo., 1972-74; human devel. counselor Regional Service Agy., Skokie, Ill., 1974-75; asst. prof. psychology, rehab. counselor Ill. Inst. Tech., Chgo., 1975—. Recipient Research award Sigma Xi, 1979, 80-81; Rehab. Services Adminstrn. Region V short-term tng. grant, 1978-79; cert. sex edn. cons.; registered psychologist, Ill. Mem. Am. Personnel and Guidance Assn., Nat. Rehab. Assn., Nat. Council Rehab. Edn., Ill. Rehab. Counseling Assn. (pres. 1979-80), Council on Rehab. Edn. (v.p. 1979-81), Kappa Beta Gamma Alumnae Assn. (nat. officer). Office: Psychology Dept Ill Inst Tech 3101 S State St Chicago IL 60616

GEIST, JAMES EUGENE, telephone co. exec.; b. Louisville, Nebr., Oct. 14, 1929; s. Alex M. and Elsie E. (Zelenka) G.; B.S. with high distinction, U. Nebr., 1960; m. Eleanor Richards, Feb. 7, 1954; 1 son, Alec James. With Southeastern Telephone Co., Tallahassee, 1956; with Lincoln Tel. & Tel. Co. (Nebr.), 1947-55, 56—, personnel coordinator, 1960-64, personnel supr., 1964-68, asst. to v.p. ops. and personnel dir., 1972-73, v.p. ops., 1973-76, exec. v.p., 1976—. Trustee, U. Nebr. Found.; bd. dirs. Lincoln Found., 1974-77, mem. adv. com., 1978—; bd. dirs. Easter Seals, 1975-80; active United Way of Lincoln, 1974-77. Served with USAF, 1950-54. Mem. Lincoln C. of C. (bd. dirs. 1975-80, pres. 1979), U.S. Ind. Telephone Assn. (pres. 1981, bd. dirs. 1973—). Methodist. Clubs: Nebr., Univ., Lincoln Country, Elks, Kiwanis (pres. 1973). Home: 1213 Crestdale Rd Lincoln NE 68510 Office: PO Box 81309 Lincoln NE 68501

GEIST, PAUL DEAN, utility co. exec.; b. Topeka, Kans., Nov. 22, 1923; s. William F. and Myrtle M. (Hardisty) G.; student Hutchinson Jr. Coll., 1941-42, Adela Hale Bus. Coll., 1941-42; m. Elnora Gwendolyn Gibbs, Nov. 24, 1948; children—Peggy Evelyn, Steven Paul. With Kans. Power & Light Co., 1946—, div. auditor, Hiawatha, 1953-58, Topeka, 1958-62, regional auditor, Hutchinson region, 1962—. Bd. dirs. ARC, Reno County, Kans., 1973-78, first aid instr., 1954-79. Served with U.S. Army, 1943-46. Mem. Hutchinson C. of C. Clubs: Moose, Carey Park Country. Home: 1204 W 31st St Hutchinson KS 67501 Office: 200 W 2nd St Hutchinson KS 67501

GELDER, MICHAEL ALLAN, health care cons.; b. Benton Harbor, Mich., July 18, 1949; s. Bert C. and Betty F. G.; B.A., Mich. State U., 1971; M.H.A., Washington U., St. Louis, 1973. Medichek regional coordinator Ill. Dept. Public Health, Chgo., 1973-75; health cons. Community Health Found., Evanston, Ill., 1975-77, project dir., 1978—; pres. Michael A. Gelder & Assos., Evanston; commr. Skokie Bd. Health; mem. exec. com. Health and Medicine Policy Research Group. Mem. Am. Public Health Assn., Am. Coll. Hosp. Adminstrs., Council on Health Promotion (dir.), Ill. Assn. Bds. Health (exec. council). Office: 3330 Lake St Evanston IL 60203

GELFAND, IVAN, investment adviser; b. Cleve., Mar. 29, 1927; s. Samuel and Sarah (Kruglin) G.; B.S., Miami U., 1950; postgrad Case-Western Res. U., 1951; grad. Columbia U. Bank Mgmt. Program, 1968; certificates Am. Inst. Banking; m. Suzanne Frank, Sept. 23, 1956; children—Dennis Scott, Andrew Steven. Accountant Central Nat. Bank of Cleve., 1950-53, v.p., mgr. bank and corp. investments, 1957-75; pres. Gelfand, Quinn & Assos. Inc., 1975-79, chmn. bd., chief exec. officer, 1979—; pres. Lindow, Gelfand & Quinn, Inc., 1976—; chief accountant Stars & Stripes newspaper, Darmstadt, Germany, 1953-55; account exec. Merrill Lynch, Pierce, Fenner & Smith, Inc., 1955-57. Instr. in investments, Cleve. Bd. Edn. adult div., 1956-58, Am. Inst. Banking 1958-68; lectr. econs., instl. portfolio mgmt., 1972—; money market columnist Nat. Thrift News, 1977-78; co-editor The Liquidity Portfolio Mgr., The Gelfand-Quinn Report, 1978-81, The Gelfand-Quinn Analysis-Money Market Techniques, 1981—. Mem. Greater Cleve. Growth Assn., 1968—; mem. investment com. United Torch of Cleve., 1972-74; study-rev. team Lake Erie Regional Transp. Assn., 1973-77. Mem. exec. fin. com. Cuyahoga County Republican Com.; mem. investment and bond com. Jewish Community Fedn., Cleve. Served with AUS, 1945-47. Mem. Cleve. Soc. Security Analysts, Les Politiques. Jewish. Clubs: Masons; Mid-day, Commerce, Univ. (Cleve.); Oakwood Country. Home: 2900 Alvord Pl Pepper Pike OH 44124 Office: Leader Bldg Cleveland OH 44114

GELLEN, ALEX, graphic designer; b. Budapest, Hungary, Apr. 30, 1941; s. S. and B. Gellen; grad. Art Acad. Cin., U. Cin.; m. Carol Flignor; children—Laurence, Scott. Owner, prin. A. Gellen Design, Cin. Mem. adv. bd. Ret. Sr. Vol. Program; exec. v.p. City of Hope, Cin. Served with USAF. Mem. Art Dirs. Club of Cin. (pres.), Am. Inst. Graphic Arts, Cin. Media Profls., Advt. Club Cin. Club: B'nai B'rith (past local pres.). Office: 405 Executive Bldg 35 E 7th St Cincinnati OH 45202

GELLER, ROBERT DENNIS, internist; b. N.Y.C., Apr. 5, 1941; s. Martin Max and Elvira Joan (Reich) G.; B.Met.E. cum laude, N.Y. U., 1962; M.D., Cornell U., 1966; m. Karen Hannk Greshes, Feb. 7, 1974; children—Meredith Anne, Evan Scott. Intern, Bellevue Hosp., N.Y.C., 1966-67, resident in medicine, 1967-68; resident in medicine North Shore U. Hosp., 1968-70; practice medicine specializing in internal medicine, cons. infectious disease, Manhasset, N.Y., 1972-77; practice medicine specializing in internal medicine, cons. infectious disease Freeport (Ill.) Clinic, S.C., 1977—, pres., chmn. bd., 1981—; clin. asst. prof. medicine Cornell U.; mem. med. malpractice panel N.Y. State Supreme Ct., Mineola, 1976; peer rev. com., bd. dirs. No. Ill. Profl. Standards Rev. Orgn., Rockford, 1978. Served with USPHS, 1970-72. Diplomate Am. Bd. Internal Medicine. Fellow A.C.P.; mem. Am. Heart Assn., Am. Soc. Microbiology, Am. Fedn. Clin. Research, AMA, Ill., Stephenson County med. socs. Contbr. articles on Coccidioidin skin test sensitivity to Am. Rev. Respiratory Diseases, 1972-73. Office: 1036 W Stephenson St Freeport IL 61032

GELLERSTED, HARRY WALTER, JR., investor; b. Chgo., Jan. 30, 1922; s. Harry W. and Mildred D. (Wilson) G.; grad. Ill. Wesleyan U., 1942; m. Marilyn Skillman, June 26, 1976; children—Diane C., Richard H. Pvt. investor, Chgo., 1972—. Served with USCG, 1942-46. Sigma Chi Alumni Assn. Chgo. Clubs: Bond, Rotary One Chgo., Execs. (Chgo.), Westmoreland Country, Tavern. Home: 570 Winnetka Ave Winnetka IL 60093

GELMAN, WARREN JAY, metals trading corp. exec.; b. Newark, Dec. 20, 1932; s. Nathan and Gertrude (Novergrad) G.; B.A. in Econs., Trinity Coll., Hartford, Conn., 1955; m. Susan E. Schwarz, Mar. 30, 1963; children—Joshua, Gregg, Wendy, Matthew, Herbert. With Gimbel's Dept. Store, N.Y.C., 1955; salesman York Litho, N.Y.C., 1957-58; purchaser raw materials Reading Metals Refining, 1958-61; pres. Web Trading, N.Y.C., 1961-62; partner Arrow Furniture, Cin., 1962-65; asst. dir. metal purchasing Cerro Copper & Brass, St. Louis, 1965-68; v.p. raw materials Diversified Industries Corp., St. Louis, 1968-72, pres. Diversified Metals Corp. subs., 1978—; v.p. Gerald Metals, N.Y.C., 1972-78. Served to capt. USAF, 1955-57. Mem. Nat. Assn. Recycling Industries (dir., v.p. metal dealers div.), Inst. Scrap Iron and Steel, Delta Kappa Epsilon. Republican. Jewish. Home: 25 Oakleigh Ln Ladue MO 63124 Office: 1034 S Brentwood Blvd Saint Louis MO 63117

GELMAN, WAYNE KENNETH, corp. ofcl.; b. Chgo., June 2, 1952; s. Sol D. and Shirley B. (Zimbler) G.; B.A. with honors, Northeastern Ill. U., 1974; postgrad. John Marshall Law Sch., 1976-78, Keller Grad. Sch. Mgmt., 1980. With purchasing dept. Ill. Atty. General's Office, Chgo., 1976-78; mgr. corporate purchasing Trans Union Corp., Chgo., 1976—. Active Young Republicans Orgn. Mem. Purchasing Mgmt. Assn. Chgo., Nat. Assn. Purchasing Mgmt., Internat. Assn. Purchasing Mgt. Home: 8653 Niles Center Rd Skokie IL 60077 Office: 111 W Jackson Blvd Chicago IL 60604

GELVIN, JOHN TIETGE, psychotherapist; b. Kansas City, Kans., Nov. 15, 1937; s. Lloyd Jay and Fon Bernice (Tietge) G.; A.A., Trenton Jr. Coll., 1973; B.S., N.E. Mo. State U., 1976, M.A., 1976; m. Ruth Ann Schreiner, Apr. 23, 1960; children—Geni Maria, Matthew Rome, Christine Louise. Mgr., Vumore Co., Brookfield, Mo., 1967, Trenton (Mo.) Cable TV, 1968-71; psychotherapist Kirksville (Mo.) Osteo. Hosp., 1976—. Campaign chmn. Linn County (Mo.) March of Dimes, 1966-68; dir. Adair County (Mo.) Civil Def., 1968-69; scoutmaster Boy Scouts Am., 1976-79; bd. dirs. Transitional Care Center, Inc., 1981—. Served in USN, 1956-59. Cert. psychologist. Mem. Am. Coll. Neuropsychiatry, Am. Psychol. Assn., Am. Personel and Guidance Assn., Assn. to Advance Ethical Hypnosis, Am. Mental Health Counselors Assn. Clubs: Lions, Elks. Home: Rural Route 2 Box 595 Kirksville MO 63501 Office: 800 W Jefferson St Kirksville MO 63501

GENGE, RAMESH BALABHAI, state ofcl.; b. Ahmedabad, India; came to U.S., 1963, naturalized, 1975; s. Balabhai J. and Kanta B. (Patwa) G.; BA., Gujerat Coll.; B.S., Husson Coll., Bangor, Maine, 1966; M.B.A., Suffolk U., 1969; m. Saroj K. Patel, July 1, 1970; children—Meelan, Ronuk. Asst. acctg. mgr. New Eng. Conf. Co., Cambridge, Mass., 1969-72; coast analyst Sanders Assos., Manchester, N.H., 1972-74; cost accounts mgr. Automation Ind. Co., Danbury, Conn., 1974-76; fiscal officer Ill. DAS, Springfield, 1976—. Gen. sec. India Assn. Greater Boston, 1970; pres. India Assn. Springfield, 1979. Mem. Am. Soc. Pub. Adminstrn., Assn. Govt. Accts. Home: 625 Rickard Rd Springfield IL 62704 Office: 703 Stratton Bldg Springfield IL 62702

GENIS, ALAN PAUL, elec. engr.; b. Chgo., Apr. 13, 1951; s. Peter Paul and Mary Ann (Nemeth) G.; B.S., No. Ill. U., 1973, M.S., 1977; Ph.D., Colo. State U., 1980; m. Carol Ann Van Der Marel, May 24, 1980. Lab. asst. Sherman Williams Labs., Chgo., 1968-69; grad. research asst. No. Ill. U., De Kalb, 1973-77, instr., 1975-77, mem. faculty dept. industry and tech., 1981—; grad. research asst. Colo. State U., Ft. Collins, 1977-81, cons. Colo. Crystal Corp., 1979-80. Mem. IEEE, Internat. Soc. for Hybrid Microelectronics, Electron Device Soc. Republican. Contbr. articles to profl. jours. Office: Dept Industry and Tech No Ill U DeKalb IL 60115

GENTES, JULIE L., trust co. exec.; b. Paxton, Ill., Nov. 3, 1947; d. Donald L. and LaVera A. (Leenerman) G.; B.S. in Mktg., U. Ill., 1969. Programmer, No. Trust Co., Chgo., 1969-72, program/system analyst, 1972-74, project leader/div. mgr., 1974-78, systems officer, 1974-81, standards/acctg./planning officer, 1978-81, bus. systems planning mgr., 2d v.p., 1981—. Mem. Am. Mgmt. Assn., Am. Inst. Banking, U. Ill. Alumni Assn., Cactus and Succulent Soc., Lincoln Park Zool. Soc., Ford County Hist. Soc. Contbg. author: Advances in Computer Programming Management, 1980. Home: 2700 N Hampden Ct Chicago IL 60614 Office: 125 S Wacker Dr Chicago IL 60675

GENTHE, WALTER ALFRED, mfg. co. exec.; b. Ludwigshafen, Germany, Mar. 20, 1926; s. Max Ferdinand and Hildegard (Ebbecke) G.; came to U.S., 1953; naturalized, 1958; Baccalaureat, Heidelberg (Germany) U., 1948; student Wayne State U., 1960; m. Marga Schimmer, July 24, 1945; children—George, Peter J., Michael W. Prodn. engr. Fisher Body div. Gen. Motors Corp., 1953; mgr. Meldrum Tool & Mfg. Co., Ferndale, Mich., 1953-59; v.p., gen. mgr. Worman Pilliant Co., Warren, Mich., 1959-63; gen. mgr. mfg. Paramount Fabricatings Co., automobile parts, Detroit, 1963-67; v.p., gen. mgr. Sparton Mfg. Co.; v.p. Sparton Corp. auto components, Flora, Ill., 1967-78, also dir.; pres., dir. Hella N.Am., Inc., 1978—. Mem. Flora High Sch. Bd. Edn., 1971-73; mem. vocat. tech. occupations adv. com. Ill. Eastern Jr. Colls., 1973-79. Mem. Ill. Mfrs. Assn., Soc. Automotive Engrs., Automobile Service Industry Assn., Flora C. of C., Clay County Arts Guild (pres. 1975-76). Republican. Lutheran. Elk. Clubs: Clay County Country; Fairlane (Dearborn, Mich.). Patentee automotive luggage carrier. Home: RFD 2 Flora IL 62839 Office: Box 399 Flora IL 62839

GENTILE, DANIEL JOHN, foundry exec.; b. Pitts., Sept. 15, 1926; s. Michael and Theresa (La Morte) Gugliemucci; indsl. engr. diploma Fenn Coll., 1953; B.B.A., Cleve. State U., 1967; M.A. in Econs., Case Western Res. U., 1977; m. Helen C. Curtis, June 30, 1956; children—Michael Charles, Charles Michael. Supr. indsl. engring. Lake City Malleable Co., Cleve., 1947-54; chief indsl. engring. Wellman Bronze & Aluminum Co., Cleve., 1954-59; mgr. mfg. engring. Superior Foundry Co., Cleve., 1959-61; with Elyria Foundry div. Chromalloy Corp., Elyria, Ohio, 1961—, v.p. adminstrn., 1977—. Served with USMC, 1945-46. Registered profl. engr., Calif. Mem. Am. Inst. Indsl. Engrs., Am. Foundrymen's Soc. (sec.-treas. 1969-75, chmn. N.E. Ohio chpt. 1979-80), Foundry Cast Metals, Ohio Cast Metals. Author tech. publs. including Foundry Industrial Engineering Handbook, 1974. Office: Elyria Foundry 120 Filbert St Elyria OH 44035

GENTILINI, JOSEPH MICHAEL, rehab. counselor; b. Columbus, Ohio, Aug. 22, 1948; s. Celso and Marie Elizabeth (Verhoff) G.; B.A. cum laude, Ohio Dominican Coll., 1970; M.A., Ohio State U., 1974; postgrad. Ohio U., 1978—. Tchr., Bishop Watterson High Sch., Columbus, 1970-71; cert. rehab. counselor Ohio Rehab. Services Commn., Columbus, 1972—. Mem. Am. Personnel and Guidance Assn., Nat. Rehab. Assn. (bd. mem. Central Ohio chpt. 1975-77), Nat. Rehab. Counseling Assn., Am. Rehab. Counseling Assn., Phi Kappa Phi. Democrat. Roman Catholic. Home: 2727 Westmont Blvd Columbus OH 43221

GENTLEMAN, JULIA BROOKS, state senator; b. Des Moines, Aug. 24, 1931; d. J. Woodson and Marguerite (Palcho) Brooks; B.S., Northwestern U., 1953; m. Gregor J. Gentleman, 1954; children—Karen Gentleman Powlen, Marcia Gentleman Frenell, Katherine B., J. Brooks, Mac Gregor. Mem. Iowa. Ho. of Reps. 1975-78; Iowa Senate, 1979. Office: State Senate Des Moines IA 50319

GENTLING, PHILLIP HENRY, dentist; b. New Orleans, Jan. 19, 1918; s. Gregory Phillip and Agnes Priscilla (Postier) G.; B.S., Tulane U., 1941; D.D.S., Northwestern U., 1944; m. Mary Jane Holmes, Sept. 9, 1942; children—Kirk, Colin, Linda, Nancy. Pvt. dental practice, Rochester, Minn.; pres. Doctors Gentling Ltd., 1946—; pres., dir. Rochester Mustang Hockey Assn., 1947-52. Bd. dirs. Rochester Softball Assn., 1948; bd. dirs. Bethany Lutheran Home, 1968-81, pres., 1979-81; bd. dirs. and planning bd. United Fund, 1962-70; bd. dirs. Samaritan-Bethany Nursing Home, 1975—; bd. dirs. Rochester YMCA, 1976—, chmn. world service com., 1978-79; bd. dirs., mem. personnel com. YMCA Camp Olson, 1977-80. Served with USNR, 1942-46. Mem. ADA, S.E. Minn. Dist. Dental Soc. (pres. 1974-75, del. to state dental assn. 1973-76), Zumbro Valley Dental Assn. (dir. 1975-78), Am. Legion. Mason, Lutheran (trustee 1956-62, pres. trustees 1961). Clubs: Exchange (dir. 1949-51, pres. 1950), Shriners. Home: 2221 Baihly Ct SW Rochester MN 55901 Office: 2210 N Broadway Rochester MN 55901

GENTRY, JAMES EDWARD, video center exec.; b. Mpls., Jan. 13, 1945; s. James and Thirza Gentry; student speech U. Minn., 1966; m. Carol W. Soper, Oct. 28, 1965; children—Christopher, Elizabeth, Emily. Asst. sales promotion mgr. Dayton's Dept. Store, Mpls., 1966-67; pres. Multimedia, Inc., Mpls., 1967-70; v.p. mktg. services Sun Newspapers, Mpls., 1970-71; dir. promotional services Dayton-Hudson, Mpls., 1971-76; gen. mgr. The Multimedia Forum, Hallmark Cards, Inc., Kansas City, Mo., 1976—. Mem. Nat. Assn. Broadcasters, Nat. Assn. TV Program Execs., Assn. Multi-Image, Advt. Club. Republican. Presbyterian. Author: Chief, 1981; also TV pilots. Home: 5257 N Baltimore Ave Kansas City MO 64118 Office: 2450 Grand Ave Suite 400 Kansas City MO 64108

GEO-KARIS, ADELINE JAY, state senator; student Northwestern U., Mt. Holyoke Coll.; LL.B., DePaul U. Admitted to Ill. bar; founder Adeline J. Geo-Karis and Assos., Zion, Ill., 19—; former mcpl., legis. atty. Mundeline, Ill., Vernon Hills, Ill., Libertyville (Ill.) Twp., Long Grove (Ill.) Sch. Dist.; justice of peace; former asst. state's atty.; former mem. Ill. Ho. of Reps.; mem. Ill. Senate. Served with USNR.; comdr. Res. ret. Recipient Americanism medal DAR; named Woman of Yr., Daus. of Penelope, Outstanding Legislator Ill. Fedn. Ind. Colls. and Univs., 1975-78, legis. award Ill. Assn. Park Dists., 1976. Address: PO Box 33 Zion IL 60099*

GEORGE, CAROL LAVONNE, data processing exec.; b. Omaha, Jan. 4, 1952; d. Max P. and Cloe Beth (Armstrong) Liebers; student Schweiter Tech., 1977-78, Okla. State U., 1980; m. Melvin Leroy George, Dec. 24, 1977; children by previous marriage—Steven LeeRoy Hannawald, Tarasa LyNe Hannawald, Tamara LaVonne Hannawald. Data processing dir./systems analyst City of Liberal, Kans., 1978—. Mem. adv. com. Seward County Community Coll. Baptist. Office: 325 N Washington St Liberal KS 67901

GEORGE, EMERY EDWARD, educator, poet; b. Budapest, Hungary, May 8, 1933; s. Larry Hofbauer and Julianna (Deutsch) G.; came to U.S., 1946, naturalized, 1954; A.B., U. Mich., 1955, M.A., 1959, Ph.D., 1964, Ottendorfer Meml. fellow, 1961-62; m. Mary Gertrude Wiedenbeck, May 9, 1969. Instr., U. Ill., Urbana, 1964-65, asst. prof., 1965-66; asst. prof. U. Mich., Ann Arbor, 1966-69, asso. prof., 1969-75, prof. Germanic langs. and lit., 1975—; faculty research fellow, grantee, 1969; guest Hungarian PEN Club, Budapest, 1979; IREX Exchange Fellow to Hungary, 1981. Served with U.S. Army, 1955-58. Recipient Avery Hopwood award in Poetry, 1960. Fellow Internat. Acad. Poets (founder, Cambridge, Eng.); mem. MLA, Holderlin-Gesellschaft (Tubingen, W. Ger.), Poetry Soc. Am., Internat. PEN, Internat. Poetry Soc., Shelley Soc. N.Y. (hon.), Spoon River Poetry Soc., Goethe Soc. N. Am., U. Mich. Research Club. Author: Holderlin's Ars Poetica, 1973; Mountainwild: Poems, 1974;

Black Jesus, 1974; A Gift of Nerve: Poems, 1978; Kate's Death: A Book of Odes, 1980; editor: Friedrich Holderlin, 1972; Husbanding the Golden Grain, 1973; translator: Subway Stops (Miklos Radnoti), 1977, The Complete Poetry (Miklos Radnoti), 1980; founding editor Mich. Germanic Studies, 1975—; asso. editor Russian Lit. Triquarterly, 1973—; editorial bd. Germano-Slavica, 1973—; editor, pub. Kylix Press, 1974—; editorial bd. Mich. Monographs in the Humanities, 1979—; contbr. poems, articles, translations, revs. Office: Univ Mich 3142 Modern Langs Bldg Ann Arbor MI 48109

GEORGE, GARY RAYMOND, state senator; b. Milw., Mar. 8, 1954; s. Horace Raymond and Audrey C. (Chevalier) G.; B.B.A., U. Wis., 1976; J.D., Mich. Law Sch., 1979; m. Mary Cook, Aug. 26, 1978; 1 son, Alexander Raymond. With Tax Dept., Arthur Young & Co., Milw., 1979-81; Wis. State senator from 6th Senate Dist., Madison, 1981—. Democrat. Roman Catholic. Office: 319 S State Capitol Madison WI 53702

GEORGE, HAROLD EUGENE, osteo. physician; b. Lancaster, Mo., Jan. 25, 1923; s. Frederick Milton and Opal (Darby) G.; B.S., N.E. Mo. State Coll., 1949; D.O., Kirksville Coll. Osteo. Medicine, 1951; children by previous marriage—Frederick Maurice, Robert Eugene, Jane Ann; m. 2d, Betty Doss Power; children—John Scott, Susan Virginia, Mary Evelyn, Carol Anne. Gen. practice osteo. medicine and surgery, Mt. Vernon, Mo., 1951—; health officer Lawrence County, Mo., 1953—; staff Jane Chinn Meml. Hosp., Webb City, Mo., 1951—, Springfield Gen. Osteo. Hosp., 1951—; chmn. profl. staff Springfield Gen. Osteo. Hosp., 1962-65; owner, dir. Mt. Vernon Clinic, 1957—; v.p. Three V Corp., 1978—; pres. Buffalo Foods div. 4 S Corp., Buffalo, Mo. Mem. med. care adv. com. Mo. Div. Welfare, 1963—; v.p. George & Harding, Inc., Joplin, Mo. Bd. dirs. Mo. Health Care Found., 1972-73. Served with USAAF, 1943-46. Fellow Am. Clin. Soc. Arthritis; mem. Am., Mo., Ozark Mo. osteo. assns., Am. Soc. Sclerotherapy, Mo. Assn. Osteo. Physicians and Surgeons (mem. pub. relations com. 1965—, mem. com. pub. health del.), Mo. Heart Assn. (dir.), Am. Coll. Gen. Practicioners (pres. Mo. chpt. 1972-73), Am. Coll. Preventive Medicine. Mason (Shriner). Home: Lane Tree Farms Route 1 Box 98 Mount Vernon MO 65712 Office: Mt Vernon Clinic East Ave and Hwy 166 Mount Vernon MO 65712 also H & B Import Bus Loop I-44 Route 1 Box 3H Mount Vernon MO 65712

GEORGE, JOHYNE OUIDA, restaurant exec.; b. Blytheville, Ark., June 3, 1949; d. John and Bernice Lee (Aiken) Hamra; B.A., Memphis State U., 1971; m. Donald George, July 8, 1973. Asso. buyer Goldsmith's, Memphis, 1971-72; store mgr., buyer Hamra's Dept. Store, Dexter, Mo., 1972-73; instr. Am. Inst. Mdse., Memphis, 1973-74; v.p. adminstrn. Wendy's Old Fashioned Hamburgers Kansas City, Inc., 1975—; asso. dir. Traders Nat. Bank of Kansas City. Mem. Greater Kansas City C. of C., Conv. and Vis. Bur. Greater Kansas City, Mo. Restaurant Assn. Methodist. Home: 5520 State Line Rd Mission Hills KS 66208 Office: 6528 Raytown Rd Suite B Raytown MO 64133

GEORGE, ROBERT JAMES, physician; b. Youngstown, Ohio, Dec. 4, 1941; s. Michael Charles and Virginia Teresa (Nassar) G.; B.S., Youngstown U., 1964; D.O., Kans. City Coll. Osteo. Medicine, 1968; m. Goldie A. Rogan, June 8, 1968; children—Michael, Mark, Michelle. Intern, Green Cross Gen. Hosp., 1968-69; resident, 1969-72; dir. med. edn. Cuyahoga Falls Gen. Hosp., 1972-76, 79—, med. dir., 1976—; dir. edn., med. dir. Doctors Hosp., Massillon, Ohio, 1976-79; asso. prof. family medicine Kans. City Coll. Osteo. Medicine, W.Va. Coll. Osteo. Medicine, Ohio U. Coll. Osteo. Medicine. Program dir. Am. Cancer Soc. Summit County, 1974; mem. program com. Summit County chpt. Am. Heart Assn., 1977-78. Diplomate Am. Bd. Family Practice, Am. Bd. Gen. Practice. Fellow Am. Acad. Family Physicians, Am. Coll. Gen. Practice in Osteo. Medicine and Surgery; mem. Am. Osteo. Assn., Ohio Osteo. Assn., Am. Acad. Family Practice, Am. Coll. Gen. Practice, Soc. Tchrs. in Family Medicine, Am. Coll. Emergency Physicians. Democrat. Roman Catholic. Home: 661 Olentangy Circle Akron OH 44313 Office: 1900 23d St Cuyahoga Falls OH 44223

GEORGE, WALTER, commn. dir., former state senator Nebr.; b. Gudensberg, Ger., Apr. 23, 1929; s. Carl and Margarethe (Dott) G.; student U. Heidelberg, U. Marburg, U. N.C.; M.A., U. Nebr., 1956—; m. Ann A. Harms, Aug. 26, 1955; children—Eric H., Stephen W. Prof., Dana Coll., Blair, Nebr., 1966-74; mem. Blair City Council, 1972-74; mem. Nebr. Senate, 1974-80, chmn. Urban Affairs Com., vice-chmn. Edn. Com., Govt. Com., Telecommunications Com.; Neb. rep. Nat. Conf. State Legislators Indian Affairs Task Force; dir. European Office, Old West Regional Commn., 1980—. Sec. Midwest Task Force for Beef Export Inc., 1975—. Fulbright scholar, 1954-55. Republican. Lutheran. Home: 3065 College Dr Blair NE 68008 Office: Old West Regional Commn Capim Center Rossmarkt 15 6000 Frankfurt/M1 West Germany

GEORGES, ROBERT EUGENE, univ. dean, educator; b. Manhattan, Kans., Nov. 3, 1921; s. Theodore John and Pauline Marie G.; B.B.A. summa cum laude, Ohio State U., 1956; M.B.A., George Washington U., 1965; postgrad. Ohio State U., 1965-68; student Air War Coll., 1965, Air Command and Staff Coll., 1953; m. Ethel Ilene Janzen, Oct. 3, 1942; children—Robert Eugene, Janet Sue, Judy K., Debra A., Ted M., Gregory L., Richard D., Steven B. Commd. 2d lt., pilot, U.S. Air Force, 1942, advanced through grades to lt. col., 1942-65; ret., 1965; with Ohio State U., 1965—, asso. dean for undergrad. programs in bus. and acctg., 1970—, asso. prof. mgmt. sci. Coll. Adminstrv. Sci., 1971—; cons. Am. Council Edn., Washington. Bd. dirs. Regional Jr. Achievement; mem. Regional Small Bus. Adv. Council; mem. Mayor's Salary Bd., Columbus; chmn. Ohio State U. chpt. United Appeal, 1975. Mem. Air Force Assn., Ret. Officers Assn., Am. Personnel and Guidance Assn., Beta Gamma Sigma, Alpha Kappa Psi, Beta Alpha Psi, Delta Sigma Pi, Phi Alpha Kappa, Phi Eta Sigma, Phi Delta Kappa. Roman Catholic. Clubs: Faculty, Officers. Home: 7265 Cooper Rd Westerville OH 43081 Office: Coll Adminstrv Sci Ohio State Univ Columbus OH 43081

GEORGESON, MENAS E., osteo. physician; b. Webb City, Mo., Sept. 29, 1920; s. Emmanuel M. and Mary (Galactos) Georgopulos; B.S., Wayne State U., 1943; D.O., Coll. Osteo. Medicine and Surgery, 1948; children—Christopher, Maria. Pharmacist, 1943-45; osteo. physician, individual practice, Detroit, 1950—. Trustee NW Gen. Hosp., Detroit, 1966—. Served with USNR, 1943-44. Fellow Hypnosis Found. (life); mem. Am., Mich., Wayne County osteo. assns., Am. Soc. Bariatric Physicians. Greek Orthodox. Clubs: Masons, Shriners. Home: 28235 Forestbrook Ct Farmington Hills MI 48018 Office: 19621 W 7 Mile Rd Detroit MI 48219

GEPHARDT, RICHARD ANDREW, congressman; b. St. Louis, Jan. 31, 1941; s. Louis Andrew and Loreen Estelle (Cassell) G.; B.S., Northwestern U., 1962; J.D., U. Mich., 1965; m. Jane Ann Byrnes, Aug. 13, 1966; children—Matthew, Christine, Katherine Hope. Admitted to Mo. bar, 1965; partner firm Thompson & Mitchell, St. Louis, 1965-76; alderman 14th ward, St. Louis, 1971-76; mem. 95th-97th Congresses from 3d Dist. Mo., 1977—, mem. Ways and Means com., Budget com. Pres., Children's United Research Effort, Inc., 1974-76; mem. devel. bd. St. Louis Children's Hosp., 1975-76; Democratic committeeman 14th ward St. Louis, 1968-71; bd. dirs. St. Louis council Boy Scouts Am., 1975—. Recipient Better Downtown award City of St. Louis, 1973; Disting. Service award St. Louis Jaycees, 1974. Mem. Mo. (chmn. young lawyers sect. 1972-73), St. Louis (chmn. young lawyers sect. 1971-72) bar assns., Am. Legion, Young Lawyer's Soc. (chmn. 1972-73). Clubs: Kiwanis, Mid-Town (St. Louis). Home: 4121 Fairview St Saint Louis MO 63116 Office: 209 Cannon House Office Bldg Washington DC 20515

GERARD, WILLIAM GENE, fin. co. exec.; b. Decatur, Ill., Dec. 10, 1932; s. William Alexander and Pauline Katherine (Brown) G.; B.A., Dartmouth Coll., 1955; M.B.A., Northwestern U., 1957; m. Georgette M. Schroeder, Sept. 30, 1960; children—Jennifer, Lisa, Kathleen. Investment banker White & Co., St. Louis, 1961-68; v.p. fin. Liberty Loan Corp., St. Louis, 1970-74; sr. v.p., treas. ITT Fin. Corp., St. Louis, 1975—. Mem. adv. bd. Mo. Baptist Hosp. Served with U.S. Army, 1956-60. Mem. Fin. Analysts Fedn., Fin. Execs. Inst., Nat. Consumer Fin. Assn., Dartmouth Coll. Alumni Council. Club: St. Louis. Office: 700 Community Federal Center St Louis MO 63131

GERBER, EUGENE J., bishop; b. Kingman, Kans., Apr. 30, 1931; s. Cornelius John and Lena Marie (Tiesmeyer) G.; B.A., St. Thomas Sem., Denver; B.S., Wichita State U.; B.S.Th., Catholic U. Am.; S.T.L., Angelicum, Rome. Ordained priest Roman Cath. Ch., 1959; asst. chancellor, Wichita Diocese, 1963, sec. to bishop, 1964, vice chancellor, 1967, mem. diocesan bd. adminstrn., 1973, diocesan cons., 1973, chancellor, 1975; chaplain, mem. governing bd. Holy Family Center for Mentally Retarded; bd. dirs. Cursillo; pastor Blessed Sacrament Parish, Wichita, bishop of Dodge City, Kans., 1976—. Office: Chancery Office 910 Central Ave PO Box 849 Dodge City KS 67801

GERBER, GEORGE ROBERT, obstetrician-gynecologist; b. Detroit, Feb. 15, 1934; s. William John and Signe W. (Wallin) G.; B.S., U. Detroit, 1956; M.D., Wayne State U., 1960; M.B.A., Oakland U., 1981; m. Mary Ann Kalwinski, Nov. 26, 1959; children—David John, Lisa Marie, Mary Jo. Intern, Mt. Carmel Hosp., Detroit, 1960-61, resident in ob-gyn., 1963-67; practice medicine specializing in ob-gyn., Rochester, Mich., 1967—; adj. asso. prof. health sci. Oakland U., 1976—; mem. staff Crittenton Hosp., Rochester, 1967—. Served with U.S. Navy, 1961-63. Diplomate Am. Bd. Obstetrics and Gynecology. Fellow Am. Coll. Obstetricians and Gynecologists; mem. Oakland County Med. Soc., Mich. Med. Soc. Roman Catholic. Home: 350 Beechview St Rochester MI 48063 Office: 83 E Avon St Rochester MI 48063

GERBER, HERBERT EGBERT, ednl. adminstr.; b. Saginaw, Mich., July 13, 1935; s. Arthur John Gerber and Henrietta (Mitchell) Stearns; B.A. in Bus. Adminstrn., Alma Coll., 1957; teaching cert. Wayne State U.; M.A., Central Mich. U., 1963; postgrad. Mich. State U., 1971-72; m. Elizabeth Marie Harvey, July 30, 1966; children—Anna Katherine Marie, Arthur John. With Saginaw Public Schs., 1959—, now asst. prin. for pupil personnel. Mem. Nat. Assn. Secondary Sch. Prins., Mich. Assn. Secondary Sch. Prins., Saginaw Assn. Secondary Sch. Prins., Assn. Supervision and Curriculum Devel., Saginaw Edn. Assn., Mich. Edn. Assn., NEA, Mich. Council English Tchrs., Central Mich. U. Alumni Assn., Jr. C. of C., Phi Delta Kappa, Tau Kappa Epsilon. Republican. Presbyterian. Clubs: Fordney, Tawas Bay Yacht, Great Lakes Sportsman, Toastmasters, Elks. Home: 4740 Hepburn Pl Saginaw MI 48603 Office: 3115 Mackinaw St Saginaw MI 48602

GERDE, PRISCILLA MURPHY, found. adminstr.; b. Indpls., Dec. 5, 1949; d. Moris Leon and Josephine (Clark) Murphy; B.A., Purdue U., 1972; postgrad. Ind.-Purdue U., Indpls., 1978; m. Carlyle Noyes Gerde, July 4, 1976. Dir. publs. Ind. Dept. Commerce, 1972-73; coordinator editorial services Eli Lilly & Co., 1973-76; sec. Eli Lilly & Co., Found., Indpls., 1976-79, 79—; Lilly sales rep., Pittsfield, Mass., 1979. Bd. dirs. Ind. chpt. Arthritis Found., 1977—, Met. Arts Council of Indpls., 1981—; regional dir. Women's Soc. of Indpls. Symphony Orch., 1978—. Named Outstanding Woman in Lafayette, Lafayette (Ind.) Bus. and Profl. Women, 1978. Mem. Women in Communications, Indpls. C. of C., Lafayette Bus. and Profl. Women (dist. officer 1980—). Republican. Club: Tippecanoe County. Home: Lakehurst Battle Ground IN 47920 Office: 307 E McCarty St Indianapolis IN 46285

GERDES, JERRELL FOSTER, hosp. adminstr.; b. Benkelman, Nebr., July 22, 1948; s. Foster Finley and Lucille Maxine (Mulvany) G.; student George Washington U., 1976-78, Trinity U., 1978; m. Charline Lou Ham, May 21, 1966; children—Patrick, Shelley, Brian. Adminstr., Hitchcock County Hosp., Stratton, Nebr., 1971-73, Oxford Home for Sr. Citizens, 1973-78, Fritzer Meml. Hosp., Oxford, Nebr., 1973—; mem. faculty Central Tech. Community Coll. Pres. Oxford Bd. Edn., 1979; sec.-treas. Nebr. Rescue and Emergency Care Assn., 1972-77. Adm. Great Navy of Nebr.; hon. lt. col. aide-de-camp State of Ala. Mem. Am. Guild Patient Acct. Mgrs., Am. Coll. Nursing Home Adminstrs., Hosp. Fin. Mgmt. Assn. Republican. Methodist. Clubs: Masons, Shriners, Elks. Home: 509 Ewing St Oxford NE 68967 Office: 811 Howell St Oxford NE 68967

GERDES, LOUIS GEORGE, editor; b. Hamlin, Iowa, Jan. 14, 1919; s. Louis George and Mable (Hunt) G.; B.J., U. Mo., 1941; m. Helen M. Swank, July 9, 1941; 1 son, Stephen Lee. Sports editor Grand Island (Nebr.) Herald, 1937; reporter Grand Island Bull., summers 1938, 39; editor Jefferson County (Wis.) Union, 1941; sports copy editor Omaha World-Herald, 1941-43, govtl. and polit. reporter, 1943-51, city editor, 1951-66, exec. editor, from 1966, v.p., 1969-79, editor editorial pages, 1979—, dir., 1966—. Bd. dirs. Nebr. Crippled Children's Soc., Omaha Found. Public Giving. Mem. Am. Soc. Newspaper Editors. Mem. United Ch. Christ. Club: Omaha. Author booklets on mcpl. govt., parking. Home: 1326 S 91st Ave Omaha NE 68124 Office: Omaha World Herald 14th and Dodge Sts Omaha NE 68102*

GEREAU, RICK, elec. mfg. co. exec.; b. Sioux City, Iowa, Dec. 30, 1930; s. Jesse and Bertha (Lorenz) G.; B.A., S.D. State U., 1978; m. Elizabeth Ann Kroeger, Feb. 7, 1953; children—Kim, Roxanne, Tracy, Rick Gene. Sportscaster, then gen. sales mgr. in radio broadcasting, 1954-76; engaged in banking, 1976-78; system designer Northeast S.D., Motorola, Inc., Watertown, 1978—. Commr., Pheasant council Boy Scouts Am., 1964-65, S.D. Amateur Baseball, 1961-63. Served with USMCR, 1948-50. Recipient various service awards; Disting. Service award S.D. High Sch. Athletic Assn., 1979. Mem. Watertown Area C. of C., Watertown Ambassadors Club, Watertown Downtown Bus. Assn. Roman Catholic. Clubs: Watertown Quarterback (pres. 1959, 60; Quarterback of Year award 1968), Magic Mile Lions (pres. 1975, 76), Watertown Elks (exalter ruler 1962, pres. S.D. 1971). Address: 872 Hidden Valley Dr Watertown SD 57201

GERG, CARL ARTHUR, business exec.; b. Niagara Falls, N.Y., Feb. 19, 1947; s. James Arthur and Marjorie Louise (Jorgensen) G.; student Ind. U., 1965-67; B.S., Duquesne U., 1973; M.B.A., U. Denver, 1974; m. Joanne S. Bozoukoff, Aug. 4, 1967; 1 son, James B. Unit mgr. Plastic Applicators, Inc., Harvey, La., 1976-77; indsl. engr. Ingalls Shipbuilding div. Litton Industries, Pascagoula, Miss., 1977-78; corp. sec. Polydimensional Service Systems, Inc., Oceans Springs, Miss., 1978; project adminstr. Northrop DSD Corp., Rolling Meadows, Ill., 1978-79; lead fin. systems analyst G.D. Searle & Co., Skokie, Ill., 1979-80; sr. fin. systems analyst N. Am. Philips Corp., Itasca, Ill., 1980; sr. fin. systems analyst Underwriters Labs., Inc., Northbrook, Ill., 1980—. Pres., Hickory Hill Country Club Homeowners Assn., 1977-78. Served with USN, 1967-70. Mem. Am. Mgmt. Assn., Assn. M.B.A. Execs., Omicron Delta Epsilon. Home: 2002 E Crabtree Dr Arlington Heights IL 60004 Office: 333 Pfingsten Rd Northbrook IL 60062

GERHART, JUDITH ANN, ednl. adminstr.; b. Indpls., Apr. 6, 1946; d. Elmer H. and Ruth E. (Geier) Cox; student Ind. U., 1965-67; B.S., DePaul U., 1969, M.Ed., 1972; Ed.D., Nova U., 1976. Instr., Bremen High Sch., Midlothian, Ill., 1969-71, Central YMCA Community Coll., Chgo., 1969-71, Thornton High Sch., Lansing, Ill., 1970-71; instr. secretarial sci. Oakton Community Coll., Morton Grove, Ill., 1971-72, asst. prof. secretarial sci. program, 1972-78, asso. prof. office systems tech. and word processing, 1978—, chmn. dept. office systems tech. and word processing, 1972—, coordinator coll.-wide faculty and staff devel. program, 1980—; coordinator Midwest cluster Inst. Higher Edn., Nova U., Fort Lauderdale, Fla., 1976—; condr. word processing and communications workshops, 1974—. Named Young Career Woman of Yr., Bus. and Profl. Women's Assn., 1975. Mem. Am. Assn. Higher Edn., Am. Vocat. Assn., Ill. Vocat. Assn., Am. Mgmt. Soc., Am. Soc. Tng. and Devel., Council of Women, Internat. Word Processing Assn., Nat. Secretaries Assn., Nat. Bus. Edn. Assn., Ill. Bus. Edn. Assn., Delta Pi Epsilon, Kappa Delta Pi. Republican. Mem. Christian Ch. Home: 600 Gillick St Park Ridge IL 60068 Office: 1600 Golf Rd Des Plaines IL 60016

GERLITZ, FRANK EDWARD, biomed. engr.; b. Phila., May 31, 1948; s. Frank Edward and LaNieta Vivian (Souden) G.; B.S., Bucknell U., 1970; B.S., U. Wis., Madison, 1973, M.S., 1977. Biomed. engr. Madison Area Tech. Coll., 1975-76, Otto Hiller Co., Madison, 1973—, U. Wis., Madison, 1973—. Mem. ASCE, ASME, Am. Engring. Model Soc., Biomed. Engring. Soc. Home: 1625 Madison St Madison WI 53711

GERMANN, RICHARD P(AUL), chemist, business exec.; b. Ithaca, N.Y., Apr. 3, 1918; s. Frank E. E. and Martha Mary Marie (Knechtel) G.; B.A., Colo. U., 1939; student Western Res. U. (Naval Research fellow), 1941-43, Brown U., 1954; m. Malinda Jane Plietz, Dec. 11, 1942; 1 dau., Cheranne Lee. Chief analytical chemist Taylor Refining Co., Corpus Christi, 1943-44; research devel. chemist Calco Chem. div. Am. Cyanamid Co., 1944-52; devel. chemist charge pilot plant Alrose Chem. Co. div. Geigy Chem. Corp., 1952-55; new product devel. chemist, research div. W. R. Grace & Co., Clarksville, Md., 1955-60; chief chemist soap-cosmetic div. G.H. Packwood Mfg. Co., St. Louis, 1960-61; coordinator chem. product devel. Abbott Labs., North Chicago, Ill., 1961-71; internat. chem. cons. to mgmt., 1971-73; pres. Germann Internat. Ltd., 1973—; pres. Ramtek Internat. Ltd., 1973—; real estate broker, 1972—. Rep. Am. Inst. Chemists to Joint Com. on Employment Practices, 1969-72. Vestryman, St. Paul's Episcopal Ch., Norwalk, Ohio, 1978-81, also chmn. adminstrn. and long range planning commn., 1980-81. Fellow Am. Inst. Chemist (chmn. com. employment relations 1969—), Chem. Soc. (London), AAAS; mem. Am. Chem. Soc. (chmn. membership com. chem. mktg. and econs. div. 1966-68, chmn. program com. 1968-69, del. at large for local sects. 1970-71, councilor, 1971-73, chmn. 1972-73; chmn. Chgo. program com. 1966-67, chmn. Chgo. endowment com. 1967-68, dir. Chgo. sect. 1968-72; chmn. awards com. 1972-73; councilor 1971-73; sec. chem. mktg. and econs. group Chgo. sect. 1964-66, chmn. 1967-68), Internat. Sci. Found., Sci. Research Soc. Am., Comml. Chem. Devel. Assn. (chmn. program com. Chgo. conv. 1966, mem. fin. com. 1966-67, ad hoc com. of Comml. Chem. Devel. Assn.-Chem. Market Research Assn. 1968-69, co-chmn. pub. relations Denver conv. 1968, chmn. membership com. 1969-70), Chem. Market Research Assn. (mem. directory com. 1967-68, employment com. 1969-70), Midwest Planning Assn., Midwest Chem. Mktg. Assn., Internat. Platform Assn., Water Pollution Control Fedn., Lake County Bd. Realtors, World Future Soc., Sigma Xi, Alpha Chi Sigma (chmn. profl. activities com. 1968-70, pres. Chgo. chpt. 1968-70). Clubs: Lions (sec. Allview, Md. 1956-57), Kiwanis, Masons, Rotary; Chemists (N.Y.C., Chgo.); Torch. Patentee in organic and pharm. field. Home: PO Box 67 Willard OH 44890 Office: 6 Vinewood Dr Norwalk OH 44857

GERMINO, FELIX JOSEPH, food co. exec.; b. N.Y.C., July 14, 1930; s. Thomas and Philomena (DeClemente) G.; B.S., Fordham U., 1952; M.B.A., U. Chgo., 1972; grad. advanced mgmt. program Harvard U., 1977; m. Faith E., Oct. 11, 1952; children—Thomas, F. Wilford, F. Joseph, Gregory G., Mary Therese, Kevin Paul, Faith Marie. Ass. chemist Gen. Foods Tech. Center, 1954-59; asso. chemist Morehead Patterson Research Center, Am. Machine & Foundry Co., 1959-64; project leader carbohydrate chems. Argo, Corn Products Co., 1964-71; dir. com. devel CPC Internat., Argo, Ill., 1971; asso. dir. Pet Foods, Barrington, Ill., 1972-74, dir., 1974-76, v.p., 1976-79; v.p. foods research and devel. Quaker Oats Co., Barrington, Ill., 1979-81. Served to cpl. U.S. Army, 1952-54. Mem. N.Y. Acad. Food Tech. Roman Catholic. Contbr. articles to profl. jours.; patentee in field. Office: 617 W Main St Barrington IL 60010

GERMOVNIK, FRANCIS, librarian, educator; b. Vodice, Slovenia, Sept. 27, 1915; s. Joseph and Frances (Kosec) G.; came to U.S., 1946, naturalized, 1952; Juris Canonici Doctor Angelicum, Rome, 1945; Baccalaureate, Our Lady of the Lake Coll., San Antonio, Tex., 1948-50; M.A. in L.S., Rosary Coll., River Forest, Ill., 1967. Prof. librarian St. John's Sem., San Antonio, Tex., 1946-52, Assumption Seminary, San Antonio, 1952-54, St. Mary's Sem., Perryville, Mo., 1954-64, DeAndreis Sem., Lemont, Ill., 1964—. Mem. Canon Law Soc. of Am., ALA, Catholic Library Assn. Address: DeAndreis Seminary 511 E 127th St Lemont IL 60439

GERNES, PATRICIA MARY, children's spty. store exec.; b. San Francisco, Mar. 4, 1944; d. J. Paul and Mary Eleanor McMahon; student U. Minn., 1962-64; B.S., Mankato State U., 1967; m. Norbert Joseph Gernes, Mar. 9, 1973; children—Megan Pat, Danielle Renee, Corrine Naviv, Zachary Norbert. Tchr. 5th grade St. Austin's Parochial Sch., Mpls., 1967-70; tchr. 6th. grade Eden Prairie (Minn.) Public Sch., 1970-78, coordinator alternative edn. program, 1973; co-owner, operator Discovery Shop, children's splty. store, Eden Prairie, 1977—. Mem. Minn. Edn. Assn. Home: 6990 Alpine Trail Eden Prairie MN 55344

GERONIMO, JOSEPH, chem. co. exec.; b. San Francisco, Feb. 19, 1932; s. Anthony and Mary (Fernandez) G.; B.S., U. Calif., Davis, 1959, M.S., 1961; Ph.D., Purdue U., 1963; m. Georgia Marie Tamplen, June 14, 1957; 1 dau., Antonia. Vis. asst. prof. biol. scis. Purdue U., 1963-64; research plant physiologist Dow Chem. Co., Walnut Creek, Calif., 1964-72, field research sta. mgr., 1972-77, agro-vet. research and devel. mgr. Dow Quimica Mexicana, 1977-78, product devel. mgr. Dow Chem. Co., Midland, Mich., 1978-80, regional mgr. tech. service and devel., Shawnee Mission, Kans., 1980—. Served with USN, 1950-54. NSF fellow, 1961-62. Mem. Am. Soc. Agronomy, Soil Sci. Soc. Am., Crop Sci. Soc. Am., Weed Sci. Soc. Am., Council Agrl. Sci. and Tech., Phi Beta Kappa, Sigma Xi. Phi Kappa Phi. Contbr. articles to profl. jours.; patentee in field. Home:

11615 Woodward St Overland Park KS 66210 Office: 10890 Benson Dr Shawnee Mission KS 66210

GERRICK, EDNA M., graphic arts co. exec., artist; b. Peoria, Ill., Apr. 7, 1939; d. Stephen Jerome and Maureen Alice (O'Grady) B.; B.A., U. Ill., Champaign-Urbana, 1959; M.B.A., Loyola U., Chgo., 1961; 1 son, Andre. Comml. artist Terra Arts, Inc., Chgo., 1961-63, creative dir., 1963-66, v.p. production, 1966-71; owner, pres. Dezign, Ltd., 1971—; instr. graphic design Northwestern Evening Div., Chgo., 1966—; exhibited in numerous one-man and group shows. Democratic precinct capt., 1970—; bd. dirs. D.A. Smythe Found., 1970—. Mem. Am. Assn. Graphic Artists. Democrat. Roman Catholic. Clubs: K.C., Rotary, Kiwanis, Ill. Athletic. Author: Graphic Design for the Novice, 1972. Home: 420 W Belmont #28-D Chicago IL 60657

GERSTENECKER, FRANK, city mgr.; b. Troy, Ill., Apr. 26, 1934; s. Edward and Edna (Stark) G.; B.A., So. Ill. U., 1962; M.Govtl. Adminstrn. (Fels fellow), U. Pa., 1963; m. Janet L. Oestrike, June 10, 1961; children—Gregory G., Kristin K. Subcontract purchase planner McDonald Aircraft Co., St. Louis, 1962; asst. to city mgr. Oshkosh (Wis.), 1963-65; city mgr. Ishpeming (Mich.), 1965-70, Troy (Mich.), 1970—. Mem. Gt. Lakes Innovations Group, 1980; mem. curriculum adv. group Ferris State Coll., 1974—; mem. S.E. Mich. Council on Regional Devel., 1978-80; mem. urban affairs com. Mich. Mcpl. League, 1979-80. Served with U.S. Army, 1954-56. Mem. Am. Acad. Polit. and Social Scientists, Internat. City Mgmt. Assn., Nat. Mcpl. League, Mich. Mcpl. League. Presbyterian. Clubs: Masons, Shriners, Rotary. Office: 500 W Big Beaver Troy MI 48084

GERSTNER, ELIZABETH JANE WILLARD, pub. co. exec.; b. Chgo., Aug. 7, 1932; d. Robert Irving and Harriet Grace (Ensign) Willard; B.S., Northwestern U., 1954, M.M., 1981; m. Robert William Gerstner, Feb. 8, 1958; children—Charles Willard, William Mark. Various mgmt. positions Time Inc., Chgo., 1954—, dir. divisional services, 1981—. Mem. Am. Soc. Tng. and Devel., Assn. Computing Machinery, Assn. Systems Mgmt., Chgo. Data Processing Edn. Council, Data Processing Mgmt. Assn., Soc. Data Educators, DAR, P.E.O., Nat. Soc. Women Descs. of Ancient and Honorable Arty. Co., Alpha Gamma Delta. Office: Time Inc 541 N Fairbanks Ct Chicago IL 60611

GERSTNER, ROBERT WILLIAM, educator; b. Chgo., Nov. 10, 1934; s. Robert Berty and Martha (Tuchelt) G.; B.S., Northwestern U., 1956, M.S., 1957, Ph.D., 1960; m. Elizabeth Willard, Feb. 8, 1958; children—Charles Willard, William Mark. Instr., Northwestern U., Evanston, Ill., 1957-59, research fellow 1959-60; asst. prof. U. Ill., Chgo., 1960-63, asso. prof., 1963-69, prof., 1969—; structural engr. cons., 1959—. Pres. Riverside Improvement Assn. Bd. dirs., v.p. Ravenswood Conservation Commn. Registered structural and profl. engr., Ill. Mem. ASCE, Concrete Inst., Am. Soc. for Engring. Edn., AAAS, AAUP, ACLU. Contbr. articles to profl. jours. Home: 2628 Agatite St Chicago IL 60625

GERSZEWSKI, RICHARD, govt. ofcl.; b. Minto, N.D., Nov. 13, 1915; s. Felix John and Julia (Lizakowski) G.; student U. N.D., 1939-42, Mankato State U., 1973-75; m. Lorraine Torkelson, May 5, 1943; children—Suzanne, James, Donald. Co-owner, mgr. Hewitt Motor Co., Minto, 1950-52; internat. chief adviser FAA, Mpls., 1957-63, prin. opns. insp., 1963-78, chief flight standards, air carrier office, 1978—. Bd. dirs. Gt. Basin Youth Services, Salt Lake City. Served to lt. comdr. USN, 1942-50, 52-57, to capt. USNR, 1957-76. Decorated Air medal. Mem. Am. Legion. Clubs: Fort Snelling Officers, Marine Meml. Home: 4509 W 88th St Minneapolis MN 55437 Office: 6201 S 34th St Minneapolis MN 55450

GERTZ, THOMAS ERWIN, orgn. exec.; b. Chgo., Dec. 4, 1944; s. Erwin August Henry and Camille Bertha (Eschenbach) G.; M. of Human Sexuality, Inst. Advanced Study of Human Sexuality, 1976, now postgrad. Adminstrv. asst. Midwest Population Center, Chgo., 1972-73; adminstrv. asst. Richard L. Bennett, M.D., Akron, Ohio, 1973-80; adminstrv. dir., sexologist Akron Forum, Inc., 1973-80; founder, pres. Thomas Gertz & Assos., Inc., 1980—, Akron Sex Forum, 1980—; mem. faculty Inst. Advanced Study of Human Sexuality, profl. sch., San Francisco, 1976-77. Past pres. Mattachine Midwest, Inc., Chgo.; bd. dirs. Akron Rape Crisis Center, sec., 1979, v.p., 1979-80, exec. com., 1980-81; trustee Mental Health Assn. Summit County, 1979-80. Mem. Am. Assn. Sex Educators, Counselors and Therapists (life, dir., treas. 1980—, cert. sex educator, cert. sex therapist), Assn. Sexologists, Sex. Info. and Edn. Council of U.S., Soc. for Sci. Study of Sex, Inc., Am. Coll. Sexologists (cert.), Harry Benjamin Internat. Gender Dysphoria Assn., Inc. (charter), U.S. Consortium for Sexology (dir., treas. 1981—). Home: 786 Hampton Ridge Dr PO Box 1803 Akron OH 44309 Office: Suite 104 3200 W Market St Akron OH 44313

GERWIN, RONALD PAUL, dir. mktg. co. exec.; b. Toledo, Sept. 16, 1933; s. Harry Adam and Delia Amelia (Suprise) G.; B.B.A., U. Toledo, 1955; postgrad. U. Pa., 1969; m. Shirley Ann Hart, Apr. 9, 1955; children—Scott Edward, Stuart Glenn. Editor, OMI Pub. Co., Toledo, 1955-56, 58-59; public relations mgr. Gladieux Corp., Toledo, 1959-63; public relations dir. Linton's Food Services, Phila., 1963-65; copy supr., v.p. Mel Richman, Inc., Phila., 1965-70; program dir., v.p. philatelics, v.p. mktg. internat. The Franklin Mint, Franklin Center, Pa., 1970-78; v.p. philatelics and spl. projects Calhoun's Collectors Soc., Mpls., 1978-80, v.p. mktg., 1980—. Served with U.S. Army, 1956-58. Mem. Am. Philatelic Soc., Am. Topical Assn., Am. Stamp Dealers Assn., Internat. Fedn. Stamp Dealer Assns., Collectors Club of N.Y., Direct Mail Mktg. Assn., Sigma Alpha Epsilon. Republican. Lutheran. Home: 6837 Point Dr Edina MN 55435 Office: Calhouns Collectors Soc 7275 Bush Lake Rd Edina MN 55435

GESELL, INEZ PATRICIA, concrete co. exec.; b. Fosston, Minn., Feb. 25, 1917; d. Elmer Olof and Esther Marie (Peterson) Solberg; student public schs.; m. William John Gesell, Dec. 31, 1938 (dec. 1975); children—William Lester, Gary John, Mary Ann. With Gesell Concrete Products Inc., Bagley, Minn., 1945—, pres., 1975—. Treas. ladies aux. St. Ann Roman Catholic Ch., Bagley. Home: Route 3 Box 74 Bagley MN 56621 Office: Gesell Concrete Products Inc Route 2 Bagley MN 56621

GETTINGER, MARIBETH, educator; b. La Porte, Ind., July 2, 1953; d. Robert Strock and Irma Eleanor (Williams) G.; B.A., Hanover Coll., 1975; M.A. (NIMH Trainee in Sch. Psychology), Columbia U., 1976, M.Ed., 1977, Ph.D., 1978. Research asso. Research Inst. for Learning Disabilities, Teachers Coll., Columbia U., N.Y.C.. 1978-80, adj. asst. prof. sch. psychology, 1979-80, research fellow Research Inst. for Learning Disabilities, 1978-80; asst. prof. ednl. psychology, U. Wis., Madison, 1980—; cons. sch. psychologist N.Y.C. Bd. Edn., 1979, cons. Resource Room Program, 1978-80. Grad. Sch. U. Wis. research grantee, 1981-82. Mem. Am. Psychol. Assn., Am. Ednl. Research Assn., Assn. for Supervision and Curriculum Devel., Council for Exceptional Children, Internat. Reading Assn. Contbr. writings to profl. publs. Office: Ednl Psychology Dept U Wis 1025 W Johnson St Madison WI 53706

GETTYS, LOYD BRYANT, numismatist; b. Lincoln, Nebr., Oct. 19, 1893; s. James Robert and Cora E. (Scofield) G.; A.B., Neb. Wesleyan Univ., 1916; m. Eloine Crosthwaite, June 27, 1917; 1 son, Robert Loyd. With Mut. Life Ins. Co. of N.Y., 1915, mgr. agency, Sioux City, Iowa, 1925-36, Davenport, Ia., 1936-50, ret. 1950; now profl. numismatist. Served with 350th Machine Gun Co., France, 1917-18, World War 1. Awarded Medaille de Verdun; Medal of Merit, Gold medal Am. Numis. Assn. Mem. U.S. 1953 Assay Commn. Mem. Davenport Life Underwriters Assn. (past pres.), Nat. Assn. Life Underwriters, Gen. Agts. and Mgrs. Assn. (past pres.), Am. Numis. Assn. (past pres., Goodfellowship award 1974), Am. Legion, V.F.W., Zeta Psi. Republican. Methodist. Clubs: Masons, Shriners. Lectr. on U.S. paper money. Home: 483 10th St David City NE 68632 Office: PO Box 378 David City NE 68632

GETZ, JAMES HENRY, II, ednl. adminstr.; b. Massillon, Ohio, Sept. 12, 1936; s. James Henry and Ollie Elizabeth (Meiner) G.; B.A., Heidelberg Coll., 1958; M.Ed., Bowling Green State U., 1964; Ph.D., Toledo U., 1976; m. Nancy Lee Gresser, June 11, 1955; children—James Henry, Kelly. High sch. tchr. and coach, Marion, Ohio, 1958-60; elem. supr., Fremont, Ohio, 1960-63; elem. prin., Fremont, 1964-65; prof., coach Heidelberg Coll., Tiffin, Ohio, 1965—, chmn. dept. health and phys. edn., dir. athletics, 1967—. Mem. Nat. Assn. Athletic Dirs., Profl. Golf Assn., Phi Delta Kappa. Clubs: Lions, Elks, Eagles. Contbr. articles to profl. jours. Office: Heidelberg Coll Tiffin OH 44883

GEWECKE, PATRICIA LOU, telephone co. exec.; b. Lexington, Nebr., Nov. 7, 1949; d. Harry Lane and Jeanne Erma (McMillan) Hart; B.A., Hastings Coll., 1972. Math. tchr., Portland, Maine, 1972-73, Platsmouth, Nebr., 1973-74; computer programmer Mut. of Omaha, Omaha, 1974-75; computer designer, programmer Northwestern Bell Telephone Co., Omaha, 1975-78, staff mgr., 1978—. Mem. Assn. for Systems Mgmt. Democrat. Methodist. Home: 514 Piedmont Dr Omaha NE 68154 Office: Room 1430 Douglas Northwestern Bell Telephone Co 100 S 19th St Omaha NE 68102

GEZELLA, FREDERICK STANLEY, steel co. exec.; b. Chgo., Aug. 28, 1938; s. Frank and Rose G.; B.S. in Metall. Engring., Ill. Inst. Tech., 1961, M.S. in Metall. Engring., 1963; m. Joanna Galante, Sept. 8, 1962; children—Kenneth, Daniel, Steven, Anthony, Jennifer. With Republic Steel Corp., Chgo., 1962—, asst. chief metallurgist, 1968-76, chief metallurgist, 1976-78, mgr. quality control and metall. services, 1978-79, gen. supt., 1979—. Mem. Am. Soc. Metals. AIME, Am. Inst. Steel Engrs. Republican. Roman Catholic. Office: 116th St and Burley Ave Chicago IL 60617

GEZON, HOWARD JAMES, automotive engr.; b. Seattle, Apr. 25, 1919; s. Martin L. and Mina Willamina (Roesink) G.; B.S. in Indsl. Engring., Mich. State U., 1955; M.B.A., Western Mich. U., 1967; m. Dorothy Smitter, Aug. 7, 1943; children—Lyndel, Kathleen, Vicki, Judy, Mary Ann, Debra. Tool and die maker Fisher One, Grand Rapids, Mich., 1937-41, 52-55; store mgr. Good Housekeeping Shop, Grand Rapids, 1946-52; sr. process engr. div. diesel equipment Gen. Motors Co., Grand Rapids, 1955-71, 73—; engring. mgr. Anchor Fasteners, Cleve., 1971-73. Served with U.S. Army, 1941-46. Mem. Soc. Automotive Engrs. (chmn. sect. 1979-80). Home: 2037 Osceola St Grand Rapids MI 49506 Office: 2100 Burlingame St Grand Rapids MI 49501

GHANTOUS, ROBERT NICHOLAS, chem. engring. co. exec.; b. Marj'oyoun, Lebanon, Mar. 23, 1939; s. Nicholas Simon and Saida (Bassit) G.; came to U.S., 1956, naturalized, 1964; student Toledo U., 1957-62; m. Patricia Ann Langer, Sept. 4, 1957; children—Robert Nicholas, Michael Eric, Tonya Sue. Lab. technician Maumee Chem. Co., Toledo, 1959, process engr., Cin., to 1965; instrument engr. Chem. & Indsl. Corp., Cin., 1965; with Devel. Cons.'s, Cin., 1965-69; sr. systems engr. Foxboro Co. (Mass.), 1969-70; engr., pres. Ghantous Corp., Cin., 1970—. Registered profl. engr. Ohio. Mem. Instrument Soc. Am., Nat. Soc. Profl. Engrs. Home: 767 Cedarhill Dr Cincinnati OH 45240 Office: 767 Cedarhill Dr Cincinnati OH 45240

GHIA, KIRTI N., aerospace engr.; b. Bombay, India, Feb. 20, 1939; s. Narottamdas K. and Prankaur N. (Parekh) G.; came to U.S., 1961, naturalized, 1979; B.S. with distinction, U. Gujarat, Bombay, 1960; M.S., Ill. Inst. Tech., 1965, Ph.D., 1969; m. Urmila Agarwal, Aug. 30, 1970; children—Kasturi, Usha Kiran. Research and devel. engr. Premier Automobiles, Ltd., India, 1960-61; instr., research and teaching asst. Ill. Inst. Tech., Chgo., 1961-64, research asst. Aerospace Research Labs. project., 1964-66, NASA project, 1966-69; asst. prof. aerospace engring. and applied mechanics U. Cin., 1969-74, asso. prof., 1974-78, prof., 1978—; vis. scientist Flight Dynamics Lab., Wright-Patterson AFB, Ohio, 1976, 77; vis. asso. prof. aerospace engring. Poly. Inst. N.Y., 1978; cons. in field. Recipient numerous sci. grants, 1970—. Mem. Am. Inst. Aeros. and Astronautics, ASME, Am. Soc. Engring. Edn. Club: Cin. Faculty. Contbr. articles to profl. jours. Office: Mail Loc #70 U Cin Cincinnati OH 45221

GIANDOMENICO, ADAM MICHAEL, educator; b. Steubenville, Ohio, May 30, 1933; s. Adam and Mary (Puzzuole) G.; B.A., Ohio State U., 1959; M.Ed., Duquesne U., 1963; Ph.D., Case Western Reserve U., 1970; m. Sylvia Margaret Harding, Dec., 22, 1958; children—Carol, George, Daryl, Lisa. Employment counselor Ohio Bur. Employment Security, Steubenville, 1960-63; instr. communication Coll. Steubenville, 1963-66; asso. prof. hearing speech scis. Ohio U., 1967—; speech pathologist Eastern Ohio Speech Hearing Center, Steubenville, 1969-73; dir., cons. Psychol. Services Inst., Steubenville, 1970-78. Mem. Mingo Junction (Ohio) Zoning Appeals Bd., 1972-75; Bd. trustees Upper Ohio Valley Kidney Found., Ming Jct., 1974-78, pres., 1976-77; mem. Mingo Junction Health Bd., 1975—. Served with USAF, 1951-55. NIH grantee, 1966. Mem. Am. (certificate clin. competence), Ohio speech hearing assns. Democrat. Roman Catholic. Home: 121 Montgomery Ln Mingo Junction OH 43938 Office: Ohio University Belmont Campus St Clairsville OH 43950

GIANINNO, SUSAN MCMANAMA, research psychologist; b. Boston, Dec. 25, 1948; d. John Carroll, Jr. and Barbara Frances (Magner) McManama; B.A. in English Lit. and Psychology cum laude, Boston Coll., 1970; M.A. in Ednl. Psychology, Northwestern U., 1973; postgrad. in behavioral scis. U. Chgo.; m. Lawrence John Gianinno, June 7, 1970; 1 dau., Alexandra Christin. Psychiat. asst. Quinn Psychiat. Pavilion, St. Elizabeth's Hosp., Brighton, Mass., 1967-70; research asso. com. human devel., dept. behavioral scis. U. Chgo., 1973-79; resident adv. U. Chgo. Housing System, 1979—; research asso., then research supr. Needham, Harper and Steers, Advt., Inc., Chgo., 1979-80, dir. spl. projects, 1981—; cons. in field. Univ. scholar U. Chgo., 1975-77. Mem. Am. Psychol. Assn., Assn. Consumer Research, Nat. Council Family Relations, Am. Mktg. Assn., Midwest Assn. Public Opinion Research, Mass. Tchrs. Assn. Author papers, reports in field. Home: 5454 South Shore Dr Chicago IL 60615 Office: 3 Illinois Center 303 E Wacker Dr Chicago IL 60601

GIBAS, GRACE BRADEN, editor, publisher; b. Santiago, Chile, Aug. 14, 1916; d. Charles Samuel and Grace (McMurray) Braden (parents Am. citizens); B.A., Northwestern U., 1939; m. Andrew C. Gibas, June 11, 1939; children—Murray Albert, Allen Henry, Barbara Jane, Rebecca Gibas Gepner. Mem. staff World Christianity, Chgo., 1938-39; co-pub., co-editor Circulating Pines, Circle Pines, Minn., 1959—. Mem. exec. com. Minn. Am. Friends Service Com., 1972-81, exec. com. N. Central region, 1976-81. Recipient 2d pl. best feature story Nat. Editorial Assn. newspaper contest, 1963; 1st pl. excellence in investigative reporting Minn. Newspaper Assn. Better Newspaper Contest, 1968, in sports reporting, govtl. reporting, women's reporting, 1973, govtl. reporting, 1974; 1st pl. for interview Minn. Press Women Contest, 1975, others. Office: 9201 Lexington Ave Circle Pines MN 55014

GIBB, CLARK RAYMOND, mfrs. rep. co. exec.; b. Cottonwood, Minn., Sept. 5, 1914; s. Raymond J. and Huldah (Pettersen) G.; B.B.A., U. Minn., 1940; m. Margaret L. Foucault, June 30, 1954. Sales engr. Despatch Oven Co., Mpls., 1941; mem. prodn. control staff Gen. Mills, Mpls., 1941-42; owner Aurex Minn. Co., Mpls., 1946-51; partner A & G Chip Steak Co., Mankato, Minn., 1947-61; v.p. Chip Steak & Provision Co., Mankato, 1961-65, pres., owner, 1965—; pres. Clark R. Gibb Co., Mpls., 1952-79, GIBBCO Sci., Inc., 1974-79; owner Wooddale Farms, Yellow Medicine County, Minn.; developer ClarMar Woods, Washburn County, Wis., 1975—. Served with AUS, 1942-46, 51-52. Mem. U. Minn. Alumni Assn., Minn. Alumni Club, Electronic Reps. Assn. (chmn. bd., past pres.), Am. Legion. Republican. Presbyn. Elk. Clubs: Electronic VIP (past pres.), Mankato (Minn.) Golf; Minneapolis Athletic. Home: 2020 Cedar Lake Blvd Minneapolis MN 55416 Office: 11100 Bren Rd W Minnetonka MN 55343

GIBBONS, ALAN CLARK, educator, underwriter; b. N.Y.C., Mar. 25, 1938; s. Maurice Clark and Josefina (Abad) G.; B.A., Carleton Coll., 1959; B.D., U. Chgo., 1963; Ph.D. (Fulbright scholar to Germany, 1963-64, 64-65, fellow Deutscher Akademischer Austauschdienst, 1965-69, 71), Albert-Ludwigs-Universitaet, Freiburg, Germany, 1969; m. B. Gail Hester; children—David, Steven, Adrienne. Instr., Lenoir Rhyne Coll., Hickory, N.C., 1969-70; asst. prof. dept. philosophy East Carolina U., Greenville, N.C., 1970-75, asso. prof., 1975-81; prin. The Gibbons Assn., Edina, Minn., 1981—. Mem. Internat. Husserl and Phenomenological Research Soc., Internat. Phenomenological Soc., Soc. Phenomenology and Existential Philosophy, So. Soc. Philosophy and Psychology, Soc. Philosophic Study Sport. Author: Religion und Sprache, 1970. Office: 7450 France Ave S Suite 120 Edina MN 55435

GIBBONS, JAMES JOSEPH, chemist, educator; b. Springfield, Mo., Oct. 31, 1946; s. John Robert and Francis Jane (Hardy) G.; A.B. cum laude in Chemistry and Math., Drury Coll., Springfield, 1968; Ph.D. in Analytical and Inorganic Chemistry, La. State U., Baton Rouge, 1974. Research chemist Hoffman-Taff div. Syntex Pharms., Inc., Springfield, 1968-69; grad. teaching asst., dept. chemistry La. State U., 1971-74; dir. Drury Research Inst., Springfield, 1974—; asst. prof. chemistry Drury Coll., 1975-79, asso. prof., 1980—; vis. scientist Kalyani (India) U., Jadavpur U., Calcutta, 1976. Mem. youth edn. council St. Paul United Methodist Ch., 1975-77; scoutmaster Troop 1, Thunderbird Dist., Boy Scouts Am., Baton Rouge, 1973-74, Cornerstone Tng. award, 1974, scoutmaster Troop 13, Gt. Oaks Dist., Springfield, 1975-76, Scouters Tng. Award medal, 1976, mem. dist. com., 1977-78, Scouters Key Award medal, 1978, asst. dist. commr., 1977—, Order of Arrow, 1976, Arrowhead Honor award, 1978. Served as lt., Med. Service Corps, U.S. Army, 1969-71. Decorated Soldiers medal, Army Commendation medal; recipient Gen. Electric Coll. Bowl Varsity Scholar medal, 1966, DuPont award for excellence in teaching, 1972. Fellow Am. Inst. Chemists; mem. Am. Chem. Soc. (treas. Ozark sect., faculty sponsor Drury Coll. student affiliate chpt., Drury Coll. Outstanding Chemistry Sr. award 1968), N.Y. Acad. Sci., Mo. Acad. Sci., AAAS, AAUP, Chemists Club (N.Y.), Springfield Acad. Sci. (past pres.), Jaycees (Outstanding Young Educator award Springfield 1980), Sigma Xi, Alpha Chi Sigma (past alumni sec.), Phi Eta Sigma, Omicron Delta Kappa, Phi Lambda Upsilon (past treas.), Sigma Pi Sigma (Outstanding Phys. Chemist award 1973). Clubs: Masons (worshipful master 1981, venerable master 1981), K.T., Shriners (Grand Lodge achievement award for Mo. 1981). Contbr. chpts. to Thermodynamic Behavior of Electrolytes in Mixed Solvents, 1979; contbr. articles to sci. jours. Home: 511 E Normal St Springfield MO 65807 Office: Drury Coll LAY 303 900 N Benton St Springfield MO 65802

GIBBONS, JOEL CLARKE, economist, educator; b. Boston, Apr. 30, 1942; s. Francis Joseph and Helen (Hanlon) G.; B.S. with honors, Georgetown U., 1964; Ph.D. in Math., Northwestern U., 1970, M.B.A., 1974; Ph.D. in Bus., U. Chgo., 1979; m. Crispina Montifolca, Aug. 26, 1967; children—Eileen Hope, Marcus Aurelius, Hugh Montifolca. Asst. prof. math. Chgo. State U., 1972-75; lectr. U. Chgo., 1975-76, research asso., 1977-79; instr. Ill. Inst. Tech., Chgo., 1976-79, asst. prof. econs., 1979—; propr. Gibbons Econometrics; cons. economist The Nika Corp.; cons. Argonne Nat. Lab. Ill. Inst. Tech. Faculty research grantee, 1980-81. Mem. Am. Math. Soc., Am. Econs. Assn., Midwest Econ. Assn., Western Econs. Assn., Beta Gamma Sigma. Republican. Roman Catholic. Home: 143 S Hawthorne St Elmhurst IL 60126 Office: Dept of Economics Ill Inst Tech IIT Center Chicago IL 60616

GIBBONS, MRS. JOHN SHELDON (CELIA VICTORIA TOWNSEND), editor, publisher; b. Fargo, N.D.; d. Harry Alton and Helen (Haag) Townsend; student U. Minn., 1930-33; m. John Sheldon Gibbons, May 1, 1935; children—Mary Vee, John Townsend. Advt. mgr. Hotel Nicollet, Mpls., 1933-37; contbg. editor children's mags., 1935—; partner Youth Assos. Co., Mpls., 1942-65; pub. art dir. Mines and Escholier mags., 1954-65; founder Bull. Bd. Pictures, Inc., Mpls., 1954, pres., 1954—; founder Periodical Litho Art Co., Mpls., 1962, pres., 1962-65; artist Cath. Boy mag., 1938; chief photographer Cath. Miss mag., 1955. Mem. Women's aux. Mpls. Symphony Orch.; mem. Fort Lauderdale (Fla.) Art. Mus. Republican chairwoman Golden Valley, Minn., 1950; alternate del. Hennepin County Rep. Conv., 1962. Mem. Mpls. Inst. Arts, Internat. Inst., St. Paul Arts and Sci., Art Guild Boca Raton, Delta Zeta. Clubs: Woman's; Minikahda; Deerfield Beach Women's. Home: 1416 Alpine Pass Tyrol Hills Minneapolis MN 55416 Office: 1057 A-1-A Hillsboro Beach FL

GIBBONS, LARRY VALGENE, research and devel. co. exec.; b. Harrisburg, Ill., Mar. 18, 1932; s. Jesse and Oma (Tison) G.; B.A., Washington U., St. Louis, 1954; M.S., So. Ill. U., 1958, Ph.D., 1970; m. Ann Wilson, Aug. 21, 1954; children—Valerie, Lisa, Cathy, Grant. Research supr. biol. sci. lab., Universal Match. Corp., Ferguson, Mo., 1958-63; physiologist advanced spacecraft design McDonnell-Douglas, St. Louis, 1963-68; asso. dir. research Intersci. Research Inst., Champaign, Ill., 1968-70; research dir. Unidynamics, Phoenix, 1970-71; pres., lab. dir. ARDL, Inc., Mt. Vernon, Ill., 1971—. Served with U.S. Army, 1954-56. Mem. Ill. State Acad. Sci. (pres. 1980-81), AAAS, Nat. Fedn. Ind. Businessmen, Sigma Xi. Home: 1016 Maple St Mount Vernon IL 62864 Office: 1801 Forest St Mount Vernon IL 62864

GIBBS, JOHN G(AMBLE), educator; A.B., Davidson Coll., 1952; M.Div., Union Theol. Sem., Richmond, Va., 1955, Th.M. (fellow), 1958; postgrad. (Union theol. Sem. fellow) U. Basel (Switzerland), 1955-56; Ph.D., Princeton Theol. Sem., 1966. Research asst. in N.T.,

Princeton Theol. Sem., 1962-63; interim instr. in religion Macalester Coll., 1964-65; tchr. Latin, Blake Sch., prep. sch., Mpls., 1965-67; asst. prof. humanities Moorhead State U., 1967-72, asso. prof., 1972-78, prof., 1978—; mem. part-time grad. faculty Charis Ecumenical Inst. at Concordia Coll., 1971—; fellow Inst. Ecumenical and Cultural Research, St. John's Abbey, Collegeville, Minn., 1973-74; lectr. U. Winnipeg (Man., Can.), 1974, 75. Moorhead State U. grantee, 1972, 79; Tri-Coll. U. Humanities Forum grantee, 1973; Nat. Endowment Humanities summer seminar fellow, 1980. Mem. Studiorum Novi Testamenti Societas, Soc. Biblical Lit. Author: Creation and Redemption, A Study in Pauline Theology, 1971; Christian Origins: A Study Guide, 1978; contbr. articles, revs. to profl. publs. Office: Moorhead State U Moorhead MN 56560

GIBBS, WALTER MANNING, JR., aluminum co. exec.; b. Chgo., Nov. 22, 1923; s. Walter Manning and Josephine (Pickens) G.; B.S. in Bus. Adminstrn., Northwestern U., 1947; m. Jeanne Marjorie Becker, June 18, 1947; children—Susan Jeanne, Carolyn Jo, David Wesley; m. 2d, Margaret Muir Pinkerton, Sept. 23, 1972. Salesman, Winchester Repeating Arms Co., New Haven, 1947-49; salesman Kaiser Aluminum & Chem. Corp., Chgo., 1949-50, br. mgr., Wichita, Kans., 1951, product mgr., Chgo., 1952-57, asst. to v.p., Oakland, Calif., 1958-59, asst. gen. sales mgr., 1960, mktg. mgr., 1961, gen. mgr. sheet and plate div., 1963-65, v.p. industry and product sales, 1965-68, v.p. bus. mktg. and planning, 1968-70; v.p. mill products and reduction ops. Martin Marietta Aluminum, Torrance, Calif., 1970-74; dir. corporate planning CONALCO, Inc. (name now Consol. Aluminum Corp.), St. Louis, 1974-76, v.p. ops., 1976-80; chmn., chief exec. officer Conalco Contract Carrier, Inc., 1977-80; dir. Alusuisse of Am. Served lt. (j.g.) USNR, 1944-46. Mem. Acacia. Republican. Presbyterian (elder, trustee). Home: 998 Claygate Ct Manchester MO 63011 Office: 301 Sovereign Ct Manchester MO 63011

GIBBS, WILLIAM CULLEN, JR., govt. ofcl.; b. Chgo., Apr. 30, 1925; s. William Cullen and Minnie Clyde (Harris) G.; student Thornton Jr. Coll., Wilson Jr. Coll., Roosevelt U., U. Chgo.; B.S., 1947; m. Eththelle Faye Byoune, June 29, 1946; children—Spencer Craig, Marvin Kent, William Cullen III. With U.S. Postal Service, 1947—, clk., Chgo., 1947-48, letter carrier, 1948-59, letter carrier, Harvey, Ill., 1959-63, civil service examiner, 1963-64, hearing officer-investigator, 1964-65, asst. br. supt., Markham, Ill., 1965-66, contract compliance examiner, Chgo., 1966, postal service officer, 1966-67, employee relations officer, Chgo., 1967-68, mgr. employee relations br., 1968-71, dist. dir. support, Springfield, Ill., 1971-75, dir. fin., Chgo., 1975—. Chmn. supt. adv. com. Sch. Dist. 205, 1969; pres. Harvey Civic Improvement Assn., 1959-61. Mem. Democratic Nat. Com., 1968-74. Methodist Episcopal. Mem. Kappa Alpha Psi. Home: 16139 S Wolcott Ave Markham IL 60426 Office: 433 W Van Buren St Chicago IL 60607

GIBLIN, EDWARD J., corp. exec.; b. 1917; B.S., Fordham U.; M.B.A., N.Y. U.; married. With Peat, Marwick, Mitchell & Co., C.P.A.'s, prior to 1953; with Ex-Cell-O Corp., 1953—, v.p., treas., 1968-69, exec. v.p., 1969, pres., chief exec. officer, 1970-78, chmn. bd., chief exec. officer, 1978—, also dir.; dir. Detroit Bank and Trust Co., Tecumseh Products Co., Detroit Edison Co. Address: Ex-Cell-O Corp 2855 Coolidge Troy MI 48084

GIBSON, CATHERINE WILLIAMS, ednl. adminstr.; b. Florence, S.C., June 12, 1920; d. James Schuler and Geneva Williams; B.S., W.Va. State Coll., 1947; M.S., Western Res. U., 1954; postgrad. (scholar) U. Boston, 1961-62; Ph.D. in Edn., U. Akron, 1977; m. Ervine A. Gibson (dec.); 1 son, Ervin Stanley. Tchr., Cleve. Public Schs., 1947-65; dir. primary/secondary edn. AID, Washington; assigned to Ministry of Edn., Kenya, East Africa, 1965-67; tchr. Cleve. Public Schs., 1967-70; research asso. U. Ariz., Tucson, 1970-73; Instr. grad. asst. U. Akron, 1973-75; prin. Charleston Elem. Sch., Lorain (Ohio) City Sch. Dist., 1976-79, pres., 1980-81, on-site inservice coordinator tchr. corps project, 1979-82; asso. prof. Coll. Edn., Margai Tchr. Tng. Coll., Freetown, Sierra Leone, summer 1964. Counselor, Girl Guides; Sunday sch. tchr. St. Andrew's Episcopal Ch.; vol. ARC; mem. Women's Civic League Cleve.; bd. dirs. Erie Shores council Girl Scouts U.S.A., Lorain County Drug and Alcohol Abuse Council; mem. Cleve. Council Human Rights. Recipient Tchr. award PTA, Educator of the year award, Lorain chpt. Negro Bus. & Profl. Women's Club, 1980; cert. of achievement Nat. Acad. of Am. Assn. of Sch. Execs., 1982. Mem. NEA, Ohio Adminstrs. Assn., Assn. Supervision and Curriculum Devel., Internat. Reading Assn., Ohio Reading Assn., Ohio Edn. Assn., Am. Assn. Sch. Adminstrs., NAACP, Urban League, Nat. Council Negro Women, Nat. Assn. Female Execs., Phi Delta Kappa, Kappa Delta Pi, Delta Sigma Theta. Clubs: Quota Internat.

GIBSON, CURTIS A., aircraft systems engr.; b. Springfield, Ohio, Nov. 5, 1929; s. Frank Z. and Helen W. (Cox) G.; Chem.E., U. Cin., 1952; Ph.D. in Religion, D.D. (hon.), Universal Life Ch., 1979. Chem. engr. Sylvania Elec. Products Co., Emporium, Pa., 1952-54; chem. engr. U.S. Air Force, Wright-Patterson AFB, Ohio, 1956-59, mech. engr., 1959-70, life support systems engr., 1970-79, aircraft systems engr., 1979—. Active Boy Scouts Am. Recipient Silver Beaver award Boy Scouts Am., 1973. Mem. Am. Def. Preparedness Assn., Air Force Assn., Internat. Acad. Profl. Bus. Execs. Home: 2806 Oxford Dr Springfield OH 45506

GIBSON, DAVID NORMAN, state ofcl.; b. San Francisco, July 25, 1942; s. James F. and Edith (Berger) G.; B.A., San Jose State U., 1964; M.A., Sacramento State U., 1966; M.A.,Ph.D., Wash. State U., 1970; m. Linda Dash, May 16, 1981; 1 son by previous marriage, David Howard. With N.Y. Dept. Transp., Albany, 1970-77; with Ill. Commerce Commn., Springfield, 1978—, mgr. transp. div., 1978—. Mem. Am. Economics Assn., Am. Soc. for Public Adminstrn., Am. Mgmt. Assn. Republican. Contbr. articles in field to profl. jours. Home: 520 S 2d St Apt 1704 Springfield IL 62701 Office: Illinois Commerce Commission 527 E Capitol Ave Springfield IL 62706 also 160 N LaSalle St Chicago IL 60601

GIBSON, FLOYD ROBERT, judge; b. Prescott, Ariz., Mar. 3, 1910; s. Van Robert and Katheryn Ida (Weitzel) G.; A.B., U. Mo., 1931, J.D., 1933; m. Gertrude Lee Walker, Apr. 23, 1935; children—Charles R., John M., Catherine L. Admitted to Mo. bar, 1932; partner firm Gibson & Kirtley, Independence, Mo., 1933-37; county counselor Jackson County (Mo.), 1941-42; partner firm Cloud, Loomis & Gibson, Kansas City, Mo., 1939-52, Stubbs, McKenzie, Williams & Gibson, Kansas City, 1952-54, Johnson, Lucas, Bush & Gibson, Kansas City, 1954-61; judge U.S. Dist. Ct., Kansas City, 1961-62, chief judge, 1962-65; judge U.S. Circuit Ct. of Appeals, Kansas City, 1965—, chief judge, 1974-80; pres. Nat. Legis. Conf., 1960; mem. Mo. Ho. of Reps., 1940-46; mem. Mo. Senate, 1946-61, majority leader, 1952-56, pres. pro tem 1956-60; bd. dirs. Jacob L. and Ella C. Loose Found.; trustee U. Kansas City; bd. mgrs. Council State Govts. Fellow Am. Bar Assn.; mem. Appellate Judges Conf. (chmn. 1973-74, chmn. Jud. Adminstrv. div. 1979-80, chmn. Conf. of Sect. Chmn. 1980-81), Nat. Conf. Commrs. on Uniform State Laws (commr.), Fed., Kansas City (Achievement award 1980) bar assns., Lawyers Assn. Kansas City (v.p.), Inst. Jud Adminstrn., Jud. Conf. of U.S., Chief Judges Conf. (chmn. 1977-78), Mo. Law Sch. Alumni Assn. (citation of merit 1975), Mo. Acad. Squires, Order of Coif, Phi Delta Phi, Phi Kappa Psi (Man of Year 1974). Clubs: Univ., Carriage, Mercury of Kansas City. Recipient Faculty-Alumni award U. Mo., 1968; named 2d Most Valuable Mem. Mo. Legislature; Globe-Democrat award, 1958, Most Valuable Mem., 1960; Spurgeon Smithson award Mo. Bar Found., 1978. Home: 11521 Winner Rd Independence MO 64052 Office: 837 US Courthouse 811 Grand St Kansas City MO 64106

GIBSON, GEORGE WARRINER, JR., automotive mfg. co. exec.; b. Detroit, Oct. 23, 1922; s. George Warriner and Vivian E. (Schulte) G.; B.S. in Elec. Engring., Washington U., St. Louis, 1947; M.Automotive Engring., Chrysler Inst. Engring., 1949; m. Betty Ann Doyle, June 14, 1947; children—Anne Marie, Michael Doyle, Celia Marie, Lisa Marie. Chief engr. Dodge div. Chrysler Corp., Highland Park, Mich., 1958-63, dir. corp. product planning, 1963-68; v.p., dir. product devel. and ops. staff Chrysler Internat., Eng. and Switzerland, 1968-73; v.p. engring. Monroe Auto Equipment div. Tenneco Inc., Monroe, Mich., 1973-80; v.p., dir. corp. devel. Newcor, Inc., Warren, Mich., 1980—; asst. dir. Grad. Sch., Chrysler Inst., 1951-53; asst. prof. elec. engring. Lawrence Inst. Tech., 1948-54. Served with U.S. Army, 1943-46. Recipient Disting. Service medal Xavier U., Cin., 1980; registered profl. engr., Mich. Mem. Soc. Automotive Engrs., Nat. Soc. Profl. Engrs., Mich. Assn. of Professions, Am. Soc. for Engring. Edn., Engring. Soc. Detroit. Club: Country of Detroit. Home: 41 Stonehurst Rd Grosse Pointe Shores MI 48236 Office: Newcor Corp Devel Office 12434 Twelve Mile Rd Warren MI 48093

GIBSON, HAROLD WAYNE, univ. adminstr.; b. Gallipolis, Ohio, May 23, 1922; s. Dallis Roy and Mollye Hodge (Bedford) G.; student Morehead (Ky.) State U., 1941-43; A.B., Miami U., Oxford, Ohio, 1948, M.Ed., 1957; m. Phyllis Marie Bender, July 17, 1949; children—Wayne Scott, Robert Todd, Randall Evan. Head football coach Sidney High Sch., 1948-49; backfield coach football U. Buffalo, 1949-50; head football coach Gallia Acad. High Sch., 1950-51, Sidney High Sch., 1951-55; backfield coach Miami U., 1956-63, asst. dir. athletics, 1964-76, asso. dir. athletics, asso. prof., 1976-79. Chmn. adminstv. bd. Methodist Ch. Served with USNR, 1943-46. Recipient cert. of appreciation City of Oxford, 1976, Miami U. Sr. Class, 1970, Talawanda Local Sch. Dist. Bd. Edn., 1978; inducted into Miami U. Hall of Fame, 1981. Mem. Nat. Athletic Dirs. Assn., Miami Cradle of Coaches Assn. (exec. v.p.), Coll. Athletic Bus. Mgrs. Assn., Beta Theta Pi (Alpha chpt.). Republican. Clubs: Univ., Elks, Sidney (Ohio) Kiwanis. Home: 100 Hilltop Rd Oxford OH 45056 Office: Millett Hall Miami U Oxford OH 45056

GIBSON, LEWIS EDWARD, nursing adminstr.; b. Staten Island, N.Y., Apr. 3, 1943; s. Lewis Edward and Celia Marie (Piraino) G.; Asso. Nursing, Cuyahoga Community Coll., 1975; student Dyke Coll., 1980. Orderly, St. Luke's Hosp., Cleve., 1970-75, staff nurse, 1975-77, nurse recruiter, 1977-79, mgr. nurse recruitment, 1979—. Mem. Nat. League Nursing, Am. Nurses Assn., Nat. Assn. Nurse Recruiters (bd. dirs. 1980-81, chmn. East North Central Region), Greater Cleve. Assn. Nurse Recruiters (founder, pres. 1980). Home: 1010 Literary Rd Cleveland OH 44113 Office: 11311 Shaker Blvd Cleveland OH 44104

GIBSON, MARK ALBERT, city mgr.; b. Painesville, Ohio, Oct. 27, 1948; s. Grant Albert Gibson and Joyce Ella (Pratt) Gibson Lintern; B.G.S., Ohio U., 1974; M.P.A., U. Dayton, 1977; m. Virginia Faye Hogan, Oct. 13, 1979; children—Lori, Mindy, Brandon. Adminstrv. asst. City of Athens (Ohio), 1974-76; adminstrv. asst. City of Miamisburg (Ohio), 1976-77, asst. city mgr., 1977-79, city mgr., 1979—; exec. dir. Tri County Community Action Agy., Athens, 1976. Pres., Miamisburg Community Improvement Corp., 1980—; mem. Citizens for Quality Edn.; mem. Montgomery County Animal Adv.; mem. Arson Task Force Commn. Served with U.S. Army, 1969-71. Decorated Bronze Star medal, Air medal. Mem. Internat. City Mgmt. Assn., Am. Soc. Public Adminstrn., Nat. Public Employee Labor Relations Assn., Ohio City Mgmt. Assn., Montgomery County Mayors and Mgrs. Assn., Am. Legion. Club: Rotary. Home: 2312 Oakbark St Miamisburg OH 45342 Office: 10 N 1st St Miamisburg OH 45342

GIBSON, MILTON EUGENE, cardiologist; b. Laporte, Ind., July 11, 1939; s. Maurice Wayne and Mary Leola (Reinhardt) G.; B.A., Valparaiso U., 1961; M.D., Ind. U., 1965; m. Gloria Jean Birky, Aug. 12, 1961; children—Kevin Scott, Bradley Mark. Resident in internal medicine Methodist Hosp., Indpls., 1968-70, fellow in cardiology, 1970-72; practice medicine specializing in cardiology Cardiology Assos., Inc., South Bend, Ind., 1972—, pres., 1981—; med. dir. Cardiac Catheterization Lab., Meml. Hosp., South Bend, 1975—, dir. Cardiology Services, 1976—, chmn. dept. medicine, 1977-80; co-dir. CCU, St. Joseph's Hosp., South Bend, 1978—; instr. Ind. U. at Meml. Hosp. Pres., Ind. affiliate Am. Heart Assn., 1977-79; mem. adv. council Midwest Chamber Orch., 1978-80. Served to capt. U.S. Army, 1966-68. Decorated Bronze Star medal. Fellow Am. Coll. Cardiology, Am. Heart Assn. (council clin. cardiology; pres., chmn. med. and sci. programs Ind. affiliate, chmn. research allocations com., membership and nominating com.); mem. A.C.P. Contbr. articles in field to med. jours. Home: 5707 S Bridgeton Ln South Bend IN 46614 Office: 919 E Jefferson Blvd South Bend IN 46622

GIBSON, ORPHA RAY, educator; b. Blue Eye, Mo., Feb. 20, 1934; s. Claude Bertrum and Sylvia Jane (Hudson) G.; B.S. in Edn., S.W. Mo. State U., 1961; M.Ed., U. Ark., 1964, Ed.D., 1968; m. Nancy Lou Lawson, Dec. 23, 1962; children—Gregory Ray, Nancy Ann, Bethany Jane. Tchr., coach Blue Eye (Mo.) Public Schs., 1960-61, Bradleyville, Mo., 1961-62, Waynesville-Fort Leonard Wood, Mo., 1962-66; asst. in secondary edn. U. Ark., 1966-67; asso. prof. edn. S.W. Baptist Coll., 1967-71; supt. Pleasant Hope (Mo.) Public Schs., 1971-72, Cabool (Mo.) Public Schs., 1972-73; prof. edn. Sch. of Ozarks, Point Lookout, Mo., 1973—. Sec. Bd. Edn., Blue Eye Public Schs., 1974—. Served with U.S. Army, 1956-58. Mem. Mo. State Tchrs. Assn., Mo. Sch. Bds. Assn., Mo. Assn. Ednl. Communication and Tech., Gideons Internat., Fellowship of Christian Athletes, Phi Delta Kappa, Kappa Delta Pi. Baptist. Clubs: Lions, Kiwanis. Home: Rt 1 Box 100 Blue Eye MO 65611 Office: Sch of the Ozarks Point Lookout MO 65726

GIBSON, ROBERT WILLIAM, social work adminstr.; b. Columbus, Ohio, Jan. 22, 1937; s. Robert Henry and Eloise (Cornell) G.; B.S. in Social Sci., Capital U., 1961; M.A. in Social Services, Ind. U., 1966; m. Helen Garner, Sept. 6, 1959; children—Keith, Diane, Brenda. Caseworker, Franklin County Welfare Dept., Columbus, Ohio, 1961-62, supr. intake and legal dept., 1966-68; probation officer Franklin County Juvenile Ct., Columbus, 1962-64; dir. ct. sers. Franklin County Domestic Relations Ct., Columbus, 1968-69; exec. dir. Travelers Aid, Columbus, 1969-71; asso. dir. Assn. for Developmentally Disabled, Columbus, 1971-73, exec. dir., 1973—; adj. instr. Coll. Social Work Ohio State U. Chmn. Columbus City Council Community Living Task Force, 1978—; lic. lay speaker Bethel United Meth. Ch. Recipient recognition award Ohio Ho. of Reps., 1978. Mem. Nat. Assn. Social Workers, Am. Assn. on Mental Deficiency (speaker nat. conf. 1979). Ohio Pvt. Residential Assn. (past pres.), Acad. Cert. Social Workers. Home: 5266 Cape Cod Ln Columbus OH 43220 Office: 1395 W 5th Ave Columbus OH 43212

GIBSON, ROBERT WILLIAM, JR., sci. corp. librarian; b. Canova, S.D., Mar. 15, 1923; s. Robert William and Mary (Zollinger) G.; student Ohio State U., 1945-49, Yankton Coll., 1944; m. Wilma Jeanne Caster, Oct. 31, 1948; children—Lisa Anne, Mary Melissa, Nancy Jeanne. Chemist Maytag Washing Machine Co., Newton, Iowa, 1944; asst. supr.-librarian Battelle Meml. Inst., Columbus, Ohio, 1944-62; asst. librarian IBM-Thomas J. Watson Research Center, Yorkton Heights, N.Y., 1962-65; head library dept. Gen. Motors Research Labs., Warren, Mich., 1965—; mem. Engring. Index, Inc.; mem. Mich. Interorganization Com. for Continuing Library Edn. Mem. AAAS, Am. Chem. Soc., Am. Library Assn., Am. Soc. for Info. Sci., Continuing Library Edn. Network and Exchange, Spl. Libraries Assn. (past pres.), Mich. Library Assn. Contbr. writings in field to profl. publs., papers to profl. confs. Office: General Motors Tech Center Warren MI 48090

GIBSON, ROSE CAMPBELL, social sci. researcher; b. Detroit, May 30, 1925; d. John Henry and Lela Gertrude (Long) Campbell; B.A., Wayne State U., 1946; M.A., U. Mich., 1968, Ph.D., 1977; m. Ralph Milton Gibson, Dec. 31, 1947; children—Ralph, John. Lectr., U. Mich., Ann Arbor, 1977, research asso., 1978, research investigator, 1979—. Vice chmn. Octagon House bd. dirs., 1979; mem. Ann Arbor mayor's com. on urban renewal, 1957; bd. dirs. Mich. Children's Aid Soc., 1956; chmn. Nat. Inst. Edn., HEW, sub-group review panel, 1979. Recipient USPHS research fellow award, 1979. Mem. Am. Psychol. Assn., AAUP, Biofeedback Soc. Am., AAAS, AAUW, Delta Sigma Theta. Club: Links. Researcher test anxiety in med. students, elderly women, counseling anxiety.

GIBSON, SCOTT WILBERT, agronomist; b. St. Charles, Ill., Feb. 27, 1948; s. Wilbert and Dorothy Elaine (Kemp) G.; M.S. in Plant and Soil Sci., So. Ill. U., 1978; m. Dec. 31, 1976 (div.); 1 dau., Jessica Sekhet. Farm worker W. Gibson and Sons, 1974-76; teaching asst., researcher So. Ill. U., 1976-78; area field mgr., agronomist Velsicol Chem. Co., Princeton, Ill., 1978-80; agrl. research scientist 3M Co., Princeton, 1980—; guest speaker for numerous colls., govt. agys. Mem. Plant Growth Regulator Working Group, Weed Sci. Soc. Am., Internat. Plant Protection Congress, Am. Soc. Agronomy, Council Agrl. Sci. and Tech., Internat. Grassland Congress, North Central Weed Control Soc., Ill. Acad. Sci. Methodist. Author book; contbr. articles to profl. publs. Home and office: 6 N Cherry St Princeton IL 61356

GIDDINGS, WAYNE ALVAN, appliance co. exec.; b. Sabula, Iowa, Nov. 13, 1922; s. Alvan James and Anna Dora Marie (Bruse) G.; student N.C. State Coll., Navy Diesel Sch., 1945; B.S. in Mech. Engring., U. Wis., 1947; postgrad. Purdue U., 1951; m. Brenda Jane Mercer, May 30, 1975; children—Catherine, Dwight. With tng. program Gen. Electric, Schenectady, N.Y., Erie, Pa., Fort Wayne, Ind., 1947-48, design engr. air conditioning dept., Fort Wayne, 1948-52; supr. engring. lab. and model shop Amana Refrigeration, Inc., Amana, Iowa, 1952-55, chief engr. refrigeration systems, 1955-57, chief engr. white goods, 1957-58, dir. engring., 1958-63, v.p. mfg. and engring., 1963-69, sr. v.p. mfg., 1969—, also dir. Served with U.S. Navy, 1942-46. Mem. C. of C., ASHRAE. Republican. Methodist. Club: University Athletic. Patentee in field. Home: 2105 Glendale Rd Iowa City IA 52240 Office: Main St Amana IA 52204

GIEBELHAUSEN, GUSTAV WILLIAM, surgeon; b. Peoria, Ill., Sept. 27, 1918; s. Jacob and Martha (Rosinski) G.; B.S., U. Ill., 1942, M.D., 1944; m. Martha H. Mugrage, June 13, 1943; children—Jane, Richard, Dean. Intern, St. Francis Hosp., 1944-45, resident, 1945-46; practice medicine specializing in surgery, Peoria, 1948—; asst. clin. prof. surgery U. Ill. Sch. Medicine in Peoria. Served with U.S. Army, 1946-48. Fellow ACS; mem. AMA, Peoria Med. Soc., Ill. Med. Soc., Ill., Midwest surg. assns., Mid-State Med. Found. Home: 5826 N Briarwood Ln Peoria IL 61614 Office: 1101 Main St Peoria IL 61606

GIELEN, MICHAEL ANDREAS, condr.; b. Dresden, Germany, July 20, 1927; s. Josef and Rose (Steuermann) G.; student U. Dresden, 1936, U. Berlin, 1937, U. Vienna, 1940, Buenos Aires U., 1950; m. Helga Augsten, May 20, 1957; children—Claudia, Lucas. Coach, Teatro Colón, Buenos Aires, 1947-50; condr. Vienna State Opera, 1950-60, Stockholm Royal Opera, 1960-65; free lance condr., Cologne, Germany, 1965-68; mus. dir. Belgian Nat. Orch. Brussels, 1969-73; chief comdr. Netherlands Opera, 1973-75; music dir., gen. mgr. Frankfurt (Germany) Opera House, 1977—; music dir. Cin. Symphony Orch., 1980—; prin. guest condr. BBC Symphony Orch., London; guest condr. Washington Nat. Symphony, Chgo. Symphony, Pitts. Symphony, Minn. Orch., Detroit Symphony, others. Composer: 4 Gedichte von Stefan George, 1958, Variations for 40 Instruments, 1959, Un dia Sobresale, 1963, die glocken sind auf falscher spur, 1969; Mitbestimmunes Modell, 1974. Office: Cin Symphony Orch 1241 Elm St Cincinnati OH 45210

GIENAPP, JOHN CHARLES, assn. exec.; b. Milw., Feb. 3, 1939; s. John Henry and Anne Marie (Bahde) G.; B.A. magna cum laude, Concordia Sr. Coll., 1961; M.Div., Concordia Sem., 1965; Ph.D. (NDEA Title IV fellow), U. Kans., Lawrence, 1970; m. Katie Ann Berg, Aug. 22, 1964; children—Anne A., John W. Asst. prof. history of sci. Concordia Sr. Coll., 1968-74, asso. prof., 1974-77, dir. coll. relations, 1971-75; vis. asst. prof. Coll. Edn. U. Ill., Urbana, 1977-78; asst. dir. grad. med. edn. AMA, Chgo., 1978-79, asso. dir., 1979-81, dir., 1981—. Mem. History of Sci. Soc., AAAS. Lutheran. Asst. editor for sci. and tech. The Cresset, 1977-78. Office: 535 N Dearborn St Chicago IL 60610

GIER, DONALD ALDON, soil scientist; b. Bloomington, Ind., Jan. 8, 1935; s. Herschel Thomas Gier and Wilma Hobson Gier Alexander; B.S., Kans. State U., 1957, M.S., 1967; Ph.D., Iowa State U., 1978; m. Mary Ann Havel, July 8, 1961; children—Mary Jo, Donna J. With USDA, Soil Conservation Service, various locations, 1955—, soil scientist, Marysville, Kans., 1973-79, Westmoreland, Kans., 1979—. Leader, Boy Scouts Am., 1954-65; mem. Marysville Bicentennial Com., 1976; leader Girl Scouts U.S.A., 1974—; sec. treas. Marysville P.R.I.D.E. Com., 1978-80; instr. CPR, 1st aid ARC, 1956-67, 78—; pres. Marysville Community Choir, 1974—. Served with AUS, 1957-58, 61-62. Hon. Dist. farmer FFA; recipient Scouters award, Scouters Key, God and Country award, Boy Scouts Am. Cert. Professional Soil Scientist (soil classifier), professional agronomist, Am. Registry of Cert. Professionals in Agronomy, Crops and Soils (ARCPACS). Mem. Am. Soc. Agronomy, Soil Conservation Soc. Am., Kans. Assn. Profl. Soil Classifiers (pres. 1980-82), Alpha Zeta. Republican. Presbyterian. Clubs: Kiwanis (lt. gov. 1980-81, adminstr. Circle K dist. 1981—), Kans. Campers Assn. Home: 507 N 11th St Marysville KS 66508 Office: Box 246 Westmoreland KS 66549

GIERE, FREDERIC ARTHUR, biologist; b. Galesville, Wis., Dec. 10, 1923; s. Arthur F. and Agnes (Peterson) G.; A.B., Luther Coll., 1947, M.S., Syracuse U., 1951; Ph.D., U. N.Mex., 1953; m. Hazel Marie Teien, June 11, 1955; children—Nils, John, Martha. Instr. to asso. prof. biology Luther Coll., Decorah, Iowa, 1947-62; asso. prof. Lake Forest (Ill.) Coll., 1962-70, prof., 1970—; cons. Argonne Nat. Labs., 1967—, Abbott Labs., 1978—. Bd. dirs. Iowa div. Am. Cancer Soc., 1958-62, Ill. div., 1973—. Served with USNR, 1943-46. USPHS fellow, Arbeidsfysiologisk Institutt, Oslo, 1968-69. Mem. AAAS, AAUP, Am. Physiol. Soc., Am. Soc. Zoology, Soc. Exptl. Biology and

Medicine, Sigma Xi, Beta Beta Beta, Phi Sigma. Home: 321 E Washington St Lake Bluff IL 60044 Office: Lake Forest Coll Lake Forest IL 60045

GIERING, RICHARD HERBERT, computerized infor. systems co. exec.; b. Emmaus, Pa., Nov. 27, 1929; s. Harold Augustus and Marguerite (Bruder) G.; B.S. in Engring. and Math., U. Ariz., 1962; m. Carol Alice Scott, Aug. 16, 1959; children—Richard Herbert, Scott K. Joined U.S. Army, 1947, commd. 2d lt., 1963, advanced through grades to capt., 1965; sect. chief data processing Def. Intelligence Agy., Washington, 1965-67; ret., 1967; with Data Corp. (name changed to Mead Tech. Labs. 1968), Dayton, Ohio, 1967-77, v.p. tech. ops., 1970-71, dir. info. systems, 1971-77; pres., chief exec. officer DG Assos., Inc., 1974—; mng. partner Infotex Assos., 1977—; instr. data processing U. Ariz., Tucson, 1962-63. Mem. Assn. Computing Machinery, Am. Soc. Info. Scis. Inventor data/central (used to establish electronic newspaper libraries). Home: 5460 Royalwood St Dayton OH 45429 Office: 1476 Route 725 Dayton OH 45459

GIERS, THOMAS RAYMOND, electric co. exec.; b. Chgo., Dec. 30, 1952; s. Raymond Walter and Irene (Rejczyk) G.; A.A., Moraine Valley Community Coll., 1972; B.A., Lewis U., 1977; cert. in advanced rate analysis Triton Community Coll., 1981; m. Mary Alice Baker, Apr. 21, 1979. Transp. and phys. distbn. planner/analyst R.D. Werner Co., Franklin Park, Ill., 1979-81; transp. asso. Western Electric Co., Lisle, Ill., 1981—; cons. in field. Democrat. Roman Catholic. Home: 304 Nelson Ct Bolingbrook IL 60439 Office: 4513 Western Ave Lisle IL 60435

GIERTZ, ROBERT WILLIAM, heavy equipment mfg. co. exec.; b. Clifton, Ill., Mar. 24, 1925; s. William Chris and Emma Louise (Meyer) G.; B.S., U. Ill., 1950; postgrad. Mass. Inst. Tech., 1964; m. Vera Rosalie Herrmann, Nov. 30, 1946; children—Deborah (Mrs. Thomas Staack), Nancy (Mrs. Scott Natvig), Norman, James, Julie. Mechanical engr. John Deere Waterloo Tractor Works of Deere & Co., Waterloo, Iowa, 1950-64, chief engr., 1964-67, gen. mgr., 1967-74, dir. mfg., Moline, Ill., 1974—; dir. Iowa Pub. Service Co., Nat. Bank of Waterloo. Mem. Dist. Judicial Nominating Commn., 1969-75; mem. Waterloo Indsl. Devel. Assn., 1968-75; past mem. United Services of Black Hawk County. Trustee, Schoitz Meml. Hosp., 1968-74, Mt. Mercy Coll., Cedar Rapids, Iowa, 1979—; bd. govs. Iowa Coll. Found., vice chmn., 1976, chmn., 1977; bd. govs. U. No. Iowa Found., pres. 1973-75; past dir. Waterloo Civic Found.; bd. dirs. Quad City World Affairs Council, pres., 1980-81. Served with USAF, 1946-47. Registered profl. engr., Ill. Mem. Soc. Automotive Engrs., Am. Soc. Agrl. Engrs., Am. Mgmt. Assn. Republican. Lutheran. Clubs: Sunnyside Country, Crow Valley Golf, Symposium. Home: 2410 Eagle Circle Bettendorf IA 52722 Office: Deere & Co John Deere Rd Moline IL

GIERUT, MARTIN PAUL, architect; b. Chgo., Apr. 7, 1946; s. Stanley Marion and Elizabeth Margret (Bardo) G.; diploma De LaSalle Inst., 1964; student Wright Jr. Coll., 1964-67; B.A., So. Ill. U., 1969; m. Petra Wollert, Sept. 20, 1969; children—Katherine, Kristina, Paul. Sr. draftsman Chgo. Park Dist., 1969-74, archtl. designer, 1974—; works include Lincoln Park Zoo New Mall, Grant Park Band Shell, Burnham Park Soldier Field remodeling; prin. architect M.P. Gierut & Assos. Architects, Cary, Ill., 1978—; mem. archtl. design rev. bd. Village of Oak Wood Hills, 1974—, planning commn., 1978-81, bd. zoning appeals, 1978-81. Registered architect, Ill. Mem. Soc. Am. Registered Architects. Democrat. Roman Catholic. Home and Office: 215 Woody Way Cary IL 60013

GIESEN, RICHARD ALLYN, pub. co. exec.; b. Evanston, Ill., Oct. 7, 1929; s. Elmer J. and Ethyl (Lillig) G.; B.S., Northwestern U., 1951; m. Jeannine St. Bernard, Jan. 31, 1953; children—Richard Allyn, Laurie J., Mark S. Research analyst new bus. and research depts. Glore, Forgan & Co., Chgo., 1951-57; asst. to pres. Gen. Dynamics Corp., N.Y.C., 1957-60, asst. treas., 1960-61, asst. v.p. ops. and contracts, 1961-63; fin. cons. IBM Corp., 1963, exec. asst. to sr. v.p., 1964-65; treas. subs. Sci. Research Assos., Inc., Chgo., 1965-66, v.p. fin. and adminstrn., 1966-67, exec. v.p., chief operating officer, 1967-68, pres., chief exec. officer, 1968—, also dir.; now pres., chief exec. officer Field Enterprises Inc., Chgo., dir. Sci. Research Assos. (Can.), Ltd., Sci. Research Assos. Ltd. (U.K.), Sci. Research Assos. (Pty.) Ltd. (Australia), Societe de Recherche Appliquee a l'Education (France), Stone Container Corp., Chgo. Mem. bus. adv. council Chgo. Urban League; trustee Roosevelt U., Chgo., TV Sta. WTTW; mem. pres.'s council Nat. Coll. Edn., Evanston, Ill.; mem. Midwest adv. bd. Inst. Internat. Edn., Chgo. Mem. Young Pres.'s Orgn., Alpha Tau Omega, Beta Gamma Sigma. Clubs: Chicago; Glen View (Golf, Ill.). Office: Field Enterprises Inc 401 N Wabash Ave Chicago IL 60611

GIFFEN, DANIEL H., lawyer; b. Zanesville, Ohio, Feb. 11, 1938; s. Harris MacArtor and Louise (Crawford) G.; A.B., Coll. William and Mary, 1960; M.A. in History of Art, U. Pa., 1963; Ph.D. in Am. Civilization, 1967; 1967; J.D., Case Western Res. U., 1973; m. Jane Louise Cayford, Nov. 23, 1963 (div. 1970); children—Sarah Louise, Thomas Harris; m. 2d, Linda S. Eastin, Aug. 19, 1972. Corp. asst. Lippincott Library, U. Pa., Phila., 1961-63; asso. curator La. State Mus., 1963-64; dir. N.H. Hist. Soc., Concord, 1964-69, also sec.; asst. dir. Arents Research Library, State U. N.Y., Syracuse, 1969-70; v.p. Village Press Publs., Inc., Concord, 1969-74; editor Walter H. Drane Co., Cleve., 1974-76; individual practice law, Cleve., asst. prof. Cleve. State U., 1976-79; asst. prof. Kent State U., 1980—. Vice pres. N.H. Antiquarian Soc. 1966-68, lectr. 1968; dir. Assn. Hist. Socs. N.H. 1967; mem. faculty Monadock (N.H.) Community Coll., 1968-69; life mem. pres.'s council Coll. William and Mary. Mem. Am., Ohio, Cleve. bar assns., Cleve. Restoration Soc., Am. Assn. Museums, Am. Assn. State and Local Historians, Nat. Trust, Soc. Am. Archivists, Soc. Archtl. Historians, Rushlight Club, Pewter Collectors Club. Author: Adventures in Vermont, 1969; Adventures in Maine, 1970; The New Hampshire Colony, 1970. Editor: Hist. N.H. mag. Contbr. profl. jours. Home: 292 Corning Dr Bratenahl OH 44108 Office: Nixson Hall Kent State U Kent OH 44242

GILBERT, ANNE WIELAND, journalist; b. Chgo., May 1, 1927; d. David and Joy (Arnold) Wieland; B.S., Northwestern U., 1949; m. George Gale Gilbert III, Apr. 7, 1953; children—Douglas, Christopher. Columist, Chgo. Daily News, 1971-76, also syndicated in N.Y. News, 1973—, San Francisco Chronicle, 1973—; reporter NBC-TV Sunday in Chgo., 1973; guest expert NBC-TV, N.Y.C. Today, 1974—; producer WSNS-TV spl. Collectors World, 1971; performer TV programs KETC-TV, St. Louis; owner syndicated radio spot The Antique Detective. Mem. Chgo. Press Club, Alpha Gamma Delta. Presbyterian. Author: Antique Hunters Guide: For Freaks and Fanciers, 1974; Collecting the New Antiques, 1977; How to Be an Antiques Detective, 1977.

GILBERT, BRUCE FREDERIC, business exec.; b. Whitehall, Wis., Dec. 23, 1932; s. Frederic B. and Louise E. (Hahn) G.; B.S., Marquette U., 1958; m. Ellen F. Strachan, June 28, 1968; children—James, Eric, Heidi, Sarah. Salesman, Tews Lime & Cement Co., Milw., 1958-64; pres., sec., dir. Cedar Lake Sand & Gravel Co., Inc., Hartford, Wis., 1962—; sec., dir. Pioneer Materials Inc., Fond Du Lac, Wis., 1975—; officer, dir. Cedar Lake Constrn. Co. Inc., Hartford, 1970—, Lake Materials, Inc., Hartford, 1980—; dir. Frontier Materials, Inc., Jebs Farms Ltd., Cedar Lake Co. Inc. Trustee, Pilgrim Evang. Lutheran Ch. Mem. Asso. Builders and Contractors of Wis., Wis. Cattleman's Assn., Tex. Longhorn Cattleman's Assn. Republican. Club: Safari Internat. Home: 5189 Hwy K Hartford WI 53027 Office: Cedar Lake Sand & Gravel Co Hwy 41 and Aurora Rd Hartford WI 53027

GILBERT, EDWARD GEORGE, ins. agy. exec.; b. Kansas City, Mo., Jan. 11, 1923; s. Edward H. and Camille S. G.; A.B., Grinnell Coll., 1942; M.B.A., U. Chgo., 1943; m. Marilyn G. Rothschild, Mar. 7, 1977; children—Richard, Robert, Charles, Katherine. Research asst. Sch. of Bus., U. Chgo., 1943; with personnel dept. Walgreen Drugs, Chgo., 1943-44; with Uhlmann Grain Co., Kansas City, Mo., 1944-47; with Edgar J. Stern/Assos. Thomas McGee & Sons, Kansas City, 1947-61, partner, 1956-61; pres. Edward G. Gilbert Agy., Kansas City, 1961—, Gilbert-Magill Co., Kansas City, 1961—. Bd. dirs. NCCJ, 1950-53, 57-60; bd. overseers Grinnel Coll., 1964-69; bd. councillors Menorah Med. Center; v.p. Urban League, Kansas City, 1960. C.P.C.U., C.L.U. Mem. Ind. Ins. Agts. Am., Assn. Internat. Ins. Agts. (dir.), Assurex Internat. (dir.), Million Dollar Round Table, Casualty and Surety Assn., Mo. Ins. Agts. Assn. (treas. 1973), Kansas City Assn. Ind. Ins. Agts. (pres. 1973), Kansas City Chartered Property Casualty Underwriters (treas. 1960), Phi Beta Kappa. Office: Commerce Tower PO Box 13265 Kansas City MO 64199

GILBERT, GWENDOLYN CYNTHIA, social worker; b. Bartlesville, Okla., Feb. 12, 1937; d. Byrdie T. Crawford; B.S. in Edn., Grambling (La.) Coll., 1958; M.S.W., Ohio State U., 1960; Ph.D. (NIMH grantee 1975-77), Case Western Res. U., 1979; m. Walter Gilbert, Sept. 6, 1959; children—Jocelyn Gwenette, Rosalyn Patrice, Robyn Michelle. Program dir. Christ Child Settlement House, Washington, 1960-61, Central Community House, Columbus, Ohio, 1961-63; research asso. dept. pediatrics, div. child devel. Ohio State U. Coll. Medicine, 1964-67, asso. prof. Coll. Social Work, 1968—; v.p. Center Change and Leadership, Battelle Chair, Columbus Urban League, 1978-81; bd. dirs. v.p. Southside Settlement, 1968-72. Bd. dirs. United Christian Center, Columbus, 1972-74, Columbus Area Internat. Program, 1979-81, Met. Women's Center, 1980—, Mayor's Econ. Devel. Council, 1980—. Mem. Acad. Cert. Social Workers, Nat. Assn. Social Workers, Nat. Conf. Social Welfare, Council Social Work Edn., Nat. Black Child Devel. Inst. Democrat. Methodist. Club: Columbus Met. Office: 1947 N College Rd Columbus OH 43210

GILBERT, HELEN LOUISE, nurse, family planning adminstr.; b. Grand Rapids, Mich., Sept. 21, 1927; d. Reginald George and Jessie Louis (Hilton) Read; diploma U. Mich. Sch. Nursing, 1949; asso. degree Marshalltown Community Coll., 1972; cert. Family Planning Specialist, U. Nebr., 1973; m. Kenneth Robert Gilbert, Feb. 1, 1947; children—Kristin Louise Gilbert Strittmatter, Mark Alan, William Walter. Sch. office hosp. nurse ARC, 1950-58; staff nurse, in service coordinator Community Hosp. Marshalltown, Iowa, 1969-71; family planning nurse Mid-Iowa Community Action, Ames, 1971-73; founder, nurse, exec. dir. Central Iowa Family Planning Inc., Marshalltown, 1973—; instr. understanding human behavior Area Coll. Adult Edn. Dept. Mem. Am., Iowa nurses assns., Nurses Assn. of Am. Coll. Obstetricians and Gynecologists (certificate excellence in practice in maternal, gynecol., neonatal nursing 1976). Home: Union Grove Lake Garwin IA 50632 Office: PO Box 375 704 May St Marshalltown IA 50158

GILBERT, HERMAN CROMWELL, state ofcl.; b. Mariana, Ark., Feb. 23, 1923; s. Van Luther and Cora (Allen) G.; student LaSalle Extension U., 1940-41, Internat. Bus. Machines Ednl. Center, 1957-72; m. Ivy McAlpine, July 19, 1949; children—Dorthea Ruth, Vincent Newton. Program coordinator AFL-CIO, United Packinghouse Workers Am., Chgo., 1955-57; with Ill. Dept. Labor, Bur. Employment Security, 1947-55, 57-81, chief data processing adminstr., 1971-73, dep. adminstr., 1973-81; chief of staff Congressman Gus Savage, 2d Dist., Chgo., 1981—; exec. v.p. Path Press, 1968—; mng. editor Westside Booster, Chgo., 1959-60, Citizen Newspapers, Chgo., 1965-67. Publicity dir. Chgo. League Negro Voters, 1958-65, Protest at the Polls, 1965-68; mem. Joint Fed.-State Com. Automated Systems, Interstate Conf. Employment Security Agencies, 1969-73; chmn. task force data elements standardization Interstate Conf. Employment Security Agencies, 1970-73; vice chmn. Assembly of Black State Execs., 1973-77; mem. Black concerns com. Ill. Employment and Tng. Council, 1977—, mem. spl. concerns com., 1978—. Served with USAAF, 1943-46. Author: The Uncertain Sound, 1969. Home: 11539 S Justine St Chicago IL 60643 Office: 1743 E 87th St Chicago IL 60617 also 1233 Longworth House Office Bldg Washington DC 20515

GILBERT, HOWARD ALDEN, econ Central Bible Inst., Springfield, Mo., 1957; postgrad. Everett (Wash.) Jr. Coll., 1959; B.S. (Danforth fellow), Wash. State U., 1961, M.A., 1962; Ph.D., Oreg. State U., 1967; postgrad. S.D. State U., 1969-70, Vanderbilt U., 1971; m.; four children. Research asst. dept. agrl. econs. Wash. State U., 1961-62; research asst. dept. agrl. econs. Oreg. State U., 1962-65, asst. in agrl. econs., 1965-66; asst. prof. dept. econs. S.D. State U., Brookings, 1966-73, asso. prof., 1973-76, prof., 1976—, chmn. campus ednl. aids com., 1969-72, student affairs sub-com. on orgns., 1970-72, goals and objectives com., 1973-74, faculty welfare com., 1974-75, citizens high sch. curriculum evaluation com., 1974-75; co-dir. econs. dept. internship program, 1974—, chmn. econs. dept. teaching and curriculum com., 1974—, acad. senate ad hoc com. on univ. core in social sci., 1976. Named Outstanding Tchr. of Year, S.D. State U., 1969-70, Coll. Agr., S.D. State U., 1978-79; NSF grantee Vanderbilt U., summer 1971, Clark Coll., 1976-77. Mem. Am., Western agrl. econs. assns., Am., Western econ. assns., Am. Sci. Affiliation, Phi Kappa Phi, Pi Gamma Mu, Gamma Sigma Delta, Alpha Zeta, Omicron Delta Epsilon. Contbr. articles on econs. to profl. publs. Home: 605 9th St Brookings SD 57006 Office: Dept Econs SD State U Brookings SD 57007

GILBERT, RICHARD GEOFFREY, savs. and loan assn. exec.; b. Chgo., Apr. 7, 1920; s. George and Marie (Bensley) G.; B.S., Northwestern U., 1947; LL.D. (hon.), Malone Coll., 1971; m. Wynifred I. Shull, Nov. 11, 1961; children—Pamela Landefeld, Rene Nichols, Jeffrey, Dana Boyd. With Fed. Res. Bank, Chgo., 1938; with Cleve. Trust Co., 1939-41; instr., asst. investment fund mgr. Northwestern U., Evanston, Ill., 1945-47; with Citizens Savs. Assn., Canton, Ohio, 1947—, now chmn., pres.; former vice chmn. Fed. Home Loan Bank of Cin.; dir. Investors Mortgage Ins. Co., Sun Savs. and Loan, Loveland, Colo. Chmn. Central Canton Devel. Assn., 1959-77; bd. dirs. Aultman Hosp., Malone Coll. Served with USN, 1941-45. Mem. U.S. League Savs. Assn. (past pres.), Ohio League Savs. Assn. (past pres.), Greater Canton C. of C. (trustee). Republican. Presbyterian. Clubs: Canton, Brookside Country; Mayacoo Lakes Country (Palm Beach, Fla.). Office: Citizens Savings Assn 100 Central Plaza S Canton OH 44702

GILBERT, RONALD RHEA, lawyer; b. Sandusky, Ohio, Dec. 29, 1942; s. Corvin E. and Mildred (Milligan) G.; B.A., Wittenberg U., 1964; J.D., U. Mich., 1967, postgrad. in bus., 1967-68; postgrad. Wayne State U. Law Sch., 1973-74; m. Marilynn Davis, Aug. 26, 1966; children—Elizabeth, Lynne, Lisa. Trainee trust dept. Nat. Bank Detroit, 1967-68; asso. firm Cozad, Shankle & Smith, Detroit, 1968-69; asst. prosecutor County of Wayne (Mich.), 1969; admitted to Mich. bar, 1968; asso. firm Rouse, Selby, Dickinson, Shaw & Pike, Detroit, 1969-72; mem. firm Charfoos, Christensen, Gilbert and Archer, P.C., Detroit, 1972—; instr. history, polit. sci. Madonna Coll., Detroit, 1977—; faculty Inst. Continuing Legal Edn., Ann Arbor, Mich., 1977—. Mem. Econ. Club. Detroit, Detroit Council World Affairs (dir. 1968-72), Wittenberg Alumni Council, Detroit Bar Assn. (chmn. young lawyers 1970-72), Mich. State Bar Young Lawyers (sec.-treas. 1971), Am. Bar Assn. (del. young lawyers sect. 1970-72), Am. Judicature Soc., Detroit Art Inst. (patron). Clubs: Country Detroit, Detroit Athletic, Renaissance, U. Mich. Contbr. articles to profl. jours. Home: 290 McKinley St Grosse Pointe Farms MI 48236 Office: Charfoos Christensen Gilbert and Archer 4000 City National Bank Bldg Detroit MI 48226

GILBERT, SIDNEY, dentist; b. Westfield, N.J., Apr. 15, 1917; s. Alexander and Bessie (Sobel) G.; D.D.S., Ohio State U., 1942; m. Eileen H. Bradford, Sept. 27, 1980; children—Stephen Lee, Donald Bernard, Marilyn Sue, Dorothy Audrey. Gen. practice dentistry, Akron, Ohio, 1946-63, Mogadore, 1963—; owner horse breeding farm, Canfield, Ohio, 1973—. Served to maj. USAAF, 1942-46; CBI. Decorated Presdl. citation. Mem. Am., Ohio dental assns., Am. Inst. Orthodontics, Stark County Dental Soc., Am. Endodontic Soc., Am. Morgan Horse Assn., Buckeye Saddlebred Futurity (trustee 1973—), Ohio Saddlebred Horse Assn. (bd. dirs. 1972-74), Alpha Omega, Am. Legion. Mason (Shriner), Elk. Home: 11860 Green Beaver Rd Canfield OH 44406 Office: 60 S Cleveland Ave Mogadore OH 44260

GILBERT, WILLIAM FREDERICK, elec. engr.; b. South Haven, Mich., Mar. 9, 1924; s. Angus and Alice Marie (Rohloff) G.; B.E.E., Mich. Tech. U., 1945, M.E.E., 1950; m. Elaine Montgomery, May 6, 1944; children—Sandra, Richard, Barbara, Patricia, Susan, Russell. Mem. faculty Mich. Tech. U. at Houghton, 1945-60, asso. prof. physics, 1955-60; asso. elec. engr., mgr. ednl. nuclear reactors labs. Argonne (Ill.) Nat. Lab., 1960-72; tng. coordinator Cooper Nuclear Station, Nebr. Pub. Power Dist., Brownville, 1972—. Mem. Am. Nuclear Soc. Methodist. Clubs: Auburn Country, Elks. Home: 2315 Lynch Ave Auburn NE 68305 Office: PO Box 98 Brownville NE 68321

GILBERTSON, LOWELL HENRY, vet. drug co. exec.; b. Audubon, Minn., Jan. 24, 1920; s. Alfred and Dena G.; student Am. Acad. Accountancy, St. Paul; m. Idabelle E. Kohler, Aug. 5, 1944; children—Lowell Dean, Deborah Deane. Successively store mgr. B.F. Goodrich Co., Sioux Falls, S.D., Austin, Minn., Mpls., St. Paul, 1944-57; Iowa sales rep. Nelson Lab., Sioux Falls, S.D., 1957-75, pres., 1975—, also dir.; mem. S.D. Task Force for Product Liability Revision; del. White House Conf. on Small Bus. Served with U.S. Army, 1940-44; PTO. Mem. Nat. Assn. Wholesalers, Am. Vet. Distbrs. Assn. (pres. 1981—), S.D. C. of C., Sioux Falls C. of C. Democrat. Lutheran. Clubs: Rotary (Sioux Falls); Masons. Office: Nelson Labs 1000 Benson Rd Sioux SD 57101

GILBOE, DAVID DOUGHERTY, educator; b. Richland Center, Wis., July 13, 1929; s. Harvey Bernard and Margaret Lucille (Dougherty) G.; B.A., Miami U., 1951; M.S., U. Wis., 1955, Ph.D., 1958; m. Myrtle Marie Kroll, Aug. 18, 1951; children—Andrew J., Sarah A. Instr. surgery and physiol. chemistry U. Wis., Madison, 1959-61, asst. prof., 1961-67, asso. prof., 1967-73, prof. surgery and physiology, 1973—; ad hoc referee Am. Jour. Physiology; cons. Neurology B Study Sect., NIH, 1980—. Served with USN, 1951-54. NIH grantee, 1965—; Wis. Alumni Research Found. fellow in surgery, 1958-59; Fulbright lectr. in Med. Sci., U. Chile, Santiago, 1970. Mem. Am. Physiol. Soc., Am. Soc. Biol. Chemists, Am. Soc. for Neurochemistry, Internat. Soc. for Neurochemistry, Soc. for Neuroscience, AAUP, Sigma Xi. Roman Catholic. Clubs: Rotary. Contbr. articles and book chpts. in field of metabolism and physiology of isolated canine brain preparation. Home: 409 Blue Ridge Pkwy Madison WI 53705 Office: 4630 Med Scis Center 1300 University Ave Madison WI 53706

GILCHRIST, (VERA) JANE, assn. exec.; b. Oklahoma City, June 2, 1945; d. Ralph E. and LaVonta T. (Goode) G.; B.S., Wichita (Kans.) State U., 1968. With Carson/Roberts Advt., Los Angeles, 1968-72, Mace Advt., Kansas City, Mo., 1972-73, Boothe Advt., Wichita, 1973-76; dir. Wichita State U. Alumni Assn., 1976—. Mem. Nat. Press Women, Council Advancement and Support Edn., Am. Mgmt. Assn. Democrat. Home: 324 N Roosevelt St Wichita KS 67208 Office: 1944 N Yale St Wichita KS 67208

GILDEHAUS, GERALD CLEMENS, restaurant exec.; b. Washington, Mo., July 22, 1943; s. Leo George and Noemi Barbara (Buhr) G.; student parochial schs., Washington, Mo.; m. Oma Louise Bradley, Mar. 22, 1975; children—Gerald Clemens, Glenda, Gina, Gayle, Mary Nell, Thomas John. With Kellwood Co., New Haven, Mo., 1962-79, mgr. indsl. engring., 1977—; owner, mgr., operator Cowan's Cafe, Washington, Mo., 1977—. Mem. Downtown Washington Shopping Center, Inc., 1977—. Mem. Downtown Mchts. Assn. Roman Catholic. Home: 301 Williams St Washington MO 63090 Office: 114 Elm St Washington MO 63090

GILDEHAUS, THOMAS ARTHUR, mfg. co. exec.; b. Little Rock, Sept. 29, 1940; s. Arthur F. and Susanna (Packham) G.; B.A., Yale U., 1963; M.B.A. with distinction, Harvard U., 1970; m. Barbara Quimby, Oct. 29, 1960; children—Elizabeth Q., Thomas Arthur, Charles L. Christopher, Allen P. Mgr., Citibank, P.R., 1963-68; v.p. Temple, Barker & Sloane, Inc., Lexington, Mass., 1970-80; v.p. bus. planning Deere & Co., Moline, Ill., 1980—, sr. v.p., 1980—. Trustee, St. Katharine's/St. Mark's Sch., Bettendorf, Iowa, 1981—. Home: 935 26th Ave Moline IL 61265 Office: John Deere Rd Moline IL 61265

GILES, HOMER WAYNE, lawyer; b. Noble, Ohio, Nov. 9, 1919; s. Edwin Jay and Nola Blanche (Tillison) G.; A.B., Adelbert Coll., 1940; LL.B., Western Res. Law Sch., 1943, LL.M., 1959; m. Zola Ione Parke, Sept. 8, 1948; children—Jay, Janice, Keith, Tim, Gregory. Admitted to Ohio bar, 1943; mem. firm Davis & Young, Cleve., 1942-43, William I. Moon, Port Clinton, 1946-48; pres. Strabley Baking Co., Cleve., 1948-53; v.p. French Baking Co., Cleve., 1953-55; law clk. 8th Dist. Court Appeals, Cleve., 1955-58; partner Kuth & Giles, law firm 1958-68, Walter, Haverfield, Buescher & Chockley, 1968—; pres. Clinton Franklin Realty Co., Cleve., 1958—, Concepts Devel., Inc., 1980—; sec. Holiday Designs, Inc., Sebring, Ohio, 1964—. Trustee, Teamster Local 52 Health and Welfare Fund, 1950-53; mem. Bakers Negotiating Exec. Com., 1951-53; troop com. chmn. Skyline council Boy Scouts Am., 1961-63. Trustee, Hiram House Camp, Florence Crittenton Home, 1965; chmn. bd. trustees Am. Econ. Found., 1973-80, chmn. exec. com., 1973-80. Served with AUS, 1943-46; ETO. Mem. Am. Bar Assn., World Law Assn. (founding), Am. Arbitration Assn. (nat. panel arbitrators), Com. on Econ. Reform and Edn. (life mem.), Inst. on Money and Inflation, Speakers Bur. Cleve. Sch. Levy, Citizens League (nationalities service com. 1965), Cleve. Hist. Soc., Delta Tau Delta, Delta Theta Phi. Unitarian (trustee 1965-68). Clubs: Cleveland Skating, Harvard Business. Editor: Banks Baldwin Ohio Legal Forms, 1962. Contbr. articles to profl. publs. Home: 2588 S Green Rd University Heights OH 44122 Office: 1215 Terminal Tower Cleveland OH 44113

GILES, JACK L., religious educator; b. Melrose Park, Ill., Apr. 27, 1951; s. Joseph Ambros and Elsie F. (Schmidt) G.; B.A., Concordia Tchrs. Coll., River Forest, Ill., 1973, M.A. in Edn. (grad. asst. 1973-74), 1976; m. Celeste D. Manichia, Aug. 10, 1974. Dir. edn. Good Shepherd Lutheran Ch. Mo. Synod, Palos Heights, Ill., 1974-76; admissions counselor Governors State U., Park Forest South, Ill., 1976-77; asst. dir. admissions No. Ill. U., DeKalb, 1977-79; minister youth and parish edn. St. Paul Luth. Ch., Addison, Ill., 1979—; leader workshops. Mem. Adult Edn. Assn. U.S.A., Ill. Adult and Continuing Educators Assn., Luth. Edn. Assn., Religious Edn. Assn., Theol. Educators in Asso. Ministries, No. Ill. Dist. Dirs. Christian Edn. Conf. (pres.). Home: 14 N Iowa Ave Addison IL 60101 Office: 37 Army Trail Rd Addison IL 60101

GILES, WILLIAM ELMER, publishing exec.; b. Somerville, N.J., July 5, 1927; s. Elmer and Mary Jane (Reed) G.; A.B. in Govt., Columbia U., 1950, M.S. in Journalism, 1951; m. Gloria Mastrangelo, June 4, 1949; children—William J., Michael E., Richard H. and Paul L. (twins), Joseph R. Reporter, Plainfield (N.J.) Courier-News, 1946-47; copyreader, reporter Wall St. Jour., 1951-58, mng. editor S.W. edit., Dallas, 1958-61, news editor Washington bur., 1961; an organizer nat. weekly newspaper Nat. Observer, 1961, editor, 1962-71; asst. gen. mgr. Dow Jones & Co., Inc., pub. Wall St. Jour. and Nat. Observer, 1971-76, dir. mgmt. programs, mem. Dow Jones mgmt. com., 1972-76; disting. editor in residence Baylor U., 1976; exec. editor Detroit News, 1976-77, editor, v.p., 1977—. Mem. Sigma Delta Chi. Home: 1014 Bishop Rd Grosse Pointe Park MI 48230 Office: Detroit News 615 Lafayette Blvd Detroit MI 48231*

GILFILLEN, GEORGE C., JR., mktg. co. exec.; b. Dayton, Ohio, Oct. 31, 1919; student Cornell U., Ithaca, N.Y.; children—George C., Mary K. Gilfillen Coughnour. Chmn. bd. E.F. MacDonald Co., Dayton, also affiliate cos. Unique Golf Products, Cathedral City, Calif., MacDonald Creative Mktg., Dayton, MacDonald Motivational Research Center, Dayton, E.F. MacDonald Showroom Sales Centers, Inc., Dayton and Columbus, Ohio, Richmond, Ind. and Lexington, Ky., Mail-A-Way, Inc., Dayton, E.F. MacDonald Travel Co., San Francisco and Dayton, E.F. MacDonald Stamp Co., Dayton, E.F. MacDonald Incentive Co., Dayton; dir. 3d Nat. Bank & Trust Co., Dayton. Bd. regents Mercersburg (Pa.) Acad.; bd. dirs. Boys' Clubs Am., Dayton Philharm. Orch. Assn.; trustee Dayton Art Inst., Miami Valley Hosp., Dayton; mem. 8th Dist. Congl. Club, Dayton Area Progress Council, Aviation Hall of Fame; mem. com. Ohio Found. Ind. Colls., Dayton; mem. steering com. U. Dayton New Horizons Fund; corp. mem. United Health Found., Dayton; mem. steering com. YMCA; mem. devel. com. Mercersburg Acad.; mem. adv. bd. Miami Valley council Boy Scouts Am.; mem. fin. resource devel. council United Way Dayton; mem. Dayton Devel. Council, Staff Assistance for Employers Com., Dayton. Mem. Dayton Area C. of C. (dir.), Am. Def. Preparedness Assn. (chpt. dir.), Newcomen Soc. N. Am. Clubs: One Hundred, Dayton Country, Dayton Bicycle, Y Athletic, Foreman's, Moraine Country, Dayton Racquet, Shriners, Mimami Valley Skeet, Masons (32 deg.) (Dayton); Mission Hills Country (Rancho Mirage, Calif.); N.Y. Athletic (N.Y.C.); Detroit Athletic (Detroit). Office: 129 S Ludlow St Dayton OH 45402*

GILGER, REBECCA LEE, educator; b. Toledo, Mar. 5, 1944; d. Hollis Ray and Esther Anna (Rundle) G.; B.A., Adrian Coll., 1966; M.Ed., U. Toledo, 1977. Tchr. Monroe (Mich.) Public Schs., 1966-77; teaching asst. U. Toledo, 1977-80, instr. elem. edn., 1981—; instr. Owens Tech. Coll., Toledo, 1980-81. Mem. Assn. Ednl. Communications and Tech., Nat. Soc. Performance and Tech., Phi Delta Kappa, Alpha Phi. Home: 3925 Torrance St Apt 1 Toledo OH 43612

GILL, DONALD GEORGE, state ofcl.; b. O'Fallon, Ill., Dec. 3, 1927; s. Fred Kenneth and Anna (Mayer) G.; A.B., Ill. Coll., 1951, LL.D. (hon.), 1981; Ed.M., U. Ill., 1954, Ed.D., 1969; m. Betty Jo Brummal, Dec. 28, 1952; children—Donald Bruce, Ann Brummal, Gay Ellen. Tchr., Waverly, Ill., 1950-52; elem. and jr. high sch. prin., Taylorville, Ill., 1952-60; asst. dir., dir. lab. schs., prof. edn. Eastern Ill. U., Charleston, 1960-74; supt. schs. Volusia County Schs., DeLand/Daytona Beach, Fla., 1974-80; supt. of edn. State of Ill., Springfield, 1980—; asso. chmn. Ill. state com. North Central Assn. Colls. and Schs.; chmn. Ill. Tchr. Cert. Bd.; pres. bd. trustees Ill. Tchr. Retirement System; Ill. commr. Edn. Commn. of States. Mem. Charleston Twp. Bd., 1964-74; edn. subcom. 6th Ill. Constrnl. Conv., 1970. Served with USNR, 1945-46. Recipient award for conspicuous service Nat. Assn. Secondary Sch. Prins., 1962, presdl. citation for service to edn. and sch. adminstrn. Ill. Assn. Sch. Adminstrs., 1970. Mem. Fla. Assn. Dist. Sch. Supts., Nat. Fedn. Urban-Suburban Sch. Dists. (exec. bd.), Fla. Tchr. Edn. Council, Am. Assn. Sch. Adminstrs., Council Chief State Sch. Officers, Phi Delta Kappa. Democrat. Methodist. Club: Century. Author: Philosophy and Functions of the Junior High School, 1959; The Elementary Principalship in Illinois, 1967; Fundamental Junior High/Middle School, 1972; A State Board of Education for Illinois, 1973; The Vanishing Laboratory School, 1974; Schools for Today's World, 1974; Art Education: A School Superintendent's Perspective, 1980; Florida State Capitol Outlay Program: Where Is It Going?, 1980. Office: 100 N 1st St Springfield IL 62777

GILL, HENRY HERR, photojournalist; b. Detroit, July 21, 1930; s. Henry Herr and Esther (King) G.; student Vincennes (Ind.) U., 1948, Northwestern U., 1949, Ind. U., 1951, McNeese State U., La., 1952, U. Miami, 1962; m. Mary Jane Brown, Aug. 26, 1957. Mem. publ. staff U. Miami, 1960; fgn. service photographer, then dir. photography Chgo. Daily News, 1976; dir. photography Chgo. Sun-Times, 1978—; lectr. in field, exhibitor of photographs, 1964—. Recipient photo reporting award on Vietnam, Nat. Headliners Club, 1967, Overseas Press Club award, 1967, Emmy award for documentary Nat. Acad. TV Arts and Scis., 1965, Best News Picture of Year award Inland Press Assn., 1968, 69, Faculty citation Vincennes U., 1979. Mem. Chgo. Press Photographers Assn., Sigma Delta Chi (Disting. Journalism award 1965). Clubs: Chgo. Press, Headliner (Chgo.). Co-author: Mississippi Notebook, 1964; photographer film A War of Many Faces, 1965. Office: 401 N Wabash Ave Chicago IL 60611

GILL, LYLE BENNETT, lawyer; b. Lincoln, Nebr., May 11, 1916; s. George Orville and Ruth (Bennett) G.; B.A., Swarthmore Coll., 1937; LL.B., Nebr. Coll. Law, 1940; m. Rita M. Cronin, Aug. 28, 1975; children by previous marriage—George, Valerie, Marguerite. Admitted to Nebr. bar, 1940; practice law, Fremont, 1945—; city atty. Fremont, 1959-62, 67—. Vice chmn. A.R.C., Dodge County, 1953-59. Chmn., Dodge County Republican Com., 1945-51. Served with USNR, 1942-45, 1951-52; lt. comdr. (ret.). Mem. Am., Nebr., Dodge County (pres. 1962) bar assns., Trial Lawyers Assn., V.F.W., Am. Legion. Episcopalian. Home: 524 E Linden Ave Fremont NE 68025 Office: First Nat Bank Bldg Fremont NE 68025

GILL, MABEL CHARLENE, ret. cartographer; b. Alton, Ill., July 3, 1924; d. Charles Baker and Katherine Freda (Dehne) Meisenheimer; B.A., Tarkio Coll., 1976; m. Fred L. Gill, Feb. 3, 1946; children—Charles Winfield, Frederic Kent. Cartographic aide Aero. Chart Plant, St. Louis, 1948-53; cartographer Aero. Chart & Info. Center, St. Louis, 1953-62, supervisory cartographer, 1962-70; program mgr. Def. Mapping Agy. Aerospace Center, St. Louis, 1970-80, ret., 1980. Chmn. for Mid-Continent Region, ERA, 1981-82; founder Alton (Ill.) Mus. History and Art, 1971, bd. dirs., 1971-82; sec. Landmarks Preservation Council of Ill./SW, 1980—; regional mgr. Federally Employed Women, 1978-79, charter pres. Arsenal '76 chpt., 1976; mem. continuing com. Internat. Women's Year. Recipient 1st pl. award for community service Fed. Women's Program Council, 1976; Equal Opportunity award Def. Mapping Agy., 1978; named Woman of Yr., Aero. Chart & Info. Center, 1966. Mem. Am. Soc. Photogrammetry (award 1977, pres. 1977-78), Am. Congress of Surveying and Mapping (dir. 1969-70), AAUW, LWV, Mo. Coalition for ERA (treas. 1980-82), NOW, Women's Register of Mo., Toastmasters Internat. (ednl. v.p. 1981-82), Homemakers Equal Rights Assn. (Mo. state organizer 1981-82), Landmarks Preservation Council Ill. Methodist. Club: Zonta (St. Louis Club v.p. 1980, pres. 1981-82). Editor Newsletter of Photogrammetric Engring. & Remote Sensing, 1974-79, Apocalypse, 1972-75. Home: 4244 Lasata Dr Saint Louis MO 63123 Office: Def Mapping Agy Aerospace Center Saint Louis AFS MO 63118

GILL, SAFDAR ALI, civil engr.; b. Tharrawaddy, Burma, Nov. 21, 1931; came to U.S., 1965, naturalized, 1972; m. Habib Ali and Fatima Bibi G.; B.Sc. with honors, Govt. Coll. Engring. and Tech., Lahore, Pakistan, 1953; M.S., Northwestern U., 1962, Ph.D., 1970; m. Parveen Hira, Nov. 23, 1963; children—Kamran, Raheela, Aneela, Nabeela. Engr., Govt. of West Pakistan, Lahore, 1953-59, asst. dir. designs and research, 1959-61, 63-65; design engr. Kaiser Engrs., Chgo., 1962; design engr. Greeley & Hansen, Chgo., 1962-63, 65-70; sr. project engr. Soil Testing Services, Northbrook, Ill., 1970-71, asst. chief engr., 1972-75, chief engr., 1975—, also dir. Fulbright fellow, 1961-62. Fellow ASCE, Inst. Civil Engrs. (London); mem. Brit. Geotech. Soc., Structural Engrs. Assn. Ill. (dir.). Muslim. Contbr. articles to profl. jours. Home: 9107 Samoset Skokie IL 60076 Office: 111 Pfingsten Rd Northbrook IL 60062

GILLE, SUSAN VIRGINIA, educator; b. Tampa, Fla., July 31, 1942; d. Joseph Richmond and Lucile (Olney) Cason; B.S. in Nursing, U. Mo., 1964, M.S. in Public Health, 1970; m. George L. Gille, Aug. 22, 1964; 1 son, George Benjamin. Staff nurse Shriners Hosp. for Crippled Children, St. Louis, summer 1964; staff nurse pediatrics, operating room nurse, head nurse medicine U. Mo. Med. Center, Columbia, 1964-70; faculty N.W. Mo. State U., Maryville, 1970—, sch. nurse, 1970-71, coordinator Sch. Practical Nursing, 1971-75, chmn. Dept. Nursing, 1975—, mem. Vocat. and Continuing Edn. adv. bd., 1978—. Mem. Area II Health Systems Agy., Moberly, Mo., 1976—, chmn., personnel com., 1976-78, review com., 1976-78, chmn. planning com., 1978—; adv. com. Maryville Vo-Tech. Sch. Health Occupations, 1977—. N.W. Mo. State U. grantee, 1976—, others. Mem. Mo. Nurses Assn. (dir. 1973-75, 77-78, mem. legis. com. 1976—, chmn., 1978-79), Mo. Vocat. Assn., Am. Nurses Assn., Am. Public Health Assn., Mo. Public Health Assn., Am. Vocat. Assn. Contbr. articles to profl. jours. Home: 220 Clayton St Maryville MO 64468 Office: 235 Garrett Strong NW Mo State Univ Maryville MO 64468

GILLES, KENNETH ALBERT, educator; b. Mpls., Mar. 6, 1922; s. Albert Peter and Alma (Stodghill) G.; student Augsburg Coll., 1940-42; B.S., U. Minn., 1944, Ph.D., 1952; postgrad. Columbia, 1944; m. Beverly Elaine Barrows, July 1, 1944; children—Jeffrey Alan, Diane Elaine. Research engr. Pillsbury Co., Mpls., 1946-49; instr., research fellow U. Minn., St. Paul, 1949-52; project leader Gen. Mills, Inc., 1952-61; prof. cereal chemistry, chmn. cereal chemistry and tech. dept. N.D. State U., Fargo, 1961-69, v.p. agr., 1969-81; adminstr. Fed. Grain Inspection Service, U.S. Dept. Agr., Washington, 1981—. Chmn. City Planning Commn., Roseville, Minn., 1955-60, Park Bd., 1960-61; bd. dirs. Fargo Indsl. Devel. Corp., 1977—. Served to lt. (j.g.) USNR, 1944-46. Named Man of Year Roseville C. of C., 1961. Fellow A.A.A.S.; mem. Am. Assn. Cereal Chemists (pres. 1971-72, Geddes award 1976), Am. Chem. Soc., Inst. Food Tech., Assn. Operative Millers, Fargo C. of C. (mem. agrl. com. 1968—, dir. 1974—), Sigma Xi. Mason (Shriner). Editor-in-chief Cereal Chemistry, 1961-68. Contbr. chpts. to books, articles to publs. Home: 925 Park Dr Fargo ND 58103

GILLESPIE, JAMES LAURENCE, historian; b. Cleve., Apr. 5, 1946; s. James Joseph and Elizabeth A. M. (Koch) G.; A.B., Kenyon Coll., 1968; B.S. in Edn., Kent State U., 1973; M.A. (fellow), Princeton U., 1970, Ph.D. (fellow), 1973. Lectr., St. Mary's Coll. of Queen's U., Belfast, No. Ireland, 1971-72; asst. prof. Appalachian State U., Boone, N.C. 1974-75, Lakeland Community Coll., Mentor, Ohio, 1975-76, U. Minn., Duluth, 1976-77, Catawba Coll., Salisbury, N.C., 1977-81; legal writer Squire, Sanders & Dempsey, Cleve., 1980—; reader on medieval English history for Albion publ., 1975—; mem. organizing com. Ohio Conf. Medieval Studies, 1975-76. Vestryman St. Paul's Episcopal Ch., Cleve., 1976-79; mem. exec. bd. Carolinas Symposium on Brit. Studies. Mem. Am., So. hist. assns., Cleve. Medieval Soc., Phi Beta Kappa, Kappa Delta Pi, Phi Alpha Theta. Author: A Series of Commentaries on the Sacraments, 1977; also articles; reviewer Library Jour. Home: 956 Roanoke Rd Cleveland Heights OH 44121 Office: Squire Sanders & Dempsey Cleveland OH 44115

GILLESPIE, PHILLIP EARL, contractor; b. Indpls., Aug. 14, 1940; s. Earl Phillip and Mildred Jane G.; m. Veda Gillespie, May 30, 1981; children—Mark P., Lorri A. With Brad Snograss, Inc., Indpls., 1968—, v.p., 1979—. Mem. ASHRAE. Office: 2514 Bethel Ave Indianapolis IN 46203

GILLETTE, HALBERT SCRANTON, publisher; b. Chgo., June 29, 1922; s. Edward Scranton and Clarebel (Thornton) G.; B.S., Mass. Inst. Tech., 1944; m. Mary Livingston, Feb. 12, 1949 (dec.); children—Anne Livingston, Susan L; m. 2d, Karla Spiel, June 8, 1963; children—James McCall, Halbert George, Edward Scranton II. Space buyer for Andrews Agy., 1946-48; advt. mgr. Good Roads Machinery Co., Minerva, Ohio, 1948; exec. v.p. Gillette Pub. Co., Chgo., 1949-60; pub. The Reuben H. Donnelley Corp., 1960-70, Trade Periodicals, 1970-72; pres. Scranton Gillette Communications Inc., Chgo., 1972-78; chmn. bd. Occidental Ins. Co. N.C., 1973-74, McMillen Corp., Peninsula Life Ins. Co., 1974-77; chmn. bd., dir., pres. The Doctor's Tax Letter, Inc., Publisher's Paper Co., Inc., Ednl. Screen Inc., The Diapason, Inc., Piano Trade Pub. Co., Inc., Seed World, Inc. Alderman, City of Lake Forest (Ill.), 1979. Served with USNR, 1943-46. Mem. Phi Gamma Delta. Episcopalian. Club: Onwentsia. Home: 255 Foster Pl Lake Forest IL 60045 Office: 380 North West Hwy Des Plaines IL 60016

GILLETTE, JERRY MARSHAL, engr., engring. consulting co. exec.; b. Dyersburg, Tenn., Aug. 17, 1939; s. Auvergne Richard and Christine (Nabors) G.; B.S.E.E., Ill. Inst. Tech., 1978; m. Paulletta D. Gillette, July 31, 1971; children—Darlene Rachele, Nykole Davieá, Darrell Rodney. Specification detailer Western Electric, Chgo., 1959-65; elec. designer Johnson & Johnson, Chgo., 1965, CKS Engrs., Chgo., 1965-66, Lester B. Knight & Assos., Chgo., 1966; elec. engr. C.F. Murphy Assos., Chgo., 1966-71; elec. engr., owner Elec. Design & Graphics, Chgo., 1971-77; elec. engr. W.B. Dolphin & Assos., Chgo., 1977-79; pres. Consulting Consortium, Inc., Chgo., 1979—. Mem. Nat. Tech. Assn., Western Soc. Engrs., Ill. Soc. Profl. Engrs., Nat. Soc. Profl. Engrs., IEEE, Instrument Soc. Am., Consulting Engrs. Council Ill., Nat. Orgn. Minority Architects, Water Pollution Control Fedn., Constrn. Specifications Inst., Air Pollution Control Assn., Am. Consulting Engrs. Council. Methodist. Office: 205 W Randolph St Chicago IL 60606

GILLIAM, THOMAS HOWARD, hosp. engring. mgr.; b. Greenup, Ky., Dec. 28, 1933; s. Richard Arville and Mary Florence (Jones) G.; A.S., Hancock Coll., Santa Maria, Calif., 1967; postgrad. U. Tex., El Paso, 1970, U. Dayton, 1952-55; m. Madylon Gail Wahl, Aug. 4, 1973; children—Lisa Gail, Edward Roy. Project engr. electromechs. WacLine, Inc., Dayton, Ohio, 1955-59; field engr. Ford Aerospace Corp., Anchorage, 1959-61, AF Western Test Range, Vandenberg, Calif., 1961-68, White Sands Missile Range, N.Mex., 1968-71, Peace Ruby Project, Tehran, Iran, 1971-72; biomed. instrumentation engr. Riverside Meth. Hosp., Columbus, Ohio, 1972-78, asst. dir. plant and engring., 1978—; gen. mgr. BIOHIO Systems, Columbus, 1977—; moderator Preventive Maintenance Round Table, 1979; lectr. Boys Club of Lompoc (Calif.), 1966. Cert. clin. engr. Am. Bd. Clin. Engring.; lic. amateur radio operator, pvt. pilot. Mem. Assn. Advancement Med. Instrumentation, Emergency Care Research Inst., Soc. Biomed. Equipment Technicians, Dayton Area Biomed. Equipment Tech. Assn., IEEE, Instrument Soc. Am., Am. Radio Relay League, Central Ohio Med. Equipment Technicians Assn. (founder, pres.). Republican. Unitarian. Author: Handbook of Precision Measurements, 1966; editor COMETA Newsletter, 1976—; art adv. SBET News, 1977—; contbr. creative graphic arts and illustrations to profl. jours. Home: 1320 Francisco Rd Columbus OH 43220 Office: 3535 Olentangy River Rd Columbus OH 43214

GILLIES, JEAN KAY, educator; b. Watertown, S.D., May 4, 1954; d. Ray Harold and Betty Joan (Dahl) Bunde; B.S., S.D. State U., 1976; M.S., No. State Coll., 1980; m. Larry Lee Gillies, Aug. 23, 1975. Sales personnel Pred's, Aberdeen, S.D., 1976-77; tchr. home econs. Warner (S.D.) Sch., 1977-80; counselor New Beginnings Center, Aberdeen, S.D., 1980; tchr. comml. foods Hub Area Vocat. Sch., Aberdeen, 1977—. Supr. children Boy's Club, Aberdeen, 1980; adv. bd. guidance/counseling No. State Coll., Aberdeen, 1980-81. Mem. S.D. Edn. Assn., S.D. Vocat. Assn., Aberdeen Home Econs. Assn., Phi Upsilon Omicron. Democrat. Lutheran. Address: 1519 Marsie Circle Aberdeen SD 57401

GILLILAND, ROBERT LYNN, elec. engr.; b. Napoleon, Ohio, Oct. 1, 1942; s. Robert Edward and Madeline Faye (Eberle) G.; B.S., Gen. Motors Inst., 1965; m. Karen Marie Burill, May 11, 1963; children—Rochelle Elaine, Melinda Marie. With Gen. Motors Co., 1960—, sr. engr. central foundry div., 1973-75, maintenance supt., 1975-76, sr. engr. major projects, 1976—. Mem. Ayersville High Sch. Athletic Boosters; mem. elec. engring. adv. bd. N.W. Tech. Coll. Registered profl. engr., Ohio. Mem. Soc. Profl. Engrs., Am. Foundrymen's Soc., Defiance Area C. of C. Republican. Mem. United Ch. of Christ. Clubs: Masons, Elks. Home: 1711 Crestwood Defiance OH 43512 Office: Rt 281 E Defiance OH 43512

GILLIS, ROBERT ELLIOT, food co. exec.; b. Lincoln, Maine, June 7, 1938; s. Hugh Allen and Helen (Bucknell) G.; B.A., Pacific U., 1961; postgrad. Grad. Sch. Internat. Relations and Law, U. Conn.; m. Shirley Diane Smith, June 21, 1958; children—Jeffry Todd, Michael Darron, Lauren Ashley. Adminstrv. asst. United Fruit Co., Boston, 1961-62, mgr. export, 1962-63, mgr. sales adminstrn., 1963-65, dir. mktg., 1966-68; pres. Intermarket Internat., Inc., Boston, 1965-66; pres. Concept Foods Corp., Chgo., 1968-70; mgmt. cons./investor, Stowe, Vt., also Dallas, 1970-76; gen. mgr. food service group Central Soya Co., Inc., Fort Wayne, Ind., 1976-77, gen. mgr. food div., 1977, v.p., 1977-80, group v.p., 1980—; chmn. bd. J.H. Filbert, Inc. subs. Central Soya Co., 1979—, pres. J.H. Filbert, Inc., 1977-79; dir. Sunmark Cos. Bd. govs. Med. Center Hosp., Burlington, Vt., 1974—; trustee Pacific U., Forest Grove, Oreg., 1978—. Mem. Internat. Foodservice Mfg. Assn. (dir. 1978—, vice chmn.), Nat. Restaurant Assn. (action com. 1973-75). Republican. Home: 5523 Sherington Rd Fort Wayne IN 46804 Office: 1300 Fort Wayne Bank Bldg Fort Wayne IN 46802

GILLIS, RUTH JEANETTE KATHAN, librarian; b. Tulsa, July 26, 1921; d. William Wallace and Edith Viola (Parrish) Kathan; student Wayne State U., 1948-52, Barnard Coll., 1953; B.A., U. Minn., 1960, M.A., 1964; Ed.D., Ind. U., 1977; m. Frank James Gillis, Sept. 13, 1943; 1 son, Christopher Jay. Librarian, Univ. Elementary Sch., U. Minn., Mpls., 1962-64; librarian Univ. Elementary Sch., Ind. U., Bloomington, 1964—, univ. vis. lectr., 1969—. Served with WAC, 1943-45. Mem. ALA, Nat. Council Tchrs. English, NEA, Ind. Tchrs. Assn., Assn. Ind. Media Educators, Beta Phi Mu, Pi Lambda Theta (chpt. v.p. 1979-80), Phi Delta Kappa. Democrat. Author: Children's Books for Times of Stress, 1978; contbr. articles to profl. jours. Home: 3508 Morningside Dr Bloomington IN 47401 Office: University Elementary School 930 State Rd E Highway 46 Bypass Bloomington IN 47401

GILLMAN, RAY WALLACE, appliance mfg. co. exec.; b. Smithville, Ohio, Mar. 17, 1922; s. John B. and Jennie May (Smith) G.; B.A., Coll. Wooster, 1948; postgrad. U. Md., 1948, Washington Sch. Protocol, 1969; m. Virginia E. Ritter, Jan. 19, 1946; children—Jeffrey Paul, Janet Louise. Methods analyst Hoover Co., N. Canton, Ohio, 1948-53, gen. office mgr., 1953-54, asso. to pres., 1954-64; v.p. pub. affairs Hoover Worldwide Corp., N. Canton, 1964—; owner, operator Holiday Valley Farm, Millersburg, Ohio, 1965—. Mayor, Canal Fulton (Ohio), 1950-51; mem. adv. bd. Malone Coll., 1969—, chmn., 1977-79; adv. bd. Akron U. Coll. Fine and Applied Arts, 1979; mem. adv. bd. Akron U. Center for Econ. Edn., 1975—; trustee Canton Symphony Orch., 1964—, Canton Civic Opera Assn., 1981—. Served to capt. U.S. Army, 1942-46. Mem. Internat. Pub. Relations Assn., Pub. Relations Soc. Am. (regional coordinator 1978-80, exec. com. corp. sect. 1980—), European Public Relations Roundtable, Nat. Press Club, Am. Legion, Ohio Found. Ind. Colls. (Stark County chmn. 1970—, trustee 1978—), C. of C. Clubs: Masons, Oakwood Country. Office: The Hoover Co North Canton OH 44720

GILLMING, KENNETH EUGENE, clergyman, educator; b. Kearney, Nebr., June 15, 1925; s. Ralph Allen and Ona Elvesta (Brannan) G.; B.A. in Edn., Nebr. State U., Kearney, 1950; Th.M., Dallas Theol. Sem., 1954; m. Norma Jean Lewis, June 13, 1948; children—Virginia, Kenneth, Keith, Mark. Ordained to ministry, Bapt. Ch.; youth dir. Liveoak Bapt. Ch., Dallas, 1951-54; pastor Bethel Bapt. Ch., Strathroy, Ont., Can., 1954-58, Cherry Street Bapt. Ch., Springfield, Mo., 1959—; prof. Bapt. Bible Coll., Springfield, 1958—, also chmn. theol. dept., acad. dean. State chmn. Moral Majority of Mo., 1980-81. Office: Baptist Bible Coll 628 E Kearney Springfield MO 65802

GILLMOR, PAUL EUGENE, state legislator; b. Tiffin, Ohio, Feb. 1, 1939; s. Paul M. and Lucy J. (Fry) G.; B.A., Ohio Wesleyan U., 1961; J.D., U. Mich., 1964; m. Aug. 11, 1962 (dec.); children—Linda, Julie. Admitted to Ohio bar, 1965; mem. Ohio Senate, 1967—, asst. minority leader, 1975-78, majority leader, 1978—, pres., 1981—. Served with USAF, 1965-68. Mem. Am. Bar Assn. Home: 2253 Sand Rd Port Clinton OH 43452 Office: 88 S Washington St Tiffin OH 44883

GILLMORE, ALVER JAMES, III, lawyer; b. Newton, Kans., May 25, 1947; s. Alver James and Orva Rachel (Buller) G.; B.A., Wichita State U., 1969; J.D., U. Kans., 1972; LL.M., George Washington U.; m. Pamela Diane Caldwell, Jan. 24, 1970. Admitted to Kans. bar, 1972; asso. firm Smith, Rushfelt, Mueller & Lamer, Prairie Village, Kan., 1972-73; atty. ICC, Bur. of Enforcement, Washington, 1973-75; partner Speir, Stroberg & Sizemore, Newton, Kans., 1975—; dir. Sedgwick (Kans.) State Bank, 1977—; dir. Jay Energy Devel. Corp., Hesston, Kans., 1980—. Mem. Kans. Ho. of Reps., 1977-79; vice chmn. Harvey County Republican Party, 1980—; pres. Harvey County Hospice, 1979—; bd dirs. Harvey County Day Care Center, 1980—; chmn. Harvey County Am. Cancer Crusade, 1979—. Mem. Harvey County Bar Assn., Kans. Bar Assn., Am. Bar Assn. Mennonite. Clubs: Optimist, Elks. Home: 215 SW 7th St Newton KS 67114 Office: 809 Main St Newton KS 67114

GILLOGLY, CHARLES OWEN, motor carrier co. exec.; b. White Sulphur Springs, Mont., Jan. 15, 1919; s. Hugh Frederick and Bessie Albert (Rader) G.; student Mont. State Coll., 1935-36; B.A., U. Mont., 1941; postgrad. Am. U., 1948-49; m. Emma Laura Rush, Apr. 22, 1941; children—Hugh James, Brian Francis, Margaret Jo (Mrs. Jerry L. Bishop), Laura Teresa (Mrs. Dan J. Brothers), Kevin Rush. Salesman, S.W. Sales Service, Gallup, N.M., 1941; traffic clk. Wingate Ordnance Depot, Gallup, N.M., 1942-44; br. chief Bur. Ordnance, Navy Dept., Washington, 1945-52; exec. v.p. C.I. Whitten Transfer Co., Washington, 1952-68; pres. USAC Transport, Inc., Joplin, Mo., 1969-70; exec. v.p. Tri State Motor Transit Co., Joplin, Mo., 1970—; pres. Huntington Assos. Am., Inc., 1953-64; exec. v.p. Hughes Transp., Inc., 1968-70. Practitioner, ICC, 1949—. Served with USNR, 1944-46. Recipient Certificates of Appreciation, Nat. Defense Transp. Assn., 1955, 68, Delta Nu Alpha, 1956, Traffic Club Washington, 1963. Mem. Munitions Carriers Conf., Inc. (mem. exec. com. 1952-72), Am. Ordnance Assn., Am. Legion, Assn. ICC Practitioners, Sigma Phi Epsilon. Republican. Elk, K.C. (4 deg.), Rotarian. Clubs: Touchdown (Washington); Columbia Country (Chevy Chase, Md.); Twin Hills Country (Joplin, Mo.). Home: 3219 Moorhead Dr Joplin MO 64801 Office: PO Box 113 Joplin MO 64801

GILLUM, JACK DEAN, cons. structural engr.; b. Salina, Kans., Nov. 21, 1928; s. Charles Z. and Lillian D. (Mulnix) G.; student Wichita U., 1946-47; B.S., U. Kans., 1950; m. Alice A. Reese, Dec. 1, 1951 (dec. July 1971); children—Jack A., Timothy, Richard, Traci, Charles, Chris; m. 2d, Judith L. Hoffmann, June 1, 1973. Designer, Stearn Roger, Denver, 1952-55; cons. engr. Jack D. Gillum & Assos., Denver, 1955-69, Chgo., 1969-72, St. Louis, 1972—; chmn. bd. Gillum-Colaco, St. Louis; pres. GKC Internat.; partner Gillum-Polk & Assos., Webster Groves, Mo., also Chgo. Active Boy Scouts Am. Served as lt. C.E., AUS, 1951-52; Korea. Recipient Spl. citation Am. Inst. Steel Constrn., 1975; 2d place award in engring. excellence Cons. Engring. Council Mo., 1975, others; registered profl. engr., Calif., 22 other states. Mem. Nat. Soc. Profl. Engrs., ASCE, Prestressed Concrete Inst. (award 1975), Am. Concrete Inst., St. Louis Regional Commerce and Growth Assn. Christian Scientist. Clubs: Masons (32 deg.), Shriners. Home: 13682 Peacock Farm Rd St Louis MO 63131 Office: 100 N Broadway St Louis MO 63102

GILLYON, ROY BERNARD, cartographer; b. St. Louis, Aug. 21, 1942; s. Nicholas and Georgianna (Meier) G.; B.S., St. Louis U., 1964, M.A. (Univ. fellow), 1966; postgrad. U. Mich., 1966-67, U. Okla., 1970. Tchr. Incarnate Word Acad., St. Louis, 1969-70; service mgr., tng. coordinator Stix, Baer & Fuller, St. Louis, 1973-76; cartographer Def. Mapping Agy. Aerospace Center, St. Louis, 1977—. Pres., Bevo Housing and Edn. Corp., 1976—; v.p. Bevo 2001 Inc., 1976—; v.p. Bevo Long Community Sch., 1976-81, pres., 1981—. Served with C.E., U.S. Army, 1967-69. Mem. Am. Def. Preparedness Assn., St. Louis U. Alumni Assn., Am. Legion. Democrat. Roman Catholic. Home: 3904 Eiler St Saint Louis MO 63116 Office: St Louis Air Force Station 2nd and Arsenal Sts Saint Louis MO 63116

GILMOR, RICHARD LUTHER, neuroradiologist; b. Wooster, Ohio, Oct. 8, 1939; s. C. Luther and Orpha (King) G.; B.S., Baldwin Wallace Coll., 1961; M.D., Ohio State U., 1965; m. Sharon K. Radant, June 14, 1968; children—John Richard, Katherine Elizabeth. Intern in surgery Ind. U. Sch. Medicine, 1965-66, resident in neurol. surgery, 1968-72, resident in diagnostic radiology, 1974-76; practice medicine specializing in neurol. surgery, Springfield, Ohio, 1972-74; fellow in neuroradiology U. Calif., San Francisco, 1976-77, instr. dept. radiology, 1976-77; asst. prof. radiology and neurosurgery, chief of neuroradiology Ind. U. Sch. Medicine, Indpls., 1978—. Served with USNR, 1966-68. Diplomate Am. Bd. Radiology, Am. Bd. Neurol. Surgery. Mem. A.M.A., Ind. State Med. Soc., Marion County Med. Soc., Am. Assn. Neurol. Surgeons, Congress of Neurol. Surgeons, Central Neurosurg. Soc., Ind. Neurosurg. Soc., Radiol. Soc. N. Am., Ind. Roentgen Soc., Am. Coll. Radiology, Am. Soc. Neuroradiology. United Methodist. Office: Ind U Sch Medicine Univ Hosp Dept Radiology 1100 W Michigan St Indianapolis IN 46223

GILMORE, HELEN CAROL, mfg. co. exec.; b. Trenton, N.J., Aug. 7, 1940; d. Louis Alfred and Catherine (Peto) Fennimore; student Rider Coll., 1969, Purdue U., 1977-78, St. Mary-of-the Woods Coll., 1980—; m. Lester Wayne Gilmore, Oct. 18, 1963; 1 son, Matthew Todd; 1 son by previous marriage, Warren Jeffery Russell. Stenographer, USAF, McGuire AFB, N.J., 1958-63; investigative recorder, 1963-65; asso. realtor Faherty Real Estate, Bordentown, N.J., 1969-74; asst. terminal mgr. G&G Tank Transport Co., Inc., Columbus, N.J., 1969-74; adminstrv. asst. to asso. dean Krannert Grad. Sch. of Mgmt., Purdue U., West Lafayette, Ind., 1976-78; cons. Secs., Inc., Oak Brook, Ill., 1979; adminstrv. asst. to dir. materials Amphenol N.Am., Bunker Ramo Corp., Broadview, Ill., 1979-80, inventory specialist/product planner, 1980—. Recipient Sustained Superior Performance award USAF, 1960; Kiwanis Acad. Excellence award, 1958; cert. prodn. and inventory control practitioner. Mem. N.J. Assn. Realtors, Am. Bus. Womens Assn., (chpt. v.p. 1979), Am. Prodn. and Inventory Control Soc., Nat. Honor Soc. Office: 2801 S 25th Ave Broadview IL 60153

GILMORE, JAMES STANLEY, JR., broadcasting co. exec.; b. Kalamazoo, June 14, 1926; s. James Stanley and Ruth (McNair) G.; student Culver Mil. Acad., Western Mich. U., Kalamazoo Coll., 1945; Litt.D. (hon.), Nazareth Coll.; m. Diana Holdenreide Fell, May 21, 1949 (dec.); children—Bethany, Sydney, James Stanley III, Elizabeth, Ruth; m. 2d, Susan C. Maggio, Sept. 13, 1980. Owner, pres. Jim Gilmore Enterprises, Kalamazoo, 1960—; chmn. bd., chief exec. officer Jim Gilmore Enterprises, Gilmore Broadcasting Corp., Jim Gilmore Investments, Inc.; chmn. bd. Gilmore Advt., Inc., Green Turtle Seafood & Cannery, Inc., Turtle Trax, Islamorada, Fla.; chmn. bd., pres. Continental Corp. Mich., Inc.; v.p. Jim Gilmore Cadillac-Pontiac Datsun Inc., Gilmore Racing Team, Inc., (A.J. Foyt, driver); v.p., dir. Holiday Inn-Continental Corp. Mich.; asst. sec., dir. Fabri-Kal Plastics Corp. Kalamazoo; partner Greater Kalamazoo Sports, Inc. (hockey franchise), Kalamazoo Stadium Co.; owner Anthony Abraham Chevrolet, Miami, Fla. Car Rental, Miami; dir., mem. trust com. First Nat. Bank & Trust Co., Kalamazoo; dir. First Nat. Bank Fin. Corp., presdl. advisor Republic Airlines. Mem. Pres.' Citizens Adv. Com. on Environmental Quality; dir. Fed. Home Loan Bank Bd., Indpls.; mem., past chmn. Mich. Water Resources Commn.; mem. Mich. Gov.'s Forum; mem. nat. adv. cancer council HEW; mem. Nat. Assn. Broadcasters' adv. com. to Corp. for Pub. Broadcasting. Pres. Kalamazoo County Young Rep. Club, 1947-49; mayor, Kalamazoo, 1959-61; past mem. Kalamazoo County Bd. Suprs.; past chmn. Kalamazoo County Rep. Exec. Com.; del. Rep. Nat. Conv. Asso. bd. dirs. Boys Clubs Am.; bd. dirs., past chmn. Kalamazoo County chpt. A.R.C.; former chmn. bd. trustees Nazareth Coll.; trustee, mem. finance com. Greater Mich. Devel. Found.; mem., chmn. bldg. com. fund dr. Constance Brown Speech and Hearing Center; past trustee Kalamazoo Coll., mem. adv. group Center Urban Studies and Community Services; trustee past vice chmn. Kalamazoo Nature Center; mem. bldg. and exec. coms. Bronson Hosp., also chmn. ad hoc legis. com.; past trustee, past v.p. Mich. Found. for Arts, Detroit; life dir. Family Service Center Kalamazoo; mem. Mich. bd. dirs. Radio Free Europe; nat. sponsor Ducks Unlimited; life mem. March Dimes; chmn. spl. reorganizational com. United Fund; mem. fund raising com. Pres. Ford Library/Mus.; hon. trustee Mich. Alvin Bentley Charitable Found. Served with USAAF, 1943-46. Named Kalamazoo Young Man of 1960, One of Mich.'s 5 Young Men of 1960, hon. citizen of Houston and Indpls.; recipient Ann. Service to Mankind award Sertoma Club; Man of Yr. award Mich. Auto Racing Fan Club, Auto Racing Found. Frat.; honors Hoosier Racing Assn., Auto Racing Frat. Found., Inc., Milw. Mem. Kalamazoo County (past pres., past dir.; mem. exec. com. of indsl. devel. com.), Mich. (mem. law and order com.) chambers commerce, N.A.M., Mich. Acad. Sci., Arts and Letters. Episcopalian (mem. bd. diocese Western Mich., chmn. cathedral drive, mem. com. Bishop Whittemore Found.). Clubs: Capitol Hill (Washington); Park (past dir.) (Richland, Mich.); Mid-America (Chgo.); Otsego Ski (Gaylord, Mich.). Home: 1550 Long Rd Kalamazoo MI 49008 also 5040 Woodlawn Beach Gull Lake Hickory Corners MI 49060 Office: Jim Gilmore Enterprises 202 Mich Bldg Kalamazoo MI 49006

GILMORE, MARY HOLMES, social worker; b. Syracuse, N.Y., Mar. 5, 1915; d. Carlton H. and Margaret E. (Robinson) Holmes; B.A., Smith Coll., 1936; M.S., Columbia U., 1946; Ed.D., Temple U., 1954; 1 dau., Susan N. Supt., Woods Haven Sch. for Delinquent Girls, Claymont, Del., 1946-48; cons. on children's instns., Harrisburg, Pa., 1949-51; exec. dir. Allegheny County Mental Health Assn., Pitts., 1956-59; supt. McGregor Home for Aged, East Cleveland, Ohio, 1959-61; mem. faculty Sch. Applied Social Scis., Case Western Res. U., Cleve., 1961-71; exec. dir. Geauga County Community Mental Health Bd., 1969-80; lectr. U. Pitts., Kent State U., Hiram Coll.; propr. Tanrydoon Antiques Shop; lectr. early Am. antiques, 1973—. Recipient Profl. Manpower Tng. grants, 1969-80. Mem. Nat. Assn. Social Workers, Am. Public Health Assn., Council Social Work Edn., Gerontol. Assn., LWV. Democrat. Presbyterian. Club: Rushlight. Home: 8269 Summit Dr Lake Lucerne Chagrin Falls OH 44022 Office: 9519 E Washington St Chagrin Falls OH 44022

GILMORE, RICHARD HORTON, dentist; b. Allentown, Pa., Aug. 5, 1920; s. Richard Clare and Helen Miriam (Horton) G.; student Hiram Coll., 1938-40; D.D.S., U. Pitts., 1943; M.S. in Orthodontics, U. Mich., 1951; m. Alma Marie Williams, Feb. 6, 1946; 1 son, Richard Scott. Practice dentistry, New Castle, Pa., 1946-49; practice orthodontics, Saginaw, Mich., 1951—; pres. Center Road Corp., 1976—; dir., treas. Delta Dental Plans Mich., 1968-74; dir. Mega-Media and Tri Media Corps., 1971—. Bd. control Saginaw Valley State Coll., 1973—; bd. dirs. E. Central Mich. Health Systems Agency, 1976—. Served with U.S. Army, 1943-46. Fellow Am. Coll. Dentists; mem. ADA, Mich. Dental Assn., Am. Assn. Orthodontists, Mich. Soc. Orthodontists, Mich. Assn. Professions. Republican. Congregationalist. Clubs: Saginaw, Germania, Rotary. Home: 1149 Arclair Pl Saginaw MI 48603 Office: 595 N Center Rd Saginaw MI 48603

GILMORE, ROBERT EUGENE, earthmoving machinery co. exec.; b. nr. Peoria, Ill., May 4, 1920; s. Myron E. and Lillian G. (Mallm) G.; grad. high sch.; m. Marguerite A. Best, May 1, 1948; children—Christine Ann, Scott Eugene. With Caterpillar Tractor Co., Peoria, 1938—, pres. Caterpillar France, Grenoble, 1963-68, gen. mgr. worldwide mfg. and facilities planning, 1968, gen. mgr. U.S. mfg. plants, 1968-69, v.p. U.S. mfg. plants, 1969-73, exec. v.p., 1973-77, pres., chief operating officer, 1977—, also dir.; dir. Santa Fe Industries, Security Savs. & Loan Assn., Peoria. Bd. dirs. Proctor Hosp. Served to 1st lt. USAAF, 1943-45; ETO. Decorated Air medal with 4 oak leaf clusters. Mem. Soc. Automotive Engrs., NAM (dir.), Nat. Exec. Service Corps. (mem. council). Republican. Lutheran. Clubs: Peoria Country; Union League (Chgo.); Masons. Home: 7316 N Edgewild Dr Peoria IL 61614 Office: 100 NE Adams St Peoria IL 61629

GILMORE, ROBERT KARL, univ. adminstr.; b. Springfield, Mo., June 6, 1927; s. Herbert F. and Beulah M. (Whitehead) G.; B.S., S.W. Mo. State Coll., 1950; M.A., St. Louis U., 1954; Ph.D., U. Minn., 1961; m. Martha M. Lyons, Aug. 7, 1950; children—Julie, Tom, Michael. Tchr. public schs., St. Louis County, Mo., 1949-57; instr. U. Minn., 1957-59; asst. prof. speech and theatre S.W. Mo. State U., 1959-61, asso. prof., 1961-65, prof., 1965—, head dept. speech and theatre, 1965-67, dean Sch. Arts and Humanities, 1967-71, provost, dean of faculties, 1971—. Served with USN, 1945-46. Mem. North Central Assn. Acad. Deans, Speech Communication Assn., Central States Speech Assn. Lutheran. Club: Rotary. Office: 901 S National St Springfield MO 65802

GILMORE, ROBERT WITTER, charitable assn. exec.; b. Hamilton, Ohio, Sept. 6, 1933; s. Robert Foster and Frances Elizabeth (Witter) G.; B.S., Miami U., Oxford, Ohio, 1955; M.S.W., Ohio State U., 1957; m. Sara Louise McIntosh, Dec. 23, 1956; children—Susan Lynne, Robert Riley, Christopher Edwin. Asso. exec. United Fund, Wheeling, W.Va., 1960-61; exec. dir Community Chest and Council, Massillon, Ohio, 1961-64; exec. dir. United Fund and Community Council, St. Joseph, Mo., 1964-68; asso. dir. United Way, Dayton (Ohio) area, 1969-72, exec. dir., 1972-78; exec. dir. Community Chest and Council/United Appeal Greater Cin., 1978—. Served to 1st lt. Med. Services, U.S. Army, 1957-60. Named Outstanding Man of Year, St. Joseph Jr. C. of C., 1967. Mem. Sigma Chi. Presbyterian. Clubs: Queen City, Rotary. Home: 8767 Tanager Woods Dr Cincinnati OH 45242 Office: 2400 Reading Rd Cincinnati OH 45202

GILPATRICK, ROBERT LEE, ednl. adminstr.; b. Springfield, Mass., Aug. 30, 1944; s. Robert Lee and Adrienne (Jacques) G.; B.S., U. Wis., Whitewater, 1966; M.E., U. Wis., Madison, 1969; m. Barbara Jean Riemer, Aug. 20, 1966; children—Kristin Lee, Shelly Jean. Tchr., Edgerton (Wis.) Public Schs., 1966-69; dir. elem. edn. Baraboo (Wis.) Public Schs., 1969-73; prin. elem. sch. Cedarburg (Wis.) Public Schs., 1973—; instr. U. Wis. Ext., Madison, 1972. Pres., Wis. Cystic Fibrosis Found., 1980-82; mem. Gov.'s Task Force on Women's Issues, 1980-81; mem. Wis. Gov.'s Com. on Higher Edn., 1965-66. Mem. So. Wis. Edn. Assn. (pres.), NEA, Assn. Childhood Edn., Assn. Supervision and Curriculum Devel., So. Wis. Ednl. Inservice Orgn., Assn. Wis. Sch. Adminstrs., Cedarburg Jaycees. Methodist. Home: 656 Hillside Ln Cedarburg WI 53012

GILPIN, HAROLD DEAN, retail exec.; b. Fort Worth, Sept. 20, 1953; s. Harold D. and Marian Janet (Keoughan) G.; B.B., Western Ill. U., 1976; A.S., Spoon River Jr. Coll., 1974; m. Wendy L. Badie, Nov. 12, 1981. Stock supr. Store for Men, Marshall Field & Co., Vernon Hills, Ill., 1976-79, sales mgr. Store for Men, Hawthorn Center, 1980-81, sportswear buyer State St., 1981—. Adv., Jr. Achievement, 1976-79. Republican. Roman Catholic. Home: 1971 Buckley Rd Libertyville IL 60048 Office: Marshall Field & Co 111 N State St Chicago IL 60090

GILPIN, JOHN STEPHEN, veterinarian; b. Kalamazoo, Aug. 30, 1941; s. Gerald Merle and Mildred Elaine (Davidson) G.; D.V.M., Purdue U., 1966. Veterinarian, Gateway Animal Hosp., Glendale, Calif., 1966-67. County Line Animal Hosp., La Habra, Calif., 1970-71, specializing in small animal practice, Highland (Ind.) Animal Hosp., 1971—. Served to capt. U.S. Army, 1967-69; Vietnam. Deocrated Bronze Star. Mem. Am., Ind., Calumet (Ind.) Area veterinary med. assns., Ind. Acad. Vet. Medicine, Delta Sigma Phi. Republican. Episcopalian. Home: 1114 Reyome Apt I Griffith IN 46319 Office: 9308 Indianapolis Blvd Highland IN 46322

GILSINAN, JAMES FRANCIS, III, educator; b. Chgo., Aug. 11, 1945; s. James Francis and Erma Mary (Becvar) G.; B.S., Loyola U., 1967, M.A., 1970; Ph.D., U. Colo., 1974; m. Christine Wessel, May 23, 1970; 1 son, James Francis. Instr. sociology, Regis Coll., Denver 1969-71; asst. prof. Regis Coll., 1971-76, chmn. dept. sociology, 1970-76; criminal justice statistician Denver Police Dept., 1973-74; asso. prof. Center for Urban Programs, St. Louis U.; cons. Francis Heights Sr. Citizens Center, Denver, 1975, Denver Police Dept. Tng. Bur., 1974-76, Behavioral Research and Evaluation Corp., Boulder, Colo., 1973; discussant KMOX Radio's Exploring series, 1977, KTVI-TV's World of Ideas, 1977, Danforth Found. St. Louis Leadership program, 1977; lectr. St. Louis Metro. Police Acad., 1977—; co-moderator KMOX-TV's Eye on St. Louis, 1978, others. Chmn. KMOX-TV Citizen Adv. com. on community involvement in crime control, 1977-79; participant St. Louis Police Dept.'s Town Hall meeting, 1977; mem. State of Colo. Mental Health Task Force on Identification of Mentally Retarded Offender 1975; chmn. citizens adv. com. on police training, Denver 1974-76. Recipient Regis Coll. Merit award for excellence in teaching, 1975; Loyola U. teaching assistantship, 1968-69; U.S. Dept. Labor grantee, 1978—, others. Mem. Mo. Assn. Criminal Justice Educators, Am. Sociol. Assn., ACLU, Acad. Criminal Justice Sci., Phi Sigma Tau. Democrat. Roman Catholic. Contbr. articles in field to profl. jours. Home: 7041 Cornell St University City MO 63130 Office: 221 N Grand St Saint Louis MO 63103

GILSON, M. DESALES, oil co. ofcl.; b. Fremont, Ohio, Aug. 16, 1945; d. Richard C. and Mercedes C. (Ziebold) Grachek; student Bowling Green State U., 1964-66, Ursuline Coll., 1976-78, St. Mary-of-the-Woods Coll., 1978-79, Antioch Sch. Law, 1981; m. J. Richard Gilson, Jan. 31, 1970. Customer service rep. Toledo Edison Co., 1963-67; programmer Standard Oil Co. Ohio, Cleve., 1967-70, successively analyst, tng. coordinator, mgr. personnel devel. corp. adminstrn. employee relations, 1971—; owner Ampersand & Friends, typesetters; Sumi painter; lectr. Trustee, Light. Recipient Woman of Achievement award YWCA, 1976. Mem. Assn. Humanistic Psychology, Am. Soc. Tng. and Devel. Club: Cleve. Women's City. Home: 3400 Wooster Rd Rocky River OH 44116 Office: 1448 Midland Bldg Cleveland OH 44115

GILTNER, SISTER ANDREA, counselor; b. Kewanee, Ill., Aug. 8, 1928; d. Horace and Winifred Agnes (Maupin) Giltner; B.A., St. Ambrose Coll., 1964; M.Ed., U. Ill., 1969. Joined Order St. Benedict, Roman Catholic Ch., 1946; tchr. St. Marys Sch., Moline, Ill., 1948-50, St. Anthony Sch., Atkinson, Ill., 1950-52, St. Roch Sch., LaSalle, Ill., 1953-55, St. Columbia Sch., Chgo., 1955-57, St. Boniface Sch., Peoria, Ill., 1957-59, Holy Family Sch., Peoria, 1960-62, St. Thomas More Sch., Munster, Ind., 1963-64, 67-69, Immaculate Conception Sch., Monmouth, Ill., 1964-65, 69-72; counselor Assumption High Sch., Davenport, Iowa, 1971-80, Columbus High Sch., Marshfield, Wis., 1980—. Corr. sec. Sisters Council, Davenport, 1972-75, pres., 1975-77. Mem. Am. Personnel and Guidance Assn., Am. Vocat. Guidance Assn., Internat. Personnel and Guidance Assn. Nat. Cath. Guidance Assn., Nat. Assembly Women Religious, AAUW, Phi Delta Kappa. Contbr. articles to religious ednl. jours. Home: St Mary Priory Nauvoo IL 62354

GIN, JACKSON, architect; b. Chgo., June 11, 1934; s. Frank Tsue and Jennie Shee (Pang) G.; B.A., U. Ill., 1958; m. Jayne Ping Kan, Oct. 5, 1963; children—Paul L., Michael F., Daniel. Designer, Milton M. Schwartz, architect, Chgo., 1958-60; project architect Greenberg & Finfer, architect, Chgo., 1960-62, Hausner & Macsai, architects, Chgo., 1962-67; project architect, partner Dubin, Dubin, Black & Moutoussamy, architects, Chgo., 1967-77; partner Mann, Gin, Ebel & Frazier, architects-engrs., Chgo., 1977—. Bd. dirs. Neighborhood Redevel. Assistance, 1972-74, Chinese Am. Civic Fedn., Euclid Lake Assn.; trustee Chinese Christian Union Ch., 1968-70. Mem. AIA, Builders Club Chgo. Home: 1332 Peachtree Ln Mount Prospect IL 60056 Office: 30 S Michigan Ave Chicago IL 60603

GINDHART, ROSEMARY FRANCES, educator; b. Indpls., May 10, 1925; d. Joseph Richard and Irene Susan (Benges) Love; B.S., Ball State U., 1965, M.A., 1969; children—Lawrence, Dana, Debra, Denise, Daphne, Hank. With Delaware Community Sch. Corp., Muncie, Ind., 1965—, tchr., supr. social studies dept. Delta High Sch., 1967—; owner P.D.Q. Print Shop, Muncie, 1980—. Vice precinct committee woman Republican Party, 1978-80. Recipient Econ. scholarship Ball State Univ., 1974-75. Mem. Ind. Council Social Studies (sec., mem. exec. bd.), Nat. Council Social Studies, NEA, Classroom Tchrs. Assn., Ind. State Tchrs. Assn., LWV, Pi Beta Phi. Republican. Roman Catholic. Home: 2108 W Jackson St Muncie IN 47303 Office: Rural Route 1 Box 225 Muncie IN 47302

GINDHART, WILLIAM ZIEGLER, JR., mfg. co. exec.; b. Swedesboro, N.J., Jan. 13, 1947; s. William Ziegler and Marie Elizabeth (Miller) G.; student Taylor U., 1965-67, 72; m. Sandra Lynn Falconero, Aug. 9, 1969; children—Heather Lynn, Lisa Marie. Buyer, expeditor Pierce Govenor Co., Upland, Ind., 1973, asst. purchasing agt., 1973, purchasing agt., 1973-74; purchasing agt. Hart Carter Co., Mendota, Ill., 1974-80; dir. purchasing Swenson Spreader Co., Lindenwood, Ill., 1980—. Chief umpire Mendota Little League, 1976-78, LaMoille Little League and Pony League, 1979; bd. dirs. Wholistic Health Center Mendota. Served with USAF, 1968-72; Vietnam. Mem. Nat. Assn. Purchasing Mgmt., Purchasing Mgmt. Assn. Rock River Valley. Republican. Baptist. Club: Moose. Home: 6168 Bristlecone Ln Rockford IL 61109 Office: PO Box 127 Lindenwood IL 61049

GINGISS, BENJAMIN JACK, formal clothing stores exec.; b. St. Paul, Feb. 27, 1911; s. Samuel and Betty (Illiewitz) G.; student U. Ill., 1929-32, Northwestern U., 1934, Ill. Inst. Tech., 1941; m. Rosalie Eisenschiml, Apr. 20, 1940; children—Peter, Joel, Randall. Co-founder Gingiss Bros., Inc., Chgo., 1936 (name later changed to Gingiss Formalwear, Inc.), now chmn. Gingiss Formalwear, Inc.; chmn. Gingiss Internat., Inc. Chmn., Fedn. for an Open Lakefront, Chgo., 1967; pres. Ill. Humane Soc., 1960, U.S.O. of Chgo., 1969, 73-74; v.p. Welfare Council Met. Chgo., 1968; commr. Lake Mich. and Adjoining Lands Study Commn., 1969—; mem. Urban Action Commn. YMCA, 1969; city commr. Commn. on Youth Welfare, 1966; chmn. men's clothing div. Combined Jewish Appeal, 1959. Bd. dirs. Big Bros., Goodwill Industries, Union Am. Hebrew

Congregations, Chgo. Better Bus. Bur., Lyric Opera of Chgo., 1977; chmn. bd. dirs. U.S.O. Chgo.; bd. dirs., sec. Ill. Humane Soc., pres., 1977; trustee Rosary Coll.; bd. assos. DePaul U. Recipient Phoenix award DePaul U., 1969, Prime Ministers medal State of Israel, 1968, Navy Certificate Merit, 1969, also commendations and awards from U.S. Army, U.S. Navy, USCG, U.S. Air Force, USO. Mem. C. of C. Clubs: City (pres., dir.), Tavern, Executives (Chgo.). Home: 175 E Delaware St Chicago IL 60611 Office: 180 N LaSalle St Chicago IL 60601

GINGRAS, ROBERT ALLAN, loss control engr.; b. Springfield, Mass., Aug. 27, 1947; s. Richard Edward and Barbara (Guertin) G.; A.S., Dean Jr. Coll., 1969; B.S., Colo. State U., 1971; m. Susan Virginia Eaton, Aug. 29, 1970; children—Brian Robert, Shari Lynn, Bradford Allan. With U.S. Fidelity & Guaranty Co., Dixon, Ill., 1971—, ins. engring. and audit supt., 1981—. Mem. Am. Soc. Safety Engrs. Home: Rural Route 3 Lowell Heights Dixon IL 61021 Office: 841 N Galena Ave Dixon IL 61021

GINN, ALEXANDER, lawyer; b. Cleve., Jan 2, 1913; s. Frank Hadley and Cornelia (Root) G.; B.A., Princeton U., 1934; postgrad. Oxford U., 1934-35; LL.B., Yale U., 1938; m. Helen Marie Vilas, June 28, 1938; children—Frank Hadley, Mary Cornelia, Patricia (Mrs. Michael J. Feeney), Walter Pope. Admitted to Ohio bar, 1939; partner Jones, Day, Reavis & Pogue, Cleve., 1953-77. Trustee Univ. Sch., Cleve. Served to lt. USNR, 1942-45. Republican. Episcopalian (former vestryman). Home: 3482 Roundwood Rd Chagrin Falls OH 44022 Office: 1700 Union Commerce Bldg Cleveland OH 44115

GINN, DONNA LYNETTE, mgmt. cons.; b. Middletown, Ohio, Sept. 1, 1948; d. Donald Jerome and Audrey Elaine (Scroggins) G.; B.A. in Psychology, Miami U., Oxford, Ohio, 1966-71, U. Cin., 1976; postgrad. Nat. Tng. Labs., 1977-79. Lab technician Middletown (Ohio) Hosp., 1965-67, Kettering (Ohio) Meml. Hosp., 1967-68; research technician Ind. U.-Wright Patterson AFB, Ohio, 1968, Miami U., 1968-71, St. Louis U. Med. Sch., 1971-73; research technician Procter & Gamble, Miami Valley Labs., Cin., 1973-77, mgr. orgnl. devel. cons., 1977—. Vol. counselor Butler County Mental Health Assn., 1977—; founder, pres. Daus. of Sophia, 1976—; dir., moderator Black Student Action Assn. radio and TV program, 1968-71; mem. youth motivation task force Nat. Alliance Bus., 1979—, Black Exec. Exchange program, 1979—; active Big Sisters, Cin., 1968-71. Am. Assn. Clin. Pathology-Middletown Hosp. acad. scholar, 1966; Martin Luther King fellow, 1970; recipient Letters of Appreciation, Minority Counselor, Middletown High Sch., 1976, Dept. Air Force, 1969; named Outstanding Young Woman Am., 1979. Mem. Am. Soc. Tng. and Devel., Orgnl. Devel. Network, Am. Mgmt. Assn., AAAS. Baptist. Club: Girls Assembly Order Eastern Star (sec. 1960-64). Office: PO Box 39175 Cincinnati OH 45239

GINN, H(ORACE) MARVIN, publishing co. exec.; b. Miller, Mo., Jan. 17, 1914; s. Horace Maynard and Jurley (Ward) G.; student S.W. Mo. State Coll., 1934-35, Northwestern U., 1947; m. Laura Marie Birzele, Apr. 16, 1942; children—Marcia Eleanor, Sheila Margaret, Sandra. Tchr., Union Hall Sch., Halltown, Mo., 1936-38; salesman Crowell-Collier Pub. Co., N.Y.C., 1939-42; promotion mgr. Opportunity Mag., Chgo., 1946-50, Irving-Cloud Pub. Co., Chgo., 1950-55; sales mgr. Pubs. Devel. Corp., Skokie, Ill., 1955-61; chmn., pres. H. Marvin Ginn Corp., Chgo., 1961—. Served with inf. AUS, 1942-46; PTO. Decorated Bronze star medal. Mem. Chgo. Assn. Bus. Pubs., Internat. Assn. Fire Chiefs, Fire Equipment Mfrs. and Services Assn. (dir.), Chgo. Advt. Club. Author: How to Be An Executive Salesman, 1953. Home: 1959 W Hood St Chicago IL 60660 Office: 625 N Michigan Ave Chicago IL 60611

GINN, ROBERT MARTIN, electric utility co. exec.; b. Detroit, Jan. 13, 1924; s. Lloyd T. and Edna S. (Martin) G.; B.S. and M.S. in Elec. Engring., U. Mich., 1948; m. Barbara R. Force, 1948; children—Anne, Martha, Thomas. With Cleve. Electric Illuminating Co., 1948—, controller, 1959-62, v.p. gen. services, 1963-70, exec. v.p., 1970-77, pres., 1977—, also dir.; dir. Soc. Corp., Soc. Nat. Bank Cleve., Ferro Corp. Mem., past pres. Shaker Heights Bd. Edn., 1968-75; pres. Welfare Fedn. Cleve., 1968-69. Served with USAAF, 1943-46. Office: Cleve Electric Illuminating Co 55 Public Sq PO Box 5000 Cleveland OH 44101

GINSBERG, NORMAN ARTHUR, physician; b. Chgo., May 28, 1946; B.A., So. Ill. U., 1968; postgrad. Ill. Coll. Pharmacy, 1968-69, U. Guadalerjara, 1969-72; M.D., Chgo. Med. Sch., 1974; m. Denise Ginsberg; children—Melinda, Sara. Intern, Michael Reese Hosp. and Med. Center, Chgo., 1974-75, resident in obs-gyn., 1975-79, staff mem., 1979—; practice medicine specializing in obs-gyn., Chgo. Fellow Am. Coll. Obs-Gyn.; mem. Am. Fertility Soc., AMA, Chgo. Med. Soc. Home: 1520 Eastwood Highland Park IL 60035 Office: Association for Women's Health Care Ltd 30 N Michigan Ave Suite 607 Chicago IL 60602

GINSBURG, SHELDON HARVEY, accountant; b. Chgo., Mar. 22, 1938; s. Max L. and Sophie L. (Schwimmer) G.; B.S., DePaul U., 1959; m. Kathleen; children—Howard, Linda, Steven. Sr. partner Sheldon H. Ginsburg & Co., C.P.A.'s, Skokie, Ill., 1961—; chmn. bd. Shell Devel. Corp., 1969—; chmn. bd. Pick Fisheries, Inc., Vistana Resort, Inc.; trustee Food Handlers Local 55 Health and Welfare Fund. C.P.A., Ill. Mem. Am. Inst. C.P.A.'s, Ill. Soc. C.P.A.'s, Beta Gamma Sigma, Pi Gamma Mu, Beta Alpha Psi. Office: 4849 W Golf Rd Skokie IL 60077

GINSBURG, SIGMUND G., univ. adminstr.; b. N.Y.C., Oct. 12, 1937; s. Saul and Rose Ginsburg; B.A. magna cum laude, Dartmouth Coll., 1959; postgrad. London Sch. Econs., 1959-60; M.P.A., Harvard U., 1961; m. Judith Ann Jacobson, July 4, 1965; children—Beth Alison, David Grant. Mgmt. intern Office of Sec. of Def., Washington, 1961-62; asst. to pres. Hudson Inst., 1964; asst. mgr. personnel adminstrv. services, mgmt. analyst Port Authority of N.Y. and N.J., 1964-66; sr. mgmt. cons. and spl. asst. to dep. mayor, Office of the Mayor, N.Y.C., 1966-67, asst. city adminstr., 1967-72; v.p. for adminstrn. and planning, treas. Adelphi U., Garden City, N.Y., 1972-78; asso. dir. CICCO and Assos., 1977—; v.p. for fin., treas. U. Cin., 1978—, adj. prof. higher edn. adminstrn., 1980—; adj. asso. prof. mgmt. Adelphi U., 1972-78; lectr., adj. asst. prof. City U. N.Y., 1966-72; mgmt. commentator Sta. WGUC, Nat. Public Radio, Cin., 1980—. Mem. City Mgr.'s Working Rev. Com., Cin. 2000 Plan, 1979-81; mem. citizen's adv. com. Wyo. Bd. Edn., 1980—. Served to lt. U.S. Army, 1962-64. Recipient Merit award City of N.Y., 1969. Mem. Phi Beta Kappa. Co-author: Managing the Higher Education Enterprise, 1980; author: Management: An Executive Perspective, 1981; contbr. articles to profl. jours. Office: 300C Administration Bldg Univ of Cin Cincinnati OH 45221

GIOIOSO, JOSEPH VINCENT, psychologist; b. Chgo., Mar. 6, 1939; s. Vincent James and Mary (Bonadonna) G.; B.A., DePaul U., 1962, M.A., 1963; Ph.D. summa cum laude, Ill. Inst. Tech., 1971; m. Gay Powers, Dec. 28, 1963; children—Joseph, Randy Marie, Danielle. Psychologist, Sch. Assn. for Spl. Edn. in DuPage County, Wheaton, Ill., 1964-67; pvt. practice as clin. psychologist, Chgo. and Downers Grove, Ill., 1966—; clin. psychologist J.J. McLaughlin, M.D., Profl. Corp., Chgo., 1970—. Founder dept. psychology Ill. Benedictine Coll., Lisle, 1968, chmn. dept. psychology, prof., dir. testing, 1968-71; cons. psychologist Chicago Ridge (Ill.) Sch. Dist. 127 1/2, 1973-76, Cath. Charities Counseling Service, Chgo., 1963-66, St. Laurence High Sch., Oak Lawn, Ill., 1963-64, Oak Lawn-Hometown Sch. Dist. No. 123, 1967-68, Addison (Ill.) Sch. Dist. 4, 1969-72; vis. prof. psychology Inst. Mgmt., Lisle, 1968-69, George Williams Coll., Downers Grove, 1970-71; chief psychologist Valley View Sch. Dist. 365U, Bolingbrook, Ill., 1971-73; dir. Pub. Program for Exceptional Children, Lisle, 1969-71; mem. Nat. Register Health Service Providers in Psychology, 1975—. Bd. dirs. Ray Graham Assn. for Handicapped, DuPage County, Ill., 1970-73; adv. bd. Care and Counseling Center DuPage County, 1977—. DePaul U. publ. grantee, 1959-61, Fitzgerald Bros. Found. grantee, 1969-71. Mem. Am., Midwestern, Ill. psychol. assns., Soc. Pediatric Psychology, Alpha Phi Delta. Clubs: Lakeside Country (Downers Grove); Racquet (Hinsdale, Ill.). Author: Completion Intelligence Test, 1963; Children's Emotional Symptoms Inventory, 1979. Contbr. articles to profl. jours. Office: 6800 S Main St Downers Grove IL 60516

GIORDANO, AUGUST THOMAS (GUS), choreographer, dancer, educator; b. St. Louis, July 10, 1923; s. Paul and Rose (Tedesco) G.; B.A., U. Mo., 1950; student Buckman Dancing Sch., St. Louis, 1932-40; m. Peggy Ann Thoelke, Oct. 14, 1950; children—Patrick Nelson, Marc August, Nan Elizabeth, Amy Paul. Dancer at Roxy Theater, N.Y.C., summers 1948-49; appeared as choreographer-dancer in On the Town, 1953; dancer-choreographer on Perry Como Show, 1954, Ed Sullivan Show, 1954, Colgate Comedy Hour, 1955; film conv. coordinator Film Council Am., 1953-56; propr., dir. Gus Giordano Dance Center, Evanston, Ill., 1953—, choreographer, 1953—; dir., choreographer Gus Giordano Jazz Dance Chicago Co., 1968—; choreographer Goodman Theatre, Chgo., 1978—, Sta. WTTW-TV, Chgo., 1968—, NBC, Chgo., 1969—, ABC-TV, Chgo., 1972-74; concert tours in U.S. and Europe, 1975—; producer various stage and indsl. shows, 1955—. Served with USMC, 1944-46. Recipient Emmy TV award, 1968, 1975, 1978, Dance Masters of Am. award, 1978, Outstanding Dancer award Boston Dance Masters, 1970, Chgo. Nat. Assn. Dance Tchrs. award, 1974, NET-TV Award of Excellence, 1969, Ill. Gov.'s award, 1971. Mem. Lambda Chi Alpha. Roman Catholic. Editor: Anthology of American Jazz Dance, 1976; originated the Giordano technique of jazz dance form. Home: 311 3d St Wilmette IL 60091 Office: 614 Davis St Evanston IL 60201

GIRON, OTILIA, coll. public relations exec.; b. San Antonio, Jan. 14, 1946; d. Louis Tellez and Aurelia (Hernandez) G.; A.A., San Antonio, Coll., 1966; B.A. in Polit. Sci., U. Iowa, 1973, M.A. in Journalism (John P. Murray scholar), 1975; children—Chuck Camacho, Deborah Camacho. Testing clk. United Services Automobile Assn., San Antonio, 1969, jr. analyst, 1970-71; cashier Pacific Gas and Electric Co., Montery, Calif., spring, 1972, Iowa Book and Supply Co., Iowa City, 1974-75; coder U. Iowa, 1972-74, teaching asst., 1974-75; reporter Daily Iowan, Iowa City, 1972-74, Iowa City Press-Citizen, 1974, The Light San Antonio, 1975-77; community relations dir. Joliet Jr. Coll., 1977—. Co-recipient 2d Pl. award for local govt. news Inland Daily Press Assn., 1974. Mem. Ill. Coll. Relations Conf., Will-Grundy Counties Public Relations Soc., Nat. Council Community Relations, Sigma Delta Chi, Kappa Tau Alpha. Club: Toastmasters. Office: 1216 Houbolt Ave Joliet IL 60436

GIRVIN, RICHARD ALLEN, rec. co. exec.; b. Chgo., Feb. 10, 1926; s. Harry J. and Esther (Easter) G.; Mus.B., Chgo. Mus. Coll., 1950, Mus.M., 1954; D.F.A., Ga. State Tchrs. Coll., 1954; m. Sharon Hillertz, June 9, 1968; children—Gregory, Kimberly, Scott. Instr. music Bob Jones U., 1950-52; tchr. high sch., Chgo., 1954-56; dir. radio and TV, NBC, Chgo., 1956-57; prodn. dir. Coronet Inst. Films, Chgo., 1957-62; producer Gilbert Altschul Prodns., Chgo., 1962-64; freelance producer, writer, Chgo. and Hollywood, Calif., 1964-65; v.p. Zenith Cinema Service, Inc., Chgo., 1965-73, owner, 1973—; pres. Dick Girvin Prodns., Chgo., 1967—; owner, operator Typing Unltd., Timbrewood Prodn. Music Co., Sharilda Pub. Co., Phas 5 Prodns., Studio Electronics Co., DB Studios, Inc., Zenith Cinema Service (all Chgo.), 1967—; instr. film sound Columbia Coll., Chgo., 1973—. Served to 1st lt. USAAF, 1943-45. Recipient Cannes Film Festival award for writing Wine of Morning, 1957, Freedom Found. award, 1961, Cine Golden Eagle award 1964-67, Indsl. Arts award, 1964-74, Atlanta Silver award, 1971, Internat. Film Festival silver award, 1971-74. Fellow Brit. Internat. Audio Soc.; mem. Nat. Assn. TV Arts and Scis., Soc. Motion Picture Engrs. and Technicians, Audio Engring. Soc., Aircraft Owners and Pilots Assn., Internat. Brotherhood Magicians, Broadcast Music Inc. Composer: The Seventh Psalm, 1953; film scores for Macbeth, 1951, Pound of Flesh, 1952, numerous films, TV programs, Wild Kingdom TV series, 1973—. Office: 676 N LaSalle St Chicago IL 60610

GISH, EDWARD RUTLEDGE, physician; b. St. Louis, Sept. 5, 1908; s. Edward C. and Bessie (Rutledge) G.; A.B., Westminster Coll., 1930; M.D., St. Louis U., 1935, M.S., 1939; m. Miriam Schlicker, July 8, 1938; children—Ann Rutledge, Mary Priscilla. Intern, St. Louis U. Hosps., 1935-36; resident in surgery St. Mary's Group Hosps., St. Louis, 1936-39; pvt. practice medicine specializing in surgery, Fulton, Mo., 1946—; staff mem. Callaway Meml. Hosp., Fulton. Bd. dirs. Mo. Symphony Soc., pres., 1981; med. dir. Callaway County CD. Served from maj. to lt. col., AUS, 1943-46; lt. col. ret. Res. Hon. col. Gov.'s Staff Mo. Fellow A.C.S.; mem. Royal Soc. London (affiliate), Internat. Coll. Surgeons, A.M.A., Mo., Callaway County med. socs., Mo. Red Poll Breeders Assn. (pres.), Am. Law Enforcement Officers Assn., Delta Tau Delta, Alpha Omega Alpha. Contbr. articles to profl. jours. Home: 7 W 10th St Fulton MO 65251 Office: 5 E 5th St Fulton MO 65251

GIST, SYLVIA REEDY, educator; b. Lexington, Miss., Sept. 4, 1946; d. John and Laurie (Campbell) Reedy; B.S., Chgo. State U., 1971, M.S., 1976; postgrad. U. Chgo.; m. Edwin S. Gist, Aug. 24, 1974; 1 dau., Jennifer. Tchr. bus. edn. St. Procopius High Sch., Chgo., 1975-76; instr. Chgo. State U., 1977-78, asst. prof. automotive mechanics, 1977—; contact person for coordinating CETA activities, Chgo., 1981—; liaison person between Chgo. State U. and vocat. edn. dept. Springfield, Ill., 1981—; mem. Rosemoor Community Assn., Chgo., 1977-79. Served with USAF, 1973-75. Mem. Am. Vocat. Assn., Ill. Vocat. Assn., Ill. Guidance and Vocat. Services Assn., Epsilon Pi Tau. Contbr. articles to profl. jours. Office: 95th St at King Dr Chicago IL 60628

GITZ, JAMES L., state senator; b. Stephenson County, Ill., Sept. 19, 1948; B.A. in Econs., Sangamon State U.; postgrad. in bus. U. Ill. Staff asst. Sci. Analysis Corp., San Francisco, 1970-72; exec. dir. Assn. Ill. Student Govt. Assn., 1972-73; staff asst. to Ill. Gov. Dan Walker, 1974; legis. liaison Ill. Capitol Devel. Bd., 1973-76; mem. Ill. Senate, 1978—. Bd. dirs. Com. Ill. Govt. Democrat. Office: State Capitol Springfield IL 62706*

GIVAN, RICHARD MARTIN, chief justice Ind. Supreme Ct.; b. Indpls., June 7, 1921; s. Clinton Hodell and Glee (Bowen) G.; LL.B., Ind. U., 1951; m. Pauline Marie Haggart, Feb. 28, 1945; children—Madalyn Givan Hesson, Sandra Givan Chenoweth, Patricia Givan Gross, Elizabeth. Partner firm Givan & Givan, 1952-59, Bowen, Myers, Northam & Givan, 1959-69; pub. defender, Ind., 1952-54; dep. atty. gen. State of Ind., 1954-65; dep. pros. atty., Marion County, Ind., 1965-67; mem. Ind. Ho. of Reps., 1967-68; judge Ind. Supreme Ct., 1969—. Served with USAAF, 1942-45. Mem. Am., Indpls., Ind. bar assns., Ind. Trial Lawyers Assn., Ind. Judges Assn., Ind. Soc. Chgo., Newcomen Soc. N.Am., Sigma Delta Kappa. Mem. Soc. of Friends. Clubs: Arabian Horse; Indianapolis Press. Office: Office of the Chief Justice Indiana Supreme Ct Indianapolis IN 46204 Address: 6726 S White Lick Creek Rd Indianapolis IN 46231

GIVEN, RONALD CARL, univ. adminstr.; b. Topeka, Aug. 12, 1948; s. Carl Myron and Thelma Bernice (Lovseth) C.; student Drake U., 1967-68; B.A. in Psychology, U. Mo., Kansas City, 1972, postgrad., 1976—; m. Mary Jane Grisham, Aug. 23, 1969; 1 son, Michael Lee. With assembly div. Gen. Motors Co., Kansas City, Kans., 1973-75; admissions counselor U. Mo., Kansas City, 1975-76, coordinator office of vets. affairs, 1976-78, coordinator student fin. aids office, 1978-79; mgr. mail equipment div. Miller and Assos., 1979-80; account exec. Victor Bus. Products, 1980—. Mem. student adv. com. Kansas City Bapt. Assn., 1978—; bd. dirs. Region IV, Mo. Spl. Olympics, 1980—, treas., 1981—. Served with USAFR, 1970-76. Mem. Nat. Assn. Student Fin. Aid Adminstrs., Nat. Assn. Concerned Vets. (dir. 1978-79, nat. conv. coordinator 1979), U. Mo.-Kansas City Alumni Assn. (life), Independence Jaycees (v.p. community devel. 1981—). Democrat. Baptist. Home: 5108 McCoy St Independence MO 64055 Office: 1535 Broadway Kansas City MO 64108

GIVENS, DOUGLAS RANDALL, archaeologist, educator; b. St. Louis, May 4, 1944; s. Glenn Stuart and Helena Katherine (Neff) G.; B.A. in Anthropology, So. Ill. U., 1967, M.A., 1972; m. Linda Louise West, Mar. 29, 1969; 1 son, Clayton West. Research asst. So. Ill. U., Edwardsville, 1970-72; instr. anthropology St. Louis Community Coll., Meramec, 1972-74, asst. prof., 1974-80, asso. prof. anthropology, 1980—, chmn. dept. behavioral sci., 1980—; sec. Internat. Inst. for Advanced Studies, 1974-81. Served with USAF, 1967-70. Decorated Air Force Commendation medal; named outstanding tchr. and scholar St. Louis Community Coll.-Meramec, 1978. Fellow Am. Anthrop. Assn. (asso. Wenner-Gren Found. for Anthrop. Research); mem. Soc. Am. Archaeology, AAAS, Internat. Soc. for Study of Time, Ill. Assn. for Advancement of Archaeology, Mo. Archaeol. Soc., Am. Assn. for Phys. Anthropology, Lambda Alpha. Methodist. Club: Elks (Granite City). Author: An Analysis of Navajo Temporality, 1979; Processual Papers in Archaeometric Dating: Potassium-Argon (K40/Ar40) and Radiocarbon (C14) Techniques, 1981; condr. research in field. Office: Dept Behavioral Science St Louis Community College-Meramec 11333 Big Bend Blvd Saint Louis MO 63122

GJERTSEN, EDWARD WALTER, design cons. co. exec.; b. Chgo., Nov. 19, 1941; s. Edward John and Berniece (Branfalt) G.; M.B.A., U. Chgo., 1973; m. Carol J. Kortas, Dec. 29, 1962; children—Joyce, Janice, Edward Walter. Personnel supr. Household Fin. Corp., Chgo., 1963-68; v.p. ISD Inc., Chgo., 1969-77; pres. Interiors Inc., Chgo., 1977—, pres., dir. affiliate firm Realty Services, Inc., 1981—; dir. Planning Systems, Inc., Chgo. Commr., Met. Sanitary Dist. Greater Chgo., 1979—. Served with U.S. Army, 1960-63. Mem. Ill. State C. of C., Chgo. Assn. Commerce and Industry. Republican. Club: Lions (pres.). Home: 658 S Elm St Palatine IL 60067 Office: 224 S Michigan Ave Chicago IL 60604

GLABE, ELMER FREDRICK, food scientist; b. Chgo., Apr. 3, 1911; s. Fred John and Holdina (Jennrich) G.; B.S. in Chemistry, Ill. Inst. Tech., 1942; m. Marjorie Browne; children—John E., Lynne Glabe Mueller, David H. Analytical chemist W.E. Long Co., Chgo., 1931-38; research chemist, tech. dir. Stein Hall & Co., Chgo., 1938-45; founder, 1946, since pres. Food Tech., Inc., Chgo.; founder, pres. Food Tech. Lab., Food Tech. Products. Recipient Outstanding Service award Am. Council Indsl. Labs. Mem. Inst. Food Technologists, Am. Chem. Soc., Am. Assn. Cereal Chemists, Am. Soc. Bakery Engrs. Lutheran. Author numerous tech. papers; holder 93 patents in field. Office: 5901 Northwest Hwy Chicago IL 60631

GLAD, WAYNE ROLAND, psychologist; b. Chgo., Feb. 6, 1950; s. Roland E. and Elaine E. Glad; B.A., Ind. U., 1972; M.S., U. Wis., 1974, Ph.D., 1978. Clin. intern psychology U. Wis., Milw., 1975-76, Chgo. Read Mental Health Center, 1976-77; dir. research and evaluation Marianjoy Rehab. Hosp., Wheaton, Ill., 1977-79, cons. chronic pain program, 1979; pvt. practice clin. psychology, Northfield, Ill., 1978, Oakbrook Terrace, Ill., 1978-79, Libertyville, Ill., 1979—; adj. clin. prof. dept. psychology U. Ill., Chgo., 1978-79; dir. mental health screening unit Lake County (Ill.) Juvenile Probation Dept., Waukegan, Ill., 1978—; clin. psychologist Lake Forest (Ill.) Hosp. Pain Treatment Center, 1978—; clin. psychologist North Shore Psychol. Services, Ltd., Libertyville, 1979—; participant 3rd World Conf. on Smoking and Health, N.Y.C., 1975. Mem. Am. Psychol. Assn., Ill. Psychol. Assn. (health adv. bd. 1981—), Soc. Clin. and Exptl. Hypnosis, Midwest Soc. for Study of Pain, Phi Beta Kappa. Roman Catholic. Contbr. articles to psychology jours. Home: 3365 A Beacon St Apt 13 North Chicago IL 60064 Office: North Shore Psychological Services Ltd 1641 N Milwaukee Suite 10 Libertyville IL 60048

GLADSTONE, WILLIAM SHELDON, JR., radiologist; b. Des Moines, Dec. 19, 1923; s. William Sheldon and Wanda (Rees) G.; B.A., State U. Iowa, 1954, M.D., 1947; m. Ruth Alice Jensen, June 19, 1944; children—Denise Ann, William Sheldon, Stephen Rees. Intern. Hurley Hosp., Flint, Mich., 1947-48; gen. practice medicine, Iowa Falls, Iowa, 1948-49; asst. dept. pathology State U. Iowa Coll. Medicine, Iowa City, 1949-50; resident in radiology Univ. Hosp., Iowa City, 1950-51, 53-54; practice medicine specializing in radiology, Kalamazoo, 1954—; exec. v.p. Kalamazoo Radiology; clin. asst. prof. radiology Mich. State U. Coll. Human Medicine; chief radiology Bronson Meth. Hosp., Kalamazoo, 1973-75, 77-79. Bd. dirs. Kalamazoo County Tb Soc., 1955-59, Mich. Children's Aid, 1960-62, Am. Cancer Soc., Kalamazoo, 1964-66. Served with AUS, 1943-46; served to capt. USAF, 1951-53. Diplomate Am. Bd. Radiology. Fellow Am. Coll. Radiology; mem. Kalamazoo Acad. Medicine, AMA, Mich. Radiologic Soc. (pres. W. Mich. sect. 1976), Mich. State Med. Soc., SW Mich. Surg. Soc., Am. Roentgen Ray Soc., Phi Beta Kappa (pres. SW Mich. chpt. 1963). Republican. Episcopalian. Clubs: Kalamazoo Country, Masons, Shriners. Home: 1029 Essex Circle Kalamazoo MI 49008 Office: 524 S Park St Kalamazoo MI 49007

GLASER, JOSEPH, mgmt. cons.; b. N.Y.C., Aug. 29, 1938; s. Morris and Fannie Glaser; student Cornell U., 1956-57; B.S., CCNY, 1962; postgrad. George Washington U., 1963; M.S., N.Y. U., 1967; children—Donna, Laura, Alison, Valerie. Asst. actuary Postal Life, N.Y.C., 1957-63; dir. ops. research Am. Airlines, N.Y.C., 1964-69; v.p., sec.-treas. Systems Audits, Inc., N.Y.C., 1969-71; dir. corp. research Montgomery Ward, Inc., Chgo., 1971-77, also pres. subsidiary Marcor Mktg. Services, Inc., Chgo., 1973-77; pres. J. Glaser & Co., Inc., Chgo., 1975—. Mem. Am. Mktg. Assn., Ops. Research Soc. Am., Assn. for Computing Machinery, Inst. Mgmt. Sci., Chgo. Council on Fgn. Relations. Club: Ill. Athletic. Contbr. articles to profl. jours. Home: 1200 Dartmouth Ln Deerfield IL 60015 Office: J Glaser and Co Inc 332 S Michigan Ave Chicago IL 60604

GLASER, JUNE ARLENE FRIESZ, research specialist, educator; b. Keytesville, Mo., June 6, 1928; d. Arthur L. and Mabel (Voss) F.; B.S. (Sears scholar), U. Mo., Columbia, 1950, M.Ed., 1972, Ed.S., 1975; vocat. cert. in home econs. Lincoln U., 1972; m. Edwin Herman Glaser, Sept. 4, 1949; children—Robert Edwin, Richard Friesz, Randall Scott. Home economist U. Mo. Extension Service, 1950-54; tchr., tutor, Cole County, Mo., 1968-70; instr., tchr. educator Lincoln U., 1972-74, research asst., 1976, instr., research specialist, 1979—; instr., tchr. educator William Woods Coll., Fulton, Mo., 1976-77; instr. home econs. Russellville (Mo.) High Sch., 1977-78; officer Extension Council. Vice pres., trustee Wesley Found.; officer United Methodist Ch.; pres. United Meth. Women Circles, United Ch. Women; sponsor Future Homemakers Am.; bd. dirs. Boy Scouts Am. Mem. Am. Home Econs. Assn. (del.), Mo. Home Econs. Assn. (dir.), South Central Home Econs. Assn. (dir.), Am. Vocat. Assn., Mo. Vocat. Assn., Mo. Home Econs. Tchrs. Assn., Mo. Home Econs. Alumni Assn., PTA (officer), AAU (bd. dirs.), Extension Homemakers (officer), Phi Upsilon Omicron, Sigma Epsilon Sigma, Kappa Omicron Phi, Delta Rho. Home: 1505 Stadium Blvd Jefferson City MO 65101 Office: Lincoln University Human Nutrition Lab Jefferson City MO 65101

GLASS, CAROLE ANNE, advt. agy. exec.; b. Milw., Dec. 29, 1949; d. Edmund Frank and Anne Judith (Kowalczewski) Modjeski; B.F.A., U. Wis., Milw., 1972; postgrad. Annenberg Sch. Communications, U. So. Calif., 1978-79, Marquette U., 1980; m. Adam M. Glass, Aug. 26, 1972. Public relations asst. Alverno Coll., Milw., 1972-73; account exec., art dir. Spectrumedia Communications, 1974-78; asso. editor Milw. Impressions mag., 1976-78; dir. advt. Tobias Kotzin Co., Los Angeles, 1978-79; dir. Spectrumedia, Milw., div. Marcus Corp., 1979-81; account exec. R.L. Meyer Advt., Milw., 1981—; communications cons., photographer, 1972—. Mem. Milw. Advt. Club, Fedn. Am. Advt. Agys. Home: 730 S Lois Ave Brookfield WI 53005 Office: 2051 W Wisconsin Ave Milwaukee WI 53233

GLASS, JAMES WILLIAM, theatre pipe organ installer; b. Oak Park, Ill., Dec. 13, 1946; s. Louis James and Grace Marie (Whaples) G.; B.S. in Elec. Engring., Ill. Inst. Tech., 1968. Electronic design engr. in data communications Gen. Telephone & Electronic Automatic Electric Labs., Inc., Northlake, Ill., 1968-72; self-employed as theatre pipe organ installer, Hinsdale, Ill., 1972—. Mem. Audio Engring. Soc., Am. Theatre Organ Soc., Owl Cinema Organ Guild (pres., chmn. bd. 1971—), Eta Kappa Nu. Home: 7823 Eleanor Clarendon Hills IL 60514 Office: 29 E 1st St Hinsdale IL 60521

GLASS, MICHAEL ANDREW, chemist; b. N.Y.C., Jan. 7, 1949; s. James Richard and Frieda Bette (Hess) G.; B.S. in Biology, Aquinas Coll., Grand Rapids, Mich., 1971; M.S. in Anatomy, U. Mich., Ann Arbor, 1973; m. Sara Elizabeth Adams, Feb. 4, 1978. Mem. staff Mich. Dept. Agr. Lab., 1975-77; instr. photography Lansing (Mich.) Community Coll., 1974-76, instr. human anatomy, 1978—; water quality control chemist Lansing Bd. Water and Light, 1977—. Mem. Am. Water Works Assn., Am. Soc. Quality Control, Nat. Rifle Assn., Beta Beta Beta. Republican. Roman Catholic. Club: Capitol City Rifle (Lansing). Home: 909 W Ionia St Lansing MI 48915 Office: Dye Water Conditioning Plant Lansing MI 48901

GLASSBURN, CARL LEONARD, paint corp. exec.; b. Bargersville, Ind., Oct. 29, 1920; s. David Denzil and Glenna Murl (Scott) G.; grad. Lain Bus. Coll., 1940; m. Laversa Jean Simerly, Sept. 7, 1952 (dec.); children—Carl Randell, Stephanie Anne, Cynthia Louise. With Standard Paints Inc. (formerly Standard Enamel & Paint Corp.), Indpls., 1940—, exec. v.p., 1971—. Pres. Barrington Health Adv. Bd., 1980-81; sec. Indpls. Council Neighborhood Health Centers, 1980-81; vice chmn. bd. elders Bluff Creek Christian Ch. Served with USCG, 1942-46. Mem. Indpls. Paint Prodn. Club (pres. 1966-67, 72-73), Ind. Paint & Coatings Assn. (sec., treas.), Cin.-Dayton-Indpls.-Columbus Soc. of Fedn. of Socs. for Coatings Tech. Club: Masons (Bargersville). Home: 5148 W Olive Branch Rd Greenwood IN 46142 Office: 1502 S Keystone Ave Indianapolis IN 46203

GLASSCOCK, TERRANCE LYNN, savs. and loan exec.; b. Clinton, Mo., Mar. 26, 1948; s. William Robert and Frances Geraldine (Sperry) G.; B.S., Kans. State U., 1971; m. Marlene K. Moyer, May 30, 1970; children—Cori Ashley, Kelly Lynn. Owner, operator, dir. Kans. Lumber Co., Manhattan, 1971—; owner, operator Ridgeview Farms, Clinton, Mo., 1971—; owner, operator Truman Devel. Properties, Clinton, 1975—; owner, developer Knollwood Shopping Center, Manhattan, 1977—; sr. v.p. First Nat. Bank Manhattan, 1978-81; pres. Valley Fed. Savs. and Loan, Hutchinson, Kans., 1981—. Adviser, Kans. State U. chpt. Mortar Bd., 1976—; mem. Manhattan City Commn., 1977—, mayor pro tem, 1978-79, mayor, 1979—; bd. dirs. United Way Manhattan, Manhattan chpt. ARC, 1977—; mem. Gov.'s State Bldg. Commn., 1978—; charter mem. Leadership Kans. Program. Named regional comdr. Kans. Cavalry, 1977. Served to capt., inf., U.S. Army, 1971-72. Republican. Club: Rotary (dir. 1977-78, pres.-elect 1981—) (Manhattan). Home: Hutchinson KS 67501 Office: Valley Federal Savs & Loan PO Box 1307 Hutchinson KS 67501

GLAZER, SIDNEY, educator; b. Quincy, Mich., Nov. 1, 1905; s. Max and Mildred (Thal) G.; A.B., Wayne U., 1927; M.A., U. Mich., 1929, Ph.D., 1932. Asst. dept. history U. Mich., 1928-30; instr. Wayne State U., Detroit, 1930-37, asst. prof., 1937-48, asso. prof., 1948-55, prof., 1955—. Mem. Orgn. Am. Historians, Am., Mich. hist. socs., Econ. History Assn., A.A.U.P., Phi Beta Kappa. Author: (with M. M. Quaife) From Primitive Wilderness to Industrial Commonwealth, 1948; Industrial Detroit, 1951; The Middle West, 1962; Detroit: A Study in Urban Development, 1965. Contbr. articles to hist. revs. and mags. Home: Sheraton-Cadillac Hotel Detroit MI 48231

GLAZZARD, CHARLES DONALDSON, psychiatrist; b. Cleve., Apr. 10, 1928; s. Charles Earl and Kathleen Hazel (Donaldson) G.; student U. Miami, 1946-48; A.B., U. Mich., 1951, postgrad., 1951-52; M.D., Wayne State U., 1956; m. Margaret Hughes Leoni, Aug. 2, 1974; children by previous marriage—Charles F., Eric D., Kim E., Teri L.; stepchildren—Dan, Linda and Bill Leoni. Intern, St. Vincents Hosp., Toledo, 1956-57; gen. practice medicine, El Cajon, Calif., 1960-61; resident Menninger Sch. Psychiatry, Topeka, 1961-64; practice medicine, specializing in psychiatry, Kansas City, Mo., 1971-72, Olathe, Kans., 1974—; clin. asst. prof. psychiatry U. Kans. Med. Center, 1980—; med. dir. Midcontinent Psychiat. Hosp., 1972-74; mem. staffs various hosps.; asst. sect. chief VA Hosp., Topeka, 1964-67; psychiatrist Forbes AFB, Topeka, 1967-71; acting med. dir. Johnson County Mental Health Center, Olathe, 1974-75, bd. dirs., 1976-79; dir. Psychiat. and Edn. Center of Olathe; mem. adv. com. Family Ct. of Johnson County, 1980. Mem. Olathe Human Relations Commn., 1974-77; bd. dirs. Cedar House, 1980. Served with USNR, 1958-60; qualified submarine med. officer. Diplomate Am. Bd. Psychiatry and Neurology. Comml. pilot. Mem. AMA, Am., Kans. Dist., Mid Continent psychiat. assns., Pan Am. Med. Assn., AAAS, Royal Soc. Health, Johnson County Med. Soc., Flying Physicians Assn., Airplane Owners and Pilots Assn. Rotarian. Home: 14301 Locust St Olathe KS 66062 Office: 407 Clairborne St Olathe KS 66062

GLEASON, STEPHEN CHARLES, physician; b. Leon, Iowa, June 30, 1946; s. Charles Gerald and Ferne Louise (Pollard) G.; B.S., Iowa State U., 1971; D.Osteopathy, Coll. Osteo. Medicine and Surgery, 1974; m. Lisa Ann Corcoran, Aug. 22, 1981; children—Michael John, Timothy Charles, Christian Kelly. Resident in family practice, Meml. Med. Center, Corpus Christi, Tex., 1974-75; family practice medicine, West Des Moines, Iowa, 1975—; chmn. dept. family practice Mercy Hosp. Med. Center, Des Moines, 1979—; med. dir. West Suburban Center, West Des Moines; pres. Talent Mgmt. Ltd., West Des Moines, 1979-80; dep. med. examiner, Polk County, Des Moines, 1976—; adj. clin. prof. family practice Coll. Osteo. Medicine and Surgery, Des Moines, 1979—; regional med. adv. Emergency Med. Tng. Program Central Iowa, 1975-76; med. dir. emergency medicine, Clive, Iowa Fire Rescue, 1976-78, West Des Moines Fire Rescue, 1976-79; physician adv. Iowa Found. Med. Care, Profl. Standards Review Orgn., West Des Moines, 1978—; faculty instr. Iowa Heart Assn., Des Moines, 1978—; mem. papal med. security team Pope John Paul's Am. Pilgrimage, 1979. Mem. nat. com. Republican party, 1978-79; mem. nat. Rep. Senatorial Com., U.S. Senatorial Club, 1979. Diplomate Am. Bd. Family Practice. Mem. Am. Acad. Family Physicians, Am. Coll. Emergency Physicians, AMA, Iowa Acad. Sci., Iowa Med. Soc., Iowa Acad. Family Practice, Polk County Med. Soc., Sigma Alpha Epsilon, Sigma Sigma Phi. Republican. Office: 1000 73d St Suite 20 Des Moines IA

GLEIM, MICHAEL LEE, retail co. exec.; b. Columbus, Ohio, Jan. 25, 1943; s. Doyle Howard and Doris Allene (Winebrenner) G.; student Columbus Bus. U., 1960-62; m. Catherine Aileen Mowery, Mar. 7, 1964; children—Michael Todd, Timothy Scott, Christina Deann. With F&R Lazarus Co., Columbus, 1962—, dir. mdse. info. systems, 1969-76, corp. dir. mgmt. info. services Federated Dept. Stores, Inc., Cin., 1976—. Mem. evaluation task force Community Chest, 1979. Mem. Nat. Retail Mchts. Assn. Presbyterian. Club: Masons. Home: 5707 Highland Terrace Dr Milford OH 45150 Office: 7 W 7th St Cincinnati OH 45202

GLEITZ, ROGER WAYNE, educator; b. Corydon, Ind., Dec. 22, 1951; s. James Edward and Catherine Elizabeth (Keller) G.; B.S. in Agr., Purdue U., 1974, B.S. in Edn., 1978, M.S. in Agr. Edn., 1980; m. Kathy Sue Goldman, June 1, 1974; 1 son, Ryan Michael. Timber mgr. Stem Veneer Corp., New Albany, Ind., 1973; naturalist Wyandotte Caves, Ind. Dept. Natural Resources, Leavenworth, Ind., 1974; lumber buyer Keller Mfg. Co., Corydon, Ind., 1974-76; instr. Nat. Hardwood Inspection Sch., Memphis, 1976; insp. Ohio Valley Container, Evansville, Ind., 1976, Jobe's, Leopold, Ind., 1977; tchr. agr. Crawford (Ind.) County Schs., 1978-81; naturalist-maintenance Wyandotte Cave State Recreation Area, Ind. Dept. Natural Resources, 1981—; advisor Future Farmers. Asst. supt. Sunday Sch., Leavenworth Presbyn. Ch., 1979—; leader 4-H; scoutmaster Boy Scouts Am. Cert. vocat. tchr. Mem. Crawford County Classroom Tchrs. Assn., NEA, Ind. State Tchrs. Assn., Ind. Vocat. Assn., Am. Vocat. Assn., Ind. Vocat. Agr. Tchrs. Assn., Ind. Hist. Soc., Ancestral Trails Soc., So. Ind. Geneal. Soc. (organizer 1979, v.p. 1979, pres. 1980). Republican. Editor, Denbo Cousins newsletter, 1977—. Home: Rural Route 1 PO Box 12-R Leavenworth IN 47137

GLENDENNING, EUGENE AUSTIN, clin. social worker; b. Ainsworth, Nebr., June 14, 1930; s. Perry G. and Norma Gladys (Havens) G.; B.R.E., Bartlesvilles (Okla.) Wesleyan Coll., 1954; B.A., Chadron (Nebr.) State Coll., 1969; M.S.W., U. Nebr., 1971; m. Velma June Minor, July 25, 1951; children—Earnest Eugene, Kenneth Ray, Evan Duane. Ordained to ministry Ch. of Nazarene, 1959; pastor Wesleyan Ch., Western Nebr., 1954-59; caseworker Cheyenne County (Nebr.), 1958-60; welfare dir. Dakota County (Nebr.), Dakota City, 1960-63; field rep. Nebr. Dept. Public Welfare, Lincoln, 1963-71, 72, tng. officer, then chief med. services, 1971-72; dep. dir. Kenosha County (Wis.) Dept. Social Services, 1972-79; therapist Jackson County (Ohio) Mental Health Clinic, 1979—; field instr. U. Wis., Milw.; lectr. Carthage Coll., Kenosha; pres. Pineridge Council Social Living, 1967-69; vol. crisis counselor Switchboard, Kenosha, 1974-76, bd. dirs., 1975-76; pvt. practice social work, 1974—. Mem. Acad. Cert. Social Workers, Nat. Assn. Social Workers. Home: 160 Anderson Dr Jackson OH 45640

GLENN, CLETA MAE, lawyer; b. Clinton, Ill., Sept. 24, 1921; d. John and Mattie Sylvester (Anderson) Glenn; B.S., U. Ill., 1947; J.D., DePaul U. Coll. Law, 1976; m. Rex Eugene Loggans, Sept. 3, 1948 (div.); 1 dau., Susan. Real estate builder, developer, 1959-69; communications dir. Transp. Research Center, Northwestern U., Evanston, Ill., 1969-72; admitted to Ill. bar, 1977; practice law, Chgo., 1977—; lectr. Assn. Trial Lawyers Am., John Marshall Law Sch. Served with U.S. Navy, 1943-59. Recipient Real Estate Humanitarian award Kislak Co., Miami, Fla., 1962. Mem. Am. Bar Assn. (com. chmn.), Ill. Bar Assn. (assembly rep., mem. standing com. on traffic laws and cts.), Chgo. Bar Assn., Assn. Trial Lawyers Am., Ill. Trial Lawyers Assn., Lex Leggio, Phi Alpha Delta. Editor: Collective Bargaining and Technological Change in American Transportation, 1979; contbr. articles to profl. publs. Home: 1313 Ritchie Ct Chicago IL 60610 Office: 69 W Washington St Chicago IL 60602

GLENN, JOHN HERSCHEL, JR., U.S. senator; b. Cambridge, Ohio, July 18, 1921; s. John Herschel and Clara (Sproat) G.; student Muskingum Coll., 1939, D.Sc., 1961; naval aviation cadet U. Iowa, 1942; grad. flight sch. Naval Air Tng. Center, Corpus Christi, Tex., 1943, Navy Test Pilot Tng. Sch., Patuxent River, Md., 1954; m. Anna Margaret Castor, Apr. 1943; children—Carolyn Ann, John David. Commd. 2d lt. USMC, 1943, advanced through grades to col.; assigned 4th Marine Aircraft Wing, Marshall Islands campaign, 1944, 9th Marine Aircraft Wing, 1945-46; with 1st Marine Aircraft Wing, North China Patrol, also Guam, 1947-48; flight instr. advanced flight tng., Corpus Christi, 1949-51; asst. G-2/G-3 Amphibious Warfare Sch., Quantico, Va., 1951; with Marine Fighter Squadron 311, exchange pilot 25th Fighter Squadron USAF, Korea, 1953; project officer fighter design br. Navy Bur. Aero., Washington, 1956-69; nonstop supersonic transcontinental Flight, July 16, 1957; astronaut Project Mercury, Manned Spacecraft Center NASA, 1959-64, pilot Mercury-Atlas 6, orbital space flight launched from Cape Canaveral, Fla., Feb., 1962; v.p. corporate devel. and dir. Royal Crown Cola Co., 1962-74; U.S. Senator from Ohio, 1975—. Trustee Muskingum Coll. Decorated D.F.C. (five), Air medal (18), Astronaut medal USMC, Navy unit commendation; Korean Presidential unit citation; Disting. Merit award Muskingum Coll.; Medal of Honor, N.Y.C. Mem. Soc. Exptl. Test Pilots, Internat. Acad. of Astronautics (hon.). Democrat. Presbyterian. Co-author: We Seven 1962. Author: P.S., I Listened to Your Heart Beat. Office: 2235 Dirksen Senate Office Bldg Washington DC 20510

GLENN, ROBERT BRUCE, univ. adminstr.; b. Kalamazoo, July 9, 1927; s. Winfield Church and Helen Grace (McCarty) G.; B.A., Western Mich. U., 1949; M.A., U. Mich., 1953, Ph.D., 1961; m. Rosemary Ann Kent, Aug. 5, 1950; children—Tama Delne Martini, Minde Char Pretzer, Deri Sabra Glenn. Asst. prof. SUNY, Cortland, 1956, asso. prof., 1963, asso. dean, 1963-66; acad. dean U. Mich., Flint, 1967-71; dean arts and scis. No. Mich. U., Marquette, 1971-74, provost, acad. v.p., 1974—. Treas., Upper Peninsula Health Edn. Corp., 1974-79, chmn. bd., 1980-82. Am. Council Edn. fellow, 1966-67. Mem. Mich. Acad. Sci., Arts and Letters (pres. 1980), MLA, Linguistic Soc. Am., Nat. Council Tchrs. English, Am. Assn. for Higher Edn., Phi Delta Kappa, Golden Key. Presbyterian. Club: Rotary. Author: (with Stewart A. Kingsbury and Z.P. Thundy) Language and Culture, 1974. Home: 32 E Nicolet Blvd Marquette MI 49855 Office: No Mich Univ Marquette MI 49855

GLENN, ROY JOHNSON, manufactured housing exec.; b. Birmingham, Ala., Dec. 23, 1920; s. Willis and Maggie (Johnson) G.; student acctg. Massey Bus. Coll., 1938-39; student engring. Auburn U., 1941-42; m. Sammie Lee Spradling, Feb. 14, 1941; children—Ellen Glenn Andersen, Jerry Alan. Mold loftsman, Higgins Industries, New Orleans, 1943-44; partner Glenn Constsn. Co., Birmingham, Ala., 1946-50; profl. golfer, 1950-57; pres. Crab Orchard Golf Club, Inc., Carterville, Ill., 1958-63; sec., treas. Cavaness-Glenn-Storme, Inc., Carterville, 1964-75; pres. Glenn & Co., Inc., Carterville, 1963-76; sec. Component Building Systems, Inc., Carbondale, Ill., 1976—; cons. various golf and country clubs; designer golf courses and bldgs. Bd. trustees John A. Logan Coll., 1968-70. Served with USN, 1944-46. Mem. Component Mfrs. Council of Truss Plate Inst., Associated Gen. Contractors. Republican. Baptist. Designer underground and above ground recirculating sewage filtering system, 1974. Home and Office: Route 2 Carbondale IL 62901

GLENNER, RICHARD ALLEN, dentist, dental historian; b. Chgo., Apr. 14, 1934; s. Robert Joseph and Vivian (Prosk) G.; B.S., Roosevelt U., 1955; B.S. in Dentistry, U. Ill., 1958, D.D.S., 1959; m. Dorothy Chapman, July 13, 1957; children—Mark Steven, Alison. Gen. practice dentistry, Chgo., 1962—; cons. on dental history to Smithsonian Instn., various corps., libraries, univs., museums, dental jours. Served to capt. AUS, 1960-62. Mem. Am., Ill. dental assns., Chgo. Dental Soc., Assn. Mil. Surgeons U.S., Am. Acad. Dental History, Fed. Dentaire Internationale, Alpha Omega. Cons. editor A Bicentennial Salute to Am. Dentistry, 1976; scriptwriter TV documentary on the history of dentistry; contbr. articles on dental history to profl. jours. Home: 6715 N Lawndale Ave Lincolnwood IL 60645 Office: 3414 W Peterson Ave Chicago IL 60659

GLENNIE, DONALD MORGAN, seed co. exec.; b. Missouri Valley, Iowa, Mar. 23, 1923; s. James and Anne McPherson (Morgan) G.; B.A., U. Iowa, 1949; m. Gloria Agnes Satterlee, Sept. 1, 1946; children—Elizabeth Ann, Donald Lachlan, Mary Irene, James M. Retail sales mgr. Am. Field Seed Co., Chgo., 1949-56; regional sales mgr. Berry Seed Co., Clarinda, Iowa, 1956-62; v.p. sales Lowe Seed Co., Kankakee, Ill., 1962-71; v.p. mktg. Jacques Seed Co., Prescott, Wis., 1971—. Served with USNR, 1942-46. Mem. Am. Seed Trade Assn., Sales and Market Execs. Assn., Am. Mgmt. Assn., Am. Mktg. Assn., Nat. Agrl. and Mktg. Assn., Internat. Platform Assn. (Gold Key award 1979), St. Andrews Soc., Am. Legion, Sigma Phi Epsilon. Presbyterian (elder). Home: 407 Lake St Prescott WI 54021 Office: 720 St Croix Prescott WI 54021

GLICKMAN, DANIEL ROBERT, Congressman; b. Wichita, Kans., Nov. 24, 1944; B.A., U. Mich., 1966; J.D., George Washington U., 1969; m. Rhoda Yura, 1966; children—Jonathan, Amy. Practiced law, Washington; trial atty. SEC, 1969-70; partner firm Sargent, Klenda & Glickman, 1973-76; mem. 95th-97th congresses from 4th Kans. Dist., mem. agr. com., sci. and tech. com., judiciary com., chmn. subcom. on transp., aviation and materials. Mem. Wichita Sch. Bd., 1973-76, pres., 1975-76; active Arthritis Found., Big Bros.-Big Sisters. Democrat. Office: Room 1507 Longworth House Office Bldg Washington DC 20515

GLICKSON, DAVID, retail clothing stores chain exec.; b. Devils Lake, N.D., June 6, 1914; s. Julius and Ida G.; B.B.A., U. Minn., 1936; m. Sarae Hallock, Apr. 11, 1948; children—Irene, Jeannie, James; m. 2d, Dorothy Halper, Oct. 8, 1972. Partner, Glickson's Men's Wear, Devils Lake, 1936-56, owner, pres., 1957-79; chmn. bd. Straus-Glickson Corp., men's store chain, N.D., 1981—; dir. First Nat. Bank, Devils Lake. Mem. exec. bd. Boy Scouts Am.; mem. Lake Region Jr. Coll. Bd., 1970-77. Served with Q.M.C., U.S. Army, 1942-45. Mem. N.W. Buyers and Jobbers (pres.), Menswear Retailers Am. (dir.), Devils Lake C. of C. (pres. 1952). Republican. Jewish. Clubs: Devils Lake Country (pres. 1975-77), Elks, Eagles, Masons, Shriners. Home: 1012 5th St Devils Lake ND 58301 Office: 402 4th St Devils Lake ND 58301

GLIDDEN, IRIS OLSEN (MRS. JOHN MOULTON GLIDDEN), librarian; b. Winchester, Wis., Dec. 4, 1917; d. Oscar Wilhelm and Violet Sarah (Rammel) Olsen; B.A., Northland Coll., Ashland, Wis., 1962; M.A., U. Wis.-Milw., 1971; m. John Moulton Glidden, Apr. 16, 1938 (dec.); children—Bonnie (Mrs. Robert C. Buchanan), Janice (Mrs. Patrick Scanlon), Marcia (Mrs. Thomas D. Parker), John Moulton. Acting instr. Kenwood Library, U. Wis., Milw., 1961-62; head librarian West Bend (Wis.) High Sch., 1962-70; dir. library services West Bend Pub. Schs., 1970—. Bd. dirs. West Bend Community Meml. Library, 1970—. Mem. Friends of U. Wis. Library, Wis. Intellectual Freedom Coalition. Mem. Am., Wis. library assns., Wis. Assn. Sch. Librarians (chmn. 1971-72), Assn. Ednl. Communications and Tech., Internat. Inst. Milwaukee County, AAUW (state bd. dirs.), Wis. Acad. Scis., Arts and Letters, Wis. Audiovisual Assn. (dir.), League Women Voters, Library Council Met. Milw., U. Wis.-Milw. Alumni Assn., Delta Kappa Gamma. Episcopalian. Club: West Bend Country. Home: Big Cedar Lake 4792 Highland Park Dr Slinger WI 53086 Office: 697 S 5th Ave West Bend WI 53095

GLIDDEN, JOHN REDMOND, lawyer; b. Sanford, Maine, July 24, 1936; s. Kenneth Eugene and Kathryn (Gilpatrick) G.; student U. Wis., 1954-55; B.S., Coe Coll., 1958; LL.B., U. Iowa, 1961; m. Jacqueline R. Scales, Aug. 6, 1964; children—Ian, Claire, Jason. Admitted to Iowa bar, 1961, Ill. bar, 1965; asso. firm Williams & Hartzell, Carthage, Ill., 1965-67; partner firm Hartzell & Glidden, 1967-72, Hartzell, Glidden & Tucker, 1972-77, Hartzell, Glidden, Tucker & Neff, 1977—; city atty., City of Carthage, 1969—. Served with USAF, 1961-65. Mem. Fed., Am., Ill., Iowa, Hancock County bar assns., Am., Ill. (governing bd. 1973-80) trial lawyers assns., Am. Legion, Phi Delta Phi, Sigma Nu. Clubs: Keokuk Country, Carthage Golf (dir. 1967—). Home: Rural Route 3 Carthage IL 62321 Office: PO Box 70 Carthage IL 62321

GLIME, RAYMOND GEORGE, lawyer; b. Highland Park, Mich., Feb. 15, 1931; s. George Henry and Edna Grace (Yutzy) G.; B.S., Wayne State U., 1954, J.D., 1957; M.B.A., U. Mich., 1958; m. Gretchen Ross, Apr. 3, 1954; children—Elizabeth Rae, Rebecca Lee. Admitted to Mich. bar, 1957; asst. pros. atty. Macomb County, Mich., 1958-59; mem. firm. Glime, Daoust, Wilds, Rusing and Widlak, Mount Clemens, Mich. Mem. State Bar Mich., Am., Macomb County (dir. 1970—, pres. 1975-76) bar assns., Nat. Sch. Bd. Attys.' Assn., Nat. Orgn. Legal Problems in Edn., Wayne State U. Law Alumni Assn. (dir. 1965— pres. 1972). Contbr. articles to profl. jours. Home: 37119 Tall Oak Dr Fraser MI 48026 Office: 25 N Gratiot Ave Mount Clemens MI 48043

GLOE, DONNA SUE OSBORN, family therapist, histotechnologist; b. Moberly, Mo., Apr. 24, 1951; d. James Frederick and E. Emogene (Semones) Osborn; B.A., U. Mo., 1973; M.Ed.,

Lincoln U., 1977; m. Lloyd R. Gloe, Feb. 14, 1975; children—Darin Robert, Leslie Renee. Lab. technician dept. pathology U. Mo., Columbia, 1974-75, dept. opthalmology sr. research technician, 1975-76; dept. head histology and cytology lab. Lester E. Cox Med. Center, Springfield, Mo., 1976-77; family therapist D.E. Burrell Community Mental Health Center, Inc., Marshfield, Mo., 1979—. Nat. Merit scholar, 1969; Regents scholar, 1969. Mem. Am. Personnel and Guidance Assn., Nat. Soc. Histotechnologists, Am. Soc. Clin. Pathologists, AAUW. Baptist. Home: Route 2 Box 171 Marshfield MO 65706

GLOMMEN, HARVEY HAMILTON, social work cons., counselor; b. Suttons Bay, Mich., Mar. 25, 1928; s. Lars Louis and Serena Sadie (Rorem) G.; B.A., Concordia Coll., 1953; postgrad. U. Minn., 1953-54, 60, 61, 62, U. Chgo., summer 1959; M.S.W., U. Mich., 1964; m. Ina Mae Wollertson, June 24, 1951; children—Brent, Barbara, Beth, Brenda. Social worker Hennepin and Anoka counties (Minn.) Welfare Bds., 1954-58; county welfare dir. Cottonwood County (Minn.) Welfare Dept., Windom, 1959-60; dir. Aitkin County (Minn.) Welfare Dept., Aitkin, 1960-63; tng. cons. for exec., supervisory tng. Minn. Dept. Pub. Welfare, St. Paul, 1964-65, supr. adoptions, 1965-66; dir. foster grandparents program Adminstrn. Aging, HEW, Washington, 1966-67; exec. dir. Minn. Assn. Retarded Citizens, Mpls., 1967-69; practice marriage and family counseling, cons. in human service, Mpls., 1972—; incorporator, pres. Our Place, emotionally disturbed facility, Blaine, 1977—; owner, operator Circus Candy Co., Mpls., 1972—, 1048 Residence, Blaine, Minn., 1968—. Mem. city charter commn., Blaine, 1974—; chmn. Blaine City Charter Commn., 1976-79; mem. constn. commn. Minn. Dem.-Farmer-Labor Party, 1976-78, fin. dir. Minn. Senate Dist. 47, 1975-78, chmn., 1978-80; treas. Anoka County Assn. for Retarded Citizens, 1949-51, bd. dirs., 1969-72; bd. dirs., incorporator Anoka County Family Service Assn., 1970-72. Served to 2d lt. AUS, 1946-50; Germany. Minn. Tng. fellow, 1963. Mem. Minn., Nat. pub. health assns., Minn., Nat. vocat. rehab. assns., Phi Kappa Phi. Democrat. Lutheran (youth bd. 1970-73, ch. council 1970-73). Home and office: 1048 87th Ave NE Blaine MN 55434

GLOOR, WILBUR TELL, cons. mech. engr.; b. Cleve., July 27, 1918; s. Walter Tell and Louisa Hedwig (Walther) G.; B.M.E., Case Sch. Applied Sci., 1940, M.M.E., 1947; m. Dorothy Duane Sandridge, Jan. 17, 1948; 1 dau., Catherine Duane (Mrs. Victor W. Simmons, Jr.). Lab. engr. Hoffman Specialty Co., Stamford, Conn., 1940; jr. mech. engr. A. H. Emery Co., Stamford, 1940-45, supervisory engr., New Canaan, Conn., 1950-56; chief research engr. Motch & Merryweather Machinery Co., Cleve., 1945-46, mgr. div. cutting tools, 1947-49, mgr. tech. promotion, 1949-50; product engr. Baldwin Testing Equipment Co., Waltham, Mass., 1956-60, King of Prussia, Pa., 1960-66; sr. mech. cons. Gilmore Industries, Beachwood, Ohio, 1966-72; pres. Gloor Inc., Aurora, Ohio, 1972—; project engr. Stock Equipment Co. unit Gen. Signal, Chagrin Falls, Ohio, 1981—; lectr. in machine design. Advanced gifts chmn. ARC, Norwalk, Conn., 1953-54; chmn. plant com. Sudbury (Mass.) Sch. Survey, 1958-60. Registered profl. engr., Conn., Mass. Mem. ASME, ASTM, Case Alumni Assn., Sigma Xi. Republican. Congregationalist. Patentee materials testing equipment; inventor three thread weaver. Home and Office: 257 Aurora Hudson Rd Aurora OH 44202

GLOSSBERG, JOSEPH BERKSON, investment counsellor; b. Chgo., Apr. 2, 1941; s. J. William Pearl (Berkson) G.; B.S. in Econs., Wharton Sch., U. Pa., 1963, M.B.A. in Fin., 1965; 2 sons, Jonathan William, David Louis. Dir. Gofen and Glossberg, Inc., Chgo., 1965—. Pres. Med. Research Inst. Council, 1972-74, bd. dirs., 1977—; bd. dirs. U. Pa. Alumni Council on Admission, 1977-78; trustee U. Pa., 1979—. Served with USCG, 1965. Recipient Alumni award of merit U. Pa., 1977; chartered fin. analyst; chartered investment counsellor. Mem. Investment Analysts Soc. Chgo., Fin. Analysts Fedn. Am., Investment Counsel Assn. Am. Republican. Clubs: Standard, City (Chgo.); U. Pa. Alumni Assn. Chgo. (pres. 1974-79); New Buffalo Rod and Gun. Home: 1303 N Sutton Pl Chicago IL 60610 Office: 401 N Michigan Ave Chicago IL 60611

GLOSSER, RONALD DEAN, banker; b. Conesville, Ohio, Apr. 17, 1933; s. Henry and Anna M.; B.A., Ohio Wesleyan U., 1955; grad. Stonier Grad. Sch. Banking, 1965; m. Lily Glosser; 1 son, Jeffrey A. Trust officer Cleve. Trust, 1957-68; v.p., sr. trust officer Goodyear Bank, Akron, Ohio, 1968-74, pres., chief exec. officer, 1974—. Past pres. Akron Regional Devel. Bd.; vice chmn. bd. trustees Ohio Wesleyan U.; dir. Robert Schuller Ministries, Guideposts. Served with USAF, 1955-57. Mem. Cleve. Young Presidents Orgn. (chmn.), Ohio Bankers Assn. (dir.). Clubs: Portage Country, Mayflower, Akron City. Office: 1177 E Market St Akron OH 44305

GLOVER, KENNETH FREDERICK, govt. ofcl.; b. Honolulu, Dec. 23, 1946; s. John Earl and Yolonda (Frederick) G.; B.S., Kans. State U., 1970, M. Regional and Community Planning, 1973; m. Nancy Johns, June 5, 1971. Planning intern Memphis and Shelby County Planning Commn., 1972; regional planner Nebr. Office of Planning and Programming, Lincoln, 1973-75; exec. dir. Mid-State Regional Planning Commn., McPherson, Kans., 1975—. Mem. Am. Planning Assn. (sec. Kans. chpt. 1978—), Am. Inst. Cert. Planners (charter), Nat. Model R.R. Assn. Democrat. Methodist. Office: 115 E Kansas Ave PO Box 963 McPherson KS 67460

GLOVER, REX BURR, real estate exec.; b. Conneaut, Ohio, Jan. 16, 1921; s. James N. and Anna (Frazier) G.; certificate real estate U. Mich., 1968; m. Georgia Lee Richardson, June 29, 1970. Supt., Gerity Mich. Corp., Adrian, Mich., 1951-54; founder, pres., chmn. bd. Glover Real Estate, Inc., Adrian, 1954—, Trade-A-Plan, Inc., Adrian, 1966—; founder, partner Glover Woods Assos., Alma, Mich., 1969—, West Terrace Apts., Adrian, 1970—; pres. Felonoff Industries, Inc., Adrian; founder, partner Rexell Devel. Co., Kalamazoo, 1979—. Served with M.P., AUS, 1943-46; PTO. Decorated Bronze Star. Mem. Nat. Assn. Realtors, Mich. Assn. Farm and Land Inst. (pres. 1970), Mich. Assn. Realtors (dir.), Real Estate Polit. Edn. Com. (life mem.), Lenawee Realtors Assn. (pres. 1961, 62, 68-70), Real Estate Alumni Mich. (pres.), Am. Legion. Republican. Presbyterian. Clubs: Elks, Rotary. Home: 4383 Evergreen Dr Adrian MI 49221 Office: 1579 W Maumee St Adrian MI 49221

GLOVER, RICHMOND WILLIAM, steel co. exec.; b. Wheeling, W.Va., Nov. 10, 1941; s. Richmond Nesbitt and Lorena Theresa (Strauss) G.; B.S., W. Liberty State Coll., 1963; m. Eileen R. O'Brien, Dec. 17, 1967; children—Erin, Scott, Megan, Molly. Resident salesman Wheeling-Pittsburgh Steel Corp., Conn., 1963-72; nat. sales mgr. Hille & Mueller, Cheshire, Conn., 1972-76; dir. sales and purchasing Rafferty Brown Steel Co., East Longmeadow, Mass. and Waterbury, Conn., 1974-75; v.p. sales, mktg., traffic Thomas Steel Strip Corp., Warren, Ohio, 1975—; dir. Avalon Golf Courses, Inc., Warren, 1980—, mem. exec. bd., treas., 1980—. Mem. Republican Town Com., Cheshire, Conn., 1971. Served to lt. (j.g.) USN, 1964-68; Vietnam. Recipient Key Man award Jr. C. of C., 1972. Mem. Warren Area C. of C. (dir., exec. bd., treas.), Trumbull County Indsl. Mgmt. Assn., Cold Rolled Steel Strip Assn. Club: Tippecanoe Country. Home: 3683 Barber Dr Canfield OH 44406 Office: Delaware Ave NW Warren OH 44485

GLOVER, ROBERT EDWARD, ice cream mfg. co. exec.; b. Frankfort, Ind., Nov. 13, 1930; s. Foster Robert and Virginia Mary (Oldshoes) G.; B.S., U. Ark., 1952; m. Virginia M. Mann, Oct. 3, 1954; children—Robert Stephen, Thom Scott, Beth Marie. Pres., Glover's Ice Cream, Frankfort, Ind. Served with AUS, 1952-53. Mem. Sigma Chi. Clubs: Jesters, Masons, Shriners, Elks, Rotary, Moose, Symposiarchs, Country (Frankfort). Home: 609 Harvard Terr Frankfort IN 46041 Office: 705 W Clinton St Frankfort IN 46041

GLOVER, WILLIAM BYRON, broadcasting exec.; b. Columbus, Ohio, Apr. 11, 1937; s. Paul L. and Jean L. (Ogle) G.; student U. Western Ont., 1954-55, Ohio State U., 1956-57; m. Nancy Lee Parker, Oct. 29, 1975; children—Nancy Jean, Suzanne Louise. Various advt. and sales positions Regina Leader-Post, Can., 1955-56, Youngstown (Ohio) Vindicator, 1957-58, Niles (Ohio) Daily Times, 1958-59, Sta. WEAM, Arlington, Va., 1959-60, No. Va. Sun, Arlington, 1960-61; gen. sales mgr. Sta. WHOT and WSRD-FM, Youngstown, 1961—; guest lectr. Sch. Bus., Youngstown State U. Chmn. phys. com. YMCA, Youngstown. Mem. Retail Advt. Club, Radio Advt. Bur. Home: 4851 Westchester Sq Austintown OH 44515 Office: Station WHOT 401 N Blaine Ave Youngstown OH 44505

GLUSAC, MICHAEL M., automobile co. exec.; b. Highland Park, Mich., July 28, 1930; B.A., Wayne State U., 1953, J.D., 1956. Admitted to Mich. bar, 1956; individual practice law, Highland Park, Mich., 1956-70; corp. counsel City of Detroit, 1970-74; exec. dir. SE Mich. Council Govts., Detroit, 1974-82; dir. govt. affairs Chrysler Corp., Detroit, 1982—. Councilman City of Highland Park, 1963-65, mayor, 1965-68, council pres., 1968-70; instr. bus. adminstrn. Wayne State U., 1959-61; exec. chmn. Detroit-Wayne County Criminal Justice System Coordinating Council, 1972-73; mem. Gov.'s Spl. Commn. on Local Govt., 1971-72, bd. dirs. Nat. Assn. Regional Councils, 1979-82; mem. Mich. Econ. Action Council, 1975-76; pres. Mich. Mcpl. League, 1969-70; mem. Wayne County Bd. Suprs., 1967-68. Mem. Am. Judicature Soc., Am., Mich., Detroit, Highland Park (past pres.) bar assns. Office: Chrysler Corp Oakland Ave Detroit MI 48203

GNAEDINGER, JOHN PHILLIP, civil engr.; b. Oak Park, Ill., Jan. 11, 1926; s. Robert Joseph and Edna (Metz) G.; B.S., Cornell U., 1946; M.S., Northwestern U., 1947; m. Elizabeth Williams, March 15, 1956; children—John Phillip, Sarah Elizabeth. Structural designer Shaw Metz & Dolio, 1946-48; founder, 1948, since pres. Soil Testing Services, Inc., Chgo. Past chmn. bldg. research adv. bd. Nat. Acad. Sci.-NRC; mem. senate Monmouth Coll. Registered structural engr., Ill., profl. engr., Ind., N.Y., Iowa, Wis., Conn., Calif., Va., Ky. Mem. Western Soc. Engrs. (past pres.), ASCE, Chief Execs. Forum, ASTM, Ill. Engring. Council (past pres.), Asso. Soil and Found. Engrs. Inc. (past pres.), Hwy. Research Bd., Cornell Soc. Engrs. Chgo. (past pres.), Fed. Constrn. Council (past chmn.), Sigma Xi, Tau Beta Pi, Sigma Chi. Clubs: Cornell (past pres.), University (Chgo.); Exmoor Country. Home: 160 Sheridan Rd Kenilworth IL 60043 Office: PO Box 1009 Northbrook IL 60026

GNAU, JOHN RUSSELL, JR., public relations exec.; b. Detroit, Mar. 3, 1930; s. John Russell and Constance L. Gnau; B.A. in Journalism, U. Detroit, 1952; m. Margaret Maher, July 25, 1952; children—Kathleen, Russell, Michael, Margaret, Julie. With sales and promotion dept. Sta. WWJ-TV, Detroit, 1951-54; gen. agt. Ohio State Life and Columbus Mut. Ins. Co., 1954-68; v.p. Alexander Hamilton Life Ins. Co., Farmington, Mich., 1968-71; pres., chmn. bd. Gnau-Carter-Jacobsen, Washington, 1979—. State chmn. for Mich., Reagan campaign, 1976, 80; mem. Oakland County (Mich.) Road Commn., 1972—; trustee Bloomfield Twp., 1972-76. Named Man of Yr., Ohio State Life Ins. Co., 1967. Address: 3894 Peabody Dr Bloomfield Hills MI 48013

GNEUHS, CHARLES OSCAR, banker; b. Cleve., Feb. 16, 1949; s. Robert Edward and Mary Jane G.; B.A., Cleve. State U., 1973; m. Pamella Eldridge, June 9, 1978; 1 dau., Faith Ann. Mgmt. intern NASA Research Center, Cleve., 1972-73; adminstrv. specialist Cuyahoga County Welfare Dept., Cleve., 1974-75; asst. mgr. G.E. Evendale Fed. Credit Union, Cin., 1976-78; loan service mgr. Am. Savs. & Loan Assn., Middletown, Ohio, 1978-80; mgr. Norwalk (Ohio) Area Fed. Credit Union, 1980; pres. N.W. Parish Credit Union, Chgo., 1980-81; pres. Sears Employees Credit Union, Chgo., 1981—; dir., asst. sec. Elderlot Inc., Cleve., 1974—. Mem. spl. gifts campaign com. Cath. Charities. Mem. Ohio Credit Union League, Cleve. Jaycees (dir. 1975—), Cin. Jaycees (dir. 1976—), Internat.-Platform Assn. Republican. Roman Catholic. Home: PO Box 587 Middletown OH 45042 Office: Sears Employees Credit Union Sears Tower Chicago IL 60684

GOAD, LINDA SICKO, research scientist; b. Highland Park, Mich., Sept. 21, 1948; d. Donald and Alfreda (Flasinski) Sicko; B.S., Wayne State U., Detroit, 1970; Ph.D., CUNY, 1974; m. Earl G. Goad, June 1, 1974. Research asso. Gt. Lakes research div. U. Mich., Ann Arbor, 1974-76, asst. research scientist, 1976-78, asso. research scientist, 1978—. Mem. Electron Miscroscopy Soc. Am., Am. Soc. Cell Biology, Can. Soc. Microbiology, Phycological Soc. Am., N.Y. Acad. Scis., Am. Soc. Limnology and Oceanography, Internat. Assn. Gt. Lakes Resgarch, Sigma Xi. Contbr. articles profl. jours. Office: Gt Lakes Research Div Univ Mich Inst Sci and Tech Ann Arbor MI 48109

GOBER, JOHN LEWIS, constrn. equipment mfg. co. exec.; b. Franklin County, Mo., Dec. 5, 1935; s. Allen Lee and Mary Kathryn (Pebeck) G.; student S.W. Bapt. Coll., 1954-55; m. Clara Mae Owens, June 11, 1960; children—Deana Lynn, Brian Keith. Head, engring. services Vernon L. Goedecke Co., Inc., St. Louis, 1957-75; v.p. mktg. Ho-Vert Systems, Inc., St. Louis, 1975-77, 81—; project mgr. Binkley Co., St. Louis, 1977-80. Served with U.S. Army, 1955-57. Baptist. Club: Mason. Home: 221 Smith Ave Kirkwood MO 63122 Office: Ho-Vert Systems Inc 9738 Gravois Rd Saint Louis MO 63123

GOCHNAUER, LENA SUE, educator; b. Massillon, Ohio, Nov. 30, 1947; d. Lester Lee and Isa Mae (Hostetler) Gochnauer; B.S. in Edn., Ashland Coll., 1969; M.A. in Edn., Ohio State U., 1975. Supr. activity therapists Zonal Project 13, Apple Creek (Ohio) State Inst., 1969-70; tchr. John R. Lea Intermediate Sch., Apple Creek, 1970—. Mem. Mohican Dist. Sci. Fair Council, 1970—. Tchr. grantee, 1978-79. Mem. NEA, S.E. Local Edn. Assn. (pres.), Ohio Edn. Assn., Ohio Middle Sch. Assn., Nat. Assn. Core Curriculum, Alpha Theta. Mem. United Ch. of Christ. Club: 4-H. Home: PO Box 488 3778 S Millborne Rd Apple Creek OH 44606 Office: John R Lea Intermediate Sch 9130 Dover Rd Apple Creek OH 44606

GODDERZ, DAVID EUGENE, data processor; b. Aberdeen, S.D., Oct. 13, 1938; s. Hernando Walter and Lois Lenore (Blethen) G.; B.S., No. State Coll., Aberdeen, 1964; M.S., N.J. Inst. Tech., Newark, 1968; Ph.D., U. Minn., 1978; m. Georgeann Elizabeth Kersteter, Nov. 21, 1970. Tchr. math. Watchung Hills High Sch., Warren, N.J., 1964-67; programmer/analyst, then mgr. program and analysis dept. Control Data Corp., Mpls., 1967-70; instr. data processing, chmn. dept. Lakewood Community Coll., White Bear Lake, Minn., 1970—; tchr. seminars in field. Served with USMC, 1956-59. NSF fellow, summer 1964, 65. Mem. NEA, Minn. Community Coll. Faculty Assn. Home: 6312 Pheasant Ct Edina MN 55436 Office: 3401 Century Ave N White Bear Lake MN 55110

GODFREY, LINDA S., paper products co. exec.; b. Bush, Ill., Dec. 31, 1948; d. Robert J. and Naomi N. (Goshen) Carter; student Morraine Valley Community Coll., 1975; m. David C. Godfrey, Dec. 3, 1977; children—Sandra Kloos, Christopher Godfrey. With Schwab Paper Products, Chgo., 1970—, office mgr., 1972-75, sales adminstr., 1975-76, gen. mgr., 1976—. Mem. Chgo. Assn. Commerce and Industry. Office: 3742 S Ashland Chicago IL 60609

GODFREY, OLLIN, oil and banking exec.; b. Cin., Dec. 10, 1930; s. Ollin and Mattie (Clemmons) G.; student Edward Waters Jr. Coll., Jacksonville, Fla., 1949, Malcolm-King Coll., N.Y.C., 1968-71; m. Joan Jarboe, June 10, 1953; children—Ollin, Mark, David. Vice pres. East Harlem Community Corp., N.Y.C., 1969-71; pres. United Leadership Consultant Services, Inc., N.Y.C., 1972—; now exec. cons., Cin.; cons. Massive Neighborhood Devel. Corp., 1970-72. Past bd. dirs. Malcolm King Coll. Served with U.S. Navy, 1950-53. Recipient certificate of appreciation Republican Nat. Com., 1977. Mem. Am. Security Council (adv. bd.), Nat. Rep. Congressional Com. (sponsor), Internat. Bankers Assn., Internat. Businessmen's Assn., Nat. Rep. Senatorial Com. Baptist. Host; Minorities Sta. WNYC, N.Y.C., 1970-73. Address: 825 William Howard Taft Rd Cincinnati OH 45206

GODFREY, ROBERT GORDON, physician; b. Wichita, Kans., June 11, 1927; s. Henry Robert and Pearl Madeline (Gaston) G.; B.A., U. Wichita, 1952; M.D., U. Kans., 1958; m. Margaret Scott Ingling, June 22, 1951; children—Timothy, Katherine, Gwendolyn, Melissa. Intern, Boston City Hosp., 1958-59; resident in internal medicine Peter Bent Brigham Hosp., Boston, 1959-60, Colo. Gen. Hosp., Denver, 1961-63; asst. in medicine Peter Bent and Robert Brigham Hosp., Harvard Med. Sch., 1959-61; fellow in rheumatology Robert B. Brigham Hosp., 1960-61, U. Colo., Denver, 1963-64; instr. medicine, U. Kans. Med. Center, Kansas City, 1964-65, asst. prof. medicine, 1965, staff physician, chief arthritis sect., 1965-75; asso. chief staff for ambulatory care VA Med. Center, Kansas City, Mo., 1976—; practice medicine specializing in rheumatology; mem. staff U. Kans. Med. Center, Kansas City VA Med. Center. Served with M.C., U.S. Army, 1945-48. Recipient Disting. Service award Kans. Arthritis Found., 1975. Mem. AMA, Am. Rheumatism Assn., Am. Soc. Clin. Rheumatology, A.C.P., Sigma Xi, Alpha Omega Alpha. Republican. Office: VA Med Center 4801 Linwood Blvd Kansas City MO 64128

GODING, CARL VERNON, service co. exec.; b. Berwyn, Ill., Apr. 19, 1922; s. Carl William and Hulda Louise (Johnson) G.; B.E.E., Ill. Inst. Tech., 1949; m. Arlene Junice Carlson, Sept. 7, 1946; children—James William, John Mark, Bonnie Lynn, David Robert. Owner, mgr. Goding Electric Co., Berwyn, Ill., 1949-72, pres., Glendale Heights, Ill., 1972—. Served with AUS, USAAF, 1942-45. Decorated Air medal. Mem. Nat. Fedn. Ind. Businesses, Elec. Appratus Service Assn., Nat. Rental Ops. Assn. (past pres.). Republican. Baptist (trustee Midwest Bapt. Conf., 1969—, trustee Bapt. Gen. Conf., mem. exec. com. Bapt. Gen. Conf. 1978—). Home: 1611 E Columbine Dr Schaumburg IL 60194 Office: 686 E Fullerton Ave Glendale Heights IL 60137

GODING, CHARLES ARTHUR, chem. co. exec.; b. Aurora, Ill., Aug. 13, 1934; s. Arthur Walter and Lillian (Berg) G.; B.A., U. Ill., 1956; grad. with honors Inst. Advanced Advt. Studies, 1965; m. Corinne Doris Dau, Aug. 31, 1957; children—Charles Arthur, Craig Jon, Cynthia Lynn. Copywriter J. Walter Thompson Co., Chgo., 1956-61, Campbell-Mithun Inc., Chgo., 1961-64; account exec., supr. Marsteller Inc., Chgo., 1964-70; dir. advt. Nalco Chem. Co., Chgo./Oak Brook, Ill., 1970—. Task force com. Sch. Dist. 205, 1975—; mem. Racket Sports Adv. Commn.; pres. Oak Brook Ride Sharing Coop. Inc.; mem. Redeemer Luth. Ch. Sch. Bd.; bd. dirs. Elmhurst Instrumental Music Boosters; active Jr. Achievement, Boy Scouts Am. Mem. Bus. Profl. Advt. Assn. (life, pres. Chgo. chpt. 1975-76, pres. internat. assn. 1980-81), Oak Brook Assn. Commerce and Industry (pres. 1981—), Delta Upsilon. Republican. Lutheran. Home: 259 Cottage Hill Elmhurst IL 60126

GODLEWSKI, MICHAEL PATRICK, physicist; b. Detroit, Oct. 9, 1938; s. Michael Stephen and Anna Katherine (Bush) G.; B.S., U. Detroit, 1960, M.S., 1964; m. Carol Anne Sowa, July 20, 1963; children—Kathleen, Jennifer, Michael. Aerospace technologist NASA, Lewis Research Center, Cleve., 1962-64, nuclear engr., 1964-68, physicist, 1968—, mgr. univ. grants. Recipient Cleve. Fed. Exec. Bd. Personal Merit award, 1974. Mem. Am. Phys. Soc., IEEE (sr. mem.), Solar Energy Soc., AAAS, Sigma Pi Sigma. Contbr. articles to profl. jours.; co-editor IEEE-Electron Devices spl. publ., 1977. Home: 337 Kraft St Berea OH 44017 Office: 21000 Brookpark Rd Cleveland OH 44135

GOEBEL, CARL WILLIAM, allergist; b. Ft. Wayne, Ind., Mar. 17, 1921; s. Carl John and Kathryn Ann (Eckart) G.; A.B. in Chemistry, Ind. U., 1942, M.D., 1944; m. Virginia Ann Cooper, Aug. 21, 1944; children—Ann, Susan, Lynn, Brenda, Cecilia. Intern, Ind. U. Med Center, 1944-45; chief resident, fellow in allergy U. Minn. Hosp., 1946-47; practice medicine specializing in allergies, Ft. Wayne, 1984—; mem. staff Luth. Hosp., St. Joseph Hosp., both Ft. Wayne; mem. asso. teaching staff Ind. U. Sch. Medicine, Ft. Wayne. Served with U.S. Army, 1942-44, 45-47, USAF, 1950. Diplomate Am. Bd. Pediatrics, Am. Bd. Allergy and Immunology. Fellow Am. Acad. Pediatrics; mem. Am. Acad. Allergy, AMA, Ind. State Med. Assn., Ft. Wayne-Allen County Med. Soc., Phi Beta Kappa, Alpha Omega Alpha. Republican. Roman Catholic. Home: 4903 Old Mill Fort Wayne IN 46807 Office: 2828 Fairfield Fort Wayne IN 46807

GOEHLE, DONNA GENE, educator; b. Mt. Lake, Minn., Mar. 12, 1946; d. Herman C. and Genevieve G. (Anderson) Goehle; B.A., U. Minn., 1968; M.B.A., So. Ill., U., 1973; Ph.D., Mich. State U., 1978. Chpt. cons. Chi Omega Sorority, Cin., 1968-71; adminstrv. asst. to dean of students So. Ill. U., Carbondale, 1971-72, dir. European travel and study program, 1972-73; asst. prof. mktg. Western Mich. U., Kalamazoo, 1976-78; asst. prof. mktg./internat. bus. Mich. State U., E. Lansing, 1978—. Mem. Am. Mktg. Assn., Acad. Internat. Bus., Acad. Mktg. Sci., Chimes, Beta Gamma Sigma, Chi Omega. Club: W. Mich. World Trade. Author: Decision-Making in Multinational Corporations, 1980; Current Readings in International Business, 1981. Office: Grad Sch Bus 320 Eppley Center Mich State Univ East Lansing MI 48824

GOEHRING, MABEL FAYE, educator; b. Bala, Kans., Jan. 9, 1929; married, 3 children. B.S. in Elementary Edn., Kans. State U., Manhattan, 1963, M.S. in Elementary Edn., 1969, in Learning Disabilities, 1978. Classroom tchr. Pottawatomie County Rural Schs., Westmoreland, Kans., 1946-51; classroom tchr. Wamego (Kans.) Unified Sch. Dist. 320, 1951-53, 55-66, reading cons., 1966—. Mem. Internat. Reading Assn. (pres. North Central Kans. 1975-76), NEA, Wamego Tchrs. Assn., Delta Kappa Gamma. Certified tchr., prin., learning disability tchr., reading tchr., lang. arts tchr., Kans.

GOERING, LARRY ELDON, educator; b. Newton, Kans., Mar. 25, 1945; s. Eldon Clarence and Bonnie Luella (Tangeman) G.; student Bethel Coll., 1963-65; B.S. in Agr., Kans. State U., 1968, M.S. in Agr. Edn., 1981; m. Margaret Rosine Hooper, June 24, 1967; children—Sandra, Kevin, Suzanne. Dir. agrl. and community devel. Mennonite Central Com., Mex., 1968-70; tchr. vocat. agr. Marion (Kans.) High Sch., 1970-74; instr. Bethel Coll., North Newton, Kans., 1975-77; tchr. vocat. agr. Unified Sch. Dist. 423, Moundridge, Kans., 1974—; farmer, Twin Pines Farm, 1971—. Adult leader 4-H Club, Marion, 1972-74. Mem. Kans. Vocat. Agr. Tchrs. Assn. (Outstanding Young Man award 1975), Nat. Vocat. Agr. Tchrs. Assn., Kans. Vocat. Assn. (Outstanding Young Vocat. Educator award 1975), Am. Vocat. Assn., Farm Bur. Mennonite (deacon). Home: Route 1 PO Box 20 Newton KS 67114 Office: Moundridge High Sch Moundridge KS 67107

GOETTIG, RAYMOND JOHN, accountant; b. Fulda, Minn., Mar. 9, 1927; s. John Henry and Marie Agnes (Brown) G.; Accountant, LaSalle Extension U., 1963; m. Doris Catherine Platz, Oct. 29, 1947; children—Gwyn (Mrs. Scott Erickson), Mary (Mrs. John Murphy), Ruth. Master mechanic, custom flooring, design and installation Rehkamp Furniture, Marshall, Minn., 1947-52; self-employed as pub. and tax accountant, Sleepy Eye, Minn., 1957—. City treas. Sleepy Eye, 1961-71. Served with AUS, 1946-47. Mem. Nat. Assn. Enrolled Agts. (nat. treas. 1973-75, dir. 1976-78, 1st v.p. 1978-79, pres. 1979-80), Minn. Soc. Enrolled Agts. (co-founder, dir. 1979-80, 81-82, pres. 1980-81), Nat. Soc. Pub. Accountants, Nat. Fedn. Ind. Bus., Nat. Adv. Council, Am. Legion, Minn. Assn. Pub. Accountants. K.C., Eagle, Lion. Home: 628 2d Ave NE Sleepy Eye MN 56085 Office: 104 W Main St Sleepy Eye MN 56085

GOFF, STEPHEN CHARLES, retail and real estate exec.; b. St. Paul, Sept. 21, 1945; s. Stillman Reese and Marion Emma (Zinsmeister) F.; B.S., Bradley U., 1967; M.B.A., No. Ill. U., 1967-69; m. Donna Jean Domnick, Mar. 9, 1969; children—Dale, Donald. Grad. resident adv. No. Ill. U., DeKalb, 1968-69; cons. Thorolf Gregerson A/S, Oslo, Norway, 1968; market research dir., planner Nash Finch Co., retail trade, St. Louis Park, Minn., 1969-78; mktg. dir. Musicland Group, Am. Can Corp., St. Louis Park, 1978-81; pres. U.S. Renovation Corp., Mpls., 1980—; v.p. U.S. Devel. Corp., 1980—; guest lectr. U. Minn., Ohio State U. Adv. HELP, minority bus. cons., St. Paul Model Cities, 1971-73; faculty Met. State U., 1975—. Pres. Social Innovations, Mpls., 1971—; liaison mem. Bldg. Block Nursery Sch. and Day Care Center, Mpls., 1971—. Del. local precinct Republican Party, 1972. Mem. Am. Mktg. Assn. (nat. minority bus. assistance com.), North Central Corp. Planning Soc. (officer 1978), Nat. Assn. Edn. Young Children, Nat. Assn. Retail Grocers (conv. lectr.), Internat. Shopping Center Council, Nat. Assn. Record Mfrs., Retail Bakers Am., Minn. Minority Bus. Cons., Food Mktg. Inst. (adv. bd.; conv. lectr.), Food Distbn. Research Soc. (conv. lectr.), Day Care and Child Devel. Council Am., Greater Mpls. Day Care Assn., Greater St. Paul Council Coordinated Child Care, Minn. Assn. Edn. Young Children, Minn. Jr. C. of C. (state dir. drug edn. 1971-72), Golden Valley Jr. C. of C., Minn. Wine Tasting Soc. (pres. 1973), Sigma Chi. Author: Computerized Food Shopping, 1974; Super Marketing in Japan, 1977; Super Marketing in Soviet Union, 1978; Need for Strategic Market Planning, 1978; Super Marketing in South America, 1979. Home: 1820 Du Pont Ave S Minneapolis MN 55403

GOFF, WILLIAM LEE EDWARD, chem. co. ofcl.; b. Batesville, Ark., Feb. 6, 1925; s. William Jennings Bryan and Tiny Ledona (Rosenbaum) G.; student continuing edn. courses Kans. U., 1965-78; m. Helen Wilberta Staggs, June 24, 1945; children—Donnie Lee, Bradley Edward. Delivery man Batesville Ice Co., 1940-43; carpenter, 1946-51; water operator Hercules Powder Co., 1951-58; power supr. E.I. duPont Co., Topeka, 1958—. Chmn., Eudora (Kans.) Bd. Zoning Appeals, 1973-81. Served with USMC, 1943-46. Cert. water supply operator, waste water treatment operator, Kans. Mem. Water Pollution Control Fedn., Am. Water Works Assn, Nat. Rifle Assn. Democrat. Methodist. Club: Eudora Lions. Home: 615 Main St Eudora KS 66025 Office: PO Box 481 Topeka KS 66601

GOGATE, ANAND BALKRISHNA, cons. engr., educator; b. Rangoon, Burma, Jan. 28, 1935; s. B.S. and Sushila B. (Phadke) G.; came to U.S., 1962, naturalized, 1970; B.E., U. Poona, 1958; M.S., U. Iowa, 1963; Ph.D., Ohio State U., 1977; m. Shashi Gogate, June 20, 1962; children—Gita, Soniya, Sanjay. Engr., Koyna project, Hindustan Contrn. Co., India, 1958-59; asst. engr. Municipal Corp. of Delhi, India, 1959-62; design engr. Peterson & Appel Engrs., Des Moines, 1963-65; structural designer PDM, Des Moines, 1966-67; chief structural engr. A.E. Stilson & Assos., Columbus, Ohio, 1967-72, Elgar Brown Engrs., Worthington, Ohio, 1972—; asso. prof. dept. architecture Ohio State U., 1981—. Recipient award for highest grade in exam. Ohio Soc. Profl. Engrs., 1968. Fellow ASCE (State of the Art award 1974, Raymond C. Reese award 1976); mem. Am. Concrete Inst. Author book; contbr. articles to profl. jours. Hindu. Home: 6112 Sedgwick Rd Worthington OH 43085

GOGGIN, JOHN EDWARD, county ofcl.; b. Chgo., Oct. 20, 1923; s. John Patrick and Sara (McCabe) G.; student U. Ill., 1941-42, DePaul U., 1946-47; B.S.C. Chgo. Kent Coll. Law, 1953; m. Helen Marie McSweeney, Dec. 29, 1945; children—John, Michael, Terrence, Brian, Kevin, Trudi, Daniel. Personal bailiff to judge municipal ct., 1946-53; ins. broker, Chgo., 1950—; pub. relations mgr. Gen. Outdoor Advt., Chgo., 1953-56, regional dir., 1956-64; asso. clk. Circuit Ct. Cook County, Ill., 1965—; sec. GHJ Transport Co., 1956-60. Cons. advt. and pub. relations Cook County Democratic Central Com., 1965-72. Mem. pres. council St. Xavier's Coll. Trustee Ill. Benedictine Coll. Served to capt., AUS, 1943-46; CBI. Decorated Soldier's medal, Bronze Star with cluster, Combat Infantry Badge; knight Order St. Lazarus. Mem. Inf. Assn., Mil. Order World Wars, Ill. Mfrs. Assn., Ill. Assn. Commerce, Chgo. Assn. Commerce and Industry (com. chmn. 1956-61), Chgo. Athletic Assn., Am. Legion, Alpha Delta Phi, Phi Delta Theta. Clubs: K.C., Federated Advertising (Chgo). Home: 7700 Augusta St River Forest IL 60305 Office: Daley Center Chicago IL 60602

GOHAR, MOHAMED MAHMOUD, chemist; b. Damanhoor, Egypt, June 8, 1945; came to U.S., 1971, naturalized, 1976; s. Mahmoud I. and Atteyat M. (Nasra) G.; B.Sc., Alexandria U., 1966; M.S., Ohio State U., 1975; m. Randa Barazi, Sept. 23, 1972; children—Aladin, Basil. Analytical research specialist El-Nasr Pharm. Co., Cairo, 1966-71; grad. research/teaching asso. Ohio State U., Columbus, 1971-74; mem. faculty dept. chemistry Ohio No. U., Ada, 1974-75; chief chemist State of Ohio Arson Crime Lab., Reynoldsburg, 1975—; mem. faculty Nat. Inst. Arson, 1980—; mem. nat. steering com. Arson Analysis Concensus Standards, 1981—; Bd. dirs. Ohio Arson Sch., 1975—; mem. Summerfield Civic Assn. Recipient cert. of appreciation No. Va. Joint Com. on Fire & Arson Investigation, 1976, Internat. Assn. Arson Investigators, 1977, Internat. Homocide Seminar, 1981. Mem. AAUP, Am. Chem. Soc., Am. Soc. Crime Lab. Dirs., Soc. Sci. Detection of Crime, Central Ohio Chromatographic Assn. Author: (with others) Fire Investigation Handbook, 1980; contbr. articles to profl. jours. Home: 10233 N Crosset Hill Pickerington OH 43147 Office: 8895 E Main St Reynoldsburg OH 43068

GOHIL, PRATAP, podiatric physician and surgeon; b. Tanga, Tanzania, May 26, 1950; B.A., M.S., U. Mo., 1975, 76; D.P.M., Ohio Coll. Podiatric Medicine, 1980. Instr. biomechanics and orthopedics Ohio Coll. Podiatric Medicine, Cleve., 1977-81, research asst. anatomy, mem. research com., 1980-81; asso. in podiatric medicine and surgery Podiatry Clinic, Kokomo, Ind., 1981—. Faculty advisor and clinician Kappa Rho Collective and Alpha Gamma Kappa, City of Cleve. Clinics, 1979-81; active Am. Diabetes Assn., ARC. Recipient Dr. Kaplan award Am. Coll. Foot Surgeons, 1980; Syntex award in dermatology, 1979. Mem. Am. Podiatry Assn., Ind. Public Health Assn., Ohio Public Health Assn., Am. Public Health Assn., Am. Coll. Podopediatrics. Hindu. Author: (with Young and Clarke) Hypertensive Ischemic Ulcers of Legs, 1981; (with Young and Graham) Tension Fibrositis of the Legs, 1981. Home: 3603 Robin Ct Kokomo IN 46901 Office: 320 E Taylor St Kokomo IN 46901

GOLBECK, AMANDA LORRAINE, statistician; b. Milw., May 25, 1952; s. Harvey F. and Gladys (Mateer) G.; B.A. (scholar), Grinnell Coll., 1974; M.A. in Anthropology (Univ. fellow), U. Calif., Berkeley, 1977, M.A. in Stats. (Regents fellow), 1979; m. Craig A. Molgaard, Aug. 11, 1979. Statis. cons. rural health research project Wash. State U., Pullman, 1979-80; research statistician, dir. research Inst. Population Research and Analysis, Planned Parenthood of Minn., St. Paul, 1980—. USPHS trainee, 1978-79. Mem. Am. Statis. Assn., Population Assn. Am., Soc. Med. Anthropology (asso.), Sigma Xi. Home: 1500 Randolph St Apt 3 Saint Paul MN 55105 Office: 1965 Ford Pkwy Saint Paul MN 55116

GOLD, GEORGE MYRON, lawyer, editor; b. Bkln., June 28, 1935; s. Harry and Rose Miriam (Meyerson) G.; A.B., U. Rochester, 1956; J.D., N.Y. U., 1959; m. Bunny Winters, Dec. 24, 1960; 1 son, Seth Harris. Admitted to N.Y. State bar, 1960; practiced in N.Y.C., 1960-64; legal editor Prentice-Hall, Inc.; Englewood Cliffs, N.J., 1960-62; asso. firm Speiser, Shumate, Geoghan & Law, N.Y.C., 1962-64; asso. editor Research and Review Service Am., Inc., Indpls., 1964-67; dir. publs., mng. editor Estate Planners Quar., Farnsworth Pub. Co., Inc., Rockville Centre, N.Y., 1967-69; editor-in-chief Trusts & Estates, N.Y.C., 1969-75; editor, house counsel Ronald Press, N.Y.C., 1976; mng. editor Trust News, N.Y.C., 1976-78; dir. news publs. and info. Am. Bar Assn., Chgo., 1978—; asst. to research counsel N.Y. Temp. State Commn. Estates, 1962-64. Mem. Soc. Law Writers (dir. 1972-75), Am. N.Y. State bar assns., Assn. Bar City N.Y., Chgo. Bar Assn., Estate Planning Council N.Y.C., Soc. Bus. Press Editors, Kappa Nu, Pi Alpha Lambda. Club: KP. Author: Investments by Trustees, Executors and Adminstrators, 1961; What You Should Know About Intestacy, 1962; What You Should Know About the Common Disaster, 1962; The Powers of Your Trustee, 1962; What You Should Know About the Antenuptial Agreement, 1963; Who May Be the Beneficiary of Your Will, 1963; What You Should Know About the Spendthrift Trust, 1963; Comprehensive Estate Analysis, 1966; You're Worth More Than You Think, 1966; Medicare Handbook, 1966; The ABCs of Administering Your Estate, 1966; The Will: An Instrument for Service and Sales, 1966; A Tax-Sheltered Pension Plan for the Close-Corporation Stockholder, 1968; Social Security Law in Nutshell, 1968; What You Should Know About Custodial Gifts to Minors, 1968; The Short-Term Trust and Estate Planning, 1976; The Importance of a Will, 1976; The Need for an Experienced Executor, 1976; Tax Tips-99 Ways to Reduce the Bite, 1976. Editor: Fundamentals of Federal Income Estate & Gift Taxes, 1965; Tax-Free Reorganizations, 1968; Guide to Pension and Profit Sharing Plans, 1968; A Life Underwriter's Guide to Equity Investments, 1968; The Tired Tirade, 1968; How to Use Life Insurance in Business and Estate Planning, 1969; Human Drama in Death and Taxes, 1970; Don't Bank On It, 1970; The Feldman Method, 1970; Directory of Trust Instns. (ann.) Home: 41W161 Colson Dr Saint Charles IL 60174 Office: 77 S Wacker Dr Chicago IL 60606

GOLDBERG, ARTHUR LEWIS, corp. exec.; b. N.Y.C., Feb. 23, 1939; s. Geroge and Rachel (Ablon) G.; B.B.A., CCNY, 1959; J.D., N.Y.U., 1962, LL.M., 1967; m. Bernice Guller, May 31, 1964; 1 dau., Deborah Ruth. Admitted to N.Y. State bar, 1962, Ohio bar, 1978; tax asst. Arthur Andersen & Co., N.Y.C., 1962-63; asso. firm Gordon, Brady, Keller & Ballen, N.Y.C., 1963-67; asso. firm Langer & Sternfield, N.Y.C., 1967-68; sr. tax atty. CBS, Inc., N.Y.C., 1968-69; asst. to chief fin. officer, sec., gen. counsel Condec Corp., Old Greenwich, Conn., 1969-77; asst. to pres., controller NRM Corp., Akron, Ohio, 1977-79; v.p. fin. and adminstrn. Conval Internat. Ltd., Chgo., 1979-80; dir. adminstrn. and ops. analysis Flow Control group Condec Corp., 1980—; instr. Grad. Sch. Bus., U. Conn., 1971-72. Served with U.S. Army, 1962-63. C.P.A., N.Y., Ohio, Ill. Mem. Am. Bar Assn., Ill. C.P.A. Soc. Contbr. articles to profl. jours. Home: 2731 Orchard Ln Wilmette IL 60091 Office: Suite 4130 875 N Michigan Ave Chicago IL 60611

GOLDBERG, DAVID JAIME, psychiatrist, educator; b. Buenos Aires, Argentina, Mar. 8, 1941; s. Herschel and Maria H. (Fizbin) G.; came to U.S., 1968; B.S., Esteban Etcheverria (Argentina), 1959; M.D., U. Buenos Aires, 1966; m. Martha Haydee Kagel, Oct. 18, 1968; children—Corinne Leilani, Nisse Aloma. Pvt. practice medicine, Buenos Aires, Argentina, 1966-68; intern, Kuakini Hosp., Honolulu, 1969; resident in psychiatry U. Hawaii, Honolulu, 1970-72, chief resident, 1971; staff psychiatrist Aiea Clinic, Hawaii Dept. Health, 1973-74; clin. teaching asst. psychiatry U. Hawaii Sch. Medicine, Honolulu, 1971-73; psychiatric cons. Leeward and Wahiawa Gen. Hosps., Aiea, 1973-74; asst. prof. psychiatry U. Nebr. Coll. Medicine, Omaha, 1974—; chmn. dept. psychiatry Richard Young Hosp., Omaha, 1978-79; cons. to cancer team Luth. Hosp. Charter mem. Menninger Found., 1978; cons. Douglas County Bd. Mental Health. Recipient Physician's Recognition award Am. Med. Assn., 1976, 80. Mem. Am. Psychiat. Assn. (sec.-treas. Nebr. dist. 1979), Nebr. Psychiat. Soc., Assn. for Acad. Psychiatry, Am. Assn. Geriatric Psychiatry, Omaha Mid-West Clin. Soc. Club: Rotary. Home: 2605 S 95th St Omaha NE 68124 Office: 2566 St Mary's Ave Omaha NE 68105

GOLDBERG, DAVID PHILLIP, physician; b. Chgo., Nov. 16, 1939; s. David Charles and Hazel Esther (Gottstein) G.; B.A., Northwestern U., 1961; M.D., Chgo. Med. Sch., 1965; m. Patricia Ann Full, Sept. 23, 1972; children—Robert Jay, Cary Trent. Intern, Michael Reese Hosp., Chgo., 1965-66, fellow in nuclear medicine, 1967-68, resident in radiology, 1968-71; staff radiologist Englewood Hosp., Chgo., 1971—, dir. nuclear medicine, 1971—; staff radiology, dir. med. edn. Palos Community Hosp., Palos Heights, Ill., 1972—, dir. nuclear medicine, 1972—; asso. prof., med. dir. radiologic technology program Moraine Valley Community Coll., Palos Hills, 1973—. Mem. Chgo., Ill. med. socs., AMA, Inst. Medicine, Am. Coll. Radiology, Am. Coll. Nuclear Medicine, Soc. Nuclear Medicine, Phi Delta Epsilon, Kappa Nu, Phi Eta Sigma. (v.p. 1975-77). Home: 16201 S 118th Ave Orland Park IL 60462 Office: 123d & 80th Ave Palos Heights IL 60463

GOLDBERG, ELLIOTT MARSHALL, physician; b. N. Adams, Mass., Dec. 18, 1930; s. Jack and Ida (Lenhoff) G.; A.B. with high honors, U. Rochester (N.Y.), 1952; M.D., Tufts U., Medford, Mass., 1956; m. Darlis Nell Ray, Apr. 17, 1966; children—Brett, Carey, Sandra, Jeffrey, Dara. Intern, D.C. Gen. Hosp., 1956-57; resident in

---

internal medicine Meml. Worcester, Mass., 1960-61, Univ. Hosps., Madison, Wis., 1962-63; practice medicine specializing in internal medicine, Flint, Mich., 1965—; mem. staff, chief medicine Hurley Hosp; chief medicine Hurley Hosp.; prof. medicine Mich. State Coll. Human Medicine. Bd. dirs. Medgar Evers Found. Served to capt., M.C., AUS, 1957-59. Endocrine fellow U. Wis., 1961-62; NIH fellow, 1963-64; recipient Outstanding Tchr. award Mich. State U., 1972-73; Humanitarian award NAACP, 1974. Diplomate Am. Bd. Internal Medicine. Fellow A.C.P.; asso. Royal Coll. Surgeons; mem. Endocrine Soc., Am. Fedn. Clin. Research, Am. Diabetes Assn., Mass., Mich., Genesee County med. socs., Am. Assn. Med. Edn. (pres. 1972-75). Author: (novels) The Karamanov Equations, 1972; The Anatomy Lesson, 1974; Critical List, 1978; Skeletons, 1979; Nerve, 1981; also med. papers. Book editor Physicians Radio Network, 1972—. Home: 2151 Crestline Dr Burton MI 48509 Office: Hurley Medical Center Flint MI 48502

GOLDBERG, KAREN JOY, optical co. exec.; b. Evergreen Park, Ill., Apr. 2, 1942; d. A.F. and E. R. (Davison) Knauf; student U. Chgo., U. Ill., Lawrence Inst. Tech.; m. H.D. Goldberg, Nov. 22, 1970; children—Marc Steven, Cydney Anne. Asst. traffic dir. marine products dept. Mitsubishi Internat. Corp., Chgo., 1961-63; asst. Barton Distilling Co., Chgo., 1963; asst. to pres., clinic coordinator, asst. registrar Chgo. Coll. Osteo. Medicine, 1964-70; pres. Multi Corp Ops., Hamtramck, Mich., 1977—; dir. Automated Eyecare Corp., Informatrix Corp. Recipient merit cert. City of Hamtramck, 1979. Mem. C. of C. (dir. 1981—), Mich. Profl. Women's Network (dir. 1981—), Am. Optometric Assn., Mich. Soc. Ophthalmic Dispensers, Nat. Assn. Female Execs., Am. Soc. Profl. and Exec. Women. Clubs: Hadassah, B'nai B'rith (life). Office: Multi Corp Ops 9727 Joseph Campau Hamtramck MI 48212

GOLDBERG, MARCY JO, ins. co. exec.; b. Detroit, Aug. 23, 1945; d. George Joseph and Terry (Epps) Reinitz; B.S., Northwestern U., 1967; C.L.U., Purdue U., 1973; postgrad. DePaul U., 1975; m. Joseph M. Goldberg, Oct. 20, 1968; 1 dau., Rachel Ann. Life underwriter Guardian Life Ins. Co., Chgo., 1971-73; life underwriter, corp. fringe benefit analyst Coordinated Fin. Programming, Chgo., 1973-75; founder, pres. Creative Compensation Plans, Chgo., 1975—; speaker ins. industry, 1972—. Bd. dirs. young leadership div. Jewish United Fund, 1973—; sec., 1974-75, pres., 1979-80, mem. profl. adv. bd. 1978-79; active Wiesenthal Center for Holocaust Studies, 1979—, United Jewish Appeal, 1977—, Chgo. Symphony Soc., 1971—, Art Inst. Chgo., 1971—, Lyric Opera Guild, 1971—, Public TV Channel WTTW, 1971—; mem. day sch. exec. com. Anshe Emet Synagogue, 1972—. Recipient Nat. Quality award Nat. Assn. Life Underwriters, 1974—. Mem. Am. Assn. C.L.U.s (dir. Chgo. chpt. 1975-77), Nat. Assn. Advanced Life Underwriting, Chgo. Estate Planning Council (founding mem.), Top of Table, Million Dollar Round Table, Five Million Dollar Forum. Contbr. articles to newspapers, Chgo. Bus. Rev. Office: Creative Compensation Plans 10 S LaSalle St Chicago IL 60603

GOLDBERG, SAMUEL IRVING, educator; b. Toronto, Ont., Can., Aug. 15, 1923; s. Jacob L. and Rachel (Berkovitz) G.; B.A., U. Toronto, 1948, M.A., 1949, Ph.D., 1951; student Cambridge (Eng.) U., 1945-46; m. Sheila Richmond, Nov. 11, 1951; children—Julia Anna, Barry Howard, Jay Michael. Sci. officer Def. Research Bd., Valcartier, Que., Can., 1951-52; asst. prof. math. Lehigh U., Bethlehem, Pa., 1952-55; asso. prof. Wayne State U., Detroit, 1955-61; asso. prof. U. Ill., Urbana, 1960-65, prof., 1965—; vis. prof. U. Toronto, 1968, Cambridge U., 1979, Collège de France, 1979; Queen's Quest prof. Queen's U. (Can.), 1980—. Served with Canadian Army, 1943-46. Recipient medal Collège de France, 1979; Sci. Research Council vis. fgn. scientist U. Liverpool (Eng.), 1973; Harvard research fellow, 1959-60; Lady Davis fellow Israel Inst. Tech., 1979. Mem. Am. Math. Soc. Author: Curvature and Homology, 1962; (with R.L. Bishop), Tensor Analysis on Manifolds, 1968; (with W.C. Weber) Conformal Deformations of Riemannian Manifolds, 1969. Home: 24 Greencroft Dr Champaign IL 61820 Office: Dept Math U Ill Urbana IL 61801

GOLDBERG, STEVEN MARK, social worker; b. Milw., Dec. 4, 1948; s. Ben and Syrene C. G.; B.A. in Sociology, U. Wis., 1971; M.S.W., Fla. State U., 1973; m. Janice K. Schroeder, July 11, 1969; children—Matthew Aaron, Elisabeth Laura. Psychiat. social worker Family Counseling Center, Kenosha, Wis., 1973-77, Psychol. Assos., Kenosha, 1977—, Kenosha Counseling and Psychiat. Clinic, 1977—. Sec. bd. dirs. Bet Shalom Religious Sch., Kenosha. Mem. Wis. Soc. for Clin. Social Workers. Social Workers. Office: 5910 39th Ave Kenosha WI 53142

GOLDBERG, TERRY EUGENE, clin. child psychologist; b. N.Y.C., Jan. 21, 1950; s. Aaron and Lillian Goldberg; B.A. with distinction (James B. Angell scholar), U. Mich., 1972, Ph.D., 1978; m. Lynette Ruth Gilbert, Mar. 7, 1976. Asst. prof. pediatrics Children's Hosp. of Mich., Wayne State U., 1979—; head dept. psychology Mich. Osteo. Med. Center, 1980—. Mem. Am. Psychol. Assn., Internat. Neuropsychol. Soc. Office: Childrens Hospital of Michigan 3901 Beaubien St Detroit MI 48201

GOLDEN, CONSTANCE JEAN, aerospace exec.; b. Highland Park, Ill., June 8, 1939; d. Herman William and Chrystle O'Linda (Tolley) Leuer; B.S., Beloit Coll., 1961; A.M., Harvard, 1962; M.S., Stanford, 1970; m. Charles Joseph Golden, June 13, 1962; 1 dau., Kerri Lynn. Scientist/engr. research and devel. div. Lockheed Missiles & Space Co., Sunnyvale, Calif., 1962-68, sr. scientist/engr. Palo Alto research labs., 1968-74, mgr. planning requirements, missile div., Sunnyvale, 1975-78; program mgr. manned space ops. Ford Aerospace, Palo Alto, 1978-79, corp. strategy mgr., Detroit, 1980—; mem. adv. council for sci. and math. Mills Coll., 1976—. NSF fellow, 1961-62; named Distinguished Woman of Yr., Lockheed, 1976. Mem. Am. Inst. Aeros. and Astronautics (pub. policy com.), Armed Forces Communications and Electronic Assn. (sect. dir.), AAAS, Soc. Women Engrs. (past pres. San Francisco Bay Area sect., past nat. scholarship chmn.), Jr. Achievement, Phi Beta Kappa. Club: Toastmasters (past club pres.). Contbg. author: Second Careers for Women, 1975. Office: Ford Aerospace and Communications Corp 300 Renaissance Center PO Box 43342 Tower 300 20th Floor Detroit MI 48243

GOLDEN, FREDERIC, clin. psychologist, educator; b. Bklyn., Apr. 21, 1947; s. Solomon and Julie (Hoffman) G.; B.S., Bklyn. Coll., 1967; M.A., W.Va. U., 1970, Ph.D., 1972. Clin. practicum, staff psychologist Western State Sch. and Hosp., Cannonsburg, Pa., 1968; clin. practicum W.Va. U. Student Counseling Service, 1969, dept. behavioral medicine and psychiatry, 1969; staff psychologist Human Resources Assn. Counseling Center, Fairmont, W.Va., 1970-71; intern Malcolm Bliss Mental Health Center, St. Louis, 1971-72; staff psychologist, coordinator community programming Children's Center for Behavioral Devel., East St. Louis, Ill., 1972-74, clin. dir.; cons. St. Clair County Parochial Schs., 1972-74 Call for Help Crisis Center, Belleville, Ill., 1973-75, Madison County Assn. Retarded Citizens, 1977—, Specialized Living Center, 1980—, East St. Louis Sch. Dist., 1979—; Collinsville Sch. Dist., 1981; ancillary staff DePaul Hosp., 1979—; asst. prof. St. Louis Community Coll. at Forest Park, 1972—; adj. asst. prof., vis. lectr. So. Ill. U., Edwardsville, 1974—.

Cert. psychologist, Mo., Ill. Mem. Am., Mo. psychol. assns., St. Clair County Child Advocacy Council (dir. 1975—), Nat. Council Health Service Providers. Contbr. articles in field to Behavior Therapy, Corrective and Social Psychiatry and others. Home: 1621 Red Bud Dr Collinsville IL 62234 Office: 353 N 88th St East Saint Louis IL 62203

GOLDENBERG, RONALD EDWIN, educator; b. Hammond, Ind., Aug. 14, 1931; s. James Abraham and Edna Sarah (Hirsch) G.; B.S., M.S., Washington U., 1956; Ed.D., Okla. State U., 1971; m. Carolyn Sachs, Dec. 25, 1955; children—Mark Robert, Cheryl G. Cardon. Tchr. public schs., Normandy, Mo., 1956-59; prin. elementary sch., University City, Mo., 1963-68; asst. prof. elementary edn. U. Ga., 1970-73, asso. prof., coordinator student teaching, 1973-78; prof., dean Sch. Edn. U. Evansville (Ind.), 1978-80, prof., dean Sch. Grad. Studies, 1980—. Bd. dirs. Raintree Council Girl Scouts Am. Served with U.S. Navy, 1951-55. Mem. Assn. Tchr. Educators, Council Grad. Schs., Assn. Supervision and Curriculum Devel., Am. Assn. Colls. Tchr. Edn., Phi Kappa Phi. Editor Children and Youth, 1978—; mem. adv. bd. Jour. Alternative Higher Edn., 1977—; adv. editor Harcourt-Brace Pub. Co. Contbr. chpts. to books, also articles. Club: Rotary (dir.). Office: PO Box 329 U of Evansville Evansville IN 47702

GOLDENHERSH, JOSEPH HERMAN, chief justice state supreme ct.; b. East St. Louis, Ill., Nov. 2, 1914; s. Benjamin and Bertha (Goldenberg) G.; LL.B., Washington U., St. Louis, 1935; m. Maxyne Zelenka, June 18, 1939; children—Richard, Jerold. Admitted to Ill. bar, 1936; pvt. practice law, East St. Louis, 1936-64; judge Appellate Ct. Ill., 1964-70; justice Supreme Ct. Ill., 1970-78, chief justice, 1979—. Chmn. Initial Gifts United Fund East St. Louis, 1952-53; dir. Mississippi Valley council Boy Scouts Am., 1952-58; pres. Jewish Fedn. So. Ill., 1949-51. Trustee emeritus Christian Welfare Hosp., East St. Louis. Mem. Appellate Judges Conf. (exec. com. 1969-70), East St. Louis (pres. 1962-63), Am., Ill. bar assns. Mason (33 deg., Shriner). Club: Missouri Athletic (St. Louis). Home: 7510 Claymont Ct Belleville IL 62223 Office: 6464 W Main St Suite 3A Belleville IL 62223

GOLDFARB, BERNARD SANFORD, lawyer; b. Cleve., Apr. 15, 1917; s. Harry and Esther (Lenson) G.; A.B., Adelbert Coll., Case Western Res. U., 1938, J.D., 1940; m. Barbara E. Brofman, Jan. 4, 1966; children—Meredith Stacy, Lauren Beth. Admitted to Ohio bar, 1940; practice law, Cleve., 1940—; partner firm Goldfarb & Reznick; spl. counsel to atty. gen. Ohio, 1950, 71-74. Mem. Ohio Commn. for Uniform Traffic Rules, 1973—. Served with USAAF, 1942-45. Mem. Am., Ohio, Cleve. bar assns. Contbr. articles to profl. jours. Home: 39 Pepper Creek Dr Pepper Pike OH 44124 Office: 1800 Illuminating Bldg 55 Public Sq Cleveland OH 44113

GOLDFEDER, HOWARD, dept. store exec.; b. N.Y.C., Apr. 28, 1926; s. Herman and Betty (Epstein) G.; B.A., Tufts U., 1947; m. Helen Wiggs; children—Carole, Joan. From buyer to v.p. and mdse. mgr. Bloomingdale's, N.Y.C., 1947-67; exec. v.p. Famous-Barr, St. Louis, 1967-69; pres. May Co., Los Angeles, 1969-71; pres., then chmn. Bullock's, Los Angeles, 1971-77; vice chmn. Federated Dept. Stores, Inc., Cin., 1977-80, pres., 1980—, chief exec. officer, 1981—, also dir.; dir. Champion Internat. Corp., Conn. Mut. Life Ins. Co. Mem. Bus. Com. for Arts. Recipient Nat. Brotherhood award NCCJ, 1981. Mem. Nat. Retail Mchts. Assn. (dir., exec. com.), Bus. Roundtable. Clubs: Commercial, Queen City, Losantiville Country (Cin.). Office: Federated Dept Stores Inc 7 W 7th St Cincinnati OH 45202

GOLDING, BRAGE, univ. pres.; b. Chgo., Apr. 28, 1920; s. Leon M. and Viola B. (Brage) G.; B.S., Purdue U., 1941, Ph.D., 1948; LL.D., Wright State U., 1975; m. Hinda F. Wolf, Dec. 21, 1941; children—Brage, Susan, Julie. Asso. dir. research Lilly Varnish Co., Indpls., 1948-57, dir. research, 1957-59; research asso. Purdue U., 1948-57, vis. prof. engring., 1957-59, head Sch. Chem. Engring., 1959-66; v.p. Ohio State U. also Miami U., 1966; founding pres. Wright State U., Dayton, Ohio, 1966-72; pres. San Diego State U., 1972-77; pres. Kent (Ohio) State U., 1977—. Cons. to industry. Mem. Am. Chem. Soc., Am. Inst. Chem. Engrs., Soc. Plastic Engrs., Am. Soc. Engring. Edn., AAAS, Phi Beta Kappa. Club: Rotary. Author: Polymers and Resins, 1959; also articles. Home: 1100 E Main St Kent OH 44240

GOLDMAN, HARVEY S., clergyman; b. Malden, Mass., Jan. 15, 1935; s. Samuel A. and Mildred (Wallach) G.; A.B., Boston U., 1961; M.A., Hebrew Union Coll., 1966; D.M., Colgate Rochester Div. Sch., 1977; m. Judith Zimmerman Heiber, Sept. 6, 1981; children—Joel, Steven, Karen, Harlan, Darren, Jordan. Ordained rabbi, 1966; rabbi Main Line Reform Temple, Wynnewood, Pa., 1966-69, Temple Sinai, Rochester, N.Y., 1969-78; sr. rabbi Temple Israel, Columbus, Ohio, 1978—. Mem. Human Rights Adv. Commn., N.Y.; dir. Planned Parenthood, Columbus; mem. adv. com. Nat. Jewish Community; mem. Columbus Jewish Fedn. Bd. Served with USN 1953-57. Mem. Am. Assn. Marriage and Family Therapists, Am. Orthopsychiat. Assn., Am. Assn. Sex Educators, Counselors and Therapists, Central Conf. Am. Rabbis, Columbus Bd. Rabbis. Home: 271 Tallowood Dr Westerville OH 43081 Office: 5419 E Broad St Columbus OH 43213

GOLDMAN, JOSEPH RICHARD, polit. scientist, historian; b. Bogota, Colombia, May 24, 1943; s. Israel and Bina (Brannover) G.; came to U.S., 1946, naturalized, 1951; B.A., U. Minn., 1965, M.A. 1967, Ph.D., 1971; postgrad. U. Kans., 1976. Vis. asst. prof. history U. Minn., Mpls., 1972-74, U. Kans., 1978-79; instr. mil. history U.S. Army Command and Gen. Staff Coll., Ft. Leavenworth, Kans., 1974-76; asst. instr. polit. sci. U. Kans., Lawrence, 1976-78; asst. prof. polit. sci. Miami U., Oxford, Ohio, 1980—; vis. prof. Jewish history Jewish Community Center Mpls., 1973-74; lay tchr. Jewish studies Jewish chapel, Ft. Leavenworth, Kans., 1974-76. McMillan fellow to Austria, U. Minn., 1969. Recipient Distinguished Civil Service award U.S. Civil Service Commn., 1976; named outstanding young man of yr. Kansas City Jaycees, 1977. Mem. Am. Hist. Assn., Am. Polit. Sci. Assn., Midwest Polit. Sci. Assn., So. Polit. Assn. Democrat. Clubs: Kiwanis, B'nai B'rith, Masons, Shriners. Lectr. profl. orgns. Home: 2834 Raleigh Ave S Minneapolis MN 55416 Office: Dept Polit Sci Miami U Oxford OH 45056

GOLDMAN, LINDA GAIL, mfg. co. exec.; b. Cleve., Jan. 21, 1946; d. Kenneth and Suzanne Ellen Water (Bergman) G.; B.A. in Mktg., John Carroll U., Cleve., 1967; m. Jerrold Goldman, May 20, 1977. Feature writer, reporter Fairchild Publs., Inc., Cleve., 1963-67; asst. account exec., copywriter Dix & Eaton, Inc., Cleve., 1967-71; mgr. consumer relations Club Products Co. div. Standex Internat., Cleve., 1971-74; mgr. advt. public relations and sales promotion Hauserman, Inc., Cleve., 1974-77; communications program mgr., mktg. communications group Herman Miller, Inc., Zeeland, Mich., 1977-79, program mgr. market programs group, 1979-80; corp. dir. communications and mgmt. devel. Am. Seating Co., Grand Rapids, Mich., 1980—. Mem. Am. Mktg. Assn., Public Relations Soc. Am. Home: 2885 Lake Dr SE East Grand Rapids MI 49506 Office: 901 Broadway NW Grand Rapids MI 49504

GOLDMAN, RICHARD STUART, indsl. engr.; b. N.Y.C., Dec. 26, 1951; s. Irving Leo and Ruth (Spector) G.; B.S. in Civil Engring., Lowell Tech. Inst., 1973. Nuclear structural engr. Electric Boat div. Gen. Dynamics, Groton, Conn., 1974-75, nuclear refueling engr., 1975-77, Trident constrn. facility engr., supt., 1977-78, mfg. facilities planning, sr. indsl. engr. Convair Aerospace div., San Diego, 1978-80, supr. indsl. engring.; corp. mgr. facilities planning Gen. Dynamics Corp., St. Louis, 1981—; lectr. in field. Mem. ASCE, Nat. Mgmt. Assn. (asst. dir. programs), Nat. Ski Assn. Am. Club: Far West Ski. Office: 7733 Forsyth Suite 1607 Saint Louis MO 63105

GOLDNER, LOUIS B., retail and service co. exec.; b. Akron, Ohio, July 27, 1924; s. Ben and Goldie (Weisman) G.; student U. Akron, 1942, 46. m. Rosalie Baskin, July 18, 1948; children—Gary, Mark, Bruce, Laura Beth. Partner, Sun Formal Wear, Akron, 1950-56; owner, founder Cleveland Tux and parent co. Tuxamerica, Inc., Macedonia, Ohio, 1956—. Served with U.S. Army, 1942-46. Mem. Black Tie Hall Fame, 1975. Mem. Am. Formalwear Assn. (founding pres. 1974). Democrat. Jewish. Club: Masons. Office: 440 E Highland Rd Macedonia OH 44056

GOLDSTEIN, AARON ABRAHAM, clin. social worker, psychotherapist; b. Detroit, June 26, 1936; s. Max and Irene Esther (Walber) G.; B.S. in Bus., Wayne State U., Detroit, 1960; M.S.W., Mich. State U., 1963, Ph.D., 1974; cert. psychoanalytic group psychotherapy Postgrad. Center Mental Health, N.Y.C., 1975; m. Judith Lee Cohen, Apr. 28, 1968; children—Deborah Ruth, Daniel Eli. Part-time dist. dir. Out-County Dist., Family Service Detroit and Wayne County, Livonia, Mich., 1967-75; pvt. practice individual and group psychotherapy, Southfield, Mich., 1968-75; clin. dir., group psychotherapy supr., individual and group psychotherapy Triad Mental Health Services, Birmingham, Mich., 1975—; adv. bd. U. Detroit Sch. Social Work, 1975-81; workshop staff Postgrad. Center Mental Health, 1975—. Cert. social worker, Mich. Mem. Acad. Cert. Social Workers, Am. Orthopsychiat. Assn., Am. Acad. Psychotherapists, Conf. Advancement Pvt. Practice in Social Work, AAAS, Am. Group Psychotherapy Assn. (dir. 1980—), Nat. Assn. Social Workers, Eastern Group Psychotherapy Soc., Mich. Soc. Clin. Social Work, Mich. Group Psychotherapy Soc. Office: 555 S Woodward Suite 614 Birmingham MI 48011

GOLDSTEIN, IRA M(URRAY), retail clothing co. exec.; b. Bklyn., Jan. 24, 1924; s. Joseph J. and Lena (Schneider) G.; student N.Mex. A&M U., 1942; B.A., Bklyn. Coll., 1949; m. Pauline R., Aug. 26, 1961. Asst. buyer S. Klein, N.Y.C., 1948-50, buyer, 1951-79; with Lane Bryant Co., 1951—, gen. mdse. mgr., N.Y.C., 1970-77, gen. mgr. Cleve., Akron, Youngstown and Columbus, Ohio areas, 1977—; mem. exec. com. Bus. Council, Growth Assn. Cleve.; mem. adv. com. Cleve. Schs. Distributive Edn.; mem. Euclid Ave Improvement Com., Cleve. Served with U.S. Army, 1942-46. Decorated Bronze Star. Democrat. Jewish. Office: 696 Euclid Ave Cleveland OH 44140

GOLDSTEIN, NORMAN RAY, distillery exec.; b. Chgo., Nov. 20, 1944; s. Max and Rose (Weiner) G.; A.A., Wright Jr. Coll., 1965; B.S., No. Ill. U., 1967; postgrad. DePaul U., 1968; m. Bonnie Ann Brod, Aug. 31, 1969; children—Russell, Matthew, Jamie. Gen. bus. mgr. Greenstreet Corp., Whiting, Ind., 1967; wholesale credit mgr. Atlantic Richfield Co., Chgo., 1968-74; dir. fin. planning Barton Brands, Ltd., Chgo., 1974—, asst. treas. Barton Distilling Assos., Inc., Chgo., 1979—; dir., pres. IECO Corp., 1971-75; dir., v.p. Consort Corp., 1971-80; dir., pres. Arco Fed. Credit Union, 1973-74. Fellow Nat. Inst. Credit; mem. Distillers, Importers and Vintners Credit Mgmt. Assn. (chmn.), Cash Mgmt. Practitioneers Assn. Chgo., N.Y. Credit and Fin. Mgmt. Assn., Credit Research Found., Nat. Assn. Credit Mgmt., Chgo.-Midwest Credit Mgmt. Assn. Contbr. articles to profl. publs. Office: Suite 1710 55 E Monroe St Chicago IL 60603

GOLDSTEIN, ROBERT VERNON, mfg. co. exec.; b. Omaha, Nebr., Apr. 1, 1937; s. Arthur Harold and Ruth Marie (Cohen) G.; B.A. magna cum laude, Harvard U., 1959; postgrad. U. Chgo. Grad. Sch. Bus., 1959-61; m. Nancy Sue Barron, June 29, 1958; children—Lawrence J., Blaine H., Jeffrey I. With Procter and Gamble Co., Cin., 1961—, project mgr. spl. products, 1977, gen. advt. mgr., 1979, v.p. advt., 1979—. Vice-pres. Jewish Fedn. Cin., 1979—; pres. No. Hill Synagogue, 1971-72, 74-75; dir. Jewish Community Center, 1963—. Mem. Nat. Assn. Advertisers (bd. dirs.), Advt. Council (dir.), Harvard U. Alumni Assn., U. Chgo. Alumni Assn. Club: Queen City. Office: PO Box 599 Cincinnati OH 45202

GOLDSTONE, SIDNEY RICHARD, physician, surgeon; b. Rock Island, Ill., Nov. 28, 1924; s. Morris and Fannie (Borenstein) G.; B.S., U. Ill., 1945; M.D. with honors, 1947; m. Muriel Glabman, Dec. 22, 1946; children—James R., Rande Goldstone Shapiro, Meri Ellen. Intern, Cook County Hosp., Chgo., 1948, preceptor in surgery, 1948-50; pvt. practice surgery, Gary, Ind., 1952—; chief of surgery MacDill USAF Hosp., Tampa, Fla., 1950-52; pres. Physicians and Surgeons Liability Ins. Co., Munster, Ind., 1976—. Pres. Civil Aviation Med. Examiners; commr. Gary Airport bd., 1964-70, pres., 1966-67. Served with AUS, 1944-46, to capt. USAF, 1950-52. Diplomate Am. Acad. Family Practice. Fellow Am. Geriat. Soc.; mem. Flying Physicians Assn. (dir. 1974, v.p. 1978-79), Am. Soc. Abdominal Surgeons, Aerospace, Civil Aviation (pres. 1977-78) med. socs. Clubs: Masons, Shriners. Home: 9129 Elmwood Dr Munster IN 46321 Office: 535 W 35th Ave Gary IN 46408

GOLICZ, LAWRENCE JOHN, appraisal corp. exec.; b. Detroit, Feb. 21, 1944; s. Anthony John and Estelle Ann (Rogowski) G.; B.A., (Regents scholar), U. Mich., 1966; M.A. (teaching asst.), Wash. State U., 1968; Ph.D. (teaching asst., scholar), U. Maine, 1973; spl. student U. Wis., 1970-72; m. Peggy L. Erickson, Aug. 3, 1968; children—Eric John, Karl Peter, Mark Joseph. Pres., Am. Appraisal Feasibility Corp., Madison, Wis., 1973—; tchr. real estate Madison Area Tech. Coll., part-time 1976-80; instr. Soc. Real Estate Appraisers, 1980—; pres. Total Realty, Inc., Madison, 1974—; partner Madison Mut. Investors, 1979—. Social Sci. Research Council grantee, 1970-71. Mem. Soc. Real Estate Appraisers (pres. Madison chpt.), Am. Inst. Real Estate Appraisers (nat. sch. outreach com.), Madison Bd. Realtors, Internat. Assn. Assessing Officers, Internat. Order Foresters (trustee local chpt.). Home: 1619 Elderwood Circle Middleton WI 53562 Office: 6510 Schroeder Rd Madison WI 53711

GOLICZ, PEGGY LOUISE, real estate appraiser; b. Washington, May 21, 1946; d. Ernest P. and Alicia A. (Peter) Erickson; student Wash. State U., Pullman, 1968; m. Lawrence J. Golicz, Aug. 3, 1968; children—Eric John, Karl Peter, Mark Joseph. Various secretarial and adminstrv. asst. positions, 1968-74; engaged in real estate, 1974—; broker, v.p. property mgmt., dir. Total Realty, Inc., Madison, 1978—; v.p. Am. Appraisal & Feasibility Corp., Madison, 1978—, also dir.; cons. in field. Cert. assessor II, Wis. Mem. Nat. Center Housing Mgmt., Inst. Real Estate Mgmt., Soc. Real Estate Appraisers (asso.), Nat. Assn. Realtors, Greater Madison Bd. Realtors, Am. Inst. Real Estate Appraisers, Nat. Assn. Female Execs., Westmoreland Youth Hockey Assn., Alpha Phi, Alpha Sigma Epsilon. Clubs: Order Eastern Star, Order Forresters. Author papers in field. Home: 1619 Elderwood Circle Middleton WI 53562 Office: 6510 Schroder Rd Madison WI 53711

GOLIN, MILTON, writer, pub., editor; b. Oak Park, Ill., Apr. 2, 1921; s. Joseph and Rose (Stein) G.; student Wright City Coll., 1939-41, Central YMCA Coll. (now Roosevelt U.), 1941-42; m. Carol Florence Thurnau, Dec. 12, 1975; 1 son, James Milton. Founding radio-TV news editor City News Bur. Chgo., 1949-56; asst. editor Jour. AMA, 1956-59; founding editor Medicine at Work, 1956-67; asst. to pres. Pharm. Mfrs. Assn., Washington, 1960-67; founding editor Ob-Gyn News, Pediatric News, Diagnosis News, Washington, 1966-67, Med. Group News, Adolescent Medicine, CME Today and Surgery Update, Chgo., 1968—; tchr. creative writing; speaker, cons. in field. Co-founder Park Forest (Ill.) Civic Music Assn., 1951, dir. public relations, 1953-56. Served to 1st lt. USAAF, 1942-46. Decorated Air medal with four oak leaf clusters; recipient citation for starting nation's first met. area broadcast news service Editor & Pub., 1954. Mem. Assn. Sci. Writers, AAAS, Am. Med. Writers Assn. Sigma Delta Chi. Republican. Presbyterian. Clubs: Nat. Press, Chgo. Press, M.W. Pharm. Advt. Contbr. numerous articles to mass-circulation mags. Home: 490 Hazel Ave Glencoe IL 60022 Office: PO Box 36 Glencoe IL 60022

GOLLINGS, ROBERT HARRY, data processing cons.; b. Pitts., July 4, 1931; s. Chester Lyman and Lorena Elizabeth (Grady) G.; B.B.A., U. Pitts., 1953, M.B.A., 1961; postgrad. U. Ill., Chgo., 1979-80; m. Marilyn Campbell, Sept. 19, 1959 (dec. Apr. 1981); children—Anne, Graham. Systems analyst Westinghouse Electric Corp., Pitts., 1956-65; supr. systems and programming Joy Mfg. Co., Pitts. and Michigan City, Ind., 1965-67; project mgr. Standard Oil Co. (Ind.), 1967-75; project mgr., lead anlayst G.D. Searle & Co., Skokie, Ill., 1975-78; sr. mgr. Comsi, Inc., Oak Brook, Ill., 1978-79; coordinator mgmt. systems U. Ill., Chgo., 1979-80; data processing cons., owner RHG Systems, 1981—. Chmn., Parks and Recreation Bd., Park Forest, Ill., 1978—; bd. dirs. Community Chest, Park Forest-Richton Park, 1973—, pres., 1975; bd. dirs. South Suburban Symphony, 1975-78, Park Forest Symphony, 1978—. Served to 1st lt. USAF, 1953-56; Korea. Mem. Assn. Systems Mgmt. Republican. Presbyterian. Club: Chgo. Bus. Sch. Alumni Club of U. Pitts. (sec.). Office: 22335 Governors Hwy Richton Park IL 60671

GOLOFF, ALEXANDER ALEXANDROVICH, JR., agrl. research adminstr., agronomist; b. Peoria, Ill., Aug. 16, 1943; s. Alex and Ruth (Scherff) A.; B.S. in Botany, U. Ill., 1966, M.S. in Plant Ecology, 1972, Ph.D., 1973; m. Caren Collver, June 28, 1970. Teaching asst. dept. botany U. Ill., Urbana-Champaign, 1969-74; plant physiologist corp. research dept. Union Carbide Corp., Tarrytown, N.Y., 1974-80, mgr. research programs, 1975-80; mgr. seed div. quality assurance research Cargill, Inc., Aurora, Ill., 1980—; cons. Keystone Seed Co., Hollister, Calif. and Twin Falls, Idaho, 1975-79. Served to lt. USN, 1966-68; Vietnam. Mem. Am. Soc. Agronomy, Crop Sci. Soc. Am., Soil Sci. Soc. Am., Am. Soc. Plant Physiologists, Soc. Comml. Seed Technologists, Assn. Ofcl. Seed Analysists, Internat. Seed Testing Assn., AAAS, N.Y. Acad. Scis. Home: 43 W 835 Oakwood Dr Elburn IL 60119 Office: Cargill Seed Research Station PO Box 470 Aurora IL 60507

GOMETZ, MODESTO SALVADOR, physician; b. Ypacarai, Paraguay, June 15, 1937; came to U.S., 1968, naturalized, 1980; s. Florentin and Isidora (Villalba) G.; B.S., Nat. Sch. Commerce, Paraguay, 1951-54; B.S., Nat. Coll., Paraguay, 1957; M.D., Nat. U., Paraguay, 1963; m. Nilda Dora Aranda, Sept. 21, 1967; children—Eric Alexander, Edward Daniel. Intern, National U., Paraguay, 1964; resident in pediatrics Univ. Hosp., Paraguay, 1965-66, chief Premature Ward, 1967-68; intern Norwalk (Conn.) Hosp., 1968-69; resident in pediatrics Kans. U. Med. Center, 1969-71; staff physician Parsons State Hosp. and Tng. Center, 1971-72, dir. Child Devel. Services, 1972-75, clin. dir., 1972-74; research asso. U. Kans., Lawrence, 1972; adj. prof. psychology, counselor edn. Pittsburg (Kans.) State U., 1973-76; pvt. practice medicine specializing in pediatrics, Pittsburg, Kans., 1975—; asso. in pediatrics Kans. U. Med. Center, 1973—; clin. asst. prof. pediatrics U. Kans. Med. Sch., Wichita, 1977—. Diplomate Am. Bd. Pediatrics. Fellow Am. Acad. Pediatrics, Internat. Coll. Pediatrics; mem. AMA, Kans. Med. Assn., Crawford County Med. Soc., Am. Assn. Mental Deficiency. Clubs: Crestwood Country, Pittsburg Rotary. Home: 2607 California St Pittsburg KS 66762 Office: 909 E Centennial St Pittsburg KS 66762

GOMEZ, FELIX, restauranteur; b. Mexico, Aug. 28, 1928; s. Pablo and Mariana (Magdaleno) G.; came to U.S., 1951, naturalized, 1978; student Acapulco schs.; m. Miquelina Cosme, Feb. 28, 1954; children—Maria, Esther, Debra, Teresa, Felix. Bus boy El Mirador Hotel, Acapulco, 1945-47, office boy, 1947, bell boy, 1945-53; with Superior Concrete, 1953; waiter Americana Hotel, 1953-62, Holiday Inn, 1962-66, Chgo. Club and Armandos, 1962-69; owner Mi Casa Su Casa Restaurant, Chgo., 1969—, also pres. Mem. Liquor Assn., Chefs of Ill., Chgo. Exec. Club. Club: Lions (sec., dir., Mem. of Year 1970). Home and Office: 2524 N Southport Ave Chicago IL 60618

GOMMEL, JACQUELINE JAYNE, interior designer; b. DeKalb, Ill., Nov. 5, 1952; d. William Karl and Martha Ann (Montgomery) G.; B.F.A. magna cum laude (Yale R. Burge Meml. scholar), No. Ill. U., DeKalb, 1975. Designer, McLane and McLane Architects, Dixon, Ill., 1974-75; freelance designer, 1975-76; dir. interiors C. Edward Ware Assos. Inc., Architects, Rockford, Ill., 1976—. Mem. Am. Soc. Interior Designers (profl.), Phi Kappa Phi. Methodist. Home: 806 N Court St Apt 207 Rockford IL 61103 Office: 415 Y Blvd Rockford IL 61107

GOMMERMANN, ANDREAS, educator; b. Mucsi, Hungary, Oct. 20, 1928; came to U.S., 1965, naturalized, 1970; s. Sebastian and Eva (Fadl) G.; student Coll. St. Georgen, Frankfurt/Main, W. Ger., diploma postal adminstrn., 1954; M.A., Marquette U., Milw., 1967; Ph.D. (Regent's fellow 1969), U. Nebr., Lincoln, 1975; m. Dora Maercz, Apr. 7, 1955; children—Richard, Norbert. Asso. personnel dir. Fed. Republic Ger., Wiesbaden, 1954-65; mem. faculty Creighton U., Omaha, 1967—, asso. prof. German, 1978—, chmn. dept. modern langs., 1976-77, coordinator modern langs., 1977—. Mem. Am. Assn. Tchrs. German, MLA, Soc. German-Am. Studies, Nebr. Fgn. Lang. Assn., Delta Phi Alpha. Roman Catholic. Author articles on history and lang. of German immigrants from Hungary to Milw. Home: 9922 Orchard St Omaha NE 68127 Office: 2500 California St Omaha NE 68178

GOMOS, PETER D., physician; b. Tubod, Lanao del Norte, Philippines, June 29, 1942; came to U.S., 1966; s. Modesto B. and Apolonia S. (Dimpas) G.; A.A., Cebu Inst. Tech., 1961, M.D., 1966; m. Anecita G. Bacus, Sept. 7, 1968; children—Julie, Peter B., Janette. Rotating intern St. John's Episcopal Hosp., Bklyn., 1967; resident in gen. practice Warren Hosp., Phillipsburg, N.J., 1968, Norwegian Am. Hosp., Chgo., 1968-69; resident in surgery St. Alexis Hosp., Cleve., 1969-73; practice medicine specializing in gen. surgery, Cleve. and Euclid, Ohio, 1973—; mem. active staff St. Alexis Hosp., Euclid Gen. Hosp.; cons. to industry. Diplomate Am. Bd. Surgery. Fellow Internat. Coll. Surgeons, A.C.S., AMA, Ohio Med. Assn., Cleve. Acad. Medicine, Cleve. Surg. Soc., Philippine Am. Soc. Ohio, Assn. Philippine Practicing Physicians in Am. Home: 760 Coy Ln Russel Twp OH 44022 Office: 25701 N Lakeland Blvd Euclid OH 44132 also 2808 Clark Ave Cleveland OH 44109

GONDA, GREGORY JOSEPH, data communications corp. exec.; b. Joliet, Ill., Oct. 6, 1951; s. Aloys A. and Beverly J. (Gualdoni) G.; A.A., N.Mex. State U., 1974; Asso. Sci., Parkland Coll., 1976; B.S., U. Ill., 1978; m. Christine Lynn Vickrey, June 2, 1979. Owner, New Lenox Tax Service (Ill.), 1970; tax cons. H & R Block Co., Bloomington, Ill., 1971; computer operator Colwell Co., Champaign, Ill., 1976-77; fin. officer Synervest Corp., Monticello, Ill., 1978-79; chief acctg. officer, treas. Compre Comm, Inc., Champaign, 1980—; tax, acctg. cons., 1970—. Served with USAF, 1972-75. Republican. Club: Rotary. Office: Compre Comm Inc 3200 Farber Dr Champaign IL 61821

GONG, MERY LEE, data processor; b. Cleve., June 14, 1931; d. Wing and Shee (Woo) Gong; B.S., Ohio State U., 1954. With Ohio State U. Instruction and Research Computer Center, Columbus, 1954—, computer operator, 1954-56, programmer, cons., 1956-61, ops. supr., 1961-65, adminstrv. asst., 1965-72, asst. dir., 1972-80, asso. dir., 1980—. Computer cons. Cole-Layer-Trumble Co.; instr. Ohio State U. continuing edn. Children's Hosp., Columbus, 1969. Mem. Ohio Commn. on Status of Women. Mem. Am. Mgmt. Assn., Assn. Computing Machinery, Data Processing Mgmt. Assn., Air Force Assn., Assn. Systems Mgmt., Ohio State U. Alumni Assn., Northwest Area Council for Human Relations, LWV, Upper Arlington Civic Assn., Columbus Area Civil Rights Council. Club: Quota (Columbus). Home: 1776 Ridgecliff Rd Columbus OH 43221 Office: 1971 Neil Ave Columbus OH 43210

GONZALEZ, DIANE KATHRYN, social worker; b. Cin., Aug. 20, 1947; d. Joseph Curtis and Kathryn Mary (Diskin) Gonzalez; B.A. in Social Work, U. Dayton, 1969; A.M. in Social Work, U. Chgo., 1973; m. Thomas Connolley Leibig, July 5, 1974; 1 dau., Abigail. Social worker Hamilton County Welfare Dept., Cin., 1969-71; social worker obstetrics dept. and prenatal clinic social service dept. St. Francis Hosp., Evanston, Ill., 1973-78; rap group leader Teen Scene, Planned Parenthood Assn., Chgo., part-time, 1979-80; social worker Chgo. Comprehensive Care Center, 1980—; chmn. adv. com. Evanston Continuing Edn. Center, 1978-80. Cert. social worker, Ill. Mem. Nat. Assn. Social Workers, Acad. Cert. Social Workers. Roman Catholic. Home: 218 W Menomonee St Chicago IL 60614 Office: Chgo Comprehensive Care Center 3639 S Michigan Ave Chicago IL 60653

GONZÁLEZ, JOSÉ GAMALIEL, muralist; b. Iturbide, Mex., Apr. 20, 1933; came to U.S., 1938, naturalized, 1955; s. Gamaliel and Conception F.; B.F.A. (Milward and Florence James Adams scholar, Art Students League scholar), Sch. Art Inst. Chgo., 1970; postgrad. (art grad. scholar) U. Notre Dame, 1970-71; m. Mary Kay Vaughan, June 25, 1977; 1 dau., Luz Alicia. Art prodn. dir. A.J. Rosenthal, Chgo., 1966-67; chmn. Movimiento Artistico Chicano, Chgo., 1976-77, dir., 1978; art dir. Revista Chicano Riquena, Ind. U. N.W., Gary, 1973-80; regional coordinator Great Lakes, Hispanic Task Force, NEA, 1978-80; mem. visual panel Ill. Arts Council, 1977, ethnic panel, 1978, multimedia panel, 1979; mem. Hispanic art adv. com. Mus. Sci. and Industry, Chgo., 1974-78; tchr. Elmhurst Coll. Extension, 1978-80; cons. Canto Cultural, WTTW-TV, 1977; contbg. curator Raices y Visiones, 1977-79; guest curator Mus. Contemporary Art, Chgo., 1979. Served with AUS, 1953-55. Mem. Facets Multi Media. Roman Catholic. Work pub. in: Chicago Murals: Yesterday and Today, 1978. Home and Office: 567 W 18th St Chicago IL 60616

GONZALEZ-MENOCAL, PABLO, hosp. adminstr.; b. Havana, Cuba, May 7, 1939; s. Eulogio Fernando and Maria Josefa (Menocal) Gonzalez; came to U.S., 1957, naturalized, 1972; B. Indsl. Engring., Ga. Inst. Tech., 1963; postgrad. U. Mich., 1968; m. Ilse Ursula Steinbrecher, June 9, 1960; children—Sylvia Maria, Evelyn Ruth, Helen Louise. Materials handling engr. Constrn. Machinery div. Allis Chalmers, Springfield, Ill., 1963-66, Consol. Packaging Corp., Monroe, Mich., 1967-68; mng. dir. Community Systems Found., cons., Ann Arbor, Mich., 1968-72; v.p. Community Mgmt. Service, Denver, 1972-73; cons. Chi Systems Inc., Ann Arbor, 1973-76; dir. corp. planning Health and Hosp. Corp. of Marion County, Indpls., 1976-79; asso. D.J. Sullivan and Assos., cons., Ann Arbor, Mich., 1979-81; asso. adminstr. Hillcrest Hosp., Mayfield Heights, Ohio, 1981—; instr. Iowa Western Community Coll., Council Bluffs, 1973; lectr. in field. Trustee, End Measles, Inc.; mem. com. health and welfare Urban League; vol. emergency med. technician; vol. CPR instr. Am. Heart Assn. Recipient Key Man award Springfield Jaycees, 1965, Spoke award, 1966. Fellow Royal Soc. Health; mem. Am. Inst. Indsl. Engrs. (sr.), Am. Hosp. Assn. Contbr. articles to nat. and internat. profl. jours. Office: 6780 Mayfield Rd Mayfield Heights OH 44124

GOO, ABRAHAM MEU SEN, aircraft co. exec.; b. Honolulu, May 21, 1925; s. Tai Chong and Lily E.W. (Dai) G.; B.S.E.E., U. Ill., 1951; postgrad. M.I.T., 1975; m. Shin Quon Wong, June 12, 1950; children—Marilynn, Steven, Beverly. With Boeing Co., 1951—, chief engr. B-1 Avionics, 1972-74, program mgr. B-1 Avionics, 1975-77, v.p., gen. mgr. aircraft armament div., 1977, v.p. mil. systems Boeing Wichita Co., 1977-79, exec. v.p. Boeing Mil. Airplane Co., Wichita, 1979—. Served with USAAF, 1946-47. Mem. Assn. Unmanned Vehicle Systems (hon. trustee), Air Force Assn., Am. Security Council, Am. Def. Preparedness Assn., Assn. Armed Forces Communications and Electronics, Airlift Assn., IEEE, AIAA, Nat. Aero. Assn., Army Aviation Assn. Home: 1507 Blue Sage Circle Wichita KS 67230 Office: 3801 S Oliver St Wichita KS 67210

GOOCH, DONALD BURNETTE, artist, educator; b. Bloomingdale, Mich., Oct. 17, 1907; s. Milford Henry and Nina Pearl (Burnette) G.; student Western Mich. U., 1923-25; B.S., U. Mich., 1935, M. Design, 1939; postgrad. Am. Sch. Painting (France), 1937; m. Marjorie Gilchrist, June 26, 1937; children—Nancy Jane, Peter Gilchrist. Tchr. pub. schs., Bloomingdale, 1925-27; instr. Detroit Sch. Lettering, 1928-32; instr. Detroit Art Acad., 1933-35; art tchr. pub. schs., Washington, 1936; instr. U. Mich., Ann Arbor, 1936-45, asst. prof., 1945-52, asso. prof., 1952-59, prof. design, 1959-73, prof. emeritus, 1974—. Advt. design cons.; exhibited paintings Detroit Inst. Arts, 1936-48, San Francisco Cow Palace, 1940, Am. Fedn. Arts, 1941, Pepsi Cola Paintings of Year, 1947, Pa. Acad., 1947. Recipient Alumni prize Am. Acad. Rome, 1935; Founders prize Detroit Inst. Arts, 1947. Horace H. Rackham grantee, 1960, 65. Mem. Mich. Watercolor Soc., Mich. Acad. Arts, Sci. and Letters, Internat. Inst. Arts and Letters, Nat. Soc. Lit. and Arts, Phi Kappa Phi, Alpha Rho Chi, Tau Sigma Delta. Editor: American Taste in Advertising, 1956; Search for Certainty in Advertising, 1959; Theatre and Main Street, 1964; Research in Pictographic Communication for Non-Literates in Nepal, 1961, 67. Address: 1633 Laird St Ann Arbor MI 48105

GOOD, LINDA LOU, educator; b. Zanesville, Ohio, May 30, 1941; d. John Robert and Alice Laura (Fulkerson) Moore; B.S. in Elem. Edn., Ohio U., 1964; m. Larry Alvin Good, Jan. 11, 1964; children—Jason (dec.), Alicia and Tricia (twins), Amy Jo. Tchr., West Muskingum Sch. Dist., 1962-64; first grade tchr., Bellevue, Ohio, 1964-68, 2d grade tchr., Zanesville Sch. System, 1970—. Co-chmn. Zane Trace Commemoration. Mem. NEA, Ohio Edn. Assn., Zanesville Edn. Assn., Eastern Ohio Tchrs. Assn. Methodist.

GOOD, MARY LOWE (MRS. BILLY JEWEL GOOD), business exec.; b. Grapevine, Tex., June 20, 1931; d. John W. and Winnie (Mercer) Lowe; B.S., Ark. State Tchrs. Coll., 1950; M.S., U. Ark., 1953, Ph.D., 1955, LL.D. (hon.), 1979; m. Billy Jewel Good, May 17, 1952; children—Billy, James. Instr., Ark. State Tchrs. Coll., Conway, summer 1949; instr. La. State U., Baton Rouge, 1954-56, asst. prof., 1956-58, asso. prof., New Orleans, 1958-63, prof., 1963-80, Boyd prof. materials sci., div. engring. research, Baton Rouge, 1979-80; v.p., dir. research UOP, Inc. Des Plaines, Ill., 1980—; chmn. Pres.'s Com. for Nat. Medal Sci., 1979—; mem. Nat. Sci. Bd., 1980—. Bd. dirs. Oak Ridge Asso. Univs. Recipient Agnes Faye Morgan research award, 1969; Distinguished Alumni citation U. Ark., 1973. AEC tng. grantee, 1967; NSF internat. travel grantee, 1968; NSF research grantee, 1969—. Fellow Am. Inst. Chemistry, Chem. Soc. London; mem. Am. Chem. Soc. (1st woman dir. 1971-74, regional dir. 1972—, chmn. bd. 1978—, Garvan medal 1973, Herty medal, 1975, award Fla. sect. 1979), Phi Beta Kappa, Sigma Xi, Iota Sigma Pi (regional dir. 1967—). Club: Zonta (past pres. New Orleans club, chmn. dist. status of women com. and nominating com.; chmn. internat. Amelia Earhart scholarship com.). Contbr. articles to profl. jours. Home: 295 Park Dr Palatine IL 60067 Office: UOP Inc Ten UOP Plaza Des Plaines IL 60016

GOOD, MILTON BILLINGS, neurologist; b. Berwyn, Ill., Mar. 12, 1939; s. Henry Harmon and Mildred Gertrude (Billings) G.; B.S. in Chemistry, Bowling Green (Ohio) State U., 1961; M.D.Ind. U., 1965; m. Donna Marie DeWitz, Nov. 30, 1963; children—Jean Marie, Karen Lynn, Amy Beth. Intern, Bronson Methodist Hosp., Kalamazoo, 1965-66; resident in neurology Cleve. Clinic, 1966-69, mem. neurology staff, 1969-74; practice medicine specializing in neurology, Rocky River, Ohio, 1974—; mem. staff Fairview Gen. Hosp., Cleve., Lakewood (Ohio) Hosp. Served to capt., M.C., USAR, 1966-72. Diplomate Am. Bd. Psychiatry and Neurology. Mem. AMA, Am. Acad. Neurology, Am. Epilepsy Soc., Am. EEG Soc. Lutheran. Home: 20638 Morewood Pkwy Rocky River OH 44116 Office: 18099 Lorain Ave Cleveland OH 44111

GOOD, ROY SHELDON, fin. exec.; b. Cleve., Dec. 13, 1924; s. Julius and Sally (Sharpe) G.; B.B.A., Western Res. U., 1948, M.B.A., 1951; children—Jeri Good Rollin, Michael. Mgr. tax dept. Touche, Ross & Co., 1952-61; asst. controller Am. Motors Corp., 1961-68; mgr. employee benefits financial adminstrn. Chrysler Corp., Detroit, 1968-77, mgr. investment rev., 1977-78, mgr. investment rev. and spl. financing, 1978-80; v.p. Alexander & Alexander of Mich., Inc., 1981—; lectr., author employee benefits and pension fund investment mgmt., 1970—. Served with AUS, 1943-46; ETO. C.P.A., Mich., Ohio. Mem. Am. Inst. C.P.A.'s, Mich. Assn. C.P.A.'s, Midwest Pension Conf., Beta Alpha Psi. Republican. Jewish. Clubs: Beverly Hills Racquet. Home: 24435 Evergreen Rd Southfield MI 48075 Office: 600 Fisher Bldg Detroit MI 48202

GOOD, SHELDON FRED, realtor; b. Chgo., June 4, 1933; s. Joseph and Sylvia (Schwartz) G.; student Drake U., 1951; B.B.A., U. Ill., 1955; m. Lois Kroll; children—Steven, Todd. Sales mgr. Baird & Warner Real Estate, Chgo., 1957-65; pres. Sheldon F. Good & Co. Realtors, Chgo., 1965—; guest lectr. Northwestern U., U. Chgo., U. Calif., Wharton Grad. Sch., U. Pa., Vanderbilt U., U. Ill.; staff instr. Central YMCA City Coll., Chgo.; cons. in field. Chmn. real estate divs. Chgo. Crusade Mercy, United Settlement Appeal, Chgo., YMCA Edn. Library Drive, Chgo., Chgo. Jewish United Fund. Bd. dirs. Child, Inc.; pres. Gastrointestinal Research Found., U. Chgo., 1979. Served with AUS, 1955-57. Recipient Levi Eshkol Premier medal State Israel, 1967, Crown of A Good Name award Jewish Nat. Fund, 1972; named one of 10 outstanding young men Chgo., 1968. Mem. Chgo. Real Estate Bd., Nat. Assn. Real Estate Bds., Chgo. Better Bus. Bur., Chgo. Assn. Commerce and Industry, Alpha Epsilon Pi, Lambda Alpha, Omega Tau Rho. Author: How to Sell Apartment Buildings; Techniques of Investment Property Exchanging; How to Lease Suburban Office Buildings; The Real Estate Auction as a Marketing Tool. Home: 180 E Pearson St Chicago IL 60611 Office: 11 N Wacker Dr Chicago IL 60606

GOODEN, KENNETH EUGENE, ch. ofcl.; b. Wichita, Kans., Feb. 26, 1939; s. Clyde O. and Dorothy (Frazier) G.; grad. Miltonvalle Wesleyan Coll., 1959; B.A., Friends U., 1961; B.D., Asbury Theol. Sem., 1964, Th.M., 1965; postgrad. U. Chgo., 1969, U. Ky., 1971-73; m. Verna L. Campbell, June 24, 1961; children—Beth Eugenia, Brian Keith. Ordained to ministry, Wesleyan Ch., 1966; pastor Belleville (Kans.) Wesleyan Ch., 1965-68; ordained elder Wesleyan Ch. in Kans. Dist., 1966; instr. religion Miltonvale Wesleyan Coll., 1966-68, Marion Coll., 1968-70; dir. Wesleyan Sem. Found., Wilmore, Ky., 1970-77; lectr. Wesleyan history Asbury Theol. Sem., Wilmore, 1972-77; exec. dir. Coop. Ministries of the John Wesley Sem. Found. and Wesleyan Sem. Found., Wilmore, 1973-74; gen. dir. estate planning Wesleyan Ch., Marion, Ind., 1977—; cons. Nat. Cons. on Fin. Devel., 1981—. Recipient Spl. Jr. C. of C. Threshold award, 1975. Mem. Nat. Soc. Fund Raising Execs., Central Ind. Council Fund Raising Execs. Club: Rotary. Contbr. articles to profl. jours.

GOODHART, ROBERT EDWARD, mfg. co. exec.; b. Phila., Aug. 11, 1942; s. Arthur Aaron and Mary Hale (Long) G.; B.S., Rider Coll., 1964; m. Elizabeth Catherine Stendardo, Aug. 13, 1966; children—Gregory Thomas, Denise Anne. Sales trainee Westvaco Corp., N.Y.C., 1965-66; sales rep. Eastman Kodak Co., Balt., 1966-69; partner Micro Records Corp., Balt., 1969-72; sales rep. Borroughs div. Lear Siegler Corp., Balt., 1972-73, nat. sales mgr., Kalamazoo, 1973-75; gen. sales mgr. Perma Steel Co., Bklyn., 1975-77; regional sales mgr. Reflector Hardware Corp., N.Y.C., 1977-79, nat. sales mgr., Melrose Park, Ill., 1979—. Area capt. United Fund, Balt., 1969. Mem. Rider Coll. Alumni Assn. (chmn. Balt. 1969-71), Nat. Assn. Store Fixture Mfrs., Inst. Store Planners. Republican. Mem. Ch. of Brethren. Home: 845 Proud Clairon Ct Naperville IL 60540 Office: 1400 N 25th Ave Melrose Park IL 60160

GOODHUE, JACKSON LYLE, petroleum co. exec.; b. Riverton, N.J., Mar. 31, 1935; s. Lyle David and Helen Elizabeth (Hamaker) G.; B.A., Wesleyan U., Middletown, Conn., 1957; m. Jane Shelton, June 29, 1957; children—Christine, Cynthia, Michael. Coordinator service sta. investment and devel. EXXON U.S.A., Boston, 1963-64, asst. dist. mgr., 1964-66, sect. head, economic analysis, Balt., 1966-67, economic and bus. analysis mgr., 1967-69, sr. planning specialist, corp. planning, Houston, 1969-71, mktg. advisor, 1971-74, ops. coordinator wholesale fuels, 1975; gen. sales mgr. Ecol Ltd., Houston, 1975-76; reseller sales mgr. wholesale mktg. Marathon Oil Co., Findlay, Ohio, 1977—; v.p., dir. Stewart Oil Co.; Webster Service Stations, Inc.; Pilot Oil Corp. Mem. Am. Petroleum Inst., Am. Mktg. Assn., Am. Mgmt. Assn., Soc. Ind. Gasoline Marketers, Nat. Petroleum Refiners Assn., Nat. Oil Jobbers Council. Republican. Methodist (mem. adminstrv. bd. 1960-63, 76-77, chmn. 1963). Office: 539 S Main St Findlay OH 45840

GOODKIN, HELEN FAIRBANK, rehab. specialist; b. Chgo., Mar. 6, 1945; d. John Young and Laverne L. (Dulfer) Fairbank; A.B., Bryn Mawr Coll., 1967; postgrad. Grad. Sch. Bus., U. Chgo., 1969; m. Michael Goodkin, Oct. 1, 1971; children—Graham Laird, Nathalie Fairbank. Securities analyst Continental Ill. Nat. Bank, 1968-72; membership coordinator Better Govt. Assn., 1972-73; dir. Access Chgo., Rehab. Inst. Chgo., 1973-74; prin. Helen F. Goodkin & Assos., 1975—; spl. asst. on disabled Chgo. Transit Authority, 1980—; mem. Ill. Gov.'s Com. Employment of Handicapped, 1974-75; cons. White House Conf. on Handicapped Individuals, 1976-77; mem. transp. com. Mayor's Office for Senior Citizens and Handicapped, Chgo., 1978; mem. arts and edn. com. Chgo. Planning Council on Aging and Rehab., 1978. Bd. dirs. Chgo. Area Project, 1969-71, asst. treas., 1971; bd. dirs. Rec. for the Blind, 1980—; co-chmn. Sculpture in the Park, Art Inst. Chgo., 1974, mem. libraries com., 1977, chmn. Burham Library subcom., 1978; mem. resources com. Bryn Mawr Coll., 1977. Mem. Chgo. Soc. Composers (trustee 1978—). Episcopalian. Clubs: Friday, Racquet, Casino. Author: A Guide to Community Action for the Handicapped, 1976; Eliminating Transportation Barriers, 1976; co-author: Environmental Aspects of Rehabilitation, 1979; editor: Access Chicago: A Guide to the City, 1973; Architect's and Designer's Handbook of Banier-Free Design, 1974. Office: 537 W Arlington Pl Chicago IL 60614

GOODKIN, MICHAEL, pub. co. exec.; b. N.Y.C., June 10, 1941; s. Harold and Rose (Mostkoff) G.; B.A., Harvard U., 1963; postgrad. U. Chgo. Bus. Sch., 1964; m. Helen Graham Fairbank, Oct. 1, 1971; children—Graham Laird, Nathalie Fairbank. Trainee, Random House, 1964-65; asst. dir. Simulmatics, N.Y.C., 1966-67; account exec. World Book Enterprises, Inc., Chgo., 1967-70, research dir., 1970-73, v.p. mktg., 1973-76, v.p., gen. mgr. mail order div., 1976—, pres. World Book Ency. Inc., 1979—, exec. v.p. World Book Childcraft Internat., 1979—. Trustee Art Inst. Chgo., 1975—, pres. aux. bd., 1975-77; bd. dirs. Chgo. Area Project. Served with Army N.G., 1963-69. Mem. Direct Mail Advt. Assn., Modern Poetry Assn. (trustee). Clubs: Racquet, Casino, Harvard (N.Y.C.); Harvard (Boston). Office: Room 446 Merchandise Mart Plaza Chicago IL 60654

GOODMAN, CHUCK W., state senator, retail exec.; b. Mpls., Dec. 29, 1927; s. Dewey and Lydia (Weber) G.; B.A., U. N.D., 1949; m. Avonne Skarsbo, June 12, 1948; children—Vicki, Dan, Douglas. Farmer; pres. Goodman's Home Furnishings, Grand Forks, N.D., Goodman's of Grafton (N.D.); mem. N.D. Senate, 1972—; dir. Community Nat. Bank, Med. Park Corp. Bd. dirs. N.D. Diabetes Assn. Served with U.S. Army, 1946-47. Recipient Community Leadership award, 1981; Boss of Yr. award, 1967. Mem. N.D. Retail Assn. (pres. 1971). Republican. Lutheran. Club: Elks. Office: 1605 S Washington St Grand Forks ND 58201*

GOODMAN, DONALD JOSEPH, dentist; b. Cleve., Aug. 14, 1922; s. Joseph Henry and Henrietta Inez (Mandel) G.; B.S., Adelbert Coll., 1943; D.D.S., Case-Western Reserve U., 1945; m. Dora May Hirsh, Sept. 18, 1947; children—Lynda (Mrs. Barry Allen Levin), Keith, Bruce; m. 2d, Ruth Jeanette Weber, May 1, 1974. Pvt. practice dentistry, Cleve., 1949—; pres. Holiday Inns Trav-l-Park, Sandusky, Ohio, 1971—. Served with Dental Corps, USNR, 1946-48. Mem. Am. Acad. Gen. Dentistry, Am., Ohio State dental assns., Cleve. Dental Soc., Fedn. Dentaire Internationale, Cleve. Council on World Affairs, Phi Sigma Delta, Zeta Beta Tau, Alpha Omega. Clubs: Masons (32 deg.), Shriners. Home: 29099 Shaker Blvd Pepper Pike OH 44124 Office: 2031 W 25th St Cleveland OH 44113

GOODMAN, JAMES LESLIE, elec. supply co. exec.; b. Coalmont, Ind., Nov. 2, 1926; s. Leslie Hartford and Emma Rebecca (Stoops) G.; student Chgo. Tech. Inst., 1948-52; m. Mary Ellen Harrison, Aug. 5, 1944; 1 son, James Leslie. With Radio Specialty Co., Phoenix, 1952-60; with Midland Splty. Co., Albuquerque, 1960-64; with L. B. Walker Radio Co., Denver, 1964-70; with Elec. Supply Co., Green River, Wyo., 1970-72; mgr., pres. Farrell Argast Electric Co., Indpls., 1972—. Served with AUS, 1944-48. Mem. Electric League Ind., Purchasing Mgmt. Assn. Ind., Nat. Bus. Mgmt. Achievement Assn. Republican. Mem. Pentecostal Ch. (lay evangelist, dir., past deacon). Home: 921 Fry Rd Greenwood IN 46142 Office: 7482 Madison St Indianapolis IN 46227

GOODMAN, JESS THOMPSON, mktg. cons., mfg. co. exec., educator, ret. naval officer; b. Joplin, Mo., Jan. 18, 1936; s. Walter Raymond and Opal Mae (Tanner) G.; A.B., U. Mo., 1959; postgrad. George Washington U., 1968; M.A., Naval Postgrad. Sch., 1975; postgrad. Naval War Coll., 1976; Ph.D. candidate U. Hawaii, 1979—; m. Yvonne Vasquez, May 27, 1972; 1 son, Walter Raymond II. Commd. ensign, U.S. Navy, 1959, advanced through grades to lt. comdr., 1967; anti-submarine warfare acad. and inflight tactics/weapons/avionics instr. Fleet Airborne Electronics Tng. Unit, Atlantic, 1966-69; aide, flag sec. to Comdr. Carrier Div. 7, 1969-70; patrol squadron, mission comdr. P3B Aircraft and exec. asst., head tng. and adminstrv. dept., 1970-73; ops. intelligence analyst and spl. projects officer Intelligence Center Pacific and comdr. in Chief Pacific, 1978; Cincpac rep. to Dept. Def., 1978; tchr. sci. Carl Junction (Mo.) Sch. Dist., 1979-80; prodn. supr., quality assurance mgr. Electronics div. Eagle-Picher Industries, 1980—. Mem. World Affairs Forum of Hawaii, 1975-79, World Affairs Council of Pitts., 1978-82; nat. coordinator, founder Mensa Spl. Interest Group in Internat. Affairs, 1978-79. Decorated Navy Commendation Medal, Navy Achievement medals (2). Mem. Air Force Assn., Acad. Polit. Sci., AAAS, Am. Acad. Polit. and Social Sci., Am. Def. Preparedness Assn., Am. Entrepreneurs Assn., Am. Film Inst., Am. Legion, Am. Mgmt. Assn., Am. Mensa Ltd., Am. Mil. Inst., Am. Mus. Natural History, Am. Polit. Sci. Assn., Am. Security Council Edn. Found., Am. Soc. Internat. Law, Am. Soc. for Quality Control, Am. Univs. Field Staff, Asso. Nat. Archives, Arms Control Assn., Center for Study of Presidency, Common Cause, Fedn. Am. Scientists, Fgn. Policy Assn., Humanist Assn., Internat. Entrepreneurs Assn., Internat. Inst. for Strategic Studies, Internat. Platform Assn., Fgn. Policy Research Inst., Internat. Studies Assn., Mil. Order World Wars, Nat. Geog. Soc., Nat. Mil. Intelligence Assn., Nat. Rifle Assn., Overseas Devel. Council, Retired Officers Assn., Security and Intelligence Fund, Smithsonian Inst., Soc. Mfg. Engrs., U. Mo. Alumni Assn., U.S. Naval Inst., U.S. Strategic Inst., VFW, World Future Soc., Pi Kappa Alpha. Democrat. Methodist. Clubs: Masons, Shriners, Kiwanis. Editor, pub.: The Mintas' Hoot, 1970. Home: 2725 Schifferdecker Joplin MO 64801 Office: 1927 W 4th St Joplin MO 64801

GOODMAN, MARK DAVID, clin. psychologist; b. Boston, Mar. 22, 1949; s. Harry Edward and Shirley Adeline (Hootstein) G.; B.A., Franklin-Pierce Coll., 1971; Ph.D. in Clin. Psychology, Brigham Young U., 1975. Predoctoral intern The Devereux Found., Devon, Pa., 1974-75; postdoctoral resident U. N.C., Chapel Hill, 1975-76; dir. child and adolescent services Mental Health Inst., Hutchinson, Kans., 1976—; pvt. practice clin. psychology Hutchinson Psychol. and Family Services, 1979—; mem. faculty McPherson Coll., 1977-78. NIMH fellow, 1975-76. Mem. Am. Psychol. Assn., Kans. Psychol. Assn., Nat. Register Health Service Providers in Psychology. Jewish. Club: Psychology (pres. 1970-71). Contbr. articles to profl. jours. Address: 1701 E 23rd St Hutchinson KS 67501

GOODMAN, NANCY TORIAN, nurse; b. Paducah, Ky., Jan. 6, 1941; d. George Willard and Velda Gray (Milam) Torian; R.N. diploma Highland Park Gen. Hosp. Sch. Nursing, 1962; B.S.N., Wayne State U., 1969, postgrad., 1980-82; m. James B. Goodman, Sept. 11, 1965; children—Jennifer Beth, Jocelyn Brooke, Jonathan

Bryce. Staff nurse Highland Park Gen. Hosp., 1962-63, part-time charge, 1963-66; public health nurse Detroit Vis. Nurse Assn., 1963-66, 67-68; staff nurse post partum E.H. Sparrow Hosp., Lansing, Mich., 1966-67; childbirth educator and monitrice Childbirth Without Pain Edn. Assn., Detroit, 1969-71; parent educator Childbirth Edn. Assn., Dayton, 1972—; staff nurse St. Elizabeth Med. Center, Dayton, 1972-76, maternity clinician, 1976-80, nursing adminstrv. coordinator maternity, 1980—; cons. bd. Childbirth Without Pain Edn. League, Riverside, Calif., 1973-76, Lamaze Edn. Assn. Greater Detroit, 1972-76, Dayton Childbirth Edn. Assn., 1979—. Named Ohio March of Dimes Nurse of Yr., 1979, Woman of Yr., Childbirth Edn. Assn., Dayton, 1978. Mem. Am Nurses Assn., Ohio Nurses Assn., Nurses Assn. Am. Coll. Ob-Gyn (cert. ob-gyn, neonatal nursing Nurses Assn.), Ohio Perinatal Assn., Internat. Childbirth Edn. Assn., Sigma Theta Tau. Home: 526 Koerner Ave Englewood OH 45322 Office: 601 Miami Blvd W Dayton OH 45408

GOODMAN, RONALD, pub. relations counsel; b. Chgo., June 3, 1920; s. Morris Goodman and Anna (Mautner) G.; Ph.B., Northwestern U., 1948; m. Ethel A. Weiss, Oct. 8, 1949; children—Anne Margaret, Victoria, Amy, Peter Kirk, Ellen. Sr. mem. The Mitchell Mc Keown Orgn., Chgo., 1947-54; pres. Ronald Goodman Pub. Relations Counsel, Inc., Chgo., 1954-67, The Pub. Relations Consortium, Chgo., 1967-75; pres. Ronald Goodman & Co., Inc., pub. relations counseling and mgmt. cons. firm, Des Moines, 1975—; mng. partner Mgmt. Cons. Group, Carl Byoir & Assos., Inc., Chgo./Des Moines, 1982—. Dir. Gateway House Found. Inc., Chgo., 1967-74; trustee N. Shore Unitarian Ch., Deerfield, Ill. Served with USAF, 1942-46. Mem. Pub. Relations Soc. Am. (Silver Anvil 1963, dir. Chgo. chpt., accredited pub. relations counselor, founding mem. counselors sect., past mem. exec. com.), Internat. Pub. Relations Assn. Club: Tower of Chgo. Author publs. in field. Home: 3505 SW 27th St Des Moines IA 50321 Office: 800 2d Ave PO Box 1712 Des Moines IA 50306

GOODMAN, SIDNEY RICHARD, computer service co. exec.; b. Cleve., June 29, 1940; s. David H. and Rose W. (Woolman) G.; B.S., Miami U., 1962; m. Diane Susan Katz, Aug. 12, 1962; children—Martin, Wendy, Tracey. Accountant Ernst & Ernst, 1962-65; exec. v.p. Becker C.P.A. Review Course, 1965; asst. to controller Foseco, Inc., Cleve., 1966-68; controller Arby's Northfield Systems, Cleve., 1968-69; pres. Datassistance Corp., Cleve., 1969-71; pres. Mgmt. Reports, Inc., Beachwood, Ohio, 1971—. Bd. govs. Temple Emanuel, 1973—, treas., 1975, v.p., 1976. Mem. Ohio Soc. C.P.A.s, Am. Inst. C.P.A.s Jewish. Patentee in field. Home: 32400 Chestnut Ln Pepper Pike OH 44124 Office: 23945 Mercantile Rd Beachwood OH 44122

GOODMAN, VIRGINIA KAY, psychologist; b. Conway, Ark., Apr. 12, 1944; d. M. Otto and Delma (Rickett) Turner; B.A., U. Ark., Fayetteville, 1966, M.Ed., 1969; Ed.D. (NIMH fellow), U. Ill., Urbana, 1976; m. Walter Goodman, Jan. 20, 1973; children—Kim L., W. Tony. Sch. psychologist Little Rock Public Schs., 1966-69; counselor Upward Bound-Ark. Poly. Inst., summer 1969; sch. psychologist Duluth (Minn.) Public Schs., 1971—; instr. dept. sch. psychology U. Wis., Superior, 1975—. Mem. Am. Psychol. Assn., Minn. Psychol. Assn., Nat. Assn. Sch. Psychologists, Minn. Sch. Psychologists Assn.

GOODRICH, ELIZABETH ANNE, bus. educator; b. Seattle; d. Frank Allen and Hildegarde Anne (Hoffman) G.; secretarial cert. Western Mich. U., 1961, B.B.A., 1963; M.A., Mich. State U., 1968; Ph.D., U. Colo., 1975. Secretarial position Inst. Social Research, U. Mich., Ann Arbor, 1963-64, Downtown Kalamazoo Assn., 1964-66; instr. Lansing (Mich.) Community Coll., 1967; grad. asst., instr. bus. law and office adminstrn. dept. Mich. State U., East Lansing, 1966-68; tchr., chmn. bus. dept. Grand Ledge (Mich.) High Sch., 1968-72; instr., officer adminstr. dept. U. Colo., Boulder, 1972-75; prof. bus. edn. and adminstrv. services dept. Central Mich. U., Mt. Pleasant, 1975—. Cert. profl. sec. Inst. Cert. Secs.; permanent secondary teaching cert. bus. edn. Mich. Dept. Edn.; vocat. edn. permanent teaching cert. Mich. Bd. Edn. Mem. AAUW, NEA, Nat., N. Central bus. edn. assns., Profl. Secs. Internat., Adminstrv. Mgmt. Soc. Internat., Mich. Bus. Edn. Assn., Mich. Edn. Assn., Delta Pi Epsilon, Pi Omega Pi. Contbr. articles to profl. jours. Office: Sch Bus Adminstrn Central Mich U Mount Pleasant MI 48859

GOODRICH, GLENN A., elec. contractor, state legislator; b. Orson, Iowa, Feb. 22, 1925; s. Walter H. and Susie W. G.; B.S., Creighton U., 1949; m. Gaynelle F. Tusha, June 15, 1950; children—D'Arcy, Gregory, Chris. Asst. v.p. Comml. Savs. & ioan Assn., Omaha, 1953-64; real estate developer, Omaha, 1964-70; owner, pres. Indsl. Elec. Works, Inc., Omaha, 1979—; mem. Nebr. Legislature, 1971—. Served with AUS, 1943-46. Democrat. Lutheran. Office: 1509 Chicago St Omaha NE 68102

GOODRICH, NICK HAROLD, sound equipment mfg. co. exec.; b. Kennett, Mo., May 25, 1944; s. Luther H. and Enyvonne G. (Howell) G.; A.S. in Data Processing, State Tech. Coll., Memphis, 1967; student Three Rivers Jr. Coll., 1974; teaching cert. South County Inst. Tech., St. Louis, 1979; m. Pamela Jean Stephenson, Feb. 5, 1977. Data processing mgr. McFadden Cotton Co., Memphis, 1967-68, Poplar Bluff Computer Center (Mo.), 1969-76; mgr. info. systems Garvey-Labelmatic Corp., St. Louis, 1976-78; mgr. von Weise Gear Co., St. Louis, 1978-79; data processing mgr. Soundolier, Inc., Crestwood, Mo., 1979—, mem. mgmt. team, 1980—, Vice pres. Region 8, Mo. Jaycees, 1974; v.p. Mcpl. Airport Devel. Bd., Poplar Bluff, 1976; mem. exec. bd. Poplar Bluff C. of C., 1975-76; adv. Explorer Post 386 Boy Scouts Am., 1970; vol. Mo. Bd. Parole and Probation, Richmond Heights, Mo., 1978-81. Served with USAF, 1962-67. Recipient Speakup award Mo. Jaycees, 1973, 74, named Outstanding Regional V.P., 1975; recipient award of distinction Vols. in Corrections, 1979, 80. Mem. Small Systems Users Group (v.p. 1979-80, pres. 1980-81), Data Processing Mgmt. Assn., Am. Prodn. and Inventory Control Soc.

GOODSMITH, DALE HAROLD, mech. engr.; b. Detroit, July 27, 1929; s. Harold Carl and Eva Elizabeth (Jones) G.; B.S., Lawrence Inst. Tech., 1971; m. Mavis Ruth Macomber, July 8, 1950; children—Mark Dale, Paul Alan, Glenn Richard. With Diversified Products, Detroit, 1949-51; aircraft technician Mich. N.G., Romulus, 1952-56; lab. technician Vickers, Inc., Troy, Mich., 1956-64, project engr., Troy, 1964-71; project engr. Multifastener Corp., Detroit, 1971-76, asst. chief engr., 1976—. Served to capt. USAF, 1951-52. Mem. Soc. Automotive Engrs., Soc. Mfg. Engrs., Am. Soc. Metals, Nat. Geographic Soc. Republican. Lutheran. Patentee in field. Home: 31743 Middleboro St Livonia MI 48154 Office: 12668 Arnold St Detroit MI 48239

GOODSTEIN, SANDERS ABRAHAM, scrap iron co. exec.; b. N.Y.C., Oct. 3, 1918; s. Samuel G. and Katie (Lipson) G.; student Wayne State U., 1934-36; A.B., U. Mich., 1938, M.B.A., 1939, J.D., 1946; postgrad. Harvard, 1943; m. Rose Laro, June 29, 1942; children—Peter, Esther, Jack, Rachel. Admitted to Mich. bar, 1946; sec., Laro Coal & Iron Co., Flint, Mich., 1946-60, pres. 1960—; owner, operator Paterson Mfg. Co., Flint, 1953—; gen. partner Indianhead Co., Pontiac, Mich., 1955-70, pres., 1965-70; sec. Amatac Corp., Erie, Pa., until 1969; chmn bd. Gen. Foundry & Mfg. Co., Flint, Mich., 1968— pres., 1970—; pres. Lacron Steel Co., Providence, 1975—; mem. corp. body Mich. Blue Shield, 1970-76. Served to lt. comdr. USNR, 1942-46. Mem. Fed. Bar Assn., Am. Bar Assn., Bar Mich., Am. Pub. Works Assn., Am. Foundrymen's Soc., Order of Coif, Beta Gamma Sigma, Phi Kappa Phi. Jewish. Home: 2602 Parkside Dr Flint MI 48503 Office: 6301 Dort Hwy Flint MI 48507

GOODWIN, BUDD RETAN, assn. exec.; b. Adrian, Mich., July 23, 1927; s. Budd A. and Eleanor (Retan) G.; m. Patricia E. Malloy, June 17, 1950; children—Thomas, Mary, William, Janet. Formerly with J.C. Penney; former v.p. Garfields, Inc., H.B. Garwin, Inc.; owner Goodwin's Fabrics; exec. sec. Lions Clubs Internat., State of Mich., Lansing, 1966—. Mem. Gov.'s Jobs for Teens Com., 1968; mem. Service Clubs Bicentennial Com., 1975-76. Served with USNR, 1945. Recipient Presdl. award (5), Lions Internat. Mem. Mich. State U. Alumni Assn. Roman Catholic. Club: Lions. Home: 2648 Melville Dr East Lansing MI 48823 Office: 309 Civic Center Lansing MI 48933

GOODWIN, JAMES HARVEY, III, social worker; b. Gloucester, Mass., Jan. 11, 1944; s. James Harvey and Doris Adeline (Wilmoth) G.; B.S., Springfield Coll., 1965; M.S.W., Mich. State U., 1967; m. Nancy Lee Morse, June 12, 1966; children—Brandon James, Ann Marie. Asso. dir. Cheshire County YMCA, Keene, N.H., 1967-68; psychotherapist Whaley Outpatient Psychiat. Clinic, Flint, Mich., 1973—; caseworker, residential sch. coordinator Whaley Center, Flint, 1968-77, dir. clin. services, 1977-79; instr. Mich. Assn. Children's Agencies, 1971-75; cons. Goodwill Industries, Flint, 1970-77. Precinct del. Dem. Party, 1970-74; 7th Dist. treas. McGovern for Pres. com., 1972; Minore State Senate campaign, treas. 1974. Mem. Nat. Assn. Social Workers, Soc. for Clin. Social Workers, Mich. Assn. Children's Agencies, Urban League of Flint. Home: 3087 Beechtree Ln Flushing MI 48433 Office: 1201 N Grand Traverse St Flint MI 48503

GOODWIN, JESSE FRANCIS, clin. chemist, city ofcl.; b. Greenville, S.C., Feb. 7, 1929; s. Jesse and Francis (Byrd) G.; B.S. in Pharmacy cum laude, Xavier U., 1951; M.S., Wayne State U., 1953, Ph.D., 1957; m. Della M. McGraw, Dec. 26, 1959; children—Gordon Francis, Paula Therese, Jesse Stephen. Research asso. Detroit Receiving Hosp., Wayne State U. Coll. Medicine, Detroit, 1958-59; biochemist Wayne County Gen. Hosp., Eloise, Mich., 1959-63; staff biochemist Children's Hosp. Mich., Detroit, 1963-73, also dir. Core Lab. Clin. Research Center for Children, Wayne State U. Sch. Medicine, Children's Hosp. Mich., 1963-73; dir. clin. labs. Detroit Dept. Health, 1973—. Instr. Wayne State U. Sch. Medicine, 1964-66, asst. prof., 1966-73. Mem. edn. com. New Detroit Inc., 1971—; trustee Marygrove Coll., 1977—; bd. dirs. Detroit Osteo. Hosp. Corp., 1980—, mem. corp., 1977—, chmn. unit bd., 1980—; mem. devel. fund adv. com. Archdiocese of Detroit, 1972-75, mem. pastoral council, 1973-77. Fellow Am. Inst. Chemists; mem. NAACP (chmn. edn. com. Detroit br., dir. 1968—, 2d v.p. 1979—), Am. Assn. Clin. Chemists (Mich. sect. chmn. 1967), Am. Chem. Soc., AAAS, N.Y. Acad. Sci., Assn. Analytical Chemists, Engring. Soc. Detroit, Sigma Xi, Phi Lambda Upsilon, Rho Chi, Alpha Kappa Mu, Alpha Phi Alpha (pres. chpt. 1972-75). Roman Catholic. Club: Detroit Renaissance Lions (charter). Contbr. articles to profl. jours. Home: 19214 Appoline St Detroit MI 48235 Office: Detroit Health Dept 1151 Taylor St Detroit MI 48202

GOODWIN, NORMAN J., state senator; b. Austin, Minn., Jan. 5, 1913; s. Nels and Nellie G.; B.S., U. Minn., 1936, M.S., 1945; m. Marion Blomgren, 1936; 3 children. Extension dir. Clinton County (Minn.), 1951-78; now mem. Iowa Senate. Recipient Bereford-Quaife award, 1967; Iowa Cattlemen's award, 1969; named hon. master pork producer, 1971; Liberty Bell award, 1975; R. K. Bliss extension citation, 1976. Mem. Iowa Assn. County Extension Service Dirs. (pres. 1965), Nat. Assn. Agrl. Agts. (pres. 1975), Farm Bur., Cattlemen's and Pork Producers Assn. Methodist. Clubs: Lions, Masons, Toastmasters. Office: State Senate Des Moines IA 50319*

GOODWIN, RICHARD HARVEY, paper bag mfg. co. exec.; b. Bklyn., Sept. 10, 1922; s. Frank Alexander and Sophia (Scheubner) G.; B.A. in Econs., Depauw U., 1947; M.A. in Accounting, Ohio State U., 1952; m. Helen Dorothy Hiteshew, Nov. 20, 1965; children—Christine Sue Goodwin Oster, Thomas Bradley. Grad. asst. accounting dept. Ohio State U., Columbus, 1951-52; auditor Ernst & Ernst, Columbus, 1953-55; comptroller Buckeye Steel Castings Co. (name now Buckeye Internat.), Columbus, 1955-64; controller Grote Mfg. Co., Madison, Ind., 1964-69; v.p. fin. Duro Paper Bag Mfg. Co., Ludlow, Ky., 1969—; dir. 1st Nat. Bank, Ludlow. Bd. dirs. United Appeal, Columbus, 1963-64, Madison, 1965; treas. Heart Fund, Columbus, 1962. Served to lt. (j.g.) USN, 1943-46; PTO. C.P.A., Ohio. Mem. Fin. Execs. Inst., Nat. Assn. Accountants, Beta Alpha Psi. Home: 9518 Croton Dr Cincinnati OH 45242 Office: Duro Paper Bag Mfg Co Davies and Oak Sts Ludlow KY 41016

GOODWIN, WILLIAM FREDERICK, coll. adminstr.; b. Dover, Ohio, July 11, 1931; s. William and Ada Lydia (Pheiffer) G.; B.A., Heidelberg Coll., 1956; m. Norma M. Fant, Apr. 9, 1955; children—William Frederick, Susanne Renee. Life underwriter Commonwealth Life Ins. Co., Tiffin, Ohio, 1955-56; dist. exec. Boy Scouts Am., Sandusky, Ohio, 1957-58, Elyria, Ohio, 1958-62, Akron, Ohio, 1962-65; alumni dir. Heidelberg Coll., Tiffin, 1965-75, dir. annual fund and planned giving, 1975-80, dir. devel./public affairs, 1980—. Scoutmaster, Boy Scouts Am., Tiffin, 1967-70; div. chmn. United Fund, Tiffin, 1975; bd. trustees YMCA, Tiffin, 1972-75, Mercy Hosp., Tiffin, 1975-78, Girl Scouts U.S.A., Sandusky, 1976-78. Served with USMC, 1948-52. Named Outstanding Man in Public Service, City of Elyria, 1960. Mem. Council for Advancement and Support of Edn. Mem. United Ch. of Christ. Clubs: Elks, Columbia Boosters (pres. 1974-75). Home: 294 Melmore St Tiffin OH 44883 Office: Heidelberg Coll Tiffin OH 44883

GOOGASIAN, GEORGE ARA, lawyer; b. Pontiac, Mich., Feb. 22, 1936; s. Peter and Lucy (Chobanian) G.; B.A., U. Mich., 1958; J.D., Northwestern U., 1961; m. Phyllis Elaine Law, June 27, 1959; children—Karen Ann, Steven George, Dean Michael. Admitted to Mich. bar, 1961; atty. Marentay, Rouse, Selby, Fischer & Webber, Detroit, 1961-62; asst. U.S. atty., Detroit, 1962-64; mem. firm Beier, Howlett, McConnell, Googasian & McCann, Bloomfield Hills, Mich., 1964-81, firm Googasian, Hopkins & Forhan, 1981—. Chmn., Oakland County Democratic Com., Pontiac, 1964-70; state campaign chmn. Sen. Philip A. Hart, 1970; bd. dirs. Big Bros. Oakland County, 1968-73. Fellow Am. Coll. Trial Lawyers; mem. State Bar Mich., Am., Oakland County (dir.) bar assns., Am. Judicature Soc. Presbyterian. Home: 3750 Orion Rd Rochester MI 48063 Office: 74 W Long Lake Bloomfield Hills MI 48013

GOOKINS, ELMER FRANKLIN, JR., mfg. co. exec.; b. Zanesville, Ohio, Dec. 14, 1940; s. Elmer Franklin and Augusta Kathryn (Zandlo) G.; grad. Ohio U., 1962; postgrad. Muskingum Coll., 1964; m. Sandra Lee Starkey, Apr. 20, 1968; children—Kimberly, Jason, Bradley. Sr. project engr. Cooper Industries, Mount Vernon, Ohio, 1964-68; mgr. quality assurance Lear Siegler, Elyria, Ohio, 1968-71; dir. corp. quality Kirkwood Industries, Cleve., 1971-79; mgr. group reliability Bendix Corp., Elyria, 1979—; mem. faculty Cleve. State U., 1972-77, Lorain Community Coll., 1968—, mem. engring. adv. com., 1970—. Served with U.S. Army, 1958. Recipient Outstanding Service award Lorain Coll., 1978. Registered profl. engr., Calif. Mem. Am. Statis. Assn., Am. Soc. Quality Control (Outstanding Service award 1979). Democrat. Roman Catholic. Club: K.C. Author: Qualibility, 1980. Home: 511 Whitman Blvd Elyria OH 44035 Office: 901 Cleveland St Elyria OH 44035

GOOLD, FLORENCE CHARLOTTE, newspaper editor; b. Bklyn., Oct. 10, 1928; d. Isidor and Anna (Rittenberg) Unterberg; A.B., Bklyn. Coll., 1947; m. Oliver Goold, Sept. 15, 1946; children—Eric, Jmes, Margaret. Public relations counsel, journalist, 1955-63; editor Hyde Park Herald, Chgo., 1963-66, 77—; trade journalist, public relations counsel, 1967-77. Bd. dirs. Hyde Park-Kenwood Devel. Co. Recipient nat. newspaper awards, 1965, 66. Mem. Chgo. Headline Club, U. Chgo. Service League, Sigma Delta Chi. Office: 5240 S Harper Ave Chicago IL 60615

GOOLD, FLORENCE WILSON, occupational therapist; b. Chgo., Aug. 26, 1912; d. Frank Elmer and Marie Louise (Walker) Wilson; student U. Wis., 1934; B.A., Boston Sch. Occupational Therapy, 1936; m. Robert Charles Goold, Dec. 28, 1938; children—Frances Louise Goold Felty, Nancy Jean, Elizabeth Jane Goold Ill., Robert Charles. Occupational therapist Ypsilanti (Mich.) State Hosp., 1936-40, Michael Reese Hosp., Chgo., 1940-42, DuPage County Easter Seal Center, Villa Park, Ill., 1959-62; dir. occupational therapy Hinsdale (Ill.) Sanitarium and Hosp., 1962-71, Marianjoy Rehab. Hosp., Wheaton, Ill., 1971-73, Central DuPage Hosp., Winfield, Ill., 1972-73, Royal Oak Convalescent Home, Oak Park, Ill., 1973, Highland House Nursing Home, Downers Grove, Ill., 1973-75, St. Charles Med. Center, Aurora, Ill., 1975-78, Westmont (Ill.) Health Center, 1978-80. Pres. bd. dirs. DuPage County Easter Seal Center, 1942-59. Mem. Am., Ill. (past pres.) occupational therapy assns., Assn. Health Care Cons. Ill., Phi Mu. Episcopalian. Home: 5604 Middaugh Ave Downers Grove IL 60516

GOPPERS, VELTA MANEKS, chemist; b. Gostini, Latvia, Feb. 28, 1915; came to U.S., 1949, naturalized, 1954; d. Karlis and Milda Maneks; m. Sergejs Goppers, 1941 (div. 1947); 1 dau., Ilze; M.S., U. Riga, Latvia, 1944. Asst. U. Riga, Latvia, 1940-44; analytical chemist Farben Industries, Germany, 1944-45; instr. tech. sch. Stuttgart, Germany, 1945-47; mgr. pharmacy and chem. preparation lab. Esslingen, N. Germany, 1947-49; analytical chemist Twin City Testing and Engring Lab., St. Paul, 1949-52; chemist U. Minn., 1952-53, jr. scientist, 1953-59, sr. scientist Sch. Public Health, 1959-68, sr. scientist Space Sci. Center, 1968-70, sr. scientist Sch. Pub. Health Environ. Health, 1970—. Fellow Am. Inst. Chemists, AAAS; mem. Am. Indsl. Hygiene (asso.), Am. Chem. Soc., Am. Inst. Physics, Sigma Xi, Iota Sigma Pi, Sigma Delta Epsilon. Recipient research award Iota Sigma Pi, 1976; contbr. articles to profl. jours. Home: 5164 Abercrombie Dr Minneapolis MN 55435 Office: U Minn Sch Pub Health Environmental Health Minneapolis MN 55455

GOR, VISHNU JETHALAL, chem. engr.; b. Malpur, India, Oct. 21, 1940; s. Jethalal V. and Maniben G. (Pandya) G.; B.S. in Chemistry, St. Xavier's Coll., 1961; B.S. in Chem. Engring., U. Mo., Rolla; m. Surya D. Pandya, June 20, 1960; children—Kanak V., Niraj V., Nehal V. Research chemist Burgess Cellulose Co., Freeport, Ill., 1965-66; sr. polymer chemist Paint Research Assos. Lab., Chgo., 1966-68; research engr. Continental Can Co., Chgo., 1968-74, supr., 1974-78; v.p. Dober Lubricants, Inc., 1978-79; pres. Poly Enviro Labs., 1979—. Mem. Am. Inst. Chem. Engrs., Fedn. Paint Tech., Am. Soc. Lubrication Engrs., Am. Chem. Soc. Hindu. Club: Toastmasters (Able Toastmasters award 1975). Patentee in field. Home: 15266 Coventry Ct Orland Park IL 60462 Office: 15554 S 70th Ct Orland Park IL 60462

GORALNIK, OLIVER AARON, chain store exec.; b. Newark, June 13, 1907; s. Abe and Anna (Krugman) G.; B.S., Washington U., 1930; m. Alma Hirsch, Oct. 27, 1935; children—Barbara (Mrs. Bernard G. Kohm), Jane Ellen (Mrs. Hans Levi), Mary Beth (Mrs. Joseph H. Mohrman, Jr.). Accountant, C. B. Adams, C.P.A.'s, St. Louis, 1930-31; asst. sales mgr. Weilkalter Mfg. Co., St. Louis, 1931-36; store mgr. P.N. Hirsch & Co., Retail Jr. Dept. Stores, St. Louis, 1936-44, div. merchandise mgr., 1944-46, treas., 1946—, also dir. Bd. dirs. Jewish Employment and Vocational Service. Mem. Beta Gamma Sigma, Omicron Delta Gamma. Jewish. Home: 14 Lake Forest St St Louis MO 63117 Office: 2001 Walton Rd St Louis MO 63114

GORBY, JOHN CARL, tng. and orgn. devel. cons.; b. Tampa, Fla., June 26, 1945; s. Cecil George and Lois (Donlon) G.; B.S. in Speech, Northwestern U., 1967, M.B.A. in Mktg., 1969; m. Joana Lou Fry, June 11, 1966; children—Chad Douglas, Brittany. Asst. TV dir. Sta. WGN-TV, Chgo., 1966-68; brand mgr. Procter & Gamble, Cin., 1969-74; group v.p. Curtis Communications, Chgo., 1975-76; v.p. Jim Hooker & Co., Schaumburg, Ill., 1977-78; pres. Youngs, Walker & Co., Rolling Meadows, Ill., 1978—. Referee, coach Tri-City Soccer League, St. Charles, Ill. Served with USAR, 1968-74. Mem. Nat. Speakers Assn., Am. Soc. Tng. Devel., Ill. Tng. and Devel. Assn. Club: Toastmasters Internat. Author: How To Give Effective Criticism, 1979; How to Handle the Six Biggest Objections to Radio Advertising, 1980; How to Be an Effective Radio Sales Manager, 1981. Home: 40W737 Longshadow Ln Saint Charles IL 60174 Office: 1 Crossroads of Commerce Rolling Meadows IL 60008

GORDILLO, MANUEL E., psychiatrist; b. Lima, Peru, Aug. 29, 1930; s. Manuel E. and Lidia A. (Vasquez) G.; came to U.S., 1958, naturalized, 1963; M.D., San Marcos U., Lima, 1957; m. Ruth Ann Smith, Aug. 18, 1959; children—Gregory, Gayle, Christine, Nancy, Daniel, Mathew, Michael. Psychiat. resident U. Minn., 1963-66; practice medicine, specializing in psychiatry, Cleve., 1966—; chief of staff Woodruff Hosp., Cleve., 1973-74, also trustee; chief of psychiatry St. John's Hosp., Cleve., 1978—. Mem. Cuyahoga Mental Health Bd., 1978-82. Diplomate Am. Bd. Psychiatry and Neurology. Fellow Am. Psychiat. Assn. (peer rev. com. 1980—); mem. Ohio Psychiat. Assn. (chmn. peer rev. com. 1973— Outstanding Service award Psychiatry Council, 1976, pres. 1979-80), Am., Ohio med. assns., Cleve. Acad. Medicine, Cleve. Soc. Psychiatry and Neurology (pres. 1973-74). Contbr. articles to profl. jours. Home: 17810 Lake St Cleveland OH 44107 Office: 15644 Madison Ave Lakewood OH 44107

GORDIN, RICHARD DAVIS, univ. athletic dir.; b. South Charleston, Ohio, July 16, 1928; s. Edwin Ray and Mildred (Davis) G.; B.A., Ohio Wesleyan U., 1952; M.A., Ohio State U., 1954, Ph.D., 1967; m. Paula Alice Egan, July 23, 1949; children—Richard D. Jr., Robert H., Douglas P. Grad. asst. phys. edn. Ohio State U., 1953; dir. recreation United Cerebral Palsy, Columbus, Ohio, 1954; Instr. phys. edn. Ohio Wesleyan U., Delaware, 1954-59, asst. prof., 1959-67, asso. prof., 1967-71, prof., 1971—, dir. athletics, 1977—; ednl. cons. Nat. Golf Found., 1966—; mem. parks recreation bd. City of Delaware, 1970-77, chmn., 1974. Recipient citation Delaware City Council, 1977; named to Golf Coaches Hall of Fame, 1980. Mem. U.S. Golf Assn. (mus. com. 1981), Golf Coaches Assn. Am. (pres. 1979-80, 81-82). Co-author: Golf Fundamentals, 1973. Editor: The Golf Coach's Guide, 1975. Home: 80 Hillside Dr Delaware OH 43015 Office: Ohio Wesleyan Univ Delaware OH 43015

GORDON, ARNOLD MARK, lawyer; b. Norwich, Conn., Oct. 2, 1937; s. Barney and Rose (Bilsky) G.; B.Sc. in Bus. Adminstrn., Wayne State U., Detroit, 1959, J.D., 1962; m. Carolyn Jean Berman; children—Lori, Adam, Jennifer. Admitted to Mich. bar, 1962, since practiced as prin. partner firm Weinstein, Kroll & Gordon; arbitrator Am. Arbitration Assn., 1969—; lectr. in field. Mem. State Bar Mich. (chmn. negligence sect. 1977-78, med.-legal com. 1976—, pub. Negligence Sect. Bull.), Detroit Bar Assn. (co-chmn. trial advocacy program continguing legal edn. 1972—), Assn. Trial Lawyers Am. (exec. bd. Mich. 1967—), Mich., Detroit trial lawyers assns., U.S. Power Squadron, Tau Epsilon Rho. Club: Masons. Home: 3874 Wabeek Lake Dr W Bloomfield Hills MI 48013 Office: 701 Travelers Tower Southfield MI 48076

GORDON, EDWIN FREDERICK ROBERT, metal fabricating co. exec.; b. Oak Park, Ill., Jan. 4, 1921; s. Edwin C. and Alice (Heller) G.; B.S., Concordia Coll., 1942; M.A., Northwestern U., 1945; Ph.D., Purdue U., 1951; children—Dawn Alice, Denise Ann, E. Robert F., Allen D., Roger M., James Adams, John Robin, Jana Amanda. Pres., dir. Geuder, Paeschke & Frey Co., metal fabricating co., Milw., 1955—; dir. Gordon-Hoover & Assos., Inc., mgmt. consultants, Chgo., Capital Investments, Inc., Milw.; chmn. bd. Boyer-Rosene Moving & Storage Co., Inc., Arlington Heights, Ill., Gordon Studios, Inc., Davie, Fla.; pres. Hillsboro Land Mark, Inc., Hillsboro Beach, Fla., Gordon Studios Inc., Davie, Fla. Mem. Am. Psychol. Assn., Sigma Xi. Office: 324 N 15th St Milwaukee WI 53201

GORDON, EDWIN LAMAR, tool engring. corp. exec.; b. Auburn, Ind., June 11, 1935; s. Herbert Valentine and Wanda G.; student Ivy Tech. Coll.; m. Victoria Sue Spangler, June 13, 1980; children by previous marriage—Nicky, Jeffrey, Zania, Kristina. Draftsman, Weatherhead Co., Ft. Wayne, Ind., 1957-61, tool designer, Columbia City, Ind., 1962-64, tool engr., 1964-66, indsl. engr., 1966-68, product design engr., Syracuse, Ind., 1968-69, chief engr., Columbia City, 1969-74; v.p., dir. engring. C & A Tool Engring., Inc., Churubusco, Ind., 1974-81; with Gordon Design Service, Huntertown, Ind., 1981—. Served with AUS, 1957-59. Lutheran. Office: PO Box 57 Huntertown IN 46748

GORDON, GILBERT, chemist, ednl. adminstr.; b. Chgo., Nov. 11, 1933; s. Catherine and Walter G.; B.S., Bradley U., 1955; Ph.D. in Chemistry, Mich. State U., 1959; m. Joyce Elaine Masura; children—Thomas, Susan. Postdoctoral research asso. chemistry U. Chgo., 1959-60; asst. prof. chemistry U. Md., College Park, 1960-64, asso. prof., 1964-67, prof., 1967; prof. chemistry U. Iowa, Iowa City, 1967-73; prof., chmn. dept. chemistry Miami U., Oxford Ohio 1973—; vis. prof. Japanese Soc. Promotion Sci., Japan, 1969; cons. Nat. Bur. Standards, Halabs, Inc., Egbert Industries. Olin Corp. Mem. Am. Chem. Soc. (named Chemist of Yr. of Cin. sect. 1981), Chem. Soc. London, Faraday Soc., Sigma Xi, Phi Kappa Phi. Editor catalysis kinetics sect. Chem. Abstracts, 1970—; editorial bd. synthesis inorganic metalorganic chemistry Ohio Jour. Sci., 1971—; contbr. articles to chem. jours. Address: 190 Shadowy Hills Dr Oxford OH 45056

GORDON, HOWARD AARON, electric supply co. exec.; b. Danville, Ill., Mar. 15, 1922; s. Harold and Irene (Seifer) G.; B.S. in Gen. Engring., U. Ill., 1943; m. Vivian Miller, June 22, 1947; children—Nancy Cara, James Miller. Plant engr. Diamond Wire & Cable Co., Sycamore, Ill., 1947-50; dist. mgr. Western Tire & Auto Stores, Chgo., 1950-52; with Gordon Electric Supply, Inc., Kankakee, Ill., 1952—, pres., 1958—; dir. City Nat. Bank, Kankakee. Bd. dirs. Riverside Hosp., 1971-77, 80—, YMCA; adv. bd. St. Mary's Hosp., Kankakee; adv. bd. Kankakee Bd. Edn., 1955-57. Served as lt. (s.g.) USNR, 1943-45. Mem. Kankakee C. of C. (dir. 1970-73), Nat. Assn. Elec. Distbrs. (bd. govs.). Jewish. Clubs: B'nai B'rith, Kankakee Country, Rotary, Ravisloe Country (gov. 1978-79), Elks. Home: 2400 Brookwood Dr Flossmoor IL 60422 Office: Route 50 N Kankakee IL 60201

GORDON, HOWARD LYON, advt. and mktg. exec.; b. Chgo., Oct. 8, 1930; s. Milton Arthur and Betty Z. (Ginsburg) G.; B.S., U. Ill., 1953; M.S., Northwestern U., 1954, M.B.A., 1962; m. Lois Jean Kaufman, Aug. 21, 1955; children—Carolyn Ann, Leslie Meredith. Mktg. research mgr. Marsteller Inc., advt., Chgo., 1960-68, v.p. mktg. services, 1969-76; dir. client service Britt and Frerichs Inc., mktg. research and advt. cons., Chgo., 1977—, sr. v.p., 1978—, prin., 1979—; lectr. advt. and mktg. Northwestern U., 1963—; lectr., seminar leader Am. Mgmt. Assn., 1965-72. Regional chmn. Crusade of Mercy, Evanston, Ill., 1969. Served with AUS, 1954-56. Recipient award Dept. Def., 1956. Mem. Am. Mktg. Assn (dir., v.p. mktg. mgmt.), Sigma Delta Chi. Club: Northwestern U. Faculty. Contbr. articles to profl. publs. and mktg. texts. Home: 2025 Sherman Ave Evanston IL 60201 Office: Wrigley Bldg 410 N Michigan Ave Chicago IL 60611

GORDON, KEITH CHARLES, paint mfg. co. exec.; b. Youngstown, Ohio, May 25, 1948; s. Eugene Arthur and Alice Evelyn (DeLisio) G.; B.S. in Bus. Adminstrn., Youngstown State U., 1974; postgrad. Kent State U., Salisbury State Coll.; m. Marilou Biastro, Nov. 25, 1967; children—Michael Scott, Kelley Anne. Sales rep. Sherwin Williams Co., Cleve., 1973-75, advt. merchandising mgr. Rubberset Co. div., 1975-77, advt. merchandising mgr., speciality products div., 1977, account exec., 1977-78, mgr. mktg., spl. products div., 1979-80, nat. sales mgr. Rubberset bus. unit, 1980—. Mem. Nat. Retail Hardware Assn., Sales and Mktg. Execs. Assn., Mahoning Valley Homebuilders Assn., Painting and Decorating Contractors Am. Home: 18809 Rivers Edge W Chagrin Falls OH 44022 Office: Sherwin Williams Co 101 N Prospect Ave Cleveland OH 44115

GORDON, LEWIS ALEXANDER, electronics exec.; b. Milw., Oct. 4, 1937; s. Lewis Alexander and Verna Alma (Stocker) G.; B.S. in Mech. Engring., Purdue U., 1959; postgrad. RCA Insts., 1962, No. Ill. U., 1967-68; m. Frances Rita Dziadzio, June 4, 1960; children—Robert Alan, Richard Alan, Pamela Ann. Process engr. Ill. Tool Works, Elgin, 1959-63; chief engr. Norcon Electronics, Elgin, 1963-65; v.p. Midland Standard, Inc., Elgin, 1964-78, chmn. bd., 1967-78; pres., chief exec. officer Gt. Lakes Industries, Elgin, 1978—; del. Joint Electronics Industry Conf.; mem. adv. bd. Electronics mag., 1976—. Vice pres. bd. trustees Gail Borden Pub. Library Dist., 1971—, pres., bd. dirs. North Suburban Library System, 1971—. Bd. advisers Easter Seal Assn., Elgin, 1971-74; adv. bd. Elgin Community Coll., 1977—. Registered profl. engr., Ill., Mich. Mem. Ill. C. of C., Elgin Assn. Commerce, A.L.A., Ill. Library Assn. (automation com. 1975—), Ill. Council Library Systems Presidents (pres.), Exptl. Aircraft Assn., Ill. Soc. Profl. Engrs., Nat. Brit. Horological Inst., Kane County Farm Bur., Ill. Mfrs. Assn., Assn. Watch and Clock Collectors, Mensa, Agent-Aeronca Champion Club, Pi Tau Sigma. Lutheran. Contbr. articles to profl. jours. Patentee in field. Home: 705 Diane Ave Elgin IL 60120 Office: PO Box 801 Elgin IL 60120

GORDON, MARYBETH, social worker, therapist; b. St. Louis, July 14, 1952; d. John and Marie Gordon; B.A. in Philosophy, So. Ill. U., Edwardsville, 1975; M.S.W., Washington U., St. Louis, 1980. With Southwestern Bell Telephone Co., St. Louis, plant staff evaluator, 1975-77, plant analysis supr., chief assigner, 1977-78, research asso., 1978, plant service evaluator, 1978-79; sch. social worker Community Sch. Dist. 9, Granite City, Ill., 1979—. Mem. Nat. Assn. Social Workers, Assn. Women in Psychology, Ill. Assn. Sch. Social Workers, Am. Fedn. Tchrs. Address: care PO Box 416 Granite City IL 62040

GORDON, MICHAEL DUANE, optometrist; b. Coffeyville, Kans., Apr. 14, 1949; s. Otho Wayne and Wilma Lea (Hodges) G.; B.S. cum laude, U. Houston, 1973, O.D. magna cum laude, 1973; m. Vicki Jo Baker, May 31, 1969; children—Kimberly Michelle, Ryan Michael, Nicole Tasha. Pvt. practice optometry, Wichita, Kans., 1973—, Derby, Kans., 1977—; optometric cons. VA Hosp., Wichita, 1975—; v.p. Ro-Ta Enterprises, Inc., Derby, 1978-81, pres., 1981—; cons. Winfield State Mental Hosp., 1980—; FDA clin. investigator for Cooper Labs., 1981—, for Baush & Lomb Soflens, 1981—. Mem. Coll. Optometrists in Vision Devel., Am. Optometric Assn., Optometric Extension Program Found., Inc., Kans. Optometric Assn., Wichita Optometric Soc., Derby C. of C., Derby Jaycees. Republican. Co-inventor, patentee motorized revolving visual exam. center; co-inventor Ro-Ta module. Home: 942 Brook Forest Rd Derby KS 67037 Office: 154 S Rock Rd Wichita KS 67207 also 248 Greenway St Derby KS 67037

GORDON, RICHARD SEYMOUR, educator, cons.; b. N.Y.C., June 28, 1925; s. Jacques and Ruth (Janeway) G.; B.A., U. Rochester, 1947; A.M., Harvard U., 1954; Ph.D., Mass. Inst. Tech., 1954; m. Emily Conover Evarts, Sept. 8, 1951; children—Richard E., Elizabeth J., Jacques N., Helen E., Charlotte C. Research asso. Mass. Inst. Tech., 1951-56; dir. agrl. research Monsanto Co., St. Louis, 1951-63, dir. central research, 1963-68, v.p., gen. mgr. new enterprise div., 1968-71, chief scientist, 1970-71; pres. Inst. Urban Devel., St. Louis, 1971-76; pres. Gordon Group, St. Louis, 1976—; prof. agribus. Ariz. State U., Tempe, 1980—; dir. Regulation as an Instrument of Public Adminstrn., Kennedy Sch., Harvard U., 1976-78. Bd. dirs. St. Louis Symphony Soc., 1964—; pres. St. Louis Conservatory and Schs. for Arts, 1973-78; pres. Urban Tng. Center, 1968-74; pres. standing com. Episcopal Diocese Mo., 1967-71; mem. exec. com., agrl. bd. Nat. Acad. Scis.-NRC, 1966-72. Served with U.S. Army, 1942-46. Predoctoral fellow Com. on Growth, 1947-48; Sloan-Kettering Inst. fellow, 1947-49, Harvard U. fellow, 1949-51. Mem. Am. Chem. Soc., Am. Soc. Microbiology, AAAS, Am. Inst. Biol. Scis. (life), Poultry Sci. Assn., Animal Nutrition Research Council, N.Y. Acad. Scis. (life). Episcopalian. Clubs: Tavern (Chgo.); Cosmos, Nat. Democratic (Washington); Chemists (N.Y.C.). Co-author, editor: Issues in Health Care Regulation, 1980; contbr. 150 articles in field to books, profl. jours., related publs.; patentee in field. Home: 20 Westmoreland Pl St Louis MO 63108 Office: Div Agr Ariz State U Tempe AZ 85281

GORDON, ROBERT JAY, phys. chemist; b. N.Y.C., Feb. 29, 1944; s. Solomon and Shirley (Byers) G.; A.B., Harvard U., 1965, A.M., 1966, Ph.D. in Chem. Physics, 1970; m. Evelyn Rabinowitz, June 22, 1969; children—Ilana, Tamar, Shmuel. Research asso. Calif. Inst. Tech., 1970-72, Naval Research Lab., Washington, 1972-74; asst. prof. chemistry U. Ill., Chgo. Circle campus, 1974-78, asso. prof., 1978-80, prof., 1980—. NSF grantee, 1975—; Dept. Energy grantee, 1977—. Mem. Am. Phys. Soc., Am. Chem. Soc. Research in chem. kinetics, laser chemistry, including effects on lasers in accelerating reactions by vibrationally exciting reacting species. Office: U Ill at Chicago Circle Chicago IL 60680

GORDON, ROBERT THOMAS, surgeon; b. Chgo., Feb. 13, 1950; s. David and Eunice (Wienshienk) G.; B.S. with highest distinction in Medicine, Northwestern U., 1971, M.D. with highest distinction, 1972, gen. surgery degree, 1977; Resident dept. surgery Wesley, Passavant, Evanston, VA, Children's Meml. hosps., 1972-76, chief resident gen. surgery, 1976-77; chief resident cardio-thoracic surgery, mem. staff Northwestern U. Med. Sch., Northwestern U. Hosps., 1977—; mem. staff Luth. Gen. Hosp., Park Ridge, Ill., chmn. dept. cardiac surgery, 1979; mem. staff Holy Family Hosp., Park Ridge, Mt. Sinai Hosp., Chgo., Highland Park (Ill.) Hosp., Edgewater Hosp., Chgo., Suburban Med. Center, Hoffman Estates, Ill., Good Shepherd Hosp., Barrington, Ill.; instr. gen. surgery Northwestern U. Med. Sch., 1976-77, instr. cardio-thoracic surgery, 1977—; clin. asst. prof. surgery U. Ill. Med. Center, Chgo., 1981—; cons., researcher in field; lectr. seminars and sci. meetings; staff asso. Nat. Inst. Health HEW, 1974. Recipient Hoffman LaRoche award, 1971-72; Macy Found. Research fellow, 1967; G.D. Searle scholar and fellow, 1967-73; Med. Scientist Life Ins. fellow, 1969; Northwestern U. Med. Research fellow, 1968; Phi Beta Pi scholar, 1970; Frederick K. Rawson, Jr. scholar, 1972. Diplomate Am. Bd. Surgery, Am. Bd. Thoracic Surgery, Nat. Bd. Med. Examiners. Mem. AMA (Physician's Recognition award 1975—), Chgo. Med. Assn., Ill. State Med. Soc., Am. Coll. Chest Physicians, Flying Physicians Assn., Royal Soc. Medicine, Am. Soc. Contemporary Medicine and Surgery, Northwestern U., Northwestern U. Med. Sch. alumni assns., Ill. Jr. Acad. Scis. (hon.), U.S., Chgo. Dist. tennis assns., Internat. Platform Assn., Alpha Omega Alpha, Phi Eta Sigma. Contbr. numerous articles to profl. jours.; patentee in U.S. and fgn. countries. Office: 4936 W Estes Skokie IL 60077

GORDON, ROOSEVELT, JR., univ. adminstr.; b. Chgo., Sept. 19, 1949; s. Roosevelt and Nellie G.; B.A. in Biology and Psychology with honors (Tchr. Ednl. scholar, Service and Leadership award), Northeastern Ill. U., Chgo., 1972, M.A. in Guidance and Counseling summa cum laude, 1977; m. Ines M. Bocanegra, Dec. 30, 1972; children—Olubayo Ubaldo, Ayo Henry, Adebayo Armando. Bio-chem. research technician Loyola U. Med. Center, 1972-73; indsl. chemist Standard Sci. Hosp. Supply Co., 1973-74; tchr., counselor Northeastern Ill. U., 1974-77, coordinator Project Success, 1977—, instr. student devel., 1974—; mem. dept. human services, chmn. subcom. on edn. Garfield Park Community Service Center, Chgo. Recipient award dept. human services Garfield Park Community Service Center, 1981. Mem. Am. Personnel and Guidance Assn., Ill. Personnel and Guidance Assn., Assn. Non-White Concerns, Ill. Assn. Non-White Concerns, Council on Coll. Attendance, Concerned Counselors for Acad. Awareness, John Marshall High Sch. Alumni Assn., Northeastern Ill. U. Alumni Assn., Psi Chi. Home: 2752 W Warren Blvd Chicago IL 60612 Office: 5500 N St Louis St Chicago IL 60625

GORDON, STUART, theater producer and dir., playwright; b. Chgo., Aug. 11, 1947; s. Bernard Leo and Rosalie (Sabbath) G.; student U. Wis.; m. Carolyn Purdy, Dec. 20, 1968; 1 dau., Suzanna Katherine. Founder, producing dir. Organic Theater Co., Chgo., 1969—, dir. nat. TV show Bleacher Bums; dir. Broadway, off-Broadway, throughout U.S. and Europe. Former mem. bd. dirs. Ill. Arts Council. Recipient Emmy award for Bleacher Bums; Golden Hugo award for Bleacher Bums, Chgo. Internat. Film Festival; Joseph Jefferson awards for writing and directing. Mem. League Chgo. Theaters (dir.), Theater Communications Group (past dir.). Jewish. Office: 3319 N Clark St Chicago IL 60657

GORDON, VIRGINIA NISWONGER, coll. adminstr.; b. Dayton, Ohio, Dec. 13, 1927; d. Milo E. and Irma (Kopf) Niswonger; B.S., Ohio State U., 1949, M.A., 1972, Ph.D., 1977; m. George D. Gordon, July 21, 1950; children—David, Catherine, Robert. Instr. dental hygiene Coll. Dentistry Ohio State U., Columbus, 1949-52, academic advisor, 1972-73, coordinator career devel., acad. advisement, 1973—, also adj. asst. prof. Coll. Edn.; cons. in field. Mem. Am. Personnel and Guidance Assn., Am. Coll. Personnel Assn., Nat. Vocat. Guidance Assn., Mortar Bd. (nat. council 1964-73), Phi Delta Kappa. Author numerous publs. in field. Home: 2924 Wellesley Dr Columbus OH 43221 Office: 025 W Hall Univ Coll Ohio State Univ Columbus OH 43210

GORE, CATHERINE ANN, social worker; b. Mullens, W.Va., Feb. 2, 1937; d. Bernard Joseph and Agnes Cecilia (Spradling) G.; B.A., Thomas More Coll., 1968; M.S.W., Ohio State U., 1971, now postgrad. Caseworker, Cath. Charities, Cin., 1967-69, 71-72; psychiat. social worker Mcpl. Ct. Psychiat. Clinic, Cin., 1973; instr. psychiat. social work, social work supr., Ct. Psychiat. Center, U. Cin., 1974-77, asst. prof. psychiat. social work, coordinator consultation services, 1978-80, grad. research asso. Coll. Social Work, Ohio State U., Columbus, 1981—; cons. Hamilton County Welfare Dept.; instr. No. Ky. U. Mem. Nat. Assn. Social Workers, Acad. Cert. Social Workers. Democrat. Roman Catholic. Home: 2599 Scioto View Ln Columbus OH 43221

GORE, GEORGE JOSEPH, educator; b. Chgo., Mar. 9, 1926; s. Joseph and Agnes Gore; B.S. in Elec. Engring., U. Ill., 1949, M.S. in Mgmt., 1950; M.B.A. (teaching fellow 1954-57), U. Mich., 1956, Ph.D. in Mgmt., 1961; m. Bette Jeanne Iles, July 28, 1949. With Gen. Electric Co., 1950, DuPont Co., 1950-54; lectr. U. Mich., 1957-59; mem. faculty U. Cin., 1959—, prof. mgmt., 1965—; pres. George J. Gore & Assos., mgmt. cons., 1958—. Served with USNR, 1944-46. Fellow Nat. Acad. Mgmt. (gov. 1970-73, v.p. 1971-73, chmn. div. managerial cons. 1977, chmn. div. prodn./ops. mgmt. 1975, prof.-in-charge U. Cin. prodn. unit 1959-76, originator various acad. publs. 1971—); mem. Mensa, Theta Delta Chi (Most Promising Grad. award 1949), Beta Gamma Sigma, Sigma Iota Epsilon, Eta Kappa Nu, Sigma Tau. Republican. Presbyterian. Club: Shriners. Author: Survey of Industrial Relations in Leading Road Construction Firms, 1961; co-author: The Academic/Consultant Connection, 1979; Consultants Manual, 1980; author numerous articles, lectr. in field. Home: 610 Terrace Ave Cincinnati OH 45220 Office: Coll Bus Adminstrn U Cin Cincinnati OH 45221

GOREN, SIMON LESLIE, librarian, educator; b. Gencs, Hungary, Nov. 9, 1913; s. Ignac and Elizabeth (Klein) Grossman; came to U.S., 1959, naturalized, 1965; Matriculation certificate, Realgimnasium, Debrecen, Hungary, 1923-31; diploma of law, British Mandatory Govt. Law Sch., 1948; M.L.S., Columbia U., 1960; m. Hilda Feuerstein, Aug. 11, 1943; children—Daphne Judith, Michael. Practice of law, Haifa, Israel, 1951-59; librarian Cleary, Gottlieb, Steen & Hamilton, N.Y.C., 1960-63; asst. law librarian Cornell U. Sch. of Law, 1964-67; law librarian Case Western Reserve U., Cleve., 1967—, prof. law, 1970—. Mem. Internat. Assn. Law Libraries, Am. Library Assn., Am. Assn. Law Libraries, Order of Coif. Home: 3380 Ingleside Rd Shaker Heights OH 44122 Office: 11075 East Blvd Cleveland OH 44106

GORFINKEL, H. JOEL, cardiologist; b. Evansville, Ind., June 23, 1940; s. Joseph Abraham and Shirley (Dolgin) G.; M.D., U. Ill., 1965; m. Dana Renner, May 15, 1977; children by previous marriage—Jordan Brian, Caryn Rachel. Intern, Michael Reese Hosp., Chgo., 1965-66, resident, 1966-69; cardiology fellow U. Pa., Phila., 1969-71; chief cardiology Ireland Army Hosp., Ft. Knox, Ky., 1971-73; asst. prof. medicine, asso. dir. coronary care unit George Washington U. Med. Center, Washington, 1973-76; asso. prof. medicine and surgery, dir. cardiac catheterization lab. George Washington U. Med. Center, VA Hosp., Washington, 1977-78; practice medicine specializing in cardiology, Columbus, Ohio, 1978—; asso. clin. prof. medicine Ohio State U., Columbus, 1981—; chief dept. medicine St. Ann's Hosp., Columbus, 1981—; project dir. Advanced Cardiac Life Support Program, Washington Met. area, 1976-77. Served to maj., M.C., U.S. Army, 1971-73. Diplomate Am. Bd. Internal Medicine and Cardiovascular Diseases. Fellow ACP, Am. Coll. Cardiology, Am. Heart Assn. (dir. 1977-78); mem. Am. Fedn. Clin. Research. Home: 6703 Elmers Ct Worthington OH 43085 Office: 777 W State St Columbus OH 43222

GORHAM, EUGENE TIMOTHY, conveyor co. exec.; b. Chgo., May 2, 1935; s. Sidney Smith and Corinne (McVoy) G.; B.M.E., Stanford, 1957; m. Barbara Francis Steinke, Nov. 26, 1966; children—Jonathon Lewis, Eugene Timothy, Brooke Lee, Whitney Ann. Indsl. engr. U.S. Rubber Co., Chgo., 1959-60, Oscar Mayer Co., Chgo., 1960-61; sales engr. Olson Conveyor Co. (now div. ACCO), Franklin Park, Ill., 1962-67; v.p. sales Automotion, Inc. (Ill. Corp.), Alsip, Ill., 1967-73; v.p. AW&H Mfg. Co., 1973-78; pres. Automotion Inc. (Del. Corp.), Alsip, 1973-78, dir., v.p., 1978-81, pres., 1981—; partner AW & H Leasing Corp. Served with AUS, 1957. Mem. Internat. Material Mgmt. Soc., Material Handling Equipment Distbrs. Assn. (chmn. engineered products com. 1971-75, dir.), Am. Material Mgmt. Soc., Chi Psi. Clubs: Pentwater (Mich.) Yacht; Saddle and Cycle, Tavern (Chgo.). Home: 1201 Chatfield Rd Winnetka IL 60093 Office: 11743 S Mayfield Ave Alsip IL 60482

GORHAM, EVILLE, biologist, educator; b. Halifax, Can., Oct. 15, 1925; s. Ralph A. and Shirley A. (Eville) G.; B.Sc. in Biology, with distinction, Dalhousie U., Can., 1945, M.Sc. in Zoology, 1947; Ph.D. in Botany, U. London, Eng., 1951; came to U.S., 1962; m. Ada Verne MacLeod, Sept. 29, 1948; children—Kerstin, Vivien, Jocelyn, James. Lectr. botany U. Coll., London, Eng., 1951-54; sr. sci. officer Freshwater Biol. Assn., Ambleside, Eng., 1954-58; lectr., botany U. Toronto, Ont., Can., 1958-59, asst. prof., 1960-62; asso. prof. botany U. Minn., Mpls., 1962-65, prof., 1966—, head dept., 1967-71, prof. ecology, 1975—; prof., head dept. biology U. Calgary, Alta., Can., 1965-66; Canadian mem. Internat. Commn. on Atmospheric Chemistry and Radioactivity, 1959-62; mem. vis. com. toxicology programs Assembly Life Scis., Nat. Acad. Scis., 1974-75, coordinating com. for sci. and tech. assessment of environ. pollutants Environ. Studies Bd., 1975-78, mem. com. on med. and biol. effects of environ. pollutants Assembly Life Scis., 1976-77, Com. on atmosphere and biosphere Commn. Natural Resources, 1979-81; mem. panel on environ. impact diesel impact study com. Nat. Acad. Engring., 80-81; mem. U.S.-Can. joint sci. com. on acid precipitation environ. studies bd. Nat. Acad. Scis./Royal Soc. Can., 1981—. NSF grantee, 1962-73, 80—; NIH grantee, 1978-82; NRC Can. grantee, 1959-60, 65; AEC grantee, 1967-68; ERDA grantee, 1977-79. Fellow Scientists Inst. for Public Info.; mem. Internat. Assn. Pure and Applied Limnology, Am. Soc. Limnology and Oceanography, Ecol. Soc. Am. Contbr. articles on ecology, limnology and biogeochemistry to profl. jours.; editorial bd. Ecology, 1965-67, Limnology and Oceanography, 1970-72. Office: Univ Minn 318 Church St Minneapolis MN 55455

GORMAN, CORNELIUS FRANCIS, JR., mfg. co. exec.; b. N.Y.C., Aug. 13, 1952; s. Cornelius Francis and Madonna I. (Riendeau) G.; B.S., Marquette U., 1974; m. Rita Elaine Iris, May 21, 1974; 1 son, Cornelius Francis. Sales rep. Robertson, Inc., Milw., 1975-76, Surg. div. Parke-Davis, Madison, Wis., 1976-77, IPCO Hosp. Supply, Chgo., 1977-78, Medi, Inc., Chgo., 1978-79; regional rep. William Harvey Research Corp., Detroit, 1979—. Mem. Assn. Practitioners in Infection Control, Jaycees (v.p. internal affairs 1976, SPOKE award 1976). Roman Catholic. Home: 28423 Raleigh Crescent New Baltimore MI 48207

GORMAN, GERALD WARNER, lawyer; b. North Kansas City, Mo., May 30, 1933; s. William Shelton and Bessie (Warner) G.; A.B. cum laude, Harvard U., 1954, LL.B. magna cum laude, 1956; m. Anita Belle McPike, June 26, 1954; children—Guinevere Eve, Victoria Rose. Admitted to Mo. bar, 1956, since practiced in Kansas City; asso. firm Dietrich, Tyler, Davis, Burrell & Dicus, 1956-62, partner, 1963—; dir. North Kansas City State Bank, Musser-Davis Land Co. Bd. govs. Citizens Assn. Kansas City, 1962—; trustee Harvard/Radcliffe Club Kansas City Endowment Fund, chmn. bd., 1977—; trustee Kansas City Mus., 1967—, Avondale Methodist Ch., 1969—, Citizens Bond Com. of Kansas City, 1973—; bd. dirs. Spofford Home for Children, 1972-77. Served with AUS, 1956-58. Mem. Lawyers Assn. Kansas City (exec. com. 1968-71), Am., Mo., Kansas City, Clay County bar assns., Harvard Law Sch. Assn. Mo. (pres. 1973). Republican. Clubs: Harvard (pres. 1966), Univ., Kansas City, Old Pike Country. Home: 917 E Vivion Rd Kansas City MO 64118 Office: 1700 City Center Sq Kansas City MO 64105

GORMAN, ROBERT JAMES, lawyer; b. Chgo., Apr. 22, 1915; s. James E. and Isabel M. (O'Brien) G.; student Northwestern U., 1934-37; J.D., Chgo. Kent Coll. Law, 1940; children—Robert C., Gregory X., Candace. Admitted to Ill. bar, 1940; practice law, Chgo., 1945—; mem. firm Gorman & Gorman; atty. Roosevelt U. Served to 1st lt. C.E., AUS, 1941-45. Mem. Am., Ill., Chgo. bar assns., Nat. Assn. Coll. and Univ. Attys., Phi Alpha Delta. Democrat. Unitarian. Home: 3734 N Wilton St Chicago IL 60613 Office: 10 S LaSalle St Chicago IL 60603

GORNICK, ALAN LEWIS, lawyer, tax counsel; b. Leadville, Colo.; s. Mark and Anne (Grayhack) G.; A.B., Columbia U., 1935, LL.B., 1937; m. Ruth L. Willcockson, 1940 (dec.); children—Alan Lewis, Diana (Mrs. Lawrence J. Richard), Keith Hardin; m. Pauline Martoi, 1972. Admitted to N.Y. State bar, 1937; practiced with firm Baldwin, Todd & Young, N.Y.C., 1937-41; practiced with firm Milbank, Tweed, Hope & Hadley, 1941-47, mem. firm, 1947; asso. counsel charge tax matters Ford Motor Co., Dearborn, Mich., 1947-49, dir. tax affairs, tax counsel, 1949-64; lectr. tax matters N.Y.U. Inst. on Fed. Taxation, 1947-49, Am. Bar Assn. and Practising Law Inst. courses on fundamentals in fed. taxation, 1946-55, Am. Law Inst. courses in continuing legal edn., 1950; spl. lectr. sch. bus. adminstrn. U. Mich., 1949, 53; chmn. Otsego Ski Club-Hidden Valley, Inc., Gaylord, Mich., Perry-Davis, Inc.; pres. Meadowbrook Park Devel. Co.; v.p. Bloomfield Center, Inc., Bloomfield Hills, Mich.; dir. Brooks & Perkins, Inc. Chmn. state and fed. tax coms.; mem. Mayor's Detroit Tomorrow Com., Citizens Adv. Com. on Taxation to Mich. Senate, Detroit Bd. Commerce; chmn. Mich. tax survey adv. com. Legis. Interim Tax and Revenue Study Com., 1951-53; chmn. Mich. State Aid Survey Com.; pres. Mich. Assn. Emotionally Disturbed Children, 1962; mem. exec. bd. adv. council Detroit area council Boy Scouts Am.; v.p., trustee Detroit chpt. Archives of Am. Art; v.p. Detroit Hist. Soc., 1980; mem. fin. com. Mich. Heart Assn. Recipient Gov.'s Spl. Award State of Colo., 1952; Distinguished Alumni Accomplishment medal Columbia, 1947. Mem. Fed., Am. (mem. fed. tax com. 1954-56; chmn. subcom. on health and welfare plans, com. pension and profit sharing trusts, sect. taxation 1950, com. extra-territorial application of taxes 1951), Mich., Detroit, N.Y.C. (chmn. subcom. estate and gift taxes 1943-47) bar assns., Am. Law Inst., Tax Inst. Inc. (pres. 1954-55, dir. 1951), Nat. Tax Assn. (exec. com. 1954-56), Internat. Fiscal Assn. (council mem.; nat. reporter 6th Internat. Congress Fiscal Law, Brussels 1952), Internat. Law Assn., World Assn. Lawyers, U.S. C. of C. (mem. taxation com.), Assn. Ex-Mems. Squadron A., Nat. Fgn. Trade Council (mem. com. taxes 1950), Automobile Mfrs. Assn. (chmn. com. taxation 1961-63), Tax Exec. Inst. (pres. 1956-57), Fedn. Alumni Columbia (dir. 1946), Class of 1935, Columbia Coll. (permanent pres.), Supreme Ct. Hist. Soc. (founder mem.), N.Y. Adult Edn. Council, Inc. (dir. 1939-45), Phi Delta Phi. Clubs: Bloomfield Hills Country; Detroit, Detroit Athletic; University (Washington); Columbia University, Church (N.Y.C.); Lawyers (Univ. Mich.); Little (Gulfstream, Fla.); Columbia University Alumni of Mich. (pres. 1950). Author: Divorce, Separation and Estate Taxes, Estate Tax Handbook, 1952; Arrangements for Separation or Divorce, Handbook of Tax Techniques, 1952; Taxation of Partnerships, Estates and Trusts, rev. edit., 1952. Adv. editor Nat. Tax Jour., 1952. Contbr. articles tax matters to various law revs., profl. publs. Home: PO Box J Bloomfield Hills MI 48013 Office: PO Box J 1565 Woodward Ave Suite 8 Bloomfield Hills MI 48013

GORNY, JOHN LOUIS, printing co. exec.; b. Toledo, Oct. 14, 1914; s. John Louis and Pauline (Kinest) G.; grad. high sch.; m. Lorraine Norma Thorp, July 24, 1942; children—David, Shelley (Mrs. John Hickey Schoenherr). Partner, Gorny-Winzeler, Inc., Bryan, Ohio, 1934-42, pres., 1942-80, chmn. bd., 1980—; pres. Gorny-Winzeler Printing, Inc., 1979—; owner, Surrey Shop, Gaylord, Mich., 1960, Four Seasons Gifts, Gaylord, 1975—. Served with USAAF, 1942-45. Mem. Nat. Office Products Assn., Nat. Office Machine Dealers Assn., Nat. Assn. Printers and Lithographers, Ohio Retail Dealers Assn., Mich. Retailers Assn. (dir. gift div. 1972-76), Bryan C. of C. (dir. 1949-57, pres. 1956). Moose, K.C., Eagle. Clubs: Otsego Ski, Hidden Valley (Gaylord); Orchard Hill Country (Bryan). Home: Route 4 3548 Nowak Rd Gaylord MI 49735 Office: 110-120 S Lynn St Bryan OH 43506

GORSKE, ROBERT HERMAN, lawyer; b. Milw., June 8, 1932; s. Herman Albert and Lorraine (McDermott) G.; student Milw. State Tchrs. Coll., 1949-50; B.A. cum laude, Marquette U., 1953, J.D. magna cum laude, 1955; LL.M. (W.W. Cook fellow), U. Mich., 1959; m. Antonette Dujick, Aug. 28, 1954; 1 dau., Judith Mary. Admitted to Wis. bar, 1955, D.C. bar, 1968, U.S. Supreme Ct. bar, 1970; asso. firm Quarles, Spence & Quarles, Milw., 1955-56; atty. Allis-Chalmers Mfg. Co., West Allis, Wis., 1956-62; instr. law U. Mich. Law Sch., Ann Arbor, 1958-59; lectr. law Marquette U. Law Sch., 1963; asso. firm Quarles, Herriott & Clemons, Milw., 1962-64; atty. Wis. Electric Power Co., Milw., 1964-67, gen. counsel, 1967—, v.p., 1970-72, 76—; mem. firm Quarles & Brady, Milw., 1972-76; dir. Wis. Natural Gas Co., Racine, Wis., Wis. Mich. Power Co., Appleton. Bd. dirs. Guadalupe Children's Med. Dental Clinic, Inc., Milw., 1976—. Mem. State Bar Wis., Am. Bar Assn., Edison Electric Inst. (vice chmn. legal com. 1975-77, chmn. 1977-79). Contbr. articles to profl. jours. Editor-in-chief Marquette Law Rev., 1954-55. Home: 12700 Stephen Pl Elm Grove WI 53122 Office: 231 W Michigan St Milwaukee WI 53203

GOSKY, GARRY ALAN, physician; b. Cleve., July 13, 1946; s. Walter Franklin and Regina Claudia (Kurcz) G.; B.A., Case Western Res. U., 1968; M.D., Ohio State U., 1972; m. Patricia Lynn O'Brien, June 20, 1970; children—Ross, Brad, Jill, Paul. Intern, Rainbow Babies and Children's Hosp., 1972, resident, 1973, chief resident, 1974, pediatrician Hydrocephalus-Myelodysplasia Clinic, 1974-77, sr. instr. pediatrics, 1975-76, asst. prof., 1976-77, asst. prof. clin. pediatrics, 1977—, researcher dept. community health, 1975—; dir. pediatrics Charity Hosp., Cleve., 1977-81; mem. staff Cleve. Met. Gen. Hosp.; pediatric dir. child devel. units and Ohio residential services Aristocrat West and South Extended Care Facilities, 1976—; pediatric dir. Children's Aid Soc., PVA Group Home, 1975—; med. dir. Cleve. Devel. Center, 1980-81; cons. Fedn. Community Planning, 1978; nat. pediatric advisor Marcare Corp. Health Delivery Systems, 1977-81; mem. adv. bd. Birthright Cleve., 1978—; med. cons. Health Edn. Learning Programs, Inc., 1978—; west side coordinator Marriage Encounter, 1978-80; nat. med. cons. Producer Services, Inc., 1979-81. Johnson Found. nat. clin. scholar, 1975-77; diplomate Am. Bd. Pediatrics. Mem. Landacre Research Soc., Alpha Omega Alpha. Roman Catholic. Contbr. articles to profl. jours. Home: 17301 Fernshaw Ave Cleveland OH 44111 Office: 2101 Adelbert Rd Cleveland OH 44106 also 7th Floor Faculty Mailbox Cleveland OH 44106

GOSS, JAMES ARTHUR, botanist; b. Brigham City, Utah, May 19, 1924; s. Archie James and Mary Alberta (Pulsipher) G.; B.S., Utah State U., 1951; Ph.D., UCLA, 1957; m. Lucille Woolley, Mar. 21, 1947; children—Lawrence Arthur, Raymond Lynn, Linda Lucille, Gerald Lee, Liana Denise, Lori Jean. Jr. plant physiologist Salinity Lab., U.S. Dept. Agr., Riverside, Calif., 1951-53; research asst. atomic energy project Sch. Medicine, UCLA, 1953-56; mem. faculty div. biology Kans. State U., Manhattan, 1956-76; livestock feed analyst Scott-Pro, Inc., Scott City, Kans., 1979—; lectr. throughout world. Mem. Sigma Xi, Gamma Sigma Delta. Mormon. Author: Physiology of Plants and Their Cells; contbr. articles to profl. jours., mags., newspapers; research on plant physiology and chemistry.

GOSSER, JON WALTER, educator; b. Seattle, May 15, 1941; s. Lawrence and Ellinore (Jones) G.; B.S. cum laude, U. Wash., 1962, M.S., 1964, postgrad., 1964-65; postgrad. U. Kans., 1965-67. Reader in stats. U. Wash., Seattle, fellow research asst. in psychology, 1962-63, USPHS predoctoral research fellow NIMH, 1963-65; predoctoral trainee in ednl. research Bur. Child Research, U. Kans., Kansas City, 1965-66; tchr. psychology, logic and marriage and family relations Kansas City (Kans.) Community Jr. Coll., 1966-67; instr. psychology Delta Coll., University Center, Mich., 1967-69, asst. prof., 1970-75, asso. prof., 1975—, dir. Mid-Mich. Psychologist, Inc., 1973-76, 79—, treas., 1978—; bd. dirs., v.p. Nat. Ednl. Network, Inc., 1982—. Mem. Data Processing Mgmt. Assn. (dir. 1971-73; individual performance award 1981), Am. Psychol. Assn., AAAS, AAUP (corr. sec. Delta chpt. 1969), Am. Ednl. Research Assn., Assn. Behavior Analysis, Mich. Acad. Sci., Arts and Letters, Sigma Xi. Author: (with Harbans Lal) Research on Teaching Pharmacy: The Role of Student Ratings, 1968; A Computerized Method of Longitudinal Evaluation of Student Performance, 1969; Computerized Test Library, 1974; Longitudinal Evaluation and Improvement of Teaching: An Empirical Approach Based on Analysis of Student Behaviors, 1975; (with Packwood and Walters) The Effect of Repeated Testing on Long Term Retention and Generalization in a General Psychology Course, 1979. Home: 3200 Noeske St Midland MI 48640 Office: Delta Coll University Center MI 48710

GOSSETT, ELIZABETH HUGHES (MRS. WILLIAM THOMAS GOSSETT), civic worker; b. Albany, N.Y., Aug. 19, 1907; d. Charles Evans and Antoinette (Carter) Hughes; student Brearley Sch., N.Y.C., 1917-19, Miss Madeira's Sch., Washington, 1923-25; A.B., Barnard Coll., Columbia, 1929; LL.D. (hon.), N.Y. Law Sch., 1977; m. William Thomas Gossett, Dec. 19, 1930; children—Antoinette Carter Gossett Wardrip, William Thomas, Elizabeth G. Karaman. Former bd. dirs. Detroit Urban League; v.p. found. trustees Mich. State U., Oakland 1957-67; trustee Barnard Coll., 1953-70, Merrill-Palmer Inst., Detroit, 1957-71; mem. Jud. Fellows Commn., Washington; former bd. dirs. Kingswood Sch., Cranbrook, Brookside Sch. Cranbrook, Bloomfield Hills, Mich.; former nat. bd. dirs. NCCJ; gov. emeritus Cranbrook Acad. Art; former mem. bd. dirs. Cranbrook Ednl. Community, Bloomfield Hills, Mich. Mem. UN Assn. (past pres. Detroit), Supreme Ct. Hist. Soc. (chmn.), Jr. League. Republican. Episcopalian. Clubs: Barnard Coll. of Detroit; Sulgrave (Washington). Home: 1276 Covington Rd Birmingham MI 48010

GOSSETT, T. K., chiropractic physician; b. Mount Carmel, Ill., May 19, 1954; s. Leo and Gwen Sue (Eldridge) G.; Asso. Sci., Parkland Jr. Coll., 1974; D. Chiropractic, Logan Coll. Chiropractic, 1978; m. Alexia Marie Howard, May 31, 1980. Intern, Logan Chiropractic Coll., St. Louis, 1976-77; resident Gilbertson Clinic Chiropractic, St. Louis, 1977-78; chief staff Gossett Clinic Chiropractic, Monticello, Ill., 1978—. Recipient award Centurian Club, 1980. Diplomate Nat. Bd. Chiropractic Examiners. Mem. Am. Chiropractic Assn. (councils on orthopedics, roentgenology and sports injuries), Ill. Chiropractic Soc., Chiro Sigma Chi, Clinic Masters. Club: Lions. Home: 1D Evergreen Circle Champaign IL 61875 Office: 113 E Washington St Monticello IL 61856

GOSSMAN, THERESA DIANE, social worker; b. Decorah, Iowa, Sept. 20, 1942; d. Arland Eugene and Kathleen Mae (Knox) G.; B.A. cum laude, Briar Cliff Coll., 1967; M.A. with distinction, DePaul U., 1979. Joined Franciscan Order, 1961; tchr. elem. sch., Iowa, 1965-67, Niles, Ill., 1967-74; coordinator religious edn. St. John Brebeuf Sch., Niles, 1967-73; counsellor St. John Berchmans Sch., 1976-80, group facilitator for women, 1976-77; social worker, Cath. Charities, 1974-78, guidance counsellor, St. John Berchman's, Chgo., 1974-79; mgr.-dir. youth programs Mercy Mission Home for Boys, Chgo., 1979—; cons. to community based service groups. Co-founder Logan Sq. Community Found. Registered social worker, Ill. Mem. Am. Personnel and Guidance Assn. Roman Catholic. Office: 1140 W Jackson Blvd Chicago IL 60607

GOTHAM, BYRON ROY, mech. engr., mfg. co. exec.; b. St. Louis, Mich., Nov. 8, 1926; s. Willard E. and Rosa Ella (Langin) G.; diploma Electronics Inst., Detroit, 1949; postgrad. Lawrence Inst. Tech., Southfield, Mich., 1957-59, Schoolcraft Coll., Livonia, Mich., 1972; m. Alice Nancy Jensen, June 30, 1951; children—Janice Rose, Gregory Roy. With standards lab. Burroughs Corp., Detroit, 1957-60; mem. staff research labs. Bendix Corp., Southfield, 1960—, supr. mech. engring. lab., 1966—; participant Soc. Automotive Engrs. Conv., Detroit, 1978. Mgr. youth hockey team Livonia Hockey Assn., 1970, coach men's hockey team, 1969; counselor youth camp Livonia Public Sch., 1968. Served with USN, 1945-46. Recipient Commemorative medallion NASA, 1972. Mem. Nat. Mgmt. Assn. Clubs: Western Racquet (Livonia); Pontiac (Mich.) Ski. Author reports and invention disclosures in field. Home: 14562 Ronnie Ln Livonia MI 48154 Office: Bendix Corp Bendix Center Southfield MI 48037

GOTKIN, MICHAEL STANLEY, lawyer; b. Washington, Aug. 15, 1942; s. Charles and Florence (Rosenberg) G.; A.A., Montgomery Community Coll., 1962; B.S., Columbia U., 1964; J.D., Vanderbilt U., 1967; m. Diana Rubin, Aug. 22, 1964; children—Lisa, Steven. Admitted to D.C. bar, 1968, Tenn. bar, 1973; trial atty. Bur. Restraint of Trade, FTC, Washington, 1967-70; atty. H.J. Heinz Co., Pitts., 1970-73; partner firm Moseley & Gotkin, Nashville, 1973; atty. K.F.C. Corp., Louisville, 1974-75; v.p., gen. counsel Farley Candy Co., Skokie, Ill., 1975—, also dir.; v.p., gen. counsel, dir. T.A. White Co., Candy Products Corp., Taste-T-Sweets, Inc., Pearson Candy Co., St. Paul, Am. Flexo Inc., Skokie, So. Spirits, Inc., Montgomery, Ala. Mem. Am. Bar Assn., Inter Am. Bar Assn., D.C. Bar Assn., Tenn. Bar Assn., Montgomery Community Coll. Assn. (past pres.), Columbia U. Alumni Assn., Vanderbilt U. Alumni Assn. Clubs: Sportsman Country, B'nai B'rith. Office: 4820 Searle Pkwy Skokie IL 60077

GOTTFRIED, MAX, med. equipment mfg. co. exec.; b. Toledo, Aug. 27, 1921; s. Morris and Gussie (Yerzy) G.; student Toledo U., 1939-40, 46-48; children—Brent Morris, Mark Ellis. Sales mgr. Columbus Hosp. Supply Co., Toledo, 1951-60; v.p. Jobst Inst., Toledo, 1960-78; pres. Gottfried Med., Inc., 1981—. Served with AUS, 1940-45. Mem. Aerospace Med. Assn., Assn. for Advancement Med. Instrumentation, Health Care Exhibitors Assn. (dir.). Patentee med. products. Home: 4340 Old Lyme Rd Toledo OH 43623 Office: 5333 Secor Rd Unit 1 Toledo OH 43623

GOTTLIEB, HAROLD JORAHMIEL, hosp. accreditation orgn. exec.; b. Bklyn., Nov. 11, 1933; s. Nathan and Rose (Friedlander) G.; B.S. in Health Edn., Bklyn. Coll., 1954; M.H.A., U. Minn., 1968; m. Frances Pauline Bluthal, Feb. 20, 1955; children—Zevie B., Aryea, Tobi D., Miriam Y. Commd. 2d lt. USAF, 1954, advanced through grades to col., 1975; service in Japan; hosp. mgmt. cons. USAF, Norton AFB, Calif., 1972-75; exec. dir. health services mgmt. Office Surgeon, SAC, Offutt AFB, Nebr., 1975-81; ret., 1981; adminstr. field rep. hosp. accreditation program Joint Commn. on Accreditation Hosps., Chgo., 1981—; cons. in field. Decorated Meritorious Service medal with oak leaf cluster, Air Force Commendation medal with 2 oak leaf cluster, Legion of Merit. Fellow Am. Coll. Hosp. Adminstrs., Royal Soc. Health; mem. Am. Public Health Assn., Am. Hosp. Assn. Author papers in field. Home: 905 Sherman Circle Papillion NE 68046 Office: Hosp Accreditation Program Joint Commn on Accreditation Hosps 875 N Michigan Ave Chicago IL 60611

GOTTLIEB, REYNOLD JAMES, radiologist; b. N.Y.C., Jan. 16, 1922; s. B. J. and Irene (Mollin) G.; B.A., N.Y. U., 1943; M.D., Chgo. Med. Sch., 1950; m. Ellen Jennette Frame, Sept. 18, 1949; children—Elizabeth, John, Margaret, Laurie. Intern, U. Ill. Hosps., Chgo., 1950-51; resident in radiology St. Luke's Hosp., Chgo., 1951-53, Cook County Hosp., Chgo., 1953-54; chmn. dept. radiology Oak Forest (Ill.) Hosp., 1954—; chief radiologist Suburban Hosp., Hinsdale, Ill., 1955—; cons. in radiology Armed Forces Induction Center, Western Electric Co.; clin. asso. Loyola U. Stritch Sch. Medicine, Chgo., 1970-76; dir. Heritage Bank Oakwood, Westmont, Ill. Served with U.S. Army, 1943-46, to col. USAR, 1946—. Diplomate Am. Bd. Radiology. Mem. AMA, Am. Coll. Radiology, Am. Coll. Chest Physicians. Republican. Presbyterian. Clubs: Itasca Country, Oak Brook Polo, Execs. of Oak Brook (pres., founder). Home: 27 Brighton Ln Oak Brook IL 60521 Office: 120 Professional Bldg Oak Brook IL 60521

GOTTLIEB, SHELDON FRED, biologist, educator; b. Bronx, N.Y., Dec. 22, 1932; s. Elias and Dorothy (Gerstenfeld) G.; B.A., Bklyn. Coll., 1953; M.S., U. Mass., 1956; Ph.D. (Teaching fellow), U. Tex. Med. Br., 1959; m. Eda Judith Robin Held, Aug. 25, 1956; children—Stephen Eric, Pamela Lynn, Glenn Ira, William Scott. Research physiologist Linde div. Union Carbide Corp., Tonawanda, N.Y., 1959-64; asst. prof. physiology and anesthesiology Jefferson Med. Coll., Phila., 1964-68; prof. biol. scis. Ind. U.-Purdue U., Ft Wayne, Ind., 1968—; cons. Edn. Devel. Center, Inc., 1976—, hyperbaric unit Brooks AFB, San Antonio, 1975—, Gorsuch Scarisbrick, publishers, 1978; guest speaker various radio and TV programs, 1969—; guest lectr. various civic, ednl., religious and profl. orgns., 1968—. Chmn. com. troop 491 Boy Scouts Am., 1969-70; judge Sci. Fair, Ft. Wayne Community Schs., 1969-75, 77-79; mem. Ind. State Bd. Advs., Anti-Defamation League of B'nai B'rith, 1968—; mem. Jewish Religious Council of Ft. Wayne, 1969—; pres. B'nai Jacob Synagogue, 1972; pres. Tamarack Homeowner's Assn., 1970-71; mem. Coalition for the Environment, Ft. Wayne, 1970—, pres., 1970-71; mem. NE area adv. council No. Ind. Health Systems Agy., 1976—. Served with U.S. Army, 1954-56. Eli Lilly Found. grantee, 1968; NIH grantee, 1968; Hoffman La Roche grantee, 1977. Mem. Am. Inst. Biol. Scis., Am. Physiol. Soc., Am. Soc. Microbiology, Soc. Gen. Physiologists, Fedn. Am. Socs. for Exptl. Biology (nat. corr. 1976—), Undersea Med. Soc. (com. hyperbaric oxygen therapy 1977—), AAAS, Aerospace Med. Assn., N.Y. Acad. Scis., Izaak Walton League Am., Am. Heart Assn. (dir. NE Ind. chpt. 1972—, pres. 1974, dir. Ind. affiliate 1974—), Sigma Xi. Contbr. articles on physiology and microbiology to sci. jours. Home: 4824 Tirol Pass Fort Wayne IN 46815 Office: 2101 Coliseum Blvd E Fort Wayne IN 46805

GOTTSCHALK, ALFRED, bibl. scholar, author, coll. pres.; b. Oberwesel Germany, Mar. 7, 1930; s. Max and Erna (Trum-Gerson) G.; came to U.S., 1939, naturalized, 1945; A.B., Bklyn. Coll., 1952; B. Hebrew Lit., Hebrew Union Coll., 1954, M.A. with honors, 1956; Ph.D., U. So. Calif., 1965, S.T.D. (hon.), 1968, LL.D. (hon.), 1976; D.Litt. (hon.), Dropsie U., 1974; D.R.E. (hon.), Loyola Marymount U., 1977; LL.D. (hon.), U. Cin., 1976, Xavier U., 1981; L.H.D. (hon.), Jewish Theol. Sem., 1971; m. Deanna Zeff, Dec. 31, 1977; children by previous marriage—Marc Hillel, Rachel Lisa. Ordained rabbi, 1957; instr. Jewish history Hebrew Union Coll.-Jewish Inst. Religion, Cin., 1957-59, asst. prof. Bible, 1959-62, asso. prof., 1962-65, prof., 1965—, pres., 1971—; acting dean Hebrew Union Coll., Los Angeles, 1958-59, dean, 1959-71; vis. prof. UCLA, 1966, 68, 70, 71; mem. exec. com. Central Conf. Am. Rabbis, 1971—, Frank L. Weil Inst. Religion and Humanities, 1971—. Mem. Pres. Johnson's Com. Equal Employment Opportunity, 1964-66, Calif. Gov.'s Poverty Support Corps Program, 1965-67, Los Angeles Mayor's Community Devel. Adv. Com., 1965-70; trustee Council Religious and Interreligious Affairs, 1975-78, Albright Inst. Archaeol. Research, 1973—, Union Am. Hebrew Congregations, 1972; mem. Pres.'s Commn. on the Holocaust, 1979-80; co-chmn. coordinating com. Holocaust Meml. Council, 1980—. Recipient Human Relations award Am. Jewish Com., 1971, Los Angeles City Council award, 1971, Tower of David award for Cultural Contbn. to Israel and Am., Israel Govt., 1972, Gold Medallion award Jewish Nat. Fund, 1972, Myrtle Wreath award Hadassah, 1977, Alumnus of Year award Bklyn. Coll., 1972, Man of Year award Boys High Sch. Alumni Assn., 1976; Nat. Educators award NCCJ, 1980; Guggenheim fellow, 1969, Smithsonian Inst. grantee, 1963, 67. Mem. NEA, Soc. Bibl. Lit. and Exegesis, Am. Philos. Soc., Am. Acad. Religion, Am. Assn. Higher Edn., World Union Jewish Studies, So. Calif. Jewish Hist. Soc. (hon. pres. 1972—), Jewish Publ. Soc. Am. (publs. com. 1975), Assn. Theol. Schs. (exec. com. 1974-76), World Union Progressive Judaism (v.p. 1973—), Israel Exploration Soc., N.Y. Bd. Rabbis (hon. v.p. 1972—), World Inst. Sephardic Studies, Synagogue Council Am. (policy planning inst.), World Zionist Orgn., Am. Assn. Pres.'s of Ind. Colls. and Univs., Am. Friends of Alliance Israelite Universelle (trustee 1972—), So. Calif. Assn. Liberal Rabbis (pres. 1965-66), Zionist Fedn. Am. (organizing pres. western region 1968), Zionist Orgn. Am. (Louis Dembitz Brandeis award 1977, v.p. western region 1960-62), Delta Sigma Rho. Contbr. articles to scholarly and popular jours.; editorial bd. Hebrew Union Coll. Ann. Home: 17 Belsaw Place Cincinnati OH 45220

GOTTSCHALK, ROBERT, lawyer, cons.; b. N.Y.C., Jan. 10, 1911; B.S. in Elec. Engring., McGill U., 1931; LL.B. cum laude, St. Lawrence U., 1934; m. Elizabeth von Papen, 1934; 1 son, William P. Admitted to N.Y. bar, 1935, Ill. bar, 1946, D.C. bar, 1973, U.S. Supreme Ct. bar, 1974; asso. firm von Briesen and Schrenk, N.Y.C., 1935-41; patent and trademark counsel Corn Products Co., Chgo., 1941-46; asst. dir. devel. and patent dept., dir. of contracts and legal matters Standard Oil Co. of Ind., Chgo., 1946-61; gen. patent counsel

Canteen Corp., Chgo., 1961-65; dir. patents GAF Corp., N.Y.C., 1965-70; dep. commr. of patents U.S. Patent Office, Washington, 1970-71, commr. of patents, 1971-73; cons. to Govt. Patents Bd., 1950-55, White House Office of Telecommunications Policy, 1976, Iranian Nat. Petrochem. Co., 1976; lectr. in law U. Chgo., 1957; chmn. commn. patent policy Nat. Acad. Sci., 1962-67; mem. advisory bd. Patent Trademark and Copyright Jour., 1975—; legal and tech. cons., 1973—; head U.S. del. Vienna (Austria) Diplomatic Conf., 1973; U.S. signatory to Trademark Registration Treaty, 1973. Mem. Fed., Am., Chgo. bar assns., Am., N.Y., Chgo. patent law assns. Clubs: Nat. Lawyers (Washington); Chemists (N.Y.C.); Internat. Trade (Chgo.). Home: 183 Dickens Rd Northfield IL 60093 Office: 545 Lincoln Ave Winnetka IL 60093

GOUKE, CECIL GRANVILLE, economist, educator; b. Bklyn., Dec. 5, 1928; s. Joseph and Etheline (Grant) G.; B.A., CCNY, 1956; M.A., N.Y. U., 1958, Ph.D., 1967; m. Mary Noel, June 19, 1964; 1 son, Cecil Granville. Instr. econs. Fisk U., 1958-60; asst. prof. Grambling Coll., 1962-64, asso. prof., 1964-67; prof., chmn. Hampton (Va.) Inst., 1967-73; prof. econs. Ohio State U., 1973—; vis. lectr. U. Wis., 1970; vis. asso. prof. UCLA, 1969; economist Fed. Res. Bank N.Y., 1972; cons. U.S. Treasury Dept., 1973. Served with U.S. Army, 1947-49, 50-51. Recipient Founders Day award N.Y. U., 1967; Fulbright scholar Internat. Exchange of Scholars, 1979-80. Mem. Am. Econ. Assn., Am. Fin. Assn., Am. Statis. Assn., Indsl. Relations Research Assn., Western Econ. Assn., Nat. Econ. Assn., Hampton NAACP (exec. bd. 1968-70), Phi Beta Sigma (pres. Beta Omicron Sigma chpt. 1977). Democrat. Episcopalian. Author: Amalgamated Clothing Workers of America, 1940-1966, 1972; asso. editor Jour. Behavioral and Social Scis., 1974—. Home: 1788 Kenwick Rd Columbus OH 43209 Office: Economics Dept Ohio State U Columbus OH 43210

GOULD, JAMES JOHN, tech. cons.; b. Harlan, Iowa, Nov. 8, 1933; s. Russell T. and Florence C. (Holmquest) G.; B.S. in Bus. Adminstrn., Simpson Coll., 1957; M.A. in Guidance and Counseling, U. No. Iowa, 1971; postgrad. in counselor edn. U. Iowa, 1971-74; 1 son, John P. Insp., Retail Credit Co., Centerville, Iowa, 1962-65; tchr. Lake City (Iowa) High Sch., 1967-70; grad. asst. U. No. Iowa, Cedar Falls, 1970-71, Am. Coll. Testing Program, Iowa City, 1972-73; tech. cons. Iowa Dept. Pub. Instrn., Des Moines, 1974—. Served with U.S. Army, 1957-59. Mem. Am. Personnel and Guidance Assn., Iowa State Edn. Assn., NEA, Nat. Assn. Users of Computer Assisted Learning, Assn. Time-Share Users, Assn. Ednl. Data Systems, Nat. Vocat. Guidance Assn., Assn. Small Computer Users, Phi Delta Kappa. Democrat. Methodist. Club: Masons. Home: Box 541 Grinnell IA 50112 Office: Grimes State Office Bldg Des Moines IA 50319

GOULD, JOHN PHILIP, JR., economist, educator; b. Chgo., Jan. 19, 1939; s. John Philip and Lillian (Jicka) G.; B.S. with highest distinction, Northwestern U., 1960; Ph.D. (Earhart Found. fellow), U. Chgo., 1966; m. Kathleen J. Hayes, Sept. 4, 1963; children—John Philip, Jeffrey Hayes. Mem. faculty U. Chgo., 1965—, prof. econs., 1974—; vis. prof. Nat. Taiwan U., 1978; spl. asst. econ. affairs to sec. Dept. Labor, 1969-70; spl. asst. to dir. Office Mgmt. and Budget, Washington, 1970; past chmn. econ. policy adv. com. Dept. Labor. Recipient award Wall St. Jour., 1960, Am. Mktg. Assn., 1960. Mem. Am. Econ. Assn., Western Econ. Assn., Econometric Soc. (chmn. local arrangements 1968). Author: (with C.E. Ferguson) Microeconomic Theory, 5th edit., 1980; contbg. author: Microeconomic Foundations of Employment and Inflation Theory, 1970; editor: Jour. Bus., 1976—, Jour. Fin. Econs., 1976, Jour. Acctg. and Econs., 1978; contbr. articles to profl. jours. Home: 5514 S Kenwood Ave Chicago IL 60637*

GOULD, TERRY ALLEN, lawyer, fin. exec.; b. St. Louis, Sept. 30, 1942; s. Courtney A. and Dorothy (Bitker) G.; B.S., Miami U., Oxford, Ohio, 1965; postgrad. Grad. Sch. Bus. Adminstrn., Washington U., St. Louis, 1966; J.D. cum laude, St. Louis U., 1981; m. Patricia Ann Wolf, July 21, 1968; children—Kristine Ann, Bradford Allen. Security analyst Merc. Trust Co., St. Louis, 1965-66; mgmt. trainee Misco-Shawnee, Inc., St. Louis, 1966-68, br. mgr., 1969-72, v.p., 1972-73, exec. v.p. adminstrn., 1973-78, sec. treas., 1975-78, dir., 1976-79; trustee Misco-Shawnee Profit Sharing Trust, 1975-78; v.p., dir. GORA Investment Co., St. Louis, 1975-78; gen. partner Tera Investment Assos., 1978—; pres., dir. Tera Mgmt. Corp., 1980—; dir. Suburban Nat. Bank Elk Grove (Ill.), 1972-77. Mem. bd. mgrs., vice chmn. fin. com., mem. membership com., downtown br. Greater St. Louis YMCA. Mem. Am. Bar Assn., Mo. Bar, Bar Assn. Met. St. Louis, Delta Sigma Pi, Beta Theta Pi. Home: 1664 Foxleigh Ct Saint Louis MO 63131 Office: 755 New Ballas Rd S Saint Louis MO 63141

GOULD, WESLEY LARSON, polit. scientist, educator; b. Cleve., May 15, 1917; s. Francis E. and Helen M. (Larson) G.; A.B., Baldwin-Wallace Coll., 1939; M.A., Ohio State U., 1941; postgrad. U. Calif., Berkeley, 1941-42; Ph.D., Harvard U., 1949; m. Jean Sarah Barnard, Jan. 24, 1946; children—Francis Barnard, Sarra Marie, Margaret Elizabeth Gould Guldan, Leona Larson. Instr., Northeastern U., 1946-49; asst. prof. Purdue U., Lafayette, Ind., 1949-58, asso. prof., 1958-61, prof., 1961-67; vis. prof. Northwestern U., 1963-64; prof. polit. sci. Wayne State U., Detroit, 1967—; cons. internat. law study U.S. Naval War Coll., summer 1960; Ph.D. examiner Patna U., India, 1963-64; cons. Detroit City Charter Revision, 1972-73, Canadian Rev. of Studies in Nationalism, 1973-74; mem. adv. council on community service of continuing edn. programs Mich. Dept. Edn., 1971-72. Mem. regional structure, transp. and communications comms. Regional Citizens Project, Met. Fund, Inc., 1973-74; del. Mich. State Democratic Conv., 1971, 72; bd. dirs. Citizens Council for Land Use Research and Edn., 1974-79. Served with U.S. Army, 1942-45; PTO. Fellow, U. Liverpool, 1974-75; Am. Soc. Internat. Law grantee, 1964, Wayne U. research grantee, 1970, Earhart Found. grantee, 1974, Canadian Embassy grantee, 1979. Mem. Am. Polit. Sci. Assn., Internat. Polit. Sci. Assn., Midwest Polit. Sci. Assn., Acad. Polit. Sci., Am. Soc. Legal and Polit. Philosophy, Internat. Assn. Philosophy of Law and Social Philosophy, Am. Soc. Internat. Law (exec. council 1959-62), Ind. Acad. Social Scis. (dir. 1958-60), Am. Assn. Higher Edn., Soc. Gen. Systems, Law and Soc. Assn., London Inst. World Affairs, Internat. Studies Assn. (exec. com.), AAUP, Am. Soc. Public Adminstrn., Assn. for Can. Studies in U.S., Pi Alpha Sigma. Democrat. Episcopalian. Club: Harvard of Eastern Mich. Author: An Introduction to International Law, 1957; (with M. Barkun) International Law and the Social Sciences, 1970; contbr. articles to jours. and books on polit. sci. and law. Office: Dept Polit Sci Wayne State Univ Detroit MI 48202

GOULD, WILLIAM ALLEN, planner, architect; b. Lakewood, Ohio, Mar. 8, 1930; s. Daniel and Esther (Itlaner) G.; B.Arch., U. Mich., 1952; M.Arch., Cranbrook Acad. Art, 1956; diploma Fontainbleau (France) Acad. of Art, 1957; m. Harriet Rosenthal, June 23, 1959; children—Philip, David, Rebecca. Sr. planner City of Cleve. Planning Commn., 1953-59; prin. William A. Gould & Assos., Cleve., 1961—, pres., 1979—; asst. prof. architecture Western Res. U., 1958-61; lectr. Case Inst. Tech., 1960-61; vis. asst. prof. architecture and environ. design Kent State U., 1972-73. Mem. City Cleveland Heights Planning Commn. Served to 1st lt. USAF, 1952. Mem. A.I.A. (dir. Cleve. chpt. 1967—), Am. Inst. Planners (pres. No. Ohio chpt. 1967-69, nat. urban design com.). Works include Cascade Plaza, Akron, Ohio, Hillel Center Case Western Res. U., Wayne Gen. and Tech. Coll. U. Akron, Univ. Circle Research Center; planner Blossom Music Center, Cleve.; executed capital improvement program analysis Ohio Bd. Regents, new city plans for Barberton, Shaker Heights and Youngstown, Ohio; master plan update NASA Lewis Research Center, Cleve.; planned communities Greenwood Village, Sagamore Hills, Ohio, Riverbend East, Athens, Ga.; renovation and expansion plans Massillon (Ohio) State Hosp.; Cleve. Warehouse Dist. study; Ohio City master plan; socio-econ. study Ashtabula County; planner mine reclamation for Borden, Inc., Lakeland, Fla.; architect transit stas. Greater Cleve. Regional Transit Authority. Home: 2722 Scarborough Rd Cleveland Heights OH 44106 Office: 1404 E 9th St Cleveland OH 44114

GOULETAS-CAREY, EVANGELINE, real estate co. exec.; b. Athens, Sept. 22, 1936; came to U.S., 1946; d. Steven and Mary (Lekkas) G.; B.S., Northeastern Ill. State Coll. 1957; M.A., Ill. Tchrs. Coll., 1966; m. Hugh Carey, Apr. 11, 1981; 1 dau., Maria. Mem. math. faculty Northeastern Ill. State Coll., 1964-68; adminstr. federally funded programs Chgo. Bd. Edn., 1968; engr. in devel. Minuteman missile program N. Am. Aviation Co., Anaheim, Calif., 1962-64; prin. Am. Invsco Corp., Chgo., 1969-81; chmn. Am. Invsco Devel. Co., Chgo., 1969-81, also dir.; dir. Ambros, Inc., Chgo. Trustee DePaul U.; chmn. bd. trustees Com. for Thalassemia Concern, Chgo.; chmn. Combined Cardiac Research Women's Found., U. Chgo.; mem. exec. bd. Chgo. City Ballet; bd. dirs. Chgo. Public Library, 1980-81; chmn. Soc. Little Flower Festival Leadership Dinner, 1980, 81 Recipient awards including Gt. Am. award B'nai B'rith, 1977, Bus. Woman of Yr. award Soc. Little Flower, 1979; named Exec. Businesswoman of Year, Internat. Orgn. Women Execs., 1980; Tree of Life award Jewish Nat. Fund. Mem. Nat. Assn. Realtors, Inst. Real Estate Mgmt., Women in Real Estate, Women's Council Realtors, Am. Mgmt. Assn. (President's Assn.), Chgo. Real Estate Bd., Chgo. Assn. Commerce and Industry, Chgo. Network, C. of C. Lake View, Lincoln Park Conservation Assn. Green Orthodox. Club: Executives. Contbr. articles on real estate and corp. mgmt., women in bus. to profl. jours. Office: 120 S La Salle St Chicago IL 60603

GOVE, DONALD JAMES, mfg. co. exec.; b. Honolulu, July 3, 1938; s. James T. and Mildred W. (Giles) G.; A.A. in Bus. Adminstrn., Long Beach (Calif.) City Coll., 1967; B.S., Washington U., St. Louis, 1971; m. Joyce Ann Wolf, Aug. 19, 1961; children—Christine Marie, Yvonne Rene, Sandra Lynne. Prodn. supr. Lever Bros. Co., Los Angeles, 1961-66, safety supr./supt., Los Angeles, St. Louis, 1966-70, asst. personnel mgr., St. Louis, 1970-72, personnel mgr., 1972—; cons. St. Louis Regional Commerce and Growth Assn. Active Parkway Sch. Dist. PTA and Booster Orgns. Served with U.S. Army N.G., 1957-64. Accredited personnel mgr. Mem. Am. Soc. for Personnel Adminstrn., Indsl. Relations Assn. Greater St. Louis, Indsl. Relations Research Assn., Am. Soc. Safety Engrs., New Spirit of St. Louis (area labor and mgmt. com.), Real Estate Bd. Met. St. Louis. Republican. Methodist. Home: 1426 Timberwood Ln Creve Coeur MO 63141 Office: 1400 N Pennsylvania Pagedale MO 63133

GOVE, SAMUEL KIMBALL, educator; b. Walpole, Mass., Dec. 27, 1923; student Mass. State Coll., 1941-43; B.S. in Econs., U. Mass., 1947; M.A. in Polit. Sci., Syracuse U., 1951. Research asst. govt. and pub affairs U. Ill., 1950-51, research asso., 1951-54, mem. faculty, 1954—, prof. polit. sci., 1966—, dir. Inst. Govt. and Pub. Affairs, 1967—. Staff asst. Nat. Assn. Assessing Officers, 1949; mem. research staff Ill. Commn. Study State Govt., 1950-51; staff fellow Nat. Municipal League, 1955-56; exec. asst. Ill. Auditor Pub. Accounts, 1957; program coordinator Ill. Legis. Staff Intern Program, 1962-70; mem. com. financing higher edn. Ill. Master Plan Higher Edn., 1963; mem. Ill. Commn. Orgn. Gen. Assembly, 1965-69, 70-73, Ill. Commn. State Govt., 1965-67; cons. elections ABC, 1964, 66, 68; chmn. Champaign (Ill.) County Econ. Opportunity Council, 1966-67; state legis. research fellow Am. Polit. Sci. Assn., 1966-68; cons. Am. Council Edn., 1966-67; sec. Local Govts. Commn., 1967-69; staff dir. Ill. Constn. Study Commn., 1968-69; exec. sec. Gov. Ill. Constn. Research Group, 1969-70; mem. Ill. Constn. Study Commn., 1969-70; chmn. Citizens Task Force on Constl. Implementation, 1970-71; mem. Gov. Elect's Task Force on Transition, 1972; adv. council Ill. Dept. Local Govt. Affairs, 1969-79; chmn. Champaign-Urbana Study Commn. on Intergovtl. Coop., 1976-78. Served to lt. (j.g.) USNR, 1943-46. Mem. AAUP (past chpt. pres., mem. nat. com. R 1969-75, 78—, nat. council 1978-81), Am. Polit Sci. Assn., Am. Soc. Pub. Adminstrn. (past chpt. chmn.; chmn. univs. govtl. research conf. 1969-71), Govtl. Research Assn. (dir. 1969-71), Ill. Hist. Soc., Midwest Polit. Sci. Assn. (v.p. 1978-80), Nat. Municipal League (council 1972—). Club: Cosmos. Author numerous books, monographs and articles. Home: 2006 Bruce Dr Urbana IL 61801 Office: Inst Govt and Pub Affairs Urbana-Champaign Campus Urbana IL

GOWELL, RONDA SUE, veterinarian; b. Breckenridge, Mich., June 19, 1948; d. Samuel B. and Bessie Mae (Kellogg) Cole; D.V.M., Mich. State U., 1972; m. Elmer Burton Gowell, Mar. 22, 1974. Veterinarian, Hart, Mich., 1972-75, Rothbury, Mich., 1975—. Recipient Outstanding Service award Dairy Farmers Oceana County, 1979. Mem. Mich., Am., Women's veterinary med. assns. New Testament Baptist. Home and Office: 475 E Cleveland St Rothbury MI 49452

GOWIN, ROBERT C., bus. exec.; b. Breckenridge, Minn., Apr. 21, 1939; s. Harold O. and Mildred B. G.; student Interstate Bus. Coll., 1960-61, Dakota Bus. Coll., 1961-62; m. Aase Dahm Jakobsen, Nov. 26, 1958; children—Sandra, Kristin, Julie, William. Credit mgr., acct. Lavelle Lumber Co. (now Lavelle Co.), Fargo, N.D., 1961-76, controller, 1976-77, sec. treas., adminstrv. mgr., 1977—. Chmn. bd. deacons Olivet Luth. Ch., 1973-75, mem. ch. stewardship com., 1977-78, mem. bd. trustees, 1980—. Mem. Nat. Assn. Credit Mgmt. (pres. Fargo chpt. 1972-73), N.Central Credit Conf. (chmn. 1973), Red River Valley Nat. Assn. Accts. (dir.), Adminstrv. Mgmt. Soc. (cert.), Fargo-Moorhead Personnel Assn. Republican. Club: Elks. Home: 902 S University Dr Fargo ND 58103 Office: PO Box 2583 115 S 31st St Fargo ND 58108

GOYAL, ARVIND KUMAR, physician; b. Haryana, India, Sept. 30, 1948; came to U.S., 1972; s. Vishnu Kumar and Giriraj Kishori G.; B.Medicine and Surgery, Govt. Med. Coll., Patiala, Punjabi U., India, 1970; M.P.H., U. Ill., 1975; m. Renu, June 6, 1974; 1 child, Sapna Arvind. Intern, Postgrad. Inst. Med. Edn. and Research, Chandigarh, India, 1970, resident in medicine, 1971, resident in surgery, 1971; resident in family practice Cook County Hosp., Chgo., 1972-75, attending physician family practice residency program, 1975-76; clin. instr. family practice Abraham Lincoln Sch. Medicine and U. Ill., Chgo., 1976; family physician Comprehensive Med. Assos. and Cure Health Plan, Chgo., 1976; family practice, Arlington Heights and Rolling Meadows, Ill., 1976—; staff physician Northwest Community Hosp., Arlington Heights, 1977—, Alexian Bros. Med. Center, Elk Grove Village, Ill., 1977, Suburban Med. Center, Hoffman Estates, Ill., 1979—; asso. program dir. family practice Norwegian Am. Hosp. and Family Health Center, Chgo., 1978-80. Served with Indian Army, 1971-72. Diplomate Am. Bd. Family Practice, Am. Bd. Preventive Medicine. Fellow Am. Acad. Family Physicians, Am. Coll. Preventive Medicine; mem. AMA, Ill. Med. Soc., Chgo. Med. Soc., Am. Public Health Assn., Can. Coll. Family Physicians, Indian Med. Assn. Home: 550 E Alexandra Ct Itasca IL 60143 Office: 3407 Kirchoff Rd Rolling Meadows IL 60008

GOYAL, RAGHBIR CHAND, mech. engr.; b. Khai Kalota, India, Aug. 14, 1942; s. Ramji Dass and Jamuna Devi G.; came to U.S., 1962, naturalized, 1973; B.S., Punjab U., Chandigarh, India, 1962; student mech. engring. Ind. Inst. Tech., 1963-64; postgrad. U. Notre Dame, 1970-71; m. Diane Mary Procissi, Aug. 14, 1965; children—Rani, Anissa M. Successively draftsman, project engr., mgr. value analysis and value engring. ILG Industries, Chgo., 1964-68; devel. engr., engring. and services mgr. Kawneer Co., Franklin, Ind., 1968-81, corp. engring. data base mgr., 1981—; cons., architect in field. Mem. ASME, Nat. Mgmt. Assn., Soc. Am. Value Engrs., C. of C. of Franklin. Hindu. Clubs: Eldorado Golf and Country (dir.), Knollwood Country. Patentee automatic entrance device. Home: 16525 Baywood Ln Granger IN 46530 Office: Kawneer Co 1105 N Front St Niles MI 49120

GOYKE, GARY REGIS, state senator; b. Oshkosh, Wis., May 9, 1947; B.S., St. Mary's Coll., 1970; married. Mem. Wis. Senate, 1974—. Bd. dirs. Oshkosh Community Council; mem. Oshkosh City Plan Commn., 1973-75. Named Wis. Outstanding Young Man, Jaycees, 1975. Mem. Oshkosh Jaycees, LWV, Winnebago Conservation Club, Serra Club. Democrat. Club: Elks, KC. Address: Room 28 South State Capitol Madison WI 53702

GRABARSKI, SAM W., arts adminstr.; b. Waukegan, Ill., June 17, 1947; s. Tony and Emma G.; B.Mus.Ed., Ill. Wesleyan U., 1969; M.M., Juilliard Sch. Music, 1972; Ed.D. (Creative and Performing Arts fellow), U. Ill., 1979. Tchr., Waukegan Public Schs., 1970-71; with Conn. Commn. on Arts, 1975; exec. dir. Quincy (Ill.) Soc. Fine Arts, 1975-79, Iowa Arts Council, Des Moines, 1979—; grants adv. panelist Nat. Endowment for Arts, 1980—; performer five symphony orchs. and chamber ensembles; soloist. Recipient musicianship awards Ill. Wesleyan U., 1968, 69. Mem. Assn. Coll., Univ. and Community Arts Adminstrs. (dir.), Affiliated State Arts Agencies Upper Midwest (dir.), Des Moines Wine Group (dir.). Office: 1223 E Court Ave Des Moines IA 50319*

GRABER, VIRGIL RICH, obstetrician, gynecologist; b. Wayland, Iowa, Jan. 15, 1921; s. Joseph and Barbara (Rich) G.; B.A., State U. Iowa, 1946, M.D., 1949; m. Evelyn Louise Scarff, Aug. 13, 1944; children—Donald, Thomas, Robert, Joan. Intern, Sparrow Hosp., Lansing, Mich., 1949-50; gen. practice medicine, St. Johns, Mich., 1950-52; resident in obstetrics and gynecology Akron (Ohio) City Hosp., 1953-56; practice medicine specializing in obstetrics and gynecology, Elkhart, Ind., 1956—; mem. active staff and bd. dirs. Elkhart Gen. Hosp.; mem. cons. staff Goshen Gen. Hosp. Diplomate Am. Bd. Obstetrics and Gynecology. Mem. Ind. Obstetrics Gynecology Council, Am. Soc. Colposcopy and Colpomicroscopy, Elkhart County (Ind.) Med. Soc. (pres.), Mennonite Med. Soc. Contbr. articles to obstet. jours. Office: 1400 Hudson St Elkhart IN 46514

GRABINSKI, ROGER NEIL, educator; b. Tacoma, May 26, 1939; s. Phil and Fernande Pauline Eugene (Bouffioux) G.; student Willamette U., 1957-60; B.A., U. Oreg., 1962, M.S., 1964; Ed.D., Western Mich. U., 1972; m. Carol Joanne Huffman, Aug. 13, 1966; 1 son, Lawrence Neil. Tchr., counselor, cons. Lane County Youth Project, Eugene, Oreg., 1964-66; asst. dir. Mobilab Inservice Tng. Program, Eugene, 1966-69; grad. asst., Mott fellow Western Mich. U., Kalamazoo, 1969-72; asso. prof. dept. counseling, ednl. adminstrn. and community leadership, cons. Center Community Edn., Central Mich. U., Mt. Pleasant, 1972—; pres. Lane Human Resources, 1969, bd. dirs., 1968-69; mem. Mt. Pleasant Community Services Council, 1977—. Mem. Mich. Community Sch. Edn. Assn., Oreg. Community Edn. Assn., Nat. Community Edn. Assn., Am. Assn. Sch. Adminstrs. (Profl. Devel. award 1979), World Future Soc., Mt. Pleasant C. of C. (asso.), Phi Delta Kappa (pres. 1979-80, Leadership award 1981). Lutheran. Office: 207 Rowe Central Mich U Mount Pleasant MI 48859

GRABLE, EDWARD E., obstetrician, gynecologist; b. Canton, Ohio, Aug. 22, 1926; s. Hugh R. and Daisy M. (Myers) G.; B.S., Western Res. U., 1946, M.D., 1950. Intern, Mercy Hosp., Canton, 1950-51, resident, 1951-53, 55; resident U.S. Naval Hosp., Bremerton, Wash., 1954, Cleve. City Hosp., 1955-56; practice medicine specializing in obstetrics and gynecology, Canton, 1956—; active staff Timken Mercy Med. Center; cons. staff Molly Stark Hosp., Louisville, Ohio; courtesy staff Aultman Hosp., Canton, Massillon (Ohio) Community Hosp.; instr. obstetrics and gynecology Western Res. U., 1956-59; mem. council of chiefs Northeastern Ohio U. Sch. Medicine, 1975, asst. prof., 1977—; owner Stencil-Art Co., Inc. Trustee, Health Planning and Devel. Council Wooster (Ohio), 1965-78, Timken Mercy Hosp., 1977—. Served to lt., M.C., USNR, 1944-45, 53-54. Diplomate Am. Bd. Obstetrics and Gynecology. Fellow A.C.S., Am. Coll. Obstetricians and Gynecologists; mem. Central Assn. Obstetrics and Gynecology, Cleve. Soc. Obstetrics and Gynecology, AMA, Ohio State, Stark County (trustee 1970—, pres. 1971) med. socs., Canton Acad. Medicine (pres. 1964), Am. Fertility Soc., N.Y. Acad. Sci. Club: Congress Lake (Hartville, Ohio). Contbr. article to med. jour. Home: 351 17th St NW Canton OH 44703 Office: 2525 13th St NW Canton OH 44708

GRABLE, R(EGINALD) HAROLD, psychologist; b. Putnam County, Ind., Sept. 22, 1917; s. Reginald R. and Cecil Ruth (Jones) G.; A.B., U. Kans., 1938, tchr.'s diploma, 1940; M.A., U. Minn., 1949; m. Elizabeth Hannah Baird, Aug. 17, 1946; children—Celia, Nancy, Daniel. Group leader occupational coders Nat. Roster Sci. and Specialized Personnel, Washington, 1940-42; vocat. counselor U. Minn., Mpls., 1947; clin. psychologist trainee VA Hosp., St. Paul, 1947-49; chief clin. psychologist Willmar (Minn.) State Hosp., 1949-51, Winnebago (Wis.) State Hosp., 1951-61; clin. psychologist West Shore Mental Health Clinic (formerly Hackley Adult Mental Health Clinic), Muskegon, Mich., 1961—; pvt. practice psychology, Willmar, Minn., 1949-51, Oshkosh, Wis., 1951-61, Spring Lake, Mich., 1961—; instr. extension div. U. Wis., 1956-61; mem. profl. adv. bd. Wis. Council Mentally Retarded Children, 1956-61. First aid instr. ARC, 1963-79; exec. bd. Grand Valley council (name now West Mich. Shores council) Boy Scouts Am., 1966-76, dist. chmn., 1968-70, commr., 1972—; various offices PTA, 1953-78; active Vols. in Probation; chmn. bd. Christian Ch. (Disciples of Christ), 1970-73. Served with AUS, 1942-46. Recipient Silver Beaver award Boy Scouts Am., 1981; lic. psychologist, Mich. Mem. Am. Psychol. Assn., Mich. Assn. Children with Learning Disabilities. Home: 717 Summer St Spring Lake MI 49456 Office: 2525 Hall Rd Muskegon MI 49442

GRABOW, CAROL JEANNE, educator; b. Detroit Lakes, Minn., Dec. 4, 1951; d. Clayton Emil and Margaret Olivia (Ramstad) G.; B.S. in Gen. Home Econs., U. Minn., 1974; B.A. in Early Childhood, U. Cedar Falls, 1978. Mgmt. trainee in food service Luther Coll., 1974-76; tchr. vocat. home econs. Sioux Valley and Round Lake, Minn., 1978-80; dir. Little Peoples Day Care and Infant Center, tchr. child care South Central Vocat. Center, Blue Earth, Minn., 1980—. Lutheran. Home: 507 1/2 W 5th Blue Earth MN 56013 Office: South Central Vocat Center Blue Earth MN 56013

GRABOW, RAYMOND JOHN, mayor; b. Cleve., Jan. 27, 1932; s. Joseph Stanley and Frances (Kalata) G.; B.S. in Bus. Adminstrn., Kent State U., 1953; J.D., LL.B., Western Res. U., 1958; m. Margaret Jean Knoll, Nov. 27, 1969; children—Rachel Jean, Ryan Joseph. Admitted to Ohio bar, 1958; counsel No. Ohio Petroleum Retailers Assn., Cleve., 1965-75; counsel, trustee Alliance of Poles Fed. Credit Union, 1972, also gen. counsel Alliance of Poles of Am.; councilman City of Warrensville Heights (Ohio), 1962-68, mayor, 1969—; sec. Sam's Investment Inc. Cleve., 1965—, Atlas Sewer & Pipe Cleaning Corp., Cleve., 1962—, Wick Restaurant Inc., Cleve., 1962—. Mem. exec. com. Democratic party Cuyahoga County, 1966—, precinct com., 1966-80; trustee Brentwood Hosp.; bd. dirs. Polonia Found. Recipient award Polonia Found., 1970, other groups. Mem. Ohio State, Cuyahoga County, Greater Cleve. bar assns., Nat. Advs., Am. Judicature Soc., Assn. Trial Lawyers Am., Ohio Trial Lawyers Assn., Ohio Mayors Assn., Ohio Municipal League, other orgns. Home: 20114 Gladstone Rd Warrensville Heights OH 44122 Office: Suite 815 Superior Bldg Cleveland OH 44114

GRABOW, STEPHEN HARRIS, architect, educator; b. Bklyn., Jan. 15, 1943; s. Philip and Ida (England) G.: B.Arch., U. Mich., 1965; M.Arch., Pratt Inst., 1966: postgrad. U. Calif., Berkeley, 1966-67; Ph.D., U. Wash., 1972; m. Eileen Williams, Aug. 21, 1969; 1 dau., Nicole Elizabeth. Architect-planner U.S. Peace Corps, Tunisia, N. Africa, 1967-69; regional planning cons., Teheran, Iran, 1969; asst. prof. architecture U. Ariz., 1969-70; teaching asso. U. Wash., 1970-72; lectr. town and regional planning Duncan of Jordanstone Coll. Art, U. Dundee (Scotland), 1972-73; asst. prof. architecture and urban design U. Kans., Lawrence, 1973-76, asso. prof., 1976—, dir. architecture, 1979—; vis. fellow U. Calif., Berkeley, 1977; research and design cons. Design Build Architects, Lawrence. Recipient citation for excellence in design research Nat. Endowment Arts, 1980; Nat. Endowment Humanities fellow, 1976-77, Nat. Endowment Arts award, 1974. Home: 1616 Louisiana St Lawrence KS 66044 Office: Sch Architecture and Urban Design U Kans Lawrence KS 66045

GRABOW, WESLEY JOHN FRED, educator; b. Morgan, Minn., Aug. 23, 1921; s. Emil Paul and Alma Louise (Hecker) G.; B.B.A., U. Minn., 1944, M.A., 1950, certificate in Philosophy, 1968, Ph.D., 1970; teaching certificate Minn. Dept. Edn., 1967. Asst. sta. agt. Mpls. & St. Louis R.R., 1939-40; communication technician U. Minn., Mpls., 1946-50, audio visual materials adviser, 1951-59, dir. audio visual edn. service, 1960-70, prof. info. agrl. journalism, dir. Instructional Devel. Center, 1970—. Cons. Ency. Brit., 1970, Head Start, 1971, 4-H Exhibit Program, 1970—. Chmn., Info. Center, Twin City Film Council, 1951-59, pres., 1955, 56; bd. dirs. Film Council Am., 1956-59; chmn. adv. com. Minn. Bd. Edn., 1964-67; mem. Gov.'s Pub. Relations Commn. on Hwy. Safety, 1965. Recipient Golden Reel award, 1954; Screen Producers Guild Silver medallion, 1955; certificate of acceptance Am. Film Festival, 1956; Best Film award Marching Band Assn., 1961. Recipient award for contbn. to audiovisual edn. Ency. Brit. Ednl. Corp., 1979; Flaherty Film Study grantee, 1966. Mem. Audio Visual Communications Assn. Minn. (chmn. awards and scholarship 1958-64, pres. 1963, 64, chmn. bd. 1965, chmn. comml. liaison 1973—), Univ. Film Producers Assn., Assn. for Ednl. Communications and Tech. (nat. newsletter chmn. 1964-67, affiliate relations council 1964-67, affiliate pres. chmn. 1974, nat. confs. steering com. 1958, 72), Consortium Univ. Film Centers, Phi Delta Kappa, Gamma Sigma Delta. Club: Masons. Author: Flannelgraph, 1955; Your Audio-Visual Handbook, 1958; Cadence West, 1960; News Letter Editors Handbook, 1966; Development of Audio-Visual Education at University of Minnesota, 1970. Resources editor, mem. media rev. bd. NACTA Jour., 1976—. Home: 3100 Wendhurst Ave NE Minneapolis MN 55418 Office: Instructional Devel Center U Minn St Paul MN 55108

GRABRICK, JOHN ALAN, elec. designer; b. Wakefield, Mich., Jan. 2, 1958; s. George Joseph and Myrtle Louise (Keebaugh) G.; student Devry Inst. Tech., 1976-77; Asso. Tech., Gogebic Community Coll., 1979; m. Cheryl Ann Cerrito, Oct. 18, 1980. With Regional Sound Co., Chgo., 1976-77, J.C. Penny Co., Ironwood, Mich., 1978-79; elec. engr. 3M Co., St. Paul, 1979—, sr. elec. designer, 1980—. Democrat. Presbyterian. Club: 3M Ski. Home: 2354 Greenbrier Circle Little Canada MN 55117 Office: 3M Co 42-7W-03 900 Bush Ave Saint Paul MN 55133

GRACE, KAREN STENTZ, greeting card mfg. co. exec.; b. Lakewood, Ohio, Jan. 23, 1945; d. Milton Bayer and Donna Marjorie (Parker) S.; A.B., Wilson Coll., 1967; M.B.A., Cleve. State U., 1977; m. James A. Grace, Oct. 14, 1967. Various positions Stock Broker Pub., Cleve., 1967-69; with Club Products Co., Cleve., 1969-78; dir. advt. and sales promotion Am. Greetings Corp., 1978-80, dir. corp. communications, 1980—. Office: American Greetings Corp 10500 American Rd Cleveland OH 44144

GRACE, OLIVER DAVIES, veterinarian; b. Washington, Dec. 21, 1914; s. Oliver Joseph and Gladys Susannah (Davies) G.; D.V.M., Colo. State U., 1940; M.S., U. Ill., 1952; m. Vera Hanawalt, July 14, 1948; children—Kerstin Elaine, Edward Oliver. With U.S. Dept. Agr., N.D., Va., N.H., 1940-45; research investigator FDA, Urbana, Ill., 1946-53; head dept. veterinary medicine Baxter Labs., Morton Grove, Ill., 1953-55; mem. faculty U. Nebr., Lincoln, 1955—, prof. veterinary sci., 1963—, acting chmn dept., 1976-77. Recipient grants NIH, U.S. Dept. Agr. Mem. AVMA, Nebr. Veterinary Med. Assn. (spl. service award 1977), Am. Assn. Avian Pathologists, Conf. Research Workers in Animal Diseases, Conf. Veterinary Lab. Diagnosticians. Democrat. Methodist. Club: Kiwanis. Contbr. articles to Nat. Hog Farmer. Home: 1720 Donald Circle Lincoln NE 68505 Office: 149 Veterinary Diagnostic Center Nebr Lincoln NE 68583

GRADELESS, DONALD EUGENE, secondary sch. tchr., genealogist; b. Warsaw, Ind., Apr. 17, 1949; s. Harmon Willard and Donna Maxine (Mort) G.; B.S. in Acctg., U. Wis., Stevens Point, 1972; M.S. in Teaching, U. Wis., Eau Claire, 1975. Tchr. high schs. in Racine, Wis., 1972-77; coordinator instructional data processing Racine Unified Schs., 1973-77; mgr. constrn. Computer Control Corp., Milw., 1977; indsl. engr. Weatherhead div. Dana Corp., Columbia City, Ind., 1977-78; instr. bus. edn. Elmbrook public schs., Brookfield, Wis., 1978—. Mem. Soc. Data Educators, Nat. Bus. Edn. Assn., NEA, Wis. Bus. Edn. Assn., SAR (sec. Wis. chpt. 1977; pres. Racine chpt. 1976-77; membership award nat. society 1976-78, Silver Good Citizenship award 1978), S.R. (nat. bd. mgrs. 1979-82, pres. Wis. chpt. 1979-82, registrar Ill. chpt. 1978— Wis. chpt. 1980-82), Children Am. Revolution (sr. registrar 1976-77, 80—), Sons and Daus. of Pilgrims (counselor 1979-80), Soc. Colonial Wars (dep. sec. Wis. chpt. 1978-79), Nat. Geneal. Soc., Whitley County Hist. Soc., Soc. Indiana Pioneers, Delta Phi Epsilon. Club: Masons. Author geneal. books. Home: 1721 Edgewood Ave Racine WI 53404 Office: 3305 N Lilly Rd Brookfield WI 53005

GRADISON, WILLIS DAVID, JR., congressman; b. Cin., Dec. 28, 1928; s. Willis David and Dorothy (Benas) G.: A.B., Yale, 1948; M.B.A., Harvard, 1951, D.C.S., 1954; m. Helen Ann Martin, June 25, 1950 (div. 1975); children—Ellen, Anne, Margaret, Robin, Beth; m. 2d, Heather Jane Stirton, Nov. 29, 1980. With W.D. Gradison & Co., Cin., 1949, gen. partner, 1958—; asst. to under sec. Treasury, Washington, 1953-55; asst. to sec. HEW, Washington, 1955-57; mem. 94th-97th congresses from 1st Ohio Dist.; mem. Cin. City Council, 1961-74, mayor, 1971. Home: 2200 Victory Pkwy Cincinnati OH 45206 Office: 1117 Longworth House Office Bldg Washington DC 20515

GRADY, DENNIS OWEN, mayor; b. Canton, Ohio, Nov. 10, 1950; s. Robert and Mildred (Sharrock) G.; B.A. (Pres.'s Disting. Service award), Bowling Green State U., 1974; postgrad. U. Akron Sch. Law; m. Susan Kerman, Dec. 11, 1976. Instr., Walsh Coll., North Canton, 1979-80, Stark Tech. Coll., Canton, 1979—, with Elton Assos., polit. cons., Columbus, Ohio. Mem. Zoning Bd. Appeals, 1975, Planning Commn., 1975; v.p. City Council, 1976, pres., 1977, mayor, 1978—; Republican precinct committeeman, 1976—; active local polit. campaigns; mem. pres.'s adv. bd. Walsh Coll., 1980—; trustee Community Improvement Corp., 1980—, active United Way. Recipient Outstanding Speak-Up award Jaycees, 1975, Disting. Service award, 1981, Outstanding Young Man of Ohio Award (Jaycees) 1981; Blue Coat award North Canton K.C., 1981. Mem. C. of C., Jaycees, Mayors Assn. Stark County, Mayors Assn. Ohio, Ohio Mcpl. League, Bowling Green State U. Alumni Assn. Republican. Lutheran. Clubs: Elks; Rotary; Pro Football Hall of Fame Luncheon. Home: 352 Briar Ave NE North Canton OH 44720 Office: 145 N Main St North Canton OH 44720

GRAEF, LUTHER WILLIAM, cons. civil engr.; b. Milw., Aug. 14, 1931; s. John and Pearl (Luther) G.; B.C.E., Marquette U., 1952; M.C.E., U. Wis., 1961; m. Lorraine Linnerud, Sept. 18, 1954; children—Ronald, Sharon, Gerald. Engr., C.W. Yoder & Assos., cons. engrs., Milw., 1956-61; partner Graef-Anhalt-Schloemer, cons. engrs., Milw., 1961—; chmn. bd. Graef Anhalt Schloemer Assos., Inc., Milw., 1967—; chmn. engr. adv. com. U. Wis., Milw., also U. Wis. extensions. Active Boy Scouts Am. Chmn. bd. assessment, City of Milw., 1962—. Served to 1st lt. AUS, 1953-56. Mem. ASCE (sect. pres. 1968), Nat., Wis. socs. profl. engrs., Cons. Engrs. Council Wis. (pres. 1973-75), Engrs. Scientists Milw. (pres. 1975), Am. Legion, Marquette U. Alumni Assn., Tau Beta Pi, Pi Mu Epsilon, Chi Epsilon. Lutheran (pres. ch. council 1969). Home: 3788 S Massachusetts St Milwaukee WI 53220 Office: 6415 W Capitol Dr Milwaukee WI 53216

GRAF, FREDERIC MOSHER, research co. exec.; b. Evanston, Ill., Dec. 29, 1944; s. Franklin Henry and Laura Jane (Mosher) G.; B.A., Ripon Coll., 1966; M.B.A., Northwestern U., 1968; m. Christine Ann Oliver, Aug. 21, 1965; children—Jennifer Lynn, Glynnis Laura. Sr. statistician A.C. Nielsen Co., Chgo., 1968-70, v.p. client service, Menlo Park, Calif., 1970-78; v.p., mgr. mktg. info. system A.C. Nielsen Co., Northbrook, Ill., 1978—. Chpt pres. YMCA Father's and Daus., 1975-78; active Am. Youth Soccer Orgn., 1978—. Mem. Soc. Mgmt. Info. Systems, Am. Mktg. Assn. Republican. Presbyn. Club: Lake Forest. Home: 635 S Waukegan Rd Lake Forest IL 60045 Office: Nielsen Plaza Northbrook IL 60062

GRAF, TRUMAN FREDERICK, agrl. economist, educator; b. New Holstein, Wis., Sept. 18, 1922; s. Herbert and Rose (Sell) G.; B.S., U. Wis., 1947, M.S., 1949, Ph.D., 1953; m. Sylvia Ann Thompson, Sept. 6, 1947; children—Eric Kindley, Siri Lynne, Peter Truman. Marketing specialist, coop. agt. U.S. Dept. of Agr. and U. Wis., 1948-50; instr. agrl. econs. U. Wis., 1951-53, asst. prof., 1953-56, asso. prof., 1956-61, prof., 1961—. Mem. Gov.'s Com. on Wis. Dairy Marketing; mem. 3 man team to make marketing analysis in Nigeria for U.S. Dept. Agr., 1962, made marketing analyses in 13 Caribbean countries, 1964, also for U. Wis. in Mexico, 1965; made analysis U.S. agrl. policy for U.S. Senate, 1965-68; made marketing analysis for U.S. Ednl. Found., Finland, 1970, for Rumanian Ministry Edn., U.S. Dept. State, Rumania, 1976; made U.S. milk mktg. study for U.S. Dept. Agr., 1971; research for internat. agrl. marketing agys., 1963—. Active Cub Scouts. Bd. dirs. Univ. Houses Assn., 1955-56, Univ. Hill Farm Assn., 1958-59, Univ. Hill Farm Swim Club, 1959-60. Served with USNR, 1942-45; comdr. Res. Recipient Uhlman award Chgo. Bd. Trade, 1952; Man of Yr. award World Dairy Expn., 1976; Disting. Service award U. Wis. Extension, 1981. Mem. Am. Agrl. Econs. Assn. (Published Research award 1974), Am. Marketing Assn., Madison Naval Res. Assn. (pres. 1968—), Am. Econ. Assn., Hist. Soc., Civil War Club. Lutheran. Kiwanian (chmn. internat. relations com.). Contbr. articles to profl. jours. Applied research study for dairy firms, agrl. orgns., state and Fed. regulatory agys. and agrl. bus. firms. Home: 5022 LaCrosse Ln Madison WI 57305

GRAFF, JOHN FREDERIC, ins. agy. exec.; b. Highland Park, Ill., Dec. 1, 1933; s. Karl Von and Bernice Mildred (Mattes) G.; B.A. in Econs., DePauw U., 1955; children—Barbara Lynn, Karen Sue. Agt., Provident Mut. Life Ins. Co., Chgo., 1958-61; mem. mgmt. devel. program, Phila., 1961-62, agy. mgr., Chgo., 1962-73; owner, propr. John F. Graff & Assos., Chgo., 1973—; pres. United Corp. of Am., Inc., 1973—, Ill. Bus. Corp., 1976—. Past officer New Trier Republican Orgn.; past chmn. Village Party, Wilmette, Ill.; charter mem., pres. Greater Chgo. Ins. Council of City of Hope, 1980—. Served to lt. (j.g.) USN, 1955-58. Named Ins. Man of Yr., City of Hope, 1978; C.L.U.; registered health underwriter Nat. Assn. Health Underwriters. Mem. Nat. Assn. Life Underwriters, Chgo. Estate Planning Council, Chgo. Assn. Life Underwriters (pres. 1975-76, Disting. Service award 1979), Chgo. Chpt. Chartered Life Underwriters (pres. 1976-77, Huebner Scholar-Disting. Service award 1979), Ill. Life Underwriters Assn. (pres. 1977-78), Chgo. Assn. Health Underwriters (dir. 1975—, Edward H. O'Connor Disting. Service award 1977), Chgo. Gen. Agts. and Mgrs. Assn. (nat. com.). Republican. Methodist. Clubs: Univ. (Chgo.); Westmoreland Country. Contbr. articles to trade mags. Home: 2556 Prairie Ave Apt 15 Evanston IL 60201 Office: United Corp Am 223 W Jackson Blvd Suite 1108 Chicago IL 60606

GRAFING, KEITH GERHART, pianist; b. Hibbing, Minn., Mar. 23, 1942; s. Gerhart and Wilhelmina Emelia (Knittel) G.; A.S., Hibbing Jr. Coll., 1962; B.Mus. (coll. scholar), Bethany Coll., 1964; M.Mus., U. Mo., Kansas City, 1968, D.Mus. Arts, 1972; m. Edith Ione Miessler, Dec. 22, 1964. Tchr. vocal music Winona (Minn.) Public Schs., 1964-65; music instr. St. Paul's Coll., Concordia, Mo., 1965-68, Concordia Coll., Milw., 1968-69, Penn Valley Community Coll., Kansas City, Mo., 1973—; dir. music Trinity Luth. Ch., Mission, Kans., 1972-79; music coordinator John Knox Village, Lee's Summit, Mo., 1980—, mgr. leisure services, 1980—; music coordinator for introduction of Luth. Book of Worship met. Kansas City area. Active Kansas City Friends of Art, Kansas City Friends of the Zoo, Mo. Repertory Theatre Guild, Univ. Assos.; bd. dirs. Kansas City Luth. Center, 1974-76; benefactor Birger Sandzen Meml. Gallery, U. Mo., Kansas City Annual Fund; mem. Humane Soc. U.S. Luth. Ch.-Mo. Synod grad. grantee, 1967-68; doctoral fellow Kansas City Assn. Trusts and Founds., 1970-72. Mem. Nat. Music Tchrs. Assn., Mo. Music Tchrs. Assn., Am. Musicol. Soc., Nat. Soc. Lit. and Arts, U. Mo., Kansas City Alumni Assn. (bd. dirs., 1975—, pres., 1979—), U. Mo. Alliance Alumni Assns., Phi Mu Alpha Sinfonia, Beta Tau Sigma, Phi Theta Kappa, Pi Kappa Lambda. Episcopalian. Club: Bedlington Terrier Club Am. Contbr. sect. to book, article, review to profl. publs. in field. Home: 4545 Wornall Rd Kansas City MO 64111 Office: John Knox Village 500 N Murray Lee's Summit MO 64063

GRAHAM, CARL FRANCIS, chem. products co. exec., chemist; b. Limon, Colo., Jan. 2, 1915; s. Karl and Edith (Nesselrode) G.; B.S., Baker U., 1938; postgrad. U. Kansas City, 1938-39; m. Marjorie Ruth Killebrew, Apr. 27, 1941; children—David Carl, Nancy Lou (Mrs. J.R. Flink), Carol Ann. Head of lab. Procter and Gamble Mfg. Co., Kansas City, Kans., 1938-41; sect. head research dept. J.B. Ford Co., Wyandotte, Mich., 1941-43; supr. analytical research Wyandotte Chems. Corp. (Mich.), 1943-56, mgr. analytical research, 1956-57; dir. research and devel. Turco Products Inc., Wilmington, Calif., 1957-65; adminstrv. asst. to v.p. chem. research Purex Corp., Ltd., Wilmington, 1964-66; mgr. research and devel. Amway Corp., Ada, Mich., 1967-70, mgr. industry and govt. tech. relations, 1970-72, sr. adviser legis. and regulatory standards, 1970-76, mgr. govt. affairs, 1976—; cons. to Chem. Corps., U.S. Army, 1952-62, Chem-Biol.-Radio Agy., Edgewood (Md.) Arsenal, 1962-63. Fellow Am. Inst. Chemists; mem. Am. Chem. Soc. (com. nat. def. 1963-70), ASTM (councilor Detroit dist. 1955-57, councilor So. Calif. dist. 1962-66), Soap and Detergent Assn. (legal com. tech. and materials div. 1970-74, mem. legis. subcom. 1974—; chmn. eutrophication task force 1980-81), Cosmetic, Toiletry and Fragrance Assn. (govt. relations com. 1972-80), Chem. Splty. Mfrs. Assn. (chmn. div. com. legis. standards 1971-77, bd. govs. 1976-78, 81, chmn. state public affairs com. 1979-81, vice chmn. detergents and cleaning compounds div. 1979-80, div. chmn. 1981), Am. Def. Preparedness Assn. (tech. com. on surface preservation 1958-66), Chemists Club of N.Y. Home: 4212 Oak Forest Ct SE Apt K-1 Grand Rapids MI 49506 Office: 7575 E Fulton Rd Ada MI 49355

GRAHAM, CHARLES, research psychologist; b. Atlantic City, Nov. 21, 1937; s. Charles Leroy and Margery (Kaplan) G.; B.S., U. Md., 1966; M.S., Pa. State U., 1968, Ph.D., 1970; m. Sally Jones, Dec. 8, 1962; children—Ronna, Christopher, Glen. Research asso. Inst. of Pa. Hosp., Phila., 1970-74; instr. dept. psychiatry U. Pa., Phila., 1970-74, lectr., 1970-74; from sr. to prin. exptl. psychologist Midwest Research Inst., Kansas City, Mo., 1975—; cons. in field of cognitive psychology and psychophysiology. Served with U.S. Army, 1960-62. Recipient Henry Guze award Internat. Soc. Clin. and Exptl. Hypnosis, 1977; NIH grantee, 1975-77, 77-79, 80-82. Mem. Mo. Biofeedback Soc. (pres. 1979-80), Biofeedback Soc. Am. (chmn. exptl. div. 1980-81), Council of Prin. Scientists, Claude Bernard Soc., Am. Psychol. Assn., N.Y. Acad. Sci., Soc. for Psychophysiol. Research, Am. Pain Soc., Friends of Art-Nelson Art Mus., Sigma Xi (chpt. pres. 1980-81), Mu Delta Epsilon. Contbr. articles to profl. jours. Home: 7405 W 56th Terr Shawnee Mission KS 66202 Office: 425 Volker Blvd Kansas City MO 64110

GRAHAM, CHARLES PATTISON, JR., surgeon; b. Wilmington, N.C., June 24, 1940; s. Charles Pattison and Jean Victor (McKoy) G.; A.B. in History, U. N.C., 1961, M.D., 1965; m. Vera Ann Mingos, Dec. 30, 1967; children—Vera Michelle, Katie McKoy, Caroline Pattison and Morey McLean (twins). Intern, then resident in surgery Vanderbilt U. Hosp., 1965-71; practice medicine specializing in surgery, Decatur, Ala., 1973-74, Topeka, 1974—; mem. staff St. Francis, Stormont-Vail, Meml. hosps.; surg. cons. Menninger Found., Topeka, 1976—, Topeka State Hosp., 1976—. Served to maj. M.C., AUS, 1971-73. Decorated Army Commendation medal; John M. Morehead scholar, 1957-61. Diplomate Am. Bd. Surgery. Mem. A.C.S., Kans. Med. Soc., Womack Surg. Soc., Kansas City Surg. Soc., H.W. Scott Soc. Episcopalian. Contbr. articles to med. jours. Home: 117 Greenwood St Topeka KS 66606 Office: Continental Med Bldg 7th and Horne Sts Topeka KS 66606

GRAHAM, CLAYTON JAMES, metal finishing co. exec.; b. Oak Park, Ill., Oct. 31, 1942; s. Barclay M. and Olive W. (Carlstrom) G.; B.S., Purdue U., 1964; M.B.A., Northwestern U., 1968; M.A., Roosevelt U., 1968; m. Margaret Ann Dewenter, June 26, 1965; children—Candace, Ashley. Asso., A. T. Kearney Inc., Chgo., 1969-73; partner Graham Plating Works, Chgo., 1973—, Graham Leasing Co., Barrington, Ill., 1974—, Leaseco Internat., Barrington, 1976—; pres. TWR Service Corp., Rosemont, Ill., 1975—, Integrated Planning Corp., Chgo., Graham Internat.; speaker at profl. meetings. Mem. pres's. council Purdue U.; mem. dean's council Northwestern U. Grad. Sch. Mgmt.; pollution control and econ. adviser to Congress and the White House, 1974-76. Mem. Inst. Mgmt. Sci., Chgo. Metal Finishers Inst. (dir., pres.), World Electroless Nickel Soc. (chmn. bd.), Nat. Assn. Metal Finishers (dir.). Clubs: Barrington Hills Country; Met., Carlton (Chgo.); Meadow (Rolling Meadows, Ill.); Marco Island (Fla.) Country, Marco Island Yacht. Home: 66 Round Barn Rd Barrington Hills IL 60010 Office: 4500 W North Ave Chicago IL 60639

GRAHAM, DOUGLAS MARTIN, educator; b. Yale, Mich., Apr. 1, 1941; s. Martin L. and Helen (Weigel) G.; B.S., Mich. State U., 1964, M.A., 1968; m. Barbara Jean Crake, June 15, 1963; children—Wendy, Alan, Aaron. Tchr. vocat. agr. Mayville (Mich.) Community Schs., 1964—. Recipient hon. degree Mich. State Future Farmers Am., 1980. Mem. Mayville Jaycees, Tuscola County Fair Assn., Mich. Edn. Assn., NEA, Mich. Assn. Tchrs. Vocat. Agr., Am. Vocat. Assn. Home: 2345 E Snover Rd Mayville MI 48744 Office: 6250 Fulton St Mayville MI 48744

GRAHAM, EDWARD RODRIC, economist; b. Utica, N.Y., Oct. 9, 1931; s. William James and Doris Emma (Smith) G.; B.S., Utica Coll., 1955; student Cornell U., 1950-51; postgrad. Temple U., 1961-62, Ind. U., 1967-68; M.B.A., Syracuse U., 1955; m. Geraldine Mary Bach, Aug. 22, 1953; children—Stephen W., Laurie E., Regina M., Jocelyn A. Instr. statistics Temple U., Phila., 1956-62; scientist Westinghouse Electric Co., Lima, Ohio, 1962-68; econometric research analyst Cummins Engine Co., Columbus, Ind., 1968-71, mgr. econ. forecasting, 1971-81, dir. econ. forecasting, 1981—. Mem. Bus. Econs. Issues Council, 1979—; mem. exec. Democratic Com. Allen County (Ohio), 1964-65. Mem. Panel Internat. Economists (conf. bd. 1976-77), Nat. Assn. Bus. Economists, Chgo. Economist Group, Nat. Bus. Econs. Issues Council (a founder). Episcopalian. Club: Masons. Home: Rural Route 3 Box 233 Nashville IN 47448 Office: Gen Office Bldg Columbus IN 47201

GRAHAM, ERIC MALCOLM, broadcasting exec.; b. Sacramento, Calif., Dec. 10, 1945; s. Harold C.A. and Myrtle Agnes (Christian) G.; B.A., Walla Walla (Wash.) Coll., 1972; M.A., Calif. State U., Northridge, 1975. Producer TV prodn. Faith for Today, Los Angeles, 1973-75; mgr. sta. KBSA-TV, Los Angeles, from 1975; pres. Group Seven Media Prodns., Los Angeles, from 1974, chmn. bd., 1976—;

gen. mgr. sta. KUCV-FM, Lincoln, Nebr., 1977. Pres. bd. dirs. Lincoln Civic Orch., 1979-80; trustee Lincoln Symphony Orch. Mem. Adventist Radio Network (dir.). Home: 3448 Neerpark Dr Lincoln NE 68506 Office: 4800 S 48th St Lincoln NE 68506

GRAHAM, GEORGE WESLEY, engr.; b. Utica, N.Y., Sept. 27, 1932; s. Leon Erastus and Marion (Babcock) G.; B.M.E., Purdue U., 1959; M.S., No. Ill. U., 1971; Ph.D., Kans. State U., 1976; m. Marelu Satterley, Sept. 7, 1957; 1 dau., Rebeca. Materials engr. Micro Switch div. Honeywell Internat., Freeport, Ill., 1959-71; prof. engring. Pittsburg (Kans.) State U., 1971-77; cons. in field; chmn. vocat. edn. Plastics Ednl. Found. U.S.A., 1975-77. Precinct committeeman Republican party, Freeport, 1966-70. Served with U.S. Army, 1954-56. Mem. Nat., Kans. socs. profl. engrs., ASME, Am. Soc. Engring. Educators (campus coordinator), Soc. Plastics Engrs., Rock Valley Soc. Plastics Engrs. (past pres.), Kansas City Plastics Engrs. (Plastics Educator of Year 1976, dir. 1973—), Phi Delta Kappa. Republican. Presbyterian. Clubs: Masons, Shriners, Eastern Star. Home: 520 Utah St Pittsburg KS 66762 Office: Dept Technology Pittsburg State U Pittsburg KS 66762

GRAHAM, H. JAMES, restaurant chain exec.; b. Columbus, Ohio, Sept. 14, 1946; s. Harry Edward and Kathleen (Deitrick) G.; B.S. in Bus. Adminstrn., Xavier U., 1968; m. Sheila A. Seidel, Nov. 30, 1968; children—Brian James, Keith Edward, James Michael. Field mgr., sr. planning analyst Ford Motor Co., 1968-73; real estate analyst Deffet Cos., Columbus, 1973-74; dir. real estate Wendy's Internat., Inc., Dublin, Ohio, 1974-77, v.p. real estate, 1977—; guest lectr., speaker. Mem. Nat. Assn. Corp. Real Estate Execs. (past pres. restaurant industry council), Am. Mgmt. Assn., Internat. Council Shopping Centers, Nat. Assn. Rev. Appraisers, Ohio Assn. Realtors, Pi Sigma Epsilon. Office: PO Box 256 Dublin OH 43017

GRAHAM, JAMES DOUGLAS, TV sta. exec.; b. Xenia, Ohio, Sept. 28, 1942; s. Robert Lewis and Rachel Leona G.; student U. Dayton, 1960-61; m. Carol Ann Howard, Dec. 15, 1962; children—Robert Scott, Douglas Wendell, Lisa Geanne. With Sta. WLWD-TV, 1960-64; with Sta. WKEF-TV, Dayton, Ohio, 1964—, gen. mgr., 1981—. Office: 1731 Soldiers Home Rd Dayton OH 54518

GRAHAM, JAMES WALLACE, credit reporting agy. exec.; b. Greensburg, Pa., Feb. 7, 1926; s. Archibald Wallace and Dolta Lavonia (Shriver) G.; student U. N.C., Ga. State Coll. Bus. Adminstrn.; m. Mildred Jean Clarke, Oct. 11, 1947; children—James Wallace, Douglas Sheldon, Charlene Yvonne. Asst. credit sales mgr. Rich's, Inc., Atlanta, 1953-62; operations mgr. Credit Bur. of Atlanta, 1962-65; treas., sec. Frederick Atkins, Inc., N.Y.C., 1965-73; pres., sec. Credit Bur. Services of Greater Cleve., Inc., 1973—; chmn., dir. Greater Cleve. Consumer Credit Counselling Service. Trustee City Mission, Cleve. Served with USNR, 1944-46; PTO. Mem. Am. Mgmt. Assn., Christian Businessmen's Com. U.S.A., Asso. Credit Burs. Ohio (dir.), Asso. Credit Burs. Republican. Clubs: Cleve. Athletic, Rotary (Cleve.); Acacia Country. Home: 1042 Professor Rd South Euclid OH 44124 Office: 666 Euclid Ave Cleveland OH 44114

GRAHAM, JARLATH JOHN, magazine exec.; b. Chgo., Dec. 18, 1919; s. Jarlath John and Isabelle Marie (Corboy) G.; B.A., U. Chgo., 1949; m. Elizabeth Grace Carlson, Aug. 23, 1958; children by previous marriage—Carol, Karen. With Advt. Age, weekly bus. publ., Chgo., 1950—, editor, 1969-75; v.p. Crain Communications Inc., Chgo., 1963—; dir. editorial devel., pub. Crain Books, 1975-77, v.p. communications and editorial devel., 1977—. Served to capt. AUS, World War II. Mem. Sigma Delta Chi. Contbr. Ency. Brit., 1966-75, World Book Ency., 1979—. Home: 415 Aldine Chicago IL 60657 Office: Crain Communications Inc 740 N Rush St Chicago IL 60611

GRAHAM, MARGARET EDNA (MRS. WILLIAM B. GRAHAM), club woman; b. Weedsport, N.Y.; d. James Leo and Grace (Van Duzer) Kanaley; grad. St. Xavier Coll., 1932; m. William Burden Graham, June 15, 1940; children—William J., Elizabeth Ann (Mrs. Dennis Muckermann), Margaret Edna (Mrs. Benson Caswell), Robert Byron. Past pres. Am. Assn. Maternal and Infant Health; mem. women's bd. De Paul U.; past sec. Chgo. Chamber Music Soc.; governing mem. Chgo. Orchestral Assn.; mem. woman's bd. Mercy Hosp., Ill. Children's Home and Aid Soc., Children's Meml. Hosp., Chgo. Rehab. Inst., Loyola U., De Paul U., English Speaking Union, U. Chgo., U. Chgo. Cancer Research Found., Alliance Francaise; exec. bd. women's assn. Chgo. Symphony; mem. U.S.O.; vice chmn. women's bd., trustee Ravinia Festival; bd. govs. Ill. Club Cath. Women; mem. bd. Kenilworth Home and Garden Club. Clubs: Women's Athletic, Casino (Chgo.); Westmoreland, Mid Am., Kenilworth, Indian Hill, Eldorado Country; Lost Tree (Fla.). Home: 40 Devonshire Ln Kenilworth IL 60043

GRAHAM, RICHARD MARSTON, sculptor; b. Lynn, Mass., July 29, 1939; s. Stuart Webster and Ellen Marston (Connor) G.; B.F.A., Boston U., 1962; M.F.A., R.I. Sch. Design, 1964. Instr., Va. Commonwealth U., 1966-68; asst. prof. art Ithaca Coll., 1968-69, Old Dominion U., 1969-70; asst. prof. Mpls. Coll. Art, 1970-78, chmn. div. basic studies, 1973-75; prof., chmn. art dept. Central Mich. U., Mt. Pleasant, 1978—; one-man exhbns. include: Albany (N.Y.) Inst. Art, 1967, Paul Schuster Gallery, Cambridge, Mass., 1971-75, J. Hunt Gallery, Mpls., 1977, Luth. Brotherhood Ins. Co., Mpls., 1977, St. Norbert Coll., 1977; group shows include: So. Assn. Sculptors traveling exhbns., 1971-75, Sculptors Guild ann. exhbns., N.Y.C., 1973-76, Minn. Sculpture, Mpls., 1977; 2-person shows: Antioch Coll., 1978, Unicorn Gallery, 1978, U. Minn., 1978; represented in permanent collections: Minn. Mus. Art, St. Paul, Carleton Coll., U. Tenn., Chattanooga, Antioch Coll., Ohio, St. Norbert Coll., De Pere, Wis., Ark. Art Center, Little Rock, 1st Nat. Bank, Atlanta; fellow Macdowell Colony, 1971, 75, Yaddo, 1971, Va. Center for Arts, 1973-75. Recipient 1st prize in sculpture Festival of Sculpture, Atlanta, 1970, Carleton Coll. Invitational, 1975; citation of excellence for design in steel Am. Inst. Iron and Steel, 1973; 1st prize toys designed by artists Ark. Art Center, 1975; purchase prize Minn. Mus. Art, 1976; Blanche E. Colman Found. grantee, Boston, 1970; Am. the Beautiful grantee, 1971-73; Union Ind. Colls. Art faculty research grantee, 1972; Minn. Arts Bd. artist-in-residence program grantee Nancy Hauser Dance Co., 1972. Mem. AAUP, Art Educators Minn., Artists Equity Assn., Am. Crafts Council. Coll. Art Assn., Minn. Craftsman's Council, Nat. Art Edn. Assn., Sculptors Guild N.Y. Home: 404 S University Ave Mount Pleasant MI 48858 Office: Central Mich U Mount Pleasant MI 48859*

GRAHAM, ROBERT CLARK, state ofcl.; b. Jeannette, Pa., Jan. 3, 1924; s. Clark W. and Frances M. (Metcalfe) G.; B.S. in Commerce and Adminstrn. summa cum laude, Ohio State U., 1949; m. Martha P. Massena, May 16, 1959; children—Myra, Mary, Carol, Barbara. Gen. mgr. D.H. Lucas Co., Pitts., 1950-72; devel. office coordinator, then dir. corp. giving John Wesley Coll., Owosso, Mich., 1973-76; liaison officer, then adminstrv. asst. to dir. Genesee-Lapeer-Shiawassee Region V Planning and Devel. Commn., Flint, Mich., 1976-78, exec. dir., 1978—. Served with AUS, 1943-46. Mem. Mich. Assn. Regions, Nat. Assn. Regional Councils, Beta Gamma Sigma. Mem. United Ch. Christ. Club: Owosso Kiwanis. Home: 2381 S M52 Owosso MI 48867 Office: 1602 W 3d Ave Flint MI 48504*

GRAHAM, ROBERT GRANT, business exec.; b. Ottawa, Ont., Can., Apr. 8, 1931; s. Wilmer A. and Lylian (Wiltsie) G.; B.Com., McGill U., 1952; m. Diane K. Wilson, May 28, 1953; children—Susan Diane, Bruce Wilson. Pres., chief exec. officer Inter-City Gas Corp., Winnipeg, Man., Can.; chmn. bd. Winnipeg Jets Hockey Club; dir. mem. exec. com. Guaranty Trust Co., Traders Group Ltd., Great-West Life Assurance Co., Can. Gen. Ins. Co.; dir. Fed. Industries Ltd., Moffat Communications Ltd. Bd. dirs. Winnipeg Found.; trustee Man. Theatre Centre. Mem. Conf. Bd. Can. (dir.).

GRAHAM, RUSSELL H., ednl. adminstr.; b. Anniston, Mo., Aug. 17, 1929; s. Sam H. and Willie M. G.; B.S., SE Mo. State U., 1954; Ed.D., U. Mo., Columbia, 1966; m. Helen, June 21, 1978; children—Sandra, Michael, Kenneth, Jon, Patricia-Pamela. Exec. sec. St. Louis-San Francisco Railway Co., Springfield, Mo., 1954-58; secondary tchr. Anniston, Mo., 1958-59, prin., 1959-61; secondary prin. Perryville, Mo., 1961-64; instr. U. Mo., Columbia, 1964-66; pres. Coffeyville (Kans.) Community Coll., 1967—. Served to capt. U.S. Army, 1951-52. Mem. Am. Vocat. Assn., Kans. Vocat. Assn., SE Kans. Community Jr. Coll. Consortium, Kans. Adv. Council on Vocat. Edn., Kans. Assn. Public Community Jr. Colls., Am. Assn. Community and Jr. Colls. (exec. com.), Nat. Adv. Council on Vocat. Edn., Edn. Commn. of the States, Phi Delta Kappa. Roman Catholic. Club: Rotary. Evaluator N.Central Assn. Schs. and Colls. Office: 11th and Willow Sts Coffeyville KS 67337

GRAHAM, RUTH VOGEL, fgn. exchange co. exec.; b. Milw., Sept. 30, 1945; d. Richard Hermann and Hannah (Nachman) Vogel; B.A., Northwestern U., 1967; m. Stephen Shafton Graham, Sept. 17, 1967 (div. 1981); children—Justin Vogel, Charles Spencer. Intern, U.S. Dept. State, Washington, 1965, 66; dir. pub. info. Cook. County Hwy. Dept., Chgo., 1969-71; account supr. Janet Diederichs and Assos., Chgo., 1972-77; trading mem. Mid-Am. Commodity Exchange, Chgo., 1976-78, Internat. Monetary Market, 1978—, also mem. govt. relations com., public affairs com.; producer and host Market Basket with Ruth Graham, Sta. WCIU-TV, Chgo., 1976-81; exec. v.p. Glass Ginsburg Ltd. Mem. Nat. Acad. TV Arts and Scis., Econs. News Broadcasters Assn. (gov.), Chgo. Press Club. Clubs: (Econs. of Chgo., Arts of Chgo. Contbr. articles to fin. publs. Home: 144 Oak Knoll Terr Highland Park IL 60035 Office: 120 S Riverside Plaza Suite 460 Chicago IL 60606

GRAHAM, STEPHEN SHAFTON, lawyer, securities and commodities trader; b. Chgo., July 10, 1938; s. Sidney G. and Phyllis (Shafton) G.; A.B. cum laude, Harvard, 1960, J.D., 1963; m. Ruth I. Vogel, Sept. 17, 1967 (div. Oct. 1981); children—Charles Spencer, Justin Vogel. Admitted to Ill. bar, 1964; exec. trainee Office of Sec. Def., Washington, 1963-65; v.p., sec. dir. Nat. Soda Straw Co., Chgo., 1966-75; mem., market-maker Chgo. Bd. Options Exchange, 1974—, mem. securities com., 1976—; mem., floor trader Chgo. Bd. Trade, 1978—, mem. new products com., 1978—; pres., dir. Pacesetter Industries, Inc. Chgo., 1968-80, Optec Investments Ltd., 1974—. Mem. Com. on Ill. Govt. 1966-74, mem. edn. and housing task forces, 1966-67, bd. dirs., 1970-72; mem. exec. bd. Expt. in Internat. Living, Chgo. Council, 1966-70; mem. central com. Cook County Young Democrats, 1966-70; exec. bd. Ill. State Young Dems., 1966-70; mem. class of 1960 steering com., capital fund campaign Harvard U., 1979—. Mem. Fed., Ill., Chgo. bar assns., Council Fgn. Relations (com. on fgn. affairs), Chgo. Assn. Commerce and Industry, Harvard Law Sch. Assn. Club: Harvard (Chgo.). Office: 141 W Jackson 7th Floor Box 253 Chicago IL 60604

GRAHAM, THOMAS E., financial planner; b. Anderson, Ind., Nov. 24, 1932; s. William F. and Kathryn (Drane) G.; B.B.A., Ball State U., 1968, M.B.A., 1970; m. Loretta Quear, June 10, 1950; children—Shirley, Terry, Thomas. With Purnell-Graham Co., Inc., Anderson, 1949—, pres., 1970—; with Anaconda Corp., 1955-60, Lynch Corp., 1960-65, Spring Air of Ind., 1963-77; instr. Ball State U., 1974; sales Pleasant Valley Modular Housing, Anderson, 1964-76; pres. The Creedmoor Co., Anderson, 1979—; sec.-treas. Oncology Therapy Inc., Terre Haute, Ind., 1980—, Oncology Facilities, Inc., Danville, Ill., 1980—; v.p. Sunbelt Ltd. Inc., Pensacola, Fla., 1979—. Mem. Ind. Dept. Commerce, Anderson C. of C., Nat. Assn. Fin. Planners, World Trade Club, Nat. Rifle Assn. Republican. Mem. Christian Ch. Clubs: Anderson Country, Elks. Office: PO Box 1751 Anderson IN 46014

GRAHAM, WILLIAM ALEXANDER, JR., pathologist; b. Chgo., Oct. 12, 1936; s. William Alexander and Helen Jeanette (Bury) G.; B.S., U.S. Naval Acad., 1958; M.D., Creighton U., 1967; children—Sandra Lynne, Richard Brian, David Jeffrey. Intern, Orange County (Calif.) Med. Center, 1967-68; resident in pathology Los Angeles County/U. So. Calif. Med. Center, 1968-72; asso. pathologist San Clemente Gen. Hosp. (Calif.), 1972-73; dir. labs. and pathology East Liverpool (Ohio) City Hosp., 1973—; instr. U. So. Calif., 1970—. Served to lt. USN, 1958-63. Diplomate Am. Bd. Pathology. Fellow Coll. Am. Pathology, Am. Soc. Clin. Pathologists; mem. Ohio Assn. Blood Banks (trustee 1977—), AMA. Club: Rotary. Home: 48660 Lakeview Circle East Liverpool OH 43920 Office: 425 W 5th St East Liverpool OH 43920

GRAHAM, WILLIAM B., pharm. exec.; b. Chgo., July 14, 1911; s. William and Elizabeth (Burden) G.; S.B., cum laude, U. Chgo., 1932, J.D. cum laude, 1936; LL.D., Carthage Coll., 1974; m. Edna Kanaley, June 15, 1940; children—Elizabeth Anne (Mrs. Dennis F. Muckermann), Margaret (Mrs. Benson T. Caswell), Robert B., William J. Admitted to Ill. bar, 1936; patent lawyer Dyrenforth, Lee, Chritton & Wiles, 1936-40; mem. Dawson & Ooms, 1940-45; v.p., mgr. Baxter Travenol Labs., Inc., Deerfield, Ill., 1945-53, pres., chief exec. officer, 1953-71, chmn. bd., chief exec. officer, 1971-80, chmn., 1980—, also dir.; dir., chmn. exec. com. Bell & Howell, Inc.; dir., mem. exec. com. 1st Nat. Bank, Chgo., NW Industries; dir. Deere & Co., Borg Warner Corp.; prof. Weizmann Inst., 1978. Past pres. Community Fund Chgo.; bd. dirs. Lyric Opera Chgo.; trustee Crusade of Mercy, U. Chgo., Evanston Hosp. Recipient V.I.P. award, 1963; Disting. Citizen award Ill. St. Andrew Soc., 1974; Decision Maker of Yr. award, 1974; Marketer of Yr. award AMA, 1976. Mem. Am. Pharm. Mfrs. Assn. (past pres.), Ill. Mfrs. Assn. (dir., past pres.), Pharm. Mfrs. Assn. (dir., past chmn.), Phi Beta Kappa, Sigma Xi, Phi Delta Phi. Clubs: Chicago (pres.), Commonwealth, Mid-America, Commercial, Indian Hill, Casino, Old Elm (Chgo.); University, Links (N.Y.C.). Home: 40 Devonshire Ln Kenilworth IL 60043 Office: One Baxter Pkwy Deerfield IL 60015

GRAHAM, WILLIAM QUENTIN, computer lessor; b. Ann Arbor, Mich., Jan. 17, 1944; s. William and Marie (MacGregor) G.; B.B.A., Eastern Mich. U., Ypsilanti, 1969; m. Susan H. Scheinker, Sept. 10, 1967; children—David Aaron, Robert Lewis, Alexandria Marie. Research asst. TRW, Los Angeles, 1965; field engr. IBM, Ann Arbor, 1966-69, salesman, Detroit, 1969-73; salesman Cambridge Memories, Inc., 1973-76; large computer specialist CMI Corp., Troy, Mich., 1976-81; lessor Meridian Leasing, Birmingham, Mich., 1981—; data processing cons. and advisor. Clubs: Motor City Striders, Motor City Packards, B'nai B'rith. Home: 5709 Stonington Ct West Bloomington MI 48033 Office: 30800 Telegraph Rd Suite 2865 Birmingham MI 48033

GRAMLEY, MURIEL E., psychiat. social worker; b. Elgin, Ill., June 16, 1946; d. Ellis A. and Pearl B. (Walseth) Greyer; student Iowa State U., 1965-66; grad. cum laude, George Williams Coll., 1976, M.S.W., 1978; div. Mem. office mgmt. staff Hintzsche's, Maple Park, Ill., 1970-75; treatment coordinator Riveredge Hosp., Forest Park, Ill., 1978-80, unit mgr. adult services, 1980—; pvt. practice psychiat. social worker, 1976—; co-owner, psychiat. social worker Gramley-Mason Counseling Services, Oak Brook Terrace, Ill., 1978-80; owner, dir., psychiat. social worker Gramley Counseling Services, 1980—; cons. to divorce lawyers. Mem. Nat. Assn. Social Workers, Am. Soc. Tng. and Devel. Office: Gramley Counseling Services 1348 S Finley Rd 2A Lombard IL 60148

GRAMLING, JAMES THOMAS, machine mfg. co. exec.; b. Wichita, Kans., Feb. 3, 1944; s. Gaylord Trussel and Avis Elaine (Franklin) G.; student U. Mo., Kansas City, 1969; m. Romala Kay Warren, July 25, 1963; children—James Warren, Lori Elaine, Richard Thomas, Steven Douglas. Tool and die maker Gramling Tool and Die, Inc., Kansas City, Kans., 1966-68, machinist designer, 1968-71, mgr., 1971-75; v.p. Preco Industries, Inc., Shawnee Mission, Kans., 1975—, also dir.; pres. Gramling Mfg. Co., Inc., 1980—; cons. in field. Served with USAF, 1962-66. Republican. Inventor Preco press, Gramling rotary engine, digital to analogue converter. Home: Route 1 Box 24W Basehor KS 66007

GRAMS, WILLIAM EDMUND, ins. co. exec.; b. Antigo, Wis., Apr. 30, 1943; s. Raymond W. and Florence A. Grams; B.S., U. Wis., Stevens Point, 1967; M.S. in Safety Edn., U. Wis., Madison, 1968; m. Jacqueline Ann Weber, July 13, 1968; children—Julie, Billy, Susie, Joey. With Employers Ins. Wausau (Wis.), 1968—, regional safety and health services mgr., Milw., 1977-80, asst. v.p. regional safety and health services, Wausau, 1980—. Mem. Am. Soc. Safety Engrs. (cert. safety profl.), Am. Mut. Ins. Alliance. Home: 605 Schmidt Ave Rothschild WI 54474 Office: 200 Westwood Dr Wausau WI 54401

GRAN, VIOLA MARGARET, real estate broker; b. LaCrosse, Wis.; d. Bernard George and Margaret Caroline (Cain) Kramer; student Wis. Sch. Real Estate, 1967; grad. Realtors Inst., Mpls., 1974; student U. Wis. Bus. and Mgmt. Extension, 1966, 73; m. James K. Gran, Sept. 16, 1937 (dec. Aug. 1977); 1 son, James B.; 1 stepson, Richard Oscar. Real estate broker, La Crosse, 1967—; owner, mgr. V. M. Gran Realty, La Crosse, 1967—, La Crescent, Minn., 1969—; owner, mgr. VMG Rentals and Advt., La Crosse, 1965—; instr. Wis. Sch. Real Estate, Milw., 1968—. Mem. Nat. Assn. Realtors, Wis., Minn. (state legis. com.), realtors assns., Greater LaCrosse, Southeastern Minn. bds. realtors, Realtors Nat. Mktg. Inst., LaCrosse, LaCrescent chambers commerce, Mississippi Valley Exchange (pres.), VFW Ladies Aux., Women of Moose (publicity chmn. La Crosse 1978-80). Methodist. Office: Jackson Plaza Suite A 103 East Ave LaCrosse WI 54601

GRANAT, BRUCE ARNOLD, librarian; b. Chgo., July 21, 1939; s. Harry Jeremiah and Nettie (Small) G.; B.S. in Psychology, Roosevelt U., 1961; M.A., U. Chgo., 1964; m. Jacqueline Eliane Kraft, Aug. 26, 1962; children—Deborah Kathryn, Rebecca Jean. Librarian trainee applied sci. and tech. dept., Chgo. Pub. Library, 1961-62; reference librarian John Crerar Library, Chgo., 1962-64; head librarian bus. information service, Abbott Labs., North Chicago, 1964-65; mgr. and head librarian Continental Ill. Nat. Bank & Trust Co. of Chgo. Library, 1965-73; dir. corp. libraries and communications services G.D. Searle & Co., Skokie, Ill., 1973—; vis. lectr. Rosary Coll.; library cons. and adv. work to various orgns., 1967—; mem. governing bd. Library of Internat. Relations. NATO Advanced Study Inst. grantee on evaluation libraries and info. centers, 1975; mem. automation com. Ill. State Library, 1975—. Mem. A.L.A., Spl. Libraries Assn. (chmn. nat. consultation com. 1976—, officer nat. documentation div. 1976—), Med. Library Assn., Am. Soc. for Info. Sci., Pharm. Mfrs. Assn. (sci. info. subcom. 1975—), U. Chgo. Alumni Assn., Beta Phi Mu. Contbr. articles to profl. publs. Home: 1401 Dempster St Evanston IL 60201 Office: GD Searle & Co Box 1045 Skokie IL 60076

GRANDON, DAWN ALICE, interior design co. exec.; b. Chgo., Mar. 18, 1943; d. Edwin Frederick and Jennifer (Adams) Gordon; student Northwestern U., 1961-62, Oreg. State U., 1962-63; B.S. in Natural Sci. and Zoology, Wayne State U., 1965, postgrad. in art and graphic design, sci. illustration, 1965-67; m. Jerry Lee Grandon, June 26, 1965; children—Jeffrey Frederick, James Brian, Julia Jennifer, Matthew Hart. Oceanography researcher and instr. Oreg. State U., 1962-63; Henry Ford Hosp., Detroit, 1965-66; designer salesperson, Hillsboro Land Mark Apts., Hillsboro Beach, Fla. 1966-69; interior design cons. Grandon Interiors, Pompano Beach, Fla., 1968-72, also dir.; product design exec. Gordon Art Co. div. GPF Co., Pompano Beach, 1968-71; sec.-treas., gen. mgr. Spectrum Designs, Inc., Deerfield Beach, Fla., 1972-79, dir. design, 1975-79; product design exec. WG Pub., Milw., 1980—; mktg. and design dir. Grandon Interiors, Lighthouse Point, Fla., 1979—; realtor Century Realty, Marshfield, Mo., 1981—; comml. farm specialist. Exec. sec. bd. dirs. Intercoastal div. Children's Home Soc. Fla., 1979-81, bd. dirs., 1972—; mem. Broward County (Fla.) Sch. Adv. Com., 1976-81; active Gulf Stream council Boy Scouts Am., 1976-78; active Boy's Clubs Am. of Broward County, 1968-81; local chmn. Broward County Sch. Bd. Adr. Council, 1978, mem. area exec. com., 1979-81; exec. v.p. Bus. and Profl. Women's Assn., Pompano Beach, 1979-80. Named Outstanding Young Women Am., 1968. Mem. Nat. Home Fashions League, Am. Soc. Interior Design, Am. Craft Council, Farm and Land Inst., Greater Springfield Bd. Realtors, Smithsonian Inst., AAUW, Children's Home Soc., Delta Zeta (v.p. Gold Coast alumnae 1968-70, treas. 1972-74, South Fla. Alumni Woman of Yr. award 1974). Republican. Mormon. Home: Route 3 Box 160F Marshfield MO 65706 Office: Century Realty I-44 and Spur Dr PO Box 1 Marshfield MO 65706

GRANGAARD, DONALD ROBERT, banker; b. Rothsay, Minn., July 16, 1918; s. O. F. and Ella J. G.; B.A., U. N.D., 1939; LL.B., William Mitchell Coll. Law, 1948; grad. Advanced Mgmt. Program, Harvard Bus. Sch., 1966; m. Irene M. Hagquist, 1944; children—Cheryl Grangaard Reinertsen, John, Blake, Paul, Janet. With First Bank System and affiliates, Mpls., 1937-50; v.p. 1st Nat. Bank, Fairmont, Minn., 1950-52; v.p., dir. 1st Nat. Bank, Austin, Minn., 1952-59; v.p., then sr. v.p. 1st Bank System, Mpls., 1959-69, pres., chief exec. officer, dir., 1969-77, chmn. bd., chief exec. officer, dir., 1977-81, chmn. bd., 1981—; dir. 1st Nat. Bank, Mpls., 1st Nat. Bank, St. Paul, 1st Trust Co., St. Paul, 1st Bank, N.A., Milw., George A. Hormel & Co. Trustee Fairview Community Hosps.; regent Augsburg Coll. Served with U.S. Army, 1942-46. Mem. Assn. Bank Holding Cos. (dir.). Clubs: Mpls., Minikahda, Minn. Office: 1200 First Bank Place E Minneapolis MN 55480

GRANGER, CHARLES R., plant physiologist, educator; b. Marshalltown, Iowa, Sept. 4, 1939; s. Earl B. and Verna M. (Zhorne) G.; B.S., Iowa State U., 1962; M.S. in Sci. Edn., U. Pa., 1966, M.S. in Biology, 1967; Ph.D., U. Iowa, 1970; 1 dau., Cheryl L. Sci. tchr. South Tama County Community Sch., Tama, Iowa, 1962-65; research asst. U. Iowa Hosps., Iowa City, 1964-65; instr. U. Iowa, 1968-70; asst. for acad. affairs Cornell U., Ithaca, N.Y., 1970-71; asst. prof. biology and edn. U. Mo., St. Louis, 1971-76, asso. prof. biology and edn., 1977-81, asso. chmn. dept. biology, 1974-78, chmn., 1981—; dir. Mo.

Jr. Acad., 1972-77; dir. Summer Sci. Research Inst., 1975-77; dir. Jr. Sci., Engring. and Humanities Symposium, 1974—; pres. Granger Engring. and Research, 1971—. Recipient Excellence in Teaching award U. Mo., 1975. Mem. Am. Inst. Biol. Sci., Assn. for Edn. Tchrs. in Sci., Nat. Assn. Biology Tchrs., Nat. Assn. Research in Sci. Teaching, Nat. Sci. Tchrs. Assn., Assn. Midwest Coll. Biology Tchrs., Sci. Tchrs. Mo. (Outstanding Mo. Sci. Educator award 1981), Mo. Acad. Sci. (pres. 1978-79), Phi Delta Kappa. Author: The Pitch, 1976; editor newspaper series Sci. in Mo.; patents, publs. in field. Office: U Mo 8001 Natural Bridge Saint Louis MO 63121

GRANT, CHARLES HENRY, energy scis. co. exec.; b. Chgo., July 8, 1927; s. Alexander Richardson and Eleanor Farrel (Riley) G.; diploma mining engring. Wis. Inst. Tech., 1950; div.; children—Deborah Ann, Charles H. From asst. to chief mining engr. Minn. ore div., Jones & Laughlin Steel Corp., 1950-60; mgr. sales dir. research, mfg. ops., new explosives Dow Chem. Co., Virginia, Minn., 1960-65, gen. mgr. explosives, Midland, Mich., 1976—; pres., treas., dir. E.S.&C. Inc., 1976—; bd. govs. Inst. Makers Explosives. Mem. Am. Inst. Mining, Metall. and Petroleum Engrs. (sec. to vice chmn. Minn. sect. 1963-65, Peele award 1964). Contbr. articles in field to trade jours.; patentee in field. Home: Star RT Box 3290 Tower MN 55790 Office: Box B Biwabik MN 55708

GRANT, CHARLES TRUMAN, paper mfg. co. exec.; b. Chgo., Oct. 10, 1946; s. Charles H. and Mildred E. (Larrey) G.; B.A., DePaul U., Chgo., 1968, M.B.A. in Fin. and Acctg., 1975; 1 dau., Jordanna Lynne. Acctg. supr. and procedures analyst Washington Nat. Ins. Co., Evanston, Ill., 1970-71; dir. internal audit, gen. credit mgr. Rand McNally & Co., Skokie, Ill., 1973-75; cost and gen. acctg. mgr. V. Mueller div. Am. Hosp. Supply Corp., Chgo., 1971-73, corp. dir. acctg. and reporting Am. Hosp. Supply Corp., Evanston, 1975-77, officer and controller Am. Hosp. Supply div., McGaw Park, Ill., 1977-78; area v.p. ops. and adminstrn. Mead Corp., Hillside, Ill., 1978-80, pres., gen. mgr. Ft. Dearborn Paper div., Chgo., 1980—; dir. CEDCO Capital, Inc., 1978—. Lectr. Merit Youth Employment Council, 1976—; fin. adv. Jr. Achievement, 1971-75. Mem. N.Y. Fin. Mgmt. Assn., Inst. Internal Auditors, Nat. Black M.B.A. Assn. (pres. 1981—). Roman Catholic. Contbr. career articles to Ebony, Black Enterprise Mag. Home: 1954 Jamestown Dr Palatine IL 60067 Office: 2901 W 36th Pl Chicago IL 60632

GRANT, FREDERICH DOUGLAS, advt./pub. relations agy. exec.; b. Chgo., Aug. 25, 1932; s. Roy Everett and Rebecca (McNair) G.; A.B., Roosevelt U., 1962; B.S. in Bus. Adminstrn., Chgo. State U., 1981; certificate Boston Coll. Franchise Inst., 1968; m. Elizabeth Anne Rankin, Jan. 28, 1965; children—George Frederich, Rebecca Margaret, John David, Cory McNair. Sr. editor Cahner's Pub., Chgo., 1968; account coordinator Vince Cullers Advt., Chgo., 1968-70; exec. v.p. Communicon, Inc., Chgo., 1970-74, pres., 1975—; dir. Ehr-Grant Corp. Cons. food service edn. curricula Chgo. Bd. Edn., 1969-71; tchr. contemporary Black Am. history Chgo. YMCA, 1968. Bd. dirs. Midwest Assn. Sickle Cell Anemia, Clarence Darrow Community Center; mem. exec. com. Operation Push Expo, 1972-73. Served with USAF, 1950-56. Recipient 3 CLIO awards for radio writing, 1975. Mem. Inst. for Religion in Age of Sci. Office: 520 N Michigan Ave Chicago IL 60611

GRANT, GERARD GRAY, clergyman, educator; b. Chgo., Aug. 27, 1908; s. Samuel Thomas and Elizabeth G.; student Loyola U., Chgo., 1926-28; A.B., St. Louis U., 1934, M.A., 1934, Ph.L., 1937, S.T.L., 1941. Joined S.J., Roman Catholic Ch., 1928, ordained priest, 1940; exec. dir. Loyola U. Alumni Assn., 1942-51; asso. prof. philosophy Loyola U., Chgo., 1951-78, prof., 1978—; pres. World Federalists in Chgo., 1960-62, 81—, exec. v.p. Chgo. World Federalists, 1962-81; mem. Nat. Council World Federalists, 1958—; v.p. World Federalists, U.S.A., 1968-75, 80—; memr. Federalist World Council, 1963—; chmn. exec. com. World Assn. World Federalists, 1975-77; chmn. council World Assn. World Federalists, 1977—; chmn. Inter-Univ. Survey on World Law, 1969—, Chgo. Com. to Save Lives In Chile, 1974, Com. for Freedom in India, 1975-77. Mem. AAUP, Clergy and Laity Concerned, Chgo. Com. to Defend Bill of Rights, Am. Cath. Philos. Assn. Democrat. Author: Elevation of the Host, 1942. Home: 6525 N Sheridan Rd Chicago IL 60626

GRANT, HAROLD PETER, profl. football coach; b. Syperior, Wis., May 20, 1927; student U. Minn. Player, Mpls. Lakers, Nat. Basketball Assn., 1949-51, Phila. Eagles, NFL, 1951-52; player Winnipeg (Man., Can.) Profl. Football Team, 1953-54, head coach, 1957-66; head coach Minn. Vikings, NFL, 1968—. Coach, Can. Football League championships, 1958-59, 61-62, Super Bowl IV, VIII, IX, XI. Address: Minn Vikings 9520 Viking Dr Eden Prairie MN 55344*

GRANT, KINGSLEY B., pathologist, dermatopathologist; b. Belize, Brit. Honduras; s. Ezekiel A. and Wilhelmina E. (Morter) G.; B.S. summa cum laude, Howard U., Washington, 1955, M.D., 1959; m. Margaret Ward; children—Ward, Conrad, Maxwell. Intern, St. Luke's Methodist Hosp., Cedar Rapids, Iowa, 1959-60, resident in pathology, 1960-62, asso. pathologist, 1964-70, co-dir. pathology labs., 1970-75, dir. pathology labs., 1975—, sec.-treas. med. staff, 1979, pres. med. staff, 1981; resident Los Angeles County Harbor Gen. Hosp., Torrance, Calif., 1962-64; clin. asst. prof. pathology U. Iowa. Bd. dirs. United Way, 1966-71; mem. commn. race and religion Iowa conf. United Meth. Ch.; chmn. Cedar Rapids Human Rights Commn., 1969-71, Cedar Rapids chpt. NCCJ, 1969. Recipient Community Builder award B'nai B'rith, 1970, certificate of appreciation City of Cedar Rapids, 1974. Mem. Iowa Assn. Pathologists, Am. Soc. Clin. Pathologists, Coll. Am. Pathologists, AMA, Nat. Med. Assn., Linn County Med. Soc., Phi Beta Kappa. Clubs: Rotary, Met., Pickwick, Cedar Rapids Country. Contbr. articles to profl. jours. Office: 1026 A Ave NE Cedar Rapids IA 52402

GRANT, MICHAEL PETER, elec. engr.; b. Oshkosh, Wis., Feb. 26, 1936; s. Robert J. and Ione (Michelson) G.; B.S., Purdue U., 1957, M.S., 1958, Ph.D., 1964; m. Mary Susan Corcoran, September 2, 1961; children—James, Steven, Laura. With Westinghouse Research Labs., Pitts., summers 1953-57; mem. tech. staff Aerospace Corp., El Segundo, Calif., 1961; instr. elec. engring. Purdue U., 1958-64; sr. engr. Indsl. Nucleonics Corp., Columbus, Ohio, 1964-67, mgr. advanced devel. and control systems, 1967-72, mgr. control and info. scis. div., 1972-74, asst. gen. mgr. indsl. systems div., 1974-76, mgr. system design, 1976—. Mem. IEEE, Sigma Xi, Eta Kappa Nu, Pi Mu Epsilon, Tau Beta Pi. Contbr. articles to profl. jours. Patentee in field of automation. Home: 4461 Sussex Dr Columbus OH 43220 Office: 650 Ackerman Rd Columbus OH 43202

GRANT, PAUL ROGER, utility co. exec.; b. Logansport, Ind., Aug. 18, 1947; s. Paul Arthur and Ruby Virginia (Gooch) G.; B.S., Purdue U., 1969, M.S., 1975; m. Jane Kathryn Knoy, June 8, 1968; children—Timothy Mark, Stephanie Jane. Engr., Pub. Service Ind., Plainfield, Ind., 1969-74, sr. tech. analyst, 1974-78, tech. info. processing supr., 1978—. Mem. Assn. Computing Machinery (pres. Central Ind. chpt. 1975-76), Central Ind. OS/VS Users Group (sec. 1975). Club: Optimists (v.p. 1978-79, pres. 1979-80). Home: 2450 Avon Rd Plainfield IN 46168 Office: 1000 E Main St Plainfield IN 46168

GRANT, SANDRA LOVE SMITH, personnel exec.; b. White Plains, N.Y., Aug. 22, 1940; d. Darwin Aldridge and Harriette Augusta (Love) Smith; student Vanderbilt U., 1958-60, U. Colo., 1974-76; B.A., Ga. State Coll., 1976, M. Govt. Adminstrn., 1979; m. July 7, 1961 (div. 1967); children—Kenneth Richard, Deborah Anne. Office coordinator, v.p. HuSAC, Atlanta, 1973-74; adminstrv. asst. Atlanta Community Relations Commn., 1974-77; office mgr. United Way Met. Atlanta, 1977-79; employment mgr. Center for Human Services, Cleve., 1979—. Vol. staff, Emmaus House, 1971-75; coordinator Com. to Stop Indsl. Encroachment, 1974-77; chmn., coordinator Inman Park Restoration Zoning Com., 1974-76; mem. community council Martin Luther King Middle Sch., 1975-76; supt. music program Cathedral St. Philip, 1971-75; campaign mgr. city council candidate, 1977; supt. ch. sch. St. Philips, 1972-73. Recipient Joel award Inman Park Restoration, Inc., 1977. Democrat. Episcopalian. Home: 3279 Meadowbrook Blvd Cleveland Heights OH 44118 Office: 1001 Huron Rd Cleveland OH 44115

GRASSLEY, CHARLES E., U.S. senator; b. New Hartford, Iowa, Sept. 17, 1933; s. Louis Arthur and Ruth (Corwin); B.A., U. No. Iowa, 1955, M.A., 1956; postgrad. U. Iowa, 1957-58; m. Barbara Ann Speicher, Aug. 22, 1954; children—Lee, Wendy, Robin, Michele, Jay. Farmer, New Hartford, 1959—; mem. Iowa Legislature, 1959-74; mem. 94th-96th Congresses from 3d Dist. Iowa; U.S. senator from Iowa, 1980—. Mem. Iowa, Butler County hist. socs., Farm Bur. Baptist. Mason. Home: Route 1 New Hartford IA 50660 Office: 344 Russell Senate Office Bldg Washington DC 20510

GRATIAS, ARTHUR LOUIS, state senator; b. Nora Springs, Iowa, May 1, 1920; s. Hugo Gustav and Katharine (Ahrens) G.; B.A. magna cum laude, Wartburg Coll., 1970; M.A., U. No. Iowa; m. Alice Dissmore, 1943; children—Thomas John, James Arthur, Douglas Edward. Farmer, 1946-69; tchr. Rudd Sch., 1970-75, elem. and jr. high sch. prin., 1975-79; mem. Iowa State Senator, 1979—. Twp. chmn., mem. Republican Com., 1965-76. Served with AUS, 1942-45; ETO. Decorated Purple Heart. Mem. Am. Legion, Farm Bur., Wartburg Alumni Assn. (Community Service award), Phi Delta Kappa. Presbyterian. Club: Kiwanis (Outstanding Sec. award 1974-75). Office: State Senate Des Moines IA 50319*

GRAU, PAUL ANDREW, lawyer; b. Buffalo, Mar. 11, 1951; s. Paul Adolph and Mary Ann (Polom) G.; B.A. cum laude in Econs. (N.Y. Regents scholar), SUNY, Oswego, 1973; J.D. magna cum laude, Cleve. State U., 1976; m. Linda F. Mruk, July 14, 1973. Admitted to Ohio bar, 1976; individual practice law, Garfield Heights, Ohio, 1976-78; partner firm Reddy, Grau & Meek, Garfield Heights, 1978—; legal counsel City of Garfield Heights, 1976—, City of Brecksville, 1981—. Mem. Am. Bar Assn., Ohio Bar Assn., Cuyahoga County Bar Assn., Cuyahoga County Law Dir.'s Assn., Greater Cleve. Bar Assn., Omicron Delta Epsilon (charter). Club: Exchange (Garfield Heights) (sec.). Home: 4717 Blythin Rd Garfield Heights OH 44125 Office: RGM Comml Bldg 5039 Turney Rd Garfield Heights OH 44125

GRAVEREAU, VICTOR P., marketing cons., ret. educator; b. Thunder Bay, Ont., Can., Mar. 20, 1909; s. James and Malvina (Lemieux) G.; came to U.S., 1910, naturalized, 1934; B.A., Ohio Wesleyan U., 1936; M.A., Kent State U., 1943; M.B.A., Case Western Res. U., 1951; m. Mildred Irene Snyder, Aug. 11, 1934. Salesman, Motorists Mutual Ins. Co., Wooster, Ohio, 1936-37; tchr. of commerce Rittman (Ohio) High Sch., 1937-46; accountant Gerstenslager Co., Wooster, Ohio, 1944; asst. prof. commerce Kent (Ohio) State U., 1946-49, asso. prof. commerce, 1949-51, prof. marketing, 1951-76, prof. marketing emeritus, 1976—, coordinator coll. grad. program, 1957-60, asst. dean, 1960-61; partner Pfeiffer, Gravereau & Assos., Kent, 1954-63; dir., v.p. Clark Zimmerman & Assos., Inc., Cleve., 1971—. Recipient Pres.'s. medal Kent State U., 1977; Republic Steel Corp. Economics-in-Action fellow Case Western Res. U., 1964. Mem. Am. Mktg. Assn., Am. Acad. Advt., Nat. Assn. of Purchasing Mgmt. (faculty intern fellow 1962), Bus. Profl. Advt. Assn., Advt. Club Akron, Beta Gamma Sigma, Delta Sigma Pi, Delta Tau Delta, Kappa Delta Pi. Clubs: Masons, Kiwanis, Akron City. Author: Purchasing Management: Selected Readings, 1973; contbr. articles in field to profl. publs.; mktg. scholarship Kent State U. established in his name, 1977. Home: 212 Elmwood Dr Kent OH 44240

GRAVES, ELIZABETH STEPHENS, designer; b. Mich., Oct. 1, 1930; d. Arthur W. and Isabella (Balhoff) Stephens; student Mich. State U., 1948-51, Layton Sch. Art. 1960, 61, Louisville Art Center, 1968, 69; m. Lee Kimball Graves, July 7, 1950; children—Wendy Leary, Joy, Barbara. Dir., WHAS Gallery, Louisville, 1968, 69; designer P.L. Mahan Interiors, Inc., Birmingham, Mich., 1971-74; designer, owner Pine Tree Interiors, Birmingham, 1975—. Mem. women's com. directorship Cranbrook Art Acad./Mus.; chmn. Louisville Salutes the Arts, 1969; chmn. rental and sales gallery Milw. Art Center, 1962-66, Speed Mus., Louisville, 1967, 68. Republican. Presbyterian.

GRAVES, MELVIN MACPIKE, JR., hosp. adminstr.; b. Cleve., Jan. 3, 1941; s. Melvin MacPike and Dorothy (Fisher) G.; B.A., Johns Hopkins U., 1963; M.B.A., U. Chgo., 1965; m. Beverly Bane Woodward, Sept. 3, 1977; children—Paul Stuart, Jonathan Michael. Adminstrv. resident Univ. Hosps. of Cleve., 1964-65, adminstrv. asst., 1965-69, asst. adminstr., 1970-76; exec. dir. Finley Hosp., Dubuque, Iowa, 1976—. Mem. United Way Community Services Planning Com., 1977—; chmn. Dubuque Airport Commn.; trustee U. Dubuque; trustee United Way of Dubuque, campaign chmn., 1981-82. Mem. Am. Coll. Hosp. Adminstrs., Am. Hosp. Assn., Iowa Hosp. Assn., Dubuque C. of C. (trustee). Republican. Club: Rotary Internat. Office: 350 N Grandview Ave Dubuque IA 52001

GRAVES, REBECCA VIRGINIA, educator; b. Memphis, Aug. 13, 1941; d. Kirby and Delores (Chambliss) Houston; B.S., Chgo. State U., 1967; postgrad. Alverno Coll., 1975; M.A., DePaul U., 1971; postgrad. U. Wis., 1977; m. William Albert Graves, June 15, 1963; children—Tanya Ruth, Jason Albert. Spl. service librarian Chgo. Bd. Edn., summer 1969; art dir. Sears Camp, YMCA, Chgo., summer 1970; chmn. lang. arts dept. Chgo. Sch. Bd., 1967-73; reading specialist Milw. Sch. Bd., 1973-75; learning disabilities resource tchr. Madison (Wis.) Sch. Bd., 1975-78, Pontiac (Mich.) Sch. Bd., 1978—; guest lectr. U. Wis., Madison, 1977; dept. head No. Assistance Center, Pontiac No. High Sch., 1978—; youth page adv. Milw. Courier. PTA area council rep. Southfield (Mich.) Public Schs., 1979; v.p. PTA, McArthur Elem. Sch., 1980, 81; campaign worker Com. to Elect Sch. Bd. Member, 1979-80; bd. dirs. YWCA, Milw. and Madison, 1973-78, personnel chmn., 1976-78. Mem. Assn. for Supervision and Curriculum Devel., Mich. Assn. for Children and Adults with Learning Disabilities, Council for Exceptional Children, Detroit Assn. for Retarded Citizens, Internat. Reading Assn., Mich. Reading Assn., Inner City Arts Council, NAACP, Urban League (mem. edn. com. 1979-81), Nat. Council Negro Women, Alpha Kappa Alpha, Phi Delta Kappa, Eta Phi Beta. Democrat. Baptist. Home: 22531 Lake Ravines Dr Southfield MI 48034 Office: 1051 Arlene St Pontiac MI 48055

GRAY, BYRON EVERETT, indsl. engr.; b. St. Louis, Mar. 14, 1918; s. Bryon A. and Edna (Brueggemann) G.; B.S. in Engring. Adminstrn., Washington U., 1941; m. Marguerite Jane Westphalen, Aug. 6, 1940; children—Byron Everett, Robert W., Richard T. Field engr. Sverdrup & Parcel, St. Louis, 1940-42; materials rev. engring. supr. airframe div. Curtiss Wright Corp., St. Louis, 1942-45; engr. tanning div. Interco, St. Louis, 1945-48, chief engr. tanning div., 1948-52, mgr. product and process devel. div., 1952-58, mgr. research and devel. div., 1958-64; pvt. practice engring., St. Louis, 1964—; tech. cons. Nat. Shoe Mfrs. Assn., 1964-72, editor Tech. Jour., 1965-68; chmn. safety footwear com. Am. Nat. Standards Inst., 1969—. Bd. dirs. YMCA Greater St. Louis, 1953—, mgr. Downtown br. bd., 1963-64; pres. Village Lutheran Ch., Ladue, Mo., 1976. Registered profl. engr., Mo. Mem. ASME, Brit. Boot and Shoe Inst., Soc. Plastics Industry (chmn. shoe div. 1961-65), ASTM, Nat. Safety Council, Am. Footwear Industries Assn. Lutheran. Clubs: University, Rotary. Patentee metatarsal hinge for safety shoes, safety shoe toe box design. Home: 6 Treebrook Ln Saint Louis MO 63124 Office: 7701 Forsyth Blvd Saint Louis MO 63105

GRAY, CHARLES ELMER, lawyer; b. Elvins, Mo., July 23, 1919; s. Grover P. and Martha Elizabeth (Sullivan) G.; student Flat River Jr. Coll., 1937-38, U. Hawaii, 1940-41; LL.B, Washington U., 1947; m. Beulah Hennrich Gray, July 4, 1942; children—Karen Lee, Cecilia Jean, Bette Sue, Marsha Dawn. Admitted to Mo. bar, 1947; since practiced in St. Louis; partner Schoenbeck & Gray, 1954; partner firm Gray & Ritter; sec., gen. counsel Don V. Davis Co.; pres. Don-Ite Corp.; gen. counsel, dir. United Mo. Bank St. Louis; mem. Mo. Appellate Jud. Commn., 1969-75; mem. rules com. Supreme Ct. Mo., 1970-81. Served sgt. to capt. USAF, 1939-45. Fellow Internat. Acad. Trial Lawyers (dir.), Am. Coll. Trial Lawyers, Internat. Soc. Barristers (state chmn., dir.); mem. Am., Mo., St. Louis bar assns., Lawyers Assn. St. Louis (v.p. 1954, bd. govs.; award of Honor 1977), Phi Delta Phi. Home: 625 S Skinker Saint Louis MO 63105 also Apt 290 950 Beach Rd John's Island Vero Beach FL Office: 900 Locust Bldg 1015 Locust St Saint Louis MO 63101

GRAY, CHARLES WEBSTER, civil and mech. engr.; b. nr. Clinton, Mo., Sept. 9, 1914; s. Harvey Gant and Mary (Lay) G.; student Central Coll., 1931-33, U. Mo., 1933-36, Pittsburg (Kans.) State Coll., 1949-50; m. Frances Louise Thomas, Sept. 6, 1936; children—Mary Elizabeth (Mrs. James E. Bolin, Jr.), Charles Webster. Started as jr. engr., supr., asst. state planning engr. WPA, Jefferson City, Mo., 1936-40; design engr., field engr., asst. maintenance supt. Hercules Powder Co., Radford, Va., Wilmington, Del., 1940-46; maintenance and engring. cons., Carthage, Mo., 1946; engr., sr. engr., projects supt. Spencer Chem. Co., Quaker Valley Constructors, Inc. subs., Pittsburg, Kans. and Kansas City, Mo., 1947-53; sr. maintenance engr., maintenance supt. Am. Cyanamid Co., New Orleans, 1953-59; maintenance cons., pres. Gray Equipment, Inc., Metairie, La., 1959-61, chmn. bd., 1959—; resident engr. Barnard and Burk, Baton Rouge, Seneca, S.C., 1961-62; chief planner, project supt., project mgr. cons. Catalytic Inc., Orange, Tex., Toledo, Phila., 1962—. Mgmt. and engring. cons., 1961—. Recipient numerous commendations and certificates from industry, govt. agys. Registered profl. engr., Mo., Kans., La. Mem. Nat., Mo. socs. profl. engrs., Am. Welding Soc. (dir. 1954-55), Internat. Platform Assn., Am. Mgmt. Asso., La. Engring. Soc. Democrat. Methodist (ofcl. bd.). Elk. Home: 121 N Livingston Pl Metairie LA 70005 Office: care George Butler Assos City Center Sq 1100 Main St Kansas City MO 64105 also 1908 Dana Dr Adelphi MO 20783 also 613 S Patterson St Gibsonburg OH 43431 also Centre-Sq West Catalytic Inc 1500 Market St Philadelphia PA 19102

GRAY, DON NORMAN, chemist; b. Carlyle, Ill., July 28, 1931; s. Garold Norman and Mary Louisa (Shoupe) G.; B.S. in Chemistry, Colo. State U., 1953; Ph.D. in Chemistry, Colo. U., Boulder, 1956; m. Mary Kelly, Oct. 10, 1959; children—Christy Elizabeth, Andrew Kelly, Jane Moore. Faculty Denver U., staff Denver Research Inst., 1956-63; scientist Martin Marietta Aerospace, Balt., 1963-66; mgr. biotechnology and toxicology Owens-Illinois, Toledo, 1966—; pres. Shenandoah Research, Inc. Mem. Am. Chem. Soc., N.Y. Acad. Scis., Am. Soc. Artificial Internal Organs, Sigma Xi. Inventor Biobland plastics; contbr. writings to profl. publs.; patentee. Home: 5503 Brixton Dr Sylvania OH 43560

GRAY, GEORGE TRUMON, educator; b. Indpls., June 1, 1946; s. Trumon Lloyd and Helen Louise (McClain) G.; student Purdue U., 1964-65; B.Music Edn., Ind. U., 1968, M.S. in Edn., 1969, Ed.D., 1973; m. Beverly Diane Liebenow, Aug. 24, 1974. Asst. prof. curriculum Tenn.-Technol. U., Cockeville, 1973-75; coordinator Office Curriculum Devel. and Evaluation, Rush U., Rush-Presbyn. St. Luke's Med. Center, Chgo., 1976-79, acting dir., 1979-80, dir. Office Curriculum Devel. and Evaluation, 1980—, asst. prof. dept. family practice, 1980—; cons. to schs. nursing, bus.; vis. scholar Northwestern U., 1975-76; curriculum and evaluation cons. family practice grants, Rush Med. Coll., 1980—. Mem. Am. Ednl. Research Assn., Assn. Supervision and Curriculum Devel., Am. Philatelic Soc., Tubists' Universal Brotherhood Assn., Phi Delta Kappa. Presbyn. Contbr. articles to profl. jours. Office: 412 AF Rush-Presbyn St Luke's Med Center 600 S Paulina St Chicago IL 60612

GRAY, GEORGIA NEESE, banker; b. Richland, Kans.; d. Albert and Ellen (O'Sullivan) Neese; A.B., Washburn Coll., 1921; D.B.A. (hon.), 1966; student Sargent's, 1921-22; L.H.D., Russell Sage Coll., 1950; m. George M. Clark, Jan. 21, 1929; m. 2d, Andrew J. Gray, 1953. Began as actress, 1923; asst. cashier Richland State Bank, 1935-37, pres., 1937—; pres. Capital City State Bank & Trust Co., Topeka, 1964-74; treas. of U.S., 1949-53. Del.-at-large nat. adv. com. SBA; treas. Girls Club Topeka. Democratic nat. committeewoman, 1936-64; hon. chmn. Villages project C. of C. Bd. dirs. Kans. A.A.A., 1950—; bd. dirs., former chmn. Kans. div. Am. Cancer Soc.; mem. bd. exec. campaign and maj. gifts com. Georgetown U.; bd. dirs. Seven Steps Found., Harry S. Truman Library; chmn. Alpha Phi Found., 1962-63; mem. nat. bd. Womens Med. Coll. Pa.; chmn. bd. regents Washburn U., 1975—; mem. bd., treas. Sex Information and Edn. Council U.S. Recipient Distinguished Alumni award Washburn U., 1950. Mem. Am. Bus. Women's Assn., Topeka C. of C., Met. Bus. and Profl. Women's Club, Women in Communications, Alpha Phi (nat. trustee), Alpha Phi Upsilon. Clubs: Soroptimist (hon. life), Met. Zonta, Topeka Country. Address: 2709 W 29 St Topeka KS 66614

GRAY, GRATTAN, publisher; b. Adrian, Mich., Aug. 24, 1925; s. JS Ralph and Harriett Kimball (Taylor) G.; B.S., Northwestern U., 1947; postgrad. Fred Archer Sch. Photography, 1953; m. Amy Louise Thomas, Oct. 23, 1948; children—Stephen Thomas, Matthew Harris. Copy boy San Francisco Chronicle, 1946; reporter Monroe (Mich.) Evening News, 1947-48, city editor, 1948-49, acting mng. editor, 1949-50, editorial page editor, 1948-50, circulation mgr., 1953-58, asso. editor, 1958-72, editor, 1972-80, pub., 1980—, gen. mgr., 1977—; pres. Monroe Pub. Co., 1977—. Mem. Amateur Radio Emergency Corps, 1960—. Bd. dirs. United Fund, 1956-62, YMCA, 1956-59, Jr. Achievement, 1960-64. Served with USNR, 1943-46, 50-51. Mem. Am. Newspaper Pubs. Assn., Internat. Press Inst., Inter Am. Press Assn., Nat. Conf. Editorial Writers, Central States Circulation Mgrs. Assn. (dir. 1957-59), Mich. Press Assn. (pres. 1973), Inland Daily Press Assn. (dir. 1973-76), Mich. Asso. Press Assn. (dir. 1975—, pres. 1980), Univ. Press Club Mich., Monroe

County Radio Communications Assn. (pres. 1966-67). Home: 1929 W Hurd Rd Monroe MI 48161 Office: 20 W 1st St Monroe MI 48161

GRAY, HANNA HOLBORN, univ. pres.; b. Heidelberg, Germany, Oct. 25, 1930; d. Hajo and Annemarie (Bettmann) Holborn; B.A., Bryn Mawr Coll., 1950; Fulbright scholar Oxford U., 1950-52; Ph.D., Harvard U., 1957; hon. degrees: M.A., Yale U., 1971; L.H.D., Grinnell Coll., Lawrence U., Denison U., 1974, Wheaton Coll., 1976, Marlboro Coll., 1979, Rikkyo U., 1979, Roosevelt U., 1980, Knox Coll., 1980, Thomas Jefferson U., 1981; Litt.D., Oxford U., 1979, St. Lawrence U., 1974, Coe Coll., 1981; H.H.D., St. Mary's Coll., 1974; LL.D., Union Coll., 1975, Regis Coll., 1976, Dartmouth Coll., 1978, Trinity Coll., 1978, U. Bridgeport, 1978, Yale U., 1978, Dickinson Coll., 1979, Wittenberg U., 1979, Brown U., 1979, U. Rochester, 1980, U. Notre Dame, 1980, U. So. Calif., 1980; m. Charles Montgomery Gray, June 19, 1954. Instr., Bryn Mawr (Pa.) Coll., 1953-54; teaching fellow Harvard U., 1955-57, instr., 1957-59, asst. prof., 1959-60, vis. lectr., 1963-64; asst. prof. U. Chgo., 1961-64, asso. prof., 1964-72; dean, prof. Northwestern U., Evanston, Ill., 1972-74; provost, prof., history Yale U., 1974-78, acting pres., 1977-78; pres., prof. history U. Chgo., 1978—; dir. Cummins Engine Co., Morgan Guaranty Trust Co., J.P. Morgan & Co. Fellow Center for Advanced Study in Behavioral Scis., 1966-67, vis. scholar, 1970-71; hon. fellow St. Anne's Coll., Oxford U. Mem. Pulitzer Prize Bd.; bd. dirs. Council Fin. Aid to Edn., Andrew W. Mellon Found.; trustee Bryn Mawr Coll., Mayo Found., Center for Advanced Study in Behavioral Scis., Brookings Instn., Mus. Sci. and Industry. U. Chgo. Newberry Library fellow, 1960-61; Phi Beta Kappa vis. scholar, 1971-72. Fellow Am. Acad. Arts and Scis.; mem. Am. Hist. Assn., Renaissance Soc. Am., Chgo. Council Fgn. Relations (dir.), Am. Philos. Soc., Phi Beta Kappa (senate). Editor (with Charles Gray) Jour. Modern History, 1965-70; contbr. articles to profl. jours. Office: U Chgo 5801 Ellis Avenue Chicago IL 60637

GRAY, JOHN DOUGLAS, meat packing co. exec.; b. Evanston, Ill., Feb. 15, 1945; s. John D. and Ruth Gray; student Miami U., Oxford, Ohio, 1962-68, Grad. Sch., U. Chgo., 1966-68. With MAS div. Price, Waterhouse & Co., Chgo., 1969-71; various fin. and adminstrv. positions Esmark, Inc., Swift & Co., Chgo., 1971-78, exec. v.p. fresh meats div. Swift & Co., Chgo., 1979-80, chief fin. and adminstrv. officer, 1980—; v.p. BRK Electronics div. Pittway Corp., Aurora, Ill., 1978-79; dir. Swift Ind. Corp. Asso. trustee Rush-Presbyn.-St. Luke's Hosp.; bd. dirs., mem. exec. com. Community Renewal Soc., 1972-75. Served with USAR, 1968-74. Clubs: Chicago, Racquet Economic (Chgo.); Glen View. Office: 115 W Jackson Blvd Chicago IL 60604

GRAY, MAI EVELYN HUTSON, educator; b. Jackson, Tenn., Feb. 19; d. John Henry and Peola (Copeland) Hutson; B.S. magna cum laude, Lane Coll., 1944; M.R.E., Gammon Theol. Sem., 1946; M.A., U. Mo., Kansas City, 1969; D.H.L., Philander Smith Coll., 1981; m. C. Jarrett Gray, June 5, 1946; children—C. Jarrett, Frances L., Jon Reginald. Caseworker, Dept. Welfare Little Rock, 1952; tchr. 1st grade, public schs. Kansas City, Mo., 1953-57, St. Louis, 1957-61; tchr. 1st grade Kansas City Sch. Dist., 1961-70, cons., 1970-76; on leave as pres. Womens div. Bd. Global Ministries, United Meth. Ch., N.Y.C., 1976-80, also nat. pres. United Meth. Women. trustee St. Paul Sch. Theology. Mem. AAUW, Phi Delta Kappa, Beta Kappa Chi.

GRAY, MOSES WILLIAM, automobile mfg. co. exec.; b. Goochland County, Va., Apr. 12, 1937; s. Moses and Ida B. (Young) G.; B.S., Ind. U., 1961; postgrad. U. Mich., 1971-72, Gen. Motors Inst., 1970-78; m. Ann Marie Powell, Nov. 22, 1962; adopted children—Tamara Ann, William Bernard. Mem. N.Y. Jets Football team, 1961-62; mfg. insp. Detroit Diesel Allison, 1962-63, tool and die apprentice, 1963-68, tool and die journeyman, 1968, production foreman, 1968-69, foreman tool room, 1969-73, gen. foreman tool room, 1973-76, asst. supt. and engring. supr. mech. and elec. engring. staff, 1976-79, dir. community relations, 1979—; adoption cons. Black Child Devel. Inst., 1974-77. Participant Marion County (Ind.) Dept. Public Welfare Foster Parents Program, 1972-75; mem. Mayor's Black History Com., Indpls., 1978-79; coach Little League Football, 1968-73, Thatcher Community Center, 1968-71; coach Indpls. Caps Football team, 1974; mem. Indpls. United Way Allocation Com., 1979—; Jr. Achievement adv., 1970-73; pres. Black Adoption Com. Marion County, 1973—; adv. council Indpls. Skill Center, 1973-75; Children's Bur. Indpls., v.p., 1973—; bd. dirs. Crossroads of Am. council Boy Scouts Am., 1969—, chmn. urban affairs com., 1976-77; active Community Service Council, 1980, United Way, 1981, Central Ind. Health Systems Agy., 1981. Recipient GM award for Excellence in Community Service, 1972, 78. Mem. Child Welfare League Am. (dir. 1978—), Ind. Assn. Adoptions and Child Care Services (dir. 1973—), N. Am. Council Adoptable Children (dir. 1974—), Indpls. C. of C. (community affairs com. 1979—), Assn. for Rights of Children (founder Black adoption com. 1974). Home: 1631 Kessler Blvd West Dr Indianapolis IN 46208 Office: PO Box 894 Indianapolis IN 46206

GRAY, RICHARD GORDON, corp. exec.; b. Emmett, Idaho, Jan. 11, 1941; s. David Draper and Doris Fern (Parrish) G.; B.S., U. Idaho, 1964; M.B.A., U. Ariz., 1967; m. Catherine Lee Powell, Oct. 10, 1964. Auditor, mgmt. cons. Peat Marwick Mitchell & Co., N.Y.C., 1967-70; group controller Textron, Inc., Providence, 1971-74; asst. to pres. First Fed. Savs. and Loan, Phoenix, 1974-76; pres. SAF Systems and Forms, Chgo., 1976—, also dir. Served as capt. U.S. Army, 1964-66; Vietnam. Mem. Chgo. Assn. Commerce and Industry, Young Pres.'s Orgn., Am. Inst. C.P.A.'s, Ill. C.P.A. Soc., Inst. Fin. Edn. Republican. Club: Plaza. Home: 50 E Bellevue Pl Chicago IL 60611 Office: 111 E Wacker Dr Chicago IL 60601

GRAY, ROBERT GEORGE, ins. investigator; b. Anderson, Ind., Sept. 7, 1926; s. Robert V. and Edna V. (Howell) G.; B.S., Ball State U., 1951; postgrad. U. Louisville, 1961-62; m. Dorothy A. Study, Dec. 23, 1950; children—Robert Thomas (dec.), Marcus W., Sharon Gray Brooks, Tracy L. Claims supr. Farm Bur. Ins. Co., to 1967; founder, owner Lincoln Trails Adjusting Co., 1967—. Served with USN, 1943-46. Mem. Save the Valley. Democrat. Author: (novel) The Elephant, 1968. Home: Route 1 Hanover IN 47243 Office: 416 Main St Madins IN 47250

GRAY, SANFORD DURHAM, educator; b. Kansas City, Mo., Mar. 3, 1929; s. William Clinton and Geneva (Durham) G.; B.A., U. Mo., 1951, M.A., 1954; m. Marie Isabel Correll, June 9, 1959 (div.); children—Sharon Marie, Martin Sanford, Clinton Bruce; m. 2d, Joan Frances McConville, June 27, 1970 (div.); children—Angela Nordica, Christopher Hansford; m. 3d, Marybeth Feehan, Mar. 3, 1979; 1 son, Benjamin Oscar. Rec. engr. Artist Rec. Studios, Kansas City, Mo., 1954; grad. asst. U. Mo., 1956-58; instr. UCLA, 1958-59; rec. engr. Calvin Prodns., Inc., 1960; asst. prof. communication, dir. film prodn. U. S.D., Vermillion, 1960-80, 81—; vis. asst. prof. film, acting head film area U. Tex., Austin, 1980-81; owner Orpheus Records, Vermillion, 1957—. Recipient Calvin Notable film award, 1965; CINE Golden Eagle award, 1968; honors certificate Am. Film Festival, 1969. Mem. Internat. Platform Assn., Speech Communication Assn., Univ. Film Assn. (dir.), Soc. Motion Picture and TV Engrs., AAUP, Sigma Phi Epsilon. Presbyn. Mason (Shriner). Author mystery novels. Designer electronic devices. Home: 323 N Pine St Vermillion SD 57069

GRAY, THEODORE MILTON, state senator; b. Springfield, Ohio, Sept. 3, 1927; s. Theodore Milton and Dorothy (Whittington) G.; student Wabash Coll., 1945; B.A., Ohio State U., 1950; m. W. Marilyn Kautz, 1951; children—Scarlett Ann Lewis, Thackery Scott, Timothy, Milton, Nathan. Pres., Howe-Simpson Co., 1961—; mem. Ohio Senate. Exec. sec. Ohio League Young Republicans, 1954-55; co-chmn. Bi-Partisan Com. Reapportionment, 1967; coordinator Ohio United Citizens for Nixon, 1968; del. Rep. Nat. Conv., 1968, 72. Served with USN, 1945-46. Recipient Jaycees Disting. Service award, 1960; Ohio Gov.'s award, 1969; Legis. Leadership citation Nat. Conf. State Legislators, 1971. Mem. Am. Legion. Presbyterian. Office: State Senate Columbus OH 43216*

GRAYBAR, CRAIG LEWIS, contracting co. exec.; b. Milw., Jan. 16, 1957; s. Richard Jerome and Esther Frances Graybar; student Milw. Area Tech. Coll., 1974-75, U. Calif., Santa Barbara, 1976-78, Ventura Community Coll., 1976-79, U. Wis., Milw., 1979—. Founder, pres. Creative Contracting, Milw., 1979—. Served with Seabees, USN, 1975-79; Vietnam. Mem. U.S. Naval Inst., Am. Def. Preparedness Assn., Naval Enlisted Reservist Assn., Vietnam Vets. Am. Patentee power assisted crane boom jib. Home: 4109 S Kirkwood Ave Saint Francis WI 53207

GRAYE, GERARD EDWARD, mech. engr.; b. Detroit, Oct. 13, 1952; s. Chester Anthony and Stephanie Julia (Krzywada) Gay; B. Mech. Engring., Gen. Motors Inst., 1975; postgrad. U. Detroit, 1979—; m. Mary Christine Gerstenberg, Nov. 16, 1974. Supr. mfg. Gen. Motors Corp., Detroit, 1975-77, gen. supr. mfg., 1977-79, coordinator budget devel. and computer systems, 1979, salary employee in tng.-labor relations, 1979-80, gen. supr. mfg., 1980—. Mem. ASME. Republican. Roman Catholic. Office: 1840 Holbrook St Detroit MI 48212

GRAYSON, RICHARD CARL, r.r. exec.; b. Cuba, Mo., Dec. 16, 1920; s. William James and Lenna (James) G.; student Columbia, 1955; m. Evelyn Honey, Sept. 24, 1939; children—Susanne, Shari, Richard Carl. With St. Louis-San Francisco Ry. Co., 1941—, v.p. operations, Springfield, Mo., 1964-68, pres., 1969-73, chmn. bd., 1973-80; pres., chief exec. officer Burlington No. R.R.; pres., dir. Clarkland, Inc., Clarkland Royalty, Inc., 906 Olive Corp.; dir. Burlington No. Inc., N.Mex. & Ariz. Land Co., Alton Packaging Corp., Centerre Bank, St. Louis, Centerre Bancorp., Laclede Gas Co., St. Louis. Trustee Drury Coll., Springfield, Mo.; bd. dirs. Barnes Hosp., St. Louis. Mem. Nat. Freight Traffic Assn., Assn. Am. Railroads (dir.), Western R.R. Assn. (dir.), Assn. Southeastern Railroads (dir.), Transp. Assn. Am. (dir.). Clubs: Noonday, Bogey, St. Louis, Old Warson Country, Minn. Office: 176 E 5th St Saint Paul MN 55101

GRAY-TOFT, PAMELA ANN, med. psychologist; b. Melbourne, Australia, May 31, 1944; came to U.S., 1976; d. Kevin Alan and Reta Elizabeth Gray; B.A., U. Sydney (Australia), 1963, Dip.Ed., 1964; M.A., Macquarie U., Australia, 1977; Ph.D., Purdue U., 1979; m. Graham Toft, Dec. 18, 1964; children—Andrew, Kerrelly, Caitlin. Tchr., New South Wales Dept. Edn., 1965-66, examiner higher sch. certificate exam., 1968-70; tchr. New South Wales Dept. Tech. Edn., 1969-72; research asst. New South Wales div. Red Cross Soc., Australian Govt. Commn. Enquiry into Poverty, 1974-75; grad. teaching asst. counseling and personnel services Purdue U., West Lafayette, Ind., 1977-78, mem. core staff Psychol. Services Center, 1978-79, Meth. Hosp. fellow health services research, 1978-79; clin. research asso. dept. med. research Meth. Hosp., Indpls., 1979-81; mem. pres.'s staff Meth. Hosp., Indpls., 1981—. Recipient award New South Wales Geography Tchrs. Assn., 1964. Mem. Am. Personnel and Guidance Assn., Assn. Specialist in Group Work, Assn. Counselor Edn. and Supervision. Home: 304 Hollowood Dr West Lafayette IN 47906 Office: 1604 N Capitol Ave Indianapolis IN 46206

GRAZIANO, CHARLES DOMINIC, pharmacist; b. Cariati, Italy, June 28, 1920; s. Frank Dominic and Marianna (Bambace) G.; student Dowling Jr. Coll., 1939, 40; B.S. in Pharmacy, Drake U., 1943; m. Corrine Rose Comito, Feb. 5, 1950; children—Craig Frank, Charles Dominic II, Marianne, Kimberly Rose, Mark, Suzanne. Pharamacist Kings Pharmacy, Des Moines, 1946-47; partner Bauder Pharmacy, Des Moines, 1948-61, owner, 1962—. Mem. Des Moines Art Center. Served with AUS, 1943-45; ETO. Decorated Bronze Star. Mem. Des Moines C. of C., Nat. Assn. Retail Druggists, Iowa, Polk County pharm. assns., St. Vincent de Paul Soc., Am. Pharm. Assn., Phi Delta Chi. Roman Catholic. Office: 3802 Ingersoll Ave Des Moines IA 50312

GRAZIANO, SALVATORE JOSEPH, elec. equipment mfg. co. exec.; b. Chgo., Mar. 25, 1944; s. Sam Joseph and Angela Marie (Bruno) G.; student St. Procopius Coll., 1961-63; B.S., U. Ill., 1965; m. Marijo Halm, July 4, 1964; children—Peter Andrew, Robert Sean, Elizabeth Anne, Megan Marie. Engr. statis. quality control Western Electric Corp., 1964-67; systems analyst Motorola, Inc., 1967-69; sr. design engr. Victor Comptometer Co., Chgo., 1969-71, project mgr., 1971-75; applications engr. Intel Corp., Oak Brook, Ill., 1975-77; regional sales mgr. Monolithic Memories, Inc., Naperville, Ill., 1977-78, area sales mgr., 1978—. Pres., Cress Creek Homeowners Assn., 1980-81. Home: 981 W Bauer Rd Naperville IL 60540

GREASOR, RUSSELL EARL, telephone co. exec.; b. Logansport, Ind., May 25, 1926; s. Virgil Elmer and Margaret Ruth (Shaw) G.; student Valparaiso (Ind.) U., 1962; m. Jeanette Elizabeth Rupenthal, Jan. 20, 1951; children—Pamela Jean, Patricia Ann, Charles Russell, Roger Allen. With Gen. Telephone Co., 1947—, plant service mgr., Elkhart, Ind., 1972, customer relations mgr., Terre Haute, Ind., 1972-80, service coordinator budgets/results, 1980—. Chmn. bd. United Way Wabash Valley, 1980; pres. Jr. Achievement Wabash Valley, 1980; v.p. Wabash Valley chpt. Honor Am., 1979; Vigo County chmn. Wabash Valley council Boy Scouts Am., 1979-80; chief staff Ind. Guard Res., 1977-79; zip area coordinator U.S. Mil. Acad., 1976—. Served with AUS, 1944-46; mem. Ind. N.G., 1955-64. Decorated Bronze Star, Combat Inf. badge, Ind. N.G. Commendation medal with oak leaf cluster; recipient award merit Wabash Valley Central Labor Council, 1979. Mem. Ind. Telephone Pioneer Assn. (club pres.), Telephone Pioneers Am., Ind. Telephone Assn., Home Builders Assn. Wabash Valley, Terre Haute C. of C. Democrat. Clubs: Wabash Valley Press, Rotary (past pres. Terre Haute). Home: 922 Fulton Ave Apt 3 Fort Wayne IN 46802

GREDESKY, JOSEPH NOLAN, publisher; b. Washington, Pa., Nov. 17, 1948; s. Joseph Nolan and Leona Jane (Dixon) G.; student Kent State U., 1967-70; m. Mary Ann Siers, Nov. 23, 1974. Advt. account exec., reporter Record Pub. Co., Ravenna, Ohio, 1970-72; pub. Tribune-Gazette, Brimfield, Ohio, 1972-81, also dir.; gen. partner Ben Franklin's Printers and Pubs. Co. Active Portage County Republican Party, 1969-73; del. Ohio State Rep. Conv., 1970; sec. Brimfield Twp. Zoning Bd. of Appeals, 1974, Brimfield Zoning Commn., 1974; mem. Jetport Study Commn. for Portage County, 1975. Served with Ohio N.G., 1971-77. Recipient Osmond C. Hooper award, 1976, 78, 80; Pub. Service award Brimfield Jaycees, 1974. Mem. Ohio Newspaper Assn., Buckeye Press Assn., Brimfield C. of C. (charter mem., pres. 1978-79). Methodist. Club: Brimfield Kiwanis (dir. 1976-77). Home: 4190 Hattick Rd Rootstown OH 44272 Office: 3982 State Route 43 Brimfield OH 44240

GREELEY, SAMUEL SEWALL, lawyer; b. Winnetka, Ill., Sept. 14, 1914; s. Samuel Arnold and Dorothy (Coffin) G.; A.B., Harvard U., 1936, LL.B., 1939; m. Irene E. Mares, Oct. 28, 1945; children—Sara S., Samuel Sewall. Admitted to Ill. bar, 1939; practice in Chgo., 1939-42, 46-51; gen. counsel Masonite Corp., Chgo., 1951-69, sec., 1958-69, treas., 1961-64, fin. v.p. 1964-66, exec. v.p., 1966-69, pres., 1969-76, chief exec. officer, 1971-77, chmn., 1976—, also dir.; chmn. Masonite Can., Ltd.; dir. Masonite Africa, Signode Corp., Harris Bankcorp., Tyler Corp. Served to lt. comdr. USNR, 1942-46. Mem. Am., Ill., Chgo. bar assns., Legal Club. Clubs: Tower, Metropolitan, Economic (Chgo.); Indian Hill (Winnetka). Home: 800 Tower Rd Winnetka IL 60093 Office: 29 N Wacker Dr Chicago IL 60606

GREEN, CHARLES ADAM, psychologist, educator; b. Detroit, Oct. 17, 1927; s. Fred and Charlena (Cragwell) G.; student Highland Park Coll., 1948-50; B.A., U. Mich., 1952; M.Ed., Wayne State U., 1957; Ph.D., Wayne State U., 1974; m. Mildred Wilson, Jan. 4, 1954; children—Iris Denise, Robin Charles. Tchr. spl. edn., Detroit, 1953-58; dir. spl. edn. Northville (Mich.) State Hosp., 1958-62; psychologist Detroit Bd. Edn., 1962-68, research asso., 1968—; instr. Wayne County Community Coll., 1969—. Mem. exec. bd. Boy Scouts Am., 1973-77, United Community Services, 1977—. Served with USAAF, 1945-46. Recipient community service cert. New Detroit Inc., 1972; award Boy Scouts Am., 1976; lic. psychologist, Mich. Fellow Am. Assn. Mental Deficiency; mem. AAAS, Soc. Lic. Psychologists, Mich. Psychol. Assn., Mich. Acad. Sci., Lit. and Arts, Mich. Assn. Black Psychologists (chmn. 1978-79), Phi Delta Kappa, Alpha Phi Alpha. Home: 2900 E Jefferson St Apt 301D Detroit MI 48207 Office: Detroit Bd Edn 10100 Grand River St Detroit MI 48204

GREEN, CHRISTOPHER JOHN, interior designer; b. Denver, May 4, 1954; s. John Elliot and Mildred Witt G.; B.Environ. Design, U. Colo., 1976; postgrad. Ill Inst. Tech. Coll. Architecture, 1979—. Designer graphics and interiors Design Collective, Inc., Columbus, Ohio, 1976-78; head designer State of Ohio Bur. Workers Compensation facilities planning, Columbus, 1978-79; interior designer Skidmore Owings & Merrill, Chgo., 1979-80; teaching asst. Ill. Inst. Tech., Chgo., 1980—. Mem. ASHRAE Engrs. (student mem.), Columbus Soc. Communication Arts (student membership coordinator).

GREEN, DAVID THOMAS, evangelist; b. N.Y.C., July 28, 1925; s. David and Sarah Louise (Oldham) G.; D.D., God's Bible Sch. and Missionary Tng. Home, Cin., 1949. Evangelist, 1934—; pastoral counselor, Bible instr.; active various evangelistic assns.; locksmith, safe and alarm technician, security cons., 1980—. Served with AUS, 1946-47. Mem. Heavenly Host Missionary Baptist Assn., Noah's Ark Missionary Bapt. Assn., Nat. Locksmith Assn. Address: 1176 N Milwaukke Ave Chicago IL 60622

GREEN, DENNIS RICHARD, advt. agy. exec.; b. Detroit, Oct. 30, 1943; s. Max Edward and Mae (Jaslove) G.; B.A., Wayne State U., 1965; children—Todd, Eric. Advt. dir. Marina News, Inc., St. Clair Shores, Mich., 1969-71, Mich. Out of Doors, Lansing, 1971-73; pres., founder RPM Advt. Inc., Southfield, Mich., 1973-80; sr. v.p. account devel. Simons Michelson Zieve Inc., Troy, Mich., 1980-81; owner Dennis R. Green/Adman Co., Southfield, Mich., 1981—; advt. tchr. Barbizon Sch., 1979, Fashion Inst. Am., 1980. Mem. Mich. Advt. Agy. Council (Creative Achievement awards 1973-79), Adcraft Club Detroit, Nat. Acad. TV Arts and Scis. (programming chmn. Detroit chpt. 1980—), Mich. Advt. Industry Alliance, Tau Epsilon Phi. Club: B'nai B'rith (v.p. programming L'Chayim Lodge 1975-77). Home: 28477 Franklin Rd Apt 346 Southfield MI 48034 Office: 16910 W 10 Mile Rd Suite 2 Southfield MI 48075

GREEN, DONALD JOSEPH, analyst/programmer; b. O'Neill, Nebr., Jan. 18, 1953; s. Lyle M. and Jennie M. G.; B.S. in Computer Sci. (Air Force ROTC scholar), U. Nebr., Lincoln, 1975; m. Nancy E. Larson, June 14, 1975; 1 son, Thomas Allan. Computer cons. U. Nebr. Computer Center, 1973-75, programmer Agnet-U. Nebr., Lincoln, 1975; programmer Fed. Land Bank Computer Center, Omaha, 1976-78, Sperry Vickers, Omaha, 1978—. Mem. Am. Prodn. Inventory Control Soc. (cert. in prodn. and inventory mgmt.; treas., sec. Omaha chpt.), Assn. Systems Mgmt., U. Nebr. Alumni Assn., Upsilon Pi Epsilon. Republican. Roman Catholic. Home: 3204 S 128th Ave Omaha NE 68144 Office: 6600 N 72d St Omaha NE 68122

GREEN, DONALD THOMAS, engring. cons.; b. Moose Jaw, Sask., Can., Sept. 20, 1920; came to U.S., 1954, naturalized, 1959; s. Arthur Wellington and Emma Loretta (Mitchell) G.; B.Sc. in Engring. Physics, U. Sask., Saskatoon, 1945; m. Charlotte Jean Kathleen McTaggart, May 14, 1944; children—Janice Emily, Donald Timothy. Research asst. Nat. Research Council of Can., Ottawa, Ont., 1945-46; mgr. prodn. and engring. Atomic Energy of Can., Ltd., Ottawa, 1945-53; mgr. indsl. x-ray Picker X-Ray Corp., Cleve., 1954-69; pres. Imagex, Inc., Mentor, Ohio, 1970-78; v.p. advanced devel. Inspection Tech., Inc., Akron, Ohio, 1978-80; pres. DTG, Inc., Mentor-on-the-Lake, Ohio, 1980—; cons. radiol. health State of Ohio, 1964-65, isotope safety regulations AEC, 1966-67. Mem. Am. Soc. Nondestructive Testing, Soc. Photo-optical Instrumentation Engrs. Club: Mentor Harbor Yachting. Contbr. articles to profl. jours.; patentee in field; designer radiotherapy equipment, x-ray inspection systems. Home: 8291 Harbor Dr Mentor OH 44060 Office: 6101 Andrews Rd Menton-on-the-Lake OH 44060

GREEN, DUANE MORGAN, JR., bridge engr.; b. Peoria, Ill., July 2, 1951; s. Duane Morgan and Beverly Jean (Gummerson) G.; B.S., U. Ill., 1973; M.S., U. Mo., 1977; m. Jane Branby. Bridge engr. damage inspections, emergency repairs Howard, Needles, Tammen & Bergendoff, Detroit, Seattle, Portland, Oreg., Burlington, Iowa and Kansas City, Mo., 1973—, pres. employee fed. credit union, 1978-79, resident engr. reconstrn. Hastings R.R. Bridge L-268. Active Eagle Scouts, Boy Scouts Am. Registered profl. engr., Mo., Minn. Clubs: Tribe of Mic-O-Say, Optimists, Order of Arrow. Home: 1006 E 99 Kansas City MO 64131 Office: 1805 Grand Ave Kansas City MO 64108

GREEN, FARNO LOUIS, automotive co. exec.; b. Memphis, Nov. 29, 1919; s. Everett F. and Eva (Smith) G.; B.A., Miss. Coll., 1941; M.S., La. State U., 1949; m. Ruth Cole, Dec. 21, 1944; children—Franklin F., Walter L. Asso. prof., head dept. physics Wayland Coll., Plainview, Tex., 1948-49; head dept. physics Howard Coll. (now Samford U.), Birmingham, Ala., 1949-51; physicist Oak Ridge (Tenn.) Nat. Lab., 1951-55; sr. research physicist, group leader GM Research Labs., GM Tech. Center, Gen. Motors Corp., Warren, Mich., 1956-63, exec. engr. GM Mfg. Devel., 1966-79, mgr. reliability methods devel., 1979—; v.p., gen. mgr. Viso Corp. subs. Ex-Cello Corp., Detroit, 1963-66; cons. materials conservation Office of Tech. Assessment, U.S. Congress, Washington, 1977—. Served with U.S. Army, 1940-42, with USAAC, 1942-45, to maj. with Ala. Air N.G., 1950-51. Decorated 2 presdl. unit citations; Croix de Guerre avec palm; co-recipient Silver medal Am. Roentgen Ray Soc., 1962; registered profl. engr., Calif.; cert. mfg. engr. Mem. Soc. Mfg. Engrs.,

Am. Soc. Nondestructive Testing, Engring. Soc. Detroit, Am. Nuclear Soc., Am. Def. Preparedness Assn., Am. Soc. Quality Control. Presbyterian. Patentee in field (4); contbr. over 35 papers to profl. jours. Home: 5934 Blandford Rd Bloomfield Hills MI 48013 Office: GM Mfg Development GM Tech Center Warren MI 48090

GREEN, FRANK EARL, civil engr.; b. Joplin, Mo., Nov. 24, 1931; s. Lloyd Cuthberson and Gladys Alberta (Kennedy) G.; B.S. in Math., Southwest Mo. State U., 1953; B.S. in Civil Engring., Kans. State U., 1958; m. Joan Imogene Wheeler, July 25, 1953; children—Kevin Joe, Keely Sue. With Mo. State Hwy. Dept., 1958—, hwy. designer, 1959-65, dist. hwy. design engr., 1965—. Trustee Grandview (Mo.) United Methodist Ch. Served with U.S. Army, 1953-55. Registered profl. engr., Mo.; registered land surveyor, Mo. Mem. Nat., Mo. (dir. Western chpt.) socs. profl. engrs., ASCE (dir. Kansas City sect.), Profl. Engrs. in Govt. (sec.-treas. Western chpt.). Republican. Home: 5608 E 100th Terr Kansas City MO 64137 Office: 5117 E 31st St Kansas City MO 64128

GREEN, JAMES MERSHON, wholesale plumbing and heating co. exec.; b. Des Moines, June 26, 1922; s. Samuel Chase and Margaret (Mershon) G.; B.S. in Engring., Iowa State U., 1947; m. Susan Houston; children—Frances, Jeffrey, Martha. Instr. gen. engring. Iowa State U., 1946; pres., gen. mgr. Iowa Supply Co., Des Moines, 1947—; chmn. Iowa Plumbing and Heating Credit Exchange, 1973. Pres. Planned Parenthood Iowa, 1962-63, Iowa Children's and Family Service, 1968; chmn. Des Moines Met. Transit Authority, 1976-78. Served with C.E., AUS, 1943-46. Decorated Army Commendation medal. Mem. ASHRAE (pres. Iowa chpt. 1966-67), N. Am. Heating and Air-Conditioning Wholesalers Assn. (pres. 1979), Central Iowa Sailing Assn. (commodore 1974). Clubs: Spectator (past pres.), Reciprocity (past pres.), Des Moines Rotary (past pres.), Pioneer (past pres.) (Des Moines). Home: 411 Tonawanda Dr Des Moines IA 50312 Office: 107 SW 2d St Des Moines IA 50305

GREEN, JAY PATRICK, JR., graphics arts exec.; b. Searcy, Ark., Feb. 14, 1949; s. Jay Patrick and Mary Virginia (Bates) G.; student Brandywine Coll., 1967, 68, 69, 79, U. Del., 1969; student Grand Valley State Coll., 1973; student W. Shore Community Coll., 1974; m. Judith Eileen Rineer, Jan. 15, 1968; children—Brent Patrick, Patrick Christopher, Regina Marie, Sarah Lynn. Graphics plant mgr. Religious Book Discount House, Inc., Grand Rapids, Mich., 1965-69; pres. Plywood Market Inc., Byron Center, Mich., 1969-72; pres., gen. mgr. LKS Modular Components, Inc., Lowell, Mich., 1970-72; owner, gen. mgr. LKS Constrn., Grand Rapids, 1969-74; gen. mgr. New Religious Book Discount House, Wilmington, Del., 1975-77; prodn. mgr. Asso. Pubs. & Authors, Inc., Lafayette, Ind., 1978-79; gen. mgr., v.p. Book Factory, Inc., Lafayette, Ind., 1980—; dir. Lit. Discovery, Inc., Wilmington, 1976-78. Served with USN, 1968-69. Mem. Nat. C. of C., Am. Entrepreneurs Assn., Internat. Entrepreneurs Assn. Republican. Baptist. Office: 408 North St Lafayette IN 47901

GREEN, JERRY HOWARD, banker; b. Kansas City, Mo., June 10, 1930; s. Howard Jay and Selma (Stein) G.; B.A., Yale U., 1952; m. Betsy Bozarth, July 18, 1981. Pres., Union Chevrolet, 1955-69, Union Securities, Inc., Kansas City, Mo., 1969—, Mo. Banc-Mgmt., Inc., Kansas City; chmn. Stadium Bank, Kansas City, 1976—, Budget Rent-A-Car of Mo., Inc., 1961—, Budget Rent-A-Car of Memphis, Inc.; chmn., dir. Security Bank & Trust Co., Branson, Mo., 1979—; pres. Douglas County Bancshares, Kansas City, Taney County Bancorp., Kansas City, 1981—; chmn., dir. Citizens Bank, Ava, Mo., 1980—; dir. Aiken Engring., Inc., Kansas City, Stadium Bank, Kansas City. Bd. dirs. Boys' Clubs Kansas City; chmn. Yale Class of 1952 Reunion Gift. Served to 1st lt. USAF, 1952-55. Mem. Am. Bankers Assn. Republican. Clubs: Woodside Racquet, Kansas City, Oakwood Country. Home: 10743 Glenwood Overland Park KS 66211 Office: 8959 East New Hwy 40 Kansas City MO 64129

GREEN, JOHN LAFAYETTE, JR., univ. pres.; b. Overland Park, Kans., Apr. 3, 1929; s. John Lafayette and Edith (Howell) G.; B.A., Miss. State U., 1955; M.S., Wayne State U., 1970; Ph.D., Rensselaer Poly. Inst., 1973; m. Harriet Hardin Hill, Nov. 9, 1968; 1 son, John Lafayette, III. Adminstr., Calif. System Higher Edn., 1955-62; asst. dir. Coordinating Council of Higher Edn. Va., 1962-65; v.p. U. Ga., Athens, 1965-72; v.p. Rensselaer Poly. Inst., 1972-76; exec. v.p. U. Miami (Fla.), 1976-80; sr. v.p. U. Houston System, 1980; pres. Washburn U., Topeka, 1981—; dir. 1st Nat. Bank of Athens (Ga.), 1965-71, Marine Midland Bank-Eastern, 1972-76. Bd. dirs. Boys Club, Salvation Army, United Way, ARC; mem. exec. com. Boy Scouts Am.; mem. citizens adv. com. Topeka State Hosp. Served with U.S. Army, 1951-53. Mem. Acad. Mgmt., Soc. Planners, Nat. Assn. Coll. and Univ. Adminstrs., Topeka C. of C. (dir.), Phi Delta Kappa, Beta Alpha, Pi Kappa Alpha. Presbyterian. Author: Strategic Planning and Budgeting for Higher Education, 1979. Office: Morgan Hall Washburn U Topeka KS 66621

GREEN, MEYER H., dentist; b. Kolno, Poland, Mar. 22, 1917; brought to U.S., 1928, naturalized, 1929; s. Louis A. and Bessie (Fellander) G.; student Wayne U., 1935-40; D.D.S., U. Detroit, 1943; m. Hilda Rosenberg, Sept. 30, 1944; children—Marc Stephen (dec.), Janice Beth. Gen. practice dentistry, Detroit, 1946-51, 51—; sr. asso. attending staff, mem. med. staff teaching dental interns Sinai Hosp. Detroit, 1962—; lectr., writer oral medicine. Bd. dirs., past v.p. Young Israel of Oak Woods (Mich.). Served to capt. AUS, 1943-46. Diplomate Am. Bd. Oral Medicine, Am. Bd. Clin. Hypnosis in Dentistry. Fellow Acad. Gen. Dentistry, Royal Soc. Health, Am. Acad. Oral Medicine (hon. and acad. fellow; nat. rec. sec., trustee 1958—, nat. pres. 1978—, gen. chmn. ann. meeting 1977; cert. of merit); mem. Mich. Soc. Oral Medicine (past pres. Mich. sect.), Mich. Soc. Psychosomatic Dentistry (past pres.), Am. Med. Writers Assn., Am. Soc. Preventive Dentistry, Internat. Acad. Orthodontics, Detroit Clinic Club, Bunting Periodontal Study Club. Club: Century Univ. of Detroit. Home: 2014 Waldon's Ct West Bloomfield MI 48033 Office: 14110 Gratiot Ave Detroit MI 48205

GREEN, RICE ANDREW, telephone co. exec.; b. Hot Springs, Ark., July 15, 1928; s. Horace Jewel and Winona (Suddeth) G.; B.S. in Bus. Adminstrn., U. Ark., 1950; m. Irene Lowe Abbay, Mar. 27, 1951; children—Linda Abbay, Robert Andrew, Russell Alan. Salesman, Union Carbide Consumer Products, Little Rock, 1953-54, Oklahoma City, 1957-60, St. Louis, 1960-62, div. mgr., Dallas, 1962-69; v.p. devel. Breckenridge Hotels Corp., St. Louis, 1969-76; sec.-dir. Rodder Rd Constrn. Co., Fenton, Mo., 1970-76; pres. G & M Constrn., Inc., St. Louis, 1976; partner Green & McGuire Investment Co., St. Louis County, 1976—; owner Green Enterprises, Webster Groves, Mo., 1977; account exec., industry cons. lodging industry Southwestern Bell Telephone Co., St. Louis, 1977—. Chmn., Jefferson Twp., Webster Groves, 1962, Gravois Twp., 1970; mem. planning com. "Y" Webster Teen Center, 1972-73, mem. Webster Groves Bd. Police Commrs., 1974-80; mem. Webster Groves Bd. Public Safety, 1981—. Served with USAF, 1954-56. Mem. Am. Hotel and Motel Assn. (allied mem.), Mo. Hotel and Motel Assn. (allied mem.), U. Ark. Alumni Assn. St. Louis (dir. 1970-73, pres. 1972), Internat. Platform Assn., Webster Groves Hist. Soc., Tenn. Soc. St. Louis, Sigma Chi. Republican. Presbyterian. Club: Rotary. Home: 238 Park Rd Webster Groves MO 63119 Office: 10820 Sunset Plaza Sunset Hills MO 63127

GREEN, ROBERT DURHAM, constrn. co. exec.; b. Sullivan, Ind., May 16, 1944; s. Robert Eugene and Mary Agnes (Durham) G.; B.Ed., U. Miami (Fla.), 1966, B.B.A., 1968; m. Dorinda Lee Landi, Aug. 14, 1966; children—Marcia Lynne, Robert Durham. Freshman basketball coach U. Miami, 1966-68; foreman Green Constrn. of Ind., Inc., Oaktown, 1968, 70, supt., 1970-75, gen. mgr., 1975—. Exec. bd. Boy Scouts Am., Evansville, Ind., 1974-76, adv. council, 1976—; bd. dirs. YMCA, Vincennes, Ind., 1969—, pres., 1978-79; pres. Jr. Achievement of Knox and Lawrence Counties, 1979-80; bus. and community devel. adv. com. bd. trustees Vincennes U., 1976—. Mem. Ind. Constructors Inc., Ky. Assn. Hwy. Contractors, Ind. Mining Inst. (dir. 1981—), Ind. Coal Council (dir.), Kappa Sigma. Democrat. Methodist. Clubs: Masons, Shriners. Home: 602 State Rd 67 Vincennes IN 47591 Office: PO Box 157 Oaktown IN 47561

GREEN, RONALD STEWART, psychologist; b. Paterson, N.J., Mar. 18, 1946; s. Harry and Pearl G.; B.A. in Psychology, Franklin Pierce Coll., 1969; cert. Glassboro State Coll., N.J., 1971; M.A. in Psychology, Central Mich. U., 1973. Tchr. spl. edn. Clayton (N.J.) High Sch., 1969-70, chmn. dept. spl. edn., 1970-71; instr. spl. edn. Central Mich. U., Mt. Pleasant, 1972-73; psychologist, program dir. Mental Health and Mental Retardation Bd. Sandusky (Ohio), 1973—. Mem. Am. Psychol. Assn., Ohio Psychol. Assn., Am. Personnel and Guidance Assn., Am. Assn. Mental Deficiency. Democrat. Jewish. Research on counseling of mentally retarded. Home and Office: 2810 Park Ln Sandusky OH 44870

GREEN, RUTH MILTON, coll. adminstr.; b. Sioux City, Iowa, Feb. 29, 1924; d. John and Myrtle Alma (Phipps) Milton; student Morningside Coll., 1943-45; m. Robert Wood Green, Dec. 31, 1943; children—Robert William, Sandra Lou Green Montignani. Registrar, East High Sch., Sioux City, Iowa, 1943; acct. Buehler Bros., Iowa City, Iowa, 1947-49; asst. dir. tchr. placement Morningside Coll., Sioux City, Iowa, 1951-55, mem. staff registrar's office, 1960-65, asst. to registrar, 1965-70, dir. spl. project funding, 1971-81, dir. Title III Strengthening Devel. Institutions program, 1975—. Pres., First Congregational Ch., Sioux City, 1980. Mem. Nat. Council Univ. Research Adminstrs., Nat. Assn. Title Three Adminstrs., Nat. Council Univ. Bus. Officers, World Future Soc. Democrat. Home: 3801 6th Ave Sioux City IA 51106 Office: Morningside Coll 1501 Morningside Ave Sioux City IA 51106

GREEN, SAMUEL JAMES, spark plug mfg. co. ofcl.; b. Toledo, Dec. 4, 1928; s. Samuel James and Ada Bar (Tippet) G.; student U. Toledo, 1954-59; m. Mary Jacquline, Apr. 30, 1949; children—Christopher (dec.), Mark, Dan, Jeff, Mary, Sharon. With Ohio Bell Telephone Co., 1945-47; constrn. electrician, 1950-59; with Champion Spark Plug Co., Toledo, 1959—, research staff engr., 1965-68, electronic lab. supr., 1968-77, asst. mgr. research and devel. services, 1977—. Electronics adv. com. Monroe County Community Coll., 1970—; former unit leader, v.p. council Boy Scouts Am., recipient Silver Beaver award, 1964, and dist. award of merit, 1974. Served with USN, 1946-50. Recipient award Mfg. Engring. Cert. Inst. Mem. Soc. Automotive Engrs., Instrument Soc. Am. (sr.), Soc. Mfg. Engrs. (cert.). Republican. Patentee in field; works include: instrumentation design of 3 engine testing labs., design and supervision of constrn. of 2 lab. type bldgs. Home: 8330 Douglas Rd Temperance MI 48182 Office: 900 Upton Ave Toledo OH 43661

GREEN, WARREN HAROLD, publisher; b. Auburn, Ill., July 25, 1915; s. John Anderson Logan and Clara Christina (Wortman) G.; student Presbyn. Theol. Sem., 1933-34, Ill. Wesleyan U., 1934-36; B.M., Southwestern Conservatory, Dallas, 1938; M.M., St. Louis Conservatory, 1940, Ph.D., 1942; H.L.D., Southeastern U., New Orleans, 1981; m. Joyce Reinerd, Oct. 8, 1960. Prof. voice, composition and aural theory St. Louis Conservatory, 1938-44; program dir. USO, Highland Park, Ill., Brownwood and Orange, Tex., Waukegan, Ill., 1944-46; community service specialist Rotary Internat., Chgo., 1946-47; editor in chief Charles C. Thomas, Pub., Springfield, Ill., 1947-66; pub., pres. Warren H. Green, Inc., St. Louis, 1966—; sec. John R. Davis Assos., Chgo., 1955—; exec. v.p. Visioneering Advt., St. Louis, 1966—; mng. dir. Publishers Service Center, St. Louis and Longview, Tex., 1967—; exec. dir. Affirmative Action Register, 1974—; cons. U.S. and European pubs., profl. socs.; lectr. med. pub. and Civil War. Mem. Mayor's Com. on Water Safety; mem. Met. St. Louis Art Mus., Mo. Bot. Gardens. Recipient Presdl. citation outstanding contbn. export expansion program U.S., 1973, awards AMA, Internat. Acad. Preventive Medicine. Mem. Civil War Round Table (v.p. 1969—), Am. Acad. Criminology, Am. Acad. Polit. and Social Sci., Am. Med. Pubs. Assn., Am. Judicature Soc., Am. Soc. Personnel Adminstrn., Direct Mktg. Club St. Louis, Great Plains Hist. Soc., Co. Mil. Historians, Am. Soc. Personnel Adminstrn., University City C. of C. (pres. 1979—). Clubs: Mo. Athletic, World Trade, Elks (St. Louis). Contbr. articles and books on Civil War history, writing and editing to profl. jours. Home: 12120 Hibler Dr Creve Coeur MO 63141 Office: 8356 Olive Blvd Saint Louis MO 63132

GREENBANK, JOHN IRVING, pianist, composer, educator; b. Ashland, Ohio, Dec. 8, 1940; s. Charles Elmer and Ethel Irene (Arndt) G.; student Ashland Coll., 1959, Baptist Bible Coll., 1963-66; Mus.B., Drury Coll., 1970; postgrad. So. Mo. State U., Springfield, 1973; M.A., Central Mo. State U., Warrensburg, 1979; m. Margaret Pearl Swinehart, Apr. 20, 1962; children—John Charles, Steven Edward, Daniel Alan, Jeffrey Randolf. Choirmaster, organist Kelley Barracks, Stuttgart, Germany, 1961-63; organist, choirmaster several chs. in Springfield, Mo., 1963-69; faculty Bapt. Bible Coll., Springfield, 1969—, prof. music theory and piano, 1970—, head music dept., 1973—, also dir. Singing Men on tour; tchr., lectr. synthesized music composition; performed at Drury Coll., S.W. Mo. State U., Central Mo. State U., Bapt. Bible Coll.; judge various contests in piano performance. Served with U.S. Army, 1960-63. Recipient Jr. Class award of appreciation, Alumni award as outstanding faculty mem. Bapt. Bible Coll., 1974. Mem. Music Tchrs. Nat. Assn., Mo. Music Tchrs. Assn., Springfield Area Music Tchrs. Assn. (sec. 1980-81). Author: The Gospel Song: A History, 1973. Composer: Seal of the Black Horse, 1978. Home: 3515 Fruitwood Ln Springfield MO 65804 Office: Bapt Bible Coll 628 E Kearney St Springfield MO 65802

GREENBAUM, SHEILA, lawyer; b. Phila., Mar. 31, 1949; d. Albert and Libbie Greenbaum; B.A. Case Western Res. U., 1971; postgrad. Cleve. Marshall Coll. Law, 1971-73; J.D., U. Mo., Kansas City, 1974; m. Gary M. Wasserman. Admitted to Mo. bar, 1974; counselor ACLU Western Mo., 1974-75; asso. mem. firm Arthur A. Benson II, Kansas City, Mo., 1974-76; chief regional civil rights atty. HEW-Region VII, Kansas City, 1976-80, Dept. Edn., 1980—. Mem. Regional Task Force on Reduction of Adolescent Pregnancy, Mayors Adv. Commn. on Human Relations. Bd. dirs. Jewish Community Relations Bur. (vice chmn.), ACLU (1st v.p.), Western Mo. Mem. Fed., Kansas City, Am. bar assns., Womens Polit. Caucus, Assn. Women Lawyers, Friends of Art. Home: 4318 Rockhill Rd Kansas City MO 64110 Office: 911 Walnut St Room 2612 Kansas City MO 64106

GREENBERG, JOSEPH HERMAN, engring. co. exec.; b. Chgo., June 7, 1918; s. Charles and Bertha (Lesser) G.; B.S., Mass. Inst. Tech., 1940; M.S., Ill. Inst. Tech., 1950; m. Edith Betty Winter, Feb. 23, 1941; children—Charles Robert, Richard Lee. Plant metall. engr. Perfection Gear Co., Harvey, Ill., 1940-45; evening instr. metallurgy Ill. Inst. Tech., Chgo., 1941-80; with Boynton Engrs., Chgo., 1945-64, v.p., 1961-64; with A.J. Kearney, Inc., Chgo., 1964—, v.p., 1972—. Fellow Am. Soc. Metals; mem. Am. Inst. Mining and Metall. Engrs., Assn. Iron and Steel Engrs., Am. Foundrymen's Soc. Club: Covenant (Chgo.). Contbr. articles to trade jours. Patentee in field. Home: 6833 N Kedzie Ave Chicago IL 60645 Office: 222 S Riverside Plaza Chicago IL 60606

GREENBERG, PAUL, publ. co. exec.; b. Indpls., Aug. 4, 1921; s. Louis and Ida (Schwartz) G.; B.S., Purdue U., 1949; m. Janet Sussman, May 5, 1957; children—Beth, Amy. Research and devel. engr. Reilly Tar & Chem. Co., Indpls., 1949-51; with RCA, Indpls., 1951-75, gen. plant mgr., 1970-73, ops. mgr., 1973-75; dir. quality control Revlon, Inc., N.Y.C., 1958-59. group dir. ops. ITT Publ. Co., Indpls., 1976—. Served with USAF, 1942-46. Home: 211 Pine Dr Indianapolis IN 46260 Office: 4300 62d St W Indianapolis IN 46268

GREENBERT, HAROLD C., dentist; b. Detroit, Jan. 25, 1922; s. Max and Clara (Katz) G.; student Wayne U., 1939-43; B.S., U. N.D., 1943; D.D.S., U. Mich., 1950; m. Gloria Mae Fox, Aug. 19, 1947; children—Gail Susan, Marcy Ann, Alan Jay. Pvt. practice dentistry, Royal Oak, Mich., 1950—. Served with AUS, 1942-45. Decorated Bronze Star. Mem. Am. Dental Assn., Mich., Detroit Dist., Oakland County dental socs., U. Mich., Alumni Assn., Alpha Omega. Clubs: Tam O'Shanter Country (Orchard Lake, Mich.). Home: 28090 Tavistock Trail Southfield MI 48034 Office: 1579 W Big Beaver Bldg B-6 Troy MI 48084

GREENBLATT, DEANA CHARLENE, educator; b. Chgo., Mar. 13, 1948; d. Walter and Betty (Lamasky) Beisel; B.S. in Edn., Chgo. State U., 1969; M.A. in Guidance and Counseling, Roosevelt U., 1973; m. Mark Greenblatt, June 22, 1975. Tchr., counselor Chgo. Pub. Schs., 1969-75, City Colls. of Chgo. GED-TV, 1976; tchr. Columbus (Ohio) Pub. Schs., 1976—; participant learning exchange, Chgo. Active B'nai B'rith; vol. Right-to-Read, Columbus; mem. Community Learning Exchange, Columbus. Certified tchr. K-9, Ill., Ohio; certified personnel guidance, Ill., Ohio; certified Chgo. Bd. Edn. Mem. Am. Personnel and Guidance Assn. Democrat. Club: B'nai B'rith Women (chpt. v.p.). Home: 4083 Vineshire Dr Columbus OH 43227

GREENBLATT, MIRIAM, author, editor, educator; b. Berlin; d. Gregory and Shifra (Zemach) Baraks; B.A. magna cum laude, Hunter Coll.; postgrad. U. Chgo., Spertus Coll.; m. Herbert Halbrecht (div. 1960); m. 2d, Howard Greenblatt, Feb. 1, 1962 (div. 1978). Tchr., New Trier (Ill.) High Sch., 1978-81; editor Am. People's Ency., Chgo., 1957-58; editor Scott, Foresman & Co., Chgo., 1958-62; pres. Creative Textbooks, Glencoe, Ill., 1972—. Vice pres. Chgo. chpt. Am. Jewish Com., 1977-79, mem. nat. exec. council, 1980—; treas. Glencoe Youth Services, 1981—. Mem. Nat. Council Social Studies, Ill. Council Social Studies, Am. Hist. Assn., Chgo. Women in Publishing, Women in Mgmt. Jewish. Author: (with Jordan and Bowes) The Americans, 1982; (with Cox and Seaburg) Human Heritage, 1981; The History of Itasca, 1976; (with Larry Cuban) Japan, 1971; (with Don-chean Chu) The Story of China, 1968; edit. cons. Peoples and Cultures Series, 1976-78; contbg. editor A World History, 1979. Address: 111 Hogarth Ln Glencoe IL 60022

GREENE, CHARLES ROBERT, clergyman; b. Charlotte, N.C., Sept. 14, 1930; s. Walter Forrest and Ava Ann (Parker) G.; B.A., Wake Forest U., 1951; M.S.M., Union Sem., 1953, M.Div., 1956; D.Minn., Drew U., 1977; m. Gloria Jane Iacone, May 20, 1953; children—Claire A., Melissa B. Ordained to ministry Episcopal Ch., 1957; asst. rector St. James the Less, Scarsdale, N.Y., 1956-59; rector St. Bartholomew's Ch., Pittsboro, N.C., 1959-62; dir. program Episcopal Diocese of N.C., Raleigh, 1963-67; rector Grace Episcopal Ch., Nyack, N.Y., 1967-79; dean Cathedral of St. James, Chgo., 1979—. Mem. faculty Inst. of Theology of Episcopal Diocese of N.Y., 1974, mem. exec. com., 1971, mem. diocesan council, 1971; chmn. Ministries Commn. of N.Y., 1971; mem. adv. com., mem. bd. N.C. Council Chs., 1963-67; mem. diocesan council Diocese of N.C., 1963-67; pres. Nyack Clergy Assn., 1971-73, Rockland Interparish Council, 1969-71. Pres. bd. dirs. Nyack Daycare Center, 1968-73; bd. dirs. Community Narcotics Counseling Service, 1970-73; chmn. instnl. rev. com. Research Center, 1973—. Recipient certificate of recognition Ch. Devel. Bd., 1966. Profl. devel. grantee Diocese of N.Y., 1975-77. Republican. Clubs: Nyack Field, Rectory (N.Y.C.); Arts (Chgo.). Contbr. articles to profl. jours. Home: 1829 N Cleveland Chicago IL 60614

GREENE, EILEEN ATHERLEY, sch. adminstr.; b. Trinidad, B.W.I., Nov. 11, 1916; came to U.S., 1920; natrualized, 1941; d. Edgar H. and Wilhelmina C. (Marcado) Atherley; B.A., DePaul U., 1949, M.A., 1954; postgrad. Chgo. Conservatory of Music, 1955-57, Chgo. Sch. Expression, 1938-46, Chgo. Tchrs. Coll., 1960-65, Northwestern U., 1953; m. Theodore T. Greene, July 30, 1938; children—Raymonda Johnson, Glorianne Jackson, Marilyn Bean. With Chgo. Bd. Edn., 1949—, prin. Parker Elementary Sch., also Parker Child Parent Center, 1969—. Mem. Am. Assn. Sch. Adminstrs., Assn. Supervision and Curriculum Devel., NEA, Chgo. Prins. Assn., Chgo. Area Women Adminstrs. (pres. Ella Flagg Young Assn. 1978-79), Nat. Assn. Elementary Sch. Prins., Delta Kappa Gamma, Phi Delta Kappa, Alpha Kappa Alpha. Roman Catholic. Office: 6800 S Stewart Ave Chicago IL 60621

GREENE, GERALD MICHAEL, clin. psychologist; b. Chgo., May 7, 1940; s. Albert and Ruth (Kaplan) G.; B.A., Carleton Coll., 1961; Candidate I Diplomate Rijksuniversiteit Te Leiden (Netherlands), 1963; M.S., U. Okla., 1966, Ph.D., 1971; children—Erin Kylie, Kegan Ellery, Gavin Gregory. Asst. instr. U. Kans., Lawrence, 1966-68; chief psychologist Head Start Program of East Central Kans., Ottawa, 1967-68; asso. dir. East Central Kans. Supplementary Tng. Program, adj. instr. Emporia State Tchr's. Coll., 1967-68; instr. Rockhurst Coll., 1968-69; staff psychologist Osawatomie (Kans.) State Hosp., 1968-69; coordinator program, asst. prof. edn. and psychology Central State U., Edmond, Okla., 1969-71; mem. staff Okla. Psychol. and Ednl. Center, Oklahoma City, 1970-71; instr. phys. therapy Northwestern U. Med. Sch., 1971-72, postdoctoral fellow and intern in clin. psychology, 1971-72, project coordinator Rehab. services, 1972-73, asso. dept. psychiatry, 1972—, dept. community health and preventive medicine, 1973—, Sch. Dentistry depts. pedodontics and orthodontics, 1972—, intervention dir. Multiple Risk Factor Intervention Trial, 1973-80; pvt. practice clin. psychology, Chgo., 1972—; cons. Chgo. Bd. Mental Health, 1972-78; field supr. U. Ill. Jane Adams Sch. Social Work, 1976-78. OEO grantee, 1967-68; Office Edn. tng. grantee, 1969-71; Social and Rehab. Services grantee, 1972-76; City of Chgo. Head Start-Model Cities grantee, 1972-76; licensed clin. psychologist, Ill. Mem. Am., Ill., Midwestern psychol. assns., Council Exceptional Children, AAUP, NEA, Assn. Tchr. Educators Emotionally Disturbed Children, Council Children with Behavior Disorders, Assn. Children with Learning Disabilities, Assn. Advancement Behavior Therapy, Midwestern Assn. Advancement Behavior Therapy, Chgo. Psychol. Club, Acad. Psychologists in Marital and Family Counseling, Ill. Biofeedback Soc., Council for Nat. Register Health Service Providers in Psychology, Am. Orthopsychiat. Assn., Soc. Behavior Medicine, Council for Advancement of Psychologic Professions and Scis., Assn. for Advancement of Psychology, Soc. Police and Criminal Psychology, Am. Soc. Psychologists in Pvt. Practice, Chgo. Soc. Clin.

Hypnosis, Am. Soc. Clin. Hypnosis, Am. Group Psychotherapy Assn., Assn. Advance and Promote Hypnosis, Psychol. Soc. (Republic of Panama; hon. diplomate), Sigma Xi, Psi Chi, Phi Delta Kappa, Kappa Delta Pi. Office: 500 N Michigan Ave Suite 542 Chicago IL 60611

GREENE, GERALD MICHAEL, psychologist; b. Chgo., May 7, 1940; s. Albert and Ruth (Kaplan) G.; B.A., Carleton Coll., 1961; diploma Rijksuniversiteit Te Leiden, Netherlands, 1963; M.S., U. Okla., 1966, Ph.D., 1971; children—Erin Kylie, Kegan Ellery, Gavin Gregory. Research asst. dept. psychology U. Okla., Norman, 1965; community cons. Lawrence (Kans.) public sch. system, 1966; asst. instr. U. Kans., Lawrence, 1966-68; clin. psychologist and cons. Head Start Programs of East Central Kans., 1967, asso. dir. East Central Kans. Supplementary Tng. Program, 1967-68; instr. Rockhurst Coll., Kansas City, Mo., 1968-69; staff psychologist Osawatomie (Kans.) State Hosp., 1968-69; mem. staff Okla. Psychol. and Ednl. Center, Oklahoma City, 1970-71; asst. prof. edn. and psychology Central State U., Edmond, Okla., 1969-71, coordinator program in emotional disturbance, 1969-71; instr. dept. phys. therapy Northwestern U. Med. Sch., Chgo., 1971-72, intern clin. psychology, 1971-72; cons. clin. psychology Chgo. Bd. Mental Health, 1972-78, psychotherapist, 1972-78; asso. dpets. pedodontics and orthodontics Sch. Dentistry, Northwestern U., Chgo., 1973-78, asso. dept. psychiatry, 1972—, practicum supr. students, 1971—, asso. dept. community health and preventive medicine, 1973—, behavioral cons., 1973-80; pvt. practice clin. psychology, 1972—. Recipient Award of Excellence, President of U.S., 1977, Youth Service Recognition award YMCA, 1971, Cert. of Appreciation, Project Head Start, 1968, Human Service Contbn. award Northwestern U., 1972; registered psychologist, Ill. Mem. Am. Psychol. Assn., Assn. for Advancement of Psychology, Ill. Psychol. Assn., Midwestern Psychol. Assn., Am. Orthopsychiat. Assn., Midwestern Assn. for Advancement of Behavior Therapy, Soc. of Behavioral Medicine, Am. Soc. Clin. Hypnosis, Assn. of Children with Learning Disabilities, Chgo. Soc. Clin. Hypnosis, Internat. Soc. of Hypnosis, Council for Advancement of the Psychol. Professions in the Scis., Soc. of Police in Criminal Psychology, Am. Soc. of Psychologists in Pvt. Practice, Acad. Of Psychologists in Marital, Sex and Family Therapy, Am. Assn. of Sex Educators, Counselors and Therapists, Ill. Biofeedback Soc., Undersea Med. Soc., Am. Soc. Profl. Consultants, AAUP, Sigma Xi, Psi Chi, Phi Delta Kappa, Kappa Delta Pi. Home: 695 Vernon Ave Glencoe IL 60022 Office: 500 N Michigan Ave Suite 542 Chicago IL 60611

GREENE, HARVEY MITCHELL, lawyer; b. Shelburn, Ind., Jan. 25, 1927; s. Guy Benton and Arslee (Mitchell) G.; student Butler U., 1947-49; LL.B., Ind. U. at Indpls., 1954; m. Charlotte Elizabeth Shook, Dec. 25, 1946 (dec. Nov. 1979); children—Cheryl Greene Palmer, Guy Frederick, Cynthia Diane Greene Dicken, Carole Dawn; m. 2d, Theda L. Poole, Oct. 25, 1980. Admitted to Ind. bar, 1954; ordained to ministry Primitive Bapt. Ch., 1959; dep. prosecutor Dearborn County, Ind., 1965-66; city atty., Aurora, Ind., 1960-63, 68-71; county atty. Dearborn County, 1977-80. Pres., Aurora High Sch. Booster's Club, 1964-70. Bd. dirs. Dearborn and Ohio Counties Humane Soc., 1971-72. Served with USAAF, 1945-47. Mem. Am. Bar Assn., Dearborn and Ohio Counties Bar Assn. (pres. 1961), Assn. Trial Lawyers Am., Lawyer-Pilots Bar Assn. Club: Rotary (past pres.). Home: 110 Dawn Dr Aurora IN 47001 Office: 437 2d St Aurora IN 47001

GREENE, RALPH VERNON, lawyer; b. Cleve., Apr. 5, 1910; s. Charles Roscoe and Pauline Johanna (Desch) G.; student Cleve. Coll. of Western Reserve U., 1938-42; J.D., Cleve. Marshall Law Sch., 1946; m. Martha Florence Burwell, Aug. 12, 1939; 1 dau., Betsy Greene Vaughn. Various positions Cleve. Trust Co., 1930-43; admitted to Ohio bar, 1946; practiced in Willoughby, Ohio, 1946—; mem. firm Greene, Tulley & Jurjans, Willoughby, 1962-66, 77—; sec., dir. Feedall, Inc. Mem. Willoughby Hills (Ohio) Charter Commn., 1970-71; mem. Lake County Bd. Mental Retardation, 1971-73; mem. bd. mgrs. YMCA, 1968-78, trustee, 1975-78; trustee Willoughby Sch. Fine Arts, 1967-75. Served with AUS, 1943-45. Mem. Am., Ohio, Lake County (pres. 1956) bar assns. Methodist (pres. bd. trustees 1966-79). Home: 36951 Riviera Ridge PO Box 65 Willoughby Hills OH 44094 Office: 38052 Euclid Ave Willoughby OH 44094

GREENE, ROBERT BERNARD, JR., journalist; b. Columbus, Ohio, Mar. 10, 1947; s. Robert Bernard and Phyllis Ann (Harmon) G.; m. Susan Bonnet Koebel, Feb. 13, 1971; B.J., Northwestern U., 1969. Reporter, Chgo. Sun-Times, 1969-71, columnist, 1971-78; syndicated columnist Field Newspaper Syndicate, 1976-78; columnist Chgo. Tribune, 1978—; contbg. editor Esquire mag., 1980—; commentator CBS TV and radio. Recipient award for best newspaper column in Ill., AP, 1975; award for best sustaining feature in Chgo., Chgo. Newspaper Guild, 1976; Nat. Headliner award for best newspaper column in U.S., 1977. Author: We Didn't Have None of Them Fat Funky Angels on the Wall of Heartbreak Hotel, 1971; Running: A Nixon-McGovern Campaign Journal, 1973; Billion Dollar Baby, 1974; Johnny Deadline, Reporter: The Best of Bob Greene, 1976; (with Paul Galloway) Bagtime, 1977. Office: 435 N Michigan Ave Chicago IL 60611

GREENE, WALTER DOUGLAS, health systems cons.; b. Brunswick, Ga., Oct. 4, 1936; s. Elliotte and Anna Olivia Greene; B.A. in Internat. Relations, U. Chgo., 1959, M.B.A. in Mgmt. and Fin., 1978. Info. processing specialist IBM Corp., 1961-70; sr. mgmt. analyst Health and Hosps. Gov. Commn. and Blue Cross Assn., Chgo., 1971-73; dep. asst. dir. Office Civil Rights, HEW, 1974-76; dir. planning Provident Hosp., Chgo., 1976-77; pres. Wherewithal Group, Inc., Chgo. and Washington, 1970—; group mgr. Price, Williams & Assos., Chgo. and Washington, 1978—; cons. in field. Mem. nat. bd. Americans for Democratic Action, 1972—; bd. dirs. Chgo. Council Liberal Chs., 1973-75, Ind. Voters Ill., 1971-78; pres. Young Democrats Washington, 1965; mem. Young Dem. Nat. Com., 1964-66; congl. dist. coordinator Common Cause, 1971-73. Fellow Assn. U. Programs in Hosp. Adminstrn., 1971. Mem. Am. Public Health Assn., Nat. Assn. Health Services Execs., Am. Hosp. Assn., Hosp. Mgmt. Systems Soc., Assn. Computing Machinery, Data Processing Mgmt. Assn., Nat. Urban League, ACLU, UN Assn., NAACP, Mensa, Alpha Phi Alpha. Unitarian. Club: Exchange. Office: Wherewithal 1237 4th St SW Washington DC 20024

GREENEISEN, DAVID PAUL, marine engr., automotive components mfg. co. exec.; b. Fayetteville, N.C., June 6, 1941; s. Franklin Robert and Mildred Alida (Cassidy) G.; B.S., U.S. Naval Acad., 1963; M.S., Mass. Inst. Tech., 1968; M.B.A., St. John's U., 1970; m. Susan Dee Besgrove, June 5, 1963; children—David Geoffrey, Kirsten Lynn. Commd. ensign U.S. Navy, 1963, advanced through grades to comdr., 1977; sta. USS Wm. V. Pratt, then various shipbldg. and design activities; res., 1973; research mgr. Kelsey Hayes, Ann Arbor, Mich., 1973-75, v.p. product assurance Romulus, Mich., 1975—. Mem. IEEE, Soc. Naval Architects and Marine Engrs., Soc. Automotive Engrs., Am. Soc. Quality Control, Tau Beta Pi, Sigma Xi, Beta Gamma Sigma. Republican. Methodist. Club: Barton Hills Country. Home: 1230 Barrister Rd Ann Arbor MI 48105 Office: 38481 Huron River Dr Romulus MI 48174

GREENFIELD, JOAN ELLEN, psychologist, social worker, writer; b. Detroit, Nov. 8, 1942; d. Jack and Florence S. Gaynor; A.B., Wayne State U., 1964, M.A., 1977; postgrad. U. Mich., 1978—; m. Allen Frederick Greenfield, Jan. 10, 1965; children—Andrew Jason, Jeffrey Howard, Lisa Faye. Counselor mobile units Mich. Employment Security Commn., Detroit, 1965-67, counseling supr., 1967-69; therapist Inst. for Family Counseling, Southfield, Mich., 1975-77; therapist Counseling Assos., Inc., Southfield, 1977-78; therapist Rosenzweig Assos., Grand Rapids, Mich., 1978-80; psychologist Clin. Resources, Inc., Southfield, 1980—; columnist The Detroit News, 1980—; pres. NSF Summer Sci. Workshop, 1959; lectr. Gen. Motors Tech. Center, 1959. Area chmn. Am. Cancer Soc., 1967-77, Muscular Dystrophy Assn., 1967-77; mem. womens com. Grand Rapids (Mich.) Symphony, 1978—. Recipient Scholastic Writing awards, 1957, Scholastic Art awards, 1959, Spl. awards in chemistry Detroit Met. Sci. Fair, 1959, 60. Cert. social worker, Mich. Mem. Am. Psychol. Assn., Nat. Assn. Social Workers, Am. Personnel and Guidance Assn., Am. Rehab. Counseling Assn., Nat. Vocat. Guidance Assn., Mich. Personnel and Guidance Assn., Mich. Vocat. Guidance Assn., Mich. Assn. Specialists in Group Work, Mich. Rehab. Counseling Assn., Mich. Assn. for Children with Learning Disabilities. Clubs: Hadassah (dir. Eleanor Roosevelt Group, Met. Detroit chpt. 1975-78, v.p., dir. Grand Rapids chpt. 1979-80); Sisterhood of Temple Emanuel of Grand Rapids. Home: 4580 McEwen Dr Bloomfield Hills MI 48013 Office: Clin Resources Inc 29540 Southfield Rd Suite 100 Southfield MI 48076

GREENFIELD, JOHN CHARLES, bio-organic chemist; b. Dayton, Ohio, Apr. 10, 1945; s. Ivan Ralph and Mildred Louis (House) G.; B.S. cum laude, Ohio U., 1967; Ph.D., U. Ill., 1974. High sch. sci. instr., Dayton, 1968-71; grad. research asst. U. Ill., 1971-74; post-doctoral research fellow Swiss Fed. Inst. Tech., Zurich, 1975-76; research chemist infectious diseases research Upjohn Co., Kalamazoo, 1976—. Am.-Swiss Found. for Sci. Exchange fellow, 1975; NSF-NATO postdoctoral fellow, 1975-76. Mem. Am. Chem. Soc., AAAS, Am. Soc. Microbiology, Sigma Xi. Home: 10618 Dandale St Kalamazoo MI 49002 Office: The Upjohn Co Infectious Diseases Research Kalamazoo MI 49001

GREENLEAF, JOSEPH ANTHONY, lawyer; b. Newport, R.I., Aug. 18, 1945; s. Joseph A. and Ruth T. (Mattson) G.; B.A., Aquinas Coll., Grand Rapids, Mich., 1971; postgrad. Detroit Coll. Law, 1971-72; J.D., Thomas M. Cooley Law Sch., 1976; m. Karlene R. Smith, Aug. 23, 1974; children—Joseph A., Benjamin P., Jacob M. Admitted to Mich. bar, 1976; asst. Prosecuting Atty., Jackson County; former pres. Joseph A. Greenleaf, P.C., Holt and Lyons, Mich., 1977—. Bd. dirs. Lyons-Muir Hist. Soc., 1979-80. Served with USCG, 1963-68. Mem. Am. Bar Assn. (computer com. 1979—), State Bar Mich., Ingham County Bar Assn., Ionia-Montcalm Bar Assn., Delta Theta Phi (dean alumni senate 1979—). Contbr. articles to profl. jours.; patentee skiing field.

GREENLEE, HERBERT BRECKENRIDGE, surgeon; b. Rockford, Ill., Sept. 6, 1927; s. Harvey James and Abbie (McCathran) G.; A.B., Beloit Coll., 1951; M.D., U. Chgo., 1955; m. Shirley Claire Rurik, June 12, 1955; children—Herbert, William, Kenneth, Anne. Intern, U. Chgo. Clinics, 1956, resident in surgery, 1956-62; practice medicine specializing in surgery, Chgo., 1964-66; staff surgeon VA Hosp., Madison, Wis., 1966-67; asst. prof. surgery U. Wis., Madison, 1966-67; asst. chief surg. service VA Hosp., Hines, Ill., 1967-72, chief surg. service, 1972—; asso. prof. surgery Stritch Sch. Medicine, Loyola U., Maywood, Ill., 1967-72, prof. surgery, 1972—. Served with M.C., U.S. Army, 1962-64. Recipient Raymond W. McNealy award Chgo. Surg. Soc., 1956. Diplomate Am. Bd. Surgery. Fellow Am. Cancer Soc., A.C.S. (med. motion pictures com. 1975, coordinator gen. surgery film sessions 1976—), Inst. Medicine Chgo.; mem. Am. Gastroenterology Assn., AMA, Soc. Surgery of Alimentary Tract, Midwest Gut Club, Chgo. Soc. Gastroenterology (pres. 1973-74, counselor 1974-75), Ill. (pres. 1975-76, trustee 1976—), Chgo. (sec. 1974-77), Charles B. Puestow surg. socs., Assn. VA Surgeons, Assn. Acad. Surgery, Collegium Internat. Chirurgiae Digestivae, Western Midwest, Central surg. assns., Internat. Soc. Surgery, Pancreas Club, N.Y. Acad. Sci., Phi Beta Kappa, Sigma Xi, Alpha Omega Alpha. Author: Surgery of the Small and Large Intestine, 1973, Spanish edit. 1976; contbr. articles to sci. publs. Home: 807 Keystone St River Forest IL 6030S Office: VA Hosp 112 Hines IL 60141

GREENLEE, HUGH THOMAS, indsl. designer, educator; b. Columbus, Ohio, Sept. 28, 1927; s. Wayne Thomas and Elizabeth (Rodefer) G.; grad. Cleve. Inst. Art, 1949; m. Elizabeth Tarmichael, July 2, 1953; children—Duncan Thomas, Megan Elizabeth. Staff designer George W. Walker Cons. Designer, Detroit, 1949-52, Smith-Scherr Designers, Akron, Ohio, 1952-53; partner Greenlee-Hess Indsl. Design, Cleve., 1953—; asso. prof. indsl. design Cleve. Inst. Art, 1955-60, prof. indsl. design, 1960—; cons. designer Harris Corp., Wright Tool & Forge, Ohio Rubber Co., W.R. Grace & Co. Mem. Indsl. Design Soc. Am. Presbyn. Clubs: Chagrin Valley Racquet, Hillbrook. Office: 4160 Mayfield Rd South Euclid OH 44121

GREENSPAN, BARNEY, clin. psychologist, child psychoanalyst; b. Miami Beach, Fla., Mar. 28, 1943; Harold and Pauline (Stern) G.; B.A. in Psychology, Calif. State U., Los Angeles, 1965, M.S., 1967; Ph.D., Mich. State U., 1970; m. Laurie Judge, June 28, 1968; children—Gabriel, Joshua, Benjamin. Intern, Napa State Mental Hosp., Imola, Calif., summer, 1966; clin. intern Psychiat. Clinic of State Prison, So. Mich., Jackson, 1969-70; postdoctoral fellow in psychotherapy Advanced Behavioral Sci. Center, Grosse Point, Mich., 1970-72; dir. psychol. services Bellefaire Residential Treatment and Child Care Center, Cleve., 1972-79; pvt. clin. practice, individual psychotherapy, 1979—; clinic asso. Cleve. Center for Research in Child Devel., 1973—; reviewer child welfare programs Child Welfare Resource Info. Exchange, Children's Bur., HEW, 1978—. Cert. Rehab. Counselor; diplomate Am. Bd. Profl. Psychology. Mem. Am. Psychol. Assn., Midwestern Psychol. Assn., Ohio Psychol. Assn., Cleve. Acad. Cons. Psychologists, Cleve. Psychol. Assn., Am. Orthopsychiat. Assn. Contbr. articles and book revs. to profl. jours.; editorial bd. Jour. Clin. Child Psychology, 1977—, The Family Coordinator, 1972-75. Home: 17307 Lomond Blvd Shaker Heights OH 44120 Office: Parkway Med Center-South 3619 Park East Suite 212 Beachwood OH 44122

GREENSTEIN, MELVIN, mental health center adminstr.; b. Chgo., Feb. 28, 1920; s. David and Sarah Bella (Green) G.; B.A., U. Chgo., 1939, M.B.A., 1940; m. Pearl Barach, Dec. 28, 1940; children—Judith Carol Greenstein Sloss, Barbara Phyllis, Robert Jonathan. Vocat. counselor Jewish Vocat. Service, Chgo., 1959-61; exec. dir. Kennedy Job Tng. Center, Palos Park, Ill., 1962-70, Orchard Center for Mental Health, Skokie, Ill., 1971—. Mem. Nat. Rehab. Assn., Am. Assn. Mental Deficiency, Ill. Assn. Community Mental Health Agys. Home: 3001 S Martin Luther King Dr Chicago IL 60616 Office: 8600 Gross Point Rd Skokie IL 60077

GREENWALD, CHARLES MORTIMER, radiologist; b. N.Y.C., Dec. 8, 1924; s. Lawrence and Rose (Krauss) G.; B.A., Columbia Coll., 1945, M.D., 1948; m. Margaret Paschall, Sept. 25, 1948; children—Charles Mortimer, Amelia, Robert, Richard, Patricia. Intern, Evanston (Ill.) Hosp., 1948-49; resident Cleve. Clinic, 1951-54, staff radiologist, 1954-57; staff radiologist Mercy Hosp., Iowa City, Iowa, 1957-60, St. Cloud (Minn.) Hosp., 1960-61; dir. dept. radiology Parma (Ohio) Community Gen. Hosp., 1961—; asst. clin. prof. Case Western Reserve U., Cleve., 1978—. Pres., S.W. Community Music Assn., 1973-74. Served to lt. (sr. grade) USN, 1949-51. Fellow Am. Coll. Radiology; mem. AMA, Am. Bd. Radiology, Radiol. Soc. N.Am. (past counselor), Ohio State Radiol. Assn., Ohio State Med. Assn., Cleve. Radiol. Soc. (past pres.). Presbyterian. Clubs: Rotary (Paul Harris award, sec.) (Parma Ohio); Town and Gown (pres. 1968-70). Abstractor, Radiology Jour., 1953-76. Home: 360 Westbridge Dr Berea OH 44017 Office: 7007 Powers Blvd Parma OH 44129

GREENWALD, GILBERT SAUL, educator; b. N.Y.C., June 24, 1927; s. Morris and Celia G.; A.B. with honors, U. Calif., Berkeley, 1949; Ph.D., 1954; m. Pola Gorsky, Sept. 8, 1950; children—Susan Greenwald Waxman, Elizabeth Greenwald Jordan, Douglas. USPHS postdoctoral fellow, dept. embryology Carnegie Inst., Washington, 1954-56; mem. faculty dept. anatomy U. Wash., Seattle, 1956-61; mem. faculty U. Kans. Med. Center, Kansas City, 1961—, disting. prof., chmn. physiology dept., 1977—, prof. gynecology and obstetrics, 1964—. Mem. AAAS, Am. Assn. Anatomists, Am. Physiol. Soc., Brit. Soc. Study of Fertility, Endocrine Soc., Soc. Study of Reprodn. (pres. 1971), Soc. Exptl. Biology and Medicine, Internat. Soc. Research Neuroendocrinology, Sigma Xi. Editor in chief Biology of Reprodn., 1974-77. Office: U Kans Med Center 39th and Rainbow Blvd Kansas City KS 66103

GREENWOLD, WARREN ELDON, physician; b. Chgo., Mar. 11, 1923; s. Charles Lauritz and Leona Clare (Alexander) G.; B.S., U. Chgo., 1944, M.D., 1946; M.S., U. Minn., 1956; m. Dorothy Marie O'Neil, Sept. 28, 1946; children—Marcia, Warren Eldon, Charles L., Gail Ann. Intern, Presbyterian Hosp., Chgo., 1946-47; gen. practice medicine, Cissna Park, Ill., 1949-52; pediatric fellow Mayo Clinic, 1953-56; practice medicine specializing in pediatrics Carle Clinic Assn., Urbana, Ill., 1956—; clin. asso. Sch. Basic Med. Scis., U. Ill., 1972-80; clin. asst. prof. pediatrics U. Ill. Med. Sch., Urbana-Champaign, 1980—; Past mem. regional bd. Ill. Children's Home and Aid Soc.; trustee, past pres. Carle Found. Served with AUS, 1947-49. Diplomate Am. Bd. Pediatrics. Mem. Champaign County, Ill., Iroquois County (past pres.) med. socs., AMA, Am. Diabetes Assn., Am. Acad. Pediatrics, Central Ill. Pediatric Soc. Home: 2502 Melrose Dr Champaign IL 61820 Office: 602 W University Ave Urbana IL 61801

GREENWOOD, MARY JEAN, ednl. adminstr.; b. Onarga, Ill., Mar. 6, 1923; d. Lloyd A. and Margaret (Shear) Koritz; B.S. (scholar), U. Ill., 1945; M.S., Ill. State U., 1970; m. Don Adams Greenwood, Feb. 18, 1945; children—Robin, Pamela, Randi. Tchr., Greenwood Country Day Sch., Peoria, Ill., 1948—, prin., 1970—; asso. dir. Sky Ranch Camps, Princeville, Ill., 1969—; sec. treas. Tamarack Inc., 1966—; dir. Greenwood Diagnostic Center. Mem. Assn. Supervision and Curriculum Devel., Ill. Assn. Non-Public Schs., Kappa Kappa Gamma. Roman Catholic. Office: 2015 W Glen Ave Peoria IL 61614

GREENWOOD, ROBERT LARRY, engring. co. exec.; b. Union County, Ohio, Oct. 25, 1935; s. Robert Webb and Ruth(Hoffman) G.; B.S. in Bus. Adminstrn., Ohio State U., 1959; m. Janice Jo Earl, Sept. 16, 1956; children—Tammera DiAnn, Randy William. Sales rep. Agrico Chem. Co., Cleve., 1959-61; sales rep. Arro Expansion Bolt Co., Marion, Ohio, 1961-66; sales and mktg. mgr. Arro Expansion Products Co., Marion and Mannasquan, N.J., 1970-72; sales rep. Fairfield Engring. Co., Marion, 1966-70, mktg. mgr. storing and reclaiming group, 1972-80, sales mgr. utility coal handling group, 1980—; dir. Fairfield Transmission Co., 1972-75. Served with AUS, 1954-56. Republican. Methodist. Club: River Valley Lions. Home: 1626 Oxford Rd Marion OH 43302 Office: 324 Barnhart St Marion OH 43302

GREER, CARL CRAWFORD, petroleum co. exec.; b. Pitts., June 12, 1940; s. Joseph Moss and Gene (Crawford) G.; B.S., Lehigh U., 1962; Ph.D., Columbia U., 1966; m. Jerrine Ehlers, June 16, 1962; children—Caryn, Michael, Janet. Asso. in bus. Columbia U., 1964-66, asst. prof. banking and fin., 1966-67; retail mktg. mgr. Martin Oil Service Inc., Alsip, Ill., 1967-68, exec. v.p., 1968, pres., dir., 1968-76, chmn. bd., pres., 1976—; dir. Pullman Bank & Trust Co., Heritage Bancorp. Inc., MSV Co., VSM Co., Colo. Energy Corp. Mem. Beta Theta Pi, Tau Beta Pi, Beta Gamma Sigma, Omicron Delta Kappa. Presbyterian. Office: 4S01 W 127th St Alsip IL 60658

GREER, EUGENE, environ. technician; b. Harrisburg, Ill., Mar. 14, 1918; s. Raymondand Rosia (Farless) G.; student So. Ill. U., 1950-51; m. Clara Reta Edwards, Nov. 20, 1938; 1 son, Larry Gene. Various positions Harrisburg Water and Sewer Co. (Ill.), 1942-77, Supt., 1960-77; sr. environ. technician Environ. Protection Agy., State of Ill., Marion, 1977-79; supt. Eldorado Water Co. (Ill.), 1979-80. Served with U.S. Army, 1943. Mem. Am. Water Works Assn., So. Ill. Water and Sewage Works Assn. (pres. 1953-54), Ill. Soc. Water Pollution Control Operators, Ill. Potable Water Supply Operators Assn. (chmn. Ill. 1969, operator of yr. 1973). Democrat. Baptist. Club: Odd Fellows. Home: 205 W State St Harrisburg IL 62946

GREER, LAVERNE GRITTON, musician, ret. educator; b. Penfield, Ill., June 12, 1916; d. Shelby Lylburn and Maudie Ann (Fetters) Gritton; B.A., U. Ill., 1937; student MacPhail Coll. Music, Mpls., 1951-53; m. E. Edward Greer, Mar. 25, 1937; 1 son, Lylburn. Tchr. music Woodbine (Kans.) pub. schs., 1944-45, schs. in Ill. and Minn., 1948-54, Rantoul (Ill.) pub. schs., 1954-76; pvt. music tchr., 1945—. Mem. Nat. Guild Piano Tchrs., Internat. Soc. Music Educators, Am. Choral Dirs. Assn. (life), AAUW (br. pres.), Internat. Platform Assn., Nat. Assn. Organ Tchrs. Mem. Christian Ch. Home and Office: 513 Eden Park Rantoul IL 61866

GREER, RANDALL DEWEY, fin. analyst; b. Balt., Apr. 29, 1951; s. James Walter and Ruth Virtue (Cooper) G.; B.S. in Psychology, U. Nebr., 1973; M.B.A., U. Fla., 1975; m. Beverly Ann Smeal, May 31, 1974. Research analyst Kirkpatrick, Pettis, Smith, Polian Inc., Omaha, 1975-76, asst. v.p., 1977-78, v.p., dir. research, 1978—. Vice chmn. Nebr. Muscular Dystrophy Telethon Com., 1980. Chartered fin. analyst. Mem. Fin. Analysts Fedn., Omaha-Lincoln Soc. Fin. Analysts. Republican. Presbyterian. Clubs: Plaza, Omaha Country. Home: 9911 Pratt St Omaha NE 68134 Office: 1623 Farnam St Omaha NE 68102

GREGERSON, RICHARD O., state senator; b. Apr. 27, 1932; B.S., Augustana Coll.; LL.B., U.S.D.; married; 2 children. Former spl. agt. FBI; practice law; mem. S.D. Senate, 1978—. Chmn. bd. pensions Am. Luth. Ch. Served with USMC. Mem. Am. Bar Assn., S.D. Bar Assn., Am. Legion. Republican. Club: Elks. Office: State Capitol Pierre SD 57501*

GREGG, ALVIS FORREST, profl. football coach; b. Birthright, Tex., Oct. 18, 1933; B.S. in Phys. Edn., So. Methodist U., 1959. Player, Green Bay (Wis.) Packers, NFL, 1956, 58-70, Dallas Cowboys, 1971; asst. coach Green Bay Packers, 1969-70, San Diego Chargers, 1972-73; asst. coach, then head coach Cleve. Browns, 1974-77; head coach Toronto Argonauts, CFL, 1979, Cin. Bengals, NFL, 1980—.

Played in NFL Pro Bowl, 1960-64, 66-68, NFL Championship Game, 1960-62, 65-67, Super Bowl, 1966-67; coach Super Bowl team, 1981. Address: 200 Riverfront Stadium Cincinnati OH 45202*

GREGG, ROBERT IRA, coll. adminstr.; b. St. Louis, Nov. 29, 1921; s. Robert Ira and Edna Ollie (Wykle) G.; B.S. in Edn., So. Ill. U., 1939-46, postgrad., 1963; M.S. in Edn., U. Mo., 1954; m. Corrinne Mitchell Smith, June 6, 1947; children—Bridget Ann, James Patrick, Timothy Michael. Indsl. arts tchr. Crossville (Ill.) Community Sch., 1946-63, bldg. and grounds supt., 1954-63, supt. schs., 1963-68; dean technology Southeastern Ill. Coll., Harrisburg, 1968—. Served to 2nd lt. USAAF, 1943-46. Mem. Am. Vocat. Assn., Ill. Vocat. Assn., Phi Delta Kappa. Episcopalian. Home: 221 W Poplar St Harrisburg IL 62946 Office: Southeastern Illinois College Route 4 Harrisburg IL 62946

GREGORCY, JOHN RAYMOND, controls engr.; b. Rockford, Ill., Dec. 3, 1929; s. Stanley and Evelyn Alice; student in Indsl. Electronics, Memphis State U., 1948-52; m. Willie May Mickey, Aug. 12, 1950; children—Perry, Paul, Patricia, Pamela, Philip. Design engr. W.F. and John Barnes Co., Rockford, 1952-56; chief elec. engr. Ill. Water Treatment Co., Rockford, 1956-72; chief controls engr. Techni-Chem, Inc., Cherry Valley, Ill., 1972—. Trustee, Techni-Chem, Inc. Pension Fund. Served with U.S. Navy, 1948-52. Recipient award Foxboro Instrument Sch., 1966. Mem. IEEE, Instrument Soc. Am., Rockford Engring. Soc. Republican. Lutheran. Club: Rockford Hockey. Designer cobolt unit treatment, solid state ion exchange unit. Home: 912 Starview Dr Rockford IL 61108 Office: 6853 Indy Dr Belvidere IL 61008

GREGORY, CLAIRE DISTELHORST, TV producer; b. Chgo., Mar. 6, 1926; d. Robert Henry and Genevieve (McCall) Distelhorst; A.B., Ind. U., 1947, M.S., 1954, postgrad. 1959; children—Charles, Martha. Tchr., pub. schs., Bismarck, Rossville and Helmsburg Ind., 1947-51; grad. asst. Audio Visual Center, Ind. U., Bloomington, Ind., 1953-55, lectr., dir. Women's, Children's and Social Service Programs, Radio and TV, 1956-59; exec. dir. Community Service Council, Inc., Bloomington, 1971-75; producer, asst. supr. Instructional TV Program Devel., dir. special projects, Ind. U. Radio and TV Services, Bloomington, 1975-81. Chmn., Telecommunications Council of Bloomington, 1975-80. Treas., Blue Ridge Assn. Mem. Women in Communications, Zeta Aux. (pres.), Psi Iota Xi, Unite Way of Monroe County, Inc., 1982. Producer: Russian Revolution and the Arts, parts I and II, 1976; Teleconference on Mass Transp., 1976; Total Teach, 1977; Environment and Development, AID and the Environment, 1978; video taped programs developmental skills Internat. Devel. Inst., 1976, 77; Transportation Briefing, 1977; Getting There, 1979; Using Immediate Access, 1978-80; Living Africa, 1979-1982. Home: 2949 Ramble Rd E Bloomington IN 47401 Office: Radio and TV Bldg Ind Univ Bloomington IN 47405

GREGORY, TENICIA ANN BANKS, radio/tv sta. exec.; b. Detroit, Sept. 28, 1933; d. William Venoid and Rose (Glassman) Banks; B.S. in Edn., Wayne State U., 1955, M.A., 1960; m. Karl Dwight Gregory, June 7, 1959; children—Karin Diane, Sheila Therese, Kurt David. Tchr., Detroit Bd. Edn., 1955-60; supr. student tchrs. Wayne State U., Detroit public schs., 1955-60, 64-68; guidance counselor Detroit public schs., 1969, tchr. Greater City Gifted Children Program, 1959-60; tchr. Manpower Devel. Tng. Pilot Program, Washington, 1963; writer, tchr. Black lit. course pilot program Mumford High Sch., Detroit, 1964-69; asso. prof. English Oakland Community Coll., Farmington, Mich., 1969-75; dir. WGPR, Detroit, 1975, sta. mgr. FM radio and TV, 1976—. Bd. dirs. Feminist Fed. Credit Union, 1971-72, pres. bd. dirs., 1972-73; del. Nat. Credit Union Conv., 1974; bd. dirs. Internat. Masons, Inc., 1975; chmn. media adv. com. Detroit Election Commn., 1980; mem. vocat. tech. telecommunications adv. com., 1980. Recipient Spirit of Detroit award Detroit City Council, 1977; Nat. Black Women's Polit. Leadership Caucus award, 1980. Contbr. articles to profl. jours. Office: 3140 6 E Jefferson St Detroit MI 48207

GREIG, WALTER, lawyer, ret. coll. pres.; b. Austin, Tex., Nov. 16, 1906; s. Walter and Elizabeth (Kopperl) G.; student U. Tex., 1924-30; B.S. (hon.), Cleary Coll., 1949, B.B.A., 1960, M.B.A., 1961, Sc.D., 1962; D.C.S., Drake Coll. Fla., 1964; m. Shirley Jean Coker, Dec. 7, 1946; children—Carol Ann Greig Butler, Walter C. Admitted to Tex. bar, 1931, Fed. Ct. Bar for Western Dist. Tex., 1932, U.S. Supreme Ct. bar, 1942, Mich. bar, 1946; practice law, Austin, 1931-41, Detroit, 1946; sec. bd. trustees Cleary Coll., 1950-70, treas. bd. trustees, 1970-74, exec. v.p., 1951-70, pres., 1970-74, pres. emeritus, 1974—, also trustee. Pres. Ypsilanti Area Indsl. Devel. Corp., 1973-74. Exec. sec. Mich. Liquor Control Commn., 1947-48; Mich. indsl. ambassador, 1962-63; pres. Estabrook PTA, 1960-61; mem. Ypsilanti Bd. Commerce, Police and Firemen's Pension Commn., 1973—; chmn. Ypsilanti City Compensation Comm., 1973-80, City Tax Bd. Rev., 1977-79. Served with M.I., AUS, 1941-46; lt. col. Res. ret. Recipient honors Mich. Legislature, 1974, Mayor of Ypsilanti, 1974; named hon. Ky. col. Mem. Res. Officers Assn. (past chpt. pres.), Am. Legion (post comdr. 1977—), Internat. Platform Assn., Am. Bus. Law Assn., Mil. Order Fgn. Wars (past comdr. Mich.), NEA, Mich. Edn. Assn., Nat. Bus. Tchrs. Assn., Mich. Secondary Sch. Assn., State Bar Mich., State Bar Tex., Nat. Counter-Intelligence Corps Assn. (v.p. Mich. 1980—), Royal Order Scotland, U. Tex. Ex-Students Assn. (pres. Detroit-Toledo chpt. 1976-77). Republican. Clubs: Masons (Gold Y honor award York Rite Coll., 33 deg.; high priest, illustrious master); K.T., Shriners, Jesters, Kiwanis (Legion of Honor); Econ. (Detroit); Washtenaw High Twelve (pres. 1975-76). Author: History of Austin, Texas, 1936. Home: 1223 Washtenaw St Ypsilanti MI 48197

GREINER, EDWARD DAVID, indsl. mfg. exec.; b. Peoria, Ill., Mar. 11, 1920; s. Fritz O. and Ethel K. (Mohn) G.; student U. Ill., 1937-38; B.S., Bradley U., 1941; m. Dorothy M. Janssen, July 31, 1943; children—David (dec.), Joel, Dan, Mark A., John R. Acct., R.G. LeTourneau, Inc., Peoria, 1941-42, asst. treas., 1946-53, sec.-treas. LeTourneau-Westinghouse Co., Peoria, 1953-59; v.p. fin. Westinghouse Air Brake Co., Pitts., 1959-63; v.p. Cherry-Burrell Corp., Chgo., 1963-64; asst. to pres. Masonite Corp., Chgo., 1965-70, v.p. adminstrn., 1970-77, exec. v.p., 1977—, also dir.; dir. Binks Mfg. Co., Franklin Park, Ill. Chmn. bd. Luth. Charities No. Ill.; bd. dirs. Met. YMCA, Chgo. Served to lt. USNR, 1942-46. Home: 34 Princeton Rd Hinsdale IL 60521 Office: 29 N Wacker Dr Chicago IL 60606

GREIVE, WILLIAM HENRY, chemist; b. Bowling Green, Ohio, Dec. 30, 1933; s. Henry Fredrick and Bernadine (Hagemeyer) G.; B.A., U. Toledo, 1976; m. Teresa Mae Pierce, Nov. 16, 1957; children—Roger F., Susan L. Technician, Toledo Edison Co., 1952-59; chemist Continental Aviation & Engring. Corp., Toledo, 1959-60; chemist Owens-Ill. Inc., Toledo, 1960—; cons. Analytical Chemistry Lab.; lectr. instrumental chemistry U. Toledo; substitute instr. chemistry Community Tech. Coll., Toledo. Mem. Parks Com. Maumee (Ohio), 1975-78, Maumee Parks and Recreation Commn., 1979—; Republican precinct chmn., 1978—. Mem. Am. Chem. Soc., Soc. Plastics Engrs., ASTM, Sigma Xi. Episcopalian. Contbr. articles in field to profl. jours. Home: 1441 Bradshaw Ct Maumee OH 43537 Office: 1700 N Westwood Ave Box 1035 Toledo OH 43666

GREKO, PHILIP JOREN, chiropractic physician; b. Moline, Ill., Aug. 2, 1950; s. Richard Leland and Dorothy Alice (Kelly) G.; student Black Hawk Coll., 1969-71; B.A. cum laude, Augustana Coll., 1973; D.C. summa cum laude, Palmer Coll. of Chiropractic, 1977. Asso. instr. anatomy Palmer Coll. of Chiropractic, Davenport, Iowa, 1975-77, instr. X-ray and technique, 1977—; pvt. practice chiropractic physician, Moline, 1977—; team physician United Twp. High Sch., 1980—. Augustana Coll. scholar, 1971; Palmer Coll. of Chiropractic Presdl. scholar, 1973-77. Mem. Prairie State Chiropractic Assn., Am. Chiropractic Assn., Council on Diagnosis and Internal Disorders, Phi Theta Kappa, Beta, Beta, Beta, Pi Tau Delta. Seventh Day Adventist. Home: 4 Hilltop Dr Coal Valley IL 61240 Office: 719 16th St Moline IL 61265

GREMLING, ROBERT PAUL, newspaper mng. editor; b. Dayton, Ohio, Sept. 30, 1947; s. Richard Paul and Catherine Ann (Fecher) G.; B.A., U. Dayton, 1974. Mng. editor Beavercreek (Ohio) Daily News. Bd. dirs. Greene County chpt. Am. Cancer Soc., 1977-79. Served with AUS, 1967-70. Decorated Army Commendation medal. Office: 1342 N Fairfield Rd Beavercreek OH 45409*

GRENAWITZKE, HARRY EDWARD, county govt. public health ofcl.; b. Benton Harbor, Mich., Dec. 12, 1945; s. Harry Edward and Evelyn Louise (Heyboer) G.; A.S., Lake Mich. Coll., 1965; B.S. in Environ. Health, Ferris State Coll., 1969; M.P.H., U. Mich., 1974; m. Mary Ellen Gallagher, Oct. 16, 1971; 1 son, William Edward. Supervising sanitarian Berrien County Health Dept., Benton Harbor, Mich., 1969-73; asst. dir. environ. health Monroe County (Mich.) Health Dept., Monroe, 1974-75, dir. environ. health, 1975—; exec. bd. Center for Continuing Edn., U. Mich., 1978—; guest lectr. Sch. Public Health, U. Mich., 1980, 81. Diplomate Am. Acad. Sanitarians. Mem. Am. Public Health Assn., Mich. Public Health Assn. (chmn. environ. health div., 1979, 80), Am. Acad. Health Adminstrn., Nat. Environ. Health Assn., Mich. Environ. Health Assn., Mich. Assn. Local Environ. Health Adminstrs. Methodist. Office: 650 Stewart Rd Monroe MI 48161

GRENELL, JAMES HENRY, mfg. co. exec.; b. Mpls., Feb. 19, 1924; s. Harrison Morton and Harriet Elizabeth (Kuch) G.; B.B.A., U. Minn., 1947; grad. Advanced Mgmt. Program, Harvard, 1974; m. Naomi Betty Callerstrom, Sept. 15, 1945; children—Bonita Grenell Wolfe, Suzanne Naomi, Andrea Grenell Mendes. With Honeywell, Inc., Mpls., 1951—, accountant, 1951-56, div. controller, 1956-68, group controller, 1968-71, asst. corp. controller, 1971-74, v.p., controller, 1974—; mem. faculty Inst. Mgmt., U. Wis., 1960-69, Inst. Tech., U. Minn., Mpls., 1963-65; asso. dir. Mgmt. Center, Coll. St. Thomas, St. Paul, 1959-69. Bd. dirs. Mpls. Soc. for Blind, 1963-71, pres., 1970-71. Served to 1st lt. AUS, 1943-46; ETO. Mem. Fin. Execs. Inst., U. Minn. Coll. Bus. Adminstrn. Alumni Bd. (dir.), Alpha Kappa Psi. Republican. Congregationalist. Clubs: Harvard (Minn.); Edina (Minn.) Country. Contbr. articles to profl. jours. Home: 6200 Wyman Ave Edina MN 55436 Office: Honeywell Plaza Minneapolis MN 55408

GRESHAM, CHARLES WARN, educator; b. Dodge City, Kans., Feb. 12, 1946; s. Alvie Warn and Zora Matilda (Birney) G.; A.A., Colby Community Coll., 1976; B.S., Kans. State U., 1978, M.S., 1981; m. Linda Sharell Steele, Feb. 10, 1968; 1 son, Jeremy Warn. Mgr. feed mill Bucklin (Kans.) Coop. Exchange, 1970-74; agrl. tchr. Winfield (Kans.) High Sch., 1978—. Served with USN, 1964-70. Mem. Nat. Vocat. Assn., Kans. Vocat. Tchrs. Assn., Kans. Vocat. Agrl. Tchrs. Assn., NEA, Am. Legion, Jaycees, Alpha Tau Alpha. Republican. Presbyterian. Home: 0310 College St Winfield KS 67156 Office: Winfield High School Vocational Agriculture Dept 300 Viking Blvd Winfield KS 67156

GRETEMAN, FRANK HENRY, bishop; b. Willey, Iowa, Dec. 25, 1907; s. Bernard and Mary (Meissner) G.; A.B., Loras Coll., 1929; S.T.L., N. Am. Coll., Rome, Italy, 1932; J.C.L., Cath. U., 1937. Asst. pastor St. Augustine Ch., Spokane, Wash., 1933-35; pastor Assumption Ch., Merrill, Iowa, 1937-41, St. Michael's Ch., Sioux City, Iowa, 1941-50, Holy Spirit Ch., Carroll, Iowa, 1950-65; aux. bishop, vicar gen. Sioux City Diocese, 1965-70, bishop 1970—. Mem. Canon Law Soc. Am. Office: PO Box 1530 1821 Jackson St Sioux City IA 51104*

GRIBBLE, CHARLES EDWARD, educator, publisher; b. Lansing, Mich., Nov. 10, 1936; s. Charles P. and Elizabeth K. G.; B.A. with high honors, U. Mich., 1957; A.M. (Woodrow Wilson fellow), Harvard U., 1958; Internat. Research and Exchanges Bd. fellow and grantee Moscow State U. (USSR), 1960-61; Ph.D. in Slavic Langs., Harvard U., 1967. Lectr., instr., then asst. prof. Brandeis U., 1961-68; asst. prof. Ind. U., 1968-75; asso. prof. Slavic langs. Ohio State U., 1975—; vis. asso. prof. U. Va., 1977; pres., editor Slavica Pubs., 1966—. Am. Council Learned Socs. fellow, 1972. Mem. Linguistic Soc. Am., Modern Lang. Assn., Am. Assn. Tchrs. of Slavic and East European Langs., Linguistic Soc. Europe, Bulgarian Study Group, Am. Assn. S.E. European Studies, Soc. Slovene Studies, Soc. Polish Studies, AAUP, Phi Beta Kappa. Author: Russian Root List with a Sketch of Russian Word Formation, 1973; A Short Dictionary of 18th-Century Russian, 1976; Reading Bulgarian Through Russian, 1982; editor: Readings in the History of the Russian Language, 11th to 15th Centuries, 1974; Studies Presented to Professor Roman Jakobson by His Students, 1968; Medieval Slavic Texts, Vol. 1 Old and Middle Russian Texts, 1973; contbr. articles profl. jours. Office: Slavic Langs and Lits Ohio State University 1841 Millikin Rd Columbus OH 43210

GRIDER, JOSEPH KENNETH, clergyman, educator; b. Madison, Ill., Oct. 22, 1921; s. William S. and Elizabeth (Krone) G.; Th.B., Olivet Nazarene Coll., 1944, A.B., 1945; B.D., Nazarene Theol. Seminary, 1947; M.Div. Summa cum laude, Drew U., 1948, M.A., 1950; Ph.D., Glasgow U., 1952; postgrad Oxford (Eng.) U., 1964; m. Virginia Florence Ballard, July 4, 1942; children—Jennifer Elizabeth, Joseph Kenneth, II, Carol Christine. Ordained to ministry Church of the Nazarene, 1944; pastor chs., Ill., Mo., N.J., 1943-50, Glasgow, Scotland, 1950-51; tutor Hurlet Nazarene Coll., Glasgow, Scotland, 1950-52; asso. prof. philosophy and theology Pasadena (Calif.) Coll., 1952-53; asso. prof. theology Nazarene Theol. Seminary, Kansas City, Mo., 1953-64, prof., 1964—. Mem. Am., Wesleyan theol. socs. Author: Repentance unto Life, 1964; Taller My Soul, 1965; Entire Sanctification: The Distinctive Doctrine of Wesleyanism, 1980; author numerous poems; contbr. articles to encyclopedias, dictionaries, Bible commentaries. Office: 1700 E Meyer St Kansas City MO 64131

GRIDLEY, JOHN WILLIS, JR., mfg. co. exec.; b. Rochester, Minn., May 10, 1939; s. John Willis and Dorothy Janet (Root) G.; B.A., Hamline U., 1960; postgrad. Princeton U., 1961-62, Harvard U., 1973; m. Elizabeth Linda Lohn, Sept. 8, 1962; children—James, Janet, Richard. Securities analyst Value Line Investment Survey, N.Y.C., 1962-64; mgr. profit analysis Ford Motor Co., Dearborn, Mich., 1964-74; asst. controller Xerox Info. Products, El Segundo, Calif., 1974-76; controller TRW Energy Systems, Redondo Beach, Calif., 1976-79; v.p., controller McQuay-Perfex, Inc., Mpls., 1979—. Budget and taxation commr. City of Redondo Beach, 1976-80. Served with AUS, 1959. Mem. Fin. Execs. Inst. Republican. Congregationalist. Clubs: Harvard Bus. Sch. Minn., King Harbor Yacht, Masons. Home: 3408 Zenith Ave S Minneapolis MN 55416 Office: 5401 Gamble Dr PO Box 9316 Minneapolis MN 55440

GRIDLEY, MARK CHARLES, musician, educator, psychologist; b. Detroit, Jan. 5, 1947; s. Frederick William and Helen Lucille (Jones) G.; B.S., Mich. State U., 1969; M.S., Case Western Reserve U., 1970, Ph.D., 1977. Psychometrist, research asst. Case Western Reserve U. Hosp., Div. Neurology, 1971-73, lectr. music dept., 1971—; flutist, saxophonist Front Row Theater Orchestra, Cleve., 1974-76; free-lance jazz flutist, saxophonist, concert artist, Ohio, 1969—; cons. psychologist Cleve. Bd. Edn., 1977—; prof. psychology of music Baldwin-Wallace Coll., 1980—; vis. asst. prof. psychology John Carroll U., University Heights, Ohio, 1981—; guest lectr. jazz Ursuline Coll., John Carroll U.; jazz cons. Prentice-Hall, Worth, Ency. Brit., Cleve. Plain Dealer; jazz lectr. demonstrations Young Audiences of Greater Cleve. Recipient Best Flutist award, Notre Dame Collegiate Jazz Festival, 1968; USPHS Tng. grants, 1969. Mem. Am. Fedn. Musicians, Nat. Assn. Jazz Educators, Northeast Ohio Jazz Soc. Author: Jazz Styles, 1978; contbr. to Ency. Brit. Home: 3356 Desota St Cleveland Heights OH 44118 Office: Dept Psychology John Carroll U University Heights OH 44118

GRIES, JOHN PAUL, geologist; b. Washington, June 7, 1911; s. John Matthew and Ethel (Goff) G.; A.B. in Geology and Math., Miami U., Oxford, Ohio, 1932; M.S., U. Chgo., 1933, Ph.D. in Geology and Paleontology, 1935; m. Virginia Overbeck, July 5, 1933; children—John Charles, Donald Alan. Geologist, Ill. Geol. Survey, 1935-36; instr. S.D. Sch. Mines, 1936-37, asst. prof. geology, 1937-42, asso. prof., 1942-44, 46-49, prof., 1949-76, dean Grad. Div., 1966-76; geologist Magnolia Petroleum Co., Midland, Tex., 1944-46; geol. cons., 1976—; participant Paris Basin Study, Am. Geol. Inst., 1965. Mem. AIME, Geol. Soc. Am., Am. Assn. Petroleum Geologists, Sigma Xi. Republican. Club: Rotary. Contbr. numerous articles on geology and mineral resources of No. Great Plains and Rocky Mountain area to profl. publs. Home: 238 Saint Charles St Rapid City SD 57701 Office: care Sch Mines Rapid City SD 57701

GRIEVE, BONNIE-JO MCLEAN, physician, med. geneticist; b. N.Y.C., Jan. 1, 1949; d. Jesse Terry and Josephine (Stanton) G.; B.S., Cornell U., 1969; M.D., U. Utah, 1973; M.S. in Med. Genetics, U. Wis., 1979. Intern, U. Wis., Madison, 1973-74, resident in pediatrics, 1974-76, Stetler Found. postdoctoral fellow in clin. genetics, 1976-78, NIH postdoctoral fellow in molecular genetics, 1978-79; asst. prof. human genetics and pediatrics Med. Coll. Va., Richmond, 1979-81; asst. prof ob-gyn, Med. Sch. U. Wis., Milw., 1981—; regional med. adv., mem. Nat. Ski Patrol Systems, 1976—. Diplomate Am. Bd. Pediatrics, Am. Bd. Med. Genetics. Fellow Am. Acad. Pediatrics; mem. AMA, Am. Med. Women's Assn., Am. Soc. Human Genetics, Med. Soc. Wis., Phi Kappa Phi, Alpha Lambda Delta. Office: Mt Sinai Medical Center Milwaukee WI 53201

GRIFFIN, BOB FRANKLIN, state legislator Mo.; b. Braymer, Mo., Aug. 15, 1935; s. Benjamin Franklin and Mildred Elizabeth (Cowan) G.; B.S., U. Mo., Columbia, 1957, J.D., 1959; m. Linda Charlotte Kemper, Aug. 18, 1957; children—Julie Lynn, Jeffrey Scott. Admitted to Mo. bar, 1959; sr. partner firm Griffin, Luckenbill & Griffin, Cameron, Mo., 1962—; pros. atty. Clinton County, Cameron, 1963-70; mem. Mo. Ho. of Reps. from 10th Dist., 1970—, speaker pro tem, 1977-80, speaker, 1981—. Served with USAF, 1959-62. Decorated Air Force Commendatidn medal; recipient certificate appreciation Nat. Police Officers Assn. Am., 1972, Commerce and Indsl. Disting. Service award, 1978, Osteopathic Physicians and Surgeons Disting. Health Service award, 1978. Mem. Mo., Clinton County bar assns., Fellowship Christian Politicians (charter). Democrat. Methodist. Clubs: Rotary, Lions, Optimist, Cameron Sportsmanship. Home: 204 Benjamin Dr Cameron MO 64429 Office: 223 E 3d St Cameron MO 64429

GRIFFIN, GEORGE ANN, psychol. cons./evaluator; b. Evansville, Ind., Nov. 12, 1950; d. George Theophilus and Laura Evelyn (Burke) Griffin; B.A., U. Evansville, 1971; M. Ed., U. Louisville, 1976, doctoral candidate. Tchr., Cath. Diocese Evansville, 1971-73; computer programer/analyst Sears, Roebuck & Co., Louisville, 1973-75; counselor/tchr. Jefferson County Schs., Louisville, 1975-76; computer systems analyst Credithrift Financial Inc., Evansville, 1976-78; computer systems analyst/cons. Gaither, Koewler, Rohlfer, Luckett & Co., Evansville, 1979-80; psychol. evaluator Rehab. Center, Evansville, 1980—. Vol., Southwestern Indian Mental Health Assn., Evansville Psychiat. Children's Center; bd. dirs., mem. public policy com., chmn. edn. com. Vanderburgh County Mental Health Assn. membership chmn. Wessleman Park Nature Center Soc., 1977—. Certified sch. guidance counselor, Ky.; certified tchr., Ind. Mem. Am. Personnel and Guidance Assn., Assn. Specialists in Group Work, Phi Kappa Phi, Alpha Omicron Pi. Clubs: Jr. League (provisional com., tng. com.), Leadership Evansville, Evansville Country, Evansville Petroleum, Order Eastern Star, Order of Amaranth, Order White Shrine Jerusalem, Daus. Nile. Home: 131 Hartin Dr Evansville IN 47711 Office: 111 Main St Evansville IN 47708 also 3701 Bellemeade Ave Evansville IN 47715

GRIFFIN, JAMES ANTHONY, clergyman; b. Fairview Park, Ohio, June 13, 1934; s. Thomas Anthony and Margaret Mary (Hanousek) G.; B.A. magna cum laude, Borromeo Coll., 1954; J.C.L. magna cum laude, Pontifical Lateran U., 1963; J.D. summa cum laude, Cleve. State U., 1972. Ordained priest, Roman Cath. Ch., 1960; asso. pastor St. Jerome Ch., Cleve., 1960; sec.-notary Diocesan Tribunal, 1963-65, asst. chancellor, 1965-68, vice chancellor, 1968-73, chancellor Diocese of Cleve., 1973-78, vicar gen., 1978-79, pastor St. William, Euclid, Ohio, 1978-79, aux. bishop Diocese of Cleve., 1979—. Bd. dirs. Holy Family Cancer Home. 1973-78; bd. trustees St. Mary Sem., 1976-78; bd. dirs. Meals on Wheels, Euclid, 1978—; bd. dirs. Cath. Cemeteries Assn., 1978—. Mem. Am. Canon Law Soc., Am. Bar Assn., Ohio Bar Assn., Cath. Press Union (past sec.), Euclid Ministerial Assn. (pres. 1978-79).

GRIFFIN, JAMES EDWARD, physical therapist, educator; b. Columbus, Ohio, Dec. 17, 1922; s. Don Wallace and Belle (Eason) G.; A.B., Western Md. Coll., 1944; M.A., Duke U., 1948; Ph.D., U. Pa., 1959; m. Frances Lorraine Roberts, Sept. 22, 1948; children—Karl Edward, Bruce William, Karen Lorraine. Staff phys. therapist, Rocky Hill, Conn., 1948-53; asso. to prof. phys. therapy, U. Pa., Phila., 1953-70; prof. phys. therapy, SUNY, Buffalo, 1970-80, chmn. phys. therapy, 1970-74; prof. physiology and health sci. Ball State U., Muncie, Ind., 1980—, dir. program in phys. therapy, 1980—; nat. lectr. clin. and research aspects of ultrasound, 1970—; cons. Nat. Acad. Scis., 1974-76, FDA, 1976—. NIH grantee, 1963-65, Social and Rehab. Services grantee, 1967-70. Mem. Am. Phys. Therapy Assn. (chmn. sect. on research, 1968-70), Am. Congress Rehab. Medicine, AAAS, N.Y. Acad. Scis. Author: (with Karselis) Physical Agents for Physiçal Therapists, 1978; contbr. articles on ultrasonic energy to profl. publs. Home: Rural Route 12 Box 302 Muncie IN 47302 Office: Lucina Hall Ball State U Muncie IN 47306

GRIFFIN, JOSEPH LAWRENCE, transp. exec.; b. Utica, Miss., Sept. 5, 1951; s. Shallie, Jr., and Carrie B. (Lyle) G.; student U. Ill., 1969-71; cert. in transp. and traffic mgmt. Coll. Advanced Traffic,

1978; m. Rhonda Evans, July 28, 1970; children—Joel, Jerl, Rael, Marel. Supr. terminal ops. Consol. Rail Corp., Chgo., 1977-78, asst. terminal mgr., 1978-79; asst. terminal mgr. Pa. Truck Lines, Inc., Chgo., 1979-81; multimodal sales rep. Consol. Rail Corp., Chgo., 1981—; transp. cons., 1981—. Notary public. Mem. Intermodal Operating Com., Am. Mgmt. Assn., Piggyback Assn. Chgo., Kappa Alpha Psi. Home: 859 Greenbriar Ln Park Forest South IL 60466 Office: Room 664 Union Sta 516 W Jackson Blvd Chicago IL 60606

GRIFFIN, LLOYD MARCUS, electric utility exec.; b. Oakland, Calif., Nov. 23, 1917; s. Lloyd Marion and Louise (Frizell) G.; B.S., Va. Mil. Inst., 1939; m. Marie Bowen, May 31, 1941; children—Judith Elizabeth, Mark Lloyd, Wayne Bowen. Asst. dir. research Chesapeake & Ohio Ry. Co., Cleve., 1945-50; sr. asso. Booz, Allen & Hamilton, Chgo., 1950-58; dir. govt. sales Cummins Engine Co., Columbus, Ind., 1958-61; v.p. So. div. Pub. Service Co. Ind., Inc., Columbus, 1961-68, v.p. ops., Plainfield, 1968-78, sr. v.p. customer services, 1978—; past chmn. and dir. Food and Energy Council; chmn. Mktg. Execs. Conf. Mem. adv. bd. Central Ind. Jr. Achievement. Served to lt. col. USAAF, 1941-45. Decorated D.F.C., Air medal with four oak leaf clusters; recipient Disting. Service award Electric League Ind. Mem. Kappa Alpha. Clubs: Crooked Stick Golf, Indpls. Athletic. Office: 1000 E Main St Plainfield IN 46168

GRIFFIN, MARK HOWARD, automobile co. exec.; b. Cambridge, Ohio, June 28, 1953; s. William Howard and Wilma Arlene (Paden) G.; B.I.A., Gen. Motors Inst., 1976; M.B.A., Ohio State U., 1980. Maintenance supr. Fisher Body div. Gen. Motors Corp., Columbus, Ohio, 1976—. Asso. bd. dirs. Ohio Celebration, Inc. Mem. Am. Mgmt. Assn., Mid-Ohio Walking Horse Assn. (pres.), Buckeye Walking Horse Assn., Tenn. Walking Horse Breeders and Exhibitors Assn., Phi Delta Theta. Nazarene. Home: 4374 Hansen Dr Columbus OH 43220 Office: Fisher Body Div Gen Motors Corp 200 Georgesville Rd Columbus OH 43228

GRIFFIN, MARY VELMA SHOTWELL (MRS. JAMES LEONARD GRIFFIN), author; b. nr. Carrollton, O., Aug. 11, 1904; d. Winfield Scott and Eva Anaz (Smith) Shotwell; certificate elementary edn., Kent State U., 1925; m. James Leonard Griffin, Oct. 2, 1929. Accordionist, Radio Sta. WTAM, Cleve., 1926, Chatauqua and Lyceum circuits, 1927-28, Accordion Gypsies, 1931-48, Ringling Bros.-Barnum and Bailey Circus, 1935-36; tchr. pub. schs., Ohio, 1922-65; ret., 1965; now free lance writer. Gray lady, ARC, 1967—; bd. dirs. Bell-Herron Scholarship Found., 1965—; pres. Carroll County Hist. Soc., 1965-67, dir., 1963—, curator, 1967—. Recipient Disting. Service award Jaycees, 1979. Mem. NEA, Carroll County Ret. Tchrs. Assn., Ohio, Carroll County (pres. 1964-65) edn. assns., Ohio Hist. Soc., Ohio, Carroll County geneal. socs., Ohioana Library Assn. (county chmn. 1958—). Republican. Presbyterian. Clubs: Rebekah, Order Eastern Star. Author: Fair Prize, 1956; Circus Daze, 1957; Mystery Mansion, 1958; numerous short stories pub. in popular mags. Home: 11 Arch St Dellroy OH 44620

GRIFFIN, RAYMOND VERNON, educator; b. Paris, Ill., Jan. 24, 1925; s. Ray and Ethel (Fletcher) G.; B.S. in Edn., Eastern Ill. U., 19—, M.S., 1954; Ed.D., U. No. Colo., 1965; m. Catherine Doak, Feb. 14, 1948; children—David Ray, Janice Kay, Stephen Michael. Tchr. elementary sch. Community Unit Sch. Dist #4 Paris, Ill., 1950-58; prof. indsl. tech. Eastern Ill. U., Charleston, 1958—, coordinator student tchrs., 1972—; faculty U. No. Colo., summers 1966-67. Served with USAF, 1940-44. NDEA Inst. grantee, 1968. Mem. Am. Indsl. Arts Assn., Am. Vocat. Assn., Am. Council on Indsl. Arts Tchr. Edn., Phi Delta Kappa. Baptist. Home: Rural Route 3 Charleston IL 61920 Office: Eastern Illinois University Charleston IL 61920

GRIFFIN, ROBERT NOEL, constrn. co. exec.; b. Lapel, Ind., Jan. 15, 1923; s. Frank Thomas and Sarah Isabell (Kinder) G.; student Ind. Central Bus. Coll., 1941-43, 46; m. Rosemary Brown, June 15, 1946; children—Howard Kent, Robert Kirk. With McCalman Constrn. Co., Danville, Ill., 1946—, successively field clk., foreman, constrn. supt., 1959—. Served with AUS, 1943-46; PTO. Mem. Am. Legion. Republican. Baptist. Elk. Home: 3711 Cornell Ave Danville IL 61832 Office: Box 854 Danville IL 61832

GRIFFIN, WALTER ROLAND, historian; b. Carbondale, Pa., Nov. 20, 1942; s. Walter Joseph and Maud Loftus (Boland) G.; B.A., Loyola Coll., Balt., 1963; M.A., U. Cin., 1964; m. Mary Eleanor Armstrong, Aug. 16, 1961; children—Becky, Kathy, Shawn; m. 2d, Penni Oncken Kerr, Dec. 6, 1980. Lectr. in history Xavier U., Cin., 1965-66; asst. prof. history Mt. St. Mary's Coll., Emmitsburg, Md., 1967-68; asst. prof. history Upper Iowa U., Fayette, Iowa, 1966-67, 68—, chairperson div. of social scis. and bus. adminstrn., also chairperson history dept., 1969-78, asso. acad. dean, 1977-78, varsity tennis coach, 1979—, supr. program devel., 1981—. Mem. City Council City of Fayette, 1971-76; chairperson Fayette County Democratic Com., 1972-77, 78-80, 2d Iowa Congl. Dist. Campaign Com., 1974-77; mem. Iowa Dem. Central Com., 1974-78; Dem. candidate for sec. state Iowa, 1978. Md. State scholar, 1959-63; Taft Teaching fellow U. Cin., 1963-64; research grantee Colo., N.J. hist. socs. 1971-72. Recipient Voter Identification Program award Iowa Democratic party, 1974. Mem. Am. Hist. Assn., Orgn. Am. Historians, Soc. Historians Am. Fgn. Relations, Iowa State Hist. Soc., Iowa Higher Edn. Assn., Phi Alpha Theta, Pi Gamma Mu. Unitarian. Contbr. articles to profl. pubis. Home: PO Box 384 105 Alexander St Fayette IA 52142 Office: Upper Iowa Univ History Dept Fayette IA 52142

GRIFFIN, WILLIAM JULIAN, II, machinery mfg. co. exec.; b. Indpls., Feb. 10, 1925; s. Frank Julian Cox and Mary (Williams) G.; student Butler U., 1942-43, Citadel, 1943-44; grad. Ind. Bus. Coll., 1948; m. Mary Jane Noel, Apr. 24, 1953; children—William Julian III, Kevin L., Kirk E., Kerry J. Buyer, Griffin Realty Corp., 1946-47; prodn. mgr. Griffin Engring. Co., Worthington, Inc., 1949-51; sec.-treas., gen. mgr. Imperial Machine & Tool Corp., Worthington, 1952-53; v.p., gen. mgr., dir. So. Ind. Machine Co., Inc., Worthington, 1954-60, pres., gen. mgr., dir. Griffin Engring. div., 1961—; pres., dir. GBF Dodge, Inc., Casa Grande, Ariz., 1964—; owner, mgr. Griffin Audit Service, 1965—. Bd. dirs. Hulen Meml. Youth Center. Served with AUS, 1943-46, 50. Mem. Am. Ordnance Assn., Am. Legion (past local comdr.), D.A.V. (life), V.F.W. Mem. Disciples of Christ Ch. Mason (Shriner). Elk. Home: 208 Christian St Worthington IN 47471 Office: Southern Ind Machine Co Inc 3d and Williams Sts Worthington IN 47471 also Gila Bend Hwy Casa Grande AZ 85222

GRIFFIN, WILLIAM LESTER HADLEY, shoe co. exec.; b. Edwardsville, Ill., May 17, 1918; s. Ralph D. and Julia (Hadley) G.; A.B., Williams Coll., 1940; LL.B., Washington U., 1947; m. Phoebe M. Perry, Apr. 1, 1942; children—Dustin H. II, Lockwood Perry, Peter Burley. Admitted to Mo. bar, 1947; counsel Wohl Shoe Co., St. Louis, 1947-51, asst. sec. treas., 1950-51; sec. Brown Shoe Co. (name changed to Brown Group, Inc. 1972), St. Louis, 1954-64, v.p., 1964-66, exec. v.p., 1966-68, pres., 1968-72, chief exec. officer, 1969-72, 79—, chmn. bd., 1972—, pres., 1972-79, chmn. exec. com., 1971-79, also dir.; dir., dep. chmn. Fed. Res. Bank of St. Louis; dir. Gen. Am. Life Ins. Co., Owens-Corning Fiberglas Corp. Trustee Washington U., Williams Coll., 1975-80, Henry J. Kaiser Family Found., David Ranken Jr. Sch.; pres. St. Louis Symphony Soc., Assn.; bd. dirs. Govtl. Research Inst., Mo. Pub. Expenditure Survey, Arts and Edn. Council St. Louis; pres. United Fund Greater St. Louis, 1973, campaign chmn., 1972; pres. Civic Progress, Inc., 1972-74. Served from ensign to lt. USNR, 1941-45; as lt. comdr., Korea, 1951-52. Mem. Am. Footwear Industries Assn. (past chmn.). Republican. Home: Mason Rd Saint Louis MO 63131 Office: 8400 Maryland Ave Saint Louis MO 63105

GRIFFITH, CALVIN ROBERTSON, baseball club exec.; b. Montreal, Que., Can., Dec. 1, 1911; s. James and Jane (Davies) Robertson; adopted by Clark C. Griffith, 1923; brought to U.S., 1921; ed. Staunton Mil. Acad., 1928-32, George Washington U., 1932-35; m. Natalie N. Niven, Feb. 1, 1940; children—Clark C., N. Corinne, Clare. Sec. Chattanooga Baseball Club, 1935-37, pres., 1937, mgr., 1937; pres., mgr., treas. Charlotte Club, 1938-41; v.p. Washington, Am. League Baseball Club, 1943-55, pres., 1955-61; pres. Minn. Twins, Am. League, 1961—, also chmn. bd.; v.p. Am. League Profl. Baseball; mem. planning com. Profl. Baseball, also rules com. Named Baseball exec. of Year, 1965. Mem. Am. Legion (v.p.). Presbyterian. Address: care Minn Twins Metropolitan Stadium 8001 Cedar Ave Bloomington MN 55420*

GRIFFITHS, RICHARD LYLE, educator; b. Aberdeen, S.D., Feb. 7, 1935; s. Charles Edward and Lillian Ada (Jones) G.; B. Music Edn., U. Wichita, 1964; M. Music Edn., Wichita State U., 1966; D. Mus. Arts, U. Washington, 1979; student Douglas Robinson, Royal Opera House, London, 1966-67, Louis Halsey BBC, 1966-67, David Willcocks, Cambridge, 1967. Dir. choral activities Monmouth (Ill.) Coll., 1967—. Program chmn. Community Concert Lecture bd., Monmouth, Ill.; minister music Woodlawn Christian Ch., Wichita, Kans., 1961-66, Baptist Ch., Galesburg, Ill., 1967-71, First United Methodist Ch., Monmouth, 1971-74. Served with USAF, 1957-61. Mem. Am. Choral Dirs. Assn., Music Educators Nat. Conf., Ill. Music Educators Assn., AAUP, Coll. Music Soc. Methodist. Home: 301 N 5th St Monmouth IL 61462 Office: Music Department Monmouth College Monmouth IL 61462

GRIFFITHS, ROBERT HENRY, dentist; b. Kirksville, Mo., Aug. 29, 1921; s. Henry and Emma Catherine (Skinner) G.; student N.E. Mo. State Coll., 1939-41; D.D.S., Loyola U., 1944; m. Patricia Ellen Sanberg, Dec. 29, 1979; children—Robert Henry, Marian E., Andrew M., Margot E., Dana L. Gen. practice dentistry, Lincoln, Ill., 1947, Charleston, Ill., 1948—; resident in anesthesia Doctors Hosp., Washington, 1958-59. Mem. Dist. Bd. Edn., 1958-67, sec. bd., 1959-66. Served with Dental Corps, U.S. Army, 1944-47. Recipient Scholastic award Blue Key; named Alumnus of Yr., Loyola U. Dental Sch. Fellow Internat. Coll. Dentists, Am. Coll. Dentists, Am. Dental Soc. Anesthesia; mem. ADA (trustee, pres.), Ill. State Dental Soc. (pres.), Eastern Ill. Dental Soc. (pres., mem. dist. council), Chgo. Dental Soc., Flying Dentists, Federation Dentaire International, Am. Assn. Dental Cons. Republican. Methodist. Clubs: Carlton, Barclay, Rotary (pres., chmn. dist. conf.), Masons, Elks (lodge exalted ruler 1950-51, dist. dep. grand exalted ruler 1952-54). Office: 1063 10th PO Box 177 Charleston IL 61920*

GRIGGY, BERNADETTE AGNES, nurse, educator; b. Detroit, Jan. 6, 1924; d. Gaylord William and Nellie Avelina (Meagher) Gump; B.S., U. Akron, 1959; M.S. in Nursing Edn., U. Pitts., 1969; Ed.D., U. Akron, 1980; m. Carl E. Griggy, Feb. 1, 1947; 1 son, David E. Staff nurse Robinson Meml. Hosp., Ravenna, Ohio, 1946-47; asst. charge nurse St. Thomas Hosp., Akron, Ohio, 1947-56, coordinator basic nursing and mangerial aspects Sch. Nursing, 1953-63, dir. nursing edn., 1963-76; chmn. div. health scis. and dept. nursing Marymount Coll. of Kans., Salina, 1980—. Mem. Am. Nurses Assn., Assn. Supervision and Curriculum Devel., Nat. League Nursing, U. Akron Alumni Assn., Am. Assn. Colls. Nursing, Alpha Sigma Lambda, Phi Delta Kappa, Sigma Phi Epsilon, Sigma Theta Tau, Kappa Delta Epsilon. Roman Catholic. Club: Soroptimist Internat. (corr. sec.). Home: 534 Winn Rd Salina KS 67401 Office: Marymount Coll Kans Salina KS 67401

GRIGSBY, GEORGE RICHARD, supt. schs.; b. West Baden Springs, Ind., Sept. 2, 1927; s. Floyd H. and Eva E. (Richardson) G.; B.S., Ind. U., 1950, M.S., 1952, Ed.D., 1970; m. Carolyn Jane Bonham, Aug. 15, 1954; children—Carol Lynn, Susan Mary, Jane Elizabeth. Tchr. public schs., Gary, Ind., 1951-57; prin. Nobel Elem. Sch., Gary, 1957-62; asst. prin. Wirt High Sch., Gary, 1962-66; prin. Horace Mann High Sch., Gary, 1966-71; asst. supt. schs. Highland, Ind., 1971-75; supt. schs. Neenah (Wis.) Joint Sch. Dist., 1975—. Served with USN, 1945-46. John Hay Humanities fellow, 1966. Mem. Wis. Assn. Sch. Dist. Adminstrs., Am. Assn. Sch. Adminstrs., Nat. Elem. Sch. Prins., Ind. U. Alumni Assn. (pres. 1966), Phi Delta Kappa. Clubs: Neenah Rotary (dirs. 1980-82), Kiwanis (dir. 1966-67). Home: 1214 Glenayre Dr Neenah WI 54956 Office: 410 S Commercial St Neenah WI 54956

GRILK, ERNEST WALTER, interior designer; b. Davenport, Iowa, July 25, 1929; s. Ernst Adolf and Alma Margaret (Koster) G.; diploma interior design Chgo. Acad.Fine Arts, 1951; m. Gloria Christine Febro, July 26, 1953; children—Karen Christine, Cynthia Elizabeth, Cornelia Margaret Marie. Asst. interior design Anita Bingham, Chgo., 1951-52; interior designer, partner family firm Davenport, 1952-67; owner, operator Grilk Interiors Co., Davenport, 1967—, Grilk Fine Arts Gallery, Davenport, 1978—. Adv. bd. Interior Design dept. Scott Community Coll. pres. Village of East Davenport (Iowa) Assn., 1973-74, also bd. dirs.; active Community Drug Abuse program; bd. dirs. Davenport Family Y. Recipient Rorimer Medal, 1950, Gift and Decorative Accessories Nat. Merit award, 1969. Mem. Davenport C. of C. (dir. 1978-81), Am. Soc. Interior Designers (profl.)(treas. Nebr.-Iowa chpt. 1978-80), Internat. Y's Men Assn. (internat. council 1975-77). Republican. Methodist. Club: Rotary (chmn. world and community service com. Davenport 1978—). Home: 1525 Farnam St Davenport IA 52803 Office: 2200 E 11th St Davenport IA 52803

GRILL, JOSEPH CHARLES, electronics mfg. co. exec.; b. Chgo., Aug. 2, 1944; s. Francis Terence and Rita Ann G.; B.S., Loyola U., Chgo., 1967, M.S., 1972; m. Rose Caroline Montana, Oct. 29, 1966; children—Francis Terence, Joseph Charles, David Anthony. Staff cons. labor relations Western Electric Co., Chgo., 1970-73; mgr. benefits and compensation, mgr. manpower planning and devel. CFS Continental, Inc., Chgo., 1973-78; dir. manpower devel. Bunker Ramo Corp., Oak Brook, Ill., 1978—; sr. class instr. St. Patrick High Sch., 1968-70. Mem. Indsl. Relations Assn. Chgo., Orgn. Renewal, Inc., Am. Mgmt. Assn. Democrat. Roman Catholic. Home: 794 11th Ave Addison IL 60101 Office: 900 Commerce Dr Oak Brook IL 60101

GRIMES, DAVID LYNN, telephone co. exec.; b. Oklahoma City, June 9, 1947; s. Glenn Ross and Kathleen Sue (Starns) G.; student Oklahoma City Coll., 1970-71; B.B.A., Central State U., 1978; m. Sandra Kay Belt, Mar. 6, 1970; children—David Edwin, Emily Kathleen. With Southwestern Bell Telephone Corp., Oklahoma City, 1970-79, communications mktg. mgr., 1974-75, account exec., 1975-76, data specialist, 1976-77, account mgr., 1977-78, mgr. industry processing, 1978-79, dist. staff supr., 1979-80, dist. staff mgr., St. Louis, 1980, mktg. mgr., Kansas City, Kans., 1981—; dir. Del Paint Mfg. Corp. (Okla.). Served with U.S. Army, 1966-68. Recipient Disting. Salesman award Oklahoma City Sales and Mktg. Assn., 1975. Mem. Petroleum Electric Supply Assn, Internat. Brotherhood Magicians. Republican. Methodist. Clubs: Masons, Shriners. Home: 11811 W 99th Terr Overland Park KS 66214 Office: Southwestern Bell Telephone Corp Suite 600 Mission KS 66202

GRIMES, HUGH GAVIN, physician; b. Chgo., Aug. 19, 1929; s. Andrew Thomas and Anna (Gavin) G.; student Loyola Acad., 1943-47, Loyola U., 1947-50; B.S., U. Ill., 1952, M.D., 1954; m. Rose Anne Leahy, Aug. 21, 1954; children—Hugh Gavin, Paula Anne, Daniel Joseph, Sarah Louise, Nancy Marie, Jennifer Diane. Intern St. Joseph Hosp., Chgo., 1954-55, resident obstetrics and gynecology, 1955-58; pvt. practice obstetrics and gynecology, Chgo., 1960—; lectr. Stritch Sch. Medicine Loyola U., Chgo.; active staff St. Joseph Hosp., Chgo., also mem. exec. adv. bd., v.p. med. staff, 1977-78, pres. staff, 1979-80; courtesy staff St. Francis Hosp., Evanston, Ill.; asst. prof. clin. obstetrics and gynecology Northwestern U. Med. Sch., 1980—. Mem. lay adv. bd. Regina Dominican High Sch. Served to capt. M.C., AUS, 1958-60. Diplomate Am. Bd. Obstetrics and Gynecology. Fellow Am. Coll. Obstetrics and Gynecology, Chgo. Gynecol. Soc.; mem. Am. Assn. Maternal and Infant Health, Am. Cancer Soc. (mem. profl. edn. com. Chgo. unit), Am. Fertility Soc., A.M.A., Ill., Chgo. med. socs., Cath. Physicians Guild, Assn. Am. Physicians and Surgeons, Am. Soc. for Colposcopy and Colpomicroscopy, Am. Assn. Gynecologic Laparoscopists, Assn. Art Inst. Chgo., Assn. Field Mus., Assn. Smithsonian Instn., Pi Kappa Epsilon. Contbr. articles to profl. jours. Office: 5214 N Western Ave Chicago IL 60625

GRIMES, JOHN EDWARD, JR., psychologist; b. Murphysboro, Ill., July 16, 1933; s. John Edward and Lorene Anna (Vaughn) G.; B.A., So. Ill. U., 1955, M.A., 1962; Ph.D., U. Ariz., 1974; m. Nancy Lynn Wickiser, June 15, 1961; children—John Michael, Kathlyn Elene, Karen Elizabeth. Rehab. counselor Tex. Rehab. Commn., Houston, 1961-66; psychologist Ariz. Tng. Center, Tucson, 1966-68; psychologist Counseling Center Eastern Ill. U., Charleston, Ill., 1968-80; pvt. practice clin. psychology, 1981—; chief examiner G.E.D. Test, Charleston, 1969—; cons. psychologist Shelby County Mental Health Center, Shelbyville, Ill., 1970-71, Moultrie County Mental Health Center, Sullivan, Ill., 1975-77, Douglas County Mental Health Center, Tuscola, Ill., 1980—; psychologist Fed. Disability Program, Charleston, 1971—. Bd. dirs. Coles County Mental Health Assn., v.p., 1972, 76, pres., 1973, treas., 1975. Served to sgt. AUS, 1955-58. Mem. Am., Ill. psychol. assns., Acad. Psychologists in Marital, Sex and Family Therapy, Am. Assn. Sex Educators, Counselors and Therapists, Am. Assn. on Mental Deficiency, Am. Assn. on Suicidology, Am. Personnel and Guidance Assn., Nat., Ill. rehab. assns., Nat., Ill. rehab. counseling assns., Coles County Mental Health Assn., Coles County Assn. for Retarded, Am. Soc. Clin. Hypnosis (chmn. liaison com.). Home: 723 Olean Pl Charleston IL 61920 Office: 1510 University Dr Suite 105 Charleston IL 61920

GRIMES, ROBERT E., coll. dean; b. Chapman, Ala.; s. Felix F. and Myra (Harris) G.; B.S., Ala. State U., 1949; M.A., W.Va. U., 1963; Sc.D. (hon.), London Inst., 1972; 1 son, Robert Earl. Asst. prin. Robert L. Austin High Sch., Georgiana, Ala., 1949-64; chmn. dept. sci. Washington Jr. Coll., Pensacola, Fla., 1964-65; instr. Howard W. Black High Sch., Tampa, Fla., 1965-67; nat. teaching fellow Central State U., Wilberforce, Ohio, 1967-68, isntr., 1968-69; asst. dean for evening programs Loop Coll./City Colls. of Chgo., 1969-80, asst. dean adminstrv. services, 1980—; pres. Loretto Adult Edn. Center, 1978-80. Regional v.p. Nat. Consumers Health Council, 1972-74; sec. Greater Lawndale Conservation Commn., 1971. Served with USN, 1943-46. NSF grantee, 1959-67. Mem. U.S. Assn. Evening Students (hon. trustee), Assn. for Continuing Higher Edn., Adult Student Personnel Assn. (pres. 1975-77), Am. Coll. Personnel Assn., Alpha Phi Alpha. Democrat. Baptist. Office: Loop Coll Evening Programs 64 E Lake St Chicago IL 60601

GRIMLEY, LIAM KELLY, educator; b. Dublin, Ireland, Apr. 4, 1936; s. William and Eileen (Kelly) G.; came to U.S., 1970; B.A., Nat. U. Ireland, 1960; L.Ph., Faculté Libre, Paris, 1963; H.D.Ed., Clongowes Wood Coll., Ireland, 1964; Th.B., Inst. Philosophy and Theology, Dublin, 1968, S.T.L., 1970; M.Ed., Kent State U., 1971, Ph.D., 1973; m. Marie Sadon, Aug. 26, 1973; children—Kevin, Conor. English teacher Lycée Moderne, Le Puy, France, 1961-62; asst. dir. Summer Sch. English, Observatorio del Ebro, Tortosa, Spain, 1961-62; tchr. math. and modern langs. Clongowes Wood High Sch., Ireland, 1963-64; tchr. math. and classical langs. St. Ignatius Elementary and Secondary Sch., Galway, Ireland, 1964-66; instr. statistics and probability theory Univ. Coll., Galway, Ireland, 1965-66; prof. theology Conf. Major Religious Superiors, Dublin, 1969-70; counselor Newman Center, Syracuse U., 1970; social studies tchr. Walsh Jesuit High Sch., Cuyahoga Falls, Ohio, 1971; asst. dir. Ohio Soc. Crippled Children and Adults, Tiffin, summer 1971; intern sch. psychologist Field Local Sch. Dist., Ohio, 1972-73; research and devel. dir. lab. sch. Kent State U., 1972-73; prof. spl. edn., Ind. State U., Terre Haute, 1973—, chmn. dept., 1975-81, dir. Inst. Continuing Edn. in Psychology, 1976-78; cons. Joseph P. Kennedy Found., 1973—; mem. State Adv. Com., Div. Pupil Personnel, 1975—. Mem. Ind. State Manpower Steering Com., 1977-80. Mem. Am., Ind. psychol. assns., Nat. Assn. Sch. Psychologists. Roman Catholic. Contbr. articles to profl. jours.; editor The Sch. Psychology Digest, 1976-79; contbg. editor Growing Child. Home: 43 Allendale Terre Haute IN 47802 Office: Ednl Psychology and Sch Psychology Dept Ind State U Terre Haute IN 47809

GRIMMER, DENNIS L., educator, city ofcl.; b. Belleville, Ill., Apr. 23, 1949; s. Paul P. and Margaret G.; B.S., So. Ill. U., Edwardsville, 1971, M.S., 1975, Ed. Adminstrn. cert., 1979; m. Mary Elizabeth Stolte, Aug. 23, 1969; children—Edwin Paul, Amy Elizabeth. Tchr., coach Berekley (Mo.) Sr. High Sch., 1971-73; tchr., coach, head dept. history O'Fallon (Ill.) High Sch., 1973—; mem. adv. council to dept. history So. Ill. U., Edwardsville. Mem. O'Fallon Planning Commn., 1977-78; alderman O'Fallon City Council, 1978—. Recipient Tenco grant, 1980, Model UN Sponser Award, 1978, 81. Named Tchr. of Yr., O'Fallon High Sch., 1977. Mem. Nat. Hist. Soc., Nat. Council Social Studies, So. Ill. Mayors Council, Am. Fedn. Tchrs., Ill. Fedn. Tchrs. Roman Catholic. Democrat. Clubs: O'Fallon City Softball League, O'Fallon Boosters, O'Fallon History, O'Fallon Sportsmen. Home: 913 Juniper St O'Fallon IL 62269 Office: 600 S Smiley St O'Fallon IL 62269

GRIMMER, MARGOT, dancer, choreographer; b. Chgo., Apr. 5, 1944; d. Vernon and Ann (Radville) Grimmer; student Lake Forest Coll., 1963, Northwestern U., 1964-68. Dancer, N.Y.C. Ballet prodn. of Nutcracker, Chgo., 1956-57, Kansas City Starlight Theater, 1958, St. Louis Mcpl. Theater, 1959, Chgo. Tent House-Music Theater, 1960-61, Lyric Opera Ballet, Chgo., 1961, 63-66, 68, Ballet Russe de Monte Carlo, N.Y.C., 1962, Ruth Page Internat. Ballet, Chgo., 1965-70; dancer-choreographer Am. Dance Co., Chgo., 1972—, artistic dir., 1972—; dancer, choreographer Bob Hope Show, Milw., 1975, Washington D.C. Bicentennial Performance, 1976, Woody Guthrie Benefit Concerts, 1976-77, Assyrian Cultural Found., Chgo., 1977-78; dir.-tchr. Am. Dance Sch., 1971—; appeared in TV commls. and indsl. films for Libbys Foods, Sears, Gen. Motors, others, 1963-81; soloist in ballet Repertory Workshop, CBS-TV, 1964, dance film Statics (Internat. Film award), 1967; soloist in concert Ravinia, 1973. Ill. Arts Council grantee, 1972-74, 78, Nat. Endowment for

Arts grantee, 1973-74. Mem. Actors Equity Assn., Screen Actors Guild, Am. Guild Mus. Artists. Important works include ballets In-A-Gadda-Da-Vida, 1972, The Waste Land, 1973, Rachmaninoff: Theme and Variations, 1973, Le Baiser de la Fec and Sonata, 1974, Four Quartets, 1974, Am. Export, 1975, Earth, Wind and Fire, 1976, Blood, Sand and Empire, 1977, Disco Fever, 1978, Pax Romana, 1979, Xanadu, 1980, others. Home: 970 Vernon Ave Glencoe IL 60022 Office: 442 Central Ave Highland Park IL 60035

GRINE, FLORENCE MAY, secondary sch. tchr.; b. Sycamore, Ohio, Apr. 21, 1927; d. Murray J. and Ethel C. (Kingseed) G.; B.S., Bowling Green (Ohio) State U., 1949, M.Ed., 1966. Tchr. schs. in Ohio, 1949—; tchr. bus. edn. Tiffin (Ohio) Columbian High Sch., 1960—, chmn. dept., 1970—. Mem. NEA, Nat. Bus. Edn. Assn., Ohio Edn. Assn., N.W. Ohio Edn. Assn., Ohio Vocat. Assn., Ohio Bus. Tchrs. Assn., Tiffin Edn. Assn. (pres. 1965), Columbia Tchrs. Assn., Tiffin Bus. and Profl. Women (pres. 1955, 63), Daus. Am., Alpha Sigma (past chpt. pres.), Delta Kappa Gamma (trustee A. Margaret Boyd Scholarship Fund, chmn. various coms. Ohio chpt.). Republican. Presbyterian. Club: Tiffin Woman's. Office: 300 S Monroe St Tiffin OH 44883

GRINSTEAD, LEONARD SYLVESTER, elec. and electronics engr.; b. East Palestine, Ohio, Dec. 27, 1939; s. Sylvester Leonard and Dorothy Catherine (McClellan) G.; A.A.S. in Computer Tech., Youngstown (Ohio) State U.; m. Patricia Ann Jacobson, Aug. 22, 1961; children—Leonard Mark, Mary Patricia. Systems analyst Newark (Ohio) Air Force Sta., 1962-64; electronics technician instr. Youngstown AFB, Vienna, Ohio, 1964-65; electronics instr. A.T.E.S. Tech. Sch., Niles, Ohio, 1965-66; sr. electronics design engr. Automatic Sprinkler Corp., Cleve., 1966-68; quality control engr. Economy Engine Co., Girard, Ohio, 1968-72; sr. electronics design engr. Fox Industries, Inc., Youngstown, 1972-74; elec./electronics engr. Trumbull Cons., Inc., Canfield, Ohio, 1974-78; elec. engr. Copperweld Steel Co., Warren, Ohio, 1978—. Served with USN, 1957-60. Mem. Assn. Iron and Steel Engrs., Am. Soc. Metals, Trumbull County Indsl. Mgmt. Assn., Copperweld Mgmt. Club. Roman Catholic. Home: 245 Sleepy Hollow Dr Canfield OH 44406 Office: 4000 Mahoning Ave Warren OH 44482

GRIPARIS, JOHN GEORGE, real estate mktg. mgr.; b. Joliet, Ill., July 22, 1936; s. Geroge Andrew and Angeline G.; B.S. in Bus. Adminstrn., Ill. Wesleyan U., 1957; postgrad. U. Ill., 1957-58; m. Georgiann Kontos, Feb. 5, 1961; children—Ellen J., George S., John George. Partner, mgr. comml. div. Shreeve Realty Co., Joliet, 1967-76; comml. real estate broker, 1976-78; new home mktg. ofcl. U.S. Home, 1978-79; mktg. mgr. Parkway Devel. Co., Schiller Park, Ill., 1979—. Pres. All Saints Ch., Greater Joliet YMCA, Troy Sch. Dist. Mem. Leyden Bd. Realtors, O'Hare Group Realtors Bus. and Industry (dir.), Ill. Assn. Realtors, Nat. Assn. Realtors. Greek Orthodox. Club: Kiwanis (dir.). Office: 9950 W Lawrence Ave Schiller Park IL 60176

GRISCOM, DAVID DREW, city adminstr.; b. Macon, Ga., Nov. 9, 1947; s. John Hollingsworth and Louise Lyons (Lacy) G.; B.A. in Polit. Sci., North Ga. Coll., 1969; M.P.A., U. Mo., Kansas City, 1976; m. Margaret Ann Orvis, Jan. 22, 1972; children—Marie Louise, David Andrew. Timekeeper, Rust Engring., Perry, Ga., 1969-70; collection mgr. GAC, Inc., Atlanta, 1970-71; agt. Prudential Ins. Co., Columbus, Ga., 1972; mgr. Ed's Men's Wear, Phenix City, Ala., 1972-73; asst. mgr. Nat. Shirt Shops, Kansas City, Mo., 1973-74; asst. to dir. public works City of Independence (Mo.), 1977-81; city adminstr. Eldon (Mo.), 1981—. Mem. Mo. City Mgrs. Assn., Am. Soc. Public Adminstrn., Am. Public Works Assn., Inst. Adminstrv. Mgmt., Inst. Bldgs. and Grounds, Internat. City Mgmt. Assn. (asso.). Methodist. Club: Kiwanis. Home: Rt 1 Box 449-B Eldon MO 65026 Office: 201 E First St Eldon MO 65026

GRISHAM, H. RICHARD, hosp. adminstr.; b. Ponca City, Okla., Sept. 4, 1945; s. Harold Edward and Billie Dean (Knight) G.; B.S. with honors, U. Okla., Norman, 1968; M.S., Washington U., St. Louis, 1973; m. Carla Maxine Davis, Jan. 29, 1965; children—Richard William, Kristin Ann. Chief pharmacist, dir. intravenous services St. John's Hosp., Tulsa, Okla., 1969-71; asst. dir. Barnes Hosp., St. Louis, 1972-74; asso. dir. profl. services Barnes Hosp. Corp., St. Louis, 1974-77, corp. v.p., 1977—; adj. prof. health care adminstrn. Washington U., St. Louis, 1978—; instr. health care adminstrn. Webster Coll., St. Louis, 1979—. Served to 1st lt., M.C., U.S. Army, 1968-69. Alumni Devel. scholar, U. Okla., 1968. Mem. Am. Coll. Hosp. Adminstrs., Rho Chi. Home: 89 Edward Dr Eureka MO 63025 Office: Barnes Hosp Plaza St Louis MO 63110

GRISNIK, PAMALA ANN, banker; b. Yokohama, Japan, Sept. 10, 1947; d. Anton J. and Donna (Carr) G.; student Am. Inst. Banking, Kansas City, Mo., 1975, 76, 77, 80, 81. With Victory State Bank, Kansas City, Kans., 1965-74, teller, 1972-74, bank mgr., 1975-77; with Security Nat. Bank, Kansas City, 1974—, asst. v.p. ops., 1979—. Adviser, Jr. Achievement; bd. dirs. Santa Fe Trail council Girl Scouts U.S.A. Mem. Nat. Assn. Bank Women, Kansas City (Kans.) Womens C. of C. (dir.), Bus. and Profl. Women Kansas City Kans. (pres.-elect). Democrat. Roman Catholic. Club: Zonta. Home: 5921 Cleveland St Kansas City KS 66104 Office: 1 Security Plaza Kansas City KS 66101

GRISWOLD, KENNETH EARL, educator; b. Langdon, N.D., Mar. 18, 1928; s. Milton Alford and Beatrice (Brudahl) G.; B.S., N.D. State U., 1950; M.Ed., Coll. William and Mary, 1958; Ed.D., Tchrs. Coll., Columbia U., 1961. Tchr., Perry (N.D.) Elem. Sch., 1948-49, Washburn (N.D.) High Sch., 1950-52, Mathews (Va.) High Sch., 1956-58; mem. faculty Adelphi U., L.I., N.Y., 1958-59, Rollins Coll., Winter Park, Fla., 1961-67; mem. faculty Purdue U., Calumet, Ind., 1967—, chmn. tchr. edn. council, 1974-77, advisor elem. edn., 1977—. Served with USN, 1952-56. Phi Delta Kappa scholar, Soviet Union, 1973, 75. Mem. Assn. Supervision and Curriculum Devel., Assn. Childhood Edn. Internat., Assn. Tchr. Educators, Phi Delta Kappa, Kappa Delta Pi, Alpha Zeta. Office: Purdue U Calumet Hammond IN 46323

GRISWOLD, KENNETH WALTER, educator; b. Joliet, Ill., Nov. 2, 1937; s. Robert P. and Louise A. (Kaatz) G.; B.S., Ill. State U., 1961; M.S., No. Ill. U., 1965; m. Carole Rockwood, Feb. 3, 1962; children—Stephen R., Kent R. Tchr., coach Reed-Custer High Sch., Braidwood, Ill., 1961-64; counselor Lockport (Ill.) Central High Sch., 1964-66, Santa Ana (Calif.) Unified and Jr. Coll. Dist., 1966-67; prof. Rock Valley Coll., Rockford, Ill., 1967—. Mem. Am. Psychol. Assn., Am. Personnel and Guidance Assn., Internat. Soc. Sport Psychology. Republican. Episcopalian. Contbr. articles in field to profl. jours. Home: 3901 Spring Creek Rd Rockford IL 61111 Office: 3301 N Mulford Rd Rockford IL 61101

GROCHOWSKI, EUGENE CARL, nephrologist; b. Chgo., June 11, 1947; s. Richard S. and Wanda E. (Siniarski) G.; student John Carroll U., 1965-66; B.A. in Chemistry, Northwestern U., 1969, Ph.D. in Exptl. Pathology, 1973, M.D., 1974; m. Francine Mary Wiktor, Jan. 31, 1966; children—Eugene Victor, Bethany Bea, Jennetta Dawn, Trina Francine. Intern in medicine Mayo Grad. Sch. Medicine, Rochester, Minn., 1974-75, resident in medicine, 1975-77, resident in nephrology, 1977-79; mem. staff Bronson Meth. Hosp., Kalamazoo, 1979—; instr. medicine U. Minn. Mayo Med. Sch., Rochester, 1977-79, affiliate faculty for advanced cardiac life support, 1977—; course dir., instr. advanced cardiac life support AHA, 1977—; asst. clin. prof. medicine Mich. State U., 1980—; cons. advanced cardiac life support tng. SWM Systems, Inc., S.W. Mich. Emergency Med. Services, Kalamazoo, 1979—. Bd. dirs. Western Mich. Critical Care Symposia, Inc. Diplomate Am. Bd. Internal Medicine, also Sub-Bd. Nephrology, Nat. Bd. Med. Examiners. Fellow ACP; mem. AMA, Am. Fedn. Clin. Research, Nat. Kidney Found., Am. Soc. Internal Medicine, Am. Soc. Nephrology, Internat. Soc. Nephrology, Soc. Critical Care Medicine, Mich. Transplantation Soc., Mich. Med. Soc., Kalamazoo Acad. Medicine, Phi Lambda Upsilon. Contbr. articles to med. jours. Office: 319 W Bronson Medical Center Kalamazoo MI 49007

GRODINSKY, WILLIAM, lawyer; b. Omaha, Aug. 5, 1894; s. Henry and Bertha (Levitan) G.; J.D. cum laude, Creighton U., 1913. Admitted to Nebr. bar, 1915; partner firm Monsky, Katleman, & Grodinsky and successor firms, Omaha, 1919-71; partner firm Kutak Rock Cohen Campbell & Garfinkle, Omaha, 1971-76; of counsel firm Kutak Rock & Huie, Omaha, 1976—. Dir. Father Flanagan's Boys Home, 1947-76, v.p., 1968; chmn. State of Israel Bonds, Omaha, 1958; mem. exec. com. Jewish Fedn. Omaha; mem. pres.'s council Creighton U., 1970—. Served with U.S. Army, 1918-19. Recipient Alumni Merit award Creighton U., 1979. Mem. Am. Bar Assn., Nebr. Bar Assn. (v.p. 1942), Omaha Bar Assn., Am. Judicature Soc. Republican. Jewish. Clubs: Omaha Press, B'nai B'rith, Mason, Shriner. Home: 3000 Farnam St Omaha NE 68131 Office: 1650 Farnam St Omaha NE 68102

GROENERT, RICK ALLEN, retail menswear co. exec.; b. Indpls., Aug. 30, 1953; s. George Jack and Dorthea Louise (Mayhew) G.; student Ind. State U., 1971-72; m. Stephanie Ann Pitt, Feb. 15, 1975. With Levinson's Inc., Evansville, Ind., 1973—, dept. mgr., 1975-76, gen., mgr., 1976-77, v.p., 1977—. Mem. Menswear Retailers of Am., Mens Apparel Guild in Calif., Nat. Assn. Mens Sportswear Buyers. Methodist. Club: Sports Car of Am. Home: 6688 Springvale Ct Newburgh IN 47630 Office: 1228 Washington Sq Mall Evansville IN 47715

GROESBECK, MARK ALAN, mgmt. info. system mgr.; b. Detroit, June 16, 1951; s. Russell and Joanne (Crane) G.; B.A. in Social Sci., Mich. State U., 1973; M.P.A., Wayne State U., 1982; m. Sharyn Ann Tito, Sept. 5, 1975; children—Kara Marie, Megan Elizabeth. Crime analyst Warren (Mich.) Police Dept., 1974-78, mgmt. info. specialist, 1978-80, mgmt. info. system mgr., 1981—. Grantee, LEAA, 1979. Mem. Digital Equipment Corp. Users Soc., Law Enforcement Mgmt. System Users Group (chmn.), Macomb County Law Enforcement Mgmt. System Task Force (chmn.). Democrat. Methodist. Office: 29900 Civic Center Warren MI 48093

GROESCH, JOHN WILLIAM, JR., oil co. exec.; b. Seattle, Nov. 22, 1923; s. John William and Jeanette Morrison (Gilmur) G.; B.S. in Chem. Engring., U. Wash., 1944; m. Joyce Eugenia Schauble, Apr. 25, 1948; children—Sara, Mary, Andrew. Engr., Union Oil Co., Los Angeles, 1944-48, corp. economist, Los Angeles, 1948-56, chief statistician, 1956-62, mgr., 1962-68, mgr., Schaumburg, Ill., 1968—. Commr., Arlington Heights (Ill.) Boy Scouts Am., 1980—; treas. Scout Cabin Found., Barrington, 1977—. Served with USN, 1944-47. Mem. West Coast Marketing Research Council (chmn. 1969), Am. Petroleum Inst. (chmn. com. 1970-72). Mason. Home: 17 Shady Lane Deer Park Barrington IL 60010 Office: 1650 E Golf Rd Schaumburg IL 60196

GROFF, RICHARD LAMARR, investment counseling co. exec.; b. Lancaster, Pa., Aug. 6, 1925; s. Frank L. and Martha E. Groff; B.S. in Econs., Franklin and Marshall Coll., 1950; M.Letters in Retail Sci., U. Pitts., 1951; m. Elizabeth Mastrocolo, May 25, 1974. Buyer, The Higbee Co., Cleve., 1951-61, mgr. suburban store, 1961-71, gen. mgr. Splty. Shop div., 1971-79; investment counselor, broker Smith Barney Harris & Upham, Cleve., 1979—. Served with USAAF, 1944-46. Mem. Am. Mgmt. Assn., Sales and Mktg. Execs. Cleve. Clubs: Rotary, Masons, N.Y. Athletic. Home: 390-2 Windward Ln Aurora OH 44202 Office: 1300 E 9th St Cleveland OH 44114

GROFF, STANLEY ALLEN, social worker; b. Madison, Minn., Oct. 24, 1942; s. Sherwood Allen and Rosella Belinda Groff; B.A., U. Minn., Morris, 1965; M.S.W., Fla. State U., 1971; m. Mary Susan Behl, Sept. 19, 1964; children—Beth Ann, Stephen Allen. Social worker Crow Wing County Welfare Dept., Brainard, Minn., 1965-67; dir. McLeod County Welfare Dept., Glencoe, Minn., 1967-69; social services supr. Stearns County Welfare Dept., St. Cloud, Minn., 1971-72; dir. Faribault County Social Services and Welfare Dept., Blue Earth, Minn., 1972-75; mgmt. analyst Minn. Gov. Office Human Services, St. Paul, 1975-77; dir. div. social services Dakota County Human Services Bd., South St. Paul, 1977-80; adminstr. Steele County Community Social Service Dept., Owatonna, Minn., 1980—; mem. faculty Mankato (Minn.) State U., 1977—; mem. field faculty U. Minn. Grad. Sch. Social Work, 1977-79; pres. Blue Earth United Way, 1974; cons. Assn. Minn. Counties, 1979. Mem. Acad. Cert. Social Workers, Nat. Assn. Social Workers (dir. Minn. chpt. 1975-77), Minn. Public Health Assn. Lutheran. Home: 11105 Lower 167th St Lakesville MN 55044 Office: 590 Dannell Dr Box 890 Owatonna MN 55044

GROFF, WARREN FREDRICK, sem. pres.; b. Harleysville, Pa., June 27, 1924; s. Reinhart R. and Reba H. (Rupert) G.; B.A., Juniata Coll., Huntingdon, Pa., 1949, D.D. (hon.), 1976; B.D., Yale Div. Sch., 1952; Ph.D., Yale U., 1955; m. Ruth N. Davidheiser, Aug. 26, 1947; 1 son, David Warren. Ordained to ministry Ch. of Brethren, 1947; asst. in instrn. Yale Div. Sch., 1953-54; asso. prof. religion Bridgewater (Va.) Coll., 1954-58; asso. prof., then prof. theology Bethany Theol. Sem., Oak Brook, Ill., 1958—, dean, 1962-75, pres., 1975—; vis. scholar Harvard Div. Sch., 1965-66; trustee Juanita Coll., 1977—; mem. Faith and Order Commn., World Council Chs., 1963-65. Mem. Assn. Theol. Schs. (commn. accrediting 1968-74; Faculty fellow 1965-66), Am. Theol. Soc., Am. Acad. Religion. Club: Torch. Author: Christ the Hope of the Future: Signals of a Promised Humanity, 1971; Story Time: God's Story and Ours, 1974; co-author: The Shaping of Modern Christian Thought, 1968. Home: 18 W 625 22d St Lombard IL 60148 Office: Bethany Theol Sem Butterfield and Meyers Rd Oak Brook IL 60521

GRONEMEYER, RICHARD VINCENT, communications co. exec.; b. Chgo., Sept. 14, 1943; s. Ferdinand and Matilda (Schoefernacker) G.; B.A. in Math., Knox Coll., 1966; m. Sharon Lee Tracy, June 20, 1970; children—Bradley, Stacy. With Western Electric, 1966—, info. systems staff sr. mem. Network Software Center, Lisle, Ill., 1979-80, dept. chief, software devel., 1980—; instr. on loan Bell System Center for Tech. Edn., 1970-71. Recipient Cost Reduction award Western Electric, 1972, Info. Systems Recognition award Western Electric No. Ill. works, 1978, Speaker of Yr., 1976; named to Outstanding Young Men Am., U.S. Jaycees, 1972. Home: 1425 Briarwood Dr Naperville IL 60540 Office: 4200 Commerce Ct Lisle IL 60532

GRONET, ARTHUR THOMAS, chem. engr.; b. Bklyn., May 12, 1930; s. Gus Stanley and Helen Catherine (Szalwinski) G.; B.A., Rutgers U., 1958, B.S. in Chem. Engring., 1958; m. Shirley Madeline Orlick, Aug. 20, 1955; children—Deborah Ann, Peter Michael, Suzanne Marie. Lab. technician Mobil Chem., Metuchen, N.J., 1952-56; chemist Emulsion div. Reichhold Chem. Inc., Elizabeth, N.J., 1956-58, sales mgr., 1958-62; mgr. tech. service minerals, pigments and metals div. Pfizer Inc., Easton, Pa., 1962-72; lab. mgr. powder coatings Midland div. The Dexter Corp., Olean, N.Y., 1972-79; mgr. research and devel. Armstrong Products Co. div. Philip Morris Indsl. Co., Warsaw, Ind., 1979—; cons. to industry on surfactants, polymer emulsions and corrosion inhibition. Served with USNR, 1949-52. Mem. Nat. Assn. Corrosion Engrs. (cert. corrosion specialist), Am. Chem. Soc., ASTM, Chgo. Soc. for Coatings Tech., Seahorse Inst., Soc. Gallows Birds. Club: Rushlight. Home: Route 9 Box 102 Warsaw IN 46580 Office: PO Box 647 Warsaw IN 46580

GRONINGER, JAMES GRANT, investment banking co. exec.; b. Chgo., Mar. 25, 1944; s. Jack Miller and Nelda Jean (Roth) G.; B.S., Yale U., 1966; M.B.A., Harvard U., 1968; m. Elisabeth Rogers Jackson, June 20, 1969; children—James Hunter, Katherine Rogers. Staff mgmt. cons. Donald R. Booz & Assos., Chgo., 1968-71; corporate fin. partner William Blair & Chgo., 1971-79; v.p. Morgan Stanley & Co., Inc., 1979—. C.P.A.; chartered fin. analyst. Clubs: Yale; Harvard, Univ. (Chgo.). Home: 775 Lincoln Ave Winnetka IL 60093 Office: 115 S LaSalle St Chicago IL 60603

GRONLI, JOHN VICTOR, coll. adminstr.; b. Eshowe, S. Africa, Sept. 12, 1932; s. John Einar and Marjorie Gellet (Hawker) G.; came to U.S., 1934, naturalized, 1937; B.A., U. Minn., 1953; M.Div., Luther Theol. Sem., 1958, D.Min., 1978; M.A., Pacific Luth. U., 1975; m. Jeanne Louise Ellertson, Sept. 15, 1952; children—Cheryl Marie Mundt, Deborah Raechel Hokanson, John Timothy, Peter Jonas, Daniel Reuben. Ordained to ministry, 1958; pastor Brocket-Lawton Luth. Parish, Brocket, N.D., 1958-61; Harlowton (Mont.) Luth. Parish, 1961-66; sr. pastor St. Luke's Luth. Ch., Shelby, Mont., 1966-75; missionary Paulinum Sem., Otjimbingwe, Namibia, 1975-76; dean, chmn. dept. philosophy and humanities Golden Valley Luth. Coll., Mpls., 1976—; bd. dirs. Mont. Assn. Chs., 1973-75; sec. bd. for communications and mission support Am. Luth. Ch., 1973-75; mem. dist. council Rocky Mountain Dist., 1963-75, sec., 1963-70, mem. S.African affairs task force SEM Dist., 1978-79. Mem. personnel and guidance assns., Am., Minn. coll. personnel assns. Editor: Rocky Mountain Dist. Yearbook, 1963-70; Rocky Mountain Views, 1973-75; contbr. to Lutheran Standard, 1973-77; contbr. articles to religious jours. Home: 1321 Orkla Dr Minneapolis MN 55427 Office: 6125 Olson Minneapolis MN 55422

GRONLUND, NORMAN EDWARD, educator; b. Dollar Bay, Mich., Apr. 25, 1920; s. Jacob and Ida (Franz) G.; B.S., No. Mich. U., 1942; M.A., U. Mich., 1947, Ph.D., 1950; m. Marie Ann Landerville; children—James, Richard. Asst. prof. Western Wash. U., 1949-50; asst. to dir. Bur. Appointments, U. Mich., 1950-52; asst. prof. ednl. psychology U. Ill., Urbana, 1952-55, asso. prof., 1955-60, prof., 1960—. Served with USCG, 1942-45. Fellow Am. Psychol. Assn.; mem. Am. Ednl. Research Assn., Nat. Council Measurement in Edn. Author: Measurement and Evaluation in Teaching, 4th edit., 1981; Constructing Achievement Tests, 2d edit., 1977; Sociometry in the Classroom, 1959; Readings in Measurement and Evaluation, 1968; Stating Objectives for Classroom Instruction, 2d edit., 1978; contbr. articles to profl. jours. Office: Coll Edn Univ Ill Champaign IL 61820

GROOMS, THOMAS ALBIN, biol. chemist; b. Dayton, Ohio, Apr. 6, 1943; s. Byron Edwin and Thelma Florence (Albin) G.; B.S., Baldwin-Wallace Coll., 1965; Ph.D., U. Cin., 1973; m. Geraldine Francis Madill, Nov. 1, 1969; children—Aaron, Evan, Ian, Sarah. Postdoctoral fellow Northwestern U., 1972-73; sr. investigator Wilson Labs., Inolex Corp., Park Forest South, Ill., 1973-75; scientist Leeds and Northrup Co., North Wales, Pa., 1975-76; mgr. chemistry devel. Yellow Springs (Ohio) Instrument Co., 1976—; instr. Am. Sch. Corr., 1973, Wittenberg U., 1978—. Mem. Internat. Soc. Artificial Organs, Sigma Xi. Mem. Christian Ch. (Disciples of Christ). Contbr. articles to profl. jours. Office: Yellow Springs Instrument Co Inc Box 279 Yellow Springs OH 45387

GROSBY, HERBERT LEON, investment co. exec.; b. St. Louis, June 22, 1919; s. Herman Garzell and Sarah (Zemansky) G.; student U. Ill. at Chgo., 1940-46, N.Y. Inst. Finance, 1947; m. Audrey Elaine Spiro, Aug. 20, 1950; children—Steven E., Sara Ann. Securities agt. Credit Thrift, Evansville, Ind., 1951-54; broker Merrill Lynch Pierce Fenner & Smith, Chgo., 1946-50, Bache & Co., Chgo., 1950-55; with Firstmark Corp. (formerly CIC Corp.), also Indpls. Morris Plan, 1955—, v.p. both firms, 1968—. Past pres. IHC Brotherhood; active United Fund, Jewish Welfare Fedn., Ind. Interreligious Commn. Human Equality; bd. dirs. Anti-Defamation League, 1955-73, Jewish Community Center Indpls., Marion County Mental Health, Jewish Edn. Assn. Mem. Mental Health Bd., Crisis and Suicide Bd., 1972-73; mem. Community Relations Bd. Mem. Indpls. C. of C., Indpls. Mus. Art. Clubs: Masons, Shriners, Elks, Lions (dir. Northside club 1973, pres. 1978-79); Columbia, Econ., Exec. Home: 8225 Windcombe Blvd Indianapolis IN 46240 Office: 110 E Washington St Indianapolis IN 46204

GROSHANS, HENRY HEAFNER, elec. engr.; b. Godfrey, Ill., Dec. 22, 1919; s. Robert Henry and Charlotte Emma (Heafner) G.; B.S. in TV Engring., Am. TV Inst., 1951; postgrad. St. Louis U., 1951-56; m. Cecilia Mary Wendle, June 5, 1946; children—Patricia, Marilyn, Edward, Michael, Brenda, Vickie. With McDonnell Douglas Corp., St. Louis, 1951—, chief program engr., 1968—. Served with USAAF, 1941-45. Mem. IEEE, N.Y. Acad. Scis., V.F.W., Sigma Xi. Club: Alton-Woodriver Sportsmen. Home: 36 Frontenac St Godfrey IL 62035 Office: PO Box 516 Dept E450 Saint Louis MO 63166

GROSHANS, RUSSELL GLEN, utility exec.; b. Minot, N.D., Feb. 14, 1929; s. Louis Christian and Elizabeth Claire (Bosse) G.; B.S., U.S. Mil. Acad., 1953; M.S., Georgetown U., 1964; Ph.D., Georgetown U., 1967; m. Barbara Joan Mottley, June 27, 1953; children—Maris, Barbara, Russell Glen. Program physicist Office Aerospace Research, Washington, 1963-67; systems engr. RCA Corp., Hightstown, N.J., 1967-68, tech. adviser corp. research and engring. staff, Princeton, N.J., 1969-77; dir. market planning COMSAT Gen. Corp., Washington, 1978-79, div. dir. bus. devel., 1979-80; v.p. tech. planning and devel. Central Telephone & Utilities, Chgo., 1980—; grad. physics lectr. RCA Corp., 1968-69. Mem. Monmouth County Environ. Council, 1972-78. Served with USAF, 1953-67. Mem. IEEE, Am. Geophys. Union. Republican. Roman Catholic. Clubs: Golf (Spring Lake, N.J.); West Point Society, Georgetown Club (N.Y.C.). Home: 1 Old Coach Rd Barrington IL 60010 Office: 5725 E River Rd Chicago IL 60631

GROSKI, DONALD S., advt. agy. exec.; b. Johnston City, Ill., May 11, 1924; s. Stanley and Edith (Hoffman) G.; student DePaul U. Sch. Commerce, 1946-50; m. Helen Bazela, May 20, 1945; children—Donald S., Robert J. Staff accountant Wolf & Co., C.P.A.'s, Chgo., 1950-55; with Tatham-Laird & Kudner, Inc., Chgo., 1955-70, controller, 1965-70; v.p. finance I/MAC, Inc., 1970-73; treas. Marvin Advt. Co., 1973—, Prime Time Mktg., Inc., 1973-74; controller Kelly

Scott & Madison, Inc., 1973—. Served with AUS, 1943-46. C.P.A., Ill. Mem. Ill. Soc. C.P.A.'s. Home: 501 Deborah Ln Mount Prospect IL 60056 Office: 1 E Wacker Dr Chicago IL 60601

GROSS, BETHUEL SAMUEL (B.G.), educator, musician, composer, orgn. exec., columnist; b. Leavenworth, Kans., Mar. 7, 1910; s. Robert and Carrie (Hoefflin) G.; A.B., Mus.B., Washburn U., 1928; Mus.B., Mus.M., Northwestern U., 1930, B.Mus.Edn., 1932, Ph.D., 1941; M.A., Loyola U., 1965; pvt. study Am. Conservatory, 1931-36; postgrad. Eastman Sch. Music, 1939-40, U. Chgo., 1942-44; m. Doris Johnson, Aug. 26, 1949; children—Brent, Dean. Prof. music Tulsa U., 1929-30; dir. music George Williams Coll., 1939-41; head dept. music U. Akron, 1941-45; dir. grad. div. Ill. Wesleyan U., 1945-46; dean students, dir. music Shurtleff Coll., 1946-48; dir. tests and measurements DePaul U., 1948-50, Chgo. Conservatory, 1950-55, also dir. choral music; dir. collegium musicum, univ. organist Loyola U. Organist, dir. St. James Choir Sch., Meth. Ch., Chgo., 1937-50; minister music Buena Meml. Presbyn. Ch., Chgo., 1950-56; organist-dir. Baker Meml. United Meth. Ch., St. Charles, Ill., 1956—; minister edn. Peoples Ch. Chgo.; founder, gen. dir. South Shore Music Festival, Gary, Nat. Composers Clinic; condr. several sch., civic orchs. Bd. dirs. indsl. relations YMCA, Chgo., 1960; bd. dirs. Indsl. Services Center, Leaning Tower YMCA. Columnist, Adminstrn., Forum, Lerner and Chronicle Newspapers, Liberalists; mem. faculty Nat. Restaurant Assn. Exec. Seminars; commd. composer Nat. Fedn. Music Clubs, also WIND radio sta.; exec. sec. Northtown Indsl. Mgmt. Council, Northtown Vocational Council; moderator WGSB Town Hall of Air. Bd. dirs. Northwest Sch. Fine Arts, Suburban Mental Health Referral Center. Mem. A.S.C.A.P., Am. Psychol. Assn., Phi Delta Theta, Pi Kappa Lambda. Composer 6 organ symphonies, 11 oratorios, 2 symphonic poems, 20 anthems, 14 art songs, 10 piano works. Home: 45 Warwick Rd Winnetka IL 60093 Office: 6300 W Touhy Ave Chicago IL 60648

GROSS, CYNTHIA DOROTHY LAVERNE, civic worker; b. Green Bay, Wis., Sept. 28, 1944; d. Walter George and Loretta Wilhemina Ida (Brandt) Boettcher; B.S., U. Wis., 1966, postgrad., 1973, 78; m. Lawrence Henry Gross, June 17, 1967; children—Aaron, Rebecca. Playgroud dir. Oshkosh (Wis.) Public Schs., 1965-66; tchr. public schs., Valders, Wis., 1966-67, Pierce Sch., Milw., 1967-68, Hawthorne Sch., Milw., 1968-70, St. John's Sch., Portage, Wis., 1975-76; head Med. Foster and Emergency Receiving Home, 1978—; head dir. Day Care Center, 1980—. Mem. Headstart Policy Com. and Seven County Council, 1979-81; pres. Lincoln-Brener PTA. Mem. Wis. Edn. Assn., Wis. Fedn. Foster Parents, Shawano Jaycettes (life, state dir. 1972—, spl. service award), U.S. Jaycettes, Wis. Jaycettes. Lutheran. Author: (with Lawrence Gross and Jerry Sterneigle) Pen and the Prof, 1964. Contbr. short articles to newsletters and newspapers. Home: 224 S Andrews St Shawano WI 54166

GROSS, DAVID EARL, educator; b. Cin., Oct. 25, 1950; s. Stanley E. and Lela Gross; B.S. Ed. in Spl. Edn. of Educable and Trainable Mentally Retarded, U. Cin., 1972, M.Ed. in Spl. Edn. and Learning Disabilities and Behavioral Disorders, 1973; postgrad. Xavier U.; m. Sue Ann Gross; children—Ryan Earl, Kyra Ann. Tchr. spl. edn. Lockland Pub. Schs., Cin., 1973-75; adminstrv. asst., adult services div. Hamilton County Bd. Mental Retardation, 1976-80; prin. Rost Sch., Hamilton County Bd. Mental Retardation, Cin., 1980—. Chmn. Youth Commn., Springdale, Ohio, 1972-73. Mem. Council Exceptional Children (pres. Cin. chpt., pres. Ohio state chpt., nat. v.p.), Phi Delta Kappa. Home: 10603 Thornview Dr Cincinnati OH 45241 Office: 5858 Bridgeton Rd Cincinnati OH 45211

GROSS, DAVID LEE, geologist; b. Springfield, Ill., Nov. 20, 1943; s. Carl David and Shirley Marie (Northcutt) G.; A.B., Knox Coll., 1965; M.S., U. Ill., 1967, Ph.D. (NDEA fellow), 1969; m. Claudia Cole, June 11, 1966; children—Oliver David, Alexander Lee. Asst. geologist Ill. State Geol. Survey, Urbana, 1969-73, asso. geologist, 1973-80, geologist, 1980—, coordinator environ. geology, 1979—. Bd. govs. Channing-Murray Found., 1973-76, pres., 1976; trustee Unitarian Universalist Ch., Urbana, 1977-80, chmn., 1977-79. Registered profl. geologist, Calif. Fellow Geol. Soc. Am.; mem. Internat. Union for Quaternary Research, Am. Quaternary Assn., Interant. Assn. for Gt. Lakes Research, Soc. for Econ. Paleontologists and Mineralogists, Am. Inst. Profl. Geologists (pres. Ill.-Ind. sect. 1980), AAAS, Ill. State Acad. Sci., Sigma Xi. Club: Rotary. Contbr. numerous articles to geol. jours. Home: 3 Flora Ct Champaign IL 61820 Office: Ill State Geol Survey Natural Resources Bldg 615 E Peabody Dr Champaign IL 61820

GROSS, HAROLD GENE, city adminstr.; b. Quicksand, Ky., July 12, 1928; s. Rader and Margaret (Smith) G.; student Lees Jr. Coll., 1948; m. Janice Bush,June 12, 1954; children—Kimberly K., Harold E. Mem. survey crew Ky. State Hwy. Dept., 1950-53; with City of Dayton (Ohio), 1953—, asst. supt. water dist., 1962-67, supt. div. water dist., 1967—. Served to sgt. U.S. Army, 1951-53; Korea. Mem. Am. Water Works Assn. (seminar participant), Am. Pub. Works Assn. Mem. Ch. of God. Club: Masons. Address: 945 Ottawa St Dayton OH 45402

GROSS, HENRY EMMETT, petroleum engr., cartographer; b. Glendale, Mo., Aug. 8, 1906; s. Hugo Carl and Frieda (Bruno) G.; B.S., Mining Engr., Mo. Sch. Mines, 1928, E.M., 1934; M.S. in Mining Engring., U. Ill., 1933; m. Margrete Wilhelmine Brauer, Sept. 6, 1941. Mem. oil well drilling crew Shell Oil Co., Santa Fe Springs, Calif., 1928-29; engr. Pacific Western Oil Co., Los Angeles, 1929-31; research grad. asst. mining engr. U. Ill., 1931-33; petroleum engr. Shell Petroleum Corp., Tulsa, Okla., 1933-36; asst. prof. petroleum engring. U. Okla., 1936-38; asso. prof. petroleum engring. Tex. A. & M. Coll., 1938-42; chief reservoir engring. sec. Petroleum Adminstrn. for War Dist. 2. Chgo., 1942-45; chief petroleum engr. Kingwood Oil Co., Effingham, Ill., 1945-46; cons. engr., cartographer pub. maps, Webster Groves, Mo., 1946-72; owner H.E. Gross Maps, Webster Groves, 1946-72. Registered profl. engr., Ill., Mo., Tex. Mem. Am. Inst. Mining, Metall. and Petroleum Engrs. (sr., Legion of Honor 50-Year mem.), Am. Assn. Petroleum Geologists (emeritus), Explorers Club, Tau Beta Pi. Lutheran. Invented marine foundation that was instrumental in exploiting continental shelves for petroleum, U. Okla., 1937; set forth drilling method for deep ocean floor that foretold Glomar Challenger operations. Patentee deep ocean salvage apparatus. Home and office: 1141 S Elm Ave Webster Groves MO 63119

GROSS, JAMES DEHNERT, pathologist; b. Harvey, Ill., Nov. 15, 1929; s. Max A. and Marian (Dehnert) G.; B.S. in Biology, U. Chattanooga, 1951; M.D., Vanderbilt U., 1955; m. Marilyn Agnes Robertson, Jan. 9, 1960; children—Kathleen Ann, Terrence Michael, Brian Andrew, Kevin Matthew. Rotating intern U.S. Naval Hosp., St. Albans, N.Y., 1955-56; resident in anatomic and clin. pathology Nat. Naval Med. Center, Bethesda, Md., 1956-59; dir. labs. St. Mary's Hosp., Streator, Ill., 1962—, pres. med. staff, 1972-73; instr. pathology and microbiology U. Tenn. Med. Sch., 1960-62; bd. dirs. La Salle County br. Am. Cancer Soc., 1966-68. Mem. parish council St. Anthony's Roman Cath. Ch., Streator, 1969-72. Served to lt. comdr. M.C., USNR, 1955-68. Diplomate Am. Bd. Pathology. Fellow Am. Soc. Clin. Pathologists, Coll. Am. Pathologists, Assn. Clin. Scientists (founder); mem. AMA, Ill. Med. Soc., Am. Assn. Blood Banks, Catholic Hosp. Assn., N.Y. Acad. Scis., Sigma Chi, Alpha Kappa Kappa. Republican. Clubs: K.C., Rotary (past dir.) (Streator). Home: 54 Sunset Dr Streator IL 61364 Office: 111 Spring St St Mary's Hosp Streator IL 61364

GROSS, JOHN DONALD, engr.; b. Evansville, Ind., Sept. 28, 1951; s. Donald Robert and Sylvia Estelle (Whobrey) G.; B.S., U. Evansville, 1973; m. Donna Rae Reuter, June 21, 1975. Engr., Ashdee div. George Koch Sons, Inc., Evansville, 1973-75, project engr., 1975-79, project mgr., 1979-80, chief engr., 1980—. Mem. Soc. Automotive Engrs., ASME. Republican. Mem. United Ch. Christ. Home: 3512 Ridgeway Ave Evansville IN 47715 Office: 10 S 10th Ave Evansville IN 47702

GROSS, JOSEPH WALLACE, JR., hosp. adminstr.; b. Berwyn, Ill., June 15, 1945; s. Joseph Wallace and Patricia Geraldine (Burke) G.; B.S., Creighton U., 1968, B.A., 1968; M.S. in Pub. Health, U. Mo., 1971; m. Linda Sue Sudholt, Mar. 6, 1971; children—Joseph Wallace III, Heide Burke. Adminstrv. asst. Boone County Hosp., Columbia, Mo., 1971; asst. adminstr., v.p. ops., exec. v.p. Wausau (Wis.) Hosps., Inc., 1971-78; pres. Luther Hosp., Eau Claire, Wis., 1978—. Pres., Halfway House of Wausau, Inc., 1974-76; chmn. large firms div. United Way, 1977. Served to 1st lt., Med. Service Corps, U.S. Army Res., 1970-78. Recipient J. Merle Sweitzer award for disting. service Wausau Hosps., 1978. Mem. Am. Coll. Hosp. Adminstrs., Wis. Hosp. Assn. (H.M. Coon, M.D. Young Hosp. Adminstrs. award 1972), U. Mo. Health Service Mgmt. Alumni Assn. (pres. 1974-75), Delta Sigma Pi. Club: Rotary (Eau Claire). Office: 310 Chestnut St Eau Claire WI 54701

GROSS, NORMAN, law assn. exec.; b. Providence, May 18, 1945; s. Martin and Fania G.; student Providence Coll., 1962-63; B.A., U. R.I., 1966; J.D., Boston U., 1969. Admitted to Mass. bar, 1969; tchr. Boston Public Schs., 1969-72; asst. staff dir. Am. Bar Assn., Chgo., 1972-74, staff dir., 1975—; instr. Ill. Inst. Tech. Chgo.-Kent Sch. Law, spring 1981. Mem. nat. law exploring com. Boy Scouts Am., 1973—; bd. dirs. Young Leadership div. Jewish Fedn. Met. Chgo., 1979—. Mem. Am. Bar Assn., Nat. Council for Social Studies, Coalition for Law-Related Edn. Co-editor: Update on Law-Related Edn., 1977-80. Home: 1938 N Cleveland St Chicago IL 60614 Office: 1155 E 60th Chicago IL 60637

GROSS, PEGGY EILEEN KNUTSON, lumber mfg. co. exec.; b. Mpls., Sept. 26, 1947; d. Edwin Walter and Barbara M. (Schneider) Knutson; B.A., Coll. of St. Catherin, 1969; postgrad. (NSF grantee) U. Minn., 1970-72; m. Harvard William Gross, Jr., Mar. 29, 1969; children—Kevin, Timothy, Brian, Jeffrey, Colleen Erin. Tchr. Am. history St. Louis Park (Minn.) High Sch., 1969-70; exec. sec., translator CEA Carter Americas, Inc., Mpls., 1975-77; youth dir. YWCA, Wausau, Wis., 1977-78; adminstrv. asst. to pres. Crestline, Inc., Wausau, 1979—. Mem. Minn. Select Com. Judicial Reform, 1974-77. Vol. counselor Hotline, 1971-72; v.p. Mpls. Jaycees Convs., Inc., 1972-74; bd. dirs. Outreach Community Center, 1974-77, Wausau Newcomers, 1977-78; mem. Wausau Area Coalition for Marital Property Legis. Reform, 1979-80. Mem. LWV (state dir. 1973-76), U.S. Jaycettes (exec. com. 1976—, programming v.p. 1977-78, parlimaentarian 1978-80, named Outstanding Nat. Officer of the Year 1979), Wis. Jaycettes (dir. 1977—, Presdl. award 1978, 79), AAUW, Wausau Jaycettes (dir. 1977-78), Wausau Hockey Assn., Wausau C. of C. (mem. firm prevention com. 1977-79), NOW, Women's Polit. Caucus, Coll. of St. Catherine Alumnae Assn. (class chmn. 1969-77) Pi Delta Phi, Pi Gamma Mu. Author: (with others) Minnesota Judiciary, Structure and Procedure, 1972; Today's Woman, 1976. Home: 410 Kent St Wausau WI 54401 Office: Crestline 91D Cleveland Ave Wausau WI 54401

GROSS, SHIRLEY MARIE, farm mgr., artist; b. Beardstown, Ill., Apr. 4, 1917; d. Robert Lee and Marie Elizabeth (Ellrich) Northcutt; A.A., Stephens Coll., 1936; B.A., Ill. Coll., 1938; m. Carl David Gross, Oct. 4, 1941; children—David Lee, Susan Jean Gross Conner. Med. technologist St. John's Hosp., Springfield, Ill., 1938-41, Schmidt Meml. Hosp., Beardstown, 1957-64; librarian Beardstown Public Library, 1970-76; pvt. practice farm mgmt., Beardstown, 1958—; exhibitor various art shows, Ill., 1969—. Bd. dirs. Beardstown Hosp., Head Start. Winner art awards various shows. Mem. Am. Soc. Clin. Pathologists (med. technologist), Jacksonville Area Artist League. Democrat. Congregationalist. Clubs: Beardstown Woman's, Cass County Council for the Arts, Beardstown Bus. and Profl. Women's (pres. 1968-70). Home: 1116 Jefferson Beardstown IL 62618

GROSS, STUART DIEHL, writer, ret. coll. adminstr.; b. Vincennes, Ind., Feb. 2, 1914; s. Charles Adam and Winnie Amanda (McGillivary) G.; B.A., Hope Coll., Holland, Mich., 1936; m. Vernice Marian Lee, Aug. 5, 1939; children—Amy Kathleen Gross Grzesiak, Mary Alice Gross Daenzer. Reporter, Saginaw (Mich.) News, 1936-65, city editor, 1965-67; dir. community affairs Saginaw Valley State Coll., Saginaw, Mich., 1967-76, asst. to pres., 1976-79; cons., dir. Youth for Understanding, 1963-73; mem. Mich. Com. Financing Equitable Edn., 1975-77. Recipient Mich. Sch. Bell award Edn. Reporting, 1961. Author publs. in local history and edn. Home: 315 Kennely Rd Saginaw MI 48603

GROSS, WILLIS CHARLES, JR., dentist; b. St. Louis, June 3, 1924; s. Willis Charles and Mary Ida (Kelly) G.; A.A., Harris Jr. Coll., 1943; D.D.S., St. Louis U., 1946; postgrad. U. Detroit, 1952-53; m. Rosemarie Dorothy Horak, Feb. 14, 1948; 1 son, Alan Charles. Commd. 1st lt. Dental Corps, U.S. Army and USAF, 1946, advanced through grades to maj., 1952; ret., 1953; pvt. practice dentistry, Affton, Mo., 1954—; pres. Willis C. Gross Dental Assos.; v.p. C & W Gross Corp. Served with AUS, 1942-44. Fellow Acad. Gen. Dentistry, Royal Soc. Health (Eng.); mem. Am., Mo. dental assns., St. Louis Dental Soc., Concord Village Bus. Men's Assn., Am. Legion, V.F.W., Alpha Sigma Nu, Omicron Kappa Upsilon, Delta Sigma Delta (past pres., sec.-treas. St. Louis chpt.), Alpha Phi Omega. Republican. Mason (Shriner, chmn. temple med. staff, 32 deg.), Lion (pres. Concord Village 1965-66). Clubs: Liberty Country (dir.) (Horine, Mo.); Big Game Hunters (St. Louis). Home: 20 Dorclin Ln Saint Louis MO 63128 Office: 7 Concord Center Dr Saint Louis MO 63123

GROSSENBACHER, PAUL, mus. curator; b. Burgdorf, Switzerland, Sept. 14, 1904; came to U.S., 1929, naturalized, 1936; s. Gottfried and Sophie (Salzmann) G.; student Coll. Agr. Switzerland, 1922-24, Bus. Coll. Switzerland, 1926-27; m. Verena Magdalene Elmer, Feb. 26, 1931; children—Elmira Grossebacher Root, Pauline Grossenbacher Boss, John, Edward. Overseer, State Prison Farm, Bern, 1927-28; farm hand, U.S., 1929-35; share farmer, New Glarus, Wis., 1936-44; owner dairy farm, New Glarus, 1944-56; with Security Mut. Co., Elmira, N.Y., 1956—; curator Swiss Hist. Mus., New Glarus, 1970—. Mem. New Glarus Maennerchor, New Glarus Yodlers, Edelweiss Singers, New Glarus Sch. Bd., 1950-53, New Glarus Village Bd., 1954-58, Wilhelm Tell Guild, New Glarus, 1938-73; dir. German drama, New Glarus, 1963-73; bd. dirs. Green County (Wis.) March of Dimes, 1956-70; Swiss chmn. bd. United Ch. Christ, New Glarus, 1946-52. Recipient Disting. Service award New Glarus Jaycees, 1970. Mem. Swiss-Am. Hist. Soc., New Glarus Hist. Soc., Midwest Underwriters Assn. (v.p. 1960-68). Clubs: Masons, Lions, Order Eastern Star. Translator old hist. documents. Address: Swiss Hist Village 6th Ave and 7th St New Glarus WI 53574*

GROSSMAN, ROBERT MAYER, lawyer; b. Chgo., Oct. 16, 1934; s. Raymond Mandel and Frances Ruth (Krucoff) G.; A.B., Dartmouth Coll., 1956; LL.B., Yale U., 1961; m. Frances Ann Rosenbacher, Mar. 17, 1963; children—Theodore, Anthony, Kate. Admitted to Ill. bar, 1961; law clk. U.S. Dist. Ct. Judge Hubert L. Will, 1961-63; asso. firm Schiff, Hardin, Waite, Dorschel & Britton, 1963-66; exec. dir. Ill. Legislative Commn. Low Income Housing, 1966-67; partner firm Grossman, Kasakoff, Magid & Silverman, 1968-70, mng. partner firm Roan & Grossman, Chgo., 1970—; gen. counsel Ill. Housing Devel. Authority, 1967-69, 73-77; trustee, gen. counsel Dermatology Found., 1979—. Vice chmn. Chgo. chpt. Am. Jewish Com.; v.p., bd. dirs. Hyde Park Coop. Soc., 1977-81; mem. Hyde Park-Kenwood Conservation Community Council; campaign chmn. Alderman William S. Singer, 1969. Bd. dirs. Drexel Home. Served to lt. (j.g.) USNR, 1956-58. Mem. Am., Ill., Chgo. bar assns., Chgo. Council Lawyers. Jewish (bd. congregation). Clubs: Law, Standard (Chgo.). Home: 5529 S Kimbark Ave Chicago IL 60637 Office: 120 S LaSalle St Chicago IL 60603

GROSSWEINER, LEONARD IRWIN, physicist, educator; b. Atlantic City, Aug. 16, 1924; s. Jules Herman and Rae (Goldberger) G.; B.Chem. Engring., CCNY, 1946; M.S., Ill. Inst. Tech., 1950, Ph.D., 1955; m. Bess Tornheim, Sept. 9, 1951; children—Karen Ann, Jane (dec.), James Benjamin, Eric William. Asst. chemist Argonne (Ill.) Nat. Lab., 1947-51, asso. physicist, 1951-57; asso. prof. physics Ill. Inst. Tech., Chgo., 1957-62, prof., 1962—, prof., chmn. dept., 1970-81; vis. prof. radiology Stanford (Calif.) U. Med. Sch., 1979; cons. Michael Reese Med. Center, Chgo., Hines (Ill.) VA Hosp., Chgo. Med. Sch., Lawrence Berkeley (Calif.) Lab.; mem. U.S. Nat. Com. on Photobiology, 1978-80, chmn., 1981—. Served with AUS, 1944-45. Sang exchange lectr., 1972; Sigma Xi disting. faculty lectr., 1970. Fellow Am. Phys. Soc. (sec.-treas. div. biol. physics 1972-76, vice chmn. 1977, chmn. 1978), N.Y. Acad. Scis.; mem. Am. Soc. Photobiology (council 1977-80, sec.-treas. 1981—), Am. Chem. Soc., AAAS, Radiation Research Soc., Sigma Xi. Contbr. articles to profl. jours. Home: 231 Wentworth Ave Glencoe IL 60022 Office: Dept Physics Ill Inst Tech Chicago IL 60616

GROT, JAMES STEPHEN, psychologist, educator, cons.; b. Ottawa, Ill., Apr. 26, 1943; s. Wilbur Walter and Eleanor Dorothy (Wruck) G.; B.S., Loyola U., Chgo., 1966; M.A., No. Ill. U., 1970, Ph.D., 1973; m. Sharon Pavett, Jan. 21, 1967; children—Jonathan, Kristin, Jennifer, James, Stephan. Clin. psychology intern Galesburg (Ill.) State Research Hosp., 1970-71; staff psychologist Dixon (Ill.) Developmental Center, 1972-74, supervising psychologist, 1974—, asst. supt., 1978—; asso. prof. Sauk Valley Coll., 1973-80; partner Sauk Valley Human Services Psychiat. Clinic, 1980—; psychol. cons. Midwest Speech and Hearing Assos., Ill., 1976—. Registered psychologist, Ill. Mem. Am., Midwestern, Ill. psychol. assns., Am. Assn. Mental Deficiency, Lost Nation Lakes Assn., Sigma Xi. Contbr. articles to profl. jours. Home: 704 E 2d St Dixon IL 61021 Office: Dixon Developmental Center 2600 N Brinton St Dixon IL 61021

GROTBERG, JOHN E., cons., state senator; b. Winnebago, Minn., Mar. 21, 1925; s. Bernard G.; B.S., George Williams Coll., 1961; m. Jean Oswalt; children—Sandra Mae Grotberg Kistler, Karen Grotberg Weinberg, James Bernard; stepchildren—Melinda and Benjamin M. Oswalt. Farmer, N.D., 1942-44; theatrical and supper club entertainer and mgr., Fargo, Saint Louis, Mpls. and Chgo., 1944-47; mgr. YMCA Hotel Shop, 1948-49, 51, 59; dept. mgr. Montgomery Ward, Chgo., 1950; resident mgr. Pheasant Run Lodge, St. Charles, Ill., 1964-65; dir. public relations YMCA Hotel, Chgo., 1966-71; cons. to mgmt. Hotel Baker Retirement Home for Sr. Citizens, 1972—; corp. dir. fin. devel. YMCA Met. Chgo., 1966-71; rep. Ill. Gen. Assembly, 1973-76; mem. Ill. Senate, 1976—, now asst. Republican leader; profl. singer and actor. Chmn. bd., lay leader Baker Meml. United Methodist Ch.; founder Fox Valley Hospice; former bd. dirs. St. Charles Community Chest; past pres. and bd. dirs. Playmakers, Inc.; founder St. Charles YMCA Indian Guides; Rep. precinct committeeman; past chmn. St. Charles Twp. Rep. Party; chmn. Kane County Rep. Central Com. Mem. Assn. Profl. Dirs. YMCA, Kappa Delta Pi. Clubs: Geneva Golf, Tower (Chgo.), Rotary (Chgo.). Address: Saint Charles IL 60174*

GROTE, CHARLES NELSON, community coll. pres.; b. Oconee, Ill., Jan. 6, 1928; s. Charles E. and Ann Elizabeth Grote; B.S. in Edn., Eastern Ill. U., 1950; M.Ed., U. Mo., 1955; Ed.D., U. Ill., 1960; m. Wilma Ellen McGee, Jan. 6, 1949; children—Carol, Janice, Mark. High sch. tchr., 1950-56; supr. edn. State of Ky., 1956-58; chmn. div. applied arts, then dean Sch. Applied Sci. and Tech., Morehead (Ky.) State U., 1960-71; pres. Schoolcraft Coll., Livonia, Mich., 1971—; cons.-evaluator N. Central Assn. Colls. and Schs. Mem. Livonia Prayer Breakfast Com., 1975—; sponsor Livonia Youth Symphony, 1976—; patron Livonia Arts Commn., 1979—. Served with C.E., AUS, 1946-47. Recipient Disting. Alumnus award Eastern Ill. U., 1978, Disting. Educator award Sch. Tech., 1978. Mem. Am. Assn. Higher Edn., Am. Assn. Community and Jr. Colls. (del.), Mich. Community Coll. Assn. (dir.), Am. Vocat. Assn. (pres. 1969-70), Livonia C. of C., Livonia Hist. Soc. Presbyterian. Club: Optimist. (past dir., dist. officer, lt. gov.). Office: 18600 Haggerty Rd Livonia MI 48152

GROTE SHOEMAKER, MARY MARIE, mktg. exec.; b. Osceola Mills, Pa., June 29, 1947; d. Herman Ray and Erna Henrietta (Srock) Dunwald; student Ashland Coll., 1975, Wooster Coll., 1976; children—Donald, Jill. Writer, compositor Barberton (Ohio) Herald, 1965-66; composing rm. supr. Gowe Printing, lMedina, Ohio, 1966-70, customer service scheduler, 1970-76, sales/mktg. coordinator, 1976—. Mem. Master Printers of Am., Printing Industries of Am. Club: Supreme Emblem. Home: 3866 Nash Blvd Norton OH 44203 Office: 620 E Smith Rd Medina OH 44256

GROTZINGER, LAUREL ANN, educator; b. Truman, Minn., Apr. 15, 1935; d. Edward F. and Marian Gertrude (Greeley) G.; A.B., Carleton Coll., 1957; M.S., U. Ill., 1958, Ph.D., 1964. Instr., asst. librarian Ill. State U., 1958-62; asst. prof. Western Mich. U., Kalamazoo, 1964-66, asso. prof., 1966-68, prof., 1968—, asst. dir. Sch. Librarianship, 1965-72, dean/chief research officer Grad. Coll., 1979—. Mem. ALA (sec.-treas. Library History Roundtable 1973-74), Acad. of Mgmt., Assn. Am. Library Schs., Am. Assn. Higher Edn., Council Grad. Schs., Nat. Council Research Adminstrs., Soc. Research Adminstrs., Mich. Acad. Sci., Arts and Letters (mem. exec. com. 1980—, pres.-elect 1981-82), AAUP (sec. W.M. chpt. 1968-70), Phi Beta Kappa (pres. Southwestern Mich. Assn. 1977-78), Beta Phi Mu (v.p., pres. Kappa chpt.), Pi Delta Epsilon, Delta Kappa Gamma, Alpha Beta Alpha. Author: The Power and the Dignity, Scarecrow, 1966; mem. editorial bd. Jour. Edn. for Librarianship, 1973-77, Dictionary Am. Library Biography, 1975-77; contbr. articles to profl. jours. Home: 2729 Mockingbird Dr Kalamazoo MI 49008

GROVE, EWART LESTER, chemist; b. Greensburgh, Kans., May 31, 1913; s. William Ewart and Theo Etha (Grove) G.; B.Ed., St. Cloud State Coll., 1934-38; M.A., Ohio State U., 1945; Ph.D., Western U., 1951; m. Ethel Lucille Metcalf, June 12, 1944; children—Edward Lester, Ernest William. Tchr., Tyler (Minn.) High

Sch., 1938-40, Cuyahoga Heights High Sch., Cleve., 1940-47; instr. Fenn Coll., 1942-44, Minn. State Tchrs. Coll., St. Cloud, 1947-48; research participant Oak Ridge Nat. Lab., summers 1953-54; asso. prof. U. Ala., 1951-59; research chemist, sr. scientist, mgr. analytical chemistry research Ill. Inst. Tech. Research Inst., Chgo., 1960-70; v.p. Freeman Labs., Inc., Rosemont, Ill., 1970-75; sr. scientist Ill. Inst. Tech. Research Inst., Chgo., 1976—. Mem. Am. Chem. Soc., Soc. Applied Spectroscopy, Am. Inst. Chemists, AAAS, AAUP, Sigma Xi. Methodist. Co-author math. textbooks. Editor: Developments in Applied Spectroscopy. Editor, contbr. Analytical Emission Spectroscopy, Vols. I-II, Applied Atomic Spectroscopy, Vols. I-II. Contbr. numerous articles to profl. jours. Home: 21 W 220 Harding Rd Rd Lombard IL 60148 Office: Ill Inst Tech Research Inst Chicago IL 60616

GROVE, HELEN HARRIET, historian, artist; b. South Bend, Ind.; d. Samuel Harold and LaVerne Mae (Drescher) Grove; grad. Bayle Sch. Design, Meinzinger Found., 1937-39, Washington U., 1940-42; spl. studies, Paris, France. Owner studios of historic research and illustration, St. Louis, Chgo., 1943—; dir. archives, bus. history research Sears, Roebuck & Co., 1951-67; com. missions art and research for Northwestern U., Chgo.-Sears Roebuck & Co. Home: 6326 N Clark St Chicago IL 60626 Studio: 6328 N Clark St Chicago IL 60626

GROVE, JEROME LAWRENCE, coll. pres.; b. St. Paul, May 13, 1939; s. Siglife and Irma (D'Arcey) G.; B.A., U. Minn., 1964; B.F.A., Mpls. Coll. Art and Design, 1963; m. Nancy Wallin, Apr. 24, 1965. Product designer Brown and Bigelow Corp., St. Paul, 1964-66; dir. admissions, registrar, instr. Kansas City (Mo.) Art Inst., 1966-71, dean, v.p., 1971-77; pres. Center for Creative Studies- Coll. of Arts and Design, Detroit, 1977—. Mem. environ. arts panel Mich. Council Arts, 1978—; mem. art adv. panel Sta. WTVS-TV, 1978—. Mem. Union Ind. Colls. Arts (dir.), Univ. Cultural Center Assn. (v.p.), Nat. Council Arts Adminstrs., Am. Assn. Higher Edn., Engring. Soc. Detroit. Office: 245 E Kirby St Detroit MI 48202

GROVE, KALVIN MYRON, lawyer; b. Chgo., Aug. 27, 1937; s. Jacob S. and Hazel (Levitetz) G.; B.A., U. Mich., 1958; J.D., DePaul U., 1961; m. Eileen Dobbs, June 22, 1965; children—Pamela Joy, Jonathan. Admitted to Ill. bar, 1961; trial atty. NLRB, Tampa, Fla. and Chgo., 1962-65; pvt. practice law, Chgo., 1965—. Guest lectr. labor law DePaul U.; arbitrator Am. Arbitration Assn., Fed. Mediation and Conciliation Service. Mem. Gov. Kerner's Com. on Manpower, 1966-68. Served with AUS, 1962. Mem. Am., Ill., Fla. bar assns., Am. Judicature Soc. Contbr. articles to profl. jours. Office: Suite 7818 Sears Tower 233 S Wacker Dr Chicago IL 60006

GROVER, JAMES ROBERT, mfg. co. exec.; b. Beardstown, Ill., Sept. 10, 1935; s. Loren J. and Grace M. (Devlin) G.; B.S., Western Ill. U., 1957; M.S., Ball State U., 1958; m. DeeLight Grebe, Aug. 17, 1957; children—Lisa, Steven, Keith. Supr. edn. and tng. U.S. Steel Corp., Chgo., 1960-62; asst. to dir. indsl. relations Velsicol Chm., Chgo., 1962-64; supr. personnel Armour Pharm., Chgo., 1964-67; with Badische Anilin and Soda Fabrik, Wyandotte Corp. (Mich.), 1967-71, dir. manpower selection, devel. and orgn., 1968-71; dir. personnel Abbott Labs., 1971-73; v.p. Frye, Timmons & Asso., Worthington, Ohio, 1973—; pres. Grover and Assos., Worthington, Ohio, 1975—. Mem. Am. Soc. Personnel Adminstrn., Am. Soc. Tng. and Devel., Indsl. Relations Assn. Detroit, Delta Sigma Phi, Epsilon Pi Tau. Home: 1310 Hickory Ridge Ln Worthington OH 43085 Office: 7870 Olentangy River Rd Worthington OH 43085

GROVER, RICHARD KINSEL, dentist; b. Carson City, Mich., Oct. 7, 1921; s. Fred Otis and Lulu (Kinsel) G.; B.S., Mich. State U., 1943; D.D.S., U. Mich., 1954; m. Carolyn Rose Rourke, Oct. 9, 1954; children—Patricia Lou, Robert Rourke, Richard Kinsel, Michael David. Research chem. engr. Standard Oil N.J., Elizabeth, 1946-50; pvt. practice dentistry, Grandville, Mich., 1954—. Pres., dir. GGM Co.; dir. Century Investors, DigCo Co., LandCo Co., gen. partner GGB Assos., others. Served with AUS, 1943-46; PTO. Mem. W. Mich. Dental Soc. (past dir.), Am., Mich. dental assns., Tau Beta Pi, Omicron Kappa Upsilon, Grandville C. of C. (pres., dir. 1970), Phi Kappa Phi, Sigma Alpha Epsilon, Delta Sigma Delta. Clubs: Grandville Rotary (dir.); Sunnybrook Country; Peninsular; Tamarron (Durango, Colo.); Blythefield Country. Mem. editorial bd. of Jour. Cryobiology, 1964-65. Contbr. articles to profl. jours. Patentee in field. Home: 3628 Chickasaw Ct Grandville MI 49418 Office: 3460 Wilson St SW Grandville MI 49418

GROVES, ANN BLAKESLEY, psychologist, educator; b. Houston, Sept. 6, 1934; d. Ralph C. and Mildred L. (James) Blakesley; B.A. in Psychology, Rice U., 1956; M.A. in Social Sci., U. Chgo., 1957; Ph.D. in Psychology, Ill. Inst. Tech., 1968; children—Mariann Jama, Montgomery St. Clair. Caseworker children's div. Cook County Dept. Welfare, Chgo., 1958-59; instr. Thornton Community Coll., Harvey, Ill., 1959-62; intern Inst. Juvenile Research, Chgo., 1965-66; prof. psychology Chgo. State U., 1968—, grant adminstr., 1978—, chmn. dept., 1973-78, Recipient grants HEW, 1973, 76, Bd. Higher Edn., 1976, Dangerous Drugs Commn., 1975, 76. Mem. Am. Psychol. Assn., Am. Personnel and Guidance Assn., Chgo. Psychol. Club (pres. 1973-74). Home: 72 Shore Dr Ogden Dunes IL 46368 Office: 9500 S King Dr Chicago IL 60628

GROVES, FRANKLIN NELSON, bus. exec.; b. Mpls., Dec. 28, 1930; s. Frank Malvon and Hazel Olive (Nelson) G.; B.A., U. Minn., 1954; m. Carolyn Mary Thomas, July 31, 1954; children—Catherine Mary Groves Gangelhoff, Franklin Nelson, Elizabeth Ann. With S.J. Groves & Sons Co., Mpls., 1954—, v.p., treas., 1964-69, pres., 1969-81, chmn. bd., 1971—, also dir., pres. subs. corps., 1964—. Pres. trustees Groves Found.; bd. dirs. Groves Learning Center; trustee Mpls. Soc. Fine Arts. Served to 1st lt. USAF, 1954-56. Mem. Am. Saddle Horse Breeders Assn. (dir.), Moles, Beavers. Mem. Community Ch. Clubs: Mpls. Athletic; Thoroughbred of Am. Home: 1482 Hunter Dr Wayzata MN 55391 Office: PO Box 1267 10000 Highway 55 W Minneapolis MN 55440

GROWE, JOAN ANDERSON, state ofcl.; b. Mpls., Sept. 28, 1935; d. Arthur F. and Lucille M. (Brown) Anderson; B.S., St. Cloud (Minn.) State U., 1956; cert. in Spl. Edn., U. Minn., 1964; children—Michael, Colleen, David, Patrick. Tchr., Bloomington (Minn.) Public Schs., 1956-58; tchr. exceptional children St. Paul Public Schs., 1964-65; tchr. spl. edn. St. Anthony (Minn.) Public Schs., 1965-66; mem. Minn. Ho. Reps., 1973-74; sec. state State of Minn., St. Paul, 1975—. Mem. Minn. Assn. Retarded Citizens, Minn. Shares for Hunger, Urban Concerns, YWCA; Mem. adv. bd. Fed. Elections Commn., State Bd. Investment. Recipient Minn. Sch. Bell award, 1977; YWCA award, 1978. Mem. Minn. LWV, AAUW, Minn. Women's Polit. Caucus, Citizens League, Nat. Order Women Legislators, Democratic Statewide Elected Ofcls., Common Cause, Nat. Assn. Secs. of State (pres. 1979-80), Bus. and Profl. Women's Club. Club: Zonta. Roman Catholic. Office: 180 State Office Bldg Saint Paul MN 55155

GRUBB, MERRITT BYRON, physician; b. Indpls., Oct. 31, 1941; s. Charles William and Phyllis Jean (Bailey) G.; student Wabash Coll., 1960-61, Ind. U., 1961-62, U. Stockholm (Sweden), 1962-63; M.D., Ind. U., 1967; m. Nancy Ann Seddelmeyer, Nov. 27, 1968; children—Erik Byron, John Nelson. Intern, Bethesda Luth. Hosp., St. Paul, 1967-68; resident in dermatology Ind. U., Indpls., 1970-73; practice medicine specializing in dermatology Med. Arts Clinic, Minot, N.D., 1973, instr. U. N.D., asso. in medicine, 1973-77, clin. asso. prof., 1977—. Served with USPHS, 1968-70. Bd. dirs. Med. Arts Clinic, 1976-81, chmn. bd. dirs., 1979-81; bd. dirs. N.D. div. Am. Cancer Soc., 1976—. Diplomate Am. Bd. Dermatology; lic. guide and outfitter, N.D. Fellow Am. Acad. Dermatology, Soc. Investigative Dermatology; mem. AMA, N.D. Med. Assn., N.D. Dermatol. Soc., Minn. Dermatol. Soc., Am. Legion, Nat. Muzzleloading Rifle Assn., Nat. Assn. Promitive Riflemen, Nat. Rifle Assn., Am. Legion, Nat. Wildlife Fedn. Clubs: Ducks Unlimited, Minot Gun. Home: Rt 1 Burlington ND 58722 Office: 120 4th Ave SE Minot ND 58701

GRUBER, CHARLES LAMAR, laundry co. exec.; b. Elkhart, Ind., 1937; s. George Marlin and Lillie Ellen (Rowe) G.; B.S. in Accounting, Ball State U., 1959; m. Paula Francis Bolerjack, Aug. 22, 1959; children—Darcy, Dexter, Barton. Accountant General Motors Corp., Muncie, Ind., 1959; divisional staff accountant Kroger Co., Cin., 1960-62, plant controller, 1962-63, corp. programmer analyst, 1963-64; field auditor Montgomery Ward Co., Cin., 1964-65, met. sr. auditor, Chgo., 1965-66, supervising sr. auditor, St. Paul, 1966-68; divisional controller Sta-Rite Industries, Inc., Delavan, Wis., 1968-71, corp. dir. data processing, 1971-77; pres. Adelman Laundry & Cleaners, Inc., Milw., 1977—; police officer City of Delavan, 1975-79. Pres., Walworth County Assn. for Retarded Citizens, 1976-77, Boy Scouts Am. Served with AUS, 1960. Mem. Soc. Cert. Data Processors, Blue Key Nat. Honor Soc. Clubs: K.C., Lions. Home: 708 Tyrell Ave Delavan WI 53115 Office: 709 E Capitol Dr Milwaukee WI 53212

GRUBER, THOMAS ALLAN, restaurant co. exec.; b. Mpls., Apr. 12, 1940; s. Arthur R. and Edna M. G.; B.S., U. Minn., 1962; m. Polly Johnson, July 3, 1977. Merchandising mgr. Naegele Outdoor Advt., 1960-63; advt. sales mgr. Wall Street Jour., 1966-67; regional advt. mgr. McDonald's Corp., Oak Brook, Ill., 1967-69, nat. mktg. mgr., 1969-71; v.p., dir. mktg. McDonald's Internat., Oak Brook, 1973—; v.p. B/R/B Advt. Agy., Kansas City, Mo., 1972-73. Served to capt. Med. Service Corps, U.S. Army, 1972-76. Mem. Internat. Advt. Assn., Nat. Restaurant Assn., Beta Theta Pi. Office: McDonalds Plaza Oak Brook IL 60521

GRUENBERG, JAMES CHANDLER, surgeon; b. Chgo., Mar. 22, 1942; s. Robert Pershing and Imogene (Chandler) G.; B.S. in Chemistry, Stanford U., 1963; M.D., U. Mich., 1967; m. Jennifer Ann Klein, Sept. 10, 1966; children—Heather Jeanne, Karl Martin. Straight surg. intern U. Hosp., Madison, Wis., 1967-68, resident in gen. surgery, 1968-72; practice medicine specializing in surgery, Detroit, 1972—; mem. staff Henry Ford Hosp.; clin. instr. surgery U. Mich., 1978—. Served to maj. U.S. Army, 1972-74; Vietnam. Decorated Bronze Star. Diplomate Am. Bd. Surgery. Fellow A.C.S.; mem. Detroit Surg. Soc., S.W. Oncology Group, Detroit Surg. Assn., Acad. Surgery Detroit, Detroit Gastroent. Soc. Contbr. articles to profl. jours. Office: Dept Surgery Henry Ford Hosp 2799 W Grand Blvd Detroit MI 48202

GRUENDNER, JOSEF, JR., janitorial services co. exec.; b. Kurd, Hungary, Dec. 26, 1938; came to U.S., 1957, naturalized, 1960; s. Joseph and Elizabeth (Fuchsberger) G.; student Wright Jr. Coll., 1961-62, YMCA Coll., Chgo., 1965-66; grad. USAF Squadron Officer Sch., 1974, USAF Air Command and Staff Coll., 1975; m. Marlies Vaas, Jan. 20, 1961; children—Frank Reinhold, Marion, Monika. With Chgo. Transit Authority, 1961-68; with AT&T, Chgo., 1968-78, data processing supr., 1974-76, acctg. supr., 1976-78; owner, mgr. Gruendner Enterprises, Park Ridge, Ill., 1978—. Squadron comdr. CAP, 1975-78, group comdr., 1978-79, dep. wing comdr., 1979—. Served with U.S. Army, 1957-60. Recipient Cert. of Recognition, German Nat. Congress, 1978; Grover Loening Aerospace award CAP, 1975, Paul E. Garber award for outstanding service, 1979, Gill Robb Wilson award, 1973, Comdrs. Commendation award, 1980, Meritorious Service award, 1981, many others. Mem. German Am. Nat. Congress (chpt. pres. 1967-69, regional pres. 1969-71, nat. v.p. 1971-74), German Am. Rep. League of Ill. (pres. 1971-74), German Am. Rep. Fedn. (pres. 1972-74). Address: 641 N Northwest Hwy Park Ridge IL 60068

GRUENWALD, GEORGE HENRY, advt. agy. exec.; b. Chgo., Apr. 23, 1922; s. Arthur Frank and Helen Marie (Duke) G.; student Grinnell Coll., 1940-41, U. Florence (Italy), 1945; B.S., Northwestern U., 1947; m. Corrine Rae Linn, Aug. 16, 1947; children—Helen Marie Gruenwald Orlando, Paul Arthur. Asst. to pres. Uarco Inc., 1947-49; mdse. mgr., creative dir. Willys-Overland Motors, 1949-51; brand advt. mgr. Toni Co., 1951-53; creative dir., account exec. Edward H. Weiss Co., 1953-55; v.p., account supr. North Advt., Inc., Chgo., 1955-65, sr. v.p., mgmt. supr., dir. planning and devel., 1965-67, exec. v.p., 1967-71; pres. Pilot Products Industries, Inc., Chgo., 1964-71, Advance Brands, Inc., 1966-71; exec. v.p. Campbell-Mithun, Inc., Mpls., 1971-72, pres., dir. 1972-80, chmn. bd., 1980—, chief exec. officer, 1981—. Trustee, Chgo. Public TV, 1971-78, Minn. Public Radio, 1973-78, Mpls. Soc. Fine Arts, 1975—; trustee, chmn. exec. com. Twin Cities Public TV, 1971—; bd. dirs., exec. com. Public Broadcasting Service, Washington, 1978—, chmn. task force on tech., 1980—. Served with USAAF, 1943-45. Recipient Hermes award Chgo. Federated Advt. Clubs, 1963; Ednl. TV awards, 1969, 71. Mem. Am. Assn. Advt. Agys. (mgmt. com. 1976—), Advt. Fedn. Minn. Clubs: Canadian (N.Y.C.); Tavern (Chgo.); Mpls., Wayzata Country, Confrerie des Chevaliers du Tastevin. Contbr. articles in field to profl. jours. Home: 1725 Hunter Dr Wayzata MN 55391 also Rancho Santa Fe CA 92067 Office: Campbell-Mithun Inc 1000 Northstar Center Minneapolis MN 55402

GRULIOW, AGNES FORREST, painter; b. Davenport, Iowa, July 5, 1912; d. James and Agnes (Johnston) Forrest; B.A., Antioch Coll., Yellow Springs, Ohio, 1938; postgrad. Art Students League, N.Y.C., 1963-66; m. Leo Gruliow, Sept. 22, 1945; children—Frank Forrest, Rebecca Agnes Lindsay. Resident dir. Am. Peoples Sch., N.Y.C., 1937-41; asst. nat. sec. Nat. Fedn. Settlements, N.Y.C., 1941-43; asst. prof., asso. personnel dir. extramural program Antioch Coll., 1943-45; index editor Current Digest of Soviet Press, N.Y.C., 1949-53; freelance editor, N.Y.C., 1954-57; tchr. art City and Country Sch., N.Y.C., 1966-68; vis. fellow Woodrow Wilson Nat. Fellowship Found., 1974-80; propr. art studio, N.Y.C., 1961-69, Worthington, Ohio, 1970-72; art therapy asst. Harding Hosp., Worthington, 1970-72; one-woman exhbns. include Antioch Coll., 1967. Pres. Greenhouse Nursery Sch., N.Y.C., 1955-56; bd. dirs. Open Door Day Care Center, N.Y.C., 1954-59; mem. founding and adv. bd. East Harlem Tutoring Program, N.Y.C., 1965-70; bd. dirs. Columbus (Ohio) Area Internat. Programs, 1970-72, adv. bd., 1979—, sec. bd., 1981—. Mem. Am. Assn. Advancement Slavic Studies, AAUW, LWV, Buckeye Art Therapy Assn. Club: Order Eastern Star. Address: 163 E Lane Ave Columbus OH 43201

GRUMBLES, CARL EDWIN, educator; b. Hammond, Ind., Dec. 20, 1941; s. Edward Eugene and Frances Harriet (Moore) Grumbles; B.A., Purdue U., 1965; M.A., Northeastern Ill. U., 1976; m. Donnejean Ferner, Sept. 2, 1966; children—Jack, Dan, Scot, Chris, Amanda. Asst. editor Leader, mag. Christian Service Brigade, Wheaton, Ill., 1966-68; tchr., prin. Open Door Children's Home, Hazard, Ky., 1968-69; tchr. Lombard (Ill.) Sch. Dist. 44, 1969—. Vol. counselor Christ Ch. Oak Brook Counseling Center, 1976—, Lafayette Juvenile Delinquents, 1963-64, Bethany Children's Home, 1962-64; counselor, program dir., camp dir. Camp Kaskitowa, 1966-74; mem. precinct com. Republican party, 1976—; bd. dirs. Lombard YMCA, 1976—. Recipient award Outstanding Merit Christian Camping, Central Camping Assn., 1972, Outstanding Young Educator award Lombard Jaycees, 1972. Mem. Lombard, Nat. (life), Ill. edn. assns., Am. Personnel and Guidance Assn., Am. Sch. Counseling Assn. Home: 5709 Essex St Lisle IL 60532 Office: Sch Dist 44 Lombard IL 60148

GRUNDSTROM, DONALD WILLIAM, mfg. co. exec.; b. Taylor Ridge, Ill., Jan. 12, 1923; s. Gust Gunnar and Harriet (Carothers) G.; student Wheaton Coll., 1943; m. Betty Mae Keuter, July 26, 1956; 1 stepdau., Judith Ann. With John Deere Co., 1941—, supt. foundry, Dubuque, 1961-71, supt. foundry, Tractor Works div., Waterloo, 1971-77, works mgr., 1977-81, mgr. foundry ops., 1981—. Served with U.S. Army, 1943-46. Mem. Nat. Foundry Assn. (dir. 1979—), Am. Foundrymens Soc. (dir. 1980), Cast Metals Fedn., Foundry Ednl. Found. (trustee 1981), Metalcasters of Iowa, Am. Mgmt. Assn., Am. Def. Preparedness Assn., U.S. Power Squadron, Aircraft Owners and Pilots Assn., Waterloo C. of C. Republican. Clubs: Rotary, Julien Dubuque Yacht, Elks. Home: 3384 Monticello Ave Waterloo IA 50701 Office: 400 Westfield Ave Waterloo IA 50704

GRUNOW, MILLIE HUST, librarian; b. Bedford County, Tenn., Oct. 16, 1931; d. William B. and Georgia Mae (Elkins) Hust; B.A., George Peabody Coll. Tchrs., Nashville, 1953, M.A. in Library Sci., 1955; m. Hubert L. Near, Aug. 13, 1955; children—Elizabeth Near Hanes, Katherine Near Baize, Margaret; m. 2d, Donald A. Grunow, Mar. 17, 1973. Head cataloging dept. W.Va. Inst. Tech., Montgomery, 1967-70; coordinator tech. services U. Evansville (Ind.), 1970-72; med. librarian Deaconess Hosp., Evansville, 1972—; exec. dir. Evansville Area Health Sci. Library Consortium, 1975-79. Mem. Med. Library Assn., Midwest Health Sci. Library Network, Ind. Library Assn., Ind. Health Scis. Librarians Assn., Evansville Area Health Sci. Library Consortium. Methodist. Home: 508 S Boeke Rd Evansville IN 47714 Office: 600 Mary St Evansville IN 47747

GRUNSFELD, ERNEST ALTON, III, architect; b. Chgo., June 5, 1929; s. Ernest Alton and Mary Jane (Loeb) G.; student Art Inst. Chgo., 1947; B.Arch., Mass. Inst. Tech., 1952; m. Sally Riblett, July 10, 1954; children—Marcia, John Mace. Pvt. practice as architect, Chgo., 1954-56; partner Yerkes & Grunsfeld, Chgo., 1956-65; owner Grunsfeld & Assos., architects, Chgo., 1965-75, sr. partner, 1975—. Vice-pres. Urban Gateways, 1969-78, dir., 1968—; mem. Highland Park Plan Commn., 1969-75; bd. dirs., pres. Grunsfeld Fund, 1965—; dir. Council for Arts, Mass. Inst. Tech., 1977—, exec. com., 1978—; mem. corp. Woodlawn Hosp., 1968-70; founding life sustaining fellow M.I.T. Served as 1st lt. USAF, 1952-53. Recipient First Honor award Burlington Mills, 1968. Mem. AIA (corp. mem., Distinguished Bldg. award 1962, 69), Art Inst. Chgo. (benefactor, hon. governing mem.), Field Mus. Natural History (life), Oriental Inst. Chgo., Chgo. Symphony Soc. (hon. life). Clubs: City (dir.), Tavern, Mass. Inst. Tech. (Chgo.); Lakeshore Country (Highland Park, Ill.). Contbr. articles to profl. jours. Office: 520 N Michigan St Chicago IL 60611

GRUNWALD, ARNOLD PAUL, engring. cons.; b. Berlin, Dec. 7, 1910; came to U.S., 1952, naturalized, 1957; s. Richard Michael and Hedwig (Bamann) G.; student U. Munich (Germany), 1929-33; m. Grete Marie Gwinner, Dec. 29, 1945; children—Eva, Peter. Chief engr. WEHOBA G.m.b.H., Weilheim, Germany, 1946-49; prodn. engr., cons. Chisholm, Boyd & White, Chgo., Ethicon Inc., Chgo., others; asso. engr. Argonne (Ill.) Nat. Lab., 1958-77; chief cons. Research for Braille Communication, Chgo., 1977-80, pres., 1980—; cons. Am. Found. for the Blind, 1973-76, div. for blind Library of Congress, 1970; mgr., prin. investigator Argonne Braille project, 1968-76. Vice pres., chmn. edn. com. Parents of the Blind, Inc., 1957-67; chmn. exec. com. Argonne Senate, 1971-72. Recipient Letter of Commendation, Pres. of U.S., 1976; HEW grantee, 1969-75. Mem. Fedn. Am. Scientists, ACLU, Nat. Fedn. of the Blind, Sigma Xi. Contbr. articles to profl. jours. Address: 1236 E 85th St Chicago IL 60619

GRUTKA, ANDREW GREGORY, bishop; b. Joliet, Ill., Nov. 17, 1908; student St. Procopius Coll. and Sem., Lisle, Ill., Urban U. and Gregorian U., Rome. Ordained priest Roman Catholic Ch., 1933; moderator of lay activities Diocese of Gary (Ind.), 1955; first bishop of Gary, 1957; mem. Pontifical Marian Acad., 1970; pres. Cath. Communications Found., 1971-76, chmn. bd., 1976—. Office: PO Box 474 668 Pierce St Gary IN 46401*

GRZYWINSKI, RONALD ALOYSIUS, banker; b. Chgo., Feb. 18, 1936; B.S., Loyola U., Chgo., 1958. Pres. 1st Nat. Bank Lockport (Ill.), 1965-66, Hyde Park Bank, Chgo., 1966-69; chmn. bd. South Shore Bank, Chgo., 1973-76, 1980—, chmn. exec. com., 1976-80; chmn. loan com., dir. Nat. Consumer Coop. Bank, Washington, 1979-81. Vice chmn., chmn. fin. com. Chgo. Coll. Osteo. Medicine. Served to 1st lt. AUS, 1958-60. Adlai Stevenson Inst. Internat. Affairs fellow, 1969-72. Address: South Shore Bank Jeffrey Blvd at 71st St Chicago IL 60649

GUARNIERI, DONALD LEWIS, lawyer; b. Warren, Ohio, May 8, 1934; s. Albert A. and Elsie C. (McKay) G.; A.B., Hiram Coll., 1956; LL.B., Cleve. State U., 1960, LL.M., 1963, J.D., 1964; m., July 11, 1970; 1 son, Lewis Donald. Admitted to Ohio bar, 1960; pvt. practice law, Warren, 1960—; land developer; pres. Champion Mall Corp., Parkhurst Mall Corp., Norwalk Mall Corp. Commr., Little All-Am. Football; bd. dirs. Salvation Army, Family Service Assn., Warren Symphony, Youngstown Symphony; pres. Civic Music Assn. Served with AUS, 1957. Elk, Moose, Eagle, Kiwanian (pres. 1980—), K.C. Clubs: Mosquito Yacht (Cortland, Ohio); Olympic, Trumbull (Warren). Author: 8th Day of May, 1968. Contbr. articles to profl. jours. Home: 399 Golf Dr Warren OH 44481 Office: 149 E Market St Warren OH 44481

GUASTELLO, THOMAS, state senator, lawyer; b. Detroit, Oct. 25, 1943; s. Peter James and Barbarose (Shaw) G.; B.A., Mich. State U., 1965; J.D., Detroit Coll. Law, 1969. Admitted to Mich. bar; v.p. Village Inns, Inc., 1964—; law clk. Circuit Ct., 1967-68; practiced in Mt. Clemens, Mich.; mem. Mich. Ho. of Reps., 1969-74, Mich. Senate, 1974—. Precinct del., Sterling Heights, Mich.; past chmn.

Macomb County Young Dems. Named to Lakeview High Sch. Hall of Fame. Mem. Macomb County Bar Assn., Macomb County Pros. Attys. Assn., State Bar Mich. Mem. Utica Citizens Adv. Com., Macomb County Drug Abuse and Vocat. Edn. Commn. Roman Catholic. Office: Mich State Senate State Capitol Lansing MI 48909*

GUBRICKY, MARY ELLEN, educator; b. Chgo., Oct. 24, 1951; d. Albert John and Helen Mary (Heinlein) G.; Cert. Arts, Richard J. Daley Jr. Coll., Chgo., 1972; B.S.Ed., No. Ill. U., 1974; M.A. in Curriculum Devel., U. Conn., 1977, postgrad., 1980—. With Ill. Bell Telephone Co., Chgo., 1969-71; internat. accountant Mex. br. Ency. Brit. Ednl. Corp., Chgo., 1974-76; advt. cons. Buzz Barton & Assos., Inc., Chgo., 1977-78; varied advt. positions Dimensional Mktg. Inc., Chgo., 1979; tchr. Nativity of Our Lord Sch., Chgo., 1979; tchr. Mother McAuley High Sch., Chgo., 1979—. Mem. Nat. Council Social Studies, Ill. Council Social Studies, Nat. Hist. Soc., Smithsonian Assos., AAUP, Art Inst. Chgo., Assn. for Supervision and Curriculum Devel.

GUCKENHEIMER, DANIEL PAUL, banker; b. Tel Aviv, Oct. 10, 1943; s. Ernest and Eva Guckenheimer; came to U.S., 1947, naturalized, 1957; B.B.A. in Fin., U. Houston, 1970; cert. hosp. adminstrn., Trinity U., San Antonio, 1973; m. Helen Sandra Fox, Dec. 21, 1969; children—Debra Ellen, Julie Susan. Asst. adminstr. Harris County Hosp. Dist., Houston, 1970-76; pres. Mid Am. Investments, Kansas City, Kans., 1976; exec. dir. Allen County Hosp., Iola, Kans., 1977-78; comml. loan officer Traders Bank, Kansas City, Mo., 1979—; v.p., mgr. Traders Ward Parkway Bank, 1980, v.p., mgr. installment loans, 1981—. Bd. dirs. United Way, Iola, Kans., 1977-78; adv. bd. Country Side Estate Nursing Home, Iola, 1977-78; clinic adminstr. 190th USAF Clinic; mem. Downtown Inc., Kansas City, Mo., 1980—. Served with USAF, 1962-66, maj. Res. Mem. Am. Coll. Hosp. Adminstrs., Am. Hosp. Assn., C. of C. Kansas City, N.G. Guard Assn., Soc. Army N.G. MSC Officers. Clubs: Iola Rotary; Kansas City. Home: 10259 Caenen Lake Rd Lenexa KS 66215 Office: 1125 Grand Ave Kansas City MO 64106

GUDENAS, JOHN WAYNE, computer scientist; b. Chgo., Aug. 5, 1946; s. Andrew J. and Irene E. (Rakauskas) G.; B.S. in Physics, Ill. Benedictine Coll., 1968; M.S. in Info. Sci., Ill. Inst. Tech., 1971; m. Patricia Barlett, July 11, 1970; children—Juliet, Jean Margaret. Computer scientist Argonne (Ill.) Nat. Lab., 1968-73; sr. analyst Standard Oil Co. Ind., Chgo., 1973-77; pres., dir. Valentine Equipment Co., Inc., Bridgeview, Ill., 1977—. Mem. Assn. Computing Machinery. Contbr. articles on air quality to profl. jours. Home: 631 Glenwood Ln LaGrange IL 60525

GUDERLEY, GEORGE WARREN, JR., hwy. engr.; b. Chgo., Oct. 12, 1922; s. George W. and Alma (Matthies) G.; student Ill. Inst. Tech., 1940-49; grad. Civil Engring. Sch., Air U., 1953; m. Lois R. Christell, Sept. 3, 1949; children—Susan Gail, George W. III. Chief engr. adminstrn. Cook County Hwy. Dept., Chgo., 1946-68; exec. dir. Ill. Toll Hwy. Authority, Oakbrook, Ill., 1969-72; v.p. CEMCON, Aurora, Ill., 1981—. Mem. Ill. Hwy. Research Council, 1962-72, chmn. sub-com. for research mgmt., 1969-72; tech. adv. Northeastern Ill. Plan Commn., Flood Control and Pure Water Commn. Trustee, Village of Inverness, Ill., 1969-79; mem. exec. bd. Northwest Suburban council Boy Scouts Am., 1969-79. Served with USAAF, 1942-45, USAF, 1951-53, 62; maj. Ret. Decorated Air Medal with oak leaf cluster, Purple Heart. Mem. Chgo. Assn. Commerce and Industry, Res. Officers Assn. (pres. 1963), Computer User's Exchange Orgn. (chmn. hwy. design com. 1961), Am. Pub. Works Assn., Ill. Transp. Council (pres.), N.W. Mcpl. Conf., Internat. Bridge, Tunnel and Turnpike Assn. (chmn. adminstrv. com. 1970, engring. design com. 1971). Home: 1482 W Banbury Rd Inverness PO Palatine IL 60067 Office: 933 W Liberty Dr Aurora IL 60187

GUDMUNDSON, BARBARA JANE ROHRKE, ecologist; b. Chgo.; d. Lloyd Ernst and Helen (Bullard) Rohrke; B.A., U. Tenn., Knoxville, 1950; student U. Chgo., 1942-44; M.A., Mankato State Coll., 1965; Ph.D., Iowa State U., 1969; m. V(altyr) Emil Gudmundson, June 14, 1951; children—Holly Mekkin, Martha Rannveig. Dist. ecologist C.E., St. Paul, 1971-72; sr. ecologist North Star/Midwest Research Inst., Mpls., 1972-76; staff engr. Met. Waste Control Commn., St. Paul, 1976-77; pres. Ecosystem Research Service/Upper Midwest, Inc., 1978—; cons. ecologist and diatomist, Mpls., 1977—; mem. adv. com. Mpls. Lakes Water Quality, 1974-75; mem. task force new concepts in urban transp. Transp. Research Bd., Nat. Acad. Scis., 1972—; mem. Mississippi River canoe expdn. Coll. of Atlantic, 1979; mem. Minnehaha Creek Watershed Dist. Bd., 1979—. Asst. precinct chmn. Democratic Farmer-Labor Party, 1974-76, caucus chmn., 1976, dir. 61st dist. central com., 1978-80, del. state central com., 1980—; mem. housing devel. task force, Minn. capital long-range improvements com. Mpls. City Council, 1981. Recipient research grant Iowa Acad. Sci., 1976, Freshwater Biol. Research Found., 1979. Fellow Iowa Acad. Sci.; mem. AAAS, Minn. Acad. Sci. (sec.-treas. 1973-75), Ecol. Soc. Am. (1st pres. chpt. 1971-75), Water Pollution Control Fedn., Phycological Soc. Am., Assn. for Women in Sci., Geol. Soc. Minn. (pres. 1980), Minn. Women's Network, NOW, Sigma Xi, Phi Kappa Phi, Hekla Icelandic Club (pres. 1977-78). Unitarian. Club: Toastmasters (adminstrv. v.p. 1979). Home: 5505 28th Ave S Minneapolis MN 55417 Office: PO Box 17102 Minneapolis MN 55417

GUELICH, ROBERT VERNON, retail co. exec.; b. Dayton, Ohio, Oct. 30, 1917; s. Lewis M. and Pearl B. (Brown) G.; B.A., Ohio Wesleyan U., 1938; M.B.A., Harvard Grad. Sch. Bus., 1940; m. Jane E. Schory, Dec. 6, 1941; children—Susan Jeanne, Robert, Jr., Helen Jane. Reporter Dayton (Ohio) Jour., 1935-37; writer, editor Air Force Mag., N.Y.C., 1942-46; asst. dir. public relations Firestone Tire & Rubber Co., Akron, Ohio, 1946-57; v.p. public relations Montgomery Ward & Co., Chgo., 1957—. Bd. dirs. Nat. 4-H Service Com., 1972-76; trustee Nat. 4-H Council, 1976—, Found. for Pub. Relations Research & Edn., 1978-80; chmn. Nat. Public Relations Seminar, 1981; pres. bd. edn. New Trier Twp. High Schs., 1967-70. Served to maj. USAF, 1941-46. Recipient George Washington Honor medal Freedoms Found., 1976; Mem. Public Relations Soc. Am. (dir. 1976-78; Silver Anvil award 1968, 71, 73, Presdl. citations, Outstanding Film award 1977), Sigma Delta Chi. Republican. Presbyterian. Clubs: National Press (Washington); Headline (Chgo.); Mid-America; Chicago Yacht. Home: 380 Sterling Rd Kenilworth IL 60043 Office: Montgomery Ward Plaza Chicago IL 60671

GUELKER, ADRIENNE MENARIK, occupational therapist; b. Evanston, Ill., Nov. 20, 1953; d. Bernard A. and Helen M. (Bartley) Menarik; B.A. in Occupational Thearpy, Coll. of St. Catherine, St. Paul, 1975; m. William R. Guelker, Jan. 22, 1977; 1 dau., Jeanette Marie. Occupational therapist Alexian Bros. Med. Center, Elk Grove, Ill., 1975-77, Ebenezer Soc., Mpls., 1977—, Project Independence, United Hosp., St. Paul, 1980—. Mem. Am. Occupational Therapy Assn. (registered), Minn. Occupational Therapy Assn., Mpls. Sr. Workers. Home: 1869 Marshall Ave Saint Paul MN 55104 Office: 2523 Portland Ave Minneapolis MN 55404

GUENTHER, DENNIS ALFRED, mech. engr., educator; b. Cleve., Sept. 29, 1946; s. Alfred Edward and Ellen (Manuel) G.; B.S.M.E., Purdue U., 1968; postgrad. (fellow), Princeton U., 1968-69; M.Sc., Ohio State U., 1971, Ph.D., 1974; m. Judith Ann Hawley, Mar. 20, 1971; children—Dax Alexander, Derek Allan, Drake Andrew. Asso. prof. mech. engring. Ohio State U., Columbus, 1974—; tech. cons. Systems Engring. Assos., Columbus, Atlanta, Tampa and Detroit, 1974—. Registered profl. engr., Ohio, W.Va., Ind., Mich., Ky., Ga., N.C., S.C., Md., Pa., Fla., Tenn. Mem. Nat. Soc. Profl. Engrs., Nat. Safety Council, ASME, Am. Soc. Safety Engring. and Edn., Am. Soc. Engring. Edn., ASTM, AAUP, Acoustical Soc. Am., Soc. Automotive Engring. Presbyterian. Contbr. articles to profl. jours. Home: 1622 Cambridge Blvd Columbus OH 43212 Office: 7349 Worthington Galena Rd Columbus OH 43085 also 206 W 18 Ave Columbus OH 43210

GUENTZEL, RICHARD DALE, historian; b. Mankato, Minn., Jan. 1, 1934; s. Edgar Theodore and Harriet Louise (Dimmel) G.; B.S., Mankato State U., 1955, M.S., 1964; Ph.D. (Heitzmann fellow), U. Nebr., 1976; m. Evelyn Carol Nelson, Aug. 7, 1965; children—Melanie Jane, Heather Lynn. History tchr. Litchfield (Minn.) High Sch., 1955-57, Mound (Minn.) High Sch., 1960-64, John Marshall High Sch., Rochester, Minn., 1965-66; instr. history Austin (Minn.) Community Coll., 1967—. Served with U.S. Army, 1957-59, 60-61. Named Outstanding Social Studies Grad. Mankato State U., 1955. Mem. Minn. Assn. History Tchrs. (governing bd. 1977-81), Minn. Community Coll. Faculty Assn., Am. Hist. Assn., Nebr., Minn. hist. socs., Phi Alpha Theta. Democrat. Lutheran. Contbr. articles to profl. jours. Home: 1104 6th Ave NW Austin MN 55912

GUENTZLER, RONALD EDWARD, educator; b. Cleve., May 17, 1934; s. Edward Frederick and Mary (Prochaska) G.; B.S. in Elec. Engring., Case Inst. Tech., 1956, M.S. in Elec. Engring., 1963; children—Judy Louise, Gretchen Suzanne. Asst. engr. transmission and protection sect., gen. engring. dept. Ohio Bell Telephone Co., Cleve., 1956-60; lectr., instr. Tech. Inst., dept. elec. engring. Fenn Coll., Cleve., 1956-67; asso. prof. dept. elec. engring. Ohio No. U., Ada, 1967—. Mem. IEEE (sr.), Am. Radio Relay League, Sigma Xi, Tau Beta Pi, Eta Kappa Nu. VHF editor RTTY Jour., 1967-77. Contbr. articles to profl. jours. Home: 212 Grandview Blvd Ada OH 45810

GUERTAL, ROCHELLE, religious order adminstr.; b. Canton, Ohio, June 11, 1946; d. John Norman and Nadyne Veronica (Leahy) Guertal; B.S.E., St. John Coll., 1974; M.Ed., John Carroll U., 1978. Joined Order Sisters of Most Holy Trinity, Roman Catholic Ch., 1964; tchr. St. John Vianney Sch., Bronx, 1967-68, St. Rocoo Sch., Cleve., 1968-70, 72-75, St. Ann Sch., Bristol, Pa., 1970-71, Nativity Sch., Brandon, Fla., 1971-72; formation directress Sisters of Most Holy Trinity, Euclid, Ohio, 1975—. Mem. exec. bd. Sisters Senate, Diocesan Pastoral Council, Diocesan Liturgy Commn., Nat. Sister Vocation Conf. Mem. Am. Personnel and Guidance Assn., Am. Sch. Counselor Assn. Home: 21320 Euclid St Euclid OH 44117

GUETH, THOMAS FRANKLIN, elec. engr.; b. Columbus, Ohio, Jan. 18, 1950; s. Clarence Francis and Jacqueline (Cummins) G.; B.S. in Elec. Engring., Ohio State U., 1973; B.S. in Engring. Mgmt., U. Evansville, 1979. Elec. engr. Warrick operations Alcoa, Newburgh, Ind., 1974-77, sr. elec. engr., 1978-79; mgr. systems dep. Kinetic Systems Corp., Lockport, Ill., 1979-81, indsl. market dir., 1981—; evening lectr. U. Evansville, 1979—. Mem. IEEE, Instrument Soc. Am., Am. Mgmt. Assn., Tau Beta Pi. Home: 316 Whispering Hills Dr Naperville IL 60540 Office: 11 Maryknoll Dr Lockport IL 60441

GUIKEMA, DALE JOHN, electric co. fin. exec.; b. Grand Rapids, Mich., Dec. 29, 1940; s. Siebrand and Gertrude Esther (Brinks) G.; student Calvin Coll., 1958-60; B.B.A., U. Mich., 1963, M.B.A., 1964; m. Joan Ellen Korschot, Sept. 2, 1961; children—Susan Elizabeth, Beth Ellen, Nancy Esther. Auditor, Arthur Young & Co., Chgo., 1964-68, mgmt. cons., 1968-71, mgr., 1970-71; controller Chain div. Borg Warner Corp., Ithaca, N.Y., 1971-74; sec.-treas. Koontz-Wagner Electric Co., Inc., South Bend, Ind., 1974-80, v.p. fin., 1980—; instr. Ind. U., South Bend, 1975-76. Active United Way. C.P.A., Ill. Mem. South Bend Area C. of C., Am. Inst. C.P.A.'s., Fin. Execs. Inst., Ind. Soc. C.P.A.'s. Republican. Mem. Christian Ref. Ch. Home: 53266 Bonvale Dr South Bend IN 46635 Office: 3801 Voorde Dr South Bend IN 46628

GUILD, RONALD JOHN, lawyer; b. Geneva, Ill., Dec. 24, 1928; s. John William and Helen Jean (Earle) G.; B.S., U. Ill., 1950, LL.B., 1955; m. Marilyn Stephens, Mar. 23, 1956; children—John S., Susan E. Admitted to Ill. bar, 1956, Fed. bar, 1956; mem. firm Hubbard, Hubbard & Dorgan, Chgo., 1955-59, McDermott, Will & Emery, 1960-68, partner, 1966-68; partner Teitelbaum, Wolfberg, Guild & Toback and predecessor firms, Chgo., 1968—; dir. Brickyard Bank, Chgo. Mem. sch. bd. Wheaton-Warrenville Elementary Schs., 1969-72; active Wheaton Community Assn., 1971—, pres., 1975-76. Served to 1st lt. arty. AUS, 1951-52. Mem. Am., Chgo. (exec. com. 1963-68), Ill. bar assns., Am. Arbitration Assn. (panel), Delta Sigma Phi, Alpha Delta Sigma, Phi Alpha Delta. Democrat. Presbyterian. Club: Glen Oak Country (Glen Ellyn, Ill.). Contbg. author books pub. Ill. Inst. Continuing Legal Edn. Home: 186 W Elm St Wheaton IL 60187 Office: 39 S LaSalle St Chicago IL 60603

GUINEE, BERT THOMAS, mfg. co. exec.; b. Chgo., Jan. 14, 1945; s. Bert and Lucille (Hanaway) G.; B.B.A., Loyola U., Chgo., 1967; m. Carol Ann Munin, June 4, 1966; children—Michael, Mark, Martin, Kathleen, Kevin, Keith, Daniel. With 3M Co., Bedford Park, Ill., 1967—, product mgr., 1973-76, market devel. mgr., 1976-79, sales and mktg. mgr., 1979-82, project mgr., St. Paul, 1982—. Active Boy Scouts Am. Mem. Nat. Electric Sign Assn. Office: 3M Co 3M Center Saint Paul MN 55144

GUINIGUNDO, NOLI CONTRERAS, physician; b. Philippines, Aug. 2, 1938; came to U.S., 1963, naturalized, 1973; s. Serafin C. and Natividad Z. (Contreras) G.; pre-med. student (entrance scholar 1954-56), U. Philippines, Far Eastern U., 1956-57; M.D., Far Eastern U., 1961; m. Maria Lourdes Ulgado, Dec. 26; children—Gary, Joey. Intern Far Eastern U. Hosp., Manila, 1961-62; gen. practice medicine and surgery, Manila, 1962-63; 66-68; rotating intern, then resident in surgery Mercy Hosp., Hamilton, Ohio, 1963-66; resident in surgery Saginaw (Mich.) Gen. Hosp., 1966; house physician Ft. Hamilton Hosp., Hamilton, 1968-70; practice medicine specializing in family practice, Brookville, Ind., 1970—; mem. staffs Fayette Meml. Hosp., McCullough Hyde Hosp.; med. adv. emergency med. services Franklin County, Ind., 1972. Diplomate Am. Bd. Family Practice. Mem. AMA, Am. Acad. Family Practice, Am. Coll. Internat. Physicans, Ind.-Philippine Med. Assn., Ind. Med. Assn. (del.), Fayette-Franklin County Med. Soc. Roman Catholic. Club: K.C. (3deg.). Home: Rural Route 4 Hidden Valley Ln Brookville IN 47012 Office: Rural Route 4 Oxford Pike Brookville IN 47012

GUJU, JOHN G., physician; b. Youngstown, Ohio, June 13, 1924; s. George and Frances (Ratz) G.; B.A., Youngstown State U., 1944; M.D., Marquette U., 1947; m. Margaret Ann Poole, May 11, 1952; children—John Howard, Paula Jean, Nancy Elissa. Rotating intern Youngstown Hosp., 1947-48, asst. resident in surgery, 1948-49, later vice chief obstetrics and gynecology, now chief; resident in obstetrics and gynecology Cleve. City Hosp., 1949-50, U. Hosps., 1950-52; practice medicine specializing in obstetrics and gynecology, Youngstown, 1955—; med. dir. Planned Parenthood Fedn., Youngstown, 1960-72; clin. prof. in obstetrics and gynecology Northeastern Ohio Univs. Coll. Medicine, 1975—. Mem. youth com. YMCA, 1965—. Bd. dirs. Ohio div. Am. Assn. for Maternal and Child Health. Served from 1st lt. to capt., USAF, 1953-55. Recipient Alan F. Gutmacher award for service and dedication to Planned Parenthood of Mahoning Valley, 1976. Diplomate Am. Bd. Obstetrics and Gynecology. Fellow A.C.S., Am. Coll. Obstetricians and Gynecologists; mem. A.M.A., Am. Soc. Abdominal Surgeons, Am. Assn. Planned Parenthood Physicians, Am. Fertility Soc., Youngstown Soc. Obstetricians and Gynecologists (pres. 1977-78), Mahoning County Med. Soc. (council 1979—). Club: Youngstown Country. Home: 1350 Virginia Trail Youngstown OH 44505 Office: 435 Gypsy Ln Youngstown OH 44504

GULLAHORN, JOHN TAYLOR, sociologist, educator; b. Roswell, N.Mex., July 13, 1916; s. Jack Taylor and Laura (Rockhill) G.; A.B., U. So. Calif., 1937, A.M., 1945; Ph.D., Harvard U., 1953; m. Jeanne Erard, May 7, 1955; children—Gregory Maurice, Lorraine Lynn, Leslie Joan. Research asst. lab. social relations Harvard U., 1950-52, research asso., 1952-53, tng. fellow grad. sch. bus. adminstrn., 1952-53; asst. prof. sociology Ohio U., Athens, 1953-54; dir. study Am. students for Dept. State, Paris, 1954-55; asst. prof. sociology U. Kans., Lawrence, 1955-58; asst. prof. sociology Mich. State U., East Lansing, 1958-60, asso. prof., 1960-64, prof., 1964—; cons., research directorate System Devel. Corp., Santa Monica, Calif., 1961; vis. prof. Univ. Coll., Cardiff, Wales, 1972-73; health sci. instr. NIMH, 1979-81. Served with AUS, 1943-46. NSF postdoctoral fellow, 1965-66. Fellow Am. Sociol. Assn., AAAS; mem. Phi Beta Kappa. Home: 313 E Brookfield East Lansing MI 48823

GULLEDGE, BILLY RAY, aero. engr.; b. Poplar Bluff, Mo., Aug. 25, 1947; s. Twedell Arvil and Virginia Genevieve (Campbell) G.; student Coll. of Sch. of Ozarks, 1965-67; A.A., Austin Peay State U., 1973; B.S., Embry-Riddle U., 19—; m. Brenda Diana Hill, June 2, 1968; children—Brian Dewayne, Piper Diana. Asst. mgr. trainee J.J. Newberry Co., Poplar Bluff, Mo., 1964-67; joined U.S. Army, 1967, advanced through grades to capt., 1971, ret., 1977; asso. Keele Realty, Poplar Bluff, 1977-79; regional mgr. United Nat. Life Ins. Co., Springfield, Ill., 1978; asso. Mattingly Realty, Florissant, Mo., 1979—; engr. product support planning McDonnell Aircraft Co., St. Louis, 1979—; grad. asst. instr. Dale Carnegie course, St. Louis. Vol. fireman Sch. of Ozarks, 1965-67; radiol. monitor instr., 1965-67. Decorated Bronze Star medal with oak leaf cluster, Meritorious Service medal, Air medal with 24 oak leaf clusters, Vietnamese Cross of Gallantry; recipient Flight Safety Achievement award U.S. Army Aviation Sch., 1971, Dale Carnegie Course Human Relations award, 1978. Travel-Study Club scholar, 1965-67. Licensed real estate and life ins. agt. Mo., radiol. monitoring instr., Mo. Mem. Aircraft Owners and Pilots Assn., AMVETS, Army Aviation Assn. Am. (local treas. 1974-75), Nat. Assn. Realtors, Ret. Officers Assn., Mo. Assn. Realtors, Florissant (Mo.) Jr. C. of C. (Springboard, Speak-up, Regional First-timer awards 1978). Clubs: Business; Library; Reading; United Nat. Presidents; Century. Home: 2185 Foggy Bottom Dr Florissant MO 63031

GULLEKSON, EDWIN HENRY, JR., physician; b. Flint, Mich., May 14, 1935; s. Edwin Henry and Amy Marcella (Graves) G.; student Flint Community Coll., 1953-56; M.D., U. Mich., 1961; m. Rosemary Evelyn Leppien, May 5, 1968; children—Kathryn Dawn, Hans Edwin, Heidi M. Intern McLaren Gen. Hsop., Flint, 1961-62, resident, 1962-63; gen. practice medicine, Flint, 1963—; mem. staffs McLaren Gen., Hurley, St. Joseph, Genesee Meml. hosps. (all Flint). Served to capt. M.C., AUS, 1966-67. Upjohn Research grantee, 1958, 59, 60. Diplomate Am. Bd. Family Practice. Mem. Mich., Genesee County med. socs., A.M.A., Am. Acad. Family Practice, Mich. Acad. Gen. Practice. Patentee surg. instrument. Home: 1721 Laurel Oak Dr Flint MI 48507 Office: 2765 Flushing Rd Flint MI 48504

GULLING, DOUGLAS RAY, auditor; b. Des Moines, Sept. 30, 1953; s. Robert Dale and Dorothy Ann (Murrow) G.; B.S. in Acctg., Drake U., 1975; m. Judy Lynn Wanek, Dec. 21, 1974. Supervising sr. acct. Peat, Marwick, Mitchell & Co., Des Moines, 1975-79; asst. auditor United Central Bancshares, Inc., Des Moines, 1979-80, auditor, 1980—. C.P.A., Iowa. Mem. Am. Inst. C.P.A.'s, Iowa Soc. C.P.A.'s, Inst. Internal Auditors. Republican. Lutheran. Home: 2208 6th St SW Altoona IA 50009 Office: Suite 900 United Central Bank Bldg 6th and Locust Sts Des Moines IA 50306

GULLY, HAROLD WAYNE, pub. relations exec.; b. Winnsboro, Tex., Oct. 19, 1917; s. Holly Walton and Erma (Sheppeard) G.; student U. Tex., 1936-39, U. Md., 1951-52; m. Jean Grace Edwards, May 17, 1964; 1 son, David Neal. Reporter-photographer Austin (Tex.) Am.-Statesman, 1939-41; with NEA Service, Inc., Dallas, 1941-42; mgr. southwestern div. Acme Newspictures, Dallas, 1946-51; mgr. central div. newspictures United Press, Chgo., 1953-58; gen. European newspictures mgr. U.P.I., London, Eng., 1958-60; mgr. pub. relations Leo Burnett Co., Inc., N.Y.C., 1960, mgr. pub. relations dept., Chgo., 1961—, v.p. pub. relations, 1974—. Vice pres. Off-the-Street Club, 1980. Served with USAAF, 1942-45; served to maj. USAF, 1951-53. Decorated Air medal with cluster. Mem. Pub. Relations Soc. Am. (accrediated mem.; chpt. pres. 1973), Chgo. Headline Club, Nat. Acad. TV Arts and Scis. (dir. Chgo. chpt. 1974—), Sigma Delta Chi. Home: 645 S Waiola Ave La Grange IL 60525 Office: Leo Burnett Co Inc Prudential Plaza Chicago IL 60601

GUMBERT, JACK LEE, surgeon; b. Ft. Wayne, Ind., July 14, 1934; s. Martin Fredrick and Beulah Faye (McClain) G.; B.A., Cin. U., 1957, M.D., 1961; m. Lois Irene Scheimann, June 15, 1957; children—Jack, Lori, Brad, Grant, Joseph. Intern, Marion County Gen. Hosp., Indpls., 1961-62, resident 1962-66; practice medicine specializing in surgery, Ft. Wayne, Ind., 1968—; staff surgeon Parkview, Luth., St. Joseph hosps., Ft. Wayne, 1968—; chmn. surgery service Parkview Hosp., 1977—; asso. faculty mem. Ind. U. Sch. Medicine. Bd. dirs. Ft. Wayne YMCA, UPD Inc., Dukes Day Inc. Served to capt. M.C., U.S. Army, 1966-68. Decorated Bronze Star, Air medal (Vietnam); Army Commendation medal with oak leaf cluster; named to Ind. Basketball Hall of Fame, 1978. Diplomate Am. Bd. Surgery. Fellow A.C.S., mem. AMA, Ind. State, Ft. Wayne med.

socs., Ind. State, Ft. Wayne (pres. 1978-79) surg. assns. Lutheran. Club: Pine Valley Country (pres. 1976-77). Contbr. articles to med. jours. Home: 10810 Old Colony Rd Fort Wayne IN 46825 Office: 5010 Riviera Ct Fort Wayne IN 46825

GUNAGA, KUPPAYYA P., biochemist; b. Hegde, India, June 1, 1940; came to U.S., 1972; s. Parameshwar K. and Girija P. Gunaga; B.S. in Chemistry, Karnatak U., India, 1962; M.S. in Biochemistry, U. Bombay, India, 1967, Ph.D., 1971; postgrad. All India Inst. Med. Scis., 1967-68, U. Mich., 1972-74; m. Chitra Rao, Aug. 10, 1972; 1 son, Satheesh. Asst. research officer Inst. for Research in Reproduction, Bombay, India, 1967-70, research officer, 1970-72; Ford Found. fellow dept. pathology and ob.-gyn., U. Mich., Ann Arbor, 1972-74; research asso. Gynocologic Endocrine Lab., Women's Hosp., U. Mich., 1974-75; clin. biochemist Saginaw Gen. Hosp., Saginaw, Mich., 1975-78; asst. adj. prof. Mich. State U., dept. pathology, East Lansing, 1978—; clin. biochemist St. Lawrence Hosp., Lansing, Mich., 1978—. Mem. Am. Assn. Clin. Chemistry, Am. Fedn. for Clin. Research, Am. Soc. Med. Technologists, Midwest Radio Assay Soc. Contbr. articles on hormone and immuno-chemistry to sci. jours. Home: 1009 Touraine East Lansing MI 48823 Office: St Lawrence Hosp 1210 W Saginaw Lansing MI 48914

GUNALE, SHIVAJI RAMRAO, oncologist; b. Patoda, India, June 10, 1943; s. Ramrao N. and Kondabai R. G.; M.B., B.S., Med. Coll. Aurangabad, India, 1967, M.D., 1970; m. Vatsala S. Yerme, Feb. 25, 1965; children—Anuradha, Swati, Nikhil. Intern, Med. Coll. Hosp., Aurangabad, India, 1967, Cook County Hosp., Chgo., 1971; resident Mercy Hosp., Buffalo, N.Y., 1971-72; lectr. medicine Med. Coll. Aurangabad, India, 1969-70; fellow oncology/hematology Borgess Hosp., Kalamazoo, Mich., 1972-74; instr. medicine, oncology U. Rochester (N.Y.), 1974-75; cons. oncologist Community Hosp., Indpls., 1975—; clin. instr. internal medicine Ind. U. Sch. Medicine, Indpls., 1975-80, clin. asst. prof., 1980—. Mem. Am. Soc. Clin. Oncology, A.C.P., Assn. Community Cancer Centers. Home: 8035 Castle Lake Rd Indianapolis IN 46256 Office: 1500 N Ritter Ave Indianapolis IN 46219

GUNDERSEN, ALICE MARSHALL, ins. co. adminstr.; b. Groveton, N.H., Nov. 19, 1934; d. Daniel Weeks and Eleanor Marshall; student Fisher Jr. Coll., Boston, 1952-53, Boston U., 1956, Northeastern U., 1957-59, Madonna Coll., 1966; B.M., U. Mich., 1970; m. Carl A. Gundersen, Apr. 11, 1959; children—Daniel Carl, M. Scott. Exec. sec. with New Eng. Colls. Fund, Boston, 1956-58, with John Hancock Mut. Life Ins. Co., Boston, 1958-59; office supr. dept. human genetics U. Mich., Ann Arbor, 1964-67; adminstrv. coordinator and mgr., brokerage adminstrn. Alexander Hamilton Life Ins. Co., Farmington, Mich., 1973-75; supr. data services Delta Dental Plan of Mich., Southfield, 1976—; pres. Data-Word Services, Inc., Southfield, 1981—; part time music dir., St. Timothy Presbyterian Ch., Livonia, Mich., 1964-72, Trinity Episcopal Ch., Farmington, 1975-77; CESA cons. Presbytery of Detroit, 1975-77, mem. task force on women, 1978—; mem. Livonia City Council, 1980—; cons. women re-entering work force; systems cons. Adv. com. Livonia Sch. Bd., 1967-68; campaign coordinator City Council Candidate, 1970; active Livonia Com. for Better Human Relations, 1965-74. Named Disting. Woman of Yr., Bus. and Profl. Women, 1980. Mem. Assn. Systems Mgmt. (publicity chmn. 1978, membership chmn. 1979-80, officer 1980-81, v.p. 1981—), Women's Econ. Club Detroit (membership com., 1976, program com., 1977), Mich. Women's Polit. Caucus (polit. action chmn. 1979—, state chmn. 1981—). Home: 15715 Southampton St Livonia MI 48154 Office: 21700 Northwestern Hwy Southfield MI 48037

GUNDERSEN, GUNNAR ADOLF, physician; b. La Crosse, Wis., June 12, 1924; s. Gunnar and Mary C. (Baldwin) G.; student Yale U., 1942-43, U. N.H., 1944; M.D., Harvard U., 1948; m. Elizabeth Hanmer, Mar. 29, 1952; children—Gunnar, Lincoln, Ralph, Sven, Per. Intern in internal medicine Mass. Meml. Hosp., Boston, 1948-49; intern in surgery N.Y. Hosp., N.Y.C., 1949-50; fellow in radiology U. Minn., Mpls., 1951, 53-56; radiologist La Crosse (Wis.) Luth. Hosp. and Gundersen Clinic, La Crosse, 1956—; mem. State Bd. Med. Examiners, 1959-63. Campaign chmn. Community Chest, 1962; candidate for Congress, 1968; mem. La Crosse Bd. Edn., 1968-71. Served with U.S. Army, 1943-46; served to capt., M.C., USAF, 1951-53. Diplomate Am. Bd. Radiology, Am. Bd. Nuclear Medicine. Mem. La Crosse County, Wis. State med. socs., AMA, Wis., N.Am. radiol. socs., Am. Coll. Radiology, Soc. Nuclear Medicine. Home: Arbor Hills N 2295 Fen Lockney St La Crosse WI 54601 Office: 1836 South Ave La Crosse WI 54601

GUNDERSON, GEORGE BRUCE, food machinery co. exec.; b. Berlin, Wis., Mar. 15, 1926; s. George B. and Eva Louise (Doty) G.; Ph.B., U. Wis., 1947; m. Marjorie D. Kettelhon, Aug. 14, 1948; children—Richard, Thomas, Stuart. Salesman, sales mgr. Swift & Co., Minn., Wis., 1947-54; owner, operator Gunderson Ford & Mercury, Inc., Columbus, Wis., 1954-61; exec. v.p. Hughes Co., Inc., Columbus, 1961-69; founder, pres. Badger Food Machinery Corp., Fall River, Wis., 1970—; dir. Farmers & Mchts. Bank, Columbus. Bd. dirs. Crestwood Condominium Assn., Aspen, Colo. Mem. Food Processing Machinery and Supply Assn. (dir.), Forty Niners (dir., officer), Young and Old Guard. Republican. Club: Maple Bluff Country (Madison, Wis.). Home: Route 1 Columbus WI 53935 Office: Fall River WI 53932

GUNDERSON, HARVEY (LORRAINE), zoologist, educator; b. Gary, Minn., June 11, 1913; s. Herman and Martine (Hauer) G.; B.A., Concordia Coll., Moorhead, Minn., 1935; M.S., U. Minn., 1948; Ph.D., U. Mich., 1962; m. Erika Rogalsky, Dec. 29, 1950; children—John, James, Nancy. With W.M. Welch Sci. Supply House, Chgo., 1936-40; asst. James Ford Bell Mus., U. Minn., 1940-42, asst. scientist, 1946-50, asso. scientist, 1950-55, curator of mammals, 1956-62; asso. prof. zoology U. Nebr., Lincoln, 1962-65, prof., 1965-78, curator zoology Univ. Mus., 1962-78, asso. dir. mus., 1965-78, prof. and dir. emeritus, 1978—. Pres., N.W. Lincoln Community Assn., 1966-70, Belmont Community Assn., 1966—. Served to 1st lt. U.S. Army, 1942-46. Mem. Am. Soc. Mammalogists, Wildlife Soc., Wilson Ornithol. Club, Nebr. Ornithologists Union (past pres.), Nebr. Acad. Scis., Sigma Xi. Methodist. Author: Mammalogy, 1976; also articles. Home: 1200 Superior St Lincoln NE 68521 Office: U Nebr Lincoln NE 68588

GUNDERSON, STEVEN CRAIG, Congressman; b. Eau Claire, Wis., May 10, 1951; B.A. in Polit. Sci., U. Wis., Madison, 1973; grad. Brown Sch. Broadcasting, 1974. Mem. Wis. Ho. of Reps., 1975-79; congl. legis. dir., 1979-80; mem. 97th Congress from 3d Dist. Wis. Republican. Lutheran. Club: Lions. Address: 416 Cannon House Office Bldg Washington DC 20515*

GUNDLACH, NORMAN JOSEPH, lawyer; b. Belleville, Ill., May 23, 1907; s. Joseph E. and Bertha (Steudle) G.; B.S., U. Ill., 1928, LL.B., 1931; m. Maxine Rain, Jan. 26, 1935; children—Gayle (Mrs. Donald McLean), Frank N. Admitted to Ill., Mo. bars, 1931; partner firm Gundlach, Lee, Eggmann, Boyle & Roessler, and predecessor firms, Belleville, 1931—; dir. Bankers Trust Co., Belleville. Mem. citizens com. U. Ill.; former mem. alumni bd. U. Ill. Served with USNR, 1943-45. Fellow Am. Coll. Trial Lawyers, Am. Bar Found.; mem. Am., Ill. (pres. 1st dist. 1955), Mo., St. Clair County (pres. 1969-70), East St. Louis (pres. 1948) bar assns., Nat. Assn. R.R. Trial Counsel, Ill. Def. Counsel, U. Ill. I Men's Assn. (past pres.), Phi Delta Phi. Home: 19 S 78th St Belleville IL 62223 Office: 5000 W Main St Belleville IL 62223

GUNN, W. FRANK, radio broadcaster; b. Great Bend, Kans., July 1, 1935; s. Arthur F. and Dorothy L. G.; B.B.A., Wichita State U., 1962; m. Ramona R. Miller, Sept. 20, 1959; children—Tara L., Linda M. Announcer, Sta. KFH, Wichita, Kans., 1959-61; salesman Sta. KAKE, Wichita, 1961-64; gen. mgr. Sta. KMNS, Sioux City, Iowa, 1964-70, Sta. KWBB, Wichita, 1970-71; exec. v.p., gen. mgr. Sta. KAKE and successor Sta. KAKZ, Wichita, 1971—. Served with USAF, 1955-59. Mem. Kans. Assn. Broadcasters (pres. 1982-83), Nat. Assn. State Radio Networks (2d v.p.), Wichita C. of C. (dir.). Episcopalian. Club: Rotary (sec., v.p., dir.). Office: 1500 N West St Wichita KS 67203*

GUNNERSON, JAMES HOWARD, mus. adminstr.; b. Aurora, Nebr., Nov. 28, 1922; s. Joe E. and Mabel Muerl (Brickner) G.; B.S., U. Nebr., 1949, M.A., 1950; Ph.D., Harvard U., 1963; m. Dolores Alice Bellamy, Jan. 3, 1944; 1 son, James Lawrence. Curator, Mus. of Anthropology, U. Utah, 1954-60; asst. prof. anthropology No. Ill. U., asso. prof., prof., to 1974, dir. anthropology labs., 1968-72, dir. anthropology labs. and mus., 1972-74; prof., dir. U. Nebr. State Mus., Lincoln, 1974—. Served with USAAF, 1943-46. NSF grantee. Mem. Soc. Am. Archaeology, Am. Assn. Museums, Assn. Sci. Mus. Dirs., Mountain-Plains Mus. Assn., Nebr. Museums Assn., Plains Anthrop. Conf. Contbr. articles to profl. jours. Office: Univ of Nebr State Mus Lincoln NE 68588

GUNSAULUS, JACK LEE, social worker; b. Houston, Jan. 6, 1935; B.A., Wayne State U., 1970, cert., 1970, M.S.W., 1976; children by previous marriage—Meyra, Myron. Corrections specialist Mich. State Corrections Dept., 1970-72; eligibility examiner Wayne County Dept. Social Services, Mich., 1972-73, protective service worker, 1973-74; instl. social worker Harreld Center for Young Adults, Northville (Mich.) State Hosp., 1974; program dir. substance abuse program Downriver Growth Center, Allen Park, Mich., 1976-80, clin. dir., 1979—; social worker Cath. Social Services Detroit, 1976-78; cons. in substance abuse, 1978—; vol. group therapist Providence Hosp., Southfield, Mich., 1971-73; mem. adv. bd., cons. Toth Counseling Center, Trenton, Mich., 1978—. Mem. Nat. Assn. Social Workers, Mich. Alcohol and Addiction Assn., Mich. Assn. of Alcoholism Counselors, Mich. Assn. Marriage Counselors, Am. Group Psychotherapy Assn. Alpha Kappa Delta. Home: 7690 Ashton Detroit MI 48228

GUNTERMANN, ALFRED ERNEST, cons. engr.; b. Chgo., June 25, 1943; s. Alfred Ernest and Elizabeth Margaret (Erhart) G.; B.M.E., U. Wis., 1967; m. Elizabeth Jane Tucker, Feb. 25, 1968; children—Daniel Scott, Katharine Marie. In charge Ft. Wayne (Ind.) office Trane Co., 1967-74; pres. Energy Econs., Ft. Wayne, 1974-78; research asso. on energy The Austin Co., Cleve., 1978—, lectr. in field. Co-chmn. Bowl Down Cancer dr. Am. Cancer Soc., Ft. Wayne, 1977. Mem. ASHRAE (pres. Ft. Wayne 1974-75, Ind. moderator 1976), Nat. Soc. Profl. Engrs. (sec. 1977-78), C. of C. Congregationalist. Club: Kiwanis. Contbr. articles in field to profl. jours. Home: 46 W Orange St Chagrin Falls OH 44022 Office: Austin Co 3650 Mayfield Rd Cleveland OH 44121

GUPTA, KRISHNA CHANDRA, mech. engr., educator; b. Ajmer, India, Sept. 24, 1948; permanent resident U.S.; s. Jagat Narain and Malti Devi (Purwar) G.; B.Tech. with distinction, Indian Inst. Tech., 1969; M.S., Case Inst. Tech., 1971; Ph.D., Stanford U., 1974; m. Karuna Purwar. Grad. asst. Case Inst. Tech., Cleve., 1969-71; research asst. Stanford (Calif.) U., 1971-74; asst. prof. mech. design U. Ill., Chgo., 1974-79, asso. prof., 1979—. NSF grantee, 1977—. Mem. ASME (Best Paper award Mechanisms Conf. 1978, Henry Hess award 1979, faculty adv. student sect. 1978-80, asso. editor Jour. Mech. Design 1981—, organizing com. 1982 Mechanisms Conf.). Contbr. numerous articles on linkages, cams and manipulators to profl. jours. in U.S. and abroad. Office: Dept Materials Engring U Ill Chicago IL 60680

GUPTA, PARKASH DEV, cardiologist; b. Fazilka, India, Mar. 7, 1936; s. Gursharan Dass and Dharam Vati (Aggarwal) G.; came to U.S., 1964, M.B. B.S., Govt. Med. Coll., Patiala, India, 1958, M.B.B.S., 1958; m. Kamlesh Aggarwal, Sept. 12, 1970; children—Malini, Vikas, Vishal. Asst. registrar medicine Govt. Med. Coll., Patiala, 1960-64; resident internal medicine Louisville (Ky.) Gen. Hosp., 1965-66; fellow in cardiology Mt. Sinai Hosp., 1965-66, Hines VA Hosp., Chgo., 1966-68; fellow in pediatric cardiology Cook County Hosp., Chgo., 1968-70, resident in internal medicine, 1970-71; mem. staff, dir. ICU and CCU, MacNeal Meml. Hosp., Berwyn, Ill., 1971—; clin. asst. prof. medicine Abraham Lincoln Sch. Medicine, U. Ill., Chgo. Fellow Council Clin. Cardiology Am. Heart Assn., Royal Coll. Physicians Can., Am. Coll. Cardiology, A.C.P.; mem. AMA, Ill., Chgo. med. socs. Hindu. Contbr. articles to med. jours. Home: 3684 Downers Dr Downers Grove IL 60515 Office: 3249 S Oak Park Ave Berwyn IL 60402

GUPTA, PARSHOTAM DASS, educator; b. Ambala City, India, Feb. 5, 1936; s. Jugal Kishore and Maya Vati G.; M.S., Panjab U., India, 1959; M.S., Carnegie Inst. Tech., 1963; Ph.D., Carnegie Mellon U., 1968; m. Kamlesh Goyal, Aug. 2, 1969; children—Raymond, Sandhya. Instr. physics dept. Panjab U., India, 1959-60; project physicist, Carnegie-Mellon U., Pitts., 1963-68; asst. prof. Purdue U. Calumet Campus, Hammond, Ind., 1968-77, asso. prof., 1977—. Mem. Am. Phys. Soc., Am. Assn. Physics Tchrs., AAUP, Sigma Xi. Condr. research, contbr. articles in nuclear and particle physics; reviewer Study Guide in Physics (V. Namias), 1974, 76. Home: 1916 Bluebird Dr Munster IN 46321 Office: Purdue Univ Calumet 2233 171st St Hammond IN 46323

GURD, ALAN ROBERT, surgeon; b. Belfast, No. Ireland, Oct. 9, 1940; came to U.S., 1976; s. Robert and Evelyn M. (Ferguson) G.; student Meth. Coll., Belfast, 1945-58; M.B., Queens U., Belfast, 1964, M.Ch., 1969; m. Elizabeth Ruth Imrie, July 16, 1966; children—Andrew, Alan, Colin, David, Jennifer. Intern, Royal Victoria Hosp., Belfast, 1964-66, lectr., 1966-67, cons. surgeon, 1974-76; registrar, Musgrave Park Hosp., 1967-73; practice medicine specializing in pediatric orthopedics Toronto, Ont., Can., 1973-74, Belfast, 1974-76, Cleve., 1976—; guest lectr. Harari Hosp., Rhodesia, 1970, Birmingham (Eng.) Accident Hosp., 1971, Glasgow (Scotland) Infirmary, 1971, Sint Lucas Hosp., Amsterdam, 1971; clin. fellow Hosp. for Sick Children, Toronto, 1973-74; mem. staff Cleve. Clinic, head pediatric orthopedics, 1976—; cons. to United Cerebral Palsy Assn., 1977—. Coach soccer, basketball and baseball Jr. League, Bainbridge Twp., Ohio, 1977—; pres. Pilgrim Village Lake Community, 1980-81. Recipient Calvert Meml. award, 1967; diplomate Am. Bd. Orthopaedic Surgery. Fellow Royal Coll. Surgeons; mem. Am. Acad. Orthopedic Surgeons, Am. Acad. Pediatrics, Am. Acad. Medicine, Cleve. Acad. Medicine, Brit. Orthopedic Assn., Cleve. Orthopedic Club. Contbr. articles on pediatric orthopedic surgery to profl. jours. Home: 17754 Lost Trail Chagrin Falls OH 44022 Office: Cleveland Clinic Cleveland OH 44106

GURNEY, BENJAMIN FRANKLIN, endodontist; b. Mendota, Ill., Sept. 3, 1914; s. Frank Herbert and Millie Martha (Powell) G.; B.S., U. Chgo., 1935, M.S., 1938; D.D.S., Loyola U., Chgo., 1961; m. Jane Hebert, Sept. 30, 1939; children—Donald Lee, Jean, Kenneth Paul. Chemist-lectr. Museum Sci. and Industry, Chgo., 1939-40; asst. chief chemist high-explosives U.S. Civil Service Commn., Joliet, Ill., 1941-43; paint chemist E.I. DuPont de Nemours & Co., Inc., Chgo., 1943-44; research chemist Armour & Co., Chgo., 1944; instr. biochemistry Sch. Dentistry, Loyola U., Chgo., 1944-48; asst. prof. biochemistry Loyola U. Dental Sch., Chgo., 1948-61, asso. prof., 1961-67, prof., 1967-70; prof., chmn. dept. endodontics, Northwestern U. Dental Sch., Chgo., 1970-74, dir. grad. endodontic tng., 1974-80, prof. emeritus, 1980—; practice dentistry specializing in endodontics, Glen Ellyn, Ill., 1961—. Diplomate Am. Bd. Endodontics. Fellow Am. Coll. Dentists, Am. Inst. Chemists; mem. Am. Chem. Soc., ADA, Am. Assn. for Dental Research, Internat. Assn. for Dental Research, Fedn. Dentaire Internat., AAAS, Am. Assn. Endodontists, Sigma Xi, Omicron Kappa Upsilon. Republican. Congregationalist. Contbr. articles to various publs. Patentee chemo-therpeutic agts. in dentistry. Home: 542 Deer Path Glen Ellyn IL 60137 Office: 432 Prospect Ave Glen Ellyn IL 60137

GURNEY, FLETCHER BARNES, mfg. co. exec.; b. Chgo., Sept. 24, 1931; s. James Granville and Patricia Flora (Early) G.; B.A., Beloit (Wis.) Coll., 1955; postgrad. Northwestern U., 1961; m. Ruth Margaret Rodgers, Oct. 15, 1966; children—James, Peter, Burke, Geoffrey; stepchildren—Adrian, Robin, Heather. Sales engr. Belden Mfg. Co., Chgo., 1956-58; sales rep. Standard Oil Co., Chgo., 1959-60; spl. agt. Prudential Ins. Co. Am., 1960-61; western regional sales mgr. Teledyne McKay Co., Chgo., 1962-79; nat. sales mgr. Taylor Chem. Co., Inc., Hammond, Ind., 1979-80; nat. sales mgr. chain products Swedish Wire Corp., Chgo., 1980—. Mem. USNR, 1951-58. Mem. U.S. Tennis Assn., Am. Mgmt. Assn., Sigma Chi. Home: Unit 5E 500 W Barry Chicago IL 60657 Office: 255 Laura Dr Addison IL 60101

GURU, BHAG SINGH, electric co. exec.; b. India, Jan. 15, 1945; s. Sucha Singh and Hazur (Kaur) G.; came to U.S., 1971, naturalized, 1979; B.S., Punjab U., Chandigarh, India, 1968; M.S. (Govt. India Overseas scholar), Mich. State U., 1972, Ph.D., 1976; m. Janet Elaine Post, Mar. 21, 1975; children—Yatendra Singh, Satendra Singh. Sr. sci. asst. Ministry Def., India, 1968-71; grad. teaching asst. Mich. State U., East Lansing, 1972-73, 74-76; mgr. research group Universal Electric Co., Owosso, Mich., 1976—; tchr. motor theory Lansing Community Coll., 1980—. NSF grantee, 1974-76. Mem. IEEE, Eta Kappa Nu. Contbr. research papers to profl. lit. Home: 1676 Chinook Dr Owosso MI 48867 Office: Universal Electric Co 300 E Main St Owosso MI 48867

GUST, CAROL ANN, occupational therapist; b. Grafton, N.D., Apr. 13, 1949; d. Allen Tilford and Lillian Jeanette (Lesperance) Lysengen; B.S., U. N.D., 1971. Staff occupational therapist Med. Center Rehab. Hosp., Grand Forks, N.D., 1971-72; chief occupational therapy Deaconess Hosp., Evansville, Ind., 1972-74; supr. occupational therapy Physicians Phys. Therapy Services, Gary, Ind., 1974-77; dir. occupational therapy St. Anthony Med. Center, Crown Point, Ind., 1977—. Mem. adv. bd. Ind. Home Aid Nursing, 1977-78; sec. Ind. Home Aid Nursing adv. bd., 1977-78. HEW trainee, 1969, 71, 72. Mem. Am. Occupational Therapy Assn., Ill. Occupational Therapy Assn., Ind. Occupational Therapy Assn., N.W. Dist. Occupational Therapy Assn., Pi Theta Epsilon. Roman Catholic. Home: 963 High Meadows Apt 963 Crown Point IN 46307 Office: Main and Franciscan Rd Crown Point IN 46307

GUSTAFSON, ANITA VIRGINIA, ret. educator; b. Galesburg, Ill., Jan. 31, 1917; s. Carl Gustafson; B.S. in Elementary Edn., U. Ill., 1957; postgrad. Western Ill. U. Elementary librarian Galesburg public schs., 1939-56, coordinator elementary sch. libraries community unit Sch. Dist. 205, 1956-69, library-learning center tchr. Nielson Middle Sch., 1969-80. Mem. Am., Ill. library assns., Galesburg, Nat., Ill. edn. assn., AAUW, Bus., Profl. Women, Alpha Delta Kappa. Address: 554 Irwin St Galesburg IL 61401

GUSTAFSON, MARY JANE, journalist, editor; b. Mpls., July 1, 1921; d. John Joseph and Marie Charlotte (Jasinski) Sokolowski; B.A., U. Minn., 1942; m. Arthur W. Gustafson, Oct. 26, 1946; children—Frederick, Gretchen Gustafson Mahubani, Gail. Advt. mgr. Herberger Stores, 1942-46; with Post Newspapers, 1960--, editor Brooklyn Center Post, 1960—, women's editor 5 newspapers, 1960—; moderator Polish radio program Sta. KUXL, 1979—. Founder Brooklyn Hist. Soc., 1970, pres., 1970—; founder Polish Arts Club, 1959, pres., 1959-71. Recipient newspaper award Minn. Newspaper Assn., Minn. Press Women. Mem. Minn. Press Women (pres. 1967-78). Club: Polanie (v.p. 1979—). Home: 4935 Abbott Ave N Minneapolis MN 55429 Office: 8801 Bass Lake Rd Minneapolis MN 55428

GUSTAFSON, ROY DAVID, educator; b. Rockford, Ill., Dec. 12, 1936; s. Roy H. and Lois M. Gustafson; B.A., Beloit Coll., 1958; M.S., No. Ill. U., 1962; M.A. Teaching (NSF scholar), Rockford Coll., 1965; m. Carol Ann Groves, June 11, 1960; children—Kristy Lynn, Steven Roy. Tchr. math. Rockford West High Sch., 1958-65; prof. Rock Valley Coll., 1965-67, chmn. div. math. and humanities, 1967—; adj. prof. math. Rockford Coll., 1965—; mem. North Central Evaluation Teams for Sch. Accreditation. Mem. Rockford Bd. Edn., 1971-74, sec., 1974; bd. dirs. Rockford Symphony Orch., 1978—. Named Outstanding Young Educator, Jr. C. of C., 1965. Mem. Nat., Ill. councils tchrs. of math., Math. Assn. Am., Am. Math. Assn. of Two Yr. Colls. Presbyterian. Author: (with Frisk) Elementary Plane Geometry, 1973, College Algebra, 1980, Plane Trigonometry, 1982. Home: 6580 Glen Devon Rd Rockford IL 61111 Office: 3301 N Mulford Rd Rockford IL 61101

GUSTAVSON, ERICK BRANDT, broadcasting and publishing exec.; b. Rockford, Ill., June 2, 1936; s. Sven Ragner and Ruth E. (Johnson) G.; student Northwestern Coll., 1954-56, Cuyahoga Community Coll., 1963-64, Loyola U., Chgo., 1969-70; m. Mary Janet; children—Ruth, Timothy. Announcer WBEL, Beloit, Wis., 1953-54; announcer KTIS, Mpls., 1954-58, asst. to mgr., 1957-58; v.p. Better Choir Publs., Mpls., 1958-59; announcer, asst. mgr. WCBC, Anderson, Ind., 1959-60; announcer WCRF, Cleve., 1960-67, sta. mgr., 1961-67; gen. mgr. KAIM, Honolulu, 1967-68; dir. broadcasting Moody Bible Inst., Chgo., 1968-74, v.p., adminstr. devel., 1974—; past pres. Evang. Christian Pubs. Assn. Elder and chmn. finance com. Moody Meml. Ch.; vice chmn. Evang. Council for Fin. Accountability. Mem. Nat. Assn. Broadcasters, Nat. Religious Broadcasters (v.p. 1970-80, exec. com. 1980). Home: 110 Columbia Ave Park Ridge IL 60068 Office: 820 N LaSalle St Chicago IL 60610

GUTEK, EDWARD PHILIP, plastic surgeon; b. Wadena, Sask., Can., Jan. 1, 1941; s. Frank and Mary (Leia) G.; B.A., U. Sask., 1963, M.D., 1967; m. Donna E. Small, Aug. 29, 1975. Intern, St. Luke's, Kansas City, Mo., 1967-68, resident in gen. surgery, 1970-74; resident in plastic surgery Gen. Hosp., Kansas City, 1974-76; gen. practice medicine, Wadena, 1968-70; practice plastic surgery McCoy, Chandler & Crow, Kansas City, 1976-77, Crow Gutek Lockwood M.D.'s Inc., 1977—; mem. research staff St. Luke's, St. Mary's, St. Joseph, Trinity, Children's Mercy, Kansas City. Fellow A.C.S.; mem.

Gt. Plains Occupational Med. Assn. (v.p. 1978-79), Am. Soc. Plastic and Reconstructive Surgeons, AMA. Roman Catholic. Office: 4400 Broadway St Kansas City MO 64111

GUTERMUTH, SCOTT ALAN, accountant; b. South Bend, Ind., Nov. 24, 1953; s. Richard H. and Barbara Ann (Bracey) G.; B.S. in Bus., Ind. U., 1976; m. Susanne Pearson, May 10, 1980. With Coopers & Lybrand, Indpls., 1976—, supr. auditor, 1980—. Adv., Jr. Achievement; mem. Marion County Republican Com., 1978—, Rep. Nat. Com., 1972—. C.P.A., Ind. Mem. Am. Inst. C.P.A.'s, Nat. Assn. Accts., Ins. Acctg. and Statis. Assn., Ind. Assn. C.P.A.'s, Indpls. Jaycees. Methodist. Home: 7450 Glenview West Dr Indianapolis IN 46250 Office: One Indiana Sq Suite 2200 Indianapolis IN 46204

GUTHRIE, ELEANOR YOUNG, lawyer; b. Annawan, Ill., Aug. 12, 1915; d. James M. and Nell (Stevenson) Young; B.A., U. Ill., 1937; LL.B., Chgo.-Kent Coll. Law, 1940; m. George B. Guthrie, Dec. 26, 1941; 1 son, Richard Y. Editor, Commerce Clearing House, Inc., 1940-42; lawyer Defrees & Fiske, Chgo., 1942-52, partner, 1952—; mem. hearing bd. for atty. registration and disciplinary commn. Ill. Supreme Ct., 1973-79. Pres., Joint Com. on Woman's Ct. and Detention Home, Chgo., 1957-58; vol. worker teen-age program Erie Neighborhood House, 1954-62; mem. com. on social security Ill. C. of C.; bd. dirs., mem. loop center com. YWCA, v.p., 1974-77, pres., 1979; bd. dirs. United Way Chgo.; asst. sec. USO Chgo., 1969-73; del. Women's Share in Pub. Service, also Ill. Women's Conf. on Legislation. Mem. Women's Bar Assn. Ill. (pres. 1950-51), Nat. Assn. Women Lawyers (state del. 1952, labor law com.), Am. (vice chmn. com. on occupational health and safety 1972-73, labor law sect.; mem. fed. labor standards legislative com.), Chgo. (mem. labor law, house, grievance coms., chmn. ho. com. 1970-72) bar assns., Central Bus. and Profl. Women (v.p. 1980-81), Alliance Bus. and Profl. Women Chgo. (pres. 1964-65), Nat. Fedn. Bus. and Profl. Women (parliamentarian 1973-74), Ill. Fedn. Bus. and Profl. Women (parliamentarian 1958—), AAUW, Internat. Platform Assn., Nat., Ill. assns. parliamentarians, Zeta Phi Eta. Congregationalist. Clubs: Pilot (pres. 1955-56), Execs. of Chgo. (youth and membership coms.). Home: 547 Belleforte Ave Oak Park IL 60302 Office: 72 W Adams St Chicago IL 60603

GUTHRIE, GEORGE RALPH, JR., real estate corp. exec.; b. Phila., Mar. 12, 1928; s. George Ralph and Myrtle (Robertson) G.; B.S. in Econs., U. Pa., 1948; m. Shirley B. Remmey; children—Mary Elizabeth, Brenda Ann. With I-T-E Imperial Corp., Phila., 1948-70, controller, fin. planner, 1960-68, treas., 1968-69, v.p. fin., 1969-70; pres. N.K. Winston Corp., N.Y.C., 1970-76; exec. v.p. Urban Investment and Devel. Co., Chgo., 1976-78, pres., 1978—. Mem. Am. Mgmt. Assn. (financial planning council 1970-75), Urban Land Inst., Nat. Coll. Edn., Chgo. Assn. Commerce and Industry, Fin. Execs. Inst. Republican. Clubs: Union League (Phila.); Glen View, Jupiter Hills, Carlton, Econ., Execs. (Chgo.). Office: 845 N Michigan Ave Chicago IL 60611

GUTHRIE, MYRNA JEAN, educator; b. Newton, Iowa, June 30, 1929; d. Frank Andrew and Hazel (Dolph) Guthrie; student Central Coll., 1947-49; B.A., Drake U., 1951, M.S., 1963. Child welfare worker State of Iowa, 1951-60; guidance counselor Newton Community Schs., 1960—, counselor Upward Bound, Central Coll., Pella, Iowa, 1967; cons. Jasper County Headstart program, 1968; coordinator Newton Achievement Motivation Project, 1971-72, Futures project Newton Community Sch., 1975. Past bd. dirs. Jasper County Community Action; past pres. RMR Soc.; bd. dirs. Newton Community Orch. Recipient Maytag Found. Conv. award, 1965; named Nat. Future Problem Solving Coach of Yr., 1980. Mem. Internat. Platform Assn., Nat., Newton edn. assns., Am., Iowa personnel and guidance assns., Newton Bus. and Profl. Women's Club (past pres.), Jasper County Hist. Soc., Iowa Woman's Polit. Caucus, Newton Community Theater, Questers (past pres.), Alpha Xi Delta, Alpha Kappa Delta, Beta Sigma Phi. Republican. Methodist. Clubs: Soroptimist (past pres.) (Newton); Hazel Dell Acad. Co-pub. series Before the Colors Fade. Home: 326 E 4th St S Newton IA 50208

GUTHRIE, RICHARD ALAN, physician; b. Nov. 13, 1935; s. Merle Pruitt and Cleona Marie (Weaver) G.; A.A., Graceland Coll., 1955; M.D., U. Mo., 1960; m. Diana Fern Worthington, Aug. 17, 1957; children—Laura, Joyce, Tamara. Intern, U.S. Naval Hosp., Camp Pendleton, Calif., 1960-61; dir. dependent services U.S. Naval Hosp., Sangley Point, Philippines, 1961-63; asst. instr., resident in pediatrics U. Mo., 1963-65, NIH fellow in endocrinology and metabolism, 1965-68, asst. prof., dir. newborn services, 1968-71, asso. prof. pediatrics, 1971-73; prof., chmn. dept. pediatrics U. Kans. Sch. Medicine, Wichita, 1973-81; dir. Kans. Regional Diabetes Center, 1974—. Mem. med. adv. bd. La Leche Internat.; mem. adv. bd. Action for Children; bd. dirs. Accent on Kids. Served with USN, 1960-63. Recipient NIH grants, 1968—; Outstanding Faculty award U. Kans. Sch. Medicine, Wichita, 1976. Diplomate Am. Bd. Pediatrics. Fellow Am. Acad. Pediatrics, Am. Pediatric Soc. mem. Am. (dir. 1972-77), Kans. (pres. 1975, chmn. bd. 1976-78) diabetes assns., Kans., Sedgwick County med. socs., Soc. Pediatric Research, Lawson Wilkins Pediatric Endocrinology Soc., Midwest Soc. Pediatric Research, Internat. Study Group Diabetes in Children and Adolescents, Internat. Diabetes Fedn., Lambda Delta Sigma, Sigma Xi. Mem. health commn. bd. Reorganized Ch. Jesus Christ Latter-day Saints. Co-author: Nursing Management in Diabetes Mellitus; contbr. articles to profl. jours. Home: 4967 Hillcrest St N Wichita KS 67220 Office: 1001 N Minneapolis Wichita KS 67214

GUTHRIE, RONALD WILLIAM, ins. agt.; b. Cambridge, Ohio, June 4, 1935; s. William Leslie and Viola Mae (McMullin) G.; student Life Underwriter Tng. Council, 1971; C.L.U., Am. Coll., Bryn Mawr, Pa., 1977; m. Sharon Pauline Wheatley, Dec. 11, 1954; children—Kimberly Guthrie Conrath, Jill Guthrie Black, Robin R., Wendy A. Laborer Autoport and Cambridge (Ohio) Water Dept., 1953-54; lube and service man DeNoyer Chevrolet, Kalamazoo, Mich., 1954-55; dept. head plumbing and heating, Montgomery Ward, Cambridge, 1955-58; with Hammonds Chevrolet, New Concord, Ohio, 1958; engr. fire dept., Cambridge, 1958-65; agt. State Farm Ins., Cambridge, 1965-67; pvt. practice ins. agt., State Farm Ins., Cambridge, 1967—; speaker in field. Active fund drives YMCA, United Fund; mem. Cambridge Bd. Edn., 1973-77, v.p., 1976-78; chmn. bd. trustees First Bapt. Ch., Cambridge, 1973-78. Served with USNR, 1953-61. C.L.U. Career Achievement Club, State Farm Ins., 1966—, key man award, 1966, 68, legion of honor, 1975-77, nat. quality award, 1978, conv. qualifier, 1967-78, Mem. Cambridge Assn. Life Underwriters (pres., 1975-76), Am. Soc. C.L.U.'s, C. of C. (edn. com., banquet chmn., 1977). Republican. Clubs: Cambridge Country, Salt Fork Striders (co-founder, pres.), Elks, Lions (pres., 1975-76), Shrine (pres. Kambri, 1976-77), Masons, Scottish Rite. Completed 14 marathons, including Boston Marathon, 1972-78. Home: 1308 Edgeworth Ave Cambridge OH 43725 Office: 320 S 11th St Cambridge OH 43725

GUTIERREZ, ANGELO, business exec.; b. Havana, Cuba, July 24, 1936; s. Angel and Carmen (Fernandez) G.; came to U.S., 1967, naturalized, 1973; B.S. in Acctg., U. Havana, 1963; M.S. in Acctg., Roosevelt U., 1973; m. Martha Gonzalez, Dec. 10, 1960; children—Marta Beatriz, Elizabeth. In various mangerial positions in banking and industry, Havana, 1957-66; accountant Hartford Ins. Group, Chgo., 1967-68; cost account mgr. Continental Coffee Co., Chgo., 1968-70; cost account mgr. Dietzgen Corp., Des Plaines, Ill., from 1970, later corp. controller, v.p. fin.; instr. acctg. U. Havana, 1963-65. C.P.A., Ill. Mem. Am. Inst. C.P.A.'s, Ill. C.P.A. Soc., Ill. Mfrs. Assn., Fin. Mgmt. Assn., Beta Gamma Sigma. Club: Econ. (Chgo.). Office: 250 W Wille Rd Des Plaines IL 60018

GUTMAN, CARLTON WAYNE, govt. services ofcl.; b. Chgo., Sept. 7, 1940; s. Carl and Winifred E. (Lutz) G.; B.S. in Geology, Mich. Technol. Inst., 1962, M.S. in Bus. Adminstrn., 1963; m. Susan Lynch, May 27, 1967; 1 dau., Hally Elisabeth. With R.R. Donnelley & Sons, Inc., Chgo., 1963-68; social worker VISTA, Ft. Apache Indian Reservation, East Fork, Ariz., 1968-69; bus. mgr. Studio 22, Inc., Chgo., 1969-70; dep. dir. Alger-Marquette (Mich.) Community Action Bd., 1971-73, dir. econ. devel., 1970-77, energy mgmt. coordinator appropriate tech./alt. energy, 1980—; adminstr. and coordinator Alger County, Munising, Mich., 1971-80; communications, tech. and managerial cons., 1974—; propr., mgr. The Pick 'N' Gad, Copper Harbor, Mich., 1977-81; notary public, 1972—. Vice chmn. Marquette Youth Services, 1971-72; mem. Marquette Lower Harbor Fund Raising Com., 1979-81; chmn. Marquette Am. Revolution Bicentennial Commn., 1973-77; vice chmn. Citizens To Save Superior's Shoreline, 1971-72; bd. dirs. Marquette County Council on Arts, 1971-75. Mem. Lake Superior Arts Assn., Marquette County Hist. Soc., Mich. Assn. County Personnel Officers, Mich. Assn. County Adminstrv. Officers, Ishpeming Rock and Mineral Club (editor booklet 1972, v.p. 1972-74, pres. 1975-77, liaison officer 1978—), Cooper Harbor Improvement Assn., Delta Sigma Phi. Home: 201 W Magnetic St Marquette MI 49855 Office: 184 Hwy 41 Negaunee MI 49866

GUTMANN, ARLYNE JEANE, ednl. psychologist; b. Mpls., Aug. 9, 1947; d. Herbert and Felicitas Sylvia (Klein) G.; B.A., Lawrence U., Appleton, Wis., 1969; M.A., Western Mich. U., Kalamazoo, 1973; Ph.D., U. Minn., Mpls., 1976. Grad. asst. Western Mich. U., 1969-70; student asst. Kalamazoo State Hosp., 1969; teaching asst. dept. spl. edn. U. Minn., 1974-75, student intern dept. child and adolescent psychiatry, 1975, dept. psychoednl. studies, 1976, teaching asst. dept. psychoednl. studies, 1975-76; dir. learning village infant program Behavior Devel. Corp., Kalamazoo, 1970-71, asso. dir. Learning Village, 1971; caseworker Kalamazoo County Juvenile Ct., 1971-73; instr. div. child and adolescent psychiatry U. Minn., Mpls., 1976, asst. prof., 1977, instr. dept. psychoednl. studies, 1977, asst. prof. dept. phys. medicine and rehab., 1977-78, lectr. dept. psychoednl. studies, 1978—; adj. asst. prof. St. Mary's Coll., Winona, Minn., 1977-79; pvt. practice psychology, 1980—; vis. prof. dept. psychology Augsburg Coll., Mpls., 1981. Recipient Appreciation of Profl. Service award Mpls. Assn. Retarded Citizens, 1978. Lic. cons. psychologist, vocat. lic. care and guidance children, Minn.; cert. psychology tchr., day care tng., tng. juvenile ct. officers, Mich. Mem. Am. Psychol. Assn., Assn. Advancement Behavior Therapy, Nat. Assn. Young Children, Center Early Child Edn., Soc. Research in Child Devel., Am. Assn. Mental Deficiency, Nat. Soc. Autistic Children, Midwest Assn. Behavior Analysis, Mpls. Assn. Retarded Citizens. Jewish. Contbr. articles to profl. jours. Home: 5604 Abbott Ave S Edina MN 55410 Office: 101 Pattee Hall Dept Psychoednl Studies U Minn Minneapolis MN 55455 also 6950 France Ave Edina MN 55435

GUTOWICZ, MATTHEW FRANCIS, JR., radiologist; b. Camden, N.J., Feb. 23, 1945; s. Matthew Francis and A. Patricia (Walzak) G.; B.A., Temple U., 1968; D.O., Phila. Coll. Osteo. Medicine, 1972; m. Alice Mary Bell, June 27, 1977; 1 dau., Melissa Gorman. Intern, Mercy Hosp., Denver, 1972-73; resident in diagnostic radiology Hosp. of U. Pa., Phila., 1973-76, fellow in nuclear medicine, 1976-77; chief Dept. Radiology Fisher Titus Meml. Hosp., Norwalk, Ohio, 1978—; asst. instr. radiology U. Pa. Sch. Medicine, Phila., 1973-77. Diplomate Am. Bd. Radiology, Am. Bd. Nuclear Medicine; lic. physician, Mo., Colo., Pa., N.J., Wash., Calif., Ore., Ohio. Mem. Am. Coll. Radiology, Ohio State Radiol. Soc., Soc. Nuclear Medicine, Benjamin Franklin Inst. Sci., Huron County Med. Soc., Ohio State Med. Assn. Roman Catholic. Contbr. articles to profl. jours. Home: 91 Christie Ave Norwalk OH 44857 Office: 272 Benedict Ave Norwalk OH 44857

GUTTERMAN, MILTON M., operations research analyst; b. N.Y.C., Nov. 5, 1927; s. Benjamin and Gussie (Rothschild) G.; B.S., Coll. City N.Y., 1948; M.S., U. Chgo., 1949; m. Joan Helen Levey, Nov. 30, 1952; children—Gail Rosemary, Allen Bernard. Researcher, Inst. Air Weapons, 1952-54, Ill. Inst. Tech. Research Inst., Chgo., 1954-66; sr. operations research cons. Standard Oil Co. Ind., Chgo., 1966—. Served with AUS, 1946-47. Mem. Operations Research Soc., Assn. Computing Machinery, Math. Programming Soc., Spl. Interest Group for Math. Programming, SHARE, Chgo. Hort. Soc., Am. Contract Bridge League (life master), Am. (cons. rosarian Ill.-Ind. dist.), No. Chicagoland, Northeastern Ill. rose socs. Jewish. Editor: Computer Applications 1962, 1964; asso. editor ACM Transactions Math. Software, 1975-79. Home: 5049 Lee St Skokie IL 60077 Office: 200 E Randolph Dr Chicago IL 60601

GUTZWILLER, WILLIAM OWEN, educator; b. Cleves, Ohio, June 1, 1925; s. William Joseph and Mildred B. (Russell) G.; student Wilmington (Ohio) Coll., 1943-44, U. Cin. evening coll., 1944-46, B.S. in Chem. Engring., U. Cin., 1950; M.S., Miami U., 1967; m. Barbara Ellen Norvell, June 20, 1953; children—Brian, Michelle. With Howard Paper Mills, Dayton, Ohio, Aetna Paper div., Dayton, 1946-50, developer new paper products, 1950-51, supr. quality control, 1959-60, mill chemist Maxwell div., Franklin, Ohio, 1951-59; successively instr., asst. prof., asso. prof. paper sci. and engring. dept. Miami U., Oxford, Ohio, 1960—; summer cons. Black Clawson Corp., Middletown, Ohio, 1962, Kimberly-Clark Corp., W. Carrollton, Ohio, 1963, 64, 65, Fox Paper Co., Lockland, Ohio, 1969; cons. research and devel. various firms, 1973—; organizer, dir. summer workshop for high sch. jrs., 1972, 78, 79, 80, 81, active participant, 1973-77. Webelos leader Dan Beard council Boy Scouts Am., 1967-69; active Jaycees, 1953-60. Recipient good citizenship medal SAR, 1939; elected to Buckeye Boys' State, 1942. Mem. TAPPI (exec. com. Ohio sect. 1974-76, past chmn. edn. com.), Am. Inst. Chem. Engrs., Instrument Soc. Am. (Dist. 5 industries and scis. dept. liaison, past chmn. edn. com. Pulp and Paper Industry div., mem. Cin. sect.). Club: Lions Internat. Contbr. articles to profl. publs. Home: 6284 Timothy Ln Oxford OH 45056 Office: 119 Kreger Hall Miami U Oxford OH 45056

GUY, DANIEL SOWERS, coll. dean, lawyer; b. Columbus, Ohio, July 12, 1928; s. Ralph Julian and Mary Elizabeth (Broyles) G.; B.A., Ohio Wesleyan U., 1949; J.D., Ohio No. U., 1952; LL.M., U. Mich., 1956, S.J.D. (Cook fellow), 1970; m. Eleanor Bryenton, Dec. 22, 1962; children—Stanley, Sharon. Admitted to Ohio bar, 1952; gen. practice law, Canton, Ohio, 1956; asst. atty. gen. State of Ohio, 1957-58; asst. prof. law Ohio No. U. Coll. Law, 1959-62, asso. prof., 1962-65, prof., 1965-73, 77—, dean, 1978—; prof. Law Sch., U. N.D., 1973-77; Congl. fellow, Washington, 1961-62; fellow Inst. in Social Sci. Methods in Legal Edn., Denver, 1967; staff dir. Crime Prevention Task Force, N.D., Criminal Justice Com., 1974-75. Served with U.S. Army, 1952-54. Mem. Ohio State Bar Assn., Am. Bar Assn., Am. Judicature Soc., League Ohio Law Sch. (pres. 1968-69), Order of Coif, Phi Beta Kappa. Methodist. Clubs: Kiwanis, Masons. Author: State Highway Condemnation Procedures, 1970; contbr. articles to profl. jours. Office: Coll Law Ohio No U Ada OH 45810

GUY, DRUE SHROPSHIRE, ednl. adminstr.; b. Elyria, Ohio; d. Leander James and Christina Mae (Davis) Shropshire; B.S. (Erie Co. scholar), Ohio State U., 1957, M.A., 1965; Ph.D., (George A. Bowman fellow), Kent State U., 1979; 1 son, Christopher Daniel. Tchr., vis. tchr. Columbus (Ohio) Public Schs., 1957-64; ednl. coordinator Franklin County (Ohio) Children's Services, 1965-67; dep. dir. new careers tng. program New Careers, Columbus, 1968-69; research psychologist Battelle Meml. Inst.; urban social services specialist United Community Council, Columbus, 1969-71; asst. dir. program devel. Ohio State U. Research Found., Columbus, 1971-75; program officer Kent State Center Ednl. Devel., also Desegregation Assistance Center, Kent (Ohio) State U., 1976-79; dep. supt. Racine (Wis.) Unified Sch. Dist., 1980—; cons. ednl. problems, juvenile justice, social services, equal ednl. opportunities. Bd. dirs. Uhuru Drug Program, Columbus, 1973-75, YWCA, Girl Scouts U.S., Racine Environ. Com., Racine/Kenosha Opportunities Industrialization Center; bd. dirs. Twig 110 of Children's Hosp., Columbus, 1963-75, chmn., 1970, projects chmn., 1971; vol. city-wide solicitation, news media coordinator United Negro Coll. Fund, 1965-66; active Columbus Area Civil Rights Council, 1969-75, LWV, 1962-70. Mem. Am. Assn. Sch. Adminstrs., Am. Personnel and Guidance Assn., Nat. Alliance Black Sch. Educators, NAACP, Phi Delta Kappa, Delta Sigma Theta (certificate achievement 1978), Kappa Delta Pi, Delta Kappa Gamma. Episcopalian. Clubs: Links, Zonta. Home: 910 Montclair Dr Racine WI 53402 Office: Racine Unified Sch Dist 2220 Northwestern Ave Racine WI 53404

GUY, ERNEST THOMAS, assn. exec.; b. Detroit, May 12, 1921; s. William G. and Anna (Utas) G.; B.A., Mich. State U., 1943; postgrad. U. Ga., 1946, U. Mich., 1948; m. Bernice Louise Smith, Mar. 8, 1945 (dec.); children—E. Timothy, Cynthia Louise. State coordinator vets. tng. Ga. Dept. Edn., Atlanta, 1946-47; mgr. sta. WATL, Atlanta, 1947-48; program dir. sta. WKNX, Saginaw, Mich., 1948-50; pub. relations dir. Mich. Heart Assn., Detroit, 1950-53, exec. dir., 1953-58; exec. dir. Tex. Heart Assn., Houston, 1958-68, Chgo. Med. Soc., 1968-69, Calif. Dental Assn., San Francisco, 1969-73, So. Calif. Dental Assn., Los Angeles, 1972-73, Unified Calif. Dental Assn., 1973-74, Am. Soc. Clin. Hypnosis, Des Plaines, Ill., 1974-75; dir. meetings Am. Bar Assn., Chgo., 1975—; bd. dirs. Meeting Planners Internat.; mem. industry adv. bd. Meeting World, 1978-80. Mem. adv. com. Tex. Rehab. Assn. Faculty pub. health classes U. Mich., Ann Arbor, 1953-58; del. White House Conf. Edn., 1956; vice chmn. Fed. Service Campaign for Health Agys. in Tex., 1961-62; mem. governing council Soc. Heart Assns. Profl. Staff, 1959-62. Mem. Pres.'s Bicentennial Commn. Precinct worker Houston Republican Com.; mem. fin. com. George Bush for Pres. Campaign, 1978-80. Served to capt. AUS, 1943-46. Co-recipient Blakeslee award, 1953; recipient award of merit Mich. Heart Assn., 1958, Merit award Tex. Heart Assn., 1968, commendation award Calif. Dental Assn. Certified assn. exec. Mem. Am. Soc. Assn. Execs., Am. Pub. Relations Soc., Nat. Assn. Parliamentarians, Profl. Conv. Mgmt. Assn., Internat. Platform Assn., Am. Assn. Dental Editors, Nat. Pub. Relations Council, Nat. Assn. Exhibit Mgrs., U.S. Parachute Assn. Republican. Episcopalian (lay reader). Contbr. numerous articles to profl. publs. Home: 930 N Northwest Hwy 202 Park Ridge IL 60068 Office: 1155 E 60th St Chicago IL 60637

GUY, JOHN EDWARD, lawyer; b. Danville, Ill., July 15, 1924; s. John Milton, Jr. and Beatrice (Marks) G.; Ph.B., U. Chgo., 1947; LL.B., J.D., John Marshall Law Sch., Chgo., 1951; m. Muriel Elaine Becking, Nov. 29, 1947; children—Randall Edward, Scott Evan, Carolyn Elizabeth. Admitted to Ill. bar, 1951, U.S. Supreme Ct. bar; practiced in Chgo., 1951—; partner firm Abramson & Fox, 1977-81. Sec., Civil Betterment Party, Village of Glen Ellyn, Ill., 1976-80; adult leader local Boy Scouts Am., 1971-72. Served with AUS, 1943-46. Recipient Order of Arrow, Boy Scouts Am., 1972. Mem. Soc. Hosp. Attys., Soc. Trial Lawyers, Appellate Lawyers Assn., Am. Judicature Soc., Am. Arbitration Assn., Ill. Bar Assn., Chgo. Bar Assn., Def. Research Inst., Ill. Def. Counsel (dir. 1972—, v.p. 1979—, pres.-elect), Trial Lawyers Club Chgo., DuPage County Bar Assn. Contbr. to legal jours. Office: 1 E Wacker Dr Chicago IL 60601

GUY, JOHN MARTIN, lawyer, state senator; b. Detroit, July 16, 1929; s. Alvin W. and Ann G. (Martin) G.; B.S., Butler U., 1958; J.D., Ind. U., 1961; m. Norma J. Puterbaugh, Aug. 13, 1950; children—Janice Lynn, Robert John. Admitted to Ind. bar, 1962, since practiced in Monticello; atty. firm Siferd, Guy, Christopher and Loy, 1962—; mem. Ind. Ho. of Reps., 1971-74, house majority leader, 1973-74; mem. Ind. Senate, 1977—, majority leader, 1979-80; dir. State and Savs. Bank, Hively's Pharmacy. Pros. atty. 39th Jud. Circuit, 1963-67. Pres. White County Mental Health Assn., 1965-68. Trustee Monticello-Union Twp. Library Bd., pres., 1970-71. Served with USAF, 1951-55. Named Outstanding Republican Freshman Ind. Ho. of Reps., 1971, Ind. Senate, 1977. Mem. Am., Ind., Monticello bar assns., Am. Judicature Soc., Am. Trial Lawyers Assn., Monticello C. of C. (pres. 1975—), Am. Legion. Clubs: Masons, Shriners, Elks, Moose. Home: 201 Western Heights Dr Monticello IN 47960 Office: 115 W Broadway Monticello IN 47960

GUY, PAUL WENDELL, hosp. exec.; b. Hartford City, Ind., June 7, 1925; s. Dennis H. and Hazel G. (George) G.; student Ohio State U., 1943-44, Internat. Coll., Ft. Wayne, Ind., 1946-47, St. Francis Coll., Ft. Wayne, 1968-69; m. Mary Louise Calvin, Aug. 17, 1947; children—John Paul, Jane Anne, James Michael. Treas., gen. mgr. Galbreath Pictures, Inc., Ft. Wayne, 1958-61; office mgr. Central Soya Co., Inc., Ft. Wayne, 1962-64; dir. personnel Parkview Meml. Hosp., Ft. Wayne, 1965—; cons., speaker in field. Served with USAAF, 1944-45. Mem. Am. Soc. Hosp. Personnel Adminstrn. (pres. 1976-78), Joint Conf. Affiliated Socs. of Am. Hosp. Assn., Adminstrv. Mgmt. Soc. (v.p. 1968), Ind. Soc. Hosp. Personnel Adminstrn. (charter pres. 1968), Delta Chi. Methodist. Clubs: Masons, Scottish Rite. Home: 227 Hillcrest Dr Warren IN 46792 Office: 2200 Randallia Dr Fort Wayne IN 46805

GUZIEC, ROBERT ALAN, physician; b. Chgo., Dec. 18, 1938; s. Philip Edward and Dorothy May (Zimmer) G.; M.D., U. Ill., 1963; m. Anita Francis Peklo, June 18, 1960; 1 son, Philip Robert. Intern, Cook County Hosp., Chgo., 1963-64; gen. surgery resident Ill. Masonic Hosp., 1966-67; otolaryngology resident U. Ill. Hosp., 1967-70; attending physician, chmn. sect. otolaryngology and maxillofacial surgery Ill. Masonic Hosp., 1975—; attending physician, cons. Walther Meml., Sydney Forkosh, Martha Washington, Highland Park hosps. Served with USPHS, 1964-66. Diplomate Am. Bd. Otolaryngology. Mem. A.C.S., Am. Acad. Otolaryngology, AMA, Am. Council Otolaryngology, Internat. Soc. Aquatic Medicine, Ill. State, Cook County, Chgo. med. socs., Chgo. Laryngol. and Otological Soc., Alpha Omega Alpha. Office: Suite 1107 30 N Michigan Ave Chicago IL 60602 also Suite 108 400 Lake Cook Rd Deerfield IL 60015

GUZIK, RUDOLPH PATRICK, engring. physicist; b. Chgo., Sept. 26, 1939; s. Rudolph Frank and Patricia Ann G.; B.S. in Physics and Math., Ill. Inst. Tech., 1970; M.S. in Physics, No. Ill. U., 1975; m. Oct. 22, 1961 (div. 1981); children—Sharon Keri, Audrey Lynn, Lauren

Briana. Profl. pianist, 1956-65; various positions in engring. and electronics, 1962-67; sr. physicist dept. research APECO Corp., Evanston, Ill., 1967-74; asso. editor Electro-Optical Systems Design, Chgo., 1974; cons., pres. Imaging Tech. Consultants, Chgo., 1974-78; sr. engring. physicist Micro Imagery group Bell & Howell Corp., Chgo., 1978—, project mgr., 1979-81; mgr. advanced research Graphic Systems div. Rockwell Internat., Chgo., 1981—; vis. asst. prof. advanced tech. art Sch. Art Inst. Chgo., 1975, vis. artist lectr., 1976; tchr. in field; cons. Sch. Holography Chgo.; project judge Chgo. area Student Sci. Conf., 1973—. Chmn. Gen. Assembly, Ind. Precinct Orgn., Chgo., 1973. Mem. Soc. Photog. Scientists and Engrs. (chmn. Imaging in 70's Conf., 1971, pres. Chgo. chpt. 1973-75, Service award 1975), TAPPI, Am. Phys. Soc., Electrostatics Soc. Am., Optical Soc. Am., Soc. for Info. Display, Soc. Photo-optical and Instrumentation Engrs., World Future Soc., IEEE (indsl. applications sect.), Mensa. Editor: Imaging in the 70's Forecasting Symposium, 1972; editor and contbg. artist CHIME, 1969-70; contbr. articles to profl. pubs.; patentee applications and processes electrophotography. Home: 5751 N Richmond Chicago IL 60659

GUZZETTA, DOMINIC JAMES, univ. pres.; b. Fredonia, N.Y., July 21, 1919; s. James and Josephine (Giordano) G.; student Alfred U., 1937-38; B.A. cum laude, U. Buffalo, 1948, M.Ed., 1951, Ed.D., 1953; student U. Rochester, 1950-51, Syracuse U., 1951-52; LL.D., Akron U., 1968, Kent State U., 1971, Bellevue Coll., 1978; D.Sc., Marian Coll., 1971; L.H.D., Walsh Coll., 1972; children—JoAnne Nola, Elaine Marie. Tchr. pub. schs., 1948-51; asst. dean Millard Filmore Coll., 1951-53; supr. productivity program FOA, Washington, 1953-54; asst. dean evening and adult edn. div. U. Akron, 1954-56, dean, 1956-59, prof. edn., 1960-68, dir. summer session, 1956-59, acting dean Coll. Edn., 1958-59, dean gen. coll., 1959-62, v.p., dean adminstrn., 1962-66, sr. v.p., provost, 1966-68, coordinator research, 1959-62; pres., prof. history Marian Coll., 1968-71; pres. U. Akron (Ohio), 1971—, prof. higher edn., 1971—. Cons. evaluator higher edn. North Central Assn. Trustee Akron Children's Hosp., Akron City Hosp., Walsh Coll., Canton, Ohio, Northeastern Ohio Univs. Coll. Medicine, United Way of Summit County, Ohio Council Econ. Edn. Served from pvt. to capt. AUS, 1940-46; lt. col. Ohio N.G. Mem. Ohio Coll. Assn., Internat. Inst. Akron (pres.), Am. Assn. Sch. Adminstrs., Nat. Council on Ednl. Research, Am. Assn. State Colls. and Univs. (chmn. com. on edn. and work), Ohio Coll. Assn. (pres.), Phi Sigma Kappa, Delta Sigma Pi, Kappa Delta Pi, Alpha Sigma Lambda, Phi Delta Kappa, Chi Sigma Nu, Omicron Delta Kappa. Clubs: Cascade, Indpls. Literary, Rotary. Home: 910 Eaton Rd Akron OH 44303 Office: U Akron Akron OH 44304

GWINN, CECIL WILLIAM, physicist; b. Wheeling, W.Va., Mar. 29, 1922; s. William J.B. and Mildred (Hale) G.; student Ohio State U., 1946-49; m. Geneva Evaline Absalom, Aug. 25, 1956. Physicist, Nat. Bur. Standards, Washington, 1950-53; asst. chemist Goodyear Atomic Corp., Waverly, Ohio, 1954-55; physicist in electromagnetics Wright Patterson AFB, Ohio, 1955-60, research physicist cybernetics, 1960—; vis. lectr. cybernetics U. Nottingham (Eng.), 1966, U. Naples (Italy), 1967, U. Ariz., Tempe, 1968, U. Tenn. Space Inst., 1972. Recipient Achievement awards USAF, 1957, 62, 64, 66, 68. Mem. AAAS, Am. Math Assn., C.G. Jung Found. for Analytic Psychology, ASCAP. Contbr. articles to profl. jours. Home: 401 Kenilworth Ave Dayton OH 45405 Office: Wright Patterson AFB OH 45433

GWINN, ROBERT P., elec. appliance mfg. exec.; b. Anderson, Ind., June 30, 1907; s. Marshall and Margaret (Cather) G.; Ph.B., U. Chgo., 1929; m. Nancy Flanders, Jan. 20, 1942; children—John Marshall, Richard Herbert. With Sunbeam Corp., Chgo., 1936—, successively in sales dept., asst. sales mgr., sales mgr., v.p. sales, 1936-55, pres., gen. mgr., dir., now chmn. bd., chief exec. officer; pres. Sunbeam Appliance Service Co., Chgo., 1952—; chmn. bd., chief exec. officer Ency. Brit.; dir. Sunbeam Corp., Ltd. (Can., U.K., Argentina, Mex.); Continental Casualty Co., CNA Fin., First Nat. Bank Chgo., Riverside Nat. Bank, Continental Assurance Co., Titan Oil Co., Exploration, Inc. Trustee Hanover Coll., U. Chgo., U. Chgo. Cancer Research Found. Mem. Alpha Sigma Phi. Clubs: Riverside Country (Ill.); Mid-Am., Wine and Food Soc., Chicago, Univ., Comml., Econ. (Chgo.); Confrerie des Chevaliers du Tastevin; Mill Reef. Home: 144 Fairbanks Rd Riverside IL 60546 Office: 5400 Roosevelt Rd Chicago IL 60650

GWYNN, JOHN LEWIS, mktg. research co. exec.; b. Washington, Jan. 10, 1918; s. William Clarence and Louise Harrison (Beall) G.; B.A., Georgetown U., 1940; m. Martha McAfee Milton, Nov. 8, 1941; children—Martha, Mary, John. Vice pres. media dir. central div. Erwin, Wasey, advt. agy., Chgo., 1964; asst. to pres. A.C. Nielsen Co., Northbrook, Ill., 1964-70, v.p., 1970-78, adminstrv. v.p., 1978—, also dir.; dir. Petroleum Info. Corp. Served with U.S. Army, 1941-45. Clubs: Biltmore Country, Lake Barrington Golf. Home: 339 Island View Ln Barrington IL 60010 Office: Nielsen Plaza Northbrook IL 60062

HAAG, MAX EDWIN, educator; b. Marshall County, Ind., Oct. 5, 1929; s. Byron Edwin and Bertha Della (Lautzenhiser) H.; A.B., Valparaiso U., 1952; M.A., Ball State U., 1958; postgrad. (Wall St. fellow), U. Minn., 1960, Ind. State U., summer, 1969; m. Dorothy Louise Hankes, June 10, 1954; children—Christina, Catherine, Cynthia. Tchr. bus. edn. Union Mills (Ind.) High Sch., 1952, New Carlisle (Ind.) High Sch., 1954—, New Prairie High Sch., New Carlisle, 1969—, vocat. coordinator, head Dept. Bus. Edn., 1969—. Chmn. stewards commn. Edn. Commn. for Ch. of Brethren, South Bend and LaPorte, Ind., 1956—; mem. supervisory com. Tchr.'s Credit Union, South Bend, Ind., 1968-80. Served with U.S. Army, 1952-54. Recipient Merit award Adminstrv. Mgmt. Soc., 1977, Diamond Merit award, 1981. Mem. Ind. State Tchr.'s Assn., Nat. Bus. Edn. Assn., Am. Vocat. Assn., Ind. Vocat. Assn., Classroom Educators of Bus. and Office Edn., Ind. Bus. Edn. Assn., Adminstrv. Mgmt. Soc. (chpt. sec. 1971—), Am. Legion, VFW, Delta Pi Epsilon. Address: 418 W Chestnut St New Carlisle IN 46552

HAAGENSTAD, SONJA JOANNE, social worker; b. Maddock, N.D., Aug. 14, 1941; d. Joseph Taylor and Stella Agnes (Kleven) H.; A.B. magna cum laude, Concordia Coll., 1963; cert. of completion U. Oslo, 1962; M.S. in Social Work, U. Wis., 1967. Case worker Benson County (N.D.) Welfare Bd., Minnewaukan, 1963-65; social worker Stark County (N.D.) Welfare Bd. Dickinson, 1967-68, Minot (N.D.) Area Social Service Center, 1968-71; social work supr. Topeka State Hosp., 1971-75; social worker Shawnee Community Mental Health Corp., Topeka, 1975-81; social worker Lake Region Human Service Center, Devils Lake, N.D., 1981—; field instr. social work Kans. U., 1972. Lic. specialist clin. social worker, Kans. Mem. Nat. Assn. Social Workers, N.E. Kans. Conf. Social Welfare, Kans. Council Children and Youth, Acad. Cert. Social Workers., Audubon Soc. Lutheran. Home: Sweetwater Apts 10 West Devils Lake ND 58301 Office: Lake Region Human Service Center Hwy 2 West Devils Lake ND 58301

HAAKE, JOHN JAY, cons. archtl. woodwork; b. Waukegan, Ill., Nov. 28, 1923; s. Walter Gerhardt and Nena Mae (Falkner) H.; student U. Ill., 1947-48, 67-69; B. Gen. Studies, Roosevelt U., 1973, postgrad., 1973—; M.P.A., Roosevelt U., 1979; m. Mary Joan DeVol, Dec. 24, 1948. Apprentice, Waukegan Sash & Door Co., 1945-49, v.p., plant mgr., 1953-57, pres., 1957-67; archtl. relations rep. Chgo. chpt. Archtl. Woodwork Inst., 1968-71, archtl. woodwork cons., 1971—. Vice-pres. Waukegan Import and Export Corp., 1955-57, pres. 1957-67; v.p. Haake Inc., Waukegan, 1963-67. Adviser constrn. Triton Coll., River Grove, Ill., 1975. Mem. adv. bd. Salvation Army Waukegan, 1957-67, v.p. 1963, pres. 1964. Mem. Ill. Woodwork Assn. (sec. 1965), Am. Legion, Forest Products Research Soc., Constrn. Specifications Inst. (dir. Chgo. chpt. 1976, 77). Presbyterian (deacon). Clubs: Elks, Kiwanis (dir. 1958 Waukegan), Sturgeon Bay Yacht, Waukegan Yacht (rear commodore 1957). Address: 649E Rockland Rd Libertyville IL 60048

HAAKENSON, PHILIP NIEL, pharmacist, educator; b. Hatton, N.D., Apr. 15, 1924; s. Martin Selmer and Theodora H.; B.S. in Pharmacy, N.D. State U., 1950, M.S. in Pharmacy, 1965; Ph.D. in Pharmacy Adminstrn., U. Wis., 1972; m. Eldora Ida Robinson, June 19, 1950; children—Mary Kim, Martin Niel. Owner, Portland (N.D.) Drug, 1950-60, Hatton (N.D.) Drug, 1956-60; asst. prof. pharmacy adminstrn. N.D. State U., Fargo, 1961-65, asso. prof., 1965-70, prof., 1970—, dean Sch. of Pharmacy, 1970-80. Served with USN, 1942-45. Decorated Air medal (2); recipient Bowl of Hygiea, N.D. Pharm. Assn., 1979; named Outstanding Alumni, Kappa Psi, 1974, Pharmacist of Yr., 1977. Mem. Am. Assn. Colls. of Pharmacy, Am. Pharm. Assn., N.D. Pharm. Assn., Sigma Xi. Republican. Lutheran. Clubs: Lions, Masons, Shriners. Editor Nodak Pharmacist, 1962-74. Home: 210 28th Ave N Fargo ND 58102 Office: ND State U Sudro Hall 215A Fargo ND 58105

HAAS, EDWARD LEE, accounting firm exec.; b. Camden, N.J., Nov. 9, 1935; s. Edward David and Mildred (Wynne) H.; B.A., LaSalle Coll., 1958; postgrad. Temple U., 1960-62; m. Mary Ann Lind, Dec. 27, 1958; children—John Eric, Gretchen Lind. Mgr. systems devel. RCA Corp., Cherry Hill, N.J., 1966-71; mgr. computer tech. services The Gen. Tire & Rubber Co., Akron, Ohio, 1971-74; mgr. computer applications research and devel. Ernst & Whinney, Cleve., 1974-75, dir. nat. systems group, 1976, nat. dir. data processing and software products, 1977, nat. partner, 1978—. Mem. Greater Cleve. Growth Assn. Served to 1st lt., arty., U.S. Army, 1958-59. Mem. Soc. Cert. Data Processors, Data Processing Mgmt. Assn., Assn. for Systems Mgmt., Assn. for Computing Machinery. Republican. Roman Catholic. Clubs: Cleve. Athletic, Hudson Country, Western Res. Racquet, Hudson Tennis, Mid-day, Cotillion Soc. Cleve. Home: 111 Old Orchard Dr Hudson OH 44236 Office: 2000 National City Center Cleveland OH 44114

HAAS, HOWARD GREEN, bedding mfg. co. exec.; b. Chgo., Apr. 14, 1924; s. Adolph and Marie (Green) H.; B.B.A., U. Mich., 1948; m. Carolyn Werbner, June 4, 1949; children—Jody, Jonathan. Promotion dir. Esquire, Inc., Chgo., 1949-50; advt. mgr. Mitchell Mfg. Co., Chgo., 1950-52, v.p. advt., then v.p. sales, 1952-58; with Sealy, Inc., Chgo., 1959—, exec. v.p., 1965-67, pres., treas., 1967—, also dir.; chmn. bd. Sealy Can. Ltd., Toronto, 1978—; dir. Ind. Spring Corp. Mem. nominating com. Glencoe (Ill.) Sch. Bd., 1956; mem. print and drawing com. Art Inst. Chgo., 1978; chmn. parent's com. Washington U., St. Louis, 1977; bd. dirs. Jewish Children's Bur. Chgo., 1977; pres. orchestra of Ill., 1982. Served to 1st lt. USAAF, 1943-45; ETO. Decorated Air medal with 3 oak leaf clusters; recipient Brotherhood award NCCJ, 1970, Human Relations award Am. Jewish Com., 1977. Mem. Nat. Assn. Bedding Mfrs. (past vice chmn., trustee), Soc. Contemporary Art vis. com. U. Chgo. Sch. of Social Sers. Adminstrn., 1982. Democrat. Club: Birchwood Tennis (Highland Park, Ill.). Address: Sealy Inc Merchandise Mart Chicago IL 60654

HAAS, JAMES WAYNE, accountant; b. Merrill, Wis., Sept. 27, 1944; s. Frank Joseph and Verna Antoinette (Beilke) H.; Asso. in Accounting, North Central Tech. Inst., 1968; m. Patrice Marie Will, June 2, 1973; children—Christopher Jon, Scott James. Controller, asst. treas. House of Merrill Inc., Merrill, 1968-72; controller Semling Menke Co., Inc., Merrill, 1968-72; treas., dir. North Star Communications, Ltd., Gleason, Wis., 1971-72; pres., treas., dir. Profl. Accounting Systems, Inc., Merrill, 1975—; pres., dir. Haas Enterprises, Inc., 1971—; pres., treas., dir. Adventure Capital, Ltd., 1971—; pres., sec., dir. Haas Millwork Corp., Merrill, 1975—; v.p., treas. ops. mgr. Accounting Bookkeeping Inc., Wauwatosa, Wis., 1975-76; v.p. Marathon Mining & Mfg. Corp., Wausau, Wis., 1976, pres., 1977-79; treas., controller, prodn. mgr. Moduline Windows, Inc., Wausau, 1977-78; mng. partner Haas Properties, Medford, Wis., 1979—; owner Midwest Investments, La Crosse, Wis., 1980—. Mem. Adminstrv. Mgmt. Soc., Inst. Internal Auditors, Nat. Notary Assn., Inst. Record Mgrs. and Adminstrs., Am. Soc. Notaries, Nat. Assn. Accts., Am. Inst. Profl. Numismatists (charter mem.), Am. Acctg. Assn., Nat. Soc. Public Accts. Democrat. Roman Catholic. Clubs: K.C., Kiwanis (New Club Bldg. award), Optimists, Winona Lions. Home: 1253 W Broadway Winona MN 55987 Office: PO Box 606 La Crosse WI 54601

HAAS, JOSEPH ALAN, broadcasting exec.; b. Dover, Ohio, Dec. 4, 1920; s. Fred J. and Pearl J. (Martin) H.; B.S. in Bus. Adminstrn., Ind. U., 1947; m. Barbara R. Stulac, June 22, 1968; children—Jody, Corby. Gen. mgr. Sta. WWCA, Gary, Ind., 1960—. Served with USAF, 1942-46, 50-52. Office: 545 Broadway Gary IN 46402

HAAS, LARRY ALFRED, chemist; b. Zeeland, N.D., Nov. 28, 1935; s. August and Martha (Wagemann) H.; B.A., U. S.D., 1957; M.S., U. Minn., 1964; m. Eleanor Louise Allen, Sept. 4, 1959; children—David Larry, Douglas Allen. Chemist, Honeywell, Mpls., 1957-62; research chemist U.S. Bur. Mines, Mpls., 1962-69, project leader, 1969—. Chmn. Mpls. Area Boys Brigade, 1968-72; bd. dirs. Minn. Camping Assn., 1972—. Served with USAR, 1959-67. Mem. Am. Inst. Mining, Metal. and Petroleum Engrs., Am. Inst. Chem. Engrs., Am. Chem. Soc., Catalysis Soc. Am. Clubs: Berean Volley Ball, Christian Service Brigade, Camp Nathanael. Contbr. articles to profl. jours. Patentee in catalysis, plasma discharges and metal extraction. Home: 1037 E Crystal Lake Rd Burnsville MN 55337 Office: US Bur Mines 5629 Minnehaha Ave S Minneapolis MN 55417

HABACK, PETER LEE, real estate exec.; b. N.Y.C., July 25, 1951; s. Harry J. and Leah (Mintz) H.; B.A., Am. U., 1973; postgrad. John Marshall Law Sch., 1974-76. Office leasing cons. Helmsley-Spear, Chgo., 1976, bldg. mgr., 1976-79, asst. v.p., 1979-80, v.p., 1980—. Registered real estate broker, Ill. Mem. Bldg. Owners and Mgrs. Assn., Bldg. Mgrs. Club. Democrat. Jewish. Office: Suite 210 One N Dearborn St Chicago IL 60602

HABAK, PHILIP A., cardiologist; b. Cairo, Egypt, Sept. 24, 1937; s. Antoine and Jeanette Habak; came to U.S., 1965; naturalized, 1969; student St. Joseph Coll., Cairo, 1952-56; M.B., B.Ch., Ainshams Faculty Medicine, 1963, m. Hermina Geels, Feb. 7, 1970; children—Patricia Jane, Glenn Eric. Intern Cook County (Ill.) Hosp., 1965-66; resident Univ. Hosps., Iowa City, Iowa, 1966-69, fellow in cardiology, 1971-73; practice medicine specializing in cardiology, 1974—; asso. cardiovascular div. dept. internal medicine U. Iowa Coll. Medicine 1973-74, clin. asst. prof. dept. internal medicine, 1977—. Served to maj., M.C., U.S. Army, 1969-71. NIH grantee, 1971-73; diplomate Am. Bd. Internal Medicine. Fellow A.C.P., Am. Coll. Cardiology, Council on Clin. Cardiology, Am. Heart Assn.; mem. AMA, Iowa State Med. Soc. Research coronary primary prevention trial, Lipid Research Clin., U. Iowa, 1973-74. Office: 1706 Brady Suite 309 Davenport IA 52803

HABENICHT, DONNA JEANNE, educator; b. Manilla, Dec. 13, 1934 (parents U.S. citizens); d. Edward Newton and Cora Catherine (Garber) Lugenbeal; A.B., Andres U., 1954, M.A., 1974, Ed.D., 1977; postgrad. U. Calif., 1956, UCLA, 1957, Interam. U., 1963-64, Mich. State U., 1977; m. Herald Allen Habenicht, May 23, 1954; children—Laurence Edward, Nancy Louise. Tchr., San Bernardino (Calif.) City Schs., 1955-56, Montebello Unified Schs., 1956-57, White Meml. Union Sch., 1958; dir. child evangelism P.R. Conf. and Antillian Union, 1962-66; tchr. Bella Vista Ch. Sch., 1965-66; chmn. dept. secretarial sci. Antillian Coll., P.R., 1966-69; tchr. Lilliputian Early Learning Center, Miami, Fla., 1970; coordinator student missionary program Andrews U., Berrien Springs, Mich., 1973-75, dir. freshmen edn., 1975-76, asst. prof. ednl. psychology and counseling, 1977—, also coordinator early childhood curriculum; vis. instr. Interam. U., 1964. Mem. Am. Psychol. Assn., Am. Personnel and Guidance Assn., Am. Sch. Counselors Assn., Assn. Religious and Value Issues in Counseling, Assn. Supervision and Curriculum Devel., Berrien Cass Van Buren Counselors Assn., Phi Delta Kappa. Author: Cradle Roll Lessons for Sabbath School and Home, Vols. 1-4, 1977; Cradle Roll A Teaching Aids, 1980. Home: 1204 Kephart St Berrien Springs MI 49103 Office: Andrews University Berrien Springs MI 49104

HABERMAN, REX STANLEY, state senator, farm mgr.; b. Friend, Nebr., Jan. 23, 1924; s. George and Frances H.; student Colo. State Coll., 1942-43, U. Nebr., 1943-44; m. Phyllis Kavan, Aug. 22, 1948; children—Mary Lou, George, Rex II, Phillip. Owner, operator 5 photog. studios, 1945-67; personnel dir. Nebr. Vets. Home, 1968-70; mgr. family farms, Imperial, Nebr., 1970—; mem. Nebr. Legislature, 1979—. Mem. Adams County Bd. Suprs., 1964-68, Imperial City Council, 1974-76; del. Republican Nat. Conv., 1976; former state pres. Nebr. Jaycees; former chmn. Adams County Rep. Party, Chase County Rep. Party; former pres. Greater Nebr. Health Systems Agy.; exec. council Nebr. Episcopal Ch. Mem. Hastings C. of C. (dir.), Am. Legion, VFW. Clubs: Masons, Shriners, Elks, Eagles, Rotary. Office: State Capitol Lincoln NE 68509

HABIB, IZZEDDIN SALIM, mech. engr., educator; b. Tripoli, Lebanon, Nov. 16, 1934; came to U.S., 1960, naturalized, 1970; B.M.E., Am. U. Beirut, 1956; M.S., Va. Poly. Inst., 1961; Ph.D., U. Calif., Berkeley, 1968; m. Nuha Sukkari, Aug. 17, 1962; children—Dina, Tania. Research engr., group leader in heat transfer Chrysler Corp., Highland Park, Mich., 1964-66; asst. prof. mech. enging. U. Mich., Dearborn, 1969-70, asso. prof., 1970-73, prof., 1973—, chmn. dept., 1971-75. Mem. ASME, Sigma Xi. Author: Engineering Analysis Methods, 1975; contbr. articles to profl. jours. Office: U Mich 4901 Evergreen Rd Dearborn MI 48128

HACHTMAN, SAMUEL JOSEPH, food co. exec.; b. Chgo., Apr. 25, 1900; s. Isaac and Molly (Burr) H.; J.D., Northwestern U., 1922; emeritus degree, U. Chgo., 1971; m. Rose Cohn, Dec. 16, 1923; 1 dau., Harriet Hachtman Wallen. Admitted to Ill. bar, 1922; corporate and gen. practice law; pres. Sugarless Candy Corp. Am., Chgo., 1964—, Health Snacks, Ltd., Chgo., 1973—, Mem. Am., Ill. (sr. counsellor), Chgo. bar assns., Decalogue Soc., Am. Judicature Soc. Clubs: Masons, Shriners, East Bank. Patentee in field. Home: 408 S Oak Park Ave Oak Park IL 60302 Office: 3537 W North Ave Chicago IL 60647

HACKBARTH, CLARENCE WALTER, educator; b. West Allis, Wis., Dec. 12, 1927; s. Clarence Walter and Norma (Keikbush) H.; B.A., Elmhurst Coll., 1954; postgrad. Eden Theol. Sem., 1954-56; M.S., U. Wis., 1958; postgrad. U. Colo., 1963, Fla. State U., 1972, U. Belgrade (Yugoslavia), 1972; m. June Ellen Splittstoesser, Aug. 17, 1957; children—Richard, Scott, Mark. Counselor, Ill. State Tng. Sch. for Boys, St. Charles, 1953-54; instr. sociology Florence (Ala.) State Coll., 1958-61, Wis. State U., Superior, 1961-64; supply analyst systems mgmt. USN Electronics Supply Office, Gt. Lakes, Ill., 1964-65; prof. sociology Delta Coll., University Center, Mich., 1965—, chmn. social sci. div., 1976—. On-site asst. dir. Yugoslavia project League of Innovation in Community Colls., 1972. Mem. com. Boy Scouts Am., 1972-73, Little League, 1974-80; county chmn. Mich. Internat. Week, 1972. Served with USNR, 1945-46. Fellow League for Innovation in Community Colls.; mem. Am., Mich. sociol. assns., A.A.U.P. (chpt. sec. 1968-69, mem. state com. on student rights and responsibilities 1967-69), Nat. Orgn. Human Service Educators, A.C.L.U., Common Cause. Home: 1205 Scott St Midland MI 48640 Office: Delta Coll University Center MI 48710

HACKBIRTH, DAVID WILLIAM, aluminum co. exec.; b. Butler, Ind., Jan. 25, 1935; s. Ernest William and Bessie Mae (Snyder) H.; B.S., Ind. U., 1959; J.D., Wayne State U., Detroit, 1963, postgrad., 1965; M.B.A., U. Detroit, 1965; m. Anna Katherine Sahffer, July 19, 1959; children—Cynthia Kay, David William. Auditor, Ernst & Ernst, C.P.A.'s, Indpls., 1958-59; admitted to Mich. bar, 1963, Fed. Dist. Ct., 1964, U.S. Tax Ct., 1964; fin. and budget analyst Ford Motor Co., Dearborn, Mich., 1959-62; legal adminstr., then tax atty. Chrysler Corp., Detroit, 1962-66; tax atty. Glidden Co., Cleve., 1966-67; asst. to treas., then asst. to group v.p. ops. Alcan Aluminum Corp., Cleve., 1967-73; pres., dir. Aluminio de Colombia, S.A., 1973-75; v.p. Bldg. Products div. Alcan Aluminum Corp., Warren, Ohio, 1975-78, pres., 1978—. Served with AUS, 1954-56. Mem. Archtl. Aluminum Assn. (dir. 1979-81), Am. Bar Assn., Mich. Bar Assn., Beta Alpha Psi, Delta Theta Phi. Clubs: Country of Hudson; Cotillion Soc. (Cleve.); Walden Golf and Tennis, Western Res. Golf, Masons. Home: 290 Bicknell Dr Hudson OH 44236 Office: 280 N Park Ave Warren OH 44481

HACKENBRACHT, PHILLIP DOUGLAS, agronomist; b. Coshocton, Ohio, Mar. 2, 1950; s. Charles Earl and Margaret Dewar (Shurtz) H.; B.S., Ohio State U., 1972. Lawn specialist, power crew chief Scotts Lawn Care Service, Columbus, Ohio, 1973-74; area supr. Perf-A-Lawn Corp., Columbus, 1975-76; agronomist Na-Chors Plant Food Co., Marion, Ohio, 1976-78; farmer, Coshocton, 1978—. Mem. Am. Soc. Agronomy, Nat. Wildlife Assn. Mem. United Ch. Christ. Club: Lions (1st v.p. 1982—). Home: 51300 CR 116 Fresno OH 43824 Office: 51001 CR 115 Coshocton OH 43812

HACKER, DONALD WILBUR, mail advt. exec.; b. Ionia, Mich., June 18, 1914; s. Herman F. and Helena (Steinke) H.; grad. Chgo. Acad. Fine Arts, 1937, U. Ga., 1942-43; m. Ruby Elaine Simonson, Sept. 28, 1943; children—Eve Rulaine, David Kent, Donna Kathleen. Asst. advt. mgr. Gen. Furniture Co., Inc., Chgo., 1937-39; advt. merchandising mgr. Franc's, Davenport, Iowa, 1939-42; owner Lettercraft Co., Detroit, 1946—; pres. D.W. Hacker Co., Detroit, 1950, University Type, Inc., 1965—, Hacker-Stutz Corp., 1963—. Bd. dirs. Detroit Cerebral Center; active community drs.; bd. dirs., pres. United Cerebral Palsy Found.; pres. Living Opportunities, Inc., 1969; v.p. United Cerebral Palsy Assn. Mich. Served as dir. public relations C.E., U.S. Army, 1944-46. Mem. Mail Advt. Service Assn. Internat. (pres. 1954-57, pres. Detroit chpt. 1947-52), Advt. Fedn. Am. (dir. 1954-57). Lutheran. Clubs: Forest Lake Country (Bloomfield Hills); Detroit Execs. Assn. (sec., dir. 1955—), Recess (Detroit); Innisbrook Golf and Country (Tarpon Springs, Fla.); Rolls Royce Owners; The Club at Crayton Cove (Naples, Fla.). Home: 4778 Lahser Rd Bloomfield Hills MI 48013 also 1817 Cliff Rd Point Aux Barques MI

48467 also 4001 Gulfshore Blvd N Naples FL 33940 Office: 13131 Lyndon Ave Detroit MI 48227

HACKER, HILARY BAUMANN, bishop; b. New Ulm, Minn., Jan. 10, 1913; s. Emil and Sophia (Baumann) H.; student Nazareth Hall, St. Paul, Minn., 1928-32, St. Paul Sem., 1932-38, J.C.B., Gregorian Univ., Rome, Italy, 1939. Ordained priest Roman Cath. Ch., 1938; asst. pastor Ch. of Nativity, St. Paul, June-Oct. 1938; asst. pastor Ch. of Most Holy Trinity, Winsted, Minn., 1939-41; vice chancellor Archdiocese of St. Paul, June-Sept. 1941, chancellor 1941-45, vicar gen., 1945-56; bishop of Bismarck, N.D., 1956—. Home: 420 Raymond St Bismarck ND 58501 Office: Box 1575 Bismarck ND 58502

HACKER, SISTER ROSE ANN, educator; b. Pratt, Kans., Sept. 18, 1950; d. Emmett Bernard and Elizabeth Catherine (Younger) H.; student Pratt Community Jr. Coll., 1968-70; B.S. in Biology, Ft. Hays State U., 1972; M.S. in Biology, Wichita State U., 1980. Sci. tchr. Unified Sch. Dist. 438 Skyline Sch., Pratt, Kans., 1972-74; field advisor, camp dir. Sioux Trails council Girl Scouts U.S.A., Sioux City, Iowa, 1974-75; animal caretaker, dept. biol. scis. Wichita (Kans.) State U., 1976-80; biology tchr. Archbishop Ryan High Sch., Omaha, 1980—; nature cons.; research asst. Active Wheatbelt Area, Sioux Trails and Wichita Area councils Girl Scouts U.S.A., 1957—. Mem. Kans. Acad. Sci., Am. Malacological Union, Sigma Xi. Condr. research, contbr. writings in field. Office: 5616 L St Omaha NE 68117

HACKMAN, DONALD JON, mech. engr.; b. Youngsville, Pa., July 24, 1936; s. William and Catherine (Morgach) H.; B.S., Cleve. State Coll., 1962; M.S., Ohio State U., 1969; m. Christine Joan Barclay, Oct. 6, 1962. Engr. asst. Sylvania Elec. Co., Warren, Pa., 1957-62, design engr., 1962-64; research engr. Battelle Inst., Columbus, Ohio, 1964-74, sr. engr., 1974—; cons. on ocean engring. to USN, Recipient award for Excellence in Machine Design, Machinery Mag., 1962. Mem. ASME, Sigma Xi. Patents, publs. on underwater tools. Home: 3499 Kirkham Rd Columbus OH 43221 Office: 505 King Ave Columbus OH 43201

HACKNEY, GARY ROSS, clin. psychologist; b. Fargo, N.D., Mar. 27, 1948; s. Roy Gerald and Lillian Maragret (Syverson) H.; B.A. magna cum laude, Concordia Coll., 1970; M.A., U. N.D., 1972, Ph.D., 1975; m. Marie Elaine Smith, Sept. 8, 1973; 1 dau., Terrin Renee. Clin. dir. Juvenile Court Clinic, Sedgwick County Dept. Mental Health, Wichita, Kans., 1975-78; psychologist, pres. Family Psychol. Center, Wichita, 1978—. Mem. Am. Psychol. Assn., Am. Assn. Sex Educators, Counselors and Therapists, Kans. Psychol. Assn., Wichita Psychol. Assn., Kans. Assn. Profl. Psychologists. Lutheran. Office: Family Psychological Center 3212 E Harry St Wichita KS 67218

HACKNEY, HOWARD SMITH, county ofcl.; b. Clinton County, Ohio, May 20, 1910; s. Volcah Mann and Gusta Anna (Smith) H.; B.S. cum laude, Wilmington Coll., 1932; m. Lucille Morrow, June 28, 1933; children—Albert Morrow, Roderick Allen, Katherine Ann Becker. Farmer, Wilmington, Ohio; farm reporter Agrl. Adjustment Adminstrn., Wilmington, 1934-40, committeeman, 1940-52, office mgr., 1952-61, county exec. dir. Agrl. Stblzn. and Conservation Service, 1961—. Treas., dir. Clinton County Community Action Council; treas. Clinton County Council Chs.; mem. agrl. adv. com. Wilmington Coll.; trustee Washington Coll., Clinton County Hist. Soc. Mem. Nat. Assn. Stblzn. and Conservation Service Office Employees (awards 1970, state, regional legis. cons.), AAAS, Soil Conservation Soc. Am., Farmers Union, Ohio Duroc Breeders Assn. (pres., dir.), Ohio Acad. Sci., Ohio Acad. History, Ohio Hist. Soc., Grange, Ohio Southdown Breeders Assn., Clinton County Farm Bur. (sec., dir.), Clinton County Agrl. Soc. (treas., dir., award 1975), Clinton County Lamb and Fleece Improvement Assn. (dir.), Clinton County Hist. Soc. Republican. Quaker. Club: Masons. Home: 2003 Inwood Rd Wilmington OH 45177 Office: PO Box 509 24 Randolph St Wilmington OH 45177

HADDAD, GEORGE RICHARD, musician, educator; b. East End, Sask., Can., May 11, 1918; s. Richard and Labeeby (Salloum) H.; asso. Toronto Conservatory Music, 1931, licentiate, 1941; Mus.B., U. Toronto, 1940; M.A., Ohio State U., 1954; student Royal Conservatory Music Toronto, 1936-40, Juilliard Grad. Sch., N.Y.C., 1940-43, Paris (France) Conservatoire, 1950-52; m. Lilyan Aboud, May 20, 1949; children—Constance Haddad Frecker, Diane, Carolyn. Appeared in various recitals, guest appearances throughout U.S., Can., Europe, 1944—; tchr. piano Bay View Summer Coll. Music, summers, 1948-51; prof. Sch. Music, Ohio State U., Columbus, 1952—; guest artist leading symphony orchs. in U.S., Can. and Europe including Detroit Symphony, Toronto Symphony, Luxembourg Symphony. , Mem. Music Tchrs. Nat. Assn., Nat. Music Guild Piano Tchrs., Ohio Music Tchrs. Assn., Musicians Union, Pi Kappa Lambda. Clubs: Faculty; Kinsmen of Can.; Torch. Home: 2689 River Park Dr Columbus OH 43220

HADDEN, H. ROSS, podiatrist; b. Bloomington, Ill., June 13, 1939; s. Harold E. and Louise R. (Ross) H.; student U. Ariz., 1957-59; D.P.M., Ill. Coll. Podiatric Medicine, 1963; m. Marilyn Deanna Golden, Oct. 30, 1975; children—Michael, Jacque, Kirk. Pvt. practice podiatry, Midstate Podiatry Assos., Ltd., Bloomington, 1963—; sr. surg. staff Hopedale (Ill.) Hosp., 1966—; courtesy surg. staff Hoopeston (Ill.) Community Hosp., 1974—; mem. surg. staff Dr. John Warner Hosp., Clinton, Ill., 1977—; teaching faculty, continuing edn. in podiatry Hopedale Med. Complex, 1970—. Mem. United Fund com., McLean County, Ill., 1965. Mem. Am. Podiatry Assn., Ill. Podiatry Soc., Ill. Public Health Assn., Am. Public Health Assn. Republican. Unitarian. Contbr. articles to profl. jours. Home: Route 4 Bloomington IL 61701 Office: 2708 McGraw Dr Bloomington IL 61701

HADFIELD, JAMES PETER, mktg. exec.; b. Milw., Oct. 16, 1945; s. James John and Jeannette (Pierson) H.; B.S., U. Wis., Milw., 1972; M.B.A., U. Chgo., 1979; m. Mary Ellen Goelz, Sept. 16, 1972; 1 son, James Arnold. Asso. engr. Westinghouse Electric Corp., Lester, Pa., 1972-74; customer service rep Gen. Cable Corp., Des Plaines, Ill., 1974-76, account mgr., 1976-79, mktg. mgr., OEM sales, St. Louis, 1979—. Served with USAF, 1965-69. Mem. Tau Beta Pi, Beta Gamma Sigma. Republican. Roman Catholic. Home: 1 Marche Dr Lake Saint Louis MO 63367 Office: 502 Earth City Plaza Suite 311 Earth City MO 63045

HADLEY, LEONARD ANSON, mfg. co. exec.; b. Earlham, Iowa, July 4, 1934; s. Willard J. and Berneice (Cook) H.; B.S.C. in Acctg., U. Iowa, 1958; m. Corine Ashland, Sept. 5, 1959; children—Philip, Christine. With Maytag Co., Newton, Iowa, 1959—, asst. controller, 1975-79, v.p. corp. planning, 1979—; dir. Hardwick Stove Co. Active local Boy Scouts Am., United Fund. Served with AUS, 1954-56. Mem. Newton C. of C. (dir.). Republican. Methodist. Clubs: Rotary, Newton Country. Office: 403 W 4th St N Newton IA 50208

HAENICKE, DIETHER HANS, coll. adminstr.; b. Hagen, Germany, May 19, 1935; s. Erwin Otto and Helene (Wildfang) H.; came to U.S., 1963, naturalized, 1971; student U. Göttingen (Germany), 1955-56, U. Marburg (Germany), 1957-59; Ph.D., U. Munich (Germany), 1962; m. Carol Ann Colditz, Sept. 30, 1962; children—Jennifer Ruth, Kurt Robert. Faculty, Wayne State U., Detroit, 1963-78, prof. German, 1972-78, chmn. Romance and Germanic lang., lit., 1971-72, asso. dean Coll. Liberal Arts, 1972-75, univ. provost, 1975-78, v.p., 1977-78; prof. German, Ohio State U., Columbus, 1978—, dean Coll. Humanities, 1978—. Fulbright scholar, 1963-65. Mem. MLA, Am. Assn. Tchrs. German, Hoelderlin Gesellschaft, Phi Beta Kappa (hon.). Author: The Challenge of German Literature, 1970; Ludwig Tieck's Works, 3 vols., 1968-71; Versepos d. 20. Jahrhunderts, 1962. Contbr. articles, revs. to U.S., Canadian, German profl. jours. Home: 2827 Pickwick Dr Columbus OH 43221 Office: Coll Humanities Ohio State U 230 N Oval Mall Columbus OH 43210

HAERER, DEANE NORMAN, pub. relations exec.; b. N.Y.C., Feb. 14, 1935; s. Frederick Sidney and Florence Agnes (Jackson) H.; A.A., Boston U., 1955, B.S., 1957; postgrad. N.Y. U. Grad. Sch. Bus. and Finance, 1958-60, Drake U. Grad Sch., 1965-67; m. Polly Ann Dunn, Feb. 24, 1961; children—Jennifer A., Heather J. Account exec. pub. relations and advt. Charles Abbott Assos., Inc., N.Y.C., 1957-60; dir. alumni, community and ch. relations Iowa Wesleyan Coll., 1960-61; tech. writer J.I. Case Co., Burlington, Iowa, 1961-64; dir. publs., asst. dir. pub. relations Drake U., 1964-68; pub. relations account supr. Thomas Wolff Assos., Des Moines, 1968; dir. sch.-community relations Des Moines Pub. Sch. System, 1968-74; mktg. communications and corp. pub. relations coordinator Stanley Consultants, Inc., Muscatine, Iowa, 1974-78, dir. public relations, 1978—; guest lectr. Sch. Journalism, Drake U., 1970-74, U. Iowa, 1974-78. Bd. dirs. Heart of the Hawkeye council Camp Fire Girls, Des Moines, 1969-72. Recipient 1st place publ. award Univ. div. Mid-Am. Conf., Am. Coll. Public Relations Assn., 1965, 66; nat. awards outstanding ednl. publs. Nations Schs. and Sch. Mgmt. mags., 1972, 73. Mem. Pub. Relations Soc. Am. (accredited, charter mem., pres. 1976, bd. dirs. Iowa chpt., charter mem. del. assembly, dir. chpt. 1977—), Nat. Sch. Pub. Relations Assn., Acad. Am. Educators. Contbr. articles profl. publs. Home: Rural Route 6 PO Box 70D-3 Muscatine IA 52761 Office: Stanley Consultants Inc Stanley Bldg Muscatine IA 52761

HAFLING, ELMER ROLAND, mech. engr.; b. Greeley, Colo., Nov. 2, 1921; s. Ernst Lawrence and Mable Marie (Roach) H.; B.S. in Mech. Engring., U. Colo., 1949; m. Lona May Erich, Mar. 18, 1947; children—Larry, Michael. With A.T. & S.F. Ry. Co., Topeka, 1949—, asst. shop extension engr., 1968-69, asst. mech. engr., 1969-80, engring. asst., 1980—. Served with USNR, 1942-51; PTO. Mem. ASME, Kans. Engring. Soc., Local Home Assn. (pres. 1974), Locomotive Maintenance Officers Assn. (chmn. com. shop 1975-77). Presbyterian (deacon, pres. ch. 1974—, chmn. 1977). Mason. Home: 2711 James St Topeka KS 66616 Office: 1001 NE Atchison St Topeka KS 66616

HAGAN, PAUL WANDEL, educator, organist; b. Spencer County, Ind., Nov. 18, 1930; s. George Wandel and Cassie Alice (Byrne) H.; B. Music Edn. magna cum laude, U. Evansville, 1954; M.S., Ind. State U., 1955. Tchr., Ft. Wayne (Ind.) Community Schs., 1963-76; organist St. Joseph Ch., 1968-76; prof. St. Francis Coll., Ind. U. Extension, Ft. Wayne. Recipient govt. grants to study music with M. Dupre, J. Langlais, A. Marchal, R. Falcinelli, F. Peeters, A. Heiller, M.C. Alain. Mason. Composer: Psalm Chorale Preludes, 1970; Swedish Suite, 1975; Scottish Suite, 1975; Trois Petite Elegies, 1973; Sketches of Paris Churches, 1974; Apostolic Suite, 1976. Home: St Paul's Parish 1031 Kem Rd Marion IN 46952

HAGAN, RONALD JAMES, accountant; b. New Castle, Pa., May 21, 1948; s. James B. and Elsie I.H.; B.B.A., Ohio U., 1974; m. Barbara E. Muempfer, Apr. 25, 1970; children—Colleen A., Kelly J. Staff accountant Groner, Boyle & Quillin, Columbus, Ohio, 1974-77; asst. controller Don M. Casto Orgn., Columbus, 1977—. C.P.A., Ohio. Mem. Am. Inst. C.P.A.'s, Ohio Soc. C.P.A.'s, Nat. Assn. Accountants. Democrat. Roman Catholic. Office: Don M Casto Orgn 209 E State St Columbus OH 43215

HAGAN, WILLIAM JOHN, pub. co. exec.; b. St. Louis, Mar. 9, 1924; s. James Edward and Mary Elizabeth (Hencke) H.; B.S. in Bus. Adminstrn., Northwestern U., 1958; m. Norma McClelland, June 11, 1949; children—Kevin, Janet, Kathy, Jeanne, Patty Jo, Bill Jr. Acct., Edward Gore & Co., Chgo., 1941-47; with F. E. Compton & Co., Pubs., Chgo., 1947-66, sec., controller, 1961-64, treas., 1964-66; adminstrv. v.p. Ency. Britannica Edn. Corp., Chgo., 1966-67, v.p. ops., 1967—. Served with USAF, 1943-45. Decorated Air Medal, French Croix De Guerre with Bronze Star. Clubs: Execs., Whitehall (Chgo.); International. Home: 680 Indian Hill Rd Deerfield IL 60015 Office: 425 N Michigan Ave Chicago IL 60611

HAGEDORN, THOMAS M., congressman; b. Blue Earth, Minn., Nov. 27, 1943; grad. high sch.; div.; children—James, Heidi, Tricia. Owner grain and livestock farm, Watonwan County, Minn.; mem. 94th-97th congresses from 2d Minn. dist., mem. Agr. Com., Public Works Com., Transp. Com. Republican. Lutheran. Office: 2344 Rayburn House Office Bldg Washington DC 20515

HAGEN, ORVILLE WEST, state ofcl.; b. Watford City, N.D., Sept. 26, 1915; s. Oscar Wilhelm and Carrie (Scollard) H.; student Dickinson State Coll., 1937-38; m. Astrid Berg, Nov. 24, 1939; children—Orvis Wayne, Mylo Leroy, Ellyn Marie, Lana Jo. Mem. N.D. Senate, 1953-56; lt. gov. N.D., 1961-62; labor commr. State of N.D., 1967—. Bd. dirs. McKenzie County Meml. Hosp. Mem. Nat. Assn. Govt. Labor Ofcls. (v.p. 1980-81), Assn. Labor Mediation Agys., Sons of Norway. Lutheran. Clubs: Lions, Elks, Eagles, Moose, Odd Fellows. Office: State Capitol Bismarck ND 58501*

HAGEN, ROBERT EDWARD, safety engr.; b. Chgo., Jan. 17, 1930; s. Martin Albert and Amelia (Kitscher) H.; student civil engring. Chgo. City Coll. and Ill. Inst. Tech., 1955-62; m. Aileen Skora, Feb. 14, 1956; children—Alison Ann, Robert Edward. Jr. civil engr. City of Chgo., 1955-59; safety engr. Royal Globe Ins. Group, 1959-66, Zurich Ins. Co., 1966-67; safety engr., supr. Transam. Ins. Group, 1967-79, loss control mgr. Chgo. br., 1979—; cons., public speaker. Served with USMC, 1952-54; Korea. Registered profl. engr., Calif.; cert. safety profl. Mem. Am. Soc. Safety Engrs. Office: 585 N 1st Bank Dr Palatine IL 60067

HAGENAH, WILLIAM JOHN, JR., chewing gum mfg. co. exec.; b. Chgo., Aug. 3, 1920; s. William John and Florence (Doyon) H.; B.A., Princeton, 1942; children—William, Philip, Blanny, John; m. 2d, Marjorie Clark. With Wm. Wrigley Jr. Co., Chgo., 1945—, asst. to treas., 1953-59, v.p., asst. treas., 1959-71, v.p., treas., 1971-78, sr. v.p., 1978—, also dir.; v.p., treas. Chgo. Cubs Nat. League Ball Club, Inc., 1977; pres., chief exec. officer & treas., 1977—; dir. Wallace Bus. Forms, Wrigley Import Co., Four-Ten Corp., Chgo. Nat. League Ball Club, Inc. Served to lt. USNR, 1942-45. Office: 410 N Michigan Ave Chicago IL 60611

HAGER, CHAUNCEY WILLIAM, real estate exec.; b. St. John, Kans., 1929; student U. Kans., Lawrence, 1947-49, Wayne State U., 1954-55; B.A. in Bus. Adminstrn., Mich. State U., 1956, M.A., 1958; m. Ruth; children—Mary, Michele, Grant, Bradley. Mem. investigation staff Ford Motor Co., 1953-56; mgmt. trainee Sears, Roebuck and Co., Dayton, Ohio, 1958-59; market research analyst Chrysler Corp., Dayton, 1959-61; mgr. Ohio Bur. Employment Services, Dayton, 1961-73; pres., owner Classics Realty, Inc., Dayton, 1973—; bus. instr. Patterson Coop. Adult Night Sch., Dayton, 1965-66; bd. dirs. Mi-Val BUC Credit Union, Dayton, 1965-72, pres., 1967-68. Pres. Clayton Area Citizens Assn., 1965-68; active Nat. Trust. Served with U.S. Army, 1951-53. Mem. Ohio Hist. Soc., Montgomery County Hist. Soc., Oakwood Hist. Soc. (pres. Dayton, 1978-79), Mich. State U. Alumni Assn. (pres. Dayton chpt. 1965-66). Methodist. Club: Oakwood Optimist. Pianist, church and pvt. accompanist, recitalist.

HAGESTAD, DOUGLAS DEAN, r.r. exec.; b. Chgo., Sept. 13, 1943; s. Walther Ferdinand and Marian May (Willing) H.; B.S., Washington and Lee U., 1965; M.B.A., Northwestern U., 1966; m. Dorothy Ann Pechtel, Feb. 20, 1971; children—James Douglas, Timothy Allen, William Michael. Asst. indsl. engr. Chessie System, Balt., 1966-67; service planning analyst Ill. Central R.R., Chgo., 1969-70, systems mgr., intermodal terminal, 1970-71, asst. to pres., 1971-72; dir. mktg. Ill. Central Gulf R.R., Chgo., 1972-75, asst. v.p. market devel., 1975-79, v.p. market devel., 1979—. Served with U.S. Army, 1967-69. Mem. Am. Ry. Devel. Assn., Nat. Council on Phys. Distbn. Mgmt., Nat. Def. Transp. Assn., Transp. Research Forum, Beta Gamma Sigma. Republican. Lutheran. Clubs: Calumet Country; Traffic (Chgo.). Office: Ill Central Gulf RR 233 N Michigan Ave Chicago IL 60601

HAGGERTY, BRIDGET NANCY, freelance writer; b. Surrey, Eng., June 14, 1946; d. Edward and Helena Bridget (Kenny) O'Flaherty; came to U.S., 1963, naturalized, 1976; ed. Ursuline Convent, 1957-62; m. Russell Owen Haggerty, Oct. 5, 1963; children—Catherine, Scott, Benjamin. Typesetter, Shillito's Budget Store, Cin., 1973-74, coordinator mdse., 1974, copywriter, 1974-76, asst. mgr. advt., 1976-78, copy dir. Fin. Advt. Agy., 1978-79; copy group dir. Stockton, West, Burkhart, Inc., 1980-81; freelance writer, 1979—; mgr. comml. services Sta. WCPO-TV, 1981—. Mem. Cin. Assn. Media Profls. Home: 5670 Meryton Pl Cincinnati OH 45224

HAGGERTY, DENNIS M., podiatrist; b. Aurora, Ill., Jan. 17, 1944; R.T., Rockford Meml. Hosp. Sch. Radiologic Tech., 1964; A.S., Joliet (Ill.) Community Coll., 1966; student Aurora Coll., 1966-67; D.P.M., Ill. Coll. Podiatric Medicine, 1971; m. Rose A. Haggerty; children—Brent Michael, Ann Elizabeth. Preceptor office of Dr. John D. Shanley, Aurora, Ill., 1971-72; practice podiatric medicine and surgery, Elgin, Ill., 1972—; med. staff Northlake (Ill.) Community Hosp., 1972— N.W. Surgicare, Arlington Heights, Ill., 1976—, Hugar Foot Clinic and Surg. Center, Elmwood Park, Ill., 1976—, Harvard (Ill.) Community Meml. Hosp., 1981—, Hawthorne Pl. Surg. Center, Libertyville, Ill., 1981—. Mem. Am. Podiatry Assn., Ill. Podiatry Soc. Republican. Roman Catholic. Office: Summit Green Podiatry Center 431 Summit St Elgin IL 60120

HAGGLUND, CLARANCE EDWARD, lawyer; b. Omaha, Feb. 17, 1927; s. Clarence Andrew and Esther (Kelle) H.; student Augustana Coll., 1946-47; B.A., U. S.D., 1949; LL.B., St. Paul Coll. Law, 1953; m. Dorothy Souser, Mar. 27, 1953; children—Laura, Bret; m. 2d, Merle Peterson, Oct. 28, 1972; 1 dau., Katherine. Admitted to Minn. bar, 1955, since practiced in Mpls.; partner firm Mordaunt, Walstad, Cousineau & Hagglund, 1960-63, Wiese, Cox & Hagglund, 1964-66, Hagglund & Johnson (all Mpls.), 1966-73, Clarance E. Hagglund P.A. and predecessor firm, 1973—. Sec., Southwest, Inc., 1961-68. Served with USNR, 1945-46. Cert. civil trial specialist. Fellow Internat. Soc. Barristers; mem. Am., Minn. bar assns., Fedn. Ins. Counsel, Am. Judicature Soc., Res. Officers Assn., Toastmaster's Internat. (past chpt. pres.), Lawyer Pilots Bar Assn., U.S. Maritime Law Assn., Trial Attys. Am., Delta Theta Phi, Beta Theta Pi, Pi Kappa Delta. Club: Ill. Athletic. Contbr. articles to profl. jours. Home: 3719 Xerxes Ave S Minneapolis MN 55410 Office: Lakeview Office Park 2622 W Lake St Minneapolis MN 55416

HAGNER, GEORGE FREDERICK, physicist; b. Riverside, Calif., June 6, 1949; s. Fred Genard and Jane (Anderson) H.; B.S., Washington U., St. Louis, 1971; masters degree U. Mo., Rolla, 1973, Ph.D., 1979; m. Carolyn Sue Farris, Sept. 15, 1974; children—Christopher Michael, Kendra Michelle. Teaching asst. U. Mo., Rolla, 1971-78; instr. Kaskaskia Coll., Centralia, Ill., 1978-79; engr. Delco Electronics Co., Kokomo, Ind., 1979—. Mem. Sigma Xi. Office: Delco Electronics Co 700 E Firman St Kokomo IN 46902

HAHN, CHARLESS, publishing co. exec., philatelic specialist; b. San Antonio, Feb. 13, 1919; s. Mannel and Nancy (Coonsman) H.; student U. Wis., 1936-38; B.A., U. Chgo., 1940; m. Harriet Paine, Dec. 27, 1940; 1 dau., Padraig de Normandie Hahn Brennen. Owner, operator C. Hahn for Stamps, St. Louis, Winnetka, Ill., 1931-44; editor Weekly Philatelic Gossip, Winnetka, 1942-44; editor pub. Canterbury Press, Chgo., 1944-57; pub., pres. All Ams. Pubs. Services, Inc., Chgo., 1957—; stamp writer Chgo. Sun, Chgo. Sun-Times, 1944—. Mem. Soc. Philatelic Historians, Philatelic History Soc., Chgo. Philatelic Soc., Gt. Brit. Philatelic Soc., London Postal History Group, Travelling Post Office Soc., Disinfected Mail Soc., Am. Philatelic Soc., Soc. Philatelic Ams. (life). Clubs: Collectors Chgo. (pres.), Internat. Philatelic Press (pres.). Editor: Postal Markings, 1940-44; World Stamp Market, 1942-44; Am. Philatelist, 1956-57. Office: 222 W Adams St Chicago IL 60606

HAHN, DONNA NICHOLAS, editor; b. Marion, Iowa, Sept. 22; d. Arthur Burns and Ava Louise (Corell) Nicholas; student Coe Coll., 1933-34, Washington U., St. Louis, 1936; grad. Am. Acad., 1937; m. Norbert B. Hahn, Sept. 5, 1953. Dress designer Stix Baer Fuller Co., St. Louis, 1936; advt. mgr. Lauermans Dept. Store, Waterloo, Iowa, 1937-39; art dir. Stamats Pub. Co., Cedar Rapids, Iowa, 1940-49, editor Perfect Home Mag., 1940-82. Chmn. adv. bd. Salvation Army Cedar Rapids, 1978. Recipient Dorothy Daw award for editorial excellence, 1952, 64; Johnson award for editorial excellence, 1956. Mem. Quota Internat., Kappa Delta. Unitarian. Home: 1929 20th St NW Cedar Rapids IA 52405 Office: 427 6th Ave SE Cedar Rapids IA 52406

HAHN, GEORGE LOUIS, univ. ofcl.; b. London, Tex., Feb. 21, 1921; s. Max Edmund and Emma Zadie Pearl H.; student Draughtons Bus. Coll., 1938-39; student George Washington U., 1957; m. Mary E. Johnson, Nov. 18, 1967; children—George Louis, Kenneth, Ronald. Joined USAAF as pvt., 1940, advanced through grades to col., 1966, ret., 1969; asst. to dean Coll. Medicine, Ohio State U., Columbus, 1969-71, dir. planning and devel., 1971-81, asst. v.p. for health scis., 1981—. Decorated Legion of Merit with oak leaf cluster, Meritorious Service medal, Commendation medal. Mem. Air Force Assn. Methodist. Club: Mason. Office: Ohio State University 370 W 9th Ave Columbus OH 43210

HAHN, WILLIAM JOSEPH, chem. co. exec.; b. Manasquan, N.J., July 18, 1924; s. Walter Charles and Mary (Laffey) H.; B.S. in Chemistry, Ohio U., 1949; m. Jean Carol Hyers, July 28, 1947; children—Deborah Hahn Nordstrom, William Joseph, Jack M., Timothy. Sales, mktg. regional mgr. Johnson & Johnson Co., New Brunswick, N.J., 1953-60; v.p. Harrison & Crosfield, N.Y.C., 1960-65; pres. Bofors Steels Inc., West Caldwell, N.J., 1972-74, also dir.; pres.

Bofors Industries Inc., Linden, N.J., 1974—, also dir.; dir. Bofors Lakeway Chems. Inc. Muskegon, Mich., mem. exec. com. and dir. Bofors Lakeway Inc., Muskegon. Served with USN, 1942-45; PTO. Decorated Purple Heart. Fellow Am. Inst. Chemists; mem. Chemists Club N.Y., Sociéte de Chimíe Industrielle Inc., Chgo. Drug, Chem. Assn., Salesman Assn. Am. Chem. Industry (dir.), Ohio U. Alumni (pres. N.Y. chpt.). Home: 18796 Fruitport Rd Spring Lake MI 49456 Office: 5025 Evanston Ave Muskegon MI 49443

HAIFLICH, STEVAN RICHARD, clergyman; b. Bluffton, Ind., July 13, 1948; s. Richard Edward and Dorma Mae (Hoopingarner) H.; B.A., Taylor U., 1970; M.Div., Asbury Theol. Sem., 1974; m. Ruby May Wilcott, Dec. 18, 1977; children—Ramona, David, Philip, Andrew. Ordained to ministry United Meth. Ch., 1974; exec. dir. Calaski Parish Ch., Science Hill, Ky., 1974-77; asst. supt. Meth. Mountain Missions in Ky., Jackson, 1977-81; mem. dist. council on ministries Conf. Bd. of Ch. and Soc., 1974-81; bd. dirs. Hazard Community Ministries, 1977-79; contbr. news articles Ky. United Meth. Reporter, 1979. Bd. dirs. Pulaski County Home Health, 1976-77; first lt. Breathitt County Rescue Squad, 1979. Mem. Pulaski County Ministerial Assn. (pres. 1977), Wilmore (Ky.) Jaycees (charter; treas. 1973). Home: PO Box 14 122 W Main St Redkey IN 47373

HAIGHT, GILBERT PIERCE, JR., chemist, educator; b. Seattle, June 8, 1922; s. Gilbert Pierce and Ruth (Gazzam) H.; A.B., Stanford U., 1943; Ph.D., Princeton U., 1947; postgrad. (Rhodes scholar) Oxford U., 1947-48; m. Shirley Myers Grapek, June 30, 1946; children—Jennifer Lea, Loisanne Fox, Charlene Ellen, Charles Pierce, Stephanie Louise, Christopher Warren. Asst. prof. U. Hawaii, 1948-49, George Washington U., 1949-52, U. Kans., 1952-54; asso. prof. chemistry Swarthmore (Pa.) Coll., 1954-65; prof. Tex. A&M U., 1965-66; prof., dir. gen. chemistry program U. Ill., Urbana, 1966—; prof. inorganic and phys. chemistry Wagner Free Inst. Sci., 1956-60; vis. scientist Tech. U. Denmark, 1960-61; Dodge lectr. Franklin Inst., 1958; Christmas lectr. Philos. Soc. Washington, 1959; Chem. Confedn. lectr., South Africa, 1978; vis. fellow Australian Nat. U., 1981-82. Mem. Rhodes Scholars Selection Com. for Kans., Ill., N.D. Recipient awards in chem. edn. Mem. Am. Chem. Soc. (chmn. div. chem. edn. 1976, edn. commn., sci. commn. 1978-80), Danish Chem. Soc., Chem. Soc. London, AAAS, AAUP, Ill. Assn. Chemistry Tchrs. (pres. 1979-80), Phi Beta Kappa, Sigma Xi, Phi Lambda Upsilon. Author: Introduction to Physical Science, 1964; (with H.B. Gray) Basic Principles of Chemistry, 1967; (with R.E. Dickerson, H.B. Gray) Chemical Principles, 3d edit., 1979; contbr. articles to profl. jours. Office: Chemistry Dept Univ of Ill Urbana IL 61801

HAIGNERE, HELEN P., state ofcl.; b. Union Furnace, Ohio, Aug. 4, 1928; d. Elmer F. and Minnie H. (Tucker) Anthony; B.S., Franklin U., 1977; m. Carroll Haignere, Nov. 30, 1953; children—Linda Barr, Diane Barton, Sandra Wilson, Norma, Gary (dec.). Accounting supr. Nat. Bd. Boiler and Pressure Vessel Insps., 1972-75; gen. accounting Housing Assos., Inc., Columbus, Ohio, 1975-76; office mgr. R.A. Saunders & Co., C.P.A.'s, Columbus, 1976-78; dir. accounts sect. Bur. of Worker's Compensation, State of Ohio, Columbus, 1978—. Lic. Public accountant. Mem. Am. Soc. Women Accountants, Nat. Assn. Accountants, Inst. Mgmt. Acctg., Psi Iota Xi (state chmn. 1974). Home: 42 Orchard Ln Columbus OH 43214 Office: 246 N High St Columbus OH 43215

HAIMAN, JOHN MICHAEL, linguist; b. Timisoara, Roumania, Jan. 31, 1946; s. Leo and Emily (Czitrom) H.; B.A., U. Toronto, 1967; Ph.D., Harvard U., 1971; m. Anna Stokes Meigs, Feb. 27, 1970; children—Claire, Florence. Lectr., Australian Nat. U., 1971-75; asso. prof. dept. anthropology U. Man., Winnipeg, Can., 1975-81, prof., 1981—. Mem. Can. Linguistics Assn., Linguistic Soc. Am. Author: Targets and Syntactic Change, 1974; Hua: A Papuan Language of the Eastern Highlands of New Guinea, 1980. Asso. editor Can. Jour. Linguistics, 1978—, Studies in Typology of Languages, 1981—. Home: 164 Wildwood Park Winnipeg MB Canada Office: Dept Anthropology Univ Manitoba Winnipeg MB R3T 2N2 Canada

HAINES, LULA ALLISON, ins. co. mgr.; b. Birmingham, Ala., June 20, 1926; d. Boatman and Jeffalonie (Armstrong) Allison; B.S. in Music, Ala. State Tchrs. Coll., 1947; postgrad. Adelbert Coll., 1962, Cuyahoga Community Coll., 1977; m. John W. Haines, Nov. 27, 1965; children—Berry Hill, Jefferecia Poindexter, Ronald Hill (by previous marriage). Substitute tchr. Cleve. Bd. Edn., 1949-57; mathematician E.M. Klein & Associates, Cleve., 1957-62, supr. ins. dept., 1963-76, asst. account exec., 1977; sales rep. Met. Ins. Co., Cleve., 1977—. Dir. youth and adult choirs Starlight Baptist Ch., Cleve., 1957-59, Mt. Nebo Bapt. Ch., Cleve., 1960-62, Holy Trinity Bapt. Ch., Cleve., 1962-64. Cert. elem. tchr., Ohio. Mem. Nat. Assn. Life Underwriters, Bus. and Profl. Women of Cleve., NAACP, Forest City Vol. Assn. (pres. 1978—), Ala. State U. Alumni (treas. 1976—), Delta Sigma Theta. Democrat. Clubs: Women's City (Cleve.); Alacrity. Contbr. poetry to lit. publs. Office: 3659 Green Rd Beachwood OH 44122

HAJNEY, ALICE MARIE, community worker; b. St. Paul, Jan. 30, 1925; d. Charles H. and Lavon Gladys (Collett) Allshouse; student U. Minn., 1974-75, Lakewood Community Coll., 1975-77; cert. advanced mgmt. St. Thomas Coll., 1978; m. John Henry Hajney, Nov. 7, 1957; children—Robin James, Kevin John, Kim Marie, Shawn Jerome. Mechanic, Northwest Airlines, Holman Field, Minn., 1943-45; mem. acctg. dept. staff Montgomery Ward & Co., St. Paul, 1949-61; driver aide Ramsey Action Programs, Inc., St. Paul, 1967-70, program asst., 1970-74, center dir., 1974-78, sr. community coordinator, 1978—. Den leader coach Indian Head council Cub Scouts and Boy Scouts Am., 1966-73; 4-H leader, 1973-78; founder, treas. City-Wide Resident Council, St. Paul, 1972-73, pres., 1972; bd. dirs. Youth Service Bur., 1974—; vice chairperson Children's Placement Service, 1976-80; mem. policy adv. com. Wilder Found. Children's Services, 1978—; pres. policy adv. com. Headstart, 1967-69; pres. Roosevelt Booster Club, 1966-77, treas., 1965-66. Served with WAVES, USN, 1945-46. Recipient Outstanding Service award City-Wide Resident Council, 1974, Merit award Shorter Coll., 1978. Mem. Women's Internat. Bowling Congress. Lutheran. Contbr. articles to local newspapers. Home: 5342 Eagle St White Bear Lake MN 55110 Office: 1575 Ames Ave Saint Paul MN 55106

HAKANSON, RICHARD COLLAR, photographer; b. Conneaut, Ohio, May 25; s. Oliver Justus and Maude Myrtle (Collar) H.; student U. Pitts., 1923-24; m. Elarka Marie Towne, Dec. 30, 1933; children—Richard Harwood, Elarka Sarah Hakanson Yuen. Owner, photographer R.C. Hakanson Forensic Photographer, Cleve., 1946—. Chief instr. evidence photography Winona Sch. Profl. Photography, Winona Lake, Ind., 1966; instr. Cleve. Coll., 1945, Ga. Police Acad., Atlanta, 1972; incorporator Evidence Photographers Internat. Council, 1968, sec.-gen., 1968-77. Speaker trainer United Appeal, Cleve., 1965-70. Recipient Service award, Photog. Soc. Am., 1955; Honors award, Profl. Photographers Am., 1966, 1973; Service award Soc. Photog. Scientists and Engrs., 1972. Fellow Evidence Photographers Internat. Council, Nat. Photog. Art Soc. Sri Lanka, Inst. Inc. Photographers (Gt. Britain); mem. Soc. Photog. Scientists and Engrs., Soc. Photo-Optical Scientists and Engrs., Crime Clinic Cleve., Royal Photog. Soc. Gt. Britain (asso.), Western Res. Soc. Sons Am. Revolution (pres. 1971), Cleve. Colony Soc. Mayflower Descs. (lt. gov. 1972), Greater Books Group Bratenahl, Western Res. Hist. Soc. Christian Scientist. Clubs: Rotary, Cheshire Cheese (Cleve.); Hermit Club; Rolls-Royce Owners. Contbr. articles to profl. jours. Editor Photographic Soc. Am. Newsletter, 1952-55; Jour. Evidence Photography, 1969-77. Home: 10322 Lake Shore Blvd Bratenahl Cleveland OH 44108

HAKARINE, DUANE DENNIS, engineer; b. Virginia, Minn., Feb. 11, 1939; s. Wayne and Alice Clara (Bruneau) H.; A.S., Va. (Minn.) Jr. Coll., 1959; B. Chemistry, U. Minn., 1964; m. Connie Hatfield, Aug. 30, 1964; children—Kevin James, Kerrie Lynn. Test tech. Gould, Inc., Mendota Heights, Minn., 1964-65, materials tech., 1965-66, materials engr., 1966-67, sr. materials engr., 1967-70, sr. product design engr., 1970-74, mgr. product engring., 1974-77, original equipment sales mgr., 1977—. Treas. Bklyn. Park Snowmobile Safety Patrol, 1975-76. Mem. Soc. Automotive Engrs., Battery Council Internat. Republican. Methodist. Patentee battery safety vent, side terminal battery, battery handle. Home: 7948 Regent Ave N Brooklyn Park MN 55443 Office: PO Box 43140 Saint Paul MN 55164

HAKEL, EDWIN HENRY, clergyman; b. Silver Lake, Minn., June 2, 1909; s. Stephen and Emily (Zbitovsky) H.; student Macalester Coll., 1929, McPhail Sch. Music, Mpls., 1930-32, Mpls. Sch. Music, 1934-35, U. Minn., 1949, Western Pastor's Sch., 1956; m. Alice Vera Svihel, Aug. 16, 1946; adopted children—Pollyann, Richard. Ordained to ministry Congl. Ch., 1954; minister, St. Paul, 1945-54, Staples, Minn., 1954-60, 1st Congl. Ch., Sherburn, Minn., 1960-73, St. Matthew's United Ch. of Christ, Litchfield, Minn., 1973-81; dir. Oak Haven Retreat, Inc., Fairmont, Minn., 1981—. Tchr. Leadership Tng. Inst., 1961; registrar No. Pacific Assn. Congl. Chs., 1955-60, scribe Minn. Conf., 1961, youth adviser Southwestern Assn., 1962-63, registrar, 1962-63; registrar Southwestern Assn. United Ch. Christ, 1964, 65, 69, 70, 71; condr. Vesper Hour TV program, 1973-74; United Ch. of Christ rep. region Minn. Council Chs., 1976, 77, vice chmn. region 6E, also rep. theology of ecology com. Vice pres. Sherburn-Dunnell PTA, 1970, pres., 1971—; mem. Meeker County Community Adv. Council, 1976—; tenor Litchfield Area Male Chorus, v.p., 1976-77, pres., 1977—, also bd. dirs.; bd. dirs. Sherburn Civic and Commerce Assn., 1972-73; bd. dirs. Meeker County Concert Assn., 1976, 77; v.p. Meeker County unit Am. Cancer Soc., 1977—, pres.-elect 1978, pres., 1978-80; pres.-elect Meeker County Music and Arts Assn., 1978, pres., 1978-79. Served with AUS, 1942-45. Recipient Good Neighbor to NW award Radio Sta. WCCO, 1977; Certificate of Recognition for Bicentennial contbns. from Gov. Minn., 1977, Minn. Gov.'s cert. of commendation, 1980. Mem. Litchfield Area Ministerial Assn. (v.p. 1974-75, pres. 1975—, program com. 1978-79), Am. Legion (life mem. dist. 7; chaplain 4th dist. 1953-54, 71, chaplain 2d dist. 1972-73, chaplain 7th dist. 1976-79, state chaplain 1979—, Meritorious Service citation dist. 7, 1979), North Central Camera Club Council. Kiwanian (life mem., pres. elect Sherburn 1964, lt. gov. div. 2 Minn.-Dakotas dist. 1965, div. 5, 1977-79, v.p. Sherburn 1970, pres. 1971, dir. Litchfield 1974—, pub. relations chmn. 1975—). Clubs: Fairmont Camera (pres. 1966-67, 70-71; Gold Cup Trophy for color slide competition 1964-66, 70); Kiwanis of Fairmont (chmn. com. spiritual aims, spl. adv. to pres.). Address: Oak Haven Retreat Inc Route 3 Box 28K Fairmont MN 56031

HAKIM, AMELIA MAY, computer mfg. co. exec.; b. Detroit, May 2, 1942; d. Shaw D. and Mary (Yelda) H.; B.A., Wayne State U., 1970, M.S., 1973; m. David Bruce Smith, Mar. 3, 1979. Cosmetologist, Mich., San Francisco, 1961-67; personnel intern Burroughs Corp., Detroit, 1973, personnel research analyst, 1973-75, sr. personnel adminstr., 1975-76, regional personnel mgr., 1976-79, Bus. Machines Group mgr. Equal Employment Opportunity, 1979—; dir. Skate World of Troy, Inc. Mem. Am. Psychol. Assn., Am. Soc. Personnel Adminstrn., Am. Mgmt. Assn., Mich. Assessment Center Assn., Mich. Indsl./Organizational Psychologists, Phi Chi. Republican. Roman Catholic. Club: Burroughs Employee Ski, Toastmasters. Home: 1043 Kensington St Grosse Pointe Park MI 48230 Office: 1 Burroughs Pl Rm 2C58 Detroit MI 48232

HAKKILA, LEON FRED, architect; b. Virginia, Minn., Oct. 22, 1945; s. Fred Leonard and Miriam Marie (Saari) H.; B.Arch., U. Minn., 1969, postgrad., 1970; m. Lonnie Kaye Dean, Aug. 10, 1968; 1 son, Bryan Lee. Staff architect, St. Paul Public Schs., 1970-72; supr. planning, 1972-74; chief architect Abe W. Mathews Engring. Co., Hibbing, Minn., 1974—. Counselor design Boy Scouts Am.; mem. Hibbing Planning Commn., 1975—, chmn., 1977-81; chmn. Hibbing Bd. Variances and Appeals, 1977-80. Served with AUS, 1970. Mem. Minn. Soc. AIA (pres. elect N.E. Minn. chpt.), AIA, Constrn. Specification Inst. Lutheran. Home: 2035 E 31st St Hibbing MN 55746 Office: 555 W 27th St Hibbing MN 55746

HAKKINEN, RAIMO JAAKKO, aero. scientist; b. Helsinki, Finland, Feb. 26, 1926; s. Jalmari and Lyyli (Mattila) H.; diploma aero. engring., Helsinki U. Tech., 1948; M.S., Calif. Inst. Tech., 1950, Ph.D. cum laude, 1954; m. Pirkko Loyttyniemi, July 16, 1949; children—Bert, Mark. Came to U.S., 1949, naturalized, 1960. Head tech. office Finnish Aero. Assn., Helsinki, 1948; instr. engring Tampere Tech. Coll., 1949; design engr., aircraft div. Valmet Corp., Tampere, Finland, 1949; research asst. Calif. Inst. Tech., 1950-53; mem. research staff Mass. Inst. Tech., 1953-56; with Western div. McDonnell Douglas Astronautics Co., Santa Monica, Calif., 1956—, chief scientist phys. scis. dept., 1964-70, chief scientist flight scis. McDonnell Douglas Research Labs., St. Louis, 1970—. Lectr. engring. U. Calif. at Los Angeles, 1957-59; vis. asso. prof. aeros and astronautics Mass. Inst. Tech., 1963-64. Served with Finnish Air Force, 1944. Asso. fellow Am. Inst. Aeros. and Astronautics (mem. fluid dynamics com. 1969-71, honors and awards com. 1975—, tech. activities com. 1975-78, dir. at large 1977-79); mem. Am. Phys. Soc., Assn. Finnish Engrs., Caltech Alumni Assn., Sigma Xi. Lutheran. Contbr. articles to profl. jours. Home: 5 Old Colony Ln Saint Louis MO 63131 Office: PO Box 516 Saint Louis MO 63166

HALA, MARILYN LOUISE, mathematician, ednl. adminstr.; b. Toledo, Iowa, Nov. 20, 1937; d. Anton Ludwig and Lilliam Marie (Fetter) H.; B.A., U. No. Iowa., 1959; M.Ed. (NSF grantee), Pa. State U., 1966. Tchr. math. Columbus High Sch., Waterloo, Iowa, 1959-62; computer program librarian Collins Radio Co., Cedar Rapids, Iowa, 1962-63; tchr. math. Davenport (Iowa) Public Schs., 1963-65; asst. prof. math. Pa. State U., Sharon, 1966-72; dir. math. lab. St. Francis (S.D.) Indian Sch., 1972-76; dir. math. State of S.D., Pierre, 1976—; cons. S.D. schs., 1975—; part-time tchr.-lectr. Sinte Gleska Coll., Rosebud, S.D., 1971-76; rep. North Central region to Nat. Regional Services Com. in Math. Council, 1980—. Fund raiser Lung Assn., 1977, 78; sec. Sicangu Oyate Ho, Inc., 1973-74. Mem. Nat. Council Tchrs. Math., Assn. State Suprs. Math., Nat. Council Suprs. Math., Math. Assn. Am., Assn. Suprs. Curriculum Devel., S.D. Council Tchrs. Math. Kappa Mu Epsilon (disting. mem.). Author: A Curriculum Guideline for Mathematics, 1981. Home: 633 N Highland St Pierre SD 57501 Office: Kneip Bldg Church St Pierre SD 57501

HALAS, GEORGE STANLEY, former profl. football coach; b. Chgo., Feb. 2, 1895; s. Frank and Barbara (Poludna) H.; B.S., U. Ill., 1918; LL.D., St. Joseph's Coll., Ind., 1958; m. Minnie S. Bushing, Feb. 18, 1922; children—Virginia Marion Halas McCaskey, George Stanley. Player Gt. Lakes team in Rose Bowl Game, 1919; semi-pro football player, Hammond, 1919; with bridge dept. Burlington R.R., 1919-20; played profl. baseball with N.Y. Yankees and St. Paul Club, 1919, profl. football with Chgo. Bears, 1920-29, coach, 1920-29, 33-42, 46-55, 58-67; pres. Chgo. Bears Football Club, 1920-64, 79—, chmn., chief exec. officer, 1964—; pres. Halas & Keefe, Inc., Chgo., 1941—; dir. Michigan Ave. Nat. Bank. Pres., Nat. Football Conf. of NFL. Bd. dirs. Chgo. Heart Assn., Eye Rehab. and Research, NFL Charities, Rehab. Inst. Chgo., Met. Fair Expn. Authority, Crime Detection Inst.; trustee St. Joseph's Coll.; citizens com. U. Ill.; bd. lay trustees Loyola U.; mem. soc. fellows, bd. assos. De Paul U., Chgo. Served as ensign USN, 1918-19; capt. USNR, 1942-46. Decorated Bronze Star; recipient Navy Disting. Public Service award; named Coach of Year, A. P., U.P., Sporting News, 1963, 65; Outstanding Profl. Coach of Year, Washington Touchdown Club, 1963; Acad. Sports Editors award, 1963; J.F. Kennedy Meml. trophy Chgo. Mayor and City Council, 1963; Chicagoan of Year, Chgo. Press Club, Jr. Assn. Commerce and Industry; Alumni Achievement award U. Ill., 1965; Horatio Alger, Jr. award, 1968; Bert Bell Meml. award, Phila., 1968; Great Humanitarian award Mentally Retarded Olympian Program, 1975; Frank Leahy award U. Notre Dame, 1976; Chicagoan of Year award Chgo. Boys Clubs, 1976; Outstanding Humanitariansim and Service to Youth Through Athletics award Loyola U., Chgo., 1976; Varsity I award of yr., 1977, Outstanding Chicagoan of Today award, 1977, Mother Cabrini award, 1977, Semper Fidelis award, 1978. Mem. Nat. Profl. Football Hall of Fame (charter mem.), Mil. Order World Wars, Hundred Club Cook County, Mawan-da, Sachem, Navy League of U.S. (nat. v.p., dir., adv. council), Tau Kappa Epsilon, Sigma Tau, Theta Nu Epsilon. Roman Catholic. K.C. Clubs: Athletic Assn., Tavern, Skyline, Nine-Hundred, Execs., Mid-Am., Bob O'Link Golf. Contbr. articles to mags. Office: 55 E Jackson Blvd Chicago IL 60602

HALBERT, FREDERIC LESLIE, farmer, agrl. engring. cons.; b. Battle Creek, Mich., Mar. 14, 1945; s. Frederick P. and Esther Evelyn (Page) H.; B.S., Mich. State U., 1967, M.S., 1968; m. Sandra Edith Huhtala, Feb. 24, 1968; children—Stephanie, Kristen, Lisa. Research engr. Eastman Kodak, Rochester, N.Y., 1967-68, Dow Chem. Co., Midland, Mich., 1968-71; propr., mgr. dairy farm, Barry County, Mich., 1971—; cons. in animal nutrition, 1971—; mem. food contaminant assessment panel Office Tech., 1978-79; chmn. Mich. Toxic Substance Control Commn., 1979—. Recipient Roy Manty award for Distinguished Service to Health of People of Mich., 1977; honoree Five Outstanding Young Men program Mich. Jaycees, 1979. Mem. Am. Inst. Chem. Engrs., Am. Radio Relay League. Instrumental in discovery of a massive chem. contamination of food chain, 1974. Address: 12150 Banfield Rd Route 2 Delton MI 49046

HALE, ALLAN MCKEAG, bot. ecologist; b. Chgo., Nov. 20, 1946; s. Harold Walton and Lucille Marie (McKeag) H.; B.A., Monmouth Coll., 1968; M.A., U. Colo., 1970, Ph.D., 1971; m. Jean Marie Didier, Aug. 22, 1970; children—David, Thomas. Greenhouse supr. U. Colo., Boulder, 1969-70, teaching asst. botany, 1969-70, lab. supr. cellular and human physiology, 1970-71; bot. ecologist Dames & Moore Co., Cin., 1972—, project mgr., 1973-76, sr. bot. ecologist, 1976—. Served with Med. Service Corps. U.S. Army, 1971-72. Sigma Xi research grantee, 1969. Mem. Ohio Acad. Sci., Ind. Acad. Sci., Bot. Soc. Am., Soc. Range Mgmt. (past pres. North Central sect., mem. nat. adv. council), Greater Cin. Amateur Radio Assn., Amateur Radio Emergency Corps., Am. Radio Relay League, Amateur Radio Satellite Corp., Nat. Collegiate Players, Pi Kappa Delta, Phi Sigma. Presbyterian. Home: 1337 Leders Ln Cincinnati OH 45238 Office: 100 Technecenter Dr Suite 212 Milford OH 45150

HALE, CHARLES ADAMS, historian; b. Mpls., June 5, 1930; s. Lloyd and Elizabeth (Adams) H.; B.A., Amherst Coll., 1951; M.A., U. Minn., 1952; Diplome Superieur, U. de Strasbourg, 1953; Ph.D., Columbia U., 1957; m. Lenore Briggs Rice, Sept. 6, 1952; children—Elizabeth A., Charles R., Roger R., Caroline R. Instr. social sci. U. N.C., Chapel Hill, 1956-57; asst. prof. history Lehigh U., 1957-62; asst. prof. history Amherst Coll., 1962-66; mem. faculty dept. history U. Iowa, Iowa City, 1966—, prof., 1970—, chmn. dept., 1977-80; vis. asso. prof. Stanford U., summer 1967. Am. Council Learned Socs.-Social Sci. Research Council grantee, 1962-63, 65-66, 76-77; Nat. Endowment Humanities fellow, 1969-70; Guggenheim fellow, 1973-74. Mem. Consortium for Latin Am. Studies Program (chmn. 1975), Conf. Latin Am. History (chmn. 1979), Am. Hist. Assn., Latin Am. Studies Assn. Democrat. Congregationalist. Author: Mexican Liberalism in the Age of Mora, 1821-1853, 1968. Contbr. articles to profl. jours. Home: 250 Black Springs Circle Iowa City IA 52240 Office: Dept History U Iowa Iowa City IA 52242

HALE, CLAYTON GOULD, ret. business exec.; b. Cleve., Mar. 27, 1902; s. Jesse G. and Edith M. (Clayton) H.; A.B., U. Mich., 1924; B.B.A., Fenn Coll. (now Cleve. State U.), 1932, LL.D., 1956; student econs., 1946; LL.D., Baldwin-Wallace Coll., 1975; m. Laura Bartlett, Oct. 8, 1927; children—Sally L. (Mrs. Thales Bowen, Jr.), William C. Property ins. agt. and broker, 1924; licensed in eleven states and Province of Ont.; mng. partner Hale & Hale Co., Cleve., 1939-63, pres., 1962-67, chmn., 1967-76; pres. Basic Investments, Inc., 1961—; prof. ins. Grad. Sch. Bus. Adminstrn., U. Mich., 1949-56, lectr., 1935-49; editorial cons. for interpretation ins. statistics and trends, on staff The Spectator, 1948-52; asst. chief ins. div. Navy Dept., 1942-43; ins. cons. office sec. def., 1950-62; mem. bd. ins. advisers Munitions Bd., 1950-53; ins. cons. to Ohio Turnpike Commn., 1953-58; dir. 2 corps. Invited del. White House Com. Hwy. Safety, 1954-58. Life Trustee Cleve Met. YMCA; chmn. bd. trustees Fenn Ednl. Found., 1967-69; mem. vis. com. U. Mich. Grad. Sch. Bus. Adminstrn.; trustee Western Res. Hist. Soc. Fellow Ins. Inst. Am.; mem. Ins. Soc. N.Y., Am. Risk and Ins. Assn. (com. on gen. ins. terminology), Order Founders and Patriots Am., S.A.R., Chi Phi. Republican. Conglist. Clubs: Clifton (Lakewood, O.); Westwood Country (Rocky River, O.); Union (Cleve.). Author: An Approach to Fire Insurance, 1933. Contbr. tech. articles to various jours. Cons. editor Property and Casualty Ins. Handbook, 1962-70. Home: 1056 Kirtland Ln Lakewood OH 44107 Office: The Arcade Cleveland OH 44114

HALE, JAMES W., brewery ofcl.; b. Moulton, Ala., June 9, 1941; s. Hardie L. and Margarette M. (Hutte) H.; student Ind. Bus. Coll., 1966-67, LaSalle Extension U., 1969-75; married; 1 dau., 1 son. Shipping clk. Dartnell Publs., Chgo., 1960—; mgr. Hale's Automotive Center, Lafayette, Ind., 1961-62; project engr. Sverdrup & Parcel Engring., Lafayette, 1965-67; with Anheuser Busch, Inc., Lafayette, 1967—, mgr. transp., 1969—; instr. Ivy Tech. Inst. Chmn. transp. carriers United Way, Lafayette, 1976. Served with U.S. Army, 1962-65. Cert. supervision and mgmt. Am. Mgmt. Assn. Mem. Am. Soc. Traffic and Transp., Lafayette Transp. Club (past pres.), Indpls. Transp. Club, Am. Legion. Baptist. Club: Moose. Office: Anheuser Busch Inc PO Box 1398 Lafayette IN 47902

HALE, JOSEPH ROBERT, lawyer; b. Ridgway, Ill., June 12, 1927; s. Everett Lee and Grace (Jackson) H.; B.S., U. Ill., 1950, LL.B., 1952; children—Susan, Sally, Joseph Robert. Admitted to Ill. bar, 1952; asso. firm Bartley & Karber, Shawneetown, Ill., 1952-54, Bartley, Karber & Hale, Shawneetown, 1954-59, Bartley & Hale, Shawneetown, 1959-74, Hale & Smith, Shawneetown, 1974-80; pvt.

practice law, Shawneetown, 1980—; exec. asst., chief of staff Ill. Atty. Gen., 1981—; county judge, Gallatin County, Ill., 1954-62, asst. atty. gen., 1966-81; dir. First Nat. Bank, Shawneetown. Mem. Ill. Ho. of Reps., 1962-64; mem. Republican State Central Com., 1966—. Served with U.S. Army, 1945-46. Mem. Am. Bar Assn., Ill. Bar Assn., Am. Judicature Soc. Republican. Presbyterian. Home: 200 W Posey St Shawneetown IL 62984 Office: First Nat Bank Bldg Shawneetown IL 62984

HALEY, JOHNETTA RANDOLPH, musician, educator; b. Alton, Ill., Mar. 19, 1923; d. John A. and Willye E. (Smith) Randolph; Mus.B. in Edn., Lincoln U., 1945; Mus.M., So. Ill. U., 1972; m. David Haley, Apr. 6, 1947; children—Karen, Michael. Vocal and gen. music tchr. Lincoln High Sch., E. St. Louis, Ill., 1945-48; vocal music tchr., choral dir. Turner Sch., Kirkwood, Mo., 1950-55; vocal and gen. music tchr. Nipher Jr. High Sch., Kirkwood, 1955-71; asso. prof. music Sch. Fine Arts, So. Ill. U., Edwardsville, 1972—; adjudicator music festivals; area music cons. Ill. Office Edn., 1977-78; program specialist St. Louis Human Devel. Corp., 1968; interim exec. dir. St. Louis Council Black People, summer 1970. Bd. dirs. YWCA, 1975-80, Artist Presentation Soc., St. Louis, 1975, United Negro Coll. Fund, 1976-78; bd. curators Lincoln U., Jefferson City, Mo., 1974—, pres., 1978—; mem. Nat. Ministry on Urban Edn., Luth. Ch.-Mo. Synod, 1975-80; bd. dirs. Council Luth. Chs., Assn. of Governing Bds. of Univs. and Colls.; mem. adv. council Danforth Found. St. Louis Leadership Program, nat. chmn. Cleve. Job Corps, 1974-78. Recipient Disting. Citizen award St. Louis Argus Newspaper, 1970; Cotillion de Leon award for Outstanding Community Service, 1977; Disting. Alumnae award Lincoln U., 1977; Disting. Service award United Negro Coll. Fund, 1979, SCLC, 1981; Community Service award St. Louis Drifters, 1979; Disting. Service to Arts award Sigma Gamma Rho; named Duchess of Paducah, 1973; received Key to City, Gary, Ind., 1973. Mem. Council Luth. Chs., AAUP, Coll. Music Soc., Music Educators Nat. Conf., Ill. Music Educators Assn., Nat. Choral Dirs. Assn., Assn. Tchr. Educators, Midwest Kodaly Music Educators, Nat. Assn. Negro Musicians, Jack and Jill Inc., Friends of St. Louis Art Mus., Alpha Kappa Alpha, Mu Phi Epsilon, Pi Kappa Lambda. Lutheran. Clubs: Las Amigas Social. Home: 30 Plaza Sq Saint Louis MO 63103 Office: Box 71 So Ill U Edwardsville IL 62026

HALFPOP, ROGER LEWIS, mfg. and distbg. co. exec.; b. Goodell, Iowa, Jan. 20, 1934; s. Edward Lewis and Fanny Christina (Landon) H.; student pub. schs. Kanawha, Iowa; m. Carole Ann Holecek, Apr. 2, 1953; children—Christine, Connie, Cary. Mgr. feed div. Minn. Farm Bur., St. Paul, 1950-65; sales mgr. Mix Mill Inc., Bluffton, Ind., 1966-71; pres. Pro Mark Inc., Alexander, Iowa, 1971—; chmn. bd. Mem. Central Iowa Mktg. Execs. Republican. Methodist. Club: Belmond Country. Home: Route 1 Belmond IA 50421 Office: 200 County Rd Alexander IA 50420

HALIKAS, JAMES ANASTASIO, med. educator, psychiatrist; b. Bklyn., Nov. 26, 1941; s. Peter Simon and Olga Peter (Vavayanni) H.; B.S. (N.Y. State Regents scholar), Bklyn. Coll., 1962; M.D., Duke U., 1966; m. Anna May Van Der Meulen, Aug. 20, 1967; children—Peter Christopher, Anna Catherine. Intern, Barnes Hosp., St. Louis, 1966-67; resident psychiatry Barnes/Renard hosps., Washington U. Sch. Medicine, St. Louis, 1967-70; research fellow alcoholism and drug abuse Sch. Medicine, Washington U., St. Louis, 1969-70, instr. psychiatry, 1970-72, asst. prof., 1972-77, mem. com. on admissions, 1975-77; asso. prof. psychiatry U. Louisville Sch. Medicine, 1978, dir. div. social and community psychiatry, 1978; asso. prof. psychiatry Med. Coll. Wis., Milw., 1978—, dir. div. alcoholism and chem. dependency, 1978—; asst. psychiatrist Barnes, Renard and Affiliated hosps., 1970-77; cons. Malcolm Bliss Mental Health Center, St. Louis, 1970-77; dir. psychiat. div. Webster Coll. Student Health Service, Webster Groves, Mo., 1973-75; dir. Grace Hill Settlement House Psychiatry Clinic, St. Louis, 1973-77; clin. instr. psychiatry dept. psychiatry Mo. Inst. Psychiatry, U. Mo., St. Louis, 1972-74; mem. profl. adv. com. Judevine Center for Autistic Children, St. Louis, 1975-77; psychiat. research cons. Reproductive Biology Research Found., Masters and Johnson Inst., St. Louis, 1975-77. Mem. Mo. Gov.'s Adv. Council on Alcoholism and Drug Abuse, 1974-75; exec. com. Drug and Substance Abuse Council Met. St. Louis, 1973-77, pres., 1971-72; chmn. Children's Mental Health Services Council Met. St. Louis, 1973-74; host KMOX-TV weekly TV series Trips - the Teenage Point of View about Drugs, spring-summer 1971; adviser on drug abuse St. Louis County Juvenile Ct., 1970-72; mem. adv. bd. Drug Crisis Intervention Unit, St. Louis, 1971-77; mem. St. Louis Youth Center profl. adv. com. Mo. Dept. Mental Health, 1977; adv. on drug abuse Drug Info. Center, St. Louis, 1970-74, Human Devel. Corp., St. Louis, 1970-73, Alliance for Regional Community Health, 1972-74; asso. psychiatrist, med. dir. for alcoholism services Jefferson County Alcoholism and Drug Abuse Center for Treatment and Research, Louisville, 1978; exec. and med. dir. River Region Mental Health-Mental Retardation Bd., Ky. Region VI Community Mental Health System, Louisville, 1978; dir. Wis. Alcoholism and Drug Abuse Research Inst., Milw., 1978—; Sr. Scientist U. Wis., Milw., 1978—; attending psychiatrist, dir. med. edn. DePaul Rehab. Hosp., Milw., 1978—; dir. research and edn. in chem. dependency, sr. attending psychiatrist Milwaukee County Mental Health Complex, Milw., 1978—; sci. dir. DePaul Hosp. Found., Milw., 1978—; asso. psychiatrist U. Louisville Affiliated Hosps., 1978; attending psychiatrist Milw. Psychiat. Hosp., 1978—, Columbia Hosp., Milw., 1980—; mem. planning com. Nat. Council on Alcoholism, 1977-78, Nat. Alcoholism Forum, 1978; co-chmn. clin. research task force Nat. Drug Abuse Conf., Seattle, 1978; mem. Mental Health Assn. Louisville, 1978, Louisville Council on Alcoholism, 1978; cons. Midwestern Area Alcohol Edn. and Tng. Program, 1976-77. Bd. dirs. Mental Health Assn. Met. St. Louis, 1973-77, chmn. St. Louis State Hosp. human research com., 1976-77; bd. dirs. Tellurian South Community, Inc., Madison, 1980—; mem. exec. council DePaul Rehab. Hosp., 1979—; mem. med. appeals bd. Div. Motor Vehicles, State of Wis., 1980—; mem. City of Mequon Bd. Appeals, 1980—. Recipient NIMH Psychiatry Career Tchr. award in narcotics, drug abuse and alcoholism, 1972-75; diplomate Am. Bd. Psychiatry and Neurology, Nat. Bd. Med. Examiners. Mem. Am. Psychiat. Assn., Eastern Mo. Psychiat. Soc., Ky. Psychiat. Assn., Wis. Psychiat. Assn., Am. Med. Soc. on Alcoholism (med. edn. com. 1977-78, Wis. chmn. 1979—), Am. Psycho-Pathol. Assn., Assn. for Med. Edn. and Research in Substance Abuse, N.Y. Acad. Scis., AAAS, Ky. Med. Assn., Research Soc. on Alcoholism, Assn. for Acad. Psychiatry, Am. Acad. Clin. Psychiatrists, Kappa Nu. Greek Orthodox. Contbr. numerous articles to profl. jours. Home: 434 Post Ct Mequon WI 53092 Office: Dept Psychiatry Med Coll Wis 9455 Watertown Plank Rd Milwaukee WI 53226

HALL, ALBERT M(ANGOLD), tech. assn. exec.; b. Bklyn., Oct. 8, 1914; s. Edgar A. and Salena A. (Mangold) H.; A.B., Columbia U., 1935, B.S., Engring. Sch., 1936, Metall. Engr., 1937; m. Jean C. Lamb, Dec. 27, 1937 (dec. Oct. 1976); children—Charles H., David A., Peter A.; m. 2d Lydia W. Pollock, Aug. 15, 1978. Research engr. Huntington Alloy Products (W.Va.), 1937-45; with Battelle Meml. Inst., Columbus, Ohio, 1945-79, sr. tech. adv., 1966-69, asst. mgr. dept. metallurgy, 1969-79; exec. dir. Materials Tech. Inst. of Chem. Process Industries, Inc., Columbus, 1979—; pres. Columbus Tech. Council, 1955-56; sec. com. on effect temperature on properties of metals Joint ASTM-ASME-Metal Properties Council, 1967-73. Organizer and chmn. ARC Bloodmobile for Sharon Twp. (Ohio), 1949-50; treas., Columbus Art League, 1972-73, pres., 1969-71, 78; elder Covenant Presbyn. Ch., Columbus. Recipient various awards for craft and sculpture, 1963-70. Mem. AAAS, Am. Soc. Metals (life), AIME, ASTM, Ohio Soc. Profl. Engrs., Sigma Xi, Tau Beta Pi. Republican. Author books, most recent being: (with others) Microstructures of Heat-Resistant Alloys, 1970; contbr. numerous articles to profl. jours.; co-patentee iron-base alloys, chromium-base alloy, process to deposit cadmium on metallic surfaces. Home: 1194 Kenbrook Hills Dr Columbus OH 43220 Office: 1380 Dublin Rd Columbus OH 43215

HALL, ALLEN L., organic chemist; b. Carthage, Mo., June 12, 1942; s. James M. and Beulah A. (Alumbaugh) H.; B.S., U. Mo., Rolla, 1964; M.A., Dartmouth Coll., 1966; Ph.D., Fla. State U., 1973; m. Selina J. Wisthoff, Nov. 16, 1976; 1 dau., S. Hall. Postdoctoral fellow Purdue U., 1973-75, asst. prof., 1976; sr. chemist Emery Industries, Cin., 1977-80, group leader, 1980—. Mem. Am. Chem. Soc., AAAS, Soc. Cosmetic Chemists (sec. 1981). Contbr. articles to profl. jours. Patentee in field. Office: 4900 Este Ave Cincinnati OH 45232

HALL, B. J., hosp. adminstr.; b. Louisville, Oct. 15, 1943; s. Jean C. and Anna Joyce (Jasper) H.; B.S. in Acctg., Western Ky. U., 1966; m. Alon Whitehouse, June 6, 1964; children—Donna Marie, J. Franklin. Supr., Ernst & Whinney, Louisville, 1966-69; dir. fin. St. Anthony Hosp., Louisville, 1969-73; asst. adminstrv. Providence Hosp., Cin., 1973—; adj. prof. Xavier U., Cin., 1979—, U. Cin., 1978—. C.P.A., Ohio, Ky. Fellow Hosp. Fin. Mgmt. Assn.; mem. Am. Inst. C.P.A.'s, Ky. Soc. C.P.A.'s, Am. Coll. Hosp. Adminstrs., Ohio Hosp. Assn. Baptist. Club: Cin. Author: Auditing the Modern Hospital, 1977; Hospital Philosophy and Objectives, 1973. Home: 9282 Sagemeadow St Cincinnati OH 45239 Office: 2446 Kipling Ave Cincinnati OH 45239

HALL, CHARLES RUDOLPH, ins. co. exec.; b. Marysville, Kans., Nov. 7, 1929; s. Percy Allen and Zella (Yaussi) H.; B.S., U. Kans., 1951; postgrad. Northwestern U., 1955-57, U. Wis., 1961; m. Helen Persson, July 19, 1952; children—Charles Rudolph, Timothy P., Jeffrey P. With Continental Ill. Nat. Bank & Trust Co., Chgo., 1955-81, asst. cashier, 1957-61, 2d v.p. nat. div., 1961-64, v.p. nat. div. group G, 1964-68, v.p. personnel div., 1968-70, sr. v.p., 1970-71, exec. v.p., 1971-75, exec. v.p. trust and investment services, 1975-81; chmn. bd., chief exec. officer Rollins Burdick Hunter Co., 1981—. Asso. St. Luke's Presbyn. Hosp., Chgo., 1965-76; bd. dirs. United Way Met. Chgo., 1970—; bd. dirs., chmn. fin. devel. Am. Diabetes Assn. Greater Chgo., 1976-80; mem. adv. bd. Citizenship Council Met. Chgo., 1973—; mem. bus. adv. bd. Nat. Alliance Businessmen, 1973-78; bd. dirs., mem. audit com. Ravinia Festival Assn., 1976—; chief crusader Crusade of Mercy, 1975-76; mem. program task force United Way Met. Chgo., 1976—, mem. exec. com., 1977, chmn. personnel com., 1977; bd. dirs. John Crerar Library, 1977—; chmn. New Trier Twp. High Sch. Bd. Caucus, 1971-72. Served with USNR, 1951-54. Mem. Chgo. Council Fgn. Relations (com. 1974—). Ill. C. of C. and Industry (labor relations com. 1969-71), Phi Delta Theta, Alpha Kappa Psi, Omicron Delta Kappa. Mem. Glencoe Union Ch. (trustee). Clubs: Chicago, Mid Am., Carlton, Economic of Chicago; Skokie (Ill.) Country. Home: 800 Grove St Glencoe IL 60022 Office: 10 S Riverside Plaza Chicago IL 60606

HALL, DAVID MCKENZIE, air force officer; b. Gary, Ind., June 21, 1928; s. Alfred McKenzie and Grace Elizabeth (Crimiel) H.; B.A., Howard U., 1951; M.S., Agrl. and Tech. State U. N.C., 1966; m. Jacqueline Virginia Branch, Apr. 30, 1960; children—Glen David, Gary Duane. Commd. 2d lt. U.S. Air Force, 1953, advanced through grades to brig. gen., 1980; chief computer ops. Air Force Accounting and Fin. Center, Denver, 1967-71, Mil. Airlift Command, Scott Air Force Base, Ill., 1971-72, asst. for social actions, 1972-74, base commdr., 1974-76; asst. comptroller Wright Patterson AFB, Ohio, 1976-77; comptroller, 1977—. Chmn. troup com. Denver Area council Boy Scouts Am., 1969-71, v.p. Tecumseh council, 1980—. Decorated Legion of Merit; recipient Dist. Merit award St. Clair Dist. Okaw Valley Council Boy Scouts Am., Belleville, Ill., 1976; Merit award, Citizens of East St. Louis (Ill.), 1976; Citation of Recognition, Dept. Ill. Am. Legion, 1976; Silver Beaver award Boy Scouts Am., 1980; Key to City of Gary, 1981. Mem. Am. Soc. Mil. Comptrollers, Assn. Systems Mgmt., Data Processing Mgmt. Assn., Assn. for Computing Machinery, Air Force Assn., Kappa Alpha Psi, Alpha Phi Omega. Home: 513 Johnson Dr Wright Patterson AFB OH 45433

HALL, DENNIS C., hydrologist; b. Hurricane, Utah, May 26, 1939; s. Melvin M. and Geneva (Cook) H.; B.S., U. Utah, 1961, M.S., 1964; Ph.D., Washington U., St. Louis, 1967; m. Mary Sue Quermann, June 17, 1966; children—Jenifer Michelle, Rebecca Sue. Microbiologist, water resources div. U.S. Geol. Survey, Lakewood, Colo., 1972—, hydrologist, 1972—, project chief, 1974—. Mem. AAAS, Am. Inst. Biol. Scis., Sigma Xi. Contbr. articles to profl. publs. Home: Lecoma Star Route Lecoma MO 65540 Office: US Gell Survey 1400 Independence Rd Rolla MO 65401

HALL, DONALD H., geophysicist; b. Maple Creek, Sask., Can., Nov. 23, 1925; s. John R. H. and Gertrude A. (Reid) H.; B.Sc. with honors, U. Alta., 1948; M.A., U. Toronto, 1950; Ph.D., U. B.C., 1959; m. Esther B. Crabbe, June 2, 1955; children—Bernard J., Norman G., Judith D. Lectr. geophysics U. B.C., 1957-59; asst. prof. U. Sask., 1959-62; research officer Sask. Research Council, 1959-62; asso. prof. geophysics U. Man., Winnipeg, 1962-69, prof., 1969—, head dept. earth scis., 1978—. Served with Can. Armed Forces, 1944-45. Mem. Am. Geophys. Union, Canadian Geophys. Union, Australian Soc. Exploration Geophysicists, Canadian Soc. Exploration Geophysicists, Geol. Assn. Can. Jewish. Author: History of the Earth Sciences in the Scientific and Industrial Revolutions, 1976; contbr. articles to profl. jours.; regional editor Geoexploration, 1965—. Home: 841 Borebank Winnipeg MB R3N 1G5 Canada Office: Dept Earth Scis U Man Winnipeg R3T 2N2 Canada

HALL, DOROTHY MARIE REYNOLDS, educator; b. Columbus, Ohio, Dec. 22, 1925; d. Thomas Franklin and Nellie May (Nail) R.; student Ohio State U., 1973-79, Sinclair Community Coll., 1976; m. Grant Forest Hall; children—Stacy L., Cynthia Kay Hall Henderson, Mark Kevin. Dental asst. and office mgr., dental offices in Westerville, Ohio, 1954-68, Columbus, Ohio, 1968-70; dental asst., staff supr., clinic instr. Good Samaritan Dental Clinic, Columbus, 1970; instr., staff supr. Ohio State U. Coll. Dentistry, 1970; tchr. adult edn. Eastland Vocat. Center, Groveport, Ohio, 1969, instr. dental assisting, 1971—; examiner Ohio Commn. on Dental Testing, Inc., 1977-78, 81—; examiner Ohio Dental Assts. Commn. on Testing, Inc., 1978-81, trustee-dir. 1978—. Mem. Columbus Dental Assts. Soc. (pres. 1968-69, Dental Asst. of Yr. 1980), Ohio Dental Assts. Assn. (pres. 1978-79, 80-81), Am. Dental Assts. Assn. (cert.), Eastland Edn. Assn., Ohio Edn. Assn., NEA, Eastland Vocat. Assn., Ohio Vocat. Assn., Am. Vocat. Assn., Nat. Ret. Tchrs. Assn. (life mem.). Mem. Reformed Ch. Am. Clubs: Order Eastern Star, Pythian Sisters (Westerville). Author profl. publs.; developer, artist: A Manual of Lesson Plans for the Ohio Adult Dental Assistant Programs, 1981. Home: 4676 Big Walnut Rd Galena OH 43021 Office: 4465 S Hamilton Rd Groveport OH 43125

HALL, EDWARD DALLAS, med. educator, researcher; b. Bedford, Ohio, June 16, 1950; s. Edward Ellis and Martha Elaine (Johnston) H.; B.S., Mt. Union Coll., 1972; Ph.D., Cornell U., 1976; m. Marilynn Frances Gay, Sept. 12, 1970; children—Edward William, Christian David. Grad. fellow in pharmacology Cornell U. Grad. Sch. Med. Scis., N.Y.C., 1972-76, postdoctoral fellow in pharmacology, 1976-77; asst. prof. biol. sci. Kent (Ohio) State U., 1978—; asst. prof. pharmacology Northeastern Ohio U. Coll. Medicine, Rootstown, 1978—. Recipient Phi Sigma award, Mt. Union Coll., 1972; NIH fellow, 1972-76; Amyotrophic Lateral Sclerosis Soc. Am. grantee, 1978-81; NIMH grantee, 1978-79, 80—. Mem. Am. Soc. Pharmacology and Exptl. Therapeutics, Soc. Neursci., N.Y. Acad. Sci., AAAS, Sigma Xi. Christian Ch. Club: Lions (3d v.p. 1980-81, 2d v.p. 1981-82). Contbr. articles to profl. jours.

HALL, FRANK BRADEN, lawyer; b. Chgo., Jan. 24, 1917; s. Thrasher and Amalia (Linda) H.; B.Sc. in E.E., Ill. Inst. Tech., 1947; J.D., DePaul U., 1956; m. Joan Brockhoff, May 11, 1957; children—Braden Brock, Scott Frank. Admitted to Ill. bar, 1956, U.S. Patent Office, 1972; instr. and tech. cons. Indsl. Tng. Inst., 1948-49; engr. Beardsley & Piper Div. Pettibone Corp., 1950-52, chief engr. elec. engring. 1952-59; sr. engr. Three E Co., 1959-60; asso. elec. engr. Argonne Nat. Lab., 1960-64; chief control engr. Beardsley and Piper, 1965-72, patent atty., 1972-79; asst. corp. counsel Pettibone Corp., 1979—. Served with USAAF, 1942-44. Registered profl. engr., Ill. Sr. mem. I.E.E.E.; mem. Am. Foundrymen's Soc. (award for sci. merit 1979), Chgo. Bar Assn., Patent Law Assn. Chgo., Nat. Soc. Profl. Engrs., S.A.R., Soc. Am. Magicians. Author: Dictionary for Dismayed Defendants; contbr. articles to tech. jours. Home: 855 N Northwest Hwy Park Ridge IL 60068

HALL, GARY CHESTER, hotel exec.; b. Owosso, Mich., Sept. 10, 1946; s. Marvin Bertram and Eleanor Louise (Bacon) H.; diploma Holiday Inn U., 1974; m. Elizabeth Ann Kosick, Oct. 5, 1974; 1 son, Michael. Mem. engring. dept. Consumers Power Co., Owosso, 1965, 66; night mgr. Grand Hotel, MacKinac Island, Mich., 1971-72; trainee Hollys Inc., Grand Rapids, 1972, asst. restaurant mgr., 1973-74; innkeeper Holiday Inn, Grand Rapids, 1975-79, dist. mgr., 1979—. Co-founder, dir. Muskegon County (Mich.) Tourist Bur., 1978-79; mem. adv. panel Tourist Bur.; bd. dirs. Muskegon County Commrs. Served with U.S. Navy, 1967-71. Mem. Am. Hotel and Motel Assn., Mich. Lodging Assn., W. Mich. Tourist Assn., Nat. Restaurant Assn., Grand Rapids Lodging Assn., Muskegon County Motel Assn. Clubs: Nat. Exchange, Mason, Shriner. Home: 916 Maryland St NE Grand Rapids MI 49505 Office: 255 Colrain St SW Grand Rapids MI 49509

HALL, GEORGE EMERSON, mgr. properties; b. Sandusky, Mich., Dec. 30, 1910; s. Edwin Albert and Carrie Pearl (Bowlby) H.; student Flint Jr. Coll., 1931-33, Gen. Motors Tech. Inst., 1934; m. Hazel Marie Sampson, Oct. 20, 1942; children—Edwin Edsel, Madeline,Ann, Melva Marie, Beverly Kay, Sherry Lee, Barbara Jean. With Buick Motor div. Gen. Motors Corp., Flint, Mich., 1935-70, tool and fixture engr., 1942-45, with tool and die dept., 1946-70; owner, mgr. Hall Engring. & Mfg. Co., Flint, 1946-79; owner, mgr. indsl. and resdl. properties, Flint, 1956—. Mem. Genesee Twp. Bd. Rev., 1963—; mem. Republican Nat. Com., 1977—; treas. Genesee Twp. Democratic Club, 1972-79. Mem. Am. Soc. Tool and Mfg. Engrs., Am. Security Council (nat. adv. bd. 1978—). Lutheran. Clubs: Shriners, Order Eastern Star. Patentee drill point gage checks. Address: 3039 Alcott Ave Flint MI 48506

HALL, GEORGE SCOTT, thoracic surgeon; b. Batesville, Ark., July 21, 1943; s. Ray H. and Katheen Alice (Scott) H.; B.S., Ark. State U., 1963; M.D., U. Ark., 1967; m. Margaret Rose Smith, June 15, 1968; children—George Scott, Matthew Morris, Justin Talmadge. Intern, U. Cin. Med. Center, 1967-68, resident in surgery, 1968-76, asst. prof. surgery, 1976—; practice medicine specializing in thoracic and cardiovascular surgery, Ft. Thomas, Ky., 1977—; chief surgery St. Luke Hosp., Ft. Thomas, 1980—. Served with M.C., USAF, 1969-71. Diplomate Am. Bd. Surgery, Am. Bd. Thoracic Surgery. Fellow A.C.S.; mem. Ohio Med. Soc., Ky. Med. Soc. Methodist. Contbr. articles to med. jours. Home: 4 Cypress Garden Cincinnati OH 45220 Office: 627 Highland Ave Fort Thomas KY 41075

HALL, HAL DAVID, editor; b. Lebanon, Tenn., Mar. 7, 1943; s. Hal Turner and Mildred Frances (Durham) H.; B.S., U. Tenn., 1965; M.A., 1966; m. Suzanne Lovell, Sept. 5, 1964; children—Carson, Matthew, Amanda. With Chgo. Daily News, 1966-78, asst. fin. editor, 1970-72, Middle East corr., 1972-73, chief editorial writer, 1976-77, asst. mng. editor, 1977-78; asst. mng. editor Chgo. Sun-Times, 1978; mng. editor St. Paul Pioneer Press, 1978—. Served with U.S. Army, 1967-69. Mem. Sigma Delta Chi. Methodist. Clubs: St. Paul Athletic, Mendakota Country. Home: 467 Woodlawn Ave Saint Paul MN 55105 Office: 55 E 4th St Saint Paul MN 55101

HALL, HANSEL CRIMIEL, govt. ofcl.; b. Gary, Ind., Mar. 12, 1929; s. Alfred McKenzie and Grace Elizabeth (Crimiel) H.; B.S., Ind. U., 1953. Officer, IRS, 1959-64; gasoline service sta. operator, then realtor, Chgo., 1964-69; program specialist HUD, Chgo., 1969-73, dir. equal opportunity, St. Paul, 1973-75, dir. fair housing and equal opportunity, Indpls., from 1975; equal opportunity officer U.S. Fish and Wildlife Serivce, Twin Cities, Minn.; cons. in civil rights. Served with USAF, 1951-53, Korea. Mem. NAACP (Golden Heritage life mem.; pres. Minn.-Dakota State Conf.), Res. Officers Assn., Omega Psi Phi; mem. Am. Inst. Parliamentarians, Ind. U. Alumni Assn. Club: Toastmasters (past pres. Minnehaha chpt. 2563). Office: Fed Bldg Ft Snelling Twin Cities MN 55111

HALL, HAROLD CLIFFORD, cons. geotech. engr.; b. Springfield, Mo., Nov. 17, 1927; s. Lawrence Emanuel and Mary Avilla (Abel) H.; B.S. in Civil Engring. with honors, Iowa State U., 1953; M.S. in Civil Engring., Northwestern U., 1970; m. Elaine Audrey Hanson, Nov. 25, 1948; children—Daniel Lee, Susan Elaine, David Eugene, Nancy Corrine, Jennifer Gail, Curtis Edward. Engr., Surveyor Howard Needles Tammen Bergendoff, Kansas City, Mo., 1953-54; draftsman Pfuhl & Shideler, Kansas City, 1954-55; design engr. Black and Veatch, Kansas City, 1955-57; structural engr. Tinsley, Higgins, Lighter & Lyon, Des Moines, Iowa, 1957-58; chief structural engr. Powers & Assos., Iowa City, 1957-59; pres. Hall Engr. Services, Inc., Iowa City, 1959-62; v.p. Shive-Hall-Hattery Engr. Services, Inc., Iowa City, 1962-67; pres. Soil Testing Services of Iowa, Inc., Iowa City, 1965-67; v.p. Soil Testing Services, Inc., Northbrook, Ill., 1967-73; pres. H.C. Hall, Cons. Civil Engr., Inc., Hart, Mich., 1973—. Chmn., Soil Mechanics Lecture Series, Am. Soc. of Civil Engrs., Chgo., 1973. Bd. dirs. Silver Lake Dunes Corp. Served with U.S.N., 1944-48. Registered profl. engr., Iowa, Minn., N.D., Mich.; registered structural engr., Ill. Mem. Am. Cons. Engrs. Council, ASTM, ASCE, Cons. Engrs. Council Mich., Nat. Soc. Profl. Engrs., Tau Beta Pi. Republican. Club: Rotary. Contbr. articles to profl. jours. Home: Route 1 Mears MI 49436 Office: 49 State St Hart MI 49420

HALL, HELENE W., educator; b. Centralia, Ill., Sept. 17, 1926; d. James O. and Gladys (Hosman) Lawrence; B.S., Emporia State U., 1966, M.S., 1969, E.D.S., 1974; m. William E. Hall, June 13, 1948; children—Ronald William, Steven Charles, Jerry Victor. Sec., asst. to physicians Medical Physicians & Dentists, Kansas City, Mo.,

1966-69; tchr. Roosevelt Lab. High Sch., Emporia, Kans.; coordinator secondary sch. tchrs. Emporia State U., 1969-71, team leader Teacher Corps, 1971-73; instr., coordinator secretarial scis. Kansas City Community Coll., 1973—. Mem. Nat. Bus. Edn. Assn., Am. Vocat. Assn., Kans. Vocat. Assn., Classroom Educators Assn., Kans. Bus. Edn. Assn., Nat. Secretaries Assn., Office Edn. Assn., Delta Pi Epsilon. Home: 403 S 6th St Osage City KS 66523 Office: Kansas City Kansas Community College 7250 State Ave Kansas City KS 66112

HALL, JACK MANUEL, architect; b. Chgo., Mar. 1, 1949; s. Jack and Naomi (Nixon) H.; B.Arch., Howard U., 1972. Summer employee Met. San. Dist. Greater Chgo., 1972, asst. architect, 1974—; grad. architect Nelson A. Harris & Assos., Chgo., 1972-74. Served with U.S. Army Res., 1972—. Methodist. Home: 7729 S King Dr Chicago IL 60619 Office: 100 E Erie St Chicago IL 60611

HALL, JOHN, printing co. exec.; b. Walsall, Eng., Oct. 14, 1934; s. David and Annie (Winfield) H.; came to U.S., 1968, naturalized, 1976; m. Carol Jane Richards, May 16, 1973; children—Roberta, Robert, Nancy, Julius. Mgr. advt. and sales promotion Polypad Imports, Cleve., 1970-72; dir. mktg. Bede Aircraft, Inc., Newton, Kans., 1972-76, Branson Aircraft Corp., Denver, 1976-77; v.p. mktg. Bellanca Aircraft Corp., Alexandria, Minn., 1977-80; propr. Quality Printing Co., Alexandria, 1980—. Served with RAF, 1957-62. Mem. Aircraft Owners and Pilots Assn., Exptl. Aircraft Assn. Episcopalian. Author: Build Your Own Airplane, 1976. Home: 1303 Lakeside Dr Alexandria MN 56308 Office: 109 15th Ave E Alexandria MN 56308

HALL, JON RICHARD, color designer; b. Petoskey, Mich., Apr. 2, 1949; s. Robert L. and Helen L. (Matthews) H.; diploma Interlochen Arts Acad., 1967; B.F.A., U. Mich., 1971, M.F.A., 1973; m. Patricia L. Ford, Aug. 17, 1968; children—Matthew Jon, Dennis Ford. Exhibited in several 1-man shows; group shows Images on Paper, Springfield (Ill.) Art Assn. (purchase award), 1972, Graphics by Young Ams., Loyola U., Los Angeles, also tour U.S., Europe; represented in permanent collections; teaching fellow art U. Mich., Ann Arbor, 1972-73; instr. printmaking Haystack Sch. Crafts, Deer Isle, Maine, 1975; design, color engr. Automotive Finishes div. PPG Industries Inc., Southfield, Mich., 1975—. Recipient Nat. Gold Medal sculpture Scholastic Art Awards, 1967. Mem. Color Mktg. Group (dir. 1979-81), Inter-Soc. Color Council, Detroit Color Council (pres. 1979). Home: 422 W Washington St Howell MI 48843 Office: Automotive Finishes div PPG Industries Inc 1 Northland Plaza Southfield MI 48075

HALL, KATIE BEATRICE GREENE, state senator; educator; b. Mound Bayor, Miss., Apr. 3, 1938; d. Jeff L. and Bessie Mae (Hooper) Greene; B.S., Mississippi Valley State U.; M.S., Ind. U., postgrad.; m. John H. Hall, Aug. 15, 1958; children—Jacqueline, Junifer. Tchr., Gary (Ind.) Public Schs.; mem. Ind. Ho. of Reps.; now mem. Ind. Senate; mem. Gary Housing Authority Bd. Commrs. Sec., Ind. Democratic Central Com.; vice chairwoman Lake County (Ind.) Dem. Central Com. Recipient Numerous awards for edn., politics, religion and civic work. Mem. AAUW, Nat. Council Social Studies, Am. Fedn. Tchrs., NEA, Nat. Conf. Black State Legislators. Baptist. Office: Statehouse Indianapolis IN 46204

HALL, KENNETH, state senator; b. East St. Louis, Ill., May 5, 1915; m. Anne Rush; children—Thomas, Kenneth, Maurice, Mark. Mem. Ill. Ho. of Reps., 1966-70; mem. Ill. Senate, 1970—, asst. majority leader, 1977—. Democratic precinct committeeman; chmn. East St. Louis City Dem. Central Com. Mem. St. Clair and Madison County Urban League, NAACP. Roman Catholic. Clubs: KC (3d deg.), Kiwanis. Office: 1st Nat Bank Bldg 327 Missouri Ave East Saint Louis IL 62201*

HALL, LARRY DEAN, lawyer, utility exec.; b. Hastings, Nebr., Nov. 8, 1942; s. Willis and Stella (Eckoff) H.; B.A., Kearney (Nebr.) State Coll., 1964; J.D., U. Nebr., 1967; m. Cindy R. Crookshanks, Feb. 11, 1977; children—R. Scott, Jeff, Mike. Admitted to Nebr. bar, 1967; asso., then partner firm Wright Simmons Hancock & Hall, Scottsbluff, Nebr., 1967-71; atty., dir. regulatory affairs Kans.-Nebr. Natural Gas Co., Inc., Hastings, 1971-76, v.p. adminstrv. law, 1977—; county atty. Scottsbluff County, 1967-69; mem. legal com. Interstate Oil Compact Commn. Bd. dirs. Scottsbluff United Way, 1968-71; chmn. Scottsbluff County Democratic party, 1968-71; active YMCA. Mem. Am. Bar Assn., Fed. Energy Bar Asssn., Adams County Bar Assn., 10th Jud. Dist. Bar Assn. Presbyterian. Clubs: Masons, Elks, Lochland Country. Home: 6537 Vesuvius Rd Evergreen CO 80439 Office: Lakewood CO

HALL, LAURENCE JAMES, cons., educator; b. Cin., May 14, 1940; s. Laurence Henry and Sarah (Brodie) H.; B.A., Baldwin Wallace Coll., 1962; M.S., Case Western Res. U., 1965; Ph.D., U. Chgo., 1978; m. Lynn Madlon Straus, Oct. 7, 1978; step children—Wendy, Peter; 1 son, Trevor. Caseworker, Summit County (Ohio) Child Welfare, Akron, 1963-65; asst. dir., Center for Study of Welfare Policy, U. Chgo., 1970-71, asso. dean Sch. Social Service Adminstrn., 1971-77, asst. prof., 1977-80; cons. to numerous public and pvt. social service agys. Served to capt. U.S. Army, 1966-69. Mem. Nat. Assn. Social Workers, Am. Mgmt. Assn., Acad. Cert. Social Workers, Ill. Welfare Assn. Author: New Colleges for New Students, 1972. Home and Office: 2142 N Cleveland Chicago IL 60614

HALL, MARTHA LOUISE, educator; b. Muskegon, Mich., May 29, 1937; d. John E. and Katharine Martha (Lavely) Bloomquist; student Muskegon Community Coll., 1955-57; B.A., U. Mich., 1959; M.Ed., Grand Valley State Coll., 1979; 1 son, Edward W. Tchr., Muskegon Heights Public Schs., 1959-61; tchr. English, Muskegon High Sch., 1969-74, reading tchr., 1974-77, secondary reading coordinator Muskegon Public Schs., 1977—. Mem. Western Dunes Reading Council (past pres.), Urban League Greater Muskegon, Mich. Reading Assn., Internat. Reading Assn., Mich. Secondary Reading Interest Council, Assn. Supervision and Curriculum Devel., Phi Kappa Phi. Republican. Methodist. Home: 3830 S Dangl Rd Muskegon MI 49444 Office: 349 W Webster Ave Muskegon MI 49440

HALL, NORRIS RICHARD, mech. engr.; b. Concordia, Kans., May 7, 1937; s. Orville Richard and Georgia Alexandra (May) H.; student Washburn U., 1955-57; B.S. in Mech. Engring., Kans. U., 1959; M.S. in Engring., Purdue U., 1961; m. Carolyn D. Daves, June 8, 1956; children—Douglas, Deborah, Dianne, Bethany. Engr., Bell. Telephone Labs., Indpls., 1959-65, engring. supr., 1965-72, engring. supr. custom telephone phys. design group, 1972—. Chmn. ch. bd. Wesleyan Ch., 1965—, local ch. treas., 1965—; trustee Marion Coll., 1968—; bd. dirs. Lawrence Twp. New Sch. Bldg. Corp., 1974—. Mem. Pi Tau Sigma, Tau Beta Pi. Republican. Home: 11356 Peacock Dr Indianapolis IN 46236 Office: 2525 Shadeland Ave Indianapolis IN 46206

HALL, PHILO DAVID, hosp. adminstr.; b. Providence, Dec. 29, 1942; s. Philo I. and Mary Virginia (Nohlgren) H.; B.S., No. State Coll., 1964; student Kings Fund Coll. of Hosp. Mgmt., London (Eng.), 1970; M.H.A., U. Minn., 1971; m. Ellen Francine DiGangi, June 11, 1971; children—Philo Daniel, Nathan Frank, Kirsten Ellen. Asst. to dir. Med. Center U. Mo., Columbia, 1971-72, asst. dir., 1972-77; exec. v.p. Dakota Midland Hosp., Aberdeen, S.D., 1977—; instr. Sch. Medicine U. Mo., 1971-77; bd. dirs. Blue Cross Western Iowa and S.D., 1979—. Commr. Aberdeen Housing and Redevel. Authority, 1977—; bd. dirs. S.D. Lung Assn., 1977-79, NESD Mental Health Center, 1980—, Brown County United Way, 1980-81; active Brown County Council on Aging, 1978—; trustee Linton (N.D.) Hosp., 1979—. Served with U.S. Navy, 1964-68. Mem. Am. Coll. Hosp. Adminstrs., Am. Hosp. Assn., S.D. Hosp. Assn., Dist. II Hosp. Council, Aberdeen Area C. of C. Republican. Clubs: Rotary, Elks. Home: 1410 N Main St Aberdeen SD 57401 Office: 1400 15th Ave NW Aberdeen SD 57401

HALL, RALPH CHARLES, architect, mech. engr.; b. Lowell, Ohio, June 9, 1925; s. Joseph Ralph and Florence (Misel) H.; B.Mech. Engring., Ohio State U., 1948; M.Div., Grace Theol. Sem., 1951; m. Elizabeth Ruth Lenox, June 28, 1947; children—Nancy Elaine (Mrs. Richard Eugene Bell), Stephen Mark. Ordained to ministry Brethern Ch., 1952; pastor Riverside Brethren Ch., Johnstown, Pa., 1951-56, Meyersdale Brethren Ch. (Pa.), 1957-60; profl. engr. Brethren Archtl. Service, Winona Lake, Ind., 1960—. Instr., Ohio State U., Columbus, 1957; sec. bldg. ministries Brethern Home Missions Council. Chmn. plan commn., Winona Lake, 1972—. Registered profl. engr., Ind.; registered architect, Ohio. Mem. Nat. Fellowship Brethren Ministers, Nat., Ind. socs. profl. engrs., A.I.A., Am. Soc. Heating, Refrigerating and Air Conditioning Engrs. Author: Let Us Rise Up and Build, 1966; Custom Designed Churches, 1968. Home: Route 8 Warsaw IN 46580 Office: Box 666 Winona Lake IN 46590

HALL, REBECCA ANN, educator; b. Dayton, Ohio, July 27, 1940; s. Noel Gould and Anna Frances (Pyle) Easton; B.S., Wittenberg U., 1961; M.Ed., Miami U., Oxford, Ohio, 1964; m. Ted D. Hall, Dec. 21, 1963; 1 dau., Robin Leigh. Tchr., counselor, public schs., Brookville, Ohio, 1961-63, Carlisle, Ohio, 1963-65, Centerville City Schs., 1965—. Mem. NEA, Ohio Edn. Assn., Nat. Bus. Edn. Assn., Ohio Bus. Tchrs. Assn., Am. Vocat. Assn., Ohio Vocat. Assn., Assn. Supervision and Curriculum Devel., Delta Pi Epsilon. Mem. United Ch. Christ. Author: A History of Springboro, Ohio, 1815-1965, 1965; Personal Typing, 1979. Home: 215 W Lytle Rd Springboro OH 45066 Office: Centerville City Schools 500 E Franklin St Centerville OH 45459

HALL, RICHARD LEE, transp. exec.; b. Tiffin, Ohio, May 23, 1917; s. Elbert Carmen and Donna Lee (Neff) H.; LL.B., LaSalle Extension U., Chgo., 1950, postgrad., 1951-54, 70-73, Coll. Advanced Traffic, Chgo., 1955-57, Internat. Correspondence Schs., Scranton, Pa., 1965-68, Upper Iowa U., 1976—; m. Elizabeth Luella Reynolds, Jan. 6, 1940; 1 dau., Michelle Lee. Asst. traffic and distbn. mgr. Capehart-Farnsworth Co., Ft. Wayne, Ind., 1951-56; traffic supr. Magnavox Co., Ft. Wayne, 1956-57; asst. traffic mgr. Central Soya Co., Ft. Wayne, 1957-64; internat. traffic mgr. N.Am. Van Lines, Ft. Wayne, 1964-65; traffic mgr. Stanadyne, Inc., Garrett, Ind., 1965-75; instr. interstate commerce law, N.Am. Van Lines and Am. Soc. Traffic and Transp., 1963-65; cons. in transp. Recipient merit awards Delta Nu Alpha; admitted to practice ICC, FMC, Fed. Ma ritime Bd. Mem. Ft. Wayne Area Traffic Mgrs. Assn., Am. Soc. Traffic and Transp. (certified in transp.), Pvt. Truck Council Am., Fort Wayne C. of C. (transp. com. 1965). Episcopalian. Clubs: Ft. Wayne Transp., Mason. Author: A Study in Grain Transit, 1959. Home: 2402 Cambridge Blvd Fort Wayne IN 46808

HALL, RONALD WILLIAM, accountant; b. Plainview, Tex., Oct. 23, 1946; s. George B. and Gladys (Geistman) H.; B.A. in Econs., U. Tex., 1968; m. Frances Ann Poulson, June 24, 1967; children—William Anders, Amy Kirstin. Credit analyst Austin Nat. Bank (Tex.), 1969-71; methods accountant Southwestern Bell, St. Louis, 1972-74, asst. dist. accounting mgr. disbursement, Kansas City, Mo., 1974-76, asst. chief acct. rate and regulatory matters, St. Louis, 1976-80, div. staff mgr., chief accountant, Topeka, 1980—. Mem. Nat. Assn. Accountants, Delta Kappa Epsilon (pres. 1967). Club: Optimists (pres. 1979-80). Home: 4113 Woodbury Court N Topeka KS 66606 Office: 220 E 6th St Topeka KS 66603

HALL, STUART PHELPS, pub. relations exec.; b. Cortland, N.Y., Nov. 29, 1919; s. Glenn Schermerhorn and Helen Winifred (Phelps) H.; B.S. in M.E., Rensselaer Poly. Inst., 1940; m. Maxine Margaret McCloy, Sept. 19, 1942; children—Philip McCloy, Allan Glenn. Engr., Buick Motor div., 1940-47; asso. editor Product Engring. Mag., McGraw Hill Pub. Co., 1947-48; editor Design News Mag., Rogers Publ. Co., 1948-52; founder, pres. Hall Indsl. Publicity Inc., Troy, Mich., 1953—. Mem. applied sci. adv. council Miami U. (Ohio), 1972-76. Recipient Indsl. Advt. Service award Till Forbid Club Detroit, 1976. Mem. ASME, Soc. Automotive Engrs., Soc. Mfg. Engrs., Engring. Soc. Detroit, Sigma Xi, Tau Beta Pi, Pi Tau Sigma, Sigma Chi. Republican. Presbyterian. Clubs: Detroit Athletic, Miami U. Presidents, Elks. Home: 1060 Hall Ln Lake Orion MI 48035 Office: 2855 Coolidge Rd Suite 105 Troy MI 48084

HALL, TONY P., congressman; b. Dayton, Ohio, Jan. 16, 1942; A.B., Denison U., 1964; m. Janet Dick, 1973; children—Jyl, Matthew. Pres., Springfield Apts. Inc.; mem. Peace Corps; mem. Ohio Ho. of Reps., 1969-73, Ohio Senate, 1973-79; mem. 96th and 97th Congresses from 3d Dist. Ohio. Democrat. Clubs: Agonis, Trail's End. Office: 1728 Longworth House Office Bldg Washington DC 20515

HALL, WILLIAM RAY, ins. agt.; b. McKenzie, Tenn., Sept. 20, 1933; s. John William and Emma Lou (Scates) H.; student Bethel Coll., McKenzie, Tenn., 1951-52, Northwestern U., 1955; LL.B., LaSalle U., Chgo., 1966; m. Patricia A. Riley, June 27, 1959; children—John William, Pamela June. Engaged in ins., 1953—; pres. Am. Inst. Agy., Inc., Chgo., 1974—; dir. Equity Gen. Ins. Co. Mem. Ind. Ins. Agts. Ill. (v.p., dir. 1977-80), Chgo. Bd. Underwriters (dir. 1976-80), Marine Multi-Peril Soc. Chgo. (past skipper). Office: 223 W Jackson Blvd Chicago IL 60606

HALLA, RUTH, speech pathologist; b. Chgo., May 26, 1947; d. Richard Charles and Mildred Johanna (Kral) Halla; B.S. magna cum laude, U. Ill., 1969, M.A., 1970. Staff speech pathologist Luth. Gen. Hosp., Park Ridge, Ill., 1970-73, acting dir. speech pathology and audiology dept., 1973-74, sr. staff speech pathologist, 1974-75, dir. speech pathology and audiology dept., 1975—. Office of Edn. fellow, 1970; Edmund James scholar, 1967; certified Am. Speech and Hearing Assn. Mem. Am., Ill. (chmn. local arrangements ann. conv. 1977, 78) speech and hearing assns., U. Ill. Alumni Assn., Phi Beta Kappa, Phi Kappa Phi. Office: Speech Pathology and Audiology Dept Lutheran Gen Hosp 1775 Dempster St Park Ridge IL 60068

HALLAN, JAMES ARTHUR, soft drink co. exec.; b. Mabel, Minn., July 9, 1917; s. Arthur M. and Inez M. (Gilbert) H.; B.A., Hope Coll., 1939; postgrad. Naval Supply Corps Sch. Harvard U., 1943; m. Frances M. Price, Sept. 12, 1941; children—Roberta, Sally Jo, James P. Salesman, Gerber Products Co., 1939-41; personnel-purchasing positions Baker Furniture Inc., Holland, Mich., 1945-54; vending positions Brooks Products Inc., Holland, Mich., 1954-57, sales mgr., 1957-63, v.p. sales, 1963-70, exec. v.p., 1970-72, pres., 1972-81. Bd. dirs. Holland Sch. Bd., 1946-57, pres., 1956; active Keep Mich. Beautiful. Served with Supply Corp, USNR, 1941-45. Mem. Holland C. of C. (pres. 1968-69), Mich., U.S. chambers commerce, W. Mich. Purchasing Agts. Assn. (pres. 1952), Am. Mgmt. Assn., Mich. Mfrs. Assn., Nat., Mich. soft drink assns. Republican. Clubs: Am. Legion, Peninsular, Rotary, Elks. Home: 185 Sorrento Dr Holland MI 49423 Died Sept. 3, 1981.

HALLENBECK, JAN TRAVER, historian, educator; b. N.Y.C., Apr. 13, 1940; s. Chester Traver and Marian (Lyston) Jones H.; B.A., Kenyon Coll., 1961; M.A., N.Y. U., 1962; Ph.D., 1966; m. Carol Ann George, Sept. 7, 1963; children—Thomas Traver, Michael Stuart. Instr., Queens Coll., N.Y.C., 1962-63; asst. prof. history Ind. U., Fort Wayne, 1966-69; asst. prof. Ohio Wesleyan U., Delaware, 1969-72, asso. prof., 1972-77, prof., 1977—, chmn. dept. history, 1974-78; co-owner, chmn. Expeditions, Inc., Writing Cons., Delaware. Recipient Sherwood Dodge Shankland Teaching award Ohio Wesleyan, 1975. Mem. Am. Hist. Assn., Mediaeval Acad. Am., Am. Catholic Hist. Assn., Ohio Acad. History, AAUP. Democrat. Episcopalian. Contbr. articles to profl. jours. Home: 130 Griswold St Delaware OH 43015 Office: Dept History Ohio Wesleyan Univ Delaware OH 43015

HALLEY, PAUL DONALD, indsl. hygienist and toxicologist; b. Gallipolis, Ohio, Oct. 2, 1915; s. Henry P. and Clara D. (Sibley) H.; B.S. in Chemistry, Ohio State U., 1936; m. Frances Walker, Dec. 6, 1936; children—Carolyn Halley Bialik, Gary. Sr. chemist Bur. Indsl. Hygiene, W.Va. Dept. Health, Charleston, 1940-43, indsl. hygienist, 1944-46, asso. dir. bur., 1947-53; indsl. hygienist Standard Oil Co. (Ind.), Chgo., 1953-63, mgr. safety-indsl. hygiene, 1967-72, dir. indsl. hygiene and toxicology, 1973—; mem. Nat. Adv. Com. on Occupational Safety and Health. Supt. ch. sch. 1st Methodist Ch., Harvey, Ill., 1957-61, lay leader, 1962-63, youth counselor Meth. Youth Fellowship, 1955-60; active Boy Scouts Am., 1945-53. Mem. Am. Indsl. Hygeien Assn. (pres. 1972-73, Cummings Meml. award and lecture 1980), Am. Chem. Soc., Bd. Cert. Safety Profls., Am. Petroleum Inst. (cert. meritorious service 1975, 81), Am. Acad. Indsl. Hygeiene. Republican. Club: Moose. Author: (with P. Wolkonsky) Records and Reports in Industrial Hygiene in Indsl. Hygiene and Toxicology, Vol. I: 1978 contbr. numerous articles to profl. jours. Home: 1924 Evergreen Rd Homewood IL 60430 Office: 200 E Randolph Dr Chicago IL 60601

HALLIDAY, WILLIAM JAMES, JR., mfg. exec.; b. Detroit, Nov. 16, 1921; s. William James and Katherine Elizabeth (Krantz) H.; A.B. (scholar), U. Mich., 1943, J.D., 1948; m. Lois Jeanne Streelman, Sept. 6, 1947; children—Carol Lynn Halliday Murphy, Richard Andrew, Marcia Katherine, James Anthony. Admitted to Mich. bar, 1948; asso. firm Schmidt, Smith & Howlett and successors, Grand Rapids, Mich., 1952-56, partner, 1956-66; sec. Amway Corp. Ada, Mich., 1964—; gen. counsel, 1966-71, v.p., 1970-79, exec. v.p., 1979—, also dir.; asst. pros. atty., Kent County, Mich., 1949-51; twp. atty., Wyoming Twp., Mich., 1955-57; city atty., Wyoming, Mich., 1961-66; dir. Nutrilite Products, Inc., Mut. Broadcasting System, Inc., Mich. Nat. Bank-Central, Grand Rapids. Bd. dirs. Council Better Bus. Burs., Inc., U. Mich. Devel. Council, Better Bus. Bur. of Western Mich., Grand Rapids Met. YMCA. Served with M.I., U.S. Army, 1943-46, with JAGC, 1951-52. Decorated Bronze Star; recipient William Jennings Bryan award, U. Mich., 1943. Mem. Am., Mich., Grand Rapids bar assns., Phi Beta Kappa, Phi Kappa Phi, Delta Sigma Rho, Phi Eta Sigma. Republican. Presbyterian. Club: Kiwanis. Home: 2096 Robinson Rd S E Grand Rapids MI 49506 Office: Amway Corp 7575 E Fulton Rd Ada MI 49355

HALLONGREN, EUGENE GUSTAV, coll. adminstr.; b. Oak Park, Ill., Apr. 29, 1943; s. Gustav A. and Ann I. (Nelson) H.; B.S. in Indsl. Edn., Stout State U., Menomonie, Wis., 1965, M.S. in Guidance and Counseling, 1966; m. Dianne June Lindberg, Nov. 1, 1944; children—Brett Jericoe, Brady Eugene. Resident asst., asst. football coach Stout State U., 1965-66; counselor, tchr., coach high schs. in Wis. and Ill., 1966-69; counselor Coll. of DuPage, Glen Ellyn, Ill., 1969-73, dir. testing and alternative credit, 1973-79, asso. dean acad. alts. unit, 1979—. Mem. Elmhurst Citizen's Student Competency Task Force, 1979; vice chmn. Elmhurst Sch. Dist. Caucus, 1979, chmn., 1980; mem. steering com. Elmhurst Sch. Dist., 1981; pres. Cornille Sch. PTA, 1979. Mem. Am. Sch. Counselors Assn., Am. Coll. Testing Council (exec. bd. Ill. 1977-81, sec. 1980), Ill. Sch. Counselors Assn. (gov. bd. 1976-80), Ill. Guidance and Personnel Assn. (senate 1978-81, exec. bd. 1981—), Ill. Assn. Measurement and Evaluation (pres. 1980), Ill. Coll. Personnel Assn., DuPage County Sch. Counselors Assn. (pres. 1972), Phi Delta Kappa, Sigma Tau Gamma. Lutheran. Home: 643 Mary Ct Elmhurst IL 60126 Office: Coll DuPage Lambert Rd and 22d St Glen Ellyn IL 60137

HALLOWELL, DAVID ALAN, mgmt. cons.; b. Sheridan, Wyo., Dec. 2, 1934; s. Herman Leo and Lois Elma (Jenkins) H.; B.S. in Mgmt., U. Wyo., 1957; M.B.A., U. Colo., 1962; m. Gretchen Evelyn Hartwig, Sept. 21, 1957; children—Lori Jo, D. Bryce, Sharon. Mgmt. trainee Gen. Mills, Inc., Mpls., 1957-59; dir. personnel and public relations Tomco, Inc., Belmond, Iowa, 1961-63; personnel dir. Farmhand, Inc., Mpls., 1964-65; pres. Hallowell Assos., Inc., mgmt. cons., Mpls., 1966—; dir. Relocation Cons., Chgo., The Guide Corp., Chgo. Served with U.S. Army, 1957-58. Mem. Am. Soc. Personnel Adminstrn. (diplomate), Am. Soc. Tng. and Devel. (past dir. Minn.), Soc. Advancement of Mgmt., Twin Cities Personnel Assn. Republican. Club: LaFayette. Office: Hallowell Assos Inc Shelard Plaza S Wayzata Blvd at County Rd 18 Minneapolis MN 55426

HALLOWELL, ROBERT EDWARD, educator; b. Charleston, Ill., Aug. 30, 1918; s. Edward Everett and Elizabeth (Stockover) H.; B.S., Eastern Ill., U., 1939, Ped.D. (hon.), 1965; M.A., U. Ill., 1940, Ph.D., 1942; postgrad. U. Geneva (Switzerland), 1946-47; m. Mirzl Mueller, Aug. 11, 1949; 1 son, Eric Edward. Spl. investigator War Dept., Ger., 1945-46; instr., then asst. prof. French, U. Ill., 1948-60; asso. prof. French and Italian, U. Wis. at Milw., 1961-63, prof., 1963-68, chmn. dept., 1964-68; prof. French U. Ill. at Chgo. Circle, 1968—, acting head dept., 1970; lectr. Centre d'Etudes Superieures de la Renaissance, Tours, France, summer 1964; Fulbright sr. research fellow, France, 1966-67. Mem. Modern Lang. Assn. (chmn. French Renaissance lit. sect. 1968, mem. Del. Assembly 1974-76), Am. Assn. Tchrs. French, Renaissance Soc. Am., Assn. Internat. des Etudes Francaises, Phi Kappa Phi, Kappa Delta Pi, Pi Delta Phi. Club: Cliff Dwellers (Chgo.). Author: Ronsard and the Conventional Roman Elegy, 1954; articles and revs. in periodicals U.S. and France. French Editor: Modern Lang. Jour., 1960-64. Home: 1564 Bowling Green Dr Lake Forest IL 60045 Office: Univ Hall Univ Illinois Chicago IL 60680

HALLSTROM, RICHARD THOMAS, mfg. co. exec.; b. Vermillion, S.D., Feb. 10, 1947; s. Darold Fredrick and Margret Anne (Kyte) H.; B.A., U. S.D., 1971; m. Linda Jo Wickre, June 12, 1971. Asst. mgr. Kresge/K Mart, Chgo., 1971-74; ter. mgr. Pride Seed Co., Redwood Falls, Minn., 1974-75; advt. mgr., composition dir. Freeman (S.D.) Courier, 1975-78; composition mgr. Sioux Falls Shopping News, 1979; advt. mgr. Zip Feed Mills, Inc., Sioux Falls, 1979—. Adviser, Everyday Clothes newsletter, 1980; vol. Big Bros., 1978-80; reader for blind and physically handicapped, N.D., S.D., 1979—. Recipient 3d place photography award S.D. State Fair, 1980. Mem. Am. Feed Mfrs. Am., Sioux Falls C. of C. Clubs: Minnehaha Sportsmens Conservation (dir. public relations, editor), Dakota

Westerners. Contbr. S.D. Wildlife Fedn. newspaper, 1980—. Home: 624 N Menlo St Sioux Falls SD 57104 Office: 304 E 8th St Box 500 Sioux Falls SD 57117

HALMAN, PAUL MARK, fin. corp. exec.; b. Akron, Ohio, May 3, 1934; s. A. Paul and Ardella F. (Ford) H.; B.A., Houghton Coll., 1956; postgrad. (NSF grantee), Ohio U., summers, 1962, 63, 64; m. Diane Enid Matz, June 11, 1970; children—J. Mark, Lisa Jean, Pamela Sue. Youth dir. Sturgis (Mich.) Wesleyan Ch., 1956-57; dir. Christian edn. Central N.W. Presbyn. Ch., Detroit, 1958-59; dir. of devel., instr. Stony Brook (N.Y.) Sch., 1959-68; dir. alumni fund MacMurray Coll., Jacksonville, Ill., 1968-70; dir. trustee assos. Alma (Mich.) Coll., 1970-72; asst. to pres. First Dayton (Ohio) Corp., 1972-74; pres. Fin. Systems, Inc., Livonia, Mich., 1974—; dir. Hazen Corp., Mgmt. Systems, Inc. Republican. Clubs: Jaycees (dir. 1968), Kiwanis (pres. 1972). Home: 14393 Alexander Dr Livonia MI 48154 Office: 33150 Schoolcraft St Livonia MI 48150

HALPERIN, PHILLIP HAROLD, surgeon, educator; b. Madison, Wis., Sept. 28, 1909; s. Charles H. and Anna (Wigonetz) H.; B.S., U. Wis., 1931, M.D., 1933; M.Med.Sci. in Surgery, U. Pa., 1939; m. Dorothy Milgram, Apr. 9, 1940; children—Janice Milgram Earle, Alan Keith. Intern, Mt. Sinai Hosp., Milw., 1933-34; resident in surgery Mt. Sinai Hosp., Milw., 1934-35, Albert Einstein Hosp., Phila., 1936-37; practice medicine specializing in gen. surgery, Madison, Wis., 1937-40, Kansas City, Mo., 1940—; former chmn. dept. surgery Manorah Med. Center, Kansas City; clin. prof. surgery U. Mo., Kansas City; clin. asso. in surgery U. Kans., Kansas City. Served with M.C., U.S. Army, 1942-46. Diplomate Am. Bd. Surgery. Mem. A.C.S., Internat. Coll. Surgeons, Pan-Pacific Surg. Assn., AMA, Kansas City SW Clin. Soc., Mo., Southwestern, Kansas City (pres. 1959-60) surg. socs., Mo., Jackson County med. socs. Jewish. Club: Oakwood Country. Contbr. articles to profl. jours. Home: 8348 Somerset St Prairie Village KS 66207 Office: 6724 Troost Ave Suite 910 Kansas City MO 64113

HALQUIST, CAROL HILDA, mgmt. cons.; b. Shakopee, Minn., July 24, 1943; d. Herbert Clifford and Ethel (Stier) H.; student MacPhail Coll. Music, 1965-66; grad. U. Minn., 1971; M.B.A., Calif. Western U., 1977-79. Tchr., Del's Music Center, Mpls., 1961-64; owner, mgr. Carol's Studios, Prior Lake, Minn., 1964-67; tchr., coordinator Allied Piano & Organ Co., Mpls., 1967-70; mgr. sales Northwest Organ and Piano Co., Mpls., 1970-74; mgmt. and sales tng. cons. Lowrey Co., Lincolnwood, Ill., 1975-79; regional sales mgr. CBS Mus. Instruments/Gulbransen, Deerfield, Ill., 1979-80, merchandising mgr., 1980; v.p. mktg. and sales Jorgensen Co., Mpls., 1981—; pres. CGS, Inc., Mpls., 1981—. Mem. Am. Mgmt. Assn. Lutheran. Editor: Make Lowrey Magic, 1978. Home: 5550 Rowland Rd Minnetonka MN 55343

HALSEY, WILLIAM DOUGLAS, systems engr.; b. Middletown, Ohio, June 26, 1946; s. Elmer J. and Alta L. (Davis) H.; B.S. in B.A., Bowling Green State U., 1968; m. Judith Ann Snyder, Aug. 6, 1965; children—James Milton, William Douglas II. With Armco, Inc., Middletown, 1968—, programmer, 1968-71, asso. systems engr., 1971-72, systems engr., 1972-75, sr. systems engr., 1975-78, supr. systems computing, 1978-80, on spl. assignment, 1980, sr. staff systems engr., 1981—. Mem. Assn. Systems Mgmt., Am. Mgmt. Assn. Republican. Club: Mason. Home: 3778 Hollybrook Dr Middletown OH 45042 Office: Eastern Steel Div 703 Curtis St Middletown OH 45043

HALSTEAD, JAMES ALLEN, bus. cons., accountant; b. Mt. Pulaski, Ill., June 29, 1940; s. Roland Peter and Bonnie Elizabeth (Stopner) H.; cert. public acctg. U. Ill.; m. Mary Ellen Cowan, June 13, 1963. Tchr. math. Balt. city high schs., 1966; programmer, systems analyst Revere Copper & Brass Co., Scottsboro, Ala., 1967-70; project leader Cabot Corp., Kokomo, Ind., 1970-71; systems analyst State Farm Ins. Co., Bloominton, Ill., 1971-72; founder, owner Gen. Bus. Services, Joliet, Ill., 1972-76; mng. partner James Halstead & Assos., Joliet, 1977—; mem. faculty Joliet Jr. Coll. Served with U.S. Army, 1963-66. Cert. data processing Data Processing Mgmt. Assn.; enrolled agt. IRS. Mem. Joliet Region C. of C. Club: Lions (Joliet). Copyright on INV/BAS. Home: 103 Hammes St Joliet IL 60436 Office: 1551 Plainfield Rd Joliet IL 60435

HALSTEAD, THOMAS MICHAEL, communications research co. exec.; b. Detroit, Nov. 18, 1949; s. Charles Richard and Jacqueline Ann (Madigan) H.; B.A., U. Mich., 1971, M.Mktg., 1973; postgrad. Law Sch., U. Detroit, 1974-76; m. Gayle Guoin, Jan. 4, 1974. In-house mktg. mgr. Ford Motor Co., Dearborn, Mich., 1971-77; mgr. Baha'i Pub. Co., Wilmette, Ill., 1977-78; partner, dir. Communications Design Group, Inc., Evanston, Ill., 1978-79; pres. In-House Cons., Inc., Vernon Hills, Ill., 1979—; dir. Energy Exchange, 1980—; partner Halstead & Garson, 1981—. Bd. dirs. Youth and Family Counseling Inc., 1981—. Mem. Am. Mktg. Assn., Aircraft Owners and Pilots Assn., Direct Mail Mktg. Assn., U. Mich. Alumni Assn. Mem. Baha'i Faith. Clubs: Toastmasters, Lake County Chess. Author: Car Buying Made Easier, 1975. Home: Route 3 Box 299A Antioch IL 60002 Office: PO Box 825 Lake Forest IL 60045

HALTERMAN, DAVE JOE, small elec. appliances co. exec.; b. Cairo, Mo., Dec. 16, 1944; s. Joe A. and Beulah B. (Bratcher) H.; student public schs.; m. Norma Barnes, June 4, 1964; children—Jeff, Bryon. Asst. purchasing agt. McGraw-Edison, Moberly, Mo., 1962-73; materials mgr. McGraw-Edison Centerville, Iowa, 1973-75, plant supt., 1975-77, plant mgr., 1977—. Bd. dirs. Adult Edn. Macon Sch. Systems, 1978—, Macon C. of C. Republican. Methodist. Clubs: Macon Country; Elks; Toastmasters. Home: 1406 Saxoney St Macon MO 63552 Office: 704 S Missouri St Macon MO 63552

HALVERSON, CLAIRE B., ednl. adminstr., educator; b. Syracuse, N.Y., Aug. 23, 1936; d. Harold G. and Lucia B. H.; B.A. cum laude, St. Lawrence U., 1958; M.A., Harvard U., 1961; Ph.D. (Trainer of Tchr. Trainers fellow), U. Wis., Madison, 1973; 1 dau., Renya. Tchr., Wayland (Mass.) Public Schs., 1962-63, Halandri Middle Sch., Athens, Greece, 1963-64; tchr. Winchester (Mass.) Public Schs., 1964-67, curriculum developer, 1967-69; instr. U. Wis.-Milw., 1969-71; asso. dir. Center for Equal Edn. Opportunity, Evanston, Ill., 1973-76; asst. prof., dir. Race Desegregation Tng. Inst., Sex Equity Tng. Inst., U. Wis.-Extension, Milw., 1976—; tchr. U. Wis.-Parkside, 1976-77, 80; cons. in field. Mem. edn. com. Milw. chpt. NAACP, 1977-79. Mem. NOW, Nat. Council Social Studies (racism and social justice com., Carter-Woodson award com.), Assn. Supervision and Curriculum Devel. (com. on racism and social justice), Soc. for Psychol. Study of Social Issues. Club: Sierra. Contbr. articles to profl. pubis. Home: 3721 N Morris Blvd Milwaukee WI 53211 Office: Univ Wis-Extension 929 N 6th St Milwaukee WI 53203

HALVERSON, HAROLD W., state senator; b. Burke, S.D., Nov. 24, 1926; s. Reuben Arnold and Viola (Hauge) H.; grad. high sch.; m. Marie Christina Vosika, 1948; children—James Arnold, Marilyn Marie, Cindy Lou, John Edward. Fieldman, Mo. Valley Mut. Ins., Burke, 1957-59; with Milbank Mut. Ins. Co., 1959-60, asst. claims supr., 1960-66, dir. agy., 1966—, v.p., 1969—, also dir.; mem. S.D. Ho. of Reps., 1971-72, now S.D. Senate. Mem. S.D. State Republican central com., 1975—. Served with USN, 1945-46; PTO. Mem. Am. Legion. Methodist. Clubs: Masons, Community, Dale Carnegie. Office: State Capitol Pierre SD 75701*

HALVERSON, PAUL KEITH, publishing co. exec.; b. Evanston, Ill., May 18, 1949; s. Roger Oscar and Helen Ann H.; B.A., Elmhurst Coll., 1972. Audit staff mgmt. trainee No. Ill. Gas Co., Aurora, 1969-71; auditor M.W. regional audit office for consol. ops GTE Service Corp., Des Plaines, Ill., 1971-74, sr. auditor, 1974-75; gen. acctg. supr. Gen. Telephone Directory Co., Des Plaines, Ill., 1975-78, asst. treas., 1978-79, customer credit mgr., 1979; v.p. fin. Fox Ridge Press, Cary, Ill., 1979-80; head dept. acctg. data processing U.S. Envelope div. Westvaco, North Chicago, Ill., 1980—; pres. Halverson Assos., Des Plaines, 1981—. Mem. Maine Twp. (Ill.) Bd. Trustees, 1973-79, town clk., 1979—, twp. supr., 1981—; sec.-treas. Town Trustees Assn. Cook County (Ill.), 1973, v.p., 1974-76, bd. dirs., 1974-77; co-founder Maine Twp. Council on Alcoholism, 1974, v.p., 1974-77, pres., 1977—; mem. Maine Twp. Bd. Liaison to Maine Twp. Com. on Youth, 1978—. Mem. Chgo. Council on Fgn. Relations, Town Clks. Assn. Cook County (legis. com. 1980), Twp. Supr. Assn. Cook County, Twp. Ofcls. of Ill. Republican. Office: 2510 Dempster St Des Plaines IL 60016

HALVERSON, ROBERT MARTIN, publisher; b. Baldwin, Wis., Apr. 9, 1942; s. Willard Clarence and Antoinette Marie (Bos) H.; B.S. in Journalism and Speech, U. Wis., River Falls, 1970; children—Julie, Stephanie. Advt. asst. Am. Hoist & Derrick, St. Paul, 1970; sales rep. Advance Stamp Works, St. Paul, 1970-72; public relations dir. Minn. Fighting Saints, St. Paul, 1972-73; publ. mgr. The Webb Co., St. Paul, 1973—, mgr. Passages and Frontier mags. of N.W. Orient and Frontier Airlines. Served with U.S. Army, 1961-64. Named salesman of yr., Sales and Mktg. Execs., 1977. Participant Boston Marathon, 1979. Office: 1999 Shepard Rd Saint Paul MN 55116

HALVERSON, ROGER MICHAEL, ins. co. exec.; b. Manitowoc, Wis., May 3, 1940; s. Erwin Joseph and Wilma H.; B.S. in Econs., U. Wis., 1964; m. Deanna C. Durben, June 17, 1961; 1 son, Troy. Supr. checking dept. Allstate Ins. Co., Milw., 1965, supr. steno dept., 1965-66; asst. mgr. customer service Surg. Care Blue Shield, Milw., 1966-67, asst. mgr. Wis. Medicaid, 1967-68, mgr. Wis. Medicaid, 1968-70, mgr. Blue Shield claims, 1970-74, v.p. Blue Shield ops., 1974-77; asst. v.p., instl. benefits adminstr. Blue Cross and Blue Shield of Greater N.Y., 1977-80; v.p. claims and govt. programs Blue Cross of N.W. Ohio, Toledo, 1980—. Mem. Adminstrv. Mgmt. Soc. Home: 5843 Winslow Rd Whitehouse OH 43571 Office: Blue Cross of NW Ohio 3737 Sylvania Ave Toledo OH 43656

HALVORSEN, RICHARD ISAAC, newspaper exec.; b. Albert Lea, Minn., Sept. 22, 1926; s. Jasper Alfred and Bessie Serena (Gullickson) H.; BB.A., U. Minn., 1950; m. Sharon Kay Abel, Aug. 12, 1972; children—Steven Richard, Susan Joyce, Sandra Lynn, Scott David. Credit supr. Gamble Skogmo Co., 1950-53; with Mpls. Star and Tribune, 1953—, asst. display advt. mgr., 1963-69, display advt. mgr., 1969-71, mktg. dir., 1971-75, opns. dir., 1975-79, advt. dir., 1979-81, v.p., 1981—. Bd. dirs. Mpls. Aquatennial, 1972-76, pres., 1974-75. Served with USN, 1944-46. Minn. state doubles bowling champion, 1973, 75; mem. Mpls. Dist. Bowling Hall Fame. Mem. Am. Newspaper Publs. Assn. (prodn. mgmt. com.), Internat. Newspaper Advt. Execs., Internat. Newspaper Promotion Assn., Advt. Fedn. Minn., Internat. Circulation Mgrs. Assn., Newspaper Advt. Bur. (long range plans com.), Minn. Press Club. Lutheran. Clubs: Admirals, Minn. Alumni. Home: 268 Peninsula Rd Medicine Lake MN 55441 Office: 425 Portland Ave Minneapolis MN 55488

HALVORSEN, WILLIAM GARRETT, noise and vibration control cons. co. exec.; b. San Diego, Nov. 27, 1944; s. Merville Linn and Gladys Irene (Garrett) H.; B.S. in Mech. Engring. with honors and distinction, San Diego State U., 1967; M.S.M.E., U. Wash., 1969; postgrad. U. Pa., 1970-71; m. Marcia Lynn Rambo, July 5, 1969; children—Anne-Lise Faye, Karin Patricia. Project mgr. Structural Dynamics Research Corp., Cin., 1971-76; ind. cons. engr., Cin., 1976-77; v.p. Anatrol Corp., Cin., 1977—; lectr., condr. univ. short courses, indsl. seminars, 1972—. Chmn., Cin. Noise Com., 1977-79; mem. Cin. Environ. Adv. Council, 1976-79. Served to lt. (j.g.), Civil Engr. Corps, USNR, 1969-71. NSF trainee, 1967-69. Mem. Inst. Noise Control Engrs., Acoustical Soc. Am., Am. Inst. Physics, Pi Tau Sigma. Club: Cin. Fencing. Contbr. chpt. to book. Home: 1114 Priscilla Ln Cincinnati OH 45208 Office: Anatrol Corp Suite 227 11305 Reed Hartman Hwy Cincinnati OH 45241

HALVORSON, WILLIAM ARTHUR, cons. actuary; b. Menomonie, Wis., June 26, 1928; s. George Henry and Katherine Eileen (Dietsche) H.; student Stout Inst., 1945-46, U. Mich., 1948; B.B.A., U. Wis., 1950, M.B.A., 1951; m. Patricia Janet von Trebra, Dec. 27, 1951; children—Robert, James, Janet, Audrey, Katherine. Asst. group actuary N.Y. Life Ins. Co., N.Y.C., 1951-56; cons. actuary Milliman & Robertson, Inc., San Francisco, 1956-61, Milw., 1961—, exec. v.p., 1972-81. Served with AUS, 1946-47. Recipient Alumni award Menomonie High Sch., 1945. Fellow Soc. Actuaries (v.p. 1973-75, pres. 1977-78); mem. Wis. Actuarial Club (pres. 1964-65), Am. Acad. Actuaries (sec. 1971-73, pres. 1981—), Milw. Assn. Commerce, Midwest Pension Conf., Wis. Retirement Plan Profls. Ltd., Beta Gamma Sigma, Phi Kappa Phi, Chi Phi. Roman Catholic. Clubs: Union League (Chgo.); Oconomowoc Golf; Cherokee Golf (Madison). Contbg. author: Group Insurance Handbook, 1965. Home: 34430 Valley Rd Oconomowoc WI 53066 Office: 200 Executive Dr Brookfield WI 53005

HAM, ARTHUR CARL, state senator; b. Rapid City, S.D.; s. Arthur C. and Gladys (Chapman) H.; B.S., S.D. State U., 1934; m. Donna Ballard, 1946; 8 children. Mem. staff extension service S.D. State U., 1947-51; rancher, 1952—; mem. S.D. Ho. of Reps., 1975-78, S.D. Senate, 1978—. Mem. Pennington County Sch. Bd., Rapid City, 1964-73; Rapid City Sch. Bd., 1969—. Served with AUS, 1942-47. Decorated Bronze Star; named Outstanding Sch. Bd. Mem. S.D., 1972. Mem. Assn. Sch. Bds. S.D., S.D. Stockgrowers, VFW. Club: Elks. Office: State Legislature State Capitol Pierre SD 57501*

HAMACHER, DAVID PAUL, mgmt. cons.; b. Madison, Wis., Apr. 4, 1943; s. John M. and Mildred L. Hamacher; B.S. in Pharmacy, U. Wis., Madison, 1966; m. Marjorie L. Heibel, Aug. 30, 1965; children—Deborah, Gregory, Heather, Bradley. Vice pres. Stein Drug Inc., Menomonee Falls, Wis., 1968-72, exec. v.p., 1972-80; pres. D. P. Hamacher and Assos., Wauwatosa, Wis., 1980—. Mem. Am. Pharm. Assn., Wis. Pharm. Assn. Roman Catholic. Home: 1700 Village Green Ct Elm Grove WI 53122 Office: 11400 W Bluemound Rd Wauwatosa WI 53226

HAMALAINEN, PEKKA KALEVI, historian, educator; b. Finland, Dec. 28, 1938; s. Olavi Simeon and Aili Aliisa (Laiho) H.; A.B., Ind. U., 1961, Ph.D., 1966; m. Patricia Beth Dunlap, 1965; children—Kim Ilkka, Leija-Lee Louise Aili, Timothy Pekka Olavi, Kai Kalevi Edward. Acting asst. prof. history, U. Calif., Santa Barbara, 1965-66, asst. prof. history, 1966-70; asso. prof. history, U. Wis., Madison, 1970-76, prof. history, 1976—, chmn. Western European Area Studies Program, 1977—; Nat. Screening Com. Scandinavian Area, Inst. Internat. Edn. for Fulbright-Hays Program. Served to lt. Finnish Navy, 1957-58. Faculty research grantee, U. Calif., 1966-69, faculty summer fellow, 1969; Ford Found. grantee, 1967; faculty research grantee, U. Wis., Madison, 1970—; Am. Philos. Soc. research grantee, 1973; Am. Council Learned Socs. fellow, 1976, research grantee, 1978. Mem. Am. Hist. Assn., Soc. for Advancement of Scandinavian Study (advisory com., exec. council), AAUP, Ind. U. Alumni Assn. Author: Kielitaistelu Suomessa 1917-1939, 1968; Nationalitetskampen och sprakstriden i Finland 1917-1939, 1969; In Time of Storm: Revolution, Civil War and the Ethnolinguistic Issue in Finland, 1978; Luokka ja Kieli Vallankumouksen Suomessa, 1978; contbr. articles, revs. to publs. in field. Home: 3122 Lakeland Ave Madison WI 53704 Office: Department of History University of Wisconsin Madison WI 53706

HAMANN, DERYL FREDERICK, lawyer; b. Lehigh, Iowa, Dec. 8, 1932; s. Frederick Carl and Ada (Hollingsworth) H.; A.A., Ft. Dodge Community Coll., 1953; B.S., U. Nebr., 1956, LL.B. cum laude, 1958; m. Carrie S. Rosen, Aug. 29, 1954; children—Karl E., Daniel A., Esther E., Julie K. Admitted to Nebr. bar, 1958; partner Baird, Holm, McEachen, Pedersen & Hamann, Omaha, 1959—; chmn. Farmers & Mchts. Bank & Trust, Watertown, S.D., Fremont County State Bank, Sidney, Iowa, Decatur Co. State Bank, Leon, Iowa, Citizen's State Bank, Corydon, Iowa, Pioneer Bank & Trust Co., St. Louis; chmn. exec. com. Douglas County Bank & Trust, Omaha; sec., dir. Hawkeye Bancorp., Des Moines. Mem. exec. com. Luth. Ch. in Am. Found., N.Y.C.; trustee Midland Luth. Coll., Fremont, Nebr. Mem. Am., Nebr. bar assns., Order of Coif, Phi Delta Phi. Lutheran. Optimist (pres. breakfast 1972-73). Club: Omaha. Home: 600 Loveland Dr Omaha NE 68114 Office: 1500 Woodmen Tower Omaha NE 68102

HAMBLEN, JOHN WESLEY, computer scientist, educator; b. Story, Ind., Sept. 25, 1924; s. James William and Mary Etta (Morrison) H.; A.B. in Math., Ind. U., 1947; M.S., Purdue U., 1952, Ph.D. in Math. and Stats., 1955; m. Brenda F. Harrod, Mar. 1947 (div. 1979); 1 son, James O. Tchr. math. and sci. Kingsbury (Ind.) High Sch., 1946-48, Bluffton (Ind.) High Sch., 1948-51; asst. prof. math. Okla. State U., Stillwater, 1955-57, cons. in statis. methods for research staff Agrl. Expt. Sta., 1955-56, asso. prof. math., 1957-58, dir. Computing Center, 1957-58; asso. prof. stats., dir. Computing Center, U. Ky., Lexington, 1958-61; prof. math. and tech. So. Ill. U., Carbondale, 1961-65, dir. Data Processing and Computing Center, 1961-65; project dir. computer scis. So. Regional Edn. Bd., Atlanta, 1965-72; prof. U. Mo., Rolla, 1972—, chmn. dept. computer sci., 1972-81; cons. to research staff D-X Sunray Oil Co., Tulsa, 1957-58, Systems Devel. Corp., Santa Monica, Calif., 1965-67; mem. tech. adv. com. Creative Application of Tech. to Edn., Tex. A. and M. U., 1966-68; mem. tech. adv. panel, Western Interstate Commn. for Higher Edn., 1969-70; vis. scientist Center for Applied Math., Nat. Bur. Standards, 1981-82; chmn. program com. 1985 World Conf. on Computers in Edn. Purdue Research Found. fellow, 1954-55; NSF grantee, 1966—; Esso Edn. Found. grantee, 1966; IBM grantee, 1966. Fellow AAAS; mem. Assn. Computing Machinery (chmn. edn. com. 1964-66, reviewer for computing revs. 1968, sec. 1972-76, chmn. curriculum com. on computer sci. 1976-80, gen. chmn. 1981 computer sci. conf.), Inst. Math. Stats. (subcom. math. tables 1958-70), Assn. Ednl. Data Systems (pres. 1968-69, award 1971, sec. 1976-77, dir. 1975-79, chmn. conv. adv. com. 1977-79), Am. Fedn. Info. Processing Socs. (edn. com. 1965—, dir. 1981—, chmn. edn. com. 1971-72, 79—), Soc. Indsl. and Applied Math., Am. Statis. Assn., Math. Assn. Am., Sigma Xi, Pi Mu Epsilon, Upsilon Pi Epsilon, Alpha Chi Sigma. Editor Ednl. Data Processing Newsletter, 1964-65; asso. editor Jour. Ednl. Data Processing, 1965-67; editor Jour. of Assn. Ednl. Data Systems, 1967-68. Contbr. articles to profl. publs. Home: Route 1 Box 256A Saint James MO 65559 Office: Dept Computer Sci U Mo Rolla MO 65401

HAMBURGER, RICHARD JAMES, physician; b. Phila., Feb. 2, 1937; s. W. Charles and Margaretha Gertrude (Schwab) H.; B.S., Villanova U., 1958; M.D., Jefferson Med. Coll., 1962; m. Mary Jane Murphy, Jan. 25, 1964; children—Ellen, Joan, Mary Lou, Richard, Maureen, James. Intern, Jefferson Med. Coll., Phila., 1962-63, resident in medicine, 1963-65, fellow in nephrology, 1965-66; practice medicine specializing in nephrology, Indpls., 1968—; mem. staff Ind. U. Hosp., Wishard Meml. Hosp., VA Hosp.; asst. prof. Ind. U. Sch. Medicine, 1968-72, asso. prof., 1972-77, prof., 1977—. Trustee Kidney Found. Ind., 1970-74, mem. med. adv. bd., 1969—. Served with AUS, 1966-68. Diplomate Am. Bd. Internal Medicine. Fellow A.C.P.; mem. Ind. Soc. Internal Medicine (trustee 1975-77), N. Central Dialysis and Transplant Soc. (dir. 1972-75, 78-81), Am. Soc. Nephrology, Internat. Soc. Nephrology, Am. Soc. Artificial Internal Organs, Am. Fedn. Clin. Research, Nat. Kidney Found., Am. Soc. Internal Medicine, Renal Physicians Assn. (dir. 1977—). Roman Catholic Clubs: Indpls. Racquet, Meridian Hills Country. Contbr. articles to profl. jours. Home: 1215 Chessington Rd Indianapolis IN 46260 Office: 1100 Michigan St W Indianapolis IN 46223

HAMDY, AZIZ (HAMED), scientist; b. Cairo, Egypt, Dec. 7, 1929; naturalized U.S. citizen; s. Hamed and Nefisa (Sultan) H.; D.V.M., Cairo U., 1953; M.S., Ohio State U., 1956, Ph.D., 1958; m. Heidi H. Mawardi, Dec. 14, 1960. Instr. Ohio Agrl. Exp., Sta. Dept. Vet. Sci., 1954-58; research asso. U.S. Naval Med. Research Unit, NAMRU-3, 1958-60, asso. prof. vet. preventive medicine Ohio Agr. Research and Devel. Center and Ohio State U., 1960-66; sci. animal health research and devel. Upjohn Co., 1966—, currently sr. scientist. Diplomate Am. Coll. Vet. Microbiology. Mem. AVMA, Am. Soc. Microbiology, Conf. Research Workers, AAAS, N.Y. Acad. Sci., Phi Zeta. Rotarian. Research on bovine respiratory diseases, swine diseases, poultry diseases and mycoplasma. Home: 1781 Greenbriar Dr Kalamazoo MI 49008 Office: Upjohn Co Kalamazoo MI 49001

HAMEEDUDDIN, ANJUM, physician; b. India, Apr. 13, 1949; d. Maqbool Ahmed Ansari and Shamin Ara; came to U.S., 1972; M.B.B.S., Osmania Med. Coll., India, 1972; m. Mir, Feb. 21, 1971; children—Nasia, Asim. Intern, W. Suburban Hosp., Oak Park, Ill., 1973-74; resident in family practice, St. Joseph Hosp., Chgo., 1974-76, attending physician, 1976—, instr. residents; family practice medicine, Chgo., 1976—. Recipient best outgoing intern award W. Suburban Hosp., 1975. Diplomate Am. Bd. Family Practice. Mem. AMA, Ill. Med. Soc., Chgo. Med. Soc. Muslim. Office: 2913 N Commonwealth St Chicago IL 60657

HAMEISTER, LAVON LOUETTA, social worker; b. Blairstown, Iowa, Nov. 27, 1922; d. George Frederick and Bertha (Anderson) Hameister; B.A., U. Iowa, 1944; postgrad. N.Y. Sch. Social Work, Columbia, 1945-46, U. Minn. Sch. Social Work, summer 1952; M.A., U. Chgo., 1959. Child welfare practitioner Fayette County Dept. Social Welfare, West Union, Iowa, 1946-56; dist. cons. services in child welfare and pub. assistance Iowa Dept. Social Welfare, Des Moines, 1956-58, dist. field rep., 1959-64, regional supr., 1964-65, supr., specialist supervision, adminstrn. Bur. Staff Devel., 1965-66, chief Bur. Staff Devel., 1966-68; chief div. staff devel. and tng. Office Dep. Commr., Iowa Dept. Social Services, 1968-72, asst. dir. Office Staff Devel., 1972-79, coordinator continuing edn., 1979—. Active in drive to remodel, enlarge Oelwein (Iowa) Mercy Hosp., 1952. Mem. Bus. and Profl. Women's Club (chpt. sec. 1950-52), Am. Assn. U. Women, Nat. Assn. Social Workers (chpt. sec.-elect 1958-59), Am. Pub. Welfare Assn., Iowa Welfare Assn., Acad. Cert. Social Workers. Lutheran. Home: 1800 Grand Ave West Des Moines IA 50265 Office: State Office Bldg Des Moines IA 50319

HAMEL, LOUIS REGINALD, systems analysis cons.; b. Lowell, Mass., July 23, 1945; s. Wilfred John and Angelina Lucienne (Paradis) H.; A.A., Kellogg Community Coll., 1978; m. Roi Anne Roberts, Mar. 24, 1967 (dec.); 1 dau., Felicia Antoinette; m. 2d, Anne Louise Staup, July 2, 1972; 1 dau., Shawna Michelle. Retail mgr. Marshalls dept. Stores, Beverly, Mass., 1972-73; tech. service rep. Monarch Marking Systems, Framingham, Mass., 1973-74; employment specialist Dept. Labor, Battle Creek, Mich., 1977-78; v.p. corp. Keith Polygraph Cons. and Investigative Service, Inc., Battle Creek, Mich., 1978-79; systems analysis cons., 1975—. Mem. Calhoun County Com. on Employment of Handicapped, Battle Creek, Mich., 1977-78. Served with USN, 1963-71; Vietnam. Recipient Services to Handicapped award Internat. Assn. Personnel in Employment Security, Mich. chpt., 1978. Mem. Nat. Geog. Soc., Mich. Assn. Concerned Vets. (dir.), Nat. Assn. Concerned Vets., VFW. Democrat. Roman Catholic. Home and Office: 12240 Assyria Rd Bellevue MI 49021

HAMELINK, JERRY H., mech. engr.; b. Hamilton, Mich., Mar. 16, 1940; s. Marinus H. and Edith H.; student Hope Coll., 1958-60; B.S. in Mech. Engring., Mich. Tech. U., 1963; postgrad Brigham Young U., 1963-64, Western Mich. U., 1970-75; M.S. in Mech. Engring., Mich. Tech. U., 1967; Ed.D., W.Va. U., 1978; m. Nancy Lou Tellman, Aug. 21, 1965; children—Greg Matthew, Nathan Eric, Faith Christine, Michael Steven. Turbine insp. Consumers Power Co., Jackson, Mich., 1964-66; utilities staff engr. Upjohn Co., Kalamazoo, 1967-68; prof. mech. engring. Western Mich. U., Kalamazoo, 1968—; cons. in field. Mem. Zoning Bd. Wakeshma Twp., 1971-72; clk. Wakeshma Twp., 1973-78, supr., 1978—. NSF grantee, 1973; registered profl. engr. Mich. Mem. ASME, Am. Soc. Engring. Edn., Am. Soc. Exptl. Stress Analysis, Tau Beta Pi, Pi Tau Sigma. Author: Engineering Experimentation, 3d edit., 1981; contbr. articles to profl. jours. Home: 13305 W Ave Vicksburg MI 49097 Office: Dept Mech Engring Western Mich U Kalamazoo MI 49006

HAMILL, ARNOLD GENE, clergyman; b. Clearwater, Nebr., Feb. 1, 1940; s. Robert John and Catherine H.; B.R.E., Grace Coll. Bible, 1962; student U. Nebr., Omaha, 1963, 64, Trinity Evang. Div. Sch., 1978—; m. Inez O. Honeywell, June 17, 1961; children—Jerald Lee, Brian Gene. Ordained to ministry Evang. Free Ch., 1967; pastor Emmaus Evang. Free Ch., Funk, Nebr., 1964-71; chmn. Mid-Nebr. Youth for Christ, 1968-70; pastor East Chain Evang. Free Ch., Granada, Minn., 1971-78; 1st vice-chmn. Camp Shamineau Bible Camp, Motley, Minn., 1976-77; pastor Cary (Ill.)-Grove Evang. Free Ch., 1978—, bd. dirs. Gt. Lakes dist. Evang. Free Ch., South-West Youth for Christ in Minn.; youth rep. North Central dist. Christian Edn. Bd. Address: 506 W Ada St Cary IL 60013

HAMILTON, BETH ALLEMAN, info. scientist; b. Stewartstown, W.Va., Apr. 3, 1927; d. Hubert Charles and Gay Elizabeth (Zearley) Alleman; B.S., W.Va. U., 1948; M.A., Rosary Coll., 1969; C.A.S., U. Chgo., 1977; m. Rex Hamilton, Apr. 17, 1949; children—Shelley Hamilton Hutter, Meredith L., Eric R., Elizabeth Hamilton Gruhn, John Z. Chemist, Standard Pharmacal, Chgo., 1948-49; tech. librarian Am. Meat Inst. Found., Chgo., 1949-51; research librarian Glidden Co., Chgo., 1952-53; owner, partner Hamilton Truck Leasing, Elk Grove Village, Ill., 1957-63; editor, bus. analyst Internat. Minerals & Chem. Corp., Skokie, Ill., 1964-69; sci. librarian, asso. prof. U. Ill., Chgo., 1969-72, adj. asso. prof., 1972—; exec. dir. Ill. Regional Library Council, Chgo., 1972-79; vis. lectr. Rosary Coll., 1970-71; vis. asst. prof. U. Ill. Grad. Sch. Library Sci., Urbana, 1977—. Mem. Dist. 25 Bd. Edn., Arlington Heights, Ill., 1966-70; mem. Burr Ridge (Ill.) Bicentennial Commn., 1975-76; exec. v.p. Republican Women's Club of Lyons Twp., 1975-76; librarian, tchr. First Presbyterian Ch. of Arlington Heights, 1960-69. Mem. Am. Chem Soc., Spl. Libraries Assn. (joint task force with Nat. Commn. on Libraries and Info. Sci. on role of the Spl. library), ALA, Beta Phi Mu. Editor: Libraries and Information Centers in the Chicago Metropolitan Area, 1973; Union List of Serial Holdings in Illinois Special Libraries, 1976, 77; Multitype Library Cooperation, 1977; (with others) As Much to Learn as to Teach: Essays in Honor of Lester Asheim, 1979; contbr. articles to profl. jours. Home: 2420 Fir St Glenview IL 60025 Office: Triodyne Inc Cons Engrs 7855 Gross Point Rd Skokie IL 60077

HAMILTON, DAVID LEE, univ. adminstr.; b. Ashland, Ohio, June 25, 1935; s. Weldon Roy and Pauline Leota (Cole) H.; B.S. in Edn., Ashland Coll., 1957; M.A., Ohio State U., 1968, Ph.D. (Battelle Meml. Inst. fellow), 1977; m. Carolyn Ann Copen, Dec. 7, 1968; children—Laura Ellen, Sarah Elizabeth. Tchr. Ruggles-Troy Local Schs., 1956-57, Norton City Schs., 1957-59; tchr. Ashland City Schs., 1963-64, adminstr., 1964-68; asso. exec. Ohio Sch. Bds. Assn., 1968-69; exec. Sch. Mgmt. Inst., 1969-71; sr. researcher, mgr. Battelle Meml. Inst., 1971-77; dir. Bur. Ednl. Field Services, Miami U., Oxford, Ohio, 1978—; cons. U.S. Office Edn., U.S. AID, several state depts. edn. Served with U.S. Army, 1959-62. Mem. Am. Assn. Sch. Adminstrs., Am. Ednl. Research Assn., Buckeye Assn. Sch. Adminstrs., Nat. Soc. for Study Edn., Soc. for Advancement Mgmt., Assn. for Supervision and Curriculum Devel., Acad. Mgmt., Council Ednl. Facility Planners Internat., Phi Delta Kappa. Club: Elks. Author: Comprehensive Needs Assessment for Community and Jr. Colleges, 1973; Usher Redesign Model, 1975; School Community Climate Survey and Guide, 1976; Professional Inservice Improvement Guide, 1977. Home: 2544 Adda Ave Columbus OH 43229 Office: 311 McGuffey Hall Miami U Oxford OH 45056

HAMILTON, FRANKLIN JAMES, restaurant exec.; b. Detroit, Mar. 8, 1943; s. Howard Campbell and Janet Kathryn (Davis) H.; student Mich. State U., 1962-65; m. Johanna Steyger, Dec. 22, 1973; children—Franklin James, Jennifer Johanna. Vice pres. Janet Davis, Inc., Berkley, Mich., 1963-73; pres. Hamilton Bros., Inc., Berkley, 1973—, Original Pancake House, Inc., Berkley, 1977—; v.p. Pancake House of Grosse Pointe, Inc. (Mich.), 1977—. Mem. Nat. Restaurant Assn., Mich. Restaurant Assn., Detroit Dry Cleaning Laundry Inst., Internat. Fabricare Inst. Presbyterian. Club: Pine Lake Country. Office: 2165 Woodward Ave Berkley MI 48072

HAMILTON, GARY, soil scientist; b. Herrin, Ill., Jan. 17, 1943; s. Ulysses Simpson and Josephine (Petroski) H.; B.S., So. Ill. U., 1966, M.S., 1972; 1 dau., Julie Jo. Grad. asst. So. Ill. U., Carbondale, 1971-72; coal miner Old Ben Coal Co., Benton, Ill., 1972-74; soil scientist Soil Conservation Service U.S. Dept. Agr., Charleston, Ill., 1974—. Served with U.S. Army, 1966-68. Mem. Soil Sci. Soc. Am., Soil Conservation Soc. Am., Ill. Soil Classifiers Assn. Democrat. Lutheran. Club: Elks. Home: 931 W Polk Charleston IL 61920 Office: Rural Route 2 Box 109 Charleston IL 61920

HAMILTON, HENRY LEE, JR., printing systems co. exec.; b. Phila., Nov. 23, 1941; s. Henry Lee and Marie (Erby) H.; B.S., Va. Union U., 1967; children—Faith, Donna, Henry Lee, Joy. Tchr. sci. Richmond (Va.) Public Schs., 1967; mktg. rep. IBM Corp., Cranford, N.J., 1969-74; mktg. rep. Xerox Printing System, N.Y.C., 1974-78, br. mgr., 1978—. Democrat. Baptist. Club: Masons. Address: 5257 Wright Way E West Bloomfield MI 48033

HAMILTON, JAMES JOSEPH, orthopedic surgeon; b. Chgo., Dec. 10, 1945; s. Gene Charles and Eleanor Florence (Fordon) H.; B.A., Northwestern U., 1967; M.D., Med. Coll. Wis., 1971, M.S., 1976; m. Linda Kay Ziemer, Nov. 10, 1979. Intern, Parkland Meml. Hosp., Dallas, 1971-72; resident in orthopedics Milw. Affiliated Hosps., 1972-76; commd. maj. U.S. Army, 1976; asst. prof. anatomy and orthopedic surgery Uniformed Services U. Health Scis., Bethesda, Md., 1976-80; cons. orthopedics, course dir. Armed Forces Inst. Pathology, Washington, 1978-80; asst. prof. orthopedic surgery Georgetown U., Washington, 1979-80; asso. prof., chmn. orthopedic surgery U. Mo./Truman Med. Center, Kansas City, 1980—; med. adv. Nat. Ski Patrol System, 1972—; instr., trainer ARC, 1976—. Diplomate Am. Bd. Orthopedic Surgery. Fellow Am. Acad. Orthopedic Surgery; mem. Soc. Mil. Orthopedic Surgeons, Wash. Orthopedic Soc. Roman Catholic. Club: Nat. Ski Patrol. Home: 8736 Cherokee Ct Leawood KS 66206 Office: Truman Med Center Kansas City MO

HAMILTON, JOHN HANDLEY, machinery mfg. co. exec.; b. Streator, Ill., Sept. 1, 1925; s. James J. and Arlene M. (Diest) H.; B.S., U. Ill., 1949; m. Catherine J. Chambers, Oct. 22, 1949; children—Jeffrey, David, Susan. With Internat. Harvester Corp., now mgr. tech. advanced harvesting systems, Chgo.; agrl. engring. adviser Pa. State U., 1973-79. Served with USAAF, 1943-45; PTO. Recipient agrl. medal and diplome of distinction, French Govt., 1969. Mem. Am. Forage and Grassland Council (dir.), Am., India (U.S. dir.) socs. agrl. engrs., Council for Agrl. Sci. and Tech., N.Y. Acad. Scis., Delta Tau Delta. Home: 1105 Summit Hills Ln Naperville IL 60540 Office: 401 N Michigan Ave Chicago IL 60611

HAMILTON, LEE HERBERT, congressman; b. Daytona Beach, Fla., Apr. 20, 1931; s. Frank and Myra (Jones) H.; A.B. cum laude, DePauw U., 1952; postgrad. Goethe U., Frankfurt au Main, Germany, 1952-53; J.D., Ind. U., 1956; m. Nancy Ann Nelson, Aug. 21, 1954; children—Tracy Lynn, Deborah Lee, Douglas Nelson. Mem. firm Wilkinson, Witwer & Moran, Chgo., 1956-57; partner firm Sharpnack & Bigley, Columbus, Ind.; mem. 89th to 97th congresses from 9th Congl. Dist. Ind., mem. Fgn. Affairs Com., also mem. Post Office and Civil Service Com. Chmn. Bayh for Senator com., 1962, Citizens for Kennedy Com., 1960; treas. Bartholomew County Young Democrats, 1960-63, pres., 1963-64. Chmn., Mayor's Commn. on Human Relations, 1962-63; sec. Columbus Growth, Inc., 1961-64; mem. DePauw U. Nat. Requests Com. Recipient Distinguished Service award, Jr. C. of C., 1962. Mem. Ind. Bar Assn. Methodist. Clubs: Rotary, 89th Congress (pres. 1965—). Office: 2187 Rayburn House Office Bldg Washington DC 20515 *

HAMILTON, MILO CHARLES, bus. economist; b. Columbia, Mo., June 4, 1945; s. Milo Fowler and Katherine (Miller) H.; B.A., Stanford U., 1967; B.S. cum laude, U. Mo., 1974; M.S., U. Minn., 1976; m. Janice Auwaerter, Mar. 3, 1973; children—Laura Jennifer, Renee Christine. Farm mgr. Green Top Farms Inc., Richmond, Mo., 1972; research asst. agrl. econs., U. Minn., St. Paul, 1974-76; mng. editor Commodities mag., also editor Commodities Report, Cedar Falls, Iowa, 1976-80; research dir., sr. partner Futures Portfolio Index Services div. Hamilton and Wasendorf, also editor Futures Portfolio Advisor, Cedar Falls, Iowa, 1980-81; comml. tech. mgr. Uncle Ben's, Inc., Cedar Falls, 1981—; lectr. Center for Futures Edn.; cons. in field. Served with U.S. Army, 1969-72. Mem. Stanford Alumni Orgn., Council for Agrl. Sci. and Tech., Rate Watchers. Democrat. Lutheran. Club: Rotary. Author: Multiply Your Profits Through Commodity Speculation, 1979. Home: 2520 Alameda St Cedar Falls IA 50613 Office: 1904 Main St Cedar Falls IA 50613

HAMILTON, RICHARD ALFRED, univ. adminstr., educator; b. Pitts., Dec. 22, 1941; s. Robert Curtis and Dorothy Katherine (Sexauer) H.; B.A., Otterbein Coll., 1965; M.B.A., Bowling Green State U., 1968; D.Bus. Adminstrn. (Univ. fellow 1968-71, Marathon Oil Co. dissertation fellow 1972), Kent State U., 1973. Production rate analyst dept. indsl. engring. RCA, Findlay, Ohio, 1966-67; computer systems analyst dept. market research Marathon Oil Co., Findlay, 1967-68; teaching fellow Coll. Bus. Adminstrn. Kent State U., 1968-71; asso. dean, asso. prof. mktg. U. Mo., Kansas City, 1971—; pres. Mission Woods Cons., Inc.; univ. asso. Lawrence Leiter and Co.; dir. Fin. Equipment Trust, Inc., U.S. Mailing Equipment, Inc.; cons. U.S. Senate Permanent Subcom. on Investigation, 1973-74, Midwest Research Inst. and Office of Tech. Assessment of U.S. Congress, 1974-75; speaker to profl. orgns. Mem. Am. Acad. Advt., Am. Inst. Decision Scis., Am. Mktg. Assn., Assn. M.B.A. Execs., Sales, Mktg. Execs., Beta Gamma Sigma. Methodist. Author: (with David R. Bywaters) How to Conduct Association Surveys, 1976; Tourism U.S.A.-Marketing Tourism, Vol. 3, 1978; rev. editor Akron Bus. and Econ. Rev., 1977—. Home: 5306 Mission Woods Rd Mission Woods KS 66205 Office: Sch of Adminstrn U of Mo Kansas City MO 64110

HAMILTON, ROBERT APPLEBY, JR., ins. co. exec.; b. Boston, Feb. 20, 1940; s. Robert A. and Alice Margaret (Dowdall) H.; student Miami U. (Ohio), 1958-62; m. Ellen Kuhlen, Aug. 13, 1966; children—Jennifer, Robert Appleby, III, Elizabeth. With Travelers Ins. Co., Hartford, Conn., Portland, Maine and Phila., 1962-65; with New Eng. Mut. Life Ins. Co., various locations, 1965—, regional rep., Boston, 1968-71, regional mgr., Chgo., 1972—. Mem. Republican Town Com., Wenham, Mass., 1970-72, Milton Twp., Ill., 1973-75; mem. Wenham Water Commn., 1970-72. C.L.U. Mem. Midwest Pension Conf., Am. Soc. Pension Actuaries (asso.), Am. Soc. C.L.U., Chgo. Council Fgn. Relations, Alpha Epsilon Rho. Republican. Home: 2 S 110 Hamilton Ct Wheaton IL 60187 Office: 10 S Riverside Plaza Chicago IL 60606

HAMILTON, WOODROW WENDELL, magazine publisher; b. Canton, Ill., Dec. 26, 1917; s. Oliver Wendell and Carrie (Harding) H.; B.S. in Indsl. Engring., Northwestern U., 1941; m. Constance Kemp Booth, Aug. 26, 1944; children—Linda Kemp, Thomas Francis. Materials handling engr. Link Belt Co., Chgo., 1945-47; asst. sales mgr. Internat. Register Co., Chgo., 1947-51; sales mgr. Harold Products Co., Chgo., 1951-53; pub. Water and Sewage Works mag., Des Plaines, Ill., 1953—. Squadron comdr. CAP, 1965-69. Served to lt. col. USAAF, 1941-45. Mem. Am. Water Works Assn. (dir.), Water and Wastewater Equipment Mfrs. Assn. (dir.), Water Pollution Control Fedn., Phi Delta Theta. Presbyterian. Club: Masons. Home: 1795 Northland Ave Highland Park IL 60035 Office: 380 Northwest Hwy Des Plaines IL 60016

HAMISTER, DONALD BRUCE, electronics co. exec.; b. Cleve., Nov. 29, 1920; s. Victor Carl and Bess Irene (Sutherland) H.; A.B. cum laude, Kenyon Coll., 1947; postgrad. Stanford U., 1948-49, U. Chgo., 1957; m. Margaret Irene Singiser, Dec. 22, 1946; children—Don Bruce, Tracy. Application engr. S.E. Joslyn Co., Cin., 1947-48; regional sales mgr. Joslyn Mfg. & Supply Co., St. Louis, 1950-52, marketing mgr., Chgo., 1953-55, asst. to pres., 1956-57, mgr. aircraft arrester dept., 1958-62, gen. mgr. electronic systems div., 1962-71, v.p., gen. mgr., dir., Goleta, Calif., 1973-78, group v.p. indsl. products, 1974-78, pres., chief exec. officer, Chgo., 1978—, chmn., 1979—; dir. Porcelanas Pinco, Mex., Joslyn Can. Industries Ltd., Little, Haugland and Kerr Ltd., Can. Served to lt. USNR, 1942-46. Mem. I.E.E.E., Airline Avionics Inst. (pres., chmn. 1972-74). Club: University (Chgo.). Home: Univ Club Chgo 76 E Monroe St Chicago IL 60603 also 1141 Camino del Rio Santa Barbara CA 93110 Office: 2 N Riverside Plaza Chicago IL 60606

HAMLETT, IONA CUYLER, psychologist; b. Austin, Tex., Dec. 12, 1901; d. Robert Henry and Sarah Iona (McBryde) Cuyler; A.B., U. Tex., 1922, A.M., 1923; Ph.D., U. Ind., 1934; m. G. W. Deluz Hamlett, Aug. 29, 1923 (div. 1934); children—Iona Helen (Mrs. James Richard Mensch), Sarah Suzanne (Mrs. Gordon M. Haggard). Ednl., clin. psychologist Ft. Wayne (Ind.) State Hosp. and Tng. Center, 1934-72, dir. dept. psychol. services, 1966-72; pvt. practice psychology, Ft. Wayne, 1972—. Fellow Am. Assn. on Mental Deficiency (chmn. Gt. Lakes region 1963), Am. Psychol. Assn., Internat. Council Psychologists; mem. Ind. Psychol. Assn. (diplomate clin. psychology), Allen County Assn. Mental Health. Presbyn. Home: Box 5131 Hazelwood Sta Fort Wayne IN 46895 Office: 3010 E State Blvd Fort Wayne IN 46895

HAMLIN, ALLENE GAY, civic worker; b. Highland, Ill., May 11, 1946; d. Israel Benjamin and Margaret Virginia (Eckmann) Hiken; ed. schs. for visually handicapped, secretarial tng.; m. Leonard Albert Hamlin, Oct. 12, 1968; children—Eric Garrett, Stephen Wayne. Mem. adv. sch. bd. Sunnyside Sch., 1979-80; comdr. Red Wing chpt. DAV Aux., 1978—, chaplain state dept., 1979—, sr. vice comdr., 1977-78, publicity chmn. Minn. dept., 1978-79, patriotic instr. Minn. dept., 1980—, patriotic instr. dept. Minn., 1981—, recipient past comdrs. pin, 1979; transcriber Braille books. Republican. Baptist. Home: 1527 Central Ave Red Wing MN 55066

HAMLIN, GRIFFITH ASKEW, clergyman, educator; b. Richmond, Va., Feb. 24, 1919; s. Charles Hunter and Mary Virginia (Griffith) H.; B.A., Atlantic Christian Coll., 1939; M.R.E., Lexington Theol. Sem., 1942; B.D., Duke U., 1946; Th.D., Iliff Sch. Theology, 1953; M.S. in Edn., So. Ill. U., 1968; m. Margaret Geneva Cook, June 1, 1943; children—Griffith Askew, John Charles. Ordained to ministry Christian Ch., 1939; asso. prof. religion and philosophy Atlantic Christian Coll., 1948-50; pastor First Christian Ch., Hampton, Va., 1951-57, Goldsboro, N.C., 1957-61; chmn. div. humanities, prof. religion William Woods Coll., Fulton, Mo., 1961—, registrar, 1969-73. Active, Kingdom of Callaway Hist. Assn.; county rep. Mo. Symphony Soc., 1974; bd. dirs. Disciples of Christ Hist. Soc., 1970-71. Recipient Distinguished Prof. award, 1968, Centennial award, 1970, Alumni Appreciation award, 1971 (all William Woods Coll.); Monticello Coll. Found. award for research and writing, 1973-75. N.Y. U. fellow, summer 1965. Mem. Am. Acad. Religion, Smithsonian Assos., Internat. Council Edn. for Teaching. Club: Masons. Author: The Old Testament: Its Intent and Content, 1959; In Faith and History: The Story of William Woods College, 1965; Monticello: The Biography of a College, 1976; William Woods College: The Cutlip Years, 1981. Home: 201 Lynn Ave Fulton MO 65251 Office: William Woods Coll Fulton MO 65251

HAMLIN, JANE GREENE, curriculum specialist; b. Washington, Nov. 26, 1934; d. Roosevelt Brown and Mildred Lola (Hendrix) Greene; B.S., Purdue U., 1956; M.Ed., Nat. Coll. Ed., 1975; m. Richard Peter Hamlin, Aug. 11, 1956; children—Diane, Peter, David, Andrea. Tchr., N.W. Suburban Spl. Edn. Orgn., Palatine, Ill., 1974-80; curriculum specialist Behavior Edn. Center, Wheeling, Ill., 1980—. Mem. Northfield Village Caucus, 1981—. Office Supt. Public Instrn. fellow, 1974. Mem. Ill. Council Exceptional Children (govt. relations regional coordinator), Assn. Supervision and Curriculum Devel., NEA, Phi Delta Kappa, Phi Mu. Republican. Mem. United Ch. of Christ. Club: Les Portfolio. Office: 1001 W Dundee St Wheeling IL 60090

HAMLIN, RICHARD EUGENE, coll. pres.; b. Royal, Iowa, June 2, 1925; s. Fred E. and Nancy Jane (Schuetz) H.; student Drury Coll., 1943; B.S., George Williams Coll., 1949; M.A., U. Omaha, 1952; Ph.D., U. Nebr., 1956; m. C. Joan Dahl, Aug. 14, 1949; children—Robert E., Elizabeth Ann. Asst. camp dir., camp counselor, asst. youth sec. YMCA, 1946-49, exec. sec. South Omaha (Nebr.) YMCA, 1949-51, program sec., adult edn. dir., Omaha, 1951-53, asso. dir. research nat. bd., 1953-61; pres. George Williams Coll., 1961—; tchr. summer confs. Am. Youth Found., summer sch. U. Omaha; chmn. bd., dir. Bank Yorktown, Lombard Ill. Mem. Am. Psychol. Assn., Downers Grove C. of C. (chmn. bd. 1974-76), Fedn. Ind. Ill. Colls. and Univs. (chmn.), Alpha Omicron Alpha (past pres.). Conglist. (lay moderator). Clubs: Economic, University (Chgo.). Author: Hi-Y Today, 1955; A New Look at YMCA Physical Education, 1957. Co-editor: YMCA Yearbook, 1958-61. Home: 3908 Forest Dr Downers Grove IL 60515

HAMM, VERNON LOUIS, JR., mgmt. and fin. cons.; b. East St. Louis, Ill., Mar. 14, 1951; s. Vernon Louis and Colleen Ann Hamm; B.S., Murray (Ky.) State U., 1973; M.B.A., St. Louis U., 1975; postgrad. Stanford U., 1975. Jr. exec. corp. accounts Brown Group, Inc., St. Louis, 1973-75; group supr. APC Skills Co., Palm Beach, Fla., 1975-77; account mgr. Inst. Mgmt. Resources, Los Angeles, 1977-78; dir. mgmt. devel. Naus & Newlyn, Inc., Paoli, Pa., 1978—; mgmt.-fin. cons., 1975—; dir. Psychosystems Mgmt. Corp., N.Y.C. Mem. Am. Soc. for Tng. and Devel., Am. Prodn. and Inventory Control Soc., Murray State U. Alumni Assn. Contbr. articles to profl. publs.

HAMMEKE, THOMAS ALAN, neuropsychologist; b. Great Bend, Kans., Dec. 10, 1950; s. Melvin F. and Lorraine (Torline) H.; B.S. summa cum laude Fort Hays (Kans.) State U., 1973, M.S., 1975; Ph.D. in Clin. Psychology, U. S.D., 1978; m. Sharon L. Howard, Aug. 14, 1971; children—Megan, Erin. Psychology intern VA Hosp., Wood, Wis., 1977-78; postdoctoral fellow dept. neurology Med. Coll. of Wis., Milw., 1978-79, asst. prof. neurology and psychiatry, 1979—; lectr. neuropsychology to various community and profl. groups, 1979—. Instl. research grantee, 1980; lic. psychologist, Wis. Mem. Am. Psychol. Assn., Midwest Neuropsychol. Soc., Internat. Neuropsychol. Soc., Assn. for Advancement of Behavior Therapy. Roman Catholic. Author: (with A.D. Purisch and C.J. Golden) Experimental and Clinical Uses of the Luria-Nebraska Neuropsychological Battery, 1978; contbr. articles on neuropsychology to psychol. jours. Home: 1118 N 69th St Wauwatosa WI 53213 Office: 9001 W Watertown Plank Rd Milwaukee WI 53226

HAMMER, JOHN HENRY, II, personnel adminstr.; b. Bartlesville, Okla., Dec. 27, 1943; s. John Henry and Lucy (Macias) H.; B.B.A., St. Joseph's Coll., 1966; student U. Md. (Europe), 1968-69; m. Michele Evano, June 27, 1970; children—John Henry, Erica. Project mgr. Economic & Manpower Corp., N.Y.C., 1971-73; asst. dir. human resources St. Catherine Hosp., East Chicago, Ind., 1974-80, pres. Employees Credit Union, 1974-80; dir. personnel Lakeview Med. Center, Danville, Ill., 1980—. Chmn., De La Garza Career Center Program Com., 1974-80; chmn. Calumet Coll. Summer Festival, 1978-79. Served to capt. USAF, 1967-71. Mem. Ind. Soc. Hosp. Personnel Adminstrn. (chmn. 1976-77, dir. 1977-79, pres. 1979-80), Am. Soc. Hosp. Personnel Adminstrn., Am. Soc. Personnel Adminstrn., Am. Mgmt. Assn., Roman Catholic. Home: 1324 N Walnut Ave Danville IL 61832 Office: 812 N Logan Ave Danville IL 61832

HAMMER, RANDY LEE, psychologist; b. N.Y.C., Mar. 3, 1948; s. Burton and Annette (Greenberg) H.; B.A., Washington U., 1970, Ph.D., 1975; m. Kathryn Ann Berger, Nov. 23, 1977; children—Alison Mary, Elizabeth Anne. Research asst. Washington U., St. Louis, 1971-75; pvt. practice psychology, St. Louis, 1975—; psychologist dept. phys. medicine Jewish Hosp., St. Louis, 1975—, asst. dir. biofeedback clinic dept. psychiatry, 1975-77; asso. med. staff Washington U. Med. Sch. Hosps., St. Louis, 1977—; pres. Psychotherapy, Inc., St. Louis, 1981—; cons. St. Louis Heart Assn., Multiple Risk Factor Intervention Trial project, 1976-80. Mem. adv. council Washington U. Child Guidance Clinic, 1977-80. Lic. psychologist, Mo.; cert. sexual therapist. Mem. Mo. Psychol. Assn., Am. Psychol. Assn., Mo. Biofeedback Soc. (treas. 1978-80), St. Louis Soc. Psychologists, Am. Assn. Sex Educators, Counselors, and Therapists. Jewish. Club: Westwood Country. Home: 505 Bonhomme Forest Olivette MO 63132 Office: 4625 Lindell St Suite 315 Saint Louis MO 63108

HAMMER, THOMAS ALOYSIOUS, JR., banker; b. N.Y.C., Sept. 22, 1917; s. Thomas A. and Jeannette M. (McLaughlin) H.; B.A., Williams Coll., 1939; M.B.A., Harvard U., 1941; m. Patricia Fitzgerald, Apr. 27, 1946; 1 dau., Tricia F. Asst. treas, asst. controller Doehler-Jarvis Corp., Toledo, 1941-53; exec. asst. to v.p. fin. The Carrier Corp., Syracuse, N.Y., 1953-57; v.p. fin. The Mead Corp., Dayton, Ohio, 1957-73; chmn. bd. The Central Trust Co., Dayton, 1973—; cons. in field. Trustee, pres. St. Elizabeth Med. Center, Dayton, 1970—, St. Elizabeth Community Health Found., Dayton, 1980—; trustee, pres. Wegerzyn Garden Center, Dayton, 1976—; commr. Ohio Student Loan Commn., 1974-76; bd. dirs., pres. Harvard Bus. Sch. Club, Dayton, 1965-75. Served to lt., USNR, 1943-46. Mem. Fin. Execs. Inst. Republican. Roman Catholic. Clubs: Sycamore Creek Country, Racquet, Queen City. Home: 3146 Upper Bellbrook Rd Bellbrook OH 45305 Office: 112 W 2d St Dayton OH 45402

HAMMER, WILLIAM EARL, JR., chem. and processing equipment mfg. co. exec.; b. Dayton, Ohio, Oct. 25, 1939; s. William Earl and Della Eyvonne (Nickell) H.; B.I.E., U. Dayton, 1962; M.S., Ohio State U., 1968; m. Beverly Gail Houston, June 15, 1963; children—Heidi Jo, William Earl III, Mark Jeffrey. Engr., Western Electric Co., Inc., Columbus, Ohio, 1962-64, planning engr., 1964-67; sr. indsl. engr. Duriron Co., Inc., Dayton, 1967-69, mgr. systems and procedures, 1969-77, dir. info. systems, 1977—. Mem. Am. Inst. Indsl. Engrs. (sr.). Republican. Presbyterian. Club: Engrs. Office: Duriron Co Inc 425 N Findlay St Dayton OH 45401

HAMMERQUIST, DONALD WILLIAM, engring. co. exec.; b. Hill City, S.D., Apr. 25, 1920; s. Anton William and Martha Eileen (Brooks) H.; B.S., S.D. Sch. Mines and Tech., 1950; M.A., Washington U., St. Louis, 1952; m. Ardeth May Liebnow, June 2, 1951; children—Marcia Marie, David Bruce, Jane Alice, Donald Wade, James Daniel, Allen Wayne. Various positions in engring. in various locations, 1952-58; faculty S.D. Sch. Mines and Tech., Rapid City, 1958-72, asso. prof. engring., to 1972; owner, mgr. Dakota Found. and Testing, Rapid City, 1972—. Served with U.S. Army, 1943-45. Decorated Bronze Star. Registered profl. engr., S.D., Wyo., Nebr., Ill. Mem. Nat. Soc. Profl. Engrs., VFW, Am. Legion, Sons of Norway, Sigma Xi. Lutheran. Contbr. articles to profl. jours. Home: 1515 9th St Rapid City SD 57701 Office: 1220 Creek Dr PO Box 8152 Rapid City SD 57701

HAMMES, BARBARA PHILLIPS, sch. adminstr.; b. Bklyn., May 25, 1952; d. John Joseph and Margaret (Cervone) Phillips; B.S., Ill. State U., 1973, M.S., 1975; cert. of advanced study Nat. Coll. Edn., 1981—; m. Richard G. Hammes, Nov. 19, 1978. Speech and lang. pathologist Aurora, Ill., 1975-76; dir. Keeler Sch., Aurora, 1976—; owner retail clothing store, St. Charles, Ill., 1979-80. Mem. sch. adv. bds. West Aurora High Sch., Head Start, Mid-Valley Vocat. Sch. Mem. Nat. Assn. Retarded Citizens, Ill. Assn. Retarded Citizens, Am. Speech and Hearing Assn., Assn. Supervision and Curriculum Devel., Ill. Assn. Supervision and Curriculum Devel. Home: 946 Bellevue Ave Elgin IL 60120

HAMMES, GEORGE ALBERT, bishop; b. LaCrosse, Wis., Sept. 11, 1911; s. August Isidore and Caroline (Schumacher) H.; student St. Lawrence Sem., Mt. Calvary, Wis., 1925-31, St. Louis Prep. Sem., 1931-33, Kenrick Sem., St. Louis, 1933-34, Sulpician Sem., Washington, 1934-37; M.A., Cath. U. Am., 1937; L.H.D. (hon.), Mt. Senario Coll., Ladysmith, Wis., 1969. Ordained priest Roman Cath. Ch., 1937; sec. to Bishop Alexander J. McGavick, LaCrosse, Wis., 1937-43; instr. Latin and religion Aquinas High Sch., LaCrosse, 1937-42; instr. ethics and religion St. Francis Sch. Nursing, LaCrosse, 1937-46; chancellor Diocese of LaCrosse, 1943-60; pastor Parish of St. Leo the Great, West Salem, Wis., 1957-60; bishop of Superior, Wis., 1960—. Officialis, Diocesan Matrimonial Tribunal, LaCrosse, 1943-60; diocesan dir. Cath. Lawyers' Guild, LaCrosse, 1956-60, pres. Tri-state Interfaith Devel. Enterprise, Superior, 1970—. Adv. bd. Viterbo Coll., LaCrosse, 1954—, Cath. Social Service, La Crosse, 1954-60; trustee Mt. Senario Coll., Wis., 1969—; bd. dirs. Nat. Tech. Assistance Found., Mpls., 1971—. Home: Gitchinadji Dr Superior WI 54880 Office: 1201 Hughitt Ave Superior WI 54880

HAMMES, RICHARD GEORGE, psychologist; b. Sheboygan, Wis., Feb. 13, 1941; s. Sherman George and Kristine Therese (Mliner) H.; B.S., U. Wis., 1965; M.A., U. Chgo., 1968; Ed.D., No. Ill. U., 1972; m. Barbara Phillips, 1978. Mental health adminstr. Elgin (Ill.) State Hosp., 1968-74; subregional coordinator developmental disabilities Ill. Dept. Mental Health and Developmental Disabilities, Elgin, 1974-80; pres. Human Devel. Corp., Rosemont, Ill., 1980—. Part-time instr. psychology Elgin Community Coll., 1971-78, Coll. of DuPage, Glen Ellyn, Ill., 1972—. Served with AUS, 1959, 61-62. Mem. Am., Midwest, Ill. psychol. assns., Nat. Assn. Social Workers, Acad. Cert. Social Workers, Am. Mgmt. Assn. Author: The Myth of Education in the University, 1976. Home: 667 Grand Ave Elgin IL 60120 Office: 6400 Shafer Ct Rosemont IL 60018

HAMMITT, COURTNEY CLARK, retail co. exec.; b. McKeesport, Pa., Feb. 5, 1915; s. Courtney Clark and Catherine Agnes (Brannan) H.; B.S., Ohio State U., 1939; student Northwestern U., 1942; m. Hannah Marie Reese, Sept. 7, 1947; 1 dau., Mary. Retail and wholesale salesman C.G. Conn Co., Elkhart, Ind., Boston and Chgo., 1939-42; dept. mgr., buyer Strouss Dept. Store div. May Co., New Castle, Pa., 1946-50, divisional mdse. mgr., Warren, Ohio, 1950-51, Youngstown, Ohio, 1951-70, 71-79, v.p. br. stores, gen. mgr. So. Park Mall, Boardman, Ohio, 1946—; dir. Met. Savs. & Loan Co., Youngstown. Chmn. retail and gen. bus. div., chmn. exec. com. United Appeal, 1973-79, campaign chmn., 1981; bd. dirs. Goodwill Industries, pres., 1976-78; active Boy Scouts Am. Served to lt. USNR, 1942-46; PTO. Mem. Westminster Coll. Parents' Assn. (past. pres.), Ohio State Alumni Assn. (pres. Mahoning County 1975-76), So. Park Mall Mchts. Assn. (dir., pres. 1976), Phi Kappa Psi. Baptist. Clubs: Youngstown, Youngstown Country. Home: 173 Alburn Dr Youngstown OH 44512 Office: 7401 Market St Youngstown OH 44512

HAMMITT, JOHN MICHAEL, data processing mgr.; b. Chgo., Sept. 21, 1943; s. John Melvin and Catherine (Ivanuski) H.; B.S. in Chem. Engring., Ill. Inst. Tech., 1970; M.B.A., U. Chgo., 1976. Engring. and research technician Moffett Research Lab., CPC Internat., 1962-67, mgr. process control computer Argo plant, 1968-70; sr. systems analyst Morton-Norwich Products, Inc., Chgo., 1970-72, mgr. corp. info. services, 1972-80, dir. info. mgmt., 1981—; cons. use of computers in lab. automation, 1968-71. Mem. Soc. Mgmt. Info. Systems, Chgo. Council Fgn. Relations, Chgo. Geog. Soc., Phi Theta Kappa. Clubs: Young Execs., Union League. (Chgo.). Home: 312 E Lincoln Barrington IL 60010 Office: 110 N Wacker Dr Chicago IL 60606

HAMMOND, JOHN FARNSWORTH, III, mfg. co. exec.; b. New Orleans, Apr. 27, 1927; s. John Farnsworth and Elizabeth (Raub) H.; student U. Va., 1947-48; B.S., Purdue U., 1960; postgrad. Goshen Coll., 1961; m. Iola Ann Atterberry, Nov. 23, 1957; children—Jacqueline Ann, William Claude. Expediter, Inland Steel Co., Indiana Harbor, Ind., 1948-58; asso. pharmacologist Miles Labs., Elkhart, Ind., 1960-62; pharm. med. rep. Abbott Labs., Oak Park, Ill., 1962-75; lab. med. sales rep. Lancet Med. Industries, Inc., Des Plaines, Ill., 1975-76; lab. med. sales rep. Brown Clin. Labs., Inc., Mt. Prospect, Ill., 1976-80, Parke DeWatt Clin. Lab. Inc., Chgo., 1980—. Pres. Washington Irving Sch. P.T.A., Oak Park, Ill., 1969-71; mem. Indian Guide program YMCA, 1972—; mem. Oak Park Twp. Revenue Sharing Adv. Com., 1973-75; chmn. Oak Park Twp. Revenue Sharing Adv. Task Force, 1973. Served with USNR, 1945-47. Mem. A.A.A.S., Am. Soc. for Microbiology, Purdue U. Alumni Assn. Democrat. Presbyterian (deacon 1968-74). Moose. Club: Purdue. Home: 1163 S Ridgeland Ave Oak Park IL 60304 Office: 111 N Wabash St Chicago IL 60602

HAMMOND, LEE CUSTER, mfg. co. exec.; b. Bristol, Pa., Aug. 19, 1910; s. W. Custer and Mabel E. (Lee) H.; A.B., U. Mich., 1932; m. Hazel M. Hinga, Aug. 25, 1934; children—Steven L., Robert E. Vice pres. Hammond Machinery, Inc., Kalamazoo, 1932-41, pres., 1941—; dir. Am. Nat. Bank & Trust Co., Am. Nat. Holding Co. (both Kalamazoo). Co-trustee Hammond Found.; past trustee Bronson Methodist Hosp., Kalamazoo. Mem. Kalamazoo C. of C.

HAMMONS, KENNETH R., service co. exec.; b. Valeen, Ind., Aug. 1, 1937; s. K. Ernest and Lilly Mable (Early) H.; B.S., Wayne State U., 1970; postgrad. Eastern Mich. U., 1971; m. Angela G. King, Aug. 13, 1960; children—Kenneth R., Gary J., Katrina A., Gregory S., John R. Founder, chief exec. Hammons Maintenance Service Inc., Union Lake, Mich., 1972—. Served with USAF, 1955-59. Home: 10275 Cedar Island Rd Union Lake MI 48085

HAMMONTREE, ROBERT JAMES, civil engr.; b. Akron, Ohio, Dec. 16, 1933; s. Robert James and Helen Martha (Cully) H.; B.C.E., U. Akron, 1957; m. Irene F. Marcinkoski, Sept. 14, 1957; children—Robert J., Charles F., Hope M., Barbara H. Design engr. Howard Needles, Tammen & Bergendoff, Cleve., 1959-64; engr. City of N. Canton, Ohio, 1964-66; pres. Hammontree & Friedl, Consulting Engrs., Canton, 1966-71; chmn. Hammontree & Assos. Ltd., Canton, 1971—; chmn. bd. Morris Knowles, Inc., Cons. Engrs., Pitts., 1980—. Councilman, Village of Hills and Dales (Ohio), 1980—. Served with U.S. Army, 1957-59. Mem. Nat. Soc. Profl. Engrs., Profl. Land Surveyors Ohio, Ohio Assn. Consulting Engrs., Am. Congress on Surveying and Mapping, ASCE. Roman Catholic. Clubs: Brookside Country, Rotary, K. of C. Home: 2824 Brentwood Close NW Canton OH 44708 Office: 5233 Stoneham Rd North Canton OH 44720

HAMPTON, GLEN RICHARD, environ. engr.; b. Detroit, June 11, 1948; s. LaVerne P. and Virginia M. Hubbard; B.S. in Engring., Mich. Tech. U., 1973; m. Jane E. Fenlon, Jan. 30, 1981. Project engr. Granger Engring., Inc., Cadillac, Mich., 1973-79; exec. v.p., dir. Chippewa Architects & Engrs., Inc., Kincheloe and St. Ignace, Mich., 1979—; cons. environ. engring., civil engring., pollution control and solar energy. Registered profl. engr., Mich., Ky., Minn., Wis. Mem. Nat. Soc. Profl. Engrs., Mich. Soc. Profl. Engrs., ASCE (pres. N.W. Mich. chpt. 1980—), Mich. Water Pollution Control Fedn., Mich. Soc. Civil Engrs., Nature Conservancy (trustee), Nat. Audubon Soc. Club: Kiwanis. Home: Route 2 Box 130 A Saint Ignace MI 49781 Office: 272 S State St Saint Ignace MI 49781

HAMRA, DONALD EDD, dentist; b. Memphis, Nov. 26, 1931; s. Richard Albert and Nellie (Hodge) H.; A.B., Central Methodist Coll., 1954; D.D.S., U. Tenn., 1962; m. Shirley Louise George, Nov. 22, 1962; 1 dau., Olivia Carole. Practice gen. dentistry, Malden, Mo., 1962—. Mem. Malden Zoning Commn.; adminstrv. adviser Boy Scouts Am., 1965-66. Served with Dental Corps, AUS, 1955-58. Mem. Malden Inner City Bus. Assn. (pres. 1972), Am., S.E. Mo. (chmn. bd. of censors 1980) dental assns., Malden C. of C. (pres. 1977-78, 81—), Xi Psi Phi, Sigma Alpha Chi. Democrat. Methodist (vice chmn. trustees). Lion (pres. Malden 1966-67, zone chmn. 1968-69). Researcher in thrombocellulitis and herpes simplex. Home: 907 Park St Malden MO 63863 Office: Box 252 110 W Howard St Malden MO 63863

HAMRA, SAM FARRIS, JR., lawyer, food service co. exec.; b. Steele, Mo., Jan. 21, 1932; s. Sam Farris and Victoria Hamra; B.S. in Bus., U. Mo., 1954, LL.B., 1959; m. June Samaha, Apr. 1, 1956; children—Sam Farris, III, Karen E., Michael K., Jacqueline K. Admitted to Mo. bar, 1959, practiced in Springfield, Mo., 1959—; mem. firm Miller, Fairman, Sanford, Carr, and Lowther, 1959-65, individual practice law, 1965—; spl. asst. to atty. gen. Mo., 1966-68; pres., chmn. bd. Wendy's of Mo., Inc., 1977—, Pizza Time Theatres of Mo. Chmn., United Fund Kickoff Campaign, 1966; mem. Mo. Savs. and Loan Commn., 1977-83; chmn. 7th Dist. Democratic Com., 1970-72; del. Dem. Nat. Conv., 1972, 80; mem. fin. com. Dem. State Com., 1972-74, treas., 1980-82; mem. fin. com. Dem. Nat. Com., 1976-80; Mo. fin. coordinator Carter-Mondale presdl. campaign, 1976, co-chmn. fin., 1980; mem. vestry, clk., lay reader St. James Episcopal Ch., Springfield, 1962-64, 69-71; bd. dirs. Jr. Achievement of Middle Am., Inc., 1978-81, Mo. Inst. for Justice, Inc., 1980, U. Mo. Devel. Fund, 1981—; mem. (Mo.) Gov.'s Labor and Employment Com., 1980. Served as 1st lt., arty. U.S. Army, 1954-56. Named Springfield's Outstanding Young Man of Yr., 1966, Mo.'s Outstanding Young Man of Yr., 1967. Mem. Mo. Bar Assn. (mem. corp. com. 1963-80), Am. Bar Assn., Greene County Bar Assn. (treas. 1966-67 dir. 1974-77), Springfield C. of C. (dir. 1971-77, chmn. City Council Liaison Com. 1974-75 chmn. sidewalk and st. improvements bond issue com. 1977-78, chmn. hwy. com. 1977, chmn. bldg. fund dr. 1979), Legal Aid Assn. (pres. 1976-77), U. Mo. Alumni Assn. (athletic com. 1981—), Jaycees (pres. Springfield 1963-64, state legal counsel 1964-65, internat. senator 1964), Phi Delta Phi (pres. 1958-59). Clubs: Masons, Shriners, Hickory Hills Country (chmn. bldg. renovation com. 1979-80), Cedars of Ozarks (v.p. 1981), Rotary (pres. 1967-68). Home: 3937 St Andrews Dr Springfield MO 65804 Office: Two Corporate Sq Suite 200 Springfield MO 65804

HAMRICK, EDITH JOANNE, nursing adminstr.; b. Bureau County, Ill., Sept. 16, 1935; d. Orland LaVerne and Helen B. (Malmberg) Gloden; R.N., St. Francis Sch. Nursing, 1956; student Baylor U., 1965-66; m. Richard Lewis Hamrick, Oct. 7, 1967; 1 son, Richard Edward. Charge nurse Burnham City Hosp., Champaign, Ill., 1956-58; staff nurse Perry Meml. Hosp., Princeton, Ill., 1958-59; operating room supr. Louise G. Wallace Hosp., Lebanon, Mo., 1959-61; staff nurse Perry Meml. Hosp., Princeton, Ill., 1961-65, operating room staff nurse, 1967-68, patient care coordinator emergency room outpatient unit, 1968—; operating room staff nurse Madison (Wis.) Gen. Hosp., 1966-67. Mem. Emergency Room Nurses Assn., Am. Operating Room Nurses Assn., Bureau County Ambulance Assn. Club: Order Eastern Star. Home: 100 E North St Wyanet IL 61379 Office: 530 Park Ave East Princeton IL 61356

HAMRICK, WILLIAM JEAN, ednl. adminstr.; b. Vigo County, Ind., Nov. 27, 1924; s. Floyd James and Kathryn Amy (Russell) H.; student Rose-Hulman Inst., 1943, 1946, Iowa Wesleyan Coll., 1944; B.S., Ind. State U., 1948, M.S., 1951; postgrad. Ind. U., 1960; m. Mary Claire Thomas, June 30, 1956; children—Charles Robert, Sally Antoinette. Tchr., counselor pub. schs., Terre Haute, Ind., 1950-60, asst. principal, 1960-61; asst. state dir. pupil services Ind. State Dept. Instns., Indpls., 1968-69; coordinator guidance and special edn. Vigo County Sch. Corp., Terre Haute, 1961-68, dir. pupil services, 1969-71, asst. supt. sch., 1971—, acting supt. sch., 1974-75; chmn. Region 7 Planning Com. Mental Retardation; mem. State Adv. Council Title IV-C. Bd. dirs. Katherine Hamilton Mental Health Center, 1965—, Vigo County Assn. Retarded Children, 1968-71, United Fund, 1967-69, Vigo County United Cerebral Palsy, 1966-69, Vigo County Hist. Soc., 1968-72. Served with USAAF, 1943-45. Recipient Acad. Fellows Distinguished Edn. award Charles F. Kettering Found., 1976-77; Human Devel. award Ind. Psychol. Assn., 1975; Outstanding Merit award State Supt. Pub. Instruction, 1974. Mem. NEA, Am., Ind. personnel and guidance assns., Am. Counselor Educators and Suprs., Nat. Assn. Pupil Personnel Adminstrs., Council for Exceptional Children, Ind. Sch. Adminstrs. Assn., Nat. Assn. Supervision and Curriculum Devel., Phi Delta Kappa, Lambda Psi Sigma. Methodist. Clubs: Kiwanis, Ind. Schoolmen's, Elks. Author: Psychological Evaluation and Prescription Development Handbook, 1971; contbr. articles in field to profl. jours. Home: 6 Monroe Blvd Terre Haute IN 47803 Office: 961 Lafayette Ave Terre Haute IN 47807

HANAFY, HAN MOHAMED, urologist; b. Egypt, Feb. 17, 1936; came to U.S., 1967, naturalized, 1974; s. Mohamed and Mariem A. H.; M.B. B.Chir., Alexandria (Egypt) U., 1961; m. Hoda A. Arafa, June 8, 1967; children—Deena, Karim. Intern, Miriam Hosp., Providence, 1967-68; resident in surgery R.I. Hosp., Providence, 1968-69; resident in urology Coll. Physicians and Surgeons, Columbia U., N.Y.C., 1969-72; co-chief urology So. Ill. Med. Center, Mt. Vernon, 1972-74; chief urology, Harrisburg (Ill.) Med. Center, 1974—; urol. cons. Pearce and Ferrell Hosps., Eldorado, Ill., 1974—, VA Hosp., Marion, Ill., Hamilton Meml. Hosp., McLeansboro, Ill.; clin. asso. in urology, So. Ill. U. Sch. Medicine, Carbondale. Diplomate Am. Bd. Urology. Mem. Am. Urol. Assn., A.C.S., Internat. Coll. Surgeons, AMA, Ill. Med. Soc. Clubs: Rotary, Kiwanis. Contbr. articles to med. jours., exhibits to profl. convs. Office: 203 N Vine St Harrisburg IL 62946

HANAS, OREST JOSAPHAT, electronics co. exec.; b. Zboiska-Lviv, Ukraine, Nov. 13, 1931; came to U.S., 1949, naturalized, 1952; s. Roman and Sydonia H.; B.S.E.E., U. Md., 1960; M.S.E.E., Drexel U., 1964; m. Christine Jane Dasho, July 7, 1960; children—Aleksandra R., Anna M., Teresa C. Design engr. Philco, Phila., 1960-61; sr. design engr. RCA, Camden, N.J., 1961-69; with AII Systems, Moorestown, N.J., 1969-76, dir. engring., 1974-76; v.p. Satellite Communications, Inc., Moorestown, 1976; engring. mgr. RCA Aestroelectronics, Princeton, N.J., 1976; dir. engring. CATV div. Oak Communications, Inc., Crystal Lake, Ill., 1971-79, v.p. engring. CATV div., 1979-80, v.p. satellite systems div., 1980—. Served with USAF, 1951-55. Mem. IEEE, Soc. Cable Television Engrs., Ukrainian Engrs. Soc. Ukrainian Catholic. Patentee in field. Office: 100 S Main St Crystal Lake IL 60014

HANAWAY, DONALD JOHN, lawyer, state senator; b. Stevens Point, Wis., Dec. 25, 1933; s. John Leo and Agnes Marie (Flatley) H.; B.B.A., U. Wis., 1958, LL.B., 1961; m. JoAnn R. Gaskell, June 21, 1958; children—Patrick, James, Mary Kathleen, Michael John, Maureen Megan. Admitted to Wis. bar, 1961; asst. dist. atty. Brown County, Green Bay, Wis., 1963-64, spl. prosecutor, 1967-78; city atty. City of De Pere (Wis.), 1964-72, 76-79, mayor, 1972-74; mem. firm Condon, Hanaway & Wickert, Ltd., Green Bay, 1969—; mem. Wis. Senate, 1979—, asst. minority leader, 1981—. Active various local govtl., civic and parish coms. Served with U.S. Army, 1954-56. Mem. Wis. Bar Assn., Brown County Bar Assn., Am. Trial Lawyers Assn., Wis. Sch. Attys. Assn. (charter), De Pere C. of C. (exec. sec. 1964-69). Republican. Club: Optimist (charter) (De Pere). Office: PO Box 1126 Green Bay WI 54305

HANCE, KENNETH G., educator; B.A., Olivet Coll., 1924, M.A. 1926, L.H.D., 1961; student Harvard U., 1928-30, Columbia U., 1932; Ph.D., U. Mich., 1937. Instr. Olivet Coll., from 1924, later asst. prof., asso. prof.; asst. prof. Albion Coll., 1930-37, prof., 1937-40; asso. prof. U. Mich., 1940-45, prof., asst. dean Sch. Speech, Northwestern U., 1945-56; prof., dir. grad studies in speech Mich. State U., 1956-71, prof. emeritus, 1971—; provost Olivet Coll., 1968-71, acting acad. v.p., 1971-73, asst. pres., dir. ch. relations, 1973-74, emeritus adminstr., 1974—; adj. prof. Garrett Theol. Sem., 1945-56, Seabury Western Theol. Sem., 1945-56, Andrews U. and Theol. Sem., 1962-70, 79—; vis. prof. Calif. State U. at Los Angeles, 1966; distinguished vis. prof. Central Mich. U., 1970-72. Recipient Distinguished Alumni award Pi Kappa Delta, 1963, Delta Sigma Rho-Tau Kappa Alpha, 1964, Mich. Speech Assn., 1964; Distinguished Service award Interstate Oratorical Assn., 1973; Distinguished Alumni award Olivet Coll., 1975. Mem. Speech Assn. Am. (exec. v.p., 1955-57, pres. 1960), Mich., Ill., Central States speech assns., NEA, Mich. Edn. Assn., Am. Assn. Higher Edn., Interstate Oratorical Assn. (exec. sec. 1939-60), Delta Sigma Rho (nat. sec. 1939-50, nat. treas. 1939-72). Co-author: Principles and Methods of Discussion, 1938; Discussion in Human Affairs, 1950; Public Speaking and Discussion for Religious Leaders, 1961; sr. author: Principles of Speaking, 1962, Principles of Speaking, 2d edit., 1969; Principles of Speaking, 3d edit., 1974. Editor The Illinois Speech Journal, 1946-50; The Gavel, 1939-50; editor-author: History of Speech Education in Michigan, 1975. Contbr. articles to profl. jours. Home: 509 Ship St Saint Joseph MI 49085

HANCIK, ROBERT DAVID, airport exec.; b. Cleve., Mar. 29, 1946; s. Albin Michael and Agnes H.; B.S. in Aeros., St. Louis U., 1967; 1 son, Joshua. Various positions commuter airlines, Cleve. and Chgo., 1967-69; project mgr. aircraft elec. systems, mktg. dept. Lear Seigler Co., Power Equipment div., Maple Heights, Ohio, 1969-70; asst. to dir. aviation Indpls. Airport Authority, 1970-72; dir. aviation Springfield (Mo.) Regional Airport, 1972—. Mem. Springfield C. of C. (chmn. transp. com. 1974), Am. Assn. Airport Execs. (dir.; accredited), Airport Operators Council Internat., Alpha Eta Rho. Roman Catholic. Club: Sertoma. Home: 2140 E Raynell St Springfield MO 65804 Office: Springfield Regional Airport Route 6 Box 384 Springfield MO 65803

HANCOCK, JAMES BEATY, interior designer; b. Hartford, Ky.; s. James Winfield Scott and Hettie Frances (Meadows) H.; B.A., Hardin-Simmons U., 1948, M.A., 1952. Head interior design dept. Thornton's, Abilene, Tex., 1945-54; interior designer The Halle Bros. Co., Cleve., 1954-55; v.p. Olympic Products, Cleve., 1955-56; mgr. interior designer Bell Drapery Shops of Ohio, Inc., Shaker Heights, 1957-78, v.p., 1979—; lectr. interior design, Abilene and Cleve.; works include 6 original murals Broadway Theater, Abilene, 1940, mural Skyline Outdoor Theatre, Abilene, 1950, cover designs for Isotopics mag., 1958-60. Served with AUS, 1942-46. Recipient 2d place award for oil painting West Tex. Expn., 1940, hon. mention, 1940. Mem. Abilene Mus. Fine Arts (charter). Home: 530 Sycamore Dr Cleveland OH 44132

HAND, JOHN STEVEN, clin. psychologist; b. River Rouge, Mich., Oct. 15, 1942; s. John Taylor and Harryet Condo (Miller) H.; student Albion Coll., 1960-62; B.S., Mich. State U., 1964, postgrad., 1968-70; M.A., Western Mich. U., 1966, post grad., 1967-68; postgrad. Wayne State U., 1970-71; m. Nancy Elizabeth Yeck, Aug. 23, 1971; children—Matthew, Rebecca. Teaching fellow Western Mich. U., 1966; instr. psychology Jackson Community Coll., 1966-67; clin. psychologist State Prison So. Mich., 1967—; asst. dir. substance abuse program Mich. Corrections Dept., 1978-80, clin. psychologist Office

Health Care, 1980—, spl. cons., 1971-73; pvt. practice clin. psychology, Jackson, Mich., 1970-72, 81—; cons. Foote Hosp., Jackson, 1968-70; half-time psychol. cons. Toledo Methadole Clinic, 1973, Urban Affairs Center, Toledo, 1974; part time faculty Jackson Community Coll. and Spring Arbor Coll., 1968—; cons., condr. research in field; advisor to gov.'s council on drug abuse, 1971-72; bd. dirs. Jackson, Hillsdale, Lenawee County Substance Abuse Commn., 1980—, chmn. fin. and personnel com., 1981—. Fellow, Fed. Bur. of Justice/Nat. Corrections Council, 1979, Office Substance Abuse Services (Mich.), 1978. Mem. Am. Correctional Assn. (cons. 1981—), Am. Psychol. Assn. (cert. of merit for outstanding public service, div. 18, 1980, media resources person for public info. office), Midwest Psychol. Assn., Ill. Group Psychotherapy Soc., Alcohol and Drug Problems Assn. N.Am. (pres.), Internat. Fund for Animals, Greenpeace, Jackson Trailpacers, Save the Whales, Hanover-Horton Hist. Soc. (Mich.). Contbr. articles on sexuality and drug abuse to profl. publs.; co-founder prison programs including Corrections Specialists, 1968-71, coll. program for inmates, 1968, specialized treatment program for sex offenders, heroin addicts, 1968-77; speaker profl. confs. and workshops in field. Office: 4000 Cooper St Jackson MI 49201

HANDEL, CHARLES HAROLD, clin. psychologist; b. Cin., Jan. 2, 1947; s. Charles H. and Helen Audrey (Schlosser) H.; m. Mary Patricia Harmeier, June 15, 1973; B.S., Xavier U., Cin., 1969; M.A., U. Dayton, 1972; Ph.D., U. Cin., 1981. Clin. psychology trainee Dayton Mental Health Center, 1970-72; intern clin. psychologist Dayton Children's Psychiat. Hosp. and Child Guidance Center, 1972-74; intern clin. psychologist Mental Health Services-East, Cin., 1974-76, clin. psychologist, supervising psychotherapist, 1976—; cons. psychologist St. Ursula Acad., Cin., 1976—; cons. clin. psychologist Ct. Psychiat. Clinic, Cin., 1979; supervising clin. psychologist Springer Ednl. Found., 1979. Lic. psychologist. Fellow Am. Assn. Orthopsychiatry; mem. Am., Ohio, Cin. psychol. assns. Home: 706 Tweed Ave Cincinnati OH 45226 Office: 3322 Erie Ave Cincinnati OH 45208

HANDLEY, ROBERT EUGENE, photographer; b. Bloomington, Ill., May 23, 1945; s. Bernard A. and Edna Margarete (Manahan) H.; student So. Ill. U., 1966-67, Ill. State U., 1967-68; grad. N.Y. Inst. Photography, 1972, Winona Sch. Profl. Photography, 1974. Formerly publicity photographer Ringling Bros. and Barnum & Bailey Circus; owner Robert E. Handley, Photography, Bloomington, 1969—. Lectr. photography for nat., state, regional confs., high schs. Pres., Bloomington Down Town Council, 1979-80. Served with AUS, 1962. Recipient Excellence award Profl. Photographers Am., 1973; Ct. of Honor trophy State of Ill.; numerous other awards. Mem. Profl. Photographers Am. (Photog. Craftsman degree 1976; asst. nat. conv. mgr. 1976), Assn. Commerce and Industry Mclean County (dir. 1980), Asso. Profl. Photographers Ill., Profl. Photographers No. Ill. (dir. 1976-80), Profl. Photographers So. Ill., Profl. Photographers Calif., Profl. Photographers West, Inst. Inc. Photographers (Gt. Britain), Am. Soc. Mag. Photographers, Am. Soc. Photographers, Photog. Soc. Am., Internat. Wedding Photographers Am., Asso. Photographers Internat. (life), Winona Sch. Alumni Assn. Moose. Contbr. articles to profl. jours. Home: 1920 E Croxton Ave Bloomington IL 61701

HANDY, CHARLES BROOKS, accountant, educator; b. Coffey, Mo., Apr. 26, 1924; s. Herbert Franklyn and Laura Ada Margaret (Mueller) H.; B.A., Westminster Coll., Fulton, Mo., 1947; M.A., U. Iowa, 1956; Ph.D., Iowa State U., Ames, 1970; m. Donna Jean Peters, June 29, 1958; children—William Mark, Karen Lynne. Staff accountant McGladrey, Hendrickson & Co. (formerly McGladrey, Hansen, Dunn & Co.), Davenport, Iowa, 1955-58; instr. acctg. Iowa State U., Ames, 1958-60, asst. prof., 1960-70, asso. prof., 1970-75, prof., 1975—, chmn. supervisory com. indsl. adminstrv. scis., 1975-78, prof. in charge acctg. studies, 1977-78, chmn. dept. indsl. adminstrn., 1978-80, dir. Sch. Bus. Adminstrn., 1980—; cons. in field. Served from ensign to lt. (j.g.), USNR, 1943-46. C.P.A., Iowa. Mem. Am. Acctg. Assn., Am. Inst. C.P.A.'s, Iowa Soc. C.P.A.'s, Inst. Internal Auditors, Midwest Bus. Adminstrn. Assn., Nat. Assn. Accts., Beta Alpha Psi, Omicron Delta Epsilon, Kappa Alpha Order. Republican. Presbyterian. Club: Lions. Home: 1132 Johnson St Ames IA 50010 Office: 300 Carver Hall Iowa State U Ames IA 50011

HANDY, DRUCILLA, pub. relations counsel; b. Lynchburg, Va., Aug. 21, 1924; d. John Bryant and Allen (Steele) Handy; student Swarthmore (Pa.) Coll., 1942-45; m. Robert M. Redinger, Oct. 30, 1954. Mem. publicity dept. Metro-Goldwyn-Mayer Studios, 1945-46; editor E.I. du Pont de Nemours & Co., 1947-48; with Rosemary Sheehan Publicity, 1948-50; account group supr. Mayer & O'Brien Pub. Relations, 1950-53; pub. relations dir. Helene Curtis Industries, 1953-54; account group supr. Gardner & Jones, Inc., 1954-56; pres. Drucilla Handy Co., Chgo., 1956—. Mem. Pub. Relations Soc. Am., Fashion Group, Art Inst., Lyric Opera of Chgo. Clubs: Arts, Metropolitan, Barclay, Publicity (Chgo.). Contbr. articles to pub. relations, home furnishings and bus. publs. Office: 813 Merchandise Mart Chicago IL 60654 also 654 Madison Ave New York NY 60621

HANDY, RICHARD LINCOLN, civil engr., educator; b. Chariton, Ia., Feb. 12, 1929; s. Walter Newton and Florence Elizabeth (Shoemaker) H.; B.S. in Geology, Iowa State U., 1951, M.S., 1953, Ph.D. in Soil Engring., 1956; 1 dau., Beth Susan. Asst. prof. civil engring. Iowa State U., Ames, 1956-59, asso. prof., 1959-63, prof., also dir. Soil Research Lab., 1963—; cons. in soil engring., soil and rock testing, landslide stblzn.; v.p. W.N. Handy Co., 1958—, pres. Handy Geotech. Instruments, Inc., 1979—. Recipient faculty citation Iowa State U., 1976. Fellow AAAS, Geol. Soc. Am., Iowa Acad. Sci.; mem. ASCE, ASTM, Soil Sci. Soc. Am., Clay Minerals Soc., Internat. Soc. Soil Mech. and Found. Engrs. Author: (with M.G. Spangler) Soil Engineering, 1973, 82; also numerous articles; patentee in soils field. Office: Geotech Research Lab Iowa State U Ames IA 50011

HANES, JAMES HENRY, chem. co. exec.; b. Houston, Dec. 23, 1922; s. Ralph Davis and Mable Mae (Anderson) H.; B.S. with honors, Rose-Hulman Inst., 1944; J.D., U. Mich., 1951; m. Doris Marilyn Hall, Sept. 1950; children—Douglas, Stephen, Barbara, Constance. Admitted to Mich. bar, 1951, Okla. bar, 1955, Colo. bar, 1974, U.S. Supreme Ct. bar, 1976; with Dow Chem. Co., 1946-48, 51—, gen. mgr. Rocky Flats div., Golden, Colo., 1972-74, asso. gen. counsel, Midland, Mich., 1974—, v.p. Dow U.S., 1976—, also mem. retirement bd.; dir. Dorinco, 1st Nat. Bank, Boulder, Colo., 1973-74. Mem. ann. fund com. Saginaw Valley State Coll.; bd. dirs. Midland Hosp. Center, 1975—, chmn., 1977-79, chmn. fin. com., 1979—; bd. dirs. United Way; active Boy Scouts Am. Served to lt. (j.g.) USNR, 1944-46. Recipient Individual Contbns. award Soc. Mfg. Engrs., 1974, Safety award Life is Fragile Club, 1974. Mem. NAM (public affairs steering com.), Mich., Colo., Okla., Midland County (past pres.) bar assns., Chem. Mfrs. Assn. (lawyers com.), Nat. Legal Center for Pub. Interest (lawyers adv. com.). Presbyterian. Clubs: Rotary, Mason (32 deg.). Office: 2030 Dow Center Midland MI 48640

HANEY, DAVID G., bus. exec.; b. Lima, Ohio, Mar. 9, 1941; s. Dwight G. and Maxine R. (Danner) H.; B.Sc., Ohio State U., 1963; m. Ann Gerlinger, Aug. 31, 1963; children—Cheryl Ann, John David. Life underwriter Nationwide Ins., Columbus, Ohio, 1964-68, sect. mgr., 1968-71, div. mgr. adminstrn. and systems, 1971-78; dir. ops. Nat. Revenue Corp., Columbus, 1978—. Fellow Life Office Mgmt. Assn., Adminstrv. Mgmt. Soc.; mem. Comml. Law League Am., S.A.R. Republican. Lutheran. Clubs: Univ. (treas.), Sertoma, Businessman's (past pres.), Toastmasters (past pres.), Masons. Home: 4217 Gavin Ln Columbus OH 43220 Office: 2323 Lake Club Dr Columbus OH 43227

HANEY, WILLIAM VALENTINE, corp. exec.; b. Troy, Mich., Sept. 26, 1936; s. Raymond Charles and Madeline Sofia (Muller) H.; B.A. in English, U. Mich., 1958; m. Marcella F. Fodell, June 27, 1959; children—Mark A., Jennifer L., Patrick M., Rebecca J., Jessica C. With Rocketdyne div. N. Am. Aviation, summer 1956; with missile div. Chrysler Corp., 1958-59; with Lockheed Aircraft Corp., 1959-60; mgr. specifications and standards Bendix Aerospace Systems div. Bendix Corp., Ann Arbor, Mich., 1960-66; dir. pub., mng. editor Inst. Social Research, U. Mich., Ann Arbor, 1966-74, mng. editor, asst. dir. U. Mich. Press, 1974-77; mgr. corp. publs. Bendix Corp., Southfield, Mich., 1977-79, corp. dir. communications, 1979-80, corp. dir. pub. and advt., 1980—; ind. pub.; pvt. pub. cons. Mem. Public Relations Soc. Am., Internat. Assn. Bus. Communicators, Detroit Econ. Club. Author: From Spirit Lake to Goose Lake, 1971. Home: 9200 Island Lake Rd Dexter MI 48130 Office: Bendix Corp Bendix Center PO Box 5060 Southfield MI 48037

HANIFAN, JAMES MARTIN, coach profl. football team; b. Compton, Calif., Sept. 21, 1933; s. James and Bridget (O'Gorman) H.; B.A., U. Calif., Berkeley; m. Mariana Osuna, Dec. 26, 1958; children—Kathleen Marie, James Peter. Asst. football coach San Diego State U., 1972; asst. coach St. Louis Football Cardinals, 1973-78, head football coach, 1980—; asst. head coach San Diego Chargers, 1979. Served with U.S. Army, 1956-58. Named Asst. Football Coach of Yr., NFL, 1977. Republican. Roman Catholic. Office: 200 Stadium Plaza Saint Louis MO 63102

HANIFY, DENNIS WILLIAM, mech. engr.; b. Blue Island, Ill., Sept. 18, 1938; s. William Theodore and Lilabelle Mae (Rector) H.; B.S. in Mech. Engring., Ill. Inst. Tech., 1965, M.B.A., 1970; m. Janet Ann Habich, July 2, 1959; children—John William, Robert Dennis. Asst. to v.p. mfg. Cromwell Paper Co., Chgo., 1960-65; lead engr. Goss Co., Cicero, Ill., 1965-66; project engr. Remington Arms Co., Park Forest, Ill., 1966-67; with IIT Research Inst., Chgo., 1967-81, mgr. mech. and systems research, sr. research engr., 1973-81; mgr. mech. systems Meyercord Co., Carol Stream, Ill., 1981—; indsl. design cons.; guest lectr. various univs.; chmn., speaker numerous confs. U.S.A., Europe, Japan. Recipient citation of appreciation U. Wis., 1972, 73. Mem. Soc. Mfg. Engrs. (sr.; treas. Robotics Internat.), Soc. Automotive Engrs., Am. Def. Preparedness Assn., Sigma Xi. Home: 660 E 169th St South Holland IL 60473

HANISH, LANCE GARY, advt. exec.; b. Milw., Feb. 16, 1942; s. Stanley Michael and Margaret Mary (Franzen) H.; B.S., U. Wis., Madison, 1964; m. Ellen Francis Larson, June 10, 1967; children—Sean L., Jodi L., Kristin H. Pres., Founder Hanish Assos. Inc., Milw., 1968—, Hanish Assos. Fla., Inc., Fort Myers, 1981—, Hanish Assos. N.Y., N.Y.C., 1980—. Served to lt. cmdr. USN, 1964-66; Vietnam. Mem. Milw. Advt. Club, Am. Advt. Fedn. Clubs: Tuckaway Country (Franklin, Wis.); Useppa Island (Fla.). Office: 120 Bishop's Way Brookfield WI 53005

HANKIS, ROY ALLEN, interior designer; b. Greenville, Mich., May 24, 1943; s. John LeRoy and Nila A. (Taylor) H.; interior design diploma Kendall Sch. Design, 1964; student Cranbrook Acad. Art, 1971. Dir. design, contract design firms, Grand Rapids and Detroit, 1964-73; owner, designer Roy Allen Hankis Interiors, Troy, Mich., 1974—; instr. interior design Henry Ford Community Coll., Dearborn, Mich., 1981—; trustee JONIRO Investment Co., Southfield, Mich., 1981—. Mem. Am. Soc. Interior Designers (dir. Mich. chpt. 1974), Christian Bus. Men's Com. Detroit. Baptist. Club: Rotary. Patentee. Home and Office: 5365 Breeze Hill Pl Troy MI 48098

HANKISON, HAZEL MAE, retail office supply store exec.; b. New Lexington, Ohio, Aug. 22, 1915; d. Clem Ellsworth and Margaret Mae (Derringer) H.; student public schs., New Lexington. Sec., Snider Flautt Lumber Co., New Lexington, 1934-35, Collection Agy., New Lexington, 1936-38, Anchor Hocking Glass Corp., Lancaster, Ohio, 1939-45, R.B. Howard & Assos., Columbus, Ohio, 1946-51, Van Sickle Office Supply, Columbus, 1952-55; owner, mgr. Grandview Office Supply, Columbus, 1955—. Mem. Grandview Bus. Assn. Republican. Home: 3481 Mountview Rd Columbus OH 43221 Office: 1221 Grandview Ave Columbus OH 43212

HANLEY, JOHN PATRICK, inventor; b. St. Joseph, Mich., Feb. 23, 1925; s. John William and Elizabeth (Canavan) H.; student Loyola U., Chgo., 1941-43, 45-46; m. Catherine Mary Bartsch, Feb. 9, 1963; children—Elizabeth, John. Broker, Travelers Ins. Cos., Chgo., 1947-55; founder, exec. dir. Chgo. Air Club, Meigs Airfield, 1955-58; with aircraft hanger constrn. project with Frank Lloyd Wright, Benton, Harbor, Mich., 1958-62; area mgr. Chgo. Assn. Commerce and Industry, 1962-65; postmaster Wilmette, Ill., 1965-68; researcher natural family planning, 1968—, patentee human reprodn. indexing device; teenage pregnancy cons. Operation Push, 1979-80; dist. mgr. Bur. Census, Gt. Lakes, Ill., 1980. Bd. dirs. Kenilworth Village House, 1979-80. Served with AUS, 1943-44. Recipient ann. Brotherhood award North Shore Chgo., 1967. Mem. Assn. Population/Family Planning Libraries and Info. Centers Internat. Democrat. Roman Catholic. Address: Box 62 Kenilworth IL 60043

HANLEY, JOHN WELLER, mfg. co. exec.; b. Parkersburg, W.Va., Jan. 11, 1922; s. James P. and Ida May (Ayers) H.; B.S. in Metall. Engring., Pa. State U., 1942; M.B.A., Harvard, 1947; D.Eng. (hon.), U. Mo., Rolla, 1974; LL.D. (hon.), Maryville Coll., 1979, U. of Pacific, 1981; D.S. (hon.), Webster Coll., 1981; m. Mary Jane Reel, June 26, 1948; children—John Weller, Michael James, Susan Jayne. Metall. engr. Allegheny Ludlum Steel Corp., 1942-43; with Procter & Gamble Co., 1947-72, mgr. case soap products, 1961-63, v.p. household soap products div., 1963-67, corp. v.p., group exec., 1967-70, exec. v.p., 1970-72, also dir.; pres., chief exec. officer Monsanto Co., St. Louis, 1972—, chmn. bd., 1975—, also dir.; dir. Citicorp., May Dept. Stores Co., R.J. Reynolds Industries, Inc. Mem. Bus. Council, Washington, Bus. Roundtable, N.Y.C.; trustee Conf. Bd.; mem. adv. council on nat. affairs Salvation Army; mem. St. Louis Civic Progress Assn.; trustee Washington U., St. Louis; mem. Nat. Council U.S.-China Trade; mem. vis. com. Harvard Med. Sch. Served to lt. (s.g.) USNR, 1943-46; PTO. Recipient Distinguished Alumnus award Pa. State U., 1972; Merit award Urban League St. Louis, 1975; Alumni Achievement award Harvard U., 1980. Home: 212 N Kingshighway Saint Louis MO 63108 Office: PO Box 526 Saint Louis MO 63166

HANLON, C. ROLLINS, physician; b. Balt., Feb. 8, 1915; s. Bernard and Harriet (Rollins) H.; A.B., Loyola Coll., Balt., 1934; M.D., Johns Hopkins, 1938; D.Sc. (hon.), Georgetown U., 1976; m. Margaret M. Hammond, May 28, 1949; children—Philip, Paul, Richard, Christine, Thomas, Mary, Martha, Sarah. Intern, John Hopkins Hosp., 1939-40, W.S. Halsted fellow in surgery, 1939-40, instr. surgery, 1946-48, asst. prof., 1948-50; asst. resident, resident in surgery Cin. Gen. Hosp., 1940-41, 43-44; exchange fellow surgery U. Calif., 1941-42; prof. surgery, chmn. dept. St. Louis U., 1950-69; prof. surgery Northwestern U. Med. Sch., 1969—; chmn. surgery study sect. NIH, 1965-66; pres. Council Med. Speciality Socs., 1974-75; chmn. Coordinating Council on Med. Edn., 1976-77. Served to lt. (j.g.) M.C., USNR, 1944-46; CBI. Recipient Fleur-de-lis award St. Louis U., 1968; Statesmen in Medicine award Airlie Found., 1974. Diplomate Am. Bd. Surgery (chmn. 1966-67); founder group Am. Bd. Thoracic Surgery, 1949. Fellow A.C.S. (gov., regent 1967-69, dir. 1969—), Royal Australasian Coll. Surgeons (hon.), Royal Coll. Surgeons Ireland (hon.); mem. Am. Heart Assn. (surgery research study com. 1966-68), Internat. Cardiovascular Soc. (pres. N.Am. chpt. 1963-64), Soc. Vascular Surgery (pres. 1968), So., Central, Am. (sec. 1968-69, pres. 1981-82), Western surg. assns., Am. Assn. Thoracic Surgery (treas. 1962-68), Soc. Clin. Surgery (pres. 1968-70), Soc. Univ. Surgeons (pres. 1968), Johns Hopkins Med. and Surg. Assn. (v.p. 1975-77), St. Louis Surg. Soc., Alpha Omega Alpha. Roman Catholic. Club: Serra (1st v.p.) (St. Louis). Bd. dirs. Surgery, Gynecology and Obstetrics, 1973-74. Contbr. articles to profl. jours. Address: 55 E Erie St Chicago IL 60611

HANLON, JOHN ROBERT, state ofcl.; b. Milw., Apr. 29, 1919; s. Thomas and Lottie (Kennedy) H.; student Milw. Bus. U., 1937-38, Radio Inst. Chgo., 1945-46, U. Nebr., 1968-69; m. Kathleen Ann Moynihan, Nov. 20, 1943; children—Susan, Richard, John Robert, Kathleen, Theresa, William. Engaged in broadcasting, 1945-52, 56-74; field supr. quality control Mead Ordnance Plant (Nebr.), 1952-56; congressional dist. coordinator, 1973-79; commr. labor State of Nebr., 1979—; pres. Nebr. AP Broadcasters Assn., 1964. Mem. exec. bd. Nebraskaland Found., 1979. Served with AUS, 1940-45. Recipient various citations, certs. merit. Mem. Internat. Conf. Employment Security Agts., Nat. Assn. Govtl. Labor Ofcls. (dir.), Internat. Footprinters Assn. (chpt. dir. 1968—). Republican. Roman Catholic. Clubs: Lincoln Optimists (dir. 1976—), KC (past grand knight). Office: 550 S 16th St Lincoln NE 68509

HANN, ALAN FREDERICK, banker; b. Rapid City, S.D., Feb. 2, 1946; s. Matt Robert and Etta Emma H.; B.S. in Metall. Engring., S.D. Sch. Mines and Tech., 1969; postgrad. U. Wis. Grad. Sch. Banking, 1978; m. Mary Kay Crider, Aug. 23, 1969. System engr., mktg. rep. IBM, Boulder, Colo., El Paso, Tex., 1969-74; dir., chief exec. officer First State Bank, Buffalo, S.D., 1974—. Chmn., Buffalo Housing and Redevel. Commn., 1978—; bd. dirs. Harding County Devel. Corp.; exhibited in various photog. exhbns. Home: Buffalo SD 57720 Office: 1 Main St Buffalo SD 57720

HANNA, MARILYN CONCHA, educator; b. Chaffee, Mo., Sept. 20, 1922; d. Arthur Clarkson and Mary Thurza (Waters) H.; Asso. Fine Arts, William Woods Coll., 1941; student Cin. Conservatory Music, 1941-42; diploma Juilliard Sch. Music, 1945; Mus.B., U. Mo., 1951, M.A., 1954. Tchr. music, piano and piano lit. Stephens Coll., Columbia, Mo., 1946—. Organist, choir dir. 1st Bapt. Ch., Fulton, Mo.; choir dir. 1st Presbyn. Ch., Columbia. Mem. Phi Beta. Democrat. Presbyterian. Home: 4216 Mexico Gravel Rd Columbia MO 65201 Office: Dept Music Stephens Coll Columbia MO 65201

HANNA, MARTIN SHAD, lawyer; b. Bowling Green, Ohio, Aug. 4, 1940; s. Martin Lester and Julia Loyal (Moor) H.; student Bowling Green State U.; B.S., Purdue U., 1962; J.D., Am. U., 1965; m. Sharon Ann Higgins, Feb. 10, 1969; children—Jennifer Lynn, Jonathan Moor, Katharine Anne. Admitted to Ohio bar, 1965, D.C. bar, 1967, U.S. Supreme Ct. bar, 1969; partner law firm Hanna, Middleton & Roebke, 1965-70, Hanna & Hanna, Bowling Green, 1971—; spl. counsel for atty. gen. Ohio, 1969-71, Ohio Bd. Regents, 1974; instr. Bowling Green State U., 1970, Ohio Div. Vocat. Edn., 1970—, Ohio Peace Officer Tng. Council, 1968. Legal adviser N.W. Ohio Vol. Firemen's Assn., 1970—. State chmn. Ohio League Young Republican Clubs, 1972-73; nat. vice-chmn. Young Rep. Nat. Fedn., 1973-75, counselor to chmn., 1975-77; vice-chmn. Wood County (Ohio) Rep. Exec. Com., 1972-80, precinct committeeman, 1968—; trustee Bowling Green State U., 1976—; mem. Ohio State Fire Commn., 1979—. Recipient George Washington honor medal award Freedoms Founds. at Valley Forge, 1969, award of merit Ohio Legal Center Inst., 1973, Robert A. Taft Distinguished Service award, 1974, James A. Rhodes Leadership award, 1975. Named One of Ten Outstanding Young Men, Ohio Jr. C. of C., 1968. Mem. Am., Ohio, N.W. Ohio, Wood County, D.C. bar assns., Am. Trauma Soc. (trauma and law com.), Phi Delta Phi, Pi Kappa Delta. Presbyterian (elder, lay minister). Contbr. articles to profl. publs. Home: 506 Knollwood Dr Bowling Green OH 43402 Office: 700 N Main St Bowling Green OH 43402

HANNA, MARY MARGARET MELSON (MRS. JOHN ALDEN HANNA) librarian; b. nr. Rolfe, Iowa, Oct. 17, 1913; d. Randall and Fern Sigourney (Beers) Melson; B.A., Morningside Coll., 1934; postgrad. U. Iowa, 1936, Iowa State U., 1937, U. No. Iowa, 1956; M.A., U. Wis., 1966; m. John Alden Hanna, Aug. 17, 1938 (dec. 1963); children—Carolyn (Mrs. Gary Clinton Snell), Frank Richard, Cynthia (dec. 1947). Tchr. English, Milford (Iowa) High Sch., 1934-37; prin. Ankeny (Iowa) High Sch., 1937-38; tchr. English, Blairsburg (Iowa) High Sch., 1957-59; tchr. Am. lit. Webster City (Iowa) High Sch., 1959-64; dir. Kendall Young Library, Webster City, 1966-79; reference librarian Rust Coll., Holly Springs, Miss., 1981—. Asst. sec. Kendall Young Library and Trust Estate, 1966-79; mem. Webster City Community Sch. Bd., 1978-81. Mem. Iowa Library Assn., Bus. and Profl. Women, P.E.O. Republican. Methodist. Club: Women's (Webster City). Home: 1404 Grove St Webster City IA 50595

HANNA, RAGY BOSHRA, trading co. exec.; b. Assiut, Egypt, July 3, 1932; came to U.S., 1961, naturalized, 1977; s. Boshra Hanna and Alice Rizk (Narouz) Mishreky; B.Sc., Cairo U., 1955, Dipl. (M.Sc.) in Clin. Biochemistry, 1961; M.Sc. in Pharmacy, Columbia U., 1966; Ph.D., U. Ga., 1970; M.B.A., Rutgers U., 1975; m. Magda E. Hanna, Aug. 6, 1968; children—Joseph, Jeahan. Chemist, Dept. Health, Cairo, Egypt, 1955-63; mem. Mission in Europe with WHO, 1964; asst. tech. dir. internat. E.R. Squibb Co., Princeton, N.J., 1970-75; pvt. mktg. cons. for U.S. cos. in Middle East, 1975-77; mktg. mgr. for Middle East, Republic Steel Corp., Cleve., 1977-81; organizer, pres. Hanna Internat., Inc., Cleve., 1981—. Columbia U. fellow, 1964-66; U. Ga. fellow, 1968-70. Mem. Am. Chem. Soc., Am. Pharm. Assn., Fedn. Internationale Pharmaceutique, Am. Mgmt. Assn., Phi Kappa Phi. Contbr. articles to profl. jours. Home: 8405 Stoney Brook Dr Chagrin Falls OH 44022 Office: 32915 Aurora Rd Solon OH 44139

HANNA, SHERMAN DAVIE, consumer economist, educator; b. Los Angeles, Dec. 24, 1946; s. Parker Davie Hanna, Jr., and Joan (Oberly) Haviland; B.S., M.I.T., 1968; M.S., Cornell U., 1973, Ph.D., 1974; m. Suzanne Lindamood, Jan. 20, 1972; 1 dau., Emily. Asst. prof. So. Ill. U., Carbondale, 1973-74; asst. prof. Auburn (Ala.) U., 1974-77; asst. prof. dept. family econs. Kans. State U., Manhattan, 1977-79, asso. prof., 1979—. Mem. Am. Council on Consumer Interests, Am. Assn. Housing Educators (dir.), Am. Econ. Assn., Assn. for Consumer Research, Am. Real Estate and Urban Econs. Assn., Am. Home Econs. Assn. Co-editor Housing and Society, 1973-80; editorial bd. Jour. Consumer Affairs, 1978—; co-author textbook Housing, Society and Consumers, 1979; dir. NSF/Auburn U. survey, 1976. Home: 1719

Humboldt St Manhattan KS 66502 Office: Family Economics Dept Kansas State Univ Manhattan KS 66506

HANNA, WAFIK ABD EL AZIZ, surgeon; b. Cairo, July 28, 1940; s. Abd El Aziz and Mary (Rizk) H.; came to U.S., 1967, naturalized, 1972; cert. Oxford U. and Cambridge U., 1958; M.D., Cairo U., 1964; m. Joan Spiega, May 13, 1972. Intern rotating and gen. surgery Cairo U., 1964, MacNeal Meml. Hosp., 1967; resident U. Ill., 1970-73; mem. staff Mac Neal Meml. Hosp., Berwyn, Ill., Hinsdale (Ill.) Sanitarium, Community Meml. Hosp., LaGrange, Ill., Presbyn.-St. Luke's Hosp., Chgo., 1976; pres. Hanna Facial Cosmetic Surgery Ltd., Hinsdale, Ill., 1976—; clin. instr. otolaryngology dept. Rush Med. Sch., 1976, asst. prof., 1981—. Mem. A.C.S., Internat. Acad. Cosmetic Surgery, Am. Acad. Facial Plastic and Reconstructive Surgery, AMA, Am. Acad. Otolaryngology, Am. Assn. Cosmetic Surgery, Ill. Acad. Cosmetic Surgery, Ill. Med. Soc., Chgo. Med. Soc. Home: 820 Merrill Woods Hinsdale IL 60521 Office: 3722 S Harlem Ave Riverside IL 60546

HANNA, WAYNE ALLEN, designer, illustrator, photographer; b. Indpls., Aug. 12, 1946; s. Dale Wayne and Gertrude Susan (Cokain) H.; B.F.A., Herron Sch. Art, Ind. U., 1968; m. Rebecca Ann Yehling, Dec. 31, 1976. Production artist Ropkey Engraving Co., Indpls., 1964-70; art dir., illustrator John W. Sweemer & Assos., Chgo., 1970-77; owner, art dir., illustrator, photographer Wayne Hanna Design, Carol Stream, Ill., 1977-80; pres. Hanna & Hanna, Inc., St. Charles, Ill., 1980—. Recipient Walcott award Herron Sch. Art, 1968; Periodical of Year award Evang. Press Assn., 1974, 75, 79; Children's Reading Round Table award, 1980. Mem. Artist's Guild Chgo. (1st Place Photography Show, 1977). Illustrator: My First Books About Jesus, 4 books, 1981; Children's Bible Basics, 8 books, 1981; The Wonderful World of the Bible, vol. 1, 1981. Office: 1495 Banbury Ave Saint Charles IL 60174

HANNAFORD, JULE MURAT, III, lawyer; b. St. Paul, Nov. 4, 1912; s. Jule M. and Caroline (Schurmeier) H.; B.A., Yale U., 1935, LL.B., 1938; m. Barbara Battin, Feb. 2, 1952; children—Caroline Hannaford Pillsbury, Barbara Hannaford Steiner, Elizabeth Hannaford Battles, Jule Murat IV. Admitted to Minn. bar, 1938; mem. firm Dorsey, Windhorst, Hannaford, Whitney & Halladay, Mpls., 1938—; dir. Downtown Auto Park, Inc.; mem. adv. com. to dir. NIH, 1976—. Mem. Fgn. Policy Assn. Minn., (pres. 1946-50), St. Paul-Mpls. Com. on Fgn. Relations (chmn. 1965-71), Minn. UN Assn. (pres. 1953-55. Episcopalian. Clubs: White Bear Yacht, Mpls., Inland Lakes Yachting Assn. (commodore 1952-53); University (St. Paul); Birnham Wood Country (Santa Barbara, Calif.); Yale (N.Y.C.). Contbr. articles to profl. jours. Home: 52 Dellwood Ave White Bear Lake MN 55110 Office: 2200 1st Nat Place E Minneapolis MN 55402

HANNAH, FRANKLIN (JESSE), religious adminstr.; b. White County, Ark., Apr. 30, 1945; s. Charley Edward and Zoria Rosia (Brooks) H.; grad. in Bus. Adminstrn., Ark. State U., 1972; m. Gloria Kay Howard, Mar. 21, 1969; children—Kenneth Edward, Kevin Dewayne, Kimberley Michelle. Tchr. 5th grade Cotton Plant (Ark.) Pub. Sch., 1968-69; mgr. Butler Shoes Co., Indian Mill, Jonesboro, Ark., 1969-71; salesman, supr. ABC Termite and Pest Control Co., Searcy, Ark., 1971-72; unit mgr. Union Life Ins. Co., Wynne, Ark., 1972-74; fin. sec. div. fgn. missions Gen. Council Assemblies God, Springfield, Mo., 1974-79, outpost comdr. Central Assembly God Royal Rangers, 1975-79, regional cons. deferred giving and trust dept., 1979—; ordained to ministry Gen. Council Assemblies of God, 1979. Mem. Adminstrv. Mgmt. Soc. (pres. Springfield 1978). Club: Kiwanis (chmn. membership com. Wynne, Ark., 1973-74). Home: 3738 S Franklin St Springfield MO 65807 Office: 1445 Boonville Ave Springfield MO 65802

HANNAH, JOHN ALFRED, educator, food and agr. cons.; b. Grand Rapids, Mich., Oct. 9, 1902; s. Wilfred Steele and Mary Ellen (Malone) H.; student Grand Rapids Jr. Coll., 1912-21, U. Mich., 1921-23; B.S., Mich. State U., 1923, D.Agr., 1941; LL.D., U. Mich., 1944, U. R.I., 1954, Central Mich. U., 1955, Albion Coll., 1957, U. Conn., 1960, Colo. State U., 1963, Alma Coll., 1964, U. Maine, 1965, Howard U., 1966, U. Md., 1966, Ariz. State U., 1966, Tuskegee Inst., 1967, Kalamazoo Coll., 1967, Western Mich. U., 1967, U. S.D., 1967, Ohio State U., 1968, U. Notre Dame, 1970, Akron U., 1970, Hope Coll., 1970, U. Am., 1970; H.H.D., U. Ryukyus, 1952, Mich. State U., 1979, Oakland U., 1969; L.H.D., U. Fla., 1953; D.Sc., Mich. Tech. U., 1953, U. Nigeria, 1961, Tri State Coll., 1967; D.Litt., No. Mich. U., 1957, Grand Valley State Coll., 1968; m. Sarah May Shaw, June 22, 1938; children—Mary Elizabeth, Robert W., Thomas A., David H. With Coop. Agrl. Extension Services, Mich. State U., 1923-35; sec. bd. trustees Mich. State U., 1935-41, pres. Mich. State U., 1941-69, pres. emeritus, 1969—; asst. sec. Dept. Def., 1953-54; mng. agt. Fed. Hatchery Coordinating Com., 1933-35; Am. chmn. Permanent Joint Bd. for Def., Can. and U.S., 1954-64; chmn. U.S. Commn. on Civil Rights, 1957-69; chmn. Am. Council on Edn., 1967-68; adminstr. AID, 1969-73; dep. sec. gen. UN World Food Conf., Rome, Italy, 1974; exec. dir. UN World Food Council, Rome, 1975-78; chmn. Internat. Fertilizer Devel. Center, Muscle Shoals, Ala., 1974—; dir. Internat. Agrl. Devel. Services, 1974—. Del., Mich. Constl. Conv., 1961-62; chmn. adv. task force for State of Mich. Civil Service Reform, 1978-79. Mem. Nat. Assn. Land Grant Colls. and State Univs. (past pres., chmn. exec. com.), Phi Beta Kappa. Clubs: Cosmos (Washington); Detroit; Univ. (East Lansing, Mich.). Home: Box 215 Dansville MI 48819 Office: Mich State Univ 220 Nisbet Bldg East Lansing MI 48824

HANNAHS, JAMES ROGER, lab. exec.; b. Columbus, Ohio, Dec. 23, 1942; s. James Harvey and Dorothy (Limes) H.; B.S. in Welding Engring., Ohio State U., 1967; m. Mary E. Hemmert, Jan. 7, 1967; children—Tricia, Michael. Welding engr. Hobart Bros. Co., Troy, Ohio, 1966-73; mgr. Bowser-Morner Testing Labs., Dayton, Ohio, 1973-79; pres. Midwest Testing Labs., Piqua, Ohio, 1979—, also dir; instr. U. Dayton, Edison State Coll., Hobart Sch. Welding Tech. Mem. Garfield Skill Center Adv. Com., Dayton; mem. adv. com. Western Ohio Youth Center, Troy; chmn. adv. com. Edison State Coll., Piqua; mem. adv. com. Upper Valley Joint Vocat. Sch., Piqua. Registered profl. engr., Ohio; cert. welding insp. Mem. Am. Welding Soc. (awards; past sect. chmn.), Am. Soc. Metals (awards; sect. sec.), ASME, ASTM, Nat. Soc. Profl. Engrs., Central Ohio Metallographic Sc., Theta Tau. Club: Ohio State U. Welding Engring. Alumni (dir.). Author: Porta-Slag Welding, 1970; contbr. articles to profl. jours.; patentee in field. Office: 8598 Industry Park Dr Piqua OH 45356

HANNEMAN, RALPH DAVID, feed mill and grain elevator exec.; b. Austinburg, Ohio, Apr. 5, 1936; s. Clarence Philip and Marietta (Sibbrel) H.; student Kent State U., 1957-58; m. Aileen Ilya Harmon, July 6, 1958; children—Philip Lee, Julie Ann, Marc David, Daniel Jay. With Austinburg (Ohio) Coop. Co., 1953—, gen. mgr., 1964—, also dir., sec. bd. dirs., 1965—. Mem. agr. dept. adv. bd. Geneva (Ohio) High Sch.; mem. agr. supply adv. bd. Ashtabula County (Ohio) Joint Vocat. Sch.; bd. dirs. Austinburg County Days; active Boy Scouts Am. Served with U.S. Army, 1955-57. Mem. Future Farmers of Am., Nat. Grain and Feed Assn., Ohio Grain, Feed and Fertilizer Assn. (trustee 1975—, sr. v.p. 1980, exec. com. 1978—), Northeast Ohio Planning Com. of Grain, Beef and Dairy, Nat. Fedn. Ind. Bus., U.S. C. of C., Ashtabula Area C. of C., Ashtabula County Builders Assn. Methodist. Home: 7440 Whitewood Dr Ashtabula OH 44004 Office: 1860 Mill St Austinburg OH 44010

HANNER, LAWRENCE DON, supt. schs.; b. Effingham, Ill., Jan. 18, 1932; s. Floyd F. and Gladys H.; B.Ed., Mo. Valley Coll., 1954; M.Ed., Ill. State U., 1960; postgrad. U. Kans., 1967-68; m. Sandra Stanfield, Dec. 17, 1976; children—Lisa, Robert. Supt., with North Wayne Community Unit Sch. Dist. 200, Cisne, Ill., 1980—. Served with USMCR, 1954-57. Mem. Ill. Assn. Sch. Adminstrs., Am. Assn. Sch. Adminstrs. Clubs: Masons, Shriners, Rotary. Office: North Wayne Community Unit Sch Dist 200 Box 235 Cisne IL 62823

HANS, ROBERT LYLE, banker; b. Lincoln, Nebr., Apr. 21, 1936; s. Lyle C. and Betty L. (Friesen) H.; B.S. U. Nebr., 1958, M.A., 1965; m. Lily Marian Greve, July 7, 1962; children—Bryce Aaron, Monica Sue. With Pacific Nat. Bank, San Francisco, 1961; with Nat. Bank of Commerce Trust & Savs. Assn., Lincoln, 1962—, asst. cashier, 1964-66, asst. v.p., 1966-68, v.p., 1968-75, sr. v.p., 1975-78, exec. v.p., 1978—, mem. dirs. trust com., 1968—; dir. Peterson Bldg. Corp., Lincoln. Mem. City-County Health Adv. Bd., 1965-66, Capital Improvements Fin. Adv. Com., 1969-71, City St. Adv. Com., 1974-75, Downtown Adv. Com., 1979—; mem. City-County Planning Commn., 1977—, chmn., 1979—; mem. City-County Planning Goals and Policies Com., 1971-77, chmn., 1973-76; mem. City-County Tech. Com. Transp., 1973-76; mem. planning bd. United Community Services, 1972-75; mem. Nebr. Solar Access Resources Adv. Panel, 1979—, Nebr. Noise Control Adv. Com., 1980-81; trustee YWCA, 1971-77, vice chmn., 1972-74; bd. dirs. Youth Employment Service, Inc., 1967-70, Lincoln Found., Inc., 1981—; treas. Malone Community Center, 1968-69, trustee, 1967-70; mem. community adv. com. East High Sch., 1975-78, chmn., 1977-78. Served with USMC, 1959. Mem. Omaha-Lincoln Soc. Fin. Analysts, Nebr. Art Assn., Lincoln Symphony Assn., Lincoln C. of C., Theta Xi. Democrat. Unitarian (trustee 1967-72, pres. 1970-72). Clubs: Sertoma (dir. 1968-70), Univ., Hillcrest Country. Home: One Camden Pl Lincoln NE 68506 Office: PO Box 82408 Lincoln NE 68501

HANSELL, EDGAR FRANK, lawyer; b. Leon, Iowa, Oct. 12, 1937; s. Edgar Noble and Celestia Delphine (Skinner) H.; A.A., Graceland Coll., 1957; B.B.A., U. Iowa, 1958, J.D., 1961; m. Phyllis Wray Silvey, June 24, 1961; children—John Joseph, Jordan Burke. Admitted to Iowa bar, 1961; mem. firm Nyemaster, Goode, McLaughlin, Emery & O'Brien, Des Moines, 1964—, partner, 1968—; dir. City Center Corp., Britt Tech. Corp. Bd. dirs. Des Moines Child Guidance Center, 1972-78, pres., 1977-78; trustee Iowa Law Sch. Found., 1975—. Served with USAF, 1961-64. Mem. Iowa Bar Assn. (pres. young lawyers sect. 1971-72, gov., 1971-72, mem. grievance commn. 1973-78, recipient Merit award young lawyers sect. 1977, chmn. corp. and bus. law com. 1979—), Am. Bar Assn., Polk County Bar Assn. Mem. editorial adv. bd. Jour. Corp. Law, 1977—. Home: 4001 John Lynde Rd Des Moines IA 50312 Office: Nyemaster Goode McLaughlin Emery O'Brien Hubbell Bldg Des Moines IA 50309

HANSEN, ARTHUR GENE, univ. pres.; b. Sturgeon Bay, Wis., Feb. 28, 1925; s. Henry A. and Ruth (Anderson) H.; B.S. in Elec. Engring., Purdue U., 1946, M.S. in Math., 1948, D.Eng., 1970; Ph.D. in Math., Case Inst. Tech., 1959; D.Sc., Tri-State Coll., 1972; m., 5 children. Research scientist NASA, 1948-49, 50-58; tchr. U. Md., 1949-50; sect. head Cornell Aero. Lab., Buffalo, 1958-59; mem. faculty mech. engring. U. Mich., 1959-66; dean Ga. Inst. Tech., 1966-69, pres., 1969-71; pres. Purdue U., 1971—; prof. mech. engring. Tuskegee Inst., 1965; sr. research engr. Douglas Aircraft Co., 1964; curriculum cons. Gen. Motors Inst., 1965; cons. to industry, 1961-70; chmn. sci. and research com. Assn. Am. Univs., 1981—; cons. McDonnell-Douglas Corp.; dir. Am. Electric Power Co., Inc., Ball Corp., Internat. Paper Co., Internat. Harvester Co. Chmn., Atlanta Civic Design Commn., 1967-69; mem. Ga. Sci. and Tech. Commn., 1968-71, Ga. Ocean Sci. Center of Atlantic Commn., Atlanta, 1968-71; mem. adv. council Skidaway Oceanographic Inst. for Univ. System Ga., 1968-71; chmn. adv. council Electric Power Research Inst., 1973-79; chmn. adv. council Gas Research Inst., 1976-79, Nat. Acad. Engring. Council; mem. gen. adv. com. ERDA, 1975-76; mem. acad. adv. bd. U.S. Naval Acad., 1975-79; pres. Ind. Conf. Higher Edn., 1975; chmn. com. on minorities in engring. NRC, 1974-76; chmn. bd. visitors Air U., 1974-77; trustee Nat. Fund for Minority Engring. Students, 1975-80; bd. dirs. Nat. Action Council for Minorities in Engring.; mem. exec. com. Assn. Am. Univs. Served with USMCR, 1943-46. Registered profl. engr., Ga. Mem. Nat. Soc. Profl. Engrs., AAAS, Am. Soc. Engring. Edn. (Ind. Engr. of Year 1979), Sigma Xi, Eta Kappa Nu, Pi Tau Sigma, Tau Beta Pi, Phi Kappa Phi, Omicron Delta Kappa, Phi Eta Sigma, Kappa Kappa Psi, Sigma Delta Chi (Leather medal). Author: Similarity Analyses of Boundary Value Problems in Engineering, 1964; Fluid Mechanics, 1967. Office: Purdue U West Lafayette IN 47907

HANSEN, BARBARA PARK, city ofcl.; b. Chgo., Feb. 26, 1928; d. Thomas E. and Mildred A. (Danielson) Park; B.A., Carleton Coll., 1949; m. Julian R. Hansen, Sept. 3, 1949; children—Jane, Dicie. Pres., Family Service Barrington Area, 1971-73; chmn. Barrington Area Council Govts., 1976-78; pres. Village of Barrington Hills (Ill.), 1977—, trustee, 1973-77. Mem. woman's bd. Chgo. Hort. Soc. Mem. DAR, Colonial Dames. Clubs: Friday; Barrington Garden (pres.). Home: 94 Hawthorne Rd Barrington Hills IL 60010 Office: 112 Algonquin Rd Barrington Hills IL 60010

HANSEN, CAROL LYNN, mfg. co. exec.; b. Milw., Dec. 31, 1938; d. Victor P. and Liane M. (Johannsen) H.; B.S. in Home Econs. Edn., U. Wis., Madison, 1960. Home service rep. Wis. Electric Power Co., Milw., 1960-62; asst. dir. Dairy Council of Milw., 1962-63; asst. dir. consumer edn. Johnson Wax, Racine, Wis., 1963-67, dir., 1967-72, exec. dir. Consumer Services Center, 1972—. Bd. dirs. Racine County council Girl Scouts U.S.A., 1981—. Mem. Home Economists in Bus. (dir. 1969-76, chmn. Wis. group 1968-69), Am. Home Econs. Assn. (dir. 1977-78), Wis. Home Econs. Assn., Am. Women in Radio and TV (pres. Badger chpt. 1969-70), Soc. Consumer Affairs, Nat. Home Fashions League, Nat. Assn. Furniture Mfrs., Phi Upsilon Omicron, Sigma Epsilon Sigma. Office: 1525 Howe St Racine WI 53403

HANSEN, CHARLOTTE LORRAINE HELGESON (MRS. GORDON H. (HANSEN), editor; b. Jamestown, N.D., June 1, 1922; d. Louis Sebern and Ida Ethelyne (Clough) Helgeson; student Jamestown Coll., 1940-41; B.S., U. Minn., 1944; m. Gordon H. Hansen, Oct. 31, 1945; 1 dau., Jo-Ida Charlotte. Hematologist, Hanford Engring. Co., Richland, Wash., 1944-45; serologist Tex. Dept. Health, Wichita Falls, 1945-46; instr. microbiology Jamestown Coll., 1951-61; food editor Jamestown Sun, 1949—; sec.-treas., v.p. Hansen Bros., Inc.; dir. Jamestown Indsl. Devel. Corp., Jamestown Nat. Bank, First Bank System, Mpls. Mother adviser Rainbow Girls, 1964-73. Pres., United Fund, Jamestown council Girl Scouts U.S.A.; bd. dirs. Camp Rokiwan, James River Sr. Citizens; trustee First United Meth. Ch., Jamestown Coll. Recipient Grand Cross of Color, Rainbow Girls, 1940, Thanks badge Girl Scouts U.S.A., 1964; named Merit Mother of N.D., 1969; named Outstanding Woman of N.D. in Civics and Community Services, 1974, Outstanding Citizen of Jamestown, 1978. Mem. AAUW, Nat. Fedn. Press Women, N.D. Press Women, Am. Legion Aux., P.E.O., Zonta, Theta Tau Sigma, Delta Kappa Gamma, Sigma Delta Chi. Mem. Order Eastern Star. Clubs: Wednesday, Civic Music. Author: Kitchen Magic, 1964; Favorites of My Family, 1972; Let's Entertain. Home: 309 11th Ave NE Jamestown ND 58401 Office: 121 2d St NW Jamestown ND 58401

HANSEN, CONNOR THEODORE, ret. state justice; b. Freeman, S.D., Nov. 1, 1913; s. William Dayton and Gladdus (Hall) H.; B.Ed., Wis. State Tchrs. Coll., 1934; LL.B. U. Wis., 1937; m. Annette Phillips Ferry, June 17, 1939; children—Annette Hansen Olson, Peter C., David P., Jane Hansen LaRonge. Admitted to Wis. bar, 1937; dist. atty. Eau Claire county (Wis.), 1938-44; spl. agt. FBI, 1943-44; individaul practice law, Eau Claire, 1945-58; judge Eau Claire county, 1958-67; justice Wis. Supreme Ct., 1967-81; county judge rep. Ct. Adminstrv. Com. for Wis., 1965-67; pres. Wis. State Bd. Juvenile Ct. Judges, 1964-65; sec. Wis. State Bd. County Judges, 1967; circuit ct. commr. Eau Claire Cbunty, 1947-58. Pres., Meml. High Sch. PTA, Eau Claire, Wis., 1940-41; mem. adv. bd. Eau Claire County Youth Camp, 1940-44; pres. Eau Claire Baseball Club, 1940-42; mem. Camp Manito-wish Com., N.Central area YMCA, 1940—; state chmn. NCCJ, 1969-70; mem. Eau Claire County Bd. Suprs., 1945-49, chmn., 1948-49; bd. dirs. Eau Claire Guidance Clinic, 1960-67, YMCA, Eau CLaire, 1954-64, Wis. Welfare Council, 1968-71, Eau Claire Found., Inc., Wis. State U., 1957-65. Recipient Distinguished award Eau Claire Jr. C. of C., 1941, Crime Prevention award Eau Claire Exchange Club, 1963, Distinguished Service award NCCJ, 1970. Mem. State Bar. Wis., Wis. Dist Attys. Assn. (pres. 1942-43), Jefferson County Bar Assn., Eau Claire County Bar Assn., Northwest Peace Officers Assn. (pres. 1941-42), Alumni Assn. of Wis. State U. (pres. 1949-50, Disting. Ser. award 1967). Club: Lions (Lake Mills). Home: 340 S Main St Lake Mills WI 53551

HANSEN, FRANKLIN ALLEN, rupture disc mfg. co. exec.; b. Sioux City, Iowa, Sept. 10, 1926; s. Harold A. and Anna H.; B.S. in M.E., Kans. State U., 1949; m. Jacqueline R. Adams, July 2, 1948; children—Vicki Lee, Lynn Ellen. Jr. engr. Black Sivalls and Bryson, Kansas City, Mo., 1949-51, sr. engr., 1951-55, asso. engr., 1955-62; chief engr. Fike Metal Products Corp., Blue Springs, Mo., 1962-66; chief engr. Continental Disc Corp., Riverside, Mo., 1966—. Served with USAAF, 1944-46. Registered Profl. Engr., Kans. Mem. ASME. Methodist. Club: Exchange Club of Raytown. Patentee field tank venting and pressure vessel safety systems for oil field, petro-chem., aero space and beer industries. Home: 6001 Harris St Raytown MO 64133 Office: 4103 Riverside St Riverside MO 64150

HANSEN, GLADYS OLGA, word processing systems cons.; b. Chgo., Nov. 19, 1920; d. Charles and Olga (Kubis) Vlas; grad. Bryant and Stratton Bus. Coll., 1938; student Wright Jr. Coll., 1941-42, Coll. of Lake County, 1978; m. Robert Roy Hansen, Mar. 2, 1947 (div. Dec. 1963); children—Gail Melody, James Drew, Lynn Diane (dec.), Diane Kathleen, Karen Lynn. Exec. sec. to pres. Universal Equip. Co., Chgo., 1964-68; sec. to chmn. bd., pres. No. Electric Co., Chgo., 1968-69; word processing mgr. Baxter Travenol Labs., Inc., Deerfield, Ill., 1969-79; word processing cons., Deerfield, 1979—; pub. Kamely Press, Deerfield, 1980. Mem. adv. com. Oakton Community Coll., Morton Grove, 1976-80, Loop Coll., Chgo., 1977-78; sec.-treas. Union Drainage Dist. 1 of W. Deerfield Twp., 1973-78; pub. chmn. PTA, Aurora, Ill., 1957; active Boys Scouts Am., Girl Scouts U.S.A. Mem. Word Processing Mgmt. Assn. Chgo. (sec. 1978-79), Internat. Word Processing Assn., Nat. Assn. Women Bus. Owners, Am. Mgmt. Soc., Women in Mgmt., Am. Soc. Profl. Cons.'s, Waukegan/Lake County C. of C., Deerfield C. of C. Republican. Presbyterian. Clubs: Questers (v.p. 1979-80), Order Eastern Star. Author: Word Processing Systems Manual for Originators and Support Staff, 1976, rev. 1980; Word Processing Systems Manual for Support Staff, 1976, rev. 1980. Home: 1150A W Osterman Pl Deerfield IL 60015 Office: 65 E Palatine Rd Suite 117 Prospect Heights IL 60070

HANSEN, GRACE VIOLET DOUGHERTY, dance dir.; b. Milw., Apr. 18; d. Charles Arnold and Flora E. (Ernst) Dougherty; tchrs. certificate Gladys Height Dance Tchr. Acad., Chgo., 1938; student Chgo. Tchrs. Coll., summers 1949-50; grad. Chgo. Nat. Assn. Dance Masters, 1950, masters degree in dance, 1953; student Ernest Flatt, Louis DePron, Donald Sawyer Fred Kelly; m. John Charles Forbes, July 27, 1971; 1 dau. by previous marriage, Judy Ellen Wilkin. Dance dir. Met. YMCA's of Chgo. and Suburbs, 1953—; tchr. dance Chgo. Bd. Edn., 1955-63; mem. faculty Chgo. Nat. Assn. Dance Masters, 1953—, Dance Masters of Wis., 1962-63, Tex. Dance Tchrs. Assn., 1964, Dance Educators Am., N.Y.C., 1953-78; judge numerous dance contests; examiner U.S. Ballroom Council, 1965-78. Mem. Pres.'s Council on Youth Opportunity, 1967. Mem. Dance Educators Am. (midwest regional dir. 1978—).

HANSEN, JAMES OTTO, ednl. adminstr.; b. Lead, S.D., Sept. 21, 1928; s. Harold J. and Lillian (Mattson) H.; B.S., Black Hills State Coll., 1952; M.A., U. No. Colo., 1956; Ed.D., U. S.D., 1968; m. Dora Laura Helmer, May 28, 1950; children—Linda Kay Hansen Reierson, Diana May Hansen Buseman, June Doreen. Tchr., prin. public schs., Philip, S.D., 1952-55; supt. schs., Wessington, S.D., 1956-60; supt. schs., Gregory, S.D., 1961-67; supt. schs., Madison, S.D., 1968-76; asst. supt. instrn. State of S.D., Pierre, 1976-77, dept. state supt., 1978-79, state supt. of elem. and secondary edn., 1979—. Served with USAF, 1946-49. Mem. NEA, Council Chief State Sch. Officers, Sch. Adminstrs. S.D. (Adminstr. of Yr., 1979), Phi Delta Kappa. Republican. Congregationalist. Clubs: Kiwanis, Rotary, Masons, Elks. Office: Kneip Bldg Pierre SD 57501

HANSEN, JOHN JARRETT, social services exec.; b. Effingham, Ill., July 11, 1942; s. Stephen John and Dorothy Saville (Mohr) H.; B.A., So. Ill. U., 1965; M.A., Eastern Ill. U., 1975; m. Vera Irene Nattier, Nov. 8, 1968; 1 dau., Dori Rene. Elem. guidance counselor, Ullin, Ill., 1965-66; planning dir. OEO, Effingham, 1968-70; counselor Mental Health Center, Effingham, 1970-75; exec. dir. Effingham County Mental Health, 1975-80; exec. dir. Comprehensive Services Inc., Mt. Vernon, Ill., 1980—. Served with AUS, 1966-68. Decorated Bronze Star. Mem. Am. Psychol. Assn., Ill. Psychol. Assn., Ill. Assn. Masters Level Psychologists. Author: A Didactic Group Therapy Program for the Treatment of Depression, 1976. Home: 2813 Apple St Mount Vernon IL 62864 Office: PO Box 428 Mount Vernon IL 62864

HANSEN, KATHRYN GERTRUDE, former state ofcl., assn. editor; b. Gardner, Ill., May 24, 1912; d. Harry J. and Marguerite (Gaston) Hansen; B.S. with honors, U. Ill., 1934, M.S., 1936. Personnel asst. U. Ill., Urbana, 1945-46, supr. tng. and activities, 1946-47, personnel officer, instr. psychology, 1947-52, exec. sec. U. Civil Service System Ill., also sec. for merit bd., 1952-61, adminstrv. officer, sec. merit bd., 1961-68, dir. system, 1968-72; lay asst. firm Webber, Balbach, Theis and Follmer, P.C., Urbana, Ill., 1972-74. Bd. dirs. U. YWCA, 1952-55, chmn., 1954-55; bd. dirs. Champaign-Urbana Symphony, 1978-81. Mem. Coll. and Univ. Personnel Assn. (hon., life mem., editor Jour. 1955-73, Newsletter, Internat. pres. 1967-68), Annuitants Assn. State Univs. Retirement System Ill. (state sec.-treas. 1974-75), Pres.'s Council U. Ill. (life), U. Ill. Alumni Assn. (life), U. Ill. Found., Campus Round Table U. Ill., Nat. League Am. Pen Women, Am. Assn. U. Women (state 1st v.p. 1958-60), Bus. and Profl. Women's Club, Champaign-Urbana Symphony Guild, Secretariat U. Ill. (life), Fortnightly Club Urbana, Medra, Delta Kappa Gamma (state pres. 1961-63), Phi Mu (life), Kappa Delta Pi, Kappa Tau Alpha.

Presbyterian. Clubs: Order Eastern Star, Monday Writers (Champaign-Urbana). Author: (with others) A Plan of Position Classification for Colleges and Universities; A Classification Plan for Staff Positions at Colleges and Universities, 1968. Editor: The Illini Worker, 1946-52; Campus Pathways, 1952-61; This is Your Civil Service Handbook, 1960-67. Author, lectr., cons., editor publs. on personnel practices. Home: 1004 E Harding Dr Apt 307 Urbana IL 61801

HANSEN, LOWELL C., II, lt. gov. S.D.; b. Oct. 11, 1939; B.S. in Bus. Adminstrn., U. Nebr. Mem. S.D. Ho. of Reps., 1972-78, speaker pro tem, 1974, speaker, 1976; lt. gov. State of S.D., Pierre, 1979—. Mem. Sioux Falls Outstanding Young Man of Yr., 1972, Outstanding Young Man of Am., 1972. Mem. Sigma Alpha Epsilon. Republican. Office: Office of Lt Gov State Capitol Bldg Pierre SD 57501*

HANSEN, MARY ANN KAUFMANN, banker; b. Albany, N.Y., Mar. 7, 1944; d. William and Charlotte Margaret Kaufmann; B.A., Wheaton Coll., 1966; m. Dennis Hansen, Feb. 14, 1981. Asso. buyer B. Altman & Co., N.Y.C., 1966-69; asst. bus. mgr. Nat. Assembly, N.Y.C., 1969-70; asst. to dir. client relations CBS, N.Y.C., 1970-71; asst. account exec. Muller Jordan Herrick, Inc., 1971-74; advt. officer U.S. Trust Co. of N.Y., 1974-79; asst. v.p., advt. mgr. 1st Bank of Mpls., 1979—. Mem. Advt. Fedn. Minn., Internat. Advt. Assn. (dir. Minn. chpt.), Bank Mktg. Assn., Direct Mktg. Assn. Office: First Bank of Minneapolis 120 S 6th St Minneapolis MN 55480

HANSEN, NIKOLAS FORBES, physician; b. Detroit, Oct. 22, 1932; s. Harvey Robert and Elizabeth Forbes (MacDonald) H.; B.A., Wayne State U., 1960, M.D., 1968; m. Jean Gunderson, July 11, 1953; children—Catherine, Kendall, Cynthia, Clarissa, Christopher. Chem. salesman E. I. duPont de Nemours & Co., Wilmington, Del., 1960-64; rotating intern Detroit Gen. Hosp., 1968-69; practice medicine specializing in family practice, Valparaiso, Ind., 1970—; mem. staff Porter Meml. Hosp., Valparaiso, 1970—; bd. govs. Porter County (Ind.) chpt. Am. Cancer Soc., 1976-78. Served with USN, 1952-56. Diplomate Am. Bd. Family Practice. Fellow Am. Acad. Family Physicians; mem. AMA (Physician's Recognition award 1974-79), Ind. State Med. Assn., Porter County Med. Soc. Republican. Episcopalian. Home: 3902 Sleighbell Ln Valparaiso IN 46383 Office: 2102 E Evans Ave Valparaiso IN 46383

HANSEN, SARA MARGARET, educator; b. Grinnell, Iowa, Mar. 4, 1948; d. Harold A. and Alice (Kingery) Lofgreen; B.A. in Spl. Edn., U. No. Iowa, Cedar Falls, 1970, M.A. in Spl. Edn., 1977; m. Larry L. Hansen; 1 dau., Sara Beth. Learning disabilities resource tchr. Marshalltown (Iowa) Schs., 1970—. Mem. adv. bd. Head Start, 1974-78, Day Care Center, 1974-76. Mem. NEA, Ia. State, Marshalltown edn. assns., Council for Exceptional Children, Assn. for Children with Learning Disabilities. Certified in spl. edn., Ia. Home: 1111 S 4th St Marshalltown IA 50158 Office: Anson Elementary Sch S 3d Ave Marshalltown IA 50158

HANSEN, WILLIAM JAMES, ins. co. exec.; b. Rhinelander, Wis., Jan. 5, 1928; s. Sophus William and Martha LaBarr (Dunning) H.; B.S. in Fire Protection Engring., Ill. Inst. Tech., 1952; C.P.C.U., Am. Inst. for Property and Liability Underwriters, 1973; m. Dorothy Mildred Anderson, July 31, 1954; 1 son, David Arthur. Engr., Factory Ins. Assn., Mnpls., 1952-54; mgr. engring. dept. Charles W. Sexton Co., Mnpls., 1954-62; dist. mgr. Protection Mut. Ins. Co., Mnpls., 1962-66, regional v.p., Milw., 1966-69, v.p. mktg., Park Ridge, Ill., 1969—. Served with U.S. Army, 1946-48. Mem. Soc. Fire Protection Engrs., Newcomen Soc. N.Am., Soc. C.P.C.U. Clubs: Metropolitan, Park Ridge Country Toastmasters Internat. Home: 21277 N Woodland Ave Barrington IL 60010 Office: 300 S Northwest Hwy Park Ridge IL 60068

HANSER, THEODORE HENRY, ret. surgeon; b. St. Louis, July 29, 1896; s. Rudolph and Marie Margaret (Schenkel) H.; grad. St. Paul's Coll., Mo., 1916; B.S., Washington U., St. Louis, 1920, M.D., 1922; LL.D., Concordia Theol. Sem., 1977; m. Edna A. Ulrich, Feb. 3, 1932 (dec. Jan. 1981); children—Naomi Hanser McCann, Mary Beth Hanser Neiger, David T. House officer Mass. Gen. Hosp., Boston, 1922-25; practice medicine specializing in surgery, St. Louis, 1925-65; mem. staff Lutheran Med. Center, St. Louis; med. dir. Anheuser-Busch Inc., St. Louis, 1925-65, med. cons., 1965-77; pres. emeritus Grandel Med. Group, St. Louis, 1925—; physician and surgeon Washington U. Sch. Medicine, St. Louis, 1925-27. Bd. dirs. Blue Shield, 1952-61; with SSS, 1939-43. Served to 2d lt. U.S. Army, 1918. Recipient Certificate of Appreciation, Pres. Franklin D. Roosevelt, 1943, Apostle Paul award St. Paul's Coll., 1966; Christus Vivit Hon. medallion Concordia Sem., 1979. Diplomate Nat. Bd. Med. Examiners. Fellow A.C.S. (med. record honor certificate 1933); mem. St. Louis Surg. Soc., St. Louis City Med. Soc., AMA. Republican. Evang. Lutheran. Clubs: Mo. Athletic, Knights of the Cauliflower Ear. Home: 12505 Village Circle Dr Apt 386G Saint Louis MO 63127 Office: 3555 Sunset Office Dr Saint Louis MO 63127

HANSES, EDWARD HENRY, ecologist; b. Chgo., May 29, 1924; s. George William and Anna Antoinette (Droste) H.; student Ill. Inst. Tech., 1942, Notre Dame U., 1943; B.S., Mich. State U., 1950, B.S.F., 1951; m. Gladys Irene Miller, Feb. 5, 1949; children—Mark, Patrick, Daniel, Ann, Mary, Teresa, Andrew, John, Susan. Forester Green Bay Paper & Pulp Co., 1950; dist. forester BLM, Montrose, Colo., 1951; forester City of Dayton, Ohio, 1953-54; pvt. practice farm forester, Minn., 1955-62, Ill., 1962-65; with C.E., U.S. Army, 1965—, chief environ. and social analysis br., Chgo., 1975—; lectr. in field. Active Boy Scouts Am. Served with USNR, 1943-46. Registered forester, Mich. Mem. Soc. Am. Foresters, Sierra Club. Roman Catholic. Club: K. C. (4th deg.).

HANSON, ALDEN WADE, chemist; b. Jennings, Mich., June 19, 1910; s. Yorgan and Goldie (Fairchilds) H.; B.S., Alma Coll., 1934, D.Sc. (hon.) 1980; m. Helen Laurine Bennett, Feb. 22, 1930; children—Peter W., Helen Laurine, Chris Alden, Alden Bennett. Chemist, Dow Chem. Co., Midland, Mich., 1934-39, project leader, 1939-41, group leader, 1941-54, dir. nuclear and basic research lab., 1954-73; cons., dir. Hanson Industries, Inc., 1970—, Alden Labs., 1980—, Regents of U. Calif., Livermore, 1956-62. Mem. Am. Chem. Soc., ASTM, AAAS, Sigma Xi. Clubs: Midland Country; Otsego Ski; Hidden Valley (Gaylord, Mich.). Contbr. articles on indsl. use of nuclear power, chem. research on plastics and nuclear waste disposal to profl. jours.; patentee plastic processes, mech. apparatus and snow making processes. Home: 3124 Valley Dr Midland MI 48640 Office: 1702 Bldg The Dow Chem Co Midland MI

HANSON, CHARLES EASTON, JR., mus. ofcl.; b. Holdrege, Nebr., Apr. 4, 1917; s. Charles Easton and Irene Hazel (Adkins) H.; student Kearney State Coll., 1934-35, U. Colo., 1949-50; m. Eva Marie Phillips, Apr. 18, 1936; children—Charles Easton, William Raymond, James Austin. Adminstrv. engr. 7th Service Command, Sioux City, Iowa, 1942-43, Bur. Reclamation, McCook, Nebr., 1946-51, USAF, Wiesbaden, Germany, 1952, Dept. Agr., Casper, Wyo. and Washington, 1954-69; dir. Mus. Fur Trade, Chadron, Nebr., 1969-72, 74—, cons. dir., 1960-68, editor mus. quar., 1965—. Spl. lectr. various colls., hist. confs.; hist. cons. for museums and major pubs. Hon. chmn. Alexander Culbertson Meml. Com., Orleans, Nebr., 1951. Bd. dirs. Mus. Assn. Am. Frontier, Chadron. Recipient Post Comdr. citation Liberal Army Airfield for exceptional civilian service, 1943; James L. Sellers Meml. award Nebr. Hist. Soc., 1977. Fellow Co. Mil. Historians; mem. Nebr. Museums Assn. Potomac Westerners (sheriff 1965), Md. Arms Collectors, Am. Soc. Arms Collectors, Phi Tau Gamma. Republican. Methodist. Author: The Northwest Gun, 1955; The Plains Rifle, 1960; co-author: The Early Fur Trade in Northwest Nebraska, 1976; The Hawken Rifle—Its Place in History, 1979; contbr. articles to profl. jours. Home: Route 2 PO Box 18 Chadron NE 69337

HANSON, DONALD WILLIAM, cons. engr., state senator; b. Fargo, N.D., Oct. 17, 1935; s. Harry William and Naomi Helen (Peterson) H.; student N.D. State U., 1953-57; m. Marilyn L. Johnson, Aug. 25, 1956; children—Deon Ruth, Mark, Kirk. Design engr. Mooney, Henning & Assos., Fargo, 1956-65; partner, cons. engr. Elken, Geston & Hanson, Moorhead, Minn., 1965-71; partner, cons. engr. Geston & Hanson, Fargo, 1971—; mem. N.D. State Senate, 1976—. Served with Air NG, 1953-57. Mem. ASHRAE, N.D. State U. Alumni Assn. (pres.), Am. Legion. Republican. Lutheran. Clubs: Fargo Rotary (pres. 1981-82), Elks. Office: 711 2d Ave N Fargo ND 58102

HANSON, FRED T., lawyer; b. Wakefield, Nebr., Feb. 25, 1902; s. Peter H. and Hannah Ulrika (Anderson) H.; LL.B., U. Nebr., 1925; m. Helen Elizabeth Haddock, Nov. 12, 1928; 1 son John Fredrik. Admitted to Nebr. bar, 1925, since in pvt. practice; probate judge, 1931-42, pros. atty., 1927-30, 51-54; spl. asst. to U.S. atty. gen., 1954-62; life mem. Nat. Conf. Commrs. Uniform State Laws from Nebr., com. on uniform probate code. Bd. dirs. Nebr. dist. Luth. Ch.-Mo. Synod, 1976-80. Served as capt. AUS, 1942-46. Mem. Am. Judicature Soc., Am. Coll. Probate Counsel (regent), Am., Nebr., local bar assns., Am. Legion. Office: 316 Norris Ave Mc Cook NE 69001

HANSON, JEAN THOMPSON, ednl. adminstr.; b. Parker Prairie, Minn., May 9, 1942; d. Elmer Milton and Mabel Alida (Eggen) Thompson; B.S., N.D. State U., 1964, M.S., 1971; m. Algie Hanson, Nov. 17, 1962; children—Jill, Mark. Tchr., Oak Grove High Sch., Fargo, N.D., 1963-64, Red Lake Falls (Minn.) High Sch., 1964-72; dir. East Polk-Red Lake County Vocat. Center, Red Lake Falls, 1972-77; dir. Pine to Prairie Coop. Center, Red Lake Falls, 1977-81; Bush Leadership fellow, 1981-82; guest instr. S.D. State U., N.D. State U. Bd. dirs. Agassiz Health Systems Agy., Grand Forks, N.D., 1976-80; pres. bd. dirs. Red Lake Falls Children's Center, 1976-80; mem. N.D. Health Coordinating Council, 1977-79; mem. corp. bd. United Hosp., Grand Forks, 1979-80. Recipient Good Neighbor award Sta. WCCO, 1975; Alumni award 4-H, 1979. Mem. Am. Vocat. Assn. (pres., v.p. 1981-82), Minn. Vocat. Assn. (pres.), Am. Home Econs. Assn., Minn. Home Econs. Assn., Nat. Council Local Adminstrs., Minn. Council Local Adminstrs., Assn. Supervision and Curriculum Devel., Minn. Assn. Secondary Vocat. Adminstrs., Home Economists in Edn., Minn. Future Homemakers Am. (hon.), Alpha Gamma Delta, Phi Kappa Phi, Kappa Delta Pi. Lutheran. Club: Toastmasters (regional and dist. awards, public speaking 1979). Home: 132 Demont Ave E Saint Paul MN 55117

HANSON, JEAN THOMPSON, ednl. adminstr.; b. Parkers Prairie, Minn., May 9, 1942; d. Elmer Milton and Mabel Alida (Eggen) T.; B.S., N.D. State U., 1963, M.S., 1971; m. Algie Hanson, Nov. 17, 1962; children—Jill, Mark. Tchr., Oak Grove High Sch., Fargo, N.D., 1963-64, Red Lake Falls (Minn.) High Sch., 1964-72; dir. East Polk Red Lake County Vocat. Center, Red Lake Falls, 1972-77, Pine to Prairie Coop. Center, Red Lake Falls, 1977-81; adj. prof. Moorhead (Minn.) State U. Bd. dirs. Agassiz Health Systems Agy., Grand Forks, 1976-80; pres. bd. dirs. Red Lake Falls Children's Center, 1976-81; mem. N.D. Health Coordinating Council, 1977-79. Recipient Good Neighbor award Sta. WCCO, 1975; Alumni award 4-H, 1979; Bush Leadership fellow, 1981-82. Mem. Am. Vocat. Assn. (dir. 1976-81, v.p. 1976-80 pres. 1981-82), Minn. Vocat. Assn. (pres. 1975-76), Am. Home Econs. Assn., Minn. Home Econs. Assn., Nat. Council Local Adminstrs., Assn. Curriculum and Devel., Minn. Assn. Secondary Vocat. Adminstrs., Home Economists in Edn., Alpha Gamma Delta. Lutheran. Club: Toastmasters. Home: 132 Demont Little Canada MN 55117 Office: 116 Classroom Office Bldg U Minn Saint Paul MN 55108

HANSON, JUDITH PARKS, advt. dir.; b. Richmond, Va., Mar. 26, 1953; d. Robert James and Judith Ann (Robertson) Parks; student Alma Coll., 1971-73; cert. Kendall Sch. Design, 1975; B.F.A., Eastern Mich. U., 1980; m. John Gottfried Hanson, May 1, 1976. Display artist Jacobson's Inc., Saginaw, Mich., 1976-77; advt. design, typesetter, composer Pioneer Press, Big Rapids, Mich., 1978; designer Bookcrafters, Inc., Chelsea, Mich., 1979; advt. dir. Home Appliance Mart, Ann Arbor, Mich., 1980—. Home: 6834 Ardsley Dr Canton MI 48187 Office: Home Appliance Mart 2019 W Stadium Blvd Ann Arbor MI 48103

HANSON, MARVIN B., state senator; B.S. with honors, 1966; J.D., Columbia U., 1969. Farmer; mem. Peace Corps, 1962-64; mem. Minn. Senate, 1976—. Mem. Democratic-Farmer-Labor party. Office: 205 State Capitol Saint Paul MN 55155*

HANSON, ROBERT ALFRED, educator; b. El Paso, Tex., June 22, 1945; B.S., U. Wis., LaCrosse, 1968; M.A., Ball State U., Muncie, Ind., 1975. Counter-intelligence agt. U.S. Army Intelligence Command, 1968-73; criminal investigator U.S. Army Criminal Investigation Command, 1973-76; instr. criminal justice No. Mich. U., Marquette, 1976-78, coordinator regional criminal justice tng. center, 1976-78, dir. tng., cons. criminal justice dept., 1978—, established Internat. Law Enforcement Diving Inst., 1978—. Mem. Task Force on Spouse Abuse; mem. public relations com. Michigan Domestic Violence Prevention and Treatment Bd. Mem. Am. Assn. Correctional Officers (nat. exec. sec. 1979—), Mich. Assn. Chiefs Police, Am. Soc. Tng. and Devel. Editor: Keeper's Voice. Office: Criminal Justice Tng Center Northern Michigan University Marquette MI 49855

HANSON, ROBERT ARTHUR, mfg. co. exec.; b. Moline, Ill., Dec. 13, 1924; s. Nels A. and Margaret L. (Chapman) H.; B.A., Augustana Coll., 1948; m. Patricia Ann Klinger, June 25, 1955. With Deere & Co., Moline, Ill., 1950—, v.p. overseas ops., 1972, sr. v.p. overseas div., 1973, exec. v.p., 1975, pres., 1978, pres., chief operating officer, 1979—, also dir.; dir. Davenport Bank & Trust Co., Dun & Bradstreet Corp., Internat. Council Morgan Guaranty Trust Co. Bd. dirs. Augustana Coll., 1975—, Agribus. Council, 1974—; bd. trustees Com. for Econ. Devel., 1980—; mem. adv. com. on bus. programs, Brookings Inst., 1978—. Served with USMC, 1943-46. Mem. Farm and Indsl. Equipment Inst. (dir. 1977—). Republican. Home: 2200 29th Ave Ct Moline IL 61265 Office: Deere & Co John Deere Rd Moline IL 61265

HANSON, ROBERT LEONARD, office supply co. exec.; b. Chgo., May 19, 1937; s. James Levoid and Thyra Hildegard (Johnson) H.; A.A., Northwestern Mich. Coll., 1956; B.S., Ferris State Coll., 1958; m. Mary Frances Filomeno, Nov. 18, 1961; children—Linda, Michael, Jeffrey, Karyn, Tracy. Sr. accountant Arthur Andersen & Co., 1958-66; controller ACCO div. Gary Industries, Chgo., 1966-69; v.p., gen. mgr. ACCO Canadian, Toronto, Ont., 1969-72; v.p. materials mgmt., asst. to pres. ACCO Internat., Wheeling and Northbrook, Ill., 1972—. Mem. Wheeling Indsl. Devel. Bd.; chmn. scouting Skokie Valley dist. Boy Scouts Am., 1977-79; coach Northbrook (Ill.) Bantam AA Hockey Club, 1977-80; mem. Northbrook Vol. Pool, 1978-81; bd. dirs. N.W. Community Hosp. Found., 1978-81, Harper Community Coll. Ednl. Found., 1981—; gen. mgr. North Suburban Jr. Varsity Hockey League; treas. Chgo. Met. Hockey League. Served with U.S. Army, 1961. Mem. Assn. Internal Mgmt. Cons., Assn. for Systems Mgmt., Constrn. Specifications Inst., Cert. Rev. Appraisers, Wheeling C. of C. (dir., past pres.), Windham Homeowners Assn. (dir., pres.). Clubs: Rotary (dir., past pres., Paul Harris fellow) (Wheeling); Northbrook Hockey; Scarboro Golf (Toronto). Home: 3010 Margo Ln Northbrook IL 60062 Office: 770 S Acco Plaza Wheeling IL 60090 also 2215 Sanders Rd Northbrook IL 60062

HANSON, ROBERT PAUL, newspaper exec.; b. Chgo., May 22, 1944; s. John Peter and Margaret (Russell) H.; student DePaul U.; m. Virginia Marie Scholl, Aug. 28, 1965; children—Margaret, Jennifer, Robert, Erica. Asst. treas. Am. Foundrymen Soc., 1962-64; salesman Des Plaines (Ill.) Pub. Co., 1967-69; regional accounts mgr. Field Enterprises, Elk Grove, Ill., 1969-71; sales mgr. Paddock Publications, Arlington Heights, Ill., 1971-76; Midwest sales mgr. U.S. Suburban Press, Schaumburg, Ill., 1976-77, Eastern sales mgr., 1977-78, v.p. sales, pres., 1978—. Office: 945 N Plum Grove Rd Suite B Schaumburg IL 60195

HANSON, ROLAND JOHN, educator; b. Rockford, Ill., Jan. 4, 1933; s. Lloyd B. and Ella M. (Larson) H.; B.S., U. Wis., Platteville, 1959; M.S., U. Wis., Madison, 1965; children—James R., Jill E. Vocational-agr. instr. Stratford (Wis.) High Sch., 1959-64; spl. young and adult farmer instr. New Richmond (Wis.) High Sch., 1964-66; vocational-agr. instr. East Troy (Wis.) High Sch., 1966—, dept. head., 1966—. Served with USAF, 1951-55; ETO. Named Outstanding Jaycee, New Richmond Jr. C. of C., 1966. Mem. Nat. Vocational Agr. Tchrs. Assn., Am. Vocat. Assn., Wis. Assn. Vocat. Agr. Instrs. (teaching scholar 1979), Wis. Assn. Vocat. Educators, Walworth County Profl. Agr. Workers, DAV (life). Republican. Lutheran. Clubs: Alumni Platteville Lettermen's, Masons. Office: East Troy High Sch East Troy WI 53120

HANTON, WILLIAM HENRY, indsl. psychologist; b. Detroit, July 26, 1948; s. John Thomas and Catherine Isabel (Watt) H.; B.S. with distinction, U. Mich., 1972; Ph.D., U. Minn., 1977; m. Peggy Jo Sisson, Mar. 17, 1973; children—David Nathaniel, Andrew William. Research asst. Personnel Decisions, Inc., Mpls., 1975-76; instr. Ill. Inst. Tech., Chgo., 1976-77; asst. prof. psychol. scis. dept. Purdue U., West Lafayette, Ind., 1977-79; asst. v.p. The Marine Corp., Milw., 1979—. Regents alumni scholar U. Mich., 1966-67; Eva O. Miller fellow U. Minn., 1975-76, Mem. Am. Psychol. Assn., Am. Soc. Personnel Adminstrn., Acad. Mgmt. Mem. Ch. of Jesus Christ of Latter-day Saints. Office: 111 E Wisconsin Ave PO Box 481 Milwaukee WI 53201

HANWAY, DONALD GRANT, agronomist, educator; b. Broadwater, Nebr., Aug. 6, 1918; s. Frank Pierce and Emma Terrissa (Twist) H.; B.S., U. Nebr., 1942, M.S., 1948; Ph.D., Iowa State Coll., 1954; m. Blanche Elizabeth Larson, Sept. 26, 1942; children—Donald Grant, Wayne Edward, Janice Kay. Tchr. rural schs. Morrill County, Nebr., 1936-40; faculty dept. agronomy U. Nebr., Lincoln, 1947—, also extension agronomist, chief of party univ. mission to Ataturk U., Erzurum, Turkey, 1965-67; agronomic cons. Nigeria, Colombia, Morocco, Tunisia. Served with USAAF, 1942-46. Named to Nebr. Hall of Agrl. Achievement. Fellow Am. Soc. Agronomy, AAAS; mem. Crop Sci. Soc. Am., Soil Conservation Soc. Am., Am. Inst. Biol. Scis., Phi Beta Kappa, Sigma Xi, Alpha Zeta, Gamma Sigma Delta. Republican. Episcopalian. Contbr. articles to profl. jours. Home: 6025 Madison Ave Lincoln NE 68507 Office: Dept Agronomy U Nebr Lincoln NE 68583

HANZLICK, WILLIAM P., state govt. ofcl.; b. Gt. Bend, Kans., Sept. 23, 1936; s. George A. and Margaret E. Hanzlick; B.S. in Biology, Ft. Hays (Kans.) State U., 1958, M.S. in Zoology, 1959; m. Neva Kay Huddleston, June 2, 1957; children—Blakes, Linda, Juli. Wildlife biologist, then supr. Western region Kans. Fish and Game Commn., 1959-80, dir. commn., Pratt, 1980—. Wildlife scholar, 1958. Mem. Am. Range Soc., Wildlife Soc., Wildlife Fedn. Kans. (Wildlife Conservationist of Year award 1976). Address: Route 2 Box 54A Pratt KS 67124

HAPP, LAWRENCE RAYMOND, metal engr.; b. Mendota, Ill., Mar. 11, 1945; s. Albert William and Mary (Becker) H.; B.S. in Metall. Engring., U. Ill., 1968; m. Susan Jean Beste, Mar. 4, 1971; children—Brian, Donald, Debra, Gregory. Supr. welding devel. labs. Caterpillar Tractor Co., Peoria, Ill., 1968-69; welding engr. Trane Co., LaCrosse, Wis., 1969-73, sr. welding engr., quality control mgr., Burlington, Iowa, 1973-74; welding and materials engr., supt. tank shop Paul Mueller Co., Springfield, Mo., 1974-81; welding and materials engr. APV-Crepaco Inc., Lake Mills, Wis., 1981—. Mem. Cursillo Movement, Birthright, Right to Life; active Scripture Study groups. Registered profl. engr., Mo. Mem. Mo. Solar Energy Assn., Am. Welding Soc. (chmn. Ozark sect. 1974-78, mem. numerous coms.), Am. Soc. Metals, Nat., Mo. socs. profl. engrs., ASME, ASTM. Roman Catholic. Club: Jaycees. Developer welding fabrication methods and equipment. Home: Route 1 Box 40A Johnson Creek WI 53038 Office: 100 South CP Ave Lake Mills WI 53551

HAPPACH, BERNARD CHARLES, hosp. mgmt. sers. adminstr.; b. Peoria, Ill., Oct. 3, 1930; s. Bernard Marius and Mildred Alma (Holliger) H.; B.S., Bradley U., 1955; m. Marlene R. Schroeder, Dec. 31, 1974; children—Rhonda, Karen, Tamara, Benjamin. Mgr., Comml. Credit Corp., Peoria, Ill., 1956-62; bus. mgr. St. Francis Hosp., Peoria, 1962-67; gen. credit mgr., corp. dir. patient accounts Sisters of the Third Order of St. Francis, Peoria, 1967—. Bd. dirs. Children's Center Tazewell County Inc. Served with USMC, 1947-51. Decorated Purple Heart; recipient Frederick T. Muncie Merit award, 1980. Nat. cert. mgr. of patient accounts, consumer credit exec. Mem. Nat. Hosp. Fin. Mgmt. Assn. (William G. Follmer merit award 1971, Robert A. Reeves merit award 1975, Robert M. McMahon achievement award 1975, life membership meritorious award 1978), Soc. Cert. Consumer Credit Execs., Ill. Assn. Hosp. Attys. Republican. Roman Catholic. Author: Collecting Receivables-How to get the Job Done, 1977; Managing Cash Flow, 1980. Home: 127 E Oakwood St Morton IL 61550 Office: 1124 N Berkeley Peoria IL 61603

HAQUE, PROMOD, elec. engr.; b. Simla, India, Apr. 20, 1948; s. Alexander and Phulwanti (Gangaram) H.; B.S. in Elec. Engring., U. Delhi, 1969; M.S. in Elec. Engring., Northwestern U., 1974, Ph.D., 1976, M.B.A., 1982; m. Dorcas Ann Daniels, July 15, 1978. Sales engr. Siemens India Ltd., New Delhi, 1969-72; sr. engr. EMI Med. Inc., Northbrook, Ill., 1976-77, lab. dir., 1977-80; v.p. Emergent Corp. of Anaheim, Calif., Northbrook, 1980—. Mem. IEEE, Am. Assn. Physicists in Medicine. Republican. Mem. Evang. Free Ch. Am. Home: 2541 Asbury St Evanston IL 60201 Office: 3605 Woodhead Dr Northbrook IL 60062

HARASEVYCH, MARIA S., author, lit. critic; b. Ukraine, Oct. 14, 1918; d. Sava and Iryna (Hannocha) Bilous; came to U.S., 1949, naturalized, 1955; philologist diploma, Kiev State U., 1941; m. Bohdan W. Harasevych, Jan. 24, 1944. Dir. studies, acting high sch. prin. in Russia, 1941-42; mem. bd. edn. Mineralny Vody, Kaukasus, USSR, 1942; dir. dept. ednl. methods and supervising insp. high schs., Mineralny Vody, 1942; wording redactor for novelists, translator and lectr., 1945-49; lit. critic, writer, journalist, tchr., cons. Ukrainian and Russian langs., 1949—; author: Contemporary Poetry in Ukraine, 1962; Satire and Humor in Soviet Literature, 1963; John Steinbeck, 1966; Works of M. Ponedilok, 1966-70; B. Alexandriv-Poetry, 1973; B. Lepky in Prose and Poetry, 1974; Literary Portrait of O.Veretenchenko, 1976; Literary Portrait of U. Samchuk, 1978; also articles, revs., essays; staff writer Horizon, Ukrainian quar., 1970—. Mem. Ukrainian Nat. Women's League Am., Ukrainian Writers Assn. in Exile, World Fedn. Ukrainian Women's Orgns. Mem. Ukrainian Orthodox Ch. Club: Ukrainian Community (Detroit). Address: 3061 Firestone St Sterling Heights MI 48077

HARASYMIW, STEFAN JAROSLAW, educator, adminstr.; b. Oct. 28, 1938; s. Stefan and Clara (Medynski) H.; B.A., U. Conn., 1961, M.S., 1963, Ph.D., 1971; m. Roxala Fylypowyez, Apr. 27, 1968; 1 child, Lewko. With United Aircraft Corp., 1963-66; research asso. ednl. technol. devel., research div. Ednl. Testing Service, Princeton, N.J., 1966-68; asst. prof. Boston U., 1970-75; asst. prof. dept. rehab. medicine Med. Sch. Northwestern U., Chgo., 1975—; dir. rehab. services evaluation Rehab. Inst. Chgo., 1976—. Lic. psychologist, Mass. Mem. Assn. for Computing Machinery, Council for Exceptional Children, IEEE, AAAS, Am. Congress Rehab. Medicine, Am. Public Health Assn., Am. Psychol. Assn., Nat. Rehab. Assn. Contbr. articles to profl. jours. Office: 345 E Superior St Chicago IL 60611

HARBINSON, BROTHER CAMILLUS, retarded adults home adminstr.; b. Belfast, No. Ireland, Apr. 18, 1924; s. William Edward and Elizabeth (Thompson) H.; L.P.N., St. Joseph Hosp., Albuquerque, 1953. Came to U.S., 1951. Joined Bros. of the Good Shepherd, asst. superior gen., 1969, internat. superior gen., 1977—; dir. Ozanam Inn., New Orleans, 1954-57; adminstr. St. Martin Home, Columbus, Ohio, 1957-63, Good Shepherd Manor, Wakefield, Ohio, 1963-71, Momence, Ill., 1971—. Address: PO Box 260 Momence IL 60954

HARBOUR, JEANNE DULAS, child psychiatrist; b. Labatut, France, Feb. 9, 1921; d. Pierre and Dorothy (Stafas) Dulas; M.D., Sch. Medicine, Paris, France, 1947; M.D., Wis. U., 1968; m. Howard Harbour, June 15, 1962. Came to U.S., 1958, naturalized, 1967. Sch. pub. health med. insp., France, 1948-58; intern Presbyn.-St. Luke's Hosp., Chgo., 1958-59, resident, 1959-61; clin. asst. psychiatry Ill. U., 1959-61; fellow psychiatry McGill U., 1962, Toronto U., 1963; fellow child psychiatry Chapel Hill Meml. Hosp., N.C. U., 1964-65; cons. child psychiatry North Shore Hosp., Winnetka, Ill., 1966-67, Mendota State Hosp., Madison, Wis., 1968-71; now child psychiatrist, mem. med. staff Children's Meml. Hosp., Chgo., Presbyn.-St. Luke's Hosp., Chgo.; asst. prof. psychiatry Rush-Presbyn.-St. Luke's Med. Center, Chgo. Diplomate Am. Bd. Psychiatry and Neurology, Am. Bd. Child Psychiatry. Mem. AMA, Am. Psychiat. Assn., Ill. Med. Soc., Am. Med. Womens Assn., Chgo. Council Child Psychiatry. Research on color blindness of sch. children. Home: 535 N Michigan Ave Chicago IL 60611 Office: 2335 W 103d Chicago IL 60643

HARBRON, WILLIAM ROBERT, ednl. adminstr.; b. Hamilton, Ohio, Dec. 20, 1950; s. Robert Kenneth and Elizabeth Ann (Roesel) H.; B.S. in Elem. Edn., Miami U., Oxford, Ohio, 1973, M.Ed. in Ednl. Adminstrn., 1976; m. Marilyn French, Mar. 22, 1974; children—Carrie Ann, Jayne Blythe. Tchr., Edgewood Local Sch. Dist., Trenton, Ohio, 1973-76, Greenhills-Forest Park Sch. Dist., Forest Park, Ohio, 1976-77; prin. Ross Local Schs., Hamilton, Ohio, 1977-79, Bowling Green (Ohio) City Schs., 1979—. Dist. chmn. Wood dist. Toledo Area council Boy Scouts Am., 1981—, also scoutmaster; youth dir. Village View Ch. of Christ, 1980—. Mem. Assn. Individually Guided Edn., Am. Assn. Sch. Adminstrs., Am. Soc. Curriculum Devel., Wood County Assn. Elem. Adminstrs., Gideons, Phi Delta Kappa. Home: 508 N Wintergarden St Bowling Green OH 43402 Office: 140 S Grove St Bowling Green OH 43402

HARDACRE, MARILYN LOUISE AMRINE, mayor; b. Marysville, Ohio, Mar. 14, 1935; d. William Lowell and Dosha Pauline (Gambill) Amrine; B.S. cum laude in Home Econs., Ohio State U., 1956; m. Jerry Medaris Hardacre, June 9, 1957; children—Jerry Medaris II, James Michael, Elizabeth Anne, Jeffrey Max. Vocational home econs. tchr., Groveport, Ohio, 1957-59; home econs. tchr., cafeteria mgr. Franklin Jr. High Sch., Columbus, Ohio, 1959-60; adminstrv. dietitian Mount Carmel Hosp., Columbus, 1960; mayor City of Marshfield (Wis.), 1978—. Bd. dirs. Greater Marshfield, Inc.; mem. adv. bd. Mid-Am. Convalescent Home, Marshfield; mem. State Adv. Council for Community Edn.; bd. dirs., past pres. St. Joseph's Hosp. Aux.; past mem. State Gov. Bd. Wis. Hosp. Assn.; active Am. Cancer Soc., Boy Scouts Am., Camp Fire Girls, mem. Marshfield Recreation Com., 1972-77, chmn., 1975-77. Mem. League Wis. Municipalities (bd. dirs.), Wis. League Municipalities (mem. com. finance and taxation), Wis. Valley Mayors (pres.), LWV, Marshfield Bus. and Profl. Women's Club. Methodist. Home: 512 Quentin St Marshfield WI 54449 Office: 112 E 2d St Marshfield WI 54449

HARDEN, OLETA ELIZABETH (MRS. DENNIS CLARENCE HARDEN), educator; b. Jamestown, Ky., Nov. 22, 1935; d. Stanley Virgil and Myrtie Alice (Stearns) Mc Whorter; B.A., Western Ky. U., 1956; M.A. in English, U. Ark., 1958, Ph.D. in English, 1965; m. Dennis Clarence Harden, July 23, 1966. Teaching asst. U. Ark., Fayetteville, 1956-57, 58-59, 61-63; instr. S.W. Mo. State Coll., Springfield, 1957-58, Murray (Ky.) U., 1959-61; asst. prof. English, Northeastern State Coll., Tahlequah, Okla., 1963-65; asst. prof. Wichita (Kans.) State U., 1965-66; asst. prof. English Wright State U., Dayton, Ohio, 1966-68, asso. prof., 1968-72, prof., 1972—, asst. chmn. English dept., 1967-70, asst. dean coll. liberal arts, 1971-73, asso. dean, 1973-74, exec. dir. Gen. Univ. Services, 1974-76. Wright State U. Research and Devel. grantee, 1969, Found. grantee, 1971; Nat. Endowment for Humanties nominee, 1977. Mem. Modern Lang. Assn., Coll. English Assn., AAUP. Author: Maria Edgeworth's Art of Prose Fiction, 1971. Home: 2618 Big Woods Trail Fairborn OH 45324 Office: Dept English Wright State U 7751 Colonel Glenn Hwy Dayton OH 45431

HARDER, JOSEPH C., state senator; b. Hillsboro, Kans., Feb. 1, 1916; s. David E. and Margaret (Flaming) H.; ed. Tabor Coll., Bethel Coll.; m. Maran Lee Brooks, 1939; 1 son, Brooks. Mgr. Harder Furniture Co., 1950-60; sec.-treas. Moundridge Telephone Co., 1955—, mgr., 1960—; pres. Ami, Inc., 1959—; mem. Kans. Senate. Councilman, Moundridge, 1954-58; precinct committeeman McPherson County Republican party, 1954—; bd. dirs. McPherson County Hosp., 1956-58; del. Rep. Nat. Conv., 1976. Recipient Disting. Service award Friends U. Address: Moundbridge KS *

HARDER, ROBERT CLARENCE, state govt. ofcl.; b. Horton, Kans., June 4, 1929; s. Clarence L. and Olympia E. (Kubik) H.; A.B., Baker U., Baldwin, Kans., 1951; M.Th., Perkins Sch. Theology, Dallas, 1954; Th.D. in Social Ethics, Boston U., 1958; m. Dorothy Lou Welty, July 31, 1953; children—Anne, James David. Ordained to ministry United Methodist Ch., 1959; pastor East Topeka Meth. Ch., 1958-64; research asso. Menninger Found., Topeka, 1964-65; part-time instr. Washburn U., Topeka, 1964, 68, 69; dir. Topeka Office Econ. Opportunity, 1965-67; tech. asst. coordinator Office Gov. Kans., 1967-68; dir. community resources devel. League Kans. Municipalities, 1968-69; sec. Kans. Dept. Social and Rehab. Services, 1969—; dir. Kans. Dept. Social Welfare, 1969-73; part-time instr. Kans. U. Sch. Social Welfare, 1971—. Mem. Kans. Ho. of Reps. from 31st Dist., 1961-67. Recipient Disting. Service award East Topeka Civic Assn., 1963, Romana Hood award social service, 1965, Man of Year in Religion in Kans., Midway mag., Topeka, 1965. Mem. Am. Soc. Public Adminstrn. (Public Adminstrn. Man of Year award 1980), Am. Public Welfare Assn., Kans. Council Children and Youth, Kans. Conf. Social Welfare. Democrat. Author papers in field. Office: Social and Rehab Services 6th Floor State Office Bldg Topeka KS 66612

HARDIN, EUGENE ALBERT, cons. civil and sanitary engr.; b. Ottawa, Kans., Nov. 21, 1895; s. Frank S. and Mary L. (Hyden) H.; B.A., Baker U., 1918; postgrad. U. D'Aix-Marseille, France, 1919; B.S. in Civil Engring., M.I.T., 1921; m. Gladys Eleanor Taylor, Apr. 11, 1925; children—Nancy Ann, Mary Lou. Hydraulic and structural engr. Black & Veatch, cons. engrs., Kansas City, 1921-25; asst. civil engr. in charge design water purification plants Dept. Water Supply, Detroit, 1925-32; asst. office engr. Black & Veatch, cons. engrs., 1932-36, asso. civil engr., Detroit sewage treatment plant, 1936-38; prin. engr. Consoer, Townsend & Quinlan, cons. engrs., Chgo., 1938-40; engr. in charge design and constrn. maj. program water system, Phila., 1940-47, project engr. in charge design Phila. sewage treatment project, 1947-51; asso. civil and san. engr. Parsons, Brinckerhoff, Quade & Douglas, cons. engrs., N.Y.C., 1951-75, project mgr., chief san. engr., 1965-75; engring. cons. in water supply and sewerage to engring. firms, 1975—. Served with U.S. M.C., AEF, 1917-19. Mem. ASCE (Thomas Fitch Rowland prize 1938), Am. Water Works Assn., Am. Public Works Assn., Soc. Am. Mil. Engrs., Am. Acad. Environ. Engrs, VFW, Am. Legion, Delta Tau Delta. Methodist. Club: Masons. Contbr. articles on sanitary engring. to profl. jours.; inventor shunt system of reservoir and pumping station operation, also composite bearing pile for founds. Address: 1214 Juliette Ave Manhattan KS 66502

HARDIN, MARTHA LOVE WOOD, civic leader; b. Muncie, Ind., Aug. 13, 1918; d. Lawrence Anselm and Bonny Blossom (Williams) Wood; B.S. with distinction and high honors, Purdue U., 1939; m. Clifford Morris Hardin, June 28, 1939; children—Susan Hardin Wood, Clifford Wood, Cynthia Hardin Milligan, Nancy Hardin Rogers, James Alvin. Librarian, U. Chgo., 1939-40. Chmn. Nebr. Heart Fund, 1967; vol. worker Lincoln Gen. Hosp., 1965, Clarkson Hosp., 1966; hon. chmn. Symphony Ball, Washington, 1970; mem. met. bd. YWCA, Washington, 1969-71, St. Louis, 1973—; mem. Women's Com. of Pres.'s Com. on Employment of Handicapped, 1970—, permanent mem. bd., 1970—; bd. dirs. St. Louis Speech and Hearing Clinic, St. Louis Met. YWCA; co-chmn. nat. fund-raising campaign U. Nebr. Found., 1977-80. Mem. St. Louis Geneal. Soc., DAR, PEO, Mortar Board, Phi Beta Kappa, Pi Beta Phi. Clubs: Congressional (Washington); Old Warson Country, St. Louis (St. Louis). Contbr. articles to geneal. publs. Home: 10 Roan Ln Saint Louis MO 63124

HARDIN, RUTH MARIE, county supr.; b. Osceola, Iowa, Sept. 8, 1943; d. Allen Sidney and Flora Marie (Fox) Butler; student Napa Coll., 1961-62; A.A., Vallejo Coll., 1967; postgrad. Drake U., 1969; m. Jack Lester Hardin, Nov. 30, 1963; children—Melinda, Michelle, David. With Pacific Telephone & Telegraph Co., Napa, Vallejo and Fairfield, Calif., 1962-65; mgr. farm truck and tractor tire repair bus., 1974-76; chmn. Warren County Bd. Suprs., Indianola, Iowa, 1981—. Active LWV, Questers. Mem. Am. Bus. Women's Assn. Democrat. Club: Scotch Ridge Women's (Carlisle, Iowa). Office: Warren County Courthouse Box 237 Indianola IA 50125

HARDING, DONN SCOTT, ednl. adminstr.; b. Montevideo, Minn., Apr. 9, 1943; s. Wayne Cromwell and Marian Alice (Lighter) H.; B.S., Mankato State U., 1966, M.A., 1978; m. Sharon Lynn Hanson, Oct. 12, 1974; children—Cindy Beth, Melanie Joy, Michelle Lynn. Zone rep. Internat. Harvester Co., St. Paul, 1966-68; distributive edn. coordinator Hastings (Minn.) Public Schs., 1968-72; dept. supr. Hennepin Tech. Centers, Mpls., 1972-76; dir. Carver-Scott Coop. Center, Chaska, Minn., 1976—; adj. instr. U. Minn.,x1981—.xMankatox(Minn.)xStatexU.,x1979 Mankato (Minn.) State U., 1979—, U. Minn., 1981—. Mem. Govs. Council Employment and Tng., 1980—; bd. dirs. CETA, 1978—. Mem. Minn. Assn. Vocat. Adminstrs., Minn. Assn. Distributive Educators, Am. Vocat. Assn., Minn. Vocat. Assn., Distributive Clubs Am., Hastings Area C. of C. Lutheran. Clubs: Rotary (dir. 1980—), Gavel. Home: 246 Stephens Ct Chaska MN 55318 Office: Carver-Scott Cooperative Center 401 E 4th St Chaska MN 55318

HARDING, GUY HOMER, automobile dealer; b. Pierre, S.D., Dec. 7, 1925; s. Guy Ula and Rose Marie (Kleepsies) H.; B.S., U. S.D., 1950; grad. Command and Gen. Staff Coll., 1972; m. Patricia Faye Binkley, Aug. 27, 1947; children—Teresa Lynn, Barbara Jane, Steven Guy, William Homer. Pres., owner Harding Motor Co., Pierre, 1950—; dir. 1st Nat. Bank, Pierre. Mem. S.D. Senate, 1970-81, majority leader, 1977-81; mem. Pierre Sch. Bd. Served as comdr. 147th F.A. Group, U.S. N.G., 1971-78, brig. gen. S.D. Army N.G. Recipient Quality Dealer award Time Mag., 1975; Golden Anniversary honoree U. S.D., 1977. Mem. Pierre C. of C. (pres.), Am. Legion, Izaak Walton League, VFW. Republican. Methodist. Clubs: Bus. Adv., Masons, Elks. Office: 518 E Sioux Ave Pierre SD 57501

HARDING, JAMES WARREN, finance co. exec.; b. Montoursville, Pa., Nov. 9, 1918; s. James John and Alda (Edkin) H.; B.A., Lycoming Coll., 1937-38; M.A., U. Chgo., 1940; m. Emily Sue Landes, Mar. 22, 1941; 1 dau., Connie Sue (Mrs. Richard E. Fisher). With Kemper Cos., Chgo., 1940—, accountant, 1940-50, comptroller, 1960-68, exec. v.p., 1969, pres. Kemper Corp., Am. Underwriting Corp., Central Mortgage Co., also dir.; dir. Kemper Corp.; chmn. bd., dir. Kemper Reins. Co., Kemper Fin. Services. Pres. Park Ridge (Ill.) Community Assn., 1962-63; finance chmn. Crusade of Mercy, Chgo., 1964-65. Trustee, pres. James S. Kemper Found.; trustee Mundelein Coll.; adv. bd. U. Chgo., Brigham Young U. Served with USNR, 1943-44. Recipient Hardy award Ins. Inst., 1946. Mem. Am. Mgmt. Assn., Econ Club, Financial Execs. Inst., Ins. Statis. Assn., Nat. Indsl. Conf. Bd., Ill. C. of C. (dir.), Phi Kappa Sigma. Republican. Methodist. Clubs: Chgo., University (Chgo.). Contbr. articles to ins. and trade mags. Home: 1230 Thornbury Libertyville IL 60048

HARDMAN, BERNICE ANN BRULA, educator; b. Oak Park, Ill., June 27, 1947; d. Bernard Matthew and Josephine Ann (Laxner) Brula; B.S., DePaul U., Chgo., 1969; M.Ed., Northeastern Ill. U., Chgo., 1975; C.A.S., Nat. Coll., Evanston, Ill., 1982; divorced; 1 dau., Kelley Jessica. Demonstration tchr.-trainer 3d Grade Resource Center, Follow Through Program, Waukegan, Ill., 1977-79, coordinator behavior analysis Follow Through Program, 1980—; human arwareness tchr.-trainer Waukegan Sch. Dist. 60, 1979-80. Mem. NEA, Assn. Supervision and Curriculum Devel., Ill. Assn. Supervision and Curriculum Devel. (liaison publicity chmn. 1981-82), Lake County Curriculum Resource Council (publicity chmn.), Phi Delta Kappa. Democrat. Roman Catholic. Home: 319 S Orchard St Waukegan IL 60085 Office: Carman Sch 520 Helmholz Waukegan IL 60085

HARDY, H. GUY, lawyer; b. Bloomfield, Iowa, July 18, 1918; s. Rufus Guy and Mabel (Kenworthy) H.; student Bloomfield Jr. Coll., 1936-38, B.A., State U. Iowa, 1940, J.D. 1942; LL.M., Harvard, 1947; m. Dorothy Rice, Apr. 22, 1949; children—Susan (Mrs. Michael Doland), Barbara (Mrs. Samuel Maihack), Beverly (Mrs. Scott Montgomery), Richard, Nancy. Admitted to Iowa bar, 1942, Ohio bar, 1948; practiced in Cleve., 1947—; mem. firm McDonald, Hopkins & Hardy Co., Cleve., 1947—. Dir., sec. Am. Handling Equipment Co., Harvest Life Ins. Co., Daniels Funeral Home, Inc., Jaquay Lake Park, Inc.; dir. Harvest Pub. Co., Harvest Ins. Agy., Inc., Lakewood Furnace Co. Asst. area chmn. United Appeal, Cleve., 1966-67; bd. mgrs. West Shore YMCA, 1963—; trustee Combined Health Fund Drive, Bay Village, Ohio, 1964-68; trustee Bay Village Swimming Pool Inc.; councilman Bay Village, O., 1956-61, pres., 1960-61; mem. bd. edn., Bay Village, 1964-73, pres., 1968-70. Served to capt. CIC, AUS, 1942-46, 51. Recipient Extension award Lions Club, 1953. Mem. Am. Judicature Soc., Am., Ohio State, Cleve. bar assns., Order of Coif. Episcopalian (vestryman 1963-66). Lion. Home: 28334 Osborn Rd Bay Village OH 44140 Office: East Ohio Bldg Cleveland OH 44114

HARDY, LUCIAN FREDERICK, quality assurance exec.; b. Rushford, N.Y., Dec. 12, 1934; s. Leigh Edward and LucY (Walker) H.; A.A.S. in Electronics, Erie County Tech. Inst., 1957-59; B.S. U. Buffalo, 1963; student quality mgmt. M.I.T., 1965; M.S., Ind./Purdue U., 1979; m. Barbara Ellen White, Oct. 29, 1960; children—Leigh Alfred, Charles Patrick, Lisa Marie. Mgr. quality control Sierra Research Corp., Buffalo, 1962-69; mgr. quality assurance Medlon Products div. Abbott Labs., Buffalo, 1969-77; quality assurance dir. Zimmer U.S.A., Warsaw, Ind., 1977—; asso. prof. math. Erie Community Coll., Buffalo, 1964-74. Chmn., Elma (N.Y.) Citizens Com. for Youth Center, 1968-70; mem. Latimer Tri-Town Recreation Com. Elma, 1965-74, chmn., 1968-69, 73; first aid instr. A.R.C., 1969-77, emergency med. technician, 1970-78; mem. Elma Democratic Com., 1963-74; bd. dirs. Elma, Marilla, Wales Boys Clubs, Inc., 1970-74; mem. Parish Council, St. Francis Ch. Served with USMC, 1953-56. Mem. Am. Soc. Quality Control (cert. quality engr.), Am. Ordnance Assn., Am. Statis. Assn., Hardy Family Assn. Am., Toy Train Operating Soc. Roman Catholic. Club: Kiwanis. Home: Rural Route 1 189-B Pierceton IN 46562 Office: Zimmer PO Box 708 Warsaw IN 46580

HARDY, MARIE PAULA, educator; b. Kansas City, Feb. 24, 1926; d. Russell Charles and Agnes Esther (Cunningham) H.; B.A., Saint Mary Coll., 1962; M.A. (NDEA grantee), U. Nebr., 1969; Ph.D. (Triple T fellow), U. Ill., 1972. Joined Sisters of Charity of Leavenworth, Roman Catholic Ch., 1943; elem. tchr. parochial schs., Kans., Mo., Colo., Ill., Calif., Mont., 1945-57; secondary tchr. parochial schs., Kans., Mont., Colo., Ill., 1957-68; scholar-in-residence U. Newcastle-Upon-Tyne (Eng.), 1970-71; mem. faculty Saint Mary Coll., Leavenworth, Kans., 1971—; chmn. dept. edn., 1978—; mem. drama commn. York Internat. Conf., Eng., 1971; condr. workshops, seminars in field. Recipient Outstanding Educator of Am. award, 1975; Kans. Regional Council Higher Edn. and U.S. Dept. Edn. grantee U. Baroda (India), summer 1976. Mem. Nat. Council Tchrs. English, Am. Assn. Univ. Women, NEA, Am. Assn. Coll. Tchrs. of Edn., Internat. Reading Assn., Kans. Assn. Higher Edn. Kans. Council of English Educators, Kans. Assn. Tchrs. English, Assn. Tchr. Educators, Kans. Internat. Reading Assn., Spl. Interest Group-A Network on Adolescent Literature, Nat. Assn. Elem. Sch. Prins., Nat. Assn. Secondary Sch. Prins., Kans. Reading Profls. Higher Edn., Kans. Assn. for Gifted, Talented, Creative, Assn. Ind. Liberal Arts Colls. for Tchr. Edn. Democrat. Roman Catholic. Contbr. articles in field to profl. publs. Home and Office: Saint Mary Coll Leavenworth KS 66048

HARDY, VIANN BUTERA, data processing exec.; b. Tucson, May 5, 1947; d. Nick M. and Ruth E. (Denney) Butera; B.A. in Psychology, U. Mo., 1972, M.P.A. cum laude, 1973; m. DeVon Jaxon Hardy, June 11, 1967; children—Simeon, Jaxon. Pension cons. for Jackson County, Kansas City, Mo., 1967-68; adminstr. mgmt. services Jackson County Juvenile Ct., Kansas City, 1968-77; asst. county purchasing agt. Jackson County, 1969-77; dir. data processing dept. social services State of Mo., Jefferson City, 1977—; regional rep. on info. systems mgmt. Am. Public Welfare Assn. Mem. Mo. Gov.'s Task Force on Criminal Justice Info. Systems, 1975-76. Home: 2909 Sue Dr Jefferson City MO 65101 Office: 313 W McCarty St Jefferson City MO 65101

HARFST, ERNEST DENNIS, coll. adminstr.; b. Havana, Ill., Nov. 8, 1926; s. Eilert E. and Iva W. (Thomason) H.; B.S., U. Ill., 1950; M.S., No. Ill. U., 1974; m. Betsy C. Perteit, Aug. 29, 1948; children—Sue Ann, Michael D., Patrick L. Indsl. mgmt. trainee various cos., Ill., 1950-54; design engr. Ideal Industries, Sycamore, Ill., 1954-62, lab. mgr., 1962-68; instr. electronics Kishwaukee Coll., Malta, Ill., 1968-72, chmn. indsl. tech. and pub. service occupations, 1972—; cons. in field. Active Boy Scouts Am., 1964-72. Served with USAF, 1945-46. Mem. Nat. Fire Protection Assn., Water Pollution Control Fedn., Ill. Assn. Electrical-Electronic Educators, Kishwaukee Amateur Radio Club, Nat. Rifle Assn., Am. Legion. Republican. Home: 825 Meadow Ln Sycamore IL 60178 Office: Kishwaukee Coll Malta IL 60150

HARGETT, HERBERT PECKOVER, ophthalmologist; b. Augusta, Ky., Oct. 5, 1918; s. Marmaduke and Susan Oridge (Barnhard) H.; A.B., U. Ky., 1940; M.D., U. Louisville, 1943; postgrad. in opthalmology, N.Y. U., 1947-48; m. Marion Hurlbut, June 9, 1945 (dec.); children—William Hurlbut, Kathryn (Mrs. Steven Webb), Pamela (Mrs. John W. Wheeler); m. 2d, S. June Cleveland, Aug. 3, 1974. Intern, Springfield (Ohio) City Hosp., 1943; resident ophthalmology Nichols VA Hosp., Louisville, 1948-50; practice medicine specializing in ophthalmology, Springfield, 1950-61, Jeffersonville, Ind., 1962—; head dept. ophthalmology Clark County Meml. Hosp., 1962—; pres. Clark County Optical Service, Inc., 1962—. Instr. ophthalmology U. Louisville, 1948-50. Pres. Clark County Chpt. Am. Cancer Soc., 1964. Served to capt. M.C., AUS,

1944-46. Diplomate Am. Bd. Ophthalmology. Mem. Clark County, Ind. State med. socs., AMA, Pan-Am. Ophthal. Soc., Barraquer Inst., Barcelona, Spain, Am. Acad. Ophthalmology, Internat. Eye Found., Soc. Eye Surgeons. Clubs: Elks, Lions. Home: 2304 St Andrews Rd Jeffersonville IN 47130 Office: 100 E 12th St Jeffersonville IN 47130

HARGITT, EDWIN FORRY, investment advisor; b. Indpls., Aug. 12, 1934; s. Paul Lee and Caroline Malott (Forry) H.; B.A., Wabash Coll., 1956; B.S., Purdue U., 1960, M.B.A., 1961; m. Verma Lee Steely, Nov. 26, 1966; children—Edwin Forry, Charles Victor, Russell Cushing, Danlee Malott, Marea Eden, David Edmond. Treas. Dahl Corp., Lafayette, Ind., 1961-67, Fin. Services, Inc., Lafayette, 1967-72, Dunn & Hargitt, Inc., Lafayette, 1972-73; pres. Dunn & Hargitt Investment Mgmt., Inc., Lafayette, 1973—; gen. partner Financial Futures Fund, Denver; dir. Dunn & Hargitt Research S.A., Brussels. Pres., West Lafayette High Sch. PTA; sec. West Lafayette Sch. Bldg. Corp.; co-chmn. West Lafayette Swimming Pool Com.; chmn. SME Sycamore council Girl Scouts U.S.A.; cubmaster Boy Scouts Am.; pres. Lafayette Youth Hockey; deacon, elder Covenant Ch. Registered investment adviser SEC, commodity trading advisor, commodity pool operator Commodity Futures Trading Commn. Mem. Nat. Assn. Futures Trading Advisors (founding dir.), Market Tech. Assn., Fin. Analysts Fedn., Am. Fin. Assn., Phi Delta Theta. Republican. Clubs: Lafayette Country, Rotary, Elks. Editor, pub. Market Guide, 1962—, Commodity Service, 1965—, Growing Child, 1971—, Growing Parent, 1971—, Option Charts, 1973—. Home: 128 Mohican Ct West Lafayette IN 47906 Office: 22 N 2d St Lafayette IN 47902

HARGRAVE, HAROLD, ret. educator; b. Boonville, Ind., June 10, 1908; s. Jacob Thurman and Dora (West) H.; B.S. in Edn., Oakland City Coll., 1930, LL.D., 1971; M.S. in Edn., Ind. U., 1936; m. Rowena Hullett, June 4, 1935; 1 dau., Ruth Ann. Began career as tchr. Crowe Sch., Ind., 1926-27, Kings (Ill.) Sch., 1930-31; tchr., guidance dir. pub. schs., LaPorte, Ind., 1931-56, prin., 1956-58, supt. schs., 1958-72; mem. faculty N.Y. U., 1947-49, Peabody Tchrs. Coll., 1948, Butler U., 1946-55. Pres. elect Ind. Pub. Sch. Study Council, 1971; spl. asst. to mayor 1972-80; sec. LaPorte Econ. Devel. Commn., 1972—; exec. com. Fairview Youth Treatment Center, 1973-78. Trustee Community Hosp., Roger Williams Found.; bd. dirs. Haven Hubbard Home for Ret., 1974-77. Mem. Am. Assn. Sch. Adminstrs., NEA, Ind. Assn. Pub. Sch. Supts. (v.p. 1967-68, pres. 1969-70), C. of C. (v.p. 1974-75), Phi Delta Kappa. Mason, Elk, Kiwanian (pres. 1945, lt. gov. 1947). Author: Extending Reading Skills, 1976. Home: 1808 Monroe St LaPorte IN 46350

HARGRAVE, SARAH QUESENBERRY, corporate found. exec.; b. Mt. Airy, N.C., Dec. 11, 1944; d. Teddie W. and Lois Knight (Slusher) Quesenberry; student Radford Coll., 1963-64, Va. Poly. Inst. State U., 1964-67. Mgmt. trainee Thalhimer Bros. Dept. Store, Richmond, Va., 1967-68; Central Va. fashion and publicity dir. Sears Roebuck & Co., Richmond, 1968-73, nat. decorating sch. coordinator, Chgo., 1973-74, nat. dir. bus. and profl. women's programs, Chgo., 1974-76, v.p., treas., program dir. Sears-Roebuck Found., Chgo., 1976—; mem. com. on equal opportunity for women Am. Assembly Collegiate Schs. Bus., 1977—, chmn., 1978-79, 80-81, bd. dirs., 1979—, vis. com., 1979—, fin. and audit com., 1980—, mem. task force on doctoral supply and demand, 1980—, donors' forum women's issues group, 1974—; mem. Com. for Equal Opportunity for Women, 1976—, chmn., 1978-79, 80-81; mem. bus. adv. council Walter E. Heller Coll. Bus. Adminstrn., Roosevelt U. Co-dir. Ill. Internat. Women's Year Center, 1975. Named Outstanding Young Woman of Year, Ill., 1976; Woman of Achievement, State St. Bus. and Profl. Womans Club, 1978. Mem. Assn. Humanistic Psychology, Am. Home Econs. Assn., Nat. Fedn. Bus. and Profl. Women's Clubs, Women and Founds./Corporate Philanthropy, Eddystone Condominium Assn. (v.p. 1978—). Home: 421 W Melrose St Chicago IL 60657 Office: Sears-Roebuck Found Sears Tower Chicago IL 60684

HARGRAVE, VICTORIA E(LIZABETH), librarian; b. Ripon, Wis., Aug. 22, 1913; d. Alexander Walter and Estelle Winifred (Swanson) Hargrave; A.B., Ripon Coll., 1934; library diploma U. Wis., 1938; M.A., U. Chgo., 1947; postgrad. U. Calif. at Los Angeles, 1970. Tchr. Brandon (Wis.) High Sch., 1934-37; extension librarian Iowa State Coll. Library, 1938-44; librarian Ripon Coll., 1944-46, MacMurray Coll., Jacksonville, Ill., 1947-78. Mem. adv. council librarians U. Ill. Grad. Sch. Library Service, 1962-64. Mem. ALA, AAUW. Home: 141 Caldwell St Jacksonville IL 62650

HARHAY, WARREN CHARLES, electric vehicle mfg. co. exec.; b. Cleve., Aug. 3, 1943; s. Joseph Stephen and Hedwig (Krucke) H.; student Kent State U., 1962-66; B.A., Cleve. State U., 1969; m. Marcia Lee Gibson, June 10, 1967; children—Matthew, Marshall, Mitchell. Field service engr., Ohio Sound Systems, Northeast Ohio, 1964-67; broadcast studio and transmitter engr., Stas. WERE, WJW, WMMS, Cleve., 1967-69; sr. instr. electronics, Normandy High Sch., Parma, Ohio, 1969-73; pres. Electric Vehicle Assos., Inc., Cleve., 1973—, also chief exec. officer; apptd. mem. nat. battery adv. council U.S. Dept. Energy. Ordained deacon, ruling elder, chmn. stewardship com. United Presbyterian Church. Mem. IEEE, Soc. Automotive Engrs., Cleve. Engring. Soc. Club: Rotary. Expert witness, U.S. Congress, 1974, 79, Dept. Transp., 1977; contbr. tech. papers to confs.; patentee electric vehicle drives. Home: 6374 Fry Rd Brook Park OH 44142 Office: 9100 Bank St Cleveland OH 44125

HARIMAN, DONALD GEORGE, chiropractor; b. Grand Forks, N.D., Feb. 4, 1925; s. George E. and Emma Lou (Cowger) H.; B.S., U. N.D., 1947; D.C., Nat. Coll. Chiropractic, 1950; m. Darlyne Lee Hamilton, Aug. 17, 1947; children—Robert Donald, Ann Maria, Jean Louise. Practice chiropractic medicine, The Spine Clinic, Grand Forks, N.D.; mem. postgrad. faculty in roentgenology Can. Meml. Chiropractic Coll., 1972-77. Served with USNR, 1943-46. Diplomate Am. Chiropractic Bd. Roentgenology. Fellow Can. Chiropractic Coll. Roentgenology, Internat. Coll. Chiropractors; mem. Am. Chiropractic Coll. Roentgenologists, Am. Chiropractic Coll. Consultants, Am. Chiropractic Bd. Roentgenology (sec. 1970-81), Am., N.D. (sec.-treas. 1954-66, pres. 1970-71) chiropractic assns., N.D. Bd. Chiropractic Examiners (sec. 1969-77), Grand Forks C. of C. (chmn. capital funds rev. bd. 1970-77), Sigma Alpha Epsilon, Lambda Phi Delta. Democrat. Presbyn. (elder). Mason. Club: Grand Forks Country. Home and Office: 711 N Washington St Grand Forks ND 58201

HARING, DAVID ALVIN, mfg. co. exec.; b. Akron, Ohio, Feb. 10, 1945; s. Stanley Alvin and Harriet Marie (Stark) H.; B.S., Baldwin-Wallace Coll., 1967; M.B.A., Ohio State U., 1973; m. Luella Mae Wiley, June 10, 1967; children—Douglas, Brian, Bradford. Porgrammer, systems analyst Chem. Abstracts Service, Columbus, Ohio, 1967-71; mgr. systems and programming Borden, Inc., Columbus, 1971-75; dir. mgmt. info. services Tremco, Inc., Cleve., 1975-77; dir. systems and data processing The Stouffer Corp., Cleve., 1977-80; v.p. mgmt. systems The E.F. Hauserman Co., 1980—. Recipient Theodore O. Hoffman edn. grant Borden, Inc., 1973. Club: Cleve. Easy Striders Track (dir., head coach). Home: 6713 Duneden Ave Solon OH 44139 Office: 5711 Grant Ave Cleveland OH 44105

HARKIN, THOMAS RICHARD, congressman; b. Cumming, Iowa, Nov. 19, 1939; s. Patrick and Frances Harkin; B.S., Iowa State U., 1962; J.D., Catholic U. Am., 1972; m. Ruth Raduenz, July 6, 1968; 1 dau., Amy. Mem. staff U.S. House Select Com. on U.S. Involvement in S.E. Asia, 1970; admitted to Iowa bar, 1972; mem. 94th-97th Congresses from 5th Iowa dist., mem. sci. and tech. com., agr. com. Served as lt. USN, 1962-67. Named Outstanding Young Alumnus, Iowa State U., 1974. Mem. Iowa Bar Assn. Democrat. Home: 3412 Ontario Ames IA 50010 Office: 2411 Rayburn House Office Bldg Washington DC 20515

HARKINS, JOHN JOSEPH, mfg. co. exec.; b. N.Y.C., Jan. 14, 1937; s. Michael Charles and Bridget Mary (Thompson) H.; B.E.E., B.Indsl. Engring. with honors, U. Fla., 1960; postgrad. Ill. Inst. Tech., Cleve. State U.; m. Shirley Joplin, Mar. 3, 1956; children—Randall, Timothy, Shannon. From asso. engr. to sr. products assurance engr. ITT Kellogg Co., Chgo., 1960-65; with Morton Salt Co., 1965—, asst. mining mgr., Fairport, Ohio, 1968-73, asst. plant mgr., Hutchinson, Kans., 1973-76, facility mgr., Marysville, Mich., 1976—. Pres. Leroy (Ohio) Youth Club, 1970-73; bd. dirs. Bluewater YMCA, 1980—; v.p. Manistee (Mich.) Jaycees, 1968. Recipient awards Leroy Youth Club, Manistee Jaycees. Mem. Soc. Mining Engrs., Adminstrv. Mgmt. Soc. (bd. dirs.). Roman Catholic. Club: Internat. Mgmt. Home: 4709 Lakeshore Terr Port Huron MI 48060 Office: 601 Busha Hwy Maryville MI 48040

HARKINS, JOSEPH FRANCIS, state ofcl.; b. Nowata, Okla., Dec. 5, 1938; s. Arthur Thomas and Patricia (Krampf) H.; B.A., U. Kans., 1960, M.P.A., 1962; m. Judith Ann Cary, Aug. 17, 1962; children—Ross, Jeffrey, Ellen. Asst. dir. Cancer Research Center, Columbia, Mo., 1964-68; adminstr. Wayne Miner Health Center, Kansas City, Mo., 1968-70; asst. dir. Model Cities Agy., Kansas City, Mo., 1970-71; research asso. Inst. Community Studies, Kansas City, Mo., 1971-73; asst. prof. U. Kans. Med. Sch., 1973-76; dir. div. health resources Kans. Dept. Health and Environ., Topeka, 1976-78, sec. health and environ., 1978—. Recipient Disting. Service award Dept. Polit. Sci., U. Kans., 1979. Mem. Am. Public Health Assn., State and Territorial Health Officers Assn., Kans. Public Health Assn. Office: Kans Dept Health and Environ Forbes Field Topeka KS 66670

HARKNESS, LAURENCE PATRICK, hosp. adminstr.; b. Kansas City, Mo., Sept. 8, 1941; s. George Robert and Marilu (Stokes) H.; A.B., Rockhurst Coll., 1962; M.S., U. Mo., 1971; m. Karen S. Myers, Aug. 11, 1962; children—Gregory, Elizabeth, Catherine, John. Personnel technician City of Kansas City (Mo.), 1962-66; personnel dir. U. Mo., 1966-73, dir. adminstrn. and med. edn., 1973-78; adminstr. Children's Mercy Hosp., Kansas City, 1978—; instr. Avila Coll.; cons. Appalachina Regional Health System. Chmn. Young Democrats., Kansas City, Mo., 1960-61. Mem. Am. Coll. Hosp. Adminstrs., United Way Agy. Execs., Internat. Assn. Personnel Mgmt. (cert. merit 1975), Am. Assn. Med. Adminstrs., Am. Hosp. Assn., Kansas City C. of C., Mo. C. of C. Roman Catholic. Club: Rotary. Devel. profile examination system for physician extenders, 1973-77. Home: 7400 Terrace St Kansas City MO 64114 Office: Children's Mercy Hosp 24th at Gillham St Kansas City MO 64108

HARLAMERT, ELIZABETH KAY, curriculum adminstr.; b. Shelby, Ind., Sept. 9, 1933; d. Fred Allen and Lois May (McKay) Keeling; B.A., Butler U., 1957, M.S., 1967; G.N., Ind. U., 1957; Ed.S., Ball State U., 1981; m. James Dale Harlamert, Dec. 19, 1955; children—Edward Allen, David James. Nurse, Inlow Clinic, Shelbyville, Ind., 1957, W.S. Major Hosp., Shelbyville, 1958-60, Johnson County Meml. Hosp., 1960-62; tchr. Northwestern Consol. Sch. Dist., Fairland, Ind., 1963-79, curriculum dir., 1979—. Mem. Assn. Supervision and Curriculum Devel., Triton Classroom Tchrs. Assn. (v.p. 1977, pres. 1978), Delta Kappa Gamma. Democrat. Presbyterian (Sunday sch. supt. 1966, Bible Sch. supt. 1972-74). Home: Rural Route 1 Box 34 Boggstown IN 46110 Office: Rural Route 1 Box 79Y Fairland IN 46126

HARLAN, NORMAN RALPH, builder; b. Dayton, Ohio, Dec. 21, 1914; s. Joseph and Anna (Kaplan) H.; Indsl. Engring. degree U. Cin., 1937; m. Thelma Katz, Sept. 4, 1955; children—Leslie, Todd. Pres. Am. Constrn. Corp., Dayton, 1949—, Mainline Investment Corp., 1951—, Harlan, Inc., realtors; treas. Norman Estates, Inc. Mem. Dayton Real Estate Bd., Ohio Real Estate Assn., Nat. Assn. Real Estate Bds., C. of C., Pi Lambda Phi. Home: 303 Glenridge Rd Kettering OH 45429 Office: 2451 S Dixie Hwy Dayton OH 45409

HARLEV, BEVERLY RUTH, nurse; b. New Brighton, Pa., June 18, 1940; d. William Wayne and Dorothy Elizabeth (McCully) Thompson; diploma nursing Beaver Valley Gen. Hosp., 1961; B.S.N., Greenville Coll., 1963; M.S., No. Ill. U., 1975; m. Robert W. Harlev, June 18, 1966; 1 son, Kenneth Wayne. Nurse, Greenville (Ill.) Coll., 1961-63; staff nurse Luth. Gen. Hosp., Park Ridge, Ill., 1963-65; instr. nursing Luth. Gen. and Deaconess Hosps. Sch. Nursing, 1965-75, curriculum coordinator, 1975-78, asst. dir. adminstrn., 1978—; vis. asst. prof. sociology Concordia Coll., River Forest, Ill., 1980—; chmn. by-laws com. Ill. Council Diploma Nursing Programs, 1979-81. Mem. Ill. Nurses Assn., Nat. League Nursing, Am. Nurses Assn., Assn. Supervision and Curriculum Devel. Office: 1700 Western Ave Park Ridge IL 60068

HARLOW, BARBARA ANN, mgmt. cons.; b. Kansas City, Kans.; d. James Vernon and Jennie Alice (Flint) Bigler; B.A., U. Nebr., 1970; children—Ronald Eric Harlow, Gregory Brent Harlow. Exec. dir. March of Dimes, Omaha, 1970-71, regional cons., Kansas City, Mo., 1971-73, nat. cons., 1973-74; pub. relations dir. Crown Center Hotel, Kansas City, 1974-78; corp. dir. tng. and devel. Woolf Bros., Kansas City, 1978-80; pres. Mgmt. Assos. Inc., Consultants in Human Resource Devel., 1980—; cons. women in mgmt. Active pub. relations Clark Welfare Council, Clark AFB, P.I.; counselor Neighborhood Youth Corps, Kansas City; mem. women's div. Kansas City Philharmonic Orch. Mem. Pub. Relations Soc. Am., Am. Soc. Tng. and Devel., Kansas City C. of C. Club: Kansas City Ski. Home: 7615 E Gregory Blvd Kansas City MO 64133

HARLOW, RONNEY LEOPOLD, communications co. exec.; b. Berlin, Germany, May 18, 1912; s. Leopold and Bronia (Meyer) Hamburger; student Polytechnic, London, Eng., 1927-28, Sorbonne, Paris, France, 1928-29; m. Rose Mary Meyer, May 4, 1938; children—Jacqueline Harlow Rothmann, Judi Harlow Berman. Came to U.S., 1941, naturalized, 1943. Organizer br. offices for telephone co. in Yugoslavia, 1933-35; founder Automatic Alarm, Marseilles, France, 1935, Automatic Alarm, Mpls., 1941; organizer, pres. Pvt. Tele-Communications, Chgo., 1946—, now chmn. Bd. dirs., officer N. Am. Telephone Assn., Communication and Sound Contractors Assn. Chgo. Served with AUS, 1943-45. Mem. Telephone Interconnect Assn. Ill. (officer). Club: Rotary. Home: 2900 W Greenleaf St Chicago IL 60645 Office: 1300 W Belmont Ave Chicago IL 60657

HARLOW, WILLIAM HENRY, II, sch. prin.; b. Seymour, Ind., Mar. 6, 1945; s. William H. and Wilma (Beickman) H.; B.S., Ball State U., 1967, M.A., 1969; m. Sharlene Kamman, Nov. 19, 1966; children—Denise Lynn, Brian David, Amy Diane. Tchr., Ind. Sch. for Deaf, Indpls., 1967-70; dir. presch. edn. of deaf, Michigan City (Ind.) Schs., 1970-71; dir. spl. edn. Plymouth (Ind.) Public Schs., 1972-76; prin. Luth. Sch. for Deaf, Detroit, 1976-81, resource cultivator, 1981—. U.S. Office Edn. fellow, 1970-71. Mem. Luth. Edn. Assn., Council Exceptional Children, Assn. Supervision and Curriculum Devel., Luth. Frats. Am. Club: Luth. Luncheon. Address: 22800 Liscomb St East Detroit MI 48021

HARMAN, HELEN BETTY, writer, editor; b. Chgo., Apr. 17, 1910; d. Herman Gottlieb and Barbara Marie (Heinkel) Rosenblatt; student U. Ill., 1931-33, Okla. State U., 1936; student Northwestern U., 1946-47, 54-55, U. Chgo., 1958-59, Oxford U., 1971; m. Harry Jones Harman, Sept. 5, 1931; children—Barbara Sue (Mrs. Albert Garvey), Katharine Lee Harman Pitzer. Village clk., Western Springs, Ill., 1949-52; writer-editor Argonne (Ill.) Nat. Lab., 1952-75; newsletter writer, editor Am. Nuclear Soc., La Grange Park, Ill., 1976-80. Co-chmn. Chgo. West Suburban Vols. for Adlai Stevenson, 1952; sec., bd. dirs. Theatre of Western Springs, 1946-67. Mem. Am. Assn. Nuclear Editors (sec. 1960-61, 65-66). Clubs: Graue Mill chpt. Questers Internat. (sec. 1978-79, pres. 1981—), Hinsdale Women's. Contbr. articles to nat. publs. Home: 407 Homestead Rd La Grange Park IL 60525

HARMON, ARTICE WARD, occupational therapist; b. Hughes, Ark., Oct. 2, 1940; d. William Oscar and Alice Turner (Williams) Ward; B.S., Ind. U., 1973; M.P.H., U. Ill., 1975; m. Luther L. Harmon, Dec. 5, 1959. Occupational therapy intern Helen Hayes Hosp., West Haverstraw, N.Y., 1973, St. Elizabeths Hosp., Washington, 1973; staff occupational therapist Mercy Hosp. and Med. Center, Chgo., 1973-76; dir. occupational therapy Westside Parent's Center for Exceptional Children, Chgo., 1976-77; head occupational therapy Americana Center, Champaign, Ill., 1977—; grad. teaching asso., curriculum in occupational therapy U. Ill., Urbana, 1978-79, instr., 1980-81; dir. occupational therapy program Chgo. State U., 1981—; pvt. cons. phys. rehab. and disabilities. Mem., People United To Save Humanity, 1976—. Edn. Professions Devel. Act fellowship, 1978-80. Mem. Am. Occupational Therapy Assn., Ill. Occupational Therapy Assn., Am. Public Health Assn., Ill. Public Health Assn., Am. Vocat. Assn., Ill. Vocat. Assn., Phi Delta Kappa, Kappa Delta Pi. Roman Catholic. Home: 748 E 104th St Chicago IL 60628 Office: Coll Allied Health Chgo State U 95th St at King Dr Chicago IL 60628

HARMON, DALE JOSEPH, research chemist; b. Cuyahoga Falls, Ohio, Mar. 1, 1927; s. Benny Mac and Gladies Harriet (Harter) H.; B.S. cum laude, Kent State U., 1951; M.S. in Polymer Chemistry, Akron U., 1960; m. Betty Lou Phillips, June 16, 1951; children—Phillip Vincent, Paul Victor, Perry Vance. With B.F. Goodrich Research and Devel. Center, Brecksville, Ohio, 1951—, jr. tech. man, 1951-56, tech. man., 1956-60, research chemist, 1960-63, sr. research chemist, 1963-68, research asso., 1968-79, sr. research asso., 1979—, tech. coordinator chromatography group, 1980—. Trained adult leader, committeeman, chmn. Troop 382, Old Trail council Boy Scouts Am., 1965-73. Served with USN, 1945-46, 51-54. Recipient service award Cleve./Akron Liquid Chromatography Discussion Group, 1976. Mem. Am. Chem. Soc. (sec. Akron sect.), ASTM, Res. Officers Assn. Republican. Presbyterian. Editorial staff Jour. of Liquid Chromatography; contbr. articles to sci. jours., papers to profl. confs. Home: 993 Cotswold Dr Copley OH 44321 Office: 9921 Brecksville Rd Brecksville OH 44141

HARMON, ROBERT LEE, data processing services co. exec.; b. St. Louis, Oct. 31, 1926; s. Jess G. and Lela E. (Beard) H.; B.S., Washington U., 1949; m. Carolyn Metzger, June 9, 1951; children—Robert Lee, Barbara C., Nancy K., Celia A., Julia G., Melinda M. With IBM, St. Louis, Nashville, N.Y.C. and Chgo., 1949-60; with McDonnell Douglas Corp., St. Louis, 1960—, now exec. v.p. commercial McDonnell Douglas Automation Co. and corp. v.p. McDonnell Douglas Corp.; dir. Bank Bldg. and Equipment Corp., St. Louis, 1977—. Treas., Delmar Bapt. Ch.; mem. exec. com. bd. trustees Mo. Bapt. Hosp.; mem. long range planning com., chmn. Baptists for Scouting, Boy Scouts Am. Served to lt. (j.g.), U.S. Merchant Marines, 1944-47. Mem. Sales and Execs., Inc. (past dir.), Washington U. Bus. Sch. Alumni Assn. (mem. exec. com.), Omicron Delta Kappa, Delta Sigma Pi, Beta Theta Pi (past chpt. pres.), Beta Gamma Sigma. Home: 3 Portland Dr Saint Louis MO 63131 Office: PO Box 516 Saint Louis MO 63166

HARMS, JOHN KENWOOD, clergyman, educator; b. Sibley, Iowa, May 3, 1944; s. John Lorence and Lavaughn Mary (Grush) H.; B.A. (Music scholar), Morningside Coll. (Sioux City, Iowa), 1967; M.Div., Bethel Theol. Sem., St. Paul, 1970; Th.M., Luther Theol. Sem., St. Paul, 1971; M.Litt. (Research grantee 1972-73, Theol. Research grantee 1973), Emmanual Coll., Cambridge (Eng.) U., 1977; postgrad. U. Amsterdam (Netherlands), 1977—; m. Connie Lou Strong, Aug. 15, 1967. Ordained to ministry Baptist Ch., 1970; clergyman, edu'cator, lectr., counsellor European div. U. Md., 1973—, Dependent Schs., European Area, U.S. Dept. Def., 1974—; instr. layman's insts. for ch. orgns. Recipient Arion Music award Sibley High Sch., 1962; Bethune-Baker Research grantee Cambridge U., 1972-73; Alisdair Charles MacPherson Research grantee, 1973. Mem. Am. Soc. Reformation Research, Soc. Sixteenth Century Studies, Am. Numis. Assn., Am. Hist. Assn., Phi Mu Alpha. Republican. Contbr. articles to Church Music. Home and offiee: 2401 Beaver Ave Des Moines IA 50310

HARMS, JOHN N., community coll. pres.; b. Bayard, Nebr., Feb. 17, 1940; s. Nick John and Beulah (Pappas) H.; B.A., Chadron State Coll., 1962, M.Ed., 1966; Ed.D., Mont. State Coll., 1975; m. Patricia Schmidt, July 6, 1963; children—Stacy, Susie, Nick. Tchr. public schs., Gering, Nebr., 1965; grad. asst. Chadron State Coll., 1965-66, dir. housing and fin. aid, 1966-68; dean students Northeastern Nebr. Coll., Chadron, 1968-70, dean instruction, 1970-72; dean instruction N.E. Tech. Coll., Norfolk, Nebr., 1972-73; pres. McCook Community Coll., McCook, Nebr., 1973-76; campus dir. Nebr. Western Coll., Scottsbluff, Nebr., 1976—, pres. Western Tech. Community Coll. Area, 1977—. Bd. dirs. Greater Nebr. Health Systems; bd. dirs. Southwestern Nebr. Assn. for Retarded Citizens; v.p. Scotts Bluff County Republican Party, 1980; dir. United Way, 1977-80. Mem. Am. Vocat. Assn., Am. Ednl. Tech. Assn., Scottsbluff-Gering C. of C. (dir.), Phi Delta Kappa. Greek Orthodox. Clubs: Elks, Masons. Office: 1601 E 27th St Scottsbluff NE 69361

HARMS, WILMER ALLEN, physician; b. Hillsboro, Kans., July 2, 1922; s. William W. and Anna C. (Thiessen) H.; student Tabor Coll., 1941-42, 48-50; A.B., Kans. U., 1952, M.D., 1956; certificate in basic scis. ophthalmology Harvard, 1968; m. Esther M. Ediger, Oct. 21, 1946; children—Willard Keith, Kevin Lynn. Intern, Bethany Hosp., Kansas City, Kans., 1956-57; practice gen. medicine, Hesston, Kan., 1957-68; fellow clin. ophthalmology Johns Hopkins, 1969; resident ophthalmology Okla. U. Med. Center, 1969-72; asso. Hertzler Clinic, Halstead, Kans., 1972—; pres. med. staff Bethel Deaconess Hosp., Newton, Kans., 1963, Halstead Hosp., 1975—; pres. Hesston Assos., 1962-68, Hertzler Clin. Assos., 1975-78, 81—; clin. instr. ophthalmology Med. Sch., Okla. U., 1972-76, asst. clin. prof., 1976—. Vice pres. Hesston Builders, Inc., 1965-72. Pres. Hesston Credit Union, 1961-68, 76-79; bd. dirs. Tabor Coll., 1978—, chmn. acad. affairs com., 1979—. Trustee, Kans. Fund for Ind. Colls., 1979—; bd. dirs. Hertzler Research Found., 1975—; v.p., bd. dirs. Schowalter Villa Found., 1963-69. Diplomate Am. Bd. Ophthalmology. Fellow

Am. Acad. Family Physicians; mem. AMA, Kan., Harvey County (pres. 1967), Christian med. socs. Home: 205 E 8th St Halstead KS 67056

HARNER, IVAN CHARLES, hosp. adminstr.; b. Ypsilanti, Mich., Feb. 25, 1945; s. Charles Harry and Gertrude Margaret (Green) H.; B.B.A., Eastern Mich. U., 1969, M.A., 1978; m. Margaret Ann Sayles, June 6, 1964; children—Melanie Marie, Nicole Christine. Mgmt. trainee Mich. Dept. Mental Health, 1969-70; asst. adminstrv. officer Northville (Mich.) State Hosp., 1970-71; chief adminstrv. officer Center Forensic Psychiatry, Ann Arbor, Mich., 1971-74; asst. facility dir. Hillcrest Regional Center Devel. Disabilities, Howell, Mich., 1974-81; exec. dir. Brighton (Mich.) Hosp., 1981—; cons. Nat. Assessment Juvenile Delinquency, U. Mich., 1975-76; mgmt. cons. Skills Unlimited, Ann Arbor, 1978; curriculum cons. U. Mich. Sch. Social Work, 1979. Co-founder, dir. Colombian-Am. Friends, Inc.; mem. adv. com. Title I Program, Ypsilanti Public Schs., 1978-79. Recipient Cert. of Achievement, Exec. Devel. Program Mich. State U. Sch. Labor and Indsl. Relations, 1973. Mem. Am. Assn. Mental Deficiency, Southeastern Regional Interagy. Coordinating Com. Devel. Disabilities (past pres.), Mental Health Assn. Mich., Mich. Assn. Nursing Home Community Councils (pres.), Alpha Kappa Psi (life). Mem. United Ch. of Christ. Club: Hiawatha Sportsman's. Home: 1088 Mark St Ypsilanti MI 48197 Office: 12851 E Grand River Brighton MI 48116

HARNESS, EDWARD GRANVILLE, soap products mfg. co. exec.; b. Marietta, Ohio, Dec. 17, 1918; s. Lewis Nye and Mary (McKinney) H.; A.B., Marietta Coll., 1940; m. Mary McCrady Chaney, Aug. 7, 1943; children—Frances Ann (Mrs. Daniel J. Jones), Edward Granville, Robert R. With Procter & Gamble Co., Cin., 1940—, v.p. paper products div., 1963-66, v.p.-group exec., dir., 1966-70, exec. v.p., 1970-71, pres., 1971-74, chmn. bd., 1974-80, chmn. exec. com., 1981—; dir. Exxon Corp., Caterpillar Tractor Co. Chmn. bd. trustees Marietta Coll., Ohio Found. Ind. Colls. Served with USAAF, 1942-46. Mem. Conf. Bd., Bus. Council, Bus. Roundtable. Clubs: Commercial, Camargo, Queen City, Commonwealth (Cin.). Office: 301 E 6th St Cincinnati OH 45202

HARNESS, JACK HAROLD, paper co. exec.; b. LaPorte, Ind., May 26, 1942; s. Woodrow Wilson and Grace Florence Harness; diploma in Bus. Mgmt., LaSalle U., 1967; postgrad U. Wis.; m. Suzanne G. Isaacs, Oct. 16, 1965; 1 dau., Andrea Suzanne. Mgr. quality control Plimpton Press, LaPorte, Ind., 1961-70; quality control engr. George Banta Co., Menasha, Wis., 1970-74; tech. sales service rep. Bergstrom Paper Co., Neenah, Wis., 1974—. Served with U.S. Army, 1963-69. Mem. Litho Club Central Wis. Roman Catholic. Club: Elks. Author: Paper and Printing Problems Guide, 2d edition, 1978. Home: 709 Manchester Rd Neenah WI 54956 Office: Bergstrom Rd Neenah WI 54956

HARNETT, DONALD LEE, bus. analyst, educator; b. Everett, Wash., Apr. 26, 1937; s. Arthur Lee and Anne K. Harnett; B.A., Pa. State U., 1959, M.A., 1961; Ph.D., Cornell U., 1964; m. Janet Louise Hartman, June 22, 1963; children—Kendall Lee, Kristina Louise. Asst. prof. Ind. U., Bloomington, 1964-67, asso. prof., 1968-71, prof. quantitative bus. analysis, 1971—, chmn. dept. quantitative bus. analysis, 1977—; vis. asso. prof. Harvard U., 1968-69; scholar Internat. Bus. Research Inst., Brussels, 1969-70; vis. prof. U. Hawaii. Recipient Teaching award Ind. U., 1971, 78; Ford grantee, 1968-70. Mem. Am. Inst. Decision Scis., Am. Stat. Assn., Inst. Mgmt. Scis., Phi Kappa Phi, Pi Mu Epsilon. Author Introductory Statistical Analysis, 1980; Bargaining Behavior: An International Study, 1980, others; research, publs. in field. Home: 2131 Meadowbluff Ct Bloomington IN 47401 Office: Sch Bus Ind U Bloomington IN 47402

HARNETT, JOSEPH DURHAM, oil co. exec.; b. Paterson, N.J., Aug. 23, 1917; s. James Harold and Emily (Steele) H.; B.S., Purdue U., 1939; m. Wilhelmina Nordstrom, June 21, 1941 (dec. July 1958); children—Gordon D., Linda C., Ralph H., David S.; m. 2d, Nancy Beam. With Consol. Edison Co., N.Y.C., 1939, Worthington Pump & Machinery Corp., 1940; with Standard Oil Co. (Ohio), 1941—, v.p., 1957-68; sr. v.p., 1968-70, exec. v.p., 1970-77, pres., 1977—, also dir.; pres., dir. Mountaineer Carbon Co., BP Oil Inc., Vistron Corp. Mem. Am. Petroleum Inst. (dir.). Presbyterian. Clubs: Mentor Harbor Yacht, Country, Union, Pepper Pike (Cleve.); Univ. (N.Y.C.). Home: 2799 Lander Rd Pepper Pike OH 44124 Office: Midland Bldg Cleveland OH 44115

HARNISCH, THOMAS W., state senator; b. LaCrosse, Wis., Jan. 16, 1947; B.A., U. Wis., Madison, 1969; J.D., U. Minn., 1972; married; 1 child. Auctioneer; practice law; mem. Wis. Senate. Mem. Wis. Bar Assn., Salvation Army, Neillsville C. of C., Neillsville Jaycees. Democrat. Address: Room 310 South State Capitol Madison WI 53702*

HARPER, CHARLES MICHEL, food co. exec.; b. Lansing, Mich., Sept. 26, 1927; s. Charles Frost and Alma (Michel) H.; B.S. in Mech. Engring., Purdue U., 1949; M.B.A., U. Chgo., 1950; m. Joan Frances Bruggema, June 24, 1950; children—Kathleen Harper Wenngatz, Carolyn Harper Wherry, Michel, Elizabeth Ann. Sr. methods engr. Oldsmobile div. Gen. Motors Corp., Detroit, 1950-54; dir. indsl. engring. Pillsbury Co., Mpls., 1954-60, dir. engring., 1961-66, v.p. research, devel. and new products, 1965-70, group v.p. poultry and food service, 1970-74; exec. v.p., chief operating officer ConAgra Inc., Omaha, 1974-76, pres., chief exec. officer, 1976-81, chmn., chief exec. officer, 1981—, also dir.; dir. Valmont Industries, Diamond Crystal Salt, Thomas Murphy Co., InterNorth. council Village of Excelsior (Minn.), 1965-70, mayor, 1974. Pres., Strategic Issues, Inc.; bd. dirs. Joslyn Mus., Creighton U., Nebr. Ind. Coll. Found.; trustee Bishop Clarkson Meml. Hosp. Served with AUS, 1944-46. Mem. Greater Omaha C. of C. (chmn. 1979), Ak-Sar-Ben (councillor), Beta Theta Pi. Clubs: Omaha Country, Mpls. Home: 6105 Lamplighter Dr Omaha NE 68152 Office: Kiewit Plaza Omaha NE 68131

HARPER, DONALD DEAN, educator; b. Zanesville, Ohio, Feb. 8, 1950; s. William Everett and Marie (Wilson) H.; B.S., Ohio State U., 1972; M.A. in Guidance, Xavier U., 1979; m. Patricia Jean Abele, Oct. 5, 1971; children—Douglas William, Jill Christine. Tchr. Eng., 8th and 9th grades, Milford Jr. High Sch., Cin., 1972-75, Duncan Falls (Ohio) Jr. High Sch., 1975—; cons. sch. dropouts Muskingum (Ohio) County Schs., 1975-81; participant writing clinic, Duncan Falls, 1975-79. Coach, Little League Baseball, Duncan Falls, 1975—. Recipient Curtis award for contbns. to sch. and community, Philo, Ohio, 1968; Outstanding Tchr. award, 1981. Mem. Poetry Pen Pals, NEA, Nat. Council Tchrs. of English, Ohio Assn. English Tchrs., Ohio Edn. Assn., Am. Profl. Guidance Assn., Nat. Council Writing Tchrs. Contbr. poetry to New Voices For 1978. Home: 5690 Adamsville Rd Zanesville OH 43701 Office: Mill St Duncan Falls OH 43734

HARPER, ERNEST BOULDIN, JR., indsl. cons. co. exec.; b. Kalamazoo, Aug. 7, 1924; s. Ernest Bouldin and Lyssa Desha (Chalkley) H.; B.S.E. in Elec. Engring., U. Mich., 1948; M.B.A., Harvard U., 1950; m. Catherine Matthews Weld, Oct. 7, 1961; children—Ernest Bouldin III, Catherine Matthews. Applications engr., then sales mgr. Westinghouse Electric Co., Pitts., 1950-60; v.p., gen. mgr. specialty steel H.K. Porter Co., Pitts., 1960-65; asst. to pres. ITT Corp., N.Y.C., 1965-71; pres. E.B. Harper & Co., Inc., indsl. consulting., Lake Forest, Ill., 1971—. Served with USAAF, 1943-46. Mem. Am. Mktg. Assn., Assn. Corp. Growth, Midwest Planning Assn. (past dir.). Republican. Episcopalian. Club: Duquesne (Pitts.). Home: 509 College Rd Lake Forest IL 60045 Office: 222 Wisconsin Ave Lake Forest IL 60045

HARPER, GLENN S., business cons.; b. Phila., Apr. 19, 1940; s. Glenn Samuel and Minnie Marie Harper; student U. Dayton (Ohio), 1961-65; B.A., Capital U., Columbus, Ohio, 1982; m. Mary Linda Weaver; children—Christopher, Trish. Br. mgr. Household Fin. Corp., Dayton, 1965-69; mgmt. cons. A.B. Cassidy & Assos., Ridgefield, Conn., 1969-70; v.p. sales Lin Conselyea, Inc., Medway, Ohio, 1970-72, exec. v.p., treas., dir., 1972-77; founder Val-Pak Promotions, Inc., Dayton, 1974-77, pres., chief exec. officer, 1977-79; founder Metro Maid, Inc., Dayton, 1978-79, pres., chief exec. officer, 1979—; dir., exec. v.p. San Sal Villas, San Salvador, Bahamas, 1978—; dir. Carousel Mountain Amusement Park, Owego, N.Y. Mem. Ch. of Brethren. Address: Metro Maid Inc 4336 Gorman Ave Englewood OH 45322

HARPER, ROGER WESLEY, consumer products co. exec.; b. Youngstown, Ohio, July 11, 1933; s. Harry Edward and Helen Marjorie (Young) H.; B.A., Wittenberg U., 1956. Sales rep. Shell Oil Co., Cleve., 1958-62, Chicopee Mills, Inc., N.Y.C., 1962-64; sales rep. H.H. Cutler Co., Grand Rapids, Mich., 1964-68; exec. v.p. Scharp Contemporary, Inc., Columbus, Ohio, 1968-77, now dir.; chmn., pres. Am. Leather Village, Inc., Columbus, 1977—. Served with U.S. Army, 1956-58. Lutheran. Home: 622 Indian Mound Rd Columbus OH 43213 Office: 2163 S James Rd Columbus OH 43227

HARPER, ROY W., judge; b. Gibson, Mo., July 26, 1905; s. Marvin H. and Minnie (Brooks) H.; A.B., U. Mo., 1929; LL.B., 1929; m. Ruth Butt, July 30, 1941; children—Katherine Brooks, Arthur Murray. Admitted to Mo. bar, 1929; mem. tax ins. claims dep. dept. Shell Petroleum Corp., St. Louis, 1929-30; pvt. practice law, Steele, Mo., 1931-34; mem. firm Ward & Reeves, Caruthersville, 1934-47; U.S. dist. judge of Mo., Eastern and Western dists. of Mo., 1947—; chief judge Eastern Dist. Mo., 1959-70, sr. U.S. dist. judge Eastern and Western Dists. Mo., 1971—. Mem. U.S. Judicial Conf., 1965-77, chmn. intercircuit assignment com., 1969-76; mem. Jud. Panel on Multidist. Litigation, 1977—. Chmn. Mo. Democratic Com., 1946-47. Bd. dirs. St. Louis unit Shriner's Crippled Children Hosp. Enlisted Air Corps, U.S. Army, 1942; apptd. 2d lt., Sept. 1942; served with 35th Fighter Group, Southwest Pacific, 1942—; col. Air Corps Res., 1945. Recipient DeMolay Legion of Honor, 1957, Citation of Merit Mo. U. Law Sch., 1963; Patriots award Mo. soc. SAR, 1973; George Washington Honor medal Freedoms Found., 1975. Mem. Am., Mo., Pemiscot County bar assns., Order of Coif, Delta Theta Phi. Democrat. Mason (33 deg., Shriner). Office: 1st Floor Room A US Court House and Custom House Saint Louis MO 63101

HARRAWOOD, LEO EDWARD, real estate broker; b. McCleanboro, Ill., Feb. 24, 1920; s. William Arnold and Elsie Valentine (Gregory) H.; grad. high sch.; m. Bernice Edna Wickline, Aug. 31, 1940; children—Diana Lee Harrawood Canup, Debra Lou Harrawood Kelly. Harrawood's Sales and Service 1949-63, Sales Training of Detroit 1967-75, Shirley Cash Realty 1975—. Councilman, Novi, 1967-71, pres. pro tem 1967-71. Served with M.C., U.S. Army, 1941-45; ETO. Mem. Am. Legion, DAV (life), AMVETS (regional comdr. 1950-56) VFW, Novi Businessman's Assn. (past pres.). Lutheran. Clubs: Masons (DeMolay Legion of Honor 1978, Order of Purple Cross 1977), Shriners (ambassador, potentate of Moslem-Shrine Temple 1980), KT, Jesters, Elks, Rotary (charter; past pres.; dist. gov. since 1980-82). Address: PO Box 331 Novi MI 48050*

HARRELL, JAMES THOMAS, bus. exec.; b. Newport, Ky., Oct. 21, 1936; s. William Thomas and Stella May (Jones) H.; B.B.A., U. Cin., 1960; M.B.A., Xavier U., 1969; certificate in mgmt. acctg., 1977. With Miami Margarine Co., Cin., 1963—, asst. controller, 1977—. Served with U.S. Army, 1962-63. Mem. Nat. Assn. Accts., Delta Sigma Pi, Beta Alpha Psi. Episcopalian. Home: 3044 Carroll Ave Cincinnati OH 45211 Office: 5226 Vine St Cincinnati OH 45217

HARRELL, JOHN LIMPUS, charitable inst. exec.; b. Frankfort, Ind., May 9, 1918; s. Jesse Albert and Mildred Vale (Limpus) H.; A.B., Franklin Coll., 1940; M.A., Ohio State U., 1941; m. Helen Vernon Schumacher, Nov. 23, 1943; 1 dau., Helen F. Asst. dir. Duluth (Minn.) Community Fund, 1941-43; exec. sec. Community Chest and War Chest, Green Bay, Wis., 1943-46; exec. dir. Community Chest, Watertown, N.Y., 1946-50, Cedar Rapids, Iowa, 1950-54; exec. dir. United Way of Wyandotte County, Kans., 1954-79; ret., 1979; fund-raising cons., 1980—. Med. field agt. SSS, 1943-46; treas. Kans. Conf. Social Welfare, 1964-66; mem. Human Relations Commn., Kansas City, 1966-75, vice chmn., 1970-71; mem. Manpower Planning Bd., City-County Consortia, 1975-79; mem. citizens adv. com. Kans. Dept. Social Rehab. Services, 1976-79; bd. dirs., cons. Econ. Opportunity Found., Inc., 1965-79. Recipient Silver Bow award, Boy Scouts Am., 1972, Com. award, YMCA, 1972, Service award United Way of Am., 1972; Service Appreciation award Econ. Opportunity Found., Inc., 1974, Founder's award, 1976; Community Services Adminstrn. Service award, 1980; Appreciation awards AFL-CIO Tri-County Labor Council Eastern Kans., 1979, Cath. Social Services, 1979; Charter Dir. Recognition award Kans. Citizens Council on Aging, 1980. Mem. Kappa Delta Rho. Republican. Baptist. Rotarian. Home: Rural Route 1 Box 194B Michigantown IN 46057

HARRELL, SAMUEL M., grain co. exec.; b. Indpls., Jan. 4, 1931; s. Samuel Runnels and Mary (Evans) H.; ed. Groton Sch.; B.S. in Econs., Wharton Sch., U. Pa., 1953; m. Sally Bowers, Sept. 2, 1958; children—Samuel D., Holly Evans, Kevin Bowers, Karen Susan, Donald Runnels, Kenneth Macy. Chmn. bd., chief exec. officer, chmn. exec. com. Early & Daniel Industries; pres., chmn. bd., chmn. exec. com. Gen. Grain, Inc., Indpls.; pres., chmn. bd., chmn. exec. com. Early & Daniel Co., Cin.; chmn. bd., chmn. bd., chief exec. officer, chmn. exec. com. Tidewater Grain Co., Phila.; dir. Wainwright Bank & Trust Co., Wainright Abstract Co., Nat. Grain Trade Council, U.S. Feed Grains Council; mem. Chgo. Bd. Trade, St. Louis Mchts. Exchange, Mpls. Grain Exchange, Buffalo Corn Exchange. Trustee YWCA, Indpls. bd. overseers Wharton Sch. Fin. and Commerce, U. Pa. Served with AUS, 1953-55. Mem. Young Presidents Orgn., U. Pa. Alumni Assn. (past pres. Ind.), Terminal Elevator Grain Mchts. Assn. (dir.), Millers Nat. Fedn. (dir.), Assn. Operative Millers, Am. Soc. Bakery Engrs., Nat. Grain and Feed Dealers Assn., N. Am. Grain Export Assn., Am. Finance Assn., Council on Fgn. Relations, Financial Execs. Inst., Delta Tau Delta (past pres. Ind. alumni). Presbyn. Mason (32 deg., Shriner), Rotarian. Clubs: Columbia, Indpls. Athletic, Woodstock, Traders Point Hunt, Dramatic, Players, Lambs (Indpls.); Racquet (Phila.); University (Washington); Les Ambassadors (London). Home: 5858 Sunset Ln Indianapolis IN 46208 Office: 902 W Washington Ave Indianapolis IN 46204

HARRELL, SAMUEL RUNNELS, business exec.; b. Noblesville, Ind., Nov. 25, 1897; s. Samuel and Vivian (Voss) H.; B.S. in Econs., U. Pa., 1919; LL.B., Yale, 1924; m. Mary Robertson Evans, Oct. 10, 1925 (div. Mar. 1972); children—Evans Malott, Mary Eleanor, Samuel Macy. First employed, Land Title & Trust Co., Phila.; admitted to Ind. bar, 1922; former chmn. bd., chmn. exec. com. Gen. Grain, Inc., now hon. chmn., adviser; pres. Acme Evans Co., Inc. 1945-59, chmn. bd., 1954—; pres. Acme Goodrich, Inc., 1947-52, chmn. bd., chmn. exec. com., 1952—; pres., chmn. bd. Tidewater Grain Co., Phila.; chmn. exec. com., chmn. bd., dir. The Early & Daniel Co., Cin., from 1946, now hon. chmn., adviser; dir. Cleve. Grain Co., 1950-58, pres., chmn. bd., 1955-58; pres. Harrell & Co.; dir. Terminal Elevator Grain Mchts. Assn., N.Am. Export Grain Assn., Indpls. Union Ry. Co.; Chmn. bd. dirs. Indpls. Bd. Trade; mem. Chgo. Bd. Trade. Co-chmn. Ind. adv. com. on commerce, industry, agr., pub. relations. Served with Naval Aviation Pilot Div. of Naval Res., 1918. Chmn., trustee Nat. Found. for Edn. in Am. Citizenship, trustee U. Pa., 1940-50, Wharton Sch. Finance and Commerce, 1950-54; mem. vis. com. Harvard Grad. Sch. Edn., 1941-56; mem. adv. com. U.S. Banking and Currency Com.; del. Am. Legion to Paris, 1937. Mem. exec. council, nat. treas. Am. Heart Assn., 1947-48; founder Ind. Heart Found., Sagamores of Wabash; founder, charter mem. Acropolitan Research and Cultural Center. Mem. Ind. Millers Assn., (pres.), Am. Bar Assn., Am. Econ. Assn., Am. Polit. Sci. Assn., Acad. Polit. Sci., Am. Acad. Polit. and Social Sci. Am. Soc. for Pub. Adminstrn., Citizens Com. Hoover Commn., S.R., S.A.R., Delta Tau Delta, Phi Delta Phi. Presbyn. Mason (32 deg.). Clubs: Racquet, Sharswood Law (Phila.); Harvard Faculty (Cambridge); University (Chgo., N.Y.); Contemporary, Athletic, Lawyers, Literary, Pioneer, Pennsylvania, Yale (Indpls.); Queen City (Cin.); Pendennis (Louisville). Chmn. and editor Nat. Found. Press. Publisher: Fundamental American Principles. Home: care Valley Forge Farms 10788 E 166th St Noblesville IN 46060 Office: 902 Washington Ave Indianapolis IN 46204

HARRIMAN, RICHARD LEE, educator; b. Independence, Mo., Sept. 10, 1932; s. Walter S. and M. Eloise (Faulkner) H.; A.B., William Jewell Coll., 1953; M.A., Stanford U., 1959. Instr., asst. prof. English U. Dubuque, Iowa, 1960-62; asst. prof. English William Jewell College, Liberty, Missouri, 1962, acting head English dept., 1965-69, dir. fine arts program, 1965—, asso. prof., 1966—. Served from pvt. to cpl., AUS, 1953-55. Recipient Woodrow Wilson fellowship from Woodrow Wilson Fellowship Found., 1957. Mem. Shakespeare Assn. Am., Modern Language Assn., Assn. Coll. Univ. and Community Arts Adminstrs. (nat. exec. bd. 1975-78), Nat. Council Tchrs. English, Am. Assn. U. Profs., Lambda Chi Alpha, Sigma Tau Delta, Alpha Psi Omega. Meth. Home: Route 5 Box 6 Liberty MO 64068

HARRINGER, HELEN EHRAT, social worker; b. Chgo., June 20, 1936; d. Charles William and Dorothy (Glanz) Ehrat; B.A., U. Mich., 1958; M.S.W., U. Conn., 1962; m. Olaf Carl Harringer, Dec. 20, 1975; children—H. L., Karen Hedges. Program supr. Hartford (Conn.) Neighborhood Centers, 1959-62; program dir. Evanston (Ill.) Children's Home, 1963-64; dir. student activities Evanston Twp. High Sch., 1975-76; social worker Wheaton (Ill.) Public Schs., 1977-79, Libertyville (Ill.) Public Schs., 1979-81, St. Joseph Hosp., Chgo., 1981—; leader Liberal Youth on North Shore, 1969-71; counseling cons. People Against Pornography, 1980-81. Mem. bd. Juvenile Protective Assn., 1963-68, Glenview United Fund, 1969-76, Family Service Wilmette, Glenview, Northbrook and Kenilworth, 1970-76, Grove Heritage Assn., 1979-81. Grantee Hartford Community Chest, 1960-62. Mem. Nat. Assn. Social Workers, Ill. Assn. Sch. Social Workers. Unitarian. Home: 530 Hunter Rd Glenview IL 60025 Office: 2130 N Kenmore Chicago IL 60614

HARRINGTON, ELIZABETH DALLAS, advt. co. exec., food mfg. co. exec.; b. Jackson, Miss., Nov. 9, 1942; s. William Lee and Louise (Crowder) Dallas; B.A., Cornell U., 1965; m. Robert W. Harrington, Aug. 21, 1965; children—Elizabeth Brooke, Kristin (dec.). Fashion coordinator Marshall Field & Co., Chgo., 1965; asst. brand mgr. Procter & Gamble Co., Cin., 1966-68; account exec. J. Walter Thompson Co., Chgo., 1968-72, account supr., 1972-76, v.p., 1973—; v.p., mgmt. supr. The Quaker Oats Co., Chgo., 1976-79, v.p. advt., pres. AdCom, 1979—; lectr. advt. Barat Coll. Advisor to bd. dirs. Grove Sch. for Handicapped Children, Lake Forest, Ill. Named Advt. Woman of Yr., 1980; recipient YWCA Leadership award, 1977; named Outstanding Young Bus. Woman of Yr., Glamour mag., 1977; Nutrition Edn. award Family Circle mag., 1973. Mem. Am. Advt. Fedn. (dir.), Nat. Assn. Better Bus. Burs. (dir. Children's Advt. Rev. Unit), Chgo. Network, Chgo. Advt. Club, Women's Advt. Club Chgo. Office: Merchandise Mart Plaza Chicago IL 60654

HARRINGTON, HARVEY DANIEL, II, design engr.; b. St. Paul, Sept. 26, 1941; s. Harvey Daniel and Marjorie Mary (Cusick) H.; A.A., U. Minn., 1961, A.Lang. Arts, 1977; diploma in bldg. constrn. Dunwoody Inst., 1964; m. Kathleen Joyce McIalwain, Nov. 11, 1967. Draftsman, Farmers Union Central Exchange, Inc., South St. Paul, Minn., 1965-67, design draftsman, 1967-70, chief draftsman, 1970-74; mgr. design engring. Cenex Co., St. Paul, 1974-78; dir. architecture Schipke Engrs., Mpls., 1978—; cons. Harrington Inc., Harrington Heating. Coach surburban woman's softball teams, summers 1970—. Served with USAR, 1961-67. Cert. bldg. ofcl., Minn. Mem. Smithsonian Assos., Irish-Am. Cultural Inst., Mensa. Home: 14001 Valley Creek Trail S Afton MN 55001 Office: 3101 W 69th St Edina MN 55435

HARRINGTON, JAY BRIAN, travel service exec.; b. Tacoma, Wash., Oct. 10, 1944; s. Walter Watson and Cecilia Ann (Osinski) H.; student U. Minn., 1963-67; m. Deanna Mae Pries, Aug. 20, 1971; 1 son, Todd Robert. Sr. sales rep. Scand. Airlines, Mpls., 1969-72; group sales mgr. Thomas Cook, Mpls., 1972-73; exec. v.p. Marquette-Sedard Travel, Mpls., 1973-76; dir. travel Minn. State Automobile Assn., Burnsville, 1976-79; v.p. ops. Gelco Travel Services, Eden Prairie, Minn., 1979—. Republican. Home: 3005 Long Meadow Circle Bloomington MN 55420 Office: Three Gelco Dr Eden Prairie MN 55344

HARRINGTON, LOIS GREY, curriculum developer, ednl. researcher; b. Framingham, Mass., Sept. 18, 1945; d. Robert Weston and Dorothy (Bates) H.; B.A. in English, Alfred U., 1966. Tchr. English, Southwestern City Schs., Grove City, Ohio, 1967-71; program asso. Nat. Center for Research in Vocat. Edn., Ohio State U., Columbus, 1971—; tchr. teaching methods Peace Corps vols., summer 1978. Recipient Dean Farmer Meml. Staff Recognition award, 1980; Outstanding Instructional Devel. award Nat. Soc. for Performance and Instruction, 1978. Mem. Assn. Tchr. Educators, Assn. Supervision and Curriculum Devel., Council Basic Edn., Pi Delta Epsilon. Author publs. defining performance/competency-based curriculum format; major designer and implementor of concept; author, co-author over 100 performance-based tchr. edn. modules for tng. of vocat. tchrs. Office: 1960 Kenny Rd Columbus OH 43210

HARRINGTON, RICHARD STANHOPE, community devel. cons. co. exec.; b. Wellington, Ohio, May 2, 1935; s. Frank Minor and Marie Eugene (LeGault) H.; M. in Broadcast Journalism, Northwestern U., 1965; m. Velma Jean Staley, Sept. 8, 1973; children—Pamela Diane, Daniel Mark, Melissa Anne. Commd. officer U.S. Marine Corp, advanced through grades to capt., 1969; assigned Armed Forces Radio, Korea, 1953-55; with NCOIC Radio-TV, Cherry Point, N.C., 1955-60; radio-TV dir. Marine Air Res., 1960-63; broadcaster,

WGN-Radio-TV News, Chgo., 1962-68; CO-PR cons., 1969-75; v.p. Urban Data Systems, Columbus, Ohio, 1971-75; pres. Tekton, Inc., Columbus, 1976—; v.p. McClendon Enterprises, Inc., Columbus, 1975-79. Housing adminstr. Mid-Ohio Regional Planning Commn., Columbus, 1976-78. Recipient Gold Mike award, Armed Forces Radio, 1955; Freedom Found. Television Documentary award, 1969. Mem. Bldg. Ofcls. And Codes Adminstrs. Internat., Nat. Assn. Housing and Redevel. Ofcls., Ohio Conf. of Community Devel., Canadian Assn. Redevel. Ofcls., Am. Soc. Bldg. and Construction Inspectors. Episcopalian. Clubs: Past Master Councilor, Chevalier, Order of DeMolay. Home: 4902 Dierker Rd Columbus OH 43220 Office: 1030 Dublin Rd Columbus OH 43215

HARRIS, BERNIE FRANCIS, educator, counselor; b. Wheeling, W. Va., Jan. 30; s. John and Marie H.; student Shrivenham U., Eng., 1945-46; A.B., W. Liberty State Coll., 1950; M. Ed., Miami U., Oxford, Ohio, 1963; m. Lillie Mae Grigsby, Dec. 19, 1955; children—Jeff, Dorothy. Laborer, Wheeling Steel; timekeeper Douglas Aircraft Co., 1951-52; tchr., coach Smith Twp., Ohio, 1952-53, Smithfield (Ohio) High Sch., 1957-61; tchr., coach. counselor Cedarville, Ohio, 1961-63, Kettering, Ohio, 1963—. Supr. sports City of Kettering, 1968—. Served with U.S. Army, 1942-45. Mem. Adlerian Psychol. Soc., Ohio Vis. Tchrs. Assn., Ohio Guidance Assn., NEA, Ohio Edn. Assn., Kettering Classroom Tchrs. Assn., Am. Legion, VFW. Democrat. Roman Catholic. Clubs: Lions, Elks. Home: 3632 Twinbrook Ln Kettering OH 45429 Office: 3490 Far Hills Ave Kettering OH 45429

HARRIS, BETTY CHAFFMAN, nurse, educator; b. Balt., May 2, 1928; d. David Henry and Ida Irene (Roberts) Chaffman; R.N., Columbia Union Coll., 1950; B.S.N., Incarnate Word Coll., 1969; M.S.N., U. Tex., 1971; postgrad. Ohio State U., 1974—; m. E. Vernon Harris, Sept. 24, 1950; children—Ellen, Dale, Carol, Sharon. Nurse pediatrics, orthopedics, med. and surg. nursing, also psychiat. nursing Ohio State U., Columbus, 1973—, instr. nursing, 1971—; instr. psychiat., mental health nursing Tex. Women's U., Dallas, 1971-73, coordinator psychiat. mental health studies, 1972-73, spl. rep. 1971; lectr. in field. USPHS profl. nurse trainee, 1968; NIMH grad. psychiat. mental health trainee, 1969. Mem. Am. Nurses Assn., Mid Ohio Dist. Assn., N. Area Mental Health Forum, AAUP, Assn. 7th. Day Adventist Nurses, Adventist Ladies Assn. (pres. 1981—), Sigma Theta Tau (chmn. eligibility com. 1977-79, v.p., editor Newsletter 1979—). Office: Ohio State U 1585 Neil Ave Columbus OH 43210

HARRIS, BEVERLY HOWARD, educator; b. Lee's Summit, Mo., Aug. 22, 1927; s. Howard K. and Mattie (Beggs) H.; A.A., SW Bapt. Coll., 1947; B.S., SW Mo. State U., 1949; M.A., U. Mo., 1953, Ed.D. (Curators scholar), 1963; m. Zorene Pruitt, May 21, 1950; children—Susan Annette, Steven Howard, Joy Aileen. Instr. mathematics U. Mo., Columbia, 1951-52; instr. SW Bapt. Coll., Bolivar, Mo., 1952-64, prof., chmn. dept., 1964—, scholarship coordinator, 1973—. Co-organizer, Mo. Tng. Center for Mentally Retarded Children, Bolivar, 1964; organizing com. Day Care Center So. Hills Bapt. Ch., Bolivar, 1972. Served with U.S. Army, 1946-47. Mem. Math. Assn. Am., Phi Delta Kappa. Baptist (deacon, dir. Sunday Sch.). Club: Bolivar Tennis (pres. 1975-77). Home: 910 E Division St Bolivar MO 65613 Office: 623 S Pike St Bolivar MO 65613

HARRIS, CHAUNCY DENNISON, geographer; b. Logan, Utah, Jan. 31, 1914; s. Franklin Stewart and Estella (Spilsbury) H.; A.B., Brigham Young U., 1933; B.A. (Rhodes scholar) Oxford U.; 1936, M.A., 1943, D.Litt., 1973; student London Sch. Econs., 1936-37; Ph.D., U. Chgo., 1940; D.Econ. (honoris causa), Cath. U., Chile, 1956; LL.D. (hon.), Ind. U., 1979; m. Edith Young, Sept. 5, 1940; 1 dau., Margaret. Instr. geography Ind. U., 1939-41; asst. prof. geography U. Nebr., 1941-43; asst. prof. geography U. Chgo., 1943-46, asso. prof., 1946-47, prof., 1947—, dean social scis., 1955-60, dir. Center Internat. Studies, 1966—, chmn. dept. geography, 1967-69, Samuel N. Harper disting. service prof., 1969—, spl. asst. to the pres., 1973-75, v.p. for acad. resources, 1975-78; del. Internat. Geog. Congress, Lisbon, 1949, Washington, 1952, Rio de Janeiro, 1956, Stockholm, 1960, London, 1964, New Delhi, 1968, Montreal, 1972, Moscow, 1976, Tokyo, 1980; U.S. del. 17th Gen. Conf. UNESCO, Paris, 1972; v.p. Internat. Geog. Union, 1956-64, sec.-treas., 1968-76, mem. U.S. Com., 1949-76; mem. exec. com. div. behavioral sci. NRC, 1967-70; mem. Joint Com. on Slavic Studies, 1954-65, Inter-Univ. Com. on Travel Grants, 1956-65, Joint Com. on Fgn. Area Fellowship Program, 1962-70; mem. exec. com. Internat. Research and Exchanges Bd., 1968-71; mem. adv. com. or bd. internat. orgns. and programs Nat. Acad. Scis., 1969-76. Recipient Disting. Service award Geog. Soc. Chgo., 1965; Alexander Csoma de Körösi Meml. medal Hungarian Geog. Soc., 1971; Alexander von Humboldt gold medal Gesellschaft für Erdkunde zu Berlin, 1978; named Laureat d'Honneur, Internat. Geog. Union, 1976; Japan Soc. for Promotion of Sci. fellow, 1980. Mem. Assn. Am. Geographers (sec. 1946-48, v.p. 1956, pres. 1957, Honors award 1976), Am. Geog. Soc. (council 1962-74, v.p. 1969-74), Am. Assn. Advancement Slavic Studies (pres. 1962, award for disting. contbns. to Slavic studies 1978), Social Sci. Research Council (dir. 1959-70, vice chmn. 1963-65, com. programs and policy 1959-67, exec. com. 1967-70), Internat. Council Sci. Unions (exec. com. 1969-72), Nat. Council for Soviet and East European Research (dir. 1977—), Library of Congress Council of Scholars; hon. mem. Royal Geog. Soc., geog. socs. Berlin, Frankfurt, Rome, Florence, Paris, Warsaw, Nippon Chiri Gakkai. Club: Quadrangle (Chgo.). Author: Cities of the Soviet Union, 1970; Guide to Geographical Bibliographies and Reference Works in Russian or on The Soviet Union, 1975; Bibliography of Geography: Part I, Introduction to General Aids, 1976. Editor: Economic Geography of the U.S.S.R., 1949, Internat. List of Geog. Serials, 1960, 71, 80; Annotated World List of Current Geographical Serials, 1960, 64, 71, 80; Soviet Geography: Accomplishments and Tasks, 1962; contbg. editor The Geog. Rev., 1960-73. Contbr. articles to profl. jours. Home: 5649 S Blackstone Ave Chicago IL 60637 Office: Center for Internat Studies U of Chgo 5828 University Ave Chicago IL 60637

HARRIS, CLARA LOUISE TRINDLE, dietitian; b. Kingfisher, Okla., Mar. 16, 1928; d. Robert and Elva G. (Gosline) Trindle; B.S., Okla. State U., 1951; postgrad. Iowa State U., 1959; m. Clifford Charles Harris, June 20, 1954; children—Donna Kay, Clifford Charles. Dietetic intern St. Mary's Hosp., Rochester, Minn., 1951-52; staff dietitian VA Hosps., Muskogee, Okla., 1952-53; dietitian Okla. U. Med. Center, 1953-54, Okla. Bapt. Hosp., Muskogee, 1954, VA Hosp., Murfreesboro, Tenn., 1955-57, VA Hosp., Muskogee, Okla., 1957-67; chief dietitian, Fort Lyon, Colo., 1967-70; asst. chief dietitian VA, Lexington, Ky., 1970-72; chief dietitian VA, Chillicothe, Ohio, 1970-79; chief dietetic service VA Med. Center, Consol., Cleve., 1979—, dir. dietetic internship-coordinated master's degree program, 1979; asso. prof. nutrition Case Western Res. U., Cleve., 1979—; adv. Colo. S.E. Hosp. Instl. Edn. Food Service Soc., 1968-70; nutrition adv. Parent Child Care Center, Las Animas, Colo., 1968-70; cons. dietitian Weisbord County Meml. Hosp., Eads, Colo., St. Joseph of the Plains Hosp., Cheyenne Wells, Colo., 1968-70; cons. nutrition Title VII Program, Washington Court, Ohio, 1975-79. Registered dietitian. Mem. Am. Dietetic Assn., Am. Soc. Hosp. Food Service Adminstrs., Ohio Dietetic Assn., AAUW. Presbyterian. Club: Order Eastern Star. Home: 8607 Hinckley Circle Brecksville OH 44141 Office: 10000 Brecksville St Brecksville OH 44141

HARRIS, CONNIE DENISE, systems analyst; b. Birmingham, Ala., July 26, 1953; d. Johnnie Mack and Vivian (Cook) H.; B.B.A. in Acctg., Mich. State U., 1975; postgrad. Roosevelt U., 1976—; advanced neurobiology course Marine Biol. Lab., Woods Hole, Mass., 1980. Auditor, systems analyst Arthur Andersen, Chgo., 1975-77; sr. programmer Fed. Res. Bank, Chgo., 1977; systems analyst Boeing Computer Services, Chgo., 1977-78, Tektronix, Chgo., 1979—; VM/CMS coordinator Bankers Life Casualty Co., Chgo., 1980—; founder, mgr. C&W Bldg. & Maintenance Co., 1978—; asst. mgr., co-owner Lincoln Park Pizza, Chgo.; tchr. computer classes. Mem. Am. Mgmt. Assn., Nat. Assn. Black Accts., Mortar Bd. (v.p. 1974-75), Phi Gamma Nu (pres. 1974-75), Beta Alpha Psi (rec. sec.). Author: (poetry) Poetry By Me, 1975; composer. Office: Tektronix 5350 Keystone Ct Rolling Meadows IL 60008 also 4444 W Lawrence Chicago IL 60630

HARRIS, DANIEL KEATING, med. assn. exec.; b. Chgo., Oct. 1, 1943; s. Daniel Phillip and Helen Margaret (Schillo) H.; B.S.B.A., Marquette U., 1965; M.B.A. in Personnel Adminstrn., Indsl. Mgmt., DePaul U., 1968; m. Karen Anne Stroup, Oct. 17, 1970. Systems analyst Eaton Yale & Towne, Chgo., 1965-69; cons., Booz Allen & Hamilton, Chgo., 1969-71; project mgr. Blue Cross & Blue Shield Nat. Assn., Chgo., 1971-73; asst. dir. Div. Med. Practice, AMA, Chgo., 1973-81, dir. Nat. Med. Info. Network, 1981—; trustee Symposium on Computer Applications in Med. Care, Inc., George Washington U. Med. Center; ind. cons. organizational and systems analysis, free-lance med. writer. Served with USMCR, 1962-65. Mem. Soc. for Advanced Med. Systems, Am. Assn. of Med. Soc. Execs. Clubs: Chgo. Athletic Assn. Editor-in-chief Computers and Medicine, 1974-81; contbg. editor Jour. of Med. Systems, 1977—. Home: 603 N Park Blvd Glen Ellyn IL 60137 Office: 535 N Dearborn St Chicago IL 60610

HARRIS, DAVID WILLIAM, petroleum exec.; b. Machen, Ga., Sept. 7, 1891; s. Nathaniel Edwin (ex-gov. of Ga.) and Fannie (Burke) H.; B.S. in Elec. Engring., Ga. Inst. Tech., 1912; m. Mildred Stoutenborough, July 2, 1914; children—Walter Alexander, Holton Edwin. Engr., Denver Gas & Electric Co., 1912-13; dir. budget, asst. treas. Cities Service Co., 1913-23; treas. Empire Gas & Fuel Co., 1923-27; v.p. Ind. Ty. Ill. Oil Co., 1927-28; v.p., gen. mgr. Ark. Natural Gas Corp. and subsidiary cos., pres. Ark. Natural Gas Corp., 1944-45, Orange State Oil Co., 1939-45; v.p., dir. Cities Service Def. Corp., 1941-45; pres., chief exec. officer Universal Oil Products Co., 1945-60; chmn. David W. Harris & Assos., cons., 1962—; dir. Harrel, Inc. Mem. Mid-Continent Oil and Gas Assn. (exec. com., past pres. La.-Ark. div.), Am. Gas Assn. (dir. 1941-45), Bartlesville (Okla.) C. of C., Western Soc. Engrs., Newcomen Soc. N.Am., Chi Phi. Recipient Alumni Distinguished Service award Ga. Inst. Tech., 1954. Methodist. Mason (32, K.T., Shriner). Clubs: Chicago; Glen View; Westmoreland, McGraw Wildlife Found. Home: 2305 Central Park Ave Evanston IL 60201 Office: 2530 Crawford Ave Evanston IL 60201. *In life, the straight-shooter wins!*

HARRIS, DONALD LEE, vet. pathologist, toxicologist; b. Girard, Kans., Aug. 20, 1940; s. Bud L. and Florence Ellen (Westhoff) H.; student Kans. State Tchrs. Coll. Pittsburg, 1958-61; B.S., Kans. State U., Manhattan, 1964, D.V.M., 1966; M.S., U. Wis., Madison, 1970; m. Penny Lee Corbin, Dec. 20, 1969; children—Jonathan Christopher, James Clayton, Joely Christina. Postdoctoral trainee Dept. Vet. Sci., U. Wis., Madison, 1968-70; chief pathologist/toxicologist, head pathology/clin. pathology sect. biology dept. Warf Inst., Madison, 1970-77; head pathology and clin. pathology section indsl. bio-test Wedge's Creek Research Farm, Neillsville, Wis., 1977-79; dist. mgr. No. Wis., Talbot Carlson Inc., 1979—; pres. Saddle Tromps Inc., 1980—. Chmn. Dane County Bicentennial wagon train, 1976; town chmn. Town of Pine Valley, 1981—. Served with Vet. Corps, U.S. Army, 1966-68. Mem. Am. Coll. Vet. Toxicologists, Dane County, Am. vet. med. assns., Am. Acad. Clin. Toxicology, Am. Assn. Lab. Animal Sci., Oreg. Horse Assn. (pres. 1974-78). Roman Catholic. K.C. Home: Box 138 Route 4 Neillsville WI 54456 Office: Box 26 Neillsville WI 54456

HARRIS, E. EDWARD, educator; b. West Burlington, Iowa, Nov. 15, 1931; s. Earl and Anne M. (Mollen) Harris; B.A., U. No. Iowa, 1953; M.A., U. Minn., 1959; Ed.D., No. Ill. U., 1965; m. Evonne L. Meier, May 29, 1954; children—Julie Anne, James Edward. Tchr.-coordinator office and distributive edn. Davenport (Iowa) Community Schs. 1955-63, head bus. edn. dept. West High Sch., 1960-63; asst. prof. edn. No. Ill. U., DeKalb, 1963-64, asso. prof., 1965-67, prof., 1968—, coordinator profl. devel. in occupational edn., 1970-72, chmn. bus. edn. and adminstrv. services dept., 1973—; project dir. numerous research grants. Cons. in field. Chmn., U.S. Office Edn. Region V Planning Com. Distributive Edn., 1966-69. Mem. DeKalb County Devel. Corp., 1974—. Bd. dirs. Ill. Found. Distributive Edn., 1965—. Served with AUS, 1953-55. Recipient Outstanding Service award Distributive Clubs Am., 1963, Ill. chpt., 1967; Excellence in Teaching award No. Ill. U., 1969; Man of Year award Distributive Edn. Clubs Ill., 1972, also Service award. Mem. Am. Vocat. Assn. (life, chmn. distributive edn. publs. com. 1966-74, mem. resolutions com. 1980—, chmn. evaluation com. 1980), Nat. Bus. Edn. Assn., Nat. Assn. Distributive Edn. (life), Mktg. and Distributive Edn. Assn. (pres. 1980—), Council Distributive Tchr. Educators, Ill. Co-op. Vocat. Edn. Coordinators Assn. (dir.), Ill. Secondary Mktg. and Distributive Edn. Coordinators Assn. (dir.), Delta Pi Epsilon, Pi Omega Pi. Presbyn. (ruling elder). Author: An Articulated Guide for Cooperative Occupational Education, 1971; Marketing Research, 1971, 78; Employer Preferences and Teacher Coordinator Practices, 1971; Methods of Teaching Business and Distributive Education, 3d. edit., 1972; Principles of Retailing, 6th edit., 1974, 7th edit., 1981; Handbook for Cooperative Vocational Education in Illinois, 1977; Annotated Bibliography of Instructional Materials in Cooperative Vocational Education, 1977; State of Illinois Marketing and Distributive Education Curriculum Planning Guide, 1978, Curriculum Guide in Food Marketing, 1978, in Wholesaling, 1978, in General Retail Merchandising, 1978, in Finance and Credit, 1979, in Transp. and Warehousing, 1980, in Automotive and Petroleum, 1981; author numerous articles and monographs in field. editor: Nat. Bus. Edn. Yearbook, 1976; editor mktg. and distbn. sect. Nat. Bus. Forum, 1976-77. Home: 802 Sunnymeade Trail DeKalb IL 60115

HARRIS, EDWIN FRIEDMAN, wholesale distbn. co. exec.; b. St. Paul, Oct. 9, 1913; s. Barney and Clara (Friedman) H.; B.A., Macalester Coll., 1936; m. Margery Zimmerman, July 1, 1976; children—Jon, Harris. Pres., Harris Industries, Mpls., 1938—; chmn. bd. NW Standard Products Co., Mpls., 1954—. Trustee, Mt. Sinai Hosp., Mpls., 1979—, Macalester Coll., 1964; pres., Temple Israel, Mpls., 1974-75. Served to lt. comdr., USNR, 1943-46; PTO. Mem. Nat. Remodelers Assn. Am. (nat. v.p. 1960-64), Nat. Remodelers Assn. Minn. (pres. 1960-64, man of yr. 1977). Clubs: Oak Ridge Country, Masons, Shriners. Home: 6017 Pine Grove Rd Edina MN 55436 Office: NW Standard Products Co 2907 Portland Ave Minneapolis MN 55407

HARRIS, EVELYN, hosp. ofcl.; b. Memphis, Mar. 17, 1922; d. Henry Evans and Pauline (Courtney) Elmore; student Memphis pub. schs.; m. Jesse James Harris, May 26, 1941; children—Jesse James, Jr. With Bruce Carton Co., Memphis, 1953-62; Central Service aide Flint (Mich.) Osteo. Hosp., 1953—, mgr. central service, 1968—. Mem. Internat. Assn. Hosp. Central Service Mgmt., Am. Soc. Hosp. Central Service Personnel, Mich. Soc. Hosp. Central Service Personnel, Mid-Mich. Central Supply Assn. (pres.). Baptist. Home: 2708 Ridgecliffe Dr Flint MI 48504 Office: 3921 Beecher Rd Flint MI 48504

HARRIS, FRANCES ALVORD (MRS. HUGH W. HARRIS), cons., ret. radio-TV broadcaster; b. Detroit, Apr. 19, 1909; d. William Roy and Edith (Vosburgh) Alvord; A.B., Grinnell Coll., 1929; L.H.D. (hon.), Ferris State Coll., 1980; m. Hugh William Harris, Sept. 24, 1932; children—Patricia Anne (Mrs. Floyd A. Metz), Hugh William, Robert Alvord. With advt. dept. Himelhoch Bros. & Co., Detroit, 1929-31; broadcaster as Julia Hayes, Robert P. Gust Co., 1931-34; tng. and personnel dept. Ernst Kern Co., 1935-36; broadcaster as Nancy Dixon, Young & Rubicam, Inc., 1939-42; women's editor Sta. WWJ, Detroit, 1943-64, Sta. WWJ-TV, 1947-64, spl. features coordinator Sta. WWJ-TV-AM-FM, 1964-74; prin. Fran Harris & Assos., cons. to social agys., instns., orgns., Detroit, 1974—; treas. I.C. Harris & Co., Detroit. Mem. exec. bd. Wayne County chpt. Mich. Soc. for Mental Health, 1953-63; chmn. Mental Health Week, 1958-59; mem. Wayne County Commn. on Aging, 1975—, chmn., 1976-77; publicity com. YWCA, 1945, 2d v.p., 1963; mem. publicity com. Tri-County League for Nursing, 1956-61; publicity chmn. Met. Detroit YWCA Bd. Dirs., 1961-66, exec. com., 1962-67; campaign dist. chmn. United Found., 1959, unit chmn., 1960-61, chmn. speakers bur., 1974; exec. bd. United Found. Women's Orgn., 1962-64; governing bd. United Community Services Women's Com., 1961-66; bd. dirs. United Community Services, 1964-67; bd. dirs. Homemaker Service Met. Detroit, pres., 1969-70; bd. dirs. Vis. Nurse Assn., pres., 1974-76; bd. dirs. Camp Fire Girls of Detroit, mem. nat. council, 1967-72, mem. nat. bd., exec. com., 1970-72, pres., 1978-80; bd. dirs. Well Being Service Aging, 1969-74, Sr. Center, 1971-76, Friends Detroit Pub. library, 1972-77, Friends Children's Museum, 1972-74; trustee Detroit Com. Alcoholism, 1961-64; mem. Mayor's Com. for Freedom Festival, 1959, chmn. women's activities, 1965; mem. Mayor's Com. for UN Week, 1959; mem. Gov.'s Commn. Status of Women, 1962-69, Mich. State Women's Commn., 1969-77; mem. nat. council Homemaker Service, 1970-73; mem. adv. com. to trustees Grinnell Coll.; mem. bd. control Ferris State Coll., 1968-78; mem. def. adv. com. Women in the Services, 1970-73, chmn., 1973; program chmn. Met. Detroit YMCA, 1973-75; sec.-treas. Mich. Assn. Governing Bds. State Colls. and Univs., 1975, v.p., 1976-77, pres., 1977-78. Recipient Grinnell Coll. Alumni award, 1959, Mental Health Soc. Mich. award, 1958, Theta Sigma Phi Headliner award for Mich., 1951, nat., 1952; Women's Advt. Club of Detroit Civic award, 1957; named Advt. Woman of Year, Detroit, 1958, 73, Soroptimist Woman of Year, 1965; Fran Harris Day in her honor, Detroit, 1960; Vol. State of Mich., 1975; Heart of Gold award, 1976. Mem. Am. Women in Radio and TV (pres. Detroit chpt. 1957-58, gen. chmn. nat. conv. 1966, Outstanding Community Service award 1972), Women's Advt. Club of Detroit (pres. 1959-60, mem. bd. 1974-77), UN Assn. U.S.A. (dir. Detroit chpt. 1962-65, Mich. div. bd. 1963-65), Advt. Fedn. (nat. v.p. women's activities 1964-67), Nat. Fedn. Press Women (hon.), Women in Communications (pres. Detroit 1950-51; del. to Asian-Am. Women in Broadcasting Conf. 1966, nat. 1st v.p. 1968-71, nat. pres. 1971-73, chmn. Communications Conf. Ams., 1968, del. III World Congress Women Journalists 1973), Pi Epsilon Delta. Episcopalian (communications com. local congregation and Diocese of Mich. 1965-66). Club: Women's Econ. (charter mem.; dir. 1975—, membership chmn. 1975, program chmn. 1976, public relations co-chmn. 1977, treas. 1978, sec. 1979, 1st v.p. 1980, pres. 1981) (Detroit). Author, editor: Focus: Michigan Women, 1977. Home and office: 8120 E Jefferson Detroit MI 48214

HARRIS, FRED, editor, publisher; b. Gary, Ind., Sept. 27, 1926; s. Fred and Mary (Wilson) H.; student Ind. U., 1947, Columbia U., 1949; married Feb. 11, 1951 (dec.); 1 son, Fredrick L. Disc jockey Sta.-WJOB, Gary, from 1943; editor, pub. Gary Am. newspaper. Served with Q.M.C., U.S. Army, 1943. Mem. Gary NAACP, Vets. In Politics (public relations exec.), VFW, Am. Legion (post comdr.). Democrat. Baptist. Clubs: Old Timers, Clay Mates Inc. Office: 2268 Broadway Gary IN 46407

HARRIS, FRED MILO, bus. exec.; b. Ottawa, Kans., Nov. 26, 1915; s. Fred Milo and Helen (Janes) H.; B.A., U. Kans., 1936; m. Josephine Elizabeth Burrow, Nov. 21, 1936; children—Fred Milo III, Nancy (Mrs. Ronald Lee Chandler), Cynthia Ann, David Christopher. With Chanute (Kans.) Tribune, 1936-52, asso. editor, 1942-48, pub., 1948-52, 73-81; promotion-publicity dir. KMBC-TV and Radio, Kansas City, Mo., 1955-59; mgr. S.E. Kan. Westam. Securities, Inc., Chanute, 1959-71; div. mgr. Internat Securities Corp., 1971-75; resident mgr. Weinrich, Zitzmann, Whitehead, Inc., Investment Securities, 1975—; pres., dir. Chanute Pub. Co., 1973-81, chmn., 1981—; pres. Mid-Am., Inc., 1967-68, chmn., 1968-69. Bd. advisers Gladys Kelse Sch. Bus. and Econ. Devel., Kans. State Coll., Pittsburg, 1974—; chmn. Neosho Meml. Hosp. Endowment Found., Chanute; chmn. Kans. Adv. Commn. on Alcoholism; mem. Kans. Adv. Com. on Drug Abuse. Mem. Chanute City Commn., 1964-67; mayor Chanute, 1966-67; mem. Kan. Ho. of Reps., 1968-76, chmn. House Transp. and Utilities Com., 1973-76. Trustee William Allen White Found., Sch. Journalism, U. Kans., 1974—. Served to lt. (j.g.) USNR, 1943-46. Mem. Chanute C. of C. (past dir., pres.), Am. Legion (past comdr.), Kans. Assn. Commerce and Industry (past dir.), Kans. Press Assn. (legis. coordinator), V.F.W., Nat. Council Alcoholism. Sigma Delta Chi, Phi Kappa Psi. Republican. Episcopalian. Home: 1208 W 14th Ct Chanute KS 66720 Office: 4 W Main St Chanute KS 66720

HARRIS, GALE ION, physicist; b. Arlington, Calif., Aug. 7, 1935; s. Albert Ion and Carmen Angeline (Waters) H.; B.S., U. Kans., 1957, M.S., 1959, Ph.D., 1962; S.M. (Sloan fellow), Mass. Inst. Tech., 1973; m. Bonnie Jean Hazlett, Mar. 31, 1956; children—Gayla Jean, Nathan Ward. With Aerospace Research Lab. USAF, Wright-Patterson AFB, Dayton, Ohio, 1965-74, project leader nuclear physics, 1962-72, dep. dir., sr. scientist solid state physics lab., 1973-74; dir. Office Mgmt. Research, Johns Hopkins Med. Sch., Balt., 1974-75, also adminstr. dept. radiology and asst. prof. radiology; asso. prof. radiology and physics Mich. State U., East Lansing, 1975—, asso. chmn. dept. radiology, 1980—; pres. Mich. Research Center, 1975—; cons. U.S. AEC, ERDA, FDA, Dept. Energy, 1974—. Served with USAF, 1962-65. Fellow Am. Phys. Soc., Soc. Nuclear Medicine, AAAS, Am. Assn. Physicists in Medicine, New Eng., Md. hist. socs., Sigma Xi, Sigma Pi Sigma, Sigma Tau, Tau Beta Pi. Contbr. articles to profl. jours. Home: 1312 Basswood Circle East Lansing MI 48823 Office: Dept Radiology Mich State Univ East Lansing MI 48824

HARRIS, GRENETTA MCKINSTRY, microbial geneticist; b. Birmingham, Ala., Oct. 10, 1947; d. Willie D. and Willie Gertrude McKinstry; A.B. cum laude, Biology, Stillman Coll., 1968; M.A. (NDEA fellow) in Microbiology, Ind. U., 1970; Ph.D., Ohio State U., 1979; 1 son, Robert L. Harris. Researcher, Eli Lilly Pharm. Co., Indpls., 1970-72; tech. asst. dept. microbiology Ohio State U., 1972-76, teaching asst., 1976-79; tutor European Molecular Biology

Orgn., U. Erlangen-Nurnberg (W. Ger.), 1979; postdoctoral asso. Max Planck Inst. for Molecular Genetics, West Berlin, 1979, Ohio State U., 1979; microbial geneticist Abbott Labs., North Chicago, Ill., 1980—. Mem. Am. Soc. for Microbiology, Assn. for Women in Sci., AAAS, N.Y. Acad. Scis., Sigma Xi. Baptist. Contbr. articles on microbial genetics to sci. publs. Home: 986 Peachtree Ct Vernon Hills IL 60061 Office: 1400 Sheridan Rd North Chicago IL 60064

HARRIS, HOWARD HUNTER, oil co. exec.; b. Cushing, Okla., Dec. 7, 1924; s. Oscar Hunter and Gertie Lee (Stark) H.; B.S. in Bus. Adminstrn., U. Okla., 1949, J.D., 1949; m. Gwendolyne J. Moyers, Dec. 31, 1945; children—Howard Sidney, Rodney Craig. Admitted to Okla. bar, 1949, Ohio bar, 1963; practiced law, Cushing and Stillwater, Okla., 1949-50; staff atty. Sun Oil Co., 1950-54; with Marathon Oil Co., 1954—, asso. gen. counsel, 1972-74, v.p. corporate external affairs, Findlay, Ohio, 1974—. Served with inf. U.S. Army, 1942-45. Decorated Bronze Star. Mem. Am. Bar Assn., Okla. Bar Assn., Ohio Bar Assn., Am. Petroleum Inst., Order of Coif. Episcopalian. Club: Masons. Office: 539 S Main St Findlay OH 45840

HARRIS, ILENE BARMASH, educator; b. Chgo., Jan. 21, 1944; d. Charles and Shirley (Garfinkel) Barmash; B.A., U. Chgo., 1965, M.A., 1972, Ph.D., 1979; m. Morton Edward Harris, July 9, 1967. Resident head U. Chgo., 1964-66, instr., 1972-73; tchr. social studies Chgo. Public Schs., 1966-68; author testing materials Sci. Research Assos., Chgo., 1969-73; instr. Rutgers U., 1971-72; research fellow U. Minn. Med. Sch., 1973-78, research asso., 1978—; mem. rev. panels Nat. Endowment Humanities; evaluation cons. Bush Found., 1978—. Ford Found. fellow, 1965-67. Mem. Am. Ednl. Research Assn., Am. Assn. Med. Colls., Nat. Soc. Study of Edn., Assn. Supervision and Curriculum Devel., Evaluation Research Soc. Contbr. articles to profl. jours. Home: 4375 Coolidge Ave S Saint Louis Park MN 55424 Office: Box 33 Mayo 420 Delaware St SE Minneapolis MN 55455

HARRIS, IRVING BROOKS, mfg. co. exec.; b. St. Paul, Aug. 4, 1910; s. William and Mildred (Brooks) H.; B.A., Yale U., 1931; m. June 19, 1974; children—Roxanne Harris Meyer, Virginia Harris Polsky, William W. Chmn. bd. Sci. Research Assos., 1953-58; pres. Harris Group, 1959-76; chmn. bd., dir. Pittway Corp., Chgo., 1962—; pres., dir. Standard Shares, Inc., 1963—; chmn. bd., dir. Acorn Fund, Inc., Chgo., 1970—; dir. Brand Insulations, Inc. Chmn., Prime Time Sch. TV, 1970—, Chgo. Ednl. TV Assn., 1973—; pres. Erikson Inst. for Early Edn., 1966—; trustee U. Chgo., Bush Found., Nat. Center for Clin. Infant Programs. Mem. Phi Beta Kappa. Clubs: Standard; Lake Shore Country; Mid-Day; Saddle and Cycle. Home: 209 E Lake Shore Dr Chicago IL 60611 Office: 120 S LaSalle St Chicago IL 60603

HARRIS, JEAN NOTON, music educator; b. Monroe, Wis., Feb. 21, 1934; d. Albert Henry and Eunice Elizabeth (Edgerton) Noton; B.A., Monmouth (Ill.) Coll., 1955; M.S., U. Ill., 1975, adminstrv. cert., 1980; m. Laurence G. Landers, June 7, 1955; children—Theodore Scott, Thomas Warren, Philip John; m. Edward Robert Harris, Nov. 27, 1981; stepchildren—Adrianne, Erica. Tchr. music schs. in Ohio, Ill. and Fla., 1955-76; tchr. music Dist. 54, Schaumburg, Ill., 1976—. Named Outstanding Young Woman of Yr., Jaycee Wives, St. Charles, Mo., 1968. Mem. Music Educators Nat. Conf., Ill. Music Educators Assn., NEA (life), U. Ill. Alumni Assn. (life), Am. Choral Dirs. Assn., Mortar Bd., Mensa, Phi Delta Kappa. Mem. United Ch. Christ. Home: 914 Roxbury Ln Schaumburg IL 60194

HARRIS, K. DAVID, justice Iowa Supreme Ct.; b. Jefferson, Iowa, July 29, 1927; s. Orville William and Jessie Heloise (Smart) H.; B.A., U. Iowa, 1949, J.D., 1951; m. Madonna Coyne, Sept. 4, 1948; children—Jane Harris Martino, Julie, Frederich. Admitted to Iowa bar, 1951; practiced law, Jefferson, 1951-62; county atty. Greene County (Iowa), 1958-62; judge 16th Jud. Dist. Iowa, 1962-72; justice Iowa Supreme Ct., 1972—. Served with inf. U.S. Army, 1945-46. Mem. Jefferson Bar Assn., Iowa Bar Assn., Am. Bar Assn. Republican. Roman Catholic. Contbr. poetry to mags. Office: Iowa Statehouse Des Moines IA 50319

HARRIS, LYNDON DENNY, JR., mfg. co. exec.; b. Chgo., Aug. 4, 1920; s. Lyndon Denny and Elsie Marie (Gonnermann) H.; B.S. in M.E., Lewis Inst. Tech., Chgo., 1942; m. Pauline C. Hirth, Nov. 20, 1978; children by previous marriage—Lyndon D., Kyle W. Dist. sales mgr. Continental Can Co., Chgo., 1953-63; gen. sales mgr. Speaker Sortation Systems, Brookfield, Wis., 1963-68; exec. v.p. Thor Systems, Inc., Cudahy, Wis., 1968-77; pres. Davlynne, Inc., Cudahy, 1977—. Served with USN, 1942-48. Decorated 2 D.F.C., 11 Air medals. Mem. ASME, Nat. Assn. Wholesale Distbrs., Am. Welding Soc., Nat. Welding Supply Assn. Lutheran. Clubs: Tripoli Country, Mason, Shriner. Home: 9314 N 60th St Brown Deer WI 53223 Office: 3383 E Layton Ave Cudahy WI 53110

HARRIS, MICHAEL EUGENE, mfg. co. exec.; b. Dallas, Mar. 16, 1945; s. Thomas Eugene and Lois Faye H.; B.A. in History, U. Tex., Arlington, 1970; m. Vicki Ann Toepfert, May 26, 1979. Sales rep. Trans Tex. Leisure Sales, 1975-76; retail store mgr. Am. Tool Supply, Garland, Tex., 1976; regional sales mgr. Shopsmith, Inc., Dallas, 1976-78, nat. sales mgr., Dayton, 1978-79, v.p. direct sales div., 1980—, mem. operating com., 1981—. Mem. Dayton Sales and Mktg. Exec. Club. Home: 7550 Normandy Ln Centerville OH 45459 Office: 750 Center Dr Vandalia OH 45377

HARRIS, MICHAEL PAUL, investment brokerage co. exec.; b. Rocky River, Ohio, May 24, 1952; s. Jack Paul and Marilyn Louise (Prince) H.; B.S. in Zoology, Ohio State U., 1974; M.B.A., U. Minn., 1976; m. Rebecca Sesler, June 8, 1974. Pres., Seal-Tight Co., Cleve., 1973; caretaker Mrs. John S. Pillsbury, Sr., Wayzata, Minn., 1974-75; account v.p. Paine Webber Jackson & Curtis, Inc., Mpls., 1975—; lectr. in field. Active Senator Pillsbury's polit. campaign, 1976. Mem. Stockbroker Soc. Assn., Delta Tau Delta. Republican. Clubs: Lions, Mpls. Athletic, Twin City Bond, Wayzata Country. Home: 3700 Bayside Rd Long Lake MN 55356 Office: 4545 IDS Center 80 S 8 St Minneapolis MN 55402

HARRIS, PATRICIA ANN, museum adminstr.; b. Michigan City, Ind., Oct. 8, 1934; d. Norman G. and Lillian M. (Noveroske) Gruse; student Purdue U., 1952-53, South Bend Coll. Commerce, 1954; m. William H. Harris, June 18, 1955; children—Susan M. Harris Vail, Keith A., Anita C., Kathleen R. Curator, dir. Old Lighthouse Museum, Michigan City Hist. Soc., Inc., 1973—. Leader, No. Ind. council Girl Scouts U.S.A., 1963-73; mem. steering com. Michigan City Sesquicentennial. Recipient Cert. of Appreciation, No. Ind. council Girl Scouts U.S.A., 1970, Cert. of Council Recognition, 1971. Mem. Am. Assn. State and Local History, Ind. Hist. Soc., Michigan City Hist. Soc. (trustee 1966—, sec. 1966-74), NW Ind. Geneal. Soc. (trustee 1975-81, v.p. 1977-78), Western Mich. Geneal. Soc., Pi Epsilon Kappa (grand pres. 1973-77). Author: History of St. Mary's of the Immaculate Conception Church, 1967; Lodner D. Phillips Launches First Submarine on the Great Lakes; research in local history. Home: 504 Greenwood Ave Michigan City IN 46360 Office: PO Box 512 Michigan City IN 46360

HARRIS, PATRICIA ANNE, physician; b. Lawrence, Kans., June 10, 1929; d. Earl Julian and Frata Frances (Holiday) Harris; A.B., U. Kans., 1951, M.D., 1954. Intern, St. Francis Hosp., Wichita, Kans. 1954-55; resident, 1955-56; practice medicine specializing in internal medicine, Wichita, 1956-60; postgrad. U. Pa. Grad. Sch. Medicine, 1960-61; mem. staff internal medicine dept. A.T. & S.F. Hosp., Topeka, 1961-67; asst. med. dir. Security Benefit Life Ins. Co., Topeka, 1968-70, asso. med. dir., 1970-77. Mem. N.Y. Acad. Scis., Am. Med. Women's Assn., Kans. Thoracic Soc., AMA, Kans., Shawnee County med. socs., Kans. Heart Assn., Pan Am. Med. Women's Alliance, Royal Soc. Medicine, P.E.O., Alpha Omega Alpha. Home: 1617 W 26th Topeka KS 66611

HARRIS, REGINA, counselor; b. Cin., Oct. 22, 1952; d. Harvey William and Vivian Ann (Mulder) H.; B.F.A., Ohio State U., 1974; M.F.A., U. Cin., 1980. Computer operator Cin. Police Div., 1975-77; art dir. Recreation Dept. City of Cin., 1977-78; adminstrv. asst. U. Cin. Med. Center, 1978-79; youth advocate counselor Human Involvement Project, Inc., Cin., 1980—. Baptist. Home: 4252 Georgia St Apt 209 Cincinnati OH 45213 Office: 635 E McMillan St Cincinnati OH 45206

HARRIS, ROBERT ARCH, musician; b. Rich Hill, Mo., May 8, 1928; s. Archie Lester and Edith Jeannette (Bailey) H.; B.Mus., Pittsburg (Kans.) State U., 1950, M.S., 1953; postgrad. Aspen Music Sch., 1958, 65-70; student Rosina Lhevinne, 1958, 65-70. Instr. piano, 1949—; instr. of music Our Lady of the Ozarks Coll., 1949-53, 55-57; asst. prof. piano and organ Mo. So. State Coll., 1971—; organist First United Meth. Ch., Carthage, Mo., 1955—; counselor Nat. Fedn. Jr. Music Clubs, Carthage; bd. dirs. Joplin (Mo.) Community Concerts Assn., 1971-76, chmn. artists com., 1975-76. Served with U.S. Army, 1953-55. Mem. Am. Music Scholarship Assn., Music Tchrs. Nat. Assn. (certified), Mo. Music Tchrs. Assn., Fellowship United Meth. Musicians, Nat. Fedn. Music Clubs, Carthage Music Club. Methodist. Home: 1344 S Main St Carthage MO 64836 Office: Mo So State Coll Joplin MO 64801

HARRIS, ROBERT BRUCE, lab. exec.; b. Lincoln, Nebr., Feb. 8, 1945; s. Lewis Elden and Antonietta E. (Synovac) H.; B.S., U. Nebr., 1968, postgrad., 1968-70; children—Matthew, Theodore. With Harris Labs., Inc., Lincoln, 1960—, v.p., 1970-76, chmn. bd., 1977—; founder, prin. R.B. Harris Co., Lincoln, 1975—; founder, pres. Harris Sci., Inc., Lincoln, 1973—; dir. PSA, Inc., FSI, Sci. Devel. Corp. Mem. Am. Platform Assn., Assn. Systems Mgmt., Nebr. Assn. Commerce and Industry, Fertilizer Inst., Nat. Fertilizer Solutions Assn., Am. Council Ind. Labs., Council Soil Testing and Plant Analysis, Am. Advt. Fedn., Am. Soc. Agrl. Engrs., Council Agrl. Sci. and Tech., Newcomen Soc., others. Republican. Presbyterian. Contbr. articles to profl. jours. Home: 2829 S 31st St Lincoln NE 68501 Office: 624 Peach St Lincoln NE 68501

HARRIS, ROBERT LAIRD, clergyman; b. Brownsburg, Pa., Mar. 10, 1911; s. Walter William and Ella Pearl (Graves) H.; B.S. in Chem. Engring., U. Del., 1931; postgrad. Washington U., St. Louis, 1931-32; Th.B., Westminster Theol. Sem., 1935, Th.M., 1937; M.A. in Oriental Studies, U. Pa., 1941; Ph.D., Dropsie U., 1947; m. Elizabeth Krugar Nelson, Sept. 11, 1937 (dec. June 1980); children—Grace (Mrs. Richard Duane Sears), Allegra (Mrs. Peter Laird Smick), Robert Laird; m. 2d, Anne Paxson Krauss, Aug. 1, 1981. Ordained minister Reformed Presbyn. Ch., 1936; instr. Faith Theol. Sem., Phila., 1937-43, asst. prof., 1943-47, prof. Bibl. Exegesis, 1947-56; prof. O.T. Covenant Theol. Sem., St. Louis, 1956-80, prof. emeritus, 1980—, dean, 1964-71; vis. lectr. Wheaton (Ill.) Coll., 1957-61; prof. Winona (Ind.) Summer Sch. Theology, 1964, 66, 67; prof. Near East Sch. Archaeology and Bible, Jerusalem, 1962; lectr. Japan, Korea, 1965. Recipient 1st. prize Zondervan Textbook Contest, 1955; E.I. DuPont de Nemours fellow, 1930-31. Mem. Soc. Bibl. Lit. and Exegesis, Am. Schs. Oriental Research, Am. Inst. Archaeology (sec. St. Louis chpt. 1971-73), Evang. Theol. Soc. (pres. 1961), Tau Beta Pi, Phi Kappa Phi. Author: Introductory Hebrew Grammar, 1950; Inspiration and Canonicity of the Bible, 1957; Your Bible, 1960; Man—God's Eternal Creation, 1971; editor: Theological Wordbook of the Old Testament, 1981; contbg. author books. Chmn. editorial bd. New Internat. Version of Bible, 1970-74. Home: 12304 Conway Rd St Louis MO 63141 Office: Covenant Theol Sem 12330 Conway Rd Saint Louis MO 63141

HARRIS, ROBERT NORMAN, advt. co. exec.; b. St. Paul, Feb. 11, 1920; s. Nathanial and Esther (Roberts) H.; B.A., U. Minn., 1940; m. Mildred Helen Burton, June 21, 1941; children—Claudia Dee, Robert Norman, Randolph B. With Toni Co. div. Gillette Co., Chgo., 1940-55, v.p. mktg., 1955; exec. v.p. Lee King & Partners, Chgo., 1955-60; exec. v.p. Allen B. Wrisley Co. div. Purex Corp. Ltd., Chgo., 1960-72; exec. v.p., dir. North Advt., Chgo., 1972-77; pres. Westbrook/Harris, Inc., Chgo., 1973-77, Harco Enterprises, Chgo., 1973-77; exec. v.p., gen. mgr. Creamer, Inc., Chgo., 1977-81, exec. v.p. corp. devel., 1981—, dir. Advance Corp., Los Angeles. Served with USNR, 1942-45. Mem. Nat. Assn. TV Arts and Scis., Am. Mktg. Assn., Am. Assn. Advt. Agys., Assn. Nat. Advertisers. Club: Sunset Valley Country. Contbr. articles in field to profl. jours.

HARRIS, SAMUEL GEORGE, electronics mfg. co. exec.; b. Vincennes, Ind., Feb. 6, 1924; s. Claud Othel and Mary Fern (Myers) H.; student Purdue U., 1941, Yale U., 1943; m. Mary Joan Ayers, May 25, 1946; children—David Alan, Brenda Susan. Broadcast engr. Sta. WAOV, Vincennes, 1940-41, Sta. WHOT, South Bend, Ind., 1946, Sta. WISH, Indpls., 1946-47; prodn. troubleshooter RCA, Indpls., 1947-49; with CIA, Washington, 1949-61; applications engr. Tech. Material Corp., Mamaroneck, N.Y., 1962-64; v.p., Delta Electronics, Inc., Springfield, Va., 1964-66; govt. sales mgr. Trylon, Inc., Elverson, Pa., 1966-68; cons. Chadwick Industries, Washington, 1968-71; mgr. spl. requirements Memcor div. E-Systems, Huntington, Ind., 1972—. Served with U.S. Army, 1942-46. Mem. Am. Def. Preparedness Assn., Armed Forces Communications and Electronics Assn., Army Aviation Assn. Am., Assn. U.S. Army. Republican. Clubs: Mason, Elks. Office: E-Systems 41 E Park Dr Huntington IN 46750

HARRIS, SCOTT MAYNARD, bus. forms and office equipment distbn. co. exec.; b. Davenport, Iowa, May 15, 1953; s. John Huntington and Lucille (Hanson) H.; B.A., Pomona Coll., 1975; M.B.A., Stanford U., 1979. Systems analyst Star Forms, Inc., Bettendorf, Iowa, 1975, data processing mgr., 1976-77, adminstrv. services mgr., 1977; asso. John Harris & Assos., Moline, Ill., 1978—, pres., 1979—; dir. Harris Enterprises. Mem. Data Processing Mgmt. Assn., Nat. Assn. Accountants, Upper Rock Island County C. of C., Nat. Bus. Forms Assn. Office: John Harris & Assos 4412 River Dr Moline IL 61265

HARRIS, SCOTT WALDEN, printing and packaging co. exec.; b. Chgo., Aug. 3, 1944; s. Everett Bagby and Marguerite Anita (Solberg) H.; B.S., U. Ill., 1966; M.B.A., Northwestern U., 1967; m. Nancy Marie Milas, Sept. 27, 1969; children—David Scott, Susan Marie. Salesman Gen. Foods Corp., Chgo., 1967; staff asst. Jewel Cos., Chgo., 1969-70; salesman M & D Flexographic Printers, Inc., Chgo., 1970-76, pres., 1976—. Vice pres. All Saints Lutheran Ch., Orland Park, Ill., 1980—; active Boy Scouts Am. Served to 1st lt., U.S. Army, 1967-69. Decorated Bronze Star. Named Businessman of the Year, Ashburn Civic Assn., 1978. Mem. Printing Industry of Ill., Ill. Mfrs. Assn., Ashburn Civic Assn. Lutheran. Club: Union League (Chgo.). Home: 12511 Roma Rd Palos Park IL 60464 Office: 3600 W 83rd Pl Chicago IL 60652

HARRIS, STANLEY GALE, JR., ret. banker; b. Chgo., June 19, 1918; s. Stanley Gale and Muriel (Bent) H.; student Yale U., 1936-38; certificate in indsl. adminstrn. Harvard Grad. Sch. Bus. Adminstrn., 1943; children—John Trumbull, Thomas Bartlett; m. 2, Alice Harwood, Nov. 4, 1972. With Nat. Bank Commerce, Seattle, 1939-41, Carnegie-Ill. Steel Corp., 1943-44; with Harris Trust & Savs. Bank, Chgo., from 1944, now ret., former chmn. bd., dir.; chmn. bd., dir. Harris Bankcorp Inc.; dir. Snap-On Tools Corp., Kenosha, Wis. Hon. trustee Ill. Children's Home and Aid Soc.; trustee U. Chgo. Clubs: Chicago, Commercial, Casino, Tavern, Little Wheels, Skokie Country (Chgo.); Bohemian (San Francisco). Home: 180 E Pearson St Apt 4704 Chicago IL 60611

HARRIS, STEVEN HESSE, geologist, oil co. exec.; b. Cin., Nov. 18, 1924; s. Ira and Eugenia Claire (Hesse) H.; B.A., U. Cin., 1948, M.S., 1950; m. Mary Kathleen Broderick, Oct. 6, 1955; children—Steven, Bruce, Terry, Wayne, Diane. Exploration geologist Shell Oil Co., Tulsa, 1950-52; cons. geologist Harris, Brown & Klemer, Bismarck, N.D., 1952—; pres. Camargo Corp., Bismarck, N.D., 1965—, Pradera del Norte, Inc., Bismarck; exec. v.p. Condor Resources, Inc. Served with AUS, 1942-46. Fellow Geol. Soc. Am.; mem. Ind. Petroleum Assn. Am. (regional v.p. N.D., S.D., Minn. 1978-80), N.D. Geol. Soc. (pres. 1965, 72), Am. Inst. Profl. Geologists (sect. pres. 1973-75), Am. Assn. Petroleum Geologists (sec.-treas. Rocky Mountain sect. 1981-82), Soc. Econ. Paleontologists and Mineralogists, Am. Legion, N.D. Landman's Assn., Dakota Petroleum Club (pres. 1960, 65), Sigma Xi, Sigma Gamma Epsilon, Kappa Kappa Psi. Clubs: Masons, Elks, Shriners. Contbr. articles to various publs. Home: 1120 N 1st St Bismarck ND 58501 Office: 204 W Thayer Bismarck ND 58502

HARRIS, VANESSA LEE, public affairs specialist; b. Columbus, Ohio, Jan. 8, 1948; d. Homer P. and Helen M. (Saunders) Lee; student Wilberforce Central State U., 1968; B.S. in Family and Consumer Resources, Wayne State U., 1976; organizing cert. Nat. Tng. and Info. Center, 1977; children—Kevin Maurice, David Vincent. Tchr. consumer edn. City Sch. Detroit, 1977; consumer edn. specialist Mich. Senator Jack Faxon, 1977-79; sales mgr. Bowers Realty, Detroit, 1979; public affairs specialist Project on Equal Edn. Rights, NOW Legal Def. and Edn. Fund, Milford, Mich., 1979—; co-owner Wolff-Harris Research & Cons.; cons. consumer issues and workshops. Mem. New Detroit Anti-Racism Com.; bd. dirs. Brightmoor Community Center, Detroit, Women of Wayne Child Care Center, Detroit; mem. citizen rev. com. Detroit City Planning Commn. Recipient Scholastic Achievement award Wilberforce Central State U., 1970. Mem. Awareness Inc., Consumer Credit Assn. Greater Detroit, Consumer Educators Mich., Wayne State U. Alumni Assn., Women of Wayne, Consumer Adv. Research Council, NOW, Nat. Assn. Female Execs. Democrat. Methodist. Home: 8801 Kingswood Apt 105 Detroit MI 48221 Office: City Nat Bank Bldg Suite 880 Detroit MI 48226

HARRIS, WILLIAM PAGE, investment mgr.; b. Alpena, Mich., Dec. 29, 1920; s. Clinton P. and Norma (Richardson) H.; B.A., Dartmouth Coll., 1942; postgrad. George Washington U., 1949; m. Dewilda E. Naramore, July 14, 1956; children by previous marriage—Clinton P., Nancy E. Fgn. service officer, vice-consul sec. embassy, Germany, Switzerland, 1950-54; dir. Allison Lumber Co., Bellamy, Ala., 1954-60; pres. Harris Concrete & Supply Co., Taylor, Mich., 1956-63; v.p. Detroit office Tex. Industries, Inc., 1963-64; pres., dir. Mohawk Lumber & Hardware Co., Detroit, 1965-78; mgr. investments, comml. real estate, 1978—. Served to lt. USNR, 1942-45. Recipient Sec. of State commendation Geneva Conf. Fgn. Ministers, 1954. Club: Detroit. Home and Office: 17845 Parke Ln Grosse Ile MI 48138

HARRISON, ALONZO, fin. exec.; b. Forest City, Ark., Aug. 16, 1952; s. Walter James and Doris Nell (Burnette) H.; B.A., Washburn U., 1974; M.P.A., Kans. U., 1978; postgrad. Harvard U., 1977, U. Pa., 1980; 1 child, Aliah Tishman. Systems engr. IBM, Topeka, Kans., 1974-75; public service employment mgr. Dept. Labor Services, Topeka, 1975-79; with Menninger Found., Topeka, 1979—, exec. mgmt. analysis fin. and mgmt. info. systems, 1979—; mgmt., investment and tax cons.; instr. fin. seminars. Mem. Congl. Small Bus. Adv. Bd., 1976-78; fin. advisor Nat. Alcoholic Info. Center, 1980—; mgr. Women's Slow Pitch Softball, Topeka, 1974-78; sponsor Girls AAU basketball, 1977-79. Named Outstanding Young Leader, Leadership Kans., 1979. Mem. Omega Psi Phi (vice boscilus). Writer, producer, dir. film documentary. Home: 729 Wear St Topeka KS 66607 Office: PO Box 829 Topeka KS 66601

HARRISON, BRUCE WILLIAM, architect; b. Chgo., Nov. 5, 1929; s. Joseph W. and Helen (Carson) H.; student U. Paris, 1954; B.Arch., U. Ill., 1960; M.Arch., U. Mich., 1971, M.Sociology, 1973, Ph.D. in Psychology, 1980; children—Taniella J., Giana B. Sr. archtl. designer Skidmore, Owings & Merrill, Chgo., 1961-62; chief archtl. designer, draftsperson Mark D. Kalischer Assos., Chgo., 1962-65; sr. archtl. designer Minoru Yamasaki & Assos., Troy, Mich., 1968—; architect Bechtel & Assos., P.C., Ann Arbor, Mich., 1967—; tchr. archtl. design Lawrence Inst. Tech. Active, Virginia Park Area Planning, Detroit, 1968—, Ann Arbor Model Cities Program, 1970-72. Served with USAF, 1951-55. Registered architect, Mich., Ill. Mem. Nat. Council Archtl. Registration Bds., AIA (nat. com. on architecture for justice), Am. Arbitration Assn., Mich. Soc. Architects. Home: 2439 Stone Dr Ann Arbor MI 48105 Office: 777 E Eisenhower Pkwy Ann Arbor MI 48106

HARRISON, DAVID CLARK, utility co. exec.; b. Richmond, Mo., June 10, 1927; s. David E. and Irma Faye (Clark) H.; A.A., St. Joseph Jr. Coll., 1945; B.A., U. Mo., 1951, LL.B., 1953; m. Allegra Lou Lile, June 8, 1949; children—David Lile, Laura Ann. Claims supr. MFA Ins. Co., Columbia, Mo., 1953-58; admitted to Mo. bar, 1953; pvt. practice law, Salem, Mo., 1958-61; gen. atty. Mo. Power & Light Co., Jefferson City, 1961, v.p., gen. counsel, 1967, pres., 1969; v.p., gen. counsel Mo. Edison Co., Louisiana, 1967, pres., 1969—; dir. Central Trust Bank, Central Bancompany, Jefferson City. Bd. dirs. Mo. Public Expenditure Survey, 1979—; chmn. exec. com. Missouri Valley Electric Assn., 1981-82. Served with U.S. Army, 1945-47. Recipient Disting. Service award Jefferson City Jaycees, 1963. Mem. Mo. C. of C. (pres. 1974-75), Jefferson City C. of C. (pres. 1970), Midwest Gas Assn. (dir. 1980—), Mo. Bar Assn., Cole County Bar Assn. Democrat. Presbyterian. Home: RFD 1 PO Box 183A Hartsburg MO 65039 Office: 101 Madison St Jefferson City MO 65101

HARRISON, GEORGE LOUIS, clergyman, social worker; b. Moorhead, Iowa, Oct. 24, 1928; s. Hugh and Beth (Whitehead) H.; A.B., Minn. Bible Coll., 1951; B.D., Lincoln (Ill.) Christian Sem., 1962; M.S., Ft. Hays (Kans.) State Coll., 1971; m. Francel Oliver, May 14, 1950 (dec.); children—Wayne, Emily. Lic. to ministry, Ch. of Christ, 1950; pastor Christian Churches, Iowa, Ill., Tenn., 1950-62, supply minister, Disciples of Christ and Ch. of Christ, United Ch. of Christ chs., Minn., 1963—; sr. caseworker, Minn. State Dept. Corrections, Lino Lakes, 1963—; career counselor for released inmates, 1976—. Grantee, Law Enforcement Ednl. Program, 1968-72. Mem. Am. Personnel and Guidance Assn., Am. Rehab.

Counseling Assn., Minn. Corrections Assn., Minn. Bible Coll. Alumni (area pres., 1966-67). Contbr. articles to Christian Standard mag. Home: 7661 Lake Dr Circle Pines MN 55014 Office: Box L Circle Pines MN 55014

HARRISON, HAROLD DUANE, advt. exec.; b. Detroit, Mar. 9, 1930; s. Hartley Curtis and Helen Magdalen (Bailey) H.; B.S. in Speech, Northwestern U., 1951; M.A., Ball State U., 1972; m. Joyce Irene Rohde, Feb. 19, 1955; children—Cheryl Jean, David Keith. Staff announcer, news dir. WBIW, Bedford, Ind., 1952; reporter, feature writer, columist Bedford Daily Times Mail, 1953-60; staff corr. Indpls. News, 1953-60; owner, pub. Star Jour., Hope, Ind., 1960-67; asst. dir. pub. relations Ball Corp., Muncie, Ind., 1967-72; exec. v.p., Groves & Assos. Inc., Muncie, 1972-80; owner H. Duane Harrison Public Relations/Advt., 1980—; asst. prof. journalism Ball State U., 1975—; Founding dir. Eastern Ind. Community TV Inc., 1971-72; pub. relations chmn. Delaware County United Way, 1976. Mem. Pub. Relations Soc. Am. (accredited, v.p., dir. Hoosier chpt. 1975-76, counselor's acad. 1974—), Indsl. Communication Council Inc. Clubs: Kiwanis (Muncie), Muncie Advt. (past pres.). Author articles in field. Home: 3501 N Vienna Woods Dr Muncie IN 47304 Office: PO Box 488 Muncie IN 47305

HARRISON, JOSEPH WILLIAM, state senator Ind.; b. Chgo., Sept. 10, 1931; s. Roy J. and Gladys V. (Greenman) H.; B.S., U.S. Naval Acad., 1956; postgrad. Ind. U. Law Sch., 1968-70; m. Ann Hovey Gillespie, June 9, 1956; children—Holly Ann, Tracy Jeanne, Thomas Joseph, Amy Beth, Kitty Lynne, Christy Jayne. Asst. to pres. Harrison Steel Castings Co., Attica, Ind., 1960-64, sales research engr., 1964-66, asst. sec., 1966-69, sec., 1969-71, v.p., 1971—, dir., 1968—, mem. Ind. Senate, 1966—. Mem. Attica Consol. Sch. Bd., 1964-66, pres., 1966-67. Served with USN, 1956-60. Mem. Wabash Valley Assn., Am. Legion, Sigma Chi. Republican. Methodist. Club: Elks. Home: 504 E Pike St Attica IN 47918 Office: PO Box 60 Attica IN 47918

HARRISON, MICHAEL JAY, educator, physicist, univ. dean; b. Chgo., Aug. 20, 1932; s. Nathan J. and Mae (Nathan) H.; A.B., Harvard, 1954; M.S., U. Chgo., 1956, Ph.D., 1960; m. Ann Tukey, Sept. 1, 1970. Fulbright fellow and H. Van Loon fellow in theoretical physics U. Leiden, Netherlands, 1954-55; NSF fellow U. Chgo., 1957-59; research fellow math. physics U. Birmingham (Eng.), 1959-61; asst. prof. Mich. State U., East Lansing, 1961-63, asso. prof., 1963-68, prof., 1968—, faculty grievance officer, 1972-73, dean Lyman Briggs Coll., 1973—. With Air Force Cambridge Research Center, summer 1953, M.I.T. Lincoln Lab., summer 1954, RCA Sarnoff Lab., summers 1961-63; physicist Westinghouse Labs., summer 1956; cons. RCA Lab., 1961-64, United Aircraft Co., 1964-66, U.K. Atomic Energy Authority, Harwell Lab., summer, 1960, Thailand project in Bangkok, Mich. State U.-AID, summer 1968; vis. research physicist Inst. for Theoretical Physics, U. Calif., Santa Barbara, 1980-81. Am. Council on Edn. fellow UCLA, 1970-71. Fellow Am. Phys. Soc., Sigma Xi; mem. Am. Inst. Physics, AAUP, N.Y. Acad. Scis., Phi Beta Kappa. Jewish. Clubs: Harvard of Central Michigan, Rotary. Contbr. numerous articles to U.S., fgn. profl. jours. Office: Physics Dept Mich State U East Lansing MI 48824

HARRISON, ROBERT STATLER, mech. engr.; b. Rochester, N.Y., Sept. 10, 1941; s. Robert P. and Clara S. (Statler) H.; asso. degree in applied sci., State U. N.Y., 1961; m. Susan Della Brown, Feb. 22, 1964; children—Todd, Jon, Kristen. Lab. technician Gen. Motors Co., Rochester, 1961-64; carburetor design engr. Ford Motor Co., Dearborn, Mich., 1964-71, sect. supr. advanced carburetor applications, 1971-73, supr. solid and fluid mechanics, 1973-76, systems engr. engine certification strategy, 1976-80, supr. V-8 engines, 1980-81, supr. truck engine design, 1980—. Mem. Soc. Automotive Engrs. Holder 24 patents in field automotive engring. Home: 17775 Parke Ln Grosse Ile MI 48138 Office: Ford Motor Co PO Box 2053 Dearborn MI 48124

HARROD, JOHN PRICE, JR., physician; b. Savannah, Ga., Apr. 18, 1923; s. John Price and Gladys (Still) H.; student Emory U., 1943; M.D., U. Ga., 1946; m. Kathleen L. Sheedy, Nov. 13, 1948; children—John Price III, William Joseph, Laurence Lee, Susan Byron. Intern, Gorgas Hosp., Panama, C.Z., 1946-47; resident in obstetrics and gynecology U. Hosp., Augusta, Ga., 1947, 49, Duval County Hosp., Jacksonville, Fla., 1949-50, Chgo. Lying-In Hosp., 1951-52; asst. prof. ob-gyn U. Ill., 1963—; practice medicine specializinig in obstetrics and gynecology, Chgo., 1958—; mem. active staff S. Chgo. Community Hosp., 1958—, chmn. dept. obstetrics and gynecology, 1963—, bd. dirs., 1977—, pres. staff, 1972, pres. elect 1973; cons. staff Chgo. Lying-In Hosp., 1963—; asso. staff Cook County Hosp., Chgo., 1959-61. Bd. dirs. chmn. med. adv. com. Chgo. Area Planned Parenthood Association; Served to capt. M.C., AUS, 1947-49. Diplomate Am. Bd. Obstetrics and Gynecology. Mem. AMA, Chgo. Gynecol. Soc. (sec. 1970-73, pres. 1974-75), Central Assn. Obstetricians and Gynecologists (exec. com. 1971-75, v.p. 1979-80), South Chgo. C. of C., Association Am., Med. Colls., Pan Am. Med. Soc., Am. Coll. Obstetricians and Gynecologists (dist. VI vice-chmn. 1977-80, chmn. 1980-83, exec. bd. 1980-83), Chgo. Med. Soc. (trustee 1975—, treas. 1977—), Ill. Soc. Obstetrics & Gynecology. Clubs: Mid-Am. Confreire de la Chaine des Rotisseurs, Bailli de Chgo. (pres.), Escoffier Soc., Confrerie des Vignerons de St. Vincent, Connoisseurs Internat. Home: 10014 S Seeley Ave Chicago IL 60643 Office: 2315 E 93d St Chicago IL 60617

HARROLD, JOHN ANDREW, educator; b. Ft. Wayne, Ind., July 11, 1937; s. Virgil Odell and Naoma (Roth) H.; B.S., Ind. U., 1961, M.A.T., 1967, 71; m. Anna M. Kaserman, June 7, 1959; children—John Andrew, Rebekah Ann. Tchr. schs. in Ind., 1961, 64-70; fellow social studies field agt. tng. program Ind. U., 1970-71; tchr., chmn. social studies dept. social studies field agt. Craig Jr. High Sch., Indpls., 1971-72; cons. div. curriculum Ind. Dept. Public Instrn., 1972-76, dir. div. curriculum, 1976—. Supt. ch. sch. St. John United Ch. Christ, Indpls., 1972-73; pres. adult sch. classes Cumberland United Methodist Ch., Indpls., 1976-78, mem. adminstrv. bd., council ministries, 1976-79. Served with USAR, 1961-79. Mem. Nat. Council Social Studies (ho. dels. 1973, 74, 76, chmn. Midwest regional conf. 1975-76), Council State Social Studies Specialists (chmn. nominations com. 1974), Ind. Council Social Studies (v.p. 1973-74, pres. 1975-77), Am. Assn. Sch. Adminstrs., Am. Ednl. Research Assn., Am. Mgmt. Assn., Assn. Supervision and Curriculum Devel. (curriculum com. 1981—), Social Studies Suprs. Assn., World Future Soc., Ind. Assn. Supervision and Curriculum Devel., Ind. Council Social Studies (pres. 1975-76). Home: 12256 Dunbar Circle S Cumberland IN 46229 Office: Room 229 State House Indianapolis IN 46204

HARRY, ORMSBY L., univ. adminstr.; b. Richmond, Ind., Aug. 28, 1918; s. Fern Cullers and Bess (Keselring) H.; student Kendall Coll., 1938-39; B.S., Ohio U., 1942, M.S., 1947; Ed.D., Mich. State U., 1960; m. Helen Louise Barklow, June 26, 1943; children—Howard David, Kathryn S., Anne L. Overlien, Rachel Lynne. Head resident Ohio U., Athens, 1946-47; asso. dean students U. Omaha, 1947-52; grad. asst. Mich. State U., East Lansing, 1952-53; asso. dean students, asso. prof. edn. Mich. Tech. U., Houghton, 1953-59; dean students, prof. edn. Shepherd Coll., Shepherdstown, W.Va., 1959-63, asst. chancellor student affairs, prof. psychology U. Wis.-Eau Claire, 1963—. Leadership tng. chmn. Winchester (Va.) Boy Scouts Am., 1961-63, Chippewa Valley (Wis.) Council, 1964-69. Served with USAAF, 1942-46. Mem. Am. Personnel and Guidance Assn., Am. Coll. Personnel Assn. (directorate com. VII), Danzarine Dance Club, Phi Delta Kappa, Phi Kappa Phi, Phi Eta Sigma (nat. exec. com. 1976-80), Omicron Delta Kappa, Delta Tau Delta, Alpha Phi Omega. Presbyn. (elder). Clubs: Moose, Kiwanis (dir. Houghton, Mich., 1955-58, Eau Claire, 1963—, pres. 1979-80, sec. 1980). Home: 1515 E Webster St Eau Claire WI 54701

HARSDORF, JAMES ERVIN, dairy farmer, state senator; b. St. Paul, Nov. 7, 1950; s. Ervin Albert and Eloise Vivian H.; B.S. in Animal Sci., U. Minn.; m. June 20, 1980; 1 son, Johnathan Scott. Partner, Trim-Bel Valley Dairy Farm, Beldenville, Wis., 1972—; rep. Wis. State Assembly, 1977-80; mem. Wis. State Senate, 1980—; tchr. dairy farm mgmt. and dairy evaluation U. Wis., River Falls, 1975; sec. Republican Senate Caucus. Mem. Wis. Holstein Assn., Wis. Farm Bur. Lutheran. Office: 410 S Capitol St Madison WI 53702*

HARSHBARGER, KENNETH E., dairy scientist; b. Arcola, Ill., Nov. 12, 1914; s. Harry H. and Maude Ethel H.; B.S., U. Ill., 1937, M.S., 1939, Ph.D., 1960; m. Elsie Joan Brown, Aug. 31, 1957; children—Kenneth Lee, Keven E., Kent E., Karen E. Vocational-agr. instr. LaRose (Ill.) High Sch., 1937-38; asst. dairy production U. Ill., Urbana, 1938-41, instr. dairy production, 1946, asst. prof. dairy science 1946-60, asso. prof., 1960-62, prof., 1962-63, prof. nutrition in dairy science, 1963—; asso. head dept., 1963-69, head dept. dairy science, 1969-79; dir. higher edn. projects Midwest Univs. Consortium for Internat. Activities (MUCIA), Jakarta, Indonesia, 1979—; cons. in field. Served with U.S. Army, 1941-46. Mem. Am. Inst. Nutrition, Am. Soc. Animal Science, Am. Dairy Science Assn., Alpha Zeta, Sigma Xi, Phi Kappa Phi, Gamma Sigma Delta. Home: 502 E Pennsylvania Ave Urbana IL 61801 Office: Dept Dairy Science Univ Ill Urbana IL 61801

HARSHMAN, CARL LEONARD, univ. dean; b. Dayton, Ohio, Jan. 11, 1944; s. Carl Lee and Evelyn R. (Borchers) H.; B.A., Ohio State U., 1965, Ph.D., 1972; M.S., Wright State U., 1970; m. Ellen F. McCorkle, Dec. 21, 1968; children—Todd C., Ryan D. Sales rep. Occidental Life Ins. Co., Columbus, Ohio, 1965-66; dist. scout exec. Boy Scouts Am., Columbus, 1966-67; constrn. mgr. Brochers Constrn. Co., Dayton, Ohio, 1967-68; asst. dir. admissions Wright State U., Dayton, 1968-70; instr. Ohio Dominican Coll., Columbus, 1970-72; coordinator acad. planning St. Louis U., 1972-74, prof. higher edn., 1975—, dean Met. Coll., 1975—; sr. asso. W.P. Dolan & Assos.; pres. Carl L. Harshman & Assos.; host World of Ideas KTVI-TV. Recipient dist. Spoke award Jaycees, 1967, Speak-up contest winner Ohio chpt., 1967. Mem. Am. Assn. for Higher Edn., Am. Personnel and Guidance Assn. Office: Met Coll St Louis U 221 N Grand Blvd Saint Louis MO 63103

HARSHMAN, DAVID MARTIN, physician; b. Pittsfield, Ill., Mar. 8, 1950; s. Clair LaRose and Jean (Martin) H.; B.S., No. Ill. U., 1971; M.D., U. Ill., 1975; m. Kathleen Marie McGraw, June 17, 1972; children—Ryan Christopher, Erik David. Intern, St. Louis U. Hosp., 1975-76, resident in internal medicine, 1976-77, fellow in cardiology, 1977-79, asst. clin. prof. medicine, 1979—; pvt. practice medicine, specializing in cardiology, St. Louis, 1979—; dir. cardiac rehab. Deaconess Hosp., St. Louis; cons. cardiology Lutheran Hosp., St. Anthony's Hosp., Alexian Bros. Hosp., all St. Louis. Diplomate Am. Bd. Internal Medicine. Fellow Am. Coll. Cardiology; mem. St. Louis Heart Assn., St. Louis Met. Med. Soc., Alpha Omega Alpha. Home: 18036 Turkey Bend Glencoe MO 63038 Office: 3535 S Jefferson St Saint Louis MO 63118

HARSHMAN, MORTON LEONARD, physician; b. Youngstown, Ohio, Apr. 21, 1932, s. Ben and Lillian (Malkoff) H.; B.S., Ohio State U., 1953, M.D., 1957; m. Barbara Elmore, June 21, 1957; children—Beth, Melissa. Intern Grant Hosp., Columbus, Ohio, 1957-58; practice medicine specializing in family practice, Cin., 1960—; v.p. med. staff Bethesda Hosp., 1974-75, pres., 1975-77; mem. staff Christ Hosp., Children's Hosp., Deaconess Hosp., Providence Hosp. (all Cin.). Pres., bd. dirs. Morton Harshman Inc., 880 Real Estate Co. Trustee Bethesda Hosp. and Deaconess Assn., 1972-79. Served with USNR, 1958-60. Fellow Am. Acad. Family Practice (charter); mem. Am. Bd. Family Practice (charter), A.M.A., Ohio Med. Assn. Cin. Acad. Medicine, Ohio, Southwestern Ohio acads. family practice, Kentucky Col. Assn., Phi Beta Kappa, Alpha Epsilon Delta, Club: Phi Delta Epsilon Grad. (Cin.). Home: 630 Flagstaff Dr Cincinnati OH 45215 Office: 880 Reynard Dr Cincinnati OH 45231

HART, CECIL WILLIAM, surgeon; b. Bath, Eng., May 27, 1931; s. William Theodore and Pauline Olive (Adams) H.; B.A., Dublin U., 1952, M.B., B.Ch., 1955, M.A., 1958; m. Brigid Frances Molloy, June 15, 1957; children—Geoffrey Arthur, Paula Mary, John Adams. Intern, Dr. Steevens' Hosp., Dublin, 1956; Little Company of Mary Hosp., Evergreen Park, Ill., 1957; resident in otolaryngology U. Chgo., 1959-62, NIH fellow, 1962-63; practice medicine specializing in otolaryngology, Chgo., 1963—; attending physician-surgeon Children's Meml. Hosp., Northwestern Meml. Hosp.; asso. prof. clin. otolaryngology and maxillofacial surgery Northwestern U. Med. Sch. Fellow A.C.S., Am. Acad. Otolaryngology-Head and Neck Surgery; mem. Brit. Med. Assn., AMA, Ill. State Med. Soc., Chgo. Med. Soc., Am. Neurotology Soc., Bárány Soc., Royal Soc. Medicine, Hearing Conservation Assn., Am. Cleft Palate Assn. Club: Carlton (Chgo.). Contbr. articles to profl. jours. Office: 707 N Fairbanks Ct Chicago IL 60611

HART, D. DENSMORE SHUTE, banker; b. Ulysses, Kans., Nov. 25, 1934; s. Frank W. and Clola E. H.; B.A. with honors, Mich. State U., 1956; M.B.A., U. Mich., 1959. With Kroger, Inc., Chgo., 1960-63; real estate broker Coldwell Banker & Co., Phoenix, 1964-65; with Bank of Kans., Hutchinson, 1965—, pres., chief exec. officer, pres. bank holding co., 1981—. Mem. Beta Gamma Sigma. Republican. Episcopalian. Office: Bank of Kans Financial Square PO Box 1707 Hutchinson KS 67501

HART, DAVID R., athletic dir.; b. Connellsville, Pa., May 25, 1925; s. David Henry and Janet (McCairns) H.; B.S. in Edn., St. Vincent Coll., 1951; M.Ed. and Adminstrn., U. Pitts., 1959; m. Patricia Furtney, Apr. 22, 1946; children—David, Richard, Daniel, Mary Candace. Head football coach Hurst High Sch., Mt. Pleasant, Pa., 1951-53; head football coach, athletic dir. Johnstown (Pa.) High Sch., 1954-61; asst. football coach U. Ky., 1962-63; asst. coach U.S. Naval Acad., 1964-65; head football coach U. Pitts., 1966-69; asst. to pres. Robert Morris Coll., Pitts., 1970-73; dir. athletics U. Louisville, 1973-78, dir. athletics U. Mo., Columbia, 1978—. Bd. dirs. Ky. State Fair, 1977-78, U.S. Sports Acad. Served with USAAF, 1944-45. Decorated D.F.C., air medal. Mem. Coll. Football Assn., Nat. Assn. Intercollegiate Athletic Dirs. (mem. exec. com.), Nat. Collegiate Athletics Assn. (basketball com.), Am. Radio and TV Artists. Democrat. Roman Catholic. Contbr. articles to profl. jours., mags. Office: Univ of Mo Columbia MO 65211

HART, G. GERALD, advt. exec.; b. Detroit, Aug. 7, 1944; s. G. and Marjorie (Epstean) H.; student Detroit Inst. Tech., 1963; B.B.A., Wayne State U., 1967; postgrad. in advt., Northwestern U., 1977. Mktg. asst. Security Bank & Trust Co., Detroit, 1967-69; advt. asst. Nat. Bank Detroit, 1969-70; copywriter Leo Burnett Co. of Mich., 1970-72; account exec. Yaffe Stone August, 1972-73, J. Walter Thompson, Chgo., 1974-77; account supr. G.M. Feldman & Co., 1978, J. Walter Thompson Co., Chgo., 1979; v.p., account supr. D'Arcy-MacManus & Masius, St. Louis, 1980—. Mem. Advt. Club Chgo., Internat. Brotherhood Magicians. Office: D'Arcy Advt 1 Memorial Dr Saint Louis MO 63105

HART, HARRY JAMES, paper co. exec.; b. Chgo., June 17, 1918; s. Robert J. and Peggy (Slutzker) H.; B.S., Northwestern U., 1939. Br. mgr. Nat. Bond & Investment Co., Evanston, Ill., 1939-41; with Schwarz Paper Co., Chgo., 1946—, dir., 1960—, v.p., 1967—; underwriting mem. Lloyd's of London, Sturge Syndicate, 1973—. Bd. dirs., v.p. Sr. Centers Met. Chgo., 1974—; trustee Harry J. Hart Found. Served to capt. AUS, 1941-46. Mem. Cercle Universitaire Franco Americaine, Alliance Française, English Speaking Union, Paper Club of Chgo. (pres. 1965-66). Clubs: Lake Shore Country (Glencoe, Ill.); Plaza, Monroe, Maison Française, Execs. (Chgo.). Home: 2321C N Geneva Terr Chicago IL 60614 Office: Schwarz Paper Co 8338 N Austin Ave Morton Grove IL 60053

HART, J. BING, computer scientist, chemist, toxicologist; b. Springfield, Mo., Jan. 20, 1942; s. H. Avery and Sue D. (Ellis) H.; B.A., U. Kans., 1964, Ph.D., 1971; postgrad. U. Oreg., 1964-66, U. Calif., 1966-68; m. Kathleen Louise Harrison, Sept. 26, 1979; children—Lea, Sasha. Research asso. dept. chemistry U. Kans., 1971-72; prin. investigator, project dir. Youth Projects, Inc., San Francisco, 1972-73; owner, operator Ergo Assos., Lawrence, Kans., 1973—; chief health chemistry Kans. Dept. Health and Environ., 1975; sr. analytical chemist Olin Corp., 1978-79; dir. Keltner Labs., Manhattan, Kans., 1979-80; instr. computer sci. Kans. State U., 1980-81; sr. research analyst Quincy Research Center, Kansas City, Mo., 1981—; cons., lectr. in field; expert witness testimony; trainer, cons., dir. st. drug analysis program Hdqrs., Inc. and other crisis centers, 1969—. Mem. Am. Chem. Soc., Ethnopharmacology Soc., Soc. Applied Spectroscopy, Kans. Psychol. Assn., Kans. Drug Abuse Counselors Assn. Editor: Straight Dope Analysis Newsletter, 1973—; contbr. articles to profl. jours.

HART, JAMES WARREN, profl. football player; b. Evanston, Ill., Apr. 29, 1944; s. George Ezrie and Marjorie Helen (Karsten) H.; B.S., So. Ill. U., 1967; m. Mary Elizabeth Mueller, June 17, 1967; children—Bradley James and Suzanne Elizabeth (twins), Katherine Anne. Quarterback, St. Louis Cardinals Profl. Football Team, 1966—; pub. relations rep. Tower Grove Bank & Trust Co., 1974—; radio sports personality Sta. KMOX, 1975—; head coach So. Ill. Spl. Olympics, 1973—, Mo. Spl. Olympics, 1976-78. Gen. campaign chmn. St. Louis Heart Assn., 1974-78; active St. Louis chpt. Multiple Sclerosis Soc., 1970—; chmn. Read-a-thon, bd. dirs. Nat. Sports Com., 1977—; hon. chmn. United Cerebral Palsy of Mo., 1977—. Named Most Valuable Player in Nat. Football Conf., 1974, Most Valuable Player with St. Louis Cardinals, 1973, 75, Man of Year, St. Louis Dodge Dealers, 1975, 76; recipient Byron White award; Brian Piccolo Nat. YMCA Humanitarian award, 1980. Mem. Fellowship Christian Athletes (chpt. dir.), Nat. Football League Players Assn. (Byron White award 1976), AFTRA. Republican. Co-author: The Jim Hart Story, 1977. Office: 200 Stadium Plaza Saint Louis MO 63102

HART, JAY ALBERT CHARLES, real estate broker; b. Rockford, Ill., Apr. 16, 1923; s. Jabez Waterman and Monty Evangeline (Burgin) H.; student U. Ill., 1941-42, U. Mo., 1942-43, U. Miami (Fla.), 1952-56, Rockford Coll., 1961-62; m. Marie D. Goetz, July 16, 1976; children—Dale M. (Mrs. Richard Peel Jr.), Jay C.H. Exec. v.p. Hart Oil Co., Rockford, 1947—; pres. Internat. Service Co., Pompano Beach, Fla., 1952-58; v.p. Ipsen Industries, Inc., Rockford, 1958-61; owner Hart Realtors, Rockford, 1961—; lectr. in field; trustee, sr. analyst Anchor Real Estate Investment Trust, Chgo., 1971—. Dir. Winnebago County (Ill.) CD, 1975. Chmn. Rock River chpt. ARC, 1973, nat. nominating com., 1971, disaster chmn. Illiana div., 1972—; bd. counselors Rockford Coll., 1974—; emergency coordinator 9th Naval dist. M.A.R.S., USN, 1960-68, civilian adv. council, 1968-78. Office mgr. Citizens for Eisenhower, Chgo., 1952. Served with USAAF, 1943-46. Mem. Rockford Air Guild (pres. 1974, 76-77), Tamaroa Watercolor Soc. (v.p. 1974—), Rockford Boys Club Assn. (dir.), Exptl. Amateur Radio Soc. (pres. 1960—), Internat. Council Shopping Centers, Nat. Assn. Real Estate Appraisers, Soc. Indsl. Realtors, Nat. Assn. Realtors, Phi Eta Sigma. Mason (Shriner). Clubs: Rockford Country, Mid-Day, Gaslight. Author: Real Estate Buyers and Sellers Guide, 1961. Paintings in pvt., pub. collections; illustrations in numerous publs. Home: 2406 E Lane Rockford IL 61107 Office: 3701 E State St Rockford IL 61108

HART, JEROME THOMAS, state senator; b. Saginaw, Mich., July 23, 1932; s. Bernard V. and Florence D. (Stevens) H.; Sec.-treas. Quality Seal Oil Co., Saginaw, 1954-58, Saginaw Catholic Cemetery Com., 1959-62; owner, mgr. Tiny Town Clothing, 1958-61; exec. asst. to treas. State of Mich., 1962-64; mem. Mich. Senate, 1965—, minority floor leader, 1973-75, chmn. appropriations com., 1974—. Treas. Saginaw County Democratic Com., 1954-58; chmn. 8th Congl. Dist. Dem. Com., 1962-64; del. Dem. Nat. Conv., 1968. Roman Catholic. Club: KC. Office: Box 240 State Capitol Lansing MI 48909*

HART, JOSEPH ADRIAN, machinery mfg. co. exec.; b. Hicksville, Ohio, June 27, 1920; s. Laurence E. and Leah E. (Hilliard) H.; A.B., Kent State U., 1960; M.B.A., U. Chgo., 1960; m. Mary Anne Bail, June 23, 1949; children—Anne Marie Hart Roberts, Jo Alice Hart Moody, Lawrence K., Karen Hart Bruketa. With Internat. Harvester, 1948—, plant mgr. tractor works Constrn. equipment div., Chgo., successively mgr. source and facilities planning Truck div., Chgo., mgr. mfg. ops. agrl. equipment, Chgo., v.p. mfg. and employee relations Internat. Harvester of Can., Hamilton, 1975-77, v.p. mfg. planning Components Group, Chgo., 1977—; dir. Iowa Indsl. Hydraulics. Served with USAAF, 1942-45; ETO. Republican. Roman Catholic. Clubs: Internat. Harvester Mgmt., 401. Office: 401 N Michigan Ave Chicago IL 60611

HART, MARIE MOONEY, real estate broker; b. Montgomery, Ala.; Jan. 20, 1913; d. Charles France and Marie (Kidd) Mooney; B.S. in Bus., Ind. U., 1939; student U. Wis., summer 1938; m. Arthur Leland Hart, Nov. 20, 1941; children—Jeffrey Mooney, John Scot, Anne Leslie. High sch. tchr. bus., St. Paul, Ind., 1939-41; with USAAF, Army Ordnance and IRS, 1941-50; cofounder Hart Realty Co., Evansville, Ind., 1964-74; owner, mgr. rental housing. Exec. bd. Dexter Sch., 1964. Mem. VFW Aux. Republican. Presbyterian. Club: Central Turners (Evansville). Home: 2919 Washington Ave Evansville IN 47714

HART, RICHARD HOWE, gen. surgeon; b. Battle Creek, Mich., Feb. 15, 1923; s. William Lafayette and Rose Marie (Ainsworth) H.; B.S., U. Ill., 1944, M.D., 1946; m. Vivian R. Jones, Jan. 12, 1980; children by previous marriage—Richard Howe, Steven, Linda. Intern U. Mich., Ann Arbor, 1946-47, resident in gen. surgery, 1947-53; sr. surgeon Akron (Ohio) City Hosp., 1970—; privileged surgeon Akron Children's Hosp., 1970-75; chief of staff, exec. com. Akron City Hosp., 1970-75, chief, 1974-75; individual practice medicine, specializing in gen. surgery Akron, 1953—; asso. clin. prof. surgery

Ohio State U. Coll. Medicine, Columbus, 1974—, Northeastern Ohio Colls. Medicine, 1978—. Served to capt., M.C., AUS, 1948-50. Diplomate Am. Bd. Surgery. Fellow A.C.S.; mem. AMA, Ohio, Summit County med. assns., Coller Surg. Soc., Sigma Chi, Alpha Omega Alpha, Phi Kappa Phi, Phi Eta Sigma. Republican. Mem. United Ch. Christ. Home: 624 Fairhill Dr Akron OH 44313 Office: 159 S Main St Akron OH 44308

HART, RONALD CARY, ops. researcher, tech. mgr., strategic planner; b. Norfolk, Va., Feb. 25, 1949; s. Robert Clyde and Mary Julia (Scott) H.; B.S., Va. Poly. Inst. and State U., 1971; M.S., U. Notre Dame, 1977; m. Deborah Woodruff Froehlich, Aug. 21, 1971; children—Michelle Naomi, Ronald Cary. Analyst, Computing and Software, Inc., Hampton, Va., 1971-72; systems analyst Space Radiation Effects Lab., NASA, Newport News, Va., 1972; sr. analyst Gen. Electric Co., Beltsville, Md., 1972-74; sr. ops. research analyst Miles Labs., Inc., Elkhart, Ind., 1974-77, research adminstr., 1977-78, mgr. research planning and services dept., 1978—; fin. cons., systems cons. Vol. leader No. Ind. council Boy Scouts Am., 1967—. Mem. AAAS, Am. Chem. Soc., Soc. Research Adminstrs., Am. Mgmt. Assn., N.Y. Acad. Scis., Phi Kappa Phi, Phi Eta Sigma, Sigma Pi Sigma. Contbr. articles to tech. jours. Home: 137 Bank St Elkhart IN 46516 Office: 1127 Myrtle St Elkhart IN 46514

HART, WILLIAM LEVATA, law enforcement ofcl.; b. Detroit, Jan. 17, 1924; s. Charles John and Gessener Mae (Brock) H.; student FBI Nat. Acad., 1972, Nat. Exec. Inst., 1977; B.S. in Criminal Justice, Wayne State U., 1977, M.Ed., 1978, D.Ednl. Sociology, 1981; m. Laura Elaine Johnson, Nov. 25, 1950; children—Cynthia Renee, Jennifer Lynn. Coal miner, Leechburg, Pa., 1940-43, 46-50; with Ford Motor Co., Detroit, 1950-52; with Detroit Police Dept., 1952—, insp., 1971-73, div. comdr., 1973-74, dep. chief hdqrs. bur., 1974-76, chief of police, 1976—; instr. criminal justice Wayne State U.; bd. dirs. Criminal Law Revision Com., 1976—; mem. U.S. Atty. Gen.'s Task Force on Violent Crime; chmn. bd. Criminal Justice Inst., Southeastern Mich., from 1978; mem. disaster adv. com. ARC; mem. Mich. Commn. on Criminal Justice; pres. Detroit Police Benefit and Protective Assn.; expert witness, juvenile justice subcom. Senate Judiciary Com. on Juvenile Justice and Deliquency Prevention. Mem. Detroit Mayor's Bus. and Labor Ad-Hoc Com.; chmn. Detroit United Fund Dr., 1978; bd. dirs. Boy Scouts Am., Boys Club Met. Detroit. Served with USN, 1943-46; PTO. Recipient Anthony Wayne award Wayne State U., 1979; Alumni award, 1979. Mem., Nat. Acad. Assn., Internat. Police Assn., Internat. Assn. Chiefs of Police, Mich. Assn. Chiefs of Police (chmn. crime prevention com., mem. subcom. on use of deadly force), Nat. Exec. Inst., Police Found., Am. Acad. Profl. Law Enforcement, Wayne County Assn. Chiefs of Police, Maj. City Chiefs of Police Assn., Police Exec. Research Forum, Nat. Orgn. Black Law Enforcement Execs. (exec. bd.), Wayne State Alumni Assn. Baptist. Clubs: Detroit Yacht, Masons. Office: 1300 Beaubien St Detroit MI 48226

HART, WILLIAM THOMAS, lawyer; b. Joliet, Ill., Feb. 4, 1929; s. William M. and Geraldine (Archambeault) H.; J.D., Loyola U., 1951; m. Catherine M. Motta, Nov. 27, 1954; children—Catherine, Susan, Julie, Sally, Nancy. Admitted to Ill. bar, 1951, U.S. Dist. Ct., 1951, U.S. Ct. Appeals 7th Circuit, 1954, U.S. Ct. Appeals D.C., 1977; asst. U.S. atty. No. Dist. of Ill., 1954-56, atty. DeFrees, Fiske, O'Brien & Thompson, Chgo., 1956-59; atty., partner, Schiff, Hardin, Waite, Dorschel & Britton, Chgo., 1959—. Special asst. atty. gen. Ill., Hodge Investigation and Litigation, 1957-58; spl. asst. states atty. Cook County, Chgo. Police Dept. Grand Jury Investigation, 1960. Bd. dirs., exec. com. Aurora Area Blood Bank; pres. adv. bd. Mercy Center for Health Care Service; bd. dirs. Chgo. Legal Assistance Found. Served with AUS, 1951-53; Korea. Decorated Bronze Star. Mem. Am., Ill., Chgo. (vice chmn. div. II inquiry com.), 7th Circuit bar assns., Soc. Trial Lawyers, Phi Alpha Delta. Republican. Roman Catholic. Clubs: Metropolitan, Union League (Chgo.). Home: 123 S Evanslawn Aurora IL 60506 Office: 233 S Wacker Dr Chicago IL 60606

HARTBANK, BETTY RUTH, librarian; b. Tolono, Ill., May 23, 1921; d. Frederick William and Alice Marie (Schulenberg) H.; B.S., U. Ill., 1954, M.S., 1955. Bookmobile librarian Ill. State Library, Springfield, 1948-53; reference librarian U. Notre Dame, 1955-56; lab. sch. librarian Eastern Ill. U., Charleston, 1956-66, serials librarian, 1966-67, head reference dept., 1967—. Mem. ALA, Ill. Library Assn., Am. Fedn. Tchrs. Democrat. Roman Catholic. Office: Eastern Ill Univ Charleston IL 61920

HARTER, DAVID JOHN, oncologist, radiation therapist; b. Milw., Apr. 12, 1942; s. G. Herbert and Marion Bernice (Kahl) H.; A.B., U. Wis., 1964, M.D., 1968; m. Diane Leigh Kuebler, Aug. 8, 1964; children—Renee, Andrew Charles, Susannah Lee. Intern, U.S. Naval Hosp., Bethesda, Md., 1968-69; postdoctoral fellow M.D. Anderson Hosp. and Tumor Inst., Houston, 1972-75; asst. radiation therapist Roanoke (Va.) Meml. Hosp., 1975-76; cons. oncologist, radiation therapist Columbia Hosp., Milw., 1976-77; dir. radiation oncology, cons. oncologist Bishop Clarkson Meml. Hosp., Omaha, 1977-80; clin. asso. prof. U. Nebr., Omaha, 1977—; med. dir. Immanuel Radiation Therapy Center, Omaha, 1978—. Bd. dirs. Am. Cancer Soc., 1978—, chmn. profl. edn. com. Nebr. div., 1980—. Served to lt. comdr., M.C., USN, 1967-72. Diplomate Am. Bd. Radiology. Mem. AMA, AAAS, Am. Soc. Therapeutic Radiologists (pres. Midlands chpt. 1981), Am. Radium Soc., Am. Coll. Radiology, Fletcher Soc., Greater Omaha Med. Soc., Phi Kappa Phi, Phi Beta Kappa, Alpha Omego Alpha. Republican. Presbyterian. Clubs: Doctors (Houston); Regency Lake and Country, Omaha. Contbr. articles in field to med. jours.; inventor sealed radioactive sources in synthetic absorbable suture, sealed radioactive source inserter, device to position and shield the testicle during irradiation. Home: 9927 Essex Omaha NE 68104 Office: 6901 N 72d St Omaha NE 68122

HARTER, DONALD HARRY, med. educator; b. Breslau, Germany, May 16, 1933; s. Harry Morton and Leonor Evelyn (Goldmann) H.; m. Lee Grossman, Dec. 18, 1960 (div. 1976); children—Kathryne, Jennifer, Amy, David; came to U.S., 1940, naturalized, 1945; A.B., U. Pa., 1953; M.D., Columbia, 1957. Intern medicine Yale-New Haven Med. Center, 1957-58; asst. resident, then resident neurology N.Y. Neurol. Inst., 1958-61; guest investigator Rockefeller U., 1963-66; mem. faculty Columbia Coll. Phys. and Surg., 1960-75, prof. neurology and microbiology, 1973-75; attending neurologist N.Y. Neurol. Inst., Presbyn. Hosp., 1973-75; Charles L. Mix prof., chmn. dept. neurology Med. Sch., Northwestern U., Chgo., 1975—; chmn. dept. neurology Northwestern Meml. Hosp., Chgo., 1975—. Mem. Nat. Commn. on Venereal Disease, HEW, 1970-72; mem. adv. com. on fellowships Nat. Multiple Sclerosis Soc., 1976-79, chmn., 1977-79; med. adv. bd. Am. Parkinson's Disease Assn., 1976—; mem. sci. adv. council Nat. ALS Found., 1978—; mem. med. adv. bd. Myasthenia Gravis Found., 1980—. Diplomate Am. Bd. Psychiatry and Neurology (written exam. com., neurology subcom. 1979—). Recipient Joseph Mather Smith prize Coll. Physicians and Surgeons, Columbia U., 1970, Lucy G. Moses award, 1970, 72. Mem. Am. Soc. Clin. Investigation, Am. Neurol. Assn., Am. Assn. Neuropathologists, Soc. Exptl. Biology and Medicine, Assn. Univ. Profs. Neurology, Infectious Disease Soc., Soc. Neurosci., Am. Acad. Neurology (alt. rep. to Council Med. Splty. Socs. 1979—), Am. Assn. Immunologists, Am. Soc. Microbiology, Soc. Gen. Microbiology, Phi Beta Kappa, Sigma Xi. Spl. fellow USPHS, 1963-66; Am. Cancer Soc. scholar, 1973-74; Guggenheim fellow, 1973. Editorial bd. Neurology, 1976—; adv. bd. Archives of Virology, 1975—. Home: 900 Lake Shore Dr Chicago IL 60611 Office: Dept Neurology Northwestern U Med Sch 303 E Chicago Ave Chicago IL 60611

HARTER, HUGH ANTHONY, educator; b. Columbus, Ohio, Dec. 13, 1922; s. Anthony H. and Georgiana (Hayes) H.; student Ohio Wesleyan U., 1940-41; B.A., Ohio State U., 1947, Ph.D., 1958; M.A., U. Americas (Mexico), 1951; m. Francis D. Reichman, Oct. 7, 1970. Instr., asst. prof. romance langs. Wesleyan U., Conn., 1953-59; asso. prof. Elmira Coll., 1959-60; postdoctoral Mellon fellow U. Pitts., 1960-61; asso. prof. Chatham Coll., Pitts., 1961-64; asso. prof. Loyola U., Chgo., 1964-66; prof. Ohio Wesleyan U., Delaware, 1966—, chmn. dept., 1966-80, dir. Ohio Wesleyan U. jr. year abroad program Spain, 1968—. Vice pres. Alliance Française, Columbus, 1969-75, life pres. Fundación Juan-Ruíz, Segovia, Spain, 1971—; pres. Horizons for Learning, 1974—; v.p. Delaware Heritage, 1974-76, bd. dirs., 1976—. Served with M.I., Air Transport Command, AUS, World War II ETO. Named hon. citizen Segovia (Spain), 1977. Mem. Academia de San Quirce de Segovia (corr.), Delaware Shakespeare Soc. (pres. 1980-81). Author: Gertrudis Gómez de Arellaneda, 1981; co-author: Femmes/Hombres, 1977. Editor: (with Willis Barnstone) Cervantes' Rinconete y Cortadillo, 1960; (with R. C. Allen) A First Spanish Handbook For Teachers in Elementary Schools, 1961; (with R. C. Allen) A Second Spanish Handbook, 1963. Transl.: A History of Spanish Literature (G. Diaz-Plaja), 1971; Sombra del paraíso (Vicente Aleixandre), 1979. Contbr. articles to profl. jours. Home: 52 W Winter St Delaware OH 43015 Office: Ohio Wesleyan U Delware OH 43015 also 25 Central Park W New York City NY

HARTIG, ELMER OTIS, aerospace co. exec.; b. Evansville, Ind., Jan. 28, 1923; s. Otto Ernest and Frieda Katherine (Sunderman) H.; B.S., U. N.H., 1946; M.S., Harvard U., 1947, Ph.D., 1950; m. Evelyn Ann Cameron, Aug. 21, 1949; children—Pamela Ann, Jeffery C., Gregory W., Bradley A. Mem. staff Los Alamos Sci. Lab., 1944-46; with Goodyear Aerospace Corp., 1950—, dir. research and engring. aerophysics div., Phoenix, 1955-76, v.p. research and engring., Akron, Ohio, 1976-81, v.p. ops., def. and energy, 1981—; participant in Air Force and Army ad hoc adv. studies; mem. adv. group Air Force Fgn. Tech. Div.; mem. U.S. Army Sci. Bd., 1979—. Served with U.S. Army, 1943-46. Fellow IEEE (1st Ann. Achievement award Phoenix sect. 1960); mem. AIAA. Office: 1210 Massillon Rd Akron OH 44315

HARTIG, JAMES PARSONS, designer, restorationist; b. Hagerstown, Ind., Oct. 12, 1917; s. Anthony Richard and Gladys Marie (Parsons) H.; B.A., U. Cin., 1941; postgrad. Parsons Sch. Design, N.Y.C., 1941. Tchr. archtl. drafting, Eng., 1945-46; engaged in restoration work with Ernest LoNano, 1951-52; asso. in residential design with Jack Cameron, Miami, Fla., 1953; an organizer, operator Barbara Dorn Assos., Miami, 1954; propr. bus. producing interior delineations, Miami, 1955; asso. with Henry End, Miami, 1955-59; an organizer Wilbar Evans Inc., Miami, 1959-60; head design dept. Morris Lapidus, Kornblath & Harle, architects, Miami Beach, Fla., 1960-62; reorganizer design dept. Western div. Maxwell Co., Calif., 1962; organizer Hotels Designs Inc., LaJolla, Calif., 1963-64, pres., 1964-66; exec. v.p. charge design Henry End Assos., 1966-69; restorer old homes, Hagerstown, Ind., 1969; founder, 1st pres. Historic Hagerstown, 1972; restored 1825 Fed. house, Centerville, Ind., 1976; propr. Two Jays, Centerville, 1976-79; charge design dept. Rosa's Inc., office design, Richmond, Ind., 1977—. Served with AUS, 1943-46. Decorated Bronze Star. Mem. Nat. Trust Historic Preservation, Historic Centerville, Old Richmond. Methodist. Home and office: 308 N 12th St Richmond IN 47374

HARTIG, KATHARINE ASHLEY, educator; b. Mpls., Mar. 23, 1926; d. Henry Edward and Dorothy (Ellis) H.; student UCLA, 1944-45; B.S. cum laude, U. Minn., 1948, M.A., 1955; Ed.D., No. Ill. U., 1969. Music supr. Richfield (Minn.) Public Schs., 1948-50, Robbinsdale (Minn.) Public Schs., 1950-52; spl. music tchr. Spokane Public Schs., 1952-55; music supr., tchr., dir. gifted student program Glen Ellyn (Ill.) Public Schs., 1955—. Mem. Glen Ellyn Edn. Assn., Ill. Edn. Assn., NEA, Assn. Supervision and Curriculum Devel., Sigma Alpha Iota. Club: Dist. 41 Twenty-Five. Office: 240 W Geneva Rd Glen Ellyn IL 60137

HARTIGAN, NEIL F., banker, former lt. gov. Ill.; b. Chgo.; grad. social scis. Georgetown U.; LL.B., Loyola U., Chgo.; LL.D. (hon.), Martin Luther King Coll., 1975; m. Marge Hartigan; children—John, Elizabeth, Laura, Bridget. Admitted to Ill. bar; formerly dep. adminstrv. officer City of Chgo.; legis. counsel City of Chgo. in Ill. 75th Gen. Assembly; then chief legal counsel Chgo. Park Dist.; lt. gov. State of Ill., 1972-77; pres., chief exec. officer Real Estate Research Corp., Chgo., 1977-79, dir., 1977—; head corp. affairs 1st Nat. Bank of Chgo., 1978-79, sr. v.p., area head Western hemisphere worldwide banking dept., 1979—; Democratic committeeman 49th ward, Chgo., 1968-80; former lectr. John Marshall Law Sch., Chgo.; bd. regents Georgetown U.; vis. com. on public policy U. Chgo.; bd. dirs. Chgo. Conv. and Tourism Bur., TRUST, Inc.; co-chmn. Ill. Olympic Com.; exec. com. March of Dimes, chmn. Superwalk, 1978; active Am. Cancer Soc. fund drives. Named among Ten Outstanding Young Men of Yr., Chgo. Jr. C. of C., 1967, among 200 Future Leaders Am., Time mag.; hon. pres. Spanish-speaking div. Jr. C. of C., Chgo.; hon. citizen several Latin Am. countries; recipient award Ill. Assn. Park Dists., 1972. Mem. Nat. Conf. Lt. Govs. (chmn. 1976, regional vice chmn.), Dem. Adv. Council Elected Ofcls., Council State Govts. (exec. com.), Am. Bar Assn., Ill. Bar Assn., Chgo. Bar Assn., Chgo. Assn. Commerce and Industry, Nat. Council on Aging, Chgo. Council on Fgn. Relations, Young Pres.' Orgn. Clubs: Econ., Rotary, K.C., Irish Fellowship, Cook County Hundred. Office: 1st Nat Bank of Chgo One 1st Nat Plaza Chicago IL 60670

HARTJE, GEORGE NICHOLAS, librarian; b. St. Louis, Sept. 27, 1924; s. Albert H. and Edna L. (Broeker) H.; A.B., Washington U., 1947; M.S. in Library Sci., U. Ill., 1950; postgrad. U. Mo., 1970-71; m. Virginia Ida Holt, Sept. 27, 1947; children—Edna Ann, George Nicholas, Allan Lee, David Russell. Asst. acquisitions dept. U. Ill. Library Urbana, 1948-50; cataloger Washington U. Libraries, St. Louis, 1950-53; supr. tech. services St. Louis Public Library, 1953-64; dir. libraries Northeast Mo. State U., Kirksville, 1964—, head div. Libraries and Museums, 1964—. Named Boss of the Year, Am. Bus. Womens Assn., 1978, Kiwanian of the Year, Kirksville Kiwanis Club, 1974. Mem. ALA, Mo. Library Assn. (pres. 1973-74), Bibliog. Soc. Am., Mo. Assn. Coll. and Research Libraries (pres. 1967-68), Greater St. Louis Library Club (pres. 1957-58). Presbyterian. Club: Ind. Order Odd Fellows, Kiwanis Internat. Author: Missouri Library Association, 1900-1975. Contbr. articles on library mgmt. and library resources to profl. jours. Home: Rural Route 6 Box 316 Kirksville MO 63501 Office: Northeast Missouri State Univ Pickler Memorial Library Kirksville MO 63501

HARTJES, LYLE JOSEPH, sales rep.; b. Appleton, Wis., Mar. 30, 1940; s. Norbert Martin and Josephine H.; B.S., Yale U., 1962; m. Sharon G. Flood, Apr. 20, 1963; children—Leigh J., Mark E. Sales rep. Endo Labs., Appleton, Wis., 1965-69, Syntex Labs., Mpls., 1969-73, Smith Kline Corp., Wausau, Wis., 1973-81; pres. Elhart Corp., Rothschild, Wis., 1978—, Hart Vending, Rothschild, Wis., 1981—. Served with USAF, 1961-65. Club: K.C. Address: 8913 Brian Dr Rothschild WI 54474

HARTLEY, JAMES MICHAELIS, printing co. exec.; b. Indpls., Nov. 25, 1916; s. James Worth and Bertha S. (Beuke) H.; student Jordan Conservatory of Music, 1934-35, Ind. U., Purdue U., Franklin Coll.; m. E. Lea Cosby, July 30, 1944; children—Michael D., Brent S. With Arvin Industries, Inc., 1934-36; founder, pres. J. Hartley Co., Inc., Columbus, Ind., 1937—, treas., 1972—. Pres., Columbus Little Theatre, 1947-48; founding dir. Columbus Arts Guild, 1960-64, v.p., 1965-66, dir., 1971-74; musical dir., cellist Guild String Quartet, 1963-73; founding dir. Columbus Pro Musica, 1969-74; dir. Regional Arts Study Commn., 1971-74; v.p. Ind. Council Republican Workshops, 1965-69, pres., 1975-77; pres. Bartholomew County Republican Workshop, 1966-67. Served with USAAF, 1942-46. Mem. Nat. Fedn. Ind. Bus. Office: 101 N National Rd Columbus IN 47201

HARTLEY, RICHARD GLENDALE, assn. exec.; b. Bennet, Nebr., Feb. 16, 1926; s. Charles Lynn and Hazel Myra (Williams) H.; student U. Nebr., 1945-46, Hastings (Nebr.) Coll., 1947-48; m. Wynona Elaine Smutz, Oct. 27, 1962; 1 dau., Patricia Ann (Mrs. Thomas H. Young). Mgr., Mt. Pleasant (Iowa) C. of C., 1959-62; mgr. Kearney (Nebr.) C. of C., 1962-67; mgr. membership Greater Kansas City (Mo.) C. of C., 1967-68; exec. v.p. Kansas City (Kans.) Area C. of C., 1968-72; mng. dir. Missouri Valley Electric Assn., 1972—. Served with AUS, 1944-45, 53-56. Mem. Am. Soc. Assn. Execs. Revised, edited jour. Evaluating Chamber Mgmt. Opportunities, 1966. Home: 8704 Lafayette Ct Kansas City KS 66109 Office: 3435 Broadway Suite 303 Kansas City MO 64111

HARTLEY, ROBERT FRANK, educator; b. Beaver Falls, Pa., Dec. 15, 1927; s. Frank Howell and Marie Eleanor (Theis) H.; B.B.A., Drake U., 1949; M.B.A., U. Minn., 1962, Ph.D., 1967; m. Dorothy Mayou, June 30, 1962; children—Constance Ann, Matthew. Store mgmt. S.S. Kresge Co., 1949-54, J.C. Penney Co., 1954-59; merchandising Dayton's Mpls., 1959-61; central buyer Dayton's Target subs., 1961-63; asst. prof. George Washington U., Washington, 1965-69, asso. prof., 1969-72; prof. dept. mktg. Cleve. State U., 1972—. Mem. Am. Mktg. Assn., So. Mktg. Assn., So. Case Research Assn. Author: Marketing - Management and Social Change, 1972; Retailing - Challenge and Opportunity, 1975; Marketing Fundamentals for Responsive Management, 1976; Marketing Mistakes, 1976, 2d edit., 1981; Sales Management, 1979; Retailing, 2d edit., 1980. Home: 17405 S Woodland Rd Shaker Heights OH 44120 Office: Dept Marketing Cleveland State U Cleveland OH 44115

HARTMAN, ALLEN LEROY, food co. sales exec.; b. Whittier, Calif., Aug. 26, 1944; s. Donald Leroy and Cathleen Marie (Graves) H.; student Fullerton (Calif.) Jr. Coll., 1963-65, U. Calif., Irvine, 1966-68; m. Dorothy Davis, June 3, 1977; children—Adam, Marc, Kari. Store mgr. Alpha Beta Markets, Calif., 1965-67; sales rep. Carnation Co., Calif., 1967-69, sales supr., 1969-72, asst. dist. mgr., Indpls., 1972-76, dist. mgr., Cleve., 1977-81, dist. mgr., Chgo., 1981—. Brunswick Boys baseball coach; Brunswick Peewee Football coach. Mem. Cleve. Food Dealers Assn., Cleve. Assn. Mfrs. Reps., Assn. Grocery Mfrs., Grocery Mfrs. Sales Execs., Merchandising Execs. Club of Chgo. Republican. Presbyterian. Club: Cleve. Browns Touchdown (dir., pres.). Home: 1872 Albright Ct Wheaton IL Office: 2818 Centre Circle Dr Downers Grove IL 60515

HARTMAN, EILEEN MARIE, ednl. cons.; b. Joliet, Ill., Apr. 11, 1945; d. Thomas Patrick and Anna Marie (Dunne) Gleason; B.A. in Communication Arts, No. Ill. U., 1969; M.A. in Edn., Central Mich. U., 1978; m. James E. Hartman, Sept. 2, 1967; 1 son, Aaron Michael. Public sch. tchr., Mont. and Ill., 1968-80; dir. MICRO-IDEAS, ednl. microcomputer consortium of sch. dists. in Ill., 1980—; mem. adj. faculty Nat. Coll. Edn., Evanston, Ill.; math. cons. D.C. Heath and Co. Mem. Assn. Ednl. Data Systems, Nat. Council Suprs. Math., Nat. Council Tchrs. Math., Ill. Council Tchrs. Math., No. Ill. Assn. Ednl. Research, Evaluation and Devel. Home: 359 N Raynor Ave Joliet IL 60435 Office: 1401 Greenwood Rd Glenview IL 60025

HARTMAN, JAMES LE-ROY, fin. corp. exec.; b. Goshen, Ind., Sept. 7, 1940; s. Kenneth B. and Carol K. (Marks) H.; B.S. in Bus. Adminstrn., Manchester Coll., 1962; m. Wanda F. Shamp, June 4, 1961; children—Lori Ann, Libby Sue, Lana Marie. Bus. tchr. public schs. Fostoria, Ohio, 1962-65; with Mut. Security Life Ins. Co., 1965—, Nappanee, Ind., 1965-67, group ins. rep., Elkhart, Ind., 1967-68, asst. to v.p. mktg., 1968-70, gen. agt. in charge of sales No. Ind. and So. Mich., 1970—; founder, pres. James L. Hartman, CLU, and Assos., Elkhart, 1977—; field advisory council Mut. Security Life Ins. Co., 1971-72, 75-76; counselor employee benefits various corps. Bd. trustees Manchester Coll., 1974-78. C.L.U. Mem. Am. Soc. C.L.U.'s, Nat. Assn. Life Underwriters, Am. Assn. Security Dealers, Gen. Agts. and Mgrs. Assn., Elkhart County Assn. Life Underwriters (bd. dirs., pres., 1975-76), South Bend (Ind.) Gen. Agts. and Mgrs. Assn. (bd. dirs., 1978-79, pres. 1981-82). Republican. Club: Christian Businessmen's Com. Speaker in ins. field. Home: 63512 C R 111 Goshen IN 46526 Office: 722 W Bristol Suite H Elkhart IN 46514

HARTMAN, PAUL ARTHUR, microbiologist; b. Balt., Nov. 23, 1926; s. Carl G. and Eva M. Hartman; B.S., U. Ill., 1949; M.S., U. Ala., 1951; Ph.D., Purdue U., 1954; m. Marjorie Ann Stewart, Aug. 19, 1950; children—Philip S., Helen A., Mark A. Mem. faculty Iowa State U., Ames, 1954—, prof. microbiology, 1962-72, disting. prof., 1972—, chmn. dept., 1974-81. An organizer Ames Community Pre-Sch. Center, 1969. Served with USAF, 1945-46. Grantee NIH, NSF, EPA. Mem. Am. Soc. Microbiology, Inst. Food Tech., Internat. Assn. Milk, Food Environ. Sanitarians, AAAS, Soc. Indsl. Microbiology, Soc. Gen. Microbiology, Soc. Applied Bacteriology, Sigma Xi, Chi Beta Chi, Gamma Sigma Delta, Alpha Delta Phi. Mem. Christian Ch. (Disciples of Christ). Author: Miniaturized Microbiological Methods, 1968; patentee; contbr. over 150 articles to profl. jours. Office: 205 Sci Bldg I Iowa State U Ames IA 50011

HARTMAN, SAMUEL JACOB, computer specialist; b. Waynesboro, Pa., Oct. 7, 1947; s. Raymond Kellar and Betty Mae H.; B.A. in Bus. Adminstrn., Central Mo. State U., 1969; m. Martha J., Sept. 2, 1968; children—Stacy, Erick, Jonathan. Applications analyst United Computing Systems, Inc., 1969-72; dir. data processing Am. Multi-Cinema, Inc., 1972-78; software specialist Comserv, Kansas City, Mo., 1978—. Office: Conserv 8023 Wayne Kansas City MO 64131

HARTMANN, DONALD OTTO, SR., beverage corp. exec.; b. St. Louis, Jan. 24, 1934; s. Otto Frederic and Mabel Lena (Schuessler) H.; B.S., U. Mo., 1963, M.Ed., 1964; m. Linda Lou Sparks, Sept. 8, 1962; children—Kimberly Lynn, Donald Otto, Jacqueline Marie, Michele Lee. Profl. scout exec. Boy Scouts Am., 1959-60; asst. prof. U. Mo., 1960-63; coordinator co-op. edn. Mo., 1963-67; dir. personnel, rehab. Goodwill Industries of Am., 1967-69; mgr. reprographics, supply services Anheuser-Busch, Inc., St. Louis, 1969—; tchr., counselor, cons. in graphic arts, forms design and mgmt., 1969—. Chmn. bd. Christian edn. United Ch. of Christ, St. Louis, 1974-77; bd. dirs. local bd. edn., 1972—, pres., 1973-76; active Boy Scouts Am., 1942—, Eagle Scout reviewer/presenter, 1960—; mem. community wide youth services panel United Way of St. Louis, 1970—; mem. White House Panel on Childhood Edn., Mo. Gov.'s Panel on Edn., 1977; active Lindbergh PTA, 1968—. Served with USN, 1953-59. Recipient Eagle Scout award Boy Scouts Am., 1952, Silver Explorer award, 1956, Gt. Grant award, 1962, Regional Service award, 1973; Outstanding Loaned Exec. award United Way, 1970, Community Service award Girl Scouts U.S.A. Mem. Am. Sch. Bds. Assn., Nat. Sch. Bds. Assn., Mo. Sch. Bds. Assn., St. Louis Suburban Sch. Bds. Assn., In-Plant Mgrs. Assn., Council of Reprographics Execs., Am. Mgmt. Assn., Phi Delta Kappa, Sigma Phi Epsilon (alumni bd. pres. 1963-70). Home: 4824 Gatesbury Dr Saint Louis MO 63128 Office: Anehuser-Busch Inc 2800 S 9th St Saint Louis MO 63118

HARTRIDGE, VIRGINIA BISHOP, physician; b. Milw., Mar. 29, 1919; d. Theodore Shears and Blanche (Bishop) Hartridge; B.A., Milw.-Downer Coll., 1941; M.S., U. Mich., 1942; M.D., Woman's Med. Coll. Pa., 1950. Intern, Hosp. Woman's Med. Coll., Phila., 1950-51; fellow anesthesiology Mayo Found., Rochester, Minn., 1953-56, cons. in anesthesiology, 1956—; asst. prof. anesthesiology Mayo Grad. Sch. Medicine, U. Minn., 1968-78, asso. prof., 1978—; dir. Mayo Clinic Sch. for Nurse Anesthetists, 1964—. Trustee Lawrence U. Served with Med. Specialist Corps, AUS, 1942-46. Diplomate Am. Bd. Anesthesiology, Nat. Bd. Med. Examiners. Fellow Am. Coll. Anesthesiology; mem. Am. Soc. Anesthesiologists, Internat. Anesthesia Research Soc., N.Y. Acad. Scis., Nat. Audubon Soc., Izaak Walton League, Wis. Hist. Soc., Royal Soc. Medicine (fgn. asso.), Sigma Xi. Contbr. articles to profl. jours. Home: Hawkhurst Route 2 Rochester MN 55901 Office: 200 1st St SW Rochester MN 55901

HARTZ, TERESITA SANDERSON, educator; b. Butler, Pa., Aug. 30, 1949; d. Edward Francis and Mary Helen (Bayne) Sanderson; A.A.S. in Bus. Mgmt., Butler County Community Coll., 1969; B.S. in Edn., Youngstown State U., 1971, M.S. in Edn., 1973; m. Gregory Dean Hartz, July 10, 1976; 1 dau., Kristen Marie. Tchr., Windham (Ohio) Bd. Edn., 1971-74; with Youngstown (Ohio) Bd. Edn., 1974—, now tchr. acctg. and office mgmt. program Choffin Career Center. Mem. Am. Vocat. Assn., Ohio Vocat. Assn., Ohio Office Edn. Assn., Ohio Bus. Tchrs. Assn., Youngstown Bus. Tchrs. Assn., Youngstown State U. Alumni Assn., Butler County Community Coll. Alumni Assn., Cath. Collegiate Assn.

HARVEY, KATHERINE ABLER, civic worker; b. Chgo., May 17, 1946; d. Julius and Elizabeth (Engelman) Abler; student La Sorbonne, Paris, 1965-66; A.A.S., Bennett Coll., 1968; m. Julian Whitcomb Harvey, Sept. 7, 1974. Asst. librarian McDermott, Will & Emery, Chgo., 1969-70; librarian Chapman & Cutler, Chgo., 1970-73, Coudert Freres, Paris, 1973-74; adviser, organizer library Lincoln Park Zool. Soc. and Zoo, Chgo., 1977-79, mem. soc.'s womens bd., 1976—, chmn. library com., 1977-79, sec., 1979-81, mem. exec. com., 1977—; mem. jr. bd. Alliance Francaise de Chgo., 1970-76, treas., mem. exec. com., 1971-73, 75-76, mem. women's bd., 1977-80; mem. Fred Harvey Fine Arts Found., 1976-78; hon. life mem. Chgo. Symphony Soc., 1975—; mem. Phillips Acad. Alumni Council, Andover, Mass., 1977-81, mem. acad.'s bicentennial celebration com. class celebration leader, 1978, co-chmn. for Chgo. acad.'s bicentennial campaign, 1977-79, mem. student affairs and admissions com., 1980-81; mem. aux. bd. Art Inst. Chgo., 1978—; mem. Know Your Chgo. com. U. Chgo. Extension, 1981—; mem. guild Chgo. Hist. Soc., 1978—; mem. women's bd. Lyric Opera Chgo., 1979—, chmn. edn. com., 1980, mem. exec. com., 1980—; mem. women's bd. Northwestern Meml. Hosp., 1979—, treas., chmn. fin. com., 1981—, mem. exec. com., 1981—. Clubs: Arts of Chgo., Friday (corr. sec. 1981—), Casino. Home: 1209 N Astor St Chicago IL 60610

HARVEY, LYNNE COOPER (MRS. PAUL HARVEY), broadcasting exec., civic worker; b. nr. St. Louis; d. William A. and Margaret (Kehr) Cooper; A.B., Washington U., St. Louis, 1939, M.A., 1940; m. Paul Harvey, June 4, 1940; 1 son, Paul Harvey Aurandt. Broadcaster ednl. program KXOK, St. Louis, 1940; broadcaster-writer women's news WAC Variety Show, Fort Custer, Mich., 1941-43; gen. mgr. Paul Harvey News, ABC, 1944—; pres. Paulynne Prodns., Ltd., Chgo., 1968—, exec. producer Paul Harvey Comments, 1968—; editor, compiler The Rest of the Story. Pres. woman's bd. Mental Health Assn. Greater Chgo., 1967-71, v.p. bd. dirs., 1966—; pres. woman's aux. Infant Welfare Soc. Chgo., 1969-71, bd. dirs., 1969—; mem. Salvation Army Woman's Adv. Bd., 1967; reception chmn. Community Lectures; Woman's com. Chgo. Symphony, 1972—; pres. Mothers Council, River Forest, 1961-62; charter bd. mem. Gottlieb Meml. Hosp., Melrose Park, Ill.; mem. adv. bd. Nat. Christian Heritage Found., 1964—; mem. woman's bd. Ravinia Festival, 1972—; trustee John Brown U., 1980—. Recipient Religious Heritage of Am. award, 1974. Mem. Phi Beta Kappa, Kappa Delta Pi, Phi Sigma Iota, Eta Sigma Phi. Clubs: Chicago Golf, Woman's Athletic, Nineteenth Century Woman's, Press (Chgo.); Oak Park Country. Home: 1035 Park Ave River Forest IL 60305 Office: Box 77 River Forest IL 60305

HARVEY, MORRIS LANE, lawyer; b. Madisonville, Ky., Apr. 22, 1950; s. Morris Lee and Margie Lou (Wallace) H.; B.S., Murray (Ky.) State U., 1972; J.D., U. Ky., Lexington, 1974; m. Judith Kay French, May 27, 1972; children—Morris Lane, John French. Admitted to Ill. bar, 1975; asso. firm Hanagan & Dousman, Mt. Vernon, 1975-77; partner firm Feiger, Quindry, Molt, Harvey, Fyre & Hawkins, Fairfield, 1977—; spl. asst. atty. gen. State of Ill., 1977—; adj. instr. Frontier Community Coll., Fairfield, 1977—. Chmn. Black Gold dist. Okaw Valley council Boy Scouts Am., 1976; adminstrv. bd. First United Methodist Ch., Mt. Vernon, 1977; pres. adminstrv. bd. First United Meth. Ch., Fairfield, 1979-80. Mem. Am. Bar Assn., Assn. Trial Lawyers Am., Ill. Bar Assn., Ill. Trial Lawyers Assn., Southeastern Ill. Bar Assn., Jefferson County Bar Assn. (pres. 1977), Fairfield Jaycees (v.p. 1978-79). Republican. Clubs: Rotary (dir. Mt. Vernon 1977), Elks, Woodmen of World. Home: 4 Cumberland Dr Fairfield IL 62837 Office: 115 NE 3d St Fairfield IL 62837

HARVEY, PHILIP RICHARD, ednl. measurement and evaluation specialist; b. Hillsboro, N.H., Jan. 29, 1922; s. Charles William and Ruth Cleveland (Travis) H.; A.B., Tufts U., 1948; M.A. in Edn., U. Conn., 1954, Ph.D. in Ednl. and Psychol. Measurement, 1958; m. Jean Roberta Stevenson, July 27, 1973; children by previous marriage—Greig Williams, Gary Alan. Math. tchr. Norwich (Conn.) Free Acad., 1948-51; instr. ednl. measurement Central Conn. State Coll., New Britain, 1955-56; program dir. grad. record exams. Ednl. Testing Service, Princeton, N.J., 1956-69; program dir. Colls. Podiatry Admission Testing Program, Evanston, Ill., 1969-73; dir. adv. services Ednl. Testing Service, Evanston, 1970—, acting dir. midwestern regional office, 1980-81; cons. measurement and evaluation elem. through coll. Pres., Cambridge PTA, Kendall Park, N.J.; mem. bd. governing body Six-Mile Run Reformed Ch. Served with USAF, 1942-46, 1951-53, Res., 47-50, 53-82. Mem. AAAS, Am. Assn. Higher Edn., Am. Ednl. Research Assn., Assn. Ednl. Data Systems, Ill. Assn. Measurement and Evaluation, Ill. Personnel and Guidance Assn., Midwest Ednl. Research Assn., Nat. Assn. Coll. Admissions Counselors, Nat. Council Measurement in Edn., No. Ill. Assn. Edn., Research and Devel. Club: Masons. Office: One American Plaza Evanston IL 60201

HARVEY, ROY WILLIAM, podiatrist; b. Elmwood Place, Ohio, Mar. 10, 1921; s. Roy Chester and Rose Elizabeth (Klingler) H.; student Miami U., 1939-41; D.P.M., Ohio Coll. Podiatric Medicine, 1951; student Wilmington Coll., 1946-47; children—Laura M., Jennifer Lynn. Intern, Cleve. State Hosp., resident, Civic Hosp., Detroit, 1967; pvt. practice podiatry, pres. Dr. Roy W. Harvey Co., Inc., Hamilton and Oxford, Ohio, 1952—; staff podiatrist Miami (Ohio) U., 1979—; asso. mem. McCullough-Hyde Hosp., Oxford, 1978—. Served with USAAF, 1942-46. Mem. So. Ohio Acad. Podiatry (pres. 1972-74), Ohio Podiatry Assn. (trustee bd. dirs. 1974-77), Am. Podiatry Assn., Acad. Ambulatory Foot Surgeons, Am. Acad. Podiatry Adminstrn., Am. Coll. Sports Medicine, Nat. Athletic Trainers Assn. Clubs: Oxford Country, Elks, Lions (pres. 1963-64).

HARVEY, VIRGINIA PEASELEY, cons.; b. Richmond, Va.; d. Gabriel B. and Florence V. (White) Peaseley; B.S., in Chemistry, U. Md., 1929; M.S. in Phy. Edn., U. Wis., 1932; Ed.D. in Ednl. Psychology, Western Res. U., 1963; postgrad. Temple U., 1966-67; m. E. W. Harvey, Apr. 8, 1939 (div. 1958); 1 dau., Virginia Lynn Harvey Schmitt. Instr. U. Mich., 1932-38; asst. prof. Kent (Ohio) State U., 1938-42, 44-46-54, asso. prof., 1954-64, prof., 1964-76, prof. emeritus, 1976—, faculty senate vice chairperson, 1973-74. Vis. prof. group dynamics Temple U., summer 1967; mem. Nat. Tng. Lab. Inst. Applied Behavioral Sci.; pres. Cons. for Organizational and Personal Effectiveness. Recipient Distinguished Tchr. award Kent State U., 1971, Service award Phi Delta Kappa, 1972. Amy Morris Homans fellow, 1962-63; licensed psychologist, Ohio. Mem. Am. Soc. Tng. and Devel., Orgn. Devel. Network, Kappa Kappa Gamma, Alpha Psi Omega, Delta Psi Kappa, Phi Delta Kappa, Omicron Delta Kappa. Home: 1315 Greenwood Ave Kent OH 44240

HARVILL, LARRY GENE, accountant; b. Surprise, Nebr., May 29, 1939; s. Cleo A. and Hazel M. (McElravy) H.; student Tulane U., 1957-59, Syracuse U., 1959-60; B.G.S., U. Nebr., Omaha, 1971; m. Gertrud Gericke, Nov. 28, 1963; children—Christian, Gabriele, David, Karen. Cost accountant Tip Top Products, Omaha, 1963-68; cost acctg. mgr. Omsteel Industries, Omaha, 1968-73; controller Nat. Crane Corp., Waverly, Nebr., 1973-78; corp. comptroller Nebr. Plastics, Inc., Cozad, 1978—. Master, Cub Scouts, 1969-73; advisor Jr. Achievement, 1965-68. Served with USAF, 1959-63. Mem. Inst. Mgmt. Acctg., Am. Mgmt. Assn., Mensa. Republican. Methodist. Club: Elks. Home: 621 Ave C Cozad NE 69130 Office: PO Box 45 Cozad NE 69130

HARWOOD, BETH MARGARET, univ. ofcl.; b. Milw., July 2, 1952; d. James Richard and Lillian Lorraine (Sattler) H.; student Marquette U., 1970-72, postgrad. Law Sch., 1977-78; B.S., U. Wis., Milw., 1975, M.A., 1979; m. Stephen Charles Raymonds, May 27, 1978; 1 son, Adam Harwood. Teaching asst. U. Wis., Milw., 1975-77, lectr., 1979-80, coordinator communication program, 1979—; mgmt. cons., communication specialist to area orgns., 1977—. Program coordinator Woman to Woman Conf., 1980-81, mem. adv. bd., 1980—; class rep. Divine Savior-Holy Angels High Sch., 1970—. Mem. Am. Soc. for Tng. and Devel., NOW. Clubs: Menomonee Falls (Wis.) Newcomers, Racquetball (Menomonee Falls). Home: N85 W14995 Knoll Terr Menomonee Falls WI 53051 Office: 929 N 6th St Milwaukee WI 53202

HASAN, SYED MASOOD, microbiologist; b. Hyderabad, India, June 2, 1941; came to U.S., 1968, naturalized, 1977; s. Syed Ali and Mahmooda (Bilquis) Mohsin; B.S., Osmania U., India, 1962, M.S., 1964; Ph.D., U. Hawaii, 1975; m. Amina T. Hasan, Dec. 22, 1967; children—Farah T., Javid S. Teaching asst. dept. microbiology U. Hawaii, Honolulu, 1971-74, lectr., 1974-75; research asso. dept. biochemistry U. Md. Sch. Medicine, Balt., 1975-77; product devel. scientist Lab-Tek div. Miles Labs., Inc., Lisle, Ill., 1977—. Mem. Am. Soc. Microbiology, N.Y. Acad. Scis., Ill. Soc. Microbiology, Sigma Xi. Contbr. articles in field to profl. jours. Home: 114 Cottonwood Dr Wheaton IL 60187 Office: Lab-Tek div Miles Labs Inc 4718 Yender Ave Lisle IL 60532

HASBARGEN, ARTHUR, educator; b. Kankakee, Ill., Apr. 20, 1925; s. Arthur and Zelpha (Spence) H.; B.S., No. Ill. U., 1949; M.A., Mich. State U., 1950; Ed.D., U. Ill., 1969; m. Lorayne Raguse, Aug. 24, 1946; children—James, Janet, Karen, Nancy. Dir. student personnel N.D. State U., Fargo, 1950-52; head guidance Kankakee Sch. Dist. Ill., 1952-64; tchr., counselor Am. Dependents Sch., Stuttgart, Germany, 1959-60; dir. spl. edn. Kankakee State Hosp., 1964-66, dir. mental retardation div., 1968-71; dir. programs, Coldwater (Mich.) State Home and Tng. Sch., 1971-74; spl. edn. dept. Western Ill. U., Macomb, 1974—, asso. prof.; cons. in field. Served with USAAF, 1943-46; ATO. U.S. Office Edn. fellow, 1966-68; Ill. Dept. Mental Health Employment Edn. grantee, 1966-68. Mem. Nat. Vocat. Guidance Assn., Am. Personnel and Guidance Assn., Council for Exceptional Children, Am. Assn. Mental Deficiency, Western Ill. Adminstrs. Round Table, Kappa Delta Pi, Phi Delta Kappa. Lutheran. Club: Kiwanis. Contbr. articles in field to profl. jours. Home: 813 Orchard Dr Macomb IL 61455 Office: 25C Horrabin Hall Western Ill Univ Macomb IL 61455

HASBROUCK, WILBERT ROLAND, architect; b. Mapleton, Iowa, Dec. 17, 1931; s. Russell M. and Hazel Elizabeth (Hornby) H.; B.S. in Archtl. Engring., Ia. State Coll., 1954; m. Marilyn Jean Whittlesey, Aug. 31, 1958; children—Charles Russell, John Whittlesey. Archtl. engr. Ill. Central R.R., Chgo., 1954-67; exec. dir. A.I.A., Chgo., 1968-75; Practice architecture as Office of Wilbert R. Hasbrouck, Historic Resources, 1970—. Life trustee Chgo. Sch. Architecture Found., mem. exec. com., 1966-75. Served to 1st lt. C.E., AUS, 1955-57. Recipient citation Nat. Trust for Historic Preservation, 1974. Fellow A.I.A.; mem. Soc. Archtl. Historians (past nat. dir.) Presbyn. Mason. Club: Cliff Dwellers. Author: Architectural Essays from the Chicago School, others, also articles.; editor, pub. Prairie Sch. Rev., 1964—. Home: 1115 S Plymouth Ct Chicago IL 60605 Office: 711 S Dearborn Chicago IL 60605

HASCALL, JEAN MARY TEAGUE (MRS. CARLETON CHANDLER HASCALL, JR.), artist; b. Shepherd, Mich.; d. Cassius Homer and Helen (Winegar) Teague; A.B., Wayne State U., 1940; m. Carleton Chandler Hascall, Jr., Jan. 23, 1943; children—Carleton Chandler III, John T., Mary Elizabeth. Indsl. designer George W. Walker Co., 1940; fashion illustrator Detroit Newspaper, 1941; engring. draftsman Chrysler Corp., 1942; 13 one-man shows Wayne State U., Women's City Club Gallery, Alpha Art Gallery, Lee Gallery, also others; exhibited in group shows Detroit Inst. Arts, Scarab Club Gallery, Detroit Artists' Market; represented in permanent collections Ann Arbor Mus. Arts, Marquette Library, Grosse Ile Schs., several hosps.; also pvt. collections. Vol., Rec. for Blind. Bd. dirs., pres. Community Theatre Grosse Ile (Mich.); mem. St. James Adoremus Bell Choir; bd. dirs. Archives of Am. Art. Mem. Detroit Soc. Women Painters and Sculptors (pres. 1950), Down River Guitar Club. Clubs: Grosse Ile Book (pres. 1963-64, 77-78, dir. 1975-77), Grosse Ile Golf and Country, Grosse Ile Friday Musicale (dir. 1975-77). Home: 28273 Elba Dr Grosse Ile MI 48138

HASELDEN, ELIZABETH LEE (MRS. KYLE HASELDEN), civic and religious worker; b. Charleston, S.C., Sept. 13, 1913; d. Thomas Oswald and Mary E. (Pettigrew) Lee; Mus.B., Meredith Coll., 1935; student Columbia, summer 1935, Colgate-Rochester Div. Sch., 1936-37; m. Kyle E. Haselden, Sept. 8, 1936; children—Kyle Haselden II, Alice, Thomas Lee. Tchr. English, music high sch., Florence, S.C., 1935-36; tchr. piano prep. dept. Morris Harvey Coll., Charleston, W.Va., 1959-60. Vice pres. United Ch. Women, Mpls., 1947-49, inter-faith chmn., Charleston, 1958-60, mem. nat. Christian social relations adv. com. of triennium, 1961-64; nat. chmn. Christian social relations Ch. Women United, 1964-67, nat. v.p., 1967-71; nat. dir. urban ministries Ch. Women United, 1971-80; mem. Bapt. Joint Com. Pub. Affairs, 1962-63; mem. div. Christian social concern Am. Baptist Conv., 1963-69; mem. commn. on Christian unity, mem. gen. bd. Am. Bapt. Chs. U.S.A., 1970-82, v.p., 1980-82; mem. urban policy panel Center Theology and Public Policy, 1979—; coordinator Evanston Ecumenical Action Council, 1980—. Mem. Citizen's Council for Better Schs., Charleston, 1958-60; mem. Mayor's Council on Human Relations, Mpls., 1947-50; pres. Women's Conf. on Human Relations, Mpls., 1946-50, Council on Human Relations, Rochester, N.Y., 1952-54, Charleston, W.Va., 1959-60; mem. Mayor's Community Relations Commn. Evanston. Mem. women's planning com. Japan Internat. Christian U., 1959—. Recipient Luke Mowbray Ecumenical award Am. Bapt. Chs. U.S.A., 1979; Alumna award Meredith Coll., 1981. Author study guide, articles. Home: 1507 Lincoln St Evanston IL 60201

HASELOW, JOHN HENRY, mktg. communications service firm exec.; b. Cleve., Sept. 2, 1934; s. Eugene Theodore and Ruth Elizabeth (Mans) H.; B.A., Fenn Coll., 1957; m. Lois Eileen Cattran, Sept. 21, 1959; children—Marcia Ann, Denise Carol, Douglas Scott. Mng. editor Precision Metal mag. Indsl. Pub. Co., Cleve., 1957-60; v.p. Rodgers & Co., Inc., Cleve., 1960-70, Carr Liggett Advt., Cleve., 1970-79; owner, pres. Haselow & Assos., Inc., Cleve., 1979—. Mem. univ. relations adv. com. Cleve. State U., 1979—; mem. public info. adv. com. Community for Fedn. Planning, 1980-81. Mem. Public Relations Soc. Am. Lutheran. Home: 3703 Fenley Rd Cleveland Heights OH 44121 Office: 23611 Chagrin Blvd Beachwood OH 44122

HASELWOOD, ELDON LAVERNE, educator; b. Barnard, Mo., July 19, 1933; B.S., U. Omaha, 1960; M.A. in L.S., U. Denver, 1963; Ph.D. in Ednl. Adminstrn., U. Nebr., Lincoln, 1972; m. Joan McQuiddy, 1960; children—Ann, Karen, Polly, Amy. Sec. and diesel records clk. U.P. R.R., Omaha, 1951-53, 55-57; jr. high sch. librarian Omaha Public Schs., 1960-61; jr.-sr. high sch. librarian Lewis Central Community Schs., Council Bluffs, Iowa, 1961-63; govt. documents librarian U. Omaha, 1963-66; vis. prof. U. Nebr., Lincoln, summers 1974, 75, 76, 79; chmn. dept. library sci. U. Nebr., Omaha, 1966-76, interim dir. Ednl. Tech. Center, Coll. Edn., 1977, prof. dept. tchr. edn., 1977—; mem. sch. evaluation team North Central Assn. Colls. and Schs./Nebr. Dept. Edn., 1968-73, 75-81; bd. govs. Nebr. Library Commn., 1981—; pres. Nebr. Adv. Council on Libraries, 1980; chmn. Met. Library Network Adv. Council, 1979-80. Mem. adv. bd. York (Nebr.) Coll., 1977—; elder S.W. Ch. of Christ, 1979—. Recipient Meritorious Performance award Coll. Edn., 1974-75, 75-76, 76-77, 77-78, U. Nebr. at Omaha, 1974-75, 76-77, 78-79. Mem. Nebr. Library Assn. (pres. 1982), ALA, Assn. Ednl. Communications and Tech., AAUP, Nebr. Ednl. Media Assn. (charter), Phi Delta Kappa, Omaha Met. Area Librarians Club (pres. 1979-80). Home: 9919 Pasadena Ave Omaha NE 68124 Office: U Nebr Coll Edn Omaha NE 68182

HASHIOKA, CHRISTOPHER EDWARD, real estate investment co. exec.; b. Chgo., Jan. 19, 1948; s. Edwin T. and Pauline A. Hashioka; A.B., Harvard Coll., 1970; M.B.A., U. Chgo., 1972. Asso. Blyth Eastman Dillon & Co., Chgo., 1972-73; partner The Balcor Co., Skokie, Ill., 1973—. C.P.A., Ill. Mem. Am. Inst. C.P.A.'s, Ill. Soc. C.P.A.'s, Inst. Real Estate Mgmt., Nat. Assn. Securities Dealers. Clubs: Univ. of Chgo., Harvard Chgo. Home: 3240 Lakeshore Dr Apt 12A Chicago IL 60657 Office: 10024 Skokie Blvd Skokie IL 60077

HASKELL, THEODORE JAMES, educator, former city ofcl.; b. Chgo., Oct. 11, 1926; s. Ted James and Grace (Hasenstab) H.; student St. Norbert's Coll., 1944; B.S., Mich. State U., 1949, M.S., 1966; m. Barbara Mae Bible, Sept. 16, 1950; children—Judith Lee, Bruce James, Rebecca Lynn. Ranger, Huron-Clinton Met. Authority, Milford, Mich., 1949; forestry foreman City of Lansing, Mich., 1949-55, asst. forester, 1955-59, forester, 1959-64, asst. dir. dept. parks and recreation, 1962-72, dir., 1973-76; asso. prof., extension specialist park and recreation resources Mich. State U., East Lansing, 1976—; cons. forestry 1956—; tchr. adult edn. Lansing sch. Dist., 1961-65; lectr. Mich. State U., 1960-72. Mem. (Lansing) Mayor's Com. River Improvement, 1963-72; chmn. com. adminstrv. control Mich. Grand River Watershed, 1967—, vice chmn. exec. bd., 1972-76, chmn., 1976—; del. to White House Conf. on Aging 1971. Mem. bd. Michigan Shade Tree Research Found., also pres., 1969—. Served with AUS, 1945-46. Named Forest and Park Conservationist of 1972, Mich. United Conservation Clubs; recipient Fellowship award Mich. Recreation and Park Assn., 1975. Registered forester, Michigan. Mem. Am. Inst. Park Execs. (Distinguished Service award 1965), Am. Mgmt. Assn., Internat. Shade Tree Conf. (bd. govs.), Nat. Recreation and Park Assn., Mich. Forestry and Park Assn. (pres. Honors award 1980) Mich. Acad. Sci., Arts and Letters, Scabbard and Blade, Xi Sigma Pi, Phi Kappa Phi. Conglist. (trustee). Club: Torch (Lansing). Author (with others) Basic Ground Maintenance, 1971. Contbr. to profl. manuals. Home: 1801 Harding St Lansing MI 48910 Office: Dept Park and Recreation Resources Mich State U East Lansing MI 48824

HASPEL, LAWRENCE USHER, cardiologist; b. N.Y.C., Oct. 21, 1941; s. Herman and Lee Haspel; B.S., Bklyn. Coll. Pharmacy, 1963; D.O., Chgo. Coll. of Osteopathic Medicine, 1971; m. Marcia Kalfen, Oct. 27, 1974; children—Charles, Dyan, Dorie, Jessica Lynn. Intern, Interboro Gen. Hosp., Bklyn., 1967-68; fellow in cardiology Mt. Sinai Hosp., Chgo., 1971-72; resident in internal medicine Chgo. Coll. Osteo. Medicine, 1968-70; practice medicine specializing in cardiology, Chgo., 1972—; asst. prof. medicine Chgo. Coll. of Osteopathy, 1972-75, asso. prof., 1975-80, dir. sect. cardiology, 1972-80, asso. dir. sect. cardiology, 1980—, v.p. out-reach clinic program, 1979—, dir. intern/resident tng. program, 1979—; cons. HEW, 1977—; cons. cardiologist Forkosh Meml. Hosp., Chgo., 1976—; adj. prof. health scis. Govs. State U., Chgo., 1977-79. Recipient Tchr. and Physician of Yr. award Chgo. Coll. Osteopathy, 1970, 73, 76; diplomate Am. Bd. Med. Examiners. Fellow Am. Coll. Osteo. Internists (mem. adv. council on clin. investigation 1979—), Inst. of Medicine of Chgo. (bd. govs. 1978—); mem. Am. Soc. Echocardiography, Am. Acad. Osteo. Med. Dirs. (trustee 1977—, pres. 1979—), Am. Heart Assn., Am. Assn. Colls. Osteo. Medicine, Ill. Heart Assn. (mem. steering com. 1977-78), Chgo. Heart Assn., Am. Inst. Ultrasound in Medicine, Assn. for Hosp. Med. Edn., Am. Physicians Fellowship for Medicine in Israel, Ill. Assn. Osteo. Physicians and Surgeons. Contbr. articles on cardiology to med. jours.; editorial bd. The Osteo. Physician Jour., 1978—. Home: 2124 Tennyson St Highland Park IL 60035 Office: 20201 S Crawford St Olympia Fields IL 60461

HASSELL, GORDON ELMER, personnel cons. exec.; b. Sharon, Pa., Jan. 13, 1929; s. Elmer Harry and Margaret (Weller) H.; B.S., Colgate U., 1951; student U. Pitts. Law Sch., 1951-52; m. Jean Treverton Hays, Sept. 8, 1951; children—Karen Lynne, Megan Ann. Mgr. staff employment Trane Co., LaCrosse, Wis., 1956-60; v.p. Longberry Employment Service, Inc., Niles, Ohio, 1960—. Bd. dirs., past pres. Trumbull County YMCA. Served to lt. (j.g.) USNR, 1952-56. Mem. Nat. Personnel Cons. (past pres., dir.), Nat. Employment Assn., Am. Soc. Personnel Adminstrn., Niles C. of C., Theta Chi. Republican. Presbyn. Home: 7401 Mines Rd SE Warren OH 44484 Office: Niles Bank Bldg Niles OH 44446

HASSELL, JEAN HAYS, dietitian, educator; b. Rochester, Pa., Mar. 16, 1929; d. Edson M. and Dorothy G. (Treverton) Hays; student Ohio U., 1947-49; B.S. cum laude, Syracuse U., 1951; M.S. in Foods and Nutrition, Kent State U., 1974; postgrad. Ohio State U., 1980; m. Gordon Elmer Hassell, Sept. 8, 1951; children—Karen Lynne, Megan Ann. Therapeutic dietitian Rochester (Pa.) Gen. Hosp., 1951-52; home economist H. J. Heinz Co., Pitts., 1952-54; therapeutic and teaching dietitian St. Vincent DePaul Hosp., Norfolk, Va., 1955-56; therapeutic dietitian Trumbull Meml. Hosp., Warren, Ohio, 1970-75; lectr. Pa. State U., Shenango Valley Campus, Sharon, Pa., 1975-78; instr. Youngstown (Ohio) State U., 1975-79, 80—, coordinator nutrition edn. and tng. program, 1979; cons. dietitian Gastroenterology Clinic, Warren, Ohio, 1975—; teaching dietitian Trumbull Meml. Hosp. Sch. Nursing, Warren, 1962—. Pres. Women's Panhellenic Assn. Trumbull County, 1967; bd. dirs. Am. Cancer Soc., Trumbull County unit. Kellogg med. dietetics grantee, 1980. Mem. Am. Dietetic Assn., Soc. Nutrition Edn., Ohio Dietetic Assn., Ohio Nutrition Council, Mahoning Valley Dietetic Assn., Omicron Nu, Chi Omega. Republican. Presbyterian. Home: 7401 Mines Rd SE Warren OH 44484 Office: Youngstown State U 410 Wick Ave Youngstown OH 44555

HASSELL, JOEL ANDRE, mfg. co. exec.; b. Detroit, July 23, 1937; s. Joseph Davis and Kay Enid Hassell; B.S. in Math., U. 68; m. Mariann Barbara Dempsey, Dec. 23, 1974; children—Myron, Robert, Joel, Terry, Jennifer, Deborah, Jocelyn, Jonelle, Jeryl Lyn, Joseph. Commd. 2d lt. U.S. Air Force, 1957, advanced through grades to maj., 1975; served at Hdqrs. USAF, Aerospace Def. Command, Air Force Systems Command, Office of Joint Chiefs of Staff; ret., 1977; mgr. target engagement br. BDM Corp., McLean, Va., 1977-79; mgr. Dayton Mil. Systems Group, Calspan Corp., Dayton, Ohio, 1979-81; with Arinc Research Corp., 1981—; instr. Fla. State U., 1969. Mem. Preparedness Assn., Mil. Ops. Research Soc., Alpha Pi Mu. Republican. Roman Catholic. Club: K.C. Home: 4322 Strathaven Dr Dayton OH 45424

HASSELQUIST, MAYNARD BURTON, lawyer; b. Amador, Minn., July 1, 1919; s. Harry and Anna M. (Froberg) H.; B.S. in Law, U. Minn., 1941, LL.B., 1947; m. Nov. 20, 1948; children—Mark D., Peter L. Admitted to Minn. bar, 1947; mem. tax dept. Gen. Mills, Inc., Mpls., 1946-53; sr. partner firm Dorsey, Windhorst, Hannaford, Whitney & Halladay, Mpls., 1953—; dir. Graco Inc., Mpls., Magnetic Controls Co., Mpls., Food Producers of Japan, McLaughlin Gormley King Co., Mpls. Served with U.S. Navy, 1941-46. Mem. Am., Minn., Hennepin County, Internat. bar assns., Am. Soc. Internat. Law, Japan-Am. Soc. Minn. (chmn.), Swedish Council Am. (dir.), Am. Swedish Inst. (dir.). Lutheran. Club: Mpls. Home: 2950 Dean Pkwy Minneapolis MN 55416 Office: 2200 First Bank Place E Minneapolis MN 55402

HASSEMAN, RODNEY LEE, advt. exec.; b. Uhrichsville, Ohio, Apr. 21, 1950; s. Robert Leroy and Patricia Lou (Smith) H.; B.A. in English and Comml. Art, Ohio State U., 1974; m. Christine Marie Heakin, June 19, 1971; 1 son, Kirby Lee. Freelance artist, 1967—; group mgr. stock control Mdse. Distbn. Center of Sears, Roebuck & Co., Columbus, Ohio, 1972-75; product line mgr. bus. calendar sales Shaw-Barton, Coshocton, Ohio, 1975-76, mgr. splty. sales, 1976-77, promotion coordinator, 1977-80, mgr. advt. and sales promotion, 1981—. Mem. advt. adv. bd. Coshocton County Joint Vocat. Sch., vice chmn. Coshocton County Heart Assn., 1981—. Recipient cert. of creative recognition Direct Mail/Mktg. Assn., 1980. Mem. Nat. Publ. Assn., Splty. Advt. Assn. Internat. (Silver Pyramid award 1979, 80), Sigma Nu. Democrat. Moravian. Club: Elks (officer innter guard). Editor Sales Booster mag., 1977—. Home: 1509 Orchard St Coshocton OH 43812 Office: 545 Walnut St Coshocton OH 43812

HASSENGER, RICHARD MARK, savs. and loan exec.; b. Sioux City, Iowa, Oct. 16, 1944; s. Leo Mark and Louise Viva (Gross) H.; B.A., Iowa State U. and U. Iowa, 1966; postgrad. Coll. Law, U. Iowa, 1966-67, Grad. Sch., 1967-68; m. Vickie E. Hassenger, Apr. 26, 1969; 1 dau., Torri. Vice pres. Sioux City Fed. Savs. & Loan Assn., 1968-72, exec. v.p., mng. officer, 1972-78, pres., 1978—, also dir.; pres., dir. Plaza Assos., Inc., Plaza Insurors, Inc.; chmn., Statewide Advt. Com. of Savs. and Loans of Iowa, 1978—. Mem. exec. com. Sioux City Planning and Zoning Commn. Mem. Savs. Instns. Mktg. Soc., Advt. Club Sioux City (pres. 1970), Sioux City C. of C. (chmn. task force on leadership devel.). Office: 700 4th St Sioux City IA 51101

HASSETT, PAUL ELLIOT, assn. exec.; b. Worcester, Mass., Sept. 4, 1917; s. George Edwards and Rosealind (White) H.; B.A., LaCrosse State Coll., 1940; H.H.D. (hon.), Milton Coll., 1976; m. Charlotte Mae Ariens, June 27, 1942; children—Sharon Marie, Paul Scott, Steve Alan. Tchr. high schs., Wis., 1940-48; editor Dunn County News, Menomonie, Wis., 1948-60; asst. sec. Wis. Petroleum Council, Madison, 1960-65; exec. sec. to Gov. Warren P. Knowles of Wis., 1965-70; pres. Wis. Assn. Mfrs. and Commerce, Milw., 1970—. Pres. Internat. Inst., Milw., 1972-78; curator Wis. State Hist. Soc. Served with USAAF, 1942-46, 54. Decorated Air medal with 5 oak leaf clusters. Mem. Am. Soc. Assn. Execs., NAM, U.S. C. of C., Conf. State Mfrs. Assns., Nat. Indsl. Council. Republican. Presbyterian. Clubs: Press, Athletic (Milw.); Press (Madison). Home: 1630 Capital Ave Madison WI 53705 Office: 111 E Wisconsin Ave Milwaukee WI 53202

HASSLER, DONALD MACKEY, II, educator; b. Akron, Ohio, Jan. 3, 1937; s. Donald Mackey and Frances Elizabeth (Parsons) H.; B.A. (Alfred P. Sloan scholar), Williams Coll., 1959; M.A. (Woodrow Wilson fellow), Columbia, 1960, Ph.D., 1967; m. Diana Cain, Oct. 8, 1960 (dec. Sept. 19, 1976); children—Donald, David; m. 2d, Sue Smith, Sept. 13, 1977; children—Shelly, Heather. Instr., U. Montreal, 1961-65; instr. English dept. Kent (Ohio) State U., 1965-67, asst. prof., 1967-71, asso. prof., 1971-76, prof., 1977—, dir. exptl. coll., 1973—, acting dean honors and exptl. coll., 1979-80. Co-chmn. Kent Am. Revolution Bicentennial Commn., 1974-77. Mem. Phi Beta Kappa. Presbyterian. (deacon 1971-74, elder 1974-77). Club: Kiwanis (dir. 1974-76). Author: Erasmus Darwin, 1974; The Comedian as the Letter D: Erasmus Darwin's Comic Materialism, 1973; Asimov's Golden Age: The Ordering of an Art, 1977; Hal Clement, 1982. Home: 1226 Woodhill Dr Kent OH 44240

HASTINGS, GEORGE JAMES, bus. exec.; b. Grand Forks, N.D., Aug. 23, 1931; s. Wilmoth Frances and Lillian Alice (Crorin) H.; student tech. schs.; m. Mary Joyce Ripplinger, Oct. 17, 1953; children—Robert A., Deborha A., Donald J., Mary Ann, Joan Marie. Pres., Hastings Heating and Sheet Metal Inc., Grand Forks, 1946—, Hastings Inc., Grand Forks, 1977—, Hastings Investment Corp., Grand Forks, 1968—, Minnesota-Dakota Prodns., Grand Forks, 1975—. Served with U.S. Army, 1950-52. Mem. Nat. Assn. Home Builders. Republican. Roman Catholic. Clubs: Lions (pres. club 1972-73), Am. Legion, DAV, Elks, Eagles. Office: 2516 S Washington St Grand Forks ND 58201

HASTINGS, ROBERT EUGENE, city-county ofcl.; b. Council Bluffs, Iowa, June 17, 1932; s. Elmer Wayne and Lillian Irene (Potts) H.; student appraisal courses Omaha U., Iowa State U., Iowa Western Community Coll., 1967-78; m. Marcia Ann Martin, Aug. 2, 1969. Meter reader Council Bluffs Gas Co., 1950; clk. Milw. R.R., Council Bluffs, 1951-52; with Harding Cream Co., Omaha, 1952-54; clk. Safeway Stores, Council Bluffs, 1954-56; circulation mgr. World Herald Newspaper, Eastern Nebr., 1956-58; agt. Met. Life Ins., Omaha, 1958-59; asst. county assessor Pottawattamie County, Iowa, Council Bluffs, 1959-72; city assessor Council Bluffs, 1972-74; city-county assessor Pottawattamie County, 1974—. Taxation and fin. steering com. Nat. Assn. Counties, Washington, 1974-79; pres. C of C Cee Bees (Goodwill Ambassadors), 1978; county govt. lobbyist, 1974-75. Recipient ICA degree, Iowa Inst. Certified Assessors. Mem. Internat. Assn. Assessing Officers (C.A.E. degree; contbr. report 1974; profl. admissions com. 1981-82), Nat. Assn. Review Appraisers (C.R.A. degree), Iowa State Assn. Assessors, C. of C. (dir. 1975-77). Lutheran. Clubs: Kiwanis (pres. Downtown Council Bluffs 1976-77, On-To dist. Nebr.-Iowa Dist. conv. chmn. 1979, lt. gov. div. 13, trustee Nebr.-Iowa Dist. 1981-82). Home: 72 Bellevue Ave Council Bluffs IA 51501 Office: Court House PO Box 1076 Council Bluffs IA 51501

HASTINGS, WILLIAM CHARLES, state supreme ct. judge; b. Newman Grove, Nebr., Jan. 31, 1921; s. William C. and Margaret (Hansen) H.; B.Sc., U. Nebr., 1942, J.D., 1948; m. Julie Ann Simonson, Dec. 29, 1946; children—Pamela, Charles, Steven. Admitted to Nebr. bar, 1948; with FBI, 1942-43; mem. firm Chambers, Holland, Dudgeon & Hastings, Lincoln, 1948-65; judge 3d judicial dist. Nebr., Lincoln, 1965-79; judge Supreme Ct. Nebr., Lincoln, 1979—. Pres. Child Guidance Center, Lincoln, 1962, 63; v.p. Lincoln Community Council, 1968, 69; vice chmn. Antelope Valley Boy Scouts Am., Lincoln, 1968, 69. Pres. First Presbyn. Ch. Found., Lincoln, 1968—. Served with AUS, 1943-46. Mem. Am., Nebr., Lincoln bar assns., Neb. Dist. Judges Assn., Phi Delta Phi. Republican. Presbyterian (deacon, elder, trustee). Club: East Hills Country (pres. 1959-60). Home: 1544 S 58th St Lincoln NE 68506 Office: Nebr Supreme Ct State House Lincoln NE 68509

HATCH, HENRY CLIFFORD, beverage co. exec.; b. Toronto, Ont., Can., Apr. 30, 1916; s. Harry C. and Elizabeth (Carr) H.; student St. Michael's Coll. Sch., Toronto; m. Joan Ferriss, May 1, 1940; children—Henry Clifford, Gail Elizabeth Todgham, Sheila Mary McNamara, Richard Ferriss. Salesman, T.G. Bright & Co., Ltd., Niagara Falls, Ont., 1933-37, now dir.; merchandising staff Hiram Walker, Inc., Walkerville, Ont., 1937; dir. Hiram Walker & Sons., Ltd., 1938—, asst. to v.p. in charge sales, 1946—, v.p., 1946—; v.p., dir. Hiram Walker-Gooderham & Worts, Ltd., Walkerville, 1955—, exec. v.p., 1961-64, pres., 1964-78, chmn. bd., chief exec. officer, 1978—; dir. R. Angus Alta. Ltd., Edmonton, London Life Ins. Co. (Ont.), Toronto-Dominion Bank, Bell Can., Montreal, Que. Served as comdr. Royal Canadian Navy, 1940-45, in command HMCS Drummondville, Ville de Que. Clubs: Rosedale Golf (Toronto); Essex Golf; Detroit Athletic. Home: 7130 Riverside Dr E Windsor ON N8S 1C3 Canada Office: 2072 Riverside Dr E Walkerville ON N8Y 4S5 Canada*

HATCH, MICHAEL ALAN, lawyer; b. Des Moines, Nov. 12, 1948; s. Lorenzo Rexford and Katharine Jane (Bell) H.; B.A., U. Minn., 1970, J.D., 1973; m. Patricia Peterson, July 17, 1976; children—Katharine Sarah, Elizabeth Bell. Admitted to Minn. bar, 1973; asso. firm Lifson, Kelber, Abrahamson, Breuning & Weinstein, Mpls., 1973-76; partner Kelber, Abrahamson, Weinstein & Hatch, Mpls., 1976-78; partner Kelber & Hatch, Mpls., 1978-80; of counsel Steffens, Usset & Rothnem, Mpls., 1980-81; dir. Legal Advice Clinics, 1977-78; arbitrator Am. Arbitration Assn., 1979-81. State chmn. Minn. Democratic Farm Labor Party, 1980-82. Mem. Am. Trial Lawyers Assn., Am. Bar Assn., Minn. Bar Assn., Minn. Trial Lawyers Assn. Mem. United Ch. of Christ. Home: 1042 Naumkaeg St Shakopee MN 55379 Office: Suite 200 3400 W 66th St Minneapolis MN 55435

HATCHER, HARRIS HICKOX, ins. agt.; b. Springfield, Ill., Oct. 14, 1950; s. Robert Evans and Jeanne (Hickox) H.; A.B. in English Lit., Washington U., St. Louis, 1973, M.A., 1974; m. Sharon Lynn Starkey, Nov. 27, 1976; 1 dau., Tracey Lynn. Asst. underwriter Continental Ins. Cos., St. Louis, 1975-76; field rep. Home Ins. Cos., St. Louis, 1976-77; spl. agt. N.H. Ins. Group, Springfield, Ill., 1977-79; mktg. mgr. Am. Internat. Group, Springfield, 1979—; asso. R.W. Troxell & Co., ins. brokerage, Springfield, 1980—. Chester Sikking scholar, 1977. Episcopalian. Clubs: Masons (32d deg.), Shriners. Home: 1412 Noble Ave Springfield IL 62704 Office: 300 S Grand Ave W Springfield IL 62704

HATCHER, RICHARD G., mayor; b. Michigan City, Ind., July 10, 1933; s. Carlton and Catherine H.; B.A., Ind. U.; J.D., Valparaiso U.; m. Ruthellyn; 1 dau., Ragen Heather. Admitted to Ind. bar, practiced in East Chicago; formerly dep. prosecutor Lake County (Ind.); councilman-at large Gary City Council, 1963-66; mayor of Gary, 1967—; v.p., mem. human resources com. U.S. Conf. Mayors, 1979-80, pres., 1980-81, also mem. exec. bd.; mem. steering com. human resources devel. Nat. League Cities, now chmn. com., also bd. dirs.; dir. Trans-Africa Corp. A founder Muigwithania, social and civic club, now v.p.; mem. Nat. Com. of Inquiry; chmn. edn. subcom. Ind. adv. com. U.S. Commn. Civil Rights; mem. exec. com. Nat. Urban Coalition; founder Nat. Black Caucus of Locally Elected Ofcls.; convenor Nat. Black Polit. Conv.; past pres. Nat. Conf. Democratic Mayors; mem. steering com. Nat. Black Assembly; chmn. Ind. State Black Caucus; mem. Ind. exec. bd. NAACP, legal adviser Gary chpt.; bd. dirs. Greater Gary United Fund; trustee, mem. adv. com. Gary Urban League; mem. adv. bd. Robert Woods Johnson Meml. Found.; chmn. Gary City Dem. Com.; mem. Ind. Dem. State Central Com.; vice chmn. Nat. Dem. Com., 1980—; mem. U.S. Intergovernmental Adv. Commn. on Edn. to Sec. of Edn.; convenor Nat. Conf. on a Black Agenda for the 80's, 1980; chmn. bd. Trans-Africa. Mem. Am., Ind., Gary (exec. com.) bar assns., Gary Jaycees. Address: City Hall 401 Broadway Gary IN 46402

HATCHER, THOMAS FOUNTAIN, mgmt. cons. co. exec.; b. Monroe, Mich., Dec. 26, 1931; s. Fountain H. and Cecilia E. (Boylan) H.; B.S., N.Y. U., 1968; m. Rosemary K. Downs, June 23, 1956; children—Mary Kathleen, Roberta Joan, Margaret Ann. With Equitable Life Assurance Soc., N.Y.C., 1955-71, mgr. learning systems, 1968-71; owner Thomas Hatcher Assos., Mpls., 1971-79; pres., owner Futures Unlimited, Inc., Mpls., 1979—. Mem. Nat. Speakers Assn., Am. Soc. Profl. Consultants. Roman Catholic. Author: The Definitive Guide to Long Range Planning, 1981. Home: 4916 W 82d St Bloomington MN 55437 Office: Futures Unlimited Inc 5200 W 73d St Minneapolis MN 55435

HATFIELD, MARY MOROZZO, math. cons.; b. Council Grove, Kans., Feb. 5, 1943; d. John and Emma Morozzo; B.S. in Edn., U. Kans., 1965; M.S. in Edn., 1970; Ph.D., 1976; m. Larry A. Hatfield, Dec. 28, 1965; children—Jeffrey W., Julie C. Tchr. elem. sch. Shawnee Mission, Kans., 1965-66, Lawrence, Kans., 1966-68; teaching asst. U. Kans., 1971-76, asso. prof., 1976-77; math. cons. Lawrence Public Schs., 1977—; presenter numerous ann. and regional confs.; mem. Kans. Adv. Com. in Math., 1978—. Deacon, Plymouth Congl. Ch. Mem. Nat. Council Tchrs. Math. (program com. Colorado Springs 1977, Topeka Conf. 1982), Kans. Assn. Tchrs. Math. (pres.-elect 1982-83) Assn. for Ednl. Data Systems, Research Council for Diagnostic and Prescriptive Math., Nat. Council Suprs. Math., PEO, Phi Kappa Phi, Phi Delta Kappa, Delta Kappa Gamma, Delta Gamma. Republican. Contbr. articles to profl. publs. Office: 936 New York St Lawrence KS 66044

HATHAWAY, ROBERT JOSEPH, chemist; b. Glendive, Mont., Dec. 2, 1921; s. Robert J. and Marjorie Ellen (Tubbs) H.; B.S., U. Ill., 1943; Ph.D. (fellow), Mich. State U., 1951; m. Phyllis Eileen Read, June 1, 1945; children—Ronda, Joline, Charla, Mary, Cynthia, Thomas. Technician, Abbott Labs., North Chicago, Ill., 1943-46; chemist Miles Labs., Elkhart, Ind., 1951-57; sr. research chemist A.E. Staley Co., Decatur, Ill., 1957—. Bd. dirs. Planned Parenthood, Decatur, 1975; pres. Unitarian. Fellowship, 1966. Mem. Am. Chem. Soc. (chmn. local sect. 1966), Am. Assn. Cereal Chemists, Sigma Xi. Republican. Patentee. Home: 3997 Northbrook Dr Decatur IL 62526 Office: A E Staley Co Decatur IL 62525

HATTERY, ROBERT WILBER, polit. scientist; b. Chgo., Jan. 5, 1925; s. Wilber and Ruth Adolphus H.; Ph.B., U. Chgo., 1948, M.A., 1954, Ph.D., 1961; m. Carolyn Potshke, Feb. 2, 1957 (dec. Feb. 1979); children—David Wilber, Lor Ruth, John Furer. Research asst. U. Chgo. Center Study Am. Fgn. Policy, 1952-54; asst. dir. Bur. Govt., U. Wis., Madison, 1955-62; instr. U. Wis., 1955-60, asst. prof. polit. sci., 1960-62, asst. dir. Inst. World Affairs Edn., 1961-62, asst. dir. Salzburg (Austria) Seminar in Am. Studies, 1960-61, asst. dean div. univ. extension, 1967-69; dir. Bur. Public Discussion, Ind. U., Bloomington, 1962—, asso. prof. polit. sci. Sch. Continuing Studies, 1968—, acting dir. West European Studies, 1969-71. Served with U.S. Army, 1943-45. Recipient award for profl. service Nat. U. Extension Assn., 1967. Mem. Am. Polit. Sci. Assn., Internat. Studies Assn., Soc. Citizen Edn. in World Affairs, Nat. Univ. Extension Assn., Adult Edn. Assn. Ind., AAUP, Ind. Acad. Social Sci., Ind. Polit. Sci. Assn. Unitarian. Clubs: Univ., Faculty Discussion (sec.), U.S. Canoe Assn. Author: Great Decisions, 1962, 1964; (with others) World Politics: An Independent Study Course, 1978; A Midwest World Affairs Audience, 1958; Undergraduate Readings in Political Science, 1968; Introduction to World Politics, 1973; Undergraduate Readings in Political Science, 1971. Home: 1316 S High St Bloomington IN 47401 Office: Bur Public Discussion Owen Hall 201 Indiana U Bloomington IN 47405

HATTIS, ALBERT D., business exec., educator; b. Chgo., Oct. 12, 1929; s. Robert E. and Victoria C. (Kaufman) H.; B.S. with highest distinction, Northwestern U., 1948, M.B.A., 1950; m. Fern Hollobow; children—Kim Allyson, Kay Arlene, John Elmore, Michael Allen, Sharon Beth. Vice-pres., sec.-treas. Robert E. Hattis Engrs., Inc., Hattis Service Co., Inc., Deerfield, Ill., 1950-73; co-mng. dir. Robert E. Hattis Engrs., Inc. AB, Robert E. Hattis Engrs., Inc. BV, 1950-73; v.p., sec.-treas. Servbest Foods, Inc., Highland Park, Ill., 1973-78; v.p., sec.-treas., dir. W.D. Allen Mfg. Co., Sterling Products Co., Inc., Gearex Inc., Dinachrome, Inc., Fulton Machine Co., Inc., A.C. Equipment Co., 1978-80; v.p., sec.-treas. Prime Packing Co., Inc., Haitian Am. Meat and Provision Co., Spanish-Am. Foods, Inc., Packers Provision Co., Inc., Servbest Foods of P.R., Inc., 1973-78; pres., chief exec. officer Frigidmeats, Inc., Chgo., 1978-80; pres., dir. Gits Enterprises, Inc., 1978-80, Double K Bar J Ranch, Inc., 1968—; prof. bus., holder Schwan Endowed Chair for Free Enterprise, Southwest State U., Marshall, Minn. Exec. dir. The Lambs, Inc., 1980-81; trustee Orphans of the Storm Found., 1972-74, Cobblers Found., 1972-74; mem. advisory bd. Northwestern Psychiat. Inst., 1972-74, Beta Gamma Sigma. Served to capt. USAF, 1946-48, 50-52. Republican. Roman Catholic. Club: Lions. Home: 100 E Marshall Rd Marshall MN 56258 Office: LC 129 A Southwest State U Marshall MN 56258

HAUBENSCHILD, STEVEN JAMES, safety engr.; b. Ft. Atkinson, Wis., Feb. 8, 1957; s. James Raymond and Margaret Emma (Anderson) H.; B.S. in Edn., U. Wis., 1979; m. Nancy Carroll Yoder, June 30, 1979; 1 son, Timothy Steven. Asst. safety coordinator Waukesha Foundry, ABEX Corp. (Wis.), 1979; safety dir. (engr.) Telsmith div. Barber Greene Co., Milw., 1980—; mem. exec. com. Waukesha Safety Council, 1981—. Mem. Am. Soc. Safety Engrs. (sec.-treas. Wis. chpt., exec. com.), Am. Welding Soc., Internat. Assn. for Hazard Control Mgrs., Am. Indsl. Hygiene Assn., Milw. Area Indsl. Safety Council, Milw. Area Indsl. Running Club. Roman Catholic. Home: 8568 N Servite Dr Milwaukee WI 53223 Office: 532 E Capitol Dr Milwaukee WI 53212

HAUF, BARBARA JUDITH, nurse; b. Forsyth, Mont., Nov. 27, 1926; d. Lee Nichols Edwards and Blanche Rosamond (Burdan) Edwards; B.S., Mont. State Coll., 1961, M.N., 1962; M.S. in Public Health, U. Minn., Mpls., 1970; Ed.D., U. Mont., Missoula, 1975; m. Jacob Hauf, Jr., June 5, 1946; children—Kathleen, Karen, Kandice, Steven. Staff nurse Sheridan (Wyo.) Meml. Hosp., 1946-47, 55-56; staff and head nurse VA Nueropsychiat. Hosp., Sheridan, 1956-60, Deaconess Hosp. and Florence Convalescent Home, Bozeman, Mont., 1961-70, Univ. Hosps., Adult Rehab. Center, Mpls., 1969-70; instr. to asso. prof., coordinator continuing edn. Mont. State U., Bozeman, 1962-77; asso. prof., coordinator continuing edn. U. Tex. Health Sci. Center Sch. Nursing, 1977-80; dir. continuing edn. and outreach Coll. Nursing, U. N.D., Grand Forks, 1980—. Bd. govs. Continuing Health Exchange Network. Mem. Am. Nurses Assn. (council on continuing edn.), Nat. League Nursing, AAUP, Soc. Advancement Nursing, Mental Health and Mental Retardation Assn., Epilepsy Found., Assn. for Continuing Higher Edn., NOW, Nat. Women's Polit. Caucus, N.D. Adult Edn. Assn., Internat. History of Nursing Soc., Common Cause, Pi Lambda Theta, Sigma Theta Tau. Contbr. articles to profl. jours. Office: Coll Nursing U ND Grand Forks ND 58202

HAUGAN, HAROLD WALTER, plastics engr.; b. Stoughton, Wis., June 17, 1902; s. Paul Julius and Emma (Kildahl) H.; B.S., U. N.D., 1925, M.S., 1927; Ph.D., St. Andrews U., 1959. Adminstr. chemistry physics dept. York (Nebr.) Coll., 1939-41; instr. Eau Claire (Wis.)

State Tchrs. Coll., 1941-43; research supr. U.S. ammunition plant, 1943-45; mem. research devel. staff Curtiss-Wright Research Lab., Cheektowaga, N.Y., 1945-47, Cornell U. Aero. Lab., 1947-49; devel. engr. Bell Aircraft Corp., 1949-54; prin. Harold Haugan Assos., Devel. Engrs., 1954-56; supr. plastics Mich. ordnance missile plant missile div. Chrysler Corp., 1956-63; plastics engr. space div. Chrysler Corp., New Orleans, 1963-68; promoter plastics edn. in schs. and libraries throughout U.S., 1968—; pioneer developer plastics for missiles and Saturn space boosters, 1947-68. Mem. Soc. Plastics Industry, Am. Chem. Soc., Am. Def. Preparedness Assn., AIAA, Ancient Astronaut Soc., Nat. Space Inst. Author tech. publs. in plastics engring. Home: 1396 Smith St Birmingham MI 48009

HAUGEN, ELIZABETH ANN, state ofcl.; b. Eagle River, Wis., Mar. 15, 1945; d. Cyril John and Marilouise (Dobson) Prince; B.A. in Speech Edn. and Sociology, Wis. State U., 1967; M.S. in Counseling, Stout (Wis.) State U., 1968; m. Wayne Haugen, June 27, 1970. Tchr. speech, counselor Manitowoc (Wis.) schs., 1968-70; instr. Silver Lake Coll., Manitowoc, 1970-71; counselor Work Incentive Program, Job Service, State of Wis., Manitowoc, 1971-79; equal opportunity specialist Wis. Dept. Employment Relations, Madison, 1979—. Gen. Electric Co. fellow, 1969. Mem. Am. Personnel and Guidance Assn., Nat. Employment Counselors Assn., Internat. Assn. Personnel in Employment Service, Wis. Personnel and Guidance Assn., Wis. Employment Counselors Assn., Am. Assn. for Affirmative Action, Wis. Assn. Affirmative Action and Equal Opportunity Profls., Wis. Women's Network, NOW, CAP. Democrat. Home: 5326 Milward Dr Madison WI 53711 Office: 149 E Wilson St Madison WI 53702

HAUGEN, ORRIN MILLARD, lawyer; b. Mpls., Aug. 1, 1927; s. Oscar M. and Emma (Moe) H.; B.S. in Chem. Engring., U. Minn., 1948, LL.B., 1951; m. Marilyn Dixon, June 17, 1950; children—Melissa, Kristen, Eric, Kimberly. Admitted to Minn. bar, 1951; patent lawyer Honewell, Inc., Mpls., 1951-59, Univac div. Sperry Rand, 1959-63; pvt. practice specializing in patent law Haugen & Nikolai, Mpls., 1963—. Pres. Arrowhead Lake Improvement Assn., Inc., Mpls., 1958-79. Served with USNR, 1945-46. Mem. Am., Minn. bar assns., Am. Patent Law Assn., Minn. Patent Law Assn., Minn. Acacia Alumni Assn., Inc. (pres. 1961-63), Acacia. Methodist. Kiwanian. Home: 6612 Indian Hills Rd Edina MN 55435 Office: Midwest Plaza Bldg Minneapolis MN 55402

HAUGHN, JAMES EUGENE, physician; b. Columbus, Ohio, Mar. 16, 1938; s. James Cyrus and Jeannetta Cora (Brown) H.; B.S. in Agr., Ohio State U., 1960; M.D., U. Louisville, 1967; m. Bonnie M. Grubb, June 14, 1959; children—James Eugene II, Elizabeth Anne, Ross Adam, David Noel. Intern, Marion County Gen. Hosp., Indpls., 1967-68; gen. practice medicine, Tell City, Ind., 1970-77, Wabash, Ind., 1977—; mem. staff Wabash County Hosp., Wabash, Ind.; med. dir. Millers Manor, Wabash, Vernon Manor Children's Home, Wabash. Served with USAF, 1968-70; Vietnam. Diplomate Am. Bd. Family Practice. Mem. Ind. Med. Assn., Wabash County Med. Soc., Phi Eta Sigma, Alpha Zeta. Club: Elks. Home: 654 W Hill St Wabash IN 46992 Office: 645 N Spring St Wabash IN 46992

HAUKEDAHL, OREL ELDEN, ret. govt. ofcl.; b. Madison, Wis., May 12, 1907; s. Louis A. and Mina E. (Andrus) H.; B.S. in Elec. Engring., U. Wis., 1932; m. Ellen Sorensen, Sept. 1, 1951; children—Jane E., Brian L. Engr., Civil Works Adminstrn., Madison, 1933-34; works sec. Wis. Emergency Relief Adminstrn., 1934-35; area engr. Works Progress Adminstrn., 1935-41; asst. engr. Fed. Power Commn., Washington, 1941-42, asso. engr., Atlanta, 1942-46, supervising hydraulic engr. Chgo. Regional Office, 1946-53; engr. charge River Basin work Chgo. Fed. Power Commn., 1953-57, dep. regional engr., 1957-77; alternate Souris-Red-Rainy Basin Commn., 1967-73, Great Lakes Basin Commn., 1967-77, Mo. River Basin Commn. 1972-77, Upper Miss. River Basin Commn. 1972-77. Mem. coordinating com. on The Missouri River main stem reservoir operations, 1954-77. Served from lt. (j.g.) to lt. (s.g.), USNR, 1943-46. Mem. U. Wis. Alumni Assn., Am. Soc. Pub. Adminstrn. Lutheran. Mason, Moose. Home: 360 Neola Park Forest IL 60466

HAUKEDAHL, STANLEY GEORGE, warranty co. exec.; b. Madison, Wis., June 24, 1913; s. Lois Anton and Mina (Andrus) H.; student U. Wis., 1931 37, Northwestern U. Traffic Inst., 1945, FBI Nat. Acad., Washington, 1953; m. Helen Anna Landis, Mar. 2, 1935 (dec. Apr. 1970); children—Sharon Lee Rumachik, Blane Leroy, Mark Steven, Reed Allen; m. 2d, Ruth E. Mace, May 27, 1972. Policeman, Dane County (Wis.) Police, Madison, 1938-42, Wis. State Patrol, 1942-48; chief of police, Kenosha, Wis., 1948-64; agy. v.p. 20th Century Guardian Life Ins. Co., Battle Creek, Mich.; sales adminstrn. Am. Diversified Holding Corp., Columbus, Ohio; pres. Am-Diversified Securities Co., Columbus; pres. Investment Life Ins. Co. Am., Columbus; now exec. v.p. Interstate Warranty Co., Toledo. Co-ordinator police agys. Mobile Bn. 2, Wis. CD, 1948-64; rep. police Gov.'s CD Hwy. Commn., 1948-64; mem. Kenosha Traffic Study Com., 1948-64. Mem. bd. Voters for Community Action, Calhoun County, Mich. Mem. Internat. Assn. Chiefs Police, Inc. (sgt.-at-arms 1960-63), Nat. Acad. Assos., Internat. Platform Assn., Am. Life Underwriters, Wis. F.B.I., Nat. Acad. Assn., U. Wis. Alumni Assn. Methodist. Mason (32 deg., Shriner), Kiwanian, Eagle. Club: National W. Home: 1483 Bradshire Dr Columbus OH 43220 Office: PO Box 7304 Toledo OH 43615

HAUKOOS, GERRY DURAND, scientist, educator; b. Alden, Minn., Mar. 19, 1938; s. Wallace and Marie (Soost) H.; A.A., Wessington Springs (S.D.) Jr. Coll., 1958; postgrad. Greenville (Ill.) Coll., 1958-59; B.S., State U. S.D., 1963; M.S., U. Wyo., 1970; Ph.D., U. Iowa, 1981; m. Barbara Jean Potter, Aug. 17, 1963; children—Tanya Joy, Carlenda Kae. Prof. natural and behavioral scis. Wessington Springs Jr. Coll., 1961-62; tchr. White River Schs., Buckley, Wash., 1962-64; tchr. biology Clinton (Iowa) High Sch., 1964-68; asst. botany labs. U. Wyo., 1968-69; prof. botany and biology Coll. of DuPage, Glen Ellyn, Ill., 1969-76, 77—; instr. edn. U. Iowa, 1976-77. Troop leader Boy Scouts Am., Buckley, 1962-64; dir. edn. Am. Cancer Soc., Clinton, Iowa, 1964-68; mem. Community-Sch. Adv. Bd., Wheaton, Ill., 1973-75. Jessup-McHenry grantee, 1968. Mem. Ill. Acad. Scis., Nat. Assn. Research in Sci. Teaching, Nat. Sci. Tchr. Assn., Assn. Midwestern Coll. Biology Tchrs., Sigma Xi, Phi Delta Kappa, Pi Lambda Theta. Democrat. Methodist. Contbr. articles in field to profl. jours. Home: 727 Fellows St Saint Charles IL 60174 Office: 22d St at Lambert Rd Glen Ellyn IL 60137

HAUN, ROGER ERIC, athletic dir.; b. Wooster, Ohio, Sept. 8, 1950; s. Harold Eugene and Mae Lucinda (Kropf) H.; B.S., Grace Coll., 1972; M.S., So. Ill. U., 1975; m. Nancy Kay Blackwell, July 21, 1979; 1 dau., Rachel Lucinda. Teaching asst., asst. basketball coach, head cross country coach, head golf coach Greenville (Ill.) Coll., 1972-75; admissions counselor Montreat-Anderson (N.C.) Coll., 1975-76, instr. phys. edn., 1976-77, head basketball coach, head golf coach, 1975-77; asst. prof. phys. edn., athletic dir., head basketball and head cross country coach Grand Rapids (Mich.) Baptist Coll., 1977—. Mem. North Central Christian Athletic Conf. (pres. 1978—). Republican. Baptist. Office: 1001 E Beltline NE Grand Rapids MI 49505

HAUN, STACY STRIMPLE, archtl. designer, builder; b. Shelby, Ohio, June 23, 1899; s. John Leonard and Anna Belle (Strimple) H.; student public schs., Shelby; m. Mary A. Bradley, June 23, 1920; children—Jeanne Annabelle, Catherine Pricilla, Margaret Sally. Pvt. practice archtl. designer, constrn. for residential, profl., comml. and indsl. bldgs., Shelby, 1921—; cons. in field. Recipient recognition award for outstanding performance in downtown area of Shelby, Shelby C. of C., 1973. Republican. Methodist. Clubs: Rotary, Shelby Advt., Masons (Shelby.). Home: 250 W Main St Shelby OH 44875 Office: 39 S Gamble St Shelby OH 44875

HAUSER, JON WILLIAM, indsl. designer; b. Sault Ste. Marie, Mich., June 8, 1916; s. Kenneth and Arlie (Hershey) H.; m. Jean MacCallum, Aug. 30, 1939; 1 son, Jon William II. With United Motors Co., 1936; stylist Gen. Motors Corp., 1936-41, Chrysler Corp., 1941-43, Budd Mfg. Co., 1939; dir. design Sears, Roebuck & Co., 1943-45; designer Dave Chapman, Chgo., 1945-46, Barnes & Reinecke, 1946-49, Reinecke Asso., 1949-52; pres. Jon W. Hauser, Inc., St. Charles, Ill., 1952—; dir. State Bank St. Charles; vis. prof. U. Ill., 1978-79. Del., Internat. Council Socs. Indsl. Design, 1963-65, 67; chmn. judging com. Design in Housewares awards, 1966; chmn. judging com. Wescon Indsl. Design Awards, 1968, 69; lectr. indsl. design. Bd. dirs. Delnor Hosp. Men's Found., pres. bd. trustees. Furnished two designs named in Best 100 Designs History, 1959. Mem. Indsl. Designers Soc. Am. (chmn. bd. 1968), Indsl. Designers Inst. (award 1956, pres. 1962-64, chmn. bd., fellow, mem. nat. exec. com., trustee Chgo. chpt.); Quiet Birdmen. Mason (32 deg. Shriner). Clubs: St. Charles Country, Fox Valley Shrine. Home: 3N981 Route 31 St Charles IL 60174 Office: 10 State Ave St Charles IL 60174

HAUSKEN, SALLY ANN, ednl. counselor; b. Wahpeton, N.D., Aug. 10, 1934; d. Clyde Olaf and Lois Beatrice (Mc Michael) H.; B.S., Northwestern U., 1956; M.S., U. Colo., 1967; Sec. to pres. North Central Airlines, Mpls., 1958-59; service club dir. U.S. Army, Germany, 1959-61; tchr. bus., counselor Littleton (Colo.) High Sch., 1962-66; secondary counselor Detroit Lakes (Minn.) High Sch., 1967-68; secondary counselor Minnetonka West Jr. High Sch., Excelsior, Minn., 1968—. Mem. Northwestern U. Alumni Admissions Council, 1972—. Mem. Am., Minn. personnel and guidance assns., Lake Area Counselors Assn., NEA, Minn. Edn. Assn., Minnetonka Tchrs. Assn. Episcopalian. Home: 1540 Skyview Dr Chaska MN 55318 Office: 6421 Hazeltine Blvd Excelsior MN 55331

HAUSMANN, WERNER KARL, pharm. co. exec.; b. Edigheim, Germany, Mar. 9, 1921; s. Carl and Johanna Hausmann; came to U.S., 1948, naturalized, 1954; M.S. in Chem. Engring., Swiss Fedn. Inst. Tech., 1945, D.Sc., 1947; postdoctoral fellow U. London, 1947-48; m. Helen M. Vas, Sept. 29, 1949; 1 son, Gregory. Research asso. Rockefeller Inst. Med. Research, N.Y.C., 1949-57; research group leader Lederle Labs., Pearl River, N.Y., 1957-66; asso. dir. quality control Ayerst Labs., Rouses Point, N.Y., 1966-71; dir. quality control Stuart Pharm. Co., Pasadena, Calif., 1971-74; dir. quality assurance Adria Labs., Columbus, Ohio, 1974—. Pres., Public TV Assn., Plattsburgh, N.Y., 1970-71; radiation officer CD, 1962-66. Served with Swiss Army, 1941-46. Fellow N.Y. Acad. Scis., AAAS; mem. Am. Soc. Quality Control (sr.; cert. quality engr.), Acad. Pharm. Scis., Am. Soc. Biol. Chemists, Parenteral Drug Assn., Am. Chem. Soc., Am. Soc. Microbiology. Presbyterian. Club: Sheraton Sports, Toastmasters. Contbr. articles to profl. jours.; mem. editorial bd. Food, Drug and Cosmetic News, Am. Soc. Quality Control, 1976—. Office: 5000 Post Rd Dublin OH 43017

HAUSSER, ROBERT LOUIS, lawyer; b. Cin., Apr. 3, 1914; s. Oscar and Alma J. (Ebel) H.; A.B., DePauw U., Greencastle, Ind., 1936; LL.B., Columbia, 1939; m. Dorothy Ann Oakes, Aug. 17, 1940; children—George Louis, Robert Oakes, Julia Janet Guffey and Joel Severin (twins). Admitted to Ohio bar, 1939, N.Y. bar, 1940; practice in N.Y.C., 1939-41, Marietta, Ohio, 1941—; asso. Baldwin, Todd & Young, 1939-41; pvt. practice, 1941—; v.p., dir. Ohio Bar Title Ins. Co., Dayton; dir. Dime Bank, Marietta. Instr. Wash. Tech. Coll., 1973. Pres. Washington County Hist. Soc., 1964. Judge, Marietta Police Ct., 1946-57; pres. Marietta Bd. Edn., 1963; mem. Marietta Civil Service Commn., 1967—. Served with AUS, 1944-45. Decorated Purple Heart with oak leaf cluster. Fellow Am. Coll. Probate Counsel; mem. Ohio Bar Assn. (past sect. chmn., past mem. exec. com.), Am. Legion, Phi Beta Kappa. Democrat. Presbyn. (past elder, clk. of session). Lion. Clubs: Marietta Country, Marietta Senior Reading (pres. 1961-62). Author: Ohio Real Property, 5 vols., 1952-58; (with William R. Van Aken) Ohio Real Estate Transactions, 3 vols., 1964; (with Allen B. Diefenbach) Ohio Estate Planning and Probate Administration, 2 vols., 1969. Editor: Title Topics, monthly jour. Ohio Land Title Assn., 1967—, Newsletter, Quar. bull. of real property sect. Ohio Bar Assn., 1973-76. Home: 507 8th St Marietta OH 45750 Office: New Dime Bank Bldg Marietta OH 45750

HAUVER, ROBERT CARLSON, flight surgeon; b. Cleve., Oct. 23, 1932; s. Robert Beebe and Catherine Marie (Carlson) H.; A.B., Miami U., Oxford, Ohio, 1954, M.S., 1958; M.D., Ohio State U., 1959; M.S., U. Rochester, 1965; m. Marina Rose Elliott, Feb. 4, 1964; children—Tracy, Robert, Steven. Intern, St. Luke's Hosp., Cleve., 1959-60, resident internal medicine, 1960; commd. 1st lt. USAF, 1960, advanced through grades to col., 1974; base surgeon RAF Mildenhall, 1960-61; squadron flight surgeon RAF Lakenheath, 1961-62, chief aerospace medicine, 1962-64; med. officer spl. weapons def. Air Force Weapons Lab., Kirtland AFB, N.Mex., 1965-68, asst. radiobiology research biophysics div., 1965-66, chief bionuclear group biophysics div., 1966-68; chief hosp. services, chief aerospace medicine 6550th USAF Hosp., Patrick AFB, Fla., 1968-69; dep. comdr. first med. service wing, chief flight medicine 13th Air Force Surgeon's Office, Clark AFB, 1969-70, dep. wing comdr., chief profl. services, chief disease surveillance div., 1970-71; despensary comdr., staff surgeon Space and Missile Systems Orgn., Los Angeles Air Force Sta., 1971-72; aerospace medicine resident Brooks AFB, Tex., 1972-73, Hdqrs. Air Force Logistics Command, Wright-Patterson AFB, Ohio, 1973-74, dir. aerospace medicine/dir. base med. services USAF Med. Center, Wright-Patterson AFB, 1974-77; clinic comdr. Kadena AB, Japan, 1977-80; comdr. Regional Med. Center, Clark Air Base, 1980—. Decorated Meritorious Service medal with two oak leaf clusters, Air medal, Air Force Commendation medal with 2 oak leaf clusters. Mem. Aerospace Med. Assn., AMA, Soc. USAF Flight Surgeons. Home: Cleveland OH

HAUWILLER, ROBERT PAUL, univ. adminstr.; b. St. Paul, June 24, 1934; s. Paul Heliodore and Bertha Elizabeth (Sherman) H.; B.S., St. Mary's Coll., Minn., 1956; M.S., U. Notre Dame, 1962; m. Mary Agnes Walsh, Aug. 15, 1970. High sch. tchr., Ill., 1956-63; asst. prof. math., registrar Lewis U., Lockport, Ill., 1963-68; asst. registrar Chgo. State U., 1968-70, dir. instl. research and univ. relations, 1976—, acting v.p. adminstrv. affairs, 1979—; dir. admissions and records, prof. math. Governors State U., Park Forest, Ill., 1968-76. NSF grantee, 1960-61. Mem. Am. Math. Assn., Assn. Institutional Research (com. for advancement and support of edn.), Phi Delta Kappa. Roman Catholic. Club: K.C. (4 deg.). Home: 661 Sullivan Ln Park Forest South IL 60466 Office: Chicago State Univ 95th St and King Dr Chicago IL 60628

HAVEN, CARL OLE, hosp. adminstr.; b. Detroit, July 13, 1940; s. Thomas Kenneth and Marion Lucile (Reading) H.; student Albion Coll., 1958-62; A.B., Wayne State U., 1968, M.A., 1976; postgrad. U. Mich., 1977; m. Patty Ann Foor, Aug. 3, 1975; children—Leslie, Brianne, Kathryn. With St. Joseph Mercy Hosp., Pontiac, Mich., 1956-57; operating technician, Grace Hosp., Detroit, 1960-61, adminstrv. resident, 1969-70, adminstrv. asst., 1970; emergency room, River Dist. Hosp., St. Clair, Mich., 1967; asst. hosp. dir., Harper-Grace Hosp., Detroit, 1971-81; dir. mgmt. Samaritan Health Center, Sisters of Mercy Health Corp., 1981—; pres. Pre-Paid Med. Legal Services, Inc.; cons. systems analysis and design for med. care delivery, Dominican Republic, 1977; profl. cons.; chmn. affiliated med. residency program, Wayne State U., 1973; chmn. fin. com. Associated Hosps. Processing Facility Corp., 1972; med. edn. com., Met. NW Detroit Hosp. Corp., 1978; cons. Mosman Electronics Inc. Com. chmn. Explorers Council 262, Dist. 13, Boy Scouts Am. Served with M.C., U.S. Army, 1962-65. Fellow Am. Coll. Hosp. Adminstrs.; mem. Am., Mich. (shared services com. 1978) Hosp. Assns., Greater Detroit Area Hosp. Council, Hosp. Fin. Mgmt. Assn. (advanced mem.), Alpha Kappa Delta. Contbr. articles to profl. hosp., med. jours. Home: 1365 Oakland Ave Saint Clair MI 48079 Office: Samaritan Health Center Sisters of Mercy Health Corp 660 Clinton Detroit MI 48226

HAVEN, HOWARD JOEL, clin. psychologist; b. Poughkeepsie, Feb. 24, 1943; s. Arnold Aaron and Adele Haven; A.A., Dutchess Community Coll., 1963; B.A. cum laude, SUNY, Fredonia, 1965; M.A., Bowling Green State U., 1967; Ph.D., Fla. State U., 1972; m. Doreen Frances Eddy, June 15, 1966; children—Jonathan, Juliette, Daniel. Chief psychologist, supr. Wis. Div. Corrections, 1972-80; clin. psychologist Clin. Psychology Assos., Menomonee Falls, Wis., 1973—; instr. Mt. Mary Coll., Milw., 1975-79; cons. psychologist Rosalie Manor, Brookfield, Wis., 1975-79; clin. psychologist Elmbrook Family Counseling Center, Brookfield, Wis., 1980—; cons. psychologist Wis. Dept. Vocat. Rehab., 1980—, Wis. Div. Corrections, 1981—. Lic. psychologist, Wis. Mem. Milw. Soc. Clin. Hypnosis (sec.-treas. 1980-81), Nat. Register Health Service Providers in Psychology, Am. Psychol. Assn., Wis. Psychol. Assn., Milw. Psychol. Assn., Am. Assn. Correctional Psychologists, Am. Soc. Clin. Hypnosis. Unitarian. Home: 1920 Stardust Ct Waukesha WI 53186 Office: 19305 W North Ave Brookfield WI 53005

HAVERCAMP, RICHARD PAUL, engr.; b. Muscatine, Iowa, Feb. 27, 1931; s. Paul John and Vivian Icey (Vetter) H.; B.S.E.E., U. Iowa, 1955, M.S.E.E., 1957; m. Shirley B. Marti, June 25, 1961; children—Michael, Amy, Molly, Heidi, David. Design engr. Turner Microphone Co., Cedar Rapids, Iowa, 1955-57; asso. engr. Collins Radio Co., Cedar Rapids, 1957-63, sr. asso. engr., 1965-72; staff engr. DCASO, Cedar Rapids, 1963-65; chief engr. Oaktron Industries, Monroe, Wis., 1972—, mem. mgmt. bd. Mem. Am. Loudspeaker Mfrs. Assn., Sigma Xi. Presbyterian. Clubs: Geneva Golf and Country, Masons. Home: Rural Route 2 Marion IA 52302 Office: 1000 30th Monroe WI 53566

HAVERLY, MAVIS ARLINE, educator; b. Ashley, N.D., July 10, 1927; d. John J. and Emilia (Becker) Rau; B.A., Jamestown Coll., 1948; postgrad. S.D. State U., 1967, No. State Coll.; m. Oscar Kenneth Haverly, Nov. 23, 1949; 1 son, Jon Keith. Bus. tchr. Britton (S.D.) High Sch., 1948-54, 56—. Recipient S.D. Bus. Tchr. of Yr. award, 1975; S.D. Journalism Tchrs. Founders award, 1977. Mem. NEA, Am. Vocat. Assn., S.D. Edn. Assn., Britton Edn. Assn., S.D. Bus. Office Edn. Assn. Republican. Lutheran. Home: 510 11th Ave Britton SD 57430 Office: Britton High School 759 5th St Britton SD 57430

HAWES, NANCYE ELIZABETH (MRS. GEORGE JASON HAWES), newspaperwoman; b. Somerset, Ky., Mar. 10, 1932; d. William Henderson and Ava Agnes (Foster) Smith; grad. high sch.; m. George Jason Hawes, Feb. 11, 1950; children—George Kelly, William Kevin, Kimberly Ellen. With Anderson (Ind.) Herald, 1965—, bridal editor, 1967-68, women's editor, 1968-72, editor Accent on Living, 1972-74, asst. news editor, 1974-75, city editor 1976-77, area news editor, 1977—, asso. editor, 1979—. Chmn., Mental Health Blue Bell Ball Com., 1965; asst. leader Wapehani council Girl Scouts U.S.A., 1971; public relations dir. Kikthawenund council Boy Scouts Am., 1966-70; mem. Hoosiers for Equal Rights Amendment. Bd. dirs. Madison County Assn. for Mental Health, 1965-73, Planned Parenthood Madison County, A.R.C. Recipient Unknown Scout award, 1957; award AP; certificate of merit Heart Fund Ind., 1971. Mem. Women's Orch. Guild, YWCA, NAACP, Urban League, Indpls., Press Club, Lady Elks, Women of Moose, Women in Communications, Women's Press Club Ind. (editor state newsletter, 1st v.p. 1978-79, pres. 1979-82), Nat. Fedn. Press Women, Sigma Delta Chi (pres. 1977—), Beta Sigma Phi (Girl of Year award 1964). Mem. Christian Ch. Clubs: Exchangettes (v.p. 1970-72) Soroptomist (pres. 1970-72). Home: 5122 Pearl St Anderson IN 46014 Office: PO Box 1090 Anderson IN 46015

HAWK, JEFFERY LEE, mgmt. analyst; b. Chillicothe, Ohio, Jan. 4, 1946; s. Donald Lee and Regina Ann (Breen) H.; B.A., John Carroll U., 1968; M.A., Miami U., Oxford, Ohio, 1969; postgrad. Ind. U., 1974—; m. Margaret Jennifer Schuer, Aug. 31, 1968; children—Donald Lee, Jeanne Marie. Dir. Speaker Bur., instr. speech Miami U. Oxford, 1969-70; asso. instr. speech, dir. speakers bur., dept. speech Ind. U., Bloomington, 1972-74; mgmt. analyst, orgn. materiel evaulation div., combat devel. directorate U.S. Army, Adminstrn. Center, Ft. Benjamin Harrison, Ind., 1974—, also dep. comptroller, civilian career program mgr. Office of Comptroller, U.S. Army Fin. and Acctg. Center; instr. speech Vincennes U., 1975—. Volunteer, Cleve. Welfare Fedn., 1965-67. Served as info. officer, speech writer AUS, 1970-72. Mem. John Carroll U., Miami U. alumni assns., VFW. Republican. Roman Catholic. Home: 2644 Sheffield Dr Indianapolis IN 46229

HAWKINS, DONALD WAYNE, radio sta. exec., clergyman; b. Birmingham, Ala., Nov. 22, 1945; s. James Robert and Juanita May (Edwards) H.; B.A., Southeastern Bible Coll., 1967; Th.M., Dallas Theol. Sem., 1974; m. Kathy Sue Robbins, May 11, 1966; children—Karen and Donna (twins), Brent. Ordained to ministry Conservative Bapt. Ch., 1966; pastor Faith Baptist Ch., Birmingham, 1965-66, Hueytown (Ala.) Bible Ch., 1966-69, Park Dr. Bapt. Ch., Hillsboro, Tex., 1969-73; announcer, morning air personality, news dir. Sta. KHBR AM-FM, Hillsboro, 1970-73; news corr. Sta. KRLD, Dallas, 1970-73; air personality, KDTY, Dallas, Tex., 1973, 74; pastor Moss Bluff Bible Ch., Lake Charles, La., 1973-78, Woodson Ave Bible Ch., Overland Park, Mo., 1978—; gen. mgr. Sta. KLJC, Kansas City, Mo., 1978—; asst. prof., chmn. dept. communications Calvary Bible Coll., Kansas City, 1978—; dir. Bible Conf. and Missions, Reeves, La., Effective Evangelism, Edinburg, Tex., Messianic Witness, Overland Park. Mem. Greater Kansas City Broadcasters Assn. Home: 6700 Reeds Overland Park KS 66204 Office: Calvary Bible College Kansas City MO 64147

HAWKINS, GARY CARSON, mktg. exec.; b. Poplar Bluff, Mo., Mar. 11, 1953; s. Douglas C. and Vesta I. (Crow) H.; E.M.T., St. Louis Coll. Pharmacy, 1974; B.S.N., St. Louis U., 1977; postgrad. in bus. adminstrn. So. Ill. U.; m. Karen Dawn Meyer, Nov. 1, 1975; 1 son,

Benjamin Carson. Registered nurse emergency room Luth. Med. Center, St. Louis, 1975-77; clin. coordinator County Hosp., St. Louis, 1977-79; customer service mgr., field sales adminstr. Chemetron Corp., St. Louis, 1979, mgr. mktg./sales adminstrn., 1980—. Instr., Am. Heart Assn., 1980. Mem. Am. Mgmt. Assn. Home: 2515 Pheasant Run Maryland Heights MO 63043 Office: 1720 Sublette Ave Saint Louis MO 63110

HAWKINS, GEORGE OLIVER, animal feed co. exec.; b. Antioch, Ill., Apr. 13, 1920; s. Arthur McKinley and Harriet Gertrude (Miller) H.; student U. Ill., 1938-39; m. Virginia Mae Ames, Nov. 23, 1942 (dec. 1946); 1 son, Arthur; m. 2d, Sally Elizabeth Welch, June 28, 1948; children—Lark, Scott. Owner, operator Mount Hatcheries, Antioch, 1947-57; sales mgr. FS Services, Inc., Bloomington, Ill., 1952-65; v.p., gen. mgr. Hales & Hunter Co., Inc., Chgo., 1965-69; gen. mgr. Nixon Feed div. ConAgra, Inc., Omaha, 1969-74; pres. Honeggers & Co., Inc., Fairbury, Ill., 1974—, also dir.; pres. Pioneer Pellets, 1967-69; chmn. bd. Central Farm Credit Corp., 1974-78. Mem. vestry Episcopal Ch., 1949-56; mem. Sch. Bd., Antioch, 1950-53; town auditor Antioch Twp., 1960-63; bd. dirs. Immigrant Service League, Chgo., 1966-70, Travelers Aid Soc., Chgo., 1968-70. Served with USAAF, 1942-46. Mem. Am. Feed Mfrs. Assn. (dir.), Fairbury (Ill.) Assn. Commerce (pres. elect 1980). Republican. Clubs: Masons; Antioch Lions (pres. 1959); Moose. Contbr. articles to profl. publs. Home: PO Box 297 Antioch IL 60002 Office: 201 W Locust St Fairbury IL 61739

HAWKINS, KIRK VAN, recruiting exec., mgmt. cons.; b. Dodge City, Kans., May 9, 1942; s. Marvin Eugene and Wahneta Virginia (Jones) H.; A.A., Dodge City Jr. Coll., 1963; B.S.B., Emporia State U., 1965; m. Carole Janine Tatera, Nov. 1, 1969; children—Brenda, Todd, Kip. New bus. rep. Western Power & Gas Co., Liberal, Kans., 1965-66; dir. program review Blue Cross & Blue Shield of Kans., Topeka, 1966-75; clinic adminstr. Dodge City (Kans.) Med. Center, 1975-76; self-employed as cons. in health care mgmt., Topeka, 1976—; pres. Mgmt. Recruiters Topeka, Inc., 1978—; guest lectr. Kans. U. Med. Center, Kansas City, St. Joseph Hosp. and Med. Center, Wichita, Kans., 1977-78. Active Downtown Topeka, Inc. Mem. Med. Group Mgmt. Assn., Soc. Profl. Bus. Cons., Broadcast Music Inst., Topeka C. of C. Methodist. Club: Optimist. Home: 2500 SE Faxon Dr Topeka KS 66605 Office: 700 Kansas Ave Suite 707 Topeka KS 66603

HAWKINS, ROBERT LYON, JR., chem. co. exec.; b. Cleve., Apr. 2, 1922; s. Robert Lyon and Catherine (Hanselman) H.; B.S. in Chem. Engring., Case Inst. Tech., 1947, M.S. in Indsl. Chemistry, 1956; m. Patricia O'Callaghan Boswell, Nov. 9, 1968; children—Robert Lyon III, Anne S., John W.; stepchildren—William O. Boswell, James T. Boswell. Paint chemist Empire Varnish Co. (name changed to Waterlox Chem. & Coatings Corp., 1967), Cleve., 1947-50, asso. tech. dir., 1950-56, corp. sec., 1950-60, exec. v.p., 1956-61, chmn. bd., chief exec. officer, 1961—. Bd. dirs. Cleve. Paint-Up Clean-Up Fix-Up Campaign, 1961-62. Served to 1st lt., USAF, 1942-46. Fellow Am. Inst. Chemists; mem. A.A.A.S., Am. Chem. Soc., Am. Mgmt. Assn., Cleve. Paint Varnish and Lacquer Assn. (pres. 1961-62, exec. bd. 1970-71), Cleve. Soc. Paint Tech. (exec. com. 1968-71), Citizens League Cleve., Cleve. Art Mus., Mus. Natural Hist., Alpha Chi Sigma, Beta Theta Pi. Clubs: Hermit (dir. 1976-79) (Cleve.); Mayfield Country. Patentee in field. Home: 10000 Lake Shore Blvd Bratenahl Cleveland OH 44108 Office: 9808 Meech Ave Cleveland OH 44105

HAWKINS, STEPHEN SYDNEY, psychologist; b. Fairmont, W.Va., Jan. 13, 1947; s. George Elmor and Eva Doreene (Hodgetts) H.; B.S., Eastern Mich. U., 1970, postgrad. 1971-72; M.S.W., U. Mich., 1973, Ph.D., 1977; postgrad. Mich. State U., 1978-79; m. A. Lynne Babbidge, Jan. 22, 1972; children—Aaron Joshua, Justin Aston, Whitney Taylor. With Hawthorn Center, Northville, Mich., 1967-68, Fisher Home for Children, Farmington, Mich., 1971-72; adj. lectr. U. Mich., Ann Arbor, 1977-80; mgmt. analyst Exec. Cons. Services, Farmington, 1978-79; social work cons. spl. services Farmington Schs., 1972—, dist. dept. chmn., 1977-78; staff psychologist Innervision Neuropsychiat. Center, Southfield, Mich., 1980—; cons. Mich. Dept. Edn., levels 13-15; resource cons. Sanctuary Adolescent Shelter, Pleasant Ridge, Mich., 1975—. Cert. social worker; lic. family and marriage counselor. Mem. Am. Psychol. Assn., Mich. Edn. Assn., NEA, Acad. Psychologists in Marital, Sex and Family Therapy, Am. Group Psychotherapy Assn., Tau Kappa Epsilon, Interdisciplinary Mental Health Assn. Contbr. articles to profl. jours. Home: 21835 Clover Ln Novi MI 48050 Office: 26555 Evergreen St Suite 700 Southfield MI 48076

HAWKINSON, JOHN, investment mgmt. co. exec.; b. Walker, Iowa, May 26, 1912; s. Theodore W. and Gertrude (Nietert) H.; A.B., U. Iowa, 1936; m. Florence Mallaire, Oct. 12, 1946; children—Diane, Judith. With Halsey, Stuart & Co., Inc., Chgo., 1936-41, 46-49; v.p., treas., dir. Central Life Assurance Co., Des Moines, 1950-62; pres., dir. Kemper Fin. Services, Inc., Chgo., 1962—, Tech. Fund, Inc., 1963—, Kemper Income & Capital Preservation Fund, Inc., Kemper Money Market Fund, Inc., Kemper Growth Fund, Inc., Kemper Total Return Fund, Inc., Kemper Summit Fund, Inc., Kemper Mpcl. Bond Fund, Kemper Option Income Fund, Inc., Kemper High Yield Fund, Inc., Cash Equivalent Fund, Kemper Fund for Govt. Guaranteed Securities; dir. Am. Fed. Savs. & Loan Assn. Central Iowa, Mapco, Inc., Kansas City So. Industries, Kansas City So. R.R., La. & Ark. R.R., Berkley & Co., Gen. Growth Properties, UMC Industries, Inc., Ryder System, Inc. Mem. Securities Adv. Com. to Sec. State Ill. Bd. dirs. U. Iowa Found.; bd. govs., also mem. divisional com., investment adviser div. Investment Co. Inst., Washington. Served with AUS, 1942-46; col. Res., ret. Decorated Legion Merit. Mem. Nat. Fedn. Fin. Analysts. Clubs: Glen View (Golf, Ill.); Chicago, Attic (Chgo.). Home: 660 Winnetka Mews Apt 416 Winnetka IL 60093 Office: 120 S LaSalle St Chicago IL 60603

HAWKS, GARY DALE, univ. adminstr.; b. Ypsilanti, Mich., Aug. 24, 1933; s. Earl and Lucy (Van Riper) H.; B.B.A., Mich. State U., 1958; m. Shirley J. Stinedurf, Aug. 23, 1958; children—Cheryl, Michael. With Gen. Motors Corp., Detroit, 1959-64, Ford Motor Co., Detroit, 1964; supr. accounts receivable Eastern Mich U., Ypsilanti, 1964, dir. personnel, 1964-70, exec. dir. univ. relations, 1970-72, v.p. univ. relations, 1972—. Pres., Ypsilanti Twp. Planning Commn., 1980, Visitors and Conv. Bur., 1980-81. Served with U.S. Army, 1953-55. Named Boss of Yr., Ypsilanti Jaycees, 1981, Citizen of Week, Sta. WAAM, 1981. Mem. Ypsilanti C. of C., Assn. Governing Bds. Colls. and Univs. (nat. com.). Lutheran. Clubs: Moose, Forum. Past chmn. Eastern United Fund Campaign; div. chmn. Washtenaw United Way, 1974. Home: 1323 Mesa Dr Ypsilanti MI 48197 Office: Eastern Mich U Ypsilanti MI 48197

HAWLEY, ELLIS WAYNE, historian; b. Cambridge, Kans., June 2, 1929; s. Pearl Washington and Gladys Laura (Logsdon) H.; B.A., U. Wichita, 1950; M.A., U. Kans., 1951; Ph.D. (research fellow), U. Wis., 1959; m. Sofia Koltun, Nov. 3, 1953; children—Arnold Jay, Agnes Fay. Instr. to prof. history N. Tex. State U., 1957-68; prof. history Ohio State U., 1968-69, U. Iowa, 1969—; hist. cons. Public Papers of the Presidents: Hoover, 1974-78. Served to 1st lt. inf., AUS, 1951-53. N. Tex. State U. Faculty Devel. grantee, 1967-68, U. Iowa, 1975-76. Mem. Am. Hist. Assn., Orgn. Am. Historians, So. Hist. Assn., Soc. History Edn., AAUP, Iowa Hist. Soc. Democrat. Author: The New Deal and the Problem of Monopoly, 1966; The Great War and the Search for a Modern Order, 1979; (with others) Herbert Hoover and the Crisis of American Capitalism, 1973, Herbert Hoover as Secretary of Commerce, 1981; contbr. articles profl. jours., essays to books. Home: 2524 Washington St Iowa City IA 52240 Office: Dept of History University of Iowa Iowa City IA 52242

HAWLEY, HELEN MARY CULP (MRS. ARCHIE HAWLEY), nurse; b. nr. Sinking Spring, Pa., Feb. 19, 1917; d. Allen M. and Bessie M. (Cutler) Culp; R.N., Homeopathic Hosp. Chs. of Nursing, Reading, Pa., 1938; certificate in pub. health nursing, Simmons Coll., Boston, 1940; B.S., Millikin U., Decatur, Ill., 1965; M.B.A., Sangamon State U.; m. Archie Hawley, Sept. 16, 1944; 1 dau., Margaret Louise. Staff nurse Pottstown Homeopathic Hosp., Pottstown, Pa., 1938-38, Vis. Nurse Assn., Reading, Pa., 1940-41, Vis. Nurse Assn., Wilmington, Del., 1940-41; pub. health nurse USPHS, 1941-46; supr. Vis. Nurse Assn., Decatur, Ill., 1949-56; pub. health instr. Sch. Nursing, Decatur Macon County Hosp., 1957-62; instr. Decatur Sch. Practical Nursing, 1962-65; med.-surg. coordinator sch. nursing Mennonite Hosp., Bloomington, Ill., 1965; formerly curriculum coordinator, now cons. hosp. div. Ill. Dept. Pub. Health, Springfield, Ill. Active ARC; bd. dirs. region IX, Ill. Heart Assn., 1949—, Sangamon County Vis. Nurse Assn., Springfield; mem. Macon County Mental Health Assn. Mem. Am. Nurses Assn., Am., Ill. pub. health assns., Am. Hosp. Assn., Profl. Nurse Assn. of Am. Coll. Obstetrics and Gynecology, Internat. Platform Assn., Beta Sigma Phi. Methodist. Club: Ill. Fedn. Bus. and Profl. Women's (dist. chmn. 1964-65, parliamentarian). Home: PO Box 771 Decatur IL 60525 Office: 525 Jefferson St Springfield IL 62761

HAWLEY, RICHARD ORIN, mfg. co. exec.; b. Cambridge, Kans., Aug. 16, 1944; s. George Fitzure and Elsie May (Manahan) H.; student Southwestern Coll., 1962-63; B.S., Pittsburg State U., 1966; m. Betty Burneta Luce, Aug. 12, 1962; children—Richard O., Robert Warren, Ronald Allen. Mgmt. trainee Johnson-Carper, 1966-67; area supr. Brunswick Corp., 1967-69; corp. dir. Q.C. Ward Furniture, 1969-70; with DeSoto, Inc., 1970-77, project dir., 1977; v.p., gen. mgr. Soundesign Ind., Santa Claus, 1981—. Active Boy Scouts Am. Mem. Indsl. Fire Fighters Assn., Pittsburg State U. Alumni Assn. Clubs: Christmas Lake Village Golf and Tennis, Petroleum. Home: PO Box 381 Santa Claus IN 47579 Office: PO Box 61 Santa Claus IN 47579

HAWLEY, STEVEN CARL, sch. adminstr.; b. Healdsburg, Calif., Jan. 24, 1946; s. Willis C. and Ann (Bradley) H.; A.B., U. Calif., Berkeley, 1967; M.Ed., Miami U., Ohio, 1974; postgrad. U. Cin., 1979—; m. Audrey Janice Mowitt, July 10, 1971; children—Robyn, Jason. Tchr. trainer Peace Corps, Dominican Republic, 1967-69; tchr./prin. Cerro Corp., Peru, 1969-72; research asst./instr. Miami U., Oxford, Ohio, 1973-74; tchr. Greenhills-Forest Park Sch. Dist., Cin., 1974-77, project dir. (tchr. edn. redesign, ACCS curriculum project, computer utilization, Title VI desegregation, 1977—; cons. Ohio Dept. Edn., U. Cin. Miami U., Youngstown U., U. Central Fla.; mem. coordinating com. Annehurst Curriculum Classification System Network, 1979—. Mem. Forest Park Housing Commn., 1981—. Recipient Service award, PTA, 1975-76. Mem. Am. Ednl. Research Assn., Assn. for Supervision and Curriculum Devel., Phi Delta Kappa. Republican. Methodist. Author: A School District's View of Teacher Training, 1980; ACCS Training Manual, 1980; ACCS Mathematics Directory of Topics, 1980; editor: Grad. Life, 1973, TERCey, 1976-80, TESN&N, 1977-80, ACCS Facts and Figures, 1978-80, CENTERpieces, 1980—; contbr. articles to profl. jours. Home: 10840 Carnegie Dr Cincinnati OH 45240 Office: 1501 Kingsbury Dr Cincinnati OH 45240

HAWTHORNE, DOUGLAS LAWSON, banker; b. Chgo., Feb. 10, 1942; s. Francis R. and Dorothea (Lawson) H.; B.A., Wabash Coll., 1963; postgrad. Grad. Sch. Bus., N.Y. U., 1963-69; m. Sarah Jane Archibald, Apr. 15, 1967; 1 son, Bryan Douglas. With Irving Trust Co., 1963-67; corporate credit mgr. CBS, N.Y.C., 1967-69; v.p., treas. Careers, Inc., N.Y.C., 1969-71; dir. research and planning Third Nat. Bank & Trust Co., Dayton, Ohio, 1971-74, v.p., 1974-75, sr. v.p., 1975-78, exec. v.p., dir., 1978—; dir., sec. XYOvest, Inc. subs. Third Nat. Bank & Trust Co. Trustee, treas. Miami Valley Hosp., 1976—, chmn. fin. and endowment com., 1977—; div. chmn. United Way, 1974-76; trustee, mem. exec. com., v.p. adminstrn. Miami Valley council Boy Scouts Am., 1975-78; mem. adv. bd. Inst. for Community and Organizational Devel., Wright State U. Mem. Am. Inst. Banking, Bank Adminstrn. Inst., Dayton Area C. of C., Phi Gamma Delta. Clubs: Moraine Country, Racquet, Dayton Indoor Tennis (Dayton). Office: Third Nat Bank & Trust Co 34 N Main St Dayton OH 45402

HAWVER, WILLIAM LLOYD, supt. schs.; b. Kansas City, Kans., Apr. 7, 1936; s. Lloyd Warner and Leona Agnes (Girten) H.; B.S., Rockhurst Coll., 1963; M.A., U. Kans., 1965; Ed.D., U. Nebr., 1971; m. Mary Jane Halbur, Aug. 10, 1963; children—John William, Thomas Halbur. Dir. pupil personnel services Bellevue (Nebr.) public schs., 1969-74; supt. schs. Father Flanagan's Boys Home, Boys Town, Nebr., 1974-76; post-doctoral fellow, dept. ednl. adminstrn. U. Nebr., 1976-77; supt. schs. Hutchinson (Kans.) public schs., 1977—; adj. prof. Creighton U., Omaha. Bd. dirs. Kans. Sci. and Arts Found.; trustee Mt. Michael Abbey High Sch.; mem. edn. com. Omaha Met. Planning Agy. mem. nat. bd. dirs. Jesuit Program for Living and Learning, St. Louis, 1981—. Served with USAF, 1956-60. Named one of N. Am.'s Top Ednl. Execs., Exec. Educator, 1980. Mem. Am. Assn. Sch. Adminstrs., Am. Personnel and Guidance Assn., PTA (life), Kans. Adminstrs. Club, Kans. Assn. Sch. Adminstrs., Phi Delta Kappa. Club: Rotary. Office: Hutchinson Pub Schs 1520 N Plum St Hutchinson KS 67501

HAY, RICHARD K., ednl. adminstr.; b. Parsons, Kans., Mar. 8, 1942; s. Harold V. and Marjorie L. (House) H.; B.A., Pittsburg State U., 1962; M.A., Kans. State U., 1963, Ph.D., 1969; m. Marsha Woods Finney, Jan. 10, 1981. Instr. Mo. So. Coll., Joplin, 1963-64; instr. Pittsburg (Kans.) State U., 1964-65, asst. prof., 1966-68, asso. prof., 1968-72, prof., 1972—, dean Gladys A. Kelce Sch. Bus. and Econs., 1975—; cons. in field. Mem. Am. Econ. Assn., Kans. Econ. Assn. (editor Proceedings, 1978), Acad. of Mgmt., Omicron Delta Epsilon, Phi Alpha Theta, Delta Mu Delta. Editor Pittsburg State University Business and Economic Review, 1975—; contbr. writings to publs. in field. Office: School of Business Pittsburg State Univ Pittsburg KS 66762

HAYDEN, ALLAN LEROY, mech. engr.; b. San Jose, Ill., May 17, 1930; s. William G. and Gladys G. (Potts) H.; student Bradley U., Peoria, Ill., 1962-64; m. Donna L. Stark, Aug. 5, 1962; children—Jan Eric, Noel Allan, Kimberly Elisabeth. Parts mgr. Truman Woll Implement Co., San Jose, 1948-54; service mgr. Lundberg Electric Co., Delavan, Ill., 1956-60; with Ill. Bell Telephone Co., 1960—, mgr. mech. engring., Chgo., 1978—. Served with AUS, 1954-56. Mem. Assn. Energy Engrs., Am. Mgmt. Assn. Congregationalist. Home: 8 Sir Galahad Dr Joliet IL 60436 Office: 225 W Randolph St Chicago IL 60606

HAYDEN, FRED REID, research and devel. orgn. exec.; b. Gary, Ind., Mar. 29, 1935; s. Fred Vivien and Marian Josephine (Nelson) H.; B.S., U. Ill., 1958. Adminstrv. mgr. Ill. Inst. Tech. Research Inst., Chgo., 1962-74, dir. adminstrn., Annapolis, Md., 1975; mgr. contracts Am. Gas Assn., Arlington, Va., 1976-77; dir. contracts Gas Research Inst., Chgo., 1978—; bus. mgr. NATO Advanced Study Inst., Munich, W. Germany, 1967. Served with U.S. Army, 1958-60. Mem. Nat. Contract Mgmt. Assn., Am. Mgmt. Assn. Republican. Office: 8600 W Bryn Mawr Ave Chicago IL 60631

HAYDEN, LEROY AUSTIN, state senator; b. Satanta, Kans., July 31, 1927; s. Austin Joseph and Goldie Irene (Schonlow) H.; grad. high sch.; m. Mavis Fern Gray Barker, 1958; children—Gary Lynn, Steven Ray, Robyn Barker, Marsha Kay Hayden Wood, Michael, Shawn. Owner-mgr., Hayden Clothiers, Satanta, 1961-77; mem. Kans. Senate, 1977—. Mem. Kans. Bur. Health Planning, 1969-76. Served with USN, 1945-46. Mem. Am. Legion. Club: Elks. Address: PO Box 458 Satanta KS 67870*

HAYDEN, MARJORIE SIEWERT, banker; b. Mpls., Dec. 21, 1930; d. Henry Alex and Marjorie Minkler Siewert; B.A., Carleton Coll., 1953; postgrad. U. Minn., 1957-58; children—Joseph, Grace. With First Nat. Bank, Little Falls, Minn., 1949—, pres., 1971—. Past pres. Carnegie Library Bd., Lindbergh Sch. PTA; vestry Episcopal Ch.; past vice chmn. Morrison County Democratic-Farmer-Labor Party. Mem. Nat. Assn. Bank Women, Ind. Bankers Assn., Little Falls C. of C. (dir.), Minn. Civil Liberties Union (past dir.). Office: First Nat Bank Little Falls MN 56345

HAYDEN, PAUL ALLAN, educator; b. Williston, N.D., Jan. 29, 1949; s. George L. and Ortense M. (Bernier) H.; B.A., Moorhead State U., 1971, M.S., 1972; Ph.D., Purdue U., 1975; m. Elaine M. Stauder, Aug. 16, 1975; 1 son, Daniel Joseph. David Ross research fellow Purdue U., West Lafayette, Ind., 1974-75; asst. prof. speech and lang. pathology U. Wis., River Falls, 1975—; cons. to area hosps. and nursing homes. Mem. Am. Speech and Hearing Assn. (cert.), Wis. Speech and Hearing Assn., Phi Eta Sigma, Phi Kappa Phi. Roman Catholic. Contbr. articles to profl. jours. Home: Route 1 Box 187B Ellsworth WI 54011 Office: U Wis River Falls WI 54022

HAYDEN, VIRGINIA EVA, pharm. co. cons.; b. Midland, Mich., May 20, 1927; d. Robert James and Altheda Mae (Wood) H.; B.A., Mich. State U., 1949; m. Donald Conrad, Feb. 14, 1952 (div.) Audit clk. City of Midland, Mich., summers 1945-49; stock inventory clk. Dow Chem. Co., 1949-50; budget clk. Upjohn Co., Kalamazoo, 1950-52, budget analyst, 1952-57, accountant, 1957-65, acctg. specialist, 1965-69, budget coordinator, 1969-72, budget mgr., 1972—, exec. devel. cons., 1978—; lectr. local colls.; advisor Center for Women's Services, Western Mich. U.; co-founder, advisor Grow, Orgn. for Upjohn Women. Team leader Community Communication Project; co-founder Kalamazoo Network; bd. dirs. Kalamazoo Area Alcohol and Drug Abuse Council. Recipient Upjohn award, 1970. Mem. Am. Soc. for Tng. and Devel., Altrusa Internat. (pres.), Kalamazoo Nature Center, Audubon Soc., Mich. State Univ. Alumni, Nat. Wildlife Assn. Home: 8207 Bruning Kalamazoo MI 49002 Office: 7000 Portage Rd Kalamazoo MI 49002

HAYDOCK, WALTER JAMES, banker; b. Chgo., Dec. 14, 1947; s. Joseph Albert and Lillian V. (Adeszko) H.; student Harvard Bus. Coll., 1969-71, Daily Coll., 1971-73; B.S. in Acctg., DePaul U., 1976; m. Bonnie Jean Thompson, Aug. 22, 1970; 1 dau., Nicole Lynn. Computer operator, jr. programmer Pepper Constrn. Co., Chgo., 1972-73; input analyst Continental Bank, Chgo., 1973-76, data control supr., 1976-79, corporate fixed asset adminstr., 1979—; partner Day's End Motel, Wisconsin Dells, Wis., 1977—. Mem. Wis. Innkeepers Assn., Wisconsin Dells C. of C. Home: 6054 Rob Roy Dr Oak Forest IL 60452 Office: Continental Bank 231 S LaSalle St Chicago IL 60693

HAYES, ALICE BOURKE, biologist, educator; b. Chgo., Dec. 31, 1937; d. William Joseph and Mary Alice (Cawley) Bourke; B.S., Mundelein Coll., Chgo., 1959; M.S., U. Ill., 1960; Ph.D., Northwestern U., 1972; m. John J. Hayes, Sept. 2, 1961. Researcher, Mcpl. Tb Sanitarium, Chgo., 1960-62; mem. faculty Loyola U., Chgo., 1962—, chmn. dept. natural sci., 1968-77, dean natural scis. div., 1977-80, asso. v.p., 1980—, asso. prof., 1974-77, prof., 1977—. Fellow in botany U. Ill., 1959-60, NSF, 1969-71; grantee Am. Orchid Soc., 1967, HEW, 1969, NSF, 1975, FIPSE, 1978, NASA, 1980. Mem. Am. Soc. Plant Physiology, Bot. Soc. Am., Soc. Ill. Microbiologists, Am. Soc. Microbiology, Internat. Soc. Human and Animal Mycology, AAAS, Am. Inst. Biol. Scis., Assn. Midwest Coll. Biology Tchrs. Roman Catholic. Contbr. profl. publs. Home: 6190 N Indian Rd Chicago IL 60646 Office: 820 N Michigan Ave Chicago IL 60611

HAYES, ARTHUR CHESTER, safety cons., state legislator; b. Ft. Wayne, Ind., Aug. 24, 1918; s. Walter F. and Marie P. (Hardesty) H.; B.S., Ind. U., 1948; m. Miriam E. Peck, Feb. 1, 1946 (dec. Nov. 1968); children—Arthur C., Bethany M., Gayle W. Crosby. Sales corr. Magnavox Corporation, 1948-54; supr. Budget State Hwy. Dept., 1954-58; owner Vernors Bottling Co., Ft. Wayne, 1959-63; became dist. mgr. Colonial Life & Accident Ins. Co., 1963; mem. Ind. Ho. of Reps., 1963-72, 77—, ho. mem. Ind. Statutory com. on Commn. on Protection and Advocacy for Developmentally Disabled, 1977-78; safety cons. Chmn. Interstate Cooperation Com., Recodification of Cities and Towns Commn.; mem. Sesquicentennial Commn.; chmn. speakers bur. Ind. Am. Revolution Bicentennial Commn.; mem. Ind. Am. Negro Emancipation Centennial Commn. Served with AUS, 1941-45. Mem. Ft. Wayne C. of C., Am. Legion. Clubs: Ft. Wayne Civitan (pres. 1963-68; lt. gov. Midwest 1967). Home: 2001 Oakland St Fort Wayne IN 46808 Office: State House Bldg Indianapolis IN 46204

HAYES, CHARLES EDWARD, newspaper editor; b. Evanston, Ill., Mar. 13, 1931; s. Chester K. and Dorothy (Wilger) H.; B.S., Wittenberg U., 1953; M.S. in Journalism, Northwestern U., 1955. With Paddock Publs., Inc., Arlington Heights, Ill., 1954-75, newspaper series on social problems, 1958-75, exec. editor, 1960-68, editor in chief, 1968-75, v.p., 1970-75, publisher, 1971-75; v.p., editor Area Publs. Corp., Hinsdale, Ill., 1975—. Mem. adv. com. Suburban Press Found., Inc., Chgo., 1967-69; v.p. Opportunity Council Inc., 1958-59, pres., 1959-60. Chmn. bd. dirs. Salvation Army Community Counselling Center, 1971-75, mem. 1968—; bd. dirs. Salvation Army Family Service, 1978—, vice chmn., 1979—; mem. Ill. Health Facilities Authority, 1973—. mem. consumer adv. bd. Northwest Surgicare; community leadership tng. bd. Harper Coll. Recipient Instrument Peace award Christian Family Movement, 1960; named Arlington Heights Jr. C. of C. Man of Year, 1964. Mem. Chgo. Press Club, Suburban Press Club (pres. 1980-81), Chgo. Headline Club (pres. 1969-70), Soc. Profl. Journalists-Sigma Delta Chi, Chgo. Press Veterans Assn., League United Latin Am. Citizens (hon.), Blue Key, Kappa Phi Kappa, Pi Delta Epsilon, Phi Kappa Psi. Contbr. monographs and articles to various publs. Home: 2703 Bel Aire Dr Arlington Heights IL 60004 Office: 765 N York Rd Hinsdale IL 60521

HAYES, DAVID JOHN, elec. component mfg. co. mktg. exec.; b. Indpls., July 30, 1943; s. Alfred Henry and Jean Alexander (Morrison) H.; A.B., Boston U., 1965; M.B.A., Cornell U., 1967. Mgmt. trainee Westinghouse Broadcasting Co., Chgo., 1967-68, Norwalk, Conn., 1968, Boston, 1968-71; nat. sales rep. NBC, Chgo., 1971-72; pres. Dana Enterprises, Chgo., 1972-75; v.p. mktg. Micron Industries

Corp., Stone Park, Ill., 1975—; dir. Haybec Enterprises, Inc., New Orleans Hotel Corp. Mem. Assn. M.B.A. Execs., Execs. Club Chgo., Salesmen with A Purpose (internat. v.p. 1980-81, Ill. pres. 1981-82), Ill. State Hist. Soc. (chmn. com. hist. markers 1980). Mem. Christian Ch. Clubs: Boston U. Chgo., Cornell Bus. Sch. Contbr. articles to Adminstrv. Sci. Quar. Home: 807 Wenonah Ave Oak Park IL 60304 Office: 1830 N 32d Ave Stone Park IL 60165

HAYES, DAVID JOHN ARTHUR, JR., lawyer; b. Chgo., July 30, 1929; s. David J.A. and Lucille M. (Johnson) H.; A.B., Harvard, 1952; LL.B., Chgo.-Kent Coll. Law, 1961; m. Anne Huston, Feb. 23, 1963; children—David J.A. III, Cary H. Admitted to Ill. bar, 1961; asst. sec., trust officer First Nat. Bank of Evanston (Ill.), 1962-63; gen. counsel Ill. State Bar Assn., 1963-66; asst. dir. Am. Bar Assn., 1966-68, div. dir., 1968-69, asst. exec. dir., 1969—; exec. dir. Naval Res. Lawyers Assn., 1971-75; asst. sec. Internat. Bar Assn., 1978—; capt. JAGC, USNR. Fellow Am. Bar Found.; mem. Ill. Bar Assn. (various coms.; assembly rep. 1972-76), Nat. Orgn. Bar Counsel (pres. 1967), Phi Alpha Delta. Contbr. to profl. jours. Home: 908 Pontiac Rd Wilmette IL 60091 Office: 1155 E 60th St Chicago IL 60637

HAYES, DAVID THOMAS, educator; b. Gallia County, Ohio, June 12, 1939; s. Buell D. and Ada I. (Harding) H.; B.S., Ohio U., 1961; M.A. in Teaching, Duke, 1965; Ph.D., Ohio State U., 1972; m. Nancy V. Clark, Aug. 19, 1961; children—Kari, John. Tchr. math. Lincoln High Sch., Cleve., 1961-65; instr. Riverside Sch. of Nursing, 1966-69; teaching asso. in math. Ohio State U., Columbus, 1965-69, asst. prof., coordinator of math. Lima campus, 1969-76; asso. prof. ednl. curriculum and instrn., math. edn. Bowling Green (Ohio) State U., 1976—. Recipient Outstanding Teaching award Lima campus Ohio State U., 1973. Mem. Nat. Council Tchrs. Math., Sch. Sci. and Math. Assn., Assn. for Supervision and Curriculum, Math. Assn. Two Yr. Colls., Ohio Assn. Two Yr. Colls., Nat. Council Suprs. of Math., Ohio Council Tchrs. Math., N.W. Ohio Computer Users Group, Phi Delta Kappa. Club: Exchange. Baptist. Home: 613 Pasteur Ave Bowling Green OH 43402 Office: Edn Bldg S College Dr Bowling Green OH 43403

HAYES, ERNEST A., ins., investment sales; b. New London, Iowa, Jan. 20, 1904; s. Alonzo D. and Margaret E. (Ferrell) H.; student Iowa Wesleyan Coll., 1921-24, H.H.D. (hon.), 1964; A.B., Washington Univ., 1924, M.S., 1926; m. Ruth Anita Irons, Feb. 13, 1937; children—Ruth Jo Ann (Mrs. Edmund J. Farrell), Janet Elizabeth (Mrs. Richard A. Dougherty). President of Central States Mutual Insurance, Assn., 1929-59; chmn. bd. Capitol Savs. & Loan Assn., 1937-77; pres. Hillsboro Savs. Bank (Iowa), 1950-76, Henry County Indsl. Devel. Corp.; chmn. bd. New London State Bank, 1945-76, Town & Country Bank, Quincy, Ill., 1974-76; dir. Hawkeye Bank & Trust Co., Burlington, Iowa, Hawkeye Ban Corp., Des Moines; pres. Hawkeye Nat. Investment Co., 1964-78; vice chmn. Hawkeye Nat. Life Ins. Co. (both Des Moines); sec., dir. Internat. Livestock, Inc., Fairfield, Iowa; dir. Henry Co. Savs. Bank, Mt. Pleasant, Measurements & Controls, Inc., Rolling Hills, Calif.; vice chmn. Iowa Bus. Devel. Credit Corp.; chmn. bd. Iowa Blue Cross; dir. Iowa Blue Shield; mem. exec. com. Nat. Adv. Council Hosp. Governing Bds. Mem. exec. com. S.E. Iowa council Boy Scouts Am.; mem. Burlington (Iowa) Youth Resources Bd.; vice chmn. Iowa Hosp. Found., Des Moines; mem. U.S. Hist. Adv. Com., Washington, Hoover Found.; chmn. Iowa Devel. Commn., 1962-78; regional Dir. U.S. Savs. Bond Div.; Republican State Finance Chmn., 1961-69; mem. Nat. Rep. Finance Com., 1961-69; chmn. bd. dirs. Henry County Meml. Hosp., Iowa Wesleyan College; trustee Midwest Research Inst., Kansas City. Recipient S.E. Iowa Man of Yr., 1961. Mem. Iowa Assn. Ind. Ins. Agts., Navy League, Sigma Phi Epsilon, Delta Sigma Pi, Omicron Delta Gamma. Methodist. Mason (Shriner). Moose, Elk. Clubs: Kiwanis, Des Moines, Lincoln (Des Moines). Home: 400 Broadway Mount Pleasant IA 52641 Office: Hayes Bldg Mount Pleasant IA 52641

HAYES, JAMES CARLTON, educator, cons.; b. Phila., Apr. 1, 1943; s. Joseph Carlton and Sonia Elizabeth (Banka) H.; B.S.E.E., U. Notre Dame, 1964, M.S. in Engring. Sci., 1967, Ph.D., 1970; m. Joanne Patricia Callahan, Aug. 10, 1968; children—Jeffrey, Jennifer. Elec. engr. Dept. U.S. Navy, Washington, 1964-67; research asst. Project Themis, U. Notre Dame (Ind.), 1967-70; faculty Purdue U., N. Central Campus, Westville, Ind., 1970—, asso. prof. engring., 1977—, chmn. tech./engring. unit, 1980—; engring. cons. Bd. dirs. Jr. Engring. Tech. Soc. Search Center, LaPorte and Porter County, Ind., 1972—; mem. consumer adv. panel No. Ind. Public Service Co., 1980—. Registered profl. engr., Ind. Mem. Ind. Soc. Profl. Engrs. (chmn. scholarship com. 1977-81, dir.-at-large 1981—), Nat. Soc. Profl. Engrs., Am. Soc. Engring. Edn., U. Notre Dame Alumni Assn., Sigma Xi. Clubs: South Bend Rugby Football (pres. 1974-75), Gt. Lakes Barbell, Notre Dame of Michigan City. Weight-lifting champion Ind., 1973. Contbr. articles to profl. jours. Home: 2106 Red Oak Dr Michigan City IN 46360 Office: Purdue U N Central Campus Westville IN 46391

HAYES, LARRY GENE, assn. exec.; b. Batesville, Ind., Nov. 16, 1939; s. Faye E. and Edna Pearl (DeLay) H.; B.A., Asbury Coll., 1965; postgrad. U. Ky., 1968; 1 dau., Kimberly Ann. Tchr., Woodford County Jr. High Sch., Versailles, Ky., 1965-67; prin. Nonesuch Elem./Jr. High Sch., Versailles, 1967-69; dir. Moser Sch., Chgo., 1969-74; dir. admissions Am. Inst. Real Estate Appraisers, Chgo., 1974-79, exec. v.p., 1979—. Mem. Am. Soc. Assn. Execs., Chgo. Soc. Assn. Execs., Execs. Club of Chgo. Office: 430 N Michigan Ave Chicago IL 60611

HAYES, MARCIE LYNN, music educator; b. Canton, Ill., May 6, 1951; d. Leo G. May and Betty Jean (Fanning) Hayes; student (scholar) Ill. State U., Normal; m. Lloyd Dayne Hayes, Jr., Sept. 20, 1969. Sec.-treas. Lewistown Plumbing & Heating, Inc. (Ill.); music tchr., Normal, Ill. Mem. Mensa. Home: Box 148 Danvers IL 61732

HAYES, MARY MARGARET, mfg. co. mgr.; b. St. Marys, Pa., Dec. 8, 1949; d. John Charles and Josephine Ann (Nekuza) H.; B.A., Duquesne U., 1971; M.B.A., Notre Dame U., 1976. Research asst. Republican Nat. Com., Washington, 1971-73; asst. to dir. ACTION, Washington, 1973-74; legis. asst. Sen. Dick Lugar, Washington, 1976-79; asso. brand mgr. Kraft, Inc., Chgo., 1979—. Staff asst. Labor for Heinz, 1971; research dir. Lugar for Senate, 1976. Mem. Am. Mktg. Assn. Roman Catholic. Club: Notre Dame. Home: 918 Linden Ave Winnetka IL 60093 Office: 1 Kraft Ct Glenview IL 60025

HAYES, RICHARD JOHNSON, assn. exec.; b. Chgo., May 25, 1933; s. David John Arthur and Lucille Margaret (Johnson) H.; B.A., Colo. Coll., 1955; J.D., Georgetown U., 1961; m. Mary R. Lynch, Dec. 2, 1961; children—Susan, Richard, John, Edward. Admitted to Ill. bar, 1961; with Sears & Streit, Chgo., 1961-63, Peterson, Lowry, Rall, Barber & Ross, Chgo., 1963-65; staff dir. Am. Bar Assn., Chgo., 1965-70; exec. dir. Internat. Assn. Ins. Counsel, Chgo., 1970—. Served to 1st lt. U.S. Army Res., 1955-57. Mem. Am., Ill. (chmn. jr. bar 1964—), Chgo. (mem. com. devel. law 1973—) bar assns., Beta Theta Pi. Roman Catholic. Club: Rotary/One of Chgo. Contbr. articles to legal jours. Home: 1920 Thornwood Ave Wilmette IL 60091 Office: 20 N Wacker Dr Chicago IL 60606

HAYFORD, WARREN J., mfg. co. exec.; b. 1929; B.S., U.S. Mil. Acad., 1952; married. With The Continental Group, Inc., 1955—, asst. to gen. mgr. sales metal ops., 1955-57, salesman Eastern Metal div., 1957-60, dist. sales mgr. Eastern Metal div., 1960-63, gen. mgr. new container metal ops., 1963-66, gen. mgr. mktg. and product planning, 1966-67, gen. mgr. mktg., 1967-68, v.p. mktg., 1968-69, v.p. and gen. mgr. paperboard and Kraft Paper div., 1969-71, v.p. and gen. mgr. paper sales and converting ops., 1971-73, sr. v.p. and dir. corporate staff, 1973-74, chief fin. and adminstrv. officer, 1974-75, exec. v.p., after 1974; pres. Continental Can Co. div., 1975-79; pres., chief operating officer Internat. Harvester Co., 1979—. Served as 1st lt. U.S. Army, 1946-55. Office: 401 N Michigan Ave Chicago IL 60611

HAYMES, RICHARD REUEL, psychologist; b. Springfield, Mo., Apr. 26, 1944; s. James Reuel and Helen Elizabeth (Goddard) H.; B.S. in Bus. Adminstrn., U. Mo., 1968, M.Ed., 1972, Ph.D., 1978; m. Virginia L. Humphrey, Sept. 9, 1967; children—Scott Matthew, Allyson Brook. Asso. dean students SE Mo. State U., Cape Girardeau, 1972-75; counseling psychologist in pvt. practice, Springfield, 1978—. Bd. dirs. Hospice of SW Mo., Springfield, 1980—; exec. bd. Ozark Area Psychol. Assn., 1980—. Mem. Mo. Psychol. Assn. (dir. continuing edn. 1981—), Am. Psychol. Assn., Am. Soc. Psychologists in Pvt. Practice, Phi Delta Kappa. Home: 919 E Powell St Springfield MO 65807 Office: 1443 N Robberson St Springfield MO 65802

HAYNES, FRANK MAURICE, profl. adminstrn. co. exec.; b. Kansas City, Mo., June 1, 1935; s. William John and Marguerite Ida (Brown) H.; B.B.A., U. Colo., 1958; M.B.A. with honors, Roosevelt U., 1974; postgrad. Sch. Mgmt. Northwestern U., 1974-75; m. Arlene Claire Kidd, June 25, 1966; children—Jonathan Frank and Elizabeth Arlene (twins). Owner, operator Frank M. Haynes Ins. Agy., Chgo., 1960-65; pres. Employees Union Health & Welfare Agy., Inc., Chgo., 1965-72; cons. pension, health and welfare plans, Chgo., 1972-75; exec. v.p. W. J. Haynes & Co., Inc., Chgo., 1975-80, pres., 1980—. Served with U.S. Army, 1958-59. Recipient Wall St. Jour. award, 1974; certificate of merit Prudential Ins. Co., 1964; C.L.U. Mem. Am. Risk and Ins. Assn., Am. Soc. C.L.U.'s, Internat. Found. Employee Benefit Plans, Beta Gamma Sigma. Home: 2408 Birchwood Ln Wilmette IL 60091 Office: 7045 N Western Ave Chicago IL 60645

HAYNES, HOWARD DOME, sch. adminstr.; b. Kansas City, Mo., Sept. 22, 1935; s. Howard Brawford and Evelyn (Dome) H.; B.A. in Econs., Baker U., 1957; postgrad. Washington U., St. Louis, 1957, DePauw U., 1958, Harvard, 1963; m. Faith Marise Newton, Nov. 2, 1957; children—Valerie Faith, H. Lee, Sarah-Elizabeth. Asst. dir. admissions Baker U., Baldwin, Kans., 1956-58; dir. admissions Tarkio (Mo.) Coll., 1958-61; dir. admissions U. Akron (Ohio), 1961-68, dir. housing, 1964-66; exec. dir. Grafton Sch., Berryville, Va., 1968-71; founder, dir. Questover and High Hope, homes retarded children, Kansas City, Mo., 1971—; chmn. bd. Haynes Investment Corp., Akron and Kansas City, 1963—; pres. N.Am. Riding for the Handicapped. Bd. dirs. Planned Parenthood, Wheelwright Mus., Santa Fe, Santa Fe Orch., Kansas City Philharm., Lyric Opera, Kansas City U. Conservatory, Prime Health, Historic Kansas City Found. Mem. Council for Exceptional Children, Am. Personnel and Guidance Assn., Coll. Admission Officers, Assn. Ind. Schs., Westport Hist. Soc., Nat. Trust, Friends of Art, Delta Tau Delta. Clubs: Millwood Country, University, Blue Ridge Hunt, Mission Valley Hunt. Home: Questover 3530 Charlotte St Kansas City MO 64109

HAYNES, MARY JOANNA, educator; b. Cleve., Apr. 10, 1945; d. William Elmer and Gertrude (Drautz) Lucas; B.S. in Edn., Bluffton Coll., 1967; M.Ed., Bowling Green State U., 1969; Ed.D., U. Toledo, 1973; m. Richard Arthur Haynes, Dec. 24, 1966; children—Jennifer Lynn, Michael Christopher. Tchr., Republic (Ohio) Schs., 1967-68, Tiffin (Ohio) Public Schs., 1968-73; asst. prof. edn. Bluffton (Ohio) Coll., 1973-74; asso. prof. Ohio No. U., Ada, 1974—; dir. kindergarten exemplary program Ohio Dept. Edn. Mem. Am. Assn. Colls. Tchr. Educators, Internat. Reading Assn., Am. Edn. Research Assn., Am. Assn. Educators of Young Children, Kappa Delta Pi, Phi Kappa Phi. Methodist. Home: 1305 E County Rd 16 Tiffin OH 44883 Office: 305 Dukes Suite 500 Main St Ohio No U Ada OH 45810

HAYNES, MARY KATHERINE, nurse; b. Butler County, Mo., Oct. 2, 1931; d. Hershel Evert and Eva Mae (Hester) Heifner; cert. with highest honors, L P N Sch. Nursing, Poplar Bluff, Mo., 1960; R.N. with highest honors, Three Rivers Community Coll., 1973; B.Health Sci., Stevens Coll., Columbia, Mo., 1978; m. Robert W. Haynes, Aug. 14, 1948; children—Janice Haynes Thurman, Robert Randall. Nurse, Poplar Bluff Hosp., 1957-79, dir. nursing, 1974-79, nurse epidemiologist, 1975-79; adminstr. nursing service Richland Meml. Hosp., Olney, Ill., 1979-80, asso. adminstr., 1980—. Active PTA, 1958-70; troop leader Cotton Boll council Girl Scouts U.S.A., 1960-66; parliamentarian Democratic Woman's Club, 1962-65; instr. CPR, Mo. Heart Assn.; bd. advisers Three Rivers Community Coll. Sch. Nursing; mem. area project rev. com., bd. selection Comprehensive Health Planning Council of So. Ill. Southeastern Lung Assn. grantee, 1977. Mem. Assn. Practitioners of Infection Control, Assn. Infection Control Nurses. Club: Altrusa (dir. 1978). Home: 800 N Boone St Olney IL 62450 Office: 800 N Locust St Olney IL 62450

HAYNES, THOMAS JOSEPH, assn. exec.; b. Grand Haven, Mich., Aug. 4, 1947; s. Donald W. and Betty L. (Dillinger) H.; B.A. in Polit. Sci., U. Colo., 1976; m. Wanda Lee Doerr, Aug. 17, 1968. Dir. rehab. Am. Legion Colo., 1976; dir. membership Am. Legion Nat. Hdqrs., Indpls., 1976-79, dir. internal affairs, 1979—; pres., chief exec. officer Promotion Mgmt. Co.; legis. coordinator United Vets. Colo., 1973-74. Pres., Hale Credit Union, Indpls., 1978; bd. dirs. Hope Luth. Ch., Indpls.; editor Bunker Hill Homeowners Assn., Indpls., 1977—. Served with USAF, 1965-69; Vietnam. Decorated Air Force Commendation medal; recipient cert. of appreciation Colo. Assn. Collegiate Vets, 1975, Mich. Boys State, 1978, Pa. Boys State, 1979. Mem. Direct Mail Mktg. Assn., Am. Mgmt. Assn., Nat. Writers Club, Army, Navy and Air Force Vets Can. (hon. life), Am. Legion. Democrat. Editor various Am. Legion publs. including: American Legion Officers Guide, 1980, 81; 6 vols. Am. Legion Extension Inst., 1980-81. Home: 5627 Personality Ct Indianapolis IN 46227 Office: 700 N Pennsylvania PO Box 1055 Indianapolis IN 46206

HAYREH, SOHAN SINGH, ophthalmologist; b. Kandole Kilan, Punjab, India, Nov. 6, 1927; s. Surjit Singh and Balwant Kaur (Kandola) H.; came to U.S., 1973; B. Medicine and Surgery, Med. Coll., Amritsar, India, 1951; M. Surgery Panjab U., Chandigarh, India, 1959; Ph.D., London U., 1965; m. Shelagh Bell Henderson, Sept. 18, 1971; children—Davinder J. S., Ravinder G.S. Lectr. Med. Coll. Patiala, India, 1955-59, asst. prof., 1959-61; Beit Meml. research fellow Inst. Ophthalmology, London, 1961-64; lectr. in ophthalmology U. London, 1965-69; sr. lectr. U. Edinburgh (Scotland), 1969-72, reader in ophthalmology, 1972-73; prof. U. Iowa, 1973—; cons. in field; mem. vision research program com. NIH-HEW; mem. ophthal. adv. com. FDA-HEW; Arris & Gale lectr. Royal Coll. Surgeons Eng., 1963. Served as capt. Indian Army M.C., 1952-55. Recipient Shakuntala Amir Chand prize Indian Council Med. Research, 1961, Instituto Barraquer prize, Barcelona, Spain, 1963, Watumull Found. prize and Gold medal, Honolulu, 1964, Norman McAllister Gregg prize and medal Ophthal. Soc. New South Wales, Australia, 1964, Middlemore prize Brit. Med. Assn., 1966. Fellow Royal Coll. Surgeons Eng., Royal Coll. Surgeons Edinburgh; mem. AMA, AAAS, Am. Assn. Research in Vision and Ophthalmology, Am. Acad. Ophthalmology, European Assn. Eye Research, Brit. and European Microcirculation Soc., Gonin Club, Internat. Glaucoma Com., Ophthalmol. Soc. U.K. (Nettleship prize 1971), Ophthalmol. Soc. France, Oxford Ophthalmol. Soc., Soc. Clin. Trials, Soc. Exptl. Biology and Medicine, Macula Soc., Retina Soc. Sikh. Author: Anterior Ischemic Optic Neuropathy, 1975; research, numerous publs. on glaucoma, optic nerve and blood circulation of eye in health and disease; editorial bd. Internat. Ophthalmology, 1977—; sci. reviewer to various Am. ophthalmic jours. Home: 600 River St Iowa City IA 52240 Office: Dept Ophthalmology U Hosp Iowa City IA 52242

HAYS, SUSAN JANE WALLACE, editor; b. Indpls., Mar. 19, 1933; d. Leon Harry and Anna Ruth (Haworth) Wallace; B.A., Ind. U., 1955; M.A., Columbia, 1969; m. Forbes Brock Hays, Apr. 14, 1957 (dec. 1967); children—Martha, Forbes. Researcher Time Mag., Time, Inc., N.Y.C., 1956-59; asst. to dir. spl. summer program Carleton Coll., Northfield, Minn., 1967-68; reporter, asst. to editor Northfield News, 1968-69; copy editor, state editor Bloomington (Ind.) Courier-Tribune, 1969-70; edn. editor Ind. U. News Bur., Bloomington, 1970-76, mng. editor, 1976—; mem. adv. com. to dean for women's affairs Ind. U., 1973-74. Treas. Methodist Women's Club, 1976-78. Mem. Women in Communications (pres. chpt. 1972-73), Nat. Fedn. Press Women, Pi Beta Phi, Kappa Kappa Kappa. Democrat. Clubs: University, Altrusa (chpt. v.p. 1980-81) (Bloomington), Woman's Press of Ind. Home: 1631 Pickwick Pl Bloomington IN 47401 Office: 306 N Union St Bloomington IN 47405

HAYWARD, MERLE ALVIN, metal processing co. exec.; b. Aurora, Ill., Sept. 23, 1924; s. Willard Herrick and Lucille (Harper) H.; grad. high sch.; m. June A. Balthazar, Oct. 16, 1945; children—Cynthia Hayward Warmbier, Nancy Hayward Macari, Thomas. Toolmaker, Aurora Metal Co., 1946-51; design engr. Argonne Nat. Lab., Lemont, Ill., 1951-53; pres. Phillips-Eckardt Electronic Corp., Chgo., 1953-66; v.p. Eckmar Corp., Chgo., 1966-68; pres. Apollo Metals Co., Chgo., 1968—, dir., 1969—; dir. Carus Corp., LaSalle, Ill., Danly Machine Corp., Chgo. Mem. Sch. Bd., Plainfield Consol. Dist., 1970—. Served with USN, 1942-46. Presbyterian. Club: Union League (Chgo.). Patentee low cost relay. Home: 733 N Bartlett Av Plainfield IL 60544 Office: 6650 S Oak Park St Chicago IL 60638

HAZELTINE, ROBERT EARL, ret. librarian; b. Fremont, Ohio, May 30, 1916; s. Nick A. and Catherine Henrietta (Keefer) H.; B.A., U. Akron, 1949; M.S. in L.S., Case-Western Res. U., 1950; m. Anna Theis, Sept. 6, 1947; children—Robert T., Catherine Ann, Amy Elizabeth. Asst. cataloger Bowling Green (Ohio) State U. Library, 1950-54, cataloger, 1954-55; head tech. processes Canton (Ohio) Library, 1955-60; head librarian Portsmouth (Ohio) Pub. Library, 1960-66; dir. Ashtabula County (Ohio) Dist. Library, 1966-79, ret., 1979; part-time instr. Ashtabula area campus Kent State U., 1968—; chmn. Council of Ashtabula County Libraries, 1973; pres. Northeastern Ohio Library Assn., 1973-75. Pres. Roosevelt Sch. PTA, Portsmouth, 1964-65; pres. Portsmouth PTA Council, 1965-66; mem. bd. trustees, exec. com. Ashtabula Area Devel. Assn., 1969—. Served with USAAF, 1942-45. Mem. No. Ohio Catalogers (chmn. 1955-56), Am. (state rep. recruitment com. 1964-69), Ohio (chmn. recruitment com. 1964-66) library assns. Lutheran (trustee 1964-65; sec. 1966). Kiwanian. Club: North End (Ashtabula). Home: 811 Myrtle Ave Ashtabula OH 44004

HAZELTON, LUCY REED, advt. exec., writer; b. St. Louis, Sept. 9, 1929; d. Ferdinand Maximillian and Elizabeth Emily (Benson) Schaeffer; student Washington U., St. Louis, 1947-48, St. Louis U., 1954-56, U. Colo., summer, 1968, U. Houston, summer, 1971; m. Burton W. Hazelton, Feb. 15, 1958 (dec.); children—Terence G. Reed (dec.), Deborah Lucy Reed, Ellen Frisch. Writer and artist for ednl. programming Webster Pub. Co., Crestwood, Mo., 1962-63, Scharr Printers, St. Louis, 1966-67; advt. writer Christian Bd. Publs., St. Louis, 1967-69; mgr. advt. and pub. relations A.G. Edwards & Sons, Inc., St. Louis, 1969—. Bd. dirs. Poetry Center Inc. of St. Louis, v.p., 1975-80, pres., 1980—. Recipient Marianne Moore award, 1977, Merit award Fin. World Mag., 1973-77, Fin. World Merit award, 1973-79. Mem. Acad. Am. Poets, St. Louis Writers Guild (treas. 1975), Advt. Fedn. St. Louis, Women in Communications, Advt. Prodn. Club of St. Louis. Author: (book of poetry) Three Circles and the Princess, 1976; Eros/Agape, 1979; (verse plays) The Still Point (E. Oscar Thalinger award), 1965; The River Laughs, 1966. Contbr. poetry to various lit. mags.; columnist St. Louis Arts Mag. Home: 668 Kirkshire Dr Kirkwood MO 63122 Office: 1 N Jefferson Saint Louis MO 63103

HAZELTON, ROBERT STAFFORD, diversified mfg. co. exec.; b. Cleve., Sept. 18, 1940; s. Paul and Marjorie (Stafford) H.; A.B., Princeton U., 1962; M.A., Case Inst. Tech., 1967, Ph.D., 1972. Analyst, Society Nat. Bank, Cleve., 1962-67; mgr. computer lab. Case Western Res. U., Cleve., 1964-72; sr. analyst product planning Harris Corp., Cleve., 1972-74; mgr. tech. services Eaton Corp., Cleve., 1977—. Active ARC. Mem. Am. Soc. Info. Sci., Assn. Computer Machinery, IEEE. Club: Univ. (treas., Cleve.). Contbr. to World Book Ency. Home: 3017 Essex Rd Cleveland Heights OH 44118 Office: Eaton Corp 100 Erieview Plaza Cleveland OH 44114

HAZEN, JUDITH ANN, home care exec.; b. Dumont, Minn., Oct. 20, 1942; d. Raymond Clifford and Lillian May (Heidelberger) Kurth; B.A. in Sociology, Macalester Coll., 1964; M.S. in Rehab. Counseling, Mankato State U., 1974; m. Jeffrey R. Hazen, Dec. 28, 1963; children—Brett Christopher, Angela Marie. Social caseworker Columbus (Ohio) Child Welfare, 1966-67; group worker Gads Hill Neighborhood House, Chgo., 1967-68; vocat. rehab. counselor United Cerebral Palsy of Mpls., 1975-76; sr. med. social worker St. John's Hosp. Home Care, St. Paul, 1976-79, asst. dir., 1979—. Mem. Am. Personnel and Guidance Assn., Mensa. Unitarian. Office: 2696 Hazlewood St N Maplewood MN 55109

H'DOUBLER, FRANCIS TODD, JR., physician; b. Springfield, Mo., June 18, 1925; s. Francis Todd and Alice Louise (Bemis) H'D.; student Washington U., St. Louis, 1943, Miami U., Oxford, Ohio, 1943-44; B.S., U. Wis., 1946, M.D., 1948; m. Joan Louise Huber, Dec. 20, 1951; children—Julie H'Doubler Thomas and Sarah H'Doubler Muegge (twins), Kurt, Scott. Intern, Milw. Hosp., 1948-49; resident in surgery U.S. Naval Hosp., Oakland, Calif., 1950-51; pvt. practice medicine specializing in thyroid surgery, Springfield, 1952—; dir. Battlefield Nat. Bank. Active YMCA; mem. Commn. to Reapportion Mo. State Senate, 1971; chmn. Sch. Bond and Tax Levy Com., 1958. County chmn. Republican party, 1974-75; mem. Rep. state finance com., 1972-75. Bd. dirs. Shrine Galveston Burns Inst.; bd. dirs. St. Louis Shrine Hosp. for Crippled Children, bd. dirs., trustee, chmn. long-range planning com. Imperial Council, Shrine N. Am., 1975—; mem. steering com. Wilson's Creek Battlefield Nat. Park, 1951-61; mem. pres.'s adv. council Sch. Ozarks, Point Lookout, Mo., 1975—. Served with USNR, 1943-46, 49-51, Fleet Marines, 1950. Recipient Humanitarian award S.W. Mo. Drug Travelers Assn., 1971; Distinguished Service award Mo. Jaycees, 1959. Fellow Am. Coll.

Nuclear Medicine (founder's group); mem. AMA, Greene County Med. Assn., Mo. med. soc., Southwestern Surg. Congress, Mo. Surg. Assn., Soc. Nuclear Medicine, Am. Thyroid Assn., Springfield Jr. C. of C. (past pres.), Springfield C. of C., Sigma Nu (Outstanding Alumnus nat. award 1980), Nu Sigma Nu. Mason, Shriner (imperial potentate), Order DeMolay Legion Honor (hon.). Home: 2445 Melbourne Rd Springfield MO 65804 Office: 1900 S National Suite 2950 Springfield MO 65804

HEABERG, ANDREA JEAN, county ofcl.; b. Lawton, Okla., Oct. 18, 1947; d. William A. and Phyllis J. (McMahan) Barker; B.A. in Behavioral Sci., U. Calif., Riverside, 1970; m. James H. Heaberg, Jr.; 1 dau., Rebecca Paige. Resident counselor Alta Loma (Calif.) Girls Home, 1970-73; analyst Loma Linda (Calif.) U. Med. Center, 1974-76; mgr. pub. assistance cases Dept. Public Social Services, Riverside, Calif., 1974-76; staff devel. coordinator Greene County Welfare Dept., Xenia, Ohio, 1977—; mgmt. and tng. cons. Instr. CPR, ARC. Mem. Jaycee Women, Nat. Tng. and Devel. Soc., Am. Soc. Tng. and Devel. Home: 2732 Trebein Rd Xenia OH 45385 Office: Greene County Welfare Dept 492 W 2d St Xenia OH 45385

HEABERLIN, DAVID ALLEN, banker; b. Kirksville, Mo., Aug. 12, 1949; s. James Claude and Loraine Frances (Cain) H.; B.A. in Acct., St. Ambrose Coll., 1971; m. Nancy Lee Odell, June 5, 1971. Auditor, Arthur Young & Co., Chgo., 1971-73, auditor supr., 1973-76, audit mgr., 1976-77; 1st v.p., comptroller Exchange Nat. Bank of Chgo., 1977-78, 1st v.p., chief fin. and ops. officer, 1978-79, sr. v.p., chief fin. officer, 1979—; treas., chief fin. officer Exchange Internat. Corp., parent co. of Exchange Nat. Bank, 1978—. Recipient Scholarship award state of Iowa, 1969, Acct. Achievement award Ernst & Ernst, 1970; C.P.A., Ill. Mem. Am. Inst. C.P.A.'s, Ill. Soc. C.P.A.'s, Bank Adminstrn. Inst., Am. Bankers Assn. Roman Catholic. Office: Exchange Nat Bank LaSalle and Adams Sts Chicago IL 60603

HEAD, DARSEALLE LAMAR, graphics designer; b. N.Y.C., Apr. 23, 1953; s. Nathaniel Edward and Almeda Mary H.; B.A., U. Mich., 1975; postgrad. Fashion Inst. Technology, 1976. With Market Opinion Research, Detroit, 1977—. Mem. U. Mich. Alumni Assn., U. Mich. Sch. Edn. Alumni Assn., Assn. Black Communicators. Home: 303 Covington Apt 303 Detroit MI 48203 Office: 550 Washington Blvd Detroit MI 48226

HEAD, HENRY BUCHEN, physician; b. Evanston, Ill., Nov. 24, 1933; s. Jerome Reed and Jean Helen (Milne) H.; B.A., Amherst Coll., 1955; M.D., Northwestern U., 1959; M.S. in Medicine, U. Minn., 1964; m. Suzanne Elizabeth Spletzer, Feb. 15, 1961; children—Elizabeth, Catherine, Heather, Henry, Alexander. Intern, Phila. Gen. Hosp., 1959-60; fellow in medicine Mayo Clinic, Rochester, Minn., 1960-63; fellow in gastroenterology Northwestern U., Evanston, 1963-65, instr. medicine, 1965-70, asso. medicine, 1970—; practice medicine specializing in internal medicine and gastroenterology, Chgo.; mem. attending staff Northwestern Meml. Hosp., Chgo. Served to maj. U.S. Army, 1967-69. Diplomate Am. Bd. Internal Medicine. Fellow A.C.P.; mem. AMA (Physician's Recognition award 1977), Ill., Chgo. med. socs., Inst. Medicine Chgo., Northwestern Med. Clin. Faculty Assn. (chmn. 1978). Presbyterian. Club: Tavern (Chgo.). Contbr. articles to profl. jours. Home: 1145 Sheridan Rd Evanston IL 60202 Office: 251 E Chicago Ave Chicago IL 60611

HEADLEE, WILLIAM HUGH, emeritus educator; b. Morristown, Ind., June 15, 1907; s. Walter C. and Nellie Ann (Adams) H.; A.B., Earlham Coll., 1929; M.S. (Rockefeller Found. fellow), U. Ill., 1933; Ph.D. (Rockefeller Found. fellow), Tulane U., 1935; m. Gabrielle Mills, Aug. 4, 1937; children—Joan (Mrs. Charles Barrett Bowden), Anne. Instr. biology Am. U., Cairo, Egypt, 1929-31; research asst. internat. health div. Rockefeller Found., Cairo, 1930-32; asst. prin. Friendsville Acad., Tenn., 1933-34; instr. biology Purdue U., 1935-42, asst. prof. zoology, 1942-43; asst. prof. parasitic diseases Ind. U. Sch. Medicine, Indpls., 1943-46, asso. prof., 1946-53, prof., 1953-77, prof. emeritus, 1977—; chmn. dept. biology Nat. Pedagogic Inst., Caracas, Venezuela, 1937-38; sr. scientist USPHS Res., 1953-71; med. parasitologist U.S. ops. mission Fgn. Ops. Adminstrn., 1953-55; vis. prof. med. parasitology Sch. of Medicine, Chulalongkorn U. and Thailand Sch. Public Health, Bangkok, 1953-55; coordinator, dir. Ind. U.-AID, Pakistan Project to develop Jinnah Postgrad. Med. Center, 1957-66; asso. dir. Div. Allied Health Scis., Ind. U. Sch. Medicine, 1968; cons. epidemiologist Ind. Regional Med. Program, 1969-77. Active Central Ind. Council on Aging, Commn. on Aging of State of Ind, Mayor's Adv. Com. on Aging and the Aged, Indpls.; adv. council Ind. U. Center on Aging and Aged. John and Mary Markle Found. fellow, 1943, 44. Emeritus fellow AAAS (life; council 1957-62), Ind. Acad. Sci. Royal Soc. Tropical Medicine and Hygiene; emeritus mem. AAUP (pres. Ind. Conf. 1975), Am. Soc. Parasitologists (sr.), Am. Soc. Tropical Medicine and Hygiene (emeritus), Sigma Xi (emeritus); mem. Soc. Internat. Devel., Internat. Coll. Tropical Medicine, Nat. Council on Aging, Nat. Ret. Tchrs. Assn., Ret. Profs. Ind., Soc. Ret. Execs., Am. Assn. Ret. Persons, Ind. Partners of Ams., Phi Sigma. Unitarian (bd. trustees 1953, 70-73, chmn. nominating com. 1970-71). Contbr. articles to profl. jours., including 49 publs. on epidemiology of parasite infections. Home: 762 N Riley Ave Indianapolis IN 46201

HEADRICK, JOHN ANDERSON, physician; b. Arbyrd, Mo., July 25, 1931; s. Elmer A. and Opal Marie (Shands) H.; A.B. with honors, Washington U., St. Louis, 1954, M.D., 1958; m. Barbara Ruth Hammond, June 9, 1956; children—John Anderson, Dean A. Intern, St. Luke's Hosp., St. Louis, 1958-59, resident, 1959-62; practice medicine, specializing in internal medicine, St. Louis, 1964-75; v.p. med. affairs Christian Hosps. N.E.-N.W., St. Louis, 1975—; mem. exec. com. Christian Hosp. N.W., 1969, asso. chief staff, 1974, chief staff, 1975; instr. clin. medicine Washington U. Sch. Medicine, St. Louis, 1964-68; cons. cardiology Service Mil. Acad. Bds., 1962-64; mem. adv. bd. Mo. Bapt. Hosp., 1970-75. Bd. mgrs. North County YMCA, St. Louis, 1976—; mem. adv. bd. St. Louis Jr. Coll. Dist., 1964-67. Served with U.S. Army, 1962-64. Diplomate Am. Bd. Internal Medicine. Mem. A.C.P., Am. Soc. Internal Medicine, AMA, Am. Acad. Med. Dirs., Mo. State Med. Assn., St. Louis Met. Med. Soc., N.Y. Acad. Scis., AAAS, Inst. for Critical Care Medicine, Soc. for Critical Care Medicine. Club: Florissant Rotary. Home: 24 Lourdes Ct Lake Saint Louis MO 63367 Office: 11133 Dunn Rd Saint Louis MO 63136

HEAGSTEDT, THEODORE CHARLES, mgmt. cons.; b. Chgo., Nov. 8, 1919; s. Walter Eugene and Rosa Elizabeth (Lindemann) H.; B.S. in Group Psychology, George Williams Coll., 1948; M.B.A., U. Chgo., 1966; m. Thelma Linnea Soderlind, Jan. 22, 1944; children—T. Daniel, Bruce W., Nina L. Dir. phys. edn. Southtown YMCA, Chgo., 1947-49; asst. indsl. relations mgr. Bauer & Black div. Kendall Co., Chgo., 1949-52; indsl. relations mgr. Dutch Brand div. Johns Manville Co., Chgo., 1952-57; personnel cons. A.T. Kearney & Co., Chgo., 1957-61; dir. indsl. relations Aldens, Inc., Chgo., 1961-68; cons. v.p. in personnel Westcott Assos., Chgo., 1968-71; owner, pres. Heagstedt Assos., Winnetka, Ill., 1971—, Exec. Secs. Assos., Wilmette, Ill., Blackhawk Machine Products Co., Addison, Ill.; instr. Kendall Coll., Evanston, Ill. Vice pres. edn. com. Orgn. S.W. Communities, Chgo., 1962-66. Served with USCGR, 1942-46. Mem. Am. Soc. Personnel Adminstrs., U. Chgo. Exec. Program Club (dir. 1978—), Chgo. Lit. Club (v.p. 1979). Republican. Unitarian. Clubs: Univ. Chgo., Swedish Chgo., Michigan Shores. Home: 2326 Greenwood St Wilmette IL 60091 Office: 456 Frontage Rd Northfield IL 60093

HEAKAL, M. SABRY, acct.; b. Shebin El-Koum, Egypt, Mar. 20, 1940; came to U.S., 1961; s. Mohamed E. and Ghadiga H.; B.Com. with honors, U. Cairo, 1960; M.S., U. Ill., 1965, Ph.D., 1968; m. Tity I. Kamel, Aug. 2, 1964; children—Hanan, Reem, Delilah. Asst. prof. acctg. St. Cloud State U., 1968-70, asso. prof. acctg., 1970-71, prof., chmn. acctg., 1971-78; vis. prof. acctg. U. Minn., 1975-78, lectr., 1978—; vis. prof. U. Fla., 1977-78; partner McGladrey Hendrickson & Co., Mpls., 1978—. C.P.A., Minn. Mem. Am. Acctg. Assn., Am. Inst. C.P.A.'s, Minn. Soc. C.P.A.'s. Club: Wayzata Country. Home: 2710 Everest Ln Plymouth MN 55447 Office: 4520 IDS Center Minneapolis MN 55402

HEALY, JOHN CORNELIUS, exploration geophysicist; b. Fairbury, Ill., Sept. 26, 1921; s. James Patrick and Rose (Rusterholtz) H.; B.S., U. Houston, 1951. Instr. physics U. Houston, 1947-51; jr. operator Tex. Rogers Explorations Inc., 1951, jr. seismologist Colo., Mont., Wyo., 1952-54, seismologist, Wyo., Mont., 1955-57, geophysicist, Venezuela, Libya, 1957-63, W. Tex., S.E. N.Mex., Ohio, Mich., Wyo., Okla., 1964—. Served with USAF, 1940-45; PTO. Decorated Philippine Liberation medal. Mem. Soc. Exploration Geophysicists, Permian Basin Geophys. Soc., Nat. Rifle Assn. (life), Tex. Rifle Assn. (life). Roman Catholic. Home: PO Box 65 Chatsworth IL 60921 Office: PO Box 1325 Midland TX 79702

HEAP, JAMES CLARENCE, mech. engr.; b. Trinidad, Colo.; s. James and Elsie Mae (Brobst) H.; B.S. in Mech. Engring., Ill. Inst. Tech., 1944, M.S., 1960; m. Alma Mae Swartzendruber. Sr. mech. engr. Cook Electric Research Lab., Morton Grove, Ill., 1955-56; asso. mech. engr. Argonne (Ill.) Nat. Lab., 1956-66; sr. project engr. Union Tank Car Co., East Chicago, Ind., 1966-71; sr. engr. Thrall Car Mfg. Co., Chicago Heights, Ill., 1971-77, research design engr. Graver Energy Systems, Inc., 1977-79; mech. cons. design engr. Pollak & Skan, Inc., Chgo., 1979—; cons. mech. design and stress analysis, 1965—. Served with USAF, 1946-47. Registered profl. engr., Wis. Mem. ASME. Club: Masons. Author: Formulas for Circular Plates Subjected to Symmetrical Loads and Temperatures, 1966; also tech. papers. Patentee in field. Home: 1913 Lambert Ln Munster IN 46321 Office: 2 N Riverside Plaza Chicago IL 60606

HEARD, MARY ALICE, editor; b. Gallup, N.Mex., Nov. 8, 1931; d. Henry Herbert and Lucy Georgia (Blain) H.; student U. Wyo., 1949-50, Kans. State U., 1950-52. Mem. staff Clay Center (Kans.) Dispatch, 1952—, society editor-reporter, 1952—. Sec. Clay Center chpt. ARC, 1956—; publicity dir. Clay Center chpt. Am. Cancer Soc., 1956-72; ch. sch. tchr. St. Paul's Episcopal Ch., Clay Center, 1954-79; active Clay Center Assn. Retarded Citizens. Mem. Nat. Fedn. Press Women, Kans. Press Women, Clay Center Bus. and Profl. Women (publicity dir. 1954—). Republican. Clubs: Helianthus (publicity chmn. 1969—), Sisters of Martha, Order Eastern Star. Office: 805 5th St Clay Center KS 67432

HEARD, WILLIAM ROBERT, ins. co. exec.; b. Indpls., Apr. 25, 1925; s. French and Estelle (Austin) H.; student Ind. U.; m. Virginia Ann Patrick, Feb. 6, 1951; children—Cynthia Ann, William Robert, II. With Grain Dealers Mut. Ins. Co., 1948, exec. v.p., Indpls., 1978-79, pres., chief exec. officer, dir., 1979—; pres., chief exec. officer, dir. Companion Ins. Co., 1979—; vice chmn., dir. Alliance Am. Insurers; chmn., exec. com. IRM; pres., dir. Grain Dealers Mut. Agy., Inc.; chmn. bd. 15 N. Broadway Corp. Served with USNR, 1942-46. Mem. Assn. Mill and Elevator Ins. Cos. (chmn., dir.), Ins. Inst. Ind. (dir., exec. com.), Mut. Reins. Bur. (dir.), Excess of Loss Assn. (vice chmn., dir.), Sales and Mktg. Execs. Indpls. (past pres.), Sales and Mktg. Execs. Internat. (past dir.), Fla. 1752 Club (past pres.), Ind. Insurors Assn. (dir.), Hoosierland Rating Bur. (dir.), Ind. Mill and Elevator Rating Bur. (dir.), Mill and Elevator Rating Bur. (dir.), Mill and Elevator Fire Prevention Bur. (dir.), Am. Legion, Pi Sigma Epsilon. Office: 1752 N Meridian St Indianapolis IN 46202

HEARIN, RICHARD L., univ. adminstr.; b. Highland Park, Mich., May 2, 1949; s. Richard Ames and Barbara Jean (Fields) H.; B.S. cum laude, Central Mich. U., 1971; M.A., Bowling Green State U., 1978; m. Talya Jean Foell, Aug. 14, 1971. Asst. to dir. grad. admissions Bowling Green State U., 1977-78; dir. career devel. and placement Ohio No. U., Ada, 1978-81; dir. career planning and placement Miami U., Oxford, Ohio, 1981—. Served to capt. U.S. Army, 1972-77. Decorated Army Commendation medal with oak leaf cluster. Mem. Am. Personnel and Guidance Assn., Am. Coll. Personnel Assn., Midwest Coll. Placement Assn., Sigma Chi. Office: Career Planning and Placement Office 227 Hoyt Hall Miami U Oxford OH 45056

HEARST, BELLA RACHAEL, physician, researcher, artist; b. Pitts.; d. Aba and Bertha (Alpern) Hearst; B.M., Chgo. Med. Sch., 1949, M.D., 1950; postgrad. Johns Hopkins, 1952-53, Art Inst. Chgo., 1958-68. Rotating intern Norwegian Am. Hosp., Chgo., 1949-50; jr. asst. pathologist Cook County Hosp., Chgo., 1950-52; fellow med. legal pathology U. Md., 1953-54; sr. pathology resident Charity Hosp., New Orleans, 1955-56; spl. cardiac research Armed Forces Inst. Pathology, Washington, 1956-57; dir., developer, coordinator pathologist Hosp. O'Horan, Merida, Yucatan, Mexico, 1957-58; originator, developer 1st health fair concept with Taylor Homes, Beacon House, Boys' Clubs Chgo., others; founder Bertha Hearst Found., Inc., 1958, exec. dir., 1958—; founder Diabetic Inst. Am., Inc., Chgo., 1959, exec. dir., 1959—; founder Internat. Diabetic Inst., Inc., Chgo., 1963, exec. dir., 1963-72; staff physician, asso. prof. health scis. Western Ill. U., Macomb, 1972—, adj. prof., 1972-73, dir. cardiac and exercise research project. research asso. microbiology Stritch Sch. Medicine, Loyola U., Chgo.; originated grupeutics concept and grupeutics centers, 1977—, Uptown Neighborhood Health Centers, 1977-78, Copernicus Neighborhood Center, 1978—, Lakeview Neighborhood Health Center, 1979—, Sr. Staywell Club and Geriatric Center, Chgo., 1978. Art exhibit Shuster Art Gallery, N.Y., 1966, Internat. Dermatology Congress, Munich, 1967. Dist. med. dir. Bur. Employees Compensation, U.S. Dept. Labor, Chgo., 1968—; research dir. Safety and Fire Council Chgo. developed health fair concept. Recipient 3d prize for art exhibit AMA Conv., Chgo., 1962. Fellow Am. Geriatric Soc., Am. Coll. Angiology, Internat. Coll. Angiology, Royal Soc. Pub. Health, Am. Soc. Angiology; mem. internat. Acad. Pathology, Am. Women's Med. Assn., Am. Soc. Microbiology, Am. Assn. for Study Neoplastic Diseases, U.S. Public Health Assn., Internat. Grupeutics (Italy, Ger.), Gerontol. Soc., Reticulo-Endothelial Soc. Author: Diabetes and Juvenile Delinquency, 1964; Diabetes, Early Detection, Prevention and Eradication, 1964; Diabetes and Fitness, 1964; Diabetic Statistical Research Survey, 1961-65; Diabetes and Blood Groups, 1965; Diabetes and Aging, 1965; Sex 'n Things on the Campus, 1973; Diabetes and Newborns; Your Heart, 1974. Contbr. articles related to diabetes, tumors, reticuloendotheliosis, ABO blood groups, preventive cardiac rehab., aging to med. publs; founder, editor: Archives of Diabetes, 1963—. Pioneer in early mass detection, cure, prevention, eradication of diabetes; pioneer geriatric medicine in Chgo.; developer concept that human obesity a disease with symptoms and pathology including hypertensive fat factor. Office: 8 S Michigan Blvd Chicago IL 60603 also PO Box A3579 Chicago IL 60690

HEARST, GLADYS WHITLEY HENDERSON (MRS. CHARLES JOSEPH HEARST), writer; b. Wolfe City, Tex.; d. William Henry and Helen (Butler) Whitley; student Trinity U., 1924-26; B.A., U. Tex., 1928, m. Journalism, 1928, postgrad., 1938-40; m. Robert David Henderson, May 17, 1933 (dec. 1941); m. 2d, Charles Joseph Hearst, Oct. 30, 1943 (dec. 1980). Editor, Future Farmer News, Austin, Tex., 1930-33; dir. Service Bur., Tex. Congress Parents and Tchrs., Austin, 1933-36; dir. Student Union, U. Tex., 1939-42; free lance writer, 1945—. Instr. writing Waterloo YWCA, 1966-69. Vice chmn. Black Hawk County Democratic party, 1945-57. Mem. County Extension Program Planning Com., 1965-68. Served as lt. WAVES, 1942-45. Recipient Des Moines Register Press award. Iowa Arts Council grantee, 1978. Mem. AAUW (Iowa chmn. Status of Women 1954-56, past pres. Cedar Falls br., grantee 1981), Iowa (life), Cedar Falls (life) hist. socs., Rural Readers Club, P.E.O., Women in Communications, Inc. (formerly Theta Sigma Phi) (nat. pres., Distinguished Service award 1962, 73, chmn. by-laws com. 1969-74, mem. nat. task force 1973-74, Iowa, nat. awards, 1969, historian Cedar Falls 1976—), Zeta Tau Alpha (life), Kappa Tau Alpha. Mem. United Ch. Christ (long-term planning com. 1975—, writer-editor History 1960-81). Club: Capital Gains Investment (past pres. Cedar Falls, treas. 1971-73); Wednesday. A writer Cedar Falls Centennial Pageant, 1952; writer, editor hist. book Cedar Falls Naval Station, 1942-45. Editor Northeast Iowa Family History Anthology, 1978. Address: 2511 Ashland Ave Cedar Falls IA 50613

HEASLEY, BERNICE ELIZABETH, speech pathologist; b. Kent, Ohio, Aug. 12, 1919; d. Cary D. and Hattie M. (Garber) Derry; B.A. cum laude, Kent State U., 1962, M.Ed., 1964; m. William H. Heasley, May 24, 1940; children—Dennis G., W. Derry. Speech pathologist Rehab. Center, Akron, Ohio, 1963-64; coordinator Canton (Ohio) City Deaf Program, 1964-68; supr. speech and hearing therapy Stark County Schs., Louisville, Ohio, 1968-73; dir. speech, hearing and language services Human Devel. and Counseling Assos., N. Canton, Ohio, 1973—. Mem. Am., Ohio speech and hearing assns., Am. Mortar Bd. Author: Auditory Perceptual Disorders, 1974; Listeneers and others, 1977; (with J. R. Grosklos) Programmed Lessons for Young Language-Disabled Children, 1976, Speech and Language Correction Through Perceptual Activities; (with K. K. Ward) The Ward-Heasley Evaluation of Expressive Language, 1977, Receptive Word Order Test, 1977; Auditory Processing Disorders and Remediation; Where Time Stood Still; Home: 226 Howe Rd Kent OH 44240 Office: 1421 Portage Rd North Canton OH 44720

HEASLEY, ROBERT KENNETH, TV exec.; b. Natrona Heights, Pa., May 15, 1948; s. Robert W. and Bette M. (Connolly) H.; B.F.A., U. Cin., 1971; m. Patricia Conley; children—Jill Suzanne, Robert Scott. Program coordinator Scenes, Inc., Cin., 1968-69; asst. to chief engr. U. Cin., 1968-69, instr., summer 1968; audio engr., technician Sta. WKRC-TV, Cin., 1969-70; audio engr., tech. dir. Sta. WCPO-TV, Cin., 1970-77; ops. mgr. Lighthouse Prodns., Scripps-Howard Broadcasting Co., 1977—; v.p. and gen. mgr. ER Prodns., Cin., 1980—. Mem. Nat. Assn. Broadcast Employees and Technicians (pres. local 44 1973-77). Roman Catholic. Home: 404 Mohican Dr Loveland OH 45140 Office: 26 E 6th St Cincinnati OH 45202

HEATH, GEORGE FREMONT, sales exec., rancher; b. St. Louis, Aug. 15, 1907; s. George Baldwin and Jennie Bell (Jones) H.; B.S. in Civil Engring., Mo. Sch. Mines, 1930; LL.B., Benton Coll. Law, 1936; m. Frances Jackson; children—Susan, Sarah, George Fremont. Engr., James A. Hooke & Assos., St. Louis, 1930-34; sales engr., asst. sales mgr. Laclede Steel Co., St. Louis, 1934-40; sales mgr. Cleve. Worm & Gear Corp., Farval Corp., Cleve., 1940-46; owner Geo. F. Heath Co., Inc., St. Louis, 1946—; pres. Continental Pump Co., Lancer Equipment Co., Heartland, Inc., House of Heath, Inc., Vari-Master, Inc., Fremont Investments, Inc. Mem. St. Louis C. of C., Theta Tau, Sigma Nu. Republican. Clubs: Engineers, World Trade (St. Louis). Home: Route 3 Box 103 Warrenton MO 63383 Office: 11811 Westline Industrial Dr Saint Louis MO 63141

HEATH, GORDON GLENN, univ. dean; b. Sultan, Wash., Sept. 22, 1922; s. Earle Gordon and Florence Faye (Penix) H.; B.V.S., Los Angeles Coll. Optometry, 1950, O.D., 1951; M.S., U. Calif., Berkeley, 1954, Ph.D., 1960; m. Dorothy Louis Faulkner, Jan. 29, 1954; children—Raymond, Kathleen, Douglass, Debra, Lauren. Asst. prof. optometry Ind. U., Bloomington, 1955-60, asso. prof., 1960-64, prof., 1964—, chmn. Grad. Sch. Com. Physiol. Optics, 1961-70, dean Sch. Optometry, 1970—; cons. dean U. Mo., St. Louis, 1978-80; pres. Assn. Schs. and Colls. Optometry, 1963-65; bd. dirs. Am. Optometric Found., 1975—; mem. Nat. Adv. Council on Edn. for Health Professions, HEW, 1967-71; mem. Nat. Adv. Eye Council, Nat. Eye Inst., NIH, 1977-80. Served to lt. (j.g.) USNR, 1943-46. Recipient Outstanding Service award Mo. Optometric Assn., 1970. Mem. Am. Acad. Optometry (mem. exec. council 1972—, pres.-elect 1981—), Optical Soc. Am., AAAS, Assn. Research in Vision and Ophthalmology, AAUP, Ind. Optometric Assn. Club: Rotary. Editor Ind. Jour. Optometry, 1959-64; author 2 books, numerous articles in field. Home: 1206 Longwood Dr Bloomington IN 47401 Office: Sch Optometry Ind U Bloomington IN 47401

HEATH, MARIWYN DWYER, polit. cons.; b. Chgo., May 1, 1935; d. Thomas Leo and Winifred (Brennan) Dwyer; B.J., U. Mo., 1956; m. Eugene R. Heath, Sept. 3, 1956; children—Philip Clayton, Jeffrey Thomas. Mng. editor Chemung Valley Reporter, Horseheads, N.Y., 1956-57; self-employed freelance writer, speech writer, editor Tech. Transls., Dayton, Ohio, 1966—; cons. Internat. Women's Commn., 1975-76; ERA coordinator Nat. Fedn. Bus. and Profl. Women's Clubs, 1974—; mem. polit. and mgmt. coms. ERAmerica, 1976—; mem. Gov. Ohio Task Force Credit for Women, 1973; mem. Midwest regional adv. com. SBA, 1976—; chmn. Ohio Coalition ERA Implementation, 1974-75. Bd. dirs. Dayton YWCA, 1968-74. Recipient various service awards. Mem. AAUW (dir. Dayton 1965-72; Woman of Year award Dayton 1974), Nat. Fedn. Bus. and Profl. Women's Clubs (pres. Dayton 1967-69, Ohio 1976-77; Woman of Year award Dayton 1974, Ohio 1974), Ohio Women. Republican. Roman Catholic. Address: 10 Wisteria Dr Dayton OH 45419

HEATHERINGTON, ALAN LAWRENCE, condr., violinist; b. Buffalo, Nov. 15, 1945; s. Lawrence Risley and Grace Muriel (Gould) H.; B.A., Houghton (N.Y.) Coll., 1967; M.Mus., Northwestern U., 1975; student Trinity Evang. Div. Sch., Deerfield, Ill., 1967-70; m. Janet Carol Burgess, Nov. 24, 1966; children—Christina Joy, Tara Marie. Concertmaster, asst. condr. Lake Forest (Ill.) Symphony, 1968-79, Chamber Orch. Lake County (Ill.), 1976—; mem. faculty Moody Bible Inst., Chgo., 1969-79; minister of music Northwest Bapt. Ch., Chgo., 1972-79; music dir. Chgo. String Ensemble, 1977—; violinist Delft Trio, 1969—, Testore Trio, 1978—; concertmaster Chgo. Chamber Choir, 1978—, Evanston (Ill.) Classic Chorale, 1977—; pvt. tchr., 1968—; music dir. Liberty Fremont Concert Soc., 1979—; performer Dame Myra Hess Meml. Concerts, Chgo., also solo appearances with orchs., recitals at colls. and univs. Home: 3320 Capitol St Skokie IL 60076 Office: 820 N LaSalle St Chicago IL 60610*

HEATHERSON, DAN MAURICE, mfg. co. exec.; b. La Porte, Ind., Feb. 4, 1947; s. Hugh Maurice and Florence Evelyn (Brady) H.; B.S. in Indsl. Mgmt., Purdue U., 1970; m. Patricia Louise Fogarty, Sept. 2, 1967; children—Jacqueline Anne, Danny Maurice, Michele Lee. Sect. indsl. engr. Colgate-Palmolive Co., Jeffersonville, Ind., 1970-71; sr. indsl. engr. AC Spark Plug div. Gen. Motors Corp., Flint, Mich., 1971-73; sr. indsl. engr. Joy Mfg. Co., Michigan City, Ind., 1974-76, mgr. mfg. engring., 1978-79, mgr. prodn. planning, 1979—; prodn. mgr. Penn Athletic Products Co., Phoenix, 1976-78. Founder, bd. dirs. Greater La Porte (Ind.) Pop Warner Football Assn., Inc., also head coach; pres. Lake Porter Pop Warner Football Conf.; bd. dirs. La Porte Little L League Baseball; head coach La Porte Little L League Baseball; asst. coach Kankakee Valley Little League Baseball, Springfield Twp., La Porte, 1978—; head coach La Porte (Ind.) YMCA Soccer. Served with USMC, 1968. Mem. Am. Prodn. and Inventory Control Soc., Nat. Mgmt. Assn. (dir. 1979-80), Nat. Pop Warner Football Coaches Assn. (regional pres.). Roman Catholic. Club: Elk. Home: 403 Sunrise Blvd La Porte IN 46350 Office: 900 Woodland St Michigan City IN 46360

HEATON, CHARLES LLOYD, dermatologist; b. Bryan, Tex., May 8, 1935; s. Homer Lloyd and Bessie Blanton (Sharp) H.; B.S., Tex. A&M U., 1957; M.D., Baylor U., 1961; M.A. (hon.), U. Pa., 1973. Intern, Jefferson Davis Hosp., Houston, 1961-62; resident Baylor U., 1962-65; sr. attending physician Phila. Gen. Hosp., 1965-69, chief of service, 1970-77; mem. dept. dermatology U. Pa. Sch. Medicine 66-78; asso. prof. dermatology U. Pa., 1973-78, U. Cin., 1978—. Served to lt. comdr. USPHS, 1965-67. Diplomate Am. Bd. Dermatology. Fellow Am. Acad. Dermatology, Pa. Acad. Dermatology, Phila. Dermatol. Soc., Coll. Physicians of Phila., A.C.P.; mem. Am. Venereal Disease Assn., Am. Dermatol. Assn., Chgo. Dermatol. Soc. (asso.), Cin. Dermatol. Soc. Author: Audiovisual Course in Venereal Disease, 1972; Chancroid: Current Therapy, 1975; (with D.M. Pillsbury) Manual of Dermatology, 1980; contbr. papers to profl. jours. Home: 5534 E Galbraith Rd Apt 25 Cincinnati OH 45236 Office: U Cin Coll Medicine Dept Dermatology 231 Bethesda Ave Cincinnati OH 45267

HEATON, MICHAEL TERRY, bronze corp. ofcl.; b. Toledo, May 8, 1948; s. Edwin and Ruth A. H.; B.A. in Indsl. Psychology, U. Toledo, 1970; M.B.A., Am. U., 1978; m. Susan Jane Zimmer, Aug. 28, 1970; children—Janeene Cynthia, Erin Kathleen, John Michael. Personnel mgr. United Can Co. div. Norton Simon, Inc., 1970-73; personnel dir. City Auto Stamping div. Sheller Globe Corp., Toledo, 1973-75; corp. mgr. indsl. relations Zeller Corp., Defiance, Ohio, 1975-78, also v.p. Allied Eastern Corp., Defiance, 1976-78; div. mgr. employee relations Markey Bronze Corp. div. Eagle-Picher Industries, mgr. employees relations Markey Delta, Ohio, 1978—; tchr., cons. indsl. relations. Bd. dirs. Defiance Career Devel. Program, Defiance Jr. Achievement, pres., 1978-79, recipient cert. of appreciation. Cert. in indsl. audiometry, Ohio. Mem. Am. Soc. Personnel Adminstrn., Toledo Personnel Mgmt. Assn., Nat. Foundry Soc., Cast Metals Fedn., N.W. Ohio Indsl. Relations Assn. N.W. Ohio Safety Council. Republican. Club: Elks. Author: Home Library of Unusual Facts, 1976; recording artist: Killing Floor/Basement Blues, 1969. Home: 2728 Copland Blvd Toledo OH 43614 Office: 200 208 Van Buren St Delta OH 43515

HEAVIRLAND, DONALD WAYNE, savs. and loan exec.; b. Esmond, S.D., Feb. 8, 1945; s. Kenneth LeRoy and Margaret Helen (Raether) H.; B.S., U. N.D., 1969; m. Cherie Ann Perron, Mar. 7, 1971; 1 son, Wayne Michael. Adjuster, Gen. Adjustment Bur., Bismarck, N.D., 1969-70; asst. mgr. Snoopy's Pizza & Suds, Bismarck, 1970-71; buyer Bendix Field Engring. Corp., United Tribes Ednl. Tech. Center, Bismarck, 1971-72; loan mgr. Gate City Savs. & Loan Assn., Bismarck, 1973—, asst. v.p., 1977—. Mem. citizens adv. bd. Community Blood Services, 1977—; mem. council Trinity Luth. Ch. Men., 1979-80, pres., 1980-81. Mem. Bismarck-Mandan Home Builders Assn. (sec.-treas. 1977-78), Bismarck-Mandan Bd. Realtors, Am. Jaycees (v.p., treas., dir.). Legion, Republican. Lutheran. Clubs: Optimists (dir. 1976-77, pres. 1978-79, lt. gov. 1979-80, named Outstanding Lt. Gov. 1980), Elks. Home: 918 Senate Dr Bismarck ND 58501 Office: 304 E Rosser Av Bismarck ND 58501

HEBEL, ROBERT WILLIAM, elec. equipment mfg. co. exec.; b. Detroit, Oct. 2, 1923; s. Alvin J. and Agnes (Winkel) H.; B.S.E., U. Mich., 1949, M.S.E. (fellow), 1950; m. Helen I. Knap, June 14, 1948; children—Claudia, Kurt, Susan. Cons., mgr. A.E. Bishop & Assos., Detroit, 1956-59; chief engr., Airborne Accessories Corp., Hillside, N.J., 1959-66; v.p. mktg. Power Equipment div. Lear Siegler Inc., Cleve., 1966-75, pres. Romec div., Elyria, Ohio, 1975-80, pres. Power Equipment div., Maple Heights, Ohio, 1980—. Bd. dirs. Jr. Achievement Lorain County, 1976-80; bd. govs. Associated Industries of Cleve., 1980—. Served with USN, 1943-46. Mem. Am. Mgmt. Assn., Greater Cleve. Growth Assn., Am. Def. Preparedness Assn., Cleve. Machine Trades Assn. Club: Elyria Country. Home: 32840 Creekside Dr Pepper Pike OH 44124 Office: 17600 Broadway Maple Heights OH 44137

HEBEN, GERMAINE FOX, educator; b. Cleve., Mar. 3, 1923; d. Clarence and Clara Fritch (Spitzig) Fox; B.S., Ursuline Coll., Cleve., 1944; postgrad. St. Louis U., 1944-45; M.A., Western Res. U., 1965, Ph.D., Case-Western Res. U., 1975; m. Edward J. Heben, June 18, 1949; children—Edward J., Mary Ellen, Elizabeth, Laura, Carol, Michael. Dietitian, City of Cleve., 1945-47, Berea (Ohio) City Hosp., 1947-49; tchr. Cleve. Bd. Edn., 1963-65, guidance counselor, 1965-79, guidance chmn., 1979—; instr. Cuyahoga Community Coll., 1979—; lectr. in field. Active, Common Cause; exec. com. Democratic Party Cuyahoga County, 1976-78. Grad. fellow St. Louis U., 1944-45; Martha Holden Jennings grantee, 1972. Cert. tchr. and guidance counselor, Ohio. Mem. Ohio Assn. Gifted Children (exec. bd. 1977-79), Am. Personnel and Guidance Assn., Northeastern Ohio Personnel and Guidance Assn. (sec. 1978, treas. 1979, del.-at-large 1980-81), Ohio Personnel and Guidance Assn., Am. Sch. Counselors Assn., Ohio Sch. Counselors Assn. (exec. bd., del. 1978-79), Internat. Platform Assn., Phi Delta Kappa. Roman Catholic. Home and office: 11001 Edgewater Dr Cleveland OH 44102

HEBERLEIN, GARRETT THOMAS, biologist, univ. dean; b. Milw., Apr. 11, 1939; s. Edward Garrett and Ruth Andrus H.; A.B., Ohio Wesleyan U., 1961; M.S., Northwestern U., 1963, Ph.D., 1966; postgrad. U. Gent, 1966-67; m. Donna Lee Frohm, Jan. 12, 1966; children—Wendy Ann, Edward Garrett. Asst. prof. biology N.Y. U., 1967-70, asso. prof., chmn. dept., 1970-73; asso. prof., chmn. dept. biology U. Mo., St. Louis, 1973-76; prof., chmn. biol. scis. Bowling Green (Ohio) State U., 1976-80, dean Grad. Coll., vice provost for research, 1980—. Trustee, Univ. Heights Presbyn. Ch., N.Y.C., 1969-72; trustee Univ. Heights Day Care Center, 1970-72; mem. Met. St. Louis Planning Bd., 1973-76; elder 1st Presbyn. Ch., Bowling Green, 1979—; chmn. exec. com. Junto, Bowling Green. NIH fellow, 1963-66; NIH grantee, 1963—; NSF grantee, and others. Mem. N.Y. Acad. Scis., AAAS, Am. Soc. Microbiology, Am. Inst. Biol. Scis., Am. Soc. Plant Physiologists, Nat. Sci. Tchrs. Assn., Nat. Assn. Biology Tchrs., Am. Assn. Univ. Adminstrs., Ohio Acad. Sci., Plant Growth Regulator Working Group, Sigma Xi, Phi Gamma Delta. Club: Kiwanis. Contbr. articles to profl. jours. Home: 1111 Bourgogne Bowling Green OH 43402 Office: Grad Coll McFall Center Bowling Green State U Bowling Green OH 43403

HECHT, ILENE FRAN, human resource mgmt. cons.; b. Chgo., Nov. 11, 1951; d. Harry and Janice H.; B.A., U. Ill., Chgo. Circle, 1973, M.A., 1975. Teaching asst. U. Ill., Chgo. Circle, 1972-73; with project mgmt. Chgo. Area Transp. Study, 1976; systems edn. coordinator Chgo. Title & Trust, from 1976; now cons. human resource mgmt., Chgo.; lectr. career path planning. Active Women's Am. Orgn. for Rehab. through Tng., 1978—. Mem. Am. Soc. Tng. and Devel. (Region V EDP coordinator), Ill. Tng. and Devel. Assn. (membership chmn.), IBM Guide Internat. Orgn. (project mgr.), Chgo. Orgn. for D.P. Educators. Democrat. Clubs: Snow Hawks Ski, Mid Town Tennis. Author: Compudoc Mortgage Closing Systems Brochure, 1976, mini-course in title policy prodn., 1978; Human Resource Management System, 1981; editor Mgmt. Systems Guide. Office: 311 W Monroe St Chicago IL 60606

HECHT, MORGAN KEEN, social worker; b. N.Y.C., June 24, 1944; d. Victor F. and Alice (Morgan) Keen; B.S., Colo. State U., 1966; M.S.W., U. Nebr., 1972; m. Walter R. Hecht, Feb. 22, 1969. Social worker Denver Dept. Welfare, 1966-69, Child Saving Inst., Omaha, 1969-71, Family Service Omaha-Council Bluffs, Omaha, 1972-77; social worker Meyer Children's Rehab. Inst., U. Nebr. Med. Center, Omaha, 1977—, acting dir. social service dept., 1978-79, dir. multi-handicapped children's program, 1978-80; pvt. practice therapist, cons. and trainer, 1980—; pres. Child Abuse Council Omaha, 1978-79; trainer, mem. adv. bd. Parent Assistance Line, Omaha, 1977-79; trainer, bd. dirs. Crisis Nursery, Omaha, 1979—; bd. dirs. Personal Crisis, Omaha, 1974-77. Named Vol. of Year, Family Service Omaha, 1978. Mem. Nat. Assn. Social Workers, Am. Orthopsychiat. Assn., Omaha Jr. League. Home: 13232 N River Rd Omaha NE 68112 Office: 601 N 30th St Omaha NE 68131

HECKER, LAWRENCE HARRIS, indsl. hygienist; b. Detroit, July 14, 1944; s. Joseph and Rose Vivian (Harris) H.; B.A., Wayne State U., 1965, M.S., 1967; M.S., U. Mich., 1969, Ph.D., 1972; m. Phyllis Rosalind Cohen, Mar. 29, 1966; children—Charles Aaron, David Alan. Indsl. hygiene technician Wayne State U., 1964-66; chief chemist, indsl. hygienist Environ. Health Labs., Franklin, Mich., 1966-68; asst. prof. U. Mich., 1972-78, nonresident lectr., 1978—; mgr. corp. indsl. hygiene Abbott Labs., North Chicago, Ill., 1978—; cons. environ. and indsl. health, 1970—; dir. environ. and indsl. health Environ. Research Group, Inc., 1972-76. Recipient various grants in field. Mem. Etylene Oxide Industry Council vice chmn. bd. 1981—), Air Pollution Control Assn., AAAS, Am. Chem. Soc., Am. Indsl. Hygiene Assn., ASTM (membership sec., 1976—), Health Industries Mfrs. Assn., Mich. Indsl. Hygiene Soc., Pharm. Mfrs. Assn., Sigma Xi. Contbr. sci. articles to profl. jours. Home: 4911 Oak Ln Gurnee IL 60031 Office: Abbott Labs 1400 Sheridan Rd North Chicago IL 60064

HECKMAN, BRUCE WILSON, urban planner; b. Washington, Apr. 25, 1945; s. Robert Wilson and Susan S. (Stone) H.; B.Arch., Kans. State U., 1968; M.Urban Affairs, St. Louis U., 1971; m. Irene Sue Hyman, Mar. 20, 1974; 1 son, Cary Ray. Central bus. dist. devel. cons., Independence, Mo., 1967-68; asst. dir. planning and devel. St. Louis City Plan Commn., 1968-70; dir. St. Louis Met. Urban Think Tank, 1970-71; prin. urban planner St. Louis County, 1971-73; dir. community devel., Kirkwood, Mo., 1973-76, Highland Park, Ill., 1976-79; exec. v.p. Robert B. Teska Assos., Inc., Evanston, Ill., 1979—; asso. prof. Wood Inst. Local and Regional Studies, Lake Forest (Ill.) Coll., 1977-79; lectr. urban affairs grad. program Roosevelt U., 1980—; asso. prof. Grad. Center for Urban Programs, St. Louis U., 1971-76; lectr., staff cons. Grad. Program in Urban Design, Washington U., St. Louis, 1972-76; lectr. Northeastern Ill. U., 1981—; mem. Bldg. Ofcl. Conf. Am., 1976-80; mem. exec. tech. com. Lake County Dept. Planning, Zoning and Environ. Quality, 1977-80; lectr., cons. in field. Mem. Planning and Zoning Commn., Kirkwood, Mo., 1970-73; mem. exec. bd. Heritage/St. Louis, Inc., 1969-70; mem. St. Louis Landmarks and Urban Design Commn., 1968-70; bd. dirs. Ill. Environ. Council, 1981—. Named Man of Year, Kirkwood C. of C., 1976. Mem. Am. Inst. Planners (pres. St. Louis sect. 1975), Am. Planning Assn. (pres. Chgo. sect. 1979-81, v.p. Ill. chpt. 1981—), Am. Soc. Planning Ofcls., Urban Land Inst., Am. Soc. Public Adminstrn., Met. Assn. Urban Designers and Environ. Planners, Suburban Chgo. Planners Assn. (pres. 1978-79), St. Louis Engrs. Club, Am. Soc. Profl. Cons., Blue Key, Steel Ring, Alpha Tau Omega, Tau Sigma Delta, Lambda Alpha. Author plan and analysis reports; mng. editor CRIT mag., 1966-68; editorial bd. Realty and Investment mag., 1971-75. Home: 2658 Marl Oak Dr Highland Park IL 60035 Office: 627 Grove St Evanston IL 60201

HECKMAN, HENRY TREVENNEN SHICK, steel co. exec.; b. Reading, Pa., Mar. 27, 1918; s. H. Raymond and Charlotte E. (Shick) H.; A.B., Lehigh U., 1939; m. Helen Clausen Wright, Nov. 28, 1946; children—Sharon Anita, Charlotte Marie. Prodn. mgr. Republic Steel Corp., Cleve., 1940-42; editor Enduro Era, 1946-51, account exec., 1953-54, asst. dir. advt., 1957-65, dir. advt., 1965—; partner Applegate & Heckman, Washington, 1955-56; advt. mgr. Harris Corp., Cleve., 1956-57. Chmn. bd. Marketing Communications Research Center, 1965. Permanent chmn. Joint Com. for Audit Comparability, 1968—; chmn. publs. com. Lehigh U., 1971-76; pres.'s adv. council Ashland Coll., 1966-76; mem. exec. com. A.R.C., 1968-74; mem. advt. adv. council Kent State U.; exec. com. Republican Finance Com. Served to comdr. USNR, 1942-46, 51-53, Korea. Named to Am. Bus. Press Advt. Effectiveness Hall of Fame, 1967; Advt. Man of Yr., Indsl. Marketing mag., 1970; Disting. Alumnus award Lehigh U., 1979. Mem. Indsl. Marketers Cleve. (past pres.; Golden Mousetrap award 1968), Cleve. Advt. Club (pres. 1961, Hall of Fame 1980), Cleve. Graphic Arts Council (Hall of Distinction 1981), Assn. Indsl. Advertisers (pres. 1968-69; chmn. media comparability council 1969—; Best Seller award 1966, G.D. Crain Jr. award 1973), Assn. Nat. Advertisers (dir., com. chmn.), Bus./Profl. Advt. Assn. (pres. 1968-69), Am. Iron and Steel Inst. (com. chmn. 1961-69), SAR, Western Res. Soc. (pres. 1979), Early Settlers Assn. Mil. Order World Wars (comdr. 1980), Internat. Platform Assn., Greater Cleve. Growth Assn. (chmn. indsl. advertisers com. 1973-76). Republican. Clubs: Cleve. Skating; Mid-Day; Cheshire Cheese, Cleve. Grays (trustee 1980—). Home: 13700 Shaker Blvd Cleveland OH 44120 Office: Republic Bldg Cleveland OH 44101

HEDBERG, GREGORY SCOTT, mus. curator; b. Mpls., May 2, 1946; s. Fred Gustav and Clare Astrid (Nelson) H.; B.A., cum laude, Princeton U., 1968; M.A., N.Y. U., 1970, Ph.D., 1980; m. Margaret Joyce Stewart, Sept. 24, 1969. Lectr. curatorial asst. Frick Coll., N.Y.C., 1971-74; curator paintings Mpls. Inst. Arts, 1974—. Club: Racquet and Tennis (N.Y.C.). Home: 728 Goodrich Ave St Paul MN 55105 Office: 2400 3d Ave S Minneapolis MN 55404

HEDBERG, PAUL CLIFFORD, radio sta. exec.; b. Cokato, Minn., May 28, 1939; s. Clifford L. and Florence (Erenberg) H.; student Hamline U., 1959-60, U. Minn., 1960-62; m. Juliet Ann Schubert, Dec. 30, 1962; children—Mark, Ann. Program dir. radio sta. KRIB, Mason City, Ia., 1957-58, radio sta. WMIN, Mpls., 1959; staff announcer Time-Life broadcast WTCN AM-TV, Mpls., 1959-61, Crowell Collier broadcast radio sta. KDWB, St. Paul, 1961-62; founder, pres. KBEW Radio Blue Earth (Minn.), 1963-81, KQAD Radio AM & FM, LuVerne, Minn., 1971—; pres. Sta. KMRS-AM and KKOK-FM, Morris, Minn., 1971—; founder, pres. Blue Earth Cablevision Inc., 1973—, Courtney Clifford Inc., advt. rep., Mpls., 1977-80; founder, owner Market Quoters, Inc., Blue Earth, 1974—; pres., owner KEEZ-FM, Mankato, Minn., 1977—; founder, v.p. Complete Commodity Options, Mpls., 1980—; dir. First Nat. Bank, Blue Earth. Bd. dirs. Minn. Good Roads, v.p., 1976-79, pres., 1979; bd. dirs. Blue Earth Indsl. Service Corp., pres., 1970-76. Served with USCGR, 1962-70. Recipient Distinguished Service award Blue Earth Jaycees, 1971. Mem. Minn. A.P. Broadcasters (pres. 1966, dir. 1976—), Blue Earth C. of C. (Leadership Recognition award 1967, pres. 1967), Nat., Minn. (dir. 1975-80, v.p. 1980—) assns. broadcasters, Minn. Press Council. Lutheran. Clubs: Masons, Shriners, Kiwanis. Home: 305 Oak Knoll Ct Blue Earth MN 56013 Office: Hedberg Bldg Hedberg St Blue Earth MN 56013

HEDGCOCK, GRACE HALL, physician; b. Plymouth, Ill., Nov. 16, 1897; d. Robert Sloan and Laura Ann (Bolton) Hedgcock; R.N., Chgo., Wesley Meml. Hosp., 1921; B.S., Northwestern U., 1941; M.D., Woman's Med. Coll., Pa., 1945. Intern, med. residency Queen's Hosp., Honolulu, 1945-47; asst. physician Kalaupapa, Molokai, 1948-50; med. dir. Hale Mohalu, Pearl City, Oahu, 1950-60. Mem. Nat. Republican Club; mem. Plymouth Congl. Ch., Ft. Wayne, Ind. Mem. Am., Hawaiian med. assns., Honolulu County Med. Soc., Pan-Pacific Surg. Assn. (asso.), Am. Assn. U. Women, Beta Sigma Phi. Conglist. Mem. Order Eastern Star. Home: 2209 St Joe Center Rd Fort Wayne IN 46825

HEDGCOCK, RALPH EVERETTE, constrn. co. exec.; b. Augusta, Ill., Mar. 17, 1896; s. Joseph Madison and Carrie Elizabeth (Griffeth) H.; student Knox Coll., 1915-17; B.S. in Civil Engring., U. Ill., 1922; m. Dorothy M. Loy, June 24, 1929 (dec. June 1956); 1 son, Clark Loy (dec.); m. 2d, Frances Koeberlein, Nov. 26, 1959. With Div. Hwys., State of Ill., Effingham, 1922-28; v.p. Watt Constrn. Co., Winchester, Ill., 1929-36; pres. Mautz & Oren, Inc., Effingham, 1936—. Dir., Asso. Gen. Contractors of Ill., 1969-71. Served with AEF, 1918-19. Recipient Disting. Alumnus award U. Ill. Civil Engring. Alumni Assn., 1977, Loyalty award U. Ill. Alumni Assn., 1973. Mem. Effingham C. of C. (dir. 1959-61), Asso. Gen. Contractors of Ill., Am., Nat., Ill. (pres. Ambraw chpt. 1960-61) socs. profl. engrs., Ill. Christmas Tree Growers Assn., U. Ill. Civil Engring. Alumni Assn. (dir. 1964-72), Am. Legion, V.F.W., Sigma Pi. Republican. Methodist. Mason, Elk. Home: 204 Clark Ave Effingham IL 62401 Office: 406 Jefferson Ave Effingham IL 62401

HEDGER, ROBERT WILLIS, nephrologist; b. Halliday, N.D., Mar. 4, 1939; s. Richard Allen and Agnes Hilda (Hendrickson) H.; B.S., U. N.D., 1962; M.D., Wake Forest U., 1964; m. Kay Alice Letnes, Feb. 3, 1962; children—Kristen, David. Intern Rush-Presbyn.-St. Luke's Med. Center, Chgo., 1964-65, resident, 1967-69; fellow in nephrology, 1969-71; practice medicine specializing in nephrology, 1971—; instr. medicine Abraham Lincoln Sch. Medicine, 1967-70, asst. prof. medicine, 1972—; instr. medicine Rush Med. Coll., 1971; mem. staffs St. Joseph Hosp., U. Ill. Hosps., Chgo., VA West Side Hosp., Chgo.; clin. asst. prof. medicine U. Ill. Med. Center, 1975-76, clin. asso. prof. medicine, 1976—, head sect. nephrology Columbus-Cuneo-Cabrini Hosps., Chgo., 1975; asso. attending staff Roosevelt Meml. Hosp.; mem. cons. staff Augustana, South Chicago, Resurrection, Northwest Community, Washington, Ravenswood hosps., Chgo. Served with U.S. Army, 1965-67. Named Best attending tchr. dept. medicine Columbus-Cuneo-Cabrini Med. Center, Chgo., 1976. Fellow A.C.P.; mem. Chgo. Soc. Internal Medicine, Am. Soc. Nephrology, Internat. Soc. Nephrology, Ill. Soc. Clin. Nephrologists, Renal Physicians Assn., Ill. Soc. Internal Medicine, AMA, Ill. State, Chgo. med. socs. Contbr. articles to med. jours. Home: 1013 N East Ave Oak Park IL 60302 Office: 450 E Ohio St Chicago IL 60611

HEDGES, MARK STEPHEN, clin. psychologist; b. Chgo., Feb. 15, 1950; s. Norman T. and Doris Mae (Walters) H.; B.S., Purdue U., 1972; M.A., U. S.D., 1974, Ph.D., 1977; m. Janice Finnie, Aug. 16, 1975; 1 dau., Anna. Psychology intern Western Mo. Mental Health Center, Kansas City, 1975-76; coordinator children and adolescent services, psychologist Northeastern Mental Health Center, Aberdeen, S.D., 1977—. Vice pres. New Beginning Center, 1978—. Mem. Am. Psychol. Assn. Baptist. Club: Cosmopolitan. Office: Northeastern Mental Health Center 703 3d Ave SE Aberdeen SD 57401

HEDLAND, ROBERT WILFRED, brush mfg. co. exec.; b. Youngstown, Ohio, June 23, 1928; s. Rhody W. and Margaret (Hackett) H.; B.S.B.A., Ohio State U., 1950; B.S. in Edn., Youngstown State U., 1951; grad. Advanced Mgmt. Program, Harvard Bus. Sch., 1971. Mktg. mgr. Am. Steel Wire div. U.S. Steel Corp., Cleve., 1953-58; with Wooster Brush Co. (Ohio), 1958—, v.p. mktg., 1963—. Served with USN, 1951-53. Clubs: Wooster Country; Harvard Bus. Sch. (Cleve.). Home: 3165 Country Club Dr Medina OH 44256 Office: 604 Madison Ave Wooster OH 44691

HEDLEY, WILLIAM JOSEPH, engring. cons.; b. St. Louis County, Mo., Nov. 6, 1902; s. Charles Henry and Elizabeth Frances (Smith) H.; B.S., Washington U., 1925; m. Katherine Henby, May 14, 1927; children—William Henby, Mary Anne Hedley Speer (dec. 1978). Draftsman, Miss. Valley Structural Steel Co., Maplewood, Mo., 1925; with Wabash R.R., St. Louis, 1925-57, chief engr., 1957-63, asst. v.p. exec. dept., 1963-64; asst. v.p. Norfolk & Western Ry., St. Louis, 1964-67; cons. U.S. Dept. Transp., Washington, 1968-81, Sverdrup & Parcel & Assoc., St. Louis, 1968—. Chmn., Clayton (Mo.) City Plan Commn., 1957-62; mem. St. Louis County Planning Commn., 1958-62; mayor City of Clayton, 1963-67; pres. St. Louis County Municipal League, 1966-67; trustee Washington U., St. Louis, 1959-62. Named Engr. of Year, Mo. Soc. Profl. Engrs., 1964; recipient Alumni citation Washington U., 1966; Achievement award medal Engrs. Club St. Louis, 1967; Civil Govt. award ASCE, 1969; Hoover medal Joint Bd. Engrs. Found. Soc., 1973; Alumni Achievement award Washington U., 1976. Mem. Joint Council Asso. Engring. Soc. St. Louis (pres. 1951-52), Am. Ry. Engring. Assn. (pres. 1956-57), ASCE (pres. 1965-66), Interprofl. Council on Environ. Design (chmn. 1967), Mo. Soc. Profl. Engrs., Transp. Research Bd. (exec. com. 1968-71), Am. Ry. Bridge and Bldg. Assn., Roadmasters and Maintenance of Way Assn., Am. Rd. Builders Assn., Am. Soc. Planning Ofcls., AAAS, Nat. Def. Transp. Assn., Smithsonian Assos., St. Louis Acad. Sci., Mo. Hist. Soc., Nat. Council State Garden Clubs (dir. 1954-65), St. Louis Council on World Affairs, Internat. Platform Assn., Theta Xi, Tau Beta Pi, Sigma Xi, Chi Epsilon. Republican. Presbyterian. Clubs: St. Louis, Engrs. of St. Louis (pres. 1950-51), Rotary, Circle (St. Louis); University (Washington). Author: The Achievement of Grade Crossing Protection, 1949; The Effectiveness of Highway-Railway Grade Crossing Protection, 1954; State of the Art Report on Railroad-Highway Grade Crossing Surfaces, 1973; Railroad-Highway Grade Crossing Surfaces, 1979. Home: 824 N Biltmore Dr Clayton MO 63105 Office: 801 N 11th Blvd Saint Louis MO 63101

HEDRICH, CLARA ANNA, educator; b. Laona, Wis., July 18, 1954; s. Charles Louis and Anna Clara (Mrugala) Kozlowski; B.S. in Agrl. Edn., U. Wis., River Falls, 1976, M.S., Madison, 1979; m. Larry Aln Hedrich, Aug. 5, 1978; 1 dau., Anna Clara. Vocat. agr. instr. Chilton (Wis.) High Sch., 1976—. Mem. Wis. Jr. Dairyman's Assn. (exec.

sec.), Wis. Assn. Vocat. Agrl. Instrs., Nat. Vocat. Agr. Tchrs. Assn., NEA, Chilton Edn. Assn., Sigma Sigma Sigma. Roman Catholic. Home: N3425 Harlow Rd Chilton WI 53014 Office: 509 School Ct Chilton WI 53014

HEDRICH, WILLIAM CLIFFORD, photographer; b. Chgo., June 21, 1912; s. Theodore Louis and Anna Sophia (Knudsen) H.; student U. Ill., 1930-31, Inst. Design, Chgo., 1945-46, U.S. Army Motion Picture Sch., London, 1943; m. Te'a Dora Kre'mer, June 3, 1942; children—Ronald Ted, Paul Scott, Sandi Ann. Partner Hedrich-Blessing Studio, Chgo., 1931-46; chmn. bd. Hedrich-Blessing Ltd., Chgo., 1946—, also dir.; photographer architecture and interiors, 1931—; one man shows Eastman House Photog. Exhibit, 1981, John Weber Gallery, N.Y.C., 1981; group shows with Hedrich-Blessing, Mich. Sq. Rotunda, Chgo., 1935, Offices Perkins & Will, Chgo., 1967, Archtl. Photographers Am. exhibits, 1946-62, AIA Exhibit, 1978-79; also represented in permanent collections; photographs include: Falling Water, a widely pub. archtl. photograph; owner, Hedrich-Blessing Island Homes, St. Maarten, N.A., 1970—; dir. Oyster Pond Devel. Corp., St. Maaretn, N.A. Bd. dirs. Golden Sect. Soc., Boy Scouts Am., 1922-25. Served with U.S. Army, 1942-45. Decorated Bronze Star; recipient Gold medal award AIA, 1967, Archtl. Photographers Invitational award Pitts. Plate Glass, 1973, also other awards; named to Photography Hall of Fame, Santa Barbara, Calif., 1978. Mem. Profl. Photographers Am., Chgo. Photog. Guild. Lutheran. Club: South End Gun (Granville, Ill.). Contbr. articles to publs. Office: 11 W Illinois St Chicago IL 60010

HEDTKE, DELPHINE L., educator, designer; b. Wayzata, Minn., Mar. 25, 1932; d. Herbert and Wyona Hedtke; B.S., Gustavus Adolphus Coll., 1953; M.S., U. Minn., 1968; postgrad. UCLA, 1961-62, Fashion Inst. Tech., N.Y.C., 1976; Ph.D., U. Mo., 1978. Tchr. fine arts, home econs. Minn. Public Schs., 1953-56; tchr. fine arts, adminstr. home econs. Calif. Public Schs., 1956-60; fashion apparel workshop coordinator, haute couture and theatre costume designer Coll. Edn., Home Econs. Edn., U. Minn., 1974—; dist. cons. home econs., asst. vocat. program dir. Roseville Area Schs., St. Paul, 1963—; dir. Creative Design Ltd., Calif.; lectr., cons. in field. Mem. AAUW, Am. Home Econs. Assn., Am. Vocat. Assn., Home Econs. Edn. Assn., Minn. Assn. Vocat. Adminstrs., Minn. Edn. Assn., Minn. Home Econs. Assn., Minn. Met. Council Adminstrv. Women in Edn., Minn. Assn. Vocat. Educators, Minn. Vocat. Assn., Nat. Assn. Female Execs., Nat. Council Local Adminstrs., NEA, Nat. Suprs. Home Econs., Mpls. Soc. Fine Arts, Friends of the Goldstein Gallery, Walker Art Center. Lutheran. Author: Apparel Fashion Dimensions: A Multidisciplinary Approach, 1978; illustrator: Tiny Tunes for Tiny Tots, 1976; contbr. articles to profl. jours., newspapers. Home: 1661 Western Ave N Saint Paul MN 55117 Office: Kellogg Sch 15 E County Rd B2 Saint Paul MN 55117

HEDTKE, RANDALL ROBERT, educator; b. Fairmount, N.D., Apr. 15, 1935; s. George Gustav and Lina Freda (Steffens) H.; A.S., N.D. State Sch. Sci., 1959; B.S., Valley City State Tchrs. Coll., 1961; M.S., St. Cloud State U., 1977; m. Karen Jane Schouweiler, Jan. 25, 1968; children—Neil, Melissa, Joel, Nathan, Benjamin. Tchr., Tech. High Sch., St. Cloud, Minn., 1961—. Served with U.S. Army, 1954-55. Mem. NEA, Minn. Edn. Assn., Nat. Assn. Biology Tchrs., Nat. Sci. Tchrs. Assn., Creation Research Soc. Lutheran. Inventor protozoa concentrator for lab. experiments; contbr. articles to profl. publs. Home: Route 1 Clearwater MN 55320

HEERENS, ROBERT EDWARD, physician; b. Evanston, Ill., July 2, 1915; s. Joseph and Karen (Larsen) H.; A.B., Kalamazoo Coll., 1938; postgrad. U. Ala. Med. Sch., 1939, 41; M.D., Northwestern U., 1944; m. Martha Virginia Lysne, Aug. 21, 1943; children—Kisti Lyn, Martha Jill, Nancy Ann, Robin Jan, Sara Bryce. Intern, U.S. Naval Hosp., Great Lakes, Ill., 1943-44, resident, 1946-47; gen. practice medicine, Rockford, Ill., 1947—; pres. med. staff Swedish-Am. Hosp.; mem. staffs St. Anthony, Rockford hosps.; clin. asso. prof. family medicine Rockford Sch. Medicine, also dir. ind. studies, mem. exec. com.; mem. admissions com. U. Ill. Coll. Medicine, 1970—, promotions com., 1973-75, mem. Senate Med. Center, 1975-77, also mem. acad. council, mem. adv. com. on family practice. Bd. dirs. Rockford Community Chest, 1954-60, Vis. Nurse Assn.; pres. Winnebago Tb Assn., 1960-61, Winnebago County Bd. Health, 1961-69; mem. Rockford Community Devel. Com.; mem. Community Action Com., 1969-71. Served with M.C., USN, 1942-47. Diplomate Am. Bd. Family Practice. Mem. Am. Acad. Family Physicians (Ill. del. to congress of dels. 1959-71, mem. pub. relations com. 1967-74, chmn. pub. relations com. 1971-74, dir. 1970-73, exec. com. 1972-73, v.p. 1974), Ill. Acad. Gen. Practice (pres. 1958), A.M.A., Ill. (chmn. pub. relations com. 1961-62), Winnebago County (v.p. 1965, pres. 1966) med. socs., Rockford C. of C. (pres. 1962, chmn. edn. com.), Phi Beta Pi. Home: 1910 Bradley Rd Rockford IL 61107 Office: 1309 Second Ave Rockford IL 61108

HEESCHEN, BARBARA ANN, musician; b. Gary, Ind., Dec. 22, 1931; d. William George and Irene Elizabeth (Enterline) Stuhlmacher Rea; B.A. magna cum laude, Hanover Coll., 1953; postgrad. Union Theol. Sem., summer 1956; M.Mus., Central Mich. U., 1977; m. Jerry Parker Heeschen, Sept. 30, 1956; children—William Andrew, Paul Richard, James Matern. Sec. to supt. Presbyn. Schs. Cardenas, Cuba, 1953-54; press staff World Council Chs., Evanston, Ill., 1954; dir. Christian edn. 1st Presbyn. Ch., Champaign, Ill., 1954-56; tchr. piano, recitalist, accompanist, Midland, Mich., 1960—; folksinger, 1965—; harpsichordist; dir. youth choir Meml. Presbyn. Ch., Midland, 1963—; accompanist, asst. dir. Canzona di Musica; instr. music theory Delta Coll., Midland, 1975-76; music critic Midland Daily News; lectr. in field. Sec. bd. dirs. Midland Music Soc., 1961-65, mem., 1971-77; bd. dirs. Midland Center for Arts, 1971-77, asst. sec. bd. dirs., 1974-75; mem. Saginaw Valley Arts Council, 1963-64; musical dir. for Teenage Musicals, 1969, 70, other musicals; publicity chmn. Sugnet Sch. Parent Tchr. Orgn., 1971-73. Recipient citizenship award DAR, Nat. Honor Soc., 1949, Hanover Coll. Alumni award, 1953. Mem. Nat. Guild Piano Tchrs. (bd. judges), Mich. Music Tchrs. Assn. (cert.; asst. chmn. jr. high activities 1972-74), Midland Music Tchrs. Assn. (v.p. 1966-70, 80—, student activities chmn. 1978-80), Midland Community Concert Soc. (bd. mgrs.), Alpha Delta Pi. Presbyterian. Clubs: P.E.O., Twentieth Century. Home: 4426 Gladding Ct Midland MI 48640

HEFFELFINGER, JOHN BROCK, cons. engr.; b. Arkansas City, Kans., July 27, 1917; s. John Byers and Lucile W. (Parmenter) H.; student Bethel Coll., 1934-36; B.S. in Elec. Engring., U. Kans., 1938; M.S., Ohio State U., 1940; m. Georgia Anna Shaw, Sept. 7, 1940; 1 dau., Carol Ann. Design engr. Collins Radio Co., 1940-43, chief field engr., 1943-46; sr. engr. Air Communications, Inc., Kansas City, Mo., 1945, Aireon, Inc., Kansas City, Kans., 1946; asst. prof. Park Coll., 1946-47; cons. radio and TV engr., Kansas City, Mo., 1947—. Registered profl. engr., Mo., Nebr. Mem. I.E.E.E. (sr.), Nat. Soc. Profl. Engrs., Sigma Xi, Tau Beta Pi, Sigma Tau, Eta Kappa Nu, Sigma Pi Sigma, Kappa Eta Kappa. Methodist. Home: 8401 Cherry St Kansas City MO 64131 Office: 9233 Ward Pkwy Suite 285 Kansas City MO 64114

HEFFELFINGER, RICHARD EARL, research chemist; b. Big Prairie, Ohio, Jan. 21, 1922; s. Gust Thomas and Amy Lillian (Norris) H.; student Fenn Coll., 1939-41; A.B. in Chemistry, Wooster Coll, 1949; m. Nella Alberta Brewster, June 11, 1947; children—Susan, Rebecca, Scott. Chemist, Ohio Agrl. Research and Devel. Center, Wooster, Ohio, 1949-51; successively chemist, research chemist, sr. research chemist, asso. sect. mgr., projects mgr. Battelle-Columbus Div., Columbus, Ohio, 1951—. Served with USNR, 1942-43, with USMC, 1943-46. Mem. Soc. Applied Spectroscopy, Ohio Acad. Sci., AAAS, Aircraft Owners and Piolots Assn., ASTM, N.W. Area Council Human Relations. Methodist. Contbr. articles to profl. jours. Home: 2122 Nayland Rd Columbus OH 43220 Office: Battelle Columbus Laboratories 505 King Ave Columbus OH 43201 .

HEFFERNAN, NATHAN STEWART, justice; b. Frederic, Wis., Aug. 6, 1920; s. Jesse Eugene and Pearl Eva (Kaump) H.; B.A., U. Wis., 1942, LL.B., 1948; postgrad. Harvard Bus. Sch., 1943-44; m. Dorothy Hillemann, Apr. 27, 1946; children—Katie (Mrs. Howard Thomas), Michael, Thomas. Admitted to Wis. bar, 1948; asso. firm Schubring, Ryan, Peterson & Sutherland, Madison, 1948-49; counsel Wis. League Municipalities, 1949; research asst. to Gov. Wis., 1949; pvt. practice law, Sheboygan, Wis., 1949-59; partner firm Buchen & Heffernan, 1951-59; asst. dist. atty. Sheboygan County, Wis., 1951-53; city atty. Sheboygan, 1953-59; dep. atty. gen. Wis., 1959-61; U.S. atty. Western Dist. Wis., Madison, 1962-64; justice Wis. Supreme Ct., 1964—. Lectr. municipal corps. U. Wis., Law Sch., 1961-64, lectr. appellate procedure and practice, 1971—, faculty, appellate judges seminar, N.Y. U., 1972—; chmn. Wis. Appellate Practice and Procedures Com., 1975-76. Gen. chmn. Wis. Democratic Conv., 1960, 61. Former mem. bd. Meth. Hosp., Madison; trustee U. Wis. Meml. Union, Wis. State Library; bd. visitors U. Wis. Law Sch., chmn. 1973-76; mem. U. Wis. Found. Served to lt. USNR, 1942-46. Mem. City Attys. Assn. (past pres.), Am. (spl. com. state-fed. jurisdiction), Wis., Dane County, Sheboygan County bar assns., V.F.W., Wis. Hist. Soc. (curator), Am. Legion, Am. Judicature Soc. (dir., program chmn.), Am. Law Inst., Inst. of Jud. Adminstrn., Council State Ct. Reps. of Nat. Center for State Cts. (chmn. council 1977), Order Coif, Iron Cross, Phi Delta Phi, Phi Kappa Phi. Congregationalist (past deacon). Home: 17 Thorstein Veblen Pl Madison WI 53705 Office: Supreme Ct Capitol Bldg Madison WI 53702

HEFLIN, CLARENCE H., state senator; b. Independence, Mo., Apr. 25, 1921; student Washburn U.; m. Betty Evelyn Beanland, Feb. 23, 1947; 4 children. Mem. Mo. Ho. of Reps., 1966-78, Mo. Senate, 1978—. Asst. scout master Boy Scouts Am. Served with USAF. Mem. VFW, C. of C. (past pres.). Democrat. Baptist. Clubs: Masons, Shriners. Office: State Capitol Jefferson City MO 65101*

HEFNER, ELROY M., state legislator; b. Coleridge, Nebr., Dec. 12, 1923; grad. high sch.; m. Carol Rae Wilms, June 12, 1949; children—William, Douglas, Cynthia. Pres., part owner Hefner Oil & Feed Co.; mem. Nebr. Legislature, 1976, 80—. Former Mem. Coleridge Sch. Bd.; former mayor, Coleridge; former mem. Coleridge Fire Dept. Mem. Am. Legion, Nebr. Petroleum Marketers, VFW. Club: Coleridge Comml. (past pres.). Home: Box 36 Coleridge NE 68727*

HEFNER, NEVA LAMAE, assn. exec.; b. West Point, Nebr., Apr. 29, 1930; d. Frank S. and Della A. (Prawitz) White; B.A., Midland Luth. Coll., 1956; m. Philip Hefner, May 26, 1956; children—Sarah, Martha, Julia. Sec., Cuming County Public Welfare Dept., West Point, 1947-52; sec. to exec. dir. Tuberculosis Inst. Chgo., 1957-61; exec. sec. N. Am. Soc. Adlerian Psychology, Chgo., 1975—. Active Murray Sch. P.T.A., Chgo., pres., 1973-75; mem. ch. council Augustana Luth. Ch., 1981. Home: 5318 S Hyde Park Blvd Chicago IL 60615 Office: 159 N Dearborn St Chicago IL 60601

HEGEL, JAMES EDWARD, farm co-op exec.; b. Wabash, Ind., May 4, 1943; s. Ralph Edward and Helen Viola (Landrum) H.; student Internat. Bus. Coll., Ft. Wayne, Ind., 1961-63, Manchester Coll., 1963-64; m. Patricia Louise Culver, Mar. 20, 1965; 1 son, John Edward. Partner, Haupert & Hegel, Urbana, Ind., 1964-65; v.p. Triple H Trucking Co., Inc., Urbana, 1968-71; yard foreman Wabash County Farm Bur. Co-op., 1972-73, asst. mgr. lumber yard, 1974-75, mgr. lumber yard, 1976—. Mem. Wabash County 4-H Fair Com.; lay leader, chmn. adminstrv. bd. Bethel United Methodist Ch. Served with U.S. Army, 1966-68. Decorated Army Commendation medal. Mem. Nat. Frame Builders Assn., Wabash County Home Builders Assn., North Manchester C. of C. Club: Masons. Home: Rural Route 6 Box 150 Wabash IN 46992 Office: Wabash County Farm Bur Co-op 108 S Mill St North Manchester IN 46962

HEGG, DAVID LEE, pediatrician; b. Evanston, Ill., Mar. 27, 1931; s. Manne Oscar and Eva Elizabeth (O'Donnell) H.; B.S., St. Mary's Coll., Winona, Minn., 1953; M.D., Loyola U., Chgo., 1957; m. Joan Elizabeth McKendry, July 9, 1955; children—David, Steven, Kevin, Susan, Daniel, Paul, Sharon, Chris. Commd. lt. USAF, 1957, advanced through grades to capt., 1958, discharged, 1965; intern Lackland AFB Hosp., Tex., 1957-58, resident, 1959-61; practice medicine specializing in pediatrics, Kankakee, Ill., 1965—; mem. staff St. Mary's Hosp., Kankakee, Riverside Hosp., Kankakee, Foster G. McGaw Hosp., Maywood, Ill.; cons. pediatrics Div. Crippled Children; clin. asst. prof. dept. pediatrics Stritch Sch. Medicine, Loyola U.; cons. pediatrics Ill. Bd. Vocat. Edn. Mem. Will-Grundy County Comprehensive Health Care Council; mem. exec. com., adviser Kankakee chpt. Nat. Found. March of Dimes; adv. bd. Kankakee area Salvation Army; bd. dirs. Alfred Fortin Villa Learning and Day Care Center. Diplomate Am. Bd. Pediatrics. Fellow Am. Acad. Pediatrics, Royal Soc. Health, Royal Soc. Medicine; mem. Pan. Am. Med. Assn. (diplomate mem.), A.C.P., Ill., Kankakee County med. socs., AMA (Physicians Recognition award 1971, 74, 77, 80), Am. Coll. Sports Medicine, Central Ill. Pediatric Soc. Roman Catholic. Home: Route 2 Box 2 Woodlake Rd Kankakee IL 60901 Office: 401 N Wall St Kankakee IL 60901

HEGG, PHILIP N., ins. and estate cons.; b. Sioux Falls, S.D., Apr. 27, 1946; s. Peter Ode and Margaret Pearl (Nelson) H.; student S.D. State U., 1964-68, La. State U., 1973; m. Kristi M. Thompson, Nov. 14, 1965; children—Margaret M., Joel F. Agt., Fidelity Union Life Ins. Co., Brookings, 1968-71, gen. agt., mgr. Brookings County, 1971-73, state mgr. Eastern dist., 1973-76, dist. mgr. N.D. and S.D., 1976—. Chmn. steering com. Brookings Centennial, 1978; chmn. Brookings Area Arts Council, 1976-77, Brookings Youth Council, 1972-74, Brookings United Fund, 1974; mem. County Republican Precinct Com., 1978. Mem. S.D. Assn. Life Underwriters (state pres.), Nat. Assn. Life Underwriters, Life Underwriters Polit. Action Century Club. Lutheran. Clubs: Rotary, Brookings Country, Elks. Home: 311 12th Ave Brookings SD 57006 Office: 811 Medary Ave PO Box 28 Brookings SD 57006

HEGGERS, JOHN PAUL, educator, microbiologist, ret. army officer; b. Bklyn., Feb. 8, 1933; s. John and May (Hass) H.; B.A. in Bacteriology, Mont. State U., 1958; M.S. in Microbiology, U. Md., 1965; Ph.D. in Bacteriology and Pub. Health, Wash. State U., 1972; m. Rosemarie Niklas, July 30, 1977; children—Arn M., Ronald R., Laurel M., Gary R., Renee L., Annette M. Med. technologist U.S. Naval Hosp., St. Albans, N.Y., 1951-53; bacteriologist Hahnemann Hosp., Worcester, Mass., 1958-59; commd. 2d lt. U.S. Army, 1959, advanced through grades to lt. col., 1975; mem. staff dept. bacteriology 1st U.S. Army Med. Lab., N.Y.C., 1959-60; chief clin. lab. U.S. Army Hosp., Verdun, France, 1960-63; chief virology and rickettsiology div. dept. microbiology 3d U.S. Army Med. Lab., Ft. McPherson, Ga., 1965-66; chief diagnostic bacteriology 9th Med. Lab., Saigon, Vietnam, 1966-67; chief microbiology div. dept. pathology Brooke Gen. Hosp., Ft. Sam Houston, Tex., 1967-69; lab. scis. officer Office Surgeon Gen., Washington, 1972-74; microbiologist spl. mycobacterial disease br. div. geog. pathology Armed Forces Inst. Pathology, Washington, 1973, spl. asst. to dir., 1973-74; chief clin. research lab. clin. research service Madigan Army Med. Center, Tacoma, 1974-76, asst. chief clin. investigation service, 1976-77; ret., 1977; asso. prof. dept. surgery U. Chgo., 1977-80, prof., 1980—; instr. bacteriology Basic Lab. Sch., Ft. McPherson, 1965-66; chmn. dept. microbiology U.S. Army Sch. Med. Tech., Ft. Sam Houston, 1967-69; instr. bacteriology eve. div. San Antonio Jr. Coll., 1969; instr. immunology, parasitology and mycology Clover Park Vocat. Tech. Inst., 1976-77. Decorated Bronze Star; Legion of Merit; recipient certificate of appreciation A.C.S., 1969, Armed Forces Inst. Pathology, 1974; Valley Forge Honor certificate Freedoms Found., 1974; Fisher award in med. tech. Am. Med. Technologists, 1968; Gerard B. Lambert award, 1973; diplomate Am. Bd. Bioanalysis. Fellow Am. Acad. Microbiology, Royal Soc. Tropical Medicine and Hygiene, Am. Geriatrics Soc., Am. Soc. Plastic and Reconstructive Surgery (asso.; Ednl. Found. Research award 1978); mem. Nat. Registry Microbiologists (chmn. exec. council 1976-79), Am. Soc. Microbiology (chmn. com. tellers 1974-75), Wash. State Soc. Am. Med. Technologists (pres. 1975-77), Wash. Soc. Med. Tech. (chmn. sect. microbiology sci. assembly, dir. 1975-77), Assn. Mil. Surgeons U.S., Am. Soc. Clin. Pathologists (asso.), Am. Med. Technologists (disting. achievement award 1975, exceptional merit award 1976, nat. dir. 1979-80, nat. sec. 1980—), Am. Burn Assn. (President's award 1981), Plastic Surgery Research Council, Ill. State Soc. Med. Technologists (v.p. 1979—), N.Y. Acad. Sci., Sigma Xi. Elk. Author: Current Problems in Surgery, 1973. Contbr. articles to profl. jours. Contbg. editor Jour. Am. Med. Tech., 1972—. Home: 10S-082 Lakewood Dr Hinsdale IL 60521 Office: Box 269 Dept Surgery U Chgo 950 E 59th St Chicago IL 60637

HEH, JACK CHIEN-KUO, chem. engr.; b. China, Sept. 3, 1944; s. Chia-Heng and Yen-Kuer (Shih) Ho; Ph.D., Kent State U., 1978; m. Sheau-Yen Kuo, June 28, 1969; children—Ca-May, Karen. Chem. engr. Chung Tai Rubber Goods Mfg. Co., Ltd., Taipei, Taiwan, 1970-73; instr. Central Police Coll., Taipei, 1972-73; postdoctoral fellow Marquette U., Milw., 1978-79; scientist Magnetic Peripherals, Inc., Mpls., 1979—. Mem. Am. Chem. Soc., Soc. Rheology. Home: 9485 Garrison Way Eden Prairie MN 55344 Office: 7801 Computer Ave Minneapolis MN 55435

HEHMEYER, ALEXANDER, lawyer; b. N.Y.C., Oct. 20, 1910; s. Frederick William and Catherine Enole (Schrader) H.; grad. Montclair (N.J.) Acad., 1928; B.S., Yale U., 1932; LL.B., Columbia U., 1935; m. Florence Isobel Millar, Oct. 10, 1936 (dec. 1967); children—Alexander Millar, Christine McKesson; m. 2d, Sheila Mary Vought, 1968. Admitted to N.Y. bar, 1936, Ill. bar, 1968; asso. firm Cravath, Swaine and Moore, N.Y.C., 1935-40, 44-46; asst. to chmn. Time, Inc., 1940-43; partner firm Paul, Weiss, Rifkind, Wharton & Garrison, N.Y.C., 1946-67; mem. exec. com., dir. Field Enterprises, Inc., Chgo., 1960-75, exec. v.p., gen. counsel, 1967-75; counsel firm Isham, Lincoln & Beale, Chgo., 1976—; past dir. Field Communications Corp., Field Enterprises Ednl. Corp., Field Enterprises Realty Corp., Field Ednl. Publs., Inc., Field Creations, Inc., FSC Paper Corp., Mantistique Pulp & Paper Co., World Book Ednl. Ins. Co., Met. Printing Co.; past mem. mgmt. bd. Kaiser Broadcasting Co., Field Newspaper Syndicate; Field Enterprises Charitable Corp.; dir. Pocket Books, Inc., 1950-57, Am. Research Bur., 1965-69, Telemedia, Inc.; dir, sec., exec. com. Am. Heritage Pub. Co., Inc., 1954-69; dir., v.p. Gahagan Dredging Corp., 1953-70. Legal-econ. cons. Fgn. Econ. Adminstrn., 1943-44; vice chmn., counsel U.S. Econ. Missions, West Berlin, 1952, Gold Coast, 1954. Dir., vice chmn., exec. com. Chgo. Council Fgn. Relations; pres. N.Y. Young Rep. Club, 1944-46; trustee Kent (Conn.) Sch.; trustee, chmn. Midwest adv. bd. Inst. Internat. Edn. Fellow Am. Bar Assn.; mem. Fed., Ill., N.Y. State, Chgo. bar assns., Bar Assn. City N.Y., Phi Gamma Delta. Clubs: University (N.Y.C.); Chicago, Commercial, Racquet, Mid-Day, Saddle & Cycle (Chgo.); Fairfield (Conn.) Hunt. Author: Time for Change, 1943. Home: 20 W Burton Pl Chicago IL 60610 also 57 Owenoke Park Westport CT 06880 Office: One 1st Nat Plaza 42d Floor Chicago IL 60603

HEHN, ANTON HERMAN, mech. engr.; b. Denta, Romania, Feb. 5, 1937; s. Joseph and Mary (Hochbein) H.; came to U.S., 1950; naturalized, 1955; B.S.M.E., Ill. Inst. Tech., 1958; M.S.M.E., Northwestern U., 1961; m. Violet S. Hofmann, Aug. 2, 1958; children—Margaret, Kathleen, Anton J. With Ill. Inst. Tech. Research Inst., Chgo., 1961-68, research engr., 1963-65, mgr., 1965-67, sr. scientist, 1967-68; sr. engr. Gard, Inc., div. GATX, Niles, Ill., 1968-72, program mgr., 1972-77; dir. engring. Graymills Corp., Chgo., 1977-80; pres. Hehn & Assos., Skokie, Ill., 1980—; partner firm Dynamic Technology, Inc., Skokie, Ill., 1967—. Pres. Parent Tchr. League, Skokie, 1976—. Mem. Fluid Power Soc. (pres., bd. dirs.), Soc. Automotive Engrs., Instrument Soc. Am. Lutheran. Holder numerous patents; contbr. articles to profl. jours. Home: 5100 W Conrad Skokie IL 60077 Office: 5100 W Conrad Ave Skokie IL 60077

HEIBEL, JOHN THOMAS, electronics co. exec., educator; b. Bklyn., Mar. 22, 1943; s. Gregory John and Margaret Edna (Westervelt) H.; B.S., U. Calif. at Berkeley, 1964; M.S., U. Ariz., 1967, Ph.D., 1969; m. Dorothy Anne Fitchett, Dec. 16, 1967; children—Gregory, Anne. Research chem. engr. Naval Biol. Lab., Oakland, Calif., 1964; instr., fellow U. Ariz., Tucson, 1965-69; systems engr. Indsl. Nucleonics Corp., Columbus, Ohio, 1968, cons., 1969-76; vis. prof. Ohio State U., Columbus, 1969, asst. prof. chem. engring., 1970-73, asso. prof. chem. engring., 1974-75; pres., chief engr. Indsl. Data Terminal Corp., Columbus, 1975, chief exec. officer, tech. dir., 1976-79; pres. ID Systems Corp., Dublin, Ohio, 1979—; vis. prof., scientist Max Planck Inst. fur Stroemungsforschung, Goettingen, Germany, 1973. Recipient Bausch and Lomb award, 1960; Scaife scholar, 1960; Calif. Alumni scholar, 1960; NSF fellow, 1965-69. Mem. Am. Inst. Chem. Engrs. (chmn. Central Ohio sect. 1975), IEEE, Instrument Soc. Am. (Achievement award 1964), Am. Chem. Soc., Am. Soc. Engring. Educators, Sigma Xi. Contbr. articles to profl. jours. Home: 4114 Winfield Rd Columbus OH 43220 Office: 4789 Rings Rd Dublin OH 43017

HEIDER, DAVID ARTHUR, mgmt. cons.; b. Oconomowoc, Wis., Mar. 30, 1941; s. Maynard Laverne and Marcella Florence (Schneider) H.; B.A., Swarthmore Coll., 1964; M.B.A., Harvard, 1966; m. Ann Mueller, July 30, 1966; children—Daniel Arthur, Kathryn Anne. Instr. Harvard Bus. Sch., Boston, 1966-69; asso. in bus. adminstrn. Harvard Med. Sch., Boston, 1969-72; cons. bus. mgmt. Peter Bent Brigham Hosp., Boston, 1969-72; pres. dir. Gambles Continental State Bank, St. Paul, 1972-76; asst. v.p. Gamble-Skogmo, Inc., Mpls., 1976-77, v.p., 1977-80; asso. Merrimac Assos., Inc., Mpls., 1980—; pres. Heider Research Assos., Newton, Mass., 1967-70; asso. Trident Growth Services, N.Y.C., 1970-72; research dir. Inst. for Ednl. Adminstrn., Harvard U., Boston, 1969-71; v.p., treas., dir. Specialized Legal Publs., Inc., St. Paul, 1980—; chief exec. officer Rhino Internat. of N.D., Inc., Grand Forks, 1980—; v.p., dir. Bluff House Holdings, Ltd., Bahamas; dir. Aristar, Inc., John Alden Life Ins. Co., Gambles Credit Corp. Mem. City St. Paul Bd. Appeals and Rev., 1974-79. Chmn. governing bd. Samaritan Hosp., St. Paul, 1974-79; exec. com. E. Met. Hosp. Trustees Council, St. Paul, 1977-79. Mem. Harvard Bus. Sch. Assn. Minn. (v.p., dir. 1973-79). Episcopalian (regional bd.). Clubs: Moss Creek Golf. Author: (with others) Selective Insect Control, 1966; Income Bonds Through the Looking Glass, 1974. Editor: Business and the Urban Environment, 1969. Home: 776 Fairmount Ave St Paul MN 55105 Office: 715 Florida Ave S Minneapolis MN 55426

HEIDER, LOUIS HENRY, social work educator; b. Byron, Nebr., June 5, 1914; s. William Hermann and Alma Friedericke (Heidbrink) H.; student Concordia Tchrs. Coll., Seward, Nebr., 1933-35, 39-40, B.S. in Edn., 1948; M.S. in Social Work, U. Nebr., Lincoln, 1948; m. Vera Ruth Eckhardt, Nov. 26, 1950; children—Jean, Dale, Roger, Sylvia, Arlen. Tchr., prin. elem. schs., Minn., Nebr., 1935-41; fuselage insp. and mechanic Lockheed Aircraft Industry, Burbank, Calif., 1941-42; caseworker, supr., dir. Luth. Family Service Nebr., Omaha, 1948-76; social work educator Concordia Tchrs. Coll., 1975-79; part time social work internship instr. U. Nebr., Lincoln. Charter bd. dirs. Personal Crisis Service, Omaha, 1962-67; mem. adv. bd. Nebr. Com. for Children and Youth; mem. Citizens Juvenile Ct. Com., Omaha; various coms. United Community Services of Greater Omaha; council, fund drive participant, basketball coach YMCA; mem. Eastern Mental Health Com., Greenleigh Task Force; mem. citizens adv. com. Luth. Med. Mental Health Center, Omaha. Served with USAAF, 1942-46. Mem. Nebr. Welfare Assn., Child Welfare League of Am.-Midwest, Nat. Assn. Social Workers. Lutheran. Instrumental in facilitating merger of Luth. Ch. Am. and Luth. Ch.-Mo. Synod social agencies in Nebr.; developed social work program Concordia Coll. Home: 4850 Grand Ave Omaha NE 68104

HEIDORN, DONALD GUSTAV, real estate exec.; b. Evanston, Ill., May 6, 1928; s. Gustav Frederick and Laura (Hinz) H.; B.A. in Bus. Adminstrn., Knox Coll., 1950; grad. Realtors Inst. Ill., 1967; m. Bettie Jane Rohlfsen, July 14, 1951; children—Steven, Scott, Bruce, Lisa Beth. Sales rep. Sunbeam Corp., Chgo., 1950-52; zone mgr. mut. fund sales Investors Diversified Services, Inc., Chgo., 1952-54; sales asso. Annen & Busse, Inc. Realtors, Arlington Heights, Ill., 1954-64, sales mgr., 1964-72, v.p., gen. sales mgr., 1972-76; pres. Century 21 Country Squire II, 1976—; pres. Chgo. Relocation Connection, Inc., 1980-81; mem. real estate adv. bd. Harper Coll., 1972—. Mem. exec. bd. N.W. Suburban council Boy Scouts Am., 1965-81, v.p., 1970-75. Bd. dirs. Mt. Prospect Crusade of Mercy, 1974-75. Served with AUS, 1951-53. Mem. Nat., Ill. assns. realtors, Realtors Nat. Marketing Inst., Soc. Real Estate Appraisers, Chgo. Council Homes for Living Network (pres. 1974-75), NW Surburban Bd. Realtors (dir. 1974-77, 80-82). Lutheran. Home: 517 S Main St Mount Prospect IL 60056 Office: 906 S Roselle Rd Schaumburg IL 60172

HEIDRICK, GARDNER WILSON, mgmt. cons.; b. Clarion, Pa., Oct. 7, 1911; s. R. Emmet and Helen (Wilson) H.; B.S. in Banking and Finance, U. Ill., 1935; m. Marian Eileen Lindsay, Feb. 19, 1937; children—Gardner Wilson, Robert L. Indsl. dist. sales mgr. Scott Paper Co., Phila., 1935-42; dir. personnel Farmland Industries, Kansas City, Mo., 1942-51; asso. Booz, Allen & Hamilton, Chgo., 1951-53; partner Heidrick & Struggles, Inc., Chgo., 1953—, now chmn. bd. Bd. dirs. Internat. Exec. Service Corps, Keller Grad. Sch. Mgmt.; bd. dirs., v.p. U. Ill. Found. Served with USNR, 1945-46. Recipient Pres.'s award U. Ill. Found., 1979. Mem. U. Ill. Alumni Assn. (past pres., Nat. Achievement award 1980), U.S., Am., Ill. srs. golf assns., Phi Kappa Sigma. Clubs: Chicago, Tower, Meadow (Chgo.); Hinsdale (Ill.). Golf (past pres.); University (N.Y.); Country of Fla., Ocean (Delray Beach). Home: 101 S County Line Rd Hinsdale IL 60521 Office: 125 S Wacker Dr Chicago IL 60606

HEIKER, VINCENT EDWARD, mfg. co. adminstr.; b. St. Louis, Apr. 21, 1942; s. Anthony E. and Muriel E. (Evans) H.; student St. Louis U., 1960-62; B.S. with honors in Systems and Data Processing, Washington U., St. Louis, 1972; M.B.A., So. Ill. U., Edwardsville, 1974; m. Sheryl Ann Bunevac, Sept. 13, 1969; children—Stacie Marie, Vincent Edward. Russian interpreter U.S. Army Security Agy., 1962-65; successively asst. sales mgr., market research mgr., systems analyst, order entry supr., product line mgr. Emerson Elec. Co., St. Louis, 1966-73; systems analyst Mallinckrodt, Inc., St. Louis, 1973-74; dir. mgmt. info. systems Permaneer Corp., St. Louis, 1974-77; info. systems mgr. Boise Cascade Corp., St. Louis, 1977—; pvt. cons. to mfg. firms, 1979—; career counselor, speaker. Served with AUS, 1962-65. Cert. data processor. Mem. Assn. Systems Mgmt., Am. Prodn. and Inventory Control Soc., Mensa Internat. Republican. Reviewer EDP books; contbr. articles profl. jours. Home: 6027 Hageman Rd Mehlville MO 63128 Office: 13300 Interstate Dr Saint Louis MO 63042

HEIKES, LINDA CORRINE, wholesale grocery chain advt. exec.; b. Akron, Ohio, July 29, 1947; d. Leonard and Helen Leona (Boldon) Clerkin; grad. Mpls. Bus. Coll., 1966; B.A., Bismarck Jr. Coll., 1979; 1 son, James D. Pvt. sec. Thunderbird Motel Corp., Mpls., 1966-70; exec. sec. Ezell Jones & Assos., Mpls., 1970-73; exec. sec. Heikes Art Studio, Hollywood Beach, Fla., 1973-74, Bismarck, N.D., 1975-78; advt. and sales promotion mgr. Super Valu Stores, Inc., Bismarck, 1979—. Recipient letter of commendation for promotion Gov. of N.D., 1980. Mem. Ad Mark (award for creative excellence 1979, 80, 81). Home: 1530 S Reno Bismarck ND 58501 Office: 707 Airport Rd Bismarck ND 58501

HEIL, JACK KERRIGAN, health care edn. and mgmt. cons., educator; b. Columbus, Ohio, Aug. 28, 1943; s. Jack K. and Carolyn M. Heil; B.A., Olivet Nazarene Coll., 1967; M.S. in Health Services Adminstrn., Ohio State U., 1972; Ph.D., U. Mo., 1977-81; children—Darren, Brittany. Adminstrv. asst. Ohio State U. Hosp., Columbus, 1968-70; adminstrv. resident Doctors Hosp., Columbus, Ohio, 1971; cons. Southeastern Ohio Health Planning Assn., 1971-72, Ohio Dept. Health, 1972-73, A.T. Kearney, Inc., Chgo., 1973-75, Abbott Hosp. Planning Cons., Beirut, 1975-76; mem. faculty grad. program health services mgmt. U. Mo., Columbia, 1977—; planning asso. Center for Health Planning, Columbia, 1977-80; pres. Health Studies Inst., Inc., Columbia, 1980—, cons. planning, mgmt. and edn. to health care orgns., 1980—. Mem. Am. Public Health Assn., Am. Soc. Hosp. Planners, Am. Coll. Hosp. Adminstrs., Am. Hosp. Assn. Contbr. articles on health care mgmt. and orgn. to profl. publs. Home: 11996 Charter Oak Pkwy Saint Louis MO 63141 Office: 415 Lewis Hall U Mo Columbia MO 65211

HEIL, RICHARD WENDELL, civil engr.; b. Chgo., Mar. 16, 1926; s. Ralph Waldo and Margaret (Stantesly) H.; B.S. in Civil Engring., U. Ill., 1948; postgrad. U. Chgo., 1965, 66; m. Sarah Jane Olinger, Sept. 28, 1947; children—Nancy Jo, R. Douglas, Margaret Lenore (Mrs. David Usery). Mining engr. Oliver Iron Mining div. U.S. Steel Corp., Hibbing, Minn., 1948-55; designer hwys. and bridges Hazelet & Erdal, cons. engrs., Chgo., 1955-58; prin. civil engr. Met. San. Dist. Greater Chgo., 1958—. Scoutmaster Troop 2, Boy Scouts Am., Hibbing, 1950-55; sr. partner Clarendon Hills Investment Club, 1978-79. Served with U.S. Army, 1944-46. Registered profl. engr., Ill.; registered structural engr., Ill.; registered sanitarian, Ill., 1967. Fellow ASCE (sec. Ill. sect. 1969-71); mem. Am. Inst. Chem. Engrs., Water Pollution Control Fedn., Central States Water Pollution Control Assn., DuPage County Geneal. Soc., Chi Epsilon. Presbyterian. Patentee in field. Home: 30 Arthur Ave Clarendon Hills IL 60514 Office: Met San Dist Greater Chgo 5901 W Pershing Rd Cicero IL 60650

HEILBRUN, WILLIAM C., bus. exec.; b. Punxsutawney, Pa., Apr. 19, 1918; s. Phillip Charles and Virginia Catherine (Dodson) H.; A.B., Allegheny Coll., 1939; M.A., U. Pa., 1940; m. Dorothy Fassett Alexander, Feb. 8, 1941; children—William C., Richard A. Dir. procurement Kaiser Metal Products, Inc., Bristol, Pa., 1942-62; v.p. materials Taylor Forge, Inc., Cicero, Ill., 1962-67; v.p. materials Gulf & Western Energy Products Group, Oakbrook, Ill., 1967-74; v.p. materials McGraw-Edison Co., Elgin, Ill., 1974—; mem. Gov.'s Cost Reduction Task Force, State of Ill., 1977. Mem. Nat. Assn. Purchasing Mgrs. Republican. Clubs: Meadow, Itasca Country, Elks, Masons. Office: One Continental Towers 1701 Golf Rd Rolling Meadows IL 60008

HEILMAN, JAMES HOWARD, air force officer; b. Seneca County, Ohio, Mar. 13, 1936; s. Howard Briney and Lois Mandana (Doolittle) H.; B.M.E., Ohio State U., 1959; M.S. in Nuclear Engring., Air Force Inst. Tech., 1969; m. Lynda Jane Dicken, June 28, 1959; children—Cheryl Lynn, Jeffrey James. Commd. U.S. Air Force, 1959, advanced through grades to col., 1980; instr. nav., 1960-64; navigator B-52 combat crew, 1964-66; navigator EB-66, 1969-70; nuclear research officer, 1970-74; program mgr., 1975-76; dir. strategic planning, dept. devel. planning Aero. Systems Div., Wright-Patterson AFB, Ohio, 1976-80; div. chief Space and Missile Warning Offutt AFB, Nebr., 1980—. Decorated Bronze Star, D.F.C., Air medal with 3 oak leaf clusters, Meritorious Service medal. Mem. Air Force Assn. Methodist. Home: 307 Flint Circle Papillon NE 68128 Office: SAC Hdqrs Space and Missile Warning and Surveillance Offutt AFB NE

HEIMANN, WILLIAM EDWIN, pharm. cons. co. exec.; b. St. Louis, Nov. 20, 1940; s. William Harold and Stella Fern (Spradling) H.; student Mo. Sch. Mines and Metallurgy, 1961; B.S., St. Louis Coll. Pharmacy, 1965; m. Kathleen Locklar, Sept. 30, 1972; 1 dau., Sarah Elizabeth. Vice-pres. Meramec Drugs Inc., 1963-69; pres. Heimann Pharmacy Inc., St. Louis, 1966-69; pres. Pharm. Consultants Inc., Fenton, Mo., 1969—, exec. v.p., 1972-76; adj. clin. instr. St. Louis Coll. Pharmacy, 1976—. Named Man of Yr., Kappa Psi Pharm. Frat., 1973. Registered pharmacist, Mo., Ill., Fla. Clubs: Masons. Home: 2336 Maybrook St Kirkwood MO 63122 Office: 786 Merus Ct Fenton MO 63026

HEIMBUCH, ROGER ANDREW, mfg. co. exec.; b. Mason City, Iowa, Oct. 21, 1942; s. Robert and Martha Sophia (Graff) H.; B.S. in Mech. Engring. with honors, Iowa State U., 1966; M.S., U. Mich., 1967, Ph.D. in Mech. Engring., 1970; m. Jane Carole Bartell, Feb. 28, 1965; children—Christopher Robert, David Gale, Matthew Andrew. Teaching asst., research asst. U. Mich., Ann Arbor, 1967-70; sr. staff project engr. Gen. Motors Mfg. Devel., Gen. Motors Tech. Center, Warren, Mich., 1970—; v.p., bd. dirs. Jr. Engring. Tech. Soc. Served to capt. U.S. Army, 1970-72. NSF trainee, 1966-69; Rackham fellow, 1969-70; registered profl. engr., Mich. Mem. ASME, Am. Soc. Metals, Soc. Automotive Engrs. (materials engring. activity), Phi Kappa Phi, Tau Beta Pi, Pi Tau Sigma. Lutheran. Contbr. tech. articles to profl. publs. Home: 11198 Patty Ann Ln Romeo MI 48065 Office: GM-MD Twelve Mile and Mount Rd Warren MI 48090

HEIMBURGER, IRVIN LEROY, thoracic surgeon; b. Tsinan, China, Sept. 28, 1931; s. LeRoy Francis and Margaret Coleman (Smith) H.; A.B., Drury Coll., 1953; M.D. Vanderbilt U., 1957; m. Marcia Enlow, June 30, 1963; children—Angela, Jeffrey, Christian, Jenny. Intern, Vanderbilt U. Hosp., Nashville, 1957-58; resident in thoracic surgery Ind. U. Med. Center, Indpls., 1958-63, faculty, 1964-66, asso. prof. surgery, 1966—; registrar thoracic surgery Leeds, Eng., 1963-64; individual practice medicine, specializing in thoracic surgery Evansville, Ind., 1967—; mem. staffs Deaconess Hosp., St. Mary's Hosp. Mem. A.C.S. (pres. Ind. chpt. 1977-78), Vanderburgh County Med. Soc. (pres. 1977-78), Central Surg. Assn., Soc. Thoracic Surgeons, Internat. Cardiovascular Soc. Contbr. articles to profl. publs., 1960—. Home: 7700 Newburgh Rd Evansville IN 47715 Office: 611 Harriet St Evansville IN 47710

HEIMLICH, HENRY JAY, physician, surgeon; b. Wilmington, Del., Feb. 3, 1920; s. Philip and Mary (Epstein) H.; B.A., Cornell U., 1941, M.D., 1943; m. Jane Murray, June 3, 1951; children—Philip, Peter, Janet and Elizabeth (twins). Intern, Boston City Hosp., 1944; resident VA Hosp., Bronx, 1946-47, Mt. Sinai Hosp., N.Y.C., 1947-48, Bellevue Hosp., N.Y.C., 1948-49, Triboro Hosp., Jamaica, N.Y., 1949-50; attending surgeon, div. surgery Montefiore Hosp., N.Y.C., 1950-69; dir. surgery Jewish Hosp., Cin., 1969-77; asso. clin. prof. surgery U. Cin. Coll. Medicine, 1969—; prof. advanced clin. scis. Xavier U., Cin., 1978—. Mem. Pres.' Commn. on Heart Disease, Cancer and Stroke, 1965. Pres. Nat. Cancer Found., 1963-68, bd. dirs., 1960-70; founder, pres. Dysphagia Found.; bd. dirs. Community Devel. Found., 1967-70, Save the Children Fedn., 1967-68, United Cancer Council, 1967-70. Served to lt. (s.g.) USNR, 1944-46. Recipient Ohio Gov.'s award, 1980; diplomate Am. Bd. Surgery, Am. Bd. Thoracic Surgery. Fellow A.C.S. (chpt. pres. 1964), Am. Coll. Chest Physicians, Am. Coll. Gastroenterology; mem. Soc. Thoracic Surgeons (founding mem.), AMA (cons. to jour.), Cin. N.Y. Soc. Thoracic Surgery, Soc. Surgery Alimentary Tract, Am. Gastroenterol. Assn., Pan Am. Med. Assn., Collegium Internat. Chirurgiae Digestive, Central Surg. Assn. Author: Postoperative Care in Thoracic Surgery, 1962; (with M.O. Cantor, C.H. Lupton) Surgery of the Stomach, Duodenum and Diaphragm, Questions and Answers, 1965; (with Lawrence Galton) Dr. Heimlich's Home Guide to Emergency Medical Situations, 1980; also contbr. chpts. to books, numerous articles to med. jours. Producer (films) Esophageal Reolacement with a Reversed Gastric Tube (awarded Medaglione Di Bronzo Minerva 1961); Reversed Gastric Tube Esophagoplasty Using Stapling Technique; How to Save a Choking Victim: The Heimlich Maneuver, 1976; How to Save a Drowning Victim: The Heimlich Maneuver, 1981. Mem. editorial bd. Emergency Medicine, Reporte's Medicos. Devised Heimlich Maneuver to save victims of food choking, 1974; inventor portable oxygen system, 1980; developer swallowing technique for stroke victims, 1979.

HEIN, DAVID LEON, diversified industry exec.; b. Cleve., Feb. 4, 1939; s. Oscar Gustav and Helen Rose (Gruss) H.; B.S., Bowling Green State U., 1961; m. Judith Ann Diemert, July 27, 1963; children—Susan, Cathleen, David, Matthew. Audit supr., Ernst & Whinney, Cleve., 1961-65, tax accountant, 1963-64, mgmt. cons., 1965-70; v.p. finance Brewer-Chilcote Paper Co., Cleve., 1970-75, treas., 1972-75, v.p. fin. Chilcote Co., Cleve., 1970—, treas., 1975—, also dir.; faculty Cleve. State U., 1965-67; dir., cons. Cleve. area small businesses. Adviser, Gt. Lakes Shakespeare Festival, 1964-67; chmn., vice chmn. Greater Cleve. Council Figure Skating Clubs, 1978-80. Bowling Green State U. grantee, 1958-61. C.P.A. Mem. Ohio Soc. C.P.A.'s, Alpha Tau Omega. Republican. Roman Catholic. Clubs: Cleve Skating, Cleve. Athletic, Rocky River Figure Skating (pres. 1977). Home: 21298 Endsley Ave Rocky River OH 44116 Office: 2140 2160 Superior Ave Cleveland OH 44114

HEIN, JOHN PERSHING, info. ofcl.; b. Port Washington, Wis., Feb. 16, 1919; s. John Adolph and Adela (Gall) H.; B.Sc. magna cum laude, Elmhurst Coll., 1941; postgrad. Northwestern U., 1941-43; M.B.A., U. Wis., 1949; m. Harriet Selma Geisler, May 9, 1942; children—John, Barbara, Richard, Donald, Kenneth, Charles. Public relations dir. Elmhurst Coll., Ill., 1938-43; nat. public relations dir. Goodwill Industries of Am., Milw., 1947-51; Wis. program dir. Anti-Tb Assn., Milw., 1952-57; prodn. and purchasing dir., tech. editor Robert M. Young Co., Milw., 1957-66; systems analyst Milw. County, 1966-71; instns. info. dir. Milw. County Instns., 1971—. Served with USAAF, 1944-47. Mem. Nat. Council for Health and Welfare Public Relations, Public Relations Soc. Am., Am. Hosp. Assn., Health Care Public Relations Soc. Presbyterian. Club: Toastmasters. Home: 6619 W Fremont Place Milwaukee WI 53219 Office: Milw County Institutions 8731 Watertown Plank Rd Wauwatosa WI 53226

HEIN, RONALD REED, hosp. ofcl., state legislator; b. Seneca, Kans., Nov. 7, 1949; s. Henry Allan and Evelyn K. (Price) H.; B.A. summa cum laude, Washburn U., 1971, J.D., 1974; m. Linda S. Davis, May 26, 1979. Exec. dir. Asso. Students of Kans., Topeka, 1973-74; asst. city atty., City of Topeka, 1974-76; mem. firm Sloan, Listrom, Eisenbarth, Sloan and Glassman, Topeka, 1976-79; devel. coordinator St. Francis Hosp. and Med. Center, Topeka, 1979—; mem. Kans. State Ho. of Reps., 1975-77; mem. Kans. State Senate, 1977—. Bd. trustees Kans. Nurses Found. Mem. Am. Bar Assn., Nat. Conf. State Legislatures (states and arts com.), Phi Alpha Delta, Phi Kappa Phi, Phi Delta Theta. Republican. Episcopalian. Office: 1700 W 7th St Topeka KS 66606

HEINECKE, ERNST ARTHUR, ins. co. agt.; b. Sheboygan, Wis., Apr. 17, 1926; s. Ernst F. and Lydia (Guehlstort) H.; B.A. in Bus., Valparaiso U., 1950; m. Nadine L. Bundy, Sept. 1, 1975; children—Thomas, Steven, Timothy. Ins. agt. Phoenix Mut., 1959, dist. rep. Aid Assn. Luths., West Bend, Wis., 1959-63, gen. agt., 1963—. Mem. Planning Commn., Town Kronenwetter, 1980—; chmn. Marathon County March of Dimes, 1970-71, Marathon County Heart Fund, 1965-66; bd. dirs. N. Wis. dist. Luth. Ch.-Mo. Synod, 1965-71, mem. bd. fin., 1973—. Served with U.S. Army, 1944-46. C.L.U. Mem. Gen. Agts. and Mgrs. Assn. (dir. 1980—), Wisconsin Valley Assn. Life Underwriters (pres. 1965-66), Wis. Assn. Life Underwriters (pres. 1970-71). Club: Lions (pres. 1976); Wausau Country. Home: 1737 McAddoe Pl Mosinee WI 54455 Office: 2420 Stewart Sq Wausau WI 54401

HEINEMAN, MRS. BEN W. (NATALIE), assn. exec. Past pres., now bd. dirs., mem. exec. com. Child Welfare League Am.; past pres., now bd. dirs., exec. com. Chgo. Child Care Soc.; past chmn. exec. com. United Settlement Appeal; past bd. dirs. Chgo. Fedn. of Settlements, past chmn. Citizens Com. of Adoption Info. Service State of Ill.; past bd. dirs. Council for Community Services in Met. Chgo.; bd. dirs., mem. exec. com. Erickson Inst. Advanced Study in Child Devel., United Way Met. Chgo.; past bd. dirs., exec. com. United Way Am.; mem. woman's bd. U. Chgo. Field Mus. Natural History, Northwestern U.; vis. com. U. Chgo. Sch. Social Service Adminstrn.

HEINEMAN, CHARLES EDWARD, psychologist; b. Aachen, Germany, Mar. 7, 1922; came to U.S., 1940, naturalized, 1943; s. Hermann George and Hedwig (Leffmann) H.; B.A. magna cum laude, Brown U., 1949; Ph.D., U. Iowa, 1952; m. Marianne Thomas, Aug. 7, 1952; children—Susan, Thomas. Psychologist, Child Guidance Center, Des Moines, 1953-54; staff Mental Health Center, Ft. Wayne, Ind., 1954—, coordinator outpatient dept., 1977—; mem. State Bd. of Examiners in Psychology, Ind., 1969-71. Pres. bd. trustees Unitarian Congregation, Ft. Wayne, 1969. Served with U.S. Army, 1943-46. Diplomate Am. Bd. Examiners in Psychology. Mem. Ind. Psychol. Assn. (pres. 1978), Am. Psychol. Assn., Orthopsychiat. Assn., Am. Group Psychol. Assn. Unitarian. Contbr. articles to profl. jours. Home: 3768 Ferndale St Fort Wayne IN 46315 Office: 909 E State St Fort Wayne IN 46805

HEINES, BARBARA ARTER, educator; b. Cleve., Aug. 16, 1930; d. John C. A. and Violette L. Arter; A.B., U. Mich., 1952; M.A., Kent State U., 1970, Ph.D., 1976; m. Thomas S. Heines, June 15, 1951; children—Jean Lindsey, Michael Howard. Tchr. English, public schs., Ill., Ohio, 1964-69; lectr. English, Cleve. State U., 1970-72; reading clinician Edn. Child Study Center, supr. student tchrs. Kent (Ohio) State U., 1972-75; coordinator secondary edn. Lake Erie Coll., Painville, Ohio, 1975—, asst. prof. edn., 1975—, mem. dean's task force on spl. edn. grants, 1979-82; cons. in field; workshop presentor; ednl. program evaluator. Cert. tchr. and supr., Ohio. Mem. Assn. Supervision and Curriculum Devel., Ohio Assn. Supervision and Curriculum Devel., Internat. Reading Assn., Nat. Council Tchrs. English, Am. Assn. Colls. of Tchr. Edn., Ohio Assn. Colls. of Tchr. Edn., Am. Ednl. Research Assn., AAUP, Phi Delta Kappa, Sigma Tau Delta, Alpha Omicron Pi. Research, publs. on tchr. expectations, reading. Home: 2886 Cricket Ln Wickliffe OH 44092 Office: PO Box 295 Lake Erie Coll Painville OH 44077

HEINICKE, JANET LOUISE, artist, educator; b. Richmond, Ind., June 11, 1930; d. Homer Stroud and Mary Demaris (Way) Hart; B.S. cum laude, Wittenberg U., 1952; M.S. Art Edn., U. Wis., Madison, 1956; M.F.A., No. Ill. U., 1976, Ed.D., 1977; m. Herbert R. Heinicke, June 15, 1955; children—Peter, John, Mary Elizabeth, Mark, Sarah. Supr. elem. art Goshen (Ind.) Public Schs., 1952-54; instr. art, public sch., Shaker Heights, Ohio, 1954-55; asst. prof. art Judson Coll., Elgin, Ill., 1960-62, 69-74; instr. art Elgin (Ill.) Community Coll., 1962-69; artist-in-residence, instr. art Coll. DuPage, Glen Ellyn, Ill., 1975-76; program coordinator art Kankakee (Ill.) Community Coll., 1977-81; chmn. art dept. Simpson Coll., Indianola, Iowa, 1982—. Mem. Elgin Planning Commn., 1973-74; mem. visual arts adv. panel Ill. Arts Council, 1981-82; del. White House Conf. on Children, 1970, mem. regional com., 1980. Mem. AAUW (nat. bd. dirs. 1969-73, v.p. NE region 1977-79, named gift award 1977), Assn. Curriculum and Supervision, Coll. Art Assn. (dir.), Ill. Higher Art Edn. Assn., Mortar Bd., Pi Lambda Theta, Delta Kappa Gamma, Alpha Lambda Delta. Republican. Lutheran. Represented in permanent collections Richmond (Ind.) Art Assn., Kankakee Community Coll., Caterpillar Tractor Co. Hdqrs., Bloomington, Ill., Farm Services Corp., Peoria, Ill. Home: 25 Briarcliff Ln Bourbonnais IL 60914 Office: Simpson Coll Indianola IA 52541

HEINTSCHEL, RUTHANN MARY, ednl. cons.; b. Toledo, Oct. 27, 1942; d. Vincent H. and Florence M. (Yenzer) H.; B.A., Mary Manse Coll., 1967; Ed.M., U. Toledo, 1973, Ph.D. in Edn., 1978. Tchr. primary grades Toledo Diocesan schs., 1963-66, tchr. secondary grades, 1966-73; tchr sci. and math. Columbus (Ohio) secondary schs., 1973-76, asst. prin., 1975-76; grad. asst. Coll. Edn., U. Toledo, 1974-75, grad. teaching asst., 1976-77; tchr. math. Chillicothe (Ohio) City Sch., 1977-78; research cons. div. elem. and secondary edn. Dept. Edn., State of Ohio, 1978—, sci. supr., 1980—. Vol. for March of Dimes, 1972-74, Cancer Drive, 1975-76. Cert. tchr., Ohio. Mem. Assn. Supervision and Curriculum Devel., Ohio Assn. Supervision and Curriculum Devel., Nat. Sci. Tchrs. Assn., Ohio Acad. Sci.

(Krecker award 1972, 74, named Outstanding Sci. tchr. 1974), Phi Delta Kappa. Democrat. Roman Catholic. Contbr. articles on edn. to profl. publs. Office: 65 S Front St Columbus OH 43215

HEINTZ, DUANE HAROLD, heavy equipment mfg. co. exec.; b. Des Moines, Dec. 3, 1947; s. Wayne H. and Juanita M. (Rosburg) H.; B.S., Iowa State U., 1970; M.H.A. (Hamilton award 1975), U. Minn., 1975; m. Jan C. Helland, Aug. 9, 1968; children—Christopher, Cortney. Dir. fin. Am. Public Health Assn., Washington, 1972-74; v.p. Iowa Hosp. Assn., Des Moines, 1975-78; mgr. health care service Deere & Co., Moline, Iowa, 1978—; chmn. Illowa Emergency Med. Service Council, 1978-79; mem. Iowa Hosp. Cost Containment Com., 1978-79, Ill. Task Force Cost Effectiveness, 1979-81; Iowa State Voluntary Effort Com., 1979-81; chmn. data com. Ill. Health Care Coalition, 1979-81; mem. Iowa Gov.'s Emergency Med. Services Adv. Council, 1980-81; chmn. bd. dirs. Midwest Bus. Group on Health, 1980-81. Served as officer U.S. Army, 1970-72. Decorated Army Commendation medal. Mem. Am. Hosp. Assn., Hosp. Fin. Mgmt. Assn., Iowa Hosp. Assn., Am. Arbitration Assn. (nat. panel of comml. arbitrators 1979-81). Author articles in field. Home: 2485 Crow Creek Rd Bettendorf IA 52722 Office: Deere & Co John Deere Rd Moline IL 61265

HEINTZ, ROBERT, educator; b. Pipestone, Minn., May 22, 1942; s. Edward J. and Evelyn (Hendren) H.; B.A. in L.S., U. No. Iowa, Cedar Falls, 1966; M.S. in Edn., Central Mo. U., Warrensburg, 1970; m. Mary Ellen Junko, Feb. 12, 1966; children—Brian, Julie. Display mgr. Montgomery Ward & Co., Waterloo, Iowa, 1962-64; librarian Cedar Falls Community Sch. Dist., 1964-66; media dir. Spencer (Iowa) Community Sch., 1966—. Pres., Sacred Heart Sch. Bd., 1977-79. Mem. ALA, Iowa Ednl. Media Assn., Iowa, Spencer edn. assns., Assn. Ednl. Communications and Tech., Assn. Supervision and Curriculum Devel. Home: 519 E 4th St Spencer IA 51301 Office: 800 E 3d St Spencer IA 51301

HEINTZ, WILLIAM LOWE, mfg. co. exec.; b. Lincoln, Ill., Aug. 19, 1945; s. John Robert and Winnifred Louise (Lowe) H.; B.M.E., U. Minn., 1971, M.S. in Indsl. Engring., 1973; postgrad. St. Cloud State U., 1976-79; m. Mary Linda Olson, Aug. 5, 1978; 1 dau., Anne Terina. Devel. technician Donaldson Co., Mpls., 1968-69, prodn. engr., 1969-71, quality engr., 1971-74; sr. quality engr. Pako Corp., Mpls., 1974-75; corp. quality engring. mgr. DeZurik, Sartell, Minn., 1975-79; quality control mgr. Graco Inc., Mpls., 1979-80; quality control mgr. Safeguard Engine Parts, Marinette, Wis., 1980—. Served with USN, 1964-68. Registered profl. engr., Calif., Minn. Mem. Am. Soc. Quality Control (sr.; cert. quality engr.), Am. So. Nondestructive Testing (level III examiner), ASTM, Nat. Soc. Profl. Engrs. Republican. Lutheran. Club: Elks. Home: Route 3 Box 197B Marinette WI 54143 Office: Safeguard Engine Parts 1731 Industrial Pkwy Marinette WI 54143

HEINTZELMAN, ROSS GARFIELD, state ofcl.; b. Greensburg, Pa., Jan. 2, 1917; s. Ross Garfield and Bertha Lee (Acklin) H.; B.S., Ohio State U., 1948, M.A., 1950; m. Margery Isabel Major, Mar. 17, 1945; children—Christian Lee, Diane Kay. Supr. evaluation programs Timken Co., Canton, Ohio, 1960-73, engr., 1936-60; chief labor relations State Inter-govtl. Personnel Adminstrn., Columbus, 1973-74; adminstrv. staff asst. Indsl. Commn. Ohio, Columbus, 1974—; cons. personnel relations. Councilman, Canton, Ohio, 1957-69; mem. Ohio Ho. of Reps., 1969-72. Served with USAAF, 1943-46. Recipient awards Am. Econ. Found., Polit. Sci. Acad., Police Boys Club, YMCA, Ohio Ednl. Assn.; Canton Tchrs. Man of Year award 1972; Appreciation award Ednl. Community Northeastern Ohio; Canton City Schs. award; Ohio Dental Assn. award; Mayor's citation. Home: 206 Grandview Ave NW Canton OH 44708 Office: Ross Heintzelman Cons Public Affairs 206 Grandview Ave NW Canton OH 44708

HEINZ, CURT STAFFORD, fin. planner; b. Topeka, Kans., July 31, 1946; s. Paul H. and Miriam W. Heinz; B.S. in Bus. Adminstrn., Kans. U., 1968; m. Jo L. Heinz, Sept. 23, 1972. Agt., Conn. Mut. Life Ins. Co., 1968-70; agt. Hussey Ins. Agy., Topeka, 1970-78, mgr. life div., 1974-79; partner Heinz & Van Dyke, Topeka, 1979—. Capt. United Way. C.L.U.; cert. fin. planner. Mem. Nat. Assn. Life Underwriters, Kans. Assn. Life Underwriters (v.p.), Topeka Assn. Life Underwriters (pres. 1979), Am. Soc. C.L.U.'s, Million Dollar Round Table (life), C. of C. Republican. Club: 20-30. Home: 3165 W 15th St Topeka KS 66604 Office: 1200 Mchts Nat Bank Topeka KS 66612

HEINZ, THOMAS ARTHUR, architect, photographer; b. Evanston, Ill., May 1, 1950; s. Wilbur Edward and Jeanne Elizabeth (Kelly) H.; B.Arch., U. Ill., 1972; M.S. in Civil Engring., Northwestern U., 1975. Architect, Jerome Cerny, Lake Forest, Ill., 1972, I.C.G. R.R., Chgo., 1972-76, Chgo. Hist. Resources, 1976, John Tilton Assos., Chgo., 1976-77; architect-owner Pensayer Architects, Oak Park, Ill., 1977—; chmn. I.H.C., 1978-81; v.p. Encon Engring. Corp., 1979-80; pres. Panelight Corp., 1981—; mem. faculty Northwestern U., 1979—; vis. asso. prof. architecture U. Ill., Urbana, 1980-81; bd. dirs. Frank Lloyd Wright Home and Studio Found., 1974-80. Grantee, Nat. Endowment Arts, 1978, 81, Dept. Interior, 1979. Mem. Soc. Archtl. Historians, (v.p. 1974-79), Nat. Trust. Clubs: Comml., Cliff Dwellers, Chgo. Archtl. (Chgo.). Author: Frank Lloyd Wright, 1981; Editor-pub. Frank Lloyd Wright Newsletter, 1977—; executed additions Emil Bach House, Chgo., 1979, Adelman House, Phoenix, 1979; living room of Francis Little House installed in Am. wing Met. Mus. Art, N.Y.C., 1981-82. Office: PO Box 663 Oak Park IL 60303

HEIPLE, JAMES DEE, judge; b. Peoria, Ill., Sept. 13, 1933; s. Rae Crane and Harriet (Birkett) H.; B.S., Bradley U., 1955; J.D., U. Louisville, 1957; Certificate in Internat. Law, City of London Coll., 1967; grad. Nat. Coll. State Judiciary, 1971; m. Virginia Kerswill, July 28, 1956; children—Jeremy Hans, Jonathan James, Rachel Duffield. Admitted to Ill. bar, 1957, Ky. bar, 1958, U.S. Supreme Ct. bar, 1962; partner firm Heiple and Heiple, Pekin, Ill., 1957-70; circuit judge Ill., 10th Circuit 1970-80; justice Ill. Appellate Ct., 1980—. Vice pres., dir. Washington State Bank (Ill.), 1959-66; dir. Gridley State Bank (Ill.), 1958-59; village atty., Tremont, Ill., 1961-66, Mackinaw, Ill., 1961-66; asst. pub. defender Tazewell County, 1967-70., legal clerk Ill. Appellate Ct., 1968-70. Chmn. Tazewell County Heart Fund, 1960. Pub. Adminstr. Tazewell County, Ill., 1959-61; sec. Tazewell County Republican Central Com. 1966-70; mem. Pekin Sch. Bd., 1970; mem. Ill. Supreme Ct. Com. on Profl. Responsibility, 1978—. Recipient certificate Freedoms Found., 1975, George Washington honor medal, 1976. Mem. Am., Ky., Ill. (chmn. legal edn. com. 1972-74, chmn. jud. sect. 1976-77), Tazewell County (pres. 1967-68) bar assns., Ill. Judges Assn. (pres. 1978-79), Ky., Ill., Pa. hist. socs., Nat. Rifle Assn., S.A.R., Delta Theta Phi, Sigma Nu, Pi Kappa Delta. Methodist. Mason. Clubs: Filson; Union League (Chgo.); Pekin Country; Mo. Athletic (St. Louis); Pendennis (Louisville). Home: 707 S 5th St Pekin IL 61554 Office: Tazewell County Ct House Pekin IL 61554

HEISER, CHARLES BIXLER, JR., botanist, educator; b. Cynthiana, Ind., Oct. 5, 1920; s. Charles Bixler and Inez (Metcalf) H.; A.B., Washington U., 1943, M.A., 1944; Ph.D., U. Calif., Berkeley, 1947; m. Dorothy Gaebler, Aug. 19, 1944; children—Lynn Marie, Cynthia Ann, Charles Bixler. Instr., Washington U., 1944-45; botanist U. Calif., Davis, 1946-47; mem. faculty dept. botany Ind. U., Bloomington, 1947—, Disting. prof. botany, 1979—; vis. prof. U. Tex., 1978. Guggenheim fellow, 1953; NSF fellow, 1962; recipient Gleason award N.Y. Bot. Garden, 1969. Mem. Am. Soc. Plant Taxonomists (pres. 1967), Soc. Study Evolution (pres. 1975), Soc. Econ. Botany (pres. 1979), Bot. Soc. Am. (pres. 1980), Phi Beta Kappa. Presbyterian. Author: Nightshades, The Paradoxical Plants, 1969; Seed to Civilization, 1973; The Sunflower, 1976; The Gourd Book, 1979; contbr. articles to profl. jours. Office: Dept Biology Indiana Univ Bloomington IN 47405

HEISLER, HAROLD REINHART, mgmt. cons.; b. Chgo.; s. Harold Reinhart and Beulah Mary (Schade) H.; B.M.E., U. Ill., 1954. Mgmt. cons. Ill. Power Co., Decatur, 1954—, mem. Nuclear Power Group, Inc., Argonne (Ill.) Nat. Lab., 1955-57; chmn. fossil fuel com., West Central region FPC, Chgo., 1966-68; chmn. evaluation com. Coal Gasification Group, Inc., 1971-75; chmn. Decatur Marine Inc., 1964-66; dir. Indsl. Water Supply Co., Robinson, Ill., 1975-77; pub. speaker in field; mem. Ill. Gov.'s Fuel and Energy Bd., 1970, Ill. Commerce Commn. Fuel and Energy Bd., 1971-75, Ill. Energy Resources Commn. Coal Study Panel, 1976-79, evaluation com. of kiln gas process, 1976-80; mem. power plant productivity com. Ill. Commerce Commn., 1977-79. Mem. ASME, Nat., Ill. socs. profl. engrs., U. Ill. Alumni Assn., Sigma Phi Delta. Conceptual designer power plant sites and recreational lakes, Baldwin and Clinton, Ill. Home: 1375 W Main St Decatur IL 62522 Office: 500 S 27th St Decatur IL 62525

HELBERT, JAMES RAYMOND, biochemist; b. Miles City, Mont., Aug. 4, 1918; s. Lu Roy and Maude Mae (Stevenson) H.; B.A. cum laude, St. John's U., Collegeville, Minn., 1947; M.S., Marquette U., 1958; Ph.D., Northwestern U., 1963; m. Bernice Cyganiak, July 9, 1949; children—Gregory, Helen, John, Monica. Chemist. Orthmann Labs., Inc., Milw., 1947-51; research chemist Red Star Yeast and Products Co., Milw., 1951-58; research biochemist, geriatrics research project VA Hosp., Downey, Ill., 1958-62, acting chief, 1962-63; research asso. div. clin. hematology dept. medicine Michael Reese Hosp. & Med. Center, Chgo., 1963-67; supr. biochem. and microbiol. research Miller Brewing Co., Milw., 1967-76; mgr. microbiol. research and adminstrv. affairs, 1976—; research asso. Marquette U., 1954-58; lectr. dept. biology Ill. Inst. Tech., Chgo., 1966; asst. prof. biochemistry Northwestern U., 1967-73; guest lectr. microbial biochemistry U. Wis., Milw., 1970. NIH fellow, 1960-63. Fellow Am. Inst. Chemists; mem. Am. Statis. Assn., Am. Chem. Soc., AAAS, Inst. Food Technologists, Am. Soc. Brewing Chemists. Roman Catholic. Clubs: Swedish Glee of Waukegan; Eagles. Contbr. in field. Office: 3939 W Highland Blvd Milwaukee WI 53201

HELBERT, MICHAEL CLINTON, lawyer; b. Wichita, Kans., Dec. 30, 1950; s. Robert Lee and Carrollyn Jean (Stull) H.; A.B., U. Kans., 1972, J.D., 1975; m. Sandra Sue Ziegler, Aug. 26, 1978. Admitted to Kans. bar, 1975, U.S. Supreme Ct. bar, 1980; staff intern Douglas County Legal Aid Soc., 1974-75; asso. firm Atherton, Hurt & Sanderson, Emporia, Kans., 1975-77; partner firm Guy & Helbert, Emporia, 1978-81, Guy, Helbert, Bell and Smith, 1981—; tchr. Neosho River Free Sch., Inc.; legal counsel Kansas Jaycees, Inc. Mem. adv. bd. Neosho River Free Sch., 1976-77, pres., 1977-78, dir., 1978—; dir. Big Bros.-Big Sisters, Emporia, 1977—; chmn. profl. div. United Way Emporia, 1977—; mem. adv. bd. U. Kans. Endowment Assn., 1977—. Mem. Am. Bar Assn., Kans. Bar Assn., Lyon County Bar Assn., Am. Trial Lawyers Assn., Kans. Trial Lawyers Assn., Emporia C. of C. (dir. 1980—), Emporia Jaycees (dir. 1978—), Kans. Jaycees (exec. com. 1978—), Kappa Sigma. Republican. Presbyterian. Club: Lions Breakfast (dir. 1978—). Home: 1721 Hammond St Emporia KS 66801 Office: 519 Commercial St Emporia KS 66801

HELD, ARTHUR HUGO, cons. graphic arts; b. Chgo., Apr. 18, 1913; s. Dr. William and Frances (Cossman) H.; B.S., DePaul U., 1935; m. Harriette Touff, May 29, 1941. Market analyst, 1935; organized own bus. advt. and lithographing Arthur Held, Advt., 1936; sold lithographing bus., retained advt. agency, 1941; active in supervision and mgmt. war prodn. industries since 1941. Dir., Employee Tng. Program, Lithographic Tech. Found. Cons. prodn. sales and mgmt. problems. Trustee Glenbrook San. Dist. Mem. Nat. Rifle Assn. Am., Wilmette Ill., Printer Supplymen's Guild (Chgo.). Club: Honorary mem. Lithographers (Chgo.). Formerly condr. column, pub. by Progressive Syndicate Mags. Author article, Public Relations. Home: 215 Hickory Ct Northbrook IL 60062

HELFANT, SEYMOUR MEYER, educator; b. N.Y.C., May 8, 1916; s. Henry and Esther (Alterescu) H.; B.S., City Coll. N.Y., 1937; J.D., St. John's U., 1941; M.S., N.Y. U., 1947; m. Thelma Kurinsky Dec. 21, 1947; children—Ronald, Michael, Richard. Co-owner Del Fant Shoes, Far Rockaway, N.Y., 1940-57; mgr. smaller stores div. and specialty stores div. Nat. Retail Mchts. Assn., 1957-68, v.p., mgr. ind. stores div., 1965-69; dir. edn., mgmt. mktg. and promotion services, meetings and convs. Internat. Council Shopping Centers, N.Y.C., 1969-77; asso. prof. Columbia (Mo.) Coll., 1977—; lectr. CCNY, 1947-73, Bklyn. Coll., 1951-64; adj. asso. prof. Adelphi U., 1974-77, New Sch. for Social Research, 1975-77, Fashion Inst. Tech., 1974-77; mem. N.Y. adv. council for SBA. Dir. seminars in shoe fitting and shoe therapy, promotion and mgmt., retail productivity; co-dir. Top Mgmt. Seminar. Mem. Am. Mktg. Assn., Am. Soc. for Tng. and Devel., Eta Mu Pi. Club: Masons. Author: Problems of Smaller of Smaller Stores, 1959; Retail Shoe Sales Training Manual, 1960; Operations Manual for Smaller Stores, 2 vols., 1960; The Successful Future of the Independent Retailer, 1960; Profitable Ideas for Smaller Stores, 1961; Increasing Profitability in Today's Retailing, 1963; Training and Motivating Retail Sales People, 1969; Person to Person Selling, 1969; co-author Retail Merchandising and Management with Electronic Data Processing, 1966; Small Store Planning for Growth, pub. 1966, rev. edit., 1977; Plan Your Store for Maximum Sales and Profits, 1969; contbr. monthly column to Shopping Center World. Home: 810A Fairview Rd Columbia MO 65201 Office: Columbia Coll Columbia MO 65216

HELFER, HERMAN HYMAN, glass co. exec.; b. Chgo., Dec. 6, 1919; s. Harry and Sarah (Kurlansky) H.; student Herzl Jr. Coll., 1941; certificate U. Ill. Coll. Pharmacy, 1946; B.S. in Mktg., Roosevelt U., 1973, M.B.A., 1977; m. Frieda Hershkopf, Nov. 16, 1947; children—Joel, Harvey, Gail. With Novelty Glass & Mirror Co., Chgo., 1946—, gen. mgr., sec.-treas., 1960—; pres. Columbia Glass Co., Chgo., 1969—; pres. Energipane Insulating Glass Corp.; pres. Insulating Glass Ednl. Inst., 1980-81, seminar chmn., Chgo., 1981. Instr., Boys State, Springfield, Ill., 1966; chmn. Glazier's Pension and Welfare Funds, Chgo., 1969-73; div. exec. com. Jewish United Fund, 1981. Served with USAAF, 1943-46. Recipient Dealer of Yr. award Glass Digest, 1979. Mem. Am. Legion (post comdr. 1967-68), Assn. Glazing Contractors (pres. 1957-73), Nat. Glass Dealers Assn. (exec. com., pres. 1979-80, rep. to Consumer Safety Products Commn.), Flat Glass Marketing Assn. (dir.), Nat. Assn. Store Fixture Mfrs. (asso.), Sealed Insulating Glass Mfrs. Assn. Jewish (sec., treas. synagogue). Mem. B'nai B'rith. Mason (Shriner). Contbr. articles to trade publs. Home: 8937 Forest View Rd Evanston IL 60203 Office: 4716 W Lake St Chicago IL 60644

HELFORD, IRWIN, office products distbn. co. exec.; b. Chgo., June 18, 1934; s. Martin and Hannah H.; student Roosevelt U., 1952-54; m. Betty Herren, May 12, 1956; children—Michael, Jackie. Asst. sales mgr. Wilson Jones Co., Chgo., 1956-60; with Reliable Corp., Chgo., 1960—, v.p. sales and mktg., 1978—. Dir., Elk Grove Community Service and Mental Health Bd., 1970—; pres. Elk Grove Estates Homeowners Assn., 1980—. Served with U.S. Navy, 1952-54. Mem. Am. Mgmt. Assn., Nat. Office Products Assn., Nat. Assn. Purchasing Mgrs. Club: B'nai B'rith (pres. Elk Grove). Home: 720 Wellington Ave Elk Grove IL 60007 Office: 1001 W Van Buren St Chicago IL 60607

HELGELAND, GLENN BERNARD, pub. co. exec.; b. Rice Lake, Wis., Mar. 15, 1943; s. Adolph Bernard and Gladys Iola H.; B.S., U. Wis., 1965; m. Judith Ellen Voland, Nov. 26, 1966; children—Jody Lynn, Bryant Bernard, Amanda Kay. Reporter, Winona (Minn.) Daily News, 1965-66; county govt. reporter Bur. Comml. Fisheries, U.S. Dept. Interior, Chgo., 1966-68; asso. editor Nat. Wildlife mag., Milw., 1968-70; editor, asso. pub. Archery World mag., Milw., 1970-80, Archery Retailer mag., 1976-80; pres. Target Communications Corp., Grafton, Wis., 1980—; columnist Am. Hunter, N. Am. Hunter, Archery Retailer mags. Mem. Outdoor Writers Assn. Am. (dir. 1980—), Wis. Outdoor Communicators Assn. Home: 1012 Falls Rd Grafton WI 53024 Office: 1012 Falls Rd Grafton WI 53024

HELLEBERG, REX STAAL, architect; b. Kearney, Nebr., Sept. 9, 1928; s. John Pedersen and Elena C. (Staal) H.; student Kearney State Coll., 1946-48; B.A., U. Nebr., 1952, M.Arch., 1978; grad. U.S. Army Engr. Sch., 1966; m. Marilyn Helen Morgan, Aug. 21, 1954; children—Karen, Paul, John. Draftsman, designer, insp. Helleberg and Helleberg, Architects, Kearney, 1951-56, partner, 1956-59, architect, owner Helleberg and Helleberg, Architects-Engrs., Kearney, 1969—. Mem. AIA (pres. western chpt., 1971), Nebr. Soc. Architects (pres. 1979), Nat. Council Archtl. Registration Bds., Constrn. Specifications Inst., Interfaith Forum on Religion, Art, and Architecture, Kearney C. of C. Lutheran. Clubs: Lions (pres. Kearney Evening Lions 1960-61, Kearney Noon Lions 1966-67), Ft. Kearney Shrine (pres. 1966), Tehama Shrine Band, Elks, Royal Arch, K.T., Masons, Shriners. Registered architect, ten states; author stories on bldg.; designer schs., churches, hosps., coll. bldgs. Home: 1702 W 35th St Kearney NE 68847 Office: 2412 1/2 Central Ave Kearney NE 68847

HELLER, ALICE MAURER, educator; b. Virginia, Ill., Dec. 8, 1931; d. George Otto and Charlotte Elizabeth (Suffern) Maurer; student Blackburn Coll., 1949-51, No. Ill. U., 1962; B.S. in Edn., U. Cin., 1969; M.S. in Edn., Xavier U., 1979; m. Duane Bowden Heller, Aug. 8, 1951 (dec. Apr. 19, 1968); children—Deborah Jeanne, Brenda Louise, Rebecca Sue. Tchr., Fremont Elem. Sch., Mundelein, Ill., 1961-62; elem. tchr. Forest Hills Sch. Dist., Cin., 1965-69, 70—; music tchr. Am. Sch. of Madrid (Spain), 1969-70. Asst. sponsor Am. Field Service. Mem. NEA, Am. Personnel and Guidance Assn., Ohio Educators Assn., Forest Hills Tchrs. Assn., Ohio Council Math. Tchrs. Unitarian. Home: 1602 Braintree Dr Cincinnati OH 45230 Office: Summitt Elem Sch 8400 Northport St Cincinnati OH 45230

HELLER, DOUGLAS BRIAN, sociologist, cons.; b. N.Y.C., Jan. 16, 1937; s. Alexander S. and Beatrice (Haim) H.; B.A., Syracuse U., 1960; M.A., U. Chgo., 1963, Ph.D., 1975; m. Rita McClure Cunningham, Dec. 21, 1976; children by previous marriage—Peter, Julia and Alison (twins), Noël. Asst. prof. State Univ. Coll., Buffalo, 1960; sr. dir. B/C Assos., Chgo., 1967-73; asst. prof. Coll. Medicine U. Ill., Chgo., 1974-77; exec. dir. Chgo. Health Plan, 1974-77; pres. Heller Assos., Chgo., 1977-78; v.p., dir. Sims-Heller Inc., Chgo., 1980—; cons. fed., state govts.; dir., sec. Health Care Benefits Services Inc., Ill., 1978-80; v.p., sec. Info. Services Group Inc., Md. Exec. com. Midwest region Am. Friends Service Com., 1972-75; chmn. bd. Hispano Alcoholism Services, Chgo., 1977-78. Served with U.S. Army, 1955-58. NIH tng. fellow, 1962-63; WHO traveling fellow, 1974. Fellow Am. Public Health Assn.; mem. Group Health Assn. Am., Am. Sociol. Assn., Nat. Sociol. Hon. Soc. Democrat. Mem. Soc. of Friends. Author: Omega, 1978; American Sociologist, 1978; mem. editorial bd. Inquiry, 1966-80. Office: 55 E Washington Suite 1934 Chicago IL also 696 W Irving Park Rd Chicago IL 60613

HELLEWELL, LOUIS PATTERSON, environ. engr.; b. Evanston, Wyo., Nov. 3, 1927; s. Joseph Henry Jr. and Etta Lucile (Patterson) H.; student Brigham Young U., 1947; B.S. in Zoology and Chemistry, U. Wyo., 1950; m. Lorraine Frances Bergren, Aug. 15, 1947; children—Joseph Henry III, Louis Thomas, John R, Judith Lynne, Nancy Anne, Darlene Frances. Tech. trainee Westvaco Chem. Co., Green River, Wyo., 1952-53, process engr., 1953; chem. process shift supr. Intermountain Chem. Co., Green River, 1953-56; asst. to prodn. supt. FMC Corp., 1956-58, sr. chem. process engr., 1958-65, chief chemist, 1965-69; sr. engr. Olin Corp., Baraboo, Wis., 1969-70, sr. project engr., 1970-74, prin. project engr., 1974-75, chief project engr., 1975-78, environ. coordinator, 1978—; instr. radiol. monitoring/radiation physics Madison Area Tech. Coll., 1970—. Dir., CD, Green River; radiol def. officer, Baraboo, v.p. Jim Bridger council Boy Scouts Am., 1959-63. Named Community Father of Year, 1961. Mem. Am. Assn. Measurements and Control, Nat. Mgmt. Assn. (dir. Baraboo chpt.), Sigma Nu, Alpha Epislon Delta. Mem. Ch. of Jesus Christ of Latter-day Saints. Clubs: Lions Internat. (zone chmn. 1964-65, 72-73, sec. Baraboo club 1972—), Baraboo Country, Elks. Contbr. articles in field. Baraboo WI

HELM, NELSON WALLIE, planning commn. exec.; b. Imperial, Nebr., Dec. 13, 1937; s. Walter Henry and Georgina (Nelson) H.; B.Arch., U. Nebr., 1961; m. Sharon Janell Brehm, Aug. 17, 1957; 1 dau., Lori Lee. Asst. planning engr. City of Aurora (Colo.), 1961-63; intermediate city planner Regional Planning Commn., Reno, Sparks and Washoe County, Nev., 1963-67; dir. planning Regional Planning Commn. Hall County, Grand Island and Villages of Alda, Cairo, Doniphan and Wood River, Nebr., 1967—. Bd. dirs. YMCA, 1974-80. Winner Flag Competition, City of Imperial, 1981. Mem. Am. Planning Assn., Urban Land Inst., Nebr. Planning and Zoning Assn. Democrat. Designer logo Platte River Wildlife Habitat Trust, 1980. Office: PO Box 1968 Grand Island NE 68802*

HELM, PHOEBE KNIGHT, coll. adminstr.; b. Lafayette, Tenn., May 13, 1943; d. Jesse Alfred and Martha Ellen (Hale) Knight; A.A., Freeed Hardeman Coll., 1963; B.S., Union U., Jackson, Tenn., 1965; M.Ed., Memphis State U., 1967; Ed.D., U. Ky., 1980; children from previous marriage—Tabitha, Elizabeth. Instr., Chester County Schs., Henderson, Tenn., 1966-68; instr. Jackson (Tenn.) State Community Coll., 1968-72; dir. learning services Med. Center U. Ky., Lexington, 1972-77; exec. dir. developmental edn. Triton Coll., River Grove, Ill., 1977—. Mem. adv. com. gifted edn. City of Elmwood Park (Ill.), 1978—. Mem. Ill. Assn. Personalized Learning Programs, Am. Assn. Community and Jr. Colls., Am. Assn. Woman in Community and Jr. Colls., Phi Delta Kappa. Mem. Ch. of Christ. Home: 1647 N 73d Ct Elmwood Park IL 60635 Office: 2000 Fifth Ave Triton Coll River Grove IL 60171

HELMER, JOHN ERIC, hosp. adminstr.; b. Indpls., Aug. 2, 1934; s. Oscar Marvin and Lois Ethel (Steffy) H.; student U. Chgo., 1950-52; B.A. in Psychology, Butler U., 1961, M.A. in Psychology, 1963; postgrad. Ind. U., 1963-67, 69-70, Walden U., 1978; m. Rebecca Karol Kuch, Apr. 4, 1974; children—Eric Marvin, Freyja Ann, Sven William. Research asst. in psychophysiology Inst. of Psychiat. Research, 1961-63; research asso. in neurosurgery Ind. U. Med. Center, Indpls., 1967-70; psychologist II, N.Y. State Dept. Mental Hygiene, 1970-72; treatment team leader Creedmoor Psychiat. Center, N.Y.C., 1972-73, chief of service, 1973-76; supt. Central State Hosp., Indpls., 1976—; cons. in research New Castle State Hosp.; cons. ophthalmology Ind. U. Med. Center; tech. adviser Central Ind. Health Systems Agy.; mem. adv. com. on community mental health Ind. Dept. Mental Health. Served with USAF, 1956-60. Recipient fed. and found. grants. Mem. Assn. Mental Health Adminstrs. (dep. gov. for Ind.), Am. Psychiat. Assn., Am. Hosp. Assn., Ind. Hosp. Assn., Met. Hosp. Assn. Presbyterian. Clubs: Woodstock, Indpls. Racket. Home: 4320 Kessler Blvd N Drive Indianapolis IN 46208 Office: Central State Hosp 3000 W Washington St Indianapolis IN 46222

HELMS, HAROLD EUGENE, engring. co. exec.; b. Muncie, Ind., Oct. 16, 1925; s. Orrie Dale and Addie Electa (Richards) H.; B.S. in Engring. Mechanics, Purdue U., 1948, M.S., 1950; m. Donna Louise Harvey, August 31, 1946; children—Robert Dale, John Eugene. Instr., Purdue U., West Lafayette, Ind., 1946-50; project engr. Argonne Nat. Lab., Lemont, Ill., 1950-52; chief project engr. Gen. Motors Corp., Indpls., 1952—; mgr. large govt. projects. Served with U.S. Navy, 1943-46. Registered profl. engr., Ind. Mem. ASME. Christian. Club: Optimist Internat. (past pres., lt. gov.). Contbr. articles to profl. jours. Home: 2844 Galahad Dr Indianapolis IN 46208 Office: Detroit Diesel Allison PO Box 894 T-15 Indianapolis IN 46206

HELMUTH, MERVIN RAY, educator; b. Elkhart, Ind., July 12, 1940; s. Eli H. and Frieda (Schwietert) H.; R.N., Parkview Hosp., 1966; B.S.N., Goshen Coll., 1969; M.N., U. Fla., 1970; postgrad. Western Mich. U.; m. Sharon Lea Moyer, Nov. 26, 1965; children—Timothy Paul, Todd Christopher. Staff nurse Parkview Hosp., Ft. Wayne, Ind., 1966-67; asso. prof. nursing Goshen (Ind.) Coll., 1970—; cons. in field; cons. NIH, 1975-77. Mem. bd. Elkhart County Assn. for Retarded, 1971-77; chmn. Project Early Attention of Elkhart County, 1977-78, Child and Youth Health Project, 1978—; mem. state-wide bd. to develop ednl. materials on preventive health for high sch. tchrs., 1977-80; pres. P.T.O., Goshen, 1978—. Recipient award Allen County Mental Health Assn., 1966. Mem. Nat. Assn. Retarded Citizens, Cystic Fibrosis Found., Respiratory Disease Assn., Mennonite Nurses Assn., Am. Nurses Assn. Democrat. Mennonite. Home: 211 W Garfield St Goshen IN 46526 Office: Goshen Coll Goshen IN 46526

HELSTROM, JAMES ALFRED, retail exec.; b. Hibbing, Minn., Mar. 7, 1939; s. Fred and Savelle (Lauhala) H.; B.S. in Civil Engring., U. N.D., 1961, B.S. in Bus. Adminstrn., 1962; m. Carole Hope Pajunen, Sept. 20, 1957; children—Michael, Greg, Mark. Engr., L.W. Burdick Co., cons., Grand Forks, N.D., 1960-62; buyer IBM, Rochester, Minn., 1962-64; supr. corp. purchasing Control Data Corp., Bloomington, Minn., 1964-67; gen. sales mgr. Gen. Office Products Co., Mpls., 1967-73; pres. Hibbing Office Supply Co., 1973—. Active local youth programs. Home: Star Route 4 Box 124-A Hibbing MN 55746 Office: 404E Howard St Hibbing MN 55746

HELTON, DANNY ORVILLE, chemist; b. Booneville, Miss., Oct. 5, 1944; s. Orville and Thelma Yvlette (Green) H.; B.S., U. Louisville, 1966, Ph.D., 1972; m. Sarah Frances Cole, Aug. 22, 1966; children—Raymond Orville. Asso. chemist Midwest Research Inst., Kansas City, Mo., 1973-75; sr. chemist, 1975—; lectr. U. Mo., Kansas City. Mem. Republican Nat. Com., 1980—. NDEA fellow, 1968-69. Mem. Am. Chem. Soc., Mid Am. Cancer Center Program, Phi Lambda Upsilon. Baptist. Club: Chung's Karate Sch. Pioneer in rapid assay method for N 5 rocket propellant. Home: 9626 Overhill Rd Kansas City MO 64134 Office: 425 Volker Blvd Kansas City MO 64110

HELTON, JAMES DANIEL, pharmacist; b. Nashville, July 1, 1945; s. Hillard Allen and Sallie Elizabeth (Norman) H.; B.S. in Pharmacy, U. Tenn., Memphis, 1968, D.Pharmacy, 1972; m. Carol Anne Payne, June 10, 1972; children—James Daniel, II, Lisa Katherine. Served as commd. officer USPHS, 1969-71, lt. comdr. Res., 1980—; dir. pharmacy and clin. lab. services McLaughlin (S.D.) Indian Health Center, Standing Rock Sioux Indian Reservation, 1969-71; dir. pharm. services Poplar Bluff (Mo.) Hosp., 1973-80; cons. pharmacist VA Hosp., Poplar Bluff, 1980—; asst. mgr. Super-D Drugs div. Malone & Hyde, Inc., Poplar Bluff, 1981—; chief pharmacist Haven Hills Med. Center, Poplar Bluff, 1981—; cons., owner Profl. Pharm. Services, Poplar Bluff, 1980—; co-owner, gen. mgr. Carol Helton Sch. of Dance, Poplar Bluff, 1979—; instr. Three Rivers Community Coll., Poplar Bluff, 1976—; pharmacy dir. Hosp. Pharmacies, Inc., 1974-79; cons. clin. pharmacist VA Merit Rev. Bd., 1978. Officer, Butler County Dep. Sheriff's Res., 1978-81. Mem. Am. Soc. Hosp. Pharmacists, Mo. Soc. Hosp. Pharmacists (dir. 1976-78), S.E. Mo. Hosp. Pharmacy Dirs. Assn., Tenn. Pharm. Assn. Methodist. Clubs: Poplar Bluff Country, Poplar Bluff Supper. Home: 2438 Channon St Poplar Bluff MO 63901 Office: Haven Hills Med Center Hwy 67 N Poplar Bluff MO 63901

HELTON, PAUL FREDERICK, JR., titanium co. exec.; b. Seattle, Sept. 25, 1947; s. Paul Frederick and Lois Carolyn (Ringstrom) H.; B.A., Portland State U., 1971, M.A., 1973; M.B.A., Columbia U., 1977. Chef, Greenwood Inn, Beaverton, Ores, 1973-75; supr. Payless Drug Stores N.W., Beaverton, Ore., 1975-76; cons. Inst. of Mgmt. Resources, Westlake Village, Calif., 1978-79; dir. mktg. and planning RMI Co., Niles, Ohio, 1980—, v.p., gen. mgr. affiliate Micron Metals Co., Salt Lake City, 1981—; dir. NRI Ent., Salem, Ore., 1978-80. Mobil Oil Distinguished scholar, Columbia U., 1976-77. Mem. Aerospace Industry Assn., Nat. Assn. Mfrs., Am. Mgmt. Assn., Am. Def. Preparedness Assn., Ohio C. of C., Trumbell Mfrs. Assn. Republican. Office: 1000 Warren Ave Niles OH 44446

HELWIG, RICHARD BRIAN, city adminstr.; b. Akron, Ohio, Mar. 18, 1946; s. Robert Charles and Mary Gertrude (Taylor) H.; B.S., Bowling Green State U., 1968; M.P.A., Harvard U., 1973; m. Carolyn Wright Shaver, Sept. 2, 1967; children—Trevor Shriver, Ryan Taylor. Mgmt. analyst City of Dayton (Ohio), 1973, dir. fin., 1973-76, asst. city mgr., 1976—. Bd. dirs. Charles R. Drew Community Health Center, 1974-75; chmn. Dayton Affirmative Action Task Force, 1976-77; chmn. Dayton Civil Service and Personnel Systems Rev. Com., 1978-79. Served with USN, 1968-72. Littauer fellow, 1972-73. Mem. Internat. City Mgmt. Assn. Congregationalist. Office: 101 W 3d St Dayton OH 45401

HEMBREE, JOHNNY ARTHUR, analytical chemist; b. Honolulu, May 25, 1947; s. Willard Rolland and Julia Irene (Phillips) H.; A.S., Young Harris Jr. Coll., 1967; B.S.Ph., Mercer U., 1970; M.S., U. Miss., 1974, Ph.D., 1976; m. Tempe Kay Lacy, Mar. 16, 1976; 1 son, Stephen Mills. Postdoctoral research asso. Purdue U., 1976-79; analytical chemist Procter & Gamble Co., Cin., 1979—. Mem. Am. Chem. Soc., AAAS. Democrat. Baptist. Office: PO Box 39175 Cincinnati OH 45247

HEMINGWAY, JOHN LUTHER, univ. adminstr.; b. Harvey, Ill., May 11, 1947; s. Whitney Luther and Mary Ann (Steimer) H.; B.A., Grinnell Coll., 1971; M.A., U. Iowa, 1975, Ph.D., 1979. Grad. asst. dept. polit. sci. U. Iowa, 1973-78, research asst. dept. pediatrics, 1978-79, program asso. in data mgmt. div. developmental disabilities, 1979-80, supr. student services, dept. student services, 1981—. Served with U.S. Army, 1970-73. Mem. Am. Rivers Conservation Council, Am. Canoe Assn. Democrat. Office: Student Services Iowa Meml Union U of Iowa Iowa City IA 52240

HENARD, DAVID EARL, data processing adminstr.; b. Herrin, Ill., Sept. 19, 1943; s. Don Earl and Helen Irene (Bulliner) H.; B.S. in Elec. Engring., U. Mo.-Rolla, 1965; M.S. in Indsl. Engring., U. Ill., 1971; m. Gail Ann Boatright, Nov. 10, 1968; children—Rachel Gayle, Tessa Helen, Franklin David. Asso. geophysicist Humble Oil Co., Oklahoma City, 1965-66; research asst., research asso. U. Ill., Champaign, 1969-71; data processing analyst, mgr. U. Ill., Urbana, 1971-80, asst. dir. system devel., 1979-80; dir. computer services Eastern Ill. U., 1980—. Mem. Sch. Bd., Villa Grove Unit Dist. 302, 1978—. Served to capt., U.S. Army, 1966-69. Decorated D.F.C., Bronze star, 19 Air medals; recipient Book Plate award Phi Kappa Phi; Armed Forces Communications award. Mem. Tau Beta Pi, Eta Kappa Nu, Theta Xi. Republican. Methodist. Home: Rural Route 1 Villa Grove IL 61956 Office: Student Services Bldg Charleston IL 61920

HENDERICK, ANNE CURRY, art dir.; b. Mpls., May 10, 1952; d. Carl E. and Kasey Curry; student Northeastern Ill. U., 1970-73; B.S. in Art Edn., No. Ill. U., 1976; m. Jed Henderick, May 28, 1976. Advt. designer, copywriter Helix Ltd., Chgo., 1976-78; art dir. in-house advt. dept. Cole-Parmer Instrument Co., Chgo., 1978—. Office: 7425 N Oak Park Ave Chicago IL 60648

HENDERSHOT, WALTER LEE, ins. co. exec.; b. Belpre, Ohio, Jan. 21, 1930; s. Willie Woodbridge and Bertha Louise (Heintz) H.; B.A., Park Coll., 1973; M.A., Central Mich. U., 1975; m. Patsy Ruth Bridgers, Apr. 6, 1966; children—Ronnald Lee, Janis Lynne, David Michael. Served in U.S. Air Force, 1948-68; supr. City Nat. Bank, Columbus, Ohio, 1968-69; accounting mgr. Educator & Exec. Insurers, Inc., Columbus, 1969-75; dir. acctg. JC Penney Casualty Ins. Co., Westerville, Ohio, 1975-80, dir. planning, 1980—; instr. certified profl. sec. courses Nat. Secs. Assn.; mem. vocat. advisory bd. Columbus Pub. Schs., 1974-79. Certified vocat. edn. tchr., Ohio. Mem. Ins. Accounting and Statis. Assn. (pres. Central Ohio chpt. 1975), Adminstrv. Mgmt. Soc. (designation C.A.M., pres. Columbus chpt. 1980-81), Office Edn. Assn. (bd. dirs. 1978-81, vice chmn. Nat. Bus. Advisory Bd. 1977), Internat. Accountants Soc. Methodist. Club: Kiwanis. Home: 1445 Knollwood Dr E Columbus OH 43227 Office: 800 Brooksedge Blvd Westerville OH 43081

HENDERSON, ALBERT DEAN, mfg. co. exec.; b. Chgo., July 10, 1929; s. Albert Dean and Margaret G. H.; B.S., Northwestern U., 1952; postgrad. Loyola U., Chgo.; m. Thelma Pike, Aug. 12, 1961; children—Norman, Edwin, Robert, Dean. Dir. personnel E.J. Brach & Sons, Chgo., 1956-66; with Griffith Labs., Chgo., 1966—, v.p. personnel, 1971—. Chmn. Troop 172, Boy Scouts Am., Glenview, Ill.; v.p., bd. dirs. Glenview Little League. Served with USMC, 1952-55. Registered safety dir. and engr. Mem. Indsl. Relations Assn., Am. Soc. Personnel Adminstrs., N.J. Employers Assn., Associated Employers, C. of C. Republican. Clubs: Sons of Acad., Men's. Office: 12200 S Central Ave Alsip IL 60658

HENDERSON, ERMA LOIS, social worker; b. Pensacola, Fla., Aug. 20, 1917; d. Louis and Rose Elizabeth McQueen; student Detroit Inst. Tech., 1945; M.S.W., Wayne State U., 1973; D.H.L. (hon.), Shaw Coll., 1975; children—Patrya, Philip, Charles. Exec. dir. Equal Justice Council, Inc., Detroit, 1968-79; mem. Detroit City Council, 1972—, pres., 1977—. Trustee Mich. Mcpl. League, Wayne County Community Coll., Marygrove Coll.; bd. dirs. United Community Services; founder, bd. dirs. Women's Conf. Concerns, 1973, Nat. League of Cities; chmn. citizens adv. council Wayne County Community Coll., 1975; chmn. Statewide Coalition Against Redlining, 1976; mem. adv. bd. Black United Fund; founder Detroit Action Council; co-founder Black Research Found.; bd. dirs. Mich. com. Nat. Council Crime and Delinquency; mem. urban affairs com. Mich. Mcpl. League; bd. dirs. Ams. for Dem. Action; region V dir. Nat. Black Caucus; nat. chmn. women in mcpl. govt. com. Nat. League Cities; chmn. bd. Divine Temple Mental Sci.; co-chmn. United Negro Coll. Fund. Recipient Spl. Achievement award Inter-Faith Center Racial Justice, 1977; Sojourner Truth award Nat. Assn. Negro Bus. and Profl. Women's Club, 1977; Outstanding Achievement award Afro-Am. Mus., 1978; Outstanding Community Service award Detroit Family Neighborhood Services, 1978; Woman of Year award Iota Phi Lambda, 1978; Humanitarian award Gospel Music Workshop Am., 1978, Citizen of Year award Metro Art Complex and Afro-Am. Festival, 1978, Michiganian of Year award Detroit News, 1978; named Citizen of Year award Salvation Army, 1978. Mem. Nat. Assn. Social Workers (Mich. Social Worker of Year 1978), Nat. Council Negro Women, LWV, Assn. Black Social Workers, Mich. Acad. Arts and Sci., Delta Sigma Theta (Outstanding Service award 1978). Democrat. Office: 1340 City-County Bldg Detroit MI 48226

HENDERSON, FRANK ELLIS, justice state supreme ct.; b. Miller, S.D., Apr. 7, 1928; s. Frank Ellis and Hilda (Bogstad) H.; LL.B., U. S.D., Vermillion, 1951; cert. Nat. Jud. Coll., Reno, 1976, 78, 79, N.Y. U., 1980; m. Norma Jean Johnson, Dec. 27, 1956; children—Frank Ellis III, Kimberly Jo, Andrea Lynn, Patrick Hayes, Eric Peter, John Paul, Anastasia Marie, Matthew Joel. Admitted to S.D. bar, 1951, to practice before U.S. Dist. Ct. S.D., 1953; individual practice law, 1953-74; Circuit Ct. judge, 1975-78; justice S.D. Supreme Ct., Pierre, 1979—; U.S. commr., 1963-64. Mem. S.D. State Senate, 1965-66, 69-70. Served to 1st lt. inf., AUS, 1951-53; Korea. Mem. Pennington County Bar Assn., S.D. Bar Assn., Am. Legion, VFW, DAV (past state judge adv., post comdr.). Republican. Roman Catholic. Office: State Capitol Pierre SD 57501

HENDERSON, GARY, ednl. coordinator, educator; b. Green Bay, Wis., Nov. 4, 1931; s. Wallace E. and M. Ruth (Misener) H.; B.S., Central Mich. U., 1959; M.S., Wayne State U., 1965; m. Joan Ann Albertine, Aug. 28, 1955; children—Matthew Brian, Scott Andrew. Machine operator Buick Gen. Motors Corp., Flint, Mich., 1950; constrn. worker Vesley Constrn., Lapeer, Mich., 1954; sheetmetal maintenance Ternstedt, Gen. Motors Corp., Flint, 1954-59; machine shop and crafting instr. Lamphere Public Sch., Madison Heights, Mich., 1959-65, drafting instr., trade and indsl. coordinator, 1965—; drafting instr. night staff Macomb County Community Coll., Warren, Mich., 1968—; field leader Howard & Smith, Inc., Madison Heights, summers 1960-74, part time designer, draftsman, 1966-68. Indsl. arts advisory com. to Mich. State Bd. Edn., 1971-72; chmn. Macomb chpt. Soc. Mfg. Engrs., 1976, chmn. Region III, 1977-78, liaison rep., 1978-79. Served with USN, 1950-54. Udylite Corp. grantee, 1962; Carnegie Corp. grantee, 1965-66; recipient Order of the Arrow Boy Scouts Am.; cert. mfg. engr. Mem. NEA (life), Mich. Edn. Assn. (life), Mich. Indsl. Edn. Soc. (life, pres., 1976-77, conv. chmn., 1977-78, master tchr. award, 1979), Mich. Vocat. Coordinators Assn. (pres., 1970-71), Macomb-Oakland Coordinators Assn., Mich. Edn. Occupation Assn. (Earl Bedell publicity award 1970), Am. Indsl. Arts Assn., Soc. Mfg. Engrs. (chmn. Macomb Chpt. 142, 1976, chmn. Region III, 1977-78, liaison rep., 1978-80, dir. 1980, pres.'s award Macomb Chpt. 142, 1970, 71, Pres.'s award, 1975, Region III, 1974, Merit award 1979), Mu Sigma Pi. Contbr. articles in field to profl. publs. and newspapers. Home: 4200 Adams Dr Rochester MI 48063 Office: 610 W 13 Mile Madison Heights MI 48071

HENDERSON, GEORGE TRUMBULL, airline exec.; b. Toledo, Ohio, Feb. 4, 1919; s. Clyde C. and Elsie (Norwood) H.; B.S.M.E., Purdue U., 1940; m. Norine Moody, Sept. 20, 1941; children—Larry, Tod, Linda. With United Airlines Inc., Chgo., 1940—, first officer, 1940-43, capt., 1943-55, flight mgr., 1955-63, flight operating mgr., 1963-66, dir. flight ops. devel., 1966-77, mgr. B747 ops., 1977-79, ret., 1979. Dir., Thomas Ford Meml. Library, 1960-66, pres., 1964-66; bd. mem. Community Meml. Gen. Hosp., 1970—; mem. president's council Purdue U.; trustee, vice chmn. bd. No. Bapt. Theol. Sem. Registered profl. engr. Asso. fellow AIAA (chmn. aircraft ops. com.); mem. Soc. Automotive Engrs. (vice-chmn. flight deck com.). Republican. Baptist. Clubs: Masons, Shriners. Home: 208 Briarwood Pass Oak Brook IL 60521

HENDERSON, JAMES ALAN, engine co. exec.; b. South Bend, Ind., July 26, 1934; s. John William and Norma (Wilson) H.; A.B., Princeton, 1956; Baker scholar, Harvard, 1961-63; m. Mary Evelyn Kriner, June 20, 1959; children—James Alan, John Stuart, Jeffrey Todd, Amy Brenton. With Scott Foresman & Co., Chgo., 1962; staff mem. Am. Research & Devel. Corp., Boston, 1963; faculty Harvard Bus. Sch., 1963; asst. to chmn. Cummins Engine Co., Inc., Columbus, Ind., 1964-65, v.p. mgmt. devel., 1965-69, v.p. personnel, 1969-70, v.p. ops., 1970-71, exec. v.p., 1971-75, exec. v.p., chief operating officer, 1975-77, pres., 1977—, also dir.; dir. Cummins Engine Found., Ind. Bell Telephone Co., Indpls., Inland Steel Co., Chgo., Hayes-Albion Corp., Jackson, Mich. Pres., Jr. Achievement, Columbus, 1967-69; gen. chmn. Bartholomew County United Fund Campaign, 1970; pres. Hoosier Hills council Boy Scouts Am., 1970-72, Culver Legion, Culver Alumni Assn., 1971-72; mem. selection com. Rockefeller Pub. Service awards, 1978-79; Co-mgr. Rockefeller for Pres. Campaign, 1968; trustee Princeton U.; bd. dirs. Culver Ednl. Found., Heritage Fund of Bartholomew County, Inc. Served to lt. USNR, 1956-61. Mem. NAM (dir.), Columbus Area C. of C. (pres. 1973, adv. com. 1974). Presbyn. (elder). Author: Creative Collective Bargaining, 1965. Home: 4228 Riverside Dr Columbus IN 47201 Office: PO Box 3005 Columbus IN 47201

HENDERSON, JEFFREY LEE, landscape architect; b. Warsaw, Ind., June 12, 1950; s. Leo Devon and Mary Elizabeth (Webster) H.; B.S., Ball State U., 1977, B.Landscape Arch., 1976; M.Landscape Arch., Harvard U., 1980. With Project Planning Assos. Ltd., Toronto, Ont., Can., 1972-73, Daniel B. Young & Assos., Inc., Muncie, Ind., 1974, Browning, Day, Pollak & Assos., Inc., Indpls., 1975, Am. Fletcher Nat. Bank, Indpls., 1976-78, Architects Collaborative, Cambridge, Mass., 1979, Camp, Dresser & McKee, Inc., Boston, 1979-80; prin. Henderson Assos., Indpls., 1980—; asst. prof. dept. landscape architecture Ball State U., 1981-82; agt. Simon Independent Devel. Co., 1982, constrn. adminstr. Simon Gen. Constrn., 1982. Mem. Am. Soc. Landscape Architects (cert. of merit, 1975-76), Internat. Council for Shopping Centers. Club: Indpls. Jaycees. Office: 3901 W 86th St Suite 150 Indianapolis IN 46268

HENDERSON, JERRY, JR., biologist, educator; b. Grand Chain, Ill., Aug. 16, 1942; s. Jerry and Lula Mae (McClelland) H.; B.A., So. Ill. U., 1966, M.S., 1970; m. Kathryn L. Henderson, Aug. 5, 1971; children—Hasanda-Marie, Jerry III. Tchr., Community High Sch. Dist. 218, Blue Island, Ill., 1966-69; grad. asst. biology So. Ill. U., Carbondale, 1969-70; asso. prof. biology Forest Park Community Coll., St. Louis, 1973—, chmn. dept., 1974—. Mem. East-West Gateway, regional environ. task force, 1977—; active girls' sport program. Mem. NEA, Mo. Edn. Assn., Am. Assn. for Higher Edn., AAAS, Mo. Acad. Sci., Ill. Acad. Sci., Am. Inst. Biol. Sci., Nat. Assn. Biology Tchrs., Conf. on Edn., Mo. Assn. Community Jr. Colls., Higher Edn. Coordinating Council. Home: 7000 Washington Ave University City MO 63130 Office: Forest Park Community Coll 5600 Oakland Ave Saint Louis MO 63110

HENDERSON, JOHN L., coll. adminstr.; b. Evergreen, Ala., Apr. 10, 1932; s. G. Leon and Ethel Eveline (Bryer) H.; B.S., Hampton Inst., 1955; M.Ed., U. Cin., 1968, Ed.D., 1976; m. Theresa Crittenden, June 28, 1969; children—Dana, Nina, Brent. Dir. univ. and urban affairs Xavier U., 1968-72; dean student devel. U. Cin., 1972-76, dean div. public services, 1976-79; v.p. student services Sinclair Community Coll., Dayton, 1979—; dir. Center City Minority Enterprise and Investment Corp.; sec. Ohio ACT Assembly. Bd. dirs. Miami Valley Lung Assn., Dayton Urban League, Dayton Ednl. Opportunity Center; community adv. bd. Dayton Job Corps. Served with AUS, 1955-57. Mem. Am. Assn. Higher Edn., Am. Assn. Univ. Adminstrs., Am. Coll. Personnel Assn., Am. Personnel and Guidance Assn., Urban League, AAUP, Phi Delta Kappa, Alpha Phi Alpha. Club: Sophisticates. Home: 1109 Towanda Terr Cincinnati OH 45216 Office: Sinclair Community Coll 444 W 3d St Dayton OH 45402

HENDERSON, MORRIS, health service adminstr.; b. Portageville, Mo., Oct. 31, 1926; s. Dave and Effie (Black) H.; student Stowe Tchrs. Coll., 1944; degree in commerce St. Louis U., 1952, postgrad., 1961-62; postgrad. Am. Coll. Hosp. Adminstrn., 1963; degree in mgmt. Webster Coll., 1977, M.S., 1978; also seminars; m. Lowell Verniece Battle, Feb. 27, 1947; children—Kenneth Morris, Carlton Eugene. Sales mgr. United Clothing Co., 1950-59; bus. mgr. St. Louis Chronicle Newspaper, 1959-60; with Bank of St. Louis, 1960; adminstr. Peoples Hosp., St. Louis, 1961-66; dir. community involvements Human Devel. Corp., St. Louis, 1966-68, dep. gen. mgr., 1969-70; project dir. St. Louis Comprehensive Neighborhood Health Center, Inc., 1970—. Pres. St. Louis County chpt. NAACP, 1955-59, 62-65, past v.p. Mo. conf., mem. nat. nominating com.; mem. County Human Relations Council, 1963; dist. mem. St. Louis area council Boy Scouts Am., after 1960, recipient Certificate of award, 1963; active YMCA, 1955—; mem. St. Louis Mayor's Commn. on Crime; pres. North unit Am. Cancer Soc.; bd. dirs. Ferrier Harris Home for Aged, Inner City Black Athletic Assn., Met. Sickle Cell Anemia Assn., adv. com. Jr. Coll. Dist. Served with AUS, 1945-46. Recipient Distinguished Pub. Service award Mound City Press Club, 1957,

Citizen of Year award Radio Sta. KATZ, 1963, certificate award, Jr. C. of C., 1964, numerous citations and Distinguished Service awards. Mem. Nat. Assn. Health Services Execs., Nat. Assn. Neighborhood Health Centers, Hosp. Assn. Met. St. Louis, Peoples Hosp. Assn. (pres. 1959-60), Frontiers, Health Delivery Systems (dir.) Mo. Assn. Social Welfare (dir.), St. Louis Conf. Religion and Race, Am. Pub. Health Assn., Am. Hosp. Assn., United Ch. Men (dir.), Alpha Phi Alpha (life). Baptist (trustee, deacon). Elk, Mason. Editor, St. Louis Argus, St. Louis Crusader; contbg. editor St. Louis Am., St. Louis Crusader newspapers, others. Home: 6528 Whitney St St Louis MO 63133 Office: 5471 Dr Martin Luther King Dr St Louis MO 63112

HENDERSON, ROSEMARY, librarian; b. Coffyville, Kans., July 15, 1936; d. Ray Aubrey and Irene Ora (Maxwell) Neale; A.A., Stephens Coll., 1956; B.S., Tex. Wesleyan Coll., 1959; M.L.S., Kans. State Tchrs. Coll., 1967; Ed.D., U. Kans., 1976; m. Vance John Henderson, Mar. 9, 1957 (div.); 1 dau., Jennifer Ann; m. 2d, Douglas James Keller, May 25, 1976 (div.). Asst. prof. librarianship U. N.D., Grand Forks, 1967-68; dir. learning resources Coffeyville Community Jr. Coll., 1968—; cons. in field. Mem. ALA (chmn. community jr. coll. sect. 1975-76, sect. archivist, historian 1978—, nominating com. 1979), Kans. (sec. 1972-74, mem. council 1970-74, 78—, chmn.-elect coll. and univ. libraries sect. 1981), Mountain Plains (chmn. coll. and univ. sect. 1973-74) library assns. Reviewer, Library Jour., 1970-74, Am. Reference Books Annual-Libraries Unltd., 1974—. Home: 2205 W 2d St Coffeyville KS 67337 Office: Coffeyville Community Jr Coll Coffeyville KS 67337

HENDERSON, THOMAS LEE, psychologist; b. Lone Pine, Calif., Aug. 12, 1941; s. Thomas A. and Pauline G. (Lyon) H.; B.S., Ind. U., 1963, M.A.T., 1965, Ph.D. (teaching fellow 1969-72), 1972; m. Sandra Kidd, July 24, 1965; 1 dau., Leigh Anne. Tchr., Shortridge High Sch., Indpls., 1965-69; asst. mgr. Kidd Ins. Agencies, Brazil, Ind., 1969-70; community mental health worker Katherine Hamilton Mental Health Center, Terre Haute, Ind., 1972-73, staff psychologist, program dir. Clay County Center, Brazil, 1973-74; chief psychologist, program dir. Katherine Hamilton Mental Health Center, 1974—; mem. faculty Ind. State U., 1972—, adj. asst. prof., 1974—; cons. Gibault Sch. Boys. Chmn. Clay County Young Republicans, 1977—, Red Cross Safety Com., 1960—. Named Outstanding Young Rep. in Clay County, 1978. Mem. Am. Personnel and Guidance Assn., Am. Psychol. Assn., Ind. Psychol. Assn., Phi Delta Kappa, Pi Gamma Mu, Kappa Delta Pi. Republican. Presbyterian. Club: Elks. Author papers in field. Home: Rural Route 11 Box 93 Forest Manor Brazil IN 47834 Office: 1206 E National Ave Brazil IN 47834

HENDRICKS, DONALD RICHARD, arboretum dir., found. exec.; b. Trenton, N.J., Dec. 31, 1945; s. John Robert and Mildred (Cahall) H.; A.B., Earlham Coll., 1971, diploma in exec. growth, 1975; M.S., Ball State U., 1979; m. Elaine Gandolph, Mar. 21, 1975. Resident naturalist Hayes Arboretum, Richmond, Ind., 1971-75, asso. dir., 1975-76, dir., 1976—; pres. S. W. Hayes Research Found., Inc., 1979—; cons. outdoor labs., environ. edn., starting arboreta. Served to capt. U.S. Army, 1966-80. Decorated Bronze Star, Air Medal (2). Fellow Explorers Club; mem. Assn. Interpretive Naturalists, Am. Assn. Bot. Gardens and Arboreta, Internat. Soc. Arboriculture, Ind. Acad. Sci. Quaker. Club: Masons (32 deg.). Designer, engr. Ind.'s first solar greenhouse, 1976. Office: Hayes Regional Arboretum 801 Elks Rd Richmond IN 47374

HENDRICKSON, CHARLES DANA, benefit communications and advanced underwriting co. exec.; b. Middletown, Ohio, Jan. 15, 1951; s. Charles W. and Gladys Emma (Horn) H.; B.S., Ohio State U., 1974; m. Valerie Elizabeth Jamra, Aug. 26, 1977. Agt., Penn Mut. Ins. Co., Phila., 1973-78; owner Hendrickson & Hendrickson, Inc., Columbus, 1978—. C.L.U. Republican. Methodist. Home: 2856 McCoy Rd Columbus OH 43220 Office: 1660 NW Profl Plaza Columbus OH 43220

HENDRICKSON, HERBERT CLARENCE, automotive co. ofcl.; b. LaCrosse, Wis., Apr. 29, 1931; s. Clarence T. and Min A. Hendrickson; B.S.E.E., U. Colo., 1955; M.S.E.E. (Hughes fellow), U. So. Calif., 1957; m. Sydney C. Freudenthal, June 12, 1954; 1 dau., Kimberly D. Digital computer designer Hughes Aircraft, Fullerton, Calif., 1955-59; digital interface designer Aeronutronic, Newport Beach, Calif., 1959-62; display and control system mgr. NASA Control Center, Philco, Houston, 1962-65; digital, display and controls engrng. mgr. Philco-Ford, Palo Alto, Calif., 1965-75; bus. planning mgr. Elec. and Electronics div. Ford Motor Co., Ypsilanti, Mich., 1976—; guest lectr. UCLA; gen. chmn. Soc. Info. Display Internat. Symposium, San Francisco, 1972. Mem. Eta Kappa Nu, Sigma Tau. Republican. Presbyterian. Clubs: Fairlane, Kiwanis (nat. del., sec.) (Dearborn); Western Racquet (Livonia, Mich.). Contbr. articles to Info. Display Jour. Home: 3031 Lindenwood Dr Dearborn MI 48120 Office: PO Box 412 Ypsilanti MI 48997

HENDRICKSON, WALTER BROOKFIELD, JR., author; b. Indpls., Aug. 24, 1936; s. Walter Brookfield and Marjorie Dorris (Walsh) H.; A.B., Ill. Coll., 1958; postgrad. MacMurray Coll. and U. Ill., 1958-61. Author: Handbook for Space Travelers, 1959; Pioneering in Space, 1961; Reach For the Moon, 1961; The Study of Rockets, Missiles and Space Made Simple, 1963; What's Going on in Space?, 1968; Wild Wings, 1969; Apollo 11: Men to the Moon, 1970; Who Really Invented the Rocket?, 1974; Manned Spacecraft to Mars and Venus, 1975; Illinois: Its People and Culture, 1975; Class G-Zero, 1976; contbr. articles to popular mags. and tech. publs. Mem. Am. Inst. Aeros. and Astronautics, AAAS, Authors Guild, Aviation/Space Writers Assn., Nat. Space Inst., Smithsonian Assos., Morgan County Hist. Soc. Democrat. Episcopalian. Club: Rotary Internat. Home and office: 724 W State St Jacksonville IL 62650

HENDRIX, JON RICHARD, educator; b. Passaic, N.J., May 4, 1938; s. William Louis and Velma Lucile (Coleman) H.; B.S., Ind. State U., 1960, M.S., 1963; Ed.D., Ball State U., 1974; m. Janis Ruth Rouhselange, Nov. 24, 1962; children—Margaret Susan, Joann Ruth, Amy Therese. Sci. supr. Sch. Town of Highland, Ind., 1960-71; instr. Ind. U., Gary, 1968-69; asso. prof. biology Ball State U., Muncie, 1972-80, prof., 1980—; cons. State Ind. Dept. Pub. Instrn., 1967-71, Center for Values and Meaning, 1971—; mem. Ind. Sci. Edn. Adv. Bd., Dept. Pub. Instrn., 1967-71. Recipient Outstanding Faculty award in edn. Ind. U. N.W. Campus, 1970, Outstanding Young Educator award Highland Jr. C. of C., 1968; Ball State U. fellow, 1971-73. Fellow Ind. Acad. Sci.; mem. Nat. (dir. 1969-71), Ind. (pres. 1968-69) sci. suprs. assns., AAUP, Assn. Supervisors and Curriculum Devel., Nat. Audubon Soc., Nat. Biology Tchrs. Assn., Nat. Sci. Tchrs. Assn. (life), Nat. Soc. Study Edn., Council Elementary Sci. Internat., Central Assn. Coll. Biology Tchrs., Hoosier Assn. Sci. Tchrs. Inc. (dir. 1968-71), Ind. Assn. Tchr. Educators, Ind. Assn. Supervisors and Curriculum Devel., Ind. Biology Tchrs. Assn., Kappa Delta Pi, Phi Delta Kappa. Author: The Wonder of Somehow, 1974; The Wonder of Someplace, 1974; The Wonder of Sometime, 1974; Becomings: A Parent Guidebook for In-Home Experiences with Nine to Eleven Year Olds, 1974; Becomings: A Clergy Guidebook for Experiences with Nine to Eleven Year Olds and Their Parents, 1974; contbr. articles to profl. jours. Home: 307 N Meeks St Muncie IN 47303 Office: Ball State U Biology Dept Muncie IN 47306

HENDRIX, THOMAS CLAGETT, ofcl. NLRB; b. Miraj, India, Sept. 3, 1920; s. Everett Jehu and Minnie Kate (Clagett) H.; came to U.S., 1924; B.A., Hastings Coll., 1942; J.D., Northwestern U., 1947; m. Carol Arden Crumpacker, Sept. 3, 1946 (div. Aug. 1966); children—Walker, Sarah, Anne, Kari; m. 2d, Dona Mae Farber, Oct. 2, 1981. Admitted to Mo. bar, 1948; practice law, Kansas City, Mo., 1948-53; exec. sec. J.P. Hillelson, U.S. Congressman, Washington, 1953; legal asst., to chmn. NLRB, 1954-55, field atty., St. Louis, 1955-57, regional atty., Kansas City, Mo., 1957-69, regional dir., 1969—. Served wtih USAAF, 1942-45. Home: 10439 Ash St Overland Park KS 66207 Office: Suite 616 Two Gateway Center 4th and State St Kansas City KS 66101

HENDRIX, WILLIAM HERLIE, psychologist; b. Kinston, N.C., Sept. 7, 1937; s. Herlie Rasse and Estelle Douglas (Tart) H.; A.B., E. Carolina U., 1962; M.S., Purdue U., 1969, Ph.D., 1974; m. Martha Centeno, Mar. 10, 1979; 1 dau., Tamyra Gaye. Commd. 2d lt. U.S. Air Force, 1962, advanced through grades to lt. col., 1972; pass and registration officer Scott AFB, Ill., 1962-63; minuteman missile launch officer Ellsworth AFB, S.D., 1963-64; instr. missile ops. tng. Chanute AFB, Ill., 1964-66, instr. supr. Missile Ops. Tng., 1966-67; instr. dept. psychology U.S. Air Force Acad., Colo., 1969-70; human engrng. staff officer Hdqrs. Electronics Systems div. L.G. Hanscom Field, Bedford, Mass., 1970-72; research psychologist, chief applications sect. Air Force Human Resources Lab., Lackland AFB, Tex., 1974-79; asso. prof. orgn. behavior, head dept. organizational scis. Air Force Inst. Tech., 1979—; cons. to leadership mgmt. devel. center Maxwell AFB, Ala., 1976; lectr. in statistics dept. psychology St. Mary's U., San Antonio, 1975-77, resource person in psychology for New Horizons for Women program, 1977. Decorated Air Force Commendation medal, Meritorious Service medal; recipient Nat. Arion Found. medal, 1955; Air Force Master Instr. award, 1966; Air Force Mil. Personnel Center citation for devel. of computer based person-job match system, 1976; Air Force Inst. Tech. fellow, 1972-74. Mem. Am. (chmn. div. 19, 1980-81), Rocky Mt., Midwestern, Southwestern psychol. assns. Methodist. Club: Wright-Patterson AFB Officers. Contbr. articles to profl. jours. Home: 7381 Union Schoolhouse Rd Dayton OH 45424 Office: Dept Organizational Scis (AFIT/LSB) AFIT Wright-Patterson AFB OH 45433

HENDRYX, STEVEN WAYNE, educator; b. Sterling, Ill., Sept. 5, 1951; s. Wayne Robert and Lorraine Delores (Ballard) H.; A.A., Sauk Valley Jr. Coll., 1971; B.S., Ill. State U., 1973; M.S., Bradley U., 1976; postgrad. Ind. U., 1980—; m. Barbara Jill Worden, Nov. 26, 1971; children—Holly Lynn, Allyson Elizabeth. English tchr. East Peoria (Ill.) High Sch., 1973-80; adminstrv. asst. to chmn. dept. curriculum and instrn. Ind. U., Bloomington, 1980—. Mem. Am. Ednl. Research Assn., Assn. Ednl. Data Systems, World Council for Curriculum and Instrn., Am. Soc. for Curriculum Devel., Phi Delta Kappa. Democrat. Baptist. Home: 1300 N Fess St Bloomington IN 47401 Office: 328 Dept Edn 3d and Jordan Sts Ind U Bloomington IN 47401

HENGES, RONALD EDWARD, mfg. co. exec.; b. St. Louis, Oct. 13, 1932; s. J. Gordon and Vera O. (Melsheimer) H.; B.A., Vanderbilt U., 1954; m. Anne Sterry, Sept. 18, 1954; children—Michael, Carolyn, Lawrence. Pres., Henges Mfg. Inc., Henges Assos.; v.p. Creve Coeur Camera Co., St. Louis; dir. Constrn. and Mining Services; chmn. bd. Mark Twain Chesterfield Bank. Vice pres. Good Shepherd Sch. for Children; bd. dirs. Nat. Museum of Transport, Parkway Youth Center, First Street Forum, Mo. Council Econ. Devel.; chmn. bd. Maryville Coll.; dir. C.D., Creve Coeur, 1965-75; alderman, City of Creve Coeur, 1971-73; mem. Mo. State Rep. Fin. Com.; commr. Higher Edn. Loan Authority, State of Mo. Served with U.S. Army, 1955-57. Mem. Young Pres. Orgn. Clubs: Univ., Media, Mason, Shriner. Home: 13398 Conway Rd St Louis MO 63141 Office: 12100 Prichard Farm Rd Maryland Heights MO 63043

HENKE, ALICE MARY, nun, ednl. adminstr.; b. Thorp, Wis., Oct. 30, 1923; d. Emil August and Anna Marie (Baldeschwiler) Henke; B.A. cum laude, St. Thomas Coll., 1957; M.A., Loyola U. Chgo., 1967. Joined Servants of Mary, Roman Catholic Ch., 1943; tchr. various Cath. schs., 1946-68; lectr. history Mt. Senario Coll., Ladysmith, Wis., 1968-71, asst. dir. admissions, 1971-76, dir. alumni, 1976-78, 80—; researcher history of Rusk County, 1978—; researcher Order of Servants of Mary, Ladysmith, 1978-80, archivist, 1981—. Recipient plaque for work done in admissions and with alumni Mt. Senario Coll., 1978. Mem. Wis. Council Local History (state adv. com. 1974-76), Wis. Ind. Coll. Alumni Assn. (chmn. Northwestern region 1976), Council on Advancement and Support of Edn., Wis. Assn. Ind. Colls. and Univs., State Hist. Soc. Wis., Rusk County Hist. Soc., Diocesan Council of Cath. Women.

HENLEY, TERRY LEW, computer co. exec.; b. Seymour, Ind., Nov. 10, 1940; s. Ray C. and Barbara Marie (Cockerham) H.; B.S., Tri-State U., 1961; m. Martha L. Gill, Mar. 26, 1961; children—Barron Keith, Troy Grayson. Research and devel. engr. Halogens Research Lab., Dow Chem. Co., Midland, Mich., 1961-63, lead process engr., polymer plant, Bay City, Mich., 1964, supt. bromide-bromate plants, Midland, 1964-68; nat. sales mgr. Ryan Industries, Louisville, 1968-70; internat. sales mgr. Chemineer, Inc., Dayton, Ohio, 1970-77; cons. mktg., Xenia, Ohio, 1977-78; pres. Computer Guidance, Inc., Vandalia, Ohio, 1978—. Mem. Internat. Graphoanalysis Soc., Am. Inst. Chem. Engrs., Am. Mgmt. Assn., Med. Group Mgmt. Assn., Ohio Handwriting Analysts Assn., Soc. Integration Graphology. Author: Chemical Engineering, 1976. Contbr. articles in field to profl. jours. Home: 1167 Highview Dr Beavercreek OH 45385 Office: Computer Guidance Inc 601 W National Rd Vandalia OH 45377

HENLINE, FLORENCE, pianist; b. Ft. Wayne, Ind.; d. Samuel and Caroline Dorothy (Mollet) Henline; B.M., Chgo. Musical Coll., 1928; m. Milson Jezek, Sept. 2, 1936. Made first concert appearance at age of 13; appeared with Ill. Symphony and Grant Park Orchs., Chgo. Women's Symphony (ofcl. pianist); accompanist; staff pianist, NBC network, 1930-32; pianist, soloist Chgo. Symphony String Ensemble, 1946-56, Chgo. Pops Symphonette; solo concert engagements in Chgo. and throughout U.S.; soloist Indpls. Symphony String Ensemble, 1970; artist faculty mem. Chgo. Conservatory Coll., 1959—. Judge piano solo contest auditions 35th Ann. Chicagoland Music Festival, 1964, soloists Ann. Young Judea Symphony Orch., 1965, 67. Fellow Internat. Inst. Arts and Letters (life); mem. Chgo. Artists Assn., Lake View Mus. Soc., Musicians' Club of Women, Alliance Francaise (Chgo.), Ill. Opera Guild, Art Inst. Chgo., Mu Phi Epsilon (soloist internat. conv. 1972). Club: Cordon. Home: 9715 S Vanderpoel Ave Chicago IL 60643

HENNE, MARY ANN, communications specialist; b. Tipp City, Ohio, Oct. 15, 1949; d. John Louis and Dorothea Joanne (Lyons) H.; A.S. in Med. Tech., Clark Coll., 1973; B.S. summa cum laude in Journalism, Ohio U., 1976. Sportswear mgr. F.W. Uhlman Co., 1969-71; med. lab. technologist Dettmer Hosp., Troy, Ohio, 1973-74; promotion asso. Telecommunication Center, Ohio U., Athens, 1975-76; public relations cons. Planned Parenthood of S.E. Ohio, Athens, 1975-76; graphic dir. Athens mag., 1975; editor Ohio's Tomorrow mag., 1975-76; dir. public relations, mktg. and devel. Dettmer Hosp. and Health Care Complex, Troy, 1976-81; trustee Dettmer Hosp. Found., Inc.; public relations planner Miami County Health Care Center, Miami County Mental Health Center, Tri-County Hearing and Speech Center, 1976-81; public relations cons. Gagnet Painting and Restoration; cons. public relations to various local orgns. Bd. dirs. Upper Valley Youth Services Bur. Recipient Communications award Ohio Hosp. Assn., 1977; award Ohio chpt. AAUW, 1979. Mem. Am. Soc. Clin. Pathologists (registered med. lab. technologist), AAUW (dir.), Tipp City Hist. Soc., Sigma Delta Chi, Phi Kappa Phi. Editor Dettmer Expressions mag., 1976—. Office: 121 W Main St Tipp City OH 45371

HENNEBERRY, JOHN THOMAS, business exec.; b. Chgo., May 12, 1929; s. John Joseph and Catherine Mary (Duffy) H.; student St. Bede Coll., 1948-49, Loyola U., Chgo., 1949-51; m. Nancy May Brown, Sept. 19, 1953; children—John Thomas, Martin J., Scott M., Ellen M., Catherine M. With Sears, Roebuck & Co., 1953-65, merchandise mgr., St. Joseph, Mo., 1961-63, operating mgr., Grand Island, Nebr., 1963-65; auto center mgr. Montgomery Ward & Co., Harvey, Ill., 1965-66, operating mgr. Waukegan, Ill., 1966-68, merchandise mgr., Evergreen Park, Ill., 1968-69; gen. mgr., Mobil Farm Stores, 1969-70; dir. store mktg. FS Services, Inc., Bloomington, Ill., 1970-78; pres. Thomas J. McNesh Enterprises, Bloomington, 1978-80; owner White, McNesh & Rhodes, 1980; pres., chief exec. officer Nu-Way Systems, Inc., 1981—. Active, Boy Scouts Am., 1962-65; com. chmn. Grand Island United Fund, 1964. Served with U.S. Army, 1951-53. Mem. Am. Mktg. Assn. (pres.-chmn. bd. Central Ill. chpt. 1976-77), Bloomington-Normal Advt. and Mktg. Club (pres.-chmn. bd. 1976-77, dir. 1974-81). Roman Catholic. Clubs: Ill. State U. Varsity, Ill. State U. Golf League, Four Seasons, FS Bridge, TWA Ambassadors, Elks, K.C. (4th deg.). Office: PO Box 782 Bloomington IL 61701 also PO Box 1725 Bloomington IL 61701

HENNESSY, HAROLD RICHARD, physician; b. Two Harbors, Minn., Aug. 12, 1903; s. Maurice Alexander and Sarah Maude (Ousman) H.; B.A., Carleton Coll., 1926; B.S., U. Minn., 1930, M.B., 1930, M.D., 1931; cert. in public health U. Calif., Berkeley, 1939; grad. U.S. Army Sch. of Mil. Govt., 1943; m. Helen Adele Lounsberry, July 24, 1930; children—Helen V., Irene E., Harold Richard, Marjorie J. Intern, Calif. Lutheran Hosp., Los Angeles, 1930-31; resident Los Angeles City Health Dept., 1931-32; practice gen. medicine, Los Angeles, 1932-33; organizer, dir. Sutter-Yuba Bi-County Health Unit, Yuba City and Marysville, Calif., 1939; commd. 1st lt., M.C., U.S. Army, 1930, advanced through grades to col., 1946; chief med. unit instrs. sect. 9th Corps Area Presidio of San Francisco, 1940-41; chief indsl. med. officer Hdqrs. 9th Service Command, Salt Lake City, 1942-43; chief public health officer Hdqrs. Communications Zone G-5, ETOUSA, Hdqrs. SHAEF, 1944; chief public health officer Office of Surgeon, 15th U.S. Army, Belgium and Germany, 1945; cons. to surgeon gen. U.S. Army, 1947-52; cons. Office of Surgeon, 5th U.S. Army, 1962, ret., 1963; pvt. practice public health cons., Park Ridge and Winnetka, Ill., now Highwood, Ill.; mem. staff AMA, 1946-48; asst. sec. Council Indsl. Health, exec. officer com. profl. relations A.C.S., 1949-66. Decorated Bronze Star; knight Order of Public Health (France); officer Order of Orange-Nassau with swords (Netherlands); hon. Ky. Col.; hon. mem. Indian Council, Clinton, Okla., named Chief White Arrow, 1960; named Hon. Citizen State of Tex., 1961, Hon. Col., Ala. State Militia, 1965, Hon. Adm. Tex. Navy, 1966; recipient Letter of Commendation, Pres. Harry S. Truman, 1971; Physician Recognition award AMA, 1980. Fellow Am. Public Health Assn.; mem. Am. Assn. Sr. Physicians, Internat. Health Soc. (founder, 1st pres. 1949), Ret. Officers Assn., Res. Officers Assn., Mil. Order World Wars (mem. Silver Star roll Chgo. chpt.), Order of Lafayette (charter), Phi Beta Pi. Republican. Clubs: Officers (Ft. Sheridan, Ill.); Masons (Two Harbors, Minn.). Author various geneal. pamphlets. Home and Office: 616 Sheridan Rd Apt 4-B Highwood IL 60040

HENNING, DAVID RALPH, food co. exec.; b. Elgin, Ill., May 3, 1940; s. Ralph Fredrich and Phyllis Shirley (Williams) H.; B.S. in Dairy Tech., U. Ill., 1962; Ph.D. in Microbiology, Oreg. State U., 1966; m. Diane Mary Miller, June 23, 1962; children—Julie Lynn, Gary David. Research asst. Oreg. State U., Corvallis, 1962-66; mgr. Moseley Lab., Indpls., 1968-71; lab. mgr., dairy products lab. Kraft, Inc., Glenview, Ill., 1971—. Served with U.S. Army, 1966-68. Decorated Army Commendation medal. Mem. Am. Dairy Sci. Assn., Inst. Food Technologists, Internat. Assn. Milk, Food and Environ. Sanitarians, Res. Officers Assn. Mem. United Ch. of Christ. Home: 6413 Johnsburg Rd Spring Grove IL 60081 Office: Kraft Inc 801 Waukegan Rd Glenview IL 60025

HENNING, EDWARD BURK, museum curator; b. Cleve., Oct. 23, 1922; s. Harold and Marguerite (Burk) W.; B.S. magna cum laude, Western Res. U., 1949; cert. Cleve. Inst. Art, 1949; postgrad. Acad. Julian, Paris, 1949-50; M.A., Western Res. U., 1952; m. Margaret Revacko, Dec. 31, 1942; children—Eric M., Lisa A. Henning Puzder, Geoffrey A. Instr., Cleve. Mus. Art, 1951-53, asst. curator edn., 1953-56, asso. curator edn., 1956-58, asst. to dir., 1958-70, curator contemporary art, 1970-72, curator modern art, 1972-78, chief curator modern art, 1978—; adj. prof. art history Case Western Res. U., Cleve., 1967—; cons. in field. Served with U.S. Army, 1942-46. Mem. Soc. Aesthetics, Coll. Art Assn., Am. Assn. Museums, New Orgn. Visual Arts. Author: Paths of Abstract Art, 1960; Fifty Years of Modern Art, 1966; The Spirit of Surrealism, 1980; contbr. articles to profl. jours. Office: 11150 E Boulevard Cleveland OH 44106

HENNING, GEORGE EMIL, ednl. cons.; b. Elgin, Ill., Apr. 4, 1932; s. George Emil and Theresa (Hauch) H.; B.A., Augustana Coll., 1953; M.Ed., U. Ill., 1954; postgrad. St. Louis U. Sch. Law, 1961-62; m. Harriet Zen Winter; children—Jeanne, Kathryn, William. Investigator, Dept. Def., Washington, 1954-56; tchr. Dearborn (Mich.) Public Schs., 1956-57; with Ethyl Corp., 1957-63; v.p. Augustana Coll., Rock Island, Ill., 1963-76; prin. George Henning and Assos., Inc., Rock Island, 1977—. Mem. Ill. State Scholarship Com., 1968-79, chmn. Ill. council Am. Coll. Testing Program, 1973-74; mem. unified edn. fund Luth. Ch. in Am., 1973-80. Served with U.S. Army, 1954-56. Mem. Am. Council Advancement and Support of Edn. Office: 741 34th St Rock Island IL 61201

HENNING, NELSON LOUIS, air force officer, clin. social worker; b. Evansville, Ind., Apr. 21, 1949; s. Louis Martin and Helen May H.; A.S., Highland Community Coll., 1974; B. Social Welfare, So. Ill. U., 1976; M.S.W., U. Ill., Urbana, 1977; m. Elaine Louise Jacobs, Aug. 14, 1971. Enlisted in U.S. Air Force, 1968, commd. 1st lt., 1978, advanced to capt., 1979; security policeman, 1968-72; clin. social worker Shapiro Devel. Center, Kankakee, Ill., 1977-78; clin. social worker Wright-Patterson AFB, Ohio, 1978-79, dir. Alcohol Treatment Center, 1979—; served in Vietnam, 1969-70. Decorated Cross of Gallantry with Palm Leaf (Vietnam); NIMH fellow, 1976-77. Mem. Nat. Assn. Social Workers, Nat. Assn. Christians in Social Work, Chi Gamma Iota. Home: 130 Buckeye Circle Wright Patterson AFB OH 45433 Office: Medical Center SGHAA Wright Patterson AFB OH 45433

HENNING, RANDALL MARVIN, automotive co. exec.; b. Milw., June 15, 1948; s. Marvin William and Joyce Jean (Helton) H.; student U. Wis., 1966-70; m. Kristina Louise Olson, July 3, 1971; children—Roy, Paul. Warehouse foreman Mueller Bros. Fish Co., Inc., Milw., 1966-70; pres., owner MoFoCo Enterprises, Inc., Milw., 1970—. Mem. Splty. Equipment Mfrs. Assn., Automotive Service

Industry Assn., Wis. Automotive Wholesalers Assn., Inc. Methodist. Office: MoFoCo Enterprises Inc 102 W Capitol Dr Milwaukee WI 53212

HENNINGS, ROBERT EDWARD, historian; b. Evanston, Ill., Aug. 4, 1925; s. Abraham James and Mervyna Barbara (Dolsen) H.; A.B., Oberlin (Ohio) Coll., 1950; M.A., U. Calif., Berkeley, 1957, Ph.D., 1961; m. Nancy Harriet Wensley, July 21, 1949; children— Deirdre Ellen, Robert Edward, Joseph Turner. Tchr. social studies and English pub. high schs. in Calif. and Ohio, 1953-56; instr. Am. history U. Ky., Lexington, 1961-62; mem. faculty Eastern Ill. U., Charleston, 1962—, prof. history, 1973—, chmn. dept., 1974—; chmn. council faculties to bd. govs. State Colls. and Univs. Ill., 1970-72. Pres., bd. dirs. Charleston Community Theatre, 1972-75. Served with AUS, 1944-46. Mem. AAUP (past chpt. pres.), Am. Assn. State and Local History, Am. Hist. Assn., Coles County, Ill., So. hist. socs., Nat. Trust Historic Preservation, Orgn. Am. Historians. Democrat. Contbr. profl. jours. Home: Bird Hill Route 4 Charleston IL 61920 Office: Dept History Eastern Ill Univ Charleston IL 61920

HENNINGS, THOMAS ARTHUR, restaurant chain exec.; b. Cleve., Jan. 26, 1946; s. Eugene George and Florence Ruth (Helwig) H.; B.S. magna cum laude in Mktg., Bowling Green State U., 1968; m. Melody L. Flood, Sept. 2, 1967; children—Thomas Michael, Traci Lyn. Mem. data processing sales staff IBM, Cleve., 1968; key account salesman Charles Pfizer Inc., Cleve., 1969-70; pres. Friar Tucks Party Docks Inc., North Olmsted, Ohio, 1972—, also dir.; pres. Franchise Mgmt. Inc., 1980—, Sisco Devel. Corp., 1980—; dir. S & D Advt. Inc. Ohio Masonic scholar, 1965; Sidney Frohman scholar, 1966; Nat. Food Mktg. scholar, 1967; Sales and Mktg. Execs. scholar, 1968; hon. gov. State of Ohio. Mem. Nat. Restaurant Assn., Phi Eta Sigma, Omicron Delta Kappa, Beta Gamma Sigma, Theta Chi. Lutheran. Clubs: Avon Oaks Country (Ohio); Riverbend Country (Tequesta, Fla.). Home: 31104 Roxbury Park Dr Bay Village OH 44140 Office: 30400 Detroit Rd Suite 407 Westlake OH 44145

HENRICH, EDWIN JOHN, ins. agy. exec.; b. Chgo., Dec. 22, 1936; s. Clement F. and Clara (Kaja) H.; student DePaul U., 1955-57; m. Eileen L. Schultz, Sept. 6, 1958; children—Edwin John, Joyce Ann, Jennifer Lynn. Asst. controller Am. Photocopy Equipment Co., Evanston, Ill., 1962-65; pres. Henrich Ins. Agy., Inc., Rolling Meadows, Ill., 1965—. Dir., Ins. Commn., Village of Mt. Prospect (Ill.), 1972-77. Rep. Sch. Dist. 57 Caucus, 1966-76; bd. dirs. United Way of Mt. Prospect, 1974-79, N.W. Community Hosp. Found., 1979—; dir. Evanston Rep. Club, 1963-66. Service award, Village of Mt. Prospect, 1977. Mem. Ind. Ins. Agts. of Am., Chgo. Bd. Underwriters, Profl. Ins. Agts. of Am. Roman Catholic. Clubs: Gaslight, Elks. Home: 2606 Mill Creek Ln Rolling Meadows IL 60008 Office: 1855-C Hicks Rd Rolling Meadows IL 60008

HENRICHSEN, MELVIN BURT, univ. bookstore dir.; b. Altamont, S.D., Dec. 14, 1913; s. Claus John and Alice Marie (Bauer) H.; B.S., S.D. State U., 1938; m. Alvina Kay Preuss, Apr. 7, 1939; children—Melvin John, Dean Douglas. Tchr., Elkton (S.D.) Public Sch., 1938-41; with supts. office Swift & Co., Watertown, S.D., 1941-45; dir. Pugsly Union, S.D. State U., Brookings, 1945-46, dir. housing and bookstore, 1946-65, dir. Student Assn. Bookstore, 1946—; tchr., cons. bookstore mgmt. Oberlin Coll., Calif. State U., U. Utah, Stanford U.; speaker profl. meetings. Dist. camping chmn. Boy Scouts Am.; state chmn. This is the Life, Luth. Laymen Men's Club. Recipient cert. of merit for cons. and teaching bookstore classes, 1970, student appreciation award for outstanding service, S.D. State U., 1978, award for service to Tri-State area, 1979. Mem. Nat. Assn. Coll. Stores (Mgr. of Yr. 1970), Am. Booksellers Assn., Christian Bookstore Assn., Tri-State Bookstore Assn. Republican. Club: Elephant. Home: 1625 Calumet Dr Brookings SD 57006 Office: Bookstore Univ Student Union South Dakota State U Brookings SD 57007

HENRIKSEN, CHARLES KENDALL, mech. engr.; b. Rockford, Ill., June 17, 1925; s. John H. and Edith O. (Olander) H.; B.S.M.E., Purdue U., 1948; m. Dorothy H. Hibbits, Feb. 7, 1948; children—David K., Richard L., Mark C. With Johnson Controls, Inc., Chgo., 1948-51, sales engr., Aurora, Ill., 1952-53, br. mgr., Peoria, Ill., 1954-62; cons. engr. Brown, Davis, Mullins, cons. engrs., Champaign. Ill., 1962-73, Phillips Swager Assos., Architects-Engrs., Peoria, 1973-78; exec. v.p. Asso. Engrs. III, Peoria, 1978-80; pres. H & S United Cons. Engrs., Inc., Peoria, 1980—. Sect. chmn. United Fund, Peoria. Served with USN, 1943-46. Recipient Service award Ill. Assn. Sch. Bds., 1973; registered profl. engr., Ill. Mem. Am. Soc. Plumbing Engrs. (pres. Ill. chpt. 1973-76, Merit award 1976), Ill. Assn. Sch. Bds. (chmn. exec. com. 1972-73), Ill. Soc. Profl. Engrs. (chmn. Ill. sect. exec. com. 1976-77), ASHRAE (pres. Central Ill. chpt.), Nat. Soc. Profl. Engrs., Constrn. Specifications Inst. Methodist. Club: Cosmopolitan Internat. Author: (with Jack T. Harroun) Good School Maintenance, 1976. Home: 9300 Timberlane Peoria IL 61615 Office: 8000 N Hale Ave Peoria IL 61615

HENRY, CHUCK, reporter, TV anchorman; b. Los Angeles, Jan. 1, 1946; s. Robert M. and Mildred (Coyle) H.; student Brigham Young U., 1963-66; m. Kay Shackelford, Sept. 3, 1966; children—Kristin, Jason, Ryan, Courtney. Reporter, TV anchorman KHVH-TV, Honolulu, 1966-67, 69-71, KABC-TV, Los Angeles, 1971-78, WMAQ-TV, Chgo., 1978—. Served with U.S. Army, 1967-69. Decorated Army Commendation medal; recipient TV Emmy award for spl. report Firetrap, KABC-TV, 1977; Emmy award for City Hall Here I Come, WMAQ-TV, 1979. Office: WMAQ-TV Merchandise Mart Plaza Chicago IL 60654*

HENRY, EDWARD FRANK, computer acctg. service co. exec.; b. East Cleveland, Ohio, Mar. 18, 1923; s. Edward Emerson and Mildred Adella (Kulow) H.; B.B.A., Dyke Coll., 1948; student Cleve. Inst. Music, 1972; m. Nicole Annette Peth, June 18, 1977. Internal auditor E.F. Hauserman Co., 1948-51; office mgr. Frank C. Grismer Co., 1951-52; Broadway Buick Co., 1952-55; treas. Commerce Ford Sales Co., 1955-65; nat. mgr. Auto Acctg. div. United Data Processing Co., Cin., 1966-68; v.p. Auto Data Systems Co., Cleve., 1968-70; pres. Profl. Mgmt. Computer Systems, Inc., Cleve., 1970—. Charter pres. No. Ohio Council Little Theatres, 1954-56; founder, artistic and mng. dir. Exptl. Theatre, Cleve., 1959-63; dramatic dir. various community theatres, 1955-65; actor Cleve. Playhouse, 1961-63; bd. dirs. Cleve. Philharmonic Orch., 1972-73. Served with USAAF, 1943-46; CBI. Notary public. Mem. Am. Mgmt. Assn., Nat. Assn. Accountants, Mil. Order World Wars, Heroes of '76, Ky. Cols. Republican. Presbyterian. Clubs: Rotary, Acacia Country, Hermit, Univ., Cleve. Grays, Deep Springs Trout, Nat. Sojourners (Nat. Pres.'s cert. 1977-78), Masons (33d degree), DeMolay (Legion of Honor 1970), K.T., Shriners (dramatic dir.), Jesters (dir. 1981), Grotto, Kachina. Author booklet. Home: 666 Echo Dr Gates Mills OH 44040 Office: 19701 S Miles Ave Cleveland OH 44128

HENRY, ERLAND PAUL, mfg. co. exec.; b. East Chicago, Ind., Nov. 12, 1949; s. Wayne John and Helen (Michalcik) H.; B.S., Ball State U., 1971; m. Diann L. Anderson, Feb. 27, 1971; children—Rachel Christian, Ryan Ross. Layout artist, account exec. Fleming & Harrison Advt., Michigan City, Ind., 1972-74; art dir. Don Kill Advt., Michigan City, 1974; advt. dir. Galbreath, Inc., Winamac, Ind., 1974—. Republican. Methodist. Home: 708 Roosevelt Rd Knox IN 46534 Office: Galbreath Inc PO Box 220 Winamac IN 46996

HENRY, FRED GRANT, mfg. co. exec.; b. Memphis, Aug. 16, 1946; s. Walter Worthington and Mary (Larrison) H.; B.A., Calif. Western U., San Diego, 1968; m. Gwen Askin, Dec. 5, 1973; children—Brooke, Blythe. Sales rep., sales trainer photocopier div. Smith Corona Marchant Co., Los Angeles, 1969-70; sales rep., terr. mgr. Johnson & Johnson, Los Angeles, 1970-72; terr. mgr. hospital div. Chesebrough-Ponds Co., Los Angeles, 1972-74; ind. mfrs. rep., San Diego, 1974-78; sales rep., dist. sales mgr. Cutter Biomed. Co., Barrington, Ill., 1978—. Mem. Health Industry Mfrs. Assn. (faculty). Club: Toastmasters (past club sec.). Address: 301 Beverly Rd Barrington IL 60010

HENRY, GILBERT EUGENE, real estate broker; b. Morenci, Mich., June 11, 1938; s. E. Merlin and Florence Pearl (Rowley) H.; student Olivet Coll., 1956-59; children—Tamara, Gil, Amy. With Abraham Realty Co., Adrian, Mich., 1963, v.p., 1968-72; v.p. Bob Goedert, Inc., 1973-74; organizer, pres. Gil Henry & Assos., Inc., Realtors, Profl. Appraisal and Real Estate Service, 1974—. Tchr. real estate class Lenawee Vocat. Tech. Sch., Adrian, 1972-73; chmn. Mich. Standard Forms Com., 1974-75. Active various charitable, ednl. fund drives. Bd. dirs. Tackabatchee council Camp Fire Girls Am., 1968-71. Mem. Mich. Real Estate Assn. (dir. 1973-80), Nat. Farm and Land Brokers, Nat. Inst., Nat. Assn. (exec. officers council 1969—) real estate bds., Lenawee County Bd. Realtors (Realtor of Year 1972, pres. 1971, dir. 1972-77), Am. Assn. Cert. Appraisers (sr. appraiser), Mich. Assn. Realtors (legis. com. 1979-80, bd. dirs.), Lenawee County C. of C. (v.p. Central Bus. Dist. 1980-81). Club: Masons. Home: 1389 Springville Hwy Adrian MI 49221 Office: 201 W Maumee St Adrian MI 49221

HENRY, JOSEPH PATRICK, chem. co. exec.; b. Mansfield, Ohio, Mar. 3, 1925; s. Harold H. and Louise A. (Droxler) H.; student Bowling Green State U., 1943-44; B.S., Ohio State U., 1949; m. Jeanette E. Russell, Oct. 26, 1957; 1 dau., Jeanette Louise. Ohio sales mgr. NaChurs Plant Food Co., Marion, O., 1949-55; organizer, pres. Growers Chem. Corp., Milan, 1955—, Sandusky Imported Motors, Inc. (Ohio), 1958—; co-owner Homestead Inn Restaurant, Homestead Farms; v.p. Homestead Inn, Inc. Motels, South Avery Corp. Motels; dir. Erie County Bank, Vermilion, Ohio. Served with USMCR, 1943-46; PTO. Mem. Nat. Fedn. Ind. Bus. (nat. adv. council), Ohio Farm Bur. Fedn., NAM, Milan C. of C., Aircraft Owners and Pilots Assn., Internat. Flying Farmers, Ohio Restaurant Assn., Ohio Motel-Hotel Assn., Ohio Licensed Beverage Assn., Am. Horse Show Assn., Nat. Trust for Historic Preservation, Huron County Hist. Soc., Ohio Farm Bur., (pres.), Ohio Internat. (regional dir.) Arabian horse assns., Internat. Platform Assn., Arabian Horse Registry Am. Clubs: Antique Automobile Am., Sports Car Am., N. Am. Yacht Racing Union, Sandusky Yacht, Sandusky Sailing; Ohio State Varsity O Assn. Home: 128 Center St Milan OH 44846 also Homestead Farms Route 1 Milan OH 44846 Office: Growers Chem Corp Box 1750 Milan OH 44846

HENRY, PATRICIA ANN, sales exec.; b. Fostoria, Ohio, Oct. 4, 1947; d. Joseph I. and Betty Jean (Feasel) Pocs; student St. Francis Sch. of Nursing and St. Mary of the Spring Coll., 1965-66, Ohio State Sch. Nursing, 1974; external degree in nursing State U. of N.Y., 1976; B.S. in Home Econs., Ohio State U., 1975, now postgrad. in bus. adminstrn.; realtor, Columbus Tech. Inst., 1978; 1 dau., Jennifer. Office nurse, Fredericktown, Ohio, 1966-67, Mt. Vernon, Ohio, 1969-71; nursing tech. St. Anthony Hosp., Columbus, Ohio, 1971-72; lab. tech. Ohio State U. Hosp., 1972-75; nursing coordinator Med. Evaluation Services, Columbus, 1975-76; sales rep. Ryan Homes, Inc., Columbus, 1976-78; home economist, sales mgr. Virginia Homes, Inc., Columbus, 1978-79; sales rep. Crest Communities, 1979-81; sales mgr. Landings-Klingbeil Mgmt. Group Co., Columbus, 1981—. Mem. Nat. Assn. Realtors, Ohio Bd. Realtors, Home Economists in Bus., Am. Home Econs. Assn., Ohio State U. Alumni Assn. Home: 5384 Fortress Trail Columbus OH 43230 Office: 2890 Chateau Circle Columbus OH 43221

HENRY, PAUL BRENTWOOD, state legislator; b. Chgo., July 9, 1942; s. Carl F. and H.I. (Bender) H.; B.A., Wheaton Coll., 1963; M.A. (fellow), Duke U., 1968, Ph.D., 1970; m. Karen Anne Borthistle, Aug. 28, 1965; children—Kara Elizabeth, Jordan Mark, Megan Anne. Vol. in U.S. Peace Corps, Liberia, 1963-64, Ethiopia, 1964-65; legis. asst. to Congressman John B. Anderson, 1968-69; instr. polit. sci. Duke U., Durham, N.C., 1969-70, asso. prof. Calvin Coll., Grand Rapids, Mich., 1970-78; state legislator Mich. Ho. of Reps., 1979-82, asst. minority floor leader, 1979-82. Mem. Mich. State Bd. of Edn., 1975-78; Kent County (Mich.) Republican chmn., 1975-76. Mem. Am. Polit. Sci. Assn. Republican. Mem. Christian Reformed Ch. Author: Politics for Evangelicals, 1974; (with Stephen V. Monsma) The Dynamics of the American Political System, 1970. Home: 438 Brookside Dr SE Grand Rapids MI 49507 Office: State Capital Lansing MI 48909

HENRY, RICHARD JAMES, educator; b. Monmouth, Ill., Mar. 6, 1935; s. James William and Elizabeth (Anderson) H.; B.S., Monmouth Coll., 1958; B.S., (univ. scholar), Case-Western Res. U., 1958; M.S. (Hughes fellow), U. Calif., Los Angeles, 1961; Ph.D. (NASA scholar), U. Conn., 1971; m. Sally Ann Platt, June 15, 1958; children—Mark Richard, Scott David, Keith William, Derek George. Engr., Hughes Aircraft Co., Los Angeles, 1958-62; sr. analytical engr., project mgr. Pratt & Whitney Aircraft Co., East Hartford, Conn., 1962-66; instr. math. U. Hartford, 1965-68; guest research scientist Deutsche Forschungs- und Versuchstalt für Luft-und Raumfahrt and U. Stuttgart (Germany), 1969-79; instr. to asso. prof. Black Hawk Coll., Moline, Ill., 1971—, dir. indsl. related tech. div. Pres., Warren County Swim Team Parent Assn., 1972-73, United Twp. High Sch. Band Parents, 1977—. Mem. AIAA, Instrument Soc. Am., ASHRAE, IMMS (edn. chmn.), Blue Key, Sigma Chi, Sigma Omicron Mu. Presbyterian. Club: East Moline Newcomers. Home: 2829 8th St East Moline IL 61244 Office: Black Hawk Coll 6600 34th Ave Moline IL 61265

HENRY, TERRY JAY, univ. adminstr.; b. Wheeling, W.Va., Sept. 12, 1937; s. Jay Everett and Virginia Eleanor (Dexter) H.; B.S. in Indsl. Adminstrn., U. Ill., Urbana-Champaign, 1961, M.A. in Public Adminstrn., 1970; Ph.D. in Adult and Continuing Edn., U. Nebr., Lincoln, 1981; m. Laura May Heffley, Sept. 4, 1960; children—Kimberly Ann, Judith Kay, Diane Lea. Indsl. engr., mgmt. services supr. A.E. Staley Mfg. Co., Decatur, Ill., 1967-70; city mgr. City of Lexington (Nebr.), 1970-72; univ. endowment mgr., investment officer U. Nebr. Central Adminstrn., Lincoln, 1972-74, univ. ops. auditor, 1974-77; adminstrv. asst. to asst. vice chancellor for acad. affairs U. Nebr., Lincoln, 1978-79; program dir. continuing mgmt. edn., continuing edn. and extension U. Minn., Mpls., 1979—. Treas., Personal Crisis Service, Inc., Lincoln, 1974-76; mem. budget allocations cabinet Lincoln and Lancaster County United Way, 1976-78; mem. Downtown Edn. Opportunities Community, Mpls., 1979—; mem. Ramsey County (Minn.) Civil Service Study Commn., 1980—. Served to capt. U.S. Army, 1961-67; maj. Res. Decorated Bronze Star (U.S.); Cross of Gallantry (Vietnam). Mem. Adult Edn. Assn. U.S.A., Am. Soc. Tng. and Devel., Missouri Valley Adult Edn. Assn., Minn. Assn. Continuing Adult Edn. Assn., Res. Officers Assn., Phi Delta Kappa. Presbyterian. Home: 1149 Sextant Ave W Roseville MN 55113 Office: 107 Armory 15 Church St SE U Minn Minneapolis MN 55455

HENRY, WILMA LUCILLE, ofcl. Calhoun County (Iowa); b. Winterset, Iowa, Dec. 28, 1928; d. Lester Monroe and Clara Lorena (Johnson) Yetter; student pub. schs.; m. Donald Dean Henry, June 30, 1946; children—Donella Sue, Paul Alan, Donald Mark, Teresa Jo, Matthew Charles, Specialist, Calhoun County Emergency and Med. Services, 1970-71; aide Calhoun County and Sac County Family Planning Services, 1971-72; parent coordinator Headstart Program, 1973-74; dir. Calhoun County Outreach Center, Rockwell City, 1972-79; owner, mgr. Holistic Health Resource Center, Ft. Dodge, Iowa, 1981—; charter mem. bd. dirs. Mobile Meals, Career Devel. Program, Well-Elderly Clinics, Iowa Coalition Environ. Orgns.; chmn. Calhoun County Environ. Action Group, 1968-77. Club: Rockwell City Bus. and Profl. Women's (pres. 1979-81). Home: 139 N Elm St Rockwell City IA 50579 Office: 3225 5th Ave S Fort Dodge IA 50501

HENSLEY, CARL WAYNE, educator; b. Bristol, Va., Feb. 25, 1936; s. James C. and Peggy H.; student Johnson Bible Coll., 1954-57; B.A., Milligan Coll., 1958; M.Div., Christian Theol. Sem., 1963; M.A., Butler U., 1966; Ph.D., U. Minn., 1972; m. Carol Annette Moeller, July 30, 1975; children—Angela Lynn, Steven W., Jennifer Robyn. Ordained to ministry Christian Ch., 1956; minister Christian Ch., Ellettsville, Ind., 1958-61; minister Christian Ch., Morristown, Ind., 1961-66; prof. Minn. Bible Coll., Rochester, 1966-73; aux. prof. Bethel Theol. Sem., St. Paul, 1972-77; prof. speech-communication Bethel Coll., 1973—; rapid reading instr. A.G.P., Inc. Adv. to Speakers' Bur., Minn. Soc. Prevention of Blindness, 1976-78; communication cons. to bus. orgns. Mem. Speech Communication Assn., Central States Speech Assn., Religious Speech-Communication Assn., Disciples of Christ Hist. Soc. Contbr. articles to profl. jours. Office: 3900 Bethel Dr Saint Paul MN 55112

HENSON, JOHN PORTER, equipment co. exec.; b. Girard, Kans., Sept. 25, 1922; s. John Porter and Gladys (deVenny) H.; B.S. in Mech. Engrng., Purdue U., 1946; m. Sarah Winslow Hodgdon, Sept. 27, 1947; children—Christena Margaret, John Winslow, David deVenny. Regional mgr. Bendix Westinghouse Air Brake, 1946-59; account exec. Dana Corp., Toledo, 1959-60, sales mgr., 1960-61, asst. gen. sales mgr., 1961-64; sales mgr. Kaydon Engrng. Co., Muskegon, Mich., 1964-65; product planning mgr. Clark Equipment Co., Buchanan, Mich., 1965—; exec. engr., 1965-66, v.p. engrng. axle div., 1966-72, v.p. mktg. worldwide transmission and axle divs., 1972-75, sales mgr. N.Am., axle and transmission divs., 1975-77, cons., 1977—; cons. Transmisiones y Equipos Mechanicos S.A., Queretaro, Mex., 1977—; cons., Mich. Export Co., Jackson, 1977, dir., 1981—. Served to 2d lt. USMC, 1942-46. Mem. Am. Ordnance Assn., Soc. Automotive Engrng., Mexican Sr. Golf Assn., Tau Beta Pi, Pi Tau Sigma, Sigma Chi. Home and office: 1105 Plym Rd Niles MI 49120

HENSON, PAUL HARRY, telecommunications exec.; b. Bennet, Nebr., July 22, 1925; s. Harry Elmer and Mae Vincent (Schoenthal) H.; B.S.E.E., U. Nebr., 1948, M.S.E.E., 1950; m. Betty Lorene Roeder, Aug. 2, 1946; children—Susan Henson Flury, Lizbeth Henson Barelli. Engr., chief engr. Lincoln Tel.&Tel. Co., Lincoln, Nebr., 1945-59; v.p. United Telecommunications, Inc., Kansas City, Mo., 1959-60, exec. v.p., 1960-64, pres., 1964-66, chmn. bd., 1966—; dir. Armco, Inc., Duke Power Co., Fed. Res. Bank Kansas City. Trustee, Tax Found., Nat. Legal Center for Public Interest; hon. consul for Sweden. Served with USAAF, 1942-45. Mem. Nat. Soc. Profl. Engrs., NAM, U.S. C. of C., Kansas City C. of C., IEEE, U.S. Ind. Telephone Assn. (dir. 1960-76), Armed Forces Communications and Electronics Assn., Sigma Xi, Eta Kappa Nu, Sigma Tau, Kappa Sigma. Republican. Clubs: River, Kansas City, Kansas City Country, Mission Hills Country, Chicago, Burning Tree, Castle Pines, Surf, Masons, Shriners. Office: PO Box 11315 Kansas City MO 64112

HENTHORNE, MARJORIE LUCILLE, designer, children's games mfg. exec.; b. Osawatomie, Kans., May 16, 1921; d. Benjamin F. and Mabel L. Emerson (Sturges) H.; grad. Kansas City (Mo.) Jr. Coll., 1939; student Kansas City (Mo.) Art Inst., 1940-41, William and Mary Profl. Inst., Richmond, Va., 1942-43, King-Smith Sch., Washington, 1943-45; m. Huston Burns McClurc, June 28, 1947; 1 dau., Jeanne Emerson. Free-lance fashion designer, 1939—; chief French Lend Lease Control Office, Washington, 1943-45; aide to U.S. senator for Calif., 1945-47; propr., designer J.M.H. Products, Kansas City, Mo., 1975—. Fin. chmn. We the Women of Hawaii, 1953-54. Mem. Kansas City Women's C. of C., Columbia Arts Club, Polit. Study Club Alumni Assn., Federated Women's Club. Mem. Christian Ch. Patentee games for children, designs. Address: 133 N Lawn St Kansas City MO 64123

HENTREL, BOBBIE KUYKENDALL, elem. sch. prin.; b. Batesville, Miss., Sept. 9, 1938; d. James and Ethel Kuykendall; B.S., Tenn. State U., 1960; M.Ed., 1964; Ph.D., U. Mich., 1975; m. Percy Gonya Hentrel, Jan. 15, 1965; 1 son, Michael Lovell. Tchr., Memphis City Schs., 1960-69; tchr. Grand Rapids (Mich.) Public Schs., 1969-73; lectr. U. Mich., 1973-75; asst. prin. Southfield (Mich.) Schs., 1975-79, prin., 1979—. Fulbright Hays award, Germany, 1975-76. Mem. Nat. Assn. Secondary Sch. Prins., Mich. Assn. Secondary Sch. Prins., Nat. Assn. Elem. Sch. Prins., Mich. Assn. Secondary Sch. Prins., Nat. Assn. Elem. Sch. Prins., Southfield Assn. Sch. Adminstrs., Mich. Assn. Elem. Sch. Prins., Nat. Assn. Supervision and Curriculum Devel., Delta Sigma Theta, Phi Delta Kappa. Democrat. Methodist. Home: 17577 E Goldwin St Southfield MI 48075 Office: 18575 W Nine Mile Rd Southfield MI 48075

HENZEY, THOMAS FRANCIS, cons. co. exec.; b. Cleve., Oct. 9, 1925; s. Frank Patrick and Loretta Veronica (Hearn) H.; B.B.A., John Carroll U., 1950; m. Winifred Mae Dunlap, Jan. 26, 1952; children—Thomas J., James R., Terrence F., William R., Beth Ann, Susan M. Office mgr. Cleve. Electric Illuminating Co., 1950-62; cons. Records Controls, Inc., Chgo., 1962-65; with Records & Filing Cons., Inc., Cleve., 1965—, exec. v.p. 1970—. Pres. Stongsville (Ohio) Bd. Edn., 1972-73. Served with USMC, 1942-46, 50-51. Decorated Navy Commendation medal; named Midwest Records Mgr. of Yr., 1962. Cert. records mgr. Mem. Assn. Records Mgrs. and Adminstrs., Bus. Forms Mgmt. Assn., Soc. Am. Archivists. Republican. Roman Catholic. Clubs: Lions, K.C. Home: 17470 Greenbrier Dr Strongsville OH 44136 Office: Records & Filing Consultants Inc PO Box 8818 Strongsville OH 44136

HENZLIK, RAYMOND EUGENE, zoophysiologist, educator; b. Casper, Wyo., Dec. 26, 1926; s. William H. and Adeline (Brown) H.; A.A., Northeastern Neb. Coll., 1946; B.S., U. Nebr., 1948, M.S., 1952, Ph.D., 1960; postgrad. Cornell U., 1961-62, Baylor Med. Coll., 1970-71; m. Wilma Louise Bartels, Oct. 1, 1950; children—Randall Eugene, Nancy Jo. Tchr., York (Nebr.) High Sch., 1948-50; supr. sci. teaching U. Nebr., 1951-53, asst. prof. zoology, 1959-61; tchr. Omaha North High Sch., 1953-56; instr. biology Nebr. Wesleyan U., 1957-59; asst. prof. zoology Ball State U., Muncie, Ind., 1962-67, asso. prof. physiology, 1967-69, prof. physiology, 1969—, also radiol. health officer; postdoctoral research on radioisotopes in marine food chains

Radiobiology Lab., U.S. Bur. Comml. Fisheries, Beaufort, N.C., tropical forest radioecology P.R. Nuclear Center, San Juan, 1967, radiotracer methodology Argonne Nat. Lab., 1969. Anatomy consultant Nat. Prescription Footwear Applicators Assn.; lectr. pedorthosis; cons. ednl. affairs Argonne Nat. Lab., also cons. radioecology; chmn. diabetes detection for Delaware County, Am. Diabetes Assn. Mem. Am. Ecol. Soc., AAAS, Am. Inst. Biol. Scis, Ind. Acad Sci., Muncie Tech. Soc. (pres.), Mensa, Sigma Xi, Phi Delta Kappa. Reviewer, referee Jour. Am. Biology Tchr. Research and publs. on radiation biology, ecology of animal communities, ednl. methodology. Home: 3311 Somerset Dr Muncie IN 47304

HEPLER, KENNETH MAX, mfg. co. exec.; b. Streator, Ill., Feb. 7, 1922; s. Max C. and Florence Roberta Hepler; B.S. in Mech. Engring., Ill. Inst. Tech., 1949; cert. mktg., UCLA, 1971; m. Wanda Ettamae Sines, Jan. 22, 1944; children—Kenneth F., Keith L., Kevin S., Vidabeth O. With U.S. Gypsum Co., 1949—, pres. subs., Yeso Panamericano SA de CV, Yeso Mexicana SA, Cia Terminal de Yeso SA, 1971-74, pres. U.C. Industries Co., 1977-79, corp. gen. mgr. mineral fiber div., Chgo., 1979—. Served with USNR, 1941-46. Mem. Chgo. C. of C. Republican. Clubs: Union League (Chgo.); Jonathan (Los Angeles); Masons. Office: 101 S Wacker Dr Chicago IL 60606

HERBERT, JAMES LAMAR, JR., food and energy co. exec.; b. Memphis, July 3, 1940; s. James Lamar and Annette J. (Claywell) H.; B.S., U. Tenn., 1962, postgrad., 1963; postgrad. Emory U., 1975; m. Judith K. Anderson, Apr. 12, 1963; children—Melissa, Scott. Editor, Tenn. Farmer Mag., Nashville, 1963, Poultry Meat Mag., Mt. Morris, Ill., 1964-68; v.p., gen. mgr. Food Systems, Inc., Nashville, 1969-70; gen. mgr. poultry ops. DeKalb Agresearch, Inc. (Ill.), 1970-79, corporate v.p., 1979—; dir. Sensors Inc., Ariz. Feeds, Dynapol, Calif. N.W. Fund, Farm Fish, Cal-Chix Inc. Recipient various trade assn. awards including Outstanding Leadership award Ala. Poultry and Livestock Assn., 1971. Mem. Southeastern Poultry Assn. (service award 1977), Am. Cattleman's Assn., Fish Farmers Assn., United Egg Producers. Republican. Baptist. Home: 438 Greenwood St DeKalb IL 60115 Office: DeKalb Agresearch Inc Sycamore Rd DeKalb IL 60115

HERBERT, MICHAEL KINZLY, mag. editor; b. Battle Creek, Mich., Dec. 1, 1942; s. Walter N. and Elaine F. (Hamblet) H.; student Kenyon Coll., 1961-62, Kellogg Community Coll., 1962-63; B.A., Western Mich. U., 1966; m. Lana Ann Viereg Stanton, May 7, 1966; children—Nancy Ann, Susan Elaine. Tchr. English, Orchard View High Sch., Muskegon, Mich., 1966-67; counselor, dormitory dir. Western Mich. U., Kalamazoo, 1967-68; sports reporter Chgo. Tribune, 1968-71; mng. editor Letterman Mag., Wheaton, Ill., 1971-72; editor Century Pub. Co., publishing Auto Racing Digest, Baseball Digest, Basketball Digest, Football Digest, Hockey Digest, and Soccer Digest, Evanston, Ill., 1972—. Mem. Profl. Football Writers Am., Football Writers Am., Profl. Basketball Writers Assn. Am., U.S. Basketball Writers Assn., Profl. Soccer Reporters Assn. Author: The Riddell Guide to Physical Fitness, 1977. Office: 1020 Church St Evanston IL 60201

HERBERTT, STANLEY, performing arts adminstr., choreographer; b. Chgo., Apr. 11, 1919; s. Samuel W. and Anna (Sturt) H.; grad. Herzl Jr. Coll., Chgo., 1938; B.Ed., Chgo. Tchrs. Coll., 1942; M.A., Nat. Acad. of Ballet, N.Y.C., 1960. With Chgo. Civic Opera Ballet, 1940-43, San Carlo Opera Ballet, Chgo., 1940-43, Littlefield Ballet Co., Chgo., 1941-42; soloist Ballet Theatre of N.Y., N.Y.C., 1943-47; soloist Broadway musical Carousel, 1947-49, Broadway musical Inside U.S.A., 1947-49; soloist, choreographer Cain Park Summer Theatre, Cleve., 1950-51; propr., dir. Ballet Arts Acad., St. Louis, 1951—; founder, dir. St. Louis Civic Ballet, 1959—. Lectr. St. Louis U., 1965—, Nat. Soc. of Arts and Letters, St. Louis, 1961—, Copper Coin Civic Ballet, Springfield, Ill., 1975—; mem. dance faculty Webster Coll., Webster Groves, Mo., 1976-77; participant Internat. Festival Youth Orchs. and Performing Arts, Aberdeen, Scotland, also London, 1976; choreographer Columbus (Ohio) Ballet Theatre, TV commls.; dir. musical fashion shows for Stix Baer and Fuller Dept. Stores; dir., choreographer ednl. program The History of Dance From Jig to Jet, 1967-81. Mem. dance com. Mo. State Council on the Arts, 1968—. Recipient Edn. for Arts award Stix Baer and Fuller, 1963; Plaque award St. Louis Civic Ballet, 1965; Merit award Fontbonne Coll., 1972; Maharishi award for Celebrations and Fulfillment, 1977; commendations from Mayor St. Louis, 1976, 79, Gov. Mo., 1977. Mem. Dance Workshop, Dance Masters of Am. Contbr. articles on dance and choreography to profl. publs. Home: 7620 Wydown Blvd St Louis MO 63105 Office: 7620 Wydown Blvd St Louis MO 63105

HERD, HAROLD S., state justice; b. Comanche County, Kans., June 13, 1918; A.B., Washburn U., Topeka, 1940, J.D., 1942; m. Margaret Zoe Rich; 6 children. Admitted to Kans. bar, 1943; practiced in Coldwater, Kans., 1946-79; atty. Comanche County 1954-58; justice Supreme Ct. Kans., 1979—. Past pres. Gyp Hills Devel. Com.; past chmn. Kans. Com. Humanities, 1980; mayor of Coldwater, 1950-54; mem. Kans. Senate 36th Dist., 1964-72, minority leader, 1968-72. Served with USNR, 1943-46. Mem. Kans. Bar Assn. (exec. council), Am. Legion (past post comdr.), VFW (past post comdr.), Phi Delta Kappa. Presbyterian. Clubs: Lions (past pres., zone chmn.), Shriners. Address: Kans Jud Center Topeka KS 66612

HERFINDAHL, LLOYD MANFORD, painter; b. Emmons, Minn., June 15, 1922; s. Albert and Betsy (Singlestad) H.; student Mpls. Coll. Art and Design, 1952; pupil of Adolph Dehn, also student in Paris. Co-pres. Internat. Grand Prix Painting Palm D'Or Des Beaux Arts, Palais de la Scala, Monte Carlo, Monaco, 1968; internat. cultural counselor Internat. Arts Guild, Monte Carlo, 1968; fgn. corr. Internat. Arts Bull., Monte Carlo, 1970-75; art dir. Lutheran Sentinel, 1966-69; fgn. corr. Minn. Arts Assn., 1974-77; chief dir. U.S.A. N.Y. exhbn. Festival Internat. de St-Germain-des-Pres, 1978; art cons. Boy Scouts Am., 1964; exhbns. include: Salon des Independents, Grand Palais, Paris, 1972, Soc. Acad. Des Arts Liberaux, Paris, 1972, Bertrand Russell Peace Found. Centenary, London, 1972, Festival Internat. St. Germain, Burssels, 1973, Paris, 1974-75, Mus. Modern Art, Paris, 1974, Holyland Mus., Los Angeles, 1974, Salon de l'Ecole de Thouet, Thovars, France, 1973, Luxembourg Palace, 1978, Ukrainian Inst. Am., 1978; rep. permanent collection Montbard (France) Mus. Fine Art, 1974. Chmn. ARC disaster com. Freeborn County and Albert Lea, Minn., 1966. Named Hon. Citizen of Mpls. for mural Guardians of Our Freedoms, 1976; commd. portrait King Olave V of Norway for Norse Heritage Series, 1968; decorated Order du Chevalier, Belgio-Hispanica, Paris, 1974; named personal délégué Vallobra de Grandry and Ehvoye Extra-ordinair, Belgium, 1978; recipient Queen Fabiola Gold medal Belgio-Hispanica, Belgium, 1973; Silver medal Soc. d'Encouragement au Proges, Paris, 1974; Grand Prix de Humanitaire de France, 1975; Paris Critique Palm of Gold, Acad. des Arts, Paris, 1975; Raymond and Isadora Duncan medal, 1978. Hon. mem. Minn. Artists Assn.; mem. Assn. Belgio-Hispanique, Soc. d'Encouragement au Progres, Internat. Arts Guild, Grand Prix Humanitair, Sons of Norway. Lutheran. Clubs: Kiwanis Day-Breakers (hon.) (Albert Lea). Address: 809 John Farry Pl Albert Lea MN 56007

HERGET, JAMES PATRICK, exec. search exec.; b. Cleve., Oct. 21, 1944; s. Louis E. and Dorothy R. (Whearty) H.; A.B., Holy Cross Coll., 1966; M.B.A., Case Western Res. U., 1969. Analyst, Cleve. Trust Co., 1966; sales rep. Xerox Corp., Cleve., 1967, cons., 1968-70, product mgr., Washington, 1971, social service leave, 1972, regional cons. mgr., 1973-75, mgr. sales and sales mgmt. programs, Rochester, N.Y., 1975-77, product mgr. Foward Products, 1977-78; asst. to v.p. mktg. Spencer Stuart Assos., Rochester, 1979-80, v.p., Cleve., 1980—; cons. Nat. Minority Purchasing Council, Inc., 1973-76; instr. mktg. Cleve. State U., 1970; dir. mktg. Interracial Council Bus. Opportunity, 1972; treas. Urban Small Bus. Cons., 1970. Co. location chmn. United Way, Arlington, Va., 1973-76; active Big Bros., Washington, 1972-75, Cleve., 1981; v.p. GeVa Theatre, Rochester, 1977-78; mem. Vols. in Partnership, Rochester, 1978-79. Recipient Nat. citation Nat. Center for Voluntary Action, 1971; Ace award SBA, 1970. Mem. Internat. Platform Assn., Mensa. Republican. Roman Catholic. Clubs: Playhouse, City, Univ., Skating, Ohio Holy Cross (Cleve.). Designer, producer 3 tng. programs for office of minority enterprise Commerce Dept., 1973-76. Home: 2178 Harcourt Dr Cleveland Heights OH 44106

HERMAN, CLIFF A., ency. sales mgr.; b. Kulm, N.D., Nov. 24, 1927; s. Adolph and Matilda (Tobler) H.; B.S., U. N.D., 1951, M. Sch. Adminstrn., 1957; m. Marilyn Ruth Hunter, June 15, 1952; children—Craig, Roxanne, Kevin, Holly. Tchr. social studies Wolf Point (Mont.) Public Sch., 1951-53; supt. schs., Gardena, N.D., 1954-55; sch. adminstr., Bottineau, N.D., 1955-59; tchr. rep. World Book, Inc., Bottineau, 1958-59, area and dist. mgr., Fargo, N.D., 1959-60, regional mgr., Sioux Falls, S.D., 1960-65, div. mgr., Sioux Falls, 1965-68, exec. trainee, Chgo., 1969, br. mgr., Pitts., 1969-71, br. mgr., Omaha, 1971—. Served with USN, 1945-46. Recipient Mgr. of Yr. award World Book, Inc., 1965. Mem. NEA (life), Am. Numismatic Soc., Hummel Soc., Phi Delta Kappa (life). Republican. Congregationalist. Clubs: Masons (past master, past high priest), Shriners, Eastern Star, Sertoma. Office: World Book/Childcraft Internat Inc 5004 Dodge St Omaha NE 68132

HERMAN, GARY MITCHELL, employment counselor; b. Bklyn., Jan. 10, 1952; s. Albert and Shirley Herman; B.A., SUNY, Binghamton, 1973; M.S., SUNY, Albany, 1976, Ed.S., 1976; m. Sandra Sue Came, June 2, 1974. Career and fin. aid counselor SUNY, Purchase, 1975-76; employment counselor CETA Titles II and VI, Grand Rapids, Mich., 1977-78; job developer Grand Rapids CETA Title I, 1978-79, employment devel. team supr., 1979—; cons., facilitator Grand Rapids Women's Resource Center; trainer cons. Grand Rapids Affirmative Action Program. Mem. Am. Personnel and Guidance Assn., Nat. Employment Counselor Assn. Office: 121 Franklin State SE Lower Level Grand Rapids MI 49507

HERMAN, GARY RONALD, state edn. ofcl.; b. Coatsville, Pa., Oct. 22, 1941; s. Marlin Frederick and Frances Louella Shawver) H.; B.S., Mankato State U., 1964; M.S., 1966; m. Sharon Lee Wiedemann, Sept. 21, 1961; children—Rick Dean, Terri Lyn, Randy Scott, Melissa Lee. Tchr. elem. schs., Wells, Minn., 1964-66, Faribault, Minn., 1966-68; prin. elem. sch., Olivia, Minn., 1968-73; regional dir. Right to Read, S.W./W. Central Minn., Minn. Dept. Edn., Olivia, 1973-79, basic skills specialist, Marshall, Minn., 1979—; owner, cons. Schoolmaster Ednl. Cons. Services, 1980. Sunday sch. supt. Cross of Calvary Luth. Ch., Olivia, 1971-73; clk. Olivia Bd. Edn., 1978-80. Recipient awards Multiple Sclerosis, 1976, Govs. award Regional Ednl. Planning Task Force, 1979. Mem. Internat. Reading Assn., Nat. Council Tchrs. English, Assn. Supervision and Curriculum Devel., Nat. Affiliation Literacy Advance. Author: (booklet) Not How to Have Them, But How to Raise Them: A Parents Guide to Discipline, 1980; (monographs) So You Want To...Get Those Rascals to Study, 1981; So You Want To...Get Your Students to Think and Comprehend, 1981. Home: 412 S 2d St Olivia MN 56277 Office: Coop Service Unit Southwest State U Marshall MN 56258

HERMAN, GERALD EVERETT, fin. co. exec.; b. Hays, Kans., Jan. 29, 1947; s. Henry Everett and Bertha (Dreiling) H.; student Ft. Hays (Kans.) State Coll., 1965-67; B.S., Kans. State U., 1973; m. Dianne Lee Nance, June 27, 1974; children—Stacia Lynn, Chad, Tara Lee. Auditor, Elmer Fox & Co., acctg., Wichita, 1974-76, sr. auditor, 1976; v.p., sec./treas., dir. Becker Corp., El Dorado, Kans., 1976—. Treas., mem. fin. bd., adminstrv. bd. 1st United Meth. Ch., El Dorado, 1979—. Served with U.S. Army, 1967-72; Vietnam. Decorated Bronze Star, Army Commendation medal with cluster, Air medal with 25 clusters; C.P.A. Mem. Kans. Soc. C.P.A.'s, Am. Inst. C.P.A.'s, VFW (life), Phi Kappa Phi. Republican. Clubs: El Dorado Rotary (dir.), El Dorado Country (dir.). Home: 730 Post Rd El Dorado KS 67042 Office: Becker Corp 131 N Haverhill Rd El Dorado KS 67042

HERMAN, HAROLD WILCOX, mgmt. cons.; b. Kodaikanal, India, May 22, 1913 (parents Am. Citizens); s. Harold Clyde and Winifred (Wilcox) H.; B.A., Carleton Coll., 1935; m. Georga Fern Burk, July 6, 1939; 1 dau., Haleen Louise. Publicity dir. Dayton (Ohio) YMCA, 1935-41; mem. internat. hdqrs. staff Jaycees, 1941-43, exec. v.p., Chgo., 1944-45; editor Coll. and Univ. Bus., 1945-68; v.p. Corco, 1969-72; sr. editor World Book Ency., Chgo., 1972-73; asst. to adminstr. Plymouth Pl., La Grange, Ill., 1973; v.p. mktg. Exertia, Inc., Park Ridge, Ill., 1973—; mem. faculty, short course on coll. bus. mgmt. U. Nebr., Omaha. Trustee, Vill. Oak Park (Ill.), 1969-73; pres. Oak Park Community Lectures, 1973-79. Served with USCG Temporary Res., 1943-44. Mem. Pi Delta Epsilon, Sigma Delta Chi. Clubs: Chgo. Press, Headline (Chgo.). Contbr. editorials to ednl. publs. Office: 819 Busse Hwy Park Ridge IL 60068

HERMAN, JAMES JAY, allergist; b. Ft. Worth, Nov. 28, 1947; s. Paul F. and Helen (Levy) H.; B.S. in Pharmacy with honors, U. Tex. at Austin, 1970, M.D., 1973; m. Rowena Ann Fischer, June 28, 1970; children—Hugh Mitchell, Elana Gabrielle. Research asst. pharmacognosy U. Tex. Coll. Pharmacy, 1969; intern, resident pediatrics Children's Meml. Hosp., Northwestern U.-McGaw Med. Center, Chgo., 1973-76; fellow pediatrics allergy-clin. immunology Children's Hosp. Med. Center, Harvard Med. Sch., Boston, 1976-78, instr. pediatrics, allergy-clin. immunology, 1978-79; asst. prof. pediatrics Northwestern U. Med. Sch., Chgo., 1979—; head div. allergy Children's Meml. Hosp., Chgo., 1979—; mem. med. adv. bd. Children's Research Found., 1979—. Mem. Nat. Com. Young Democrats; mem. Ill. Dist. 108 Sch. Caucus. Welch fellow U. Tex., 1967-70, NSF Summer Inst. fellow U. Tex., 1968-69. Diplomate Nat. Bd. Med. Examiners, Am. Bd. Pediatrics, Am. Bd. Allergy and Immunology. Fellow Am. Acad. Pediatrics; mem. Am. Acad. Allergy, Am. Assn. Immunology, Chgo. Immunology Assn., Ill. Allergy Soc., Chgo. Allergy Soc., AAAS, Am. Thoracic Soc., Asthma and Allergy Found. Am., Joint Council Allergy and Clin. Immunology, N.Y. Acad. Scis., Phi Eta Sigma, Rho Chi, Common Cause, Nat. Audubon Soc. Democrat. Jewish. Club: B'nai B'rith. Contbr. articles in field to profl. jours. Office: 2300 Children's Plaza Chicago IL 60614

HERMAN, JOHN ALLEN, editor; b. Willmar, Minn., Apr. 9, 1936; s. Herbert Allen and Mable A. (Boyer) H., student U. Minn., 1955-59; m. Joan Elaine Eddy, Jan. 28, 1967; children—Sarah Elizabeth, Andrew Allen. Field dir. Nat. Small Bus. Assn., Mpls., 1959-60; v.p. Minn. Small Bus. Assn., St. Paul, 1960-61; pub. relations cons., Washington, 1961-66; editor; pub. Washington County Bull., Cottage Grove, Minn., 1966—; pres. Bull. Pub. Corp., Cottage Grove, Minn., 1970—. Mem. state central com. Minn. Republican party, 1970-75; Kandiyohi County chmn. Young Reps., 1964; dep. registrar City of Cottage Grove, 1973—; Rep. candidate U.S. Senate, 1978. Recipient State Americanism award Minn. V.F.W., 1970. Mem. Nat., Minn. newspaper assns., Cottage Grove Area C. of C., Washington County, Nat., Minn. hist. socs., Minn. Dep. Registrars Assn. (v.p. 1977-78), Nat. Trust Hist. Preservation, Minn. Press Club. Club: St. Paul Rotary. Home: 6192 65th St S Cottage Grove MN 55016 Office: 7162 80th St S Cottage Grove MN 55016

HERMAN, RONALD ELWYN, mfg. co. exec.; b. Rochester, N.Y., Mar. 13, 1931; s. Elwyn and Rossie Angeline (Harer) H.; M.E., Gen. Motors Inst., 1954; m. Shirley Joann Danton, Sept. 21, 1963; children—Vicki Herman Drayer, Richard R., Teresa L., David J. From trainee to engr. carburetor devel. Rochester (N.Y.) Products div. Gen. Motors Corp., 1950-54; with Holley Carburetor div. Colt Industries Inc., 1954—, dir. engring. Holly spl. products div., Warren, Mich. from 1979, now v.p. engring. Mem. Soc. Automotive Engrs. Republican. Author patents fuel systems. Office: 11955 E Nine Mile Rd Warren MI 48090*

HERMANN, DONALD HAROLD JAMES, lawyer, educator; b. Southgate, Ky., Apr. 6, 1943; s. Albert Joseph and Helen Marie (Snow) H.; A.B. (George E. Gamble Honors scholar), Stanford U., 1965; J.D. (John Noble fellow), Columbia U., 1968; LL.M. (Law and Humanities fellow), Harvard U., 1974; M.A. (Grad. fellow), Northwestern U., 1979, Ph.D., 1981. Mem. staff, directorate of devel. plans Dept. Def., 1964-65, Legis. Drafting Research Fund, Columbia U., 1966-68; admitted to Ariz. bar, 1968, Wash. bar, 1969, Ky. bar, 1971, Ill. bar, 1972, U.S. Supreme Ct. bar, 1974; mem. faculty U. Wash., Seattle, 1968-71, U. Ky., Lexington, 1971-72; mem. faculty DePaul U., Chgo., 1972—, prof. law, 1973—, dir. acad. programs and interdisciplinary study, 1975-76, asso. dean, 1975-78; fellow law and humanities Harvard U., 1973-74; vis. prof. Washington U., St. Louis, 1974, U. Brazilia, 1976; lectr. law Sch. Edn., Northwestern U., 1974-76, Am. Soc. Found., 1975—, Christ Coll., Cambridge U., 1977; mem. faculty in law and econs. U. Rochester, 1974; lectr. dept. philosophy Northwestern U., 1978-81; fellow law and econs. U. Chgo., 1975-76; lectr. Instituto Superiore Internazionale Di Science Criminali, Italy, 1978—. Bd. dirs. Council for Legal Edn. Opportunity, Ohio Valley Consortium, 1972, Ill. Bar Automated Research Corp., 1975—, Criminal Law Consortium Cook County, 1977-80; cons. A Federacao de Comercia de Estado de Sao Paulo, Brazil; reporter Ill. Jud. Conf., 1972—; cons. Adminstrv. Office of Ill. Cts., 1974—. Nat. Endowment for Humanities fellow, 1978, 81. Mem. Am., Ill., Chgo. bar assns., Am. Law Inst., Am. Acad. Polit. and Social Sci., Soc. Phenomenology and Existential Philosophy, Am. Soc. Polit. and Legal Philosophy, Am. Judicature Soc., Am. Philos. Assn., Internat. Assn. Philosophy of Law and Social Philosophy, Soc. Writers on Legal Subjects, Soc. Am. Law Tchrs., Am. Assn. Law Schs. (del., sect. chmn.), Chgo. Hist. Preservation Soc., Evanston Hist. Soc., Art Inst. Chgo., Northwestern Alumni Assn., Signet Soc. (Harvard). Episcopalian. Clubs: Hasty Pudding (Harvard); Univ., Quadrangle (Chgo.); Univ. (Evanston); Univ. (Chgo.). Home: 1243 Forest Ave Evanston IL 60202 Office: DePaul U Coll of Law 25 E Jackson St Chicago IL 60604

HERMANN, PAUL DAVID, assn. exec.; b. Chgo., Feb. 1, 1925; s. Edgar Paul and Marjory (Alexander) H.; student Lawrence U., 1942-45; B.S. in Bus. Adminstrn., Northwestern U., 1948; m. Joan Louise Mullin, Nov. 10, 1948; children—Bruce Phillip, Susan Marie. Asst. dir. news bur. Ill. Inst. Tech., 1945-48; editor Constrn. Equipment Distbn., Chgo., 1948-49; exec. v.p. Asso. Equipment Distbrs., Oak Brook, Ill., 1950—, also pres. Asso. Equipment Distbrs. Research and Services Corp., 1974—. Certified assn. exec. Mem. Am. Soc. Assn. Execs. (pres. 1974), U.S. C. of C. (dir. 1981-83, mem. assn. com. Small Bus. Council, chmn. 1981-82; adv. council nat. chamber alliance for politics), Chgo. Soc. Assn. Execs. (pres. 1968-69), Inst. Orgn. Mgmt. (regent 1969-72), Nat. Assn. Wholesaler-Distbrs. (trustee), Pi Delta Epsilon (hon.). Delta Tau Delta. Contbr. articles to profl. jours. and textbooks. Home: 2 S 751 Ave Cherbourg Oak Brook IL 60521 Office: 615 W 22d St Oak Brook IL 60521

HERMANN, ROBERT RINGEN, packaging co. exec.; b. St. Louis, Jan. 3, 1923; s. Frederick A. and Evelyn (Ringen) H.; B.S., Princeton U., 1944; married; children—Carlotta Hermann Holton, Robert Ringen; stepchildren—Robert, Stephen, Lesley and Mark Scherer. Chmn. bd., pres. Hermann Group, Inc., and divs. Standard Container Co., Hermann Devel. Co. and subs. Anchor Mktg. Inc., Anchor Industries, Inc., Bauhaus Ltd., St. Louis, 1954—; pres. and chmn. Fair, Inc.; dir. Hermann Oak Leather Co., Hermann Pump Co., Inc., Link, C.A. Vice chmn. United Fund, 1960; chmn. Muscular Dystrophy of Mo., 1960—; bd. dirs. N.Am. Soccer League, 1968—, chmn. exec. com., 1970; bd. dirs. Barnes Med. Center, 1962, St. Louis Sports Hall of Fame, 1970; trustee Mo. Bot. Garden, 1965; trustee St. Louis Mcpl. Opera, 1965, pres., 1978—; trustee St. Louis Symphony, 1960, Jefferson Nat. Expansion Meml. Assn., 1972; bd. dirs. Theater Project. Served to lt. USN, 1943-46. Mem. Nat. Council for Arts and Edn. (mem. exec. com. 1974), Princeton Alumni Council. Clubs: Princeton of St. Louis (past pres.), St. Louis Country, Log Cabin, Yacht of St. Louis (commodore), Stadium (dir.), Frontenac Racquet (bd. dirs.). Ann. award to most valuable soccer player in U.S. named in his honor by N.Am. Soccer League. Home: 777 Cella Rd St Louis MO 63124 Office: 1750 S Hanley Rd St Louis MO 63144

HERMANSON, EDWARD HILDOR, constrn., real estate and banking exec.; b. Salem, Oreg., Apr. 15, 1936; s. Hildor Egil and Ruby Evelyn (Bjelde) H.; A.B., Cascade Coll., 1958; M.A., Tchr.'s Coll., Columbia U., 1959, Ed.D., 1965; m. Luella Marie Warkentin, June 15, 1958; children—David Hildor, Eileen Marie. Instr. in music Tchrs. Coll., Columbia U., 1960-61; mem. voice faculty Nyack (N.Y.) Missionary Coll., 1961-63; tchr. music, public schs., Mt. Vernon, N.Y., 1964-67; chmn. dept. music Taylor U., 1967-73; pres. Willman Lumber Co. and Hermanson Constrn. Co., Hartford City, Ind., 1973-77, Hermanson Enterprise's, Hartford City, 1977—; chmn. bd. First State Bank, Dunkirk, Ind., 1978, First Nat. Bank, Columbus, Ind.; baritone soloist; minister of music Lakeview Wesleyan Ch., Marion, Ind., 1975-80. Pres. Mississinewa Arts Council, Marion, 1969, Marion Philharmonic Orch., 1969-72, Ind. Higher Edn. Music Adminstrs. Assn., 1971. Named Man of Yr., Oreg. Edn. Assn., 1958, Disting. Friend, Taylor U., 1978. Mem. Upland C. of C. (v.p. 1975), NEA (life), Marion Civic Theater, Phi Delta Kappa. Republican. Club: Rotary. Author: It's Your Profession, 1958; Audio-Visual Materials in Music, 1965; The Solo Vocal Literature of Edvard Grieg, 1965. Office: 141 S Adams St Marion IN 46952

HERMSMEYER, CARL ALFRED, clin. psychologist; b. Litchfield, Ill., Sept. 28, 1928; s. Carl Christopher and Lillie (Stein) H.; B.A. summa cum laude, So. Ill. U., 1972; Ph.D., St. Louis U., 1976; children—Kay, David, Beth, Christopher; m. 2d, Carrol Eleanor Bauer, Aug. 15, 1981; children—Amanda, Frank, Deborah. With A. K. Busch & Assos., Belleville, Ill., 1973-78; pvt. practice clin. psychology, Collinsville, Ill., 1978—; pres. Internat. Rational Stress Inst., Collinsville, 1977—; adj. prof. St. Louis U., Webster Coll., Columbia, Mo., McKendree Coll., Lebanon, Ill.; mem. nat. faculty Soc. Clin. and Exptl. Hypnosis, 1979-80. Alderman, Litchfield, 1954-66. Served with inf. U.S. Army, 1946-48. Mem. Am. Psychol. Assn., Ill. Psychol. Assn., Am. Soc. Clin. Hypnosis, Soc. Clin. and Exptl. Hypnosis, Biofeedback Research Soc. Republican. Lutheran.

Contbr. articles to profl. jours. Home: Rural Route 1 Box 126A Saint Jacob IL 62281 Office: 1518 Vandalia Collinsville IL 62234

HEROLD, MORT, memory improvement cons.; b. Chgo., Nov. 13, 1925; s. Jack George and Bessie Lorraine Abrams; B.A., Roosevelt U., 1957; m. Cressida Tabb, Jan. 29, 1956; children—Richard, June. Pres. Herold Sch. Music, Chgo., 1960-70; head accordion dept. Vandercook Coll. Music, Chgo., 1962-65; dist. mgr. Lyon-Healy, Inc., Chgo., 1970-77; pres. Memory Improvement Services, Hazel Crest, Ill., 1977—; speaker, leader seminars, cons. Served with USN World War II. Mem. Nat. Speakers Assn., Calif. Memory Research Center, Internat. Brotherhood of Magicians. Author: Learning the Accordion is Fun, 1964; Herold Memory Course, 1969; cassette course: A Memory System That Works, 1980. Office: 18658 Golfview Dr Suite 334 Hazel Crest IL 60429

HERRICK, CLAY, JR., civic worker, ret. advt. agy. exec.; b. Cleveland Heights, Ohio, Dec. 15, 1911; s. C. Clay and Alice Mabel (Meriam) H.; B.A. Adelbert Coll. of Western Res. U., 1934; diploma John Huntington Poly. Inst.; m. Ruth Eleanor Penty, Apr. 27, 1935; children—Clay Herrick III, Jill. Pub. relations dir. General Tire & Rubber Co., Akron, 1940-45; creative dir. JP Smith creative printers for Eastman Kodak, Rochester, 1945-48; account exec. Fuller, Smith & Ross, Inc., 1948-58; v.p. Carpenter, Lamb & Herrick, Inc., 1958-64, pres., 1964-73; pres. Western Reserve Press, Inc., 1973—; sr. v.p. Watts, Lamb, Kenyon & Herrick Inc., 1973-74, ret., 1974. Instr. graphics Cleve. State U.; originator, 1st pres. Cleve. Printing Week celebrations; seminar leader In-Plant Printing Mgmt. Assn., 1978. Pres., Early Settlers Assn.; chmn. Cleve. Landmark Commn.; v.p. Shaker Landmarks Commn.; chmn. Cleve. Hall Fame Commn.; v.p. Cleve. Bicentennial Commn.; mem. univ. alumni council Western Res. U.; fund chmn. Cleve. Ch. Fedn.; scoutmaster, cubmaster Boy Scouts Am.; active PTA; trustee YMCA, Shauffler div. Defiance Coll.; pub. relations bd. United Appeal; chmn. task force Cleve. Ambassadors, 1978; mem. public relations com. ARC Centennial, 1981; program vice chmn. Cleve. Sr. Council, 1981-82; deacon Fairmount Presbyn. Ch., Shaker Heights, Ohio. Named Cleve. Graphic Arts Man of Year, 1965; elected to Graphic Arts Hall of Distinction, 1977; recipient Heritage award New Eng. Soc., 1978; elected to Disting. Alumni Hall of Fame, Cleveland Heights High Sch., 1981. Mem. Nat. Cartoonists Soc., Am. Assn. Advt. Agys. (chmn.), New Eng. Soc. (pres., named Man of Year 1977), Cleve. Cultural Gardens Fedn. (v.p.), Shaker Hist. Soc. (pres.). Cleve. Ad Club (v.p.), Founders and Patriots Am. (lt. gov. nat. soc.), Fine Arts Assn. (trustee), Am. Advt. Fedn. (dist gov., named Advt. Man of Year 1974), Intercomm Communications Group (1st pres.), Cleve. Graphic Arts Council (organizer, pres.), Adelbert Alumni Assn. Western Res. U. (pres.), SAR (past pres., sec.-treas. 1974—), Delta Upsilon, Sigma Delta Chi, Delta Sigma Rho, Pi Epsilon Delta. Clubs: Toastmasters Internat. (hon. life), Cheshire Cheese (past pres. 3 times). Author: But It's So, 1934; Cleveland's Rich Heritage, 1975; author monthly feature Cleveland Landmarks in Properties Mag., 1977—. Editor, pub. Graphic Artisan; editor Pioneer, others. Home: 16315 Fernway Rd Shaker Heights OH 44120

HERRICK, JOHN MIDDLEMIST, educator; b. Mpls., Aug. 21, 1942; s. John Lewis and Dorothy (Middlemist) H.; B.A. egregia cum laude, St. John's U., Collegeville, Minn., 1964; M.A., U. Minn., 1967, Ph.D., 1970; m. Kathleen Magara, Feb. 5, 1966; children—Elizabeth Jane, Kathryn Mary. Instr. dept. history Macalester Coll., St. Paul, 1969-70; instr. dept. history U. Ill., Champaign-Urbana, 1970-71; asst. prof. depts. social work and history King's Coll., U. Western Ont. (Can.), London, 1971-73; asso. prof. social work Mich. State U., 1973-80, prof., 1980—; cons. in field. Bd. dirs. The Open Door, Lansing, Mich., 1975-79, The New Way In, Lansing, 1974—, The Listening Ear, East Lansing, Mich., 1979—. Mem. Orgn. Am. Historians, Social Welfare History Group, Nat. Assn. Social Workers, Assn. Voluntary Action Scholars, Council Social Work Edn., Soc. Study Social Problems, Phi Alpha Theta, Phi Alpha, Phi Kappa Phi. Roman Catholic. Author: (with John F. Jones,) Citizens in Service, Volunteers in Social Welfare During The Depression, 1929-41, 1976. Home: 2330 Shawnee Trail Okemos MI 48864 Office: School of Social Work Baker Hall East Lansing MI 48824

HERRIN, SNYDER E., lawyer; b. Herrin, Ill., Dec. 25, 1903; s. Jeff Snyder and Louisa Clementine (Stearns) H.; student U. Mich., 1921-22; A.B., U. Ill., 1925, J.D., 1927; m. Norma Dot Keen, Aug. 16, 1930; children—Sandra Lou (Mrs. Sandra Plapp), Snyder E. II. Admitted to Ill. bar, 1927; since practiced in Herrin, Ill. Chmn. bd. Herrin Security Bank, 1957-77, atty., 1957—. Govt. appeal agt. Draft Bd., Herrin, 1940-71. Sec. Herrin Bd. Edn., 1928-31; city atty., Herrin, 1935-37, 49-53, 57-69, 76-77, Ziegler, Ill., 1934-42; village atty., Cambria, Ill., 1950-62, Bush, Ill., 1966-70; atty. Herrin Park Dist., 1955—, Herrin Mosquito Abatement Dist., 1962—. Served to capt. JAG, AUS, 1942-46. Mem. Ill., Williamson County (pres. 1940-42, 63-64) bar assns., Ill. Trial Lawyers Assn. (hon.), Ill. Assn. Park Dists. (hon.), Am. Legion (comdr. 1952-54), Herrin C. of C. (dir. 1975—), Williamson County Hist. Soc. (pres. 1957-61), Pi Kappa Phi, Gamma Eta Gamma, Phi Alpha Delta. Democrat. Baptist. Club: Rotary (pres. 1932-34). Home: 408 S 12th St Herrin IL 62948 Office: 2 Park Plaza Herrin IL 62948

HERRING, MONVILLE (LEE), county ofcl.; b. Brookhaven, Miss., May 14, 1935; s. Lonnie E. and Mildred Ada (Lea) H.; student U. New Orleans, 1945-52, U. Kans., 1963-64; 1 dau., Suzie Ray. With Woodward White Co., New Orleans, 1952; buyer, supt. material control Water Dist. #1 of Johnson County, Mission, Kans., 1962—. Served with USN, 1952-61. Mem. Nat. Wildlife Fedn., C. of C., Am. Water Works Assn., Purchasing Mgrs. Assn. (dir. 1964-65), Kansas City Purchasing Agts., Am. Legion. Baptist. Address: 5930 Beverly St Mission KS 66202

HERRIOTT, DAVID BRUCE, retail computer co. exec.; b. Urbana, Ill., June 2, 1942; s. Merle Fisher and Miriam Berniece (Fort) H.; student Ill. Comml. Coll.; m. Donna Jean Bullard, Aug. 19, 1962; children—Dean Fisher, Deborah Rene. Clk., office mgr. Lindsay-Schaub Newspapers, Urbana, 1962-66, data processing mgr., 1968-79; pub. New Port Richey (Fla.) Press, 1967; data processing mgr., v.p. Lindsay-Schaub Ill., Inc., 1976-79, Lindsay-Schaub Mich., Inc., 1976-79, Lindsay-Schaub Fla., Inc., 1976-79, Decautur (Ill.), Newspapers, Inc., 1976-79; partner, treas., dir. Main St. Computer Co., Decatur, 1979—, Mattoon's Main St. Computer Co. (Ill.), 1979—. Bus. mgr. publs. Fla. Jaycees, 1967; bd. dirs. Decatur Jaycees, 1975; deacon First Baptist Ch., Decatur, 1976-79, chmn., 1978-79; mem. Decatur Zoning Bd. Appeals, 1977—, chmn., 1981—; mem. Decatur Transit Adv. Commn., 1981—. Served with USNR, 1960-62. Republican. Club: Decatur Kiwanis. Author newspaper articles. Home: 112 Point Bluff Dr Decatur IL 62521 Office: 215 N Main St Decatur IL 62523

HERRMANN, EDWARD JOHN, bishop; b. Balt., Nov. 6, 1913; s. Walter E. and Jennie (Doyle) H.; A.B., Mt. St. Mary's Coll. and Sem., Emmitsburg, Md., 1947, LL.D. (hon.). Ordained priest Roman Catholic Ch., 1947; asst. Our Lady of Victory Parish, Washington, 1947-60, pastor, 1968-73; pastor St. Mary's Ch., Washington, 1960-68; asst. chancellor Archdiocese of Washington, 1951-62, vice chancellor, 1962-66, chancellor, 1966-72, vicar-gen., 1966-73, counsultor, 1964-73; aux. bishop Washington, titular bishop of Lamzella, 1966-73; bishop of Columbus, 1973—.

HERRMANN, THOMAS ANTHONY, civil engr.; b. St. Louis, Oct. 30, 1928; s. Anthony E. and Susan K. (Shinker) H.; B.S.C.E., Mo. Sch. Mines, Rolla, 1950; cert. USPHS, Cin., 1966; m. Mary M. Finan, Apr. 7, 1951; children—John T., Marguerite A. Field engr. Sverdrup & Parcel, Inc., St. Louis, 1950-52; design engr. Russell & Axon, Inc., St. Louis, 1952-56; profl. engr. Williamson & Assos., St. Louis, 1956-66; v.p./mgr. civil, environ. div. Zurheide-Herrmann, Inc., St. Louis, 1966—. Served to col. C.E. USAR, 1950—. Registered profl. engr., 8 states; registered land surveyor, Mo. Mem. Nat. Soc. Profl. Engrs. (nat. dir.), Mo. Soc. Profl. Engrs. (pres. 1979-80, pres. St. Louis chpt. 1969-70, St. Louis Young Engr. of Yr. 1963, St. Louis Outstanding Engr. in Pvt. Practice 1980, St. Louis Engr. of Yr. 1981), Cons. Engrs. Council, ASCE, Am. Water Works Assn. (Disting. Service ciation 1977), U. Mo. at Rolla Acad. Civil Engrs., Water Pollution Control Fedn., Mo. Water and Sewerage Conf., Soc. Am. Mil. Engrs., Res. Officers Assn., Chi Epsilon. Office: 4333 W Clayton Ave Saint Louis MO 63110

HERROLD, LLOYD WILSON, accountant; b. Evanston, Ill., Apr. 27, 1925; s. Lloyd Dallas and Phoebe Mae (Wilson) H.; Ph.B., U. Chgo., 1948; B.S., Northwestern U., 1949; J.D., Harvard U., 1952; m. Edith Rose Bannon, Dec. 16, 1948; children—Edith Anne, Lloyd Wilson, Bradley James. Staff acct., Price Waterhouse Co., Boston, 1952-56; tax acct. Arthur Andersen & Co., Milw., 1956-58; exec. v.p. Lloyd Herrold Co., Evanston, Ill., 1958-62; partner Tillman Kennedy & Herrold, Milw., 1958-62; partner firm Peat Marwick Mitchell & Co., Milw., 1962—; lectr. U. Wis., Milw., 1981—. Mem. adv. council Sch. Bus. Adminstrn. U. Wis., Milw.; pres. Milw. Art Mus., 1980—; hon. dir. Milw. Repertory Theater; pres. St. John's Home, 1971-72; sr. warden St. Pauls Ch., 1976-77, 78-79; co-chmn. Lakefront Festival Art, 1965; pres. Friends of Art, 1965-66; bd. dirs. Vis. Nurse Assn., 1969-76; trustee Fox Point Found., 1979—, Milwaukee County War Meml. Center, 1980—. Served with AUS, 1943-46. Mem. Am. Inst. C.P.A.s, Wis. Inst. C.P.A.s, Tax Club, Milw. Estate Planning Council (pres. 1975-76), Estate Counselors Forum. Republican. Episcopalian. Clubs: Milwaukee, University, Town, Hillsboro, Rotary, Masons. Contbr. articles to profl. jours. Home: 8090 N Beach Dr Milwaukee WI 53217 Office: 777 E Wisconsin Ave Milwaukee WI 53202

HERSCOE, JAMES RICHARD, bus. services co. exec.; b. Pitts., Mar. 12, 1931; s. Louis Lawrence and Adelaide (Schafer) H.; grad. Robert Morris Jr. Coll., 1959; m. Bertha Burick, Nov. 19, 1955; 1 son, Daniel Mark. Various positions Canteen Corp., Pitts., 1949-59, office mgr., 1959-65, Chgo., 1965-71, area controller, 1971-72, mgr. Midwest, 1972-76, staff v.p., 1976—. Office: Canteen Corp 1430 Mdse Mart Chicago IL 60654

HERSHBARGER, ROBERT ALLEN, educator, univ. ofcl.; b. Champaign, Ill., Aug. 30, 1932; s. Lawrence Arlington and Elizabeth Mae (Van Mefer) H.; m. Nancy J. Weeden, Dec. 18, 1954; children—Larry, Delynne, Russell, Mark; B.S., U. Ill., 1955; M.B.A., No. Ill. U., 1970; Ph.D., U. Ga., 1972. Asst. supr. ins. U. Ill., 1959-66; coordinator ins. No. Ill. U., 1966-69; instr. U. Ga., Athens, 1969-71, adviser to chmn. staff benefit com., 1969-71; asst. prof. finance and ins. U. R.I., 1971-74, mem. ins. adv. com. Extension Div., 1973-74; asso. prof. fin. U. Mo.-Columbia, 1974-81; asso. dean Coll. Bus. Adminstrn., Cleve. State U., 1981—; mem. industry risk and ins. ednl. adv. com., 1974—; cons. to pub. and pvt. orgns., 1974—. Vice pres., treas. Ins. & Fin. Cons., Inc., 1971-74; mem. adv. com. State Univs. Retirement System, State of Ill., 1965-69; mem. Police and Firemen Retirement Commn., City of Columbia, 1975—. Mem. Am., So., Western risk and ins. assns., Risk and Ins. Mgmt. Soc. Assn., Midwest Bus. Adminstrn. Assn., Central Mo. Estate Planning Council, Ins. Cons. Soc., Phi Gamma Delta, Sigma Iota Epsilon, Beta Sigma Delta, Beta Gamma Sigma, Alpha Kappa Psi. Contbr. articles to profl. jours. Office: Cleve State U Cleveland OH

HERSHBERGER, GERALD ROBERT, lawyer; b. Hamden, N.D., Jan. 6, 1917; s. George Robert and Mabel Marie (Clouse) H.; grad. indsl. engring. Gen. Motors Inst., 1939; LL.B., J.D., Wayne State U., 1958; m. Lillian Agnes Mason, Dec. 31, 1942; children—Carole (Mrs. Gary Isom), Trudy (Mrs. Terry Filer), Faye (Mrs. Jack Preston), Gregory, Helen, Gerald, Mark. Tool and die engring. defense work, 1939-43; product engring. work research devel., 1946-61; admitted to Mich. bar, 1958, U.S. patent office, 1960, U.S. Supreme Ct., 1971; practice gen. and patent law, Troy, Mich., 1958—; pres. Ponderosa Realty Co.; pres., owner Snap-Sighter Inc., mfrs. iron dual sight for rifle scopes. Served in Ordnance Corps, AUS, 1943-46. Decorated Victory medal. Recipient 10 yr. grad. key, Gen. Motors Inst., 1956. Mem. Mich. Patent Law Assn., Am., S. Oakland, Oakland County bar assns., Mich. State Bar., Delta Theta Phi. Patentee vehicle, lighting, timing and warning system, also driving light control. Home and Office: 285 E Long Lake Rd Troy MI 48084

HERSHENSON, MARVIN, human resource cons.; b. Winthrop, Mass., Aug. 30, 1945; s. Morris and Ida R. (Engorn) H.; A.B., Boston U., 1968, M.S., 1973; Ed.D., Ind. U., 1981; m. Michelle Koplow, Feb. 18, 1973; children—Jared Adam, Evan Seth. Tchr. sci. Hillside Jr. Sch., Montclair, N.J., 1968-70, also faculty adv. to sch. PTA, 1969-70; counselor Olde Firehouse, School St., Marblehead, Mass., 1971-72; tchr. sci. Clark Jr. High Sch., Lexington, Mass., 1972-73; dir. crisis prevention div., Ind. State Dept. Public Instrn., 1975-78, dir. pupil personnel services div., 1978-81; with Research & Planning Assos., Indpls., 1981—. Mem. Adult Edn. of Ind., Anti-Defamation League. Jewish. Home: 1213 Woodbridge Ln Indianapolis IN 46260 Office: Research and Planning Assos Room 320 9240 Meridian St Indianapolis IN 46260

HERSHEWAY, CHARLES EUGENE, mktg. exec.; b. Chgo., Apr. 23, 1933; s. Louis and Jean (Manfre) H.; student U. Ill., 1951-53; B.S., Northwestern U., 1959; m. Shirley Leyendecker, Jan. 19, 1957; children—Deborah Lynn, Louise Jeffrey; m. 2d, Priscilla Karas, Dec. 1, 1974. Editorial dir. Nat. Research Bur., Chgo., 1958-62; promotion mgr. Advt. Publs., Inc., Chgo., 1962-64; advt. mgr. Pfaelzer Bros. div. Armour Co., Chgo., 1964-67, marketing mgr., 1967-70, sales mgr., 1970, v.p. marketing, 1970-74; pres. United Am. Food Processors Gourmet Fare, 1974-76, Mail Market Makers, Inc., Clarendon Hills, Ill., 1976-79; v.p. Lerner Scott Corp., 1979—. Mem. Percy for Gov. Finance Com., 1965. Served with USMCR, 1952-54, USNR, 1954-58. Mem. Mail Advt. Club Chgo., Chgo. Federated Advt., Premium Industry Club, Sales Promotion Execs., Mail Advt. Author: NRB Retail Advertising and Sales Promotion Manual, vol. I, 1960, vol. II, 1961, vol. III, 1962; M.P. Brown Collection Letter Manual, 1961; Nat. Research Bur. Discount Store Manual, 1961. Contbr. articles to profl. jours. Home and Office: 270 Holmes Ave Clarendon Hills IL 60514

HERSHEY, THADDEUS MERLE, mgmt. cons.; b. Lancaster, Pa., Sept. 10, 1945; s. John David and Miriam Witmer (Shank) H.; B.S. in Mgmt. Scis., Carnegie Inst. Tech., 1967; M.S. in Indsl. Adminstrn., Carnegie-Mellon U., 1969; m. Mary Lee Jenks, Dec. 27, 1970; children—Erick Steven, Kevin Christopher. Mgmt. cons. Touche Ross & Co., Detroit, 1968-70, Mgmt. Research & Planning, Inc., Evanston, Ill., 1970-74, prin., 1974-79; prin. Mgmt. Cons. div. The Austin Co., Evanston, 1979—; controller Mgmt. Research & Planning, Inc. Chmn. fin. commn. Meth. Ch., 1978-80. Mem. Assn. Systems Mgmt., Inst. Mgmt. Scis., Ops. Research Soc. Am. Developer ops. research models. Home: 1826 Robincrest Ln Glenview IL 60025 Office: 820 Davis St Suite 310 Evanston IL 60201

HERSTEAD, LOU ANN, retail monument co. exec.; b. Scottsbluff, Nebr., Sept. 10, 1952; d. Lewis John and Doris T. (Luther) H.; A.A., Nebr. Western Jr. Coll., 1972; B.S. in Econs. (Rodeo scholar), U. Wyo., 1974, postgrad. in econs. and bus. adminstrn. (Univ. grantee), 1974-75. Stat. research asst., div. stats. Wyo. Dept. Labor, Cheyenne, 1974; grad. asst. M.B.A. program U. Wyo., 1974-75; summer intern First Nat. Bank of Bayard, Nebr., 1975; trainee Herstead Monument Co., Scottsbluff, 1976-80, exec. v.p., 1980—. Named Nat. Collegiate All-around Cowgirl, Girls Rodeo Assn., 1973, World Championship Goattyer, 1976. Mem. Rocky Mountain Monument Builders (trustee 1980—, pres. 1979, 81—), Monument Builders N. Am. Republican. Episcopalian. Club: U. Wyo. Rodeo. Writer Wyo. Econ. Indicators mag., fall 1974. Home: Route 1 Mitchell NE 69357 Office: 1319 Ave A Scottsbluff NE 69361

HERTEL, DENNIS MARK, lawyer, Congressman; b. Detroit, Dec. 7, 1948; s. John and Marie (Kaufmann) H., Jr.; B.A. cum laude, Eastern Mich. U., 1971; J.D., Wayne State U., 1974; m. Cynthia S. Grosscup, 1971; children—Heather, Heidi, Katie. Former tchr. Detroit Public Schs.; admitted to Mich. bar, 1975; mem. Mich. Ho. of Reps., 1975-80; mem. 97th Congress from 14th Dist. of Mich.; intern Office Atty. Gen., State of Mich.; aide to Ernest Browne, Detroit City Council. Head field staff for 14th dist. campaign activities Mich. Democratic Com. Mem. Mich. Bar Assn. Roman Catholic. Club: St. Matthews Men's. Office: 1017 Longworth House Office Bldg Washington DC 20515

HERTEL, LEONA, religious assn. adminstr.; b. Grand Rapids, Mich.; d. Nicholas and Dena (Timmer) Hertel; grad. high sch. Personal sec. Dr. M.R. DeHaan, founder, tchr. Radio Bible Class, weekly religious broadcast, Grand Rapids, 1941-65, editor newsletter, also contbr., 1953—, corporate sec.-treas., 1963-65, asst. sec.-treas., 1965—, also sec. finance com. Pianist, Calvary Undenominational Ch., 1950—, mem. 50th anniversary com., also sec., 1976-80; organist Mel Trotter Mission, 1959—. Contbr. monthly article Discovery Digest; contbr. Moody Monthly mag. Home: 320 Baynton NE Grand Rapids MI 49503 Office: 3000 Kraft Ave SE Grand Rapids MI 49508

HERTZ, RICHARD CORNELL, rabbi; b. St. Paul, Oct. 7, 1916; s. Abram J. and Nadine (Rosenberg) H.; A.B., U. Cin., 1938; M.H.L., Hebrew Union Coll., 1942, D.D. (hon.), 1967; Ph.D., Northwestern U., 1948; m. Mary Louise Mann, Nov. 25, 1943 (div. July 1971); children—Nadine (Mrs. Michael Wertheimer), Ruth Mann (Mrs. Alain Joyaux); m. 2d, Renda Gottfürcht Ebner, Dec. 3, 1972. Ordained rabbi, 1942; asst. rabbi North Shore Congregation Israel, Glencoe, Ill., 1942-47; asso. rabbi Chgo. Sinai Congregation, 1947-53; sr. rabbi Temple Beth El, Detroit, 1953—; adj. prof. Jewish thought U. Detroit, 1970-81, Disting. prof. Jewish studies, 1981—. Went on spl. mission for White House to investigate status Jews and Judaism in USSR 1959, mission for chief chaplains Def. Dept. to conduct retreats for Jewish chaplains and laymen, Berchtesgaden, Germany, 1973; mem. mission to Arab countries and Israel, Nat. Council Chs.-Am. Jewish Com., 1974; 1st Am. rabbi received in pvt. audience at Papal Palace by Pope Paul VI, 1963; del. to internat. conf. World Union for Progressive Judaism, London, 1959, 61, Amsterdam, 1978, bd. dirs. union, 1973—. Lectr. Jewish Chautauqua Soc.; former mem. plan bd. Synagogue Council Am.; mem. chaplaincy commn., former bd. dirs. Nat. Jewish Welfare Bd.; former mem. exec. com., vice chmn. Citizen's Com. for Equal Opportunity; mem. Mich. Gov.'s Com. on Ethics and Morals, 1963-69; mem. Mich. adv. council U.S. Commn. on Civil Rights, 1979—; mem. nat. bd. dirs. Religious Edn. Assn., adv. bd. Joint Distbn. Com.; former mem. nat. rabbinical council United Jewish Appeal; mem. rabbinic cabinet Israel Bonds, 1972—; pres. Hyde Park and Kenwood Council Chs. and Synagogues, Chgo., 1952. Dir. Am. Jewish Com., mem. nat. exec. bd., former hon. vice-chmn. Detroit chpt.; past dir. Mich. Soc. Mental Health, Jewish Family and Children's Services, United Community Services, Jewish Welfare Fedn. Detroit, Jewish Community Council Detroit; dir. United Found., Boys Clubs, Mich. region Anti-Defamation League; chmn. bd. overseers Hebrew Union Coll.-Jewish Inst. Religion, 1968-72; bd. govs. Detroit Inst. Tech., 1955-70. Served as chaplain AUS, 1943-46. Fellow Am. Sociol. Soc.; mem. Detroit Hist. Soc., Central Conf. Am. Rabbis (former nat. chmn. com. on Jews in Soviet orbit), Am. Jewish Hist. Soc., Am. Legion (dept. chaplain 1956-57), Jewish War Vets. (dept. chaplain 1958-59, 72—), Alumni Assn. Hebrew Union Coll.-Jewish Inst. Religion (past dir.), U.S. Commn. on Civil Rights. Clubs: Rotary, Economic (dir.) (Detroit); Wranglers (past pres.), Great Lakes, Standard, Franklin Hills, Knollwood, Tam O'Shanter. Author: Rabbi Yesterday and Today, 1943; This I Believe, 1952; Education of the Jewish Child, 1953; Our Religion Above All, 1953; Inner Peace for You, 1954; Positive Judaism, 1955; Wings of the Morning, 1956; Impressions of Israel, 1956; Prescription for Heartache, 1958; Faith in Jewish Survival, 1961; The American Jew in Search of Himself, 1962; What Counts Most in Life, 1963; What Can A Man Believe, 1967; Reflections for the Modern Jew, 1974; Israel and the Palestinians, 1974; Roots of My Faith, 1980; also articles in sci., popular publs. Office: Temple Beth El 7400 Telegraph Rd at 14 Mile Birmingham MI 48010

HERWIG, THELMA LANGE (MRS. THEODOR FREDRICK HERWIG), physician; b. Toledo, June 22, 1932; d. Edward Henry and Oleva Henrietta (Edler) Lange; B.S., U. Toledo, 1953; M.D., Ohio State U., 1958; m. Theodor Fredrick Herwig, June 10, 1956; children—Theodor Thomas, Nathaniel Christopher, David Edward. Intern, Mt. Carmel Hosp., Columbus Ohio, 1958-59; family practice medicine, Dublin, Ohio, 1963-67, Columbus, 1967—; employee health physician Riverside Meth. Hosp., Columbus. Diplomate Am. Bd. Family Practice. Mem. AMA, Am. Med. Women's Assn. Acad. Medicine Franklin County (med. services com.). Home: 2090 Cheltenham St Columbus OH 43220 Office: 3720 Olentangy River Rd Columbus OH 43214

HERZBERGER, EUGENE E., neurosurgeon; b. Sotchi, Russia, June 7, 1920; came to U.S., 1957, naturalized, 1964; s. Eugene S. and Mary P. Herzberger; M.D., U. King Ferdinand I, Cluj, Rumania, 1947; married; children—Henry, Monica. Intern, Univ. Hosp., Cluj, 1946-47, resident in surgery, 1947-48, resident in neurosurgery Beilinson Hosp., Tel Aviv, Israel, 1949-53; chief neurosurgeon Tel Hashomer Govt. Hosp., Tel Aviv, 1953-57; research asst. Yale U., 1958-59; instr. neurosurgery Med. Coll. Ga., 1959-60; attending neurosurgeon St. Clare Hosp., Monroe, Wis., 1960-76, Mercy Hosp., Finley Hosp. and Xavier Hosp., Dubuque, Iowa, 1976—. Diplomate Am. Bd. Neurol. Surgery. Mem. Am. Assn. Neurol. Surgeons, Central Neurosurg. Soc., AMA, Iowa M.W. Neurosurg. Soc., Congress Neurol. Surgeons, Am. Acad. Neurology, Iowa State Med. Soc. Contbr. articles to med. jours. Office: Mercy Dr Dubuque IA 52001

HERZER, DAVID GLEN, banker; b. Milw., Jan. 1, 1933; s. David O. and Laura E. (Glenzer) H.; B.B.A., U. Wis., 1954; children—Susann, Carol Ann Fronberry. Vice-pres. Marine Nat. Exchange Bank, Milw., 1956-64; exec. v.p. Midland Nat. Bank, Milw., 1965-76; pres. First Bank Milw., 1976—. Dir., Milw. Area

Tech. Coll. Found.; dir., chmn. Channel 10/36 Auction, Public Service Television, 1981. Served with U.S. Army, 1954-56. Republican. Methodist. Clubs: Metropolitan, Ocean Reef, Western Racquet, Milw. Yacht. Office: First Bank Milwaukee 201 W Wisconsin Ave Milwaukee WI 53259

HERZOG, DORREL NORMAN ELVERT (WHITEY), profl. baseball team mgr.; b. New Athens, Ill., Nov. 9, 1931. Infielder, outfielder Washington Senators, 1956-58, Kansas City (Mo.) Athletics, 1958-60, Balt. Orioles, 1961-62, Detroit Tigers, 1963; scout, then coach Kansas City Athletics, 1964-66; coach, then dir. player devel. N.Y. Mets, 1966-72; coach Tex. Rangers, 1973; coach Calif. Angels, 1974-75, interim mgr., 1974; mgr. Kansas City Royals, 1975-79; gen. mgr., mgr. St. Louis Cardinals, 1980—. Address: St Louis Cardinals Busch Meml Stadium 250 Stadium Plaza Saint Louis MO 63102*

HERZOG, GODOFREDO MAX, physician; b. Chemnitz, Germany, Jan. 12, 1931; s. Heinrich and Louise (Gittler) H.; came to U.S., 1950, naturalized, 1960; B.S., La. State U., 1953; M.D., Washington U., St. Louis, 1957; m. Eva R. Muller, Sept. 2, 1956; children—Jacques A., Patricia M., Elsa M. Intern, Jewish Hosp., St. Louis, 1957-58, Sch. Aerospace Medicine, San Antonio, Tex., 1960; resident in surgery Jewish Hosp., Cin., 1958-59; resident in gynecology and obstetrics Jewish Hosp., St. Louis, 1964-67; instr. obstetrics-gynecology Washington U., St. Louis, 1967—; individual practice medicine, specializing in obstetrics, gynecology St. Louis, 1967—; cons. in field. Med. adviser, bd. dirs. Life Seekers, Planned Parenthood, Abortion Rights Alliance. Served to capt. M.C., USAF, 1959-64. Diplomate Nat. Bd. Med. Examiners, Am. Bd. Obstetrics and Gynecology. Fellow Am. Coll. Obstetrics and Gynecology; mem. AMA, St. Louis County Med. Soc., Pan Am., Israel, Mo. med. assns., Mo., St. Louis gynecol. socs., Am. Soc. Gynecol. Laparoscopists, Am. Fertility Soc. Jewish. Contbr. articles to profl. publs. Home: 9 Wendover St St Louis MO 63124 Office: 77 Westport Plaza Dr Suite 265 St Louis MO 63141

HERZOG, SYLVIA LOUISE, speech pathologist; b. Irvington, Ill., Aug. 2, 1927; d. Julius Alfred and Laura Regina (Hake) Wacker; B.S., U. Ill., 1948, M.S., 1971; m. Roy Martin Herzog, June 27, 1948; children—Linda Herzog Mollman, Garry Steven. Speech therapist Tuscola (Ill.) Pub. Schs., 1948-52; tchr. learning disabilities pub. schs., Champaign, Ill., 1954-57; speech therapist Easter Seal Soc., Danville, Ill., 1955-58; clin. supr. dept. speech and hearing sci. U. Ill., 1973; speech and lang. pathologist Champaign Public Schs., 1957—, dept. chmn., 1976—. Pres. bd. dirs. Champaign Sch. Dist. Credit Union, 1957-69. Mem. Ill. Speech and Hearing Assn., U. Ill. Alumni Assn. (dir.), Altrusa Internat., Zeta Phi Eta, Delta Kappa Gamma. Republican. Methodist. Office: 405 E Clark Champaign IL 61820

HESBURGH, THEODORE MARTIN, clergyman, univ. pres.; b. Syracuse, N.Y., May 25, 1917; s. Theodore Bernard and Anne Marie (Murphy) H.; student U. Notre Dame, 1934-37; Ph.B., Gregorian U., 1939; postgrad. Holy Cross Coll., Washington, 1940-43; S.T.D., Cath. U. Am., 1945; hon. degrees Bradley U., LeMoyne Coll., U. R.I., Cath. U. of Santiago (Chile), Dartmouth, Villanova U., St. Benedict's Coll., Columbia, Princeton, Ind. U., Brandeis U., Gonzaga U., U. Cal. at Los Angeles, Temple U., Northwestern U., U. Ill., Fordham U., Manchester Coll., Atlanta U., Wabash Coll., Valparaiso U., Providence Coll., U. So. Calif., Mich. State U., St. Louis U., Cath. U. Am., Loyola U. at Chgo., Anderson Coll., State U., N.Y. at Albany, Utah State U., Lehigh U., Yale, Lafayette Coll., King's Coll., Stonehill Coll., Alma Coll., Syracuse U., Marymount Coll., Hobart and William Smith Coll., Hebrew Union Coll., Cin., Harvard. Entered Order of Congregation of Holy Cross, 1934; ordained priest Roman Catholic Ch., U. Notre Dame, 1943; chaplain Nat. Tng. Sch. for Boys, Washington, 1943-44; vets. chaplain U. Notre Dame, 1945-47, asst. prof. religion, head dept., 1948-49, exec. v.p., 1949-52, pres., 1952—. Former dir. Woodrow Wilson Nat. Fellowship Corp.; mem. Civil Rights Commn., 1957-72; mem. of Carnegie Commn. on Future of Higher Edn.; chmn. U.S. Commn. on Civil Rights, 1969-72; mem. Commn. on an All-Volunteer Armed Force, 1970. Chmn. bd. trustees Rockefeller Found.; former trustee Carnegie Found. for Advancement Teaching, Woodrow Wilson Nat. Fellowship Found., Inst. Internat. Edn., Nutrition Found., United Negro Coll. Fund, others. Recipient U.S. Navy's Distinguished Pub. Service award, 1959; Presdl. Medal of Freedom, 1964; Gold medal Nat. Inst. Social Scis., 1969; Cardinal Gibbons medal Cath. U. Am., 1969; Bellarmine medal Bellarmine-Ursuline Coll., 1970; Meiklejohn award A.A.U.P., 1970; Charles Evans Hughes award Nat. Conf. Christians and Jews, 1970; Merit award Nat. Cath. Ednl. Assn., 1971; Pres.' Cabinet award U. Detroit, 1971; Am. Liberties medallion Am. Jewish Com., 1971; Liberty Bell award Ind. State Bar Assn., 1971; others. Fellow Am. Acad. Arts and Scis.; mem. Internat. Fedn. Cath. Univs., Commn. on Humanities, Cath. Theol. Soc. Author: Theology of Catholic Action, 1945; God and the World of Man, 1950; Patterns for Educational Growth, 1958; Thoughts for Our Times, 1962; More Thoughts for Our Times, 1965; Still More Thoughts for Our Times, 1966; Thoughts IV, 1968; Thoughts V, 1969; The Humane Imperative: A Challenge for the Year 2000, 1974; The Hesburgh Papers, 1979. Home: U Notre Dame Notre Dame IN 46556

HESDORFFER, ALAN WALTER, sales and mktg. ofcl.; b. Mpls., Sept. 6, 1935; s. Meredith B. and Ruth (Burkhard) H.; B.A. in Psychology, U. Va., 1958; m. Mary Boyd Day, Sept. 14, 1963; children—Meredith D., Alan B. With sales and sales mgmt. Procter & Gamble Co., Davenport, Iowa, Cin. and Indpls., 1963-69, nat. sales mgr. indsl. paper sales, Cin., 1969-75; sales merchandising dir. Pillsbury Co., Mpls., 1976—; lectr. U. Minn. Served with U.S. Army, 1959-63. Republican. Episcopalian. Clubs: Coldstream Country (Cin.), Mpls. Athletic. Home: 5308 Dundee Rd Edina MN 55436 Office: Pillsbury Center Minneapolis MN 55402

HESLINGA, ROBERT EDWARD, ednl. adminstr.; b. Chgo., May 9, 1949; s. John and Josephine (Klumbis) H.; B.A., Tolentine Coll., 1972; M.R.E., Loyola U., 1977; m. Mary M. Dever, June 27, 1981. Dir. religious edn. St. Clare Parish, Grosse Point Park, Mich., 1972-73; prin., dir. religious edn. St. Colette Parish, Rolling Meadows, Ill., 1974—. Mem. Nat. Assn. Elem. Sch. Prins., Am. Assn. Supervision and Curriculum Devel., Am. Assn. Sch. Adminstrs., Nat. Forum Religious Educators. Roman Catholic. Author: One Mind, One Heart, 1972. Office: 3900 Pheasant St Rolling Meadows IL 60008

HESS, A. DEAN, educator; b. Tomahawk, Wis., Aug. 30, 1949; s. August S. and Margaret R. (Labudd) H.; B.S., U. Wis., 1972, M.S. in Curriculum and Instrn., 1980; m. Wendi E. Gutschenritter, July 21, 1973. Tchr. biology Peace Corp., Bumpe High, Bumpe, Sierra Leone, West Africa, 1973-74, DePere (Wis.) High Sch., 1974—, chmn. sci. dept., 1977-79, head girls track coach, 1978—, mem. high sch. curriculum com., 1980-83; chmn. DePere Dist. Inservice Com., 1979—, mem. dist. curriculum com., 1978-81; mem. North Central Evaluation Steering Com. for DePere Sch. Dist., 1980. Mem. NEA, Nat. Sci. Tchrs. Assn., Assn. Supervision and Curriculum Devel., Nat. Wildlife Fedn., Kappa Delta Pi. Roman Catholic. Home: 1439 Bruce Ln Green Bay WI 54304 Office: 1700 Chicago St DePere WI 54115

HESS, BARTLETT LEONARD, clergyman; b. Spokane, Wash., Dec. 27, 1910; s. John Leonard and Jessie (Bartlett) H.; B.A., Park Coll., 1931, M.A. (fellow in history 1931-34), U. Kan., 1932, Ph.D., 1934; B.D., McCormick Theol. Sem., 1936; m. Margaret Young Johnston, July 31, 1937; children—Daniel Bartlett, Deborah Margaret, John Howard and Janet Elizabeth (twins). Ordained to ministry Presbyn. Ch., 1936; pastor Effingham, Kan., 1932-34, Chgo., 1935-42, Cicero, Ill., 1942-56, Ward Meml. Presbyn. Ch., Detroit, 1956-68, Ward, U.P. Ch., Livonia, Mich., 1968-80, Presbyn. Ch., 1980—. Tchr. ch. history, bible Detroit Bible Coll., 1956—, bd. dirs., 1956—; minister radio sta. WHFC, Chgo., 1942-50, WMUZ-FM, Detroit, 1958-68, 78—, WOMC-FM, 1971-72, WBFG-FM, 1972—; missioner to Philippines, United Presbyn. Ch. U.S.A., 1961; mem. Joint Com. on Presbyn. Union, 1980. Adviser Mich. Synod council United Presbyn. Ch.; mem. com. Billy Graham Crusade for S.E. Mich., 1976. Mem. Organizer Friendship and Service Com. for Refugees, Chgo., 1940. Bd. dirs. Beacon Neighborhood House, Chgo., 1945-52, Presbyns. United for Bibl. Concerns, 1975-80; pres. bd. dirs. Peniel Community Center, Chicago, 1945-52. Named Pastor of Year, Mid-Am. Sunday Sch. Assn., 1974; recipient Service to Youth award Detroit Met. Youth for Christ, 1979. Mem. Cicero Ministers Council (pres. 1951), Phi Beta Kappa, Phi Delta Kappa. Author: (with Margaret Johnston Hess) How to Have a Giving Church, 1974; (with M.J. Hess) The Power of a Loving Church, 1977. Contbr. articles in field to profl. jours. Traveled in Europe, 1939, 52, 55, 68; also in Greece, Turkey, Lebanon, Syria, Egypt, Israel, Iraq; condr. tour of Middle East and Mediterranean countries, 1965, 67, 73, 74, 76, 78, 80; missioner, India, 1981. Home: 16845 Riverside Dr Livonia MI 48154 Office: 17000 Farmington Rd Livonia MI 48150

HESS, EDWARD ANTHONY, electromech. and solid state components co. exec.; b. Cin., Sept. 30, 1930; s. Edward August and Clara (Segers) H.; B.S., Xavier U., 1952; postgrad. LaSalle U., 1955-58, Ind. State Tchrs. Coll., 1956, U. Dayton, 1959; M.B.A., U. Calif. at Los Angeles, 1966; m. Virginia Lee Bowen, Oct. 3, 1953 (div. 1968); children—Jennifer, Andrew, Joseph, Matthew, Lynn, Amelia; m. 2d, Shirley Ann Danzeisen, Nov. 13, 1976. Exec. tng. program Pa. R.R. Freight Sales & Service, 1953-57; with Ledex, Inc., Dayton, Ohio, 1960—, product mgr., 1970-71, sales mgr. indsl. markets, 1971-72, comml. markets mgr., 1972-73, gen. sales mgr., 1973-76, mgr. product mgmt., 1976-78, internat. sales mgr., 1978—. Traffic Club Chgo. scholar LaSalle Extension U., Chgo., 1955. Mem. Am. Mktg. Assn., Electronic Industries Assn. (exec. council parts div. 1971-74), Am. Def. Preparedness Assn. Home: 4309 Glen Heath Dr Kettering OH 45440 Office: 801 Scholz Dr Vandalia OH 45377

HESS, JOHN HANS, physician; b. Soltur, Yugoslavia, Aug. 19, 1925; came to U.S., 1956, naturalized, 1961; s. Franz and Katharina (Wottreng) H.; M.D., Karl Franzens U., Graz, Austria, 1954; m. Anna Willer, July 20, 1957; children—Arthur, Lydia. Rotating intern, Austria, 1954-56; rotating intern West Suburban Hosp., Oak Park, Ill., 1956-57, resident in gen. surgery, 1957-58; gen. practice medicine, Fisher, Ill., 1958-60; family practice medicine, Rantoul, Ill., 1960—; bd. dirs. Mercy Hosp., Urbana, Ill., 1977—; med. dir. Country Health Nursing Home, Gifford, Ill., 1978—. Med. adv. Champaign County Home Health Care, 1976-77; bd. dirs. Health System Agy. Champaign and Ford County, 1975-78, Rantoul Twp. High Sch., 1976—. Diplomate Am. Bd. Family Practice. Fellow Am. Acad. Family Practice; mem. AMA, Ill. State Med. Soc., Champaign County Med. Soc. Roman Catholic. Clubs: Lions, Moose (Rantoul). Home: 224 Bethany Park Rantoul IL 61866 Office: 1419 Pine St Rantoul IL 61866

HESS, MARGARET JOHNSTON, religious writer, educator; b. Ames. Iowa, Feb. 22, 1915; d. Howard Wright and Jane Edith (Stevenson) Johnston; B.A., Coe Coll., 1937; m. Bartlett Leonard Hess, July 31, 1937; children—Daniel, Deborah, John, Janet. Bible tchr. Community Bible Classes Ward United Presbyn. Ch., Livonia, Mich., 1959—, Christ Ch. Cranbrook (Episcopal), Bloomfield Hills, Mich., 1980—. Author: (with B.L. Hess) How to Have a Giving Church, 1974, The Power of a Loving Church, 1977; Love Knows No Barriers, 1979; Esther: Courage in Crisis, 1980; Unconventional Women, 1981. Contbr. articles to religious jours. Home: 16845 Riverside Dr Livonia MI 48154

HESS, PAUL ROBERT, state senator Kan.; b. Albany, N.Y., Aug. 29, 1948; s. Robert Benjamin and Evelyn (Wortham) H.; student Wheaton Coll., 1966-68; B.A., U. Wash., 1970; J.D., U. Kans., 1974. Mem. Kans. Ho. of Reps., 1971-73; mem. Kans. Senate, 1973—. Mem. Republican State Com., from 1972. Home: 816 S Estelle St Wichita KS 67211 Office: 816 S Estelle St Wichita KS 67211*

HESS, ROBERT, JR., pvt. ambulance service exec.; b. East Cleveland, Ohio, Oct. 22, 1957; s. Robert Hess and Patricia Lou H.; student John Carroll U., 1976—, Cuyahoga Community Coll., 1977—. With Physician's Ambulance Service, East Cleveland, 1972—, v.p. in charge fin., data processing, med. assurance, 1978—; dir. Hess Enterprises, Inc., pres. North Coast Data div., 1981—; pres., Chief exec. officer Tidy Services Inc., 1980—; lectr. paramedic tng. Cuyahoga Community Coll., also mem. paramedic admissions com.; mem. Disaster Com. for Southeastern Cuyahoga County. Mem. Ohio Bd. Regents Paramedic Adv. Com., 1979—. Mem. Ohio Ambulance Assn. (pres. 1981—), Am. Ambulance Assn. (dir., fin. com.). Republican. Roman Catholic. Club: Rotary (community service com.). Office: 1765 Wymore Ave East Cleveland OH 44112

HESS, ROBERT BOND, mfg. co. exec.; b. Crystal City, Mo., Aug. 5, 1920; s. Francis J. and Anna M. (Bond) H.; B.S. in Mech. Engring., U. Mo., 1943; M.Engring. Adminstrn., Washington U., 1957; m. Mary Lou Gwinn, June 20, 1943; 1 dau., Sharon Gwinn Hess Summers. Chief components engr. Emerson Electric Co., St. Louis, 1946-59, proposal adminstr., 1959-61, mgr. market planning and research, 1961-62; sales rep. Conductron div. McDonnell Aircraft Co., St. Louis, 1962-65, mgr. product mktg., 1965-67, sales mgr., 1967-69; mgr. product devel. and acquisition Monsanto Co., St. Louis, 1969-71; pres. Low Com Systems Co., St. Louis, 1971-72; sr. v.p. ROI Controls Corp., Princeton, N.J., 1972-73; pres. Blake Assos., Inc., St. Louis, 1972-74; exec. v.p. CE Industries Corp., Belleville, Ill., 1974-75, pres., 1975—, also dir. Bd. dirs. YMCA, Belleville. Served with USAF, 1943-45. Mem. Belleville C. of C. (dir., mfrs. div. 1975-77), Engrs. Club St. Louis, Ill. Mfrs. Assn., Regional Growth and Commerce Assn. (vice chmn. So. div.). Clubs: Optimist (dir.) (Belleville); Media, Ambassadors (St. Louis); Lake St. Louis. Home: 531 N Ballas Rd St Louis MO 63122 Office: PO Box 446 1200 East A St Belleville IL 62222

HESSLER, DAVID WILLIAM, media specialist, educator; b. Oak Park, Ill., May 9, 1932; s. William Wigney and Gwendolyn Eileen (Butler) H.; B.A., U. Mich., 1955, M.A., 1961; Ph.D., Mich. State U., 1972; m. Helen Montgomery, Aug. 27, 1955; children—Leslie Susan, Laura Lynn. Comml. photographer Oscar & Assos., Chgo., 1950; equipment engr. Western Electric Co., Chgo., 1958-59; cons. and asst. dir. U. Mich. Audio-Visual Center, 1960-66; dir. libraries and media Ann Arbor (Mich.) Public Schs., 1966-67; asst. prof. edn. Western Mich. U., 1967-72, asso. prof., 1974-77; dir. instructional services U. S.C., 1973-74; prof. library sci., dir. instructional strategy services for schs. Edn. and Library Sci., U. Mich., 1977—; cons. media; instructional designer and evaluator. Served to lt. USAF, 1955-58, capt. Res. ret. Decorated Air Force Commendation medal; named Most Valuable Tchr., Chrysler Corp., 1965; Ednl. Profl. Devel. Act fellow, 1968-69. Mem. Mich. Audio Visual Assn. (sec.-treas. 1960-65), ALA, Assn. Ednl. Communications and Tech., Mich. Assn. Media in Edn., Am. Assn. Library Schs., Assn. Coll. and Research Libraries, Am. Soc. Info. Sci., Am. Assn. Sch. Librarians, Am. Soc. Tng. and Devel., Mich. Alumni Soc., Mich. State U. Alumni Assn., Phi Delta Kappa, Phi Kappa Phi. Club: U. Mich. M. Author: (with others) Student Production Guide, 1975; producer, dir. numerous films, filmstrips, TV programs and sound/slide programs for various ednl. levels. Home: 3677 Frederick Dr Ann Arbor MI 48105 Office: U Mich Sch Library Sci Ann Arbor MI 48109

HESSON, JAMES MARSH, army officer; b. St. Paul, Nov. 28, 1931; s. Floyd Edward and Hulda Olivia (Jasperson) H.; B.S., St. Benedicts Coll., 1965; M.S., George Washington U., 1973; grad. Indsl. Coll. Armed Forces, 1973; m. Joyce Lorraine Martin, Aug. 1, 1952; children—Leslie Ann, James Marsh, Jeffrey W., Laurie Jo. Commd. 2d lt. U.S. Army, 1952, advanced through grades to brig. gen., 1980; dep. comdg. gen. U.S. Army Troop Support and Aviation Materiel Readiness, St. Louis, 1979—. Served with AUS, 1950-52. Decorated D.F.C., Legion of Merit with oak leaf cluster, Air medal with 2 oak leaf clusters, Commendation medal, Bronze Star: recipient Sec. Army award for project mgmt., 1979, also award for outstanding achievement in materiel acquisition, 1979. Mem. Assn. U.S. Army, Army Aviation Assn. Home: 505 Richley Dr Ballwin MO 63011 Office: US Army Troop Support and Aviation Materiel Readiness Command 4300 Goodfellow Blvd Saint Louis MO 63120

HESTAD, BJORN MARK, metal distbg. co. exec.; b. Evanston, Ill., May 31, 1926; s. Hilmar and Anna (Aagaard) H.; student Ill. Inst. Tech., 1947; m. Florence Anne Ragusi, May 1, 1948; children—Marsha Anne Hestad Chastain, Patricia Lynn, Peter Mark. Sales corr., Shakeproof, Inc., Chgo., 1947-50; indsl. buyer Crescent Industries, Inc., Chgo., 1950-51; purchasing agt. Switchcraft, Inc., Chgo., 1951-73, materials mgr., 1973-74, dir. purchasing, 1974-77; pres. Tool King, Inc., Prospect Heights, Ill., 1977—. Mgr. youth orgns. Northfield Jr. Hockey Club, 1968-71, Winnfield Hockey Club, 1972-73; bus. mgr. West Hockey Club, 1973-74. Served as cpl. USAAF, 1944-46. Mem. Tool and Die Inst. Republican. Mem. United Ch. Christ. Lion. Home: 850 Happ Rd Northfield IL 60093 Office: 65 E Palatine Rd Prospect Heights IL 60070

HESTER, JACK W., state senator; b. Modale, Iowa, June 22, 1929; s. Everett and Clair H.; grad. high sch.; m. Joan Goshorn, 1951; 6 children. Farmer, livestock raiser; former mem. Iowa Ho. of Reps.; now mem. Iowa Senate. Mem. Neola Community Choir; bd. dirs. Westfair Bd. Served with USAF; Iowa. Mem. Farm Bur. (dir.), Pork Producers. Methodist. Office: State Senate Des Moines IA 50319*

HESTER, JAMES FRANCIS, JR., fastener mfg. co. exec.; b. Chgo., May 6, 1928; s. James Francis and Marion A. (Meservey) H.; student Marquette U., 1948; B.S. in Commerce, De Paul U., 1951; m. Doris Bauer, Nov. 17, 1951; children—James III, Timothy, Maureen, Stacie, Deidre. Credit mgr. St. Joseph Hosp., Chgo., 1950-53; with Am. Rivet Co., Inc., Franklin Park, Ill., 1953—, v.p., dir., 1960—. Served with U.S. Army, 1946-47. Mem. Franklin Park C. of C. (dir. 1967-70), Ill. Mfg. Assn., Chgo. Assn. Commerce and Industry, Purchasing Mgmt. Assn. Chgo., Nat. Assn. Purchasing Mgmt., Chgo. Midwest Credit Mgmtm. Assn., NAM, N.W. Suburban Mfrs. Assn. (dir. 1967-70, pres. 1976-77). Roman Catholic. Club: River Forest Golf (Elmhurst, Ill.). Office: 11330 W Melrose St Franklin Park IL 60131

HETH, MICHAEL LEWIS, safety engr.; b. Waterloo, Iowa, May 27, 1951; s. Herbert Lewis and Beverly Joyce (Smith) H.; B.A., U. No. Iowa, 1975; m. Jolene Frances Lyons, Aug. 23, 1971; children—Kasey, Timothy. Compliance safety and health officer Iowa Occupational Safety and Health Adminstrn., Iowa Bur. Labor, Des Moines, 1976—. Served with U.S. Army, 1970-72. Decorated Air medals (22). Mem. Am. Soc. Safety Engrs., Iowa Safety Council. Presbyterian. Home: 741 Jane St Waterloo IA 50701 Office: 307 E 7th St Des Moines IA 50319

HETHERINGTON, JAMES RICHARD, ins. co. exec.; b. Indpls., Feb. 3, 1931; s. Frederick Benjamin and Pauline (Suiter) H.; A.B., Ind. U., 1953; m. Susan Esther Bassett, Jan. 31, 1953; children—Robert Bassett, William Frederick. Reporter, Ind. news editor, Daily Mag. editor Louisville Times, 1955-61; asst. city editor Indpls. Times, 1961-63; editorial editor Sta. WFBM, 1963-74; public relations dir. Am. United Life Ins. Co., Indpls., 1974—, v.p., 1977—; lectr. broadcast newswriting Butler U., 1970-75; dir. Indpls. Public Transp. Corp. Bd. dirs. Indpls. Family Service Assn., 1969-77, 79—, pres., 1974-76. Served with U.S. Army, 1953-55. Recipient Alfred P. Sloan award, 1966; Peabody award for public service, 1969; 5 editorial awards Radio-TV News Dirs. Assn. Mem. Public Relations Soc. Am. (accredited; pres. Hoosier chpt. 1979), Indpls. Public Relations Soc., Life Ins. Advertisers Assn., Sigma Delta Chi (award 1967). Lutheran. Club: Indpls. Press (dir. 1965-68, 75-76, pres. 1967). Home: 7702 Bay Shore Dr Indianapolis IN 46240 Office: Am United Life Ins Co PO Box 368 Indianapolis IN 46206

HETLAND, LARUE E. (LOU), advt. exec.; b. Artesian, S.D., Oct. 21, 1933; s. Elmer Clarence and Edna (Lucid) H.; B.S., U. S.D., 1960; m. Lorma Jane Wittstruck, May 30, 1959; children—James, Nancy, Susan. Corp. dir. advt. Nash-Finch Co., Mpls., 1960-75; regional dir. advt. A & P, Indpls., 1975-77; v.p. McGrath & Co. Advt., Indpls., 1977-78; pres. Image Printing & Typesetting, Inc., 1978—. Pres. Hopkins (Minn.) Little League, 1973. Served to sgt. USMC, 1954-57. Mem. Internat. Platform Assn. Lutheran. Club: Advt. of Indpls. Home: 11 Highland Dr Lamb Lake Trafalgar IN 46181 Office: 611 N Park Ave Indianapolis IN 46204

HETSKO, CYRIL MICHAEL, physician; b. Montclair, N.J., May 25, 1942; s. Cyril Francis and Josephine (Stein) H.; B.A., Amherst Coll., 1964; M.D., U. Rochester, 1968; m. Barbara Lynn Stein, Nov. 24, 1978. Intern, U. Wis. Hosps., Madison, 1968-69, resident in internal medicine, 1969-72, clin. asst. prof. medicine U. Wis., 1975—; practice internal medicine Dean Clinic, Madison, 1975—. Served to maj. M.C., AUS, 1972-75. Diplomate Nat. Bd. Med. Examiners, Am. Bd. Internal Medicine. Mem. AMA, Am. Soc. Internal Medicine, Am. Soc. Microbiology, Am. Thoracic Soc., Assn. Mil. Surgeons U.S., State Med. Soc. Wis. (Councillor 1979-81, dir. 1981—), Dane County Med. Soc. (chmn. com. on prepaid health plans 1977—; Pres.'s award 1981), Wis. Soc. Internal Medicine (councillor 1981—), N.Y. Acad. Scis., New Eng. Soc. in City N.Y., Nat. Found. for Infectious Disease, Madison Acad. Medicine. Club: Madison. Home: 1114 Sherman Ave Madison WI 53703 Office: Dean Clinic 1313 Fish Hatchery Rd Madison WI 53715

HEULER, LEROY AUGUST, constrn. co. exec.; b. Milw., Apr. 28, 1931; s. Lester Arthur and Florence Ella (Spalzbury) H.; B.S.B.A., Marquette U., 1953; m. Patricia Ann Grayson, Sept. 13, 1952; children—Cheryl, James, John, Lisa. Treas., Glendale Tiles Inc., Milw., 1953-58; pres. Heuler Tile Co., Wauwatosa, Wis., 1958—. Pres., Hepatha Lutheran Ch., Milw., 1958-60; bd. dirs. Elm Grove

(Wis.) Luth. Ch., 1968-74. Mem. Tile Contractors Assn. Am., Asso. Gen. Contractors Wis., Asso. Tile Contractors Milw., Milw. Assn. Commerce, Milw. Jaycees, Luth. Layman's League, Delta Sigma Pi. Republican. Clubs: Westmoor Country, Concordia Century. Home: 1700 Legion Dr Elm Grove WI 53122 Office: 730 N 109th St Wauwatosa WI 53226

HEWITT, AMOS LATHAN, JR., mfg. co. ofcl.; b. San Francisco, Dec. 25, 1952; s. Amos Lathan and Willie M. Hewitt; B.A. in Urban Devel. and Communications, Mich. State U., 1975, M.A. in Labor and Indsl. Relations, 1977; m. Rhonda J. Raiford, June 21, 1980. Legal clk. Office Ingham County Corp. Counsel, East Lansing, Mich., 1976-77; personnel mgr. trainee Rockwell Internat., Troy, Mich., 1978, supr. personnel activities, Oshkosh, Wis., 1978-80, supr. indsl. relations, 1981—, also editor co. newspaper. Mem. adv. com., public relations com., co. chmn. United Way, Oshkosh; bd. dirs., v.p. Georgia Gardens Condominium Assn.; vol. United Cerebral Palsy Found. Mem. Appleton Valley Personnel Assn., Oshkosh Assn. Mfrs. and Commerce, Oshkosh Indsl. Safety Council, Mgmt. Club Oshkosh, Mich. State U. Alumni Assn., Kappa Alpha Psi. Democrat. Episcopalian. Home: 920 Georgia St Oshkosh WI 54901

HEWITT, JAMES WATT, lawyer; b. Hastings, Nebr., Dec. 25, 1932; s. Roscoe Stanley and Willa Manners (Watt) H.; student Hastings Coll., 1950-52; B.S., U. Nebr., 1954, J.D., 1956; m. Marjorie Ruth Barrett, Aug. 8, 1954; children—Mary Janet, William Edward, John Charles, Martha Ann. Admitted to Nebr. bar, 1956; practiced in Hastings, 1956-57, Lincoln, Nebr., 1960-61; v.p., gen. counsel Nebco, Inc., Lincoln, 1961—. Vis. lectr. U. Nebr. Coll. Law, 1970-71, adj. fellow univ. studies U. Nebr., 1978—; dir. Gateway Bank, Lincoln. Mem. state exec. com. Republican party, 1967-70, mem. state central com., 1967-70, legis. chmn., 1968-70. Bd. dirs. Lincoln Child Guidance Center, 1969-72, pres., 1972; bd. dirs. Lincoln Community Playhouse, 1967-73, pres., 1972-73; trustee Bryan Meml. Hosp., Lincoln, 1968-74, 76—, chmn., 1972-74; trustee U. Nebr. Found., 1979—. Served to lt. USAF, 1957-60. Mem. Am. (Nebr. state del. 1972-80, bd. govs. 1981—), Nebr. State (chmn. ins. com. 1972-76), Fed., Lincoln bar assns., Newcomen Soc., Am., Nebr., Lincoln rose socs., Round Table, Beta Theta Pi, Phi Delta Phi. Presbyn. (elder 1962—). Mason (Shriner). Clubs: Univ. Country of Lincoln (Lincoln). Home: 2990 Sheridan Blvd Lincoln NE 68502 Office: 1815 Y St Lincoln NE 68501

HEWITT, PATRICIA WIMAN, agriculturalist; b. Chgo., Jan. 17, 1925; d. Charles Deere and Pattie (Southall) Wiman; student Conn. Coll. for Women, 1942-44, U. Calif. at Santa Barbara, 1944-45, George Washington U., 1946-47; m. William Alexander Hewitt, Jan. 3, 1948; children—Anna Deere, Adrienne Deere, Alexander Southall. Asst. to mgr. Midvale Farms Corp., Tucson, 1945-47, dir., sec., 1945-80, half owner, 1963-80; owner, mgr. Friendship Farms, East Moline, Ill., 1955—; owner, joint mgr. Camelot Vineyards, Rutherford, Calif., 1960—; dir. Diagnostic Data Inc., Mountain View, Calif. Equestrian coach Japanese Self Def. Forces, 1967-68. Mem. Jr. League, San Francisco, 1951—; asst. to field dir. A.R.C., San Francisco, 1944-45, service cons., 1950-54; bd. dirs. YWCA, San Francisco, 1951-52, Moline Welfare Agy., 1959-69; governing mem. Arabian Horse Club Registry Am., 1963-64; trustee, pres.'s council Marycrest Coll., Davenport, Iowa, 1969-73; v.p. U.S. Modern Pentathlon Assn., 1971-76; mem. U.S. Olympic Games Com., 1970-76; mem. nat. bd. advisers Nat. Assn. for Retarded Children, 1967—; mem. Ill.-Iowa Assn. for Children with Specific Learning Problems, 1970-79; mem. Ill. State Adv. Council Edn. Handicapped Children, 1973-75; mem. exec. com. Nat. Reading Council, 1970-72; trustee Charles Deere Wiman Meml. Trust, Morris Animal Found., Lincoln Acad. of Ill., Rock Island Franciscan Hosp., Knox Coll., Galesburg, Ill., 1975—; chmn. bd. trustees Butterworth Meml. Trust; trustee Arabian Horse Owners Found., 1961-73, mem. adv. bd., 1973—; mem. women's bd. Field Mus. Natural History, Chgo., 1972—; bd. dirs. Family YMCA, Rock Island, 1975-79; mem. service council United Way Rock Island, Ill. and Scott County, Iowa, 1973-76; governing life mem. Art Inst. Chgo., 1972—; mem. Nat. Com. on U.S.-China Relations, 1974—, Ill. Racing Bd., 1973-77, Nat. Assn. State Racing Commrs., 1973-77; mem. nat. bd. dirs. U.S. Equestrian Team, 1977—; mem. citizens com. U. Ill., 1974-77, animal sci. adv. com. Coll. Agr., 1974-77; mem. mental health adv. com. Rock Island County Pub. Health Bd., 1974—; mem. adv. bd. Assn. for Retarded Children and Adults Rock Island County, 1972—; mem. corp. vis. com. for dept. psychology Mass. Inst. Tech., 1977—. Mem. Internat. Arabian Horse Assn. (dir. 1964-67), Grayson Found., Arabian Horse Racing Assn., Am. Horse Show Assn. (life, mem. drugs and medications com.). Episcopalian. Clubs: Santa Barbara Yacht; Arts (Chgo.). Home: 38th St and Blackhawk Rd Rock Island IL 61201 Office: Friendship Farms Rural Route 2 Box 612 East Moline IL 61244

HEWITT, WILLIAM ALEXANDER, mfg. exec.; b. San Francisco, Aug. 9, 1914; s. Edward Thomas and Jeannette (Brun) H.; A.B., U. Calif., 1937; m. Patricia Deere Wiman, Jan. 3, 1948; children—Anna, Adrienne, Alexander. With John Deere Plow Co., San Francisco, 1948-54, v.p., 1950-54; dir. Deere & Co., Moline, Ill., 1951—, exec. v.p., 1954-55, pres., chief exec. officer, 1955-64, chmn., chief exec. officer, 1964—; dir. Continental Ill. Corp., Continental Ill. Nat. Bank & Trust Co. of Chgo., Baxter-Travenol Labs., Inc., AT&T; mem. internat. adv. com. Chase Manhattan Bank. Founding mem. Bus. Com. for Arts, Emergency Com. for Am. Trade; trustee Calif. Inst. Tech., Nat. Safety Council, Carnegie Endowment for Internat. Peace, 1971-75, Council of Americas, St. Katharine's/St. Mark's Sch., 1965-76; bd. govs. ARC, 1967-70; vis. com. Harvard U. Grad. Sch. Bus. Adminstrn., 1962-67, Grad. Sch. Design, 1967-73, now mem. vis. com. on East Asian studies; incorporator Nat. Corp. for Housing Partnerships, 1968-70; mem. council Stanford Research Inst., 1971-79; laureate Lincoln. Acad. Ill.; hon. mem. nat. bd. Smithsonian Assos.; trustee Mus. Modern Art, N.Y.C.; mem. Nat. Endowment for Humanities, 1975-80, Trilateral Commn., 1973-81; mem. Wilson council Woodrow Wilson Internat. Center for Scholars. Served as lt. comdr. USNR, 1942-46. Fellow Am. Soc. Agrl. Engrs.; mem. Farm Indsl. Equipment Inst., The Conf. Bd., Soc. Automotive Engrs., Internat. C. of C. (trustee U.S. council), UN Assn. (dir. 1970-73), Com. Econ. Devel. (hon. trustee), Advt. Council, Inc., AIA (hon.), Bus. Council, Council Fgn. Relations, Ill. Council Econ. Edn. (governing mem. 1970-77), Bus. Roundtable, Nat. Council U.S.-China Trade (dir. 1973-80, vice chmn. 1973-75, chmn. 1975-78), U.S.-USSR Trade and Econ. Council (dir.), Asia Soc. (internat. council), Alpha Delta Phi. Clubs: Pacific-Union (San Francisco); Burlingame (Calif.) Country; Chicago (Chgo.); Bohemian; Pilgrims of U.S. Home: 3800 Blackhawk Rd Rock Island IL 61201 Office: Deere & Co John Deere Rd Moline IL 61265

HEWLETT, LELA MAE, educator; b. Horton, Kans., Mar. 5, 1949; d. Leonard Keith and Ida Mae (Ploeger) Hooper; B.S., Kans. State U., 1970; M.S., Purdue U., 1974; m. H. Stephen Hewlett, Dec. 20, 1969; children—Jennifer Diane, Casee Michele. Vocat. home econs. tchr. Ben Davis Jr./Sr. High Sch., Indpls., 1970-71; dept. chmn. South Wayne Jr. High Sch., Indpls., 1971-73; grad. asst. Purdue U., West Lafayette, Ind., 1974; vocat. home econs. tchr. Valparaiso (Ind.) High Sch., 1975-76, Morgan Twp. Jr./Sr. High Sch., Valparaiso, 1979-81; public speaker. Bd. dirs. Ind. Consumer Adv. Council, 1970-73. Named Young Career Woman of Yr., Porter Bus. and Profl. Women's Assn., 1976. Mem. Am. Vocat. Assn., Nat. Assn. Vocat. Home Econs. Tchrs., Ind. Vocat. Assn. (award of merit 1975, outstanding service award 1978, editor News and Views 1973-79), Ind. Vocat. Home Econs. Assn., Am. Home Econs. Assn., Ind. Home Econs. Assn. (editor The Voice 1981—), Future Homemakers Am. (advisor), Phi Upsilon Omicron, Omicron Nu, Alpha Delta Kappa. Mem. Church of Christ. Home: 2055 S State Rd 2 Valparaiso IN 46383

HEY, DENNIS JOHN, neonatologist; b. St. Louis, Sept. 23, 1940; s. Gustav James and Elsie Anna (Ontl) H.; student N.E. Mo. State U., 1962-65; D.O., Kansas City Coll. Osteo. Medicine, 1969; m. Gloria Lee Hainds, May 29, 1965; children—John, Sonya. Intern, Bay View Hosp., Bay Village, Ohio, 1969-70; resident in pediatrics Kansas City (Mo.) Coll. Osteo. Medicine, 1970-72, asst. prof. pediatrics, 1973—, dir. newborn and intensive care nursery unit, 1973—; head dept. pediatrics U. Health Sci., 1981—; fellow in neonatology Children's Mercy Hosp., Kansas City, Mo., 1972-73. Mem. edn. adv. com. Mo. Div. Health Bill, 1976—, State of Mo. Profession Liability Rev. Bd., 1976—. Served with USAF, 1957-62. Diplomate Am. Coll. Osteo. Pediatricians, Nat. Bd. Osteo. Examiners. Mem. Am. Osteo. Assn. (editorial reviewer Jour. 1974—), Mo. Assn. Osteo. Physicians, Jackson County Osteo. Soc. (rep. to Kansas City Public Health for Children's Immunizations Program 1978), S.W. Pediatric Soc., Midwest Neonatology Soc. Republican. Baptist. Participant revision manual Standards and Recommendations for Hospital Care for Your New Baby, 1977. Home: 3712 Beechwood Dr Lee's Summit MO 64063 Office: U Health Sci Univ Hosp 2105 Independence Blvd Kansas City MO 64124

HEYDE, EDWARD LEE, ophthalmologist; b. Etna Green, Ind., Jan. 10, 1935; s. Claude Edward and Helen Elizabeth (Forney) H.; B.S. in Pharmacy, Purdue U., 1957; M.D., Ind. U., 1967; m. Stephanie Kay Seybert, July 21, 1956; children—Craig Edward, Melissa Kay, Erin Lynn. With Phillips Pharmacy, Goshen, Ind., 1957-58; intern Meml. Hosp., South Bend, Ind., 1966-67; resident in ophthalmology Ind. U. Med. Center, 1967-70; practice medicine specializing in ophthalmology, South Bend, 1970—; mem. staff Meml. Hosp., South Bend, St. Joseph's Hosp., South Bend. Served to 1st lt. M.C., USAF, 1958-61. Mem. AMA, Am. Acad. Ophthalmology and Otolaryngology, Am. Assn. Ophthalmology, Ind. Acad. Ophthalmology. Republican. Presbyterian. Club: Shriners. Home: 17646 Woodridge Ct South Bend IN 46635 Office: 513 N Michigan St South Bend IN 44601

HEYDEGGER, H(ELMUT) ROLAND, chemist; b. Phila., Dec. 3, 1935; s. Helmut and Allyse Theresa (Paulich) H.; B.S., Queens Coll., N.Y.C., 1957; M.S., U. Ark., 1958; Ph.D. (Gen. Electric fellow), U. Chgo., 1968; m. Karen Iversen, Aug. 15, 1970. Research asso. U. Chgo., 1968-77, sr. research asso., 1978—; mem. faculty Purdue U., Hammond, Ind., 1970—, asso. prof. chemistry, 1975-81, prof., 1981—, head dept. physics and chemistry, 1979—; vis. fellow Australian Nat. U., 1976-77; cons. Argonne (Ill.) Nat. Lab., 1973-74; instr. Prairie State Coll., Chicago Heights, Ill., 1961-62; phys. chemist U.S. Bur. Mines, 1958; mem. radiation emergency response com. Ind. Bd. Health, 1973—; vis. research asso. Brookhaven Nat. Lab., Upton, N.Y., 1970; guest scientist Los Alamos Sci. Lab., 1973-78, vis. staff, 1978—; guest scientist Fermi Nat. Accelerator Lab., 1975—. Mem. Am. Chem. Soc., Am. Phys. Soc., Am. Geophys. Union, Geochem. Soc. (charter), Internat. Assn. Geochemistry and Cosmochemistry (charter), Meteoritical Soc. Co-investigator lunar sample analysis project, 1968-71. Contbr. articles to profl. jours. Office: Dept Chemistry Purdue U Hammond IN 46323

HEYMAN, SISTER MARY JEROME, librarian; b. Chgo., Dec. 14, 1914; d. Sidney M. and Anna (Ryan) Heyman; B.A., Rosary Coll., 1937; M.S. in L.S., U. Ill., 1947. Tchr., librarian Trinity High Sch., Bloomington, Ill., 1939, Cathedral High Sch., Sioux Falls, S.D., 1940; librarian Visitation High Sch., Chgo., 1940-50, Catholic High Sch., Oklahoma City, 1950-53, Edgewood Coll. of Sacred Heart, Madison, Wis., 1953—. Mem. bd. Madison Area Library Council, 1971-72, 78-80. Mem. Am. Cath., Wis. (membership chmn. 1958-60, sec. 1962-63, dir. 1967-70, com. on acad. tenure and status for librarians 1971-73) library assns. Contbr. articles to profl. jours. Home: 855 Woodrow St Madison WI 53711 Office: Edgewood Coll Library 855 Woodrow St Madison WI 53711

HIBNER, DIXIE JOHNSTON, ednl. adminstr.; b. Dawson Springs, Ky., Jan. 16, 1942; d. Euel Matthew and Ester May (Beshears) Johnston; B.S., Eastern Mich. U., 1963, M.A., 1966; postgrad. U. Mich., 1978—; m. Edward Joseph Hibner, Jr., Aug. 10, 1963; children—Bradly Alan, Michael Ryan. Tchr., Elmhurst, Ill., 1963-64, Wayne, Mich., 1964-74; curriculum cons., Wayne, Mich., 1974-77; prin., Saline, Mich., 1977—, elem. prin. Saline Area Schs., 1977—, dir. Title I programs, 1977—, coordinator profl. devel. program, 1979—, chmn. curriculum adv. com., 1979—. Mem. Assn. Supervision and Curriculum Devel., Nat. Assn. Elem. Sch. Prins., Assn. Retarded Citizens, Assn. Tchr. Educators, Mich. Assn. Supervision and Curriculum Devel. (bd. mem., pres.), Mich. Elem. Middle Sch. Prins. Assn., Mich. Council Women in Ednl. Adminstrn., Washtenaw Reading Council. Home: 44928 Gov Bradford St Plymouth MI 48170 Office: 203 Risdon Dr Saline MI 48176

HICKEY, CLARENCE DAREN, bus. exec.; b. Aurora, Ill., Oct. 23, 1925; s. Clarence P. and Marie E. (Challis) H.; B.S. in Accounting, U. Ill., 1950; postgrad. Northwestern U., 1952; m. Alice Gillette, June 7, 1947; children—Patricia Ellen (Mrs. James Zajicek), Laura Marie (Mrs. Robert Osterhoff), Mary Alice, Peter Daren, Maureen Ann, Tracy Lynn, Wendy Ann, Margaret Jo, Timothy Sean. Acting prin. mgr. Hasking & Sells Co., Chgo., 1952-63; controller James B. Beam Distilling Co., Chgo., 1963-67; v.p. and treas. Chevway Corp., Chgo., 1967-68; v.p. and controller Barton Brands, Inc., Chgo., 1968-70; v.p. fin. and adminstrn. Creative Bldg. Systems, Inc., Urbana, Ill., 1970-72; v.p., sec., treas., Nat. Student Mktg. Corp., Chgo., 1972-80; sr. v.p. fin. and adminstrn. Palm Beach, Inc., Cin., 1980—; dir. Nat. Student Mktg. Corp., Sandpaper Inc. Ill., Palm Sport Ltd., U.S. Apparel Co. Mem. Wheaton (Ill.) Community Assn.; treas. Wheaton Parent's Club; mem. St. Michael's Sch. Bd., 1969-70. Served With USNR, 1943-46. C.P.A., Ill. Mem. Am. Inst. C.P.A.'s, Ill. Soc. C.P.A.'s, Fin. Execs. Inst., Am. Mgmt. Assn., Tax Execs. Inst. Clubs: Coldstream Country; Ill. Athletic, Brookwood Country, K.C. Home: 754 WatchPoint Dr Cincinnati OH 45230 Office: 400 Pike St Cincinnati OH 45202

HICKEY, HOWARD WESLEY, educator; b. Bozeman, Mont., Oct. 20, 1930; s. Wesley Grandon and Frances Mildred (Howard) H.; B.A., Western Wash. U., 1953, Ed.M., 1958; M.A., Bowdoin Coll., 1962; Ph.D., Mich. State U., 1968; m. Kay Young, July 1, 1976; children—Darcianne, Benjamin, Morris, Stuart, Bryan; 1 dau., by previous marriage, Brooks. Dir. fed. programs Puyallup (Wash.) schs., 1962-66; asst. prof. elem. edn. Mich. State U., East Lansing, 1968-71; asso. prof., dir. Mott Inst. for Community Improvement, Mich. State U., 1971-77, prof. higher edn., 1978—; cons. in field. NSF fellow, 1958, 61-62; Mott fellow, 1966-67. Mem. Nat. Community Edn. Assn., Nat. Soc. for Study of Edn., Phi Delta Kappa. Episcopalian. Club: Rotary (pres. 1965-66). Author: (with Curt Van Voorhees) Role of the School in Community Education, 1969; asso. editor Community Edn. Jour., 1971-74; contbr. articles to profl. jours. Home: 3885 Binghampton Okemos MI 48860 Office: 420 Erickson Hall East Lansing MI 48824

HICKMAN, DAVID MICHAEL, paper tableware mfg. co. exec.; b. Salem, Oreg., Dec. 11, 1942; s. Vernon Combs and Margaret Irene (Copley) H.; student public schs.; m. Karen Joyce Cox, Aug. 24, 1968; children—Sean Michael, Shannon Lee. Terr. mgr. Brown & Williamson Tobacco Co., 1964-66, Gibson Greeting Cards, Inc., 1966-69; chain drug specialist Coty, Inc., 1970-73; pres., owner Expressions, Seattle, 1973-75; v.p. sales Paper Art Co., Inc., Indpls., 1975-78, exec. v.p., 1978—; pres., owner Paper Artery Co., Inc., 1979—, Shaniko Mktg. Co., 1978—. Served with U.S. Army, 1960-63. Republican. Presbyterian. Home: 9202 Behner Brook Dr Indianapolis IN 46250 Office: 3500 N Arlington Ave Indianapolis IN 46218

HICKOX, JOHN EKSTROM, geologist; b. Topeka, Oct. 29, 1925; s. Russel B. and Edna (Ekstrom) H.; B.S., U. Kans., 1949, M.S., 1951; m. Mary L. Parman, Nov. 6, 1949; 1 son, John Eric. Geologist, Texaco, Inc., Mid-Continent area, 1951-63; cons. geologist, 1963—; project supr. Center for Research in Engring. Sci., U. Kans., Lawrence, 1965; asst. research psychologist, Menninger Found., Topeka, 1967-73; geologist Mar-Win Devel. Co., Topeka, 1975-77; pres. Island Creek Drilling Co., Topeka, 1978—; asst. instr. U. Kans., 1949-51; lectr. Washburn U., Topeka, 1968. Served with AUS, 1943-46. Recipient Haworth honors U. Kans., 1950. Mem. Am. Assn. Petroleum Geologists, AAAS, Geol. Soc. Am., Kans. Geol. Soc., Am. Legion, Sigma Xi, Sigma Gamma Epsilon. Presbyn. (elder 1957-58). Club: Petroleum of Wichita. Author: (with others) The Permian Reef Complex of West Texas and New Mexico, 1953. Contbr. articles to profl. jours. Home: 3147 Westover Rd Topeka KS 66604 Office: 1271 Woodhull Suite 100 Topeka KS 66604

HICKS, ALFRED BARRETT, JR., civil engr.; b. Columbus, Miss., Feb. 8, 1951; s. Alfred Barrett and Mildred Marguerite (Hays) H.; B.S., Miss. State U., 1973, M.C.E., 1981; m. Pok Sin Choe; children—Alfred Barrett, Jennifer Marie. Commd. lt. U.S. Air Force, 1973, advanced through grades to capt., 1975—; chief programs br. 14th civil engring. squadron, USAF, Columbus AFB, Miss., 1978; chief engring. design sect. Red Horse squadron, Korea, 1978-79; instr. Air Force Inst. Tech., Wright-Patterson AFB, Ohio, 1979—; pres. Barrett Engring. Co., Inc., Memphis and Starkville, Miss., 1975—. Treas., social chmn. Columbus AFB Jr. Officers Council, 1977-78. Registered profl. engr., Miss.; named 14th Flying Tng. Wing Outstanding Jr. Officer Columbus AFB, Miss., 1976. Mem. Nat. Soc. Profl. Engrs., Miss. Engring. Soc., Soc. Am. Mil. Engrs., Water Pollution Control Fedn., Miss. Water Pollution Control Assn., Am. Water Works Assn., Miss. Water Pollution Control Operators Assn., Air Force Assn., Tau Beta Pi, Phi Kappa Phi. Baptist. Home: 2478 Kewanna Ln Xenia OH 45385 Office: Inst Tech Sch Civil Engring Wright-Patterson AFB OH 45433

HICKS, CHRISTOPHER, safety engr.; b. Cin., Oct. 15, 1953; s. Willie Douglas and Florene Isabell Hicks; B.S. in Safety Mgmt. and Environ. Safety, Ind. State U., 1976; m. Gloria Jean Carter, July 7, 1979. Safety engr. Laclede Steel Co., Alton, Ill., 1976-79; safety engr. II corp. research and devel. Monsanto, St. Louis, 1979—. Mem. edn. and employment com. St. Louis Urban League; active blood drive ARC, 1979. Named an Outstanding Young Man of Am., U.S. Jaycees, 1980. Mem. Am. Soc. Safety Engrs., Sigma Mu. Home: 2254 Westglen Park Dr Saint Louis MO 63043 Office: 800 N Lindbergh St St Louis MO 63166

HICKS, JAMES THOMAS, physician, lawyer; b. Brownsville, Pa., June 5, 1924; s. Thomas and Florence Julia (O'Donnel) H.; B.S., U. Pitts., 1945, A.B., 1946, M.S., 1946; Ph.D., George Washington U., 1950; M.D., U. Ark., 1956; J.D., DePaul U., 1975; m. Ellen Elliott, Aug. 25, 1950; children—Ellen, Mary Jo. Intern USPHS, Balt., 1958-60; resident VA Hosp., Pitts., 1958-60; admitted to Ill. bar, 1977, U.S. Ct. of Appeals, 1977, Pa. bar, 1977 U.S. Supreme Ct. Bar, 1980; practice medicine specializing in forensic and legal medicine, River Forest, Ill., 1964—; dir. labs. Oak Park (Ill.) Hosp., 1964—; pres. Oakton Service Corp., 1968—; Anktin Ser. Corp. of Pa. Served with USPHS, 1956-57. Fellow Nat. Cancer Inst., 1949-50. Fellow A.C.P., Internat. Coll. Surgeons; mem. AMA, Am. Bar Assn., Ill. Bar Assn., Pa. Bar Assn., Assn. Am. Trial Lawyers, Am. Assn. Hosp. Lawyers, Sigma Xi. Clubs: Univ., Whitehall, Oak Park Country, Carlton. Contbg. editor Hosp. Formulary Mgmt., 1966-70. Home: 7980 W Chicago Ave River Forest IL 60305 Office: 520 Maple Ave Oak Park IL 60304

HICKS, JOHN MARTIN, artist, educator; b. Tulsa, Dec. 15, 1930; s. Hanne J. and Laurie K. (Saxer) H.; B.S., Ind. U., Bloomington, 1957, M.S., 1968, Ed.D., 1972; m. Mary Ann Stevens, Apr. 1, 1957; children—Jon Martin, Scott Shawn. Art. instr. Sachem Schs., L.I., N.Y., 1957-59; grad. asst., teaching asso. Ind. U., Bloomington, 1959-60, teaching fellow, 1968-69; mem. faculty Drake U., Des Moines, Iowa, 1960—, prof. art and art edn., 1973—; one-man shows: Blanden Gallery, Ft. Dodge, Iowa, 1967, Bloomington, Ind., 1968, Drake U. 1972. Served with USN, 1950-54. Mem. Nat. Art. Edn. Assn., Art Educators Iowa, Assn. Supervision and Curriculum Devel., Phi Delta Kappa. Mem. Christian Ch. Editor: Western Arts Assn. Jour., 1959-60, Art Educators of Iowa Newsletter, 1969-73; contbr. articles in field to profl. publs. Home: 537 56th St Des Moines IA 50312 Office: Fine Arts Center 278 Drake U Des Moines IA 50311

HICKS, RONALD EDWARD, archaeologist, educator; b. Kingman, Ind., Aug. 26, 1940; s. Winfield Spencer and E. Genevia (Clements) H.; B.A., Purdue U., 1963; Ph.D., U. Pa., 1975; 1 son, Geoffrey. Asst. prodn. editor Prentice-Hall, 1965-66; asst. editing supr. World Publ., 1966-67; mng. editor American Anthropologist, 1968-70; teaching fellow U. Pa., Phila., 1970-71, 72-73, staff dir. univ. devel. commn., 1972, instr./lectr., 1974-76; instr. Community Coll. of Phila., 1974-76; asst. prof. Ball State U., Muncie, Ind., 1976-80, asso. prof. dept. anthropology, 1980—, dir. Archaeol. Resources Mgmt. Service, 1978—; active field research, N.J., 1970, 72, 75-76, Ireland, 1971, 73-74, 77, Scotland, 1976, Ind., 1978—; Fulbright-Hays fellow, Ireland, 1973-74; bd. dirs. Council for Conservation of Ind. Archaeology, 1977—, pres., 1979-81. Served to lt. j.g. USN, 1963-65, lt. comdr. Res. ret. Grantee Am. Council Learned Socs., 1977, U.S. Dept. Interior Heritage Conservation and Recreation Service/Ind. Div. Hist. Preservation, 1979, 80, 81. Fellow Am. Anthropol. Assn., Royal Soc. Antiquaries of Ireland, Soc. Antiquaries of Scotland; mem. Soc. Profl. Archaeologists, Archaeol. Inst. Am. (com. of European Archaeology, 1977—), Assn. for Field Archaeology, Soc. for Am. Archaeology, AAAS, Folklore Soc. Co-editor: Old World Archaeology Newsletter, 1977-81; cons. editor Archaeoastronomy, 1979—; contbr. articles to publs. including Bull. of Phila. Anthrop. Soc., Expedition, Jour. of Royal Soc. of Antiquaries of Ireland, Irish Archaeo. Research Forum, Archaeology, Mondo Archeologico. Office: Dept Anthropology Ball State Univ Muncie IN 47306

HICKS, SAMUEL IRVING, educator; b. Stormville, N.Y., Apr. 4, 1902; s. Irving J. and Elizabeth (Tripp) H.; A.B., U. Mich., 1924; M.A., Columbia, 1927; Ed.D., Columbia U., 1947; postgrad. N.Y. U., 1931-33; m. Margaret Anderson, Jan. 7, 1924; children—Eleanor (Mrs. Peter Werenfels), Virginia (Mrs. John Karl). Tchr., Boyne City

(Mich.) High Sch., 1924-26; prin. jr. and sr. high sch., Dobbs Ferry, N.Y., 1926-29; supt. schs., Central Park, N.Y., 1929-32, Pearl River, N.Y., 1932-58; coordinator services to adminstrs. citizenship edn. project Columbia U., 1954-56; prof. edn. Ohio U., Athens, 1958—, dir. Center for Ednl. Research and Service, 1960-66, coordinator ednl. placement, 1972—; dir. Inst. Edn., Ahmadu Bello U., Nigeria, 1966-70; exec. sec. SEOKWA Council Adminstrv. Leadership, 1972—. Mem. Am. Ednl. Research Assn., N.Y. State Ednl. Research Assn. (past pres.), Am. Assn. Sch. Adminstrs., Nat. Conf. Profs. Ednl. Adminstrn., Comparative and Internat. Edn. Soc., Assn. Sch. Bus. Ofcls., Am. Ednl. Fin. Assn., AAUP, Kappa Delta Pi, Phi Delta Kappa. Clubs: Athens Rotary, Rotary (Zaria, Nigeria), Pearl River (past pres.). Home: 48 Briarwood Dr Athens OH 45701 Office: Lindley Hall Ohio University Athens OH 45701

HICKSON, ROBERT COMINS, banker; b. Mt. Gilead, Ohio, Aug. 24, 1928; s. Charles C. and Marian (Sampson) H.; A.B., Ohio Wesleyan U., 1950; M.B.A., Ohio State U., 1952; m. Mary Jean Sturrock, Feb. 13, 1954; children—Robert Comins, Thomas M. With City Nat. Bank & Trust Co., Columbus, Ohio, 1950-51, Ohio Bell Telephone Co., Cleve., 1952-54; owner Hickson Ins.-Realty, Mt. Gilead, 1954—; with Peoples Bank, Mt. Gilead, 1963—, pres., 1967—, chmn. bd., 1963—; pres. Peoples Bldg. Finance and Devel. Co., Mt. Gilead, 1967—; dir. HPM Corp., 1977—; mem. Ohio Bank Bd., 1976-80, Ohio Devel. Financing Commn., 1980—. Mem. exec. com. Hardinging area council Boy Scouts Am., 1968-74, 76—, v.p. 1970-74; chmn. adv. com. Tri-River Vocat. Sch., 1974-75; sec.-treas. Morrow County Found., 1974—; chmn. Republican central com. Morrow County, 1964-68; trustee Ohio Wesleyan U., 1978—; trustee Elyria Meth. Home, 1974-78; trustee Marion Concert Assn., 1976-80; mem. citizens adv. council Marion Campus, Ohio State U., 1976-78. Named Outstanding Young Man Morrow County Jr. C. of C., 1961. Mem. Ohio Bankers Assn. (dir. 1977-80), Mt. Gilead C. of C. (past pres.), Morrow County Bd. Realtors (pres. 1977—). Methodist (local lay leader 1971-72, vice chmn. bd. ch. and society, East Ohio Conf., 1973-74). Kiwanian (past pres.). Home: 371 N Main St Mount Gilead OH 43338 Office: Public Sq Mount Gilead OH 43338

HIDVEGI, ERNEST B., orthopedic surgeon; b. Budapest, Hungary, Sept. 24, 1925; s. Istvan and Maria (Kovacs) H.; came to U.S., 1958, naturalized, 1963; M.D., Royal Hungarian U., 1949; m. Tamara Jancewycz, 1966; children—Erica, Andrea. Research asso. Presbyn. Med. Center, U. Ill., Chgo., 1959-61; intern Cook County Hosp., Chgo., 1961-62; resident in orthopedic surgery U. Cin. Med. Center, Childrens Hosp., VA Hosp., Cin., 1963-66; resident in pathology Hosp. Joint Diseases and Med. Center, N.Y.C., 1967-70; mem. attending staff orthopedic surgery Astoria Gen. Hosp., Hillcrest Gen. Hosp., Parkway Hosp., N.Y.C., 1968-70; attending orthopedic surgeon Youngstown (Ohio) Hosp. Assn., 1971—; chief sect. orthopedic surgery Ohio Permanente Med. Group Kaiser Med. Center, Cleve., Parma, Ohio, 1972—. Diplomate Am. Bd. Orthopedic Surgery. Fellow Am. Acad. Orthopedic Surgeons. Contbr. papers to med. jours. Home: 18500 S Woodland Rd Shaker Heights OH 44122

HIEBERT, ELIZABETH BLAKE (MRS. HOMER L. HIEBERT), civic worker; b. Mpls., July 18, 1910; d. Henry Seavey and Grace (Riebeth) Blake; student Washburn U., 1926-30; B.S., U. Tex. 1933; m. Homer L. Hiebert, Aug. 29, 1935; children—Grace Elizabeth (Mrs. John E. Beam), Mary Sue (Mrs. Donald Wester), John Blake, Henry Leonard, David Mark. Free lance writer. Sec. Topeka Regional Sci. Fair, 1958-60, mem. bd., 1964—; mem. bd. Topeka Welfare Planning Council, 1958-62, YWCA, 1962—, Kans. Council Children and Youth; water safety instr., swimming instr. for handicapped; active Campfire Girls, Nat. Trust for Historic Preservation, Internat. Oceanographic Found., People-to-People; Fellow Harry S. Truman Library Inst.; mem. bd. Can Help; mem. Topeka Friends of Zoo, Friends of Topeka Library, YMCA, Friends of John F. Kennedy Center Performing Arts, Los Angeles Internat. Fern Soc., Nat. League Am. Pen Women (pres. Topeka), AAAS, D.A.R., Daus. Am. Colonists (mem. bd.), Colo. Hist. Soc., AAUW (bd. mem. 1944-62, 65—, v.p.), New Eng. Women, Washburn U. Alumni Assn., Nat. Wildlife Fedn., Kans. Hist. Soc., N.E. Hist. and Geneol. Soc., Tex. U. Alumni, Am. Home Econs. Assn., Shawnee County Med. Aux., (past pres.) Nat. Audubon, Internat. Platform Assn., Topeka Civic Symphony, Met. Mus. Art, P.E.O. (past local pres. coop. bd.), Topeka Art Guild, Nat. Soc. Ancient and Hon. Arty., Cousteau Soc., Shawnee County Hist. Soc. (dir.), Oceanie Soc., Exec. Female, Delta Kappa Gamma, Delta Gamma. Republican. Methodist. Clubs: Capitol Hill, Knife and Fork. Editor children's page Household mag., 1934-39. Home: 1517 Randolph Topeka KS 66604

HIEBERT, ROBERT WAYNE, educator; b. Hillsboro, Kans., Dec. 27, 1939; s. Dan S. and Katherine (Nickel) H.; B.Music Edn., Emporia State U., 1961, M.S., 1968; m. Esther Madsen, June 1, 1960; children—Robert Edwin, Craig Jay. Tchr. music Midway Sch., Buffalo, Kans., 1961-63; tchr. music, Humboldt, Kans., 1963-67; guidance counselor, Abilene, Kans., 1967-76; child and family counselor Central Kans. Mental Health Center, Salina, 1976-78; elem. counselor Salina (Kans.) Schs., 1978—; adj. inst. extension courses Emporia (Kans.) State U., 1973—; cons. various Kans. sch. systems. Bd. dirs. Kans. Assn. for Mental Health, 1971-72. Named Abilene Outstanding Young Educator, 1973, Kans. Counselor of Yr., 1975. Mem. Am., North Central Kans. personnel and guidance assns., Kans. Sch. Counselors Assn., Am. Sch. Counselors Assn. Club: Elks. Contbr. articles to profl. jours. Home: 415 NE 9th St Abilene KS 67410 Office: 300 W Ash St Salina KS 67401

HIEGEL, JERRY M., food co. exec.; b. Davenport, Iowa, 1927; B.S., St. Ambrose Coll., 1949; M.B.A., U. Wis., 1950; married. With Des Moines Register, 1946; with Oscar Mayer & Co. Inc., Madison, Wis., 1946—, asst. v.p. and gen sales mgr. Western div., 1962-66, v.p. sales, 1966-70, v.p. mktg., 1970-71, group v.p., 1971-73, exec. v.p., 1973-77, pres., 1977—, chief exec. officer, 1980—, also dir. Served with USN, 1945-46. Office: 910 Mayer Ave PO Box 7188 Madison WI 53707

HIESTAND, THOMAS WARREN, economist, educator; b. Appleton, Wis., Sept. 17, 1945; s. Warren Good and Arlene Mary (Lopas) H.; B.A., Luther Coll., 1967; Ph.D., Kans. State U., 1974; m. Anna Marie Stallbaumer, June 7, 1969; children—Elizabeth, Thaddeus, Leeanna, Peter. Temporary instr. econs. Kans. State U., Manhattan, 1971-72; asst. prof. econs. Concordia Coll., Moorhead, Minn., 1972—, chmn. dept. econs. and bus. adminstrn., 1978—; lectr. in field, cons. Sec., Fargo-Moorhead Y's Men's, 1976, v.p., 1977-78, pres., 1979—; sec.-treas. River Oaks Assn. Inc., 1972—. Served to lt. Q.M.C., U.S. Army, 1972. NDEA fellow, 1967-70. Mem. AAUP, Mid-Continent Regional Sci. Assn., Community Devel. Soc., Am. Econ. Assn., Adminstrv. Mgmt. Soc., Omicron Delta Epsilon, Pi Gamma Mu. Republican. Lutheran. Home: Rural Route 3 Box 30 Moorhead MN 56560

HIGGINBOTHAM, WILLIAM HENRY, mgmt. cons.; b. Jefferson City, Mo., Apr. 19, 1909; s. William Barber and May (Pritchard) H.; B.S., Washington U., St. Louis, 1953; m. Mildred Catherine Winsby, Mar. 4, 1944 (dec. Dec. 1959); children—Cynthia, Pamela (dec.), Ronald; m. 2d, Suzanne Guge, Oct. 4, 1970. Personnel dir. Rice-Stix Dry Goods Co., St. Louis, 1945-50, White Rodgers Co., St. Louis, 1950-58; v.p. indsl. relations Century Electric Co., St. Louis, 1958-63; mgmt. cons., St. Louis, 1963—; faculty Ann. Inst., Creative Edn. Found., Buffalo, 1963—. Bd. dirs., Jr. Achievement Mississippi Valley, Inc. Cert. mgmt. cons. Mem. Assn. Mgmt. Consultants (nat. pres. 1977), Am. Soc. Tng. and Devel., Am. Soc. Personnel Adminstrn., Exec. Assn. Grad. Sch. Bus. Columbia U., Indsl. Relations Assn. Greater St. Louis, Inst. Mgmt. Cons., Mgmt. Devel. Study Group. Republican. Christian Scientist. Club: Rotary. Home: 890 Judson Manor Dr Saint Louis MO 63141 Office: 7701 Forsyth Blvd Saint Louis MO 63105

HIGGINS, ALAN MILLS, real estate exec.; b. Cin., Jan. 10, 1945; s. Jack and Agnes (Mills) H.; B.S., Miami U., Oxford, Ohio, 1967; m. Elaine Marie Benes, May 11, 1968; children—Scott, Jason. Site developer Standard Oil Co., Ohio, 1967-72; corp. real estate rep. Gen. Tire Realty Co., Gen. Tire & Rubber Co., 1972-74, mgr. corp. real estate, v.p., 1974-76, pres., dir., 1976—; chmn. bd., pres. Am. Realty Acquisition Cons.'s, 1978—; mem. bus. devel. council 1st Union Nat. Bank of N.C.; vice chmn. Am. Inst. Asset Mgmt.; staff U. Okla., U. Wis. schs. continuing edn.; staff U. N.C., Charlotte. Mem. Brecksville (Ohio) Charter Rev. Com., 1973. Served with AUS, 1967-69. Profl. designations include: C.R.A., F.C.A., S.I.R. Mem. Nat. Assn. Corp. Real Estate Execs. (chmn. bd. dirs.), Soc. Indsl. Realtors, Indsl. Devel. Research Council, Soc. Real Estate Appraisers, Am. Inst. Corp. Asset Mgmt. (founder). Contbr. articles to profl. jours., chpts. to tech. books; mem. editorial adv. bd. Corp. Design mag. Home: 495 Bath Hills Blvd Akron OH 44313 Office: 1 General St Akron OH 44329

HIGGINS, ALBERT JOHN, JR., educator; b. Atchison, Kans., Nov. 7, 1933; s. Albert John and Laura Marguarite (Andre) H.; B.A., Baker U., 1955; M.S., Emporia State U., 1964; m. Virginia Helen Bundy, Aug. 19, 1962. Tchr., Lakin (Kans.) Rural High Sch., 1955-56, Central High Sch., Kansas City, Mo., 1958-59; tchr. Emporia (Kans.) Sr. High Sch., 1959—, debate coach, 1959—, drama dir., 1961-65, yearbook instr., 1963-66, coordinator sch. radio and TV instructional program, 1970—. Host, local Muscular Dystrophy Telethon, 1978—; committeeman Youth Programs of Emporia Recreation Commn., 1960—; mem. steering com. Kans. Basketball Tournament, 1965—; asst. dir. Kans. Baseball Tournament, 1975—. Republican precinct committeeman, 1972-76. Served with U.S. Army, 1956-58. Named Man of Week, Emporia Gazette, 1962. Mem. Kans. Speech Communication Assn. (rep. to acad. freedom group 1978—, named Outstanding High Sch. Speech Tchr. 1978), Emporia Nat. Edn. Assn., Nat. Forensic League (Triple Diamond Key award 1977). Congregationalist. Contbr. articles to profl. jours. Home: 1548 Sherwood Way Emporia KS 66801 Office: 3302 W 18th St Emporia KS 66801

HIGGINS, ANDREW JACKSON, state justice; b. Platte City, Mo., June 21, 1921; A.B., Central Coll., 1943; LL.B., Washington U., St. Louis, 1948; m. Laura Jo-An Brown, Oct. 30, 1948; 2 children. Admitted to Mo. Bar, 1948; practice in Platte City, 1948-60; former pros. atty. Platte County; judge Mo. Jud. Circuit 6th Dist., 1960-64; commr. Supreme Ct. Mo., 1964-79, justice, 1979—. Former Mayor Platte City; bd. curators Central Methodist Coll., from 1977; mem. nat. awards jury Freedoms Found. Valley Forge, 1976. Served with USNR, 1942-46. Recipient Dist. Alumni award Central Meth. Coll., 1973. Mem. Am. Bar Assn., Mo. Bar Assn., VFW, Alumni Assn. Central Meth. Coll. (pres. 1978), Sigma Alpha Epsilon, Delta Theta Phi. Mem. Christian Ch. (Disciples of Christ). Address: Supreme Ct Mo Supreme Ct Mo Jefferson City MO 65101*

HIGGINS, FRANCIS EDWARD, educator; b. Chgo., Nov. 29, 1935; s. Frank Edward and Mary Alyce (Fahey) H.; B.S., Loyola U., Chgo., 1959, M.A., 1964; postgrad. Exeter Coll., Oxford (Eng.) U., 1962, Am. U. Beirut, 1966, McGill U., Montreal, Que., Can., 1967; adminstrn. cert. St. Xavier Coll., 1971; Ed.D., U. Sarasota, 1977. Tchr., Washington Jr. High Sch., Chicago Heights, Ill., 1959; tchr. Chgo. Vocat. High Sch., 1960-68, dept. chmn., 1964; asst. prof. social sci. Moraine Valley Community Coll., 1968-69; tchr. history Hillcrest High Sch., Country Club Hills, Ill., 1969—; instr. nursing continuing edn. St. Francis Coll., 1978—. Mem. pres.'s council St. Xavier Coll., 1978—; mem. St. Germaine Sch. Bd., 1972-73, St. Alexander Sch. Bd., 1978-84; active Chgo. council Boy Scouts Am., 1969-77, asst. dist. commr., 1971-75, mem. dist. scout com., 1976-77. Recipient Disting. Service award Chgo. council Boy Scouts Am., 1974; Brit. Univ. scholar, 1962; Fulbright fellow, summer 1966; English Speaking Union fellow, 1967. Mem. Ill. Hist. Soc., Del. Hist. Soc., Am. Cath. Hist. Soc., Nat. Council Social Studies, Ill. Council Social Studies, Nat. Curriculum and Supervisory Assn., Ill. Supervisory Assn., Chgo. Hist. Soc., Nat. Hist. Soc., Brit. Hist. Assn., Brit. Hist. Assn., Nat. Soc. Study Edn., Phi Delta Kappa, Phi Gamma Mu. Republican. Roman Catholic. Contbr. revs. to Am. Cath. Hist. Jour., History Tchr. Jour. Home: 7660 W 131st St Palos Heights IL 60463 Office: Hillcrest High Sch 175th and Pulaski Rd Country Club Hills IL 60477

HIGGINS, MARGE, state legislator; b. Lincoln, Nebr., Aug. 3, 1931; student St. Joseph's Coll., Owensboro, Ky.; m. David Higgins, Mar. 24, 1956. Formerly with radio advt. sales staff Wall St. Jour.; advt. mgr. Daily Record; owner Higgins TV & Appliances; now owner, mgr. Howell Ins. Agy., Omaha; mem. Nebr. Legislature, 1980—. Chmn., Douglas County Democratic Com., 1974-76; past chmn. Douglas County Corrections Adv. Com.; bd. dirs. YWCA; mem. jud. nominating com. Juvenile Ct. Douglas County. Mem. Am. Legion Aux. Club: Eagles. Home: 105 N 31st Ave Omaha NE 68131 Office: 6820 J St Omaha NE 68117*

HIGGINS, NORMAN GIBSON, chem. co. exec.; b. Media, Pa., June 25, 1934; s. David Lewis and Margaret (Gibson) H.; A.B., Duke U., 1959; m. Patricia McGaughey, June 19, 1957; children—Tracy, Shawn, Whitney, David, Kerry. Examiner, Labor relations Pa. R.R., 1959-61; supr. labor relations Monsanto Co., St. Louis, 1962-65, gen. supt. personnel, 1966-69, constrn. labor relations mgr., 1970-71, personnel dir. Process Chem. div., 1972-76, mgr. employee and labor relations, 1976—; lectr. So. Ill. U., W.Va. U. Bd. dirs. Ill. Heart Assn., St. Clair County, 1967-68; pres. St. Clair County Heart Assn., 1969-70. Served with U.S. Army, 1956-58. Mem. Am. Soc. Personnel Adminstrn. (dir.), Personnel Accreditation Inst. (treas. 1980, pres. 1981). Republican. Lutheran. Home: Route 1 Box 7 Millstadt IL 62260 Office: 800 N Lindbergh Blvd Saint Louis MO 63166

HIGGS, ROLLAND BRADFORD, indsl. engr.; b. St. Louis, Oct. 7, 1912; s. Walter E. and Agnes (Gilbert) H.; cert. indsl. engr. Washington U., St. Louis, 1937; m. June 23, 1938; children—Gary Kent, Jeffrey Brent; m. 2d, Rose Brischetto Nelson, June 30, 1960; 1 stepson, Robert T. Nelson. Indsl. engr. Granite City Steel Co., 1942-48; staff asst. to store mgr. Famous-Barr Co., St. Louis; then chief indsl. engr. May Co.; pres., treas. Lady Belt Co., 1953-74; indsl. engr. Jackes-Evans Mfg. Co., St. Louis, 1978—; faculty Washington U., St. Louis. Mayor, Pasadena Park, Normandy, Mo., 1972. Mem. Soc. Advancement Mgmt. (v.p.), Am. Soc. Indsl. Engrs., Alpha Pi Mu. Roman Catholic. Home: Rt 5 Box 401-A Hillsboro MO 63050 Office: 4427 Geraldine St St Louis MO 63121

HIGH, DONALD ANDREW, chem. engr.; b. Dayton, Ohio, Sept. 4, 1918; s. Louis D. and Jessie L. (Mumma) H.; B.Chem. Engring., U. Dayton, 1942; m. Susan J. Martin, Aug. 8, 1942; children—Anne M., Katherine L., Christopher L. Assembler Inland div. Gen. Motors, Dayton, Ohio, 1936-38; with Monsanto Co., Dayton, 1945—, groupleader research, 1960-66, mgr. research, St. Peters, Mo., 1966-74, supt. mfg., 1974-76, sr. research engring. specialist, 1976-81, engring. cons., 1981—. Served to 1st lt. U.S. Army, 1942-45. Mem. Am. Chem. Soc., Am. Inst. Chem. Engring., Sigma Xi. Republican. Roman Catholic. Home: 1007 Edgeworth Ave Kirkwood MO 63122 Office: PO Box 8 St Peters MO 63776

HIGHSMITH, CAROL A., banker; b. Chgo., Nov. 12, 1952; d. Edward J. and Pearl R. (Bonk) Zmich; B.A. in Psychology, Northeastern Ill. U., 1974; postgrad. various classes Am. Inst. Banking, 1979, 80; m. Stephen W. Highsmith, Mar. 22, 1975. Universal teller Plaza-Drive-In-Bank, Chgo., 1974-75; drive-in teller Mchts. Nat. Bank, Terre Haute, Ind., 1975; cashier, sr. ops. officer 1st Nat. Bank, Crown Point, Ind., 1976—; tchr. classes on banking various high schs. Lic. probation officer, Ind. Mem. Nat. Assn. Bank Women, Phi Theta Kappa (life). Home: 1851 98th Ct Crown Point IN 46307 Office: 117 E Joliet St Crown Point IN 46307

HIGHT, RALPH DALE, physicist, educator; b. San Antonio, Mar. 6, 1945; s. Rolla Angus and Virginia (Goodrich) H.; A.S., San Antonio Jr. Coll., 1964; B.S. with honors in Chemistry and Physics, N. Tex. State U., Denton, 1967, M.S. in Physics, 1969; Ph.D. in Physics, Mont. State U., Bozeman, 1975; m. Sheila Ann Loudat, June 4, 1967; 1 son, Marc Alan. Instr. chemistry N. Tex. State U., Denton, 1965-69, instr. physics, 1969-71; NDEA fellow Mont. State U., Bozeman, 1969, instr. physics, 1971-73, research asst., 1973-75; NSF postdoctoral research fellow U. Toledo (Ohio), 1975-77; instr. physics Bowling Green (Ohio) State U., 1977—; vis. asst. prof. U. Nebr., 1977-79; with dept. research and devel. Dale Electronics, Norfolk, Nebr., 1979—; NSF summer fellow La. State U., New Orleans, 1965. Recipient regional award Chem. Rubber Co., 1964. Mem. Am. Inst. Physics, Blue Key, Sigma Pi Sigma. Contbr. articles in field to profl. jours. Home: 204 Trailridge Rd Norfolk NE 68701 Office: Dept Research and Devel Dale Electronics Norfolk NE 68701

HILBOLDT, JAMES SONNEMANN, lawyer, investment adviser; b. Dallas, July 21, 1929; s. Grover C. and Grace E. (Sonnemann) H.; A.B. in Econs., Harvard, 1952; postgrad. U. Chgo., 1952-53; J.D., U. Mich., 1956; m. Martha M. Christian, Sept. 5, 1953; children—James, Katherine Ann, Susanna Jean, Thomas Christian. With comml. banking and trust depts. No. Trust Co., Chgo., 1952-53; admitted to Mich. bar, 1957; practice law, Kalamazoo, 1957—; registered investment adviser, 1971—; dir. Bond Supply Co., Kalamazoo, 1961—, sec., 1961-80; dir. Lafourche Realty Co., Kalamazoo, 1961—, pres., 1971—; chmn., dir. LRC Oil and Gas Co., 1981—; dir. Hayes-Albion Corp., Jackson, Mich., Am. Nat. Holding Co., Am. Nat. Bank and Trust Co. Mich., Kalamazoo. Pres., Community Caucus, 1964-66; treas. Kalamazoo Civic Players, 1961-64; alumni rep. sch. and scholarships com. Harvard Coll., 1968—, area chmn. Class of 1952, Fun, 1966, permanent class com. Class of 1952, 1972—, regional dir. Asso. Harvard Alumni, 1973-76. Sec., trustee Power Found., W.P. Laughlin Charitable Found.; former pres. bd. dirs. Southwestern Mich. Tennis Patrons, Inc.; bd. dirs. Kalamazoo Tennis Patrons, Inc., 1974—; former bd. dirs., treas. Chamber Music Soc. Kalamazoo. Served with USMCR, 1946-48. Recipient Barristers award U. Mich. Law Sch., 1956. Mem. Am., Mich., Kalamazoo County bar assns., Owl Club and Hasty Pudding Inst. 1770, Barristers Soc., Phi Delta Phi. Methodist (steward 1961-64). Clubs: Kalamazoo Country, Kalamazoo Figure Skating; Harvard of Western Mich. (pres. 1972-74) (Kalamazoo and Grand Rapids). Home: 4126 Lakeside Dr Kalamazoo MI 49008 Office: American Nat Bank Bldg Kalamazoo MI 49007

HILBORN, JOHN R., ins. co. exec.; b. Oak Park, Ill., Dec. 15, 1928; s. John T. and Evelyn N. (Newcomer) H.; B.A., DePauw U., 1951; M.B.A., Northwestern U., 1956; m. Shirley S. Butcher, Dec. 22, 1950; children—James, Janet, John, Jeffrey. Vice pres., treas. Easterling Co., Wheaton, Ill., 1959-63; tax mgr. Cory Corp., Chgo., 1963-68; v.p., treas. Page Engring. Co., Chgo., 1968-74; v.p. finance and personnel Map Internat., Wheaton, Ill., 1974-77; field dir. Northwestern Mut. Ins. Co., 1977—. Pres., LaGrange Highlands Civic Assn., 1957. Served to 1st lt. USMCR, 1951-53. Home: 4446 Gilbert Ave Western Springs IL 60558 Office: 600 W Hillgrove Ave Western Springs IL 60558

HILDEBRAND, DAVID JAMES, bus. exec.; b. nr. Omro, Wis., Apr. 17, 1933; s. James Henry and Leone Veronica (Burdick) H.; student U.S. Army Electronics Sch., 1954, Internat. Corr. Sch., 1957, U. Wis., 1962; m. Verna Maliske, Nov. 8, 1952; children—Dennis D., Michele A., Jeffrey G. Farmer, Wis., 1955-57; sales rep. Am. Tobacco Co., Oshkosh, Wis., 1957-60; area field rep. Winnebago Dairy Herd Improvement Assn., Oshkosh, 1960-69; dept. mgr. Chief Equipment Corp., farm equipment, Oshkosh, 1969-71; regional sales mgr. Trojan Seed Co., Pickett, Wis., 1971-76; dist. supr. Blaney Farms, Inc., West Union, Iowa, 1976—, dist. sales mgr., 1978—; owner Hilco Mktg. Fayette, Iowa; owner Imperial Coating Products Co., Fayette; owner, gen. mgr. Hawkeye Enterprises (Iowa). Served with U.S. Army, 1953-55. Recipient Outstanding Sales Achievement award Trojan Seed Co., 1974, Blaney Seed Co., 1977. Home: 308 Volga St Fayette IA 52175 Office: 345 E Main St Hawkeye IA 52147

HILDEBRAND, JAMES KARL, foundry exec.; b. Cleve., July 5, 1936; s. Wylie George and Ione Davis (Snyder) H.; B.S. in Engring. Mgmt., Case Inst. Tech., 1958; M.B.A., U. Toledo, 1968; m. Joan Otto, Feb. 1, 1958; children—Hallie Ann, Wendy Elizabeth, Andrew James. Vice pres. mfg. Buckeye Steel Castings div. Buckeye Internat. Co., Columbus, Ohio, 1968-72; v.p. mfg. valve castings Walworth Co., Columbus, 1973-74; gen. mgr. Keencast Inc., Griffith, Ind., 1975-76; gen. mgr. castings div. Ohio Brass Co., Mansfield, from 1976, now v.p., gen. mgr. ind. prodn. div.; cons. to metal working industry. Served with USAF, 1958-61. Mem. Am. Foundrymen's Soc., Foundry Ednl. Found., Iron Castings Soc., Phi Kappa Psi. Republican. Clubs: Court, Racquet. Author: Maintenance Turns to the Computer, 1970; also articles. Home: 4726 Bayford Ct Upper Arlington OH 43220 Office: 380 N Main St Mansfield OH 44902

HILDEBRAND, JUDITH ANN, educator; b. Independence, Mo., Nov. 23, 1948; d. Frank Harlan and Nina Marie (Eidson) Jackson; B.S. in Edn., Central Mo. State U., 1969; M.Reading Edn., U. Mo., 1976; 1 dau., Julie. Tchr., North Kansas City (Mo.) Pub. Schs., 1969-74; adult basic edn. coordinator CETA Manpower, Kansas City, Mo., 1976-80; reading tchr. Kansas City (Mo.) Tech. Sch., 1980—. Lobbyist, for edn. bills, Jefferson City, 1978-79. Mem. Am. Vocat. Assn., Mo. Vocat. Assn., Nat. Employment and Tng. Assn., Mo. Manpower Tng. Assn., Nat. Assn. Vocat. Edn. Spl. Needs Personnel, Mo. Spl. Needs Personnel, Am. Fedn. Tchrs. Baptist. Office: Kansas City Tech Sch 1215 Truman St Independence MO 64106

HILDEBRANDT, BRUNO F., educator; b. Goerlitz, Germany, Sept. 26, 1926; s. Otto and Selma (Lange) H.; student Goethe U. (Frankfurt, Germany), 1958; Ph.D., U. Hamburg (Germany), 1963; m. Lieselotte M. Prochnow, Apr. 7, 1949. Came to U.S., 1963, naturalized, 1972. Various teaching positions, Germany, 1960-63; asst. prof. German, U. Colo., Boulder, 1963-65; asso. prof. German, U. Ill., Chgo., 1965-69; prof. German, U. N.D., Grand Forks, 1969—, Hill Family Found. research prof., summer 1971, also dir. grad.

studies in German; vis. asso. prof. Ind. U., Bloomington, summer 1967; vis. prof. Middlebury (Vt.) Coll., summers 1968, 69, U. Chgo., 1968, U. Minn., summer 1977; dir. German Linguistic Research Lab., U. Ill., Chgo., 1967, Exam. Center, Deutsches Sprachdiplom fuer Auslaender, Goethe-Inst., U. Ill., Chgo., 1968-69, U. N.D., 1969—. U. N.D. research grantee, 1979. Mem. Found. for Univ. Studies of German People, Midwest Modern Lang. Assn., Rocky Mountain Modern Lang. Assn., Modern Lang. Assn. Am., Am. Assn. Tchrs. German, Verein fuer Niederdeutsche Sprachforschung, Linguistic Circle Manitoba and N.D. (pres. 1978-79), Linguistic Soc. Am. Author: Experimentalphonetische Untersuchungen zur Bestimmung und Wertung der "durativen Funktion" akzentuierter Vokale, 1963; Drills in German Pronunciation, 1964; Strukturelemente der deutschen Gegenwartshochsprache: Phone und Phonaden, 1976. Contbr. numerous articles to profl. jours. Home: 916 29th Ave S Grand Forks ND 58201 Office: U ND Grand Forks ND 58202

HILDEBRANDT, LIESELOTTE MARGARETE, educator; b. Stettin, Ger., Feb. 22, 1920; d. Richard Albert and Elisabeth Maria (Pechtoldt) Prochnow; came to U.S., 1963, naturalized, 1972; M.A., U. Hamburg (Ger.), 1961; m. Bruno F.O. Hildebrandt, Apr. 7, 1949. Instr. German, U. Colo., Boulder, 1963-65, U. Ill., Chgo., 1965-69; asst. prof. German, U. N.D., Grand Forks, 1969-80, asso. prof., 1980—; instr. German, Stanford U., summers 1961, 62, 64, 65, Ind. U., summer 1967, Middlebury (Vt.) Coll., summers 1968, 69, U. Minn., summer 1977. U. N.D. faculty research grantee, 1974. Mem. AAUP, Modern Lang. Assn. Am., Am. Assn. Tchrs. German, Linguistic Circle Manitoba and N.D., Fgn. Lang. Assn. N.D., Midwest, Rocky Mountain modern lang. assns. Fgn. Lang. Assn. Red River, Delta Phi Alpha (hon.). Author: Drills in German Pronunciation, 1964; Deutsche Phonetik fuer Amerikaner, 1976. Home: 916 29th Ave S Grand Forks ND 58201 Office: U ND Grand Forks ND 58202

HILDERBRAND, HENRY MICHAEL, clergyman; b. Hackensack, N.J., Nov. 10, 1947; s. Ewing Andrew and Madeliene Marie (Chenard) H.; B.A., St. Meinrad Coll. Liberal Arts, 1969; M.A., Ind. U., 1974; M.Div., St. Meinrad Sch. Theology, 1976; M.S. in Edn., Ind. U., 1976. Ordained priest Roman Catholic Ch., 1976; secondary tchr. social studies Latin Sch. Indpls., 1972-76; secondary tchr., chmn. dept. theology Our Lady of Providence High Sch., Clarksville, Ind., 1976—; adminstr. parish St. Joe Hill, Sellersburg, Ind., 1981; chaplain Camp Rancho Framasa, Nashville, 1977-81. Mem. Nat. Cath. Ednl. Assn., Am. Hist. Assn. Roman Catholic. Home: 1752 Scheller Ln New Albany IN 47150 Office: 707 W Hwy 131 Clarksville IN 47130

HILE, BARRY LEWIS, power tool co. exec.; b. Kendallville, Ind., July 14, 1947; s. Paul Erwin and Mary Elizabeth (Haid) H.; B.S. in B.A., Wright State U., 1970; m. Cylinda S. Clary, July 27, 1973; children—Todd, Heather. With NCR Corp., Dayton, Ohio, 1970-73; dir. mktg. Paramount Internat. Coin Corp., Englewood, Ohio, 1973-79; v.p., dir. mktg. Shopsmith, Inc., Vandalia, Ohio, 1979—; adj. asso. prof. mktg. Wright State U., 1980—; mem. mktg. adv. council Edison State Coll., Piqua, Ohio; lectr. in field. Mem. Direct Mail Mktg. Assn., Direct Mail Mktg. Assn. Ednl. Found., Direct Mail Mktg. Assn. Catalog Council. Home: 546 Elm Grove Dr Dayton OH 45415 Office: 750 Center Dr Vandalia OH 45377

HILE, DUANE LEWIS, mgmt. cons.; b. Findlay, Ohio, June 18, 1945; s. Dwight L. and Janice M. (Browne) H.; A.B., Wabash Coll., 1967; M.B.A. with high honors, U. Notre Dame, 1973; m. Mary Ann Rummel, Aug. 1, 1970; children—David Christopher, Kathryn Anne, Suzanne Alexis. Mktg. rep. Am. Oil Co., Detroit, 1967-68, South Bend, Ind., 1968-69; terr. mgr. Jessup Door Co. div. AJ Industries, Dowagiac, Mich., 1969-70, gen. sales mgr., 1970-71; asso. A.T. Kearney, Inc., Cleve., London, Eng., 1973-76, mgr., Chgo., 1976-78; dir. Duane L. Hile & Assos., Cleve., 1978—. Methodist. Home: 2559 Fenwick Rd University Heights OH 44118

HILER, JOHN PATRICK, Congressman; b. Chgo., Apr. 24, 1953; s. Robert J. and Fran Hiler; B.A., Williams Coll., 1975; M.B.A., U. Chgo., 1977. Mktg. dir. Charles O. Hiler and Son, Inc., also Accurate Castings, Inc., La Porte, Ind., 1977-81; mem. 97th Congress from 3d Dist. of Ind. Del., Ind. Republican Conv., 1978, 80; chmn. La Porte Rep. City Com., 1979; del. White House Conf. on Small Bus., 1980; trustee La Lumiere Sch., La Porte. Mem. La Porte C. of C. Roman Catholic. Office: River Glen Office Plaza 501 E Monroe St Room 120 South Bend IN 46601 also 1338 Longworth House Office Bldg Washington DC 20515

HILKERT, REBECCA JANE, telecommunications co. market research supr.; b. Akron, Ohio, Sept. 20, 1953; d. William Albert and Mary Louise (Ahern) H.; student Miami U., Oxford, Ohio, 1971-74; B.A. in Polit. Sci., U. Akron, 1975; M.A. in Econs., 1977. Grad. research asst. U. Akron, 1976-77; with GTE Service Corp., Stamford, Conn., 1977-78, Indpls., 1979—, regional adminstr. market research, 1979-80, regional supr. market research, 1980—; budget projects adminstr. Gen. Telephone Co. Ohio, Marion, 1978-79. Mem. Econs. Club Indpls. Roman Catholic. Research on zero based budgeting. Home: 215 Fox Circle E Noblesville IN 46060 Office: PO Box 407 Westfield IN 46074

HILL, ANN OUGRITA, market research and campaign cons. co. exec.; b. Johnson City, Tenn., Aug. 12, 1946; d. Edward and Mable Jean (Little) H.; B.S., magna cum laude, East Tenn. State U., 1966; M.A. in Journalism, Ohio State U., 1971. Polit., ednl. and regional devel. reporter, various newspapers, Tenn., Ill., Ohio, 1967-73; lobbyist Ohio AFL-CIO, Columbus, 1976-78; pres. Hill & Zoog, Columbus, 1978—. Active Democratic Party, labor movement. Recipient numerous design and writing awards, including Mead award Ohio State U. Community, 1979; Columbus Found. research grantee, 1976-77. Mem. Am. Fedn. Tchrs., Columbus Advt. Fedn., Columbus Soc. Community Arts, Columbus Area Women's Polit. Caucus, NOW, Ohio Women's Polit. Caucus, Nat. Women's Polit. Caucus, Coalition Labor Union Women, Loose Umbrella Network Assn. Author: Appalachian Culture: A Guide for Students and Teachers, 1976. Home: 777 City Park Ave Columbus OH 43206 Office: 1654 E Broad St Columbus OH 43203

HILL, CARL HENRY, data processor, systems cons.; b. Splunge, Miss., Oct. 21, 1918; s. Charles W. and Pearl (Palmer) H.; B.S. in Bus., Northwestern U., 1947; certificate Data Processing Mgmt. Assn., 1956. Vice pres. Nat. Bus. Lists, Chgo., 1960; systems and procedures U. Chgo. Hosps., 1962-74; partner Car-Wal Enterprises, Chgo., 1968-79; v.p. Harley L. Ward, Inc.; pres. Viscose, Inc.; v.p. Gallery Yolanda. Served with AUS, 1942-46. Home and office: 3712 W Montrose Chicago IL 60618

HILL, DRAPER, editorial cartoonist; b. Boston, July 1, 1935; s. L. Draper and Jean (Thompson) H.; B.A. magna cum laude, Harvard, 1957; postgrad. Slade Sch. Fine Arts, Univ. Coll., London, Eng., 1960-63; m. Sarah Randolph Adams, Apr. 22, 1967; children—Jennifer Randolph, Jonathan Draper. Reporter, cartoonist Quincy (Mass.) Patriot Ledger, 1957-60; editorial cartoonist Worcester (Mass.) Telegram, 1964-71, Comml. Appeal, 1971-76, Detroit News, 1976—. Bd. dirs. Play of the Month Guild, N.Y.C., 1958—; instr. drawing Worcester Art Sch., 1967-71; one man shows, Germantown Tenn., 1973, Brooks Meml. Art Gallery, Memphis, 1975. Mem. Assn. Am. Editorial Cartoonists (pres. 1975-76), Club: Odd Vols. Author: Mr. Gillray, The Caricaturist, 1965; Fashionable Contrasts, 1966; The Satirical Etchings of James Gillray, 1976; (with James Roper) The Decline and Fall of the Gibbon, 1974. Home: 368 Washington Rd Grosse Pointe MI 48230 Office: 615 W Lafayette Blvd Detroit MI 48231

HILL, HENRY DAVID, real estate co. exec.; b. Fillmore, Ill., Dec. 27, 1933; s. Jesse J. and Lydia H.; B.S. in Fin., U. Ill., 1961; M.S. in Taxation, DePaul U., 1976. Sr. internal auditor Union Tank Car Co., Chgo., 1961-68; asst. mgr. taxes Deltec Internat., Ltd., Chgo., 1968-71; asst. mgr. taxes Santa Fe Industries, Inc., Chgo., 1971-72, asst. to pres., 1978-79; controller Santa Fe Land Improvement Co., Chgo., 1972-78, v.p., 1979—. Served with USAF, 1954-58. Mem. Nat. Assn. Realtors. Office: 224 S Michigan Ave Chicago IL 60604

HILL, JAMES HARRY, educator; b. Buffalo Center, Iowa, Oct. 1, 1954; s. James Kenneth and Joan Margaret (Forsyth) H.; B.S. in Agrl. Edn., Iowa State U., 1977; m. Debra Marie Movick, June 16, 1978. Tchr. vocat. agr. Sentral High Sch., Fenton, Iowa, 1977-81; dir. Coop. Extension Office Hancock County, Garner, Iowa, 1981—. Adv., Sentral chpt. Future Farmers Am., 1977-81; chmn. Fenton Sweetcorn Days Parade, 1978-80. Named hon. farmer Sentral chpt. Future Farmers Am. Mem. NEA, Iowa Edn. Assn., Sentral Edn. Assn. (v.p. 1980-81, chief negotiator 1980-81, grievance chmn. 1980-81), Nat. Assn. County Agrl. Agts., Nat. Vocat. Agr. Tchrs. Assn., Iowa Vocat. Agr. Tchrs. Assn. (subdist. sec. 1978-79), Iowa State U. Extension Assn., Garner Jaycees. Club: Garner Lions. Democrat. Methodist. Active community improvements. Office: Coop Extension Office 110 E 8th St Garner IA 50438

HILL, JOHN THOMAS, plumbing and heating contractor; b. Richmond, Ind., Mar. 25, 1941; s. John T. and Norma Jean Hill; B.S. with honors, Tri-State Coll., 1964; m. Taraneh Monhandes, Dec. 16, 1961; children—Dean Ali, Tina Laleh, John Taymoor. Pres., Hill Bros. Plumbing & Heating Inc., Richmond, 1976—; pres., Tom Hill, Mech. Contractor, Richmond, 1972—; mem. faculty Richmond Vocat. Trade Sch., 1973—; football coach Richmond City Jr. High Sch., 1975-77. Mem. fundraising com. Football Hall of Fame; bd. dirs. Richmond YMCA, 1978—; plumbing examiner City of Richmond, 1967-69. Recipient Beautification award City of Richmond, 1975. Mem. Ind. Subcontactors Assn. (pres. 1978—), Plumbing and Heating Contractors Ind., Mech. Contractors Ind., Richmond C. of C. Methodist. Clubs: Elks Country, Masons. Office: Hill Bros Plumbing & Heating Inc 600 NW 2d St Richmond IN 47374

HILL, JOSEPH PAUL, JR., electronics engr.; b. Chattanooga, Apr. 23, 1948; s. Joseph Paul and Frances R. H.; student Franklin U., 1968-71. Engr., Hill Labs., Westerville, Ohio, 1974-81; with Internat. Research and Devel.-Mechanalysis, Secunda, S. Africa plant, 1981—. Mem. Ohio Ry. Mus., Assn. R.R. Passengers. Club: Central Railfans. Home and Office: 1111 Belle Meade Pl Westerville OH 43081

HILL, KEARNEY H.J., educator; b. Pawnee, Okla., Apr. 11, 1933; s. Kearney H. and Bernice (Rengle) H.; A.Sci., Okla. State U., 1963, B.S., 1965; M.S., Kans. State U., 1972; m. Rita M. Karleskint, Aug. 23, 1958. Jr. research engr. Seismograph Service, Tulsa, 1955-56; service mgr., asst. to chief inspector Aerotron Radio Corp., Tulsa, 1956-61; head Instrument div. Quality Control Dept., Midwestern Instruments, Tulsa, 1961; pres. Tultech Electronics Labs., Pawnee, Okla., 1961-65; instr. electronics and math. Classen High Sch., Oklahoma City, 1965-66; electronics instr. Oklahoma City Area Vocat.-Tech. Sch., 1966-67; prof., head dept. computer tech. dept., Kans. Tech. Inst., Salina, 1967-79, dir. Computer Center, 1967-80; asso. prof. data processing, bus. edn. dept. Emporia (Kans.) State U., 1980—; cons. to CompuServ, Salina, Kans., 1969—. Adviser computer merit badge Boy Scouts Am., Salina, 1972-74. Mem. Data Processing Mgmt. Assn. (chpt. v.p. 1969-70), Am. Soc. Engring. Edn., Assn. for Computer Machinery, Instrument Soc. Am., IEEE, Assn. Ednl. Data Systems (chpt. pres.-elect 1977-78, pres. 1978-79, dir. 1980-84), Phi Delta Kappa, Sigma Tau. Contbr. articles to profl. jours. Home: 1027 Whittier Emporia KS 66801

HILL, KENNETH MURRAY, mfg. co. exec.; b. Holland, Mich., Sept. 27, 1940; s. Murray S. and Dorothy (Aalderink) H.; student Grand Rapids Jr. Coll., 1964-69; student Mich. State U., 1976-77; grad. Maynard Mgmt. Inst., 1979; m. Emilie Waganmaker, June 2, 1971; children—Thomas Lee Phillips, Wanda Marie Phillips, Debra Eunice, Susan Ruth Phillips, Gregory M., James Michael, Matthew K. Dealer, mgr. Clark Oil & Refining Co., Holland, 1959-61; supr. Gen. Electric, Holland, 1959-61, Emco Tool & Die, Holland, 1970-73; with Haworth Mfg., Inc., Holland, 1973—, plant mgr., 1977—. Scoutmaster, Boy Scouts Am., Holland, 1962-65; mgr. Am. Legion Baseball, 1963-68, Rocket Football, 1964-67. Mem. Am. Mgmt. Assn., Soc. Mfg. Engrs., Am. Prodn. Inventory Control Soc. Club: Ottawa Sno-Dusters. Home: 612 Wedgewood Dr Holland MI 49423 Office: 545 E 32d St Holland MI 49423

HILL, LEWIS WARREN, transp. authority ofcl., Chgo.; b. Ft. Worth, Feb. 25, 1926; s. Alvin Carnes and Constance (Lewis) H.; B.A. in Math., U. Minn., 1946; B.S. in Design, Ill. Inst. Tech., 1951; LL.D. (hon.), Loyola U., 1977; m. Dorothy Mae Hey, Sept. 11, 1954; children—Mary Lew, Martha, Katherine, Thomas, David, Sara. Various supervisory positions Chgo. Land Clearance Commn., Community Conservation Bd., Chgo. Dept. Urban Renewal, 1951-65; chmn., commr. Chgo. Dept. Urban Renewal, 1965-78, commr. Dept. Devel. and Planning, 1967-78; chmn. Comml. Dist. Devel. Commn., 1976-78, Regional Transp. Authority, 1978—; lectr. Loyola U., 1964-70. Mem. Northeastern Ill. Planning Commn., Ill.-Ind. Bi-State Planning Commn., Chgo.-Cook County Criminal Justice Commn. Mem. Nat. Assn. Housing and Redevel. Ofcls., Am. Inst. Planners, Western Soc. Engrs., Lambda Alpha. Clubs: Econ., Svith Old, Tavern. Home: 5858 N Kenton St Chicago IL 60646 Office: 300 N State St Chicago IL 60610

HILL, LINDA SUE, social worker; b. Breckenridge, Tex., Jan. 4, 1950; d. John Whitman and Carolina Floella (Elkins) H.; B.A., Tarleton State U., 1971, M.A., 1972; M.S.W., U. Tex., Arlington, 1978; postgrad. U. Mich., Ann Arbor, 1980—. With Tex. Dept. Human Resources, various cities, 1973-80; social sci. rep. Rackham Student Govt. Council, U. Mich., 1981—. Mem. Nat. Assn. Social Workers, Acad. Cert. Social Workers, Am. Polit. Sci. Assn., Gamma Sigma Sigma. Democrat. Baptist. Home: 520 N Ashley St Apt 4 Ann Arbor MI 48103 Office: Sch Social Work U Mich 2078 Frieze Bldg Ann Arbor MI 48109

HILL, LLOYD RHEA, ins. co. exec.; b. Memphis, July 25, 1940; s. Thomas Bruce and Pauline (Michie) H.; B.A. in Polit. Sci., Miss. State U., 1962; m. Trudy Cress, Sept. 18, 1976; children—Thomas Alton, Paul Jackson, Margaret Rhea. Public relations dir. Athens (Ala.) Coll., 1963-64, The Birmingham (Ala.) News, 1964-66, Operation New Birmingham, 1966-68; dir. public relations Office of Vice Pres. U.S., Washington, 1968-69; v.p. Statesman-Vulcan Life Ins. Co., Des Moines, 1969—. Bd. dirs. Birmingham Mayor's Council for Youth Opportunities, 1967-68; mem. Urbandale (Iowa) Park and Recreation Commn., 1979—. Democrat. Roman Catholic. Home: 8317 Twana Dr Urbandale IA 50322 Office: 1400 Des Moines Bldg Des Moines IA 50309

HILL, MARILYN JEAN, sociologist; b. Oshkosh, Wis., June 26, 1929; d. Kenneth Leonard and Grace Evelyn (Jones) Thompson; B.A., Carroll. Coll., 1951; M.A., Marquette U., 1973; Bush Leadership fellow, U. Minn., 1977; m. Richard E. Hill, June 5, 1951; children—Mark R., Kenneth L., Richard E., Joy A., Sarah J. Dir. Indian tutoring program U. Wis., Stevens Point, 1966-69, developer Pride Upward Bound program, 1967-69; instr. sociology Concordia Coll., Milw., 1973-74; asst. prof. sociology Huron (S.D.) Coll., 1974-77; social impact analyst Donohue & Assos., Inc., 1978-79; govtl. liaison coordinator Donohue & Assos., Inc., Sheboygan, Wis., 1979—. Mem. Gov.'s Task Force for Evaluation of Wis. Dept. Natural Resources, 1979; speaker S.D. Humanities Program, 1974-76. Mem. Am. Socio. Assn., AAUW. Republican. Presbyterian. Club: P.E.O. Home: Lakeland College PO Box 359 Sheboygan WI 53081 Office: 4738 N 40th St Sheboygan WI 53081

HILL, MARION PHYLLIS, social worker; b. Lawrenceville, Va., Sept. 21, 1928; d. Vernon Algie and Harriet Ann (Rhodes) Jones; B.A., Hampton (Va.) Inst., 1948; postgrad. Atlanta U., 1948-49; M.S.W., U. Mich., 1964, cert. Inst. Gerontology, 1981; m. Walter W. Hill, Dec. 31, 1950; children—Walter W., Patricia Francine. Child welfare worker Bur. Social Services, Richmond, Va., 1949-50; sr. child placement worker dept. public welfare City of Chgo., 1951-54; nursery sch. dir. Neighborhood House Assn., Buffalo, 1960-61; clin. social worker Med. Center, U. Mich., Ann Arbor, 1964-75, sr. social worker, 1975—, field instr. social work, 1968—, social work supr., 1979—. Mem. City of Ann Arbor Recreation Bd., 1964-70, City of Ann Arbor Housing Commn., 1977—, v.p., 1979-80, mem. exec. com. Community Devel. Block Grants, 1978—. Mem. NAACP (corr. sec. 1976—), Nat. Assn. Negro Bus. and Profl. Women (founder, pres. Ann Arbor chpt. 1976-78, chmn. nat. bd. health task force 1980—), Nat. Assn. Social Workers, Acad. Cert. Social Workers, Nat. Conf. Social Welfare, Am. Burn Assn., Phi Kappa Phi, Alpha Kappa Alpha. Episcopalian. Home: 701 Sunset Rd Ann Arbor MI 48103 Office: U Mich Medical Center 1405 E Ann St Ann Arbor MI 48108

HILL, PAMELA ELLEN, psychologist, educator; b. Chgo., June 28, 1953; d. David Willis and Joan Marie (Payne) H.; B.S. in Psychology, Western Ill. U., 1974; M.Ed. in Counseling and Guidance, Loyola U., 1975; M.S. in Mktg. Communications, Roosevelt U., 1978. Family planning counselor Friendship Med. Center, Chgo., 1975; lectr. psychology Chgo. State U., Chgo., 1975—; instr. psychology Moraine Valley Community Coll., Palos Hills, Ill., from 1975; research asst. Consumer Analyst, Chgo., 1977—; clin. therapist Chgo. Div. Mental Health; cons. in field. Bd. dirs. Far South Mental Health Council. Mem. Alpha Kappa Alpha (treas. Macomb, Ill. 1973). Democrat. Roman Catholic. Home: 1081 W 108th St Chicago IL 60643 Office: Chgo Alcoholic Treatment Center 3026 S California Chicago IL 60608 Ave Palos Hills IL 60465

HILL, RUANE BURTON, educator; b. Mondovi, Wis., May 27, 1924; s. Laurence Burton and Velma (Butler) H.; A.B., Beloit Coll., 1948; M.A., Northwestern U., 1949, Ph.D., 1964; m. Marie J. Bergerson, Sept. 3, 1949; children—Gregory, Kristin, Kristofer. Asst. prof. Willamette U., Salem, Oreg., 1949-51; grad. fellow Sch. Speech, Northwestern U., 1951-52; asst. prof. speech Beloit Coll., 1952-55; gen. mgr. Sta. WFGM, Fitchburg, Mass. and Sta. WMCR, Milford, Mass., 1955-58; asst. prof., gen. mgr. Sta. WAER, Syracuse, U., 1958-63; prof. mass communications U. Wis., Milw., 1973-76, chmn. dept., 1970-73, 79—, gen. mgr. Sta. WUWM, 1963-76; mem. faculty U. Mass. extension, 1956-58; mem. Milw. Radio and TV Council, 1963-67. Active ARC, Milw., 1973—; mem. Greater Milw. Conf. on Religion and Urban Affairs, 1968—, chmn., 1970-74, 79-81; project dir. Corp. Public Broadcasting, Johnson Found., Radio-TV Internat., 1970-76, Nat. Endowment for Humanities, 1978-79. Served with USAAF, 1943-46. Mem. Nat. Assn. Ednl. Broadcasters (dir. exec. bd. 1973-74), Nat. Ednl. Radio, Assn. Public Radio Stas., Broadcast Edn. Assn., Milw. Adult Assn., Milw. Press Club, Milw. Area Broadcast News Assn. (exec. dir. 1969-75), Wis. Broadcasters Assn. (dir., sec. 1965-76). Editor: (with A. E. Koenig) The Farther Vision: ETV Today, 1967, Spanish edit., 1969, Arabic edit., 1975; moderator TV show Innerview, MTMJ-TV, 1970-79.

HILL, STEVEN PHILLIPS, educator; b. Estherville, Iowa, Apr. 25, 1936; s. Charles Kelley and Mary Ola (Phillips) H.; B.A., Stanford U., 1957; M.A. (Univ. fellow), U. Mich., 1958, Ph.D., 1965. Teaching asst. in Russian, U. Mich., Ann Arbor, 1959-61; instr. U. Ill., Urbana, 1961-65, asst. prof., 1965-69, asso. prof. dept. Slavic langs. and lits., 1969—. U. Ill. Travel grantee, 1965, 68, 76. Mem. Am. Assn. Tchrs. Slavic and East European Langs., Soc. Cinema Studies, Univ. Film Assn., Phi Beta Kappa. Author: The "N" Factor and Russian Prepositions, 1977; translator: (films) End of St. Petersburg, 1975, Earth, 1976; contbr. articles to profl. publs. Home: 506 W California Ave Urbana IL 61801 Office: Slavic Dept 3092 Foreign Languages Bldg Univ Ill 707 S Mathews St Urbana IL 61801

HILL, W. CLAYTON, mgmt. cons.; b. New Hampton, Mo., Sept. 24, 1916; s. Charles A. and Elva E. (Riggins) H.; B.S. in Bus. Adminstrn., U. Mo., 1937; m. Dorothy L. Crosby, Aug. 24, 1938; children—Charles W., Douglas L. Acct., Gen. Elec. Co., Bridgeport, Conn., 1937-41; sales mgmt. IBM Corp., 1941-50; asst. to pres. Gen. Elec. X-Ray Corp., Milw., 1950-53; v.p. Hotpoint Co. div. Gen. Elec. Co., Chgo., 1953-57; cons., mgr. planning Gen. Elec. Co., N.Y.C., 1957-62; dir. planning Am. Can Co., 1962-64; mgmt. cons. C. Hill Assos., Greenwich, Conn., 1964-80, Prairie Village, Kans., 1980—; instr. Marquette U., 1950-53; cons. RCA Corp., Sperry Co., Ford Motor Co., Pet, Inc., Gen. Elec. Co., Monsanto Co., H&R Block, Inc., Farmland Industries, Inc., United Telecommunications, Inc., others. Pres. King Merritt Community, Inc. Served with Signal Corps, AUS, 1943-46. Decorated Army Commendation Medal. Mem. Am. Mktg. Assn., Nat. Assn. Accts., Sales Exec. Club N.Y.C. Office: 8713 Catalina Dr Prairie Village KS 66207

HILLIARD, ROBERT JOHN, bakery co. exec.; b. Chgo., Nov. 10, 1924; s. Robert John and Agnes (Kelleher) H.; B.S., Northwestern U., 1948, J.D., 1951; postgrad. advanced mgmt. Harvard, 1959; m. Rita Marie Uchison; children by previous marriage—Janet, Joann, Robert, Richard. Admitted to Ill. bar; with Am. Bakeries Co., Chgo., 1953—, dir. indsl. relations, 1961-63, v.p. indsl. relations, 1963-68, pres., 1968-70, sr. v.p. indsl. relations, 1970—, dir., 1966—; dir. Gray & Co., Pilgrim Farms, Monarch Egg Co., Westnut Corp., Langendorf United Bakeries, A-Media, Am. Bakeries Domincana. Sec. Wheat and Wheat Foods Found. Trustee Bakery and Confectionery Union and Industry Internat. Pension Fund, Retail, Wholesale and Dept. Store Union Industry Pension Fund, St. Joseph's Hosp. Found.; bd. dirs. Am. Inst. Baking. Served with AUS, 1943-46. Decorated Combat Infantryman's Badge. Mem. Am. Bakers Assn. (gov.), Am., Ill. Chgo. bar assns. Home: 19 W 186 Old Tavern Rd E Oak Brook IL 60521 Office: 10 S Riverside Plaza Chicago IL 60606

HILLIARD, STANLEY EARL, statis. cons.; b. Washington, Mar. 12, 1936; s. Philip Carter and Eileen Jane (Killmon) H.; B.Chem.Engring., U. Minn., 1960; m. Barbara Ann Bicknell, Mar. 19, 1960; children—Amy Jo, Gregory Claude. Process engr. Allied

Chem. Corp., Wilmington, Del., 1960-63; prodn. chem. engr., Pottsville, Pa., 1963-64; product devel. engr. 3M Co., St. Paul, 1964-66, math./stats. analyst, 1966-70, sr. math./stats. analyst, 1970-74, systems specialist, 1974-78, tech. specialist, 1978—; instr. stats. in quality control St. Paul Tech./Vocat. Inst., 1968—. Registered profl. engr., Calif. Mem. Am. Soc. for Quality Control (cert. quality engr.), Am. Statis. Assn. Editor, Random Sampler, 1969-70; author articles on sampling plans for process and quality control. Home: 2668 N 2nd St North Saint Paul MN 55109 Office: IS & DP Statis Cons Dept 3M Center Saint Paul MN 55144

HILLIARD, THOMAS JOHN, pharm. co. exec.; b. Mpls., June 4, 1936; s. John Clyde and Francis Abby (Wicklander) H.; B.S. in Bus. Adminstrn., Macalester Coll., 1960; m. Judith Lynne Beale, Aug. 26, 1961; children—John Beale, David Thomas. Trainee, Upjohn Co., Mpls., 1960-62, supr., Phila., 1962-65, Chgo., 1965-69, mgr., Mpls., 1969-72, N.Y.C., 1972-74, Kansas City, Mo., 1974-77, regional mgr., 1977—. Served with Army N.G., 1953-61. Recipient The Upjohn award, 1971. Mem. Am. Mgmt. Assn., Nat. Assn. Credit Mgmt. Republican. Lutheran. Home: 10007 W 70th Ter Merriam KS 66203 Office: 6655 Troost St Kansas City MO 64131

HILLIS, ELWOOD HAYNES, congressman; b. Kokomo, Ind., Mar. 6, 1926; s. Glen R. and Bernice (Haynes) H.; B.S., Ind. U., 1949, J.D., 1952; m. Carol Hoyne, June 12, 1949; children—Jeffrey H., Gary L., Bradley R. Admitted to Ind. bar, 1952; mem. Ind. Ho. of Reps., 1967-69; mem. 91st to 97th Congresses from 5th Ind. Dist. Pres. Elwood Haynes Meml. Charitable Trust; Howard County United Fund, 1969. Served with USAAF, 1944-46; ETO. Mem. Am., Ind., Howard County (past pres.) bar assns., Am. Legion, VFW. Presbyterian. Clubs: Rotary, Elks, Masons, Shriners. Office: 2336 Rayburn House Office Bldg Washington DC 20515*

HILLMAN, CHARLENE HAMILTON, public relations exec.; b. Akron, Ohio; d. Charles E. and Maeton (Anderson) Hamilton; ed. Youngstown Coll., 1940-41, Ind. U. Extension, 1949, 50; 1 son, Robert E. Sales promotion and secretarial work nitrogen div. Allied Chem. Corp., Indpls., 1955-59; mem. Bob Long Assos., Indpls., 1959-62; public relations dir. Paul Lennon Advt. Agy., Indpls., 1962-63, Clowes Meml. Hall of Butler U., 1963-64; pub. relations counselor Charlene Hillman Pub. Relations Assos., Indpls., 1964-75; v.p., dir. pub. relations Caldwell-Van Riper, Inc., Indpls., 1975—. Mem. Indpls. Mayor's Communications Task Force, 1968-71. Mem. Pub. Relations Soc. Am. (pres. Hoosier chpt. 1967, 72-73, dist. chmn., nat. dir. 1975-76), Advt. Club Indpls. (Advt. Woman of Year 1969, dir.), Women in Communications, Indpls. Public Relations Soc., Ind. Soc. Assn. Execs. Club: Indpls. Press. Editor: Mayflower Warehouseman, 1965-66, Hoosier Ind., 1966—. Office: 1314 N Meridian St Indianapolis IN 46202

HILLMAN, MELVILLE ERNEST DOUGLAS, chemist; b. Winnipeg, Man., Can., Aug. 3, 1926; came to U.S., 1954, naturalized, 1976; s. Frank Ernest and Elizabeth (Grindlay) Hillman; B.A. with honors, U. B.C., 1952, M.Sc., 1954; Ph.D., Ohio State U., 1958; m. Marion Louise Pettingill, Nov. 22, 1974; stepchildren—Robert F. James, Deborah L. Wasylak, Lorraine Maillot. Research chemist E.I. DuPont de Nemours and Co., Wilmington, Del., 1958-61; research chemist Chevron Research, Richmond, Calif., 1961-64; research supr. W.R. Grace Co., Columbia, Md., 1964-68; group leader Celanese Research Co., Summit, N.J., 1968-71; program leader Ethicon, Inc., Somerville, N.J., 1971-73; prin. research scientist Battelle Columbus Labs. (Ohio), 1973-75, sr. research scientist, 1975-79, research leader, 1979—; cons. in field. Socony-Mobil fellow, 1955-56, Lubrizol fellow, 1956-57, DuPont fellow, 1957-58. Mem. Am. Chem. Soc., N.Y. Acad. Scis., N.Y. Catalyst Soc., Sigma Xi, Phi Lambda Upsilon. Baptist. Contbr. articles to profl. jours.; patentee in field. Home: 3317 Darbyshire Dr Columbus OH 43220 Office: 505 King Ave Columbus OH 43201

HILLMAN, STANLEY ERIC GORDON, diversified holding co. exec.; b. London, Eng., Oct. 13, 1911; s. Percy Thomas and Margaret Eleanor Fanny (Lee) H.; ed. Holyrood Sch., also Tonbridge Sch., Eng.; m. May Irene Noon, May 2, 1947; children—Susan Ann, Deborah Ann, Katherine Ann. Came to U.S., 1951, naturalized, 1957. With British-Am. Tobacco Co., Ltd., London and Shanghai, 1933-47; dir. Hillman & Co., Ltd., Cosmos Trading Co., FED Inc., U.S.A., Airmotive Supplies Co. Ltd., Hong Kong, 1947-52; v.p. Gen. Dynamics Corp., 1953-61; v.p., group exec. Am. Machine & Foundry Co., 1962-65; v.p., dir. Gen. Am. Transp. Corp., 1965-67; vice chmn., pres., dir. IC Industries, 1968-78; chmn., chief exec. officer Ill. Central Gulf R.R., 1976-78; bankruptcy trustee Chgo., Milw., St. Paul R.R., 1978-79; dir. Stone Container Corp., SFN Cos., Bandag Corp., Cooper Industries, Inc., Avco Corp., Bell & Howell Co., Bliss & Laughlin, Consol. Rail Corp.; trustee Gen. Growth Properties. Clubs: Mid-Am., Chicago, Onwentsia, Royal Poinciana. Home: 1001 Hawthorne Pl Lake Forest IL 60045

HILLSMAN, WILLIAM GERARD, communications co. exec.; b. Evanston, Ill., Aug. 14, 1953; s. William Gerard H.; B.A., Carleton Coll., 1975; M.S.J., Northwestern U., 1976. Sr. writer Waldbillig & Besteman Advt., Madison, Wis., 1976-80; copy chief J. Patrick Moore Advt., Mpls., 1980; asso. creative dir. J. MacLachlan & Assos., Wayzata, Minn., 1980; copywriter Bozell & Jacobs, Mpls., 1980—; lectr. in field. Scripps Howard grantee, 1976; recipient United Way of Am. Nat. Communications award, 1977; Am. Cancer Soc. Communications Vol. award, 1980. Mem. Am. Advt. Fedn. (recipient numerous Addy awards), Art Dirs. and Copywriters Club. Home: 2401 Sheridan Ave S Minneapolis MN 55405 Office: Butler Square 100 N 6th St Minneapolis MN 55403

HILLSTROM, DANIEL MICHAEL, retail co. exec.; b. Fargo, N.D., Dec. 6, 1954; s. Paul Victor and Dorothy Marilyn Joyce (Reitan) H.; B.A., Moorhead State U., 1978. With Ind. News Agy., Moorhead, 1974-81, Fargo, 1981—, gen. mgr., 1978—, mgr. bookstores, 1978—. Mem. Moorhead State U. Alumni Assn., Red River Sci. Fiction and Fantasy Club. Home: 1620 7th St S Moorhead MN 56560 Office: FM News KMart Plaza Fargo ND 58102

HILLYER, CRAIG ALLEN, savs. and loan exec.; b. Hendricks, Minn., Dec. 13, 1937; s. Clifford L. and Beatrice R. (Macknikowski) H.; B.S. in Fin., U. Notre Dame, 1959; M.B.A., U. Ariz., 1964; m. Barbara A. Lasiewicz, Aug. 18, 1968; children—Mark C., Audrey A. Exec. v.p. Brookings Internat. Life Ins. Co. (S.D.), 1959-69; analyst Bankers Life & Casualty Co., Chgo., 1969-71; v.p. Montgomery Ward Life Ins. Co., Chgo., 1971-76; pres. DGP, Inc., Brookings, 1976—, dir., 1971—; pres. Home Trust Savs. & Loan Assn., Vermillion, S.D., 1979—, dir., 1978—. Pres., Brookings United Fund, 1965-67. Served to 1st lt., Transp. Corps, AUS, 1962-63. Mem. Am. Contract Bridge League (dir.). Roman Catholic. Clubs: Rotary, Elks (treas. 1967-69), K.C. Office: 700 22d Ave S Brookings SD 57006

HILPERT, BRUNETTE KATHLEEN POWERS (MRS. ELMER ERNEST HILPERT), civic worker; b. Baton Rouge; d. Edward Oliver and Orvilla (Nettles) Powers; A.B., La. State U., 1930, B.S. in L.S., 1933; postgrad. Columbia, 1937; m. Elmer Ernest Hilpert, Aug. 1, 1938; children—Margaret Ray, Elmer Ernest II (dec.). Cataloguer, La. State U. Library, Baton Rouge, 1930-36, La. State U. Law Sch. Library, 1936-38; librarian Washington U. Law Sch. Library, St. Louis, 1940-42; reference librarian Washington U. Library, 1952-54; mem. women's adv. bd. Continental Bank & Trust Co., 1970-80. Drive capt. United Fund, St. Louis, 1956; del. White House Conf. on Edn., St. Louis, 1962, White House Conf. on Domestic and Econ. Affairs, 1975. Trustee John Burroughs Sch., 1959-63; bd. dirs. Grace Hill Settlement House, 1957-63, v.p., 1960-62; bd. dirs. Internat. Inst., 1964-68; exec. com., bd. dirs. Arts and Edn. Council, 1967—; bd. dirs. Miss. River Festival, 1969-75, Community Music Sch., 1972-74, Community Assn. Schs. for Arts, 1974-77, Artist Presentation Soc., 1974-77, Little Symphony Concerts Assn., 1975-78; exec. com., bd. dirs. Dance Concert Soc., 1977-80, St. Louis Conservatory and Schs. for Arts, 1977—; bd. dirs. St. Louis String Quartet, 1971-77, pres., 1975-79; bd. dirs. Neighborhood Health Center, 1964-67, sec., 1964-66; pres. Womens Assn. St. Louis Symphony Soc., 1969-71, dir., 1957—; exec. com., bd. dirs. St. Louis Symphony Soc., 1969—, St. Louis Inst. Music, 1971-74; exec. com. CASA Aux., also v.p., bd. dirs., 1978—; bd. dirs. Dance Concert Soc. Troup, 1979-80. Recipient Woman of Achievement award St. Louis Globe Democrat, 1967. Mem. Nat. Soc. Arts and Letters (dir. 1964-65), Delta Zeta. Republican. Presbyn. Clubs: Wednesday (rec. sec. 1963-64), St. Louis Woman's. Home: 630 Francis Pl Saint Louis MO 63105

HILSTON, CHARLES RALPH, ednl. assn. exec.; b. Girard, Ohio, Dec. 20, 1930; s. Ralph Wayne and Evelyn (Miller) H.; B.S., Mich. State Normal Coll., 1952; postgrad. Wayne State U., 1956; M.A., Eastern Mich. U., 1959; m. Luella May Cox, Oct. 17, 1959; children—Wayne Charles, Steven Fred, Thomas Christopher, Amylu, Evelyn. Tchr., Hazel Park, Mich., 1955-56, Wyandotte, Mich., 1956-63; prin., Van Wert, Ohio, 1963-65; exec. dir. Ohio Assn. Secondary Sch. Prins. and Ohio Dept. Elementary Sch. Prins., 1965-68; dir. profl. assistance Nat. Assn. Secondary Sch. Prins., Washington, 1968-71; exec. sec. Wis. Secondary Sch. Adminstrs. Assn., Stevens Point, 1971-78; exec. dir. Assn. Wis. Sch. Adminstrs., 1978—; cons., lectr. in field. Asst. mgr. Nat. Music Camp, Interlochen, Mich., summers 1957-59; cons. Ohio Sch. Dist. Orgn. Master Plan, 1966; chmn. Wis. Ednl. Goals Task Force, 1972-73, Wis. United Action Council Pub. Edn., 1973; sec.-treas. Wis. Council Sch. Adminstrv. Assns., 1972—; mem. Wis. Center Vocat. Edn., 1972—; chmn. Wis. Sch. Adminstrs., 1974—. Vice pres. Civic Music Assn., Van Wert, 1963-64; active Boy Scouts Am., 1961-63; mem. Ohio selection com. Internat. Farm Youth Exchange, 1965-68; adv. com. Wis. Ednl. Communications Bd., 1974—. Served with USNR, 1953-55. Cert. assn. exec. Mem. Phi Delta Kappa. Lutheran. Contbr. articles to profl. jours. Home: 533 Shady Wood Way Madison WI 53714 Office: 1310 Mendota St Madison WI 53714

HILTON, STANLEY WILLIAM, JR., theatrical mgr.-dir.; b. Phila., Mar. 24; s. Stanley William and Jennie (Parsons) H.; B.A., Fisk U., 1959; postgrad. Temple U.; m. Inge Himmersbach, Dec. 1962. Office mgr., resource cons., social worker Cook County Dept. Pub. Aid, Chgo., 1961-70; coordinator, ednl. and vocat. counselor Community Coll. Dist., San Francisco, 1971-74; co. mgr. prodn. Hair, San Francisco, 1969; mgr. Orpheum Theatre, San Francisco, 1970; co. mgr. prodns. No Place To Be Somebody, 1971, My Fair Lady, 1973, in San Francisco, also co-mgr. Jesus Christ Superstar, 1973; dir. park and theatre ops. Art Park, Lewiston, N.Y., 1974; exec. dir. Blackstone Theatre, Chgo., 1974—; bd. dirs. The Acad., Art, Music, Dance, Theatre, Chgo. Mem. Assn. Theatrical Press Agts. and Mgrs., Internat. Alliance Theatrical State Employees, Moving Picture Machine Operators U.S. and Can. Home: 1540 N State Pkwy Chicago IL 60610 Office: 60 E Balbo St Chicago IL 60605

HILTZ, ROBERT MURRAY, ins. co. ofcl.; b. Washington, Apr. 30, 1946; s. Kenneth Murray and Katherine Ann (Menefee) H., Jr.; student Miami U., Ohio, 1964-66; B.S. in Indsl. Edn., East Tex. State U., 1968, M.S. in Indsl. Edn., 1970; m. Carol Ann Jennings, Aug. 10, 1968; children—Jeffrey Dylan, Ryan Matthew. Instr. indsl. arts Arlington (Tex.) Ind. Sch. Dist., 1968-70; claims rep. Transam. Ins., Dallas, 1970-71; with Kemper Group, 1971—, beginning as loss control engr., Dallas, successively dist. supr. loss control engring., br. mgr., Atlanta, Dallas br. mgr., div. loss control officer, Long Grove, Ill., 1971-81, loss control safety officer, 1981—. Vestryman, St. Mary's Episcopal Ch., Crystal Lake, Ill.; active mcpl. elections. Cert. hazard control mgr.; asso. in risk mgmt. Ins. Inst. Am. Mem. Am. Soc. Safety Engrs., Sigma Tau Epsilon. Republican. Home: 110 Dartmoor Dr Crystal Lake IL 60014 Office: LCE D6 Kemper Dr Long Grove IL 60049

HIMELSTEIN, SAUL, communications co. exec.; b. Wülfratshausen, W. Ger., Dec. 1, 1948; came to U.S., 1950, naturalized, 1955; s. Samuel and Ida (Evdokimova) H.; B.S., Lynchburg (Va.) Coll., 1969; M.B.A., U. Va., 1971. Br. mgr. Avco Fin. Services, Inc., Englewood, N.J., 1969-71; with warehouse ops. dept. Western Electric Co., Inc., Union, N.J., 1970-74; owner Radio Shack store, Short Hills, N.J., 1974-77; cons. J. Limerick & Assos., Atlanta, 1977-78; gen. mgr. Ohio Mobile Telephone, Inc., Columbus, 1978—; dir. Spectrum Group, Inc.; cons. AT&T Systems Group; sponsor Vocat. Indsl. Clubs Am.; adv. N.J. Public Utilities Commn., 1974-76. Served with USAR, 1969-75. Recipient Pres.'s Health and Safety award, 1974, Tandy Achievement award, 1976. Mem. Columbus C. of C., Nat. Assn. Bus. and Ednl. Radio, IEEE, U.S. Golf Assn. Club: Kiwanis. Office: 2899 E Dublin-Granville Rd Columbus OH 43229

HINDELANG, ROBERT DAVID, air force officer, clin. psychologist; b. Carrollton, Ill., Sept. 22, 1949; s. Robert Louis and Vivian Pauline (Varble) H.; B.S., USAF Acad., 1972; M.S., Purdue U., 1972; Ph.D., U. Wyo., 1978; m. Tyann Alea Moss, June 10, 1972; children—D. Kyle, Curran J. Commd. 2d lt. U.S. Air Force, 1972, advanced through grades to capt., 1976; hosp. psychologist Keesler AFB, Biloxi, Miss., 1973-74, psychology resident, Wilford Hall, Lackland, AFB, Tex., 1977-78; staff clin. psychologist, Scott AFB, Ill., 1978—. Mem. Am. Psychol. Assn., Am. Soc. Clin. and Exptl. Hypnosis, Soc. for Air Force Psychologists. Co-author reports in field. Home: 1401 G Paegelow Scott AFB IL 62225 Office: USAF Medical Center SGHMM Scott AFB IL 62225

HINDERKS, JAMES HERMAN, mfg. corp. mgr.; b. Renville, Minn., Sept. 17, 1942; s. Herman Johnson and Tillie (Ryks) H.; B.S., St. Cloud State U., 1964; postgrad. (Macro-Econs. scholar), Mankato State U., 1965; postgrad. in Bus. Mgmt., U. Minn., 1966-73, in Acctg., North Hennepin Jr. Coll., 1974-76; m. Joyce Elsie Lange, Oct. 24, 1964; children—Julie, James Herman. Tchr. English and Am. history, Lakeville (Minn.) Public Schs., 1964-66; tech. lit. researcher Honeywell Inc., Mpls., 1966-67; life ins. salesman Luth. Aid Assn., Appleton, Wis., 1967-68; purchasing expediter, sr. buyer integrated circuits Control Data Corp., Mpls., 1968-73; sr. buyer, supr. material planning group Medtronic Inc., Mpls., 1973-77, mgr. group mech. buyers, purchasing mgr., 1977—. Chmn., Brooklyn Park Republican Party, 1973-74, del. state Rep. conv., 1972-78, alt. del., 1980; del. dist. conv. Minn. State Senate, 1972, 76; active YMCA Indian Guides program, 1974-76; com. mem. Troop 542 Viking council Boy Scouts Am., 1979-80; chmn. bd. edn. Beautiful Savior Luth. Ch., New Hope, Minn.; pres. congl. voting assembly Grace Luth. Ch., Brooklyn Park, Minn., 1978-79; del. nat. conv. Luth. Ch., Mo. Synod, 1979. Mem. Am. Mgmt. Assn., Twin Cities Purchasing Mgmt. Assn., Am. Prodn. and Inventory Control Soc. Home: 7632 Scott Ave N Minneapolis MN 55443 Office: 6972 Central Ave NE Minneapolis MN 55432

HINDERY, PHYLLIS CATHERINE, bus. exec.; b. Chgo., Oct. 1, 1947; d. John Anthony and Charlotte Mary (Hayes) Dombeck; B.A., Rosary Coll., 1969; student U. Ill., Chgo. Circle, 1969-70; m. Richard Francis Hindery, Dec. 2, 1972. Asst. personnel mgr. Sears Roebuck & Co., Chgo., 1972-76, staff asst. nat. tng. dept., 1977-79, coordinator apparel and accessories tng., 1979-80, asst. buyer misses' dresses, 1980—. Home: 1907 Sunnydale Ln Lisle IL 60532 Office: Sears Roebuck & Co 2 N LaSalle St Dept 631 Chicago IL 60602

HINDMAN, DON J., corp. exec.; b. Spearville, Kans., 1926; B.S., Ind. U., 1949; postgrad. W.Va. U. Past chmn. bd. Time Industries, Inc., Chgo.; now chmn. bd., pres. Clark Products Inc., Elk Grove Village, Ill.; dir. Barrett Bindery Co., Packaging Concepts, Inc., Smurfit Industries, Alton Packaging Corp., 1st Bank Naperville (Ill.). Address: 1850 Arthur Ave Elk Grove Village IL 60007

HINE, WILLIAM CLYDE, educator; b. Chgo., Jan. 2, 1944; s. Maynard Kiplinger and Harriett Anna (Foulke) H.; student Butler U., 1962-65; B.S., Ind. U., 1967, Ed.D., 1973; M.Div., Christian Theol. Sem., 1970; m. Elizabeth Nash, Aug. 24, 1968; children—William Clyde, Charles Foulke. Registrar, Ind. U., Richmond, 1973-75, chmn. div. applied arts and sci., 1975-80; asst. dean Coll. Alternative Programs, dir. continuing edn. U. Evansville, Ind., 1980—, prof. edn., 1980—. Mem. Am. Assn. Higher Edn., Adult Edn. Assn., Council for Advancement Exptl. Edn., Assn. for Continuing Higher Edn., Disciples of Christ Hist. Soc., Blue Key, Phi Delta Kappa, Alpha Sigma Lambda. Mem. Christian Ch. Clubs: Lions, Elks. Book reviewer, Choice, Mag. for Libraries, 1975—. Contbr. articles to profl. jours. Home: 500 Greenfield Rd Evansville IN 47715 Office: University of Evansville PO Box 329 Evansville IN 47702

HINES, DEBORAH FRANCES, ednl. adminstr.; b. St. Charles, Mo., Sept. 21, 1948; d. Marvin Horace and Marceline Elizabeth (Bloebaum) H.; B.A., Notre Dame Coll., 1970; M.A. in Spl. Edn., St. Louis U., 1977, Ph.D. in Ednl. Adminstrn., 1982. Self-contained spl. edn. tchr. St. Mary's Spl. Sch., St. Louis, 1970-75; master tchr. U. Mo., Fontbonne Coll., 1970-75; resource tchr. Francis Howell Sch. Dist., Central Intermediate Sch., St. Charles County, Mo., 1975-78, asst. prof., 1978—; instr. Lindenwood Coll., 1979, 81. Coach, Spl. Olympics, 1971-78, mem. exec. com., 1980—, regional dir., 1976-79, tng. sch. coordinator, 1981—; bd. dirs. St. Charles County Assn. Retarded Citizens, 1976-79. Recipient Citizens award Mo. Assn. Retarded Citizens, 1977; Joseph P. Kennedy Jr. scholar, 1972, Mark Fitz scholar, 1979; Coro Found. Women in Leadership grantee, 1981. Mem. Nat. Assn. Elem. Sch. Prins., Nat. Assn. State Dirs. Spl. Edn., Council Exceptional Children, Council Adminstrs. Spl. Edn., Assn. Supervision and Curriculum Devel., Mo. Assn. Adminstrs. Spl. Edn., Phi Delta Kappa. Roman Catholic. Home: 1855-105 McKelvey Hill Dr Maryland Heights MO 63043 Office: 4525 Central School Rd Saint Charles MO 63301

HINES, JACK EDWARD, newspaper exec.; b. Valpariaso, Ind., July 3, 1946; s. Lester Kenneth and Dorothy Louise (Riddell) H.; student Am. Acad. Art, Chgo., 1964-67; B.F.A., U. Akron, 1973-74; m. Jeanne Louise Kaether, July 26, 1980. Creative dir. Akron (Ohio) Beacon Jour., 1974-77; promotion mgr. Madison (Wis.) Newspapers, 1977-80; dir. promotion Kansas City (Mo.) Star Co., 1980—. Charter mem. bd. dirs. Oversight Com., Greater Kansas City Camping Connection, 1980. Mem. Internat. Newspaper Promotion Assn. (1st pl. award 1977, membership chmn. Mo. 1981-82). Home: 3906 NW 82d St Kansas City MO 64151 Office: 1729 Grand Ave Kansas City MO 64108

HINESLY, THOMAS DANIEL, soil ecologist, educator; b. San Saba, Tex., May 18, 1925; s. Marvin Henry and Mary Alice (Rohn) H.; B.S., Tex. A&M U., 1952, M.S., 1955; Ph.D., Iowa State U., 1961; m. Frances Patrick, Nov. 17, 1951; children—Thomas Christopher, Lisa Ann Hinesly Eversole. Research asst. Tex. A&M U., College Station, 1952-54; instr. Iowa State U., Ames, 1955-61; faculty U. Ill., Champaign-Urbana, 1961—, prof. soil ecology, 1976—; adv. to panel on agrl. uses water Nat. Acad. Sci., 1971-72, mem. panel on methane generation from human, animal and agrl. waste, 1977; sci. adv. civil functions div. Office Sec. Army, Washington, 1972-73; cons. EPA, U.S. Army C.E., 1973—. Served with USMCR, 1942-46. Recipient award Polish Ministry Agr., 1977. Mem. Am. Soc. Agronomy, Soil Sci. Soc. Am., Water Pollution Control Fedn., Council for Agrl. Sci. and Tech., Sigma Xi, Alpha Zeta, Gamma Sigma Delta. Republican. Roman Catholic. Club: Lincolnshire Fields Country. Contbr. numerous articles to profl. jours. Home: 2302 Staley Rd Champaign IL 61820 Office: Dept Agronomy N0225 Turner Hall U Ill Urbana IL 61801

HINKAMPER, EDWARD CHARLES, state agy. adminstr.; b. Quincy, Ill., Dec. 2, 1939; s. Frank Charles and Dorothy Elizabeth (Heckle) H.; B.S. in Bus. Adminstrn., Quincy Coll., 1961; M.A. in Child, Family and Community Service, Sangamon State U., 1977. With Dept. Children and Family Service, State of Ill., Quincy, 1965—, regional licensing coordinator, 1978—. Bd. dirs. ARC, Adams County, Ill., 1970—, chmn. first aid, 1970—. Served with U.S. Navy, 1962-64. Mem. Assn. Regulatory Adminstrn., Nat. Rifle Assn. Am. Roman Catholic. Clubs: St. Rose Men's, K.C. Home: 3721 Queen Anne Ave Quincy IL 62301 Office: 4500 S 6th St Springfield IL 62706

HINKLE, CARL, Realtor; b. Riverton, W.Va., May 19, 1921; s. Lloyd and Gettie (Hedrick) H.; A.B., Davis-Elkins Coll., 1948; M.A., W.Va. U., 1957; m. Ruth White, Nov. 25, 1953; children—Marcella Lee, Christina Rae, Thomas Carl. Tchr., Carroll County, Ohio, 1948-50; tchr., elementary supr., prin. Columbiana County Schs., 1950-58; local supt. Tuscarawas, Ohio, 1958-66; edn. cons. div. sch. finance Ohio Dept. Edn., 1966-72; supt. Ledgemont Pub. Schs., Thompson, Ohio, 1972-75; supr., prin. Heisley Christian Acad., Mentor, Ohio, 1977-78; affiliated with DeLuxe Motel, Mentor, Ohio, Stanmor Realty Co., Homes for Living. Active Ledgemont P.T.A.; mem. Tuscarawas Town Council, 1963-64. Served with USNR, 1942-45; PTO. Mem. Nat. Edn. Assn., Ohio Assn. Realtors, Lake County (Ohio) Bd. Realtors, Nat. Assn. Realtors, West Point Grange, 15th Seabee Bn. Assn. (reunion chmn. 1978, pres. 1979), Ohio Assn. Ret. Tchrs. (life), Buckeye Assn. Sch. Adminstrs. (life), Ledgemont Boosters Club. Mem. Christian Ch. (deacon, elder). Club: Men's. Home: 15559 Thompson Rd Thompson OH 44086

HINKLE, DONALD DEAN, acct., fin. cons.; b. Dayton, Ohio, Nov. 29, 1938; s. Herman Earl and Grace Beatrice (Fouts) H.; B.S. (Chrysler Found. scholar), Marquette U., 1967; m. Jacquelyn Mary Vaccaro, June 23, 1962; children—Sheila, Donna. Sr. acct. Price Waterhouse & Co., Milw., 1967-71; v.p. Robert W. Baird & Co., Milw., 1971-78; sr. v.p. Heritage Bank of Milw., 1978-79; partner Ziegert, Smaler, Kaminski & Freyberg, 1979—; mem. advisory bd. Wis. Security Commn., 1974-78, Midwest Stock Exchange Securities Trust Co., 1976-78; chmn. Milw. Bus. Showcase, 1978. Asst. treas. United Performing Arts Fund, 1978—; sect. vol. United Way campaign, 1975-77; treas., dir. Squires Grove Mgmt. Assn. and Water Trust, 1979-81. Mem. Am., Wis. insts. C.P.A.'s, Nat. Assn. Accountants (chpt. v.p. 1976-80, pres. 1981), Beta Gamma Sigma,

Beta Alpha Psi. Republican. Clubs: Westmoor Country, Grove (treas. 1980); Kiwanis. Home: 1140 Terrace Dr Elm Grove WI 53122 Office: 200 Bishops Way Suite 200 Brookfield WI 53005

HINKLE, DOUGLAS PADDOCK, educator; b. Stamford, Conn., June 9, 1923; s. Frank Leslie and Kathryn Barton (Paddock) H.; B.A., U. Va., 1952, M.A., 1954, postgrad., 1955, 61-62; postgrad. Ohio U., 1968-69; m. Rose-Marie Hecker, Apr. 14, 1966; children—Anthony Barton, Monica Kathryn. English tchr. Va. public schs., 1948-49; instr. Spanish, U. Va., 1952-55; dir. Am. Binat. Center, La Paz, Bolivia, 1955-57; asst. prof. Spanish, Sweet Briar (Va.) Coll., 1957-62, Southwestern U., Memphis, 1962-63; coll. editor Modern Langs., D.C. Heath & Co., Boston, 1963-65; asso. prof. modern langs. Eastern Ky. U., Richmond, 1965-67; lectr. Spanish lit., modern langs. Ohio U., Athens, 1967—, dir. jr. year in Spain, 1970-71; program evaluator Nat. Endowment for Humanities. Served with AUS, 1943-46. Named caballero Order of Condor of Andes, Bolivia, 1957; recipient citation newspaperman of La Paz, 1957. Mem. Raven Soc., Am. Name Soc. (jour. editorial bd. 1968-74), MLA, Am. Soc. Sephardic Studies, Phi Beta Kappa, Audubon Soc. Roman Catholic. Author: Poetry Is You, 1977; manuscript reader Modern Lang. Jour.; contbr. articles to profl. jours. Home: 60 Morris Ave Athens OH 45701 Office: 312 Ellis Hall Ohio U Athens OH 45701

HINMAN, MYRA MAHLOW, educator; b. Saginaw County, Mich., Jan. 11, 1926; d. Henry and Cynthia (Mims) Mahlow; B.S., Columbia U., 1946; M.A., U. Fla., 1954, Ph.D., 1959; m. George E. Olstead, 1948 (div. 1967); 1 son, Christopher Eric; m. 2d, Charlton Hinman, 1968 (dec. 1977); 1 stepdau., Barbara. Asst. prof. Memphis State U., 1959-61; instr. U. Kans., Lawrence, 1961-63, asst. prof., 1963-68, asso. prof. English lit., 1968—. Travel grantee Am. Council Learned Socs., 1966. Mem. MLA, Internat. Arthurian Soc., Shakespeare Assn. Am., U. Va. Bibliog. Soc., AAUP, Kans. Folklore Soc., Midwest Modern Lang. Assn., S. Atlantic Modern Lang. Assn., United Burmese Cat Fanciers, Am. Shorthair Cat Assn., Phi Kappa Phi. Asst. editor: Hinman Text, Complete Works of Shakespeare. Contbr. articles to profl. jours. Home: 1932 Maine St Lawrence KS 66044 Office: Wescoe Hall Univ Kans Lawrence KS 66044

HINSON, LEONARD FRANK, JR., mfg. co. exec.; b. East Saint Louis, Ill., Aug. 28, 1948; s. Leonard Frank and Lindell Fern L.; lic. airframe and power plant Parks Air Coll., 1967; student Washington U., St. Louis, 1979; 1 dau., Genice Marie. Pres., prin. St. Louis Fgn. Car, St. Louis, 1971-73; engring. mgr. Indee Co., St. Louis, 1974-79; ops. mgr., prin. Nutherm Internat., Mt. Vernon, Ill., 1979—. Served with U.S. Army, 1968-71. Mem. Am. Mgmt. Assn., Soc. Mfg. Engrs., Am. Inst. Indsl. Engrs. Home: 505 Halia Crest Mount Vernon IL 62864 Office: 501 S 11th St Mount Vernon IL 62864

HINTZ, JOY ALICE, mus. curator; b. Zanesville, Ohio, Feb. 7, 1926; d. James Sherman and Lela Gladys (Zink) Posey; B.A. in Biology, B.S. in Edn., Ohio State U., 1947, postgrad., 1947-49; postgrad. Capital U., 1950-51, Heidelberg Coll., 1967-76; m. Howard William Hintz, June 15, 1952; children—Loren Douglas, Constance Joy Hintz Nusbaum, Julia Kay. Tchr., Tiffin, Ohio, 1955-60; mus. curator Heidelberg Coll., Tiffin, 1956—. Pres. Seneca County (Ohio) Family Planning Services, 1969-70, outreach worker, 1969-71, bd. dirs., 1969-76, dir. program, 1976-80; mem. Ohio Gov.'s Com. on Migrant Affairs, 1974-75. Elizabeth McGee Found. grantee, 1973, 79. Mem. Midwest Fedn. Mineral Clubs, Firelands Geol. Club, Mansfield Mineral Club, Ohio Acad. Sci., Seneca County Ch. Women United (pres. 1965-68), Ch. Women United in Ohio (dir. 1971-76), AAUW (chmn. sci. group 1966-75), LWV, Com. Migrant Relations (chmn. com. on migrant relations 1970—), Auxilio y Amistad (v.p. 1976—), La Raza Unida de Ohio (dir. 1971-76, sec. 1974-76), Christian Women's Fellowship (pres. local unit 1962-63), Pi Lambda Theta. Mem. Ch. Disciples of Christ. Club: Eastern Star. Editor: An Anthology of Ohio Mexican American Writers, 1974; Anthology II: Mexican Americans Write, 1976; Seven Families: A Two Year In-Depth Study of Incomes and Job Experiences of Seven Ohio Migrant Farm Worker Families, 1976; Poverty, Prejudice, Power and Politics: Migrants Speak About Their Lives, 1981; contbr. articles to sch. and geol. jours. Home: 500 E Perry St Tiffin OH 44883 Office: Jones Collection of Minerals Heidelberg College Tiffin OH 44883

HIPPE, H. EUGENE, planning ofcl.; b. Wabasha County, Minn., July 8, 1937; s. Fred Ernest and Helen Gertrud (Sommer) H.; B.S., Mankato State Coll., 1963; postgrad. So. Conn. State Coll., U. Minn.; m. Gloria Jean Conzemius, Nov. 13, 1964; children—Eugenia Marie, Mary Elizabeth, Tyrone Eugene. Planner, interim dir. City of Hamden (Conn.), 1964-66; planning dir. City of Winona (Minn.), 1966-68; county planning dir. Rochester (Minn.), 1968-74; exec. dir. Devel. Commn. Willmar (Minn.), 1974—. Neighborhood commr. Boy Scouts Am., 1970-72; local sec. Assn. Retarded Citizens, 1968-69, pres., 1978-79, mem. state bd., 1980—, pres. elect. Minn. Assn. Retarded Citizens, 1982; founder, 1st pres. Wildlife Habitate Improvement, Inc., 1972. Mem. Am. Inst. Planners (past dir. Minn. chpt.), Roman Catholic. Club: KC. Home: Rt 1 Horseshoe Dr Willmar MN 56201 Office: 333 W 6th St Willmar MN 56201*

HIPPLE, CHARLES ALLEN, fed. govt. ofcl.; b. Dayton, Ohio, June 19, 1949; s. Robert Gene and Bernice Ardella (Allen) H.; diploma Internat. Acad., 1968, Internat. Broadcasting Sch., 1976; B.S., Wright State U., 1980; m. Roberta Ann Hecker, Nov. 9, 1975; children—Joseph Allen, Sung Kyo. Computer operator Def. Electronics Supply Center, Kettering, Ohio, 1968, 72-81, procurement agt., 1981—; real estate exec., part-time 1973-78; baseball umpire, 1973—; radio disc jockey, 1977-79. Mem. Greene County Democratic Exec. Com., 1980-81; mem. Greene County Recreation and Parks Bd., 1981—; mem. Montgomery-Greene County Transp. Coordinating Citizens Com.; mem. Xenia Bd. Edn., 1981—. Named Ohio Jaycee Family of Year, 1979. Mem. Xenia Jaycees (pres. 1981—). Home: 2290 Maryland Dr Xenia OH 45385 Office: Def Electronics Supply Center 1507 Wilmington Pike Kettering OH 45444

HIPPLER, RANDOLPH, broadcasting exec.; b. Detroit, Oct. 8, 1938; s. Ralph Roland and Monica Angela H.; B.A. in Communication Arts with honors, Mich. State U., 1960; m. Lilla A. Weigl, Oct. 28, 1967; 1 dau., Kimberly Elizabeth. Producer-dir., Sta. WNEM-TV, Saginaw, Mich., 1959-60; producer-dir. Sta. WLOF-TV, Orlando, Fla., 1960-61; sales engr. Gen. TV Network, Ferndale, Mich., 1961-65, v.p., Oak Park, Mich., 1965-70, pres., 1970—. Recipient Spirit of Detroit award City of Detroit, 1977. Mem. Acad. Video Communicators, Detroit Producers Assn., Soc. Motion Picture and TV Engrs. (chmn. Detroit sect.), Nat. Acad. TV Arts and Scis., Beta Theta Pi (Founders award 1960, pres. chpt. 1965—). Club: Trenton Outboard Racing.

HIRN, DORIS DREYER, health services adminstr.; b. N.Y.C., Dec. 3, 1933; d. James M. and Dorothy Van Nostrand (Young) Dreyer; student Colby Jr. Coll., 1951-52, Hofstra U., 1953-56, Northwestern U., 1972-74; m. John D. Hirn, Oct. 27, 1956; children—Deborah Lynn, Robert William. Asst. to adminstr., Albany (N.Y.) Med. Coll., 1962-64; propr., dir. Hickory Hill Camp, Galena, Ill., 1965-72; v.p. Home Health Service of Chgo. North Inc., 1972-74; pres., adminstr. Suburban Home Health Service, Inc., Des Plaines, Ill., 1974—; pres. Hickory Hill Mgmt. Corp., 1977—; dir. Serengeti Prodns., 1979—. Bd. dirs. Nat. Health Delivery Systems, 1973—, Fox Valley council Girl Scouts U.S., 1965-70. Served with USN, 1951-53. Mem. Am. Fedn. Home Health Agys., Ill. Council of Home Health Agys., Internat. Film Producers Assn., Am. Camping Assn. (dir. Chgo. chpt. 1968-70). Republican. Club: Chicago Yacht. Home: 1550 N Lake Shore Dr Chicago IL 60610 Office: 2250 E Devon Ave Des Plaines IL 60018

HIRSCH, LORE, psychiatrist; b. Mannheim, Germany, July 8, 1908; d. Erwin and Marie (Kiefe) Hirsch; came to U.S., 1940, naturalized, 1946; M.D., U. Heidelberg (Germany), 1937; postgrad. N.Y. U., 1942-43; m. Eugene Hesz, Jan. 25, 1958. Intern, Greenpoint Hosp., Bklyn., 1942-43; resident in psychiatry Bellevue Hosp., N.Y.C., 1943-46, sr. psychiatrist, N.Y.C., 1946-49; sect. chief psychiatry div. VA Hosp., Bronx, N.Y., 1949-54; clin. dir. psychiatry Wayne County Gen. Hosp., Eloise, Mich., 1954-55; dir. out-patient dept. Northville (Mich.) State Hosp., 1955-58, cons., 1978—; pvt. practice psychiatry, Dearborn, Mich., 1958—; staff Oakwood Hosp., Dearborn, 1958—; asst. prof. psychiatry Wayne State U., Detroit, 1954-55. Pres., Dearborn Health Council, 1960-62. Bd. dirs. YWCA, Dearborn, 1962-70. Recipient Award for leadership City of Dearborn, 1962; award in appreciation of qualities as tchr. Resident Staff Northville State Hosp., 1958. Diplomate Am. Bd. Psychiatry and Neurology. Fellow Am. Psychiat. Assn. (life fellow); mem. AMA (life mem.), Mich. Mental Health Soc., Mich. Med. Soc., Mich. Psychiat. Soc., Pan Am. Psychiat. Assn. Unitarian Universalist. Contbr. articles to profl. jours. Home: 212 S Melborn St Dearborn MI 48124 Office: 2021 Monroe Blvd Dearborn MI 48124

HIRSCH, RALPH FRED, equipment mfg. co. exec.; b. Schwinfurt, Germany, May 13, 1931; s. Harry G. and Ruth N. (Hirsch) H.; came to U.S., 1939, naturalized, 1946; B.S. in Bus. Adminstrn., Northwestern U., 1958; m. Shirley A. Abrams, 1969; children—Paula, Steve, Vicki, Teri, Ron, David. Mem. sales mgmt. staff Sears Roebuck & Co., Chgo., 1953-58; dist. sales mgr. Glaser Crawdell Co., Chgo., 1958-65; exec. nat. sales mgr. food div. DoAll Co., Des Plaines, Ill., 1965—; instr. Jr. Achievement program Sears, Roebuck & Co. Served with USN, 1949-53. Recipient Teaching award Jr. Achievement, 1956. Jewish. Clubs: B'nai B'rith, T-Bird Hunting Lodge (Wis.). Home: PO Box 82 Barrington IL 60010 Office: 254 N Laurel Ave Des Plaines IL 60016

HIRTZEL, RICHARD DALE, polit. scientist, educator; b. Chgo., Feb. 1, 1929; s. Frederich Edward and Sarah Ferne (Swank) H.; B.S. in Polit. Sci., Brigham Young U., 1956, M.S., 1962; Ph.D., U. Utah, 1967; m. Connie Kay Olsen, Oct. 16, 1964; children—Thomas Dale, Lori Anna, Tammie Kay, Carrie Brenda. Supr., office spl. courses and confs. Brigham Young U., Provo, Utah, 1957-61; civilian personnel placement and tng. officer U.S. Govt. in Utah, 1961-63, 65; asst. prof. polit. sci. Winona (Minn.) State Coll., 1966-68; asso. prof. polit. sci. Western Ill. U., Macomb, 1968—; mem. cons. faculty U.S. Army Command and Gen. Staff Coll., 1969—; guest lectr. Nat. Strategy Info. Center, 1969-74. Mem. 20th Congl. Dist. Mil. Acad. Selection Bd., 1969-72. Dir. ann. Boy Scout Merit Badge Pow-Wow, Brigham Young U., 1957-61. Served to 2d lt. U.S. Army, 1950-53; col. Res. Decorated Army Commendation medal. Mem. Res. Officers Assn. (pres. Central Utah chpt. 1960-61), Pi Sigma Alpha. Mem. Ch. of Jesus Christ of Latter-day Saints (pres. Ill. W. dist. mission 1973—). Author: Career Opportunities in Political Science, 1975. Home: 1606 Riverview Dr Macomb IL 61455

HITT, WARREN G., mfg. adminstr.; b. Bryan, Ohio, May 7, 1926; s. Prather R. and Mildred C. (Brace) H.; student public schs., Bryan; m. Babette Joan Sprunger, July 22, 1948; children—Debbie, Greg, Rebecca. With Aro Corp., 1951—, mgr. order billing dept., 1963—, govt. contract adminstr., 1964—, mgr. customer service dept., 1969—; direct distbr. Amway Corp., 1981—; curriculum cons. vocat. sch. Served with USAAF, 1944-46. Recipient cert. of appreciation 4-County Vocat. Sch., 1979, 80, 81. Republican. Lutheran. Home: Route 5 Bryan OH 43506 Office: One Aro Center Bryan OH 43506

HJALMARSON, GORDON ROSS, publishing co. exec.; b. Dauphin, Man., Can., Apr. 9, 1926; s. John I. and Holmfridur J. (Johnson) H.; came to U.S., 1942, naturalized, 1950; B.A., Pomona Coll., 1949; M.A., San Francisco State U., 1951; postgrad. U. So. Calif., 1953-54; m. Carroll L. Clark, Aug. 9, 1952; children—Gordon Ross II, Melissa Anne, John Clark, Eric Alexander. Sch., univ. tchr., 1951-58; with Houghton Mifflin, Boston, 1958-73; asso. dir. sch. depts., 1968-69, dir. dept., 1969-73, v.p., mem. exec. com., 1973, also dir., 1970-73; pres., dir. Scott, Foresman & Co., Glenview, Ill., 1973-76, chmn., chief exec. officer, 1976—; pres. chmn., chief exec. officer SFN Cos., Inc., 1980, holding co. for Scott, Foresman & Co., Silver Burdett Co., Morristown, N.J., William Morrow Co., N.Y.C., South Western Pub. Co., Cin., Fleming H. Revell, Tappan, N.J., University Park Press, Balt.; dir. GLC Ltd. of Can., Toronto, Gage Pub. Co., Toronto. Asso. pres.'s com. Northwestern U., Pomona (Calif.) Coll., Chgo. Theol. Sem., Nat. Coll. Edn., Evanston, Ill., U. Chgo., U. Ill.; trustee Pomona Coll. Recipient Disting. Alumnus of Yr., San Francisco U., 1979; named Top Chief Exec. Officer in Pub. Industry, Wall St. Transcript, 1980. Mem. Pres.'s Assos., C. of C. of U.S., Chgo. Assn. Commerce and Industry, Chgo. Com. Fgn. Relations. Clubs: Masons, Wellesley Country; Union (Boston); Chicago, Executive, Econ. (Chgo.); President's (N.Y.C.); Sunset Ridge Country (Northbrook, Ill.). Home: 119 Abingdon Ave Kenilworth IL 60043 Office: 1900 E Lake Ave Glenview IL 60025

HJELLE, JOHN ORLO, ret. editor; b. Mercer, N.D., Nov. 15, 1913; s. Ole S. and Ella T. (Myrah) H.; A.B., Luther Coll., 1936; m. Alice Marie Driver, Dec. 19, 1943; children—Ann Marie, Kathryn Lynn, Barbara, Kristin. Reporter, sports editor, telegraph editor Bismarck Tribune, 1936-41, city editor, 1941-45, editor, 1948-79; exec. sec., adminstrv. asst. to U.S. Senator M.R. Young, Washington, 1945-48. Bd. dirs. Upper Midwest Council of Mpls. Mem. Am. Soc. Newspaper Editors, N.D. Newspaper Assn. (pres. 1969-70). Lutheran. Clubs: Elks, Masons, Shriners, Rotary. Contbr. articles to profl. publs. Home: 106 W Sioux Ave Bismarck ND 58501

HO, ALAN DARRELL, structural engr.; b. Chgo., Sept. 21, 1953; s. Mon Foo and Maymie (Lee) H.; B.Arch., U. Ill., Chgo., 1977; M.S., M.I.T., 1979; m. Mary Lam, July 28, 1979. Teaching asst. U. Ill., 1974, 75-77; teaching and research asst. M.I.T., 1977-79; structural engring. specialist, computer liaison agt. Sargent and Lundy Engrs., Chgo., 1979—; adj. asst. prof. U. Ill., Chgo., 1981—. Mem. ASCE, Am. Concrete Inst., Sigma Xi. Baptist. Club: M.I.T. (Chgo.). Author curriculum materials.

HO, ALFRED KUOLIANG, educator; b. Peking, China, Mar. 12, 1919; came to U.S., 1941, naturalized, 1956; m. Yuan-Hsi and Chi-shan (Kung) H.; B.A., Yenching U., Peking, 1941; M.A., U. Wash., 1942; Ph.D., Princeton U., 1944; Ph.D., UCLA, 1968; m. Marjorie Kao, July 1, 1944; children—Jenny, Laura Ho Fineman, Henry, Laurence. Instr. polit. sci. and econs. Yenching U., Peking, 1946-49; instr. Def. Lang. Sch., Monterey, Calif., 1950-56; asso. prof. econs. Los Angeles City Coll., 1957-67; asso. prof. Western Mich. U., Kalamazoo, 1967-69, prof. econs., 1969—. Mem. Am. Econs. Assn. Democrat. Congregationalist. Author: Japan's Trade Liberalization of the 1960's, 1973; Economic Policies in the 1970's, 1972; The Far East in World Trade, 1967. Office: Dept Econs Western Mich U Kalamazoo MI 49008

HO, CHO-YEN, phys. sci. research adminstr.; b. Gueiping, Guangxi, China, Aug. 11, 1928; came to U.S., 1957, naturalized, 1972; s. Yu-Chih and Tsui-Chen (Huang) H.; M.S. in Mech. Engring., U. Ky., 1960; Ph.D., Purdue U., 1964; m. Nancy Yang Wang, June 1, 1963; children—Chris Meichung W., Chester Meihua W. Asst. sr. researcher Thermophys. Properties Research Center, Purdue U., West Lafayette, Ind., 1964-69, head reference data div., 1967—, asso. sr. researcher, 1969-74, asst. dir., sr. researcher Center for Info. and Numerical Data Analysis and Synthesis, 1974—, interim dir., 1981—; indexer Applied Mechanics Revs., 1967-72; bd. govs., treas. Internat. Thermal Conductivity Confs., 1973—, co-chmn., 1968; instr. NSF short course Pa. State U., 1973; lectr. seminar and workshop Engring. Joint Council, U. Ill., 1975. Recipient Thermal Conductivity Achievement award Internat. Thermal Conductivity Confs., 1981. Mem. Am. Phys. Soc., ASME (mem. standing com. on thermophys. properties, reviewer Jour. Heat Transfer 1968—), AAAS, Am. Soc. for Metals, Sigma Xi, Pi Tau Sigma. Author, co-author several reference books; contbr. articles on thermophysics, thermophys. and elec. properties of materials and thermoelectric power generation and conversion to sci. jours.; tech. series editor Thermophys. Properties of Matter, 1969—; co-editor McGraw-Hill/CINDAS Data Series on Material Properties, 1981—. Office: Center for Info and Numerical Data Analysis and Synthesis Purdue Univ 2595 Yeager Rd W Lafayette IN 47906

HO, GRINNY HONG CHI, obstetrician, gynecologist; b. Tai Tung, Taiwan, Dec. 25, 1941; came to U.S., 1968, naturalized, 1976; s. T.H. and C.H. (Wu) H.; M.D., China Med. Coll., 1967; m. Chun-Mei Hu, May 16, 1968; children—Christina, Eddie, Jennie. Intern, Martland Hosp. units N.J. Coll. Medicine and Dentistry, Newark, 1968-69; resident Community Hosp., Glen Cove, N.Y., 1969-70; chief resident Misericordia Hosp., Fordham Hosp., 1970-71; chmn. obstet. com. Missouri Delta Community Hosp., Sikeston, Mo., 1974—. Diplomate Am. Bd. Obstetrics and Gynecology. Fellow Am. Coll. Obstetrics and Gynecology; mem. AMA (physician recognition award 1974-80), Mo. State Med. Assn., Semo County Med. Soc. Presbyterian. Home: 325 Kennedy Dr Sikeston MO 63801 Office: 808 E Wakefield St Sikeston MO 63801

HOAG, JAMES DAVID, mfg. co. safety ofcl.; b. Downers Grove, Ill., July 14, 1924; s. Carroll I. and Goldie E. (Curry) H.; student Purdue U., 1946-49; B.S., N.Y. U., 1951; postgrad. La. State U., 1957; m. Angeline F. Freskos, Jan. 19, 1945; children—David, Dean, Kim, Daniel, Carol. Safety engr. Liberty Mut. Ins. Co., Chgo., 1949-50, Armed Forces Spl. Weapons Project, Albuquerque, 1950-52, U.S. Naval Ordnance Plant, Macon, Ga., 1952-56; safety supr. Kaiser Aluminum Corp., Baton Rouge, 1956-58; mgr. occupational safety and health Union Electric Co., St. Louis, 1960—; lectr. Washington U; v.p. Mo. Safety Council, St. Louis Safety Council. Pres. Kirkwood Theatre Guild. Served to 1st lt. USAAF, 1942-45. Decorated Air Medal with 5 oak leaf clusters. Recipient Louis H. Antoine award, 1979; profl. engr., Calif. Mem. Edison Electric Inst. (chmn. codes and standards exec. adv. com.), ASTM (com.), Am. Soc. Safety Engrs. (safety profl. of year region IV, 1980), Profl. Photographers Am. Greek Orthodox. Club: Masons. Home: 1170 Glenway Dr Glendale MO 63122 Office: 1901 Gratiot St Saint Louis MO 63166

HOAGLAND, PETER JACKSON, lawyer, state senator; b. Omaha, Nov. 17, 1941; s. Laurance Redington and Naomi Ann (Carpenter) H.; A.B., Stanford U., 1963; LL.B., Yale U., 1968; m. Barbara Erickson, Sept. 1, 1973. Summer asso. Davis Polk & Wardwell, N.Y.C., 1967; asso. firm Wald, Harkrader & Ross, Washington, 1968-69; law clk. to judge U.S. Dist. Ct., Washington, 1969-70; trial atty. Public Defender Service for D.C., Washington, 1970-73; individual practice law, Omaha, 1974—; of counsel firm McGill, Koley, Parsonage & Lanphier; now mem. Nebr. Legislature, mem. appropriations com. Served with U.S. Army, 1963-65. Mem. Omaha Bar Assn., Nebr. State Bar Assn., D.C. Bar Assn., Am. Bar Assn., Common Cause (nat. bd. govs., vice chmn. legal affairs com. 1977-78), Phi Delta Pi, Phi Kappa Sigma. Home: 5405 Nicholas St Omaha NE 68132 Office: 10010 Regency Circle Omaha NE 68114

HOAGLUND, JAMES BARRON, air conditioner mfg. co. exec.; b. Mpls., Sept. 15, 1924; s. Arthur William and Mary M. (Barron) H.; B.S. in Elec. Engring., M.I.T., 1945, B.S. in Bus. Adminstrn., 1947; m. Mary E. Lamb, Sept. 10, 1946; children—John B., Judith A., Nora Ellen. With Honeywell, Inc., Boston, Los Angeles, Phoenix, 1947-51, Boyd Engrs. Co., Phoenix, 1952-53; partner Carns-Hoaglund Co., mfrs. rep., Phoenix, 1953-62; mgr. air condition and refrigeration div. Bell & Gottett Co., Morton Grove, Ill., 1962-64; with ITT Heating and Air Conditioning Group, 1965; asst. dir. engring. ITT Environ Products Div., Phila., 1966, v.p., dir. engring., 1967-68; tech. dir. comml.-indsl. products worldwide ITT Corp., N.Y.C., 1969-72; v.p. corporate planning and devel. McQuay-Perfex Inc., Mpls., 1972-74, exec. v.p., 1979—; pres. McQuay Group, Mpls., 1974-79; bd. dirs. Air-Conditioning and Refrigeration Inst. Served as ensign USNR, 1943-46. Registered profl. engr., Ariz. Mem. ASHRAE (pres. Central Ariz. chpt. 1955-56). Republican. Clubs: Mpls., Interlachen Country. Patentee. Office: McQuay Perfex Inc 5401 Gamble Dr Minneapolis MN 55416

HOARD, ADRIENNE WALKER, painter, educator; b. Jefferson City, Mo., Jan. 22, 1949; d. Charles Mason and Yvonne (Walker) H.; B.S. cum laude, Lincoln U., 1970; M.F.A., U. Mich., 1972. One Woman shows: The Studio Mus. in Harlem, N.Y.C., 1977, Shelton Gallery, N.Y.C., 1980, Am. Embassy, Seoul, 1981; group shows include: Detroit Inst. Art, 1971, Cinque Gallery, N.Y.C., 1974, Bklyn. Mus., 1974, Aames Gallery, N.Y.C., 1975, Rockefeller Center, N.Y.C., 1977; represented in permanent collections Nat. Mus. Modern Art, Korea, Columbus (Ohio) Mus. Fine Art; asst. prof. painting U. Ark., 1972-73; instr. edn. Bklyn. Mus., 1973-75; asst. prof. fine arts and black studies Ohio State U., 1975-81; vis. prof. Hong-Ik U., 1980-81, EWha Women's U., 1980-81; set designer Sta. PBS-TV 34 WOSU, Ohio. N.Y. State Council on the Arts grantee, 1974-75; Fulbright-Hays grantee, 1980-81. Mem. Coll. Art Assn. Am. Baptist. Home: 815 E Dunklin St Jefferson City MO 65101

HOATSON, GRANT CAMERON, educator; b. Montclair, N.J., Oct. 19, 1930; s. Grant and Isobel (Cameron) H.; A.B., Wheaton (Ill.) Coll., 1953; M.A., Ohio State U., Columbus, 1958; Ed.D., Ind. U., 1978; m. Patricia Joan Witt, July 25, 1959; children—Robin Kae, Kirk Cameron, Todd Barton. Dir., film dir. sta. WLW-C, Columbus, 1955-57, sta. WPTA-TV, Ft. Wayne, Ind., 1958-59; dir. public relations Ft. Wayne Bible Coll., 1953-55, dir. instructional services, asso. prof. communications, 1975—; vis. instr. Huntington (Ind.) Coll., 1978-81; cons. in field, workshop coordinator. Served with AUS, 1953-55. Public Relation bd., Am. Assn. of Bible Colls., bd. Publs. Missionary Ch. Internat. Mem. Assn. Ednl. Communications and Tech., Evang. Press Assn., Nat. Audio-Visual Assn., Ind. Coll. Public Relations Assn. (pres. 1971), Christian Coll. Coordinating Council (sec.-treas. 1960-74). Republican. Mem. Missionary Ch. Club: Anthony Wayne Rotary (editor newsletter 1970-71). Home:

1524 Park Ave Fort Wayne IN 46807 Office: 1025 W Rudisill Blvd Fort Wayne IN 46807

HOBBS, JAMES CALVIN, communications exec.; b. Harlingen, Tex., May 1, 1938; s. Edward and Bessie Mae (Jackson) H.; student N.Mex. State U., 1955-57; B.J., U. Mo., 1959, B.A. in Math, 1961, M.A. in Journalism, 1961; m. Marijo Caposell, July 11, 1970; children—Rachel Elizabeth, Jared Charles. Publs. editor Trane Co., LaCross, Wis., 1962-65; publicist Dow Corning Corp., Midland, Mich., 1965-68; account exec., account supr. Ketchum, McLeod & Grove, Pitts., 1968-72; v.p. Dave Brown & Assos., Inc., Oakbrook, Ill., 1972—. Served with Mil. Police, U.S. Army, 1962. Recipient Golden Quill award Pitts. Communications Assn., 1971. Mem. Soc. Tech. Communicators (chmn. Pitts. 1971-72), Nat. Agrl. Mktg. Assn., Public Relations Soc. Am., Am. Med. Writers Assn., Chgo. Headline Club, Agrl. Relations Council, Am. Agrl. Editors Assn., Profl. Photographers Am., Kappa Tau, Phi Alpha Mu, Sigma Alpha Epsilon, Sigma Delta Chi. Presbyterian. Club: Elks. Contbr. articles to profl. jours. Home: 3026 W 76th St Woodridge IL 60517 Office: 900 Jorie St Suite 70 Oakbrook IL 60521

HOBBS, MARIAN LAURETTA, educator; b. Kansas City, Kans., May 1, 1920; d. Frank Burley and Mary (Olson) Hobbs; A.A., Jr. Coll. Kansas City, 1940; B.S., U. Mo., Kansas City, 1960, M.S., 1967; acctg. degree LaSalle Extension U., 1954; postgrad. (Bank Clearing House Assn. scholar) Emporia State U., summers 1968-69, U. Kans. Sch. Medicine, spring 1970, Pittsburg State U., summer 1975, Kans. State U., spring 1973. Bacteriology technician Jensen-Salsbery Labs., Kansas City, Mo., 1940-42, bacteriologist, 1964-66; bacteriology technician Peters Serum Co., Kansas City, Mo., 1942; research asst. U. Mo. at Kansas City Dental Sch., 1942-43; pvt. practice public acctg., Kansas City, Kans., 1954—; food technologist Rutherford Food Corp., Kansas City, Mo., 1960-63; tchr. sci. Kansas City (Kans.) Public Schs. United Sch. Dist. 500, 1966—; mem. Officer Retiree Adv. Council, Ft. Leavenworth, Kans., 1975—; mem. Army Chief of Staff Officer Retiree Council, 1979—. Served with Women's Army Corps, 1943-46; ETO. Recipient letter of commendation Signal Security Agy., 1945; Master Sci. Tchr. award Sigma Xi, 1974; Delta Kappa Gamma internat. scholar, 1976-77. Mem. Am. Soc. Microbiology, AAAS, NEA, Nat. Assn. Biology Tchrs., Ret. Officers Assn. (treas. chpt. 1958-63), AAUW, AAUP, Nat. Sci. Tchrs. Assns., Nat. Parks and Conservation Assn., Am. Soc. Curriculum Devel., U. Mo. at Kansas City Alumni Assn., Cousteau Soc., Smithsonian Soc., Delta Kappa Gamma (chpt. rec. sec. 1978-80). Republican. Methodist. Clubs: Scandinavian of Greater Kansas City Women's Aux., Woman's Kansas Day. Patentee smog filter, method of testing pungency, odor and flavor of organic substances. Home: 1885 State Ave Kansas City KS 66102 Office: Kansas City Public Schs United Sch Dist 500 Sumner Acad Arts and Sci 8th and Oakland Sts Kansas City KS 66101

HOBBS, MARVIN, engring. exec.; b. Jasper, Ind., Nov. 30, 1912; s. Charles and Madge (Ott) H.; B.S. in Elec. Engring., Tri-State Coll., Angola, Ind., 1930; postgrad. U. Chgo., 1932-33; m. Bernadine E. Weeks, July 4, 1936. Chief engr. Scott Radio Labs., Chgo., 1939-46; cons. engr. RCA, Camden, N.J., 1946-49; v.p. Harvey-Wells Electronics, Southbridge, Mass., 1952-54; asst. to exec. v.p. Gen. Instrument Corp., Newark, N.J., 1958-62; mgr., cons. engr. Design Service Co., N.Y.C., 1963-68, v.p. corp. devel. Gladding Corp., 1968-72, cons., 1972-79; sr. tech. editor Bell Telephone Labs., 1979—; dir. A.R.F. Products, Inc., Raton, N.Mex. Mem. Electronics Prodn. Bd., ODM, Washington, 1951-52; operations analyst Far East Air Force, 1945. Recipient Certificate of Appreciation War Dept., 1945, Certificate of Commendation, Navy Dept., 1947. Registered profl. engr., Ill. Life mem. IEEE. Author: Basics of Missile Guidance and Space Techniques, 1959, Fundamentals of Rockets, Missiles and Spacecraft, 1962; Modern Communications Switching Systems, 1974. Inventor low radiation radio receiver. Home: 655 W Irving Park Rd Chicago IL 60613 Office: Bell Labs Naperville IL 60566

HOBEN, WILLIAM JOSEPH, univ. adminstr., acct.; b. Hardinsburg, Ky., May 19, 1927; s. William Joseph and Maud H. (Smith) H.; B.S., U. Dayton (Ohio), 1950; M.B.A., Xavier U., Cin., 1960. Sr. acct. David E. Flagel & Co., Dayton, 1952-57; mem. faculty U. Dayton, 1957—, asso. prof. acctg., 1959-62, asst. dean, then acting dean, 1959-63, dean Sch. Bus., 1963—; dir. Technology, Inc., MAP, Inc., Catholic Telegraph Register. Pres., chmn. bd. dirs. Teach Fund, Inc., Dayton, 1960; bd. dirs. S.W. Ohio chpt. NCCJ, 1965—; trustee Sinclair Community Coll., Dayton, 1974-80. Served with USNR, World War II, Korean War. C.P.A., Ohio. Mem. Nat. Assn. Accountants, Nat. Bus. Tchrs., Inst. Internat. Auditors, Am. Mgmt. Assn., Ohio Inst. C.P.A.'s (dir., com. chmn. Dayton chpt. 1960), Dayton C. of C., Lima C. of C., Columbus C. of C., Alpha Kappa Psi. Roman Catholic. Clubs: Dayton Bicycle, Dayton Racquet, Dayton Rotary. Office: 300 College Park Dayton OH 45469

HOBERG, DON DWAINE, radio mgr.; b. St. Paul, Oct. 4, 1953; s. Dwaine H. and Kay N. (Nelson) H.; B.A., Moorhead State U., 1976. Gen. mgr. Sta. WEBC Radio, Duluth, Minn., 1979—. Mem. Nat. Assn. Broadcasters, Radio Advt. Bur., Duluth/Superior Advt. Club. Republican. Office: 1001 E 9th St Duluth MN 55805

HOBSON, DOROTHY LEE, data processing exec.; b. Benton, Ala., July 2, 1943; d. Charlie and Martha Ree (James) Maull; student IBM Tng. Center, 1965, St. Paul Tech. Inst., 1981, St. Catherine Coll., 1981—; m. Clarence Hobson, Sept. 23, 1980; 1 dau. by previous marriage, Pamela Jean Jones; 1 stepson, Clarence Liemandt Hobson. Supr., operator PAMAC Data Systems, N.Y.C., 1971-73; data operator Data Processing Center, St. Paul, 1973-74; asst. mgr. data preparation N.W. Airlines, St. Paul/Mpls., 1975-76; data entry supr. Econ. Labs., Inc., St. Paul, 1977—. Occupational cooperating adv. com. 916 Area Vocat. Tech., 1979, St. Paul Area Vocat. Tech., 1979-81. Mem. Data Entry Mgmt. Assn. Home: 927 Iglehart Ave Saint Paul MN 55104 Office: 370 Wabasha St Saint Paul MN 55104

HOCHWALD, WERNER, economist, educator; b. Berlin, Germany, Jan. 21, 1910; s. Moritz and Elsa (Stahl) H.; grad. U. Berlin, 1932; Ph.D., Washington U., 1944; m. Hilde Landenberger, Jan. 28, 1938 (dec. June 1958); children—Miriam Ruth, Eve Fay. Came to U.S., 1938, naturalized, 1944. Counsel, Com. on Aid and Reconstrn., Berlin, 1933-38; accountant, St. Louis, 1938-42; instr. Army Specialized Tng. Program, 1942-44; instr. econs., Wash. U., St. Louis, 1944-47, successively asst. and asso. prof., chmn. dept., prof., 1950-63, Tileston prof. polit. economy, 1963—; Kennedy Disting. prof. econs. U. of South, 1981. Cons., U.S. Office Edn., 1967—; dir. Internat. Econ. Research, 1950-55; lectr. Army Fin. Sch., 1950-52; cons. Fed. Res. Bank St. Louis, 1947-58. Mem. Citizens' Budget Com., St. Louis, 1957. Mem. Nat. Planning Assn. (dir. study local impacts fgn. trade), Am. Econ. Assn., Indsl. Relations Research Assn., Econometric Soc., Am. Statis. Assn. (nat. council 1950-52), Econ. History Assn., Am. Farm Econ. Assn., So. (pres. 1966-67). Midwest econ. assns., Conf. Research Income and Wealth, Internat. Assn. Research in Income and Wealth, Nat. Acad. Scis. (hwy. research bd. 1961-64). Author: Local Impact of Foreign Trade, 1960; Essays in Southern Economic Development, 1964; An Economist's Image of History, 1968; The Idea of Progress, 1973. Contbg. author various books, profl. jours., Ency. of Econs. Editor: Design of Regional Accounts, 1961. Home: 6910 Cornell Ave Saint Louis MO 63130 Office: Washington U Saint Louis MO 63130

HOCK, GERALD CARL, packaging co. exec.; b. Chgo., Jan. 1, 1938; s. Carl August and Ann Marie (Hermes) H.; B.B.A., U. Wis., Madison, 1960; M.B.A., U. Wis., Milw., 1977; m. Patricia A. Dalton, July 23, 1960; children—Debra, Carlton. Exec. trainee Bauer & Black div. Kendall Co., Chgo., 1960-62; prodn. mgr. Curtiss Candy Co., Chgo., 1962-64; dir., asso. dean U. Wis., Milw., 1964-76; v.p. Taxman Co., Milw., 1976-78; gen. mgr. Green Bay Packaging, Inc. (Wis.), 1979—; chmn. bd. U.S. Sports Acad.; dir. Tng. & Placement, Inc. Area chmn. United Way; state chmn. Blue Crutch Campaign; rep. from Wis., Boys Nation. Recipient Danforth award, 1955, Elks Leadership award, 1956, Black Student Union award, 1974. Fellow Am. Geog. Soc.; mem. Nat. Assn. Aux. Services, Weber Exec. Alumni Assn. (pres.), Internat. Racquetball Assn., U. Wis.-Madison Jr. Men's Hon. Soc. Home: 4568 Creek Valley Ln Green Bay WI 54155 Office: PO Box 1107 Green Bay WI 54305

HOCKENBERG, HARLAN DAVID, lawyer; b. Des Moines, July 1, 1927; s. Leonard C. and Estyre M. (Zalk) H.; B.A., U. Iowa, 1949, J.D., 1952; m. Dorothy A. Arkin, June 3, 1953; children—Marni Lynn, Thomas Leonard, Edward Arkin. Admitted to Iowa bar, 1952; asso. firm Abramson & Myers, Des Moines, 1952-58; mem. firm Abramson, Myers & Hockenberg, Des Moines, 1958-64; sr. partner firm Davis, Hockenberg, Wine, Brown & Koehn, and predecessor, Des Moines, 1964—; dir. West Des Moines (Iowa) State Bank. Pres., Des Moines Jewish Social Service Agy., 1958-60; mem. Internat. Relations and Nat. Security Adv. Council, Republican Nat. Com., 1978; chmn. Council of Jewish Fedns., Small Cities Com., 1970-71; pres. Willkie House Inc., Des Moines, 1965-66, Des Moines Jewish Welfare Fedn., 1973-74. Served with USNR, 1945-46. Mem. Des Moines C. of C. (chmn. Bur. Econ. Devel. 1979, 80), Delta Sigma Rho, Omicron Delta Kappa, Phi Epsilon Pi. Republican. Clubs: Des Moines, Pioneer, Wakonda. Home: 3920 Grand Ave Des Moines IA 50312 Office: Davis Hockenberg Wine Brown & Koehn 2300 Financial Center Des Moines IA 50309

HOCKINGS, PAUL EDWARD, educator; b. Hertford, Eng., Feb. 23, 1935; came to U.S., 1960; s. Arthur and Mary Frances (Allen) H.; B.A., U. Sydney, 1957; M.A., U. Toronto, 1960; postgrad. U. Chgo., 1961; Ph.D., U. Calif., Berkeley, 1965. Research asso. Inst. for Communications Research, Stanford (Calif.) U., 1964-65; asst. prof. anthropology UCLA, 1965-69; asso. producer MGM, Culver City, Calif., 1969; asso. prof. anthropology U. Ill., Chgo., 1970—. Adv. council Nat. Human Film Center, Smithsonian Inst., 1975—; organizer festivals for anthropol. film Field Mus. Natural History, Chgo., 1978-81; founding mem. Library-Anthropology Resource Group, 1971-81. Am. Inst. Indian Studies fellow, 1962-77; Social Sci. Research Council fellow, 1964-65; Ford Found. grantee, 1967-68; U. Ill. grantee, 1972-79. Mem. Royal Anthropol. Inst. Gt. Britain, Am. Anthropol. Assn. (fgn. fellow), Soc. for Anthropology of Visual Communication, Soc. for S. Indian Studies. Editor: Principles of Visual Anthropology, 1975; Ancient Hindu Refugees, Badaga Social History 1550-1975, 1980; Sex and Disease in a Mountain Community, 1980, A Bibliography for the Nilgiri Hills of Southern India, 1978. Home: 9255 S Winchester Ave Chicago IL 60620 Office: Dept Anthropology Univ Ill Chicago PO Box 4348 Chicago IL 60680

HODA, QAMRUL, physician; b. Jamshedpur, India, Feb. 2, 1942; came to U.S., 1969; s. Syed Anwarul and Ummatuz (Zohra) H.; I. Sci., St. Xavier's Coll., Ranchi, India, 1960; M.B.B.S., P.W. Med. Coll., Patna, India, 1965; M.D. in Pediatrics, Patna U., 1968; m. Nikhat Bano, June 14, 1972; children—Syed Tanveer, Tasnim. Intern, St. Joseph Mercy Hosp., Pontiac, Mich., 1969-70, now staff mem.; resident in pediatrics, Pontiac Gen. Hosp., 1970-72, now staff mem., cons. in pediatric nephrology, 1975—; resident Hosp. for Sick Children, Toronto, Ont., Can., 1972-73; teaching fellow in nephrology and ambulatory pediatrics Wayne County Gen. Hosp., Pontiac, 1974-75; pvt. practice medicine specializing in pediatrics and pediatric nephrology, Pontiac, 1975—. Fellow Am. Acad. Pediatrics; mem. Mich. Med. Soc., Oakland County Med. Soc., Detroit Pediatric Soc. Office: 185 Elizabeth Lake Rd Pontiac MI 48053

HODES, BARBARA, orgn. cons.; b. Chgo., Nov. 30, 1941; d. David and Tybe (Ziff) Zisook; B.S., Northwestern U., 1962; m. Scott Hodes, Dec. 19, 1961 (div. 1977); children—Brian, Valery. Partner Just Causes, cons.not-for-profit orgns., Chgo., 1979—; Chgo. cons. Population Resource Center, 1978—. Woman's bd. dirs. Mus. Contemporary Art; bd. dirs., vice chmn. Med. Research Inst. Council, Michael Reese Med. Center; bd. dirs., chmn. Midwest Women's Center; trustee Francis W. Parker Sch. Office: Just Causes 1405 N Dearborn Pkwy Chicago IL 60610

HODGE, DORIS JEAN, educator; b. Chattanooga; d. Herman Van Buren and Motis Senetta (Hester) Davis; B.S., Wayne State U., 1965, Ed.D., 1980; M.A., U. Mich., 1971; 1 dau., Angela Karen. Reading coordinator Murray Wright, Detroit Public Schs., 1971-77; reading cons. Detroit Coll. Opportunities Program, U. Detroit, 1972-75; research asst. Office Research, Evaluation and Planning, Detroit Public Schs., 1977—. Pres., Episcopal Ch. Women of Grace Ch., 1980—; active Greater Opportunities Industrialization Centers voter registration drive, 1980; campaign worker local polit. campaign; participant Tng. Urban Educators for Linking Agt. Roles project Nat. Inst. Edn., 1980-81. Recipient Spirit of Detroit award, 1980. Mem. Am. Edn. Research Assn., Internat. Reading Assn., Assn. Sch. Curriculum Devel., Detroit Assn. Univ. Mich. Women, Mich. Alliance Black Sch. Educators, Mich. Council Tchrs. of English, Mich. Edn. Research Assn., Nat. Alliance Black Sch. Educators, Detroit Women Sch. Adminstrs., U. Mich. Alumni, Wayne State U. Coll. Edn. Alumni (bd. govs. 1981—), Engring. Soc. Detroit, Eta Phi Beta, Phi Delta Kappa. Democrat. Club: Jim Dandy Ski. Home: 1913 Hyde Park Dr Detroit MI 48207 Office: 10100 Grand River Detroit MI 48204

HODGE, JAMES ROBERT, psychiatrist; b. Martins Ferry, Ohio, Jan. 28, 1927; s. Robert Gabriel and Ethel Melissa (Ashton) H.; B.S., Franklin and Marshall Coll., 1946; M.D., Jefferson Med. Coll., 1950; m. Marilyn Jane Dinklocker, June 10, 1950; children—Sharon, Scott. Intern, U.S. Naval Hosp., St. Albans, N.Y., 1950-51; resident Menninger Sch. Psychiatry, Topeka, 1951-52, USN Hosp., Oceanside, Calif., 1952-53, Univ. Hosps., Cleve., 1954-55; USPHS fellow adult psychiatry Sch. Medicine, Case-Western Res. U., Cleve., 1955-56; practice medicine specializing in psychiatry, Akron, Ohio, 1956—; head psychiatry Akron City Hosp., 1962-75, chmn., 1979—, cons. staff, 1975-79; adj. prof. psychology U. Akron, 1963—; council chiefs psychiatry Northeastern Ohio U. Coll. Medicine, Akron, 1974-76, 78—, prof. psychiatry, 1980—, program dir. psychiat. residency program, 1981—; chmn. div. mental health scis. Internat. Grad. U., 1976-79. Served to lt. USNR, 1944-45, 50-51, 52-54. Recipient spl. recognition award Ohio Psy. Assn., 1976, 81. Fellow Am. Psychiat. Assn., Am. Soc. Clin. Hypnosis, Internat. Soc. Clin. and Exptl. Hypnosis, Acad. Psychosomatic Medicine, Central Neuropsychiat. Assn., Am. Coll. Psychiatrists; mem. Ohio Psychiat. Assn. (pres. 1980-81). Author: Practical Psychiatry for the Primary Physician, 1975. Feature writer Med. Times mag. Producer movie: The Use of Hypnosis in Psychotherapy, 1975. Home: 295 Pembroke Rd Akron OH 44313 Office: Dept Psychiatry Akron City Hosp 525 E Market St Akron OH 44309

HODGES, JAMES TROY, mfg. co. exec.; b. Chgo., Dec. 5, 1949; s. Troy Manual and Peggy Ann (White) H.; student Baylor U., Waco, Tex., 1967-70; B.A., U. Ill., 1971; postgrad. U. Louisville, 1973-75; m. Pamela Sue Vance, Dec. 19, 1970; children—Rebekah Lea, James Thomas, Joseph Adam. Systems programmer City of Louisville, 1971-72; systems analyst Liberty Nat. Bank, Louisville, 1972-73; computer center mgr. Med. Sch. U. Louisville, 1973-75; pres. Bloodstock Computers Services, Lexington, Ky., 1975-79; devel. mgr. Merrell Dow Pharm. Inc., Cin., 1979—. Deacon, budget dir. First Baptist Ch. of Anderson Hills, Cin. Mem. Digital Equipment Computer Users Soc., Assn. Computing Machinery, Assn. Timesharing Users, Am. Nat. Standard Inst. Republican. Home: 537 N Revere St Cincinnati OH 45230 Office: 2110 E Glabraith Rd Cincinnati OH 45215

HODGES, LEO CHARLES, publishing exec.; b. Portland, Tenn., Jan. 31, 1946; s. Cleo Clifton and Leola (Durham) H.; B.A., Purdue U., 1968; J.D., Harvard U., 1971. Admitted to Ind. bar, 1971; asso. firm Ice Miller Donadio & Ryan, Indpls., 1971-73; practice law Savill & Hodges, Indpls., 1973; editor, editorial dept. head R&R Newkirk, Indpls., 1973-79, dir. product devel., 1980—; seminar and inst. speaker. Active Noble Schs. and Industries, Crossroads Rehab. Center, Center for Ind. Living. C.L.U. Mem. Am. Bar Assn., Ind. Bar Assn., Am. Soc. C.L.U.'s. Presbyterian. Editor-in-chief Advanced Underwriting Service, 6 vols., 1973-80; co-author, contbr. Pension Plans Service, 2 vols., 1976—, Charitable Giving Tax Service, 3 vols., 1977—, Estate Planner's Service, 3 vols., 1978—; author, co-author books and monographs including: Retirement Plans After Pension Reform, 1974; Professional Corporations Today, 1976; The Tax Reform Act Manual, 1976; The Tax Companion, 1977, 81; Unified Estate Planning, 1977, 80; One Year of Unified Tax Planning, 1977; The Revenue Act Manual, 1978; Estate Planning Highlights of 1978, 1979, 1980 (1979, 80, 81); Generation-Skipping Transfer Tax, 1979; The Living Legacy: Charitable Gifts of Life Insurance, 1979; Tax Planning for Gifts of Life Insurance, 1979; The Public Life of a Private Annuity, 1980; The Life Insurance Trust Handbook, 1980; contbr. articles to publs. Home: 2026 W 76th St Indianapolis IN 46260 Office: PO Box 1727 Indianapolis IN 46206

HODGES, NOWELL DALE, educator; b. California, Mo., July 9, 1958; s. Henry Brent and Ina Jean (Stinson) H.; B.S., U. Mo., Columbia, 1980; m. Carol Rae Crawford, Jan. 5, 1980. Vocat. agr. instr. Maries R-1 Schs., Vienna, Mo., 1980—; adv. Vienna chpt. Future Farmers Am. Mem. Maries County Fair Bd., Livestock div., 1980-81. Mem. Am. Vocat. Assn., Nat. Vocat. Assn., Nat. Vocat. Agr. Tchrs. Assn., Mo. Vocat. Agr. Tchrs. Assn., Mo. State Tchrs. Assn., Mo. Vocat. Assn. Baptist. Home: Star Route 1 Vienna MO 65582 Office: Route 42 E Maries R-1 Vienna MO 65582

HODGES, PAMELA SUE, physician; b. Harlingen, Tex., Jan. 8, 1950; d. Duvel Leo and Nannie Elfa (Hardin) Vance; B.A., U. Louisville, 1972, M.D., 1976; m. James Troy Hodges, Dec. 19, 1970; children—Rebekah Lea, James Thomas, Joseph Adam. Intern, in anesthesiology U. Ky., 1976-77; resident in ob-gyn U. Ky., 1976-80; practice medicine specializing in ob-gyn, Covington, Ky., 1980—; tchr. St. Elizabeth Med. Center, Covington. Fellow Am. Coll. Obstetrics and Gynecology; mem. Am. Women's Med. Assn., Ky. Med. Assn., Kenton-Campbell County Med. Soc., John Greene Soc., Alpha Lambda Delta, Alpha Epsilon Delta. Baptist. Home: 537 N Revere St Cincinnati OH 45230 Office: 18 N Fort Thomas Ave Fort Thomas KY 41075

HODGKINS, EARL WARNER, r.r. engring. assn. exec.; b. Woodsville, N.H., June 30, 1919; s. Earl Warner and Elizabeth (Mitchell) H.; B.S. in Civil Engring., U. N.H., 1950; m. Ruth Abbie Davison, Sept. 23, 1939; children—Earl Warner, Linda Ruth Hodgkins Jacobs, Lorraine Dawn Hodgkins Cunningham. From transferman to messenger to clk. Ry. Express Agy., Woodsville, N.H., 1936-50; structural designer B.& M. R.R., 1950-52, student supr., Greenfield, Mass., 1952; asst. supr. bridges and blgs. Maine Central R.R., Portland, 1953-54, asst. engr. structures, 1954-58; asso. editor Ry. Track and Structures mag., Chgo., 1958-64; asso. engring. editor Ry. Age Weekly, 1958-64; exec. sec. Am. Ry. Engring. Assn., Chgo., 1964-68, exec. mgr., 1968-73, exec. dir., 1974—; exec. vice chmn., engring. div. Assn. Am. R.R.'s, Chgo., 1964-71, exec. dir. engring. div., 1971—. Active local Boy Scouts Am., 1954-60. Served to 1st lt., C.A.C. and Transp. Corps, AUS, 1942-45; ETO. Mem. Am. Ry. Engring. Assn., Am. Ry. Bridge and Bldg. Assn., Roadmasters and Maintenance of Way Assn. Am., Maintenance of Way Club Chgo., Am. Soc. Assn. Execs., Am. Soc. Engring. Edn., ASCE, Council Engring. and Sci. Soc. Execs., Nat. Geog. Soc. Mem. Ch. Jesus Christ of Latter-day Saints. Office: 238 Marquette Park Forest IL 60466

HODSON, DARREL LEROY, lawyer; b. Amboy, Ind., July 20, 1912; s. Charles John and Dora Ellen (Sharp) H.; student Purdue U., 1929-30, U. Wis., 1931; B.S. in Bus. Adminstrn., U. Ind., 1935, J.D., 1937; m. Elaine Emeline Estrich, June 8, 1941; children—John Darrel, James Leroy. Admitted to Ind. bar, 1937; since practiced in Kokomo, partner firm Hodson, Lucas and Hillis, 1938-40, Winslow and Hodson, 1940-42; dir. U.S. Fgn. Claims Commns. in Europe, 1946-47; gen. practice law, 1948-62; partner firm Hodson and Osborn, 1962—; dir., pres. Imperial Properties, Inc.; city judge, Kokomo, 1938; pros. atty. 62nd Jud. Circuit, 1941-42, 55-58; county atty., 1950-52. Bd. dirs. Family Service Assn., Inc., 1971-77, United Fund, 1951-52. Served to maj. AUS, 1942-46; col. Res., ret. Decorated Bronze Star. Mem. Am. Legion, C. of C., Am., Ind., Howard County (pres. 1950) bar assns., Judge Advs. Assn. (state pres. 1954-56), Internat. Platform Assn., Res. Officers Assn. Democrat. Methodist. (dir. No. Ind. Conf. Found. 1963-68, dir. dist. missionary soc. 1959-68). Clubs: Kiwanis (v.p. 1955, sec. 1961, dir. Kiwanis Club Found. 1972-77), Elks. Home: 803 West Blvd Kokomo IN 46901 Office: 216 E Walnut St Kokomo IN 46901

HOECKER, BURDET WESLEY, banker; b. Ames, Iowa, June 7, 1942; s. Wesley H. and Grace S. (Semon) H.; B.S., B.A., U. Mo., 1965, M.S., M.B.A., 1972; m. Marilyn Sue Hughes, Oct. 29, 1977; 1 dau., Julie Anna. Vice pres. Mercantile Mortgage Co., St. Louis, 1972-77; v.p. corr. div. Mercantile Trust Co., St. Louis, 1977—, v.p. Mercantile Bancorp., St. Louis, 1980—; dir. Foremost Livestock Ranch, Columbia, Mo.; mem. faculty Penn Valley Coll., Kansas City, Mo. Served with USNR, 1965-69; Vietnam. Decorated D.F.C., Purple Heart, Air medal. Mem. Mortgage Bankers Assn., Farm Bur. Republican. Clubs: Mo. Athletic, St. Louis. Office: 1 Mercantile Center St Louis MO 63166

HOEDEL, MICHAEL ANTHONY, radio broadcaster; b. St. Louis, Feb. 13, 1945; s. Anton Alois and Violet Dolores H.; B.F.A., U. Cin., 1966; M.A., U. Mo., 1969; m. Dianne Kay Risser, Oct. 21, 1978; 1 dau., Christina Irene. Sports dir., disk jockey Sta. KJCF, Festus, Mo., 1968-69; announcer, writer, producer Sta. KSLH, St. Louis, 1969-73; gen. mgr. Sta. KQCA, Canton, Mo., 1974-75; disk jockey KOOL-FM, Phoenix, 1975; gen. mgr. Sta. KSLH, St. Louis, 1976—; tchr. Culver Stockton Coll., Canton, 1975. Mem. Public Radio in Mid-Am. Club:

Francis Park Tennis of St. Louis (past pres.). Office: 1517 S Theresa St Saint Louis MO 63104

HOEFFKEN, DEBORAH ANN, educator; b. Belleville, Ill., Apr. 27, 1952; d. Francis Martin and Ethel Mae (Bertschinger) H.; B.S. in Math., Quincy Coll., 1974; postgrad. in adminstrn. SE Mo. State U., 1976-78. Tchr., St. Vincent High Sch., Perryville, Mo., 1974-78; math. tchr. Mater Dei High Sch., Breese, Ill., 1978—, asst. volleyball coach, asst. cheerleading coach, head softball coach. Mem. Assn. for Supervision and Curriculum Devel., Nat. Cath. Edn. Assn., Nat. Council Tchrs. of Math. Roman Catholic. Home: 411 N Cherry Ct Apt 321 Breese IL 62230 Office: 9th and Plum Sts Breese IL 62230

HOEFFNER, LLOYD CARL, educator; b. Manitowoc, Wis., May 8, 1938; s. Edmund Henry and Clalie (Krueger) H.; m. Margery Jean Bell, Aug. 13, 1966; children—John, Tom. Printing instr. SUNY, Oswego, 1961-63; tchr. Manitowoc Public Schs., 1963-65, Menasha (Wis.) Public Schs., 1965-66; coordinator Graphic Arts Inst., Fox Valley Tech. Inst., Menasha, 1966-68; flexography instr., 1968—. Mem. Wis. Edn. Assn., Am. Vocat. Assn., Internat. Graphic Arts Edn. Assn., Wis. Assn. Vocat. and Adult Edn., Flexographic Tech. Assn. (dir.), Coop. Council Ind. Graphics. Lutheran. Home: 2532 S East St Appleton WI 54911 Office: PO Box 2277 Appleton WI 54913

HOEFLE, RONALD A., cons. engring. co. exec.; b. Freeport, Ill., Apr. 24, 1929; s. Everett G. and Mary Pauline H.; B.S., U. Ill., 1951; m. Shirley Ann Stegeman, June 12, 1954; children—JoEllen, Paul Ryan, Julie Lynn. Engr., Dravo Corp., Pitts., 1951-55; engr. W.E. Deuchler Assos., Inc., Aurora, Ill., 1955-65, v.p., 1965-76, v.p. engring., sec., treas., 1976—. Elder, Presbyn. Ch., 1960—. Served with USAF, 1951-53. Registered profl. engr., Ill. Mem. Nat. Soc. Profl. Engrs., ASCE, Am. Acad. Environ. Engrs., Ill. Soc. Profl. Engrs. Republican. Club: Rotary. Home: 145 S Edgelawn Dr Aurora IL 60506 Office: W E Deuchler Assos Inc 230 S Woodlawn Ave Aurora IL 60506

HOEFT, JERALD ROBERT, ins. co. exec.; b. West Bend, Wis., Sept. 3, 1942; s. Robert Herman and Dolores Cecilia (Bales) H.; B.B.A., U. Wis., Whitewater, 1964; m. Sandra Delores Schuster, June 7, 1969; children—Montgomery, Megan Marie. Cost analyst Bendix Corp., 1964-65; audit supr. Ernst & Ernst, Milw., 1965-72; v.p. fin., asst. treas. surg. care Blue Shield, Inc., Milw., 1972-79; v.p. fin., treas. Wis. Employers Ins. Co., Green Bay, 1980—. C.P.A., Wis.; cert. mgmt. acct. Mem. Fin. Execs. Inst., Am. Inst. C.P.A.'s, Wis. Inst. C.P.A.'s, Nat. Assn. Accts., Inst. Mgmt. Acctg., Ins. and Acctg. Statis. Assn. Republican. Roman Catholic. Home: 4515 Wyandot Trail Green Bay WI 54302 Office: Wis Employers Ins Co 2777 Ridge Rd Green Bay WI 54303

HOEHNE, DAVID PAUL, broadcasting exec.; b. Wacoma, Iowa, Apr. 14, 1945; s. Paul Victor and Evelyn Dorthea H.; student U. No. Iowa, 1963-64, Brown Inst. Broadcasting, 1964-65; m. Elizabeth Ann Clancy, Nov. 27, 1974; 1 son, Jonathan David. Broadcaster, Sta. WHBF, Rock Island, Ill., 1968-70, Sta. WEEL, Fairfax, Va., 1970-71; broadcaster, salesman Sta. WHMC, Gaithersburg, Md., 1971-73, Sta. WINX, Rockville, Md., 1973-74; sales mgr., exec. v.p. Sta. KRNA, Iowa City, 1974—, also dir. Mem. Iowa City C. of C. (chmn. tourism and convs. com. 1979—, mem. stash the trash com. 1979—), Iowa City Jaycees (Service award 1975, Jaycee of Month 1978, Spoke award 1977). Home: 1414 Keokuk St Iowa City IA 52240 Office: 1027 Hollywood Blvd Iowa City IA 52240

HOEKSTRA, RONALD BENNETT, ednl. adminstr.; b. Paxton, Ill., Jan. 2, 1943; B.S., U. Ill., Urbana, 1965, M.Ed., 1969; Ph.D., Ohio State U., Columbus, 1973; m. Linda Turney, June 12, 1966; 1 dau., Elizabeth Leigh. Edn. intern Office of Gov. Ohio, Columbus, 1971; adminstrv. intern Office of Supt. Schs. Saginaw (Mich.), 1972-73; ednl. policy fellow Inst. Ednl. Leadership, Washington, 1973-74; chief program planning/assessment Fairfax County (Va.) Public Schs., 1974-80; asso. dean undergrad. studies Southeastern U., Washington, 1978-80; dir. bus. affairs Westerville (Ohio) City Schs., 1980—; mgmt. cons.; lectr. in field. Mem. Am. Assn. Sch. Adminstrs., Assn. Sch. Bus. Ofcls., Ohio State Edliners, Kappa Delta Pi, Phi Delta Kappa. Club: Masons. Author articles in field, also monograph. Home: 85 Marlene Dr Westerville OH 43081 Office: 336 Otterbein Ave Westerville OH 43081

HOELLEN, JOHN JAMES, lawyer; b. Chgo., Sept. 24, 1914; s. John J. and Mame F. (Skellinger) H.; B.A., Northwestern, 1935, J.D., 1938; m. Mary Jane McMeans, Apr. 24, 1948; children—Elizabeth Hoellen Ward, Robert. Admitted to Ill. bar, 1938; practice law, Chgo., 1938-41, 47—; atty. Ill. Dept. Registration and Edn., 1946-47; dir. Lincoln Square Savs. & Loan Assn., Chgo., Bank Ravenswood, Chgo. Alderman, 47th Ward., Chgo., 1947-75. Mem. Republican Central Com. Cook County, 1964—, del. nat. conv., 1972, 76, 80; candidate for mayor of Chgo., 1975. Served as lt., USNR, 1941-46, with Naval Intelligence Service, 1941-43, aboard U.S.S. Chester T. O'Brien, 1944-46. Bd. dirs. Ravenswood YMCA; pres. Sulzer Family Found., Inc.; mem. Chgo. Transit Authority, 1979—. Recipient pub. service award YMCA, Trinity Coll., Indsl. Engring. Coll., V.F.W., Am. Vets, Lions, Kiwanis. Mem. Am., Ill., Chgo. bar assns., Am. Judicature Soc., Germania, Northcenter C. of C., Chgo. Hist. Soc., Art Inst. Chgo., Field Mus., Shedd Aquarium, Am. Legion, V.F.W., S.A.R., Chgo. Assn. Commerce & Industry, Navy League, Delta Theta Phi, Phi Beta Kappa. Clubs: Executives, Northwestern University (Chgo.). Home: 1842 W Larchmont Av Chicago IL 60613 Office: 1940 W Irving Park Rd Chicago IL 60613

HOELTING, FLOYD B., univ. adminstr.; b. Tulia, Tex., Feb. 16, 1943; s. N. A. and Mary Elizabeth Hoelting; B.A., Emporia State U., 1967; M.S.E., 1968; Ed.D., Okla. State U., 1972; m. JoEllen Greathouse, Jan. 18, 1969; children—Jason, Ryan. Grad. asst. to dean of students Emporia (Kans.) State U., 1967-69; asst. dir. housing Okla. State U., Stillwater, 1969-72; dir. residence hall programs Western Ill. U., Macomb, 1972-77; dir. Office of Residential Life, Ill. State U., Normal, 1977—. Pres., Ill. March of Dimes, 1977-79; dir. McDonough County March of Dimes, 1973-77; vol. dir. United Way, 1972-78. Served with USAF, 1961-65. Recipient Edn. and Enlightenment award Internat. Meditation Soc., 1976; Nat. award Outstanding Educators Am., 1975; Disting. Service award Nat. March of Dimes Assn., 1980. Mem. Nat. Assn. Student Personnel Adminstrs., Am. Coll. Personnel Assn., Assn. Coll. and Univ. Housing Officers, Nat. Entertainment and Campus Activities Assn. (chmn. residence life com.). Author: Residence Hall Programs, 1971; How To Do It In Residence Halls: 1001 Ways to Program, 1973; Resident Student Development, 1980. Home: RFD 1 Towanda IL 61776 Office: Office Residental Life Ill State U Normal IL 61761

HOENICKE, EDWARD HENRY, airline exec.; b. Chgo., Apr. 12, 1930; s. Edward Albert and Henrietta Christina (Hameister) H.; student Deep Springs Coll., 1946-48; A.B., Cornell U., 1950; J.D., U. Mich., 1956; m. Janice A. Gravel, Aug. 14, 1954; children—Jeanne E., Anne L. Admitted to N.Y. bar, 1957; asso. firm Cravath, Swaine & Moore, N.Y.C., 1956-59; internat. counsel Olin Corp., N.Y.C., 1959-68; v.p., gen. counsel Beech-Nut Lifesavers Corp., N.Y.C., 1968-69, pres. internat. div., 1969-75; v.p., asst. gen. counsel Squibb Corp., N.Y.C., 1975-77; sr. v.p., gen. counsel, sec. United Airlines, Inc. and VAL, Inc., Chgo., 1980—. Bd. dirs. Care, Inc., 1972—. Served with USAF, 1951-53. Mem. Am. Bar Assn. Republican. Presbyterian. Clubs: Bronxville (N.Y.) Field; Bath and Tennis (Lake Forest, Ill.). Office: United Airlines PO Box 66100 Chicago IL 60666

HOENISCH, GREG STEVEN, mfg. co. advt. mgr.; b. Wausau, Wis., June 16, 1953; s. Ernest Alfred and Rosemarie Delores (Lerch) H.; B.B.A., U. Wis., Eau Claire, 1976; m. Mary Beth Adams, Oct. 1, 1977. Account exec. Sta. WAOW-TV, Wausau, 1976-77, Sta. WRIG, Wausau, 1977-78; advt. promotion mgr. Hoffers Inc, Wausau, 1978—; cons. advt. promotion Wausau High Sch. Publicity dir. Wis. Valley Fair, Wausau, 1980—. Club: Elks (Wausau). Home: 524 S 3d Ave Wausau WI 54401 Office: 310 Bellis St Wausau WI 54401

HOEPPNER, JOHN PAUL, advt. agy. exec.; b. Cherokee, Iowa, Jan. 12, 1952; s. Paul John and Juanita Madilin (Begg) H.; B.S., U. S.D., 1974; m. Shirleen Honsbruch, July 31, 1977; children—Jennifer, Justin. Farm mgr. Hoeppner Farms, Sutherland, Iowa, 1970-72; account exec. Griffith Advt., Sioux City, Iowa, 1972-74; pres., owner Hoeppner Advt., Sioux City, 1974—; dir. Hoeppner Farms, Inc., Com Pro Prodns., Inc.; dir. communications dept. U. S.D.; guest inst. U. S.D., Morningside Coll., S.D. Bankers Assn. Bd. dirs. Sioux City Community Theater, 1979—, Rivercade, 1970—. Recipient Outstanding Public Service award Iowa Broadcasters Assn., 1976, Outstanding Tourism Promotion award Iowa Devel. Commn., 1979. Mem. Am. Assn. Advt. Agencies, Nat. Agri Mktg. Assn., Bus. and Profl. Advt. Assn., Ad Club Sioux Cities, Sioux City C. of C., Iowa Lakes C. of C., Better Bus. Bur. Republican. Methodist. Clubs: Sioux City Bus. Leaders, Sioux City Kiwanis. Office: 4409 Stone St Sioux City IA 51106

HOERNEMAN, CALVIN A., JR., educator; b. Youngstown, Ohio, Sept. 30, 1940; s. Calvin A. and Lucille A. (Leiss) H.; B.A., Bethany Coll., 1962; M.A., Mich. State U., 1964; m. Cheryl L. Morand, Aug. 10, 1973; children—David, Jennifer. Mem. faculty Delta Coll., University Center, Mich., 1966—, prof. econs., 1976—; syndicated wine columnist Detroit News, Flint Jour., Mich. Beverage News, Ariz. Beverage Guide, 1977—; cons. Prentice-Hall, Goodyear Pub. Recipient Recognition award AAUP, 1972; Bergstein award Delta Coll. Grad. Class, 1972. Mem. Am. Econ. Assn., Midwest Econ. Assn., AAUP, Wine Educators Soc. Author: Poverty, Wealth and Income Distribution, 1969; contbr. articles to various publs. Home: 5712 Lamplighter Ln Midland MI 48640 Office: Delta Coll University Center MI 48710

HOERNER, JOHN FINCH, corp. exec.; b. Versailles, Ohio, Aug. 27, 1939; s. Wilbur Franklin and Mary (Finch) H.; B.S., Ohio State U., 1961; M.B.A., Harvard U., 1965; m. Susan Caroline Hobson, July 22, 1967; children—Deborah Lynn, Barbara Ann. With Procter & Gamble Co., 1965—, personnel mgr., Dallas, 1970, Lima, Ohio, 1971-72, head corp. employee benefits, Cin., 1973-75, head corp. employee info. systems, 1975-80, head corp. employee benefits and compensation, 1981—. Maj. campaign chmn. United Appeal of Cin., 1974. Served with U.S. Army, 1961-63. Recipient Meritorious Service award Boy Scouts Am., 1979. Mem. Am. Soc. Personnel Adminstrn. (regional dir. 1970), Am. Mgmt. Assn. Presbyterian. Club: Harvard Bus. Sch. (Cin.). Home: 7856 Trailwind Dr Montgomery OH 45242 Office: Procter and Gamble Co 6th and Sycamore Sts Cincinnati OH 45202

HOFELING, HARLAN WILBUR, agronomist; b. Watseka, Ill., Sept. 14, 1955; s. Wilbur Harm and Esther Emma (Kuhlman) H.; student So. Ill. U., 1973-75; B.S. in Agronomy, U. Ill., 1977. Technician, U. Ill., Urbana, 1975-77; prodn. mgr. Peterson Soybean Seed div. Pioneer Hi-Bred Internat., Inc., Champaign, Ill., 1978-79, agronomist, Le Roy, Ill., 1980—. Mem. Am. Soc. Agronomy, Crop Sci. Soc. Am., Soil Sci. Soc. Am. Lutheran. Club: U. Ill. Rugby. Home: 408 1/2 S Chestnut St Le Roy IL 61752 Office: Rural Route 1 Box 119-A Le Roy IL 61752

HOFER, ALBERT CORNELIUS, rubber co. exec.; b. Akron, Ohio, Sept. 25, 1920; s. Ernest Edward and Emma (Straub) H.; bus. degree Actual Bus. Coll., 1938-39; student U. Akron, 1940-50; m. Helen Grace Klespies, July 31, 1942; children—Barry A., Diana L., Denise L. Accounting supr. Firestone Tire & Rubber Co., Akron, 1941-53; with Cooper Tire & Rubber Co., Findlay, Ohio, 1953—, mgr. employee services, 1975—; asst. treas. Findlay Warehouse Corp., 1972-76. Republican precinct committeeman, Findlay, 1976—; councilman-at-large City of Findlay, 1970-71, city treas., 1978—; mem. bd., pres. Winnebrenner Meml. Fund, 1975—; chmn. Task Force on Crime and Vandalism, 1976—. Served with USAAF, 1942-45. Mem. Adminstrv. Mgmt. Soc. (Merit Award key 1969, Diamond Merit award 1977), Soc. Pre-Retirement Program Planners, Findlay Area C. of C., Am. Assn. Ret. Persons, Findlay Area C. of C. Methodist. Clubs: Masons, Shriners, K.T. (Findlay). Home: 608 Yorkshire Dr Findlay OH 45840 Office: PO Box 550 Findlay OH 45840

HOFER, STEVEN LYLE, interior designer; b. Clinton, Iowa, June 22, 1945; s. Lyle Arthur and Helen Mae (Howson) H.; B.S., Iowa State U., 1967; m. Teresa Kay, 1980. Dir. design Alpine Interiors, Bettendorf, Iowa, 1967-68; dir. design Storey Kenworthy Co., Des Moines, 1968-81; pres. Environ. Interiors, Polk City, Iowa, 1977—; dir. interior design CPMI, Des Moines, 1981—; mem. faculty Drake U., 1972-73. Mem. Citizens Com. for Planning and Zoning, Ankeny, 1974-75. Mem. Inst. Bus. Designers, Tau Sigma Delta. Republican. Methodist. Home: 3769 NW 90th Pl Polk City IA 50226 Office: 2015 Grand Ave Des Moines IA 50312

HOFFBECK, JAMES RICHARD, educator; b. Ortonville, Minn., May 31, 1931; s. Arthur Herbert and Geraldine (Sparks) H.; B.S., S.D. State U., 1957; M.A., U. Minn., 1971; m. Marilyn Gwen Jensen, Aug. 15, 1954; children—Richard, Randall, Ronald, Renee. Asst. county agrl. agt. Morrison County, Little Falls, Minn., 1958-60; county agrl. agt. Aitkin County, Minn., 1960-65; county extension agt. Ramsey County, St. Paul, 1965-66; area extension coordinator Agrl. Extension Service, U. Minn., Mora, 1966-72, asst. dist. extension dir., 1972-76; prof., staff devel. leader, St. Paul, 1976—. Served with USMC, 1950-54. Mem. Minn. Assn. Continuing Adult Edn., Epsilon Sigma Phi, Gamma Sigma Delta. Presbyterian. Club: Lions. Home: 528 McLean St Mora MN 55051 Office: U Minn 260 Coffey Hall St Paul MN 55108

HOFFMAN, ALBERT ROMAINE, mgmt. cons.; b. Auburn, Ind., Dec. 27, 1918; s. Darrel Clyde and Cleora Selma (Wolfe) H.; grad. U.S. Army Command and Gen. Staff Coll., 1957; B.S., U. Md., 1964; M.S. in Bus. Adminstrn., George Washington U., 1965; grad. Indsl. Coll. of Armed Forces, 1965; m. Carol Rose Cullis, Nov. 27, 1943; children—Andrew, Alan, DeeAnn. Enlisted U.S. Army, 1942, commd. 2d lt., advanced through grades to col., 1972; batallion comdr. 806th Engrs., Korea, 1950-52; dir. Systems Def. Supply Agency, 1965-69; dep. comdr. U.S. Army Computer Systems Command, 1969-72, ret. 1972-78; mgmt. cons., 1978—; mgr. planning and devel. parts mktg. and distbn. Chrysler Corp., Center Line, Mich., 1972—. Decorated Legion of Merit with oak leaf cluster, Silver Star, Bronze Star with 3 oak leaf clusters, Army Commendation medal with 2 oak leaf clusters. Mem. Am. Mgmt. Assn., U.S.A. Engr. Hall of Fame. Home and Office: 600 Circle Dr Bryan OH 43506

HOFFMAN, ARTHUR CHARLES, publishing co. exec.; b. Wood River, Ill., Dec. 14, 1950; s. Arthur Casper and Doris Mae (Noe) H.; B.S., So. Ill. U., 1974, M.B.A., 1979; m. Marcia Ann Maxin, May 6, 1978. Asst. payroll supt. Wohl Shoe Co., St. Louis, 1974-75; account services supr. Occidental Chem. Co., St. Louis, 1975-77; cost analyst 1st Nat. Bank, St. Louis, 1977-79; gen. acctg. mgr. Concordia Pub. House, St. Louis, 1979—. Mem. Nat. Assn. Accts., Inst. Managerial Acctg., Assn. M.B.A. Execs., Sigma Tau Gamma. Democrat. Roman Catholic. Home: 6135 Tennessee St Saint Louis MO 63111 Office: Concordia Publishing House 3558 S Jefferson St Saint Louis MO 63118

HOFFMAN, CLYDE HARRIS, dean tech. inst.; b. Jamestown, N.D., Mar. 24, 1925; s. Clarence William and Ada Catherine (Gensrich) H.; B.S.E.E., U. N.D., 1950; M.S.E.E., U. Notre Dame, 1952, Ph.D. in Applied Mechanics, 1962; m. Betty Myra Ledingham, May 29, 1950. Instr. elec. engring. U. Notre Dame, 1951-52, asst. prof., 1953-62; project engr. Jack & Heintz, Inc., Cleve., 1952-53; asso. prof. elec. engring. Ill. Inst. Tech., Chgo., 1962-70, also head elec. engring. dept. Kabul (Afghanistan) U., 1966-68; mgr. IIT/TV Instructional Television Network, 1968-70; tng. mgr. Page Communications Engrs. INTS Program, Tehran, 1970-72; dir. tech. and vocat. tng. Harza Engring. Co., Chgo., 1972-73; 1st officer, program specialist UNESCO, Paris, 1973-78; mgr. transit communications systems IIT Research Inst., Chgo., 1978-80; dean acad. affairs DeVry Inst. Tech., Chgo., 1980—; evaluation panels undergrad. sci. instructional equipment program NSF, 1963-65; mem. Nat. Acad. Scis. adv. com. to electronics instrumentation div. Nat. Bur. Standards, 1965-68; trustee Nat. Electronics Conf., Inc. Sustaining mem. Republican Nat. Com.; mem. nat. adv. bd. Am. Security Council. Served with inf. AUS, 1943-46; ETO, PTO. Decorated Bronze Star; registered profl. engr., Ill., Ind., Calif. Mem. Instrument Soc. Am. (sr. mem., governing bd. 1964-65, v.p. Chgo. sect. 1980-81), Am. Def. Preparedness Assn. (life), DAV, (life), Nat. Rifle Assn. (life), Nat. Assn. Watch and Clock Collectors, Am. Soc. Tng. and Devel., Am. Legion, Inst. Radio Engrs. (chmn. South Bend sect. 1960-61), IEEE (exec. com. Chgo. 1964-65), Am. Ordnance Assn., AAAS, L'Assn. Internat. pour le Calcul Analogique, Simulations Councils, ASME, Marine Tech. Soc., Assn. Computing Machinery, Am. Soc. Engring. Edn., Nat. Electronics Conf. (dir. 1957-64), Art Inst. Chgo. Republican. Club: Elks. Contbr. numerous articles to profl. jours. Home: 184 Cascade Dr Indian Head Park IL 60525 Office: 3300 N Campbell St Chicago IL 60618

HOFFMAN, ELLEN BARKER, baking co. exec.; b. La Harpe, Kans., Oct. 12, 1920; d. Otis Earl and Gertrude Ellen (Jones) Barker; student Clark's Bus. Coll., Topeka, 1938, U. Kansas City Night Sch., 1947-48; m. Donald D. Hoffman, June 8, 1968. Continuity dir. KMBC-TV, Kansas City, Mo., 1955-58; set dir. Calvin Prodns., film producers, Kansas City, 1958-67; with Interstate Brands Corp., wholesale bakers, Kansas City, 1967—, dir. pub. and consumer communications, 1975—. Mem. rifle shot com. Rockhurst Coll., Kansas City, 1977. Mem. Am. Bakers Assn. (pub. relations com. 1977), Pub. Relations Soc. Am. (dir. Kansas City chpt. 1977-80), Kansas City C. of C. Democrat. Episcopalian. Club: Rockhill (Kansas City). Home: 3744 Warwick Blvd Kansas City MO 64111

HOFFMAN, ERIC ALLEN, purchasing exec.; b. Anderson, Ind., Mar. 30, 1950; s. Albert Laverne and Helen Lois H.; B.S., Ind. U., 1973, postgrad., 1977-78. Med. technologist St. Joseph's Hosp., Fort Wayne, Ind., 1973-74, 75-76, night supr., 1975-76, purchasing mgr., 1976—; med. technologist Lake Ave. Med. Lab., Ft. Wayne, 1974-75. Mem. Am. Soc. Clin. Pathologists, Am. Soc. Hosp. Purchasing and Materials Mgmt. Home: 4205 Winding Way Dr Fort Wayne IN 46815 Office: 700 Broadway Fort Wayne IN 46802

HOFFMAN, GEORGE WILLIAM, accountant; b. Waukegan, Ill., Nov. 19, 1939; s. Edward Richard and Anna Marie (Titus) H.; B.A. in Bus. Adminstrn., Lake Forest (Ill.) Coll., 1962; m. Janet L. Rowe, Aug. 22, 1974; 2 sons, Peter William, George William, 2 daus. Sr. accountant Price Waterhouse & Co., Inc., 1962-66; mem. treas.'s staff United Greenfield Corp., 1966-68; chief fin. officer, sec., dir. J.W. Johnson & Co., 1968-70; treas. Morse/Diesel, Inc., Chgo., 1970-76; mng. partner G. W. Hoffman & Co. P.C., Chgo., 1976—; chmn. bd. dirs. GWH, Inc., 1976—; dir., v.p., sec., treas. Maple Jackson Assos. Inc.; chmn., pres., treas. GWH Leasing Inc., GWH Mchts. Inc., GWH Realty Co.; chmn., pres. GWH Devel. Corp., Midwest Energy Corp., N. Winthrop Devel. Corp.; chmn. bd. Air Lincoln Internat., Vasi Air Express, Inc.; pres. M&H Inc.; gen. partner 2245 N. Kedzie Ltd. Partnership, 5727 N. Winthrop Ltd. Partnership, 5221 N. Hoyne Ltd. Partnership. Bd. dirs. So. Sch.; bd. dirs. Pop Warner Little Scholars; del. Republican. State Conv., 1976; mem. businessmen's adv. com. Gov. of Ill. Served with USAR, 1957-65. C.P.A., Ill. Mem. Am. Inst. C.P.A.'s, Ill. Soc. C.P.A.'s. Clubs: Union League, Met., Young Execs. (Chgo.). Home: 3100 N Sheridan Rd Chicago IL 60657

HOFFMAN, JAMES KENNETH, indsl. sales and service exec.; b. Covington, Ky., Dec. 13, 1945; s. Joseph Carl and Dolores (Schetter) H.; B.A. in Bus. Adminstrn., St. Thomas More Coll., 1965; m. Della Susan Dean, Oct. 11, 1974. Sales rep. Continental Shoe Products & Machinery Co., 1970-72, sales mgr., 1972-74, gen. mgr., 1974-75; gen. mgr. Indsl. Sales & Service Co., Dayton, Ohio, 1975-80, pres., 1980—. Served with USAF, 1966-70; Vietnam. Decorated Air Force Commendation Medal; lic. comml. pilot and flight instr. Mem. Aircraft Owners and Pilots Assn., Cin. Shoe and Leather Club. Home: 3708 Lisbon St Kettering OH 45429 Office: 4645 Gateway Circle Kettering OH 45440

HOFFMAN, JAMES PAUL, lawyer; b. Waterloo, Iowa, Sept. 7, 1943; s. James A. and Luella M. (Prokosch) H.; B.A., U. No. Ia., 1966; J.D., U. Ia., 1967; 1 dau., Tiffany Christine. Admitted to Ia. bar, 1967, since practiced in Keokuk; sr. partner firm Frazier and Hoffman, after 1967; now sr. partner firm James P. Hoffman. Lee County atty., 1973-74. Chmn. bd. HRW, Ltd.; dir. KEOWA Broadcasting, Inc. Co-Chmn. Am. Citizenship Program, 1969—; chmn. legal div. United Fund, 1968-72. Bd. dirs. Keokuk Art Center, Lee County Assn. Retarded Children, 1972, Vis. Nurses Assn., 1968-71. Mem. Iowa, Lee County bar assns., Am. Judicature Soc., Am. Trial Lawyers Assn., Jaycees (pres. 1971). Democrat. Club: Keokuk Country (pres. 1973—), Am. Inst. Hypnosis, Ill. Trial Lawyers Assn., Iowa Trial Lawyers Assn., Iowa Inst. Hypnosis (pres.). Home: Middle Rd Keokuk IA 52632 Office: Middle Rd Keokuk IA 52632-1066

HOFFMAN, JO, editor; b. Trenton, Mo., Sept. 23, 1922; d. Steward Frank and Nada (Wild) Hoffman; B.J., U. Mo., 1944, Reporter United Press, Kansas City, 1944; city editor Trenton Republican-Times, 1944-46; publ. Grundy County (Mo.) Gazette, 1946-52; mng. editor Inter-City Press, Kansas City, 1952-53; asst. prof. journalism U. So. Cal., 1953-55; Nat. Bull. Ladies Aux. of V.F.W., Kansas City, 1956-63, pub. relations dir., 1959-62; editorial cons., asst. to pres. Multicrafts, Inc., Kansas City, Mo., 1963-64; assignment editor Kansas City Star, 1966-70, asst city editor, 1970-73, dir. spl. projects, 1973-77; v.p., gen. mgr. Rahija & Assos., Inc., 1977—; dir. Cement Field Oil Co., Trenton, Mo., 1957—, v.p., 1961—. Mem. AAUP.

Home: 3345 Karnes Blvd Kansas City MO 64111 Office: 406 W 34th St Suite 106 Kansas City MO 64111

HOFFMAN, JOHN HARRY, lawyer, accountant; b. Chgo., June 18, 1913; s. Dave and Rose (Gewirtzman) H.; J.D., John Marshall Law Sch., 1938; m. Gwen Zollo, Dec. 30, 1949; children—Alana Sue Glickson, Edward Jay, Gayle Beth. Admitted to Ill. bar, 1938, U.S. Supreme Ct. bar, 1956; practiced in Chgo., 1938—; propr. John H. Hoffman & Co., 1952—; partner John H. Hoffman & Co., 1966—; pres. John H. Hoffman, P.C., 1972. C.P.A., Ill. Mem. Am., Ill., Chgo. bar assns., Decalogue Soc., Am. Inst. C.P.A.'s, Ill. Soc. C.P.A.'s. Mason (Shriner); mem. B'nai B'rith. Clubs: Covenant (Chgo.); Twin Orchard Country. Home: 239 Valley View Dr Wilmette IL 60091 Office: 221 N LaSalle St Chicago IL 60601

HOFFMAN, JULIUS J., fed. judge; b. Chgo., July 7, 1895; s. Aaron and Bertha Hoffman; student Lewis Inst., Chgo.; Ph.B., Northwestern U., 1912, LL.B., 1915, LL.D., 1955; m. Eleanor H. Greenebaum, Sept. 20, 1928. Admitted to Ill. bar, 1915; practiced in Chgo., 1915-47; judge Superior Ct. Ill., Cook County, 1947-53, U.S. Dist. Ct. for No. Dist. Ill., 1953—, now sr. U.S. Dist. judge; designated judge U.S. 7th Circuit Ct. Appeals. Vice pres., gen. counsel, dir. Brunswick-Balke-Collender Co.; mem. faculty Northwestern U. Law Sch., Evanston, Ill. Fellow Am. Bar Found.; mem. Northwestern U. Alumni Assn. (pres., merit award 1954, service award, 1962), Am. Law Inst., Fed., Am., Ill., Chgo. bar assns., Am. Judicature Soc., Northwestern U. Assos. Republican. Clubs: Standard, Tavern, Union League, Mid-Day (Chgo.); Lake Shore Country (Glencoe, Ill.). Home: 179 E Lake Shore Dr Chicago IL 60611 Office: 219 S Dearborn St Chicago IL 60604

HOFFMAN, MARY CATHERINE, nurse anesthetist; b. Winamac, Ind., July 14, 1923; d. Harmon William Whitney and Dessie Maude (Neely) H.; R.N., Methodist Hosp., Indpls., 1945; cert. obstet. analgesia and anesthesia, Johns Hopkins Hosp., 1949, grad. U. Hosp. of Cleve. Sch. Anesthesia, 1952; Staff nurse Meth. Hosp., 1945-49; research asst., then staff anesthetist Johns Hopkins Hosp., 1949-62; staff anesthetist Meth. Hosp., 1962-64, U. Chgo. Hosps., 1964-66; chief nurse anesthetist Paris (Ill.) Community Hosp., 1966-80; staff anesthetist Hendricks County Hosp., Danville, Ind., 1980—; instr. CPR, 1975—; mem. Terr. 08 CPR Coordinating Com., 1975-80. Mem. Danville Welcome Wagon. Mem. Am. Assn. Nurse Anesthetists, Am. Heart Assn., Ill. Heart Assn., Ill. Fedn. Bus. and Profl. Women's Clubs (dist. chmn. 1977-78, state found. chmn. 1978-79; found. award 1979), Ind. Fedn. Bus. and Profl. Women's Clubs. Republican. Presbyterian. Club: Indpls. B&PW. Home: 109 Adams St Danville IN 46122 Office: 1000 E Main St Danville IN 46122

HOFFMAN, MICHAEL STUART, podiatrist; b. Cleve., Nov. 12, 1945; s. Albert Eli and Shirley Fanny (Bora) H.; A.A., Cuyahoga Community Coll., 1966; D.P.M., Ohio Coll. Podiatric Medicine, 1970; m. Barbara Renae Speser, Apr. 4, 1967; children—Gary Isaac, Mark Allen, Steven Jay. Preceptor, Shelbyville, Ind., 1970-71; mem. staff Morgan County Meml. Hosp.; podiatrist Bloomington Podiatric Centre, Ind., 1970—. Pres., Bloomington Jewish Community, 1980-81. Rotary Internat. Paul Harris fellow, 1980. Mem. Ind. State Podiatry Assn., Am. Podiatry Assn., Am. Assn. Hosp. Podiatrists. Clubs: Elks, Rotary (pres. 1974-75). Office: 203 W 1st St Bloomington IN 47401

HOFFMAN, NORTON LEE, systems analyst; b. St. Louis, May 11, 1939; s. Benjamin H. and Sarah Helen (Leibson) H.; B.A., U. Pa., 1961; postgrad. Columbia U., 1962-63; m. Linda May Londe, Aug. 20, 1967; children—Amy, Jonathan. Systems programmer Am. Airlines, N.Y.C., 1963-65; systems analyst Edison Bros., St. Louis, 1966-67; mgr. info. systems Angelica Uniforms, St. Louis, 1968-70; founder, STS, Inc., St. Louis, 1969—, pres., 1970—. Mem. Metro. Census Com., St. Louis County, 1980-81; pres. Rep. Dem. Club of Clayton Twp., 1974-76; sec. Central Agy. for Jewish Edn., 1972-78. Served with U.S. Army, 1961-62. Recipient Certificate of Achievement, Jewish Fedn., 1980. Mem. Planning Execs. Inst., Ind. Computer Cons. Assn., Assn. of Time-Sharing Users, Assn. for Systems Mgmt. Jewish. Contbr. articles to profl. jours. Home: 420 S Meramec St Clayton MO 63105 Office: 7751 Carondelet Ave Clayton MO 63105

HOFFMAN, PATRICIA, telecommunication mfg. co. exec.; b. Lancaster, Pa., June 6, 1947; d. Ralph J. and Anne M. (Gentry) Reeves; B.S., Chgo. State U., 1974; M.B.A., Roosevelt U., 1976; B.D., U. Iowa, Ph.D., 1982; children—David Ellson, Sean Kevin. Mgr. support services Cedco Inc., 1969-72; regional personnel mgr. Pillsbury Corp., Elk Grove Village, Ill., 1972-74; personnel officer State of Ill., 1974-76; asst. prof. mgmt. Chgo. State U., 1976-78: mgr. personnel devel. Rockwell Internat. Co., Cedar Rapids, Iowa, 1978-80; pres. McCed Inc., Chgo., 1973-76. Bd. dirs. Berea (Ohio) Upward Bound, 1969. Named Mgr. of Yr., Jaycees, 1973. Mem. Nat. Assn. Progressive Mgrs. (v.p. 1973-78), Acad. Mgmt., Am. Soc. Tng. and Devel., Am. Soc. Public Adminstrs., Am. Mgmt. Assn. Republican. Author studies in field. Office: 427 N Monroe Columbus OH 43203

HOFFMAN, RICHARD PAUL, rail car leasing exec.; b. Evergreen Park, Ill., Nov. 15, 1942; s. Richard John and Rosemarie (Hill) H.; student Northwestern U., 1966-69, DePaul U., 1980-81; m. Jill Diane McDonald, Apr. 3, 1976; children—Michael John, Julie Anne. With acctg., fin. and engring. depts. Chgo. Rock Island & Pacific R.R. Co., 1961-68, safety, ops. and mech. depts. Chgo. & Northwestern Ry. Co., 1968-77; dir. railroad transp. Iowa Dept. Transp., 1975-76; dir. fleet mgmt. Pullman Leasing Co., Chgo., 1976—. Mem. Am. Ry. Engring. Assn., Railcar Repair Assn. (dir.). Republican. Presbyterian. Club: Union League (Chgo.). Co-author: Track Train Dynamics Accident Investigation, 1975. Home: 255 N Edgewood St Wood Dale IL 60191 Office: 200 S Michigan Ave Chicago IL 60604

HOFFMAN, ROBERT, state senator; b. Apr. 28, 1925; grad. high sch.; married; 3 children. Farmer, rancher, (nr.) Rockham, S.D.; mem. S.D. Senate, 1976—. Mem. S.D. Extension Bd., S.D. Stockgrowers and Crop Improvement Assn. Republican. Methodist. Address: State Legislature State Capitol Pierre SD 57501*

HOFFMAN, ROWLAND ROBERT; mfg. co. exec.; b. Peoria County, Ill., Apr. 4, 1917; s. William P. and Mary A. (Stevens) H.; student Alexander Hamilton Inst., 1958-59, Bradley U., 1963-64; m. Donna J. Flesner, Jan. 11, 1962; 1 dau., Jerilyn J. Hoffman Church. With Caterpillar Tractor Co., 1935—, tng. mgr., Mossville, Ill., 1963-65, mgr. program devel., gen. offices, 1965-67, asst. safety mgr., Peoria, Ill., 1967-69, corp. safety mgr., 1969—. Bd. dirs., v.p. industry Nat. Safety Council. Cert. hazard control mgr. Mem. Am. Soc. Safety Engrs. (pres. chpt. 1975-76, recipient Safety Profl. of Yr. award 1979), Central Ill. Indsl. Assn., Peoria C. of C., Am. Soc. Tool and Mgf. Engrs., Am. Def. Preparedness Assn., U.S. C. of C. (safety task force), NAM (safety task force), others. Republican. Presbyterian. Club: Rotary (dir.). Contbr. articles to profl. jours. Home: 310 Sycamore St Morton IL 61550 Office: 110 NE Adams St Peoria IL 61629

HOFFMAN, WILLIAM KENNETH, obstetrician, gynecologist; b. Milw., Jan. 18, 1924; s. William Richard and Marian (Riegler) H.; student U. Wis., 1942-43; student U. Pa., 1943-44, postgrad, 1954-55; M.D., Marquette U., 1947; m. Peggy Folsom, July 28, 1952; children—Janet Susan, Ann Elizabeth. Intern, Columbia Hosp., 1947-48, resident in obstetrics and gynecology, 1948-49, mem. staff, 1949—; preceptor R.E. McDonald, M.D., Milw., 1949-50; resident in obstetrics and gynecology U. Chgo., 1950-51; practice medicine specializing in obstetrics and gynecology, Milw., 1955-74; mem. staff, Columbia Hosp.; dir. health service U. Wis., Milw., 1974—, cons. Sch. Nursing, 1976-77, vice chmn., mem. instl. rev. bd., 1976—. Mem. Am. Coll. Obstetrics and Gynecology, Am. Coll. Health Assn., Am. Coll. Sports Medicine, Milw. Acad. Medicine, Am. Cancer Soc. (public edn. com. Milw. div.). Home: 4629 N Murray Ave Milwaukee WI 53211

HOFFMANN, LOTHAR ALBERT, designer, calligrapher; b. Penzig, Schlesien, Ger., Feb. 27, 1936; came to U.S., 1964; s. Hans Joachim and Karla (Meier) H.; student Fachschule fuer Angewandte Kunst, Berlin, 1958-60, Blochererschule, Munich, 1960-61; grad. Folkwangschule, Essen, 1961-64; m. Karin Elisabeth Breustedt, Aug. 30, 1962; children—Oliver, Elisabeth. Graphic designer Abus Industries, Koethen, Ger., 1955-58, Al Hutt Assos., Detroit, 1964-65, New Center Studios, Detroit, 1965-72; freelance designer Skidmore-Sahratian, Troy, Mich., 1972—; asso. prof. design and calligraphy Center Creative Studies, Detroit, 1972—; one-man exhbn. calligraphy Detroit Public Library, 1971; designer logos, med. books, brochures. Mem. Am. Soc. Bookplate Collectors and Designers, Graphic Artists Guild Detroit, Book Club Detroit. Lutheran. Home: 20927 Country Club Harper Woods MI 48225 Office: 2100 W Big Beaver Rd Troy MI 48084

HOFFMEYER, SUSAN SHOWALTER, educator; b. Wheeling, W.Va., June 1, 1953; d. Howard Russell and Dorothy Jeanne (Merritt) Showalter; B.S., Bowling Green State U., 1975; m. William Junior Hoffmeyer, May 2, 1981. Instr., Maplewood Area Joint Vocat. Sch., Ravenna, Ohio, 1975-78; instr. R.G. Drage Career Edn. Center, Massillon, Ohio, 1980, instr., 1978—; cons. P.R.I.D.E., Stark County Vocat. Edn., 1980-81; cons. Stark County Spl. Needs Project, Judge, Stark County 4-H Clubs, 1980-81. Mem. Ohio Vocat. Assn. (pres.-elect home econs. div. 1980—), Am. Vocat. Assn., Am. Home Econs. Assn., Ohio Home Econs. Assn., Stark County Home Econs. Assn. (v.p. 1980—), NEA, Ohio Edn. Assn., Stark Area Vocat. Educators, Marriage Encounter, Phi Upsilon Omicron, Kappa Delta. Presbyterian. Home: 611 Jeffrey NW Massillon OH 44646 Office: 6805 Richville Dr SW Massillon OH 44646

HOFMANN, JAMES MERRILL, mfg. co. exec.; b. New Albany, Ind., Dec. 14, 1953; s. Merrill E. and Margaret Ann (Evaline) H.; student Ind. U. Materials mgr. Keller Mfg. Co., Corydon, Ind., 1978-81, Culpeper, Va., 1981—. Pres., Harrison County Young Dems., 1980; alt. del. Dem. Nat. Conv., 1976, 80. Mem. Am. Acad. Polit. and Social Sci., Middle East Inst. Democrat. Ch. of Christ. Home: Rural Route 1 New Salisbury IN 47161 Office: PO Box 31 Culpeper VA 22701

HOFSTAD, RALPH PARKER, agrl. coop. exec.; b. Phila., Nov. 14, 1923; s. Ottar and Amelia (Davis) H.; student Hamline U., 1942-43, Gustavus Adolphus Coll., 1943-44, Northwestern U., 1944, U. Minn., 1946-47; B.B.A., Northwestern U., 1948; m. Adeline Smedstad, June 14, 1947; children—Diane (Mrs. Roger Dunker), Barbara (Mrs. Dan McClanahan), James, Ron, Tom, Susan. Accountant F S Services, Bloomington, Ill., 1948-51, mgmt. ops., 1953-65; pres. Farmers Regional Coop (Felco), Ft. Dodge, Iowa, 1965-70; sr. v.p. Agrl. Services, Land O' Lakes Inc., Ft. Dodge, 1970—, pres. Land O' Lakes Inc., Mpls., 1974—; dir. Mut. Service Ins. Cos., St. Paul, 1970—, Nat. Milk Producers Fedn., Washington, 1977—. Bd. dirs. Nat. Council Farmer Coops., Washington, 1973—, Goodwill Industries Am., 1977—; chmn. Internat. Energy Coop., Inc., 1979-80, bd. dirs., 1974—. Served with USNR, 1943-46. Methodist. Home: 6608 Field Way Edina MN 55436 Office: Land O'Lakes Inc PO Box 116 Minneapolis MN 55440

HOGAN, DONALD JOHN, JR., mfrs. rep. co. exec.; b. Evergreen Park, Ill., Feb. 23, 1944; s. Donald John and Jane Francis (Rumpf) H.; B.A., U. Notre Dame, 1965, M.A., 1967; m. Carolyn Vivian Smith, June 12, 1965; children—Judy, Molly, Donald III. Asst. football coach U. Notre Dame, 1964-66; mktg. analyst Shell Oil Co., Chgo., 1967; salesman Donald J. Hogan & Co., Chgo., 1967-69, pres., 1969-80, chmn. bd., dir., 1980—; pres. Maintenance of Way Supply Group of Chgo., chmn. area coms. 22 and 27, 1980—. Chmn., St. Barnabas Athletic Bd., 1969—. Mem. Am. R.R. Engring. Assn. (asso.), Chgo., Northwest maintenance of way clubs, St. Ignatius Alumni Assn. (dir.). Democrat. Roman Catholic. Clubs: Monogram (U. Notre Dame). Home: 1943 W 102d St Chicago IL 60643 Office: 327 S LaSalle St Chicago IL 60604

HOGAN, KEMPF, lawyer; b. East Grand Rapids, Mich., May 11, 1939; s. Romain Grammel and Helen Maude (Kempf) H.; B.B.A., U. Mich., 1961, M.B.A. with distinction, 1965, J.D., 1966; postgrad. Harvard U., 1962. Security analyst Detroit Bank & Trust Co., Detroit, 1961-62; tax analyst Standard Oil Co. of N.J., N.Y.C., 1964; admitted to Mich. bar, 1967; asso. firm Poole Littell & Sutherland, Detroit, 1967-71, partner, 1971-76; partner firm Butzel, Long, Gust, Klein & Van Zile, 1976—; dir. Mich. Nat. Bank-West Metro, Mich. Nat. Bank-Dearborn; mem. trust com. Mich. Nat. Bank Detroit. Bd. dirs. jr. council Detroit Inst. Arts, 1971-78, mem. adv. bd., 1979—, also patron; active Friends of U. Mich. Mus. Art; bd. dirs. mem. devel. bd. The Children's Center; bd. dirs. Planned Parenthood League, Inc., Readings for the Blind, Inc. Mem. State Bar Mich., Am., Detroit bar assns., Oakland County Bar, Founders Soc. (patron), Am. Judicature Soc., Phi Kappa Phi, Beta Gamma Sigma, Beta Alpha Psi, Beta Theta Pi, Phi Delta Phi. Presbyterian. Clubs: Harvard (Detroit); Bloomfield Hills Country. Home: 500 Hawthorne Rd Birmingham MI 48009 Office: 525 N Woodward Ave Suite 1100 Bloomfield Hills MI 48013

HOGAN, TIMOTHY SYLVESTER, judge; b. Wellston, Ohio, Sept. 23, 1909; s. Timothy Sylvester and Mary (Deasy) H.; m. Evalon Roberts, Dec. 27, 1934; children—Nancy Hogan Dutton, Margaret Hogan Wyant, Timothy Sylvester; A.B., Xavier U., 1930, LL.D. (hon.), 1976; J.D., U. Cin., 1931. Admitted to Ohio bar, 1931. Asso. firm Cohen, Baron, Druffel & Hogan, Cin., 1931-66; spl. counsel Ohio atty. gen., 1936-41, 48-50; lectr. trial practice U. Cin. Law Sch., 1950-59; judge U.S. Dist. Ct., So. Dist. Ohio, Cin., 1966—, chief judge, 1975-77. Democratic nominee Ohio atty. gen., 1946; del. at large Dem. Nat. Conv., 1952; mem. Clermont County Planning Com., 1958-60. Mem. Fed., Ohio, Clermont County, Cin. bar assns., Order of Coif, Phi Delta Phi. Home: 3810 Eileen Dr Cincinnati OH 45209 Office: 829 US Post Office and Court House Cincinnati OH 45202

HOGE, JAMES FULTON, JR., newspaper publisher; b. N.Y.C., Dec. 25, 1935; s. James Fulton and Virginia (McClamroch) H.; B.A. in Polit. Sci., Yale U., 1958; M.A. in Modern Am. and European History, U. Chgo., 1961; grad. Advanced Mgmt. Program, Harvard U. Grad. Sch. Bus., 1980; m. Alice Patterson Albright, June 2, 1962 (div. 1971); children—Alicia McClamroch, James Patrick, Robert Warren; m. 2d, Sharon King, Jan. 4, 1981. Fin. writer Chgo. Sun Times, 1958-62; Am. Polit. Sci. Assn. Congressional fellow, 1962-63; Washington corr. Chgo. Sun Times, 1963-65, city editor, 1965-67, mng. editor, 1967-68, exec. editor, 1968, editor, 1968-76; editor in chief Chgo. Sun Times and Chgo. Daily News, 1976-78; exec. v.p., editor in chief Chgo. Sun-Times, 1978-80, pub., 1980—. Chmn. exec. council Adlai Stevenson Center; adv. council Aspen Program Communications and Soc., Am. Council on Germany; mng. com. U.S.-South Africa Leader Exchange Program; mem. German Marshall Fund, Trilateral Commn.; bd. dirs. Eisenhower Exchange Fellowships, Children's Meml. Hosp., Chgo. Theatre Group (Goodman Theatre), Landmarks Preservation Council; mem. Japan-U.S. Friendship Commn.; mem. adv. bd. Inst. Internat. Edn.; mem. internat. newspaper adv. bd. UP; bd. visitors Inst. Policy Scis., Duke U.; mem. vis. com. public policy studies U. Chgo.; bd. dirs. Mus. Contemporary Art. Mem. Am. Newspaper Pubs. Assn. (journalism edn. com.), Council Fgn. Relations Chgo. (vice-chmn.; chmn. exec. com. of com. on fgn. affairs, vice-chmn.), Council Fgn. Relations N.Y.C. (dir.), Sigma Delta Chi. Clubs: Tavern, Econ., Execs., Arts, Comml., Headline (Chgo.). Office: 401 N Wabash Ave Chicago IL 60611

HOGEMAN, WYLIE BARROW, textile and chem. co. exec.; b. Baton Rouge, Mar. 20, 1931; s. Hubert Henry (dec.) and Mary Louis (West) H.; B.S. in Chemistry, La. State U., 1952, B.S. in Chem. Engring., 1956; postgrad. M.I.T., 1974; m. Lola Elizabeth Fenn, Dec. 28, 1957; children—Mary Laura, Lola Eustis. Chem. engr. Monsanto Textiles Co., Pensacola, Fla., 1956-59, chem. engr., 1959-63, sr. chem. engr., 1963-64, group leader, 1964-67, supr., 1967-68, plant engr., 1968-69, gen. supt. ops., 1969-71, plant mgr. polyester plant, Guntersville, Ala., 1971-74, dir. indsl. fibers bus. group, 1974-76, gen. mgr. mfg. div., St. Louis, 1976-80, gen. mgr. mktg. div., 1980, gen. mgr. rubber chems. div., 1981—; dir. Hale Mfg. Co., Wilmington, Del. Served with C.E., U.S. Army, 1952-54. Mem. Am. Inst. Chem. Engrs., Am. Textiles Mgmt. Assn. Republican. Episcopalian. Club: Old Warson Country (St. Louis). Patentee in field. Home: 36 Fair Oaks St Saint Louis MO 63124 Office: 800 N Lindbergh St Saint Louis MO 63166

HOGEN, MARVIS T., state senator; b. Nov. 6, 1923; student Dakota Wesleyan U.; m. Florence Brown, Oct. 28, 1943; 4 children. Rancher, Kadoka, S.D.; mem. S.D. Ho. of Reps., 1972-78, S.D. Senate, 1978—; dir. Badlands State Bank. Active numerous civic orgns. Mem. Minn.-Dakotas Retail Hardware Assn. (dir.). Republican. Lutheran. Address: State Capitol Pierre SD 57501*

HOGLE, KEITH GUY, cons.; b. Kenosha, Wis., Feb. 11, 1934; s. John Raymond and Jeannette Mary (Rasmussen) H.; B.S., U. Wis., Milw., 1960; M.S., U. Wis., Madison, 1966; m. Doris Rebecca Trangmar, Jan. 26, 1957; children—Richard John, Bonnie Rebecca, Amy Kristiane. Tchr., prin. Oconomowoc (Wis.) Public Schs., 1960-68; lectr., research asst. U. Wis., Madison, 1968-72; co-dir. Wis. Indian tchr. corps program U. Wis., Madison and HEW, 1970-72; sr. cons. CBS/Holt, Rinehart & Winston, N.Y.C., 1972—; lectr. workshops on ednl. methodology Mankato State U., U. No. Colo., Oreg. State U., Waltham, Mass., U. Miss., 1974-77. Ch. edn. supt. Our Savior's Luth. Ch., 1961—. Served with U.S. Army, 1954-56. Recipient Outstanding Achievement award Holt, Rinehart & Winston, 1975; U. Wis. fellow, 1970. Mem. Assn. Supervision and Curriculum Devel., Wis. Reading Assn., Phi Delta Kappa. Author: Inquiring about Communities, 1976; Inquiring about American History, 1976. Home: 37091 E Yale St Oconomowoc WI 53066 Office: 901 N Elm St Hinsdale IL 60521

HOHAUSER, HARVEY RONALD, coll. adminstr.; b. Newark, July 25, 1943; s. Samuel and Dorothy Carol (Dunsky) H.; B.A., Fairleigh Dickinson U., 1965; M.A., Mich. State U., 1966; Ph.D., Case Western Res. U., 1971; m. Andrea Susan Krich, Apr. 4, 1966; children—Jay, Todd, Eric. Dir. Lakewood Acad. Center, instr. sociology Cleve. State U., 1968-70; chmn. community services dept., asst. prof. Union Coll. at Cranford, N.J., 1971-73; coordinator, program mgr. univ. year for action Oakland U., Rochester, Mich., 1973-75, asso. dir. Center for Community and Human Devel., 1975-79, dir. urban programs devel., 1979-81, asso. dir. Urban Affairs Center, 1981—; adj. prof. Cuyahoga Community Coll., Cleve., summer 1970; cons. internat. div. Harcourt, Brace, Jovanovich, N.Y.C., 1972-73; sr. vis. lectr. Mich. State U., East Lansing, 1974-75; cons. Nat. Adv. Council for Vocat. and Tech. Edn., 1971-73, Oakland County Spl. Olympics, 1978; edn. cons. Area Agy. on Aging, 1976—; mem. adv. council Mich. Office on Services to Aging, 1979—. Vice pres. Turning Point, 1974-75; mem. Nat. Center for Pub. Service Internship Programs; mem. fund allocation com. United Way of Pontiac, 1973—, chmn. ednl., profl., comml. fund drive, 1975—; mem. state budget com. United Way of Mich., 1976—, bd. dirs., 1977—; chmn. Oakland County Energy Conservation Commn., 1978—, Oakland Health Edn. Program, 1978—; corp., found. coordinator Neighborhood Housing Services, 1979-80. Mem. Am. Sociol. Assn., Am. Assn. Higher Edn., Soc. for Experiential Edn. Asso. editor Vol. Adminstrn. Home: 123 Gunder Dr Rochester MI 48063

HOHENSTEIN, JAMES BRYAN, architect, graphic designer; b. Lincoln, Nebr., Aug. 7, 1948; s. William Nels and Lillian Sarah (Hunt) H.; B.Arch., U. Nebr. at Lincoln, 1972; m. Donna Rae Gruenemeier, Dec. 27, 1969; children—Heather Suzanne, James Bryan. Design architect Reynolds, Smith & Hills, Tampa, Fla., 1972-73, Bahr, Hanna, Vermeer & Haecker, Omaha, 1973-75, Henningson, Durham & Richardson, Omaha, 1975-81; head designer med. architecture Kirkham & Michael Assos., 1981—; contbg. illustrator The Landmark mag.; partner Hohenstein-Dance Studio, graphic and photographic design. Recipient Asso. Arts award AIA, 1976. Mem. Nebr. Soc., AIA. Club: Ak-Sar-Ben.

HOHWEILER, DARYL WAYNE, sociologist; b. Shattuck, Okla., Nov. 23, 1941; s. Henry C. and Lois M. (Lahann) H.; B.A., Oklahoma City U., 1964; cert. U. Frankfurt (W. Ger.), 1965; M.A., So. Meth. U., 1967; diploma U. Stockholm Internat. Grad. Sch., 1968; cert. U. Geneva, 1969; M.Social Sci., U. Uppsala, 1968, Ph.D., 1975. Asst. prof. dept. sociology U. Okla., Norman, 1969-71; Bernadotte Fund research fellow Am.-Scandinavian Found., 1971-72; asst. prof. sociology Sangamon State U., Springfield, Ill., 1972-81; asso. prof. sociology Ottawa (Kans.) U., 1981—. Rotary Internat. Found. fellow, 1964-65, Swedish State scholar, 1967-69, Allie B. Jones Found. fellow, 1965-67; recipient Silver Letzeisser award for acad. excellence, 1963, Thomas A. Jefferson award in sociology of law, 1965. Mem. Am. Sociol. Assn., S.W. Sociol. Assn., Midwest Sociol. Assn., AAAS, Am. Assn. Higher Edn., Internat. Sociol. Assn., Nat. Assn. Student Personnel Adminstrs., D.C. Sociol. Assn., Ill. Sociol. Assn., Blue Key. Author: On Women's Social and Occupational Mobility, 1975; An Enlisted Soldier's View of the Civil War, 1981. Home: 1404 S Olive Ottawa KS 66067 Office: A-309 Box 111 Ottawa U Ottawa KS 66067

HOLAN, DAVID H., service co. exec.; b. Burlington, Vt., Aug. 26, 1943; s. Arnold and Irene (Carter) H.; student Tarkio Coll., Loyola U., 1961-63; m. Hildene King, Dec. 29, 1964; children—Jodi Lynn, Scott Harold. Pres., Crystal Tips of No. Ill., Chgo., 1974—, Iceman's Ice Co., 1976—, Crystal Tips of Ill., Inc., 1981—; pres., treas. Sani-Serv of Ill., Inc., 1981—, Ice Dispensers, Inc., 1981—; v.p. Charter Beer of Am., 1973—, 1140 Corp., 1978—, Charter Imports, 1979—. Mem.

Asso. Beer Distbrs. Ill. (trustee ins. and service bd. 1981—). Contbr. articles to profl. publs. Office: 1142 S Washtenaw Chicago IL 60612

HOLBROOK, REID FRANKLIN, lawyer; b. Kansas City, Kans., Jan. 19, 1942; s. Henry Edmiston and Margaret Dorothy (Reid) H.; A.B., U. Kans., 1964; postgrad. Universidad de Guanajuato (Mexico), 1963; J.D., U. Kans., 1966; m. Mary Lynn Rogers, Feb. 24, 1968; children—Ann Rogers, Katherine Reid. Admitted to Kans. bar, 1967; probate and juvenile judge Wyandotte County, Kansas City, Kans., 1967-68, 70-71; partner law firm Fallon, Holbrook & Ellis, Kansas City, Kans., 1970—; spl. asst. atty. gen., State of Kans., 1970-78. Bd. dirs. Mid-Am. Health Systems Agy., 1976-78. Served with U.S. Army, 1968-70. Mem. Am. Bar Assn., Kans. Bar Assn., Wyandotte County Bar Assn., Am. Soc. Hosp. Attys., Am. Coll. Law and Medicine, Kans. Assn. Def. Counsel. Democrat. Home: 2005 Washington Blvd Kansas City KS 66102 Office: 727 Ann Ave PO Box 1279 Kansas City KS 66117

HOLDEMAN, RICHARD WENDELL, II, consumer goods mfg. co. exec., psychologist; b. South Bend, Ind., Feb. 19, 1938; s. Richard Wendell and Lillian Estella (Scheib) H.; B.A., DePauw U., 1960; M.S., Purdue U., 1962, Ph.D., 1965; m. Diane Marilynn Grant, Aug. 26, 1961; children—Richard Brewster, Robert Grant, Thomas Edward, John William. Research fellow, teaching asst., admissions counselor Purdue U., 1961-64; research scientist Am. Inst. Research, U. Pitts., 1964-65; v.p. personnel Cosco, Inc., Columbus, Ind., 1965—; instr. Purdue U. at Columbus, 1966-67. Bd. dirs. Opportunity, Inc., 1969-75, pres., 1973-74; bd. dirs. United Devel. Services, 1973-76, Bartholomew County Jr. Achievement, 1969-72, Bartholomew County Hosp. Found., 1971-75; bd. dirs. Children, Inc., 1973—, v.p., 1977-78, pres., 1979; exec. bd. Smith Parent Tchr. Orgn., 1976—, pres., 1977-78; trustee Columbus Coll., 1970-71. Mem. Am. Psychol. Assn., Am. Soc. Personnel Adminstrn. (accredited exec. in personnel), Am. Soc. Tng. and Devel., Midwest Coll. Placement Assn., Sigma Xi, Psi Chi. Purdue Research Found. grantee, 1964; certified pvt. practice psychologist, Ind. Author: The Evolution of Veterinary Medicine in Indiana, 1965; also Project TALENT Studies. Home: 1825 Park Valley Dr Columbus IN 47201 Office: 2525 State St Columbus IN 47201

HOLDEN, CRAIG ALLEN, devel. planner; b. Northfield, Minn., Feb. 5, 1952; s. Howard Frederick and Evelyn Ruth (Allen) H.; student Friends World Coll., 1971-72, Mankato State U., 1973-74, U. Minn., 1976-78. Dir., designer Wolf Lake Refuge, McGregor, Minn., 1972-78; master site planner, v.p. Communities for Service, Inc., Bloomington, Minn., 1976—; devel. planner, v.p. Holden Farms, Inc., Northfield, 1979—, also dir. Recipient Design award for environ. design, U. Minn. and Minn. Soc. Architects, 1977; registered emergency med. technician. Mem. Universalist Union of the Great Prairie Spirit. Home: PO Box 46 Route 1 Nerstrand MN 55053 Office: Holden Farms Inc Route 1 Northfield MN 55057

HOLDEN, EDGAR HOWARD, state senator; b. Tama, Iowa, Mar. 24, 1914; s. Glenn H. and Laura (Warner) H.; grad. high sch.; m. Rachel O. Brown, 1937. Pres., Holdens, Inc., 1949—, Central Scott Telephone Co., 1956—; sec.-treas. Edgetowner Restaurant, 1964—; mem. Iowa Ho. of Reps., 1967-75, Iowa Senate, 1978—. Served with AUS, 1943-45. Mem. Gideons, C. of C. (dir.), Am. Legion, Farm Bur. Presbyterian. Club: Rotary (dir.). Home: Davenport IA 52807 Office: State Senate Des Moines IA 50319*

HOLDER, GERALD WILLIAM, pharm. co. exec.; b. Montreal, Que., Can., Nov. 5, 1930; came to U.S., 1942, naturalized, 1950; s. Hubert Roland and Florence (Grandin) H.; B.S., Springfield (Mass.) Coll., 1954, M.S., 1955; m. Barbara J. Gallant, June 18, 1955; children—Robin Lee, Jay Gerald (dec.). Dir. personnel adminstrn. Abbott Labs., North Chicago, Ill., 1963; asst. v.p. indsl. relations Am. Home Products Co., N.Y.C., 1972-73; v.p. personnel Marion Labs., Inc., Kansas City, Mo., 1974-78, sr. v.p., 1978—, dir., 1980—; instr. Morris Harvey Coll., Charleston, W.Va., 1959-63, Rockhurst Coll., Kansas City, Mo., 1977-81; bd. dirs. Indsl. Mgmt. Inst., Lake Forest (Ill.) Coll. Deacon, First Presbyn. Ch., Libertyville, Ill., coach Little League Baseball, Kids Hockey. Served with AUS, 1955-57. Mem. Am. Soc. Personnel Adminstr. (chmn. president's council 1981), Pharm. Mfrs. Assn. (chmn. personnel sect. 1981). Republican. Club: Rotary. Office: 9221 Ward Pkwy Kansas City MO 64114

HOLDT, ROY HOWARD, mfg. co. exec.; b. Edgewood, Md., Nov. 19, 1920; s. Jacob S. and Francis (Hansen) H.; student Dyke Bus. Coll., 1941, Cleve. State U., 1947; m. Audrie Smith, Oct. 26, 1972; children by previous marriage—Linda Holdt Greene, Douglas M. With Lake Erie Chem. Co., Cleve., 1938-40, Apex Elec. Mfg. Co., 1941-56; div. controller White Consol. Industries, Inc., Cleve., 1956-58, corp. controller, 1958-61, v.p., controller, 1961-64, v.p. fin., 1964-67, sr. v.p., 1967-69, exec. v.p., dir., 1969-72, pres., chief operating officer, 1972-76, chmn., chief exec. officer, 1976—; dir. Cleve. Trust Co., Cleve. Electric Illuminating Co. Mem. bd. Fairview Gen. Hosp., Cleve. State U. Devel. Found.; trustee Dyke Coll. Served with AUS, 1942-45. Mem. Nat. Assn. Accountants, Greater Cleve. Growth Assn. (dir.). Clubs: Pepper Pike (Ohio); OSU Presidents; Westwood Country; Clevelander, Cleve. Atheletic, Mid-Day, The 50, Clifton, Union, Treasurers (Cleve.); Duquesne (Pitts.). Office: White Consol Industries 11770 Berea Rd Cleveland OH 44111

HOLE, FLOYD MARVIN, educator; b. Crawfordsville, Ind., Feb. 14, 1935; s. Virgil Wesley and Lucy Fern (Weikel) H.; B.S., No. Ariz. U., 1957, M.S. in Biology, 1964; Ed.D., Ariz. State U., 1968; postgrad. U. No. Colo., 1974-75, 80-81; m. Wanda Ruth Clements, Jan. 25, 1957; children—Marva Ruth, Carl Earl, Zetta Chesny. Med. lab., x-ray technologist Flagstaff (Ariz.) Hosp., 1961-63; med., surg. lab. equipment salesman Southwestern Surg. Supply, Phoenix, 1964-66; dir. edn. Am. Protestant Hosp. Assn., Chgo., 1970-71; asst. prof. edn. Idaho State Univ., Pocatello, 1972-74; asst. adminstrv. dean Ill. Valley Community Coll., Oglesby, 1968-69; asst. prof. vocat. edn. Pa. State U., State College, 1975-78; lectr. adult edn., health occupations edn. and vocat. edn. U. Wis., Milw., 1978—, lectr. dept. adminstrv. Leadership, 1978-81. Sec., treas. Townjacks, 1961-63; dir. Ariz. All-Stars, 1961-63. Served with U.S. Army, 1957-59. Recipient Leadership award Adult Edn. Assn. U.S.A. 1978; Leadership award Assn. Health Occupations Tchr. Educators, 1979, 80. Mem. Assn. Health Occupations Tchr. Educators (exec. com., treas.), Commn. Prof. Adult Edn., Adult Edn. Assn. U.S.A., Nat. Assn. Public and Continuing Adult Edn., Am. Vocat. Assn., Am. Soc. Manpower Edn. and Tng., Am. Soc. Allied Health Professions, AAAS, Ariz.-Nev. Acad. Sci., Blue Key, Phi Delta Kappa, Beta Beta Beta, Iota Lambda Sigma. Home: 4425 N Cramer St Shorewood WI 53211 Office: 653 Enderis Univ Wis Milwaukee WI 53201

HOLIDAY, HARRY, JR., steel co. exec.; b. Pitts., July 2, 1923; s. Harry and Charlotte Poe (Rutherford) H.; B.S. in Metall. Engring. with honors, U. Mich., 1949; m. Kathlyn Collins Watson, Sept. 6, 1947; children—Edith Elizabeth, Harry III, Albert Logan II. Spl. assignment metall. engring. adminstrn. Armco Steel Corp., Middletown, Ohio, 1949-55, asst. to supt. blast furnace, Hamilton, Ohio, 1955-57, supt. blast furnace, 1957-59, asst. gen. supt. steel plant, Middletown, 1959-64, gen. supt. steel plant, 1964-66, dir. raw materials, 1966-67, v.p. steel ops., 1967-69, exec. v.p. steel, 1969-74, pres., 1974-79, now chief exec. officer, also dir.; dir. Cin. Gas & Electric Co., Reserve Mining Co., First Nat. Bank Middletown, Nat. Cash Register. Pres., Middletown YMCA, 1955-58; pres. Moundbuilders Area council Boy Scouts Am., 1963-67. Served to capt. AUS, 1943-46. Mem. Am. Inst. Metall. Engrs. (recipient J.E. Johnson, Jr. Blast Furnace award), Am., Internat. iron and steel insts., Tau Beta Pi, Psi Upsilon. Office: Armco Inc 703 Curtis St Middletown OH 45043*

HOLIGA, LUDOMIL ANDREW, metall. engr.; b. Dayton, Ohio, Dec. 7, 1920; s. Andrew and Antonia Margaret (Sefcek) H.; Engr. asso., Sinclair Coll., 1948; B.Sc., Calgary Coll. Tech., 1974, M.M.E., 1975; m. Aryetta Lillian Mernedakis, Feb. 6, 1960; children—David, Carol, Millard, Timothy, Michael. Engr. designer Wright Patterson AFB, Ohio, 1941-54; contract designer Product Design Services, Inc., Dayton, Ohio, 1955-60; with Dayton Progress Corp., 1961—, dir. corp. devel., 1972-73, dir. research and tech. edn., 1974—. Served with USAAF, 1942-45, AUS, 1951-52. Certified mfg. engr. Mem. Soc. Mfg. Engrs. (chmn. standards com. 1963-72), Ohio Research and Devel. Found., Foremans Club, Am. Metal Stamping Assn. Lutheran. Research on cutting clearances for perforating metals in stamping dies. Home: 2025 Oak Tree Dr E Kettering OH 45440 Office: 500 Progress Rd Dayton OH 45449

HOLIHAN, FRANCIS LEONARD, health services mgmt. cons.; b. Syracuse, N.Y., Nov. 15, 1918; s. Thomas Daniel and Agnes (Maroney) H.; student Am. Inst. Banking, 1936-37, Syracuse U., 1937-40, Am. U., 1946-48; B.A., U. Md., 1960; m. Justyne Williamson, Dec. 15, 1943; children—Francis Leonard, Daniel Patrick, Patricia Kay, Michael Stephen, Kathleen Marie. Mgr. div. time sales dept. 1st Trust and Deposit Co., Syracuse, 1936-41; mgr. mortgage loan dept. Fausett & Co., realtors, Little Rock, 1946; served with med. dept. U.S. Army, 1941, advanced through grades to maj., 1945; discharged; returned as maj., Med. Adminstrv. Corps Air Transport Command U.S. Air Force, 1946, advanced through grades to col., 1959; various med. staffing and edn. positions, 1946-56; chief med. liason selection div. Hdqrs., Washington, 1956-60, chief plans and ops. support Hdqrs 15th Air Force, SAC, 1960-64; med. service, hosp. adminstr. Hdqrs 16th Air Force, SAC, Spain, 1964-67, dir. health services mgmt. Air Force Logistics Command, Ohio, 1967-72, ret., 1972; asso. exec. dir. Miami Valley Health Systems Agency, Dayton, Ohio, 1973-79; health services mgmt. adv. and cons., 1979—; mem. biomed. engring. edn. advisory com. Wright State U., 1974-75; mem. advisory com. Central Service Community, Sisters of the Precious Blood, Dayton, 1975-77. Past pres. Wright Brothers chpt. Armed Forces Mgmt. Assn., 1971. Decorated Legion of Merit. Mem. Assn. Mil. Surgeons U.S., Am. Assn. Hosp. Planning. Fed. Health Care Execs. Inst. Alumni Assn., Ret. Officers Assn., Am. Defense Preparedness Assn., Nat. Histo. Soc. Roman Catholic. Clubs: USAF Officers, Dayton Racquet. Home: 3456 S Dakar Dr Dayton OH 45431 Office: 3456 S Dakar Dr Dayton OH 45431

HOLINGER, LAUREN DRAKE, physician; b. Chgo., Aug. 9, 1942; s. Paul Henry and Julia Campbell (Drake) H.; B.S., Union Coll., 1964; M.D., Chgo. Med. Sch., 1971; m. Susan Wherry, June 26, 1976; children—Christopher, Elizabeth. Resident in surgery U. Colo. Affiliated Hosps., 1971-72, resident in otolaryngology, 1972-75; practice medicine specializing in otolaryngology, Chgo., 1975—; mem. staff Rush Presbyn.-St. Luke's Hosp., Children's Meml. Hosp., Chgo., U. Ill. Eye and Ear Infirmary; asst. prof. dept. otolaryngology and bronchoesophagology Rush Med. Coll., Rush Presbyn. St. Luke's Med. Center, Chgo., 1975—; instr. dept. otolaryngology and maxillofacial surgery Northwestern U. Med. Sch., Chgo., 1975—. Mem. AMA, Ill. Med. Soc., Chgo. Med. Soc., Am. Council Otolaryngology, A.C.S., Am. Acad. Pediatrics, Am. Acad. Otolaryngology, Am. Broncho-Esophagological Assn., Am. Coll. Chest Physicians, Soc. for Ear, Nose and Throat Advances in Children, Internat. Bronchoesophacolgical Soc., Ill. Soc. Pediatric Surgeons, Chgo. Laryngol. and Otol. Soc., Inst. Medicine Chgo. Contbr. articles to med. jours. Office: 700 N Michigan Ave Chicago IL 60611

HOLLAND, GEORGE WILLIAM, elem. sch. prin.; b. Sac City, Iowa, Nov. 25, 1951; s. Albert and Leona Lydia Holland; B.S., Mankato (Minn.) State Coll., 1973; M.S. in Elem. Edn., Wayne (Nebr.) State Coll., 1977, M.S. in Elem. Adminstrn., 1978. Elem. sch. tchr. and adminstr., Nebr. and Iowa, 1973-77; elem. sch. prin. Sergeant Bluff (Iowa)-Luton Community Schs., 1977; mem. adj. faculty Wayne State Coll.; cons. in field. Active local Cub Scouts, Big Bros./Big Sisters. Named Outstanding Elem. Sch. Tchr., South Sioux City, Nebr., 1975; life mem. Sergeant Bluff-Luton PTA, 1978, recipient Merit award, 1976, 77. Mem. Internat. Reading Assn., Assn. Supervision and Curriculum Devel., Nat. Assn. Elem. and Middle Sch. Prins., Iowa Reading Assn., Iowa Assn. Elem. Sch. Prins., Phi Delta Kappa. Democrat. Roman Catholic. Home: Box 486 407 B St Sergeant Bluff IA 51054 Office: 200 South D St Box 97 Sergeant Bluff IA 51054

HOLLAND, JOAN HARRIETT, ednl. adminstr.; b. Woodstock Twp., Mich., Feb. 15, 1934; d. Claude E. and Lillian (Schwatz) H.; A.A., Jackson Jr. Coll., 1954; B.S., Eastern Mich. U., 1960, M.A., 1965; postgrad. Mich. State U., 1967-79. Tchr., Clement Sch., Michigan Center, Mich., 1954-57, Cement City (Mich.) Schs., 1957-60, Madison Sch., Adrian, Mich., 1960-62, Cement City and Columbia Sch. Dists., Brooklyn, Mich., 1962-65; elem. prin. Cement City Public Schs., 1965-67, Columbia Sch. Dist., Brooklyn, Mich., 1967-81, Cement City, 1965—; Title 1 dir. Columbia Sch. Dist., 1980-82. Mem. Assn. Supervision and Curriculum Devel., Nat. Elem. and Middle Sch. Prins. Assn., Mich. Elem. and Middle Sch. Prins. Assn., Jackson County Middle and Elem. Sch. Prins. Assns. Democrat. Club: Bowling. Home: 104 Sheridan St Box 132 Brooklyn MI 49230 Office: 130 E Jackson St Cement City MI 49233

HOLLAND, RAY LAURIMORE, accountant; b. Rich Hill, Mo., Sept. 10, 1916; s. Ralph Lee and Florence Grace (Horton) H.; A.B., U. Mo., 1937; certificate advanced mgmt. U. Chgo., 1960; m. Thasia G. Tidd; children—Dennis L., Laurel M., Ray C. Accountant, Arthur Andersen & Co., Chgo. and Seattle, 1940-57, sr. mgr., 1947-57; controller Transunion Corp., Chgo., 1957-65; pvt. practice accounting, Arlington Heights, Ill., 1966-78; pres. Holland & Asso., Inc., Twinsburg, Ohio, 1972—; controller Indsl. Electronic Rubber Co., Twinsburg, Ohio, 1978-81; dir. The Enamel Products Co. C.P.A., Kans., Ill., Wash., Wis., Ohio. Mem. Am. Inst. C.P.A.'s. Home: 166 N Park Dr Aurora OH 44202 Office: 8589 Darrow Rd Twinsburg OH 44087

HOLLAND, RONALD WILFORD, regional govtl. exec.; b. Big Spring, Tex., May 4, 1943; s. Wilford P. and Johnnie E. H.; B.A., So. Ill. U., Edwardsville, 1973, M.S., 1974; m. Joyce E. West, May 27, 1977; children—Douglas, Paul, William. Respiratory therapist St. Joseph's Hosp., Alton, Ill., 1970-74; planner Ozark Gateway Council of Govts., Joplin, Mo., 1974-75, planning dir., 1975-78, exec. dir., 1978—; exec. v.p. Ozark Gateway Devel. Inc., Joplin, 1978—. Bd. dirs. Joplin Family Self-Help Center, Inc. Mem. Am. Soc. Public Adminstrn. Club: Exchange (dir. 1978-80, pres. 1980-81, dir. dist. 1981-82, Exchangite of Yr. 1980) Joplin). Office: 2008 Sergeant 5th Floor Joplin MO 64801*

HOLLEB, DORIS BERNSTEIN, economist, urban affairs cons.; b. N.Y.C., Oct. 26, 1922; B.A. magna cum laude, Hunter Coll., 1942; M.A. in Econs., Harvard, 1947; postgrad. U. Chgo., 1959-60, 65-66; m. Marshall M. Holleb, Oct. 15, 1944; children—Alan, Gordon, Paul. Research asst. Harvard Bus. Sch., 1942-43; economist, research div., internat. sect. Fed. Res. Bd., Washington, 1943-44; asst. editor Lake Placid News, 1945; research cons. U.S. Mut. Ins. Assn., 1953; teaching asst. Ill. Inst. Tech., 1954-55; free lance journalist, 1955-63; econ. cons. Chgo. Dept. Devel. and Planning, 1963-64; sr. research asso. Center for Urban Studies, U. Chgo., 1966—, professorial lectr., 1980—, dir. Met. Inst., 1973—, mem. adv. council Adlai E. Stevenson Center for Internat. Studies, 1975—; cons. NSF, OMB, HUD, HEW, Fed. Res. Bd., Ill. Bd. Higher Edn. Mem. citizens adv. com. Ill. Bd. Higher Edn., 1965-71, Ill. Dept. Edn., 1971-74; chmn. Frances W. Parker Sch. Ednl. Council, 1965-71, chmn. parents com., 1959-61; mem. acad. com. Center for Study Democratic Instns., 1975-80; mem. Northeastern Ill. Planning Commn., 1973-77, sec., mem. exec. com., 1974-77, chmn. housing sub-com., 1973-74, by laws sub-com., 1975-77, forcasting sub-com., 1976-77; bd. dirs. Bright New City Com., Landmarks Preservation Fund, Know Your Chgo. Com.; trustee Adlai E. Stevenson Inst., 1972-75; mem. vis. com. Oriental Inst., U. Chgo.; Ill. rep. UN Conf. on Human Settlements, 1976; mem. nat. adv. com. White House Conf. on Balanced Nat. Growth and Econ. Devel., 1978, Ill. Com. to Strengthen Community Economies, 1978-80; mem. adv. com. on internat. investment, tech. and devel. U.S. State Dept., 1979; mem. U.S. Dept. Edn. Adv. Council to Nat. Center for Research on Vocat. Edn., 1979-83; bd. dirs. U.S. Inter-Am. Found., 1980-84. Recipient Founders Day award Loyola U., 1974; elected to Hunter Coll. Alumni Hall of Fame, 1980. Mem. Am. Inst. Cert. Planners, Am. Econ. Assn., Am. Planning Assn., AAAS, Phi Beta Kappa. Club: Harvard-Radcliffe (bd. dirs.) (Chgo.), Lambda Alpha. Author: Social And Economic Information for Urban Planning, 1968; Colleges and the Urban Poor: The Role of Public Higher Education in Community Service, 1972. Mem. editorial bd. Ill. Issues. Contbr. articles to profl. jours.

HOLLEBEEK, JAMES MAYNARD, counselor; b. Grand Rapids, Mich., July 11, 1945; s. Maynard and Henrietta (Endema) H.; A.B., Calvin Coll., 1968; M.A. in Social Studies, Western Mich. U., 1974, M.A. in Counseling and Personnel, 1976; postgrad. Drake U.; m. Faye Annece Bax, Apr. 6, 1968; children—Scott James, Kimberly Anne, Eric Marten. Tchr., Maplewood Christian Sch., Holland, Mich., 1968; tchr. social studies Holland Christian Middle Sch., 1968-76; guidance counselor Pella (Iowa) Christian High Sch., 1976-80; counselor Calvin Coll., Grand Rapids, 1980—. Human Relations facilitator Heartland Area. Recipient Permanent Profl. Teaching and guidance cert., Mich., Permanent Profl. cert. in teaching and guidance, Iowa. Mem. Am. Personnel and Guidance Assn., Am. Coll. Personnel Assn., Assn. Humanistic Edn. and Devel., Assn. Humanistic Psychology, Assn. Specialists in Group Work; Mich. Personnel and Guidance Assn., W. Mich. Personnel and Guidance Assn., Mich. Assn. Humanistic Edn. and Devel., Mich. Vocat. Guidance Assn., Mich. Assn. Specialists in Group Work. Mem. Christian Reformed Ch. Home: 990 Waltham Grand Rapids MI 49506 Office: Broene Counseling Center Calvin Coll Grand Rapids MI 49506

HOLLENBERG, ROBERT LEE, controller; b. Arrowood, Alta., Can., Nov. 7, 1931; s. Quinter Earl and Florence Margaret (Wallace) H.; B.S. in Bus. Adminstrn., Manchester Coll., 1957; m. Helen Ruth Bollinger, Feb. 5, 1955; children—Robert Eugene, Cynthia Ann, William Bruce. Acctg. trainee Central Soya Co., Inc., Marion, Ohio, 1957-61; jr. acct. Essex Internat., Inc., Ft. Wayne, Ind., 1961-65, sr. acct., 1965-67, internal auditor, 1967-69, asst. controller, 1969-76; controller Tokheim Corp., Ft. Wayne, 1976—. Chmn. Grand Prairie Twp. Zoning Bd. Appeals, Marion, Ohio, 1959-61; chmn. troop com. Boy Scouts Am., Ft. Wayne, 1969-73, com. mem. Thunderbird dist., 1972-74. Served with USAF, 1951-55. Mem. Nat. Assn. Accts. (chpt. pres. 1976-77), Inst. Internal Auditors (dir. 1968-70), Ft. Wayne C. of C. Republican. Mem. Ch. of the Brethren. Clubs: Ft. Wayne Exec., Masons, Shriners, DeMolay (Hon. Legion of Honor award Internat. Supreme Council 1978, Cross of Honor 1981). Home: 3416 Trier Rd Fort Wayne IN 46815 Office: 1600 Wabash Ave Fort Wayne IN 46801

HOLLERMAN, CHARLES EDWARD, pediatric nephrologist; b. Turtle Creek, Pa., Apr. 22, 1929; s. Harry R. and Lena F. Hollerman; B.S., Allegheny Coll., Meadville, Pa., 1951; M.D., Cornell U., 1955; m. Catharine L. Smith, Aug. 22, 1953; children—James, Karen, Jeffrey, Pamela. Mem. adminstrv. staff U. S.D. Med. Sch., Vermillion, 1977—, v.p. health affairs, dean, 1979—. Served as officer M.C., USNR, 1956-59. Mem. Am. Acad. Pediatrics, Am. Soc. Nephrology, AMA, Am. Soc. Pediatric Nephrology, S.D. Med. Assn. Author: Pediatric Nephrology: Medical Outline Series, 1979. Office: Univ SD Med Sch Clark and Dakota Sts Vermillion SD 57069

HOLLEY, GERALD NEAL, broadcasting exec.; b. Warsaw, Mo., Oct. 30, 1938; s. John and Beulah Faye (Johnson) H.; B.A., Baker U., 1960; m. Aletha Jane Quellhorst, June 18, 1961; children—Pamela Jo, Mark Cameron. Announcer, Sta. WIBW-TV, Topeka, Kans., 1960-62, promotion mgr., 1962-63; gen. mgr. Sta. KSEK, Pittsburg, Kans., 1963-65, Sta. WIBW-AM-FM, Topeka, 1965-69; v.p. broadcasting Stauffer Communications, Inc., Topeka, 1977—. Bd. trustees William Allen White Found., U. Kans., mem. adv. council Sch. Radio-TV-Film; mem. alumni bd. dirs. Baker U.; bd. dirs. United Way, State Employment and Tng. Council; tech. adv. Kans. Promotion Council, Heart Fund; v.p. affiliate chpt., mem. bd. Kidney Found. Kans. and Western Mo.; mem. exec. com. Topeka Bicentennial Assn.; broadcast chmn. Inaugural Com.; mem. corp. bd. Joslin Clinic, Boston. Mem. Nat. Assn. Broadcasters, TV and Radio Polit. Action Com. (dir.), Broadcast Pioneers, TV Bd. Dirs., Kans. Assn. Commerce and Industry, Kans. Assn. Broadcasters (mem. bd., past pres.), Topeka Broadcast Council, Kans. Cavalry, Am. Quarter Horse Assn., Kans. Quarter Horse Assn., Kans. Quarter Racing Assn., Topeka C. of C. (past mem. bd. dirs., exec. com.). Republican. Methodist. Club: Rotary (past pres. Topeka Downtown). Home: 3520 SW Lincolnshire Rd Topeka KS 66614 Office: PO Box 119 Topeka KS 66601

HOLLIDAY, JACK MCKINLEY, educator; b. Danese, W.Va., Feb. 15, 1948; s. Jay McKinley and Grace Ann (McClung) H.; B.S. in History, Cedarville Coll., 1970; M.Ed., Wright State U., 1976. Tchr. history Beavercreek High Sch., Xenia, Ohio, 1970—, chmn. dept. history, 1976-80, head cross country coach, 1970—, asst. track coach, 1975—. Active Cloud for Gov. Campaign, 1970. Served with U.S. N.G., 1970-76. Named Girls Cross Country Coach of Yr. for West Central Ohio, Cross Country Coaches Assn., 1979; recipient commendation for cross country records Ohio Ho. of Reps., 1979. Mem. Am. Hist. Assn., Nat. Hist. Soc., Nat. High Sch. Athletic coaches Assn., Ohio Track and Cross Country Coachs Assn., NEA. Republican. Baptist. Home: 2472 N Aragon Ave Kettering OH 45420 Office: 2660 Dayton-Xenia Rd Xenia OH 45385

HOLLIFIELD, PERRY JAY, constrn. co. exec.; b. Roswell, N.Mex., Aug. 1, 1931; s. George V. and Edith P. Hollifield; B.S. in Mech. Engring., U. N.Mex., 1959; postgrad. U. Wash., Seattle; divorced; children—Sharon, Perry Jay. With Gen. Electric Co., 1959-74, mgr. design engring. Vallecitos Nuclear Center, Pleasanton, Calif., 1965-74; mgr. tech., cons. services div. Daniel Internat. Co.,

Greenville, S.C., 1974-76; mgr. bus. devel. Austin Power, Inc., Dallas, 1967-78; v.p., officer Fegles-Power Service Corp., Mpls., 1978—. Registered profl. engr., Tex., Calif., N.Mex. Mem. Am. Nuclear Soc., TAPPI, Northwest Electric Light and Power Assn. Republican. Methodist. Home: 8417 Amsden Ridge Dr Bloomington MN 55438 Office: 2110 Nicollet Ave Minneapolis MN 55404

HOLLINGSWORTH, HOLLY HOUSTON, statistician, educator; b. Sacramento, May 1, 1942; s. Howard Houston and Wilma Mae (Holland) H.; B.A., San Francisco State U., 1965; M.A., U. Ill., 1971, Ph.D., 1975; m. Carol Joy Shunker, Oct. 28, 1968; children—Howard Holly, Lucie Clare. Staff asso. Office Admissions, U. Ill., 1975-76; vis. prof. U. Pa. Grad. Sch. Edn., 1976-77; asso. prof. research methodology St. Louis U., 1977—; cons. Franklin Inst. Research Labs., Kirkwood Sch. Dist. Coach youth soccer, 1978—. Served with U.S. Peace Corps, 1965-68, summers 1972, 73; served with U.S. Army, 1968-70. NSF grantee, 1980. Mem. Am. Ednl. Research Assn., Am. Statis. Assn. Cons. editor Jour. Exptl. Edn., 1979—; contbr. research articles to profl. jours. Office: St Louis U Saint Louis MO 63103

HOLLINGTON, DAVID WILLIAM, banker; b. Cleve., June 9, 1944; s. Richard Rings and Annett Ewing (Kirk) H.; A.B., Univ. Sch., Franklin and Marshall Coll., 1966; postgrad. Western Res. Law Sch., 1966-67, Bus. Sch. Harvard, 1973; m. Deborah Lynn Jones, May 8, 1976; 1 dau., Courtenay L. Asst. v.p. Ohio Bank & Savs. Co., Findlay, 1968-70, sec., 1970-74, v.p., sec., 1974-76, pres., 1976—; dir. various corps. Trustee Hancock Hist. Mus., FANTAM, Hancock County United Way, Arthritis Found. of NW Ohio, 1972—. Mem. Am., Ohio bankers assns., Young Presidents Orgn. Episcopalian. Clubs: Kirtland Country, Findlay Country; Winois Point Shooting. Home: Holly Creek Farm Findlay OH 45840 Office: 236 S Main St Findlay OH 45840

HOLLINS, MITCHELL LESLIE, lawyer; b. N.Y.C., Mar. 11, 1947; s. Milton and Alma (Bell) H.; B.A., Western Res. U., 1967; J.D., N.Y. U., 1971; m. Nancy Kirchheimer, Mar. 27, 1977. Admitted to Ill. bar, 1971; asso. Sonnenschein Carlin Nath & Rosenthal, Chgo., 1971-78, partner, 1978—. Bd. dirs. Med. Research Inst. Council, Michael Reese Hosp. and Med. Center, 1978—, mem. exec. com., 1979—, sec., 1981—, chmn. jr. bd., 1978-79; asst. sec. Jr. Achievement of Chgo., 1980—; mem. info. and referral com. Comprehensive Community Services of Met. Chgo., 1981—; former bd. dirs. Young Men's Jewish Council and Young People's Div. of Jewish United Fund of Met. Chgo. Mem. Am. Bar Assn., Ill. State Bar Assn., Chgo. Bar Assn. Republican. Clubs: Standard, Lake Shore Country (Glencoe, Ill.). Home: 3000 N Sheridan Rd Chicago IL 60657 Office: Sonnenschein Carlin Nath & Rosenthal 8000 Sears Tower Chicago IL 60606

HOLLOWAY, DONALD PHILLIP, librarian; b. Akron, Ohio, Feb. 18, 1928; s. Harold Shane and Dorothy Gayle (Ryder) H.; B.S. in Commerce, Ohio U., Athens, 1950; LL.B., U. Akron, 1955; M.A., Kent State U., 1962. Title examiner Bankers Guarantee Title & Trust Co., Akron, 1950-54; accountant Robinson Clay Product Co., Akron, 1955-60; librarian Akron Pub. Library, 1962-69, head fine arts and music div., 1969-71, sr. librarian, 1972—. Payroll treas. Akron Symphony Orch., 1957-61; treas. Friends Library Akron and Summit County, 1970-72. Mem. Music Library Assn., Am., Ohio, Akron bar assns., Ohio Library Assn., ALA, Nat. Trust for Historic Preservation, Soc. Archtl. Historians, Coll. Art Assn. Club: Nat. Lawyers (Washington). Home: 601 Nome Ave Akron OH 44320

HOLLOWAY, LAWRENCE MILTON, osteo. physician; b. Kirksville, Mo., Sept. 8, 1913; s. Edward Lee and Vetta (Elmore) H.; student Kirksville Bus. Coll., 1933, NE Mo. U., 1933-36; D.O., Kirksville Coll. Osteopathy and Surgery, 1940; M.D., U. Santo Tomas, 1951; m. Roena Jane Williams, Dec. 24, 1935; children—Lawrence Milton, Lynette Jane. Intern, A.S.O. Hosp., Kirksville, 1939-40, Detroit Osteo. Hosp., 1940-42; gen. practice osteo. medicine, Byron, Mich., 1940-56, specializing in endocrinology, Flint, Mich., 1956—; examining physician Am. Pres. Life Ins. Co.; fellow in surgery Am. Coll. Osteo. Physicians and Surgeons, Byron, 1940-56; instr. Physiol. Chemistry Lab., Kirksville Coll. Osteopathy and Surgery, 1938-40; founder, chief surgeon, chief staff Lawrence Osteo. Hosp., Byron, 1942-56; dir., bus. mgr. L. M. Holloway Clinic; plastic and cosmetic surgeon Flint Gen. Hosp. Pres., L.M. Holloway Mfg. Co., Byron, 1944-47; v.p. Owosso Finance Co. (Mich.), 1952-56, pres., 1956—; adv. bd. Hamilton Internat. Life Ins. Co. Physician, Byron High Sch., 1940-54. Adviser Swartz Creek chpt. Boy Scouts Am.; sec. Orgn. for World Wide Postgrad. Study. Fellow Am. Soc. Clin. Hypnosis (life); mem. Am., Genesee County osteo. assns., Mich. Assn. Osteo. Physicians and Surgeons, Am. Coll. Osteo. Surgeons (life), Am. Soc. Endocrinology and Nutrition, Am. Soc. Clin. Arthritis, Kirksville Osteo. Alumni Assn., Future Farmers Am. (life), Psi Sigma Alpha. Clubs: Masons (32 deg.), Shriners, Elks, 750 (pres. Mich. chpt. 1958-59, 61, 64-66). Home: 10283 Corunna Rd Swartz Creek MI 48473 Office: G 5200 Corunna Rd Flint MI 48504

HOLLOWAY, LAWRENCE MILTON, JR., wholesale exec.; b. Detroit, Jan. 14, 1946; s. Lawrence Milton and Roena Jane (Williams) H.; B.S., Mich. State U., 1968; M.A., Drake U., 1977; m. Charlotte Jane Spiter, June 19, 1970; children—Tiffany Jane, Marque Spiter. Collection supr. Owosso (Mich.) Fin. Co., 1963-66; supr. med. lab. L.M. Holloway Clinic, Flint, Mich., 1966-68; lab. supr. Ferris State U., Big Rapids, Mich., 1968-69; tchr. St. Matthew Sch., Flint, 1969-70; fin. cons. Hamilton Internat. Corp., Farmington, Mich., 1970-71; v.p. Nat. Potential Devel. Co., St. Louis, 1971—; pres. Holloway House, Des Moines, 1971—; instr. Des Moines Area Community Coll., 1978-79. Active, Iowans for L.I.F.E., Inc., 1975—, mem. exec. com., 1980; bd. dirs. Des Moines Right to Life, Inc., 1978—, polit. chmn., 1979—; bd. dirs. Pro-Life Action Council, 1980—, Am. Security Council, 1980—, Rep. Nat. Com., 1980—. Recipient Notable Ams. award Hist. Preservations Am., 1976. Mem. Nat. Assn. Federally Lic. Firearms Dealers, Am. Chem. Soc., Am. Inst. Hypnosis, Am. Soc. Nondestructive Testing, Student Osteopathic Med. Assn. Iowa Soc. Osteo. Physicians and Surgeons (dir. 1980), Iowa Acad. Sci. (dir. 1980), Am. Acad. Osteopathy (dir. 1979). Republican. Mem. Evangelical Ch. Club: Masons (Shriner). Author: Dry Cell Therapy, Its Future, 1964; Biochemical Basis of Learning, 1977. Address: 818 15th St Des Moines IA 50314

HOLM, CALVIN DOUGLAS, electric co. exec.; b. Tiffin, Ohio, Dec. 27, 1948; s. Raymond Adelph and Janice Lucille (Senn) H.; student Ohio State U., 1973-76; m. Mary Shafer, June 16, 1979. Financial accountant John W. Galbreath & Co., Columbus, Ohio, 1976-77; asst. controller Wyandot Popcorn Co., Marion, Ohio, 1977-78; cost accountant Borden Chem., div. Border, Inc., Columbus, 1978-79; cost analyst ITT-North Electric Co., Galion, Ohio, 1979—. Served with USAF, 1968-72. Mem. Ohio State U. Vets. Assn. (pres. 1975-76). Methodist. Club: Masons. Home: 1450 Walnut Dr Galion OH 44833 Office: Portland Way N Galion OH 44833

HOLM, DONALD SUTHERLAND, JR., educator, univ. ofcl.; b. Highland Park, Mich., Oct. 1, 1920; s. D. S. and Louise (Hemeyer) H.; A.B., Oberlin Coll., 1941; M.B.A., Harvard U., 1947; M.A., Ind. U., 1950, Ph.D. (fellow), 1952; m. Marilynn Ruth Lamb, June 8, 1951; children—Donald Sutherland III, Elizabeth L. Asst. prof. bus. mgmt. U. Mo., Columbia, 1950-53, asso. prof., 1953-58, prof., 1958—, chmn. dept. bus. mgmt., 1962-65, coordinator M.B.A. program, 1964-65, chmn. dept. mgmt., 1965-69, dir. grad. programs in bus., 1965-70, acting asst. v.p. fin., 1972-73, asst. v.p., asst. treas., 1973-77, treas. and asst. v.p., 1977—; cons. U.S. Dept. Labor, 1960, Comptroller and Budget Dir., State of Mo., 1962, Hawthorn Co., New Haven, Mo., 1963-64, Mo. State Library, 1962-63, M.F.A. Oil Co., Columbia, 1964-65, City of Columbia, 1966, OEO, 1966-67, Mo. Dept. Revenue, 1967, Boone County Hosp., 1968, 73, Am. Coll. Hosp. Adminstrs., 1968-71, Mo. State Hwy. Commn., 1956—, Mo. Savs. and Loan League, 1972. Mem. Mo. Com. on Econ. Devel., 1960-61; chmn. City of Columbia Personnel Adv. Bd., 1963-72; mem. Task Force on Personnel Adminstrn., Mo. State Reorgn. Commn., 1970-71; chmn. Mo. Gov.'s Adv. Council on Employment Security, 1962-65. Served from ensign to lt. comdr. USNR, 1942-46, comdr. Res. ret. Recipient Outstanding Achievement award in Aerospace Edn., USAF, 1970. Mem. Acad. Mgmt., U.S. Navy League (dir. 1967-70), Nat., Central assns. coll. and univ. bus. officers. Clubs: Columbia Country (treas., gov. 1966-71); Harvard (N.Y.C.); Mo. Athletic. Author books on labor and unemployment. Contbr. articles on fin. and mgmt. to profl. publs. Home: 106 W Ridgeley Rd Columbia MO 65201 Office: 215K University Hall Columbia MO

HOLM, ROBERT ANTON, ednl. adminstr.; b. Bklyn., June 26, 1938; s. Carl Vincent and Solveig Louise (Blom) H.; B.A., Ohio Wesleyan U., 1960; m. Mary Wallace Steele, July 2, 1960; children—Robert A., Anne, David. Adminstr., Ohio Wesleyan U., Delaware, 1963—, dir. devel., 1972—. Trustee, Wesley Glen Retirement Center, 1969—, vice chmn., 1974-77; trustee Library Community Center, 1981—; adv. bd. Delaware Children's Home, 1977—. Served with USAF, 1960-63. Mem. Council for Advancement and Support of Edn. Methodist. Home: 277 N Franklin St Delaware OH 43015 Office: Ohio Wesleyan U Delaware OH 43015

HOLMAN, JAMES LEWIS, profl. assn. exec.; b. Chgo., Oct. 27, 1926; s. James Louis and Lillian Marie (Walton) H.; B.S. in Econs. and Mgmt., U. Ill., Urbana, 1950, postgrad., 1950; postgrad. Northwestern U., 1954-55; m. Elizabeth Ann Owens, June 18, 1948; children—Craig Stewart, Tracy Lynn, Mark Andrew. Traveling auditor, then statistician, asst. controller parent buying dept. Sears, Roebuck & Co., Chgo., 1951-54; asst. to sec.-treas. Hanover Securities Co., Chgo., 1954-65; fin. analyst Hales & Hunter Co., Chgo., 1965; mgmt. controller Harry F. Chaddick Assos., Inc., Chgo., 1965-66; asst. to controller chem. ops. div. Montgomery Ward & Co. Inc., Chgo., 1966-68; controller Henrotin Hosp., Chgo., 1968; bus. mgr. Julian, Dye, Javid, Hunter & Najafi, Associated, Chgo., 1969—; dir. Medtran, Inc. Sec., B.R. Ryall YMCA, Glen Ellyn, Ill., 1974-76, bd. dirs., 1968-78; trustee Gary Meml. United Methodist Ch., Wheaton, Ill., 1961-69, 74-77, Goodwill Industries Chgo., 1978-79; bd. dirs. DuPage (Ill.) Symphony, 1954-58, treas., 1955-58. Served with USN, 1944-46. Scholarship Nat. Music Camp, Interlochen, Mich., 1944. Mem. Hosp. Fin. Mgmt. Assn. Baha'i. Clubs: Kiwanis (dir. Chgo. 1956-60, bd. dirs. youth found. dir. 1957-60, pres. 1958-60), Masons. Home: 822 S Main St Wheaton IL 60187 Office: 1725 W Harrison St Chicago IL 60612

HOLMAN, WILBUR ALLEN, clergyman; b. Aug. 13, 1911; s. Stokley Allen and Laura Jane (Glidewell) H.; A.B., William Jewell Coll., 1943; B.D., Central Bapt. Theol. Sem., 1952, Th.M., 1954; m. Cordie Jane Piburn, Jan. 16, 1934. Ordained to ministry Christian Union Ch., 1942; pastor various chs., 1940—; sec. Mo. council Christian Union, 1943-51, pres., 1952-56; dir. Christian Union Extension Bible Sch., 1953-78; pres. gen. council Christian Union, 1962-71; mem. ordination bd. Mo. council Christian Union. Mem. Pi Gamma Mu. Publisher: Bible Truth Vs. the Teachings of Jehovah's Witnesses, 1958; editor: The Christian Union Directory, 1947; contbr. articles and Bible studies to Christian Union Witness, 1942-79. Home: 500 Beverly St Excelsior Springs MO 64024

HOLMBERG, RAYMON E., state senator; b. Qrand Forks, N.D., Dec. 10, 1943; s. Leslie Orwell and Nina (Marchildon) H.; B.S., U. N.D., 1965, M.S., 1976; m. Kerry Louise Hackett, 1973; children—Mariah Jay, Brady Jon. Mem. N.D. Senate, 1976—, vice-chmn. judiciary com.; public sch. tchr. Mem. NEA, N.D. Edn. Assn. Club: Elks. Home: 1701 Riverside Dr Grand Forks ND 58201*

HOLMES, CHARLES FREDERICK, mfg. co. exec.; b. Pana, Ill., May 19, 1949; s. William Albert and Genevieve Elizabeth (Singler) H.; A.S., Parkland Coll., 1971; student U. Ill., 1971-74; m. Sara Jo Rowe, June 12, 1971; children—Summer Rae, Erica Autumn, Charles Phillip. Devel. engr. Torrington (Conn.) Co., 1969; sr. research tech., Cabot Corp., Tuscola, Ill., 1973-78; plant engr. Littelfuse, Inc., Tuscola, 1978-79, plant supt., 1979-80, plant mgr., 1980—; lectr. Sangamon State U., Springfield, Ill., 1969-70. Served with Ill. N.G., 1970-76. Mem. ASME, Am. Soc. for Quality Control. Roman Catholic. Clubs: Rotary, Elks. Patentee in field. Home: 214 E Newkirk St Tuscola IL 61953 Office: 700 S Main St Tuscola IL 61953

HOLMES, DAVID S., state senator; b. Covington, Ky., Aug. 11, 1914; s. Sanford and Elizabeth (Cain) H.; B.S., Va. State Coll.; postgrad. U. Mich.; m. Avis Ernestine Greene, 1962. Former sch. tchr., Va., social worker and union organizer; mem. Mich. Ho. of Reps., 1958-76; mem. Mich. Senate, 1976—. Chmn. Mich. Black Caucus, 1966—; del. Democratic Nat. Conv., 1968, alt. del., 1976. Mem. Trade Union Leadership Council. Clubs: Masons, Bus. and Profl. Men's. Office: Mich Senate State Capitol Lansing MI 48909*

HOLMES, DEBORAH SUE, educator; b. Topeka, Mar. 21, 1953; d. Robert G. and Virginia M. (Slingerland) H.; B.S. in Edn., U. Kans., 1974, M.S. in Curriculum Devel., 1979, cert. adminstrn. instructional tech., 1980. Elem. sch. tchr., Lawrence, Kans., 1972-73, 74-79; co-coordinator Green House Child Care Center, Lawrence, 1973-74; instr. U. Kans., 1973-75; curriculum developer media, literacy project Lawrence Public Schs., 1979-80; dir. fed. programs/curriculum projects University City, Mo., 1980—; chmn. personnel com. Hilltop Child Devel. Center, Lawrence, 1975-80; cons. in field. Recipient Vicki Larason Landman Non-Sexist Teaching award U. Kans., 1975, Jayhawk Tchr. award, 1976. Mem. Assn. Supervision and Curriculum Devel., Assn. Ednl. Communications and Tech., Conf. Edn., Ninety Nines, NOW, Phi Delta Kappa, Pi Lambda Theta. Author: Thumbs Up, 1978; Nature's Way, 1980; Daily Breaks, 1981; also articles. Home: 4431 McPherson St St Louis MO 63108 Office: 725 Kingsland St University City MO 63130

HOLMES, EDNA PAULINE, univ. food service adminstr., restaurant exec.; b. Keith, Ohio, June 14, 1919; d. Willard Thomas and Mildred Marie (Lamp) Farson; B.S., Kent State U., 1940; m. Brian Ward Holmes, Apr. 4, 1942; children—Margaret Alice, Brian Farson, Gregory Ward. Dietitian, Good Samaritan Hosp., Ashland, Ohio, 1940-42; dietary clk.-typist Sta. Hosp., Camp Maxey, Paris, Tex., 1943; receptionist USO-Travel Aid, Blackstone, Va., 1944, caseworker, Akron, Ohio, 1944; supr. food service Akron div. Ohio Bell Telephone Co., 1944-47; owner, mgr. Welshfield Inn, Burton, Ohio, 1946—, v.p., sec.-treas., 1975—; mgr. food service Residence Halls, U. Akron, 1974—; instr. hospitality Community Coll. Cleve., 1973; cons. mgmt. Pres. PTA Troy Sch., Geauga, County, Ohio, 1958-60. Mem. Nat. Restaurant Assn., Geauga County Home Econs. Assn., Geauga County Hist. Soc. (trustee 1968-74), Nat. Lic. Beverage Assn., AAUW (Hiram br.), Panhellenic Club, Alpha Gamma Delta. Republican. Methodist. Clubs: Garden Center Greater Cleve., Order Eastern Star. Office: Welshfield Inn 14001 Main-Market Rd Burton OH 44021 and Robertson Dining Hall U Akron 303 Carroll St Akron OH 44304

HOLMES, GLORIA MAUDE HENDREN, educator; b. Newark, Ohio, Nov. 5, 1930; d. Walter Ebert and Corinne (Tope) Hendren; B.Ed., Ohio State U., 1952, M.Ed., 1957, postgrad., 1958—; m. Richard Lewis Holmes, July 19, 1959; children—Kimberly Sue, Sally Lou, Kathy Lynn, Jeffery Richard, Nancy Ann, David Michael, Susan Elizabeth. Tchr., Cherry Valley Elem. Sch., Newark, 1952-56; grad. asst. lab. sch. Ohio State U., 1956; asso. prof. elem. edn. Ashland Coll., also supr. elem. student teaching, acad. counselor, 1956—, founder, dir., supr. Ashland Coll. Kindergarten, 1960-63; mem. curriculum redesign com. tchr. edn. Ohio and Ashland Coll., 1976-77; cons., lectr. Bd. dirs. Ashland Community Day Care Center. Mem. Ashland City Schs. PTA, Ashland Christian Sch. PTA. Active United Appeal; hosp. Vol. ARC, 1956-59; v.p. Women's Missionary Soc. Hope Circle group III Park St. Brethren Ch., 1970-71; staff ch. sch., Bible sch. and youth activities Berean Sunday Sch. Recipient award Women's Recognition Day, State of Ohio, 1978; Jennings Research scholar, 1974-75. Recipient Adminstrs. Cert., Ohio. Mem. Ohio, Nat. edn. assns., Ohio, Nat. assns. for higher edn., Ohio Assn. for Tchr. Educators, Nursery-Kindergarten-Primary Assn., Assn. for Supervision and Curriculum Devel., Assn. for Childhood Edn., AAUW, Bus. and Profl. Women's Club, Symphony League, Assn. of Adminstrs., Guidance Assn., Assn. for Exceptional Children, Ohio State U. Alumni Assn., Ohio State U., Ashland Coll. devel. fund assns., N. Central Ohio Tchrs. Assn., Ashland Christian Bus. and Profl. Women's Club, Internat. Reading Assn., Internat. Platform Assn., Phi Delta Kappa, Alpha Delta Kappa, Beta Sigma Phi (pres. Delta Gamma chpt. 1969-70), Kappa Delta Pi (hon.), Xi Iota Alpha. Mem. Order of Eastern Star, White Shrine of Jerusalem, Altrusa Internat. Club: Ashland Coll. Faculty Club, Ashland Coll. Faculty Women's Club (pres. 1959-60), Garden. Author: Handbook for Administrators, Cooperating Teachers, Student Teachers, and College Supervisors-Ashland College, 1957; Handbook for Kindergarten Teachers, 1963; (with Richard L. Holmes) Innovations in Church School Teacher-Education Program, 1972; A Competency Based Program for Teacher Education-Children's Literature, 1974; A Competency Based Program for Teacher Education-Kindergarten Methods, 1974; Planning for the Culturally Different Learner and the Handicapped Learner in the Kindergarten Environment, 1979. Home: 439 N Woodhill Dr Ashland OH 44805 Office: Edn Dept Ashland Coll Coll Ave Ashland OH 44805

HOLMES, MARJORIE MARIE, transit authority ofcl.; b. Oakland, Calif., Nov. 25; d. Willis and Juanita (Chism) Wardlaw; A.A., Loop Coll., 1975; B.S. in Bus. Adminstrn., Roosevelt U., 1977, M.B.A., 1978; 1 dau., Lyndel Marie. Sec. to Ann Landers, Chgo. Sun-Times, 1965-67; sec. to v.p. engring. Wilson & Co., Inc., Chgo., 1967-69; supr. human relations Chgo. Transit Authority, 1979-80, dir. human relations, 1980—; instr. bus. adminstrn. Roosevelt U. Instr., Sunday sch. dept., bd. dirs., radio announcer, organist, youth leader, coordinator, lectr. retreats and seminars Shiloh Ch. Recipient YWCA ann. merit award, 1975, cert. of merit Chgo. Public Schs., 1978, Fred Hampton humanitarian award, mgmt. edn. program Chgo. Transit Authority, 1978. Mem. Chgo. Area Assn. for Affirmative Action and Compliance (sec. bd.), M.B.A. Soc., Roosevelt Alumni Assn. Co-author affirmative action program, Chgo. Transit Authority; contbr. articles to mags. and newspapers. Home: 505 N Lake Shore Dr Apt 5305 Chicago IL 60611 Office: Merchandise Mart Plaza Chicago IL 60654

HOLMES, NORMAN SINCLAIR, bank holding co. exec.; b. Chgo., Feb. 15, 1928; s. Norman Eastman and Alelle (Sinclair) H.; B.B.A., U. Wis.-Milw., 1964, M.B.A., 1970; grad. U. Wis.-Grad. Sch. Banking, 1972; m. Edith Elinor Aalto, Aug. 26, 1950; children—June Elinor, Carol Ann, Diane Lee. Vice-pres., dir. Pho-Tronics, Inc., Milw., 1962-68; asst. v.p. 1st Wis. Nat. Bank, Milw., 1967-73; v.p., mortgage officer 1st Wis. Mortgage Corp., 1974; v.p., trust officer 1st Wis. Nat. Bank, Milw., 1974-78; v.p. 1st Wis. Corp., Milw., 1978—; past dir. 1st Wis. Bank of Waukesha. Mem. bus. adv. council Milw. Area Tech. Coll., 1974—; congregation pres. St. Thomas Evang. Luth. Ch., 1979—. Mem. Assn. Systems Mgmt. (past pres. Milw. chpt.), Am. Inst. Banking, U. Wis.-Milw. Alumni Assn., Exptl. Aircraft Assn. Republican. Office: 777 E Wisconsin Ave Milwaukee WI 53202

HOLMES, PHYLLIS IRENE, educator; b. Crawfordsville, Iowa, Feb. 3, 1940; d. Thomas Julius and Irene Julie (Cassabaum) Holmes; B.S., Greenville (Ill.) Coll., 1961; M.A., U. So. Calif., 1968. Tchr. phys. edn. Winfield (Iowa) Mt. Union High Sch., 1961-64; coach, instr. phys. edn. Biola Coll., La Mirada, Calif., 1964-67; coach, prof. phys. edn. Greenville Coll., 1967—; women's basketball clinician to Sao Paulo, Brazil with Ill. Partners Assn., 1976; asst. coach Midwest women's team Nat. Sports Festival, 1978; asst. coach U.S. women's basketball team to Spartakiade Games, USSR, 1979; commr. Ill. Assn. Intercollegiate Athletics for Women, 1969—, Midwest Assn. Intercollegiate Athletics for Women, 1971-73, 76—; coordinator nat. women's basketball tournament Nat. Assn. Intercollegiate Athletics, also chmn. basketball com.; mgr. U.S.A. women's nat. team to World Univ. Games, 1981, U.S.A. women's select team to Cuba, 1981; mem. women's games com. Am. Basketball Assn. U.S.A., 1981—. Mem. AAHPER, Nat., Midwest assns. phys. edn. coll. women. Office: Greenville Coll Greenville IL 62246

HOLMES, RICHARD LEWIS, sch. adminstr.; b. Ashland, Ohio, Nov. 28, 1927; s. Lewis Mason and Evelyn Lucille (Ledyard) H.; B.S., Ashland Coll., 1965; M.Ed., Kent State U., 1968; postgrad. U. Akron, 1970, Ohio U., 1971; Ed.D (hon.), Lawford State U., 1974; m. Gloria Maude Hendren, July 19, 1959; children—Kimberly Sue, Sally Lou, Kathy Lynn, Jeffery Richard, Nancy Ann, David Michael, Susan Elizabeth. Elementary tchr. Ashland County (Ohio) Schs., 1961-62, Medina County (Ohio) Schs., 1962-67; asst. dir. audio-visual center Kent State U., 1967-68; dir. fed. program, elementary prin. Grant Sch., Wooster, Ohio, 1968-69; dir. ednl. media, coordinator-supr. vocat. edn. Ashland City Schs., 1969—; producer multi-media ednl. programs; chmn. policy adv. com. Head Start Program, Ashland, 1971; pres. Ashland Christian Sch. Parent-Tchr. Fellowship, 1975-76; mem. bd. Christian edn. First Brethren Ch., 1972-76. Served with USAF Res., 1947-55. Cert. tchr. and adminstr., Ohio. Mem. Ednl. Media Council Ohio, Assn. Communications and Tech. in Edn., NEA, Ohio Edn. Assn., Nat. Guild Hypnotists, Am. Mentalists Assn., Order of Merlin, Internat. Brotherhood Magicians, Soc. Am. Magicians, Intercontinental Biog. Assn., Phi Delta Kappa, Kappa Delta Pi. Club: Lions (pres., 1966-67). Inventor wireless didactic system for teaching, 1968. Author: Understanding School Subjects through Mnemonics, 1967; (with Gloria M. Holmes) Innovations in Church School Teacher-Education Programs, 1972. Home: Countryside Addition 439 N Woodhill Dr Ashland OH 44805 Office: 1440 King Rd Ashland OH 44805

HOLMES, RICHARD WINN, state ofcl.; b. Wichita, Kans., Feb. 23, 1923; B.S., Kans. State U., 1950; J.D., Washburn U., Topeka, 1953. Admitted to Kans. bar, 1953; individual practice law, Wichita,

1953-77; judge Wichita Mcpl. Ct., 1959-61; instr. bus. law Wichita State U., 1959-60; justice Kans. Supreme Ct., 1977—. Mem. Kans. Bar Assn., Wichita Bar Assn., Topeka Bar Assn., Am. Judges Assn. (founder 1959, bd. govs. 1980—). Office: Kansas Judicial Center Topeka KS 66612

HOLMES, ROBERT EDWARD, state justice; b. Columbus, Ohio, Nov. 14, 1922; s. Harry B. and Nora (Birney) H.; A.B., Ohio U., 1943, LL.B., 1949; children—Robert E., H. Barclay. Admitted to Ohio bar; individual practice law, Columbus, 1949-69; mem. Ohio Ho. of Reps., Columbus, 1960-69; judge 10th Dist. Ct. Appeals, Columbus 1969-78; justice Supreme Ct. Ohio, Columbus, 1978—. Bd. dirs. Boy Scouts Am., Salvation Army, Pilot Dogs, Inc., Columbus. Served with USN. Mem. Nat. Council Internat. Programs (past pres.), Am. Bar Assn., Ohio Bar Assn., Columbus Bar Assn. Clubs: Agonis, Kiwanis, Charity Newsies, Athletic. Office: 30 E Broad St Columbus OH 43215*

HOLOHAN, O. J., indsl. and interior designer; b. Detroit, Sept. 18, 1936; s. James Frances and Ernestine Flora (Neumann) H.; degree in Indsl. Designs and Interiors, Cleve. Inst. Art, 1961; m. Laurinda Anne Loewe, Oct. 25, 1969; children—Eric James, Shauna Lynn, Brian James. Illustrator to Pres. D. Eisenhower, 1957-58; art dir. TV sta., Washington, 1958-59; dir. design O.J.K. Designers div. F.W. Roberts, Cleve., 1962-67; pres. O.J. Holohan Assos., Inc., Burton, Ohio, 1967—; judge design juries. Served with U.S. Army, 1957-59. Recipient Merit award Nat. Stationary and Office Equipment Assn., 1962; Design award 2d place Nat. Office Furniture Assn., 1963; Design award, 1965; 1st and 2nd place awards Office Interior Design Mag., 1965; hon. mention award S.M. Hexter Co., 1975. Mem. Inst. Bus. Designers (founding), Zool. Assn. Am., Nat. Office Furniture Assn. Home: 2 Serenity Pk 12175 Snow Rd Burton OH 44021 Office: 1 Serenity Pk 12175 Snow Rd Burton OH 44021

HOLSEN, JAMES NOBLE, JR., chem. engr.; b. Palo Alto, Calif., June 20, 1924; s. James N. and Esther (Giltrud) H.; B.S., Princeton U., 1948; D.Sc., Washington U., St. Louis, 1954; m. Margot Martin Meyer, Nov. 11, 1977; children—James Noble III, David Edwards. Chem. engr. Olin Mathieson Chem. Corp., 1954-55; asst. prof. chem. engring. Washington U., 1955-58, asso. prof., 1958-61, prof., 1961-73; prof. chem. engring. U. Mo., Rolla, 1973-74, vis. prof. engring. mgmt., 1974-75; chem. engr. McDonnell Douglas Corp., St. Louis, 1975—; cons. chem. engring. and aerospace scis.; vis. prof. engring. Kabul U., Afghanistan, 1963-64, 69-73; mem. U.S. Engring. Team, Kabul, 1963-64, 69-73. Served with AUS, 1942-46. Registered profl. engr., Mo. Asso. fellow AIAA; mem. Am. Inst. Chem. Engrs. (chmn. St. Louis sect. 1962), Am. Chem. Soc., Am. Soc. Engring. Edn., AAAS, Sigma Xi, Tau Beta Pi. Mem. Ethical Soc. Club: Princeton Quadrangle. Research on gas phase reaction kinetics, gaseous transport properties, materials processing in space. Home: 419 E Argonne Dr Kirkwood MO 63122 Office: McDonnell Douglas Corp PO Box 516 Saint Louis MO 63166

HOLST, NORMAN DOLCY, bank holding co. exec.; b. St. Louis, Jan. 26, 1943; s. Dolcy Warren and Thelma Clayton (Avery) H.; student Okla. Bapt. U., 1961-62, Mo. Western Coll., 1962-63; B.S. in Bus. Adminstrn., U. Mo., Columbia, 1966; m. Frances Ellen Bartlett, Jan. 12, 1968; children—Jason Bradford, Adam Bartlett, Zachary Avery. Asst. city mgr. Pittsburg, Kans., 1966-67; economist Mid-America Regional Council, Kansas City, Mo., 1967-70, chief economist, 1970-72; pres. Holst & Assos., Econ. Consultants, Kansas City, Mo., 1972-73; dir. market research Commerce Bancshares, Inc., Kansas City, Mo., 1973-74, asst. v.p., mgr. corp. real estate and constrn., 1974-78, v.p., dir. corp. real estate, 1978—; guest lectr. colls. Mem. Nat. Assn. Corp. Real Estate Execs. (bd. dirs.), Am. Mgmt. Assn., Am. Inst. Banking, Bldg. Owners and Mgrs. Assn., Greater Kansas City C. of C. Republican. Condr. research studies Kansas City area; mgr. design and constrn. buildings. Office: 720 Main St Kansas City MO 64105

HOLSWORTH, THOMAS ELMAN, JR., psychologist; b. Indpls., Nov. 24, 1948; s. Thomas Elman and Patricia Louise (Miles) H.; B.A., B.S. in Edn., Taylor U., 1971; M.A. (Univ. fellow), Ind. U., 1973; M.S. in Edn., Ph.D., Purdue U., 1976; m. Shirley Ann Gick, May 26, 1973; children—Melissa Marie, Damian Thomas, Thomas Andrew. Chief psychology Trade Winds Rehab. Center, Gary, Ind., 1976-77; cons. psychologist So. Hills Mental Health Center, Jasper, Ind., 1977—, also asst. prof. psychology St. Meinrad (Ind.) Sem., 1977—; pres. Perry County Group Homes, Inc. (Tell City, Ind.); facilitator Archdiocese of Indpls. Priest Support Groups. Eli Lilly & Co. grantee, 1979. Mem. Am. Psychol. Assn. Roman Catholic. Home: Rural Route 4 Box 698H Jasper IN 47546 Office: Dept Psychology Saint Meinrad Sem Saint Meinrad IN 47577

HOLT, DONALD HENRY, utility co. exec.; b. Cleve., Jan. 22, 1941; s. Randall N. and Lolia E. (Kinciad) H.; B.S.B.A., John Carroll U., 1964; M.B.A., Case Western Res. U., 1971; J.D., U. Akron, 1976; m. Dianne Williford, May 20, 1970. Mgmt. trainee East Ohio Gas Co., Cleve., 1964, cost analyst, 1967-68, spl. asst. to pres., 1968-69, asst. to pres., 1969—; admitted to Ohio bar, 1977. Trustee Met. Gen. Hosp. Found., United Torch Services, Urban League. Served with AUS, 1965-67. Mem. Greater Cleve., Ohio, Nat. bar assns., Alpha Kappa Psi. Republican. Congregationalist. Club: Rotary. Home: 23512 Cedar Rd Beachwood OH 44122 Office: East Ohio Gas Co 1717 E 9th St Cleveland OH 44114

HOLT, DOUGLAS EMERSON, social worker, owner hotel, restaurant; b. Grand Island, Nebr., Mar. 4, 1944; s. Emerson and Elsie Ruth (Palmer) H.; student So. Meth. U., 1964; B.A., Ouachita Bapt. Coll., 1967; M.S.W., Tulane U., 1971; postgrad. Perkins Sch. Theology, 1973; m. Kathleen Marie Magouirk, July 22, 1967; children—Matthew Douglas, Christopher Lewis. Psychiat. social worker Mo. State Hosp. System, Nevada, 1968-69; adminstrv. dir. New Orleans Mental Health Center, 1969-70; program dir. Alaska Children's Service, Anchorage, 1971-72, Meth. Youthville, Newton, Kans., 1973-74; dir. Broadway, Inc. Youth Ranch, New Orleans, 1975-76; prof. social work St. Mary of the Plains Coll., Dodge City, Kans., 1976-78; pvt. practice psychiat. social work, Cimarron, Kans., 1978—; owner, operator Cimarron Hotel and Restaurant, 1978—; mgr. Chevrolet-Oldsmobile, Cimarron, 1978—; program cons. Area Mental Health, 1978—; chmn. bd. KANZ-FM Radio; now mem. Kans. State Ho. of Reps. Active, Parks and Recreation, Cimarron, 1976—. Lic. social worker, Kans. Mem. Nat. Assn. Social Workers, C. of C. Club: Kiwanis. Contbr. articles to profl. jours. Home: PO Box 633 Cimarron KS 67835 Office: PO Box 545 Cimarron KS 67835

HOLT, GARY LYNDLE, psychologist, educator; b. Livermore, Calif., June 10, 1941; B.S. in Psychology and Physiology, U. Calif., San Francisco, 1965; B.S. in Exptl. Child Psychology, Utah State U., Logan, 1967; Ph.D. in Devel. Psychology, W.Va. U., 1970; 1 dau., Diana Marie Prof. psychology SUNY, Geneseo, 1970-72; prof. Eastern Ill. U., Charleston, 1972—; pvt. practice clin. psychology, Charleston; clin. staff psychologist Moultrie County Counseling Center; exec. dir. Coles County Counseling Center. Mem. Am., Eastern, Western, Midwestern psychol. assns., Psychonomic Sci. Soc., Assn. for Advancement of Behavior Therapy; Animan Behavior Soc., Psi Chi. Office: Psychology Dept Eastern Illinois University Charleston IL 61920 also 1705 Jackson Ave Charleston IL 61920

HOLT, JOSEPH PAYNTER, JR., physician; b. Louisville, Sept. 30, 1941; s. Joseph Paynter and Myrle Elizabeth (Walter) H.; M.D., U. Louisville, 1975; m. Beatrice Guarneschelle, Oct. 22, 1966; children—Joseph P., Jennifer G., Dominic W. Resident in ob-gyn, Stanford U., Palo Alto, Calif., 1976-79; fellow in reproductive endocrinology and infertility Washington U., St. Louis; now asst. prof. ob-gyn dept. reproductive biology Case Western Res. U., Cleve. Contbr. articles to med. jours. Office: MacDonald House Univ Hosps of Cleve 2105 Adelbert Rd Cleveland OH 44106

HOLT, (WILLIAM) KERMIT, travel editor; b. Clarksburg, W.Va., Oct. 26, 1916; s. William Tilford and Emelyne (Gregory) H.; A.B., Salem Coll., 1938; M.S. in Journalism, Northwestern U., 1939; m. Gisela Leers, May 7, 1941; children—William Henry, Heidi (Michael T. Gendusa). Reporter, Clarksburg Exponent, 1937-38, City News Bur., Chgo., 1939; night editor Mil Bur. AP, 1940; reporter Chgo. Tribune, 1940-46, fgn. corr., 1946-48, copy editor, 1948-55, asst. makeup editor, 1955-60, travel editor, 1960-82. Served to lt. USMCR, 1942-45. Decorated Purple Heart; recipient Pacific Area Travel Assn. award for best newspaper articles on Pacific, 1962, 65, 70, 71, 73, 77, Trans World Airlines Travel Writing award, 1965, 68, Mark Twain Travel Writing awards, 1960-61, 62-63, George Hedmon award, 1967, Edward Scott Beck award, 1970, Strebig-Dobben Meml. award, 1970; named Salem Coll. Alumnus of Year, 1963, Distinguished W. Virginian, 1971. Mem. Soc. Am. Travel Writers (nat. pres. 1965-67, chmn. bd. 1968-69), Chgo. Press Club (bd. govs. 1965-76, pres. 1975), Sigma Delta Chi. Club: Skal. Home: 227 Parkview Rd Glenview IL 60025 Office: Tribune Sq Chicago IL 60611

HOLT, PETER NORMAN, architect; b. Ciacova, Romania, May 21, 1929; s. Frank and Magdalena (Theisz) H.; B.S.A.E., Chgo. Tech. Coll., 1970; m. Christine H. Borck, June 23, 1956; children—Lawrence, Gloria, Kathy, John, Julie. Founder, pres. Holt Constrn. Co., 1953-60; supt. Harmony Builders, Chgo., 1960-63; supt. George A. Fuller Co., Chgo., 1963-67; project architect Mittelbusher & Tourtelot, Chgo., 1967-71; asst. dir. phys. plant dept. Roosevelt U., Chgo., 1971-81, dir., 1981—. Served with C.E., U.S. Army, 1951-53. Decorated Bronze Star. Mem. AIA, Chgo. Bldg. Supts. Assn. Roman Catholic. Home: 503 Meacham Park Ridge IL 60068 Office: 430 S Michigan Ave Chicago IL 60605

HOLT, ROBERT GALE, ins. broker; b. Memphis, Jan. 21, 1950; s. Houston Leon and Florence Ruth (Howard) H.; A.A. in Forestry, Southeastern Ill. Coll., 1971; m. Elizabeth Ann Schmitt, Dec. 16, 1972; children—Heather Renee, Robert Heath, Tonya Michelle. Self employed logger, 1971; engaged in ins. sales, 1972—; owner Shawnee Hills Ins. Agy., Equality, Ill., 1976—, Cave-In-Rock, Ill., 1979—; real estate salesman, 1978—. Active local Boy Scouts Am., CAP; chmn. Equality Salt Festival, 1979, 80, 81; bd. dirs. Shawnee Town Regional Port Authority, 1981—. Served with U.S. Army Res., 1971-72. Republican. Club: Masons. Address: Box 68 Equality IL 62934

HOLT, WALDO SLY, physician; b. Omaha, July 4, 1924; s. Ralph Waldo and Fara (Sly) H.; A.B., U. Kan., 1945, M.D., 1950; m. Jane Koslowsky, Nov. 24, 1950; children—Barry Alan, Peter Scott. Intern U.S. Naval Hosp., Phila., 1950-51; resident Cleve. Clinic Hosp., 1951-52, Ochsner Found. Hosp., New Orleans, 1954-56; practice medicine specializing in internal medicine, Kansas City, Mo., 1956—; mem. staffs St. Mary's, St. Luke's, Bapt. Meml., Research hosps., Kansas City. Mem. med. edn. com. Kansas City, Mo., 1964—. Fellow A.C.P., Phi Sigma; mem. Kan. Acad. Medicine, Jackson County Med. Soc., Am. Soc. Internal Medicine, Jackson County Med. Soc., Am. Soc. Internal Medicine, Mo. Diabetes Assn. (dir.). Home: 5525 Wornall Rd Kansas City MO 64113 Office: 4620 Nichols Pkwy Kansas City MO 64112

HOLT, WILLIAM CARL, JR., mfg. co. exec.; b. Liberty, Mo., July 12, 1947; s. William Carl and Elizabeth Grace (Dearing) H.; B.S. in Chemistry, U. Ill., 1969; m. Barbara Ruth Bosworth, July 31, 1971. Research chemist UOP, Inc., Des Plaines, Ill., 1969-73, research contract adminstr., 1973-75, dist. mgr. div. automotive products, Southfield, Mich., 1976-78, internat. mktg. mgr., 1978—; exec. dir. Tech. Adv. Bd., Dept. Commerce, Washington, 1975-76. Active Young Republicans, 1969-75; mem. sci. controversy subcom. Pres's. Adv. Com. on Sci. and Tech. Mem. AAAS, Soc. Automotive Engrs. Baptist. Author: Crisis! Environment and Energy, 1972; editor East-West Technol. Trade, 1976; inventor new class of materials, condrs. organic-ceramics. Home: 1518 S Harvard Arlington Heights IL 60005 Office: 40 UOP Plaza Des Plaines IL 60016

HOLT, YALE JACOB, indsl. mfg. co. exec.; b. Youngstown, Ohio, June 23, 1927; s. Leo I. and Dora K. H.; B.S., Ohio State U., 1950; postgrad. U. Dayton; m. Donna, June 9, 1965; children—Ilene, Susan, Teri, Patricia, Jon. Vice pres. mktg. Globe Industries, Inc., 1952-68; plant mgr. TRW, 1968-71, group v.p. mktg.-bus. devel., 1971-72; mgmt. cons. Yale Co., Dayton, Ohio, 1972-75; sr. v.p. Dayflex Co. div. group Dayco Corp., Dayton, 1975—, pres. Metal Products Group, 1979—, group ops. v.p., 1981—; cons. to cos.; lectr. local univs. Served with USN, 1945-46. Recipient awards for participation in spl. confs., seminars Wharton Sch., U. Pa., 1979, U. Cin., 1978, Dayton U., 1975. Mem. Am. Mgmt. Assn., Am. Bus. Club, Dayton Exec. Club, C. of C., Dayton Philharm. Dayton Art Inst., Mus. Natural History. Club: Ohio State U. Varsity O. Office: 333 W 1st St Dayton OH 45402

HOLTER, THOMAS ROGER, broadcasting exec.; b. Chippewa Falls, Wis., Feb. 10, 1934; s. Stanley Edward and Mildred Catherine (Jennings) H.; B.A., Eau Claire State Coll., 1962; m. Dorothy Jane Celesnik, July 8, 1964; children—Linda, Michael, Kirsten, Thomas Jennings. Staff announcer, writer stas. WECL and WIBZ, Eau Claire, Wis., 1959-62; press sec. campaign staff atty gen. Wis., 1962; staff announcer sta. WATR, Waterbury, Conn., 1962-63; program dir. sta. KOLM, Rochester, Minn., 1963; news editor sta. WISM, Madison, Wis., 1964-66; pres., gen. mgr. sta. WISM-FM, Madison, 1966-69, sta. WIBU-WLVE, Madison, 1969-79. Pres. Eau Claire Community Theatre, 1960-62. Served with USNR, 1952-54. Mem. Nat. Radio Broadcasters Assn. (dir. 1971-78), Sales and Mktg. Execs. Madison (dir. 1972-74), Madison Advt. Club (dir. 1972-75). Clubs: Maple Bluff (Wis.) Country; Madison, Madison Press (pres. 1965-66). Home: 33 Harbort Dr Madison WI 53704 Office: 2041 Atwood Ave PO Box 3336 Madison WI 53704

HOLTKAMP, DORSEY EMIL, med. research scientist; b. New Knoxville, Ohio, May 28, 1919; s. Emil H. and Caroline E. (Meckstroth) H.; student Ohio State U., 1937-39; A.B., U. Colo., 1945, M.S., 1949, Ph.D., 1951, med. student, 2 1/2 yrs.; m. Marianne Church Johnson, Mar. 20, 1942 (dec. May 1956); 1 son, Kurt Lee; m. 2d, Marie P. Bahm Roberts, Dec. 20, 1957; stepchildren—Charles Timothy Roberts, Michael John Roberts. Teaching asst. in biochemistry, research asst. in biology U. Colo., 1945-46; grad. scholar (univ. fellow) U. Colo. Sch. Medicine, 1946, asst. in biochemistry, 1947-48, research fellow in biochemistry, 1948-51; sr. research scientist Biochemistry sect. Smith, Kline & French Labs., Phila., 1951-57, endocrine-metabolic group leader, 1957-58; head endocrinology dept. Merrell-Nat. Labs. div. Richardson-Merrell, Inc., Cin., 1958-70, group dir. endocrine clin. research, med. research dept., 1970-81; group dir. endocrinology, med. research dept. Merrell Dow Pharms. subs. Dow Chem. Co., 1981—. Fellow AAAS, Am. Inst. Chemists; mem. Am. Soc. Clin. Pharm. and Therapeutics, Endocrine Soc., Am. Fertility Soc., Am. Chem. Soc., Am. Soc. Pharmacology and Exptl. Therapeutics, N.Y., Ohio acads. scis., Soc. Exptl. Biology and Medicine, Reticuloendothelial Soc., Am. Inst. Biol. Scis., AMA (affiliate), Sigma Xi, Nu Sigma Nu. Republican. Presbyterian. Contbr. articles to sci. publs.; patentee in various phases endocrinology, pharmacology, tumor metabolism, fertility-sterility control, biochemistry, teratology, inflammation and nutrition. Research and devel. new drugs. Home: 9464 Bluewing Terr Cincinnati OH 45241 Office: 2110 E Galbraith Rd Cincinnati OH 45215

HOLTON, IRA JAMES, meat co. exec.; b. Cedar Rapids, Iowa, Aug. 16, 1919; s. Ed Bacon and Mabel (Donnan) H.; B.A. in Econs., U. Iowa, 1941, J.D., 1947; m. Adelaide Elizabeth Roeder, June 23, 1941; children—Janet, Brooks, Ann. Admitted to Iowa bar, 1947, Minn. bar, 1947; with Geo. A. Hormel & Co., Austin, Minn., 1947—, sec., 1956—, exec. v.p., 1968-69, dir., 1961—, pres., 1969—, chief exec. officer, 1972—, chmn. bd., 1979—, chmn. exec. com., 1981—; dir. 1st Bank System, Inc. Pres. Austin Community Scholarship Com., 1963—. Bd. dirs. Hormel Found., Mower County chpt. ARC. Served to maj., inf., AUS, 1941-45. Decorated Croix de Guerre (France). Mem. Am. Meat Inst. (past chmn. bd.), Phi Beta Kappa. Republican. Home: 403 21st St SW Austin MN 55912 Office: Box 800 Austin MN 55912

HOLTUM, EDWIN ALFRED, librarian; b. Neptune, N.J., Feb. 9, 1947; s. Alfred Gerard and Betty Louise (Larson) H.; B.A., Augustana Coll., Rock Island, Ill., 1968; M.S. in L.S. (USPHS fellow 1970-71), U. Ill., 1971; m. Marilyn Jean Hill, Aug. 13, 1967; children—Beth, Rachel. Instr., Superior (Wis.) Sr. High Sch., 1968-70; librarian I, U. Iowa Health Scis. Library, 1971-74, librarian II, 1976—; coordinator health sci. libraries in Iowa, 1974-76; adj. asst. prof. U. Iowa Sch. Library Sci., 1973—. Mem. ALA. Office: Health Scis Library U Iowa Iowa City IA 52242

HOLTZINGER, JOHN IRVIN, realty co. exec.; b. Goshen, Ind., July 25, 1942; s. Irvin C. and Mary Ellen (Diveley) H.; student Goshen Coll., 1960-62; B.S. in Bus., Ind. U., 1965; m. Connie Rae Spindler, Nov. 23, 1967; children—John Todd, Nicole Marie, Bianca Jean, Celeste Rae. Fin. auditor Arthur Young & Co., Chgo., 1964-71; corp. controller Corterra Corp., Chgo., 1972-73; Midwestern U.S. controller Centennial Industries, Chgo., 1974; adv. to Arthur Rubloff, Arthur Rubloff Co., Chgo., 1975—. C.P.A., Ind. Mem. Am. Inst. C.P.A.'s, Ind. Assn. C.P.A.'s, Internat. Council Shopping Centers. Lutheran. Home: 7220 W 138th Pl Cedar Lake IN 46303 Office: 69 W Washington St Chicago IL 60602

HOLTZMAN, ANDRE EDWIN, paper co. exec.; b. Chgo., Sept. 19, 1936; s. Bernard and Juanita (Good) H.; B.S.C., Roosevelt U., 1953-57; student John Marshall Law Sch., 1957-58; M.B.A., Loyola U., 1976; 1 dau., Elizabeth. Mgmt. cons. Booz Allen & Hamilton, 1957-68; v.p., fin., corp. controller Walter E. Heller Industries, 1969-71; pres. Investor Guaranty Corp., 1972-77; v.p. fin., treas., dir. Flint (Mich.) br. Consol. Packaging Corp., Chgo., 1978—. Mem. Fin. Execs. Inst. Republican. Presbyterian. Club: Plaza. Home: 1030 N State St Chicago IL 60610 Office: 111 E Wacker Dr Chicago IL 60601

HOLUM, JOHN ROBERT, educator; b. Tracy, Minn., Aug. 31, 1928; s. Gilbert and Sine Elvine (Lauve) H.; B.A., St. Olaf Coll., 1950; Ph.D. (NSF fellow, 1952-54), U. Minn., 1954; postgrad. Calif. Inst. Tech., 1962-63, Harvard U., 1969-70; m. Mary Elizabeth Mattill, June 10, 1950; children—Elizabeth Mary, Ann Barbara, Kathryn Marie. Chemist Eastman Kodak Co., Rochester, N.Y., 1954; asst. prof., Augsburg Coll., Mpls., 1957-58, asso. prof., 1959-64, prof. chemistry, 1965—; prof. chemistry Pacific Luth. U., Tacoma, Wash., 1958-59; cons. Control Data, 1966-67, Plastics Inc., 1967-69. Served with Chem. Corps U.S. Army, 1955-56. NSF sci. faculty fellow, 1962-63. Mem. Am. Chem. Soc. (coll. chemistry tchr. award, Minn. sect., 1973), AAAS, Minn. Acad. Sci., Midwest Assn. Chemistry Tchrs. in Liberal Arts Colls., Danforth Asso., Sigma Xi, Sigma Pi Sigma, Phi Beta Kappa, Phi Lambda Upsilon. Lutheran. Clubs: Sierra, Mpls. Audubon. Author: Introduction to Organic and Biological Chemistry, 1969; Principles of Physical, Organic and Biological Chemistry, 1969; Topics and Terms of Environmental Problems, 1978; Organic and Biological Chemistry, 1978; (with Kenneth Atkins and Arthur Strahler) Physical Science, 1978; Fundamentals of General, Organic and Biological Chemistry with study guide and (with Ruth Denison) lab. manual, 1978; Elements of General and Biological Chemistry 5th edition with study guide and lab. manual, 1979; (with James E. Brady) Fundamentals of Chemistry, 1981; advisory editor John Wiley & Sons, Inc., N.Y., 1963—. Home: 3352 47th Ave S Minneapolis MN 55406 Office: Augsburg College Minneapolis MN 55454

HOLVICK, OLAF, II, computer cons. co. exec.; b. Long Beach, Calif., June 16, 1946; s. Olaf and Elaine Margaret (Klarr) H.; B.S. in Bus. Adminstrn., Babson Coll., 1968; m. Christine Frances Fisher, Dec. 6, 1974; children—Lindsay Fisher, Tara Fisher. Mktg. rep. Statis. Analyst Corp., Detroit, 1968-69; mktg. analyst Nat. Bank of Detroit, 1969; group sales mgr. Pathfinder Internat., Detroit, 1969-70; nat. account exec. R.L. Polk & Co., Taylor, Mich., 1970-75; Eastern regional mgr. Cutler-Williams, Inc., Dearborn, Mich., 1975-78; pres. Holvick Corporation, Detroit, 1978—; dir. Interface Systems, Inc., Ann Arbor, Mich., 1972-75. Mem. Econ. Club Detroit, Engring. Soc. Detroit. Republican. Roman Catholic. Clubs: Country of Detroit, Detroit Athletic, Detroit Racquet, Racquet of Chgo. Home: 21 Renaud Rd Grosse Pointe Shores MI 48236 Office: 400 Renaissance Center Suite 2760 Detroit MI 48243

HOLZ, HARRY GEORGE, lawyer; b. Milw., Sept. 13, 1934; s. Harry Carl and Emma Louise (Hinz) H.; B.S., Marquette U., 1956, LL.B., 1958; LL.M., Northwestern U., 1960; m. Nancy L. Heiser, May 12, 1962; children—Pamela Gretchen, Bradley Eric, Erika Lynn. Admitted to Wis. bar, 1958, Ill. bar, 1960; asso. firm Sidley & Austin, Chgo., 1959-60; partner firm Quarles & Brady, Milw., 1968—; teaching fellow Northwestern U. Sch. Law, 1958-59; lectr. U. Wis. Law Sch., 1971-74; adj. prof. Marquette U. Law Sch., 1975-81; faculty mem. Wis. Bar ATS-CLE Program on Anti-Trust Law, 1975—; bd. dirs. Corp. Practice Inst., dir., lectr. continuing legal edn. programs, 1977-78. Bd. visitors Marquette U. Sch. Law, 1978. Mem. Am. Bar Assn., State Bar Wis. (sec. corp. banking and bus. law sect. 1976-77, chmn. 1978-79, dir. 1978—), Milw. Bar Assn., Bar Assn. 7th Fed.

Circuit, Woolsack Soc. of Marquette U. Sch. Law, Beta Gamma Sigma. Lutheran. Clubs: Milw. Athletic; Western Racquet. Editor-in-chief, Marquette Law Rev., 1957-58. Home: 1720 Village Green Ct Elm Grove WI 53122 Office: 780 N Water St Milwaukee WI 53202

HOLZER, RICHARD JEAN, lawyer; b. Easton, Pa., Jan. 31, 1940; s. J. A. and Ann C. (Carta) H.; B.A., Gettysburg Coll., 1961; M.B.A., U. Dayton, 1971; student N.Y. U., 1968-69; J.D., Salmon P. Chase Coll. Law, No. Ky. State U., 1975; m. Charlotte L. Branson, Aug. 15, 1964; children—Richard Jean, C. Christopher. Field rep. INA, Pitts., 1961-66; asso. R. D. Griewahn & Assos., Erie, Pa., 1966-68; mgr. compensation and benefits Curtis-Wright Corp., Woodridge, N.J., 1968-69; mgr. personnel services, McCall Printing Co., Dayton, 1969-70; labor relations adminstr. City of Dayton, 1970-75; admitted to Ohio bar, 1975; atty. pub. sector labor and corp. law Pickrel, Schaeffer and Ebeling, Dayton, 1975—; asst. prof. U. Dayton, 1976-77, Wright State U., 1979—. Com. chmn. Montgomery County Personnel Task Force, 1979—. Served with AUS, 1962-64. Mem. Am. Soc. Personnel Adminstrs., Nat. Pub. Employers Labor Relations Assn., Ohio State Bar Assn., Fed. Bar Assn., Dayton Bar Assn., Scabbard and Blade, Phi Alpha Delta, Lambda Chi Alpha. Lutheran (council 1976—, pres. council 1978-79). Home: 10887 Putnam Rd Englewood OH 45322 Office: 2700 Winters Bank Tower Dayton OH 45423

HOLZMAN, MICHAEL STANLEY, mgmt. cons., lawyer; b. Milw., Dec. 12, 1949; s. Stanley L. and Berenice D. (Del Monte) H.; B.A., Northwestern U., 1971; M.A., U. Chgo., 1973, M.A.T., 1973; J.D., Loyola U. Chgo., 1980. Social sci. tchr., 1973-74; chief planning analyst Chgo. Dept. Human Services, 1975-78; legal researcher Chgo. Title & Trust Co., 1978-79; dir. neighborhood employment study project T.R.U.S.T., Inc., Chgo., 1979-80; mgmt. cons., lawyer James H. Lowry & Assos., Chgo., 1980-81; lawyer firm Martin & Karcazes Ltd., Chgo., 1981—; dir. Westside Devel. Corp.; cons. in field. Univ. Chgo. scholar, 1971-72; fellow U.S. Office Edn., 1972-73; recipient Disting. Achievement award Loyola Law Sch. Mem. Am. Soc. Planning Ofcls., Nat. Assn. Housing and Redevel. Ofcls., Nat. Assn. Community Devel., Am. Bar Assn., Ill. Bar Assn., Chgo. Bar Assn. Democrat. Jewish. Editor Loyola U. Law Rev., 1979-80. Home: 1850 Wabansia Chicago IL 60622 Office: 10 S LaSalle St Chicago IL 60603

HOMBURG, HAROLD NORMAN, constrn. co. exec.; b. Sun Prairie, Wis., Feb. 25, 1928; s. Chris Frederick and Anita Martha (Kassabaum) H.; student public schs., Sun Prairie and Madison, Wis.; m. Shirley Landsness, June 23, 1951; children—Annette Mae, Chris Adolph, Andrew Gilbert. Truck driver Madison Sand & Gravel Co., 1944-50; with L.S. Lunder Co., Madison, 1952-71, supt., 1960-65, asst. sec., 1965-71; pres. Homburg-Olp Constrn. Co. Inc., Monona, Wis., 1971—, Homburg Equipment Co. Monona Plumbing; partner Madison Rock & Sand Co., Homburg Farms; dir. Monona Grove State Bank. Served with U.S. Army, 1950-52. Mem. Asso. Gen. Contractors, East Side Businessman's Assn., Wis. Corn Growers Assn., Monona Jaycees (hon. life), Historic Blooming Grove Hist. Soc. Club: Four Lakes Yacht. Home: 4621 Tonyawatha Trail Monona WI 53716 Office: 100 E Broadway Monona WI 53716

HOMBURGER, RICHARD HANS, educator, accountant; b. Karlsruhe, Germany, Aug. 15, 1914; s. Paul Phillip and Anna (Schuelein) H.; came to U.S., 1940, naturalized, 1945; student Faculte de Droit, Sorbonne, 1934; J.D., U. Zurich, 1937; M.S., Columbia, 1946; m. Ursula Sinell, Dec. 23, 1947; 1 dau., Ann Marie. Dir. bus. adminstrn. W.Va. State Coll., 1946-56, asst. prof., then asso. prof., 1946-56; faculty Wichita (Kans.) State U., 1956—, prof. accounting, 1961-79, prof. emeritus, 1979—, coordinator grad. studies in accounting, 1962-71. Adviser, Mayor Wichita Com. on Municipal Income Tax, 1956-57. C.P.A., W.Va. Mem. Am. Accounting Assn., Acad. Accounting Historians (1st v.p. 1974-75, trustee; program chmn. 2d world congress 1976), Am. Inst. C.P.A.'s, AAUP, Beta Gamma Sigma. Contbr. to Accountants Ency., articles, revs. to profl. jours. Editor: Wichita State U. Bus. Jour., 1967-69; asso. editor Southwestern Social Sci. Quar., 1960-62. Home: 2260 N Roosevelt Wichita KS 67220

HOMSHER, PAUL THURLOW, aero. engr.; b. Kendallville, Ind., May 10, 1922; s. Thurlow E. and Bess C. Homsher; B.S. in Aero. Engring., Purdue U., 1945; m. Jeanette Schott, June 4, 1949; children—Deborah L., Nangy G., Jeffrey Paul. Design engr. Curtiss Wright Corp., 1945; aerodyamics engr. Chance Vought Co., 1945-47; With McDonnell Aircraft Co., 1947—, program mgr., dep. gen. mgr. F-15, 1969—; v.p., gen. mgr. McDonnell Douglas Saudi Arabia, Inc., 1978—; dir. MDS, Inc. Pres. bd. deacons Kirk of Hills Presbyn. Ch., St. Louis, 1980. Recipient Disting. Alumni award Purdue U., 1980. Mem. Am. Def. Preparedness Assn., AIAA. Club: Creve Coeur Country (dir.). Office: McDonnel Douglas Saudi Arabia Riyadh Saudi Arabia

HONAKER, LINTON RICHARD, ednl. adminstr.; b. Alliance, Ohio, Sept. 29, 1924; s. George R. and Ina (Hobson) H.; B.S., Mount Union Coll., 1948; M.A., Western Res. U., 1949, Ed.D.; m. Betty Lou Baker, Aug. 24, 1947; children—Emily Jean, Diana Lee, Richard, Robert. Tchr. math. Hartville (Ohio) High Sch., 1949-58; high sch. supr. Tuscarawas County (Ohio) Schs., New Philadelphia, 1958-64, supt., 1964-80; dir. tchr. preparation Walsh Coll., 1980—. Exec. com. Agr. Extension Service; mem. State Adv. Com. for Vocat. Agr.; pres. Tuscarawas Valley Mental Health Assn., 1961-63; bd. dirs. Tuscarawas County Guidance Center; treas. Tuscarawas County Guidance Center, Tuscarawas County Crippled Children's Soc., 1964—; active Boy Scouts Am.; former deacon United Ch. Christ; pres. bd. Tuscarawas Valley Comprehensive Mental Health Center, 1977-79. Served with AUS, 1944-46. Named Hon. Ohio Chpt. Farmer, Future Farmers Am. Mem. Northeastern Ohio (pres. 1966-67), Ohio County supts. assns., E. Central Ohio Tchrs. Assn. (pres. 1968), Northeastern Ohio (past pres.), Ohio (past exec. com. mem.) assns. county suprs., NEA, Ohio Edn. Assn., Am., Ohio, Buckeye assns. sch. adminstrs., DAV, Am. Legion. Club: Lions. Home: 724 Oak St NW New Philadelphia OH 44663 Office: 261 W High Ave New Philadelphia OH 44663

HONG, CAROL ANN, microbiologist; b. Altoona, Pa., Oct. 9, 1942; d. John Irwin and Lela Frances (Miller) Kleffman; B.A., Miami U., Oxford, Ohio, 1964; M.B.A., Cleve. State U., 1981; m. Philip Fernandez Ma, Sept. 15, 1965; 1 son, Michael; m. 2d, Jong Kyu Hong, Aug. 14, 1978. Teller, Akron (Ohio) Nat Bank, summers 1960-64; vol. Peace Corps, tchr. sci., math. and English, Philippines, 1964-66; bacteriology technologist Case Western Res. U. Hosps., Cleve., 1966; med. technologist, adminstrv. supr. microbiology, mgr. lab. services Cleve. Clinic Found., 1966—, sec. subcom. infectious diseases, 1974-79, mem. safety com., 1979—, chmn. hazardous waste subcom., 1977—, mem. ops. group, 1981—. Registered med. technologist, registered specialist in microbiology Am. Soc. Clin. Pathologists. Mem. AAUW (chmn. hospitality 1975-77, dir. 1977-79), Am. Soc. Clin. Pathologists (council on microbiology 1977—), Cuyahoga Women's Polit. Caucus, Am. Soc. Microbiology, Assn. for Practitioners in Infection Control (pres. Greater Cleve. chpt. 1975-76, 76-77, dir. 1975-78, chmn. nominating com. 1977, mem. bylaws com. 1980, chmn. 1981), S. Central Assn. for Clin. Microbiology (sec. 1975, dir. area 1976-77, chmn. nominating com. 1977-80, chmn. awards com. 1979-80, membership chmn. 1981), Clin. Lab. and Mgmt. Assn. (pres. Cleve. chpt. 1975-76), Nat. Assn. Female Execs., Mensa, NOW. Club: Order of Eastern Star. Editorial bd. Lab. Medicine, 1978—. Contbr. articles to profl. publs. Home: 374 Karen Dr Chardon OH 44024 Office: 9500 Euclid Ave Cleveland OH 44106

HONG, KUHN, radiologist; b. Seoul, Korea, Aug. 27, 1946; s. Tae Joon and Moon Young (Ahn) H.; M.D., Seoul Nat. U. (Korea), 1970; m. Kyung Ok Kim, June 10, 1972; children—Timothy, Joseph, David. Intern, Gottlieb Meml. Hosp., Melrose Park, Ill., 1973-74; resident in radiology Mercy Hosp. and Med. Center, Chgo., 1974-77; fellow in nuclear medicine Rush-Presbyn. St.-Luke's Med. Center, Chgo., 1977-79; dir. nuclear medicine, dept. radiology Little Co. of Mary Hosp., Evergreen Park, Ill., 1979—; instr. Rush Med. Coll., 1977. Served with Korean Navy, 1970-73. Diplomate Am. Bd. Radiology, Am. Bd. Nuclear Medicine. Mem. AMA, Ill. State Med. Soc., Chgo. Med. Soc., Radiol. Soc. N. Am., Am. Coll. Radiology, Soc. Nuclear Medicine, Am. Inst. Ultrasound in Medicine, Am. Coll. Med. Imaging, Am. Physicians Art Assn. Methodist. Home: 24 Heatherwood Dr Lockport IL 60441 Office: 2800 W 95th St Evergreen Park IL 60642

HONIGBAUM, JOEL ALLEN, ins. co. exec.; b. St. Louis, Nov. 28, 1943; s. Arthur Jack and DeVera Estelle (Moulton) H.; B.S., Washington U., St. Louis, 1965; m. Linda Snyder, Aug. 3, 1969; children—Jodi Leigh, Brian Paul. Dir. compensation and benefits ITT Aetna Mgmt. Co., St. Louis, 1967-70; dir. personnel ITT Hamilton Life Ins. Co., St. Louis, 1970-71; dir. compensation and benefits ITT Aetna Mgmt. Co., 1971-73; dir. human resources Blue Cross Blue Shield of Ind., Indpls., 1973—; cons. in field; nat. dir. Salary Survey Consortium; guest lectr. Nat. Personnel Conf. Chmn. personnel com. United Way; past pres. Brotherhood, Indpls. Hebrew Congregation. Mem. Am. Compensation Assn., Am. Mgmt. Assn., Am. Soc. Personnel Adminstrs., Pi Lambda Phi. Jewish. Home: 7869 Sunset Ln Indianapolis IN 46260 Office: 120 W Market St Indianapolis IN 46204

HOODWIN, ROBERT LOUIS, real estate broker; b. Chgo., Feb. 25, 1916; s. Joseph W. and Mary (Kohn) H.; student public schs. Chgo.; 1 dau. by previous marriage—Judy. Property mgr. Glatt & Price, Realtors, Chgo., 1935-40; owner, prin. Hoodwin Mgmt. Co., Chgo., 1946—; owner, mgr. Saranac Hotel Co., Chgo., 1961—; partner Cornell Parking, Chgo., 1976—. Served as master sgt. USAAF, 1942-45; ETO. Jewish. Clubs: East Bank, Rotary. Home: 30 E Huron St Chicago IL 60611 Office: 5541 S Everett Ave Chicago IL 60637

HOOGESTRAAT, ARDYS RHETA YAHN, county ofcl.; b. Edgerton, Wis., Apr. 7, 1934; d. Heinrich Volbert and Hildegard Anna Kathe (Schumacher) Yahn; student Minn. Sch. Bus.; m. William Henry Hoogestraat, Feb. 25, 1956; children—Jean Marie Hoogestraat Holland, Joann Carol. With 1st Nat. Bank, Mpls., 1952-53; purchasing sec. No. Ordances Inc., Mpls., 1953-57; med. sec. Mork Clinic, Inc., Anoka, Minn., 1967-75; personnel asst. Anoka County, 1975—. Mem. Am. Soc. Personnel Adminstrn., Am. Mgmt. Soc., Anoka Personnel Assn., Internat. Personnel Mgmt. Assn. (chpt. bd. dir.). Republican. Lutheran. Home: 833 Adams St Anoka MN 55303 Office: 325 E Main St Anoka MN 55303

HOOK, CHARLES NYE, part handling systems mfg. co. exec.; b. Elyria, Ohio, July 30, 1937; s. Crosby Johnson and Jane Elizabeth (Nye) H.; B.S.C., Ohio U., 1959; postgrad. Butler U., 1964-65, Ind. U., 1968-70; m. Karen Elayne Main, Feb. 9, 1963; children—Charles Nye II, Tamra Elayne, Tig Ann. Budget analyst Allison div. Gen. Motors Corp., Indpls., 1962-65; controller trainee Allstate Ins. Co., Indpls., 1965-66; internal auditor Herff-Jones Co., Indpls., 1966-67; acctg. supr. and credit mgr. Schwitzer div. Wallace-Murray Corp., Indpls., 1968-71; controller Rough Notes Co., Inc., Indpls., 1971-74; controller Vibromatic Co., Inc., Noblesville, Ind., 1974-76, treas., 1976—, pres., 1979—, chmn. bd., 1979—. Treas. Noblesville Area C. of C., 1979, v.p., 1980-81; treas. Forest Hill Elem. Sch. Parent Tchr. Orgn., Noblesville, 1979, pres., 1980-81. Served with U.S. Army, 1959-62. Mem. Nat. Assn. Accts., Ind. Assn. Mfrs., Noblesville Area C. of C. (treas. 1979, v.p. 1980-81). Republican. Presbyterian. Club: Kiwanis (v.p. club 1980-81, pres. 1981) (Noblesville). Home: 755 Sunset Dr Noblesville IN 46060 Office: 1301 S Sixth St Noblesville IN 46060

HOOPER, FINLEY ALLISON, historian; b. London, Ont., Can., Aug. 14, 1922; s. Harry Reginald and Lola Emily (Allison) H.; B.S., Purdue U., 1947; M.A., U. Mich., 1949, Ph.D., 1951. Instr., U. Mich., 1951-52; asst. prof. history Mich. State U., 1953-57; faculty Wayne State U., Detroit, 1958—, prof. history, 1966—. Served with AUS, 1943-45. Mem. Am. Hist. Assn., Assn. Ancient Historians. Author: Funerary Stelae from Kom Abou Billou, 1961; Greek Realities, 1967; Roman Realities, 1979. Office: Dept History 807 Mackenzie Hall Wayne State U Detroit MI 48202

HOOPFER, GERALD JOSEPH, real estate broker; b. San Antonio, Nov. 9, 1940; s. Paulus D. and Josephine H.; student Ferris State Coll., 1959-60, Oakland Community Coll., 1960-61; real estate degree U. Mich., 1974; grad. Realtor Inst., 1974; m. Cara G. Howe, July 18, 1978; children—Peter Joseph, Todd Antony, Gerald Joseph, Stacey M. With Royer Realty, Oxford, Mich., 1966-69, McCullough Realty, Pontiac, Mich., 1969-71, Carter & Assos., Pontiac, Mich., 1971-73; pres., asso. broker Evans & Assos., Drayton Plains, Mich., 1973-79; asso. broker Group One, Inc., Drayton Plains, 1980—, Howard & Keating Assos., Bloomfield Hills, Mich., 1980-81. Named Dir. of Yr., Pontiac Jr. C. of C., 1977. Cert. real estate appraiser, 1980. Mem. Nat. Assn. Realtors (cert. resdl. specialist 1979), Mich. Assn. Realtors, Nat. Inst. Real Estate Brokers, N. Oakland C. of C., N. Oakland County Bd. Realtors (dir. 1976-79, pres. 1980), N. Oakland County C. of C. Republican. Roman Catholic. Clubs: Azteca, Kiwanis.

HOOPMAN, HAROLD DEWAINE, oil co. exec.; b. Lucas, Kans., July 22, 1920; s. Ira William and Mary B. (Dorman) H.; B.S. in M.E., U. Wyo., 1942; postgrad. Harvard U., 1964; LL.D. (hon.) Marietta Coll., 1979; m. Eleanor Gessner, July 6, 1946; children—Judith Kristin Hoopman Hains, David W., Michael J. Test engr. Wright Aero. Co., Patterson, N.J., 1942-43; with Marathon Oil Co., 1946—, v.p. internat. div., Findlay, Ohio, 1962-67, asst. to pres., 1967-68, v.p. prodn., 1968-69, v.p. mktg. U.S., 1969-72, pres., 1972—, chief exec. officer, 1975—, also dir.; dir. Am. Petroleum Inst., Owen-Ill., Inc., First Nat. Bank Findlay. Served with USNR, 1943-46. Office: 539 S Main St Findlay OH 45840

HOOSIN, JANICE LAUTT, social worker; b. Chgo., June 22, 1942; d. Herbert and Ruth Jean (Rubenstein) Lapine; B.A., U. Ill., 1964; M.S.W., Jane Addams Grad. Sch. Social Work, 1966; postgrad. U. Utah, summer 1977. Psychiat. social worker New Trier Twp. High Sch., East Winnetka, Ill., 1966-70; dir. day hosp. St. Vincent's Hosp., N.Y.C., 1970-73; psychotherapist (part-time) New Trier East High Sch., Winnetka, 1973-74; dir. psychiat. day hosp. dept. psychiatry Evanston (Ill.) Hosp., 1974-78, dir. partial hospitalization, 1978—; clin. asso., field work supr. U. Chgo. Sch. Social Service Adminstrn., 1974—; cons. Center for Treatment and Rehab., Sheltered Care Facilities, Ill. Div. Vocat. Rehab., 1978—; pvt. practice marital and individual psychotherapy, 1975—; leader human sexuality edn. Northwestern U. Med. Sch., Chgo., 1976—. NIMH fellow, 1964-66; cert. psychiat. social worker, Ill. Mem. Nat. Assn. Social Workers, Internat. Assn. Psychosocial Rehab., Am. Group Psychotherapy Assn. Jewish. Home: 2800 N Lake Shore Dr Chicago IL 60657 Office: Evanston Hosp Dept of Psychiatry 2650 Ridge Ave Evanston IL 60201

HOOVER, GARY EUGENE, real estate exec.; b. Lafayette, Ind., Mar. 19, 1951; s. Wilbur Charles and Judith Ellen (Rarick) H.; B.A. in Econs., U. Chgo., 1973. Securities analyst Citibank, N.A., N.Y.C., 1973-75; buyer Sanger Harris Div. Federated Dept. Stores, Dallas, 1975-77; asst. mgr. fin. planning and research May Dept. Stores Co., St. Louis, 1977-78. mgr. corporate devel., 1978-79; dir. research May Centers, Inc., St. Louis, 1979-80, v.p. mktg., planning and research, 1980—. Home: 1445 Sproule Ave Saint Louis MO 63139 Office: 611 Olive St Suite 1555 Saint Louis MO 63101

HOOVER, GARY LYNN, banker; b. Tipton, Ind., Oct. 20, 1937; s. Carmel Wayne and Virginia Ruth (Mitchell) H.; B.S., Purdue U., 1959; div.; children—Devin Page, Melissa Virginia. With First Nat. Bank, Winnetka, Ill., 1961-62; nat. bank examiner-internat. Comptroller of Currency, U.S. Dept. Treasury, Washington, 1962-70; asst. v.p. Lafayette Nat. Bank (Ind.), 1970-71; v.p.-internat. Am. Fletcher Nat. Bank, Indpls., 1971-81; with Farm Credit Adminstrn., Washington, 1981—. Bd. dirs. Indpls. Mus. Art, Indpls. Zool. Soc., Internat. Center of Indpls., Channel 20 TV; mem. Nat. Republican Com. Served with U.S. Army, 1961. Mem. Econs. Club Ind., Purdue Alumni Assn., World Trade Club, Ind. Congregationalist. Clubs: Indpls. Ski, Ambassadair Travel. Home: 12392 D Creek Run Dr Creve Coeur MO 63141 Office: 490 L'Enfant Plaza SW Suite 4000 Washington DC 20578

HOOVER, REGINA MAE, educator; b. Webster, S.D., July 10, 1921; d. Harold Valentine and Naomi Mae (Ahlers) H.; B.A., U. Wash., 1943, Ph.D., 1971; M.A., Radcliffe Coll., 1946. Social worker, Seattle, 1946-49; English tchr. Am. Sch., Tsingtao, China, 1947-49; asst. sec. Wash. State Hwy. Commn., 1951-58; ct. reporter, Pierce, Whatcom counties, Wash., 1959-64; mem. English composition faculty Central Mich. U., Mt. Pleasant, 1971—, asso. prof., 1976-80, prof., 1980—; exec. com. Conf. on Coll. Composition and Communication, 1975-78; chmn. 4C's Task Force on Testing, 1977-79; cons. freshman composition programs Southwestern Mich. Coll., Xavier U. of La., Mich. State U., 1975—. Mem. Nat. Council Tchrs. English, Conf. on Coll. Composition and Communication, Phi Beta Kappa. Author: Make Your Writing Count, 1977. Contbr. articles to profl. jours. Home: 800 Watson St Mount Pleasant MI 48858 Office: 207 Anspach Dept English Central Mich U Mount Pleasant MI 48859

HOOVER, THOMAS HENRY, univ. ofcl.; b. Wilburton, Okla., Sept. 28, 1919; s. Harry and Jessie (Jackson) H.; B.A., Pacific Lutheran U., 1959; M.A., U. Wis., 1968, Ph.D., 1970; m. Viola (Kalcik) H.; July 30, 1948 (dec. 1979); children—Kathleen, Thomas, Ruth, Chris, James; m. 2d, D. Ann Cleary, Nov., 1979. Commd. 2d lt. U.S. Army, 1942, advanced through grades to lt. col., 1962; mgmt. analyst, Ft. Benning, Ga. and Madigan Army Hosp., Washington, 1952-59, plans and ops. officer Hdqrs. U.S. Army, Europe, Heidelburg, Germany, 1959-62; ret., 1964; asso. prof. mil. sci. U. Wis., Madison, 1962-64, asst. registrar, 1964-66, registrar, 1967—. Chmn. com. on service to mil. families and vets. ARC, 1975—, bd. dirs. Dane County chpt., 1977—; bd. dirs. Wesley Found., 1966-68, M.C.S.H.U.I., Inc., sch. guidance agy., 1968-74. Mem. Am. Assn. Collegiate Registrars and Admissions Officers, Wis. Assn. Collegiate Registrars (sec. 1978-79, pres. 1980-81), Wis. Coll. Personnel Assn., Phi Kappa Phi, Phi Delta Kappa. Author: VOLAR-The Volunteer Army and Social Expectations, 1975; Nonresident Tuition in Wisconsin (with others), 1978. Office: U Wis Madison WI 53706

HOOVER, WILLIAM LEICHLITER, educator, fin. cons.; b. Brownsville, Pa., July 29, 1944; s. Aaron Jones and Edith (Leichliter) H.; B.S., Pa. State U., 1966, M.S., 1971; Ph.D., Iowa State U., 1977; m. Peggy Jo Spangler, Aug. 30, 1976; children—Jennifer Mary, Monica Susan. Research asst. Pa. State U., Iowa State U., 1970-74; asst. prof. Purdue U., West Lafayette, Ind., 1974-79, asso. prof. dept. forestry and natural resources, 1980—; sec./treas., dir. econ. and fin. analysis Tim Tech., Inc., W. Lafayette, 1978—. Served to 1st lt., C.E., U.S. Army, 1967-69. Decorated Bronze Star. Mem. Forest Products Research Soc., Am. Econ. Assn., Nat. Assn. Public Accts., Soc. Am. Foresters. Republican. Presbyterian. Asst. editor Timber Tax Jour., 1979—; author: A Guide to Federal Income Tax for Timber Owners, 1981. Home: 206 Connolly St PO Box 2257 West Lafayette IN 47906 Office: Dept Forestry Purdue U West Lafayette IN 47907

HOPKINS, B. SMITH, JR., physician; b. Waukesha, Wis., Jan. 12, 1912; s. B. Smith and Sarah Maude (Childs) H.; A.B., Albion Coll., 1932; M.D., Johns Hopkins U., 1936; m. Louise Varty, June 11, 1936; children—Stephen A., Jonathan W., B. Smith. Intern, Balt. City Hosp., 1936-37, resident in medicine, 1937-38, 39-40; resident in medicine Vanderbilt U. Hosp., Nashville, 1938-39; cons. in internal medicine and rheumatology Carle Clinic Assn., Urbana, Ill., 1940-78, mem. staff Carle Found. Hosp., trustee, 1967-71, 74-76; mem. staff McKinley Hosp., Urbana, Charleston (Ill.) Meml. Hosp.; bd. dirs. E. Central Ill. Health Systems Agy., 1974-79, pres., 1975-78; mem. Statewide Health Coordinating Council, Ill., 1976-80, exec. sec., 1980—. Mem. Champaign County Med. Soc. (past pres.), Ill. Med. Soc. (chmn. health planning com.), AMA, A.C.P., Am. Rheumatism Assn. Clubs: Urbana Exchange, Urbana Golf Country. Home: 606 W Delaware St Urbana IL 61801

HOPKINS, HARRY H., regional planner; b. Springfield, Ill., Oct. 6, 1947; s. Albert and Wanda Lee (Sexton) H.; B.A., So. Ill. U., Carbondale, 1969; m. Carol Dulak, Sept. 20, 1975. Planner, Springfield-Sangamon County Regional Planning Commn., 1970-72, chief transp. planner, 1972-77, exec. dir., 1977—. Long range planning com. United Way, 1981—; planning body YMCA, 1981—. Served with U.S. Army, 1970. Mem. Am. Planning Assn. Presbyterian. Clubs: Breakfast Optimist, Elks. Office: 703 Myers Bldg Springfield IL 62701

HOPLEY, DAVID PHILIP, mfg. co. exec.; b. Witt, Ill., Nov. 7, 1932; s. Philip and Verda Elizabeth (Jones) H.; B.A., Augustana Coll., 1954; m. Eleanor Julia Knott, Dec. 22, 1956; children—Cheryl Ann, Sara Jo, Julie Elizabeth, Susan Eileen. Auditor, Arthur Andersen & Co., 1956-59; auditor Deere & Co., 1959-62, div. controller, 1967-73, controller John Deere Des Moines (Iowa) Works, 1962-67, mng. dir. John Deere Mexico S.A., 1973-74, gen. mgr. Dubuque Works, 1974-80, v.p. mfg., Moline, Ill., 1980—; dir. Am. Trust Nat. Bank, Dubuque. Treas., Bethany Home, 1970-73. Served with U.S. Army, 1954-56. C.P.A. Mem. Augustana Coll. Alumni Assn. (pres. 1979). Republican. Lutheran. Office: John Deere Rd Moline IL 62101

HOPPER, ALICE EVELYN HEUBERGER, dietitian; b. Chapin, Iowa, Dec. 12, 1921; d. Louis Frederick and Celia Maude (Deam) Heuberger; B.S. in Foods and Nutrition, Iowa State U., 1944; m. A. Bruce Hopper, May 31, 1959. Dietetic intern Watts Hosp., Durham,

N.C., 1944-45; adminstrv. dietitian Union Meml. Hosp., Balt., 1945-47; diabetic food cons. Mayo Clinic, Rochester, Minn., 1947-49; teaching/therapeutic dietitian Presbyn. Hosp., Newark, 1949-55; dir. dietetics Mt. Sinai Hosp. Med. Center Chgo., 1955-68, dir. food service, 1968—. Recipient Silver Menu award Nat. Restaurant Assn., 1972, Bronze Menu award, 1977. Mem. Am. Soc. for Hosp. Food Service Adminstrs., Am. Dietetic Assn., Ill. Dietetic Assn., Chgo. Dietetic Assn. Presbyterian. Club: Order of Eastern Star. Home: 30 E Elm St Chicago IL 60611 Office: Mt Sinai Hosp Med Center of Chgo California Ave at 15th St Chicago IL 60608

HOPPER, CECIL HAROLD, govt. ofcl.; b. Patriot, Ind., Nov. 19, 1938; s. Cecil Courtney and Kathleen (Chapman) H.; A.Electronics, United Electronics, 1963; m. Dolores Ann Schwartz, June 3, 1967; children—Terry David, Jeffrey Stephen. With McDonald Douglas Aircraft, St. Louis, 1963-64; with Aerospace Guidance & Metrology Center, Newark, Ohio, 1964—, instrument worker foreman, 1978—; owner the Humidor, Newark, 1976—. Bd. dirs. Land of Legend Festival, 1975-76, 1st v.p., 1976-77, pres., 1977-78, 78—; chmn. Newark Downtown Tree Planting Com., 1976—; mem. San. Sewer projects, City of Newark, 1976-77; mem. parade com., United Way, 1973; active Boy Scouts Am., 1978, Babe Ruth World Series, 1978; mem. Bd. Housing Appeals, City of Newark, 1976-79; worker Diocesan Devel. Fund dr., 1968-76; spl. events chmn. Licking County Heart Fund, 1981; bd. dirs. Licking County chpt. ARC, 1980-81, mem. disaster com., 1981. Served with USMC, 1957-59. Recipient Pres. Award of Leadership, Nat. Jr. C. of C., 1975, Pres. Award of Honor, 1974; Keyman award, Newark Jr. C. of C., 1974; Govtl. Affairs award, Ohio Jr. C. of C.; Newark Mayors Civic Achievement award, 1975; Jr. C. of C. Spoke award, 1974, Spark Plug award, 1974; named Kiwanian of the Year, 1975-76, 77-78; recipient Outstanding Service award, 1976-77; Superior Performance award, Air Force, 1971-72, Outstanding Performance award, 1974-75, 77-78; recipient Air Force Assn. Community Service award, 1977-78, Jaycee Internat. Senatorship award, 1975. Mem. Newark Downtown Assn., Air Force Nat. Assn. of Suprs., Air Force Assn., Am. Retail Tobacco Assn., Downtown Bus. Mens Assn. (dir. 1977-78), Ohio Jr. C. of C. (legal counsel for internat. senate 1976-77, v.p. 1977-78, pres. 1978-79), Newark Area Jaycees (dir. 1973-74, pres. 1974-75), Newark Area C. of C. (dir. 1974-75). Republican. Roman Catholic. Club: Kiwanis of Moundbuilders (dir. 1976-78, pres.-elect 1977-78, div. membership chmn. 1979, Disting. Pres. award 1979, pres. 1978-79). Home: 537 Granville St Newark OH 43055 Office: Aerospace Guidance and Metrology Center Newark OH 40355

HOPPONEN, RAYMOND E(LLWOOD), univ. adminstr., pharm. scientist; b. New York Mills, Minn., July 6, 1921; s. Victor William and Hilma Lydia (Ruonakoski) H.; B.S., U. Minn., 1943, Ph.D., 1950; postgrad. (NIH Career Devel. fellow) U. Wis., 1962-63; m. Mary Helen Robinson, Sept. 4, 1955; children—Lisa, Andrew, Susan. Asst. prof. pharmacy U. Kans., Lawrence, 1950-55, asso. prof., 1955-62, prof., 1962-64, asst. dean pharmacy, 1964-66; dean pharmacy S.D. State U., 1966—. Bd. dirs. Dakota affiliate Am. Heart Assn., 1976—; mem. Brookings (S.D.) Area Betterment Com., 1975-77, 79—. Served with M.C., U.S. Army, 1943-46. Recipient Hon. Mention, Ebert Prize in Pharm. Research, 1953. Mem. Am. Pharm. Assn., Acad. Pharm. Scis., Am. Assn. Colls. Pharmacy (exec. com., sec. council of deans), S.D. Pharm. Assn., Rho Chi Soc. (nat. pres. 1972-74). Democrat. Methodist. Club: Kiwanis. Research in cardiac glycosides, dosage forms, organic reactions. Office: Coll Pharmacy Box 2201 SD State U Brookings SD 57007

HOPSON, THERESA MAE, educator; b. Sanford, Fla., Mar. 1, 1945; d. Henry Reynold and Annie Mae (Davis) Garrett; B.S., Eastern Mich. U., 1967, M.S., 1970; Ph.D., U. Mich., 1981; m. Robert Louis Hopson, Aug. 27, 1966; 1 dau., Gwendolyn Denise. Tchr., Jackson (Mich.) Public Schs., 1967-68, Ann Arbor (Mich.) Public Schs., 1968-69, 71—; grad. intern Inkster (Mich.) Child Devel. Center, 1969-70. HEW Early Childhood fellow, 1969-70. Mem. NEA, Ann Arbor Edn. Assn. (lang. arts rep., mem. retirement com.), Mich. Edn. Assn., World Orgn. Early Childhood Edn., Assn. Curriculum and Supervision, Phi Delta Kappa, Beta Sigma Phi. Democrat. Eckankar. Home: 1835 Franklin Ct N Ann Arbor MI 48103 Office: Carpenter Sch 4250 Central Blvd Ann Arbor MI 48104

HOPWOOD, KURT FRANZ, service co. exec.; b. Roslyn, N.Y., Dec. 31, 1948; s. Stafford Leopold and Elisabeth Anne (Knapp) H.; student Hofstra U., 1968-69, Memphis State U., 1966-68; B.A., Fairfield U., 1975; postgrad Xavier U., summer 1978; m. Pamela Aileen Morey, Oct. 4, 1975; children—Christopher Franz, Colleen Melissa. Check control clk., computer operator, shift supr. data processing opns. Fidelity Trust Bank, Stamford, Conn., 1972-74; analyst, programmer analyst Electronic Data Systems Co., Dallas, 1974-76; systems supr. asst. to regional mgr. INSCO Systems, Columbus, Ohio, 1976-78; spl. project team leader data processing systems implementation Continental Ins. Co., N.Y.C., 1978—, also sr. staff cons. productivity research and devel.; gen. mgr. exec. placement for data processing, fin. and acctg. Robert Half of Columbus. Mem. little braves program YMCA. Served with USMCR, 1969-71. Mem. Data Processing Mgmt. Assn., Nat. Assn. Accts., Jaycees, Tau Kappa Epsilon. Club: Kiwanis. Home: 1072 Timberbank Ln Westerville OH 43081 Office: 88 E Broad St Columbus OH 43215

HORAK, PENELOPE CATHERINE, engr.; b. Chgo.; d. Edward Peter and Helene Catherine (Kohes) H.; B.S., Roosevelt U., 1967, M.P.A. with highest honors, 1972, M.Ph. with highest honors, 1975. Draftsman, Engring. Services Co., Chgo., 1959-64; draftsman, engr. De Leuw Cather & Co., Cons. Engrs., Chgo., 1964-68; project engr. Nat. Gas Pipeline Co., Chgo., 1968-69; engr. Greeley & Hansen Cons. Engrs., Chgo., 1969-73; staff engr. chmn. div. Quaker Oats Co., Chgo., 1973-74; asst. head tech. services, Fermilab, Batavia, Ill., from 1974; pres. Energy Frontiers, Inc., Winfield, Ill.; instr. solar and energy conservation Elgin Community Coll. Mem. Use Energy Wisely Com. Greater Chgo. Mem. Am. Soc. Public Adminstrs., AAUW, Internat. Solar Energy Soc., No. Ill. Solar Energy Soc. (dir.), Ill. Fedn. Bus. and Profl. Women's Clubs (pres. Hinsdale 1976-77), NOW, ASCE, Soc. Women Engrs. Democrat. Office: Fermilab PO 500 Batavia IL 60510 also EFI PO Box 695 Winfield IL 60190

HORBELT, DOUGLAS VINCENT, physician; b. N.Y.C., Jan. 2, 1947; s. Vincent and Kathryn (Kost) H.; B.A. with honors, U. Tex., Austin, 1969; M.D., U. Tex., Galveston, 1972; m. Patricia Ann Butschek, June 10, 1972; children—Robert, Christopher. Resident in Ob-Gyn, Wesley Med. Center, Wichita, Kans., 1972-75, asst. dir. Ob-Gyn edn., 1975—; clin. fellow in Ob-Gyn, Wichita br. U. Kans. Sch. Medicine, 1974, asst. prof. Ob-Gyn, 1975—; practice medicine specializing in Ob-Gyn, Wichita, 1975—. Recipient Thor Jager, M.D. award, 1978; diplomate Am. Bd. Ob-Gyn. Fellow Am. Coll. Obstetricians and Gynecologists; mem. Central Assn. Obstetricians and Gynecologists, Assn. Profs. Gynecology and Obstetrics, AMA, Kans. Med. Soc., Med. Soc. Sedgwick County. Contbr. articles to med. jours. Office: 3333 E Central St Suite 301 Wichita KS 67208

HORESH, ARTHUR JAMES, pediatrician; b. Cleve., Nov. 24, 1900; s. James Fred and Nettie Mary (Tesar) H.; A.B. magna cum laude, Case Western Res. U., 1923, M.D., 1927; m. Irma Elenore Fischer, July 1, 1930; children—Jean Horesh Fisher, Carol Horesh David. Intern and resident, Univ. Hosps. Cleve., 1927-30, allergist in chief, Pediatric Allergy Clinic, 1933-55; instr. in pediatrics Case Western Res. Med. Sch., 1930-32, clin. prof. pediatrics, 1933-66; practice medicine specializing in pediatrics and pediatric allergy, Cleve., 1930-80. Active Civilian Def. Aux. Group, 1942. Traveling fellow in pediatrics Heidelburg U., 1932-33. Mem. AMA, Ohio State Med. Assn. (cert. of distinction 1977), Cleve. Acad. Medicine, No. Ohio Pediatric Soc., Ohio Pediatric Soc., Am. Acad. Pediatrics (pres. allergy sect. 1955-57, award 1960), Am. Coll. Allergists (award of merit 1977), Am. Assn. Cert. Allergists (bd. govs. 1975-81), Asthma Care Assn. Am. (trustee 1965), Cleve. Allergy Soc. (pres. 1957-58), Assn. for Care of Asthma (bd. dirs. 1965), Phi Beta Kappa, Alpha Kappa Kappa, Lambda Chi Alpha. Editorial bd. Pediatric News, 1960; contbr. writings to publs. in field. Home: 1272 Ford Rd Lyndhurst OH 44124 Office: 3609 Park E Cleveland OH 44122

HORIST, LARRY PATRICK, public affairs exec.; b. Chgo., Mar. 16, 1943; s. John P. and Lorraine (Trendel) H.; B.A. in Econs., Knox Coll., 1965; m. Karen Kelly, Oct. 10, 1970; children—William, Caroline. Communications cons. Ill. Bell Telephone, Chgo., 1965-67; account exec. Donald Young Associates, Chgo., 1967-68, Daniel J. Edelman, Inc., Chgo., 1968; asst. to v.p. public relations Motorola, Inc., Franklin Park, Ill., 1968-69; spl. cons. for White House, 1969-71; asst. info. dir. govtl. affairs Sears, Roebuck & Co., Washington, 1971-73, staff asst. nat. news office, Chgo., 1971-74, also asst. public relations dir. Sears Tower, Chgo., 1973-74; dir. communications and public affairs Capital Resources Corp., Chgo., 1974-75; pres. L.P. Horist & Associates, Inc., Evanston, Ill., 1975—, chmn. bd., 1976—. Mem. nat. adv. com. Dept. Def., 1969-76. Served with USAR. Mem. Ill. State Soc. (v.p. 1972-73, chmn. Presdl. Inaugural Reception 1973), Chgo. Area Public Affairs Group, Public Affairs Council, U.S. C. of C., Internat. Platform Soc. Address: 2708 Simpson St Evanston IL 60201

HORN, CHARLES FREDERICK, lawyer; b. Bellefontaine, Ohio, July 20, 1924; s. Huber and Mary Catherine (Stieg) H.; B.S.E.E., Purdue U., 1949; LL.B., Cleve. Marshall Law Sch., 1953; J.D., Cleve. State U., 1954; m. Shirley Farnsworth, Aug. 1, 1953; children—Holly, Charles J., Heidi. Application engr. Gen. Precision Equipment Co., Dayton, Ohio, 1951-61; admitted to Ohio bar, 1954, U.S. Supreme Ct. bar, 1969; pvt. practice law, Kettering, Ohio, 1961—; mayor City of Kettering, 1969-81; commr. Montgomery County, 1981—. Mem. Intergovtl. Sci., Engring. and Tech. Adv. Panel, 1978-81; chmn. Nat. Innovations Network, 1980; bd. dirs. Nat. League of Cities, 1978-79; chmn. Fed. Lab. Consortium Adv. Bd., 1979; chmn. adv. bd. Urban Tech. System, 1979; co-chmn. NLC-ICMA Joint Com. for Urban Planning, 1978-80; bd. dirs. Sister Cities, Internat., 1979-81; mem. Internat. Urban Tech. Exchange Program, 1977; founder Dayton Area Tech. Assistance Program, 1976; mem. adv. bd. Intergovtl. div. NSF, 1980—; chmn. steering com. on tech. transfer Pub. Tech., Inc., 1979-80; chmn. new tech. com. Ohio Municipal League, 1978-79; cons. NSF, 1978-80; chmn., organizer Miami Valley Cable TV Council, 1970—; founder, chmn. Camp for Kids Who Can't, 1969-81; del., vice chmn. Miami Valley Regional Planning Commn., 1974—; chmn., Miami Valley Open Space Com., 1975—, Montgomery County Rev. Com., 1976—; del. Montgomery County Gen. Health Dist. adv. council, 1969-81, others; mem. adv. bd. Kettering Meml. Hosp., 1979-81; chmn. municipal sect. United Way campaign; trustee Community Devel. Corp.; past trustee Kidney Soc., Leukemia Soc., Grandview Hosp., Kettering Sr. Citizens, Public Opinion Center. Recipient Michael A. DeNunzio award U.S. Conf. Mayors, 1980; Award for Volunteerism Program, 1980, 79; Environ. Quality award U.S. EPA, 1976; Citizens Legion of Merit, Pres.'s Club of Dayton, 1975; Service to Mankind award Sertoma, Community Service award, Rotary, 1973; Man of Yr. award Kiwanis, 1972, others. Mem. Montgomery County Mayors and Mgrs. Assn. (pres. 1969), Nat. Assn. Regional Councils (bd. dirs. 1978-79), Nat. Assn. Regional Councils (2d v.p. 1981). Home: 617 Enid Ave Kettering OH 45429 Office: 2185 S Dixie Ave Kettering OH 45409

HORN, RICHARD ERNEST, optometrist; b. Dayton, Ohio, Jan. 14, 1927; s. Harold Houston and Margaret Ellen (Chambers) H.; O.D., Ohio State U., 1951; m. Lois Joanne Stephens, Sept. 11, 1948; children—Richard Gregory, Kathleen Joanne, Robert Michael. Research optometrist, asst. chief vision sect. Aerospace Med. Research Lab., Wright Patterson AFB, Ohio, 1951-64; pvt. practice pediatric optometry, Dayton, Ohio, 1964—; mem. profl. adv. bd. Ohio Assn. Children with Learning Disabilities. Served with U.S. Army, 1944-46. Fellow Coll. Optometrists in Vision Devel.; mem. Ohio Assn. Children with Learning Disabilities (Talisman award 1980), Ohio Optometric Assn. (Spl. Merit award, 1981), Am. Optometric Assn. (Recognition award 1980, 81, 82), Miami Valley Soc. Optometrists, Optometric Extension Program Found., Am. Public Health Assn., Am. Sch. Health Assn., Adventures in Movement for Handicapped, Assn. Children with Learning Disabilities, Assn. for Retarded Children. Methodist. Club: Masons. Address: 315 Porter Dr Englewood OH 45322

HORNBAKER, DAVID LEE, state ofcl.; b. Hutchinson, Kans., Oct. 3, 1945; s. Lee Vaughn and Alma (Wacha) H.; B.A. in Adminstrn. of Justice, Washburn U., Topeka, 1981; m. Peggy Lou Smith, Dec. 23, 1965; children—Veronica Lee, Matthew Richard. Mem. Junction City (Kans.) Police Dept., 1966-68; mem. Kans. Hwy. Patrol, 1968—, supt., Topeka, 1980—; guest instr. Central Mo. State U., Warrensburg, Washburn U. Served with USAR, 1965-67. Named Law Enforcement Officer of Yr. in Gt. Bend (Kans.), 1975. Mem. Internat. Assn. Chiefs Police, Kans. Peace Officers Assn., Amateur Radio Relay League. Methodist. Club: White Lakes Optimist (pres. 1980-81) (Topeka). Home: 2917 SE Meadow View Dr Topeka KS 66605 Office: 2 Townsite Plaza Suite 130 200 E 6th St Topeka KS 66603

HORNICK, SANDRA JO, educator; b. Lorain, Ohio, Aug. 11, 1939; d. John and Mary J. (Malinovsky) H.; B.S. cum laude, Bowling Green State U., 1960, M.S., 1962; Ph.D., Ohio State U., 1971. Tchr., Lorain City elem. schs., 1960-67, 68-69; teaching fellow Ohio State U., Columbus, 1967-68; asst. prof. elem. edn. Kent (Ohio) State U., 1969-75, asso. prof., 1975—; cons. to various sch. dists. and ednl. orgns., 1969—. Mem. Internat. Reading Assn., Assn. for Supervision and Curriculum Devel., Orgn. Tchr. Educators in Reading (dir. 1981-82), Am. Ednl. Research Assn., Nat. Council Tchrs. English, AAUW (pres. Kent br. 1975-77), Assn. Ednl. Communications and Tech., Internat. Platform Assn., Phi Delta Kappa. Contbr. articles on edn. to profl. publs. Home: 1937 Courtland Dr Kent OH 44240 Office: 404 White Hall Kent State Univ Kent OH 44242

HORNING, ROSS CHARLES, JR., educator; b. Watertown, S.D., Oct. 10, 1920; s. Ross Charles and Harriett (Meaghan) H.; B.A., Augustana Coll., 1948; M.A., George Washington U., 1952, Ph.D. (Sanders fellow in History), 1958; postgrad. Russian, Inst. Langs. and Linguistics, Georgetown U., 1952-53. Instr., Wis. State U., Eau Claire, 1958-59; asst. prof. St. John's U., Collegeville, Minn., 1959-64; asso. prof. Russian history and internat. affairs Creighton U., 1964-68, prof. Russian, Indian and Canadian history, 1968—, chmn. athletic bd. Mem. council Nebr. com. for humanities Nat. Endowment for Humanities. Served with USAAF, 1943-46. Fulbright scholarship to India, summer 1967. Mem. AAAS, Am. Assn. For Advancement of Slavic Studies, Am. Hist. Assn., Am. Soc. Internat. Law, AAUP, Orgn. Am. Historians, Conf. on Slavic and European Studies, Assn. Profl. Baseball Players, Omaha Urban League, Joslyn Liberal Arts Soc., S.W. Am. Assn. for Advancement Slavic Studies, Western Social Sci. Assn., Am. Fgn. Service Assn., Canadian History Assn., Assn. Canadian Studies in U.S. (councillor, exec. council), Assn. for Canadian Studies Assn. Asian Studies, Omaha Symphony Assn., Assn. Canadienne de Sci. Politique, Internat. Law Assn., World Peace Through Law Center, Am. Br. Foreign Service Club (Washington), Nebr. Arts Council, Asia Soc., Opera/Omaha, Fulbright Alumni Assn., Omaha Press Club, Alpha Sigma Nu. Home: 4955 Cuming St Omaha NE 68132

HORNTHAL, PHILIPP RICHARD, mgmt. cons.; b. Chgo., Feb. 25, 1950; s. William J. and Sally (Schultz) H.; B.S. in Indsl. Engring., Purdue U., 1972, M.S. in Indsl. Engring., 1972; m. Sheila Maureen, Apr. 21, 1974; children—Jennifer Lynn, David Adam. Mgmt. cons., Arthur Andersen & Co., Chgo., 1973—, mgr. mgmt. info. and cons. div., 1978—. Mem. fund drive com. Jr. Achievement; mem. Northbrook Civic Found. Mem. Am. Prodn. and Inventory Control Soc. (flight chmn. 1974, 75, cert. in inventory mgmt., speaker internat. conf. 1980), Am. Inst. Indsl. Engrs., Ops. Research Soc. Am., Am. Materials Mgmt. Soc. (flight chmn. 1979-80, dir.). Home: 2727 Quail Ln Northbrook IL 60062 Office: 33 W Monroe St Chicago IL 60603

HORSLEY, JACK EVERETT, lawyer; b. Sioux City, Iowa, Dec. 12, 1915; s. Charles E. and Edith V. (Timms) H.; A.B., U. Ill., 1937, LL.B., 1939, J.D., 1965; m. Sallie Kelley, June 12, 1939 (dec.); children—Pamela, Charles Edward; m. 2d, Bertha J. Newland, Feb. 24, 1950 (dec.); m. 3d, Mary Jane Moran, Jan. 20, 1973; 1 dau., Sharon. Admitted to Ill. bar, 1939, since practiced law in Mattoon, Ill.; sr. counsel Craig & Craig, attys. for Ill. Central Gulf R.R. Co., C. & E.I. R.R. Co., Penn Central R.R. Co., Internat. Harvester Co. and other cos.; specializes in defensive trial work; vice chmn. bd., dir. Central Nat. Bank, 1976—; mem. lawyers adv. council U. Ill. Law Forum, 1960-63; lectr. Practising Law Inst., N.Y.C., 1967-73, Ct. Practice Inst., Chgo., 1974—, U. Mich. Coll. Law Inst. Continuing Legal Edn., 1968; vis. lectr. Duquesne Coll., Pitts., 1970, chmn. rev. com. Ill. Supreme Ct. Disciplinary Commn., 1973-76. Pres. bd. edn. Sch. Dist. 100, 1946-48; bd. dirs. Moore Heart Research Found., 1969—; narrator Poetry Interludes, WLBH-FM. Served with J.A.G.D., A.C., 1942-46; disch. as lt. col. Fellow Am. Coll. Trial Lawyers; mem. Am., Ill. (mem. exec. council ins. law 1961-63, lectr. ins. law course for attys. 1962, 64, 65), Coles-Cumberland (v.p. 1968-69, pres. 1969-70, chmn. jud. inquiry com. 1976—) bar assns., Assn. Bar City N.Y. (non-resident mem. emeritus), Am. Arbitration Assn. (nat. panel arbitrators), U. Ill. Law Alumni Assn. (pres.), Ill. Def. Counsel Assn. (dir. 1966-67, pres. 1967-68), Soc. Trial Lawyers (chmn. profl. activities 1960-61; dir. 1961-62), Adelphic Debating, Assn. Ins. Attys., Internat. Assn. Ins. Counsel (membership com. 1966-67), Am. Judicature Soc., Appellate Lawyers Assn., Scribe, Delta Phi (mem. exec. com. Alumni Assn. 1960-61), Sigma Delta Kappa. Republican. Mason (32 deg.). Author: Trial Lawyer's Manual, 1967; Voir Dire Examinations and Opening Statements, 1968; Current Development in Products Liability Law, 1969; Illinois Civil Practice and Procedure (textbook), 1970; The Medical Expert Witness, 1973; The Doctor and the Law, 1975; The Doctor and Family Law, 1975; The Doctor and Business Law, 1976; The Doctor and Medical Law, 1977. Contbr. Ill. Bar Jour., Def. Law Jour.; contbr. jury instructions and special defenses articles Fedn. of Ins. Council Quar. and Ill. Law Forum, 1958; cons., contbr. Med. Econs., 1969—; legal cons. Mast-Head, 1972—; contbr. RN Mag., 1976—. Home: 50 Elm Ridge Mattoon IL 61938 Office: 1807 Broadway Mattoon IL 61938

HORSMAN, LENORE LYNDE, soprano; b. Saginaw, Mich., Apr. 21, 1937; d. George Clark and Gwendolyn (Steele) McNabb; B.S., Ind. U., 1956, M.A., 1957; vocal student, Eng., 1965, Accademia Musicale di Chigiana, Accademia di Virgiliana Italy, 1976, 77, 78, 79, Salzburg Mozarteum, 1977, 78, 79; m. Reginald Horsman, Sept. 3, 1954; children—John, Janine, Mara. Leading roles in operas, operatta, musicals, plays, also operas on TV; singer premier TV performance of Greed Under a Tree, 1954; Am. TV premier Angelique, 1974; dir., tchr. Gads Hill Community Center, Mu Phi Epsilon Sch. Music, Chgo., 1976—; dir. Mt. Clemens (Mich.) Studio, Music, 1950; tchr. voice and piano Milw. Conservatory Music, 1964—; founder, staff dir., designer Milw. Opera Theatre, 1966, Opera for Two, 1975, Cameo Prodns., 1974; 1st chmn. steering com., 1st pres. Wis. Women in Arts, Milw., 1973-76; vocal coach opera dept. U. Wis., Madison, 1969-70; Theatre X, 1977; performer Artreach, 1977; tchr., dir. Northshore Theatre, 1978—. Bd. dirs. Internat. Women's Year Festival, Milw., 1975. Recipient Career Achievement award Milw. Panhellenic Assn., 1978. Mem. Nat. Women in Arts, Nat. Assn. Tchrs. Singing, AAUW, Modern Dance Council, Wis. Music Tchrs. Assn., Mu Phi Epsilon, Theta Alpha Phi. Presbyterian. Address: 3548 N Hackett Ave Milwaukee WI 53211 also 1919 W Fullerton Chicago IL 60608

HORTON, FRANK E., univ. adminstr.; b. Chgo., Aug. 29, 1939; s. Elba Earl and Mae Pauline (Prohaska) H.; B.S. in Bus. Adminstrn., Western Ill. U., 1963; M.S. in Geography, Northwestern U., 1964, Ph.D. in Geography, 1966; m. Nancy Horton, Aug. 26, 1960; children—Kimberley, Pamela, Amy, Kelly. Asst. prof. to prof. geography, U. Iowa, Iowa City, 1966-75, dir. Inst. Urban and Regional Research, 1968-72, dean for advanced studies, 1972-75; v.p. acad. affairs and research So. Ill. U., Carbondale, 1975-80; chancellor U. Wis., Milw., 1980—. Served with U.S. Army, 1957-60. Mem. AAAS, Assn. Am. Geographers. Author, editor: (with B.J.L. Perry) Geographic Perspectives on Urban Systems with Integrated Readings, 1970, Urban Environmental Management: Planning for Pollution Control, 1974; editor: Geographical Perspectives on Contemporary Urban Problems, 1973. Office: U Wis Milwaukee WI 53201

HORTON, JOSEPH JULIAN, JR., educator; b. Memphis, Nov. 7, 1936; s. Joseph Julian and Nina (Williams) H.; A.A., Lon Morris Jr. Coll., 1955; B.A., N.Mex. State U., 1958; M.A., So. Meth. U., 1965, Ph.D., 1968; postgrad. (research fellow) Harvard U., 1970-71; m. Linda Anne Langley, May 30, 1964; children—Joseph Julian, Anne Adele, David Douglas. Claims examiner Social Security Adminstrn., Kansas City, Mo., 1958-60, claims authorizer, 1960-61; with FDIC, Washington, 1967-71, fin. economist, 1967-69, coordinator merger analysis, 1969-71; prof., chmn. dept. econs. and bus. Slippery Rock State Coll. (Pa.), 1971-81; vis. fin. economist Fed. Home Loan Bank Bd., Washington, 1978-79; prof., chmn. commerce div. Bellarmine (Ky.) Coll., 1981—; asst. prof. George Washington U., Washington, 1968-69, U. Md., College Park, 1969-70; pres. Pa. Conf. Economists. Ford Found. dissertation fellow, 1966-67; NSF grad. fellow, 1964-66; Bank Adminstrn. Inst. Clarence Lichtfeldt fellow, 1981; recipient Cokesbury award So. Meth. U., 1965. Mem. Am. Econ. Assn., Am. Fin. Assn., N. Am. Econ. Studies Assn. (dir., v.p.). Bd. editors Eastern Econ. Jour.; contbr. to profl. jours.

HORTON, RALPH GRIDER, JR., hosp. adminstr.; b. Flatriver, Mo., Oct. 12, 1941; s. Ralph Grider and Monica Irene (Mann) H.; B.S., St. Louis Coll. Pharmacy, 1963; M.A. in Health Services Adminstrn., Webster Coll., 1980; m. Linda Daisy Grover, June 9, 1962; children—Kimberly, Kelly, Kara. Owner-mgr. Missler-Horton Drugs, Terrell, Tex., 1963-66; staff pharmacist St. John's Mercy Med.

Center, St. Louis, 1966-71; asst. dir. pharmacy Incarnate Word Hosp., St. Louis, 1971-75; dir. pharmacy services DePaul Community Health Center, St. Louis, 1975-81, asst. adminstr., 1981—; instr. hosp. pharmacy St. Louis Coll. Pharmacy, 1975-78, adj. clin. prof., 1978-81. Mem. Am. Soc. Hosp. Pharmacists, Am. Assn. Colls. Pharmacy, Mo. Soc. Hosp. Pharmacists (dir. 1979—), St. Louis Soc. Hosp. Pharmacists (Outstanding Hosp. Pharmacist of Year 1978, mem. instl. pharmacy liaison com. to Mo. State Bd. Pharmacy 1980—), Am. Coll. Hosp. Adminstrs. Club: Elks. Contbr. articles to profl. jours. Home: 10716 Forest Circle Dr Saint Louis MO 63128 Office: 12303 DePaul Dr Bridgeton MO 63044

HORTON, SHERMAN ELBERT, ins. co. exec.; b. Indpls., Oct. 6, 1947; s. Edward Lee and Mildred Janett (Mitchell) H.; B.A., S.W. Bapt. Coll., 1972; m. Ellen Catherine Wilson, Oct. 14, 1966; children—Sharon Sue, Carolyn Denise. Tchr., coach Collins Elem. Sch., Collins, Mo., 1972-75; ins. field underwriter N.Y. Life Ins. Co., Bolivar, Mo., 1975-77, asst. mgr., Springfield, Mo., 1977—. Mem. Polk County Community Bd., 1976-77. Recipient Nat. Quality award Life Ins. Mktg. and Research Assn., Nat. Assn. Life Underwriters, 1977; 1977, 78; Health Quality award, various life ins. socs., 1977. Mem. Nat. Assn. Life Underwriters (Nat. Sales Achievement award 1977, 78), Springfield Assn. Life Underwriters, Springfield C. of C., Jr. C. of C. (Outstanding Young Man award 1980, 81). Baptist. Home: 3551 S Westwood St Springfield MO 65807 Office: Bank of Springfield Bldg Suite 400 300 S Jefferson Ct Springfield MO 65806

HORTON, YVONNE, home economist, writer, educator; b. Orwell, Ohio; d. Edmund Earl and Stella (Jenks) Horton; B.S. in Edn., Kent State U., 1943; vocational home econs. certification Ohio State U., 1944; M.S. in Home Econs., Syracuse U., 1950; postgrad. in edn. U. Nev., 1963-64, U. N.H., 1976, Mich. State U., 1980-81; m. Stanley Kolsan, Dec. 29, 1951 (div. 1963); children—Vera Suzanne, Helen Jane. Home econs. tchr., secondary schs., No. Ohio, 1944-48; teaching asst. Syracuse U., 1948-50; asst. dir. Hoover Home Inst., North Canton, Ohio, 1950-51; asst. home econs. editor Plain Dealer, Cleve., 1952-54; lang. arts tchr. secondary schs., Clark County, Nev., 1963-66; staff home economist Christian Sci. Monitor, Boston, 1966-70, writer Candid Consumer column, 1967-70; home econs. tchr. secondary schs., Mass., 1970-72, 75-76; ednl. cons. N.H. Dept. Edn., 1976; food instr. Sch. Nursing Tenacre Found., Princeton, N.J., 1977-78; resident dir. Asher religious living unit Mich. State U., East Lansing, 1979—; editor, writer Co-ed mag., N.Y.C., 1973. Mem. Frontier council Girl Scouts U.S.A., 1964, 65; mem. Boston Mus. Fine Arts, 1967-76, Friends Old Sturbridge Village, 1968-72. Recipient Alma award Assn. Home Appliance Mfrs., 1967, 68, 69. Mem. Nat. Council Tchrs. English (life), Religious Advisers Assn. of Mich. State U., Friends of Concord (Mass.) Free Public Library (life). Address: Box 892 East Lansing MI 48823

HORVATH, CECILE PATRICIA, word processing mgr.; b. East Chicago, Ind., Sept. 15, 1939; d. Albert Paul and Victoria Bernadette H.; grad. parochial schs. Biller, clerk-typist CNA Ins., Chgo., 1957-60; typist Internat. Assn. Lions Clubs, Oak Brook, Ill., 1960-73, sec., 1963-70, supr., 1970-73; mgr. Word Processing Center, Ryan Ins. Group, Inc., Chgo., 1973—. Mem. Internat. Info. Word Processing Assn., Word Processing Mgmt. Assn. Chgo. Office: 222 N Dearborn St Chicago IL 60601

HORVATH, JAMES JAY, orthopaedic surgeon; b. Detroit, Apr. 16, 1916; s. Julius Frank and Mary Veronica (Ujfalusi) H.; B.S. in Liberal Arts, Wayne State U., 1944, M.D., 1945; m. Leola H. Montag, Sept. 21, 1946; children—James C., Thomas C., William C., Vikki Lee. Intern, Highland Park (Mich.) Gen. Hosp., 1945-46; resident in gen. surgery St. Joseph Mercy Hosp., Detroit, 1949, resident in orthopedic surgery Harper Hosp., 1951, Children's Hosp., Detroit Gen. Hosp. 1952 (all Detroit); pvt. practice medicine specializing in orthopedic surgery, Detroit, 1953—; chief orthopedic surgery Highland Park Gen., 1958-72, pres. staff, 1960; mem. staff Rehab. Inst., Detroit, pres., 1972; staff Harper, 1953—, chief orthopedic surgery outpatient dept., 1958-68; staff Children's, Detroit Gen., Jennings Meml. hosps., 1953— (all Detroit). Clin. asso. prof. orthopedic surgery Wayne State U. Sch. Medicine, Detroit, 1960—, asst. dean clin. faculty, 1972—. Served with AUS, 1943-45, 46-48. Fellow A.C.S., Clin. Orthopedic Soc., Detroit Acad. Orthopedic Surgeons (pres. 1965); mem. Royal Coll. Medicine-Eng., Am. Acad. Orthopedic Surgeons, Middle Eastern and Mediterranean Orthopedic and Traumatology Soc., Wayne State U. Sch. Medicine Alumni Assn. (pres. 1972), Phi Beta Pi (pres. Kappa chpt. 1956). Mason (Shriner). Contbr. articles to profl. jours. Home: 776 Berkshire Rd Grosse Pointe Park MI 48230 Office: 15035 E Seven Mile Rd Detroit MI 48205

HORVATH, STEPHEN JOHN, JR., supt. schs.; b. Chgo., Sept. 3, 1933; s. Steve John and Sophie (Bartus) H.; B.S. in Edn., No. Ill. U., 1955, M.S. in Edn., 1956; postgrad. Loyola, Chgo., 1964, U. Ill., 1965—; m. Theresa Marie Moscinski, June 20, 1959; children—Stephen John, Jeffrey Paul, Curt, Paul. Freshman advisor Miami U., 1958-60; counselor pub. schs., Orland Park, Ill., 1960-62; guidance dir. DeLaSalle Inst., Chgo., 1962-65; bus. mgr. Cook County Sch. Dist. 127, 1965-70; asst. supt. Cook County Supt. Schs., 1970-71; supt. Fairmont Sch. Dist. 89, Will County, 1971-75, Atwood Heights Dist. 125 Cook County, 1975—. Chmn. Worth Youth Commn., 1962-64; mem. dist. 127 Bd. Edn., 1964-65; alderman City of Palos Heights, Ill., 1979—. Served with AUS, 1956-58. Recipient Silver Beaver award Boy Scouts Am. Mem. Ill. Counselor Educators and Supervisors Assn., Am. Sch. Adminstrs. Assn., Assn. Ednl. Negotiators, Ill. Sch. Counselors Assn. (pres.), Ill. Guidance and Personnel Assn. (mem. exec. bd., conv. coordinator), No. Ill. U. Alumni Assn. (pres.), Am. Sch. Counselors Assn., No. Ill. U. Found. (pres.), Ill. Assn. Sch. Adminstrs. Home: 12133 S 75th Av Palos Heights IL 60463 Office: Dist 125 3900 W 116th Pl Alsip IL 60658

HORWITCH, MARILYN DOLORES, educator; b. Chgo., June 7, 1927; d. Sol and Toby (Cohn) Holzman; A.B., U. Chgo., 1947; B.A., Roosevelt U., 1948; M.A., Northeastern Ill. U., 1972; m. Edward Horwitch, Sept. 3, 1948; children—Marc Jerome, Ilene Gail, Neal Lawrence. Tchr. pub. schs., Wheeling, Ill., 1948-49; tchr. pub. schs., Chgo., 1949-54, 64-72, tchr., counselor, 1972—, prin. Copernicus Elem. Sch. Recipient Rose Maremont Schutz Dedicated Tchr. award Swift Sch. PTA, 1974, 75; Dedicated Tchr. award Chgo. region PTA, 1976. Mem. Ill. Edn. Assn. (dir. 1954-56), Am. Personnel and Guidance Assn., Am. Sch. Counselor Assn., Jennie Singer League for Pediatric Research, AAUW, Phi Beta Kappa. Jewish. Address: 645 LeClaire Ave Wilmette IL 60091

HORWITT, MAX KENNETH, biochemist; b. N.Y.C., Mar. 21, 1908; s. Harry and Bessie (Kenitz) H.; B.A., Dartmouth Coll., 1930; Ph.D., Yale U., 1935; m. Frances Levine, 1933 (dec. 1973); children—Ruth Ann Horwitt Singer, Mary Louise Horwitt Goldman; m. 2d, Mildred Gad Weitzman, Jan. 1, 1974. Research fellow in physiol. chemistry Yale U., 1935-37, lab. asst., 1932-34, asst., 1934-35; dir. biochem. research lab. Elgin (Ill.) State Hosp., 1937-59, L.B. Mendel research lab., 1960-68, hosp. dir. research, 1966-68; asso. dept. biol. chemistry U. Ill. Coll. Medicine, 1940-43. asst. prof., 1943-51, asso. prof., 1951-62, prof., 1962—; prof. dept. biochemistry St. Louis U. Sch. Medicine, 1968-76, prof. emeritus, 1976—; vis. prof. dept. internal medicine Rush Med. Sch., 1979—; acting dir. div. research services Ill. Dept. Mental Health, Chgo., 1967-68; field dir. Anemia and Malnutrition Research Center, Chiang Mai Med. Sch., Thailand, 1968-69; cons. in human nutrition Rush Med. Sch., Chgo., 1967—; mem. com. of dietary allowances Food and Nutrition Bd., NRC, 1980—; mem. expert group on vitamin E, WHO, Geneva, 1981—; chmn. St. Louis U. Institutional Rev. Bd., 1980—. Pres., Kneseth Israel Congregation, Elgin, 1965. Recipient Osborne and Mendel award Am. Inst. Nutrition, 1961. Diplomate Am. Bd. Clin. Chemistry, Am. Bd. Nutrition. Fellow Gerontol. Soc., AAAS, N.Y. Acad. Scis., Am. Inst. Chemists; mem. Am. Soc. Biol. Chemists, Am. Soc. Clin. Nutrition, Soc. Exptl. Biology and Medicine, Soc. Biol. Psychiatry, Assn. Vitamin Chemists, Am. Chem. Soc. Editorial bd. Jour. Nutrition, 1967-71; co-editor Am. Jour. Clin. Nutrition, 1974. Contbr. more than 150 articles in biochemistry, psychopharmacology and clinical nutrition to profl. publs. Home: 18 York Hills Brentwood MO 63144 Office: St Louis U Sch Medicine 1402 S Grand Blvd Saint Louis MO 63104

HORWITZ, HARRY, physician; b. London, Mar. 20, 1927; s. Benjamin and Doris H.; came to U.S., 1960, naturalized, 1965; M.D., U. London, 1950; m. Jeanna Dorren Segal, Mar. 18, 1958; children—Ruth, Caroline. Intern, Met. Hosp., London, 1950-51, St. Bartholomew's Hosp., London, 1951-52; resident St. Bartholomew's Hosp., 1954-58; sr. resident Addenbrooke's Hosp., Cambridge, Eng., 1958-60; fellow Mt. Sinai Hosp., N.Y.C., 1959; prof. radiology U. Cin., 1960—; pres. Oncology Assos., Inc., Cin., 1972—. Bd. dirs. Am. Cancer Soc., 1967—. Served with RAF, 1952-54. Am. Cancer Soc. grantee, 1960-63, USPHS grantee, 1961, 62, 63. Diplomate Am. Bd. Therapeutic Radiology. Fellow Royal Coll. Radiology; mem. AMA, Brit. Med. Assn., Am. Coll. Radiology, Am. Roentgen Ray Soc., Radiol. Soc. N.Am., Am. Soc. Clin. Oncology, Cancer Control Council, Radiol. Soc. Greater Cin. (past pres.). Clubs: Queen City (Cin.); Lodge of Hospitality. Contbr. articles in field to med. jours. Home: 9355 Holly Hill Cincinnati OH 45243 Office: 3120 Barnet Ave Suite 103 Cincinnati OH 45229

HORWITZ, ROBERT HENRY, polit. scientist; b. El Paso, Tex., Sept. 3, 1923; s. David and Louise (Mendelsohn) H.; B.A., Amherst Coll., 1949; M.A., U. Hawaii, 1950; Ph.D., U. Chgo., 1954; m. Noreen Margaret Surti, Jan. 1948; children—Susheila Louise, David D. Asst. prof., researcher U. Hawaii, 1948-51; research asst. com. for study citizenship edn. U. Chgo., 1953-55; from asst. prof. to prof. polit. sci. Mich. State U., 1956-66; prof. polit. sci., chmn. dept. Kenyon Coll., Gambier, Ohio, 1966—, dir. Public Affairs Conf. Center, 1976—. Served with AUS, 1942-46; ETO, PTO. Decorated Bronze Star, Combat Inf. badge. Fellow Emil Schwarzhaupt Found., 1953-55, Rockefeller Found., 1959, Ford Found., 1956-58, Nat. Endowment Humanities, 1973-76. Mem. AAUP, Am. Polit. Sci. Assn., Am. Soc. Polit. and Legal Philosophy. Jewish. Co-author: John Locke's Questions Concerning the Law of Nature, 1981; editor: The Moral Foundations of the American Republic, 1977; contbr. to profl. publs. Home: 214 Kokosing Dr Gambier OH 43022 Office: Dept Polit Sci Kenyon Coll Gambier OH 43022

HOSMANEK, JOHN JOSEPH, ednl. adminstr.; b. Oak Creek, Wis., Jan. 24, 1926; s. Joseph Rudolph and Susan H.; B.S., U. Wis., 1950; M.Ed., Marquette U., 1955, D.Ed., 1975; m. Angeline J. Wolsey, Aug. 28, 1948; children—Thomas J., Joan, Jane, Mark, Jean. Asst. jr. high sch. prin., Sheboygan, Wis., 1956-60; asst. prin. Lincoln Jr. High Sch., Kenosha, Wis., 1960-62; prin. Lance Jr. High Sch., Kenosha, 1962-66, Tremper High Sch., Kenosha, 1966-70; asst. supt. Kenosha Unified Sch. Dist., 1970-79, supt., 1979—. Served with USMC, 1943-46. Ford Found. fellow, 1952-53. Mem. Am. Assn. Sch. Adminstrs., Nat. Sch. Public Relations Assn., Wis. Library Assn., Phi Delta Kappa. Club: Elks. Contbr. articles in field to profl. jours. Home: 8023 19th Ave Kenosha WI 53140 Office: Kenosha Unified School District 625 52nd St Kenosha WI 53140

HOSTETLER, DAVID ROLAND, chemist; b. Lima, Ohio, Jan. 31, 1928; s. Waldo Lee and Lesta Mae (Basinger) H.; B.S. in Chemistry, Bowling Green State U., 1951; M.S. in Chemistry, Toledo U., 1958; m. Laurie Pflug, Apr. 15, 1950; children—Dan, Susan, Dean, Dirk, Sally. Chemist, Sun Oil Co., Toledo, 1951-65, lab. mgr. tar sand field test unit, Alta., Can., 1965-66, supr. lab. Toledo Refinery, 1967—; instr. analytical chemistry Toledo U., 1968—; speaker on petrochems. to tech., schs. and community groups. Wood County (Ohio) chmn. Bus. and Profl. People for Kennedy-Johnson, 1960; mem. budget com. Toledo Community Chest, 1970—; chmn. bd. dirs. Sun Oil Responsible Citizens Program, 1976—. Served with USNR, 1945-46. Recipient Silver Beaver award Toledo council Boy Scouts Am., 1975. Mem. Am. Chem. Soc., Am. Inst. Chemists (accredited profl. chemist), Am. Soc. Quality Control, Nat. Mgmt. Assn. Democrat. Home: 227 E Front Perrysburg OH 43551 Office: PO Box 920 Toledo OH 43693

HOUCK, MARK HEDRICH, civil engr., educator; b. Balt., May 14, 1951; s. Walter Clifton and Ruth Marie (Hedrich) H.; B.E.S., Johns Hopkins U., 1972, Ph.D., 1976; m. Margaret Ann Nolan, Sept. 1, 1972; 1 son, Timothy Daniel Nolan. Research asst. prof. dept. civil engring. U. Wash., Seattle, 1975-77; asst. prof. Sch. Civil Engring. Purdue U., West Lafayette, Ind., 1977—. Registered profl. engr., Ind. Mem. ASCE, Am. Geophys. Union, Inst. Mgmt. Sci., Ops. Research Soc. Am., Sigma Xi. Contbr. articles to profl. jours. Office: Sch Civil Engring Purdue U West Lafayette IN 47907

HOUGEN, THERESE YVONNE, mfg. co. exec.; b. Fall River, Mass., Nov. 15, 1922; d. Victor Joseph and Ida Donalda (Riel) Perrault; grad. high sch., 1941; m. Everett Douglas Hougen, July 5, 1941; children—Douglas S., Victor L., Randall B., Bradley R. With Wright Aero., Paterson, N.J., 1943-44, Quackenbushes, Paterson, N.J., 1944-45; with Blair Equipment Co., Flint, Mich., 1953-59, corp. sec., treas., 1959-73, dir., 1977—; with Hougen Mfg. Co., Inc., Flint, 1970—, exec. v.p., 1974—, dir., 1976—. Del., PTO. Mem. U.S. C. of C., Mich. C. of C. Club: East Bay Country (Largo, Fla.). Home: 1184 Normandy Terr Flint MI 48504 Office: G-5072 Corunna Rd Flint MI 48504

HOUGER, N. WILLIAM, transp. co. exec.; b. Cleve., Dec. 20, 1942; s. Norman William Burdette and Margaret Harriet (Baltes) H.; B.A., Kent State U., 1970, M.A., 1978; m. Adele Kay Friedt, June 6, 1975; 1 dau., Kerri Lyn. Grad. asst. dept. philosophy Kent (Ohio) State U., 1970-71; co-mgr. Kroger Co., Akron, Ohio, 1971-73, store mgr. Akron and Massillon, Ohio, 1973-74; with Miller Transfer & Rigging, Akron, 1974, v.p. spl. commodities div., Youngstown, Ohio, 1974-78, v.p. adminstrn., Akron, 1978-80, v.p. ops. and adminstrn., 1980—. Served with USAR, 1961. Mem. Akron Traffic Club, Delta Nu Alpha. Home: 2144 Yellow Creek Rd Akron OH 44313 Office: PO Box 322 Cuyahoga Falls OH 44222

HOUGH, FREDERICK JOHN, II, chiropractic coll. ofcl.; b. Chgo., Sept. 14, 1936; s. Frederick John and Eleanora Francis (Cyra) H.; A.A., Coll. of DuPage, 1975; B.A., Elmhurst Coll., 1976; m. Lorraine Sacher, July 3, 1957; children—Frederick, Michael, Neil, Linda, Laura. Cost acct. Wilson Sporting Goods Co., 1957-58; office mgr. Howell Tractor and Equipment Co., 1958-60; pres. Great Lakes Sci. Corp., Lombard, Ill., 1960-74; comptroller, mem. faculty Nat. Coll. Chiropractic, Lombard, 1974—; instr. investing, fin., bus. and law, 1974—; lectr., bus. and investment adv., 1974—. Served with USMC, 1954-57. Mem. Adminstrv. Mgmt. Soc., 1st Marine Brigade, Fleet Marine Force, VFW (chpt. treas.), Delta Mu Delta. Republican. Methodist. Club: Ill. Athletic. Author: Investing and Financing, 1980. Home: 326 S Monterey St Villa Park IL 60181 Office: Nat Coll Chiropractic 200 E Roosevelt Rd Lombard IL 60148

HOUGH, JOHN physician; b. Mt. Clemens, Mich., Mar. 24, 1948; s. Walter Wells and Rose Adeline (York) H.; B.S. with honors in Zoology, U. Mich., Ann Arbor, 1970, M.D., 1974; m. Cheryl Sue Metcalf, July 21, 1973; 1 son, John Benjamin. Intern, N.C. Bapt. Hosp., Winston Salem; surgeon Nat. Health Service Corps, Hamlin, W.Va., 1975-78, also cons. Bd. Rev. for Disability, Vocat. Rehab., 1976-78, and clin. instr. family medicine Marshall U., Huntington, W.Va., 1976-78; asst. prof. family and community medicine Hershey Med. Center of Pa. State U., 1979-80; asst. dir. family practice program Midland (Mich.) Hosp. Center, 1980—; rep. Health Services Agy., 1978; sch. physician, Hamlin, 1975-78, Halifax, Pa., 1979; physician Tri-State Golden Gloves Tournament, 1978. Served with USPHS, 1975-78. Recipient Physicians Recognition award AMA, 1977; award Southwestern Community Action, Huntington, 1978; award Rotary Club, 1979, diplomate Am. Bd. Family Medicine. Mem. Am. Acad. Family Physicians. Author: Radiographic Visualization of Arterial Lesions, 1971; Cholesterol Kinetic Analyses, 1975; Rubella Immunization Effectiveness, 1979. Office: Family Practice Program Midland Hosp Center Midland MI 48640

HOUGLAND, SYLVIA, state ofcl.; b. Saginaw. Mich., Oct. 12, 1938; d. Seymour and Fritzi Seltzer; M.P.A., U. So. Calif., 1976; m. Curtis Rives Hougland, July 9, 1960; children—Kimberly, Curtis Rives. Coordinator, Nat. Sr. Citizens Law Center; dir. services to aged Jewish Family and Children's Services, Kansas City, Mo.; dir. Legal Assistance for Sr. Adults, 1977; sec. on aging Kans. Dept. Aging, Topeka, 1980—; bd. dirs. Legal Services for Elderly; mem. Task Force Older Women's Issues, Status of Women Commn. Mem. Am. Soc. Public Adminstrn., Western Geront. Soc., Mid Am. Congress Aging, Older Women's League. Author papers in field. Office: 610 W 10th St Topeka KS 66612

HOULTON, LOYCE, dance theatre dir.; b. Duluth, Minn.; B.A., Carleton Coll., Northfield, Minn.; M.A., N.Y. U.; pupil of Louis Horst, Martha Graham, Doris Humphrey, Nina Fonaroff; m. William Houlton; 4 children. Tchr. modern dance U. Minn., Mpls., 1959-62; founder, dir. Contemporary Dance Playhouse, Mpls., 1962-69; artistic dir. Minn. Dance Theatre, Mpls., 1969—. Address: Minn Dance Theatre 528 Hennepin Ave Minneapolis MN 55403*

HOUPIS, CONSTANTINE HARRY, elec. engr.; b. Lowell, Mass., June 16, 1922; s. Harry John and Metaxia (Gourokous) H.; student Wayne U., 1941-43; B.S., U. Ill., 1947, M.S., 1948; postgrad. Ohio State U., 1952-56; Ph.D., U. Wyo., 1971; m. Mary Stephens, Aug. 28, 1960; children—Harry C., Angella S. Spl. research asst. U. Ill., 1947-48; devel. elec. engr. Babcock & Wilcox Co., Alliance, Ohio, 1948-49; instr. elec. engring. Wayne U., 1949-51; prin. elec. engr. Battelle Meml. Inst., Columbus, Ohio, 1951-52; prof. elec. engring. Air Force Inst. Tech., Wright-Patterson AFB, Ohio, 1952—; guest lectr. Nat. Tech. U. Athens, 1958. Served with AUS, 1943-46. Recipient Outstanding Engr. award Dayton area Nat. Engrs. Week, 1962. Mem. IEEE, Am. Soc. Engring. Edn., Am. Hellenic Edn. Progressive Assn., Tau Beta Pi, Eta Kappa Nu, Sigma Chi. Mem. Greek Orthodox Ch. Author: (with J.J. D'Azzo) Feedback Control System Analysis and Synthesis, 1960, 2d edit., 1966; Principles of Electrical Engineering: Electric Circuits, Electronics, Energy Conversion, Control Systems Computers, 1968; Linear Control Systems Analysis and Design: Conventional and Modern, 1975, 2d edit., 1981; (with J. Lubelfeld) Outline of Pulse Circuits; also articles on automatic controls in profl. jours. U.S., Eng., Greece. Home: 1125 Brittany Hills Dr Centerville OH 45459 Office: Air Force Inst Tech Wright-Patterson AFB OH 45433

HOUSER, ROBERT NORMAN, ins. co. exec.; b. Bloomfield, Iowa, Sept. 21, 1919; s. Charles B. and Venna C. (Bartholomew) H.; B.A. summa cum laude, U. Iowa, 1947; m. Doris V. Miller, Dec. 18, 1943; children—Theodore Alan, Judith Eileen, James Robert. With Bankers Life Co., 1936-38, 40-43, 47—, asst. actuary, 1953-60, assoc. actuary, 1960-63, 2d v.p., actuary, 1963-68, v.p., actuary, 1968-71, v.p., chief actuary, 1971-72, sr. v.p., chief actuary, 1972-73, pres., 1973—, pres., chief exec. officer, 1975—; chmn. bd., pres. BLC Growth & Income Funds, BLC Fund, Inc.; chmn. bd. BLC Equity Mgmt. Co., BLC Equity Services Corp.; dir. BLC Ins. Co. Bd. dirs. Drake U., Mercy Hosp., United Way Greater Des Moines; bd. govs. Iowa Coll. Found. Served to 1st lt. USAAF, 1943-45, USAF, 1951-52. Decorated D.F.C., Air medals. Fellow Soc. Actuaries; mem. Greater Des Moines C. of C. (dir.), Am. Council Life Ins. (dir.). Office: 711 High St Des Moines IA 50307

HOUSLEY, CHARLES EDWARD, hosp. adminstr.; b. LaFollette, Tenn., Mar. 29, 1939; s. John R. and Hazel Ellen (Byrd) H.; B.S., U. Tenn., 1964; M.B.A. in Hosp. Adminstrn., Xavier U., Cin., 1967; postgrad. health adminstrs. devel. program Cornell U., 1967. Asst. adminstr. East Tenn. Children's Hosp., Knoxville, 1964-65; adminstrv. resident St. Anthony Hosp., Columbus, Ohio, 1966-67, asst. adminstr., 1967-69, asso. adminstr., 1969—. Lectr. on hosp. materiel mgmt. throughout U.S., 1970—; clin. instr. hosp. and health services adminstrn. Ohio State U., Columbus, 1973—, lectr. health care adminstrn., 1972—; preceptor program in hosp. and health services adminstrn. Xavier U., 1968—; vice chmn. shared services com. Franklin County Adminstrv. Council, 1973-74; mem. task force on environ. health concerns on health care facilities Ohio Health Dept., 1975—. Chmn. hosp. div. United Way Campaign, 1973; chmn. hosp. div. Community Health Fair, 1974; active Big Bro. Assn. Trustee, Isabel Ridgway Home for Aged, 1970-75. Recipient appreciation award Columbus Police Dept., 1971, certificate of appreciation United Way Campaign, 1972. Mem. Am., Ohio (materiel mgmt. com. 1975—, Monsignor Griffin award for lit. 1975), Catholic hosp. assns., Am. Coll. Hosp. Adminstrs., Ohio Pub. Health Assn., Nat. Mgmt. Assn., Columbus Acad. Med. (courtesy, disaster planning com. 1969—), Young Adminstrv. Colloquium of Central Ohio (past pres.), Columbus C. of C. (fire prevention com. 1975—). Author: Hospital Materiel Management, 1978; contbr. articles to profl. jours. Home: 146 Glen Circle Worthington OH 43085 Office: St Anthony Hosp 1450 Hawthorne Ave Columbus OH 43203

HOUSTON, JOHN CARL, civil engr.; b. Graceville, Minn., Aug. 10, 1937; s. Howard A. and Thelma E. (Swingen) H.; B.S., N.D. Agrl. Coll., 1960; M.S., N.D. State U., 1962; m. Carol Mae Schmiesing, Dec. 21, 1958; children—Mark, Kristi, Michael. Civil engr. Civil engr. Kirkham, Michael & Assos., Fargo, N.D., 1958-61; hwy. engr. Dept. Transp., 1961-71; cons. engr. Houston Engring. Co., Burnsville, Minn., 1971-78; pres. Gt. Stock Corp., Apple Valley, Minn., 1973—, dir., 1975—; pres. Houston Constrn., Inc., Apple Valley, 1975—, dir., 1980—; dir. Magnusystem Corp. Pres. Farquar Lake Homeowners Assn., 1975—; precinct chmn. Apple Valley Democrat Farm Labor Party, 1980—. Mem. ASCE, Tau Beta Pi. Unitarian. Home and Office: 13009 Diamond Path W Apple Valley MN 55124

HOUSTON, MURRAY, foods corp. exec.; b. Chgo., Aug. 23, 1926; s. Sam, II, and Anna (Sherman) H.; children—Barbara, Gregory. Owner Mickey Houston, Inc., Chgo., 1945-53; owner Houston Foods, Inc. Ltd. (merged into J.M. Smucker Co., Orrville, Ohio 1971, acquired by CFS Continental, Chgo. 1979, subs. CFS Continental), Chgo., 1953-70, mem. corp. mgmt. team CFS Continental, 1980-81; steering com. Nat. Fancy Food Show; splty. food cons., U.S. govt., 1952-60; foodmarket cons. Home TV Show, 1958; vis. prof. Hotel and Restaurant Sch., Cornell U., Mich. State U., 1976. Active City of Hope. Served with U.S. Army, World War II. Named Overseas Buyer of Decade, 1970-80, Fancy Food Industry Man of Year, 1977, Gourmet Food Industry Gift Packer Man of Year, 1974. Mem. Nat. Assn. Spl. Food Trade. Clubs: Bryn Mawr Country (Chgo.), La Gorce Country (Miami Beach, Fla.), Palm Bay (Miami), Outrigger Canoe (Honolulu), Internat. (Chgo.), Racquet (Palm Springs). Office: 4245 N Knox Chicago IL 60641

HOUSTON, PAUL DENNIS, county ofcl.; b. Warrick County, Ind., Apr. 16, 1921; s. Gurney Earl and Lenora Evelyn H.; student schs., Boonville, Ind.; m., Nov. 13, 1943; children—Donna Jean Houston Barnett, Jay Bradford, Kent Earl. With engring. dept. Peabody Coal Co., 1941-53; partner Houston Mining Co., 1953-57; police chief Boonville, 1957-63; Warrick County assessor, Boonville, 1971—, sheriff Warrick County, 1963-71. Chmn., Warrick County Democratic Central Com., 1967-81. Served with U.S. Army, 1941-43. Recipient Jaycees Public Servant award, 1977. Mem. Ind. Sheriffs Assn. (life), Ind. County Assessors Assn., Am. Legion (comdr. post 1951-52), VFW. Clubs: Boonville Lions (pres.), Masons, Shriners. Home: 1016 E Monroe St Boonville IN 47601 Office: PO Box 562 Court House Boonville IN 47601

HOUSTON, WILLIAM ROBERT MONTGOMERY, ophthalmic surgeon; b. Mansfield, Ohio, Nov. 13, 1922; s. William T. and Frances (Hursh) H.; B.A., Oberlin Coll., 1944; M.D., Western Res. U., 1948; m. Marguerite LaBau Browne, Apr. 25, 1968; children—William Erling Tenney, Marguerite Elisabeth LaBau, Selby Cabot Truitt Vanderbilt. Intern, Meth. Hosp. Bklyn., 1948-49, Ill. Eye and Ear Infirmary, Chgo., 1949-50; resident N.Y. Eye and Ear Infirmary, 1950-52; practice medicine specializing in ophthalmic surgery, Mansfield, 1952—; mem. staffs Mansfield Gen. Hosp., Peoples Hosp., Mansfield, N.Y. U. Bellevue Med. Center, N.Y.C.; asso. prof. clin. ophthalmology N.Y. U. Sch. Medicine. Pres. Mansfield Symphony Soc., 1965-68, Mansfield Civic Music Assn., 1965; mem. Mansfield City Sch. Bd., 1962-65, v.p., 1965. Served to capt. M.C. USAF, 1952-55. Diplomate Am. Bd. Ophthalmology. Recipient Honor award Acad. Ophthalmology. Fellow Internat. Coll. Surgeons; mem. SAR (color guard 1961-71), Ohio Hist. Soc. (life), N.Y. Geneal. and Biog. Soc. (life), Ohio Geneal. Soc. (trustee 1955—). Editor, Ohio Records and Pioneers Families, 1970—. Address: 456 Park Ave W Mansfield OH 44906

HOUTCHENS, ROBERT AUSTIN, JR., chemist; b. Denver, Mar. 31, 1953; s. Robert A. and Lorna G. (Smyth) H.; B.S. in Engring. Sci., Colo. State U., 1975; Ph.D. (Boettcher Found. fellow), 1980; m. Cynthia Susan Barth, July 24, 1976. Grad. research asst. biochemistry dept. Colo. State U., Ft. Collins, 1976-80; sr. research chemist Dow Chem. Co., Midland, Mich., 1980—. Mem. Am. Chem. Soc., AAAS, Sigma Xi, Tau Beta Pi. Contbr. articles on biochemistry to profl. jours. Home: 2008 Laurel Ln Midland MI 48640

HOUTTUIN, ERIK, surgeon; b. Djakarta, Indonesia, Mar. 11, 1936; came to U.S., 1976; s. Wiebe Laurens and Johanna Hendrika (Westerbeke) H.; M.D., Gemeentelyke Universiteit (Amsterdam), 1959; Ph.D., U. Toronto (Can.), 1972; m. Carolyn M. MacDonald, May 9, 1963; children—Monica Joan, Christiaan Bernard, Robert Jan, Erika Marie, Roland Maarten. Intern, St. Rita's Hosp., Lima, Ohio, 1960-61, Toronto Gen. Hosp., 1967-68; resident in surgery U. Mich., Ann Arbor, 1962-64, U. Chgo., 1964-66; resident in surgery U. Toronto (Ont., Can.), 1966-67, resident in urology, 1973-76; practice medicine specializing in urology and surgery, St. Louis, 1976—; asst. prof. Dept. Surgery, St. Louis U., 1980—; staff St. Louis U. Hosp., St. Louis City Hosp., St. Mary's Hosp., St. Francis Mercy Hosp., Bethesda Meml. Hosp., Cardinal Glennon Childrens Hosp. Served with Netherlands Army. Diplomate Am. Bd. Urology; cert. Royal Coll. Surgeons of Can.; Med. Research Council of Can. fellow, 1968-72. Fellow A.C.S.; mem. AMA, Mo. Med. Assn., Acad. Medicine of Toronto, Franklin Gasconade County Med. Soc. (pres.). Club: Spirit of St. Louis Working Dog Assn. (pres. 1977-81). Contbr. articles in field to profl. jours. Home: Route 1 PO Box 136 Labadie MO 63055 Office: 1325 S Grand St Saint Louis MO 63104

HOVDA, MARY LOU, librarian; b. Tyler, Minn., Aug. 8, 1927; d. Lloyd Ellsworth and Grace Jerusha (Combes) Haburn; B.A., Northwestern Coll., Roseville, Minn., 1953; B.A., Macalester Coll., St. Paul, 1962; M.A. in L.S., U. Minn., 1965; m. Wilford Murrel, July 6, 1968. Asst. librarian Northwestern Coll., 1954-59, 64-67, head librarian, 1972—; student asst. Macalester Coll., 1959-62, acquisitions asst., 1962-64; adminstrv. librarian Mpls. Community Coll., 1969-72; vis. lectr. Faith Mission Tng. Sch., Edinburgh, Scotland, summer 1966; asst. librarian Wycliffe Bible Translators, Brasilia, Brazil, 1977-78; indexer Christian Periodical Index, 1972—. Mem. ALA, Assn. Christian Librarians (sec. 1976-77), Awana Clubs. Republican. Baptist. Home: 339 N Finn St Saint Paul MN 55104 Office: 3003 N Snelling Ave Roseville MN 55113

HOVDE, RUSSELL JAMES, banker; b. Madison, Wis., Oct. 27, 1927; s. Ingvald and Joseffa O. (Anderson) H.; B.S., U. Wis., 1950; postgrad. Northwestern U., 1955-65; m. Betty Lou Dunn, Feb. 24, 1951; children—David, Martha. Realtor, I. Hovde Realty Co., Madison, 1950-53; asst. to pres. No. Moulding Co., Franklin Park, Ill., 1954-58; Midwest rep., homes div. U.S. Steel Corp., Chgo., 1958-61; with Continental Ill. Nat. Bank & Trust Co., Chgo., 1961—, v.p., 1970—, v.p., mgr. U.S. cash mgmt. div., 1972-80, v.p. controllers div., 1981—; dir. Correct Craft, Inc., Orlando, Fla. Village trustee, fin. chmn., Fontana, Wis., 1975—. Served with USN, 1945-46. Mem. Fin. Mgrs. Assn. Chgo., Bank Adminstrn. Inst. (vice-chmn. 1980, nat. cash mgmt. council), Phi Kappa Phi, Phi Eta Sigma, Beta Gamma Sigma, Alpha Chi Rho. Republican. Clubs: U. Wis. (Chgo.); Lake Geneva (Wis.) Country. Home: 372 N Lake Shore Dr Fontana WI 53125 Office: 231 S LaSalle St Chicago IL 60693

HOVELL, DARLA JEAN, editor; b. Burlington, Iowa, Oct. 13, 1944; d. Duane K. and Darlene Juanita Engle; student public schs., New London, Iowa; m. Richard Leon Hovell, Oct. 5, 1963; children—Darren, Tina, Timmy, Brandon. Corr., Dispatch News, Woodway, Tex., 1973; editor Whitewright (Tex.) Sun, 1974-77; society editor Knoxville (Iowa Jour.-Express, 1979-80, news editor, 1980—. Recipient First Place award Tex. Press Assn., 1975, awards N.E. Tex. Press Assn., 1974, 75, 76, 77, Cert. of Recognition, VA, 1979. Mem. Nat. Fedn. Press Women, Tex. Press Women, Iowa Press Assn., Whitewright C. of C. (v.p. 1977), Beta Sigma Phi. Baptist. Clubs: Hist. Soc., Rebekah. Home: PO Box 218 Hamilton IA 50116 Office: 122 E Robinson St Knoxville IA 50138

HOVINGA, PETER, office equipment co. exec.; b. Jenison, Mich., July 31, 1930; s. David and Martha (DeKraker) H.; grad. high sch.; m. Hildred Ann Baar, Sept. 6, 1951; children—James Peter, Lynne Marie. Metal finisher Gezon Motors, Grand Rapids, Mich., 1948-50; self-employed carpenter, 1950-52, home contractor, Grand Rapids, 1952-53; service mgr. Ditto Inc., Grand Rapids, 1953-63; material handling engr. Rapistan Inc., Grand Rapids, 1963-65; pres. Hovinga Bus. Equipment Inc. and Hovinga Leasing Co., Inc., Grandville, Mich., 1965—; owner, pres. Mich. Marine Co. Inc., 1975-77; founder Cell-U-Save Mfg. Insulation Co. Inc., 1978-79. Mem. Jenison Bd. Edn., 1958-62, sec., 1960-62; bd. dirs. Mich. Cystic Fibrosis Found., 1956-58; pres. publicity com. Reformed Ch., Grand Rapids, 1972-75; bd. dirs. T.E.L.L. (Evang. Lit. League), 1964-68. Served with U.S. Army, 1949-50. Mem. Mich., Grand Rapids, Grandville chambers of commerce, Mich. Mfrs. Assn. Republican. Mem. Reformed Ch. in Am. Home: 4820 Green Moor Ct Hudsonville MI 49426 Office: 4390 Chicago Dr Grandville MI 49418

HOWARD, BARRY SHAWN, candy broker; b. Beech Grove, Ind., Jan. 3, 1954; s. Willis R. and Ruby L. (Daron) H.; B.A., Ind. Central U., 1976; m. Paula Annette Thornburg, Aug. 7, 1976; 1 son, Shawn Matthew. Loan officer, loan supr. Railroadman Fed. Savs. and Loan Assn., Indpls., 1976-78; sales rep. Fairley Brokerage Co., Zionsville, Ind., from 1978, now 2d v.p. Mem. Nat. Candy Wholesalers Assn. Republican (precinct fin. chmn. 1980). Lutheran. Home: 6414 Marble Ln Indianapolis IN 46227 Office: 70 E Cedar St Zionsville IN 46077

HOWARD, BENJAMIN WILLIAM, foundry exec.; b. Walla Walla, Wash., Mar. 20, 1938; s. Percival Gilbert and Esther Clara (Washburn) H.; A.A., Blackhawk Coll., 1963; m. Carol Anne Stiegel, Sept. 24, 1955; children—Troi Anne, Randall William, Stephanie Wynne, Monica Lea. Prodn. clk. John Deere Planter Works, Moline, Ill., 1956-57; lab. technician John Deere Malleable Works, East Moline, Ill., 1958-59, indsl. engr., 1959-63, quality control supr., 1963-65; quality control mgr. Blackhawk Foundry, Davenport, Iowa, 1965-69; sales mgr. J&J Splty. Machining Co., Milan, Ill., 1969—; v.p. ops. Bloomfield Foundry (Iowa), 1970—; pres. Vermilion Iron Corp., Hoopeston, Ill., 1977—. Mem. Am. Foundrymen's Soc. (past dir. Quad-City chpt.), Nat. Foundry Assn. (dir.), Ill. Cast Metals Assn. (dir.), Metalcasters of Iowa (past co-chmn.), Iowa-Ill.-Nebr. Foundry Mgrs. Group (past chmn.). Republican. Clubs: Moose, Viking, Mill Creek Country, Hubbard Trail Country. Office: J&J Splty Machining Co 630 W 4th St Milan IL 61264

HOWARD, HAZEL BLAND, sch. adminstr.; b. St. Louis, Jan. 21, 1947; d. Hayden and Johnnie Mae (Williams) Bland; B.S., So. Ill. U., 1969, M.Ed., 1973; m. Willie James Howard, June 10, 1977; children—Lamondes Darian, Lucillious Damone (twins). Tchr. Sch. Dist. 189, East Saint Louis, Ill., 1969-70; tchr. Promise Center for the Developmentally Disabled, East Saint Louis, 1970-73, adminstr., 1973—. Sec. Friends of the Metro-East Arts, East Saint Louis, 1978-81, chmn. grants com., 1980-81. Mem. Nat. Council Negro Women; Kappa Delta Pi, Sigma Gamma Rho. Democrat. Baptist. Clubs: East St. Louis Civic, Women of Essence Civic. Home: 8 Hillside Dr East Saint Louis IL 62203 Office: 2900 State St East Saint Louis IL 62205

HOWARD, MATTHEW ALOYSIUS, retail chain exec.; b. Columbus, Ohio, May 7, 1940; s. Francis Patrick and Elsie (Casey) H.; B.A., Ohio State U., 1962; m. Elizabeth J. O'Leary, Apr. 28, 1962; children—Matthew, Patricia, Molly. With Sears Roebuck, Chgo., 1962—; gen. mdse. office asst., 1967-68, buyer, nat. buying office, 1969-70, mktg. mgr. men's apparel, 1970-74, buying coordinator men's apparel, 1975-78, nat. mdse mgr. Sears lawn and garden, Christmas trim, pet supplies and house plants, 1978-81, nat. mdse. mgr. draperies, curtains, bedspreads and window hardware, 1981—. Bd. dirs. Gen. R.E. Wood Boys Club; v.p. Cress Creek Home Owners Assn., Naperville, Ill. Home: 1036 Royal Bombay Ct Naperville IL 60540 Office: Sears Tower Dept 671 Chicago IL 60684

HOWARD, THOMAS CLEMENT, surgeon; b. Austin, Tex., May 7, 1943; s. Walter Burke and Virginia H.; B.A., Stanford U., 1965; M.D., Yale U., 1969; m. Paula Cheryl Greenwald, June 7, 1969; children—Jennifer, Michael. Intern, Yale-New Haven Hosp., New Haven, 1969-70; resident in surgery Yale-New Haven Hosp., 1970-74; instr. in surgery Sch. of Medicine, Yale U., New Haven, 1973-74; asst. prof. surgery, Med. Center U. Nebr., Omaha, 1976—. Served with M.C. U.S. Army, 1974-76. Diplomate Am. Bd. Surgery. Fellow A.C.S., Midwestern Vascular Surg. Soc.; mem. AMA, Assn. for Acad. Surgery, Southwestern Surg. Soc., Assn. VA Surgeons. Presbyterian. Clubs: Colonial Order of the Crown (fellow), Magna Charta Barons, Hugenot Soc., SAR. Home: 1750 S 85th St Omaha NE 68124 Office: 509 Doctors Bldg Omaha NE 68131

HOWARD, WALTER BURKE, chem. engr.; b. Corpus Christi, Tex., Jan. 22, 1916; s. Clement and Nell (Smith) H.; B.A., U. Tex., 1937, B.S. in Chem. Engring., 1938, M.S., 1940, Ph.D., 1943; m. Virginia Kentucky Freeman, Feb. 14, 1942; children—Thomas Clement, Virginia Ann. From asst. to sr. chem. engr. Bur. Indsl. Chemistry, U. Tex., Austin, 1939-52; from sr. engr. to scientist Monsanto Chem. Co., Texas City, Tex., 1952-64; mgr. process safety/sci. fellow to disting. fellow Monsanto Co., St. Louis, 1965-81; process safety tech. cons. Vice-pres., Texas City Sch. Bd., 1963-64; chmn. bd. dirs. Mainland Opportunity Sch., 1958-61; mem. area council Boy Scouts, 1958-60; active P.T.A. Trustee Austin Presbyn. Theol. Sem., 1961-64. Fellow Brit. Instn. Chem. Engrs., Am. Inst. Chem. Engrs. (dir.), Am. Chem. Soc., Combustion Inst. Internat., Austin Engrs. Club (past dir.), Phi Beta Kappa, Sigma Xi, Phi Lambda Upsilon. Presbyn. (elder). Contbr chpts. to books, articles to profl. jours. Patentee in field. Home and office: 1415 Bopp Rd Saint Louis MO 63131

HOWARD, WILLIAM LIPPOLD, research engr.; b. Bklyn., July 31, 1941; s. Kenneth Painter and Norma Louise (Lippold) H.; B.A. in History, The Citadel, 1964; B. Engring. Tech., U. S. Fla., Tampa, 1979; student mil. service schs. Sales rep. Sun Oil Co., 1970-72; claims rep. Liberty Mut. Ins. Co., 1972-76; ordnance tech. research engr. Battelle Columbus (Ohio) Labs., 1980—. Served to lt. col. U.S. Army, 1964-70. Decorated Bronze Star, Army Commendation medal, others. Mem. SAR (pres. Cadet chpt.), Engring. Tech. Soc. (sec.), Assn. U.S. Army, Nat. Def. Preparedness Assn., Nat. Rifle Assn., Res. Officers Assn., Air Force Assn., Armor Assn., Mil. Order World Wars, Assn. of Century. Republican. Episcopalian. Editor: (with others) European Safety, 1966; Evacuation of U.S. Forces from France, 1967; author army booklets. Home: 309 Old Spring Ct Dublin OH 43017 Office: 505 King Ave Columbus OH 43201

HOWARTH, RALPH PERCIVAL, JR., assn. exec.; b. Cleve., July 12, 1934; s. Ralph Percival and Esther (Wells) H.; student U. Dubuque (Iowa), 1961. With Jr. Achievement, 1962—, dir. adminstrv. services, Chgo., 1973-75, exec. dir., Moline, Ill., 1975-78, Central Ill., Inc., Peoria, 1978-81; area dir. Nat. Inst. Career Advancement, Cleve., 1981—. cons. to dir. Office Career Edn., U.S. Office Edn. Served with U.S. Navy, 1953-57. Recipient Horace A. Moses award Jr. Achievement, 1977. Mem. Am. Soc. Assn. Execs. Episcopalian. Club: Rotary. Office: PO Box 22904 Beachwood OH 44122

HOWE, JONATHAN THOMAS, lawyer; b. Evanston, Ill., Dec. 16, 1940; s. Fredrick K. and Rosalie C. (Volz) H.; B.A. with honors, Northwestern U., 1963; J.D. with distinction, Duke U., 1966; m. Lois H. Braun, July 12, 1963; children—Heather C., Jonathan Thomas, Sara E. Admitted to Ill. bar, 1966, D.C. bar, 1976, Supreme Ct. bar, 1970; partner firm Jenner and Block, Chgo., 1966—; lectr. Ill. Inst. for Continuing Legal Edn., 1967, 68, 70, 72, 73, Am. Law Inst., 1968, Nat. Sch. Bds. Assn., 1973—, Practising Law Inst., 1974—. Mem. Bd. Edn., Dist. 27, Northbrook, Ill., 1969—, sec., 1969-73, pres., 1973—; mem. exec. com. Northfield Twp. Republican Orgn., 1967-71; Congressional campaign mgr. 13th Congressional Dist., Ill., 1969; mem. bd. deacons Village Presbyn. Ch. of Northbrook, 1975-78, trustee, 1981—. Mem. Am. (chmn. young lawyers sect. environ. law com. 1967-70, mem. antitrust sect. 1967—), Ill. (co-editor antitrust newsletter 1968-70), Chgo. (chmn. judiciary and bench bar relations com. 1971-72, mem. exec. com. young lawyers sect. 1971-72), D.C. bar assns., Am. Judicature Soc., Am. Soc. Assn. Execs., Nat. Sch. Bds. Assn. (dir. 1979—, exec. com. 1981—), Ill. Assn. Sch. Bds. (pres. 1977-79, dir. 1971—), Chgo. Athletic Assn., Northwestern U., Duke U. alumni assns. Republican. Presbyterian. Clubs: Chgo. Athletic Assn., Plaza, Legal, Law, Mid-America, Execs. (Chgo.); Barristers; Sunset Ridge Country (Northbrook, Ill.). Author: (with Thomas P. Sullivan) Briefs, Illinois Civil Practice , 1967, rev., 1976; (with Philip W. Tone) Illinois Appellate Practice, 1970, rev. edit., 1973; Real Estate Sales People in the United States, 1977; Liability of Real Estate Brokers, 1977; Law of Real Estate Management, 1978; Operating Considerations for Not for Profit Corporations, 1981; contbr. articles to law jours. Home: 3845 Normandy Ln Northbrook IL 60062 Office: One IBM Plaza Chicago IL 60611

HOWE, RICHARD RAY, lawyer; b. Decatur, Ill., Aug. 23, 1932; s. Elbert Davis and Marie (Harris) H.; A.B., U. Mo., 1954, J.D., 1959; m. Elaine Bondurant, Apr. 17, 1954; children—Richard R., Scott W., Dale A., Tracy. Admitted to Mo. bar, 1959, since practiced in Canton. Mem. Canton Bd. Edn., 1962-68, sec., 1962-67, v.p., 1967-68. Pros. atty. Lewis County (Mo.), 1969-72; commr., also chmn. Commn. to Reapportion Mo. Legislature, 1971. Mem., vice chmn. Mo. Commn. on Human Rights, 1974-76. Chmn., Republican Central Com. Lewis County, 1971-76, 79—; chmn. 9th Congl. Dist. Rep. Com., 1974-76. Trustee Canton Pub. Library, 1961-70. Served with USAF, 1955-57. Mem. Am. Bar Assn., Assn. Trial Lawyers Am., Am. Judicature Soc., Alpha Tau Omega, Phi Alpha Delta. Mason, Kiwanian. Home: Rural Route 2 Canton MO 63435 Office: 436 Lewis St Canton MO 63435

HOWE, ROBERT WILSON, educator; b. Klamath Falls, Oreg., July 9, 1932; s. Fred Philip and Adelaide Alice H.; B.A., Willamette U., 1954; M.S., Oreg. State U., 1960, Ed.D., 1964; m. Alma Ann Felton, Mar., 1955; children—Jeanine Adele, Jeffrey Philip. Grad. asst. Willamette U., 1954-55; tchr., counselor Arlington (Wash.) Pub. Schs., 1955-60; instr. Oreg. State U., 1961-63; asst. prof. Ohio State U., 1963-66, asso. prof., 1967-70, prof., 1970—, chmn. dept. faculty of sci. and math. edn., 1969-77; dir. ERIC Clearinghouse, 1969—; cons. fed. agencies, schs., state govts. Sec., bd. trustees Center of Sci. and Industry, Columbus, Ohio. NSF fellow, 1959, 60, 61; EPA grantee, 1977—. Fellow Ohio Acad. Sci.; mem. Nat. Sci. Tchrs. Assn., Am. Ednl. Research Assn., Assn. Educators Tchg. of Sci., Nat. Assn. for Research in Sci. Tchg., Phi Delta Kappa, others. Methodist. Contbr. articles to profl. jours. Author, co-author books, monographs. Mem. editorial bd. Jour. of Science Education, 1970—. Home: 283 Weydon Rd Worthington OH 43085 Office: 1200 Chambers Rd Columbus OH 43212

HOWE, WILLIAM HUGH, artist; b. Stockton, Calif., June 18, 1928; s. Edwin Walter and Eugenia (Mercanti) H.; A.B., Ottawa (Kans.) U., 1951. Exhibited paintings of butterflies at Philbrook Art Center, Tulsa, Ft. Worth Children's Mus., Witte Meml. Art Mus., San Antonio, Anthropology Mus., Chapultepec Park, Mexico City; represented in permanent collections: Smithsonian Instn., Washington, Cranbrook Inst., Bloomfield Hills, Mich., U. Mich. Exhibits Mus., Ann Arbor, Oak Knoll Mus., Clayton, Mo., Hax Art Center, St. Joseph, Mo., Am. Mus. Natural History, N.Y.C., Central Mo. State Coll., Warrensburg, Mich. State U., East Lansing, U. Wyo. Art Mus., Laramie, San Diego Mus. Nat. History, Balboa Park, U. Ariz., Tucson, Ill. State Mus. Art, Springfield, Mont. Hist. Soc., Helena, Wyo. State Art Mus., Cheyenne, Ariz. State U., Tempe, Milw. Pub. Mus., State Capitol Bldg., Denver, Denver Pub. Library, Kansas City (Mo.) Mus. History Sci., Presdl. Palace, Tamazunchale, San Luis Potosi, Mexico, Ottawa (Kans.) Jr. High Sch., others. Mem. Jour. Lepidopterists Soc., Burroughs Nature Club, Audubon Soc. Mo., Central States Entomo. Soc., Los Angeles County Mus. Democrat. Episcopalian. Author-artist: Our Butterflies and Moths, 1964; The Butterflies of North America, 1975; Butterfly Chart of North America, 1979. Address: 822 E 11th St Ottawa KS 66067

HOWELL, JOHN DERWIN, materials engr.; b. Portsmouth, Va., Aug. 5, 1942; s. Orland Reed and Margaret Mary (Hagan) H.; B.S. in Metall. Engring., U. Mo., Rolla, 1966. Metall. engr. Crane Co., Chgo., 1966-69, Ferraloy Foundry, Wichita, Kans., 1969-70; chief materials engr. ARCO Petroleum Products Co., Harvey, Ill., 1970—. Registered profl. engr., Ill., Calif. Mem. State Micros. Soc. Ill., Am. Petroleum Inst., Nat. Assn. Corrosion Engrs., Hist. Metall. Soc. Gt. Britain, Am. Soc. Metals, AIME, Soc. for History of Tech., Internat. Inst. for Conservation of Historic and Artistic Works. Home: 1255 N Sandberg Terr Apt 1809 E Chicago IL 60610 Office: 400 E Sibley Blvd Harvey IL 60426

HOWLAND, ANN, clin. psychologist; b. Cleve., Jan. 7, 1944; d. Richard Moulton Howland and Natalie (Fuller) Howland Merrill; adopted d. William Fessenden Merrill; B.A., Goucher Coll., 1965; M.A., U. Fla., 1971, Ph.D., 1973; children—Andrea Merrill, Joshua Howland. Clin. psychologist, treatment dir. clin. services Mt. St. Mary's Hosp., Nelsonville, Ohio, 1973-75; clin. psychologist, pvt. practice Ann Howland, Ph.D. & Assos., Athens, Ohio, 1975—; chmn. psychology service O'Bleness Hosp., 1976-78; cons. Parkersburg (W.Va.) Head Start; instr. Case Mgmt. Mental Health Technicians, 1975. Peace Corps vol., Colombia, 1966-68. Mem. Am., Ohio, Southeastern Ohio psychol. assns., Nat. Register Health Service Providers in Psychology, Athens County Humane Soc., Animal Protection Inst., Phi Kappa Phi. Democrat. Clubs: Sawgrass, Ponte Vedra (Fla.) Country. Home and Office: Rte 3 Box 163 Athens OH 45701

HOWLAND, JUANITA MAE, fire protection equipment co. ofcl.; b. Kirbyville, Mo., Sept. 7, 1929; d. Thomas Raymond and Ruth Marie (Rowley) Edwards; m. John David Howland, Mar. 24, 1949; children—Juanita Joan Howland Portier, John David, Jerri Ann. Various secretarial and office positions, 1947-72; adminstrv. asst. systems div. Edcor Safety Co., Kansas City, Mo., 1972-77; sales rep. B-H Electronics Co., Kansas City, Mo., 1977-78; pres. Able II Fire Protection Co., Toledo, 1979—. Mem. Am. Bus. Women's Assn. (chpt. pres. 1980-81), Nat. Assn. Women in Constrn. (chpt. v.p. 1979-81), Toledo C. of C., Sylvania C. of C. (dir.), Nat. Assn. Female Execs. (network dir.). Methodist. Home: 7012 Orvieto Dr Sylvania OH 43560 Office: 709 S Bryne Rd Toledo OH 43609

HOWLAND, WILLARD J., radiologist; b. Neosho, Mo., Aug. 28, 1927; s. Willard Jay and Grace Darlene (Myrphy) H.; A.B., U. Kans., 1948, M.D., 1950; M.A., U. Minn., 1958; m. Kathleen V. Jones, July 28, 1945; children—Wyck, Candice, Charles, Thomas, Heather. Intern, U.S. Naval Hosp., Newport, R.I., 1950-51; gen. practice medicine, Kans., 1951-55; resident Mayo Clinic, Rochester, Minn.,

1955-58; radiologist Ohio Valley Gen. Hosp., Wheeling, W.Va., 1959-67; prof., dir. diagnostic radiology U. Tenn. Med. Units, Memphis, 1967-68; dir., chmn. dept. radiology Aultman Hosp., Canton, Ohio, 1968—, pres. med. staff, 1978; prof., chmn. radiology council NE Ohio U. Coll. of Medicine, Rootstown, 1976—, program dir. integrated radiology residency, 1976—. Served with U.S. Army, 1945-46, with USN, 1950-51. Fellow Am. Coll. Radiology; mem. AMA, Radiol. Soc. N. Am., Am. Roentgen Ray Soc., Ohio State Radiol. Soc. (pres., 1980-81). Republican. Presbyterian. Club: Masons. Author, co-author two books and research papers in field. Home: 4445 Market Ave N Canton OH 44714 Office: Aultman Hospital 2600 6th St SW Canton OH 44710

HOWLETT, PHYLLIS LOU, educator; b. Indianola, Iowa, Oct. 23, 1932; d. James Clarence and Mabel Louella (Fisher) Hickman; B.A., Simpson Coll., 1954; m. Jerry H. Howlett, Jan. 2, 1955 (dec. 1972); children—Timothy Alan, Jane Ann; m. 2d, Ronlin L. Royer, Dec. 30, 1977. Tchr. phys. edn. Oskaloosa (Iowa) High Sch., 1954-55; psychometrist Drake U., Des Moines, 1956-57, asst. to athletic dir. men, 1974-79; asst. athletic dir. U. Kans., 1979—. Chmn. Iowa Commn. on Status Women, 1976-79; nat. pres. Assn. Vol. Burs., 1972-73; pres. Arts and Recreation Council Greater Des Moines, 1975-76; pres. Iowa Children's and Family Services, 1973. Mem. Council Coll. Women Athletic Adminstrs., Nat. Assn. Dirs. Collegiate Athletics. Republican. Mem. Jr. League. Home: 1613 Kasold Dr Lawrence KS 66044 Office: U Kans Allen Fieldhouse Lawrence KS 66045

HOWLETT, ROBERT GLASGOW, lawyer; b. Bay City, Mich., Nov. 10, 1906; s. Lewis Glasgow and Anne Lucille (Hurst) H.; B.S., Northwestern U., 1929, J.D., 1932; m. Barbara Withey, Sept. 19, 1936; children—Eleanor Howlett Burton, Craig G., Douglas W. Admitted to Ill. bar, 1932, N.Y. bar, 1940, D.C. bar, 1944, Mich. bar, 1947; mem. firm Schmidt, Howlett, Van't Hof, Snell & Vana, Grand Rapids, 1949—; mem. Mich. Employment Relations Commn., 1963-76, chmn., 1964-76; chmn. Fed. Service Impasses Panel, 1976-78; vice-chmn. Fgn. Service Impasse Disputes Panel, 1976-78, chmn., 1981—; industry mem. shipbldg. commn. Nat. War Labor Bd., 1963-65; spl. asst. atty. gen., dept. aeronautics State of Mich., 1957-61; vis. prof. Mich. State U., East Lansing, 1972, 75. Chmn. Kent County Rep. Com., 1956-61; del. Rep. Nat. Conv., 1960. Mem. Am., Grand Rapids (pres. 1962-63) bar assns., State Bar Mich., Nat. Acad. Arbitrators, Indsl. Relations Research Assn. (pres. Detroit chpt. 1978-79), Soc. Profls. in Dispute Resolution (pres. 1974-75), Assn. Labor Relations Agys. (pres. 1977-78). Clubs: Kent Country, Peninsular (Grand Rapids). Contbr. articles to profl. jours. Home: 2910 Oak Hollow Dr SE Grand Rapids MI 49506 Office: 700 Frey Bldg Grand Rapids MI 49503

HOWLEY, LEE CHRISTOPHER, lawyer; b. Cleve., June 16, 1910; s. Christopher J. and Emily A. (Smith) H.; B.A., Wittenberg Coll., 1932; LL.B., Western Res. U., 1935; m. Jean H. Hauserman, June 5, 1937; children—Tim (dec.), Dan, Kate, Lee, Tom. Admitted to Ohio bar, 1935, practiced in Cleve., 1935-39; asst. U.S. dist. atty., 1939-45; law dir. City of Cleve., 1945-51; v.p., gen. counsel Cleve. Electric Illuminating Co., 1951-75; partner firm Weston, Hurd, Fallow, Paisley & Howley, 1975—; chmn. bd. Elyria Spring & Splty. Co.; dir. E.F. Hauserman Co., Cardinal Fed. Savs. & Loan, Wenham Trucking Co.; chmn. bd. Revco, D.S., Inc., 1969—; trustee U.S. Realty Investments. Past pres., dir. Catholic Charities Corp.; mem. exec. com., past pres., past dir. Cleve. Conv. and Visitors Bur.; bd. dirs. Kaiser Found. Health Plans, Hosps.; chmn. bd. dirs. Kaiser Community Health Found. Recipient certificate of recognition for achievements in field of good govt. Cleve., U.S. Jr. chambers commerce, 1954; named hon. commr. Cleve. Mounted Police; hon. bn. chief City of Cleve. Fire Dept. Mem. Am., Ohio, Cuyahoga County, Cleve. bar assns., Ohio C. of C., Ducks Unlimited (exec. com., past chmn. bd.), Phi Gamma Delta, Delta Theta Phi. Clubs: Cleveland Athletic, City, Union, Vermilion Yacht. Home: 5430 Portage Dr Vermilion OH 44089 Office: 2500 Terminal Tower Cleveland OH 44113

HOXIE, ROY CLIFTON, JR., spice co. exec.; b. Bay City, Mich., Oct. 7, 1926; s. Roy Clifton and Margaret (Gibson) H.; grad. Food Exec. Program, Cornell U., 1966; m. Virginia Ida Feddick, Nov. 3, 1951; 1 dau., Susan Jan. With Campbell Soup Co., various locations, 1953-67; with Oscar Mayer & Co., Ill. and Wis., 1967—, sales mgr. subs. OM Ingredients Inc., Madison, 1972—. Served to 1st lt. U.S. Army, 1944-46. Decorated 2 Bronze Stars. Mem. Sales and Mktg. Execs., Inst. Food Technologists. Republican. Lutheran. Home: 106 Quarterdeck Dr Madison WI 53705 Office: 1910 Roth St Madison WI 53704

HOY, CLAUDE W(ILFORD), restaurant exec.; b. Laredo, Tex., Feb. 19, 1947; s. Robert C. and Frankie G. Hoy; student Kent State U., 1965-68; m. Patricia L. O'Brien, June 12, 1970; 1 son, Brandon J. Mgr., Perkins Pancake, Parma Heights, Ohio, 1968-69; field service rep. Famous Recipe Fried Chicken, Dayton, Ohio, 1969-71, owner, operator restaurants, Vermilion, Ohio, 1971—; food advisor Sandusky Sailing Club, 1976-81. Aux. dep. sheriff Sheriff's Dept. of Erie County (Ohio), 1970-71. Recipient Sales awards Famous Recipe Fried Chicken Co. Mem. Famous Recipe Franchise Holders Assn. (nat. chmn. 1978-81, bd. dirs. for nat. advt. 1971-75, 1978-80), Internation Famous Recipe Franchisee Assn. (sec. 1980). Republican. Methodist. Clubs: Optimists (sec.-treas. club 1979-81, Most Valuable Optimist, Sandusky 1980); Masons. Office: PO Box 403 Vermilion OH 44035

HOYLAND, JANET LOUISE, govt. ofcl.; b. Kansas City, Mo., July 21, 1940; d. Robert J. and Dora Louise (Worley) H.; B.A., Carleton Coll., 1962; postgrad. in music (Mu Phi Epsilon scholar 1966) U. Mo. at Kansas City, 1964-67; M.L.A., So. Meth. U., 1979. Policy writer Lynn Ins. Co., Kansas City, 1963-64; music librarian U. Mo. at Kansas City, 1966-68; benefit authorizer Social Security Adminstrn., Kansas City, Mo., 1969-75, tech. specialist, 1976-79, claims authorizer, 1980—; piano tchr. Leta Wallace Piano Studio, Kansas City, 1963, 68; piano accompanist Barn Players, Overland Park, Kans., 1972-75, Off Broadway Dinner Playhouse, Inc., Kansas City, 1973, Resident Theatre, Kansas City, 1979. Co-chmn. Project Equality work area, 1971; work area chmn. on ecumenism Council on Ministries, 1969-70; sec. fair housing action com. Council on Religion and Race, Kansas City, 1968. Active ward and precinct work Democratic Com. for County Progress, 1968. Mem. Women's Div. Kansas City Philharmonic, Friends of Art Kansas City, Fellowship House Assn. Kansas City, Internat. Platform Assn., Kansas City Mus. Club (chmn. composition dept. 1967-68), Mu Phi Epsilon (v.p. Kansas City 1968, sec. 1971, pres. 1975-76), Pi Kappa Lambda. Methodist. Home: 4322 Rockhill Rd Kansas City MO 64110

HOYT, GEORGE SAYRE, mfg. co. exec.; b. Bainbridge, N.Y., Apr. 17, 1943; s. Richard Wilson and Dorothy Mae (Corcoran) H.; B.S. in I.E., Purdue U., 1967; M.B.A., U. Chgo., 1975; m. Marie Louise Syracuse, Nov. 12, 1966; 1 son, Richard Wilson. Quality engr. Sundstrand Corp., Rockford, Ill., 1966-72, materiel systems mgr., 1972-74, mfg. systems mgr., 1974-78, prodn. planning mgr., 1978-79, materiel training mgr., 1979—; owner Hoyt Video Prodns., 1981—; project bus. cons. Mem. adv. bd. No. Ill. U.; mem. curriculum adv. bd. Rock Valley Coll., 1979—, chmn., 1981—. Cert. quality engr., Am. Soc. Quality Control, 1972; cert. fellow Am. Prodn. and Inventory Control Soc., 1977—, cert. chmn., 1979—. Mem. Am. Soc. for Tng. and Devel., Am. Film Inst., Am. Prodn. and Inventory Control Soc., Alpha Pi Mu. Home: 6292 Graydon Rd Rockford IL 61109 Office: 4747 Harrison Ave Rockford IL 61101

HOYT, KENNETH LOYD, public relations fund raising exec.; b. Ashtabula, Ohio, July 24, 1948; s. John F. and Orletta A. Hoyt; B.A. in Bus. Adminstrn., Baldwin-Wallace Coll., 1970; M.A. in Journalism, Ohio State U., 1978; m. Marcia Swigart, Apr. 6, 1974. Asst. to public relations dept. Baldwin-Wallace Coll., Berea, Ohio, 1966-70, asst. to exec. v.p. coll. relations and adminstrn., 1970-74; asst. to exec. v.p. merchandising Internat. Artware Corp., Cleve., 1970, also dir. advt., 1970; dir. devel. Otterbein Coll., Westerville, Ohio, 1974-75; dir. public relations and devel. Ohio Presbyn. Homes, Columbus, 1975—. Mem. Public Relations Soc. Am., Nat. Assn. Fund-Raising Execs. (founder central Ohio chpt. 1979, pres. 1978-79), Ohio Council Fund-Raising Execs., Columbus C. of C. Republican. Home: 3266 Lansmere Rd Shaker Heights OH 44122 Office: 6800 N High St Columbus OH 43085

HOYT, RICHARD COMSTOCK, econs. consulting co. exec.; b. St. Paul, Sept. 30, 1939; s. Charles Richardson and Minnie (Comstock) H.; B.S., Kans. State U., 1961; M.S., U. Minn., 1968, Ph.D., 1972; m. Ingrid Langensiepen, Oct. 24, 1964; children—Monika Anna, Derek Richard. Milling engr. Tennant & Hoyt Co., Lake City Minn., 1971-72, pres., 1972; research asst. U. Minn., 1968-71; pres. Analytics, Inc., Excelsior, Minn., 1973—; lectr. in field. Served with C.E., U.S. Army, 1962-65. Mem. Am. Econ. Assn., Am. Agrl. Econ. Assn., Mgmt. Sci. Assn. Republican. Contbr. articles in field to profl. jours. Home: 5975 Ridge Rd Excelsior MN 55331 Office: 464 2d St Excelsior MN 55331

HOZIAN, JACOB MARTIN, interior designer; b. Chgo., Feb. 17, 1934; s. Martin James and Gertrude Dorothy (Houska) H.; diploma Chgo. Sch. Art and Design, 1964-67. Staff, C.D. Peacock Co., Chgo., 1950, Tiffany and Co., N.Y.C., 1951; featured performer skating soloists Holiday on Ice Shows, N.Y.C., 1952-56; performer Blvd. Room Ice Show, Chgo., 1958-67; interior designer Delores Miller & Assos., Chgo., 1967-69; Contract Interiors for Bus., Chgo., 1969—. Served with U.S. Army, 1956-58. Office: 500 N Orleans St Chicago IL 60610

HRACHOVINA, FREDERICK VINCENT, osteo. physician and surgeon; b. St. Paul, Sept. 2, 1926; s. Vincent Frank and Beatrice (Funda) H.; B.A. in Chemistry, Macalester Coll., 1948; D.O., Kirksville (Mo.) Coll. Osteopathy and Surgery, 1956; m. Joan Halverson, July 2, 1955. Chemist, Twin City area, 1948-51; intern Clare (Mich.) Gen. Osteo. Hosp., 1956-57; pvt. practice, Mpls., 1957—; founder Physician Placement Service, 1975—. Smith, Kline & French Labs. grantee, 1973. Mem. Am. (council fed. health programs, drug enforcement adminstrn. prescribers working com. 1974-75), Minn. (pres. 1965-66, exec. dir. 1966-74, pub. relations dir. 1974-75) osteo. assns., Assn. Osteo. State Exec. Dirs. (pres. 1970-71, dir. 1971-74), Am. Coll. Gen. Practitioners Osteo. Medicine and Surgery (lectr. Mo. soc.), Am. Acad. Osteopathy, Am. Assn. Sr. Physicians, Am. Blood Resources Assn., Minn. Gymnastic Assn. (founder 1962-72), Twin City Model A Ford Club. Mason (Shriner). Clubs: Breakfast, Optimist (dir. Mpls. 1959-62, 69-72, pres. 1970-71, gen. chmn. floor exercise gymnastic program 1959-65), Antique Auto Am., Minn. car, Classic Car Am. (membership chmn. Upper Midwest Region 1977, sec. 1978), Cadillac La Salle (founder, treas. North Star Region). Author: Microscopic Anatomy, 1952; Methods of Development for New Osteopathic Medical Colleges in the Next Millennium, 1977. Contbr. articles to profl. jours. Home: 3655 47th Ave S Minneapolis MN 55406 Office: 202 Inland Bldg 1000 2d Ave S Minneapolis MN 55403

HRASTICH, THOMAS ANTHONY, chem. engr.; b. St. Louis, Nov. 25, 1943; s. Anthony Christian and Amy Louise (Heege) H.; B.S. in Chem. Engring., U. Mo., Rolla, 1965; postgrad. U. Mo., Columbia, 1965-68, Jacksonville (Ala.) State U., 1971-72, St. John's U., 1972-73; children—Jeffrey, Thomas. Asst. plant mgr. BASF Wyandotte Corp., Troy, Mich., 1974-75, plant mgr., 1975-79, sr. project engr., 1979-80; ops. mgr. Motor Oils Refining Co., 1980—. Served to capt., U.S. Army, 1968-73. Decorated Bronze star, air medals. Mem. Am. Chem. Soc., Am. Inst. Chem. Engrs., AAAS. Office: 7601 W 47th St McCook IL 60525

HRINKO, JEAN AYR, educator; b. Goes, Ohio, Mar. 20, 1923; B.S. in Elementary Edn., Wittenberg Coll., Springfield, Ohio, 1968; postgrad. in spl. edn. U. Dayton, Kent (Ohio) State U.; married; 1 child. Tchr., Mad-River Green Sch., Enon, Ohio, 1964-68; tchr. Springfield Pub. Sch., 1968—; mem. Ohio Low Incidence Curriculum Com. Vol. info. desk Mercy and Community hosps., also St. John's Convalescent Home, Springfield. Mem. Civic Opera Guild, 1974—. Mem. NEA, Ohio Edn. Assn., Springfield Tchrs. Assn. Ohio Deaf Tchrs. Assn., Quota Internat. for Deaf, Theta Phi Gamma, Alpha Iota. Jennings scholar, 1970-71. Certified, Ohio; specialist in field of hearing impaired, educable mentally retarded. Home: 3641 Troy Rd Springfield OH 45504 Office: 1452 S Wittenberg Ave Springfield OH 45506

HROMATKO, WESLEY VINTON, clergyman; b. Slayton, Minn., Oct. 2, 1947; s. Annel J. and Maybelle (Moffatt) H.; B.A. cum laude, U. Minn., 1969, M.A., 1971; D. Ministry, Meadville Theol. Sch., Lombard Coll., 1973; m. Marilyn Blitzstein, Sept. 17, 1978. Ordained to ministry Unitarian Universalist Ch., Oaklandon, Ind., 1973; pastor Oaklandon Universalist Ch., Indpls., 1973-75, First Unitarian Ch., Hobart, Ind., 1975—; instr. Sem. of the Community, Chgo., Gary, Ind., 1980—. Founding mem. Ind. Religious Coalition for Abortion Rights, 1974-75; mem. Eastern Lawrence Twp. Planning Commn., Ind., 1974-75; mem. Hobart (Ind.) Am. Revolutionary Bicentennial Com., 1976; bd. dirs. Unitarian Universalist Council, Chgo. area; bd. dirs. Oaklandon Civic Assn., Indpls., 1974-75; bd. dirs. Ind. Civil Liberties Union, Calumet, 1980—, treas., 1980—; adv. bd. Lake County (Ind.) CETA, v.p., 1980-81. Recipient Entemann Ohanian award Unitarian Universalist Service Com., 1975. Mem. Unitarian Universalist Ministers Assn., Unitarian Universalist Hist. Soc., Internat. Assn. Religious Freedom, Hobart Ministerial Assn. (v.p. 1980-81), Religious Humanists, Unitarian Hist. Soc., Meadville Theol. Sch. Alumni. Co-editor: Appeal of the Irreligious, 1980; contbr. articles to religious publs. Home: 1310 Garfield St Hobart IN 46342 Office: PO Box 291 5th and Main Sts Hobart IN 46342

HRUBY, PAUL JAMES, sales and mktg. services exec.; b. Cleve., July 30, 1927; s. John and Jennie (Matousek) H.; B.B.A., Western Res. U., 1951, M.B.A., 1967; m. Theresa M. Tulcewicz, Oct. 3, 1964; children—Maria, Faith Ann, Paul James. Asst. product mgr. Harshaw Chem. Co., Cleve., 1951-61; mktg. analyst Shell Oil Corp., Cleve., 1962; tech. sales rep. N.Am. Mogul Products Co., Cleve., 1963-64; mktg. and sales mgr. Marlin Mfg. Corp., Cleve., 1964-76; pres., owner Pathon Co., Cleve., 1976—. Active Big Bros., 1963-67; former cons., judge Jr. Achievement. Served with USNR, 1945-46. Mem. Sales and Mktg. Execs. Internat., Soc. Plastic Engrs., Cleve. Bd. Area Realtors. Republican. Roman Catholic. Club: Cayomaw (hon., past pres., trustee). Home and Office: 4352 Brendan Ln North Olmsted OH 44070

HRUBY, THOMAS JOSEPH, sales ofcl.; b. St. Jospeh, Mo., Aug. 21, 1934; s. V. George and Katherine Helen H.; B.B.A., Gen. Motors Inst., 1957; m. Joan Marie Fisher, Oct. 20, 1956; children—Jodie Kay Hruby Beggs, Jill Marie, John Thomas, Thomas Joseph. With Central Foundry div. Gen. Motors, 1956—, supervisory positions, Defiance (Ohio) plant, 1956-62, market forecaster, div. offices, Saginaw, Mich., 1962-66, direct sales rep., 1966-76, mgr. sales ops., 1976—. Active, Mich. Republicans; sustaining mem. Rep. Nat. Com. Recipient achievement award United Fund Saginaw County, 1977. Mem. Am. Foundrymen's Soc., Indsl. Exec. Club, C. of C. Clubs: Gen. Motors Inst. Alumni, K.C. Office: 77 W Center Saginaw MI 48605

HRUSKA, JAMES EMIL, museum founder, dir.; b. Waterville, Minn., June 16, 1912; s. Emil and Minnie Mabel (Belden) H.; student W.H. Dunwoody Inst., Minn., 1930; m. Dorothy Irene Gartamaker, Sept. 20, 1941; 1 son, David Kent. Postoffice worker, Waterville, 1931-73; dir. Le Sueur County Hist. Soc. Museum, Elysian, Minn.; adult edn. tchr. Waterville-Elysian Schs., 1976-79; lectr. Lake Sakata State Park, Waterville. Mem. Civil Defense dir., 1960-64; mem. Cannon Valley Developmental Assn., bd. dirs., 1970; mem. adv. com. Minn. Agrl. Interpretive Center, 1977-78; adv. bd. LeSueur County Arts Council, 1978—. Mem. Minn. Territorial Pioneers (life; pres. 1980-81), Minn. State Hist. Soc., Le Sueur County Hist. Soc. (life mem., pres. 1968-70, 72—, bd. mem. 1968-71), Minn. State Archeol. Soc., Pioneerland Hist. Assembly (v.p. 1972-73, pres. 1974-75), So. Minn. Hist. Assembly (dir. 1977—). Roman Catholic. Club: K.C. Established Le Sueur County Hist. Soc. Mus.; asso. editor Stepping Stones 76; contbg. author LeSueur County Atlas, 1975; contbr. to Minn. Territorial Pioneers' Pioneer Chronicles, Remember When. Home: 306 W Lake Waterville MN 56096 Office: Box 557 Elysian MN 56028

HSIA, JOHN YUAN, restaurant owner; b. Kaohsiung, Taiwan, Feb. 24, 1948; came to U.S., 1971, naturalized, 1981; s. Yu-Tse and Chao-Sun (Sue) H.; B.S., Taiwan Cheng-Kung U., 1970; M.S., U. Miss., 1974; m. Mary Tai, Mar. 26, 1974; 1 dau., Annie. Capt., House of Hunan, Chgo., 1976-78; pres., mgr. House of Hunan, Cin., 1978—; owner, mgr. House of Hunan, Louisville, 1981-82. Office: 34 W 7th St Cincinnati OH 45202

HSIEH, PAUL I-PO, engring. specialist; b. Canton, China, Sept. 12, 1938; s. Lin Yui and Hwan Lai H.; Ph.D., U. Ga., 1978; 1 son, Mike Y. Asst. prof. N.Mex. State U., Las Cruces, 1977-78; research asso. Carnegie-Mellon U., Pitts., 1978-79; sr. reliability engr. Bechtel Power Corp., Ann Arbor, Mich., 1979—. Mem. adv. com. New Pride Project, Nat. Inst. Juvenile Justice and Delinquency Prevention, 1979—. Mem. Am. Statis. Assn., Am. Nuclear Soc., Am. Soc. Quality Control, Phi Kappa Phi, Pi Mu Epsilon. Roman Catholic. Home: 2962 Birch Hollow Dr 1-B Ann Arbor MI 48104 Office: 777 E Eisenhower Pkwy Ann Arbor MI 48106

HSU, CHEN CHAO, chemist; b. Changhwa, Taiwan, June 29, 1940; came to U.S., 1967, naturalized, 1976; s. Shui Y. and Pin (Yang) Hsu; B.S. in Chemistry, Nat. Taiwan Normal U., 1963; M.S. in Phys. Chemistry, Brigham Young U., 1969; Ph.D., U. Utah, 1972; m. Nancy F. Lai, Jan. 13, 1966; children—Samuel, Sandra. Teaching asst. Brigham Young U., Provo, Utah, 1967-69; teaching and research asst. U. Utah, Salt Lake City, 1969-72; postdoctoral research asso. U. Chgo., 1972-74; software engr. Bell & Howell, Pasadena, Calif., 1974-75; phys. chemist Argonne (Ill.) Nat. Lab., 1975—; cons. in field. Pres., Parent Adv. com., Head Start Day Care Center, Salt Lake City, 1972; v.p. Taiwanese Credit Union of Chgo., 1979-80, sec., 1980-81. Taiwan Provincial Govt. scholar, 1967-72. Mem. Am. Chem. Soc. (mem. com. profl. relations and status, Chgo. sect., 1977-78), Electrochem. Soc., Taiwanese Assn. Am. (dir., pres. Greater Chgo. chpt. 1980-81), Sigma Xi. Club: Taiwanese Toastmasters. Contbr. articles to profl. jours. Home: 8217 Westview Ln Woodridge IL 60517 Office: Argonne Nat Lab 9700 S Cass Ave Argonne IL 60439

HSU, DEH YUAN, environ. engr.; b. Shan-si, China, Jan. 1, 1943; s. Jen Tsi and Shen Shian H.; B.S., Nat. Taiwan U., 1964; M.S., Northwestern U., 1968, Ph.D., 1973; m. Lillian L.C. Wang, May 20, 1971; 1 son, Andrew S.L. Research asso. McGill U., Montreal, Que., Can., 1972-74; asst. prof. Wayne State U., Detroit, 1975-78; process engr. Greeley & Hansen, Chgo., 1978—. Registered profl. engr., Mich., Taiwan. Mem. ASCE, Am. Water Works Assn., Water Pollution Control Fedn., Chinese Engr. Assn. Office: Greeley & Hansen 222 S Riverside Plaza Chicago IL 60606

HSU, JAMES PEI-LIANG, orthopedic surgeon; b. Taipei, Taiwan, May 6, 1942; s. Shui-Te and Chun-Tzu (Lee) H.; M.D., Taipei Med. Coll., 1966; m. Yeh-Sun W. Hsu, Oct. 17, 1976; 1 son, Timothy W. Intern, Cook County Hosp., Chgo., 1967-68; resident in pathology Wayne State U., 1968-69, in general surgery Good Samaritan Hosp., 1969-70, in orthopedic surgery U., Cin., 1970-73; Handfellow U. Louisville, 1973-74; practice medicine specializing in orthopedic and hand surgery, Cin., 1974—; mem. staffs Bethesda Hosp., Children's Hosp., Christ Hos., Deaconess Hosp. Fellow A.C.S., Am. Acad. Orthopedic Surgeons; mem. AMA, Ohio Orthopedic Soc., Ohio Med. Assn., Tristate Orthopedic Soc. Home: 11907 Montgomery Rd Cincinnati OH 45242 Office: 9030 Montgomery Rd Cincinnati OH 45242

HSU, JOHN J., psychiatrist; b. China, Oct. 14, 1919; s. Ku Chin and Juen-Mei (Shih) H.; M.D., Coll. Medicine Nat. Central U., Nanking, China, 1944; m. Elizabeth Chang, Oct. 14, 1946; children—James, Nancy, Timothy, Esther, John R. Asst. dept. physiology Coll. Medicine Nat. Central U., 1945-49; pvt. practice, Taipei, Formosa, 1950-54; resident physician Camden (N.J.) County Hosp., 1954-56; resident Pontiac (Mich.) State Hosp., 1957-60, dir. male in-patient dept., 1960-62, dir. research, 1962-65, dir. alcoholism program, 1961-65; pvt. practice psychiatry, Pontiac, 1965-74, Bloomfield Hills, Mich., 1974—; mem. staff dept. psychiatry Pontiac Gen. Hosp., 1963—, chmn. dept. psychiatry, 1973-75; mem. staff St. Joseph Mercy Hosp., 1965-75. Pres., Com. on Alcoholism, Pontiac, 1965-66, Oakland County (Mich.) Com. on Alcoholism, 1966-67; bd. dirs. Alcoholics Anonymous, Pontiac, 1965—; mem. med. bd. City Drug Abuse Treatment Program, 1970-74. Fellow Am. Assn. Social Psychiatry; mem. AAAS, Am. Psychiat. Assn., Mich. Psychiat. Soc., AMA, Am. Soc. Clin. Hypnosis. Contbr. articles in field to med. jours. Home: 7224 Old Mill Rd Birmingham MI 48010 Office: 10 W Square Lake Rd Suite 104 Bloomfield Hills MI 48013

HSU, KUANG-LIANG, library educator; b. Honan, China, Jan. 11, 1931; s. Wen-ching and Feng-Wei (Ling) H.; came to U.S., 1963, naturalized, 1972; M.L.S., George Peabody Coll. for Tchrs., 1965, Ph.D., 1972; m. Susie Nok-sau, Dec. 24, 1961; children—Ting-yu Tim, May Chun, Sophia Chun, Kean Yu. Asst. librarian Valley City State Coll., 1965; head cataloger, asst. prof. library sci. Willamette U., 1966-68; Doctoral fellow, research asso. Internat. Center, George Peabody Coll. for Tchrs., 1969-70; asst. prof. East Tex. State U., 1971-72, asso. prof., 1972-73; asso. prof. Ball State U., 1973-76, prof., 1976—, chmn. Asia studies com., 1980-81. Faculty Assn. grantee, 1981. Mem. Assn. Ednl. Communications and Tech., Ind. Assn. Ednl. Communications and Tech. (dist. program chmn. 1974-75, dist. dir. 1975-76), Chinese-Am. Librarians Assn. (chmn. Midwest chpt. 1981-82), Assn. Am. Library Schs., Phi Delta Kappa, Phi Tau Phi.

Baptist. Author: Chinese Education and Society: A Bibliographic Guide, 1972; Library and Information Sciences: Textbooks-in-Use: A Master Checklist, 1976. Office: Room 300 NQ Bldg Ball State U Muncie IN 47306

HUANG, JOSEPH JUIN-SHYONG, structural engr.; b. Taiwan, China, Nov. 20, 1941; s. Huang Chuan Shou and Huang Juan Hsu; came to U.S., 1966, naturalized, 1977; B.S. in Civil Engring., Nat. Taiwan U., 1965; M.S., Lehigh U., 1968, Ph.D., 1973; m. Vivian Weiwei Wang, June 20, 1970; children—Peter B., Andrew B. Post-doctoral research asso. Lehigh U., Bethlehem, Pa., 1973; sr. structural engr. Skidmore, Owings & Merrill, Chgo., 1973-75; sr. structural engring. specialist Sargent & Lundy, Chgo., 1976—. Recipient A.F. Davis Silver medal Am. Welding Soc., 1971; registered profl. and structural engr., Ill. Mem. ASCE, Am. Concrete Inst., Structural Engrs. Assn. Ill., Sigma Xi, Contbr. engring. articles to profl. jours. Home: 806 N East Ave Oak Park IL 60302 Office: Sargent & Lundy 55 E Monroe St Chicago IL 60603

HUANG, NELSON SHIANG-LUNG, coll. adminstr.; b. Anxi, Fujian, China, June 9, 1941; s. Chun Sen and Chian Wan H.; B.A., Wayland Bapt. Coll., 1967; M.A., Colo. State U., 1969. Instr. behavioral scis. humanities div. State Community Coll., East St. Louis, Ill., 1970-76, chmn. behavioral scis. humanities div., 1976-78, coordinator Title III project, 1978-81, coordinator planning and research, 1981—. Mem. Am. Mgmt. Assn. Baptist. Office: 417 Missouri Ave East Saint Louis IL 62201

HUBBARD, ALAN EUGENE, mktg. exec.; b. Manito, Ill., July 6, 1937; s. George H. and Amy L. (Runyon) H.; B.S. in Mktg., Bradley U., 1959; m. Barbara E. Heyl, Nov. 28, 1957; children—George Alan, James Wesley, Constance JoAnne. Credit sales mgr. Sears, Roebuck & Co., Marion, Ind., 1960-62, regional credit supr., Chgo., 1963-64, Midwest territorial supr., 1965-68, credit central mgr., Peoria, Ill., 1969-70, Louisville, 1971-74, Midwest territory credit mktg. mgr., Skokie, Ill., 1974—; v.p., sec. Catering By George, Northbrook, Ill.; co-propr. Baskin-Robbins, Northbrook, Ill. Mem. Ky. Consumer Credit Assn. (pres. 1973-74), Soc. Consumer Credit Execs., Ky. C. of C., Ky. Assn. Ky. Cols., U.S. Power Squadron, Northbrook C. of C., U.S. C. of C. Clubs: Elks, Sertoma. Home: 152 Bertling St Winnetka IL 60093 Office: 7447 Skokie Blvd Skokie IL 60077

HUBBARD, DAVID STEVENS, mfg. co. exec.; b. Pitts., Sept. 16, 1944; s. George S. and Janet (Goodwin) H.; B.S. in Engring., Cornell U., 1966, M.S. in Chem. Engring., 1967; m. Aug. 26, 1967; 1 dau., Ashlie Anne. Product devel. engr. Procter & Gamble, Cin., 1967-72, sect. mgr., 1972-75, mgr. product devel., Frankfurt, W. Ger., 1975-78, asso. dir. shortening and oil products Food div., Cin., 1978—. Small bus. co-chmn. United Appeal of Cin., 1974. Mem. Am. Oil Chemists Soc. Republican. Presbyterian. Office: 6071 Center Hill Rd F2A10 Cincinnati OH 45224

HUBBARD, DEAN LEON, coll. pres.; b. Nyssa, Oreg., June 17, 1939; B.A., Andrews U., 1961, M.A., 1962; Ph.D., Stanford U., 1979; m. Aleta Ann Thornton, July 12, 1959; children—Melody, Paul, Joy. Ordained to ministry Seventh-day Adventist Ch., 1966; pastor, Rice Lake, Wis., 1962-66; dir. Korean Union Ministerial Assn., 1966-71; founder, dir. English lang. schs., Korea, 1969-71; cons. Bd. Higher Edn., N. Am. div. Seventh-day Adventists, 1972-74; cons. Exxon Edn. Found., 1975-78; acad. dean, dir. instl. research Union Coll., Lincoln, Nebr., 1976-80, pres., 1980—. Chmn. planning Bd. Nebr. Ednl. TV Council for Higher Edn., 1979-80. Mem. North Central Assn. Colls. and Schs. (commr. 1980—), Am. Assn. Higher Edn., Soc. Coll. and Univ. Planning, Assn. Instl. Research, Phi Delta Kappa. Club: Rotary. Office: 3800 S 48th St Lincoln NE 68506

HUBBARD, EDWARD EARL, edn. devel. co. exec.; b. Cleve., June 23, 1953; s. Bennie and Geneva Hubbard; B.A., Ohio State U., Columbus, 1974, M.A., 1975; Ed.D. (hon.), Addison State U., Ont., Can., 1980; divorced; 1 son, Edward Earl, II. Computer programmer Xerox Corp., Columbus, 1974; with computer ops. dept. Battelle Meml. Inst., Columbus, 1975-76; adminstrv. asso. Ohio State U., 1975, dir. developmental edn., 1975-78; edn. cons. Davis Assos., Columbus, 1975-80; with computer ops. support dept. Xerox Corp., 1975; edn. devel. specialist Informatics, Inc., Columbus, 1978-81; pres. Fin. Info. and Resources Mgmt. Co., 1981; vis. prof. Denison U., Granville Ohio; cons. Dow Chem. Co.; mem. Devel. Edn. Commn., Ohio Bd. Regents. Chmn. fundraising com. Fedn. Community Orgns. Columbus, 1981. Recipient various service awards. Mem. Am. Soc. Tng. and Devel., Am. Fedn. Musicians. Author handbook. Home: 4008 Gateway Dr Englewood OH 45322

HUBBARD, FREDERICK CONGDON, warehouse co. exec.; b. St. Louis, Mich., May 25, 1916; s. Benjamin Congdon and Mary Paul (Garrett) H.; A.B., U. Chgo., 1938; m. Millicent McElwee, July 12, 1947; children—Thomas Frederick, Amy Louise. Cost accountant Am. Seating Co., Grand Rapids, Mich., 1939-41; with Elston-Richards Storage Co., Grand Rapids, 1946—, v.p., 1949-55, pres., 1955-79, chmn. bd., 1979—; pres. Asso. Warehouses Inc., Chgo., 1964-65. Vice pres. Friends of Aquinas Coll. Library, 1971-73, pres., 1974-75. Bd. dirs. Mich. State Accident Fund, 1955—, vice-chmn., 1968-79, chmn. bd., 1979—; bd. dirs. Grand Rapids Civic Theatre, v.p., 1964-70; bd. dirs. Community Health Service, 1979—, Vis. Nurses Assn., 1979—. Served to capt. C.E., AUS, 1941-46; ETO. Recipient (with wife) Clay award Grand Rapids Civic Theatre, 1969. Mem. Mich. (dir. 1947-53), Ohio (dir. 1972-74), Ind. (pres. 1976-78) wholesale assns., U. Chgo. Alumni Club (pres. 1940-41). Republican. Episcopalian (vestryman). Mason. Club: University (Grand Rapids). Home: 3211 Lake Dr SE Grand Rapids MI 49506 Office: 3739 Patterson Ave Grand Rapids MI 49508

HUBBARD, PAUL LEONARD, orgn. exec.; b. Cin., Oct. 31, 1942; s. Paul William and Sylvia Lenora H.; B.S., Ohio U., 1965; postgrad. Wayne State U., 1971; 1 son, Paul Anthony. Coordinator distbv. edn. Northwestern High Sch., Detroit, 1965-69; asso. dir. Family and Neighborhood Services of Western Wayne County, Inkster, Mich., 1971-74; v.p. New Detroit, Inc., 1974—. Treas. bd. dirs. Homes for Black Children, 1970-76, Project Child, 1974—; vice chmn. State of Mich. Examiners Bd. of Social Workers, 1972-74; mem. Gov.'s Task Force on Violence and Vandalism in Schs., chmn. subcom. on social and community resources. Mem. Nat. Assn. Black Social Workers (nat. conf. chmn. 1977-78). Baptist. Home: 14350 Forrer St Detroit MI 48227 Office: 1010 Commonwealth Bldg 719 Griswold St Detroit MI 48226

HUBBARD, WILLIAM NEILL, JR., pharm. co. exec.; b. Fairmont, N.C., Oct. 15, 1919; s. William Neill and Mary Emma (Fenegan) H.; A.B., Columbia U., 1942; postgrad. U. N.C. Sch. Medicine; M.D., N.Y. U., 1944; m. Elizabeth Terleski, Dec. 28, 1945; children—William Neill III, Michael J., Mary E., Elizabeth A., Susan E. Mem. house staff 3d med. div. Bellevue Hosp., N.Y.C., 1944-50; instr. medicine N.Y. U., 1950-53, asst. prof., 1953-59, asst. dean, then asso. dean N.Y. U. Coll. Medicine, 1951-59; dean U. Mich. Med. Sch., 1959-70, asso. prof. internal medicine, 1959-64, prof., 1964-70, dir. U. Mich. Med. Center, 1969-70; gen. mgr. pharm. div., v.p. Upjohn Co., 1970-72, exec. v.p., 1972-74, pres., 1974—, dir., 1968—; dir. 1st Am. Bank Corp., Hoover Universal Inc., Consumers Power. Cons. USPHS; mem. Nat. Adv. Commn. on Libraries, 1966-68; med. adv. com. W.K. Kellogg Found., 1959-67; mem. Gov.'s Adv. Com. on Edn. Health Care, 1965-69; chmn. Gov.'s Action Com. on Corrections, 1972-73; mem. panel ednl. consultants Commn. on Edn. for Health Adminstrn., 1973-75; mem. com. on med. edn. Brown U., 1974-77; mem. nat. sci. bd. NSF, 1974—; mem. bd. sci. and tech. for internat. devel. Nat. Acad. Scis., 1978—, Council on Sci. and Tech. for Devel., 1978—; bd. visitors in East Asian studies U. Mich., 1976—; bd. overseers Morehouse Coll., 1976—; bd. dirs. Nat. Med. Fellowships, Inc., 1973-75, Nat. Fund. Med. Edn., 1962-75; trustee Kalamazoo Coll., 1973-78; mem. bd. regents Nat. Library of Medicine, 1963-67, 72-76, chmn., 1965-67, 74-76, cons., 1976—; bd. dirs. Am. Near East Refugee Aid, 1977—. Fellow A.C.P.; mem. Harvey Soc., N.Y. Acad. Medicine, Soc. Alumni Bellevue Hosp., Mich. Med. Soc. (council 1960-62), AMA, Kalamazoo Acad. Medicine, Am. Soc. Clin. Pharmacology and Therapeutics, Assn. Am. Med. Colls. (pres. 1966-67), Sigma Xi, Alpha Omega Alpha. Home: 1401 Lama Rd Kalamazoo MI 49008 Office: 7000 Portage Rd Kalamazoo MI 49001

HUBBELL, ROGER SHERMAN, mfg. co. exec.; b. Fayette, Iowa, Sept. 9, 1916; s. Roger Sherman and Rose Fernietta (Dunbar) H.; student Upper Iowa Coll., 1933-36; B.S.E.E., U. Wis., 1940; m. Opal Handy, May 2, 1936 (dec.); children—Roger Sherman, Sandra, Jonathan, Margaret; m. Janet M. Schmit, Dec. 30, 1965. With Allis Chalmers, Milw., 1940-76, corp. compensation mgr., 1961-76; dir. corp. compensation and benefits Fiat-Allis, 1976-79; dir. corp. compensation Nat. Can Corp., Chgo., 1979—. Asso. chmn., project leader Wis. Com. on Improved Expenditure Mgmt., 1965; chmn. Wis. Legis. Compensation Council, 1968-75. Recipient Cert. of Merit, Warren P. Knowles, Gov. of Wis., 1965, Mayor Henry Maier, Milw., 1976. Fellow Soc. for Advancement of Mgmt.; mem. Am. Compensation Assn., Indsl. Relations Assn. of Chgo., Exec. Compensation Inst. (founder). Home: 1672 Clendenin Ln Riverwoods IL 60015 Office: 8101 Higgins Rd Chicago IL 60631

HUBER, RITA NORMA, civic worker; b. Cin., July 16, 1931; d. Andrew Elwood and Mary Gertrude (Hille) Stewart; student Cin. Coll. Conservatory Music, 1949-50, Berlitz Sch., Cin., 1951-52; m. Justin G. Huber, July 17, 1954; children—Monica Ann, Sarah Marie, Rachel Miriam. Tchr. Russian lang. for officers' Wives, Ft. Sill, Okla., 1955-56; bd. dirs. United Community Services, Cedar Rapids, Iowa, 1969; founder, chairperson Linn County Consumers League, 1969-70; founder, pub. relations dir. Cedar Rapids Rape Crisis Services, 1974—; vice chmn. Linn County Bd. Health; chairperson Linn County Democratic Women's Club, 1966-67, Linn County com. Eugene McCarthy for Pres., 1967-68; campaign mgr. Delores Cortez for Iowa Legislature, 1968, Jan V. Johnson for Iowa Legislature, 1970, Stanley Ginsberg for county supr. Linn County, 1974, E.L. Colton for Cedar Rapids pub. safety commr., 1977; chairperson Linn County Dem. Central Com., 1976—; state coordinator Jerry Brown for Pres., 1976; mem. Iowa and Nat. Women's Polit. Caucus; instr. parliamentary procedures Cedar Rapids Women's Community Leadership Inst., 1975-77; mem. Linn County Steering Com. Carter Re-election, 1979-80; lectr. local colls. and service orgns.; tchr. conversational Russian, Pierce Elementary Sch., Cedar Rapids, 1976. Roman Catholic. Composer: She is Risen, 1973. Home: 2050 Glass Rd NE Cedar Rapids IA 52402

HUBER, THOMAS HENRY, army officer; b. Pitts., Jan. 25, 1938; s. Michael and Helen Catherine (Welte) H.; B.S., U.S. Mil. Acad., 1960; M.S., Purdue U., 1966; M.B.A., L.I. U., 1976; m. Patricia Collier, June 20, 1960; children—Kathleen, Michael, Elizabeth, Jennifer. Commd. 2d lt. U.S. Army, 1960, advanced through grades to col., 1980; dep. comdr., lab. chief and program dir. Mobility Research and Devel. Center, Ft. Belvoir, Va., 1968, research/devel. staff Hdqrs., Pentagon, Washington, 1971, asst. prof. dept. engring., U.S. Mil., Acad., West Point, N.Y., 1974, dir. tank-automative concepts lab., Warren, Mich., 1978—. Decorated Legion of Merit, Bronze Star; recipient spl. award for leadership Mobility Research & Devel. Center, 1970; Buhl found. scholar, 1955-56; registered profl. engr., Va. Mem. Soc. Automotive Engrs., Am. Assn. Engring. Edn., AIAA, Assn. U.S. Army, Am. Def. Preparedness Assn. Roman Catholic. Contbr. articles to profl. jours. Home: 2353 Chalet Dr Rochester MI 48063 Office: TACOM DRSTA-Z Warren MI 48090

HUBER, WALTER GLENN, ret. judge; b. Irvington, Nebr., Dec. 24, 1908; s. George F. and Amanda A. (Borup) H.; student U. Omaha, 1926-28; B.A., U. Nebr., 1930, LL.B. cum laude, 1932, J.D. with distinction, 1968; m. Anna M. Hansen, Aug. 24, 1935. Admitted to Nebr. bar, 1932; pvt. practice law, Blair, Nebr., 1939-72; dist. judge 6th Jud. Dist. Nebr., Blair, 1972-80. County atty., Washington County, Nebr., 1940-46; city atty., Blair, 1941-42. Pres. Nebr. State Rose Soc., Inc., Lincoln, 1973-75. Chmn. Washington County Democrat Party, 1958-60. Bd. trustees U. Nebr. Found., Lincoln, 1972—. Recipient Silver Beaver award Mid-Am. council Boy Scouts Am., 1958. Mem. Washington County Bar Assn. (pres. 1968-72), Phi Beta Kappa. Lutheran. Club: Golf (Blair). Author: Deprivation of Parents' Right to Custody of Children in Civil Actions, 1948. Home: Box 530 Blair NE 68008 Office: 1570 Washington St Blair NE 68008

HUBER, WILLIAM EVAN, II, lawyer; b. Celina, Ohio, Mar. 10, 1943; s. William Evan and Genevieve Rose (Jenkins) H.; B.S. in Edn., Ohio No. U., 1965, J.D., 1968; m. E. Marie Schwaberow, June 25, 1966; children—Michael David, Mark William. Tchr. history St. lMary's (Ohio) city schs., 1968-69; admitted to Ohio bar, 1968, U.S. Dist. Ct. For No. Ohio, 1972, U.S. Supreme Ct., 1972; mem. firm Barrett G. Kemp, St. Mary's, Ohio, 1968-69; asso. law firm Kemp & Huber, St. Mary's, 1969-72, partner, 1972—; solicitor Village of Ft. Recovery (Ohio), 1969-78; asst. prosecutor Auglaize County, Ohio, 1969-76; dir. Community Savs. & Loan St. Marys. Profl. chmn. United Fund dr., St. Mary's, 1969, gen. chmn., 1970; chmn. St. Mary's Recreation Adv. Bd., 1976-81, mem. sesquicentennial com., 1973; pres. St. Mary's Nat. Little League, 1970-81; chmn. St. Mary's Medic Search, 1977—; trustee Community Improvement Corp., 1969—, St. Marys Community Found., 1981; chmn. bd. trustees St. Marys Youth Center, 1980—. Mem. Auglaize County Bar Assn. (pres. 1975), Am. Assn. Hosp. Attys., St. Mary's C. of C. (pres. 1977, 78), Phi Alpha Delta. Clubs: Eagle, St. Mary's Outing. Home: 119 S Ash St Saint Marys OH 45885 Office: Suite 203 Central Trust Bldg Saint Marys OH 45885

HUBERT, THOMASYNE CAMPBELL, investment banking co. exec.; b. Chgo., Dec. 7, 1946; d. John William and Bernetta Elizabeth (Garrity) Campbell; B.A., Rosary Coll., 1967; M.S., Kans. State U., 1970; m. James Bland Hubert, Sept. 19, 1970; 1 son, Thomas. Systems cons. URS, Oak Brook, Ill., 1970; systems analyst State of Iowa, Des Moines, 1970-72; programmer analyst A.G. Becker, Chgo., 1973-74, project leader, 1974-77, supr., 1977-78, v.p. program mgr., 1978-81, mgr. programming, 1981—. NIH fellow, 1967-69. Mem. Nat. Assn. Securities Dealers, Kans. State Alumni Assn. Home: 1817 Basswood Ln Mount Prospect IL 60056 Office: 2 First National Plaza Chicago IL 60603

HUCKLE, JAMES EARL, newspaper exec.; b. Cadillac, Mich., Apr. 3, 1946; s. Earl Thomas and Audrey Ruth H.; B.S., Mich. State U., 1968; postgrad. Wayne State U., 1971; m. Diana Tefft, Dec. 12, 1970; children—Renee, Martha. Mgmt. trainee Gen. Motors, Warren, Mich., 1969-71; personnel specialist City Nat. Bank of Detroit, 1971-72; bus. mgr. Cadillac (Mich.) Evening News, 1972-76; pub., pres. Ionia (Mich.) Sentinel-Standard, 1976—, South Haven (Mich.) Daily Tribune, 1978—, Ionia County News, 1976—, Lake Odessa (Mich.) Wave, 1978—. Pres., United Way of Ionia, 1979-80; chmn. Ionia Revitalization, 1979—. Mem. Mich. League Home Dailies Press Assn. (pres. 1977), Mich. Newspapers Inc. (dir. 1977—), Am. Newspaper Pubs. Assn., Nat. Newspaper Assn., Inland Daily Newspaper Assn., Mich. Press Assn., Internat. Newspaper Advt. Execs., Internat. Newspaper Promotion Assn. Methodist. Clubs: Rotary, Hunt and Fish, Country. Office: 114 N Depot St Ionia MI 48846

HUDACKO, ANDREW ROBERT, lawyer; b. East Cleve., Mar. 25, 1943; s. Andrew J. and Vilma Rose (Toth) H.; B.A., Kent State U., 1966; J.D., Cleve. State U., 1971; m. Andrea Lee Collins, June 28, 1969; children—Kimberly Ann (dec.), Rebecca Lynn, Deborah Jean. Newspaper reporter The Daily Legal News, Cleve., 1967-75; admitted to Ohio bar, 1976; adjudicator Regional Office, VA, Cleve., 1975-76; life ins. salesman Sun Life of Can., Cleve., 1976; asso. firm Thomas M. Shaughnessey, Cleve., 1976-77; field rep. Ohio Assn. of Public Sch. Employees, Columbus, 1977—; legal counsel Mayfield Hist. Soc., 1976—; atty. vol. Cuyahoga County Juvenile Ct. Offender Program, 1976—. Lay minister St. Francis Assissi Ch., Gates Mills, Ohio, 1972—. Recipient Am. Jurisprudence award, 1971, numerous civic awards. Mem. Ohio State Bar Assn., Greater Cleve. Bar Assn., Cuyahoga County Bar Assn., Mayfield Jaycees (trustee 1975-76), Mayfield Jaycees (sec. 1977-78), Phi Alpha Delta. Democrat. Roman Catholic. Home: 6776 Seneca Rd Mayfield OH 44143 Office: 5151 Warrensville Center Rd Maple Heights OH 44137

HUDELSON, ANNA LOUISE, educator; b. Greenville, Ohio, Mar. 15, 1952; d. Eldean Lee and Mary Louise (Strobel) Hamilton; B.S. in Edn., Bowling Green State U.; M.S. in Edn., Wright State U., 1981; m. Dennis Lee Hudelson, Aug. 10, 1974; 1 dau., Angela Marie. Tchr. bus. edn. Ft. Loramie (Ohio) High Sch., 1974-76, Upper Valley Joint Vocat. Sch., Piqua, 1976—. Named Outstanding Young Women Am., 1979. Mem. Am. Vocat. Assn., Ohio Vocat. Assn., Nat. Bus. Edn. Assn., Ohio Bus. Tchrs. Assn., Piqua Bus. and Profl. Women (corr. sec. 1979-81, 2d v.p. 1981—; Outstanding Bus. Woman for 1981). Home: 120 Garnsey St Piqua OH 45356 Office: 8811 Career Dr Piqua OH 45356

HUDGINS, DUDLEY RODGER, lab. exec.; b. Chgo., Nov. 4, 1937; s. Dudley Wallace and Helen (Sterling) H.; B.A. in Psychology, Kans. U., 1959; m. Pegge Resch, Aug. 8, 1975; children—Brian, Randy; stepchildren—Todd Woods, Mianne Woods. With Marion Labs., Inc., 1961—, tng. mgr., also bids and contracts mgr., 1970-72, dir. sales tng. and devel., Kansas City, Mo., 1972—; cons. in field. Formerly active local Jr. Achievement, Birthright; pres. Zion Lutheran Ch., 1980; hon. dir. Rockhurst Coll., Kansas City, Mo. Served with AUS, 1960. Recipient Builder award Marion Labs., 1979. Mem. Nat. Soc. Pharm. Sales Trainers (past chpt. treas., pres. 1978—, nat. pres. 1979-80), Am. Security Council (nat. adv. bd.). Home: 12817 Sagamore St Leawood KS 66209 Office: 10236 Bunker Ridge Rd Kansas City MO 64137

HUDNUT, WILLIAM HERBERT, III, mayor, former congressman, univ. adminstr.; b. Cin., Oct. 17, 1932; s. William H. and Elizabeth (Kilborne) H.; A.B. magna cum laude, Princeton U., 1954; B.D. summa cum laude, Union Theol. Sem., 1957; D.D., Hanover Coll., 1967, Wabash Coll., 1969; D.Litt., Ind. Central U., 1981; LL.D., Butler U., 1980; m. Susan Greer Rice, Dec. 14, 1974; children by previous marriage—Michael, Laura, Timothy, William H. IV, Theodore. Ordained to ministry Presbyn. Ch., 1957; asst. minister Westminster Ch., Buffalo, 1957-60; pastor 1st Ch., Annapolis, Md., 1960-63, 2d Ch., Indpls., 1963-72; mem. 93rd Congress from 11th Ind. Dist.; dir. dept. community affairs Ind. Central U., Indpls., 1975; mayor, Indpls., 1976—. Pres., Anne Arundel County Mental Health Assn., 1961-63, Marion County Mental Health Assn., 1965-67, Westminster Found. Purdue U., 1967-72; mem. Central Area council Boy Scouts Am. (1964-72); mem. bd. Safety Indpls., 1971. Bd. dirs. Goodwill Industries; bd. dirs. Nat. League of Cities, 1977—, pres., 1981; trustee Ind. Central U., 1976—; pres. bd. trustees Darrow Sch., 1965-75; pres. Ind. Assn. Cities and Towns, 1979, Ind. Rep. Mayors Assn., 1980. Recipient travelling fellowship Union Theol. Sem., 1957. Mem. Phi Beta Kappa. Presbyn. Republican. Clubs: Indpls. Columbia, Woodstock, Princeton. Editor: Union Sem. Quar. Rev., 1956-57. Home: 722 Pine Dr Indianapolis IN 46204 Office: City County Bldg 200 E Washington St Indianapolis IN 46204

HUDSON, DEAN ALLEN, savs. and loan assn. exec.; b. Greensburg, Pa., Dec. 20, 1935; s. Harold Baird and Lucy May (Baldridge) H.; student U. Pitts., 1962-63, 65-66; m. Nancy Jean LoBuono, Aug. 16, 1963; children—Ellen Dawn, Brian Wesley, Gayle Suzanne. Sr. systems analyst Robertshaw Controls Corp., New Stanton, Pa., 1963-64; pvt. practice acctg., Irwin, Pa., 1964-72; sec.-treas., mgn. officer, dir. First Fed. Savs. and Loan Assn. of Irwin, 1964-72; v.p. fin. and adminstrn. Heritage Fed. Savs. and Loan Assn., Daytona Beach, Fla., 1972-78; pres., dir. Hometown Fed. Savs. and Loan Assn., Delphi, Ind., 1978—. Bd. dirs. Norwin Public Library Assn., 1970-72, Norwin Community Found., 1971-72. Mem. Am. Inst. C.P.A.'s, Pa. Inst. C.P.A.'s, Inst. Fin. Edn. Republican. Mem. Christian and Missionary Alliance Ch. Club: Rotary. Home: 5940 Battleview Dr West Lafayette IN 47906 Office: 215 E Main St Delphi IN 46923

HUDSON, HAROLD DON, veterinarian; b. Audrain County, Mo., Nov. 22, 1943; s. Harold F. and Greta Arlene (Boyd) H.; A.A., Hannibal (Mo.) La Grange Coll., 1963; B.S., U. Mo., 1967, D.V.M., 1970; m. Carole Jacqueline Spence, Aug. 30, 1964; children—Dale Brent, Kim Marie. Asso. Clarinda (Iowa) Vet. Clinic, 1970-71, Bethany (Mo.) Vet. Clinic, 1971-72, Vet. Clinic, Mexico, Mo., 1972—. Mem. AVMA, Mo. Vet. Med. Assn., Am. Assn. Bovine Practitioners, Am. Assn. Swine Practitioners. Baptist. Home: 933 Emmons St Mexico MO 65265 Office: 1624 Hwy 54 E Mexico MO 65265

HUDSON, LORNA KRUEGER, indsl. safety engr.; b. Independence, Mo., Feb. 10, 1955; d. Thomas Leroy and Saundra Lea (Petersen) Krueger; A.A.S., Longview Community Coll., 1975; B.S., Central Mo. State U., 1979, M.S., 1982; m. Scott Kellogg Hudson, Feb. 8, 1976. Staff mem. Stewart Indsl. Hygiene Service, Inc., Kansas City, Mo., 1980—; sr. loss control rep. U.S. Ins. Group, Crum and Forster Orgn., Mission, Kans., 1979—. Mem. Am. Soc. Safety Engrs., Am. Indsl. Hygiene Assn. Home: General Delivery Lone Jack MO 64070 Office: U S Ins Group Suite 700 5700 Broadmoor St Mission KS 66202

HUDSON, RANDOLPH HOYT, educator; b. Cleve., Apr. 12, 1927; s. Hoyt Hopewell and Margaret Calvert (Dille) H.; B.A., Stanford U., 1950, Ph.D., 1963; M.A., Cornell U., 1953; student U. Paris and U. Poitiers, 1948-49; m. Jan Pinkerton, Aug. 1, 1967; children—Laura, Lucy, Andrea, Hoyt, Roy. Acting instr. Stanford U., 1956-59; asst. prof. English, Humboldt State Coll., 1959-62; asso. prof. U. Colo., 1962-67; chmn. dept. English, Central State U., Ohio, 1967-69; dean arts and scis. Northeastern Ill. U., Chgo., 1969-79, prof. English, 1979—; cons. in field; founder, chief exec. officer Winnetka Fin.

Services. Served with USN, 1945-46; with U.S. Army, 1953-55. Mem. Colo. Lang. Arts Soc. (exec. officer), AAUP, Nat. Council Tchrs. of English, Am. Fedn. Tchrs. Author: Technology, Culture, and Language, 1967; A Modern Handbook of American English, 1967; mem. exec. com., editorial bd. College Composition and Communications; contbr. articles and revs. to profl. jours. Home: 943 Oak St Winnetka IL 60093 Office: Dept English Northeastern Illinois Univ Chicago IL 60625

HUE, JOHN EMMET, printing co. exec.; b. Chgo., Aug. 4, 1930; s. Herman E. and Laurella Marilyn H.; B.S. with honors in Econs., U. Ill., 1956, M.S., 1957; m. Carmella Trinchese, Jan. 29, 1955; children—William, Antonette. With Kimberly-Clark Corp., 1957-67, dir. personnel, personnel mgr. Modine Mfg. Co., LaPorte, Ind., 1967-69; dir. indsl. relations George Banta Co., Inc., Menasha, Wis., 1969—, mem. exec. com., 1972—. Served with U.S. Army, 1948-51, USAF, 1951-53. Mem. Am. Soc. Personnel Adminstrn., Artus, Phi Eta Sigma, Chi Gamma Iota. Republican. Episcopalian. Home: 192 Adella Beach Neenah WI 54956 Office: Curtis Reed Plaza Menasha WI 54952

HUEBNER, LLOYD OTTO, coll. pres.; b. Manitowoc, Wis., Mar. 7, 1925; s. Carl and Erna (Glaeser) H.; B.A., Northwestern Coll., Watertown, Wis., 1947; M.Div., Wis. Lutheran Sem., Mequon, 1951; m. Inez F. Wahl, June 17, 1951; children—Janet, James, Barbara, David, Gary. Ordained to ministry Wis. Evang. Lutheran Synod, 1951; parish pastor Zion Luth. Ch., Akaska, S.D., 1951-54, St. John's Luth. Ch., Wood Lake, Minn., 1954-58; prin. Lakeside Luth. High Sch., Lake Mills, Wis., 1958-67; dean of students Dr. Martin Luther Coll., New Ulm, Minn., 1967-80, pres., 1980—. Bd. dirs., treas. Heritagefest, 1975—. Mem. Nat. Assn. Ind. Colls. and Univs., Am. Assn. Pres.'s Ind. Colls. and Univs. Club: Rotary (past pres.) (New Ulm). Home: 225 S Highland St New Ulm MN 56073 Office: Dr Martin Luther College New Ulm MN 56073

HUEBNER, RUSSELL HENRY, physicist, sci. research ofcl.; b. Indpls., Jan. 24, 1941; s. Alvin Walter and Julia Helen (Ryza) H.; student U. Dayton, 1958-60; B.S. in Physics (Alcoa Aluminum Co. sr. scholar), Purdue U., 1962; M.S. (AEC Health Physics fellow), Vanderbilt U., 1965; Ph.D. (USPHS radiol. physics fellow), U. Tenn., 1968; student Exec. Program, U. Chgo., 1981—; m. Elaine Marie Luthman, Aug. 31, 1963; children—Karl Andrew, Bradley Stephen, Kathryn Angela, Russell Henry. Research fellow Oak Ridge Nat. Lab., 1963-68; radiol. physicist, div. biology and medicine AEC, Washington, 1968-70; guest scientist, optical phys. div. Nat. Bur. Standards, Washington, 1970; vis. scientist, radiol. and environ. research div. Argonne (Ill.) Nat. Lab., 1970-71, asst. physicist, 1971-75, physicist, 1975-77, program coordinator biomed. and environ. research Office of Dir., 1977—; lectr. NATO Advanced Studies Inst., Netherlands, 1976, Italy, 1977. Lisle Twp. Republican election judge, 1981. Physics Soc., Am. Phys. Soc., Radiation Research Soc. (program com., 1971), Sigma Xi, Sigma Pi Sigma. Roman Catholic. Clubs: Purdue Alumni Assn., Joliet Marriage Encounter Council (1976-77). Author (with W.H. Bradley) Nuclear Spectrometer Applications, 1962; asso. editor Radiation Research, 1979—; contbr. chpts. to books in field.

HUEBSCH, TONY LOUIS, communications exec.; b. McGregor, Iowa, May 12, 1929; s. Fredric George and Abbie Mae H.; B.A., U. Iowa, 1951, M.B.A., 1972; m. Suzanne Tagge, Nov. 4, 1951; children—Scott, Rebecca, Katherine. Mem. editorial staff Omaha World-Herald, 1953-54; editor indsl. publs. Collins Radio Co., Cedar Rapids, Iowa, 1954-60, advt. mgr. Tex. div., Dallas, 1960-61; advt. mgr. Collins Avionics divs., Cedar Rapids, 1961-79; dir. communications avionics group Rockwell Internat., Cedar Rapids, 1979—. Bd. dirs. Cedar Rapids Community Theater, Cedar Rapids Symphony. Served with USAF, 1951-53. Mem. Aviation Space/Writers Assn. (awards chmn.), Am. Advt. Fedn., Cedar Rapids C. of C. Presbyterian. Clubs: Cedar Rapids Mgmt., Optimists, U.S. Power Squadrons. Home: 359 Pleasant Dr SE Cedar Rapids IA 52403 Office: 400 Collins Rd Cedar Rapids IA 52498

HUELSBECK, CHARLES JOSEPH, ret. tech. librarian and non-tech. editor; b. Dedham, Iowa, Jan. 29, 1920; s. Herman Joseph and Mary Anne (Werner) H.; B.A., U. No. Iowa, 1946; M.S., U. No. Colo., 1948; Library certificate, Emporia (Kans.) State U., 1952; M.S. in L.S., U. Wis., 1953, postgrad., summers 1955, 57, 59; postgrad. U. Iowa, summers 1951, 56, Northwestern U., summer 1960. Instr. English, Creighton U., Omaha, 1947-49, St. Ambrose Coll., Davenport, Iowa, 1949-51; dir. library, publs. adviser U. Maine, Presque Isle, 1953-56; asst. prof., asso. prof. English, guidance cons. Merrimack Coll., North Andover, Mass., 1956-71; dir. Ames Free Library, North Easton, Mass., 1973-74; librarian-editor Iowa Geol. Survey, Iowa City, 1975-80; writer, 1980—. Served with AUS, 1942-43. Mem. Geoscience Info. Soc., Kappa Delta Pi, Pi Gamma Mu. Roman Catholic. Author: (with Jayne Harbaugh and Suzan M. Stewart) Iowa Water Resources Data Systems Catalog, 1977. Editor: Iowa Geol. Survey Newsletter, 1975-78; Iowa Geology, 1979-80; contbr. book revs. to America, Catholic World, Sign, 1967-72.

HUENEFELD, THOMAS ERNST, banker; b. Cin., July 7, 1937; s. Carl Ernst and Catherine Louise (Messer) H.; B.S. in Bus. Adminstrn., U. Fla., 1961; grad. Nat. Comml. Lending Grad. Sch., U. Okla., 1975; m. Catherine Ann Cogburn, Feb. 5, 1960; children—Richard Ernst, Amy Cogburn. Mgmt. trainee Huenefeld Co., Cin., 1961-62, asst. sec., buyer, 1963-65; credit analyst First Nat. Bank Cin., 1966-68, asst. cashier, 1968-69, asst. v.p., 1969-75, v.p., 1975—; dir. Wolf Machine Co., S. Eastern Materials Corp., Ninth St. Garage, Inc. Bd. mgrs. Emanuel Community Center, Cin., 1965-70, pres., 1968-70; trustee Huenefeld Meml., Inc., Cin., 1965-72, treas., 1965-69; trustee Funds for Self Enterprise, Cin., 1972-76, pres., 1973-76; trustee Cin. Musical Festival Assn., 1976—, mem. exec. com., 1977-79; trustee Community Ltd. Care Dialysis Center, Cin., 1978—, Cin. Hist. Soc., 1979—, Mercantile Library, 1979—. Cert. comml. lender Am. Bankers Assn. Mem. Am. Fin. Assn. (life), Fin. Mgmt. Assn. (life), Robert Morris Assos., Cin. Assn. Credit and Fin. Mgmt. (dir. 1972-76), Am. Inst. Banking, Newcomen Soc. N. Am., Ohio (life), Cin. (life) hist. socs., Cincinnatus Assn. Sigma Chi. Republican. Methodist. Clubs: Cin. Country, Univ., Queen City, Bankers, The Assemblies (chmn. 1972-73), Fanfare (pres. 1979-80). Home: 3440 Principio Ave Cincinnati OH 45226 Office: 111 E 4th St Cincinnati OH 45202

HUESER, ROBERTA JEAN, city govt. ofcl.; b. Dallas, Iowa, Oct. 3, 1932; d. Carl Robert and Lucille Julia (Logue) Wheeler; student Wayne (Nebr.) State Coll., Colo. State Coll., Greeley, Northwestern Coll., Orange City, Iowa; m. William Joseph Hueser, June 1, 1956; children—Kyle Robert, Jon William. Sch. tchr. in Iowa, 1953-63; city clk. George (Iowa), 1977—. Chmn. bd. George Bicentennial Mus., 1976-81; adv. bd. George Good Samaritan Center, 1978-81. Mem. Lyon County Mcpl. League (sec.-treas. 1977-78). Democrat. Mem. Ch. of Christ. Club: Facts and Fun (pres. 1978-80). Co-author: In and Around George 1872-1912. Home: 402 E Minnesota Ave George IA 51237 Office: City Hall S Main St George IA 51237

HUEY, ARTHUR SANDMEYER, real estate and investments, ind. petroleum landman; b. Van Buren, Ark., May 18, 1913; s. Richard King and Adele (Sandmeyer) H.; A.B., Amherst Coll., 1935; postgrad. U. Wis., 1939; m. Helen Dorothy Mautz, June 17, 1935; children—Richard King II, Arthur Ticknor, Adele Susan, Sara Louise. Asst. dir. Leelanau Schs., Glen Arbor, Mich., 1935-43, headmaster, owner, 1943-54, pres., owner, 1954-64, pres. emeritus bd. trustees; asst. dir. Camp Leelanau, Glen Arbor, 1935-43, camp dir., 1943-54, pres., owner, 1954-72; mgr. Leelanan Homestead Guest Inn, Glen Arbor, 1935-54, owner, 1943-72, pres., 1954-72; pres. ASH, Inc., 1972-79; ind. petroleum landman. County chmn. Republican Party, 1956-58, finance chmn., 1951-56. Nat. adv. bd. Interlochen Arts Acad.; mem. East Central Regional Bd.-area 2, Boy Scouts Am., Rotary Camps Inc.; bd. dirs. Rotary Charities, Traverse City. Recipient Silver Beaver and Silver Antelope awards Boy Scouts Am. Mem. Mich. State C. of C. (past dir., vice chmn.), Traverse City Area C. of C. (Disting. Service award 1969), U.S. Ski Assn., Mich. Hotel and Motor Hotel Assn. (past pres., past chmn. exec. bd.), Mich. Skeet Assn., Delta Kappa Epsilon. Mason (32 deg., Shriner, past master Blue Lodge), Rotarian. Clubs: Traverse City Golf and Country; Detroit Gun. Home: Overbrook North Glen Arbor MI 49636

HUFF, RUSSELL JOSEPH, business exec.; b. Chgo., Feb. 24, 1936; s. Russell Winfield and Virgilist Marie (McMahon) H.; B.A. cum laude, U. Notre Dame, 1958; S.T.B., Cath. U. Santiago (Chile), 1960; M.A. in Communication Arts, U. Notre Dame, 1968; m. Beverly Diane Staschke, 1 dau., Michelle Lynn. Exec. editor Cath. Boy, and Miss, Notre Dame, Ind., 1963-68; mng. editor Nation's Schs., McGraw Hill, Chgo., 1968-70; v.p. pub. affairs Homart Devel. Co., Chgo., 1971-76; dir. public relations Sears, Roebuck Co. Internat. Ops., Chgo., 1976—, dir. public affairs Sears Roebuck Found. Internat. Projects, 1981—; v.p., sec. TOP, Inc. of Fla. Recipient Outstanding Mag. award Cath. Press. Assn., 1965, 67; named for Best Cover, Nation's Schs., 1968; cert. jr. coll. tchr., Calif. Mem. Pub. Relations Soc. Am. (accredited, mem. accreditation com. Chgo. chpt.), Nat. Fgn. Trade Council, Public Affairs Council, Conf. Bd., Internat. Bus. Council, Internat. Visitors Center Chgo., Partners of the Ams. (adv. council), Sao Paulo Partners (dir. Ill.), Chgo. Chamber of Commerce and Industry, U.S.-Spanish C. of C. of Middle West (dir.), War Memorabilia Collectors Soc. (exec. dir.). Roman Catholic. Author: Come Build My Church, 1966; On Wings of Adventure, 1967; contbr. articles to family mags. Home: 25 Princeton Rd Hinsdale IL 60521

HUFFINE, COY LEE, chem. engr.; b. Knoxville, Tenn., Apr. 2, 1924; s. Coy Mann and Inez Belle (Story) H.; B.S., U. Tenn., 1945, M.S., 1947; Ph.D., Columbia U., 1953; m. Virginia Elizabeth Browne, Mar. 31, 1951; children—Jeremy Bennett, Lucinda Jane. Prin. engr. Gen. Electric Co., Oak Ridge and Cin., 1951-59; research ceramist Gen. Electric Research Lab., Schenectady, 1959-60; project mgr. devel. and mfg., space systems div. Avco Corp., Lowell, Mass., 1960-67; with IBM, Rochester, Minn., 1968—, mgr. component tech., info. systems div. 1980—. Served with USN, 1945-46. Mem. Am. Inst. Chem. Engrs., AIME, Nat. Inst. Ceramic Engrs., Am. Ceramic Soc., N.Y. Acad. Scis., Sigma Xi. Home: 2247 5th Ave NE Rochester MN 55901 Office: IBM Corp 3605 Hwy 52 N Rochester MN 55901

HUFFMAN, BILL J., state senator; b. Estelle, Ga., Dec. 27, 1924; married; children—Marvin, Krisaundra, Beth. Former mem. City Council Madison Heights (Mich.), former mayor 1 term; mem. Mich. Ho. of Reps., 1962-76, Mich. State Senate, 1976—. Del., Democratic Nat. Conv., 1980. Served with USN, 1942-47. Club: Kiwanis. Office: Mich State Senate State Capitol Lansing MI 48909*

HUFFMAN, EDITH DEETTE, occupational therapist; b. Jamestown, N.Y., Dec. 24, 1922; d. Allan William and Lillian Ethel (Middleton) Firth; B.S. in Occupational Therapy, U. Kans., 1963; M. Ednl. Psychology, Wichita State U., 1973; m. Richard E. Huffman, June 28, 1968; children by previous marriage—Stephen R., Thomas R. and Deborah Page, Lynne D. Worthington. Dir. occupational therapy Capper Found. Crippled Children, Topeka, 1963-66, Wesley Med. Center, Wichita, 1966-75; vocat. evaluator Kans. Elks Tng. Center for Handicapped, 1976-78; occupational therapy cons. mentally retarded and geriatric nursing homes, 1976-80; chief occupational therapist VA Center, Wichita, 1980—. Bd. dirs. Sedgwick County Mental Health Assn. Mem. U. Kans. Alumni Assn., Wichita State U. Alumni Assn., Am. Occupational Therapy Assn., Kans. Occupational Therapy Assn. (Occupational Therapist of Yr. 1977), Am. Diabetes Assn., Multiple Sclerosis Soc., World Fedn. Occupational Therapists, NOW, AAUW, Edn. for Ministry, Wichita Ind. Scholars, St. Francis Homes, Phi Delta Gamma (treas. 1981—). Episcopalian. Club: Fairfield Bay (Ark.) Community. Author: Adapted Group Exercise Program, 1979; book reviewer Am. Jour. Occupational Therapy, 1968—. Home: 339 N Rutan St Wichita KS 67208 Office: 5500 E Kellogg St Wichita KS 67218

HUFFMAN, JAMES FLOYD, educator; b. Kalamazoo, May 1, 1922; s. Floyd Sampson and Carrie Myrtle (Booker) H.; B.S., Northwestern U., 1948, M.A., 1949; Ph.D., Mich. State U., 1966; m. Martha Alice Neal, June 9, 1946; children—David, Ann. Instr. speech Northwestern U. instr. Iowa State U., Evanston, Ill., 1949; prof. humanities and communication Gen. Motors Inst., Flint, Mich., 1974—, Rodes prof., 1978-79, del. to English Indsl. Revolution Bicentennial Commemoration, 1979, recipient Distinguished Service award; cons. Banking Inst. Am., 1964. Served to 1st. lt. USAF, 1942-45. Decorated 5 battle stars and Air medal. Mem. U.S. Naval Inst., Am. Acad. Polit. Social Sci., Am. Assn. State Local Historians, Nat. Trust for Hist. Preservation, Nat. Office Mgmt. Assn., Beta Theta. Pi (chief dist. 9). Clubs: Kiwanis Internat. Contbr. film documentaries in field. Home: 1059 W Hemphill St Flint MI 48507 Office: Gen Motors Inst Flint MI 48502

HUFFMAN, NANCY ANNE, city ofcl.; b. McAlister, Okla., Dec. 26, 1942; d. Eustace Wright and Margaret Marcelle (Miller) Carlton; B.S., Spring Hill Coll., 1965; student Pensacola Jr. Coll., 1968-69; m. William Eugene Huffman, Nov. 26, 1966; children—Eugenia Anne, Carlton Eugene. Claims examiner Social Security Payment Center, Birmingham, Ala., 1965-68; councilwoman Springboro (Ohio) Village Council, 1974-77, 78—, pres. council, 1978, dep. mayor, 1979—, past mem. street com., now legal com.. fin. com., salary and wage com., rep. to Warren County HUD Rehab. Bd., 1976-78, chmn. fin. com. 1976—. Joint mem. Ohio Mcpl. League of Cities and Villages. Republican. Methodist. Author: One Chance for Happiness, 1963. Home: 165 Pinecone Ln Springboro OH 45066 Office: Springboro Mcpl Bldg 280 W Central St Springboro OH 45066

HUFFMAN, PATRICK JOHN, chemist; b. Peoria, Ill., May 8, 1948; s. Patrick Howard and Jane Francis (Hoey) H.; m. Carol Anne Dresch, June 20, 1970; children—John, Jeffrey, Anne Marie; B.S., Ill. State U., 1970, M.S., 1973. Cert. class A waste treatment operator, Ill., cert. pesticide control operator, Ill. Tech. cons. Hawthorne House, Inc., Bloomington, Ill., 1971-72; quality control mgr. Paul F. Beich Co., Bloomington, 1971-73, gen. supr., 1973-74, ops. mgr., 1974—. Mem. Am. Chem. Soc., Environ. Mgmt. Assn., Am. Assn. Candy Techs., Nat. Confectioners Assn., Ill. State Acad. Sci. Recipient Boss of Year award Con Brio chpt. Nat. Secs. Assn; author: Silver Complexes Containing Pyrazine N-oxides as Ligands, 1974. Office: Beich Rd Bloomington IL 61701

HUFFMAN, WILLIAM EUGENE, chem. co. exec.; b. Birmingham, Ala., Sept. 15, 1943; s. Dempsey Eugene and Mary Elizabeth (Davis) H.; B.S., Auburn U., 1965; postgrad. U. West Fla., 1969-72; m. Nancy Anne Carlton, Nov. 26, 1966; children—Eugenia Anne, Carlton Eugene. Mgmt. trainee, engr. U.S. Steel Co., Birmingham, Ala., 1965-66; process engr., maintenance and ops. supr. Allied Chem., Birmingham, 1966-68; with Monsanto Co., 1968—, utilities ops. mgr., Miamisburg, Ohio, 1979—. Mem. exec. bd. Dayton Miami Valley Safety Council, 1978—. Mem. Am. Inst. Chem. Engrs. (internat. cert. as hazards control mgr.), Dayton C. of C. (legis. and govtl. affairs com. 1979—). Methodist. Home: 165 Pinecone Ln Springboro OH 45066 Office: Monsanto Research Corp PO Box 32 Miamisburg OH 45342

HUGE, THOMAS ARNOLD, advt. co. exec.; b. Alliance, Ohio, Oct. 8, 1944; s. Edwin Oscar and Dorathea Marie Louise (Auman) H.; B.S., Ball State U., 1982; m. Saundra Lou Haseman, May 24, 1972; children by previous marriage—Rene D., Thomas Aaron. Film editor, asst. dir. sta. WFBM-TV, Indpls., 1967-68; disc-jockey, program dir., continuity dir., music dir. sta. WBMP-FM, Elwood, Ind., 1968; disc-jockey sta. WCSI-AM/FM, Columbus, Ind., 1968-72; mgr. studio ops. Soundstage, Indpls., 1972-74; ops. mgr. Tapemasters Studio, Indpls., 1974-76; v.p., sec.-treas. Soundwriters, Inc., Indpls., 1976; pres. Huge Co., Inc., Indpls., 1977—. Mem. Aircraft Owners and Pilots Assn. Safety Found., Exptl. Aircraft Assn., AFTRA, Screen Actors Guild, E.A.A. Ultralight Assn., Internat. Aerobatic Club, Theta Xi, Alpha Chi Omega. Presbyterian. Clubs: Advt. of Indpls. (Addi awards 1978, 81, 82), Art Dirs. Indpls. (Silver Medal award 1981). Office: 6331 N Carrollton Ave Indianapolis IN 46220

HUGGINS, CHARLES BRENTON, physician; b. Halifax, N.S., Can., Sept. 22, 1901; s. Charles Edward and Bessie (Spencer) H.; B.A., Acadia U., 1920, D.Sc., 1946; M.D., Harvard, 1924; M.Sc., Yale, 1947; D.Sc., Washington U., St. Louis, 1950, Leeds U., 1953, Turin U., 1957; Sigillum Magnum, Bologna U., 1964; D.Sc., Trinity Coll., 1965, Wales, 1967, U. Mich., 1968, Med. Coll. Ohio, 1973, Gustavus Adolphus Coll., 1975, Wilmington Coll., 1980, U. Louisville, 1980; LL.D., U. Aberdeen, 1966; D.P. S., George Washington U., 1967; LL.D. (hon.), York U. (Can.); hon. doctorate, U. Calif. at Berkeley, 1968; m. Margaret Wellman, July 29, 1927; children—Charles Edward, Emily Wellman (Mrs. Fine). Intern in surgery U. Mich., 1924-26, instr. surgery, 1926-27; instr. surgery U. Chgo., 1927-29, asst. prof., 1929-33, asso. prof., 1933-36, prof. surgery, 1936—, dir. Ben May Lab. for Cancer Research, 1951-69, William B. Ogden Distinguished Service prof., 1962; Macewan lectureship U. Glasgow, 1958; Chancellor Acadia U., Wolfville, N.S., 1972-79. Trustee Worcester Found. Exptl. Biology; hon. trustee Jackson Lab., Bar Harbor, Maine; bd. govs. Weizmann Inst. Sci., Rehovot, Israel. Recipient Charles L. Meyer award for cancer research Nat. Acad. Sci., 1943; Am. Urol. Assn. award for research on male genital tract, 1948; Francis Amory award for cancer research, 1948; AMA gold medals for research, 1936, 1940; Société Internationale d'Urologie, 1948; Am. Cancer Soc. award, 1953; Bertner award M.D. Anderson Hosp., 1953; award Am. Pharm. Mfrs. Assn., 1953; Gold medal Am. Assn. Genito-Urinary Surgeons, 1955; Borden award Assn. Am. Med. Colls., 1955; Cartwright medal Columbia U., 1975; decorated Order Pour le Merite, Germany, 1958, Order of The Sun, Peru, 1961; recipient Comfort Crookshank award Middlesex Hosp., London, 1957; Charles Mickel fellow Toronto U., 1958; Cameron prize Edinburg U., 1958; Valentine prize N.Y. Acad. Medicine, 1962; Hunter award Am. Therapeutic Soc., 1962; Lasker award for med. research, 1963; Gold medal for research Rudolf Virchow Soc., 1964, Passano award, 1965; Ramon Guiteras medal and award Am. Urol. Assn., 1966; Centennial medal Acadia U., 1967; Bigelow medal Boston Surgical Soc., 1967; Nobel prize for physiology and medicine, 1966; James Ewing Soc. award, 1975, others. Fellow A.C.S. (hon.), Royal Coll. Physicians (London), Royal Coll. Physicians (Edinburgh), Royal Coll. Surgeons (Can.; hon.); mem. Am. Philos. Soc., Nat. Acad. Scis., Canadian Med. Assn. (hon.), Am. Assn. Cancer Research (hon.), Alpha Omega Alpha. Home: 5807 S Dorchester Chicago IL 60637 Office: 950 E 59th St Chicago IL 60637

HUGGINS, CHARLOTTE SUSAN HARRISON, educator; b. Rockford, Ill., May 13, 1933; d. Lyle Lux and Alta May (Bowers) H.; student Knox Coll., 1951-52; A.B. magna cum laude, Radcliffe Coll., 1958; M.A., Northwestern U., 1960, postgrad, 1971-73; m. Rollin Charles Huggins, Apr. 26, 1952; children—Cynthia Charlotte, Shirley Ann, John Charles. Asst. editor Hollister Publications, Inc., Wilmette, Ill., 1959-65; tchr. advanced placement English New Trier High Sch. East, Winnetka, Ill., 1965—, asst. sponsor yearbook, 1979—; pres. Harrison Farm, Inc., Lovington, Ill., 1976—. Mem. women's bd. St. Leonard's House, Chgo., 1965-75; Central Sch. PTA Bd., Wilmette, 1960-64; mem. jr. bd. Northwestern U. Settlement, Chgo., 1965-75. Recipient DAR Citizenship award, 1953, Phi Beta Kappa award, 1957; Am. Legion award, 1959; named Master Tchr., New Trier High Sch., 1979. Mem. NEA, Ill. Edn. Assn., New Trier Edn. Assn., Nat. Council Tchrs. English, Ill. Assn. Tchrs. English, MLA, Northwestern U. Alumni Assn., Jr. Aux. Chgo. Cancer Research Bd., Mary Crane League, Pi Beta Phi. Clubs: Nat. Huguenot Soc., Ill. Huguenot Soc., Womans' of Wilmette, Univ. of Chgo., Mich. Shores, Knox Coll., Radcliffe Coll. of Chgo. Author: A Sequential Course in Composition Grades 9-12, 1979; editor: A History of New Trier High Sch. Twp. and Communities, 1981. Home: 700 Greenwood Ave Wilmette IL 60091 or Ptarmigan Meadows Creede CO 81130 Office: 385 Winnetka Ave Winnetka IL 60093

HUGHES, CALVIN HOOVER, psychiatrist; b. Clearfield, Pa., Dec. 12, 1928; s. James P. and Bertha Mae (Hoover) H.; B.S., Grove City Coll., 1951; M.D., U. Mich., 1960; m. Wanda Arlena Davis, June 20, 1953; 1 dau., Tammy J. Research asso. Wayne State U., 1951-52; head of mech. heart project research staff Gen. Motors Corp., 1952-56; gen. rotating intern Detroit Meml. Hosp., 1960-61; resident in psychiatry Lafayette Clinic, 1961-64; pvt. practice medicine specializing in psychiatry Harper Woods, Mich., 1964—; attending staff Cottage Hosp., 1974—, acting chief of psychiatry, 1973-74; sr. attending staff Detroit Meml. Hosp., 1970—, acting chief of psychiatry, 1973-74, chmn. continuing med. edn. com.; sr. attending staff South Macomb Hosp.; chief psychiatry Detroit-Macomb Hosps. Assn.; attending staff St. John's Hosp.; chief of psychiatry Holy Cross Hosp., 1980—; cons. Saratoga Hosp., Warren Meml. Hosp.; clin. asst. prof. psychiatry Wayne State U., 1973—; mem. Mich. Bd. Licensing and Regulation Marriage Counselors. Mem. Macomb County Mental Health Bd., 1965-67; bd. dirs. hosps. and homes div. Methodist Ch., 1965-70. Served with U.S. Army, 1946-47. Recipient Outstanding Alumni Achievement award Grove City Coll., 1970. Diplomate Am. Bd. Psychiatry and Neurology. Fellow Am. Psychiat. Assn.; mem. AMA, Mich. Psychiat. Soc. (chmn. pub. info. com.), Mich., Wayne County med. socs., Port Huron Power Squadron. Republican. Presbyn. Clubs: Bayview Yacht (fleet surgeon), Masons. Address: 19959 Vernier Rd Harper Woods MI 48225

HUGHES, CAROLYN SUE, ednl. adminstr.; b. Peoria, Ill., Mar. 20, 1938; d. Eldon Eugene and Bernadine Vivian (Thompson) Houghton; B.S., Miami U., 1961, M.Ed., 1964; Ph.D., Kent State U., 1971; m. J. Edward Hughes, Nov. 29, 1957; children—Laura Beth, Lisa Kay,

Ronald Lee. Tchr., Dayton, Ohio, 1961, Eaton, Ohio, 1962-63, Wooster, Ohio, 1964-68; doctoral fellow Kent (Ohio) State U., 1968-71; asst. prof., dir. grad. reading program Youngstown (Ohio) State U., 1971-73; cons., supr. elem. edn. Parma (Ohio) City Sch. Dist., 1973-81; prin. Ludlow Sch., Shaker Heights, Ohio, 1981—; vis. prof. Baldwin Wallace Coll., 1976, 80, 82. Trustee, Cleve. Christian Children's Home, 1974-81. NDEA fellow, 1968-71; recipient Disting. Service award Ohio Assn. for Supervision and Curriculum Devel., 1981. Mem. Ohio Assn. for Supervision and Curriculum Devel. (pres. 1976-77), Nat. Assn. for Supervision and Curriculum Devel. (dir. 1976—, exec. council 1980—), Internat. Reading Assn., Nat. Soc. for Study of Edn., Ohio Assn. Elem. Sch. Adminstrs., Phi Delta Kappa, Kappa Delta Pi. Mem. Christian Ch. Author: Achievement and Self Concept as Related to Elementary School Reporting Instruments, 1971; Expanding Reading Comprehension Skills: Figurative Language, 1981. Home: 15925 Van Aken Blvd Apt 101 Shaker Heights OH 44120 Office: Ludlow School 14201 Southington Rd Shaker Heights OH 44120

HUGHES, JEROME MICHAEL, state senator Minn.; b. St. Paul, Oct. 1, 1929; s. Michael Joseph and Mary (Malloy) H.; B.A., Coll. St. Thomas, 1951; M.A., U. Minn., 1958; Ed.D. (Mott fellow), Wayne State U., 1970; m. Audrey Magdalen Lackner, Aug. 11, 1951; children—Bernadine, Timothy, Kathleen, Rosemarie, Margaret, John. Tchr., St. Paul Bd. Edn., 1951-62, counselor, 1963-66, edn. cons., 1966—; mem. Minn. Senate from 50th Dist., 1966—, chmn. Edn. Com., 1973—, pres. pro tem, 1981. Chmn. Minn. Community Sch. Adv. Council, 1971-74; commnr. Edn. Commn. of States. Dist. committeeman Boy Scouts Am. Chmn. Village of Maplewood Police Commn., 1964-66. Mem. Phi Delta Kappa. Democrat. Home: 1978 Payne St St Paul MN 55117 Office: State Capitol Bldg St Paul MN 55155

HUGHES, MARGARET CYRENA, ret. assn. exec.; b. Springfield, Ill.; d. Thomas Patrick and Elizabeth (Donelan) Hughes; student Springfield Jr. Coll., U. Ill. Campaign chmn. Community Fund Assn., 1947-51; exec. dir. Sangamon County Tb Assn., Springfield, 1951-70; exec. dir. Lincoln Land Tb and Respiratory Disease Assn., 1970-76. Pres. Friends of Library, 1956. Exec. com. Sangamon County Council Social Agys., 1940-41; pres. Ill. State Assn. Women's Divs. Chambers of Commerce; bd. dirs., sec., treas. Springfield Safety Council, 1978—, trustee, 1976; bd. dirs. Sangamon County Mental Health, 1948-53, Ret. Sr. Vol. Program (R.S.V.P.), Sr. Citizens of Sangamon County; Cath. adv. com. Girl Scouts, 1946-51, nat. resettlement adv. com. 1948-53; bd. dirs. St. John's Sanitorium Aux. Recipient Pro Ecclesia at Pontifice medal. Mem. Assn. Commerce and Industry (pres. women's div. 1961-62), Ill. C. of C. (v.p. women's div.), Ill. Conf. Tb Workers (pres. 1961-62), Dioceasen Council Cath. Women (past pres.; dir.), Nat. Council Cath. Women (past provincial dir.; chmn. youth com. 1944-51), Louise de Marillac Guild, Sacred Heart Acad. Alumni Assn. (past pres.), Cathedral Altar Soc. (pres. 1956-57), Symphony Guild. Clubs: Zonta (pres. Springfield 1962, area dist. dir. 1963-64); Cotarle (dir. 1943-44); Springfield Women's (dir., chmn. safety com., v.p. 1971—, pres. 1973-75). Home: 417 E Canedy St Springfield IL 62703

HUGO, NORMAN ELIOT, plastic surgeon, educator; b. Beverly, Mass., Sept. 23, 1933; s. Victor Joseph and Helen Bernadette H.; A.B., Williams Coll., 1955; M.D., Cornell U., 1959; m. Geraldine P. Tonry, Oct. 10, 1959; children—Helen, William, Geraldine, Norman, Catherine. Intern, resident Cornell Surg. Service, Bellevue Hosp., N.Y.C., 1959-63; resident N.Y. Hosp.-Cornell Med. Center, 1963-65; chief plastic and reconstructive surgery Michael Reese Hosp., Chgo., 1969-71, Passavant Hosp., Chgo., 1971-79; instr. surgery Cornell U., 1965-66; asst. prof. Ind. U., 1966-67, asst. chief plastic surgery, 1966-67; asso. prof. U. Chgo., 1967-69, Northwestern U., 1971—; dir. plastic surgery Lakeside VA Hosp., 1971-77. Served to maj. M.C., AUS, 1967-69. Diplomate Am. Bd. Plastic and Reconstructive Surgery. Mem. Am. Soc. Plastic and Reconstructive Surgeons (trustee 1981, bd. dirs. Ednl. Found.), A.C.S., Am. Assn. Plastic and Reconstructive Surgery, Am. Soc. Aesthetic Plastic Surgery (sec. 1979—), Chgo. Soc. Plastic Surgery (sec. 1979-81, v.p. 1981—), Plastic Surgery Research Council, Am. Cleft Palate Soc., Assn. Acad. Surgery, Soc. Head and Neck Surgeons, N.Y. Acad. Sci., AMA, Am. Burn Soc. Clubs: Williams (N.Y.C.); Univ. (Chgo.). Home: 1023 Woodland Ave Barrington IL 60010 Office: 707 Fairbanks Ct Chicago IL 60611

HUGULEY, JENNIE REBECCA, welding supply co. exec.; b. Tupelo, Miss., Sept. 5, 1941; d. Leonard Forest and Lena Mae (Sheffield) Isbell; student Morton Coll., 1979—; m. Robert C. Huguley, Nov. 1, 1960; children—Rebecca Lynn, Joseph Michael. Keypunch operator Victor Dana Corp., Chgo., 1965-68; tax cons. H & R Block, Berwyn, Ill., 1971-75; sec. Barton Welding Supply Co., Cicero, Ill., 1972—, bookkeeper, 1973—, cost accountant, 1974-75, office personnel dir., 1975—; corp. officer, sec., treas. Cylinders & Equipment Co., Inc., Cicero, Ill., 1977—. Youth dir. Cicero-Berwyn Assembly of God, 1963-68, treas., 1965-71; trustee Morton East High Sch. Music Bd., 1978, 79-80. Mem. Welding Distbr. Assn., Nat. Welding Supply Assn., Cicero Mfrs. Assn., Cicero C. of C. Home: 5113 W 29th St Cicero IL 60650 Office: 5919 W Ogden Ave Cicero IL 60650

HUHEEY, MARILYN JANE, ophthalmologist; b. Cin., Aug. 31, 1935; d. George Mercer and Mary Jane (Weaver) H.; B.S. in Math., Ohio U., Athens, 1958; M.S. in Physiology, U. Okla., 1966; M.D., U. Ky., 1970. Tchr. math. James Ford Rhodes High Sch., Cleve., 1956-58; biostatistician Nat. Jewish Hosp., Denver, 1958-60; life sci. engr. Stanley Aviation Corp., Denver, 1960-63, N. Am. Aviation Co., Los Angeles, 1963-67; intern U. Ky. Hosp., 1970-71; emergency room physician Jewish Hosp., Mercy Hosp., Bethesda Hosp., Cin., 1971-72; ship's doctor, 1972; resident in ophthalmology Ohio State U. Hosp., Columbus, 1972-75; practice medicine specializing in ophthalmology, Columbus, 1975—; mem. staff Univ. Hosp., Grant Hosp., St. Anthony Hosp., 1975-79, Children's Hosp.; clin. asst. prof. Ohio State U. Med. Sch., 1976—, dir. course ophthalmologic receptionist/aides, 1976. Diplomate Am. Bd. Ophthalmology. Fellow Am. Acad. Ophthalmology and Otolaryngology; mem. AAUP, Am. Assn. Ophthalmologists, Ohio Ophthalmol. Soc., Franklin County Acad. Medicine (profl. relations com. 1979—, legis. com. 1981—, edn. com. 1981—), Ohio Soc. Prevent Blindness (chmn. med. adv. bd. 1978-80), Ohio State Med. Assn., Columbus EENT Soc., LWV, Internat. Council Mid-Ohio, Phi Mu. Clubs: Columbus Met., Mercedes Benz (dir. 1981—). Home: 2396 Northwest Blvd Columbus OH 43221 Office: 1275 Olentangy River Rd Columbus OH 43212

HUI, PETER WING-TAK, hand surgeon; b. Canton, China, May 23, 1946; s. Kam-Chun and Wen-Yu (Siu) H.; came to U.S., 1971, naturalized, 1978; M.D., Nat. Def. Med. Center, Taipei, 1970; married; children—Anna, Anthony, Andrew. Intern, Mt. Sinai Hosp., Chgo., 1971-72, resident in surgery, 1972-76; fellow in hand surgery Cook County Hosp., Chgo., 1976—; practice medicine specializing in hand surgery, Elmhurst, Ill., 1977—; attending hand surgeon Cook County Hosp., 1977—; clin. instr. surgery Rush Med. Coll., Chgo., 1978—. Fellow A.C.S.; mem. Am. Assn. for Hand Surgery, AMA, Chgo. Soc. Surgery of the Hand, Ill. Med. Soc., DuPage Med. Soc., Chgo. Soc. Indsl. Medicine and Surgery. Roman Catholic. Address: 135 S Kenilworth St Elmhurst IL 60126

HUIZENGA, DONALD LEE, mfg. co. exec.; b. Muskegon, Mich., Nov. 8, 1946; s. Donald Irving and Anita J. (Wraalstad) H.; B.S., Drake U., 1968; m. Alice Jane Petersen, Aug. 23, 1968; children—Jason Donn, Jaime Lynn. With Old Kent Bank & Trust, Grand Rapids, Mich., 1968-77, v.p. trust ops., 1976-77; pres. Cedar Springs Castings, Inc. (Mich.), 1977—. Bd. dirs. Grand Rapids (Mich.) chpt. Am. Cancer Soc., 1975-77. Served with U.S. Army, 1968-70, USAR, 1970-74. Mem. Cedar Springs C. of C. (bd. dirs. 1980—), Foundry Assn. Mich. (bd. dirs. 1979—), Am. Inst. Banking (pres. 1976-77), Am. Foundrymens Soc. Republican. Lutheran. Clubs: Rotary (bd. dirs. 1980—), Lions (pres. 1972-73). Office: 69 W Maple St Cedar Springs MI 49319

HUKILL, WILLIAM VIRGIL, architect; b. Washington, Sept. 11, 1930; s. William V. and Maybelle Ella (Burt) H.; B.S. in Archtl. Engring., Ia. State U., 1952; m. Nancy Lee, Mar. 21, 1953; children—Craig, Linda, Sue, Molly, Brook, Jill, Eric. With Gerald I. Griffith, architect, Des Moines, 1955-56, N Clifford Prall, architect, 1956-59, Kohlman & Eckman, architects, Cedar Rapids, Ia., 1959-60; mem. firm Kohlmann-Eckman-Hukill architects, 1960-68; mem. firm Hukill, Pfiffner, Alexander, Duenow, architects and engrs., 1969-71; Sr. partner Design Asso., Architects, and Engrs., 1971—; vis. lectr. Indian Hills Community Coll., 1978—, Coe Coll., 1979—, Mt. Mercy Coll., 1981; pres. dir. Mill Grove Corp., Cedar Rapids; pres., dir. Hek, Ltd., Cedar Rapids; participant Environmen. Planning Inst., Palo Alto, Calif., 1969. Mem. Bd. Appeals, Cedar Rapids, 1963-69. Bd. dirs. Camp Wapsie, Central City, Iowa, YMCA, Cedar Rapids, 1962—. Served with C.E., AUS, 1953-55. Recipient honor award Ch. Archtl. Guild Am., 1964, honor award Nat. Council Schoolhouse Constrn., 1966, DIDACTA internat. exhibit, Switzerland, 1976. Registered profl. engr. and architect, Ia. Mem. A.I.A. (chpt. treas. 1964-67), Nat. Sch. Facilities Council, Am. Assn. Sch. Adminstrs., Assn. Sch. Bus. Ofcls., Council Ednl. Facilities Planners, Nat. Guild Religious Architecture, Cedar Rapids C. of C., Phi Delta Theta, Phi Eta Sigma. Mem. Christian Ch. (deacon 1955-57, elder 1958-59). Optimist (Golden Circle award). Author: Winning Bond Elections; guest editorial writer Cedar Rapids Gazette, 1978—. Home: 1112 Norwood Dr Cedar Rapids IA 52403 Office: 610 10th St SE Cedar Rapids IA 52403

HULBERT, SAMUEL FOSTER, coll. pres.; b. Adams Center, N.Y., Apr. 12, 1936; s. Foster David and Wilma May (Speakman) H.; B.S. in Ceramic Engring., Alfred U., 1958, Ph.D. in Ceramic Engring., 1964; m. Joy Elinor Husband, Sept. 3, 1960; children—Gregory, Samantha, Jeffrey. Asst. varsity and freshman football coach Alfred (N.Y.) U., 1959-61; lab. instr. N.Y. State Coll. Ceramics, Alfred, 1958-59; instr. math. and physics Alfred U., 1960-64; asst. prof. ceramic and metall. engring. Clemson (S.C.) U., 1964-68, head div. interdisciplinary studies, asso. prof. materials and bioengring., 1968-71, asso. dean for engring. research and interdisciplinary studies, prof. materials engring. and bioengring., dir. materials engring. and bioengring., 1970-73; prof. bioengring., dean Sch. of Engring., Tulane U., New Orleans, 1973-76; pres.-designate, spl. asst. to pres. Rose-Hulman Inst. Tech., Terre Haute, Ind., 1976, pres., 1976—. Pres. Terre Haute Com. Area Progress, 1979; mem. exec. com. Wabash Valley chpt. Boy Scouts Am. Recipient medal Italian Soc. Orthopaedics, 1973, Delitala medal Instituto Ortopedico Rizzoli, 1973; registered profl. engr., La. Mem. Am. Soc. for Artificial Internal Organs, Biomed. Engring. Soc., Soc. for Biomaterials (dir. 1974—, pres. 1975-76), Am. Ceramic Soc., Nat. Inst. Ceramic Engrs., Am. Soc. for Engring. End., Assn. for Advancement of Med. Instrumentation, Independent Colls. and Univs. Ind., Associated Colls. of Ind., Ind. Conf. Higher Edn., Assn. Independent Engring. Colls. (sec.-treas. 1977—), Am. Assn. Presidents of Independent Colls. and Univs., Vigo County Hist. Soc. (dir. 1979—), Keramos, Blue Key, Sigma Xi. Republican. Club: Rotary. Mem. editorial bd. Annals of Biomed. Engring., 1974, Jour. of Biomed. Materials Research, 1970—, Jour. Internat. Soc. Artificial Organs, 1977—; contbr. articles in field of biomaterials and artificial organ design to profl. jours. Office: 5500 Wabash Ave Terre Haute IN 47803

HULESCH, WILLIAM STANLEY, physician; b. Cleve., Apr. 28, 1946; s. Stanley and Beatrice R. (Suchma) H.; B.S., U. Dayton, 1968; M.D., Loyola U., Chgo., 1972; m. Jane S. Liebel, Aug. 9, 1969. Resident in family practice MacNeal Hosp., Berwyn, Ill., 1972-75; practice medicine specializing in family practice, Downers Grove, Ill., 1975—; clin. asso. prof. U. Ill.; past chmn. family practice dept. Good Samaritan Hosp.; chmn. family practice dept. Hinsdale Hosp.; mem. faculty George Williams Coll., Hinsdale Hosp. Family Practice Residency. Advisor, Downers Grove Sch. System. Diplomate Am. Bd. Family Practice, Nat. Bd. Med. Examiners. Fellow Am. Acad. Family Physicians; mem. AMA (Physicians Recognition award), Ill. Acad. Family Physicians (pres.), Alpha Epsilon Delta. Republican. Editorial research bd. Sports Medicine. Office: 6800 Main St Downers Grove IL 60515

HULETT, JOHN MASON, III, resort hotel exec.; b. Ithaca, N.Y., Feb. 15, 1947; s. John Mason, II and Mary Marguerite (Storrs) H.; B.S., Fla. State U., 1969. Sales mgr., then v.p. food ops. Grand Hotel, MacKinac Island, Mich., 1972-78, v.p., 1978—. Served with U.S. Army, 1969-72. Decorated Joint Service Commendation medal. Mem. Hotel Sales Mgmt. Assn., Meeting Planners Internat., Mich. Soc. Assn. Execs., Mackinac Island C. of C. (v.p. 1979, pres. 1981). Republican. Presbyterian. Clubs: Mackinac Island Yacht; Mackinack Assos. Address: Grand Hotel Mackinac Island MI 49757

HULL, ALVENIA RHEA, urban coalition exec.; b. Pocahontas, Va., July 6, 1947; d. Herbert Jackson Rhea; B.S. in Edn., Ohio State U., 1969, M.A. in Guidance and Counseling, 1974. Tchr. public schs., Columbus, Ohio, 1970-72, Worthington, Ohio, 1972-74; counselor Ohio Wesleyan U. Teenage Drug Inst., 1974; program devel. specialist div. drug misuse Miss. Dept. Mental Health, 1974-75; cons. minority affairs Miss. Council on Human Rights, Jackson, 1975-76; asst. dir. services for community-based corrections Project S.T.A.R.T., Detroit, 1976-77, asso. dir. project, 1977-79, dep. dir. project, 1979; dir. community self determination and community relations and devel. New Detroit, Inc., 1979—; cons. grantsmanship. Bd. dirs. Mich. Council Govts., Detroit Repertory Theatre; mem. Southeastern Mich. Transp. Authority; mem. Detroit Mayor's Task Force on Hunger and Malnutrition. Recipient Disting. Service award Miss. Council on Human Relations, 1975; Meritorious Speakers award Booker T. Washington Businessmen's Assn., 1977; Program Achievement award Project S.T.A.R.T., 1976, 77, 78, Outstanding Service award, 1979. Mem. Am. Personnel and Guidance Assn., Nat. Assn. Blacks in Criminal Justice, Mich. Corrections Assn., NAACP, Urban League, Nat. Assn. Exec. Women, YWCA, Alpha Kappa Alpha. Baptist. Office: 719 Griswold 1010 Commonwealth Bldg Detroit MI 48226

HULL, GRAFTON HAZARD, JR., educator; b. Great Bend, Kans., Nov. 24, 1943; s. Grafton Hazard and Mary Kathryn (Hagerty) H.; B.S., U. Wis., 1967; M.S.W., Fla. State U., 1969; Ed.D., U. S.D., 1979; m. Judith Susan Diehl, June 10, 1967; children—Michael, Patrick. Chief social work sect. Mental Hygiene Clinic, Ft. Knox, Ky., 1969-71; foster care coordinator Manitowoc (Wis.) County Social Services, 1971; social work supr. I, Manitowoc County Social Services, 1972-74; dir. criminal justice programs Morningside Coll., Sioux City, Iowa, 1974-77, chmn. dept. sociology and social work, 1977-79., asso. prof., chmn. dept. social welfare U. Wis., Whitewater, 1979—; cons. Sioux City Police Dept., 1979 N.W. Iowa Area Crime Commn., 1978-79. Mem. Siouxland Continuing Edn. com., 1977-79; bd. dirs. Vista Adv. Group, 1977-79, Community Service Club, 1977-78. Served with U.S. Army, 1969-71. Recipient Cert. of Achievement, Ireland Army Hosp., Ft. Knox. Mem. Nat. Assn. Social Workers, Council on Social Work Edn. (mem. ho. of dels. 1978—), Acad. Cert. Social Workers, Wis. Council on Edn. for Social Work (sec. 1980-81). Democrat. Club: Kiwanis. Editor: Readings in Criminal Justice, 1975; contbr. articles to profl. publs. Home: 122 N Esterly Ave Whitewater WI 53190 Office: 800 W Main St Whitewater WI 53190

HULL, LOIS ANN, hosp. social service ofcl.; b. Detroit, Aug. 12, 1932; d. Joseph Guy and Cora Blanche (Daoust) Winefordner; student Black Hawk Jr. Coll., 1967-70; B.A., Marycrest Coll., 1972; M.S.W., U. Iowa, 1975; m. Ward Kenneth Hull, Aug. 11, 1951; children—Richard, Randall, Russell, Daniel, Jonathan. Dir. social services Hammond Henry Dist. Hosp., Geneseo, Ill., 1972—; instr. biofeedback Black Hawk Jr. Coll., Moline, Ill.; mental health and social work counselor fields of alcohol and drug abuse. Treas. Henry County Mental Health Assn., 1973-75; founding bd. Growth Incorp Day Care, 1972-73, Marriage and Family Counseling, Geneseo, 1973—; bd. dirs. Clinic on Alcohol and Drugs, 1977-78; founding bd., v.p. Good Shepherd Found., 1978—; pres. Jr. Women's Club, Geneseo, 1966-67. Cert. alcoholism counselor, Ill. Mem. Nat. Assn. Social Workers (certified), Ill. Alcohol and Drug Dependence Assn., Ill. Welfare Assn., Ill. Biofeedback Soc., Am. Assn. Biofeedback Clinicians (certified), Am. Hosp. Assn. of Social Work Dirs. Roman Catholic. Home: Rural Route 4 Geneseo IL 61254 Office: Hammond Henry Dist Hospital 210 W Elk St Geneseo IL 61254

HULSE, MERLIN D., state senator; b. Clarence, Iowa, Sept. 21, 1923; s. Richard and Eleanor H.; grad. high sch.; m. Darelene Prange, 1945; children—Patricia, Denny. Farmer; chmn. Lean Line Feeder Pig Corp.; dir. Clarence Savs. Bank; mem. Iowa Senate. Chmn. United Ch. of Christ; chmn. Community Ambulance Assn., County Fair Bd., County Extension Ser. Named Master Swine Producer. Mem. Farm Bur., County Cattleman's Assn. Republican. Home: Clarence IA 52216 Office: State Capitol Des Moines IA 50319*

HULT, THERESA MARIE, interior designer; b. Chgo., May 5, 1950; d. Einar Axel and Marjorie Alice H.; B.S., So. Ill. U., 1972. Interior designer Spitzer's Office Furniture, Chgo., 1973, Slater Co., Chgo., 1973-75, Hult Floor Covering Co., Kankakee, Ill., 1975—; lectr. in field. Mem. Am. Soc. Interior Designers. Office: 125 S Washington St Kankakee IL 60901

HULTGREN, DENNIS EUGENE, farmer; b. Union County, S.D., Mar. 19, 1929; s. John Alfred and Esther Marie (Johnson) H.; grad. high sch.; m. Nelda Ethelyn Olson, Aug. 3, 1957; children—Nancy (Mrs. Bruce Klemme), Jean (Mrs. Dene Doty), Jahn Dennis, Ruth Dorothy (Mrs. Scott Henneman). Farmer, Union County, 1953—; commr., chmn. Union County Planning and Zoning Bd., 1972—. Pres. bd. Union Creek Cemetery, 1958—; pres. bd. mgrs. Union-Sayles Watershed Dist., 1965-70. Treas., Sioux Valley Twp., Union County, 1980—; treas., bd. dirs. W. Union Sch., 1957-67; chmn. Union County Sch. Bd., 1961-68; pres. Alcester (S.D.) Sch. Bd., 1970-77; chmn. Alcester PTA, 1967-68; mem. tech. bd. rev. Southeastern Council Govts., Sioux Falls, S.D., 1976-77; bd. dirs. Siouxland Interstate Met. Planning Council, Sioux City, Iowa, 1977—, sec. council ofcls., 1978—; bd. dirs. Old Opera House Community Theater, Akron, Iowa; Republican precinct committeeman, 1970—; mem. Union County Rep. Central Com., 1970—. Served with AUS, 1951-53; Korea. Decorated Combat Inf. badge; recipient Best Actor award Old Opera House Community Theatre, 1976. Mem. Farm Bur., Farmer's Union, S.D. Livestock Feeders Assn., Asso. Sch. Bds. S.D. (Merit award 1976), Am. Legion (exec. bd. Akron 1978—, comdr. Akron 1980-81). VFW. Lutheran (mem. bd. 1967-70, lay chmn. 1970, chmn. centennial com. 1974). Address: Hulteboda Farm Box 147 Route 2 Akron IA 51001

HULTGREN, LENNART SVEN, educator; b. Ludvika, Sweden, Mar. 18, 1950; came to U.S., 1974; s. Sven Olof and Beerie Lilian (Eriksson) H.; B.S. in Engring. Physics, Uppsala U., 1973; M.S. in Aero. and Astronautical Engring., M.I.T., 1975, PH.D., 1978. Research engr. Aero. Research Inst. of Sweden, Stockholm, 1973-74; research asst. M.I.T., Cambridge, 1974-78, postdoctoral asso., 1978-79; vis. asst. prof. Ill. Inst. Tech., Chgo., 1979-80, asst. prof., 1980—; cons. Aero. Research Inst. of Sweden, Stockholm. Mem. Am. Phys. Soc. (fluid dynamics div.), AIAA, Sigma Xi. Office: 3300 S Federal St Chicago IL 60616

HULTMAN, CALVIN O., state senator; b. Omaha, May 24, 1941; s. Oscar and Lola H.; student Dana Coll.; B.S., Iowa State U., 1965; m. Charlene Maines, 1968; children—Calvin O., Daniel A. Businessman; mem. Iowa Senate, majority leader; adminstrv. asst. to Congressman William H. Scherle. Mem. Red Oak C. of C., Acacia. Republican. Lutheran. Clubs: Masons, Elks. Home: 701 Joy St Red Oak IA 51566 Office: State Capitol Des Moines IA 50319*

HUME, HORACE DELBERT, mfg. co. exec.; b. Endeavor, Wis., Aug. 15, 1898; s. James Samuel and Lydia Alberta (Sawyer) H.; student pub. schs.; m. Minnie L. Harlan, June 2, 1926 (dec. May 1972); 1 son, James; m. 2d, Sarah D. Lyles Rood, Apr. 6, 1973. Stockman and farmer, 1917-19; with automobile retail business, Garfield, Wash., 1920-21, partner and asst. mgr., 1921-27; automobile and farm machine retailer, Garfield, partner, mgr., 1928-35, gen. mgr. Hume-Love Co., Garfield, 1931-35, pres., 1935-57; partner, gen. mgr. H.D. Hume Co., Mendota, Ill., 1944-52; pres. H.D. Hume Co., Inc., 1952—; partner Hume and Hume, 1952-72; pres. Hume Products Corp., 1953—; pres., dir. Hume-Fry Co., Garden City, Kans., 1955-73. Mayor, Garfield, Wash., 1938-40. Bd. dirs. Mendota Hosp. Found., 1949-73, pres., 1949-54; bd. dirs. Mendota Swimming Pool Assn.; mem. City Planning Commn., 1953-72, chmn., 1953-69; mem. Regional Planning Commn., LaSalle County, Ill., 1965-73, chmn., 1965-71; mem. Schs. Central Com., 1953—, LaSalle County Zoning Commn., 1966—, LaSalle County Care and Treatment Bd., 1970-73; chmn. Mendota Watershed Com., 1967-73. Mem. Am. Soc. Agrl. Engrs., Eagle River (Wis.) C. of C. (pres., dir. 1962-63), Mendota C. of C. (pres. 1948-49, dir. 1946-49). Republican. Presbyterian (elder). Clubs: Kiwanis (pres. 1953, dir. 1954), Masons, Shriners, Order Eastern Star, Elks; Lakes (Sun City, Ariz.). Patentee in various fields. Home: 709 Carolyn St Mendota IL 61342 Office: 1701 1st Ave Mendota IL 61342

HUMES, THOMAS HAROLD, JR., homebuilder, developer; b. Cin., Jan. 5, 1949; s. Thomas and Jane (Day) H.; B.B.A., U. Cin., 1971, M.A., 1976; m. Marcia Allen Roberts, June 16, 1973; children—Jamie, Scott. Asst. to dean Evening Coll., U. Cin., 1971-72, asst. dir. devel., 1972-73, dir. alumni services, 1973-74, asst. exec. v.p., 1975-78 asst. to pres., 1977-78; pres. and partner Cin. Environs Corp., 1979—; cons. mktg. and communications U. Cin., 1978—. Pres. S.E. Ohio Easter Seals Soc., 1981, treas., 1979; trustee U. Cin. Athletic

Fund, 1979-81; bd. dirs. Clifton Town Meeting, 1980—; campaign dir. Cin. Public Schs. Tax Levy, 1977, U. Cin. State Affiliation Campaign, 1976; active Leadership Cin., 1981—. Mem. Homebuilders Assn. Greater Cin., Delta Tau Delta (v.p. No. div.), Sigma Sigma. Presbyterian. Club: Rotary. Home: 780 Lafayette Ave Cincinnati OH 45220 Office: 4181 Crossgate Dr Cincinnati OH 45236

HUMITA, TIBERIUS TED, educator; b. Cluj, Romania, Dec. 20, 1913; s. Teodor and Teodosia (Abrudan) H.; student U. Bucharest (Romania), 1937-39, U. Rome (Italy), 1946-50; B.A., Wayne State U., 1958, M.A. in Polit. Sci., Tchrs. Coll., 1960, secondary teaching certificate, 1961; m. Sophie Kisch, Sept. 20, 1954. Came to U.S., 1951, naturalized, 1956. Sec., v.p. Romanian Polit. Refugee Welfare Com., Rome, Italy, 1948-50; worker, timekeeper, payroll clk. Chrysler Corp., Highland Park, Mich., 1951-60; tchr. fgn. langs. Detroit Pub. Schs., 1961—. Corr., Romanian News America, Cleve., 1964—. Romanian cons. Greater Detroit Ethnic Group Project, 1968—. Candidate, Mich. Constl. Conv., 1961; chmn. Romanian sect. nationalites div. Mich. Democratic Com., 1960—, v.p., 1965-66, treas., 1968—. Contbg. mem. Iulia Maniu Found., N.Y., 1965—. Served to 1st lt. Romanian Army, 1939-40; polit. prisoner, Buchenwald, Germany, 1942-44. Recipient Service award Nationalites div. Mich. Dem. Com., 1967; M. Banciu award Romanian of Year, 1978; Aron Cotrus award, 1979; Fonds European Secour Etud. Etranger, Switzerland scholar, 1949-50; Nat. Def. Edn. Act grantee N.Y. State U., 1963; Fed. grantee, P.R., 1966. Mem. Internat., Am. polit. sci. assns., Am. Fedn. Tchrs., Am. Acad. Polit. and Social Sci., Mich. Fgn. Lang. Assn., Am. Council Fgn. Lang. Tchrs. Editor Bull. Romanian Am. Nat. Com., Detroit, 1958-63; dir. sci. book exhibit Internat. Congress Dialectology. Louvain, Belgium, 1960. Home: 16424 Lincoln St East Detroit MI 48021

HUMMEL, GEORGE HENRY, air freight co. exec.; b. Bklyn., Apr. 9, 1945; s. Herbert W. and Katherine (Wulpern) A.; B.A., Muhlenberg Coll., 1967; B.D., Hamma Sch. Theology, 1971, M.Div., 1972, S.T.M., 1972; cert. clin. pastoral edn., 1968; m. Jeanette K. Inbody, July 6, 1968; children—Elissa, Seth. Ordained to ministry Lutheran Ch., 1971; asst. pastor Bethesda on the Bay Luth. Ch., Bay Village, Ohio, 1971-74; pastor Triumphant Cross Lutheran Ch., Trotwood, Ohio, 1974-77; dir. adult programs Wright State U., Dayton, 1977-79; tng. and devel. specialist Monarch Marking—Pitney Bowes, Miamisburg, Ohio, 1979-81; supr. mgmt. tng. and devel. Emery Air Freight, 1981—; pres., chmn. bd. Devel. Learning Program, Inc., Dayton, 1976-79; adj. faculty Hamma Theol. Sch., 1971-79. Mem. econ. devel. com. Miami Valley Regional Planning Commn., 1974-78; chmn. bd. Trotwood-Madison Com. on Youth, 1975-79, Montgomery County Fine Arts Commn., 1977, Montgomery County Adv. Bd. on Community Devel., 1978; chmn., Trotwood Action Commn., 1975-79; dir. Project Intercept-Trotwood Police, 1975-79; treas. Day-Mont West Mental Health Corp., 1975-77; mem. Montgomery County Democratic Central Com., 1977—; councilman at large City of Trotwood, 1979—. Recipient Lutheran Brotherhood award, 1970, Leadership award Aid Assn. Lutherans, 1971, Trotwood/Madison Outstanding Community Service award, 1979. Mem. Am. Soc. Tng. and Devel. Home: 9 N Sunrise Ave Trotwood OH 45426 Office: Dayton Internat Airport Dayton OH 45401

HUMMEL, ROBERT PAUL, surgeon; b. Bellevue, Ky., Sept. 17, 1928; s. Robert Paul and Clara (Rechtin) H.; B.S., Xavier U., 1947; M.D., U. Cin., 1951; m. Helen Beam, June 26, 1954; children—Claire, Molli, Robert Paul. Intern, Duke U. Hosp., Durham, N.C., 1951-52; surg. resident Cin. Gen. Hosp., 1952-54, 56-59, chief surg. resident 1959-60; instr. surgery U. Cin. Med. Sch., 1959-63, asst. prof., 1963-67, asso. prof., 1967-76, prof., 1976—; asst. attending surgeon Cin. Gen. Hosp., 1959-64, clinician, surg. out-patient dept., 1960—, attending surgeon, 1965—; attending surgeon Children's Hosp. Cin., 1964—; cons. Shriners Burns Inst., Cin., 1967—; mem. active staff C. R. Holmes, Our Lady of Mercy hosps.; mem. courtesy staff Bethesda, Christ hosps. Served in U.S. Army, 1954-56. Diplomate Am. Bd. Surgery. Mem. Am. Surg. Assn., Am. Assn. Surgery of Trauma, Am. Burn Assn., A.C.S. (bd. govs. 1979—), AMA, Am. Trauma Soc., Internat. Soc. Burn Injuries, Societe Internationale de Chirurgie, Soc. Surgery of Alimentary Tract, Central Surg. Assn. (treas. 1978—), Ohio Med. Assn., Cin. Acad. Medicine (sec. 1977, pres. 1981), Cin. Surg. Soc. (pres. 1977), U. Cin. Grad. Surg. Soc., Sigma Xi, Alpha Omega Alpha. Republican. Roman Catholic. Clubs: Univ., Country (Cin.), Office: 231 Bethesda Ave Cincinnati OH 45267

HUMPHREY, ALBERT S., planning corp. exec.; b. Kansas City, Mo., June 2, 1926; s. Albert S. and Margaret Elizabeth (Benton) H.; B.S. with high honors in Chem. Engring., U. Ill., 1946; M.S. in Chem. Engring., M.I.T., 1949; M.B.A. in Fin., Harvard U., 1955; m. Virginia Potter, Oct. 7, 1957 (div.); children—Albert S., Virginia Potter, Johnathan Benton Cantwell, Heidi. Chem. engr. Esso Standard Oil Co., 1948; chief chem. and protective group Office of Chief Chem. Officer, U.S. Army Chem. Corps, 1952-55; asst. to pres. Penberthy Instrument Co., 1955; chief product planning Boeing Airplane Co., 1956-60; mgr. value analysis Small Aircraft Engine Div. Gen. Electric, 1960; Mgr. research and devel. planning P.R. Mallory & Co. Inc., 1961-64; head mgmt. audit for improved ops. Gen. Dynamics, 1964-65; sr. economist Stanford Research Inst., 1965-69; chmn. bd. Bus. Planning and Devel., London, Eng., and Kansas City, Mo., 1969—; faculty, extension sch. for adult edn. U. Wash., 1955-58, USNR Officers Tng. Sch., 1955-60; dir. Treasured Products Inc., Triade Inc., Galley West Inc., Aqua Media Inc., Delta Control Inc., Integrated Graphics Inc., Coffenco Internat., London, Petras Petrochemische Anwendungssysteme GmbH, Nurnberg, Germany, Tower Lysprodukter a/s, Oslo, Tower Lamps Ltd., Eng.; cons. Lear Siegler Inc., Ottawa Silica Sand, J.C. Carter, Gen. Dynamics Centrifugal Products, Continental Coffee Co., Faultless Starch Co., W.H. Smith & Son Ltd. (Can. and Eng.), J. Lyons Groceries Ltd., Lyons-Tetley Ltd., Intertext Group Ltd., J.W. French Ltd., Anglia Canners Ltd., Burda Mapleton's Foods Ltd., Bramah Tea & Coffee Co. Ltd., Singer Bus. Machines, Bemrose Corp., Am. Steriliser Co., Erie Technol. Products Inc., Givaudin Corp., Appleton Mills, Appleton Coated Paper Co., G.D. Searle & Co., Unitog, the Burndy Corp., Jack E. Falve Enterprises, Givaudin et Cie, United Recorded Tape, Corpo Mex S.A., Ansul Co., No. Ill. Gas, Foremost Foods, Coca Cola Co., Fireman's Fund Inc., Western Litho Trade Services Inc., Phila. Sci. Center, Norbury Packaging Co., Pricerite Ltd., Coffenco Internat. Ltd., J. Lyons Soft Drinks Div., Roche Products Ltd., Caledonian Tractor & Equipment Co. Ltd., Rist Wire and Cable Co. Ltd., Rolls-Royce Ltd., 1971, Allied Computer Tech., Aqua Media Corp., Delta Control Inc., Integrated Graphics Corp., Leckenby Co., Internat. Bus. Forum, Hambledon Press, Kalamazoo Ltd., Kearley & Tonge Ltd., L. Noel & Sons Ltd., Metal Box Ltd., Ardel og Sunndal Verk Seguros America Benamex S.R., NASA Office Advanced Research and Tech. Served to lt. comdr. USNR, 1944-47, 50-52. Mem. Am. Inst. Chem. Engrs., Brit. Inst. Dirs., Sci. Research Soc. Am., Brit. Inst. Mktg., Sigma Xi, Tau Beta Phi, Sigma Tau. Republican. Mem. Ch. of Eng. Clubs: M.I.T. Alumni, Ill. U. Alumni, Harvard Bus. Sch. Alumni. Contbr. articles to profl. publs. in field U.S., U.K. Home and Office: 4030 Charlotte St Kansas City MO 64110

HUMPHREY, HUBERT HORATIO, III, state senator; b. Mpls., June 26, 1942; s. Hubert Horatio and Muriel F. (Buck) H.; B.A., Am. U., 1965; J.D., U. Minn., 1969; m. Nancy Lee Jeffrey, 1963; children—Florence Christine, Pamela Katherine, Humbert Horatio IV. Admitted to Minn. bar, practiced law; mem. Minn. Senate, 1973—. Del. state conv. Democratic-Farmer-Labor party, 1970, nat. conv., 1980. Mem. Insterstate Coop. Commn., Am., Minn. bar assns., Citizens League, Am. Judicature Soc. Club: Optimists. Office: 301 State Capitol Saint Paul MN 55155*

HUMPHREY, LOREN JENKINS, surgeon, educator; b. Springfield, Ill., May 4, 1931; s. Merle G. and Alma (Jenkins) H.; B.A., Albion (Mich.) Coll., 1953; M.D., U. Ill., Chgo., 1956, M.S., 1960; Ph.D. in Immunology, SUNY, Buffalo, 1967; m. Janice Pederson, Dec. 19, 1953; children—Peter, Mark, Paul, Lori. Intern, Ill. Research and Edn. Hosp., Chgo., 1956-57, asst. resident, 1959-62, resident, 1962-63; asso. prof. surgery, microbiology Emory U., 1969-71; prof. dept. surgery U. Kans., 1971-76, chmn. surgery, 1971-76; prof. U. Mo., Kansas City, 1977—, dir. surg. oncology, 1977—; pres. Mid-Am. Immunotherapy and Surg. Research Found., Kansas City, Kans., 1978—; pres. Humphrey Med. Clinic and Tumor Inst., Shawnee, Kans., 1981—, Surg. Oncology Chartered, Shawnee, 1977—. Bd. dirs. Lake Quivira, Inc., 1981—. Served with M.C., U.S. Army, 1957-59. Am. Cancer Soc. fellow, 1963, Nat. Cancer Inst. fellow, 1963-66; grantee in field. Fellow A.C.S.; mem. Am. Assn. Physicians and Surgeons, Assn. Acad. Surgery, Central Surg. Assn., Soc. Univ. Surgeons, Transplantation Soc., AMA, Christian Med. Soc., Ga. Surg. Soc., Am. Thyroid Assn., Soc. Head and Neck Surgeons, Soc. Surgery Alimentary Tract, So. Med. Assn., Am. Assn. Cancer Research, So. Surg. Assn., Soc. Univ. Chmn., Am. Assn. Cancer Edn., Am. Surg. Assn., Kansas City Surg. Soc., Sigma Xi. Republican. Lutheran. Editor: Am. Journal of Surgery, 1975—, Jour. Surgical Oncology, 1971—, Iranian Jour. Surgery, 1975—, Oncology Times, 1979—; contbr. articles to profl. jours. Home: 470 Terr Trail E Lake Quivira KS 66106 Office: 7312 Antioch St Shawnee Mission KS 66204

HUMPHREY, OWEN EVERETT, ret. ednl. adminstr.; b. Wautoma, Wis., Oct. 25, 1920; s. Marion Arthur and Flora Agnes (Helms) H.; B.S., Wis. State Coll., 1947; M.S., U. Ark., 1949; Ed. Specialist, U. Ill., 1954; m. Billye Allene Cox, Apr. 6, 1946; children—Reba (Mrs. James Rick), Ivye. Tchr., Plainfield, Wis., 1941-42, Sheboygan, Wis., 1947-48; prin. Lincoln Elementary Sch., Mattoon, Ill., 1950-55; supervising prin., Peotone, Ill., 1955-57; tchr. Nameoki Elementary Sch., Granite City, Ill., 1957-59; prin. Maryville Sch., Granite City, 1959-67; curriculum coordinator, Granite City, 1967-79; adminstrv. asst. Madison County ESR, 1979-81; cons. Citizens Adv. Com. for Local Dist. Ednl. Planning, 1972-79. Dir., P.T.A. Area Council Mothersingers, Mattoon, Ill., 1951-54, Granite City Area Council Mothersingers, 1958-63. Served with 95th Inf., AUS, 1941-45; ETO. Decorated Bronze Star medal. Mem. Internat. Platform Assn., Nat. Edn. Assn. (life mem.), Assn. Supervision and Curriculum Devel., Ill. Assn. Supervision and Curriculum Devel., Am. Assn. Sch. Adminstrs., Am. Ednl. Research Assn., Madison County Curriculum Council. Musical compositions: I Should Have Told You, 1965, It Doesn't Matter Now, 1965, Think Kindly of Me, 1966, The Resurrection, 1959; New Jerusalem, 1960; I Will Hold My Master's Hand, 1974; I Remember It All, 1977. Contbr. articles to ednl. jours. Home: 18 W Wilson Park Dr Granite City IL 62040

HUMPHREY, RONALD RICHARD, endocrinologist; b. Detroit, Mar. 24, 1930; s. James Edward and Elizabeth Ann (Rancilio) H.; B.S., Aquinas Coll., 1951; M.S., U. Mich., 1953; m. Gaye Hellene Hilliard, May 28, 1971. Research biologist Army Chem. Center, Md., 1953-55; research pharmacologist Parke Davis Co., Detroit, 1955-71; research scientist in endocrinology, Ann Arbor, 1971-76; research asso. Warner Lambert Co., Ann Arbor, 1976-78, scientist in teratology, 1978—; cons. Bio Engring. Cons., Whitmore Lake, Mich., 1968—. Served with AUS, 1953-55. Mem. AAAS, Am. Soc. Andrology, Soc. Exptl. Biology and Medicine, Soc. Study Reproduction, N.Y. Acad. Scis. Republican. Roman Catholic. Clubs: U. Mich. (Detroit); Town of Ann Arbor. Contbr. articles to profl. jours. Home: 2220 Copley St Ann Arbor MI 48104 Office: PO Box 1047 Warner Lambert Ann Arbor MI 48106

HUMPHREY, SUZANNE W., ednl. cons.; b. Terre Haute, Ind., Sept. 19; d. Charles H. and Juliette A. (Phillip) Wilson; B.S. in Edn., Ind. State U., 1953; M.S. in Ednl. Adminstrn., So. Ill. U., Edwardsville, 1979; postgrad. in curriculum and instrn. State U.; m. Robert D. Humphrey, June 21, 1953; children—Julie, Elise, Jacquie, Laurie. Elem. tchr., public schs., Lafayette, Ind., 1953-54, New Castle, Ind., 1963-69; substitute tchr., public schs., Litchfield, 1969-75; asst. dir. mgmt. programs Ill. Assn. Sch. Bds./Sch. Mgmt. Found. Ill., Springfield, Ill., 1979—. Sec., Litchfield (Ill.) Sch. Dist. Bd. Edn., 1978, pres., 1979; mem. bldg. com. Litchfield Community Center, 1972-80. Mem. Ind. State U. Alumni Council (v.p. 1977, pres. 1978), Assn. Supervision and Curriculum Devel., Ill. Women Adminstrs., Soc. Educators and Scholars (1980 Conf. dir., pres. 1980-81), Pamarista, Kappa Delta Pi, Alpha Omicron Pi (cert. of honor 1979). Methodist. Clubs: Zonta, Women's Federated, Litchfield Woman's (pres. 1975-77). Home: Rural Route 3 Litchfield IL 62056 Office: 1209 S 5th St Springfield IL 62703

HUMPHRIES, BEVERLY NELL (MRS. DONALD R. HUMPHRIES), librarian; b. Gatesville, Tex., July 3, 1930; d. E.B. and Nora H. (Nelson) Harris; A.A., Clifton Jr. Coll., 1946-48; B.S., N. Tex. State U., 1950; M.S., So. Ill. U., 1971; m. Donald R. Humphries, May 27, 1951; children—Brett, Joel. Elementary tchr. Balmorhea (Tex.) Pub. Schs., 1948-49; res. librarian Tex. Technol. U., Lubbock, 1950-51; elementary tchr. Fairbanks (Alaska) Sch. Dist., 1952-54; serials and documents librarian Tex. A. and M. U., College Station, 1954-57; periodicals librarian Davenport (Iowa) Pub. Library, 1957-59; librarian Monticello Coll., Godfrey, Ill., 1965-71, Lewis and Clark Community Coll., Godfrey, 1971—. Bd. dirs. Greater Alton Concert Assn., 1968-80. Mem. Am., Ill. library assns. Club: Zonta (bd. dirs. 1980—). Home: 4810 Chateau Dr Godfrey IL 62035 Office: Lewis and Clark Community College Godfrey IL 62035

HUNDELT, CRAIG THOMAS, constrn. co. exec.; b. St. Louis, Oct. 23, 1947; s. Lester W. and Lydia P. (Hamill) H.; student St. Louis U., 1967-68, 72-73; B.S. in Bus. Adminstrn., U. Denver, 1975; m. Norma Colón-Muñoz, Feb. 14, 1976; 1 son, Miguel. Broker, researcher domestic and fgn. markets in agrl. and energy commodities James McClain Corp., St. Louis, 1975-76; pres. Consol. Engring. & Sheet Metal Co., St. Louis, 1976—; v.p. Consol. Mechanicals, Inc., St. Louis, 1976—, gen. mgr. heating, ventilating, air conditioning dept., 1977—. Mem. Sons of Bosses, fundraising orgn., St. Louis, 1979-81. Served with M.C., U.S. Army, 1968-71. Mem. Sheet Metal and Air Conditioning Contractors Nat. Assn., ASHRAE, Am. Mgmt. Assn., Mo. C. of C., Assn. Energy Engrs., St. Louis Art Mus., Mo. Bot. Garden Soc., Ambassadors of St. Louis. Republican. Office: 1430 Kingsland St Saint Louis MO 63133

HUNDT, RICHARD MICHAEL, hosp. safety ofcl.; b. Mpls., Mar. 6, 1953; s. Ronald Emory and Janet Barbara Trembley; student Normandale Jr. Coll., 1971-72, U. Nebr., 1976; numerous trade courses. Police intern Burnsville (Minn.) Dept. Public Safety, 1971-72; chief security officer Dayton Hudson Properties, Mpls., 1974-78; dir. safety and security Hennepin County Med. Center, Mpls., 1978—; adult edn. instr.; cons. Mem. Mpls. Central Community Planning Council, 1979-81. Nominee, Mpls. Citizens award, 1975. Mem. Internat. Assn. Hosp. Security, Nat. Fire Protection Assn., Internat. Assn. Arson Investigators, Am. Soc. Indsl. Security, Am. Soc. Safety Engrs. Republican. Greek Orthodox. Office: 701 Park Ave Minneapolis MN 55415

HUNGATE, CARROLL PAUL, ret. physician, naval officer; b. Emporia, Kans., July 31, 1904; s. John T. and Meta Bena (Paulson) H.; student Nebr. Wesleyan U., 1921-22, Baker U., 1922-23; A.B., U. Kans., 1925, B.S., 1928, M.D., 1928; postgrad. Harvard, 1929, U. Munich, Vienna, Komenskeho, 1930-31; m. Mary Agnes Patterson, June 23, 1928; children—Mary Agnes Hungate Grubb (dec.), Annabel Hungate Christy. Intern, Chelsea Naval Hosp., (Mass.), 1928-29, resident, 1929-30; commd. lt. (j.g.), M.C., 1928, capt., 1945; med. officer, 1938-47, sr. med. officer Naval Air Sta., Olathe, Kans., 1948-59; ret., 1959; practice medicine, Kansas City, Mo., 1931-40, 47—; ret. physician Ford Motor Co., Kansas City, Mo.; surg. staff Research Bapt., St. Joseph's, St. Luke's hosps., Kansas City; former instr. preventice medicine Sch. Pharmacy, U. Mo. at Kansas City. Past chmn. health services adv. com. U.S. Civil Def. Council; past cons. AEC, USPHS; mem. bd. Kansas City Council on Alcoholism, 1965—, v.p., 1966; former mem. Mo. Gov.'s Com. Occupation Health and Safety; chmn. Edward Holman Skinner Meml. Trust Fund. Trustee Mo. Valley Coll. Recipient awards Jackson County Med. Soc., U.S. Civil Def. Council, U.S. Civil Def. Adminstrn.; Pfizer award Surgeon Gen. USPHS; Pioneer of Ky. award Harrodsburg (Ky.) Hist. Soc.; keys to cities of Harrodsburg and New Orleans; named Hon. Flight Surgeon, Brazilian Air Force, Wisdom Hall of Fame. Diplomate Am. Bd. Preventive Medicine. Fellow Am. Coll. Preventive Medicine; mem. AMA, Am. Social Health Assn. (past dir.), Mo. (former disaster med. care com.), Jackson County (former mem. emergency med. care com.) med. socs., Mil. Surgeons Assn., Kansas City Social Health Soc. (past pres.), Great Plains (past pres.), Kansas City (past pres.) indsl. med. assns., Am. Occupational Medicine Assn., Am. Med. Writers Assn., AAAS, Am. Assn. Med. History. Am. Soc. Geneology, Mil. Order World Wars, Am. Legion, SR (surgeon gen. U.S. 1979—), Kansas City S.W. Clin. Soc. (pres. 1957), Navy League (dir. Kansas City), Hungate Hist. Soc. (pres. 1976-78). Presbyn. Clubs: Univ. (Kansas City, Mo.), Rotary, Masons. Author: History of Hungate Family, Vols. I-V, 1972-75; How to Trace Your Ancestors, 1977. Contbr. articles to profl. jours. Developed traveling exhibit on civil def. and nuclear energy, 1949-50 (now in mus. of physics dept. U. Kans.). Home: 6845 Oak St Kansas City MO 64113

HUNGERFORD, LUGENE GREEN, nuclear co. exec.; b. Birmingham, Ala., Sept. 1, 1924; d. Wesley Cornith and Anna Mae (Majors) Green; student U. Ala. Law Sch., part-time 1946-48, 1953, 55, U. Tenn., Wayne State U., 1956, 60, Purdue U., 1966, 68; B.S., Birmingham So. U., 1946; M.S., U. Ala., 1950; m. Herbert Eugene Hungerford, Jr., Nov. 4, 1949. Instr., Snead Jr. Coll., Boaz, Ala., 1948; tchr. math. adult edn., Knoxville, Tenn., 1953-54; substitute tchr. Knoxville and Knox County, 1951-53, 54-55; pvt. cons., tutor, 1956-59, 61-64; instr., then asst. prof. physics Wayne State U., 1955-56, 59-60, from adminstrv. asst. to v.p., treas. Calif. Nuclear Co., 1963-68; v.p., treas. Nuclear Mgmt., Inc., Lafayette, Ind., 1968—; dir. Nuclear Engring. Co., 1969-72; sec., treas., dir. Bio-Service, Inc., 1969—; sec., treas. Mediatech, Inc., 1972-76, dir., 1977—; treas., dir. Chemtree Corp., Central Valley, N.Y., 1973-79. Nat. 2d v.p. Ch. Periodical Club of Episcopal Ch., 1964-67, diocesan dir., 1957-60, provincial dir., 1961-64. Mem. Am. Nuclear Soc., Health Physics Soc., Atomic Indsl. Forum, Am. Phys. Soc., Sigma Xi, Sigma Pi Sigma. Republican. Clubs: Lafayette Country, Purdue Women's. Contbr. articles to profl. jours. Home: 7 Knoll Crest Ct West Lafayette IN 47906 Office: 601 N 4th St Lafayette IN 47906

HUNNICUTT, THOMAS EDGAR, ins. agy. exec.; b. Wells County, Ind., Aug. 26, 1945; s. Carl Leo and Mary (Mead) H.; B.S., Ball State U., 1970; M.S. in B.A., Ind. U., 1975; m. Karen Kay Johnson, Sept. 1, 1968; children—Heath, Lisa. With Howard Johnson's Restaurants, Midwest region, 1965-70; systems analyst, data processing systems cons. Lincoln Nat. Life Ins. Co., Ft. Wayne, Ind., 1970-76; pres. Hunnicutt Ins. Agy., Warren, Ind., 1976—; ind. bus. systems cons. Served with U.S. Army, 1965-67. Mem. Warren C. of C. (pres. 1981). Republican. Club: Masons (sec. Huntington County Scottish Rite Club). Home: Route 3 PO Box 46A Warren IN 46792 Office: PO Box 475 Warren IN 46792

HUNSSINGER, EDWARD FREDERICK, JR., brokerage co. exec.; b. Chgo., Sept. 20, 1949; s. Edward Frederick and Celopha F. (Smith) H.; student Loyola U., Chgo., 1967-71; m. Susan M. Malloy, Aug. 21, 1971; children—Michael Malloy, Mary Malloy. Sales rep. Weiss Brokerage Co., Chgo., 1971-74; v.p. sales Bachner Frozen Foods, Chgo., 1974-75; pres. Midland Brokerage Co., Inc., Orland Park, Ill., 1976—; chief exec. officer Silver Lake Farms Inc., Orland Park, 1979—. Bd. dirs. Alumni St. Rita High Sch., Chgo., S.W. Suburban Montessori Schs., Palos Park, Ill., 1980—. Home: 8517 W Golfview Dr Orland Park IL 60462 Office: 62 Orland Square Dr Orland Park IL 60462

HUNSTIGER, CYNTHIA ANN, nurse; b. St. Cloud, Minn., Aug. 24, 1948; d. William Henry and Patricia Jane (Fisher) H.; R.N., St. Mary's Hosp., Rochester, Minn., 1969. Mem. nursing staff St. Mary's Hosp., 1969-73, health service supr., 1973-77, asst. dir. materials mgmt., 1977-80, dir. central service, 1980—; cons., vol. in field. Recipient Pearl Eusterman award St. Mary's Sch. Nursing, 1969; named Young Career Woman, Rochester Bus. and Profl. Women, 1977. Mem. Am. Soc. Hosp. Central Service, St. Mary's Alumni Assn. (dir., past pres.). Author papers in field. Office: 1216 2d St SW Rochester MN 55901

HUNT, CHARLES KELLOGG, educator; b. Detroit, June 3, 1907; s. Harry Edward and Katherine Harman (Kellogg) H.; B.S., U. Mich., 1929, M.A., 1930, Ph.D., 1934; m. Ednamae Fisher, Dec. 10, 1929; children—Norman, Diana (Mrs. James Taylor). Teaching fellow U. Mich., Ann Arbor, 1930-34; fellow Mellon Inst. Indsl. Research, Pitts., 1934-35; research chemist Gulf Research & Devel. Corp., Harmarville, Pa., 1935-36; group leader Pitts. Plate Glass Co., Columbia Chem. Div., Barberton, Ohio 1936-37; sect. head Sharples Chems., Inc., Wyandotte, Mich., 1937-44, sales research dir., 1944-49; editor, publisher Investment Adv. Services Summarized, Wyandotte, 1949-51; asst. prof. phys. scis. U. Ill., Chgo., 1951-57, asso. prof. chemistry, 1957-64, prof., 1964-74, prof. chemistry emeritus, 1974—. Cons. McGean Chem. Co., Cleve., 1934; field rep. Babson's Reports, Inc., Chgo., 1954-57; cons. Com-Bar, Inc., Chgo., 1957-58, dir., 1958. Cub Scout pack chmn. Boy Scouts Am., 1946-49, scout committeeman, 1949-50, Sea-Scout committeeman, 1947-50; state dir. Westinghouse Sci. Talent Search, 1966-69. Recipient Honor Scroll award Am. Inst. Chemists, Chgo., 1972. Fellow AAAS, Am. Inst. Chemists (chmn. Chgo. chpt. 1968-69); mem. Am. Chem. Soc. (chmn. Detroit sect. 1948, chmn. Chgo. sect. 1966-67, sponsor student affiliate chpt. 1951-72, nat. councilor 1947, 49-51, 62-73, nat. council com. on constitution and by-laws 1967-73, joint bd. council ad-hoc com. on investments 1974-75), Chgo. Chemists Club, Fedn. Am. Scientists, Ill. Acad. Sci. (v.p. 1969-70), Chgo. Acad. Scis., Sigma Xi, Alpha Chi Sigma; hon. mem. Wyandotte Y's Men's Club, Ill. Jr.

Acad. Sci. Author: Quinoidation of Triarylmethyl Chlorides, 1934; Nonchlorinated Compounds Derived from Monochloropentanes, 1943; Hindered Phenols, 1945; Inhibitor for Steel Pickling Baths, 1946; contbr. to vols. 1, 2 and 3 Ency. Chem. Tech., 1947-49. Home: 307 W 6th St Hinsdale IL 60521

HUNT, EARL WILBUR, chemist; b. Brainerd, Minn., Mar. 12, 1926; s. Ralph Ernest and Alisemon Ione (Harris) H.; student public schs., Crosby, Minn.; m. Vera Lorraine Knuppel, June 12, 1948; children—Valli Marie, Terry Earl. Research chemist Manganese Chem. Corp., Riverton, Minn., 1953-62, 3M Co., St. Paul, 1962—. Served with USN, 1944-46. Mem. Wilderness Soc., Nat. Wildlife Fedn. Methodist. Author: The Living Wilderness, 1977. Home: 397 Sherrie Ln Woodbury MN 55125 Office: 3M Center Saint Paul MN 55101

HUNT, JAMES FREDERICK, advt. agy. exec.; b. Osborn, Ohio, Apr. 5, 1945; s. James F. and Mary E. (Chamberlain) H.; B.S. in Journalism, Ohio U., 1967; m. Bonnie A. Haire, July 6, 1968; children—Marcy, Katie. Account asst. Ketchum, MacLeod & Grove, Inc., Pitts., 1969-70, account exec., 1970-72, account mgr., 1972-77; product mgr. Andrew Jergens Co., Cin., 1977-79; account supr. Wyse Advt. Inc., Cleve., 1979—. Adv., Jr. Achievement; coordinator United Fund, Pitts., 1976. Served with Transp. Corps., U.S. Army, 1967-69. Decorated Bronze Star; recipient award Freedoms Found., 1968. Republican. Home: 26604 Jefferson Ct Bay Village OH 44140 Office: Wyse Advt Inc 24 Public Sq Cleveland OH 44113

HUNT, LAMAR, profl. football team exec.; b. 1933; grad. So. Meth. U.; m. Norma Hunt; children—Lamar, Sharon, Clark. Founder, pres. Kansas City Cheifs of Nat. Football League, 1959—; founder, pres. Am. Football League, 1959 (became Am. Football Conf. Nat. Football League 1970), pres. Am. Football Conf., 1970; pres. Kansas City Chiefs to 1977, chmn., 1977—; dir. Great Midwest Corp., Interstate Securities, Traders' Nat. Bank. Bd. dirs. Profl. Football Hall of Fame, Canton Ohio. Named Salesman of Year, Kansas City Advt. and Sales Execs Club, 1963, Southwesterner of Year, Tex. Sportswriters Assn., 1969. Address: care Kansas City Chiefs One Arrowhead Dr Kansas City MO 64129*

HUNT, MARGARET MARY, educator; b. Gary, Ind., Nov. 29, 1934; d. Albert Edward and Margaret Mary Marconi; B.S. in Elem. Edn., Ind. U. Northwest, 1970, M.S., 1972; cert. sch. library and audio-visual scis., Purdue U., Hammond, Ind., 1974; Ed.S. in Ednl. Adminstrn. and Supervision, Ind. State U., 1980; m. Joseph Howard Hunt, Feb. 5, 1960; 1 dau., Alice Jane. Staff extension and circulation depts. Gary-Lake County Public Library, 1952-62; mem. staff Hobart (Ind.) Twp. Community Sch. Corp., 1970—, media specialist, curriculum coordinator, 1976-80, ofcl. presentor Utah Systems Approach to Individualized Learning, 1978—. Trustee Lake County Public Library, 1978—. Mem. Assn. Supervision and Curriculum Devel., Internat. Reading Assn., ALA, Am. Library Trustees Assn., AAUW, NEA, Ind. Library Assn., Ind. Assn. Supervision and Curriculum Devel., Ind. Library Trustees Assn., Ind. Tchrs. Assn., Assn. Ind. Media Educators, Friends of Library, Ind. Polit. Action Com. Edn. Roman Catholic. Author, editor media and elem. curriculum guides. Home: 103 Fraser Ln Hobart IN 46342 Office: 3334 Michigan Ave Hobart IN 46342

HUNT, MARK ALAN, assn. exec.; b. Topeka, Kans., May 21, 1949; s. Ira B. and Marjorie May (McConnell) H.; B.A. (Wiseman scholar, Washburn scholar), Washburn U., 1971; M.A., Cooperstown Grad. Programs, 1982; m. Cynthia E. Rush, Feb. 21, 1976; 1 son, Alexander Rush. Nat. Endowment for Humanities intern Am. Assn. State Local History, 1974-75; mus. dir. Plymouth (Mich.) Hist. Mus., 1976; curator exhibits Kans. State Hist. Soc., Topeka, 1976, asst. mus. dir., 1976-79, dir. State Hist. Mus., 1979—; cons. Menninger Found., 1980; faculty mem. summer inst. Public History Program, U. Calif., Santa Barbara, 1980. Recipient God and Country award, Boy Scouts Am., 1962, Eagle award, 1963; Clark fellow, 1973-74; recipient membership award Am. Assn. for State and Local History, 1977. Mem. Am. Assn. for State and Local History (nat. edn. com. 1981—, state membership chmn. 1976—), Mt. Plains Mus. Assn. (dir., Kans. rep. 1977), Kans. Mus. Assn. (pres. 1978-80), Am. Assn. Mus., Kans. State Hist. Soc., Kappa Sigma. Republican. Methodist. Contbr. articles to profl. jours. Office: 120 W 10th St Topeka KS 66612

HUNT, MARVIN WRIGHT, dietitian; b. Manhattan, Kans., Oct. 16, 1930; s. Orville Don and Lovey Alta (Wright) H.; B.S. in Home Econs., Kans. State U., 1956; m. Jean Lewis, Nov. 26, 1967; children—Paige Justine, Christine Wright, Alan Curtis. Catering mgr. Kans. State Union, Kans. State U., Manhattan, 1957-61; sr. supr. food service Boeing Co., Wichita, Kans., 1961-65; dir. food service Research Hosp. and Med. Center, Kansas City, Mo., 1965-68; dir. food service St. Louis U., Food Service Mgmt., Inc., 1968-72; area mgr. Servomation, Inc., Atlanta, 1972-77; dir. food service Incarnate Word Hosp., St. Louis, 1977—; vis. lectr. Kans. State U., 1963-67. Served with U.S. Army, 1949-53. Decorated Combat Inf. badge. Ky. Col. Mem. Am. Dietetics Assn., Am. Soc. Hosp. Food Service Adminstrs. Clubs: Elks; Mo. Athletic. Office: 3545 Lafayette St Saint Louis MO 63104

HUNT, RICHARD HOWARD, sculptor; b. Chgo., Sept. 12, 1935; s. Cleophus Howard and Etoria Inez (Henderson) H.; studied sculpture with Nelli Bar, 1950-53; student U. Chgo., 1953-55; B.A.E., Art Inst. of Chgo.; m. Betty Marjorie; 1 dau., Cecilia Elizabeth. Exhibited Artists of Chgo. and Vicinity exhbn., 1955-56, 62d, 63d, 64th Am. exhbns. Art Inst. Chgo., also 1971, Carnegie Internat. Pitts., 1958, Mus. Modern Art, N.Y.C., 1959, 71; one-man shows: Alan Gallery, N.Y.C., 1960, B.C. Holland Gallery, Chgo., 1963, Dorsky Gallery, N.Y.C., 1971; represented in permanent collections: Mus. Modern Art, N.Y.C., Whitney Mus., N.Y.C., Mus. 20th Century, Vienna, Austria; vis. artist Yale, 1964, Chovinard Art Sch., 1964-65. Trustee, Am. Acad. in Rome, 1980—. Served with U.S. Army. Recipient Frank G. Logan medal and prize, 1956, Pauline Palmer prize, 1957, James Nelson Raymond traveling fellowship, 1957, Logan medal and prize Artists of Chgo. and Vicinity show, 1961; John Simon Guggenheim fellow, 1962-63. Office: 1017 W Lill Ave Chicago IL 60614*

HUNT, ROBERT PAUL, mfg. co. exec.; b. Wooster, Ohio, June 22, 1944; s. Paul Robert and Ruth Irene (Hooser) H.; student Bowling Green U., 1962-63, Ohio State U., 1963-64, Alaska U., 1968; m. Bette Rae Chitwood, Sept. 9, 1972; children—Alexis Leann, Carla Rae. With Ohio Brass Co., Mansfield, Ohio, 1963-66, 69—, transp. mgr., 1970—. Served with USAF, 1966-69. Mem. Central Ohio Traffic Club (dir. 1973-75), Transp. and Distbn. Assn., Nat. Rifle Assn., Am. Legion. Republican. Methodist. Home: 71 Yorkshire Rd Lexington OH 44904 Office: Ohio Brass Co 380 N Main St Mansfield OH 44902

HUNT, ROGER SCHERMERHORN, hosp. adminstr.; b. White Plaines, N.Y., Mar. 7, 1943; s. Charles Howland and Mildred Russell (Schermerhorn) H.; B.A., DePauw U., 1965; M.B.A., George Washington U., 1968; m. Mary Adams Libby, June 19, 1965; children—Christina, David. Adminstrv. resident Lankenau Hosp., Phila., 1966-68; asst. adminstr. Hahnemann Med. Coll. and Hosp., Phila., 1968-71, hosp. dir., 1971-74, asso. v.p., hosp. adminstr., 1974-77; dir. Ind. U. Hosps., Indpls., 1977—; pres. United Hosp. Services, Inc., 1979—; chmn. Alliance of Indpls. Hosps., 1981—; mgr. bd. trustees, sec.-treas. Delaware Valley Hosp. Laundry, 1969-77; bd. trustees Nat. Benefit Fund of Nat. Union Hosp. and Health Care Employees, 1973-77, Phila. Blood Center, 1972-74; asso. prof. hosp. adminstrn. Ind. U. Sch. Medicine, 1977—. Vice chmn. Pa. Emergency Health Services Council, 1975-77; pres. Chester County Emergency Med. Service Council, 1971-77; v.p. Wayne Area Jr. C. of C., 1969-70, pres., 1970-71, state dir., 1971-72. Fellow Am. Coll. Hosp. Adminstrs. (Postgrad. tng. award 1968): mem. Am. Hosp. Assn., Ind. Hosp. Assn. Office: Ind U Hosps 1100 W Michigan St Indianapolis IN 46202

HUNT, RUTH CECELIA, pub. co. exec.; b. Chgo., Apr. 5, 1923; d. Leslie Edward and Gladys Esther (Pratt) Hunt; B.S., Loyola U. Chgo., 1943, M.A., 1969, Ph.D., 1975. Asst. editor Am. Osteopathic Assn., Chgo., 1946-48, acting editor, 1948-51; advt. coordinator J.B. Roerig Co., Chgo., 1951-52; copy editor Jordan-Sieber & Assos., Chgo., 1952-53; sci. editor Am. Peoples Ency., Chgo., 1953-57, mng. editor, 1957-59, editor-in-chief, 1959-63; editorial dir. La Salle Extension U., Chgo., 1963-65; freelance writer, editor, Chgo., 1965-75; adminstr., research and evaluation Am. Coll. Obstetricians and Gynecologists, Chgo., 1974-76; med. evaluator Planned Parenthood - World Population, N.Y.C., 1976-79; mng. editor Riverside Pub. Co., Iowa City, Ia., 1979—; lectr. edn. Loyola U. Chgo., 1969-80; cons. in psychometrics. Mem.-at-large Nat. Accreditation Bd. for Continuing Edn., Am. Nurses Assn., 1975-79. HEW fellow, 1967-69. Mem. AAAS, Am. Statis. Assn., Am. Ednl. Research Assn., Nat. Council for Measurement in Edn., MLA, N.Y. Acad. Sci., Nat. Soc. for Study of Edn., Am. Assn. Sex Edn. Counselors and Therapists, Phi Delta Kappa. Republican. Episcopalian. Author: Job Tests for Women, 1980; editor Jour. Am. Assn. Sex Educators, Counselors and Therapists, 1979—.

HUNTER, DONALD FORREST, lawyer; b. Mpls., Jan. 30, 1934; s. Earl Harvey and Ruby Cecelia Hunter; B.A. cum laude, U. Minn., 1961, LL.B., 1963; m. Maryls Ann Zilge, June 2, 1951; children—Jeffrey, Cheri, Kathryn. Admitted to Minn. bar, 1963; asso., then partner Gislason, Dosland, Hunter & Malecki, New Ulm, Minn., 1963-76; exec. v.p., sec., gen. counsel, dir. Wirtz Prodns., Ltd., also Shipstads and Johnson Ice Follies, Inc. and Holiday on Ice, Chgo., 1976-79; partner firm Gislason, Dosland, Hunter & Malecki, Mpls., 1978—; dir. Chgo. Milw. Corp., Chgo., 1978—, chmn. bd., 1980—. Mem. Am. Bar Assn., Minn. Bar Assn. (alt. gov. 1973-76), Minn. Def. Lawyers Assn. (dir. 1976), 5th Dist. Bar Assn. (pres. 1971-72), Hennepin County Bar Assn. Club: Decathleon Athletic (Mpls.). Office: 460 Shelard Plaza Minneapolis MN 55426

HUNTER, DONALD H., state justice; b. Anderson, Ind., Oct. 21, 1911; LL.B., Lincoln Law Sch., 1937. Admitted to Ind. bar, 1937; practice law, LaGrange, Ind., 1946-48; dep. hearing examiner Ind. Public Service Commn.; judge LaGrange Circuit Ct., 1948-62; judge Ind., Appellate Ct. 1963-66, then chief justice ct.; acting presiding judge Ct. of Appeals, 2nd Dist., Ind., acting chief justice of Ct.; justice Ind. Supreme Ct., 1967—, now chief justice; mem. Ind. Jud. Council on Legal Edn. and Competence at the Bar, 1976—; chmn. Lake County Jud. Nominating Commn., 1973-76; jud. mem. Com. for Revision of Adoption Laws, Adv. Com. on Probation and Parole for Ind. Citizens Council; vol. instr. Ind. State Police Acad., Bloomington, 1972-74; guest lectr. various civic orgns. and legal assns.; mem. Constl. Revision Commn., 1967-71; chmn. com. creating disciplinary commn. financed by attys., 1970-71. Mem. Ind. Ho. of Reps., 1943-44. Served with inf., U.S. Army, 1943-46; ETO. Decorated Bronze Star, Purple Heart; Belgique Fouragere. Mem. Ind. State Bar Assn., Madison County Bar Assn., Ind. Council of Freedoms Found. (mem. Distinguished awards jury 1967-68, 70-72), VFW, Am. Legion, Phi Delta Phi (hon. mem.), Phi Alpha Delta (hon. mem.), Tau Kappa Epsilon. Methodist. Club: Masons. Home: 1719 Costello Dr Anderson IN 46011 Office: Supreme Ct 304 State House Indianapolis IN 46204

HUNTER, JOHN O., coll. pres.; b. Newfane, N.Y., Mar. 17, 1933; s. Alexander and Jane (Robertson) H.; B.A., U. Buffalo, 1959; M.A., SUNY, Buffalo, 1964, Ed.D., 1968; m. Lyla Beth Brown, Aug. 31, 1957; children—Elaine, John, Suzan, Elizabeth. Dean of coll. Niagara Community Coll., Sanborn, N.Y., 1969-78; pres. Coll. of Lake County, Grayslake, Ill., 1978—. Bd. trustees Nioga Library, Niagara Falls, N.Y., 1973-78; dir. Clara Abbott Scholarship Found., 1979—; bd. dirs. United Way of Lake County, 1979—. Served to 1st lt. U.S. Army, 1954-57. Mem. World Future Soc., Am. Assn. Higher Edn., Ill. Council Community Coll. Presidents. Club: Lion. Author: Values and the Future: Models of Community College Development, 1977. Home: 405 Berwick Waukegan IL 60085 Office: College of Lake County Grayslake IL 60030

HUNTER, LANE WILLIAM, sales exec.; b. Chgo., June 23, 1952; s. Robert William and Mattie Lee (Thomas) H.; student Elmhurst Coll., 1971-72, Trinity Christian Coll., 1972-73; grad. in history Moraine Valley Coll., 1973-74; m. Kristine Ann Johnson, Oct. 2, 1971; children—Jason Erik, Michelle Noel. With Stone Container Corp., Chgo., 1971—, asst. sales service mgr., 1976, sales rep., 1976-79, field sales mgr., 1979-80, gen. sales mgr., 1980—. Nat. Merit scholar, 1970-73; Ill. State scholar, 1970-73. Mem. Am. Mgmt. Assn. Democrat. Club: Chgo. Health. Home: Route 5 Box 36H Liberty MO 64068 Office: 933 S Kent Liberty MO 64068

HUNTER, LEE, automotive equipment mfg. co. exec., inventor; b. St. Louis, Apr. 27, 1913; s. Lee and Ollie (Stark) H.; ed. Westminster Coll., Fulton, Mo., Washington U., St. Louis; m. Jane Franklin Brauer, 1959; stepchildren—Arthur J. Brauer, Stephen F. Brauer. Draftsman, designer Herman Body Co., 1935-36; founder Lee Hunter Jr. Mfg. Co., 1936; pres. Hunter-Hartman Corp., 1937-42; pres. Hunter Engring. Co., Bridgeton, Mo., 1947-55, chmn. bd., chief exec. officer 1955—; pres. Hunter Aviation Co., 1955-60; hon. consul of Belgium, St. Louis; adv. dir. St. Louis County Nat. Bank, County Nat. Bancorp. Bd. dirs. Webster Coll., Junior Achievement, YMCA; trustee Westminster Coll., Fulton, Mo. Served to 1st lt. C.E., AUS, 1942-46. Recipient Alumni Achievement award Westminster Coll., 1972. Mem. Mo. C. of C., Phi Delta Theta. Presbyterian (trustee). Clubs: Le Mirador (Switzerland); St. Louis, Bellerive Country, Racquet, Strathalbyn, Engineers (St. Louis). Inventor: 1st rapid battery chargers; dynamic lever theory balancing; 1st on car mech. wheel balancer; 1st discharged battery analyzer, wheel alignment, automotive equipment. Patentee in field. Home: Hunter Farms 13501 Ladue Rd Saint Louis County MO 63141 Office: Hunter Engring Co 11250 Hunter Dr Bridgeton MO 63044

HUNTER, MIRIAM EILEEN, artist, educator; b. Cin., June 6, 1929; d. James R. and Bertha (Oberlin) Hunter; B.S., Ball State Tchrs. Coll., 1951, M.A. in Art, 1957; M.A. in Christian Edn., Wheaton Coll., 1958; Ed.D., Nova U., 1979. Tchr. art and English, Madison-Marion Consol. Sch., 1951-52; tchr. art Wheaton Coll., 1952—, chmn. art dept., 1969-70, 75-79; asst. prof. art Fine Arts Gallery, Chgo., then asso. prof., 1971—; free lance art cons. Vol. Cook County Hosp., Chgo., 1955-58; mem. Wheaton Human Relations Orgn., 1965-67. Recipient Ingersol award for paintings, 1946, 47, 2d place award DuPage Sesquecentennial, 1968; Outstanding Alumnus award Ball State U., 1975. Mem. Ill. Art Edn. Assn., Midwest Art Conf., Nat. Soc. Lit. and the Arts, Art Inst. Chgo., Delta Phi Delta, Sigma Tau Delta, Kappa Delta Pi. Home: 530 Aurora Way Wheaton IL 60187

HUNTER, RONALD WESLEY, lawyer; b. Kingsley, Iowa, Jan. 3, 1930; s. Albert W. and Dorothy M. (Barkley) H.; student Waldorf Coll., 1948-49; B.A. magna cum laude, Nebr. State Tchrs. Coll., 1951; B.S., U. Nebr., 1953, J.D. cum laude, 1955; m. Stephanie M.; children—Mark, Steven, Ronald, Ann, Thomas, Heather. Admitted to Nebr. bar, 1955, Iowa bar, 1958; asso. firm Swift & Brown, Des Moines, 1957-61; atty. Swanson Enterprises, Omaha, 1961-64; individual practice law, Omaha, 1964—; pres., Western Heritage Mus., Omaha, 1975—. Served with CIC, AUS, 1955-57. Club: Rotary. Editor U. Nebr. Law Rev., 1954-55. Home: 509 Ridgewood Dr Bellevue NE 68005 Office: 7100 W Center Rd Omaha NE 68106

HUNTLEY, RICHARD ALLEN, physician; b. Chgo., May 7, 1932; s. Joseph Edward and Emily Rose (Beran) H.; B.S., U. Ill., 1954, M.S., 1956; M.D., U. Bern, Switzerland, 1961. Intern, Hackley Hosp., Muskegon, Mich., 1962; practice medicine specializing in gen. practice, Muskegon, 1963—; mem. staffs Mercy Hosp., Hackley Hosp., Muskegon. Contbr. Muskegon Area Assn. Retarded Children, Indian Funds; patron Hackley-House Heritage Assn., West Shore Symphony Orch.; bd. dirs. Mich. Heart Assn. Archaeol. Indian excavations with Mus. No. Ariz. Fellow Royal Soc. Health (Eng.); mem. AMA, Mich., Muskegon County med. socs., Am. Assn. Foreign Med. Grads., Stratford Festival Assn. Can., Swiss Benevolent Soc. Chgo., Internat. Platform Assn., Mus. No. Ariz. (life), Smithsonian Instn., Chgo. Council on Fgn. Relations, Forum for Contemporary History, Nat. Trust for Historic Preservation, Nat. Hist. Soc. Club: Muskegon Rifle and Pistol. Home: 3685 Farmwood Dr Muskegon MI 49441 Office: 1704 W Sherman Blvd Muskegon MI 49441

HUNTOON, RICHARD BENSON, ops. analyst; b. Moline, Ill., Nov. 27, 1932; s. Benson Elsworth and Ella Louise (Gralow) H.; student Monmouth Coll., 1950-52; B.Sc., U. Ill., 1954; postgrad. Capital U. Music Conservatory, 1969-73; M.B.A., Capital U., 1980; m. Norma Jean Robb, June 20, 1953; children—Ben Lambert, Ann Kristen, John Richard. Field engr. missile div. Chrysler Corp., 1958-59; human factors specialist, project leader heavy mil. electronics dept. Gen. Electric Co., Syracuse, N.Y., 1959-64; sr. research engr., project engr., group leader N. Am. Rockwell, Columbus, Ohio, 1964-70; internal auditor Western Electric Co., Columbus, 1970-74; mem. tech. staff Rockwell Missile Systems div., Columbus, 1974-80; engr./scientist Rockwell Collins Govt. Avionics div., Cedar Rapids, Iowa, 1980—; instr. human factors engring. Gen. Electric Co., 1962-64. Mem. presidential selection com. Capital U., 1978-79. Served with U.S. Army, 1954-58. Mem. Inst. Mgmt. Scis., Theta Chi. Lutheran. Home: 3324 Wenig Rd NE Cedar Rapids IA 52402 Office: 400 Collins Rd NE Cedar Rapids IA 52498

HUNTRESS, BETTY ANN, music store propr.; b. Poughkeepsie, N.Y., Apr. 29, 1932; d. Emmett Slater and Catherine V. (Kihlmire) Brundage; B.A., Cornell U., 1954; m. Arnold Ray Huntress, June 26, 1954; children—Catherine, Michael, Carol, Alan. Tchr. high sch., Bordentown, N.J., 1954-55; part-time asst. to prof. Delta Coll., Northwood Inst., Midland, Mich., 1958-71; part-time tchr. Midland Public Schs., 1968-79; owner, mgr. The Music Stand, Midland, 1979—. Bd. dirs. Midland Center for Arts, 1978—; v.p. MCFTA (Arts Center), 1981—; mem. charter bd. mgrs. Matrix Midland Ann. Arts and Sci. Festival, 1977-80; cons. Girl Scouts Am., 1964-76; mem. Mich. Internat. Council, 1975-76. named (with husband) Midland Musician of Yr., 1977. Mem. Music Soc. Midland Center for Arts (dir. 1971—, chmn. 1976-79), AAUW (dir. 1962-73, pres. 1971-73, mem. Mich. state div. bd. 1973-75, outstanding woman as agt. of change award 1977, fellowship grant named in her honor 1976), Midland Symphony League Soc, Community Concert Soc., Kappa Delta Epsilon, Pi Lambda Theta, Alpha Xi Delta. Republican. Presbyterian. Home: 5316 Sunset Dr Midland MI 48640 Office: 6 Ashman Circle Midland MI 48640

HURD, RICHARD NELSON, pharm. co. exec.; b. Evanston, Ill., Feb. 25, 1926; s. Charles DeWitt and Mary Ormsby (Nelson) H.; B.S., U. Mich., 1946; Ph.D., U. Minn., 1956; m. Jocelyn Fillmore Martin, Dec. 22, 1950; children—Melanie Hurd Brown, Suzanne DeWitt. Chemist, Gen. Electric Co., Schenectady, 1948-49; group leader, research and devel. group Koppers Co., Pitts., 1956-57; chemist, Mallinckrodt Chem. Works, St. Louis, 1956-63, group leader, 1963-66; group leader Comml. Solvents Corp., St. Louis, 1966-68, sect. head, 1968-71; mgr. sci. affairs G.D. Searle Internat. Co., Skokie, Ill., 1972-73; dir. mfg and tech. affairs, 1973-77; v.p., Elder Pharms., Inc., Bryan, Ohio, 1977—. Mem. Ferguson—Florissant (Mo.) Sch. Bd., 1964-66; bd. dirs. United Fund Wabash Valley, 1969-71. Served with USN, 1943-46, 53-55. duPont fellow, 1956. Mem. Am. Chem. Soc., N.Y. Acad. Scis., AAAS, Am. Acad. Dermatology, Soc. Tropical Dermatology, Regulatory Affairs Profl. Soc., Soc. Investigative Dermatology, Am. Pharm. Assn., Acad. Pharm. Scis., Sigma Xi. Republican. Presbyterian. Clubs: Michigan Shores (Wilmette, Ill.), Pine Valley (Fort Wayne). Patentee in field; contbr. articles to profl. jours. Home: 1537 Ransom Dr Fort Wayne IN 46825 Office: 705 E Mulberry St Bryan OH 43506

HURL, RODNEY BECK, physician; b. Shelby, Ohio, Feb. 25, 1930; s. Robert Davis and Esther Helen (Beck) H.; B.S., Bethany (W.Va.) Coll., 1951; M.D., Temple U., 1955; m. Judith Rothrock, July 17, 1959; children—Megan, Marcy, Jeffrey. Rotating intern Mt. Carmel Hosp., Columbus, Ohio, 1955-56, resident in family practice, 1959; practice medicine specializing in family practice, Marysville, Ohio, 1959—; pres. R.B. Hurl M.D. Inc., 1970—; mem. staff Meml. Hosp., Marysville; v.p., dir. Marysville Rest Homes, Mildon Park Assos. Inc.; dir. Marysville Newspapers Inc., Mid-Ohio Corp. Trustee Bethany Coll., 1971—, chmn. devel. com., 1974—; mem. Union County Mental Health Bd., 1970-80, pres., 1978-80; pres. Marysville City Parks and Recreation Commn., 1974-78. Served to capt. M.C., USAF, 1956-58. Recipient Outstanding Alumni Service award Bethany Coll., 1978; diplomate Am. Acad. Family Practice. Mem. AMA, Am. Acad. Family Practice, Ohio Med. Assn., Ohio Acad. Family Practice, Central Ohio Acad. Family Practice (dir. 1979-80), Union County Med. Assn. Republican. Lutheran. Club: Masons. Home: 381 Hickory Dr Marysville OH 43040 Office: 211 Stocksdale Dr Marysville OH 43040

HURLEY, JAMES DONALD, JR., lawyer; b. LaSalle, Ill., June 11, 1935; s. James Donald and Emily Elizabeth (Reinhard) H.; B.A., U. Ill., 1957, LL.B., 1959; m. Judith A. Hurley; children—Katherine, Mary, James Donald III, Ellen. Admitted to Ill. bar, 1959, also U.S. Cts. Appeals, Fed. Dist. Ct., U.S. Tax Ct.; mem. firm Hollerich, Hurley & Banich, LaSalle, 1959—; dir. 1st Nat. Bank, Peru, Ill. City atty., LaSalle, 1968-72. Trustee Hollerich Trust. Recipient Distinguished Service award U.S. Jr. C. of C., 1970, Community Service award Ill. Valley Area C. of C., 1970. Mem. Am., Ill., LaSalle bar assns., Ill. Valley C. of C. (pres. 1967-68). Elk, Lion. Home: 617 Fifth St LaSalle IL 61301 Office: 654 First St LaSalle IL 61301

HURLEY, JAMES WILLIAM, diversified holding co. exec.; b. St. Cloud, Minn., July 4, 1939; s. James Warren and Margaret Caroline (Kapphahn) H.; B.S., So. Ill. U., 1967; M.B.A., Northwestern U.,

1974; m. Kathleen A. Krol, Aug. 26, 1978. Sr. auditor Arthur Andersen & Co., Chgo., 1968-72; mgr. taxes Oak Industries, Inc., Crystal Lake, Ill., 1972-74; asst. treas. Trans-Union Corp., Lincolnshire, Ill., 1974—. C.P.A., Ill. Mem. Am. Inst. C.P.A.'s, Ill. C.P.A. Soc. Home: 3100 Scotch Ln Riverwoods IL 60015 Office: 90 Half Day Rd Lincolnshire IL 60015

HURRY, JOAN LUCILLE, educator; b. Faribault, Minn., May 31, 1932; d. Henry Albert and Lucille (Gutknecht) Guth; B.S. magna cum laude, Mankato State U., 1980; m. Dennis Hurry, Oct. 29, 1950; children—Susan, Steven. Tchr. related services Mankato Area Vocat. Tech. Inst. (Minn.), 1968—. Instr. 1st aid, CPR, 1st aid for children, personal mgmt.; mem. Mankato Energy Subcom., 1980-81. Mem. Am. Vocat. Assn., Minn. Vocat. Assn., NEA, Minn. Edn. Assn., Mankato Tchrs. Assn., Mankato Vocat. Assn., Am. Home Econs. Assn., Minn. Home Econs. Assn. (state council 1980-83, dist. pres.-elect 1981-82), Phi Upsilon Omicron, Phi Kappa Phi. Evang. Lutheran. Home: 310 Dane St Mankato MN 56001 Office: 1920 Lee Blvd North Mankato MN 56001

HURSH, HESTER JO, surgeon; b. Macoun, Sask., Can., Oct. 31, 1935; d. Benjamin B. and Hester Maud (Bicknell) H. (parents U.S. citizens); B.S., George Williams Coll., 1958; M.D., U. Ill., 1964; grad. advanced cardiac life support provider, 1979; div.; 1 dau., Cindy. Intern, Cook County Hosp., Chgo., 1964-65, resident in gen. surgery, 1965-69, fellow in hand surgery, 1969-71; practice medicine specializing in hand surgery, Northeastern Ill., 1970-75; attending hand surgeon MacNeal Hosp., Berwyn, Ill., 1970-75, Hinsdale (Ill.) Hosp., 1971-75; cons. surgeon, Downers Grove and Joliet, Ill., 1970-75; indsl. surgeon, cons. Sears Roebuck Nat. Office, Chgo., 1971-75; indsl. hand surgeon, cons. John Deere Tractor Works, Waterloo, Iowa, 1975—; resident in occupational medicine U. Cin., 1980-81; attending hand surgeon Schoitz Meml. Hosp.; lectr. trauma assessments and hand surgery Allen Hosp. Sch. Nursing. Mem. Am. Occupational MedMed. Assn., AMA, Blackhawk County Med. Soc. Roman Catholic. Research on effects of vibration on hand vasculature. Home: 426 Ivanhoe Rd Waterloo IA 50701 Office: Medical Dept PO Box 270 Waterloo IA 50704

HURST, HOYT, editor, publisher; b. Carlisle, Ind., Feb. 27, 1913; s. Roy Eugene and Clara Mae (Winkler) H.; A.B., Ind. State U., 1935; M.S., Medill Sch. Journalism, Northwestern U., 1942. Tchr. public schs., Gery, Ind., 1936-42; editor Implement & Tractor, Kansas City, Mo., 1945-51, Farm Implement News, Chgo., 1952-55, Vance Publs., Chgo., N.Y., 1955-57; editor, pub. Modern Jeweler, Kansas City, Mo., 1958—; instr. jewelry store mgmt. workshops. Recipient Golden Nuggets award, 1966, Israeli medal of Merit Israeli Diamond Inst., 1980; Ky. col. Mem. Overseas Press Club Am., Soc. Profl. Journalists, 24 Karat Club N.Y.C., 24 Karat Club So. Calif. Democrat. Mem. Disciples of Christ Ch. Address: Modern Jeweler 15 W 10th Kansas City MO 64105

HUSAR, JOHN PAUL, newspaper columnist; b. Chgo., Jan. 29, 1937; s. John Z. and Kathryn (Kanupke) H.; A.A., Dodge City Coll., 1958; B.S. in Journalism, U. Kans., 1962; m. Louise Kay Lewis, Dec. 28, 1963; children—Kathryn, Laura. Reporter, Clovis (N.Mex.) News-Jour., 1960; night wire editor Okinawa Morning Star, 1961; city editor Pasadena (Tex.) Daily Citizen, 1962; bus. editor Topeka Capital-Jour., 1963; regional news editor Wichita (Kans.) Beacon, 1963-65; sports columnist and writer Chgo. Tribune, 1966—. Chmn., Village of Willow Springs (Ill.) Zoning Commn., 1975-77; mem. Ill. Forestry Adv. Com., 1981—. Served with U.S. Army, 1960-62. Recipient 1st pl. award in sportswriting Ill. UPI, 1977; 1st pl. award in feature writing Bowling mag., 1979; environ. reporting award Chgo. Audubon Soc., 1979; 2d pl. award for public service reporting Ill. AP, 1980, 2d pl. award for sports column writing, 1981; spl. writing award Chgo. Tribune, 1980; Jacob A. Riis award Friends of Parks, 1981. Mem. Golf Writers Assn. Am. (past dir.), Baseball Writers Assn. Am., Phi Kappa Theta. Office: 435 N Michigan Ave Chicago IL 60611

HUSARIK, ERNEST A., ednl. adminstr.; b. Gary, Ind., July 2, 1941; married, 2 children. B.A. in History, Olivet Nazarene Coll., Kankakee, Ill., 1963; M.S. in Ednl. Adminstrn., No. Ill. U., DeKalb, 1966; Ph.D. in Ednl. Adminstrn. and Curriculum Devel., Ohio State U., Columbus, 1973; m. Elizabeth Ann Bonnette; children—Jennifer, Amy. Supt., Ontario (Ohio) Pub. Schs., 1973-75; supt. Euclid (Ohio) Pub. Schs., 1975—; adj. prof. Grad. Sch., Cleve. State U.; chmn. Cuyahoga Spl. Edn. Service Center, 1978. Mem. Euclid Gen. Hosp. Assn.; sec., trustee Euclid Devel. Corp. Mem. Am., Buckeye (dir.) assns. sch. adminstrs., Nat., Ohio assns. supervision and curriculum devel., Greater Cleve. Sch. Supts. Assn. (past pres.), Mid-Am. Assn. Sch. Supts., Euclid C. of C. (v.p. community affairs), Olivet Nazarene Coll. Alumni Assn. (alumni bd. dirs.), Phi Delta Kappa (past chpt. pres.), Sigma Tau Delta. Club: Kiwanis (dir., com. chmn.). Contbr. articles in field to profl. jours. Home: 25600 Breckenridge Dr Euclid OH 44117 Office: 651 E 222 St Euclid OH 44123

HUSBAND, LORETTA, publicist; b. Chgo., June 2, 1941; d. William and Katherine Mabel (Shipp) H.; student Central YMCA Community Coll., 1968. Systems rep., adminstr. Burroughs Corp., Chgo., 1969-73; prin. Lori Husband & Assos., Chgo., 1973—; publicist Fujii Assos., Inc., Chgo., 1977-80; book prodn. cons. and writer. Founding mem., dir. public relations Women's Bd., Washington Park YMCA; corr. sec. Women's Bd., Cook County Hosp., 1978-80, co-dir. public relations, 1976-77; mem. Chgo. adv. council SBA; mem. procurement subcom. Chgo. Minority Bus. Opportunity Com., U.S. Dept. Commerce. Mem. Chgo. Women in Publishing, Women in Mgmt., Nat. Assn. Media Women, LWV. Democrat. Lutheran. Prodn. coordinator: Illustrated Home Reference, 1973; prodn. cons.: Black History, Vol. 4, 1973, 1,000 Successful Blacks, 1973; byline columnist Hyde Park Herald, 1973-75; news editor Christ the Mediator Luth. Ch., 1978-80; polit. reporter Chgo. Jour., 1981. Home: 601 E 32d St Chicago IL 60616 Office: 203 N Wabash Ave Chicago IL 60601

HUSBAND, RICHARD LORIN, SR., bus. exec.; b. Spencer, Iowa, July 28, 1931; s. Ross Twetten and Frances Estelle (Hall) H.; A.A., Rochester State Community Coll., 1953; arts degree U. Minn., 1954; m. Darlene Joyce Granberg, 1954; children—Richard Lorin, Thomas Ross and Mark Thurston (twins), Julia Lynn, Susan Elizabeth. Pres., Orlen Ross Inc., Rochester, Minn., 1962—; partner The Gallery, European antiques, china, gifts, Rochester, 1968—, Millenium III, home furnishings, Rochester, 1975—. Active Episcopal Diocese of Minn., 1951-52, 58—, nat. dept., 1969-73, alt. dept., 1973-75; trustee Seabury Western Theol. Sem., 1975—, exec. com., 1976—; founder Rochester Arts Council, Rochester PTA Community Coll. Scholarship Program, H.D. Mayo Meml. Lecture in Philosophy, others; pres. Olmsted County (Minn.) Hist. Soc., 1976-77; bd. dirs. Rochester Symphony Orch., Choral, Opera, 1970-78, pres., 1974-75; del. Olmsted County Republican Party, 1974—. Recipient Disting. Service award Rochester Jaycees, 1965, Fifty Mem. award YMCA, 1968, award for Minn. Bicentennial, Gov. Minn., 1976; named 1 of Minn's, 10 Outstanding Young Men, Minn. Jaycees, 1966. Mem. Minn. Home Furnishings Assn. (pres. 1976-79, trustee 1968—), First Dist. Hist. Assembly Minn. (pres. 1969-71), Minn. Retail Fedn. (trustee 1972—), Olmsted County Archeology Soc. (founder), Rochester Civil War Roundtable (founder), Rochester Revolutionary War Roundtable (founder), Rochester Arts Council (founder), Am., Nat. (charter), Minn., Norwegian/Am. hist. socs., Minn. Archeology Soc., Am. Assn. State and Local History, U. Minn. Alumni Assn., U. Minn. Alumni Club (charter) Rochester C. of C., Alpha Delta Phi Alumni Assn., Soc. Mayflower Descs. (trustee Minn.), SAR (Minn. pres.), Descs. Colonial Clergy, Sons Union Vets of Civil War, Minn. Territorial Pioneers (trustee 1978—, pres. 1981—). Clubs: Rotary (historian) (Rochester); Sertoma (Austin) (founder). Public speaker. Home: 1820 26th St NW Rochester MN 55901 Office: Orlen Ross Inc 105 N Broadway Rochester MN 55901

HUSE, DIANE MARIE, nutritionist; b. Mpls., June 21, 1944; d. Gordon Simmons and Mildred Lillian (Johnson) H.; student St. Olaf Coll., Northfield, Minn., 1962-64; B.S. in Dietetics, U. Minn., 1966; M.S. in Clin. Nutrition and Biochemistry, U. Minn., 1972. Dietetic intern Henry Ford Hosp., Detroit, 1966-67; therapeutic dietitian St. Barnabas Hosp., Mpls., 1967-68; nutritionist, dept. pediatrics and clin. dietetics sect. Mayo Clinic and Found., Rochester, Minn., 1971—; instr. nutrition Mayo Med. Sch., Rochester, 1976—; coordinator nutrition edn. project Rochester Public Schs. Mem. Am. Dietetic Assn. (registered), Minn. Dietetic Assn. (sec. 1977-79), Rochester Dist. Dietetic Assn. (mem. exec. bd. 1972-80, pres. 1975-76), Dietitians in Pediatric Practice Group, Am. Coll. Sports Medicine, Minn. Nutrition Council, Sigma Xi. Republican. Lutheran. Office: Mayo Clinic 200 SW 1st St Rochester MN 55901

HUSK, DONALD ESTEL, state ofcl. Ind.; b. Oakland City, Ind., Dec. 10, 1925; s. George Raymond and Hazel Rita (Ashley) H.; grad. high sch.; m. Velma Cunningham, June 7, 1946; children—Robert, Mark. With Hoosier Cardinal, Inc., Evansville, Ind., 1949; asst. cashier English State Bank (Ind.), 1949; with Ind. Dept. Financial Instns., 1953—, sr. examiner, 1958-70, supr. div. banks and trust cos., Indpls., 1970—. Served with USNR, 1943-46. Certified fin. examiner. Mem. Hist. Record Assn., Soc. Fin. Examiners. Clubs: Masons, Plainfield Optimists. Home: 424 Wayside Dr Plainfield IN 46168 Office: 1024 State Office Bldg Indianapolis IN 46204

HUSS, EDWARD HARRY, JR., metallurgist; b. New Brunswick, N.J., Sept. 22, 1925; s. Edward Harry and Margaret (Hauth) H.; student U. Wis., 1945-46, Georgetown U., 1945-46, Ia. State. Tchrs. Coll., 1949; children—Joseph Edward, James Harold. Chemist, John Deere Waterloo (Ia.) Tractor Wks., 1948-50; metallurgist Viking Pump Co., Cedar Falls, Ia., 1950-66, 67—, metallurgist, dept. head, 1956—; metallurgist Doerfer Engring., Cedar Falls, 1966-67; cons. in field; lectr. in field. Pres. bd. AMVET Home, Cedar Falls, Iowa, 1955. Served with U.S. Army, 1943-46. Decorated Bronze Star medal, Purple Heart. Mem. ASTM, Am. Soc. for Metals, Am. Foundrymans Soc., Smithsonian Inst., Metal Treating Inst., Am. Olympic Com., Am. Legion, VFW, AMVETS. Republican. Anglican. Club: Masons. Contbr. articles to profl. jours. Home: 904 W 10th St Cedar Falls IA 50613 Office: 4th and State St Cedar Falls IA 50613

HUSSEINY, ABDO AHMED, engr.; b. Estanha, Egypt, July 7, 1936; s. Ahmed and Fahima (Sabbah) H.; B.S., Alexandria (Egypt) U., 1963; M.S., U. Wis., 1967, Ph.D., 1970; postgrad. Queen Mary Coll., London, 1964; engring. tng. sch. Argonne (Ill.) Nat. Lab., 1966; Mass. Inst. Tech., 1973. m. Zeinab Abdel-Salam Sabri, Sept. 23, 1964. Registered profl. engr. Egypt. Asst. engr. Brown Boveri, Vienna, Austria, 1962; instr. Sacred Heart Girl's Coll., Alexandria, 1963-64; instr. elec. engring. U. Alexandria, 1963-64; research asso. U. Wis., Madison, 1970-71; cons. Saudi Arabia and Kuwait, 1971-72; asst. prof. nuclear engring. U. Mo., Rolla, 1972-73; asst. prof. Carnegie-Mellon U., Pitts., 1973-75; cons. Los Alamos (N.Mex.) Sci. Lab., 1974; with Devel. Cons. Assn., Heliopolis, Egypt., 1973; asso. prof. nuclear engring. Iowa State U., Ames, 1975-78, adj. prof. Engring. Research Inst., 1978-79; mgr. decision analysis and advanced systems div. Sci. Applications, Inc., Ames, 1978—; mgr. Sci. Applications Saudi Arabia, Jeddah, Riyadh; cons. Engring. and Tech. Cons. Assos., Alexandria, 1976—; chmn. bd. Tech. Internat. Inc., Arlington, Va., 1977—; tech. chmn. 1st Internat. Conf. and Workshops on Iceberg Utilization, 1977—; bd. editors Desalination, The Internat. Jour. of the Sci. and Tech. of Water Desalting and Purification, 1977—. Mem. IEEE, Am. Nuclear Soc. (first chmn. Iowa/Nebr. sect. 1977-78), Am. Phys. Soc., Am. Soc. Engring. Edn., Brit. Nuclear Energy Soc., Inst. Physics (London), Sigma Xi. Author: Modern Vector Analysis, 1963; Iceberg Utilization, 1978; Icebergs for Survival, 1979; contbr. articles to profl. jours. Home: 2144 Ashmore Ct Ames IA 50010 Office: 125 S 3d St Ames IA 50010

HUSTAD, THOMAS PEGG, mktg. educator; b. Mpls., June 15, 1945; s. Thomas Earl Pegg and John Charles and Dorothy Helen (Anderson) H.; B.S. in Elec. Engring., Purdue U., 1967, M.S. in Indsl. Mgmt., 1969, Ph.D. in Mktg., 1973; m. Sherry Ann Thomas, Jan. 30, 1971; children—Kathleen, John. Vis. asst. prof. Purdue U., West Lafayette, Ind., 1971-72; asst. prof. Faculty of Adminstrv. Studies, York U., Toronto, 1972-74, asso. prof., 1974-76, asso. prof., mktg. area coordinator, 1976-77; asso. prof. mktg. Sch. Bus., Ind. U., Bloomington-Indpls., 1977-82, prof., 1982—; cons. N. Am. corps., Can. Govt.; condr. seminars for U.S., Can. and Venezuelan industry. Mem. Am. Mktg. Assn. (award 1973), Assn. Consumer Research, Product Devel. and Mgmt. Assn. (program chmn. 3d ann. conf., v.p. confs. 1979, pres. elect 1980, pres. 1981), Phi Eta Sigma, Tau Beta Pi, Beta Gamma Sigma. Author: Approaches to the Teaching of Product Development and Management, 1977; contbr. articles to books and profl. jours. Home: 8931 Butternut Ct Indianapolis IN 46260

HUSTAK, THOMAS LEONARD, clin. psychologist; b. Trenton, N.J., Apr. 28, 1949; s. Leonard and Harriet Helen (Patykula) H.; B.S. cum laude, Mt. St. Mary's Coll., 1971; M.A. magna cum laude, Fairleigh Dickinson U., 1974; Ph.D. in Clin. Psychology, U. So. Miss., 1977; m. Nancy Jean Wyllie, June 19, 1971; 1 son, Keith Thomas. Coordinator mobile evaluation units Bur. Spl. Needs and Coop. Edn., State Dept. Edn., Trenton, N.J., 1971-72; teaching asst. exptl. psychology Fairleigh Dickinson U., Madison, N.J., 1972-73; psychology extern Ellisville (Miss.) State Sch. for the Retarded, 1974; cons. Speech and Hearing Clinic, U. So. Miss., Hattiesburg, 1974-75, psychology extern, 1974-75; psychology extern VA Hosp., Gulfport, Miss., 1975; instr. psychology (part-time) Fed. Correctional Inst., Danbury, Conn., 1975-76; clin. psychology intern Fairfield Hills Hosp., Newtown, Conn., 1975-76; instr. psychology (part time) Northwestern Bus. Coll., Lima, Ohio, 1977-78; coordinator St. Marys Mental Health Clinic, Lima, Ohio, 1976-79; dir. psychol. services G.F. Aukerman Med. Center, Jackson Center, Ohio, 1979—; mem. exec. com. Social Services Council, Lima, 1977-78. Mem. Assn. for Advancement of Behavior Therapy, Am. Psychol. Assn., Ohio Psychol. Assn., Inst. for Rational Living, Auglaize County Mental Health Assn., Alpha Mu Gamma, Psi Chi. Roman Catholic. Club: Elks. Contbr. articles on clin. psychology to profl. jours. Home: 4900 Pheasant Dr Elida OH 45807 Office: GF Aukerman Med Center W Pike St PO Box Drawer A Jackson Center OH 45334

HUSTON, DONALD BRUCE, research and devel. exec.; b. Colorado Springs, Colo., July 29, 1938; s. Arthur and Anna Elvira (Henderson) H.; A.B., Colo. State Coll., 1961; M.S., Stout State U., 1966; m. Diane Mary Le Roux; 1 son, Eric Norman. Quality control trainee George Banta Co., 1966, plant quality control mgr., 1966-69, project mgr. charge lab. facilities, 1969-74, corp. research mgr., Menasha, Wis., 1974—; vocat. tchr. Menasha Tech. and Vocat. Sch. Served to lt. (j.g.) USNR, 1961-64. Recipient certificate of appreciation Stout State U., 1971. Mem. Graphic Arts Tech. Found., TAPPI, Tech. Assn. of Graphic Arts, Res. Officers Assn., Naval Res. Assn., YMCA. Clubs: Twin City Rod and Gun, Elks, Masons. Patentee spirit duplicating master; inventor invisible ink process for instant response programmed learning, low cost durable coating method for books used in sch., offset process to print styrene and polyester. Home: 1741 Oakridge Ct Menasha WI 54952 Office: George Banta Co Inc Curtis Reed Plaza Menasha WI 54952

HUSTON, GEORGE RUSSELL, JR., mfg. co. exec.; b. Salem, Ohio, Mar. 19, 1933; s. George Russell and Mabel Marie Huston; B.S. in Bus. Adminstrn., Ohio State U., 1955; m. Helen Louise Heil, Nov. 27, 1954; children—Linda L., George R., James R. Gen mgr. AP parts div. Questor Corp., 1970-75; mgr. product distbn., then mgr. distbn. ops. DeVilbiss Co., Toledo, 1975-78, dir. employee relations, 1978—. Served with AUS, 1955-57. Mem. Nat. Mgmt. Assn. (adv. bd.), Employers Assn. Toledo, Toledo C. of C., Toledo Personnel Mgrs. Assn., Ohio State U. Alumni Assn., Delta Sigma Pi. Republican. Episcopalian. Home: 5723 E Candlestick Ct Toledo OH 43615 Office: PO Box 913 Toledo OH 43692

HUTCHESON, JOHN MARVIN, JR., med. illustrator; b. Birmingham, Ala., Oct. 13, 1930; s. John Marvin and Bertha Lee (Bryan) H.; B.A., Birmingham So. Coll., 1955; M.S., Med. Coll. Ga., 1958; m. Sharie Lee Clark, Dec. 29, 1967; children—Yancey Bryan, Shelby Lee. Med. illustrator audiovisual sect. Communicable Disease Center, USPHS, Atlanta, 1958-59, dept. med. illustration U. Fla. Coll. Medicine, Gainesville, 1959-61, sect. med. graphics Mayo Clinic, Mayo Found., Rochester, Minn., 1961—. Mem. Mayo Centennial Commemorative Stamp Com., 1964; sub-chmn. steering com. Rochester Festival of the Arts, 1965; project advisor Rochester's adoption of the 173d Airborne Brigade, 1966; dir. Am. Revolution Bicentennial Commn. Olmsted County, 1975-77. Served with USNR, 1951-53. Recipient Tom Jones award AMA, 1969, Billings Gold medal AMA, 1961, Certificate of Merit, AMA, 1968, Hektoen Bronze medal AMA, 1969. Mem. Assn. Med. Illustrators (editorial bd. 1963-65), Am. Med. Writers Assn., Olmsted County Hist. Soc., History of Medicine Soc., Lambda Chi Alpha. Republican. Methodist. Elk. Clubs: Rochester Coin, Rochester Stamp (pres. 1973-76). Cinematographic co-director movie, Tetanus and its Prevention, 1963. Designed the offcl. cachet cover for the Doctors Mayo commemorative postage stamp, 1964. Numerous contributions to med. texts and jours. Home: 625 6th St SW Rochester MN 55901 Office: 200 First St SW Rochester MN 55901

HUTCHINGS, THOMAS WILLIAM, hosp. exec.; b. Columbus, Ohio, May 27, 1943; s. Walter John and Minerva Margaret (Williams) H.; B. Indsl. Engring. (Am. Inst. Indsl. Engrs. scholar), Ohio State U., 1967; M.B.A., U. Hawaii, 1969; m. Charlotte Lynne McCaleb, Nov. 28, 1964; children—Deborah, Andrew, Theresa. Mgmt. service staff mem. Ernst & Ernst, Honolulu, 1968-69; adminstrv. analyst St. Francis Hosp., Honolulu, 1969-70; sr. mgmt. engr. Midtown Hosp. Assn., Denver, 1970-72; dir. mgmt. engring. Bethesda Hosps., Cin., 1972-73; mgr. facility planning and constrn., 1973-79; asst. exec. dir. Children's Hosp., Columbus, 1979—; pvt. practice mgmt. cons., 1976—. Mem. St. Vincent Ferrer Sch. Bd. Edn. Mem. Ohio Soc. Profl. Engrs., Nat. Soc. Profl. Engrs., Am. Soc. Hosp. Engrs., Planning Exec. Inst. Roman Catholic. Home: 1278 Crestview St Reynoldsburg OH 43068 Office: 700 Children's Dr Columbus OH 43205

HUTCHINGS, U(RBAN) WILLIAM, credit union exec.; b. St. Louis, Jan. 25, 1932; s. Ralph McKinley and Bertie Ruth (Harville) H.; A.B., U. Mo., 1953; M.Div., Lexington Theol. Sem., 1956; postgrad Tarkio Coll., Henry Ford Community Coll.; m. Gloria Gwendolyn Moreillon, May 25, 1974; 1 dau., Judith Renee. Ordained to ministry Christian Ch. Disciples of Christ, 1956; asso. minister Overland (Mo.) Christian Ch., 1956-57; minister, 1st Christian Ch., Tarkio, Mo., 1957-59, asso. minister Wyatt Park Christian Ch., St. Joseph, Mo., 1959-62, Central Christian Ch., Dallas, 1962-63, Waco, Tex., 1963-66; asso. minister Central Woodward Christian Ch., Detroit, 1966-72; sr. edn. specialist Mich. Credit Union League, Detroit, 1972—. Bd. mgrs. Christian Ch. Mich. Region, 1970-72; bd. dirs. North Woodward Interfaith Corp., 1968-72; mem. cabinet Central Woodward Christian Ch., 1978-80. Mem. Am. Soc. Tng. and Devel. (past pres.), Mich. Soc. Instructional Tech., Nat. Soc. Performance and Instrn. Democrat. Home: 2783 Roundtree Dr Troy MI 48084 Office: 15600 Providence Dr Southfield MI 48075

HUTCHINS, CHARLES WILLIAM, state senator; b. Guthrie County, Iowa, Mar. 21, 1931; s. Jack and Hazel H.; grad. high sch.; m. JoAnn Reser, 1955; 4 children. Mem. Iowa Ho. of Reps., 1973-76, Iowa Senate, 1976—. Mem. Vol. Fire Dept., 1963-81. Mem. C. of C., Am. Legion. Methodist. Democrat. Club: Lions. Home: 902 Prairie St Guthrie Center IA 50115 Office: State Senate Des Moines IA 50319

HUTCHINS, RONALD CHARLES, sound and video co. retail exec.; b. Broken Bow, Nebr., June 26, 1949; s. Charles Lester and Virginia Dolores (Willard) H.; student Kearney State Coll., 1968-72; m. July 31, 1971; children—Seraphine Theresa, Amanda Jane. Vice pres. retail div. and repair dept. Stanal Sound Ltd., Kearney, Nebr., 1969—. Mem. Kearney Vol. Fire Dept., 1976—; bd. dirs. Kearney Community Theater. Clubs: Rotary (dir.), Elks. Baptist. Home: 4102 Palamino Rd Kearney NE 68847 Office: 3817 2d Ave Kearney NE 68847

HUTCHINSON, KENNETH LEE, electronics mfg. co. exec.; b. Evansville, Ind., June 11, 1928; s. Thomas G. and Mina M. (Lacke) H.; B.S. in Elec. Engring., U. Evansville, 1953; m. Carolyn Weber, Aug. 25, 1951; children—Thomas Lee, Kenneth Bradley. With Magnavox Co., Fort Wayne, Ind., 1953—, projects engr., 1953-58, product mgr., 1958-68, v.p. marketing, 1971—; v.p. marketing planning Magnavox Govt. and Indsl. Electronics Co., Ft. Wayne, 1975—; pres. Magnavox Overseas, Ltd., Fort Wayne, 1971—. Served with USMC, 1946-49. Named Outstanding Engr. of Year, U. Evansville, 1948. Mem. C. of C., Electronics Industries Assn., Nat. Security Indsl. Assn., Assn. Old Crows, Am. Mgmt. Assn., Univ. Evansville Alumni (dir.), Sigma Pi Sigma, Phi Beta Chi. Home: 6040 Ranger Trail Fort Wayne IN 46815 Office: 1313 Production Rd Fort Wayne IN 46808

HUTCHISON, ALDEN CRAIG, trailer mfg. co. exec.; b. Algona, Iowa, Aug. 14, 1926; s. Horace James and Mabel Emma (King) H.; B.S.M.E., U. Mo., Rolla, 1950; m. Jacqueline Nadine Adams, June 6, 1948; children—Mary Luanne, Susan Lynn, David Craig; m. Martha Ann Ward, Sept. 2, 1977. Sales engr. Springfield Body & Trailer Co. (Mo.), 1950-55, Custom Trailers, Springfield, 1955-61; founder, engr., purchasing agt., fin. officer Acro Tank Co., Springfield, 1961-76; Acro Corp. founder, sec.-treas. and Acro Trailer Co., Springfield, 1976—; partner M.H.E. & G., owners and leasers machinery, Springfield, 1976—. Mem. Springfield Park Bd., 1964-71, v.p., 1970, pres., 1971. Served with USAAF, 1944-46. Registered profl. engr., Mo. Mem. Truck/Trailer Mfrs. Assn., Nat. Soc. Profl. Engrs., Mo. Soc. Profl. Engrs. (v.p. Ozark chpt. 1959-60, pres. 1961), U.S. C. of C. Republican. Baptist. Clubs: Kiwanis, Lions, Masons. Office: 2320 N Packer Rd Springfield MO 65803

HUTCHISON, JANIE RUTH, broadcaster; b. Shreveport, La., Aug. 31, 1943; d. Rufus and Josephine (McGinthy) Martin; B.A., Columbia Coll., 1975; m. William E. Hutchison (dec.); children—William, Natalie Roxanne, Tamara Renee. Office mgr. Jack Benny Center for Arts, Waukegan, Ill., 1968-70; dir. Nightline, sales sec. Sta. WBBM-FM, Chgo., 1974-76; adminstrv. asst., communications dir. Chgo. Met. Council on Alcoholism, 1976-77; public affairs dir. Sta. WLOO-FM, Chgo., 1977-81. Chmn. adv. com. North Chgo. Sch. Dist. 64, 1974. Recipient YWCA Leadership award in media/communications, 1980; Outstanding Accomplishment award in communications State of Ill., 1980. Mem. ASCAP. Baptist. Club: AWRT. Home: 509 Lakehurst Rd #1-R Waukegan IL 60085

HUTMACHER, EDWARD JAY, mgmt. cons.; b. Kansas City, Mo., Feb. 12, 1953; s. George and Ruth Anita (McClure) H., Jr.; B.B.A. cum laude, Southwestern Coll., 1979; postgrad. Wichita State U., 1979—; m. Betty L. Evans, Feb. 28, 1975; children—Sonia, Aaron, Andrea. Fin.-adminstrv. analyst NCR Corp., Wichita, Kans., 1979-80; coordinator energy research, planning and program devel. SER, Inc., Wichita, 1980-81; mng. partner Environs, mgmt. cons., Wichita, 1981—; energy cons. state and local govts., cons. on program devel. for non-profit orgns., 1980—. Adminstrv. aide to speaker Kans. Ho. of Reps., 1977-78. Served with USMC, 1972-75. Mem. Am. Mgmt. Assn., Am. Planners Assn., Kans. Solar Energy Soc., Nat. Assn. Parliamentarians, Am. Enterprise Inst., Kans. Assn. Parliamentarians, Pi Gamma Mu. Republican. Mem. Orthodox Christian Ch. Author: Quantitative Analysis of Quality Control Process in a Manufacturing Operation, 1976; Rural and Small Town Energy Planning, 1981. Office: PO Box 2577 Wichita KS 67201

HUTSON, DON, lawyer; b. Kansas City, Mo., Nov. 4, 1931; s. Alpha Henry and Lola (Walmer) H.; A.B. with honors, Central Coll., Fayette, Mo., 1953; postgrad. U. Mo., 1954; J.D. with honors, George Washington U., 1958; m. Betty Jane Switzer, Sept. 7, 1952; children—Eric, Sheila, Robin, Heather. Ordained to ministry Internat. Conv. Christian Chs., 1949; minister Oak Grove (Mo.) Christian Ch., 1949-53; tchr., coach various Mo. schs., 1952-54; staff asst. to Sen. Stuart Symington, 1955-59; admitted to Mo. bar, 1958; since practiced in Kansas City; mem. firm Hutson, Schmidt, Hammett & Yates, P.C., 1958—. Asst. pros. atty. Jackson County, 1959-63. Mem. Am., Fed., Kansas City bar assns., Am. Judicature Soc., Am., Mo. trial lawyers assns., Kansas City C. of C., Sigma Epsilon Pi, Phi Alpha Delta (internat. justice 1974-76), Pi Kappa Delta. Democrat. Home: 6409 E 64th St Kansas City MO 64133 Office: Traders Bank 1125 Grand Ave Kansas City MO 64106

HUTSON, RONALD PHILLIP, librarian; b. Hamilton, Ohio, Aug. 10, 1942; married, 4 children. B.S. in Econs., So. Ill. U., Edwardsville, 1965, M.S. in Instructional Tech., 1974. Tchr., Worden (Ill.) Pub. Sch., 1966-68; tchr., librarian Meissner Sch., Bunker Hill, Ill., 1968-73; media service dir. Community Unit Dist. 8, Bunker Hill, 1973—. Pres. bd. dirs. Bunker Hill Pub. Library, 1969-75; mem. library tech. adv. com. Lewis and Clark Community Coll., 1975—; mem. instructional tech. adv. council So. Ill. U., Edwardsville, 1980-81. Mem. Ill. Assn. Ednl. Communications and Tech., Gateway Media Roundtable (pres. 1976-78). Certified tchr. K-6, media specialist K-12, Ill. Home: 212 N Union St Bunker Hill IL 62014 Office: Community Unit Dist 8 Box Y Bunker Hill IL 62014

HUTTIE, JOSEPH J., JR., communications ofcl.; b. Allentown, Pa., Nov. 20, 1942; s. Joseph and Irene A. H.; B.S. in Journalism, Northwestern U., Evanston, Ill., 1964, M.J., 1968. Editor, Am. Youth Mag., Gen. Motors Corp., 1968-70; program dir. World Press Inst., St. Paul, 1970-71; media cons., 1971-80; dir. corp. communications Ellerbe, Inc., Bloomington, Minn., 1980—; media cons. State of Minn., City of St. Paul. Served with U.S. Army, 1965-67. Decorated Army Commendation Medal; recipient grants So. Regional Council, Russell Sage Found., Black Econ. Research Center, Emergency Land Fund. Clubs: Minn. Press, Decathlon. Author: Great Space Race (film); contbr. articles to periodicals. Home: 841 Laurel Ave Saint Paul MN 55401 Office: 1 Appletree Sq Bloomington MN 55420

HUTTON, EDWARD LUKE, corporate exec.; b. Bedford, Ind., May 5, 1919; s. Fred and Margaret (Drehoble) H.; B.S. with distinction, Ind. U., 1940, M.S. with distinction, 1941; m. Kathryn Jane Alexander, Dec. 22, 1942; children—Edward Alexander, Thomas Charles, Jane Clarke. Dep. dir. Joint Export Import Agy. U.S.-U.K., Berlin, 1945-47; v.p. dir. World Commerce Corp., N.Y.C., 1948-51; asst. v.p. W.R. Grace & Co., N.Y.C., 1951-53; cons. internat. trade, finance, 1953-54; v.p., dir. New York & Cuba Mail S.S. Co., N.Y.C., 1954-61, fin. v.p., 1958-59; v.p. and group exec. W.R. Grace & Co., 1969-71; exec. v.p., gen. mgr. DuBois Chem. div. W.R. Grace & Co., 1964-68; pres. E. L. Hutton, Assos., Inc., 1954-69; pres., chief exec. officer Chemed Corp., 1971—; chmn. and dir. Omnicare dir. Chemed Corp., W.R. Grace & Co., Am. States Ins. Co., Am. States Life Ins. Co., Am. Economy Ins. Co., Daylin, Inc., The Veratex Corp., Lubrizol, Inc., 1978-80; dir., mem. exec. com. Investors Diversified Services, 1973-75. Trustee Village Bronxville, 1965-68. Trustee Millikin U. Mem. Newcomen Soc. Served from pvt. to 1st lt. AUS, 1943-46. Methodist. Clubs: Downtown Assn., Economics, University, Princeton (N.Y.C.); Queen City, Bankers (Cin.). Home: 6680 Miralake Dr Cincinnati OH 45243 also Harris Rd East Orleans MA 02643 Office: 1114 Ave of Americas New York NY 10036 also 1200 DuBois Tower Cincinnati OH 45202

HUTTON, JOHN THOMAS, physician; b. Kansas City, Mo., Dec. 26, 1945; s. John Howard and Adele Katherine (Greenway) H.; B.A., Tex. Tech U., 1968; M.D., Baylor U., 1972; Ph.D., U. Minn., 1980; m. Sarah Gertrude Plunket, June 8, 1969; children—John Andrew, Sarah Katherine. Intern, Hennepin County Gen. Hosp., Mpls., 1972-73; resident dept. neurology U. Minn., Mpls., 1973-74, 75-77; fellow U.S.-USSR Health Profl. Exchange Program to Burkenko Neurosurg. Inst., U. Moscow, 1974-75; practice medicine, specializing in neurology, Mpls., 1977—; staff physician VA Med. Center, Mpls., 1977—, co-dir. Behavioral Neurology sect., 1977-79, med. dir., Geriatric Research Edn. and Clin. Center, 1979-81, asst. chief neurology service, 1979-80; instr. dept. neurology U. Minn., Mpls., 1977-80, asst. prof., 1980—; cons. in field. NIH student research fellow, 1971; Minn. Med. Found. grantee, 1979—; Nat. Inst. Aging grantee, 1979—; lic. physician, Tex., G.B., Minn.; diplomate Am. Bd. Neurology. Mem. Am. Acad. Neurology, Internat. Neuropsychology Soc. Methodist. Contbr. articles to profl. jours. Home: 8739 Lakeview Rd Bloomington MN 55438 Office: 54th St and 48th Ave Minneapolis MN 55417

HWANG, KYU-JEONG, physician; b. Seoul, Korea, Sept. 28, 1941; s. Doo-Seong and Jae-Yeol (Chang) H.; came to U.S., 1968, naturalized, 1975; B.A., Seoul Nat. U., 1961, M.D., 1965; m. Jeong-Sun Bae, Jan. 4, 1969; children—Joanne, Brian. Rotating intern St. John Hosp., Detroit, 1968-69; resident physician Dept. Ob-Gyn, Wayne State U., 1969-73; partner R. R. Licker & K. J. Hwang, P.C., Port Huron, Mich., 1973—; mem. med. staff Port Huron and Mercy hosps. Served with Korean Navy, 1965-68. Diplomate Am. Bd. Ob-Gyn. Fellow Am. Coll. Obstetricians and Gynecologists; mem. A.M.A., Mich. Med. Soc., St. Clair County Med. Soc. Office: 2425 Military St Med Village Port Huron MI 48060

HYATT, BEVERLY CAROL, nurse; b. Sedalia, Mo., Apr. 13, 1942; d. Stuart King and Audrey Virginia (Marshall) H.; R.N., St. Lukes Hosp. Sch. Nursing, Kansas City, Mo., 1963. Instr., staff nurse St. Lukes Sch. Nursing and St. Lukes Hosp., Kansas City, 1963-67; office nurse Dr. George Thiele, Kansas City, 1967-68; charge nurse Menorah Med. Center, Kansas City, 1968-73, asst. dir. nursing, 1973-78, nurse recruiter, 1978—, I Care Employee award, 1978. Mem. Nat. Student Nurses Assn. (sustaining), Nat. Assn. Nurse Recruiters, Kansas City Area Nurse Recruiters. Mem. Christian Ch. Club: Jobs Daughters (hon. life mem.). Office: 4949 Rockhill Rd Kansas City MO 64110

HYATT, HUDSON, lawyer; b. Cleve., Jan. 1, 1914; s. Harry Cleve and Rose Evelyn (Miller) H.; A.B. cum laude, Adelbert Coll., Western Res. U., 1937, LL.B., 1939; m. Helen Fulmor, Feb. 3, 1940; children—David Hudson, Margaret (Mrs. Ross J. Dixon), Nancy (Mrs. Michael A. Schwartz), Shirley. Admitted to Ohio bar, 1939; asso. Davis & Young, 1939-40; adjudicator Social Security Bd., 1940-42; law clk. U.S. Dist. Ct., 1942-44; atty. Erie R.R. Co., 1946-52; practiced in Cleve., 1952-54; regional atty. SBA, Cleve., 1954-63, asst. regional counsel, 1963-66, dist. atty., 1966-71, dist. counsel, 1971-77; lectr. law Coll. Law, Cleve. State U., 1976. Pres., Cleve. Masonic Employment Bur., 1960-63, 1969-70, v.p., 1963-69; pres. Greater Cleve. Vets. Council, 1952-53; bd. control Cleve. Freedom Council, 1961—. Trustee C.L. Jack Meml. Fund, Shaker Masonic Bldg. Assn.; trustee Cleveland Heights Local Devel. Corp., pres., 1981. Served from ensign to lt (j.g.), USNR, 1944-46. Mem. Fed. (1st v.p. Cleve. chpt. 1965-66, pres. Cleve. chpt. 1966-67), Am. (chmn. small bus. com. 1965-69), Cleve. Cuyahoga County (editorial bd. bull. 1962-73; chmn. editoral com. 1965-66; contbg. editor 1979-81) bar assns., S.A.R., Am. Legion, V.F.W. (nat. judge adv. gen. 1947-48). Clubs: Masons, Shriners, Ripon. Contbg. editor Baldwin's Ohio Legal Forms, 1963, 70, 73, Baldwin's Kentucky Legal Forms, 1963; Carroll and Whiteside's, Forms for Commercial Transactions, 1963. Home: 2648 Euclid Heights Blvd Cleveland Heights OH 44106

HYBBEN, LOIS BRITTA ANDERSON, nursing adminstr.; b. Faribault, Minn., Feb. 18, 1936; d. Carl E. and Hattie I. (Paulson) Anderson; R.N., Northwestern Hosp. Sch. of Nursing, 1956; B.A., Met. State U., 1975; M.A., St. Thomas Coll., 1979; m. John W. Hybben, Sept. 14, 1957; children—Lori, William, Robert. Staff nurse Northwestern Hosp., 1956-58, Fairview Southdale, 1968-70; ednl. instr. Met. Med. Center, Mpls., 1970-71, super-ambulatory care, 1971-73, dir. med.-surg. nursing, 1973-76, dir. patient edn./staff devel., 1976-77; dir. nursing services Mt. Sinai Hosp., Mpls., 1977—, asst. dir. hosp., 1979-80, v.p. patient care services, 1981; v.p. patient care services Mercy Med. Center, Mpls., 1981—; mem. community faculty Met. State U.; clin. faculty U. Minn. Sch. Public Health. Mem. bd. evangelism Christ Lutheran Ch., 1980-81. Registered nurse, Minn. Mem. Am. Hosp. Assn. of Nursing Service Adminstrn., Am. Acad. Med. Adminstrs., Twin City Soc. Nursing Service Adminstrs. (pres.-elect 1981—), Met. State U. Assn. Grads. and Friends (dir. 1981—). Home: 1862 Gold Trail Eagan MN 55122 Office: Mercy Med Center 4050 Coon Rapids Blvd Minneapolis MN 55433

HYDE, GEORGE CHARLES, JR., broadcasting co. exec.; b. Providence, Nov. 28, 1947; s. George Charles and Margaret Mary (Monahan) H.; A.B., Brown U., 1968; M.B.A., York Coll., 1980; m. Kathleen Marie Fusco, Oct. 16, 1971; 1 son, Douglas Andrew. Announcer, newsman, asst. to gen. mgr. Sta. WICE, Providence, 1965-72; asst. to sr. v.p., dir. sales devel. radio div. Susquehanna Corp., York, Pa., 1972-77, v.p. mktg. and devel., 1977-79; v.p., gen. mgr. Sta. WRRM, Cin., 1979—; mem. adj. faculty Coll. Mt. St. Joseph, Cin. Dir., Vol. Action Center, Cin. Mem. Advt. Club Cin. (2d v.p.). Club: Rotary. Office: 1223 Central Pkwy Cincinnati OH 45244

HYDE, HENRY JOHN, lawyer, Congressman; b. Chgo., Apr. 18, 1924; s. Henry Clay and Monica Therese (Kelly) H.; student Duke U., 1943-44; B.S., Georgetown U., 1947; J.D., Loyola U., Chgo., 1949; m. Jeanne M. Simpson, Nov. 8, 1947; children—Henry J., Robert, Laura, Anthony. Admitted to Ill. bar; mem. Ill. Ho. of Reps., 1967-74, majority leader, 1971-72; mem. 94th to 97th Congresses from 6th Ill. Dist. Served with USNR, World War II; comdr. Res., ret. Mem. Am., Ill., Chgo. bar assns. Home: 1004 Argyle Bensenville IL 60106 Office: 1203 Longworth Bldg Washington DC 20515*

HYETT, EVANGELINE SHEIBLEY, educator; b. Ottawa, Ohio, Aug. 27, 1906; d. Albert Franklin and Agnes Elizabeth (Preisendorfer) Sheibley; A.B. summa cum laude, Marygrove Coll., 1929; M.A., Cath. U. Am., 1930; M.S.S.A., Case Western Res. U., 1943; postgrad. U. Mich., 1930-49, Wayne State U., 1933-45. With Bur. Cath. Welfare, Detroit, 1930-31, Children's Center, Detroit, 1931-33, Cath. Home Bur., N.Y.C., 1933-34, Detroit Orthopedic Clinic, 1934-36, Wayne County Gen. Hosp. and Psychiat. Clinic, Detroit, 1936-45; exec. dir. Family Services of Montgomery County, Dayton, Ohio, 1945-48; sec. family and child welfare fedns. United Community Services of Met. Detroit, 1948-52; asst. prof. Wayne State U. Sch. Social Work, Detroit, 1952-54, asso. prof., 1954-69, acting dean, 1963-64, dir. admissions and placement, 1954-69, prof. emeritus, 1969—. Mem. Mich. Mental Health Commn., 1951-61, chmn., 1956, 61. Recipient award of merit Met. Detroit chpt. Nat. Assn. Social Workers, 1958; Mother Domitilla award Marygrove Coll., 1958. Mem. Nat. Assn. Social Workers (nat. bd. 1952-56, nat. exec. com. 1953-55), Marygrove Coll. Alumni Assn., Cath. U. Am. Alumni Assn., Case Western Res. U. Alumni Assn., Honor Soc. Women's Colls., Kappa Gamma Pi. Roman Catholic. Contbr. articles to profl. jours. Address: 630 Merrick St Detroit MI 48202

HYMEN, MARY LOUISE, occupational therapist; b. San Francisco, June 21, 1944; d. Leo Vincent and Louise Carter (Brown) H.; B.S. with honors in Occupational Therapy, U. Puget Sound, 1966; M. Occupational Therapy, U. Wash., 1973. Staff therapist U. Wash. Med. Sch. Hosp., 1967-68, sr. therapist, 1968-73; supr. occupational therapy Santa Clara Valley Med. Center, 1973-79; dir. occupational therapy Rehab. Inst. Chgo., 1979—; clin. instr. U. Wash., 1968-78; instr. rehab. medicine Northwestern U., 1979—. Precinct committeewoman, Seattle, 1971; Rehab. Services Adminstrn. grantee, 1977-80. Mem. Am. Congress Rehab. Medicine, Am. Occupational Therapy Assn. (fellow), Ill. Occupational Therapy Assn., Wash. Occupational Therapy Assn., Occupational Therapy Assn. Calif. (pres. 1975-78, Outstanding Therapist in Calif. award 1978), Nat. Assn. Exec. Women, Women in Mgmt. Home: 2326 N Sheffield St Chicago IL 60614 Office: Rehabilitation Institute of Chicago 345 E Superior Chicago IL 60611

HYNES, PATRICIA ANN, dental clinic adminstr.; b. Milw., Dec. 22, 1953; d. William Joseph and Catherine Shirley (McGovern) H.; B.B.A. with honors, U. Wis., Milw., 1976. Office mgr. Pediatric Dental Clinic, Milw., 1976—; corporate treas. Rallye Imports, Ltd., Wauwatosa, Wis., 1978—. Mem. Beta Gamma Sigma. Home: 2564 N 124th St Wauwatosa WI 53226 Office: 5019 W North Ave Milwaukee WI 53208

HYUN, KUN SUP, chem. engr.; b. Seoul, Korea, Feb. 25, 1937; s. Yong Han and Sam Soon (Ahn) H.; came to U.S., 1960, naturalized, 1973; B.S. in Chem. Engring., Seoul Nat. U., 1959; M.S., U. Mo., Columbia, 1962, Ph.D., 1966; m. Sung Za Lee, Aug. 5, 1973; children—Eileen, Phillip Joonsuk, Paul Joonki. Sr. research engr. Dow Chem. U.S.A., Midland, Mich., 1966-69, research specialist, 1969-79, sr. research specialist, 1979-80, research asso., 1980—; abstractor Am. Chem. Abstract Service, 1967-75. Vice pres. Adams Sch. PTO, 1974-75; mem. com. Boy Scouts Am., 1976—. Served with Korean Air Force, 1958-60. Mem. Mid Mich. Korean Soc. (pres. 1970-71), Am. Inst. Chem. Engrs., Am. Chem. Soc., Soc. Plastics Engrs., Soc. Rheology, Internat. Microwave Power Inst., Korean Scientists and Engrs. Assn. Am. (v.p. 1981-82), Sigma Xi. Mormon. Contbr. articles to profl. jours.; patentee in field. Home: 613 Nakoma Dr Midland MI 48640 Office: Dow Chem Co Bldg 1603 Midland MI 48640

IACOBELLI, JOHN LOUIS, economist; b. Cleve., Dec. 24, 1931; s. Joseph and Theresa (Caporaso) I.; B.S., Kent State U., 1955, M.A., 1965; Ph.D., U. Tex., Austin, 1969; m. Eleanor M. Mandale, Sept. 3, 1956; children—Joseph, Andrew, Christopher. Sr. sales rep., ter. mgr. NCR, Cleve., 1957-64; asst. prof. labor and indsl. relations Cleve. State U., 1968-71, asso. prof. mgmt. and labor, 1971-76; prof. econs. Wright State U., 1976-78, chmn. dept., 1976-78; pres. Delphi Assos., Inc., Cleve., 1972-75; economist, spl. rep. August DiVito and Assos., Cleve., 1980—; cons. in field. Served with U.S. Army, 1955-57. U.S. Dept. Labor grantee, 1967-68; HUD and Nat. League of Cities grantee, 1973-74. Mem. Am. Econ. Assn., Indsl. Relations Research Assn., Acad. Mgmt., Christian Family Movement, Christ Renews His Parish. Contbr. articles to profl. jours. Home: 19953 Idlewood Trail Strongsville OH 44136 Office: 6659 Pearl Rd Cleveland OH 44130

IACOCCA, LIDO ANTHONY (LEE), automotive co. exec.; b. Allentown, Pa., Oct. 15, 1924; s. Nicola and Antoinette (Perrotto) I; B.S., Lehigh U., 1945; M.E., Princeton U., 1946; m. Mary McCleary, Sept. 29, 1956; children—Kathryn Lisa, Lia Antoinette. With Ford Motor Co., Dearborn, Mich., 1946—, successively mem. field sales staff, various merchandising and tng. activities, asst. dirs. sales mgr., Phila., dist. sales mgr., Washington, 1946-56, truck mktg. mgr. div. office, 1956-57, car mktg. mgr., 1957-60, vehicle market mgr., 1960, v.p. Ford Motor Co., gen. mgr. Ford div., 1960-65, v.p. car and truck group, 1965-67, exec. v.p. of co., 1967-68, pres. of co., 1970-78, also pres. Ford N. Am. automobile ops.; pres., chief operating officer Chrysler Corp., Highland Park, Mich., 1978-79, chmn. bd., chief exec. officer, 1979—. Wallace Meml. fellow Princeton U. Mem. Tau Beta Pi. Club: Detroit Athletic. Office: Chrysler Corp 12000 Lynn Townsend Dr Highland Park MI 48231*

IANNONE, LIBERATO ALESSANDRO, cardiologist; b. Winnipeg, Man., Can., Mar. 13, 1941; s. Giuseppe Luigi and Julia (Valentino) I.; came to U.S., 1945, naturalized, 1956; B.S. cum laude in natural sciences, Niagara U., 1963; M.D., State U. N.Y., Buffalo, 1967; m. Delores Patricia Torres, 1971; children—Timothy, Christopher, Sonya, Sophia. Intern Buffalo Gen. Hosp., 1967-68, resident, 1968-69; cardiology fellow Walter Reed Army Med. Center, 1969-71; staff cardiologist, dir. coronary care unit William Beaumont Army Med. Center, El Paso, Tex., 1971-73, dir. cardiac catherterization lab., 1971-73; staff cardiologist Geisinger Med. Center, Danville, Pa., 1974, practice medicine specializing in cardiology, 1974—; dir. coronary care unit, dir. cardiac rehab. Mercy Hosp., Des Moines; dir. coronary care unit, dir. cardiovascular lab., dir. cardiology teaching service, chmn. acute care com. Iowa Luth. Hosp., Des Moines; mem. staff Meth. Hosp., Des Moines. Served with U.S. Army, 1969-73. Diplomate Am. Bd. Internal Medicine. Fellow Am. Coll. Cardiology, Am. Coll. Angiology, Council Clin. Cardiology, Am. A.C.P., Coll. Chest Physicians; mem. AMA, Iowa, Polk County med. socs., Am. Heart Assn. Contbr. articles to med. jours. Home: 1400 Casady Dr Des Moines IA 50315 Office: 943 19th St Des Moines IA 50314

IBBOTSON, ROGER G., fin. co. exec., educator; b. Chgo., May 27, 1943; s. Arthur E. and Margaret B. (Wenthrich) I.; B.S., Purdue U., 1965; M.B.A., Ind. U., 1967; Ph.D., U. Chgo., 1974. Bond portfolio mgr. Office of Treas., U. Chgo., 1971-75, asst. prof. fin. Grad. Sch. Bus., 1975-79, sr. lectr. in fin., 1979—, exec. dir. Center for Research in Security Prices; pres. R.G. Ibbotson & Co. Recipient Graham and Dodd award, 1980. Mem. Am. Fin. Assn., Am. Econ. Assn., Fin. Mgmt. Assn. Asso. editor Financial Management; author: Stocks, Bonds, Bills, and Inflation: The Past and the Future, 1977, 2d edit., 1979, 3d edit., 1982. Home: 2500 Lakeview Chicago IL 60614 Office: R G Ibbotson & Co 8 S Michigan Ave Suite 707 Chicago IL 60603

IBENDAHL, CALVIN FREDERICK, farmer; b. Oakdale, Ill., Nov. 12, 1924; s. Arthur Herman and Lena Louise (Brammeier) I.; A.A., Moline Jr. Coll., 1953; student So. Ill. U., 1956-58; m. Jean Ayres Towell, Dec. 31, 1958. Shipping clk. Mpls.-Moline Implement Co., 1948-50; pvt. practice farming, Tamaroa, Ill., 1958—; reporter Ill. Crop Reporting Service, 1960—; mem., past v.p., sec., treas. Perry County (Ill.) Farm Bur. Served with USN, 1944-46, 50-52. Named Hon. Farmer, Tamaroa High Sch. chpt. Future Farmers Am., 1967, Hon. Pork Producer, Ill. Pork Producers, 1975; recipient Outstanding Farmer of Am. award Apollo Pub. Co., 1971. Mem. Pyramid Pork Producers (pres.), Nat. Corn Growers Assn., Top Farmers Am., Profl. Farmers, No-Till Farmers Assn. Methodist. Home and Office: Route 1 Tamaroa IL 62888

IDLEBURG, DOROTHY ANN BELL, substance abuse counselor; b. Tunica, Miss., Aug. 17, 1951; d. Earnest and Queen Ether (Mann) Bell; student (scholar) U. Wis., 1970-72; B.A., Jackson State U., 1975, M.A. (Nat. Inst. on Alcohol Abuse and Alcoholism scholar), 1976; M.S.W. (NIMH fellow in primary prevention), Washington U., St. Louis, 1979; m. W.D. Idleburg, Jr., Aug. 19, 1972; children—Sonia, Gary Lenard. Receptionist, Afro-Am. Center, U. Wis., Madison, 1970-72; youth supr. Miss. Dept. Youth Services, Jackson, 1972-73; mgr. Nat. Convenience Stores, Inc., Jackson, 1974-76; alcohol/drug counselor Region 1 Mental Health Center, Clarksdale, Miss., 1976-78; outreach counselor drug treatment program Jackson Mental Health Center, 1978-79; teaching asst., adviser master's program students Washington U., 1979—. Vol. worker univ. Hosp., 1972-73. Mem. Nat. Assn. Social Workers, Mid-South Sociol. Assn., Council Social Work Edn., Nat. Black Alcoholism Council, Miss. Alumni Assn. Schs. of Alcohol and Drug Studies, Delta Sigma Theta (rec. sec. 1974). Democrat. Baptist. Clubs: Homemakers, YWCA. Home: 405 Roosevelt Circle Jackson MS 39213 Office: GWB Sch Social Work Box 1196 Washington U Saint Louis MO 63130

IENNACCARO, LOUISE ROSE, adminstr.; b. Kansas City, Mo., Apr. 22, 1944; d. John James and Mollie M. (Sorrentino) I.; B.A., Avila Coll., 1968; M.A., Webster Coll., 1979; children—Glenn Anthony, Dionne Marie, Jason Andrew. Dir. social work dept. St. Luke Hosp., Kansas City, Mo., 1969-75, Bros. of Mercy Extended Care Facility, Kansas City, 1975-76; adminstr. Rockhill Care Center, Kansas City, 1976-79; asso. dir. Center for Mgmt. Assistance, Kansas City, 1979—; mem. faculty Avila Coll., 1973; field supr. coop. social welfare program Kansas City Coll. for Higher Edn., 1974-78. Mem. adv. bd. social work dept. Avila Coll.; mem. adv. bd. Cath. Family and Community Services Home Health Agy., 1970-75; mem. Mayor's Task Force on Devel. of Inner City Homemaking Program, 1973-74. Lic. nursing home adminstr., Mo. Mem. Am. Hosp. Assn. Soc. for Hosp. Social Work Dirs., Am. Coll. Nursing Home Adminstrs., Mo. Assn. Home Health Agys., Greater Kansas City Area Hosp.

Coordinators (founder). Office: Center for Mgmt. Assistance One W Armour Blvd Suite 302 Kansas City MO 64111

IGLEBURGER, ROBERT MARTIN, ret. city ofcl.; b. Dayton, Ohio, Dec. 19, 1909; s. Charles Martin and Cora Belle (Bickel) I.; student Ohio State U., 1929-31; student police adminstrn. Northwestern U., 1954-55; M.Pub.Adminstrn., U. Dayton, 1976; m. Eve Hartman, Nov. 23, 1946; children—Lois Elaine, Debra Gayle; 1 stepson, Gary Tanner. With Dayton Police Dept., 1939-73, capt. in charge traffic sect., 1961-63, capt. in charge uniformed patrol sect., 1963-65, maj. in charge line operations, 1965-67, dir. of police, 1967-73, ret.; resident police adminstr. U. Wis. Law Sch., 1973-74; dir. Dayton Pilot City LEAA Program, 1974-76. Served to sgt. AUS, 1942-46; PTO. Mem. Am. Soc. Pub. Adminstrn., Internat. Assn. Chiefs Police. Club: Foreman's (Dayton). Home: 932 Westminster Pl Dayton OH 45419

IGOE, PHILIP ANDREW, lawyer, corp. cons. co. exec.; b. Muskegon, Mich., Dec. 12, 1950; s. Philip Andrew and Lilliam Ann (Bomher) I.; B.S., U. Ill., 1972; M.S., Roosevelt U., 1977; J.D., Chgo.-Kent Coll., 1977. Admitted to Ill. bar, 1977; asst. dir. engring. div. Perma-Line Corp. of Am., Chgo., 1970-74; in-house legal cons. to Ill. Sec. of State, 1978—; asst. to Ill. State Senator John Merlo, 1979-80; asst. to Chgo. Rep. Party chmn. Louis J. Kasper, 1981—; design cons. J.P. Constrn. Co. Vice pres. 44th ward Young Reps., 1981-82. Strawn fellow, 1975; recipient Patrick Henry award, 1970. Mem. ASTM, Am. Chem. Soc., Decalogue Soc., Am., Ill. State, Chgo. bar assns. Nichiren Shoshu Buddhist. Home: 645 W Barry Ave Chicago IL 60657 Office: 134 N LaSalle St Suite 818 Chicago IL 60602

IHLE, HERBERT DUANE, internat. food co. exec.; b. Ames, Iowa, July 8, 1939; s. Joe and Martha Marie (Larson) I.; A.A., Waldorf Jr. Coll., 1957-59; B.A., Concordia Coll., 1961; M.S., U. Minn., 1963; m. Catherine Eileen Klein, Dec. 27, 1959; children—Brenda Kirsten, Valerie Anne, Michael David. With Pillsbury Co., Mpls., 1963-79, 80—, dir. control fin. consumer group, 1976-78, v. p. fin. consumer group, 1978-79, 80-81, v.p., corp. controller, 1981—; sr. v.p. fin. Burger King Corp., Miami, Fla., 1979-80. Mem. Fin. Execs. Inst., Planning Execs. Inst., Nat. Assn. Accts. Republican. Lutheran. Office: MS 1366 608 2d Ave S Minneapolis MN 55402

ILER, ROBERT LAWRENCE, conductor; b. Highland Park, Mich., Apr. 2; s. Earl Bruce and Lois Minnie (Towne) I.; grad. Moody Bible Inst., 1949; student Am. Conservatory Music, 1949-51. Music dir., youth leader, office mgr. Salem Bapt. Ch., Chgo., 1949-61; asst. to dir., concert mgr. sacred music dept. Moody Bible Inst., Chgo., 1961—, condr. Moody Men's Glee Club, 1974—; condr./organizer King's Couriers Ensemble, 1963-73, South Side Choral Group, 1963—. Mem. Intercollegiate Mus. Council, Chgo. Choral Condr.'s Club. Republican. Baptist. Office: 820 N LaSalle Dr Chicago IL 60610

ILLMER, RUTH (MRS. NORMAN ROUSSEAU), psychologist, educator; b. Festus, Mo., May 31, 1918; d. Joseph B. and Bertha (Martin) Landau; A.A., Flat River Jr. Coll., 1937; B.A., U. Mo., Kansas City, 1959, M.A., 1966, Ph.D., 1974; m. Herman Illmer, Aug. 25, 1937; children—Charles Richard, Paula Jane (Mrs. Clyde J. West). Elementary tchr. Seemel Sch., Jefferson County, Mo., 1937-38; kindergarten tchr. Porter Sch., Prairie Village, Kans., 1959-64, mem. curriculum com., 1960-62, grade level chmn., 1963-64; teaching fellow U. Mo., Kansas City, 1964-66, instr. elementary edn., 1966-68; lectr. elementary edn., 1966-68; elementary counselor, Grandview, Mo., 1966-68, ednl. cons., 1968-70; ednl. cons. hearing and speech dept. Menorah Med. Center, 1970-72; ednl. cons., dir. Ruth Illmer Assos., 1972—; chmn. dept. edn. Park Coll., Kansas City, Mo., 1974-79; cons. psychologist Crittenton Center, 1979—; project dir. Title VI Project, Implementation of Comprehensive Ednl. Program for Children with Learning Disabilities. Mem. alumni bd. dirs. U. Mo. Life mem. Prairie Village P.T.A. Mem. AAUW (past chmn.), Sch. Edn. Alumni Assn. (pres.), Mo. Assn. for Edn. Young Children (past sec.), Assn. for Children With Learning Disabilities (mem. profl. adv. bd. Kansas City council), Am. Sch. Counselor Assn., Mo. Tchrs. Assn., Am. Personnel and Guidance Assn., Profl. Counselors Assn., Am. Psychol. Assn., Mo. Psychol. Assn., Kans. Psychol. Assn., Council Exceptional Children, Orton Soc. (mem. bd.). Unitarian. Author: (with Jack Katz) Auditory Problems in Children with Learning Disabilities; No Longer Ignored, Evaluation Diagnosis and Educational Planning for Children with Learning Disabilities. Home: 9671 Reeder Overland Park KS 66214

ILTIS, JOHN FREDERIC, advt.-public relations co. exec.; b. Chgo., Dec. 14, 1940; s. Frederic and Alice Henrietta (Nachman) I.; student Lincoln Coll., 1962; A.A., Bradley U., 1964; m. Gillian Ann Cane, Nov. 20, 1976; children—Claire Alexandra, Annika Leigh. Advt., public relations asst. Balaban & Katz Theatres, Chgo., 1965-68; midwest dir. advt., public relations Universal Pictures, Chgo., 1968-69, field ops. dir., N.Y.C., 1969-70; owner, operator film prodn. and mktg. co., London, 1971-73; pres. John Iltis Assos., entertainment, advt. and public relations, Chgo., 1973—; instr. public relations Columbia Coll., Chgo. Mem. adv. bd. Wisdom Bridge Theatre, Chgo., Oak Park (Ill.) Festival Theatre; bd. dirs. Variety Club Ill. Served with U.S. Army, 1964. Mem. Publicity Club Chgo., Chgo. TV Acad., Publicists Guild. Home: 3844 N Kenmore Chicago IL 60613 Office: 233 E Erie St Chicago IL 60611

IMES, JOHNIE MCBRIDE, accountant, educator; b. Stephenville, Tex., Aug. 9, 1922; d. Lonnie Daniel and Annie Evangeline (Carter) McBride; R.N., Mo. Methodist Hosp., 1943; B.A., N.W. Mo. State U., 1966, M.A., 1970; postgrad. U. Mo.; m. Elvin D. Imes, June 25, 1941; children—Pamela Kathyrn, Carolyn Elizabeth. Surg. nurse Deaconess Hosp., Evansville, Ind., 1943-46; adminstr. health services Head Start Program, N.W. Mo., 1964-75; asst. prof., coordinator acctg. and fin. N.W. Mo. State U., Maryville, 1979—, chmn. dept. fin., 1975—. Chmn., Nodaway County Blood Bank, 1967-77; vice chmn. Nodaway County Republican Com.; sec. 6th Dist. Rep. Com.; mem. Mo. State Rep. Com.; bd. dirs. Womens Mo. Golf Assn. Registered nurse. Mem. Am. Accounting Assn., Fin. Mgmt. Assn., Acad. Mgmt., Mo. Assn. Accounting Educators (pres., dir.). Methodist. Club: Order Eastern Star. Home: 151 N Country Club Rd Maryville MO 64468 Office: Colden Hall 235 NW Mo State U Maryville MO 64468

IMESCH, JOSEPH LEOPOLD, bishop; b. Grosse Pointe Farms, Mich., June 21, 1931; s. Dionys and Margaret (Margelisch) I.; B.S., Sacred Heart Sem., 1953; student N. Am. Coll., Rome, 1953-57; S.T.L., Gregorian U., Rome, 1957. Ordained priest Roman Catholic Ch., 1956; sec. to Cardinal Dearden, 1959-71; pastor Our Lady of Sorrows Ch., Farmington, Mich., 1971-77; aux. bishop of Detroit, 1973-79; bishop of Joliet (Ill.), 1979—; asst. bishop N.W. Region, 1977-79. Office: Chancery Office 425 Summit St Joliet IL 60435

IMHOF, ANTON B., logging contractor; b. International Falls, Minn., Nov. 12, 1927; s. Otto B. and Mary (Weiss) I.; grad. high sch.; m. Zelah C. Popejoy, June 23, 1951; children—Lynn Anthony, JoAnn Marie, Michael Lee, William Otto. Partner, Otto Imhof & Son, Logging Contractors, Littlefork, Minn., 1951-68, owner Anton Imhof Logging Contractor, 1968—. Mem. Sch. Bd. Littlefork, 1965—. Served with USNR, 1945-47. Mem. Am. Legion. Roman Catholic. Club: K.C. Address: Box 50 Rural Route 1 Littlefork MN 56653

IMHOFF, JOHN CLAWSON, hosp. adminstr.; b. Lorain, Ohio, Nov. 5, 1925; s. Grover Cleveland and Sadie I.; B.Sc., Ohio State U., 1949; postgrad. Baldwin Wallace Coll., 1949-50; M.B.A., U. Chgo., 1952; postgrad. Cleveland Marshall Law Sch., 1953-54; m. Vera Louise Chance, July 19, 1952; children—Jeffrey C., Judson C., Jane C. Adminstrv. resident Cleve. City Hosp., 1951-52, asst. adminstr., 1952-54; adminstr. Polyclinic Hosp., Cleve., 1954-62; adminstr. Shadyside Hosp., Pitts., 1962-67; exec. v.p. Mountainside Hosp., Montclair, N.J., 1967-78; pres., chief exec. officer Galion (Ohio) Community Hosp., 1978—; chmn. Hosp. Council Western Pa., 1964-65; bd. dirs. Ohio Health Systems Agy. Mem. Olmsted Falls (Ohio) Council, 1958-61, pres., 1960-61; pres. Community Ch., Olmsted Falls., 1960-61. Served with USMC, 1944-46. Recipient citation for public service Alumni Assn. U. Chgo., 1962. Mem. Am. Hosp. Assn., Ohio Hosp. Assn. (dir. polit. action com.), N.J. Hosp. Assn. (trustee), Am. Coll. Hosp. Adminstrs., Am. Occupational Therapy Assn., Ohio PSRO (dir.). Presbyterian. Clubs: Elks, Rotary, Kiwanis (pres. club 1961-62) (Olmsted Falls). Home: 125 Switzer Dr Galion OH 44833 Office: Galion Community Hosp Portland Way S Galion OH 44833

IMHULSE, DIANE MERGLER, assn. exec.; b. Cin., July 21, 1934; d. Wilton Henry and Mildred (Pulliam) Mergler; B.S., U. Cin., 1956; M.S., So. Ill. U., 1962. Tchr., public schs., Cin., 1956-62, Herrin, Ill., 1962-63, Urban, Ill., 1963-65; asso. dir. ednl. services Chgo. Lung Assn., 1965-68; mgr. sch. and coll. women's depts. Nat. Safety Council, Chgo., 1968—. Del., White House Conf. on Children, 1970. Mem. Assn. Supervision and Curriculum Devel., Am. Assn. Sch. Adminstrs. Author: Child Safety Club, 5 vols., 1979-81. Home: 5701 N Sheridan Rd Apt 21B Chicago IL 60660 Office: 444 N Michigan Ave Chicago IL 60611

IMMEL, WILLIAM RAYMOND, accountant; b. Columbus, Ohio, Jan. 30, 1926; s. Raymond Frederick and Helen Barbara (Dietlin) I.; B.S., Franklin U., 1963; m. Mary Katherine Bower, Nov. 23, 1949; children—Gregory, Karen. Payroll clk. Comml. Motor Freight, Columbus, 1948; asst. controller Atlas Linen Supply, Columbus, 1948-61; pvt. practice pub. accounting, Columbus, 1961—; pres. Established Shoe Data, Inc., Columbus, 1972; chmn. bd., sec.-treas. Typog. Press, Inc. Served with AUS, 1945-47. C.P.A., Ohio. Mem. Pub. Accountants Soc. Roman Catholic. Clubs: Columbus Maennerchor, Shamrock, Sertoma. Home: 68 Amazon Pl Columbus OH 43214 Office: 4666 Indianola Ave Columbus OH 43214

IMUNDO, LOUIS VICTOR, JR., mgmt. cons., educator; b. Bronx, July 10, 1942; s. Louis V. and Ursula H. (Kurzmann) I.; B.S. in Indsl. Engring., C.W. Post Coll., L.I.U., 1964; M.B.A., Adelphi U., 1966; Ph.D. in Mgmt., U. Okla., 1971; children—Louis III, Lawrence, Daniel. Indsl. engr. Grumman Corp., Bethpage, N.Y., 1964-66; asst. mgr. indsl. engring. Martin Marietta Corp., Denver, 1966-67; grad. asst. dept. mgmt. U. Okla., Norman, 1967-70; instr. in mgmt. Central State U., Edmond, Okla., 1970-71; asst. prof. mgmt. Wright State U., Dayton, Ohio, 1971-75, asso. prof. mgmt., 1975-79; pres. Mgmt. Perspectives Inc.; cons. Wright State U.; mem. roster of arbitrators Fed. Mediation and Conciliation Service. Research grantee, 1972-79. Mem. Am. Arbitration Assn. (comml. and indsl. arbitration panels), Beta Gamma Sigma. Author: The Effective Supervisor's Handbook, 1980; The Arbitration Game, 1982. Contbr. cases, articles on labor relations and mgmt. to acad. and profl. jours. Home: 1040 Green Timber Trail Spring Valley OH 45370

INATOME, RICK, computer co. exec.; b. Detroit, July 27, 1953; s. Joseph T. and Atsuko Nan (Kumagai) I.; B.A. in Econs., Mich. State U., 1976; m. Joyce Helen Kitchen, Aug. 18, 1979; 1 dau., Dania Lynn. Vice pres., gen. mgr., founder Computer Mart, Inc., Clawson, Mich., 1976—; lectr., cons. computers; instr. Marygrove Coll., Macomb Community Coll. Mem. Engring. Soc. Detroit, Am. Mgmt. Assn., Assn. Computer Machinery, Phi Delta Theta. Home: 5726 Sussex Troy MI 48084 Office: 1824 W Maple Troy MI 48084

INGERSLEW, NEILL DENNIS, printing co. exec.; b. Kirksville, Mo., Oct. 6, 1934; s. John P. and Lissa (Madsen) I.; B.S. in Edn., U. Mo., 1958; m. Shirley Ann Bareis, Oct. 8, 1954; children—John, Susan, Cheryl, Nancy. With Western Pub. Co., Hannibal, Mo., 1956—, sales engr., 1964-65, preparatory supt., 1965-67, prodn. mgr., 1967-69, mgr. Data Page div., St. Charles, Mo., 1969-77; sr. v.p., gen. mgr. Lincoln (Nebr.) ops. Metromail, 1977—. Republican. Lutheran. Clubs: Masons (32 deg.), Shriners. Home: 404 Lincoln St Seward NE 68434 Office: 901 W Bond St Lincoln NE 68521

INGRAHAM-PARSON, VIVIAN JUNE LOWELL, city ofcl.; b. Omaha, June 1, 1922; d. John Calvert and Pearl Mabel (Whitscell) Lowell; student schs. Omaha; m. Clarence Parson, Sept. 7, 1969; children—Richard D. Ingraham, Leroy Lowell Ingraham, John Edwin Ingraham, Jeffrey Scott Ingraham. Supr. customer service Met. Utilities Dist., 1940-46; news reporter sta. KBON, Omaha, 1962-67; med. transcriber VA Hosp., Omaha, 1971-73; exec. dir. Gt. Plains Council Girl Scouts U.S.A., Omaha, 1973-75; job developer City of Omaha, 1976—. Exec. com. Mid-Am. Council Boy Scouts Am., 1960—, Fontenelle Dist. Boy Scouts Am., 1958-76; youth coordinator Douglas County ARC, 1965-70; dist. II dir. Nebr. State PTA, 1964-68; v.p. Omaha PTA Council, 1966-68; pres. Walnut Hill Sch. PTA, 1958-60, Monroe Sch., 1965-67, Fontenelle Schs., 1962-64; dist. del. Rep. party; state PTA hon. life mem. Recipient hon. nat. life PTA award, 1972, Good Neighbor award Ak-Sar-Ben, 1970, Brotherhood Week-Good Neighbor award NCCJ, 1967, service award ARC, 1968-71; nat. officer (Stewards) Nat. Presbyn. Mariners, 1960-66; hon. adm. Nebr. Navy; Outstanding Citizen award Omaha Public Schs. Mem. Profl. Assn. Girl Scout Execs. Presbyterian. Panelist: Discrimination and Its Effect on Children, 1970; author booklet: A Look at PTA, 1966; contbr. articles to religious mags. Office: 5002 S 33rd St Omaha NE 68107 also PO Box 4315 Benson Station Omaha NE 68104

INGRAM, KENNETH EUGENE, civil engr.; b. Maysville, Ky., Feb. 2, 1932; s. Cecil Walker and Pearl Lee (Barnett) I.; B.S. in C.E., U. Ky., 1958; m. Mary Lowe Batchelor, Jan. 29, 1955; children—Stephen Craig, Rebecca Lowe. Structural engr. McDonnell Aircraft, St. Louis, 1958-59; asst. city engr. St. Charles (Mo.), 1959-60; v.p. Maran-Ingram-Cooke, Inc., St. Charles, 1960-71; hwy. engr./planning dir. St. Charles County, 1971-73; v.p. Russell & Axon, St. Louis, 1973-77; pres. Ingram-Kiethline-Wehmeyer, Inc., St. Charles, 1977—. Chmn., Mayor's Adv. Com., St. Charles, 1979—; advisor St. Charles County Planning/Zoning Commn., 1971-73; bd. dirs. St. Charles County Regional Sewer Dist., 1972-73, St. Charles County Home Builders, 1979-80, St. Charles Boys Club, 1971-73, 78—; del. St. Charles Community Council, 1977—. Served with USMC, 1950-54. Registered profl. engr., Mo., Fla., Ky., Ark., Conn., Pa., Ill. Mem. Nat. Soc. Profl. Engrs., Am. Cons. Engrs. Council, ASCE, Water Pollution Control Fedn., Home Builders Assn. Christian Ch. Clubs: Bogey Hills Golf and Country, Masons, Shriners. Home: 3205 Yale Blvd Saint Charles MO 63301 Office: 6 Westbury Dr Saint Charles MO 63301

INGRAM, LOIS SWINTON, pharmacist; b. Galesburg, Ill., Oct. 13, 1934; d. Wayne and Hope Gurnee (Giddings) Swinton; B.S., St. Louis Coll. Pharmacy, 1963; m. William Ingram, Mar. 21, 1954; children—Susan, William Scott. Pharmacist, Bakers Rexall Drug Store, Keokuk, Iowa, 1963-69; dir. pharacy Graham Hosp., Keokuk, 1969-74; pharmacist Osco Drug Store, Keokuk, 1974-75; dir. pharmacy St. Lukes Hosp. West, Chesterfield, Mo., 1975—. Mem. Am. Soc. Hosp. Pharmacists, Mo. Soc. Hosp. Pharmacists, St. Louis Soc. Hosp. Pharmacists. Republican. Episcopalian. Home: 710 Wild Walnut St Manchester MO 63011 Office: 232 Woodsmill Rd Chesterfield MO 63017

INGRAM, MORD-ESSIE MAYO, ednl. adminstr.; b. Greenwood, Miss., Jan. 15, 1936; d. Willie and Jessie B. (McCoy) Mayo; B.S., Wayne State U., 1967, M.A., 1970, Edn. Specialist, 1980; m. James Hilton Ingram; children—Diane Jessie, Denise Darchelle. Tchr., Detroit Public Schs., 1967-74, reading coordinator, 1974-79, counselor, 1979-80, staff coordinator, adminstr., 1979-81, active tutoring and counseling programs. Corr. sec. St. Peter Claver Aux., 1979-81; program chmn. Sickle Cell Anemia Detection Center, 1978. Recipient bd. of gov.'s award Wayne State U., 1966; favorite tchr. award, 1968. Mem. Assn. for Supervision and Curriculum Devel., Am. Personnel and Guidance Assn., Guidance Assn. Met. Detroit, Pi Lambda Theta, Phi Delta Kappa, Alpha Kappa Alpha (police dept. vol., 1978-81). Roman Catholic. Club: Progressive Women. Home: 16585 Stansbury Detroit MI 48235

INGRAM, ROBERT PALMER, investment co. exec.; b. Norfolk, Va., July 21, 1917; s. Robert Palmer and Margaret (Wible) I.; student Washington and Lee U., 1935-36, U. Pitts., 1936-37; m. Mary Elizabeth Renfro, Sept. 30, 1949; children—Marsha Jill, Robert Palmer. Salesman, Anchor Hocking Glass Corp., Grand Rapids, Mich., 1943-44, Kansas City, Mo., 1945-46; pres. Robert P. Ingram & Co., Kansas City, 1946—, Tracy Devel. Co., Ten Main Center, Mo., 1963—, Ingram Investment Co., 1964—, LaSalle Leasing Co., 1971—, stas. KXTR and KBEA, Rigby Co., Kansas City Bus. Advt. Co. (all Kansas City); dir. Rubbermaid Inc., Harzfelds Inc., Am. Cablevision of Kansas City; met. chmn. Nat. Alliance Businessmen, 1969. Mem. com. on capital requirements for public schs. Kansas City, 1969; chmn. fin. com. Jackson County Republication Party, 1966; trustee U. Mo., Kansas City, M.W. Research Inst.; bd. govs. Starlight Theatre Assn.; bd. dirs. Civic Council Greater Kansas City. Mem. Kansas City C. of C. (past pres), Downtown Inc. (pres. 1970-72), Am. Royal Assn. (bd. govs.). Clubs: Kansas City, Carriage (Kansas City). Office: 306 E 12 St Kansas City MO 64106

INNES, DONNA LORRAINE, ednl. adminstr.; b. Beloit, Wis., Aug. 8, 1945; d. William Joseph Innes and Lorraine Margaret (Swetland) Innes Angstrom; B.S.Ed., Marian Coll., 1967; M.S. in Ed., U. Dayton, 1976; postgrad. Marquette U., 1968-69, U. Wis., Milw., 1969, Alverno Coll., 1969-70, Coll. Steubenville, 1970, Marion Coll., 1973-74, 75, 79, St. Thomas Coll., 1980, St. Cloud State U., 1980. Joined Congregation of St. Agnes, Roman Catholic Ch., 1963; tchr. St. Jude the Apostle Sch., Wauwatosa, Wis., 1967-71, St. Joseph Sch., Fond du Lac Wis., 1971-75; tchr. Saints Mary and Joseph Sch., Fond du Lac, 1975-80, bldg. prin., 1977-80; curriculum coordinator Archdiocese of St. Paul/Mpls., 1980—; chmn. process edn. coms. Fond du Lac Consortium, 1971-75; chmn. Milw. Archdiocesan Sisters Council, 1976-80; mem. exec. bd. Milw. Archdiocesan Pastoral Council, 1979-80; mem. summer sch. faculty St. Thomas Coll., 1981; mem. adv. bd. Center for Econ. Edn., St. Thomas Coll., 1980—. Mem. Cable TV Selection Com., City of Fond du Lac, 1978-79. Recipient John Philip Sousa award Beloit Cath. High Sch., 1963; cert. tchr., Wis. Mem. Nat. Cath. Ednl. Assn., Assn. Supervision and Curriculum Devel., Sisters Council St. Paul/Mpls. Home: 14400 Cameo Ave Rosemount MN 55068 Office: Cath Edn Center 328 W 6th St Saint Paul MN 55102

INNIS, RALPH, indsl. engr.; b. Alden, Mich., July 30, 1921; s. William James and Neila Mae (Black) I.; m. Helen Esther Wellman, Jan. 19, 1941; children—Arla Jean, Terry, Patty Lou, Rose. Machine operator Simpson Mfg. Co., Litchfield, Mich. (name changed to Simpson Industries, Inc.), 1942-47, foreman, 1947-53, supt., 1953-63, inter plant mfg. coordinator, 1963-70, prodn. engr., 1970-75, mgr. indsl. engring., 1975—. Vice pres. Sch. Bd., 1967-75. Served with USNR, 1943-46. Republican. Baptist. Home: 308 N Chicago St Litchfield MI 49252 Office: 917 Anderson Rd Litchfield MI 49252

INY, GEORGE SALIM, retail co. exec.; b. Teheran, Iran, Sept. 18, 1933; s. Salim J. and Daisy Farah (Djedda) I.; came to U.S., 1948, naturalized, 1959; B.S. in Indsl. Engring., Johns Hopkins U., 1955; B.S. in Bus. Mgmt., U. Balt., 1957; m. Karen Louise Teeven, Dec. 3, 1976. Credit unit mgr. Standard Oil Co., Chgo., 1959-66; asst. v.p. First Nat. Bank of Chgo., 1966-72; sr. v.p. ops. Olympic Savs. & Loan Assn., Chgo., 1974-76; corp. credit mgr. Madigan Bros., Inc., River Forest, Ill., 1972-74, v.p., chief fin. officer, 1976—; guest lectr. Am. Mgmt. Assn., 1971, Morton Coll., 1974-76, Chgo. Midwest Credit Mgmt. Assn. Mem. Internat. Consumer Credit Assn., Nat. Assn. of Credit and Fin. Mgmt., Nat. Retail Mchts. Assn., Chgo. Retail Fin. Execs. Assn. Clubs: Order Eastern Star, Masons. Office: 7440 W Central River Forest IL 60305

IQBAL, ZAFAR, biochemist, neurochemist; b. Lucknow, India, July 12, 1946; s. Shujaat Ali and Saleha (Begum) Siddiqui; came to U.S., 1972, naturalized, 1979; B.S., Lucknow U., 1961, M.S., 1963, certificate proficiency in French, 1965; Ph.D., All India Inst. Med. Scis., New Delhi, 1971; m. Bernida Lucile Jasiewicz, Nov. 27, 1974; m. C. Jameel, Jan. 18, 1979; 1 child, Shirin. Jr. research fellow Council Sci. and Indsl. Research, India, 1963-66, research fellow, 1967-68; research scholar Directorate Gen. Health Services, India, 1966-67; asst. research officer Indian Council Med. Research, 1968-71; research asso. in physiology, investigator Ind. U. Sch. Medicine, Indpls., 1972—; asst. prof. med. biophysics, 1977—, biochemistry, 1979—. NIH research grantee, 1973-77, Muscular Dystrophy Assn. Am. research grantee, 1975-77; Am. Cancer Soc. research grantee, 1979—; Am. Diabetes Assn. research grantee, 1980. Mem. Internat. Brain Research Orgn., Internat. Soc. Neurochemistry, Soc. Neurosci., Am. Soc. Neurochemistry, AAAS, Ind., N.Y. acads. scis., Biophys. Soc., Soc. Exptl. Biology and Medicine, Sigma Xi. Contbg. author: Macromolecules in Storage and Transfer of Biological Information, 1969; Macromolecules and Behavior, 1972; Growth and Development of the Brain, 1975; Mechanism, Regulation and Special Function of Protein Synthesis in the Brain, 1977; Peripheral Neuropathies, 1978; Neurochemistry and Clinical Neurology, 1980; Calcium-Binding Proteins, 1980; Axoplasmic Transport, 1981; contbr. articles to profl. jours. Home: 8511 N College Ave Indianapolis IN 46240 Office: Physiology Dept Ind U Med Center Indianapolis IN 46223

IRIE, ROBERT KEITH, med. mfg. co. exec.; b. Springfield, Ohio, Jan. 3, 1918; s. Charles William and Jenny Alice (Webster) I.; A.B. in Econs., Miami U., Oxford, Ohio, 1940; m. Bertharae Hohenstein, Nov. 19, 1944; children—Mary Lou, Joseph, Jean Ann, Robin Janis, Susan. Mgr., Sears Roebuck & Co., Inc., Fostoria, Ohio, 1950-53, Massillon, Ohio, 1953-54, Lancaster, Ohio, 1954-57, Ashland, Ky., 1957-64, Bloomington, Ind., 1964-75; pres. Vance Products, Spencer, Ind., 1980—; v.p. Noble Roman's, Bloomington, 1976-78; v.p. Cook

Group, Inc., Bloomington, 1979—; v.p. Brandon Pizza, 1978—, Lindale Pizza, 1980—, Compton Pizza, 1979—, Cook Pacemaker, 1981—; dir. Hughes Med., Melbourne, Australia, William Cook Europe, Copenhagen, Cook Surg., Bjaverskov, Denmark, K-Tube Corp., San Diego, Western Research, Denver, Baxa Corp., Northbrook, Ill., Sabin Corp., Bloomington, others. Pres., Mchts. Assn., Massillon, Ohio, 1954, Easter Seal Assn., Lancaster, Ohio, 1956-57, Mchts. Assn., Ashland, Ky., 1960-61; v.p. Tri-State council Boy Scouts Am., 1961-64; pres. United Fund, 1962-63, Coll. Mall Mchts. Assn., Bloomington, 1965-67; bd. dirs. United Fund, Bloomington, 1970-74; mem. Human Rights Commn., Bloomington, 1972-74; campaign chmn. United Fund, Bloomington, 1973; mem. adv. bd. Jr. Achievement, Bloomington, 1969-78; mem. City Planning Commn., Bloomington, 1976—, v.p., 1979; mem. County Planning Commn., 1981; mem. adv. bd. City Hosp., Bloomington, 1981—; head usher First United Meth. Ch., Bloomington, 1978—. Served to 1st lt. U.S. Army, 1941-46. Decorated Purple Heart. Named Outstanding Store Mgr. of Yr., Mall Mchts. Assn., 1974. Mem. C. of C. (pres. 1974-75). Club: Rotary (pres. 1973-74). Home: 920 Meadowbrook St Bloomington IN 47401 Office: 925 Curry Pike Bloomington IN 47401 also 165 S Main St Spencer IN

IRISH, GARY DON, securities firm exec.; b. Topeka, Kans., Nov. 10, 1933; s. Roland C. and Martha L. (Stachelback) I.; B.S. in Fin., U. Kans., 1955; m. Barbara Ley, Oct. 21, 1961; children—Michael Shawn, Kelly Ann, Megan Lee. Securities analyst Bankers Life Co., Des Moines, 1958-59; instl. security sales E.F. Hutton & Co. Inc., Kansas City, Mo., 1959—, asst. v.p., 1968-69, asso. br. mgr., 1969-71, v.p., 1971-80, 1st v.p., 1980—; dir. Blakemore Bros. Bldg. Co., Inc., House of Commons, Inc.; ann. guest prof. bus. U. Kans. Bd. dirs. Sigma Nu House Corp. Served with USN, 1955-58. Recipient Wall St. Jour. Excellence in Finance award, 1955. Republican. Presbyterian. Clubs: Kansas City, Indian Hills Country. Home: 2108 Arno Rd Shawnee Mission KS 66208 Office: 920 Baltimore St Kansas City MO 64105

IRIZARRY, JOSEPH HENRY, educator; b. Bklyn., June 13, 1931; s. Joseph Antonio and Celina (Velez) I.; A.A.S., Inst. Applied Arts and Scis., SUNY, 1954; B.A. in Lang. Arts, Greenville (Ill.) Coll., 1968; M.A. in Spanish, U. Ill., 1972; B.A. in Bible, Moody Bible Inst., 1978; m. Joan Smith Snyder, Nov. 28, 1964; children—Joan Sophia, Joseph Daniel. Occupational instr. Central Islip (N.Y.) State Hosp., 1957-59; tchr. Spanish and English Greenville (Ill.) Public Schs., 1968-69, Worth (Ill.) Public Schs., 1969-74; bilingual instr. Bible, Moody Bible Inst., Chgo., 1974-78, 79—; bilingual instr. Radio WMBI, Moody Bible Inst., 1980—; lectr. in Spanish Trinity Coll., Deerfield, Ill., 1978—; tchr. Spanish, Midwestern Christian Acad., Chgo., 1980—; vol. Spanish tchr. Salem Christian Sch., Inner-City Impact. Bd. dirs. Salem Christian Sch., 1972-76, Inner-City Impact, 1978—; active Chgo. Area Spanish Evangelism, Inc., 1975—, v.p., 1979—. Mem. Am. Assn. Tchrs. Spanish and Portuguese, Inter-Am. Soc. Mem. Plymouth Brethren Ch. Contbr., editor various publs. Moody Bible Inst.; translator pamphlets. Home: 2046 N California Chicago IL 60647

IRONS, LINDA DORIS, occupational therapist; b. St. Joseph, Mich., July 18, 1951; d. Frederick and Sophia Ann (Palmer) Yauch; Asso. Sci., Lake Mich. Coll., 1976; B.S. with honors, Western Mich. U., 1978; m. Richard V. Irons, Aug. 2, 1973; children—Tori, Tara, Jenni. Rehab. specialist Internat. Rehab. Assos., Phila., 1979-81, sr. specialist Midwest region, S.W. Mich., Stevensville, 1981—. Clark Equipment Co. scholar, 1974-76; Western Mich. U. scholar, 1977; Social and Rehab. Services Outstanding student trainee, 1977-78. Mem. Am. Occupational Therapy Assn., Mich. Occupational Therapy Assn. Baptist. Home and Office: 4753 Ridge Rd Stevensville MI 49127

IRVIN, HELEN ARLENE BOWSER, home economist; b. Perry County, Ohio, May 30, 1932; d. Frank Harold and Frankie Louise Bowser; B.Sc. in Home Econs. Edn., Ohio State U., 1955; postgrad. Ohio U., 1979—; m. Charles A. Irvin, Dec. 23, 1956; children—Elizabeth C., Bonnie L., Robert D. Tchr. home econs. Keene High Sch., Coshocton County, Ohio, 1955-57, Maysville High Sch., Muskingum County, Ohio, 1957-59; tchr. nutrition, diet therapy, family living in practical nurse program Muskingum Area Vocat. Sch., 1970-74, project coordinator Family Life Edn. program, 1974—. Mem. Zanesville Community Concert Assn., Friends of Zanesville Art Inst., Zanesville Band Boosters; tchr. Sunday Sch., Coburn U. Meth. Ch. Mem. Am. Vocat. Assn., Ohio Vocat. Assn., Am. Home Econs. Assn., Ohio Home Econs. Assn., Ohio State U. Home Econs. Alumni Assn., Ohio State U. Sch. Home Econs. Key Alumni, Phi Upsilon Omicron, Omicron Nu. Republican. Methodist. Author: (with others) Ohio Family Life Education Curriculum Guide, 1979. Home: 1255 Pfeifer Dr Zanesville OH 43701 Office: 400 Richards Rd Zanesville OH 43701

IRVIN, WILLIAM THOMAS, safety specialist; b. Evansville, Ind., July 20, 1950; s. Joe Thomas and Sophronia I.; B.A., Knoxville Coll., 1975; m. Cynthia Tawanda Beal, June 17, 1977; 1 dau., Chloé Noir. City info. aide City of Knoxville, Tenn., 1974-75; equal employment opportunity investigator, 1975-76, OSHA compliance officer, 1976-77; dir. safety Hollywood Brands div. Consol. Foods Corp., Centralia, Ill., 1977-79; safety engr. Alcoa, Davenport, Iowa, 1979-80; safety cons., Evansville, 1980—. Community organizer Evansville chpt. Ind. State Black Polit. Caucus, 1973. Mem. Nat. Safety Mgmt. Soc., Am. Soc. Safety Engrs., Am. Indsl. Hygiene Assn., Tenn. Safety and Health Assn., Indsl. Safety Engrs. Assn. Quad Cities. Baptist. Club: Masons. Home: 634 E Maryland St Evansville IN 47711

IRVING, DONALD J., art adminstr.; b. Arlington, Mass., May 3, 1933; ed. Mass. Coll. Art, 1955; student Columbia U. Tchrs. Coll., 1956, Ed.D., 1963; m. Jewel P. Irving; children—Kevin William, Todd Lawrence. Tchr. art White Plains (N.Y.) High Sch., 1958-60; instr. art SUNY, Oneonta, 1960-62; prof. art, dean Moore Coll. Art, Phila., 1963-67; chmn. art dept., dir. Peabody Mus. Art, George Peabody Coll. Tchrs., Nashville, 1967-69; dir. Sch. Art Inst., Chgo., 1969—; mem. U.S. del. Conf. Nat. Soc. Edn. Through Art, Prague, Czechoslovakia, 1966; cons. ednl. TV series Art Now, WRCV-TV, Phila. Mem. Nat. Assn. Schs. Art (treas., dir. 1975-77), Union Ind. Colls. Art (chmn., dir.), Nat. Council Art Adminstrs. (dir.), Fedn. Ind. Ill. Colls. and Univs. (dir.), Nat. Art Edn. Assn. (officer Eastern region 1966-68), Eastern Arts Assn. (council 1964-66, mgr. conv. 1959-64), Nat. Council Arts in Edn. Internat. Soc. Edn. Through Art, Coll. Art Assn., Phi Delta Kappa. Author: Sculpture Material and Process, 1970; contbr. articles to profl. jours. Home: 1019 Superior St Oak Park IL 60302 Office: Sch Art Inst 200 S Columbus Dr Chicago IL 60603*

IRWIN, GEORGE EARLE, JR., radiologist; b. Kankakee, Ill., Mar. 24, 1919; s. George Earle and Ruth (McBroom) I.; B.S., Northwestern U., 1940, M.S., 1943, M.D., 1944; m. Marguerite Imle, Sept. 19, 1942; children—Patricia McConnell, George Stephen, Janet Johnson. Intern, Evanston (Ill.) Hosp., 1943; resident Wesley Meml. Hosp., Chgo., 1945-48; chief dept. radiology Brokaw Hosp., Normal, Ill., 1948-80; attending radiologist Mennonite Hosp., Bloomington, 1948—, St. Joseph Hosp., 1948—; clin. asso. U. Ill. Coll. Medicine, 1973—; active McLean County Health Dept. Served with AUS, 1944-46. Fellow Am. Coll. Radiology; mem. Radiol. Soc. N. Am., Ill. Radiol. Soc., AMA, Phi Beta Kappa, Alpha Omega Alpha. Presbyterian. Club: Bloomington Country. Home: 44 Sunset Rd Bloomington IL 61701 Office: 703 N East St Bloomington IL 61701

IRWIN, MITCHEL LAMOUR, state senator; b. Sault Ste. Marie, Mich., July 8, 1952; s. Frank Lamour and Mildred (Holt) I.; B.A., Lake Superior State Coll., 1974; m. Cynthia K. Williams, June 21, 1975; 1 son, Jeffrey Mitchel. Tchr., coach, juvenile counselor Rudyard (Mich.) Area schs., 1972-74, St. Mary's Grammar Sch., Sault Ste. Marie, 1970-71, Transition House, Inc., Sault Ste. Marie, 1972-74, Lake Superior State Coll., 1976-77; regional planner Eastern Upper Peninsula Regional Planning and Devel. Commn., Sault Ste. Marie, 1974-77; adminstr. Chippewa County (Mich.) Econ. Devel. Corp., 1977-78; Mich. Senate, Lansing, 1979—. Vice chmn. Chippewa County ARC. Mem. Mich. Park and Recreation Assn. Democrat. Roman Catholic. Office: 765 Senate Office Bldg Lansing MI 48909*

IRWIN, RICHARD LOREN, assn. exec.; b. Los Angeles, Dec. 8, 1924; s. Loren Wilson and Letty Elizabeth (Tate) I.; student Lockyear's Bus. Coll., 1942-43, 46-48; m. Martha Louise Sutton, Dec. 15, 1945; children—Martha Jean, Carol Ann. Mgr. machine accounting U. O. Colson Co., Paris, Ill., 1949-55; founder Nat. Machine Accountants Assn., 1951, internat. pres., 1954-55, exec. sec., Paris, Ill., 1955-60; asst. adminstrv. dir. Am. Optometric Assn., St. Louis, 1960-62; exec. dir. Assn. Systems Mgmt., Cleve., 1962—. Served with USNR, 1943-46. Mem. Am. Soc. Assn. Execs. (cert.), Data Processing Mgmt. Assn. (life), U.S. C. of C., Am. Legion. Republican. Presbyterian. Clubs: Masons, Shriners, Elks, Moose. Home: 156 Sunset Dr Berea OH 44017 Office: 24587 Bagley Rd Cleveland OH 44138

ISAAC, MARGRETHE GLORIA, educator; b. Chgo., May 6, 1927; d. Merle J. and Margrethe D. (Lehmann) Isaac; B.Ed., Chgo. Tchrs. Coll., 1947; M.A., Northwestern U., 1950, Ph.D., 1962. Tchr., Chgo. public schs., 1947-58; instr. TV Tchrs. Coll., WGN-TV, Chgo., 1958-59; asst. prof. Chgo. Tchrs. Coll., 1959-61; asso. prof. Northeastern Ill. U., Chgo., 1961—, asso. chmn. dept. early childhood edn., 1968-71, 73-80, chmn., 1980—. Vis. faculty Northwestern U., summer 1964. Mem. exec. com. Elem. Sch. sect. Nat. Safety Council, 1972-81, vice-chmn., 1975-76, chmn., 1976-77, mem. exec. com. Sch. and Coll. div., 1976-81, bd. dirs., 1977-80, Outstanding Service award, 1977; book reviewer Ill. Reading Service, 1971-76; advisory com. Child Safety Club, 1977—. Mem. Chgo. Public Schs. Kindergarten-Primary Assn. (pres. 1954-56), Ill. Edn. Assn. (pres. Chgo. div. 1964-65, Disting. Service award 1967), Ill. Assn. Higher Edn. (pres. 1968-69), Assn. Childhood Edn. Internat., (chmn. various coms. 1954—, v.p. Chgo. area br. 1973-77), NEA, AAUP, AAUW, Assn. Tchr. Educators, Nat. Assn. Edn. Young Children, Alpha Delta Kappa (pres. Ill. Alpha Epsilon chpt. 1957-59, Ill. historian 1958-60, Ill. rec. sec. 1964-66), Pi Lambda Theta (rec. sec. Alpha Zeta chpt. 1965-67, corr. sec. Chgo. area chpt. 1973-77, pres. Chgo. area chpt. 1977-81), Delta Kappa Gamma (chpt. music chmn. 1972-76), Phi Delta Kappa (chpt. historian 1977-79). Research on profl. problems of beginning tchrs. Home: 700 Victoria Rd Des Plaines IL 60016 Office: Dept Earl Childhood Edn Northeastern Ill U Bryn Mawr at St Louis Ave Chicago IL 60625

ISAACS, GERALD LOUIS, EDP adminstr.; b. St. Paul, June 25, 1947; s. Gerald Dewitt and Otellia Ida (Horbach) I.; B.S. in Math., U. Minn., 1969; M.S. in Computer Sci., U. Iowa, 1973, Ph.D. in Stats. and Measurement, 1978; m. Linda Kay Berg, Aug. 24, 1974; children—Joey Allen, Roberta Ann, Robert Paul, Gerald Louis, Nicole Lee. Programmer, 3M Co., St. Paul, 1968-69; programmer software devel. Collins Radio Co., Cedar Rapids, Iowa, 1969-72; programmer analyst Am. Coll. Testing, Iowa City, 1972-73; leader systems devel. project U. Iowa, Iowa City, 1973-78; computer dir., chmn. computer sci. dept. Carroll Coll., Waukesha, Wis., 1978—; cons. NSF, 1978—, Nat. Enforcement Adminstrn. Agy., Dept. Justice, 1978—; computer and statis cons. Conduit, Westinghouse Learning Corp., U. Iowa. Author publs. in computer sci. and stats. Home: 1644 W Shore Dr Delafield WI 53018 Office: Carroll Coll 100 N East Ave Waukesha WI 53186

ISAACS, KENNETH S(IDNEY), psychoanalyst, educator; b. Mpls., Apr. 7, 1920; s. Mark William and Sophia (Rau) I.; B.A., U. Minn. 1944; Ph.D., U. Chgo., 1956; postgrad. Inst. Psychoanalysis, 1957-63; m. Ruth Elizabeth Johnson, Feb. 21, 1950 (dec. 1967); m. 2d, Adele Rella Bodroghy, May 17, 1969; children—Jonathan, James; step-children—John, Curtis, Peter and Edward Meissner. Intern, Worcester (Mass.) State Hosp., 1947-48; trainee VA Hosp., Chgo., 1948-50; chief psychologist-outpatient clinic system Ill. Dept. Pub. Welfare, 1949-56; research asso. (asso. prof.) U. Ill. Med. Sch., Chgo., 1956-63; practice psychoanalysis, Evanston, Ill., 1960—; supr. psychiat. residency program Evanston Hosp., Northwestern U., 1972—. Cons. schs., hosps., clinics, pvt. practitioners. Served with AUS, 1943-45; ETO. Mem. Am. Psychol. Assn., AAAS, Chgo. Psychoanalytic Soc., N.Y. Acad. Sci., Sigma Xi. Contbr. articles to profl. publs. Office: 636 Church St Evanston IL 60201

ISABELLE, FRANK EDWARD, obstetrician-gynecologist; b. Canton, Ohio, May 21, 1939; s. Woodrow Jean and Jenny Marie (Babbo) I.; B.S., U. Notre Dame, 1961; M.D., Ohio State U., 1966; m. Sharon Rose Mahan, July 25, 1964; children—Frank Edward, Kristina Kay. Intern, Great Lakes (Ill.) Naval Hosp., 1966-67; resident in ob-gyn. Ohio State U., Columbus, 1971-75; fellow in maternal-fetal medicine, Ohio State U., 1975-76; practice medicine specializing in ob-gyn., Columbus, 1976—; staff physician Dept. Ob-Gyn., Central Ohio Med. Clinic, Columbus, 1976—, dir., 1971—; teaching staff Ohio State U. Hosp., Columbus, 1976—, Mt. Carmel Hosp., Columbus, 1976—, Grant Hosp., Columbus, 1976—. Served with USN, 1966-71. Fellow Am. Coll. Obstetricians and Gynecologists; mem. Franklin County Obstetrical and Gynecol. Soc., Ohio Med. Assn., A.C.S. Producer film: Cesarian Section, with QUBE TV, 1978; producer slide: Cesarian Section, 1978. Office: 497 E Town St Columbus OH 43215

ISDALE, CHARLES EDWIN, chem. engr.; b. DeQuincy, La., Mar. 10, 1942; s. Vester Edwin and Katherine Gwendolyn (Wincey) I.; B.S., La. State U., 1965; M.B.A., So. Ill. U., 1977; m. Myrna Lucille Brown, Aug. 26, 1962; children—Charles Edwin, Jennifer Denise. Chem. engr. Firestone Synthetic Rubber & Latex Co., Lake Charles, La., 1965-69, A.E. Staley Mfg. Co., Decatur, Ill., 1969-72; dir. engring. and maint. Viobin Corp., Monticello, Ill., 1972-80; cons., prin. Charles Isdale & Assos., Champaign, Ill., 1980—. Mem. Am. Inst. Chem. Engrs. (Central Ill. sect. chmn. 1974), Nat. Soc. Profl. Engrs., Ill. Soc. Profl. Engrs., Am. Oil Chemists Soc. Home: 902 Stratford Dr Champaign IL 61820 Office: Country Fair Box 3226 Champaign IL 61820

ISELY, JOHN J., mfg. co. exec.; b. New Philadelphia, Ohio, Nov. 14, 1926; s. John H. and Frieda I.; B.B.A. in Acctg., Western Res. U., 1952; m. Rose Marie Isely, Sept. 13, 1951; children—Cindy, Jeff, Jim, Bob. Cost analyst Am. Steel & Wire, 1955-58; budget dir. Ferro Corp., 1958-59; cost analyst Chrysler Corp., 1959-60; budget dir. Clevite Corp., Cleve., 1960-69; group fin. planning dir. Gould, Inc., Chgo., 1969-70, group controller govt. systems, 1970-72, dir. fin. info., 1975-77, v.p., controller valve and fittings div., 1977—. Asso. dir. Firelands dist. Boy Scouts Am. Served with U.S. Army, 1945-46. Mem. Nat. Assn. Accts. (past asso. dir. Cleve. chpt.), Planning Execs. Inst. (past pres. Cleve. chpt.), Fin. Execs. Inst. Office: 6300 W Howard St Niles IL 60648

ISO-AHOLA, SEPPO ENSIO, educator; b. Saarijärvi, Finland, Nov. 11, 1948; came to U.S., 1971; s. Aaro Matti and Sylvi (Ruuska) Iso-Ahola; B.S. (honors scholar, 1970-71), U. Jyväskylä (Finland), 1971, M.S., 1973; M.S., U. Ill., 1972, Ph.D., 1976; m. Leena Riitta Koskela, Sept. 2, 1972; children—Vikke, Ville. Grad. teaching asst. U. Ill., Urbana-Champaign, 1971-72, grad. research asst., 1973-76; grad. teaching and research asso. U. Jyväskylä, Finland, 1972-73; asst. prof. U. Iowa, Iowa City, 1976-80, asso. prof., 1980—; invited organizer, chmn. research symposia on psychology of leisure Nat. Recreation and Park Assn. Conv., 1978, 79, 80; invited evaluator edn. research projects Bur. Edn. for Handicapped, N.Tex. State U., 1980. Served to 2d lt. Finnish Army, 1968-69. Travel and research grantee Ministry of Edn., Finland, 1971, 73; Old Gold summer fellow, U. Iowa, 1978, 79; devel. assignment award U. Iowa, 1980. Mem. Am. Psychol. Assn. Author: The Social Psychology of Leisure and Recreation, 1980; editor: Social Psychological Perspectives on Leisure and Recreation, 1980; cons. editor, reviewer Jour. of Leisure Research and Leisure Sciences, 1980—; contbr. sci. research articles to books and sci. jours. Home: 3051 Wayne Ave Iowa City IA 52240 Office: W619 East Hall U Iowa Iowa City IA 52242

ISRAELSTAM, DAVID MICHAEL, psychiatrist; b. Chgo., July 20, 1939; s. Alfred William and Beatrice (Ruden) I.; B.S., U. Chgo., 1959; M.D., Western Res. U., 1963; Ph.D. in Med. Physics, U. Calif., Berkeley, 1971; 1 dau., Shana Rebecca. Intern, Presbyn. Med. Center, San Francisco, 1963-64; resident in psychiatry U. Calif., Berkeley, Cowell Hosp., 1967; staff psychiatrist Napa (Calif.) State Hosp., 1968-69; staff psychiatrist, dir. adolescent program DeWitt State Hosp., Auburn, Calif., 1970-71; liaison, corp. med. office G.D. Searle & Co., Skokie, Ill., 1971-75; program physician Sonoma State Hosp., Eldridge, Calif., 1975-77; med. dir. Anoka (Minn.) State Hosp., 1979; clin. dir. St. Peter (Minn.) State Hosp., 1979-80; physician, specialist Mendota Mental Health Inst., Madison, Wis., 1980—; staff psychiatrist Jefferson County Human Services Dept., Jefferson, Wis., 1980—; chief med. cons. corp. fitness div. Forest Hosp. Found., 1978-79. NIH postdoctoral and spl. fellow, 1964-67; recipient Alumni/Deans Men's award U. Chgo., 1959. Mem. Am. Coll. Nuclear Physicians, AAAS, Sigma Xi. Contbr. articles to profl. jours. Home: 1525 Troy Dr Madison WI 53704

ISSARI, MOHAMMAD ALI, film maker, educator; b. Esfahan, Iran, Aug. 13, 1924; s. Abbas Bek and Qamar (Soltan) I.; B.A., U. Tehran (Iran), 1963; M.A., U. So. Calif., 1968, Ph.D., 1979; m. Joan Gura Aamodt, 1953; children—Scheherezade, Katayoun, Roxana. Films officer Brit. Embassy, Brit. Council Joint Film Div., Tehran, 1944-50; asst. motion picture officer USIS, 1950-65; cons. to various Iranian Govt. ministries on film and TV devels., 1950-78; prof. cinema, coll. communication arts and scis. Mich. State U., East Lansing, 1969-81, dir. instructional film and multimedia prodn., 1969-78; producer over 1000 ednl., instructional and documentary films, 1956-81, including: Earthquake Village, 1963, Roxana, 1967, Life-Long Education, 1972, The Tasks of Teaching, 1973, Life on the Iranian Plateau, 3000-800 B.C., The First World Empire, 800-530 B.C., 1976-78; free lance film reporter Telenews, UPI, Iran, 1959-61; film adviser to Iranian Oil Operating Cos. in Iran, 1963-65; spl. cons. on edn. and instructional TV, Saudi Arabian Ministry of Info., 1972; project dir., exec. producer Iran Film Series, 1974-78; dir. film prodn. workshops Cranbrook Inst., Detroit, 1973-74; tchr. Persian lang. Iran—Am. Soc., Tehran, 1949-59. Founder, Youth Orgn. of Iran, 1951-52; v.p. Rugby Football Fedn., Iran, 1952-53, pres., 1954-55. Recipient Cine Golden Eagle award, 1975, Meritorious Honor award USIA, 1965; decorated Order of Cavalieres (Italy); Order of Oranje Nassau (Holland); Orders of Kooshesh and Pas (Iran); Order of Esteghlal (Jordan); Order of Sancti Silvestri Papae, Pope John 23d, 1951-76. Mem. Anglo-Iranian Dramatic Soc. (dir. 1943-50), Mich. Film Assn. (co-founder 1972, dir. 1972-73), Soc. Motion Picture and TV Engrs., Assn. Ednl. Communication and Tech., Delta Kappa Alpha. Author: (with Doris A. Paul) A Picture of Persia, 1977; What is Cinema Verité?, 1979; contbr. articles on ednl. communication and audio-visual instruction to periodicals and profl. jours.; introduced audio-visual edn. in Iran, 1951; established first film festivals in Iran. Home: 4454 Seneca Dr Okemos MI 48864

ISSERMAN, ANDREW MARK, economist, educator; b. N.Y.C., June 28, 1947; s. Manfred Alexander and Ellen Sophie (Kann) I.; B.A., Amherst Coll., 1968; M.A. (NSF trainee), U. Pa., 1970, Ph.D. (Mellon fellow), 1975; m. Ellen Lise Jacobsen, July 23, 1977; 1 son, Jacob David. Instr. econs. Pa. State U., 1972-73; lectr. U. Ill., 1973-75, asst. prof. planning and econs., 1975-77, asso. prof., 1977-81; asso. prof. planning, geography and econs. U. Iowa, Iowa City, 1981—; vis. asso. prof. planning U. So. Calif., 1977-78; cons. in field. Am. Statis. Assn. research fellow, 1979-81; HUD grantee, 1978-80. Mem. Am. Econs. Assn., Regional Sci. Assn. (editor Internat. Regional Sci. Rev. 1976—, mem. N. Am. program com. 1979-81), Assn. Am. Geographers, Am. Statis. Assn. (conf. dir. 1982). Author: (with Marilyn Brown) Suburban Need and Distress, 1981; bd. editors Jour. Am. Planning Assn., 1979—, Central Ill. Econ.-Bus. Rev., 1979-81, Jour. Planning Edn., 1981—; contbr. articles to profl. jours. Office: 347 Jessup Hall U Iowa Iowa City IA 52242

ISZLER, HARRY EUGENE, state senator; b. Street, N.D., Sept. 11, 1930; s. Gottlieb M. and Mary (Wolt) I.; student N.D. State Sch. Sci., 1950-51; m. Leona Hoffer, 1953; children—Bernadean Iszler Ketterlin, Holly Iszler Becker, Michael, Mary Jean, Timothy. Farmer, rancher, 1953—; mem. N.D. Senate, 1974—. Served with AUS, 1952-53; Korea. Decorated Bronze Star. Mem. N.D. Stockmen Assn., Am. Legion, Farm Bur., Am. Nat. Cattlemens Assn. Methodist. Club: Elks. Home: Street ND 58483 Office: ND Senate State Capitol Bismarck ND 58505*

ITIN, ROBERT BRUCE, JR., oil co. exec.; b. Batavia, Ohio, Sept. 15, 1931; s. Robert B. and Carrie I.; B.S.C., Ohio U., 1953; m. June C. Rucker, Sept. 5, 1953; children—Robin, Janel. Mem. sales staff Shell Oil Co., 1955-61; various sales mgmt. positions Texaco, Inc., 1961-69; pres. Itin Oil Co., Dearborn Heights, Mich., 1969—, Dearborn Wheels Inc., 1974—. Pres. Dearborn Inter Service Club Council, 1981. Served to 1st lt. U.S. Army, 1953-55. Mem. Delta Sigma Pi, Sigma Nu. Republican. Presbyterian. Clubs: Kiwanis (pres. 1979, lt. gov. Div. 4 Mich. Dist. 1981) (Dearborn, Mich.); Masons, Shriners. Home: 646 Mohawk St Dearborn MI 48124 Office: Itin Oil Co 6425 N Telegraph St Dearborn Heights MI 48127

ITIN, SHIRLEY BESEMER, new ventures and export co. exec.; b. Ithaca, N.Y., Feb. 11, 1936; d. Martin Charles and Josephine Sarah (Palmer) B.; student Cornell U., 1953-55, 57, U. Md., 1960-62; m. Thomas William Itin, Jan. 28, 1955; children—Dawn Elizabeth, Timothy Sean. With TWI Internat., Inc., Southfield, Mich., 1968—, exec. v.p. 1978—. Mem. U.S. Ski Assn. Republican. Presbyterian. Clubs: Cornell, Houston City. Office: TWI International 29621 Northwestern Hwy Southfield MI 48034 also 5201 Bayard St Houston TX 77006

ITOH, SEIICHI, banker; b. Tokyo, Japan, June 24, 1933: s. Doki and Mie (Sugimori) I.; M.B.A., Tokyo U., 1956; m. Michiko Kato, Nov. 26, 1961. Sr. v.p., br. mgr. Bank of Tokyo Trust Co., N.Y.C., 1974-76; sr. regional mgr. Bank of Tokyo, Tokyo, 1976-78; chmn. bd., pres. Chgo.-Tokyo Bank, Chgo., 1979—. Clubs: Econ., Exec., University (Chgo.). Office: 40 N Dearborn St Chicago IL 60602

IVENS, VIRGINIA RUTH, educator; b. Decatur, Ill., July 27, 1922; d. John Raymond and Dessie Lenora (Underwood) I.; B.S., U. Ill., 1950. Tracer blueprints Caterpillar Mil. Engine Co., Decatur, 1941-45; mem. faculty Coll. Veterinary Medicine, U. Ill., Urbana, 1950—, asso. prof. veterinary parasitology, 1979—, chmn. curriculum com. dept. veterinary pathobiology, 1976-78; chmn. 9th Ann. Conf. Coccidiosis, 1972. Mem. Am. Soc. Parasitologists (transl. com. 1963-71, 80, 81), Soc. Protozoologist, Am. Inst. Biol. Scis., Entomol. Soc. Am., League Women Voters, Sigma Xi, Phi Zeta. Translator Russian articles on parasitology; contbr. articles to profl. jours. and co-author three monographs; sr. author: Principal Parasites of Domestic Animals in the U.S., 1978. Home: 608 S Edwin St Champaign IL 61820 Office: 1101 W Peabody Dr 303 Veterinary Medicine Annex U Ill Urbana IL 61801

IVERSEN, JAMES TERRY, polit. scientist; b. Worland, Wyo., Apr. 5, 1939; s. John and Josephine Roberta (Snyder) I.; B.A. Internat. Affairs, U. Wyo., 1961, M.A. Polit. Sci., 1962; postgrad. U. Denver, 1963-66; m. Judith A. Bingeman, May 12, 1979. Instr. polit. sci. Drake U., Des Moines, 1962-63; instr. polit. sci./internat. affairs U. Wyo., Laramie, 1965-67, chmn. internat. affairs acad. program, 1966-67; instr. dept. polit. sci. U. Ill., Urbana-Champaign, 1967-73, head continuing edn. in internat. affairs, 1967—, world affairs conf. dir., 1968—, chmn. com. for public service in internat. affairs, 1973—. Grad. fellow, 1962, 64, 65. Mem. Internat. Studies Assn., Nat. Univ. Extension Assn., Nat. Council World Affairs Orgns., Chgo. Assn. Commerce and Industry, Ill. Dist. Export Council. Club: Kiwanis (Champaign-Urbana). Home: 906 W Columbia St Champaign IL 61820 Office: 205 Arcade Bldg 725 S Wright St U Ill Champaign IL 61820

IVINS, RICHARD ORVILLE, chem. engr.; b. Chgo., Nov. 1, 1934; s. Julian Phillip and Agnes Delores I.; B.S. in Chem. Engring., Northwestern U., 1958, M.S. in Chem. Engring., 1960; M.B.A., U. Chgo., 1979; m. Leila Ann Phillips, May 29, 1971; children—Dana H., Alexander B.; stepchildren—Christopher Allen, Gregory Allen. With Argonne (Ill.) Nat. Lab., 1959—, dep. dir. storage programs, 1974-76, dep. and acting dir. coal, 1976-78; dep. for commercialization Energy and Environ. Systems div., 1978-80, dir. Office of Indsl. Mktg. Scis., 1980—. Mem. AICE, Am. Nuclear Soc., Am. Inst. Chemists, Phi Lambda Upsilon. Contbr. articles to profl. jours. Office: 9700 S Cass Ave Argonne IL 60439

IVY, CONWAY GAYLE, business exec.; b. Houston, July 8, 1941; s. John Smith and Caro (Gayle) I.; student U. Chgo., 1959-62; B.S. in Natural Scis., Shimer Coll., 1964; postgrad. U. Tex., 1964-65; M.B.A., U. Chgo., 1968, M.A. in Econs., 1972, postgrad. 1972-74; m. Diane Ellen Cole, May 25, 1973; 1 son, Brice McPherson. Geol. asst. John S. Ivy, Houston, 1965-72; securities analyst Halsey Stuart & Co. and successor Bache & Co., Chgo., 1973-74, Winmill Securities Inc., Chgo., 1974; econ. and fin. cons., Chgo., 1974-75; dir. corp. planning Gould Inc., Rolling Meadows, Ill., 1975-79; v.p. corp. planning and devel. Sherwin-Williams Co., Cleve., 1979—; pres. Ivy Minerals Inc., 1978—. Mem. Am. Econs. Assn., N.Y. Acad. Scis., Phi Gamma Delta. Republican. Author of numerous analytical reports for brokerage industry. Home: 37475 Jackson Rd Moreland Hills OH 44022 Office: Sherwin-Williams Co 101 Prospect Ave NW Cleveland OH 44115

IWANSKI, MARIE IDA, rehab. counselor; b. Wisconsin, Rapids, Wis., Oct. 13, 1948; d. Adam John and Mary Elizabeth (McNamee) I.; B.S., U. Wis., 1974, M.S., 1978. Record keeper, personnel clk., cost accounting clk. Consol. Papers, Inc., Wisconsin Rapids, Wis., 1966-71; child care worker, dorm head Norris, Inc for boys, Mukwonago, Wis., 1974-76; adminstrv. sec. U. Wis., Madison, 1978-79; planning analyst III dept. health and social services Wis. Div. Health, Madison, 1979—. Mem. Nat. Rehab. Assn., Am. Rehab. Counseling Assn., Am. Personnel and Guidance Assn., Nat. Spinal Cord Injury Assn. (corr. sec. Wis. chpt. 1981). Roman Catholic. Office: Dept Health and Social Services Div Health Room 244 1 W Wilson St Madison WI 53702

IZANT, ROBERT JAMES, JR., pediatric surgeon; b. Cleve., Feb. 4, 1921; s. Robert James and Grace (Goulder) I.; A.B., Amherst Coll., 1943; M.D., Western Res. U., 1946; m. Virginia Lincoln Root, Sept. 27, 1947; children—Jonathan G. II, Mary Root, Timothy Holman. Gen. surgery resident U. Hosp. of Cleve., 1946-47, 49-52; pediatric surgery residency Boston Children's Med. Center, 1952-55; asst. prof. pediatric surgery Ohio State U., 1955-58; prof., dir. divs. pediatric surgery Case Western Res. U., 1958—; dir. div. pediatric surgery Univ. Hosps. of Cleve., Rainbow Babies and Children's Hosp., also Cleve. Met. Gen. Hosp. Mem. med. adv. bd. Ohio State Services for Crippled Children, exec. com ., 1972—; trustee Am. Cancer Soc. Served to lt. (j.g.) M.C., USNR, 1947-49. Diplomate Am. Bd. Surgery. Fellow A.C.S., Am. Acad. Pediatrics; mem. Central Surg. Assn., Am., Ohio med. assns., Am. Assn. for Surgery of Trauma, Cleve. Surg. Soc. (sec.-treas. 1965-68, pres. 1971-72), Cleve. Acad. Medicine (dir. 1971-74), Am. Trauma Soc., Teratology Soc., Lilliputian Surg. Soc., No. Ohio Pediatric Soc., Brit. Assn. Pediatric Surgery, Pediatric Surgery Biology Club, Pediatric Surg. Assn., Western Res. U. Sch. Medicine Alumni Assn. (pres. 1961-62), Am. Burn Assn., Sigma Xi. Alpha Omega Alpha, Nu Sigma Nu, Delta Kappa Epsilon. Co-author: The Surgical Neonate; contbr. articles to profl. jours. Home: 2275 Harcourt Dr Cleveland Heights OH 44106 Office: University Hospitals of Cleveland University Circle Cleveland OH 44106

JABLONSKI, LUCIAN STANLEY, physician; b. Toledo, July 20, 1920; s. Anthoni and Helena Josephine (Nowak) J.; B.S., U. Toledo, 1939; Dr. Osteopathy, Kirksville Coll. Osteo. Medicine, 1942; children—Wanda Marie (Mrs. Terry Hatmaker), Helena Angeline. Intern, Research Hosp., Kansas City, Mo., 1942-43; resident Parkview Hosp., Toledo, 1952-57; practiced medicine, specializing in internal medicine, Toledo, 1955—; chmn. dept. internal medicine Parkview Hosp., 1962—. Sch. physician Dupont High Sch., Bradner High Sch., Lake High Sch., Clay High Sch., Start High Sch., Toledo, 1947—; chmn. dept. sports medicine Ohio AAU, 1965—; pres. physician World Wrestling Championships, 1962, 66, 73, 75. Bd. dirs. NW Ohio Heart Assn., 1976—. Recipient Educator of Year award Parkview Hosp., 1973-74, Meritorious Service award Fedn. Internat. Lutte Amateur, 1962, Gold Key award Amateur Hall of Fame, 1968, Meritorious certificate U.S. Olympic Com., 1960, World Cup, 1973, Soul City Dedicated Service award, Toledo, 1970, Letter of Appreciation, Japanese Army, 1965, Distinguished Service award Japan Gen. Seiichi Yoshie, 1966; knight's cross of honor, comdrs. cross Legion of Merit Fedn. Internationale Des Luttes Amateur, 1976; also 3 certificates of distinction AAU of U.S. Mason (Shriner). Home and office: 1925 Parkwood Av Toledo OH 43624

JABLONSKI, PHILIP JOHN, occupational therapist; b. Jackson, Mich., June 21, 1950; s. Stanley Walter and Esther Agnes (Ratkowski) J.; A.A., Jackson Community Coll., 1971; B.S. in Occupational Therapy, Western Mich. U., 1975; m. Margaret R. Dodd. Occupational therapist VA Med. Center, Northport, N.Y., 1974, Mt. Sinai Hosp., Cleve., 1974, Wyandotte (Mich.) Gen. Hosp., 1975; supr. occupational therapy VA Med. Center, Marion, Ind., 1975—, chmn. handicapped employment com.; cons. in field. John George scholar, 1972. Mem. Am. Occupational Therapy Assn., Ind. Occupational Therapy Assn., Pi Theta Epsilon. Roman Catholic. Club: K.C. Home: 4128 W Magers Dr Marion IN 46952

JACHIM, DAVID PAUL, psychologist; b. Hinsdale, Ill., Jan. 24, 1949; s. George John and Lillian (Trayer) J.; B.A., Knox Coll., 1971; M.A., Eastern Ill. U., 1972; Ph.D., Ill. Inst. Tech., 1978. Clin. psychologist Family Service and Community Mental Health Center, 1972-74, 75; grad. asst. team leader Ill. Inst. Tech., 1977-78; clin. psychologist Chgo. Cath. Charities, 1977, DuPage County Health Dept. Wheaton, Ill., 1978-81, Met. Rehab. Services, Mpls., 1981—; instr. Coll. of DuPage, 1979. Registered psychologist, Ill. Mem. Ill. Psychol. Assn., Am. Psychol. Assn. Home and Office: 1900 Colfax St S Minneapolis MN 55403

JACK, DONALD EUGENE, policeman; b. Coles County, Ill., Mar. 15, 1946; s. Vernon E. and Evelyn M. Jack; B.S. in Bus. Adminstrn., Millikin U., Decatur, Ill., 1976; postgrad. U. Ill., Eastern Ill. U.; M.A. in Police Adminstrn., Sangamon State U.; m. Janice F. Mintel, June 12, 1976; 1 dau., Anastasia Marie. Patrol officer City of Decatur Police Dept., 1968-72, police liaison officer, 1972—; tchr. classes in field. Active local Boy Scouts Am., A.R.C. Served with USAR, 1965-68; Vietnam. Decorated Army Commendation medal. Mem. Internat. Arson Investigators Assn., Internat. Juvenile Officers Assn., Internat. Police Chiefs Assn., Ill. Policemen's Benevolent and Protective Assn. (exec. bd.), Ill. Police Assn., Decatur Police Benevolent and Protective Assn. (sec. 1973—). Methodist. Author articles in field. Home: 1816 S Country Club Rd Decatur IL 62521 Office: 707 E Wood St Decatur IL 62521

JACKAMONIS, EDWARD GEORGE, state legislator Wis.; b. New Britain, Conn., Oct. 19, 1939; s. Edward George and Sophie (Horosik) J.; B.A. magna cum laude, Northeastern U., 1962; M.A., U. Wis. at Madison, 1964; m. Barbara Bastenbeck, Aug. 26, 1962; children—April Marie, Jason Scott. Project asst. Inst. Govtl. Affairs, Madison, Wis., 1962-64; teaching asst. polit. sci. dept. U. Wis., Madison, 1964-65; instr. sci. U. Wis., Waukesha, 1966-71; mem. Wis. Assembly, 1971—, speaker pro tempore, 1975-76, assembly speaker, 1977—. Chmn., LaFollette for Gov. Com. Waukesha County, 1968; sec. Waukesha County Democratic Party, 1969; chmn. 9th Congl. Dist. Lindsay for Pres. Com., 1972; del. Wis. Dem. Conv., 1968-81. Mem. Waukesha County Mental Health Assn., Waukesha Assn. Retarded Citizens, Wis. Acad. Scis., Arts and Letters, Waukesha Environ. Action League, The Women's Center, La Casa de Esperanza, Pi Sigma Alpha, Phi Alpha Theta. Home: 622 Greenmeadow Dr Waukesha WI 53186 Office: State Capitol Bldg Madison WI 53702

JACKLIN, WILLIAM THOMAS, county ofcl., educator; b. Chgo., Dec. 26, 1940; s. Robert Theodore and Florence Carrie (Dombrow) J.; B.S., Roosevelt U., 1967; M.S. in Bus., Ind. U., 1968; m. Bonnie Joy Winquist. Vice pres. Du Page Corp., Lombard, Ill., 1970-73; instr. bus., Coll. Du Page, Glen Ellyn, Ill., 1969—. Chief dep. auditor DuPage County, 1973, county auditor, 1973—; v.p. DuPage County Employees Credit Union, 1978-79, pres., 1979-80. Mem. Ill. Prairie Path; mem. DuPage County Republican Central Com.; sec. York Twp. Rep. Orgn., 1978-80; treas. Highland Hills Assn., 1975-78; chmn. DuPage County com. Gerald R. Ford presdl. campaign, 1976; mem. fin. mgmt. project com. Ill. Dept. Commerce and Community Affairs, 1980—; mem. 1st Ch. of Christ, Scientist, Downers Grove. Recipient High Scholastic Achievement award Ind. U., 1968; named Most Outstanding DuPage County Pub. Ofcl., Young Republicans, 1976. Mem. Inst. Internal Auditors (govt. and public affairs com. 1976—), Nat. Assn. Accountants (asso. dir.), Am. Accounting Assn., Ill. Assn. County Auditors (sec.-treas. 1976-78, v.p. 1978-80, pres. 1980—), Phi Delta Kappa. Club: Masons (sec. lodge 1979-80). Home: 411 E 17th St Lombard IL 60148 Office: DuPage Center 421 N County Farm Rd Wheaton IL 60187

JACKOWAY, MARLIN KAY, ednl. adminstr.; b. St. Louis, May 15, 1924; s. Samuel Charles and Sadie (Holiner) J.; B.S.B.A., Washington U., St. Louis, 1948, M.A., 1964; Ph.D., St. Louis U., 1971; m. Goldie Duhov, Sept. 1, 1947; children—Judith Lee Newmark, Marcia Gay. With Westcher Hat Co., St. Louis, 1949-59, asst. to v.p., 1955-59; tchr. Pattonville Sch. Dist., Maryland Heights, Mo., 1959-62, counselor, 1962-66, dir., 1967-79, asst. to supt. pupil personnel, 1980—. Vice pres. Mo. P.T.A., 1978-80; chmn. educators task force St. Louis Anti-Defamation League. Served with U.S. Army, 1943-46. Decorated Bronze Star. State Dept. Edn. grantee, 1967-70, 71-73, 74-77. Mem. Am. Personnel and Guidance Assn., Am. Ednl. Research Assn., Nat. Assn. Pupil Personnel Adminstrs., Am. Vocat. Edn. Research Assn., Mo. Personnel and Guidance Assn. (treas. 1975-78), Mo. Guidance Assn., Suburban Guidance Assn., St. Louis Personnel and Guidance Assn. (past pres.), Pattonville Community Tchrs. Assn. (past pres.), Kappa Delta Pi, Phi Delta Kappa. Jewish. Club: B'nai B'rith (mem. nat. edn. com.). Author: Current Concepts in Dyslexia, 1971. Home: 11105 Schuetz St St Louis County MO 63141 Office: 115 Harding St Maryland Heights MO 63043

JACKSON, A(MOS) HENRY, analyst, programmer computer systems; b. Mt. Orab, Ohio, July 3, 1944; s. J(ohn) Pierce and Ocie Rebecca (Howlette) J.; B.S., SW Mo. State U., Springfield, 1975. Programmer, Fasco Industries, Eldon, Mo., 1975-76, Rowlette and Assos. Acctg. Services, Eldon, 1976; programmer EDP coordination Office of Adminstrn., State of Mo., Jefferson City, 1976-78; programmer, analyst Info. Systems Div. Mo. Dept. Revenue, Jefferson City, 1979—. Served with U.S. Army, 1965-68; ETO. Mem. Adminstrv. Mgmt. Soc., Pi Omega Pi. Mem. Ch. of God. Home: Route 1 Holt's Summit MO 65043 Office: Info Systems Div Mo Dept Revenue Jefferson Bldg Jefferson City MO 65101

JACKSON, BILLY MORROW, artist, educator; b. Kansas City, Mo., Feb. 23, 1926; s. Alonzo David and Opal May (Morrow) J.; B.F.A., Washington U., St. Louis, 1949; M.F.A., U. Ill., 1954; m. Blanche M. Trice, June 12, 1949; children—Lon Allan, Robin Todd, Aron Drew, Sylvia Marie. Prof. dept. art and design U. Ill., Champaign, 1954—; asso. mem. Center for Advanced Study, U. Ill., 1967-68; one-man shows of paintings and/or drawings include: Peoples Art Center, St. Louis, 1952, Millikin U., Decatur, Ill., 1956, Art Mart, St. Louis, 1956, 58, 60, 62, Arnold Finkel Gallery, Phila., 1962, Banfer Gallery, N.Y.C., 1963, 64, Antique Gallery, Champaign, Ill., 1963, Kenmore Galleries, Phila., 1964, Lehigh U., Bethlehem, Pa., 1966, Premier Art Gallery, Springfield, Ill., 1966, Menemsha Gallery, Martha's Vineyard, Mass., 1966, St. Louis Gallery, 1966, Haslem Gallery, Madison, Wis., 1966, 69, 70, 71, 73, 76, Decatur (Ill.) Art Center, 1966, 4 Arts Gallery, Evanston, Ill., 1967, Lakeview Center of Art, Peoria, Ill., 1967, Martha's Vineyard Nat. Bank, Chilmark, Mass., 1968, 72, Krannert Art Mus., U. Ill., Champaign, 1968, Swope Mus., Terre Haute, Ind., 1970, 75; numerous group shows, latest being: McClung Mus. Gallery, U. Tenn., Knoxville, 1966, 67, Flint (Mich.) Inst. Arts, 1966, Fine Arts Gallery, San Diego, 1966, Smithsonian Institution, Washington, 1970, Nat. Gallery of Art, Washington, 1971, Worlds Fair, Spokane, Wash., 1974, Phila. State Coll., 1974, Mitchell Art Mus., Mt. Vernon, Ill., 1974; represented in numerous permanent collections including: Nat. Gallery Art, Washington, Smithsonian Instn., Washington, Met. Mus. Art, N.Y.C., Library of Congress, Washington, Evansville (Ind.) Mus. Arts and Scis., Butler Inst. Am. Art, Youngstown, Ohio, Sheld Meml. Gallery, U. Nebr., Lindoln, Wichita (Kans.) Art Mus., Swope Mus., Terre Haute, Ind. Served with USMC, 1944-45. Recipient numerous awards, latest being: Hon. Mention award Ark. Art Center, 1966, Best of Show award Marietta Coll., 1971, Merit award Bluegrass Exhibit, 1977, Bellinger award Chatauqua Art Assn., 1966. Home: 608 S Prospect Champaign IL 61820 Office: 130 Fine Arts Univ Illinois Champaign IL 61820

JACKSON, C(LARENCE) LINDLEY, JR., hosp. adminstr.; b. Dixfield, Maine, Apr. 26, 1926; s. Clarence Lindley and Katharine Helena (Thurston) J.; B.S., St. Michael's Coll., Wiwooski, Vt., 1949; M.A., U. Vt., 1951; M.S. in Hosp. Adminstrn., Northwestern U., 1953; postgrad. Cleve.-Marshall Law Sch., 1958-60; 1 son, Angel Denegri. Resident in hosp. adminstrn., U. Colo. Hosps., 1952-53; adminstr. Holden Methodist Hosp., Carbondale, Ill., 1953-56, Brightlook Hosp., St. Johnsbury, Vt., 1956-57, Hawthornden (Ohio) State Hosp., 1957-60, Cleve. State Hosp., 1960-62; supt. hosp. ship Project Hope, Peru, 1962-63; cons. N.Y. State Bur. Adult Instns., Albany, 1963-65; v.p. John G. Steinle and Assos., Garden City, N.Y., 1965-73; supt. Dr. Pila Community Health Care Center, Ponce, P.R., 1972-73; exec. v.p. Gordon A. Friesen Internat., Washington, 1973-76; dir. health care cons. Hosp. Bldg. & Equipment Co., St. Louis, 1976—; v.p. HOSPCO Del., 1968-73; pres. HOSPCO P.R., 1971-73, C.L. Jackson, Inc., 1973—. Served with AUS, 1944-45. Decorated Purple Heart. Fellow Am. Coll. Hosp. Adminstrs., Am. Public Health Assn., AAAS, Acad. Health Care Cons. (pres. 1969-73), Royal Soc. Health; mem. Am. Hosp. Assn. Author articles in field. Home: 1230 Postgrove Dr St Louis MO 63141 Office: 717 Office Pkwy St Louis MO 63141

JACKSON, CARL ROBERT, obstetrician, gynecologist; b. Mpls., Jan. 8, 1928; s. Carl J. and Mildred J. (Johnson) J.; B.A., Gustavus Adolphus Coll., 1951; M.D., Jefferson Med. Coll., 1956; m. Ann Flesch, Dec. 26, 1967; children—Amy, Carrie, Tom. Intern, St. Mary's Hosp., Duluth, Minn., 1956-57; resident and postdoctoral fellow in obstetrics gynecology U. Wis., Madison, 1957-61; practice medicine specializing in obstetrics gynecology, Madison, 1961—; mem. active staff Madison Gen. Hosp., 1961—, vice chief staff, 1972-74; mem. attending staff Univ. Hosps., Madison; asso. clin. prof. obstetrics gynecology U. Wis., 1971—, mem. high risk obstet. team, 1974-75; chmn. Physicians Alliance, Dane County, Wis. Am. Cancer Soc. fellow, 1960-61; diplomate Am. Bd. Obstetrics Gynecology. Mem. Am. Coll. Obstetrics Gynecology, Central Assn. Obstetricians Gynecologists. Republican. Lutheran. Office: Madison Med Center 20 S Park St Madison WI 53715

JACKSON, CURTIS MAITLAND, metall. engr.; b. N.Y.C., Apr. 20, 1933; s. Maitland Shaw and Janet Haughs (Dunbar) J.; B.S. in Metall. Engring., N.Y. U., 1954; M.S., Ohio State U., Columbus, 1959, Ph.D. (Battelle staff fellow), 1966; m. Cordelia Ann Shupe, July 6, 1957; children—Carol Elizabeth, David Curtis. Prin. metall. engr. Columbus div. Battelle Meml. Inst., 1954-61, project leader, 1961-67, asso. chief specialty alloys, 1967-77, asso. mgr. phys. and applied metallurgy, 1977—. Mem. troop com. Boy Scouts Am., 1975—, asst. scoutmaster, 1978—; advisor Order of DeMolay, 1954-57, 78—; mem. ch. ofcl. bd. Meth. Ch., 1957-66. Registered profl. engr., Ohio; recipient IR-100 award Indsl. Research Mag., 1976, cert. of appreciation Soc. Mfg. Engrs., 1977; Legion of Honor, Order of DeMolay, 1978. Mem. Wire Found. (dir. 1974—), Wire Assn. Internat. (v.p. 1973-76, pres. 1976-77, dir. 1970-78, Mordica Meml. award 1977, J. Edward Donnellan award 1978, meritorious tech. paper award 1981), N.Y. U. Metall. Alumni Assn. (pres. 1966-68), Am. Inst. Mining, Metall. and Petroleum Engrs. (chmn. Ohio Valley sect. 1964-66), Am. Soc. Metals, Am. Vacuum Soc., N.Y. U., Ohio State U. alumni assns., Sigma Xi, Alpha Sigma Mu, Phi Lambda Upsilon. Chmn. bd. Wire Jour., 1976-77, dir., 1973-78. Contbr. tech. articles profl. jours. Research on metall. tech. Home: 1667 Barrington Rd Columbus OH 43221 Office: 505 King Ave Columbus OH 43201

JACKSON, DAVID ARTHUR, metals co. exec.; b. Dublin, Ireland, Feb. 22, 1909 (parents Am. citizens); s. Asher and Edith (Goldwater) J.; B.S., Ill. Inst. Tech., 1937; m. Lauraine Grace Schachter, Nov. 23, 1932; children—Carol Ann Jackson Rice, Sandra Abbie Jackson Cohen, Joan Aileen. Chemist, Interstate Steel Co., 1928-30; chemist, assayer R.W. Hunt Co., Chgo., 1930-37; supt. Div. Lead Co., Chgo., 1937-39; pres. Inland Metals Refining Co., Chgo., 1939-81, chmn. bd., 1981—; pres. Lake Calumet Smelting Co., Chgo., 1939—; cons. Ames Metal Products Co., Chgo., 1960—; farmer nr. South Haven, Mich., 1962—. Chem. foundry div. Chgo. Community Fund, 1941; co-chmn. metals div. United Jewish Appeal, 1948—; past treas. South Shore Temple. Registered profl. engr., Ill. Mem. Am. Inst. Mining, Metall. and Petroleum Engrs., Am. Soc. Metals, United Inventors and Scientists Am., Mich. Blueberry Growers Assn. Club: B'nai B'rith. Patentee in field. Home: 5801 N Sheridan Rd Chicago IL 60660 Office: 651 E 119th St Chicago IL 60628

JACKSON, DOUGLAS NORTHROP, psychologist, educator; b. Merrick, N.Y., Aug. 14, 1929; s. Douglas Northrop and Caya (Cramer) J.; B.Sc., Cornell U., 1951; M.Sc., Purdue U., 1952, Ph.D., 1955; m. Lorraine Jean Morlock, July 28, 1962; children—Douglas Northrop III, Lori Diana, Charles Theodore VI. Research psychologist Menninger Found., Topeka, 1952-53, postdoctoral fellow, 1955-56; clin. psychologist intern U.S. VA, 1951-52, 53-55; asst. prof. psychology Pa. State U., University Park, 1956-61, asso. prof., 1961-64, vis. prof., 1978-79; vis. asso. prof. psychology Stanford U., 1962-64; sr. prof. psychology U. Western Ont., London, 1964—; cons. Ednl. Testing Service, Princeton, N.J., 1958-64, vis. scholar, 1971-72; cons. Research Psychologists Press, Inc., Port Huron, Mich., 1967—. USPHS research fellow, 1955-56; NIMH spl. research fellow, 1962-63, 71. Fellow Am. Psychol. Assn., Can. Psychol. Assn.; mem. Psychometric Soc., Soc. Multivariate Exptl. Psychology (pres. 1975-76), Am. Personnel and Guidance Assn., Sigma Xi. Author: Personality Research Form, Jackson Personality Inventory, Jackson Vocat. Interest Survey; editor: (with Samuel Messick) Problems in Human Assessment, 1967; contbr. numerous articles to profl. jours. Office: Dept Psychology U Western Ont London ON N6A 5C2 Canada

JACKSON, ERNEST HARDING, genealogist, publisher; b. Pollard, Ark., Oct. 13, 1920; s. James William and Minnie Mae (Holcomb) J.; student Harvard U., 1940-41; B.A., U. Albuquerque, 1954; M.A., U. N.Mex., 1955; m. Anna Amalia Hofflund, Aug. 5, 1951. Enlisted U.S. Air Force, 1942, advanced through grades to chief warrant officer, 1968; 35 combat missions, ETO, World War II; assigned to Berlin Air Lift, 1949-50, Spl. Weapons Command, 1951-56; staff supply officer 11th Air Div., Alaskan Air Command, 1956-60; supply officer SAC bases, 1960-68; ret., 1968; asst. prof. English, Rock Valley Jr. Coll., Rockford, Ill., 1968-74. Decorated Air medal with silver and bronze oak leaf clusters, Purple Heart. Mem. Nat. Geneal. Soc., Ill. Geneal. Soc., Am. Studies Assn., North Central Ill. Geneal. Soc. (charter mem., pres.), Phi Delta Kappa. Pub.: Jacksoniana - A Jackson Family Newsletter, 1977; compiler: Marriages of Union County, Illinois, 1818-1880, 1977; compiler, pub.: Federal Census of Union County, Illinois, 1820-1880, 1978; editor: Combined Atlases of Winnebago County, Illinois, 1981. Home and Office: 730 Parker Woods Dr Rockford IL 61102

JACKSON, ETHEL CURRY (MRS. RAYMOND T. JACKSON), civic worker; b. Mineral Point, Wis.; d. William Jenkin and Adeline (Argall) Curry; student Northwestern U.; m. Raymond T. Jackson, Sept. 30, 1918 (dec.). Hon. fellow Harry S Truman Library Inst.; mem. U.S. Olympic Com. Mem. Cleve. Council on World Affairs, Cleve. Museum Art, Cleve. Health Mus., Cleve. Mus. Natural History, Musical Arts Assn., Garden Center of Greater Cleve., Women's Com. Cleve. Orch., Northwestern U. Alumni Assn., Cleve. Women's City Club Found., Western Res. Women's Rep. Club, Western Res. Hist. Soc. Cleve., Cleve Inst. Music, Met. Mus. Art N.Y., Friends of Cleve. Library, Friends of Cleve Zool. Soc., Holden Arboretum, Cleve. Play House (women's com.), UN Assn. U.S.A., Smithsonian Assos. (charter), Nat. Hist. Soc. Methodist. Republican. Clubs: Women's City, Union, Country. Home: 13901 Shaker Blvd Cleveland OH 44120

JACKSON, EUNICE, security specialist; b. Laurel County, Ky., July 18, 1921; d. William Herbert and Mamie (Houston) J.; B.S., Eastern Ky. State U., 1944; M.A., Central Mich. U., 1977. Sec., U.S. Air Force, Wright-Patterson AFB, Ohio, 1953, clk., stenographer, 1953-54, personnel security specialist, 1954-79, security specialist, 1979—, recipient various profl. awards. Mem. Am. Def. Preparedness Assn., Am. Bus. Women's Assn. (past treas., corr. sec.), Am. Assn. Ret. Persons, Federally Employed Women (treas. regional conf., 1979). Republican. Home: 4073 Forest Ridge Blvd Dayton OH 45424 Office: USAF (ASD/SP) Wright Patterson AFB OH 45433

JACKSON, JAMES AVELON, JR., educator; b. Granite City, Ill., June 5, 1942; s. James Avelon and Ruby Cleona (Lee) J.; B.S., So. Ill. U., 1970; M.A., Sangamon State U., Springfield, Ill., 1973; postgrad. St. Louis U.; children—James Avelon, Jay Allen. Juvenile officer Madison County Sheriff's Office, Edwardsville, Ill., 1970-73; dir., instr. law enforcement program Muscatine (Iowa) Community Coll., 1973-75; asst. prof. Minot (N.D.) State Coll., 1975-76; dir. Inst. for Adminstrn. of Justice McKendree Coll., Lebanon, Ill., 1976-78; coordinator criminal justice and community service programs Southeastern Community Coll., West Burlington, Iowa, 1979-81; chmn. dept. criminal justice St. Louis Community Coll. at Forest Park, 1981—. Mem. Am. Assn. Univ. Adminstrs., Acad. Criminal Justice Scis., Iowa Criminal Justice Educators Assn. (pres. 1981), Ill. Assn. Criminal Justice Scientists, Midwestern Assn. Criminal Justice Educators (exec. com.), So. Ill. Criminal Justice Educators Assn. (founder), Ill. Community Edn. Assn., Am. Soc. Criminologists, Anglo-Am. Acad., Lambda Alpha Epsilon. Home: 327 E Schuetz Lebanon IL 62254 Office: St Louis Community Coll at Forest Park Saint Louis MO 63110

JACKSON, JAMES MAURICE, banker; b. St. Joseph, Mo., Apr. 9, 1922; s. Grover Cleveland and Sarah (McMaster) J.; student Iowa State Coll., 1939-40; B.S., Mo. State Tchrs. Coll., 1943; m. Betty Jean Lynch, Oct. 17, 1943; children—James Maurice, Michael Todd. Head farm mgmt., loan dept. Central Nat. Bank of Peoria, Ill., from 1953, asst. v.p., from 1960; asst. v.p., head cattle loan div., corr. officer City Nat. Bank, Kansas City, Mo., 1960-62; pres., chief exec. officer El Paso Nat. Bank (Ill.), 1963-64; v.p. Mchts. Nat. Bank, Indpls., 1964-66; pres., chief lending officer Onarga State Bank (Ill.), 1966-71, Cardinal Bancorp., Greenville, Ill., 1st Bank & Trust Co., Greenville, Ill., 1971—; pres., mgr. Farmers & Mchts. Bank of Vandalia, Ill, 1978—, Old Capitol Bancorp., Inc., Vandalia, 1978—; pres., chief exec. officer 1st Bank & Trust Co., O'Fallon, Ill., 1981—; chmn. Salem (Ill.) Nat. Bank, 1981; mem. Ill. Banking Bd., 1970-73. Exec. com. Boy Scouts Am., 1973—. Served with AUS, 1943-45. Mem. Am. Soc. Farm Mgrs. Republican. Presbyterian. Clubs: Greenville Country; Mo. Athletic (St. Louis). Home: 14 Spring Dr Greenville IL 62246 Office: 1st Bank & Trust Co 210 W Main St Greenville IL 62246

JACKSON, JAMES SIDNEY, psychologist, educator; b. Detroit, July 30, 1944; s. Pete James and Johnnie Mae (Wilson) J.; B.S., Mich. State U., 1966; M.A., U. Toledo, 1970; Ph.D., Wayne State U., 1972; m. Toni C. Antonucci, Dec. 1, 1979; 1 dau., Ariana Marie. Probation counselor Lucas County Juvenile Ct., Toledo, 1967-68; teaching and research asst. Wayne State U., Detroit, 1968-71; asst. prof. U. Mich., Ann Arbor, 1971-76, asso. prof. psychology, 1976—. Bd. dirs. Public Com. on Mental Health, 1978—. Urban Studies fellow, 1969-70. Mem. Am. Psychol. Assn., AAAS, Gerontol. Soc., Assn. Black Psychologists, Assn. for Advancement Psychology, Soc. Psychol. Study Social Issues. Contbr. articles to profl. jours. Home: 517 Fairview Ypsilanti MI 48197 Office: U Mich 5271 Inst Social Research Ann Arbor MI 48106

JACKSON, JEANNE ANNE, sch. adminstr.; b. Lakewood, Ohio, Aug. 21, 1922; d. Edward Adam and Elsa Wilhelmina (Stengel) Roege; A.B., Hiram Coll., 1944; M.A., Kent State U., 1962; Ph.D., Case-Western Res. U., 1970; m. Stuart Ray Jackson, July 12, 1946; children—Stuart Clinton, Philip Clay. With Nat. City Bank Cleve., 1944-47, Geneva Savs. & Trust Co. (Ohio), 1947-52; tchr. Geneva Area City Schs., 1954-68; tchr., guidance counselor Kirtland (Ohio) Middle Sch., 1969-70; adminstv. asst. Ashtabula (Ohio) County Joint Vocat. Sch., 1970-75; prin., adminstrv. asst. Geneva Area City Schs., 1975—; asst. prof. Kent (Ohio) State U., 1980—. Trustee, Hiram Coll.; v.p. United Way Ashtabula County; pres. 1st Ch. of Christ Scientist, Geneva. Recipient Status of Women award Zonta 1981. Mem. AAUW, Women's Service League Ashtabula, LWV, Assn. Supervision and Curriculum Devel., Am. Assn. Sch. Adminstrs., Internat. Reading Assn., Mensa, Nat. Council Tchrs. English, Delta Kappa Gamma. Republican. Clubs: Eastern Star (past matron), Zonta. Home: 1634 Highland Ln Ashtabula OH 44004 Office: Geneva Secondary Schs Sherman St Geneva OH 44041

JACKSON, JESSE LOUIS, clergyman, civic leader; b. Greenville, N.C., Oct. 8, 1941; s. Charles Henry and Helen Jackson; student U. Ill., 1959-60; B.A. in Sociology, A. and T. Coll. N.C., 1964; postgrad. Chgo. Theol. Sem., D.D. (hon.); m. Jacqueline Lavinia Brown, 1964; children—Saniita, Jesse Louis, Jonathan Luther, Yusef DuBois, Jacqueline Lavinia. Ordained to ministry Baptist Ch., 1968; founder (with others) Operation Breadbasket joint project SCLC, Co-ordinating Council Community Orgns., Chgo., 1966, nat. dir., 1966-71; founder, exec. dir. Operation PUSH (People United to Save Humanity), Chgo., 1971—. Active Black Coalition for United Community Action, 1969. Recipient Presdl. award Nat. Med. Assn., 1969; Humanitarian Father of Year award Nat. Father's Day Com., 1971. Address: 930 E 50th St Chicago IL 60615*

JACKSON, JOHN HENRY, psychologist; b. Macon, Ga., Sept. 21, 1922; s. Monroe and Nettie (Taylor) J.; B.S., U. Wis., Milw., 1946; A.M., U. Chgo., 1948, Ph.D., 1957; m. Cynthia Audrey Dorothy Fletcher, Dec. 24, 1959. Psychologist spl. project U. Wis., Milw., 1964-66; lectr. Marquette U., 1966-73; sch. psychologist Dept. Psychol. Services, Bd. Sch. Dirs., Milw., 1962-66, supr. dept., 1966-68, coordinator dept., 1968-78, coordinating head dept., 1978—; pvt. practice cons. psychology, 1966—; mem. Wis. Psychology Examining Bd., 1974-80, vice chmn., 1974-76, sec., 1976-78, chmn., 1978-79; 1st v.p. Planning Council Mental Health and Social Services, Milw., 1979-82, bd. dirs., 1976—. Diplomate Am. Bd. Profl. Psychology. Mem. Am. Psychol. Assn. (council reps. 1981—, monitor standards Div. Sch. Psychology 1977-80, mem. exec. council div. 1977-80, 81—), Milw. Area Psychol. Assn. (pres. 1981-82), Am. Orthopsychiat. Assn., Nat. Assn. Sch. Psychologists, Wis. Psychol. Assn., Milw. Area Psychol. Assn., Clin. Child Psychology, Soc. Pediatric Psychology, Nat. Register Health Service Providers in Psychology, Kappa Delta Pi, Phi Delta Kappa. Author: (with Margaret Bernauer) Skills for Comprehensive and Effective Psychological Services in Large Urban School Districts, 1975; editor: (with Margaret Bernauer) The School Psychologist As A Therapist, 1968; editorial cons. Jour. Sch. Psychology, 1971—. Home: 10405 W Grantosa Dr Wauwatosa WI 53222 Office: PO Drawer 10K Milwaukee WI 53201

JACKSON, LESTER BODE, cons. co. exec.; b. San Antonio, June 6, 1932; s. Wilmer and Alice J.; B.J., U. Mo., 1953, M.A., 1954; M.B.A., U. Houston, 1961. Dir. personnel and public relations Conoco, Europe, 1963-66; dir. employee relations Far East div. Singer Co., 1967-69; mgr. exec. compensation policy and planning ITT, N.Y.C., 1970-75; corp. dir. compensation, benefits, and planning Motorola Inc., Schaumburg, Ill., 1975-78; v.p., corp. dir. human resources Foote Cone & Belding, Chgo., 1978-81; co-founder Jackson & Rimsky, compensation cons., Bensenville, Ill., 1981—. Served with U.S. Army, 1954-56. Mem. Am. Compensation Assn. (pres. 1979-80, chmn. 1980-81, symposium leader 1975-81), Am. Soc. Personnel Adminstrn. Author: How To Select a Long Range Incentive Plan, 1981; co-author: Elements of Sound Base Pay Administration, 1981. Office: 765 Route 83 North Suite 117 Bensenville IL 60106

JACKSON, LYDIA OCTAVIA, poet; b. Grafton, N.D., Mar. 5, 1902; d. Karl Olaf and Inga (Schellstad) Svarte; student pub. schs., N.D.; m. Arthur F. Jackson, Dec. 20, 1920; 1 dau., Elizabeth Marjean (Mrs. Leonard Fagerholt). Author: Rhymes for Every Season, 1943; also numerous poems in all types of publs. Publicity chmn. Poetry Day, 1950. Treas. Grafton sch. dist. 22, 1931-61. Recipient Nat. Writers award Farmers Union Ednl. Dept., 1950; named co-asso. poet laureate of N.D., 1975, co-poet laureate, 1979. Mem. Walsh County Sch. Officers Assn. (treas. 1945-62), Midwest Fedn. Chaparral Poets (state regent 1950-51), Nat. League Am. Pen Women, Am. Poetry League, Poetry Soc. of London, Am. Poets Fellowship Soc. (poet laureate 1972-73), World Poetry Day Assn. (membership chmn. N.D. and S.D. 1963—), N.D. Pen Women (past chmn., compiler Peace Garden of Verses 1967), World Poetry Soc. Intercontinental, Centro Studie Scambi Internazionali (Rome) (recipient Bronze medal 1965, Silver medal 1967). Presbyn. Mem. Order of Eastern Star. Clubs: Riverside Woman's (sec. 1955-57, 59-61, v.p. 1957-59), Sigma Rho Study (v.p. 1950-52, pres., 1952-54, sec., treas., 1958—). Author: Selected Poems, 1962; Pardon My Gaff, 1965. Home: Route 2 Grafton ND 58237

JACKSON, M. MORRIS, state senator; b. Ga., 1920; ed. Cleve. Coll.; married; 2 children. Real estate broker; mem. Ohio Senate, 1967—, asst. pres. pro tem. Del., Democratic Nat. Conv., 1972, 76; mem. Dem. Nat. Com., 1972—. Office: State Senate Columbus OH 43216*

JACKSON, MARJORIE ANN, mathematician; b. New Castle, Pa., Oct. 15, 1930; d. Frank August and Mary Ellen (Truby) Mielke; B.Ed., Slippery Rock State Coll., 1951; postgrad. U. Louisville, 1952-53, Ind. U., 1970, (NSF grantee) Notre Dame U., 1974-75, Bradley U., 1976; M.Ed., Butler U., 1970; m. George Ronald Jackson, Aug. 16, 1952; children—Sharon (dec.), Deborah, Cynthia, Catherine. Tchr., East Lawrence (Pa.) Consol. High Sch., 1951-52, Fern Creek High Sch., Louisville, 1952-54, Greensburg (Ky.) High Sch., 1955-56, Charleston (W.Va.) High Sch., 1961-63, Sharon (Pa.) Public Schs., 1957-59; tchr. Indpls. Public Schs., 1967-74, math. cons., 1974—; editorial cons. Harcourt Brace Jovanovich, N.Y.C., 1978—; mem. adv. council Ind. Dept. Public Instrn., 1981. Troop leader Charleston council Girl Scouts U.S.A., 1964-65; pres. Charleston Parent Tchrs. Orgn., 1963. Mem. Nat. Council Tchrs. Math, Ind. Council Tchrs. Math, Nat. Assn. Supervision and Curriculum Devel., Ind. Assn. Supervision and Curriculum Devel., Indpls. Assn. Adminstrs., Suprs. and Consultants, Kappa Delta Pi, Phi Delta Kappa. Republican. Presbyn. Scottish Rite Ladies (pres. exec. council 1980—). Club: Riviera. Author: T.E.-4th Grade Heath Math Program, 1979; editorial cons. Learning to Compute I and II, 4th edit., 1980-81; Growth in Mathematics, Books 1 through 8, 1979-80. Home: 4901 Kessler Blvd N Indianapolis IN 46208 Office: Education Center 120 E Walnut St Indianapolis IN 46204

JACKSON, PATRICIA DIANE, human resource specialist; b. Indpls., June 26, 1951; d. Richard Avis and Lillie Mae (Edmonds) Matchen; B.A., Ind. U., 1973, grad. fellow, 1973-74, M.S., 1981; m. Arthur Charles Jackson, Jan. 28, 1974. Coordinator coop. edn. U. South Fla., Tampa, 1974-76; counselor Opportunity Industrialization Center, Inc., Miami, Fla., 1976-77, project coordinator safer sch. environ. through parent involvement, 1977-78; project dir./coordinator coop. edn. Ind. Tech. Coll., Indpls., 1978-79; vocat. cons., 1973—; coordinator Office of Affirmative Action, State of Ind., 1981. State sec. Ind. chpt. NAACP, 1964-65; bd. dirs. Tampa Commerce and Industry Council, 1975-76; exec. bd. Greater Miami Cultural Alliance Council, 1976-77, v.p., 1977; vol. United Way, 1976—. Certified Acad. Mgmt. Tng. Mem. Am. Personnel and Guidance Assn., Assn. Coop. Edn., Nat. Employment Counselors Assn., Am. Soc. for Tng. and Devel., DAR. Mem. Disciples of Christ Ch. Club: Ind. U. Women's. Research, publs. in field. Home: 3314 Fallcreek Way E Indianapolis IN 46205

JACKSON, REGINALD SHERMAN, pub. relations counselor; b. Newport, R.I., Dec. 25, 1910; s. Sherman Clinton and Gertrude (Miller) J.; student U. Toledo, 1929-34; m. Frances Holland, Jan. 20, 1941; 1 son, Reginald Sherman, Jr. Reporter, Toledo (Ohio) News-Bee, 1937; pub. relations dir. Ohio N.G., 1939-40; account exec. Flournoy & Gibbs, Inc., Toledo, 1945-51, 53-63, v.p., 1963-75, treas., 1967-75. Bd. dirs. Toledo-Lucas County Pub. Library; mem. adv. com. Mobile Meals of Toledo. Served from 1st lt. to lt. col. AUS, 1940-46; lt. col. USAR, 1951-60. Decorated Bronze Star with two oak leaf clusters. Mem. Res. Officers Assn. (pres. Toledo 1949), Am. Legion (Toledo post comdr. 1949), Pub. Relations Soc. Am. (accredited; pres. N.W. Ohio chpt. 1963, dir., nat. treas. 1972), Toledo Area C. of C. (trustee 1973-75), Beta Gamma Sigma, Alpha Phi Gamma. Congregationalist. Clubs: Masons, Rotary, Toledo, Hermits, Toledo Press. Home: 3707 Richlawn Dr Toledo OH 43614

JACKSON, RICHARD HOMER, mfg. co. exec.; b. Pontiac, Mich., Nov. 2, 1942; s. Homer Corneilus and Grace Marie J.; B.S., U. Mich., 1964, M.B.A., 1967; m. Kathleen Marie Kaliher, Feb. 13, 1965; children—Sharon, Carolyn, Margaret. Fin. analyst Litton Industries, Inc., Beverly Hills, Calif., 1967-69, asst. controller Litton Microwave Cooking, 1969-73, sr. v.p. fin. and adminstrn., 1973-79; v.p., corp. controller Toro Co., Mpls., 1979—. Pres. bd. dirs. Childrens Theatre Co. and Sch., 1978-80; pres. Plymouth Civic League, 1977. Mem. Fin. Execs. Inst., Assn. Corp. Growth. Republican. Roman Catholic. Club: Five Fifty Five. Office: 8009 34th Ave S Minneapolis MN 55420

JACKSON, ROBERT HOWARD, lawyer; b. Cleve., Dec. 12, 1936; s. Herman Herbert and Frances (Goldman) J.; A.B., U. Ill., 1958; J.D., Case Western Res. U., 1961; m. Donna Lyons, Mar. 22, 1959; children—Karen, Douglas. Admitted to Ohio bar, 1961, since practiced in Cleve.; fin. trial atty. SEC, Cleve., 1961-66; partner firm Kohrman and Jackson, 1969—; dir. Mor-Flo Industries, Inc.; lectr. law Case Western Res. Sch. Law, Cleve., 1967-69. Mem. Am. (chmn. subcom. proxy solicitations, shareholders proposals, fed. securities com. 1970-73), Fed. (chmn. Cleve. chpt. fed. securities com. 1972-73), Internat., Cleve. bar assns. Club: Rowfant. Contbr. articles to legal jours. Home: 10 Lyman Circle Shaker Heights OH 44122 Office: 1600 Central Nat Bank Bldg Cleveland OH 44114

JACKSON, ROBERT LEON, psychologist; b. Bond, Miss., Mar. 1, 1939; s. Robert S. and Helen R. Jackson; B.A., Miss. Goll., 1961; M.A., Baylor U., 1963; Ph.D., E. Tex. State U., 1967; postdoctoral fellow U. Colo. Med. Sch., 1972-73; m. Mamie Willingham, Aug. 19, 1961; children—Stacey Lynette, Jeffrey Noel. Child clin. psychologist Shreveport (La.) Mental Health Center, 1962-64; asst. prof. psychology and guidnce Delta State U., Cleveland, Miss., 1967-72; asso. prof. Sangamon State U., Springfield, Ill., 1973-74; asso. prof. psychiatry So. Ill. U. Med. Sch., Springfield, 1974—; pvt. practice clin. psychology, Springfield, 1973—; mem. family stress consutation team Ill. Dept. Children and Family Services. Mem. Am. Psychol. Assn., Am. Personnel and Guidance Assn., Ill. Psychol. Assn., Am. Assn. Family Therapists, Soc. Clin. and Exptl. Hypnosis, Am. Soc. Clin. Hypnosis, Nat. Rehab. Soc., Soc. Pediatric Psychology. Office: PO Box 3926 Springfield IL 62708

JACKSON, RONALD STEPHEN, advt. agy. exec.; b. Morehead, Ky., Nov. 1, 1948; s. George Wallace and Aurola Kegley J.; B.A. with distinction, Morehead State U., 1969; m. Adrienne Emily Ridey, Feb. 21, 1981. Dir. creative writing The Living Arts Center, Dayton, Ohio, 1969-72; project dir. Community Schs. Program, Dayton, 1972; chmn. bd. Jackson/Ridey & Co., Inc., Cin., 1970—. Recipient Gold award, Merit award Am.Advt. Fedn., 1980. Mem. Cin. C. of C., Lewisburg C. of C. Republican. United Brethren. Office: 424 E 4th St Cincinnati OH 45202

JACKSON, WADE MOSBY, assn. exec.; b. Brinkley, Ark., Jan. 30, 1916; s. Alfred Mosby and Claude Keturah (Hallum) J.; student William Jewell Coll., 1933-37, A.B., 1937; student Marquette U., 1958-61, M.B.A., 1961; m. Evelyn Westover Byrd, Jan. 18, 1942; children—Sterling Byrd, Wade Mosby, Kent Turnbull. Commd. 2d. lt. U.S. Marine Corps, 1937, advanced through grades to col., 1957; co. and bn. comdr. 3d. Marine Div., 1942-44; comdr. Inf. Troop Leaders Sch., 1944-45; asst. chief staff Fleet Marine Force, Western Pacific, 1945-47; comdr. 4th Marines, 1953-54; dir. indsl. relations Marine Corps Air Bases, 1954-57; ret., 1957; dir. corporate tng. Allis-Chalmers Mfg. Co., Milw., 1957-61; v.p. mktg. Bank of Milw. & Trust Co., Milw., 1961-64; dir. adminstrn. and planning Bendix Corp., Dayton, Ohio, 1964-71; bus. mgr. Dayton Art Inst., 1972-74; state treas., trustee Ohio Right to Life Soc. Inc., Clin., 1970—; fin. mgmt. adv. to Nat. Right-to-Life Com. and Christian Action Council, 1977—; cons. mem. Service Corps Ret. Execs.; lectr. in field. Chmn. U.S. Civil Service Security Screening Bd., 1954-57; mem. N.C. Gov.'s Safety Council, 1955-57; regional adviser SBA, 1958-61; regional del. Boy Scouts Am., 1954-63. Decorated Silver Star. Mem. Nat. Machine Tool Builders Assn., Dayton C. of C., Soc. Advancement Mgmt., Republican. Baptist. Clubs: Twin Base Rod and Gun, William Jewell Coll. Century, Wright-Patterson Officers. Editor Principles and Practices of Bus. Mgmt., 1960-61. Contbr. articles to profl. publs. Home: 917 Garrison Ave Dayton OH 45429 Office: Nat Press Bldg Washington DC 20045

JACKSON, WILLIAM ELMER, JR., packaging co. mgr.; b. Washington, Pa., Oct. 25, 1935; s. William Elmer and Hazel Celestine (Moore) J.; B.S. in Indsl. Engring., Okla. U., 1966; M.B.A. in Fin., U. Mo., Kansas City, 1970; children—Randall Lee, Barry Howard. With Sealright Co. Inc., Kansas City, Kans., 1966—, corp. econ. evaluation engr., 1966-69, process engr. central div., 1969-72, profit evaluation specialist, central div., 1972-74, corp. mgr. econ. evaluation, 1974-75, corp. ops. analysis mgr., 1975-78, adminstrv. mgr. central div., 1978-81, mfg. and control mgr. central div., 1981—, chmn. eastern div. operational study project, 1976, chmn. corp. mfg. info. requirements study project, 1978, mem. bus. profile study team. Com. chmn., merit badge counselor Troop 278 Heart of Am. council Boy Scouts Am., 1972-74; adv. Jr. Achievement of Greater Kansas City, 1974-75; caravan dir. Overland Park Nazarene Ch., 1968-74, ch. bd., 1976-79, ch. treas., 1977-78, fin. com., 1976-78, house com., 1978-79, mem. choir, 1968-81; chmn. adv. bd. mid-mgmt. program Penn Valley Community Coll., Kansas City, Mo., 1980—; mem. Johnson County Assn. Retarded Citizens. Served with USAF, 1955-59. Republican. Club: Fishing Club Am. Home: 5322 Foster Dr Overland Park KS 66202 Office: 2925 Fairfax Rd Kansas City KS 66115

JACOB, H. JOHN, otolaryngologist; b. Detroit, Sept. 29, 1941; s. David G. and Esther (Selzer) J.; B.A., U. Mich., 1963; M.D., Wayne State U., 1967; m. Constance G. Wineman, June 21, 1966; children—Catherine, David. Intern, Michael Reese Hosp., Chgo., 1967-68, resident, 1968-69; resident Wayne State U., Detroit, 1971-73, now asst. clin. prof.; practice medicine specializing in otolaryngology, Southfield, Mich. Served with USNR, 1969-71. Mem. AMA, A.C.S., Am. Acad. Otolaryngology. Club: Detroit Golf. Patentee nasal septal plug. Office: 21700 Northwestern St Southfield MI 48075

JACOB, KANNAMPALLY L., urologist; b. Pariyaram, India, Jan. 26, 1931; came to U.S., 1971; M.D., Kastusba Med. Coll., Mangalore, Mysore, India, 1959; m. Lizzie Eapen, June 2, 1960; children—Anita, Tessa, John, Eapen. Intern, St. Luke's Hosp., Cleve., 1971-72; resident Huron Rd. Hosp., Cleve., 1973-76; chief of surgery, supt. Little Flower Hosp., Angamally, India, 1963-71; practice medicine specializing in urology, El Dorado, Kans., 1976—; mem. staff Allen Meml. Hosp. Diplomate Am. Bd. Urology. Mem. AMA, South Central Urol. Assn., Kans. Med. Soc., Butler-Greenwood County Med. Soc. Roman Catholic. Clubs: El Dorado Country, Rotary (El Dorado). Home: 820 Delmar St El Dorado KS 67042 Office: 123 N Atchison St El Dorado KS 67042

JACOBS, ANDREW, JR., congressman; b. Indpls., Feb. 24, 1932; s. Andrew and Joyce (Wellborn) J.; B.S., Ind. U., 1955, LL.B., 1958; m. Martha Elizabeth Keys. Practiced law in Indpls., 1958-65, 73-74; mem. 89th to 92d, 94th to 97th congresses from 11th Ind. dist. Mem. Ind. Ho. of Reps., 1959. Served with inf. USMCR, 1950-52; Korea. Mem. Am. Legion, Indpls. Bar Assn. Democrat. Office: 1533 Longworth Office Bldg Washington DC 20515*

JACOBS, GLORIA BOHM, sch. adminstr.; b. Akron, Ohio, Jan. 7, 1942; d. Samuel and Sarah (Stearn) Bohm; R.N., Montefore Hosp. Sch. Nursing, 1962; B.A., U. Mo., 1973, M.P.A., 1975; children—Robin Rebecca, Daniel Geoffrey. Registered nurse, 1962-73; instr. Kansas City (Kans.) Community Coll., 1973-76; dir.

Choffin Sch. Practical Nursing, Youngstown, Ohio, 1976—; mem. ad hoc com. on edn. Ohio State Bd. Nursing, 1981—. Mem. Lic. Practical Nurses Assn. Ohio (advisor 1976-81, accreditation visitor 1977-80), Am. Vocat. Assn., Tri-County Nursing Adminstrs. and Educators Council, Mahoning Shenango Area Health Edn. Network, Ohio Orgn. Practical Nurse Educators. Home: 2860 Dade Ave Youngstown OH 44505 Office: 200 E Wood St Youngstown OH 44503

JACOBS, HOWARD MATTHEW, pediatrician; b. Chgo., July 26, 1907; s. John Martin and Nellie Almeda (Anderson) J.; B.S., U. Ill., 1929, M.D., 1931; m. Loretta B. May, Sept. 28, 1935; children—Richard, William, Robert, Donald. Intern and resident Cook County Hosp., Chgo., 1931-34, asso. attending pediatrician, 1934-42, asso. to chief of staff, 1934-41; attending pediatrician, Ravenswood Hosp., 1934-56, chmn. dept. pediatrics, 1954-56; attending pediatrician St. Vincent's Infant Hosp., 1934-72, chief of staff, 1948-68, dir. edn. and research, 1968-72; attending pediatrician St. Joseph Hosp., 1934—, chmn. dept. pediatrics, 1952-61, 69-78, dir. residency tng. program, 1969-78, pres. staff, 1954-55; sr. attending pediatrician Resurrection Hosp., Chgo., 1960—; practice medicine specializing in pediatrics, Chgo.; asst. in pediatrics Coll. Medicine, U. Ill., 1934-37, instr. pediatrics, 1937-42; instr. pediatrics Med. Sch., Northwestern U., 1942-50; asst. clin. prof. Stritch Sch. Medicine, Loyola U., Chgo., 1951-54, asso. clin. prof., 1954-58, clin. prof., from 1958, clin. prof. emeritus, 1982; asst. chief bur. child welfare Bd. Health, 1935-37. Served to maj., M.C., USAAF, 1942-46. Decreed papal knight of St. Gregory, 1957; recipient first Friend of Children award Child Care Assn. Ill., 1969; award of merit Stritch Sch. Medicine, Loyola U., 1951-79; Howard M. Jacobs, M.D., Pediatric Endowment Fund created St. Joseph. Hosp., 1980. Diplomate Am. Bd. Pediatrics. Fellow AMA, Am. Acad. Pediatrics, Inst. Medicine; mem. Ill. Med. Soc., Chgo. Med. Soc., Chgo. Pediatric Soc. (disting. service award 1979), Los Angeles Pediatric Soc. Republican. Roman Catholic. Club: Northshore Country (Glenview, Ill.). Contbr. articles to profl. publs. Home: 6750 N Wildwood Ave Chicago IL 60646 Office: 7447 W Talcott Ave Chicago IL 60631

JACOBS, IRWIN LAWRENCE, diversified enterprises exec.; b. Mpls., July 15, 1941; s. Samuel and Rose H. Jacobs; student public schs.; m. Alexandra Light, Aug. 26, 1962; children—Mark, Sheila, Melinda, Randi, Trisha. Pres., chief exec. officer Jacobs Industries, Inc., Mpls., 1977—; chmn. bd. Fed. Fin. Corp., Mpls., 1976—; chmn. Arctic Enterprises, Inc., Thief River Falls, Minn., 1977—, Watkins Products, Winona, Minn., 1978—; owner Grain Belt Properties, 1976—, Countryside Estates, 1978—; chmn. bd. Jacobs Bag Corp., 1977—; pres. Northwestern Bag Corp., Mpls., Harper-Crawford Bag Co., Charlotte, N.C., 1978—; v.p. JYJ Corp., Mpls. Shareholders Co., 1976—, Regional Accounts Corp., Mpls., 1976—, FFC Realty, 1977—, Nationwide Collection Service, Inc., 1977—, Nationwide Accounts Corp., 1977—; chmn. Kodicor, Inc., Mpls., 1979—. Clubs: Mpls., Mpls. Athletic, Lafayette Country, Belle Aire Yacht, Oakridge Country. Office: Jacobs Industries Inc 1215 Marshall St NE Minneapolis MN 55413

JACOBS, JAMES AVROM, advt. co. exec.; b. Cin., Dec. 2, 1927; s. Louis A. and Rhea (Nathan) J.; B.S., U. Cin., 1949; m. Barbara M. Bein, June 5, 1955; children—Robin S., Thomas A. Artist, Pease Co., Cin., 1949-50; advt. prodn. mgr. Ruthrauff & Ryan, Inc., Cin., 1950-51; sales promotion mgr. Fashion Frocks, Inc., Cin., 1953-54; account exec. Sive Asso., 1954-59; sr. writer, v.p., creative dir. Stockton, West, Burkhart, Inc., 1959-68; pres. James A. Jacobs, Inc., Cin., 1968—; co-owner Sta. WAVV-FM, Vevay, Ind. Bd. dirs. Jewish Community Relations Council, Cin., 1981—, Glen Manor Home for Aged, Cin., 1981—. Served with U.S. Army, 1951-53. Clubs: Losantiville Country, Masons, Advertisers. Home: 8580 Concord Hills Circle Cincinnati OH 45243 Office: James A Jacobs Inc 225 E 6th St Cincinnati OH 45202

JACOBS, JAMES NAJEEB, supt. schs.; b. Tonawanda, N.Y., Mar. 4, 1930; s. Leo and Sofea Jacobs; B.A. in Psychology, Mich. State U., 1951, M.A. in Guidance and Counseling, 1952, Ed.D. in Founds. Edn., 1957; m. Suzanne Hetzel; children—Lance, Thor, Lars. Thcr., Fletcher Elementary Sch., Tonawanda, 1951; grad. teaching asst. Mich. State U., 1953; mem. staff Clin. public schs., 1954—, dir. div. program research and design, then asst. supt. dept. research and devel., 1965-76, supt. schs., 1976—; asso. prof. U. Cin. Coll. Edn., 1960; lectr. Miami U., Oxford, Ohio, 1960, Xavier U., Cin., 1960; vis. asst. prof. U. Md., 1960; adj. asso. prof. Ohio State U., 1971; cons. in field, mem. various profl. adv. bds.; bd. dirs. sta. WCET-TV, Center Econ. Edn., Cin.; adv. council Miami U. Mem. Am. Personnel and Guidance Assn., Nat. Council Measurement Edn., Am. Ednl. Research Assn., Am. Assn. Sch. Adminstrs., Ohio Assn. Supervision and Curriculum Devel. Presbyterian. Author articles in field; mem. editorial bds. profl. jours. Home: 5283 Adena Trail Cincinnati OH 45230 Office: 230 E 9th St Cincinnati OH 45230

JACOBS, JEFFREY DAVID, lawyer; b. Chgo., Feb. 23, 1950; s. Leslie and Lorelei (Belson) J.; B.A., Bradley U., 1971; J.D., Loyola U., 1974. Admitted to Ill. bar, 1974; partner firm Foos, Meyers & Jacobs, Ltd., Chgo., 1976-80; sr. partner firm Foos, Jacobs, Malk & David Asso., Chgo., 1981-82, Engerman, Erlich, Jacobs & Berman, Ltd., Chgo., 1982—; lectr. Chgo.-Kent Coll. Law, 1981. Mem. Am. Bar Assn. (sports com.), Ill. Bar Assn., Chgo. Bar Assn. Monthly columnist on sports law Pro Football Weekly. Office: 55 W Monroe St Chicago IL 60603

JACOBS, JOEL BERNARD, chem. co. exec.; b. Lakewood, N.J., May 22, 1942; s. Roland Arthur and Julia May (Breeskin) J.; student Rutgers U., 1960-61; B.S., Newark Coll. Engring., 1965; m. Dorothy Donahue Jacobs, Aug. 20, 1972; children—Jennifer, Geoffrey. With FMC Corp., 1965—, tech. supt., Carteret, N.J., 1972-73, mfg. coordinator, N.Y.C., 1973-74, gen. supt., Lawrence, Kans., 1974-77, resident mgr. phosphorus chems. div., 1977—, dir. Cottonwood, Inc. Pres., Jr. Achievement of Lawrence, 1978-79, chmn. bd., 1979—; bd. dirs. Boys Club of Lawrence, 1980-81, Lawrence Arts Center, 1981. Mem. Am. Inst. Chem. Engring., Kans. Assn. Commerce and Industry, Lawrence C. of C. (chmn. mfg. council 1979—, dir.). Jewish. Clubs: Rotary, Breakfast, Cosmopolitan. Patentee chem. mfg. field. Home: 214 Providence Rd Lawrence KS 66044 Office: FMC Corp 9th and Maple Sts Lawrence KS 66044

JACOBS, LEO EDWARD, business exec.; b. Chgo., Feb. 15, 1893; s. David and Paulina (Robinson) J.; ed. public schs.; m. Harriet H. McKeon, Sept. 19, 1922; 1 dau., Nancy H. Jacobs Botbyl. Vice pres. Charles H. Besly Co., Chgo., 1907-1948; pres. Titan Abrasives, Chgo., 1948-71, ret., 1971. Mem. Soc. Mfg. Engrs. (life). Died Aug. 15, 1981. Home: 14994 Bignell Dr Grand Haven MI 49417

JACOBS, LOUIS SULLIVAN, architect, engr., planner; b. Chgo., June 11, 1917; s. Morris and Mary Jacobs; B.S. in Architecture and City Planning, Armour Inst. Tech., 1940; M.S. in Indsl. Engring., Ill. Inst. Tech., 1952, Ph.D. in Indsl. Engring., 1958; Sc.D. in Safety, Ind. No. U., 1972, Ph.D. in Human Engring., 1974; M.S. in Profl. Mgmt., 1980. Pres., Louis S. Jacobs & Assos., Architects, Engrs. and Planners, Chgo., 1946—; prof. archtl. engring. Loop Coll., Chgo., 1967—, coordinator engring., archtl. and tech. services dept. applied scis., 1975—; prof. indsl. engring. Ill. Inst. Tech., 1948-58, 67; prof. architecture U. Ill., Chgo., 1968; prof. engring. Chgo. Citywide Coll., 1980. Bd. dirs. Old Town Boys Club, 1951—; trustee Chgo. Sch. Architecture Fedn., 1967. Served as lt. USN, 1942-46. Recipient award of merit Office CD, State of Ill., 1957; citation Gov. State of Ill., Office Emergency Services, 1964; citation for Outstanding public services Office of Pres. U.S., U.S. Emergency Resources Bd., 1967; registered profl. engr., Ill., Del., Calif.; registered indsl. engr., safety engr., mfg. engr., Calif.; registered architect, Ill.; cert. in materials handling, materials mgmt., indsl. hygiene. Fellow Am. Soc. Registered Architects, Nat. Soc. Profl. Engrs.; mem. AIA, Ill. Soc. Architects (dir. 1976-78 v.p. 1978-80, pres. 1980-82), Ill. Soc. Profl. Engrs. (v.p. 1976—), System Safety Soc. (pres. 1980—), ASCE, Western Soc. Engrs., Am. Soc. Mil. Engrs., Am. Soc. Safety Engrs., Internat. Materials Mgmt. Soc., Am. Inst. Indsl. Engrs., Soc. for Gen. Systems Research, Standards Engring. Soc., Soc. Mfg. Engrs., Vets. Safety, Constrn. Safety Assn. Am. (v.p. 1976—), Am. Soc. Environ. Engrs. (diplomate), Nat. Safety Mgmt. Soc., Nat. Assn. Fire Investigators, Nat. Fire Protection Assn., Nat. Safety Council, Mil. Order World Wars, Naval Order U.S., Res. Officers Assn., Tau Beta Pi, Sigma Iota Epsilon, Alpha Phi Mu, Tau Epsilon Phi. Editor: Vector, 1968. Office: 2605 W Pratt Blvd Chicago IL 60645

JACOBS, MICHAEL ROBERT, ins. co. exec.; b. Terre Haute, Ind., June 5, 1946; s. Robert and H. Louise J.: B.A., DePauw U., 1969; M.B.A., Ind. State U., 1973; m. Diane Mayo, Aug. 17, 1968; children—Karen, Daniel. Audit sr. Price Waterhouse & Co., Chgo., 1973-79; controller James S. Kemper & Co., Chgo., 1979, v.p. fin., 1980—, chief fin. officer, 1980—. C.P.A., Ill., Ind. Mem. Execs. Club Chgo., Am. Inst. C.P.A.'s, Ill. Soc. C.P.A.'s. Club: Tower. Home: 825 Glenmore Ct Naperville IL 60540 Office: 20 N Wacker Dr Chicago IL 60606

JACOBS, NORMAN JOSEPH, pub. co. exec.; b. Chgo., Oct. 28, 1932; s. Herman and Tillie (Chapman) J.; B.S. in Math., U. Ill., 1954; m. Jeri Kolber Rose, Jan. 2, 1977; 1 son, Barry Jacobs; children by previous marriage—Carey, Murray, Dale. Display salesman Chgo. Daily News, 1954-57; dist. mgr. Davidson Pub. Co., Chgo., 1957-62; v.p. Press-Tech, Inc., Evanston, Ill., 1962-69; pres. Century Pub. Co., Evanston, 1969—. Served with USNR, 1951-59. Mem. Alpha Delta Sigma, Tau Epsilon Phi. Jewish. Club: B'nai B'rith. Office: 1020 Church St Evanston IL 60201

JACOBS, PAUL D., indsl. psychologist; b. Akron, Ohio, Oct. 12, 1939; s. Joseph Paul and Anna Elizabeth (Roth) J.; B.A. in Psychology, Baylor U., 1962, Ph.D. in Indsl. Psychology, 1967; m. Peggy S. Young, Feb. 7, 1970; stepchildren—Jerri S. Turner, Bradford H. Turner. Intern comparative psychology USAF, 1962-63; instr. to adj. asso. prof., U. Okla., 1967-78; chmn. Jacobs, Hillgren & Assos., Dallas, 1972-74; human resources mgr. R.R. Donnelley & Sons Co., Chgo., 1974—; pvt. practice cons., Oklahoma City, 1969-72; cons. govt. agys., 1968-73, City of Dallas, 1972-73. Lic., cert. psychologist, Okla., Tex., Ill. Mem. Am. Psychol. Assn. (Div. 4 profl. affairs com., 1979-80). Co-author: Perceived Stress Index, 1970, Organization Attitude and Satisfaction Inventories, 1970; co-patentee cosmetic; contbr. papers to profl. publs. and confs. Office: 2223 King Dr Chicago IL 60613

JACOBS, RICHARD DEARBORN, marine engring. cons. co. exec.; b. Detroit, July 6, 1920; s. Richard Dearborn and Mattie Phoebe (Cobleigh) J.; B.S., U. Mich., 1944; m. Mary Lou Hammel, Sept. 16, 1971; children—Richard, Margaret, Paul, Linden, Susan. Engr., Detroit Diesel Engine div. Gen. Motors, 1946-51; mgr. indsl. and marine engine div. Reo Motors, Inc., Lansing, Mich., 1951-54; chief engr. Kennedy Marine Engine Co., Biloxi, Miss., 1955-59; marine sales engr. Nordberg Mfg. Co., Milw., 1959-69; marine sales mgr. Fairbanks Morse Engine div. Colt Industries, Beloit, Wis., 1969-81; pres. R.D. Jacobs & Assos., cons. naval architects and marine engrs., Roscoe, Ill., 1981—. Served with AUS, 1944-46. Registered profl. engr., Ill., Mich., Miss. Mem. Soc. Naval Architects and Marine Engrs. (chmn. sect. 1979-80), Soc. Automotive Engrs., Am. Soc. Naval Engrs., Soc. Am. Mil. Engrs., ASTM, Navy League U.S., Assn. U.S. Army, Propeller Club U.S. Unitarian. Clubs: Country (Beloit); Rockford Polo, Masons. Home: 7887 Louella Dr Roscoe IL 61073 Office: 11405 Main St Roscoe IL 61073

JACOBS, ROSEMARIE, clin. lab. mgr.; b. Lincoln, Nebr., Oct. 25, 1943; d. Jacob, Jr., and Darleen Rose (Worster) J.; B.S., U. Nebr., 1965; children—Michael Jacob and Douglas Henry Schwabauer. Staff med. technologist Shawnee Mission (Kans.) Hosp., 1965-66, Pediatric Profl. Assn., Shawnee Mission, 1971-73, Shawnee Mission Med. Center, 1976-77, lab. mgr., 1977—; dir. Jacobs Constrn. Co., Inc., Kansas City Milk Bank. Internal coordinator United Way campaign, 1980, 81; adminstrv. bd. Valley View United Methodist Ch., 1981-83, chair work area on worship, mem. Council on Ministries, 1981-83; pres. Shawnee Mission Women's Chorale, 1974-76. Cert. Am. Soc. Clin. Pathologists, Nat. Cert. Agy. Mem. Cons./Trainers S.W., Am. Soc. Med. Technologists, Kans. Soc. Med. Technologists, Clin. Lab. Mgmt. Assn., Am. Soc. Clin. Pathologists (affiliate), U. Nebr. Alumnae Assn., Alpha Xi Delta. Office: Shawnee Mission Medical Center 74th and Grandview Sts Shawnee Mission KS 66201

JACOBS, TIMOTHY WILLIAM, educator; b. Chgo., Aug. 29, 1942; s. William Edward and Margaret Lucille (Hogan) J.; student Loyola U., Chgo., 1963; B.A., DePaul U., 1966, M.A., 1970; m. Madelynn Corbett, June 18, 1966; children—Maureen Elizabeth, Anastasia Eileen, Timothy Corbett. Cashier, City of Chgo., 1961-64; accountant Roto Processing Co., Chgo., 1964-67; tchr. Chgo. Bd. Edn., 1967—, Westinghouse Vocat. High Sch., 1968—. Bd. dirs. Ravenswood Manor Improvement Assn., 1975-76. Mem. Am. Hist. Assn., Chgo. Sch. Architecture Found., Chgo. Tchr.'s Union. Roman Catholic. Home: 4529 N Francisco Ave Chicago IL 60625 Office: 3301 W Franklin Blvd Chicago IL 60618

JACOBS, VERNON KENNETH, acct., fin. cons.; b. Chgo., June 25, 1936; s. Jerome and Marguerite B. (Brown) J.; B.B.A., Wichita State U., 1962; m. Marcia Lynn Mountain, July 2, 1960; children—Deanne Lynn, Laura Ruth. Auditor, Deloitte Haskins & Sells, Kansas City, Mo., 1962-66; accounting mgr. Old Am. Ins. Co., Kansas City, 1966-72, v.p., controller, 1972-79; pvt. practice fin. cons., Prairie Village, Kans., 1979—; pres. Syntax Corp., Prairie Villa, 1978—. Served with USN, 1954-58. C.P.A., Kans. Mem. Am. Inst. C.P.A.'s, Am. Coll. C.L.U.'s, Internat. Assn. Fin. Planners. Author: The Taxpayers Audit Survival Manual, 1980; The New Taxpayer's Counterattack, 1980; newsletter editor Tax Angles, 1977—; newsletter editor, pub. Fin. Systems Report, 1980—. Home and Office: 4500 W 72d Terr Prairie Village KS 66208

JACOBSEN, DOROTHY HELEN CALDWELL, occupational therapist; b. Algona, Iowa, Aug. 19, 1935; d. Harry Vincent and Beulah Ramona (Larsen) Caldwell; B.A. in Occupational Therapy, U. Iowa, 1957; m. Eric Kasner Jacobsen, Mar. 30, 1957; 1 son, Steven Keith. Occupational therapist St. Louis County (Mo.) Spl. Dist. of Edn. for Severely Handicapped Children, Brentwood, 1960-64; dir. occupational therapy St. Luke's Hosp., St. Louis, 1964-69; instr. U. Kans., 1970-71; pvt. practice occupational therapy, phys. dysfunction and sensory dysfunction, Chargrin Falls, Ohio, 1971—; cons. in field. Bd. dirs. ABC Day Care Center, Chargrin Falls, 1976—. Registered, licensed profl. therapist. Mem. Am., Ohio occupational therapy assns., Center for the Study of Sensory Integrative Dysfunction. Presbyterian. Home: 16 Louise Dr Chagrin Falls OH 44022

JACOBSEN, ERIC KASNER, cons. engr.; b. N.Y.C., July 21, 1932; s. Henry and Caroline (Kasner) J.; B.S.C.E., U. Iowa, 1956; m. Dorothy H. Caldwell, Mar. 30, 1957; 1 son, Steven. Structural engr. Stanley Engring. Co., Muscatine, Iowa, 1956-59; asso. dept. mgr. R. W. Booker & Assos., St. Louis, 1959-63; plant mgr. Tri-Cities Terminal div. Nat. Marine Service, Inc., Granite City, Ill., 1963-65; sr. engr. Monsanto Co., 1965-69; chief structural engr. Weitz-Hettalsater Engrs., Kansas City, 1969-72; supr. structural and archtl. engring. Austin Co., Cleve., 1972-78; mgr. Engring. Mining and Metals div., 1978—; cons. engr. structural and archtl. engring., 1960—. Recipient Eagle Scout award Boy Scouts Am., 1951; registered profl. engr., Ill., N.Y., Iowa, Mo., Wis. Mem. ASCE, ASME, Cleve. Engring. Soc., Chi Epsilon. Presbyterian. Home: 16 Louise Dr Chagrin Falls OH 44022 Office: 1245 E 222d St Cleveland OH 44117

JACOBSEN, GREGG WILLARD, constrn. co. mktg. ofcl.; b. Erie, Pa., July 28, 1947; s. Arthur Willard and Dorothy Jean (O'Brien) J.; B.A. in Psychology, Kent State U., 1969; m., July 15, 1967; children—Kristin, Erik, Paul. Pvt. practice fin. planning, Kent, Ohio, 1976-78; quality control technician Norandex, Inc., Cleve., 1978-79; office mgr. The Ruhlin Co., Akron, Ohio, 1979-80, adminstrv. asst., 1980, mktg. coordinator, 1980—. Cert. fin. planner. Home: 617 Yacavona Dr Kent OH 44240 Office: The Ruhlin Co 3 Cascade Plaza Akron OH 44308

JACOBSEN, HOWARD, metal products mfg. co. exec.; b. N.Y.C., Aug. 12, 1921; s. Richard Bernhart and Aagot (Hansen) J.; student N.Y. U., 1940-43, 46-47; m. Betty Pernilla Anderson, June 19, 1943; children—Christine Jacobsen Muenchinger, Howard Emil, Carl Lawrence. Field rep., supr. engring. test dept. Sperry Gyroscope Co., Great Neck, N.Y., 1939-44; salesman Nat. Gypsum Co., Mpls., 1947-49, asst. sales mgr., Chgo., 1951-54, dist. mgr., Detroit, 1954-61; gen. mgr. wholesale div. Nichols Aluminum Co., Davenport, Iowa, 1962-63, v.p. sales, Hinsdale, Ill., 1963-69; v.p., gen. mgr. Amax Aluminum Bldg. Products, Inc., Evansville, Ind., 1969-74; product mgr., mktg. devel. mgr. Allied Tube & Conduit Corp., Harvey, Ill., 1974—. Served with USN, 1944-46. Home: 1600 Fox Bend Ct Naperville IL 60540 Office: Allied Tube & Conduit Corp 16100 S Lathrop Harvey IL 60426

JACOBSON, DOUGLAS LYMAN, clergyman, social worker; b. St. James, Minn., Mar. 14, 1913; s. John O. and Amanda Josephine (Gjervik) J.; B.A., Augustana Coll., Sioux Falls, S.D., 1935; B.Th., Luther Seminary, St. Paul, 1939; postgrad. U. Chgo., 1949; M.S.W., State U. Iowa, 1957; m. Gretchen Norby, June 14, 1940; children—Jo Ann, Jon Douglas, Gretchen Marie, Martha Jane. Ordained to ministry Am. Luth. Ch., 1939; pastor St. Paul Luth. Ch., Cut Bank, Mont., 1939-42, Elk Point (S.D.) Luth. Parish, 1942-46, Grace Luth. Ch., San Francisco, 1946-48; exec. dir. Beloit of Iowa, Ames, 1949-58; psychotherapist Northeast Psychiat. Clinic, Waterloo, Iowa, 1958—; chaplain Mental Health Inst., Independence, Iowa, 1958—. Bd. dirs. Parents Without Partners, 1973—; bd. dirs. Psychiat. Outpatient Centers Am., 1975—, treas., 1977, pres., 1979. Mem. Nat. Assn. Social Workers, Assn. Mental Health Clergy, Assn. Clin. Pastoral Edn. Democrat. Home: 3128 Grand Blvd Cedar Falls IA 50613 Office: 1st National Bldg Waterloo IA 50703

JACOBSON, JOHN STEPHEN, hosp. adminstr.; b. Sioux Falls, S.D., May 1, 1945; s. Edwin Gerald and Alexandra King (Smyrak) J.; B.S. in Journalism, S.D. State U., Brookings, 1972; m. Mary Elizabeth Leander, June 12, 1970; children—Kevin John, Anna Marie, Erik Gerald, Carrie Christine. Reporter, Sioux Falls Argus-Leader, 1972-73, state editor, 1973-75, asst. city editor, 1975-76; public relations dir. McKennan Hosp., Sioux Falls, 1976—. Bd. dirs. Sioux Falls Community Blood Bank; loaned exec. Sioux Empire United Way, 1979-80, 80-81; vice chmn. maj. firms United Way, 1981-82; chmn. public relations council Presentation Health System, 1980-82. Served with U.S. Army, 1966-69. Winner 2d place S.D. AP news contest in spot news category, 1974. Mem. Am. Soc. Hosp. Public Relations (S.D. rep. to Region VI), S.D. Assn. Hosp. Public Relations (pres. 1981-82), Sioux Falls Area Press Assn. Roman Catholic. Club: Sioux Falls Sertoma (dir. 1974-76, 79-81, GEM award, 1st and 2d degree Gold Eagle award). Contbr. articles to newspapers. Home: 212 E 29th St Sioux Falls SD 57105 Office: 800 E 21st St Sioux Falls SD 57101

JACOBSON, LILLIAN ELEANORE, ret. librarian; b. Fingal, S.D., Aug. 23, 1919; d. Halvor P. and Ida B. (Maasjo) Langemo; B.A. in Edn., Valley City (N.D.) State Tchrs. Coll., 1940; B.S. in L.S., U. Denver, 1947; summer student U. Minn., 1965; m. Allen John Jacobson, Feb. 1, 1957. Librarian high sch. in N.D., 1940-46, Minn., 1949-50; library asst. Pacific Lutheran Coll., Parkland, Wash., 1946-49; asst. librarian Moorhead (Minn.) State Coll., 1950-51; circulation librarian No. Ill. State Coll., 1951-56; campus sch. librarian Valley City State Coll., 1956-65, head librarian, 1965-80. Mem. ALA, N.D. Library Assn., Delta Kappa Gamma. Republican. Lutheran.

JACOBSON, LOREN JOEL, obstetrician, gynecologist; b. Parshall, N.D., Oct. 28, 1923; s. Phillip Melvin and Nora (Blessum) J.; student U. Willamette, 1944-45; B.S., U. Minn., 1946, M.B., 1948, M.D., 1949; m. m. Anna Mae Kling Orozco, Nov. 15, 1980; children by previous marriage—Laurie Jo, Janel Noreen, Steven John, Julie Ann. Rotating intern U. Minn., Mpls., 1948-50; ltd. practice medicine, specializing in obstetrics and gynecology, Mpls., 1952-59; resident in obstetrics and gynecology Mayo Clinic, Rochester, Minn., 1959-61; mem. staff Mpls. Obstetrics and Gynecology Assos., Ltd., 1961—; active staff North Meml. Med. Center, Mpls., Fairview Southdale Hosp. Served as flight surgeon USAF, 1950-52. Mem. Minn. Obstet. and Gynecol. Soc. (pres. 1976), Am. Coll. Obstetricians and Gynecologists (chmn. Minn. sect. 1975-77, dist. sec. 1978-83). Republican. Lutheran. Office: 3366 Oakdale Ave N Minneapolis MN 55422

JACOBSON, MICHAEL HAROLD, educator; b. Lajunta, Colo., Feb. 16, 1945; s. Irving Ralph and Bernice Marie (Rubin) J.; B.S., Loyola U., Chgo., 1967; LL.B., LaSalle U., 1971; M.A., Northeastern Ill. U., 1970; Ph.D., Sussex Coll. (Eng.), 1973; L.H.D. honoris causa, London Inst., 1974. Tchr., Chgo. Bd. Edn., 1967-71, counselor, 1971-76; pres. Chgo. Counseling Assos., 1971-74; regional coordinator Chgo. Region, Effectiveness Tng. Assos., 1972-73; Ill. state rep. Universal Life Ch., 1975—; prof. psychology Foster G. McGaw Grad. Sch., Nat. Coll. Edn., Chgo., 1975—; dir. guidance services Orr High Sch., Chgo., 1976-78; asso. prin. Dunbar Vocat. High Sch., 1978-79, Phillips High Sch., 1979-80; prin. Abbott Elem. Sch., Chgo., 1980—. Dist. commr. Boy Scouts Am., Chgo., 1975—, asst. dist. commr., 1973-75; staff officer public edn. USCG Aux. Recipient Dist. award of Merit Boy Scouts Am., 1976, Wood badge, 1977, named explorer advisor of the year, 1974; decorated Knight Sovereign Order of Lichstenstine; Knight commdr. Order Sursum Corda; Knight Order of Constantine. Mem. Am., Ill. personnel and guidance assns., Am., Ill. sch. counselor assns., Am. Assn. Sex

Educators Counselors and Therapists, Assn. for Supervision and Curriculum Devel., Chgo. Prins. Assn., Chgo. Personnel and Guidance Assn., U.S. Coast Guard Aux. (dist. staff officer 1980—), Mensa, Psi Chi, Phi Delta Kappa, Alpha Phi Omega (nat. exec. alumni com. 1974—). Contbr. articles to profl. jours. Home: 4124 N Clarendon Ave Chicago IL 60613 Office: 3630 S Wells St Chicago IL 60609

JACOBSON, PAUL, agrl. engr.; b. Harcourt, Iowa, Oct. 23, 1909; s. Frank A. and Pauline (Jacobson) J.; B.S. in Agrl. Engring., Iowa State U., 1932; m. Marion E. Jensen, June 3, 1934; children—Ann Jacobson Arden, Mary Jacobson Kimsey, Jean Jacobson Marx, Paul A. Area engr. Soil Conservation Service, Shenandoah, Iowa, 1934-44, dist. conservationist, Ft. Dodge, Iowa, 1944-45, zone conservationist, Milw., 1945-54, state cons. engr. for Iowa, Des Moines, 1954-64; drainage and soil conservation specialist Harza Engring. Co., Chgo., 1964—; irrigation specialist spl. mission to Iraq FAO, 1975. Recipient Soil and Water award Am. Soc. Agrl. Engrs., 1973. Fellow Am. Soc. Engrs. (recipient Doerfer Engring. Concept of Yr. award 1981); mem. Gamma Sigma Delta. Editor sect. on soil and water Agricultural Engineering Handbook, 1965. Developed system of push-up terraces with tile outlets. Home: Rural Route 1 Dow City IA 51528 Office: Harza Engring Co 150 S Wacker Dr Chicago IL 60606

JACOBSON, ROBERT MANFRED, hospital adminstr.; b. Chisholm, Minn., June 17, 1930; s. Clarence and Edna Jesse (Johnson) J.; B.A. in Econs., St. Olaf Coll., 1952; M.H.A., U. Minn., 1954; m. Helen Syverson, Dec. 27, 1953; children—Mark, Daniel, Peter, Joanna, Deanna, Sarah. Asst. adminstr. Lutheran Hosp., Ft. Dodge, Iowa, 1957-63; adminstr. Deaconess Hosp., Grand Forks, N.D., 1963-70; faculty U. N.D., 1968-79; exec. v.p. United Hosp., Grand Forks, 1971-76, pres., 1976—; faculty, ind. study program preceptor U. Minn., 1971—; clin. faculty Concordia Coll., 1969—; sec. Grand Forks Med. Park Corp., 1971—; bd. dirs., mem. exec. com. Agassix Health Systems Agy.; bd. dirs. Upper Midwest Hosp. Conf.; bd. dirs., mem. plan devel. com. N.D. Health Coordinating Com. Sunday Sch. tchr., trustee Lutheran Ch., 1959-62, 68-71; active Grand Forks Council on Alcoholism, 1965-69; pres. United Fund, 1967; chmn. citizens' adv. com. to mayor Grand Forks, 1968; bd. dirs. YMCA, 1981—. Served to 1st lt. USAF, 1954-57. Mem. Am. Hosp. Assn. (del.), N.D. Hosp. Assn. (dir., treas., v.p., pres.), Am. Assn. Hosp. Planning (dir.), Am. Coll. Hosp. Adminstrs., Nat. League Nursing (v.p. N.D.), Grand Forks C. of C. (v.p. 1978). Club: Rotary. Home: 1015 Reeves Dr Grand Forks ND 58201 Office: 1200 S Columbia Rd Grand Forks ND 58201

JACOBSON, STEVEN LEE, civil engr.; b. Chgo., May 29, 1942; s. Vernon Hans and Esther Margaret (Colson) J.; grad. Suburban Bldg. Ofcls. Conf. Tng. Inst., 1961; B.S.C.E., Ill. Inst. Tech., 1974; M.B.A., Roosevelt U., 1980; grad. Dale Carnegie Inst., 1977; m. Shirley Jeanne Carlson, July 20, 1963; children—Sheryl Jeanne, Scott Eric. Engring. aide Village of Glenview (Ill.), 1960-64; civil engr. Village of Wilmette (Ill.), 1964-66; civil engr., asso. Murry & Moody, Palatine, Ill., 1966-74; staff specialist in civil engring. Davy McKee Corp., Chgo., 1974—. Recipient Young Profls. award, 1979. Registered profl. engr., Ill., Ind.; registered land surveyor-in-tng., Ill. Mem. Nat. Soc. Profl. Engrs., ASCE. Club: McKee Employees (pres. 1978—). Home: 1330 Huber Ln Glenview IL 60025 Office: Davy McKee Corp 10 S Riverside Plaza Chicago IL 60606

JACOBY, ROBERT EDWARD, II, physician; b. DuQuoin, Ill., Mar. 4, 1946; s. Robert Edward and Melba (Scherle) J.; B.A. with distinction in Chemistry (Summerfield Scholar), U. Kans., Lawrence, 1968; M.D., Johns Hopkins U., 1972; Resident in family medicine Sch. Medicine U. Kans., Kansas City, 1972-75, pres. house staff assos., 1973-74, clin. asst. prof. dept. family practice, 1976—; practice medicine specializing in family practice, Topeka, Kans., 1975-76; med. dir. family practice group St. Francis Hosp. and Med. Center, Topeka, 1977—; mem. staff St. Francis Hosp., Stormont-Vail Hosp., Meml. Hosp.; mem. physician utilization rev. panel Kans. Blue Cross-Blue Shield. Mem. central budget com. United Way of Greater Topeka, 1978—; bd. dirs. Counseling and Consulation Service, Topeka, Topeka Civic Symphony Soc.; asst. organist First Presbyterian Ch., Topeka. Mem. AMA, Am. Guild Organists, Am. Acad. Family Physicians, Kans. Med. Soc., Shawnee County Med. Soc. and Med. Found., Organ Hist. Soc., Phi Beta Kappa, Alpha Kappa Lambda. Club: Rotary (Topeka). Home: 3520 NW 43d Ct Topeka KS 66618 Office: 631 Horne St Suite 340 Topeka KS 66606

JACOX, JOHN WILLIAM, engring. and consulting co. exec.; b. Pitts., Dec. 12, 1938; s. John Sherman and Grace Edna (Herbster) J.; B.S. in M.E., Carnegie Mellon U., 1962, B.S. in Indsl. Mgmt., 1962; 1 son, Brian Erik. Mfg. engr., Nuclear Fuel div. Westinghouse Elec. Co., Pitts., 1962-65; data processing salesman IBM, Pitts., 1965-66; mktg. mgr. nuclear products MSA Internat., Pitts., 1966-72; v.p. Nuclear Consulting Services, Inc., Columbus, Ohio, 1973—; v.p. NUCON Internat., 1981—; dir. NUCON Europe Ltd.; London; cons., lectr. Nat. Center for Research in Vocat. Edn., 1978—. Coop. edn. adv. com. Otterbein Coll. Mem. ASME (code com. nuclear air and gas treatment, exec. com., legis. services commn., chmn. subcom. testing), Am. Nuclear Soc. (pub. info. com.), Nat. Rifle Rifle Assn. (life), Sun Bunch (pres. 1980-81). Home: 5874 Northern Pine Pl Columbus OH 43229 Office: PO Box 29151 Columbus OH 43229

JACQUEMIN, JOHN NICHOLAS, educator; b. Hamilton, Ohio, Dec. 6, 1950; s. Leroy Paul and Rita Mary (Hangbers) J.; B.S., Ohio State U., 1975, M.S., 1978; m. Linda Grace Cast, June 9, 1978; 1 dau., Jodi Marie. Tchr. vocat. agr. Lakota High Sch., West Chester, Ohio, 1975—. Served with N.G., 1969-78. Mem. NEA, Nat. Vocat. Assn., Nat. Vocat. Agrl. Tchrs. Assn., Ohio Vocat. Agrl. Tchrs. Assn., Ohio Vocat. Assn., Ohio Edn. Assn., Lakota Edn. Assn. Democrat. Roman Catholic. Club: Optimist (dir. 1980—). Home: 6986 Logsdon Rd Hamilton OH 45011 Office: Lakota High School 5050 Tylersville Rd West Chester OH 45069

JAEGER, FRED KARL, engring. co. ofcl.; b. Racine, Wis., May 16, 1931; s. Fred Franz and Lydia Emma (Kraft) J.; student U. Wis.; m. Beverly K. Gehrig, Dec. 25, 1955; children—Heidi Lynn, Lisa Marie. Tool and die maker E.C. Styberg Engring. Co., Racine, Wis., 1951-55, gen. sales mgr., 1969—; test technician Walker Mfg. Co., Racine, 1957-58; process engr. J.I. Case Co., Racine, 1958-59; plant engr. Bardon Rubber Co., Union Grove, Wis., 1959-60; dist. sales mgr. Dumore Co., Racine, 1960-65, E.L. Essley Machinery Co., Chgo., 1965-69. Deacon Plymouth Congl. Ch. Served with USN, 1955-57. Mem. Mfrs. Assn. Racine (mktg. council), Ferrari Club Am. Home: 33701 Academy Rd Burlington WI 53105 Office: 1600 Goold St Racine WI 53404

JAFARI, JAFAR, educator; b. Isfahan, Iran, Nov. 18, 1942; came to U.S., 1967; s. Mehdi M. and Aghdass (Sadre-Hashemi) J.; B.A. in English, U. Isfahan, 1965; B.S., Cornell U., 1970, M.S. in Hotel Adminstrn., 1973; m. Fariba Ketabi, Aug. 17, 1976; 1 dau., Sheherazade. Instr. dept. habitational resources U. Wis.-Stout, Menomonie, 1973-75, asst. prof., 1975—; founder, editor-in-chief Annals of Tourism Research: A Social Sci. Jour., 1973—. Recipient Outstanding Service award World Tourism Orgn., 1975. Mem. Assn. Internationale d'Experts Scientifiques du Tourisme, Am. Anthrop. Assn., Travel and Tourism Research Assn. (chmn. CenStates chpt., 1980-82), Assn. for the Anthropological Study of Play, Soc. Internat. Devel., Soc. Applied Anthropology, Phi Kappa Phi. Muslim. Asso. editor: Handbook of Travel and Tourism Management and Research, 1982; mem. editorial bd. Jour. Travel Research; contbr. tourism articles to profl. and academic lit. Home: 1421 15th St E Apt 5 Menomonie WI 54751 Office: Dept Habitational Resources U Wis-Stout Menomonie WI 54751

JAFFE, KAREN LESLIE, clin. psychologist; b. N.Y.C., Mar. 21, 1952; d. Herbert Charles and Selma (Wollenberg) J.; A.B., Boston U., 1973; M.A.Ed., Washington U., St. Louis, 1974; postgrad. U. Va., 1974; Psy.D., Ill. Sch. Profl. Psychology, 1980; m. Alan M. Jaffe, Oct. 20, 1979. Counselor, Moraine Valley Community Coll., Palos Hills, Ill., 1975-79, asst. prof. psychology; clin. psychology intern Forest Hosp.; now cons. psychologist and in pvt. practice. Mem. Am. Psychol. Assn., Ill. Psychol. Assn., Chgo. Assn. for Psychoanalytic Psychology. Psi Chi. Home: 2020 Lincoln Park W Chicago IL 60614 Office: 30 N Michigan Ave Suite 1316 Chicago IL 60602

JAFFEE, JAMES A(RTHUR), pharm. co. exec.; b. N.Y.C., Aug. 2, 1915; s. Leo H. and Catherine T. (Kruse) J.; B.S. in Bus. Adminstrn. cum laude, Syracuse U., 1941, postgrad., 1941-42; postgrad. N.Y. U., 1949, Marquette U., 1961-62; m. Virginia C. Tempest, Dec. 31, 1938; children—Lynne C. Jaffee Pensa, Joan K. Jaffee Pfirrmann, Patricia L. Jaffee Ramseyer. Bus. rep., internat. rep. Internat. Brotherhood of Firemen and Oilers, 1935-42; asso. dir. N.Y.C. region NLRB, 1951-57; dir. indsl. relations Mack Truck Co., 1957; labor arbitrator, 1958—; dir. personnel realtions Cutler Hammer Inc., Milw., 1959-70; v.p. personnel relations Parke Davis Co., Detroit, 1970—; lectr. Rutgers Inst. Mgmt.-Labor Relations, 1948-58; mem. adv. bd. Wis. Indsl. Relations Research Assn., 1965-70, v.p., pres., 1963-65; dir. Blue Cross Blue Shield of Mich. Served with airborne troops U.S. Army, 1945-46. Mem. Am. Soc. Personnel Adminstrn., Indsl. Relations Research Assn. Detroit (adv. council), Soc. Profls. Dispute Resolution, Am. Arbitration Assn., Internat. Labor Law Assn. Club: Detroit Boat. Office: Parke Davis PO Box 118 Detroit MI 48232

JAGELS, RONALD RAYMOND, clothing co. exec.; b. Detroit, Apr. 10, 1938; s. Raymond Stephen and Jeanette Helen (Wroblewski) J.; B.A., John Carroll U., 1960; m. Jane Kathleen Clifford, June 17, 1961; children—Thomas, Laura, James, Patricia. Salesman, Hudson Paper & Pulp Co., N.Y.C., 1960-63; mgr. telephone program Bobbie Brooks, Inc., Cleve., 1963-64, mgr. customer relations, 1964-73, mgr. mil. sales, 1973—, dir. marketing ops., 1975—; cons. in field. Advisor, Jr. Achievement, Cleve., 1967-69; advisor, leader Boy Scouts Am., Cleve., 1973-76; adult advisor C.Y.O. Youth Orgn., Cleve., 1978-79; area capt. Cath. Charities fund raising drives, 1974-79. Mem. Am. Mgmt. Assn., Am. Logistics Assn. Democrat. Roman Catholic. Clubs: Ch. Couples (pres. 1974-76), Booster (treas. 1975-78), K.C., 3 Gal. Doner of ARC. Home: 4651 Bradford St South Euclid OH 44121 Office: 3830 Kelley Ave Cleveland OH 44114

JAGER, LEE EDWARD, state govt. ofcl.; b. Grand Rapids, Mich., July 12, 1933; s. Louis and Kathryn (Boone) J.; B.S. in Civil Engring., U. Mich., 1955; m. Katherine Gore, June 6, 1954; children—Louis Lee, Kathy Ann. Cons. engr., 1955-56, 59-62; adminstr. Mich. Air Pollution Control Program, 1971-77; chief Mich. Bur. Environ. and Occupational Health, 1977—. Served with AUS, 1956-59. Registered profl. engr., Mich. Mem. Am. Public Health Assn., Am. Water Works Assn., Am. Pollution Control Assn. Mem. Reformed Ch. Am. Address: PO Box 30035 3500 N Logan St Lansing MI 48909

JAGGERS, LAWRENCE EARL, chiropractic physician; b. Decatur, Ill., June 18, 1948; s. Harold D. and Catherine C. (Yarama) J.; B.S. in Zoology, Lincoln Coll., 1969; B.S. in Human Anatomy, Nat. Coll. Chiropractic, 1972; m. Patricia Ann Brown, Jan. 27, 1973; children—Amanda Jo, Nicholas Adam. Chiropractic physician specializing in orthopedics, neurology, acupuncture, Indpls., 1972—; mem. staff, instr. acupuncture Lincoln Nat. Postgrad. Sch. Edn.; chmn. bd. Total Solar Energy Systems. Fellow Internat. Acad. Clin. Acupuncture; mem. Am. Chiropractic Assn., Ind. State Chiropractic Assn. (dir.). Club: N.E. Exchange (dir.). Office: 6502 E 56th St Indianapolis IN 46226

JAGODZINSKI, BENJAMIN ANDREW, physician, surgeon; b. Warsaw, Poland, Feb. 12, 1937; s. Matthew and Marie (Goscinski) J.; B.S., St. Peter's Coll., 1958; M.D., Loyola U., 1962; m. Judith M. Norka, May 26, 1962; children—Susan, Sharon, Caryn, Christine. Intern, Monmouth Med. Center, Long Branch, N.J., 1962-63; obstetrics-gynecology resident Little Co. of Mary Hosp., Evergreen Park, Ill., 1963-64, 66-68, sr. attending physician, cons. 1968—; active attending physician, cons. Christ Hosp., Oak Lawn, Ill., 1968—, Palos Community Hosp., Palos Heights, Ill., 1968—; asso. prof. obstetrics-gynecology Rush Med. Coll.-Presbyn.-St. Luke's Hosp., Chgo., 1970—. Served to capt. M.C., U.S. Army, 1964-66. Diplomate Am. Bd. Obstetrics and Gynecology. Mem. AMA (physicians recognition award 1974-77, 78-81), Am. Coll. Obstetricians and Gynecologists (award 1979, 80), Am. Fertility Soc., Internat. Coll. Surgeons, Am. Assn. Gynecol. Laparascopists, Ill. State, Chgo. med. socs., Chgo. Gynecol. Soc. Roman Catholic. Club: Elks. Office: 3900 W 95th St Evergreen Park IL 60642

JAHN, HELMUT, architect; b. Nuremberg, Germany, Jan. 1, 1940; came to U.S., 1966; s. Wilhelm Anton and Karolina (Wirth) J.; Dipl. Ing.-Architect, Technische Hochschule, Munich, W. Ger., 1965; postgrad. Ill. Inst. Tech., 1966-67; D.F.A. (hon.), St. Mary's Coll., Notre Dame, Ind., 1979; m. Deborah Ann Lampe, Dec. 31, 1970. With P.C. von Seidlein, Munich, 1965-66; with C.F. Murphy Assos., Chgo., 1967—, partner in charge of design, 1973—. Winner nat. competition for Minn. Capitol Expansion, 1977. Mem. AIA (Nat. Honor award for Kemper Arena 1975, St. Mary's Athletic Facility 1978, progressive architecture citation 1976-78, Chgo. chpt. award 1975-78). Roman Catholic. Clubs: Arts, Chgo. Athletic. Prin. works include Kemper Arena, Kansas City, Mo., 1975, Auraria Learning Resources Center, Denver, 1975, Richmond (Va.) Courts Bldg., 1976, Kansas City (Mo.) Conv. Center, 1976, Maywood (Ill.) Cts. Bldg., 1976, Michigan City (Ind.) Library, 1977, St. Mary's Coll. Athletic Facility, South Bend, Ind., 1977, Rust-Oleum Hdqrs., 1977, Xerox Centre, 1978. Home: 2400 Lakeview Chicago IL 60614 Office: 224 S Michigan Ave Chicago IL 60604*

JAICKS, FREDERICK G., steel co. exec.; b. Chgo., 1918; ed. Cornell U., 1940. Pres., dir. Inland Steel Co., 1966-72, chmn. bd., chief exec. officer, 1972—; dir. R.R. Donnelley & Sons Co., 1st Nat. Bank Chgo., Carson Pirie Scott & Co., Champion Internat. Corp. Served with USN, 1942-45. Office: Inland Steel Co 30 W Monroe St Chicago IL 60603

JAKEWAY, EDWIN WILLIAM, JR., lawyer; b. Flint, Mich., Dec. 7, 1936; s. Edwin William and Lucille (Hodge) J.; A.A., Genesee Community Coll., 1955-57; B.A., Eastern Mich. U., 1958; J.D. (Kiwanis scholar), Detroit Coll., 1961; m. Suzanne Henry, June 23, 1963; children—Craig Edwin, Morgan Henry, Sally Pamela, Brooke Song. Admitted to Mich. bar, 1961; asso. firm Ransom and Fazenbaker, Flint, 1962-63, McTaggart and Lattie, Flint, 1964-65; partner firm Neal, Keil, Jakeway and Fazenbaker, Flint, 1965-70, Jakeway, Fazenbaker, Henry & Lawniczak, Grand Blanc, Mich., 1970—; asst. prosecutor Genesee County, 1962-63; lectr. various schs. and chs., 1968—. Served with Mich. N.G., 1955-62. Cert. civil trial advocate Nat. Bd. Trial Advocacy. Mem. Trout Unltd. (pres. Flint chpt. 1971-74), Gideons Internat., Am., Mich., Genesee County (dir. 1971-75, pres. 1978-79) bar assns., Am., Mich. trial lawyers assns. Home: 7338 McCandlish Rd Grand Blanc MI 48439 Office: 8161 S Saginaw Rd Grand Blanc MI 48439

JAKLE, KENNETH RICHARD, broadcasting exec.; b. Effingham, Ill., Aug. 7, 1942; s. Kenneth Dean and Kaythryn Joan (Loy) J.; B.S. in Communications, U. Ill., 1964; m. Sharon S. James, Jan. 12, 1980; children by previous marriage—Ann Elizabeth, Joellen Kaythryn, Richard Edward. Sales mgr. Sta. WKEI, Kewanee, Ill., 1964-65; gen. mgr. Sta. WCRA, Effingham, 1965-66; mng. owner Sta. WRMN-FM-AM, Elgin, Ill., 1966-74, pres., 1974—; pres. Sta. WJKL, Elgin, 1974—; v.p. Sta. WBEV-AM-FM, Beaver Dam, Wis., 1973—, Sta. WXRO, Beaver Dam, 1976—; v.p., dir. Clinton (Ill.) Daily Jour. and Public, 1979—; dir. Elgin Nat. Bank, San Jose Tri-County Bank. Bd. mgrs. Sherman Hosp., Elgin; chmn. Elgin Econ. Devel. Commn., 1975-77; pres. Elgin YMCA, 1972-73; bd. dirs. Elgin Downtowner, Easter Seal Assn., Upper Kane County Heart Assn., Larkin Home for Children, Salvation Army. Served with USNG, 1964-66. Recipient Disting. Service award Jaycees, 1969. Mem. Nat. Assn. Broadcasters, Nat. Radio Broadcasters Assn., Ill. Broadcasters Assn., Elgin Hist. Soc. (dir.), Elgin C. of C. Methodist. Clubs: Rotary, Masons, Shriners. Home: 731 Carlton St Elgin IL 60120 Office: WRMN and WJKL 18 1/2 Douglas Ave Elgin IL 60120

JAKOVLJEVIC, IVAN M., research scientist; b. Volos, Greece, June 25, 1916; came to U.S., 1959, naturalized, 1964; s. Males J. and Leposava (Leshcinski) J.; grad. U. Zagreb (Yugoslavia), 1940; M.S., U. Belgrade (Yugoslavia), 1942; children—Milica, Alexandar. Asst. prof. U. Belgrade, 1940-44; dir. analytical research labs. Prolek, Pharm. Co., Belgrade, 1944-57; adv. Royal Pharm. Assn. of Holland, 1958-59; analytical chemist Squibb Co., New Brunswick, N.J., 1959; research scientist Eli Lilly Co., Indpls., 1959—. Pres., Ind. Com. for Captive Nations, 1960-70. Recipient Eisenhower medal for promoting freedom Captive Nations Com., 1970. Mem. Am. Pharm. Assn., Pharm. Acad. Sci. Serbian Orthodox Ch. Contbr. chpts. to books, articles to profl. jours. Home: PO Box 664 Indianapolis IN 46206 Office: PO Box 618 Indianapolis IN 46206

JALIL, MAZHAR, entomologist; b. India, Nov. 2, 1938; s. Mohammad Ahmad and Safia (Khatoon) J.; came to U.S., 1967, naturalized, 1973; B.Sc. in Agr., U. Agra (India), 1952, M.Sc. in Agr. in Zoology and Entomology, 1954; M.Sc. in Agrl. Zoology (Lord Belper postgrad. scholar), U. Nottingham (Eng.), 1963; Ph.D. in Biology, U. Waterloo, Can., 1967; postdoctoral U. Ky., 1967-69; m. Betty Ann Lunsford, Feb. 28, 1970; children—Tariq, Khalid. Farm supt. R.A.K. Agrl. Inst., Sehore, India, 1955-56; tchr., lectr. Govt. Coll., Sehore, India, 1956-60; instr. U. Nottingham, 1962-64, U. Waterloo, 1964-67; research asso. U. Ky., 1967-69; entomologist and microbiologist Ohio Dept. Health, Columbus, 1969—; UN devel. program cons. to NIH, Govt. of Pakistan, 1980-81. Mem. Acarological Soc. Am., Entomol. Soc. Am., Am. Registry Profl. Entomologists, Islamic Found. Central Ohio. W.V.S. travelling scholar U. Nottingham, 1964; teaching fellow U. Waterloo, 1964-67, Ont. grad. fellow, 1965-67. Contbr. articles to profl. jours. Home: 2769 Heston Ct Columbus OH 43220 Office: Ohio Dept Health PO Box 2568 Columbus OH 43216

JAMES, ARMINTA SUSAN, ednl. adminstr.; b. Erie, Pa., May 1, 1924; d. Leonard S. and Alice R. Martin; A.B., Fisk U., 1946; M.A. in Ednl. Adminstrn., Roosevelt U., 1965; m. Walter R. James, Jr., June 30, 1951. Health edn. sec. Erie County Tb Assn., 1946-48; child placement worker Chgo. Welfare Dept., 1946-52; elem. tchr. North Chicago (Ill.) Dist 64, 1955-65, prin. Forrestal Sch., 1965—, co-chmn. sch. dist. EEO awareness team. Bd. dirs. Lake County Urban League; mem. Panel Am. Women, North Shores Community Service League, Nat. Council Negro Women. Mem. Nat. Assn. Elem. Sch. Prins., Ill. Prins. Assn., Nat. Alliance Black Sch. Educators, Alpha Kappa Alpha (pres. chpt. 1979-81). Episcopalian. Home: 1316 14th St Waukegan IL 60085 Office: Forrestal School Washington St Great Lakes IL 60088

JAMES, ERNEST WILBUR, lawyer; b. N.Y.C., July 21, 1931; s. Ernest Leaman and Lola Maude (Clancy) J.; B.S., U.S. Naval Acad., 1956; M.S.A.E., U.S. Naval Postgrad. Sch., 1964; J.D., St. Louis U., 1979; m. Jane Gallagher; children—Ernest Jude, Sean Patrick, Patrick Logan, Sharon Ann; 1 stepdau., Susan Bartsch. Title examiner Queens County Registrar's Office, N.Y.C., 1949-51; commd. ensign U.S. Navy, 1956, advanced through grades to comdr., 1971; aviation maintenance mgmt., 1956-69; maintenance mgmt. engr. planning, 1969-76; ret., 1976; admitted to Mo. bar, 1979; atty., claims and litigation Bi-State Devel. Agy., St. Louis, 1979—; adj. prof. safety Central Mo. State U. Active Maryville Homecoming Assn.; vol. fire insp. Maryville Fire Dept. Decorated D.F.C., Air medal (3), Navy Commendation medal. UMTA grantee, 1978. Mem. Am. Bar Assn., Mo. Bar Assn., Met. St. Louis Bar Assn., Met. St. Louis Safety Council, Naval Acad. Alumni Assn., U.S. Naval Inst., Am. Def. Preparedness Assn., Met. St. Louis Lawyers Club, VFW. Home: 12 W Perry Ave Maryville IL 62062 Office: 3869 Park Ave Saint Louis MO 63110

JAMES, FRANCIS EDWARD, III, investment analyst; b. Harlingen, Tex., June 28, 1953; s. Francis Edward and Iris Rae (Senn) J.; B.A., Rice U., 1979; m. Margaret Lovena Jenkins, Aug. 27, 1977. Research asso. James Investment Research Inc., Alpha, Ohio, 1975—; pres. James Computer Systems, Inc., Alpha, 1981—, also dir. Officer, youth devel. Ch. of God. Nat. Merit scholar, 1971-75. Mem. Dayton C. of C., Am. Mgmt. Assn. Conservative. Home: 2348 Kewanna Ln Xenia OH 45385 Office: Box 8 Alpha OH 45301

JAMES, GERALDINE YVETTE-MARIE JENNINGS, hosp. ofcl.; b. Chgo., Dec. 19, 1936; d. James C. and Masceola Christine (Wilson) Jennings; degree in Nursing, Fresno State Coll., 1956; B.S. in Med. Tech., Wayne State U., M.S., 1975; m. Rudolph James, Dec. 19, 1966 (dec. Aug. 11, 1981); children—Ronald, Rudolph, Donna, Roland. Labor and delivery nurse, supr. central supply room Merced County Hosp., Merced, Calif., 1956-57; research technologist Parke-Davis Co., Ann Arbor, Mich., 1962-63; devel. immunologist Hutzel Hosp., Detroit, 1964-69, sect. head devel. immunology, 1969-74; ednl. coordinator Oakwood Hosp., Dearborn, Mich., 1974—; adj. instr. immunology Wayne State U.; adj. instr. Mich. State U., Mich. Technol. U., Eastern Mich. U., Lake Superior State Coll., Saginaw Valley State Coll.; immunology-genetic cons., ednl. cons. Mary Grove Coll. Leader, Girl Scouts U.S.A., 1962-65; mem. Detroit Internat. Ethnic Bicentennial Com., 1974-76; mem. vicariate sch. bd., 1974-76; sec. parish council, 1974-77; precinct chmn. various polit. campaigns. O. Brines scholar, 1975; Regents scholar, 1959-60. Mem. Am. Assn. Blood Banks, Mich. Assn. Blood Banks, Am. Soc. Met. Tech., Mich. Soc. Med. Tech., Detroit Soc. Med. Tech., Am. Soc. Clin. Pathologists, Mich. Soc. for Health Manpower Edn. and Tng., Am. Soc. for Tng. and Devel., Detroit Staff Devel. Educators, Wayne State U. Alumni Assn. Med. Tech. Group (pres. 1978-79), Alpha Kappa

Alpha. Clubs: Order Eastern Star, Daus. of ISIS. Office: Oakwood Hosp 18101 Oakwood Blvd Dearborn MI 48124

JAMES, GORDON DAVID, ret. educator; b. Warren, Ohio, Nov. 27, 1920; s. David R. and Carolyn (Schisler) J.; B.S., Youngstown U., 1942; student Ohio State U., 1947-48, Kent State U. 1958, Columbia U., 1964; m. Mary E. Evans, Mar. 31, 1946; children—Candace Lee (Mrs. Michael Richmond), Timothy Alan, D. Kevin. Tchr. Lordstown High Sch., Warren, 1941-42, 46-52, prin., 1952-58; supt. Gordon D. James Career Center and Lordstown Schs., 1958-79. Councilman, Loudstown Village, 1979—. Served with M.C., AUS, 1942-46. Mem. Am., Buckeye assns. sch. adminstrs., Ohio Assn. Local Sch. Supts. (exec. com. 1967-69, pres. 1970, rec. sec. 1972), Ohio Assn. Sec. Sch. Adminstrs., Nat. Assn. Secondary Sch. Adminstrs., Am., Buckeye assns. sch. adminstrs., Ohio Sch. Bds. Assn., Trumbull County Supts. Assn. (pres. 1966-67). Presbyterian (ordained elder). Home: 2835 Hallock-Young Rd Warren OH 44481

JAMES, JANE EMERSON, psychologist; b. Creston, Iowa, Oct. 5, 1920; d. Stephen Ray and Meta Florence (Raney) Emerson; B.A., U. Mo., Kansas City, 1968, M.A., 1970; Ph.D., Union Grad. Sch., Ohio, 1977; m. Fred Allen James, Sept. 15, 1945; children—John William, Meta Elizabeth. Surveyor, free-lance writer Kansas City (Mo.) Star, 1971-72; counselor Nevada (Mo.) State Hosp., 1972, Nat. Council on Alcoholism, Kansas City, 1972-77; cons. Midwest Research Inst., Kansas City, 1976—; founder, pres. Task Force for Women Alcoholics, Inc., 1975-76; dir. Jan Clayton Center, 1977-79; trustee Kansas City area Nat. Council on Alcoholism. Mcpl. judge City of Lake Winnebago, Mo., 1977-78. Recipient award N.Am. Women's Commn. on Alcohol and Drug Abuse, 1979. Mem. Am. Psychol. Assn., Mo. Psychol. Assn., Mo. Assn. Alcoholism Counselors, Kans. Assn. Alcoholism Counselors, P.E.O., U. Mo. Kansas City Alumni Assn., Mensa. Author: Alcoholism in the Future - Views from Four Delphis, 1978; editorial referee Jour. of Studies on Alcohol, 1972—. Home: 432 Winnebago Dr Lake Winnebago MO 64034

JAMES, MARION RAY, editor; b. Bellmont, Ill., Dec. 6, 1940; s. Francis Miller and Alma Lorraine (Wylie) J.; B.S., Oakland City Coll., 1964; postgrad. U. Evansville, 1966; M.S., St. Francis Coll., 1978; m. Janet Sue Tennis, June 16, 1960; children—Jeffrey Glenn, David Ray, Daniel Scott, Cheryl Lynne. Sports and city editor Daily Clarion, Princeton, Ind., 1963-65; English tchr. Jac-Cen-Del High Sch., Osgood, Ind., 1965-66; indsl. editor Whirlpool Corp., Evansville and LaPorte, Ind., 1966-68; indsl. editor Magnavox Govt. and Indsl. Electronics Co., Fort Wayne, Ind., 1968-79; pres., editor, pub. Bowhunter mag. Blue-J Pub. Co., Fort Wayne, 1971—; instr. Ind.-Purdue U., Ft. Wayne, 1980—. Recipient Best Editorial award United Community Services Publs., 1970-72. Mem. Outdoor Writers Assn. Am., Fort Wayne Assn. Bus. Editors (Fort Wayne Bus. Editor of Year 1969, pres. 1975-76), Alpha Phi Gamma, Alpha Psi Omega, Mu Tau Kappa. Club: Toastmasters (Able Toastmaster award). Author: Bowhunting for Whitetail and Mule Deer, 1975; editor: Pope and Young Book World Records, 1975; Bowhunting Adventures, 1977-81. Home: 9713 Saratoga Rd Fort Wayne IN 46804 Office: 3808 S Calhoun St Fort Wayne IN 46807

JAMES, PAULINE, court reporter; b. Chgo.; d. Claude and Bertha (Walker) Dixon; student Roosevelt U., 1951-53, 65-66, 76-78, Chgo. Coll. Commerce, 1958-60, 63-64; m. Goldwyn James, Feb. 10, 1952; children—Pamela M., Goldwyn H., Karen L., Keith Edward. Sec. to head dept. pedodontics U. Ill. Dental Sch., 1958-60; sec. U. Chgo. Law Sch., 1960-61; sec. to Luis Kutner, internat. law specialist, 1961-63; office mgr. Ill. Inst. Tech. Research Inst., 1963-66; owner James Sec. Service, 1966-72; ct. reporter, office mgr. U.S. Dist. Ct., 1969-72; owner Pauline James, Inc., Chgo., 1972-74; owner Pauline James & Assos., Ct. Reporters, Chgo., 1975—. Active Nat. Urban League. Mem. Nat. Women Bus. Owners (mem. ednl. seminars com.), LWV, Ill. Ct. Reporters Assn. (editor newsletter), Nat. Assn. Shorthand Reporters, Ill. State C. of C. (exec. com.). Club: Order Eastern Star. Home: 2218 E 99th St Chicago IL 60617 Office: 219 S Dearborn St Chicago IL 60604

JAMES, WALTER, state ofcl.; b. Mpls., June 8, 1915; s. James Edward and Mollie (Gress) Smoleroff; B.Ch.E., U. Minn., 1938, postgrad, 1945-60; m. Jesse Ann Pickens, Dec. 27, 1948; 1 son, Joel Pickens. Process designer Monsanto Chem. Co., St. Louis, 1940-45; instr. math U. Minn., Mpls., 1945-60, extension div., 1950—; researcher computer based applied math. 3M Co., St. Paul, 1960-68; info. systems planner State of Minn., St. Paul, 1968—. Mem. Am. Math. Assn., AAAS, Sigma Xi. Contbr. articles to profl. jours. Home: 6228 Brooklyn Dr Brooklyn Center MN 55430

JAMES, WARREN EDWARD, educator, musician; b. Xenia, Ohio, Oct. 29, 1922; a. Joshua Byford and Millie (McCoy) J.; student Muskingum Coll., 1940-41; B.S., Ohio State U., 1947, M.A., 1949, Ph.D., 1957; m. Betty M. Smith, 1946 (div.); 1 child, Terri Jan Holderman; m. 2d, Claire Y. Jackson, 1957 (div. 1962); children—Weston Eric, Carson Willard; m. 3d, Martha Boulton, 1968. Instr., Cornell U., 1951-52; instr. Ohio State U., 1952-57; asst. prof. Rutgers U., 1957-59; dir. alcoholism unit Ohio Dept. Health, Columbus, 1960-61; prof. sociology Central State U., Wilberforce, Ohio, 1962-79, ret., 1979, conductor workshops in improvised music, ethnomusicology, 1976—; flutist, composer; owner Nada Records, Yellow Springs, Ohio, 1972—. Served with U.S. Army, 1943-46. Mem. Soc. Ethnomusicology, N.Central Sociol. Assn., Assn. Humanistic Psychology, Living Tao Found. Author: Alcoholism in Ohio, 1950; editor: Sick Man in Society, 1967; composer: Summer Rain, 1962, Latino, Circles I, Circles II, Electronic Wham, Electronic Bam, 1972-73, From Here to There, 8 plus 2, 1979, Floating on a Dark Wind, 1980; composer-producer record album Intersections, 1973, Floating on a Dark Wind, 1981. Address: 251 Whitehall Dr Yellow Springs OH 45387

JAMES, WILLIAM ELLERY SEDGWICK, physician; b. N.Y.C., June 1, 1920; s. Ellery Sedgwick and Louise Russell (Hoadley) J.; B.A., Yale, 1942; M.D., Columbia, 1945; m. Mary Ladds, Nov. 18, 1950; children—Sarah L.S., Laura Ladds., Emily Preston. Intern, Mary Imogene Bassett Hosp., 1945-46; asst. resident in medicine Univ. Hosps., Cleve., 1948-49; resident in internal medicine Cleve. VA Hosp., 1949-51; demonstrator dept. preventive medicine Case Western Res. U. Med. Sch., Cleve., 1951-52, now sr. instr. medicine; practice medicine specializing in internal medicine, Cleve. and Shaker Heights, 1952—; active staff St. Luke's Hosp., Cleve.; sch. physician Shaker Heights Schs., 1952-77. Pres. Margaret Wagner House, 1967; vestryman St. Pauls Ch., Cleveland Heights, Ohio, 1981—. Served as lt. (j.g.) USN, 1946-48. Eddie Painton fellow in rheumatic fever, 1952-55. Diplomate Am. Bd. Internal Medicine. Mem. ACP, AMA, Ohio Med. Assn., Cleve. Acad. Medicine, Cleve. Diabetes Assn. (trustee 1962-69), Nu Sigma Nu. Republican. Episcopalian. Clubs: Kirtland Country, Montserrat Golf. Home: 2266 Chatfield Dr Cleveland Heights OH 44106 Office: 3461 Warrensville Center Shaker Heights OH 44122

JAMES, WILLIAM JOSEPH, chemist; b. Providence, Sept. 17, 1922; s. Christopher and Rose (Petit) J.; B.S., Tufts U., 1949; M.S., Iowa State U., 1952, Ph.D., 1953; m. Arlene Carll, Aug. 23, 1942; children—Varie Linda James Lynch, Candice Lynn James Metcalf. Predoctoral research fellow in corn products Iowa State U., 1949-53; NIH fellow Pa. State U., 1952; asst. prof. chemistry U. Mo., Rolla, 1953-57, asso. prof., 1957-64, prof., 1964—, dir. grad. center materials research, 1964-75, asso. dir. grad. center materials research, 1975-76, dir. center, 1981—, mem. staff Inst. Chem. and Extractive Metallurgy, sr. investigator materials research, 1976—; indsl. cons., 1957—; abstractor Am. Chem. Soc., 1963—; dir., pres., treas. Mead Technologies Corp., Rolla, 1975—; v.p., dir. Brewer Science, Inc., Rolla; Fulbright research prof. U. Grenoble (France), 1961-62; pres., dir. Rare Earth Research Confs., 1979-81, sec., dir., 1981—. Mem. tech. adv. com. St. Louis Regional Council for Growth and Commerce, 1975—. Served with USAAC, 1941-46; PTO. Decorated Air medal; recipient Outstanding Tchr. award Circle K, U. Mo., Rolla, 1965, Outstanding Research award, 1968, Alumni Merit award for research, 1970; 10 Years Service award Chem. Abstracts, 1972. Fellow Am. Inst. Chemists; mem. Am. Crystallographic Assn., Electrochem. Soc., Mo. (pres. 1968—), N.Y. acads. scis., Newcomen Soc., Keramos, Alpha Chi Sigma, Sigma Pi Sigma, Phi Lambda Upsilon, Sigma Xi, Alpha Sigma Mu, Phi Kappa Phi, Kappa Sigma. Contbr. articles to profl. publs. Home: PO Box 45 Rolla MO 65401 Office: Materials Research Center U of Mo Rolla MO 65401

JAMES, WILLIAM W., banker; b. Springfield, Mo., Oct. 12, 1931; s. Will and Clyde (Cowdrey) J.; A.B., Harvard U., 1953; m. Carol Ann Muenter, June 17, 1967; children—Sarah Elizabeth, David William. Asst. to dir. overseas div. Becton Dickinson & Co., Rutherford, N.J., 1956-59; stockbroker Merrill Lynch, Pierce, Fenner & Smith, Inc., St. Louis, 1959-62; with trust div. Boatmen's Nat. Bank of St. Louis, 1962—, v.p. in charge estate planning, 1972—; dir. Heer-Andres Investment Co., Springfield. Mem. gift and bequest council Barnes Hosp., St. Louis, 1963-67, St. Louis U., 1972-78. Served with U.S. Army, 1953-55. Mem. Estate Planning Council St. Louis, Mo. Bankers Assn., Bank Mktg. Assn., Am. Inst. Banking. Republican. Clubs: Harvard (pres. 1972-73), Noonday (St. Louis). Office: PO Box 7365 Saint Louis MO 63166

JAMESON, LEE MERLE, dentist; b. Peoria, Ill., May 28, 1946; s. Donovan Edward and Josephine May (Wolf) J.; B.S. in Biology, Bradley U., 1968; D.D.S., Loyola U., Chgo., 1974, M.S. in Oral Biology, 1976; m. Loretta Joan Cuder, July 12, 1975. Sci. tchr. Central High Sch., East Peoria, Ill., 1968-70; gen. practice dentistry, Darien, Ill., 1974-76, Palos Heights, Ill., 1977—; clin. instr. dept. fixed prosthodontics Loyola Dental Sch., Chgo., 1975-78; asso. prof., dir. postgrad. prosthodontics Northwestern U. Dental Sch., Chgo., 1978—. Mem. ADA, Ill., Chgo. dental socs., Am. Coll. Prosthodontists (1st place Research Competition 1977), Xi Psi Phi (dep. supreme pres. 1980), Blue Key. Home: 728 E Berkshire Lombard IL 60148 Office: 7600 College Dr Palos Heights IL 60463

JAMIESON, MATTHEW WATT, utilities co. exec.; b. Dumbarton, Scotland, Sept. 20, 1922; came to U.S., 1926, naturalized, 1931; s. William Wallace and Annie Dempster (Neil) J.; B.Comml. Scis., Detroit Bus. Inst., 1950; m. Margaret H. Willis, Apr. 22, 1945; children—Gregory Allen, Gary Thomas, Grant Matthew. With Detroit Edison Co., 1939—, budget supr. control dept., 1965-75, project controller air and water quality projects, 1975-77, adminstrv. budget and mgmt. info. services ops., 1977—; instr. Detroit Bus. Inst., 1952-59. Chmn. trustees Mich. Vets. Trust Fund, 1979-80, trustee, 1978—. Served with USAAF, 1942-46. Mem. Nat. Assn. Accts., Engring. Soc. Detroit, Am. Legion (nat. vice comdr. 1980-81, comdr. State of Mich. 1970-71). Republican. Clubs: Elks, Masons, Past Comdrs. Am. Legion. Office: 2000 2d Ave Detroit MI 48226

JAMISON, KENNETH WALTER, SR., ednl. adminstr.; b. Ashtabula, Ohio, Jan. 8, 1952; s. William Robert and Alberta May (Thompson) J.; asso. degree Lakeland Community Coll., 1975; m. Miriam Lynne Newness, Apr. 23, 1977 (div. 1981); 1 son, Kenneth Walter. Stock man, sales mgr. Carlisle's, Geneva, Ohio, 1969-70, display mgr., sales mgr., Madison, Ohio, 1970-73, group mgr., Ashtabula, Ohio, 1973-76, ops. mgr., Stuebenville, Ohio, 1976-77; adult edn. coordinator Ashtabula County Joint Vocat. Sch., 1977—. Dir. Bicentennial Celebration, 1976; bd. dirs. Big Bros., 1977—; adv. Ashtabula Vocat. Sch. Ski Club, 1977—; 2d v.p. Western Res. Bus., Industry and Edn. Consortium, 1980—; mem. Ashtabula County CETA Youth Adv. Com., 1980—, CETA Adv. Council, 1981—; mem. emergency med. technician ambulance adv. com. State of Ohio, 1981—; mem. PIC Council, 1981—, Planning Commn., 1981—, ARC Safety Com., 1981— (all Ashtabula County). Mem. Am. Vocat. Assn., Ohio Vocat. Assn. (sec. adult div. 1978, 79, pres.-elect 1979, 80, pres. 1980-81), Parents and Alumni for Vocat. Edn., Ashtabula Area C. of C., Arrowhead Bus. Assn. (dir. 1975, 76), Ohio Assn. Adult Educators (dir. 1980-81), Ashtabula Jr. C. of C. (dir. 1976, 78, 79, pres. 1979-80, Disting. Service award 1976), Greater Ohio Showmen's Assn. Republican. Clubs: Kiwanis (dir. 1976), NorthEnd (dir. 1979, 80, v.p. 1980-81, pres. 1981-82). Home: 4458 Jamison Ln Geneva OH 44041 Office: Ashtabula County Joint Vocat Sch 1565 State Route 167 Jefferson OH 44047

JAMISON, WALLACE NEWLIN, clergyman, coll. dean; b. Alexandria, Egypt, Aug. 1, 1918; s. William Brainerd and Gertrude May (Newlin) J. (parents Am. citizens); B.A., Westminster Coll., Pa., 1940, L.H.D. (hon.), 1976; Th.B., Princeton Theol. Sem., 1943; Ph.D., U. Edinburgh, 1948; m. Ruth Dean Galloway, Nov. 16, 1943; children—Kathryn M., Robert N., Mary E., James W. Ordained to ministry United Presbyn. Ch. U.S.A., 1943; pastor United Presbyn. Ch., Indianola, Iowa, 1948-51; chmn. dept. history, dean chapel Westminster (Pa.) Coll., 1951-56; prof. ch. history New Brunswick (N.J.) Theol. Sem., 1956-63, pres., 1963-69; dean coll. Ill. Coll., Jacksonville, Ill., 1970—. Served with Chaplain Corps, USNR, 1943-46. Mem. Am. Hist. Assn., Am. Assn. Acad. Deans, Phi Alpha Theta. Republican. Rotarian. Author: The United Presbyterian Story, 1958; Religion in New Jersey, 1964. Home: 112 Park St Jacksonville IL 62650

JANECEK, LENORE ELAINE, chamber of commerce exec.; b. Chgo., May 2, 1944; d. Morris and Florence (Bear) Picker; M.A.J. in Speech Communications (talent scholar), Northeastern Ill. U., 1972; postgrad. (Ill. Assn. C. of C. Execs. scholar) Inst. for Organizational Mgmt., U. Notre Dame, 1979-80; m. John Janecek, Sept. 12, 1964; children—Frank, Michael. Adminstrv. asst., exec. dir. Ill. Mcpl. Retirement Fund, Chgo., 1963-65; personnel mgr. Profile Personnel, Chgo., 1965-68; personnel rep. Marsh Instrument Co., Skokie, Ill., 1971-73; restaurant mgt. Gold Mine Restaurant and What's Cooking Restaurant, Chgo., 1974-76; pres., owner Secretarial Office Services, Chgo., 1976-78; founder, exec. dir. Lincolnwood (Ill.) C. of C. and Industry, 1978—; rep. 10th dist. U.S. C. of C., 1978—. Mem. mktg. bd. Niles Twp. Sheltered Workshop; pres. Lincolnwood Sch. Dist. 74 Sch. Bd. Caucus; bd. mem., officer, founder Ill. Fraternal Order Police Ladies Aux.; bd. mem., officer Lincolnwood Girl's Softball League, PTA; mem. sch. curriculum com. Lincolnwood Bd. Edn. Mem. Am. C. of C. Execs., Ill. Assn. C. of C. Execs., Women in Mgmt., Nat. Assn. Female Execs., Am. Notary Soc., Ill. LWV, Nat. Council Jewish Women, Hadassah, City of Hope. Jewish. Home: 6707 N Monticello St Lincolnwood IL 60645 Office: 6731 N Lincoln Ave Lincolnwood IL 60645

JANIAK, THOMAS ANTHONY, educator; b. Oak Park, Ill., July 16, 1949. A.S. in Media, Coll. DuPage, Glen Ellyn, Ill., 1971; B.A. in Communications, Sangamon State U., Springfield, Ill., 1973, M.S. in Ednl. Adminstrn., Nat. Coll. Edn., Evanston, Ill., 1979. Media technician Sch. Dist. 201, Cicero Ill., 1969-71; dir. media activities, supr. performing arts Argo High Sch. Dist. 217, Summit Ill., 1973—; gen. mgr. WARG Broadcast Services, 1975—; project dir. Resource Devel. and Mgmt. Inst. of Chgo., 1980—; ind. cons. on cable TV, 1980—. Asst. dist. commr. Boy Scouts Am., 1970-72, post advisor, 1972-78, chmn., 1979-80; bd. dirs. Hull House Desplaines Valley Community Center, 1975-76. Mem. ALA, Ill. Library Assn., Am. Assn. Supervision and Curriculum Devel., Assn. Ednl. Communication and Tech., Nat. Assn. Broadcasters, Nat. Assn. Ednl. Broadcasters. Home: 1516 S 59th Ct Cicero IL 60650 Office: 7329 W 63rd St Summit IL 60501

JANICEK, RAYMOND PETER, lawyer; b. Chgo., Jan. 31, 1916; s. Emanuel A. and Mary T. (Pfeiffer) J.; A.A., Central YMCA Coll., Chgo., 1938; J.D., John Marshall Law Sch., Chgo., 1942; m. Annabelle M. VonEsh, Sept. 29, 1945; children—Raymond Peter, Judith M. Janicek Watson. Clk., U.S. Ct. Appeals, Chgo., 1936, firm Bell, Boyd & Marshall, Chgo., 1938-64; admitted to Ill. bar, 1942; partner firm Janicek & Novotny, Berwyn, Ill., 1964-70; pvt. practice, Berwyn, 1968—; mem. law faculty Morton Coll., Chgo., 1965-70. Bd. dirs. Bradley U. Dad's Assn., 1964-66, MacNeal Meml. Hosp., Berwyn, 1964-77; chmn. Berwyn Police Pension Bd., 1953-79, St. Leonard Sch. Bd., Berwyn, 1970-80; trustee West Suburban Mass Transit Dist.-BN Rd., 1970—, chmn., 1978—; trustee Fenwick High Sch. Bd., Oak Park, Ill., 1968—. Mem. Ill. Bar Assn., Chgo. Bar Assn., W.Suburban Bar Assn., Bohemian Lawyers Assn., Soc. Hosp. Attys. (charter), Am. Hosp. Assn. Roman Catholic. Home: 110 Rugeley Rd Western Springs IL 60558 Office: 3322 S Oak Park Ave Berwyn IL 60402

JANIS, MICHAEL JAMES, zoo dir.; b. Chgo., Apr. 2, 1947; s. Fabian S. and Phyllis J. (Underwood) J.; grad. Zoo Mgmt. Sch., N.C. State U., 1979; m. Victoria Elizabeth Christie, Dec. 23, 1967; 1 dau., Jennifer Lynn. Naturalist, Kingwood Center, Mansfield, Ohio, 1967-68, Forest Preserve Dist. DuPage County (Ill.), Lombard, 1968-69, Fla. State Parks, Ft. White, 1969-70; curator of birds Balt. Zoo, 1970-71; dir. Bolingbrook (Ill.) Park Dist., 1971-73; dir. outdoor edn. Hutchinson (Kans.) Recreation Commn., 1973-75; dir. Harvey County (Kans.) Parks Dept., Newton, 1975-77; dir. Akron (Ohio) Zool. Park, 1977—. Recipient Distinguished Service award Ill. Assn. Kiwanis Clubs, 1966; named Youth Conservationist of Year, Ill. Wildlife Fedn., 1966; others. Mem. Nat. (certified), Kans. (certified; dir. 1976-77, chmn. pub. info. com. 1976-77), Ohio (certified) recreation and parks assns., Am. Assn. Zool. Parks and Aquariums, Assn. Interpretive Naturalists, Ohio Mus. Assn., Natural Sci. for Youth Found., Kans. Assn. Biology Tchrs., Nat. Audubon Soc., Sand Hills Audubon Soc. (co-founder, dir. 1973-76). Contbr. articles to profl. jours. Office: Akron Zoological Park 500 Edgewood Ave Akron OH 44307

JANKE, OTTO MARTIN, hosp. adminstr.; b. Freystadt, Ger., Aug. 11, 1925; s. Martin and Alice (Gehring) J.; came to U.S., 1925, naturalized, 1933; B.A., Hamline U., St. Paul, 1952; M.H.A., U. Minn., 1954; J.D., William Mitchell Coll. Law, St. Paul, 1963; m. Inez I. Loverude, June 24, 1950; children—Cheryl Ann, Cynthia Rae, Paul G., Mark D., David T. Mem. staff Asbury Hosp., Mpls., 1947; chief admitting officer St. Barnabas Hosp., Mpls., 1947-52; purchasing agt., then adminstrv. resident Abbott Hosp., Mpls., 1952-54; mem. adminstrv. staff St. Paul Ramsey Hosp. and Med. Center, 1954-68, exec. dir., supt., 1968; adminstr. St. Paul-Ramsey Hosp. Community Mental Health Center, 1968-73; dir. hosps. and clinics Sacramento Med. Center, also asso. dean U. Calif. Med. Sch., Davis, 1973-75; v.p., adminstr. Christ Hosp., chmn. joint mgmt. com. Rush U. Sch. Medicine-Christ Hosp., Oak Lawn, Ill., 1976—; mem. Mayor St. Paul Task Force Central Data Processing for City of St. Paul and County of Ramey, 1966-73, Minn. Civil Service Oral Interview Bd., 1961-73, Inter Govt. Council, 1969-72; mem. faculty Bethel Coll., St. Paul, 1968, Xavier U., Cin., 1968, U. Minn., 1955-74; adj. faculty Northwestern U., Chgo., Govs. State U., Chgo., 1977—; v.p. Evang. Hosp. Assn., 1976. Bd. dirs. S.W. Cook County YMCA, 1977—, Nat. Residency Matching Bd., 1981—; mem. com. public policy United Ch. of Christ Health and Welfare Council, 1982. Served with USAAF, 1944-47. Mem. Am. Hosp. Assn., Met. Hosp. Planning Council, Am. Assn. Med. Colls., Nat. League Nursing, Am. Assn. Med. Adminstrs. (charter), Christian Soc. Health Care Execs. (exec. com., treas. 1981—), Oak Lawn C. of C. (dir.). Club: Rotary. Address: Christ Hosp 4440 W 95th St Oak Lawn IL 60453

JANKLOW, WILLIAM JOHN, gov. S.D.; b. Chgo., Sept. 13, 1939; B.S., J.D., U. S.D.; m. Mary Dean; children—Russell, Pamela, Shawna. Staff atty., later directing atty. and chief officer S.D. Legal Services System, 1967-73; chief prosecutor Office Atty. Gen. of S.D., 1973-74, atty. gen., 1975-78; gov. of S.D., 1979—; practice law, Pierre, S.D., 1972-73. Served with USMC, 1956-59; Vietnam. Mem. Am., S.D. trial lawyers assns., Am. Judicature Soc., Am., S.D. bar assns. Recipient Nat. award for Legal Excellence and Skill, Office of Equal Opportunity Legal Services. Office: Office of Gov State Capitol Pierre SD 57501*

JANOVER, ROBERT H., lawyer; b. N.Y.C., Aug. 17, 1930; s. Cyrus J. and Lillian D. (Horwitz) J.; B.A., Princeton U., 1952; J.D., Harvard U., 1957; m. Mary Elizabeth McMahon, Oct. 23, 1966; 1 dau., Laura Lockwood. Admitted to N.Y. State bar, 1957, U.S. Supreme Ct. bar, 1961, D.C. bar, 1966, Mich. bar, 1973; practice law, N.Y.C., 1957-65; cons. Office of Edn. HEW, 1965, legis. atty. Office of Gen. Counsel, HEW, 1965-66; asst. gen. atty. Mgmt. Assistance, Inc., N.Y.C., 1966-71; atty. Ford Motor Credit Co., Dearborn, Mich., 1971-74; mem. firm Freud, Markus, Slavin, Toohey & Galgan, Troy, Mich., 1974-79; individual practice law, Detroit, 1979—. Bd. dirs. Oakland Citizens League, 1976—, v.p., 1976-79, pres., 1979—; bd. dirs. Civic Searchlight, 1979—. Served to 1st lt. U.S. Army, 1952-54. Mem. Mich. State Bar, Am., N.Y. State, Detroit bar assns., Bar Assn. D.C., Assn. Bar of City of N.Y. Clubs: Univ., Players (Detroit); Harvard (N.Y.C.). Home: 685 Ardmoor Dr Birmingham MI 48010 Office: 1970 City Nat Bank Bldg Detroit MI 48226

JANOWICH, VINCENT ROBERT, data processing co. exec.; b. Cleve., Dec. 29, 1939; s. William Andrew and Frances M. Janowich; B.B.A., Cleve. State U., 1977; children—Jeffrey, Brian, Lisa. Indsl. engr. White Motor Co., Cleve., 1958-67; from systems analyst to asst. sec.-treas. Wolf Envelope Co., Cleve., 1967-78; v.p. Project Career, Inc., Cleve., 1978—; v.p., treas., dir. Creative Computing Co., Independence, Ohio, 1978—; sr. mgmt. cons. Greater Cleve. Growth Assn., Council Small Enterprises. Corp. rep. United Torch campaign, 1975. Mem. Assn. Systems Mgmt., Data Processing Mgmt. Assn., Cleve. Area Bd. Realtors, Am. Inst. Indsl. Engrs. (asso.). Republican. Roman Catholic. Home: 19577 Misty Lake Dr Strongsville OH 44136 Office: 4500 Rockside Rd Suite 130 Independence OH 44131

JANSEN, BERNARD JOSEPH, engr.; b. Rockville, Minn., Aug. 10, 1927; s. Barney C and Blanche (Brinkman) J.; B.A. cum laude, St. Johns U., Minn., 1950; M.A., St. Louis U., 1952; m. Sarah Kathryn Knight, Dec. 17, 1955; children—Kathryn L., Bernard Joseph,

Stephen T., David E. Teaching asst. St. Louis U., 1950-52; mathematician Ballistics Research Lab., Aberdeen (Md.) Proving Ground, 1953-54, summer 1955; instr. math. St. Johns U., Collegeville, Minn., 1954-56; with Univac Def. Systems Co., div. Sperry Rand Corp., St. Paul, 1956—, program mgr., 1967-76, staff cons. engr., 1976—; lectr. math. St. Thomas Coll., St. Paul, 1960-61; mem. com. spaceborne digital computers NASA, 1968-71. Active local Boy Scouts Am., 1946—; pres. home/sch. assn. Highland Cath. Sch., 1974-75; bd. dirs. Highland Cath. Sch. Bd., 1972-74; pres. parish council St. Leo's Ch., 1980-81. Served with USNR, 1945-46, AUS, 1952-54. Mem. Math. Assn. Am., Sigma Xi, Pi Mu Epsilon. Co-author papers, monograph. Home: 1859 Hillcrest Ave Saint Paul MN 55116 Office: care Sperry Univac Univac Park Saint Paul MN 55165

JANSEN, MERLE EUGENE, utilities co. exec.; b. Madison, Nebr., Mar. 17, 1934; s. Herbert F. and Agnes A. (Bartak) J.; A.A., Norfolk Jr. Coll., 1953; B.S. in Mech. Engring., U. Nebr., 1956; postgrad. U. Omaha, 1959; m. Darlene Ann Ebel, May 23, 1965; children—Michael Ellis, Julie Ann. Draftsman, Central Electric & Gas Co., Norfolk, Lincoln, Nebr., 1951-55, heating engr., Lincoln, 1955-56, dist. engr., 1956-60; div. utilization engr. Western Power & Gas Co., Columbus, Nebr., 1960-69; dist. mgr. Central Telephone & Utilities Corp., Norfolk, Nebr., 1969-75; S.D. region mgr. Minn. Gas Co., Sioux Falls, S.D., 1975—. Pres., Norfolk United Way, 1973; sec.-treas. Sioux Falls Downtown Devel. Corp.; sec. Jr. Achievement, Sioux Falls; mem. Sioux Falls Devel. Found.; bd. dirs. Sioux council Boy Scouts Am. Served with U.S. Army, 1956. Registered profl. engr., Nebr. Mem. Profl. Engrs. Nebr. (pres. 1970), Am. Gas Assn., Midwest Gas Assn., S.D. Engring. Soc., ASME, Sioux Falls C. of C. (pres. 1980). Republican. Lutheran. Clubs: Rotary (pres. 1974), Jaycees (v.p. Nebr., 1965-66), Minnehaha Country, Elks. Home: 4201 Birchwood Ave Sioux Falls SD 57103 Office: 114 S Main Ave Sioux Falls SD 57102

JANSMA, THEODORE JOHN, JR., psychologist; b. Phila., Apr. 17, 1943; s. Theodore John and Ruth Virginia (Gezon) J.; B.S., Calvin Coll., 1965; M.A., Mich. State U., 1967; Ph.D., Ill. Inst. Tech., 1971; m. Jo B. Battiston, June 28, 1969. Mental health rehab. counselor Chgo. State Hosp., 1967-69; staff psychologist Charles F. Read Zone Center, Chgo., 1969-71, adminstrv. psychologist, clin. chief service, 1971-72; staff psychologist Pine Rest Christian Hosp., Grand Rapids, Mich., 1972-80; dir. dept. psychology, 1977-80; pvt. practice psychology, Grand Rapids, 1980—; asst. clin. prof. psychiatry Mich. State U., 1974—. Exec. dir. Project Talk, 1970-72, Chgo. Registered psychologist, Ill.; lic. cons. psychologist, Mich.; Nat. Rehab. Study grantee, 1965-67. Mem. Am. Psychol. Assn., Mich. Psychol. Assn., Christian Assn. Psychol. Studies, Grand Rapids Area Psychol. Assn. (chmn. ethics com. 1979-80). Mem. Christian Reformed Ch. Home: 7434 Thornapple River Dr Caledonia MI 49316 Office: 3330 Claystone St SE Grand Rapids MI 49506

JANSSEN, DONALD PHILLIP, telephone co. exec.; b. Stuart, Iowa, Mar. 20, 1924; s. Philip Bernard and Catherine Margaret (Happe) J.; student Iowa State U., 1942-43, 46-48; m. Katherine Ellen Hulsizer, Apr. 29, 1951 (dec. Apr. 1979); children—Lynn Marie, Kevin Charles; m. 2d, Caroline Beth Thompson, July 19, 1980; stepchildren—Cynthia, Mary, Jean, Chris, Robert, Katherine. Lineman, Northwestern Bell Telephone Co., Marshalltown, Iowa, 1950-51, engr., 1951-60, dist. engr., 1960-79; owner, pres. Pentz Appliance & TV Inc., Marshalltown, 1979—. Vice pres. N.E. Council Alcoholism, 1967-71, pres., 1972—; councilman, Cedar Falls, Iowa, 1966-72. Served with USAAF, 1943-45. Mem. Marshalltown C. of C. Clubs: Sertoma, Elks (Cedar Falls). Home: 1320 W Main St Marshalltown IA 50158 Office: 13 S Center St Marshalltown IA 50158

JANSSEN, GAIL EDWIN, banker; b. Oconto, Wis., Dec. 11, 1930; s. Ernest Harold and Helen (Jelinske) J.; B.S. in Agr., U. Wis., 1960, B.S. in Mech. Engring., 1962; m. Janice F. Detaeje, May 23, 1953; children—Gary, Joel. Operator dairy farm, Wis., 1949-57; advisor farm electrification Wis. Public Service Corp. of Green Bay, 1960-61; design engr., asst. chief engr. Gehl Co., West Bend, Wis., 1962-68; chief engr., v.p. engring. Badger Northland, Inc. subs. Massey-Ferguson, Kaukauna, Wis., 1968-71; pres., gen. mgr., 1971-77; pres., chmn. bd. F&M Bank, F & M Bancorp., Inc., Kaukauna, 1977—. Dir., Nat. Agrl. Communications Bd., Wis.-Agri-Bus. Council; pres. Wis. 4-H Found. Recipient Engr. of Year award Am. Soc. Agrl. Engrs., Wis. sect. 1973. Mem. Nat. Soc. Profl. Engrs., Wis. Soc. Profl. Engrs., Am. Soc. Agrl. Engrs. (chmn. Wis. sect., vice chmn. Wis.-Ill. region, chmn. 1968-71). Clubs: Rotary, Kiwanis, KC. Office: F&M Bank 4th St Plaza Kaukauna WI 54130

JANSSEN, TERRANCE ERNEST, real estate developer, assn. exec.; b. Yankton, S.D., Oct. 18, 1942; s. Ernest A. and Kathryn S. (Markeson) J.; student public schs.; m. Glenna J. Milander, Apr. 29, 1961; children—Terasa, Ross, Joel. Automobile salesman, then ins. salesman, mortgage banker, 1960-72; pres. Golden West Corp., South Sioux City, Nebr., 1972-74, Janssen/Dak. Corp., Beresford, S.D., 1974-79, Janssen Cos., Beresford, 1979-80, Hudson, Wis., 1980—, Am. Council Continuing Edn., Stillwater, Minn., 1981—; charter pres. S. Sioux City Home Builders Assn., 1972-74. Past pres., bd. dirs. Beresford Bus. and Indsl. Devel. Corp. Mem. Nat. Assn. Home Builders (various awards), Am. Soc. Planning Ofcls., Rural Am. Republican. Presbyterian. Clubs: Hudson Country, Southview Country, Rotary. Home: Riverview Acres Route 2 Box 116 Hudson WI 54016 Office: PO Box 8 Stillwater MN 55082

JANZEN, NORINE MADELYN QUINLAN, med. technologist; b. Fond du Lac, Wis., Feb. 9, 1943; d. Joseph Wesley and Norma Edith (Gustin) Quinlan; B.S., Marian Coll., 1965; med. technologist St. Agnes Sch. Med. Tech., Fond du Lac, 1966; M.A., Central Mich. U., 1980; m. Douglas Mac Arthur Janzen, July 18, 1970; 1 son, Justin James. Med. technologist Mayfair Med. Lab., Wauwatosa, Wis., 1966-69; supr. med. technologist Dr.'s Mason, Chamberlain, Franke, Klink & Kamper, Milw., 1969-76, Parkview Med. Assos., Ltd., 1976—. Substitute poll worker Fond du Lac Democratic Com., 1964-65; mem. Dem. Nat. Com., 1973—. Mem. Nat., Wis. (chmn. awards com. 1976-77, co-chmn. Southeastern suprs. group 1976-77, pres.-elect 1981-82, dir. 1977—), Milw. (pres. 1971-72; dir. 1972-73) socs. med. technologists, Communications of Wis. (originator, chmn. 1977-79), LWV, Alpha Delta Theta (nat. dist. chmn. 1967-69; nat. alumnae dir. 1969-71), Methodist. Home: N 98 W 17298 Dotty Way Germantown WI 53022 Office: 1004 E Sumner St Hartford WI 53027

JARACZ, RONALD FRANK, Realtor; b. East Chicago, Ind., Apr. 26, 1931; s. Frank Stanley and Julia (Kubacki) J.; B.S., Ind. U., 1957; m. Janice Pandak, June 25, 1959 (div. May 1963); 1 son, John Ronald; m. 2d, Pamela DuFrain, Mar. 18, 1972; 1 dau., Julia Avis. Mgr., Wieklinski Realty Co., East Chicago, Ind., 1957-62, Elks Realty Co., East Chicago, 1964-68; owner Jaracz Realty Co., East Chicago, 1962—; v.p., dir. Elks Realty Co. Mem. Ind. Selective Service Bd., 1964—, now pres.; mem. real estate adv. bd. Ind. U., 1966—; chief land appraiser for North Twp. re-assessment, 1969-70, 78-79; mem. East Chicago Plan Commn., 1973—, v.p., 1975-78, pres., 1978—. Asst. county chmn. Republican Party, 1963-67. Served with AUS, 1952-54. Mem. Ind. Real Estate Assn. (dir.), East Chicago Bd. Realtors (pres. 1960-72). Roman Catholic. Rotarian, Elk (exalted ruler 1963-64). Home: 7541 Woodmar Ave Hammond IN 46323 Office: 809 W Chicago Ave East Chicago IL 46312

JARDON, OSCAR MAX, orthopedic surgeon; b. Long Island, Kans., Dec. 23, 1931; s. Robert Fredrick and Dorothy Dee (Yantiss) J.; B.S., Nebr. State Coll., Kearney, 1953; M.D., U. Nebr., 1957; children—Karla K., Eric M. Practice medicine specializing in orthopedic surgery, Omaha, 1969-77; chief of med. staff Sacred Heart Hosp., Loup City, Nebr., 1961-68; chief resident in orthopedic surgery service U. Nebr., Omaha, 1968-71; asso. prof. dept. orthopedic surgery, 1971—; cons. orthopedic surgery Omaha VA Hosp., 1971—; bd. dirs. Nebr. Arthritis Found., 1971—. Mem. Nebr. Republican Central Com., 1962-67. Served as capt. M.C., U.S. Army, 1958-61; col. USAF Res. Decorated Meritorious Service medal; recipient Outstanding Community Service award Loup City C. of C., 1968; R. Shrock award as outstanding orthopedic surgery resident U. Nebr., 1970; Sir Henry Wellcome medal and prize, 1981. Diplomate Am. Bd. Orthopedic Surgery. Mem. ACS, Am. Acad. Orthopedic Surgery, Assn. Mil. Surgeons U.S. Contbr. articles to med. jours.; research on muscle disease. Home: 5603 Oak Hills Dr Omaha NE 68137

JARETT, IRWIN M., acct., educator; b. Lubbock, Tex., Apr. 28, 1930; s. Jerry and Nellie (Bloomberg) J.; B.A., Tex. Tech. Coll., 1958, M.B.A.; Ph.D. in Acctg., La. State U., 1964; m. Rhoda Goldman, May 28, 1952; children—Andrew Robert, Debra Hope, Alex Scott. Instr., Tex. Tech. Coll., 1957-58; mgr. adminstrv. services div. Arthur Andersen & Co., St. Louis, 1962-68; chmn. acctg. So. Ill. U., Edwardsville, 1968-71, asso. dean health care planning Med. Sch., Springfield, 1971-75, prof. med. econs., 1975-81; founder, pres. Irwin M. Jarett C.P.A. Ltd., 1979—; adj. prof. Tulane U. Sch. Public Health, New Orleans, 1974-80. C.P.A., Mo., Ill., La., Tex. Mem. Am. Inst. C.P.A.'s, Ill. Soc. C.P.A.'s (chmn. state of the art), Continuing Profl. Edn. Found. Mem. editorial bd. Computer Graphics for Mgmt., 1981—; contbr. articles to profl. jours. Office: 960 Clock Tower Dr Springfield IL 62704

JARICH, CAROLE DOLORES, phys. therapist; b. Milw., June 19, 1939; d. Bernard and Angeline Regina (Kordas) Shaleski; B.S. in Phys. Therapy, U. Wis., 1962; m. Nicholas Jarich, June 1, 1963; children—Danielle, Peter. Staff phys. therapist St. Luke's Hosp., Milw., 1962-66; chief phys. therapist St. Annes Home for the Aged, Milw., 1966—; pres., dir., chmn. bd. Phys. Therapy Services, Inc., Greenfield, Wis., 1967—; owner, mgr. Needle in the Haystack, Minocqua, Wis., 1971-73, Harbor Stitchery, Greenfield, 1975-77; cons. for Volunteers of Am., Retirement Community Center and Schs. Benefactor, Little Sisters of the Poor, 1966—; volunteer naturalist Wehr Nature Center, Milw., 1979—. Mem. Am. Phys. Therapy Assn., Wis. Phys. Therapy Assn., Am. Assn. on Mental Deficiency, Southeastern Wis. Health System and Agy., Wis. Lung Assn., Am. Heart Assn., C. of C., Am. Forestry Assn., Nat. Audubon Soc., Nat. Wildlife Fedn. Roman Catholic. Clubs: Sierra, YWCA, Nat. Fedn. Bus. and Profl. Women. Home: S 58 W22495 Weiland Dr Waukesha WI 53186 Office: 7517 W Coldspring Rd Greenfield WI 53220

JAROS, KEVIN LARSON, food co. exec.; b. Virginia, Minn., Aug. 29, 1951; s. Floyd D. and Joyce Marilyn (Larson) J.; A.B. (N.W. Paper Found. scholar 1969-73), Brown U., 1973; M.B.A. (fellow, 1974-76), Harvard U., 1976; m. Margaret Helen Bernhard, Nov. 3, 1979. Asst. to controller NW Paper div. Potlatch Corp., Cloquet, Minn., 1973-74; mktg. asst. Flour div. Gen. Mills, Mpls., 1976-77, asst. product mgr., Cereal div., 1977-78, product mgr. New Cereals Group, Big "G„ div., Mpls., 1979—; tutor Harvard Bus. Sch., Cambridge, Mass., 1975-76. Mem. Delta Phi Omega. Home: 14027 Orchard Rd Minnetonka MN 55343 Office: PO Box 1113 Minneapolis MN 55440

JARRELL, ROBERT HOMER, ednl. adminstr.; b. Harrisburg, Ill., July 16, 1923; s. John L. and Catherine (Grace) J.; B.S., U. Ill., 1946; M.S., Ill. Inst. Tech., 1961; m. Elizabeth Jane Beidelman, Feb. 26, 1949; children—Katherine, Michael, Steven, Peter. Accountant, Ill. Farm Supply Co., 1947-50; asst. comptroller Ill. Inst. Tech., 1950-54, comptroller, 1954-62, bus. mgr., 1962—, lectr. in accounting, 1961—; treas. Argonne U. Assos., 1979—. Chmn. edn. div. Ill. Cancer Crusade, Am. Cancer Soc., 1960-63, 65, 66; mem. adv. bd. Salvation Army Settlement, Chgo., chmn., 1975-77; mem. pub. edn. com. Chgo. unit Am. Cancer Soc., vice chmn., 1974-79, chmn., 1979—; mem. adv. com. Sch. Dist. 203, 1967, 71-72; town clk. Lisle Twp., 1973—; jury commr. 18th Jud. Dist. Ill., 1975—, chmn., 1979—; chmn. Lisle Twp. Republican Orgn., 1976-78; mem. exec. com. Du Page County Central Rep. Com., 1976-78. Mem. Fin. Execs. Inst. (sec. 1964-65), Nat. Assn. Ednl. Buyers (sec.-treas. Ill.-Wis. sect. 1969, chmn. 1971), Nat., Central assns. coll. and univ. bus. officers, Alpha Kappa Psi, Delta Sigma Rho. Republican. Congregationalist. Club: Rotary. Home: 1204 Cardinal Ln Naperville IL 60540 Office: 3300 S Federal St Chicago IL 60616

JARRETT, JERRY VERNON, banker; b. Abilene, Tex., Oct. 31, 1931; s. Walter Elwood and Myrtle Elizabeth (Allen) J.; B.B.A., U. Okla., 1957; M.B.A., Harvard U., 1963; m. Martha Ann McCabe, June 13, 1953; children—Cynthia Ann, Charles Elwood, Christopher Allen, John Carlton. Gen. sales mgr. Tex. Coca-Cola Bottling Co., Abilene, 1957-61; exec. v.p. Marine Midland Bank, N.Y.C., 1963-73; exec. v.p. Cleve. Trust Co., 1973-76, vice-chmn., 1976-78, pres., 1978—; pres. Cleve. Corp. Served with USAAF, 1950-54. Mem. Phi Gamma Delta. Co-author: Creative Collective Bargaining, 1964. Office: AmeriTrust 900 Euclid Ave Cleveland OH 44101

JARVIS, EDGAR ALLAN, telephone co. exec.; b. Ulysses, Kans., Nov. 16, 1928; s. Edgar Wilson and Lora Leone (Hoss) J.; B.S. in Bus. Adminstrn., U. Kans., 1951. With Southwestern Bell Telephone Co., 1951—, traffic supr., Topeka, 1966-69, div. mgr. operator services, Wichita, Kans., 1969—. Gen. campaign chmn. United Way Wichita and Sedgwick County, 1978, pres., 1980; pres. Health Systems Agy. S.E. Kans., 1975-77; chmn. Kans. Statewide Health Coordinating Council, 1976-80, Kans. Emergency Med. Services Council, 1979-80. Served with AUS, 1946-47. Recipient cert. award Kans. Dept. Health and Environ., 1981. Mem. Am. Public Health Assn., Am. Health Planning Assn., Mental Health Assn. Kans., Kans. Assn. Commerce and Industry, Wichita Area C. of C., U.S. C. of C. Republican. Club: Topeka. Home: 341 N Crestway St Wichita KS 67208 Office: 154 N Broadway Room 1210 Wichita KS 67202

JARVIS, JOHN EDMUND, bank exec.; b. Winfield, Kans., Dec. 25, 1908; s. George L. and Jess B. (Lynn) J.; A.B., U. Kans., Lawrence, 1931; m. Shirley Johnson, Feb. 14, 1940; children—Ed, Paul. With First Nat. Bank, Winfield, 1931—, exec. v.p., 1961-67, pres., 1967—, also dir.; dir. Kans. Bankers Surety Ins. Co., 1962. Mem. exec. bd. dirs. Quivira council Boy Scouts Am., 1964, recipient Silver Beaver award, 1969; trustee Snyder Research Found., Winfield, 1960. Served to lt. USNR, 1946-52. Commd. col. aide-de-camp Gov. N.Mex., 1962. Mem. Am., Kans. ind. bankers assns., Bankers Adminstrn. Inst., Bank Mktg. Assn., Inst. Community Bankers, VFW, Am. Legion, Nat. Cowboy Hall of Fame (charter mem.), Sigma Alpha Epsilon. Republican. Presbyterian (trustee). Club: Winfield Country. Office: 900 Main St Winfield KS 67156

JARVIS, PHILLIP ROBERT, insulated products mfg. co. exec.; b. Winfield, Kans., Feb. 27, 1942; s. Robert Henry and Alta Mae (Dunbar) J.; student U. Kans., 1960-63; B.A., Southwestern Coll. at Winfield, 1964; children—Jeffrey Phillip, David Alan, Kieran Brian, Brendan Duncan. Mgr. data processing Jarvis Auto Supply Inc., Winfield, 1963-73; mgr. info. services Gott Corp., Winfield, 1973-81, mgr. employee benefits and ins., 1981—; mem. data processing adv. com. Cowley County Community Jr. Coll. Instl. rep. Boy Scouts Am.; bd. dirs. Winfield United Way, pres., 1980; elder, mem. Christian edn. com., chmn. worship com. Presbyn. Ch. Mem. Nat. Assn. Accountants, Winfield Jr. C. of C. (v.p. 1965-66), Nat. Assn. System 3 Users, Wichita Area Assn. System 3 Users, Data Processing Mgmt. Assn., Risk and Ins. Mgmt. Soc., U.S. Angus Assn., Kans. Angus Assn., Winfield C. of C. (chmn. housing com., mem. long-range planning com.). Club: Winfield Country. Home: 402 E 12th St Winfield KS 67156 Office: 1616 Wheat Rd Winfield KS 67156

JASKOVIAK, PAUL ANTHONY, chiropractor; b. Evergreen Park, Chgo., Dec. 6, 1946; s. Larry James and Ina Janet (Lindsay) J.; B.S., Loyola U., Chgo., 1968; D.C., Nat. Coll. Chiropractic, Lombard, Ill., 1975; div.; children—Debra, Jennifer, Laura. Clk., anatomy and chemistry Nat. Coll. Chiropractic, Lombard, Ill., 1974-75, dir. acupuncture research program, 1975—, dir. chiropractic asst.'s programs, 1978—, acting chmn. dept. physiol. therapeutics, 1977—, asst. prof., 1978—, dean postgrad. div., 1978—; research asso. Argonne (Ill.) Nat. Labs., 1975-77; individual practice chiropractic, Villa Park, Ill., 1977-78; lectr. on acupuncture. Item reviewer, mem. physiotherapy test bd. Nat. Bd. Chiropractic Examiners, 1977—; chiropractic assts. com. Council on Chiropractic Edn., 1978—; team mem. Cosmetology Accrediting Commn., 1978—. Served with U.S. Army, 1969-72. Recipient Clyde Martin ann. award, 1978. Fellow Internat. Coll. Chiropractors; mem. Ill. Chiropractic Soc. (chmn. medicare com. 1978, chiropractic assts. com. 1979—), Am. Chiropractic Assn. (pres. Council on Neurology 1978—), Ill. Acad. Sci. Republican. Roman Catholic. Club: Am. Legion. Home: 606 Glendale Glen Ellyn IL 60137 Office: Nat Coll Chiropractic 200 E Roosevelt Rd Lombard IL 60148

JASPER, A. WILLIAM, farm orgn. exec.; b. Phila., June 3, 1925; s. G. Leonard and Jessie Edna Jasper; B.Sc. in Agr., U. Vt., 1950; M.Sc., Ohio State U., 1951; Ph.D., Cornell U., 1954; m. Dorothy Irene Moore, Feb. 16, 1946; children—William Mark, Peggy Joy; m. 2d, Dolores M. Van Loan, July 11, 1980. Mktg. specialist Dept. Agr., Washington, 1951-52, Ithaca, N.Y., 1952-54; mng. editor Poultry Tribune, Mt. Morris, Ill., 1954-57; asso. prof. mktg. and farm mgmt. Cornell U., 1977-78; dir. promotion Poultry and Egg Nat. Bd., Chgo., 1958-59; asst. dir. comodity div. Am. Farm Bur. Fedn., Chgo., 1959-66; mgr. poultry div. Am. Agrl. Mktg. Assn., Chgo., 1963-71; successively asst. sec. market devel. and research, dir. poultry dept. Am. Farm Bur. Fedn., Park Ridge, Ill., 1971-79, dir. mktg. div., 1979—; gen. mgr. Am. Agrl. Mktg. Assn., Park Ridge, 1979-81; dir. tech. services, internat. v.p. Agrimerica, Inc., Northbrook, Ill., 1981—; cons., lectr. FAO. Mem. Mt. Morris High Sch. Bd. Edn., 1956-57, Citizens Adv. Com. Pleasant Hill, DuPage County, Ill., 1960-65. Served with AUS, 1943-46. Decorated officier l'Ordre du Merite Agricole (France); named Disting. Alumnus, Ohio State U., 1978; recipient Gold medal Soc. d'Aviculture de France, 1978. Mem. Am. Poultry Hist. Soc. (past pres.; award of merit 1966), Poultry Sci. Assn., Quartermaster Assn., Am. Farm Econs. Assn., World Poultry Sci. Assn. (past pres.). Republican. Club: Australian-Am. Wine (Chgo.). Author: The Poultry Industry, 1958, Poultry History, 1823-1973 (Marketing), 1974; also articles, bulls. Home: 927 S Dryden Pl Arlington Heights IL 60005 Office: 1829 Stanley St Northbrook IL 60062

JASPER, ELBERT BAKER, veterinarian; b. Berea, Ohio, May 11, 1923; s. Jay Elbert and Marion Bethia (Baker) J.; student Baldwin Wallace Coll., 1941-42; D.V.M., Ohio State U., 1949; m. Carolyn Agatha Beach, Oct. 27, 1951. Area veterinarian U.S. Dept. Agr., Ohio, 1949-54, Kans., 1955-56, asst. veterinarian in charge State of N.J., 1956-59, asst. veterinarian in charge State of Tenn., 1959-61, mem. program appraisal staff, Washington, 1961-63, veterinarian in charge State of Md., 1963-65, mem. import export staff, Hyattsville, Md., 1965-71; gen. practice veterinary medicine specializing in small animals, Berea, 1973—. Served with Veterinary Corps, U.S. Army, 1944-46; CBI. Mem. Am., Ohio veterinary med. assns., Cleve. Acad. Veterinary Medicine, U.S. Power Squadron. Methodist. Club: Masons. Home and Office: 84 West St Berea OH 44017

JAUTOKAS, VICTOR, electronics engr.; b. Rietavas, Lithuania, Nov. 29, 1929; s. Zigmas and Emilia (Jokubaitis) J.; came to U.S., 1950, naturalized, 1954; B.S. in Elec. Engring., Ill. Inst. Tech., 1963; m. Ruth Kerelis, Aug. 30, 1958; children—Paul, Raminta. Design engr. Chgo. Ry. Equipment Co., 1957-63; project engr. Nat. Video Corp., Chgo., 1963-69; circuit designer Verson Allsteel Press Co., Chgo., 1969-72; communications engr. Chgo. Police Dept., 1972—; cons. to Facilities Design, Ltd. Served with U.S. Army, 1951-53. Registered profl. engr., Ill. Mem. Nat. Soc. Profl. Engrs., Associated Pub. Safety Communications Officers, Am.-Lithuanian Engrs. and Architects Soc., Am. Legion. Democrat. Roman Catholic. Editor: Engineering Word, 1974—; author tech. articles in field. Home: 5859 S Whipple St Chicago IL 60629 Office: 1121 S State St Chicago IL 60605

JAVINSKY, PHILLIP ERWIN, engring. co. exec.; b. Mpls., Feb. 13, 1941; s. Simon and Molly (Weinshenker) J.; student Northwestern Electronics, 1964-66; m. Marie Lahusky, Apr. 23, 1962; children—Phillip, Donna, Diane, Stephen. Tech. rep., Honeywell, Inc., Fla., Minn., 1965-72; pres., chmn. bd. J & W Instruments, Inc., St. Paul, 1972—. Served with USAF, 1962. Mem. Soc. Die Casting Engrs. Home: 59 E Golden Lake Rd Circle Pines MN 55014 Office: 4800 Mustang Circle Saint Paul MN 55112

JAWADEKAR, MAKARAND SHRINIWAS, educator; b. Nasik, India, Jan. 14, 1951; s. Shriniwas Mahadev and Meena Shriniwas (Bhadkamkar) J.; came to U.S., 1976, naturalized, 1976; M.Pharm., Bombay U., 1974; postgrad. U. Minn., 1976—. Jr. research fellow U. Bombay (India), 1972-74; exec. prodn. pharmacist May & Baker Ltd., Bombay, 1975-76; research asst. U. Minn., Mpls., 1976-81, project asst., teaching asso. I, 1977—; research scientist Pfizer Central Research, 1982—; participant World Sanskrit Conf., Paris, 1977, Weimar, E. Ger., 1979, Varanasi, India, 1981. Singhanee Research fellow, 1972-73; Council of Sci. and Indsl. Research, Govt. of India research fellow, 1973-74; J.N. Tata fellow, 1975-76. Mem. Am. Name Soc., Indo-Am. Assn., Minn. Acad. Sci., Am. Pharm. Assn., Indian Pharm. Assn. Contbr. articles to profl. jours.; appeared in movie Foolin' Around, 1978. Home: 614 Ontario St Minneapolis MN 55414 Office: Coll Pharmacy Univ of Minn Washington Ave Minneapolis MN 55455

JAWADI, MUHAMMED HUSAIN, physician, educator; b. Warangal, India, Aug. 25, 1946; came to U.S., 1971, naturalized, 1978; s. Muhamed and Najmunnaisen (Begum) Ghouse; student Saifabad Sci. Coll., 1964; M.B.B.S., Osmania Med. Coll., 1971; m. Jameela Hameed, June 9, 1974; children—Haroon, Khalid. Med. resident St. Peter's Hosp., Albany, N.Y., 1971-72; resident internal medicine St. Mary's Health Center, St. Louis, 1972-73, Phila. Gen.

Hosp., U. Pa., 1973-74; fellow endocrinology and metabolism U. N.Mex., Albuquerque, 1974-75, U. Colo. Med. Sch., Denver, 1975-77; staff physician VA Hosp., Wichita, Kans., 1977—; asst. prof. dept. internal medicine U. Kans. Sch. Medicine, Wichita, 1977—; mem. screening com. Am. Heart Assn., 1978. Mem. A.C.P., Am. Soc. Internal Medicine, Am. Coll. Clin. Pharmacology. Islam. Contbr. articles to profl. jours. Home: 6713 E 32d St Ct Wichita KS 67226 Office: 1001 N Minneapolis St Wichita KS 67214

JAYABALAN, VEMBLASERRY, nuclear medicine physician, radiologist; b. India, Apr. 3, 1937; s. Parameswara and Janakay (Amma) Menon; came to U.S., 1970; B.Sc., Madras (India) Christian Coll., 1955; M.B., B.S. Jipmer U., India, 1961; Diploma in Med. Radiodiagnosis, U. Liverpool (Eng.), 1967; m. May 2, 1963; children—Kishore, Suresh. Intern, Jipmer Hosp., Pondicherry, India, 1961-62; resident in cardiology K.E.M. Hosp., Bombay, India, 1962-63; resident in radiology Mt. Sinai Hosp., Chgo., 1970-72; fellow in nuclear medicine Michael Reese Hosp., Chgo., 1972-73; dir. nuclear medicine Hurley Med. Center, Flint, Mich., 1973—; asst. clin. prof. radiology Mich. State U. Diplomate Am. Bd. Radiology, Am. Bd. Nuclear Medicine. Fellow Internat. Coll. Physicians; mem. Mich. Coll. Nuclear Medicine (mem. legis. com.), Genesee County Med. Soc. (mem. credential and membership com.), Mich. Med. Soc., Radiol. Soc. N.Am., Am. Coll. Nuclear Medicine, Am. Coll. Nuclear Physicians, Brit. Inst. Radiology, Royal Coll. Radiology, Soc. Nuclear Medicine (mem. program com. Central chpt.). Home: 5495 Floria Dr Swartz Creek MI 48473 Office: Hurley Med Center Flint MI 48502

JAYCOX, KATHLEEN MARIE, coll. dean; July 2, 1948; d. Richard Edward and Eileen Katherine (Penn) J.; B.A., U. Ill., Chgo., 1969, M.A., Urbana, 1972, postgrad., 1975-78. Tchr. English and biology Visitation High Sch., Chgo., 1969-71; instr. English, Western Ill. U., Macomb, 1972-75; instr. Lincoln (Ill.) Coll., 1978-79, dir. Tri-County Programs, 1979-81; asst. dean continuing edn. Morton Coll., Cicero, Ill., 1981—. Mem. Nat. Council Tchrs. English, Conf. Coll. Composition and Communications, Adult Edn. Assn. U.S., Ill. Council Continuing and Higher Edn., LWV, Phi Delta Kappa. Roman Catholc. Office: 3801 S Central Cicero IL

JAYDOS, ROBERT ANTHONY, architect; b. Chgo., Feb. 5, 1938; s. Anthony Walter and Angeline Rita J.; B.Arch., U. Ill., 1968; children by former marriage—Robert Anthony, Christine Marie, Shari Anne. Designer, Perkins & Will, Chgo., 1968-69; designer, asst. job capt. Loebl, Schlossman, Bennett & Dart, Chgo., 1969-71; draftsman Graham, Anderson, Probst & White, Chgo., 1971-72; job capt. Marshall Lieb & Assos., Chgo., 1972-73; pres., design cons. Smith & Jaydos Inc., Elk Grove Village, Ill., owner, operator Robert A. Jaydos & Assos., Ltd., Elk Grove Village, 1973-80, pres., 1980—. Served with USAF, 1955-59. Lic. comml. pilot. Mem. U. Ill. Alumni Assn. (life), Chgo. Assn. Commerce and Industry, AIA (asso.), Art Inst. Chgo. Club: Kiwanis. Office: Crystal Towers 1747 Crystal Ln Mount Prospect IL 60056

JAYE, DAVID ROBERT, hosp. exec.; b. Chgo., Aug. 15, 1930; s. David Robert and Gertrude J.; B.S., Loyola U., Chgo., 1952; M.H.A., Northwestern U., 1954; m. Mary Ann Scanlan, June 6, 1953; children—David, Jeffery, Kathleen. Asst. adminstr. Sharon (Pa.) Gen. Hosp., 1957-60; asst. adminstr. St. Josephs Hosp., Joliet, Ill., 1960-65; adminstr. Sacred Heart Hosp., Allentown, Pa., 1965-69; pres. St. Josephs Hosp., Marshfield, Wis., 1969—. Bd. dirs. North Central Health Planning Assn. Served to 1st lt. Med. Service Corps, USAF, 1954-57. Fellow Am. Coll. Hosp. Adminstrs. (bd. regents); mem. Am. Hosp. Assn., Wis. Hosp. Assn. (trustee, chmn. 1977-78), Catholic Hosp. Assn. (trustee), Marshfield C. of C. (dir.). Roman Catholic. Clubs: Rotary; K.C.; Elks; Riveredge Country. Contbr. articles to profl. jours. Home: 1125 Ridge Rd Marshfield WI 54449 Office: St Josephs Hosp Marshfield WI 54449

JEANMARIE, MARY RUTH MARIA, ednl. adminstr.; b. McCormick, S.C., Jan. 22, 1935; d. Joseph and Irene Gilchrist; B.S., Wayne State U., 1959, M.A., 1962, Ed.D., 1978; m. Henry Jeanmarie, June 18, 1961; 1 child. Tchr., U. Mich., Ann Arbor, 1959-62; reading specialist Region 7, Detroit, 1962-67; asst. prin. Courtis Elem. Sch., Detroit, 1968-75, prin., 1975—. Scholarship chmn. Wayne State U., 1980-81. Recipient Humanitarian award God's Humanitarian Garden, 1978, Achievement award Right-to-Read Project, 1979; 4 A's award Courtis Sch. PTA, 1980; Resolution award from Senate, State of Mich., 1981. Pi Lambda Theta. Roman Catholic.

JEANNE, DONALD JOSEPH, sch. counselor; b. New Orleans, Sept. 1, 1937; s. Charles Joseph and Myrtle Estelle (Simmons) J.; B.S. in Biol. Scis., Xavier U., New Orleans, 1962; M.Ed. in Psychology, U. Ill., 1976; Seminarian Congregation of Missions, Vincentian Fathers, 1952-58, postgrad., 1979—; m. Maria R. Alicea, June 25, 1966; children—Donald Patrick, John Paul and Robert Vincent (twins). Epidemiologist, USPHS, 1963-64; tchr. math. Crane High Sch., Chgo., 1964-65, counselor, 1965, 69—, tchr. biology adult edn. center, 1968-73, faculty liaison to Alumni Assn.; tchr. adult edn. Benito Juarez Center, Chgo. City Coll.; counselor/coordinator Neighborhood Youth Corps, 1965-69; dist. 9 CETA coordinator, Chgo. Bd. Edn., 1976—. Pres., P.R.O.S. Neighborhood Orgn., 1977, 79, 80, 81—; pres. N.W. Community Orgn., 1978, 79, fin. chmn., 1981, 82; mem. 13th dist. steering com. Chgo. Police Dept. Mem. Am. Fedn. Tchrs., Chgo. Tchrs. Union, Phi Delta Kappa. Democrat. Roman Catholic. Home: 2322 W Grand Ave Chicago IL 60612 Office: 2245 W Jackson Blvd Chicago IL 60612

JECK, HOWARD SHEFFIELD, surgeon; b. N.Y.C., July 14, 1921; s. Howard Sheffield and Norine Harriet (Lever) J.; A.B., Yale U., 1942; M.D., Cornell U., 1945; m. Eileen Isabel McLellan, May 13, 1950; children—H. Sheffield, III, Allister M., Lynne T. Intern in surgery N.Y. Hosp., 1945-46; asst. resident in neurosurgery, 1948-49; asst. resident surgery Cornell div. Bellevue Hosp., N.Y.C., 1949-50; asst. resident surgery VA Med. Teaching Group Kennedy Hosp., Memphis, 1950-52, sr. resident surgery, 1952-53; practice medicine specializing in surgery, Torrington, Conn., 1953-54, St. Joseph, Mo., 1954-56, Oxford, Ohio, 1956—; bd. trustees and dirs. McCullough Hyde Meml. Hosp., Oxford, 1962-69, chmn., 1964-66; asst. prof. clin. surgery Wright State U. Sch. Medicine, 1975—; pres. med. adv. council Blue Cross of Southwestern Ohio. Served to lt. (j.g.) USN, 1946-48. Diplomate Am. Bd. Surgery. Fellow A.C.S. (chmn. community hosp. com. Ohio chpt.); mem. AMA, Ohio State Med. Assn., Butler County Med. Soc. (pres. 1976-77), R. F. Bowers Surg. Soc., Assn. Yale Alumni (rep.). Republican. Presbyterian. Clubs: Rotary (Oxford), Oxford Country, Net-Set Tennis; Cin. Yale. Home: 4141 Reily Rd Oxford OH 45056 Office: 5995 Fairfield Rd Oxford OH 45056

JECMEN, JOHN JOSEPH, mfg. co. exec.; b. Chgo., Jan. 16, 1916; s. James and Marie (Steker) J.; student DePaul U., 1933-37, Ill. Inst. Tech., 1942; m. Betty R. Malek, June 18, 1938. Pres., chmn. bd. Harris Preble Co. mfg. elevator doors, Cicero, Ill., 1933—. Mem. NAM, DePaul U. Assos., Nat. Assn. Elevator Contractors, Ill. Mfrs. Assn., Internat. Bus. Council, Execs. Club Chgo., Chgo. Assn. Commerce and Industry, Briarwood Lakes Community Assn., French-Am., Finnish-Am., Mid-Am. Arab chambers commerce, C. of C. U.S., U.S., Western golf assns. Moose. Club: Butterfield Country (Oak Brook, Ill.). Patentee in field. Home: 210 Briarwood Pass Oak Brook IL 60521 Office: 4608 W 20th St Chicago IL 60650

JEFFERIES, ROBERT AARON, JR., lawyer, furniture co. exec.; b. Richmond, Ind., June 30, 1941; s. Robert A. and Roberta June (Hart) J.; student Earlham Coll., 1959-63, A.B. with honors, 1963; J.D. (Herman C. Krannert scholar) with distinction, Ind. U., 1966; m. Sylvia Mae Gilmore, Apr. 16, 1962; children—David Eric, Michael Scott, Stephen Robert. Admitted to Ohio bar, 1966, Ind. bar, 1966, Mo. bar, 1970, Ill. bar, 1970; asso. firm Shumaker, Loop and Kendrick, Toledo, Ohio, 1966-69; staff atty. The May Dept. Stores Co., St. Louis, Mo., 1969-72, asst. gen. counsel, 1972-77, asst. sec., 1973-77; v.p., gen. counsel, sec. Leggett & Platt, Inc., Carthage, Mo., 1977—. Mem. Am. Bar Assn., Ohio Bar Assn., Ind. Bar Assn., Ill. Bar Assn., Mo. Bar Assn., St. Louis Bar Assn., Order of Coif. Contbr. articles to legal jours.; editorial bd. Ind. Law Jour., 1965-66.

JEFFERS, DEAN W., ret. ins. co. exec.; b. Woodsfield, Ohio, Sept. 7, 1916; grad. Ohio U., 1936, LL.D. (hon.), 1976; H.H.D., Ohio Dominican Coll., 1976, Springfield Coll., 1978; m. Ruth Workman. Gen. chmn., chief exec. officer Nationwide Ins. Cos. and affiliated cos., also Nationwide Corp., ret., 1981; dir. Orange-co, Inc., Columbus, Ohio Bell Telephone Co. Trustee Springfield (Mass.) Coll., Ohio U. Served with USMCR, 1943-45. Recipient Ohio Gov.'s award for outstanding citizen's career achievement, 1975; Horatio Alger award Am. Schs. and Colls. Assn., 1975; named Alumnus of Year, Ohio U., 1976. Home: 2600 Clairmont Ct Columbus OH 43220 Office: Two Nationwide Plaza Columbus OH 43216

JEFFERS, GERALD LOUIS, business exec.; b. Newark, Ohio, Apr. 7, 1935; s. Andrew and Catherine Olive (Foley) J.; m. Joan Francis Merryman, Oct. 17, 1959; children—Sabrina Ann, Gerald Louis. Partner, Louis Jeffers & Sons, Inc., wholesale produce bus., Newark, Ohio, 1964—, pres., 1964—; pres. Louis Jeffers & Sons Real Estate Co., Inc. Pres., St. Edwards Parish Council, Granville, Ohio. Mem. Granville Preservation Assn. (treas. 1981), Central Ohio Restaurant Assn., United Comml. Travelers Assn. Clubs: Elks, Moose, Kiwanis, Coachmen (pres. Midwest 1977-78, nat. dir. 1979). Home: 3160 Milner Rd Granville OH 43023 Office: Rear 45 S 3d St Newark OH 43055

JEFFERSON, ARTHUR, ednl. adminstr.; b. b. Ala., Dec. 1, 1938; B.S., Wayne State U., 1960. M.A. in Polit. Sci., 1963, Ed.D. in Curriculum Leadership, 1973; m. Marion Martin; children—Mark, Michael. Asst. region supt. Detroit pub. schs., 1970-71, region supt., 1971-75, interim gen. supt., 1975, gen. supt., 1975—. Mem. Nat., Mich. councils social studies, Assn. Supervision and Curriculum Devel., Am. Assn. Sch. Adminstrs., Mich. Assn. Supervision and Curriculum Devel., Council Basic Edn., Met. Detroit Soc. Black Ednl. Adminstrs., Nat. Alliance Black Sch. Educators, ACLU, NAACP, Wayne State U. Edn. Alumni Assn. (gov. 1968-71), Wayne State U. Alumni Assn. (trustee 1968-71), Phi Sigma Alpha. Home: 19445 Gloucester St Detroit MI 48203 Office: 5057 Woodward Ave Detroit MI 48202*

JEFFERSON, MELVIN DORSEY, fire commr. Detroit; b. Phila., July 5, 1922; s. Charles and Leona J.; student Temple U.; m. Helen Cuzzens, July 5, 1947; children—Joyce, Melvin. Pres., Superior Beauty and Barber Supply Co., Inc., Detroit; mem. Detroit Bd. Fire Commrs., 1969-74, fire commr., 1974—, exec. commr. Detroit Fire Dept.; mem. Detroit Bd. Suprs.; dir. Johnson Products. Bd. dirs. Econ. Devel. Corp., Coop. Assistance, Boy Scouts Am., North Detroit Gen. Hosp., United Found.; past mem. Detroit Airport Commn.; past bd. dirs., treas. Detroit Urban League. Served to lt. USAF. Mem. NAACP (life), Detroit C. of C. Club: One Hundred. Episcopalian. Office: 250 W Larned St Detroit MI 48226*

JEFFREYS, JAMES VICTOR, aero-mech. engr., air force officer; b. Nashville, June 28, 1938; s. James Terry and Jean Young (Stewart) J.; B.M.E., Vanderbilt U., 1961; M.S. in Aero-Mech. Engring., Air Force Inst. Tech., 1967; m. Carolyn Virginia Beam, Sept. 7, 1960; children—Mark, Kathryn, Clara. Commd. 2d lt. U.S. Air Force, 1961, advanced through grades to lt. col., 1981; mech. engr. USAF Security Service, Washington, 1961-65; aero. engr. Warner Robins Air Logistic Center, Robins AFB, Ga., 1967-69; dep. comdr. Detachment 4 Air Force Procurement Region Far East, Saigon, Vietnam, 1969-70; chief Air Force Logistics Command Corrosion Mgmt. Office, Robins AFB, 1970-74; asst. chief div. tech. services Def. Constrn. Supply Center, Columbus, Ohio, 1974-78; group leader, directorate of inertial engring. Aerospace Guidance and Metrology Center, Newark Air Force Station, Ohio, 1978—. Active Central Ohio council Boy Scouts Am. Decorated Bronze Star, Meritorious Service medal, Joint Services Commendation medal, Air Force Commendation medal (U.S.); Cross of Gallantry with palm (Vietnam); registered profl. engr., Calif. Mem. ASME, Nat. Assn. Corrosion Engrs. (accredited), Soc. Am. Mil. Engrs. (pres. Columbus post 1975), Nat. Rifle Assn. (life), Nat. Eagle Scout Assn., Air Force Assn., SCV, Sigma Nu. Methodist. Clubs: Masons (32 deg.), K.T., Shriners. Home: 306 Jennie Dr Gahanna OH 43230 Office: Aerospace Guidance and Metrology Center AGMC/SNA Newark Air Station Newark OH 43055

JEFFREYS, RICHARD EUGENE, biochemist; b. Uniontown, Pa., July 2, 1942; s. Robert Earl and Mary Jane (Cooley) J.; B.S., W.Va. U., 1964, M.S. in Biochemistry, 1966, Ph.D. in Biochemistry, 1969; m. Kathy J. Becilla, Aug. 28, 1965; children—Dwight Douglass, Rachel Marie. Research asst. Samuel Roberts Noble Found., Ardmore, Okla., 1969-71; asst. prof. Mo. Baptist Coll., 1971-75; chmn. dept. biology Grace Coll., 1975—. Served with USN, 1968. Mem. AAAS, Nat. Assn. Biology Tchrs., Am. Inst. Biol. Scis., Sigma Xi. Home: Rural Route 8 Box 392 Indian Village Warsaw IN 46580 Office: Grace Coll Winona Lake IN 46590

JEFFRIES, CHARLES DEAN, scientist, educator; b. Rome, Ga., Apr. 9, 1929; s. Andrew Jones and Rachel Lucinda (Ringer) J.; B.S., N. Ga. Coll., 1950; M.S., U. Tenn., 1955, Ph.D., 1958; postgrad. Purdue U., 1955-56; m. Virginia Mae Alford, Sept. 6, 1953. Technician, Ga. Pub. Health Dept., Rome, 1950-51; instr. microbiology Wayne State U., Detroit, 1958-60, asst. prof., 1960-65, asso. prof., 1965-70, prof., 1970—, acting chmn. dept., 1972-73, asso. dermatology, 1968—, asst. dean for curriculum affairs, dir. grad. programs Sch. Medicine, 1975-80; guest researcher Center for Disease Control, USPHS, Dept. Health and Human Services, Atlanta, 1980-81. Fulbright-Hays lectr., Cairo, Egypt, 1965-66; examiner bacteriology Bd. Basic Scis. State Mich., 1967-72, v.p., 1970-72; councilor Am. Assn. Basic Sci. Bds., 1970-72; mem. sci. adv. bd. Mich. Cancer Found., 1970-79. Served with AUS, 1951-53. NIH grantee, 1958-70; NSF grantee, 1959-69. Fellow Am. Acad. Microbiology; mem. Am. Soc. for Microbiology (councilor 1976-78, chmn. med. mycology div. 1977-78), Nat. Registry Microbiologists, Soc. Gen. Microbiology, Soc. Exptl. Biology and Medicine, Internat. Soc. Human and Animal Mycology, Sigma Xi. Contbr. articles to profl. jours. Home: 22513 Raymond Ave St Clair Shores MI 48082 Office: Dept Immunology and Microbiology Sch Medicine Wayne State U 540 E Canfield Detroit MI 48201

JEFFRIES, EVA BELLE, counselor; b. Appleton, Wis., Nov. 10, 1923; d. Robert Henry and Amy Taylor Hannum; B.A., Park Coll., 1944; M.A., U. Ill., 1950; m. Bernard C. Jeffries, Sept. 27, 1947; children—Connie, Barbara. Tchr. elem. schs., Benton Harbor, Mich. and Franklin, Ind., 1947-51; tchr. English, guidance counselor Jacksonville (Ill.) High Sch., 1956-60, St. Joseph Acad., Green Bay, Wis., 1966-70, Western Wis. Tech. Inst., La Crosse, 1970-81, guidance counselor, 1976—. Served with WAC, U.S. Army, 1946-48. NDEA fellow, 1960. Mem. Wis. Adult Vocat. Edn. Assn. Office: Western Wis Tech Inst 6th and Vine Sts La Crosse WI 54601

JEFFRIES, JAMES E., Congressman; b. Detroit, June 1, 1925; student Mich. State U.; m. Barbara Cray, 1947; children—James Thomas, Jeri Lee, Gregory Alan. Grain and livestock farmer, 1947-50; market researcher and salesman, 1950-70; investment counselor, 1970—; mem. 96th and 97th Congresses from 2d Dist. Kans. Served with USAAF, 1943-45. Mem. Am. Legion, Am. Security Council. Republican. Presbyterian. Clubs: Masons, Shriners. Office: 424 Cannon House Office Bldg Washington DC 20515

JEFFS, J. DALE, psychologist; b. Pekin, Ind., Oct. 7, 1931; s. Raymond Hosea and Dora Mae (Matthews) J.; B.S. with distinction, Ind. U., 1953; M.B.A., U. Mich., 1959, Ph.D. (Rackham grantee), 1972; m. Marilyn Goldstein, Sept. 4, 1965. Tng. dir. Ypsilanti (Mich.) State Hosp., 1966-67; program coordinator U. Mich., Ann Arbor, 1974-75; clin. psychologist Fed. Correctional Inst., Milan, Mich., 1975-80, VA Med. Center, Allen Park, Mich., 1980—; vol. counselor Crisis Walk-In Center, Ann Arbor, 1973-74, Child and Family Services, Ypsilanti, 1973. Served to lt. (j.g.) USN, 1953-56. Mem. Am. Psychol. Assn., Mich. Psychol. Assn., Internat. Neuropsychol. Soc., Am. Assn. Correctional Psychologists, Delta Sigma Pi, Theta Xi, Phi Delta Kappa, Beta Gamma Sigma. Home: 1400 Harbrooke Ann Arbor MI 48103 Office: VA Med Center Allen Park MI 48101

JELINEK, RICHARD CARL, hosp. mgmt. cons. co. exec.; b. Czechoslovakia, Apr. 3, 1937; s. Jindrich Henry and Jarmila Jana (Zizka) J.; came to U.S., 1959, naturalized, 1972; B.S. in Indsl. Engring. (Univ. fellow), U. Mich., 1961, M.B.A., 1962, Ph.D. in Indsl. Engring. (W.K. Kellogg fellow), 1964; m. Linda Graves, June 24, 1972; children—Valerie Susan, Richard Michael, Hope Linda. Project engr. St. Joseph's Hosp. and U. Mich. Med. Center, Ann Arbor, 1959-63, Ypsilanti (Mich.) State Hosp., 1961-62; lectr. U. Mich., Dearborn Center, 1963-64; asst. prof. indsl. engring. and hosp. adminstrn., U. Mich., Ann Arbor, 1964-67, asso. prof., 1968-70, dir. health systems mgmt., 1966-69; v.p. The Medicus Corp., Evanston, Ill., 1970-72, pres. Medicus Systems Corp., Evanston, 1972-74, pres., chief exec. officer, 1974—; prof. coll. nursing and allied health, Rush U., Chgo., 1973-75, dept. health systems mgmt., 1975—; cons. Am. Coll. Radiology, 1968-69, VA, Washington, 1965-67, others; various HEW grants; mem. research adv. com. Am. Nursing Found., 1969-72; mem. Health Program Systems Center Adv. Council and USPHS Div. Indian Health, 1967-72; prin., co-prin. investigator various HEW grants. Mem. Young Presidents Orgn., Ops. Research Soc. Am. (chmn. nat. meeting 1970, geog. sect. com. 1971-73, council health applications sect. 1970-72), Am. Inst. Indsl. Engrs., Hosp. Mgmt. Systems Soc., Am. Public Health Assn., Am. Hosp. Assn., Alpha Pi Mu, Beta Gamma Sigma, Phi Kappa Phi. Author monographs; contbr. articles to profl. publs. Home: 1722 Judson St Evanston IL 60201 Office: 990 Grove St Evanston IL 60201

JELINEK, WARREN DOUGLAS, plastic pipe and fittings mfg. co. exec.; b. Grand Island, Nebr., Sept. 29, 1939; s. Edwin and Alice Marie J.; B.S. in Chem. Engring., Ill. Inst. Tech., 1963; m. Joyce Marie Vrana, June 5, 1976; 1 son, Jimmy. Various engring. assignments Celanese Plastics Co., Batavia, Ill., Columbus, Ohio, Belvidere, N.J., 1962-72; plant mgr. Central Foundry, Holt, Ala., 1972-74, Carlon Co., Clinton, Iowa, 1974-77; ops. mgr. Plexco, Fairfield, Iowa, 1978—; cons. Amoco, Stow, Ohio, 1977. Mgr., bd. dirs. Little League. Mem. Fairfield Mfg. Assn. Republican. Club: Rotary. Office: Plexco 1806 W Stone Ave Fairfield IA 52556

JELKS, EDWARD BAKER, archeologist, educator; b. Macon, Ga., Sept. 10, 1922; s. Oliver Robinson and Lucille (Jarrett) J.; B.A., U. Tex., 1948, M.A., 1951, Ph.D., 1965; m. Juliet Elizabeth Christian, Aug. 12, 1944; 1 son, Edward Christian. Archeologist, Smithsonian Instn., 1950-53; research scientist U. Tex., Austin, 1958-65; asso. prof. anthropology So. Meth. U., Dallas, 1965-68; prof. anthropology Ill. State U., Normal, 1968—, dir. Midwestern Archeol. Research Center, 1981—; active archeol. field research Tex., La., Ill., Va., Mo., Nfld., Micronesia. Served with USN, 1942-44. Smithsonian Instn. research fellow, 1968. Fellow AAAS, Am. Anthropol. Assn.; mem. Soc. Profl. Archeologists (pres., 1976-77), Soc. Hist. Archaeology (pres., 1968-69), Am. Soc. for Conservation Archaeology, Soc. for Am. Archaeology, Assn. Field Archaeology, Archaeol. Inst. Am. Co-author: Handbook of Texas Archeology, 1954; Trick Taking Potential, 1974; The Joachim De Brum House, Likiep, Marshall Islands, 1978; author: Archaeological Explorations at Signal Hill, Newfoundland, 1973. Home: 605 N School St Normal IL 61761 Office: 105 Edwards Hall Ill State U Normal IL 61761

JELLISON, JAMES LOGAN, II, mktg. exec.; b. Chgo., June 3, 1922; s. James Logan and Ethel (Reynolds) J.; Ph.B., DePaul U., Chgo., 1943; B.M.E., Northwestern U., 1948; M.B.A., U. Louisville, 1959; m. Charlotte Jean Scott, Oct. 20, 1951; children—James Logan, Jeanene Lynn, Jennifer Lee. Mgr. mktg. research Gen. Electric Co., Holland, Mich., 1961—. State and County Conv. del. Republican Party, 1964—; vice chmn. bd. govs. Fountain St. Ch., Grand Rapids, Mich. Served to 1st lt. AUS, 1943-46, ETO. Decorated Bronze Star, Purple Heart; registered profl. engr. Mem. Am. Mktg. Assn. (pres. W. Mich. chpt. 1970-71), Am. Legion, Elfun Soc., Kappa Sigma. Republican. Club: Holland Country. Home: 729 Lugers Rd Holland MI 49423 Office: 570 E 16th St Holland MI 49423

JELLISON, RICHARD MARION, educator; b. Muncie, Ind., Dec. 26, 1924; s. Carl R. and Leora Melvina (Folkner) J.; B.S., Ball State U., 1948; A.M., Ind. U., 1949, Ph.D., 1953; m. Kathleen Elizabeth Frick, May 5, 1945; children—Richard G., Stephanie L., Leslie N. Instr. history Ind. U., 1952-56; instr. Mich. State U., 1956-58; asso. prof. Eastern Ill. U., 1958-62; prof. Miami U., Oxford, Ohio, 1962—, chmn. dept. history, 1971—; lectr. U. Berlin, 1966, U. Siena, Italy, 1968, Budapest, Hungary, 1974. Served with U.S. Navy, 1942-44. Colonial Williamsburg summer research fellow, 1958-62. Mem. Am. Hist. Assn., Inst. Early Am. Culture, Am. Assn. History Medicine, Orgn. Am. Historians, Internat. Soc. History Medicine, Ohio, Ind., S.C. hist. socs., AAUP (pres. Miami U. chpt. 1967). Author: Society, Freedom & Conscience: The American Revolution in Virginia, Massachusetts and New York, 1976. Contbr. articles to profl. jours. Home: 6345 Fairfield Rd Oxford OH 45056 Office: History Department Miami University Oxford OH 45056

JENEFSKY, JACK, wholesale exec.; b. Dayton, Ohio, Oct. 27, 1919; s. David and Anna (Saeks) J.; B.S. in Bus. Adminstrn., Ohio State U., 1941; postgrad. Harvard Bus. Sch., 1943; M.A. in Econs., U. Dayton, 1948; m. Beverly J. Mueller, Feb. 23, 1962; 1 dau., Anna Elizabeth; 1 stepdau., Cathryn Jean Mueller. Surplus broker, Dayton, 1946-48; sales rep. Remington Rand-Univac, Dayton, 1949-56, mgr. AF account, 1957-59, br. mgr. Dayton, 1960-61, regional marketing cons.

Midwest region, Dayton, 1962-63; pres. Bowman Supply Co., Dayton, 1963—. Selection adv. bd. Air Force Acad., 3d congressional dist., chmn., 1974—; chmn. 3d. dist. screening bds. Mil. Acad., 1976—; coordinator Great Lakes region, res. assistance program Civil Air Patrol, 1970-73. Served from pvt. to capt. USAAF, 1942-46; CBI; maj. USAF, 1951-53; col Res. Mem. Air Force Assn. (comdr. Ohio wing 1957-58, 58-59), Res. Officers Assn. (pres. Ohio dept. 1956-57, nat. council 1957-58, chmn. research and devel. com. 1961-62), Dayton Area C. of C. (chmn. spl. events com. 1970-72), Ohio State U. Alumni Assn. (pres. Montgomery County, Ohio, 1959-60), Nat. Sojourners (pres. Dayton 1961-62). Jewish. Clubs: Harvard Bus. Sch. Dayton (pres. 1961-62), Northmoor (Dayton), Lions. Home: 136 Briar Heath Circle Dayton OH 45415 Office: 225 N Irwin St Dayton OH 45403

JENKINS, CHARLES FRANKLIN, educator; b. Kansas City, Mo., Sept. 20; s. Festus Earl and Winnifred Chasteen (Nicholson) J.; A.A., Kansas City Jr. Coll., 1945; B.A., U. Mo., 1948, M.A., 1951, postgrad. summers, nights 1951-52, 72-74; postgrad. summers Cornell U., 1953, 54; Ed.S., Central Mo. State U., 1971; Ed.D., U. Kans., 1979. Tchr. sci. and math. Raytown (Mo.) Jr. High Sch., 1951-54, Paseo High Sch., Kansas City, Mo., 1954-58; tchr. math Basehor (Kans.) Jr. High Sch., 1964-68, Old Mission Jr. High Sch., Shawnee Mission, Kans., 1968-77; tchr. sci. Raytown High Sch., 1977-78, Lewis Middle Sch., Excelsior Springs, Mo., 1978-79; spl. edn. tchr., homebound program Kansas City (Mo.) Public Schs., 1979—. Served with AUS, 1946-47. Mem. Nat. Council Tchrs. Math, Research Council Diagnostic and Prescriptive Math, NEA (life), Assn. Supervision and Curriculum Devel., Phi Delta Kappa. Democrat. Methodist. Clubs, Masons, dance. Home: 1608 Poplar St Kansas City MO 64127 Office: Gen Offices Bd Edn Bldg Kansas City Public Schools 1211 McGee St Kansas City MO 64106

JENKINS, CHARLES HERBERT, greeting card co. ofcl.; b. Butler, Mo., Sept. 22, 1944; s. Charles William and Laura Maxine Jenkins; B.F.A., Kans. State Coll., 1968; m. Linda Jo Wynes, Jan. 22, 1966; children—Tracy Jo, Leslie Deane. Art tech. Nevada (Mo.) Rural Vocat. Schs., 1966; layout artist Jones Store Co., 1967-69; art dir., advt. mgr. Russell Stover Candies, Kansas City, Mo., 1969-77; advt. mgr. Crown Center Redevel. Corp., Hallmark Cards, Inc., Kansas City, Mo., 1977—. City councilman, Lake Winnebago, Mo., 1980-81. Served with U.S. Army, 1968-69. Mem. Advt. Club Kansas City (Mo.). Methodist. Office: 2440 Pershing Rd Kansas City MO 64108

JENKINS, DALE STEVENS, dentist; b. Orient, Ill., Dec. 11, 1915; s. Llewellyn E. and Effie (Stevens) J.; B.S., Blackburn Coll., 1935; D.D.S., Chgo. Coll. Dental Surgery, 1939; m. Maude Elizabeth Wheeler, Aug. 30, 1942; 1 son, Richard. Pvt. practice dentistry, DeKalb, Ill., 1939—; dir. Kishwaukee Community Health Services. Bd. dirs., div. mental health The Kids Place; committeeman Fox River Valley Peer Rev. Served with USAAF, 1943-46. Mem. Acad. of Dentistry, ADA, Ill. (del. 1967, mem. pub. relations com. 1970—, mem. peer rev. com.), Fox River Valley (pres. 1968-69, dir. 1965-70) dental socs., Ill. Dental Service (committeman 1972—). Club: Elks. Home: 1630 N 1st St DeKalb IL 60115 Office: 1606 Sycamore Rd DeKalb IL 60115

JENKINS, E(THEL) VALERIE, ret. media specialist; b. Amherst, Ohio, Sept. 7, 1913; d. Frank A. and Ethel E. (Dute) Eppley; student Hiram Coll., 1932; B.A., Baldwin-Wallace Coll., 1936; postgrad. Western Res. U., 1936, 41, 66, State U. Iowa, 1938-39, Ohio State U., 1960; M.A., Kent State U., 1962; m. William J. Jenkins, Aug. 13, 1944 (div. May 1964). Dir. dramatics Baldwin-Wallace Coll., Berea, Ohio, 1936-38; tchr. English and speech St. Elmo (Ill.) High Sch., 1939-42; tchr. English, speech, dir. dramatics Clearview-Lorain (Ohio) High Sch., 1942-57, librarian, 1949-57; library coordinator Amherst (Ohio) Pub. Schs., 1957-80, drama dir., 1957-60, 75-77; instr. Kent State U., 1963-66; instr. speech Cleve. State U., 1966-70; lectr. costumes for theatre; owner, operator children's theatre, also costume rental; cons. Amherst Pub. Library Bldg. Program, 1972-73. Founder Workshop Players, Inc., 1948, trustee, 1948—, pres., 1948-49, 56-58, 60, 75-80; mng. dir. Workshop Theatre, 1980—; mem. bd. Amherst Pub. Library, 1962—, pres., 1963-65. Mem. Nat., Ohio (life) edn. assns., Am. Theatre Assn., ALA, Ohio Ednl. Library Media Assn. (dir. NE chpt. 1974-76), Amherst Tchrs. Assn. (pres. 1962-64), Internat. Platform Assn., Delta Kappa Gamma, Phi Mu. Republican. Conglist. Home: 439 Shupe Ave Amherst OH 44001 Office: 450 Washington St Amherst OH 44001

JENKINS, GEORGE HENRY, educator; b. Shanghai, China, Oct. 24, 1929 (parents Am. citizens); s. Clarence O. and Efransinia M. (Pomorenkoff) J.; grad. N.Y. Inst. Photography, 1952; student Purdue U., 1952-55; student Ind. U., 1955-58, B.B.A., Ind. No. U., 1972; M.Ed., Wayne State U., 1976, postgrad., 1976—; m. Madge Marie Vickroy, Aug. 19, 1967. Photographer, Ft. Wayne (Ind.) Jour.-Gazette, 1952-55; computer programer Gen. Electric Co., Ft. Wayne, 1955-61; data processing mgr. Columbia Record Club subs. CBS, Terre Haute, Ind., 1961-63; adminstrv. coordinator Capital Record Club, Scranton, Pa. and Toronto, Ont., Can., 1963-64; mktg. systems analyst Xerox Corp., Detroit, 1964-66; dir. systems and data processing Nicholson File Co., Anderson, Ind., 1966-69; hosp. adminstr. Wayne County Gen. Hosp., Eloise, Mich., 1969-78; asst. prof. bus. Western Washington U., Bellingham, 1978-80; asst. prof. Lima (Ohio) Tech. Coll., 1980—; freelance photographer, 1969—; Chmn. supervisory bd. Eloise Credit Union, 1972-76. Served with USAF, 1948-52. Cert. data processor, data educator. Mem. Photog. Soc. Gt. Britian, Photog. Soc. Am., Assn. System Mgmt., Human Factors Soc., Am. Soc. Tng. and Devel., Am. Inst. Indsl. Engrs., Acad. Mgmt., Assn. Ednl. Communications and Tech. Presbyterian. Clubs: 8-16 Cine, Detroit Yacht (both Detroit); Hogg Creek Toastmasters (Lima). Home: 710 W Main St Cairo OH 45820 Office: Lima Tech Coll Lima OH 45804

JENKINS, HAROLD RICHARD, library adminstr.; b. Pottstown, Pa., Aug. 23, 1918; s. Stanley Frederick and Flora (High) J.; B.A., Ursinus Coll., 1953; M.A. in L.S., U. Mich., 1956; m. Margaret Houston Leech, Nov. 1, 1957; children—M. Elizabeth, Richard H. Catalog librarian Washington and Lee U., Lexington, Va., 1956-58; dir. Kingsport (Tenn.) Pub. Library, 1958-59, Wise County (Va.) Regional Library, 1959-61, Pottstown Pub. Library 1961-63, Lancaster County (Pa.) Library, 1963-74, Kansas City (Mo.) Pub. Library, 1974—. Bd. dirs. Lancaster Goodwill Industries, 1973-74. Lancaster County Hist. Soc., 1972-73. Served with C.E., AUS, 1941-52. Mem. Mo. Library Assn. (pres. 1977-78), Pa. Library Assn. (2d v.p. 1967-68), Beta Phi Mu, Pi Gamma Mu. Rotarian. Author: Management of a Public Library, 1981. Contbr. articles to profl. jours. Home: 5700 Wyandotte St Kansas City MO 64113 Office: 311 E 12th St Kansas City MO 64106

JENKINS, HARRY GHLEE, ret. retail sales exec.; b. Smithfield, Ill., Sept. 22, 1900; s. Fred Ashton and Lela Sarah (Totten) J.; B.S., Knox Coll., 1928; m. Ruth Jeanette Ramp, Dec. 25, 1928; children—Mary Jane (Mrs. Lloyd Ogilvie), Harry Ghlee. Rural sch. tchr., Fulton County, Ill., 1920-22, Knox County, 1922-23; salesman Wake Electric Co., Galesburg, 1927-28; salesman Montgomery Ward & Co., Galesburg, 1928-29, asst. mgr., 1929-31, store mgr., Burlington, Iowa, 1931-33; plater Casket Hardware Co., Galesburg, Ill., 1933-34; with Sears, Roebuck and Co., 1934-64, successively salesman Davenport, Iowa, asst. mgr., Moline and Decatur, Ill., mgr. Lafayette, Ind. and Waukegan, Ill., 1934-54, gen. mgr. 6 stores, Milw. area, 1954-64; dir. M.T. Linens, Inc., Carlyle, Ill. Chmn. war savs. staff Tippecanoe County, Ind., 1941-43, state chmn. retail div., 1943, co-chmn. Lake County, 1943-45; pres. Community Chest, Waukegan-N. Chgo., 1950-52, bd. dirs., 1944-54, chmn. drive, 1954; chmn. Mayor's Com. for Off-Street Parking, Waukegan, 1953; chmn. drive Victory Meml. Hosp. Bldg. Program, 1953; bd. dirs. Waukegan-N. Chgo. Council Chs., 1951-54; chmn. retail div. Lafayette C. of C., 1940-41, bd. dirs., 1943; pres. Waukegan-N. Chgo. C. of C., 1947-48, chmn. comml. div., 1943-45, bd. dirs., 1945-49; chmn. urban renewal com. Greater Milw. Com., 1961-65, bd. dirs., 1961-65, asso. mem., 1965—; bd. dirs., v.p. Milw. Hosp. Area Planning Com., Inc., 1963, 67; planning adv. council Wauwatosa, 1967-70; mem. Comprehensive Health Planning Agy. Southeastern Wis., Milw. state chmn. Wis. payroll savs. retail div. U.S. Savs. Bonds, 1963; bd. dirs. Better Bus. Bur., 1955-64, v.p., 1957; bd. dirs. mem. exec. com. Milw. chpt. ARC, 1964-66. Mem. Lake County Civic League (dir. 1954), YWCA of Waukegan (chmn. adv. com. 1954), Wis. C. of C. (dir. 1955-57, pres. 1959-60). Methodist (chmn. Capital fund drive spl. gifts div. Eastern Wis. Conf. 1964, trustee, chmn. bldg. com.). Clubs: Masons (32 deg.), Shriners, Wisconsin. Home: 7500 W Dean Rd Apt 312 Milwaukee WI 53223

JENKINS, HULEN FRANK, grain processing co. exec.; b. Kansas City, Kans., Nov. 6, 1937; s. George Barker and Nancy Fern (Boring) J.; B.S., U. Kans., 1959; m. Patricia Mae Thornburgh, July 12, 1958; children—Nancy Jan, Marny Jan. Rep., Gen. Am. Life Ins. Co., St. Louis, 1966-68; from gen. foreman to prodn. mgr. Olin Corp., East Alton, Ill. and St. Mark's, Fla., 1968-72; plant mgr. Plastics Extrustion div. Western Textile Products Co., St. Louis, 1972-74; indsl. relations mgr. Mallinckrodt, Inc., St. Louis, 1974-78; mgr. plant services A.E. Staley Mfg. Co., Decatur, Ill., 1978—. Dist. commr. St. Louis council Boy Scouts Am., 1977-78; founding pres. Decatur Employee Assistance Council, 1979-80. Served to capt. USMC, 1959-66; Vietnam. Mem. St. Louis Indsl. Relations Assn. (program chmn. 1978). Home: 4525 Baker Woods Pl Decatur IL 62521 Office: 2200 E Eldorado St Decatur IL 62525

JENKINS, JAMES GEORGE, II, chem. co. exec.; b. Midland, Mich., May 15, 1938; s. James George and Lois Love (McKieth) J.; B.S., Central Mich. U., 1964; M.S., Mich. State U., 1966; m. Tona Kozlow, Dec. 28, 1979; children—David, Susan, Mary Sue, Ann, Steve, James George III. Engr., Dow Chem. Co., Midland, Mich., 1966-70, dist. mgr. consumer products div., 1971-75, project purchasing agt., 1975-78, research specialist, 1978-80, purchasing agt. Mich. div., 1980—. Mem. Midland City Planning Commn., 1968-73, vice-chmn., 1971, chmn., 1972; chmn. loaned exec. program United Way, 1976; bd. mem. Alcohol Service, 1979-80, vice-chmn., 1981. Mich. State U. acad. grantee, 1965. Mem. Grocery Mfrs. Am. (mem. distbn. and warehousing com. 1972-74). Republican. Episcopalian. Club: Elks. Home: 3701 Greenbrier St Midland MI 48640

JENKINS, MICHAEL JAMES, fast food chain communications exec.; b. Mt. Clemens, Mich., June 19, 1948; s. Robert William and Rita Patricia (McCartan) J.; B.A. in Journalism, Mich. State U., 1976; m. Nancy Beth Larkin, June 14, 1974. Community relations asst. Wyandotte (Mich.) Gen. Hosp., 1976, acting dir. community relations, 1976-77, dir. community relations, 1977-78; editor Burger Chef Systems, Inc., Indpls., 1978-79, communications mgr., 1979-81, mgr. communications and corp. affairs, 1981—. Ofcl. photographer Indpls. Soap Box Derby, 1979; Burger Chef Systems chmn. United Way Campaign, 1978, 79, 80. Served with USN, 1968-71. Recipient graphic arts awards, Printing Industries Am., 1979, 80. Mem. Internat. Assn. Bus. Communicators (communications chmn. U.S. Dist. 7 1981-82, gold quill award of merit, 1978, U.S. Dist. 7 award of excellence, 1980, 81, award of merit 1981), Public Relations Soc. Am., Ind. Bus. Communicators (evaluations chmn., 1980, Excellent Performance in Communications award, 1980), Sigma Delta Chi. Office: PO Box 927 Indianapolis IN 46206

JENKINS, ROBERT RICHARD, ser. co. exec.; b. Chgo., June 1, 1938; s. Matthew N. and Marion (Shelby) J.; B.S., Loyola U., 1960, M.A., 1962; m. Mary Ellen Thulis, May 31, 1969; children—Tracy Jane, David Robert. Product mgr. Nat. Steel Corp., Evanston, Ill., 1965-69; sales mgr. Xerox Corp., Chgo., 1969-71; regional mgr. Gelco Corp., N.Y.C., 1971-77, v.p. mktg., Eden Prairie, Minn., 1977-80; v.p. mktg. The Van Arnem Co., Bloomfield Hills, Mich., 1980—. Mem. Planning Commn. City of Westport, Conn., 1975-77. Served with USNR, 1963-65. Mem. Sales Exec. Club N.Y., Am. Equipment Leasing Assn., Sales & Mktg. Exec. Mpls., Am. Automotive Leasing Assn. Clubs: Decathlon, Mpls. Athletic, Northwest Racquet. Editor: Guide, 1978-80. Office: 100 W Long Lake Rd Bloomfield Hills MI 48013

JENKINS, ROGER CARL, mfg. co. exec.; b. Van Wert, Ohio, July 1, 1942; s. Roger Ellis and Mary Elizabeth (Sharpe) J.; grad. Chrysler Inst., 1980; m. Katherine M. Lantz, May 17, 1974; children—Theresa Sue, Angela Marie. With various retail aubomobile companies, 1965-74; quality control and prodn. supr. Essex Controls Co., Logansport, Ind., 1974-79; prodn. supr. Chrysler Corp., Kokomo, Ind., 1979—. Served with USAF, 1961-65. Mem. Nat. Mgmt. Assn., VFW, Am. Legion, Am. Motorcycle Assn., GoldWing Rd. Riders Assn. Club: Eagles. Home: Box 108 Hemlock IN 46937 Office: Rural Route 6 Logansport IN 46947

JENKINS, THOMAS NELSON, fin. cons.; b. Balt., Mar. 15, 1933; s. Glenn Llewellyn and Serena Elizabeth (Forberg) J.; B.S., Purdue U., 1957; cert. fin. planner Coll. Fin. Planning, 1975; m. Carol Louise Snelling, June 6, 1954; children—David Glenn, Stephen Ralph. Vice pres. Loeb Rhoades Hornblower, Cleve., 1962-80; pres. Thermox Corp., Cleve., 1969—, Conceptual Fin. Planning Inc., Cleve., 1975—, Enersource Mgmt. Corp., 1980—; chmn. Resource Properties Inc., Youngstown, Ohio, 1978—; cons. in field. Post adv. Greater Cleve. council Boy Scouts Am. Served with U.S. Army, 1953-55. Registered investment adv. Mem. Internat. Assn. Fin. Planners, Inst. Cert. Fin. Planners, Ohio Soc. Fin. Counselors (pres. 1977—), Purdue Alumni Assn. (pres. 1970-72). Clubs: Rotary, Cheshire Cheese, Toastmasters Internat. Author, Jenkins Tax Incentive Investment Newsletter. Home: 1544 St Charles Ave Lakewood OH 44107 Office: Box 07210 1609 Onondaga Ave Lakewood OH 44107

JENKS, DOWNING BLAND, railroad exec.; b. Portland, Oreg., Aug. 16, 1915; s. Charles O. and Della (Downing) J.; B.S., Yale U., 1937; m. Louise Sweeney, Nov. 30, 1940; children—Downing B., Nancy Randolph. Chainman, Spokane Portland & Seattle Ry., Portland, 1934-35; asst., engr. corps Pa. R.R., N.Y. div., 1937-38; successively roadmaster, div. engr., trainmaster various divs. G.N. Ry., 1938-47, div. supt., Spokane, Wash., 1947-48; gen. mgr. C. & E.I. R.R., 1949-50; asst. v.p. ops. Rock Island Lines, Chgo., 1950-51, v.p. ops., 1951-53, exec. v.p., dir., 1953-55, pres., 1956-61; pres. M.P.R.R., 1961-71, chmn., 1972—, also dir.; chmn., chief exec. officer, dir. Mo. Pacific Corp., 1971—; dir. 1st Nat. Bank, St. Louis, Bankers Life Co., 1st Union Bancorp. Life trustee Northwestern U.; nat. pres. Boy Scouts Am., 1977-80. Served from 1st lt. to lt. col. 704th Ry. Grand Div., AUS, 1942-45; ETO, MTO. Mem. Tau Beta Pi. Home: 8 Greenbriar St Louis MO 63124 Office: Mo Pacific Bldg St Louis MO 63103

JENKS, HALSEY DENTON, retail gas and automotive co. exec.; b. Ypsilanti, Mich., Sept. 2, 1937; s. Halsey Barnes and Rosa Lena (Griggs) J.; A.B., Spring Arbor Coll., 1970; postgrad. Western Mich. U., 1972—. Joined U.S. Army, 1956, advanced through grades to sgt. 1st class, 1965, ret. 1966; partner Arbor Oil Co., Concord, Mich., 1973—; substitute tchr. Concord Middle Sch., 1972-74. Trustee Village of Concord, pres., 1978—; chmn. Concord-Pulaski Police Assn., 1971-72. Mem. Orgn. Am. Historians, Concord Heritage Assn. (pres. 1971-73), Concord High Sch. Alumni Assn. (pres. 1977-78). Club: Masons. Home: 216 Hanover St Concord MI 49237 Office: 230 E Jackson St Concord MI 49237

JENKS, SETH ALLEN, coll. dean; b. Batavia, N.Y., Dec. 31, 1941; s. Robert Stephen and Martha Francis (Allen) J.; B.A., Westminster Coll., 1963; M.A., Case Western Reserve U., 1972; m. Carol Jane Holroyd, Aug. 15, 1964; children—Edward Allen, Laura Carol. Tchr., Avalon (Pa.) Public Schs., 1964-65; adminstr. admissions and fin. aid Case Western Res. U., Cleve., 1968-73; v.p., dean students Kansas City (Mo.) Art Inst., 1973-77, v.p., dean coll., 1977—. Mem. Citizens Com. to Save the Philharmonic. Served with U.S. Army, 1966-68. LaRue fellowship grantee Claremont Higher Edn. Mgmt. Inst., 1979. Mem. Am. Craft Council, Assn. Fine Arts Deans, Union Ind. Colls. Art, Am. Assn. Higher Edn., Mo. Assn. Student Fin. Aid Personnel (past dir.), Kansas City Regional Council Higher Edn. Office: 4415 Warwick Blvd Kansas City MO 64111

JENNER, ALBERT ERNEST, JR., lawyer; b. Chgo., June 20, 1907; s. Albert Ernest and Elizabeth (Owens) J.; m. Nadine Newbill, Mar. 19, 1932; 1 dau., Cynthia Lee; J.D., U. Ill., 1930; LL.D., John Marshall Law Sch., 1952, Northwestern U., 1975, Columbia Coll., 1974, U. Notre Dame, 1975, William B. Mitchell Sch. Law, 1976, U. Mich., 1976; Admitted to Ill. bar, 1930; mem. firm Jenner & Block, Chgo., 1933—; prof. law Northwestern U., 1952-53; dir. Gen. Dynamics Corp., United Bank of Am. Spl. asst. to atty. gen. Ill., 1956-68; chmn. U.S. Supreme Ct. Adv. Com. on Fed. Rules of Evidence, 1965-75; chmn. Ill. Commn. on Uniform State Laws, 1951—; mem. Nat. Conf. Commn. on Uniform State Laws in U.S., pres., 1969-71; mem. U.S. Supreme Ct. Adv. Com. Fed. Civil Rules, 1960-70; mem. Nat. Conf. Bar Assn. Pres. U.S., pres., 1952-53; mem. U.S. Loyalty Rev. Bd., 1952-53; mem. council U. Ill. Law Forum, 1948-51; sr. counsel Presdl. Commn. to Investigate the Assassination Pres. Kennedy (Warren Commn.), 1964; law mem. Ill. Bd. Examiners Accountancy, 1948-51; mem. Pres.'s Nat. Commn. on Causes and Prevention of Violence in U.S. (Eisenhower Commn.), 1968-69; chief spl. counsel to minority Ho. of Reps. Judiciary Com. Conducting Impeachment Inquiry on Pres. Nixon, 1974. Bd. dirs. Center for Study Democratic Instns., 1975—; trustee Fund for Republic, recipient Robert Maynard Hutchins Disting. Service award, 1976; trustee, sec. U.S. Navy Found., 1977—; bd. dirs. or trustee Evanston Glenbrook Hosp., Roosevelt U., Columbus Coll., Walter E. Heller Found. Recipient Disting. Service award for outstanding public service Chgo. and Ill. Jr. chambers commerce, 1939, U. Ill. Disting. Alumnus award, 1962, Disting. Civic Achievement award Am. Jewish Com., 1973, Disting. Citizens award N.Y. U., 1975; named Chicagoan of Yr., Chgo. Press Club, 1975, laureate Lincoln Acad. of Ill. Fellow Am. Coll. Trial Lawyers (bd. regents, pres. 1958), Internat. Acad. Trial Lawyers; mem. Ill. Soc. Trial Lawyers, Nat. Assn. Def. Lawyers in Criminal Cases, Am. (Ill. state del. ho. of dels. 1948-75, state del. 1975-78, chmn. standing com. on fed. judiciary 1965-68, chmn. sect. on individual rights and responsibilities 1973-74, mem. council, sect. on legal edn. 1967-75, bd. govs. 1977-80), Ill. (pres. 1949-50), Chgo. (sec. 1947-49) bar assns., Am. Judicature Soc. (pres. 1958, recipient Herbert Harley award 1981), Am. Inst. Jud. Adminstrn., Bar Assn. U.S. Ct. Appeals (gov.), Am. Law Inst., ACLU (dir. 1976), Order of Coif, Alpha Chi Rho, Phi Delta Phi. Clubs: Skokie Country, Law, Legal, Chgo. Press, Tavern, Chicago. Author, co-author: Ill. Civil Practice, Annotated; Smith-Hurd Ill., Annotated Statutes, 1934-77, 6 vols. on Pleading and Practice Procedure. Mem. permanent editorial bd. Uniform Commercial Code. Contbr. articles to law revs., legal publs. Home: 119 Tudor Pl Kenilworth IL 60043 Office: One IBM Plaza Chicago IL 60611

JENNER, WILLIAM ALEXANDER, govt. ofcl., meteorologist; b. Indianola, Iowa, Nov. 10, 1915; s. Edwin Alexander and Elizabeth May (Brown) J.; A.B., Central Meth. Coll., Mo., 1938; certificate meteorology U. Chgo., 1943; M.Ed., U. Mo., 1947; postgrad. Am. U., 1951-58; m. Jean Norden, Sept. 1, 1946; children—Carol Beth, Paul William, Susan Lynn. Instr. U. Mo., 1946-47; research meteorologist U.S. Weather Bur., Chgo., 1947-49; staff Hdqrs. Air Weather Service, Andrews AFB, Md., 1949-58, Scott AFB, Ill., 1958—, dir. tng., 1960—. Mem. O'Fallon (Ill.) Twp. High Sch. Bd. Edn., 1962—, sec., 1964-71, pres., 1971—; mem. O'Fallon Planning Commn., 1973—, sec., 1979-81, sub-div. chmn., 1978—. Served with AUS, 1942-46. Recipient Distinguished Service award O'Fallon PTA, 1968. Mem. Am. Psychol. Assn., Wilson Ornithological Soc., Am. Philatelic Soc., Am. Meteorol. Soc., AAAS, Nat. Soc. Study Edn., Am. Legion, Phi Delta Kappa, Psi Chi. Clubs: Masons, Shriners, O'Fallon Sportsmen's, Toastmasters Internat. Home: 307 Alma St O'Fallon IL 62269 Office: Scott AFB IL 62225

JENNINGS, EDWARD HARRINGTON, univ. pres.; b. Mpls., Feb. 18, 1937; s. Edward G. and Ruth (Harrington) J.; B.S., U. N.C., 1959; M.B.A., Western Res. U., 1963; Ph.D. (NDEA Title IV fellow), U. Mich., 1969; m. Mary Eleanor Winget, Nov. 4, 1954; children—William Francis, Steven Winget. With Deering Milliken Service Corp., 1959-61, Merck & Co., 1959-61, Merck & Co., 1963-65; acad. positions at various instns., 1967-74; chmn. dept. bus. adminstrn. U. Iowa, 1974-75, asst. dean faculties, dir. summer sessions, 1975-76, prof. fin., 1976-79, v.p. for fin. and univ. services, 1976-79; pres. U. Wyo., Laramie, 1979-81; pres. Ohio State U., Columbus, 1981—; bd. dir., Ohio Bell, Columbus C. of C.; exec. com. Board of Electors Ins. Hall. Presbyterian. Club: Rotary (Columbus). Author: (with R.A. Stevenson) Fundamentals of Investments, 1976. Office: Office of Pres Ohio State U Columbus OH 43210

JENNINGS, FRANK LAMONT, pathologist, educator; b. Mpls., Apr. 25, 1921; s. Frank L. and Helen (Germond) J.; A.B., Ind. U., 1942, M.D., 1947; m. Beverly K. Carlson, Dec. 15, 1948; children—Frank Lamont, III, Kathryn Eleanor, Paul Ernest, Mark Oliver. Fellow, U. Chgo. Hosps., 1947-51, intern, 1951-52; instr. then asst. prof. U. Chgo. Clinics, 1954-60; mem. faculty U. Tex. Med. Br., Galveston, 1960-77, prof. pathology, chmn. dept., 1963-75; prof., chmn. dept. pathology Wright State Sch. Medicine, 1977—; sec. Gulf Coast Waste Disposal Authority, 1970-77. Bd. dirs. Tex. div. Am. Cancer Soc., 1963-77. Served with M.C., AUS, 1955-57. Mem. AMA, Am. Soc. Clin. Pathologists, Coll. Am. Pathology (gov. 1975—), Am. Assn. Pathologists, and Bacteriologists, Internat. Acad. Pathology, Am. Soc. Exptl. Pathology, Am. Assn. Cancer Edn., Radiation Research Soc. Office: Dept Pathology Greene Meml Hosp Xenia OH 45385

JENNINGS, JAMES BLANDFORD, historian; b. Ironwood, Mich., Jan. 23, 1922; s. Blandford and Anne (Heise) J.; B.E., Ill. State U., 1947, M.Ed., 1948; postgrad. U. Wis., 1950-51, Washington U.,

1956, Ripon Coll., 1961, Northwestern U., 1965, Southern Ill. U., Edwardsville, 1970, 71. Instr. polit. sci. and econs. Mc Kendree Coll., Lebanon, Ill., 1948-49; tchr. social studies high sch., Pleasant Hope, Mo., 1950; tchr. history Howe (Ind.) Mil. Sch., 1951-52; tchr. social studies Center Twp. Sch., LaPorte, Ind., 1952-54; tchr. history East High Sch., Aurora, Ill., 1954-67, Maine Twp. High Sch. West, Des Plaines, Ill., 1967-69; instr. history State Community Coll. East St. Louis, 1969—, chmn. humanities, 1972-75. Co-chmn. Search for the Am. Dream in East St. Louis, 1976. Served with AUS, 1943-45. Decorated Bronze Star, Purple Heart with 2 oak leaf clusters. Mem. Nat. Forensic League (dist. chmn. 1962-65), Aurora Edn. Assn. (pres. 1961-62), NEA, Ill. Community Coll. Faculty Assn. (editor newsletter), Am. Hist. Assn., Abraham Lincoln Assn., AAUP, Pi Kappa Delta, Pi Gamma Mu. Home: 7746 Rannells Maplewood MO 63143 Office: 417 Misouri Ave East St Louis IL 62201

JENNINGS, WILLIAM GRANGER, real estate and financial exec., investor; b. Evanston, Ill., Aug. 10, 1928; s. Archibald Granger and Florence (Johnson) J.; B.S., Cornell U., 1951; M.B.A., Harvard, 1955; m. Betty Ann Swanson, Apr. 9, 1960; children—Robert William, Elizabeth Ann. With Stewart-Warner Corp., Chgo., 1955-63, with Quinlan & Tyson, Inc., Evanston, 1964—, chmn., 1978—, pres., 1980—; chmn. Quinlan & Tyson Mortgage Corp., 1973—; chmn. Quinlan & Tyson Real Estate Investment Advisors, Inc., 1973—; pres. Quinlan & Tyson Securities, Inc., 1978—, Quinlan & Tyson Holdings, Inc., 1980—; dir. Community Bank & Trust Co. of Edgewater. Mem. Chgo. Real Estate Bd., North Side Real Estate Bd., Evanston-North Shore Bd. Realtors. Trustee, bd. dirs., vice chmn. Goodwill Industries, Chgo. Served to 1st lt. USAF, 1951-53. Mem. ASME, Cornell Soc. Engrs., Inst. Real Estate Mgmt. (cert. property mgr.), Real Estate Securities and Syndication Inst., Harvard Bus. Sch. Assn. Clubs: Cornell, Union League (Chgo.); Westmoreland Country, University (Evanston); Kenilworth; Dairymen's, Rotary, Adventurers. Patentee in field. Home: 508 Brier St Kenilworth IL 60043 Office: 1569 Sherman Ave Evanston IL 60204

JENNY, HANS HEINRICH, coll. adminstr.; b. Ennenda, Switzerland, Apr. 11, 1922; came to U.S., 1947, naturalized, 1957; m. Sebastian and Gertrude J.; B.A., Ecole Superieure de Commerce, Lausanne, Switzerland, 1942; postgrad. U. Lausanne, 1942-43; Lic. rer. pol., U. Bern (Switzerland), 1947, Dr. rer.pol., 1950; postgrad. George Washington U. Law Sch., 1947, Yale U., 1948-49. Instr. dept. econs. Coll. of Wooster (Ohio), 1949-51, asst. prof., 1951-54, asso. prof., 1954-59, prof., 1959-62, dir. instl. research, 1962-66, v.p. budgetary affairs, 1966-69, v.p. fin. and bus., 1969—; bd. dirs. Nat. Center for Higher Edn. Mgmt. Systems; commr. N. Central Assn. for Colls. and Schs. Mem. Assn. Instl. Research (treas.), Inst. for Mgmt. Scis. Club: Rotary. Author: The Golden Years, 1970; The Turning Point, 1972; The Consolidated Net Worth of Private Colleges, 1973; The Bottom Line, 1978; Financial Viability in Postsecondary Education, 1979; Institutional Financial Assessment, 1979; Another Challenge: Age 70 Retirement in Higher Education, 1979; Hang-Gliding, or Looking for an Updraft: A Study of College and University Finance in the 1980's - The Capital Margin, 1980. Office: Coll of Wooster Wooster OH 44691

JENSEN, CARL ARTHUR, judge; b. Sleepy Eye, Minn., Dec. 11, 1920; s. Jens and Hulda (Hansen) J.; B.S.L., U. Minn., 1948, LL.B., 1949; m. Lorraine Lucille Johnson, Jan. 3, 1948 (dec. Dec. 1975); children—Steven, Karen, Scott, Paul, Bruce; m. 2d, Patricia Passman Glenn, June 14, 1977; stepchildren—Mona, Rich, John. Admitted to Minn. bar, 1949, Fed. Dist. Ct., Minn., 1950; former atty. Minn. Bankers Assn. and Minn. Assn. Twp. Officers; city atty., Sleepy Eye, 1962—; mem. Minn. Ho. of Reps. from Brown County, 1950-60, Minn. Senate from 28th Dist., 1966-80; judge Minn. Tax Ct., St. Paul, 1980—. Served with USAAF, 1944-46. Mem. Am., Minn. bar assns., Sleepy Eye PTA, Ish Tak Ha Ba Investment Club, Indsl. Devel. Corp. Sleepy Eye, Am. Legion, Sleepy Eye C. of C. Republican. Lion. Club: Sleepy Eye Golf; Sportsmen (Sleepy Eye). Home: 3530 Ridgewood Rd Arden Hills MN 55112 Office: Minn Tax Ct Space Center Saint Paul MN 55101

JENSEN, CHARLES WAGNER, appliance mfg. co. public relations mgr.; b. Waterloo, Iowa, July 4, 1920; s. Sam and Bertha C. (Jensen) J.; student Iowa State Tchrs. Coll., Cedar Falls, 1939-41; B.A., cert. in journalism, U. Iowa, 1943; m. Margaret Jean Subra, Dec. 21, 1947; children—Andrea Gale and Christine Ann (twins). Editor of sales mag. Maytag Co., Newton, Iowa, 1946-57, mgr. public relations activities, 1957—. Moderator Congl. Ch., Newton, 1972, trustee, sec. bd. dirs., 1980; pres. Am. Field Service, 1972; bd. dirs. Newton Salvation Army, 1977-79; exec. bd., nat. council rep. Mid-Iowa council Boy Scouts Am., 1964, vice chmn. Newton, 1964, chmn. Scout show, 1960; bd. dirs. YMCA, 1958-59; promotion chmn., county orgn. Republican Party, 1958; banquet chmn. Nat. Field Days, 1956; bd. dirs. Jasper County Hist. Soc., 1980—; promotion chmn. Newton United Way campaign, 1961-67; bd. dirs. Mus. Natural History, 1968; program chmn. Iowa Coll. Public Relations Conf., 1963. Served with USMC, 1942-46. Recipient Silver Beaver award, Boy Scouts Am., 1965. Mem. Iowa Indsl. Editors Assn. (pres., 1950), C. of C. Newton (chmn. public relations 1960-64, dir. 1959-61, 67, chmn. indsl. relations com. 1959, chmn. coms., 1959, 76—). Clubs: Elks (ruler 1958), Rotary (pres. 1968), Am. Legion (Newton historian 1948, adj. 1946), Maytag Mgmt. (dir., chmn. program com., 1948), Maytag Speech (pres. 1960). Home: 2900 S 3rd Ave E Newton IA 50208 Office: Maytag Co Newton IA 50208

JENSEN, EILEEN MARIE, assn. sec.; b. Ravenna, Ohio, Jan. 4, 1919; d. Alfred Frederick and Pearl M. (Cox) Jensen; student Western Res. U., 1936-37, Wilcox Sch. Bus., Cleve., 1942. Hostess, Cafe Rouge Statler Hotel, Cleve., 1939-41; sec. to chief engr. Hollenden Hotel, Cleve., 1941-46; sec. to purchasing agt. Milner Electric Co., Cleve., 1946-49; personnel mgr. Superior Carbon Products Co., Cleve., 1950-53; sec. solicitations dept. Greater Cleve. Growth Assn. (formerly Cleve. C. of C.), 1953-54, sec. to v.p. and sec., 1954-58, sec. to pres., 1959-68, adminstrv. asst., 1968-72, mgr. co. data center, 1972-74, mgr. fin. support rev., 1975—; office sec. Cleve. Tool, Die & Machine Shops Assn. (now Cleve. chpt. Nat. Tool, Die and Precision Machining Assn.), 1953-59, exec. sec., 1969-74; office sec. Soc. No. Ohio Profl. Photographers, Cleve. Soc. Profl. Photographers, 1953-60, exec. sec., 1970-74; office sec. Lake Erie Internat. Vacationland Assn., Cleve., 1954-60. Mem. Am. Bus. Women's Assn. (pres. Moses Cleveland Chpt. 1960, 64, Woman of Year award 1959, Merit award for outstanding service 1964), Exec. Secs. Inc. (v.p. Cleve. chpt. 1969, pres. 1969-70). Clubs: Order Eastern Star, Women's City (Cleve.). Home: 4133 W 143d St Cleveland OH 44135 Office: 690 Union Commerce Bldg Greater Cleve Growth Assn Cleveland OH 44115

JENSEN, EMMANUEL TRANBERG, cons. civil engr.; b. Council Bluffs, Iowa, Nov. 26, 1910; s. Lars Peter and Christina Sophia (Lindhardt) J.; B.S., Iowa State U., 1933, M.S., 1948; postgrad. U. Minn., 1960-62; m. Wilma Mary Westburg, Aug. 15, 1947. Chief engr. Western Contracting Corp., Sioux City, Iowa, 1938-44; project engr. Al Johnson Constrn. Co., Mpls., 1948-50; civil engr. Guy F. Atkinson Co., South San Francisco, Calif., 1950-51; project engr. Donovon-Lovering-Boyle, Pickstown, S.D., 1951-56; civil engr., Winston Bros. Co., Mpls., 1956-58; pvt. cons. civil engr., Minnetonka, Minn., 1958—. Instr. civil engring. U. Minn., 1936-37, structural engring. Iowa State U., 1947-48. Vice pres. Nat. Luth. Alumni Fellowship, 1936-38. Serve to lt. USNR, 1944-45. Fellow ASCE (pres. N.W. sect. 1970-71, dir. 1971-73, vice chmn. nat. constrn. div. 1973-75, chmn., 1975-76, chmn. nat. publs. com. 1971-73), Nat. Model R.R. Assn. (nat. model contest judge 1968), Am. Arbitration Assn. (nat. panel), World Brotherhood Exchange, Phi Kappa Phi. Lutheran. Address: 3620 Fairlawn Dr Minnetonka MN 55343

JENSEN, ERLING N., ret. coll. pres.; b. Des Moines, Sept. 3, 1908; s. Jens Lars and Efra (Nielsen) J.; A.B., Drake U., 1932, LL.D. (hon.), 1969; A.M. (Lydia Roberts fellow), Columbia U., 1933; Ph.D., Iowa State U., 1947; Litt.D. (hon.), Lafayette Coll., 1962; LL.D. (hon.), Muhlenberg Coll., 1969, Lehigh U., 1969; m. Ruth McElhinney, Aug. 9, 1936; children—Richard Erling, Carl Harold, Edward Erik, David Paul. Sci. instr., high sch., prin., 1934-35; prof. sci. Grand View Coll., Des Moines, 1935-43; prof. physics, sr. physicist Inst. for Atomic Research, Iowa State U., 1943-61, prof. physics, 1969-73, prof. emeritus, 1973—; pres. Muhlenberg Coll., Allentown, Pa., 1961-69, pres. emeritus, 1969—. Chmn., Joint Commn. on Lutheran Unity Com. on Colls., 1960-61; chmn. nat. conv. Am. Evang. Ch., 1943-62; del. Luth. World Fedn., Helsinki, Finland, 1963; mem. exec. com. Nat. Luth. Council, 1963-66; del. Luth. Ch. in Am. convs., 1964, 66, 68; del., mem. exec. com. Luth. Council in U.S.A., 1966-69; pres. council Luther Meml. Ch., Des Moines, 1941-42; mem. council St. Pauls Luth. Ch., Allentown, 1962-68; bd. dirs. Luth. Student Found. at Iowa State U.; treas., bd. dirs. Iowa Luth. Campus Mission; mem. Charter Study Commn., Allentown, 1966; mem. exec. com. Commn. on Ind. Colls. and Univs. in Pa., 1965-68, Citizens Com. for Progress Lehigh County (Pa.), 1966-69; active liaison com. from pvt. colls. and univs. Pa. Council Higher Edn., 1967-69; adviser Council Higher Edn., Pa. Bd. Edn., 1969; chmn. bd. dirs. Grand View Coll. and Grand View Sem., 1951-62; bd. dirs. Indsl. Devel. Corp. of Lehigh County, 1964-69, Muhlenberg Med. Center, 1962-69, United Fund of Lehigh County, 1964-69, Allentown-Lehigh County C. of C., 1965-68, Distinguished Service award, 1969, pub. adv. com. Lehigh Valley Hosp. Planning Council, 1969; trustee Grand View Coll. Endowment Fund, 1951-62. Recipient Distinguished Service award, 1965, Double D award, 1968 both from Drake U.; Iowa Tennis Hall of Fame, 1974. Fellow Am. Phys. Soc., Iowa Acad. Sci. (chmn. physics sect. 1946-47); mem. Am. Assn. Phy scis. Tchrs., Am. Fedn. Scientists, Phi Beta Kappa, Sigma Xi, Phi Kappa Phi, Kappa Phi Kappa, Pi Mu Epsilon. Author: College Physics Laboratory Manual, 1944. Contbr. articles on nuclear physics to profl. jours. Home: 2522 Pierce Ave Ames IA 50010

JENSEN, FRED CHARLES, research and devel. mech. engr.; b. Mpls., Jan. 11, 1947; s. Hays Hamilton and Hedwig Elizabeth (Ball) J.; B.S. in Engring. Sci., Fla. State U., 1970; postgrad. Cleve. State U., 1978—; m. Barbara Elizabeth Adamczyk, Sept. 13, 1969. Lab. instr. Fla. State U., Tallahassee, 1968-70; project engr. Tocco div. Park Ohio, Cleve., 1970-72; engring. design dept. head Life Systems, Inc., Cleve., 1972-77; NASA cons. W.L. Tanksley and Assos., Inc., Cleve., 1977-79; founder (with wife), pres. Patriot Engring. Co., Chagrin Falls, Ohio, 1979—. Bd. dirs. diversified coop. tng. program Kenston High Sch. Recipient achievement award Lyndon B. Johnson Space Center, 1980; registered profl. engr., Ohio. Mem. Am. Soc. Metals, Am. Nuclear Soc., Am. Mgmt. Assn., Nat. Soc. Profl. Engrs., ASME, Cleve. East Soc. Profl. Engrs. (chmn. community action com. 1975-78, pres. 1978-79, dir. 1974—, state dir. 1979-80, cert. of appreciation 1979). Republican. Roman Catholic. Contbr. articles to profl. jours. Patentee in field. Home and Office: 1607 Bell St Chagrin Falls OH 44022

JENSEN, JAMES ROBERT, educator, dentist; b. Mpls., Mar. 17, 1922; s. Ernest William and Edith Ann (Norstedt) J.; B.A., U. Minn., 1944, D.D.S., 1946, M.S., 1950; m. Alvern Halverson, Mar. 24, 1945; children—Thomas, Mark, James, Elizabeth. Teaching asst. U. Minn., 1948-50, asst. prof., 1950-53, asso. prof., 1953-57, prof., chmn. div. operative dentistry and endodontics, 1957-69, asst. dean acad. affairs, 1969-74, asso. dean acad. affairs, 1974—, prof., chmn. div. endodontics, 1969—; part time practice specializing endodontics; cons. endodontics VA Hosps., St. Cloud, Minn. and Mpls.; team leader operative dentistry and endodontics Project Vietnam of AID; cons. dental health Pan Am. Health Orgn., WHO; cons. to council on dental edn. Am. Dental Assn. and Hosp. Dental Service; mem. staff Hennepin County Gen. Hosp., Univ. Hosp. of U. Minn.; postgrad. faculty Universidad Autonoma de Nueva Leon, Monterrey, Mexico. Served with U.S. Army, 1943-44, as capt. Dental Corps, 1946-48; res. dental surgeon USPHS and Assn. Res. Officers. Diplomate Am. Bd. Endodontics. Fellow Am., Internat. colls. dentists; mem. Am., Minn. dental assns., Mpls. Dist. Dental Soc., Internat. Assn. Dental Research, Dental Materials Group, Internat. Assn. Dental Research, Am. Assn. Endodontists, Fedn. Dentaire Internationale, Am. Assn. Dental Schs. Author: (wtih Thomas P. Serene and Fernando Sanchez) Fundamentos Clinicos de Endodoncia, 1977; (with Thomas P. Serene) Fundamentals of Clinical Endodontics, 7th edit., 1977; Effective Dental Assisting, 5th edit., 1978. Contbr. articles profl. jours. Home: 2167 N Rosewood Ln Saint Paul MN 55113 Office: Sch of Dentistry Univ Minnesota Minneapolis MN 55455

JENSEN, JERRY KIRTLAND, food co. exec.; b. Chgo., Sept. 27, 1947; s. Harry Dybdahl and Violet May (Nowak) J.; B.S. (John McMullen scholar 1965-69), Cornell U., 1969, M.Indsl. Engring., 1971. Pres., Jensen's Cinema 16, Western Springs, Ill., 1970—; indsl. engr. Gen. Foods, Chgo., 1970-72, sr. indsl. engr., 1972-73, prodn. scheduling supr., 1973-74, prodn. control mgr., 1974-76; mgmt. systems specialist Beatrice Foods Co., Chgo., 1976-77, operating services project mgr., 1977-79, mgr. indsl. engring., 1980—; v.p., sec. Country Residential, Inc., Western Springs and Crystal Lake, Ill. Film festivals chmn. Western Springs Recreation Commn., 1969-70, 73-81. Cert. in prodn. and inventory mgmt. Mem. Am. Prodn. and Inventory Control Soc., Great Lakes English Springer Spaniel Breeders Assn. (pres. 1979-81), Alpha Phi Omega, Beta Theta Pi. Clubs: Cornell, Variety. Author: (with Dr. Joel Ross) Productivity, People and Profits, 1981; contbr. (with Ted Olson) Productivity Improvement: Case Studies of Proven Practice, 1981. Home: 4524 Howard Ave Western Springs IL 60558 Office: 2 N LaSalle St Chicago IL 60602

JENSEN, JOHN W., state senator; b. York, Nebr., Mar. 26, 1926; s. Matthias and Bessie J.; grad. high sch.; Myrtle L. Shipp; 5 children. Farmer, Plainfield, Iowa; fieldman Butler County Farm Bur., 8 yrs.; mem. Iowa Senate. Past pres. Plainfield Community Sch. Bd. Served with USMC, World War II. Mem. Farm Bur., N.E. Iowa Angus Assn., Iowa Angus Assn., Bremer County Beef Producers, Bermer County Pork Producers. Republican. Baptist. Home: Route 1 Box 103 Plainfield IA 50666 Office: State Capitol Des Moines IA 50319*

JENSEN, RAYMOND ANDREW, lawyer; b. St. Paul, June 30, 1923; s. Einer Nordall and Laura Camille (Hansen) J.; student U. Wis., 1941-43, U. Calif. at Los Angeles, 1943-44; J.D., U. Chgo., 1950. Admitted to Ill. bar, 1950; atty. Office of Solicitor, U.S. Dept. Labor, Chgo., 1951-53; asst. cashier City Nat. Bank & Trust Co. Chgo., 1953-58; with Dovenmuehle, Inc., Chgo., 1958-73, v.p., 1960-72, counsel, 1958-73, sr. v.p., 1972-73; partner firm Burditt & Calkins, Chgo., 1974—. Mem. Mechanic's Lien Law and Constrn. Financing Study Comm., Ill., 1969-71, Mayor's Adv. Com. Community Renewal Program, Chgo., 1963-68; mem. adv. com. Uniform Land Transactions Act, Nat. Conf. Commrs. Uniform State Laws, 1969-76. Mem. Am. (chmn. real estate financing com. 1968-71, council real property, probate and trust law 1976—), Ill. State, Chgo. (chmn. real property law com. 1968-69), Fed., bar assns., Chgo. Mortgage Attys. Assn. (pres. 1963-64), Lambda Alpha. Clubs: Univ. (Chgo.), Cliff Dwellers, Monroe. Contbr. articles to publs. Home: 1555 N Dearborn Pkwy Chicago IL 60610 Office: 135 S La Salle St Chicago IL 60603

JENSEN, SHIRLEY WULFF, bus. exec.; b. Kingsbury County, S.D., Jan. 12, 1925; d. Ferdinand and Karen Margaret (Jensen) Wulff; honor grad. Chillicothe Bus. Coll., 1943; m., Nov. 23, 1975; 1 son, Fred Monroe Smith, Jr. Legal sec., New Port Richey, Fla., 1959-63; sec. to pres. Huron (S.D.) Coll., 1947-50; ins. agt., bd. dirs., mgr. Farm Mut. Fire Ins. Co. of Kingsbury County, De Smet, S.D., 1972-75; exec. sec. Beresford (S.D.) C. of C. and Beresford Bus. and Indsl. Devel. Corp., 1976-78; partner, office mgr., sales asst. Black Angus Ranch and Jensen Appliances, Beresford, 1979—. City commr. De Smet, 1974-75; Kingsbury County chmn. Easter Seal Soc., 1973-75; sec. ch. council Emmanuel Luth. Ch., Beresford; mem. S.D. Women's Caucus. Mem. S.D. Assn. Mut. Ins. Cos. (bd. dirs.), Beresford C. of C. Clubs: Christian Women's, Am. Legion Aux. First woman bd. dirs. S.D. Assn. Mut. Ins. Cos.; first woman city commr. De Smet. Home and Office: Route 3 Box 11 Beresford SD 57004

JENSEN, THEODORE ROBERT, business exec.; b. Bemidji, Minn., June 16, 1943; s. Melvin Eward and Olive Mae (Bradseth) J.; B.A., North Central Bible Coll., 1968; Dipl., Spartan Sch. Aeros., 1972; m. Judith Ann Reed, Aug. 7, 1965; children—Kevin Lee, Karla Rae, Kerri Mae. Ordained to ministry Assembly of God Ch., 1967; pastor Casino Assembly of God, Pillager, Minn., 1967-70, Ashland (Wis.) Assembly of God, 1974-76; mgr., fixed base operator Ashland Air Service, 1976-80; with Snap-On Tools, Prentice, Wis., 1980—. Mem. CAP, Nat. Small Bus. Assn., Exptl. Air Craft Assn., Aircraft Pilots and Owners Assn., Wis. Airports Mgrs. Assn. Address: PO Box 248 Prentice WI 54556

JEPSEN, ROGER WILLIAM, Senator; b. Cedar Falls, Iowa, Dec. 23, 1928; s. Ernest Emil and Esther (Sorensen) J.; student U. No. Iowa, 1945-46; B.A., Ariz. State U., 1950, M.A., 1953; m. Dee Ann Delaney, 1958; children—Jeffrey, Ann, Craig, Linda, Deborah, Coy. Counselor, Ariz. State U., 1950-53; ins. agt. Am. United Life Ins. Co., 1954-56; br. mgr. Conn. Gen. Life Ins. Co., 1956-72; exec. v.p. Agridustrial Electronics Co., 1973-76; pres. pvt. mktg. co., 1976-78; supr. Scott County, 1962-65; mem. Iowa Senate, 1966-68; lt. gov. State of Iowa, 1968-72; mem. U.S. Senate from Iowa, 1978—. Served with U.S. Army, 1946-47; capt. Res. (ret.). Mem. Nat. Assn. Life Underwriters. Republican. Lutheran. Clubs: Shriners, Jesters. Office: 110 Russell Senate Office Bldg Washington DC 20510

JEPSON, DARRELL EDWARD, vets. orgn. exec.; b. Sioux City, Iowa, May 13, 1935; s. Edward R. and Florence G. (Cook) J.; B.S., Morningside Coll., 1962; m. Beverly Ann Brown, Mar. 13, 1954; children—Chris, Charles, Cheri. Cattle buyer Raskin Packing Co., Sioux City, 1967; cattle rancher, 1964-74; owner Sportsmen's Recreation, Lennox, S.D., 1971-75; S.D. state dir. White House Conf. on Handicapped Individuals, Sioux Falls, 1975-78; regional adv. dir. Paralyzed Vets. Am., Tea, S.D., 1978-81, recipient Disting. Service award, 1979. Bd. dirs. S.D. Easter Seal Soc., 1979-81, East River Legal Services, 1979-81, Sioux Vocat. Sch., 1978-81; chmn. S.D. Vocat. Rehab. Bd., 1978-81; commr. Lincoln County, 1978-81; chmn. Southeastern Mental Health Center Bd., 1979-81; mem. State Manpower Bd., 1979-81, State Planning Council, 1979-81, Gove.'s Handicapped Adv. Com., 1980-81, S.E. Area Home Health Care Bd., 1979-81; chmn. Internat. Year of Disabled Persons for City Sioux Falls, S.D., 1980-81; mem. Lincoln County Extension Bd., 1979-81, Southeastern Council Govts. Urban Devel. Bd., 1979-81, Southeastern Criminal Justice Bd., 1979-81; mem. Lennox Dist. 100 Sch. Bd., 1972-77, chmn., 1976-77. Recipient Disting. Service award Mayor of Sioux Falls, 1980. Mem. Nat. Assn. Counties (nat. 504 adv. com. 1979-81). Lutheran. Office: PO Box 98 Tea SD 57064

JEPSON, ROBERT SCOTT, JR., internat. investment banking specialist; b. Richmond, Va., July 20, 1942; s. Robert Scott and Inda (Hodges) J.; B.S., U. Richmond, 1964, M.Commerce, 1975; m. Alice Finch Andrews, Dec. 28, 1964; children—Robert Scott III, John Steven. With Va. Commonwealth Bankshares, Richmond, 1966-68; v.p. corp. fin. Birr Wilson & Co., Inc., San Francisco, 1968-69; with Calif. Capital Mgmt. Corp., Irvine, 1970-73; pres. Calcap Securities Corp., Los Angeles, 1970-73; v.p., dir. corp. fin. Cantor Fitzgerald & Co., Beverly Hills, Calif., 1973-75; dir. corp. planning and devel. Campbell Industries, San Diego, 1975-77; v.p., mgr. merger and acquisition div. Continental Ill. Bank, Chgo., 1977—; asst. prof. fin. Nat. U., 1976. Served to 1st lt. Mil. Police Corps, AUS, 1964-66. Mem. Omicron Delta Kappa, Alpha Kappa Psi. Republican. Clubs: Mid-Am., Chgo. Home: 65 Hills and Dales Rd Barrington Hills IL 60010 Office: 231 LaSalle St Chicago IL 60693

JERATH, SUKHVARSH, structural engr.; b. Khaur, Pakistan, May 27, 1942; came to U.S., 1971, permanent resident, 1978; s. Ram Partap and Raj Rani J.; B.E., Birla Engring. Coll., Pilani, India, 1962; M.E., Birla Inst. Tech. and Scis., Pilani, 1968; M.S., Brigham Young U., 1972; Ph.D., U. Ill., Urbana, 1977; m. Saroj Shahi, Oct. 1, 1968; children—Aradhana, Rahul. Asst. prof. civil engring. Birla Inst. Tech. and Scis., Pilani, India, 1962-71; teaching asst. U. Ill., Urbana, 1972-74, 75-77; research asst. U.S. Army Constrn. Engring. Research Lab., Champaign, Ill., 1974-75; sr. engr. Custodis Constrn. Co., div. Research Cottrell, Inc., Terre Haute, Ind., 1977-80; asst. prof. civil and environ. engring. Wash. State U., Pullman, 1980—. Merit scholar Brigham Young U., 1972. Mem. ASCE, ASME, Sigma Xi, Phi Kappa Phi. Registered profl. engr., Ill., Ind. Contbr. articles to profl. jours. Home: NW 1705 Turner Dr Pullman WA 99163 Office: Dept Civil and Environmental Engring Wash State U Pullman WA 99164

JERMYN, CHARLOTTE CALDWELL MOSS, civic and polit. worker; b. Richmond, Ind., May 22, 1932; d. Warrington Caldwell and Katherine (Smead) Moss; student Henry Ford Community Coll., 1963-64; m. Walter Driscoll, May 22, 1950 (div. Feb. 1967); m. 2d, William Palmer Harrington, July 3, 1968 (div. Mar. 1972); children—Charles Spencer, Robert Wylie, Alice Warrington, William Ward; m. 3d, Willis Franklin Keiser, Aug. 12, 1972 (div. 1975); m. 4th, Thomas D. Jermyn, Apr. 17, 1976. Freelance photo-illustrator, 1981—; program coordinator City of Dearborn Pub. Info. Exchange. Sec., PTA, 1961-62, vice chmn., 1965-66; leader Girl Scouts U.S.A., 1969—; sec. Young Republicans, 1960-61, 1961-63; sec. East Dearborn Rep. Club, 1963; sec. West Dearborn Rep. Club, 1964-67, vice chmn., 1965-66, 67-68, chmn., 1969—; vice chmn. Congressional Dist. Rep. Com., 1965-69; mem. Mich. Rep. Central Com., 1969—; Rep. precinct del., 1960-64, 66—; del. Mich. Rep. Conv., 1960—; mem. Rep. Task Force on Human Rights, 1969—; mem. exec. com. Reps. of Dearborn, 1972—; mem. organizing com. 16th Congressional Dist. Women's Polit. Caucus, 1972, vice chmn., 1972—; precinct del. chmn. Dearborn Rep. Com., 1972; bd. dirs. Midwestern Wayne County NOW Speakers Bur., arrangements chmn. Nat. Conf., 1977; dir. vols. Detroit chpt. Nat. Hemophilia Found., 1968-69. Mem. Mensa (v.p. S.E. Mich. 1977-78, pres. 1978-81, coordinator central S.C. chpt. 1981—). Congregationalist (mem. social activities com. and

Christian edn. 1970, planning bd. 1971—, supt. ch. sch., del. Mich. Conf.). Home: 6 42d Ave Isle of Palms SC 29451

JEROME, NORGE WINIFRED, nutritionist, anthropologist; b. Grenada, W.I., Nov. 3, 1930; d. Mc Manus Israel and Evelyn Mary (Grant) J.; came to U.S., 1956, naturalized, 1973; B.S. magna cum laude, Howard U., 1960; M.S., U. Wis., 1962, Ph.D., 1967. Asst. prof. U. Kans. Med. Sch., 1967-72, asso. prof., 1972-78, prof., 1978—; dir. ednl. resource centers U. Kans. Med. Center, 1974-77, dir. community nutrition div., dept. community health, 1981—; cons. Children's TV Workshop, 1974-77; chmn. adv. bd. Teenage Parents Center, 1971-75; mem. planning and budget council, children and family services United Community Services, 1971—; mem. panel on nutrition edn. White House Conf. on Food, Nutrition and Health, 1969; mem. bd. dirs., health care com. Prime Health, 1976-79; bd. dirs. Council on Children, Media and Merchandising, Washington, 1977—; mem. consumer edn. task force Mid-Am. Health Systems Agy., 1977-78. Bd. dirs. Kansas City Urban League, 1969-77, Crittenton Center, Kansas City, Mo., 1979—. Decorated Dau. British Empire. Fellow Am. Anthrop. Assn. (chairperson com. on nutritional anthropology 1974-77), Soc. Applied Anthropology; mem. Am. Pub. Health Assn. (food and nutrition council 1975-78), Am. Inst. Nutrition, Am. Soc. Clin. Nutrition, Soc. Med. Anthropology, N.Y. Acad. Scis., Am. Men and Women of Sci., Nat. Acad. Scis. (world food and nutrition study panel), Soc. Nutrition Edn., Am. Dietetic Assn. Contbr. articles to profl. jours.; asso. editor Jour. Nutrition Edn., 1971-77, nat. adv. council, 1977—; editor Nutritional Anthropology Communicator, 1974-77; editorial adv. bd. Med. Anthropology: Cross Cultural Studies in Health and Illness, 1976—; mem. editorial bd. Nutrition Planning, 1977—. Home: 14402 W 68th St Shawnee KS 66216 Office: 39th and Rainbow Sts Kansas City KS 66103

JEROME, ROBERT THEODORE, JR., educator; b. Balt., June 7, 1950; s. Robert Theodore and Margaret Esther (Atkinson) J.; B.A., Tex. Christian U., 1972; A.B.D. (Gov.'s fellow 1973-74), U. Va., 1976, postgrad. 1973—; m. Margaret Ann Stoops, Jan. 6, 1973. Instr. econs. U. Va., Charlottesville, 1977-78; asst. prof. econs. St. Joseph's Coll., Rensselaer, Ind., 1978-80; vis. instr. econs. Notre Dame (Ind.) U., 1980—; cons. in field; lectr. in field. Organist, Presbyn. Ch., Rensselaer, 1979—. E. Europe area study fellow, HEW, 1976-77. Mem. Am. Econs. Assn., Ind. Acad. Social Sci., Assn. for Comparative Econ. Systems. Presbyterian. Editor, Va. Essays in Econs., 1974-76. Home: 618 E Grace St Rensselaer IN 47978 Office: Dept Econs Notre Dame Univ Notre Dame IN 45560

JERREL, BURTON BLANCHARD, film producer; b. Oskaloosa, Iowa, Dec. 31, 1907; s. Burt Owen and Rose (Blanchard) J.; B.A., Oberlin-Iowa U., 1929; LL.B., J.D., Harvard U., 1934; m. Dorothy Palmer, Oct. 12, 1935 (dec. Feb. 1970); children—Valerie Jerrel Armstrong, Louise Jerrel Kirke, Jean Jerrel Carlson; m. 2d, Rosalyn McKinnie, Feb. 5, 1972. Newsreel and documentary film producer, 1935-56; landowner, mgr. Jerrel Bldgs. 2d Farms, 1937—; pres. Inter-State Film Corp., Des Moines, 1935-45; producer La. News Flashes, 1935-43; owner, producer Tele-Topics Pro Football Shorts, 1944-54; partner Chgo. Bears, 1944-53; owner, producer Southland Newsreel, 1948-56; chmn. bd. Inter-State Film Corp.; partner Televisual Prodns.; mem. Nat. Film Adv. Bd.; originator, producer Iowa News Flashes, Tele-Topics, Southland Newsreel; midwest rep. Pathe Newsreel, March of Time; producer documentaries including Iowa Comes of Age; producer more than 1000 newsreel subjects. Mem. Drake Relays Com., 1935-44; mem. Iowa Wilkie Com., 1940, Dewey Com., 1948; active Iowa Arthritis Found., Iowa Soc. Prevention Blindness, Nat. Umpires Assn., 1952-54; mem. Iowa Treasury Bond Com., World War II, U.S. Treasury Bond Com., World War II. Recipient Iowa Disting. Artists award, 1942; award of merit Nat. Film Adv. Bd., 1944; GI Movies award, 1944-45; U.S. Treasury award, 1945. Mem. Iowa Bar Assn., Harvard Law Assn. (life), Iowa U. Alumni Assn. (life), Oberlin Alumni Assn. (life), Sigma Delta Chi, Phi Kappa Psi. Republican. Clubs: Harvard (N.Y.C.); Ill. Athletic; Des Moines, Wakonda Country, Bohemian (Des Moines); U. Iowa Athletic (Iowa City); Chancery Pitney Law (Cambridge, Mass.). Big 10 high jump champion, 1927. Home and Office: PO Box 4746 2d Ave Des Moines IA 50318

JERRITTS, STEPHEN G., electronics co. exec.; b. New Brunswick, N.J., 1925; B.M.E., Rensselaer Poly. Inst., 1947, M.S., 1948; married. With IBM, to 1967; gen. mgr. peripheral div. Gen. Electric Co., 1967-68; with Honeywell Inc., Mpls., 1970—, mng. dir. Honeywell Info. Systems Ltd., 1974, v.p and gen. mgr. U.S. info. systems group, 1977-80, pres. info. systems, 1980—. Office: Honeywell Inc Honeywell Plaza Minneapolis MN 55408*

JESKE, PHYLLIS MYERS, real estate exec.; b. Carmi, Ill.; d. Frank M. and Ruby P. (Lee) Myers; student public schs.; grad. Realtors Inst. Ill., 1975; m. Thomas N. Jeske, Nov. 23, 1966. Engaged in real estate, 1971—; with Baird & Warner Inc., 1973—, sales mgr., St. Charles, Ill., 1976—, asst. v.p., 1978-81, v.p., 1981—. Grad. Realtors Inst. (GRI), Cert. Residential Specialist (CRS). Mem. Nat. Assn. Realtors, Ill. Assn. Realtors (v.p. Dist. 12), Fox Valley Bd. Realtors (pres. 1980), Women in Mgmt., Am. Soc. Profl. and Exec. Women, St. Charles C. of C. Home: 5N251 Elm Rd Box 434 Wayne IL 60184 Office: 1564 E Main St PO Box 1011 St Charles IL 60174

JESSEPH, JOHN ERVIN, educator, surgeon; b. Pasco, Wash., Nov. 6, 1925; s. Harry Ervin and Eula Victoria (Ledgerwood) J.; A.B., Whitman Coll., 1949, D.Sc. (hon.), 1975; M.D., U. Wash., 1953, M.S., 1956; m. Marley M.G. Austin, June 20, 1948; children—Steven A., Jerry M. Intern, King County Hosp., Seattle, 1953-54; resident in surgery U. Wash. Affiliated Hosps., Seattle, 1954-59; asst. prof. surgery U. Wash., Seattle, 1959-62; scientist Brookhaven Nat. Lab., 1962-65; faculty Ohio State U., Columbus, 1965-71, prof., 1967-71; prof. surgery, chmn. dept. Sch. Medicine, Ind. U., Indpls., 1971—. Served with USMCR, 1944-46, col. M.C., USNG. USPHS research grantee, 1955-58. Diplomate Am. Bd. Surgery (dir.), Am. Bd. Family Practice. Mem. Am. Surg. Assn., A.C.S., other orgns. Mason. Editor, contbg. author med. books; contbr. articles to profl. publs. Home: 5230 N Meridian St Indianapolis IN 46208 Office: 1100 W Michigan St Indianapolis IN 46202

JESSUP, ROGER L., educator, state senator; b. Fairmount, Ind., Feb. 23, 1929; s. Donald B. and Elizabeth L. (Leach) J.; B.S., Purdue U., 1950; M.A., Ball State U., 1959; m. Geraldine A. Mitchener, June 5, 1954; children—Karen, Rita, William, Mary Beth. Formerly tchr. vocat. agr. Blackford and Grant County schs.; then dean of boys Jones Jr. High Sch., sci. tchr. Marion Community Schs.; dir. research project in vocat. edn., 1973—; dir. assessment and planning project vocat. edn. div. Mississinewa (Ind.) Community Schs., 1977—; Ind. state rep., 1967-72; Ind. state senator, 1972—. Served with USAF. Mem. NEA, Nat. Assn. Sch. Adminstrs., Am. Vocat. Assn., Ind. Vocat. Assn., Nat. Soc. Legislators, Grant County Taxpayers Assn., Am. Legion, AMVETS. Republican. Quaker. Clubs: Columbia, Masons. Home: 3831 E 1200 S Summitville IN 46070 Office: State Legislature Indianapolis IN 46204*

JESUNAS, KENNETH PAUL, physician; b. Chgo., May 31, 1941; s. Paul and Sophie (Ambrose) J.; B.S., U. Ill., 1963, M.D., 1967; intern Cook County Hosp., Chgo., 1967-68; resident Northwestern U., 1968-72; m. Carolyn Carr, Jan. 4, 1969; children—Jason, Jocelyn. Asst. chief otolaryngology Brooke Army Med. Center, 1972-74; practice medicine, specializing in otolaryngology, Joliet, Ill., 1974—; mem. staff St. Joseph Hosp., Silver Cross Hosp. Diplomate Am. Bd. Otolaryngology, Nat. Bd. Med. Examiners. Fellow A.C.S.; mem. AMA, Am. Acad. Facial Plastic and Reconstructive Surgery, Soc. Mil. Otolaryngologists, Am. Acad. Ophthalmology and Otolaryngology, Am. Pharm. Assn., U. Ill. Alumni Assn., Will-Grundy County Med. Soc., Chgo. Laryngol. and Otol. Soc., Alpha Kappa Kappa, Rho Chi, Phi Delta Chi. Home: 110 Rebecca St Joliet IL 60435 Office: 3077 W Jefferson St Joliet IL 60435

JETER, HAROLD COOPER, oil co. exec.; b. Ironton, Ohio, Nov. 30, 1920; s. William Bransford and Lillian (Grady) J.; student public schs., Ironton; m. Mabel Marie Stewart, Nov. 21, 1959; children—Carole A. Jeter Broughton, Harold Stewart. Personnel asst. Henrite Products Corp., Ironton, 1940-46, personnel dir., 1946-56; personnel asst. Ashland Oil, Inc., (Ky.), 1956-69, employment supr., 1969, mgr. non-exempt employment, 1969-77, equal employment opportunity specialist, 1977—. Served with USAAF, 1942-45. Ky. col. Mem. Tri-State Personnel Assn. (past pres.), Nat. Mgmt. Assn., Inst. Cert. Profl. Mgrs., Ashland Area C. of C., Grange. Democrat. Home: Route 5 Box 457 South Point OH 45680 Office: Ashland Oil Inc PO Box 391 Ashland KY 41101

JETTKE, HARRY JEROME, govt. ofcl.; b. Detroit, Jan. 2, 1925; s. Harry H. and Eugenia M. (Dziatkiewicz) J.; B.A., Wayne State U., 1961; m. Josefina Suarez-Garcia, Oct. 22, 1948; 1 dau., Joan Lillian Jettke Sorger. Owner, operator Farmacia Virreyes/Farmacia Regina, Toluca, Mex., 1948-55; intern pharmacist Cunningham Drug Stores, Detroit, 1955-63; drug specialist, product safety specialist FDA, Detroit, 1963-73; acting dir. Cleve., U.S. Consumer Product Safety Commn., 1973-75, compliance officer, 1975-78, supr., investigations, 1978—. Served with Fin. Dept., U.S. Army, 1942-43. Drug specialist FDA. Mem. Am. Soc. for Quality Control (sr., chmn. Cleve. sect. 1977-78, cert. quality technician, cert. quality engr.), Asociación Nacional Mexicana de Estadística y Control de Calidad. Roman Catholic. Home: 25715 Yoeman Dr Westlake OH 44145 Office: US Consumer Product Safety Commn 1404 E 9th St Cleveland OH 44114

JEVNE, LOUISE PRISCILLA ARMSTRONG, genealogist; b. Ward County, N.D., Jan. 1, 1910; d. Joseph Robert and Valentine Emma (Butterfield) Armstrong; grad. Minot State Tchrs. Coll., 1964; m. Harry Oscar Jevne, Mar. 21, 1932; children—Henry Eugene, Vallie Ann, Donald Harry, Terry Byron. Tchr., Van Buren 3, Lansford, N.D., 1929-31, 49-54, Clay Center Consol. Sch., Lansford, 1931-32, Mercer County Rural Sch., Hazen, 1937-39, Nedrose Rural Sch., Minot, N.D., 1954-58, Minot (N.D.) pub. schs., 1958-71; writer biographies, tchr. family history, 1971-80. Dir. Van Buren Sch. Dist., 1948-49. Mem. N.D. Congress Parents and Tchrs. (life), Nat. Ret. Tchrs. Assn., Renville County Hist. Soc. (dir., life mem.), N.D. Hist. Soc., Red River Valley Hist. Soc., Valdres Samband, DAR, Garrett County (Md.) Hist. Soc., Soc. of Mareen Duvall Descendants, Red River Valley Genealogy Soc., Wis. State Geneal. Soc., Mouse River Loop Genealogy Soc., Erie County (Pa.) Soc. for Geneal. Research, DAR (N.D. state regent 1981-83), Delta Kappa Gamma. Mem. Ch. of Nazarene. Club: Vansign Homemakers. Author: Drane Families of Maryland, 1973; Teachers and Pupils, 1979; compiler: Methodist Church Records of Renville County, North Dakota, 1980. Home: Route 1 Box 17 Lansford ND 58750

JEWELL, HELEN STEVENS, educator; b. Elkhart, Iowa, Sept. 10, 1920; d. Ralph William and Ethel Eleanor (Peters) Stevens; A.S., Drake U., 1941; B.S.A., Western Ill. U., 1972, M.S.A., 1975; m. Louis C. Jewell, Dec. 7, 1942 (div.); children—H. Richard, Janis I.; m. 2d, Stanley S. Sims, Jan. 2, 1980. Tchr. primary grades, Iowa, 1943-45; substitute tchr., Monmouth, Ill., 1965-77; tchr. Harding Sch., Monmouth, 1972-77; coordinator curriculum, instr. early childhood edn. Carl Sandburg Community Coll., Galesburg, Ill., 1976—. Mem. exec. bd. Girl Scouts U.S.A., 1965-75, leader, 1965-77; mem. bldg. fund com. YMCA. Mem. AAUW, AAUP, Ill. Children's Assn., Nat. Assn. Edn. Young Children, Phi Kappa Phi. Republican. Presbyterian. Club: Garden. Home: Rt 4 Monmouth IL 61462

JEWELL, JOYCE BENGE, steel co. exec.; b. Franklin, Ohio, Mar. 6, 1934; d. Thomas and Bess (Gillen) Benge; student Miami U., Oxford, Ohio, 1953, 54, 55, 59; m. James Wey Jewell, Aug. 20, 1965; 1 dau., Paula. With Mound Labs., U.S. AEC, Miamisburg, Ohio, 1952-53; adminstrv. asst. Armco Steel Corp., Middletown, Ohio, 1953-70; supr. corr. support and services Armco, Inc., Middletown 1970-81, word processing cons., corp. info. resources mgmt., 1981—. Apptd. mem. Warren County Children Services Bd., 1970-81; mem. adv. council Warren County Joint Vocat. Schs., 1978—, Scarlet Oak Vocat. Sch., 1976—. Mem. South Western Ohio Word Processing/Adminstrv. Support Group (dir., 1st pres., co-founder), Internat. Info./Word Processing Assn., Word Processing Soc. Republican. Methodist. Order Eastern Star. Home: 2758 Audubon Dr Middletown OH 45042 Office: 703 Curtis St Middletown OH 45043

JHA, CHANDRA K., constrn. mgmt. co. exec.; b. India, July 2, 1928; come to U.S., 1953, naturalized, 1967; s. Lakshmi K. and Yogmaya J.; B.Sc., Bihar Coll. Engring., India, 1950; M.S., Ill. Inst. Tech., 1957; M.B.A., U. Chgo., 1962; m. Hekmat Elkhanialy, Dec. 20, 1969; 1 dau., Lakshmi E. Design engr. Harza Engring. Co., Ranchi, India, 1950-53, design engr., Chgo., 1953-55; sr. design engr. McDonald Engring. Co., Chgo., 1955-56; staff engr. John Mohr & Sons, Chgo., 1957-64; mgr. sci. mgmt. services Lester B. Knight & Assos., mgmt. cons., Chgo., 1964-67; v.p. Tishman Realty & Constrn., Chgo., 1967-77; pres. PSM Internat. Corp., Chgo., 1977—; former condr. seminars project mgmt. UCLA, Ill. Inst. Tech., U. Ill., Stanford U., Constrn. Mgmt. Inst., Zurich, Switzerland. Mem. India League Am. (founder, pres. 1972-76, dir.), ASCE, Project Mgmt. Inst., Ops. Research Soc. Am., Inst. Mgmt. Sci., Am. Mgmt. Assn. Club: Metropolitan. Author: (with Goldhaber) Construction Management: Principles and Practices, 1977. Office: 200 W Monroe St Chicago IL 60606

JHAMB, TEJ BAHADUR, engineer; b. India, Apr. 1, 1934; came to U.S., 1968, naturalized, 1978; s. Jamna Dass and Thirthi Devi (Wadhwa) J.; B.A., Punjab U., India, 1954, B.M.E., 1959; M.S. in Indsl. Engring., Wayne State U., 1974; m. Chander Malik, Nov. 29, 1962; children—Gagan, Aalok. Process engr. Hindustan Motors Ltds., Hoogly West Bengal, India, 1960-62, project engr., 1962-64, sr. project engr., 1964-66, asst. to works mgr., 1967, asst. to prodn. mgr., 1968; prodn. supr. Auto. div. Budd Co., Detroit, 1969-70, prodn. control supr., 1971, asst. to prodn. mgr., 1972, spl. assignment, 1973-74, asst. gen. supr. indsl. engring., 1975-77, asst. mgr. indsl. engring., 1978-79, mgr. indsl. engring., 1980—. Pres. Community Action Com., Hooghly West Bengal, 1961-66; mem. organizing com. cub scout pack 269 Clinton Valley council Boy Scouts Am., 1970-74; bd. dirs. Detroit-Eastside YMCA; mem. organizing com. India Culture Soc., 1970-80. Cert. mfg. engr. Mem. Am. Inst. Indsl. Engrs. (sr.), Engring. Soc. Detroit (industry ambassador). Mem. Sikh Soc. Michigan, Bhartia Temple. Club: Budd Mgmt. Office: 12141 Charlevoix Detroit MI 48215

JHAWAR, SHIV RATAN, investment and tax cons.; b. Bikaner, Rajasthan, India, Aug. 13, 1948; came to U.S., 1973; s. Dhanraj Harakhchand and Ratan Devi (Bajaj) J.; B.Commerce with 1st class honors, U. Calcutta, 1968; chartered acct. Inst. Chartered Accts. India, 1971; M.Acctg. Sci., U. Ill., Urbana, 1974. Articled apprentice Inst. Chartered Accts. India, 1967-71; research asst. Grad. Sch. Bus., U. Ill., 1973; prof., dir. studies Walton Sch. Commerce, Chgo., 1974; chief acct. spl. projects div. CBS TV, Chgo., 1975; owner, investment and tax specialist SRJ Cons., Chgo., 1975—; lectr. income tax and acctg. Registered investment adv. SEC; enrolled to practice before IRS; gen. securities registered rep. Mem. Am. Acctg. Assn., Acad. Acctg. Historians, Nat. Soc. Public Accts., Assn. Internat. Accts., Inst. Chartered Accts. India, Malabar Hill Jaycees (treas. 1972). Contbr. articles to profl. jours. Office: 120 S LaSalle St Suite 1161 Chicago IL 60603

JILANI, ATIQ AHMED, mfg. co. exec.; b. Amroha, India, Feb. 1, 1948; s. Siddiq Ahmed and Nasima (Khatoon) J.; B.E., N.E.D. Engring. Coll., Karachi U., 1969; M.S., Tuskegee Inst., Ala., 1971; m. Khalida Bano Naqvi, Dec. 25, 1975; children—Hussain, Ibrahim. Script writer Karachi (Pakistan) TV, 1967-70; mem. research staff AEC, Tuskegee, Ala., 1970-71; design engr. Lummus Industries, Columbus, Ga., 1971-73; product engr. Borg-Warner Corp., Chgo., 1974-78, mem. cost and productivity com., 1976, mgr. engring. Chgo. Marine Containers div. Sea Containers, Broadview, Ill., 1978-80; v.p., gen. mgr. Borg-Erickson Corp., Chgo., 1980—; cons. in industry and agr. UN, including work in S. Asia, 1981. Registered profl. engr., Ill.; cert. mfg. engr.; cert. plant engr. Mem. Nat., Ill. socs. profl. engrs., Am. Soc. Agrl. Engrs., ASME, Assn. Energy Engrs. (charter), Thinkers Forum (pres. 1967-70). Muslim. Contbr. articles to profl. jours. Patentee (U.S. and internat.) in field agrl. equipment. Home: PO Box 2461 Glen Ellyn IL 60137

JIMERSON, JAMES COMPERE, SR., toxicologist; b. Little Rock, Oct. 10, 1936; s. George Alexander and Lois (Compere) J.; B.A., B.S., Ouachita Bapt. Coll., 1958; postgrad. U. Ark., 1959; m. Ina Sue Jones, Aug. 18, 1957; children—Martha LeAnn, James Compere. Lab. instr. Ouachita Bapt. Coll., Arkadelphia, Ark., 1957-58; teaching asst. U. Ark., Fayetteville, 1958-59; sr. chemist Allied Chem. Corp., Metropolis, Ill., 1959-62; analytical chemist Tech. Service Labs., P.R. Mallory & Co., Indpls., 1962-65; engring./research group leader Mallory Capacitor Co., Indpls., 1965-72; toxicologist, dept. pathology Wishard Meml. Hosp., Indpls., 1972-79, adminstrv. dir. dept. pathology, 1979—; affiliate instr. Ind. Vocat. Tech. Coll. Sr. staff/communication coordinator Office of Civil Def., Indpls. and Marion County, 1965—; bd. dirs. Crossroads of Am. council Boy Scouts Am., 1973—, v.p., mem. exec. com., 1975-80, commr., 1969-72, tng. chmn., 1972-73, dist. chmn., 1973-76; bd. dirs. Marion County unit Am. Cancer Soc. Recipient Silver Beaver award Boy Scouts Am., 1976; Pub. Service award Am. Radio Relay League, 1966, 74; named Man of Yr., Civil Def., 1976. Fellow Am. Inst. Chemists, Am. Acad. Forensic Scis.; mem. Am. Chem. Soc., Soc. for Applied Spectroscopy, Coblentz Soc., Central Ind. Clin. Biochem. Forum, Am. Soc. Analytical Toxicologists, Nat. Eagle Scout Assn. (Silver Wreath award 1979), Central Ind. VHF/UHF Club. Republican. Baptist (deacon). Clubs: Masons, Scottish Rite. Patentee. Home: 1820 Fairhaven Dr Indianapolis IN 46229 Office: 1001 W 10th St Indianapolis IN 46202

JOB, RICHARD WILLIAM, mech. engr.; b. Freeport, Minn., Dec. 12, 1939; s. Ralph Leo and Wilhelmina (Wensman) J.; B.M.E., Mich. Technol. U., 1963; m. Jane E. Friberg, May 26, 1962; children—Reba Nell, Sara Jean. Quality control engr. Clinton Engines Corp., Maquoketa, Iowa, 1963-64; design engr. J. I. Case Co., Racine, Wis., 1964-67; project engr. Avco New Idea, Coldwater, Ohio, 1967-70; sr. project engr. Hesston Corp. (Kans.), 1970; sr. project engr. Twin Disc Inc., Racine, Wis., 1970-71; chief engr. test and devel. White Farm Equipment Co., Libertyville, Ill., 1971-79; chief test engr. Harnischfeger Corp., Escanaba, Mich., 1979—. Mem. Soc. Automotive Engrs. Roman Catholic. Home: 527 S 29th St Escanaba MI 49829 Office: 2525 14th Ave Escanaba MI 49829

JOBE, CECILIA AUBURN, designer; b. Denver, Aug. 13, 1949; d. Cecil Elbert and Alien Joyce (Hudson) J.; B.S. in Bus. Adminstrn., Roosevelt U., 1973, postgrad., 1978—. Mgmt. analyst Washington Nat. Ins. Co., Evanston, Ill., 1973-76, work measurement analyst, 1976-78, layout and design analyst, 1978-80, layout and design supr., 1980—. Adviser, Jr. Achievement, 1976-77. Mem. Assn. M.B.A. Execs., Southend Jr. C. of C. Women's Assn. (internal v.p. 1973-74). Roman Catholic. Home: 8232 S Michigan Ave Chicago IL 60619 Office: Washington Nat Ins Co 1630 Chicago Ave Evanston IL 60619

JOBES, ALVIN ROY, cons. engr.; b. Roscoe, Pa., Aug. 3, 1925; s. Edgar Robert and Ethel (Langford) J.; student Bethany Coll. (W.Va.), 1943-46; B.S., E.M., W.Va. U., 1950; m. Carol Sarah Bier, May 7, 1948; children—Deborah Ann, Edward Alan, Robert Landon. Engr., sect. foreman Valley Camp Coal Co., 1950-54; design engr., project engr., div. 5 ops. engr. Ohio Dept. Hwys., 1954-63; cons. engr., owner A. R. Jobes and Assos., Inc., 1963-69; pres. Jobes, Henderson & Assos., Inc., 1969—. Served with AUS, 1943-45, ETO. Registered profl. engr. and surveyor, Ohio; profl. engr., W.Va. Mem. Nat., Ohio socs. profl. engrs., Nat., Ohio socs. homebuilders, C. of C., Alpha Sigma Phi. Democrat. Presbyterian. Clubs: Masons (32 deg.), Shriners, Moundbuilders Country. Home: 1574 Russet Ln Newark OH 43055 Office: 80 Westgate Dr Newark OH 43055

JOBST, CAROLINE BRIGGS, mfg. co. exec.; b. Asheville, N.C., May 7, 1919; d. Horace Gladstone and Erma Parham Briggs; student Cecil's Coll., 1937-38; m. Conrad Jobst, June 16, 1941 (dec.). Pres., chief exec. officer Jobst Inst., Inc., Toledo, Ohio, 1957—; dir. Toledo Trust Co. Bd. dirs. Community Chest; mem. Pres. Council, Toledo Mus. Art; Golden Baton asso. Toledo Symphony Orch. Mem. Am. Mgmt. Assn., Aerospace Med. Assn., Nat. Mgmt. Assn. (mem. adv. bd., Silver Knight award 1980), Nat. Assn. Hosiery Mfrs., Employers Assn. Toledo, Toledo Area C. of C. (bd. dirs.). Episcopalian. Club: Toledo. Home: 418 Riverside Dr Rossford OH 43460 Office: 653 Miami St Toledo OH 43605

JOCZ, PATRICIA ELEANOR, ednl. adminstr.; b. Milw., Dec. 4, 1935; d. David John and Eleanor (Goertz) Goggins; B.A., Mt. Mary Coll., 1958; m. Martin Anthony Jocz, Aug. 2, 1958; children—Martin, Victoria, Thomas. Tchr., S. Div. High Sch., Milw., 1958-59; dir. religious edn. St. Matthias Parish, Milw., 1968-75; asso. dir. field edn. Sacred Heart Sch. Theology, Hales Corners, Wis., 1972-75, dir. field edn., 1975—, adv. bd., 1976—. Sec. to Senate Dist. 8, Citizens for Ednl. Freedom, 1967-70; v.p. 88th St. Home and Sch., 1967-68, pres., 1968-69; mem. St. Matthias Home and Sch. Bd., 1968-74, St. Matthias Bd. Edn., 1968-75, St. Matthias Parish Council, 1970-75. Mem. Nat. Cath. Edn. Assn., Assn. Theol. Field Educators (sec.-treas. 1979—), Assn. Clin. Pastoral Edn. (standards com. North Central region, dir. North Central region 1981—, sem. relations task force 1981), Assn. Profl. Edn. for Ministry, Midwest Assn. Theol. Schs. Roman Catholic. Office: Sacred Heart Sch Theology 7335 S Lovers Ln Hales Corners WI 53130

JODELKA, EDWARD STEFAN, mfg. co. exec.; b. Emsdetten, Germany, Sept. 26, 1949; came to U.S., 1951, naturalized, 1966; s. Stefan and Maria (Budnik) J.; B.S. indsl. Edn., Chgo. State U., 1971, postgrad., 1971, 72-73; m. Deborah Lee Boykovsky, July 3, 1971; children—Melissa Lynn, Thomas Edward. With Radiant Products Co., Inc., Chgo., 1965—, v.p. 1978—; vocat. guidance counselor, sch. programmer, tchr. Gregier Vocat. High Sch., Chgo., 1972-74. Mem. Internat. Entrepreneurs Assn., Am. Entrepreneurs Assn., Am. Mgmt. Assn. Republican. Office: Radiant Products Co Inc 6224 S Oakley Ave Chicago IL 60636

JOHANN, EDWARD WRIGHT, physicist; b. Hannibal, Mo., Mar. 4, 1949; s. George Edward and Junia Florence (Wright) J.; B.S. in Physics, NE Mo. State U., 1971, B.S. in Sci. Edn., 1971; A.A., Hannibal LaGrange Jr. Coll., 1969; M.S., U. Wyo., 1973; m. Deborah Payne, Aug. 21, 1970; children—George Raymon, Paul Edward. Grad. intern Jefferson County Public Schs., Lakewood, Colo., 1971-73; tchr. Hannibal (Mo.) Public Schs., 1973-78; project engr. Maxon Corp., Muncie, Ind., 1978—; tchr. electronics Ind. Vocat. Tech. Coll., 1979—. Dist. camping com. Boy Scouts Am., Hannibal, 1976-77; active United Way, 1979-80; advisor Jr. Achievement, 1979; v.p. Hannibal Photo Club, 1976-77. NSF fellow, 1971-73. Presbyterian. Contbr. articles to profl. jours.; inventor solar heat and cool system, 1977; electronic back pressure controller, 1981. Home: 1900 Norwood St Muncie IN 47304 Office: 201 E 18th St Muncie IN 47302

JOHANNSEN, GAIL CORRINE, educator; b. Wagner, S.D., June 23, 1940; d. T. Raymond and Cora Grace (Eitemiller) Duncanson; B.S., S.D. State U., 1959, postgrad., 1961-62; postgrad. U. S.D., 1972-80; m. James A. Johannsen, Mar. 31, 1962; children—Julie, Todd, Tim. Tchr. home econs. Wagner, 1962-63, 66—, Lake Andes, S.D., 1965-66; advisor Future Homemakers Am. Organizer, participant rodeos, jamboree, edn. programs March of Dimes, Am. Cancer Soc., Heart Fund, Good Samaritan Home. Named Tchr. of Yr., 1972. Mem. NEA, S.D. Edn. Assn., Wagner Edn. Assn., S.D. Home Econ. Tchrs. Assn., Am. Vocat. Assn., Future Homemakers Am. (hon. mem. state, regional, local). Republican. Methodist. Clubs: Wagner Saddle, Ruth Circle of Meth. Ch., Bus. and Profl. Women. Home: Rural Route 2 Box 65 Wagner SD 57380 Office: Wagner Heights Wagner SD 57380

JOHANSEN, ROBERT, artist; b. Kenosha, Wis., Mar. 30, 1923; s. Johan and Dorthea (Nelson) J.; grad. Layton Sch. Art, 1945-47; m. Kathleen Flynn, Jan. 29, 1949; children—Christine, John, Ann, Roberta, Lawrence, Paul. One man shows at Kenosha Mus., Marine Bank, Milw., Bergstrom Art Center, Neenah, Wis.; group shows include Wis. Watercolor Soc., Watercolor Wis., Wustum Mus., Racine Invitational, Am. Watercolor Soc. Traveling Show, Salmagundi, N.Y., Nat. Acad., Acad., Watercolor U.S.A., Rocky Mountain Nat. Watermedia; in permanent collections at Borg-Warner, Standard Oil, Marine Bank, Wustum Mus., U. Wis.-La Crosse, Johnson's Wax Can. comml. artist Eisenberg Studios, Milw. Served with U.S. Army, 1943-45. Recipient award of merit Midwest Watercolor Show. Mem. Wis., Midwest watercolor socs. Featured in book 40 Watercolorists and How They Work. Home: 3017 Taylor Ave Racine WI 53405

JOHN, ELMER ROY, mgmt. cons.; b. St. Paul, July 28, 1916; s. Gustav H. and Anna (Siering) J.; A.A., Bethel Coll., 1937; B.S. cum laude U. Minn., 1945, M.A., 1952; m. Evelyn C. Rutz, July 22, 1944; children—Gloria Gail, Patricia Ann, Douglas Rychner. Instr., lectr. U. Minn., 1945-49; dir. personnel Midland Coops. Mpls., 1948-59; corporate dir. personnel Gen. Mills, Inc., Mpls., 1959-69; pres. Elmer R. John Assos., Inc., 1969—; pres. Midland Metro Services, Mpls.; chmn. bd., dir. Modern Service Ins. Co., Mut. Service Ins. Cos.; pres., exec. dir. Mantread, Inc., 1976—; pres. Seminar Clearinghouse Internat., Inc., 1981—; dir. Personnel Decisions, Inc., Mpls. Faculty mem. Minn. Met. State U., 1972—; asso. clin. prof. U. Minn., 1972—. Past mem. exec. council Viking council Boy Scouts Am.; pres. adv. council Indsl. Relations Center, U. Minn.; mem. Gov.'s Adv. Com. on Mgmt. Devel.; chmn. Gov.'s Task Force on Model Personnel Law; past pres. Twin City chpt. Council Ind. Mgrs., Mpls. Certified Consulting Psychologist, Minn. Fellow Internat. Soc. Advancement Mgmt.; mem. Am. Psychol. Assn. Club: Athletic (Mpls.). Home: 2110 Fairmount Ave St Paul MN 55105 Office: Suite 1100 Minnesota Bldg St Paul MN 55101

JOHN, KAVANAKUZHIYIL VARUGHESE, biochemist, educator; b. Kerala, India, May 12, 1940; s. P.V. and Aleyamma (Easow) Varughese; came to U.S., 1969, naturalized, 1974; m., July 4, 1968; children—Lijo V., Jean E., Abie J. Research asso. Okla. Med. Research Found., Oklahoma City, 1971-75; research asso. biochemistry Med. Coll. Wis., Milw., 1975-77, instr., 1977-78, asst. prof., 1978—; dir. research Clin. Pathology Lab., St. Joseph's Hosp., Milw., 1978—. NIH grantee, 1978—. Mem. Am. Chem. Soc., Sigma Xi. Home: 1075 Vista View Dr Brookfield WI 53005 Office: St Joseph's Hosp 5000 W Chambers St Milwaukee WI 53210 also Dept Biochemistry Med Coll Wis 8701 Watertown Plank Rd Wauwatosa WI 53226

JOHNS, GENE, state senator; b. Carrer Mills, Ill., Oct. 6, 1927; grad. So. Ill. U.; m. Eve Prince; children—Mark, Daredan, Dane. Prin. schs., Saline County, Ill.; adminstr. Dept. Bus. and Econ. Devel., Herrin, Ill.; mem. Ill. Senate. Bd. dirs. So. Ill. Inc. Served with USN. Mem. Am. Legion. Democrat. Baptist. Clubs: Shriners, Elks, Eagles. Office: State Capitol Springfield IL 62706*

JOHNS, R(OBERT) POWELL, JR., advt. exec.; b. Boston, Dec. 25, 1937; s. Robert Powell and Barbara (Green) J.; B.A., Wesleyan U., 1960; m. Yvonne Mendonca, June 11, 1961; children—Robert Powell, Douglas Mendonca, Laura Hardenbrook. With Robert Powell Johns Corp., N.Y.C., 1960; asst. buyer Lord & Taylor, N.Y.C., 1961-62; asst. program adminstr. Sikorsky Aircraft Co., Stratford, Conn., 1961-62; account exec. BBDO Advt., N.Y.C., Chgo., 1964-66; v.p. Leo Burnett Co., Chgo., 1966-74; pres. Dawson, Johns & Black, Inc, Chgo., 1974—. Served with USAR, 1960-61. Mem. Chgo. Advt. Club (dir.), Am. Assn. Advt. Agencies. Episcopalian. Home: 1017 Lee St Evanston IL 60202 Office: 500 N Michigan Ave Chicago IL 60611

JOHNS, ROBERT HORACE, constrn. co. exec.; b. Cleve., Oct. 13, 1927; s. James Edmond and Antoinette (Height) J.; student Oberlin Coll., 1946-47, Bowling Green State U., 1947-48, Case Western Res. U., 1949; B.B.A., U. Mich., 1950; student Harvard Bus. Sch., 1976; m. Ruth S. Schwendler, Mar. 11, 1950; children—Jeffrey W., Jill Antoinette, J. Richard, Courtney B. and Whitney A. (twins). Sales trainee Tremco Mfg. Co., Cleve., 1950-51; mgmt. trainee Pollock Paper Corp., Columbus, Ohio, 1951-53; owner, pres. Robert H. Johns Co., Columbus, 1953—; lectr. high schs. and colls.; dir. Skyline Commuter Air Transport, Inc., Max & Ermas Inc. Councilman Village of Marble Cliff, 1972—; mem. Columbus Bd. Lic. Appeals, 1975—; merit badge counselor Boy Scouts Am., 1967—; mem. Greater Columbus Devel. Com. Mem. Asso. Builders and Contractors (nat. dir.), Ohio Asso. Builders and Contractors (v.p.), Builders Exchange Columbus. Republican. Clubs: Columbus Rotary, Leather Lips Sailing, Univ., Sandusky Sailing. Office: PO Box 1557 Columbus OH 43216

JOHNS, THOMAS LATHERN, charitable orgn. exec.; b. Rhodell, W.Va., July 24, 1929; s. Willie Lathern and Margaret Rose May (Bolen) J.; B.A., U. Wis., 1965; M.Div., Garrett-Evang. Theol. Sem., 1969; m. Kathryn Joy Goehring, June 13, 1971; children—Deborah, Rebecca, Thomas Lathern, Daniel, Benjamin, Karis. Store mgr. Quality Store, Oak Hill, W.Va.; dept. mgr. J.C. Penney Co., Beckley, W.Va.; Midwest sales mgr. Fogleman-Jefferies Corp., Wis., Minn., N.D., S.D., Nebr., 1957-61; pastor Evang. United Brethern Ch., Van Dyne and Eldorado, Wis., 1963-65, United Meth. Ch., North Fond du Lac, Wis., 1966-70; ordained to ministry, United Meth. Ch., 1969; lectr. U. Wis., Fond du Lac, 1974-75; cons. in field; exec. dir. Community Training & Devel., Inc., Fond du Lac, 1970—. Chmn., Assn. Commerce, Oak Hill, 1958; sec. Coalition for War on Poverty, 1973-75; v.p. Community Council on Human Concerns, 1979-80. OEO grantee, 1970; U.S. Community Services Adminstrn. grantee, 1979. Mem. Conf. Wis. United Meth. Chs., NAACP (life), Am. Soc. for Tng. and Devel. Clubs: Fond du Lac Yacht, Century. Contbr. articles to profl. jours. Home: 126 3rd St Fond du Lac WI 54935 Office: 41 S Main St Fond du Lac WI 54935

JOHNSEN, GORDON NORMAN, hosp. adminstr.; b. Concord, Mass., Sept. 18, 1926; s. Olaf Magnus and Esther Victoria J.; B.B.A., U. Wis., 1950, M.S., 1953; M.H.A., U. Minn., 1955; postgrad. Harvard U., 1974; m. Barbara Ann Haddon, July 7, 1951; children—Carrie, Paul, Victoria, Peter. Asst. adminstr. Iowa lMethodist Hosp., Des Moines, 1956-57; adminstr. Madison (Wis.) Gen. Hosp., 1958-75, pres., 1975—; asst. clin. prof. dept. preventive medicine U. Wis. Med. Sch., 1974; dir. Viking Ins. Co. Trustee, Trinity Coll., Deerfield, Ill., Edgewood Coll., Madison. Served with USAAF, 1945-46. Recipient Merit award Tri-State Hosp. Assembly, 1970. Fellow Am. Coll. Hosp. Adminstrs.; mem. Am. Hosp. Assn. (trustee 1974-77), Wis. Hosp. Assn. (pres. 1968-69), Am. Public Health Assn. Methodist. Clubs: Rotary; Madison; Blackhawk Country. Home: 1102 Willow Ln Madison WI 53705 Office: 202 S Park St Madison WI 53715

JOHNSON, A. ARNOLD, retail kitchen supply co. exec.; b. Des Moines, Iowa, June 25, 1920; s. Carl Alfred and Sarah Elizabeth (Mossberg) J.; grad. Lincoln Aero. Inst., 1942; m. Vera Marie Pilmer, Nov. 6, 1943; 1 son, James Arnold. Mechanic, Glen L. Martin Aircraft, Omaha, 1942. Iowa Airplane Co., Des Moines, 1942-45; chief mechanic, govt. aircraft maintenance insp. Am. Aviation Co., Des Moines, 1945-54; owner, pres. Johnson Constrn. Co., Des Moines, 1955-59, Kitchen Center, Inc., Des Moines, 1959—. Served with U.S. Army, 1942-44. Lic. aircraft and engine mechanic, U.S. Govt.; cert. kitchen designer. Mem. Am. Inst. Kitchen Dealers (program chmn. 1981), Home Builders Assn. Des Moines (pres. remodelers council 1962), Greater Des Moines C. of C., Better Bus. Bur. of Des Moines, Fedn. Ind. Businessmen. Democrat. Lutheran. Clubs: Masons, Am. Union of Swedish Singers, Men's Garden, Full Gospel Businessmen's Fellowship. Home: 4114 Leonard Pl Des Moines IA 50310 Office: PO Box 4000 Des Moines IA 50333

JOHNSON, A. W., broadcasting co. exec.; b. Insinger, Sask., Can., Oct. 18, 1923; B.A. in Polit. Sci. and History, U. Sask., 1942; M.A., U. Toronto, 1945; Ph.D. (Littauer fellow) in Polit. Economy, Harvard U., 1963; LL.D. (hon.), U. Regina, 1977, U. Sask., 1978; married; 4 children. Adminstrv. asst. Budget Bur., Govt. Sask., 1946-49, dir. adminstrv. mgmt. div., 1949-52; dep. provincial treas. Govt. Sask., 1952-64; asst. dep. minister fin. Govt. Can., 1964-68, econ. adv. to prime minister on the constn., 1968-70, sec. treasury bd., Govt. Can., 1970-73, dep. minister of welfare dept. nat. health and welfare, 1973-75; pres. Canadian Broadcasting Corp., 1975—; mem. research staff (part time) Royal Commn. on Banking and Fin., 1962; pres. Inst. of Public Adminstrn. of Can., 1962-63. Mem. Nat. Film Bd. of Can., 1970—; bd. dirs. U. Sask. Hosp., 1957-64, Nat. Arts Centre, 1975—. Decorated Order of Can.; recipient Gold Medal award Profl. Inst. of Public Service of Can., 1975, Vanier Medal, Inst. Public Adminstrn. of Can., 1976. Mem. Ottawa Polit. Economy Assn. (pres. 1969-70), Canadian Polit. Sci. Assn. (mem. exec. council 1963-74), Commonwealth Broadcasting Assn. (standing com.), Nat. Arts Center. Contbr. articles on public adminstrn. to profl. jours.; editorial bd. Canadian Public Policy, 1974-75. Office: CBC PO Box 8478 1500 Bronson Ave Ottawa ON K1G 3J5 Canada

JOHNSON, ALBERT EDDIE, publisher; b. Chgo., Dec. 10, 1932; s. Albert Elwood and Evelyn Margret Jessie (Morgan) J.; student Loop Jr. Coll., Chgo., 1962-63, U. Chgo., 1963, Inst. Contemporary Latin Am. Studies, 1968; m. Annette Dial, Nov. 15, 1955; children—Martin, Charles, Michael, Albert, Aquanette, Audray, Toni. With Ill. Bell Telephone Co., Chgo., 1957-70, community relations mgr., 1968-70; pres. Al Johnson & Assos., Inc., Chgo., 1970—; chmn. bd. Act V Prodns., Inc., 1965; pub.-editor Chgo. Shoreland News, weekly, 1975—; dir. Ebony Talent Assos., Inc.; cons. Mem. Coalition Community Action, Black Strategy Center; bd. dirs. Sears YMCA, Midwest Community Council. Served with AUS, 1950-53. Decorated Purple Heart; recipient Nat. Lane Bryant award, Joint Action Dirs. award, Vision Found. for Blind Youth award, Maury Hoffberg Meml. Found. award, Nat. Eye Research Found. award, Philander Smith Coll. award, Jobs for Youth Service award, BMI Pubs. award, Black Media Reps. award, Sears YMCA Service award, Chgo. I Will award. Mem. Nat. Black Media Inc., Nat. Newspaper Pubs. Assn. Creator, author: Time's Running Out, 1969; Where Do I Go From Here?, 1967; The Easter Story, 1966; The Easter Story Record, 1966; The Johnson's View. Office: 1020 S Wabash Ave Chicago IL 60605

JOHNSON, ALSCE, JR., ednl. adminstr.; b. Orangeburg, S.C., Feb. 10, 1939; s. Alsce and Mary J. Johnson; B.S., S.C. State Coll., 1963; Ed.M., Wayne State U., 1969, Ed.S., 1972; Ph.D., Mich. State U., 1977. Tchr. carpentry and mech. drawing Washington (Ga.) Central High Sch., 1965-68; tchr. woodshop and crafts Wilson Jr. High Sch., Detroit public schs., 1969-73; instr. metals and woods Mich. State U., East Lansing, 1973-75; tchr. metal shop Longfellow Middle Sch., Detroit, 1975-79; adminstr. Detroit public schs., 1979—; gen. mgr. Alvito's Inc., Detroit, 1969—. Mem. exec. bd. Longfellow PTA, 1975-81. Served with U.S. Army, 1963-65. Mem. Am. Indsl. Arts Assn., Nat. Assn. Indsl. and Tech. Tchr. Educators, Mich. Assn. Supervision and Curriculum Devel., Assn. Supervision and Curriculum Devel., NAACP, Mich. Indsl. Edn. Soc., Met. Detroit Alliance of Black Sch. Educators (polit. action chairperson 1981), Phi Delta Kappa. Baptist. Home: 3910 Somerset Detroit MI 48224 Office: Longfellow Middle School 13141 12th St Detroit MI 48224

JOHNSON, (MARY) ANITA, physician;, med. service adminstr.; b. Clarksburg, W.Va., Oct. 18, 1926; d. Paul F. and Mary Elizabeth (Harris) Johnson; B.S., North Tex. U., 1946; M.D., Woman's Med. Coll. of Pa., 1950; m. Lawrence J. Ciessau, Aug. 22, 1959 (div. 1974); children—Matthew A., Susan E., Sharon L., Mark A.; m. 2d, Ralph Allen Fretwell, Dec. 18, 1976. Intern, Baylor U. Hosp., Dallas, 1950-51, resident, 1951-54; practice medicine specializing in internal medicine, Dallas, 1954-58, Chgo., 1958—; instr. internal medicine Southwestern Med. Coll., U. Tex., Dallas, 1954-58; med. dir. YWCA, Dallas, 1955-58; physician infant welfare Chgo. Bd. Health, 1960-63; house physician, emergency physician St. Mary of Nazareth Hosp. Center, Chgo., 1963-81, instr. for nurses intensive care unit, 1963-80, asst. cardiologist, 1963—, sec. med. staff 1974-75, treas., 1980, pres.-elect, 1981, pres., 1982; med. dir. Family Care Center, 1973-74; nat. med. dir. Nat. Cath. Soc. Foresters Ins. Co., Chgo., 1975-77; chief med. clinics St. Mary of Nazareth Hosp. Center, 1977-78; cons. internal medicine Lisbon VA Hosp., Dallas, 1955-56. Lectr. to community elementary sch. students on opportunities in health field, 1967—. Named Med. Woman of Year, St. Mary of Nazareth Hosp. Center, 1973. Mem. AMA, Ill., Am. socs. internal medicine, Am. Coll. Angiology, Am. Med. Woman's Assn. (regional dir. 1955-58, pres.-elect br. 2, 1981, 82). Ill., Chgo. (councillor 1980-81, del. to Ill. Med. Soc. 1981) med. socs., Zeta Phi. Club: Pilot. Home: 1146 N Ashland Ave River Forest IL 60305

JOHNSON, ANITA K., library adminstr.; b. Wilmington, Del., May 12, 1947; d. Harold Steen and Vera Anuta (Enss) Kemp; B.A. in English, Wittenberg U., 1969; M.S.L.S., Case Western Res. U., 1975; m. Byron R. Johnson, Dec. 26, 1970. Reference librarian Otterbein Coll. Library, 1971-74; adult services and reference librarian Mentor (Ohio) Public Library, 1975-77; library dir. Notre Dame Coll., Cleve., 1977—. Mem. Ohio Library Assn., Acad. Library Assn. Ohio, Cath. Library Assn. Office: Notre Dame Coll Library 4545 College Rd Cleveland OH 44121

JOHNSON, ARTHUR SUNE, veterinarian; b. Mpls., Aug. 13, 1927; s. Richard E. and Marie (Johanson) J.; B.S., U. Minn., 1953, D.V.M., 1955; m. Carol Lou Stedman, July 21, 1951; children—Ann Marie, Arthur Mark. Veterinarian, small animal practice All Pets Hosp., Mpls., 1958—; pres. Arthur S. Johnson Corp., investments, 1965—, chmn. bd., 1965—; ordained to ministry Pentecostal Ch., 1969; radio evangelist Selby Gospel Broadcasting, Inc., St. Paul, 1970—; evangelist Harvest Field Mission, Mpls., 1967—, Northside Outreach Worker Program, Mpls., 1971. Precinct chmn. Rep. party, 1966-69; bd. dirs. Kings Acad., Young Am. Encounter. Served with USMCR, 1945-46. Mem. AVMA, Minn. Veterinary Med. Assn., Am., Met. animal hosp. assns., Am. Pub. Health Assn., Nat. Assn. Professions, Full Gospel Businessmen Fellowship Internat., Am. Legion, Gideons Internat. (Bible sec. 1968-71). Clubs: Kiwanis; Forest Hills Golf (Forest Lake, Minn.). Home: 907 51st Ave NE Minneapolis MN 55421 Office: 5100 Central Ave NE Minneapolis MN 54421

JOHNSON, AUDREY JEAN, educator; b. Milbank, S.D., July 28, 1950; d. Herbert Allen and Marcella Madge (Manning) J.; B.A., Dakota Wesleyan U., 1972; M.A., U. S.D., 1981. Elem. classroom tchr., Kyle, S.D., 1975-76; Title IV, IEA project asso. Batesland (S.D.) Pine Ridge Reservation, 1976-78; metric edn. program dir. Batesland (S.D.) Pine Ridge Reservation, 1978-79, Title IV, IEA project asso., 1979—. Mem. NEA, Nat. Council Tchrs. Math., Assn. Supervision and Curriculum Devel., S.D. Edn. Assn., S.D. Indian Edn. Assn., Epsilon Sigma Alpha. Democrat. Methodist. Home: PO Box 144 Martin SD 57551 Office: PO Box 578 Batesland SD 57716

JOHNSON, BARBARA COE, med. librarian; b. Detroit, Jan. 19, 1923; d. Harrison Thomas and Ann (Mack) Coe; B.A., Bryn Mawr Coll., 1944; B.S. in L.S., U. Calif., Berkeley, 1951. Patients' librarian VA Hosp., Palo Alto, Calif., 1951-53, med. librarian 1953-56; dir. libraries Harper Hosp., Detroit, 1956—; mem. Biomed. Library Rev. Com., Nat. Library of Medicine, 1978-82. Mem. Med. Library Assn. (bd. dirs. 1968-71, pres. 1974-76), Spl. Libraries Assn. (profl. cons. 1959—). Quaker. Contbr. articles to profl. jours. Home: 2075 Hyde Park Dr Detroit MI 48207 Office: 3990 John R St Detroit MI 48201

JOHNSON, BARBARA JANE, sales rep.; b. Chgo., Aug. 19, 1946; d. Sidney and Norma Mona Shaffer; B.A. in Sociology and Psychology, U. Ill., 1968; postgrad. M.B.A. program, Roosevelt U., 1971-72; m. Gary Johnson, Aug. 25, 1968. Asst. personnel dir. Associated Mills, Chgo., 1967-69, Scholl Mfg. Co. Inc., Chgo., 1969-71; nurse recruiter Cook County Hosp. Governing Com., Chgo., 1971-73; recruiter Mt. Sinai Hosp., Chgo., 1973-76; sales rep. Stryker Corp., Kalamazoo, 1976—, area trainer; founder Chgo. Area Nurse Recruiters; cons. positions as nurse recruiter. Vice pres. Budlong Community Action Group, 1979—; advisor Jr. Achievement, 1969-72; auction com. Ednl. TV. Recipient Lee Stryker sales award, 1979. Mem. Assn. of Operating Room Nurses (sponsor). Recipient first place Recruitment Brochure for Chgo. Area Bus. Communicators, 1975; salesman of year, 1979; first woman to achieve nat. award, 1979. Office: 420 W Alcott St Kalamazoo MI 49001

JOHNSON, BARBARA SPEARS, ednl. adminstr.; b. Chgo., May 24, 1932; d. William and Sadie (Fennoy) Spears; A.B., U. Chgo., 1952; B.E., Chgo. Tchrs. Coll., 1954; M.Ed., Loyola U., Chgo., 1967; m. John G. Johnson, July 29, 1967; children—Steven, Jeri-Lynn. Tchr., Chgo. Pub. Schs., 1954-70, counselor, 1966-70; dir. Resource-Skills Center, Kennedy-King Coll., Chgo., 1970—, pres. Kennedy-King Faculty Council, 1976-78; mem. exec. com., treas. Ill. Assn. Personalized Learning Programs, 1976-81. Den mother Boy Scouts Am., 1965-67; social action coordinator United Meth. Women, 1975-76; county chairperson Mothers Assn. U. Ill., Urbana, 1976-81; mem. planning adv. com. Ill. Community Coll. Bd., 1980-81. Mem. NEA, Ill. Edn. Assn., Ill. Community Coll. Assn. for Instrn. Tech., Ill. Community Coll. Faculty Assn. (pres. 1981-82), Ill. Reading Council, Nat. Reading Assn., Am. Bridge Assn., Alpha Kappa Alpha. Home: 8610 S Vernon Ave Chicago IL 60619 Office: 6800 Wentworth Ave Chicago IL 60621

JOHNSON, BARRY LEE, clergyman; b. Bloomington, Ill., July 28, 1943; s. James Robert and Elizabeth Carol (Schultz) J.; B.A. in History, Wheaton Coll., 1965; M.Div., Evang. Theol. Sem., 1968; m. Celeste Jane Hoppe, June 10, 1965; children—Tracy Michelle, Dane Christian. Ordained to ministry United Meth. Ch., 1968; asso. minister Bethany United Meth. Ch., Aurora, Ill., 1967-68; sr. minister Bensenville (Ill.) United Meth. Ch., 1968-71, Shiloh Ch., Dayton, Ohio, 1975—; exec. dir. EURISKON, Inc., Chgo., 1971-75; sec. bd. evangelism No. Ill. Conf. United Meth. Ch., 1969-72; cons. United Meth. Ch. Bd. Evangelism, Alaska, Mich., N.Y. confs. Mem. Bensenville Youth Commn., 1969-71. Recipient civic club recognition Rotary, 1969, 75, 77, Lions, 1970, 77, Optimists, 1975, 76, 77, Sertoma, 1976. Mem. Nat. Assn. United Meth. Evangelists, Family Counselors Assn., Bensenville Home Soc., Alcoholic Counselors Assn. Club: Optimists (Dayton). Author: EURISKON'S Personal Planning Manual, 1972; Sometimes There's a Hole in the Ceiling, 1975; Getting to Know Who!?!, 1981; contbr. articles to profl. jours. Home: 4165 Colemere Circle Dayton OH 45415 Office: 5300 Philadelphia Dr Dayton OH 45145

JOHNSON, CAROL JAYNE, elem. sch. prin.; b. Ohio, May 16, 1943; d. Arnold Q. and Viola Jayne (Stewart) Hashman; B.A., Oakland U., Rochester, Mich., 1971, M.A., 1976; m. Richard Taft Johnson, Dec. 29, 1962; children—Mark Richard, David Taft. Owner, mgr. Baskin Robbins Ice Cream Store, Pontiac, Mich., 1969-70; elem. sch. tchr., then dir. elem. curriculum Bloomfield Hills (Mich.) Public Schs., 1971-79; prin. Conant Elem. Sch., Bloomfield Hills, 1979—; cons. in field. Mem. Am. Assn. Sch. Adminstrs., Assn. Supervision and Curriculum Devel., NEA (del. 1978), Mich. Edn. Assn., Mich. Assn. Supervision and Curriculum Devel., Oakland County Assn. Gifted and Talented Edn., Bloomfield Hills Edn. Assn. (v.p. 1977-78), Bloomfield Hills Assn. Gifted and Talented Edn., Delta Kappa Gamma (com. chmn. 1978—). Author papers in field. Home: 3156

Long Lake St West Bloomfield MI 48033 Office: 4100 Quarton St Bloomfield Hills MI 48013

JOHNSON, CECIL AUGUST, lawyer; b. Stratford, Iowa, June 9, 1905; s. Franklin A. and Louise (Erickson) J.; student Iowa State Coll., 1922-23; LL.B., Southeastern U., 1936, M.P.L., 1938, B.S.C., 1939; LL.M., Columbus U., Washington, 1937; LL.D. (hon.), Midland Lutheran Coll., 1964; m. Esther M. Nelson, June 30, 1926 (dec. Aug. 1959); children—Newell D., M. Nadyne, Franklin C., Richard A.; m. 2d, Harriet L. Paige, Sept. 1, 1960. Pvt. bus., Ames, Iowa, 1926-33; exec. asst. A.A.A., U.S. Dept. Agr., 1933-35, dir. commodity loans, 1935-38; sec. and asst. mgr. Fed. Crop Ins. Corp., Washington, 1938-42; directed reorgn. Office Civilian Def., Washington, 1942, asst. to gov. FCA, Kansas City, Mo., 1942-44; admitted to Iowa bar, 1936, D.C. bar, 1937, Ill. bar, 1945, Nebr. bar, 1950; partner law firm Ekern, Meyers & Matthias, Chgo., 1944-51; mem. firm Barton & Johnson, Washington, 1951-66, Johnson & Hunter, Omaha, 1951-64, Johnson & Ilich, 1964-73, Johnson & Fike, 1973-76; gen. counsel C. A. Swanson & Sons, Omaha, 1951-55, Butter Nut Foods Co., 1955-64, Swanson Enterprises, Omaha, 1955-79; dir. Yellow Freight Co., Omaha Pub. Power Co. Dir. adv. bd. indsl. alcohol prodns., govt. alcohol plant, 1944-49; lay mem. Nat. Adv. Council for Neurol. Diseases and Blindness, USPHS, 1950-51. Trustee Immanuel Med. Center; chmn. bd. trustee Lutheran Ch. Am. Found., 1963-71, U. Nebr. Found.; chmn. bd. trustees Midland Luth. Coll.; bd. dirs. Am. Missions Luth. Ch. Am., mem. mgmt. com. office adminstrn. and finance. Mem. Am., Iowa, Ill., Nebr., Chgo. bar assns., Am. Judicature Soc., Theta Chi. Democrat. Lutheran. Mason. Co-author Fed. Crop Ins. act and Nat. All Risk Crop Ins. program. Home and Office: 8717 Capitol Ave Omaha NE 68114

JOHNSON, CHARLES PHILIP, agrl. cons. co. exec.; b. Darien, Wis., May 9, 1922; B.A., U. Wis., 1947, L.L.B., 1949; m. Frances V. Huber, June 17, 1944; children—Philip C., Jennifer S., Kristi L., Jay L., Craig R. Admitted to Wis. bar, 1949; partner-operator Johnson Farms, Darien, 1950-69, Jon-Dyke, Inc., Agri-Bus., Darien, 1969-75, Johnson & Danielson, Inc., Ins. and Real Estate, Darien, 1954-74, Darien Hardware Co., 1961-73; prin. C. Phil Johnson, Agcons., Darien, 1976—. Pres. Village of Darien, 1951-52; treas. Darien Consol. Schs., 1960-64, pres., 1965-69; treas. Walworth County March of Dimes, 1950-58; mem. exec. com Walworth County Farm Bur., 1955-59; dir. Wis. div. Nat. Farmers Orgn., 1965-69; area rep. Tri County State Line council Boy Scouts Am., 1954-66; bd. dirs. Family Motor Coach Assn., 1972-80, v.p., 1972-73, pres., 1974-77; bd. dirs. Wis. Vocat. and Tech. Adult Edn., 1972-78, pres., 1976-78; bd. dirs. Wis. Higher Edn. Aids, 1973-80, Wis. Regents, 1976-78, Coop. Edn. Service Agy., 1967-71; pres. Wis. Found. Vocat., Tech. and Adult Edn., 1977—. Home: 239 E Jackson St Darien WI 53114 Office: Starview Capital Co Inc 105 N Walworth Ave Williams Bay WI 53191

JOHNSON, CHARLES SILAS, banker; b. Muscatine, Iowa, Mar. 1, 1909; s. Raymond E. and Edna I. (Ryan) J.; student Drake U., 1926-29; m. Orpha B. Christian, July 28, 1928; children—Sally Ann (Mrs. Gerald Schomers), Raymond C., Nancy K. (Mrs. Harry Mooney). With Des Moines Nat. Bank, 1924-29; bank examiner State of Iowa, 1929-40; pres. First Nat. Bank of Perry (Iowa), 1940-58; exec. v.p. Brenton Banks, Inc., Des Moines, 1958-74, cons., dir., 1974—; chmn. exec. com., dir. South Des Moines Nat. Bank, 1962—, First Nat. Bank of Perry, 1962—; vice chmn. various Brenton banks in Iowa; chmn., pres. Iowa Bus. Devel. Credit Corp., Des Moines. Chmn. Herman L. Rowley Meml. Masonic Home; pres. Perry Ind. Sch. Dist., 1948-51; chmn. Republican Central Com., Dallas County, 1952-58. Chmn. Dallas County Hosp. Bd., 1952-58. Recipient Outstanding citizen award Kiwanis, 1953, Legion of Honor award Iowa DeMolay, 1969. Mem. Perry C. of C. (pres. 1946, 47). Lutheran. Clubs: Masons (grand treas. Iowa 1978-79), Moose, Rotary (pres. 1950), Elks, Des Moines, Embassy, Bohemian. Home: 7004 Bellaire Ave Des Moines IA 50311 Office: 550 39th St PO Box 5005 Des Moines IA 50306

JOHNSON, CURTIS MILTON, educator, ednl. adminstr.; b. St. Paul, Feb. 29, 1928; s. Vivian W. and Emma (Bethke) J.; B.S., St. Cloud State U., 1952, M.A., St. Thomas Coll., 1965; A.B.D., Ohio U., 1974; m. Jewel M. Troyer, July 22, 1949; children—Wendy, Cheryl, Brant, Jay, Dana, Todd. Indsl. arts tchr. Clarkfield (Minn.) Schs., 1952-56; indsl. arts tchr., chmn. dept. Sibley Sr. High Sch., West Saint Paul, Minn., 1956-66; adminstrn. fellowship Ohio U., 1966-67, dir. continuing edn., 1967-69, dir. Ext. Div., 1969-80, dir. internat. edn., 1980—, asst. prof. engring. graphics, 1976—. Pres., South St. Paul (Minn.) Public Schs. Bd. Edn., 1964-66; chmn. Dakota County (Minn.) Jr. Coll. Com., 1965-66; chmn. Athens Twp. Zoning Commn., 1973-74; dir., pres. Athens County Regional Planning Commn., 1975—. Served with USCGR, 1946-47. Recipient Nat. Ford Indsl. Arts award, Bush Found. Leadership fellow. Mem. Nat. Univ. Continuing Edn. Assn., Ohio Coll. Assn., Ohio Adult Edn. Assn., Ohio Council on Higher Continuing Edn., Phi Delta Kappa. Rotarian. Home: Route 1 Box 48F Athens OH 45701 Office: 302 Tupper Hall Ohio Univ Athens OH 45701

JOHNSON, DEAN EVAN, ins. exec.; b. Kiester, Minn., Aug. 16, 1931; s. Ingvard M. and Annette A. (Kapplinger) J.; B.S., Ill. Inst. Tech., 1953; m. Margaret L. Mentink, Mar. 24, 1951; children—Stephanie, Kevin. Insp., engr., asst. mgr. Iowa Inspection Bur., 1953-66; with Protection Mut. Ins. Co., Park Ridge, Ill., 1966—, v.p., dir. underwriting, 1970—, v.p., dir. ops., 1973-76, exec. v.p., 1976-78, pres., chief exec. officer, 1978—, also dir.; pres. Park PM Corp., Park Ridge, 1978—; dir. Factory Service Corp., Factory Mut. Service Bur., Factory Mut. Engring. Assn., Factory Mut. Engring. Corp., Factory Mut. Research Corp. (all Norwood, Mass.), Factory Mut. Internat., London. Mem. Nat. Fire Protection Assn., Soc. Fire Protection Engrs., Soc. Chartered Property and Casualty Underwriters, Salamander Hon. Fire Protection Engring. Soc., Newcomen Soc. N. Am., Theta Xi. Clubs: Chgo. Athletic Assn., Park Ridge Country. Home: 15 Nottingham Dr Deerfield IL 60015 Office: 300 S Northwest Hwy Park Ridge IL 60068

JOHNSON, DENNIS LESTER, ednl. cons. co. exec.; b. Hampton, Iowa, Oct. 23, 1938; s. Royden Lester and Lorraine Anita (Rhoades) J.; B.A., Parsons Coll., 1960; m. Carolyn Louise Campbell, Aug. 18, 1963; children—Dené Lynn, Laurie Anne. Admissions officer Parsons Coll., Fairfield, Iowa, 1960-63, regional dir., 1963-65, dir. of admissions counselors, 1965-67; founder Johnson Assos., Inc., Oak Brook, Ill., 1967, pres., 1967—, chmn. bd., 1967—. Bd. dirs. United Cerebral Palsy of Chgo., 1977—, Du Page County (Ill.) Easter Seal Treatment Center, 1975-76. Mem. Am. Assn. for Higher Edn., Am. Mktg. Assn., Am. Mgmt. Assn., Am. Personnel and Guidance Assn. Presbyterian. Club: Oak Brook Bath and Tennis. Contbr. articles on edn. and mktg. to profl. publs.; columnist Nation's Schools and Colleges, 1974—. Home: 1103 Fairview Ave Lombard IL 60148 Office: 1301 W 22d St Oak Brook IL 60521

JOHNSON, DON BAKER, maintenance services co. exec.; b. Provo, Utah, Aug. 26, 1943; s. Don LaRell and Grace Yvonne (Baker) J.; student Brigham Young U., 1961-65, N.Mex. State U., 1968; B.S., Pittsburg State U., 1977, M.S., 1978; m. Kathy Diane Mueller, Jan. 18, 1974; children—William LaRell, Pauline Mary, Don Baker II. Dispatcher, Aero Mayflower Transit Co., Indpls., 1969-70, Atlas Van Lines, Evansville, Ind., 1970-73; propr., decorating contractor Johnson's Painting Service, Evansville, 1973-74; field service rep. United Mine Workers Health and Retirement Funds, Pittsburg, Kans., 1975-76; pres., gen. mgr. Pittsburg Custom Service, Inc., 1977—. Mem. Neighborhood Rehab. Com., Pittsburg, 1978-79; counselor to bishop Ch. of Jesus Christ of Latterday Saints, 1978-80. Mem. Am. Personnel and Guidance Assn., N.Am. Soc. Adlerian Psychologists, Phi Delta Kappa, Psi Chi. Address: 418 E 11th St Pittsburg KS 66762

JOHNSON, DONALD LEE, sr. agronomist; b. Butler, Mo., Sept. 13, 1935; s. Ralph Lee and Helen Opal (Baldwin) J.; B.S., U. Mo., 1957; m. Patricia Gayle Roberts, Sept. 2, 1956; children—Barbara Elaine, Scott Wade. Salesman agrl. sales Spencer Chem. Co., Cedar Falls, Iowa, 1959-62; dist. sales mgr. Me-Jon, Inc., Oxford, Iowa, 1962-64; salesman Employed Allied Chem. Corp., Omaha, 1964-67, regional promotion mgr., 1967-69, regional promotion agronomist, 1969-71, zone agronomist, 1971-74, mgr. agronomy services, 1974-79, sr. agronomist, 1979—. Served with U.S. Army, 1957-59. Mem. Nat. Fertilizer Solutions Assn. (chmn. com.), Am. Soc. Agronomy, Am. Registry Cert. Profls. in Agronomy, Crops and Soils, U.S. Army Reserve Officers Assn., Nat. Rifleman Assn. Republican. Presbyn. Clubs: Prairie Lane Community (pres.); Valley View Booster (v.p.). Patentee in field. Home: 2924 S 113th St Omaha NE 68144 Office: 9706 Mockingbird Dr Omaha NE 68127

JOHNSON, DOROTHY GREENE, historian; b. Chgo., June 6, 1921; d. Louis Greenberg and Mildred (Brody) Greenberg; B.A., U. Chgo., 1942, M.A., 1951, Ph.D., 1956; m. June 14, 1947. Propaganda analyst Office Coordinator Inter-Am. Affairs, Washington, 1942-43; field program officer in charge Central Am. and Caribbean cultural centers U.S. Dept. State, 1944-47; lectr. Western civilization U. Chgo., 1957-67; historian-archivist, index editor Jane Addams papers, U. Ill., Chgo., 1977—. Pres., Womens Scholarship Assn., Roosevelt U., Chgo., 1972-75, bd. dirs., v.p., 1969-72. Honors scholar U. Chgo. Mem. Historians of Met. Chgo., Midwest Conf. Brit. Studies. Home: 5545 S Kimbark St Chicago IL 60637 Office: Hull House Univ Ill Chicago IL 60680

JOHNSON, DOROTHY PHYLLIS, counselor, art therapist; b. Kansas City, Mo., Sept. 13, 1925; d. Chris C. and Mabel T. (Gillum) Green; B.A. in Art, Ft. Hays State U., 1975, M.S. in Guidance and Counseling, 1976, M.A. in Art, 1979; m. Herbert E. Johnson, May 11, 1945; children—Michael E., Gregory K. Art therapist High Plains Comprehensive Mental Health Assn., Hays, Kans., 1975-76; art therapist, mental health counselor Sunflower Mental Health Assn., Concordia, Kans., 1976—, co-dir. Project Togetherness, 1976-77, coordinator partial hospitalization, 1978—; dir. Swedish Am. State Bank, Courtland, Kans., 1960—, sec., 1973-77. Mem. Kans., Am. art therapy assns., Am. Mental Health Counselors Assn., Am. Personnel and Guidance Assn., Assn. Specialists in Group Work, Phi Delta Kappa, Phi Kappa Phi. Contbr. articles to profl. jours. Home: Box 183 Courtland KS 66939 Office: 520 B Washington St Concordia KS 66901

JOHNSON, DOUGLAS J., state senator; b. Cook, Minn., Aug. 17, 1942; A.A., Va. Jr. Coll.; B.S., U. Minn.-Duluth; M.E., Wis. State U. Guidance counselor; mem. Minn. Ho. of Reps., from 1970, Minn. Senate, 1976—. Mem. Iron Range Legis. Del., Iron Range Resources and Rehab. Bd., Tax Study Commn.; mem. legis. adv. commn. Legis. Audit Commn. Recipient Outstanding Future Tchr. award, 1964. Mem. Kappa Delta Pi, Phi Alpha Theta. Mem. Democratic-Farmer-Labor party. Office: 205 State Capitol Saint Paul MN 55155*

JOHNSON, EARL JOHN, regional govt. exec., former ednl. adminstr.; b. Clay Center, Ohio, June 7, 1911; s. Carson and Mayme (Jensen) J.; B.E., U. Toledo, 1936, M.A., 1951. Elem. tchr., public schs., 1932-34; elem. tchr., prin., 1934-42, 45-47; high sch. tchr., 1947-53; high sch. prin., 1953-56; elem. and secondary supr., 1956-69; supt. schs. Ottawa County (Ohio) Public Schs., 1969-79, ret., 1979; suburban-rural mail carrier U.S. Postal Service; supr. Ottawa Soil and Water Conservation Dist., 1970—; mem. Ottawa Regional Planning Commn., pres., 1979. Bd. dirs. Michael J. Owens Tech. Coll., 1979—. Served with U.S. Army, 1942-45. Recipient Silver Beaver award Boy Scouts Am. Mem. Buckeye Assn. Sch. Adminstrs., Am. Assn. Sch. Adminstrs., Ottawa County Farm Bur., Ottawa County Ret. Tchrs. Assn., Ohio Ret. Tchrs. Assn. Democrat. Lutheran. Club: Grange. Contbr. articles on migrant edn. in Ohio to profl. jours. Office: 315 Harrison St Port Clinton OH 34352*

JOHNSON, EARLE BERTRAND, ins. co. exec.; b. Otter Lake, Mich., May 3, 1914; s. Bertrand M. and Blanche (Sherman) J.; B.S., U. Fla., 1937, J.D., 1940; m. Peggy Minch Rust, Apr. 30, 1972; children by previous marriage—Earle Bertrand, Victoria, Julia, Sheryl. With State Farm Ins. Cos., Bloomington, Ill., 1940—, regional agy. dir., 1958-60, regional v.p., 1960-65, v.p., sec. State Farm Mut. Automobile Ins. Co., 1965-80, dir., 1967—, also mem. exec. com., chmn. bd. State Farm Life Ins. Co., 1970—, also mem. exec. com.; dir. State Farm Fire & Casualty Co., State Farm Internat. Services, Inc., 1967—; dir. State Farm Gen. Ins. Co. First v.p., dir. S.W. Ins. Information Service, 1963-65; mem. U. Tex. Ins. Adv. Bd., 1964; trustee Life Underwriter Tng. Council. Mem. Agy. Officers Round Table (exec. coms.), Am., Fla. bar assns., Phi Alpha Delta, Phi Kappa Tau. Home: 215 Imperial Dr Bloomington IL 61701 Office: One State Farm Plaza Bloomington IL 61701

JOHNSON, EDITH MYRTLE, med. social worker; b. Anita, Iowa, Feb. 24, 1923; d. Anton Marius and Amalia (Olesen) Nielsen; B.A. magna cum laude, U. Minn., 1948, M.S.W., 1971; m. John Alexander Johnson, Aug. 31, 1946; children—Margaret, Nancy, Tony, Jean. Dir. social service Crestview Lutheran Home, Mpls., 1971-72; social worker family counseling div. Luth. Social Service, Mpls., 1971-73; sr. social worker social service dept. U. Minn. Hosps., 1973—, chmn. com. hospice concepts, 1978—, prin. social worker Masonic Cancer Center, 1981—; mem. faculty U. Minn. Sch. Social Work, 1975—, clin. asst. prof., 1978—. Served with Cadet Nurse Corps, 1945-46. Mem. Acad. Cert. Social Workers, Nat. Assn. Social Workers, Coalition Terminal Care, Minn. Council Family Relations, Women's Internat. League Peace and Freedom (exec. sec. 1973). Mem. Democratic-Farm-Labor Party. Unitarian. Home: 104 Malcolm Ave SE Minneapolis MN 55414 Office: 424 Harvard St SE Minneapolis MN 55455

JOHNSON, ERVIN VICTOR, music co. exec., entertainer; b. Racine, Wis., Sept. 3, 1938; s. Victor and Alice (Hansen) J.; grad. Elsmo Sch. Music, Racine, 1961; m. Karen Sue Peterson, Oct. 16, 1965. Owner, Happiness Music Co., 1961—; sales mgr. Elsmo Music, Inc., Racine, Wis., 1962-65, Johnson's Music, Inc., Racine, 1965-76; pvt. organ and piano tchr., Racine, 1963—; tchr. Bob Ploetz Organ and Piano Studios, Kenosha, Wis., 1976—. Lutheran. Composer. Address: 4200 Taylor Ave Racine WI 53405

JOHNSON, FRANKLIN A., ins. co. exec.; b. Anderson, Ind., Feb. 15, 1947; s. Franklin C. and Vera R. (Eastburn) J.; B.S., Ball State U., 1969; m. Susan Mahony, Aug. 12, 1972. Producer, Fidelity Union Life Ins. Co., 1970-71; personal lines mgr. Kirkpatrick Sursa, Muncie, Ind., 1971-73; producer Ins. and Risk Mgmt., Ft. Wayne, Ind., 1973-78, chief adminstr. comml. ins. div., partner, 1978—. Bd. dirs. United Cerebral Palsey Central Ind., Inc., Downtown Bus. Council, Muncie. Mem. Soc. Chartered Property and Casualty Underwriters, Am. Mgmt. Assn., Assn. Internat. Ins. Agts., Assurex, Independent Ins. Agts. Ind., Ind. Ins. Agts. Muncie, Ind. (v.p.), Ball State U. Coll. Bus. Alumni Assn. (pres.), Lambda Chi Alpha. Methodist.

JOHNSON, FRANKLYN MCQUEEN, business exec., fin. planner; b. Rockford, Ill., Mar. 25, 1930; s. Franklyn Herbert and Rosemary (McQueen) J.; B.A., Knox Coll., 1952; m. Carol Lou Johnson, June 9, 1956; children—Mark, Susan, Linda. Trainee, underwriter Firemen's Fund Ins. Co., Rockford, Ill., 1952-54, field rep., Flint, Mich., 1954-58, service office mgr., Grand Rapids, Mich., 1958-61; account exec., v.p. Brady-Schirmer Co., Saginaw, Mich., 1961-71; v.p., treas. Saginaw Underwriters, 1971-76, pres., treas., chief exec. officer, 1976—; registered rep. Mut. Services Co., 1980—; continuing edn. instr. Mich. State U., E. Lansing, 1957-61. Adv. bd. St. Mary's Hosp. Saginaw, 1976—, vice chmn., 1979-80, chmn., 1980-81; bd. dirs. Big Bros. of Saginaw, 1962-66, pres., 1963-64; bd. dirs. Home for Aged, Saginaw, 1965—, now v.p.; treas. Saginaw Downtown Improvement Co., 1965-70; mem. Com. of 50 Local Polit. Action, 1966-70; treas. United Saginaw Citizens Polit. Action, 1970-78. Mem. Mich. Assn. Ind. Ins. Agts., Nat. Assn. Ind. Ins. Agts., Profl. Ins. Agts. Am., Greater Saginaw C. of C. (treas. 1976-77, dir. 1974-77). Presbyterian (elder). Club: Saginaw (dir. 1976-79, sec. 1977-79), Saginaw Country. Office: 1213 S Washington St Saginaw MI 48601

JOHNSON, FREDERIC HENRY, anatomist; b. Geneva, Ill., May 23, 1926; s. Leonard Walter and Helena Elizabeth (Henry) J.; A.B., Cornell U., 1948, A.M., 1950, Ph.D., 1951; children by former marriage—Gary Richard, Frederic Henry. Research asst. Naval Arctic Research Lab., Point Barrow, 1948; research asso. Inst. Research, Walter Reed Army Med. Center, Washington, 1951-52; asst. prof. anatomy U. Oreg., Portland, 1952-53; research asso. Neuropsychiat. Inst., U. Ill., Chgo., 1953-59; dir. neurophysiology lab. Research Inst., U. Buffalo, 1959-61; research neurophysiologist Med. Scis. Research Lab., Miles Lab., Elkhart, Ind., 1961-63; asst. prof. anatomy Temple U., Phila., 1963-67; research asso. neurology Children's Meml. Hosp., Chgo., 1967-69; asso. prof. anatomy Loyola U., Chgo., 1969-70; scholar in residence, also staff Newberry Library, Chgo., 1970-71; scholar Crerar Library, Chgo., 1971—. Pres. Chgo. Ballet Guild, 1961-63. Served with AC, USNR, 1944-46. Mem. Am. Assn. Anatomists, Physiol. Soc. Phila., Am. Soc. Zoologists, Am. Inst. Biol. Sci., AAAS, Am. Soc. Coll. Profs., Fedn. Am. Scientists, Pa. Med. History Soc., Sigma Xi, Phi Kappa Psi, Alpha Kappa Kappa (hon.). Moose. Author: The Anatomy of Hallucinations; Brain Tracts. Home: 519 S Humphrey Ave Oak Park IL 60302

JOHNSON, GARY DENNIS, nursing home adminstr.; b. Milw., Feb. 5, 1943; s. Alvin L. and Norma M. (Jergonsen) J.; B.S., U. Wis., River Falls, 1965; M.S. in Social Work, U. Wis., Madison, 1967; postgrad. U. Wis., Oshkosh; m. Kathleen L. Capelle, July 1, 1972; 1 dau., Michelle Denise. Child welfare supr. Clark County Dept. Social Services, Neillsville, Wis., 1967-69, dir. dept., 1969-76; program dir., nursing home adminstr. St. Croix Health Center, New Richmond, Wis., 1976—; ad hoc instr. U. Wis., Eau Claire and LaCrosse; cons. Neillsville Meml. Nursing Home. Bd. dirs. United Way, New Richmond, 1980-83. Mem. Nat. Assn. Social Workers, Acad. Cert. Social Workers, Wis. Assn. County Homes (sec.-treas. 1978-79, v.p. 1979-80, pres. 1980-81), New Richmond C. of C., Kappa Delta Pi. Democrat. Club: New Richmond Kiwanis (dir. 1980-81). Home: Rural Route 3 Box 290B New Richmond WI 54017 Office: St Croix Health Center Rural Route 2 Box 16A New Richmond WI 54017

JOHNSON, GEORGE E., cosmetic mfg. co. exec.; v. Richton, Miss., June 16, 1927; s. Charles D. and Priscilla (Thigpen) J.; D.B.A. (hon.), Xavier U., Cin., 1973; H.H.D. (hon.), Clark Coll., Worcester, Mass., 1974; D.Comml.Sci. (hon.), Coll. of Holy Cross, Worcester, 1975; LL.D. (hon.), Babson Coll., Wellesley, Mass., 1976; L.H.D. (hon.), Chgo. State U., 1977; m. Joan B. Henderson, Mar. 18, 1950; children—Eric, John, George, Joan Marie. Pres. Johnson Products, Inc., Chgo., 1954—; past chmn. bd. Independence Bank Chgo.; dir. Commonwealth Edison Co., Chgo.; bd. govs. U.S. Postal Service, 1971. Vice pres. Jr. Achievement Chgo.; bd. dirs. Chgo. Urban League, Chgo. Northwestern Meml. Hosp., Howalton Day Sch., Lyric Opera Chgo., Chgo. Area council Boy Scouts Am.; mem. corp. Babson Inst. Clubs: Economic (dir.), Commercial (Chgo.); Tres Vidas Country (Acapulco, Mex.); Runaway Bay (Jamaica). Address: 8522 S Lafayette St Chicago IL 60620*

JOHNSON, GEORGE ROBERT, govt. ofcl.; b. Grand Forks, N.D., Sept. 30, 1927; s. Sam A. and Olga (Bjorge) J.; Ph.B., U. N.D., 1949, postgrad. 1963; postgrad. George Williams Coll., 1950, Oreg. State U., 1950-52, U. So. Calif., 1952-53, George Washington U., 1972; m. Marjorie F. Dorsher, Nov. 24, 1948; children—Sam, Margie, Peter, Kari, Robert. With YMCA, 1941-52, gen. sec., Kelso, Wash., 1950-52; research dir. John Danz Found., Seattle, 1952; intern, placement dir. Sch. Public Adminstrn., U. So. Calif., Los Angeles, 1952-53; staff fed. personnel programs, various orgns., 1953—, chief classification officer Bur. Indian Affairs, Aberdeen, S.D., 1978—. Served with U.S. Army, 1946-47. Recipient Service awards Classification and Compensation Soc., 1970, Down's Syndrome Congress, 1978. Mem. Classification and Compensation Soc. (founder, 1st pres. 1969-70), Aberdeen Personnel Assn. (pres. 80-81), Down's Syndrome Congress (one of the founders), Am. Assn. on Mental Deficiency, Assn. Retarded Citizens, ARC Brown county (treas. 79-81), Nat. Apostolate with Mentally Retarded Persons, V.F.W., Am. Legion. Club: Sons of Norway. Contbr. articles to profl. jours.; founder, 1st editor Down's Syndrome News; co-founder Down's Syndrome Papers and Abstracts, People with Spl. Needs. Home: 1409 N 1st St Aberdeen SD 57401 Office: Fed Bldg BIA Personnel Aberdeen SD 57401

JOHNSON, GEORGE TAYLOR, aircraft co. exec.; b. Kansas City, Mo., Jan. 12, 1930; s. George Dewey and Geneva (Van Leu) J.; B.A., Columbia Coll., 1977; m. Pamela Kay Cole, Aug. 30, 1981; children—Van L., Victoria L., Wendell O., Marcella Johnson Bruce. Enlisted in U.S. Army, 1947, served to 1967; chief instr. rotary wing sect. U.S. Army Transp. Sch., Ft. Eustis, Va., 1965-67; ret., 1967; group leader aerospace publs. Beech Aircraft Corp., Wichita, Kans., 1968-79, adminstr. aerospace logistics programs, 1979—. Mem. Community Action Agy., Wichita, 1973-75. Served with U.S. Army, 1947-67. Decorated D.F.C., Air medal with V and four oak leaf clusters. Mem. Negro Airmen Internat. (state dir.), Nat. Bus. League, NAACP, Army Aviation Assn. Am., Assn. U.S. Army, Soc. Logistics Engrs., V.F.W. Baptist. Club: Optimist. Home: 1919 N Spruce Wichita KS 67214 Office: 9709 E Central Wichita KS 67201

JOHNSON, GORDON GILBERT, clergyman; b. St. Paul, Nov. 19, 1919; s. Gilbert Oliver and Myrtle Isabel (Bjorklund) J.; diploma Moody Bible Inst., Chgo., 1938-41; B.A., U. Minn., 1945; B.D., Bethel Theol. Sem., St. Paul, 1946; Th.M., Princeton Theol. Sem., 1950; Th.D., No. Baptist Theol. Sem., Oakbrook, Ill., 1960; postgrad. research scholar Yale Div. Sch., 1969; m. Alta Fern Borden, May 21, 1945; children—Gregg Allen, Gayle Ellen Johnson Boyd. Ordained to ministry Bapt. Ch., 1946; pastor chs. in Wis., N.J. and Ill., 1946-59; prof. preaching Bethel Theol. Sem., 1959—, dir. field edn., 1959-64, v.p., dean, 1964—; moderator Bapt. Gen. Conf., 1958; mem. gen. council Bapt. World Alliance, 1965—. Served with USNR, 1944-45. Assn. Theol. Schs. grantee, 1976, 78-79. Mem. Assn. Profl. Edn. for Ministry, Religious Speech Communication Assn., Am. Acad. Homileticians. Author: My Church, 15 edit., 1957; also articles. Office: 3949 Bethel Dr Saint Paul MN 55112

JOHNSON, HAROLD KENNETH, assn. exec.; b. Hanover, Mass., Oct. 20, 1941; s. Harold Forrest and Marjorie Ruth (French) J.; A.A., Stockbridge Sch. Agr., U. Mass., 1962; B.S. (Ralphs S. Lovett scholar), Ohio State U., 1965; M.S. (Conn. State scholar), U. Conn., 1970; m. Dawn Robie Foote, Sept. 7, 1963; children—Mark Kenneth, Elizabeth Jane. Supr. quality control lab. Dinner Bell Foods, Defiance, Ohio, 1966-67; mgr. quality control Stop & Shop, Inc., Marlboro, Mass., 1969-72; dir. meat merchandising Nat. Live Stock & Meat Bd., Chgo., 1972-74, exec. dir. food sci. div., 1974-78, v.p. meat sci. div., 1978—; cons. processing and mktg. meats, 1974—. Recipient Disting. Alumni award Ohio State U., 1981. Mem. Am. Meat Sci. Assn. (sec.-treas. 1975—, archivist 1974—, chmn. mktg. com. 1973, Signal Service award 1981), Am. Soc. Animal Sci., Inst. Food Technologists, ASTM, Council Agrl. Sci. and Tech., Gamma Sigma Delta. Editor: Meat Management and Operations, 1975; meat co-editor Supermktg. Mag., 1976—. Club: Masons. Contbr. articles to profl. jours. Home: 1907 E Illinois St Wheaton IL 60187 Office: 444 N Michigan Ave Chicago IL 60611

JOHNSON, HENRY CLYDE, mfr., engr., lawyer, fin. exec.; b. Niagara Falls, N.Y., June 18, 1914; s. Willis Oscar and Della R. (Hagerty) J.; S.B., S.M., M.I.T., 1936; J.D., Harvard U., 1940; m. Dorothy Diedre Montagu, Feb. 11, 1955; 1 stepdau., Martha Browning (Mrs. Robert T. Mast). Admitted to Mass. bar, 1940, N.Y. bar, 1940, U.S. Supreme Ct. bar, 1944; asso. firm Phipps, Durgin & Cook, Boston, 1940-41; div. purchasing agt., mgr. planning dept. on staff pres. Philco Corp., Phila., 1946-50; mem. central finance staff, engring. bd., controller engring. div. Ford Motor Co., Dearborn, Mich., 1950-58; chmn. bd., pres., owner Phil Wood Industries Ltd. (formerly Gar Wood Industries of Can. Ltd.), Windsor, Ont., Can., 1958-69, hon. chmn., 1969—. Mem. Windsor Econ. Com.; benefactor, mem. Founder Soc., Detroit Inst. Arts; patron mem. Detroit Symphony Orch.; maj. donor Meadowbrook Festival; mem. pres.'s club Oakland U.; life mem. Am. Mus. in Britain, Cranbrook Inst. Sci., Detroit Hist. Soc.; mem. Archives Am. Art; trustee, chmn. ednl. policy com., mem. exec. com. Detroit Inst. Tech., 1972-78. Served to col. Signal Corps, AUS, 1941-46. Decorated Army, Navy commendation medals, registered profl. engr., Pa.; FAA rated instrument, comml. pilot; FCC amateur extra class radio lic. Sr. mem. IEEE (life); mem. Am. Bar Assn., Am. Mgmt. Assn. (Personal plaque 1960), AAAS (life), Aircraft Owners and Pilots Assn., Am. Radio Relay League (life), Mich. Acad. Sci., Arts and Letters, English Speaking Union, Quarter Century Wireless Assn. (life), Sigma Alpha Epsilon, (founder mem.). Episcopalian. Clubs: Econ. (sustaining mem.), M.I.T., Detroit Athletic (Detroit); Otsego (Mich.) Ski; Circumnavigators (life) (N.Y.C.); Harvard (Mich.); Cranbrook Tennis (Bloomfield Hills, Mich.). Patentee automatic tripping snow plow. Home: 3000 Quarton Rd Bloomfield Hills MI 48013

JOHNSON, J. THOMAS, state ofcl.; b. DeKalb, Ill., Nov. 27, 1946; s. Owen A. and Irene K. (Hart) J.; B.S. in Acctg., No. Ill. U., 1968; postgrad. DePaul U., 1970-71. Mgr. gen. acctg. and fin. analysis Field Enterprises Ednl. Corp., Chgo., 1968-71; auditor County of DeKalb, 1971-74, adminstrv. aide to bd., 1974-77; dir. Dept. Local Govt. Affairs, State of Ill., Springfield, 1977-79, asst. dir. Dept. Revenue, 1979-80, dir., 1980—. Pres. DeKalb Community Council, 1975-76. Mem. Ill. Soc. C.P.A.s. Republican. Roman Catholic. Club: Elks. Office: 1500 S 9th St Springfield IL 62708

JOHNSON, JAMES DUKE, mfg. co. exec.; b. St. Louis, Jan. 21, 1941; s. James Monroe and Frances Miriam (Duke) J.; B.A., Washington U., St. Louis, 1959-63; children—James Michael, James Duke. With Duke Mfg. Co., St. Louis, 1961—, v.p. mktg., 1968-71, pres., chief exec. officer, 1971—. Active Jr. Achievement, St. Louis, 1970-81; fund raiser Boy Scouts Am., St. Louis, 1975—. Mem. Nat. Assn. Food Equipment Mfrs., Food Equipment Distbrs. Assn., Young Presidents Assn. Episcopalian. Clubs: Glen Echo Country, St. Louis, Mo. Athletic. Patentee in field. Office: 2305 N Broadway Saint Louis MO 63102

JOHNSON, JAMES FREEMAN, office furniture mfg. co. exec.; b. Cedar Rapids, Iowa, Oct. 30, 1932; s. Freeman and Marie Rose Johnson; B.A., Knox Coll., 1954; m. Kathleen Keane, Mar. 17, 1968. Salesman, Am. Chicle Co., Minn., 1954-57; advt. mgr., Toronto, Ont., Can., 1962-65; regional sales mgr. Warner Lambert, Chgo., 1969-71; dir. sales, mgr. Europe, Am. Optical Co., South Bridge, Mass., 1971-75; dir. nat. sales Am. Chicle div. Warner Lambert, Morris Plains, N.J., 1976-79; v.p. sales and mktg. The HON Co., Muscatine, Iowa, 1979—. Served with AUS, 1954-56. Home: 516 W 2d St Muscatine IA 52761 Office: The HON Co 200 Oak St Muscatine IA 52761

JOHNSON, JAMES HARDING, educator; b. Perry, Iowa, Sept. 26, 1940; s. Richard Harding and Dorothy Margarite (Nelson) J.; B.A., U. Wash., 1963; Ph.D., U. Minn., 1972; m. Kathy Novak, Dec. 27, 1980; children by previous marriage—Jennifer Lynn, James Harding. Asst. prof. U. Utah, Salt Lake City, 1975-77, dir., div. psychology Med. Sch., 1976-77; asso. prof., vice chmn. dept. psychiatry, E. Va. Med. Sch., Norfolk, 1977-79; chmn. Va. Consortium for Profl. Psychology, Norfolk, 1978-79; prof., dir. clin. psychology Ill. Inst. Tech., Chgo., 1979—; dir. Psych Systems, Inc., Balt., 1980—. Recipient Rush Bronze Medal award, Am. Psychiat. Assn., 1975; lic. psychologist, Utah, Va., Ill. Mem. Am. Psychol. Assn., Am. Psychopath. Assn., Soc. for Personality Assessment, Psychonomic Soc. Author: Mental Health in the 21st Century, 1979; Technology in Mental Health Care Delivery Systems, 1980; contbr. articles to profl. jours.; editorial bd. Behavior Research Methods and Instrumentation, 1977—. Home: 3200 Highland Ave Downers Grove IL 60515 Office: Dept Psychology Ill Inst Tech Chicago IL 60616

JOHNSON, JANET LESAN, bank exec.; b. Denver, June 1, 1929; d. Walter Glen and Jenne Mae (Richardson) Lesan; student Roosevelt U.; 1 dau., Karen Lee McBride; m. Floyd A. Johnson, June 13, 1958; 1 stepson, Floyd McKenzie. Office mgr. No. Petrochem. Co., Des Plaines, Ill., 1968-72; mgr. mktg. adminstrn., domestic and internat. Advanced Systems, Inc., Elk Grove Village, Ill., 1972-76; mgr. optigraphics dept. Chgo. Title & Trust Co., 1976—. Mem. Adminstrv. Mgmt. Soc. (officer), Nat. Micrographics Assn. (officer), Assn. Records Mgrs. and Adminstrs., Data Processing Mgrs. Assn., Computer Micrographic Tech. (dir.), Internat. Platform Assn. Office: 30 N LaSalle St Suite 3700 Chicago IL 60602

JOHNSON, JENNIFER MARIE, store fixtures mfg. co. exec.; b. Toledo, Oct. 27, 1951; d. Frank Vernon and Dora Jean Johnson; B.S. in Edn., Bowling Green (Ohio) State U., 1973, M.A. in Coll. Student Personnel, Coll. Adminstrn. and Counseling, 1976. Elem. tchr. Defiance (Ohio) City Bd. Edn., 1973-75; asst. to v.p. student affairs, area coordinator residence hall Findlay (Ohio) Coll., 1975-76; asst. dean students Dana Coll., Blair, Nebr., 1976-79; tng. dir. Lozier Corp., Omaha, 1979-80, user systems analyst, 1980—. Loaned exec. United Way, Omaha, 1979, 80, sect. chmn. comml. div., 1980, team capt., 1981, mem. Speakers Bur., 1980-81, solicitor tng. cons. and trainer, 1980—, also mem. planning and allocations com.; CPR and first aid instr. ARC, 1980—; solicitor Fontenelle Forest Operation Fund, 1981; job placement cons. Omaha Opportunity Industrialization Center, 1981; career cons. Jr. Achievement, 1981; mem. career fashion bd. Zoeb's, 1981; mem. racism/sexism task force, role of women task force Am. Luth. Ch., 1979; author, facilitator membership drive tng. sch. Omaha Symphony, 1981. Recipient Pres.'s Disting. Service award Bowling Green State U., 1973, others, Faculty Growth scholar, 1978, 79. Mem. Am. Soc. for Tng. and Devel. (membership chmn. Omaha chpt. 1980—, dir. 1980—, Rookie of Yr. award 1981). Republican. Lutheran. Club: Omaha Sports. Home: 11381 Evans St Apt 10 Omaha NE 68164 Office: 2201 N 21st St Omaha NE 68110

JOHNSON, JOHN ARTHUR, greeting card co. exec.; b. Dayton, Ohio, July 8, 1947; s. Arthur Eugene and Effsivia Sylvia (Hornis) J.; B.S., U. Cin., 1971; postgrad. Cleve. State U., 1975—; m. Kathleen Anne Clarke, July 9, 1948; children—Gwendolyn, Nathan. With Booz, Allen Hamilton, Landrum & Brown, Inc., Cin., 1970-73; mgr. product devel. dept. Am. Greetings Corp., Cleve., 1973—; cons. product design, devel., 1967—. Mem. Soc. Plastic Engrs., Point-of-Purchase Advt. Inst. (Ann. Design awards 1977, 78), Indsl. Designers Soc. Am. Design patentee packaging, enclosure cabinets, elec. boxes, bus. machine enclosures. Office: Am Greetings Corp 10500 American Rd Cleveland OH 44144

JOHNSON, JOHN FOWLER, dentist; b. Wolcott, N.Y., Sept. 23, 1917; s. John F. and Mary (Hay) J.; B.S., U. Mich., 1939, D.D.S., 1950; m. Anne Rynearson, Nov. 15, 1957; children—John Fowler, Jeremy Ann, James Bruce. Tchr. physiology U. Mich. Med. Sch., Ann Arbor, 1939-42; gen. practice dentistry, Flint, Mich., 1950—. Pres. Flint Planned Parenthood, 1967. Served with USAAF, 1941-45, with U.S. Army, 1950-52 to col., 1962, ret. Res., 1970. Fellow in physiology U. Mich., 1939-42. Mem. Am., Mich., Genesee County dental assns., MENSA (sec. Flint 1966). Pioneer in dentistry techniques including use of high speeds with equipment of his own design, full-flow, low vacuum suction. Producer filmed travelogs. Home and Office: 608 Welch Blvd Flint MI 48503

JOHNSON, JOHN HAROLD, mag. publisher; b. Arkansas City, Ark., Jan. 19, 1918; s. LeRoy and Gertrude (Jenkins) J.; student U. Chgo., Northwestern U.; LL.D., Shaw U., Benedict Coll., Carnegie-Mellon Inst., Central State Coll., Eastern Mich. U., Hamilton Coll., Lincoln U., Malcolm X Coll., Morehouse Coll., N.C. Coll., N.C. A. and T. State U., Upper Iowa Coll., Wayne State U., Pratt Inst.; m. Eunice Rivers Walker, June 21, 1951; children—John Harold, Linda Eunice. Pres., pub. Johnson Pub. Co., pubs. Ebony, Jet, Black Stars Ebony Jr.!, mags., Chgo., 1942—; pres. Sta. WJPC, Chgo.; dir. Marina Bank, Greyhound Corp., Twentieth-Century-Fox Film Corp., Zenith Radio Corp. Bd. dirs. Harvard Grad. Sch. Bus., United Negro Coll. Fund, NCCJ, Chgo., United Negro Coll. Fund; trustee Art Inst. Chgo. Named 1 of 10 outstanding young men of yr. U.S. Jaycees, 1951; recipient Henry Johnson Fisher award Mag. Pubs. Assn., 1972; Communicator of Year award U. Chgo. Alumni Assn., 1974; Columbia Journalism award, 1974; Horatio Alger award, 1966. Fellow Sigma Delta Chi; mem. Mag. Pubs. Assn., Opportunities Industrialization Centers. Home: 1040 Lake Shore Dr Chicago IL 60611 Office: 820 S Michigan Ave Chicago IL 60616 also 1750 Pennsylvania Ave NW Washington DC 20006 also 3600 Wilshire Blvd Los Angeles CA 90005 also 1270 Ave of Americas New York NY 10020

JOHNSON, JOHN HAROLD, analytical chemist; b. Chgo., May 17, 1946; s. Harold Charles and Karin Elizabeth (Hamm) J.; B.A. in Chemistry, Monmouth (Ill.) Coll., 1968; Ph.D. in Organic Chemistry, U. Ark., 1974; m. Karen Ann Senew, Aug. 15, 1970; children—Eric, Michael, Patricia. Environ. chemist EPA, 1973-77; sr. chemist Nalco Environ. Scis., 1977-78; sr. research investigator Searle Labs., Skokie, Ill., 1978-80, Am. Critical Care, McGaw Park, Ill., 1980—; cons. Argonne Labs., Center Ednl. Affairs. Coach Libertyville Soccer Assn., 1979—. Served to capt., ordnance AUS, 1972-78. Recipient Lubrizol award, 1967, Cliff Struthers Hamilton prize, 1968, spl. achievement award EPA, 1975; Conoco fellow, 1971-72. Mem. Am. Chem. Soc., Am. Pharm. Assn., Am. Inst. Chemists, Chicagoland Discussion Group (dir.). Office: 1600 Waukegan Rd McGaw Park IL 60085

JOHNSON, JOSEPH BERNARD, lawyer; b. Cambridge, Minn., July 6, 1919; s. Joseph B. and Ruth (Barker) J.; student Carleton Coll., 1938-41; LL.B., J.D., U. Mich., 1948; m. Kathryn M. Dabelstein, Feb. 20, 1943; children—Joseph Bernard III, Christine Ruth. Admitted to Minn. bar, 1948; asso. Holmes, Mayall, Reavill & Neimeyer, Duluth, Minn., 1948-51; partner Reavill, Neimeyer, Johnson, Fredin, Killen & Thibodeau, and predecessor firms, Duluth, 1951-74; pres., sr. mem. firm Johnson, Fredin, Killen, Thibodeau & Seiler, profl. assn., 1974—. Corporate officer, dir. Atwood Larson Co., Halvorson of Duluth Inc., Arrowhead Electric Inc., W.P. & R.S. Mars Co., Lincoln Stores, Inc., Daugherty Howe Inc., Polar Gas, Inc., Conveyor Belt Service, Inc., Duluth Photographics Inc., Anderson Well-Drilling Inc., Easy Housing Inc., Alley Homes Inc.; dir. First Nat. Bank Duluth. Vice chmn. Minn. Bd. Law Examiners, 1956-59. Chmn. budget com. Duluth Community Chest, 1952-63; chmn. Duluth Welfare Council, 1967-70. Bd. dirs. Duluth YMCA, pres., 1977-79, chmn. bd. trustees, 1979—; mem. Nat. Council YMCA's; bd. dirs. St. Luke's Hosp., Duluth, 1970-76; trustee Hunt Scholarship Fund, 1957-69, chmn., 1967-69; bd. dirs., v.p. United Way of Duluth. Served to capt. AUS, 1941-45; now lt. col. Res. Decorated Bronze Star medal with two oak leaf clusters, Purple Heart with two oak leaf clusters (U.S.); Croix de Guerre (France); Fiurre de Gurre (Belgium); Order of Holland (Netherlands). Fellow Am. Coll. Probate Counsel; mem. Am. (taxation sect., probate and trust law sect.), Minn. (bd. govs. 1967-70, chmn. jud. selection com. 1969-73), 11th Dist. (pres. 1966-67) bar assns., Am. Judicature Soc., Duluth C. of C. (chmn. tax and tax laws com.), Duluth Jr. C. of C. (v.p. 1950-51). Republican. Lutheran (chmn. finance, bldg. coms., trustee, exec. com., ch. council). Clubs: Northland Country (pres. 1962-63), Kitchi Gammi, Rotary (chmn. jud. com.). Home: 3715 Greysolon Pl Duluth MN 55804 Office: 811 First Nat Bank Bldg Duluth MN 55802

JOHNSON, JOYCE MARIE BETTS, stockbroker, columnist; b. East Chicago, Ind., Jan. 18, 1938; d. Hobart and Mattie (Upshaw) Betts; B.S. magna cum laude, U. Md., 1976; m. Emmitt Johnson, July 6, 1959; children—Roderick, Terence. Tchr. shorthand Univ. Lang. Center, Taipei, Taiwan, 1963; adminstrv. asst. exec. sec. U.S. Army Intelligence, Munich, Germany, 1969-73; tchr. McArthur Jr. High Sch., Ft. Meade, Md., 1974-75; bus. mgr. The Reading Center, Gary, Ind., 1976-77; stockbroker A. G. Edwards Co., Merrillville, Ind., 1977—; columnist Info Newspaper, Gary, Dollars & Sense mag., Post Tribune newspaper, Gary, Chgo. Defender. Bd. dirs. Women's Assn. NW Ind. Symphony Soc., 1978, Friends Lake County Library, 1978; mem. adv. bd. Businesswomen's Ednl. Programs; mem. Vol. Council, Am. Symphony Orch. League; mem. NW Ind. Opera Theatre Bd. Mem. Nat. Council Negro Women, AAUW (dir. Gary-Merrillville br. 1977—), Am. Soc. Women Accts., Nat. Soc. Registered Reps., League Black Women, Phi Kappa Phi, Alpha Sigma Lambda, Delta Sigma Theta. Club: Civitan Internat. Office: 8300 Mississippi St Merrillville IN 46410

JOHNSON, JULIE M(ARIE), lawyer; b. Aberdeen, S.D., Aug. 7, 1953; d. Howard B. and Jerauldine M. J.; B.A., U. S.D., 1974, J.D., 1976, M.A., 1976; m. Terry J. Sherman, June 17, 1977. Admitted to S.D. bar, 1977; legal intern S.D. Atty. Gen.'s Office, 1975; asso. firm Siegel, Barnett, Schutz, O'Keefe & Jewett, Aberdeen, 1976, 77; law clk. Fifth Jud. Circuit Ct., Aberdeen, 1977-78; partner firm Maloney, Kolker, Fritz, Hogan & Johnson, Aberdeen, 1978—; pres. Shogon, Inc. doing bus. as Brown County Abstract Co.; treas. Johnson Motor Co., Inc. Bd. dirs. Aberdeen Resource Center for Women, 1978—, Aberdeen Area Child Protection Team, 1978—; sec. bd. dirs. YWCA, Aberdeen, 1978-80, 1st v.p., 1980-81, pres., 1981-82, chmn. 1979 Fantasy of Trees; loaned exec. Brown County United Way, 1979, co-chmn. profl. div., 1980; co-chmn. Aberdeen Arts Festival Com., 1978-81; mem. Aberdeen Area Arts Council, S.D. Found. for Arts; active S.D. Polit. Action Com. Mem. S.D. Bar Assn. (com. on profl. responsibility), S.D. Trial Lawyers Assn., Am. Bar Assn., Nat. Assn. Women Laywers, Aberdeen Bus and Profl. Women (pres. 1979-80, parliamentarian 1980-81, legis. chmn. 1981-82), S.D. Bus. and Profl. Women (bylaws chmn. 1979-80, rec. sec. 1980-81, 2d v.p. 1981-82), S.D. Women's Caucus (pres. 1978-79), AAUW (topic chmn. 1979-81, legis. chmn. 1981-82), Aberdeen Area C. of C. (state govt. chmn. 1980—), N.E. S.D. Women's Caucus (coordinator 1977-79), LWV, Brown County Republican Women (pres. 1980-81). Republican. Lutheran. Clubs: Zonta (dir.), Moccasin Creek Country (dir. 1979—). Home: 4138 Greenwood Ln Rural Route 1 Aberdeen SD 57401 Office: 205 Berkshire Plaza 405-8th Ave NW Aberdeen SD 57401

JOHNSON, KAREN LEE, nurse; b. Toledo, Oct. 5, 1940; d. Richard F. and Roberta M. (Wunder) Krause; diploma Maumee Valley Hosp. Sch. Nursing, Toledo, 1962; B.S., U. Toledo, 1976, postgrad., 1976-79; postgrad. U. Mich., Ann Arbor, 1980. Staff public health nurse Lucas County (Ohio) Health Dept. 1962-66, 71-72, field nurse cons. Bur. Crippled Children Services, 1972-76, dir. nursing service, Toledo, 1976—; dir. social services North Staff Borough, Community Action Agy., Fairbanks, Alaska, 1968-69; Mem. exec. com. March of Dimes, Toledo, 1978—. Mem. Toledo Dist. Nurses Assn., Ohio Nurses Assn. (chmn. sect. public health 1977-79), Am. Nurses Assn., NW Ohio Public Health Assn., Ohio Public Health Assn. (chmn. sect. nursing 1977), Am. Public Health Assn., Nat. League Nursing, Ohio Council Home Health Agys., NW Ohio Health Planning Assn., NOW, Nat. Assn. Female Execs., Am. Motorcyclists Assn. Democrat. Lutheran. Office: 129 21st St Toledo OH 43624

JOHNSON, KEITH LIDDELL, food products co. exec.; b. Darlington, U.K., July 22, 1939; s. Arthur Henry and Beatrice (Liddell) J.; came to U.S., 1948, naturalized, 1958; B.A., U. Mich., 1960; m. Margaret Elaine Meston, Aug. 29, 1959; children—Leslie Margaret, Kevin Liddell, Gregory Norman, Kathleen Elaine. Chem. technician Ajem Labs., Livonia, Mich., 1956-60; research chemist Swift & Co., Labs., Chgo., 1960-63, project mgr., 1963-67, group leader research and devel. center, Oak Brook, Ill., 1967-71, adminstrv. asst. to exec. v.p., Chgo., 1971-72, quality assurance mgr., refinery div. Swift Edible Oil Co., Chgo., 1972-73, corporate quality assurance mgr., 1973-74, quality assurance dir., 1974-78; group mgr. plant quality assurance, 1978—; mem. Chgo. Manpower Area Planning Com., 1971. Mem. Chgo. Chemists Club, Chem. Arts Forum Chgo. (v.p. 1980, pres. 1981), Am. Chem. Soc., Am. Oil Chemists Soc., Am. Soc. Quality Control, Chgo. Jr. Assn. Commerce and Industry (dir. 1968, v.p. 1969, exec. v.p. 1970, pres. 1971), U.S. (dir. 1972), Ill. (v.p. 1972) jr. chambers commerce. Episcopalian. Contbr. articles to profl. jours. Holder 17 U.S. and 25 Fgn. patents. Home: Route 1 Box 68 Matteson IL 60443 Office: 1919 Swift Dr Oak Brook IL 60521

JOHNSON, KENNETH ODELL, systems engr., exec.; b. Harville, Mo., Aug. 31, 1922; s. Kenneth D. and Polly Louise (Wilson) J.; B.S. in Aero. Engring., Purdue U., 1950; m. Betty Lou Jones, Aug. 5, 1950; children—Cynthia Jo, Gregory Alan. Engr., design, quality and production mgmt. Gen. Lamp Co., Elwood, Ind., 1950-51; mem. staff aircraft gas turbine engine design Allison div. Gen. Motors Corp., Speedway, Ind., 1951-66; mem. marine, indstl. gas turbine engine design mgmt. staff Gen. Electric Co., 1966—. Served as pilot USAF, 1942-45. Fellow Am. Inst. Aeros. and Astronautics. Republican. Methodist. Patentee in field. Home: 8360 Arapaho Ln Cincinnati OH 45243 Office: Gen Electric Co M/D G20 Cincinnati OH 45215

JOHNSON, KENNETH STUART, publisher and printer; b. Chgo., Aug. 22, 1928; s. William Moss and Lucille (Carsellio) J.; student Wright Jr. Coll., 1949-50, U. Ill., 1951-52; m. Mary Joan Kerber, Aug. 8, 1953; children—Cynthia Diane, Randall, Andrew, Peter. Dir., chmn. Free Press, Inc., Carpentersville, Ill., 1965—. Served with U.S. Army, 1946-47. Recipient Man and Boy award of Year, 1963. Mem. Cook County Pubs. Assn. (pres. 1963, dir.), Profl. Journalistic Soc., Nat. Editorial Assn., Sigma Delta Chi. Address: Free Press Inc Carpentersville IL 60110

JOHNSON, LAURA STARK, educator; b. Unityville, S.D., Jan. 9, 1913; d. Fred Hartman and Catherine (Culver) Stark; B.A., Dakota Wesleyan U., 1937; M.A., Northwestern U., 1966; postgrad. Northeastern Ill. U., 1968-75; M.S., No. Ill. U., 1982; m. Falk Simmons Johnson, June 11, 1940; children—Mark, Bruce, Martha, Craig (dec.). Tchr. pub. schs., Unityville S.D., 1932-36; tchr. McIntosh (S.D.) High Sch., 1937-38, Washington Sch., Wauwatosa, Wis., 1938-40, Mark Twain Sch., Des Plaines, Ill., 1964-65, Maine S. High Sch., Park Ridge Ill., 1965-69, Evanston (Ill.) High Sch. and Adult Continuing Edn., 1969—; lectr. Northeastern Ill. U., 1974-76; tchr. Oakton Community Coll., 1977-79; instr. Triton Community Coll., 1981—; writer Ency. Brit. Films, 1958-59; writer, editorial cons. Coronet Instructional Media, 1974-80; speaker 6th World Congress on Reading, Singapore, 1976. Mem. Nat. Assn. Pub. Continuing and Adult Edn., Internat. Reading Assn. (mem. publs. com. 1976-79), Ill. Reading Council (treas. 1970-71), Suburban Reading Council (past pres.), S.D. Hist. Soc., Alaska Hist. Soc., Kappa Delta Pi. Editor: Reading and the Adult Learner, 1980; contbr. articles to profl. jours., textbooks; mem. editorial adv. bd. Jour. of Reading, 1973-76. Home: 7624 Maple St Morton Grove IL 60053

JOHNSON, LOUISE CLAYTON, social worker; b. Kansas City, Mo., June 15, 1923; d. John R. and Susan T. Clayton; B.A. magna cum laude, Syracuse U., 1958; M.S.W., U. Conn., 1962; children—Nancy Emmert, Charlotte. Dir., Waterbury (Conn.) Girls Club, 1962-64; supervising psychat. social worker Connecticut Valley Hosp., Middletown, Conn., 1964-68; asst. prof. social work U. Iowa, Iowa City, 1968-74; asso. prof., dir. social work program U. S.D., Vermillion, 1974—. Local chmn. United Ministries in Higher Edn., Am. Bapt. Ch., 1979—, diaconate 1st Bapt Ch. chmn., 1981; mem. Sr. Citizens Outreach Com. Vermillion, 1981; mem. Successful Living Center, Sioux Falls, S.D., 1981. Cert. gerontologist Acad. Cert. Social Workers; winner S.D. White House Conf. on Aging Research Competition, 1981. Mem. Nat. Assn. Social Workers, Council on Social Work Edn., Assn. Baccalaureate Program Dirs. (vice chmn. 1979—), Am. Public Welfare Assn., LWV, Alpha Delta Mu, Alpha Kappa Delta, Delta Kappa Gamma. Democrat. Contbr. articles to profl. jours. Home: 220 Sycamore St Apt 40 Vermillion SD 57069 Office: Social Work Program U SD Vermillion SD 57069

JOHNSON, LOWELL C., state legislator; b. Dodge County, Nebr., June 12, 1920; B.S. in Mech. Engring., U. Nebr., 1942; m. Ruth Marion Sloss, June 21, 1943; children—Mark C., Kent R., James S., Nancy L. Farm and property mgmt. exec.; pres. Johnson-Sloss Land Co., North Bend, Nebr.; mem. Nebr. Legislature, 1980—. Former trustee Meml. Hosp. Dodge County; former mem. adv. council Nebr. Dept. Labor; former mem. citizens adv. com. Immanuel Hosp., Omaha; former mem. County Sch. Reorgn. Com.; former field rep. Congressman Charles Thome; former pres. bd. dirs. North Bend Sr. Citizens Home. Mem. Am. Legion, Fremont C. of C. Clubs: Masons, Rotary. Address: RFD 2 North Bend NE 68649*

JOHNSON, LUCIE JENKINS, social worker, educator; b. Elizabethtown, Ky., Feb. 10, 1927; d. Alex Heady and Mary Lee (Igleheart) Jenkins; B.A. magna cum laude, Wake Forest U., 1949; M.S.W., Tulane U., 1953; postgrad. Va. Poly. Inst. and State U., 1974-80; m. Glenn E. Johnson, Oct. 24, 1952; children—Alexander, Rebecca, Catherine, Elizabeth. Psychiat. social worker with families in public/pvt. service, 1952-67; chief psychiat. social worker Youth Services, Va. Dept. Welfare and Instns., Richmond, 1967-69; asst. prof. Va. Commonwealth U., 1969-74; asst. prof., coordinator continuing edn. in social work Wayne State U., Detroit, 1977-81; supr. oncology social work Harper Hosp./Wayne State U., Detroit. Mem. Nat. Assn. Social Workers, Acad. Cert. Social Workers, Mich. Soc. Clin. Social Work, AAUP. Democrat. Home: 79 Kenwood Rd Grosse Pointe Farms MI 48236 Office: Harper Hosp Wayne State U 3990 John R St Detroit MI 48201

JOHNSON, M(ICHAEL) DAVID, civil engr.; b. Terre Haute, Ind., Sept. 29, 1945; s. Herbert Norman and Doris Mae (Nolan) J.; B.S., Ill. Inst. Tech., 1975, M.B.A., 1977; certificates in lighting design, wiring design and motor control design Chgo. Elec. Assn., 1972, in mgmt. and supervision pub. services Inst. of City Colls. of Chgo., 1976, in sewage treatment plant ops. Calif. State U., Sacramento, 1978, in storm water detention U. Wis., 1978; m. K(athryn) Heather Gillett, July 4, 1969; children—Stephen Matthew, Stephanie Anne. Engring. aide City of San Jose (Calif.), 1965-67; engring. designer Cons.'s & Designers Inc., Palo Alto, Calif. and Chgo., 1967-68; engring. designer Intermatic, Inc., Spring Grove, Ill., 1968-71; design engr. Met. San. Dist. Greater Chgo., 1971-74, engring. constrn. mgr., 1974-77, govt. ofcl., 1978—; village engr. Village of Villa Park (Ill.), 1977-78. Adv. mem. U.S. Consumer Product Safety Commn., 1975—. Served with USNR, 1964. Registered profl. engr., Calif., Ill. Mem. Nat. Soc. Profl. Engrs., Ill. Soc. Profl. Engrs. (bd. dirs., past pres. North Shore chpt.), Water Pollution Control Fedn., ASCE, Am. Pub. Works Assn. (cert. in erosion control 1978), Costeau Soc., U.S. Chess Fedn., Nat. Model R.R. Assn. Mem. Evangel. Covenant. Home: 442 Michael Manor Glenview IL 60025 Office: 100 E Erie St Chicago IL also PO Box 485 Glenview IL 60025

JOHNSON, SISTER MARIE INEZ, librarian; b. Mitchell, S.D., June 2, 1909; d. Charles and Inez L. (Williams) Johnson; B.A. in English, Coll. St. Catherine, 1929, B.S. in L.S., 1939; M.S., in L.S., Columbia, 1940; postgrad. U. Denver, 1951-52, U. So. Calif., 1953-54. Joined Sisters St. Joseph Carondolet, 1926; tchr. elementary schs. St. Paul, 1930-38; librarian Coll. St. Catherine, St. Paul, 1940-42, head librarian, 1942—. Mem. steering com. U. Minn. Workshop for Librarians, 1956; library cons. survey Mt. Mercy Coll., Cedar Rapids, Iowa, 1963-64; bldg. cons. Fontbonne Coll., St. Louis, 1964—. Mem. Conf. Am. Folklore for Youth, St. Paul Speakers Bur., com. standard catalog for high sch. Cath. Support, Children's Lit. TV Series. Butler Fgn. Study fellow Coll. St. Catherine, 1958. Named Minn. Librarian of Year, 1967. Mem. Am. (various coms.), Cath. (various coms.) library assns. Editor column Cath. Library World, 1954—. Contbr. articles to profl. jours. Address: Coll St Catherine St Paul MN 55105

JOHNSON, MARTIN WESLEY, athletic dir.; b. Fargo, N.D., Nov. 27, 1941; s. William L. and Hazel (Lee) J.; B.S. in Edn., Mayville State Coll., 1966; M.Ed., U. Ariz., 1968; Ph.D., Ohio State U., 1972; m. Diane Kliniske, Aug. 3, 1968. Tchr., coach Morenci (Ariz.), 1968-69; recreation dir. Wyandotte Communities, Columbus, Ohio, 1969-71; student tchr. supr. Mayville (N.D.) State Coll., 1971-73; curriculum writer Tri-County Career Edn. Project, Eastern Ariz. Coll., Thatcher, 1973-74; athletic dir., chmn. div. health, phys. edn. and recreation Mayville State Coll. City auditor, Portland, N.D., 1978-80; alderman City of Portland, 1980—. Served with USMC, 1960-63. Mem. NEA, N.D. Edn. Assn., AAHPERD, N.D. Assn. Health, Phys. Edn. and Recreation, Nat. Assn. Intercollegiate Athletics, Athletics Dirs. Assn. Republican. Roman Catholic. Clubs: Masons, Eagles. Office: Mayville State Coll Mayville ND 58257

JOHNSON, MARVIN BRUCE, educator; b. Duluth, Minn., May 11, 1950; s. Bruce Elmer and Dorothy Eleanor (Tallakson) J.; B.A. in Econs., Carleton Coll., 1972; Ph.D., Syracuse U., 1976; m. Terri Zook, Nov. 22, 1972. Asst. prof. agrl. econs. U. Wis., Madison, 1976-80, asso. prof., 1980—. Ford Found. fellow, 1972-75. Mem. Am. Econs. Assn., Nat. Tax Assn., Am. Agrl. Econs. Assn. Contbr. articles to profl. jours. Home: 2008 Vilas Ave Madison WI 53711 Office: 1450 Linden Dr Madison WI 53706

JOHNSON, MARVIN MELROSE, indsl. engr.; b. Neligh, Nebr., Apr. 21, 1925; s. Harold Nighram and Melissa (Bare) J.; B.S., Purdue U., 1949; postgrad. Ill. Inst. Tech., 1953; M.S. in Indsl. Engring., U. Iowa, 1966, Ph.D., 1968; m. Anne Stuart Campbell, Nov. 10, 1951; children—Douglas Blake, Harold James, Phyllis Anne, Nighram, Melissa. Quality control supr., indsl. engr. Houdaille Hershey, Chgo., 1949-52; sr. indsl. engr. Bell & Howell, Chgo., 1952-54; with Bendix Aviation Corp., Davenport, Iowa, 1954-64, successively chief indsl. engr., staff asst., supr. procedures and systems, 1954-63, reliability engr. Pioneer Central Div., 1963-64, cons., 1964—; lectr. indsl. engr. State U. Iowa, 1963-64; instr. indsl. engring. U. Iowa, 1965-66; asso. prof. U. Nebr., 1968-73, prof., 1973—; U.S. AID adviser mgmt. engring. and food processing Kabul (Afghanistan) U., 1975-76. NSF trainee U. Iowa, 1964-67. Served with AUS, 1943-46, ETO. Registered profl. engr., Iowa, Mo., Nebr. Fellow Am. Inst. Indsl. Engrs.; mem. Am. Soc. Engring. Educators, Am. Statis. Assn., ASME, Ops. Research Soc. Am., Inst. Mgmt. Sci., Sigma Xi, Tau Beta Pi, Pi Tau Sigma, Pi Mu. Presbyterian. Home: 2507 Ammon Ave Lincoln NE 68507 Office: 175 Nebraska Hall U Nebr Lincoln NE 68588

JOHNSON, NORMA JEANETTE, sheep farmer; b. Dover, Ohio, Aug. 30, 1925; d. Jasper Crile and Mildred Catherine (Russell) J.; student Heidelberg Coll., 1943; cert. drafting techniques Case Sch. Applied Sci., 1944; student Western Res. U., 1945-47, Ohio State U., 1951, Muskingum Coll., 1965; A.A., Kent State U., 1979; m. Robert Blake Covey, Oct. 7, 1951 (div. 1960); 1 dau., Susan Kay. Instr. arts and crafts Univ. Settlement House, Cleve., 1944; mech. draftswoman Nat. Assn. Civil Aeros., Cleve., 1944-46; mfrs. rep. Nat. Spice House, 1947-49; tchr. econs., English, math, history, high sch., Tuscarawas County Sch. System, New Philadelphia, Ohio, 1962-69; owner, mgr. Sunny Slopes Farm, producer of specialty wools, Dover, Ohio, 1969—. Tchr., Meth. Sunday Sch., 1956-61; chaplain Winfield PTA, 1960; program dir. Brandywine Grange, 1960-62; troop leader Girl Scouts, U.S.A., 1961-70; mem. Tuscarawas County Jail Com., 1981. Recipient Ohio Wildlife Conservation award Tuscarawas County, 1972. Mem. Mid States Wool Growers, Select-Sires Inc., Am. Angus Assn., Internat. Platform Assn. Club: Nat. Grange. Home and office: Rt 1 Box 398 Dover OH 44622

JOHNSON, ORA J., religious ofcl.; b. Oakland City, Ind., Aug. 31, 1932; s. Ora F. and Thelma Pauline (Julian) J.; B.S., Oakland City Coll., 1971; m. Wanda Mae Lockamy, Aug. 11, 1952; chidlren—David Russell, Kent Alan, Vicki Jeanne. Ordained to ministry Baptist Ch., 1966; sales rep., staff sales mgr. Western & So. Ins. Co., Evansville, Ind., 1956-70, also pastor Corydon (Ky.) Gen. Bapt. Ch., 1965-68, Wadesville (Ind.) Gen. Bapt. Ch., 1968-70, North Haven Gen. Bapt. Ch., Evansville, 1970-75; nat. dir. evangelism and ch. growth Gen. Bapt. Hdqrs., Poplar Bluff, Mo., 1976—; producer, dir. weekly TV program Moments of Worship, 1973-74; pres. Greater Evansville Sunday Sch. Assn., 1975; pres. Gen. Bapt. Home Mission Bd., 1972-73, Gen. Bd. Gen. Bapts., 1972-73; pres. Evansville Clergy Assn., 1975-76. Named Outstanding Theolog of 1971, Gen. Bapt. Brotherhood; recipient Good Shepherd award Boy Scouts Am., 1980. Mem. Christian Resource Assos., Inc., Evangelization Forum, Nat. Assn. Evangelicals. Club: Kiwanis (dir. Evansville 1975, pres. Poplar Bluff 1982—). Home: 2026 N Meadows Rd Poplar Bluff MO 63901 Office: General Baptist Headquarters 100 Stinson Dr Poplar Bluff MO 63901

JOHNSON, OSCAR, JR., farms operator; b. St. Louis, Aug. 18, 1905; s. Oscar and Irene (Walter) J.; ed. pvt. schs.; m. Eloise Long Wells, July 12, 1946; 1 dau., Irene Walter Johnson Barnes; stepchildren—Samuel Wistar Polk, Jr., Eloise Wells Polk Spivy. Pres., St. Albans Farms, Inc. (Mo.), 1946—. Pres. St. Louis Symphony Soc., 1933-55, v.p., 1955—; trustee Jacob L. Babler Perpetual Endowment Trust Fund, 1954-70. Recipient award for civic service St. Louis Jr. C. of C., 1936; key to City of St. Louis for service to St. Louis Symphony Soc., 1941. Served with AUS, 1941-42; to lt. comdr., USNR, 1942-45. Mem. Am. Meteorol. Soc., St. Louis Astron. Soc. Republican. Presbyterian. Clubs: St. Louis Country, Racquet, Univ., St. Louis (St. Louis); Cypress Point (Pebble Beach, Cal.); Old Capitol (Monterey, Calif.); Trans-Pacific Yacht (Los Angeles). Home: Saint Albans MO 63073 Office: 611 Olive St Suite 1400 Saint Louis MO 63101

JOHNSON, PAUL EDWARD, advt. agy. ofcl.; b. Detroit, Feb. 8, 1948; s. Charles Edward and Ruth Dorothy (Brown) J.; B.A., U. Mich., 1970; M.B.A., Eastern Mich. U., 1976; m. Deborah Jean Robertson, Nov. 25, 1972. Faculty, Detroit Coll. Bus., Flint, Mich., 1976-77; with Amrigon, Inc., Detroit, 1977-81, research analyst, 1977-79, sr. program dir., 1980-81; research supr. Young & Rubicam, Detroit, 1981—. Mem. Penninsular Soc., Alpha Delta Phi. Office: 200 Renaissance Center Suite 1000 Detroit MI 48243

JOHNSON, PERRY, state ofcl.; b. Rocky Rapids, Alta., Can., May 27, 1931; s. Harl and Mary (Alport) J.; B.S. in Police Adminstrn., Mich. State U., 1955, M.S. in Corrections Adminstrn., 1977; m. Uyvonne Teske, Feb. 17, 1951; children—Kathleen, Stephen, Randal, Penny, Julayne. Prison counselor State Prison So. Mich., Jackson, 1955-59; prison camp supr. Mich. Dept. Corrections, Lansing, 1959-63, adminstrv. asst. to warden State Prison So. Mich., 1963-64, dep. warden, 1967-69, warden, 1970-72, asst. dep. warden Marquette Br. Prison, 1964-67, dep. dir. Bur. Correctional Facilities, Lansing, 1969-70, dir. Mich. Dept. Corrections, 1972—; asst. adj. prof. criminal justice Mich. State U. Recipient award for disting. service Nat. Govs. Conf., 1977. Mem. Am. Correctional Assn. (govs. 1980-82), Assn. State Correctional Adminstrs. (pres. 1980-81, dir. 1977), Mich. Commn. Criminal Justice, Mich. Corrections Assn. Home: 3670 Bayou Pl Holt MI 48842 Office: Mich Dept Corrections Stevens T Mason Bldg Lansing MI 48913

JOHNSON, PHYLLIS AUDREY, banker; b. Darwin, Minn., July 25, 1923; d. John Emmanuel and Emma Elizabeth (Schneidegger) Nelson; B.A., Met. State U., St. Paul, 1973; B.Applied Sci., U. Minn., 1974; diploma U. Wis. Grad. Sch. Banking, 1973; cert. Am. Inst. Banking, 1975; m. Ellsworth Orr Johnson, Apr. 6, 1943; children—Elwood Oren (dec.), Christine Marie Johnson Wilbur, Elizabeth Ann Johnson Milne, Eric Christian (adopted). Asst. cashier Farmers State Bank, Darwin, 1941-42; asst. cashier State Bank Anoka (Minn.), 1944; cost accountant Red Wing Boast Works (Minn.), 1956-57; banking generalist First Bank Southdale, Edina, Minn., 1960-70; asst. v.p. ops., personnel and purchasing S.W. Fidelity State Bank, Edina, 1970-71; auditor First Nat. Bank Glenwood City (Wis.), 1973—, Hiawatha Nat. Bank, Hagen City, Wis., 1973—; employment mgr., personnel officer Bank Shares, Inc., Mpls., 1973-77; mortgage loan officer St. Anthony Park State Bank, St. Paul, 1978-79; mem. adv. com. bus. mgmt. program Mpls. Tech. Inst., 1975—, instr. bus. mgmt., 1979—; adv. com. banking program Suburban Hennepin Tech. Inst., White Bear Lake, Minn., 1972-77; speaker in field, 1974—. Precinct chmn. Edina Ind. Republicans, 1970-74; chmn. service unit, mem. coms., leader Edina and Red Wing councils Girl Scouts, 1958-68; sec. Edina United Fund, 1963-64; pres. St. Paul's Lutheran Ch., Mankato, Minn., 1965-67, St. Paul's Luth. Ch., Red Wing, 1950-58, Bethlehem Luth. Ch., Mpls., 1959—. Mem. Am. Banking Assn., Nat. Assn. Women Bus. Owners, Am. Bus. Women's Assn., Nat. Bus. Edn. Assn., Am. Vocat. Assn., Minn. Bus. Edn. Assn., Minn. Vocat. Assn. Clubs: Normandale Tennis, Winterset and Marti Grau Dance, Interlachen Country. Home: 5301 Ayrshire Blvd Edina MN 55436 Office: 1415 Hennepin Ave S Minneapolis MN 55403

JOHNSON, RAYMOND JOEL, state ofcl.; b. Duluth, Minn., Sept. 23, 1925; s. Joel and Dorthy May (Sutherland) J.; B.B.A., U. Minn., 1950, S.C.I.E., 1953; M.Ed., Nat. Coll. Edn., 1963; m. Lynnaea Jean Olson, June 25, 1949; children—Scott, Bruce, Mark, Kathryn. Project engr. Champion Motors Co., Mpls., 1951-54; chief indsl. engr. Streater Industries, Spring Park, Minn., 1954-58; exec. dir. CAP and Aviation Edn. Bur., Ill. State Div. Aeros., Chgo., 1958—. Vice pres. Balloons & Things, Inc. Exec. sec. Ill. Aerospace Edn. Com., Chgo., 1966—. Mem. Libertyville (Ill.) Dist. 70 Bd. Edn., 1964-76; exec. dir. Ill. Wing Civil Air Patrol, 1958—. Served with USAAC, 1944-45. Recipient Crown Circle award Nat. Congress on Aerospace Edn., 1981. Mem. Chgo. Soc. Assn. Execs. (dir.), Am. Soc. Assn. Execs., Aviation/Space Writers Assn., Brit. Balloon and Airship Club, Am. Soc. Aerospace Edn. (dir., Disting. Aerospace Educator award 1980), Univ. Aviation Assn. Mem. Editor: Illustrated Ency. of Aviation and Space. Home: 817 S 4th St Libertyville IL 60048 Office: 33 W Jackson Blvd Chicago IL 60604

JOHNSON, RAYMOND NAVARRO, landscaping co. exec.; b. Harrisburg, Ill., Aug. 27, 1932; s. Ray B. and Velma A. (Cole) J.; Ph.D., U. Ill., 1958; m. Olive H. Norman, May 12, 1960; children—Rene, Donna. Pres., Interstate Landscaping Co., Inc., Harrisburg, Ill., 1962—; pres., owner, cons. engr. Raymond N. Corp., 1971—. Served to lt. (j.g.) USN, 1951-55. Mem. Ill. Assn. Gen. Contractors of Ill., Profl. Engrs. Assn. Office: Interstate Landscaping Co US Route 45 North Harrisburg IL 62946

JOHNSON, RICHARD DEAN, bus. exec.; b. DeKalb, Ill., July 8, 1936; B.S. in Pharmacy, U. Calif. at Berkeley, 1960; Pharm.D., U. Calif. Med. Center, San Francisco, 1961, M.S. in Pharm. Chemistry, 1962, Ph.D. in Pharm. Chemistry, 1965; m. Paula Jennings, July 26, 1969; children—Janet, Julie, Richard Dean, Brodie. Practicing pharmacist, San Francisco, 1960-65; teaching asst. phys. chemistry U. Calif., San Francisco, 1962-64, research asst., 1964-65; sect. head pharm. research and devel. Allergan Pharms., Irvine, Calif., 1965-67; asso. dir. regulatory affairs Syntex Labs., Palo Alto, Calif., 1967-73; dir. licensing Marion Labs., Kansas City, Mo., 1973-79, v.p. licensing, 1979—; presdl. interchange exec. Dept. Commerce, Washington, 1970-71; lectr. Sch. Bus. Adminstrn., U. S.C., Columbia, 1975-78. Registered pharmacist Calif. Fellow Am. Found. Pharm. Edn., Am. Inst. Chemists, Sir Henry S. Wellcome Meml.; mem. AAAS, Acad. Pharm. Scis. (chmn. membership econ. adminstrn.), Nat. Formulary (com. specifications). Contbr. articles to profl. jours. Home: 5330 Ward Pkwy Kansas City MO 64112 Office: 9221 Ward Pkwy Kansas City MO 64114

JOHNSON, ROBERT ALAN, lumber co. exec.; b. Joliet, Ill., Aug. 5, 1947; s. Arthur Leslie and Alice Katherine (Simpson) J.; B.S., No. Ill. U., 1969; M.B.A., Lewis U., 1980; m. Kathleen Joan Doyle, Nov. 17, 1973; children—Lorie Anne, Michael Alan. Accountant, Ernst & Ernst, Chgo., 1969-74; ops. and systems mgr. Edward Hines Lumber Co., Chgo., 1974—. Served with U.S. Army, 1970-71. Mem. Am. Mgmt. Assn. Home: 29 W 281 Mark Dr Naperville IL 60540 Office: Edward Hines Lumber Co 200 S Michigan Ave Chicago IL 60604

JOHNSON, ROBERT HAROLD, advt. agy. exec.; b. Dayton, Ohio, Oct. 23, 1931; s. Robert Harold and Virginia Louise (Lambert) J.; B.S. in Journalism, Bowling Green State U., 1953; m. Linda Louise Kitzmiller, Aug. 23, 1973; children—Mark, Robin, Zachary. Vice-pres., creative dir. Caldwell-Van Riper, Inc., Indpls., 1970-75; pres. Carr-Johnson Advt., Toledo, Ohio, 1975-78; v.p., creative dir. Baker, Abbs & Klepinger Inc., Birmingham, Mich., 1978-80, Bayless-Kerr & Palm, Inc., Cleve., 1980—. Served with USN, 1953-57. Recipient Best Public Service Film award Am. Advt. Fedn., 1976. Mem. Nat. Acad. TV Arts and Scis., Am. Advt. Fedn., Cleve. Soc. Communicating Arts, Cleve. Advt. Club. Home: 1181 Orchard Park Dr Rocky River OH 44116 Office: 1166 Hanna Bldg Cleveland OH 44115

JOHNSON, ROBERT LESLIE, chem. engr.; b. Chgo., June 23, 1916; s. Arthur E. and Gertrude (Zeiger) J.; B.S. in Ch.E., Mich. State U., 1939; m. Irene L. Turiansky, Aug. 9, 1975; 1 dau., Rebecca Sue; stepchildren—Edward S. Czekaj, Paul A. Czekaj. Chem. engr. So. Calif. Gas Co., Los Angeles, 1946-47; chem. engr. Consumers Power Co., Jackson, Mich., 1947-54, supr. chem. div. research and testing lab., 1954-76, dept. supr. engring. and research lab., 1976—. Owner, mgr. Color Aids Co., Jackson, 1959—. Served with AUS, 1941-46; to major USAR. Decorated Bronze Star medal. Registered Profl. Engr., Mich.; Cert. Corrosion Specialist. Mem. Am. Soc. Testing Materials, Reserve Officers Assn. (exec. council Mich.), Congress Interallied Officers of Reserves (commn.), Mich. State U. Engring. Alumni Assn., German-Am. Nat. Congress. Republican. Baptist. Club: Vasa Order. Inventor oxygen comparator.

JOHNSON, ROBERT OLIVER, JR., jr. high sch. prin.; b. Galesburg, Ill., Mar. 10, 1940; s. Robert Oliver and Veda Margaret J.; B.S., Western Ill. U., 1963, M.S., 1968, Ed.S., 1972; Ed.D., Western Colo. U., 1975; m. Patricia Ann O'Field, Apr. 7, 1979; children—Ray, Greg, William. Tchr., adminstr. Ill. schs., 1963—; prin. Knoxville (Ill.) Jr. High Sch., 1973—, curriculum coordinator, 1970—; mem. Ill. Curriculum Council. Trustee, Main St. Congl. Ch., Galesburg; chmn. Christian edn. com. E. Main Congregational Ch., Galesburg. Mem. Ill. Jr. High Sch. Assn. (pres. elect 1981), Assn. Ill. Middle Schs. Club: Masons. Home: 208 W North St Knoxville IL 61448 Office: 700 E Mill St Knoxville IL 61448

JOHNSON, ROBERT OSCAR, educator; b. Detroit, May 7, 1926; s. Jalmar Oscar and Lydia (Evans) J.; B.S. in Elec. Engring., U. Mich., 1946, in Math., 1946, M.S. in Physics, 1949; M.S. in Math., U. Ill., 1952; Ph.D. in Math., Ohio State U., 1975; m. Hannelore Haselbarth, May 5, 1960; children—Norbert, Dean, Karen. Sr. engr. Internat. Tel.&Tel. Labs., Nutley, N.J., 1950-52; procurement engr. Republic Aviation, Farmingdale, N.Y., 1954; adminstrv. engr. Bendix Corp., Teterboro, N.J., 1954-58; proposal mgr. aerospace div. Walter Kidde & Co., Bellville, N.J., 1958-62; mgr. advanced design Arde Inc., Paramus, N.J., 1963; research specialist N.Am. Rockwell, Columbus, O., 1964-68; engr. Ohio Dept. Transp., Columbus, 1969-75; prof. Franklin U., Columbus, 1968—, chmn. div. engring. tech., 1981—; prof. Park Coll., Rickenbacher AFB, Ohio, 1975—; ednl. cons. to various colls. and cos., 1975—. Mem. dist. council Boy Scouts Am. 1974. Served with AUS, 1946-47. Mem. Nat. Soc. Profl. Engrs., Am. Soc. Engring. Edn., Math. Assn. Am., Am. Assn. Physics Tchrs., Inst. Math. Statistics, Tau Beta Pi. Contbr. articles to tech. publs. Home: PO Box 30722 Gahanna OH 43230 Office: 201 S Grant Ave Columbus OH 43215

JOHNSON, ROBERT THANE, state senator; b. Kansas City, Mo., Sept. 5, 1945; B.S., Central Mo. State U., 1967, M.A. in Bus., 1968; m. Susan McConnell, Oct. 20, 1967; 1 child. Homebuilder, Lee's Summit, Mo.; mem. Mo. Ho. of Reps., 1972-76; Mo. Senate, 1979—. Mem. adv. com. Lee's Summit (Mo.) Sch. Dist., 1974—; bd. regents Central Mo. State U., 1977-79. Mem. Lee's Summit C. of C., Central Mo. State U. Alumni Assn. Presbyterian. Republican. Office: State Capitol Jefferson City MO 65101

JOHNSON, ROGER BERNOLD, food co. ofcl.; b. Bottineau, N.D., Nov. 11, 1941; s. Berthel John and Clara Beatrice (Wierson) J.; student schs., Grand Forks, N.D.; m. Gloria Ann Thompson, Feb. 9, 1963; children—Kimberly Ann, Bradley. Produce mgr. Millers Superfair, Emerado, N.D., 1963-65, Disgo Foods, Grand Forks, 1965-67, Spies Super Valu, Pierre, S.D., Breckinridge, Minn., 1967-79; stock control mgr. Red Owl, Grand Forks, 1969-73; gen. mgr. Country Kitchen, Crookston, Minn., 1973—; treas., gen. mgr. Crookston Inc.; cons. Hotel, Restaurant Inst., U. Minn., Crookston. Served with USN, 1959-62. Mem. Nat. Fedn. Small Bus., Minn. Restaurant Assn., Crookston C. of C. (retail com.). Republican. Lutheran. Clubs: Polk County Hist. Soc., Kiwanis (charter Crookston Breakfast Club). Home: 2008 Meadowlark Ln Emporia KS 66801 Office: PO Box 432 Crookston MN 56716

JOHNSON, ROLAND EDWARD, appliance co. exec.; b. Kenosha, Wis., May 14, 1931; s. Edward R. and Clara A. (Blank) J.; B.S., U. Wis., 1953, M.B.A., 1957; m. Mable L. Muller, Aug. 27, 1955; children—Keith E., Carol L. Personnel research specialist Esso Research & Engring. Co., Linden, N.J., 1957-59; mgr. personnel research Whirlpool Corp., Benton Harbor, Mich., 1959-62, dir. of personnel research, 1962-64, dir. orgn. planning, 1964-68, dir. of adminstrv. ops., 1968—; instr. Fairleigh Dickinson U., 1957-59, Mich. State U., 1959-64. Served with U.S. Army, 1953-55. Recipient Research award Indsl. Relations Center, U. Minn., 1960. Mem. Am. Mgmt. Assn., Am. Soc. of Personnel Adminstrs. Club: Elks. Co-editor: Ency of Mgmt., 1978. Home: 4645 Terra Ln St Joseph MI 49085 Office: Administrative Center Whirlpool Corp Benton Harbor MI 49022

JOHNSON, RONALD DELYNN, librarian; b. Minden, Nebr., Mar. 4, 1939; s. Olof and Eva Isabell (Jacobs) J.; B.A., Dana Coll., Blair, Nebr., 1961; M.L.S., Emporia (Kans.) State U., 1962; m. Bodil Strom, July 17, 1962; children—Lisa Lynn, Eva Marie. Asst. librarian, then library dir. Bethany Coll., Lindsborg, Kans., 1962-66; library dir.

Dana Coll., 1966—. Future Faculty fellow Am. Library Ch., 1961. Mem. ALA, AAUP, Am.-Scandinavian Found., Nebr. Library Assn. (pres. coll. and univ. sect. 1967). Democrat. Lutheran. Office: Dana Coll Blair NE 68008

JOHNSON, RONALD HARRY, educator; b. Moline, Ill., May 17, 1931; s. Harry Carl and Jane Agatha (Young) J.; B.A. in Bus. Adminstrn., St. Ambrose Coll., 1954; M.A. in Bus. Edn., U. Iowa, 1964; postgrad. U. Santa Clara, 1975, Western Ill. U., 1976, 80; m. Ruth Beverly Ashton, June 10, 1955; children—Michael James, Andrew Ashton, Daniel Ronald. In shipping and receiving positions Sears Roebuck & Co., Moline, 1946-52, salesman, 1952-54; mgr. sporting goods dept., Davenport, Iowa, 1954-57, mgr. automotive dept., Moline, 1957-62, mgr. automotive service, 1962-63; tchr. bus. Central High Sch., Davenport Community Sch. Dist., 1964—. Instr., ARC, 1961—; active Boy Scouts Am., 1965-76, scout master troop 4 Illowa council, 1971-76; swim ofcl. Iowa AAU, 1962—; head scorer 1st Iowa Girls Swim Meet, Iowa Girls High Sch. Athletic Union, 1967; chmn. fin. Sacred Heart Roman Catholic Parish Council, Davenport, 1980—, v.p. council, 1981-82. Served to cpl. arty. U.S. Army, 1951-52. Mem. Davenport Edn. Assn. (pres. 1968-69, exec. bd. 1969-78), Iowa Edn. Assn. (exec. bd. 1974-78), NEA (rep. del. assembly 1974-78), Adminstrv. Mgmt. Soc. (edn. chmn. Quad-Cities chpt. 1970-71, exec. bd. 1970-71, 79-80), Iowa Bus. Edn. Assn. (S.E. Dist. Outstanding Bus. Tchr. award 1969, treas. and mem. exec. bd. 1974-75), Pi Kappa Alpha, Delta Pi Epsilon. Clubs: Sky Cats Flying (treas., exec. bd.), K.C. Home: 2627 Middle Rd Davenport IA 52803 Office: 1020 Main St Davenport IA 52803

JOHNSON, S. L., life ins. exec.; b. Waseca, Minn., May 26, 1933; s. Clarence N. and Leona L. Johnson; C.L.U., 1978; m. Joyce E. Baumgartner, May 16, 1953; children—Sherry, Terry, Diane, Kristine, Marc. Cost analyst Wilson & Co., Albert Lea, Minn., 1951-63; agy. mgr. Lutheran Mut. Life Ins. Co., Albert Lea, 1963—. Past pres. council Salem Luth. Ch., Albert Lea; pres. Freeborn County Agr. Soc., 1964-80; Freeborn County commr., 1980—. Recipient various service awards. Mem. Nat. Assn. Life Underwriters (Appreciation award 1968), Tri-County Life Underwriters Assn., Albert Lea-Austin Life Underwriters Assn. (nat. com.). Clubs: Lions (dir.), Masons, Shriners, Eagles, Elks, Moose. Home: Route 1 Box 200 Albert Lea MN 56007 Office: 1001 S Broadway PO Box 527 Albert Lea MN 56007

JOHNSON, SHERYL JOY, mfg. corp. adminstr.; b. Mpls., Dec. 5, 1947; d. Mervin Oscar and Gladys Millicent (Herje) Seashore; B.A. in Social Sci., Trinity Coll., Deerfield, Ill., 1969; M.S. in Edn. Counseling, U. Wis., River Falls, 1980; m. Bill Heilhecker, Aug. 21, 1981. children—Aliya Joy (adopted Korean), Kristina Gayle. Tchr., Morrison Acad., Taichung, Taiwan, 1970-72; receptionist Mpls. Clinic Psychiatry and Neurology, 1973-74; eligibility technician Hennepin County Welfare Dept., Mpls., 1975-76; career edn. specialist Wis. Indianhead Tech. Inst., New Richmond, 1977-81; mgr. div. adminstrv. services Doboy Packaging Machinery, New Richmond, 1981—; condr. workshops and tng. programs for industries; counselor, cons. in career growth. Active human services coordinating com., St. Croix County, Wis., 1978-81. Mem. Am. Personnel and Guidance Assn., Wis. Assn. Vocat. and Adult Edn. Democrat. Founder, developer career center; developer, dir. programs in career areas public community and businesses. Home: Route 4 Box 180 Amery WI 54001 Office: Doboy Packaging Machinery New Richmond WI 54017

JOHNSON, STANLEY EDWIN, civil engr.; b. Columbus, Ohio, June 14, 1946; s. Edwin Clarence and Helen Catherine (Jones) J.; B.C.E., Ohio State U., 1970, M.S., 1973, M.B.A., 1981; postgrad. Ohio U., 1976-77, Marietta Coll., 1976-77, Ohio Dominican Coll., 1975; m. Linda Louise Bayliss, Aug. 18, 1979. Engr., Burgess & Niple, Ltd., Columbus, Ohio, 1970-76, chief engr., Parkersburg, W.Va., 1976-78, Columbus, 1978—. Advisor in civil engring. Explorers post Central Ohio council Boy Scouts Am., 1971; mem. Franklin County Dep. Sheriff Scuba Diving Squad, 1978—; mem. credit com. Burgess & Niple Employees Credit Union, 1975-76, asst. treas., 1979, treas., 1980, pres., 1981. Grad. trainee, Office of Water Programs EPA, 1972-73; registered profl. engr., Ohio; registered profl. surveyor, Ohio; cert. fallout shelter analyst. Mem. ASCE (pres. Central Ohio Sect., 1978, numerous coms., 1972—), Nat. Soc. Profl. Engrs., Ohio Soc. Profl. Engrs. and Franklin County Chpt. (judge State Sci. Fair Day, 1972, chmn. intersoc. relations, 1972), Am. Water Works Assn., Profl. Land Surveyors of Ohio, M.B.A. Assn., Ohio State U. Alumni (life), Franklin County Alumni Club of Ohio State U., Chi Epsilon. Republican. Methodist. Clubs: Sertoma Internat. (Gem award 1970, Silver Honor Club award 1974, pres. Columbus Breakfast Club 1974, chmn. bd. dirs. 1975, bd. dirs. N.W. Club 1978), Colbre Clown Unit, Masons. Home: 6983 Ardelle Dr Reynoldsburg OH 43068 Office: 5085 Reed Rd Columbus OH 43220

JOHNSON, SUE HOLLAND, mgmt. cons.; b. Cleve., June 27, 1942; d. Walter Beck and Sue Antoinette Holland; B.A., Case Western Res. U., 1964; M.Ed., Cleve. State U., 1975; 1 dau., Heidi Lynne. Reading cons., English tchr. Cleve. Public Schs., 1964-78; project coordinator Cleve. Bd. Edn., 1978, project cons., 1978-79; employee devel. coordinator Univ. Hosps., Cleve., 1979-81; owner, pres. Sue Johnson & Assos., Inc. Mem. Ohio Citizens Advocacy Adv. Bd., 1980—. Mem. Am. Soc. Tng. and Devel., Nat. Assn. Female Execs., Working Women's Exchange, Women Bus. Owners Assn., WomenSpace, Delta Sigma Theta. Presbyterian. Club: Women's City. Author, editor: Department of Dietetics Orientation Program for New Employees, 1981; author: On Becoming a Reformed Coward, 1982. Office: 3696 Riedham Rd Shaker Heights OH 44120

JOHNSON, SUSAN MARJAMAA, ednl. cons.; b. Newark, Jan. 16, 1945; d. Robert Oscar and Jane Albertina (Long) Marjamaa; B.S. with honors in Biology, Bates Coll., 1966; M.A., Johns Hopkins U., 1968; Ph.D., U. Tex., Austin, 1975; m. Lathrop Park Johnson, Aug. 4, 1973. Tchr., Balt. County pub. sch. system, 1967-69; instr. Essex Community Coll., Balt., 1968-69; teaching asst. U. Tex., Austin, 1972-73; asst. prof. curriculum research and devel. U. Fla., Gainesville, 1974-79, asso. prof., 1979; edn. cons., Muncie, Ind., 1980—. Mem. Am. Assn. Colls. Pharmacy (Lyman award 1978), Health Edn. Media Assn., Nat. Assn. for Research in Sci. Teaching, Fla. PLATO Users Group, Phi Kappa Phi. Author: An Astronomy Bibliography-Selected and Annotated for the Layman and the Sci. Teacher, 1972; (with M.W. McKenzie) The Medication History Interview, a Self-Instructional Module, 1976; contbr. articles to pharm. jours. Home: 1002 Shellbark Rd Muncie IN 47304

JOHNSON, VARD ROYCE, state senator; b. Kansas City, Mo., Mar. 11, 1939; s. Wilbur Louis and Jean Allison (Browder) J.; B.A., Yale U., 1960; LL.B., Harvard U., 1964; m. Loretta Turner, Jan. 26, 1963; children—Samuel Eliot, Schuyler Elizabeth. Admitted to Nebr. bar, 1964; asso. firm Young, Holm, McEachen & Hamann, Omaha, 1964-68; atty., dep. dir. Dinebeiina Nahiilna Be Agaditahe, Inc., Window Rock, Ariz., 1968-69; dir. Legal Aid Soc. Omaha, 1969-76, staff atty., 1977-81; partner firm Broom and Johnson, Omaha, 1982—; adj. prof. Creighton U. Law Sch., Omaha; mem. Nebr. Senate from 8th Legis. Dist., 1979—. Chmn. Douglas County Welfare Adv. Com., 1974-77. Recipient numerous community and service awards. Fellow Internat. Inst. Public Mgmt.; mem. Nebr. Bar Assn. Republican. Unitarian. Home: 2707 Fontenelle Blvd Omaha NE 68104 Office: 254 Continental Bldg Omaha NE 68102

JOHNSON, WALLACE, army officer; b. Oklahoma City, Aug. 8, 1939; s. Carroll Wallace and Pauletta (Bibbs) J.; B.S., U. Okla., 1961; M.B.A., Ala. A&M U., 1973; m. Lela Mae Johnson, Dec. 25, 1959; children—Wallace, Steven, Valerie Lynne, Sharon Denise. Commd. 2d lt. U.S. Army, 1961, advanced through grades to lt. col., 1978; exec. officer 101st Ordnance Bn., Heilbronn, W. Ger., 1976-78; surety insp. Office of Insp. Gen., Heidelberg, W. Ger., 1978-79; logistics instr. Command and Gen. Staff Coll., Ft. Leavenworth, Kans., 1979—; instr. U.S. Army service shcs. Decorated Combat Inf. Badge, Bronze Star, Army Commendation medal, Meritorious Service medal. Mem. Assn. U.S. Army, Am. Def. Preparedness Assn. Democrat. Baptist. Clubs: Jaywalkers of Ft. Leavenworth (v.p. 1980-81), Sertoma (pres. 1981-82). Home: 2 Buckner Dr Fort Leavenworth KS 66027 Office: Dept Combat Support US Army Command and Gen Staff Coll Fort Leavenworth KS 66027

JOHNSON, WALLACE DEVON, investment banker; b. Etna Green, Ind., July 15, 1926; s. Devoe Ward and Pauline Magdalene (Burgh) J.; B.A., Lake Forest Coll., 1950; m. Barbara Mary Smail, June 6, 1950 (div.); children—Anne J. (Mrs. James W. East, Jr.), Mary S. (Mrs. Robert Salzarulo), Joseph S. With Baker, Walsh & Co., Chgo., 1950-52, Farwell Chapman & Co., Chgo., 1952-60; partner David A. Noyes & Co., Chgo., 1960-64; pres. Howe, Barnes & Johnson, Inc., Chgo., from 1965, now chmn. emeritus. Bd. commrs. Chgo. Transit Authority, 1970-76; mem. adv. bd. high speed ground transp. Fed. R.R. Commn., U.S. Dept. Transp., 1973-77. Del., Republican Nat. Conv., 1964. Bd. dirs., pres., mem. finance com. Home for Destitute Crippled Children, 1966-78; trustee, mem. exec., athletic and student affairs com. Lake Forest Coll.; bd. dirs., treas., fin. cons. Scottish Rite Cathedral Assn., Chgo. Valley; bd. dirs., chmn. investment com. Presbyn. Home, Evanston, Ill.; trustee, chmn. bd. Indiana Soc. Chgo. mem. exec. com. of adv. bd. Salvation Army; mem. citizens bd., council of Salvation Army's Booth Meml. Hosp.; mem. citizens bd., finance com. Ill. Masonic Med. Center; mem. trustees com. on hosps. and clinics U. Chgo. Served with USNR, 1944-46. Recipient Disting. Service citation Lake Forest Coll., 1975. Mem. Chgo. Assn. Stock Exchange Firms (chmn. 1970-71), Securities Industry Assn. (chmn. exec. com. Mid-Continental dist. 1977). Mason (Shriner, 33 deg.), Rotarian (pres. Rotary One 1976). Clubs: Bond (sec., dir. 1969-70), University, Attic, Quadrangle (Chgo.). Author articles on transp. Home: 111 E Chestnut St 56-D Chicago IL 60611 Office: 135 S LaSalle St Chicago IL 60603

JOHNSON, WILLARD HAVEN, hosp. adminstr.; b. Wilmington, Del., Nov. 6, 1944; s. Willard and Margaret (Ellis) J.; B.A., Coll. of Wooster, 1966; M.H.A., U. Mich., 1969; m. Gale Ann Maynard, Sept. 16, 1967; children—Meredith Lynn, Melissa Ann, Lindsay Elizabeth, Daniel Ellis. Adminstrv. resident Wilmington Med. Center, 1967-68; asst. adminstr. U. Nebr. Med. Center, Omaha, 1968-71; v.p. St. Peter's Hosp., Albany, N.Y., 1971-75; adminstr. Chelsea (Mich.) Community Hosp., 1975—. Mem. Am. Coll. Hosp. Adminstrs., Am. Hosp. Assn., Mich. Hosp. Assn. Club: Inverness Country. Home: 14410 Stofer Ct Chelsea MI 48118 Office: Chelsea Community Hosp 775 S Main St Chelsea MI 48118

JOHNSON, WILLIAM BENJAMIN, bus. exec.; b. Salisbury, Md., Dec. 28, 1918; s. Benjamin A. and Ethel (Holloway) J.; A.B. maxima cum laude, Washington Coll., 1940, LL.B. (hon.), 1975; LL.B. cum laude, U. Pa., 1943; m. Mary Barb, Dec. 19, 1942; children—Benjamin H., Kirk B., John P., Kathleen M. Admitted to Md. bar, 1943, Pa. bar, 1947; atty. U.S. Tax Ct., 1945-47; asst. solicitor Pa. R.R., 1947-48, asst. gen. solicitor, 1948-51, asst. to gen. counsel, 1951-52, asst. gen. counsel, 1952-59; pres., dir. REA Express (formerly Ry. Express Agy., Inc.), N.Y.C., 1959-66, chmn. bd., 1966; pres., chief exec. officer, dir. Ill. Central Industries and I.C. R.R., 1966-68; chmn., pres., chief exec. officer Ill. Central Industries, 1968-72, chmn., chief exec. officer, 1972—; chmn., chief exec. Officer I.C. R.R., 1969-72, chmn. exec. com., 1972-76; dir. Continental Ill. Corp., Chgo., Continental Ill. Nat. Bank, Chgo., Abex Corp., N.Y.C., Ill. Central Gulf R.R., Midas-Internat., Chgo., Esmark, Chgo., Pet Inc., St. Louis, Pepsi-Cola Gen. Bottlers, Inc., Chgo. Bd. dirs. Chgo. Central Area Com.; trustee Com. for Econ. Devel., U. Chgo.; mem. Northwestern U. Assos.; bd. visitors Tulane U. Served as spl. agt., Security Intelligence Corps, AUS, 1943-45. Mem. Am., Phila. bar assns., ICC Practitioners Assn., Juristic Soc., Conf. Bd., Newcomen Soc. N.Am., Transp. Assn. Am. (dir.), Assn. Am. Railroads (dir.), Nat. Def. Transp. Assn. (life; past chmn. bd.), Md. Soc. Pa., S.A.R., Order of Coif, Kappa Alpha, Omicron Delta Kappa. Clubs: Sky, Economic, Links (N.Y.C.); Commercial, Economic, Chicago, Executives, Metropolitan, Mid-America (Chgo.); Onwentsia (Lake Forest); Old Elm (Highland Park). Editor-in-chief U. Pa. Law Rev. Office: Room 2700 111 E Wacker Dr Chicago IL 60601

JOHNSON, WILLIAM CUMMING, JR., civic worker, former educator; b. Memphis, June 26, 1904; s. William Cumming and Evangeline (Harvey) J.; B.S., Princeton U., 1925; E.E., Rensselaer Poly. Inst., 1927; postgrad. in engring. Gen. Electric Co., 1927-30; m. Mayo Crew, Feb. 5, 1926; children—Kenn Harvey, Carel Crew, EveAnne. With Gen. Electric Co., Schenectady, 1927-33; asst. prof. Rensselaer Poly. Inst., 1933-39; asso. prof. Va. Poly. Inst., 1939-43; research and devel. Goodyear Aerospace Corp., Akron, Ohio, 1943-65; asst. prof. Kent State U., 1965-74; vol. Western Res. Hist. Soc., Cleve., 1970-81; registrar Ohio soc. Order Founders and Patriots Am., 1977-81. Mem. AIAA, Ohio Geneal. Soc. (v.p. 1974-80), Phi Beta Kappa, Sigma Xi. Quaker. Developed method for calculation stresses in helicopter rotor blades. Home: 11687 Vaughn Rd Hiram OH 44234

JOHNSON, WILLIAM DAFOE, constrn. co. exec.; b. Flint, Mich., Sept. 5, 1941; s. Orr H. and Donna G. (Dafoe) J.; student Wheaton Coll., 1959-61; B.S. in C.E., U. Mich., 1964; m. Marcia Louise Cogswell, Aug. 1, 1964; children—Kristi, Kevin. With William M. Johnson, Gen. Contractor, Inc., Flint, 1964—, chief exec. officer, 1979—; founder Rhoads & Johnson Constrn. Co., Flint, 1968, sec.-treas., 1969—; founder Jonmarkley Corp., Flint, 1971, pres., 1971—; partner Silver Lake Centre, Flint, 1978—, C.J.R. Co., Flint, 1979—, Rhoads & Johnson Bldg., Flint, 1972—; guest lectr. Mott Community Coll., 1977—; cons. in field. Bd. dirs. Victorious Christian Youth, Flint, 1966-76, chmn., 1970-76; chmn. bd. dirs. Trinity Missionary Ch., Flint, 1973-76; treas. Here's Life Flint, Inc., 1978; bd. dirs. Calvary United Meth. Ch., Flint, 1979—. Home: 5435 S Sycamore St Burton MI 48509 Office: 5125 Exchange Dr Flint MI 48507

JOHNSON, WILLIAM RAYMOND, clergyman; b. Chgo., Feb. 6, 1951; s. Raymond Gottfried and Ruth Elinor (Mathae) J.; B.A., Augustana Coll., Rock Island, Ill., 1973; M.A., State U. Iowa, Iowa City, 1975, Ph.D., 1977; M.Div., U. Dubuque Theol. Sem., 1979; m. Helen Ann Eckhoff, June 9, 1973; children—Sarah, Seth. Terminal operator Augustana Coll. Computer Center, 1971-73; computer-based edn. asst. State U. Iowa, 1973-75; dir. computer resources Loras Coll., Dubuque, 1975-77, acting dir. computer resources, 1977-78; ordained deacon United Meth. Ch., 1978, elder, 1981; pastor Greeley (Iowa) United Meth. Ch., 1977-79, St. Paul's United Meth. Ch., Waukon, Iowa, 1979-81, St. John's United Meth. Ch., Dorchester, Iowa, 1979-81; asst. gen. sec. systems and procedures Gen. Council on Fin. and Adminstrn., United Meth. Ch., Evanston, Ill., 1981—; computer cons. U. Dubuque Theol. Sem.; mem. bd. edn. Iowa conf. United Meth. Ch., also mem. div. higher edn., mem. computer task force, chmn. info. and adminstrv. self-study com., mem. superintendency com. Dubuque dist. Cert. tchr. secondary sch. math., Iowa, Ill.; E. Craig Brandenburg scholar of United Meth. Ch. Mem. Assn. Ednl. Data Systems, Assn. Devel. Computer-Based Instructional Systems, Assn. Computing Machinery, Allamakee County Clergy Assn. (pres.), Internat. Platform Assn., Pi Lambda Theta, Phi Delta Kappa. Home: 139 E Blodgett Lake Bluff IL 60044 Office: 1200 Davis St Evanston IL 60201

JOHNSTON, CHARLES NICKELL, JR., mental health center adminstr.; b. Honolulu, Aug. 24, 1941; s. Charles Nickell and Bess Lorena (Redbarn) J.; B.S., Ind. State U., 1963; M.S. in Social Work, Mo. U., 1966; m. Ella Jo Crouch, Sept. 2, 1967; children—Aaron Garth, Micah Stuart. Social worker Singer Zone Center, Rockford, Ill., 1966, 68-69; dir. clin. services Springfield (Ill.) Mental Health Center, 1969—; staff affiliate dept. psychiatry St. John's Hosp.; asso. dept. psychiatry Sch. Medicine, So. Ill. U., 1974—; instr. Lincolnland Community Coll.; cons. Goodwill Industries, 1972—, Mary Bryant Home for Blind, 1977—. Pres., Sangamon County (Ill.) Case Coordinating Commn., 1975; bd. dirs. Land of Lincoln council Girl Scouts U.S.A., 1976—, mem. grievance com., 1978—, chmn. nominating com., 1981-82; mem. Bd. Health Menard County (Ill.), 1978—, pres., 1980-81. Served with U.S. Army, 1966-68. Mem. Nat. Assn. Social Workers (Social Worker of Yr., Springfield 1981). Presbyterian. Home: 108 W Washington St Petersburg IL 62675 Office: 707 N Rutledge St Springfield IL 62702

JOHNSTON, HOWARD DARRELL, mfg. exec.; b. Milton, Wis., Feb. 22, 1937; s. John and Bertha Ann (Wenslaff) J.; B.S. in Indsl. Engring., Gen. Motors Inst., 1960; m. Dorothy Hazel Gray, Sept. 12, 1959; children—Michael Howard, Cheryl Lynn. Co-op student Chevrolet-Saginaw Grey Iron Foundry, 1955-60; supr. melting dept. Chevrolet-Saginaw, 1961-62, plant engr., Chevrolet, 1962-63; project engr. Chrysler Corp., Indpls., 1963-65, quality control mgr., 1965-67; mfg. engring. mgr., Detroit, 1967-71; mfg. mgr. P.R. Mallory & Co., Inc., Indpls., 1971-73, div. mgr., 1974-78; pres., chmn. bd., owner CMW, Inc., Indpls., 1978—. Mem. Am. Welding Soc., Resistance Welding Mfrs. Assn., Metal Powders Industries Fedn., Ind. C. of C., Indpls. C. of C., Econ. Club Indpls., Am. Mgmt. Assn. Republican. Baptist. Club: Columbia (Indpls.). Home: 3217 Albright Ct Indianapolis IN 46268 Office: PO Box 2266 70 S Gray St Indianapolis IN 46206

JOHNSTON, JAMES ROBERT, library adminstr.; b. Aurora, Ill., June 3, 1947; s. Robert William and Betty Sue (Townsend) J.; B.A., U. Notre Dame, 1969; M.S. in L.S., Fla. State U., 1973; m. Carol Ann Trezza, June 14, 1969; children—Steven James, Julie Marie. Head librarian Grande Prairie Library Dist., Country Club Hills, Ill., 1973-76; chief librarian Joliet (Ill.) Public Library, 1976—. Mem. Heritage com. Country Club Hills Bicentennial Commn.; mem. City of Joliet Land Use Planning Com., 1977-78; mem. staff rev. com. City of Joliet Capitol Improvement Program, 1978—. Mem. Ill. Library Assn. (pres. public library sect. 1978-79, mem. exec. bd. 1978-79), ALA, Library and Media Assn. Greater Will County, Library Adminstrs. Conf. No. Ill., Jaycees (past state dir.), Beta Phi Mu. Club: Kiwanis. Office: 150 N Ottawa St Joliet IL 60431

JOHNSTON, JOHN ANDREW, air force officer; b. Ont., Can., Jan. 30, 1923; s. Robert Andrew and Rebecca Ellen (McKenzie) J.; grad. Air Force Command Staff Coll., 1955, Armed Forces Inst., 1962; m. Dorothy L. Crabb, Aug. 17, 1945; children—Robert H., Susan L., James J., William G. Commd. 2d lt. USAAF (named changed to USAF 1947), 1942, advanced through grades to maj. gen., 1974; base comdr. Detroit Met. Airport, 1952-60; asst. adj. gen. Mich., 1960-74, adj. gen. Mich., dir. Mich. Dept. Mil. Affairs, 1974—. Bd. dirs. St. Lawrence Hosp., Lansing, Mich., 1972—; mem. Dept. Def. Policy Bd. Decorated Air medal with 16 oak leaf clusters, Purple Heart. Mem. N.G. Assn. U.S., N.G. Assn. Mich., Am. Legion, Am. Def. Preparedness Assn., Air Force Assn. Clubs: Rotary, Quiet Birdmen. Home: 1708 Briarwood Rd Lansing MI 48917 Office: 2500 S Washington Lansing MI 48913

JOHNSTON, LEO LORRAINE, constrn. co. pres.; b. Sidney, O., June 1, 1920; s. Leo Cargill and Anna Dolores (Elliott) J.; B.S., Ohio U., 1942; m. Fern Maxine Camplin, Jan. 30, 1942; children—Kay, Cheryl. Founder, pres. Midwest Constructors, Inc., Mansfield, O., 1946—. Chmn., Midwest Utility Service Corp., Mansfield, O., 1967-70, Profl. Bldg. Corp., Mansfield, 1960-63; dir. Richland Trust Co., Mansfield. Chmn. Lake Erie Council Carpenters Benefit Fund, 1966—, Ohio State chmn., 1976-77, Joint Apprenticeship and Tng., 1966—. Bd. dirs. Mansfield Mental Health Center, 1972—, Am. Cancer Soc., 1977—. Served with USNR, 1942-46; ETO. Registered profl. engr., Iowa. Mem. Am. Soc. C.E. (dir. 1972-73), N. Central O. Builders Assn. (pres. 1966-67), Ohio Contractors (chmn. labor relations div. 1969), Nat., Ohio socs. profl. engrs., Cleve. Soc. Engrs. Mason (32 deg., Shriner), Kiwanian (past pres.). Clubs: University, Westbrook Country (pres. 1977). Home: 550 Palomar Dr Mansfield OH 44906 Office: 210 N Illinois Ave Mansfield OH 44905

JOHNSTON, LLOYD DOUGLAS, psychologist; b. Boston, Apr. 18, 1940; s. Leslie D. and Madeline B. (Irvin) J.; B.A. in Econs., Williams Coll., 1962; M.B.A., Harvard U., 1965, postgrad. 1965-66; M.A. in Social Psychology, U. Mich., 1971, Ph.D., 1973; 1 son, Douglas Leslie. Research asst. Grad. Sch. Bus. Adminstrn., Harvard U., Boston, 1965-66; asst. study dir. Inst. for Social Research, U. Mich., Ann Arbor, 1966-73, asst. research scientist, 1973-75, asso. research scientist, 1975-78, research scientist and program dir., 1978—; cons. to WHO, UN, White House, fed. agys. and various univs., 1979—; mem. adv. com. Drug Abuse Epidemiology Data Center, Tex. Christian U., 1974—; mem. various coms. Nat. Inst. on Drug Abuse, 1975—. Mem. Am. Psychol. Assn., Soc. for Psychol. Study of Social Issues (sec.-treas. 1976-79), AAAS. Author: Drugs and American Youth, 1973; various monographs on drug use among American high school students, 1972-80; contbr. chpts. to books, articles to profl. jours. Home: 4231 Shetland Dr Ann Arbor MI 48104 Office: Inst for Social Research Univ of Michigan Ann Arbor MI 48109

JOHNSTON, MICHAEL L., state senator; b. Parsons, Kans., July 29, 1945; s. William Lewis and Jean Marie (McClarnan) J.; B.S., Kans. State Coll., 1971; M.S., U. Kans., 1976. Agt., Washington Nat. Ins. Co., 1977—; mem. Kans. Senate, 1977—. Served with U.S. Army, 1965-71. Roman Catholic. Club: Elks. Address: Parsons KS*

JOHNSTON, ROD, state senator; b. Milw.; B.S., U.S. Naval Acad.; J.D., George Washington U. Commd. ensign U.S. Navy; mem. Wis. Assembly, 1975-79, Wis. Senate, 1979—. Address: Room 314 South State Capitol Madison WI 53702*

JOHNSTON, WALTER WESLEY, data processor; b. Chgo., May 20, 1946; s. Walter George, Jr. and Elsie Marie (Subert) J.; B.S. in Math. cum laude (De Kalb Ogle Co. Sci. scholar 1966), No. Ill. U.,

DeKalb, 1967; M.A. in Math., Sangamon State U., Springfield, Ill., 1974, M.A. in History, 1981; postgrad. math. and computer sci. U. Ill., 1967-69; m. Guadalupe Maria De Leon, Dec. 30, 1968; children—Martha, Walter Wesley II. With State of Ill., 1969—, mgr. data processing for health services Dept. Public Health, 1977—; geneal. researcher, lectr., 1975—; treas., dir. Alba Cottage Industries, Inc., 1978-79. Cert. geneal. record searcher. Mem. Ill. Hist. Soc. (life), Ill. Geneal. Soc. (life, long-range planning com. 1980—), Chgo. Hist. Soc. (life), Chgo. Geneal. Soc. (life), Sangamon County Geneal. Soc. (life, 2d v.p. 1976, trustee 1978-80), Ont. Hist. Soc. (life), Ont. Geneal. Soc. (life), Soc. Genealogists London, Cornwall Family History Soc., Devon Family History Soc., Sangamon County Hist. Soc. (life), Brown County (Minn.) Hist. Soc. (Life), Holland (Mich.) Geneal. Soc., Utah Geneal. Soc., Concordia Hist. Inst. Club: Springfield Road Runners. Contbr. articles to profl. publs. Editor and pub. Butson Family Newsletter, 1979—. Home: 1524 S Holmes Ave Springfield IL 62704 Office: 535 W Jefferson St Springfield IL 62706

JOHNSTON, WILLIAM WALTER, lawyer, state ofcl.; b. Harrisburg, Pa., Dec. 15, 1945; s. Paul Waldo and Eleanor Tatum (Kuhn) J.; B.A. in Econs., Ohio State U., 1967, LL.B., 1970; m. Pamela Kelch, Apr. 9, 1976; 1 stepdau., Lisa Kelch. Admitted to Ohio bar, 1970; asso. firm Crabbe, Brown, Jones, Potts & Schmidt, 1972-76; chmn. Indsl. Commn. Ohio, Columbus, 1976—. Served to 1st lt., F.A., AUS 1970-72. Republican. Presbyterian. Office: 246 N High St Columbus OH 43215

JOHNSTONE, CECELIA ALTA TAYLOR (MRS. PAUL NUGENT JOHNSTONE), poet; b. Gainesville, Mo.; d. John David and Elizabeth (Smith) Taylor; student U. Mo., 1921-22, Johns Hopkins, 1925-26, U. Mo., 1965-66; Ph.D. (hon.), Colo. State Christian Coll., 1973; m. Paul Nugent Johnstone, Dec. 20, 1919; children—Emma-Jean (Mrs. Ray), Paul Nugent. Author childrens stories, plays, also many poems in mags., newspapers, 1949—, also poetry book, 1977. Active Children's Community Theater, Kansas City (Mo.) Young Matrons, 1935—; mem. women's auxs. Jackson County Med. Soc., 1935—, Research Hosp. and Med. Center, Kansas City, 1950—, Internat. Coll. Surgeons, 1953—. Recipient various poetry awards, 1965-67, 70-72, 76-78, state awards, 1969, 72, juvenile story awards, 1970-73. Mem. Nat. League Am. Pen. Women (pres. 1952-54, workshop chmn. Kansas City br. 1966-68, 69—). Mem. Christian Ch. Clubs: Women's City, Coll. Club Kansas City, Carriage. Address: 117 W 69th Terrace Kansas City MO 64113

JOHNSTONE, DONALD FREDRICK, mfg. co. exec.; b. Ocean City, N.J., May 25, 1930; s. Lari and Helen F. (Bielicki) J.; B.S., Cornell U., 1953; M.B.A., Harvard U., 1957; m. Mar. 27, 1977; children—David, Dwight, Helen, Eileen. With Gen. Electric Co., Louisville, 1957-79, gen. mgr. TV div., 1971-74, gen. mgr. range div., 1975-79; v.p. mktg. Litton Microwave, Mpls., 1980—. Served to 1st lt. U.S. Army, 1953-55. Home: 3345 Eagle Bluff Dr Minnetrista MN 55364 Office: 1045 Xenium Ln N Minneapolis MN 55440

JOLLIFF, CARL R., clin. biochemist, lab. adminstr.; b. Lakewood, Ohio, July 2, 1926; s. Gaither Franklin and Selma Edna (Wolfe) J.; B.S., State U. Iowa, 1949, postgrad., 1949-51; m. Shirley Ann Abbott, June 5, 1948; children—Kathy Lynne Jolliff Harvey, Anne Elizabeth Jolliff Saber. Co-dir. Hastings-Lincoln (Nebr.) Med. Labs., 1951-58; dir. clin. labs. Hastings State Hosp., 1953-56, Lincoln Clinic, 1958—; vis. prof. biology Nebr. Wesleyan U., Lincoln, 1972—; lectr., cons. in field. Sec.-treas. Lincoln Med. Research Found., 1964—. Served with AUS, 1944-46. Am. Cancer Soc. research fellow, 1950. Fellow Royal Soc. Health (London); mem. Am. Acad. Microbiology (specialist microbiologist), Am. Assn. Clin. Chemists (chmn. midwest sect. 1959, 73), N.Y. Acad. Scis., Am. Chem. Soc., Am. Assn. Clin. Chemists, Am. Soc. Microbiology, Sigma Xi. Club: Exec. (pres. Lincoln 1968). Author: (with others) Chemistry for Medical Technologists, 1976; contbr. articles to profl. publs. Home: 1400 Crestline Dr Lincoln NE 68506 Office: Clin Labs Sect Lincoln Clinic PO Box 81009 Lincoln NE 68501

JONAS, GLENN FRANKLIN, exec. search cons.; b. Door County, Wis., May 29, 1934; s. Fred Karl and Esther Cora (Honold) J.; B.M.E., U. Wis., 1961, B.B.A., 1963; m. Rita Marie Koss, June 8, 1963; children—Jory Lynn, Jamey Lea, Glenda Sue, Fredric. Prodn. mgr. indsl. controls div. Square D Co., Milw., 1963-69; materials mgr. and mfg. mgr., switchgear and control div. Allis Chalmers Corp., W. Allis, Wis., 1969-71; planning and control mgr. Johnson Controls Co., Milw., 1970-73; owner, chief exec. officer Jonas & Assos., Inc., Milw., 1973—; guest lectr. U. Wis.-Whitewater, 1973—. Mem. Brown Deer Sch. Bd., 1975—. Served with U.S. Army, 1953-55. Mem. Sales and Mktg. Execs. Milw. (v.p.-edn. 1977-78, bd. dirs. 1978—), Met. Assn. Commerce, Pi Sigma Epsilon. Lutheran (past pres. ch. council). Club: Milw. Kiwanis. Home: 9173 N Alpine Ln Brown Deer WI 53223 Office: 3333 N Mayfair Rd Milwaukee WI 53222

JONCKHEERE, ALAN MATHEW, physicist; b. Howell, Mich., Feb. 12, 1947; s. August Peter and Elizabeth Gertrude (Nash) J.; B.S. (NSF fellow), Mich. State U., 1969; M.S., U. Wash., 1970, Ph.D., 1976; m. Barbara Jean Minter, Aug. 16, children—Jessica Susan, Laura Jean and Amanda Jean (twins). Instr. physics dept. U. Wash., Seattle, 1969-70, research asst., 1970-76; research asso., physics dept. Fermi Nat. Accelerator Lab., Batavia, Ill., 1976-78; staff physicist Fermilab, 1978—, asso. dept. head meson dept., 1981—; researcher elem. particle physics Stanford Linear Accelerator Center, Lawrence Berkeley Lab. (Calif.). Contbr. papers to physics publs. Home: 637 Church St Batavia IL 60510

JONES, A. CLIFFORD, state senator; b. St. Louis, Feb. 13, 1921; s. Wilbur B. and Irene (Clifford) J.; A.B., Princeton U., 1942; J.D., Washington U., St. Louis, 1948; children—A. Clifford, Irene, Wesley, Janet; m. 2d, Nan Thornton, Nov. 1974. City clk. Ladue (Mo.), 1948-50; mem. Mo. Ho. of Reps., Jefferson City, 1950-58, minority floor leader, 1956-58; mem. Mo. Senate, Jefferson City, 1964—, minority floor leader, 1968-76; pres. Mo. Polaris Corp., Aluminum Truck Bodies, Inc.; sec.-treas. Hewitt-Lucas Body Co., Inc. Pres. Mo. Assn. for Social Welfare, 1953-54; trustee St. Louis Country Day Sch., 1948-50. Served with USNR, 1942-46; ETO, PTO. Recipient award Jaycees of St. Louis, 1952, Globe Democrat award for pub. service, 1958, 65, 69, 76. Mem. Mo., St. Louis (Bicentennial award) bar assns., Am. Legion, John Marshall Club. Republican. Congregationalist. Clubs: Masons (32 deg.), Shriners, Rotary. Home: 7 Willow Hill Ladue MO 63124 Office: State Capitol Bldg Jefferson City MO 65101

JONES, ADRIENNE EILEEN, sch. prin.; b. Hamtramck, Mich., Dec. 7, 1946; d. Sidney Minrose and Rosa Eileen (McKinney) J.; B.A., U. Mich., 1969, M.A., 1973; m. John William Crockett, June 27, 1981. Tchr., Bloomfield Hills (Mich.) Schs., 1969-77, adminstrv. intern, 1977-78, prin., 1978—. Vice pres. Bloomfield Hills Adminstrv. Council, 1980-81. Organist, St. Peters African Meth. Episcopal Zion Ch., 1974-79; fin. sec., treas. Brazeal Dennard Chorale, 1973—; dir. Christian edn. bd., St. Peters, 1980—. Recipient Opportunity grant U. Mich., 1965-69. Mem. Internat. Reading Assn., Nat. Assn. Elem. Sch. Prins., Mich. Elem. and Middle Sch. Prins Assn., U. Mich. Alumni Club, One Hundred Club U. Mich. Home: 22950 Mapleridge St Southfield MI 48075 Office: 1101 Westview St Eastover Sch Bloomfield Hills MI 48013

JONES, ALAN PORTER, JR., meat packing co. exec.; b. Milw., Feb. 27, 1925; s. Alan Porter and Eleanor Pratt (Bright) J.; B.A., Harvard U., 1948, M.B.A., 1950; m. Jean E. Drummond, Sept. 12, 1953; children—Richard, Susan, Cynthia, Alexandra. With Jones Dairy Farm, Ft. Atkinson, Wis., 1950—, asst. treas., 1953-61, treas., 1961-74, v.p. and treas., 1974—, also dir.; pres. Uncle Josh Bait Co., 1978—; dir. Bank Ft. Atkinson, PDQ Corp. Bd. dirs. Dwight Foster Pub. Library; mem. Wis. citizens environmental council 1980—; Fort Atkinson Sch. Bd., 1968-69; trustee Ripon (Wis.) Coll., 1974-77. Served with inf. U.S. Army, 1943-45. Decorated Bronze Star, Combat Inf. badge. Mem. Mid Am. Com., Newcomen Soc. Nat. Audubon Soc., Sierra Club. Republican. Congregationalist. Home: 433 Adams St Fort Atkinson WI 53538 Office: Jones Dairy Farm Fort Atkinson WI 53538

JONES, ALICE HANSON, economist; b. Seattle, Nov. 7, 1904; d. Olof and Agatha Marie (Tiegel) Hanson; A.B., U. Wash., Seattle, 1925, M.A., 1928; Ph.D., U. Chgo., 1968; m. Homer Jones, Apr. 21, 1930; children—Robert Hanson, Richard John, Douglas Coulthurst. Teaching fellow U. Wash., 1927-28; fellow, research asst. econs. U. Chgo., 1928-29, 32-34; asst. editor Ency. Social Scis., N.Y.C., 1930; researcher, writer Pres.'s Com. Social Trends, N.Y.C., 1931; economist, asst. chief Cost of Living div. Bur. Labor Stats., Washington, 1934-44; economist div. statis. standards Bur. Budget, Washington, 1945-48; sec. com. nat. accounts Nat. Bur. Econ. Research, Washington, 1957; supervising economist, cons. Dept. Agr., Washington, 1958-61; lectr. econs. Washington U., St. Louis, 1963-68, asst. prof., 1968-71, asso. prof., 1971-73, adj. prof., 1973-77, prof. emeritus, 1977—; prin. investigator Social Sci. Inst., 1969—; adj. prof. econs. Claremont Men's Coll., 1973-74; econ. adviser Bank of Korea, AID, 1967-68. Named Woman of Achievement, St. Louis Globe-Dem., 1980; NSF research grantee, 1969-75; Nat. Endowment Humanities research grantee, 1970-76. Mem. Am. Econ. Assn., Econ. History Assn. (v.p. 1976-77, pres.-elect 1981-82), Orgn. Am. Historians. Internat. Assn. Research in Income and Wealth, Social Sci. History Assn., Mortar Bd., Phi Beta Kappa, Delta Zeta (Nat. Woman of Yr. 1981), Omicron Delta Epsilon. Congregationalist. Author: American Colonial Wealth: Documents and Methods, 3 vols., rev. edit., 1978; Wealth of a Nation to Be: The American Colonies on the Eve of the Revolution, 1980. Home: 404 Yorkshire Pl Webster Groves MO 63119 Office: Dept Economics Washington U Saint Louis MO 63130

JONES, ANABEL RATCLIFF, anesthesiologist; b. Lafayette, Ind., Sept. 6, 1933; d. Frank William and Mary Rovene (Holt) Ratcliff; A.B., Ind. U., 1955, M.D., 1959; m. Wiley A. Jones, Oct. 4, 1975; 1 son by previous marriage, Warren Lee. Intern, Meth. Hosp., Indpls., 1959-60; resident anesthesiology Ind. U. Med. Center, Indpls., 1960-62; staff anesthesiologist VA Hosp., Indpls., 1962-63; practice medicine, specializing in anesthesiology, Lafayette, 1963—; mem. staff St. Elizabeth Hosp., Home Hosp., Purdue U. Hosp.; instr. Ind. U. Med. Center, Indpls., 1962—. Piano accompanist civic chorus, also combined civic vocal groups; mem. governing bd. Lafayette Symphony Orch., 1971—. Diplomate Am. Bd. Anesthesiology. Mem. Am. Soc. Anesthesiologists, Internat. Anesthesia Research Soc., Ind. Med. Assn., Ind. Soc. Anesthesiologists, AMA, DAR (gen. Lafayette chpt.), Kappa Kappa Kappa, Delta Delta Delta. Methodist. Home: 3301 Cedar Ln Lafayette IN 47905 Office: Life Bldg Lafayette IN 47901

JONES, B. J., lawyer; b. Iowa City, Iowa, Sept. 28, 1920; s. M.P. and M.E. Jones; B.Sc., State U. Iowa, 1942; M.A., U. Miami, 1946, Ph.D., 1948; LL.B., UCLA, 1952, J.D., 1954; m. Estelle Perry, June 3, 1950 (dec. 1960). Founder, pres., chmn. bd. Exec. Consultants Inc., Miami Beach, Fla., 1953-78; dir. indsl. relations and labor law, v.p. Internat. Harvester, 1946-53; founder, developer, pres., chmn. bd. Paradise Haven Villa, La Jolla, Calif., 1978—, founder KCID-TV/AM-FM, Iowa City. Personnel dir., asst. city mgr., Berkeley, Calif., 1945-48. Served to maj. USAF, 1942-45. Decorated Purple Heart with 6 clusters, Congressional Medal of Honor with 3 clusters. Mem. Personnel and Indsl. Relations Execs. Assn. (past pres.), Indsl. Relations and Labor Law Execs. Club (Los Angeles, past pres.). Clubs: Rotary (past pres.), Kiwanis (past pres.), U. Iowa Athletic, K.C. (4th deg., grand knight), Lions. Author numerous books in field. Home: 715 N Van Buren St Iowa City IA 52240 also La Jolla CA 92123

JONES, BARBARA SMITH, employment counselor; b. St. Louis, Feb. 20, 1942; d. William Osceola and Alice Lillian (Allen) Smith; A.A., Kankakee (Ill.) Community Coll., 1974; B.S., Olivet Nazarene Coll., 1976; m. Walter Jones, Jr., May 10, 1960; children—Terry, Walter, Kim, Verran. Social service Olivet Student Placement Agy., Kankakee, Ill., 1976; counselor Kankakeeland Community Action Program, Inc., Kankakee, 1976-77; employment counselor, adminstr. Kankakee Community Coll., 1978—. Election Judge, Kankakee County, 1966, 69. Mem. Am. Personnel and Guidance Assn. Methodist. Poet, composer song Who Will Love Me, 1964. Home: Route 1 Box 94 Momence IL 60954 Office: PO Box 888 River Rd Kankakee IL 60901

JONES, BEAU FLY, curriculum developer, ednl. researcher; b. Memphis, Aug. 28, 1938; d. Wilson and Doré D. (Beauchamp) Fly; B.A. with honors in Sociology, Newcomb Coll., 1960; M.A. in Sociology, McGill U., Can., 1964; Ph.D. in Ednl. Psychology, Northwestern U., 1976; m. Peter d'Alroy Jones, June 10, 1961 (div. 1980); children—Kathryn Beauchamp Fly, Barbara Collier. Lectr. dept. sociology Smith Coll., Northampton, Mass., 1964-68, dept. sociology Kendall Coll., Evanston, Ill., 1970-73; cons. public schs. in Phila., N.Y.C., Dallas, Tex., Cleve., San Diego, Calif., Kansas City, Mo., 1977—; curriculum researcher and developer Chgo. Mastery Learning Reading Program, Chgo. Public Schs., 1977—; adv. to Center for Study of Reading, U. Ill., Champaign-Urbana, 1980—, Wis. Research and Devel. Center, U. Wis., Madison, 1980—; appeared in ednl. program ABC-TV, 1981. Mem. Assn. for Supervision and Curriculum Devel., Internat. Reading Assn., Am. Ednl. Research Assn., Am. Assn. Sch. Adminstrs. Reviewer, contbr. Jour. Ednl. Psychology, 1980—. Home: 774 Green Bay Rd Winnetka IL 60093 Office: Chicago Public Schs 228 N LaSalle St Chicago IL 60601

JONES, BEVERLY JEAN, nurse, educator; b. Macon, Mo., July 31, 1935; d. Joseph Ellsworth and Elsie Marie (Glass) Henry; student Quincy Coll., 1953-56; R.N., St. Mary's Hosp., 1956; postgrad. St. Louis U., 1963-65, Mo. U., 1978-81, N.E. Mo. State U., 1979-81; m. Victor T. Jones, Feb. 14, 1968; 1 son, Michael Patrick. Staff nurse Pike County Hosp., Louisiana, Mo., 1956-58; head nurse Bethesda Hosp., St. Louis, 1963-64, dir. nursing service, 1964-68; health occupations instr. for spl. needs students Lewis and Clark AVTS, St. Charles (Mo.) Sch. Dist., 1978—; mem. adv. com. Health Occupations Aide; pres. Skilled Nursing Facilities, Ariz., 1974-75, N.E. Mo. Dist. for Health Occupations. Mem. Am. Vocat. Assn., Mo. Vocat. Assn., Assn. Disadvantaged and Handicapped. Mem. United Ch. of Christ. Home: 820 Elmhurst Saint Charles MO 63301 Office: 2400 Zumbehl Saint Charles MO 63301

JONES, BRUCE EDWARD, Realtor; b. Anderson, Ind., Nov. 21, 1947; s. George Lewis and Hazel Marie (Crull) J.; B.S., Ball State U., 1970, M.A., 1974; m. Laura Dona Harrell. Tchr., Pendleton (Ind.) Community Schs., 1970-74; tchr. Ball State U.-Burris Lab. Sch., 1974-75; res. dep. sheriff, Madison County, Ind., 1972-74; pres. Bernard Realty Co., Anderson, 1974—; pres. BEJ Cattle Ranch; mgmt. broker VA. Precinct election judge, insp., poll taker, Anderson. Served as comdr. USCG Aux., 1977-78. Named Tchr. of Yr., Current Events Club, 1974. Lic. prin., Ind.; cert. hunter instr., boating instr. Mem. AAUP, Nat. Rifle Assn., Chief Ind. Tng. Officers, Nat. Assn. Realtors, Anderson Bd. Realtors, Am. Assn. Cert. Appraisers (lic. appraiser), Nat. Assn. Realtors, Phi Delta Kappa. Republican. Baptist. Clubs: Fall Creek Valley Conservation (chmn. bd. trustees), Lincoln, Moose Lodge, Young Republicans (officer 1968-70). Home: 4231 W Cross St Anderson IN 46011 Office: 424 Citizens Bank Bldg Anderson IN 46016

JONES, C. W., banker; b. Murdock, Kans., Oct. 20, 1921; s. Claude C. and Ina (Silvius) J.; student Kansas City Jr. Coll., 1942-43, Park Coll., 1943-44; m. Helen Johnson, Sept. 15, 1946; children—Marcia A. (Mrs. James R. Steele III), Mark A., Jeffrey L. With Jones Investment Corp., Independence, Mo., 1955—; with Jomaco, Inc., Independence, Mo., 1958—; pres. Chrisman-Sawyer Bank, Independence, Mo., 1962—. Life mem. hon. bd. Baptist Hosp., Kansas City. Mem. Am. Bankers Assn., Home Builders Assn., Mo. Bankers Assn. Baptist. Office: 201 W Lexington St Independence MO 64051

JONES, C. WAYNE, coll. adminstr.; b. Corbin, Ky., Aug. 4, 1941; s. William Clifford and Margie Marie (Black) J.; A.A., Sue Bennett Coll., 1961; B.S., Eastern Ky. U., 1964; M.A., Ohio State U., 1968, postgrad., 1972-75; postgrad. U. Cin., 1976-79; m. Shirley Lou Lockaby, Apr. 18, 1964; children—Courtney Wayne, Stephanie Leigh. Tchr., So. Ohio Manpower Tng. Center, Jackson, 1964-67; asst. tchr. educator Vocat. div. Ohio Dept. Edn., Columbus, 1968; chmn. dept. bus. Urbana (Ohio) Coll., 1968-74, controller, bus. mgr., 1974-76; campus dir. So. State Community Coll., Wilmington, Ohio, 1976—; pres., dir. Lake Cowan Enterprises. Chmn. ednl. dept. United Way, 1980; co-chmn. Am. Cancer Soc., 1981. Hon. Ky. Col.; faculty devel. grantee Urbana Coll., 1972; Ohio State U. fellow, 1967-68. Mem. Am. Vocat. Assn., Ohio Vocat. Assn., Ohio Bus. Tchrs. Assn., Am. Soc. Tng. and Devel., Delta Pi Epsilon (past chpt. pres.). Republican. Methodist. Clubs: Rotary, Optimist, Masons. Home: 260 Silver Creek Dr Wilmington OH 45177 Office: 2698 Old State Rt 73 Wilmington OH 45177

JONES, CECILY ANNE WILDER, hosp. public relations dir.; b. Ste. Genevieve, Mo., Apr. 17, 1929; d. David Lambert and Gertrude Mary (Sutherby) Wilder; B.J., U. Mo., 1951; m. Apr. 26, 1952 (div.); children—Michael, Theresa, Christopher, Juliana, Daniel, David. Public relations dir. Montini High Sch., Lombard, Ill., 1969-71, Phelps County Regional Med. Center, Rolla, Mo., 1976—; writer, editor Suburban Life newspapers, LaGrange Park, Ill., 1972-74. Past program chmn. PTA, Downers Grove. Recipient 1st place awards (2) Mo. Press Women Communications Contest, 1978, 79 (3); 1st place award Nat. Fedn. Press Women, 1981. Mem. Am. Soc. Hosp. Public Relations, Mo. Assn. Hosp. Public Relations (charter; dir. region 4, vice chmn.), Am. Hosp. Assn., Nat. Fedn. Press Women, Mo. Press Women. Roman Catholic. Club: Toastmasters Internat. Contbr. articles to various publs. Home: Edgar Star Route Box 356 Rolla MO 65401 Office: Phelps County Regional Med Center 1000 W 10th St Rolla MO 65401

JONES, CHARLES LEWIS, assn. exec.; b. Springfield, Mo., May 12, 1928; s. Charles Archibald and Marie Ethel (Rook) J.; B.A. in English and Journalism, Drury Coll., Springfield, 1954; postgrad. edn. Adelphi U., 1958-62; m. Jeanette Barnett, July 4, 1954; children—Dana Marie, Craig Alan, Angela Sue. Instr. English, drama, speech and journalism high schs., Ill., Mo., N.Y., 1954-68; exec. dir. Mo. Optometric Assn., Jefferson City, 1968-70; exec. v.p. Mo. Hotel and Motel Assn., Jefferson City, 1970—. Eastern N.Y. dir. Nat. Thespian Soc., 1958-64; editor Best of Broadway column Dramatics mag., 1959-64, pres. Little Theatre Jefferson City, 1974. Served with USAAF, 1946-49. Named Hon. citizen of Cork, Ireland, 1974. Mem. Am., Mo. socs. assns. execs., Internat. Soc. Hotel Assn. Execs. (pres. 1979), Ark.-Mo.-Kans.-Okla. Lodging Assn. (sec.-treas. 1974-75), Am. Hotel and Motel Assn. (dir. 1979), Mo. Travel Council (treas. 1979). Home: Renns Lake Rd Jefferson City MO 65101 Office: 119 Madison St Jefferson City MO 65101

JONES, CHARLES PRESTON, educator; b. Birmingham, Ala., July 21, 1934; s. Charlie Preston and Lucile Elizabeth (Nelson) J.; B.S., Ala. A&M Coll., 1956; M.Ed., Wayne State U., 1960, Ed.D., 1981; m. Willie Mae Thomas, May 25, 1953; 1 dau., Jamese Annetta. Tchr. social studies, English, Public Schs., Union Springs (Ala.), 1956-59, Russell County (Ala.), 1959-62, Yeshiva Schs., Detroit, 1964-65; quality control insp. Chrysler Corp., Detroit, 1965-70. reading tchr. Highland Park (Mich.) Sch. System, 1970—. Mem. Internat. Reading Assn., Mich. Reading Assn., Assn. Supervision and Curriculum Devel., Omega Psi Phi. Democrat. Home: 15700 Providence Dr Southfield MI 48075

JONES, CURTIS H., state senator; b. Mar. 2, 1934; grad. high sch.; married; 4 children. Farmer, Britton, S.D.; mem. S.D. Senate, 1970—. Planning commr., Marshall County, S.D. Mem. Nat. Farmers Orgn., Farmers Union. Democrat. Presbyterian. Office: State Capitol Pierre SD 57501*

JONES, DONNA M., trucking co. ofcl.; b. Chgo., Apr. 12, 1948; d. William C. and Juanita Jones; A.S., Moraine Valley Coll., 1975; A.S., John Marshall Law Sch., 1967. With P-I-E Trucking, 1966-81, office mgr., Chgo., 1974-78, terminal mgr., Grand Rapids, Mich., 1978-81; office mgr. Associated Truck Lines, Grand Rapids, 1981, office mgr. and Chgo. Valuliner mgr., 1982—. Mem. Grand Rapids Motor Carriers Assn., Grand Rapids Transp. Club, Kalamazoo Transp. Club, Holland (Mich.) Traffic Club, Ladies Transp. Club Chgo., Am. Trucking Assn., W. Mich. Freight Claim Prevention Council, Delta Nu Alpha. Home: 7553 W 62d Pl Argo IL 60501 Office: 1415 W 35th St Chicago IL 60509

JONES, E(BEN) BRADLEY, steel co. exec.; b. Cleve., Nov. 8, 1927; s. Eben Hoyt and Alfreda Sarah (Bradley) J.; B.A., Yale U., 1950; m. Ann Louise Jones, July 24, 1954; children—Susan Robb, Elizabeth Hoyt, Bradley Hoyt, Ann Campbell. With Republic Steel Corp., Cleve., 1954—, asst. dist. sales mgr., Chgo., 1964-65, asst. mgr. sales flat rolled div., 1965-67, sr. asst. mgr. sales flat rolled div., Cleve., 1967, mgr., 1967-71, v.p. mktg., Cleve., 1971-74, v.p. comml., 1974-76, exec. v.p., 1976-79, pres., 1979-81, pres., chief operating officer, 1981—, also dir.; vice chmn., dir. Republic Supply Co.; v.p., dir. Union Drawn Steel Co. Ltd.; dir. Mooney Aircraft Corp., Republic Bldgs. Corp., Nat. City Bank Cleve., Nat. City Corp.; pres., dir. Ga. Tubing Corp.; dir. Republic Hibbing Corp., Republic Builders Products Corp., Res. Mining Co. Mem. exec. bd. Greater Cleve. council Boy Scouts Am.; trustee, v.p., mem. exec. com. Cleve. Clinic Found.; trustee, exec. com. Univ. Sch., Cleve.; bd. dirs. INROADS/Cleve., Inc.; adv. bd. Case Inst. Tech., Cleve. Served with U.S. Army, 1950-53. Mem. Am. Iron and Steel Inst, Delta Kappa Epsilon. Office: PO Box 6778 Cleveland OH 44101*

JONES, EARLE CHESTER, hosp. engr.; b. Yakima, Wash., Mar. 2, 1919; s. Giles Filley and Cora Marie (Horton) J.; asso. degree in aircraft maintenance engring. Parks Coll., St. Louis U., 1939. Field engr. Wildhagen Machine & Supply Co., St. Joseph, Mo., 1946-49; revenue acct., claim agt. Mid-Am. Truckline, Inc., St. Joseph, 1949-52; purchasing agt., plant engr. St. Joseph Structural Steel Co., 1952-66; dir. plant services Meth. Med. Center, St. Joseph, 1966-81, asst. adminstr. support services, 1981—. Bd. dirs. St. Joseph Safety Council, 1976—; cert energy auditor Mo. Dept. Natural Resources. Served with USAAF, 1941-45. Mem. Am. Soc. Hosp. Engring. Fellow mem. faculty continuing edn. service), Kansas City Hosp. Assn., Mo. Soc. Hosp. Engring., Refrigeration Service Engrs. Soc., Nat. Fire Protection Assn., Bldg. Ofcls. and Code Adminstrs. Internat., Nat. Rifle Assn., Nat. Wildlife Fedn., Mo. Conservation Fedn., Am. Legion. Roman Catholic. Club: Optimist (life mem.). Home: 2709 Doniphan Ave Saint Joseph MO 64507 Office: Meth Med Center 7th to 9th on Faraon St Saint Joseph MO 64501

JONES, EDWARD COLE, meat packing co. exec.; b. Fort Atkinson, Wis., May 10, 1902; s. Edward C. and Charlotte W. (Brown) J.; student Dartmouth, 1920-22, U. Wis., 1922-24; m. Helen E. Schlosser, Jan 23, 1926; children—Frances Cole (Mrs. F.J. Paddock), Deborah Wells (Mrs. Malcolm Donaldson), Edward Cole. With Jones Dairy Farm, Ft. Atkinson, 1922—, pres., 1966—. Bd. dirs. Am. Meat Inst., 1948—, treas., 1964-68, chmn. bd., 1968-71, recipient Community Relations award, 1958; pres. Wis. Live Stock and Meat Council, 1963-81. Pres. bd. trustees Ft. Atkinson Meml. Hosp., 1943-76; bd. dirs. Center for Study of Presidency. Recipient award outstanding service and leadership Wis. Live Stock Breeders Assn., 1964; hon. recognition U. Wis., 1967; award distinguished community service Ft. Atkinson Lions Club, 1968; recognition and appreciation award, Wis. Live Stock and Meat Council, 1969; Hon. Am. Farmer award Future Farmers Am., 1973; Distinguished Service award Am. Meat Inst. Mem. N.A.M. (past dir.), Wis. Mfrs. Assn. (past dir.; recognition outstanding service to Am. bus. 1969), Def. Orientation Conf. Assn. (pres. 1968-70, dir. 1956—), Sigma Chi. Republican. Episcopalian. Clubs: University (Milw.); Madison; Chicago, Union League, Tavern (Chgo.); Rolling Rock (Ligonier, Pa.); Lake Zurich (Ill.) Golf. Home: 424 W Milwaukee Ave Fort Atkinson WI 53538 Office: PO Box 25 Fort Atkinson WI 53538

JONES, ELIZABETH BROWN, author, editor; b. Kansas City, Mo., Sept. 27, 1907; d. James Riley and Agnes Julia (Gammage) Brown; student U. Mo.; m. C. Hartley Jones, June 4, 1929; children—Elizabeth Ann, Sara Denise, David Hartley, Phyllis Elaine. Sec., Riley Brown Paint Co., Knasas City, Mo., from 1927, also office mgr.; free-lance writer, 1939—; editor Ch. of the Nazarene, Kansas City, Mo., 1962-78; cons. in curriculum, 1977-79; author of twenty books including: When You Need a Bible Story, 1966, Teaching Primaries Today, 1974, Because God Made Me, 1975, The Story of God's Love, 1976, Stories of Jesus, 1977; Let the Children Come, 1979; contbr. over 500 poems and short stories for children. Mem. Ch. of the Nazarene.

JONES, ERNEST, ednl. adminstr.; b. St. Louis, Jan. 26, 1929; s. Phillip Clinton and Christine C.; B.A., Stowe Tchrs. Coll., St. Louis, 1950; M.A., Washington U., St. Louis, 1955; Ph.D., St. Louis U., 1977; m. Dorothy W. Jones; children—Karla M., Janice L. Tchr., St. Louis Public Schs., 1950-56, asst. prin., 1956-57, reading clinician, 1957-58, adminstrv. asst. to dist. supt. Banneker Dist., 1958-62, prin., 1962-64, prin., 1964-67, dir. city-wide federally-funded programs, 1967-68, dir. elem. edn. Banneker Dist., 1968-69; prin. Work Study High Sch., St. Louis, 1969-70; dep. supt. Mo. Public Schs., St. Louis, 1970-71, acting supt., 1971-72, dep. supt., 1972-75, exec. dep. supt., 1976-79; supt. schs. Gary (Ind.) Community Sch. Corp., 1980—; lectr. Bd. dirs. United Way, St. Louis, 1972-75, Gary, 1980—. Served with U.S. Army, 1950-53. Recipient NAACP Freedom Fund Dinner Service award; St. Louis Police Acad. Service award; St. Louis Bd. Edn. Resolution of Appreciation; St. Louis Council PTA Citation of Appreciation; Mem. Nat. Assn. Secondary Sch. Prins., Nat. Alliance Black Sch. Educators, Assn. Supervision and Curriculum Devel., Am. Assn. Sch. Adminstrs., Ind. State Supts. Assn., Gary C. of C. (dir.). Office: 620 E 10th Pl Gary IN 46402

JONES, EUNECE RITA BOEHLER, constrn. machinery co. exec.; b. Springfield, Ill., Oct. 8, 1946; d. Lawrence John and Alma Elizabeth (House) Boehler; A.A. in Bus. Adminstrn., Central YMCA Community Coll., 1976; B.A. in Human Resources Mgmt., Sangamon State U., 1978; m. Richard Earl Jones, June 26, 1965. With Fiat-Allis Constrn. Machinery Inc., Springfield, Ill., 1966—, personnel and salary adminstr., 1980—. Mem. cert. profl. sec. adv. com., mem. resource and referral adv. com. Lincoln Land Community Coll.; mem. Right to Read adv. council Ill. Office of Edn. Recipient Sec. of Yr. award Nat. Secs. Assn., 1972; cert. of appreciation Ill. Welfare Assn., 1978; cert. of merit Sangamon State U., 1979; cert. of recognition Springfield Mental Health Assn., 1979; cert. profl. sec. Mem. Am. Mgmt. Assn., Am. Personnel Assn., C. of C. Home: 112 N Wilson St Girard IL 62640 Office: Fiat-Allis Constrn Machinery Inc 3000 S 6th St Springfield IL 62710

JONES, EVAN ARTHUR, chem. engr.; b. Chgo., Mar. 18, 1923; s. Evan and Nancy (Price) J.; B.S., Northwestern U., 1949; m. Arlene Joyce Saline, Aug. 19, 1950; children—Joyce, Janis, Jeanne. With Process div. UOP, Des Plaines, Ill., 1949—, dir. process and computer engring., 1974—. Served with inf. U.S. Army, 1943-45. Decorated Purple Heart; registered profl. engr., Ill. Mem. Am. Inst. Chem. Engrs. Republican. Club: Masons. Patentee in field. Office: UOP Process Div 20 UOP Plaza Des Plaines IL 60016

JONES, FRANCIS ARTHUR, III, lawyer; b. Iowa City, Oct. 9, 1935; s. Francis Arthur, Jr., and Dorothea Moore (Niles) J.; B.A., U. Colo., 1958; J.D., Wayne State U., 1961; m. Judith Sheryl Hartman, Aug. 9, 1958; children—Deborah Ann, Francis Arthur IV. Admitted to Mich. bar, 1961; asso. firm Hartwig & Crow, 1961-63; partner firm Hartwig, Crow & Jones, 1963-71, Hartwig, Crow, Jones & Postelli, St. Joseph, Mich., 1971—. Chmn. Mich. State Officers Compensation Commn., 1975-78, 4th Congl. Dist. Com., 1970-78, Republican State Com., 1972-78; chmn. Berrien County Republican Com., 1968-72, vice chmn., 1980—; vestryman, sr. warden St. Paul's Episcopal Ch., 1973-77; pres. Humane Soc. Southwestern Mich., 1968-80; v.p. Lakeland Choral Soc., 1980—; dir. Twin City Sailors, 1963-68. Recipient Gold Key Scholarship award, 1961, Am. Jurisprudence Labor Law award, 1961; decorated Bishop's Cross. Mem. Am. Bar Assn., Berrien County Bar Assn., Mich. Bar Assn., Am. Arbitration Assn., Delta Tau Delta. Clubs: Berrien Hills Country, Hidden Valley, South Shore Racquet, Econ. of Southwestern Mich. Home: 227 N Sunnybank St Saint Joseph MI 49085 Office: 206 Court St Saint Joseph MI 49085

JONES, FRANK WARREN, township ofcl.; b. LaHarpe, Kans., Dec. 4, 1922; s. Jason Wilson and Bertha (Filson) J.; student Emporia State Coll., 1939-41; B.S. in Civil Engring., Kans. State U., 1943; M.S., U.S. Naval Postgrad. Sch., 1963; m. Mary Catherine Randell, July 23, 1944 (div. Feb. 1967); children—Terry Lee, Dennis Warren, Shirley Kaye, Steven Allen, Connie Linn, Kenneth Stanley, Karl Curtis; m. 2d, Martha Lee Albritton Taylor, Nov. 28, 1969. Engring. draftsman N.Am. Aviation, Inc., Kansas City, 1943-44; civil engr. div. water resources Kans. Dept. Agr., 1946; resident engr. Kan. Hwy. Comm., Hutchinson, 1946-51; now mgr. Saginaw Twp., Mich. Served from ensign to lt. (j.g.) USN, 1944-46, recalled 1951, advanced through grades to comdr., 1963, pub. works officer Naval Air Engring Center, Phila., 1965-70. Mem. nat. adv. bd. Am. Security Council. Registered profl. engr., Kans., Colo. Mem. Navy League U.S. (pres. Tri-Cities council 1976-78), Ret. Officers Assn., Fleet Res. Assn., Assn. Navy Civil Engr. Corps Officers, Am. Assn. Ret. Persons, Mich. Public Purchasing Officers Assn., V.F.W., Am. Legion, Kans. State U. Alumni Assn., Emporia State U. Alumni Assn. Baptist. Clubs: Rotary Internat., Masons. Home: 5335 Nottingham Dr N Saginaw MI 48603 Office: 4980 Shattuck Rd Saginaw MI 48603

JONES, FRED ALLEN, assn. exec.; b. McMinnville, Tenn., Apr. 23, 1943; s. John A. and Louise S. J.; student Middle Tenn. State U., 1961-63; B.S. in Journalism, U. Tenn., Knoxville, 1965; postgrad. U. Mo., St. Louis, 1969-70. With Concordia Pub. House, St. Louis, 1965-66, Volkswagen Ins. Co., St. Louis, 1966-67; with ITT Aetna Mgmt. Co., St. Louis, 1968-75; advt. mgr. Am. Optometric Assn., St. Louis, 1975-80; advt. sales promotion mgr. Hosp. Progress jour. Cath. Health Assn. U.S., St. Louis, 1980—. Mem. Am. Soc. Assn. Execs., Advt. Fedn. St. Louis, Advt. Club Greater St. Louis, Studebaker Drivers Club (pres. Mo.-Ill. chpt. 1980-81). Club: Press (St. Louis). Editor: The Steering Wheel newsletter Mo.-Ill. chpt. Studebaker Drivers Club, 1974-78. Home: 3444 Keokuk St Saint Louis MO 63118 Office: Cath Health Assn US 4455 Woodson Rd Saint Louis MO 63134

JONES, GARY HADEN, clergyman; b. Santa Barbara, Calif., Dec. 30, 1944; s. Charles Haden and Eileen Rose Jones; B.A., San Francisco State Coll., 1969; grad. Sch. Ministerial and Religious Studies, Unity Village, Mo., 1971; postgrad U. Mo., Kansas City, 1978-81. Ordained to ministry Unity Ch., 1971; asso. minister Christ Unity Ch., Sacramento, 1971-72; minister, Unity Ch., Palo Alto, 1972-74; sr. minister Unity West Ch., Milw., 1974-77; chmn. faculty Unity Ministerial Sch., Unity Village, 1977—. Chmn., Task Force on Aging, Kansas City, Mo., 1979-80. Mem. Assn. Supervision and Curriculum Devel. Contbr. articles to religious periodicals. Home: 9828 Willow St Kansas City MO 64134 Office: Unity Ministerial Sch Unity Village MO 64065

JONES, GARY R., railroad exec.; b. Wellsville, N.Y., Nov. 11, 1947; s. Harold R. and Pauline L. (Mattison) J.; B.S. in Bus. Adminstrn., Pa. State U., 1969; m. Janice Gelber, June 21, 1968 (div. 1981); children—G. William, Scott L., Timothy J.; m. 2d, Christine Gosselin, 1981. Mgmt. trainee Bessemer & Lake Erie R.R., Pitts., 1969-71; research analyst lumber and wood products Union Pacific R.R., Omaha, 1971-73, market devel. analyst, 1973-75, asst. market mgr. energy resources, 1975-76; dir. market research Detroit, Toledo & Ironton R.R., Dearborn, Mich., 1976-77, dir. market devel., 1977-78, dir. mktg. services, 1979-80; mgr. tech. support Grand Trunk Western/Detroit, Toledo & Ironton R.R., Detroit, 1980—. Mem. Am. Mktg. Assn. Republican. Photographs on cover Progressive Railroading mag., also various indsl. publs. Home: 23245 Edward St Dearborn MI 48128 Office: 131 W Lafayette Detroit MI 48226

JONES, GEORGE STEVEN YOVICICH, civil engr.; b. Belgrade, Yugoslavia, June 2, 1927; s. Steven and Dzagica J.; B.S. in Civil Engring., Northwestern U., 1951, M.S., 1956, Ph.D. in Bus. Adminstrn., 1958; D.Econs. (hon.), U. Fla., 1972; Ph.D. (hon.), Hamilton State U., 1972; m. Sofia, 1960; 1 son. Civil engr. Hollabird & Root, Chgo., 1956-57; project engr., gen. mgr. Arcadia Engring. Internat. Inc., Skokie, Ill., 1956-70, chmn. bd. dirs., 1970—; prof. structural engring. Northwestern U., Evanston, 1957-74; chmn. dept. econs. U. Ill., Chgo.; v.p., gen. mgr. Whithfield Constrn. Co., Palm Springs, Calif., 1978—; chmn. bd. dirs. Oakton Coll.; pres. Hamilton State U., 1971-76, Tetrakear & Assos., Inc.; dir. First Nat. Bank of Chgo. Legis. asst. Gen. Assembly Ill., 1969—, mem. coms., 1970-79; Bd. dirs. Skokie Community Hosp. Served to capt. C.E. U.S. Army, 1951-54. Mem. ASCE, Nat. Soc. Profl. Engrs. Author: The Pneumatic Tube Goes Modern, 1958; Opportunities in Construction, 1960; Management and Labor, 1962; contbr. articles to Engring. News Record. Office: Arcadia International Inc PO Box 712 Skokie IL 60076

JONES, HOWARD HERMAN HUNTER, tool and die co. exec.; b. Dayton, Ohio, Jan. 11, 1931; s. Lee Warren and Ruth Marion J.; B.A., Yale U., 1955; m. Samantha Wilkin, June 11, 1955; children—Virginia, Paige, Hunter, Lee. With Vulcan Tool Co., Dayton, Ohio, 1955—, pres., 1968—, chmn. and pres. Prodn. Tool Cutting, 1959—. Chmn., Dayton area chpt. ARC, 1975-76; bd. dirs., sec. United Appeal, Dayton, 1970—; bd. dirs. Dayton Area Heart Assn., 1965-77. Served with USN, 1951-52. Recipient L. A. Sommer award Nat. Tooling and Machining Assn., 1978. Mem. Nat. Tool, Die and Precision Machining Assn. (pres. 1974), Alliance Metalworking Industries (chmn. 1974-75), Dayton Tool and Die Mfrs. Assn. (pres. 1960), Dayton C. of C. (dir. 1973—). Clubs: Miami Valley Hunt and Polo (pres. 1969-70), Ye Buz Fuz (bencher 1975—), Dayton Polo Team (capt., pres. 1963-74), Yale (pres. 1971-75) (Dayton). Home: 55 Walnut Ln Dayton OH 45419 Office: 730 Lorain Ave Dayton OH 45410

JONES, HUGH EDWARD, psychologist; b. Holly Springs, Miss., July 31, 1943; s. Levite and Ever Lee (Faulkner) J.; B.A., Coll. of Emporia, 1965; M.Div., McCormick Theol. Sem., 1970; M.S.W., U. Ill., 1970; M.A., Mich. State U., 1972, Ph.D., 1975; m. Vernell Thomas, Apr. 16, 1966; children—Gilbert, Derrick. Dir. counseling/guidance Mary Holmes Coll., West Point, Miss., 1970-71; chief psychologist Bixby Hosp., Adrian, Mich., 1975-76; program supr. counseling and cons. services Ingham Community Mental Health Center, Lansing, Mich., 1976-81; staff psychologist Counseling & Referral Services, Steelcase, Inc., Grand Rapids, Mich., 1981—; asso. clin. prof. psychology, psychiatry and social work Mich. State U., East Lansing, 1976—; pvt. practice psychology Center for Wholistic Medicine, East Lansing, 1976—. Bd. dirs. Office of Young Children, Ingham County, 1977-79; mem. Lansing Public Schs., curriculum and Title IX task forces, 1975-77; cubmaster Boy Scouts Am., 1972-75, 76-78; active PTA, 1971-78. Rockefeller Trial Year Theol. fellow, 1966; NIMH fellow, 1971-74; USPHS trainee, 1968-70. Mem. Nat. Registry Health Service Providers in Psychology, Nat. Assn. Black Psychologists, NAACP, Urban League, Am. Psychol. Assn. Mem. Trinity A.M.E. Ch. Club: Gideons. Home: 4144 Thackin Dr Lansing MI 48910 Office: PO Box 67 Grand Rapids MI 49508

JONES, JACQUELINE LEE, occupational therapist; b. Ironton, Ohio, Aug. 30, 1934; d. Leslie Marion and Victoria Louise (Greenlee) J.; B.S., Milw. Downer Coll., 1956; M.S., Fla. Internat. U., 1975; postgrad. U. Ill., 1979—; 1 dau., Victoria Lee Cooke. Dir. occupational therapy dept., asst. prin. children's div. S. Fla. State Hosp., Hollywood, 1969-76; sr. instr. occupational therapy program Palm Beach Jr. Coll., Lake Worth, Fla., 1976-79; asst. prof. U. Ill. Med. Center, Chgo., 1979—. Served with USAF, 1957-60. Mem. Am. Occupational Therapy Assn., AAUP, Am. Soc. Allied Health Professions, Ill. Occupational Therapy Assn., Adult Edn. Assn. Am., Ill. Adult and Continuing Educators Assn., AAUW, Phi Delta Kappa. Republican. Presbyterian. Office: U Ill Medical Center Dept Occupational Therapy 1919 W Taylor St Chicago IL 60612

JONES, JAMES CLINTON, journalist; b. Paul, Idaho, Dec. 17, 1922; s. James Clinton and Marilla Lucile (Houghtaling) J.; B.A., B.J., U. Mo., 1949; m. Barbara Ann Nancarrow, June 10, 1950; children—James Clinton, Michael A., Cynthia Ann. Corr., Bus. Week mag., 1949-53; chief Detroit bur. McGraw-Hill Pub. Co., 1953-55, Newsweek mag., 1955—. Served with USMCR, 1942-45, 50-51. Mem. Sigma Delta Chi. Clubs: Detroit Athletic, Press (medallion for public service 1979, 9 awards excellence in journalism), Renaissance (Detroit). Office: 100 Renaissance Center 19th Floor Detroit MI 48243

JONES, JAMES EDWARD, mfg. co. ofcl.; b. Portsmouth, Ohio, Oct. 9, 1949; s. Harold Edward and Agnes Mae J.; B.A., Piedmont Coll., 1971; postgrad. Ball State U., 1975-79; m. Cristina Lucia Fennell, July 24, 1971; 1 son, Kyle Edward. Tchr., coach Sacred Heart Sch., Coshocton, Ohio, 1971-74; mfg. adminstrv. asst. Warner Gear Div., Muncie, Ind., 1974-75, asst. unit. mgr., 1975-76, sales engr., product distbn. mgr., 1976-80, inventory control supr., 1980-81, plant layout and facilities engr., 1981—. Pres. St. Lawrence Sch. Bd., 1977; v.p. St. Lawrence Men's Orgn., 1981. Mem. Nat. Assn. Purchasing Mgmt. Roman Catholic. Club: Elks. Office: PO Box 2688 Muncie IN 47302

JONES, JAMES PAUL, foundry exec.; b. Evansville, Ind., Oct. 6, 1936; s. Sheridan A. and Kathleen (Taylor) J.; B.S., U. Detroit, 1958; J.D., Detroit Coll. Law, 1962; m. Dorothy Ellen Green, Aug. 4, 1957; children—Michael, David, Robert, Kathleen. Admitted to Mich. and fed. bars, 1958; indsl. engr. King Seeley Corp., Ann Arbor, Mich., 1959-60, Gen. Motors Corp., Pontiac, Mich., 1960-61; labor relations staff Ford Motor Co., 1961-67; foundry mgr. Colt Industries, Beloit, Wis., 1967-73; gen. mgr. foundries Rockwell Internat., 1973-77; div. mgr. Sibley Machine & Foundry Corp., South Bend, Ind., 1977—; cons. Drex Assos., 1976-77. Served with USMCR, 1956-62. Mem. Am. Foundryman's Soc. Home: 51872 Old Mill Rd South Bend IN 46637 Office: 206 E Tutt St South Bend IN 46623

JONES, JAMES WESLEY, clergyman; b. Lake Commerant, Miss., Oct. 30, 1935; s. Robert Jand Ester Lean (Patton) J.; student (Oratorial scholar 1956), Detroit Bible Coll., 1959-61, Am. Baptist Theol. Sem., 1964-65; m. Annie Catherine Proctor, Jan. 2, 1965; 1 son, James Wesley. Ordained to ministry Baptist Ch., 1959; asso. pastor New Liberty Bapt. Ch., Detroit, 1959-64; pastor Mt. Moriah Bapt. Ch., Cin., 1965—; exec. producer, creator public affairs programming sta. WLW-TV, WKRC-TV, WCPO-TV, Cin., 1971-80; pres. Cin. chpt. So. Christian Leadership Conf., 1970-75, nat. dir., 1971-78; chmn. Coalition of Blacks for Justice and Equality in Media, 1971-80; pres. Black Cultural Prodn., Inc., 1971-80. Pres. Mt. Moriah Devel. Corp., 1970—. Recipient various service and appreciation awards. Mem. World Bapt. Alliance, Nat. Bapt. Conv. U.S., Ohio Bapt. Gen. Assn., Cin. Missionary Bapt. Conv. Assn., Ohio Council Chs., Cin. Council Christian Communions. Author articles in field. Home: 7608 Castleton Pl Cincinnati OH 45237 Office: 1169 Simmons St Cincinnati OH 45215

JONES, JERALD FRANKLIN, broadcasting co. exec.; b. Jackson, Minn., Feb. 2, 1934; s. Byron Spencer and Anna Laura J.; student Internat. Corr. Schs., 1957; m. Betty Darlene Hoffman, Feb. 5, 1956; children—Craig, Dennis, Julie. Transmitter, studio engr. KGLO TV, Mason City, Iowa, 1955-69; asst. chief engr. KAAL-TV, Austin, Minn., 1969-70, chief engr., 1970-71, v.p. engring., 1972—; v.p. KAAL-TV Inc., 1981—. Mem. on site evaluation group Minn. Vocat. Sch. High Sch. Occupational Adv. Com., Austin; chmn. mem. adv. bd. for electronics Austin Vocat. Tech. Inst. Certified sr. broadcast engr. Mem. Soc. Broadcast Engrs., Soc. Motion Picture and TV Engrs., Popular Rotorcraft Assn., S.E. Minn. Amateur Computer Soc. Home: 306 3d Ave SW Austin MN 55912 Office: 1701 10th Pl NE Austin MN 55912

JONES, JERREL WILLIAM, communications co. exec.; b. Milw., July 30, 1939; s. Jesse and Mary Ellen (Brady) J.; student Milw. Area Tech. Coll., 1959-61; m. Earnestine Jones, June 13, 1959; children—Lynda, Stacey, Jerrel, Earnest, Mary Ellen. Pub., Milw. Courier, Inc., 1964—, Milw. Star, 1968—, Racine Courier, 1970—; gen. mgr. Sta. WNOV, Milw., 1973—; pres. Courier Communications Corp., Milw., 1973—; dir. North Milwaukee State Bank, 1978—. Bd. dirs. Med. Coll. Wis., 1979—, Greater Milw. chpt. ARC, 1979—; mem. Gov.'s Com. on Minority Bus. Recipient service award Am. Nat. Red Cross, 1974, Am. Cancer Soc., 1976; recognition service award League of Martin, 1974; humanitarian award Sister Clara Muhammad Prep. Sch., 1978, community service award, 1979; community service award United Black Community Council, 1978; Dr. Martin Luther King, Jr. award, 1979. Mem. Nat. Newspaper Pubs. Assn. (1st v.p. 1976-78), Wis. Press Assn., Nat. Assn. Broadcasters, Met. Milw. Assn. Commerce, SCLC (cert. of appreciation 1979), NAACP. Office: 3815 N Teutonia Ave Milwaukee WI 53206

JONES, JOHN BENTON, chem. engr.; b. Naples, Tex., Nov. 12, 1938; s. Wilbert and Phronie (Wearing) J.; B.S., Tex. A&M U., 1962; M.S., Stanford U., 1964; M.B.A., U. Chgo., 1975; student law John Marshall Law Sch., 1979—; m. Rhonda Sue Fike, Dec. 31, 1975; children—Keith, Kevin, Kristofer Jason. Commd. 2d lt., U.S. Army, 1962, advanced through grades to lt. col., 1973; resigned, 1973; sr. engr. Peoples Energy Corp., Chgo., 1975-76, field supt., 1976-77, labor adminstr., 1977-78, adminstrv. asst. to pres. natural gas pipeline, 1978-80, supt. dist. ops., 1980—; chmn., chief exec. officer Lawndale Packaging Corp. Bd. dirs. Boy Scouts Am., 1981, Gen. Jones Fellowship Found., 1981. Decorated Silver Star, Legion of Merit, Bronze Star; recipient Recognition award YMCA, 1979. Mem. Am. Gas Assn., Assn. Ind. Boxmakers. Democrat. Presbyterian. Author: Coping with Racism in America, 1970. Home: 2721 W Jerome St Chicago IL 60645 Office: 122 S Michigan Ave Chicago IL 60603

JONES, JOHN DAVID, cons. engr.; b. Nanty Glo, Pa., Oct. 4, 1923; s. Joseph Louis and Jennie Gertrude (Beutman) J.; student U. Mich., 1949-50; B.S. in Civil Engring., U. Akron, 1952; m. Rose Capriola, Dec. 24, 1942; children—James Steven, Lynn Marie, Stephanie Ann. Field engr. AT & T, Cin., 1952-53, city of Akron, 1953-55, Firestone Tire and Rubber Co., Akron, 1955-58, individual practice cons. engring., Cuyahoga Falls, Ohio, 1958—; pres. John David Jones and Assos., Inc., 1970—, chmn. bd., 1979—. Bd. dirs. Green Cross Gen. Hosp.; elder United Presbyn. Ch.; former trustee Cuyahoga Valley Christian Acad. Served with U.S. Army, 1942-45. Decorated Bronze Star medal, Purple Heart with oak leaf cluster. Registered profl. surveyor, Ohio, Pa.; registered profl. engr., Ohio, Pa., Ind., Va., W.Va. Mem. ASCE, Nat. Soc. Profl. Engrs., Am. Congress on Surveying and Mapping, Profl. Engrs. Ohio, Ohio Assn. Constrn. Engrs., Water Pollution Control Fedn., Am. Water Works Assn., Phi Sigma Tau, Tau Beta Pi. Mason (32 deg.), Lion. Club: University (Akron). Home: 3192 Hudson Dr Cuyahoga Falls OH 44221 Office: 2162 Front St Cuyahoga Falls OH 44221

JONES, JOHN EDWIN, ednl. adminstr.; b. Oneida, N.Y., Feb. 25, 1934; s. William Grant and Marie Cooper J.; B.S., Cortland State Tchrs. Coll., 1957; M.S., Syracuse U., 1965, cert. advanced study, 1968, Ph.D., 1973; children—David, Meredith. Coordinator, Utica Internship Project, Syracuse (N.Y.) U., 1967-68; asst. to dir. Center Advanced Study Ednl. Adminstrn., U. Oreg., Eugene, 1968-70, asst.

dir., 1970-75; dir. ednl. services Loess Hills Area Edn. Agy., Council Bluffs, Iowa, 1975—. Fin. com. chmn. Nishnabotna Girl Scout Council, 1975-81. Mem. Am. Assn. Sch. Adminstrs., Nat. Staff Devel. Council, Assn. Supervision and Curriculum Devel. Republican. Clubs: Rotary, Mason. Home: 14 Nall Rd Council Bluffs IA 51501 Office: PO Box 1109 Council Bluffs IA 51501

JONES, JOHN LACEY, city ofcl.; b. Boone, Iowa, July 26, 1947; s. Lytle Raymond and Mary Johanna (Garvey) J.; B.A. in Polit. Sci., Drake U., 1969, postgrad. 1975; m. Kathie Ann Christianson, Nov. 26, 1971; children—Michael Lee, Jessica Lyn. With Des Moines (Iowa) Police Dept., 1969—, dir. research and devel., 1973—. Bd. dirs. Polk County Rape/Sexual Assault Care Center, 1976-78, Alcohol and Drug Abuse Services, Inc., 1977-78; rep. Iowa Commn. for Law Enforcement Standards and Goals, 1977. Mem. Internat. Assn. Chiefs of Police, Assn. Public Safety Communications Offiers, Iowa Policemen's Assn. Home: 1637 Northwest Dr Des Moines IA 50310 Office: E 1st and Court Ave Des Moines IA 50309

JONES, JOHN PAUL, probation dept. adminstr.; b. Blanchard, Mich., July 23, 1944; s. Lawrence John and Thelma Blanche (Eldred) J.; B.S., Central Mich. U., 1970, M.A., 1974; Ph.D., Wayne State U., 1980; m. Joan Margret Bruder, Aug. 18, 1972. Mgr., F.W. Woolworth Co., Bay City, Mich., 1970; probation officer Oakland County, Pontiac, Mich., 1970-74, probation officer supr., 1974-78, dir. probation spl. programs, 1978-80; instr. Oakland U., Rochester, Mich., 1978—. Served with U.S. Army, 1966-68. Cert. social worker; lic. psychologist, Mich. Mem. Oakland County Corrections Assn., Am. Corrections Assn., Mich. Psychol. Assn. Republican. Lodge: Fraternal Order of Police. Home: 3249 Woodside Ct Bloomfield Hills MI 48013 Office: 1200 N Telegraph Rd Adminstrv Annex II Pontiac MI 48053

JONES, JOHN PAUL, community planner; b. N.Y.C., July 4, 1921; s. Ottis Clyde and Wilhelmina Blanch Deborah (Rouark) J.; student William and Mary Coll., 1940-41; B.S., U. Va., 1950; m. Carrie Ward, Feb. 18, 1944; children—Peggy Allyn Brayman, Van Allen. Asst. planning engr. City of Norfolk (Va.), 1945-52; regional planning officer Fed. Housing and Home Finance Agy., 1952-57; planning dir. Ebasco Services, Inc., N.Y.C., 1958-60; city planning dir., Grand Rapids, Mich., 1960-70; profl. community planner Williams & Works, Inc., Grand Rapids, 1970-80; owner J. Paul Jones Assos., Greenville, Mich., 1981—; vis. lectr. Mich. State U., 1971-75; mem. Grand Rapids Environs Tech. Study, 1965-70; chmn. Profl. Community Planner Registration Bd., 1978—. Mem. Mich. Cultural Commn., 1961-62, Mich. State Council Arts, 1966-67, Grand Rapids Housing Commn., 1967-70, Pub. Transp. Council, 1973-75. Served with U.S. Army, 1941-44. Mem. Am. Planning Assn. Republican. Episcopalian. Home and Office: 13209 Old 14-Mile Rd Route 4 Greenville MI 48838

JONES, JOSEPH REDFERN, JR., fire protection engr.; b. Columbus, Ohio, June 9, 1922; s. Joseph Redfern and Nell Margaret (Hamilton) J.; B.S. in Civil Engring., Va. Mil. Inst., 1947; postgrad. Ohio State U., 1948; m. Janet Marilyn Wehe, June 14, 1944; children—Stephanie, Julia, Andrew. Product devel. engr. Armstrong Furnace Co., 1947-48; insp. Ohio Inspection Bur. (name changed to Ins. Services Office of Ohio 1971), 1947-51, 54-71, supr. public protection dept., 1971—; spl. agt. Aetna Ins. Co., Columbus, Ohio, 1951-53; agt. Mahon Ins. Agy., Columbus, 1953-54; mem. Ohio Adv. Com. Firefighter and Fire Safety Insp. Tng., chmn., 1981; mem. adv. com. Ohio State Fire Sch., hon. dean, 1979; mem. State Fire Marshal's Ohio Fire Code Rev. Com. Served with Field Arty., U.S. Army, 1943-46. Mem. Am. Water Works Assn., Internat. Fire Service Tng. Assn., Ohio Fire Chief's Conf. Republican. Presbyterian. Club: Masons. Home: 4237 Kendale Rd Columbus OH 43220 Office: PO Box 1290 Columbus OH 43216

JONES, LARRY LEE, structural engr.; b. Niles, Mich., May 23, 1944; s. Lawrence Ernest and Audrey Olive (McCullen) J.; B.S., Western Mich. U., 1969; m. Annie Ruth Boswell, Nov. 17, 1973. Machinist Henco Enterprises, Niles, Mich., 1966; engring. coop. student Clark Equipment Co., Buchanan, Mich., 1967-69, test engr., 1971—, also supervisory engr. for structures and field testing; applications engr. Hyster Co., Danville, Ill., 1970-71. Registered profl. engr., Mich. Mem. Soc. Automotive Engrs., Nat., Mich. socs. profl. engrs. Home: 608 River St Box 21 Buchanan MI 49107 Office: 324 E Dewey Buchanan MI 49107

JONES, LEANDER CORBIN, media specialist; b. Vincent, Ark., July 16, 1934; s. Lander Corbin and Una Bell (Lewis) J.; A.B., U. Ark., Pine Bluff, 1956; M.S., U. Ill., 1968; Ph.D., Union Grad. Sch., 1973; m. Lethonee Angela Hendricks, June 30, 1962; children—Angela Lynne, Leander Corbin. Tchr. English pub. high schs., Chgo. Bd. Edn., 1956-68; vol. English-as-fgn. lang. tchr. Peace Corps, Mogadiscio, Somalia, 1964-66; TV producer City Colls. of Chgo., 1968-73; communications media specialist Meharry Med. Coll., 1973-75; asso. prof. Black Americana Studies Western Mich. U., 1975—, chmn. African studies program, 1980—; dir. 7 art workshop Am. Negro Emancipation Centennial Authority, Chgo., 1960-63. Mem. Mich. Commn. on Crime and Delinquency. Served with U.S. Army, 1956-58. Mem. Nat. Assn. Ednl. Broadcasters, DuSable Mus. African Am. History, Assn. for Study African-Am. History (exec. com. K 280), NAACP, Prisoners Progress Assn. (dir.), Theatre Arts (pres.), Broadcasting Skills Center, AAUP, Bus. and Academia Dialog, Mich. Orgn. African Studies, Nat. Council Black Studies, Popular Culture Assn., South African Solidarity Orgn. Dir. for South Side Center of Performing Arts, Chgo., 1968-69, Progressive Theatre Unltd., Nashville, 1974-75; writer, producer, dir. TV drama: Roof Over my Head, Sta. WDCN, Nashville 1975; designer program in theatre and TV for hard-to-educate; developer edn. programs in Ill. State Penitentiary, Pontiac, and Cook County Jail, Chgo., 1971-73. Writer, dir. 10 Score!, 1976, Super Summer, 1978; dir. Trouble in Mind, Black Theatre of Kalamazoo Civic Players, 1979, chmn. Black Theatre com., 1980-82, also bd. dirs.; chmn. Kalamazoo Community Relations Bd., 1978, mem. bd., 1979-80; featured in Great White Hope, Civic Auditorium, Kalamazoo, 1979, in Moon on a Rainbow Shawl, Kalamazoo Carver Arena, 1980. Home: 2226 S Westnedge Ave Kalamazoo MI 49008 Office: Black Americana Studies Western Mich U Kalamazoo MI 49001

JONES, LESTER TYLER, JR., research scientist; b. Des Moines, Dec. 5, 1939; s. Lester Tyler and Bertha Marie (Tigges) J.; B.S. with honors and distinction, U. Iowa, 1961; Ph.D. (NDEA fellow), Wash. State U., 1966; m. Ardith Gayle Brocka, Apr. 9, 1962; children—Trent Tyler, Lance David, Kevin Neal. With Central Research Labs., 3M Co., St. Paul, 1965—, sr. chemist, 1965-71, research specialist, 1972-73, supr., 1973-74, mgr. biotech. research, 1974—, mem. tech. forum, 1965—, chmn., 1976-77. Pres., Gall Sch. PTA, 1970-72; sustaining membership solicitor YMCA, 1975; zone chmn. sustaining membership Indianhead council Boy Scouts Am., 1976; co-chmn. Vols. for Hamill, 1980; judge 31st Internat. Sci. and Engring. Fair, 1980. Mem. Am. Chem. Soc. (chmn. edn. com. Minn. sect. 1973-74, chmn. profl. activities com. 1974-75), Alpha Chi Sigma, Delta Tau Delta, Phi Lambda Upsilon, Phi Alpha Mu. Conglist. Mason (Shriner). Office: Central Research Labs 3M Co PO Box 33221

JONES, LINDA NELL, real estate broker; b. Bonham, Tex., Sept. 17, 1939; d. Lowell Curn and Elta Agnes (Ridings) Shuler; student U. Mich., 1969; m. John David Jones, Sept. 6, 1957 (div. Oct. 1980); children—Angela Kay, Randal David. Salesperson, Arbor Oaks Realtors, Ann Arbor, Mich., 1969; salesperson Larson & Gillies, Ann Arbor, 1970-72; partner/broker Gillies Co., Ann Arbor, 1972-75; owner, broker Century 21-Arbor Homes, Inc., Ann Arbor, 1975—. Sec., bd. dirs. met. council Century 21 of Mich., 1977—. Grad. Realtors Inst.; cert. residential specialist. Mem. Ann Arbor Bd. Realtors (pres. women's council 1976) Mich. Assn. Realtors, Nat. Assn. Realtors, Real Estate Alumni of U. Mich. Baptist. Club: U. Mich. Faculty Women's (dir. 1970). Home: 4345 Crestline St Ann Arbor MI 48103 Office: 1829 W Stadium Blvd Ann Arbor MI 48103

JONES, LORETTA, educator; b. Tuscaloosa, Ala., July 8, 1950; d. L. C. and Lois Elizabeth (Harris) Hall; B.S. in Elem. Edn., Ala. A&M U., 1972; m. Joe Eddie Jones, Sept. 10, 1974; children—Joanna Michelle, Tamara LaChelle. Tchr. 4th grade Lorain (Ohio) Bd. Edn., 1975-76, 3d grade, 1976-77, 6th grade, 1977—, coordinator black history program, 1980-81, now tchr. gifted/plus students; dir., organizer plays for PTA programs. Active Girl Scouts U.S.A., Little League; mem. sr. usher bd., pres. jr. usher bd. New Bethel Primitive Baptist Ch., Lorain. Recipient cert. of excellence Safety Patrol Program, 1979, 81; cert. Right to Read Program, 1980; cert. tchr., Ohio. Mem. Lorain Edn. Assn., Ohio Edn. Assn., NEA. Research on teaching banking, internat. study. Home: 791 Alameda Ave Sheffield Lake OH 44054 Office: 1850 Oakdale Ave Lorain OH 44052

JONES, MARGARET EILEEN ZEE, physician, educator; b. Swedesboro, N.J., June 24, 1936; d. Wilmer and Elsie (Schober) Zee; B.A., U. Pa., 1957; M.D., Med. Coll. Va., 1961; m. John Walker Jones, Aug. 29, 1959; children—John Stewart, Mary Cassaday, Amanda Worthington. Intern, U. Wash., Seattle, 1962-63, resident in pathology and neuropathology 1963-65; resident in pathology Med. Coll. Va., Richmond, 1966-67, instr. pathology, 1967-68, acting dir. div. neuropathology, 1967, 68-69, asst. prof. 1968-69; asst. prof. pathology Mich. State U., East Lansing, 1969-73, asso. prof., 1973-78, prof., 1978—, dir. Regional Neuromuscular Diagnostic Lab., 1972—. Lectr. neurosurgery Med. Sch., Yale, 1969—. Recipient Disting. Faculty award Mich. State U., 1978, Teaching award, 1981; A.D. Williams summer fellow, 1959, 60; Nat. Inst. Neurol. Diseases and Blindness-NIH fellow, 1970-71; Nat. Endowment for Humanities fellow, 1979; NIH grantee, 1980-83. Fellow Am. Soc. Clin. Pathologists; mem. Am. Assn. Neuropathologists (Weil award 1980), Am. Fedn. for Clin. Research, Soc. Neurosci. (pres. chpt. 1974—). Contbr. articles to tech. jours. Office: Dept Pathology Mich State University East Lansing MI 48824

JONES, MARTHA LOUISE, home economist; b. Greenville, Ohio, Jan. 15, 1941; d. James Samuel and Virginia Louise Hair; B.S. in Edn., Miami U., Oxford, Ohio, 1962, postgrad., 1963-64; m. Daniel Morgan Jones, Mar. 25, 1967; 1 dau., Meridith Melissa. Tchr. vocat. home econs. New Lebanon (Ohio) High Sch., 1962-67, Logan (Ohio) High Sch., 1967-68, Gen. Sherman Jr. High Sch., Lancaster, Ohio, 1968-69, Ansonia (Ohio) High Sch., 1969-70, Lancaster High Sch., 1971-72; vocat. home econs. job tng. tchr. Lancaster High Sch., 1974—; adviser Future Homemakers Am./Home Econs. Related Occupations. Mem. Am. Vocat. Assn., Delta Kappa Gamma. Presbyterian. Club: Rushville-Union Lioness (pres. 1980-81). Home: 2799 W Rushville Rd Lancaster OH 43130 Office: 1312 Granville Pike Lancaster OH 43130

JONES, MICHAEL DAVID, guidance counselor; b. Yokohama, Japan, Dec. 31, 1948 (parents Am. citizens); s. James Nicholas and Mildred Adelaide (Schaefer) J.; B.A., U. S.C., 1970, M.Ed., 1973; postgrad. (fellow) Mich. State U., 1980; m. Betty Gaskin, Sept. 5, 1969; children—Christopher, David. Sch. counselor, then dir. guidance C.E. Williams Middle Sch., Charleston, S.C., 1973-75; human relations specialist Charleston County (S.C.) Sch. Dist., 1975-76; sr. grad. asst. Mich. State U., E. Lansing, 1976—, instr. spl. topic seminar, coordinator psychiatry clerkship program; pres. Charleston Adlerian Soc., 1976. Gen. Electric Co. guidance fellow, 1974; recipient Outstanding Service award S.C. Personnel and Guidance Assn., 1975. Mem. Am. Sch. Counselors Assn. (Meritorious Service award 1975), Am. Personnel and Guidance Assn., Assn. Non-White Concerns. Roman Catholic. Author: A Practical Guide for Organizing toward Effective School Self-Improvement, 1978; contbr. articles to profl. jours. Home: 808 J Cherry Ln East Lansing MI 48823 Office: Room A236 Dept Psychiatry East Fee Hall Mich State U East Lansing MI 48824

JONES, NANCY THOMPSON, singer, educator; b. Humansville, Mo., Oct. 31, 1938; d. Guy Hill and Noveta Luella (Brown) Thompson; B.M., Cin. Coll. Conservatory of Music, 1960; M.S. in Music, Kans. State U., 1962; postgrad. S.W. Mo. State U., 1960-61; m. Russell Ransom Jones, June 23, 1962; children—Beverly Diane, Steven Russell. Pvt. instr. in voice, Kans. and Mo., 1956—; singer, actor St. Louis Mcpl. Opera, 1959, 60; instr. voice Baker U., 1967-71, Park Coll., 1972-74, St. Mary Coll., 1973-76; artist-instr. William Jewell Coll., Liberty, Mo., 1975—; lectr., clk. Weight Watchers of Greater Kansas City, 1972-75; solo recitalist, opera singer, 1955—; resident artist Kansas City Lyric Opera, 1967—; traveling cons. preparation for operatic auditions; lectr. women's achievement activities and Career Days; guest adjudicator singing competitions; featured soloist RCA Red Seal rec., 1975, Desto rec., 1973, Sound Trek rec., 1981; created roles in three operatic premieres by Am. composers, 1958, 73, 75; guest artist, opera, oratorio, recital and musical comedy throughout U.S. Pi Kappa Lambda scholar, 1959; Barrows Travel grantee, 1976; William Jewell Coll. grantee, 1979, 81; Nat. Fedn. Music Clubs scholar, 1957. Mem. Nat. Assn. Tchrs. Singing, Kansas City Musical Club, Am. Guild Mus. Artists, William Jewell Coll. Aux., Mu Phi Epsilon (Nat. Sterling Achievement award), Delta Kappa Gamma. Methodist. Research and publs. on vocal pedagogy, vocal lit., piano accompaniment, fgn. langs., poetry and dramatic lit., opera theater and prodn., diction pedagogy, aria and art song interpretation, music history. Home: 2301 Strader Terr Saint Joseph MO 64503 Office: William Jewell College Liberty MO 64068

JONES, NELSON, marketing cons.; b. Chgo., May 21, 1947; s. George and Rosa Mae (Grant) J.; B.S. in B.A., Roosevelt U., 1969; M.B.A. (Mgmt fellow), U. Chgo., 1974; m. Valerie Ann Hughes, June 21, 1966 (div. 1973); children—Selene Tess, Nelson, Manuel. Sales trainee/sales trainee mgr. Gen. Foods Corp., Chgo., 1968-70; computer marketing rep. IBM, Chgo., 1971-73; program marketing analyst Xerox Corp., Rochester, N.Y., 1973-75; industry account exec. 3M Co., Chgo., 1975-76; asso. dir. mktg. Nat. Minority Purchasing Council, Chgo., 1976-78; mktg. exec. NCR Corp., 1978-80; Midwest regional sales mgr. Blackfeet Indian Writing Co., 1981—; mktg. cons. computer systems/word processing. Mem., supporter WTTW/Channel 11, Chgo. Pub. TV, 1977—, Easter Seal Soc., Chgo., 1977—, Masca-Sickle Cell Anemia, 1977—. Boost fellow, Roosevelt U., 1965-69. Mem. Am. Marketing Assn., Assn. of MBA Execs., Nat. Specialty Merchandisers Assn., Air Force Mus. Found., Grant Park Concerts Assn., Mus. Sci. and Industry, Internat. Platform Assn. Contbr. articles in field to profl. jours. Home and Office: 333 E Ontario St Chicago IL 60611

JONES, NORMA LOUISE, educator; b. Poplar, Wis.; d. George Elmer and Hilma June (Wiberg) Jones; B.E., U. Wis.; M.A., U. Minn., 1952; postgrad. U. Ill., 1957; Ph.D., U. Mich., 1965. Librarian, Grand Rapids (Mich.) pub. schs., 1947-62; Grand Rapids (Mich.) Pub. Library, 1948-49; instr. Central Mich. U., Mt. Pleasant, 1954, 55; librarian Benton Harbor (Mich.) pub. schs., 1962-63; lectr. U. Mich., Ann Arbor, 1954, 55, 61, 63-65, asst. prof., 1966-68; asst. prof. dept. library sci. U. Wis.-Oshkosh, 1968-70, asso. prof., 1970-75, prof., 1975—; mem. com. on certification of sch. librarians State of Wis., 1972—. Mem. ALA (chmn. reference conf. 1975—), Wis. Library Assn., Am. Assn. Sch. Librarians, Spl. Libraries Assn., Soc. Am. Archivists, Phi Beta Kappa, Phi Kappa Phi, Pi Lambda Theta, Beta Phi Mu, Sigma Pi Epsilon. Home: 1220 Maricopa Dr Oshkosh WI 54901

JONES, PAXTON LANE, obstetrician and gynecologist; b. Youngstown, Ohio, Oct. 23, 1921; s. Maurice Paxton and Elizabeth (Lane) J.; M.D., Duke U., 1944; m. Margaret Swanton, Aug. 18, 1945 (dec. 1977); children—Deborah, Rebecca; m. Anita B. Andrews, 1980; stepchildren—Jack, Joanne. Rotating intern Albany (N.Y.) Hosp., 1944-45; resident in obstetrics and gynecology Syracuse (N.Y.) Med. Center, 1947-50; practice medicine specializing in obstetrics and gynecology, Youngstown, 1950—, practice ltd. to gynecology, 1971—; pres. staff Youngstown Hosp., 1966, dir. dept. obstetrics and gynecology, 1967. Served to lt. (j.g.) M.C., USNR, 1945-47. Diplomate Nat. Bd. Med. Examiners, Am. Bd. Obstetrics and Gynecology. Fellow Am. Coll. Obstetricians and Gynecologists, ACS; mem. Youngstown Soc. Obstetricians and Gynecologists, Ohio Med. Soc., Mahoning County Med. Soc. Republican. Episcopalian. Club: Youngstown Country. Office: 841 Boardman-Canfield Rd Youngstown OH 44512

JONES, PHILIP ALAN, TV broadcasting exec.; b. Cairo, Ill., June 27, 1944; s. Charles E. and Doris E. (Hogendobler) J.; B.J., U. Mo., Columbia, 1966; grad. exec. program Harvard U., 1976; m. Lynnsay Williams, Sept. 6, 1967; children—Whitney Jones, Spencer. Salesman and sales mgr. radio and TV stas. in Kansas City, Mo., 1966-74; TV gen. sales mgr. Sta. WTAF-TV, Phila., 1974-76; gen. mgr. Sta. WGR-TV, Buffalo, 1976-79; v.p., gen. mgr. Sta. KCMO-TV, Kansas City, Mo., 1979—; dir. CBS Affiliates Bd. Bd. dirs. Kansas City March of Dimes, 1980-81, Conv. Bur. Greater Kansas City, 1980—; bd. dirs., exec. com. Starlight Theatre, Kansas City, 1980—; mem. communications com. Kansas City United Way, 1979—; bd. govs. Am. Royal, 1980—; mem. Nelson Gallery Soc. Fellows, Kansas City, 1980—. Mem. Nat. Assn. Broadcasters, TV Bur. Advt., Assn. Maximum Service Telecasters, United Minority Media Assn. (adv. bd.), Mo. Broadcasters Assn., Kans. Broadcasters Assn., Advt. Club Kansas City, C. of C. Greater Kansas City (dir. 1980—), Ducks Unlimited, Alpha Delta Sigma, Phi Delta Theta. Methodist. Clubs: Carriage, Woodside Racquet, Overland Park Racquet. Office: 4500 Johnson Dr Fairway KS 66205

JONES, PHILLIP ERSKINE, univ. adminstr.; b. Chgo., Oct. 26, 1940; s. Dorothy Ruth J.; B.S., U. Ill., 1963; M.A., U. Iowa, 1967, Ph.D., 1975; m. Jo Lavera Kennedy, Jan. 18, 1964; children—Phyllis Lavera, Joel Erskine. Social worker Chgo. Youth Centers, 1963-64; tchr. high sch., Flint, Mich., 1967-68, coll. admissions counselor, 1968-70; spl. services dir. U. Iowa, Iowa City, 1970-75, asst. v.p., 1975-76, dir. affirmative action, 1976-78, asso. dean student services, asst. prof. edn., 1978—; cons. Office of Edn., HUD. Mem. Iowa City Human Rights Commn., 1971-74, chmn., 1973-74; mem. community adv. com. public broadcasting stas. WSUI/KSUI, 1977—. Mem. Am. Assn. Higher Edn., Nat. Assn. Student Personnel Adminstrs., Nat. Assn. State Univs. and Land-Grant Colls., Soc. Internat. Devel., NAACP. Office: Univ of Iowa 105 Jessup Hall Iowa City IA 52242

JONES, RAMONA LEE CHILDS, state agy. exec.; b. Milw., Oct. 8, 1940; d. Lorenzo Will and Lucille Campbell Childs; B.S., Winona State U., 1962; M.Ed., Northeastern Ill. U., 1969; 1 dau., Nadená Wenonáh. Tchr. public schs., Kenosha, Wis., 1962-63, Waukegan, Ill., 1963-64, Mpls., 1964-67, Chgo., 1967-72; instr. Northeastern Ill. U., Chgo., 1969-74, Bemidji (Minn.) State U., 1974-79; govt. civil rights and research specialist HEW, 1972-74, Desegregation Inst., 1972-74; co-dir. Independent Consultings, nat., regional and local, Welch, Minn., 1967-79; Indian and rural housing devel. specialist Minn. Housing Fin. Agy., St. Paul, 1979—. Bd. dirs. Community Program for Arts and Scis., St. Paul, 1977—, Prairie Island Project Inc., 1979—; commr. City of Red Wing Adv. Planning Commn., 1977-78; bd. dirs. Minn. Women of Color, 1977—. Mem. AAUW, Minn. Planning Assn., United Indian Planners Assn., Internat. City Mgrs. Assn., Nat. Congress Am. Indians. Nat. Assn. Female Execs., Nat. Urban Indian Council, Dakota Tribe. Home: Route 2 Box 72 Welch MN 55089 Office: 333 Sibley St Suite 200 Saint Paul MN 55101

JONES, RAYMOND CHARLES, health service orgn. exec.; b. Balt., Nov. 30, 1931; s. Raymond C. and Pearl Mildred (Noell) J.; B.S. in Mktg., U. Balt., 1959; M.S., Case Western Res. U., 1977; postgrad. George Washington U., 1964-65; m. Elizabeth L. Schwarzmann, Apr. 8, 1961; children—Jeffrey Noell, Christopher Ryan, Patrick Damien. Asst. to public relations mgr. Am. Oil Co., Balt., 1953-62; dir. personnel and office services Md. Blue Cross, Inc., Balt., 1962-65, dir. personnel and manpower devel., 1965-72; dir. orgn. devel. Blue Cross of N.E. Ohio, Cleve., 1972-75, v.p. corp. services, 1975—; mem. adv. coms. Nat. Blue Cross and Blue Shield, 1965—; mem. faculty Cuyahoga Community Coll., 1977-78, Cleve. State U., 1978, Baldwin Wallace Coll., 1978—. Cub Scout den dad, Balt., 1971-72; chmn. adult edn. com. Immaculate Heart of Mary Ch., 1971-72. Accredited personnel exec. Mem. Am. Soc. Personnel Adminstrn. (regional v.p. 1969, 80—, v.p. edn. 1979), Cleve. Personnel Assn. Democrat. Roman Catholic. Contbr. articles on indsl. relations to profl. publs. Home: 30500 Manhassett Dr Bay Village OH 44140 Office: 2066 E 9th St Cleveland OH 44115

JONES, RAYMOND EDWARD, JR., brewing exec.; b. New Bern, N.C., Jan. 27, 1927; s. Raymond Edward and Ellen LaVerne (Mallard) J.; B.S., U. Md., 1953; LL.B., U. Balt., 1962; m. Sarra Gordon O'Bryan, Aug. 29, 1958; children—Leslie Anne, Raymond Edward III. Office mgr. Hopkins Furniture Co., Annapolis, Md., 1953-55; sr. v.p. legal, sec. Nat. Brewing Co., Balt., 1956-75 (merged with Carling Brewing Co. 1975), sr. v.p. legal and indsl. relations, dir. Carling Nat. Breweries, Inc., 1975-78; sec., asso. gen. counsel Miller Brewing Co., 1978—; house counsel and/or officer Divex, Inc., Laco Products, Inc., Laco Corp., C.W. Abbott, Inc., Pompeian, Inc., Interhost Corp., Solarine Co., Balt. Baseball Club, Inc.; 1967-75; admitted to Md. bar, 1962. Bd. dirs. Soc. Preservation Md. Antiquities, 1969—. Served with USNR, 1942-45. Mem. U.S. Brewers Assn., Am., Md., Balt. City bar assns., Sigma Chi, Sigma Delta Chi. Democrat. Presbyterian. Home: 7749 Hawthorne Rd Mequon WI 53092 Office: 3939 W Highland Blvd Milwaukee WI 53208

JONES, RICHARD CYRUS, lawyer; b. Oak Park, Ill., Oct. 20, 1928; s. Ethler E. and Margaret S. (Stoner) J.; Ph.B., DePaul U., 1960, J.D., 1963; children—Richard C., Carrie, William. Admitted to Ill. bar, 1963; dept. mgr. Chgo. Title & Trust Co., 1947-64; mem. firm Sachnoff, Schrager, Jones, Weaver & Rubenstein Ltd. and predecessor firms, Chgo., 1964—. Instr., Real Estate Inst., Chgo., 1970—. Served with U.S. Army, 1951-52. Decorated Bronze Star, Combat Inf. badge.

Mem. Am., Ill., Chgo. (com. chmn. real property law 1970-72, 76-81) bar assns., Chgo. Council Lawyers, Delta Theta Phi. Kiwanian. Home: 1044 Forest Ave River Forest IL 60305 Office: One IBM Plaza 47th Floor Chicago IL 60611

JONES, RICHARD LEE, data processing exec.; b. Pitts., Feb. 16, 1931; s. Carl Grover and Emma Ruth (Cramer) J.; B.S., Ohio U., 1953; m. Marilyn Jean Betz, June 1, 1954; children—Sandra, Craig, Scott, Joyce. Underwriter Ohio Casualty Ins., 1953-54; sales rep. Ohio Bell Telephone, 1956; asst. data processing mgr., 1957-62; data processing mgr. Shenango China, 1962-72; project mgr. Tappan Co., 1973-76; data processing mgr. R.G. Barry Co., Pickerington, Ohio, 1976-79; project mgr. ITT-North Electric, Galion, Ohio, 1979—; chmn., pres. Data System and Services; pres. ASM Corp. Served with USAF, 1954-56. Mem. Assn. Systems Mgmt., Data Processing Mgmt. Assn. Republican. Methodist. Office: PO Box 688 Galion OH 44833

JONES, ROBERT D., III, heavy equipment co. exec.; b. Kankakee, Ill., July 22, 1949; s. Robert D. and Velma Jane (Schroeder) J.; B.A. in Sociology, So. Ill. U., 1975; M.S. in Indsl. Ops., Bradley U., 1976; m. Kathleen Ann Norton, Sept. 1, 1973; 1 dau., Melissa. With Morton Caterpillar Distbn. System (Ill.), 1973-76; parts salesman, gen. offices Caterpillar Tractor Co., Peoria. Ill., 1976-78, product rep. for Mex., 1979—; mem. faculty Ill. Central Coll. Served with U.S. Army, 1968-74. Mem. Am. Mgmt. Assn. Office: Caterpillar Tractor Co 100 NE Adams St Peoria IL 61629 also Mexico City Mexico

JONES, ROBERT LEE, petroleum co. exec.; b. Hutchinson, Kans., Apr. 13, 1927; s. Ralph Wilson and Bertha Christina (Peterson) J.; A.B., M.A., U. Kans., 1949; children—Mary Christina, Michael Allen. Founder, pres. Amco Petroleum Co., Chgo., 1954—, Apco Records, Chgo., 1958—; pres. Amco Stores Corp., Chgo., 1962—; founder, pres., chmn. bd. Amco Tire Corp., Chgo., 1966—; founder Am. Nat. Opera Co., Chgo., 1962; owner, operator Consultants Internat., Inc., Chgo., Washington, Bellevue, Nebr. Served with AUS, 1945-46. Mem. Retail Store Assn., Tire Mktg. Assn., Petroleum Mktg. Inst. Republican. Methodist. Author: The Jew and the Gentile, 1960; The Man Who Played God, 1962; War in the City; The Second Civil War; The New Presidency-The New United States. Home: 1902 Gregg Rd Bellevue NE 68005 Office: PO Box 126 Bellevue NE 68005 also PO Box 8329 Chicago IL 60680

JONES, ROBERT STANLEY, psychologist; b. Cin., Jan. 27, 1936; s. Robert Stanley and Ann Louise (Curtis) J.; B.A., Xavier U., 1958, M.A., 1966; Psy.D., Central Mich. U., 1981; m. Ruth Lee Weinstein, Nov. 26, 1971; children—Debora, Dorothy, Robert, Diana, Sandra, William, Mary, Jonathan. Staff psychologist Hamilton County Juvenile Ct., Cin., 1966-67; psychologist Longview State Hosp., Cin., 1967-68; staff psychologist Midland-Gladwin Mental Health Clinic, Midland, Mich., 1968-69; dir. inpatient psychiat. unit Midland (Mich.) Hosp., 1969-77; psychology intern Hurley Hosp., Mott Children's Health Center, Flint, Mich., 1980—. Mem. Am. Psychol. Assn., Mich. Psychol. Assn., Midwestern Psychol. Assn. Home: 128 W Livingston Ct Midland MI 48640 Office: 806 W 6th Ave Flint MI 48503

JONES, RONALD DAVID, audio-visual learning aids co. exec.; b. Kankakee, Ill., July 31, 1949; s. David Joseph and Rose Marie Jones; B.S., Murray State U., 1971; m. Lesley Joan Stamper, June 7, 1973; children—Lisa Marie, Maria Angela. Tchr. public schs., Kankakee County, 1972; with Imperial Internat. Learning Corp., Kankakee, 1973—, nat. sales mgr., 1975-79, v.p. mktg., 1979—. Mem. Nat. Audio Visual Assn. (exec. com. software council), Nat. Sch. Supply and Equipment Assn. Roman Catholic. Home: 975 S Yates Kankakee IL 60901 Office: Box 548 Kankakee IL 60901

JONES, RUSSELL EUGENE, agrl. mfg. co. exec.; b. Hallsville, Ohio, Aug. 24, 1930; s. Lowell Dwight and Tessie Marie J.; student public schs., Chillicothe, Ohio; children—Connie Sue, Russell Eugene, Vickie Ann, Linda Kae. Mechanic, Jones Implement, Hallsville, Ohio, 1948-53; owner Russ Jones Garage, Hallsville, 1955-67; owner, pres. Floater Vehicle, Inc., 1967—. Trustee, Ross County Water Co., 1979—. Served with Mil. Police, U.S. Army, 1953-55. Patentee in field. Home: 13601 Marietta Rd Kingston OH 45644 Office: Floater Vehicle Inc 6694 State Rd 180 Hallsville OH 45633

JONES, STEWART, advt. agy. exec.; b. Terre Haute, Ind., Feb. 10, 1919; s. Edward James and Mary Jane (Stewart) J.; B.A. in Journalism, U. Kans., 1940; m. Martha Ann Watson, July 11, 1952; children—Dennis David, Candace Ann, James Stewart, Elizabeth Wuichet. City editor Anderson Countian, Garnett, Kans., 1940-41; successively publns. editor, community relations mgr., asst. dir. public relations Champion Papers, Inc., Houston and Hamilton, Ohio, 1947-63; v.p. Rowe & Wyman, advt., Cin., 1963-66; pres. Brewer, Jones & Fedlman, Inc., Cin., 1966—. Past elder Front St. Presbyn. Ch., Hamilton; past bd. dirs. Boys Club Hamilton. Served to maj. USAAF, 1941-46. Recipient Schott award journalism U. Kans., 1939. Mem. Am. Assn. Indsl. Editors (past v.p.), Ohio Valley Direct Mktg. Club (past pres.), Cin. Indsl. Editors Assn. (past pres.), Cin. Indsl. Advt. Assn. (past pres.) (dir.), Spiritual Forum Hamilton (past chmn.). Home: 10 Hillcrest Dr Hamilton OH 45013 Office: 7507 Reading Rd Cincinnati OH 45037

JONES, SYLVIA JEANNE KIRBY, ednl. adminstr.; b. Canton, Ohio, June 1, 1926; d. Judson Taylor and Edna Barbara (Schwartzwalder) Kirby; A.A. in Math., U. Toledo, 1948, B.Ed., 1971, M.Ed., 1974, Ed.S. in Adminstrn., 1980; m. Robert Laurence Jones, Oct. 3, 1971; children by previous marriage—Bufford A. Parker, Holli Reed Parker Shelton. Job analyst LaSalle and Koch Co., Toledo, 1948-50; sec. with First Fed. Savs. & Loan Assn., West Palm Beach, Fla., 1950-52; exec. asst. to pres. 1st S.E. Corp., Palm Beach, 1956-60; bookkeeper Fla. Airmotive, Lantana, 1960-61; treas.-comptroller Tilford Flying Service, West Palm Beach, 1961-67; tchr. educable mentally retarded Toledo Public Schs., 1968-70, prin., program coordinator Crittenden Sch., 1970-74, state coordinator Major Cities Project, 1974-78, program developer state and fed. programs, 1978—; mem. spl. edn. task force Ohio Dept. Edn., 1977. Participant Second Nat. Conf. on Juvenile Justice, 1975; mem. governing bd. Lucas County Juvenile Ct. Vol. Probation Counselor Program, 1975-77, Project Mgmt. Bd. Low Incidence Handicapped Project, 1976-77, Project 419, Tchr. Edn. Redesign, State of Ohio, 1978-80. Recipient Golden Nike award, Ohio Fedn. Bus. and Profl. Women, 1972. Mem. Phi Delta Kappa, Phi Kappa Phi, Kappa Delta Pi, Pi Lambda Theta. Episcopalian. Club: Women of Moose. Contbr. writings in field to profl. publs. Home: 3150 Springbrook Dr Lambertville MI 48144 Office: Manhattan and Elm Streets Toledo OH 43608

JONES, TREVOR OWEN, automobile co. exec.; b. Maidstone, Kent, Eng., Nov. 3, 1930; s. Richard Owen and Rudy Edith (Martin) J.; came to U.S., 1957, naturalized, 1971; Higher Nat. Certificate in Elec. Engring., Aston Tech. Coll., Birmingham, Eng., 1952; Ordinary Nat. Certificate in Mech. Engring., Liverpool (Eng.) Tech. Coll., 1957; m. Jennie Lou Singleton, Sept. 12, 1959; children—Pembroke Robinson, Bronwyn Elizabeth. Student engr., elec. machine design engr. Brit. Gen. Electric Co., 1950-57; project engr., project mgr. Nuclear Ship Savannah, Allis-Chalmers Mfg. Co., 1957-59; with Gen. Motors Corp., 1959-78, staff engr. in charge Apollo computers, 1967, dir. electronic control systems, 1970-72, dir. advanced product engring., 1972-74, dir. Gen. Motors Proving Grounds, 1974-78; v.p. engring., automotive worldwide TRW Inc., 1978-81, v.p., gen. mgr. transp. electronics ops., 1981—; vice chmn. Motor Vehicle Safety Adv. Council, 1971; chmn. Nat. Hwy. Safety Adv. Com., 1976. Trustee Lawrence Inst. Tech., 1973-76; mem. exec. bd. Clinton Valley council Boy Scouts Am., 1975; gov. Cranbrook Inst. Sci., 1977. Served as officer Brit. Army, 1955-57. Recipient Safety award for engring. excellence U.S. Dept. Transp., 1978. Registered profl. engr., Wis.; chartered engr., U.K. Fellow Brit. Instn. Elec. Engrs. (Hooper Meml. prize 1950), IEEE (exec. com. vehicle tech. soc. 1977—), Soc. Automotive Engrs.; mem. Soc. Automotive Engrs. (Arch T. Colwell paper award 1974, 75, Vincent Bendix Automotive Electronics award 1976), Engring. Soc. Detroit and Cleve. Republican. Episcopalian. Clubs: Birmingham (Mich.) Athletic; Capitol Hill (Washington); Kirtland Country; Cleve. Skating. Author, patentee automotive safety and electronics. Home: 18400 Shelburne Rd Shaker Heights OH 44118 Office: TRW Inc 30000 Aurora Rd Solon OH 44139

JONES, WILLIAM HUGH, newspaper editor; b. Marinette, Wis., May 23, 1939; s. Hugh Fred and Mildred (Festge) J.; B.S. in Journalism with sr. honors, U. Wis.-Milw., 1964; M.S., Northwestern U., 1965; m. student Advanced Mgmt. Program, Harvard U., 1978; Virginia Marie Murphy, Aug. 22, 1964; children—William Hugh, Michael Joseph, Megan Kathleen. Mng. editor Chgo. Tribune, 1965—. Served with USMC, 1958-61. Recipient Pulitzer prize for local reporting, 1971, Nat. Headline Club award, 1968, more than 20 other journalism awards; Civic award Civic Found., Northbrook, 1971; award of merit Northwestern U. Alumni Assn., 1972; Distinguished Alumnus award U. Wis.-Milw., 1975. Home: 515 Jackson Ave Glencoe IL 60022 Office: 435 N Michigan Ave Chicago IL 60611

JONES, WILLIAM MOSES, ophthalmologist; b. Earle, Ark., Nov. 12, 1898; s. Thomas Caanan and Nancy Emma (Conyers) J.; A.B. in Math. with honors, Fisk U., 1922; M.D., U. Chgo., 1932; m. Geneva May Lacy, Dec. 27, 1934; 1 dau., Jean Andre. Intern, Kansas City (Mo.) Gen. Hosp., 1931-32; resident in ophthalmology U. Chgo.-Billings Meml. Hosp., 1932-37; practice medicine specializing in ophthalmology, Chgo., 1937—; cons. Jackson Park, Woodlawn, Provident, Tamarack hosps.; asso. prof. U. Chgo. Med. Sch., 1954-55; co-owner Walnut Grove Camp, Sturgis, Mich. Mem. Am. Acad. Ophthalmology and Otolarygnology, A.C.S., AMA, Nat. Med. Assn., N.Y. Acad. Scis., Chgo. Med. Soc., Cook County Physicians Assn., Alpha Phi Alpha. Democrat. Conglist. Home: 5234 S Michigan Ave Chicago IL 60615 Office: 7531 Stony Island Ave Chicago IL 60049

JONES, WILLIAM SANFORD, JR., ins. salesman; b. Ft. Thomas, Ky., Nov. 19, 1934; s. William S. and Leigh C. (Simpson) J.; B.S., U. Nebr., 1964; m. Carolyn Ann Greiner, June 17, 1955; children—Barbara Leigh, Deborah Ruth. Staff, Lancaster County Sheriff's Dept., Lincoln, 1958-64; field underwriter N.Y. Life Ins. Co., Lincoln, Nebr., 1964—, asst. mgr. Lincoln Gen. Office, 1971-73. Active Trinity Luth. Ch., Lincoln, 1955—; bd. dirs. Lincoln Luth. Jr. High Sch.; bd. dirs. Lincoln Luth. Sch. Assn., 1981. Mem. Lincoln Assn. Life Underwriters Nebr. Assn. Life Underwriters, Nat. Assn. Life Underwriters, Million Dollar Round Table. Republican. Home: 640 N 54th St Lincoln NE 68504 Office: NY Life Ins Co Suite 1506 233 S 13th St Lincoln NE 68508

JOO, PILJU KIM, seed physiologist; b. Korea, Sept. 9, 1937; came to U.S., 1962, naturalized, 1971; d. Myunglyon and Okjin (Chu) Kim; B.S., Seoul (Korea) Nat. U., 1960; M.S., Miss. State U., 1964; Ph.D., Cornell U., 1970; m. Young Don Joo, Nov. 27, 1963; children—Michael Wuchung, Thomas Wuil, Eungie. Research asst. Miss. State U., Cornell U. and Pa. State U., 1962-69; research asst. U.S. Plant Soil and Nutrition Lab., Cornell U., Ithaca, N.Y., 1969-70, postdoctoral research asso., 1971-73, 73-75; dir. seed sci. research and seed quality assessment lab., Northrup King Co., Mpls., 1975—; chairperson ad hoc ednl. com. Vigor Com., Assn. Official Seed Analysts. Pres., Women's Assn., Korean Presbyterian Ch. of Twin Cities, Mpls., 1979-80; prin. Korean Inst. Minn., Mpls. Mem. Am. Soc. Agronomy, Crop Sci. Soc. Am., Soc. Comml. Seed Tech., AAAS, Grad. Women in Sci., N.Y. Acad. Sci., Council Agrl. Sci. and Tech., Minn. Chromatography Forum, Am. Soc. Plant Physiology, Sigma Xi. Research, publs. in field. Home: 1128 Karth Lake Dr Arden Hills MN 55112 Office: 1500 Jackson St NE Minneapolis MN 55413

JOOS, LOYAL WILSON, ednl. adminstr.; b. Alma Center, Wis., Dec. 2, 1917; s. Alfred and Charlotte (Rather) J.; B.S., U. Wis., 1941; M.S., U. Minn., 1957, Ph.D., 1959; m. Mary Tupper, Nov., 16, 1941; children—Heidi Louise, Margaret Winifred Joos Moran, Miriam Elizabeth Joos Curtis. Tchr. agr., secondary schs. in N.D., 1941, Wis., 1946-48, Minn., 1948-57; instr. U. Minn., 1957-58; dir. research and planning Baltimore County (Md.) Schs., 1959-64; dir. research, evaluation and planning Oakland Schs., Pontiac, Mich., 1964—. Served with U.S. Army, 1943-46. Recipient Coffman Meml. award U. Minn. Coll. Edn., 1958. Mem. Assn. for Ednl. Data Systems, Mich. Ednl. Research Assn. (pres. 1973-74), Phi Delta Kappa. Republican. Methodist. Club: Masons. Contbr. chpt. to book, writings in field to publs., computer programs. Office: 2100 Pontiac Lake Rd Pontiac MI 48054

JORDAN, EARL CLIFFORD, ins. co. exec.; b. Austin, Minn., Dec. 29, 1916; s. Chester R. and Gladys (Ray) J.; A.B., U. Wis., 1939; m. Marion Brannon, Aug. 31, 1940; children—Robert Earl, Julie Ann. Group supr. Aetna Life Ins. Co., Chgo., 1939-43, asst. gen. agt., Chgo., Albany, N.Y., 1946-48; gen. agt. Mass. Mut. Life Ins. Co., Chgo., 1948—; pres. Planned Futures, Inc.; dir. Nasco Internat., Inc., Ft. Atkinson, Wis., Weatherby Inc., Prehler, Inc.; past pres. Life Agy. Mgmt. Conf. Trustee Ill. Children's Home and Aid Soc., past pres.; bd. dirs. U. Wis. Found., Elvehjam Art Center Council U. Wis. Served from pvt. to 1st lt., AUS, 1943-46. Mem. Gen. Agts. and Mgrs. Assn. (pres. Chgo.), Life Ins. and Trust Council Chgo., Chgo. Assn. Life Underwriters, Manila Alumni Assn. (founder, 1st pres.), U. Wis. Nat. Alumni Assn. (past pres., chmn. bd.), Sigma Alpha Epsilon, Fellowship Christian Athletes (treas., dir.), Mass. Mut. Gen. Agts. Assn. (past pres.), Internat. Gen. Agts. and Mgrs. Conf. (past pres.). Mason (32 deg.). Clubs: U. Wis., Bob-O-Link Country, Bob-O-Link Golf (pres.), Westmoreland Country, Union League, Execs. (Chgo.); Tucson Nat. Golf; Shikar-Safari Internat.; One Shot Antelope Hunt Adventurers; Elgin Golf (Morayshire, Scotland). Home: 3 Ct of Connecticut River Valley Wood Creek Cts Lincolnshire IL 60015 Office: 69 W Washington St Chicago IL 60602

JORDAN, FRANCES JEAN, psychotherapist, counselor; b. Savannah, Ga., Sept. 9, 1932; d. Dellmar Clinton and Frances Perkins Jordan; B.S. in Psychology, Ill. Inst. Tech., 1955, M.S., 1979; L.P.N., San Francisco Sch. Nursing, 1970; postgrad. Armstrong Coll., Savannah, 1950-52, San Francisco State U., 1964-68, Diocesan Sch. for Ministers, U. Calif., Berkeley, 1980—, Gestalt Inst., Chgo., 1979-80; m. James C. DuBois, Dec. 21, 1974; children—Charlean Gerling, Jeanie DeVaney. Freelance writer, 1950—; adminstr. U.S. Army and Navy, 1950-54; tchr. spl. edn. Akron (Ohio) Schs., 1956-59, San Francisco Schs., 1969-74; vol. counselor, Phalabora, S. Africa, 1962-64; rehab. counselor Rehab. Inst., Chgo., 1977—; counselor Gestalt Clinic, Evanston, Ill., 1979—. Vol., Suicide Prevention Bur., San Francisco, 1966-68. George Drew and Nautha Perkins Trust grantee, 1977—. Mem. Am. Personnel and Guidance Assn., Ill. Rehab. Assn., Council Exceptional Children, Nat. Rehab. Assn., Psi Chi, Kappa Phi Delta, Beta Sigma Phi, Phi Delta Epsilon, Beta Sigma Phi, 3d Order St. Francis. Episcopalian. Clubs: Eastern Star, United Daus. Confederacy, DAR. Home: 600 N McClurg Ct Chicago IL 60611 also 111 Lighthouse Ln Daly City CA 94014 Office: 345 E Superior St Chicago IL 60611

JORDAN, GENE MORRISON, aerospace co. exec.; b. Los Angeles, Aug. 26, 1931; s. Eugene Morrison and Wilhelmina (Warner) J.; B.S., Calif. Inst. Tech., 1953; M.S., UCLA, 1959; m. Neva Maye Vervalin, Oct. 30, 1951; children—Alan G., Donna J., Gary W., Steven R. Engr., U.S. Naval Ordnance Test Sta., Pasadena, Calif., 1952-53; head instrumentation group U. So. Calif. Engring. Center, Naval Missile Center, Point Mugu, 1953-56, univ. instr., 1954-55; mgr. systems analysis Bendix Pacific div., North Hollywood, Calif., 1956-59, dir. systems analysis, Ann Arbor, Mich., 1959-62; v.p. Veda Inc., Ann Arbor, 1962-71; pres., dir. First Ann Arbor Corp., 1971—; partner Jordan, Belcher, Eisenhardt & Douthat, Ann Arbor, 1971—, Group 214, Ann Arbor, 1980—; cons. Nat. Space Council, 1965-66. Scoutmaster, Boy Scouts Am., Ann Arbor, 1964-69; publicity chmn. March of Dimes, Ann Arbor, 1964-65, Meritorious Service award, 1965; pres. Abbott Sch. PTA, 1964-65, Dexter Schs. PTA, 1975; pres., dir. Loch Alpine Improvement Assn., 1972-75, Econ. Devel. Corp. Scio Twp., Mich., 1980—. Named An Outstanding Young Man of Am., Nat. Jaycees, 1966. Mem. AIEE, Am. Security Council, Am. Def. Preparedness Assn., Ann Arbor C. of C. (legis. com. chmn. 1966). Republican. Episcopalian. Club: Ann Arbor Country (treas. 1976-79, pres. 1978). Contbr. articles, papers to profl. lit. Home: 4772 Sunset Ct Ann Arbor MI 48103 Office: First Ann Arbor Corp 214 E Huron St Ann Arbor MI 48104

JORDAN, JACK DENNIS, newspaper publisher; b. Xenia, Ohio, Aug. 12, 1921; s. Leslie Lawrence and Marie Alta (Jenner) J.; student Rollins Coll., Fla., 1943, U. Ga., 1943; m. Inez Gilley Blair, July 16, 1976; children—Michael W., Julie Jordan Wedderburn, Constance Blair, Lesa Blair. Reporter, sports editor, city editor, mng. editor Xenia (Ohio) Daily Gazette, 1939-50, editor/gen. mgr., 1951-77, pub., 1978-79; pub. Middletown (Ohio) Jour., 1980—, also gen. mgr.; past v.p. ops., dir. Chew Newspapers of Ohio. Pres., Spirit of 74 Com., Xenia, 1974-76, Dayton/Miami Valley Better Bus. Bur., 1978-80, Xenia YMCA, 1958-59. Served as lt., aviator USNR, 1942-45; PTO. Recipient F. M. Torrence Community Service award, 1966; Xenia Daily Gazette received Pulitzer prize for gen. news reporting in 1975. Mem. Am. Soc. Newspaper Editors, Am. Newspaper Pubs. Assn., Ohio Newspaper Assn., Newcomen Soc. N. Am., Fraternal Order of Police Assos., Am. Legion (past post comdr.), Xenia Area C. of C. (past pres.), Sigma Delta Chi. Methodist. Home: 122 Euclid St Middletown OH 45042 Office: 289 City Centre Mart Middletown OH 45042

JORDAN, JESSIE MAE, educator; b. Leadwood, Mo., May 25, 1921; d. Thomas and Dora J.; B.S. in Elem. Edn., U. Mo., Columbia, 1948, M.Ed. in Spl. Edn. and Reading, 1956; postgrad. in learning disabilities Fontbonne Coll., St. Louis. Tchr. grade 3 Leadwood (Mo.) Sch. R-IV, 1944-52; tchr. spl. edn. Leadwood Sch., 1952-71; reading specialist West County RIV Public Schs., 1971—. Active, East Side Ch. of God. Mem. St. Francois County, Mo. State tchrs. assn., Council Exceptional Children (nat., local-mem. chmn.), Internat. Reading Assn. (past pres. Mineral area chpt., mem. research com., treas. 1981-82). Specialist in spl. edn., educable mentally retarded, home-bound cerebral palsy, emotionally disturbed, reading specialist. Home: 205 E 9th St Leadwood MO 63653 Office: West County RIV Public Schs 1124 Main St Leadwood MO 63653

JORDAN, LEMUEL RUSSELL, hosp. exec.; b. Smithfield, N.C., Oct. 21, 1924; s. Thomas and Sophronia Lee (Creech) J.; B.A., Amherst Coll., 1947; M.A., Columbia U., 1949; postgrad. mgmt. U. N.C., 1949-50, 51-54, Ernest H. Abernathy fellow, 1953; m. Jean Marrow, Dec. 15, 1951; children—Jean H., Rebecca, Judy. Instr. personnel relations Sch. Bus. Adminstrn., U. N.C., 1954-55; asst. dir., asst. prof. hosp. mgmt. Duke U. Med. Center, 1955-59; dir. teaching hosps. and clinics, asso. prof. mgmt. Coll. Bus. Adminstrn., J. Hillis Miller Health Center, U. Fla., Gainesville, 1959-65, asso. prof. health and hosp. adminstrn. Coll. Health Related Professions, chmn. grad. program health and hosp. adminstrn., 1963-65; exec. dir., chief exec. officer Baptist Med. Center, Birmingham, Ala., 1965-71, pres., chief exec. officer, 1971-74; pres., chief exec. officer Alton Ochsner Med. Found., New Orleans, 1974-78; chmn. bd., chief exec. officer Eye, Ear, Nose and Throat Hosp. and Clinics, New Orleans, 1976-78; pres., chief exec. officer, dir. Miami Valley Hosp., Dayton, Ohio, 1978—; adj. prof. U. Ala., Birmingham, 1969—, Washington U., St. Louis, 1971—, Sch. Public Health and Tropical Medicine, Tulane U., 1975—, Wright State U., 1979—; Kellogg Found. vis. prof., San Salvador, 1964; chmn. Accrediting Commn. Edn. Health Services Adminstrn., 1975-77; adv. com. Robert Wood Johnson Community Hosp.-Med. Staff, Washington, 1974—. Served as officer USAAF, World War II, Korea. L.R. Jordan Library dedicated at Ida V. Moffett Sch. Nursing, Birmingham, 1975; L.R. Jordan Health Care Mgmt. Soc. founded as nat. ednl. soc., New Orleans, 1978; named hon. alumnus Duke U., U. Ala., Birmingham, George Washington U. Fellow Am. Coll. Hosp. Adminstrs. (chmn. com. article-of-year awards 1969-70); mem. Am. Heart Assn., Dayton Area Heart Assn. (dir.), Am. Hosp. Assn., Am. Mgmt. Assn., Am. Public Health Assn., Nat. League Nursing, Alpha Kappa Psi (nat. pres. 1959-65, dir. found. 1965-72, 76—; Disting. Service award 1952, 62, 63). Republican. Presbyterian. Clubs: Racquet, Dayton Country, Rotary (Dayton). Author papers in field. Office: 1 Wyoming St Dayton OH 45409

JORDAN, MARGARET WILKINSON, state ofcl.; b. Madison, N.J., July 1, 1922; d. Harry Rockerfellow and Mary (Wolf) Wilkinson; B.S. in Elec. Engring., Rutgers U., 1948, B.S. in Mech. Engring., 1949; J.D., U. Mo.-Kansas City, 1965; m. Ben B. Jordan, Sept. 17, 1944; children—Bradley, Marsha. Engring. asst. Western Electric Co., 1941-44; archtl. designer David Ludlow, A.I.A., Summit, N.J., 1954-57; admitted to Kans. bar, 1965; practiced in Johnson County, 1965-73; dist. atty. 10th Jud. Dist. Kans., Olathe, from 1973; now exec. dir. Metropolitan Organization to Counter Sexual Assault (MOCSA), OCSA Asst. Center. Mem. Mid-Am. Drug Forum, Region I Kans. Drug Abuse Council; mem. nat. adv. com. Rape Treatment and Prevention, Kans. Chmn. Gov.s Task Force on Rape Prevention State of Mo. Nat. Asso. of Criminal Justice Planners, Nat. Assn. Drug Abuse and Alcohol Problems. Com. Criminal Justice Standards and Goals. Councilman, Leawood, Kans., 1969-71, mayor, 1971-72, Bd. dirs., regional rep. Johnson County Drug Abuse Council. Recipient Community Leadership award U. Mo.-Kansas City, 1971. Mem. Am. Bar Assn. (Women and Criminal Justice Com.), Kans. Bar Assn., Johnson County Bar Assn. (treas. 1972-73), Nat. Dist. Attys. Assn., Kansas County and Dist. Attys. Assn., Met. Chiefs and Sheriffs Assn. (asso.), Johnson County Chiefs of Police (asso.), Kans. Citizens Advisory Com. on Drug Abuse (past chmn.); pres. Johnson County Mental Health Center, Johnson County Bench-Bar com. for Family, Phi Alpha Delta. Club: Perry Yacht (gov.). Home: 2515 W 91st St Leawood KS 66206 Office: PO Box 728 Olathe KS 66061

JORDAN, ROBERT ARLO, electronic mfg. co. exec.; b. St. Cloud, Minn., Mar. 13, 1946; s. Arlo Evert and Lillian Cecil (Olson) J.; student St. Cloud State U., 1964-66, U. Minn., 1972, 79; B.S. in Bus. Adminstrn., Met. State U., 1979; postgrad. U. Chgo., 1980, Wharton Sch. Fin. With Sperry Univac, Roseville, Minn., 1967-73, product adminstr., 1970-72, material status supr., 1972-73; materials mgr. Solid Controls Inc., Mpls., 1973-80, dir. mfg. ops., 1980—; prin. Jordan & Assos. Baseball coach Babe Ruth League, 1974-76; mem. City Council, Minn. Cities Planning Commn.; mem. adv. bd. Dept. Natural Resources; chmn. Park and Recreation Bd. Office: Solid Controls Inc 6925 Washington Ave S Minneapolis MN 55435

JORDAN, THOMAS EDWARD, ednl. adminstr.; b. Leeds, Eng., July 23, 1929; came to U.S., 1947, naturalized, 1954; Ed.D., Ind. U., 1955. Asso. vice chancellor, grad. dean, U. Mo., St. Louis, 1975—. Fellow Royal Soc. Health (London) (Starkey research prize 1981); mem. Am. Ednl. Research Assn., Soc. Study of Human Biology. Author: The Mentally Retarded, 1961, 66, 72, 76; Exceptional Child, 1962; Perspectives in Mental Retardation, 1966; America's Children, 1974; Development in the Preschool Years, 1980; Child Development, Information and the Formation of Public Policy, 1982. Office: Univ Missouri Saint Louis MO 63131

JORDAN, ZEMA LOUISE, ednl. adminstr.; b. Huntsville, Ala.; d. Willie Davey and Hattie (Jobe) Jordan; B.A., Tenn. A&I State U., 1953; M.Ed., Wayne State U., 1963, now doctoral candidate. Instr. English, Liberty (Miss.) High Sch., 1953-54; instr. English, part-time guidance counselor Wilson Jr. High Sch., Florence, S.C., 1954-64; instr. English, Hutchins Jr. High and Southwestern High Sch., Detroit, 1964-68; head English dept. Farwell Jr. High Sch., Detroit, 1968-75; instr. English, Wayne County Community Coll., Detroit, part-time, 1969—; adminstrv. unit head Richard Middle Sch., Detroit, 1976-77, Von Steuben Middle Sch., Detroit, 1977—; curriculum cons. Profl. Growth Center, Detroit Pub. Schs., Wayne State Univ., 1980—. Active Adult Great Books Discussion Group, Detroit, 1965—. Mem. Orgn. Sch. Adminstrs. and Suprs., Met. Detroit Alliance Black Sch. Educators, Nat. Alliance Black Sch. Educators, Tchrs. English to Speakers Other Langs., Nat. Council Tchrs. English, Mich. Council Tchrs. English, Met. Detroit Reading Council, NAACP, Delta Sigma Theta, Pi Lambda Theta. Methodist. Contbr. articles to profl. jours. Office: Von Steuben Middle Sch 12300 Linnhurst St Detroit MI 48205

JORFI, JOSEPH JOHN, JR., univ. adminstr.; b. Lebanon, Pa., Nov. 22, 1941; s. Joseph John and Margaret Rosemary (Erdei) J.; student Washtenaw Community Coll., 1974-77; m. Beverly Jean Braatz, Nov. 22, 1971; children—Brenda Jean, Rebecca Jane. Enlisted U.S. Air Force, 1959, ret., 1968; machine operator Hoover Ball & Bearing Co., Ann Arbor, Mich., 1969; faculty Eastern Mich. U., Ypsilanti, Mich., 1970-76, 77—, asst. dir. undergrad. admissions, 1980—; programmer analyst U. Mich., Ann Arbor, 1976. Mem. Mich. Assn. Coll. Admissions Counselors, Mich. Coll. Personnel Assn., Mich. Personnel and Guidance Assn., Assn. for Computing Machinery, VFW. Republican. Home: 546 Archwood Dr Ann Arbor MI 48103 Office: Eastern Mich U 214 Pierce Hall Ypsilanti MI 48197

JORGENS, THOMAS PHILLIP, regional planner; b. Bertha, Minn., July 14, 1947; s. Joseph Anthony and Anna Marie (Fjeld) J.; B.A., U. Minn., 1969, M.A., 1971; m. Michal Kulenkamp, June 13, 1970; children—Gwendolyn Anna, Amber Blythe. Instr. econs. and history U. Minn., Mpls., 1970-73, researcher, 1974-75; planning dir. Upper Minn. Valley Regional Devel. Commn., Appleton, 1975-79; exec. dir. N.W. Regional Devel. Commn., Crookston, Minn., 1979—; mem. Intergovtl. Info. Systems Adv. Council, 1980—. Bd. dirs. Appleton Cultural Affairs Com., 1976-79. McMillan fellow, 1972-73. Mem. Minn. Planning Assn., Soil Conservation Soc. Am., Minn. Waterfowl Assn., Phi Alpha Theta. Democrat. Club: Ducks Unltd. (chpt. dir. 1980—). Author: The Fiscal Impact of Federal and State Waterfowl Production Areas on Local Units of Government in West Central Minnesota, 1979. Home: 309 Leonard Ave Crookston MN 56716 Office: 425 Woodland Ave Crookston MN 56716

JORGENSEN, GERALD THOMAS, psychologist; b. Mason City, Iowa, Jan. 15, 1947; s. Harry Grover and Mary Jo (Kollasch) J.; B.A., Loras Coll., 1969; M.S., Colo. State U., 1970, Ph.D., 1973; m. Mary Ann Reiter, Aug. 30, 1969; children—Amy Lynn, Sarah Kay, Jill Kathryn. Psychology intern Counseling Center, Colo State U., 1971-72, VA Hosp., Palo Alto, Calif., 1972-73; psychologist Loras Coll., Dubuque, Iowa, 1973-76, Clarke Coll., Dubuque, 1973-76; asst. prof. psychology, psychologist Loras Coll., Dubuque, 1976-80, dir. Center Counseling and Student Devel., 1977—, asso. prof., 1981—; cons. and supervising psychologist Dubuque Jackson County Mental Health Center, 1978—; mem. Iowa Bd. Psychology Examiners, 1981—. Treas., Dubuque County Assn. Mental Health, 1975—; ordained deacon Roman Cath. Ch., 1979, asst. dir. for diaconate formation, 1981—. NDEA fellow, 1969-72. Mem. Am. Psychol. Assn., Am. Personnel and Guidance Assn., Am. Coll. Personnel Assn., Iowa Psychol. Assn. Democrat. Home: 2183 St Celia Dubuque IA 52001 Office: Loras Coll Dubuque IA 52001

JORGENSEN, KAY SUSAN, state legislator; b. Winner, S.D., May 25, 1951; d. Arnold and Twyla Vivian Jorgensen; B.S. in Edn., Black Hills State Coll., 1974; m. Michael R. Pangburn, July 5, 1975. Auctioneer, 1968—; page adv., tchr. S.D. Legislature, Pierre, 1975-78; co-owner, mgr. Bell Boy Drive Inn, Spearfish, S.D., 1976-77; mgr. food concession Passion Play, Spearfish, 1976-80; exec. dir., trustee High Plains Heritage Soc., Spearfish, 1979—; mem. S.D. Ho. of Reps., 1978—, mem. tax com., 1979—, state affairs com., 1981—. Mem. Black Hills State Coll. Alumni Assn. (pres. 1978-79), S.D. Restaurant Assn., AAUW, Bus. and Profl. Women's Club, Epilepsy Found., Am. Quarter Horse Assn., Community Concert Assn., Delta Kappa Gamma. Republican. Office: Box 385 Spearfish SD 57783

JORGENSEN, LAVERNIA MAE, educator; b. Luck, Wis., Mar. 2, 1918; d. George and Alice (Christensen) J.; B.S., River Falls (Wis.) State Tchrs. Coll., 1939; M.Ed., U. Minn., 1950; dir. phys. edn. Ind. U., 1955, P.E.D., 1960. Tchr. English and phys. edn., Plummer, Minn., 1941-43, history and phys. edn., Sleepy Eye, Minn., 1943-46; girls' phys. edn., Detroit Lakes, Minn., 1946-49; teaching asst. U. Minn., Mpls., 1949-50; health and phys. edn. Manchester Coll., 1950-55, Ind. U., Bloomington, 1955-56; tchr. health and phys. edn. Eastern Mich. U., 1956-58, U. S.D., 1958-61, Augustana Coll., 1961-63, U. N.D., Grand Forks, 1963—. Recipient honor awards N.D., Central Dist. assns. health, phys. edn. and recreation, 1972; Outstanding Woman N.D. award, 1973; Distinguished Alumnus award U. Wis.-River Falls, 1977. Fellow Am. Sch. Health Assn., AAHPER; mem. AAUP, Am. Corrective Therapy Assn., AAUW, N.D. Health, Phys. Edn., Recreation and Coaches Assn., Nat., N.D. assns. for phys. edn. coll. women, Nat. Recreation and Parks Assn., Soc. Parks and Recreation Educators, Am. Camping Assn., N.D. Park and Recreation Assn., Nat. Found. for Health, Phys. Edn. and Recreation, Am. Numismatic Assn., Ind. U. Alumni Assn., Royal Soc. Health, Internat. Platform Assn., Internat. Recreation Assn., Am. Acad. Sports Medicine, Phi Sigma Alpha (Woman of Year award N.D. Gamma chpt. 1974), Delta Psi Kappa. Republican. Lutheran (deacon). Club: River Bend Country. Contbr. articles in field to profl. jours. Home: 2007 2d Av N Grand Forks ND 58201

JORNS, DANIEL ALAN, psychol. counselor; b. Shawnee, Okla., Apr. 14, 1953; s. Victor L. and Nancy H. (Pollard) J.; B.A., Okla. State U., 1975, M.S., 1976. Group worker Payne County Correctional System, Stillwater, Okla., 1975-76; outpatient counselor ADAPT, Des Moines, 1976-77; sr. counselor Alcohol and Drug Abuse Services, Inc., Des Moines, 1977-78, outpatient coordinator, 1978-80; program coordinator Nat. Council on Alcoholism, Central Assessment Center, Des Moines, 1980—; pvt. practice psychol. counseling, Des Moines; group co-facilitator Westminsterhouse, Des Moines; mem. Substance Abuse Com. on Cert., State of Iowa, 1980—; bd. dirs. Employment Assistance for Recovered Drug Abusers, Inc., 1980—. Mem. Am. Personnel and Guidance Assn., Internat. Transactional Analysis Assn., Central Iowa Transactional Analysis Soc., Sigma Alpha Epsilon. Democrat. Home: 2318 35th St Des Moines IA 50310 Office: Suite 517 Fleming Bldg 218 6th Ave Des Moines IA 50310

JORNS, RAYMOND MICHAEL, mktg. dir.; b. St. Louis, Aug. 21, 1940; s. George Michael and Jeanette (Meier) J.; B.S. in Commerce, St. Louis U., 1961; m. Maria Elizabeth Calderon, Nov. 4, 1961; children—Michael, Lisa, Stephen, David. Area sales mgr. Lever Bros. Co., 1961-67; sales promotion mgr. Eversweet Foods div. Capitol Foods, Chgo., 1967-68; dir. corp. mktg. CFS Continental, Chgo., 1968—. Mem. Am. Mktg. Assn., Am. Mgmt. Assn., Internat. Food Mfrs. Assn., Nat. Restaurant Assn. Home: 1260 Fairmont Rd Hoffman Estates IL 60194 Office: 2550 N Clybourn St Chicago IL 60614

JOSAITIS, MARVIN, business exec.; b. Detroit, Dec. 27, 1941; s. Frank W. and Margaret Agnes (Girard) J.; B.A., Sacred Heart Sem. Coll., 1963; M.A., Eastern Mich. U., 1970, U. Detroit, 1971; postgrad. St. Louis U., 1965, St. John's Provincial Sem., 1963-67; Ph.D., U. Mich., 1977; m. Donna Marie Rimer, Mar. 25, 1970; children—Kateri, Ta'mara, Tarik. Ordained priest Roman Catholic Ch., 1967; asso. pastor St. Michael's Ch., Monroe, Mich., 1967-69; asso. prof. philosophy, English, Monroe County (Mich.) Community Coll., 1969-76; edn. coordinator Alcohol and Drug Abuse program The Ford Motor Co., 1976-78; indsl. relations analyst Ford Motor Co., 1978, labor relations analyst, 1978-80, indsl. relations unit supr., 1980-81, sect. supr. salaried personnel and tng., 1981; employee resource mgr. Massey-Ferguson, Inc., 1981—. Mem. Monroe County Planning Commn., 1975-76. Named Best instr. Monroe County Community Coll., 1970. Home: 2917 Aspen Lane Bloomfield Hills MI 48013 Office: Massey-Ferguson Inc N Am Tractor Div 12655 Southfield Rd Detroit MI 48223

JOSCELYN, KENT BUCKLEY, research scientist, lawyer; b. Binghamton, N.Y., Dec. 18, 1936; s. Raymond Miles and Gwen Buckley (Smith) J.; B.S., Union Coll., 1957; J.D., Albany Law Sch., 1960; m. Mary A. Komoroske, Nov. 20, 1965; children—Kathryn Anne, Jennifer Sheldon. Admitted to N.Y. State bar, 1961, U.S. Ct. Mil. Appeals, 1962, D.C. bar, 1967, Mich. bar, 1979; atty., adviser Hdqrs. USAF, Washington, 1965-67; asso. prof. forensic studies Coll. Arts and Scis. Ind. U., Bloomington, 1967-76, dir. Inst. Research in Pub. Safety, 1970-75; head policy analysis div. Hwy. Safety Research Inst., U. Mich., 1976-81, dir. transp. planning and policy, urban and regional planning program, 1981—; partner firm Joscelyn & Treat, P.C., 1981—; cons. Law Enforcement Assistance Adminstrn., U.S. Dept. Justice, 1969-72; Gov.'s appointee as regional dir. Ind. Criminal Justice Planning Agy., also vice chmn. Ind. Organized Crime Prevention Council, 1969-72; commr. pub. safety City of Bloomington, 1974-76. Served to capt., USAF, 1961-64. Mem. Transp. Research Bd. (chmn. motor vehicle and traffic law com.), Nat. Acad. Sci., NRC, Am. Soc. Criminology, AAAS, Soc. Automotive Engrs., Am. Soc. Pub. Adminstrn., Acad. Criminal Justice Scis., Am., D.C., Mich., N.Y. State bar assns., Internat. Assn. Chiefs Police (asso.), Nat. Safety Council, Sigma Xi. Editor Internat. Jour. Criminal Justice. Home: 2255 Blueberry Ln Ann Arbor MI 48103 Office: 3131 S State St Ann Arbor MI 48104

JOSEF, NORMA CASTRO, psychiatrist; b. Manila, Philippines, Apr. 18; came to U.S., 1964; d. Tomas Gozon and Teofila Mendoza (Castro) J.; M.D. cum laude, U. Santo Tomas, Manila, 1963; m. R. John Kinkel. Intern, Albert Einstein Med. Center, Phila., 1964-65; resident in internal medicine Wayne State U., Detroit, 1965-66, William Beaumont Hosp., Royal Oak, Mich., 1971-72; gen. practice medicine, med. missionary, Asia and Africa, 1968-71; resident in gen. psychiatry Lafayette Clinic, Detroit, 1972-75, head adult in-patient service, 1977—; asst. prof. Coll. Medicine, Wayne State U.; med. missionary Soc. Catholic Med. Missionaries, 1966-78. Diplomate Am. Bd. Psychiatry and Neurology. Mem. Mich. Psychiat. Soc., Am. Psychiat. Assn., Am. Med. Women's Assn. Speaker World Congress of Psychiatry, 1977. Office: 951 E Lafayette St Detroit MI 48207

JOSEPH, ALBERT M., inst. exec.; b. Cleve., Sept. 5, 1928; s. Hyman and Lillian (Hirsch) J.; B.F.A., Ohio U., 1953; m. Dylene Madorsky, Nov. 1, 1953; children—Paul, William, Cynthia. Mag. editor Penton IPC Corp., Cleve., 1955-65; pres. Internat. Writing Inst., Cleve., 1965—; vis. lectr. Case-Western Res. U., Cleve., 1960-65; dir. Plain Talk, Inc., 1979—. Trustee, Youth Enrichment Services, Inc., Cleve., 1980—. Served with U.S. Army, 1949-53. Recipient Am. Mgmt. Assn. Outstanding Service award, 1979. Mem. Am. Soc. Tng. and Devel. (James J. Graven Meml. award 1976), Nat. Council Tchr. English, Am. Bus. Communications Assn., Am. Bar Assn., Mensa. Author: Put It in Writing; The New English. Home: 15815 Shaker Blvd Shaker Heights OH 44120 Office: Hanna Bldg Cleveland OH 44115

JOSEPH, CHARLES EDWARD, periodontist, research scientist; b. Springfield, Ill., Jan. 22, 1949; s. Peter C. and Mary L. Joseph; B.S., Loyola U., Chgo., 1971, U. Ill., 1973; D.D.S., U. Ill., 1975, M.S., 1977, Ph.D., 1981; m. Jean M. Curley, June 28, 1975. Instr. periodontics U. Ill. Med. Center, Chgo., 1975-76, instr. periodontal sr. surgery, 1976-77, research scientist oral pathology, 1977—; practice dentistry specializing in periodontics, Chgo., 1975—; tchr., cons. Nat. Inst. Dental Research fellow, 1977-81; Am. Cancer Soc. fellow, 1971-73; recipient Honor of Lincoln award, 1975, award Am. Acad. Oral Pathology, 1975, Dr. Robert Savage Meml. award, 1975, Leadership award U. Ill., 1975. Mem. Am. Acad. Periodontology, Ill. Soc. Periodontists, Midwest Soc. Periodontology, ADA, Chgo. Dental Assn., Am. Assn. Dental Research, Midwest Soc. Electron Microscopists, AAAS, Nutrition Today Soc., Ill. Nutrition Com., Sigma Xi. Contbr. articles to sci. jours. Office: 5850 N Clark St Chicago IL 60660 also 64 Old Orchard Rd Skokie IL 60076

JOSEPH, EARL CLARK, computer co. exec.; b. St. Paul, Nov. 1, 1926; s. Clark Herbert and Ida Bertha (Schultz) J.; A.A., U. Minn., 1947, B.A., 1951; m. Alma Caroline Bennett, Nov. 19, 1955; children—Alma (Mrs. Richard Chadner), Earl, Vincent, René. Mathematician/programmer Remington Rand Univac, Arlington, Va., 1951-55, supr., St. Paul, 1955-60, systems mgr. Sperry Univac, St. Paul, 1960-63, staff scientist-futurist, 1963—; chmn. bd. Future Systems. Vis. lectr. U. Minn., Mpls., 1971—; mem. Sci. and Mgmt. Adv. Com., U.S. Army, 1972-74. Futurist-in-residence Sci. Mus. of Minn., 1973—; chmn. bd. Future Systems; pres. Anticipatory Scis. Chmn., Met. Young Adult Ministry, 1967-69; mem. Gov.'s Planning Commn. for City Center Learning, 1968. Served with USNR, 1944-46. Distinguished lectr. I.E.E.E. Computer Soc., 1971-72, 76-82, Assn. Computer Machinery. Mem. I.E.E.E. (sr.), Minn. Futurists (founder, dir., past pres.), World Future Soc., Soc. for Gen. Systems Research, Assn. Computer Machinery (gen. chmn. 1975, pres. chpt. 1976-77), AAAS, Data Processing Mgmt. Assn., Beta Phi Beta. Patents, publs. in field; co-author 30 books; founding editor jour. Futurics; editor Future Trends Newsletter, System Trends Newsletter; adv. editor Jour. Cultural and Ednl. Futures. Home: 365 Summit Ave St Paul MN 55102 Office: Univac Park PO Box 3525 St Paul MN 55165

JOSEPH, MARGUERITE WILSON, state ofcl.; b. Camden, O., Mar. 26, 1919; d. Roeloff H. and Grace D. (Gilpin) Wilson; student Miami U., Oxford, O., 1936-37, 44-45, Baldwin-Wallace Coll., 1937-38; m. Kenneth L. Joseph, Sept. 9, 1938 (div. June 1948); 1 dau., Claudia F. (Mrs. Raymond Hampton). Social worker Ohio State Aid for Aged, Hamilton, 1945-47, Fla. Dept. Welfare, Jacksonville, 1947-48; mgr., owner West Side Drugs, St. Augustine, Fla., 1948-50; radiol. technician St. Joseph's Hosp., Mishawaka, Ind., 1954-56, McCullough-Hyde Hosp., Oxford, 1957-60, Christ Hosp., Cin., 1960-62; test examiner Ohio State Employment Service, Hamilton, 1962-69; coordinator Butler County W.I.N., 1969—. Mem. adv. bd. Miami Valley Tech. Sch., Hamilton, 1967—. Mem. Internat. Assn. Personnel in Employment Security, Nat. Wildlife Assn., Aircraft Owners and Pilots Assn., Soc. Radiol. Technologists, Ohio Civil Service Employees Assn., Internat. Platform Assn. Mem. Order Eastern Star. Contbr. poems to anthologies, mags. including Etude, Silhouette, Am. Poetry, others. Home: 119 N Campus Ave Oxford OH 45056 Office: 112 N 2d St Hamilton OH 45012

JOSEPH, PAMELA BOLOTIN, educator; b. Chgo., May 16, 1947; d. Jack R. and Claire B. Bolotin; B.A., Lawrence U., 1969; M.A.T., Northwestern U., 1971, Ph.D. (Univ. fellow), 1978; m. David A. Joseph, Aug. 24, 1969; children—Daniel, Jordan, Gabriel. Tchr., Taft High Sch., Chgo., 1969-70, Dempster Jr. High Sch., Mt. Prospect, Ill., 1970-73; supr. M.A.T. program and tutorial clin. program Northwestern U., 1974-75; instr. Northeastern U., Chgo., summer 1977; mem. adj. faculty Nat. Coll. Edn., 1979—; mem. expert pool Sch. Dist. #111, Highland Park-Highwood, Ill. Co-chairperson legis. com. Dist. #111 Sch. Bd.; mem. PTA Legis. Round Table, 1981-82; observer LWV. Mem. Nat. Council Social Studies, Ill. Council Social Studies, Assn. Supervision and Curriculum Devel., Phi Delta Kappa.

JOSEPH, RAMON RAFAEL, physician, educator; b. N.Y.C., May 17, 1930; s. Felix R. and Helen (Espinet) J.; B.S., Manhattan Coll., 1952; M.D., Cornell U., 1956; m. Mary Ann Kowalchik, June 16, 1956; children—Ricardo George, Maria Ann, Lisa Marie. Intern, Meadowbrook Hosp., Hempstead, N.Y., 1956-57, resident, 1957; resident Wayne County Gen. Hosp., Westland, Mich., 1959-62; practice medicine, specializing in internal medicine and gastroenterology 1962—; dir. gastroenterology Wayne County Gen. Hosp., 1962—, asst. dir. internal medicine, 1964-73, dir., 1973—, pres. med. staff, 1971-72; cons. Annapolis Hosp.; instr. internal medicine U. Mich., 1962-65, asst. prof., 1965-69, asso. prof., 1969-74, prof., 1975—, asst. dean, 1973—; cons. gastroenterology St. Mary Hosp., Livonia, Mich., 1966—. Commr. Community Commn. on Drug Abuse, Livonia and Westland, Mich., 1970-73; mem. Mich. Dept. Edn. Council on Drug Abuse; cons. on drug abuse pub. schs., Livonia, 1968-74; pres. Livonia Sch. Bd. Adv. Council, 1970-71. Served as capt. U.S. Army, 1957-59. Diplomate Nat. Bd. Med. Examiners, Am. Bd. Internal Medicine. Fellow A.C.P.; mem. Am. Fedn. for Clin. Research, Am. Gastroenterol. Assn., A.A.A.S., Assn. Am. Med. Colls., A.M.A., N.Y. Acad. Scis., Detroit Gastroenterol. Soc. (pres. 1969-70), Mich., Wayne County med. socs., Am. Assn. Lab. Animal Sci., Am. Soc. for Gastrointestinal Endoscopy, Mich. Endoscopic Soc. (pres. 1982-83), Mich. Assn. Professions, Assn. Program Dirs. in Internal Medicine. Roman Catholic. Contbr. articles in field to profl. jours. Home: 5593 Stratford Dr West Bloomfield MI 48033 Office: Wayne County Gen Hosp Westland MI 48185 also U Mich Med Sch Ann Arbor MI 48104

JOSEPHS, HAROLD, tech. co. exec.; b. N.Y.C., Feb. 16, 1937; s. Louis and Dora (Wolf) J.; B.S., U. Pa., 1959; M.S., Villanova U., 1964; m. Bette Ruth Shear, Nov. 23, 1961; children—Syril Penina, Fayga Zipporah, Nacham Moshe, Meira Rachel, Zev Azriel. Program dir. Biodynamics div. Comar Corp., Birmingham, Mich., 1969-72; research engr. Ford Motor Co., Dearborn, Mich., 1972-74; mgr. water systems div. Foster Chems. Co., Detroit, 1974-76; pres. Kehilla Assos. Inc., Berkley, Mich., 1976—; lectr. dept. mech. engring. Lawrence Inst. Tech.; cons. in field. Chmn. bd. P'Tach, Detroit, 1979—; bd. dirs. Yeshiva Beth Yehudah. Registered profl. engr., Mich.; cert. safety profl. Mem. Am. Soc. Safety Engrs., Nat. Soc. Profl. Engrs., Mich. Soc. Profl. Engrs. (sec. chpt. 1979-80), Soc. Automotive Engrs. (dir. chpt. 1980—), System Safety Soc., Am. Soc. Quality Control. Office: Box 1012 Berkley MI 48072

JOSEPHS, LYMAN COLT, III, aerospace exec.; b. Newport, R.I., Oct. 5, 1920; s. Lyman Colt, Jr., and Dorothy Stott (Pearson) J.; B.S., Harvard Coll., 1941; postgrad. Harvard Grad. Sch. Engring., 1941; A.M.P., Harvard Bus. Sch., 1969; m. Marion Roberts Newell, Oct. 6, 1945; children—Elizabeth Josephs Kelly, Janet C., Anne C. Josephs Pottinger. Project engr., chief engr., dir. engring., program dir. Chance Vought Aircraft (later LTV, Inc.), 1946-65; dir. aircraft devel. Martin-Marietta, Balt., 1965-67; dir. advanced systems, v.p., gen. mgr. Convair Div., Gen. Dynamics, v.p., program dir. F-16, Gen. Dynamics, Ft. Worth, 1967-76, corp. v.p. internat., Gen. Dynamics Corp., St. Louis, 1976—. Served with USN, 1942-46. Fellow AIAA; mem. ASME, Soc. Automotive Engrs., Navy League, Air Force Assn., Am. Defense Preparedness Assn., Nat. Aero. Assn. Republican. Episcopalian. Clubs: St. Louis, Old Warson Country, Internat. Club of Washington, Harvard Club of St. Louis, Harvard Bus. Sch. Club of St. Louis. Office: Pierre Laclede Center Saint Louis MO 63105

JOSHI, AZHIKATH NINAN, mech. engr.; b. Madras, India, June 23, 1934; s. Ninan Thomas and Elizabeth Joshua; came to U.S., 1966; B.E. in Mech. Engring., U. Madras, 1955; M.S., S.D. State U., 1975, Ph.D., 1976. Jr. engr. River Valley Project, Madras, 1955-58; lectr. mech. engring., then head dept. Central Poly., Madras, 1958-69; asso. prof. S.W. State U., Marshall, Minn., from 1969, now prof.; vis. asso. prof. S.D. State U., 1976—. Mem. ASME, AAAS, Minn. Edn. Assn., S.D. Order Engrs., Tau Beta Pi. Author papers in field. Home: Box 194 Marshall MN 56258 Office: SW State Univ Marshall MN 56258

JOSLYN, WALLACE DANFORTH, psychologist; b. Cape Girardeau, Mo., Apr. 13, 1939; s. Lewis Danforth and Margaret Bernice (Gallup) J.; B.A., U. Va., 1961; Ph.D., U. Wis., 1967; m. Moreen Virginia Drescher, May 26, 1979. Research asso. Oreg. Regional Primate Research Center, Beaverton, 1967-71; adj. asst. prof. U. Oreg. Med. Sch., Portland, 1970-71; staff clin. psychologist VA Med. Center, Knoxville, Iowa, 1972—. NIMH fellow, 1962-63. Mem. Am. Psychol. Assn., Soc. Personality Assessment, Assn. Advancement Psychology. Republican. Contbr. articles to profl. jours. Home: 1003 W 3d Ave #32 Indianaola IA 50125 Office: 1515 W Pleasant St Knoxville IA 50138

JOSLYN-BISHOP, LINDA MAY, clin. psychologist; b. Los Angeles, Dec. 14, 1941; d. Allyn Morgan and Dorothy (Yockel) Joslyn; B.A., UCLA, 1964; M.A., Calif. State U., 1967; Ph.D., U. Kans., 1976; m. Riley Bishop; 1 dau., Sarah. Intern clin. psychology Western Mo. Mental Health Center, Kansas City, 1970-71; staff psychologist adolescent service Western Mo. Mental Health Center, Kansas City, Mo., 1971-79, adolescent unit coordinator, 1973-75; cons. Jackson County Juvenile Ct., Kansas City, Mo., 1974, 76, Florence Crittenton Center, Kansas City, 1977-78; pvt. practice clin. psychology, Personal and Family Devel. Assos., Kansas City, Mo., 1976—; instr. Avila Coll., Kansas City, 1977-78; lectr. U. Kans., Lawrence, 1978-80. Bd. dirs. Alternative Opportunities, Inc., Kansas City, Mo., 1976-79, Nat. Register Health Service Providers in Psychology. Cert. psychologist, Kans.; lic. psychologist, Mo. Mem. Am., Kans., Mo. (chmn. profl. standards rev. com.) psychol. assns., Am. Soc. Group Psychotherapy and Psychodrama, Assn. Advancement Psychology, Am. Bus. Women's Assn. Contbg. author Sensitivity Training and the Laboratory Approach, 3d edit., 1977. Office: 4400 Broadway Suite 112 Kansas City MO 64111

JOUETT, RICHARD LEE, JR., ednl. adminstr.; b. Carrolton, Ill., Oct. 6, 1949; s. Richard Lee and Doris Jean (Wyatt) J.; B.S. in Edn., So. Ill. U., Edwardsville, 1972, M.S. in Counseling, 1976; m. Cheryl Rosann Ferguson, Apr. 29, 1972. Tchr., St. Elizabeth's Sch., Granite City, Ill., 1972-73; coordinator supportive services Office Manpower Devel., Edwardsville, 1974-76; sr. personnel rep. Shippers Car Line, St. Charles, Mo., 1976-77; dir. Career Guidance Center, Lewis and Clark Community Coll., Godfrey, Ill., 1977-81, dir. career planning and placement, 1981—; bd. dirs. Consortium Vocat. Educators and Employers. Served with USAF, 1973-74. Mem. Am. Personnel and Guidance Assn., Nat. Assn. Career Edn., Ill. Vocat. Assn., Nat. Council on Community Services and Continuing Edn., Phi Delta Kappa. Democrat. Home: 173 10th St Wood River IL 62095 Office: 5800 Godfrey Rd Godfrey IL 62035

JOYCE, FLORENCE V. MIENERT (MRS. GEORGE T. JOYCE), civic worker; b. Fosston, Minn., Feb. 13, 1923; s. William P. A. and Clara (Lindfors) Mienert; R.N., Ancker Hosp. Sch. Nursing, St. Paul, 1944; student U. Minn., 1944-45; m. George T. Joyce, Aug. 8, 1946; children—Roberta Eileen Joyce Dreyer, Elizabeth Anne. Bd. dirs. N. Central Iowa chpt. ARC, 1960-66, 67-73, nursing services chmn., 1967—; pres. Vols. Service League, St. Joseph Mercy Hosp., Mason City, Iowa, 1959-61; leader Girl Scouts U.S.A., 1948-66; sec. family and children's services com. Community Planning Council, 1971; bd. dirs YWCA, 1963-66; precinct chmn. Cerro Gordo County Republican Central Com., 1974—. Recipient Community Achievement award Mason City YWCA, 1979. Mem. Am. Nurses Assn., Iowa Nurses Assn., Iowa 10th Dist. Nurses Assn. (dir. 1981—), Nat. Trust Historic Preservation, Cerro Gordo County Med. Aux., Ancker (Hosp.) Alumni Assn., Charles H. MacNider Art Guild (chmn. 1971-72, mems. council 1975-80). Club: Mason City Woman's (dir. 1965-75, 76-77, 81— pres. 1969-70). Roman Catholic. Home: 259 N Crescent Dr Mason City IA 50401

JOYCE, JEREMIAH E., state senator; b. Chgo., Jan. 4, 1943; B.S.; M.A. in Edn.; LL.B., DePaul U.; m. Mairsey; children—Daniel, Michael, Jerry, Kevin. Admitted to Ill. bar; former asst. state's atty., Cook County, Ill.; mem. faculty St. Xavier Coll., John Marshall Law Sch.; mem. Ill. Senate, 1981—. Alderman, Chgo., 1974-78. Mem. Am. Bar Assn., Chgo. Bar Assn., Chgo. Patrolmen's Assn., AAUP, Mensa, Nat. Dist. Attys. Assn. Democrat. Clubs: Kiwanis, Lions, KC. Office: State Capitol Springfield IL 62706*

JOYCE, JEROME J., state senator; b. June 14, 1939; grad. high sch.; m. Janet Meece; 4 children. Farmer; mem. Ill. Senate. Mem. Kankakee County Bd. Suprs., 1969-74; Essex Twp. supr., 1959-74. Mem. Kankakee County Farm Bur., Ill. Wildlife Fedn., Ill. Twp. Ofcls. Assn. Democrat. Roman Catholic. Club: Essex-South Wilmington Sportsmen's. Office: State Capitol Springfield IL 62706*

JOYCE, JOSEPH FRANCIS, sports arena exec.; b. N.Y.C., Apr. 8, 1929; s. Joseph F. and Dorothy (Devere) J.; A.B., Coll. Holy Cross, 1951; LL.B., Fordham U., 1957; m. Elizabeth Trotter, Sept. 11, 1954; children—Elizabeth Ann, Mary, Joseph, Eugene, Jane, Ellen, John, Teresa, Paul, Maura, Timothy, Patrick, Michael. Admitted to N.Y. State bar, 1957; counsel Precision Components div. Norden Ketay Corp., Commack, N.Y., 1957-59; partner firm Steinbugler, Joyce & Scully, N.Y.C., 1959-61, Joyce & Malloy, Smithtown, N.Y., 1961-71; individual practice acctg., Commack, 1961-64; exec. v.p. N.Y.C. Off-Track Betting Corp., N.Y.C., 1971-74; sr. v.p., dir. Madison Square Garden Corp., N.Y.C., 1974—; chmn. bd., dir. Roosevelt Raceway, Inc., Westbury, L.I., N.Y.; chmn. bd., pres. Arlington Park-Washington Park Race Tracks Corp.; v.p., dir. Harness Tracks of Am.; pres. Amsterdam Fund, Inc., 1959-61; bd. dirs. Racing Industry Charitable Found., Inc., 1979—. Served to capt. USMC, 1951-53. Recipient Man of Year award Chgo. div. Horseman's Benevolent Protective Assn., 1976; Off-Track Betting Industry award, 1976; Frank Leahy All Am. award, 1980. Mem. N.Y. Trial Lawyers' Assn., N.Y. State, Suffolk County bar assns., Thoroughbred Racing Assn. (gov.), Aircraft Owners and Pilots Assn. Home: 400 Forest Ave Oak Park IL 60302 Office: Arlington Park-Wash Park Race Tracks Corp PO Box 7 Arlington Heights IL 60006

JOYES, ALDON WESLEY, regional planning adminstr.; b. Plentywood, Mont., Mar. 27, 1949; s. Arnold Edward and Iris Vivian (Vogt) J.; student Eastern Mont. Coll., 1966-68; B.A. in Geography, U. Mont., 1970; M.A. in Geography, Bowling Green State U., 1973; m. Pamela Marie Ruemmele, June 24, 1979. Asso. planner South Central Dakota Regional Council, Jamestown, N.D., 1973-76, planning dir., 1976-78, exec. dir., 1978—; mem. N.D. Water Devel. Com. Vice pres. Jamestown chpt. Nat. Audubon Soc., 1980, pres., 1981. Mem. N.D. Planning Assn. (v.p. 1979, pres. 1980), N.D. Assn. Regional Councils (v.p. 1981), Am. Planning Assn., Jamestown C. of C. (community devel. research com. 1981), Nature Conservancy. Office: 1921 9th Ave SE Jamestown ND 58401

JOYNER, DEE ANN, planning ofcl.; b. Alton, Ill., Feb. 26, 1947; d. Turner Claxton and Dorothy Marie (Troeckler) Burroughs; B.A. in Govt. (Ill. State Tchrs. scholar 1967), So. Ill. U., 1971, M.S. in Govt., 1973; m. Orville DeLong Joyner, Mar. 15, 1973. Faculty adminstr. So. Ill. U., Edwardsville, 1970-72; staff asso. Marshall Kaplan, Gans & Kahn, Washington, 1972-73; dir. community and public affairs East-West Gateway Coordinating Council, St. Louis, 1973-78; bd. dirs. Coro Found., St. Louis, 1980—, exec. dir., 1978-80; dir. planning St. Louis County Govt., 1980—; sec. St. Louis County Local Devel. Co., 1979. Participant, St. Louis Leadership Program, 1976-77; v.p. Central Metro unit Am. Cancer Soc., 1978-79; bd. dirs. Metro St. Louis Forum, 1979-81; chmn. Service Agy. Council, United Way, 1979, mem. Planning Council, 1981; mem. pres.'s adv. council Greater St. Louis council Girl Scouts U.S.A., 1981. Mem. Am. Planning Assn., LWV. Office: 7900 Forsyth St Clayton MO 63105

JOYNER, H. SAJON, physicist, med. cons.; b. Ft. Worth, June 6, 1939; s. Howard Warren and Arista (Arnold) J.; student U. Tex. at Arlington, 1957-60; B.S., U. Tex. at Austin, 1962, M.A., 1964; M.S., U. Mo. at Rolla, 1967, Ph.D., 1970; m. Mary Ellen Yankoff, June 15, 1969; children—Mary Elizabeth, Arista Elia, Patricia Danielle. Nuclear engr. Gen. Dynamics, Fort Worth, 1964; asst. prof. dept. mech. engring. Wichita (Kans.) State U., 1969-75, dir. planning, research and devel. U. Kans. Sch. Medicine, Wichita, 1975-77; pres. Kinetic Corp., 1977—. Mem. Am. Phys. Soc., ASME, N.Y. Acad. Scis., Sigma Xi, Pi Tau Sigma, Sigma Pi Sigma, Tau Beta Pi, Phi Kappa Phi. Episcopalian. Home: 16406 E 37th St N Route 1 Towanda KS 67144

JUDD, DOROTHY HEIPLE, educator; b. Oakwood, Ill., May 27, 1922; d. Eldridge Winfield and Mary Luciel (Oliphant) Heiple; B.A., Ind. U., 1944; M.Ed., U. Toledo, 1971; Ed.S., Troy State U., 1976; Ed.D., No. Ill. U., 1981; m. Robert Carpenter Judd, Sept. 19, 1964; children by previous marriage—Patricia Ann Konkoly, Catherine Rafferty, Deborah Brown, Nancy Lee Arrington; stepchildren—Dianna Kay Judd Carlisi, Nancy Carol Judd Wilber, Linda Judd Marinaccio. Head lang. arts dept. Eisenhower Jr. High Sch., Darien, Ill., 1961-70; instr. devel. edn. Owens Tech. Coll., Perrysburg, Ohio, 1971-73; instr. edn. Troy State U., Montgomery, Ala., also right-to-read coordinator State of Ala., 1975-76; core dept. chair Community Consol. Sch., Dist. 15, Palatine, Ill., 1977-79; instr. curriculum and instrn. No. Ill. U., 1979—; pres. R.C. Judd & Assos., Bloomingdale, Ill., 1980—. Mem. Assn. Ednl. Data Systems, Assn. Supervision and Curriculum Devel., Assn. Tchr. Edn., Internat. Council Computers in Edn., Internat. Reading Assn., Nat. Council Social Studies, Nat. Council Tchrs. of English, Pi Lambda Theta. Contbg. editor Ednl. Computer mag., 1981—; contbr. articles to profl. jours. Home: 1990 Flagstaff Ct Glendale Heights IL 60137

JUDGE, JOHN EMMET, mktg. cons.; b. Grafton, N.D., May 5, 1912; s. Charles C. and Lillian (Johnson) J.; B.S., U. N.D., m. Clarita Garcia, Apr. 18, 1940; children—Carolyn (Mrs. Samuel Stanley), J. Emmet, Maureen, Eileen, Susan. Asst. to adminstr. Fed. Works Agy., Washington, 1939-42; staff mem. Wallace Clark & Co., mgmt. cons., 1942-46; v.p. Morgan Furniture Co., Asheville, N.C., 1946-48; mgr. financial analysis Lincoln Mercury div., Ford Motor Co., 1949-53, asst. gen. purchasing agt., 1953-55, merchandising mgr., 1955-58, mgr. Mercury mktg., 1958-60, mgr. product planning office, 1960-62; v.p. mktg. services Westinghouse Electric Corp., Pitts., 1963-67; v.p. marketing Indian Head Inc., 1967-68; mktg. cons., Birmingham, Mich., 1968—. Dir. Intertek Industries Inc., Kratos Inc. Mem. nat. adv. com. mktg. to sec. commerce. Chmn. library study com., Birmingham, Mich., 1957; dir. Boysville of Mich., 1957. Mem. Am. Def. Preparedness Assn., Soc. Advancement Mgmt., Engring. Soc. Detroit, Am. Soc. M.E., Nat. Assn. Accountants, Soc. Automotive Engrs., U.S. C. of C. (consumer com.), N.A.M. (mktg. com.), Newcomen Soc. N.Am., Sigma Tau, Alpha Tau Omega. Roman Catholic. Clubs: Detroit Athletic, Economic (Detroit); Orchard Lake County (dir.). Address: Shore Dr Harbor Springs MI 49740

JUDGE, JOHN ROBERT, pathologist, virologist; b. Sharon, Pa., May 13, 1933; s. Nicholas A. and Carmella (Taliano) J.; B.A., Case Western Res. U., 1955, M.S., 1957; M.D., Ohio State U., 1961; m. Helen Louise Kapl, Jan. 8, 1955; children—Michael Raymond, Judith Anne. Intern, St. Lukes Hosp., Cleve., 1961-62; resident Cleve. U. Hosps., 1964-66; resident St. Lukes Hosp., Cleve., 1966-68, mem. staff, 1968-69; dir. pathology Lakewood (Ohio) Hosp., 1970—; asst. clin. prof. pathology Case Western Res. U.; med. cons. Am. Cancer Soc. (local branch). Served with M.C., USN, 1962-64, S.E. Asia. Diplomate Am. Bd. Pathology. Fellow NIH, Am. Cancer Soc.; mem. Cleve. Soc. Pathologists, Cleve. Acad. Medicine, Ohio State Path. Assn., Ohio State Med. Assn., Coll. Am. Pathologists, Am. Soc. Clin. Pathologists, Internat. Acad. Pathology. Republican. Roman Catholic. Clubs: Cleve. Yachting. Author numerous profl. papers; research viral etiology of cancer, 1964-70. Home: 20710 Saratoga Dr Fairview Park OH 44126 Office: 14519 Detroit Ave Lakewood OH 44107

JUDSON, LYMAN SPICER VINCENT, speech pathologist, educator; b. Plymouth, Mich., Mar. 27, 1903; s. Ernest W. and Fannie Louise (Spicer) J.; A.B. in Biol. Scis., Albion Coll., 1925; M.S. in Med. Scis., U. Mich., 1929; Ph.D., U. Wis., 1933; postgrad. S.E. Mich. U., 1926, U. Iowa, 1929-30, U. So. Calif., 1927, Harvard U., 1942, U. San Francisco, Palma, Mallorca, Spain, 1967; m. E. Ellen MacKechnie, 1933 (dec. 1964); m. 2d, S. Adele H. Christensen, 1968. Chmn. dept. sci. Las Vegas (Nev.) High Sch., 1925-27; instr. speech, studio dir. Sta. KUSD, U. S.D., 1927-28; instr. speech U. Mich., 1928-29; research asso. speech pathology U. Iowa, 1929-30; asso. prof. Kans. State Tchrs. Coll., summers 1929, 30; chmn. dept. speech Ala. Poly. Inst., Auburn, 1930-31; asst. prof. speech U. Ill., 1933-35; prof. speech Kalamazoo Coll., 1936-42; chief motion picture and visual edn. divs. Pan Am. Union, OAS, 1946-50; served to comdr. USNR, 1942-65; mem. joint bd. control USN tng. films, 1944-46; chmn. dept. speech, dir. public relations Babson Coll. Bus. Adminstrn., 1950-55; vis. prof. Latin Am. affairs Assn. Am. Colls., 1952; speech writer Hon. Christian A. Herter, 1954-57; asst. to pres. Alfred U., 1955-57; dir. devel. Ripon Coll., 1957-63; lectr. U. Wis., 1963-64; prof. speech Minn. State U., Winona, 1964-71; chmn. bd., treas. Am. Fine Arts Found., Rochester, Minn., 1971—; staff Supreme Allied Comdr. Atlantic, liaison officer staff Supreme Allied Comdr. Europe and European Hdqrs., dir. gen. NATO, 1953-54; spl. mission Vietnam and 7th Fleet, 1966; TV cons. Johnson Found., 1963-64; devel. and long-range planning cons., 1965—; Mem. Explorers Scout bd., cabinet mem., bd. mem., exec. com. mem., treas. Twin Lakes council Boy Scouts Am., 1972-73. Fellow Am. Geog. Soc.; mem. AAAS, Inter-Am. Soc. Anthropology and Geography, Soc. Am. Archeology, Am. Soc. Agrl. Scis., Am. Acad. Polit. and Social Scis., Public Relations Soc. Am., Wis. Arts Council, Boston Athenaeum (propr.), Explorers Club (N.Y.C.), Archeol. Inst. Am. (pres. Winona-Hiawatha Valley chpt.), Friends of Library Oshkosh, Navy League, Sigma Xi, Alpha Phi Omega, Delta Sigma Rho (nat. sec., nat. editor), Tau Kappa Alpha, Pi Kappa Delta, Sigma Delta Chi, Sigma Chi. Episcopalian. Clubs: Rotary; Cosmos (Washington). Author: Electrodynamic Recorder, 1930; Objective Studies on the Influence of the Speaker and the Listener, 1930; Combining the Breathing Undae of Speaker and Listener, 1932; Preliminary Study of the Offerings of Speech-Content Courses in the Technical Colleges of the United States, 1932; The Vegetative Versus the Speech Use of Biological Systems, 1932; Basic Speech and Voice Science, 1933; The Fundamentals of the Speaker-Audience Relationship, 1934; Modern Group Discussion, 1935; Manual of Group Discussion, 1936; Public Speaking for Future Farmers, 1936; After-Dinner Speaking, 1937; Winning Future Farmers Speeches, 1939; The Student Congress Movement, 1940; The Monroe Doctrine and the Growth of Western Hemisphere Solidarity, 1941; Voice Science, 1942, rev. edit., 1965; The Judson Guides to Latin America, including: Let's Go to Colombia, 1949, Let's Go to Guatemala, 1950, Let's Go to Peru, 1951, Your Holiday in Cuba, 1952; Report of Command Information Bureau 47 on Operation Inland Seas, 1959; The Interview, 1966; The Business Conference, 1969; Vincent Judson: The Island Series, 1973; Solution: PNC and PNCLAND, 1973; The AQUA Declaration, 1976. Address: PO Box 277 Rochester MN 55903-0277

JUDY, BERNARD FRANCIS, newspaper editor; b. Grove City, Pa., Mar. 20, 1920; s. Francis Xavier and Catherine Veronica (Toomey) J.; B.S. in Commerce, Grove City Coll., 1941; A.B. in Econs., Washington and Lee U., 1947; M.S. in Journalism, Columbia U., 1948; m. Jane Elizabeth Urey, Apr. 3, 1945; children—Kathleen, Cynthia, Jill, Mark. Reporter, Toledo (Ohio) Blade, 1948-60, asso. editor, 1960-73, editor, 1973—; dir. Toledo Blade Co. Served with USAAF, 1942-44, U.S. Army, 1944-45. Mem. Phi Beta Kappa, Sigma Delta Chi. Roman Catholic. Club: Toledo Press. Home: 3405 Kenwood Blvd Toledo OH 43606 Office: Toledo Blade 541 Superiro St Toledo OH 43660

JUERGENS, JOHN LOUIS, internist; b. Belle Plaine, Minn., Mar. 29, 1925; s. Herman M. and Leona E. J.; student U. Louisville, U. Minn., 1945-47; M.D., Harvard U., 1949; postgrad. U. Minn., 1953-56; m. Kristy Olsen, Sept. 2, 1948; children—Carol, Anne, Kristy, Laura. Practice medicine, Belle Plaine, 1952-53; fellow Mayo Found., Rochester, Minn., 1953-56; cons. internal medicine sect. cardiovascular diseases Mayo Clinic and Mayo Found., Rochester, 1956—; mem. Expert Adv. Panel on Cardiovascular Drugs. Served with USNR, 1950-52. Fellow Council Arteriosclerosis, Council Circulation, ACP; mem. Minn. Soc. Internal Medicine, Minn. Heart Assn., Am. Heart Assn., Sigma Xi. Author: (with J.A. Spittell and J.F. Fairbairn) Peripheral Vascular Diseases, 1980; editor Mayo Clinic Procs., 1977-81. Office: 200 1st St SW Rochester MN 55905*

JUERGENSMEYER, ELIZABETH BOGART (MRS. JOHN ELI JUERGENSMEYER), biologist; b. Columbia, Mo., May 28, 1940; d. Ralph and Frances (Warbritton) Bogart; B.S., Oreg. State U., 1962; M.S. (NSF fellow), U. Ill., 1964, Ph.D., 1967; m. John Eli Juergensmeyer, Sept. 10, 1963; children—Margaret Ann, Frances Elizabeth. Teaching and research asst. U. Ill., Chgo. Circle, 1965-68; asst. prof. biology William Rainey Harper Coll., Palatine, Ill., 1968-69; asso. prof. biology Judson Coll., Elgin, Ill., 1969-79, prof., 1979—. Mem. citizens adv. bd. U46 Sch. Dist.; lay leader, mem. adminstrv. bd. Wesley Methodist Ch., Elgin; mem. Commn. on Higher Edn. and Campus Ministry, No. Ill. conf. United Meth. Ch. Mem. AAAS, Am. Soc. Zoologists, Genetics Soc., Am. Soc. Protozoologists, Am. Inst. Biol. Sci., N.Y. Acad. Sci. Home: 401 Hazel Dr Elgin IL 60120

JUGENHEIMER, DONALD WAYNE, journalist; b. Manhattan, Kans., Sept. 22, 1943; s. Robert William and Mabel Clara (Hobert) J.; B.S., U. Ill., 1965, M.S., 1968, Ph.D. in Communications, 1972; m. Bonnie Jeanne Scamehorn, Aug. 30, 1970; 1 dau., Beth Carrie. Instr. advt. U. Ill., 1967-71; mem. faculty William Allen White Sch. Journalism, U. Kans., 1971—, prof., 1980—, chmn. advt. sequence, 1974-78, dir. grad. studies and research, 1978—; cons. advt., public relations, communications and research. Served with USAF, 1962-68. Finalist sr. class teaching award U. Kans., 1977, 78, teaching award, 1971-72; recipient numerous research grants and awards. Mem. Am. Acad. Advt. (treas.), AAUP, Assn. Edn. in Journalism (head advt. div.). Author: Basic Advertising, 1979; Advertising Media, 1980; Strategic Advertising Decisions, 1976; Advertising Media Sourcebook, 1975, 81; Problems and Practices in Advertising Research, 1981; contbr. numerous articles and revs. to profl. jours. Home: 1200 Lawrence Ave Lawrence KS 66044 Office: Flint Hall U Kans Lawrence KS 66045

JUGENHEIMER, ROBERT WILLIAM, educator; b. Scott County, Iowa, Nov. 6, 1904; s. William and Frances (Linder) J.; B.S., Iowa State U., 1934, M.S., 1936 Ph.D., 1940; m. Mabel Hobert, June 17, 1933; children—Robert William, Donald Wayne. Agt., U.S. Dept. Agr., Ames, Iowa, 1928-38, asso. agronomist, Manhattan, Kans., 1938-44; research dir. Pfister Associated Growers, El Paso, Ill., 1944-45; prof. plant genetics U. Ill., Urbana, 1945-72, asst. dean, asst. dir. and coordinator internat. programs, 1959-62, dir. overseas projects, 1962-68, dir. overseas projects and spl. programs, 1970-72, prof. emeritus, dir., 1972—; research adminstrn. adv. Pant U., India, 1968-70; cons. in field. Recipient Curtiss Medal for scholarship Iowa State U., 1927, Disting. Achievement citation, 1978. Fellow Am. Soc. Agronomy, AAAS; mem. Sigma Xi, Gamma Sigma Delta, Alpha Zeta. Republican. Presbyterian. Contbr. numerous articles to profl. jours. Author: Corn: Improvement, Seed Production and Uses, 1976. Office: S12 Turner Hall U Ill Urbana IL 61801

JULIAN, ROBERT LYNN, chemist; b. Wyandotte, Mich., Mar. 10, 1950; s. James Marvin and Gertrude Elanor (Smith) J.; B.A., Kalamazoo Coll., 1972; Ph.D., U. Wis., Madison, 1976; m. Maryanne Sammons, Aug. 4, 1973. Lab. technician Monsanto Co., Trenton, Mich., 1969; asst. plant mgr. Hardy Salt Co., Salt Lake City, 1970; sr. applications chemist Nicolet Instrument Co., Madison, Wis., 1976-78, Fourier transform infrared product mgr., 1979—. Mem. Madison Civic Repertory, Madison Theatre Guild. Recipient Lemeul Smith award Kalamazoo Coll., 1972. Mem. Am. Chem. Soc., Soc. Applied Spectroscopy, Sigma Xi. Democrat. Methodist. Contbr. articles to profl. jours.; editor FT-IR Spectral Lines, 1979. Home: 4938 Raymond Rd Madison WI 53711 Office: 5225 Verona Rd Madison WI 53711

JUMP, TERESA LAYNE, educator; b. Muncie, Ind., Apr. 7, 1952; d. William Lee and Betty Jenette (Licht) J.; B.S. in Early Childhood Edn., Ball State U., 1974; M.S. in Elem.-Early Childhood Edn., Ind. U., Indpls., 1978; postgrad. in edn. Ind. U., Bloomington, 1979—; m. Michael Lee Coppes, Sept. 23, 1979. Tchr. elem. sch., basketball coach jr. high sch. Indpls. Public Schs., 1974-79; asso. instr. Ind. U., Bloomington, 1979—, supr. student tchrs., Navajo Indian Reservation, 1979-80, Indpls., 1980—; pvt. early childhood cons. to Head Start, day care centers, parent edn. groups; grad. cons. Ind. U. Sch. Edn. Commn. on Women. Mem. Nat. Assn. Educators of Young Children, Assn. Supervision and Curriculum Devel., Nat. Council Family Relations, NOW, Phi Delta Kappa, Pi Lambda Theta. Democrat. Methodist. Office: Ind U Sch Edn 323 Bloomington IN 47401

JUNAID, RAJA MUHAMMAD, psychiatrist, educator; b. Gujranwala, Pakistan, July 2, 1939; s. Raja Asgharali and Fatima (Bibi) Khan; came to U.S., 1964; M.D., King Edward Med. Coll., U. Punjab (Pakistan), 1963; m. Susan Mary Nejdl, Dec. 30, 1974; children—Jeffrey, Jon, Sara, Adam. House surgeon, physician Mayo Hosp., Lahore, Pakistan, 1963-64; intern Glens Falls (N.Y.) Hosp., 1965; resident psychiatry Fairfield Hills Hosp., Newtown, Conn., 1966-68; fellow psychiatry and neurology Yale Med. Sch., 1967-68; psychiatrist Mental Health Inst., Independence, Iowa, 1968-69, asst. chief adult psychiatry, 1969-73, dir. profl. edn. and research, 1973-77; dir. psychiatry div. Black Hawk Area Family Practice Residency Program, Waterloo, Iowa; pvt. practice psychiatry, Waterloo, 1976—; mem. staff Allen and St. Francis hosps., Waterloo. Clin. instr. U. Iowa, Iowa City, 1973—. Diplomate Am. Bd. Psychiatry and Neurology. Mem. Am. Psychiat. Assn., AMA, Iowa Psychiat. Soc., Iowa Med. Soc., Black Hawk County Med. Soc., Am. Assn. Dirs. Psychiat. Residency Tng., Pakistan Med. Assn. Club: Rotary. Home: 922 Sheridan Rd Waterloo IA 50701 Office: 610 First Nat Bldg Waterloo IA 50703

JUNGHANS, RICHARD PAUL, bldg. co. exec.; b. Fort Atkinson, Wis., Sept. 11, 1925; s. Paul, Jr. and Rosina V. (Billings) J.; B.S. in Econs., U. Wis., 1950; m. Eleanor R. Archer, June 9, 1956; children—Richard Paul, Brian V., Steven A. Sales engr., Highway Trailer Co., Edgerton, Wis., 1950-52; branch mgr., Trailmobile, Inc., Cin., 1952-55, Freuhauf Trailer Co., Terre Haute, Ind., 1955-56; personnel dir., U.O. Colson Co., Paris, Ill., 1957-59; owner, mgr., The Building Specialties Co., Paris, 1959—. Served in U.S. Army, 1942-46. Mem., Am. Inst. Kitchen Dealers (pres. chpt. 1974-75, OutstandinService award, 1975-76), Council Certified Kitchen Designers, Nat. Assn. Home Builders. Clubs: Kiwanis (pres. 1975-76, lt. gov. 1977-78, recipient Disting. Lt. Gov. award 1978, Internat. Excellence award 1979) (Paris), Masons, Shriners. Home: Rural Route 1 Tucker Beach Rd Paris IL 61944 Office: PO Box 505 Paris IL 61944

JUNK, PAUL EDWIN, univ. provost; b. Plymouth, Ill., July 9, 1929; s. A. Lee and Grace L. Junk; B.A., Blackburn Coll., Carlinville, Ill., 1951; M.A. (Henrietta Hermans fellow 1953-54), Washington U., St. Louis, 1954; Ph.D., Northwestern U., 1962; m. Mary E. Boring, June 13, 1953; children—David, Robert, Scott, Denise. Research asst. Northwestern U., 1954-56; economist Fed. Res. Bank Chgo., 1957-58; mem. faculty U. Mo., Columbia, 1958-73, prof. econs., 1965-73, chmn. dept., 1970-72; prof. econs., dean Sch. of Bus., Washburn U., Topeka, 1973-79; vice provost acad. adminstrn. U. Minn., Duluth, 1979—; cons. in field. Served as officer AUS, 1951-53; Korea. Decorated Commendation medal. Mem. Am. Econ. Assn., Am. Fin. Assn., Midwest Econ. Assn. (1st v.p. 1977), Mo. Valley Econ. Assn. (pres. 1976), Omicron Delta Epsilon. Editor: Selected Articles by Harry Gunnison Brown, The Case for Land Value Taxation, 1981. Contbr. articles to profl. jours. Home: 424 Aspen Ln Duluth MN 55804 Office: U Minn Duluth MN 55812

JUNK, SHALON JEAN, personnel adminstr.; b. Fort Wayne, Ind., Sept. 27, 1945; d. Edwin C. and Jean Opal Ezzelle; m. Richard Ellis Junk, Aug. 22, 1964; children—Richard Edwin, Scott Michael. Sec., Gen. Telephone Co., 1966-72; with Super Market Service, Fort Wayne, Ind., 1974—, personnel mgr., 1975-76, human resource mgr., 1976—. Mem. Am. Soc. Personnel Adminstrn., Ind. Personnel Assn., Ft. Wayne Personnel Assn. (v.p.), Delta Sigma Kappa. Baptist. Home: 2109 Kentucky Ave Fort Wayne IN 46805

JUNKINS, LOWELL LEE, state senator, constrn. co. exec.; b. Ft. Madison, Iowa, Mar. 9, 1944; s. Ralph Renaud and Selma J. (Kudeheh) J.; student Iowa State U., 1962-63; m. Linda Lee Decker, 1963; children—Kristina Lynne, Kara Dyann. Vice pres., treas. Golden Acres, Inc.; partner Junkins, Hunold, Junkins Constrn. Co.; v.p. Lee County Ambulance Service, Inc., 1967—; mem. Iowa Senate, 1973—. Councilman, Montrose, Iowa, 1969-70, mayor, 1972-73; chmn. Montrose Planning and Zoning Commn., 1970-71; Democratic committeeman, Iowa, 1970—; chmn. North Lee County Areawide Health Planning Council, 1971-72; vice chmn. Lee County Dem. Com., 1971-72. Presbyterian (elder). Clubs: Eagles, Lions (1st v.p. Montrose), Masons. Office: State Senate State Capitol Des Moines IA 50319*

JUNTUNE, JOYCE ELAINE, assn. exec.; b. Carlton, Minn., Jan. 13, 1944; d. John Harold and Berniece Catherine (Finifrock) Bergstrom; B.A., Bethel Coll., St. Paul, 1966; M.S., St. Cloud (Minn.) State U., 1978; cert. in creative studies SUNY at Buffalo, 1981; m. Daniel Leonard Juntune, June 11, 1966. Elementary classroom tchr., Minn. and Calif., 1966-74; dir. Project REACH Minn., 1974-80; ednl. cons., 1974—; exec. dir. Nat. Assn. Gifted Children, St. Paul, 1979—; tchr. grad. courses Coll. St. Thomas, St. Paul, Bemidji (Minn.) State U., Bethel Coll.; speaker in field. Recipient Outstanding Alumni award Bethel Coll., 1981, Colleague award Creative Edn. Found., Buffalo, 1981. Mem. NEA, Nat. Assn. Gifted Children, Creative Edn. Found., Assn. Gifted, Council Exceptional Children, Assn. Supervision and Curriculum Devel., Nat. Soc. Study Edn., Minn. Council Gifted and Talented (pres. 1979; recognition cert. 1981), Minn. Edn. Assn., Alpha Delta Kappa. Republican. Baptist. Author, editor in field. Office: 2070 County Rd H St Paul MN 55112

JUNTUNEN, MICHAEL EDWARD, acct.; b. Grand Forks, N.D., Oct. 29, 1951; s. Robert Lee and Helen A. (Haberstroh) J.; B.S. in Acctg., U. N.D., 1975, postgrad. Law Sch., 1980-81; m. Karen Adelle Lund, June 26, 1971; children—Michelle, Bryan, Erika. Product packaging operator Pillsbury Co., Grand Forks, 1972-75; sr. acct. Schauer, Bartholomay & Fuchs, Ltd., Jamestown, N.D., 1975-78, officer and shareholder, 1979—; dir. U. N.D. Vol. Income Tax Assistance Program, 1980-81. Coach youth hockey Jamestown Park Bd., 1976-79; coach jr. varsity Jamestown High Sch., 1978-79; head ofcl. Jamestown Hockey Hockey Ofcls., 1977-79. C.P.A., N.D. Mem. Am. Inst. C.P.A.'s (regional rep. to nat. legis. com. 1980-81), N.D. Soc. C.P.A.'s, N.D. Assn. Hockey Ofcls., Mcpl. Fin. Officers Assn., Nat. Assn. Life Underwriters, Jamestown Jaycees. Lutheran. Club: Jamestown Optimist. Home: 404 State St Grand Forks ND 58201 Office: 406 1st Ave N Jamestown ND 58401

JUREK, BERNARD JAMES, JR., mech. engr.; b. St. Cloud, Minn., Aug. 19, 1925; s. Ben Joseph and Naomi Louisa (Latteral) J.; B.S.M.E., U. Minn., 1946; m. Eileen Mary Dahl, Feb. 25, 1946; children—Thomas Jon, William Robert, Cherilyn Sue, Connie Louise. With Chevrolet div. Gen. Motors Co., various locations, 1949—, plant mgr., Bay City, Mich., 1967-72, Detroit, 1972-77, mgr. Chevrolet mfg. research and devel., 1977—. Served with USN, 1943-46. Mem. Hamtramck C. of C. (dir.), Soc. Automotive Engrs. Republican. Baptist. Clubs: Masons, Shriners, Huron River Hunting and Fishing. Home: 35675 Congress Rd Farmington Hills MI 48018 Office: 30007 Van Dyke St Warren MI 48090

JURGENSEN, GEORGENE FAY, newspaper advt. exec.; b. Sheldon, Iowa, Apr. 4, 1948; d. George Eugene and Marian Evangeline (Syverson) Dunn; student Mt. Marty Coll., 1970; m. Russell Vernon Jurgensen, June 4, 1965; children—Trevor Mark, Tara Michelle. With Yankton (S.D.) Press and Dakotan, 1970—, advt. dir., 1978—. Mem. Am. Soc. Profl. and Exec. Women, Yankton C. of C., Yankton Hist. Preservation Soc. Republican. Methodist. Clubs: Yankton Women's, Hillcrest Country. Home: 303 Golf Ln Yankton SD 57078 Office: 319 Walnut Yankton SD 57078

JURICH, ANTHONY PETER, educator; b. Mineola, N.Y., July 9, 1947; s. Peter Paul and Clara Mary (Kaftanski) J.; B.S., Fordham U., 1969; M.S., Pa. State U., 1971, Ph.D., 1972. Instr. family and child devel. Pa. State U., 1970-72; asst. prof. family and child devel. Kans. State U., 1972-76, asso. prof., 1976—; supr. dirs. Manhattan (Kans.) Teen Outreach; sec. Manhattan Youth Care. Recipient Kans. State Outstanding Tchr. award, 1976.; cert. marriage and family therapist, sex therapist. Mem. Am. Assn. Marriage and Family Therapists, Kans. Assn. Marriage and Family Therapists, Am. Assn. Sex Educators, Counselors and Therapists, Nat. Council on Family Realtions, Am. Psychol. Assn., Am. Sociol. Assn. Contbr. articles to profl. jours. Home: 1428 McCain Ln Apt 338 Manhattan KS 66502 Office: Dept Family and Child Development Kans State U Manhattan KS 66506

JURKOWITZ, CAROLYN MARY ANN, sch. adminstr.; b. Medford, Mass., Nov. 28, 1950; d. Andrew Francis and Norma Elvira (Scalingi) De Gregory; B.A., U. Akron, 1971; M.A., St. Louis U., 1974; Ph.D., Case Western Res. U., 1978; m. Paul M. Jurkowitz, Dec. 29, 1972; 1 son, Joseph Andrew. Tchr., Burnswick (Ohio) City Schs., 1971-72, St. Joseph Acad., St. Louis, 1972-73, Rosary High Sch., St. Louis, 1973-74; co-adminstr. St. Benedict Acad., Erie, Pa., 1974-79; secondary and elem. sch. coordinator Diocese of Columbus (Ohio), 1979-80, asst. supt. schs., 1980—; lectr. Case Western Res. U., 1978-79. Mem. Chief Adminstrs. Catholic Edn. Contbg. editor Pvt. Sch. Monitor, 1980—. Home: Route 2 2318 MC Rd 194 Fredericktown OH 43019 Office: 197 E Gay St Columbus OH 43215

JUSTESEN, DON ROBERT, exptl. psychologist, educator; b. Salt Lake City, Mar. 8, 1930; s. Richard C. and Elizabeth A. (Gustafson) J.; B.A., U. Utah, 1955, M.A., 1957, Ph.D. with distinction, 1960; m. Patricia Ann Larson, Feb. 14, 1957; children—Lyle Richard J., Jonille Jacelyn, Tracy Ann, Anthony Ray. Asst. prof., head dept. psychology Westminster Coll., Salt Lake City, 1959-62; lectr. dept. psychology U. Mo., Kansas City, 1963-66, asso. prof., 1966-68, prof., 1968-75; vis. prof. psychology U. Colo., 1965; asst. prof. psychiatry U. Kans. Sch. of Medicine, Kansas City, 1963-66, asso. prof., 1966-71, prof., 1971—, mem. grad. faculty, 1964—; dir. neuropsychology and behavioral radiology labs., VA Med. Center, Kansas City, Mo., 1962—; cons. to NASA, 1969-72; mem. adv. panel on microwave radiation in relation to satellite power systems, NASA/EPA, 1978-80; mem. ad hoc adv. com. on non-ionizing radiation Office of Sci. and Tech. Policy, Exec. Office of the President, 1978-79. Elected Prof. of the Year, Westminster Coll., 1961; recipient Career Research Scientist award U.S. VA, 1980. Fellow Am. Psychol. Assn., AAAS; mem. IEEE (chmn. com. on man and radiation 1977-80), Internat. Microwave Power Inst. (bd. govs. 1977-81), Fedn. of Am. Scientists, Psychonomic Soc., Bioelectromagnetics Soc., Soc. for Neuroscis., Nat. Acad. Scis. (URSI commn. on metrology; del. to 19th gen. assembly of Internat. Union Radio Sci. 1978), Brit. Soc. for Philosophy of Sci. Contbr. articles on biol. effects of microwave radiation to sci. jours.; asso. editor Jour. of Microwave Power, 1975—; editorial bd. Bioelectromagnetics, 1979—. Home: 12416 Ewing Circle Grandview MO 64030 Office: 4801 Linwood Blvd Kansas City MO 64128

JUSTIS, ROBERT TRACY, educator; b. Aurora, Colo., Apr. 6, 1944; s. Guy Reynolds and Ardis Caroline (Larson) J.; B.A., Brigham Young U., 1967, M.B.A., 1969; D.B.A., Ind. U., 1972; m. Susan Rae Zimmerman, May 29, 1969; children—Jill Frances, Jeri Ann. Mem. faculty dept. bus. adminstrn. Tex. Tech. U., Lubbock, 1972-77; mem. faculty Coll. Bus. Adminstrn., U. Nebr., Lincoln, 1977—, asso. prof. mgmt. and dentistry, 1977—, dir. Small Bus. Center, 1977—. Bd. dirs. Jr. Achievement. Mem. Acad. Mgmt., Am. Psychol. Assn., Small Bus. Inst. Dirs. Assn., Internat. Council Small Bus., Midwest Acad. Mgmt. Mormon. Club: Rotary. Author: Managing Your Small Business, 1981; Dynamics of American Business, 1982; editor, Am. Jour. Small Bus., 1980—. Home: 2501 Winchester North Lincoln NE 68512 Office: Coll Bus Adminstrn U Nebr Lincoln NE 68588

KAATZ, HERBERT WILHELM GOTTFRIED, aviation mfg. co. exec.; b. Cleve., Apr. 25, 1920; s. Herbert R. and Pauline (Dregalla) K.; A.B., Oberlin Coll., 1958; m. Mildred N. Fischer, May 3, 1941; children—William H., Lynn R., Donald W. Owner, Photo Shop, Elyria, Ohio, 1939-41; project engr. Romec Pump Co., Elyria, 1941-45; pres. Kenco Products Inc., Lorain, Ohio, 1946-55; pres. Airborne Mfg. Co., Elyria, 1958-80, also dir.; pres. Universal Hydraulics, Inc., Willoughby, Ohio, Tronco Inc., North Ridgeville, Ohio, Tronair, Inc., Toledo; chmn. bd. E-S Pacific Corp., San Bruno, Calif.; dir. E-S Pacific Devel. & Constrn. Co., Hamilton, Bermuda. Founder Lake Ridge Acad., North Ridgeville, Ohio, 1963, pres., 1964-65, trustee, 1963—. Served with USN, 1945-46. Mem. Am. Phys. Soc., Cleve. Engring. Soc., Gen. Aviation Mfrs. Assn. (dir.), Black River Astron. Soc., Am. Orchid Soc. Lutheran. Clubs: Elyria Country; Beaver Creek Hunt. Patentee in field. Home: 878 Chamberlain Rd Grafton OH 44044 Office: 711 Taylor St Elyria OH 44035

KABINS, LAURENCE J., elec. appliance co. exec.; b. Chgo., Mar. 23, 1927; s. Max and Lillian (Hornung) K.; B.S., U. Ill., 1949; M.B.A., Northwestern U., 1951; m. Joan Phyllis Robinson, June 3, 1950; children—Jeffrey Scott, Susan Lorel, Melissa Beth. Copywriter, Sherman & Marquette Advt. Agy., Chgo., 1949-50; advt. mgr. Ill. Upholsterer's Supply, Chgo., 1950-51, Cumming-Chgo., 1951-54, Cummings Portable Tool Div. John Oster Mfg. Co., Milw., 1954-60; dir. advt. sales promotion and public relations Oster Corp., 1960-77; v.p., advt. dir. Sunbeam Corp., Oak Brook, Ill., 1977—; tchr. advt. budgeting Am. Mgmt. Assn., 1967. Mem. Wis. Gov.'s Communications Task Force, 1966-68; mem. public relations adv. council Marquette U., 1972—. Served to 1st lt. USAAF, 1944-46. Mem. Public Relations Soc. Am., Tau Epsilon Phi (pres. 1945). Clubs: Advt., Press (Milw.). Home: 7266 N Pierron Rd Glendale WI 53209 Office: 2001 S York Rd Oak Brook IL 60521

KACHIK, DAVID JOSEPH, mining engr., geologist; b. Bellefonte, Pa., Jan. 1, 1922; s. Andrew Joseph and Ella (De Brasky) K.; B.S. in Mining Engring., Pa. State U., 1943, M.S. in Mining and Geology, 1949; m. Rosemarie Teresa Bula, Sept. 5, 1961; 1 son, Timothy A. Instr., research asst. in mining engring. Pa. State U., 1946-49; jr. engr., geologist Paul Weir Co., Chgo., 1949-60, sr. engr., geologist, 1960-66, v.p., 1966—. Served with USNR, 1943-46. Mem. Am. Inst. Mining, Metall. and Petroleum Engrs., Ill. Mining Inst., Coal Mining Inst. Am., Sigma Gamma Epsilon. Republican. Roman Catholic. Club: Tower (Chgo.). Contbr. articles to tech. jours. Home: 648 N Inverway Inverness Palatine IL 60067 Office: Paul Weir Co Room 2828 20 N Wacker Dr Chicago IL 60606

KACHRU, BRAJ BEHARI, linguist, educator; b. Srinagar, Kashmir, India, May 15, 1932; s. Shyam Lal and Shobhavati Tulsidevi (Tutu) K.; came to U.S., 1963, naturalized, 1969; B.A. with honors, U. Kashmir, India, 1952; M.A., U. Allahabad, India, 1955; diploma applied linguistics U. Edinburgh, Scotland, 1959, Ph.D. (Brit. Council fellow), 1961; m. Yamuna Keskar, Jan. 22, 1965; children—Amita, Shamit. Research fellow Deccan Coll. Research Inst., Poona, India, 1957-58; asst. prof. Lucknow U., India, 1962-63; research asso. U. Ill., Urbana, 1963-64, mem. faculty, 1964—, prof. linguistics, 1970—, head of dept., 1969-79, coordinator div. applied linguistics, 1976—; dir. summer program in S. Asian studies, 1967; chmn. regional varieties of English com. Assn. Commonwealth Lit. and Lang., Brisbane, Australia, 1968; mem. lang. com., cons. Am. Inst. Indian Studies, 1971—; cons. Ford Found., 1974-75; mem. lang. and lit. com. S. Asian Regional Council, 1977-78; chmn. Internat. Com. on S.Asian Langs. and Linguistics, 1980—. Research fellow Am. Inst. Indian Studies, 1967-68, 70-71, 81, trustee, 1980—; research fellow Center Advanced Study U. Ill., 1971-72, 79-80. Mem. Linguistic Soc. Am. (dir. Linguistic Inst. 1978), Linguistic Soc. India, Am. Oriental Soc., Linguistic Assn. Can. and U.S., Assn. Tchrs. of English to Speakers of Other Langs. Author: A Reference Grammar of Kashmiri, 1966; An Introduction to Spoken Kashmiri, 1973; Studies in Language Learning, 1978; Kashmiri Literature, 1981; The Indianization of English: The English Language in India, 1982; editor: Dimensions of Bilingualism: Theory and Case Studies, 1976; Aspects of Sociolinguistics in South Asia, 1978; The Other Tongue: English Across Cultures, 1982; editor Lang. and Devel.: An Internat. Perspective, 1980—; editorial bd. Papers in Linguistics, 1969—, Studies in the Linguistic Scis., 1970—, Internat. Jour. Sociology of Lang., 1978—, Studies in Lang. Learning, 1978, Jour. S. Asian Lits., 1980—; editorial adv. English World-Wide: A Jour. of Varieties of English, 1980—; Jour. Applied Lang. Study, 1981—; World Lang. English, 1981—; editorial dir. Ann. Rev. Applied Linguistics, 1980—. Home: 2016 Cureton Dr Urbana IL 61801 Office: Dept Linguistics U Ill Urbana IL 61801

KACMARCIK, THOMAS, mfg. co. exec.; b. Ironwood, Mich., Sept. 28, 1925; s. Mathew T. and Mary (Murra) K.; E.E., U. Ga., 1944; m. Josephine Tody, June 19, 1948; children—Sharon, Karen, Thomas, Shirley, James. Pres. F.W. Busch Co., Grafton. Wis., 1960-68; treas., dir. Cargo Ties Co., Cedarburg, Wis., 1968—; pres., dir. Milsted Products Co., Cedarburg, 1964—, Ataco Steel Products Co., Grafton, 1964—; pres. Continental Mfg. Co., Kapco Inc. (both Grafton); v.p. prodn. Stamping Corp., Milw.; dir. Snow Mobile Accessories, Inc. Mem. adv. com. Cedarsburg Sch., 1968—. Served as pilot USNR, 1943-48. Mem. Personal Mgmt. Assn. Lion (pres. 1969), Kiwanian (dir.). Home: 9413 Western Ave Cedarburg WI 53012 Office: 1046 Hickory St Grafton WI 53024

KADER, AMIN, educator; b. Egypt, Sept. 24, 1938; came to U.S., naturalized, 1974; s. Mohamed and Naima (Elgindy) K.; B.A., U. Cairo, 1960; M.B.A., U. Mich., 1966; postgrad. U. S.C., 1972-73; m. Khairat Elsedawy, Nov. 24, 1966; children—Khalid, Dina. Instr., U. Cairo, 1960-63; asst. prof. Tenn. State U., 1968-69; asso. prof. S.C. State Coll., 1969-71; cost acct. Xerox Corp.; asso. prof. bus. adminstrn. Augsburg Coll., Mpls., 1974—; cons. S.C. Nursing Homes, internat. mktg.; vis. prof. U. S.C. Mem. Am. Acctg. Assn., Nat. Assn. Accts. Democrat. Home: 8101 Ewing Ave N Minneapolis MN 55443 Office: Augusburg College Minneapolis MN 55414

KADERABEK, DALE EDWARD, educator; b. Cresco, Iowa, Feb. 16, 1941; s. Edward Joseph and Louise Marie (Gilbert) K.; m. Jeanie Ann Byrnes, Sept. 4, 1965; children—Kimberley, Kris. On-air personality radio sta. KAUS, Austin, Minn., 1965-68; advt. and mktg. officer Northwestern State Bank, Austin, 1968-73; account exec., on-air personality Sta. KAAL-TV, Austin, 1973-75; mgr. Northland Piano & Organ, Austin, 1975-77, Lord's Diamond Center, Austin, 1977-79; sales mgr. Charles F. Fox Co., Austin, 1979-80; instr. small bus. mgmt. and profl. sales Austin Vocat. Inst., 1980—; cons. Past exec. dir. Miss Minn. Pageant; past nat. bd. dirs. Miss Am. Pageant. Served with USAF, 1959-63. Mem. Austin Area C. of C. (chmn. Ambassadors). Roman Catholic. Home: 1104 9th St NW Austin MN 55912

KADLUBOWSKI, MICHAEL GEORGE, business exec.; b. Reno, Feb. 17, 1945; s. Stanley Laurance and Constance Sadie (Colby) K.; B.A. in Accounting with honors, North Eastern Ill. U., Chgo., 1978; children—Michelle Leigh, Jeffrey Kurtis. Chief accountant Pyle Nat. Corp., Chgo., 1969-72; corp. controller Doncor, Inc., Chgo., 1972-73; controller Emconite div., Chgo., 1973-77; corp. controller, chief fin. officer, v.p. Bearcat Tire Co., 1977-81; v.p. ops. and adminstrn. Singer SVE Corp., Chgo., 1981—. Served with USN, 1965-69. Mem. Am. Accounting Assn., Am. Mgmt. Assn., Shellback Fraternity, Beta Alpha Psi. Home: 2210 S Grace St Apt 406 Lombard IL 60148 Office: 1345 W Diversey Pkwy Chicago IL 60614

KADOW, RUTH ELEANORE, ednl. adminstr.; b. Cleve., Apr. 14, 1921; d. Walter Jacob and Clara Leona (Kobabe) K.; B.S., Kent State U., 1948, M.A., 1957, Ed.S., 1974; postgrad. U. Ariz., Tucson, 1959-70. Tchr., Marion (Ohio) Harding High Sch., 1948-50, Maple Heights (Ohio) High Sch., 1950-51; Medina (Ohio) High Sch., 1951-55, Parma (Ohio) Public Schs., Pleasant Valley Jr. High Sch., Valley Forge Sr. High Sch., 1956-66; asso. prof. Lorain County Community Coll., Elyria, Ohio, 1966-75; ednl. adminstrv. specialist Padua High Sch., Parma, Ohio, 1981—. Mem. NEA (life), Nat. Ret. Tchrs. Assn., Assn. Supervision and Curriculum Devel., Assn. Ednl. Communications Tech., Ohio Ret. Tchrs. Assn. (life). Office: 6740 State Rd Parma OH 44134

KADRMAS, EDWIN E., publishing co. exec.; b. Dickinson, N.D., Feb. 18, 1934; s. William J. and Emilie A. Kadrmas; B.S., N.D. State U., 1956; postgrad. Mont. State U.; m. Melda Pfenning, Aug. 16, 1955; children—Ronald L., Robert R., Russell W., Roger J. Instr. bus. Rosebud (Mont.) High Sch., 1956-58, Dawson County (Mont.) High Sch., 1958-59, Dawson County Jr. Coll., Glendive, Mont., 1958-59; coll. and gen. rep. South-Western Pub. Co., 1959-67, asst. regional mgr., West Chicago, Ill., 1967-78, regional v.p., 1979—. Chmn., West Chicago Crusade of Mercy, 1974-75; pres. United Way of West Chicago, 1975-77; pres. Suburban Mgmt. Assn., 1974, top mgmt. adv. com., 1975—; div. pres. Internat. Mgmt. Council, 1974-76. Cert. profl. mgr. Mem. Ill. State C. of C., Ill. Bus. Edn. Assn., Am. Vocat. Assn., Nat. Bus. Edn. Assn., Chgo. Bus. Edn. Assn. Republican. Club: Rotary (gov.'s rep. 1977-80, dist. gov. 1981-82). Home: 25 W 360 Plamondon Wheaton IL 60187 Office: 355 Conde St West Chicago IL 60185

KAEDING, WILLIAM FREDERICK, educator; b. Benton Harbor, Mich., Feb. 28, 1949; s. Arthur Frederick and Adeline Marie (Zilke) K.; B.S., Ferris State Coll., 1971; M.A. in Bus., Western Mich. U., 1975; m. Janice Mae Winn, July 3, 1971; children—William A., Robert J. Tchr. bus. edn. Benton Harbor High Sch., 1972—, chmn. dept., 1976—; adult edn. tchr. Benton Harbor Area Schs., 1972—, also cons. for Title IV Planning Center. Mem. Mich. Bus. Edn. Assn., NEA, Mich. Edn. Assn., Bus. and Office Edn. Club Mich., Delta Pi Epsilon. Lutheran. Office: Benton Harbor High School 870 Colfax Ave Benton Harbor MI 49022

KAEGEL, RAY MARTIN, real estate and ins. broker; b. St. Louis, Dec. 7, 1925; s. Ray E. and Loyola (Mooney) K.; B.S. in Secondary Edn., Washington U., St. Louis, 1948, M.B.A., 1955; m. Daniel Marilyn Dugger, July 2, 1943. Mgr., St. Louis Amusement Co., Inc., 1941-43, 46-52; gen. mgr. Md. Real Estate & Ins. Agy., Inc., Granite City, Ill., 1953-60; pres., gen. mgr., dir. Kaegel Real Estate & Ins. Agy., Inc., 1961—; sec. Granite City Bd. Realtors, 1959-63, 66-77, pres., 1964-65, 79-81; sec.-treas. Granite City Multiple Listing Service, 1971—. Served to lt. (j.g.) USNR, 1943-46. Mem. Nat. (exec. officer's council 1959-77), Ill. assns. real estate bds., Tri-Cities Ind. Ins. Assn. Agts. (pres. 1970-73), Ind. Ins. Agts. Ill., Tri-Cities C. of C. Club: Noonday Optimist. Home: 11255 Ladue Rd Saint Louis MO 63141 Office: 2721 Madison Ave Granite City IL 62040

KAERICHER, JOHN CONRAD, artist, educator; b. Springfield, Ill., June 6, 1936; s. John Henry and Edna Ann (Beckett) K.; B.F.A., Millikin U., 1959; M.F.A., U. Iowa, 1963; student under Mauricio Lasansky, Stuart Edie, James Lechay, David Driesbach. Asst. prof. art Northwestern Coll., Orange City, Iowa, 1963-65, asso. prof., 1965—, chmn. art dept., 1963—, dir. art gallery, 1966—, chmn. fine arts collection acquistions, 1964—; lectr., cons. in field; exhibited in several one-man shows including Kirkland Fine Arts Center, Millikin U., 1972, Sioux City Art Center; numerous group shows including Central Ill. Ann. Show, Decatur, 1961, Sioux City Ann. Show, 1965, Iowa Gov.'s Office, Des Moines, 1971, Kottler Galleries, N.Y.C., 1973, Paper works, Waterloo (Iowa) Ann. Shows, 1975, Benjamin Galleries, Chgo., 1976, Va. Poly. Inst. Invitational Show, 1976; represented in pvt. and pub. collections. Northwestern Coll. grantee, 1966, 69, 75, 77. Mem. Mid-Am. Coll. Art Assns., Iowa Print Group. Mem. Christian Ch. Home: 615 Arizona Ave SW Orange City IA 51041 Office: 720 Delaware Ave SW Orange City IA 51041

KAFARSKI, MITCHELL I., chem. processing co. exec.; b. Detroit, Dec. 15, 1917; s. Ignacy A. and Anastasia (Drzazgowski) K.; student U. Detroit, 1939-41, Shrivenham (Eng.) Am. U., 1946; m. Zofia Drozdowska, July 11, 1967; children—Erik Michael, Konrad Christian. Process engr. Packard Motor Car Co., Detroit, 1941-44; organizer, dir. Artist and Craftsman Sch., Esslingen, Germany, 1945-46; with Nat. Bank of Detroit, 1946-50; founder, pres. Chem. Processing Inc., Detroit, 1950-65, also dir.; chmn. bd., pres., treas. Aactron Inc., Madison Heights, Mich., 1965—; treas. Detroit Magnetic Insp. Co., 1960-65, also dir.; v.p. KMH Inc., Detroit, 1960-64, also dir.; treas. Packard Plating Inc., Detroit, 1962-67, also dir. Commr. Mich. State Fair, 1965-72; mem. com. devel. and planning to build Municipal Stadium, State of Mich., 1965-69; patron, mem. Founders Soc. Detroit Inst. Arts, 1965—, chmn. Art of Poland Galerie, 1981—; sponsor, host world celebrity for World Preview Mich., 1965-66; mem. dist. adv. council SBA, 1971-73; del. White House Conf. on Aging, 1971; White House rep. to opening of first U.S. Trade Center, Warsaw, Poland, 1972; chmn. fund raising Bloomfield Arts Assn., Birmingham, Mich., 1973-74, dir., 1973—; vice chmn. Republican State Nationalities Council Mich., 1969-73; bd. dirs. Pennsylvania Ave. Devel. Corp., Washington, 1973-81; trustee Straight Meml. Hosp., Southfield, Mich., 1971—, chmn. bd., 1977; trustee Detroit Sci. Center, 1972—; bd. dirs. Friends of Kresge Library, Oakland U., 1973—; organizer, treas. Mich. Reagan for Pres. Com., 1980; alt. del. to Rep. Nat. Conv., 1980; mem. Rep. Congl. Leadership Council, Washington, 1980—, Space Theater Consortium, Inc., Seattle, 1981—; bd. regents Orchard Lake (Mich.) Schs., 1981—. Served with AUS, 1944-46; ETO. Decorated knight's cross Order of Poland's Rebirth Polonia Restituta; recipient Nat. award for war prodn. invention War Prodn. Bd., 1943. Mem. Nat., Mich. (dir., pres. 1976) assns. metal finishers, NAM, Am. Electroplaters Soc., Cranbrook Acad. Arts, Am.-Polish Action Council (chmn. 1971-76). Clubs: Otsego Ski; Capitol Hill (Washington); Detroit Athletic; La Coquille (Palm Beach, Fla.); Oakland U. President's. Home: 240 Chesterfield Rd Bloomfield Hills MI 48013 Office: 29306 Stephenson Hwy Madison Heights MI 48071

KAGEY, F(LORENCE) EILEEN, educator; b. Lima, Ohio, July 29, 1925; d. Joseph Leonard and Florence Elizabeth (Niles) K.; B.S. in Edn., Ball State U., 1952; M.S. in Edn., Ind. U., 1955. Sec., Gen. Electric Co., Ft. Wayne, Ind., 1943-45, 48-49, Farnsworth Telephone and Radio Corp., Ft. Wayne, 1945-49; H.A. Jeep prof. Ball State U., 1949-52; elem. tchr. Harmar Sch., Ft. Wayne, 1952-54, Emerson Sch., Gary, Ind., 1954-58, Sch. 52, Indpls., 1959-61, George Kuny Sch., Gary, 1961—; sec. to v.p. Research and Rev. Service of Am., Indpls., 1958-59. Chmn. public relations Calumet Corner chpt. Sweet Adelines, Inc., Munster, Ind., 1980—, bd. dirs., 1981—. Mem. NEA (life), Am. Fedn. Tchrs. (bldg. rep. Local 4 1979—), Ind. State Tchrs. Assn., Assn. Supervision and Curriculum Devel., Ind. Assn. Supervision and Curriculum Devel., AAUW (v.p. charge program chpt.), Kappa Delta Pi. Democrat. Roman Catholic. Author: (juvenile) Jeremy: the People-Dog, 1974. Home: 3040 W 39th Pl Gary IN 46408 Office: 5050 Vermont St Gary IN 46409

KAH, RALPH EDWARD, gynecologist; b. Middletown, Ohio, Apr. 26, 1933; s. Ralph Edward and Zelma May (Sargeant) K.; B.A., M.A., Miami U., 1955; M.D., Ohio State U., 1959, M. Med. Sci., 1964; Ph.D., Calif. Western U., 1979; m. Deeann Haney, July 14, 1962; 1 dau., Kathryn Lee. Intern, Ohio State U. Hosps., Columbus, 1959-60, resident in obstetrics and gynecology, 1960-64; practice medicine specializing in gynecology Gynecologic Cons., Inc., Middletown, Ohio; asst. clin. prof. Wright State U. Served to capt. U.S. Army, 1964-66. Mem. AMA (Physicians Recognition award 1976), Ohio State Med. Assn., Am. Coll. Gynecologists, Am. Fertility Soc., Am. Bd. Ob-Gyn, Am. Assn. Gynecologic Laparoscopists, Gynecologic Urology Soc. Episcopalian. Home: 3209 Milton Rd Middletown OH 45042 Office: 20 S Breiel Blvd Middletown OH 45042

KAHLE, MARTIN F., state legislator; b. Kearney, Nebr., Apr. 6, 1916; ed. public schs.; m. Faye Larson, June 11, 1939; children—Ronald, Alton, Sharilyn Hartman, LaNita Johnson. Farmer-stockman; mem. Nebr. Legislature, 1980—. Supr., Kearney County, 1969-77, also former chmn.; mem. local 1st dist. drainage dist.; mem. Nebr. Environ. Control Council, 1975-76; former mem. Kearney County Zoning Bd., 4-H Council. Mem. Kearney County Livestock Feeders Assn. Lutheran. Address: Rural Route 4 Kearney NE 68847*

KAHLENBECK, HOWARD, JR., lawyer; b. Fort Wayne, Ind., Dec. 7, 1929; s. Howard and Clara Elizabeth (Wegman) K.; B.S. with distinction, Ind. U., 1952; LL.B., U. Mich., 1957; m. Sally A. Horrell, Aug. 14, 1954; children—Kathryn Sue, Douglas H. Admitted to Ind. bar, 1957; partner Krieg, DeVault, Alexander & Capehart, Indpls., 1957—; sec., dir. Maul Tech. Corp. (formerly Buehler Corp.), indsl. equipment mfg., Indpls., 1971—, Am. Monitor Corp., med. equipment mfg., Indpls., 1971—, Am. Interstate Ins. Corp. Wis., Milw., 1973—, Am. Interstate Ins. Co. Ga., 1973—, Am. Underwriters, Inc., ins. holding corp., Indpls., 1973—. Served with USAF, 1952-54. Mem. Am., Ind., Indpls. bar assns., Alpha Kappa Psi, Delta Theta Phi, Beta Gamma Sigma, Delta Upsilon Internat. (dir. 1971—). Lutheran. Home: 6320 Old Orchard Rd Indianapolis IN 46226 Office: 2800 Indiana National Bank Tower Indianapolis IN 46204

KAHLENBERG, JOHN BABOR, marine products mfg. exec.; b. Two Rivers, Wis., Nov. 19, 1915; s. John Ludwig and Pauline (Babor) K.; B.S. in Mech. Engring., Purdue U., 1938; m. Norma Cherney, May 2, 1942; children—Charles J., Peter A. With Kahlenberg Bros. Co., Two Rivers, 1938-40, 45—, pres., chief exec. officer, 1979—. Pres., Manitowoc Tax Payers Assn., 1972. Served to capt. ordnance dept., AUS, 1941-45. Mem. Am. Soc. Naval Engrs., ASCE, Ret. Officers Assn., Purdue U. Alumni Assn. Republican. Presbyterian. Clubs: Sturgeon Bay (Wis.) Yacht, Rotary (chpt. pres. 1978), Elks, Shriners. Home: 1925 30th St PO Box 304 Two Rivers WI 54241 Office: 1700 12th St PO Box 358 Two Rivers WI 54241

KAHLER, VERN ROBERT, packaging co. exec.; b. Grand Rapids, Mich., Feb. 4, 1928; s. Vern Leo and Lucille Mildred (Randall) K.; B.S. with honors, Mich. State U., 1950; m. Norma Louise Baas, Sept. 1, 1950; children—Boyd, Terri, David. Research chemist Sinclair Research Labs., 1950-55; research group leader Packaging Corp. Am., Grand Rapids, Mich., 1956-71, mktg. mgr. corp. mktg., 1973-79, product devel. mgr. paperboard div., 1979—; mktg. mgr. Tenneco Chems., 1971-73. Mem. Carded Packaging Inst. Patentee in field. Home: 4263 Caddo Grandville MI 49418 Office: 470 Market Grand Rapids MI 49502

KAHN, CHARLES HOWARD, architect, educator; b. Birmingham, Ala., Feb. 10, 1926; s. Benjamin Arthur and Dorothy (Goldman) K.; A.B., U. N.C., 1946; B.C.E., N.C. State U., 1948, B.Arch., 1956; M.S., M.I.T., 1949; Fulbright grantee Inst. di Urbanistico, Rome, 1957-58; m. Annette Lee, May 12, 1956; children—Kathryn Lauren, Sarah Elizabeth, Benjamin Arthur. With Robert and Co., architects and engr., Atlanta, 1949-51, Fredrick Snare Corp., N.Y.C., 1951-52, F. Carter Williams, AIA, Raleigh, N.C., 1952-54; propr. Charles Howard Kahn and Assos., architects and engrs., Lawrence, Kans., 1959—; prof., dean U. Kans. Sch. Architecture and Urban Design, Lawrence, 1968-80, prof. architecture, 1980—, dir. Community Devel. Center, 1968—, dir. Environ. Research and Devel. Found., 1968; pres. Design/Planning Assos., Lawrence; mem. Kans. Bldg. Commn., 1978-80; prin. works include Carter Stadium, N.C. State U., 1966, Minges Auditorium, E. Carolina Coll., 1967, Poliedro, Caracas, Venezuela, 1973. Fulbright vis. research scholar Gt. Britain, 1977-78. Mem. AIA, Assn. Collegiate Sch. Architecture, Phi Kappa Phi, Phi Beta Kappa, Sigma Xi, Tau Beta Pi. Democrat. Jewish. Office: Sch Architecture and Urban Design 114 Marvin Hall Lawrence KS 66045

KAHN, JAN EDWARD, metall. engr.; b. Dayton, Ohio, Aug. 29, 1948; s. Sigmond Lawrence and Betty Jane K.; B.S. in Metall. Engring., U. Cin., 1971; m. Deborah Ann Deckinga, Nov. 28, 1975; 1 son, Jason Edward. Mgmt. trainee U.S. Steel Corp., Gary, Ind., 1971-72; plant metallurgist Regal Tube Co., Chgo., 1972-74, gen. foreman draw-over-mandrel, 1974-76, supt., 1976-77, mgr. tech. service, 1978-80, materials mgr., 1980-81; mgr. quality control Standard Tube Co., Detroit, 1977-78; dir. ops. Boye Needle Co., Chgo., 1981—. Mem. Am. Soc. Metals (Outstanding Young Mem. Calumet chpt. 1973, past mem. exec. com.), AIME, ASTM, Welded Steel Inst., Nat. Fluid Power Assn. Republican. Christian Reformed Ch. Club: Triangle. Home: 15315 S Treetop St Orland Park IL 60462 Office: 4343 N Ravenswood Chicago IL 60613

KAHN, MARK LEO, economist, educator; b. N.Y.C., Dec. 16, 1921; s. Augustus and Manya (Fertig) K.; B.A., Columbia U., 1942; M.A., Harvard U., 1948, Ph.D., 1950; m. Ruth Elizabeth Wecker, Dec. 21, 1947 (div. Jan. 1972); children—Ann Mariam, Peter David, James Allan, Jean Sarah. Asst. economist U.S. OSS, Washington, 1942-43; teaching fellow Harvard U., 1947-49; dir. case analysis U.S. WSB, Region 6-B Mich., 1952-53; econs. faculty Wayne State U., Detroit, 1949—, prof., 1960—, dept. chmn., 1961-68, dir. indsl. relations M.A. Program, 1978—; arbitrator union-mgmt. disputes, specializing in airline industry. Bd. govs. Jewish Welfare Fedn. Detroit, 1976—; trustee Mich. Quality of Work Life Council, 1978—. Served to capt. AUS, 1943-46. Decorated Bronze Star. Mem. Indsl. Relations Research Assn. (chpt. pres. 1956, exec. sec. 1979—), Am. Econ. Assn., AAUP (past chpt. pres.), Nat. Acad. Arbitrators (bd. govs. 1960-62, v.p. 1976-78, chmn. membership com. 1979—). Co-author: Collective Bargaining and Technological Change in American Transportation, 1971; contbr. articles to profl. jours. Home: 4140 2d Ave Detroit MI 48201

KAHN, STEVEN, psychologist; b. N.Y.C., Dec. 26, 1951; s. Paul and Edith (Goldfarb) K.; B.A., Stony Brook Coll., 1973; M.A., Ohio State U., 1976; Ph.D., Peabody Coll., 1978. Psychologist, Golden Valley Psychiat. Clinic, Mpls., 1978-79; clin. dir. Inst. Human Growth, St. Paul, 1979-80; psychologist Jamestown Treatment Found., Stillwater, Minn., 1979—. NIMH fellow, 1974-76. Mem. Am. Psychol. Assn., Minn. Psychol. Assn. Home: 265 Silver Lake Rd New Brighton MN 55112 Office: 11550 Jasmine Trail N Stillwater MN 55112

KAIMAN, ARNOLD GARTH, clergyman; b. Omaha, Mar. 30, 1933; s. William E. and Esther K. (Platt) K.; A.A., Yale, 1951; B.A. magna cum laude, U. Cin., 1953; M.A., U. Omaha, 1955; M. Hebrew Letters, Hebrew Union Coll., Cin., 1957; m. Judith Fox, June 3, 1956 (div. July 1972); children—Joshua, Kimberly; m. Dory Self, Sept. 7, 1977. Rabbi, 1957; asst. rabbi Reform Congregation Keneseth Israel, Phila., 1959-62, asso. rabbi, 1962-65, rabbi, 1965-67; dir. adult edn. Fedn. Jewish Agys. U.S., Philadelphia, 1967-68; rabbi Larchmont (N.Y.) Temple, 1968-71; asso. dir. Pacific Southwest council Union Am. Hebrew Congregations, Los Angeles, 1971-72; partner Ohalim Supper Club, Los Angeles, 1971-72, rabbi Congregation Kol Ami, Chgo., 1973—. Mem. faculty Rosemont Coll., (Pa.), 1961-65; mem. faculty Gratz Coll., Phila., 1967-68; vis. lectr. Marymount Coll. (N.Y.), 1968; host WIND radio show Ask The Rabbi; Jewish Chaplain asso. Northwestern Meml. Hosp.; chmn. adv. bd. Central Mental Health, City of Chgo.; founding chmn. Northwestern Community Mental Health Center; mem. nat. exec. council Am. Jewish Com. Chmn. com. on Israel, Anti Defamation League of Westchester County, N.Y., 1968-71; chmn. Com. on the Spl. Child Union Am. Hebrew Congregations, 1968-72; pres. North Loop Clergy, Chgo., 1973—; chaplain B'nai B'rith Lodge 5060, 1975. Bd. dirs. Central Mental Health, City of Chgo., 1975. Served 1st lt. USAF, 1957-59. Home: 2909-11 A 600 N McClurg Chicago IL 60611 Office: 233 E Erie St Chicago IL 60611

KAINLAURI, EINO OLAVI, architect; b. Lahti, Finland, June 13, 1922; came to U.S., 1947, naturalized, 1954; s. William and Eva K.; student Finland Inst. Tech., 1945-47; B.Arch., U. Mich., 1950, M.Arch., 1959, Ph.D., 1975; m. Genevieve Marjorie Mobley, Aug. 20, 1949; children—John Stanford, William Eino, Mary Ann. Draftsman, U. Mich. Architect's Office, Ann Arbor, 1951-55; dealer systems planner Ford div. Ford Motor Co., Livonia, Mich., 1955-56; partner, gen. mgr. Davis, Kainlauri & MacMullan, architects-engrs.-planners, Ann Arbor, Mich., 1956-59; pres. KMM Assos., architects-engrs.-planners, Ann Arbor, 1959-75; prof. architecture Iowa State U., Ames, 1975—. Bd. dirs. Des Moines chpt. Am. Scandinavian Found.; adv. bd. Class A energy audits Iowa State Energy Policy Council. Served to 1st lt. Finnish Army, World War II. Decorated Cross and Medal of Liberty; Fulbright-Hayes sr. scholar, 1973-74. Mem. AIA (mem. nat. com. on profl. devel.), Am. Planning Assn., ASTM, Am. Nat. Metric Council, Internat. Soc. Housing Sci., Nat. Trust Historic Preservation, Nat. Inst. Bldg. Sci. (cons. council). Lutheran. Clubs: Optimist (life), Lions. Author: Multinational Cooperation in Regional Planning for Lapland, 1976. Prin. archtl. works include Finnish Cultural Center, Farmington, Mich., schs., chs. Home: 1305 Wisconsin Circle Ames IA 50010 Office: 290 Coll Design Iowa State U Ames IA 50011

KAISER, CLARENCE JAMES, agronomist; b. Eckerty, Ind., May 28, 1930; s. Clarence Edward and Selma June (Esarey) K.; B.S., Purdue U., 1952; M.S., Ind. U., 1959; Ph.D., U. Mo., 1971; m. Doris June Snider, Feb. 9, 1951; children—Jacquelyn Sue, Katharine Ann, Millicent Marie, James Edward. Tchr. Milltown (Ind.) High Sch., 1954-56; supt. Purdue U. So. Ind. Forage Farm, Dubois, 1957-68; research asst. dept. agronomy, U. Mo., Columbia, 1968-70; asst. prof. agronomy U. Ky., Lexington, 1970-72; asso. prof. agronomy, dir. Dixon Springs Agrl. Center, U. Ill., Urbana-Champaign, 1973—; cons. USIA; lectr. Bucharest and Cluj, Romania, 1976-77. Coordinator Pope County, Ill., Emergency Services and Disaster Agy., 1979—; chmn. DuBois Soil and Water Conservation Dist., Jasper, Ind., 1963-65. Served with U.S. Army, 1952-54, Res., 1949—; served to col. Army N.G., 1960-80. Cert. profl. agronomist, crop scientist, soil specialist. Mem. Internat. Soc. Soil Sci., Am. Soc. Agronomy, Crop Sci. Soc. Am., Soil Sci. Soc. Am., Soc. for Range Mgmt., Am. Forage and Grassland Council, Soil Conservation Soc. Am., Council Agrl. Sci. and Tech., Ill. Forage and Grassland Council, Ill. Acad. Sci., Sigma Xi, Gamma Sigma Delta. Methodist. Clubs: Rotary (Golconda, Ill.); Masons (Newton Stewart, Ind.); Scottish Rite (Madisonville, Ky.). Contbr. articles to profl. publs. Home: Route 1 Box 132 Simpson IL 62985

KAISER, DORIS JEAN, ednl. adminstr.; b. St. Clair County, Ill., Jan. 14, 1931; d. Leonard Andrew and Luella Lillian K.; B.S. Ed., Miami U., Oxford, Ohio, 1953, M.Ed., 1960. Tchr., Public Schs. Aurora (Colo.), 1953-54; tchr. Oak Hills Local Sch. Dist., Hamilton County, Ohio, 1954-63, intermediate supr., 1963-68, T.E.S.T. Project curriculum specialist, 1968-70, tchr. S.W. Local Sch. Dist., 1970-72; curriculum coordinator Sycamore Community Schs., Cin., 1972—; mem. tchr. edn. redesign com. Miami U., Oxford, 1979-81; mem. adv. com. Grad. Sch. Adminstrn., Xavier U., Cin., 1977-81. Mem. Assn. Supervision and Curriculum Devel., Council Exceptional Children, Cin. Council Social Studies (pres. 1978), Kappa Alpha Theta Methodist. Club: Quota. Home: 5343 Foley Rd Cincinnati OH 45238 Office: Sycamore Community Schs 4881 Cooper Rd Cincinnati OH 45242

KAISER, JEFFREY STEVEN, educator; b. Buffalo, Dec. 15, 1943; s. Norman; A.A.S., SUNY, Buffalo, 1964, B.S., 1966, Ed.M., 1969, S.E.A., 1972, Ph.D., 1973; m. Diane Sara Greenberg, Dec. 25, 1966; children—Deborah Lauren, Joshua Lawrence. Lectr., Monash U., Melbourne, Australia, 1973-74; asst. prof. Marquette U., Milw., 1976-78, asst. dean, 1978-80; prof. ednl. adminstrn. Govs. State U., Park Forest South, Ill., 1980—; cons. orgn. behavior to corps., univs., sch. systems. Mem. AAUP, Eastern Ednl. Research Assn., Am. Ednl. Research Assn. Co-author: Complete Guide to Administering School Services, 1980; contbr. articles to profl. jours. Office: Govs State U Park Forest South IL 60466

KAISER, JOSEPH MATTHEW, constrn. co. exec.; b. Belleville, Ill., Nov. 11, 1948; s. Louis Joseph and Janice Marie (Weber) K.; B.S. with highest honors, U. Ill., Urbana, 1970, M.S., 1971; m. Patricia Ann Sanders, Jan. 30, 1971; children—Douglas, Gregory, Bradley. Project engr., United Parcel Service, Omaha, 1976-78; project mgr. Ty-Mar Industries Ltd., Beloit, Wis., 1978-80, constrn. mgr., 1980—. Bd. dirs. Eucharistic Ministers Cath. Ch., Guam, 1974. Served to lt. USNR, 1971-76. Ill. State scholar, 1966, Universal Oil Products scholar, 1969, Edmund B. James scholar, 1967-70; U. Ill. fellow, 1970-71, W.E. O'Neil fellow, 1971; registered profl. engr., Wis., Ill. Mem. ASCE (award 1970), Nat. Soc. Profl. Engrs., Ill. Soc. Profl. Engrs., Chi Epsilon, Phi Eta Sigma, Sigma Tau. Roman Catholic. Author articles in field. Home: 627 Valley Forge Trail Rockton IL 61072 Office: Ty-Mar Bldg Beloit WI 53511

KAISTHA, KRISHAN KUMAR, toxicologist; b. Sulah, Himachal Pradesh, India, Apr. 6, 1926; s. Mangat Ram and Tara Devi (Mahajan) K.; came to U.S., 1959, naturalized, 1974; B.S. in Chemistry, Punjab (India) U., 1947, B.S. in Pharmacy with honors, 1951, M.S., 1955; Ph.D., U. Fla., 1962; m. Swarn L. Kaistha, Feb. 22, 1948; children—Anita Kaistha Mahajan, Vivek, Vinek. Analytical chemist Punjab (India) Govt. Med. Directorate, 1952-57, chief pharmacist, 1957-59; research fellow State U. N.Y., Buffalo, 1962-63; head pharm. and phytochem. research lab. Punjab Govt., 1964-66; research scientist food and drug directorate Dept. Nat. Health and Welfare, Ottawa, Ont., Can., 1966-69; dir. toxicology labs. State Ill. Dept. Mental Health Drug Abuse Programs, Chgo., 1969-74; chief toxicologist State Ill. Dangerous Drugs Commn., Chgo., 1974—. Research asso. dept. psychiatry U. Chgo., 1969-75. Recipient 1st prize, Lunsford-Richardson award, 1962; Gov.'s Economy Incentive award State Ill., 1973. Diplomate Am. Bd. Forensic Toxicology; certified clin. chemist Nat. Registry Clin. Chemistry. Fellow N.Y. Acad. Sci., Am. Acad. Forensic Scis., Nat. Acad. Clin. Biochemistry; mem. Am. Acad. Clin. Toxicology, Am. Assn. Clin. Chemists, Am. Soc. Pharmacology and Exptl. Therapeutics, Rho Chi, Phi Kappa Phi, Rho Pi Phi. Contbr. numerous research articles to profl. jours. Home: 542 Ashbury Ave Bolingbrook IL 60439 Office: care IIT Research 10 W 35th St Chicago IL 60616

KALARAS, JOHN NICK, educator; b. Corinth, Greece, Jan. 29, 1948; came to U.S., 1972, naturalized, 1978; s. Nickolas John and Bessy Nick K.; B.S., U. Athens, 1970; M.S., Grad. Sch. Indsl. Studies, Greece, 1972; M.B.A., Roosevelt U., 1975. Food and beverage dir. McCormick Inn., Chgo., 1975-77; regional dir. sales and mktg. N.Y. Life Ins. Co., Chgo., 1977-80; pres. Bus. Tng. Inst., Chgo., 1980—; prof. DeVry Coll., Chgo., 1980—; faculty adult edn. program Chgo. City Coll., 1981—; mktg. cons. N. Am. Investment Group Inc., Chgo. Exec. v.p. United Hellenic Voters of Am., regional dir., 1977—; treas. Hellenic Congress, 1979—. Mem. Am. Soc. Tng. and Devel., M.B.A. Execs. Assn., Hellenic Profl. Soc. Greek Orthodox. Author: Inventory Methods, 1975; Management Skills, 1981; Professional Teaching, 1981. Home: 6845 W Leland Ave Harwood Heights IL 60656 Office: 3300 N Campbell St Chicago IL 60618

KALB, BEN DAVID, steel co. exec.; b. Frankfort, Mich., Apr. 29, 1948; s. Carl Duane and Francis Blanche (Van der Vort) K.; student Macomb County Community Coll., 1967-70, Wayne State U., 1974—; m. Ruth Ann Guerney, Apr. 11, 1970; children—Trena Marie, Rebecca Ann. Indsl. forecaster Sperry Vickers, Troy, Mich., 1967-69; prodn. scheduler Production Steel, Detroit, 1969-71; supr. inventory control Whittaker Steel, Detroit, 1971-73, supr. prodn. control, 1973-77, mgr. planning-prodn. control, 1977-80; ops. mgr. Namasco, Inc., Roseville, Mich., 1980-81; gen. mgr. Caine Steel Co., Detroit, 1981—. Mem. Am. Mgmt. Assn., Nat. Council Phys. Distbn. Mgmt. Mo. Synod Lutheran. Home: 16802 Josephine St Fraser MI 48026 Office: 30360 Edison Dr Roseville MI 48066

KALB, CHESTER HARRY, II, educator; b. Cin., Nov. 12, 1945; s. Chester and Marie E. Kalb; B.S. with honors, U. Cin., 1967, B.S. in Edn., 1968; M.S. with distinction, Xavier U., 1974; m. Jill Kay Rice, Aug. 26, 1967. Tchr., Woodward High Sch., Cin., 1967-71, Schroeder Jr. High Sch., Cin., 1971-72; tchr. Woodward High Sch., 1972—, head dept. math., 1975—. Coach swimming Amberley Swim and Tennis Club, 1968-72. Recipient Disting. Tchr. Service award Cin. Bd. Edn., 1979. Mem. Nat. Council Tchrs. of Math., Assn. Supervision and Curriculum Devel. Clubs: Ohio River Roadrunners, Funmakers

Bowling League (sec. 1978—). Home: 10008 Howard Rd Harrison OH 45030 Office: 7001 Reading Rd Cincinnati OH 45237

KALBERLOH, RALPH JUNIOR, trade assn. exec.; b. Excelsior Springs, Mo., July 21, 1925; s. Albert Henry and Goldie (Hatfield) K.; student Lincoln U., 1956-57, Mich. State U., 1962-69; m. Joann Fry, Sept. 11, 1943; 1 dau., Kim J.R. Spl. agt. Farm Bur. Ray County, Richmond, Mo., 1952-55; exec. v.p. Mo. Jr. C. of C., Jefferson City, 1955-57; exec. mgr. Mo. Limestone Producers Assn., Jefferson City, 1957-59; exec. dir. Mo. Safety Council, Jefferson City, 1959-61; exec. v.p. Mo. Automobile Dealers Assn., Jefferson City, 1961—; dir. Mark Twain Life Ins. Co., Mo. Acceleration Corp. Campaign chmn. Jefferson City, Cole County United Fund, 1968-69; chmn. mayor's adv. commn. reapportionment, 1967-69; sec. Jefferson City Planning and Zoning Commn., 1963-68; mem. Gov.'s Interim Legislative Com., 1960, 68; mem. Home Rule Study Commn., 1960-68, chmn. charter drafting com., 1968; chmn. Greater Jefferson City Trafficways Com., 1968-74; co-chmn. Payroll Bond Issue com., Jefferson City, 1968—. Chmn. bd. regents Inst. Orgn. Mgmt., 1975; pres. Meml. Community Hosp., 1977—; pres. Yesterdays Children Inc. Served to sgt. USAF, 1943-45; ETO. Mem. Automotive Trade Assn. Mgrs. (sec. 1969-70, v.p. 1970-71, pres. 1971-72), Mo. Hwy. Users Conf. (sec. 1966—), Mo. Safety Council (dir. 1961—, treas. 1974, v.p. 1975, 80), Jefferson City (pres. 1960-61), Richmond (pres. 1954-55) jr. chambers commerce, Jefferson City C. of C. (pres. 1965-66), Orgn. Execs. Jefferson City (pres. 1957-58), Am. (dir. 1976-77, v.p. 1978), Mo. (pres. 1975) socs. assn. execs., Cole County Hist. Soc. Episcopalian. Rotarian (pres. 1971—), Mason (Shriner). Club: Jefferson City Country. Home: 300 Old Gibler Rd Jefferson City MO 65101 Office: 205 E Capitol St Jefferson City MO 65102

KALES, ROBERT GRAY, mgmt., finance, mfg., real estate exec.; b. Detroit, Mar. 14, 1904; s. William R. and Alice (Gray) K.; B.S., Mass. Inst. Tech., 1928; M.B.A., Harvard U., 1933; m. Jane Webster, Nov. 27, 1932; children—Jane (Mrs. William H. Ryan), Robert Gray, William R., Anne W. (Mrs. Jeffrey Howson); m. 2d, Miriam Wallin, Jan. 6, 1945; 1 son, David Wallin; m. 3d, Herma Lou Boyd, Mar. 6, 1951; m. 4th, Shirley L. McBride, Feb. 14, 1961; children—John Gray, Nancy Davis. With Whitehead & Kales Co., Detroit, 1928-31, 43—, v.p., 1943-77, chmn. bd., River Rouge, Mich., 1977—, also dir.; with Union Guardian Trust Co., Detroit, 1933-34; analyst, sec.-treas. Investment Counsel, Inc., Detroit, 1934-35; organizer Kales Kramer Investment Co., Detroit, 1935, pres., dir., 1935—; pres., dir. Indsl. Resources, Inc., 1955-74, Automotive Bin Service Co., Inc., 1955—, Jefferson Terminal Warehouse, 1934-80, Kales Bldg. Co., 1944-73, Kales Realty Co., 1935-73, Midwest Underwriters, Inc., 1938—, Modern Constrn., Inc., 1938-60 (all Detroit); v.p., dir. Basin Oil Co., Metamora, Mich., 1947-75; dir. Independent Liberty Life Ins. Co., Grand Rapids, Mich., Atlas Energy Corp., Dallas. Chmn. vets. com. Detroit Armed Forces Week. Adv. bd. Patriotic Edn., Deland, Fla.; chmn. trustees, pres. Kales Found., 1977. Served to lt. comdr. USNR, 1942-45; capt. Res. Mem. Am. Legion, Navy League U.S. (pres. Southeastern Mich. council), Mil. Order World Wars (past nat. comdr.-in-chief), Nat. Sojourners, Naval Order U.S., S.A.R., U.S. Naval Inst., Sigma Chi. Episcopalian. Clubs: Army and Navy, Univ., Capitol Hill (Washington); Bayview Yacht, Detroit Country, Detroit Athletic, Detroit, Curling, Detroit Power Squadron, The Players, St. Clair Yacht, Scarab, Univ. (Detroit); Black River Ranch (Onaway, Mich.); Longwood Cricket, Union Boat (Boston); Stone Horse Yacht (Harwich, Mass.); Triton Fish and Game (Quebec, Can.); Grosse Pointe (Mich.) Hunt, Grosse Pointe Yacht; Otsego Ski; Pelee; Masons, Shriners, K.T. Home: 87 Cloverly Rd Grosse Pointe Farms MI 48236 Office: 1900 E Jefferson St Detroit MI 48207

KALES, SHIRLEY MCBRIDE (MRS. ROBERT GRAY KALES), club woman; b. Detroit, Feb. 18, 1927; d. Goerge L. and Elsie J. (Storey) McBride; student Wayne State U., 1946-48; student Detroit Conservatory Music, 1948-50; m. Robert Gray Kales, Feb. 14, 1961; children—John Gray, Nancy Davis. Advt. staff Detroit Evening News Assn., 1949-55; mem. advt. and publicity staff Bielfield Agy., Detroit, 1955-59; mem. advt. and sales dept. Mich. Bell Telephone Co., Detroit, 1959-60; mem. sales promotion and advt. staff Mich. Consol. Gas Co., Detroit, 1960-61. Mem. Detroit Mus. Art Founders Soc., Fine Arts Soc. Detroit, Mich. Anti-Cruelty Assn., Navy League U.S. (pres. Detroit women's council). Clubs: Women's City (chmn. program com.), Country, Review (pres.), (Detroit); Grosse Pointe (Mich.) Yacht. Home: 87 Cloverly Rd Grosse Pointe Farms MI 48236 Office: 1900 E Jefferson Ave Detroit MI 48207

KALIHER, PAUL LARKIN, mfg. co. exec.; b. Little Falls, Minn., Aug. 2, 1946; s. Earl Larkin and Anne K.; B.E.E., U. Minn. Inst. Tech., 1968; M.B.A., Coll. St. Thomas, 1978; m. Susan Ann Hermanson, June 22, 1968; children—Kevin Paul, Kristi Ann. Elec. engr. Motorola Corp., Schaumburg, Ill., 1968-69; elec. engr. 3M Co., St. Paul, 1969-73, engring. supr., 1973-75, market devel. supr., 1975-79; mktg. mgr. Teradyne Central, Inc., Northbrook, Ill., 1979—. Alworth Meml. Fund scholar, 1964-68. Mem. Theta Chi. Clubs: Lake County Camera, YMCA Indian Guides, U.S. Jaycees (internal dir. White Bear Lake Minn. chpt. 1973). Patentee electrosurg. unit. Home: 306 Cypress Ln Libertyville IL 60048 Office: 3368 Commercial Ave Northbrook IL 60062

KALIKOW, ALBERT, advt. agy. exec.; b. Lynn, Mass., Jan. 23, 1918; s. Barnet and Ethel (Meirovitz) K.; B.B.A., Boston U., 1941; m. Betty Lee Pucker, May 19, 1946; children—Harvey E., Nancy, Barbara. Account exec. Reeves Advt. Co., Kansas City, Mo., 1946-47; owner, account exec. Kalikow Advt. Co., Kansas City, Kans., 1947—. Mgr. Jewish Community Choral Group, 1968-73; mem. Kansas City (Kans.) Civic Choral Group, 1974-79. Served with AUS, 1941-45. Mem. Am. Legion Band (dir. 1955-65). Club: B'nai B'rith. Home: 12001 W 100th Terr Lenexa KS 66215 Office: 812 N 5th St Kansas City KS 66101

KALISCH, PHILIP A., educator; b. Omaha, Apr. 3, 1942; s. Philip E. and Geneva (Meredith) K.; B.S., U. Nebr., 1963, M.A., 1964; Ph.D., Pa. State U., 1967; postgrad. Johns Hopkins U., 1967-68; m. Beatrice J. Petersen, Apr. 17, 1964. Instr. history and social sci. N.W. Mo. State U., 1964-65, Pa. State U., 1965-66; asst. prof. social sci. W. Tex. State U., 1969-71; asso. prof. history, dir. interdisciplinary social sci. program U. So. Miss., Hattiesburg, 1971-74; asso. prof. nursing research, co-prin. investigator Bur. Health Manpower grants and contracts to study various aspects history and politics of nursing U. Mich., Ann Arbor, 1974-78, prof. history and politics of nursing, co-prin. investigator Bur. Health Professions, 1974—; adj. asso. prof. nursing Wayne State U., Detroit, 1977-79. Recipient grants from NIH, 1972, Bur. Health Manpower, 1974, Health Resources Adminstrn., 1977, Div. Nursing, 1979. Mem. Nat. League Nursing, Am. Public Health Assn., Am. Hosp. Assn., Am. Assn. History Medicine, History Sci. Soc., Am. Hist. Assn., AAAS, Hastings Inst. Soc., Ethics and Life Scis., Phi Alpha Theta. Author: The Advance of American Nursing, 1978; Nursing Involvement in Health Planning, 1978; Impact of Federal Aid on Schools of Nursing in the United States in the 1940's, 1974; Nurturer of Nurses, 1977; Politics of Nursing, 1981. Home: 5663 Glen Oak Ct Saline MI 48176 Office: U Mich Sch Nursing 609 E Liberty St Ann Arbor MI 48109

KALJOT, VICTOR, physician; b. Tartu, Estonia, June 15, 1925; s. Voldemar and Marie (Gruenbaum) K.; M.D., U. Vt., 1955; m. Linda Roose, Aug. 25, 1949; children—Kaarel T., Lena M., Lisa A., Tiina. Came to U.S., 1950, naturalized, 1955. Intern, Mary Fletcher Hosp., Burlington, Vt., 1955-56; resident in internal medicine U. Vt., 1956-57, Boston VA Hosp., 1958-59; resident in cardiology Letterman Gen. Hosp., 1962-63; practice medicine specializing in cardiology Trinity Med Center, Minot, N.D., 1965—, chief med. staff, 1975-77, bd. dirs., 1975—. Served to maj., M.C. U.S. Army, 1957-65. Diplomate Am. Bd. Internal Medicine with subsplty. bd. cardiovascular disease. Fellow A.C.P., Am. Coll. Cardiology, Council Clin. Cardiology, Am. Heart Assn., Am. Coll. Chest Physicians. Lutheran. Home: 2111 11th Ave NW Minot ND 58701 Office: 500 Trinity Profl Bldg Minot ND 58701

KALLAS, JAMES GUS, coll. pres.; b. Chgo., Dec. 15, 1928; s. James Gus and Lillian Kallas; B.A., St. Olaf Coll., 1950; B.Th., Luther Sem., 1955; Ph.D., U. So. Calif., 1967; D.D., U. Redlands, 1975; m. Darlean Quernemoen, June 3, 1950; children—James, III, Paris, Jacqueline, Kingsley. Missionary Am. Luth. Ch., West Africa, 1955-61; prof. religion Calif. Luth. Coll., 1961-78; mem. faculty Dana Coll., Blair, Nebr., now pres. Rockefeller scholar; Fulbright scholar. Mem. Phi Beta Kappa. Author: The Satanward View: A Study in Pauline Theology, 1966; Jesus and the Power of Satan, 1968; The Story of Paul, 1966; A Layman's Introduction to Christian Thought, 1969; Revelation-God and Satan in the Apocalpse, 1973. Office: Dana Coll Blair NE 68008

KALLET, HENRY ABRAHAM, pathologist; b. Chgo., Mar. 26, 1935; s. Sam and Kate (Gordon) K.; A.B., U. Chgo., 1954, B.S., 1955; M.D., Northwestern U., 1959; m. Beverley Jean Frommert, July 22, 1967. Intern, U.S. Naval Hosp., San Diego, 1959-60; resident U. Mich. Med. Center, Ann Arbor, 1964-68; instr. pathology U. Mich., Ann Arbor, 1969; dir. lab. W. A. Foote Hosp., Jackson, Mich., 1969-76; asso. prof. pathology Mich. State U., Lansing, 1976—; dir. clin. pathology Jackson Lab. Clin. Pathology, 1977-79; dir. pathology Chelsea Med. Labs. (Mich.), 1979—. Served to lt., M.C., USN, 1959-63. Mem. Coll. Am. Pathology, Am. Soc. Clin. Pathologists, Soc. Nuclear Medicine. Home: 3324 Bluett St Ann Arbor MI 48105 Office: 775 S Main St Chelsea MI 48118

KALLICK, MAUREEN, social research adminstr.; b. Chgo., Chgo.; d. Irving M. and Jeannette (Welcher) Kallick; student Brandeis U., Ohio State U.; B.A., U. Akron, 1961, M.A., 1962; Ph.D., Purdue U., 1964; Project dir. Kenyon & Eckhardt Advt. Co., N.Y.C., 1964-66, asso. research dir., 1966-67, v.p., dir. research services, 1973-74; v.p. Dimensions for Decisions, N.Y.C., 1967-69; v.p., sr. asso. research dir. SSC & B Advt. Co., N.Y.C., 1969-73; research scientist, program dir. econ. behavior program U. Mich. Survey Research Center, Inst. for Social Research, Ann Arbor, 1974—; vis. prof. Baruch Coll., N.Y.C., 1965-69. Bd. dirs. Person-to-Person, N.Y.C., 1967-71. Mem. Am. (sec.-treas. div. consumer psychology 1973-76, pres. 1977-78), Midwestern psychol. assns., Am. Acad. Polit. and Social Sci., Am. Mktg. Assn., Am. Assn. Public Opinion Research. Author: Gambling in America, 1977; The Postal Mail Stream, 1978, 80; Pollution Control and Employment, 1979; Coping with Inflation, 1980; Effects of the Minimum Wage Increase on Inflation and Employment, 1981; contbr. articles on consumer and econ. psychology to profl. jours. Home: 1160 Pauline Ann Arbor MI 48103 Office: U Mich Survey Research Center Ann Arbor MI 48109

KALLSTROM, DAVID H., real estate exec.; b. Akron, Ohio, Mar. 6, 1928; s. Gust R. and Norma P. (Peterson) K.; student Case Inst. Tech., 1945-47; B.S., Ohio State U., 1949; m. Jacqueline V. Kallstrom; children—James D., Neil G. Vice pres. Gust Kallstrom, Inc., builders and developers, Akron, 1949-60; pres. Kallstrom Realtors, Akron, Kallstrom Ins. Agy., Inc., Kallstrom's Comml. & Investment Real Estate, Inc., 1961—, Kallstrom Tele Video Prodns., Kallstrom Realty Assos., Inc.; guest lectr. Kent State U., 1963-68; cons. Cleve. Trust Co., 1970—. Chmn., Cuyahoga Falls YMCA Bldg. drive, 1960; mem. exec. com. Tri County Regional Planning Commn., 1963-65; mem. Com. of 100, Goals for Greater Akron Area, 1973; mem. adv. commn. to Summit County Govt., 1973. Mem. Appraisal Inst., Soc. Real Estate Appraisers (pres.), C. of C., Akron Area Bd. Realtors. Home: 316 W Streetsboro Rd Hudson OH 44236 Office: 141 Broad Blvd Cuyahoga Falls OH 44221

KALP, KARL REX, supt. schs.; b. Frankfort, Ind., Mar. 8, 1920; s. Karl Leslie and Euphemia (Henderson) K.; student U. Cin., 1941; B.S., Butler U., 1948, M.S., 1952, LL.D., 1973; postgrad. Columbia U., summer 1969, Yale U., 1970-71; m. Marcella Downey, Feb. 16, 1941; children—Jeanne Kalp McNew, Janet Kalp Jackson, Joanne. With B.F. Goodrich Tire Co., Rushville, Ind., 1938-40; cost acct. Herring-Hall-Marvin Safe Co., Hamilton, Ohio, 1941-42; successively tchr. elem. and high sch., dir. guidance, vice prin., asst. supt., asso. supt., gen. supt. Indpls. Public Schs., 1972—. Served to capt. AUS, 1942-46, 50-52. Decorated Silver Star, Bronze Star, Army Commendation medal, Purple Heart; recipient Am. Educators medal Freedoms Found., 1973; Yale fellow in urban adminstrn., 1970-71. Mem. Am. Assn. Sch. Adminstrs., Nat. Assn. Secondary Sch. Prins., Nat. Assn. Elem. Sch. Prins., Ind. Assn. Public Sch. Supts., Am. Legion, DAV, Phi Delta Kappa, Kappa Delta Pi. Clubs: Masons, Rotary. Home: 5501 Culver St Indianapolis IN 46226 Office: 120 E Walnut St Indianapolis IN 46204

KALSEM, MILLIE E., former hosp. dietitian, investment co. exec.; b. Huxley, Iowa; d. Ole J. and Anna (Nelson) Kalsem; B.S., Iowa State U., 1921; dietetic internship Michael Reese Hosp., Chgo., 1922-23; post grad. student U. Ill. Med. Sch., 1935-36. Tchr. home econs. and physiology, Monticello High Sch., Monticello, Iowa, 1921-22; dietitian Beaver Valley Gen. Hosp., New Brighton, Pa., 1922-23, Iowa Meth. Hosp., Des Moines, Iowa, 1923-27, Ill. Tng. Sch. for Nurses and Cook Co. Sch. Nursing, 1927-38; chief dietitian Cook County Hosp., 1936-62; dir., v.p. Lorraine L. Blair, Inc., investments. Selected by Carrie Chapman Catt as one of 100 Women, Women's Centennial Congress, 1940; recipient Alumni merit award, Iowa State Coll., 1946, Alumni Medal, 1956. Mem. Am. Dietetic Assn. (v.p. 1946-47), Ill. Dietetic Assn. (organizer and 1st pres.), Finance Forum Am. (research chmn. 1954-57), Art Inst. Chgo., Order Knoll (gov. Iowa state found.), Omicron Nu, Phi Kappa Phi, Chi Omega. Club: Altrusa (pres. Chgo. 1959-61). Home: 111 Lynn Ave Ames IA 50010 Office: 11 S LaSalle St Chicago IL 60603

KALTHOFF, FREDERICK ROBERT, TV sta. sales rep. co. exec.; b. Chgo., Oct. 12, 1931; s. Frederick Casper and Genevieve Margaret (Finnegan) K.; B.S., U. Ill., 1956; postgrad. U. Nebr., 1966, Harvard U. Grad. Sch. Bus., 1970; m. Dianne Margaret Black, Jan. 13, 1979; children—Kenneth Robert, Karen Lynn. With Avery Knodel TV, Inc., Chgo., 1956—, exec. v.p. advt., 1968—, also dir. Asst. master N.W. Suburban council Boy Scouts Am., Chgo., 1969-71; bd. dirs. Culver Ednl. Found., 1981—. Served with USAF, 1950-54. Mem. Broadcast Advt. Club of Chgo., Sta. Rep. Assn. (pres. 1960), Broadcast Pioneers (dir. 1979—), Nat. Assn. Farm Broadcasters, TV Bur. Advt., Culver Summer Sch. Alumni Assn. (dir. 1977—, 1st v.p. 1979-81, pres. 1981—). Presbyterian. Office: 2600 Prudential Plaza Chicago IL 60601

KALTON, ROBERT RANKIN, crop scientist; b. Mpls., Oct. 28, 1920; s. Martin Edmund and Eva Lucinda (Rankin) K.; B.S., U. Minn., 1941; M.S., Iowa State Coll., 1945, Ph.D., 1947; m. Vivian W. Wiltsey, Oct. 9, 1942; children—JoAnne, Barbara, Bonnie, Robert, Martin. Asso. agronomist Tex. Research Fedn., Renner, Tex., 1947-49; asso. prof. to prof. farm crops Iowa State U., 1950-60; research dir. Rudy-Patrick Seed Co., Ames, Iowa, 1960-70; dir. agronomic research Land O' Lakes, Inc., Webster City, Iowa, 1970—. Active Ames Community Chest, 1950's; troop committeeman, leader Webelos, Mid-Iowa council Boy Scouts Am., 1960's; treas., v.p. Beardshear PTA, Ames, 1950's; county committeeman Hamilton County Republicans, 1974-78. Recipient Merit cert. Am. and Iowa Forage and Grassland Councils. Fellow Am. Soc. Agronomy, AAAS; mem. Crop Sci. Soc. Am., Am. Genetics Assn., Am. Seed Trade Assn., Iowa Seed Assn. (pres., dir.), Iowa Crop Improvement Assn., Nat. Council Comml. Plant Breeders (pres., dir.), Sigma Xi. Republican. Methodist. Club: Elks. Home: 814 N Terrace Dr Webster City IA 50595 Office: Land O' Lakes Inc Rural Route 2 Webster City IA 50595

KAMAKA, SISTER ELISSA, educator, nun; b. Honolulu, Mar. 5, 1932; d. James H. Lopailani and Elizabeth Sau Hong (Pang) Kamaka; B.A., Holy Family Coll., 1960; M.S.T., U. Wis., 1971; Ph.D., St. Louis U., 1981. Entered Franciscan Sisters of Charity, Roman Cath. Ch., 1951; elem. tchr. St. Paul Sch., Manitowoc, Wis., 1954-58, Immaculate Conception Sch., Yuma, Ariz., 1958-66, St. John Vianney Sch., Kailua, Hawaii, 1966-68, St. Agnes Sch., Green Bay, Wis., 1968-71; faculty Silver Lake Coll., Manitowoc, Wis., 1971—, chmn. Dept. Edn., dir. tchr. edn., 1973—; cons. in edn. Ford Found. fellow, 1979-80; EPDA fellow, 1970-71. Mem. Wis. Assn. Tchr. Educators, Assn. for Supervision and Curriculum Devel., Wis. Assn. Supervision and Curriculum Devel., Nat. Assn. for Gifted, Assn. of Creative Innovators, Am. Assn. Colls. Tchr. Edn., Wis. Assn. Tchr. Educators. Address: 2406 S Alverno Rd Manitowoc WI 54220

KAMIKOW, NORMAN B., publishing co. exec.; b. Chgo., Dec. 25, 1943; s. Howard M. and Ethel (Morris) K.; B.A. in Journalism, Drake U., 1967; m. Sheri Greenfield, June 18, 1969; children—Jeffrey R., David A. Account exec. Chgo. Tribune, 1967-69; account exec., dir. sales devel. Branham Newspapers, Chgo., 1969-72; asso. Chgo. mgr. Seventeen mag., 1972-76; Midwest advt. dir. Penthouse Internat., Chgo., 1976—; dir. D.E.K. Properties; guest lectr. U. Ill. Mem. Chgo. Advt. Club (trustee). Clubs: Plaza, East Bank, Agate. Office: 303 E Wacker Dr Chicago IL 60601

KAMINKOWITZ, GRACE, advt. and public relations co. exec.; b. N.Y.C., May 23, 1935; d. Louis and Gertrude (Noachs) K.; B.A., U. Iowa, 1955; postgrad. Northwestern U., 1956-58. Advt. copywriter Montgomery Ward, Chgo., 1955-57; advt. copywriter May Co., Los Angeles, 1957; retail advt. mgr. major appliances Montgomery Ward, Chgo., 1957-61; advt. copy chief Helene Curtis, Chgo., 1961-70, dir. mktg., 1970-73, v.p. mktg., 1973-75; v.p. New Dimensions Mktg., Chgo., 1975-77, pres., 1977—; v.p., sec. Am. Sch. Needlework, Northbrook, Ill., also dir. Vice pres. ERA Ill., 1980—; mem. Ill. Gov.'s Adv. Com. on Health and Fitness; regional adv. council to Gov.'s Spl. asst. for Women. Mem. Women in Communications, Inc. (pres. Chgo. chpt. 1966-67, regional dir. 1968-69), Fashion Group, Chgo. Women in Govt. Relations, Publicity Club of Chgo. Home: 1143 S Plymouth Ct Chicago IL 60605 Office: 111 E Wacker Dr Suite 2928 Chicago IL 60601

KAMINSKI, WILLIAM ARTHUR, hair stylist; b. Brainerd, Minn., May 30, 1944; s. Steve Stanley and Mildred K.; student St. Paul Barber Coll., 1965, Minn. Sch. Real Estate, 1975, Sassoon Sch. Hair Styling, 1977; m. Susan Marie Ellstrom, June 1, 1966; children—Stacey, Steve. Hair stylist, barber The Modern Barbershop, Mpls., 1967; hair stylist The Barbers, Mpls., 1968, owner, stylist, Rochester, Minn., 1972, Madison, Wis., 1977—; pres. Split Hair Ltd.; Square Hair Ltd. Recipient 28 trophies, awards for hairstyling, Midwest, S.D., Iowa, Wis. Mem. Internat. Hairstyling Assn., Assn. Barbers and Beauticians Am., Minn. Barbers Union (chmn. state conv.), C. of C., Nat. Hairdressers, Cosmetologist Assn. Roman Catholic. Clubs: Sertoma, Jaycees, Toastmasters, Elks. Home: 3805 Valley Ridge Rd Middleton WI 53562 Office: 324 Westgate Mall Madison WI 53711

KAMINSKY, DANIEL BENJAMIN, agronomist; b. Niles, Mich., July 8, 1950; s. Daniel Benjamin and Imogene Kaminsky; B.S., Purdue U., 1972, M.S., 1975; m. Donita Louise Baker, Aug. 24, 1975; 1 son, Benjamin David. Agronomist, Pulaski County Farm Bur. Coop., Winamac, Ind., 1975—; mem. agr. com. Arrowhead Regional Planning Commn., 1980—. Mem. com. Tri County Child Evangelism Fellowship, 1976—; youth dir. Bethel Bible Ch., 1975—. Served with AUS, 1976. Mem. Am. Soc. Agronomy, Soil Sci. Soc. Am., Alpha Zeta, Gamma Sigma Delta, Ceres. Home: Rural Route 4 Box 416 Winamac IN 46996 Office: PO Box 346 Winamac IN 46996

KAMM, CARL JACOB, greenhouse co. exec.; b. Rocky River, Ohio, Dec. 18, 1914; s. Jacob and Minnie (Christensen) K.; A.B., Baldwin Wallace Coll., 1937; m. Jean Roth, Sept. 14, 1944; children—Carl II, Lauren, Karen. Pres., Rocky River Greenhouse Co., 1948-64; sec-treas. Am. Growers, Inc., Huron, Ohio, 1950—; treas. Lorain Ave. Greenhouse Co., Cleve. 1950-72; dir. Cleve. Quarries Co., 1956-61, treas., 1960-61; dir. Silica Chems., Inc., Amherst, Ohio, 1956-61; Cleve. Stone Co., 1958-61. Trustee Berlin-Milan Library Bd. Mem. Ohio Grange, Alpha Sigma Phi. Mem. Soc. of Friends. Mason (Shriner). Club: University of Cleveland. Home: 7310 Kamm Farms Dr Huron OH 44839

KAMM, HERBERT, newspaper editor; b. Long Branch, N.J., Apr. 1, 1917; s. Louis and Rose (Cohen) K.; student Monmouth Jr. Coll., 1935; m. Phyllis I. Silberblatt, Dec. 6, 1936; children—Laurence R., Lewis R., Robert H. Reporter, sports editor Asbury Park (N.J.) Press, 1935-42; with AP, 1942-43; with N.Y. World-Telegram and Sun, 1943-66, successively rewrite man, picture editor, asst. city editor, feature editor, mag. editor, asst. mng. editor, 1943-63, mng. editor, 1963-66; exec. editor N.Y. World Jour. Tribune, 1966-67; editorial cons. Scripps-Howard Newspapers, 1967-69; asso. editor Cleve. Press, 1969-80, editor, 1980—; radio and TV news commentator and panelist, 1950—; TV talk show host, 1974—; instr. journalism Case Western Res. U., 1972-75. Bd. overseers Case Western Res. U., 1974-78. Mem. AFTRA, Sigma Delta Chi. Jewish (bd. dirs. temple 1957-60). Clubs: Cleve. City (pres. 1981-82), Nat. Press. Contbr. articles mags. Editor Jr. Illus. Ency. Sports, 1960, rev. edit., 1963, 66, 70, 74. Home: 1 Bratenahl Pl Bratenahl OH 44108 Office: 901 Lakeside Ave Cleveland OH 44114

KAMM, JACOB OSWALD, economist; b. Cleve., Nov. 29, 1918; s. Jacob and Minnie K. (Christensen) K.; A.B., Baldwin-Wallace Coll., 1940; LL.D., 1963; Litt.D., Erskine Coll., 1971; A.M., Brown U., 1942; Ph.D., Ohio State U., 1948; m. Judith Steinbrenner, Apr. 28, 1965; children—Jacob Oswald Kamm II, Christian Philip. Asst. in econs. Brown U., 1942; instr. Ohio State U., 1945; instr. Baldwin-Wallace Coll., 1945-46, asst. prof., 1947-48, asso. prof., 1948, prof., dir. Sch. Commerce, 1948-53; exec. v.p. Cleve. Quarries Co., 1953-55, pres., dir., 1955-67, chmn., chief exec. officer, 1967—; dir., exec. com. United Screw & Bolt Corp.; exec. v.p., treas., dir., then pres. Am.

Shipbldg. Co., 1967-69, 73-74; vice chmn., dir. Cardinal Fed. Savs. & Loan Assn. Cleve., MTD Products Inc., Electric Furnace Co., McDonald Money Market Fund, Inc., Nordson Corp., Bibb Co., Oatey Co., United Western Corp. Hon. mem. mental health com. Ohio Mental Health Assn.; trustee, mem. exec. com., chmn. investment com. Baldwin-Wallace Coll., 1953-78, hon. trustee, 1979—; bd. regents State of Ohio; bd. counselors Erskine Coll.; mem. grad. com. on research and edn. Brown U., 1978-80; life fellow Cleve. Zool. Soc., St. Lukes Hosp. Assn. Mem. Am. Econ. Assn., Am. Fin. Assn., Ohio Mfrs. Assn. (chmn. bd. trustees), Royal Econ. Soc., AAUP, Indsl. Assn. N. Central Ohio (pres. 1960), World Wide Acad. Scholars, Assn. Ohio Comdrs., Nat. Alumni Assn. Baldwin-Wallace Coll. (pres. 1961-63), Newcomen Soc. N.Am., John Baldwin Soc., Phi Beta Kappa, Delta Phi Alpha, Delta Mu Delta. Methodist. Clubs: Masons (33 deg., trustee, treas. Scottish Rite bodies of Cleve.; DeMolay (hon. Legion of Honor); Shriners; Brown U. (N.Y.C.); Clifton (Lakewood, Ohio); Union (Cleve.); Duquesne (Pitts.); Pres.'s Ohio State U. Author: Economics of Investments, 1951; Making Profits in the Stock Market, 1952, rev., 1959, 61, 66; Investor's Handbook, 1954; contbg. editor Webster's New World Dictionary; contbr. articles to profl. publs. Office: PO Box 261 Amherst OH 44001

KAMMER, KERRY KENNETH, state senator; b. Detroit, Aug. 13, 1948; s. Kenneth W. and Betty Lou (Aebel) K.; B.A., Wayne State U., 1970; m. Carole Busch, 1972. Claims examiner Zurich Ins. Co., 1966-70; spl. aide to fisheries div. Mich. Dept. Natural Resources, Lansing, 1971; regional claims supr. Mut. Benefit Life Ins. Co., Detroit, 1971-73; city clk. Pontiac (Mich.), 1973-74; mem. Mich. Senate, 1975—. Del., Democratic Nat. Conv., 1980. Mem. Pontiac Jaycees, Pontiac Urban League. Club: Oakland County Sportsmen's. Office: Mich State Senate State Capitol Lansing MI 48933*

KAMP, LINDA JEANNE GATES, occupational therapist; b. Belle Plaine, Iowa, Dec. 22, 1942; d. Maynard Cecil and Ladye Arlillian (Gould) Gates; B.S., U. Iowa, 1965, cert. in occupational therapy, 1966; m. Thomas Nicholas Kamp, June 4, 1966; children—Thomas Gates, David Nicholas, Kathryn Lynn. Dir. occupational therapy Mercy Hosp., Davenport, Iowa, 1966-67; supr. stroke unit occupational therapy sect. St. Anthony's Hosp., Rock Island, Ill., 1968-72; cons. to med. dir. Franciscan Hosp. Rehab. Unit, Rock Island, 1977; instr. Scott Community Coll., Bettendorf, Iowa, 1973—; pvt. practice cons. health care facilities, Davenport, 1978—; dir. Illowa Health Systems Agy., 1976—, pres., 1979—; mem. Statewide Health Coordinating Council, 1976—; mem. Joint Standards Com. for Cert. of Need, 1978—, vice-chmn., 1980—. Bd. dirs. Iowa Easter Seals Soc., 1974-80, pres., 1979-80; mem. adv. bd. Good Samaritan Center, 1978—; mem. Jr. Bd. Scott County, 1972—. Mem. Am. Occupational Therapy Assn., Iowa Occupational Therapy Assn. (mem. exec. commn. 1977-80), Dist. V Iowa Occupational Therapy Assn. (pres. 1977-79). Clubs: Davenport, Scott County Bar Aux., Tri-Cities Garden. Home and office: 40 Edgehill Terrace Davenport IA 52803

KAMRA, SURJIT SINGH, sci. co. exec.; b. Mailsi, India (now Pakistan), Apr. 12, 1939; s. Tarlok Singh and Raj Kaur (Sandhu) K.; came to U.S., 1970; B.S., Punjab U., 1962; M.S., U. Alta., 1967, M.B.A., 1971; m. Nirmaljit Chawla, Jan. 7, 1969; 1 son, Ajaypreet Singh. Tech. supt. H.M.M. Ltd., Nabha, India, 1962-65; prodn. foreman Palm Dairies, Edmonton, Alta., Can., 1967-69; mgr. quality control Beecham Inc., Racine, Wis., 1971-75; dir. tech. services Foulds Inc., Libertyville, Ill., 1975-78; gen. mgr. Copper Country Dairy Inc., Dollarbay, Mich., 1978—; cons. product devel. E. Indian ethnic foods. Rep. Mayor Citizens Com. Desegregation Racine Schs., 1974. Merit scholar Nat. Dairy Research Inst., Karnal, India, 1959, 61. Mem. Inst. Food Technologists (profl.), Am. Assn. Cereal Chemists (profl.). Club: Rotary (sec. Nabha 1965, pres. Hancock, Mich. 1981-82). Home: 747 Green Acres Houghton MI 49930 Office: Copper Country Dairy Dollar Bay MI 49922

KAMRIN, MICHAEL ARNOLD, chemist; b. Bklyn., Aug. 5, 1940; s. Benjamin Barnett and Bessie Kamrin; B.A., Cornell U., 1960; M.S., Yale U., 1962, Ph.D., 1965; m. Ritva Anneli Nieminen, July 19, 1964; children—Kari Allan, Edward Juhani. Research asso. Oak Ridge Nat. Lab., 1963-66; NIH postdoctoral trainee Hopkins Marine Sta., Stanford U., Pacific Grove, Calif., 1966-67; prof. dept. natural sci. Mich. State U., East Lansing, 1967—; vis. scientist legis. office of sci. advisor, Lansing, 1980-81; vis. prof. U. Turku (Finland), 1973-74. Pres. Haslett Edn. Boosters; mem. Haslett Community Edn. Adv. Bd. Recipient U. Turku Meml. Medal, 1974. Mem. AAAS, Sigma Xi. Home: 2037 Haslett Rd Haslett MI 48840 Office: Michigan State Univ East Lansing MI 48824

KAMY, EUGENE MITCHELL, mgmt. cons.; b. Chgo., May 9, 1927; s. Matthew and Marie (Polanski) K.; B.S., U. Ill., 1951; M.S., Loyola U., Chgo., 1957; postgrad. Roosevelt U., 1951-57, Ill. Inst. Tech., 1954-55, DePaul U., 1956-57; m. Margaret Ocsai, Sept. 3, 1949; children—Deborah Ann, Elizabeth. Vice pres. Chgo. Hardware Foundry, N. Chicago, Ill., 1960-67; pres. Eugene M. Kamy & Assos., Inc., 1962—; pres., founder Tolerance Mfg. Co., Waukegan, Ill., 1966-67; pres., treas., founder Profl. Growth Counselors, 1973—; lectr. Sch. Bus. Northwestern U., Evanston, Ill., 1958—; professorial lectr. Grad. Sch. Roosevelt U. Bd. dirs. Indsl. Engring. Coll., Chgo. Registered profl. engr., Calif., Can.; certified mfg. engr., U.S., Can. Mem. Am. Inst. Indsl. Engrs., Nat. Soc. Profl. Engrs., Ill. Soc. Profl. Engrs., Lake County Soc. Profl. Engrs., No. Ill. Indsl. Assn. (Work Improvement Inst.), Am. Prodn. and Inventory Control Soc., Soc. Mfg. Engrs., Ill. Alumni Assn. (life), Delta Sigma Pi, Phi Chi Theta, Psi Chi. Clubs: Chgo. Farmers, Rotary of McHenry. Office: 4723 W Elm St McHenry IL 60050

KANAGA, CLINTON WILLIAMSON, JR., ins. broker; b. Kansas City, Mo., Feb. 28, 1921; s. Clinton W. and Ruth (Smith) K.; B.A., U. Kans., 1942; m. Nina Louise Green, Apr. 30, 1949; children—Stephen C., Carolyn M., William G. With Gambrel Stubbs (merged with Mann-Kline), 1946-49; exec. v.p. Mann-Kline, 1949-68; v.p. Haas & Wilkerson, Kansas City, 1968-78; ins. v.p. Reed Shaw Stenhauce, 1978—; chmn., presiding agt. Jackson County Ins. Commn.; dir. Grandview (Mo.) Bank. Commr., Kansas City Area Transp. Authorily, 1973-77, chmn., 1976, 77; pres. Kansas City Bd. Police Commrs., 1977-81. Served to maj. USMCR; PTO. Named Outstanding Young Man in Kansas City, Mo., Jaycees, 1954; P.E.O. Northland Man of Year, 1977, Eagle Scout, 1936. Mem. U. Kans. Alumni Assn. (nat. dir. 1971-76), Internat. Assn. Chiefs of Police. Democrat. Congregationalist. Clubs: Mercury, Vanguard, Mission Hills Country, K Club, Rotary. Home: 1208 W 65 St Kansas City MO 64113 Office: Suite 222 127 W 10th St Kansas City MO 64105

KANAROWSKI, STANLEY MARTIN, chemist, chem. engr., govt. ofcl.; b. Beausejour, Man., Can., Dec. 12, 1912; s. Joseph and Caroline K.; came to U.S., 1923, naturalized, 1928; B.S., U. Toledo, 1934; postgrad. Ohio State U., 1938-42, U. Akron, 1943-47, N.Y. U., 1954, Xavier U., 1969; m. Pearl Lewus, Aug. 8, 1936; children—Stanley Martin, Janice Ellen, Nancy Carol Kanarowski Cioffari. Chemist, chief chemist Ohio Dept. Liquor Control, Columbus, 1936-42; sr. cons. chemist Nebr. Ordnance Plant Firestone Tire and Rubber Co., Fremont, 1942-43; asst. dir. corp. gen. lab., chief factory product, chem. engr., research and devel. compounding engr. Firestone Tire and Rubber Co., Akron, Ohio, 1943-49; lab. dir., asst. research and devel. mgr. Fremont Rubber Co. (Ohio), 1949-52; research and devel. chem. engr. Glass Fibers, Inc., Waterville, Ohio, 1952-53; chief research and devel. chemist-engr., mgr. quality control Dairypak Butler, Inc., Toledo, 1953-60; chief chemist No. Ohio Region Lab. Liquor Control Enforcement Div., State of Ohio, Cleve., 1960-62; research and devel. chemist-engr. Consol. Paper Co., Monroe, Mich., 1962-63; chemist City of Toledo, 1963-64; project engr., head chemist investigations sect. Ohio River Div. Labs., U.S. Army Engr. Div. C.E., 1964-69; project leader, prin. investigator U.S. Army Constrn. Engring. Research Lab., Champaign, Ill., 1969—. Mem. U. Ill. Illini Symphony Orch., 1970—. Recipient Army-Navy E award, 1943. Mem. Am. Inst. Chem. Engrs., Am. Chem. Soc. (mem. rubber div. 1954—), Am. Def. Preparedness Assn. Office: PO Box 4005 Champaign IL 61820

KANE, CAROL ANN, advt./mktg. co. exec.; b. Los Angeles, Mar. 22, 1946; s. Edwin T. and Carolyn A. (Kajer) Richter; B.A., Marquette U., 1968; m. Christopher Edward Kane, Aug. 31, 1968. Public relations account exec., staff writer William F. Grimshaw Co., 1968-69; advt. audio visual writer, live prodns. coordinator D.P. Brother & Co., 1969-70; partner, creative dir. Christopher Kane Assos./Advt. & Mktg. Counselors, Detroit, 1970—. Mem. Mich. Advt. Agy. Council (pres. 1977-78, dir. 1974-77), Direct Mail Mktg. Assn., New Girls Network, Franklin Hist. Soc. Home: 26875 Charles Ln Franklin MI 48025 Office: Kane & Kane Advt Inc 183 1/2 Oakland St Birmingham MI 48009

KANE, DAVID SHERIDAN, ins. co. exec.; b. Deadwood, S.D., July 12, 1940; s. Arthur Sheridan and Grace Marie K.; Ph.B., U. N.D., 1964. Agt., Fidelity Union Life Ins. Co., Grand Forks, N.D., 1963-65, gen. agt., 1965; pres., founder D.S. Kane & Assos., Inc., Fargo, N.D., 1968—; pres. Coll. Agy. Mgmt., Inc., Fargo, 1971—; pres., founder, dir. Midwest Internat. Life Ins. Co., Fargo, 1976—; nat. dir. sales ITT Life, 1980—; dir. Target Energies. Mem. Nat. Assn. Life Underwriters, Fargo-Moorhead Life Underwriters Assn. (pres. 1980), Am. Soc. C.L.U. Lutheran. Office: D S Kane & Associates Inc PO Box 5676 University Station Fargo ND 58105

KANE, JACK ALLISON, physician; b. Meadville, Pa., Feb. 28, 1921; s. Thomas Emery and Mildred May (McMahon) K.; B.S., Allegheny Coll., 1944; M.D., Case Western Res. U., 1949; m. Virginia Joan Gasque, Sept. 28, 1946; children—Jeffrey, Marsha, Sharman, Cheryl. Intern, U.S. Naval Hosp., St. Albans, N.Y., 1949-50; fellow in indsl. medicine U. Mich., 1950-51; plant physician Frigidaire div. Gen. Motors Corp., Dayton, 1950-52, med. dir. Central Foundry div., Defiance, Ohio, 1954—; mem. exec. staff Defiance Hosp.; mem. occupational health com. Am. Foundrymen's Soc., Des Plaines, Ill. Pres. Defiance County Tb and Health Assn., 1959-72, Defiance County Bd. Health, 1960—. Served with USNR, 1942-45, 52-54. Diplomate Am. Bd. Preventive Medicine. Fellow Am. Occupational Med. Assn.; mem. AMA, Am., Ohio thoracic socs., Ohio Med. Assn., Defiance County Med. Soc., N.W. Ohio Health Planning Assn. Republican. Home: 2 Mirival Ln Defiance OH 43512 Office: Central Foundry Division General Motors Corp Defiance OH 43512

KANE, LAWRENCE JOHN, clin. psychologist; b. Chgo., Feb. 2, 1943; s. John Joseph and Mildred K.; A.B. with honors, Xavier U., Cin., 1965; M.A. in Philosophy cum laude, U. Ottawa, Can., 1968; M.S. in Counseling Psychology magna cum laude, George Williams Coll., 1972; Ph.D., U.S. Internat. U., 1976; m. Lisa F. Pew, Aug. 11, 1973; 1 dau., Kristin. Asst. prof. philosophy Coll. of St. Francis, Joliet, Ill., 1967-72, asso. prof. psychology, 1972-74; staff counselor Counseling in Human Relations Center, part-time instr. psychology George William Coll., Downers Grove, Ill., 1972-74; clin. psychology intern Dept. Health and Social Services, Div. Corrections, Madison, Wis., 1977, staff psychologist Waupun (Wis.) Correctional Inst., 1977, acting chief psychologist-supr., 1978, chief psychologist-supr., 1979—; pvt. practice clin. psychology Capitol Sq. Psychotherapy Assn., Madison. Trustee Family Service, Madison. Mem. Am. Psychol. Assn., Wis. Psychol. Assn., Nat. Register Health Service Providers, Am. Soc. Clin. Hypnosis. Home: 3002 Oakridge Ave Madison WI 53704 Office: Capitol Sq Psychotherapy Assn Suite 149 1400 E Washington St Madison WI 53703

KANE, MICHAEL MYRON, architect-planner, internat. cons.; b. Cleve., Mar. 10, 1922; s. Abraham J. and Anne J. (Solomon) K.; B. in Interior Design, U. Mich., 1943, B. Arch., 1949; student Western Res. U., Case Inst. Tech., 1946, U. Paris, 1960-61, Ecole du Louvre, Scola Cantorum, Paris, 1960-61; m. Edith Smith, Dec. 24, 1975; children—Anina Jo Kane-Van Alstine, Carol. Prin., propr. Michael M. Kane & Assos., architects, planners, Cleve., 1950-62, Lorain, Ohio, 1955-60, Buena Park, Calif., 1959-62; architect-engr. adv. for schs., housing, planning and health facilities, AID, Central and S. Am., Africa, Caribbean, 1962-64; regional architect for Central Am. and Panama, Am. Inst. Free Labor Devel., 1964-67; cons. architect World Bank, Nigeria, 1963-64; adv. campus and facilities planning City U. of N.Y., Queensborough Community Coll., 1968-70, exec. dir. community action programs, 1968-70; vis. lectr. urban environment City U. N.Y., N.Y.C., 1968; chief architect Kingdom of Lesotho, 1975-76; pvt. practice interior design, architecture and planning; also housing market analyst; state architect of Ohio Farmers Home Adminstrn., U.S. Dept. Agr., 1978—; cons. and adv. archtl. project devel. in U.S. V.I., 1970-75, Dominican Republic 1962-67, Haiti, 1962—; dir. Greater Ashtabula (Ohio) Realty Co., Town Top Inc.; founder Self Help Inc., U.S. V.I., 1971; exhibited archtl. projects: Columbus (Ohio) Gallery of Art, 1957, Cleve. Mus. of Art, 1953; numerous archtl. works including: Warehouse Realty Co., Cleve., 1951, Cerebral Palsy Found. Sch., Cleveland Heights, Ohio, 1954, City of Cleve. Mcpl. Golf Course Clubhouse, 1955, Fire Station, Sheffield Lake, Ohio, 1956, Byron Jr. High Sch., Shaker Heights, Ohio, 1957; major planning projects include: Community Center, Recreation and Park, Cleve., 1950, Regional Shopping Center, Cleve., 1952, housing, comml. and recreational facilities Avon Lake, Ohio, 1953. Mem. Mayor's Com. on Housing, Cleve., 1950-52; mem. Ohio Senate Shelter Housing Com., 1979—; bd. dirs. Celo Co-op Community and Arthur Morgan Sch., N.C., 1963-68, Cerebral Palsy Found. Sch., 1952-54. Served to lt. USN, World War II; PTO, ETO. Recipient Merit award Ch. Archtl. Guild of Am., 1960, Turtle award Student Assn. of Queensborough Community Coll., 1970; Fulbright travel and French Govt. grantee, 1960-61. Mem. AIA, Am. Inst. Planners, Ohio Soc. Architects, Soc. for Coll. and Univ. Planners, U.S. V.I. Assn. Architects, Engrs. and Land Surveyors, Am. Assn. Jr. Colls., Soc. for Internat. Devel., Pi Lambda Phi. Contbr. articles on architecture and planning to profl. jours. Home: 290 E South St Worthington OH 43085

KANE, RALPH EDGAR, savings and loan exec.; b. Akron, Ohio, July 16, 1921; s. Albert Anton and Ida Martha (Golz) K.; student U. Akron, 1940-42, 46-47, S.D. State Coll., 1943-44; achievement certificate Am. Savs. & Loan Inst., 1953; m. Alice Mabel Zantow, July 2, 1945; children—Paul Anton, Elisabeth Ann. With B.F. Goodrich Co., Akron, 1940-42, 46; with First Fed. Savs. and Loan Assn., Wooster, 1947—, treas., 1950-78, fin. v.p., 1978—, advt. mgr., 1960—. Chmn., Citizens Com. for Study Local Taxation, Wooster, 1965, Citizens Com. Reapportionment of Wooster, 1968, 71; chmn. bldg. com. Wooster Municipal Bldg., 1960-61; unit treas. Am. Cancer Soc., 1948-52. Councilman-at-large, Wooster, 1958-61. Trustee, Wooster Cemetery Assn., 1960-73. Served with U.S. Army, 1943-46. Named man of the year 20-30 Club Wooster, 1961; recipient award Clipper Graphic Arts, 1973, 74. Mem. Nat. Soc. Savs. and Loan Financial Officers (br. operations com. 1963-65), Am. Savs. and Loan Inst. (achievement award 1951), Ohio Savs. and Loan League, Wayne County Builders Exchange, U.S. C. of C., Wayne County Hist. Soc. (treas. 1965-70), Internat. Platform Assn. Republican. Lutheran (endowment treas. 1948—). Kiwanian (pres. 1969). Clubs: 20-30 (pres. 1950, emeritus mem.), Century (pres. 1971-72, emeritus mem.) (Wooster). Author: 25 Years of Christmas Poems, 1965; (play) A Modern Version of the Christmas Story, 1967; (play) T.H.E.A.T.R.E., 1975; 42 Years of Poems, 1979; (play) T.H.E.R.A.P.Y., 1979. Home: 315 Oakley Rd Wooster OH 44691 Office: PO Box 385 135 E Liberty St Wooster OH 44691

KANEKO, THOMAS MOTOMI, chemist; b. Tokyo, Japan, Aug. 14, 1914; s. Bert Yosaburo and Miwako (Tokunaga) K.; B.S. in Chem. Engring., U. Utah, 1936, Ph.D., 1956; m. Yoko Moro, Mar. 16, 1957. Assayer, Kennecott Copper Corp., Ruth, Nev., 1936-39; research engr. Mitsubishi Chem. Industries, Tokyo, 1939-41; liaison engr. Mitsubishi Rayon Co., Tokyo, 1950-52; research metallurgist Union Carbide Corp., Niagara Falls, N.Y., 1956-57, Nat. Distillers & Chem. Corp., Cin., 1957-59; sr. research chemist BASF Wyandotte Corp., Mich., 1959-78, research asso., 1978—. AEC fellow, 1953-56. Fellow A.A.A.S., Am. Inst. Chemists; mem. N.Y. Acad. Scis., Am. Chem. Soc. (editor Detroit chemist 1967-69), Am. Inst. Chem. Engrs., Am. Inst. Mining and Metall. Engrs., Sigma Xi, Sigma Pi Sigma. Contbr. articles to profl. jours. Patentee in field. Home: 1579 Boxford Rd Trenton MI 48183 Office: 1419 Biddle Ave Wyandotte MI 48192

KANET, ROGER EDWARD, polit. scientist; b. Cin., Sept. 1, 1936; s. Robert George and Edith Mary (Weaver) K.; Ph.B., Johannes Berchmanskolleg, Pullach-bei-Muenchen, Germany, 1960; A.B., Xavier U., Cin., 1961; M.A., Lehigh U., 1963; M.A., Princeton U., 1965, Ph.D., 1966; m. Joan Alice Edwards, Feb. 16, 1963; children—Suzanne Elise, Laurie Alice. Asst. prof. polit. sci. U. Kans., Lawrence, 1966-69, asso. prof., 1969-74; asso. prof. U. Ill., Urbana-Champaign, 1974-78, prof., 1978—, fellow Inst. Advanced Study, 1981-82. Columbia U. joint sr. fellow Russian Inst. and Research Inst. on Communist Affairs, 1972-73; Am. Council Learned Socs. grantee, 1972-73, 78; Internat. Research and Exchanges Bd. grantee, 1976. Mem. Am. Polit. Sci. Assn., Am. Assn. Advancement Slavic Studies, Internat. Studies Assn., Internat. Polit. Sci. Assn. Roman Catholic. Editor books, the most recent being: Background to Crisis: Policy and Politics in Gierek's Poland, 1981. Home: 1007 S Victor St Champaign IL 61820 Office: 361 Lincoln Hall 702 S Wright St Urbana IL 61801

KANG, BANN, physician; b. Kyungnam, Korea, Mar. 4, 1939; d. Dae Ryong and Buni (Chung) K.; came to U.S., 1964, naturalized, 1976; M.D., Kyung Buk Nat. U., 1963; m. Ung Yun Ryo, Mar. 30, 1963. Intern, L.I. Jewish Hosp./Queens Hosp. Center, N.Y.C., 1964-65, resident in medicine, 1965-67; resident in medicine Kyung Buk Nat. U., Teagu, Korea, 1967-70; fellow in allergy and immunology Creighton U./St. Josephs Hsp., Omaha, 1970-71, Henry Ford Hosp., Detroit, 1971-72, U. Mich. Med. Center, Ann Arbor, 1972-73; asst. prof. Chgo. Med. Sch., 1973-74, Rush Med. Sch., Chgo., 1975—; chief div. allergy and clin. immunology Mt. Sinai Hosp., Chgo., 1973—; practice medicine specializing in allergy/immunology, Chgo., 1973—; mem. staff Mt. Sinai Hosp.; cons. Edgewater, St. Anthony hosps. Diplomate Am. Bd. Internal Medicine, Am. Bd. Allergy and Clin. Immunology. Fellow ACP, Am. Acad. Allergy; mem. Chgo. Allergy Soc., AMA, Am. Fedn. Clin. Research. Contbr. articles to profl. jours. Home: 1555 Astor St Chicago IL 60610 Office: Mt Sinai Hosp 15th St at California Ave Chicago IL 60608

KANG, TAI KYUN, psychiatrist; b. Kwangju, Korea, Oct. 15, 1933; s. Pan Suck and Ae Bock (Yoon) K.; came to U.S., 1964, naturalized, 1968; M.D., Chunnam U., 1959; m. Won-Sook Hong, Dec. 17, 1971; children—Sora, Sumi, Daniel. Intern, Worcester (Mass.) Meml. Hosp., 1964-65; resident in psychiatry Conn. Valley Hosp., Middleton, Conn., 1965-68; dir. psychiat. unit Mt. View Hosp., Lockport, N.Y., 1968-69; program dir. Genesee County Community Mental Health Services, Flint, Mich., 1969-72; dir. methodone program Genesee County Regional Drug Abuse Commn., City of Flint, also chief methadone investigator HEW, Flint, 1970-72; practice medicine specializing in psychiatry, Flint, 1972—; asst. clih. prof. Mich. State U., East Lansing, 1972—; chmn. dept. psychiatry McLaren Gen. Hosp., Flint, 1980—; mem. mental health com. G.L.S. Health Systems, Inc., 1980—; critical care cons. Region V Council, Mich. Emergency Med. Service. Chmn. treatment and rehab. sub-com. Citizens Narcotic Action Com., Flint, 1969-70. Served to capt. Korean Army, 1959-64. Research grantee Sandoz Pharm. Co., 1971, Lederle Labs., 1975. Diplomate Am. Bd. Psychiatry and Neurology. Mem. Korean Am. Assn. Flint (pres. 1979—), Chunnam U. Med. Sch. Alumni Assn. Am. (pres. Mid-eastern chpt. 1979—, pres. assn. 1980—), AMA, Genesee County Med. Assn., Mich. Med. Assn., Mich. Psychiat. Assn., Am. Psychiat. Assn., Am. Acad. Psychosomatic Medicine. Clubs: Rotary, Lions, Flint Swimming and Racquet, Shussmeister Ski, Warwick Hills Country. Home: 9395 Burning Tree Grand Blanc MI 48439 Office: 2765 Flushing St Flint MI 48504

KANNENBERG, JOHN L., mayor; b. Texas, Wis., Dec. 16, 1919; s. Ernest F. and Rosine G. (Fischer) K.; student U. Wis.; m. Ella Rose Parent, Sept. 23, 1939; children—Raymond, Lloyd and Loren (twins), Anthony. Salesman, Kannenberg Real Estate, 1946-64; co-propr. Kannenberg Granite Co., 1949-63; city alderman Wausau (Wis.), 1954-64, mayor, 1964—; mem. adv. bd. Sta. WSAU-TV. Pres., United Cerebral Palsy Assn. Wis. Valley; sec. rules and resolutions com. Wis. Conservation Congress; dep. sheriff Marathon County (Wis.); mem. N. Central Wis. Regional Planning Commn., 1974—, vice chmn., 1980-81; mem. Wis. Rail Service Adv. Com., 1978; mem. adv. council Wausau Hosps., Inc. Named Boss of Year, Nat. Secs. Assn., 1972. Mem. Nat. League Cities (small cities adv. com. 1979—), Alliance of Cities (v.p.), Assn. Wis. Planners (pres. 1969-70), Wis. Valley Mayors and Chamber Execs. (pres. 1978-79), Nat. Assn. Regional Councils (intergovtl. affairs policy com. 1981), League Wis. Municipalities (pres. 1973-74, chmn. fin. com. 1980-82), Wausau Area C. of C. Clubs: Elks, Optimist, Moose (state pres. Wis. 1956-57, Pilgrim Degree of Merit 1966). Office: Wausau Water Utility City Hall 407 Grant St Wausau WI 54401

KANO, STANLEY FRANCIS, orgn. exec.; b. Little Rock, Jan. 4, 1944; s. Henry H. and Jean F. (Harvey) K.; B.A., Calif. Lutheran Coll., 1966; m. Alice M. Johnson, July 19, 1969; children—Erech Steven, Tei Lea Marie. Tchr., Good Shepherd Sch., Addis Ababa, Ethiopia, 1966-68; asst. editor Am. Lutheran Ch., Mpls., 1968-71; exec. dir. Helping Industry Resolve Employment Disabilities, Mpls., 1971—; founder Creative Options, Inc., 1980; cons. in field. Bd. dirs. Urban Coalition of Mpls., 1976—; bd. dirs., co-founder Minn. Council for Exoffender Employment, 1972-78; mem. Nat. Interreligious Task Force on Criminal Justice, chmn. joint strategy and action com., 1981; sec. Hennepin County Pvt. Industry Council, 1980-81; mem. Winnetka Elementary Parents Adv. Council; mem. adv. task force Minn. state auditor. Recipient commendation Office Pres. U.S., 1971.

Mem. Am. Mgmt. Assn., Am. Soc. Personnel Adminstrs., Minn. Community Corrections Assn., Am. Vocat. Assn., Am. Correctional Assn. Author: Quest, 1972; Family Vacation Bible Sch., 1970. Home: 11620 52d Ave N Plymouth MN 55442 Office: 1009 Nicollet Mall Minneapolis MN 55403

KANTER, GERALD ALAN, ins. agy. exec.; b. Detroit, Jan. 6, 1931; s. Phillip L. and Florence (Blumberg) K.; B.A., Mich. State U., 1952; m. Marilyn D. Kates, Apr. 10, 1956; children—Susan G., David M., Sharyn H. Exec. v.p. P.L. Kanter Agy., Inc., 1955-72; pres. N.Am. Assn. Underwriters Corp., Southfield, Mich., 1970-75; v.p. Penn Gen. Agys. of Mich., Inc., Southfield, 1972-76; pres. N.Am. Agys., Inc., Bloomfield Hills, Mich., 1977—; chmn. Radcliffe Adminstrs., Inc., Bloomfield Hills; ins. counsel to assns. and spl. risks. Served as 1st lt. U.S. Army, 1953-55; Korea. Named Man of Yr., Life Ins. Leaders Assn., 1961. Mem. Ind. Ins. Agts. Assn., Zeta Beta Tau (pres. 1950-51). Republican. Jewish. Clubs: Masons, Shriner, B'nai Brith; Met. Detroit Ins.; Hamilton Pl. (Southfield); Cricket (Miami, Fla.); Fairlane (Dearborn, Mich.). Home: 1332 Northview Ln Rochester MI 48063 Office: 2550 S Telegraph Rd Bloomfield Hills MI 48013

KANTER, MORTON JAY, editor; b. Chgo., Apr. 7, 1942; s. Isadore and Esther Barbara (Holtzman) K.; B.S. with honors, U. Ill., 1963, Ph.D. (NIH fellow 1963-66), 1966; m. Linde L. Anderson, Nov. 22, 1966; 1 dau., Traci. Research scientist Texaco Research Co., Beacon, N.Y., 1966-68; sr. asso. editor Chem. Abstracts Service, Columbus, Ohio, 1968—; dir. Nat. Center for Pet Info. Jewish. Club: B'nai B'rith. Home: 103 S Dawson Rd Columbus OH 43209 Office: PO Box 3012 Columbus OH 43210

KANTOR, DAVID ALAN, computer services co. ofcl.; b. Bklyn., Nov. 5, 1951; s. Lewis Kantor and Bertha Kantor (Friedman) Gershman; B.A. in Econs., Queens Coll., CUNY, 1973; M.B.A., U. Pa., 1975. Economist, N.Y. State Power Authority, N.Y.C., 1975-76; mgr. mktg. Allied Van Lines, Broadview, Ill., 1976-80; dir. mktg. Amherst Assos. Inc., Chgo., 1980—; adj. prof. Elmhurst (Ill.) mgmt. program Elmhurst Coll., 1980—. Mem. Am. Mktg. Assn. Co-author: The Labor Relations Climate and Management Rights in Urban School Systems, 1975.

KANTOR, HARVEY SHERWIN, physician, educator; b. N.Y.C., Apr. 30, 1938; s. Jack and Henrietta (Feingold) K.; student U. Miami, 1955-58; M.D., Washington U., 1962; postgrad. M.I.T., 1966-69. Intern, Barnes Hosp., St. Louis, 1962-63; asst. medicine Washington U., St. Louis, 1962-63; asst. resident medicine Boston City Hosp., 1963-64; research fellow infectious diseases New Eng. Med. Center Hosps., Boston, 1966-67, chief resident infectious disease service, 1967-68, research fellow in infectious disease, 1968-69; asst. medicine Tufts U., Boston, 1966-69; instr. medicine U. Miami (Fla.) Sch. Medicine, 1969-71; attending physician dept. medicine and infectious diseases Jackson Meml. Hosp., Miami, 1969-71; asso. dir. dept. infectious diseases Cook County Hosp., Chgo., 1971-72, attending physician, 1971-74; asst. prof. medicine U. Ill. Med. Center, Chgo., 1971-75, asst. prof. microbiology, 1971-75; acting dir. dept. infectious diseases Cook County Hosp., Chgo., 1972-74; staff physician sect. infectious diseases West Side VA Hosp., Chgo., 1974-75; chief infectious disease sect. VA Hosp., North Chicago, Ill., 1975—; asso. prof. medicine U. Health Scis., Chgo. Med. Sch., 1975—, dir. div. infectious Diseases, 1975—, asso. prof. pathology, 1978—; lectr. Cook County Grad. Sch. Medicine, Chgo., 1977—. Served to capt. M.C., U.S. Army, 1964-66. NIH fellow, 1966-69; research and edn. asso. VA, 1969-71, research awards, 1976, 79; AMA Physicians Recognition award, 1977; U. Health Scis./Chgo. Med. Sch. Bd. Trustees Research award, 1977; lic. physician, Mo., Mass., Fla., Ill.; diplomate Am. Bd. Internal Medicine. Fellow Royal Soc. Medicine (London), A.C.P., Infectious Disease Soc. Am.; mem. Am. Soc. Microbiology, Lake County Med. Soc., Am. Fedn. Clin. Research, Ill. Med. Soc., AMA, N.Y. Acad. Sci., Sigma Xi. Contbr. numerous articles to med. jours. Home: 1 Kingswood Ct Riverwoods IL 60015 Office: Chgo Med Sch Dept Medicine North Chicago IL 60064

KANZIGG, RAYMOND WILLIAM, coal co. exec.; b. Belmont County, Ohio, Sept. 12, 1922; s. William C. and Eula M. K.; student Ohio U., 1948, Coll. of Steubenville, 1967-68; m. Cynthia L. Ferguson, June 18, 1977; 1 dau., Cythia Rae; 1 dau. by previous marriage, June I. Kanzigg Baker. With N.Am. Coal Corp., Cleve., 1947—, chief shipper, 1964-67, personnel asst., 1967-68, div. personnel mgr., 1968, 69, mgr. indsl. relations, 1969-71, corp. personnel mgr., 1971—. Instl. rep. Nat. Trail council Boy Scouts Am.; disaster chmn. Belmont County chpt. ARC; v.p., pres. Bd. Edn., 1956-68; chmn. Community Planning Commn., 1963-64; tech. adv. vocat. sch., 1969-71. Served with U.S. Army, 1942-46. Accredited personnel mgr. Personnel Accreditation Inst. Mem. Am. Soc. Personnel Adminstrs. Clubs: Rotary, Masons, Shriners. Home: 9040 Portage Pointe Dr Streetsboro OH 44240 Office: N Am Coal Corp 12800 Shaker Blvd Cleveland OH 44120

KAO, STEPHEN SHENG-TE, engineer; b. Hupeh, China, June 8, 1921; s. Shong Yin and Chi San (Lee) K.; came to U.S., 1959, naturalized, 1968; M.S., U. Colo., 1948, Carnegie Mellon U., 1961; m. Jean C.H. Tung, Dec. 5, 1948; children—Hugh, June. Prof., chmn. dept. indsl. mgmt. Nat. Cheng-Kung U., Tainan, Taiwan, 1950-59; devel. engr. Blackstone Co., Jamestown, N.Y.. 1961-68; sr. engr. Modine Co., Racine, Wis., 1968—. Mem. Ops. Research Soc. Am., ASME. Republican. Author: Operations Research, 1959; Quality Control, 1958; Production Control, 1957; Application of Operations Research to Optimize Heat Transfer Surface, 1977; Proposed Presidential Performance Index, 1981. Patentee in field (2). Home: 30 Illinois St Racine WI 53405

KAPACINSKAS, JOSEPH, engr., author; b. Mazuciai, Lithuania, Oct. 20, 1907; came to U.S., 1949, naturalized, 1956; s. George and Teofile (Baskeviciute) K.; Engr., Tech. Coll., Ausburg, Germany, 1948; student Ill. Inst. Tech., 1950-51; B., Allied Inst. Tech., Chgo., 1960; m. Marie Kulikauskas, Dec. 27, 1952; 1 son, Joseph-Vytautas. Employee, City of Kaunas Municipal Govt., Lithauania, 1929-39, Nat. R.R., Lithuania, 1939-44, Nat. R.R., Treuchtlingen, Germany, 1944-45; instr., chief electrician UNRRA, Weissenburg, Germany, 1946-47; electrician Burlington No. R.R., Inc., Chgo., 1951-72; editor Sandara, weekly Lithuanian League newspaper, Chgo., 1973-76. Mem. Am. Lithuanian Engrs. and Architects Assn., Lithuanian Journalists Assn., Am. Tool and Mfg. Engrs., AAAS, Internat. Platform Assn., Intercontinental Biog. Assn., Lithuanian Alliance of Am. Author: Siaubingos Dienos-Horrifying Days, 1965; Iseivio Dalia-Emigrant's Fate, 1974; Spaudos Baruose-Within the Press, 1979. Contbr. articles on Lithuanian culture and social life to newspapers. Home: 6811 S Maplewood Ave Chicago IL 60629

KAPILA, VED PARKASH, engineer, surveyor, builder; b. Lopon, India, Dec. 27, 1932; s. Baboo Ram and Amravati (Vasishta) K.; came to U.S., 1963; naturalized, 1977; student Punjab U., India, 1949-51; Civil engring. Sch., Lucknow, Ind., 1951-53; B.S. in Civil Engring., U. Mich., 1964, M.S. in Civil Engring., 1965; M.B.A., Wayne State U., 1970, value engring. orientation, 1970; m. Pushpa Pipat, Nov. 18, 1952; children—Shashi, Rajnish, Rita, Renu. Engring. sect. officer Punjab State Public Works Dept., India, 1953-63; design, engr. Ayres, Lewis, Norris & May, Ann Arbor, Mich., 1964-65; Obenchain Corp., Dearborn, Mich., 1965-66; v.p., chief civil and structural engr. O. Germany, Inc., Warren, Mich., 1966-76; dir. project services and chief planning and scheduling, chief quality assurance, chief client purchasing Hoad Engrs., Inc., Ypsilanti, Mich., 1976-78; pres. Kapila Constrn. Co., Inc., Kapila Contracting Co., Inc., Kapila & Assos., 1968—. Registered profl. engr. Mich., Ga., Va., Punjab State (India); registered land surveyor, Mich.; licensed builder, Mich.; certified Nat. Council Engring. Examiners. Mem. ASCE, Am. Concrete Inst., Am. Inst. Steel Constrn., Mich. Soc. Registered Land Surveyors, Am. Soc. Quality Control, Soc. Am. Value Engrs., Nat. Soc. Profl. Engrs. Home: 25039 Branchaster Farmington Hills MI 48018 Office: 7439 Middlebelt Rd Suite 2 West Bloomfield MI 48033

KAPLAN, ETHAN ZADOK, urban planner-analyst; b. Pontiac, Mich., May 9, 1935; s. Morris J. and Certie (Bock) K.; B.A., U. Chgo., 1955, M.A., 1958; postgrad. Washington U. at St. Louis, 1960-62; m. Jane B. Breese, Dec. 23, 1958; children—Mark, Alan. Sr. planner St. Louis County Planning Com., 1962-66, prin. planner, 1967-69; chief advanced planning City Alexandria, Va., 1966-67; research planner Health and Welfare Council St. Louis, 1969-75; pvt. cons., 1975-78; exec. dir. Southeast Kans. Regional Planning Commn., 1978—. Served with AUS, 1958-60. Mem. Am. Inst. Cert. Planners, Nat. Con. Social Welfare, Am. Planning Assn., Am. Sociol. Assn. Home: 630 S Evergreen St Chanute KS 66720

KAPLAN, FRANK, food service exec.; b. Chgo., July 16, 1927; s. Edward and Anna (Gordon) K.; grad. chef's program Washburn Trade Sch., 1954; H.M.M., Oakton Community Coll., 1978; m. Marilyn Reznick, Dec. 18, 1949; children—Edward, Bonnie, Leslie. Employed with various restaurants, hotels and instns., 1961; night chef Key Club, Chgo., 1961-65; sous chef Kon Ti-Ki Ports Restaurant, Chgo., 1965-68; chef tng. supr. Food Service Industry Tng. Project, Chgo., 1968-69; first sous chef Conrad Hilton Hotel, Chgo., 1969-70, 70-73; chef ARA Services, Phila.; mfg. rep. Modern Maid Food Products, Chgo., 1973; food service mgr. Interstate United Corp., Chgo., 1973-77; food service dir. Frances W. Parker Sch., Chgo., 1977-79; chef Continental Bank, Chgo., 1979—. Served with USNR, 1945-46. Mem. Am. Culinary Fedn. (cert. exec. chef), Chefs of Cuisine Assn. Chgo., Les Amis D'Escoffier. Home: 3843 W Harvard Terr Skokie IL 60076 Office: Continental Bank 230 Clark St Chicago IL 60604

KAPLAN, HOWARD GORDON, lawyer; b. Chgo., June 1, 1941; s. David I. and Beverly Kaplan; B.S., U. Ill., 1962; J.D., John Marshall Law Sch., Chgo., 1967. Acct., Chgo., 1962-67; admitted to Ill. bar, 1967, U.S. Supreme Ct. bar, 1971, D.C. bar, 1980; practiced in Chgo., 1967—; partner firm Angell, Kaplan, Zaidman & Gomberg, 1975—; asst. prof. Chgo. City Colls., 1967-78; field editor Pollution Engring. mag., 1970—. C.P.A., Ill. Mem. Am. Bar Assn., Ill. Bar Assn., Chgo. Bar Assn., Bar Assn. 7th Circuit, Decalogue Soc., Am. Inst. C.P.A.'s, Ill. Soc. C.P.A.'s. Clubs: Chgo. Athletic Assn., Covenant (Chgo.); B'nai B'rith; Friars (Los Angeles). Author papers in field. Office: 105 W Madison St Chicago IL 60602

KAPLAN, KIPTON, health care adminstr.; b. Fort Wayne, Ind., May 11, 1940; s. Max and Mary Louise (Helms) K.; A.B., Ind. U., 1961; M.G.A., U. Pa., 1963; m. Martha Ann Kiessling, June 6, 1959; children—Corinne, Caroline, Kipton, Carlene, Kevin, Catherine. Exec. dir. N.W. Ind. Comprehensive Health Planning Council, Inc., Highland, 1970-76; project dir. health planning projects Purdue U. Calumet Campus, Hammond, Ind., 1969-70; dir. spl. programs, sr. asso. City Planning Assos., Inc., subs. Computer Scis. Corp., Mishawaka, Ind., 1967-69; planning dir., asst. city mgr., acting city mgr. City of Port Huron, Mich., 1964-67; exec. dir. No. Ind. Health Systems Agy., Inc., South Bend, 1976—; pres., chief exec. officer No. Ind. Found. for Health Inc., South Bend, 1981—; tchr. dept. sociology and anthropology U. Notre Dame, 1980-81. Active United Way. Fels Inst. scholar, 1961-62, Fels Inst. fellow, 1961-62. Mem. Am. Health Planning Assn., Am. Planning Assn., Am. Hosp. Assn., Soc. Hosp. Planning, Am. Soc. Public Adminstrn., Ind. Soc. Public Adminstrn., Ind. Health Planning Assn. Jewish. Club: Univ. of Notre Dame. Home: 16833 Barrington Ct Granger IN 46530 Office: 900 E Colfax Ave South Bend IN 46617

KAPLAN, MARTIN F., social psychologist, educator; b. Bklyn., Apr. 20, 1940; s. Ben and Bebe (Wulinsky) K.; B.B.A., CCNY, 1960, M.A., 1962; Ph.D. (research fellow NIMH 1962-64), U. Iowa, 1965; m. Lydia Eagle, July 9, 1960; children—Jonathan, Jeremy, Jaymie. Psychology asst. VA, Iowa City, Iowa, 1964-65; asst. prof. No. Ill. U., De Kalb, 1965-68, asso. prof., 1968-75, prof., 1975—; vis. scholar U. Calif., San Diego, 1970-71; research visitor U. N.C., Chapel Hill, 1981; cons. Elgin State Hosp., 1966-70. NIMH, NSF research grantee. Fellow Am. Psychol. Assn., Midwestern Psychol. Assn., Soc. Exptl. Social Psychologists, Soc. for Advancement of Social Psychology, Psychonomic Soc., Am. Law-Psychology Soc., Sigma Xi. Jewish. Author: Human Judgment and Decision Processes, 1975; Human Judgment and Decision Processes in Applied Settings, 1977; contbr. articles to research pubIs. Home: 1503 Carlisle Ln De Kalb IL 60115 Office: Northern Illinois Univ De Kalb IL 60115

KAPLAN, MORTON HARVEY, public relations firm exec.; b. Chgo., Nov. 26, 1931; s. Charles C. and Mabel (Schack) K.; B.S., DePaul U.; children—Robin, Maebeth, Nancy. With Julius Klein Public Relations; exec. v.p., creative dir. Herbert M. Kraus & Co.; dir. public info. Ill. Public Aid Commn.; now pres. Morton H. Kaplan Assos. div. Ketchum Public Relations, Chgo.; instr. Columbia Coll., Chgo.; cons. to Gov. of Ill., also to U.S. senator. Trustee Kate Maremont Found.; pres. Ill. Arts Alliance. Served with CIC, U.S. Army, 1953-55. Home: 333 E Ontario St Chicago IL 60611 Office: 405 N Wabash Ave Chicago IL 60611

KAPLAN, ROBERT, steel co. exec.; b. Chgo., Jan. 20, 1907; s. Max S. and Jennie K.; Ph.B., U. Chgo., 1929; m. Virginia M. George, July 1, 1943; children—Miriam Kaplan Schwartz, Donna L. Kaplan Rautbord, Patricia K. Mem. Midwest Stock Exchange, 1929-37; pres. Filshie Lead Head Nail Co., Chgo., 1935-39; v.p. Paumar Engring. Co., Gary, Ind., 1939-43; pres. Sun Steel Co., Chicago Heights, Ill., 1943—; dir. M.S. Kaplan Co. Bd. dirs., v.p. Nat. Found. for Progressive Relaxation. Mem. Am. Assn. for Advancement Tension Control (dir.). Clubs: Presidents (U. Chgo.), Standard. Patentee lead head nails, vinyl coating sheet steel, reclamation of steel from slag. Home: 1040 Lake Shore Dr Chicago IL 60611 Office: 2500 Euclid Ave Chicago Heights IL 60411

KAPNAS, MICHAEL GEORGE, public relations and advt. co. exec.; b. Gary, Ind., June 24, 1926; s. George M. and Virginia (Asimakis) K.; B.S., Northwestern U., 1948; m. Helen I. Tsatsos, June 5, 1949; children—George M., II, Irene B. (dec.). Dir. public relations Whiteco Industries, Inc., Merrillville, Ind., 1972-80; pres. Michael G. Kapnas Assos., Inc., Merrillville, 1980—; lectr. Valparaiso U., 1974, Ind. U. Northwest, 1976. Vice pres. Northwest Ind. Council Econ. Growth, 1977—; bd. dirs. Crisis Center. Served to comdr. U.S. Navy, 1943-46. Mem. Communicators Northwest Ind. (dir., pres.), Merrillville C. of C. (pres. 1978), N.W. Ind. Navy League (pres.), Res. Officers Assn. (pres.). Greek Orthodox. Club: Rotary. Home: 225 W 49th Ave Gary IN 46408 Office: Twin Towers South Suite 516 Merrillville IN 46410

KAPPES, PHILIP SPANGLER, lawyer; b. Detroit, Dec. 24, 1925; s. Philip Alexander and Wilma Fern (Spangler) K.; B.A. cum laude, Butler U., 1945; J.D., U. Mich., 1948; m. Glendora Galena Miles, Nov. 27, 1948; children—Susan Lea, Philip Miles, Mark William. Admitted to Ind. bar, 1948, U.S. Supreme Ct. bar, 1970; practiced in Indpls., 1948—, asso. firm Armstrong and Gause, 1948-49; asso. law offices C. B. Dutton, 1950-52; partner firm Dutton, Kappes & Overman, 1952—; chmn. bd., mem. exec. com. dir. Lab. Equipment Corp.; sec., dir. SW, Inc., Midwest Food Center, Inc., Meml. Properties, Creston Corp.; asst. sec., dir. Wellman Dynamics Corp.; partner Shadeland Properties; instr. bus. law Butler U., 1948-49. Counselor, chmn. trust and legal coms. Crossroads of Am. council Boy Scouts Am., 1959—, bd. dirs., exec. com., v.p. adminstrn., 1976—, v.p. fin., 1975-76, pres., 1977-79; trustee Children's Mus. Indpls., Washington Twp. Sch. Found., 1967-76. Mem. Am. Judicature Soc., Am. (ho. dels. 1970-71, chmn. lawyers title guaranty fund com. 1971-73), Ind. (ho. dels. 1959—, sec. 1973-74, bd. mgrs. 1975— nominating com., chmn. public relations exec. com.), Indpls. (treas. 1959, 1st v.p. 1965, pres. 1970, bd. mgrs. 1976-77) bar assns., Lawyers Assn., Indpls. Legal Aid Soc., Indpls. Jr. C. of C. (past 1st v.p.), Butler U. (bd. govs., past pres.), Mich. alumni assns., Phi Delta Theta, Tau Kappa Alpha. Republican. Presbyterian (pres. bd. trustees, deacon, ruling elder). Clubs: Masons (32 deg., past master), Scottish Rite (sr. warden chpt. Rose Croix); Shriners; Lawyers, Gyro (past pres.); Meridian Hills Country. Home: 7450 North Park Ave Indianapolis IN 46240 Office: Guaranty Bldg Indianapolis IN 46204

KAPSALIS, THOMAS, city ofcl.; b. Chgo., Mar. 9, 1933; s. George and Harriet (Gkikas) K.; B.S., Purdue U., 1956; postgrad. Grad. Sch. Bus., U. Chgo.; m. Patricia Ann Surgalski, Sept. 12, 1964; children—William, Alexandra. With dept. aviation City of Chgo., 1958-62, with dept. city planning, 1962-77, dir., 1965-77, adminstrv. aide to mayor, 1977, exec. dir. Chgo. urban transp. dist., 1977-78, commr. dept. planning, city and community devel., 1978-79, mgr. O'Hare Airport, coordinator aviation planning, dept. aviation, 1979-80, commr. aviation, 1980—; former chmn. Comml. Dist. Devel. Commn.; former co-chmn. coordinating com. Chgo. Community Devel. Program; former sec., mem. Chgo. Plan Commn.; former sec. Public Bldg. Commn.; former mem. Ill.-Ind. Bi-State Commn., Northeastern Ill. Planning Commn., Chgo. Econ. Devel. Commn., Chgo Commn. on Hist. and Archtl. Landmarks; former mem. Chgo. constrn. coordinating com. Dept. Labor. Mem. Am. Hellenic Democratic Council Ill. Served with U.S. Army, 1956-58. Recipient cert. of appreciation U.S. Dept. Labor, 1976; Inst. Human Relations award Am. Jewish Com., 1980. Mem. Am. Assn. Airline Execs., Airport Operators Council Internat., Purdue U. Alumni Assn., Lambda Alpha. Club: Economic (Chgo.). Office: Dept Aviation City Hall 121 N LaSalle St Room 1111 Chicago IL 60602*

KARAYANNIS, NICHOLAS MARIOS, chemist; b. Athens, Greece, May 30, 1931; s. Marios L. and Antiopi M. (Horsch) K.; came to U.S., 1965; B.S., Nat. Tech. U., Athens, 1955; Ph.D. (Greek Chem. Products & Fertilizers Co. scholar), U. Coll., London, England, 1960; m. Alexandra E. Manolakis, Oct. 1, 1955; children—Marios, Yannis. Sci. adviser Greek Nat. Defense Gen. Staff, Athens, 1961-62; sci. adviser Greek Ministry Coordination, Athens, 1962-65; fuels and lubricants tech. instr. Nat. Tech. U., Athens, 1963-65; research asso. Johns Hopkins, Balt., 1965-67, Drexel U., Phila., 1967-70; sr. research chemist Amoco Chem. Corp., Naperville, Ill., 1970-76, research asso., 1976—. Served with Greek Army, 1959-61. NIH research asso. grantee, 1965-67; U.S. Army Edgewood Arsenal research asso. grantee, 1967-70. Mem. Am. Chem. Soc., N.Y. Acad. Scis., A.A.A.S., Greek Tech. Chamber, Ramsay Soc. Chem. Engrs., Phi Lamda Upsilon. Club: Pebblewood Swim and Racquet. Patentee in field. Home: 15 Pebblewood Trail Naperville IL 60540 Office: Amoco Chemicals Corporation Naperville IL 60566

KARDAS, BARBARA JEAN, coll. dean; b. N.Y.C., Mar. 7, 1931; d. Robert Andrew and Helen Frances (MacNaughton) Cotil; B.S., N.Y. State Univ. Coll., Oswego, 1952; M.A., Hunter Coll., N.Y.C., 1956; Ph.D., Northwestern U., 1969; m. Julian Kardas, Feb. 24, 1957; 1 dau., Janine. Elementary sch. tchr., 1952-67; mem. faculty Chgo. State U., 1967—, prof. edn., 1974—, dean Coll. Edn., 1974—; proposal reader Nat. Endowment Humanities, 1979; pres. Chgo. Consortium Colls. and Univs., 1979—. Pres. Epis. Ch. Women, mem. vestry Holy Nativity Ch. Recipient Disting. Alumnus award SUNY, Oswego, 1975. Mem. AAUP, Am. Assn. Colls. Tchr. Edn., Ill. Assn. Colls. Tchr. Edn. (exec. bd.), Nat. Council Adminstrv. Women (bd. dirs. Ella Flagg Young chpt.), Am. Assn. Higher Edn., Ill. Curriculum Council, Kappa Delta Pi, Phi Delta Kappa. Episcopalian. Author: Teacher Aides, 1969; also articles. Office: Chgo State Univ 95th and King Dr Chicago IL 60628

KARDASZ, JOHN THOMAS, sales mgr.; b. New Brighton, Pa., Oct. 10, 1945; s. Joseph F. and Beatrice J. (Gill) K.; A.A., Burlington County Community Coll., 1973; B.S., Rutgers U., 1976; m. Deborah M. Schultz, Feb. 10, 1968; children—Kevin Michael, Timothy John, Kelly Lynn, Patrick James. Systems rep. RCA Graphic Systems, Dayton, N.J., 1968-69; systems mgr. Am. Computer Graphics, Cinnaminson, N.J., 1969-71; project mgr. Internat. Computaprint Corp., Ft. Washington, Pa., 1971-78; sales mgr. Datacomp Corp., Cleve., 1978—. Served with USAF, 1964-67. Mem. Am. Mgmt. Assn., Council of Smaller Enterprises (Cleve.), Greater Cleve. Growth Assn. Roman Catholic. Home: 400 Caladonia Ave Akron OH 44313 Office: 2342 E 9th Cleveland OH 44115

KARIM, M. REZA-UL, microbiologist, educator; b. Noakhali, Bangladesh, India, Nov. 1, 1941; came to U.S., 1963, naturalized, 1974; student Ahsannauallah Engring. Coll., Pakistan, 1956-58; B.Sc. with honors in Microbiology (gold medalist), U. Karachi (Pakistan), 1962; M.S., U. Minn., 1966; Ph.D., U. Mont., 1974; m. Agnes A. Mullenbach, Feb. 4, 1967; children—Lisa Mona, Sarah Ranee. Teaching asst. dental microbiology U. Minn., 1963-64; instr. Bengali lang. Peace Corps Tng. Program, 1963-64; instr. biology U. Wis., Eau Claire, 1966-67; asst. prof. gen. biology, physiology and microbiology No. State Coll., Aberdeen, S.D., 1968-70, research and teaching asst. virology U. Mont., Missoula, 1970-71; asso. prof. organic chemistry, gen. biology dept. natural scis. No. State Coll., Aberdeen, S.D., 1972-75, prof., 1975—, also chief health professions advisor, 1976—, coordinator health scis. program and health scis. research, 1981—; dir. DeVries project on quality control of milk, 1969; dir. various workshops on sanitation and public health, 1973-75. Mem. Am. Acad. Microbiology, Am. Soc. Microbiology, Pakistan Soc. Microbiology, NEA, S.D. Edn. Assn., S.D. Assn. for Health Educators and Practitioners, S.D. Acad. of Sci., Central Assn. Advisors for Health Professions, S.D. Cancer Soc., Gerontology Assn. of S.D., N.Y. Acad. Sci., Minn. Alumni Assn., Sigma Xi, Phi Sigma. Clubs: Elks, Cosmopolitan. Contbr. articles to sci. jours. Home: 1714 S 8th St Aberdeen SD 57401 Office: Northern State College Aberdeen SD 57401

KARIOTIS, JOSEPH ANTHONY, ednl. adminstr.; b. Chgo., July 13, 1931; s. Anthony John and Stella (Kourakis) K.; student No. Ill. U., 1950-51, M.S. in Edn., 1961; B.A., Elmhurst Coll., 1958; Ph.D., Walden U.; m. Anne Paraschos, Sept. 7, 1952; children—Shelley, Anthony, Alexander. Tchr., Roy Sch., North Lake, Ill., 1958-63; prin. Queen Bee Sch., Wheaton, Ill., 1963-64; supt. schs. Dist. 16, Wheaton,

1964—. Served with USAF, 1951-53. Mem. NEA, No. Ill. Prins. Roundtable, No. Ill. Supts. Roundtable, Sch. Assn. Spl. Edn. DuPage County (dir.), Am.-Hellenic Ednl. Progressive Assn. Home: 886 Bryan St Elmhurst IL 60126 Office: 1560 Bloomingdale Rd Glen Ellyn IL 60137

KARKLYS, JOSEPH, elec. engr.; b. Kaunas, Lithuania, Dec. 28, 1927; s. Klemensas and Jolanta (Svarcaite) K.; came to U.S., 1949, naturalized, 1956; B.S. in Elec. Engring., Ill. Inst. Tech., 1957; m. Elvira Kriauciunaite, June 9, 1956; 1 child, Rimas J. Devel. engr. Motorola, Inc., 1957-58; sr. devel. engr. ITT, 1958-63; sr. design engr. Gen. Dynamics Electronics Co., Rochester, N.Y., 1963-66; with Whirlpool Research & Engring. Center, Benton Harbor, Mich., 1966—, sr. research engr., 1971—. Served with Signal Corps, U.S. Army, 1950-52. Mem. Am. Legion, IEEE, Sigma Xi. Republican. Roman Catholic. Office: Whirlpool Research and Engring Center Monte Rd Benton Harbor MI 49022

KARKUT, ANN LOUISE, editor; b. Bellwood, Ill., June 30, 1924; d. Walter and Anna (Jacobs) Knippenberg; student LaSalle U.; m. Edward Karkut, Mar. 20, 1943; children—Patricia, Edward, Stanley, Susan, Christopher. Asst. editor, Lockport (Ill.) Herald, 1960-63, editor, 1963-69; asst. editor Naperville (Ill.) Sun, 1969-70; editor Joliet (Ill.) Circle, 1970; editor Pointer Publs., Riverdale, Ill., 1970-72; asst. editor Lisle (Ill.) Sun, 1972-74; asst. editor Big Farmer mag., Frankfort, Ill., 1974—. Sec., Homer Fire Dept. Aux., 1962, Dist. 92 Band Parents, 1967; mem. Homer Republican Precinct Com., 1976—; clk. Homer Twp., 1981—, also editor twp. newsletter. Mem. Lockport Bus. and Profl. Women's Club (charter mem., past pres., named Woman of Yr. 1979), Ill. Bus. and Profl. Women's Club, Ill. Press Women's Assn. Roman Catholic. Club: Waa-Shee Riders (pres.). Home: Rt 2 Box 26 Gougar Lockport IL 60441 Office: Rt 1 Box 375-A Lockport IL 60441

KARL, GREGORY PAUL, acct.; b. Saginaw, Mich., Feb. 7, 1950; s. Harry F. and Mary E. (Knox) K.; B.S. in Acctg. magna cum laude, U. Detroit, 1971; m. Mary Rose Capizzo, July 15, 1972; children—Sheri Lynn, Matthew John, Joseph Harry. Sr. tax acct. Ernst & Ernst, Saginaw, 1971-74; asst. controller J.P. Burroughs & Son, Inc., Saginaw, 1974-75, controller, 1975-79; corporate staff Gen. Motors Corp., 1979-80; controller Wickes Engineered Materials, Saginaw, 1980—. Mem. acctg. curriculum adv. com. Delta Coll., University Center, Mich. C.P.A., Mich. Mem. Am. Inst. C.P.A.'s, Mich. Assn. C.P.A.'s, Mich. Assn. Professions, Am. Acctg. Assn., Am. Mgmt. Assn., Am. Inst. Corp. Controllers, U.S. Yacht Racing Union, Boat Owners Assn. U.S. Home: 315 Holbrook St Saginaw MI 48603 Office: 1621 E Holland St Saginaw MI 48601

KARLI, WADE MARION, sch. prin.; b. Sioux Falls, S.D., Nov. 27, 1949; s. Palmer LeRoy and Wanda Eris K.; student Buena Vista Coll., 1968-69, B.A., Augustana Coll., Sioux Falls, 1972; cert. edn. deaf Lady Spencer Churchill Coll., Eng., 1976; M.A., Calif. State U., Northridge, 1978; postgrad. U. Nebr., Lincoln; m. Barbara Louise Rist, Apr. 2, 1971; children—Rebecca Ruth, Scott Palmer. Tchr. secondary lang. arts Minn. Sch. for Deaf, Faribault, 1972-75, 76-77; asst. prin. Iowa Sch. for Deaf, Council Bluffs, 1978-79, curriculum dir., 1978—, prin. community oriented skills tng. program, 1980—; coordinator sci. career program for hearing impaired Iowa State U., 1982, Pride-Fest, arts festival for handicapped, Council Bluffs, 1982. Bd. dirs. Met. Edn. Planning Agy., Omaha, Bluffs Arts Council, Council Bluffs. Rotary Found. fellow, 1975-76; Nat. Leadership Tng. Program fellow, 1978, Nat. Com. Arts for Handicapped grantee, 1982. Mem. Assn. Supervision and Curriculum Devel., Conv. Am. Instrs. of Deaf, Phi Delta Kappa. Lutheran. Club: Rotary Internat. Home: 4 Victoria Dr Council Bluffs IA 51501 Office: 1600 S Hwy 275 Council Bluffs IA 51501

KARLIN, GARY LEE, ins. co. exec.; b. Chgo., Jan. 18, 1934; s. Jack and Pearl (Malin) K.; student U. Ill., 1951-52, Roosevelt U., 1952; m. Cheryl Daneman; children—David, Paige. With Mut. of N.Y., 1956-62, sales mgr., Chgo., 1958-62, regional trainer, 1962-63; pres. Exec. Motivation, Inc., Rolling Meadows, Ill., 1964—; cons. in field. Mem. Chgo. Assn. Life Underwriters, Nat. Assn. Life Underwriters (life) Million Dollar Round Table (Top of Table). Contbg. editor Profl. Mgmt. Mag., 1965-77; contbr. articles to profl. jours.; also narrator ins. film (award). Home: 1497 Lake Shore Ct Barrington IL 60010 Office: Suite 309 1 Crossroads Rolling Meadows IL 60008

KARLOWSKI, THOMAS RAYMOND, internist; b. Detroit, Jan. 6, 1943; s. Stanley and Sophie (Sohacki) K.; B.S., Wayne State U., 1965, M.D., 1969; m. Diana Lambert, June 21, 1968; children—Thomas Michael, Maria Ann, Christina Rose. Intern, William Beaumont Hosp., Royal Oak, Mich., 1969-70; resident in internal medicine Mayo Clinic, Rochester, Minn., 1972-74; practice medicine specializing in internal medicine, Waterloo, Iowa, 1974—; mem. staff St. Francis Hosp., Allen Hosp., Schoitz Hosp.; med. advisor ARC. Served with USPHS, 1970-72. Diplomate Am. Bd. Internal Medicine. Mem. AMA (Physician Recognition awards 1969-72, 72-75, 75-78, 78-81, 81-84), Am. Coll. Physicians, Iowa State Med. Soc., Waterloo C. of C. Roman Catholic. Clubs: Kiwanis, Elks. Research, publs. on vitamin C and common cold. Home: 216 Lovejoy Ave Waterloo IA 50701 Office: 622 W 4th St Waterloo IA 50701

KARLSON, BEN EMIL, kitchen design co. exec.; b. Hedemora, Sweden, Aug. 27, 1934; came to U.S., 1954, naturalized, 1960; s. Emil W.J. and Ester Linnea (Hellman) Karlsson; student bus. mktg. Alexander Hamilton Inst., N.Y.C., 1967, Am. Inst. Kitchen Designers, 1972; grad. Dale Carnegie Inst., 1972; m. Susan Jo Kaupert, Feb. 7, 1958; children—David, Kristine, Thomas. Salesman, Edward Hines Lumber Co., Chgo., 1954-63; v.p., gen. mgr. Lake Forest Lumber Co. (Ill.), 1963-67; pres. Karlson Home Center, Inc., Evanston, Ill., 1967—, Poggenpohl-Midwest/USA, Inc., Evanston, Atag USA Corp., Evanston; dir. tng. U.S. Poggenpohl, Herford, W. Ger., 1981—; pres. Bank Lane Investors, Lake Forest, 1971-72; founder chmn. Evanston Home Show, 1973, 74; judge, Nat. Design Contest, 1974; showroom design cons., Ill., Poggenpohl Kitchens Germany. Mem. steering com. Covenant Meth. Ch., Evanston, 1968-69; bd. dirs. Evanston Family Counseling Service, 1973-75, Evanston United Community Services, 1974-75, mid-Am. chpt. No. region ARC, 1974; chmn. bus. div. Evanston United Fund, 1974, gen. campaign chmn., 1975. Recipient awards for community service. Cert. kitchen designer. Mem. Am. Inst. Kitchen Designers (pres. 1975-76), Evanston C. of C. (dir. 1973-74, v.p. 1975, pres. 1976), Nat. Fed. Ind. Bus., Mid-Am. Swedish Trade Assn. Club: Evanston Rotary. Contbr. kitchen designs to nat. mags. Home: 2311 Central Park Ave Evanston IL 60201 Office: 1815 Central St Evanston IL 60201

KARMAZIN, JOSEPHINE ROSE, Realtor; b. N.Y.C., Feb. 9, 1922; d. John and Rose Marie (Mares) K.; grad. Bradford Jr. Coll., 1941. Personnel mgr. Kline's Store, Detroit, 1945-53; asst. buyer and advt. Hutzel Store, Ann Arbor, Mich., 1953-55; v.p. personnel and labor relations Karmazin Products Corp., 1955-69; now co-owner So Wayne Realty Inc., Trenton, Mich. Chmn. bd. mgmt. Downriver YWCA, 1970-73, 81-83; chmn. Camp Cavell com. YWCA Met. Detroit, 1974, chmn. expansion com., 1975-78, 2d v.p., 1978—, mem. planning and devel. com., 1980—; sec. Wyandotte Community Theatre Relocation Com., 1980; mem. bd. mgmt. Family Neighborhood Services, 1958-68; del. Mich. Republican Conv., 1978. Presbyterian (deacon). Clubs: Women's Econ. (Detroit); Grosse Ile Yacht; Soroptimist (pres. 1961, 63) (Wyndotte, Mich.). Home: 22085 Thorofare Grosse Ile MI 48138 Office: 3010 Van Horn Rd Trenton MI 48183

KARNES, GEORGE DAVID, dentist; b. Galatia, Ill., June 18, 1936; s. Cloyd Edmund and W. Wilma (Smith) K.; D.D.S., U. Ill., 1961; m. Mary Alice Mitchell, Sept. 14, 1957; children—Mark David, Kathy Lynn, Mitchell Scott. Pvt. practice dentistry, Carbondale, Ill., 1966—. Pres. Green Earth Inc. Chmn., Bd. Fire and Police Commrs., City of Carbondale, 1969-70; mayor pro-tem, councilman, Carbondale, 1971-73; bd. dirs. So. Ill. Airport Authority; sec.-treas. bd. Mid-Continent Energy Systems, Inc.; cons. in field. Served to capt. USAF, 1961-66. Mem. Am., Ill., So. Ill. dental socs., Leonard S. Fosdick Dental Study Club (pres. 1970-71, 73-74). Baptist (deacon 1967—, chmn.). Home: Rural Route 3 Carbondale IL 62901 Office: 1225 E Grand St Carbondale IL 62901

KARNS, ANTHONY WESLEY WARREN, geol. cons.; b. Kansas City, Mo., Dec. 15, 1936; s. Anthony Wesley and Madge Pearl (Hill) K.; A.A., Coffeyville (Kans.) Coll., 1956; B.S. in Geology, Colo. State U., 1960; M.S. in Geology, Okla. U., 1961; children—Anthony Wesley, Shawn Michelle. With Mobil Oil Co., U.S., North Africa and Can., 1961-68, Magellan Petroleum, Australia, North Africa, N.Z., Tonga, Fiji, 1968-71; pres., founder Earth Scientists, Ltd., Australia, N.Z., Can., U.S. and New Hebrides, 1971—. Mem. Am. Assn. Petroleum Geologists, Geol. Soc. Am., Am. Assn. Scientists, N.Z. Geol. Soc., Four Corners Geol. Soc., Sigma Xi, Sigma Gamma Epsilon. Republican. Contbr. chpt. in book. Home: Route 1 Box 15AA Coffeyville KS 67337 Office: 806 Hickman St Coffeyville KS 67337

KARNS, MARGARET PADELFORD, educator; b. Winchester, Mass., Oct. 14, 1943; d. Norman Judson and Helen (Proctor) Padelford; B.A., Denison U., 1965; M.A., U. Mich., 1966, Ph.D., 1975; m. David Alan Karns, Apr. 29, 1967; 1 son, Paul Alan. Research asst. in defense analysis program Brookings Instn., Washington, 1969-70; instr. SUNY, Cortland, 1970-71; asst. to the dean Cornell U., Ithaca, N.Y., 1971-72; asst. prof. govt. Wells Coll., Aurora, N.Y., 1972-73; asst. prof. polit. sci. U. Dayton (Ohio), 1976—. Mem. steering com. World Trade Council, 1979—. Mem. Internat. Studies Assn., Am. Polit. Sci. Assn., Midwest Polit. Sci. Assn., Nat. Collegiate Conf. Assn. (dir. 1975). Office: Dept Political Science University of Dayton Dayton OH 45469

KARON, BERTRAM PAUL, clin. psychologist; b. Taunton, Mass., Apr. 29, 1930; s. Harold Banny and Celia (Silverman) K.; B.A., Harvard U., 1952; M.A., Princeton U., 1954, Ph.D. (USPHS fellow), 1957; m. Mary K. Mossop, 1958; 1 son, Jonathan Alexander; stepchildren—Brent Armstrong, Blake Armstrong. Research fellow psychometrics Ednl. Testing Service, 1952-55; intern in direct analysis John M. Rosen, M.D., 1955-56; sr. clin. psychologist Annandale (N.J.) Reformatory, 1958; research psychologist Phila. Psychiat. Hosp., 1958-59; USPHS postdoctoral fellow Phila. Psychiat. Hosp., 1959-61; asst. prof. psychology Mich. State U., East Lansing, 1962-63, asso. prof., 1963-68, prof., 1968—; project dir. Mich. State Psychotherapy Research Project, 1966—; research cons. dept. psychiatry U. Pa., 1963, U.S. Naval Hosp., Phila., 1963; lectr. psychiatry Ypsilanti (Mich.) State Hosp., 1964-65; cons. psychology Allen Park (Mich.) VA Hosp., 1966—, Ann Arbor (Mich.) VA Hosp., 1971. Lic. psychologist, Mich., Calif.; diplomate Am. Bd. Profl. Psychology. Fellow Am. Psychol. Assn.; mem. Midwest Psychol. Assn., Mich. Psychol. Assn., Am. Statis. Assn., Soc. Psychotherapy Research, Psychologists Interested in Study of Psychoanalysis. Author: The Negro Personality, 1958; Black Scars, rev. ed., 1975; (with G.R. Vandenbos) Psychotherapy for Schizophrenia: The Treatment of Choice, in press; editor: Affect, Imagery and Consciousness, Vol. I, 1962, Vol. II, 1963; contbr. articles to profl. jours., chpts. in books. Home: 420 John R St East Lansing MI 48823 Office: Psychology Research Bldg Michigan State University East Lansing MI 48824

KARPMAN, MAX, fur stylist; b. Chgo., July 9, 1917; s. Abraham and Mollie (Schectman) K.; ed. high sch.; m. K. Marie Rogers, Nov. 10, 1936; children—George Alan, Helena Kae Potash. Owner, operator fur store Springfield, Ill., 1946-49; lessee fur dept. Altman's (later Berger-Siegel), Springfield, 1949-78; owner, operator fur dept. Myers Bros., Springfield, 1978—; chmn. bd. People's Nat. Bank Springfield, 1976—. Served with USNR, 1944-46, 50-51; PTO. Jewish. Clubs: Jewish War Vets. (comdr. post 1965), Navy Sangamon (comdr. post. 1969), Sangamon, Masons, Shriners. Home: 2201 W Washington Rd Unit 11 Springfield IL 62702 Office: 101 S 5th St Springfield IL 62701

KARR, DONALD LEE, educator; b. Friendship, Ohio, Jan. 26, 1934; s. William C. and Bessie M. (Hicks) K.; B.S., Ohio U., 1959; M.A., U. Cin. 1962; Ph.D., Ohio State U., 1969; m. Ellen L. Treece, Apr. 7, 1979; children by previous marriage—Lee M., Lou Ann. Auto. tchr. Portsmouth (Ohio) High Sch., 1957-62; supr. trade and indsl. edn. West Clermont Local Sch. Dist., Amelia, Ohio, 1962-64; faculty Ohio State U., Columbus, 1964-70, U. Ga., Athens, 1970-71; asso. prof. Cleve. State U., 1972—. Served with USN, 1954-56. Recipient Centennial medal Ohio State U., 1970. Mem. Am. Vocat. Assn., Ohio Vocat. Assn., Iota Lambda Sigma. Republican. Methodist. Home: 16416 Fernway Rd Shaker Heights OH 44120 Office: UT 1405 22d St and Euclid Ave Cleveland OH 44115

KARR, GERALD LEE, agrl. economist, state senator; b. Emporia, Kans., Oct. 15, 1936; s. Orren L. and Kathleen M. (Keller) K.; B.S., Kans. State U., 1959; M.S. in Agrl. Econs., So. Ill. U., 1962, Ph.D. in Econs., 1966; m. Sharon Kay Studer, Oct. 18, 1959; children—Kevin Lee, Kelly Jolleen. Livestock mgr. Eckert Orchards Inc., Belleville, Ill., 1959-60; grad. asst. So. Ill. U., Carbondale, 1960-64; asst. prof. econs. Central Mo. State U., Warrensburg, 1964-67; asst. prof. agrl. econs., head dept. Njala U., Sierra Leone, West Africa, 1967-70; asst. prof. agrl. econs. U. Ill., Urbana, 1970-72; asso. prof. agrl. econs., chmn. dept., mgr. coll. farms Wilmington (Ohio) Coll., 1972-76; farmer, Emporia, Kans., 1976—; dir. Chase County Nat. Farmers Union, L and M Pork Producers; mem. Kans. Senate, 1981—; research advisor Bank of Sierra Leone, Freetown, summer 1967; agrl. sector cons. Econ. Mission to Sierra Leone, IBRD, 1973. Mem. Am. Agrl. Econs. Assn., Lyon County Farm Bur., Lyon County Livestock Assn., Omicron Delta Epsilon, Farm House. Contbr. articles to profl. jours. Democrat. Methodist. Club: Kiwanis.

KARRAKER, LOUIS RENDLEMAN, appraisal co. exec.; b. Jonesboro, Ill., Aug. 2, 1927; s. Ira Oliver and Helen Elsie (Rendleman) K.; B.A., So. Ill. U., 1949, M.A., 1952; postgrad. U. Wis., 1951-52, Washington U., 1954-56; m. Patricia Grace Stahlheber, June 20, 1952; children—Alan Louis, Sharon Elaine. Asst. prof. Augustana Coll., 1956-60, acting chmn. div. social scis., 1960-61, asst. to pres., 1962-64; personnel mgr. Parker Pen Co., Janesville, Wis., 1964-67, personnel mgr., asst. to chmn., 1967-68, gen. asst. to chmn., 1968-69; v.p. personnel Am. Appraisal Assos., Inc., Milw., 1969-73, v.p. adminstrn., 1973-74, group v.p., dir., 1974-77, exec. v.p., dir., 1977-79, pres., dir., 1979—. Served with USNR, 1952-53. Republican. Lutheran. Clubs: Milw., Univ., Rotary (Milw.). Home: 3035 Applewood Ct Brookfield WI 53005 Office: 525 E Michigan St Milwaukee WI 53201

KARRER, RATHE STEVENS, psychophysiologist; b. Cleve., Mar. 8, 1930; s. Enoch and Ethel (Walther) K.; B.A., La. State U., 1953; M.A., New Sch. Social Research, 1957, Ph.D., 1966; m. Betty MacKune, Aug. 15, 1971; children—Dana, Phillip, Tana. Research psychologist Vineland (N.J.) Tng. Sch., 1957-66; research scientist Ill. Pediatric Inst., Chgo., 1966-74; asso. div. psychology Northwestern U. Med. Sch., Chgo., 1968—; sr. research scientist Ill. Inst. Devel. Disabilities, 1974—, asso. dir. research, 1979—; asst. to prof. psychology U. Ill., Chgo., 1974—; vis. lectr. Roosevelt U., 1968-70; cons. research proposals NIMH, Nat. Inst. Child and Human Devel., March of Dimes. Research grantee NIMH, Nat. Inst. Child and Human Devel. Mem. Am. Psychol. Assn., Eastern Psychol. Assn., Soc. Psychophysiol. Research, Soc. Neurosci., AAAS, N.Y. Acad. Scis., Soc. Research Child Devel., Am. Assn. Mental Deficiency, Am. Acad. Mental Retardation, Animal Behavior Soc., Am. Primatological Soc. Author: Physhophysiology of Mental Retardation, 1976; cons. editor Am. Jour. Mental Deficiency, 1973-75, 79-81; contbr. numerous articles to profl. jours. Home: 411 Woodland Rd Highland Park IL 60035 Office: 1640 Roosevelt Rd Chicago IL 60608

KARRYS, WILLIAM GEORGE, mech. engr.; b. Milw., Nov. 13, 1923; s. George W. and Callope (Stathas) K.; B.S., U. Wis., 1947; m. Effie T. Tarachas, Nov. 25, 1956; children—Kathryn, George, Michael. Indsl. engr. A.O. Smith Corp., Milw., 1947-54; chief indsl. engr. Mech. Handling Systems, Detroit, 1954-55; plant engr. U.S. Steel Corp., Chgo., 1955-56; with Pollak & Skan, Inc., Rosemont, Ill., 1956—, adminstrv. engr., v.p., 1956-72, pres., 1972—, dir. Served with USNR, 1944-46. Mem. Nat., Ill. socs. profl. engrs., ASME, IEEE. Club: Carlton. Home: 150 Eddy Ln Northfield IL 60093 Office: 9575 Higgins Rd Rosemont IL 60018

KARSTENSEN, ELMER LELAND, transp. exec.; b. Lincolnville, Kans., May 18, 1934; s. Karl John and Ernestine Mathilda (Westphal) K.; B.S., Kans. State U., 1956; M.Urban Affairs, Wichita State U., 1979; m. Bernice Fry, July 3, 1960; children—Brian, John. Reporter, Beatrice (Nebr.) Daily Sun, 1959-61; printer The Cheney Sentinel (Kans.), 1961-68; asst. to city mgr. City of Wichita (Kans.), 1970-76; exec. dir. Wichita Met. Transit Authority, 1977—. Served with U.S. Army, 1957-58, 68-69. Decorated Bronze Star medal. Mem. Am. Public Transit Assn., Internat. City Mgmt. Assn. Lutheran. Home: 908 Robin Rd Wichita KS 67212 Office: 1825 S McLean Blvd Wichita KS 67213

KARWAND, ELWOOD CHARLES, educator; b. Fargo, N.D., Jan. 12, 1931; s. Edwin Carl and Bertha (Olson) K.; B.A., Hamline U., 1957; M.A., U. Minn., 1964, postgrad., 1965—; m. Barbara Sprenger, July 20, 1957; children—Eldon Craig, Kim Carolyn, Kaye Leslie, Colleen Heather. State corr. Mpls. Tribune, St. Paul Pioneer Press, 1950-51, A.P., 1956-57; dir. athletic pub. relations Hamline U., St. Paul, 1956-57; high sch. tchr. English, journalism, Hibbing, Minn., 1957-60; tchr., journalism supr. Beloit (Wis.) Pub. Schs., 1960-64; chmn. journalism dept. U. Wis.-Eau Claire, 1964—. Faculty journalism U. Minn., Mpls., summers 1962-66, 68, U. Wis., Madison, summer 1963; dir. Minn. high sch. journalism workshops U. Minn., 1964-72; dir. Wis. pub. workshops, 1973—; mem. Wis. Freedom Info. Council. Pub. relations dir. United Givers Campaign, Beloit, 1963. Served with USAF, 1951-53. Wall St. Jour. fellow, 1961. Named Outstanding Wis. Tchr.-Adviser, U. Wis., 1966; recipient Nat. Achievement award Wall Street Jour., 1961; Nat. Scholastic Press Journalism Pioneer award, 1970; Jour. Recognition award U. Mich., 1971. Mem. Journalism Edn. Assn. (nat. exec. sec. 1964—; Carl Towley award 1969), Chippewa Valley Sch. Press Assn. (exec. sec. 1964—), Assn. for Edn. in Journalism (chmn. secondary sch. div. 1967-69), Wis. Journalism Tchr.-Adviser Council (v.p. 1962, pres. 1963-65), Nat. Council Publs. Advisers (citation 1967, mem. commn. freedom coll. press 1968—, state chmn. 1969-70), Am. Assn. Journalism Sch. Adminstrs., A.A.U.P., Western Wis. Press Club (v.p. 1975), Wis. Press Assn., Sigma Delta Chi, Pi Delta Epsilon, Alpha Phi Omega, Phi Delta. Methodist. Scholastic editor Am. Ency. Edn., 1967-68. Contbr. articles to profl. jours. Home: 3105 State St Eau Claire WI 54701

KASHUL, WILLIAM NICHOLAS, telecommunications co. exec.; b. Chgo., Oct. 7, 1933; s. Nicholas and Julia (Marchuk) K.; M.B.A., U. Chgo., 1969; m. Christine Karnazes, Sept. 15, 1956; children—William Nicholas, Steve, Tom, Deborah, Laura, Susan. Equipment engr. Automatic Electric Co., Chgo., 1956-59; applications engr. ITT Corp., Chgo., 1959-62; project engr. Alpha Engring. Co., Mt. Prospect, Ill., 1962-67; sales engr. Stromberg Carlson Co., Chgo., 1967-72; regional sales mgr. No. Telecom, Inc., Elk Grove, Ill., 1972—. Served with AUS, 1953-56; Korea. Mem. Am. Mgmt. Assn. Roman Catholic. Home: 1521 Belle Plaine Park Ridge IL 60068 Office: 401 S Busse Rd Elk Grove Village IL 60007

KASLEY, SAMUEL JOHN, chem. co. exec.; b. Wheeling, W.Va., May 8, 1938; s. Samuel John and Helen Lillian (Ulrich) K.; B.S. in Chem. Engring., W.Va. U., 1961; M.S., Clemson U., 1964, Ph.D., 1967; m. Doris Jane Walters, Sept. 23, 1961; children—Samuel John, David Marcalan, Susan Jane. With Dow Chem. Co., Midland, Mich., 1966—, project supt., 1974-76, prodn. plant supt., 1977-79, project mgr. Ludington, Mich., 1979—. Chmn. Young Republicans Clemson U., 1964, precinct chmn., 1964; co chmn. fund raising PBS, 1979—. USPHS trainee, 1963-66. Mem. Am. Inst. Chem. Engrs., Nat. Mgmt. Assn., Mensa. Republican. Clubs: Elks., Masons. Patentee polymer prodn. Home: 7470 M-116 Ludington MI 49431 Office: Dow Chem Co S Madison St Ludington MI 49431

KASMER, WILLIAM JOHN, JR., corp. plant engr.; b. Youngstown, Ohio, Mar. 28, 1949; s. William John and Irene (Sebest) K.; B.Engring., Youngstown State U., 1972; m. Rolayne Dawn Smith, Sept. 6, 1975. Maintenance engr. Kaiser Refractories div. Kaiser Aluminum and Chem. Corp., Columbiana, Ohio, 1973-74, mech. engr., 1974-76, sr. mech. engr., 1976-78, plant engr., 1978—; pres. K & K Racing Design; cons. dust and fume collection; instr. continuing edn. courses in indsl. ventilation N.C. State U. Mem. ASME. Democrat. Roman Catholic. Club: Sports Car Am. Home: 1336 Humbolt St Youngstown OH 44502 Office: 41728 Esterly St Columbiana OH 44408

KASNY, DON-FRANKLYN RAMMEL, clin. psychologist; b. Chgo., Oct. 16, 1949; s. Raymond J. and Loretta (Rammel) K.; B.A. in Psychology and Sociology, Milton (Wis.) Coll., 1972; postgrad. Roosevelt U., Chgo., 1972-73, North Park Coll., 1973-74; M.S., Nat. Coll. of Edn., Evanston, Ill., 1976; Ph.D., Calif. Western U., Santa Ana, 1977; m. Faustina H. Landicho, Apr. 5, 1975; 1 dau., Kimberly Landicho. Head dept. adjunctive therapy Forest Hosp., Des Plaines, Ill., 1971-75; clin. therapist Children's Center for Learning, Evanston, 1975-76, student therapeutic Edn. Program Drug Rehab. Center, Mt. Prospect, Ill., 1976-77; clin. cons. Elgin (Ill.) Psychol. Center, 1977—; dir. developmental disabilities program Ray Graham Assn. for the Handicapped, Hinsdale, Ill., 1977-78; pvt. tchr. percussion, 1974—; tchr. karate/self-defense Maine Oakton Niles Adult Continuing Edn. Program, Morton Grove, Ill., 1977—; pvt. practice clin. psychology,

Hoffman Estates, Ill., 1978—; clin. cons. Northwest Community Hosp., Arlington Heights, Ill., 1978—; dir. psychol. services Sch. Dist. 15, Palatine, Ill., 1978—; lectr. on marriage, children and preventive mental health to various community groups or orgns., 1977—. Recipient numerous trophies for Karate competitions, 1971—; cert. tchr., Ill. Mem. Am. Psychol. Assn., Ill. Psychol. Assn., Soc. Pediatric Psychology, Am. Assn. Biofeedback Clinicians, Assn. Advancement of Behavior Therapy, Profl. Assn. Scuba Diving Instrs., Japan Karate Assn., Am. Tae-Kwon-Do Karate Assn. Midwest karate champion, 1975; Ill. State karate champion, 1975-77; karate world champion, 1980; U.S. nat. karate champion, 1981. Home: 4085 N Victoria Dr Hoffman Estates IL 60195

KASPER, DANIEL JACK, machine tool accessory mfg. co. exec.; b. Cleve., Feb. 7, 1946; s. Joseph and Caroline (Schoeck) K.; B.M.E., Cleve. State U., 1969; M.S. in Mgmt., Case-Western Res. U., 1972; m. Janet Fedorka, June 29, 1968; children—Dawn, Kristy, Danny. With Warner Swasey Co., 1964—, mgr. engring. Balas div., Cleve., 1976-79, mgr. ops. div., 1979-81; mgr. ops. Balas div. Sandvik Inc., Cleve., 1981—. Registered profl. engr., Ohio. Mem. ASME, Soc. Automotive Engrs., Soc. Mfg. Engrs. (cert. mfg. engr.). Patentee force measuring device for collet or chuck. Office: 1557 E 27th St Cleveland OH 44114

KASPER, LARRY JOHN, accountant; b. Springfield, Ohio, Apr. 17, 1947; s. Billy David and Phyliss Mae (McCauley) K.; B.S. in B.A., Ohio State U., 1969; M.B.A., U. Mich., 1971; M.Acctg., Ohio State U., 1975; m. Helen Lydia Harrison, Dec. 22, 1976. Econometrician, Dean Witter & Co., Inc., N.Y.C., 1971; economist Battelle Meml. Inst., Columbus, Ohio, 1971-75; mgmt. cons. Touche Ross & Co., Columbus, 1976; pvt. practice acctg., Columbus, 1976—. lectr. in acctg. Ohio State U., Columbus, 1977, 78; speaker SBA, 1978-81; expert witness as economist in personal injury and wrongful death claims, 1981. Chmn. audit com. Victorian Village Soc., 1977-78. Recipient cert. of merit for article pub. in Mgmt. Acctg., 1977. Mem. Nat. Assn. Accts. (chpt. bd. dirs. 1978-81, profl. devel. seminar leader), Ohio Soc. C.P.A.'s. Club: Sertoma (treas. 1978-79). Office: 773 Dennison Ave Columbus OH 43215

KASPER, ROBERT EUGENE, radiologist; b. Sioux Falls, S.D., Sept. 19, 1926; s. Thomas C. and Clara B. (Lillesve) K.; student U. Minn., 1944-46, postgrad., 1953-55; M.D., Marquette U., 1949; m. Rita May Armstrong, July 2, 1954; children—Ann, David, Thomas. Intern Mpls. Gen. Hosp., 1949-50; resident Boston City Hosp., 1952-53, U. Minn. Hosps., Mpls. VA Hosp., 1953-56; practice medicine specializing in radiology, Mpls., 1956—; mem. staffs Swedish Hosp., Waconia Ridgeview, 1956-66; clin. instr., then asst. prof. radiology U. Minn., 1956-67. Served to lt. M.C., USN, 1950-52. Mem. AMA, Minn., Hennepin County med. socs., Mpls. Acad. Medicine, Am. Coll. Radiology, Am. Roentgen Ray Soc., Radiol. Soc. N. Am., Minn. Radiol. Soc. Episcopalian. Club: Minikahda. Contbr. articles to med. jours. Home: 1705 Morgan Ave S Minneapolis MN 55405

KASPROWICZ, EDWARD HENRY, sculptor, educator; b. Detroit, Apr. 8, 1941; s. Henry and Gladys (Osinski) K.; B.F.A., Wayne State U., 1965, M.F.A., 1970; M.A., Mich. State U., 1966, teaching cert., 1967; student Soc. Arts and Crafts, Detroit, 1970. Archtl. designer, draftsman MGM Constrn. Co., Detroit, 1965-69; teaching fellow U. Mich., Ann Arbor, 1968; race car builder, driver Mich. Internat. Speedway, Watkins Glen, N.Y., Indpls. Raceway Park, Road Atlanta, Mid-Ohio, Elkhart Lake, Wis., Milw. State Fairgrounds, Nelson Ledges, Ohio, 1968—; instr. Wayne County Community Coll., Detroit, 1970-73; tchr. Cass Tech. High Sch., Detroit, 1970-80; instr. Mercy Coll., Detroit, 1981—; sculptor Arwin Galleries, Detroit, 1967-81; harpsichord builder, Detroit, 1971—; free-lance comml. artist Detroit Bd. Edn., 1977—; exhibited at Detroit Inst. Arts, 1967; life-size stone sculpture bought by Wayne State U. grad. class, 1965; life-size bronze sculpture Top of the Ponch at Pontchartrain Hotel, Detroit, 1968, bronze sculpture at Gospel Music Workshop Am., Detroit, 1970, seven-foot bronze Ballerina purchased by Gen. Motors Corp., also other life-size bronze figures, stone carvings and woodcarvings in pvt. collections; designer, builder world's largest harpsichord at Detroit Orch. Hall, 1981; aerobatic pvt. pilot, 1959—; also designer, builder race cars. Recipient 40 automobile racing trophies including 16 for 1st place; 1st place trophies in Detroit Classic and Southeastern Mich. Open, U.S. Chess Fedn. Chess Tournaments; cert. of achievement Detroit Bd. Edn., 1978. Mem. Aircraft Owners and Pilots Assn., U.S. Chess Fedn., U.S. Tennis Assn., Sports Car Club Am., Fedn. Internationale de Automobile. Home: 1130 Chicago Blvd Detroit MI 48202

KASSABAUM, GEORGE EDWARD, architect; b. Atchison, Kans., Dec. 5, 1920; s. George A. and Dorothy (Gaston) K.; B. Arch., Washington U., 1947; m. Marjory J. Verser, Jan. 22, 1949; children—Douglas, Ann, Karen. Faculty, Washington U., St. Louis, 1947-50; asso. firm Hellmuth, Yamasaki & Leinweber, St. Louis, 1950-55, prin. Hellmuth, Obata & Kassabaum, 1955—. Dir. Tower Grove Bank. Bd. dirs. YMCA, St. Louis, 1970—, Downtown St. Louis Inc., St. Louis Symphony; trustee Washington U., St. Louis. Served with USAAF, 1944-45. Named Mo. Architect of Yr., 1978; registered profl. architect, Mo., Kans., Pa., Ohio, Fla., D.C., Mass., N.Y., Alaska, Wis., Calif., Md., Colo., N.C., Tex., N.J. Fellow AIA (pres. St. Louis chpt. 1964, nat. pres. 1968-69, chancellor 1978); mem. Sociedad Colombiana de Arquitectos (hon.), La Sociedad de Arquitectos Mexicanos, Royal Archtl. Inst. Can. (hon.), Sigma Chi. Clubs: Noonday, Racquet, Media, Old Warson, St. Louis Country, Bogey Country (St. Louis). Prin. archtl. works include: Terminal, Dallas-Ft. Worth Airport, Equitable Bldg., St. Louis, Smithsonian Air-Space Mus., Washington, Squibb Hdqrs., Lawrenceville, N.J., Duke Hosp., Durham, N.C., McAuto Computer Center, St. Louis, Conv. Center, San Francisco, U. Riyad, Riyadh, Saudi Arabia, Riyadh Airport, Saudi Arabia, Exxon Research and Engring. Facilities, Clinton, N.J. Contbr. articles to profl. jours. Home: 761 Kent Rd Saint Louis MO 63124 Office: 100 N Broadway Saint Louis MO 63102

KASSEL, RAYMOND LEE, transp. cons. co. exec.; b. Mason City, Iowa, Feb. 27, 1926; s. Henry and Eva (Kahley) K.; B.S.C.E., U. Colo., 1950; M.Engring. in Transp. Engring., Iowa State U., 1972; m. Opal Wood, Sept. 18, 1949; children—Kevin, Rosalyn, Stephanie. Engr., Iowa Hwy. Commn., Decoyah, 1951-57, with central planning and programming dept., 1957-71, dir. planning, 1974-77; dep. dir. Iowa Dept. Transp., Ames, 1977-78, dir., 1978-82; exec. sec. Iowa Ry. Fin. Authority, 1980-82; pres. Kassel Services Corp., Nevada, Iowa, 1982—; mem. Transp. Research Bd., Nat. Acad. Scis., 1978; chmn. Iowa Govt. Communications Adv. Council, 1978-80; mem. Gov.'s Mgmt. Tng. Bd., Gov.'s Mgmt. Adv. Council, 1981-82, Iowa Legis. Environ. Agy. Group, 1978-82. Served with USN, 1944-46. Recipient H.W. Hartmann award Am. Concrete Paving Assn., 1978; award Iowa Conservation Commn., 1978; Audio Visual Achievement award Nat. Council for Disadvantaged, 1979; award Fed. Hwy. Adminstrn., 1980; recognition award Nat. Soc. Profl. Engrs., 1980. Mem. Am. Assn. State Hwy. and Transp. Ofcls. (policy com., exec. com., standing com. on planning), Mississippi Valley Conf. State Hwy. and Transp. Ofcls., Council State Dept. Transp. Ofcls., Am. Public Works Assn., ASCE, Iowa Engring. Soc. (Iowa Govt. Profl. Devel. award 1980), Am. Legion. Republican. Mem. Christian Ch. Address: 913 11th St Nevada IA 50201

KASSELMANN, ROBERT LEO, health care mgmt. exec.; b. St. Louis, Feb. 1, 1936; s. Julius Henry and Marie Ida K.; B.S. in Mech. Engring., Gen. Motors Inst., 1959. Supr., Gen. Motors Co., 1954-63; mgr. Alexander Proudfoot Co., Chgo., 1963-68; v.p. SDS Mgmt. Services Co., Peoria, Ill., 1968-74; v.p. contracts Comprehensive Care Corp., Earth City, Mo., 1974—. Bd. dirs. St. Louis Area Council on Alcoholism, 1979. Mem. Am. Hosp. Assn., Hosp. Mgmt. Systems Soc., U.S. Power Squadron. Roman Catholic. Home: 87 Meadowbrook Country Club Dr Ballwin MO 63011 Office: 12255 DePaul Dr 5th Floor Bridgeton MO 63044

KAST, KEVIN FRANCIS, health services adminstr.; b. Louisville, Jan. 18, 1950; s. Conrad V. and Mary Ann (Reardon) K.; B.A. in Sociology, U. Mo., Kansas City, 1973, M.A. in Communications, 1975, M.P.A. in Health Services Adminstrn.; m. Janet Marie Hopper, Feb. 17, 1973. Cafeteria mgr. Menorah Med. Center, Kansas City, Mo., 1971-73; food prodn. mgr. Bapt. Meml. Hosp., Kansas City, 1973-74, asst. food service dir., 1974-75, food services dir., 1975-80; exec. v.p. Affiliated Health Services Inc., 1980—; instr. organizational communication Avila Coll.; instr. theories of communications Columbia Coll. Bd. govs. Bapt. Meml. Hosp. Mem. Am. Soc. for Hosp. Food Service Adminstrs. (pres. Heart of Am. chpt. 1979). Roman Catholic. Home: 9845 Overhill Rd Kansas City MO 64134 Office: Affiliated Health Services Inc 4405 Noland Rd Kansas City MO

KASTEN, ROBERT W., JR., U.S. Senator; b. Milw., June 19, 1942; s. Robert W. and Mary (Ogden) K.; B.A., U. Ariz., 1964; M.B.A., Columbia U., 1966. With Genesco, Inc., Nashville, 1966-68; dir., v.p. Gilbert Shoe Co., Thiensville, Wis., 1968-75; mem. Wis. Senate, 1972-75, mem. joint fin. com., 1973-75, chmn. joint survey com. on tax exemptions, after 1973; designee Eagleton Inst. Politics, 1973; mem. 94th-95th Congresses from 9th Wis. Dist.; mem. U.S. Senate from Wis., 1980—. Alt. del. Republican Nat. Conv., 1972, del., 1976. Mem. Milw. Council Alcoholism, Milw. Soc. Prevention of Blindness; regional dir. Milw. Coalition for Clean Water. Served to 1st lt. USAF, 1967-72. Named Jaycee of Year, 1972, Legis. Conservationist of Year, 1973. Mem. Nat. Audubon Soc., Sigma Nu, Alpha Kappa Psi. Office: 221 Russell Senate Office Building Washington DC 20510

KASTENMEIER, ROBERT WILLIAM, congressman; b. Beaver Dam, Wis., Jan. 24, 1924; s. Leo H. and Lucille (Powers) K.; LL.B., U. Wis., 1952; m. Dorothy Chambers, June 27, 1952; children—William, Andrew, Edward. Branch office dir. Claims Service, War Dept., Philippines, 1946-48; admitted to Wis. bar, 1952; practiced Watertown, Wis., 1952-58; justice of peace, 1955-58. Mem. 86th-97th Congresses from 2d Dist. Wis.; mem. house jud., interior and insular affairs coms.; chmn. judiciary subcom. on cts., civil liberties and adminstrn. of justice. Served from pvt. to 1st lt. Inf., AUS, 1943-46. Philippines. Home: Sun Prairie WI 53590 Office: 2232 Rayburn House Office Bldg Washington DC 20515

KASTETTER, MARY M., med. technologist; b. Hartford City, Ind., Nov. 2, 1927; d. Joseph William and Jessie May (Corder) K.; B.S., Purdue U., 1950. Intern. Springfield (Ohio) City Hosp., 1950-51; supr. blood bank Springfield City Hosp., 1951-52; supr. hematology White Cross Hosp., Columbus, Ohio, 1953-55, supr. blood bank, 1955-61; supr. blood bank Riverside Meth. Hosp., Columbus, 1961—. Cert. med. technologist. Mem. Ohio Assn. Blood Banks (bd. dirs. 1965-67), Central Ohio Soc. Med. Technologists (pres. 1956-57), Am. Assn. Blood Banks, Am. Soc. Med. Tech., Am. Soc. Clin. Pathologists. Club: Order Eastern Star, White Shrine. Home: 6396 Middleshire St Columbus OH 43229 Office: 3535 Olentangy River Rd Columbus OH 43214

KASTNER, CURTIS LYNN, food technologist, educator; b. Altus, Okla., Sept. 21, 1944; s. Carlus and Alma Darlene (Shield) K.; B.S., Okla. State U., 1967, M.S., 1969, Ph.D., 1972; m. Rebecca Jon Diltz, Aug. 6, 1966; children—Jason Lynn, Justin Jon. Research asst. Armour Food Co., Oak Brook, Ill., summer, 1967; grad. research and teaching asst. dept. animal scis. and industry Okla. State U., Stillwater, 1967-71; asst. prof. food sci. and tech. Wash. State U., Pullman, 1972-75; asso. prof. dept. animal sci. Kans. State U., Manhattan, 1975—; cons. to Inst. de tecnología de Alimentos, San Paulo, Brazil, 1978, also cons. to industry and govt. agys. Served as capt. U.S. Army, 1971-72. Recipient Tchr. award Wash. State U., 1975. Mem. Inst. of Food Technologists, Am. Meat Sci. Assn., Am. Soc. Animal Sci., Council for Agrl. Sci. and Tech., Sigma Xi, Phi Kappa Phi, Gamma Sigma Delta. Republican. Mem. Ch. of Christ. Contbr. numerous articles on food tech. to popular and profl. publs. Home: 1124 Village Dr Manhattan KS 66502 Office: Dept Animal Sciences and Industry Weber Hall Kans State U Manhattan KS 66506

KASTOR, TINA BENNETT, linguist; b. La Mesa, Calif., Feb. 8, 1954; d. Clayton Leon and Patricia Jean (Howard) Bennett; B.F.A., Calif. Inst. Arts, 1973; M.A., U. So. Calif., 1976, Ph.D., 1978; m. Frank Sullivan Kastor, Oct. 28, 1979; 1 dau., Kristina Rebecca. Teaching asst. linguistics dept. U. So. Calif., 1975-78, research asst., 1975-76; research asso., co-dir. research John Tracy Clinic, Los Angeles, 1977; research cons. R. M. Lencione, U. Calif. Rehab. Center, Los Angeles, 1977; asst. prof. English and linguistics Wichita (Kans.) State U., 1978—. Recipient Wichita State U. research award, 1979-80. Mem. AAAS, Linguistic Soc. Am., MLA, Nat. Council Tchrs. English, N.Y. Acad. Scis. Episcopalian. Contbr. articles to profl. publs. Home: 4726 E English Wichita KS 67218 Office: Dept English Wichita State Univ Wichita KS 67208

KATIMS, MICHAEL ALLEN, sch. adminstr.; b. Pasadena, Calif., July 11, 1946; s. Seymour Katims and Fredi Beard; B.A., U. Calif., Santa Barbara, 1969; teaching cert. UCLA, 1971; postgrad U. Chgo., 1971—; m. Nancy Klastorin Naron, Mar. 21, 1980. Project dir., Chgo. mastery learning reading program, dept. research and evaluation Chgo. Public Schs., 1975-78, coordinator mastery learning program devel., dept. curriculum, 1978—. U. Chgo. tuition scholar, 1971-73. Mem. Am. Ednl. Research Assn. (program chmn. mastery learning spl. interest group 1981), AAAS, Assn. Supervision and Curriculum Devel., Phi Delta Kappa. Democrat. Contbr. articles to profl. jours. Home: 1314 Main St Evanston IL 60202 Office: 228 N LaSalle St Chicago IL 60601

KATT, LINDA KAY, occupational therapist; b. Niles, Mich., Jan. 31, 1950; d. Clayson E. and Betty Jane (Wadsworth) Cooper; B.S., Western Mich. U., 1972; m. Peter C. Katt, Dec. 16, 1972; 1 dau., Erinn Elizabeth. Staff occupational therapist Kalamazoo State Hosp., 1972-74, Ohio State Dodd Hall Rehab. Center, Columbus, 1974-76, Charleston (W.Va.) Med. Center, 1976-77; dir. occupational therapy Charleston (W.Va.) Med. Center, 1977-78, Henry Ford Hosp., Detroit, 1978—. Mem. Am. Occupational Therapy Assn., Mich. Occupational Therapy Assn., North Met. Occupational Therapy Assn., Detroit Occupational Therapy Assn. (chmn. council on practice), Southeastern Mich. Dirs. Occupational Therapy Assn., Alpha Phi. Episcopalian. Club: Sq. Lake Racquet. Home: 604 Fox River Dr Bloomfield Hills MI 48013 Office: Henry Ford Hospital 2799 W Grand Blvd Detroit MI 48202

KATTIJA-ARI, MANO, phys. chemist; b. Bangkok, Thailand, June 3, 1949; came to U.S., 1972; s. Manoonsiri and Dorothy Fariola (de Rozzoli) Kattija-Ari; student Baker U., 1973-75; B.S. with honors in Chemistry and Biology, U. Kans., 1976, M.S. in Chemistry, 1980; m. Kathleen Marie Hoskins, June 28, 1980. Forensic chemist regional criminalistics lab. Kansas City (Mo.) Police Dept., 1981—. Recipient award NSF, 1974. Mem. Am. Chem. Soc., AAAS, N.Y. Acad. Scis., Sigma Xi, Alpha Delta Sigma. Roman Catholic. Contbr. articles to profl. jours. Office: 2100 N Noland Rd Independence MO 64051

KATUBIG, CORNELIO PATAWARAN, JR., pathologist; b. Dagupan City, Philippines, Nov. 15, 1939; s. Cornelio and Barbara K.; M.D., U. of the East, Quezon City, 1963; m. Carmencita Rivera, June 16, 1964; children—Cornelio III, Christina, Catherine. Intern, Oakwood Hosp., Dearborn, Mich., 1964-65; resident in internal medicine Huron Rd. Hosp., Cleve., 1965-66; resident in pathology Cleve. Met. Gen. Hosp., 1966-70; resident in anatomic pathology Cleve. VA Med. Center, 1970-71; staff pathologist, chief blood bank Aultman Hosp., Canton, Ohio, 1971-72; dir. lab. Marion Meml. Hosp. and VA Med. Center (Ill.), 1972—; pres. med. staff Marion Meml. Hosp., 1975-76; clin. asst. prof. So. Ill. U. Med. Sch., Carbondale, 1979—. Fellow Coll. Am. Pathologists, Am. Soc. Clin. Pathologists; mem. Williamson County Med. Soc. (pres. 1976-77), AMA, Ill. Med. Soc., Am. Assn. Blood Banks, Assn. VA Chiefs of Labs., So. Ill. Med. Assn., Ill. Soc. Pathology. Roman Catholic. Clubs: Lion, K.C. Home: 305 Lakeview Rd Marion IL 62959 Office: 917 W Main St Marion IL 62959

KATZ, A(DOLPH) EDWARD, psychologist; b. Phila., June 22, 1926; s. Jacob and Sadie (Kaplan) K.; B.S., Purdue U., 1949; Ph.D., U. Chgo., 1956; m. Jeanette Ann Best, June 30, 1951; children—Judith Barbara, Margaret Ann (Mrs. James Pickering), David Martin, Jonathan Eric. Research asst. dept. psychology U. Chgo., 1953-55; psychologist Jewish Vocat. Service, Chgo., 1955-56; psychologist Hawthorn Center, Northville, Mich., 1956-61, asso. dir. dept. psychology, 1961-71, dir., 1971—; psychol. cons. Waterford Twp. (Mich.) Pub. Schs. Reading Center, Davis Clinic, Farmington Hills, Mich., Neuroednl. Clinic, William Beaumont Hosp., Royal Oak, Mich. Founder, Livonia (Mich.) Citizens for Better Human Relations, 1963, chmn., 1974-78; trustee Livonia Bd. Edn., 1964-72, pres., 1968-69. Served to 1st lt. Q.M.C., AUS, 1944-47. Lic. psychologist, Mich. Mem. Mich. Psychol. Assn. (exec. council 1964-68, 76-80). Home: 16008 Oak Dr Livonia MI 48154 Office: 18471 Haggerty Rd Northville MI 48167

KATZ, ARTHUR STANLEY, mktg. consulting co. exec.; b. Kansas City, Mo., Oct. 8, 1937; s. Sol and Minnie P. Katz; B.J., U. Mo., Columbia; m. Barbara S. Pittell, June 14, 1959; children—Leslie, Gary. Account exec. Sher & Jones, Inc., 1961-64; pres. Katz & Assos., 1964-71; partner, sr. v.p. Bernstein Rein & Boasberg, Kansas City, Mo., 1972-79; pres. The Mktg. Group, Kansas City, Mo., 1979—; guest lectr. U. Mo., Kansas City and Columbia. Served with U.S. Navy, 1959-61, USNR, 1961-66. Bd. dirs. Beth Shalom Synagogue, Kansas City, Jewish Family and Children's Service, Kansas City. Club: Homestead Country. Contbr. articles in field. Home: 11100 Walnut St Kansas City MO 64114 Office: 1160 City Center Sq Kansas City MO 64105

KATZ, LAWRENCE MARSHALL, ednl. adminstr.; b. Norfolk, Va., May 6, 1954; s. Carl J. and Juliet A. Katz; student Hebrew U., 1974-75; B.A., Columbia U., 1976; M.A., Jewish Theol. Sem., 1978; postgrad. John Carroll U., 1979—; m. Marilyn Spitalny, July 12, 1981. Fell in Jewish ednl. leadership Cleve. Bur. Jewish Edn., 1978-80, dir. community services, 1980—. Mem. Assn. for Supervision and Curriculum Devel., Jewish Educators Assembly, Coalition for Alternatives in Jewish Edn., Judiaca Hist. Philatelic Soc. Jewish. Office: 2030 S Taylor Rd Cleveland Heights OH 44118

KATZ, MYER, indsl. metals co. exec., educator, biologist, historian; b. Winona, Minn.; s. William Udell and Anna Sara (Schochett) K.; B.E. in Biol. Sci. and History, U. Wis.; M.A. in Biol. Scis., George Washington U.; postgrad. U. Wis., U. Minn., U. Chgo., Am. U., Western Wis. Tech. Inst. Sec.-treas., Katz Indsl. Metals, Inc., La Crosse, Wis., 1959—; exec. v.p. Gateway Plastics Corp., La Crosse, 1965-69; instr. bus. mgmt. Western Wis. Tech. Inst., La Crosse, 1969-71; instr. am. history and gen. scis. Central High Sch., La Crosse; research biologist and writer U.S. Dept. Agr., Washington, U.S. Dept. Interior, Washington; office mgr. Wis. Dept. Hwys., Madison; guest lectr. U. Wis. Library Sch., 1972-73; lectr. local, state and Jewish history to various sch., civic and ch. groups in Wis., 1970-81; editorial writer La Crosse Tribune, 1977-79, spl. writer, 1980-81. Pres., La Crosse Public Library Friends, 1969-71; mem. Mayor's Bicentennial Commn., La Crosse, 1975-76, chmn. heritage div., 1975-76; mem. U. Wis. Bicentennial Commn.; mem. La Crosse City Historic Sites Commn., 1973-78, chmn., 1973-78; bd. curators New Swarthout Hist. Mus., 1975—; bd. dirs. Congregation Sons of Abraham, La Crosse, 1974-76, La Crosse Public Library, 1968-72; bd. dirs. Mississippi River Sci. and Industry Center, La Crosse, 1979—, hist. adv., 1979—; bd. dirs. Wis. Libraries Friends, 1969-72; del. Wis. Gov.'s Conf. on Libraries, 1978. Served with U.S. Army Mil. Welfare, field dir. ARC. Recipient Bronze Plaque award La Crosse County Hist. Soc., 1976; award of Recognition Luther Rice Soc., George Washington U., 1972; Blue Ribbon for meritorious contbns. to Am. Bicentennial Year, 1976; nat. award of Commendation, Am. Assn. State and Local History, 1977; award of Merit, State Hist. Soc. Wis., 1974; 1st citizen award City of La Crosse, 1980. Mem. Am. Bibl. Archeol. Soc., Wis. Archeol. Soc., Coalition for Regional Environ. Studies, Washington Biol. Soc., AAAS, Wis. Soc. Jewish Learning, Wis. Acad. Scis., Art and Letters, Am. Ornithologists Union, Nat. Audubon Soc., Smithsonian Instn., La Crosse Writers Club, U. Wis. Alumni Assn., George Washington U. Alumni Assn., La Crosse County Hist. Soc. (dir. publs. 1973-77, pres. 1975-76, museum dir. 1973-75), Wis. State Hist. Soc., Tau Alpha Omega. Club: B'nai B'rith. Author: History of Jews and Judaism in La Crosse Area (State award), 1974; Pictorial History of Mayors of La Crosse, 1974; History of Rabbinate of La Crosse, 1979; History of Onalaska, Wis., 1974; The Caves of Barre Mills, Wis., 1975; History of Hebrew Chirography, The Hirshheimer Saga, 1976; contbr. articles on local and state history to scholarly publs. Home: 1525 State St La Crosse WI 54601 Office: 2535 E Ave South La Crosse WI 54601

KATZ, ROBERT LAWRENCE, otolaryngologist; b. Cleve., July 12, 1937; s. Bernard and Florence (Gavronsky) K.; B.A., Northwestern U., 1959; M.D., Western Res. U., 1963; m. Linda Moritz, June 19, 1965; children—Peter, Douglas. Intern in medicine and surgery Mt. Sinai Hosp., Cleve., 1963-64, resident in gen. surgery, 1964-65; resident in otolaryngology Mass. Eye & Ear Infirmary, Boston, 1965-68; practice medicine specializing in otolaryngology, South Euclid, Ohio; mem. staff Case Western Res. U., Mt. Sinai, Cleve. Clinic Found.; asst. clin. prof. Case Western Res. U., Cleve., 1973—. Trustee, Montifiore Home for Aged. Served to maj. M.C., USAF, 1968-70. Mem. AMA, Am. Acad. Otolaryngology, Am. Soc. for Head and Neck Surgery, Am. Acad. Pediatrics, Am. Cleft Palate Assn., Ohio Med. Assn., Cleve. Acad. Medicine, N. Eastern Ohio Otolaryngology and Maxillofacial Surgery Club, Alpha Omega Alpha. Jewish. Home: 22099 Parnell Rd Shaker Heights OH 44122 Office: 1611 S Green Rd South Euclid OH 44121

KATZEL, JEANINE ALMA, journalist; b. Chgo., Feb. 20, 1948; d. LeRoy Paul and Lia Mary (Arcuri) Katzel; B.A. in Journalism, U. Wis., 1970; M.S. in Journalism, Northwestern U., 1974. Publs. editor U. Wis. Sea Grant Program, Madison, 1969-72; editor research div. agrl. sch. U. Wis., Madison, 1972; research editor Prism mag. AMA, Chgo., 1972-73; free lance writer, 1974-75; lit. editor Plant Engring. mag. Tech. Pub. Co., Barrington, Ill., 1975-76, news editor, 1976-77, asso. editor, 1977-79, sr. editor, 1979—. Recipient Elsie Bullard Morrison prize in Journalism, U. Wis., 1969. Mem. Women in Communications, Am. Soc. Bus. Press Editors (pres. Chgo. chpt. 1977-78), Soc. Profl. Journalists, Soc. Fire Protection Engrs., Am. Inst. Plant Engrs., Assn. Energy Engrs., Nat. Audubon Soc., Nat. Fire Protection Assn. (tech. com. on fire pumps), Am. Soc. Safety Engrs., Phi Kappa Phi. Home: 16 Boxwood Ln Cary IL 60013 Office: 1301 S Grove Ave Barrington IL 60010

KATZMAN, MAURICE, fin., mktg., tech. exec.; b. Detroit; Samuel and Sofie K.; B.S. in Mech. Engring., Lawrence Inst. Tech., Southfield, Mich., 1956; B.S. in Elec. Engring., 1960; M.B.A. in Fin. and Mktg., U. Mich., 1961; m. Barbara A. Halprin, Aug. 15, 1961; 3 children. Cons. engring. supr. Migdel & Layne Cons. Engrs., 1954-57; project mgr. missile and space vehicles div. Chrysler Def. Co., 1957-60; Western regional field mgr. Inland Steel Corp., 1960-62; sr. sales engr. Consol. Electrodynamic Corp., 1962-64; Eastern regional mgr. Cook Electric Co., 1964-65; sr. mktg. rep. Ampex Corp., Redwood City, Calif., 1965-68; nat. automotive industry mgr. Univac div. Sperry Rand, 1968-71, Digital Equipment Corp., 1971-73; Eastern and central regional mgr. Bendix Corp. Advanced Tech. div., 1973-75; Midwest regional mgr. Sykes Datatronics, Inc., Southfield, Mich., 1975-79, sr. mgr. systems engring. labs., 1979; sales mgr. Aydin Controls and Computer Systems, 1980-81; area mgr. Megatech Corp., 1981—. Served with USAF, 1957-58, USAFR, 1958-63. Mem. Engring. Soc. Detroit, Jewish Community Center. Jewish. Clubs: B'nai B'rith, Investment, Masons, Hamilton Place Health and Country. Home: 30200 Northgate Dr Southfield MI 48076

KAUFFMAN, EWING MARION, pharm. co. exec., baseball exec.; b. 1916; s. John S. and Effie May (Winders) K.; Asso. Sci., Kansas City Jr. Coll.; D.Sci., Union Coll.; m. Muriel Irene McBrien, Feb. 28, 1962; children—Larry, Sue, Julia Moore. Founder, chmn. bd. Marion Labs., Inc., Kansas City, Mo., 1950—; owner, pres. Kansas City Royals Baseball Club, 1969—; founder Royals Baseball Acad., Sarasota, Fla., 1970. Mem. Civic Council Kansas City, Kansas City Sports Commn., Mayor's Corps of Progress; pres. Ewing M. Kauffman Found. Served with USN. Recipient Horatio Alger award Am. Schs. and Colls. Assn.; Man of Year award Mensa; Mktg. Man of Year Sales and Mktg. Execs. Internat.; Distinguished Service award Fellowship Christian Athletes; named to Mo. Sports Hall of Fame. Clubs: Indian Hills Country, Kansas City, Eldorado Country. Home: 5955 Mission Dr Shawnee Mission KS 66208 Office: Marion Labs Inc 10236 Bunker Ridge Rd Kansas City MO 64137

KAUFFMAN, JOHN DALE, testing co. exec.; b. Chicago Heights, Ill., May 15, 1940; s. Merle Maurer and Mildren Joan (Langbehn) K.; B.S., Bradley U., 1962, M.A., 1964; Ph.D., U. Iowa, 1970; m. Marilyn Joy Goodson, Dec. 27, 1964; children—Heidi Anne, Kirsten Johanna. Math. tchr. pub. schs., Flint, Mich., 1962-63, Lakewood, Ohio, 1963-65; counselor Sudlow Jr. High Sch., Davenport, Iowa, 1965-67; field cons. Iowa Testing Programs U. Iowa, Iowa City, 1967-69; dir. test services Houghton Mifflin Co., Geneva, Ill., 1969-72, coordinator spl. projects-tests, Boston, 1972-74; dir. field services Scholastic Testing Service, Inc., Bensenville, Ill., 1974-77, v.p. mktg., 1977—. Mem. Am. Personnel and Guidance Assn., Assn. for Measurement and Evaluation in Guidance, Council for Exceptional Children, Nat. Council on Measurement in Edn., Phi Delta Kappa. Lutheran. Home: 326 Clearwater Ct Carol Stream IL 60187 Office: 480 Meyer Rd Bensenville IL 60106

KAUFMAN, ALAN STEPHEN, psychologist, educator; b. N.Y.C., Apr. 21, 1944; s. Max and Blanche Kaufman; A.B., U. Pa., 1965; M.A., Columbia U., 1967, Ph.D., 1970; m. Nadeen Bengels, Dec. 20, 1964; children—Jennie Lynn, David Scott, James Corey. Asst. dir. The Psychol. Corp., N.Y.C., 1968-74; asso. prof. U. Ga., Athens, 1974-79; asso. prof. U. Ill., Chgo., 1979-80; prof. sch. psychology Foster G. McGaw Grad. Sch., Nat. Coll. Edn., Evanston, Ill., 1980—; research cons. Rutland Psychoednl. Center, Athens, 1976—. Recipient Outstanding Research award Ariz. Sch. Psychologists Assn., 1980. Mem. Am. Ednl. Research Assn., Am. Psychol. Assn., Council Exceptional Children, Nat. Assn. Sch. Psychologists, Phi Beta Kappa, Sigma Xi, Phi Delta Kappa. Author: Clinical Evaluation of Young Children with the McCarthy Scales, 1977; Intelligent Testing with the WISC-R, 1979; contbr. articles to profl. jours., chpts. in books. Home: 1030 Williamsburg Dr Northbrook IL 60062 Office: 2840 Sheridan Rd Evanston IL 60201

KAUFMAN, ALBERT NICK, mfg. exec.; b. Warsaw, Ind., May 16, 1924; s. Emanuel Kaufman; student Ind. U., 1948; m. Gwendolyn Ione, May 1, 1943; children—Victoria Joyce, Timothy N. With Arnolt Corp., Indpls., 1942-62, advancing through various positions and serving as v.p. mfg., dir., 1953-62; pres. K-T Corp., 1962—; pres., chmn. bd. Kaufman Enterprises, Inc., 1977—; sec.-treas. Kaufman Energy Devel. Corp.; v.p. Splty. Products Group, ALCO Standard Corp.; pres. ALCO Aerospace Co., 1981—. Vice pres. bd. pensions Ch. of God Anderson, Ind. Served with USNR, World War II. Mason (Shriner). Home: 6220 N Chester Ave Indianapolis IN 46220 Office: 850 Elston St Shelbyville IN 46176

KAUFMAN, IRA J., business exec.; b. Chgo., Mar. 4, 1928; s. Hyman and Gertrude (Schwartz) K.; student U. Ill., 1945-46; m. Audrey Becker, Jan. 12, 1969; children—Stephen, Stacy, Elizabeth, John. With Rodman & Renshaw Inc., Chgo., 1958—, pres., 1969-79, chmn. bd., 1979—; chmn. bd. Exchange Nat. Bank, Chgo., 1979—, Exchange Internat. Corp., 1979—; mem. Chgo. Bd. Trade, Midwest Stock Exchange, Chgo. Bd. Options Exchange. Trustee, exec. adv. bd. St. Joseph Hosp., Chgo. Clubs: Standard, Chgo. Yacht, Attic (Chgo.); Palm Bay (Miami, Fla.); Ocean Reef (Key Largo, Fla.). Home: 2479 Woodbridge Ln Highland Park IL 60035 Office: 120 S La Salle St Chicago IL 60603

KAUFMAN, IRMA ELINOR, hosp. public relations adminstr.; b. Escanaba, Mich., May 6, 1918; d. John Warner and Johanna Claudine (Johnson) Okerlund; student Cloverland Coll., 1936-38, Mich. State U., 1966-70, Lansing Community Coll., 1970-72; m. Robert Wright Kaufman, July 11, 1949; children—Alan, Susan. Writer, sec. bd. dirs., Mich. United Conservation Clubs, Lansing, 1959-63; free-lance writer, 1965-70; public relations dir. Ingham Med. Center, Lansing, Mich., 1970—; writing cons. Mich. Med. Soc., 1978-79. Mem. public relations com. Girl Scouts U.S.A., 1974, leader, 1963-66; leader Lansing 4-H, 1966-68. Mem. Mich. Hosp. Public Relations Assn. (pres. 1976-77), Am. Soc. Hosp. Public Relations, Public Relations Assn. Mich. (pres. 1982), Beta Sigma Phi, Lansing Area Writers Club. Republican. Methodist. Contbr. articles to nat. mags. Office: 401 W Greenlawn Ave Lansing MI 48909

KAUFMAN, JOANNE PAULA KLEIN, urban reports corp. exec.; b. Cleveland; d. Joseph E. and Martha (Ulmer) Klein; A.B. with honors, Western Res. U., 1958, M.A., 1963; m. James S. Kaufman, 1946; children—Martha J. Kaufman Stone, Peter, Thomas. Manpower program analyst, anti-poverty program Office Equal Opportunity, Dept. Labor, Washington; cons. U.S. Dept. Commerce, Washington; cons. Cleve. Dept. Pub. Health and Welfare, Cleve. Dept. Community Devel., Cleve. Commn. Higher Edn., Amtrak, Office of Edn. and Manpower Tng., HEW, Washington; mem. advance staff Vice Pres. Walter F. Mondale, Washington, 1977-80; lectr. western civilization Cuyahoga Community Coll., Cleve. State U.; pres. Urban Reports Corp., Joanne Kaufman Travel. Mem. advance staff Carter-Mondale presdl. campaign; participant White House Conf. on Balanced Growth and Econ. Devel., 1978, White House Conf. on Small Bus., 1980; trustee Child Conservation Council Greater Cleve. Mem. Nat. Women's Polit. Caucus, Cuyahoga Women's Polit. Caucus (founder). Clubs: Univ., City (Cleve.) Editor: Work and the Nature of Man (Frederick Herzberg), 1964. Home: 2676 E Overlook Rd Cleveland Heights OH 44106 Office: 1030 Euclid Ave Cleveland OH 44115

KAUFMAN, KIESL KARL, physician; b. Milw., Feb. 22, 1921; s. Aaron and Ida (Cherney) K.; student U. Wis., Milw., 1939-40; B.S., Marquette U., 1943, M.D., 1946; m. Yetta Bodner, Mar. 10, 1946; children—Jay Stuart, Lynne Gail, Jill Kaye. Intern, Mt. Sinai Hosp., Milw., 1946-47; resident in internal medicine, pulmonary disease VA Hosp., Wood, Wis., 1949-52; asso. clin. prof. medicine Med. Coll. Wis., Milw., 1952—; asso. attending staff chest service Milw. Gen. Hosp., 1952—; attending staff Muridale Sanitarium, Milw., 1954-58; asso. clin. prof. medicine Med. Sch., U. Wis., Madison, 1974—; med. dir. sch. inhalation therapy Mt. Sinai Med. Center, Milw., med. dir. respiratory therapy/pulmonary physiology, chief pulmonary diseases, attending staff; cons. staff Deaconess, Family hosps., Milw. Served to capt. U.S. Army, 1947-49. Diplomate Am. Bd. Internal Medicine, Am. Bd. Pulmonary Disease. Fellow A.C.P., Am. Coll. Chest Physicians, Israel Med. Assn. (Am. Physicians fellow); mem. AMA, Med. Soc. Milw. County, State Med. Soc. Wis., Am. Soc. Internal Medicine, Am. Thoracic Soc., Royal Soc. Medicine, Wis. Lung Assn., Wis. Heart Assn., Milw. Acad. Medicine. Contbr. articles to sci. publs. Home: 7760 N Regent Rd Milwaukee WI 53217 Office: 1218 W Kilbourn Ave Suite 207 Milwaukee WI 53233

KAUFMAN, LESLIE MICHAEL, chem. mfg., retailing exec.; b. St. Louis, Aug. 9, 1946; s. Hyman and Betty (Margulis) K.; student London Sch. Econs., 1966-67; B.A., U. Wis., 1968; M.B.A., U. Chgo., 1974; m. Marilyn Slein, Jan. 18, 1970; children—Lisa Victoria, Laura Carolyn. Midwest sales mgr. Datapage div. Western Pub. Co., Chgo., 1971-75, gen. mgr. Datapage div., St. Louis, 1976-78, dir. sales devel., comml. products div., Racine, Wis., 1979; exec. v.p., chief operating officer Progressive Industries Corp., Dayton, Ohio, from 1979, also dir.; now with Sigma-Aldrich Corp., St. Louis. Mem. Phi Beta Kappa, Sigma Alpha Mu. Office: 3500 DeKalb St Saint Louis MO 63102

KAUFMANN, FELIX, technol. and planning cons.; b. Berlin, July 4, 1918; s. Bruno P. and G. Edith (Seligsohn) K.; came to U.S., 1954, naturalized, 1968; B.S. with honors, U. London, 1940, D.I.C., 1943; grad. Brit. Inst. Mgmt., 1952; hon. diploma Instituto Politécnico Nacional de México, 1981; m. Maureen Kallick; children—Ruth, Michael, Julian, Cornelia. Dir. med. research EGH Labs. Ltd., Manchester, Eng., 1947-51; cons. WHO, Geneva, 1952-55; head makeup dept. Revlon Inc., N.Y.C., 1956; exec. v.p. Kerr Internat. Inc., Detroit, 1957-62; pres. Kerr Italia, SpA, Scafati, Italy, 1959-62; dir. futures program Hudson Inst., Croton, N.Y., 1962-65; mgr. corp. planning Hoffman-LaRoche, N.J., 1965-71; pres. Sci. for Bus. Inc., N.Y.C., 1971—; dir. internat. strategic planning Bendix Corp., Southfield, Mich., 1974-77; cons. to govts. U.S., N.Y. State, India, Pakistan, Romania, Egypt, also to WHO, UNITAR, AT&T, Ciba-Geigy, Hoffmann-La Roche, Johnson & Johnson, Marshall Foods Inc., Merck, Sharp & Dohme Internat., Storck U.S.A.; instr. courses grad. sch. bus. U. Pitts., 1972, New Sch. for Social Research, N.Y.C., 1972-73, 73-74, Am. Mgmt. Assn., 1977, 78, Grad. Sch. Bus. Adminstrn., U. Mich., 1975, 76, 79-82. Cited in resolution State of Mich. Ho. of Reps. for contbns. to Internat. Congress of Tech. Assessment, 1976. Mem. AAAS, Am. Acad. Polit. and Social Sci., Am. Chem. Soc., N.Y. Acad. Scis., N.Am. Soc. Corp. Planning, World Future Soc., Newark Center for Tech. Assessment (asso.). Author: Decisions, 1972; Organizational Decisions, 1972; World Government and the U.S. National Interest, 1965; (with others) Hypercryogenics, 1963; contbr. articles in field to publs. Home and office: 1160 Pauline Blvd Ann Arbor MI 48103

KAUFMANN, JOHN DENNIS, lawyer; b. Berwyn, Ill., June 7, 1940; s. John Joseph and Rosalie Barbara (Franek) K.; B.E.E., Marquette U., 1962; J.D., Georgetown U., 1966; m. Ellen Theresa Pease, Aug. 10, 1963; children—Anne Therese, Matthew John, Katherine Ellen. Admitted to D.C. bar, 1967, N.Mex. bar, 1973; patent trainee Western Electric Co., Washington, 1962-66; patent atty. Western Electric Co., Kearney, N.J., 1966-67, Princeton, N.J., 1967-70, N.Y.C., 1970-72; gen. atty. Sandia Corp., Albuquerque, 1972-74; patent atty. Teletype Corp., Skokie, Ill., 1974-76; gen. counsel S & C Elec. Co., Chgo., 1976—; instr., lectr. Practising Law Inst., Seminar Services Internat., S.W. Legal Found. Mem. Practising Law Inst., Engring. Knights of Marquette, Def. Research Inst., Sigma Phi Delta, Delta Theta Phi. Roman Catholic. Republican. Author: (with others) Mechanics of Patent Claim Drafting, 1974, Patents, Copyright, Trademarks and Trade Secrets for Corporate Counsel and General Practitioners, 1979, U.S. Patent Law and Practice, 1976, Patent Law Annual, 1976, PLI Patent Bar Review Course, 1970—. Home: 733 Charlemagne Dr Northbrook IL 60062 Office: 6601 N Ridge Blvd Chicago IL 60626

KAUFMANN, ROBERT JOHN, physician; b. Chgo., Feb. 10, 1921; s. John H. and Anna (Schoenenberger) K.; A.B., James Millikin U., 1943; M.D., U. Ill., 1946; m. Majory Ann Magill, June 15, 1946; children—Suzanne (Mrs. Marc Tomlinson), Philip, Stephen, John, Thomas. Resident, MacNeal Meml. Hosp., 1949-51; physician, surgeon, adminstr. Pahala Hosp., Hawaii, 1951-58; med. dir. Maytag Co., Newton, Iowa, 1958-62; dir. Med. Services Am. Samoa, Dept. Interior, 1962-65; with AEC Health Found., Richland, Wash., 1965-66; practice medicine, Martinez, Calif., 1966-69; pres. staff Martinez Community Hosp., 1969; pvt. practice, Renton and Redmond, Wash., 1969-70; adminstrv. head emergency physicians Auburn (Wash.) Gen. Hosp., 1970-76, sec., med. staff, 1973-74, treas., 1972-76; tng. Brooks AFB Sch. Aerospace Medicine, 1976-77; dir. aerospace medicine Maxwell AFB, Ala., 1976-78; hosp. comdr. Wurtsmith AFB (Mich.) Hosp., 1978—; reviewing physician local draft bd., 1967-69; mem. planning bd. King County Puget Sound Health Planning Council, 1972-76. Mem. local council Boy Scouts Am., 1967-69. Served as lt. (j.g.) USNR, 1946-49; lt. col. to col., M.C., USAF, 1976—. Decorated Meritorious Service medal. Mem. Am., Indsl., Iowa, King County (com. emergency services) med. assns., Am. Geriatrics Soc., Pan Pacific Surg. Assn., Am. Coll. Emergency Physicians (charter mem. N.W. div. mem. chpt. exec. bd. 1972, sec. 1973-74), AMA, Assn. Mil. Surgeons U.S., Air Force Assn., Renton Hist. Soc., U. Ill. Alumni Assn., James Milliken U. Alumni Assn., Ft. Steilecoom Running Club, Oreg. Road Runners, Marathon Runners Club, Sigma Zeta. Roman Catholic. Clubs: Montgomery Track, Troy Track. Home: 8413 Power Dr Wurtsmith AFB MI 48753 also Renton WA Office: Wurtsmith AFB Hosp Wurtsmith AFB MI 48753

KAUFMANN, STELLA MIRIAM BUTCHER (MRS. KENNETH KAUFMANN), religious Worker; b. Clinton, Ind., Sept. 22, 1922; d. Aaron Edward and Frances Hannah (Phipps) B.; student Greenville Coll., 1940, Terre Haute Comml. Coll., 1942, Ind. State Tchrs. Coll., 1943-45, Aurora Coll., 1949-50, U. Ill., 1950-54; B.A., Greenville Coll., 1954; m. Marion Kenneth Kaufmann, Aug. 24, 1948; children—Kenneth Walter, Bruce Gregory, Donald Alan, Gary Bryan, Stella Louise, Sheryl Lyn, April Dawn. Various positions, Terre Haute and Seymour, Ind., 1941-42; accountant Kroger's Dist. Office, Terre Haute, 1942-47; bookkeeper Greenville (Ill.) Coll., 1947-49; tchr. East View Sch. Dist. 115, Aurora, Ill., 1949-52; accountant, husbands med. bus., Greenville, 1956—. Co-dir. Christian Youth Crusader, Akron, Ohio, 1956-59, Greenville, 1959-63; chmn. hosp. bazaar, 1980, 81. Mem. W.C.T.U. (state sec. 1968-69, county pres. 1966-68, chpt. treas. 1969-70), Ill. Acad. Gen. Practice Aux., Ill. Med. Soc. Aux., Utlaut Meml. Hosp. (pres. 1968-70, hos. aux. program chmn. 1970-72, chmn. Bazaar 1972), Carolyn Winslow Women's Missionary Circle (v.p. 1968-69). Methodist. Editor: Christian Youth Crusader-Heralds, 1960-68. Home: 933 N Elm St Route 3 Box 29 Greenville IL 62246

KAUL, MOHAN LAL, social worker, educator; b. Kashmir, India, 1929; s. Mahanand and Tarawati Kaul; came to U.S., 1969, naturalized, 1976; B.Sc., Panjab U., 1947; Govt. India grantee Delhi Sch. Social Work, 1957-58; M.S.W. (Ford Found. fellow 1965-67), U. Pitts., 1967; Ph.D. (NIMH grantee 1974-75), Case Western Res. U., 1977; m. Jai Kishori Nagari, Aug. 8, 1950; children—Rajiv, Sanjiv, Prerna. Successively community organizer, chief community organizer, dir. dept. urban community devel., Delhi, 1959-65; asst. dir. Delhi Dept. Community Services, 1967-69, East Akron Community House, Akron, Ohio, 1969-71; mem. faculty Kent (Ohio) State U., 1971—, asso. prof. 1977—; site visitor to conduct on campus evaluations of social work programs, 1981. cons. in field. Bd. dirs. Akron Fair Housing Contact Service, 1972, Portage County (Ohio) Child Abuse and Neglect Project, 1977, Portage County Community Action Council, 1978. Mem. Acad. Cert. Social Workers, Council Social Work Edn., Nat. Assn. Social Workers, Kent State U. Profl. Assn., Homestead St. Block Club. Author articles in field. Home: 1158 Morningview Dr Tallmadge OH 44278

KAUL, TEJ KISHAN, economist, econometrician, educator; b. Srinagar-Kashmir, India, Dec. 13, 1947; came to U.S., 1976; s. Prithvi Nath and Rupa (Sahib) K.; B.Sc., Jammu and Kashmir U., Srinagar, India, 1967; M.Sc., South Gujaret U., Surat, India, 1970; Ph.D., Birla Inst. Tech. and Sci., Pilani, India, 1976; m. Rita Pathak, Nov. 9, 1976. Research asso. Center for Sci., Tech. and Devel., Council Scientific and Indsl. Research, New Delhi, 1976; economist Birla Inst. Scientific Research, New Delhi, 1976; postdoctoral research asso. dept. econs. Iowa State U., Ames, 1976-80, asst. prof. dept. quantitative and info. scis. Western Ill. U., Macomb, 1981—; cons. NSF Research Project, 1976. University Grants Commn. India Jr. Research fellow, 1970-75. Mem. Am. Econ. Assn., Econometric Soc., Soc. Econ. Dynamics and Control, Soc. Policy Modeling. Author: (with Karl A. Fox) Intermediate Economic Statistics, Vol. II: A Guide to Recent Developments and Literature, 1968-78, 1980; contbr. articles to profl. jours. Home: 369-13 Eggers Dr Macomb IL 61455 Office: Dept Quantitative and Info Scis Western Ill U Macomb IL 61455

KAUP, SHERRY DAWN, educator; b. Aberdeen, S.D., Oct. 29, 1947; d. Charles Aaron and Frieda Carolina (Steinwand) Kirnan; B.S., No. State Coll., Aberdeen, 1969; M.S., U. Nebr., 1977; m. Randall Allan Kaup, June 10, 1972. Tchr., elem. schs., Merle Beattie Sch., Lincoln, Nebr., 1969-75, reading coordinator, 1975-77, coordinator Clare McPhee Lab. Sch., 1977—. Recipient Outstanding Tchr. award Lincoln Public Schs., 1976. Mem. NEA, Nebr. Edn. Assn., Lincoln Edn. Assn., Assn. Supervision and Curriculum Devel., Assn. Tchr. Educators, Alpha Delta Kappa, Phi Delta Kappa, Internat. Reading Assn., Nebr. Assn. Tchr. Educators. Democrat. Roman Catholic. Home: 301 SW 92d St Lincoln NE 68502 Office: 820 S 15th St Lincoln NE 68508

KAUTZ, RICHARD CARL, chem. and feeds co. exec.; b. Mucatine, Iowa, Aug. 1, 1916; s. Carl and Leah (Amlong) K.; student U. Ariz., 1936-37; B.S. with high distinction, U. Iowa, 1939; D.H.L., George Williams Coll., 1973; m. Mary Elda Stein, Dec. 24, 1939; children—Linda, Judith (Mrs. J. David Curb), John Terry, Thomas R., Susan E. (Mrs. Donald C. Teeple), Sarah J. (Mrs. Harold Aavang), Mary Catherine (Mrs. Jay S. Huff), Jennifer W. (Mrs. Donald W. Kreger). Supr. in fin. dept. Gen. Electric Co., 1939-43; with Grain Processing Corp. and Kent Feeds, Inc., Muscatine, 1943—, chmn. bd., dir., mem. exec. com., 1966—. Mem. U. Iowa Pres.'s Club; mem. citizens com. Rock Island dist. U.S. Army Engrs.; chmn. bd. trustees mem. exec. com. Herbert Hoover Presdl. Library Assn., 1976—; chmn. bd. Nat. Council YMCA, 1970-73, now mem., mem. exec. com. and bd.; N.Am. regional v.p. World Alliance YMCA's, 1973—, mem. pres.'s com., exec. com.; mem. Bd. Trustees YMCA's; trustee Center for Study of Presidency, 1977—; sec.-treas. Bus.-Industry Polit. Action Com., 1977—. Mem. NAM (dir., chmn. exec. com. 1977, chmn. fin. com. 1978, vice chmn. 1975, chmn. 1976), Iowa Mfrs. Assn. (dir.), Muscatine C. of C., DeMolay Legion of Honor, Beta Gamma Sigma (dirs. table), Sigma Chi (named Significant Sig.). Presbyn. Mason (Shriner), Elk, Rotarian. Clubs: Union League (Chgo.); Met., Capitol Hill (Washington); Marco Polo, Met., Canadian (N.Y.C.); University Athletic (Iowa City); Des Moines, Lincoln (Des Moines). Home: Rural Route 4 Box 201 Muscatine IA 52761 Office: 1600 Oregon St Muscatine IA 52761

KAVANAGH, THOMAS GILES, state supreme ct. justice; b. Bay City, Mich., Aug. 14, 1917; A.B., U. Notre Dame, 1938; LL.B. cum laude, U. Detroit, 1943; m. Mary Mahoney, 1939; children—Joseph Hayes, Kathleen Kavanagh Doherty, Thomas Giles, Kervin Pedraic. Judge, Mich. Ct. Appeals, 1964-68; justice Mich. Supreme Ct., 1968—. Bd. dirs. Cardinal Newman Found., Wayne State U. Mem. State Bar Mich., Oakland, Detroit bar assns., Catholic Lawyers Soc., Notre Dame Law Assn. Roman Catholic. Office: Supreme Ct Law Bldg Lansing MI 48909*

KAWATRA, SURENDRA KOMAR, educator; b. Peshwar, India, June 3, 1944; came to U.S., 1977, Amar Nath and Sushila K.; Ph.D., U. Queensland, 1975; m. Geeta, Jan. 5, 1977. Asst. prof. Mich. Technol. U., Houghton, Mich., 1977-79, asso. prof. dept. metallurgy, 1979—. Mem. Am. Nuclear Soc., Am. Inst. Mining and Metallurgy. Contbr. articles in field to profl. jours. Home: 1212 E 5th Ave Houghton MI 49931 Office: Michigan Technological University Dept Metallurgy Houghton MI 49931

KAY, DICK (RICHARD D. SNODGRASS), TV reporter; b. Delrose, Tenn., July 24, 1936; s. Keby Joe and Ida Belle (Thompson) Snodgrass; B.S. in Speech Edn., Bradley U., 1962; m. Kay Sue Johnson, Apr. 16, 1960; children—Steven Anthony, Eric Charles, Brett Alan. Announcer, WSIV, Pekin, Ill., 1960; news and program dir. Radio Sta. WAAP, Peoria, Ill., 1960-63; reporter WTVH-TV, Peoria, 1963-65; news dir. WFRV-TV, Green Bay, Wis., 1965-68; writer-producer NBC News, Chgo., 1968-70; reporter WMAQ-TV, NBC News, Chgo., 1970—. Served with USN, to 1957. Recipient 6 Emmy awards Chgo. chpt. Nat. Acad. TV Arts and Scis., 1976-78.

Mem. North Side Jaycees (hon. dir.; life mem. internat. senate 1977—). Office: NBC News Merchandise Mart Chicago IL 60654

KAY, DONALD JOHN, engring. and service co. exec.; b. Chgo., June 19, 1928; s. John Lawrence and Mary (Dzubinski) Kwiatkowski; student Allied Inst. Tool Design; M.E., Chgo. Tech. Coll.; m. Marion Zivan, Sept. 4, 1954; children—Gregory, Kathleen, Bradley. Tool designer Falcon Tool & Engring., Chgo., 1951-52; project mgr. Tammen & Dennison, Chgo., 1952, then field mgr., salesman, to 1960; pres., dir. Kay & Assos., Inc., Mt. Prospect, Ill., 1960—. Served with U.S. Army, 1946-47. Club: Rolling Green Country. Office: 800 E Northwest Hwy Mount Prospect IL 60056

KAY, FRANCIS SUTTON, govt. ofcl.; b. Atlanta, Oct. 8, 1949; s. James David and Charlotte Kay; B.S. in Indsl. Mgmt., Ga. Inst. Tech., 1971; m. L. Darnell Shaw, Sept. 14, 1968; children—Shelley, Andrew, Robin. Career intern U.S. CSC, Atlanta, 1971-72, personnel mgmt. specialist, Atlanta, 1973-76; ops. mgmt. officer surveillance, hazard evaluations and field studies div. Nat. Inst. Occupational Safety and Health, Cin., 1976—. Mem. Loveland Sch. Bd.; active Loveland Stage Co. Methodist. Office: 4676 Columbia Pkwy Cincinnati OH 45226

KAY, JOHN FRANK, materials engr.; b. Bklyn., Aug. 15, 1950; s. John Frank and Agnes Mary (MaKoske) K.; B.S., Rensselaer Poly. Inst., 1972, M.S., 1974, Ph.D., 1977. Postdoctoral asso. Rensselaer Poly. Inst., Troy, N.Y., 1978; sr. engr., advanced composites systems Owens Corning Fiberglas Corp., Granville, Ohio, 1978—. Mem. Am. Chem. Soc., Soc. Biomaterials, Soc. Advancement Materials and Process Engrs., Am. Helicopter Soc., AIAA, Am. Def. Preparedness Assn., Sigma Xi. Contbr. articles to profl. jours. Home: 1572 Lonsdale Rd Columbus OH 43227 Office: Tech Center Owens Corning Fiberglas Corp Granville OH 43023

KAYAFAS, NICHOLAS, transp. co. exec.; b. New Kensington, Pa., May 6, 1931; s. Steve and Mary K.; B.B.A., U. Pitts., 1954, M.B.A., 1960; m. Helen Herouvis, July 8, 1956; 1 dau., Stephanie Ann. Indsl. engr. Crucible Steel Co. Am., Pitts., 1956-60; programmer and systems analyst Nat. Steel Corp., Portage Ind., 1960-63; chief indsl. engr., GATX Corp., Chgo., 1963-68, terminal engr., 1968-72, plant safety dir., 1972-78, mgr. indsl. hygiene and safety, 1978—; chmn. Orgn. Resources Counselors Task Force on OSHA Marine Terminal Regulations, Washington. Served with AUS, 1954-56. Cert. hazard control mgr. Mem. Am. Soc. Safety Engrs., Am. Welding Soc., Am. Indsl. Hygiene Assn. Greek Orthodox. Home: 612 E Wilson Rd Lombard IL 60148 Office: 120 S Riverside Plaza Chicago IL 60606

KAYE, JOEL EDMUND, radiologist; b. Cleve., Jan. 21, 1933; s. Norman and Mary (Arnoff) K.; B.S., Ohio State U., 1955, M.D., 1960; m. Monica Bradley, May 6, 1965; children—Ann Kathleen, Clare Monica, Louis David. Intern, Mt. Sinai Hosp., Cleve., 1960-61, resident in radiology, 1961-64; instr. radiology Ohio State U., 1964-65; practice medicine specializing in radiology, Mansfield, Ohio, 1965—; trustee Mansfield Gen. Hosp., 1977, pres. med. staff, 1976—, chmn. dept. radiology, 1981—; med. dir. Mansfield Cancer Clinic. Diplomate Am. Bd. Radiology, Am. Bd. Nuclear Medicine. Mem. AMA, Ohio, Richland County (sec.-treas. 1979, v.p. 1980, pres. 1981) med. assns., Am. Coll. Radiology, Am. Roentgen Ray Soc., Am. Coll. Nuclear Medicine (sec. Ohio chpt.), Soc. Nuclear Medicine, Radiol. Soc. N.Am., Cleve., Ohio radiol. socs., Soc. Computed Tomography. Clubs: Westbrook Country; Rotary. Home: 551 Forest Hill Rd Mansfield OH 44907 Office: 335 Glessner Ave Mansfield OH 44903

KAYE, KENNETH PETER, psychologist; b. Bklyn., Jan. 24, 1946; s. Saul and Juanita Jose (Kane) K.; A.B., Harvard U., 1966, Ph.D., 1970; m. Rosalind Charney, Sept. 24, 1976; 1 son, Lev Dylan. Knox fellow Cambridge (Eng.) U., 1969-70; asst. prof. U. Wash., Seattle, 1970-71; asst. prof. U. Chgo., 1971-78, asso. prof., 1978-81; asso. prof. Northwestern U. Med. Sch., 1981—; pvt. practice family therapy, Chgo., 1981—. Mem. AAAS, Am. Psychol. Assn., Soc. Research Child Devel. Club: Harvard of Chgo. Author: The Mental and Social Life of Babies, 1981. Contbr. articles to profl. jours. Office: 4810 S Dorchester Ave Chicago IL 60615

KAYE, RALPH ELMO, contract packaging co. exec.; b. Boston, Mar. 24, 1923; s. Ralph E. and Hazel B. (Libby) K.; B.Engring., Yale U., 1944; postgrad. Princeton U., M.I.T.; m. Mary S. O'Brien, Oct. 27, 1944; children—Joan Kaye Sandrik, William R., Sarah J. Kaye Kirk. Vice pres. G. Barr Co., Niles, Ill., 1965-69; v.p. Prodn. Controls div. U.S. Industries, Inc., Chgo., 1969-74, pres., 1974-75; chmn. bd., pres. Kaye Contract Packaging Corp. (formerly Prodn. Controls, Inc.), Chgo., 1975—. Commr., Highland Park (Ill.) Park Dist., 1963-67; plan commr. City of Highland Park, 1964-66; bd. dirs., treas. Hist. Pullman Found., 1979—. Served to lt. USNR, 1943-46, 51-52. Mem. Chgo. Perfumery, Soap and Extract Assn. (hon. mem., past pres.), Ill. Mfrs. Assn., Ill. C. of C. Republican. Presbyterian. Clubs: Singapore Yacht, Michigan City Yacht, Shriners. Office: 340 E 138th St Chicago IL 60627

KAYNE, JON BARRY, indsl. psychologist; b. Sioux City, Iowa, Oct. 20, 1943; s. Harry Aaron and Barbara Valentine (Daniel) K.; B.A., U. Colo., 1973; M.S.W., U. Denver, 1975; Ph.D., U. No. Colo., 1978; m. Bunee Ellen Price, July 25, 1965; children—Nika Jenine, Abraham. With spl. services Weld County Sch. Dist. 6, Greeley, Colo., 1975-77; forensic diagnostician Jefferson County (Colo.) Diagnostic Unit, 1977-78; asso. Dow Center, asst. prof. psychology Hillsdale (Mich.) Coll., 1978—; pres. Jon B. Kayne, P.C., Hillsdale, 1980—. Bd. dirs. Domestic Harmony, 1979—; dir. religious sch., Greeley, 1975-77; candidate for sheriff of Boulder County, 1974. Served with USAR, 1962. Mem. Am. Psychol. Assn., Am. Soc. Clin. Hypnosis, Am. Statis. Assn., Internat. Neuropsychol. Soc., Mich. Soc. Investigative and Forensic Hypnosis (chmn. bd.), N.Y. Acad. Scis., Phi Delta Kappa, Psi Chi, Alpha Gamma Sigma. Home: 220 Osseo Rd Osseo MI 49266 Office: Dow Center Hillsdale College Hillsdale MI 49242

KEAIRNS, RAYMOND EARL, dentist; b. nr. Jackson, Ohio, July 27, 1912; s. Gus Earl and Ethel Jane (McClure) K.; student Rio Grande Coll., 1931-33, Ohio State U., summers, 1934-37, 39; D.D.S., Ohio State U., 1943; m. Alice Genevieve Poston, Aug. 21, 1946. Tchr. elementary schs., Jackson County, Ohio, 1933-39; pvt. practice dentistry, Logan, Ohio, 1946—. Pres., Keairns, Inc., Spic and Span Laundromat, Lancaster, Ohio, U-Do-It Laundromat, Logan, Speed Queen Coin-Op Laundry, McArthur, Ohio, U Pick Strawberry Operation. Served with AUS, 1943-46. Mem. Nat. Automatic Laundry and Cleaning Council, Am., Ohio, Logan dental assns., Logan Area C. of C. Presbyn. Kiwanian (dir. 1955-57, 62-64). Club: Square Dance. Home: 36660 Hocking Dr Logan OH 43138 Office: 9 E 2d St Logan OH 43138

KEANE, JOHN G., business cons.; A.B. in Russian, Syracuse U.; B.S.C. in Bus. Adminstrn., U. Notre Dame; M.B.A. in Mktg., Ind. U.; Ph.D. in Econs., U. Pitts. With U.S. Steel Corp.; later with Booz, Allen & Hamilton; v.p. research and planning J. Walter Thompson, Inc., Chgo.; pres. Managing Change, Inc., Barrington, Ill., 1972—. Mem. Internat. Platform Assn., World Future Soc., N.Am. Soc. for Corporate Planning, Am. Mktg. Assn. (nat. pres. 1976), Indiana Soc. Chgo., Econ. Club of Chgo. Contbr. articles to profl. jours. Address: 106 Fox Hunt Trail Barrington IL 60010

KEATING, DONALD JOHN, electronics engr.; b. Flandreau, S.D., Dec. 30, 1925; s. John Harvey and Verna Anna (Waxdahl) K.; B.S. in Elec. Engring., S.D. State U., 1956, postgrad., 1956-57. Farmer, nr. Flandreau, 1943-50; teaching asst. S.D. State U., 1955-56; devel. engr. Wright Patterson AFB, Ohio, 1956; instr. elec. engring. S.D. State U., 1956-57; devel. engr. Def. Systems div. Sperry Univac div. Sperry Rand Corp., St. Paul, 1957—, staff engr., group leader, 1974—. Ch. del. Merriam Park Community Council, St. Paul, 1977—. Served with U.S. Army, 1950-52. Mem. IEEE, Nat. Rifle Assn., Antique Aircraft Assn., Aircraft Owners and Pilots Assn., Smithsonian Assos., Tau Beta Pi, Eta Kappa Nu, Phi Kappa Phi. Republican. Methodist. Clubs: Masons (32 deg.), K.T., Shriners. Home: 1765 Carroll Ave Saint Paul MN 55104 Office: Sperry Univac PO Box 3525 MS U2T22 Saint Paul MN 55165

KEATING, JAMES WILLIAM, real estate exec.; b. Warren, Ohio, Sept. 5, 1948; s. Walter Leo and Louise (Heltzel) K.; B.S., Youngstown State U., 1973; postgrad. Kent State U.; m. Bernadette Massacci, June 26, 1971; children—Brendan James, Ryan Patrick. Youth counselor Trumbull County (Ohio) Juvenile Ct., Warren, 1976-78; exec. dir. Trumbull County Pretrial Diversion Agy., Warren, 1978—; now v.p. Natale Co. Councilman, City of Warren, 1978—; mem. Northeastern Ohio Youth Commn. Recipient cert. of achievement Grantsmanship Inst., 1978; Ohio Farm and Home Safety award, 1968. Mem. Ohio Correctional and Ct. Services Assn., Ohio Pretrial Services Assn., Jaycees. Democrat. Roman Catholic. Club: Elks, K.C. Home: 206 Central Pkwy SE Warren OH 44483 Office: 123 W Market St Rm 125 Warren OH 44481

KEATING, MICHAEL JACK, advt. exec.; b. Liberal, Kans., June 1, 1950; s. James Bryce and Wylma Aletha (Bloom) K.; student Ft. Hays State Coll., 1969, Seward County Community Coll., 1970; B.S. magna cum laude in Bus. and Pub. Adminstrn., U. N.D., 1972; m. Geraldine Marie Staggs, May 17, 1970; children—Michelle Jeanette, Marla Jane. Sales contact supr. Cessna Aircraft Co., Wichita, Kans., 1972-75, sales promotion supr., 1977, multi-engine advt. mgr., 1978-80; with The Agency, Inc., Wichita, 1980—; corporate pilot Builders, Inc., Wichita, 1976. Mem. Kans. Dist. 375 bd. edn. chmn. bd. adminstrn. Benton Methodist Ch. Mem. Benton Jr. C. of C. (v.p.), Alpha Eta Rho. Home: Rural Route 1 Box 84-2B Benton KS 67017 Office: The Agency Inc 8080 E Central St Wichita KS 67206

KEATING, WILLIAM JOHN, newspaper exec., former congressman; b. Cin., Mar. 30, 1927; s. Charles H. and Adele (Kipp) K.; B.B.A., U. Cin., 1950, J.D., 1950, LL.D., 1975; m. Nancy Nenninger, Sept. 22, 1951; children—Nancy Keating Roe, William J., Michael K., Daniel N., Susan Keating Lame, Thomas J., John S. Admitted to Ohio bar, 1950; asst. atty. gen. Ohio, 1957-58; judge Cin. Municipal Ct., 1958-65, presiding judge, 1962-63; judge Ct. Common Pleas, Hamilton County, Ohio, 1965-67; mem. Cin. City Council, 1967-70, majority leader, chmn. finance com.; mem. 92d-93d congresses from 1st Dist. Ohio, 1970-74; pres. Cin. Enquirer, Inc., 1973-79, pres. and pub., 1979—; dir. Fifth Third Bank. Bd. dirs. AP, Kenton County Airport, Zool. Soc. Cin. Served wtih USNR, World War II. Mem. Ohio Newspaper Assn. (dir.), Greater Cin. C. of C. (sr. council), Am. Newspaper Pubs. Assn., Am. Soc. Newspaper Editors, Former Mems. Congress, Am. Legion, Sigma Chi. Office: 617 Vine St Cincinnati OH 45201

KEATS, ROGER ALAN, state legislator, banker; b. Cleve., Aug. 12, 1948; s. Robert L. and Margaret Anne (Achelpohl) K.; B.A., U. Mich.; M.A., U. Ill. Formerly mem. Ill. Ho. of Reps., now mem. Ill. Senate; banker. Served with armor br. U.S. Army, 1972-74. Republican. Christian. Office: PO Box 305 Kenilworth IL 60043

KECK, GREGORY CHARLES, social worker, educator, cons.; b. Shelby, Ohio, Jan. 13, 1949; s. Donald S. and D. Jane (Howell) K.; B.A., U. Akron, 1971; M.S. in Social Adminstrn., Case Western Res. U., 1973; Ph.D., Union Grad. Sch., Cin., 1978. Youth counselor Ohio Youth Commn., Cleve., 1973-75; social worker Indian River Sch., Massillon, Ohio, 1975-77; asst. dir. staff devel. and tng. Cuyahoga County (Ohio) Juvenile Ct., 1977; coordinator social services tech. Wayne Coll., U. Akron, 1978-79; sr. research asso. human services design lab. Case Western Res. U., 1979-80; asst. dir. Office Mental Health and Substance Abuse, City of Cleve., 1980-81, dir., 1981—; chief tng. cons. Cuyahoga County Youth Services Coordinating Council, 1980—; cons. Commn. on Accreditation for Corrections, 1980—; pvt. practice clin. social work, Cleve., 1977—. Recipient Ohio Youth Commn. Disting. Service award, 1974. Mem. Nat. Assn. Social Workers, Acad. Cert. Social Workers, AAUP, Phi Sigma Alpha, Alpha Kappa Delta, Sigma Delta Pi. Clubs: Cleve., Cleve. City, Citizens League Greater Cleve. Editor: Jour. Internat. Differential Treatment Assn., 1978-79. Home: 48 Lexington Sq Cleveland OH 44143 Office: 6688 Ridge Rd Cleveland OH 44129

KECK, JAMES MOULTON, advt. agy. exec., ret. air force officer; b. Scranton, Pa., Sept. 4, 1921; s. R. L. and Helen Louise (Walker) K.; m. Barbara Brown Fleck, June 2, 1943; children—Bonnilyn Brown, Thomas James, Allison Sarah; student Brown U., 1939; B.S., U.S. Mil. Acad., 1943; postgrad. Naval War Coll., 1952, Nat. War Coll., 1960. Commd. 2d lt. USAAF, 1943, advanced through grades to lt. gen. USAF, 72; dep. dir. OPS. Strategic Air Command, 1969-70; dep. dir. ops. USAF, 1970-71, dir. plans, 1971-72; comdr. 2d Air Force, 1972-73; vice comdr. Strategic Air Command, 1973-77; ret., 1977; sr. v.p. corporate affairs Bozell & Jacobs, advt. agy., Omaha, 1977—. Vestryman, Episcopal Ch., 1978-81; active United Way, Boy Scouts Am., ARC. Decorated D.S.M., Legion of Merit, D.F.C., Air medal. Mem. Air Force Assn., Rotary. Home: 911 S 113th St Omaha NE 68154 Office: 10250 Regency Circle Omaha NE 68114

KECK, JOSEPH JAMES, innkeeper; b. Morris, Ill., Mar. 5, 1953; s. Harold Arthur and Kathryn Margaret (Walsh) K.; A.Liberal Arts, Joliet Jr. Coll., 1973; student St. Bede Acad., 1968-71. Asst. innkeeper Holiday Inn of Morris (Ill.), 1973-80, Holiday Inn LaSalle-Peru (Ill.), 1980—; cons. in field. Recipient St. Bede Radio award, 1971, Service award, 1971. Mem. Grundy Area Jr. C. of C. (treas. 1973-75), Pub. TV of Chgo., Smithsonian Inst., Nat. Soc. of Lit. and the Arts, U.S. Jr. C. of C. Roman Catholic. Office: Holiday Inn PO Box 555 LaSalle IL 61301

KECK, ROBERT CLIFTON, lawyer; b. Sioux City, Iowa, May 20, 1914; s. Herbert A. and Harriet (McCutchen) K.; A.B., Ind. U., 1936; J.D., U. Mich., 1939; L.H.D., Nat. Coll. Edn., 1973; m. Ruth P. Edwards, Nov. 2, 1940; children—Robert Clifton, Laura E. Keck Simpson, Gloria E. Keck Sauser. Admitted to Ill. bar, 1939; practiced in Chgo., 1939—, mem. firm Keck, Mahin & Cate, 1939—, partner, 1946—; dir. 1st Ill. Corp., Evanston, Union Spl. Corp., Rust-Oleum Corp., Schwinn Bicycle Co., Signode Corp., Methode Electronics, Inc. Chmn. bd. trustees Nat. Coll. Edn.; bd. dirs. Sears Roebuck Found., 1977-79. Served with USNR, 1943-45. Mem. Fed., Am., Ill., Chgo. bar assns., Bar Assn. 7th Fed. Circuit (past pres.), Am. Coll. Trial Lawyers, Phi Gamma Delta. Republican. Clubs: Masons; Westmoreland Country (Wilmette, Ill.); Chgo., Met., Law, Legal, Econ., Execs. (Chgo.); Biltmore Forest Country (Asheville); Glen View (Golf, Ill.). Home: 1043 Seneca Rd Wilmette IL 60091 Office: 233 Wacker Dr Chicago IL 60606

KEECH, ELOWYN ANN, interior designer; b. Berrien County, Mich., Oct. 5, 1937; d. Earl Docker and Elizabeth Hall (Paullin) Stephenson; 1 son, Robert Earl. Print designer, copywriter newspaper accounts, dept. stores, resorts, service orgns., industry, 1957-75; freelance interior designer St. Joseph, Mich., 1975—. Bd. dirs. Blossomland United Way, 1981—; goal and allocations panel chmn. United Way Mich., 1976—, bd. dirs., 1980—; mem. Meml. Hosp. Aux. Designer interiors 1st. Fed. Savs. & Loan Assn., Three Oaks, Mich., 1975, Holland (Mich.) Central Trade Credit Union, 1978, 1st. Fed. Savs. & Loan Assn., Holland, 1978, Yonker Realty, Co., Holland, 1979, People's Bank of Holland, 1979, others. Mem. Ft. Miami Heritage Soc., Nat. Trust Historic Preservation, St. Joseph Art Assn. Home and Office: 375 Ridgeway Saint Joseph MI 49085

KEEFE, JOHN, state senator; b. Chgo., May 28, 1928; student Macalester Coll.; B.A., U. Minn.; LL.B., William Mitchell Coll. Law; married; children—John, Lynn, Lisa, Stephen. Admitted to Minn. bar; practiced law; mem. Minn. Ho. of Reps., from 1966, Minn. Senate, 1972—; mcpl. judge. Mem. Minnetonka-Hopkins (Minn.) Recreation Commn. Mem. Am. Legion. Republican. Clubs: Lions, KC Office: 124 State Capitol Bldg Saint Paul MN 55155*

KEEFNER, KENNETH ROBERT, pharmacist, educator; b. Chgo., Oct. 3, 1940; s. Emil Charles and Violet Rose (David) K.; student Coll. Pharmacy, U. Ill., Chgo., 1958-62, J. Sterling Morton Jr. Coll., 1961-62; B.S. in Pharmacy, N.D. State U., 1964; M.S. in Physiology, U. N.D., 1969, Ph.D. in Physiology, 1971; m. Mary Elizabeth Ryan, Aug.20, 1966; children—Kristen Anne, Michael Timothy, Peter Charles. Apprentice pharmacist Reisa Pharmacy, Chgo., 1956-58, LaVergne Pharmacy, Cicero, Ill., 1959-62; pharmacist Young Drug, Inc., Grand Forks, N.D., 1964-66; chief pharmacist Med. Center Rehab. Hosp. Pharmacy, U. N.D., Grand Forks, 1967-71; asst. prof. clin. pharmacy St. Louis Coll. of Pharmacy, 1971—, dir. div. clin. pharmacy, 1978—; cons. to hosp. pharmacies. Trustee Park West Subdiv., St. Louis, 1976-79. Registered pharmacist, N.D., Ill., Mo. Mem. Am. Assn. Colls. of Pharmacy, Am. Soc. Hosps. Pharmacists, Mo. Soc. Hosp. Pharmacists, St. Louis Soc. Hosp. Pharmacists, Sigma Xi (asso.). Roman Catholic. Club: K.C. Home: 52 Sun Valley Dr Creve Coeur MO 63141 Office: 4588 Parkview Pl Saint Louis MO 63110

KEELEY, MARGARET, mgmt. cons.; b. Mpls., May 21, 1921; d. Gordon Lewis and Dorothy (Badger) K.; B.A., Macalester Coll., 1942; postgrad U. Minn., 1965-66. Tchr., public schs., Minn., 1942-49; exec. dir. council Girl Scouts U.S.A., 1949-54; mgmt. cons., Chgo., 1954—. Mem. Ill. Adv. Com. Youth Camp Safety, 1974—; Republican Precinct chairwoman, 1965-66, del. Minn. State Conv., 1966. Decorated Ancient Order of Chammori (Guam). Mem. Assn. Girl Scout Profl. Workers, AAUW. Presbyterian.

KEEN, JOYCE, psychologist; b. Davenport, Va., Aug. 22, 1941; d. Perry A. and Helen (Wampler) K.; A.A., Va. Intermont Coll. Sch. Nursing, 1961; B.A. with honors, U. Ala., 1974; Ph.D. in Clin. Psychology, Nova U., 1978; children—Lance, Nichole, Trevor. Staff nurse VA Hosp., Memphis, Tenn., 1961-63, Wadsworth, Kans., 1963-65; charge nurse Huntsville (Ala.) Mental Health Center, 1973-75; counselor children's assessment and treatment program Nova U., Fort Lauderdale, Fla., 1976-78, counselor adult therapy Psychol. Clinic, 1976-78, adj. prof. physiol. psychology dept. psychology, 1977-78, adj. prof. pharmacology and therapeutics, 1977-78; psychology intern Ohio State U., Med. Center, Columbus, 1978-79; part-time pvt. practice psychotherapy, 1979-80; chief psychologist Southeast Community Mental Health Center, Columbus, Ohio, 1979-80; research clinician Ohio State U., Columbus, 1979-80; clin. psychologist Iowa Meth. Med. Center, Des Moines, 1980—. Mem. Am. Psychol. Assn., Assn. Advancement Behavior Therapy, Soc. Behavioral Medicine, Biofeedback Soc. Am. Contbr. articles to jours. in psychology. Home: Rural Route 1 PO Box 307 Norwalk IA 50211 Office: Psychology Dept Iowa Methodist Medical Center 1200 Pleasant St Des Moines IA 50308

KEEN, MARIA ELIZABETH, educator; b. Chgo., Aug. 19, 1918; d. Harold Fremont and Mary Eileen Honore (Dillon) Keen; A.B., U. Chgo., 1941; postgrad. U. Wyo., summer 1943, U. Mich., 1957; M.A., U. Ill., 1949. Tchr. high sch., Wyo., 1942-43, Mich., 1943-44; tchr. Am. Coll. for Women, Istanbul, Turkey, 1944-47; mem. faculty U. Ill., Urbana, asst. prof. English as 2d lang., also edn. adminstrn., 1967—. Mem. Champaign Community Devel. Com.; mem. coms. YWCA, YMCA. Mem. AAUP (treas.), Animal Protection Inst., Defenders of Wildlife, LWV, Nat. Assn. Fgn. Student Advisers, Am. Inst. Biol. Scis., U. Ill. Athletic Assn. (sec.), Ont. Geneal. Soc., AAAS, Phi Kappa Epsilon. Baptist. Home: 608 S Edwin St Champaign IL 61820 Office: 3054 Fgn Langs Bldg U Ill Urbana IL 61801

KEEN, STEPHEN, book distbg. co. exec.; b. Chgo., June 1, 1945; s. Gilbert Roland and Eleanor (Shapiro) K.; B.A., Mich. State U., 1967; M.B.A., DePaul U., 1969; m. Gerry Ann Heyman, Dec. 16, 1967; children—Robert Adam, Richard Jacob. Mgr. edn. div. Charles Levy Circulating Co., Hillside, Ill., 1968, book buyer, 1971-72, gen. mgr. computer book service, 1972-73, book circulation mgr., 1973-77, asst. v.p., book merchandising dir., 1977—. Home: 1144 Bob-O-Link St Highland Park IL 60035 Office: Charles Levy Circulating Co 4201 Raymond Dr Hillside IL 60162

KEENAN, DANIEL JOSEPH, automotive exec.; b. Joliet, Ill., Feb. 18, 1929; s. Daniel Francis and Agnes Elizabeth (Webb) K.; student Kent State U., 1962-64, U. Detroit, 1964-74; B.S. in Bus. Adminstrn. and Mgmt., W.Va. State Coll., 1976; m. Elizabeth Therese Rapp, June 20, 1953; children—Daniel P., Therese A., Melanie M., Timothy M. Prodn. supr. Gen. Motors Corp., Chgo., 1954-57; prodn. control supt. Chrysler Corp., Twinsburg, Ohio, 1957-64, div. material mgr., Detroit, 1964-65, prodn. control mgr., 1965-69; ops. mgr. Hoover Universal, Ann Arbor, Mich., 1969-70; corp. prodn. control mgr. Am. Motors Co., Detroit, 1970-78; corp. mgr. material handling engring. and equipment Volkswagen of Am., Warren, Mich., 1978—. Mem. Soc. Packaging and Handling Engrs., Am. Prodn. and Inventory Control Soc. Roman Catholic. Club: Kiwanis (Rochester Mich.). Office: 27621 Parkview Blvd Warren MI 48092

KEENAN, JAMES AUGUSTINE, JR., coll. adminstr.; b. Waterbury, Conn., Apr. 29, 1932; s. James Augustine and Anna Frances (Harmon) K.; B.S., Coll. Holy Cross, 1954; J.D., Georgetown U., 1957; m. Mary Louise Crane, Sept. 7, 1957; children—John, Anne, Patricia, James. Spl. agt. FBI, 1957-63; dir. annual giving Coll. of the Holy Cross, St. Paul, 1963-69; dir. devel. Coll. St. Thomas, St. Paul, 1969-71, v.p., 1971—. Trustee Minn. Mus. Art; chmn. Minn. Coll. and Univ. Devel., 1971. Mem. Council for Advancement and Support of Edn., St. Paul C. of C. (chmn. edn. com. 1979), Phi Alpha Delta. Clubs: University, Minnesota, Serra. Home: 650 Goodrich Ave St Paul MN 55105 Office: 2115 Summit Ave St Paul MN 55105

KEENER, JEFFERSON WARD, JR., rubber co. exec.; b. Akron, Ohio, Sept. 29, 1932; s. Jefferson Ward and Marian Grace (Feudner) K.; B.A., Amherst Coll., 1954; M.B.A., Case Western Res. U., 1956; postgrad. Ohio State U., 1959; m. Kathleen Margaret Cullinan, Apr. 19, 1958; children—Marian Margaret, Patricia Lee, Elizabeth, Jefferson Ward. Asst. to treas. Mohawk Rubber Co., Akron, Ohio, 1959-65, corp. sec., 1966-76, v.p. ops., 1969-76, pres. Mohawk

Internat., 1965-76; mgmt. cons. A.T. Kearney, Inc., Cleve., 1976-78; pres. Chardon Rubber Co. (Ohio), 1978—, also dir.; dir. Hardware and Supply Co., Akron. Mem. Pres.'s Com. on Employment of the Handicapped, 1968-76; mem. adv. com. Coll. Bus. Adminstrn., U. Akron, 1961—; mem. exec. bd. United Found., Summit County, 1964-69, hon. trustee, 1969—; trustee Family and Children's Service Soc. Summit County, 1960-73, pres., 1969-71, mem. adv. com., 1973—; treas., trustee Western Res. Acad., Hudson, Ohio; trustee Akron Gen. Med. Center. Served with USNR, 1956-59. Republican. Lutheran. Clubs: Portage Country, Akron City, Mayflower. Office: 373 Washington St Chardon OH 44024

KEENER, PATRICIA ANN, pediatrician; b. Urbana, Ill., Apr. 6, 1942; d. Edward Holland and Helen (Bibart) Fowler; M.D., Ind. U., 1968; m. Gerald Theron Keener, Jr., May 18, 1968; children—Kristina Kathleen, Leslie Lynn, Nicholas Edward. Intern, Wishard Meml. Hosp., Indpls., 1969; resident in pediatrics Riley Hosp. for Children, Indpls., 1969; resident Med. Coll. S.C., Charleston, 1969-71, chief resident, 1971; asso. prof. pediatrics Riley Hosp. for Children, Ind. U., Indpls., 1972-78, clin. asso. prof., 1978—, dir. undergrad. pediatric med. edn., 1972-78; dir. nurseries and pediatrics Community Hosp. Indpls., Inc., 1973—, cons. neonatologist Reid Meml. Hosp., Jasper County Hosp., Ball Meml. Hosp. Adv. bd. NeoFight Inc.; chmn. profl. adv. bd. March of Dimes, 1981—. Named Outstanding Prof. Pediatrics, Ind. U. Sch. Medicine, 1976, 77; recipient Edwin Gresham Meml. award for advances in neonatology, 1981. Diplomate Am. Bd. Pediatrics. Fellow Am. Acad. Pediatrics (Bronze award 1974, treas. Ind. dist. 1981—); mem. Ind. Neonatal Soc. (sec.-treas. 1980—). Editor: Introduction to Pediatrics, vol. 1, 1974; editorial bd. Perinatal Press, 1978—; contbr. articles to profl. jours. Home: 5455 N Pennsylvania St Indianapolis IN 46220 Office: 1500 N Ritter St Indianapolis IN 46219

KEFAUVER, WELDON ADDISON, publisher; b. Canal Winchester, Ohio, Apr. 3, 1927; s. Ross Baker and Virginia Marie (Burtner) K.; B.A., Ohio State U., Columbus, 1950. Mem. faculty Columbus Acad., 1956-58; mng. editor Ohio State U. Press, 1958-64, dir., 1964—; pres. Assn. Am. Univ. Presses, 1977-78; mem. U.S. del. 2d Asian Pacific Conf. Publs., Taiwan, 1978. Served with AUS, 1945-46. Recipient citation Ohioana Library Assns., 1974. Mem. AAUP. Clubs: Torch, Crichton, Ohio State U. Faculty (Columbus). Home: 675 Eastmoor Blvd Columbus OH 43209 Office: 2070 Neil Ave Columbus OH 43210

KEGEL, PAUL LINKEN, coll. adminstr.; b. Milw., July 28, 1935; s. Paul William and Volga Louise (Linken) K.; B.A., Ripon Coll., 1957; M.S., U. Wis., Madison, 1958, 63, Ph.D. in English, 1976; m. Ann Catherine McGarry, June 12, 1965; children—Patrick, Brian, Thomas, Lynn Ann. English instr., student activities dir. U. Wis., Marshfield, 1965-68; dir. student affairs U. Wis., Washington campus, 1968-69; dean students Worthington (Minn.) Community Coll., 1970-77; dean, pres. Marshalltown (Iowa) Community Coll., 1977—; mgr. Wis. Telephone Co., 1961-62. Mem. Minn. Gov.'s. Task Force on Public Radio, 1975; mem. Worthington (Minn.) Park Bd., 1975-77; mem. S.W. Minn. Arts and Humanities Council, 1974-76; pres. Worthington Montessori Sch., 1972; mem. Central Com. Marshall County Democratic party, 1980-82; div. leader ann. membership/fund drive YMCA; bd. dirs Marshalltown Area Council for Arts; mem. Community Relations Com.; del. county and state convs. Dem. party, 1980, precinct chmn. Marshall County Dem. party. Served with USNG, 1959. Mem. Iowa Assn. Lifelong Learning, Iowa Archeol. Soc., Ripon Coll. Alumni Assn. (dir. 1978—). Club: Rotary. Contbr. articles to profl. jours. Home: 1904 Blossom Ln Marshalltown IA 50158 Office: 3700 S Center St Marshalltown IA 50158

KEGERREIS, ROBERT JAMES, univ. pres.; b. Detroit, Apr. 2, 1921; s. Irl George and Adah Marguerite (Merry) K.; B.A. in Econs., Ohio State U., 1943, B.Sc. in Fgn. Trade, 1943, M.B.A. in Mktg. Mgmt., 1947, Ph.D. in Bus. Adminstrn., 1968; LL.D. (hon.), Central State U., Wilberforce, Ohio, 1977; m. Katherine Louise Falknor, Oct. 30, 1943; children—Robert Duncan, Melissa Ann. Sr. researcher Fed. Res. Bank Cleve., 1947-49; market researcher Donald R.G. Cowan Agy., Cleve., 1949; partner Kegerreis Stores, Woodsfield, Ohio, 1950-60; v.p., treas. KBK Devel. Corp., Woodsfield, 1954-60; mgmt. cons., 1966—; dir. Robbins & Myers, Inc., Systems Research Labs., Inc., Dayton Power & Light Co., Chemineer, Inc., Winters Nat. Bank and Trust Co., Dayton, Ranco, Inc., Progressive Industries Corp.; asso. prof. bus. adminstrn., chmn. dept. Ohio U., Athens, 1967-69; prof. mktg., dean Coll. Bus. and Adminstrn., 1969-71, v.p., dir. adminstrn., 1971-73; pres. Wright State U., Dayton, 1973—. Trustee, Dayton Art Inst., Engring. and Sci. Found., Otterbein Coll., Westerville, Ohio, Dayton-Miami Valley Consortium, Meth. Theol. Sch. Ohio. Served as officer USNR, 1943-46. Mem. AAUP, Assn. Consumer Research, Am. Inst. Decision Scis., Am. Psychol. Assn., Am. Mktg. Assn., Acad. Mgmt., Am. Assn. Univ. Adminstrs., Am. Assn. Higher Edn., Ohio Coll. Assn., Sphinx, Beta Gamma Sigma, Phi Delta Kappa. Methodist. Clubs: Dayton Rotary, Dayton Bicycle, Dayton Racquet, Moraine Country. Author articles. Home: Rockafield House Wright State U Dayton OH 45435 Office: Office of President Wright State U Dayton OH 45435

KEHN, EDWIN CLARK, ranching corp. exec.; b. Burke, S.D., Sept. 12, 1942; s. Edwin Elmer and Alta Maxine (Whitley) K.; B.S., S.D. State U., 1965; m. Bonnie L. Vawser, Dec. 28, 1963; children—Jeffrey Clark, Scott Lee, Bradley David. Vice pres. Kehn Ranch Inc., St. Charles, S.D., 1970—. Asst. leader 4-H Club. Republican. Methodist. Clubs: Odd Fellows, Rebekahs, Order of Eastern Star, Masons, Shriners, Elks. Home and Office: Rural Route 1 Saint Charles SD 57571

KEISTER, DOUGLAS CHARLES, psychologist; b. Akron, Ohio, May 12, 1950; s. Harold Morton and Ellen Elizabeth (Miller) K.; B.S., Mt. Union Coll., 1972; postgrad. Kent State U., 1974; M.A., Ball State U., 1977, psychometrist license, 1979; m. Martel Louise Bahn, July 16, 1977. Advisor/dir. recreational activities for mentally retarded Weaver Sch., Tallmadge, Ohio, 1975; clin. psychology intern alcohol/drug abuse Marion (Ind.) VA Hosp., 1975; clin. psychology intern New Castle (Ind.) State Hosp., 1975-76; behavioral clinician for area services E. Central Ind., New Castle State Hosp., 1976—; behavior mgmt. cons.; coordinator, tng. on epilepsy program, psychometrist New Castle Community Schs., 1978-79. Recipient Cert. of Disting. Merit New Castle State Hosp., 1978; Disting. Service award Ind. Bd. Health, 1979. Mem. Internat. Neuropsychol. Soc., Ind. Psychol. Assn., Am. Assn. on Mental Deficiency. Republican. Methodist. Editorial adv. bd. Jour. Clin. Neuropsychology, 1979; contbr. articles in field to profl. jours. Home: Rural Route 6 PO Box 3E New Castle IN 47362 Office: 100 Van Nuys Rd New Castle IN 47362

KEISTER, FRED D., III, mfg. co. exec.; b. Ionia, Mich., Jan. 27, 1927; s. Fred D. and Katherine (Gauss) K.; B.A. in Journalism, U. Mich., 1950; m. Barbara Jean Robinson, June 26, 1948; children—Katherine Ruth, Fred, Lawrence Bruce, Christopher Bill, Jeffrey David. Editor, publisher Ionia (mich.) County News, 1950-65; mgr. publ. and engring. services Mech. Products, Inc., Jackson, Mich., 1966; dir. public relations and advt. Sparton Corp., Jackson, 1967—. Mem. Ionia Bd. Edn., 1956-65; mem. Ionia County Tax Allocation Bd., 1961-64. Served with U.S. Army, 1945-46. Club: Elks. Home: 584 Birchwood St Jackson MI 49203 Office: 2700 E Ganson St Jackson MI 49202

KEITEL, GLENN HOWARD, engr.; b. Chgo., Feb. 16, 1930; s. Fred and Harriet (Johnson) K.; B.S. magna cum laude, U. Wash., 1952, M.S., 1954; Ph.D., Stanford U., 1955; postgrad. Cambridge (Eng.) U., 1955-56; m. Laurel Josephine Lund, June 12, 1953; children—Kristin Marie, Karin Anne. Mem. tech. staff Gen. Electric Co., Palo Alto, Calif., 1956-59; mgr. communications scis. dept. Philco Corp., Palo Alto, 1959-62, prof. elec. engring., chmn. dept. San Jose (Calif.) State Coll., 1962-69; electronics liaison scientist U.S. Office Naval Research, London, 1963-64; prof. elec. engring., chmn. dept. Drexel U., 1969-71; dean Coll. Engring., Bucknell U., Lewisburg, Pa., 1971-79; dir. engring. CPT Corp., Eden Prairie, Minn., 1980-81; pres. Office Automation Consultants, Inc., Mpls., 1981—; cons. Mem. Am. Mgmt. Assn., Phi Beta Kappa, Sigma Xi, Tau Beta Pi, Eta Kappa Nu, Pi Mu Epsilon. Office: 511 11th Ave S Suite 205 Minneapolis MN 55415

KEITH, DONALD MORTON, ret. army officer, found. dir.; b. Chgo., Apr. 24, 1935; s. Myron and Jennette (Porter) K.; B.B.A. cum laude, U. Wis., 1956; postgrad. U. Hawaii, 1957-58; M.B.A. summa cum laude, Monmouth Coll., Long Branch, N.J., 1973; postgrad. N.Y. U., 1974; m. Phyllis Beryl Markuson, Mar. 24, 1963; children—Nina Susan, Paula Dorit. Enlisted in U.S. Army Res., 1954, commd. 2d lt., 1956, advanced through grades to lt. col., 1971; dep. comdr. U.S. Army Security Agy. Material Support Command and dir. Nat. Maintenance Point, 1974-77; ret., 1977; logistics mgr. CALCULON Corp., cons., Washington, 1977—; chmn. bd. dirs., exec. dir. Center for Study of Multiple Birth, Northwestern U. Med. Sch., Chgo./Prentice Women's Hosp. and Maternity Center, 1977—; research asst. Am. Assn. Gynecol. Laparoscopists, 1973-78, staff asst. sci. program com., 1973-78; participant symposia. Decorated Bronze Star (2), Meritorious Service medal, numerous others; Armed Forces Communications Electronics Assn. scholar, 1957; cert. profl. logistician, profl. resource mgr. Fellow Internat. Soc. Twin Studies, Soc. Advanced Med. Systems, Soc. Logistics Engrs. (chmn. tech. communications workshop 1978); mem. Am. Public Health Assn., Am. Assn. Gynecol. Laparoscopists (asso.), Am. Coll. Hosp. Adminstrs. (asso.), Am. Hosp. Assn., Assn. U.S. Army, World Population Soc. (charter). Club: Masons. Office: Suite 463-5 333 E Superior St Chicago IL 60611

KEITH, KENNETH DWIGHT, psychologist; b. Council Bluffs, Iowa, July 8, 1946; s. Delbert Dwight and Loraine Mae (Pollitt) K.; B.A., N.W. Mo. State U., 1967; M.A., Pittsburg State U., 1968; Ph.D., U. Nebr., 1975; m. Constance Anne Bishop, Dec. 18, 1966; children—David Wesley, Heather Elaine. Unit psychologist Glenwood (Iowa) State Hosp., 1968-69; asso. psychologist Beatrice (Nebr.) State Home, 1969-70, psychologist, I and co-dir. staff devel., 1970-71; instr. dept. ednl. psychology U. Nebr., Lincoln, 1971-72; dir. research/planning Beatrice State Home, 1972-73; instr., U. Nebr. System, Lincoln, 1973-77, asst. prof., 1977-80; pres. Center for Human Resource Devel., Lincoln, 1978—; vis. asso. prof. dept. psychology Nebr. Wesleyan U., Lincoln, 1980-82; pvt. practice psychology, Lincoln, 1975—. Mem. human and legal right com. on edn. Nebr. Assn. for Retarded Citizens, 1973-77, chmn. 1974-77; mem. public edn. com. Am. Cancer Soc., 1975—, Nebr. div. chmn., 1977-80; mem. ednl. services study com. Eastern Nebr. Community Office Retardation, 1977-78; mem. regionalization evaluation task force Lancaster Office Mental Retardation, 1977; bd. dirs. Nebr. div. Am. Cancer Soc., 1977—, chmn., 1981-82; lectr. Nebr. Forum on Human Values, U. Nebr. and Nebr. Wesleyan U., 1979-80. Lic. psychologist, Nebr. Mem. Am. Psychol. Assn., Nebr. Psychol. Assn., Assn. Advancement of Behavior Therapy, Assn. Behavior Analysis, Nat. Assn. for Retarded Citizens, Nebr. Assn. for Retarded Citizens, Capital Assn. for Retarded Citizens, Am. Humanist Assn., Soc. Behavioral Medicine, Nebr. Soc. Profl. Psychologists, Lancaster County Psychol. Soc., Psi Chi. Democrat. Scientific Humanist. Contbr. articles to profl. jours. Home: 1541 Manatt St Lincoln NE 68521 Office: 770 N Cotner St Suite 201 Lincoln NE 68505

KEITH, LOUIS GERALD, physician; b. Chgo., Apr. 24, 1935; s. Myron and Jennette K.; B.S., U. Ill., 1956; M.D., Chgo. Med. Sch., 1960; m. Gail Elayne Gersh, July 14, 1968. Intern, Cook County Hosp., Chgo., 1960-61, resident in ob-gyn, 1961-64; mem. faculty dept. ob-gyn Northwestern U. Med. Sch., 1975—, prof., 1975—; attending physician dept. ob-gyn Prentice Women's Hosp. and Maternity Center, Chgo., 1978—; lectr. ob-gyn Cook County Grad. Sch. Medicine, 1977—; cons. dept. ob-gyn Ponce (P.R.) Sch. Medicine, 1980—; pres. Center for Study of Multiple Gestation, 1978—; research cons. Charles A. Fields Med. Found., Ltd., 1981, bd. dirs., 1978—; exec. dir. Center for Advancement of Reproductive Health, Chapel Hill, N.C., 1979—. Served to lt. comdr. USPHS, 1964-66. Diplomate Am. Bd. Ob-Gyn. Fellow Internat. Coll. Surgeons (exec. council U.S. sect. 1977—), Am. Coll. Obstetricians and Gynecologists, ACS, Am. Fertility Soc., Royal Soc. Health, Inst. Medicine Chgo., Am. Acad. Reproductive Medicine, Royal Soc. Medicine (London); Chgo. Gynecol. Soc.; mem. Assn. Profs. Ob-Gyn, Internat. Soc. Twin Studies (founding mem., chmn. working party on multiple pregnancy 1980—, dir. 1973—), Am. Assn. Maternal and Neonatal Health (dir. 1980—), Am. Public Health Soc., Am. Assn. Med. Writers, Am. Assn. Planned Parenthood Physicians, Am. Assn. Gynecol. Laparoscopists (founding mem.), Am. Soc. Colposcopy and Colpomicroscopy, Am. Med. Soc. Vienna (life), Am. Assn. Blood Banks, Med. Soc. Study of Venereal Diseases (London), Am. Gynecol. Soc. Study of Breast Diseases, Internat. Growth Fedn. (steering com.), Sigma Xi, Alpha Omega Alpha, Phi Delta Epsilon, Omega Beta Pi. Asso. editor Acta Geneticae Medicae et Gemellologiae, 1972—, Jour. Reproductive Medicine, 1973—, Acta Medica Auxologica, 1975—, Internat. Surgery, 1976—, Compendium Drug Therapy, 1979—, Current Problems in Obstetrics and Gynecology, 1981—. Editor (with others): Gynecological Laparoscopy: Principles and Techniques, 1974; Laparoscopy, 1977; Chronogenetics: The Inheritance of Biological Time, 1977; Endoscopy in Gynecology, 1978; The Care of Twin Children: A Common Sense Guide for Parents, 1978; The Safety of Fertility Control, 1980; Second Trimester Abortion: Perspective after a Decade of Experience, 1981; author (with others): Sexually Transmitted Diseases, 1978; IUDs and their Complications, 1979; Postabortal Contraception, 1979; Vaginal Contraceptives, 1981; contbr. articles to profl. jours. Office: 333 E Superior St Chicago IL 60611

KEITHLEY, BONNIE LOUISE, ednl. adminstr.; b. Cleve., Mar. 10, 1947; d. Harvey Matthew and Elaine (Finger) Weiss; B.S. in Edn., U. Mo., 1969; m. William C. Keithley, Feb. 9, 1969; children—Adam Justus, Rachel Leona. Tchr. bus. edn., Aberdeen, Md., 1969-71; sec. U. Mo., Columbia, 1972; adminstrv. sec. MFA, Inc., Columbia, 1972-73; clk.-typist program adminstr. CETA, Columbia; seminar instr. Mem. Mo. Employment and Tng. Assn. (pres. 1977-78), Am. Vocat. Assn., Mo. Vocat. Assn., Nat. Employment and Tng. Assn., Columbia Adult Edn. Coordinators Council. Office: 310 N Providence Rd Columbia MO 65201

KEITHLEY, RICHARD ERNEST, lawyer; b. Kansas City, Kans., Mar. 12, 1948; s. Marion C. and Elsie V. (Hatch) K.; A.A., Donnelly Coll., 1968; B.A., Kans. U., 1970, J.D., 1974; m. Lydia Lois Brewer, Aug. 6, 1977; children—Shannon Eileen, Heather Dawn. Admitted to Kans. bar, 1974, Fed. bar, 1974, U.S. Supreme Ct. bar, 1977, U.S. Ct. of Appeals bar for 10th Circuit, 1977; clk. to Dist. Judge Kenneth Harmon, Leavenworth, Kans, 1973; individual practice law, Kansas City, 1974-75; asst. city atty. City of Kansas City, 1975-77; now pvt. practice; lectr. in field. Democratic nominee Kans. Ho. of Reps., 1972. Mem. Kansas City Jaycees, Phi Alpha Delta, Delta Sigma Phi. Democrat. Episcopalian. Home: 4218 Lathrop Ave Kansas City KS 66104 Office: 430 Brotherhood Block Kansas City KS 66101

KELADA, NABIH PHILOBBOS, chemist; b. Cairo, Egypt, Nov. 12, 1930; came to U.S., 1969, naturalized, 1975; s. Philobbos Bey and Fahima (Takla) K.; B.Sc. in Chemistry and Biology, Cairo U., 1951; spl. diploma in edn. Ain-Shams U., Cairo, 1957; M.Sc. in Chemistry, Am. U. in Cairo, 1968; grad. fellow Tech. U. Denmark, 1969; M.S. in Environ. Chemistry, U. Mich., 1971, Ph.D., 1972; children—Reda, Samir. Tchr. sci. high schs., Egypt, 1952-64; sci. rep. and head public relations Wyeth Internat. Sci. Office, Cairo, 1964-68; research asso. Tech. U. of Denmark, Lyngby, 1968-69, Nat. Sanitation Found., Ann Arbor, Mich., 1969-71; prin. investigator environ. chemistry U. Mich., Ann Arbor, 1971-72, research asso. Sch. of Public Health, 1972-73; chief environ. Labs., Ohio State Public Health Lab., Columbus, 1973-74; head methodology and instrumentation R&D Labs., Met. Sanitary Dist. of Greater Chgo., 1974—; cons. to industry and govt. agys., 1973—. Mem. Am. Chem. Soc., ASTM, Sigma Xi. Mem. Christian Coptic Orthodox Ch. Club: Glen Ellyn Tennis. Contbr. articles to profl. jours.; patentee in cyanide systems.

KELEDJIAN, EDWARD JAMES, real estate exec.; b. Detroit, Nov. 25, 1942; s. Edward and Fern (Ickes) K.; B.S., Eastern Mich., U., 1966; M.Urban Planning, Wayne State U., Detroit, 1969; m. Helen Lawlor, Dec. 28, 1968; children—Alex, Kate. Planner, City of Chgo., 1969-73; acquisition dir. real estate Multi-Vest Inc., Detroit, 1973-75; investment officer Life Investor, Inc., Cedar Rapids, Iowa, 1975-77; regional v.p. acquisition Robert A. McNeil Corp., Chgo., 1977-81; exec. v.p. VMS Realty Inc., Chgo., 1981—; instr. Roosevelt U., Chgo., 1972-73. Served with USMCR, 1963-64. Mem. Real Estate Securities Inst. (dir. Ill. chpt.), Chgo. Multi-Famliy Housing Assn. (dir.), United Armenian Cultural Assn.; asso. mem. Internat. Council Shopping Centers, Ill. Mortgage Bankers Assn. Office: 69 W Washington St Chicago IL

KELKAR, MANOHAR SHANKAR, physician; b. Dahanu, Maharashtra, India, Oct. 16, 1932; s. Shankar Trimbak and Yamuna Shankar (Marathe) K.; came to U.S., 1962. Intern, Paterson (N.J.) Gen. Hosp., 1962-63; pres. Manohar S. Kelkar, M.D., Inc., Solon, Ohio, 1975—. Pres., Marathi Cultural Assn., Solon, 1976. Diplomate Am. Bd. Family Practice. Fellow Am. Acad. Family Physicians; mem. Acad. Medicine Cleve., Ohio Med. Assn., India Assn. Cleve. Author: Ten Minutes of Asans for Physical Fitness, 1974. Home: 5800 Ledgebrook Ln Solon OH 44139 Office: 34420 Aurora Rd Solon OH 44139

KELLAMS, DARRELL FRANK, educator; b. Salina, Kans., July 1, 1926; s. Perry C. and Ruth E. Kellams; B.S. in Edn., Emporia (Kans.) State U., 1951; M.Ed., U. Kans., 1955, Ed.D., 1964; m. Elizabeth Marie Lincoln, Feb. 7, 1948; children—David Michael, John Keith, Robert Andrew. From elem. sch. tchr. to jr. high sch. prin., Shawnee Mission, Kans., 1951-64; mem. faculty U. Nebr., Omaha, 1965—, prof. ednl. adminstrn., chmn. dept., 1968—. Served with AUS, 1944-46. Profl. Devel. fellow U. Nebr. System, 1979. Mem. Am. Assn. Sch. Adminstrs., Nat. Assn. Core Curriculum, NEA, Nebr. Council Sch. Adminstrs., Nebr. Schoolmasters Club, Am. Legion, Phi Delta Kappa (Nebr. area coordinator). Lutheran. Author articles, chpt. in handbook. Office: Univ Nebr 60th and Dodge Sts Omaha NE 68182

KELLER, BRENDA JO, jr. high sch. tchr.; b. Clay Center, Kans., Apr. 7, 1942; d. Paul Wilson and Florence Dolly (Hudson) Griffith; B.S., Kans. State U., Manhattan, 1964; M.S. in Sci. Edn., U. Iowa, 1970; M.Ed. in Curriculum and Supervision, Wright State U., Dayton, Ohio, 1980; m. Harold W. Keller, Mar. 7, 1965; children—David Bryant, Brian Lee. Teaching asst. Kans. State U., 1962-64; mgr. city swimming program, Manhattan, 1964; swimming instr. YWCA, Atlanta, 1965-67; instr. Santa Fe Jr. Coll., Gainesville, Fla., 1971-72; tchr. Fairborn (Ohio) city schs., 1972—; tchr. life & earth scis. Central Jr. High Sch., 1972—; sci. dept. coordinator Fairborn City Schs., 1975—. Recipient Acker award Ohio Acad. Sci., 1981; Martha Holden Jennings tchr./scholar, 1981. Mem. Nat. Sci. Suprs. Assn., Nat. Sci. Tchrs. Assn., Assn. Supervision and Curriculum Devel., NEA, Am. Women Sci., Ohio Sci. Edn. Assn., Fairborn Edn. Assn. (Disting. Service award 1976-77), Kappa Delta Pi, Phi Delta Kappa. Address: 1732 Hillrose Pl Fairborn OH 45324

KELLER, CARL EDWARD, educator; b. Shelbyville, Mo., Sept. 1, 1934; s. Carl Albert and Thekla (Wild) K.; B.S. in Edn., N.E. Mo. State U., 1955; m. Joyce Darlene Woods, Aug. 24, 1953; children—Linda Irene, Carl Robert, James Edward. Tchr., Shelbina (Mo.) public schs., 1955-64; tchr. indsl. edn. Shelby County R-IV Schs., Shelbina, 1964—. Mem. Mo. Tchrs. Assn., Community Tchrs. Assn. Republican. Lutheran. Home: Shelbyville MO 63469 Office: Shelby County R-IV Schs Shelbina MO 63468

KELLER, DAVID COE, dept. store exec.; b. Warren, Ohio, Jan. 30, 1921; s. David Claude and Minnie Corlin (Furgerson) K.; B.B.A., Cleve. State U., 1943; m. Gladys Marie Carstens, Jan. 6, 1945; 1 dau., Anne Marie. Staff accountant Touche Ross & Co., Cleve., 1946-49; asst. controller M. O'Neil Co., dept. store, Akron, Ohio, 1950-56; controller, treas., dir. F.N. Arbaugh Co., dept. store, Lansing, Mich., 1956-59; v.p., treas., dir. Wurzburg Co., dept. store, Grand Rapids, Mich., 1959-72; chief financial officer, v.p., treas. Wieboldt Stores Inc., Chgo., 1972—. Bd. dirs. Jr. Achievement, Grand Rapids, 1961-69, Civic Fedn. Chgo., 1974. Served to 1st lt. USMCR, 1943-45. Named Grand Rapids Boss of Year, Am. Women's Clubs, 1969. Mem. Ill. Retail Mchts. Assn. (dir., treas.), State St. Council (tax com. 1974—), Tau Kappa Epsilon. Clubs: Masons, Shriners. Office: Wieboldt Stores Inc 1 N State St Chicago IL 60602

KELLER, HAROLD WILLIAM, chem. co. exec.; b. Grand Forks, N.D., Aug. 24, 1922; s. Charles Earl and Margaret Ann (Carlson) K.; student U. N.D., 1940-42, 46-48; m. S. Betty Larsen, Oct. 31, 1947; children—Charles William, Kenneth Earl. Asst. dir. research Ill. Water Treatment Co., Rockford, 1952-68, service mgr., 1968-69, mgr. market devel., 1969-72; v.p. Techni-Chem, Inc., Cherry Valley, Ill., 1972-77, pres., 1977—, also corporate exec., dir. Served with USAAF, 1942-46. Mem. Am. Chem. Soc., Am. Oil Chemists Soc., Am. Inst. Chem. Engrs., Am. Soc. Sugar Beet Tech., Lambda Chi Alpha. Home: 7633 Lucky Ln Rockford IL 61108 Office: 6853 Indy Dr Belvidere IL 61008

KELLER, JOHN FREDERICK, educator; b. Harvey, N.D., Sept. 25, 1930; s. Fred August and Martha (Martin) K.; B.S., Valley City (N.D.) State Coll., 1955; M.S., U. N.D., 1960, Ed.D., 1973. Tchr. high schs. in N.D., 1955-65; mem. faculty Dawson Jr. Coll., Glendive, Mont., 1965-67, Mayville (N.D.) State Coll., 1967-68; mem. faculty

Valley City State Coll., 1968—, prof. bus., 1974—, chmn. div. bus., 1970—; curriculum cons., 1970—. Vice pres. Valley City Troubadors, 1978, pres., 1979. Served with AUS, 1951-53. Decorated Meritorious Service award. Mem. Nat. Bus. Edn. Assn., NEA, Mountain Plains Bus. Edn. Assn. (pres. 1979—; Outstanding Leadership in Bus. Edn. award 1979), N.D. Bus. Edn. Assn., N.D. Edn. Assn., N.D. Assn. Higher Edn., N.D. Coll. Tchrs. Acctg., Am. Legion, VFW, Phi Delta Kappa, Delta Pi Epsilon, Pi Omega Pi. Republican. Baptist. Clubs: Elks, Eagles. Home: 330 College St SW Valley City ND 58072 Office: Valley City Coll Valley City ND 58072

KELLER, KATHRYN ANN, mfg. co. exec.; b. Plainwell, Mich., Oct. 3, 1946; s. Robert Sherman and Margaret May (Russell) Melvin; student Kalamazoo Valley Community Coll. 1979-80; m. John Charles Keller, Oct. 23, 1965; children—Elizabeth Ann, John Charles. With Parker Hannifin Corp., various locations, 1964-65, 72—, graphic arts specialist pneumatic div., Otsego, Mich., 1977-78, advt. sales mgr., 1978—. Mem. Am. Soc. Profl. and Exec. Women, Indsl. Marketers W. Mich. Home: 1387 E M 89th St Otsego MI 49078 Office: 601 S Wilmott St Otsego MI 49078

KELLER, LARRY LEE, coll. pres.; b. Lincoln, Nebr., Aug. 5, 1939; s. Elton R. and Alta J. K.; B.S., U. Nebr., 1966; M.S., U. Wis., 1970; m. Shirley, Aug. 16, 1959; children—Mark L., Laura A. Machinist, Sharpnack Engring., Lincoln, 1957-59; prototype machinist, toolmaker Bruning Mfg. Co., Lincoln, 1959-60, 63-66; faculty Central Tech. Community Coll. Area, Grand Island, Nebr., 1966—, pres. Grand Island Campus, 1978—. Served with USN, 1960-63. Mem. Am. Vocat. Assn., Adult and Continuing Edn. Assn. Nebr., Missouri Valley Adult Edn. Assn., Soc. Mfg. Engrs. Republican. Lutheran. Clubs: Masons, Rotary. Office: Central Community College PO Box C Grand Island NE 68802

KELLER, LEONARD, mfg. co. tng. exec.; b. Phila., May 8, 1931; s. Nathan and Ann K.; B.A.Ed., Ariz. State U., 1954; M.S. in Adult Edn., Supervisory Leadership and Adminstrn., U. Wis., Milw., 1979; m. Christa Maria Schuberth, Feb. 3, 1965; children—Michael, Hobert, Debra, Steven, Ronald, Stanley, David. Commd. 2d lt. Chem. Corps, U.S. Army, 1954, advanced through grades to lt. col., 1969; assignments U.S., Ger., Vietnam; ret., 1969; area mgr., mfrs. rep. Indsl. Electronics Corp., Denver, 1969; mgr. tng. and devel. Ball Corp., Lakewood, Colo., 1970-74; mgr. tng. container div. Joseph Schlitz Brewing Co., Milw., 1974-78; mgr. sales and mgmt. tng. Eaton Corp., Milw. Ops. and Tech. Center, 1978—; cons. tng. Mem. Greater Milw. Civic/Religious Council, 1979. Decorated Bronze Star with oak leaf cluster, Air medal with oak leaf cluster, Army Commendation medal with oak leaf clusters; recipient Spl. Recognition cert. Boy Scouts Am., 1978. Mem. Am. Soc. Tng. and Devel., Nat. Soc. Sales Tng. Execs., Mensa, Internat. Legion Intelligence. Republican. Club: Aviation (Denver). Home: 5640 S 104th St Hales Corners WI 53130 Office: 4201 N 27th St Milwaukee WI 53219

KELLER, REED T., physician, educator; b. Aberdeen, S.D., May 26, 1938; s. Emil T. and Maybelle K.; B.A., U. N.D., 1959, B.S., 1961; M.D., Harvard U., 1963; m. Mary Ann Larsen, June 14, 1959; children—Kristen, Laura, Julie. Asst. prof. Case-Western Res. Sch. Medicine, 1970-73; chief medicine U. N.D. Rehab. Hosp., Grand Forks, 1973—; prof., chmn. dept. medicine U. N.D. Med. Sch., Grand Forks, 1973—. Served with USAF, 1968-70. Fellow Am. Coll. Gastroenterology, A.C.P.; mem. Soc. Exptl. Biology and Medicine, N.D. Commn. on Med. Edn., Assn. Profs. Medicine, Am. Soc. Gastrointestinal Endoscopy, AMA, Phi Beta Kappa, Alpha Omega Alpha. Contbr. articles to med. jours. Office: Dept Medicine U ND Grand Forks ND 58202*

KELLER, ROBERT HOWARD, JR., physician; b. Bklyn., Oct. 3, 1942; s. Robert Howard and Christine Marie (Bode) K.; B.A., Fordham U., 1964, M.S., 1966; M.D. cum laude, Temple U., 1970; m. Joan Theresa Flaherty, June 29, 1968; children—Stacy Lynn, Chiara Lynn, Megan Beth, Robert Howard III. Intern, resident in internal medicine U. Rochester-Strong Meml. Hosp., 1970-74; research fellow in immunology Mayo Grad Sch. Medicine, Rochester, Minn., 1974-76, sr. research fellow, 1976-77, asst. prof. immunology, 1977, asso. cons., 1977; asst. prof. medicine Med. Coll. Wis., Milw., 1977-80, asso. prof. pediatrics, 1980—; clin. asso. prof. health scis. U. Wis., 1980—; chief immunology Milw. Children's Hosp., 1980—; dir. immunology Midwest Children's Cancer Center, 1980—; dir. cell surface analysis lab. Med. Center S.E. Wis., 1980—. Recipient Career Devel. award Vets. Adminstrn., 1978-81. Diplomate Am. Bd. Internal Medicine; Nat. Arthritis Found. fellow, 1975-78; Am. Cancer Soc. grantee, 1976-77, 78-80; Nat. Cancer Inst. grantee, 1981—. Fellow A.C.P.; mem. AAAS, Am. Assn. Immunology, Am. Soc. Hematology, Am. Fedn. Clin. Research, N.Y. Acad. Scis., Alpha Omega Alpha. Roman Catholic. Contbr. articles to profl. jours. Office: 750 N 18 St Milwaukee WI 53120

KELLER, ROBERT JOHN, educator; b. White Bear Lake, Minn., May 25, 1913; s. John Joseph and Lillie Elsie (Olson) K.; B.E., Winona State Tchrs. Coll., 1937; M.A., U. Minn., 1940, Ph.D., 1947; LL.D., Yonsei U., Seoul, Korea, 1973; m. Alice Maurine Fawcett, Dec. 29, 1943; children—Janet Maurine, Marilyn Jean. Tchr., Washington County, Minn., 1931-32; tchr., prin. elem. schs., Ramsey County, Minn., 1932-38; tchr. high sch., North St. Paul, 1938-40; teaching, research asst. U. Minn., 1940-42, 45-46; research psychologist Lackland AFB, Tex., 1946-47; asst. prof. U. Minn., 1947-48, asso. prof. edn., 1948-51, prof., 1951—, dir. Univ. High Sch., U. Minn., 1956-64, dean Coll. Edn., 1964-70; Carnegie Found. vis. prof. U. Hawaii, 1957-58, 70-71; cons. Ministry of Edn., Korea, 1971-73, 74, 77, 79. Served with USAF, 1942-45. Mem. Am. Assn. Higher Edn. (pres. 1969-70), Am. Psychol. Assn., Am. Ednl. Research Assn., North Central Assn. Colls. and Schs. (bd. dirs. 1960-77), NEA, Psychometric Soc., Am. Assn. Community and Jr. Colls. Presbyterian. Author works in field. Home: 1989 W Shryer Ave Saint Paul MN 55113 Office: 236 Health Services Univ of Minn Saint Paul MN 55108

KELLEY, BENNETT WALLACE, chem. engr.; b. Kansas City, Mo., Jan. 10, 1926; s. William Lafayette and Maude S (Belshe) K.; A.S., Kansas City Jr. Coll., 1948; B.S. in Chem. Engring., Kans. State U., 1950; m. B. Louise Senior, July 12, 1947; children—William Albert, Kathryn Louise. Chem. engr. Black & Veatch, Cons. Engrs., Kansas City, Mo., 1950-52; process engr. Remington Arms Co., Inc., Independence, Mo., 1952-61; chief devel. and explosives Thiokol Chem. Corp., Brigham City, Utah, 1961-63; sr. prin. engr. Honeywell, Inc., Hopkins, Minn., 1963-67, product area mgr., 1969-75, prin. engr., 1979—; chief engr. Tech. Ordnance, Inc., St. Louis Park, Minn., 1967-69; owner, pres. Applied Energies Inc., 1975—; mktg. dir. Stetter Assos., Menlo Park, Calif., 1975-77; exec. v.p. Pyro Kinetics, Inc., Roberts, Wis., 1977-79; prin. Bennett W. Kelley, P.E., cons. in pyrotechnics, explosives, explosive-related components, 1969, 75-77, 79. Scoutmaster Kansas City Area and Viking councils Boy Scouts Am., 1950-52, 64-68, asst. dist. commr. Norseman dist., 1967—, vice chmn. dist., 1968; moderator various chs. United Churches of Christ, Minn., Utah, Mo., 1957-66; vice chmn. precinct Independent Republicans, Plymouth, Minn., 1969. Served with USMC, 1943-46. Recipient Parents award Boy Scouts Am., 1969; registered profl. engr., Kans. Mem. Am. Preparedness Assn., Am. Def. Preparedness Assn. (seminar presenter 1975, 76, 77), Profl. Engrs. in Industry, Minn. Soc. Profl. Engrs. Club: Mean Old Men's (pres. 1964-81). Home: 6840 Chaparral Ln Chanhassen MN 55317 Office: MN 50-2060 600 2d St NE Hopkins MN 55343

KELLEY, DENNIS BRACKEN, diesel engine co. exec.; b. Evanston, Ill., June 30, 1950; s. Herbert Matthew and June Audrey (Bracken) K.; B.A., DePauw, U., 1972; M.Internat. Mgmt., Am. Grad. Sch. Internat. Mgmt., 1974. Rep. internat. mktg. Europe-Mid East Cummins Engine Co., Columbus, Ind., 1974-75, regional mgr. Middle East, 1975-77, mgr. internat. mktg., 1977-78, mgr. China bus., 1978-80, dir. China ops., 1981—. Mem. Nat. Council for U.S.-China Trade. Home: 3825 Lakeside Dr Columbus IN 47201 Office: 1000 5th St Columbus IN 47201

KELLEY, DONALD EDMOND, ins. co. exec.; b. Greenwich, Conn., Dec 9, 1943; s. Charles Carleton and Dorothy Loyola (Jordan) K.; B.F.A., U. Conn., 1967, C.L.U., 1972; m. June Smith, Sept. 9, 1967; children—Michael, Raymond, Ryan, Megan. Lectr. music U. Conn., Storrs, 1970-75; coll. unit dir. Northwestern Mut., Storrs, 1970-72, asst. gen. agt., Hartford, Conn., 1972-76, dir. coll. mktg., Milw., 1976-77, asst. regional dir., 1977-78, gen. agt., Akron, 1978—. Mem. Nat. Assn. Life Underwriters, Ohio Life Underwriters, Akron Life Underwriters Assn., Gen. Agts. and Mgrs. Assn. (treas. 1980). Republican. Roman Catholic. Club: Tallwood Country (pres. 1974). Home: 226 Scenic View Dr Copley OH 44321 Office: Suite 1512 Ohio Edison Bldg Akron OH 44308

KELLEY, EDGAR ALAN, educator; b. Bath, Mich., Aug. 1, 1940; s. Clarence E. and Cora (Bollinger) K.; B.A., Mich. State U., 1961, M.A., 1965, Ph.D., 1970; m. Marie Elaine Foerch, Aug. 10, 1963; 1 son, Wesley Lynn. Tchr., Ovid Elsie (Mich.) Area Schs., 1961-67; sch. adminstr. Colon (Mich.) Community Schs., 1967-69; asst. prof. ednl. adminstrn. and secondary edn. Tchrs. Coll., U. Nebr., Lincoln, 1970-74, asso. prof. ednl. adminstrn. and curriculum and intrn., 1974-79, prof., 1979—. Recipient Disting. Teaching award U. Nebr., 1969. Mem. Assn. Supervision and Curriculum Devel. (exec. bd. 1978—), Nat. Assn. Secondary Sch. Prins. (Disting. Service award), Nebr. Assn. Supervision and Curriculum Devel. (Disting. Service award), Nat. Soc. Study Edn., Assn. Tchr. Educators, Nebr. Council Sch. Adminstrs., Phi Delta Kappa (Outstanding Young Leaders in Edn. award 1981). Editor: Catalyst, 1977—; contbr. articles to profl. jours. Home: 2701 S 75th St Lincoln NE 68506 Office: Tchrs Coll U Nebr Lincoln NE 68588

KELLEY, EDWARD GLENN, artist; b. Nashville, Dec. 17, 1922; s. Michael Francis and Gertrude Louise (Hess) K.; student Watkins Art Inst., 1938-41, Chouinard Art Inst., 1946-48, Ill. Inst. Tech., 1950-53. One-man shows: Chgo. Pub. Library, Riccardo, Dubuque Art Assn., Feingarten Gallery (Chgo.), Monroe St. Gallery, Old Town Art Center, Lake Forest Acad.; exhibited in group shows: Art Inst. Chgo., Pasadena Art Inst., Rockford Art Mus., Frank Oehlschlaeger Gallery, Main St. Gallery, many others; represented in permanent collections: Art Inst. Chgo. Rental and Sales Gallery, Gillman Galleries, Chgo., Vincent Price-Collection; instr. art, Galena, Ill., 1964-68; owner E.G.K. Collectibles and Antiques, Galena. Served with USAAF, 1943-46. Recipient awards Chgo. Magnificent Mile Festival, 1953, 54, 61, Union League Club Chgo., 1959. Life mem. Art Inst. Chgo., Artists Guild Chgo. (awards 1952, 55, 57, 62, 64), Arts Club Chgo., Galena Hist. Soc. Home and office: 305 S Main St Galena IL 61036

KELLEY, FRANK JOSEPH, atty. gen. Mich.; b. Detroit, Dec. 31, 1924; s. Frank Edward and Grace Margaret (Spears) K.; pre-law cert. U. Detroit, 1948, J.D., 1951; m. Josephine Palmisano, June 30, 1945; children—Karen Ann, Frank Edward, Jane Francis. Admitted to Mich. bar, 1952; practice law, Detroit, 1952-54, Alpena, Mich., 1954-61; public adminstr. Alpena County, Mich., 1956; atty., Alpena, 1958-61; atty. gen. Mich., 1962—; instr. econs. Alpena Community Coll., 1955-56; instr. real estate law U. Mich. extension, 1957-61. Mem. Alpena County Bd. Suprs., 1958-61; founding dir., 1st sec. Alpena United Fund, 1955; founding dir., 1st pres. Northeastern Mich. Child Guidance Clinic, 1958; pres., dir. Northeastern Mich. Cath. Family Sers. Council, 1956. Mem. Am., 26th Jud. Circuit (pres. 1956) bar assns., State Bar Mich., Internat. Movement Atlantic Union, Nat. Assn. Attys. Gen., Alpha Kappa Psi. Club: K.C. (4 deg.). Office: Law Bldg 525 W Ottawa Lansing MI 48913*

KELLEY, JERRY JOHN, reading specialist; b. Detroit, Feb. 26, 1943; s. Chester A. and Marion D. (Farmer) K.; B.A., Oakland U., 1965; M.A., Mich. State U., 1970, Ed.S., 1979; m. Diana Kay Klaput, July 31, 1970; children—Bryon Kristofor, Jeffrey Jay. Asst. dir. Royal Oak Boys Club, 1964-65; tchr., dir. Learning Reading Resource Center, Beecher Jr. High Sch., Hazel Park, Mich., 1968-81; prin. Capac (Mich.) Middle Sch., 1981—. Served with AUS, 1967-68; Vietnam. Decorated Bronze Star; named Optimist of Yr., 1980. Mem. Oakland Schs. Tchr. to Tchr. Network, Mich. Assn. Middle Sch. Educators, Assn. Supervision and Curriculum Devel., Mich. Elem. and Middle Sch. Prins. Methodist. Club: Optimists (dist. lt. gov. 1981-82, disting. club pres. 1979-80). Home: 309 N Glassford St Capac MI 48014 Office: 2001 N Neeper St Capac MI 48014

KELLEY, JOHN PAUL, mfg. co. exec.; b. Columbus, Ohio, May 12, 1919; s. John Adrian and Josephine Nash K.; B.S. in Journalism, Ohio State U., 1941; M.B.A., Harvard U., 1946; m. Dorothy Rose Peters, July 31, 1942; children—John M., Ann, Daniel, Peter. Sales promotion mgr. Seiberling Rubber Co., 1946-48; account exec. Batten, Barton, Durstine and Osborn, 1948-51; advt. mgr. consumer products div. Monsanto Chem. Co., 1951-55; pres. Mumm, Mullay & Nichols Advt. Agy., Columbus, 1955-59; dir. advt. Goodyear Tire and Rubber Co., Akron, Ohio, 1961-72, v.p. advt., 1972—. Vice-pres. Summit County Hist. Soc., 1973-74. Served with U.S. Army, 1942-46. Mem. Assn. Nat. Advertisers (chmn. 1969-70), Advt. Council (chmn. 1979-80), Am. Trucking Assn. Found. Republican. Roman Catholic. Clubs: Advt. of Akron, Portage Country. Office: 1144 E Market St Akron OH 44316

KELLEY, MARIE ELAINE, ednl. adminstr.; b. St. Johns, Mich., Feb. 6, 1941; d. Berl Louis and Doris Louise (Tait) Foerch; B.A. (Mich. Bd. Edn. scholar), Central Mich. U., 1963; M.A., Mich. State U., 1965, Ph.D. (Grad. Faculty scholar), 1973; Ed.S., U. Nebr., Lincoln, 1976; m. Edgar Alan Kelley, Aug. 10, 1963; 1 son, Wesley Lynn. Tchr., Ovid Elsie (Mich.) Area Schs., 1963-67, Colon (Mich.) Community Schs., 1967-68, Lincoln (Nebr.) Public Schs., 1970-78; asst. prin. instrn. Lincoln East-Jr. Sr. High Sch., 1978—; vis. prof. U. Nebr., Lincoln, 1976, 77, 80, 81; originator, 1st dir. Lincoln Writing Lab., 1975-78. Mem. Nat. Council Tchrs. English, Nat. Assn. Secondary Sch. Prins., Assn. Supervision and Curriculum Devel., Nebr. Council Sch. Adminstrn., Mortar Board, Phi Delta Kappa, Delta Kappa Gamma, Alpha Lambda Delta. Contbr. articles to profl. jours. Home: 2701 S 75th St Lincoln NE 68506 Office: 1000 S 70th St Lincoln NE 68510

KELLEY, MICHAEL GARHART ROOSEVELT, historian; b. Cambridge, Mass., July 25, 1943; s. John Joseph and Elisabeth Ann Roosevelt (Garhart) K.; A.B., Boston U., 1966, M.A., 1967; Ph.D. (postgrad. fellow 1969-71), U. Edinburgh (Scotland), 1973; m. Barbara Gunwaldsen, June 26, 1971. Prof. history Blackburn Coll., Carlinville, Ill., 1974—, acting chmn. dept., 1976-77; Midwest Faculty fellow U. Chgo., 1979. Organizer, dir. Bicentennial Celebration Carlinville, 1975-76; organizer sesquicentennial celebration of Carlinville and Macoupin County (Ill.), 1979. Nat. Endowment Humanities summer fellow U. Calif. at Berkeley, 1980. Fellow Augustan Soc., 1968; mem. Am. Hist. Assn., AAUP, St. Andrews Soc. Author articles in field. Office: Blackburn Coll Carlinville IL 62626

KELLEY, PIERRE JOSEPH, railroad exec.; b. Sioux City, Iowa, June 8, 1935; s. Vincent A. and Anna L. (Hansen) K.; B.G.S., U. Nebr., Omaha, 1979, M.B.A., Lincoln, 1981; m. Mary Ann Dixon, June 7, 1958; children—Mike, Jody, Tom, Mary Pat. With Union Pacific R.R. Co., Omaha, 1958—, chief draftsman, 1969-72, technician realty, 1972-73, supr., 1973—. Chmn. security and crowd control Cerebral Palsy Telethon, Omaha, 1978. Served with U.S. Army, 1959-60, USAR, 1960—. Recipient Omaha Softball Assn. Spl. Services award, 1968. Mem. Internat. Mgmt. Council, Res. Officers Assn. U.S. Army (pres. Gt. Plains chpt. 1978-80), U.S. Army Armor Assn., Omaha Softball Assn., Omaha C. of C. Republican. Roman Catholic. Home: 4604 N 83d Ave Omaha NE 68134 Office: 1416 Dodge St Omaha NE 68179

KELLEY, VERNON EDWARD, ret. labor union ofcl.; b. Tappen, N.D., Jan. 31, 1914; s. Charles E. and Helen C. (Dagan) K.; grad. high sch.; grad. Trade Union Program, Harvard U., 1957; m. Ruby, 1940; children—Charles R., Cynthia C. Thornton. Bus. agt. local 13 Hotel and Restaurant Employees and Bartenders Internat. Union, 1940-41; personnel mgr. Stone & Webster Engring., 1941-44; with Aluminum Workers Internat. Union, 1953—, sec.-treas. local 205, 1947-53, research and edn. dir., 1953-67, exec. asst. to pres., 1967-75, pres., 1975-77. Served in USMC, 1944-46. Home: 4507 39th St Zachary LA 70791

KELLMAN, JEROLD LEE, editor; b. Chgo., Mar. 3, 1945; s. Bernard and Bertha Lillian (Goldberg) K.; A.B., U. Mich., 1967; M.A. (Ford Found. fellow), U. Calif., 1968, Ph.D. (Ford Found. fellow), U. Calif., 1972; m. Nancy Lou Holleb, May 28, 1967; children—Gabriel, Gayle. Editor, Publs. Internat. Ltd., 1972-74, mng. editor, 1974-75, sr. mng. editor, 1975-77, exec. editor, 1977, editor-in-chief, 1978-80; pres., pub. Writer's Guide Publs. div. Gabriel House, Inc. Author: Presidents of the United States, 1975; A Writer's Guide to Chicago-Area Publishers, 1979; contbg. author: Ency. Brit. Micropaedia, 1972, 81, Ency. Brit. Yearbook, 1977, 78, 79, 80, 81, Peoples Almanac, 1974, Peoples Almanac 2, 1977; contbr. to other publs. Home: 9329 Crawford Ave Evanston IL 60203 Office: 5045 Oakton St Suite 7 Skokie IL 60077

KELLNER, CYNTHIA ANN, credit union exec.; b. Milw., Nov. 4, 1948; d. Robert Q. and Alice (Barcz) K.; student U. Wis., Milw., 1970-72, Mt. Mary Coll., 1979-82. Sec., Marquette U. Sch. Dentistry, 1966-68; sec., receptionist Edwards Advt. Agy., Inc., Milw., 1969-70, name changed to Edwards Commo-Net, Inc., sec. to pres., 1970-71, asst. to pres., 1971-73, v.p. charge ops., dir., 1973-80; mktg. dir. State Central Credit Union, Milw., 1980, sr. v.p. in charge mktg., Milw. and West Bend, 1981—; speaker. Mem. Nat. Assn. Female Execs., Nat. Assn. Exec. Secs., Am. Mktg. Assn., Am. Soc. Profl. and Exec. Women. Home: 5250 N Shoreland Ave Whitefish Bay WI 53217 Office: 10015 W Greenfield Ave Milwaukee WI 53214

KELLNHAUSER, BART F., communications exec.; b. Menasha, Wis., Nov. 8, 1923; s. Henry Anthony and Myrtle Amelia (Heroux) K.; m. Patricia Sturtevant, Nov. 15, 1957; children—John, Arleen. Film dir. Sta. WSAU-TV, Wausau, Wis., 1954-56, program dir., 1956-63, exec. v.p., 1963-75, pres., gen. mgr., 1975—. Bd. dirs. Central Wausau Progress, N. Central Tech. Inst. Found.; mem. Wausau Tax Increment Financing Com.; mem. planning com. United Way Campaign; mem. Wausau Shop and Park Com., Wausau Conv. Task Force Com., Wausau Downtown Devel. Council; mem. adv. bd. U. Wis.; past pres. Marathon County Devel. Corp., Community Services Bldg. Corp.; past bd. dirs. Wausau Story Drum & Bugle Corp, Marathon County United Way, ARC, Boy Scouts Am., Family Counseling Services, Friends of Wausau Civic Symphony. Recipient Outstanding Citizen of Yr. award N. Central Tech. Inst., 1975; Citizen of Yr. award Vets. Labor Day Corp Celebration, 1978. Mem. Wis. Broadcasters Assn. (dir., sec., scholarship and awards com., chmn. public TV liaison com.). Home: 421 10th St Wausau WI 54401 Office: 1114 Grand Ave Wausau WI 54401

KELLOGG, EUGENE JAMES, family center exec.; b. Harvey, Ill., Feb. 20, 1926; s. Henry Joe and Ella Mae (Riley) K.; student Art Inst. Chgo., 1948-52, Air Brush Art Sch., 1949, Columbia Coll., 1953-54. Illustrator, air brush artist Filmack Studios, Chgo., 1952-59; photographer, animator Trueline Studios, Hollywood, Calif., 1960-63; advt. dir. White Front Stores, Los Angeles, 1963-69; freelance air brush artist May Co., Los Angeles, 1967-69; advt. and promotion dir. Mays Family Centers, Schererville, Ind., 1970—. Recipient 3d place award for advt. excellence Retail Advt. Conf., 1972, 2d prize for best retail advt., 1974. Mem. Communicators of N.W. Ind., Inc. (charter). Methodist. Office: Route 30 and Route 41 Schererville IN 46375

KELLOGG, PHILLIP LEE, printing co. exec.; b. Monmouth, Ill., June 24, 1961; s. Buster LaVerne and Mary Rose K.; student Western Ill. U., 1979—. On-air broadcaster, promotion dir. WDRL/FM, Monmouth, Ill., 1977-80; paste-up artist Los Angeles Times, 1980; art dir. Kellogg Printing Co., Monmouth, Ill., 1977—; cons. mktg. dir. Western Ill. U., 1979—. Advt. dir. Bur. Cultural Affairs, Macomb, Ill., 1979-80, pres., 1980-81. Ill. Legislature grantee, 1979-80; Western Ill. U. Talent grantee, 1979—. Mem. Lambda Chi Alpha. Office: 95 Public Sq Monmouth IL 61462

KELLY, ARTHUR LLOYD, steel co. exec.; b. Chgo., Nov. 15, 1937; s. Thomas Lloyd and Mildred (Wetten) K.; B.S. with honors, Yale U., 1959; M.B.A., U. Chgo., 1964; m. Diane Rex Cain, Nov. 25, 1978; children—Mary Lucinda, Thomas Lloyd, Alison Williams. With A.T. Kearney, Inc., 1959-75, mng. dir., Dusseldorf, W.Ger., 1964-70, v.p. for Europe, Brussels, 1970-73, internat. v.p., London, 1974-75, partner, dir., 1969-75, mem. exec. com., 1972-75; pres., chief operating officer, dir. LaSalle Steel Co., Chgo., 1975—; dir. Snap-on Tools Corp., Kenosha, Wis., Twin Disc Inc., Racine, Wis., Otto Dürr, Stuttgart, W.Ger. Mem. vis. com. div. phys. scis. U. Chgo.; mem. adv. council Ditchley Found., Oxford, Eng. Mem. Chgo. Council Fgn. Relations (dir.), Com. Fgn. Affairs (exec. com.), Young Pres.'s Orgn., Beta Gamma Sigma. Clubs: Chgo., Racquet (Chgo.); Yale (N.Y.C.). Office: PO Box 6800 A Chicago IL 60680

KELLY, DALE EMERY, cons. engr.; b. Centuria, Wis., Aug. 6, 1923; s. Arthur Emery and Helga Rosemine (Rasmussen) K.; student River Falls State Tchrs. Coll., 1941-42; B.E.E., U. Wis., 1948. With Carl C. Crane, Inc., cons. engrs., 1949-65; owner, mgr. Dale E. Kelly Co., cons. engrs., Belleville, Wis., 1965—; owner, operator Kelly Field, airport, Belleville. Served with USAAF, 1943-45. Decorated Air medal with three oak leaf clusters. Address: Route 2 Belleville WI 53508

KELLY, DONALD PHILIP, holding co. exec.; b. Chgo., Feb. 24, 1922; s. Thomas Nicholas and Ethel M. (Healy) K.; student Loyola U., Chgo., 1953-54, De Paul U., 1954-55, Harvard U., 1965. Mgr.

tabulating United Ins. Co. Am., 1946-51; mgr. data processing A.B. Wrisley Co., 1951-53; mgr. data processing Swift & Co., 1953-65, asst. controller, 1965-67, controller, 1967-68, v.p. corp. devel., controller, 1968-70, fin. v.p., dir., 1970-73; fin. v.p., dir. Esmark, Inc., Chgo., 1973, pres., chief operating officer, 1973-77, pres. chief exec. officer, 1977—, also dir.; dir. McGraw-Edison Co., G.D. Searle & Co., Harris Bankcorp., Inc., Harris Trust & Savs. Bank, Inland Steel Co. Bd. dirs. Lyric Opera, Chgo.; trustee Michael Reese Hosp. and Med. Center, Chgo., St. Norbert Coll., De Pere, Wis., Ill. Inst. Tech. and IIT Research Inst., Chgo., Com. for Econ. Devel., Washington, Mus. Sci. and Industry, Chgo.; mem. citizens bd. U. Chgo. Served in USNR, 1942-46. Mem. Fin. Execs. Inst., Chgo. Council Fgn. Relations (dir.), Chgo. Assn. Commerce and Industry (dir.). Clubs: Chgo., Comml., Econ. (Chgo.). Office: 55 E Monroe St Chicago IL 60603

KELLY, EARL PATRICK, social services agy. adminstr.; b. Newton, Iowa, Feb. 17, 1940; s. Earl Patrick and Ismene Beatrice (Bianchi) K.; B.A., U. Iowa, 1962; M.S.W., St. Louis U., 1966; Ed.D., Drake U., 1978; m. Madleine Carol Vivone, Aug. 11, 1962; children—Anne, Kathleen, Michael. Tchr. public schs., Sheboygan, Wis., 1962-63; staff social worker Cath. Social Services, Des Moines, 1963-69; with Orchard Place, Des Moines, 1969—, exec. dir., 1975—; instr. Drake U., 1971—. NIMH grantee, 1965-66. Mem. Nat. Assn. Social Workers. Home: 1335 SW Thornton St Des Moines IA 50315 Office: 925 SW Porter Ave Des Moines IA 50315

KELLY, EDWARD FRANCIS, broker; b. Chgo., Nov. 14, 1949; s. Edward Robert and Frances Mary (Burianek) K.; student Wilbur Wright Jr. Coll., 1969. Clk., Ralph W. Davis Co., Chgo., 1969-70, 72-73, v.p., 1973-75; mgr. floor Chgo. bd. options exchange Goldman, Sachs & Co., Chgo., 1975—. Active Republican Party. Served with U.S. Army, 1970-72. Mem. Chgo. Bd. Options Exchange. Roman Catholic. Club: Union League Chgo. Home: 200 Menomonee St W Chicago IL 60614 Office: Goldman Sachs & Co 6000 Sears Tower Chicago IL 60606

KELLY, JERRY BOB, county ofcl.; b. Chgo., Feb. 6, 1942; s. Robert Lee and Mildred Florence (Griffin) K.; B.S. in Acctg., Roosevelt U., 1968; m. Diane Joyce Wilburn, Nov. 29, 1969; children—Jerold Robert, Joycelyn Renae. Br. mgr. Chgo. Econ. Devel. Corp., 1970-77; acct. Weather Bloc Mfg. Co., Chgo., 1967-68; programmer Morton Salt Co., Chgo., 1968-69; mgr. adminstrn. Suburban Cook County Area Agy. on Aging, Chgo., 1979—. Treas. Day Care Crisis Council Met. Chgo., 1973-76, appreciation award; 1st v.p. West Side Health Planning Orgn., 1974-76, appreciation award. Served with AUS, 1964-67. Recipient appreciation award Chgo. Black Caucus, Am. Fedn. Tchrs., Chgo. Bd. Election Commrs., Comprehensive Health Planning Orgn. Chgo. Mem. Nat. Caucus on Black Aged, Inc., Asso. Photographers Internat. Baptist. Club: Elks (2d v.p. Ill.-Wis., past grand exalted ruler). Research on redevel. plans for East Garfield. Home: 133 N Mason St Chicago IL 60644 Office: 223 W Jackson Blvd Chicago IL 60606

KELLY, JOHN ALVIN, psychiat. social worker; b. South Charleston, W.Va., Sept. 2, 1949; s. James, Jr. and Lily Van (Sykes) K.; B.A. in Sociology, W.Va. State Coll., 1973; M.S.W., W.Va. U., 1977. Social service worker W.Va. Dept. Welfare, Charleston, 1974-77; crisis intervention counselor People Reaching Out, Logan-Mingo Area Mental Health, Williamson, W.Va., 1977-78; psychotherapist City-County Clinic Johnstown (Pa.), 1978; sr. therapist adult outpatient unit Jefferson County Comprehensive Mental Health Center, Steubenville, Ohio, 1978-79; coordinator SE Canton Outreach Program, Central Stark County Mental Health Center, Canton, Ohio, 1979—. Mem. Am. Mental Health Counselors Assn., Nat. Assn. Social Workers, Urban League, NAACP, U.S. Jaycees, Acad. Cert. Social Workers. Author papers in field. Office: 201 9th St NW Canton OH 44702

KELLY, JOHN FRANCIS, state senator; b. Detroit, Sept. 6, 1949; s. Robert and Margaret (Murphy) K.; A.B. with honors, U. Mich., 1972; M.P.A., Wayne State U., 1974, postgrad., 1974-78; postgrad. Georgetown U., 1975-76, Detroit Coll. Law, 1976-78; m. Toni Plotzke, May 5, 1972; children—Dana, Rebecca. Instr. dept. polit. sci. Wayne State U., 1972-78; mem. Mich. Senate, 1978—. Served to lt. U.S. Army, 1972-78. Mem. Detroit Council Fgn. Relations (chmn. banking and econ. devel. com.), Grosse Pointe Jaycees. Office: PO Box 30036 State Capitol Lansing MI 48909

KELLY, JOHN TERENCE, architect; b. Elyria, Ohio, Jan. 27, 1922; s. Thomas Alo and Coletta Margaret (Conrad) K.; B.Arch., Carnegie Mellon U., 1949; M.Arch., Harvard U., 1951, M.Landscape Architecture (Charles Eliot Norton fellow), 1952. Prin., John Terence Kelly, architect, Cleve., 1954—; vis. critic, lectr. U. Mich., U. Cin., Case Western Res. U., McGill U. Bd. dirs. Nova. Served with inf. AUS, 1943-46. Fulbright fellow, Munich, Germany, 1953. Recipient Cleve. Arts prize in Architecture, 1968. Mem. AIA (nat. com. on design), Am. Inst. Landscape Architects, Am. Inst. Planners, Am. Soc. Planning Ofcls., Western Res. Hist. Soc. Home: 2646 N Moreland Blvd Cleveland OH 44120 Office: 13125 Shaker Sq Cleveland OH 44120

KELLY, JOSEPH FRANCIS, JR., broadcasting co. exec.; b. Bklyn., July 24, 1941; s. Joseph F. and Mary Genevive (Griffin) K.; B.S., Fordham U., 1965; M.B.A., N.Y. U., 1969; m. Sharon Parke, Dec. 26, 1965; children—Steven, Deborah, Michael, David. Bus. mgr. ABC Radio Network, various divs., N.Y.C., 1962-72, account exec., Detroit office, 1972-74, Chgo. office, 1974-75, sales mgr., Detroit Officer, 1975—, v.p., 1977—, regional sales mgr., 1975—; treas., dir. Detroit Radio Adv. Group, 1975—, v.p., 1980, 81. Pres., Moms and Dads Club, St. Mary Prep., Orchard Lake, Mich., 1981-82; chmn. Roman Cath. Cable TV Access Com., Troy, Mich., 1981-82. Mem. Am. Mktg. Assn. (membership chmn. Detroit chpt., pres. 1981-82). Republican. Roman Catholic. Clubs: K.C., Lions, Recess, Bloomfield Open Hunt. Home: 5766 Bingham St Troy MI 48098 Office: 20777 W Ten Mile Rd Southfield MI 48075

KELLY, LESLIE ANN, tng. and devel. cons.; b. Hammond, Ind., June 13, 1945; d. Philip C. and Esther A. (Lardie) K.; B.S., Northwestern U., 1967; M.S. summa cum laude, Ind. U., 1973; m. Raymond S. Battey, Aug. 10, 1968; children—Christine Anna, Raymond Sutton. Tchr. and debate coach Belleville (Ill.) West High Sch., 1967-71; asso. faculty dept. speech, theatre and communications Ind. U.-Purdue U., Indpls., 1973—; pres. Kelly & Assos., Indpls., 1979—, tng. and devel. cons., 1978—; instr. St. Louis U. Summer High Sch. Speech Program, 1973. Recipient Outstanding Tchr. award Am. Legion, Belleville, 1971. Mem. Am. Soc. for Tng. and Devel., Am. Soc. for Personnel Adminstrs., Am. Bus. Communication Assn., Central States Speech Assn. (Outstanding Young Tchr. award 1971), Network of Women in Bus. (Bus. Woman of Yr. 1980), Soc. for Tech. Communication, Am. Mgmt. Assn. Quaker. Author: Individual Events Guide, 1969; Group Organization Guide, 1975; Packaging Yourself for Real Estate Success, 1979; Childbirth Education Manual, 1979; contbg. author various manuals and handbooks on tech. report writing. Office: 6125 Graham Rd Indianapolis IN 46220

KELLY, RALPH DONALD, wholesale co. exec.; b. Grand Island, Nebr., Dec. 6, 1920; s.Martin J. and Elva M. (Howard) K.; student U. Nebr., 1939-40, Utah State U., 1943; m. Patricia J. Stone, Nov. 24, 1941; children—Michael R., Erin C., Michele A. Vice pres. Kelly Supply Co., Grand Island, 1946—; sec.-treas. Lakeview Homes, Inc., Grand Island, 1963-75; v.p., sec. Kelly Supply Co., Norfolk, Nebr., 1968—; dir. First Nat. Bank of Grand Island; senator Nebr. Unicameral Legislature, 1973-81. Vice chmn. Grand Island Civil Service Commn., 1968-72; bd. dirs. YMCA, 1955-68, Teen Chance, 1980—; sec. Nebr. Water Resources Assn., 1980—. Served with USAAF, 1942-50. Decorated D.F.C., Air medal with oak leaf cluster; named Boss of Yr., Grand Island Jaycees, 1960; recipient Better Life award Nebr. Health Care Assn., 1980; Govt. award Central Platte Natural Resource Dist., 1976. Mem. Nebr. Wholesalers Assn., Am. Supply Assn. (nat. edn. chmn. 1966-68, dir. 1964-68), Nebr. Plumbing and Heating Wholesalers Assn. (pres. 1966-68), Am. Supply Assn., V.F.W., Am. Legion. Republican. Roman Catholic. Clubs: Riverside Golf, Leiderkranz Soc. Home: 2015 W John St Grand Island NE 68801 Office: 1004 W Oklahoma Ave Grand Island NE 68801

KELLY, RAYMOND RANSOME, JR., ret. ednl. adminstr.; b. Chgo., Sept. 9, 1912; s. Raymond Ransome and Bessie Mae (Case) K.; A.B., Ill. Coll., 1935, LL.D., 1969; M.S., Ind. U., 1946; m. Lois Eileen McNeely, Dec. 10, 1938. Tchr. Jr. Mil. Acad., Chgo., 1935-36; head English dept. boxing coach Mo. Mil. Acad., Mexico, 1936-39; English tchr. Howe Mil. Sch., Howe, Ind., 1939-43, head English dept., 1946-48, headmaster, 1948-65, supt., 1965-81, supt. emeritus, 1981—. Served to lt. (j.g.), USNR, 1943-45. Recipient Educator's medal, Freedoms Foundn., 1974. Mem. Assn. Mil. Colls. and Schs. (pres. 1974-75). Home: 602 Union St Howe IN 46746 Office: Academy Pl Howe IN 46746

KELLY, RAYMOND THOMAS, JR., ednl. adminstr.; b. Chgo., Jan. 7, 1939; s. Raymond Thomas and Marie Ann (Parent) K.; B.S., Loyola U., Chgo., 1961, Ed.D., 1982; M.S.Ed., Chgo. State U., 1968; M.A., DePaul U., 1972. Probation officer Family Ct. Cook County, 1961, 64-65; with Chgo. Bd. Edn., 1965—, head librarian, audio-visual coordinator Bogan High Sch., 1967-69, dir. media services, 1979—. Served with AUS, 1962-64. Mem. Chicagoland Assn. Media in High Schs. (pres.), ALA, Ill. Library Assn., Am. Assn. Sch. Adminstrs., Assn. Supervision and Curriculum Devel., Kappa Delta Pi, Phi Delta Kappa. Clubs: K.C. (sec. Cook County chpt.); South and South Suburban Grand Knights and Past Grand Knights (pres.); St. Augustine Frat. of Secular Franciscan Order (vice-prefect).

KELLY, ROBERT DONALD, exec. and mgmt. cons.; b. Chgo., Sept. 14, 1929; s. Donald Francis and Irene Sarah (Gardner) K.; B.S. Indsl. Engring., Iowa State U., 1951; M.S., Purdue U., 1955, Ph.D., 1957; m. Kay Romayne Black, Apr. 25, 1959; children—Kim Robert, Kris Donald, Candis Elizabeth. Faculty, Purdue U., Lafayette, Ind., 1953-57; with A.T. Kearney, Inc., Chgo., 1957-80, v.p., dir., 1968-80; mng. partner-personnel Arthur Andersen & Co., Chgo., Geneva, Switzerland, 1980—; dir. Allied Farm Equipment, Duff Truck Line, Smith Transp. Co. Pres. bd. edn. Dist. 86, Hinsdale (Ill.) High Sch., 1976—; chmn. bd. trustees Presbyterian Ch., Clarendon Hills, Ill., 1969-72, chmn. bd. deacons, 1966-69. Served to 1st lt. USAF, 1951-53. Mem. Am. Psychol. Assn., Inst. Mgmt. Cons., Sigma Xi. Clubs: Economic, Univ. (Chgo.). Home: 120 S Elm St Hinsdale IL 60521 Office: 69 W Washington Chicago IL 60602 also 18 Quai Général Guisan/1211 Geneva Switzerland

KELLY, ROBERT DUANE, publishing co. exec.; b. Los Angeles, Oct. 16, 1933; s. Lawrence Bernard and Ruth Marie (Reddinger) K.; B.S., U. So. Calif., 1959; m. Anne Margret Halpin, Apr. 4, 1964; children—Kathleen, Patricia. Mgmt. trainee Foote, Cone & Belding, advt. agy., Los Angeles, 1959-62; asso. nat. advt. dir. Wall Street Jour., N.Y.C., 1962-74; midwest regional mgr. Chilton Pub. Co., Chgo., 1974-77; western sales mgr. Progressive Farmer Co., Chgo., 1977—. Served with U.S. Army, 1954-56. Mem. Nat. Agri Mktg. Assn., Farm Harvest Assn., U. So. Calif. Midwest Alumni Club. Republican. Roman Catholic. Home: 4150 Lawn Ave Western Springs IL 60558 Office: Progressive Farmer Co 120 S Riverside Plaza Chicago IL 60606

KELLY, ROBERT EMMETT, sch. prin.; b. Flushing, N.Y., Aug. 20, 1947; s. Robert Emmett and Lucille Ann (Shell) K.; B.A., Northwestern U., 1969; postgrad. Coll. Law, U. Ill., 1969-70, Coll. Law, U. Cin., 1970-71, 72-73; M.Ed., Xavier U., 1974; m. Trena Christine Ciabay, Aug. 23, 1969; children—Briana, Alison. Athletic dir. Cardinal Pacelli Sch., Cin., 1971-74; tchr. sci. St. Williams Sch., Cin., 1973-74; prin. St. Peter's Elem. Sch. and St. Peter's Montessori Preschool, Mansfield, Ohio, 1974—; cons. Sci. Curriculum Improvement Study, NSF; founder St. Peter's Montessori Sch., 1976; mem. Diocese Toledo Kindergarten Commn. Trustee, Mohican Outdoor Sch., 1975—, exec. com., 1976—; bd. govs. N. Central Ohio Spl. Edn. Regional Resource Center, 1979—; v.p. Children's Theatre Found., 1981—. Named Educator of Yr., Diocese Toledo, 1980; NSF grantee, summer 1975. Mem. Assn. Supervision and Curriculum Devel., Ohio Assn. Elem. Sch. Adminstrs., Ohio Catholic Edn. Assn., Ohio Council Social Studies, Nat. Council Social Studies, Nat. Sci. Tchrs. Assn., Stratford Shakespearean Festival Found. Can., Toledo Diocesan Prins. Assn. Democrat. Roman Catholic. Club: Serra. Office: 63 S Mulberry St Mansfield OH 44902

KELMAN, STEPHEN JAY, chiropractor; b. Louisville, Feb. 11, 1944; s. Ben and Billie Ethel (Hark) K.; A.A., U. Louisville, 1968; D.Chiropractic magna cum laude, Palmer Coll. Chiropractic, 1971; m. Delores Sue Callaway, Feb. 11, 1968; children—Jason David, Rachel Leah. Dir., Chiropractic Arts Center, Fort Wayne, Ind., 1971-72; owner, Three Rivers Chiropractic Center, Fort Wayne, Ind., 1972—. Bd. dirs. Allen County chpt. Am. Cancer Soc., 1976-79. Rep., Fort Wayne Jewish Fedn., 1975—; bd. dirs. N.E. Subarea adv. council No. Ind. Health Systems Agy., 1977—; bd. dirs. B'nai Jacob Synagogue, 1973-76, 78-79, 80—, pres. Men's Club, 1978-79; advisor B'nai B'rith Youth Orgn., 1972-79. Served with U.S. Army, 1964-66. Recipient Service awards Ind. State Chiropractic Assn., 1974, 75, 81; Service award B'nai Jacob Synagogue, 1980; Merit award B'nai B'rith Youth Orgn., 1981; Ky. Col. Mem. Am. Chiropractic Assn. (alt. state del. 1977—), Ky. Assn. Chiropractors, Ky. Chiropractic Soc., Ind. State Chiropractic Assn., Inc. (dir. 1973-81, 2d v.p. 1977-78, 1st v.p. 1978-79, pres. 1979-80, chmn. council on ins. 1981—), Allen County Chiropractic Soc. (pres. 1973-75), Delta Delta Pi, Pi Tau Delta. Jewish. Mem. B'nai B'rith. Home: 7408 Kingsway Dr Fort Wayne IN 46809 Office: 3310 E State Blvd Fort Wayne IN 46805

KELNER, MARVIN IRA, lawyer; b. N.Y.C., June 8, 1931; s. Joseph L. and Pearl K.; B.S. in Bus. Adminstrn., Ohio State U., 1953; J.D. cum laude, Cleve. State U., 1960; m. Ileen Schneider, Feb. 20, 1955; children—Paul, David Matthew. Admitted to Ohio bar; appeals officer IRS, Cleve., 1955-58; asso. firm Lane, Krotinger & Santora, Cleve., 1959-62; pres. Shelter Equities Co., Cleve., 1971-75; chmn. Investment Assos., Inc., Cleve., 1975-79; asso. firm Benesch, Friedlander, Coplan and Aronoff, Cleve., 1962—; adj. faculty Sch. of Law, Cleve. State U., 1973—; lectr. tax matters and tax sheltered investments; cons. to industry on federally financed and subsidized housing. Mem. Am. Bar Assn., Ohio State Bar Assn., Cleve. Bar Assn. Jewish. Club: Hawthorne Valley Country. Asso. editor Cleve. State Law Rev., 1959; contbr. articles to profl. jours. Home: 25032 Maidstone Ln Beachwood OH 44122 Office: 1100 Citizens Bldg Cleveland OH 44114

KELPIN, DONALD WAYNE, motel exec.; b. Payette, Idaho, Jan. 1, 1949; s. Arthur John and Kathaleen Marie (Woerman) K.; Asso. Sci., Treasure Valley Community Coll., 1969; student Boise State U., 1969-71; m. Linda Elaine Himes, Oct. 19, 1974; children—Chad Eric, Marlys DaNae. Bartender, Downtowner Motel, Boise, Idaho, 1972-73; bar mgr. Ramada Inn, Boise, 1973, asst. gen. mgr., 1973-74; gen. mgr. Drake Best Western Motel, Chattanooga, Tenn., 1974-75, Ramada Inn, Springfield, Mo., 1975-77, Sheraton Inn, Aberdeen, S.D., 1977—. Chmn. exec. com. Sand Lake council Boy Scouts Am. Mem. S.D. Restaurant Assn., Aberdeen Retail Liquor Dealers, Aberdeen C. of C., Aberdeen Jr. C. of C. Republican. Lutheran. Club: Elks (Ontario, Oreg.). Home: 719 N 3d St Aberdeen SD 57401 Office: 1400 8th Ave NW Aberdeen SD 57401

KELSAY, CURTIS DWIGHT, mech. engr.; b. Treynor, Iowa, July 25, 1933; s. Curtis E. and Mildred Delores (Addison) K.; B.S. in Mech. Engring., Iowa State U., 1959; postgrad. bus. adminstrn. U. No. Iowa, 1975-77; m. Fern F. Taylor, Feb. 15, 1953; children—Curtis G., Mark Allan, Ann E. Product engr. Delavan Mfg. Co., Des Moines 1959-60; mgr. engring. ops. for Nebr., Becton, Dickinson & Co., Columbus, Nebr., 1960-70; dir. engring. Doerfer Corp. div. Container Corp. Am., Cedar Falls, Iowa, 1970-77, gen. mgr. research and devel. Container Corp., St. Louis, 1977-81, group mgr. corp. research and devel., 1981—. Served with AUS, 1953-55; Korea. Registered profl. engr., Nebr., Iowa. Mem. Mo. Soc. Profl. Engrs., ASME. Republican. Lutheran. Club: Sertoma (sec., dir.). Home: 1737 Fawnvalley St Saint Louis MO 63131 Office: 3235 S Big Bend Blvd Saint Louis MO 63143

KELSAY, JERI DIANE, state ofcl.; b. Marion, Ind., Aug. 18, 1931; d. Hugo L. and Honey (Roepke) Kuester; B.S., Western N.Mex. U., 1952; M.S., No. Ill. U., 1974, Ed.D., 1978; children—Kathi Dawn, Bruce David. Tchr. English and speech, Flowing Wells Pub. Schs., Tucson, 1960-62; tchr. English, Deming (N.Mex.) pub. schs., 1962-66; dir./tchr. retarded class Santa Fe (N.Mex.) Assn. for Retarded, 1967-68; tchr. social maladjusted class Sch. Dist. 45, Village of Villa Park (Ill.), 1969; dir. children's services Ray Graham Asso., Addison, Ill., 1970-76; extension instr. spl. edn. No. Ill. U., DeKalb, 1975; vis. instr. U. Ill., Chgo. Circle, 1975; instr. spl. edn. No. Ill. U., 1976-77, Ill. State U., 1981; spl. edn. specialist Ill. Office Edn., Springfield, 1977-78, asst. mgr., 1978—, mem. task force on severely and profoundly handicapped, 1976-77. Chmn. adv. bd. for Human Services Div., Coll. of DuPage, 1975-76; chmn. Madden Zone Pavilion 11 adv. bd., 1976. Music Edn. Nat. Conf. scholar, 1948-49; Alpha Psi Omega scholar, 1948-49; Edn. Policy Fellowship program, Nat. Inst. Edn. fellow, George Washington U., 1978-79. Mem. Ill. Assn. for Retarded Citizens, Am. Assn. on Mental Deficiency, Ind. Program Dirs. Assn. (sec. 1975-76), Nat. Assn. for Retarded Citizens, Assn. for Spl. Edn. Tech., Am. Assn. for Edn. of Severely/Profoundly Handicapped, Council for Exceptional Children, Pi Lambda Theta, Phi Delta Kappa, Delta Kappa Gamma. Lutheran. Contbr. articles in field to profl. jours. Home: 704 S Grand St W Springfield IL 62704 Office: 100 N 1st St Springfield IL 62777

KELSEY, ROLAND JACK, mfg. co. exec.; b. Barrington, Ill., Dec. 10, 1920; s. Harold D. and Theresa K.; B.S., U. Ill., 1942; m. Maxine M. Kelley, June 16, 1945; children—Robert J., James A., Susan M. Mem. fin. staff, Bendix Co., 1943-46, Drake Mfg. Co., 1947-50, Ford Motor Co., 1951-52, Aeroquip Co., 1953-58, Unistrut, 1959—; sr. partner McGladrey Hendrickson & Co., Barrington, 1960-79; pres. Kelco Industries, Inc., Woodstock, Ill., 1980—. C.P.A., Ill. Mem. Ill. C.P.A. Soc. (dir. 1973-74; chpt. pres. 1972), Barrington C. of C. (pres. 1962, dir. 1969-79), Econ. Club Chgo., Am. Inst. C.P.A.'s, Chgo. Estate Planning Council. Republican. Clubs: Barrington Hills Country, Elks. Home: 666 Park Dr Barrington IL 60010 Office: 9210 Country Club Rd Woodstock IL 60098

KELSO, HAROLD GLEN, physician; b. Newport, Ky., Apr. 1, 1929; s. Harold Glen and Alvina Marie (Hehl) K.; B.S., U. Dayton (O.), 1951; M.D., St. Louis U., 1955; m. Janet Rae Cooper, Aug. 12, 1950; children—Harold Glen III, Susan Annette. Intern St. Elizabeth Hosp., Dayton, 1955-56; practice medicine specializing in family practice, Centerville, O., 1956—; mem. teaching staff St. Elizabeth Hosp., Dayton, O.; mem. staff Kettering (O.) Meml. Hosp., chief staff, 1975-76; chief staff Sycamore Med. Center, 1978-79; clin. prof. family practice Wright State U.; mem. faculty Kettering Coll. Med. Arts; med. dir. Kettering Convalescent Center. Pres., vice mayor, Centerville, O., 1960-62; pres. Bd. Edn., Centerville city schs., 1969-72; trustee Western O. Found. Med. Care, Kettering Med. Center, Sycamore Med. Center. Served with U.S. Army, 1957-59. Diplomate Am. Bd. Family Practice. Fellow Am. Acad. Family Practice; mem. Am., Ohio, Montgomery County (sec. 1970) med. assns., Phi Chi. Rotarian (pres. local club 1974-75, Paul Harris fellow 1979). Home: 2212 E Alex-Bellbrook Rd Centerville OH 45459 Office: 330 N Main St Centerville OH 45459

KELSO, JAMES JUDE, obstetrician, gynecologist; b. Washington, July 2, 1933; s. Arthur David and Helen Margaret (Taylor) K.; B.S., U. Md., 1956, M.D., 1958; m. Greta Joyce Johnson, Sept. 3, 1955; children—Leslie Ann, Elizabeth Ann, Karen Leigh, Arthur David, Marianne, Suzanne, James Francis. Intern, Youngstown (Ohio) Hosp., 1958-59; resident in obstetrics and gynecology Georgetown U. Hosp., Washington, 1961-64; practice medicine specializing in obstetrics, gynecology, Des Moines, 1964—; chief med. staff Mercy Hosp., 1973, chief dept. obstetrics and gynecology, 1977—; chief dept. obstetrics, gynecology Broadlawns Hosp., Des Moines, 1977—; dir. Mercy Hosp. Found., Economy Data Products. Served to lt. comdr. USN, 1959-61. Mem. AMA, Iowa State, Polk County med. socs., Am. Coll. Obstetrics and Gynecology, Am. Bd. Obstetrics and Gynecology, Am. Infertility Soc., Iowa Found. Med. Care (dir.). Clubs: Embassy, Wakonda Country. Home: 2324 Terrace Rd Des Moines IA 50312 Office: 1410 Woodland Ave Des Moines IA 50309

KELSON, ALLEN HOWARD, editor, dining critic, video-electronics writer; b. Chgo., May 4, 1940; s. Ben and Esther Mae (Ashkin) K.; student U. Ill., Chgo., 1957, U. Ill., Urbana, 1958; B.A. in English, Roosevelt U., Chgo., 1965; m. Carla S. Lipson, Aug. 18, 1966; children—David Lauren, Melina Elisabeth. Catalog copywriter Sears, Roebuck & Co., Chgo., 1962-64, sales promotion writer, 1964-67, spl. projects dir., catalog advt. div., 1967-68; editor-in-chief WFMT Guide, Chgo. Guide, Chgo. mag. WFMT, Inc., Chgo., 1968—; pub. relations and advt. mgr. WFMT, Inc., 1968-70, v.p., dir., 1974—; editor-in-chief, asso. pub. Chgo. mag., 1977—; editor Chgo. Guide. Prin. Kelson Kapuler Advt., 1962-68; editor Chgo. GuideBook, 1972-73; lectr. Nat. Retail Mchts. Assn., 1973, Nat. Restaurant Assn., 1975. Mem. adv. staff Walt Disney Magnet Sch., Chgo. Bd. Edn., 1974-75; judge Ill. Women's Press Assn., 1976. Mem. adv. council Internat. Visitors Center, Chgo.; bd. regents Roosevelt U. Alumni Assn. Recipient Merit award Chgo. Advt. Club, 1965, Designer awards Chgo. 4, 1973, 74; award Am. Inst. Graphic Arts, 1976, Chgo. '78, 1978, N.Y. Art Dirs. Club, 1979, Chgo. 3, 1980, 81; Clarion award, 1981; hon. mem. Duncan Hines Meml. Fellowship, 1971. Mem. Am. Soc. Mag. Editors. Club: East Bank. Office: Three Illinois Center Chicago IL 60601

KELTNER, RAYMOND MARION, JR., surgeon, educator; b. Springfield, Mo., Apr. 15, 1929; s. Raymond Marion and Othello Mary (Forgey) K.; B.S., Drury Coll., 1950; B.S. in Medicine, U. Mo., 1955; M.D., Washington U., St. Louis, 1957; m. Carla Ann Clark, May 10, 1974; children—Aintre B., Raymond M., Merl K., Albert D., Gisela W. Practice medicine specializing in surgery, Houston, 1962-63, Houghton, Mich., 1966-68; mem. faculty Washington U. Sch. Medicine, 1963-66; asst. prof. surgery St. Louis U. Sch. Medicine, 1968-71, asso. prof., 1971-76, prof., 1976—, attending surgeon St. Louis U. Hosp., 1968—; chief surgery St. Louis City Hosp. Fellow A.C.S.; mem. Western Surg. Assn., AMA (Service Recognition award). Contbr. articles to surg. jours. Office: 1325 S Grand Ave Saint Louis MO 63104

KELTS, KEITH ALAN, pediatrician, neurologist; b. Norwich, N.Y., Feb. 16, 1942; s. Keith Roy and Gladys Amanda (Wheeler) K.; B.A., Ohio Wesleyan U., 1964; M.D., U. Rochester, 1971, Ph.D., 1971; m. Susan Margaret Sims, May 1, 1977; children—Eric Alan, Amanda Jean. Intern, U. Wash., Seattle, 1971-72, resident in pediatrics, 1972-73; resident in child neurology U. Colo., Denver, 1973-76; asst. prof. U. Alaska, Fairbanks, 1972-73; asst. prof. neurology and pediatrics Stanford U., 1976-79; asso. prof. pediatrics U. S.D., Sioux Falls, 1979-81; pvt. practice medicine specializing in neurology, Rapid City, S.D., 1981—. Mem. med. exec. com. S.D. chpt. Muscular Dystrophy Assn. Diplomate Am. Bd. Pediatrics, Am. Bd. Psychiatry and Neurology. Mem. Am. Acad. Pediatrics, Am. Acad. Neurology, Neurosci. Soc., Child Neurology Soc. Democrat. Club: Masons. Research on autonomic nervous system.

KELTY, PAUL DAVID, physician; b. Louisville, Oct. 2, 1947; s. William Theadore and Mary Frances (Hinton) K.; B.E.E., U. Louisville, 1970; M.S., Ohio State U., 1971; M.D., U. Louisville, 1978. Mem. tech. staff Bell Labs., Whippany, N.J., 1970-72; design engr. Gen. Electric Co., Louisville, 1972-74; intern St. Mary's Med. Center, Evansville, Ind., 1978-79, resident in Ob-Gyn, 1979—. Mem. AMA, N.Y. Acad. Scis., Sigma Xi, Phi Kappa Phi, Tau Beta Pi, Sigma Tau, Sigma Pi Sigma, Eta Kappa Nu, Gamma Beta Phi, Omicron Delta Kappa. Roman Catholic. Home: 1901 Coker Ave Evansville IN 47714 Office: St Marys Med Center Evansville IN 47750

KEMP, ARNOLD RAYMOND, mech. engr.; b. Champaign, Ill., Nov. 22, 1918; s. Arnold Raymond and Helen Ruth (Dillon) K.; student U. Ill., 1937-38, Knox Coll., 1938-40; B.S., Bradley U., 1946; m. Mary Elizabeth Quick, Sept. 20, 1941. Mech. engr. John Deere Co., Moline, Ill., 1947-48; design engr. Beling Engring. Cons., Moline, 1948-60; office mgr., Burlington, Iowa, 1961—. Trustee YWCA, 1972—; mem. Bd. Elec. Examiners, Burlington, 1970—. Served with AUS, 1942-45. Mem. Burlington Engrs. Club, Illuminating Engrs. Soc. Methodist. Clubs: Lions, Eagles. Home: 2900 Sunnyside Ave Burlington IA 52601 Office: 214 1/2 N 4th St N Burlington IA 52601

KEMP, CYNTHIA LEE, nursing adminstr.; b. Cleve., Sept. 14, 1935; d. Coleman Larry and Victoria Mae (Gaines) Shields; R.N., Mt. Sinai Hosp. Sch. Nursing, Cleve., 1957; m. James Kemp, Nov. 21, 1959, (div.); 1 dau., Frances Michelle. Staff nurse Mt. Sinai Hosp., Cleve., 1957-59, asst. head nurse, 1959-60; staff nurse Cedars of Lebanon Hosp., Hollywood, Calif., 1961-63, head nurse, 1963-64; night supr. Mt. Sinai Hosp., Cleve., 1964-65, head nurse emergency room, 1965-71, part-time supr., 1971-72; night and day supr. Woman's Gen. Hosp., Cleve., 1972-73; day supr. Huron Rd. Hosp., East Cleveland, 1973-75, asst. dir. nursing service, 1975—. Mem. 21st Congl. Dist. Caucus, Inc. Mem. Nat. Black Nurses Assn., Nat. League Nursing, Cleve. Area League Nursing, Am. Soc. Nursing Adminstrs., Nat. Black Nurses Assn. Democrat. Baptist. Home: 13504 Casper Rd Cleveland OH 44110 Office: 13951 Terrace Rd East Cleveland OH 44112

KEMP, JOHN BERNARD, state ofcl.; b. Scobey, Mont., Aug. 14, 1918; s. John Bert and Margaret Antoinette (Little) K.; student No. Mont. Coll., 1935-36; B.A. in Econs. and Sociology, Mont. State U., 1940; B.S. in Gen. Engring., Iowa State U., 1947, M.S. in Engring. Valuation and Econs., 1949; m. Kathryn Elinor Lally, July 22, 1944 (dec. Dec. 1950); children—Kathryn JoAnn Kemp Lehmann, John Daniel, Mary Elizabeth Kemp Titus; m. 2d, Elizabeth Jean Berscherd Stacey, Feb. 7, 1970; stepchildren—Susan Louise and Elizabeth Ann Stacey. Axeman survey crew Mont. Hwy. Dept., summers 1936-37, rodman, 1940-41; engring. aide WPA, 1938-39; engring. aide C.E., 41-42, instr., vets. counselor, 1948-49; hwy. engr. U.S. Bur. Public Rds. and Fed. Hwy. Adminstrn., 1949-52, planning engr., St. Paul, 1952-63, planning dist. and div. engr., Bismarck, N.D., 1963-67, chief systems and location div., Washington, 1967-68, regional Fed. hwy. adminstr., Kansas City, 1968-79; sec. transp. State of Kans., Topeka, 1979—. Served to lt., USNR, 1942-46. Recipient Gold medal Dept. of Transp., 1971, Silver medal, 1965, Bronze medal, 1979; Bronze medal Fed. Hwy. Adminstrn., 1969; registered profl. engr., Iowa. Fellow ASCE; mem. Nat. Soc. Profl. Engrs., Kans. Engrs. Soc., Am. Soc. Public Adminstrn. Roman Catholic. Club: K.C. Office: Room 756W State Office Bldg Topeka KS 66612

KEMP, JOHN STEPHEN, ednl. adminstr.; b. Pana, Ill., July 9, 1935; s. Charles Delbert and Mildred Lucy (Kopp) K.; B.S. with honors, U. Ill., 1957, M.Ed., 1961, Ed.D., 1967; m. Martha Lee White, June 16, 1962; children—Michelle Lynette, Julia Suzanne. Chemist, USI Chems. Corp., Tuscola, Ill., 1958; tchr. chemistry Eisenhower High Sch., Decatur, Ill., 1958-63, asst. prin., 1962-63; asst. univ. coordinator sch. and coll. relations U. Ill., 1963-72; asso. state chmn. North Central Assn., 1963-72, state dir., 1972—; univ. coordinator sch. and coll. relations, prof. ednl. adminstrn. U. Ill., Champaign, 1972—; Pres. Adv. Com. on Edn. in Ill., 1969-71. Served with U.S. Army, 1957-58. Mem. Ill. Assn. Sch. Adminstrs. (dir.), Am. Assn. Sch. Adminstrs., Nat. Assn. Secondary Sch. Prins., Ill. Prins. Assn., Assn. Supervision and Curriculum Devel., Nat. Soc. Study of Edn., Phi Delta Kappa. Presbyterian. Club: Champaign County Torch. Home: 1203 McHenry St Urbana IL 61801 Office: Suite 314 409 E Chalmers St Champaign IL 61820

KEMPA, ROY G., market research co. exec.; b. Chgo., June 27, 1945; s. Anthony and Jean (Bolsinga) K.; B.A. in Bus. Adminstrn., St. Ambrose Coll., 1967; M.S. in Mktg., No. Ill. U., 1969; m. Marilyn Kranz, Feb. 8, 1969; children—Maureen Lynn, Carolyn Ann, Sherilee. Instr. in bus. orgn. and mgmt. U. Wis., Platteville, 1969-71; dir. market research Chgo. Suburban Paddock Newspapers, Arlington Heights, Ill., 1971-75; mgr. client services Mid-Am. Research Co., Chgo., 1975-80; v.p./account exec. D.S. Howard & Assos., Inc., Chgo., 1980—; mktg. cons. Paddock Corp., Arlington Heights, 1977-78. Lay minister St. Hubert Roman Cath. Ch., Hoffman Estates, Ill., 1980—. Mem. Am. Mktg. Assn. Home: 829 Pinehurst Ln Schaumburg IL 60193 Office: 307 N Michigan Ave Chicago IL 60606

KEMPE, ROBERT ARON, instrument co. exec.; b. Mpls., Mar. 6, 1922; s. Walter A. and Madge (Stoker) K.; B.Chem. Engring., U. Minn., 1943; postgrad. Case Western Res. U., 1946-49; m. Virginia Lou Wiseman, June 21, 1946; children—Mark A., Katherine A. Research engr., divisional sales mgr. TRW, Inc., Cleve., 1943-53; v.p. Metalphoto Corp., Cleve., 1954-63, pres., 1963-71; v.p., treas. Horizons Research, Inc., Cleve., 1970-71; pres. Allied Decals, Inc., Cleve., 1963-68; pres. Reuter-Stokes, Inc., Cleve., 1971—. Vice pres. Miles Ahead, Inc. Served to lt. (j.g.) USNR, 1944-46. Mem. Chemists Club N.Y.C., Am. Nuclear Soc. (chmn. No. Ohio sect.), Sigma Chi. Club: Country (Hudson, Ohio). Patentee in field. Home: 242 Streetsboro St Hudson OH 44236 Office: 18530 S Miles Pkwy Cleveland OH 44128

KEMPEN, JOSEPH FRANCIS, foundry exec.; b. Green Bay, Wis., Sept. 6, 1952; s. Francis Joseph and Ann Marie (Schmidt) K.; B.B.A., U. Wis., 1974, M.B.A., 1978; m. Dianne T. Heiland, Aug. 23, 1975; 1 son, Scott Phillip. Personnel mgr. Barclay Foundry, Neillsville, Wis., 1974-78, div. mgr., 1978-80, controller, Milw., 1980—; controller Motor Castings Co., Milw., 1980—. Mem. Phi Kappa Phi, Alpha Kappa Lambda. Home: 807 S 105th St West Allis WI 54214 Office: 1323 S 65th St Milwaukee WI 53214

KEMPER, CHARLES SAMUEL, dentist; b. Joplin, Mo., Mar. 12, 1933; s. Charles B. and Catharine (Walker) K.; student Joplin Jr. Coll., 1951-52, Washington U., St. Louis, 1952-53, Drury Coll., Springfield, Mo., 1953-54; D.D.S., U. Mo., 1958; grad. Famous Writers Sch., 1976; m. Mary Maurine George, Sept. 20, 1958; children—Kristina Lynn, Samantha Sue. Gen. practice dentistry, Blue Springs, Mo., 1958—; organizer, sole operator charity dental clinic Don Bosco Youth Center, Kansas City, Mo. Mem. Acad. Gen. Dentistry, Blue Springs C. of C., Kappa Alpha, Psi Omega. Prebyn. (elder). Rotarian. Home: 48 D Lake Tapawingo Blue Springs MO 64015 Office: Med Center Blue Springs 900 North Woods Chapel Rd Blue Springs MO 64015

KEMPER, LAURA LANE, banker; b. Kansas City, Mo., Dec. 5, 1948; d. James M. and Mildred K.; B.A., Wellesley Coll., 1970; m. Michael Fields, Dec. 18, 1980. Dir., camera operator St. Joseph Cablevision (Mo.), 1971-72; mem. staff admissions office Harvard U., 1971; mktg. asst. Commerce Bancshares, Inc., Kansas City, Mo., 1972-75, mktg. officer, 1975-77, v.p., dir. advt., 1980—; v.p., dir. mktg. Commerce Bank of Kansas City, 1977-80. Bd. dirs. Kansas City Public TV, 1973-79, v.p. exec. com., 1975-79; bd. dirs. Kansas City Corp. for Indsl. Devel., 1978-80, chmn. public relations com., 1978-80; bd. govs. Kansas City Philharmonic Assn., 1977-80, v.p., chmn. public relations com., 1978-79; bd. dirs. Learning Exchange, Inc., Kansas City, 1976—; mem. exec. com. Performing Arts Found., 1977—; bd. govs. Am. Royal Horse Show, 1977—. Office: Commerce Bancshares Inc 720 Main St Kansas City MO 64105

KEMPER, YVES JEAN, automotive engr., research exec.; b. Paris, Feb. 29, 1936; came to U.S., 1976; s. Frederic and Jacqueline (Rigaut) K.; grad. Ecole Poly., Lausanne, Switzerland, 1964; m. Anne Brigitte Marie Petry, June 19, 1965; children—Frederic, Stanislas, Helene, Guillaume. Cons. engr. Battelle Inst., Geneva, 1965-66; project engr. SNECMA, Villaroche, France, 1966-68; dir. research and devel. Sambron Sarl, Ponchateau, France, 1968-71; chief exec. officer DEMECA, Maisons Lafitte, France, 1971-76; pres. Vadetec Corp., Troy, Mich., 1976—; asst. instr. Inst. de Thermodynamique and Ecole Poly. Federale, Lausanne, 1964-68; mem. chmn.'s com. U.S. Senatorial Bus. Adv. Bd. Mem. ASME (com. on traction drives), Engring. Soc. Automotive Engring., Engring. Soc. Detroit. Patentee automotive engines and transmissions. Home: 841 Glengarry Birmingham MI 48010 Office: 2681 Industrial Row Troy MI 48084

KEMPIN, LINDA JEANNE, interior design cons.; b. Chgo., June 5, 1951; d. Emil August and Margaret Mary (Pierorazio) K.; student U. Ill., 1969-71; B.F.A., No. Ill. U., 1974; postgrad. Keller Grad. Sch. Mgmt., 1978—. Layout editor, asst. prodn. mgr. No. Star, DeKalb, Ill., 1972-74; advt. and promotional dir. Group Travel Enterprises, Chgo., 1973-74; design asst. 3M Nat. Advt., Chgo., 1974; designer, asso. art dir. R.R. Donnelley & Sons, Chgo., 1975-79; communications cons. Saga Communications Group, Greenwich, Conn., 1979-81; cons., sr. project mgr. PCS Reports, Ltd., Oakbrook, Ill., 1981—. Past v.p., publicity chmn. Southeast Lakeview Neighbors. Mem. Soc. Typog. Arts, Nat. Assn. Female Execs., Internat. Platform Assn., Bus. and Profl. Women Chgo. Home: 517 W Oakdale Ave Apt 303 Chicago IL 60657 Office: Box 1098 Chicago IL 60690

KEMPINERS, WILLIAM LEE, state ofcl.; b. Oak Park, Ill., Jan. 26, 1942; s. Wilbur Henry and Margaret E. (Hardesty) K.; B.A., Augustana Coll., 1964; postgrad. U. Iowa, 1964-66; m. Virginia Bromley Wrather, July 5, 1978; children—J.J., Jeffrey. Pres. Westin & Assos., Inc., Wheaton, Ill., 1968-70; legis. asst. Ill. State Med. Soc., Chgo., 1970-72; mem. Ill. Ho. of Reps., Springfield, 1973-79; dir. Ill. Dept. Public Health, Springfield, 1979—. Bd. dirs. Augustana Coll., 1978—. Served with U.S. Army, 1966-68. Decorated Army Commendation medal. Mem. Ill. Public Health Assn., Am. Heritage Soc., Nat. Trust Historic Preservation, Assn. State and Territorial Health Officers. Republican. Lutheran. Home: 102 Ridge Dr Shorewood IL 60435 Office: 535 W Jefferson St Springfield IL 62761

KEMPINERS, WILLIAM LEE, state ofcl.; b. Oak Park, Ill., Jan. 26, 1942; s. Wilbur Henry and Margaret (Hardesty) K.; B.A., Augustana Coll., Rock Island, Ill., 1964; postgrad. U. Iowa, 1964-66; m. Virginia Bromley Wrather, 1978; children—James J., Jeffrey T. Chmn. bd. Ill. Coop. Health Data Systems, Inc.; mem. Ill. Ho. of Reps., 39th Dist., 1973-79; dir. Ill. Dept. Public Health, 1979—. Bd. dirs. East Seal Rehab. Center Will County and Augustana Coll. Served with U.S. Army, 1966-68. Decorated Commendation medal; named Best Freshman Rep., Ill. Polit. Reporter, 1973, Outstanding Freshman Legislator, Ill. Edn. Assn., 1973, Best Legislator award Ind. Voters Ill., 1974. Lutheran. Address: Dept Public Health 535 W Jefferson St Springfield IL 62761

KENDALL, DONNA JOYCE, coll. ofcl.; b. Milan, Ill., Jan. 15, 1929; d. Orville Daniel and Mare Grace (Hansen) K.; A.A., Stephens Coll., 1948; B.A., State U. Iowa, 1950. Reporter, Milan Ind., 1950-56; pub. relations asst. Modern Woodmen of Am., Rock Island, Ill., 1956-57, publs. editor, 1957-60, asst. to pub. relations mgr., 1960-63; corporated pub. relations asst. Title Ins. & Trust Co., Los Angeles, 1963-69; mktg. officer Comml. & Farmers Nat. Bank, Oxnard, Calif., 1969-71; pub. info. dir. Western Ins. Info. Service, Los Angeles, 1971-73; corp. relations mgr., asst. v.p. Lloyds Bank, Los Angeles, 1973-74; pub. relations dir. Palmer Coll. Chiropractic, Davenport, Iowa, 1974—. Free-lance pub. relations cons. in areas of real estate and politics. Recipient Achievement award Los Angeles Advt. Women, 1968. Mem. Pub. Relations Soc. Am. (dir. Los Angeles 1966-67, v.p. Quad City chpt. 1978—), Los Angeles Advt. Women (dir. 1967-69, rec. sec. 1972-73, 1st v.p. 1973-74), Los Angeles C. of C. (dir. women's div. 1967-69, 71-74), Calif. Assn. Real Estate Tchrs. (dir. 1965-69), Davenport C. of C., Am. Advt. Fedn., DAR, Alpha Delta Pi, Gamma Alpha Chi. Republican. Methodist. Home: 1804 16th St Rock Island IL 61201 Office: 1000 Brady St Davenport IA 52803

KENDALL, GEORGE PRESTON, ret. ins. co. exec.; b. Seattle, Aug. 11, 1909; s. George R. and Edna (Woods) K.; B.S., U. Ill., 1931; m. Helen A. Hilliard, Sept. 30, 1933; children—George Preston, Thomas C., Helen R. With Washington Nat. Ins. Co., Evanston, Ill., 1931-76, sec., 1950-76, exec. v.p., 1956-62, pres., 1962-67, chmn. bd., 1968-76, also chief exec. officer, dir.; chmn. bd., chief exec. officer, dir. Washington Nat. Corp., 1969-76; dir. State Nat. Bank, Evanston. Served from 2d lt. to 1st lt., inf. AUS, 1942-45. Decorated Purple Heart. Mem. Northwestern U., Assos., Nat. Coll. Edn. Assos., Kendall Fellows of Kendall Coll., Theta Chi. Mason (K.T. Shriner). Clubs: Univ. (Evanston); Westmoreland Country (Wilmette, Ill.); Bankers (Chgo.).

KENDALL, ROBERT LLEWELLYN, contractor; b. Mishawaka, Ind., May 3, 1923; s. Harold E. and Jessie (Pettengill) K.; student pub. schs., Cadillac, Mich.; m. Betty Louise Powers, July 23, 1943; children—Stephen, Jane, Kay, Holly, David, Roberta. Owner, Kendall Constrn. Co., Cadillac, 1945-63, Cadillac Lumber Co.; pres. Robert Kendall, Inc.; v.p. Hungerford Constrn. Co., Jackson, Mich. Mayor, Cadillac, 1953-55; mem. Wexford County Bd. Suprs., County Social Welfare Bd., County and City Planning Bds.; chmn. Bd. Edn., 1948-50; pres. Mich. Extended Care Bldg. Corp.; dir. phys. plant services, mem. adminstrv. staff Chelsea Community Hosp. Served from pvt. to capt. USAAF, 1942-45; ETO. Mem. C. of C. (pres. 1958-60), Am. Soc. Hosp. Engring., Am. Soc. Profl. Cons. Am. Legion. Presbyterian (deacon). Club: Elks. Home: 340 Edward St Jackson MI 49201 Office: Chelsea Community Hosp 775 S Main St Chelsea MI 48110

KENDIG, LANE HOMER, county planning exec.; b. N.Y.C., Feb. 16, 1939; s. Robert S. and Pauline L. K.; B.Arch., U. Mich., 1962; M.S. in City and Regional Planning, U. N.C., 1968; married; 1 dau., Heather. Dir. local planning Bucks County (Pa.) Planning Commn., 1968-76; dir. Lake County (Ill.) Dept. Planning, Zoning and Environ. Quality, 1976—. Mem. Am. Planning Assn. (chmn. environ. div.), Urban Land Inst. Author: Performance Zoning, 1980. Office: 18 N County St Waukegan IL 60085

KENDRICK, MAURINE LAJUINE, educator; b. Magna, Utah, June 20, 1920; married, 1 child. B.A. in Edn., LaVerne (Calif.) Coll., 1943; M.S. in Edn., Purdue U., Hammond, Ind., 1971; adminstrv. endorsement Purdue U., 1978. Jr. high sch. reading tchr. Ben Franklin High Sch., Kenmore, N.Y., 1963-65; elementary reading specialist Dist. 149, Dolton, Ill., 1965-66; English tchr. South High Sch., Dist. 215, Lansing, Ill., 1967-70; dist. reading cons. Thornton Fractional Twp. High Sch., Dist. 215, Calumet City, Ill., 1970—; adj. instr. Nat. Coll. Edn. Mem. task force State Supts. Right to Read Adv. Council in Ill., 1974-75, 75-76; coordinator jr./sr. high sch. reading specialists meetings; trustee Community Council Greater Hammond, 1975-77. Mem. Internat., Suburban (corr. sec.) reading assns., Ill. Tchrs. English Assn. Home: 325 Belden Pl Munster IN 46321 Office: Adminstrv Center 1601 Wentworth Ave Calumet City IL 60409

KENDRO, RICHARD JOSEPH, steel co. exec.; b. Canton, O., Dec. 15, 1931; s. Joseph Francis and Anne Marie (Kvasnick) K.; grad. Embry-Riddle Sch. Aviation, 1952; B.S., Kent State U., 1958; m. Barbara Ann Goedicke, July 7, 1956; children—Margo E., Colby E. Display artist C.N. Vicary Co., Canton, 1949-51; salesman Standard Oil Co., Canton, 1955-56; cost analyst E.W. Bliss Co., Canton, 1956-58; plant mgr. Sparta Ceramic Co., East Sparta, O., 1958-66; plant mgr. Good Roads Machinery Corp., Canton, 1966-67; plant mgr. Cleaver-Brooks Co. div. Aqua-Chem., Inc., 1967-71, v.p. mfg. water tech. div., Milw., 1971-73, exec. v.p. water tech div., 1973-74, pres. Cleaver-Brooks div., 1974, v.p. parent co., 1974-76, sr. v.p., 1976-79, exec. v.p., chief operating officer, 1979—, also dir.; v.p., dir. Cleaver Brooks De Mexico, 1976—, Aqua-Chem, Pty (Australia), 1976—, VP C-B Sales & Service, 1976—; v.p. Maintek, Inc., 1966-68. Exhibited in group shows at Canton Art Inst., 1948, 49, North Canton Art Gallery, 1949, 50; instr. Indsl. Edn. Inst., Inst. for Better Confs. Exec. dir., asst. scoutmaster Buckeye council Boy Scouts Am., 1956-57; pres. P.T.A., 1966-67. Bd. dirs. Community Chest, 1966-67, Am. Boiler Mfrs. Assn., 1975—, Weight Watchers of Wis., 1979—; bd. dirs. United Way, 1979-80, now vice chmn. Served with USAF, 1951-55. Named to Pa. Sports Hall of Fame. Mem. Internat. Platform Assn., Indsl. Mgmt. Club. Clubs: St. Michaels Mens, Toastmasters (past pres.), Lebanon Country. Office: PO Box 421 Milwaukee WI 53201

KENDZIOR, ROBERT JOSEPH, fast food chain mktg. dir.; b. Chgo., Mar. 24, 1952; s. Joseph W. and Josephine R. Kendzior; B.Arch., Ill. Inst. Tech., 1975. Account supr. Burger King Corp., Rogers Merchandising, Inc., Chgo., 1975-77; account exec. Walgreen Corp., Eisaman, Johns & Laws Advt., Inc., Chgo., 1977-78; dir. mktg. Midwest region, Dunkin' Donuts Am., Inc., Park Ridge, Ill., 1978—. Mem. Triangle Fraternity, Chgo. Advt. Club. Home: Glencoe IL 60022 Office: 1550 Northwest Hwy Park Ridge IL 60068

KENIG, NOE, electronics co. exec.; b. Warsaw, Poland, June 5, 1923; came to U.S., 1974; naturalized, 1980; s. Lazaro Hersz and Felisa (Elenbogen) K.; diploma mech. and elec. engring., Nat. U. La Plata, Buenos Aires, Argentina, 1951; mech. technologist diploma, Nat. Indsl. Sch. Luis M. Huergo, Buenos Aires, 1951; m. Ida Melnik, Apr. 17, 1948; children—Jorge Alberto, Carlos Eduardo. Licensee, Westinghouse Electric Corp., Argentina, 1941-49, Bendix Home Appliance Corp., Argentina, 1949-67; dir. Philco Argentina Corp., 1959-62; asst. pres., group gen. mgr. subs. Nat. Distillers and Chem. Corp., Argentina, 1958-72; with Motorola Inc., 1972—, v.p. multinat. ops., regional dir. Americas, Schaumburg, Ill., 1980—, also dir. subs. Office: 1303 E Algonquin Rd Schaumburg IL 60196

KENLEY, WILLIAM ALTON, county ofcl.; b. Holland, Mo., Feb. 28, 1917; s. Samuel Clelley and Alice (King) K.; B.S., Washington U., St. Louis, 1965; m. Mary Dorothy Marsic, June 2, 1947; children—Elizabeth L., William Alton, Alice S., James M., Timothy A., Steven G. Enlisted U.S. Navy, 1940, served hosp. corps, 1940-60, chief hosp. corpsman, 1945-60, ret., 1960; with dept. community health and med. care St. Louis County, Mo., Clayton, 1960—, supr. public health sanitarians food inspection sect., 1965—. Trustee St. Louis County Employees Pension Plan, 1965-70. Mem. Nat. Environ. Health Assn., Internat. Food, Milk and Environ. Assn., Mo. Milk, Food and Environ. Health Assn. Club: Nat. Fleet Res. Assn. Home: 1555 Night Dr Florissant MO 63031 Office: 801 S Brentwood St Clayton MO 63105

KENLY, GRANGER FARWELL, holding co. exec.; b. Portland, Oreg., Feb. 15, 1919; s. F. Corning and Ruth (Farwell) K.; A.B. cum laude, Harvard U., 1941; m. Suzanne Warner, Feb. 7, 1948 (div. Nov. 1977); children—Margaret Farwell, Granger Farwell; m. 2d, Stella B. Angevin, Oct. 8, 1978. Adminstrv. asst. to v.p. Poole Bros., Inc., Chgo., 1941-42; asst. advt. mgr. Sunset Mag., San Francisco, 1946-47; pub. relations, sales promotion mgr. Pabco Products, Inc., San Francisco, 1947-51; v.p., mgmt. supr. Needham, Louis & Brorby, Inc., Chgo., 1951-60; mgr. mktg. plans dept. Pure Oil Co., Palatine, Ill., 1961-62, v.p. pub. relations, personnel, 1962-66; v.p. pub. affairs Abbott Labs., North Chicago, Ill., 1966-71; v.p. corporate and investor relations IC Industries, 1971—. Mem. 22d Ann. Global Strategy Conf., U.S. Naval War Coll., 1970; mem. public affairs council Am. Productivity Center. Bd. dirs. Evanston Hosp., Lawson YMCA, Chgo.; trustee Ill. Soc. Prevention Blindness, 1958-74, Off-the-Street Boys Club, Chgo. Served to maj. USAAF, 1942-46; ETO. Mem. Newcomen Soc. N.Am., Pub. Relations Soc. Am., Chgo. Assn. Commerce, New Eng. Soc. N.Y.C., Pub. Relations Seminar. Republican. Congregationalist. Clubs: Chgo., Econ., Univ., Execs. (Chgo.); Glen View (Golf, Ill.); Onwentsia (Lake Forest, Ill.); Harvard

(N.Y.C.). Home: 1160 N Sheridan Rd Lake Forest IL 60045 Office: 111 E Wacker Dr Chicago IL 60601

KENNA, JOHN THOMAS, public relations exec.; b. Bklyn., July 19, 1919; s. John J. and Nadja Louise (Leahy) K.; student St. Charles Coll., Balt., 1938-40; A.B. in English and Philosophy, St. Mary's U., 1943. Regional dir. NCCJ, Kans., 1949-51, Ky., 1951-56, asso. dir., Ill., 1956-57; dir. religious activities Nat. Safety Council, Chgo., 1957-60; dir. leadership devel. Nat. Council Cath. Men, Washington, 1960-62; info. officer President's Com. on Youth Employment, Washington, 1962-63; spl. asst. Family Life Bur., Nat. Cath. Welfare Conf., Washington, 1963-66; regional dir. Nat. Soc. Crippled Children and Adults, Chgo., 1966-67; pres. Fund Raising Orgn. and Graphics Service, Chgo., 1967-69; dir. info. services Mt. Sinai Hosp. Med. Center, Chgo., 1969-71; dir. public relations and devel. Augustana Hosp., Chgo., 1971—. Bd. dirs. Safer Found., 1979—. Recipient MacEachern award Acad. Hosp. Public Relations, 1979. Mem. Public Relations Soc. Am., Assn. for Hosp. Devel. Chgo. Press Club, Nat. Soc. of Fund Raising Execs. Democrat. Roman Catholic. Home: 2223 N Bissell St Chicago IL 60614 Office: 411 W Dickens St Chicago IL 60614

KENNEDY, BELA ELLIS, state legislator Mich.; b. Bangor, Mich., July 8, 1918; s. Bela G. and Ada P. (Briggs) K.; B.S. in Agrl. Econs., Mich. State U., 1941; m. Eleene Price, Sept. 2, 1941; children—Cindra (Mrs. R. Dean Bishop), Dawne (Mrs. John Speeter). Rural rehab. supr. FSA, 1941-43; owner fruit farm, Bangor, 1955—; dist. sales mgr. Haviland Agrl. Chem. Co., 1966; pres. Blossomland Bus. Analysis Corp., Benton Harbor, Mich., 1969. Mem. Mich. Ho. of Reps. from 45th Dist., 1971—. Mem. hort. adv. com. Mich. State U., 1962-67; v.p., dir. Mich. Pesticide Assn., 1971; agrl. adv. com. Southwestern Mich. Coll., 1968-71; 4-H Club leader. An organizer Van Buren Young Republican Club, 1950; sec. Van Buren County Rep. Com., 1955-60; del. county convs.; mem. Bangor Sch. Bd., 1955-67. Bd. dirs. South Haven (Mich.) Hosp. Mem. Van Buren Artificial Breeders Assn. (sec. mgr.), Mich. Hort. Soc., Van Buren County Farm Bur., Southwestern Mich. Profl. Fieldmen's Assn., Mich. Asparagus Assn. (past pres.). Methodist (mem. bd., Sunday sch. tchr.). Mason (32 deg., K.T.); mem. Order Eastern Star. Home: Route 2 Box 122 Bangor MI 49013 Office: PO Box 30014 State Capitol Bldg Lansing MI 48909

KENNEDY, CHRISTOPHER ROBIN, ceramist; b. Ottawa, Ont., Can., June 25, 1948; s. Robert Alvin and Ruth Christina (Downie) K.; B.S., Rutgers U., 1969; M.S., Pa. State U., 1971, Ph.D., 1974; m. Christine Willa Wayman, Jan. 28, 1978; 1 son, Scott Wayman. Asst. ceramist Argonne (Ill.) Nat. Lab., 1974-79, ceramist, 1979—. Mem. Am. Ceramic Soc., Nat. Inst. Ceramic Engrs., Keramos, Sigma Xi. Contbr. articles in field to profl. jours. Home: 7 Vermont Circle Bolingbrook IL 60439 Office: Bldg 212 9700 S Cass Ave Argonne IL 60439

KENNEDY, CORYA JEAN, television communications specialist; b. Noblesville, Ind., June 27, 1948; d. James Blair and Bebita Corya K.; student Butler U., 1966-67; B.S., Ind. U., 1975, M.S., 1980. Tchr., Monroe County Sch. Corp., Bloomington, Ind., 1975-77; promotion mgr. Sta. WNDU-TV, South Bend, Ind., 1978; mgr. sales and services, producer of vidiocel computer animation Computer Creations, Inc., South Bend, Ind., 1978—. Chmn. publicity com. Hotline, a United Way Agy., 1980-81. Mem. Videotape Prodn. Assn., Broadcast Promoters Assn., Ind. U. Alumni Assn., Alpha Epsilon Rho, Kappa Kappa Kappa, Alpha Chi Omega. Episcopalian. Home: 623 Portage Ave South Bend IN 46616 Office: 1657 N Commerce Dr Suite 1-B South Bend IN 46628

KENNEDY, FORTUNE TAM, nurse; b. Philippines, Oct. 14, 1940; d. Tomas Tam and Felicidad (Rasco Tam) Kwong; B.S.N., Far Eastern U., 1964; M.S.N., Loyola U. Chgo., 1975; doctoral candidate in edn. No. Ill. U.; m. James P. Kennedy, June 18, 1966; 1 dau., Jennifer Marie. Operating rm., recovery rm., labor and delivery room nurse, 1962-64; head nurse Wesley Pavilion Northwestern Meml. Med. Center, Chgo., 1969-71, Resurrection Hosp., Chgo., 1971-72; mem. faculty Wesley Passavant Sch. Nursing, 1972-74; mem. faculty Lewis U., 1975—, asso. prof., 1980—. Cert. cardiac rehab., CPR instr. Mem. Am. Critical Care Nurses Assn. Philippine Nurses Assn. Chgo. (pres. 1965-66), Assn. Supervision and Curriculum Devel., Am. Nurses Assn., Nat. League Nursing, Assn. Operating Rm. Nurses, Am. Assn. Critical Care Nurses, Sigma Theta Tau. Republican. Roman Catholic. Club: Chgo. Health. Home: 20W227 Pleasantdale Dr Lemont IL 60439 Office: Route 53 Romeoville IL 60441

KENNEDY, GEORGE DANNER, natural resource co. exec.; b. Pitts., May 30, 1926; s. Thomas Reed and Lois (Smith) K.; student Williams Coll., 1947; m. Valerie Putis; children—Charles Reed, George Danner, Jamey Kathleen, Susan Patton, Timothy Christian. With Scott Paper Co., 1947-52, Champion Paper Co., 1952-65; exec. v.p. Brown Co., 1965-71, also dir.; exec. v.p. Internat. Minerals & Chem. Corp., Northbrook, Ill., 1971-78, pres., 1978—, also dir.; dir. Brunswick Corp., Riegel Textile Corp., SCM Corp. Bd. dirs. Children's Meml. Hosp., Chgo.; bd. adv. Orch. Soc. of Chgo. Symphony; mem. Chgo. Com.; mem. bus. adv. council Grad. Sch. Indsl. Adminstrn., Carnegie-Mellon U., Pitts.; mem. Ill. council Boy Scouts Am. Served with U.S. Navy. Mem. Econs. Club Chgo., Chgo. Assn. Commerce and Industry (bd. dirs.). Clubs: Mission Hills Country (Northbrook); N.Y. Athletic, Bd. Room (N.Y.C.); Sleepy Hollow Country (Scarborough N.Y.); Larchmont (N.Y.) Yacht; Skokie Country (Glencoe, Ill.). Office: 2315 Sanders Rd Northbrook IL 60062

KENNEDY, GEORGE FRANCIS, publishing co. exec.; b. Providence, Sept. 23, 1936; s. Amos Huntington and Theresa Catherine (Glancy) K.; B.A., Brown U., 1958; M.A., U. Mich., 1959, Ph.C., 1965. Teaching fellow U. Mich., 1960-63; editor U. Mich. Inst. Sci. and Tech., 1963-66, mng. editor, 1966-68, head publs. 1968-69; publs. dir., pub. info. dir., dir. curriculum devel. High/Scope Ednl. Research Found., Ypsilanti, Mich., 1970-72; gen. mgr. Prakken Publs., Inc., Ann Arbor, 1972—. Mem. adv. council on vocat. edn., mem. summer sch. program com. Ann Arbor Schs., 1976—. Mem. Am. Mgmt. Assn., Am. Bus. Communication Assn., Soc. Tech. Writers and Pubs., Phi Beta Kappa, Phi Kappa Phi. Democrat. Roman Catholic. Home: 921 Raymond Ann Arbor MI 48103 Office: 416 Long Shore Dr Ann Arbor MI 48107

KENNEDY, GORDON JAMES, research engr.; b. Crawford County, Ohio, Mar. 7, 1927; s. Milford Joseph and Mildred Marie (Kimble) K.; B.S. in Bus. Adminstrn., Ohio State U., 1951; B.S. in Elec. Engring., Ohio No. U., 1957; postgrad. U. Toledo, 1963-64, Wayne State U., 1973; m. Doris Mae Holsinger, Sept. 9, 1950; children—Suzanne, Margaret, Dwight. With Battelle Meml. Inst., Columbus, Ohio, 1949-51; design engr., cost analyzer, Shunk Mfg. Co., Bucyrus, Ohio, 1951-52; chief engr. Transp. Co., Bucyrus, 1952; electro-mech. design engr. No. Electric Co., Galion, Ohio, 1952-55; process instrument engr. Gen. Electric Co., Cleve., 1957-63; instrumentation engr. NASA, Sandusky, Ohio, 1963-71; mech. engr. EPA, Ann Arbor, Mich., 1971—; instr. elec. engring. Cleve. State U., 1961-63. Pres. N.E. Property Owners Civic Assn., Cleve., 1960; precinct committeeman, Cleve., 1960-61. Served with U.S. Army, 1945-49. Registered profl. engr., Ohio. Mem. Soc. Automotive Engrs. Presbyterian. Club: Masons. Intervened in AEC hearing on constrn. of Davis-Besse Nuclear Power Sta., Port Clinton, Ohio, 1970, 71. Home: 1534 Barrington Pl Ann Arbor MI 48103 Office: EPA 2565 Plymouth Rd Ann Arbor MI 48105

KENNEDY, JAMES A., interior design cons.; b. Mexico, Mo., Jan. 2, 1938; s. James Robert and Florence L. (Owens) K.; B.A., N.E. Mo. State U., 1959; B.S., U. Mo., Kansas City, 1962; postgrad. U. Colo., 1965-67, U. Denver, 1967-68; m. Mary Patricia Supple, Nov. 30, 1968; 1 son, Timothy James. Dir. youth services Christian Chs. of Mo., 1957-62; interior design cons., Boulder, Colo., 1963-72; owner, design dir. Kennedy & Assos., Design Cons., Kansas City, Mo., 1972-80; family therapist Div. Family Services, 1980—. Chmn. bd. Community Counseling Services, 1972-74; chmn. diocesan scouting activities, 1979—. Served with M.C., U.S. Army, 1956-59. Mem. Inst. Bus. Designers (dir. 1976-78), Kansas City C. of C. (speakers bur.). Roman Catholic. Club: Optimist (pres. Crown Center 1978). Home: 317 E 70th St Kansas City MO 64113 Office: Mo State Office Bldg 615 E 13th St Kansas City MO 64106

KENNEDY, JOHN BRIAN, med. technologist; b. Bluffton, Ind., July 4, 1929; s. Dwight Franklin and Kathryn (Reed) K.; A.B. in Zoology, Ind. U., 1957; M.S. in Biology, St. Lawrence U., Canton, N.Y., 1971; Ed.D., U. Nev., 1980; m. Patricia Cherry, Nov. 15, 1952; children—Robert Brian (dec.), Steven John, Denise Anne, John Douglas. Lab. and teaching supr. St. Joseph's Hosp., Syracuse, N.Y., 1965-68; program dir., asso. prof. med. lab. tech. SUNY, Canton, 1969-77; asst. prof. hematology, immunochematology and clin. chemistry U. Nev., Reno, 1977-81, program dir., 1980-81; dir. med. tech. program, asst. prof. hematology Bowling Green (Ohio) State U., 1981—. Bd. dirs., chmn. rehab. and service Am. Cancer Soc., Canton, 1975-77; pres. St. Mary's Home and Sch. Assn., Canton, 1975-76. Served to capt. USAF, 1958-65. Mem. Am. Soc. Med. Tech., Sigma Xi, Beta Beta Beta. Roman Catholic. Author articles. Home: 876 Champagne Ave Bowling Green OH 43402 Office: Med Tech Program Bowling Green State U Bowling Green OH 43403

KENNEDY, JOHN JOSEPH, educator; b. Cortland, N.Y., Sept. 13, 1914; s. John Austin and Anna Gertrude (Ryan) K.; B.A., U. N.Mex., 1936; A.M., Columbia U., 1938, Ph.D., 1954; m. Elizabeth Carol Riordan, Aug. 19, 1942; children—John Christian, Kathryn Kennedy Bueno. Liaison officer internat. activities Pub. Adminstrn. Clearing House, Chgo., 1938-41; regional specialist Latin Am., Dept. State, Washington, 1941-42, 46-48; vis. prof. U. P.R., 1949-50; asst. prof. polit. sci. U. Notre Dame, 1951-56, asso. prof., 1956-59; prof. U. Va., Charlottesville, 1959-64; prof., dir. Latin Am. studies program Notre Dame (Ind.) U., 1964—; vis. prof. CCNY, 1960; cons. Ford Found., Peru and Chile, 1964, Rockefeller Found., 1978-80; Rockefeller Found. affiliate, vis. prof. U. del Valle, Colombia, 1968-71. Served to lt. comdr. USNR, 1942-46. Nat. Council on Religion in Higher Edn. fellow, 1937; postdoctoral fellow Council on Fgn. Relations N.Y., 1958-59. Mem. Am. Polit. Sci. Assn. Democrat. Roman Catholic. Author: Catholicism, Nationalism and Democracy in Argentina, 1958; Over All Development in Chile, 1969. Home: 1937 Inglewood Pl South Bend IN 46616 Office: Box 201 Notre Dame IN 46556

KENNEDY, JOHN XAVIER, banker; b. Chgo., June 10, 1918; s. R. Emmett and Bernadine (Galvin) K.; student Northwestern U., 1946-47; certificate Wharton Sch. Fin. U. Pa., 1964; m. Mary Ann Luke, Nov. 6, 1948; children—J. Luke, Mark, Matthew, Pete, Paul, Kristine. With United Air Lines, Chgo., 1937-41, 46; with Stifel, Nicolaus & Co., Inc., Chgo., 1946-53, bond salesman, 1946-51, buyer, 1951-53; with White Weld & Co., Chgo., 1953-72, municipal bond buyer, 1953-58, mgr. revenue bonds, 1959-63, v.p., 1964-72; v.p. fixed income securities F.S. Moseley & Co., 1972-74; pres. U.S. Securities Corp., 1974-76; v.p. John Nuveen & Co., 1977-78, Paine, Webber Jackson & Curtis, 1979, Securities Corp. Iowa, 1979; v.p., dir. Stanley Luke Farm, Inc. Mem. devel. bd. Sisters of St. Joseph, La Grange, Ill.; mem. corporate support DePaul U., 1965-66. Served with USAF, 1942-45. Decorated Air medal. Mem. Securities Industry Assn. (chmn. municipal securities com. Central States 1965, mem. municipal fed. legis. com. 1969-71, municipal securities com. 1972), Municipal Fin. Forum, Washington, Bond Club Chgo., Municipal Bond Club Chgo. (past dir.). Home: 10101 5th Ave La Grange IL 60525 Office: 307 N Michigan Ave Chicago IL 60601

KENNEDY, LEILA MAY, lawyer; b. Marysville, Ind., Nov. 9, 1895; d. John Conrad and Katharine Elizabeth (Reis) Hartling; LL.B., Benjamin Harrison Law Sch., 1936, Ind. U., 1944; m. Roy Kennedy, May 14, 1913 (dec.); children—Roy Albert, Dorothea Leila Kennedy Powers. Sec., Herbert Foltz & Sons, Indpls., 1933-37; admitted to Ind. bar, 1940; registrar Ind. Law Sch., Indpls., 1937-44; law librarian Ind. Supreme Ct. Library, Indpls., 1944-50; referee Juvenile Ct., Indpls., 1950-53; real estate broker Irvington Realty Co., Indpls., 1953-60; pvt. practice law, Indpls., 1960—. Mem. Bus. and Profl. Woman's Club, Ind. U. Alumni Assn., Ind. U. Women's Assn., Mut. Service Assn., Phi Alpha Delta. Presbyterian. Clubs: Pilot (pres. Indpls. 1940), Order Eastern Star. Home and Office: 1314 N Emerson Ave Indianapolis IN 46219

KENNEDY, LOIS EVELYN, mfg. co. exec.; b. Toledo, Sept. 2, 1931; d. Wallace Clifton and Una Hope (Hartman) Edwards; student U. Toledo, 1949-51; m. Donald A. Kennedy, Aug. 1, 1951 (div. June 1972); children—David Edward, Douglas James. Exec. sec. Kaiser Jeep Corp., Toledo, 1958-64; exec. sec. to pres. Dana Corp., Toledo, 1966-71, adminstrv. asst. to chmn., 1972-76, mgr. state govt. relations, 1976-78, mgr. govt. relations, 1978—. Bd. dirs. Women Involved in Toledo, 1977-81; trustee U. Toledo, 1980—. Mem. Mich. C. of C. (dir. 1977-81), Toledo Area C. of C. (dir. 1978—), Toledo Econ. Planning Council (dir. 1978, exec. bd. 1979—), Ohio C. of C. (dir. 1981—), U.S. C. of C., Pi Beta Phi. Republican. Home: 3910 Sheffield Ct Toledo OH 43623 Office: Dana Corp PO Box 1000 Toledo OH 43697

KENNEDY, STEPHEN JOSEPH, stockbroker; b. Chgo., Oct. 21, 1943; s. David J. and Josephine B. (Serpico) K.; B.A. in Econs., U. Chgo., 1967; m. Sheila P. Folino, Sept. 10, 1966; children—Stephen Charles, Brian Scott. With Marquis Who's Who, Chgo., 1963-69, mng. editor World Who's Who in Sci., dir. names research Who's Who in Am., asso. dir. prodn. Marquis Who's Who Inc.; exec. recruiter Mgmt. Recruiters, Inc., 1969-72; stockbroker Bacon Whipple & Co., Chgo., 1972-74, mgr. options sales, 1977—; stockbroker William Blair & Co., 1974-75, A.G. Becker, 1976-77; mem. Glen Ellyn (Ill.) Plan Commn. Mem. Jaycees. Office: 135 S LaSalle St Chicago IL 60603

KENNEDY, WILLIAM JOSEPH, instrument mfg. co. exec.; b. Ponca City, Okla., Oct. 9, 1932; s. William Joseph and Dovie Lee (Bridges) K.; B.M.E. cum laude, U. Okla., 1955; M.B.A., Harvard U., 1960; m. Mary Louise Rusin, Dec. 26, 1960; children—Elizabeth B., William Joseph. Controller. treas. Dorsett Electronics, Norman, Okla., 1960-63; sr. asso. Booz, Allen & Hamilton, Chgo., 1963-67; dir. mgmt. services Baxter Labs., Inc., Morton Grove, Ill., 1967-70; v.p. Miller & Co., Chgo., 1970-72; v.p. Ill. Tool Works, Inc., Chgo., 1972-79; pres., chief exec. officer, dir. Alnor Instrument Co., Chgo., 1979—. Mem. allocations com. Community Fund of Chgo., 1974-75, agy. and ops. com. 1976-77; group chmn. capital campaign Field Mus. History, 1973-74; mem. capital fund campaign com. Met. YMCA, Chgo., 1976—; asst. chmn. United Settlement Appeal Fund, 1975; capital fund campaign com. Chgo. Met. Crusade of Mercy, 1977; vice chmn. Met. membership standards com. United Way of Met. Chgo., 1977—, chmn. new applicants com., 1977—; bd. dirs., chmn. Duncan YMCA; vice-chmn. Marianjoy Rehab. Inst. Served with USAF, 1955-58. Mem. Harvard Bus. Sch. Assn. (mem. exec. council 1972-73), Assn. Corp. Growth, Am. Mktg. Assn., Am. Mgmt. Assn., Ireland-U.S. Council for Commerce and Industry. Clubs: Harvard Bus. Sch. Chgo. (pres. 1972-73, sr. adv. com. 1968-77), Econ. of Chgo. (chmn. membership com., exec. com. 1974-75), Univ. of Chgo. (Chgo.); Chgo. Golf (Wheaton, Ill.); Harvard (N.Y.C.). Home: 571 Hill Ave Glen Ellyn IL 60137 Office: 7301 N Caldwell Ave Niles IL 60648

KENNEL, ARTHUR JOHN, physician; b. Lancaster County, Pa., Apr. 26, 1929; s. John E. and Anna M. (Summers) K.; B.S., Eastern Mennonite Coll., Harrisonburg, Va., 1952; M.D., Hahnemann Med. Coll., Phila., 1957; M.S., U. Minn., 1973; m. Lois Landis Ruth, Aug. 21, 1954; children—Susan Elizabeth, Kurt Arthur. Intern, St. Luke's Hosp., Bethlehem, Pa., 1957-58; gen. practice medicine, N.C. and Va., 1958-63; resident in internal medicine Mayo Clinic, Rochester, Minn., 1963-65; practice medicine specializing in internal medicine, Stuart, Va., 1965-67; head dept. cardiology Kinshasa (Zaire) Gen. Hosp., 1970-72; asso. cons. internal medicine Mayo Clinic, Rochester, 1972-73, cons., 1973—; asst. prof. medicine Mayo Med. Sch., 1973—. NIH fellow in cardiology U. Pa., 1969; diplomate Am. Bd. Internal Medicine, Am. Bd. Cardiovascular Disease. Mem. Internat. Soc. Cardiac Research, AMA (Physicians Recognition award 1969, 72, 76), Am. Coll. Chest Physicians, Am. Coll. Cardiology, Mennonite Med. Assn. (pres. 1978-79), Minn. Med. Assn. Club: Rochester Rotary (dir. 1980—). Author: Your Body and You, 1964; also articles. Home: 702 23d St SW Rochester MN 55901 Office: Mayo Clinic 200 1st St SW Rochester MN 55901

KENNEY, CATHERINE MCGEHEE, educator; b. Memphis, Oct. 3, 1948; d. J. D. and Norma McGehee; M.A. (fellow), Loyola U., Chgo., 1970, Ph.D., 1974; m. John P. Kenney, June 1, 1968. Faculty, Loyola U., Chgo., 1968-72, Mundelein Coll., Chgo., 1976—, chmn. dept. English and communications, 1978—; writing cons. Chgo. area corps. and univs. Mem. MLA, Midwest MLA, AAUP. Office: Mundelein College 6363 N Sheridan Rd Chicago IL 60660

KENNEY, DORINE THELMA, hosp. ofcl.; b. Mt. Olive, Ill., Mar. 27, 1926; d. Arthur R. and Edna J. (Ruhlander) Heusler; student public schs.; m. Thomas F. Kenney, Nov. 27, 1943; children—Kathleen, Thomas A., Kevin John. Various clerical positions, 1943-50, 60-69; dir. vol. services Chgo. Coll. Osteo. Medicine, Hosp. and Clinics, 1969—; cons. seal com. Nat. Ostep. Found.; condr. workshops, 1965—. Sec., treas., supr. primary and jr. dept., mem. choir Community Covenant Ch. Calumet Park, 1966—. Mem. Am. Soc. Dirs. Vol. Services, Assn. Adminstrs. Vol. Service, Nat. Assn. Parliamentarians, Nat. Osteo. Guild Assn. (life, past pres.), Ill. Soc. Dir. Vol. Services, Ill. Assn. Parliamentarians (pres. 1981—), Chgo. Council Dirs. Hosp. Vols. Clubs: Zonta (v.p. program 1977-79, pres. 1979—), Rebekah. Author articles in field. Office: 5200 S Ellis Ave Chicago IL 60615

KENNEY, ROBERT LYLE, city ofcl.; b. Boonville, Mo., July 17, 1941; s. Cecil T. and Juanita Virginia (Wolfe) K.; B.S.B.A., U. Mo., Columbia, 1965; m. Betty Caroline Gieger, June 25, 1967; children—Pamela, Patrick. Cost acct. Remington Arms Co., Lake City Army Ammunition Plant, Independence, Mo., 1966-67; property acct. Independence Power & Light Co., 1967; acctg. supr. City of Independence, 1967-71, budget and systems supr., 1971, dir. fin., 1971—. Served with USAFR, 1965-66. C.P.A., Mo. Recipient Curators award U. Mo., Columbia, 1959. Mem. Mcpl. Fin. Officers Assn. (Mo. chmn., career devel. com.), Nat. Assn. Accts., Mo. Mcpl. League (revenue and tax com.), Mo. (dir.), Western Mo. (treas.) city clks. and fin. officers assns. Home: 14608 E 36th Terr Independence MO 64055 Office: 103 N Main St Independence MO 64050

KENNEY, RUTH HELENE, civic worker; b. Marion County, Iowa, Oct. 29, 1903; d. Frank and Nancy Ann (Snyder) Woodle; grad. Drake U., 1959; m. Norris Kenney, Mar. 4, 1933; 1 dau. from previous marriage, Mildred Ann Flanagan. Elementary tchr. rural schs. Marion County, Iowa, 1923-25, elementary schs. Knoxville, Iowa, 1944-60, ret., 1960. Spl. mem. Women's Soc. Christian Service, 1972—, historian, 1965-71; mem. United Meth. Women; chmn. refreshments com. Iowa City Crippled Children's Clinic, 1963-80. Recipient medal for history, DAR, 1923. Mem. Knoxville Ret. Tchrs., Daus. Union Vets. of Civil War (Iowa historian 1972-80), DAR (Mary Marion chpt. past treas., vice regent 1968-70). Republican. Clubs: Knoxville Woman's (pres. 1963-64), Progressive Garden, Farm Bur., Rebekah, Odd Fellows. Contbr. Genealogy of Desc. of Jenkins Stafford. Home: Route 4 Box 110 Knoxville IA 50138

KENNON, GARY LLOYD, publishing exec.; b. Springfield, Mo., May 1, 1939; s. Leslie Lorne and Edna May (Freeman) K.; student SW Mo. State U., 1957-60, So. Ill. U., 1961-62. Asst. to dir. public relations and econs. Ill. Med. Soc., 1967-69; polit. writer, legis. corr. Springfield (Mo.) Newspapers Inc., 1969-71; news dir. KICK-AM, Springfield, 1971-78; asso. editor Muffler Digest Mag., Springfield, 1978-80; v.p., mng. editor, dir. MD Publs. Inc., Springfield, 1980—. Mem. Greene County Republican Central Com., 1980—; vice chmn. 149th Dist. Rep. Legis. Com., 1980—. Mem. Greater Springfield Press Club (pres. 1974), Internat. Motor Press Assn., Nat. Assn. Noise Control Ofcls. (asso.), Exhaust Systems Profl. Assn. (asso.) Am. Soc. Bus. Press Editors, Sigma Delta Chi. Roman Catholic. Home: 600 E Loren St Springfield MO 65807 Office: 304 E Pershing St Springfield MO 65806

KENNY, PHILIP THOMAS, railroad exec.; b. Omaha, Jan. 18, 1930; s. Lee Roy and Clare Gertrude (Connor) K.; student parochial schs., Omaha; m. Jean Marie Welch, June 2, 1956; children—Kathleen Ann, Thomas James, Jane Elizabeth. With Union Pacific R.R., Omaha, 1949—, asst. exec. dir. Nebr. R.R. Assn., 1972-76, exec. dir. assn., 1976—. Served with U.S. Army, 1951-53. Mem. Omaha C. of C., Nebr. Tax Research Council, Nebr. Tax Forum, Nebr. Water Resources Assn., Nebr. Farm Bur. Democrat. Roman Catholic. Clubs: Lincoln Country, Lincoln U., Sunset Valley Country, Nebraska, Omaha Press; Capitol Hill (Washington), K.C. Home: 310 S 56th St Omaha NE 68132 Office: Nebr RR Assn 1416 Dodge St Omaha NE 68179

KENNY, PHILIP WILLIAM, assn. exec.; b. Chgo., June 14, 1935; s. William and Lillian Elizabeth (Mount) K.; B.A., St. Bonaventure U., 1958, M.A., 1966; S.T.L., Cath. U. Am., 1963; Ph.D., Marquette U., 1974; m. Gaye Frances Salerno, Dec. 20, 1972. Tchr., adminstr. Joliet Cath. High Sch., 1963-67, Mt. Carmel Coll., Niagara Falls, Ont., 1967-68; tchr., counselor, adminstr. Marquette U., Milw., 1968-73; adminstr. Joliet Jr. Coll., 1973-74; adminstr. Rosary Coll., River Forest, Ill., 1974-78; asst. dir. dept. grad. med. evaluation AMA, Chgo., 1978—. Mem. James Joyce Soc., MLA, Phi Beta Kappa. Democrat. Roman Catholic. Home: 1540-E Franklin Ave River Forest IL 60305 Office: 535 N Dearborn St Chicago IL 60610

KENT, A. ROBERT, real estate broker; b. Elizabeth, Pa., Dec. 8, 1911; s. John W. and Mary K. (Oriol) K.; B.A., Ohio U., 1933; postgrad. Biarritz Am. U., France, 1945; m. Mary Jo Wintermute, Oct. 20, 1943. Mgr. advt. and mktg. depts. several newspapers and bus., Cleve., Weirton, W.Va. and Ambridge, Pa., 1933-52; owner Kent Real Estate, Columbus, Ohio, 1953—; dir. R.R. Savs. and Loan Co., Columbus; pres. Kent Community Sales, Inc., 1964—, Kent Co-ops., Inc., 1962—, 4000, Inc., 1958— (all Columbus). Active Columbus Gallery Fine Arts, 1965—, Columbus Symphony Orch., 1961—, Central Ohio council Boy Scouts Am., United Way Pacesetters Club, 1966—; bd. dirs. House of Hope, Columbus, 1965—, v.p., 1973—. Served with AUS, World War II; ETO. Recipient Grand awards for Advt. Achievement Columbus Dispatch and Citizen Jour., 1973, 74, 75; certificate of Merit Columbus Bd. Realtors, 1960. Mem. Columbus Bd. Realtors, Nat. Assn. Realtors, Columbus Area C. of C., Rolls-Royce Owners Club, Excalibur Assn., Delta Sigma Pi. Republican. Methodist. Clubs: Scioto Country, Pres.'s Ohio State U., Ohio State U. Faculty Athletic (Columbus). Home: 4000 Old Poste Rd Columbus OH 43220 Office: Fishinger at Riverside Dr Upper Arlington Columbus OH 43221

KENT, ANNABELLE HASSELSON, social work adminstr.; b. Chgo., Dec. 4, 1909; d. Benjamin and Fannie (Kollitz) Hasselson; B.A., Roosevelt U., Chgo., 1937; M.A. in Social Work, Northwestern U., 1940; postgrad. U. Chgo., 1940-42; m. Frank E. Kent, Dec. 6, 1934; Caseworker, Chgo. Welfare Dept., 1938-41, med. worker, 1941-42; med. social worker and supr. Crippled Children's Services, D.C. Health Dept., 1942-44; med. social cons. D.C. Rehab. Service, 1944-47, supr. phys. restoration, 1946-47; instr. Army Edn. Center, Tokyo, Japan, 1947; chief public welfare sect. Mil. Govt., Saitama Prefecture, Japan, 1948-49; public welfare adv. Tokyo Regional Office Kanto Civil Affairs Region, Gen. Hdqrs., Supreme Comdr. for Allied Forces, 1949-50; social service cons. Ill. Public Aid Commn., 1950-51; adminstr. Children's Convalescent Hosp., Washington, 1951-59; med. social cons. div. standards and procedures State Dept. Social Welfare, Iowa, 1959-62; asso. dir. dept. social work Temple U. Hosp., Phila., 1962-77, ret., 1977. Mem. health sect. United Community Services, Washington, 1951-59. Mem. Nat. Assn. Social Workers (chmn. med. social work sect. Washington chpt. 1955-57), Am. Public Welfare Assn. (mem. health policy com. 1975—), AAUP. Address: Gross Point Towers 9240 Gross Point Rd Skokie IL 60077

KENT, LEE ANNE, lawyer; b. Evergreen, Ala., Nov. 10, 1926; d. Prinus and Daisy Mae Bradley; B.A., Wayne State U., 1972, M.S. in L.S., 1973, J.D., 1976; m. Earl Kent, Feb. 4, 1950 (div. Mar. 1956). Admitted to Mich. bar, 1976. Stenographer, Internat. Union, UAW, Detroit, 1953-74; librarian Walter P. Reuther Library, Wayne State U., 1974-76; individual practice law, Detroit, 1976-77; hearing officer City of Detroit, 1974—, asst. corp. counsel, 1977—. Pub. mem. Mich. State Elec. Adminstrv. Bd. Mem. Am., Mich., Detroit bar assns., Spl. librariies Assn., Am. Arbitration Assn., Indsl. Relations Research Assn. Home: 1940 Hyde Park Dr Detroit MI 48207 Office: 1010 City-County Bldg Detroit MI 48226

KENWORTHY, JOHN RICHARD, ins. agt.; b. Dayton, Ohio, Aug. 1, 1932; s. E. Leonard and Merle Christina (Gibson) K.; B.S. in Edn., Wittenberg U., 1955; m. Carolyn Beard, Dec. 27, 1952; children—Christine, Carol, Paul. Tchr., coach Northridge High Sch., Dayton, 1955-57; field rep. Horace Mann Ins. Group, Ft. Wayne, Ind., 1957-59, Ind. state mgr., Indpls., 1959-65, asst. v.p. mktg., Springfield, Ill., 1965-69; supt. agencies Franklin Life Ins. Co., Springfield, 1969-70, regional mgr., Grand Rapids, Mich., 1970—. Bd. dirs. Goodwill Industries of Grand Rapids; blood and leukopheresis donor. Recipient nat. quality award Nat. Assn. Life Underwriters, 1972-79; life mem. Franklin Million Dollar Conf.; C.L.U. Mem. Grand Rapids Assn. Life Underwriters, Grand Rapids Gen. Agts. and Mgrs. Assn. (pres. 1976-77), Life Leaders of Mich., Am. Bus. Clubs (pres. S. Kent chpt. 1978-79, dist. gov. 1981-82). Republican. Congregationalist. Home: 308 Arlington Dr SE East Grand Rapids MI 49506 Office: 4362 Cascade Rd SE Grand Rapids MI 49506

KENWORTHY, MERRELL T., systems analyst; b. Kokomo, Ind., Aug. 11, 1946; s. Wayne R. and Naomi Gertrude (Henderson) K.; S.B., Mass. Inst. Tech., 1968; postgrad. Syracuse (N.Y.) U., 1968-70; m. Rosalea Kay Farris, Oct. 28, 1974. Programmer, Gen. Electric Corp., Syracuse, 1968-70; instr. Ind. Vocat. Tech. Coll., Kokomo, 1970-73; systems analyst Kokomo Tribune, 1973-78; programmer/analyst Penn-Dixie Steel Corp., 1978—. Mem. Assn. Computing Machinery, Math. Assn. Am., Kokomo Mental Health Assn., Kokomo Civic Theatre, Howard County Hist. Soc., Kokomo Community Concerts Assn. Presbyterian. Club: Kokomo Kiwanis. Home: 3110 Orleans Ct Kokomo IN 46901 Office: 1111 S Main St Kokomo IN 46901

KEOGH, CHARLES RALPH, ednl. adminstr.; b. St. Louis, Nov. 16, 1927; s. Charles Ambrose and Irene (Swanard) K.; B.S., Moorhead State U., 1959; M.S., Tri Coll. U., 1980; m. Carol Mae Johnson, Sept. 14, 1951; children—Steven Lee, Peggy Lynn, Danny Charles, Lisa Jane, Kathy Irene. Tchr., Waubun (Minn.) High Sch., 1960-75, 77-78, asst. prin., 1978—. Mem. council Trinity Luth. Ch., 1952-54, supt. Sunday sch., 1955-58, pres. ch. council, 1980—. Served with AUS, 1946-47. Decorated Purple Heart. Mem. Nat. Assn. Secondary Sch. Prins., Minn. Assn. Secondary Sch. Prins., Assn. Supervision and Curriculum Devel. Club: Mahnomen Country. Home: Route 1 Waubun MN 56589 Office: Waubun High Sch Waubun MN 56589

KEOGH, JEANNE MARIE, librarian; b. Toledo, Sept. 20, 1924; d. Thomas Leroy and Agnes Mary (Wenzler) Keogh; B.A., Mary Manse Coll., 1946; B.L.S., Western Res. U., 1947. Asst. librarian tech. dept. Toledo Pub. Library, 1946-54; tech. librarian Libbey Owens Ford Co., Toledo, 1954—. Established library Riverside Hosp. Nursing Sch., Toledo, 1950-51; grey lady ARC, Toledo, 1966-70; mem. Transp. Safety Info. Com., 1972—; mem. fin. com. Mary Manse Coll., Toledo, 1972-75. Chmn. bd. Ecumenical Library Toledo, 1976—. Mem. Ohio, Catholic librarian assns., Spl. Libraries Assn. (scholarship com. 1968-74, chmn. 1960-70, 72-74, chmn. Detroit conf. hospitality com. 1970, chmn. metals/materials div. 1977-78), Mary Manse Coll. Alumni Assn. (dir. 1971-76, pres. 1972-73). Club: Quota (Toledo). Home: 3634 Rugby Dr Toledo OH 43614 Office: 1701 E Broadway Toledo OH 43605

KEOWN, WILLIAM ARVEL, clergyman, educator; b. Clinton, Ind., June 4, 1920; s. James Edward and Lula Nettie (Jackson) K.; Th.B. cum laude, God's Bible Sch. & Coll., Cin., 1949; M.A., Butler U., Indpls., 1956; cert. in edn. Ind. State U., 1961; m. Jewel Cook, Mar. 25, 1950; children—Evelyn Jewel, Deborah Anne, William S., A. Duane, Wayne A. Ordained to ministry Ch. of God (Anderson affiliated), 1957; dean of men God's Bible Sch., 1948-49; pastor Nazarene Ch., Evansville, Ind., 1950-52, Nazarene Ch., Clinton, Ind., 1952—; instr. Frankfort Coll., 1954-57, dean of men, 1954-55; tchr. S.Vermillion Middle Sch., Clinton, 1957-79, coach basketball, 1967-70; pastor Ch. of God, Terre Haute, Ind., 1970-80; instr. Anderson (Ind.) Day Treatment Center, Ind. Dept. Corrections, 1979—; cons. in field. Served with U.S. Army, 1942-46. Mem. NEA, Ind. State Tchrs. Assn., Classroom Tchrs. Assn., Internat. Platform Assn., Correctional Edn. Assn., Internat. Ministers Assn. of Ch. of God, Ind. State Ministers Assn. of Ch. of God, Kingdom Bldrs. Assn. Home: Route 2 Box 26 Clinton IN 47842 Office: 2316 Mounds Rd Anderson IN 46013

KEPNER, HENRY SIEBER, JR., mathematician, educator; b. Chgo., May 22, 1940; s. Henry Sieber and Inez (Madsen) K.; B.S. in Math., U. Iowa, 1962, M.S., 1964, Ph.D. in Math. Edn., 1970. Instr. math. Univ. Sch., Iowa City, 1963-72; asst. prof. U. Iowa, 1970-72; mem. faculty U. Wis., Milw., 1972—, asso. prof. math. edn., 1975—; dir. summer insts. tchrs. NSF; pres., treas., exec. bd. Wis. Math. Council. Treas., v.p., deacon Lake Park Lutheran Ch., Milw. Mem. Nat. Council Tchrs. Math. (com. chmn.), Math. Assn. Am., Sch. Sci. and Math. Assn., Am. Ednl. Research Assn., Milw.-Area Math. Council, Eastern Wis. Ofcls. Assn. (pres. 1979), Wis. Umpires Assn. (exec. bd. 1974—). Author books, articles, tests. Home: 4211 N Prospect Ave Milwaukee WI 53211 Office: Dept Curriculum and Instrn U Wis Milwaukee WI 53201

KER, CHARLES ARTHUR, furniture and indsl. products mfg. co. exec.; b. Warsaw, Ind., May 29, 1934; s. Charles Hoskins and Jessie Marie (Anglin) K.; B.A., DePauw U., 1956; M.B.A., Northwestern U., 1957; m. Alice Ann Steele, Sept. 8, 1957 (div.); m. Connie Louise Collier, Oct. 3, 1981; children—Kelly, Karen, Kristin. Cost accountant, financial analyst Eli Lilly & Co., Indpls., 1957-61, head receipts and disbursements Elanco Products div., 1962-65; asst. treas. Dalton Foundries, Inc., Warsaw, 1965-67; treas., 1968-74; pres. Endicott Industries, Warsaw, 1975—; pres. Endicott Ch. Furniture div. Dalton Foundries, Inc., Winona Lake, 1971-74; dir. Lake City Bank, 1973—. Bd. dirs. United Fund of Kosciusko County (Ind.), 1966-76, pres., 1968, chmn. bd., 1969, chmn. gen. campaign, 1974; bd. dirs. Jr. Achievement, Warsaw, 1968-71, pres., 1969-70, treas., 1968-69; bd. dirs. Baker Boys Club, 1966—, treas., 1966-74; past deacon (moderator), trustee, pres., sec. and elder Presbyterian Ch.; bd. dirs. Kosciusko Community YMCA, 1967-68, 77-79, Lakeland council Girl Scouts Am., 1969-71; bd. dirs. No. Ind. Lung Assn., 1977—, treas., 1979-81, v.p., 1981-82; bd. dirs. Am. Lung Assn. Ind., 1979—, treas., 1980—; bd. dirs. Am. Diabetes Assn. Ind., 1979—, treas., 1980-81, vice-chmn., 1981—; bd. dirs. Am. Diabetes Assn. Kosciusko County, 1978—, pres., 1978-79, treas., 1981—. Recipient Disting. Service award Warsaw Jr. C. of C., 1968, Warsaw Man of Yr. award, 1975. Mem. Warsaw C. of C. (dir. 1968-72, pres. 1970-71, dir. indsl. bd. 1974-76), Financial Execs. Inst. (dir. Ft. Wayne chpt. 1971-73, pres. 1972-73), Ch. Furniture Mfrs. Assn. (dir. 1974-75, pres. 1975), Christian Bus. Men's Com. Republican. Clubs: Rotary (pres. 1975-76, dir. 1968-70, 72-77). Home: 202 Tyner Dr Warsaw IN 46580 Office: Endicott Industries 765 W Market St Warsaw IN 46580

KERBER, LINDA KAUFMAN, historian, educator; b. N.Y.C., Jan. 23, 1940; d. Harry Hagman and Dorothy (Haber) K.; A.B. cum laude, Barnard Coll., 1960; M.A., N.Y. U., 1961; Ph.D. (Danforth Found. Kent fellow), Columbia U., 1968; m. Richard Kerber, June 5, 1960; children—Ross Jeremy, Justin Seth. Instr., asst. prof. history Stern Coll., Yeshiva U., N.Y.C., 1963-68; asst. prof. history San Jose (Calif.) State Coll., 1969-70; vis. asst. prof. history Stanford (Calif.) U., 1970-71; asst. prof. history U. Iowa, Iowa City, 1971-75, prof., 1975—. Barnard Coll. alumnae fellow, 1964-65; Am. Philos. Soc. grantee, 1971; Am. Bar Found. grantee, 1975; Am. Council Learned Socs. grantee, 1975; Nat. Endowment for Humanities fellow, 1976. Mem. Orgn. Am. Historians, Am. Hist. Assn., Am. Studies Assn., Am. Soc. for Legal History, Berkshire Conf. Women Historians. Jewish. Author: Federalists in Dissent: Imagery and Ideology in Jeffersonian America, 1970, paperback edit., 1980; Women of the Republic: Intellect and Ideology in Revolutionary America, 1980; co-editor: Women's America: Refocusing the Past, 1982; mem. editorial bd. Jour. Am. History, Signs: Jour. Women in Culture and Society; contbr. articles and book revs. to profl. jours. Office: Dept History U Iowa Iowa City IA 52242

KERESZTES, GERALD WAYNE, aerospace engring. designer; b. South Bend, Ind., July 27, 1947; s. Floyd Casimer and Katherine Anne Keresztes; Asso. Engring., Acme Inst. Tech., 1968. Tool and die designer Adams Engring. Co., Inc., South Bend, 1968-70, Niles Engring. Co. (Mich.), 1970-71; tool, die designer Weldun Internat., Bridgman, Mich., 1971-72; machine, plastic mold designer Martin Machine Co., Inc., South Bend, 1972-75; engring. designer in aerospace, energy controls div. Bendix Corp., South Bend, 1975—. Mem. Aircraft Owners and Pilots Assn. Clubs: Business Fliers, St. Joseph Valley Ski, Daves Gym and Health. Developer prodn. designs of fuel control systems for fighter aircraft. Home: 1822 Coachmans Trail South Bend IN 46637 Office: Bendix Corp 717 N Bendix Dr South Bend IN 46620

KERFOOT, EDWARD JAMES, toxicologist; b. Detroit, July 28, 1941; s. Gerald and Winifred M. (Abram) K.; B.S., Detroit Inst. Tech., 1968; M.S., Wayne State U. Sch. Medicine, 1970, Ph.D. (USPHS fellow), 1974; m. Ellen M. Debbaudt, Aug. 8, 1964; children—Daniel, David, Jeffrey, John, Martha. Instr. in toxicology and indsl. hygiene Wayne State U. Sch. Medicine, 1973-74, asst. prof. indsl. toxicology and indsl. hygiene, 1974-80, asso. prof., 1980—; guest lectr. U. Mich.; asso. prof. chemistry Oakland U.; dir. toxicology and indsl. hygiene BASF Wyandotte Corp. (Mich.), 1974—. Mem. adv. bd. Ferris State Coll. Nat. Inst. Occupational Safety and Health grantee, 1972-73. Mem. Am. Acad. Clin. Toxicology, Am. Coll. Toxicology, Am. Indsl. Hygiene Assn. Am. Conf. Govt. Indsl. Hygienists, Inst. Occupational Hygienists (Eng.), Mich. Indsl. Hygiene Soc., Am. Chem. Soc., Sigma Xi. Contbr. articles to profl. jours. Office: 1609 Biddle St Wyandotte MI 48192

KERMES, KENNETH NEAL, food co. exec.; b. Lafayette, Ind., May 21, 1935; s. Frank T. and Jane O. (Nicalo) K.; B.A., Amherst Coll., 1957; postgrad. N.Y. U., 1960-63, Harvard U., 1976-77; m. Susan Pennock, Mar. 8, 1958; children—Suzanne, Robert. Second v.p. Chase Manhattan Bank, N.Y.C., 1960-65; asst. treas. Gen. Foods Corp., White Plains, N.Y., 1966-71; corp. treas. Monsanto Co., St. Louis, 1971-75; gen. mgr. detergent and phosphate div., 1975-77; sr. v.p. chief fin. officer Lone Star industries, Greenwich, Conn., 1977-79; sr. v.p., chief fin. officer Ralston Purina Co., St. Louis, 1979—. Past pres. Parents Assn., DePauw U., Greencastle, Ind.; pres. Rowayton (Conn.) Civic Assn., 1968-70; chmn. Darien (Conn.) United Way, 1978-79; mem. exec. bd. St. Louis Met. YMCA, 1975-77, 79—; mem. exec. com. Hobart Coll. Parents Assn., Geneva, N.Y., from 1980; bd. dirs., treas. 1st Street Forum, St. Louis, 1980—; bd. dirs. Good Shepherd Sch. for Children, St. Louis, 1980—. Served to lt. (j.g.) USN, 1957-60. Mem. Fin. Execs. Inst. Presbyterian. Clubs: Mo. Athletic, Woodsmill Racquet, Log Cabin, Amherst (St. Louis). Home: 7 Warridge St Saint Louis MO 63124 Office: Ralston Purina Co 835 S 8th St Saint Louis MO 63102

KERN, JOHN CHARLES, cons.; b. Chgo., May 22, 1925; s. Herbert Arthur and Edith (Speckman) K.; S.B., Mass. Inst. Tech., 1950; postgrad. Harvard U., 1951-53, Northwestern U., 1969-70; m. Anne Rumsey Moreland, Sept. 13, 1958; children—Elizabeth Anne, John Charles, Louise Moreland. Mem. staff div. indsl. cooperation Mass. Inst. Tech., 1951-53; asst. to v.p. research and devel. Royal McBee Corp., West Hartford, Conn., 1954-58; div. mgr. advanced planning and mktg. research Sperry Rand Corp., N.Y.C., 1959-63; dir. planning and devel. Coleman Instruments div. Perkin-Elmer Corp., Oakbrook, Ill., 1964-69; pres. Familia Kern, Inc. Advising trustee Kern Found.; trustee, sec., exec. com. First Ill. Religious and Charitable Risk Pooling Trust; trustee Theosophical Investment Trust; vice chmn. Calif. Inst. Integral Studies; bd. dirs., mem. exec. com. Northwestern Mil. and Naval Acad.; trustee Mus. Contemporary Art, Chgo., Council for Arts at Mass. Inst. Tech.; mem. sch. com. Happy Valley Found., Ojai, Calif. Served with U.S. Army, 1943-46; ETO. Mem. Sigma Xi, Beta Theta Pi. Clubs: Hinsdale Golf; Cliff Dwellers (Chgo.). Address: 3712 Adams Oakbrook IL 60521 also Palmas del Mar Humacao PR 00661

KERNAN, EDWARD JAMES, law firm adminstr.; b. Two Harbors, Minn., Mar. 22, 1926; s. Edward James and Edith A. (Scott) K.; B.S., U. Minn., 1948; M.Ed., U. Wis., 1962; m. Barbara Louise Iverson, Aug. 28, 1948; children—Edward J., Barbara Lee, James E. Coach, athletic dir. Robbinsdale (Minn.) High Sch., 1948-53; coach, athletic dir. Northland Coll., Ashland, Wis., 1954-64; placement dir. U. Minn., Duluth, 1965; adminstrv. and personnel mgr. Price Waterhouse, Cleve., 1966-73; adminstrv. dir. Sidley & Austin, Chgo., 1974—. Pres., Ashland (Wis.) Little League, 1958-63; chmn. Citizens Com. for Sch. Bond Issue, Rocky River, Ohio, 1973. Served with USAAF, 1944-45. Mem. Law Office Mgrs. Assn. (bd. dirs. 1976-79), Assn. Legal Adminstrs. (bd. dirs. 1977-80). Roman Catholic. Clubs: Brookwood Country (bd. govs.), Ill. Athletic, Midwest Spaniel. Home: 1205 Candlewood Hill Northbrook IL 60062 Office: 1 First National Plaza Chicago IL 60603

KERNAN, JOHN TERENCE, corp. exec.; b. Balt., Feb. 17, 1946; s. Anthony Eugene and Mildred Mary (Farson) K.; B.S., Loyola Coll., Balt., 1969; m. Dianne Mary Ruminski, May 11, 1973; 1 dau., Amy Beth. Project mgr. G.W. Stephens & Assos., Towson, Md., 1962-69; systems analyst McCormick & Co., Balt., 1969-73, mgr. info. services, 1973-75, dir. systems services, 1976-77; dir. info. systems Borden Foods div. Borden, Inc., Columbus, Ohio, 1977-79; v.p. product devel. Deltak, Inc., 1979—. Served to 1st lt. Md. NG, 1965-72. Mem. Assn. Systems Mgmt., Am. Mktg. Assn., Am. Prodn. and Inventory Control Soc. Home: 6463 Cape Cod Ct Lisle IL 60532 Office: 1220 Kensington Rd Oak Brook IL 60521

KERNDT, THOMAS MARTIN, banker; b. Lansing, Iowa, July 22, 1917; s. Moritz and Mary (Martin) K.; student Columbia Coll. (now Loras Coll.), 1935-37; B.S., Marquette U., 1939; m. Patricia Ann Reynolds, Feb. 3, 1945; children—Mary Patricia (Mrs. Patrick Ahern), Kathleen Ann (Mrs. Michael Higgins), Gustave William, Thomas Moritz, Peter Reynolds, Ann Louise (dec.), Margaret Mary, Susan Marie, Gretchen Marie, James Michael. With Kerndt Bros. Savs. Bank., Lansing, 1939-42; spl. agt. FBI, 1942-47; with Kerndt Bros. Savs. Bank, 1947—, pres., 1964—; officer, dir. Med. Offices, Inc., 1965—, Lansing Marina, Inc., 1962—. Active various town coms., zoning com., devel. com., Lansing, 1971—. Bd. advisers Viterbo Coll., LaCrosse, Wis., 1960—. Recipient Distinguished Service award Lansing Jr. C. of C., 1969, Pope John XXIII award Viterbo Coll., La Crosse, Wis., 1980. Mem. Delta Sigma Pi. Republican. Roman Catholic (trustee high sch. 1958-71). K.C. (4 deg.), Kiwanian (pres. 1965). Home: RFD Lansing IA 52151 Office: Main St Lansing IA 52151

KERNS, GERTRUDE YVONNE, sch. psychologist; b. Flint, Mich., July 25, 1931; d. Lloyd D. and Mildred C. (Ter Achter) B.; B.A., Olivet Coll., 1953; M.A., Wayne State U., 1958; Ph.D., U. Mich., 1979. Sch. psychologist Roseville (Mich.) Public Schs., 1958-68, Grosse Pointe (Mich.) Public Schs., 1968—; pvt. practice psychology, 1980—; instr. psychology Macomb Community Coll., 1959-63. Mem. Mich., Am. psychol. assns., Mich., Nat. socs. sch. psychologists, NEA, Psi Chi. Home: 28820 Grant St St Clair Shores MI 48081 Office: 389 St Clair Ave Grosse Pointe MI 48230

KERPER, RICHARD JOHN, truck dispatch co. exec.; b. Dubuque, Iowa, Dec. 6, 1950; s. Harold Clarence and Rita Mary (Berens) K.; student Iowa State U., 1969-70; B.A., U. No. Iowa, 1973, M.A., 1978. Instr., asst. track coach U. No. Iowa, 1977-78; transp. broker, asst. comptroller Am. Truck Dispatch, Omaha; head track coach No. Iowa Track Club. Served with USAF, 1973-77. Recipient 7 athletic awards U. No. Iowa. Mem. Nat. Joggers Assn., Am. Alliance for Phys. Edn. and Recreation, U.S. Track Coaches Assn. Democrat. Roman Catholic. Home: 4413 N 127th Ct Box 108 Omaha NE 68164 Office: 7811 L St Suite 110 Omaha NE 68127

KERR, FREDERICK HOHMANN, hosp. adminstr.; b. Pitts., July 11, 1936; s. Nathan F. and Laura (Hohmann) K.; B.A., Pa. State U., 1958; M.P.A., U. Pitts., 1961; 1 dau., Linda Jean; m., Phyllis Jensen, Aug. 21, 1970. Planning intern Allegheny County Planning Commn., Pitts., 1958-59; exec. sec. Fayette County br. Pa. Economy League, Uniontown, 1959, Armstrong County br., Kittanning, 1959-62; exec. sec. Woodbury County Tax Research Conf., Sioux City, Iowa, 1962-65; public service dir. City Sioux City, 1965-66; asst. adminstr. St. Luke's Med. Center, Sioux City, 1966-69, asso. adminstr., 1969-71; adminstr. Meml. Hosp., Michigan City, Ind., 1971-75; pres. St. Luke's Hosp., Maumee, Ohio, 1975—; part-time instr. public fin. and mgmt. Morningside Coll., Sioux City, 1963-66. Dir. N.W. Ohio Data Center, 1975—, pres., 1976-79, 81—; dir. Clin. Engring. Center N.W. Ohio, 1975-78; mem. Sioux City Community Appeals Rev. Bd., 1969-71, chmn., 1970; v.p. LaPorte County (Ind.) Health Planning Council, 1972-74, pres., 1974-75; bd. dirs. Sioux City Council Community Services, 1965-70; bd. dirs. Hosp. Council N.W. Ohio, 1975—, v.p., 1977-78, pres., 1978-80; bd. dirs. Siouxland United Way, 1970-71, chmn. planning div., 1970; bd. dirs. No. Ind. Sch. Radiol. Tech., 1971-75, pres., 1972; bd. dirs. Ohio Hosp. Mgmt. Services, 1976—; bd. dirs. Ohio Hosp. Ins. Co., 1978—, treas., 1981—; bd. dirs. Health Planning Assn. N.W. Ohio, 1977-81, v.p., 1980-81. Served to 2d lt. U.S. Army, 1958-59. Fellow Am. Coll. Hosp. Adminstrs.; mem. Am. Soc. Public Adminstrn. (pres. Siouxland chpt. 1963-64, nat. council 1966-69), Am. Inter-profl. Inst. (pres. Sioux City chpt. 1968-69), Sioux City Hosp. Council (sec. 1967), Am. Protestant Hosp. Assn. (council health and religious values), Am. Hosp. Assn., Photog. Soc. Am., Federation Internationale de l'Art Photographique, Pi Sigma Alpha. Home: 1526 Cherrylawn Dr Toledo OH 43614 Office: 5901 Monclova Rd Maumee OH 43537

KERR, FREDRIC ARTHUR, state senator, farmer; b. Spearville, Kans., Dec. 29, 1940; s. Fredric Henry and Eleanor Mills (Barrett) K.; student Southwestern Coll., Winfield, Kans., 1959-61; B.A., Okla. State U., 1963; m. Nancy Jeanne Okerberg, July 24, 1965; children—Kathryn, Alan. Farmer, stockman, Pratt, Kans., 1964—; mem. Kans. Senate, 1976—. Republican. Methodist. Office: State Capitol Bldg Topeka KS 66612

KERR, LLOYD, salesman; b. Oxford, Miss., Nov. 20, 1946; s. Lonzo and Leloia (Buford) K.; B.S., Colo. State U., 1969; Certificate of Lang., U. Leige, Leige, Belgium, 1970; m. Maggie Jean White, Aug. 10, 1968; children—Lloyd, Jr., Schin Anwar. Tchr. Washington High Sch., South Bend, Ind., 1970-71; field worker Human Relation Commn., South Bend, 1971; salesman Cutter Labs., Chgo., 1971-73; area mgr. DWS, Inc., Portland, Ore., 1974-75, product, sales mgr., 1975-78, sr. salesman, 1978—, salesman B D Drake-Willock, Chgo., 1975-81; salesman Deseret Co., Sandy, Utah, 1981—. Mem. Am. Assn. Nephrology Nurses and Technicians, Kappa Alpha Psi. Mem. Christian Ch. Club: Presidents. Office: 9450 South St Sandy UT 84070

KERR, WILLIAM EDWARD, JR., author, publishing co. exec.; b. Dalhart, Tex., Jan. 25, 1929; s. William E. and Norma Lucretia (Wightman) K.; B.A., Highlands U., 1951; m. Margaret Elizabeth Dahlbo, Aug. 15, 1953; children—Richard, Kendra. Tchr., Los Alamos High Sch., 1951-52; mem. sales staff South-Western Pub. Co., Cin., 1953-62, advt. mgr., 1962-67, dir. ednl. media dept., 1967—; lectr. audiovisual teaching techniques U. Denver, U. Colo., No. Colo. State U.; author: Dictionary of Accounting Terminology, 1977; (with wife) Think Metric, 1980; co-author: Metric Guide for Educational Materials, 1977; author, dir., producer filmstrips, films, slides, videotapes and audio cassettes in bus., consumer and metric edn.; specialist in ednl. media design; metric cons. ednl. materials sector com. Am. Nat. Metric Council. Served to lt. (j.g.) USNR, 1948-50. Recipient Student of Yr. award NAM, 1950; Service award Jour. Bus. Edn., 1952. Home: 7859 Ayerdayl St Cincinnati OH 45230 Office: 5101 Madison Rd Cincinnati OH 45227

KERRIGAN, JOHN JOSEPH, ins. co. exec.; b. Chgo., Nov. 6, 1944; s. John Joseph and Margaret Agnes (Christie) K.; B.S., Loyola U., 1967, M.A., 1970, M.S.I.R., 1974, postgrad., 1977—; m. Mary Ann Cook, July 14, 1973; children—John Alexander, Mary Margaret. Tchr., Kenwood High Sch., 1971-77; coordinator developmental econ. edn. Chgo. Bd. Edn. and Ill. Council on Econ. Edn., 1977-80; coordinator Center for Econs. and Bus. Studies Chgo. Bd. Edn. and Continental Bank, 1977-80; sr. tng. program developer Allstate Ins. Co., Northbrook, Ill., 1980—; cons. in field. Mem. Ill. Guidance and Personnel Assn., Ill. Council on Econ. Edn. (cert. of honor in econ. edn. 1979), Am. Soc. Tng. and Devel., Ill. Tng. and Devel. Assn., Phi Delta Kappa. Home: 6202 S Karlov St Chicago IL 60629 Office: Allstate Insurance Company Allstate Plaza S IG Northbrook IL 60062

KERSHAW, BEULAH FRANCES (MRS. BRYAN KERSHAW), music tchr., poet; b. Cloride, Miss., Jan. 9, 1921; d. William Washington and Esther Matilda (Bone) Warren; student pub. schs.; m. Bryan Kershaw, July 10, 1965; children—Georgia Verdon, Sandra Kershaw Gentry. Tchr. piano, organ, guitar and drums, 1962—; writer poetry, 1942—; rec. artist. Vol. worker in rest homes; mem. Republican Com., Evansville, Ind., Carmi, Ill., 1967—. Recipient awards Mental Health Assn. of Ill. Mem. Internat. Platform Assn. Author: Poems by Beulah, Vol. I, 1968, Vol. II, 1973. Composer: It Hurts to be Hurt, 1939; Your Woman, 1964; Santa Kissed Me. Home: Route 1 Crossville IL 62827

KESKITALO, WALLACE ALBERT, county agt.; b. Republic, Mich., Sept. 3, 1913; s. John O. and Hilda W. (Anttila) K.; B.S., Mich. State U., 1940, M.S., 1956; m. Olive Gwendolynn Kelsey, Sept. 26, 1941 (dec. Nov. 1973); children—John, Patricia Keskitalo Newton, Stewart, Peggy Keskitalo Binoniemi, Pamela; m. 2d, Joyce M. Kalen, Sept. 7, 1976; stepchildren—Gary, David, Brian and Jim Kalen. Tchr., Kellogg Consol. Sch., Augusta, Mich., 1940-42, Shepherd (Mich.) High Sch., 1942-43; loan supr. Farm Security Adminstrn., Ontonogon, Mich., 1943-47; county extension agt. Mich. State U., Houghton, 1947—; mem. Houghton County Soil Conservation Dist. Bd., 1960—, Houghton County Overall Econ. Devel. Dist. Com., 1972—. Chmn. career edn. planning council Houghton, Keweenaw and Baraga County Schs.; mem. bd. edn. Portage Twp. Schs., Houghton, 1958-62, Osceala Twp., 1976; chmn. Houghton County Planning Commn., 1962-81; bd. rev. Torch Lake Twp., 1978-79; mem. Copper Country Intermediate Sch. Bd., 1979; chmn. Regional Ednl. Media Center Bd. of Western Upper Peninsula. Recipient Disting. Service award Houghton-Keweenaw Soil and Water Conservation Dist., 1977. Mem. Nat. Assn. County Agrl. Agts. (Disting. Service award 1974), Epsilon Sigma Phi, Alpha Gamma Rho. Episcopalian (mem. vestry 1974-79). Club: Dollar Bay Lions. Home: Box 173 Dollar Bay MI 49922 Office: Courthouse Houghton MI 49931

KESLER, DARREL JOE, educator; b. Portland, Ind., Sept. 21, 1949; s. David Gordon and Lucille Marie (Bullock) K.; B.S., Purdue U., 1971, M.S., 1974; Ph.D., U. Mo., 1977; m. Cheryl Scaletta, May 26, 1973; children—Cheralyn Elizabeth, Darrel Phillip. Teaching asst. Purdue U., West Lafayette, Ind., 1971-74; research asst. U. Mo., Columbia, 1974-77; asst. prof. reproductive physiology, U. Ill., Urbana, 1977-81; asso. prof., 1981—. Active, Univ. YMCA. Cited for excellence in teaching by students U. Ill., Urbana, 1978, 80, 81. Mem. Soc. Study Reproduction, AAAS, Am. Soc. Animal Sci., Am. Dairy Sci. Assn., Nat. Assn. Colls. and Tchrs. Agr., Soc. Theriogenology, Sigma Xi, Gamma Sigma Delta. Presbyterian. Contbr. articles in field to profl. jours. Home: 111 Willard St Urbana IL 61801 Office: 101 Animal Genetics Urbana IL 61801

KESSE, VICTOR EDMUND, JR., systems analyst; b. Atchison, Kans., Aug. 2, 1948; s. Victor Edmund and Pauline Mary (Maday) K.; student Copenhagen U., 1968; B.S., Washburn U., 1970; m. Debra Renee Claussen, Sept. 29, 1979. With Bankers Life Co., Des Moines, 1970—, EDP analyst, 1974-76, sr. systems analyst, 1976—. Fellow Life Office Mgmt. Assn.; mem. Assn. for Systems Mgmt. Home: 4008 SW 13th St Des Moines IA 50315 Office: Bankers Life 711 High St Des Moines IA 50307

KESSINGER, HOWARD DAVID, editor, publisher; b. Wellington, Kans., Oct. 25, 1932; s. Jesse Harrison and Grace (Johnson) K.; student Wichita State U., 1950-52; B.S., Kans. State U., 1957; m. Sharon L. Totten, Sept. 29, 1962; children—Hannah Ann, Sarah Ruth, Mary Catherine, Michael David. Reporter, advt. man Junction City (Kans.) Republic, 1955-58; advt. mgr. Abilene (Kans.) Reflector-Chronicle, 1958-61; mng. editor Oberlin (Kans.) Herald, 1961-66, editor-pub., 1966-75; editor-pub. Marysville (Kans.) Adv., 1975—. Trustee, William Allen White Found. Served with C.E., U.S. Army, 1953-55. Mem. Oberlin C. of C. (pres., 1967, 68), Kans. Press Service (pres. 1976), Kans. Press Assn. (dir. 1968-70, 80-81), Kans. State U. Alumni Assn. (dir. 1977-80, v.p. 1980), Kansas State U. Found. Bd., 1981—, Sigma Delta Chi. Republican. Episcopalian. Club: Rotary. Home: 1103 Elm St Marysville KS 66508 Office: 107 S 9th St Marysville KS 66508

KESSINGER, MARGARET ANNE, internist; b. Beckley, W.Va., June 4, 1941; d. Clisby Theodore and Margaret Anne (Ellison) Kessinger; B.A., W.Va. U., 1963, M.D., 1967; m. Loyd Ernst Wegner, Nov. 27, 1971. Intern, U. Nebr., 1967-68; resident in internal medicine U. Nebr. Hosp., 1968-70, fellow med. oncology, 1970-72; asst. prof. internal medicine U. Nebr., 1972-77, asso. prof., 1977—; Am. Cancer Soc. fellow, 1971-72; clin. cancer tng. grantee USPHS, 1970-72. Diplomate Nat. Bd. Med. Examiners, Am. Bd. Internal Medicine. Fellow A.C.P.; mem. Am. Soc. Clin. Oncology, Am. Fedn. Clin. Research, Nebr., Greater Omaha med. socs., AMA, Assn. Cancer Edn., Sigma Xi. Republican. Methodist. Home: Route 1 Scribner NE 68057 Office: Nebraska Medical Center Omaha NE 68105

KESSLER, CLEMM CROMWELL, III, mgmt. cons.; b. Hartford, Conn., Mar. 12, 1941; s. Clemm Cromwell, Jr. and Elizabeth (Graf) K.; A.B., Bucknell U., 1963; M.S., Western Res. U., 1965; Ph.D., Case Western Res. U., 1967; m. Patricia Jane Catherman, Aug. 31, 1963; children—Dawn Elizabeth, Danielle Ursula. Asst. to asso. prof. U. Nebr., Omaha, 1967-77; v.p. personnel Pacesetter Corp., Omaha, 1977-80; partner Kessler, Kennedy & Assos., Omaha, 1980—. Mem. Am. Psychol. Assn., Midwestern Psychol. Assn., Nebr. Psychol. Assn. Home: Route 2 Glenwood IA 51534 Office: Kessler Kennedy & Assos 6818 Grover St Omaha NE 68106

KESSLER, JOHN EDWARD, mfg. co. exec.; b. Champaign, Ill., Aug. 29, 1941; s. Louis M. and Helen Elizabeth (Smith) K.; B.S., U. Ill., 1963, M. Accounting Sci., 1965; m. Nancy Jane Rolfe, Aug. 31, 1963; children—Sherri Marie, Edward Lawrence. Sr. accountant Haskins & Sells, 1965-69; asst. to sr. v.p. adminstrn. Hart Schaffner & Marx, Chgo., 1969-70; regional controller N.Am., IMS Am., Ltd., Des Plaines, Ill., 1970-73; v.p., controller Cummins-Allison Corp., Glenview, Ill., 1973-77; sec.-treas., gen. mgr. Ames Supply Co., Downers Grove, Ill., 1977—. Recipient Outstanding Young Man Am. award, 1974, Elijah Watt Sells certificate of hon. mention, C.P.A. exam., 1964, bronze tablet U. Ill., 1963, Haskins & Sells Found. award, 1962. Mem. Fin. Execs. Inst., Alpha Kappa Psi (scholarship medallian), Beta Alpha Psi, Phi Alpha Mu, Phi Eta Sigma, Phi Kappa Phi, Sigma Iota Epsilon, Beta Gamma Sigma, Alpha Kappa Lambda, Delta Sigma Pi (scholarship key). Presbyterian (elder, trustee). Home: 913 69th St Darien IL 60559 Office: 2537 Curtiss St Downers Grove IL 60515

KESSLER, LAWRENCE W., scientist, sci. instrument co. exec.; b. Chgo., Sept. 26, 1942; s. Michael C. and Sue (Sniader) K.; m. Gloria M. Lerman, Aug. 23, 1964; children—Jeffrey, Brett, Corey, Brandy; B.S.E.E., Purdue U., 1964; M.S., U. Ill., 1966, Ph.D., 1968. Mem. research staff Zenith Radio Corp., Chgo., 1968-74; pres. Sonoscan, Inc., Bensenville, Ill., 1974—; adj. prof. info. engring. U. Ill., Chgo.; organizer 7th Internat. Symposium Acoustical Imaging and Holography, 1976; mem. statutory adv. com. FDA, 1973-75. Mem. IEEE (sec.-treas. sonics and ultrasonics div. 1969-71, pres. div. 1971-73, nat. lectr. 1981-82), Am. Inst. Ultrasound in Medicine, Acoustical Soc. Am., Am. Soc. Non-destructive Testing, Sigma Xi, Eta Kappa Nu. Editor: Procs. Ultrasonics Symposium, IEEE, Inc., 1970; Acoustical Holography, Vol. 7, 1977. Contbr. articles to tech. jours. Patentee acoustical microscopy, Bragg diffraction imaging, also liquid crystal device. Home: 418 Warren Rd Glenview IL 60025 Office: Sonoscan Inc 530 E Green St Bensenville IL 60106

KESSLER, MILTON, mfg. co. exec.; b. E. Pitts., Nov. 2, 1917; s. Harry and Rose (Hirsch) K.; m. Justine Heselov, Nov. 16, 1947; children—Ronald N., Kathyann, Wendy, Brian. Pres., Kessler Products Co., Inc., Youngstown, Ohio, 1940—, Kessler Inc., Youngstown, 1955—, Dover Molded Products, Dover, Ohio, 1958—, Youngstown Kitchens, 1975—, Anderson (S.C.) Textile, 1974—; chmn. bd. Space Links, Youngstown, 1975—. Bd. dirs. Heritage Manor, Youngstown, 1960. Mem. Am. Mgmt. Assn., Young Pres. Orgn., Youngstown C. of C., Soc. Plastics Industry, Soc. Plastics Engrs. Republican. Jewish. Clubs: Squaw Creek Country (bd. dirs. 1977), B'nai B'rith, Masons (32 degrees). Inventor in field. Home: 6690 Harrington St Boardman OH 44512 Office: 302 McClurg Rd Youngstown OH 44512

KESSLER, NEIL JAY, aircraft co. mgr.; b. St. Louis, Feb. 6, 1938; s. Maury and Mollie (Schwartz) K.; B.S.E.E., Washington U., 1959, M.S., 1961; m. Diane G. Schachter, Nov. 5, 1961; 1 son, Robert. Lectr. elec. engring. Washington U., St. Louis, 1959-61; engr. N. Am. Aviation, Los Angeles, 1961-63; sr. engr. McDonnell Aircraft Co., St. Louis, 1963-66, sect. chief electronics, 1970—; group engr. Emerson Electric, St. Louis, 1966-70. NSF fellow, 1960. Mem. Am. Def. Preparedness Assn. (sec. steering com. avionics sect., chmn. avionic systems session, avionics sect. symposium, 1979), Sigma Xi, Tau Beta Pi, Eta Kappa Nu. Author articles on automatic control systems and future fire control armament systems. Home: 568 Hickory View Ln Ballwin MO 63011 Office: PO Box 516 St Louis MO 63166

KESSLER, WINIFRED BEAM-FLAUTT, personal and orgn. devel. cons.; b. Memphis, May 1, 1934; d. George Lee and Winifred Antoinette (Peek) Beam; A.B., U. Calif., Berkley, 1956; M.Ed. (sholar), Xavier U., Cin., 1968; A.B.D., U. Cin., 1973; m. Thomas J. Flautt, 1955 (div. 1970); children—Madeleine T., David G.; m. 2d, Adriaan Kessler, Nov. 2, 1972; stephchildren—Glenn, Sylvia, Marc. Sec. to pres. Maryville Coll., St. Louis, 1952-54; asst., office dean students U. Calif., Berkeley, 1956-57; tchr. Latin and English, Acad. Sacred Heart, Cin., 1957-60; tchr., counselor Convent of Good Shepherd, Cin., 1967-68; tchr. English and Latin, Public Schs. Cin., 1968-71; instr. counseling and ednl. psychology U. Cin., 1971-76; prin. WBFK Assos., Cin., 1976—; staff exec. Womon Ways, Inc., Cin., 1977—. Bd. dirs., edn. chairwoman Cin. Human Relations Commn., 1963-67; bd. dirs., exec. com. Citizens Sch. Com. Cin., 1969—; bd. dirs. Christ Child Day Care Center, Cin., 1960-64; pres. Catholic Interracial council, Cin., 1965-67; bd. dirs. St. Johns Unitarian Ch., 1974-76; mem. priorities com. Community Chest, Cin., 1975-78; Maryville Coll. scholar, 1952-55. Mem. Orgn. Devel. Network, Am. Psychol. Assn., Am. Personnel and Guidance Assn. Democrat. Unitarian. Clubs: Woman's City, Clifton Meadows Swim/Tennis, Colonial Racquet. Home: 3674 Clifton Ave Cincinnati OH 45220 Office: PO Box 20145 Cincinnati OH 54220

KESTEL, GWEN CECELIA, home furnishings accessories exec.; b. Laurens, Iowa, Apr. 25, 1948; d. Harold Joseph and Syvilla Catherine (Bedel) K.; B.A. in Journalism, Creighton U., Omaha, 1970. Reporter, Home Furnishings Daily, Chgo., 1970-72, midwest bur. chief, 1972-77; asst. nat. accounts sales mgr. Disston, Inc., Chgo., 1977-78; nat. accounts sales mgr. Burwood Industries, Chgo., 1978-80, dir. sales and mktg., 1980—. Mem. Housewares Club Chgo. Republican. Roman Catholic. Contbr. articles to Chgo. Sun-Times. Home: 2800 N Lake Shore Dr Chicago IL 60657 Office: 4655 W Chase Ave Chicago IL 60646

KESTNBAUM, ROBERT DANA, mgmt. cons.; b. Chgo., Aug. 5, 1932; s. Meyer and Gertrude (Dana) K.; A.B., U. Chgo., 1951; A.B., Harvard U., 1953, M.B.A., 1955; m. Kate Trynin, June 10, 1957; children—Ellen Jean, Meyer II. Coordinator spl. sales Bell & Howell Co., Chgo., 1959-61, co-founder Robert Maxwell div., 1961, v.p., asst. gen. mgr., 1962-64, gen. mgr., 1964-66; direct mail mgr. Montgomery Ward & Co., 1966-67; pres. R. Kestnbaum & Co., direct mktg. cons., Chgo. Bd. dirs. North Side Boys' Clubs, 1960-67, pres., 1965-67; bd. dirs., mem. exec. com. Chgo. Youth Centers, v.p., 1969-71, adminstrv. v.p., 1971-72; vice chmn. campaign for Chgo., U. Chgo. Alumni Fund, 1969-71; bd. dirs. U. Chgo. Alumni Found.; founding co-chmn. Chgo. Forum; founding treas., incorporator Inner City Fund; mem. adv. com. on correctional services Ill. Youth Commn., 1969-70; mem. Gov.'s Adv. Council State of Ill., 1969-72; mem. citizens rev. com. Ill. Bd. Higher Edn., 1971—; vice chmn. operating effectiveness com. Community Fund Met. Chgo., 1972-75, chmn. 1975-77, mem. agy. services com., 1972-77, vice-chmn., 1975-77; pub. mem. devel. com. Jewish Vocat. Service, 1972—; bd. govs. Republican Citizens League of Ill., 1961-63. Served from ensign to lt. (j.g.), USNR, 1955-58. Mem. Chgo. Assn. Direct Mktg. (dir. 1975—), Soc. Contemporary Art, Harvard Bus. Sch. Assn. Chgo. (Ill.). Jewish (trustee congregation 1968—, v.p. 1969-75, treas. 1975—). Clubs: Harvard (dir. 1976—), Mid Am. (Chgo.). Home: 442 Wellington Ave Chicago IL 60657 Office: 221 N LaSalle St Chicago IL 60601

KETTERMAN, CLARK STUART, sch. adminstr.; b. Madison, Ind., Jan. 11, 1931; s. and Ella Agnus (Stuart) K.; B.A., Hanover Coll., 1952; M.S., Butler U., 1956, Ed.S., 1963; Ph.D., Purdue U., 1966; m. Sylvia Dan, June 29, 1952; children—John David, Joan Stuart Ketterman Defabis. Jr. high sch. math. tchr., Plainfield, Ind., 1952-53; spl. edn. tchr. Harry E. Wood High Sch., Indpls., 1954-56, counselor, 1957-59, dir. guidance, 1959-64; dir. pupil personnel Met. Sch. Dist. of Washington Twp., Indpls., 1966-80, coordinator vocat. curriculum and guidance services, 1981—. Deacon, St. Andrew's Presbyn. Ch., 1959-62, pres. Men's Assn., 1963; pres. bd. dirs. Public Action in Correctional Efforts, 1971; chmn. fund raising Hanover Coll., 1974-78, mem. pres.'s adv. council, 1974-77; bd. dirs. Tri-County Mental Health Found., 1976—; gov.'s appointee as state dir. Selective Service, Ind., 1981—. Served to col. N.G., 1948—. Decorated Army Commendation medal; recipient Alumni Achievement award Hanover Coll., 1979. Mem. NEA, Am. Personnel and Guidance Assn., Assn. Counselor Educators and Supervisors, Ind. Personnel and Guidance Assn. (pres. 1969), Central Ind. Personnel and Guidance Assn. (pres. 1968), Nat. Guard Assn., Hanover Coll. Alumni Assn. (pres. 1979), Phi Delta Kappa, Phi Gamma Delta. Presbyterian. Contbr. articles to profl. jours.

KETTERMAN, SYLVIA DAN, sch. counselor; b. Indpls., Feb. 11, 1931; d. George and Sylvia (Taflan) Dan; A.B., Hanover Coll., 1952; M.S., Butler U., 1963; cert. Fgn. Lang. Inst., 1965; cert. U. Strasbourg (France), 1966; cert. Fgn. Lang. Inst. of Ind. State U., 1967; m. Clark Stuart Ketterman, June 29, 1952; children—John David, Joan Stuart Ketterman DeFabis. Tchr. for gifted John Marshall High Sch., Indpls., 1959-65, tchr. French, 1965-68, tchr. French and Spanish, 1968-70; tchr. French and Spanish, Crispus Attucks High Sch., Indpls., 1970-71, counselor, 1971-80; counselor Spl. Service Team, Indpls. Public Schs., 1980—. Chairperson fundraising Hanover Coll. Fulbright scholar, 1966; Ind. honors grantee; recipient Alumni Achievement award Hanover Coll., 1979. Mem. Am. Assn. Tchrs. French (pres. chpt. 1970), Fulbright Alumni Assn., Ind. Personnel and Guidance Assn. (chmn. archives), Hanover Coll. Alumni Assn. (bd. dirs. 1969-72, Indpls. chmn. 1967), Clowes Hall Women's Com., Phi Mu Found. (treas. 1976-80, v.p. 1972-84), Delta Kappa Gamma (chpt. pres. 1980-82). Presbyterian. Club: Ind. N.G. Wives. Contbr. articles to profl. jours. Home: 4521 Lincoln Rd Indianapolis IN 46208

KETTLER, FREDERICK DELVAUX (DEL), aerospace co. exec.; b. Wichita, Kans., July 11, 1926; s. Frederick Charles and Blanche (Delvaux) K.; B.F.A., Wichita State U., 1949; m. Patricia Eileen Smith, Sept. 16, 1950; children—Christian, Von. With Boeing Co., Wichita, 1949—, mgr. illustration group, product support, 1953—. Past bd. dirs. Wichita Art Mus.; past mem. Wichita Met. Arts Bd. Republican. Mem. Unity Ch. Clubs: 20-30, Cosmopolitan (co-founder Wichita Mid-way 1968, pres. 1975, regional gov. 1977-79, Mo.-Kans. fedn. Cosmopolitan of Yr. 1975, internat. v.p. 1980-81), Boeing Mgmt. (pres. 1981-82). Established Clayton Staples art scholarship Wichita State U., 1972.

KEVITT, MARK BUCKLIN, social worker; b. South Weymouth, Mass., Dec. 1, 1949; s. Chester B. and Elizabeth M. (Kesselring) K.; A.B., Franklin Coll., 1971; postgrad. Ind. U., 1978—; m. Cynthia Schroeder, June 12, 1971. Music dir., account exec. WIFN-FM, Franklin, Ind., 1971-74; caseworker Interlocal Assn., Franklin, 1975-78, job readiness counselor, career edn. and media coordinator, New Castle, Ind., 1978—; staff asst. Congressman Dave Evans, 6th Dist. Ind., Indpls., 1975—. Mem. exec. bd. These Orgns. United Can Help; Franklin Twp. coordinator Johnson County Democratic Com., 1976-78, mem. precinct com., 1976—; pres. Johnson County Young Democrats, 1977-80; sec. Franklin City Dem. Central Com., 1979; Johnson County coordinator Dave Evans for Congress Com., 1974, 76, 78, 80. Recipient recognition cert. Atterbury Job Corps, 1977; cert. of appreciation Nat. Hemophilia Found., 1974; Franklin Citizen award Franklin Coll., 1977. Mem. Nat. Wildlife Fedn., Nat. Hist. Soc., Nat. Trust for Historic Preservation, ACLU, Franklin C. of C., Franklin Jr. C. of C., Johnson County Assn. for Retarded Citizens (sec.), Phi Omega Psi (past pres.), Phi Alpha Theta (past treas.). Mem. United Ch. of Christ. Home: 898 E Jefferson St Franklin IN 46131 Office: 150 S Water St Franklin IN 46131

KEYES, EDWARD LAWRENCE, JR., electric co. exec.; b. N.Y.C., Apr. 19, 1929; s. Edward Lawrence and Emily (Shepley) K.; B.A. cum laude, Princeton, 1951; m. Margaret Combs, July 21, 1981; 1 dau., Elisabeth Elliott. Asst. to pres. Emerson Electric Co., St. Louis, 1961-64, asst. v.p. adminstrn., 1964-65, v.p. adminstrn. Emerson Motor div., 1965-67, exec. v.p., dir. Day-Brite Lighting div., 1967-69, pres. Builder Products div., 1970; pres. Chromalox Comfort Conditioning div., 1970, Day-Brite Lighting Co. div., St. Louis, 1971-73, corp. group v.p., 1973-74, exec. v.p., ops. and group exec., 1974-76, exec. v.p. ops., 1976-77, pres., chief operating officer, 1977—; dir. Emerson Electric Co., 1st Nat. Bank Clayton (Mo.), Central Bancompany. Mem. adv. bd. St. John's Mercy Med. Center. Served to 1st lt. USAF, 1951-56. Republican. Roman Catholic. Clubs: Cottage (Princeton); Saint Louis Country, Racquet (St. Louis), Log Cabin, Univ. Home: 33 Deerfield St Louis MO 63124 Office: 8000 W Florissant St Louis MO 63136

KEYES, JAMES LYMAN, JR., diesel engine distbr.; b. Peru, Ind., Apr. 27, 1928; s. James Lyman and Mary Edith (Weigel) K.; A.B., Wabash Coll., 1950; M.B.A., Harvard U., 1952. Mgr. Mesabi Range Distributorship, Cummins Engine Co., Inc., Hibbing, Minn., 1958-59, gen. mgr. Cummins Diesel Sales Corp., Columbus, Ind., 1959-61, dir. marketing services, 1961-66, gen. sales mgr., 1966-69, v.p. engine sales, 1969-70, v.p. nat. accounts, 1971-72, v.p. indsl. mktg., 1973-76, pres. Cummins Central Ohio, Inc., Columbus, 1976—. Bd. dirs., exec. com. Nat. Assn. for Retarded Children, 1964-73, v.p., 1969-73. Pres. Ind. Assn. Retarded Children, 1962-65, Columbus Landmark Found., 1977—; trustee Wabash Coll., 1980—. Served to 1st lt. USAF, 1952-54. Mem. Nat. Assn. Wabash Coll. Men (dir. 1970-79, pres. 1974-76). Republican. Presbyn. (elder). Mason (32 deg., Shriner). Home: 1467 B Lake Shore Dr Columbus OH 43204 Office: 101 Phillipi Rd Columbus OH 43228

KEYES, JOSEPH BERNARD, psychologist; b. Chgo., Mar. 20, 1948; s. Bernard Francis and Josephine K.; B.S., Loyola U., Chgo., 1970; M.A., La. State U., 1971, Ph.D. (NDEA fellow), 1974; postdoctoral fellow in pediatric psychology, Johns Hopkins U., 1974-75; m. Catherine Ryan, Mar. 21, 1981. Staff psychologist Dixon (Ill.) Devel. Center, 1975-79; chief psychologist Regional Intake and Habilitative Assessment Program, Chgo. Region, 1979-80; treatment evaluation coordinator Dixon (Ill.) Devel. Center, 1980—; pvt. practice clin. psychology, Dixon, 1980—; cons. Lee County Juvenile Probation Dept., 1976-77; instr. Saulk Valley Coll., 1977, No. Ill. U., 1978. Registered psychologist, Ill. Mem. Am. Assn. Mental Deficiency, Johns Hopkins Med. and Surg. Assn., Am. Psychol. Assn., Midwestern Psychol. Assn., Sigma Xi. Research on basic memory processes and programming of mentally retarded. Home: 419 W Graham Dixon IL 61021 Office: 2600 N Brinton Dixon IL 61021

KEYES, MARION ALVAH, IV, mfg. co. exec.; b. Bellingham, Wash., May 11, 1938; s. Marion Alvah and Winnefred Agnes (Nolte) K.; B.S. in Chem. Engring., Stanford U., 1960; M.S. in E.E., U. Ill., 1968; M.B.A., Baldwin Wallace Coll., 1981; m. Loretta Jean Mattson, Nov. 17, 1962; children—Marion A., Zachary Leigh, Richard. Teaching asst. dept. math. Stanford U., 1958-59, technician Stanford Aerosol Labs., 1957-59; chem. engr. Ketchikan (Alaska) Pulp Co., 1960-63; dir. engring. Control Systems div. Beloit Corp. (Wis.), 1963-70; gen. mgr. digital systems div. Taylor Instrument Co., Rochester, N.Y., 1970-75; v.p. engring. and contract engring. Bailey Controls Co., Wickliffe, Ohio, from 1975, now pres. Bd. advisors Fenn Coll. Engring. Cleve. State U., United Cerebral Palsy, Rochester; bd. dirs. Boy Scouts Am., Cleve. United Cerebral Palsy. Registered profl. engr., Calif., Wis., N.Y., Ill., Ohio. Mem. Am. Mgmt. Assn., IEEE, U.S. Automation Research Council, TAPPI, Am. Automatic Control Council, Instrument Soc. Am., Am. Inst. Chem. Engrs., Am. Chem. Soc., Wis. Acad. Arts, Scis. and Letters. Republican. Lutheran. Club: Willoughby Men's Athletic. Editor: A Glossary Of Automatic Control Terminology, 1970. Contbr. articles to profl. jours. Patentee in field. Home: 120 Riverstone Dr Chagrin Falls OH 44022 Office: 29801 Euclid Ave Wickliffe OH 44092

KEYHANI, MAJID, mech. engr.; b. Tehran, Iran, Dec. 11, 1952; came to U.S., 1973; s. Mohammad H. and Batool (Haddad) K.; B.S. in M.E., Tri-State U., Angola, Ind., 1977; M.S. in M.E., Ohio State U., 1979. Research asso. Ohio State U., 1978, teaching asso., 1978-79, research asso., 1979—. Mem. ASME, Sigma Xi, Pi Tau Sigma.

KEZON, PETER P., assn. exec.; b. Chgo., Dec. 14, 1946; s. Peter P. and Elizabeth (Wanat) K.; B.B.A., Loyola U., Chgo., 1973; m. Diane M. Whelan, May 12, 1979. Staff coordinator Am. Bar Endowment, Chgo., 1973-77, asso. adminstr. charge fin. and planning, 1977—. 47th Democratic ward coordinator McGovern for Pres., Chgo., 1972. Served with U.S. Army, 1969-74. Roman Catholic. Home: 441 W Oakdale Ave Chicago IL 60657 Office: 1155 E 60th St Chicago IL 60637

KHABBAZ, NICHOLAS GEORGE, educator; b. Becharre, Lebanon, June 21, 1951; came to U.S., 1974, permanent resident, 1981; s. George and Marie (Succar) K.; M.S., U. Mich., 1975, Ph.D. in Computer Engring., 1980. Asst. prof. computer sci. Wayne State U., Detroit, 1980; asst. prof. info. systems U. Cin., 1980—. Mem. IEEE, Assn. Computing Machinery, Soc. Mgmt. Info. Systems, Sigma Xi. Office: Quantitative Analysis Dept Mail Location 130 U Cin Cincinnati OH 45221

KHAMBATA, ADI JEHANGIR, electronics engr., educator; b. Bombay, India, Apr. 8, 1922; s. Jehangir M. and Najoo J. (Vakil) K.; came to U.S., 1956, naturalized, 1959; B.A., U. Bombay, 1944; B.S.E.E. (R.D. Sethna scholar), Milw. Sch. Engring., 1950; m. Ruth Elizabeth Flopper, Mar. 7, 1954; children—Jimmy Adi, Soonoo Ruth, Danny Adi. Customer engr. IBM World Trade Corp., Bombay, 1953-55; jr. cons. Beacons Ltd., Bombay, 1955-56; with Sperry Univac div. Sperry Rand Corp., St. Paul, 1956-75, engring. mgr., 1965-69, staff engr., 1969-75; tchr. St. Paul Tech.-Vocat. Inst., 1960—; tchr. Ramsey Engring. Co., St. Paul, 1975-76, U. Minn., Mpls., summer 1978. Pres. Grove Elementary Sch. PTA, St. Paul Park, Minn., 1962-63. Mem. IEEE, Am. Mgmt. Assn., Aircraft Owners and Pilots Assn., Kappa Eta Kappa. Clubs: Southview Country (West St. Paul, Minn.); Rotary (St. Paul). Author: Introduction to Integrated Semiconductor Circuits, 1963 (German transl. 1968); Introduction to Large-scale Integration, 1969 (German transl. 1971, Japanese transl. 1970); Microprocessors/Microcomputers: Architecture, Software and Systems, 1982; Introduction to the ZILOG Z-80 Microcomputer, 1982. Home: 19 Cutler St Saint Paul MN 55119

KHAMIS, HARRY JOSEPH, statistician; b. San Jose, Calif., Dec. 20, 1951; s. Thomas Dodd and Joy (Rogers) K.; A.A., San Jose Community Coll., 1972; B.S., Santa Clara U., 1974; M.S., Va. Poly. Inst., 1976, Ph.D., 1980. Grad. teaching asst., statis cons. Va. Poly. Inst., 1974-80; asst. prof. statistics Wright State U., Dayton, Ohio, 1980—; cons. for research physicians. Recipient cert. of teaching excellence Va. Poly. Inst., 1978. Mem. Am. Statis. Assn., Biometric Soc. Clubs: Yugoslav, Miami Valley Folkdance (Dayton). Office: 420 Fawcett Hall Wright State U Dayton OH 45325

KHAN, MOHAMMED NASRULLAH, physiologist, veterinarian; b. Hyderabad, India, Oct. 11, 1933; s. Ghouse Mohammed and Hayath (Khatoon) K.; B.V.Sc., Osmania U., India, 1955; M.S., La. State U., 1963, Ph.D., 1970; m. Soraya Khan, Mar. 3, 1957; children—Mahmood, Faiz. Practice vet. medicine, Hyderabad, 1955-58; asst. lectr. Vet. Sch., Rajendranagar, 1958-61; research asst. La. State U., 1961-63, 67-70; instr. Vet. Colls., Hyderabad and Tirupati, 1963-67; asst. prof. City Colls. of Chgo., 1970-72; asso. prof. Lewis U., Schs. of Nursing South Chgo. Hosp., Little Company of Mary Hosp., and Michael Reese Hosp., Chgo., 1972-77; coordinator biology dept. Central YMCA Coll., Chgo., 1974; asst. prof. Truman Coll., 1977—. Mem. Andhra Pradesh Vet. Assn. (mng. com. 1960-61), AAUP, AAAS, World Poultry Sci. Assn. H.E.H. The Nizam's fellow, 1961; Ford Found. scholar U. Delhi, 1966; contbr. sci. articles to profl. jours. Home: 2904 W Greenleaf Ave Chicago IL 60645

KHARADIA, VIRABHAI CHELABHAI, economist; b. Laxmipura, Gujarat, India, Jan. 21, 1939; s. Chelabhai Manabhai and Joitiben Velabhai (Thumbadia) K.; came to U.S., 1969; B.Commerce (Nat. Merit scholar, V.Y. Kolhatkar gold medal), U. Baroda (India), 1964, M.Commerce (V.Y. Kolhatkar gold medal), 1966; M.S. in Econs. (Univ. fellow), 1971, Ph.D. (Univ. fellow), 1973; m. Kokila Kugasia, May 1955; children—Shanta, Geeta, Bharat. Lectr. banking U. Baroda, 1966-69; mem. faculty N.W. Mo. State U., Maryville, 1973—, prof. econs., 1977—, chmn. dept., 1979—. Mem. Am. Fin. Assn., Midwest Econs. Assn. Contbr. articles to profl. jours. Home: Route 4 Maryville MO 64468 Office: Northwest Missouri State Univ Maryville MO 64468

KHAZEI, AMIR HASSAN, surgeon; b. Tehran, Iran, Jan. 12, 1932; s. Gasem and Esmat (Khaligazam) K.; came to U.S., 1957, naturalized, 1968; B.S., U. Lausanne (Switzerland), 1953, M.D., 1957, Certificat d'Etude Medicale, 1957; m. Mona, June 20, 1958; children—Kimberly, Deborah, Brent, Eric. Intern in internal medicine Hospital Universitaire Nestle, Lausanne, 1955; intern in gen. surgery Centre Hospitalier de Nice (France), 1955; rotating intern Menorah Med. Center, Kansas City, Mo., 1957-58, jr. resident in gen. surgery, 1959-60; surgeon, mem. med. team Internat. Red Cross to Congo, 1961; asst. resident in gen. surgery U. Man. (Can.), Winnipeg, 1960-62, chief resident, teaching fellow in gen. surgery, 1962-63; asso. resident in thoracic and cardiovascular surgery U. Md., 1963-64, chief resident in thoracic and cardiovascular surgery, 1964-65; instr. U. Md. Hosp., 1965-68, asso. dir. shock trauma units, 1966-68; chief thoracic and cardiovascular surgery South Balt. Gen. Hosp., 1965-68; practice medicine, specializing in thoracic and cardiovascular surgery, Elgin, Ill., 1968—; mem. staff Sherman Hosp., St. Joseph Hosp., Elgin. Diplomate Am. Bd. Surgery, Am. Bd. Thoracic Surgery. Fellow A.C.S., Am. Coll. Chest Physicians; mem. AMA, Md. Surg. Soc., N.Y. Acad. Scis., Ill. State (Gold medal award 1969, Bronze award 1971), Kane County (Ill.) med. socs., Soc. Thoracic Surgeons, Am. Coll. Angiology, Am. Trauma Soc. Author: (with others) Biochemical Engineering Symposium, 1966; contbr. articles to profl. jours.; co-author profl. films. Home: Rural Route 3 Box 218 A Elgin IL 60120 Office: 860 Summit St Elgin IL 60120

KHO, EUSEBIO, surgeon; b. Philippines, Dec. 16, 1933; s. Joaquin and Francisca (Chua) K.: came to U.S., 1964; A.A., Silliman U., Philippines, 1955; M.D., State U. Philippines, 1960; fellow in surgery, Johns Hopkins, 1965-67; m. Grace C. Lim, May 24, 1964; children—Michelle Mae, April Tiffany, Bradley Jude, Jaclyn Ashley. Intern in surgery Balt. City Hosp., 1964-65, resident in gen. surgery, 1965-67; research asso. pediatric surgery U. Chgo. Hosps., 1967-68; resident in gen. surgery, then chief resident U. Tex. Hosp., San Antonio, 1968-70; hosp. surgeon St. Anthony Hosp., Louisville, 1970-72; practice medicine specializing in surgery, Scottsburg, Ind., 1972—; chmn. dept. surgery Scott County Meml. Hosp., 1973—; cons. surgeon Washington County Meml. Hosp., Salem, Ind., also Clark County Meml. Hosp., Jeffersonville, Ind., 1973—; courtesy surgeon Suburban Hosp., Louisville, 1973—; gen. surgeon U.S. Army Hosp., Louisville, 1980—. Served to maj. M.C., USAR, 1980—. Diplomate Am. Bd. Surgery. Fellow A.C.S.; mem. Am. Coll. Internat. Physicians (founding mem., trustee 1974—), AMA (Physician's Recognition award 1969, 72), Ind., Ky., Philippine med. assns., Internat. Coll. Surgeons, Soc. Philippine Surgeons in Am. (life), Assn. Philippine Practicing Physicians in Am. (life), Assn. Mil. Surgeons of U.S., Res. Officers Assn. of U.S. Presbyterian. Clubs: Optimists, Masons. Home: 14 Carla Ln Scottsburg IN 47170 Office: 137 E McClain Ave Scottsburg IN 47170

KHOOBLALL, KHEM LALL, cardiologist; b. Port-Louis, Mauritius, July 25, 1937; s. Motee Lall and Radhika (Neerunjun) K.; B.Sc., U. Cambridge (Eng.), 1956; M.D., Royal Coll. Surgeons Ireland, 1964; m. Navina Ramphul, July 23, 1977; 1 dau., Vanessa. Intern, Ellis Hosp., Schenectady, 1964-65; resident in internal medicine St. Kevins Hosp., Dublin, 1965-67, Regional Chest Hosp., Dublin, 1967-68, VA Hosp., Hines, Ill., 1968-69, Cleve. Clinic, 1969-73; fellow in clin. cardiology Cleve. Clinic Found., 1971-73, Univ. Hosp., Geneva, 1973-74; pvt. practice medicine, specializing in cardiology and internal medicine, Mauritius, 1974-80, Strongsville, Ohio, 1980—; mem. staff St. Vincent Charity Hosp., Cleve., Parma (Ohio) Community Gen. Hosp., Medina (Ohio) Community Gen. Hosp.; clin. tutor Loyola U., Chgo., 1968-69. Diplomate Royal Coll. Physicians (Ireland). Recipient Physicians' Recognition award AMA, 1971, 74, 77. Fellow Internat. Coll. Angiology, Am. Coll. Cardiology; mem. Am. Coll. Cardiology, Internat. Soc. Cardiology, Am. Coll. Angiology, Royal Soc. Health (London). Office: Parmatown Med Bldg South 6688 Ridge Rd Suite 1215 Parma OH 44129

KHOSH, JOHN GHOLAM HOSEIN, physician; b. Meshed, Iran, Apr. 21, 1929; s. Hessam and Fatemeh (Tabas) Khoshnevisan; came to U.S., 1957, naturalized, 1970; M.D. summa cum laude, U. Meshed, 1955; postgrad. U. Pa., 1960; m. Mary Nell Sivert, Sept. 1, 1961; children—Sheila June, Deanna June, Lisa June, Lora June. Intern, Cook County Hosp., Chgo., 1957-58; resident in surgery Deaconess Hosp., Cleve., 1959-60, in ob-gyn St. Thomas Hosp., Akron, 1959-62, in pathology St. Joseph's Hosp., Hamilton, Ont., 1962-63, in surgery Hamilton Gen. Hosp., 1963-64; practice medicine specializing in ob-gyn, Strongsville, Ohio, 1965—; mem. staff Fairview Gen. Hosp., Cleve., S.W. Gen. Hosp. Diplomate Am. Bd. Ob-Gyn. Fellow Am. Coll. Ob-Gyn; mem. Am. Soc. Laparoscopists, Am. Fertility Soc., Cleve. Acad. Medicine, Cleve. Obstetrics and Gynecol. Soc., Ohio Med. Assn. Democrat. Club: Rotary. Office: 12563 Pearl Rd Strongsville OH 44136

KHOSH, MARY SIVERT, psychologist; b. Akron, Ohio, July 28, 1942; d. Floyd Calvin and Mattie Paul (Milwee) Sivert; B.A., U. Akron, 1966, M.S., 1970; Ph.D., Kent State U., 1976; m. John G. H. Khosh, Sept. 1, 1961; children—Sheila June, Deanna June, Lisa June, Lora June. Career counselor Baldwin-Wallace Coll., Berea, Ohio, 1974-75, asst. dir. counseling and advising center, 1975-76, asso. dir., 1976-78, dir., 1978-80, dir. career counseling and field experience, 1980—, dir. articulation project, 1976-77; practice psychology, 1977—; cons. in field. Vice pres. SW Gen. Hosp. Jr. Bd., Berea, 1969; guest organist Akron United Meth. Ch., 1961. Mem. SW Gen. Hosp. Med. Wives, 1966-76, pres. 1968-70, Am., Ohio, Cleve. psychol. assns., Cleve. Cons. Psychol. Assn., Nat., Ohio assns. women deans, adminstrs. and counselors, Am. Personnel and Guidance Assn., Am. Coll. Personnel Assn., Fairview Gen. Hosp. Women's Aux. Democrat. Methodist. Contbr. articles to profl. jours. Office: #118 Adminstrn Bldg Baldwin-Wallace Coll Berea OH 44017

KHWAJA, JAVAID RASHID, economist; b. Delhi, India, Jan. 11, 1942; s. Ghulam Jilani and Fatima (Begum) K.; B.A., U. Panjab, Lahore, Pakistan, 1960; M.A., Duke U., 1968, Ph.D., 1978. Lectr. econs. Govt. Intermediate Coll., Jhelum, Pakistan, 1962-63; probationary officer United Bank Ltd., Karachi, Pakistan, 1963-64; research officer Social Sci. Research Center, U. Panjab, Lahore, 1964-65; asst. prof. East Carolina U., Greenville, N.C., 1968-69; research analyst Community Action Agy., Akron, Ohio, 1977; asst. prof. econs. U. Akron, 1978, Ohio No. U., Ada, 1979-80; dir. Pakistan Inst. Econ. Research, 1980—; cons. Research Triangle (N.C.) Inst. Mem. Pakistan Am. League, Am. Econ. Assn., Econometric Soc., Am. Cultural Assn., Assn. Voluntary Action Scholars. Muslim. Home: 725 Excelsior St Apt 4 Akron OH 44306

KIANI, REZA, physician; b. Shahmirzad, Iran, Feb. 23, 1939; s. Farjollah and Salemeh K.; came to U.S., 1968, naturalized, 1973; M.D., Pahlavi U., Iran, 1966; m. Mashid Z. Kiani; children—Katayoun, Maryam, Cyrus, Daryoush. Rotating intern New Rochelle (N.Y.) Hosp., 1968-69; resident in internal medicine U. Cin. Gen. Hosp., 1969-70, sr. resident in internal medicine, 1970-71; fellow in endocrinology and metabolism Northwestern U. Med. Center, Chgo., 1971-72; fellow in endocrinology and metabolism, instr. medicine, U. Ill. Med. Center, Chgo., 1972-73, asso. in medicine, 1973-74, asst. prof. medicine, attending physician, 1974-79, asso. prof. clin. medicine, 1979—; practice medicine specializing in endocrinology and metabolism, Chgo., 1974—; dir. outpatient clinic emergency room, cons. endocrinology, and metabolism Community Gen. Hosp., Sterling, Ill., 1973-74. Recipient Pilz award, Tchr. of Yr. award U. Ill. Hosp./W. Side VA Hosp., 1979; diplomate Am. Bd. Internal Medicine. Mem. AMA, (Physician Recognition award, 1971, 73-76), A.C.P. Contbr. articles to med. jours. Home: 360 Versailles Dr Northbrook IL 60062 Office: Dept Medicine Abraham Lincoln Sch Medicine 840 S Wood St PO Box 6998 Chicago IL 60680

KIBBE, JOHN CARTER, lawyer; b. California, Mo., Nov. 2, 1924; s. Edgar Allen and Bess (Carter) K.; student Central Coll., Fayette, Mo., 1941-43, Oreg. U., 1943; A.B., Mo. U., 1948, LL.B., 1950; m. Barbara Hadley, Dec. 26, 1950; children—Ann Kibbe Matthews, John David, Barbara Jane Blank. Admitted to Mo. bar, 1950; since practiced in California, pros. atty. Moniteau County, 1951-64; spl. counsel City of California, 1963-65, city atty., 1965-70; v.p., gen. counsel Moniteau Mills, Inc., 1964-72, pres., 1972-75; mem. firm Kibbe, Kay & Cartwright and predecessor firm, California, Mo., 1973—; pres. Mo. Abstract Co., California, 1974-77, Mo. Abstract & Title Co., 1980—; dir. The Farmers & Traders Bank; mem. bar com. 26th Jud. Circuit, 1962-70. Chmn. adv. com. trust Elia B. Paegelow; trustee Wood Place Library, 1969—. Served from pvt. to technician AUS, 1943-46. Mem. Am., Moniteau County bar assns., Assn. Trial Lawyers Am., Mo. Integrated Bar, Mo. Assn. Trial Attys., Acad. Polit. Sci., Am. Acad. Polit. and Social Sci., VFW (comdr. Post 4345, 1967-68), Am. Judicature Soc., Am., Mo., Moniteau County (dir. 1966) hist. socs., Alumni Assn. Mo. U. (chmn. Moniteau County 1964—), Internat. Soc. Law and Sci., Internat. Platform Assn., Order High Priesthood Mo., Phi Alpha Delta, Alpha Phi Omega. Mem. Christian Ch. (trustee). Club: Masons (past master). Home: Lake St California MO 65108 Office: Kibbe Kay & Cartwright California MO 65108

KICKELS, MARY KAY, coll. adminstr.; b. Chgo., Aug. 16, 1939; d. Gordon J. and Florence M. (McGraw) Kickels; B.A., Rosary Coll., River Forest, Ill., 1961; M.A., Cath. U. Am., 1966; postgrad. (Ford Found. fellow) George Washington U., 1972-73; Ed.D., No. Ill. U., 1982; m. Donald L. Chase, Nov. 8, 1975. Chmn. dept. speech/theatre Nazareth High Sch., La Grange, Ill., 1961-71; media program coordinator/producer, writer Ill. Office of Edn., Springfield, 1971-72; asso. researcher Council Chief State Sch. Officers, Washington, 1972-73; asst. dir. Ednl. Facilties Center, Chgo., 1973-74; chmn. inter-visions dept. Triton Coll., River Grove, Ill., 1975-78, dir. admissions, 1978-79; asst. dean of students, 1979-81, dean Sch. of Univ. Transfer, 1981—; cons. humanities div. Ency. Brit., 1975—; spl. workshop leader Chgo. Consortium Colls. and Univs., 1974—; mktg. cons., mem. Johnson & Assos.; lectr. women's programs and women in mgmt. Adv. bd. Nat. Indian Employment Council, 1977—; mem. nat. identification program Am. Council on Edn., 1981—. Danforth Found. grantee, 1971. Mem. AAHE, Nat. Assn. Curriculum Devel., Assn. Gen. and Liberal Studies, AACJC, Nat. Assn. ednl. Tech., Phi Delta Kappa, Rosary Coll. Alumni Assn. (sec., bd. dirs.). Scriptwriter endl. films. Home: 3 N 658 Woodland Dr West Chicago IL 60185 Office: 2000 5th Ave River Grove IL 60171

KIDDER, RONALD CURTIS, psychologist; b. Lansing, Mich., July 9, 1948; s. Thomas Alva and Agnes Maria (Schaible) K.; B.S., Mich. State U., 1970, M.A., 1972, Ph.D., 1976; m. Tefra Robinson, June 13, 1970; 1 son, Aaron Curtis Kidder. Teaching asst. and research asst. Mich. State U., E. Lansing, 1970-75; psychologist Muskegon (Mich.) Regional Center, 1976-78, chief psychologist, 1979—; cons. in field. Lic. psychologist, Mich. Mem. AAUP, Am. Psychol. Assn., Am. Assn. on Mental Deficiency, AAAS, Mich. Assn. Profl. Psychologists, Sigma Xi, Phi Kappa Phi, Psi Chi. Home: 416 Glen Oaks St Apt 2B Muskegon MI 49442 Office: 1903 Marquette St Muskegon MI 49442

KIDDLE, LAWRENCE BAYARD, educator; b. Cleve., Aug. 20, 1907; s. Bayard Taylor and Emma Melvina (Volmar) K.; B.A. magna cum laude, Oberlin (Ohio) Coll., 1929; M.A., U. Wis. at Madison, 1930, Ph.D., 1935; m. Allene Cornelia Houglan, June 29, 1932; children—Sue (Mrs. Edward Frederick Meyer), Mary Ellen. Teaching asst. Spanish and French, U. Wis., 1929-35; instr. U. N.Mex., Albuquerque, 1935-37, asst. prof., 1937-38; instr. Spanish, Princeton, 1938-40; asst. prof. Romance langs. Tulane U., New Orleans, 1940-41, asso. prof., 1941-43; asst. prof. Spanish, Romance linguistics U. Mich., Ann Arbor, 1947-48, asso. prof., 1948-54, prof., 1954-78, prof. emeritus, 1978—. Fulbright prof. linguistics Instituto Caro y Cuervo, Bogota, Colombia, 1963-64. Served to lt. comdr. USNR, 1943-47. Decorated comandante Orden Militar De Ayacucho (Peru). Mem. Hispanic Soc. Am. (corr.), Modern Lang. Assn. Am., Am. Assn. Tchrs. Spanish and Portuguese (pres.), Linguistic Soc. Am. Democrat. Editor: (with J.E. Englekirk) Los de Abajo (Mariano Azuela), 1939; Veinte Cuentos Hispanoamericanos del Siglo Veinte, 1956; El Libro de Las Cruzes (Alfonso El Sabio), 1961; Cuentos Americanos y Algunas Poesias, 1970; La Barraca (Blasco Ibanez), 1961. Home: 2654 Englave Dr Ann Arbor MI 48103

KIEFER, JOSEPH HENRY, med. educator; b. Chgo., Aug. 20, 1910; s. Michael Nicholas and Mary Anna (Seiler) K.; B.S., Northwestern U., 1931, B.M., 1934, M.D., 1935; m. Marie Manning Kinser, July 7, 1945; children—Joseph Henry, Harry K., Marianna S. Intern, then resident urology Cook County Hosp., Chgo., 1935-37; pvt. practice urol. surgery, Chgo., 1937-73; mem. faculty U. Ill. Coll. Medicine, 1937—, prof. urology, 1944-78, prof. emeritus, 1978—, chmn. div., 1945-60, acting chmn. div., 1968-71; sr. cons. Univ. Ill. Hosps., 1971—; mem. emeritus staffs St. Joseph Hosp., Augustana Hosp., 1971—; Belfield lectr. Chgo. Urol. Soc., 1971. Recipient Distinguished Service award U. Ill. Dept. Surgery, 1959; Centennial award St Joseph Hosp., Chgo., 1969; Alumni Service award DePaul U., Chgo., 1972. Mem. AMA, A.C.S., Ill. (sci. exhibit award 1957), Chgo. (past pres. N. Shore br.) med. socs., Inst. Medicine Chgo., Am. Urol. Assn. (1st prize med. history exhibit 1970, Wirt B. Dakin award 1971), Chgo. Urol. Soc. (past pres.), Am. Assn. Genito-Urinary Surgeons, Soc. Internat. d'Urologie, Soc. Univ. Urologists, Soc. Pediatri Urology, Urology Corr. Club, Soc. Med. History Chgo. (pres. 1978-80), Am. Assn. History Medicine, AAAS, Soc. Internat. d'Histoire de Medicine, Ill. Soc. Med. Research, Catholic Physicians Guild Chgo. (past pres.), Chgo. Historians Medicine and Sci., Sigma Xi. Club: Caxton (Chgo.). Author and editor: Davis Memorial Volumne in Medicine History, 1965. Contbr. numerous articles to profl. jours. Donor, Joseph H. Kiefer collection of 2500 books on history of urology and medicine to U. Ill. Library Med. Scis. Home: 1240 W North Shore Ave Chicago IL 60626

KIEFER, WILLIAM LEE, computer mktg. exec.; b. St. Louis, Aug. 19, 1946; s. A.A., St. Louis Community Coll., 1971; B.S., U. Mo., St. Louis, 1975; m. Joyce Ann Cwiklowski, Aug. 15, 1970; children—Jason Lee, William Andrew. Ins. agt. Liberty Mut. Ins. Co., St. Louis, 1973-75; Democratic dir. elections City of St. Louis, 1975; mktg. specialist GAF Corp., Lincolnwood, Ill., 1976-79; now with Microdata Corp., St. Louis. Ward committeeman Dem. party City of St. Louis, 1976-79, mem. ward steering com., 1974-79, campaign mgr., 1974-76. Served with USMC, 1965-69. Mem. Internat. Computer Consultants Assn., Engring. Reprographics Soc., Data Processing Mgmt. Assn., St. Louis Jaycees, North Park Neighborhood Assn. (chmn.), Assn. Computer Users, VFW, Am. Legion, Am. Vets., U. Mo.-St. Louis Alumni Assn., U. Mo.-St. Louis Bus. Alumni Assn. (pres. 1980-81). Democrat. Roman Catholic. Clubs: Sargents, St. Louis Advt. Home: 1656 Grape St Saint Louis MO 63147 Office: Microdata Corp 1864 Craig Rd Saint Louis MO 63141

KIEHM, TAE GEE, physician; b. Seoul, Korea, Mar. 12, 1944; s. Byung-Ho and Pil Kyo (Kim) K.; M.D., Seoul Nat. U., 1968; m. Hee Cheong Shin, Apr. 15, 1972; children—Kelly J., Brady J. Resident in internal medicine Bklyn.-Cumberland Med. Center, 1973-75; fellow in endocrinology U. Ky. Med. Center, Lexington, 1975-77; practice medicine specializing in internal medicine and med. endocrinology, Mishawaka, Ind., 1977—; attending physician St. Joseph's Hosp., Mishawaka, Ind., Meml. Hosp., South Bend, Ind., 1977—. Served to 1st lt. Republic of Korea Air Force, 1968-71. Diplomate Am. Bd. Internal Medicine. Mem. AMA, A.C.P., Am. Soc. Internal Medicine, St. Joseph County Med. Soc. Research on correlation between high fiber-high carbohydrate diet in diabetic patient. Home: 50700 Trails North Granger IN 46530 Office: 303 S Main St Mishawaka IN 46544

KIELY, PATRICK JAMES, state legislator, investment broker; b. Anderson, Ind., Sept. 23, 1951; s. William Griffin and Mary Louise (Doyle) K.; B.S., Ball State U., 1973; student U. Notre Dame, 1976-78; m. Mary Patricia Harrold, Aug. 31, 1974; 1 son, Ryan Patrick. Dir. research Anderson C. of C., 1973-77, exec. v.p., 1978; account exec. Thomson & McKinnon Securities, Anderson, 1978—. Mem. Ind. Ho. Reps., 1978—, mem. ways and means com., ins. and corps. com., chmn. sch. fin. Named Outstanding Freshman Legislator of Yr., 1979; registered rep. Security Exchange Commn.; commodity license Chgo. Bd. Trade. Mem. Anderson C. of C., Beta Theta Pi. Republican. Roman Catholic. Clubs: K.C., Chesterfield Optomists. Home: 2304 Beth St Anderson IN 46011 Office: 936 Meridian St Anderson IN 46015

KIENTZ, WILLIAM DESHLER, ins. exec.; b. Columbus, Ohio, May 18, 1922; s. Harvey A. and Goldie (Deshler) K.; B.S. in Indsl. Engring., Ohio State U., 1947; m. Jean Bonner, Feb. 28, 1952; children—William Deshler II, Andrew B. Engr., FIA, Columbus, 1947-51; partner McElroy Minister Agy., Columbus, 1951-77; founder, pres., chmn. Kientz & Co., Columbus, 1977—, Crump Kientz Co., 1977—, Kientz Corp., 1981—. Chmn. trustees First Congregational Ch., 1965-66; chmn. Citizens Research Inc. Served with AUS, 1943-47; ETO. Decorated Bronze Star. Mem. Ohio Agts. Assn. (v.p., trustee 1958-62), Nat. Assn. Casualty Surety Agts. (sec. 1981), Phi Gamma Delta. Clubs: Scioto Country (pres. 1981), Athletic (dir. 1965-70), Muirfield Country, Masons. Home: 2670 Edington Rd Columbus OH 43221 Office: 1328 Dublin Rd Box 451 Columbus OH 43216

KIEP, JOHN WILLIAM, state govt. ofcl.; b. Joliet, Ill., Feb. 11, 1930; s. John Michael and Ann Mary (Kaffer) K.; B.A. in Acctg., St. Ambrose Coll., Davenport, Iowa, 1953; M.S. in Bus. Adminstrn., No. Ill. U., DeKalb, 1967; m. Marjery June Seppi, Jan. 24, 1953; children—Michael John, Julie Ann. Controller, Amax Aluminium Extrusions, Inc., St. Charles, Ill., 1955-68; treas. BW Constrn. Co., Chgo., 1968-71; v.p., treas. Kaiser Ducett Corp., also Kaiser Ducett Internat., Inc., N. Aurora, Ill., 1971-77; mgr. fin., then mgr. fin. and spl. asst. to exec. dir. Ill. State Toll Hwy. Authority, Oak Brook, 1977-80, acting exec. dir., 1980—; instr. No. Ill. U., 1967-68, St. Dominic's Coll., St. Charles, Ill., 1968, Aurora Coll., 1970-71. Chmn., Wheaton (Ill.) Housing Commn., 1977-78; mem. Wheaton Plan Commn., 1978—; bd. dirs. Marianjoy Rehab. Hosp., Wheaton, 1978—, chmn., 1980—. Served with AUS, 1953-55. Mem. Nat. Credit Mgmt. Assn., Nat. Assn. Cost Accts., Am. Public Works Assn., Internat. Bridge, Tunnel and Turnpike Assn. Roman Catholic. Club: K.C. (3 deg.). Office: 2001 W 22d St Oak Brook IL 60521

KIEPERT, DONALD ROBERT, JR., pharmacist; b. Johnstown, Pa., Mar. 21, 1948; s. Donald Robert and Anna Jean (Escherich) K.; B.S., Purdue U., 1971, M.S., 1973, also postgrad.; m. Cathy Ann Jones, June 7, 1969; children—Christopher Todd, Matthew Robert. Resident pharmacy Ind. U., Indpls., 1971-72; grad. asst., football coach Purdue U., Lafayette, Ind., 1973-78, affiliate asst. prof. clin. pharmacy dept., 1973-78; dir. pharmacy Lafayette Home Hosp., 1973-78; tech. affairs asso. pharmacy Baxter Travenol Labs., Deerfield, Ill., 1978-79, clin. nutrition mgr. Travacare services, 1979-80, mgr. Travacare services, 1980—. Mem. Am. Soc. Hosp. Pharmacists, Am. Soc. Parenteral and Enteral Nutrition, Ind. Soc. Hosp. Pharmacists. Methodist. Club: Rotary. Contbr. articles to profl. jours. Home: 503 Mallard Ln Deerfield IL 60015 Office: Baxter Travenol Labs 6301 Lincoln Ave Morton Grove IL 60013

KIERNAN, EDWARD HENRY, mktg. exec.; b. Bronx, Nov. 5, 1941; s. Edward and Ester (Savola) K.; B.S., N.Y. U., 1964, M.B.A., 1967; m. June 17, 1964; children—Edward, Kerry, Carolyn. With Colgate Palmolive, N.Y.C., 1966-69; product mgr. H.J. Heinz, Pitts., 1969-70; with Dow Chem. Co., Indpls., 1970—, mgr. mktg. services, 1980—. Mem. Assn. Nat. Advertisers (fin. com. 1980-81). Home: 795 Sugerbush Dr Zionsville IN 46077 Office: PO Box 68511 Indianapolis IN 46268

KIESEWETTER, FRANK HOWARD, ret. design engr.; b. Covington, Ky.; s. Frank John and Lynda (Pursifull) K.; student U. Cin.; B.S. in Engring., U. Ky.; m. Evelyn Vaught Cundiff (dec.); 1 son by previous marriage, Frank Reid. Ret. sr. design engr. Emery Industries, Cin. Past pres. Green Twp. Sch. Bd.; past v.p. Oak Hill Bd. Edn., recipient Appreciation plaque; active Boy Scouts Am.; mem. dist. com. Henry Clay Meml. Found. Served to maj. USAF, World War II. Recipient Scouter award. Registered profl. engr., Ohio. Mem. Am. Soc. Heating, Refrigeration d Air-Conditioning Engrs., U. Ky. Alumni Assn. (life), Blue Grass Trust Hist. Preservation, Nat. Buckley Hills Audubon socs., Demolay Legion of Honor, Cin. Opera Guild, Ky. Admirals, Ky. Civil War Round Table, Nat. Hist. Soc., Nat. Trust for Historic Preservation, Met. Opera Guild, Lexington Mus. Theatre, Central Ky. Concert and Lecture Series, U.S.S. Constitution Mus. Found., Res. Officers Assn., Boat Owners Council Am. (charter). Presbyn. (deacon, trustee). Mason. Club: Spindletop Hall Country. Home: Via Manor 7370 State Route 128 Apt 1C Cleves OH 45002

KIETHLINE, DAVID RAY, cons. engr.; b. Berwick, Pa., June 20, 1942; s. Charles Willard and Bernice (Curwood) K.; student Pa. State U., 1960-61; B.T. in Structural Engring., Washington U., St. Louis, 1974; m. Katherine Sue Claxton, July 12, 1964; children—Charles David, Brian Scott, Rebecca Sue. Draftsman, Sterling Aluminum Products, St. Charles, Mo., 1962-63, Maran & Assos., 1963-66, resident engr., 1969-72; design engr. Maran Cooke, Inc., St. Charles, 1972-74, exec. v.p., 1974-78; prin. Ingram, Kiethline, Wehmeyer, Inc., St. Charles, 1978—; v.p. Roberts Engring., Inc., 1980—; pres. WIK Constrn., Inc., 1981—. Mem. St. Charles Bicentennial Commn., 1975-76; bd. dirs. Wonderland Camp for Handicapped in Mo.; v.p. Nat. Ch. Residences of St. Charles, 1978—; chmn. steering com. Sect. 202 Housing for Elderly. Served with U.S. Army, 1966-69. Registered profl. engr., Mo., W.Va., Miss., Pa., Oreg. Mem. Nat. Soc. Profl. Engrs., Mo. Soc. Profl. Engrs., Cons. Engrs. Council, Am. Forestry Assn., Mo. Water Pollution Control Assn., Am. Water Works Assn., St. Charles Jaycees (pres. 1975-76, Keyman for Mo. 1975). Methodist. Home: 613 Concordia Ln Saint Charles MO 63301 Office: 6 Westbury Dr Saint Charles MO 63301

KILBURN, RICHARD FRIEND, veterinarian; b. Lodi, Ohio, July 13, 1944; s. Friend Le Roy and Stella Julia (Larsen) K.; D.V.M., Iowa State U.. 1968; m. Mary Helen Osth, May 26, 1968; children—Erin Leigh, David Friend. Asso. veterinarian Belmont (Mass.) Animal Hosp., 1968-70, Bulger Animal Hosp., North Andover, Mass., 1970-71; owner, mgr. County Line Animal Hosp., Naperville, Ill., 1971—, Our Animal Hosp., Chgo., 1972-74; dir. Emergency Vet. Services, Ltd., 1976—, sec., 1977—, treas., 1978—. Councilor, Juvenile Probation of DuPage County, 1976-77. Mem. AVMA, Ill. (People-to-People del.), DuPage vet. med. assns., Am. Animal Hosp. Assn. (asso.), Vet. Radiol. Soc. Republican. Methodist. Clubs: Bus. Men's Flying (dir. 1979-80), Flying Veterinarian, Kiwanis (pres. Naperville chpt. 1977-78, dir. 1950-81, lt. gov.). Home: 2204 S Washington St Naperville IL 60540 Office: 2200 S Washington St Naperville IL 60540

KILCREASE, MYRTLE ALLEN, educator; b. Howell, Ky.; d. Brentis and Estell (Coleman) Allen; A.B., Ky. State Coll., 1954; M.Ed., Loyola U., Chgo., 1977; postgrad. Chgo. Tchrs. Coll., 1956-59, Nat. Coll. Edn., 1972-74, U. London, summer 1976; m. James W. Kilcrease, Aug. 5, 1961. Elem. tchr. Chgo. Bd. Edn., 1955-72, reading resource tchr., 1972-78, reading specialist Access to Excellence, 1978—. Recipient Tchr. of Yr. award Hookway Elem. Sch. P.T.A., Chgo., 1969; Reading Resource Tchr. award Chgo. Bd. Edn., 1973. Mem. Internat. Reading Assn., Ill. Reading Council, Assn. Supervision and Curriculum Devel. Conglist. Contbr. articles in field to profl. publs.

KILDEE, DALE E., congressman; b. Flint, Mich., Sept. 16, 1929; s. Timothy Leo and Norma Alicia (Ullmer) K.; B.A., Sacred Heart Sem., 1952; tchr.'s certificate U. Detroit, 1954; M.A., U. Mich., 1961; postgrad. (Rotary Found. fellow) U. Peshawar (Pakistan), 1958-59; m. Gayle Heyn, Feb. 27, 1965; children—David, Laura, Paul. Tchr., U. Detroit High Sch., 1954-56, Flint Central High Sch., 1956-64; mem. Mich. Ho. of Reps. from 81st Dist., 1964-74; mem. Mich. Senate from 29th dist., 1975-76; mem. 95th-97th Congresses from 7th Mich. dist., 1977—. Mem. Am. Fedn. Tchrs., Urban League, Phi Delta Kappa. Clubs: K.C., Optimists. Home: 1434 Jane Ave Flint MI 48506 Office: 314 Cannon House Office Bldg Washington DC 20515 also 400 N Saginaw St Flint MI 48502

KILEY, DAN EDWARD, psychologist; b. Pontiac, Ill., Nov. 10, 1942; s. Jerome and Genevieve Agnes (Monahan) K.; B.S., St. Ambrose Coll., 1964; M.A., U. Ill., 1966, Ph.D., 1969; m. Nancy Garlock, Feb. 13, 1978; 1 son, D. Patrick. Psychology intern VA Hosp., Danville, Ill., 1966-68; research asst. U. Ill., 1967, counselor, 1968; staff psychologist Mental Health Clinic, Danville, 1969; psychologist, adminstr. Ill. Dept. Corrections, 1970-75, staff cons., 1977; therapist Ill. Wesleyan U., 1975; pvt. practice clin. psychology, Decatur, Ill., 1977-81, Wheaton, Ill., 1981—. Mem. Ill. Psychol. Assn., Am. Psychol. Assn. Contbr. articles to profl. jours., nat. mags. Office: Suite 201 213 W Wesley St Wheaton IL 60187

KILEY, JAN, broadcasting research exec.; b. Urbana, Ill., Jan. 31, 1952; d. George Lowell and Jeanne Adaline (Grismer) K.; B.A. cum laude with distinction, U. Ill., 1974. Research asst. Midwest TV, Inc., Stas.-WCIA-TV, Champaign, Ill., WMBD-AM-TV and WKZW-FM, Peoria, Ill., KFMB-AM-FM-TV, San Diego, 1969-74, researcher, 1974-75, dir. research, 1975—. Counselor, Illini Girls State, 1971, staff advisor, asst. to dir., sec. corp., 1972-76. Mem. Am. Assn. Public Opinion Research, Midwest Assn. Public Opinion Research, Am. Mktg. Assn. (bd. dirs. Central Ill.), Ill. News Broadcasters Assn., Am. Women in Radio and TV (pres. River City chpt.), AAUW, Alpha Lambda Delta, Kappa Delta Pi, Phi Alpha Theta, Phi Kappa Phi. Methodist. Clubs: Order Eastern Star, Am. Legion Aux. (pres. club 1976-77). Home: 715 S Lynn Champaign IL 61820 Office: 509 S Neil Champaign IL 61820

KILGARIN, KAREN DENISE, state senator; b. Omaha, Mar. 12, 1957; d. Bradford Michael and Verna Jane (Will) K.; B.A. in Polit. Sci. and Journalism, Kearney State Coll., 1979. Agt., Real Estate Assos., Omaha, 1979—; mem. Nebr. Senate, 1980—. Trustee, Nebr. State Coll., 1977. Mem. Nat. Assn. Realtors, Nebr. Assn. Realtors, Omaha Bd. Realtors, Omaha Women's C. of C., Omaha Jaycees. Clubs: S.E. Civic, Q-Street Mchts. Office: State Capitol Lincoln NE 68509

KILGORE, JAMES COLUMBUS, educator; b. Ansley, La., May 2, 1928; s. James Wilson and Ruth B. (Armstrong) K.; B.A., Wiley Coll., 1952; M.A. in English, U. Mo. at Columbia, 1963; m. Alberta Gunnels, June 20, 1960; children—Steven, Sheila, Kenneth. Instr., English, Langston High Sch., Hot Springs, Ark., 1954-58, A.M. and N. Coll., Pine Bluff, Ark., 1958-59, Fairlawn (N.J.) High Sch., 1959-60, Central High Sch., Hayti, Mo., 1960-61; instr. Southwest High Sch., Kansas City, Mo., 1963-66; prof. English, Cuyahoga Community Coll., Cleve., 1966—; adj. prof. Afro-Am. lit. Akron (O.) U., 1972; cons. in field, lectr. Black lit. Participant Bread Loaf Writers' Conf., 1970, Cleve. State U. Poetry Center, 1966—. Served with AUS, 1952-54. Recipient So. Edn. Found. award, 1957, Higginsbottom Found. award U. Mo., 1962, Clem award, 1978. Mem. Nat. Council Tchrs. English, MLA, Soc. Study Midwestern Lit., Internat. Platform Assn., Renaissance Soc. Am., Ohio Poets' Assn., Phi Beta Sigma. Baptist. Author poetry books. Contbr. numerous stories, articles, poems to mags. and jours. Home: 2531 Richmond Rd Beachwood OH 44122

KILGORE, JOE MOFFATT, editor; b. Clifton, Tex., Sept. 9, 1916; s. Walter Louis and Mary Alice (Gallagher) K.; B.J. magna cum laude, Temple U., 1950; M.S.J., UCLA, 1951; m. Cathryn McCormick, Feb. 4, 1965; 1 dau., Linda Kilgore Brandon. Mng. editor Three Sons Publ. Co., Niles, Ill., 1961—; realtors asso. Century 21 Grant, Assos., Inc., Lake Zurich, Ill. Mem. Constl. Amendment Conv., 1977. Served with USN, 1939-46. Mem. Nat. Assn. Realtors, Lake County Bd. Realtors. Home: 134 Eastwood Ln Route 4 Barrington IL 60010 Office: 6311 Grosse Pointe Rd Niles IL 60068

KILLENBERG, GEORGE ANDREW, editor; b. St. Clair County, Ill., Mar. 30, 1917; s. George W. and Lavinia Helen (Ruhl) K.; B.A., St. Louis U., 1954, M.A., 1958; m. Therese M. Murphy, June 3, 1943; children—George M., Mary C., John A., Terry M., Susan M. News bur. dir. St. Louis U. Athletic Dept., 1935-39; with Thomas W. Parr Corp., St. Louis, 1939-40; reporter St. Louis Globe-Democrat, 1941-50, day city editor, 1950-56, city editor, 1956-66, mng. editor, 1966-79, exec. editor, 1979—. Served with U.S. Army, 1942-46. Mem. Am. Soc. Newspaper Editors, A.P. Mng. Editors Assn., Mid Am. Press Inst. (chmn.), Sigma Delta Chi. Office: 710 N Tucker Blvd Saint Louis MO 63101

KILLIAN, WILLIAM PAUL, mfg. co. exec.; b. Sidney, Ohio, Apr. 26, 1935; s. Ray and Erie K.; B.Chem. Engring. with honors, Ga. Tech. Inst., 1957; M.Engring.-Adminstrn. with honors, U. Utah, 1968; m. Beverly Ann Buchanan, Sept. 7, 1957; children—William, Katherine, Michael. Chem. engr. Esso, Baton Rouge, 1957-58; mgr. research and devel. Thiokol Corp., Brigham City, Utah, 1958-64, project engring. dir., 1964-68; mgr. corp. project mgmt. Masonite Corp., Chgo., 1968-70, mgr. new bus. ventures, 1970-73; mgr. strategic planning, chem. and metall. group Gen. Electric Co., Columbus, Ohio, 1973-77; v.p. corp. planning and devel. Hoover Universal, Inc., Ann Arbor, Mich., 1977—. Mem. Assn. Corp. Growth, N. Am. Soc. Corp. Planners, Am. Mgmt. Assn., Mensa, Koseme Soc., Tau Beta Pi, Omicron Delta Kappa, Phi Kappa Phi, Pi Delta Epsilon, Phi Eta Sigma. Clubs: Travis Pointe Country, Ann Arbor Court, Liberty Racquet. Office: 825 Victors Way Ann Arbor MI 48104

KILLIGREW, MARY CATHERINE, food service mgmt. cons.; b. Gary, Ind., May 6, 1928; s. John William and Alvina Marie K.; B.S. in Dietetics, Rosary Coll., River Forest, Ill., 1950; M.S. in Instl. Adminstrn., Mich. State U., 1968. Intern in dietetics Good Samaritan Hosp., Cin., 1950-51; dietitian St. Lukes Hosp., Chgo., 1951-53; chief dietitian Ferguson-Droste-Ferguson Hosp., Grand Rapids, Mich., 1953-56; area mgr. sch. food service Gary Schs., 1957-58, dir. food service, 1958-69; sch. mgmt. cons. Mich. Dept. Edn., 1970-72, supr. child nutrition programs, 1972-75, editor food and nutrition newsletter, 1970-75; dir. sch. food service Penn-Harris-Madison Sch. Corp., Osceola, Ind., 1979; food service mgmt. cons., 1979—; cons AID, Panama, 1966; mem. adv. council Ind. Dept. Public Instrn.'s Div. Sch. Food and Nutrition Programs. Mem. Queen of Peace Parish Altar Soc., Osceola. Mem. Am. Dietetic Assn. (life), Am. Sch. Food Service Assn. (nat. exec. bd. 1969-71), Am. Home Econs. Assn., Ind. Sch. Food Service Assn. (pres. 1963-64), Ind. Dietetic Assn. Club: Altrusa (Gary). Contbr. articles to Sch Food Service Jour. Home: 610 Vistula Terr E 21 Mishawaka IN 46544

KILLINGBECK, JANICE LYNELLE (MRS. VICTOR LEE KILLINGBECK), journalist; b. Flint, Mich., Nov. 11, 1948; d. Leonard Paul and Ina Marie (Harris) Johnson; B.A., Mich. State U., 1970; postgrad. Delta Coll., 1971-72; m. Victor Lee Killingbeck, Sept. 26, 1970; children—Deeanna Dawn, Victor Scott. Tourist counselor Mich. Dept. State Hwys., Clare, 1969; copy editor Mich. State News, East Lansing, 1969-70; gen. reporter Midland (Mich.) Daily News, 1970; tchr. Saginaw (Mich.) Public Schs., 1971; public relations teller 1st State Bank of Saginaw, 1971-75; crew leader spl. census in Buena Vista Twp., Detroit Regional Office, U.S. Bur. Census, 1976, interviewer ann. housing survey-standard met. statis. areas, 1977-78, interviewer on-going health surveys, 1979—. Mem. Women in Communications, Sigma Delta Chi. Methodist. Home and Office: 4946 Hess Rd Saginaw MI 48601

KILLION, DIANE KELLEY, educator; b. Chgo., Apr. 18, 1946; d. Wayman E. and Hattie M. (Woosley) Kelley; B.S., So. Ill. U., 1970; M.A. (fellow), Washington U., St. Louis, 1975, postgrad., 1976-77; m. James H. Killion, III, July 27, 1968 (div. 1981); children—James Harrison IV, Kimya. Tchr., Sch. Dist. of University City (Mo.), 1970—; prin. Elem. Summer Study Center, University City, 1978; founder St. Paul Kinder-Coll., St. Louis, 1974, chmn. bd. dirs., 1974-75; coordinator community workshops for parents, 1978-79. Den leader St. Louis council Cub Scouts Am., 1978-79; 2d v.p. Nathaniel Hawthorne Sch. Parent-Tchr. Orgn., 1978-79. Mem. Mo. Fedn. Tchrs. (Membership Growth award 1979, sec. 1980—), Assn. Supervision and Curriculum Devel., University City Fedn. Tchrs. (pres. 1979—), Mo. State Labor Council, St. Louis Labor Council, Delta Sigma Theta. Methodist. Editor University City Union Tchr. Newsletter, 1979—. Home: 6953 Etzel St University City MO 63130 Office: 1351 N Hanley Rd University City MO 63130

KILLPACK, JAMES ROBERT, banker; b. Persia, Iowa, Aug. 11, 1922; s. James Marion and Dorothy (Divelbess) K.; B.S., Miami U., Oxford, Ohio, 1946; m. Norma Hewett, June 11, 1949; children—James, John, Steven. With Peat, Marwick, Mitchell & Co., Cleve., 1946-58; treas. Ferro Corp., Cleve., 1958-66; fin. v.p. Island Creek Coal Co., Cleve., 1966-68; dir. corp. planning Eaton Corp. (formerly Eaton Yale & Towne Inc.), Cleve., 1968-69, v.p. corp. planning, 1969, v.p. adminstrn., 1970, v.p. fin., 1970-78, exec. v.p. fin. and adminstrn., 1978; pres., dir. Nat. City Bank, Cleve., 1979, Nat. City Corp., 1981—; dir. Sherwin-Williams Co., 1979. Served with AUS, 1942-45. C.P.A., Ohio. Mem. Fin. Execs. Inst. (dir. Cleve. chpt., pres. 1970-71), Am. Inst. C.P.A.'s. Mem. Christian Ch. Clubs: Tavern, Union (Cleve.); Shaker Country (Shaker Heights, Ohio); Pepper Pike. Home: 13901 Shaker Blvd Cleveland OH 44120 Office: 1900 E 9 St 35th Floor Cleveland OH 44114

KILMAN, JAMES WILLIAM, cardiovascular surgeon, med. sch. and hosp. adminstr.; b. Terre Haute, Ind., Jan. 22, 1931; s. Arthur and Irene Louise (Piker) K.; B.S., Ind. State U., 1956; M.D., U. Ind., 1960; m. Priscilla Margaret Jackson, June 21, 1968; children—James W., Julia Ann, Jennifer Irene. Intern, U. Ind. Med. Center, Indpls., 1960-61, resident in cardiovascular surgery, 1961-66; asst. prof. surgery Ohio State U., Columbus, 1966-73, prof., 1973—, dir. div. thoracic surgery, 1976-80, pres. med. staff Univ. Hosp., 1975—; chmn. dept. thoracic surgery Children's Hosp., Columbus, pres., 1977—. Fellow A.C.S., Am. Coll. Cardiology, Am. Acad. Pediatrics, Am. Coll. Chest Physicians; mem. Acad. Medicine Columbus (pres.), Am. Surg. Assn. Republican. Presbyterian. Contbr. papers to profl. jours.; researcher cardiovascular bypass for infants and children and peripheral vascular flow. Home: 4231 Jackson Pike Grove City OH 43123

KILMORE, MEARL ANTHONY, physiologist, pharmacologist; b. Cumberland County, Pa., Jan. 24, 1937; s. Weir and Evelyn (Anthony) K.; B.S., Franklin and Marshall Coll., 1957; M.S., Jefferson Med. Coll., 1960, Ph.D., 1964; m. Hazel Catherine Derr, Sept. 4, 1957; children—Renee, Allen, Donna. Instr. physiology Temple U. Dental Sch., Phila., 1962-64; head performance sect. of nutrition br. U.S. Army Natick Labs., Natick, Mass., 1964-67; asst. prof. dept. pharmacology Coll. Osteo. Medicine and Surgery, Des Moines, 1967-70, asso. prof., 1970-72, prof. physiology and pharmacology, 1972—; cons. to Am. Osteo. Assn., 1974—; mem. adv. bd. for tng. med. secs. Des Moines Area Community Coll., 1977—. Mem. Am. Soc. Clin. Pharmacology and Therapeutics, Am. Coll. Clin. Pharmacology, Assn. for Gnotobiotics, Am. Assn. Lab. Animal Sci., Soc. for Exptl. Biology and Medicine, Am. Acad. Clin. Toxicology, Am. Coll. Toxicology, AAAS, Sigma Xi. Democrat. Mem. Christian Ch. Contbr. articles on exptl. medicine, pharmacology and phsiology to sci. jours. Home: 8409 Ridgemont Dr Urbandale IL 50322 Office: College Osteo Medicine and Surgery 3200 Grand Ave Des Moines IA 50312

KILPATRICK, PATRICIA BALDWIN, univ. ofcl.; b. Cleve., May 19, 1927; d. Leland Stanford and Agnes Mildred (Sweeney) Baldwin; student Ohio Wesleyan U., 1945-47; A.B., Case Western Res. U., 1949, M.A., 1951; m. Rufus Hall Kilpatrick, June 9, 1951; children—Timothy Leland, Catherine Louise, Rufus Hall III. Tchr., Lorain (Ohio) High Sch., 1951-52; instr. Case Western Res. U., Cleve., 1962-65, asst. prof. phys. edn., 1965-72, chmn. dept., 1970-72, asst. dean Flora Stone Mather Coll., 1965-72, asso. dean univ., 1972-77, asst. sec. univ., 1977-79, sec., 1979—. Layreader, Episcopal Ch., 1972—, mem. council Ohio Diocese, 1977, v.p. council, 1979, mem. various coms. Mem. Nat. (profl. standing com.), Ohio (treas. 1965-67, 79—) assns. women deans, adminstrs. and counselors, AAHPER, Kappa Alpha Theta (coll. dist. pres. 1965-67). Contbr. sect. to Ency. Edn., 1970. Home: 33 Division St Hudson OH 44236 Office: Case Western Res U 2040 Adelbert Rd Cleveland OH 44106

KILSDONK, MARTIN SEXTON, mfrs.' rep.; b. Detroit, June 3, 1926; s. Martin J. and Catherine Ann (Sexton) K.; B.S. in Mech. Engring., U. Notre Dame, 1947; m. Catherine Lee Considine, Nov. 8, 1958; children—Martin W., James R. Mgmt. trainee Clark Equipment Co., 1947-50; systems analyst Ford Motor Co., 1950-55;

sales engr. Rollway Bearing Co., 1955-58; dist. mgr. Kaydon Engring. Corp., 1958-61; mfrs. rep. F.W. Lynch Co., Southfield, Mich., 1961—, dir., 1968—. Served with USN, 1944-46, 51-53. Mem. Soc. Automotive Engrs. Roman Catholic. Clubs: Edgewood Country, Fairlane, Notre Dame. Home: 1832 Long Lake Shores Bloomfield Hills MI 48013 Office: PO Box 2089 Southfield MI 48037

KIM, CHUL, physician; b. Chon Ju City, Korea, Apr. 6, 1943; s. Kyu Seung and Boo Yong K.; M.D., Chon Nam U. Med. Sch., Kwang Ju, Korea, 1967; came to U.S., 1972, naturalized, 1978; m. Martha Meekyung Yoon, May 18, 1970; children—Isidor Jung-yoon, Paul Sug-yoon. Intern, Chon Nam U. Hosp., Kwang Ju, Korea, 1967-68; chief Imsil County Public Health Center, Chon Buk, Korea, 1971-72; physician Chon Buk Province Public Health Dept., Chon Buk, Korea, 1972; intern Shadyside Hosp., Pitts., 1972-73, resident in internal medicine, 1974-76, fellow in endocrinology and metabolism, 1976-78; practice medicine specializing in internal medicine, endocrinology and metabolism, Poplar Bluff, Mo., 1978—; mem. staff Poplar Bluff Hosp., Lucy Lee Hosp.; mem. adv. com. Ozark Foothills Home Health Agy. Served as capt. M.C., Korean Army, 1968-71. Lic. physician, Mo., Pa., Korea; diplomate Am. Bd. Internal Medicine. Mem. A.C.P., AMA, Mo. Med. Assn., Four County Med. Soc. Roman Catholic. Club: K.C. Home: 2143 Autumn Rd Poplar Bluff MO 63901 Office: 217 Oak St Poplar Bluff MO 63901

KIM, DONG-SOO, pediatrician; b. Korea, Aug. 8, 1940; s. Jong-Kwan and Mae-Saol (Shin) K.; came to U.S., 1966, naturalized, 1977; M.D., Chonnam Nat. U., Korea, 1966; m. Sook-Hee Kim, Dec. 9, 1972; children—Ihan, Seran. Intern, St. Peter's Hosp., Albany, N.Y., 1966-67; resident in pediatrics Springfield (Mass.) Hosp. Med. Center, 1967-69; research scientist Birth Defects Inst., N.Y. State Health Dept., Albany, 1969-73; staff physician Hillcrest Center, 1973-79, McPherson Community Health Center, Howell, Mich., 1973—; instr. Albany Med. Coll., 1969-72; asst. clin. prof. dept. human devel. Mich. State U. Diplomate Am. Bd. Pediatrics. Mem. AMA, Mich. Med. Soc., Am. Soc. Human Genetics, Am. Acad. Pediatrics. Contbr. articles in field to med. jours. Home: 510 Aberdeen Way Howell MI 48843 Office: 711 Byron Rd Howell MI 48843

KIM, EUHONG, radiologist; b. Seoul, Korea, Jan. 10, 1937; s. Dong Jin and Gil Su (Kwack) K.; came to U.S., 1969, naturalized, 1975; M.D., Seoul Nat. U., 1964; m. Suncho Kim, Mar. 30, 1978. Intern, Trumbull Meml. Hosp., Warren, Ohio, 1969-70; resident St. Elizabeth Hosp., Youngstown, Ohio, 1970-72, Youngstown Hosp. Assn., 1972-75; attending radiologist Providence Hosp., Sandusky, Ohio, 1975-77; dir. radiology dept. East Liverpool (Ohio) City Hosp., 1978—. Mem. AMA, Am. Coll. Radiology. Club: Kiwanis. Office: Dept Radiology East Liverpool City Hosp East Liverpool OH 43920

KIM, HYUNG KON, educator; b. Korea, Nov. 18, 1927; came to U.S., 1954, naturalized, 1968; s. Myung Hee and Aae Jin Kim; B.S., U. Wash., 1956, M.B.A., 1958, Ph.D., 1967; m. Bockim Im, Oct. 26, 1952; children—Lisa Hyangmi, Mimi Eunmi, Ronald Min. Faculty, U. Minn., Duluth, 1965—, prof. fin., internat. bus., 1973—, chmn. dept. bus. adminstrn., 1973-74, acting dean Sch. Bus. and Econs., 1974-75, asso. dean, 1978—, dir. M.B.A. program, 1978—. Bd. dirs. Miller-Dwan Hosp. and Med. Center, 1975—. Recipient Outstanding Bus. Faculty of Yr. award, 1970, cert. of appreciation Korean Bus. Adminstrn. Assn., 1972; research grantee U. Minn. Mem. Am. Fin. Assn., Fin. Mgmt. Assn., Midwest Fin. Assn. Presbyterian. Home: 3911 Rockview Ct Duluth MN 55804 Office: Sch Bus and Econs U Minn 2400 Oakland Ave Duluth MN 55812

KIM, MANOK, biochemist; b. Seoul, Korea, Mar. 1, 1936; came to U.S., 1965, naturalized, 1978; s. Changjern and Whasil (Hong) K.; B.S., Seoul Nat. U., 1960; M.Sc., U. Wis., 1976, Ph.D., 1979; m. Rhee Okkyung Lee; children—Julie, Allis, Jimmy. Research and devel. chemist Yu-Han Chem. Co., Seoul, Korea, 1962-66; med. technologist St. Mary's Hosp., Racine, Wis., 1966-69; tech. dir. Chem-Bio Co., Milw., 1979—. Mem. AAAS, Am. Chem. Soc., Am. Public Health Assn., Am. Assn. Clin. Chemistry, ASTM, Sigma Xi. Home: 5111 Denton Pl Madison WI 53711 Office: 140 E Ryan Rd Oak Creek WI 53154

KIM, MOON HYUN, physician, educator; b. Seoul, S. Korea, Nov. 30, 1934; s. Jae Hang and Kum Chu C. (Choi) K.; M.D., Yonsei U., 1960; m. Yong Cha Pak, June 20, 1964; children—Peter, Edward. Sr. Instr. obstetrics and gynecology Yonsei U., Seoul, 1967-68; intern Md. Gen. Hosp., Balt., 1961-26; resident in obstetrics and gynecology, Cleve. Met. Gen. Hosp., 1962-66; fellow in reproductive endocrinology U. Wash., Seattle, 1966-67, U. Toronto (Ont., Can.), 1968-70; asst. prof. obstetrics and gynecology, also chief endocrinology and infertility U. Chgo., 1970-74; asso. prof. obstetrics and gynecology Ohio State U., Columbus, 1974-78, prof., 1978—, chief div. reproductive endocrinology, 1974—. Recipient McClintock award U. Chgo., 1975; named Prof. of Yr., Ohio State U., 1976. Diplomate Am. Bd. Obstetrics and Gynecology. Fellow Am. Coll. Obstetrics and Gynecology; mem. Korean Med. Assn. Am. (chmn. sci. and edn. subcom. obstetrics and gynecology 1977—), Am. Fertility Soc., Chgo. Gynecol. Soc., Endocrine Soc., Soc. for Study of Reprodn., Soc. for Gynecol. Investigation, other orgns. Contbg. author books, contbr. articles to profl. publs. Home: 4331 Donington Rd Columbus OH 43220 Office: 410 W 10th Ave N-613 Columbus OH 43210

KIM, NHAK HEE, dentist; b. Seoul, Korea, Apr. 15, 1929; s. Chung Mok and Bo (Sung) K.: came to U.S., 1954, naturalized, 1972; D.D.S., Seoul Nat. U., 1951. postgrad. Baylor U., 1966; D.D.S., N.Y. U., 1959; m. Oak Sook Chun, June 29, 1957; children—Bill, Jim, Heidi. Asst. prof. dept. periodontics Baylor U., Dallas, 1966-67; pvt. practice dentistry, Muscatine, Iowa, 1970—; adj. asst. prof. U. Iowa, Iowa City, 1972—. Bd. dirs. Muscatine Shelter Work Shop. Mem. Am. Dental Assn., Am. Acad. Periodontology, Am. Coll. Dentists, Korean Acad. Periodontology (founder, pres. 1961). Club: Kiwanis. Home: 19 Colony Dr Muscatine IA 52761 Office: 502 Laurel Bldg Muscatine IA 52761

KIM, SUNG CHUL, mech. engr.; b. Seoul, Korea, Mar. 23, 1934; s. Yu Moon and Eun Dong (Sung) K.; came to U.S., 1957, naturalized, 1968; student Seoul Nat. U., 1953-56; B.S., Bradley U., 1960; M.S., U. Mo., 1962; m. Marilyn Hiroko Suzuki, June 26, 1964; children—Rodney James, Alice Kay. Sr. product engr. heat transfer ITT Bell & Gossett Co., Morton Grove, Ill., 1962—. Served with Korean Army, 1956-57. Mem. ASME, Am. Inst. Chem. Engrs., Korean Engrs. and Scientists Assn. in Am. Patentee in field. Home: 310 W Norman Ct Des Plaines IL 60016 Office: 8200 N Austin Ave Morton Grove IL 60053

KIM, YOU-SAH, surgeon; b. Nagoya, Japan, Feb. 25, 1941; s. Byung-Hun and Sook-Ja (Kang) K.; M.D., Kyungpook Nat. U., Daegu, Korea, 1965; m. Yang-Ja Lee, June 26, 1968; children—Ju-Hyun, Jung-Dong, Jae-Dong. Intern, St. Joseph Hosp., Chgo., 1969-70; resident in surgery Northwestern U. Med. Center, 1970-71, Loyola U. Affiliated Hosps. and VA Hosp., Hines, Ill., 1971-74; attending surgeon Northwoods Hosp., Phelps, Wis., 1974—; dir. Northwoods Hosp. Assn., 1974-79. Served with Republic of Korea Navy, 1966. Diplomate Am. Bd. Surgery. Fellow ACS; mem. AMA, State Med. Assn. Wis., Oneida-Vilas County Med. Assn. Presbyterian. Home: Route 1 Phelps WI 54554 Office: Northwoods Clinic Phelps WI 54554

KIMBALL, P. TOBIN, public relations exec.; b. Austin, Minn., Nov. 18, 1954; s. Paul Williams and Gwen Elizabeth (Lageson) K.; A.A., Normandale Coll., 1974; B.A., No. Ariz. U., 1976. Asst. public relations dir. Minn. Edn. Assn., St. Paul, 1973-75; asst. dir. Austin (Minn.) C. of C., 1975; sales mgr. KNAU Radio, Flagstaff, Ariz., 1975-76; v.p. public relations Delta Dental Plans, Mpls., 1976—; teaching cons. St. Cloud State U., 1978—. Mem. Public Relations Soc. Am., Sigma Delta Chi. Democratic/Farmer-Labor. Club: Tower. Home: 1200 Nicollet Mall Minneapolis MN 55403 Office: 4570 W 77th St Edina MN 55435

KIMBLE, M(ARCUS) ALLEN, minister, instn. adminstr.; b. Sussex, N.J., Oct. 30, 1920; s. Marcus Lynn and Wilhelmina (McConnell) K.; student U. Va. Law Sch., 1941-42; A.B., Wheaton Coll., 1943; M.Div., Princeton Theol. Sem., 1946; D.D., Lake Forest Coll., 1976; L.H.D., Nat. Coll. Edn., 1976; m. Sara Elizabeth Rogers, Aug. 28, 1945; children—Carolyn, Beverly. Ordained to ministry Presbyn. Ch.; asst. minister First Presbyn. Ch., Westfield, N.J., 1946-47; minister Presbyn. Ch., Lawrenceville, N.J., 1947-59, Calvary Presbyn. Ch., Wyncote, Pa., 1959-72; sr. v.p., now chmn. bd., chief exec. officer Presbyn. Home, Evanston, Ill.; master religion Lawrenceville Boys' Sch., 1947-54; moderator Presbytery of New Brunswick; vice moderator Synod of N.J.; mem. gen. assembly com. on budget rev. United Presbyn. Ch. U.S. Trustee Presbytery Phila., Presbytery Chgo. Clubs: Univ. (Chgo.); Westmoreland Country (Wilmette, Ill.). Contbr. articles to profl. jours. Home: 865 Hiawatha Ln Riverwoods IL 60015 Office: 3200 Grant St Evanston IL 60201

KIMBROUGH, DORIS DANIELS, telephone co. exec.; b. Wetumpka, Ala., Mar. 11, 1938; d. Thomas and Novella Naomi (Saxton) Daniels; B.S., Ala. State U., 1957; M.A., Webster Coll., 1978; children—Yolanda Leshell, Darlene Benita. Tchr. high sch. math. Linden (Ala.) Acad., 1957-59, Druid High Sch., Tuscaloosa, Ala., 1959-60, Wetumpka (Ala.) High Sch., 1960-62; cartographer Aero. Chart & Info. Center, St. Louis, 1962-67; sci. programmer/analyst Def. Mapping Agy., St. Louis, 1968-77; asst. staff mgr. data systems Southwestern Bell Telephone Co., St. Louis, 1977—. Vice-pres. Black Awareness Group, Def. Mapping Agy. Aerospace Center, 1971-72, chmn. exec. bd., 1971-72; bd. dirs. Ethical Soc. West, 1972; asst. adv. University City Girl Scouts, 1973; acctg. adv. Jr. Achievement Mississippi Valley, 1973; bd. dirs. Faith Acres, Inc., 1977-79. NSF scholar, 1952, Masonic/Eastern Star scholar, 1952-57. Mem. Assn. Computing Machines, Alpha Kappa Alpha. Baptist. Home: 8014 Malibou Ct University City MO 63130

KIMBROUGH, WILLIAM JOSEPH, library adminstr.; b. Bowling Green, Ky., Apr. 21, 1930; s. William Joseph and Mary Alice (Sexton) K.; A.B., Western Ky. U., 1952; M.A. in L.S., Ind. U., 1956; m. Ann Cecil Cornett, Nov. 25, 1954; children—Charles Madison, Howard David. Reference asst. Grosse Pointe (Mich.) Public Library, 1956-58; head librarian Sturgis (Mich.) Public Library, 1958-60; supr. adult services Lansing (Mich.) Public Library, 1960-66, chief librarian, 1966-69; asst. librarian, dir. public service Denver Public Library, 1970-75; dir. Mpls. Public Library and Info. Center, 1975—; chmn. program Minn. Gov.'s Conf. on Library and Info. Services, 1978. Served to 1st lt. U.S. Army, 1952-54. Mem. Am. Library Assn. (pres. library adminstrn. div. 1973-74), Mich. Library Assn. (pres. 1968), Minn. Library Assn., Minn. Assn. Continuing and Adult Edn. Clubs: Skylight, Ampersand (Mpls.). Editor: (with others) Requiem For The Card Catalog, 1979. Office: 300 Nicollet Mall Minneapolis MN 55401

KIMBROUGH, WILLIAM WALTER, III, psychiatrist; b. Cleve., Sept. 26, 1928; s. William Walter and Minerva Grace (Champion) K.; student Cornell U., 1945-46; B.S., U. Mich., 1948, M.D., 1952; m. Jo Ann Greiner, July 6, 1953; children—Elizabeth, Douglas. Intern, Ohio State U. Health Center, Columbus, 1952-53; resident U. Chgo. Clinics, 1955-56, Ypsilanti (Mich.) State Hosp., 1956-59; asso. psychiatrist U. Mich. Health Service, Ann Arbor, 1959-61; practice medicine specializing in psychoanalytic psychiatry, Ann Arbor, 1961—; cons. Atty. Gen. U.S., 1958—, Center for Forensic Psychiatry, 1974—, Brighton Found. for Alcoholism, 1961—, Washtenaw County (Mich.) Community Mental Health Services, 1978—, Mich. Dept. Social Services, 1978—. Served to col. USPHS(R), 1953-81. Recipient Physicians Recognition awards AMA, 1972-81. Fellow Am. Acad. Psychiatry and Law, Am. Soc. Psychoanalytic Physicians; mem. Am. Acad. Psychotherapists, Am. Psychiat. Assn., Ann Arbor Psychiatric Assn., Mich. Psychiat. Assn., N.Y. Acad. Sci., AAAS, Hon. Order Ky. Cols., Sigma Alpha Epsilon, Phi Rho Sigma. Clubs: Ann Arbor Town, Ann Arbor Racquet, Univ., Travis Pointe Country (Ann Arbor); Little Harbor (Harbor Springs, Mich.). Home: Fair Oaks Ann Arbor MI 48104 Office: 1231 Ferdon Rd Ann Arbor MI 48104

KIMM, JAMES WILSON, cons. engr.; b. Huron, S.D., Sept. 26, 1925; s. Arthur A. and Mary (Fry) K.; B.S., U. Iowa, 1950; m. Dorothy A. Madsen, Aug. 16, 1952; children—Mary L., Jill A., Tobias J. Pub. health engr. Iowa State Dept. Health, Des Moines, 1950-55; head san. engring. report sect. Stanley Engring. Co., Muscatine, Iowa, 1955-61; pres. Veenstra & Kimm, Inc., Engrs. and Planners, West Des Moines, Iowa, 1961—, West Des Moines Devel. Corp. Served with AUS, 1943-45. Named Engr. Distinction, Engrs. Joint Council. Mem. Iowa Water Pollution Control Assn. (past pres.), Iowa Engring Soc., Nat. Soc. Profl. Engrs., C. of C., Cons. Engrs. Council Iowa, Water Pollution Control Fedn. (dir.), Tau Beta Pi, Chi Epsilon. Presbyterian (elder). Contbr. articles and papers to profl. jours. Home: 3932 Ashworth Rd West Des Moines IA 50265 Office: 300 West Bank Bldg 1601 22 St West Des Moines IA 50265

KINCAID, MARY ELIZABETH, author, illustrator; b. Cleve., June 4, 1923; d. George Walter and Elizabeth (Phillips) Getz; B.A., U. Mich., 1944; m. William Harold Kincaid, Dec. 26, 1945; children—Judith Elizabeth, Jay Alexander, Rebecca Lee. Author-illustrator fgn. lang. comic strip Contes Français, various Am. newspapers, 1962-66; author, designer, dir. audiovisual film Lang. Strips, 1973-76; co-author bilingual radio series French Minutes, 1973-76; cons. and speaker audiovisual fgn. lang. instructional techniques; contbr. articles to mags. newspapers. Recipient award Mich. Council Arts, 1975-76. Home: 3550 Woodland Rd Ann Arbor MI 48104

KINDNESS, THOMAS NORMAN, congressman; b. Knoxville, Tenn., Aug. 26, 1929; s. Norman G. and Christine (Gunn) K.; A.B. in Polit. Sci., U. Md., 1951; LL.B., George Washington U., 1953; m. Ann G. Hosman, Sept. 15, 1951; children—Sharon L., David T., Glen J., Adam B. Admitted to D.C. bar, 1954; practiced in Washington, 1954-57; asst. counsel Champion Internat. Corp., Hamilton, O., 1957-73; mem. 94th-97th Congress from 8th dist. Ohio, 1975—, mem. judiciary, govt. operations coms. Mem. Hamilton City Council, 1964-69, mayor, 1964-67; mem. Ohio Ho. of Reps., 1971-74. Republican. Home: 328 South D St Hamilton OH 45013 Office: Room 2434 Rayburn House Office Bldg Washington DC 20515

KINDRICK, ROBERT LEROY, educator; b. Kansas City, Mo., Aug. 17, 1942; s. Robert William and Waneta LeVeta (Lobdell) K.; B.A., Park Coll., 1964; M.A., U. Mo., 1967; Ph.D., U. Tex., 1971; m. Carolyn Jean Reed, Aug. 20, 1965. Instr., Central Mo. State U., Warrenburg, 1967-69, asst. prof., 1969-73, asso. prof., 1973-78, prof. English, 1978—, head dept. English, 1975-80; dean Coll. Arts and Scis., also prof. English, Western Ill. U., Macomb, 1980—. Chmn. bd. dirs. Mo. Com. for Humanities, 1979-80. U. Tex. fellow, 1965-66; Am. Council Learned Socs. travel grantee, 1975; Nat. Endowment for Humanities summer fellow, 1977; Mediaeval Acad. Am. grantee, 1976; Mo. Com. for Humanities grantee, 1975-76; Assn. for Scottish Lit. Studies grantee, 1979. Mem. Mo. Assn. Depts. English (pres. 1978-80), Mo. Philological Assn. (founding pres. 1975-77), Medieval Assn. Midwest (councillor 1977—), Mediaeval Acad. Am., Mid-Am. Medieval Assn., Rocky Mt. Modern Lang. Assn., Assn. for Scottish Lt. Studies, S. Central Modern Lang. Assn., Mo. Assn. Depts. English, Early English Text Soc., Societe Rencesvals, Internat. Arthurian Soc., Sigma Tau Delta, Phi Kappa Phi. Club: Rotary. Author: Robert Henryson, 1979; A New Classical Rhetoric, 1980; contbr. articles to profl. jours. Home: 700 Western Ave Macomb IL 61455 Office: Coll Arts and Scis Western Ill U Macomb IL 61455

KINDT, WALTER HEINZ, religious orgn. exec.; b. Schneidemuehl, Germany, Nov. 15, 1923; came to U.S., 1952, naturalized, 1957; s. Johannes E.P. and Frieda E.L. (Fritz) K.; student land surveying trade sch., 1937-40; m. Roswitha M. Steinmann, June 8, 1955; children—Christopher, Timothy, Stephan, Laurie, Sabina, Melissa, Joshua. Missionary, E. Ger., 1946-51; bishop Ch. of Jesus Christ of Latter-day Saints, Milw., 1956-61, councilor to stake pres., 1961-69, pres. Mission, Dusseldorf, W. Ger., 1969-72, regional rep., Germany, 1972-74, Pa., 1974-76, New Eng., 1976-78, Minn., Wis., 1978-80, councilor to mission pres., Milw., 1980—; prodn. mgr. Sight & Sound Internat., Inc., music pub. co., New Berlin, Wis., 1973—. Served with German Army, 1941-45. Mem. Milw. Advt. Club. Home: 5696 Gladstone Ln Greendale WI 53129 Office: 3200 S 166th St New Berlin WI 53151

KINDWALL, ERIC POST, physician; b. N.Y.C., Jan. 17, 1934; s. Josef Alfred and Anna Linnea (Post) K.; B.A., U. Wis., 1956; M.D. (NSF fellow, NIH fellow), Yale U., 1960; m. Betsy Fernald, Sept. 12, 1964 (div. 1975); children—Kristina, Alexander; m. 2d, Marilyn MacArthur, Aug. 5, 1978. Intern, U. Va. Hosp., Charlottesville, 1961-62; resident in psychiatry Mass. Mental Health Center, Harvard U. Med. Sch., 1962-65; pvt. practice psychiatry, Boston, 1965-66; dir. dept. hyperbaric medicine St. Luke's Hosp., Milw., 1969—; asst. adj. clin. prof. pharmacology, div. environ. medicine Med. Coll. Wis., 1969—; chmn. Wis. state code com. for work in compressed air, 1970—; cons. hyperbaric oxygen to Chinese Navy, Taiwan, 1976—, Indonesian Navy, 1981—; cons. Nat. Inst. for Occupational Safety and Health, 1975-76, FDA, 1977, OSHA, 1976, 10 diving and constrn. cos.; Midwest regional dir. Diving Accident Network, NOAA, 1980—. Served to comdr. USNR, 1966-69. Fellow in diving physiology Karolinska Inst., Stockholm, 1960-61; prin. investigator Office Naval Research, 1972-74. Mem. Undersea Med. Soc. (sec.-treas. 1971-73, v.p. 1978-79, pres. 1981-82, chmn. com. on hyperbaric oxygenation 1976-80), AAAS, AMA, Marine Tech. Soc., Am. Occupational Medicine Assn., Aerospace Med. Assn. Contbr. articles on diving and submarine medicine, caisson work and hyperbaric medicine to sci. jours., chpt. to Occupational Medicine, 1975. Home: 13020 Oriole Ln Brookfield WI 53005 Office: 2900 W Oklahoma Ave Milwaukee WI 53215

KING, ARTHUR THOMAS, air force officer; b. Greensboro, Ala., Feb. 10, 1938; s. Harvey James and Elizabeth (Williams) K.; B.S. in Biology, Tuskegee Inst., 1962; M.S. in Econs., S.D. State U., 1971; Ph.D. in Econs., U. Colo., 1977; m. Rosa Marie Bryant, June 24, 1962; children—Donald, Kevin. Commd. 2d lt. U.S. Air Force, 1962, advanced through grades to lt. col., 1979; asst. prof. econs. U.S. Air Force Acad., 1970-74; ops. planner, Davis-Monthan AFB, Tucson, 1975-76, strategic planner/energy economist, Wright-Patterson AFB, Ohio, 1977-79, asso. prof. econs. Air Force Inst. Tech., 1979—. Mem. Am. Econ. Assn., Nat. Econ. Assn., Soc. Govt. Economists, Air Force Assn. Baptist. Author articles in field. Home: 234 Chatham Dr Fairborn OH 45324 Office: AFIT/LSY Wright Patterson AFB OH 45433

KING, CHARLES MURRAY, mgmt. and tng. cons.; b. Columbia, S.C., Feb. 2, 1934; s. David Abenedab and Susie Clark K.; B.S., A&T State U., Greensboro, N.C., 1956; M.Ed., Kent State U., 1968; postgrad. U. Pa., 1969; m. Jessie M. Burch, Apr. 9, 1955; children—Anthony, Charles Murray, Aaron J., David. Exec. dir. Mansfield (Ohio) Opportunities Indsl. Center, 1968-71; salesman, instr. Motivational Co., Akron, Ohio, 1971-72; pres. Goald, Inc., Cuyahoga Falls, Ohio, 1972—. Chmn. Cuyahoga Valley Community Mental Health Center; bd. dirs. WCRF. Served from 2d lt. to capt. U.S. Army, 1956-67. Recipient Student Achievement award Wall St. Jour., 1956. Mem. Am. Soc. Tng. and Devel., Am. Mgmt. Assn. Republican. Clubs: Rotary (Akron). Contbr. articles to profl. jours. Home: 3921 Greentree Rd Stow OH 44224 Office: 1060 Graham Rd Stow OH 44224

KING, CHARLES ROSS, physician; b. Nevada, Iowa, Aug. 22, 1925; s. Carl Russell and Dorothy Sarah (Mills) K.; student Butler U., 1943; B.S. in Bus., Ind. U., 1948, M.D., 1964; m. Frances Pamela Carter, Jan. 8, 1949; children—Deborah Diane, Carter Ross, Charles Conrad, Corbin Kent. Dep. dir. Ind. Pub. Works and Supply, 1949-52; salesman Knox Coal Corp., 1952-59; rotating intern Marion County Gen. Hosp., Indpls., 1964-65; family practice medicine, Anderson, Ind., 1965—; sec.-treas. staff Community Hosp., 1969-72, pres. elect, dir., chief medicine, 1973—, also bd. dirs., 1973-75; sec.-treas. St. John's Hosp., 1968-69, chief medicine, 1972-73, chief pediatrics, 1977—; dir. Rolling Hills Convalescent Center, 1968-73; pres. Profl. Center Lab., 1965—. Vice-chmn. Madison County Bd. Health, 1966-69; dir. First Nat. Bank Madison County, Anderson. Bd. dirs. Family Service Madison County, 1968-69, Madison County Assn. Mentally Retarded, 1972-76; chmn., bd. dirs. Anderson Downtown Devel. Corp., 1980—. Served with AUS, 1944-46. Diplomate Am. Bd. Family Practice. Recipient Physician's Recognition award AMA, 1969, 72, 75, 78. Fellow Royal Soc. Health, Am. Acad. Family Practice (charter); mem. AMA, Ind., Pan Am. med. assns., Am. Acad. Gen. Practice, Madison County (pres. 1970), 8th Dist. (sec.-treas. 1968) med. socs., Anderson C. of C. (dir. 1979—), Indpls. Mus. Art (corp. mem.). Phi Delta Theta Alumni Assn. (pres. 1952), Phi Delta Theta, Phi Chi. Methodist. Club: Anderson Country (dir. 1976-79). Home: 920 N Madison Ave Anderson IN 46011 Office: 1933 Chase St Anderson IN 46014

KING, CHARLES THOMAS, assn. exec.; b. Nashville, Mar. 4, 1943; s. Leslie Thomas and Freddie Faye (Collier) K.; B.S., Eastern Mich. U., 1966; M.A., Wayne State U., 1968, Sp.Edn., 1972; Ph.D., Mich. State U., 1978; m. Barbara Jean Harrison, Apr. 9, 1966; children—Kiersten Faye, Kyla Ann. Tchr., Romulus (Mich.) High Sch., 1965-69; instr. social sci. dept. Kellogg Community Coll., Battle Creek, Mich., 1969-70, dir. Afro-Am. studies, 1970-72; cons. human relations Mich., Edn. Assn., East Lansing, 1972-74, coordinator profl. excellence, 1974—. Mem. Mich. Assn. Supervision and Curriculum Devel. (bd. dirs.), NEA, Mich. Edn. Assn. (past dir.), Assn.

Supervision and Curriculum Devel., Nat. Alliance Black Sch. Educators, Assn. Tchr. Educators, Nat. Assn. Human Right Workers, Nat. Staff Orgn., Mich. Alliance Black Sch. Educators. Democrat. Club: Masons. Home: 4165 Marmoor Dr Lansing MI 48917 Office: 1216 Kendale Blvd East Lansing MI 48823

KING, CHRISTINE B., transp. co. exec.; b. Chgo., Jan. 14, 1951; d. Edward John and Irene Mary (Parkes) K.; B.S. in Edn., No. Ill. U., 1972; m. Barry L. Aronson, Sept. 25, 1975. With Continental Air Transport Co., Inc., Chgo., 1973-81, dir. sales, 1975-78, v.p. sales, 1978-81; sr. v.p. sales and mktg. Keeshin Charter Service, Chgo., 1981—. Mem. Hotel Sales Mgmt. Assn. (dir.-at-large 1976-78), Chgo. Assn. Soc. Execs., Meeting Planners Internat., Chgo. Area Meeting Planners, Am. Soc. Travel Agts., Midwest Passenger Traffic Assn., Chgo. Conv. and Tourism Bur., Sales and Mktg. Execs. Club (bd. dirs. Chgo. chpt.), Nat. Assn. Exposition Mgrs., Airline Passengers Assn., Women's Transp. Assn. Roman Catholic. Clubs: Chgo. Women's Travel, Ill. Athletic. Office: Keeshin Charter Service 705 S Jefferson Chicago IL 60607

KING, DAN L., educator; b. Detroit, July 2, 1947; s. Don L. and Doris K.; B.A., Madonna Coll., 1973; M.A., U. Detroit, 1975; Ed.D., Wayne State U., 1979; m. Denise Murray, Jan. 25, 1975; children—Joshua James, Andrew John. Tchr., Britton, Mich., 1969-70, Detroit, 1970-72; edn. dir., Mora, Minn., 1973-75; prin. high sch., Royal Oak, Mich., 1976-78; asst. prof. edn. Loras Coll., Dubuque, Iowa, 1979—. Mem. citizens adv. com. South Redford (Mich) Public Schs., 1972, Mora Community Sch. Dist., 1974-75. Mem. Am. Assn. Sch. Adminstrs., Assn. Instl. Research, Assn. Tchr. Educators, Nat. Assn. Secondary Sch. Prins., Assn. Supervision and Curriculum Devel., Phi Delta Kappa. Home: 595 Clarke Dr Dubuque IA 52001 Office: Dept Edn Loras Coll Dubuque IA 52001

KING, DENISE MARGARET MURRAY, coll. adminstr.; b. Detroit, Mar. 20, 1953; d. Roy F. and Margaret Murray; B.S., Eastern Mich. U., 1977, M.S., 1980; m. Dan L. King, Jan. 20, 1975; children—Joshua James, Andrew John. Tchr., St. Andrew High Sch., Detroit, 1977-79; dir. activities, coach Loras Coll., Dubuque, Iowa, 1981—. Mem. AAHPER, Council Exceptional Children, Iowa Student Personnel Assn., Nat. Soc. Study of Edn. Home: 595 Clarke Dr Dubuque IA 52001 Office: Loras Coll Dubuque IA 52001

KING, EDWARD ALVIN, city ofcl.; b. Pratt City, Ala., Sept. 4, 1919; s. Fred Elijah and Phyllis Ann (Robertson) K.; A.B., Del. State Coll., 1943; M.S.W., Atlanta U., 1947; m. Beatrice Pitts, Nov. 14, 1980; children by previous marriage—Linda Ann, Antone J. Scrivens, Daniel Scrivens. Dir. group work, community relations Grand Rapids (Mich.) Urban League, 1947-53; community relations specialist Boston Urban League, 1953-57; exec. dir. Dayton (Ohio) Human Relations Council, 1963—; instr. U. Dayton, 1968-71. Bd. dirs. Johnson C. Smith Sch. Theology, 1975—; sr. elder Trinity United Presbyn. Ch., 1973—. Served with AUS, 1943-46. Recipient Public Service awards Rotary Club, 1973, Kiwanis Club, 1979, U. Dayton, 1979, Optimist Club, 1974, Dayton Bd. Edn., 1980. Mem. Internat. Assn. Ofcl. Human Rights Agys., Nat. Assn. Human Rights Workers, NAACP, Alpha Phi Alpha. Club: Kiwanis (dir. 1976-80). Home: 1828 Ruskin Dr Dayton OH 45406 Office: Dayton Human Relations Council Suite 721 40 S Main St Dayton OH 45402

KING, JAMES EARL, psychiat. social worker; b. Lima, Ohio, July 10, 1925; s. Benjamin D. and Slylvia Margaret K.; B.Th., Owosso (Mich.) Coll., 1950; B.A., Kletzing Coll., 1951; M.A., Butler U., 1956; postgrad. Mich. State U., 1960-65, M.S.W., 1981; LL.D., John Wesley Coll., 1972; m. Janet K. Baker, Oct. 29, 1970; children—Carol Ann DesAutels, Robert. Dean of men Owosso Coll., 1956-57, dean of students, 1958-67; pastor Wesleyan Ch., 1967-69; prof. psychology, counselor John Wesley Coll., Owosso, 1969-77; therapist Anderson Counseling Clinic, Owosso, 1977—. Served with USN, 1942-46. Mem. Am. Personnel and Guidance Assn., Mich. Council Family Relations, Christian Assn. for Psychol. Studies. Author: Heretical Movements of the Second and Third Centuries, 1956; Psychology of Religious Experiences, 1978. Home: 6734 Highland Dr Laingsburg MI 48848

KING, JAMES EDWARD, mfg. co. exec.; b. Toledo, Sept. 12, 1944; s. Edward Earl and Lizzette Elizabeth (Schmitt) K.; student U. Toledo, 1962-72; m. Cheryl Lee Gray, June 30, 1979; children—Joseph James, Jeffrey Allen, Jennifer Lynn. With Owens-Ill. Inc., Toledo, 1965—, worldwide mgr. TV glass sealant sales, 1978-81, worldwide mgr. indsl. materials sales, 1981—. Mem. Toledo Area C. of C. Patentee in low temperature glass sealants, oxidation materials, glass sealant pastes, vehicle systems for pastes. Home: 4903 Fleet Rd Toledo OH 43615 Office: Owens-Ill Inc One Seagate Toledo OH 43666

KING, JEROME LEWIS, assn. exec.; b. Bklyn., Mar. 16, 1938; s. Bernard and Shirley K.; B.A., U. Mich., 1959; M.B.A., Columbia U., 1961; m. Dale Anne Reiss, Mar. 5, 1979; children—Stacey, Mitchell, Matthew. Market researcher Reuben H. Donneley, N.Y.C., 1962-66; v.p. CNA Ins., Chgo., 1966-76; pres. Jerome L. King & Assos., Chgo., 1977-80; v.p. YMCA Met. Chgo., 1980—. Active United Way Met. Chgo. Served with U.S. Army, 1960-61. Mem. Am. Mktg. Assn., Soc. Ins. Research. Office: 140 S Dearborn St Chicago IL 60690

KING, JERRY WAYNE, chemist; b. Indpls., Feb. 19, 1942; s. Ernest E. and Mariam (Sanders) K.; B.S., Butler U., 1965; Ph.D., Northeastern U., 1973; postgrad. (fellow), Georgetown U., 1973-74; m. Bettie Maria Dunbar, Aug. 8, 1965; children—Ronald Sean, Valerie Raquel, Diana Lynn. Research chemist Union Carbide Corp., Bound Brook, N.J., 1968-70; asst. prof. dept. chemistry Va. Commonwealth U., Richmond, 1974-76; research scientist Arthur D. Little, Inc., Cambridge, Mass., 1976-77; research asso. Am. Can Co., Barrington, Ill., 1977-79; research scientist CPC Intern., Summit-Argo, Ill.; guest lectr. various sci. groups and meetings, 1964-81. Research Corp. grantee, 1975-77; NSF fellow, 1973-74. Mem. Am. Chem. Soc., ASTM, Va. Acad. Scis., Soc. Plastics Engrs., AAAS. Contbr. articles on chromatography to sci. jours. Home: 211 Sunset Terrace Crystal Lake IL 60014

KING, JOAN CARNAHAN, publisher, communications cons.; b. Pitts., Sept. 4, 1930; d. J. Lloyd and Eva Ferne (Riddle) Carnahan; B.A., Westminster Coll., 1953; children by previous marriage—Peter John Koenig, Christina Joan Koenig. Researcher, Ketchum, McLeod & Grove Advt., Pitts.; copywriter Joseph Horne Co., Pitts., 1954-59; community relations ofcl. Coll. of DuPage, Glen Ellyn, Ill., 1973-76; asso. dir. devel., public relations Meml. Hosp. of DuPage County, Elmhurst, Ill., 1976-79; pub. Memo, Women in Mgmt. mag.; freelance writer, cons. public relations. Mem. Women in Mgmt. (Oakbrook chpt. newsletter editor). Address: 1045 Wheaton Oaks Dr Wheaton IL 60187

KING, JOHN JOSEPH, mfg. co. exec.; b. Toledo, Jan. 12, 1924; s. Walter and Frances (Gwozd) Kawecka; B.S. in M.E. magna cum laude, U. Toledo, 1957, M.S. in Indsl. Engring., 1961; m. Joy G. Mohler, Jan. 28, 1950; children—Catherine M., Carolyn S., David J., Michael R., Mark A.R. Draftsman, Tecumseh Products Co., 1941-42; die designer Bingham Stamping Co., 1942-46; tool designer Spicer Mfg. Co., 1946-47; product designer Am. Floor Surfacing Co., 1947-50; founder, mgr. engr. Kent Industries, 1950-52; mech. engr. Owens Ill. Inc., Toledo, 1953-63; mgr. research and devel. Permaglass Inc., Genoa, Ohio, 1963-69; founder, pres. Ashur Inc., Rossford, Ohio, 1969—, also chmn. bd. Registered profl. engr., Ohio. Mem. Am. Ceramic Soc., Soc. Mfg. Engrs., Tau Beta Pi, Phi Kappa Phi. Republican. Roman Catholic. Clubs: Devils Lake Yacht, Ukranian Am. Citizens, K. of C. Patentee glass making machinery. Home: 1111 Elm Tree Rd Rossford OH 43460 Office: 1117 Elm Tree Rd Rossford OH 43460

KING, JOSEPH CLEMENT, physician; b. Colorado Springs, Colo., Aug. 20, 1922; s. Charles Clement and Gladys (Ascher) K.; B.S., Tulane U., 1944, M.D., 1946; m. Margie Freudenthal Leopold, Apr. 2, 1947; 1 son, Leopold Ascher. Instr. zoology, Tulane U., 1941-42; rotating intern Michael Reese Hosp., Chgo., 1946-47, resident in internal medicine, 1947-50; asso. with Dr. Sidney Portis, Chgo., 1950-51; practice medicine specializing in internal medicine, Chgo., 1953-77, Palm Springs, Calif., 1977-79; attending staff Desert Hosp., 1977-79; med. dir. Life Extension Inst., Chgo., 1979-80, Continental Ill. Nat. Bank, Chgo., 1980—; asst. to asso. clin. prof. internal medicine Northwestern U. Med. Sch., Chgo., 1954-67; clin. asst. prof. medicine Abraham Lincoln Sch. Medicine U. Ill., 1973-77, clin. asst. prof. preventive medicine and community health, 1980—. Served to capt. M.C., AUS, 1944-46, 1951-53. Diplomate Am. Bd. Internal Medicine. Fellow A.C.P., Am. Coll. Geriatrics; mem. Chgo. Soc. Internal Medicine, Chgo. Med. Soc., Am., Ill. med. assns., Am., Chgo. heart assns., Am. Rheumatism Assn., Ill. Soc. Med. Research, AAAS, Am. Occupational Med. Assn., Am. Geriatric Soc., Tulane Med. Alumni Assn. (dir.), Phi Beta Kappa, Beta Mu, Alpha Omega Alpha. Club: Chgo. Tulane Alumni (pres.). Contbr. numerous articles in field to med. jours. Home: 1100 Lake Shore Dr Chicago IL 60611 Office: 231 S LaSalle St Room 2048 Chicago IL 60693

KING, LAURA JANE, former home economist; b. Pemberville, Ohio, Jan. 19, 1947; d. Richard D. and Jessie Florence (Brown) Zepernick; B.A., Bowling Green (Ohio) State U., 1969, M.Ed., 1976; m. Bruce William King, June 17, 1972; 1 son, Christian Andrew. County extension agt. home econs. Ohio Coop. Extension Service, Paulding County, 1970-77; mem. PRIDE com., vocat. home econs. dept. Paulding Exempted Village, 1975—; instr. genealogy Office Continuing Edn., Bowling Green State U. Mem. Paulding County Bicentennial Commn., 1975-77; organist 1st Presbyterian Ch., Pemberville, ruling elder, 1978-81. Recipient Tenure award Coop. Extension Service, 1975. Cert. geneal. record searcher. Mem. Ohio, Wood County hist. socs., Ohio, Wood County (pres., dir.) geneal. socs., DAR (vice regent chpt. 1975-77, regent 1979-82; state vice chmn. pages 1977-80, state chmn. lineage research 1980—; state and div. outstanding jr. mem. 1980), U.S. Daus. of 1812, First Families Ohio, Daus. Union Vets., Bus. and Profl. Women's Club (pres. Paulding 1975-76, v.p. 1974-75). Club: Order Eastern Star. Genealogy columnist Bowling Green Sentinel-Tribune. Home: 14553 N River Rd Pemberville OH 43450

KING, LEROY HARRY, JR., physician; b. Paducah, Ky., Sept. 4, 1937; s. LeRoy Harry and Goldia Elmarene (Fletcher) K.; A.B., Duke, 1959; M.D., Ind. U., 1964; m. Carol Jane Henzie, July 4, 1974; children—Stephen Lee, Heather Lee, Brandon Williams, Carson Tyler, Travis Warren. Intern Ind. U. Med. Center Hosps, Indpls., 1964-65, resident in internal medicine, 1965-67, fellow in nephrology, 1967-68; instr. dept. medicine Ind. U. Med. Center Hosps., 1968-69: practice medicine specializing in internal medicine and nephrology, Indpls., 1971—; mem. staff Meth. Hosp. of Ind., Indpls., 1971—, asst. med. dir. renal dept., 1971—, attending physician, 1971—; mem. staffs Community Hosp. Indpls., 1973—, Winona Hosp., Indpls., 1972—. Served as maj. MC, U.S. Army, 1969-71. Diplomate Am. Bd. Internal Medicine. Fellow A.C.P.; mem. AMA, Am. Heart Assn., Internat., Am. socs. nephrology, Am. Soc. Artificial Internal Organs, Nat. Kidney Found., Am. Fedn. for Clin. Research, Am. Soc. Internal Medicine, Ind. Med. Assn., Marion County Med. Soc., Kidney Found. of Ind. (trustee), Ind. U. Men's Club of Indpls., Beta Theta Pi, Nu Sigma Nu. Republican. Contbr. articles to profl. jours. Home: 7610 Cape Cod Circle Indianapolis IN 46250 Office: 1633 N Capitol St Suite 722 Indianapolis IN 46202

KING, RALEIGH WAYNE, beauty sch. exec.; b. Camden, N.J., Oct. 18, 1945; s. Travis Greer and Eva Virginia K.; student U. Md., 1969-71, Belleville Area Coll., 1972-74. Instr., Coiffure Sch. Beauty Culture, Belleville, Ill., 1978-79, dir., 1979—; educator Revlon-Realistic, 1981—. Bd. dirs. Ill. Assn. Cosmetology Schs., 1981. Served with USAF, 1965-76. Mem. Nat. Hairdressers and Cosmetologists Assn. (pres. affiliate 40 1979-80). Home: 211 S 59th St Belleville IL 62223 Office: Coiffure Sch Beauty Culture 402 E Main St Belleville IL 62220

KING, ROBERT HOWARD, publisher; b. Excelsior Springs, Mo., June 28, 1921; s. Howard and Nancy Eaton (Henry) K.; student Kenyon Coll., Gambier, Ohio, 1942; m. Nancy Brown, 1946; children—John McFeeley, Mary Nan King Murphy, Sarah Ann; m. 2d, Marjorie Kerr, Mar. 15, 1975. Vice pres. sales Ency. Brit., Chgo., 1946-61; pres. Spencer Internat. Press, Chgo., 1961-66; v.p. Dill Clitherow & Co., Palatine, Ill., 1966-68; pres. Time-Life Libraries, Palatine, 1968-79; chmn. bd., chief exec. officer World Book-Childcraft Internat., Inc., Chgo., 1979—. Served to capt. AUS, 1942-46. Mem. Direct Selling Assn. (past chmn. bd.), World Fedn. Direct Selling Assns. (past chmn. Bd.), Direct Selling Ednl. Found. (past chmn. bd.), Sales and Mktg. Execs. Internat., Internat. Bus. Council. Clubs: Chicago; Lighthouse Point Yacht (Fla.); Ocean Reef (Key Largo, Fla.). Home: 155 Harbor Point Chicago IL 60603 Office: 510 Merchandise Mart Plaza Chicago IL 60654

KING, ROBERT JAMES, psychologist; b. Logansport, Ind., May 8, 1932; s. William John and Margaret Patricia (Vallely) K.; m. Jane Kemper, Oct. 17, 1959; children—Robert, David, Jane, Michael, John; B.S., Loyola U., Chgo., 1955, M.S., 1961; Ph.D., Ill. Inst. Tech., 1973. Asst. personnel mgr. Gen. Foods Corp., Chgo., 1958-60; personnel mgr. Kaiser Engrs., Chgo., 1960-61; employment mgr. Motorola, Inc., 1961-63, personnel mgr., 1963-65, corp. mgr. personnel testing, 1965-73, corp. dir. human resources, 1973—; lectr. U. Mich. Indsl. Relations Bur., Loyola U. Grad. Sch. Bus. and Inst. Indsl. Relations, Ill. Inst. Tech. Grad. Sch. Psychology; lectr., cons. Midwest Indsl. Relations Assn. Registered psychologist, Ill., 1973, Ariz., 1974. Mem. Am., Ill., Ariz. psychol. assns., Indsl. Relations Assn. Chgo. Extensive research in psychometric testing and orgn. planning and devel. Home: 1521 S Prospect Ave Park Ridge IL 60068 Office: Motorola Center 1303 E Algonquin Rd Schaumburg IL 60196

KING, THOMAS JOSEPH, physician; b. Chgo., Aug. 17, 1920; s. Thomas and Norah Catherine (Nash) K.; B.S., Xavier U., 1938-42; M.D., Loyola Med. Sch., 1945; m. Agnes Therese Bush, Oct. 30, 1943; children—Thomas, John, Therese (Mrs. Richard Vincent Malak), Gerald, Dennis, Elizabeth, Catherine. Intern Little Co. of Mary Hosp., Evergreen Park, Ill., 1945-46, staff, 1960—, dir. emergency room, 1966-73; practice medicine, Chgo., and Evergreen Park, 1948-58. Athletic dir. Mendel Cath. High Sch., 1960-69. Served with M.C. U.S. Army, 1946-47. Mem. Am., Ill., Chgo. med. socs., Am. Med. Soc. on Alcoholism, Am. Legion (comdr. 1964, 65). Elk. Home: 6241 Forestview Dr Oak Forest IL 60452

KING, THOMAS VAN DYKE, wholesale buying center adminstr.; b. Cin., Mar. 9, 1924; s. Thomas H. and Lula (Van Dyke) K.; student Mich. State U., 1942-43; B.A., U. Mich., 1946; m. Barbara Ann Scott, Sept. 17, 1955; children—Shelley Jean Coble, Thomas V. Profl. basketball player Detroit Falcons, 1945-46; dir. public relations Arthur Wirtz Enterprises, Chgo., 1946-55; dir. advt. and sales promotion The Merchandise Mart, Chgo., 1955-60, gen. mgr. Merchandise Mart/The Apparel Center, 1960—. Pres. bd. dirs. Mercy Hosp. and Med. Center, Chgo., 1972-76; trustee Evans Scholars Found.; mem. exec. com. NCCJ; pres. United Cerebral Palsy of Greater Chgo., 1977-80; vice chmn. Chgo. Mortgage Bond Com., 1977; trustee John Marshall Law Sch., Chgo., 1976-80; mem. Chgo. Crime Commn., 1978-80; bd. dirs. March of Dimes; mem. capital devel. bd. State of Ill., 1981—. Served to capt. USMC, 1942-45, 50-51. Named Man of Year, Modern Floor Coverings, 1974. Mem. Better Bus. Bur. Met. Chgo. (past chmn.), Chgo. Conv. and Tourism Bur. (past chmn.), Chgo. Assn. Commerce and Industry (dir.), Ill. Sprots Council, Floor Covering Industry Edn. Found. (dir.). Episcopalian. Clubs: Evanston Golf (past pres.), Western Golf Assn. (past pres.), Mchts. and Mfrs. (exec. v.p.), Mich. State U. Alumni, U. Mich. Alumni). Office: 830 The Merchandise Mart Chicago IL 60654

KING, (JACK) WELDON, photographer; b. Springfield, Mo., Jan. 19, 1911; s. Clyde Nelson and Mary Blanche (Murphy) K.; B.A., Drury Coll., 1934, Mus.B., 1934. Chief still photographer African expdns. including Gatti-Hallicrafters Expdn., 1947-48, 12th Gatti Expdn., 1952, Wyman Carroll Congo Expdn., 1955, 13th Gatti Expdn., 1956, 14th Gatti Expdn., 1957; also free-lance photog. expdns., Africa, 1960, 66, 76-77; trips for GAF Corp. to S.Am., 1962, 63, 77-78, Australia and N.Z., 1972-73, also numerous assignments throughout U.S. Served as photographer with Coast Arty. Corps, U.S. Army, 1941-42; PTO; Japanese prisoner of war, 1942-45. Decorated numerous service ribbons and battle stars. Mem. Space Pioneers, Am. Theatre Organ Soc., Humane Soc. U.S., Friends Animals, Nat. Parks and Conservation Assn., Animal Protection Inst. Am., African Wildlife Leadership Found., World Wildlife Fund, Am. Defenders of Bataan and Corregidor, Am. Ex-Prisoners War, Lambda Chi Alpha. Democrat. Roman Catholic. Contbr. to numerous art books including Africa is Adventure, 1959, also French and German edits.; Primitive Peoples Today, 1956; Africa: A Natural History, 1965; South American and Central America, 1967; Animal Worlds, 1963; Living Plants of the World, 1963; The Earth Beneath Us, 1964; Living Trees of the World; The Life of the Jungle, 1970; Living Mammals of the World. Contbr. photographs to mags., encys., textbooks. Address: 1234 E Grand Ave Springfield MO 65804

KINGERY, ELDRED EUGENE, bldg. contractor; b. Greene, Iowa, Jan. 22, 1945; s. Orval Henry and Alice Virginia (Hunter) K.; B.S., McPherson Coll., 1972; postgrad. Kans. State Coll., 1971, Wichita State U., 1971, Ill. State U., 1972; m. Leah Mae Standafer, Jan. 19, 1969; children—Barry Edward, Dennis Wayne. Tchr. indsl. arts, Pratt, (Kans.) public schs., 1972-73, Worthington (Minn.) public schs., 1973-74; owner, mgr. Kingery Constrn., Preston, Minn., 1974—; remodeling cons. Trustee McPherson Coll., 1977—. Served with USN, 1963-67. Mem. Ch. of Brethren. Address: Rural Route 2 PO Box 152 Preston MN 55965

KINGSRITER, DOUGLAS JAMES, real estate co. exec.; b. Little Falls, Minn., Jan. 29, 1950; s. Arvid Carl and Marian (Menzie) K.; B.A. (NCAA scholar 1971-72), U. Minn., 1973, postgrad. 1981—; m. Deborah Patton, Jan. 5, 1974; children—Lauren Beth, Barrett Douglas. Tight end Minn. Vikings, 1973-77; mgr. Harvey Hansen Realtors, Burnsville, Minn., 1978, gen. mgr., Edina, Minn., 1979-80, pres., 1980—; lectr. in field. Mem. Gov.'s Commn. for Phys. Fitness, Minn., 1981—. Mem. Mpls. C. of C., Mpls. Bd. Realtors. Clubs: Fellowship of Christian Athletes, Decathelon Athletic, U. Minn. "M", Mpls. Dunkers, Parents for Heart, Order of Ky. Cols. Home: 5708 Parkwood Ln Edina MN 55436 Office: 5307 Vernon Ave Edina MN 55436

KINKADE, DONALD RAY, respiratory care adminstr.; b. St. Louis, Apr. 26, 1946; s. Roy Lee and Marie Clara (Kofron) K.; grad. Cook County Grad. Sch. Medicine Sch. of Respiratory Therapy, 1967; B.A., Govs. State U., 1978, postgrad., 1978—. Respiratory therapist Jewish Hosp., St. Louis, 1963-65, DePaul Hosp., St. Louis, 1965-66; respiratory therapy intern Presbyn.-St. Luke's Hosp., Chgo., 1966-67; dir. respiratory therapy Meml. Hosp., Belleville, Ill., 1967-74; dir. respiratory therapy-pulmonary physiology labs Columbus-Cuneo-Cabrini Med. Center, Chgo., 1974—. Served with USMC, 1966-72. Registered respiratory therapist, cert. respiratory therapy technician Nat. Bd. for Respiratory Therapy. Mem. Am. Coll. Hosp. Adminstrs., Am. Assn. for Respiratory Therapy, Ill. Soc. for Respiratory Therapy, Am. Heart Assn., Chgo. Heart Assn., Chgo. Thoracic Soc. Home: 2414 W Lunt Ave Chicago IL 60645 Office: Columbus-Cuneo-Cabrini Med Center 2520 N Lakeview St Chicago IL 60614

KINLEY, GEORGE RAYMOND, state senator; b. Akron, Ohio, June 4, 1937; s. Raymond Frank and Marie (McCormick) K.; B.A., Drake U., 1960; m. Carolyn Ann Pritchard, 1958; children—Raymond, Kathryn, Frank, Elizabeth. Mem. Iowa Ho. of Reps., 1971-72; mem. Iowa Senate, 1973—, majority leader, 1975—; owner Airport Golf Range, 1955—. Mem. Izaak Walton League. Roman Catholic. Club: Dowling. Office: Iowa Senate State Capitol Des Moines IA 50319*

KINNEBREW, JOSEPH EDWIN, IV, sculptor, designer; b. Tacoma, Oct, 12, 1942; s. Joseph Edwin and Elaine (Montgomery) K.; B.A., Syracuse U., 1964; M.F.A., Mich. State U., 1971, postgrad., 1971; m. Ellen Carol McKittrick, June 28, 1970; children—Heather Christine, Peter Joseph Tobias. Commns. include: Mich. Consol. Gas Co., Grand Rapids, Joint Arts Commn. of Wayne State U., Harris Bank & Trust Co., Mich. Dental Assn., State of Mich., City of Lansing (Mich.), City of Janesville (Wis.), Knapp & Vogt Co.; represented in permanent collections: Guggenheim Mus., N.Y.C., Met. Mus. Art, N.Y.C., Library of Congress, Montreal Mus. Fine Arts, Bklyn. Mus.,

Detroit Inst. Arts; set designer Ariz. State Opera, 1970; artist-in-residence Nat. Endowment for Arts, 1972-73, project dir. air-supported structures, 1973; mng. dir. Jacquot Ltd., St. Lucia, West Indies. Co-chmn. visual arts adv. panel Mich. Council Arts, 1976, mem. bicentennial com., 1976, chmn. panel on aid to individual artists, 1977. Work selected as One of Mich.'s 50 Most Hist. Significant Archtl. Structures, Mich. chpt. AIA; recipient Mich. Gov.'s Arts award Mich. Found. for Arts, 1976; Mich. Week Community Achievement of Yr. award, 1976; Nat. award Concrete Reinforcing Steel Inst., 1977. Mem. Indsl. Designers Soc. Am. (product of yr. award). Contbr. articles to profl. jours.; work pub. various books and periodicals. Address: 13300 Beckwith Dr NE Lowell MI 49331

KINNEY, EARL ROBERT, food co. exec.; b. Burnham, Maine, Apr. 12, 1917; s. Harry E. and Ethel (Vose) K.; A.B., Bates Coll., 1939; postgrad. Harvard U., 1940; children—Jeanie Elizabeth, Earl Robert, Isabella Alice. Founder, North Atlantic Pack Co., Bar Harbor, Maine, 1941, pres., 1941-42, treas., dir., 1941-64; with Gorton Corp. (became subs. Gen. Mills, Inc. 1968), 1954-68, pres., 1958-68; v.p. Gen. Mills, Inc., 1968-69, exec. v.p., 1969-73, chief fin. officer, 1970-73, pres., chief operating officer, 1973—, now chmn., chief exec. officer; dir. Nashua Corp., Honeywell, Inc., Jackson Lab., Bar Harbor, Sun Co.; trustee 11 various Putnam Funds. Trustee Bates Coll., also chmn. alumni drives, 1960-64; bd. dirs., mem. exec. com. Mpls. YMCA. Mem. Conf. Bd., Com. for Econ. Devel., Bus. Roundtable (exec. com.). Office: PO Box 1113 Minneapolis MN 55440

KINNEY, JAMES LEWIS, mgmt. cons.; b. Columbus, Ohio, Oct. 7, 1911; s. James E. and Bertha (Rankin) K.; B.A., Ohio Wesleyan U., 1932; M.B.A., Harvard U., 1935; m. Virginia H. Thalman, Aug. 25, 1973; children—Margaret F. (Mrs. John Akin), Elizabeth Ann Kinney, John Redfield Thalman, James Randall Kinney, James Charles Thalman, Carol (Mrs. George Henry), Margaret Rankin Kinney, Robert William Thalman, Anne Elizabeth Thalman. Mktg. specialist lamp div. Gen. Electric Co., Nela Park, Cleve., 1935-38; field salesman, Buffalo, St. Louis, Nashville, Jackson, Miss., 1938-56, sales exec., Cleve. office, 1956-60; retailer Marketing Services, Inc., Cleve., 1960-76; pres., propr. Marketing Services Co., Cleve., 1976—; instr. marketing Case Western Res. U., Cleve., 1960-61; instr. in bus. Cuyanoga Community Coll., 1961-62. Bd. dirs. Northeast YMCA, 1967-78, Heights YMCA, 1978—. trustee Fairmount Presbyn. Ch., 1975-78, deacon, 1972-75; trustee Cleve. Sr. Council, 1979-81. Served with Ordnance Corps, U.S. Army, 1942-46. Mem. Sales Mgmt. Execs. Internat., Elec. Bd. of Trade. Republican. Clubs: Shaker Heights Country; Cleveland Skating and Tennis; Naples Bath and Tennis; Masons. Address: 20350 N Park Blvd Shaker Heights OH 44118

KINNICK, AUGUST EDWARD, real estate broker; b. Coon Rapids, Iowa, Aug. 18, 1928; s. Paul Harold and Dorothy Christina (Sorensen) K.; grad. high sch.; m. Collen JoAnn Davis, June 23, 1948; children—Marcia, Cynthia, Lon, Bryan. Salesman, Armour Agrl. div. W.R. Grace, Bayard, Ia., 1964-67, Am. Cyanamid, Bayard, 1974; dist. sales mgr. Golden Harvest Co., Bayard; farmer/rancher, Bayard, 1949—; real estate broker, Bayard, 1969—. Mem. Bayard Sch. Bd., 1972. Served with U.S. Army, 1946-48. Mem. Nat. Real Estate Bd., Internat. Platform Assn., Am. Legion. Mason, Odd Fellow. Methodist. Address: Rural Route 1 Box 58 Bayard IA 50029

KINSELL, ANNE SEAGROATT, assn. exec.; b. Indian River City, Fla., Nov. 23, 1927; married, 3 children. B.S. in Edn., Ind. U., Bloomington, 1951; M.S. in Edn., Purdue U., W. Lafayette, Ind., 1959; m. Richard Byron; children—Kandice, Theresa, Kimberly. Tchr. English, social studies, phys. edn., librarian Wadena High Sch., Fowler, Ind., 1957-59; tchr. English, librarian Pine Village (Ind.) High Sch., 1960-62; tchr. Burtsfield Elementary Sch., W. Lafayette, Ind., 1962-69; librarian, dir. audio-visual dept. W. Lafayette (Ind.) High Sch., 1969-80; exec. sec. Ind. Land Improvement Contractors Assn., West Lafayette, 1980—. Vestry, St. John's Episcopal Ch., 1974-77. Mem. W. Lafayette Edn. Assn. (past pres.), AIME, Unified Profls. Author, Purdue Dept. Edn's. 1st curriculum guide. Certified in elementary edn., librarianship, audio-visual aides, social studies, English. Home and Office: 2000 Indian Trail Dr West Lafayette IN 47906

KINSELLA, JAMES JOSEPH, holding co. exec.; b. Peoria, Ill., Sept. 14, 1921. Prin., James J. Kinsella Enterprise Inc., holding co., Peoria, 1977—; founder, mgr. Key Resort Club Am., Peoria, 1977—; founder, owner, pres. U.S. Enterprises Corp., Peoria, 1977—, also dir.; owner, founder U.S. Enterprise Holding Corp.; notary public. Mem. Common Cause, Nat. Resources Def. Council. Republican. Clubs: Eagles, Playboy, Loom, Sea World Dolphin, Enterprise, Inc. Home and Office: PO Box 315 Peoria IL 61651

KINSMAN, ROBERT DONALD, art mus. adminstr.; b. Bridgeport, Conn., Sept. 13, 1929; s. Cummings Sanborn and Sarah Elizabeth (Barton) K.; B.S., Columbia U., 1958, M.A. in Art History, 1966, A.B.D. in Art History; m. Patricia Ann Mulreed, Oct. 3, 1953. Asst. curator Nat. Gallery Art, Washington, 1961-62; instr. art history Mary Washington Coll., U. Va., Fredericksburg, 1962-63; curator contemporary art Detroit Inst. Arts, 1963-65; asst. prof. art history and dir. duPont Art Galleries, Mary Washington Coll., 1966-68; asst. prof. art history SUNY, Albany, 1968-77; dir. Sheldon Swope Art Gallery, Terre Haute, Ind., 1978—. Bd. dirs. Arts Illiana, Inc., 1981—. Served with U.S. Army, 1951-53. Mem. Am. Assn. Museums, AAUP, Coll. Art Assn. Am. Contbr. articles to profl. jours. Home: 4591 Dixie Bee Rd Terre Haute IN 47802 Office: 25 S 7th St Terre Haute IN 47807

KINZER, DONALD LOUIS, historian; b. Kent, Wash., Nov. 9, 1914; s. Addison Louis and Lois Minerva (Fay) K.; B.A., Western Wash. Coll., 1942; B.A., U. Wash., 1947, M.A., 1948, Ph.D., 1954; m. Kathryn Jane Tipton, Aug. 20, 1955; 1 son, William Tipton. Instr., U. Wash., 1954-55; instr. U. Del., 1955-58; asso. prof. Trenton State Coll., 1958-66; asso. prof. Ind. U.-Purdue U., Indpls., 1966-70, prof., 1970—, chmn. dept., 1970-80. Served with USAAF, 1942-46. Mem. Am. Hist. Assn., Orgn. Am. Historians, Ind. Hist. Soc., AAUP. Author: An Episode in Anti-Catholicism: The American Protective Association, 1964. Home: 5610 Central Ave Indianapolis IN 46220 Office: Dept History Cavanaugh Hall Ind U Purdue U Indianapolis IN 46202

KINZIE, JEANNIE JONES, physician; b. Gt. Falls, Mont., Mar. 14, 1940; d. James Wayne and Lillian Alice (Young) Jones; B.S., Mont. State U., 1961; M.D., Washington U., St. Louis, 1965; m. Joseph Kinzie, Mar. 25, 1965; 1 son, Daniel Joseph. Intern in surgery U. N.C., Chapel Hill, 1965-66; resident in radiology (radiation therapy) Washington U. Sch. Medicine, St. Louis, 1968-71, instr. radiology, 1971-73; Am. Cancer Soc. advanced clin. fellow, 1971-74; asst. radiologist Barnes Hosp., St. Louis, 1971-73; cons. radiology Homer G. Phillips Hosp., St. Louis, 1971-73; mem. med. records com., asst. prof. radiology Med. Coll. Wis., 1973-74; asso. attending staff Milw. County Gen. Hosp., 1973-74; head radiation therapy dept. Wood (Wis.) VA Hosp., 1973-74; cons. in radiology Community Meml. Hosp., Menomonee Falls, Wis., 1974; radiology staff West Allis (Wis.) Meml. Hosp., 1973-74; asst. prof. radiology U. Chgo., 1975-78, asso. prof., 1978-80; asso. prof. Wayne State U., Detroit, 1980—. N.I.H. grantee, 1974-76, mem. radiation studies sect., 1981-85. Diplomate Am. Bd. Radiology. Mem. AMA, Am. Coll. Radiology, Detroit Med. Soc., Am. Soc. Therapeutic Radiologists, AAAS, AAUP, Am. Soc. Clin. Oncology, Alpha Lambda Delta, Phi Kappa Phi, Mortar Bd., Sigma Xi. Republican. Lutheran. Home: 436 Lakeland Grosse Pointe MI 48230 Office: Radiation Oncology Center 4201 St Antoine Detroit MI 48201

KINZIE, RAYMOND WYANT, lawyer, banker; b. Chgo., Oct. 20, 1930; s. Raymond Allen and Florence Ethelyn (Wyant) K.; B.A., Carleton Coll., 1952; LL.B., Yale U., 1955, J.D., 1967; m. Dorothy Cherry Beek, Sept. 17, 1955; children—Diana Louise, Dorothy Donley, Susan Hawthorne (dec.), Raymond Wyant. Admitted to Ill. bar, 1956, U.S. Supreme Ct., 1964; asso. firm McBride Baker, Chgo., 1955-56; asso. trust counsel Continental Ill. Nat. Bank & Trust Co., Chgo., 1956-59; asst. trust officer Lake View Trust & Savs. Bank, Chgo., 1959-65, asst. v.p. loans and credit, 1965-71, v.p., trust officer, head trust dept., 1971—, also chmn. dirs.'s trust com.; dir. RHC Title Holding Co.; Ravenswood Health Corp.; mem. trust com. W.N. Lane Interfin. Inc.; lectr., media commentator fin. planning, law, taxation, trusts and estates, govt. Sec., bd. dirs., exec. com. Ravenswood Hosp. Med. Center, Chgo.; adv. bd. Nat. Coll. Edn., Evanston, Ill. Mem. Chgo. Bar Assn., Am. Bar Assn. (bd. dirs.), Land Trust Council Ill., Chgo. Assn. of Commerce and Industry, Bank Adminstrn. Inst. Republican. Presbyterian. Clubs: Oak Park Tennis; Yale of Chgo. Home: 1027 N Marion St Oak Park IL 60302 Office: 3201 N Ashland Ave Chicago IL 60657

KIONKA, EDWARD JAMES, lawyer; b. Oak Park, Ill., Feb. 18, 1939; s. Edward Frederick and Antoinette (Harcus) K.; B.S., U. Ill., 1960, J.D., 1962; LL.M. (Krulewitch fellow), Columbia U., 1974; m. Sandra Sellers, Aug. 17, 1958 (div. Apr. 1974); children—Thomas Edward, Meridith Ann, David James. Admitted to Ill. bar, 1962, Mo. bar, 1977; asso. firm Leibman, Williams, Bennett & Baird (now Sidley & Austin), Chgo., 1962-64; instr. U. Mich. Law Sch., 1964-65; dir. Ill. Inst. for Continuing Legal Edn., Springfield, 1965-67; asst. dean, asst. prof. law U. Ill. Coll. Law, 1967-71; cons. atty., Ill., 1971-72, 75-76; asso. prof. law So. Ill. U., Carbondale, 1973-75, 76-77, prof., 1977—; vis. prof. law Washington U., St. Louis, 1979-80; spl. counsel gen. govt. com. 6th Ill. Constl. Conv., 1970; mem. com. rules of evidence Ill. Supreme Ct., 1977-79, reporter com. jury instrns. in civil cases, 1979—; cons. to lawyers on civil trials, appeals; bd. dirs. Ill. Inst. for Continuing Legal Edn., 1967-72, 73—, mem. exec. com., 1967-71, 80—, treas., 1980-82. Mem. Am., Ill. (publs. com. 1979—), Chgo., Jackson County bar assns., Bar Assn. Met. St. Louis, Assn. Trial Lawyers of Am., Appellate Lawyers Assn. (treas. 1974-75, sec. 1975-76, v.p. 1976-77, pres. 1977-78), Am. Judicature Soc., Order of Coif, Scribes, Phi Delta Phi. Author: Tort Law in a Nutshell, 1977; Practitioners Handbook for Appeals to the Illinois Supreme and Appellate Courts, 1978, 2d edit., 1980. Asso. editor-in-chief U. Ill. Law Forum, 1961-62; gen. editor, chpt. author Illinois Civil Practice After Trial, 1970, 75. Home: 601 W Main St Carbondale IL 62901

KIPKA, ROSS ALBIN, lawyer, pharm. co. exec.; b. Cleve., Apr. 11, 1930; s. Ross Eugene and Marion Varian (Albin) K.; B.A., Yale U., 1952; J.D., U. Mich., 1957; m. Mary Josephine Harder, May 28, 1965; children—Kathryn Harder, Julia Kirby. Admitted to Ohio bar, 1957; with firm Baker, Hostetler & Patterson, Cleve., 1957-66; with Eli Lilly Internat. Corp., Indpls., 1966-70, asst. sec., counsel, 1970-79; asst. counsel Eli Lilly and Co., 1979—. Bd. dirs. Indpls. Settlements, Inc., 1975—; pres. bd. dirs. Concord Center Assn., Indpls., 1974—. Served with USAF, 1952-54. Mem. Am., Ohio, Cleve. bar assns., Zeta Psi, Phi Delta Phi. Republican. Episcopalian. Clubs: Columbia (Indpls.); Yale (N.Y.C.); Cleve. Athletic; Small Point (Maine). Sr. editor Mich. Law Rev., 1956-57. Home: 6161 N Meridian W Dr Indianapolis IN 46208 Office: PO Box 32 307 E McCarty St Indianapolis IN 46208

KIPP, DEBORAH SHARPLES, educator; b. Fall River, Mass., Feb. 16, 1955; d. Irving William and Doreen Marie (Senechal) Sharples; B.S., Providence Coll., 1977; M.S., S.D. State U., 1979; m. William John Kipp, Feb. 10, 1978. Lab. teaching asst. Providence (R.I.) Coll., 1975-77; research asst. S.D. State U. dairy sci. dept., Brookings, 1978-79; supr. Dairy Herd Improvement Assn., Renville County, Minn., 1979-80; instr. agr. Willmar Area Vocat. and Tech. Inst., (Minn.), 1980—. Adviser Willmar E.A.R.T.H. Club. Mem. Am. Diary Sci. Assn., NEA, Nat. Agr. Instrs. Assn., Minn. Edn. Assn., Minn. Agr. Instrs. Assn., Willmar Edn. Assn., Willmar Vocat. Tech. Faculty Assn. (treas.), Union Concerned Scientists, Nat. Wildlife Fedn., Friends of Earth. Clubs: Sierra; Willmar Ag Sales. Home: Box 40F Rural Route 1 New London MN 56273 Office: Agr Dept Willmar Area Vocational and Tech Inst Willmar MN 56201

KIPPER, DAVID ABRAHAM, clin. psychologist; b. Tel Aviv, Israel, Mar. 24, 1939; s. Shlomo and Hulda Kipper; B.A., Bar-Ilan U., Israel, 1964; Ph.D. in Psychology, U. Durham (Eng.), 1969; m. Barbara Rose Levy, Sept. 9, 1974; children—Talia Rose, Tamar Yudit. Dir. group psychotherapy, psychodrama and sociometry, Moreno Acad., Beacon, N.Y., 1967; lectr. dept. psychology, coordinator clin. program, coordinator Psychology Clinic, Bar-Ilan U., 1969-72, sr. lectr., 1974-76, 78—, head clin. program, 1978-80; postdoctoral fellow in behavior modification SUNY, Stony Brook, 1972-73; sr. lectr. dept. psychology Tel-Aviv U., 1975-76; vis. research psychologist Indsl. Relations Center, U. Chgo., 1976-78, research asso.-psychologist, dir. behavior simulation unit Human Resources Center for Research, Edn. and Tng., 1979—; trainer, tchr., practitioner Am. Bd. Examiners in Psychodrama, Group Psychotherapy and Sociometry, 1979—. Registered psychologist, Ill.; lic. clin. psychologist and supr. psychotherapy, Israel. Mem. Am. Psychol. Assn., Brit. Psychol. Soc., Assn. for Advancement Behavior Therapy, Am. Soc. Group Psychotherapy, Psychodrama and Sociometry, Israel Psychol. Assn. (clin. div., accredited supr. psychotherapy). Mem. internat. cons. bd. Small Group Behavior; co-exec. editor: Jour. Group Psychotherapy, Psychodrama and Sociometry; contbr. articles to profl. jours. Office: Human Resources Center U Chgo 1225 E 60th St Chicago IL 60637

KIRACOFE, JOHN HARMON, city mgr.; b. Gomer, Ohio, Feb. 8, 1921; s. Chester Harmon and Martha Jane (Watkins) K.; B.S. in Civil Engring., Ohio No. U., 1954; grad. program in nat. econs. Indsl. Coll. Armed Forces, 1957; cert. in chem. engring. Ohio State U., 1958, cert. in traffic engring., 1962; cert. U. Md. Law Enforcement Inst., 1965; postgrad in tech. of mgmt. Am. U., 1966; diploma Internat. City Mgmt. Assn. Tng. Inst., 1974; M.Public Adminstrn., Nova U., 1977, D.Public Adminstrn., 1978; m. Adeena Mary Miller, Aug. 18, 1946; children—Gregory Lee, Douglas Eugene. Sr. engr. Standard Oil Co. (Ohio), Lima, 1948-60; city engr., Lima, 1960-63, dir. planning, 1963-64; town mgr., Aberdeen, Md., 1964-65; city mgr. Bowie, Md., 1965-69, Berkley, Mich., 1969—; vis. lectr. public fin. U. Md., 1966; lectr. public works Wayne State U., 1980; instr. public adminstrn. Eastern Mich. U., 1981; participant seminar Nat. Endowment Humanities, 1980. Mem. Lima Community Devel. Com., 1953; v.p. PTA, 1957; pres. Ottawa Watershed Assn., 1958; chmn. Lima Mayor's Tax Study Com., 1958, Lima Traffic Com., 1960; chmn. Lima Regional Area Transp. Planning Coordinating Com., 1964; bd. dirs. Greater Bowie Bd. Trade, 1966-68; mcpl. cons. Md. Constl. Conv., 1967; mem. Md. Assn. Housing & Renewal Agys., 1966; chief adviser, bd. dirs. Jr. Achievement, Lima, 1960; bd. dirs. Beaumont Hosp. Authority, Royal Oak, Mich.; mem. phys. edn. com. YMCA; trustee, chmn. Southeastern Oakland County Water and Incinerator Authorities, 1969—; treas. Greater Oakland Cable TV Authority, 1981. Del. to gen. assembly, mem. council on regional devel. S.E. Mich. Council of Govts., 1981. Served with USAAF, 1941-45. Recipient Engring. award Lincoln Arc Welding Found., 1953-54, Distinguished Service award Lima Soc. Profl. Engrs. Registered profl. engr., Ohio, Md., Fla., Mich., D.C.; registered profl. community planner, Mich. Mem. Lima (past pres.), Ohio (vice chmn. engrs.-in-industry functional group 1957, chmn. young engrs. com. 1958, trustee 1960) socs. profl. engrs., Lima Refinery Foremen's Club (pres. 1956), Md. City Mgrs. Assn. (pres. 1967), Internat. City Mgmt. Assn., Mich. City Mgmt. Assn. (chmn. 1979-80), Am. Inst. Planners, Mich. Municipal League (transp. com. 1974—, employee tng. adv. com. 1976, 77, workman's compensation ins. adv. com. 1976, public works adv. com. 1980), Order Engr. Ohio No. U., Mich. Engring. Soc., Am. Acad. Polit. and Social Sci., Am. Soc. Public Adminstrn., Acad. Polit. Sci., Inst. Transp. Engrs., So. Mich. Water and Sewer Utilities Assn., Bldg. Ofcls. and Code Adminstrs. Internat., Am. Legion, VFW. Clubs: Masons (32 deg.), Shriners, Elks, Lions (1st v.p.), Toastmasters Internat. (past area gov., pres., recipient Distinguished Service award 1957). Presbyterian (elder). Contbr. articles to profl. jours. Patentee in field. Home: 4218 Cumberland St Berkley MI 48072 Office: 3338 Coolidge Hwy Berkley MI 48072

KIRBERGER, WILLIAM ALFRED, purchasing exec.; b. Mpls., Mar. 9, 1928; s. Alfred William and Grace L. K.; student U. Minn., 1951-55; m. Bernice M. Moe, Oct. 21, 1950; children—Carrie, Randy. Safety and prodn./inventory control mgr. Perfection Pump & Milking Machine Co., 1951-55; purchasing and inventory supr. Sewall Gears, St. Paul, 1955-59; purchasing dir. Hartzell Mfg., St. Paul, 1959-63; mgr. purchasing, materials and services Minco Products, Mpls., 1963—; dir., v.p. bd. Rise, Inc., Spring Lake Park, Minn., 1974-76; cons. in field of procurement and inventory practices. Bd. govs. Mpls. YMCA; former v.p. bd. dirs. N.E. Mpls. YMCA; former dir. Camp Bd. Luth. Ch. of Am.-Minn. Synod. Served with U.S. Army, 1946. Mem. Nat. Assn. Purchasing Mgmt. (disting. profl. person award, treas. nat. materials mgmt. group), Twin City Purchasing Mgmt. Assn. (pres.), Fridley C. of C. (dir. edn. com., public service award), Gideons Internat., Am. Law Enforcement Officers Assn., Citizens Band Radio Patrol, Good Sam Recreational Vehicle Club, Nat. Camper Hikers Assn., DAV. Home: 163 16th Ave NW New Brighton MN 55112 Office: 7300 Commerce Ln Fridley MN 55432

KIRBY, KENT BRUCE, artist; b. Fargo, N.D., Dec. 31, 1934; s. Harold Ely and Vida Nicole (Vennerstrom) K.; B.A., Carleton Coll., 1956; M.A., U. Dakota, 1959; M.F.A., U. Mich., 1970; m. Lynn Rennetha Schutte, Sept. 1, 1956; children—Kalin Louise, Jeffrey Bruce, Kirstin Beth. Tchr., Benjamin Franklin Jr. High Sch., Fargo, 1956-59; instr. art, acting head dept. art Muskingum Coll., 1959-61; instr. Wilkes Coll., 1961-62; faculty dept. art Alma (Mich.) Coll., 1962—, prof., 1971—, chmn. dept. art and design, 1962—, chmn. div. fine arts, 1973-75, Charles A. Dana prof. art, 1976; one-man shows include: Grand Rapids (Mich.) Art Mus., 1981, U. N.Mex., 1981; group shows include: Mich. Printmakers Biennial Exhibition, Detroit Inst. Arts, 1977, 20th N.D. Annual Printing and Drawing Exhibition, Grand Forks, 1977; represented in permanent collections: Guggenheim Mus., N.Y.C., Chgo. Art Inst., Met. Mus. Art, N.Y.C., Detroit Art Inst.; chmn. museums com., council mem. Mich. State Council for Arts, 1966-67; research fellow Newberry Library, Chgo., 1974. Mich. Council for Arts grantee, 1975, 78, 80; Nat. Endowment Arts grantee, 1976. Mem. AAUP, Coll. Art Assn., Nat. Council Art Adminstrs. Office: 614 W Superior St Alma MI 48801

KIRCHMAN, MARGARET MARY, occupational therapist, educator; b. Bay City, Mich., Mar. 26, 1922; s. Frank Joseph and Mary Ann (Auman) K.; A.A. cum laude, Bay City Jr. Coll., 1941; B.S. in Occupational Therapy (Univ. scholar), Eastern Mich. U., 1951; M.A., U. So. Calif., 1964; Ph.D., U. Mich., 1973. Staff therapist sect. occupational therapy U. Mich., 1952-64, asst. chief div. occupational therapy, 1964-70, grad. asst. Inst. for Study Mental Retardation, 1972, adminstrv. intern Inst. Study Mental Retardation, 1972-73, guest lectr. in spl. edn. U. Mich., Dearborn, 1972-73; lectr. occupational therapy curriculum Eastern Mich. U., 1970-72; asso. prof. occupational therapy, head grad. study and research for curriculum in occupational therapy Sch. Asso. Med. Scis., U. Ill., Chgo., 1974-76, asso. prof., asst. dept. head, dept. occupational therapy Coll. Asso. Health Professions, 1976-80, asso. prof. grad. study and research, dept. occupational therapy Sch. Public Health, 1980—; mem. Coalition on Aging, 1976—; mem. Task Force on Age Discrimination, 1977—; trainee U. So. Calif., 1963-64, U. Mich., Ann Arbor, 1970-73. Recipient Research award Am. Occupational Therapy Found., 1972, Outstanding Therapist award Mich. Occupational Therapy Assn., 1974. Mem. Am. Occupational Therapy Assn. (project cons. 1971-73, named to Roster of Fellows 1976), Ill. Occupational Therapy Assn., Ill. Centro Metro Occupational Therapy Dist., Am. Public Health Assn., Arthritis Found. Roman Catholic. Research on personality of rheumatoid arthritic patient. Home: 903 S Ashland Blvd Apt 418B Chicago IL 60607 Office: 1919 W Taylor St Room 325 Chicago IL 60612

KIRCHNER, CHARLES, mgmt. cons.; b. Havana, Ill., Nov. 15, 1930; s. Joseph Louis and Greta Alice (Nollsch) K.; B.S. in Arch., U. Ill., 1953, M.B.A., 1977; m. Jean House, July 6, 1962; 1 dau., Andrea Paige. Archtl. designer, 1953-57; city planner/asst. exec. dir. Springfield-Sangamon County (Ill.) Regional Planning Commn., 1957-61; chief Div. of Local and Regional Planning, State of Ill., Springfield, 1962-71; city coordinator City of Springfield, 1971-73; spl. asst. to dir. Ill. Dept. Local Govt. Affairs, Springfield, 1973-77; spl. cons. Ill. Dept. Local Govt. Affairs, 1977-79; spl. cons. Ill. Dept. Commerce and Public Affairs, 1979—; pres. Environments Plus, Inc., 1979—; vis. prof. U. Ill., 1979. Mem. exec. com. Central Ill. Health Planning Council, 1970-75; adv. com. Coll. of Phys. Edn., U. Ill., 1970-71; bd. dirs., treas. Springfield Urban League, 1970-76, 78-80; mem. Community Service and Continuing Edn. council, Ill. Bd. Higher Edn., 1969-71; mem. Springfield Area Council for Pub. Broadcasting, 1975—; mem. Capital City R.R. Relocation Authority steering com., 1975—; bd. dirs. Springfield Arts Council, 1978—. Mem. Am. Inst. Cert. Planners, Am. Planning Assn. (treas. Ill. chpt. 1979-81), Springfield C. of C. (dir. 1970-72). Editor: Local and Regional Planning Notes, 1967-71; contbr. numerous articles to profl. jours. Home: 3 Country Pl Springfield IL 62703 Office: 222 E College St Springfield IL 62706

KIRCHNER, JAMES WILLIAM, elec. engr.; b. Cleve., Oct. 17, 1920; s. William Sebastian and Marcella Louise (Stuart) K.; B.S. in Elec. Engring., Ohio U., Athens, 1950, M.S., 1951; m. Eda Christene Landfear, June 11, 1950 (dec. May 1977); children—Kathleen Ann, Susan Lynn. Instr. elec. engring. Ohio U., 1950-52; mgr. liaison engring. Lear Siegler Inc., Maple Heights, Ohio, 1952-64; coordinator engring. services Case Western Res. U., Cleve., 1964-72, gen. mgr. Med. Center Co., 1972—. Mem. Portage County Republican exec. com., 1961-62; treas. Aurora (Ohio) PTA, 1963-65, v.p., 1965-66; trustee ch., 1963-65, deacon, 1978—. Served with USAAF, 1942-45; PTO. Registered profl. engr., Ohio. Mem. Cleve. (dir. 1969-71), Nat., Ohio socs. profl. engrs., Cleve. Engring. Soc. (chmn. environ. com.

1976), IEEE (sr.), Am. Pollution Control Assn., ASEE. Home: 140 Aurora Hudson Rd Aurora OH 44202 Office: 2250 Circle Dr Cleveland OH 44106

KIRCHNER, JOHN HOWARD, psychologist; b. Passaic, N.J., Dec. 28, 1933; s. John Howard and Anita Gladys (Smith) K.; A.B., U. Ill., 1955; M.A., Northwestern U., 1956, 60, Ph.D., 1964; postgrad. Bradley U., 1965-68; m. Nora Ilse Kuehne, June 16, 1956; 1 son, John Douglas. Tchr., high sch., Evergreen Park, Ill., 1956-57, Park Ridge, Ill., 1959-61; asso. prof. Ill. State U., Normal, 1964-71, psychologist, 1965-71; pvt. practice Cashen & Kirchner, Normal, 1969-71; chief psychologist Wood County Mental Health Clinic, Bowling Green, Ohio, 1971-75; exec. dir., chief psychologist Gt. River Mental Health Center, Muscatine, Iowa, 1975-79, Jasper County Mental Health Center, Newton, Iowa, 1979—. Served with U.S. Army, 1957-59, 61-62. Diplomate in clin. psychology Am. Bd. Profl. Psychology. Mem. Am., Iowa psychol. assns., Phi Beta Kappa, Phi Delta Kappa, Delta Phi Alpha. Contbr. articles to profl. jours. Home: 300 E 30th St South Newton IA 50208 Office: 2009 1st Ave E Newton IA 50208

KIRCHNER, RICHARD JAY, educator; b. Schenectady, Feb. 17, 1930; s. Richard Jacob and Leah (Williams) K.; B.S., U. Wis., 1952, M.S., 1955, postgrad., 1956; Ed.D., Mich. State U, 1962; m. Barbara Ann Crane, Feb. 2, 1952; children—Richard Alec, Barbara Jayne, Carolyn Diane, Robert Jay, Kathleen Kay. Instr. wrestling and track coach St. Cloud (Minn.) Tchrs. Coll., 1955-56; asst. prof., coaching staff Central Mich. U., Mt. Pleasant, 1956-62, prof. recreation, chmn. dept., 1962—, chmn. pres.'s adv. com.; camp program dir., camp dir. Elkton-Pigeon-Bayport Sch. Camp, Caseville, Mich., 1962; municipal recreation dir. Petoskey (Mich.), 1963, cons., 1964-74; vice chmn. citizens adv. com. Recreation Services div. Mich. Dept. Conservation, 1966-67. Pres. Mt. Pleasant Intermediate Sch. PTA, 1968-69; chmn. tech. planning com. Mt. Pleasant Recreation Commn. Served to capt. USMCR, 1952-54. Mem. AAHPER (v.p. Mich. 1966-67, v.p. Midwest dist. 1973-74), Nat Recreation and Parks Assn., Am. Assn. Leisure and Recreation (nat. pres. 1976-77, nat. accreditation council 1978—, vice chmn. 1979-81, chmn. 1981-82), Am. Camp Assn., Mich. Soc. Gerontology, Outdoor Edn. and Camping Council (charter), Mich. Recreation and Parks Assn. (v.p. 1968-70), Phi Eta Sigma, Phi Epsilon Kappa, Phi Delta Kappa. Home: 6953 Riverside Dr Mount Pleasant MI 48858

KIRK, MILDRED THOMAS, educator; b. St. Louis, Apr. 1, 1927; d. Robert and Annie Laura (Poole) Thomas; B.S., U. Mo., 1975; m. Isaac Wilson Kirk, Apr. 10, 1948; 1 son, Isaac Douglas. Acctg. clk. Southwestern Bell Telephone Co., St. Louis, 1950-75; tchr. Buder Sch., St. Louis, 1976—. Mem. Assn. Supervision and Curriculum Devel., Mo. Tchrs. Assn., U. Mo. Alumni Assn., Am. Fedn. Tchrs., Nat. Writers Club. Lutheran. Author: A Different Kind of Birthday, 1980. Home: 5919 Evergreen St Saint Louis MO 63134 Office: 5319 Lansdowne St Saint Louis MO 63109

KIRK, WILLIAM EDWARD, child psychiatrist, mental health services facility adminstr.; b. Erie, Pa., May 7, 1933; s. Cecil Rayne and Ruth Elizabeth (Weindorf) K.; B.A., Gannon Coll., 1955; M.D., St. Louis U., 1959; m. Jean Marie Vickey, July 19, 1958; children—Douglas, Kathleen, Cynthia, Karen, Jeanmarie, Mary Patrice, Susan, Kristen, Michelle, Sharon. Intern, St. Francis Gen. Hosp. and Rehab. Inst., Pitts., 1959-60; resident in gen. psychiatry Warren (Pa.) State Hosp., 1960-62; fellow in child psychiatry Children's Psychiat. Hosp., U. Mich., 1962-64; dir. York Woods Center, Ypsilanti, Mich., 1964-77, tng. dir. child psychiatry fellowship program, 1974-76; pvt. practice medicine specializing in psychiatry and child psychiatry, Ann Arbor, Mich., 1972—; mem. staff York Woods Center, Detroit; staff Mt. Carmel Mercy Hosp., Detroit, dir., chmn. dept. child psychiatry, 1977-80; dir. child psychiatry program Wyandotte (Mich.) Gen. Hosp., 1981—. Recipient award for excellence in natural sci. Gannon Coll., 1955; diplomate Am. Bd. Psychiatry and Neurology. Fellow Am. Psychiat. Assn., Am. Orthopsychiat. Assn., Am. Acad. Child Psychiatry; mem. Mich. Psychiat. Soc. (pres.). Roman Catholic. Club: Racquet of Ann Arbor. Contbr. articles to profl. jours. Home: 2900 Provincial St Ann Arbor MI 48104 Office: Wyandotte Gen Hosp 2333 Biddle St Wyandotte MI 48192

KIRKHUS, HAROLD PRESTON, ret. educator; b. Leland, Ill., July 31, 1910; s. Burton Maynard and Ida (Kittleson) K.; A.B., Bradley U., 1933; M.A., U. Ill., 1938; student Miami U., 1948; m. Ruth Susan Mathre, June 25, 1936; children—John Mark, Mary Jane Kirkhus Hinshaw, Sue Elizabeth Kirkhus Swanson, Karen Jean Kirkhus Mason. Tchr., prin. Newark (Ill.) Pub. Schs., 1933-38; prin. Oswego (Ill.) Consol. Elementary Schs., 1938-43; with Peoria (Ill.) Pub. Schs., 1944-73, tchr., 1944-57, dir. adult edn., 1954-60. dir. ednl. research, 1957-73, ret., 1973. Chmn. pub.-pvt. edn. unit United Fund, 1957-61; exec. sec. steering com. that established Ill. Central Coll., 1966; mem. restoration com. Jubilee Coll.; bd. dirs. Peoria Neighborhood House Assn., 1976-77. Recipient merit award Peoria Pub. Sch. System, 1973, certificate of appreciation Peoria Bd. Edn., 1973; Restoration Service award Jubilee Coll., 1976. Mem. Ill. (past pres. Peoria div.), Peoria (past pres.) edn. assns., NEA, Kendall County Tchrs. Assn. (past pres.), Adelphic Nat. Lit. Soc., Am. Ednl. Research Assn., Sons of Norway, Phi Delta Kappa (Distinguished Service Key Edn. 1946, 67, Emeritus Membership award 1973), Kappa Phi Kappa, Pi Kappa Delta, Beta Sigma Mu. Lutheran. Republican. Club: Kiwanis. Home: Old Orchard Trace 6024 Imperial Dr 403 Peoria IL 61614

KIRKPATRICK, CHARLES DAVID, clergyman; b. Rockford, Ill., Apr. 16, 1921; s. Charles and Ollie Jane (Eustice) K.; student Wessington Springs Jr. Coll., S.D., 1939-43, Platteville (Wis.) U., 1943-44; A.B., Seattle Pacific U., 1946, D.D. (hon.), 1965; postgrad. Fuller Theol. Sem., 1975; m. Ivanelle Lois Bendorf, Sept. 16, 1947; children—Barbara Kirkpatrick Landis, Pamela Kirkpatrick Endicott. Ordained to ministry Free Meth. Ch. N. Am., 1943; pastor, Platteville, Wis., 1943-44, Portland, Oreg., 1947-49, Seattle, 1949-56; supt. Pacific N.W. Conf., 1956-64; gen. missionary sec., Gen. Missionary Bd., Winona Lake, Ind., 1964—; dir. World Relief Commn., Wheaton, Ill., 1965—; observer Congress on Evangelism, Berlin, Germany; del. Congress on World Evangelization, Lausanne, Switzerland, Consultation on World Evangelization, Thailand; mem. bd. adminstrn. Free Meth. Ch. N. Am., 1960-64. Mem. N. Am. Panel World Evang. Fellowship, Evang. Fgn. Missions Assn. (dir., past pres.), World Fellowship Free Meth. Ch. (N. Am. panel), Nat. Assn. Evangs. (dir., 1974-76). Club: Rotary. Contbr. articles to religious publs. Home: 526 Crestlane Dr Warsaw IN 46580 Office: Gen Missionary Bd 901 College Ave Winona Lake IN 46590

KIRKPATRICK, CLAYTON, newspaper editor; b. Waterman, Ill., Jan. 8, 1915; s. Clayton Matteson and Mable Rose (Swift) K.; A.B., U. Ill., 1937; m. Thelma Marie De Mott, Feb. 13, 1943; children—Pamela Marie (Mrs. Foy), Bruce, Eileen Bea, James Walter. Reporter, City News Bur., Chgo., 1938; mem. staff Chgo. Tribune, 1938—, day city editor, 1958-61, city editor, 1961-63, asst. mng. editor, 1963-65, mng. editor, 1965-67, exec. editor, 1967-69, editor, 1969-79; v.p. Chgo. Tribune Co., 1967-77, exec. v.p., 1977-79, pres., 1979—, chief exec. officer, 1980—. Served with USAAF, 1942-45. Decorated Bronze Star medal; recipient Elijah Parish Lovejoy award Colby Coll., 1978; William Allen White award U. Kans., 1977; Fourth Estate award Nat. Press Club, 1979. Mem. Phi Beta Kappa, Sigma Delta Chi. Republican. Methodist. Clubs: Chicago, Tavern, Chgo. Press, Commercial, Glen Oak Country, Butler Nat. Golf. Home: 156 Sunset Ave Glen Ellyn IL 60137 Office: Chgo Tribune 435 N Michigan Ave Chicago IL 60611*

KIRKPATRICK, GARY LEE, accountant, computer program exec.; b. Davenport, Iowa, Feb. 14, 1945; s. William E. and Ruby B. (Bernauer) Kirkpatrick; student Palmer Jr. Coll., 1966-67, U. Iowa, 1967-69. Tax. cons. H. & R. Block, Davenport, 1970, Tax Corp. Am., Moline, Ill., 1971; owner, operator Kirkpatrick Enterprises, Davenport, 1972—. Served with USNR, 1964-66. Gordon H. Clarke scholar, 1967-69. Mem. U.S. Chess Fedn. (sustaining). Roman Catholic. Clubs: Quad-City Computer (pres.), Toastmasters, Illowa Chess (sec. 1976-77), Mensa. Home: 230 W 3d St Apt 5 Davenport IA 52801 Office: 515 Putnam Bldg Davenport IA 52801

KIRKPATRICK, JAMES C., state ofcl., newspaper publisher; b. Braymer, Mo., June 15, 1905; s. Ray N. and Lena L. (Rea) K.; student Central Mo. State U., U. Mo. Sch. Journalism; m. Jessamine Elizabeth Young, Aug. 18, 1927; 1 son, Don W. Editor, Warrensburg (Mo.) Daily Star-Jour., Jefferson City (Mo.) Post-Tribune and Daily Capitol News; pub. Windsor (Mo.) Rev., 1954-72, Lamar (Mo.) Daily Democrat, 1972-74; former adminstrv. asst. to gov. of Mo.; sec. state State of Mo., Jefferson City, 1965—. Campaign dir. Missourians for Progress, 1962; mem. Mo. Gov.'s Com. on Commerce and Indsl. Devel., 1961-65; mem. Fed. Elections Commn. Advisory Panel, 1975-77. Mem. Mo. Democratic State Exec. Com., from 1973; hon. chmn. Mo. March of Dimes, 1977. Bd. dirs., past chmn. Mo. 4-H Found.; trustee, pres. Central Mo. State U. Recipient Honor scroll Mo. Good Rds. and Sts. Assn., 1968; Honor medal U. Mo. Sch. Journalism, 1969, U. Mo. Faculty-Alumni award, 1972. Mem. Mo. (past pres.), Central Mo. (past pres.) press assns., Nat. Assn. Secs. State (pres. 1973-74), Dem. Editors Mo. (past pres.), Mo. Acad. Squires, Windsor C. of C. (past pres.). Rotarian (past 1st v.p. Jefferson City), Lion (past pres. Windsor). Home: 602B Norris Dr Jefferson City MO 65101 Office: Sec of State Capitol Bldg Jefferson City MO 65101*

KIRKPATRICK, PAUL WILLIAM, psychologist; b. Lafayette, Ind., Aug. 3, 1950; s. Paul Alfred and Emily (Acquaroli) K.; B.A., Ind. U., 1972; Ph.D., U. Tex., 1977. Clin. dir. Coastal Bend Youth City, Corpus Christi, Tex., 1976-78; clin. psychologist Harris County Mental Health/Mental Retardation Assn., Houston, 1978-80; pvt. practice clin. psychology, Houston, 1979-80; cons. psychologist Hobert-Martin Cons. Psychologists, Inc., Mpls., 1980—; lectr. in field. Author Metz Disting. scholar, 1968-72; NIMH fellow, U. Tex., 1972-73. Mem. Am. Psychol. Assn., Minn. Psychol. Assn., Nat. Register of Health Service Providers in Psychology, Phi Beta Kappa. Office: 4428 IDS Center Minneapolis MN 55402

KIRSCHENBAUM, STUART EDWARD, podiatrist; b. Bklyn., Jan. 23, 1945; s. Albert Barry and Eleanor K.; B.S., Mich. State U., 1965; D.P.M., N.Y. Coll. Podiatric Medicine, 1970; m. Janice Beardslee, July 27, 1967; children—Jennifer Robin, Storm Tyler. Resident in foot surgery Grand Community Hosp., Detroit, 1970-71; gen. practice podiatry, Detroit, 1970—; founder, pres. Foot Surgeons of Detroit, P.C., 1970—; chief podiatry services, trustee Monsignor Clement Kern Hosp. for Spl. Surgery; nat. lectr. in field; bd. dirs. Mich. Foot Health Found.; Profl. and amateur boxing judge Mich. Athletic Commn.; judge World Boxing Assn.; team podiatrist women's basketball team Shaw Coll., Detroit. Diplomate Am. Bd. Podiatric Surgery, Nat. Bd. Podiatry Examiners. Fellow Royal Soc. Health, Am. Coll. Foot Surgeons, Am. Soc. Podiatric Medicine; mem. Am. Podiatry Assn., Mich. Podiatry Assn. (ethics com.), Mich. Pub. Health Assn., Am. Pub. Health Assn., Am. Med. Writers Assn., Am. Coll. Sports Medicine (chmn. boxing com.), Acad. Podiatric Medicine, World Med. Assn., Am. Soc. Podiatric Sports Medicine, Am. Soc. Podiatric Dermatology, Am. Acad. Podiatric Acupuncture, Internat. Platform Assn., Internat. Vet. Boxers Assn. (podiatry cons.), Internat. Acupuncture Research Assn. Author publs. on foot surgery and sports medicine. Home: 27080 Wellington Rd Franklin MI 48025 Office: 8339 Mack Ave Detroit MI 48214

KISELA, JAMES FRANCIS, agrl. chem. co. exec.; b. Chgo., July 12, 1942; s. Frank and Helen K.; M.B.A., U. Chgo., 1973; m. Kathe R. Rieger, June 14, 1969; children—David, Donald, Douglas. Various personnel mgmt. positions to dir. personnel and orgn. CNA Fin. Corp., Chgo., 1964-75; dir. personnel Terra Chems. Internat., Inc., Sioux City, Iowa, 1975-76, v.p. personnel, 1976—; mem. adj. faculty Morningside Coll., Sioux City, Briar Cliff Coll., Sioux City. Bd. dirs. Friends of FM 90, United Way of Siouxland; chmn. Citizens Com. for the '80's, Sioux City Community Sch. Dist., 1979; officers compensation com. Ill. State C. of C., 1973; trustee 1st Unitarian Ch. Accredited personnel mgr. Personnel Accreditation Inst. Mem. Am. Compensation Assn., Am. Soc. Tng. and Devel., Am. Soc. Personnel Adminstrn., Interprofl. Inst. Unitarian. Club: Kiwanis. Office: PO Box 1828 Sioux City IA 51102

KISER, WILLIAM SITES, surgeon; b. Romney, W.Va., Jan. 27, 1928; B.S., U. Md., 1949, M.D., 1953; m. Eugenia Crow, May 1, 1954; children—William Sites, Jonathan Van Lieu, Stephen Graham. Intern, U. Hosp., Balt., 1953-54, asst. resident in surgery, 1957-58, asst. resident in urology, 1958-60, resident in urology, 1960-61; sr. investigator and staff urologist Nat. Cancer Inst., NIH, Bethesda, Md., 1961-64; practice medicine specializing in urology, Cleve., 1964—; staff urologist Cleve. Clinic Found., 1964-73, bd. govs., 1972—, exec. sec., 1973-74, vice chmn. ops., 1974-76, exec. vice chmn., 1976, chmn. bd. govs., 1977—. Served to maj., M.C., USAF, 1954-57. Diplomate Am. Bd. Urology. Fellow Am. Coll. Physician Execs. (regent); mem. ACS, Am. Assn. Clin. Urologists, Am. Urol. Assn., Cleve. Urol. Assn., Nat. Urologic Forum, Soc. of Univ. Urologists, Acad. Medicine of Cleve., Am. Soc. Nephrology, Transplantation Soc., AMA, Am. Acad. Med. Dirs., Societe Internationale D'Urologie, Societe Internationale D'Nephrologie, Am. Mgmt. Assn., Alpha Omega Alpha (pres. Beta chpt. 1953), Phi Eta Sigma, Phi Kappa Phi. Contbr. articles on nephrology and transplantation to profl. jours. Office: Cleveland Clinic Found 9500 Euclid Ave Cleveland OH 44106

KISH, ELMER ANTHONY, cons. engr.; b. Glens Run, O., May 24, 1913; s. Antal and Theresa (Horvath) K.; diploma elec. engring. Am. Sch., 1937; postgrad. Oberlin Coll., 1940-41, Detroit U., 1944-47, Case Inst. Tech., 1949-51; m. Theresa Popp, July 16, 1938; children—Karen Jean, Roger Anthony. Elec. supt. Albert Kahn, Asso. Architects and Engrs., Inc., Detroit, 1942-43; elec. designer Austin Co., spl. engring. div., Cleve., 1941; chief elec. engr. Brooker Engring. Co., Detroit, 1944-47; constrn. mgr. Harley, Ellington & Day, architects and engrs., Detroit, 1947-48; constrn. engr. C. Iber & Sons, gen. contractors, Peoria, Ill., 1948; constrn. mgr. Fulton, Krinsky & DelaMotte, architects, Cleve., 1949-50; asst. chief elec. engr. J. Gordon Turnbull, Inc., cons. engrs., Cleve., 1950-53; chief elec. engr. Arthur G. McKee & Co., indsl. div., Cleve., 1954; owner Kish Engring. Co., Lyndhurst, O., 1955—. Registered profl. engr., Ohio, N.Y., Mich., Mo. Mem. Am. Inst. Plant Engrs., Am. Soc. Heating, Refrigeration and Air Conditioning Engrs., Cleve. Engring. Soc., Energy Conservation Council, Nat. Fire Protection Assn. Mason (Shriner). Address: 4837 Fairlawn Rd Lyndhurst OH 44124

KISHPAUGH, ALLAN RICHARD, mech. engr.; b. Dover, N.J., Aug. 31, 1937; B.S. in Mech. Engring., N.J. Inst. Tech., 1967; m. Maryann M. Bizub, July 31, 1965. Engring. technician Stapling Machines Co., Rockaway, N.J., 1956-65; design engr. Airoyal Engring. Co., Livingston, N.J., 1965-66; project engr. Simautics Co., Fairfield, N.J., 1966-67; design engr. Pyrofilm Resistor Mfg. Co., Cedar Knolls, N.J., 1967-68; sr. engr., project mgr. Packaging Systems div. Standard Packaging Corp., Clifton, N.J., 1968-77; sr. machine design engr. Travenol Labs., Round Lake, Ill., 1977-79; dir. engring. TEC, Inc., Alsip, Ill., 1979-80; mgmt. cons., machine developer, Palos Heights, Ill., 1980—; expert Expertise Adv. Service, Inc., 1980—; owner Ark Internat., 1981—. Councilman, Borough of Victory Gardens (N.J.), 1969-71, council pres., 1971, police commnr., 1970-70, chmn. fin. com., 1970; pres. Pompton River Assn., Wayne, N.J., 1976-77; mem. Wayne Flood Control Commn., 1976-77; past deacon, elder, Sunday sch. tchr. and supt. local Presbyn. chs. Served with Air N.G., 1960-61, 62-65, with USAF, 1961-62. Registered profl. engr., N.J., Ill. Mem. ASME (vice chmn. N.J. sect. 1973-74, numerous other regional offices), Nat. Soc. Profl. Engrs. Patentee mechanism for feeding binding wire, wirebound box-making machine, method packaging granular materials, others in field. Address: 6118 W 123d St Palos Heights IL 60463

KISIEL, ROSEMARY ANN GOSSE, ins. brokerage exec.; b. Chgo., Jan. 22, 1954; d. William A. and Sadie M. Gosse; student Triton Coll., 1972-76; B.A. in Psychology, Elmhurst Coll., 1978; M.S. in Adminstrn. and Orgnl. Behavior, George Williams Coll., 1981; m. Terrence L. Kisiel, Aug. 24, 1974. With Stineway Ford Hopkins Drug Co., Melrose Park, Ill., 1972-74, Hoffmann-La Roche, Inc., Des Plaines, Ill., 1974-76; adminstrv. asst. fin. adminstr. Aparacor, Inc., Evanston, Ill., 1976-79, asst. mgr. acctg. systems control, 1979-80; adminstrv. mgr., orgnl. devel. exec. Exec. Ins. Services, Elmhurst, Ill., 1980—. Recipient Meritorious Service award Crusade of Mercy, 1979; Ill. State Scholar, 1976-78. Mem. Am. Soc. Personnel Adminstrn., Am. Mgmt. Assn., Am. Legion Aux., Psi Chi. Roman Catholic. Home: 10315 Medill Ave Melrose Park IL 60164 Office: Exec Ins Services PO Box 372 Elmhurst IL 60126

KISKIS, JAMES MATTHEW, process engr.; b. Springfield, Ohio, Mar. 25, 1932; s. George Charles and Dorothy Jane (Van Gundy) K.; ed. pub. schs., spl. courses; m. Norma Beulah Powell, May 9, 1979; children—Brenda, James, Thomas, Kenneth, Karen, Daniel, Elaine. Apprentice electrician Internat. Harvester Co., Springfield, Ohio, 1949-53; electrician Robbins & Myers, Inc., Springfield, 1954-61, process engr. pump div., Gallipolis, Ohio, 1961-67, inspection supr., quality control mgr., 1967-75, process engr., 1975—. Lic. amateur radio operator, 2d class comml. radiotelephone operator FCC. Republican. Methodist. Club: Mid Ohio Valley Amateur Radio. Research and innovations in elec. motor manufacture and design. Home: 525 Magnolia Dr Gallipolis OH 45631 Office: Box 502 Gallipolis OH 45631

KISPERT, DONALD EUGENE, engring. dept. mgr.; b. Clinton, Ind., Sept. 1, 1928; s. Ortie Curtis and Euphemia (Broatch) K.; B.S. in Civil Engring., Ind. Inst. Tech., 1951; m. Nancy Marie Berghoff, Aug. 27, 1950; children—Robert Calvin, Donna Jean, Linda Sue. Field project engr. E.I. DuPont Co., Ind., Ga., N.J., 1951-54, 55-56; constrn. supr. Socony Mobil Oil Co., New Goshen, Ind., 1954-55; field supt. Fruin-Colnon Constrn. Co., Indpls., 1956-59; design engr. Clyde Williams & Assoc., Indpls., 1956-59, E.R. Hamilton & Assos., 1959-60; bldg. and maintenance mgr. R.R. Donnelley & Sons Co., Warsaw, Ind., 1960-70, mgr. plant engring., 1970-78, quality and services mgr., 1978—. Bd. dirs. Warsaw YMCA, 1965-72. Served with U.S. Army, 1946-48. Licensed profl. engr., Ind. Mem. Nat., Ind. socs. profl. engrs. Republican. Presbyterian. Clubs: Optimists, Masons. Home: 1933 E Clark St Warsaw IN 46580 Office: RTE 30 W Warsaw IN 46586

KISS, JANOS, music educator, composer, condr.; b. Hungary, Mar. 21, 1920; s. Andras and Maria (Laszlo) K.; came to U.S., 1956, naturalized, 1973; teaching diploma Bela Bartok Conservatory of Music, Budapest, 1954; conducting diploma People's Ednl. Inst., Budapest, 1956; Franz Liszt Acad. Music, Budapest, 1954-56; student music edn. sci. Western Res. U., 1960-64; m. Josephine Anna Recse, July 27, 1963. Tchr. brasses Cleve. Music Sch. Settlement, 1964-79; chmn. music dept. St. Luke Sch., Lakewood, Ohio, 1966-70; dir. orch., composer in residence, tchr. instruments Western Res. Acad., Hudson, Ohio, 1967-72; tchr., composer in residence St. Edward High Sch., Lakewood, Ohio, 1968-74; composer in residence Luth. High Sch., Rocky River, Ohio, 1973-76; chmn. music dept. Holy Family Sch., Parma, Ohio, 1974—, St. Ann's Sch., Cleveland Heights, 1974-75; co-founder, condr., music dir. West Suburban Philharmonic Orch., 1969—; hon. mem. Zoltan Kodaly Acad. and Inst., Chgo. Mem. Am. Soc. Univ. Composers, Nat. Assn. Composers U.S.A., Music Tchrs. Nat. Assn., Ohio Music Tchrs. Assn., Cleve. Fedn. Musicians, Am. Music Center, ASCAP. Composer: Spring-At-Las, 1970; String Bass Concerto, 1970; Flute Concerto, 1970; Concerto for Trombone, 1971; On the Wing, for flute and guitar, 1972; Josepha, quintet for alto recorder with violin, viola, cello and harp, 1973; Concerto for B-Flat Clarinet, with orch., 1974; Celebration and Challenge, for wind ensemble with electronics, 1974; Western Legend, rhapsody for harp and orch., 1975; Twilight Mist, for string quartet and organ, 1975; Impression, for trumpet and piano, 1975; Adagio for Viola, with two violins, cello and harp, 1975; Silent Presence, tone poem for clarinet, viola and organ, 1975; winter's Sonnet, flute-harp-organ, 1975; Ballet for Harps, 1975; Concerto for violoncello and orch., 1976; Lexington '76, Bicentennial Rhapsody for Orch., 1976; Divertimento, solo violin, solo viola, solo string bass, harp and chamber ensemble, 1977; Episode for oboe, french horn, bassoon and harp, 1977; In Homage for harp ensemble, 1977; Suite in Stilo Antico for orch. with harpsichord, 1977; Salute-in Retrospect, cimbalo solo with orch., 1977; Chorale Prelude, organ, 1977; Via Lactea (The Galaxy), symphonic fantasy, 1978; Rhapsody for Cimbalom and Orch., 1978; Dance of Colors on the Black Hills of South Dakota, for harp ensemble, 1978; Sinfonia Atlantis, for orch., 1979; Canzone da Sacra for string quartet, 1979; Let Me Be Near for voice and orch., 1980; Las Vegas (The Meadows), cimbalom solo with orch., 1980; Ave Maria for voice and organ, 1980; Benedictus Dominus for orch. and mixed voices, 1981; Mount of Atlantis clarinet solo with synthesizer and orch., 1981; Agnus Dei for orch. and mixed voices and organ, 1981. Office: Holy Family Sch 7367 York Rd Parma OH 44130

KISSLING, CHARLES DANIEL, clin. psychologist; b. Cleve., Feb. 7, 1919; s. Charles John and Mary Catherine (Schaefer) K.; B.S.M., Baldwin-Wallace Coll., 1940; M.A., Case-Western Res. U., 1942, Ed.D., 1962; postgrad. Fenn Coll., 1946-48; m. Marjorie Jeanne Dreher, Nov. 20, 1948; children—Mary Catherine, Charles Daniel, Judith Anne, Patricia Louise. Counselor, psychologist Cleve. Catholic Diocese, 1958-62; sch. psychologist Lorain (Ohio) Bd. Edn., 1962-67, chief psychologist, 1967-69, psychol. evaluator, 1969-70; asst. prof. dept. psychology John Carroll U., 1971-74; instr. dept. psychology Cleve. State U., 1965-70; lectr. Lorain County Community Coll., 1964, 69-74; music supr. St. Ignatius Sch. Ch., Cleve., 1942-62; cons.

psychologist St. Raphael Sch., Bay Village, Ohio, 1968-70, St. Mary's Elem. and High Schs., Lorain, 1968-69, St. Angela Merici Sch., Fairview Park. Ohio, 1974—; pvt. practice clin. psychology, Rocky River, Ohio, 1964-73, Westlake, Ohio, 1973—; allied staff mem. Bay View Hosp., Bay Village, Ohio, 1975—; mem. profl. adv. bd. Parents Without Partners, Cleve., 1968—. Served with U.S. Army, 1942-45. Licensed psychologist, Ohio. Mem. Am., Midwest, Ohio, Cleve. psychol. assns., Nat., Cleve. assns. sch. psychologists, Am. Soc. Clin. Hypnosis, Assn. for Advancement of Ethical Use of Hypnosis, Internat. Soc. for Profl. Hypnosis, Ohio, Cleve. acads. cons. psychologists, Phi Delta Kappa, Phi Mu Alpha Sinfonia. Home: 3630 Trails End Dr Medina OH 44256 Office: 24700 Center Ridge Rd Westlake OH 44145

KITAZUMI, MARIE NAKAMURA, religious assn. exec.; b. Sacramento, Feb. 5, 1921; d. Iwazo and Kishino (Yamamto) Nakamura; student Merritt Sch. Bus., Oakland, Calif., 1939-41, Ind. U. Extension, 1944-46, U. Chgo. Extension, 1955-56, Northwestern U. Extension, 1964-66; m. Tadasu Kitazumi, Dec. 12, 1942 (div. 1962); children—Anita Lin, Constance Marie, Lisa Kishino. Jr. relocation officer War Relocation Authority, Indpls., 1944-46; asst. to chief research analyst Nuermberg Trials, Germany, 1947; office mgr. Chgo. Pottery Co., Chgo., 1950-55; owner Kitazumi Ins. Agy., Waukegan, Ill., 1959-62; adminstrv. asst. Gen. Council on World Service and Fin., United Methodist Ch., Evanston, Ill., 1962-72, asst. gen. sec. Council on Fin. and Adminstrn., 1973—; sec. adminstrv. bd. 1st United Meth. Ch., Evanston, 1970-71; mem. staff parish relations com. Kingswood United Meth. Ch., Buffalo Grove, Ill., 1979-81. Bd. dirs. MABC Credit Union, 1976—. Home: 1425 Sandpebble #336 Wheeling IL 60090 Office: 1200 Davis St Evanston IL 60201

KITCHEN, DENIS LEE, publisher, artist; b. Milw., Aug. 27, 1946; s. Benjamin Luthor and Margaretha (Margert) K.; B.J., U. Wis. at Milw., 1968; m. Irene Frances Nonnweiler, Feb. 13, 1971 (div. 1977); children—Sheena, Scarlet; m. 2d, Holly Gene Brooks, Aug. 15, 1980. Pres., Kitchen Sink Press comic book div. Krupp Comic Works Inc., Princeton, Wis., 1970—, pres. parent co., 1970—, editor-in-chief all periodicals published by Kitchen Sink Press; co-founder Bugle-Am., newspaper, 1970-78; art dir. Cartoon Factory, Princeton, 1972—; co-pub., art dir. Fox River Patriot, newspaper, 1976-80; pres. Yesteryear Publs., Inc., 1979-80; one-man shows: Priebe Art Gallery, Oshkosh, Wis., 1976, Jewish Community Center, Milw., 1977, Reeve Meml. Union, Oshkosh, 1978, Ripon Coll., 1978, 79, Wis. State Hist. Soc., 1979; editor Comix Book, Marvel Comics, N.Y.C., 1974-75, Dope Comix, 1978—; instr. history of comics U. Wis. at Milw., 1972. Socialist Labor party candidate lt. gov. Wis., 1970. Mem. United Cartoon Workers Am. (pres. local). Co-author: (with Catherine Yronwode) The Art of Will Eisner, 1981; editor Spirit mag., 1978—; co-editor, co-pub. Yesteryear, monthly antique newspaper, 1979-80. Home: Route 1 Box 329 Princeton WI 54968 Office: 2216 Old Green Lake Rd Princeton WI 54968

KITCHENMASTER, ROBERT WESLEY, acct., mgmt. co. exec.; b. Luverne, Minn., Jan. 8, 1948; s. Wesley Emil Albert and Alma Margarite (Funck) K.; B.S., Mankato State U., 1969; m. Karen Kristine Aklestad, June 5, 1976; 1 son, Karl Robert. Mem. staff Touche Ross & Co., Denver, 1969-70; pres. Clapper Kitchenmaster & Co., Mankato, Minn., 1972—; co-founder, pres. Diversified Systems, Inc., Mankato, 1974—; co-founder, dir. Profl. Mgmt. Systems, Inc., Madison, Wis., 1974—; speaker, presenter numerous seminars, 1972—. Treas., pres. Messiah Luth. Ch., 1978-79; chmn. Luth. Council Chs. of Greater Mankato area. Served with USN, 1970-72. C.P.A., Minn. Mem. Am. Inst. C.P.A.'s, Minn. Soc. C.P.A.'s (1st v.p. So. Minn. chpt. 1979-80, pres. 1980-81), Internat. Assn. Fin. Planners, Nat. Assn. Accts., Mankato Area C. of C. (legis. com. 1979—). Republican. Club: Key City Sertoma (charter pres. 1975-76, Sertoman of Yr. award 1976). Home: 1620 Sherwood Ct North Mankato MN 56001 Office: 209 S 2d St Mankato MN 56001

KITT, MICHAEL, fin. exec.; b. Phoenix, Oct. 19, 1950; s. Carl N. and Barbara A. Kitt; B.S. in Bus. Adminstrn., Roosevelt U., 1975. With account mgmt. Lester Witte & Co., C.P.A.'s., Chgo., 1970-77, Arthur Meyerhoff Advt., Chgo., 1977-78; with fin. mgmt. Benton & Bowles Advt., Chgo., 1978—; fin. planner, cons. small bus. Active Off the Street Club, Chgo. Boys Club, Chgo. Area council Boy Scouts Am., Chgo. Mem. Am. Advt. Assn., Am. Assn. Advt. Agys., Nat. Assn. Accts. (dir., 1975), Am. Advt. Fedn. (dir. scholastic div., 1975-76). Episcopalian. Pub. Fiscal Management Training Manual, Ill. Ind. Youth Services Agys., 1977. Home: 5728 N Kenmore Chicago IL 60660 Office: 233 N Michigan Ave Chicago IL 60660

KITTELL, THEODORE HARMON, hosp. exec.; b. Bloomfield, N.Mex., Jan. 19, 1934; s. Arthur Cullen and Virginia Anne (Harmon) K.; B.B.A., U. N.Mex., 1955; M.H.A., U. Minn., 1963; Ph.D., Walden U., 1975; m. Martha H. Kittell, Nov. 30, 1958; 1 dau., Mary. Commd. 2d lt. U.S. Air Force, 1957; advanced through grades to capt., 1963; bus. mgr. Malcolm Grow U.S. Air Force Hosp., Elmendorf, Alaska; adminstrv. resident U.S. Air Force Hosp., San Antonio; adminstrv. officer, Eglin AFB, Fla.; ret., 1967; pres. Pulaski Meml. Hosp., Winamac, Ind., 1967-80, Apple River Valley Meml. Hosp., Amery, Wis., 1980—; mem. Ind. Health Careers Bd., 1973-76. Internat. Farm Youth Exchange fellow, 1956. Mem. Am. Coll. Hosp. Adminstrs., Am. Public Health Planning Assn., Am. Hosp. Assn. Methodist. Clubs: Lions, Mason, Shriner. Home: 705 Harriman St S Amery WI 54001 Office: 221 Scholl St Amery WI 54001

KITTERMAN, CHARLES THOMAS, bldg. contractor; b. Earl Park, Ind., July 6, 1931; s. Charles Howard and Mary Naomi (Richey) K.; student law enforcement, Ind. U., Kokomo, 1972-75; m. Virginia Lee Wolfe, Oct. 5, 1949; children—Cheryl, Carol, Rick, Randy. Self-employed bldg. contractor, Earl Park, 1964—; water supt. Town of Earl Park, 1973-79, marshal, 1973-79, mem. town bd., 1961-73; mem. Region IV policy adv. com. 208 Water Quality Mgmt. Plan, 1978—. Elder, Earl Park Presbyn. Ch., 1957-59, 61-63, 67-69, 79—; cubmaster, asst. scoutmaster Boy Scouts Am., 1956-67. Served with Ind. N.G., 1948-52. Mem. Am. Water Works Assn., Ind. Police League, Nat. Sheriff's Assn. Clubs: Masons, Order Eastern Star. Address: 106 6th St Earl Park IN 47942

KITTNER, EDWIN HENRY, mfg. co. exec.; b. Utica, N.Y., Mar. 7, 1925; s. Emanuel Joseph and Genevieve Victoria (Rybicki) K.; B.S. in M.E., Kans. State U., 1950; m. Mary Elizabeth Totten, Oct. 20. 1950; children—Jane Elizabeth, Katherine Ann, Joseph Andrew, John David. Plant engr. Certain-Teed Products Co., Blue Rapids, Kans., 1950-57; chief project engr. Bestwall Gypsum Co., Blue Rapids, 1957-61, project engr. central engring. dept., Paoli, Pa., 1961-63; supt. engring. and maintenance Georgia-Pacific Corp., Blue Rapids, 1963—; lectr. local univs.; participant nat. confs. Mem. exec. bd. Jayhawk Council Boy Scouts Am., Topeka, Kans., 1950—; mayor, councilman City of Blue Rapids, 1954-61, 71—. Recipient Silver Beaver award, 1969. Registered profl. engr., Kans. Mem. Nat. Soc. Profl. Engrs., Kans., Tri-Valley (pres. 1980) engring. socs. Republican. Roman Catholic. Clubs: Lions (pres. 1955, 65, zone chmn. 1956). Am. Legion, V.F.W. Contbr. articles in field to profl. jours. Home: 604 E Ave Blue Rapids KS 66411 Office: Box 187 Blue Rapids KS 66411

KITTO, LOIS ANN, ednl. program designer; b. Platteville, Wis., Sept. 19, 1947; d. Ambrose Stephen and Marie Anna (McClain) Wunderlin; B.S. in Edn., U. Wis., Platteville, 1969; M.Ed. in Instrn. and Curriculum, Va. Commonwealth U., 1975; m. John, June 1, 1968. Elem. tchr. public schs., Mineral Wells, Tex., 1969-70, Dubuque, Iowa, 1970-72, Platteville, Wis., 1972-74, Chesterfield, Va., 1975-76, unit leader, 1971-74; staff devel. dir. Tchr. Center coordinator for curriculum devel., tchr., public schs., Little Chute, Wis., 1976-81; program design and developer, Mpls., 1981—; cons. staff devel., math. instrn. Recipient award for most outstanding profl. growth program in Wis., Wis. Assn. Tchr. Educators, 1980. Mem. Nat. Staff Devel. Council, Am. Soc. Tng. and Devel., Nat. Council Tchrs. Math., U.S. Metric Assn., Phi Delta Kappa. Author: Metric Measuring Program, Part I and II, 1980; Shopping Spree Book, 1980; computer literacy program developer, 1981; A Small School District Staff Development, 1981. Home: 2928 Dean Pkwy #2K Minneapolis MN 55416

KITZMILLER, KARL WILLIAM, dermatologist; b. Cin., Sept. 23, 1931; s. Karl Vivien and Mary Agnes (McDevitt) K.; student Xavier U., Cin., 1949-50; B.S., U. Cin., 1953, M.D., 1960; m. Alice Ann Meehan, Jan. 29, 1955; children—Sue Ann, William John, Daniel Joseph, Sarah Mary, Kevin William (dec.), Brian Andrew. Intern, Cin. Gen. Hosp., 1960-61; fellow in dermatology Mayo Clinic, Rochester, Minn., 1961-64; practice medicine specializing in dermatology, Cin., 1964—; asso. clin. prof. dermatology Coll. Medicine U. Cin., also asst. clin. prof. family medicine; attending staff, chief dermatology Good Samaritan and Deaconess hosps.; cons. Longview State Hosp., Wright Patterson AFB, Dayton, Ohio; courtesy staff Our Lady of Mercy and Holmes hosps.; mem. staffs Children's, Bethesda, Hillsboro hosps.; attending staff Christ Hosp., Cin., 1976—, sec. dept. dermatology, 1977—; attending physician Jewish Hosp., 1966—, sec. dept. dermatology, 1977—; attending physician Cin. Gen. Hosp., 1966—; courtesy staff Margaret Mary Hosp., Batesville. Trustee, So. Ohio chpt. Leukemia Soc. Am.; dir. Mt. Lookout Civic Club, 1970-73, 1st v.p., 1972-73. Served to lt. USAF, 1954-56. Recipient Physicians Recognition award AMA, 1969-73. Diplomate Am. Acad. Dermatology; lic. physician, Ind. Fellow A.C.P.; mem. Am., Ohio State (sec. sect. dermatology 1974—) med. assns., Noah Worcester Dermatol. Soc. (chmn. membership com.), Acad. Medicine Cin., Soc. Dermatol. Surgery, Chgo., Central States, Cin. (sec. 1973-75, pres. 1975-76) dermatol. socs., Assn. Ohio Commodores, Kidney Found., Cin. C. of C. Roman Catholic. Clubs: Cin. Tennis, Cin. Rotary, Cin. Country. Contbr. articles to med. jours. Office: 8040 Reading Rd Cincinnati OH 45237

KIVETT, MARVIN F., anthropologist; b. Nebr., Mar. 10, 1917; s. Thomas and Murl (Mark) K.; A.B., U. Nebr., 1942, M.A., 1951; m. Caroline Ritchey, Sept. 12, 1941; 1 son, Ronald Lee. Archeologist, Smithsonian Instn., 1946-49; mus. dir. Nebr. Hist. Soc., Lincoln, 1949-63, adminstrv. dir., 1963—. Served with AUS, 1942-46. Editor: Nebraska History, 1963—. Contbr. articles to profl. jours. Home: 5425 Franklin Lincoln NE 68506 Office: 1500 R Lincoln NE 68508

KIZILOS, APOSTOLOS PETER (TOLLY), human resources devel. ofcl.; b. Athens, Greece, May 10, 1935; came to U.S., 1953, naturalized, 1962; s. Peter and Marina (Laskos) K.; B.S., M.I.T., 1957, M.S., 1958; M.F.A., U. Iowa, 1971; m. Betty M. Ahola, June 7, 1958; children—Peter, Paul, Mark. With Honeywell, Inc., Mpls., 1961—, prin. research engr., research dept., 1961-70, ombudsman, research dept. Systems and Research Center, asst. to dir., 1971-76, human resources devel. mgr., 1976-80, human resources devel. corp. cons., human resources devel. mgr. Systems and Research Center, 1981—; lectr. U. Minn., 1979; interviewer Bush leadership fellows program; lectr. writers' confs; speaker in field. Central com. Dem. Farm Labor Party. Bush leadership fellow, 1970. Greek Orthodox. Mem. Am. Hellenic Edn. Progressive Assn. Condr. sci. research in aerodynamic controls; patentee in field; contbr. book revs. to Mpls. Tribune, paper to profl. publ.; author novel: Dwarf's Legacy, 1977. Home: 2841 Mayfield Rd Wayzata MN 55391 Office: 2600 Ridgway Pkwy Minneapolis MN 55413

KLAAS, ROBERT JAMES, banker; b. Evergreen Park, Ill., May 18, 1957; s. John R. and Lois M. (Johnson) K.; B.S. in Communications, Northwestern U., 1979; m. Renay H. McNitt, Sept. 22, 1979. With Harris Trust and Savs. Bank, Chgo., 1979—, mktg. mgr. Charge Card div., 1979—. Methodist. Office: 311 W Monroe St Chicago IL 60606

KLAER, FRED HARLAN, JR., geologist, hydrologist; b. Phila., Nov. 28, 1914; s. Fred Harlan and Mary W. (Howland) K.; B.A., Amherst Coll., 1935; M.S., Northwestern U., 1937; m. Edith H. Snyder, June 1, 1940; children—Susan, Judith, Barbara. Geologist, groundwater div. U.S. Geol. Survey, Washington, Reading, Ohio and Indpls., 1937-51; dir. surveys and research Ranney Method Water Supplies, Columbus, Ohio, 1951-62; cons. geologist and hydrologist Fred H. Klaer, Jr. & Assos., Columbus, 1962—. Mem. Plain Twp. (Ohio) Zoning Bd., 1974-78. Cert. profl. geologist. Fellow Geol. Soc. Am.; mem. Nat. Water Well Assn. (dir. tech. div. 1960-63, vice chmn. 1963), Assn. Profl. Geol. Scientists (chmn. Ohio sect. 1967-68), Am. Water Works Assn. (life). Contbr. articles to profl. jours. Home: 6320 Kitzmiller Rd New Albany OH 43054 Office: 4620 Indianola Ave PO Box 14307 Columbus OH 43214

KLARREICH, SUSAN FRIEDMAN, career program devel. cons.; b. Cleve., Jan. 14, 1929; d. Maurice David and Matilda (Saks) Friedman; B.A., U. Mich., 1950; M.A., Case Western Res. U., 1964, Ph.D., 1973; m. Harold Leopold Klarreich, Oct. 28, 1950 (dec. Dec. 1978); children—Karin, Betsy, Kathie, Beth. Ednl. testing cons. Cleveland Heights-University Heights Bd. Edn. (Ohio), 1965-67, Community Action for Youth, Cleve., 1966-67; dir. program devel. Jewish Vocat. Service, University Heights, 1968-78; dir. Met. Savs. Assn.; guest lectr. Case Western Res. U., Cleve. State U.; project coordinator HEW career equity promotion project. Trustee, Mt. Sinai Hosp., 1979, Jewish Vocat. Service, 1980. Mem. Am. Personnel and Guidance Assn., Nat. Vocat. Guidance Assn., Ohio Personnel and Guidance Assn., Am. Arbitration Assn., B'nai Brith Hillel Found. Contbr. articles to profl. jours. Home: 1546 Oakwood Dr Cleveland Heights OH 44121

KLASEK, CHARLES BERNARD, ednl. adminstr., ednl. cons.; b. Wilber, Nebr., Dec. 28, 1931; s. Bernard Jacob and Sylvia Frances (Smrz) K.; B.S. with distinction, U. Nebr., 1954; cert. (Fulbright scholar) Inst. Internat. Ednl. Research, Germany, 1955; M.A., U. Nebr., 1956, Ph.D. in Ednl. Adminstrn., 1971; m. Lila Lee Wanek, Aug. 9, 1953; children—Terese Ann, Steven Charles, Joseph Mark. Tchr. of English, speech and German, Lincoln (Nebr.) Public Schs., 1958-69; exec. dir. Nebr. Council for Ednl. TV, U. Nebr., Lincoln, 1960-63; dir. instructional TV, Santa Ana (Calif.) Unified and Jr. Coll. Dists., 1963-67; instr. evening classes Calif. State Coll., Fullerton, 1965-67; dir. edn. Ky. Ednl. TV Network, Lexington, 1967-71; instr. instructional TV utilization U. Ky., Lexington, 1968-69; asst. prof. dept. instructional materials So. Ill. U., Carbondale, 1971-76, asso. prof., 1976-81, prof., 1981—, acting departmental exec. officer of curriculum, instrn. and media, 1977, mem. Univ. Task Force on Internat. Edn., 1976-77, dir. Office Internat. Edn.; UNESCO cons. in utilization and evaluation of ednl. radio and TV, Ministry of Edn., Malaysia, 1974, 75, 72-73; cons. to various pub. schs., San Diego, 1965, New Orleans, 1970, Ill. State U., 1977, Appalachian Ednl. TV Satellite Project, U. Ky., 1977, Nat. Instructional TV Center, Bloomington, Ind., 1967, 68, 69. Mem. Carbondale Bicentennial Commn., 1975-76, Freedom Fest Com., Carbondale, 1976; v.p. council Epiphany Lutheran Ch., Carbondale, 1973, 75, 76-77. Served with U.S. Army, 1954-58. Recipient Academic Excellence award So. Ill. U., 1976; Disting. Service award City of Carbondale, 1977; named Tchr. of Yr., Coll. Edn., So. Ill. U., 1977. Mem. Nat. Assn. Ednl. Broadcasters (field coordinator 1969-71), Assn. Ednl. Communications and Tech. (dir. 1969-72, cert. com. 1975-77), Ill. Audiovisual Assn., Phi Delta Kappa. Club: Kiwanis. Author: Instructional Media in the Modern School, 1972; The Use of Radio Broadcast for Formal and Non-Formal Education in Developing Nations, 1978; contbr. articles on ednl. communications to profl. jours.; editor: Action with Kentucky's Children and Youth, 1971. Home: 208 Pine Ln Carbondale IL 62901 Office: Woody B-106 So Ill U Carbondale IL 62901

KLASHNA, MICHAEL JOSEPH, JR., marine transp. cons.; b. East Chicago, Ind., Feb. 21, 1941; s. Michael Joseph and Agnes Marie (Lambert) K.; B.S. in Bus. Adminstrn., So. Ill. U., 1968; M.B.A., Washington U., St. Louis, 1975; m. Carolyn Sue Gueldner, June 3, 1972. With Monsanto Co., St. Louis, 1968-79, distbrn. analyst, 1968-71, tanker ops. mgr., 1971-76, mgr. barge ops., 1976-79; marine transp. cons., St. Louis, 1979—; partner Brentwood Marine Investments, Mudcat Diversified Investments; chief fin. officer Barge Mgmt., Inc., 1981—. Served with USAF, 1958-62. Named Man of Yr., Meadowbrook Farm Assn., 1976. Mem. St. Louis Port and Harbor Assn. (dir.), Nat. Council Phys. Mgmt., St.Louis Milling and Grain Club, St. Louis Coal Club., Propeller Club St. Louis. Republican. Roman Catholic. Club: Yacht (St Louis). Home: 16452 Horseshoe Ridge Rd Chesterfield MO 63017 Office: 2510 S Brentwood Blvd St Louis MO 63144

KLASS, JOSEPH BENJAMIN, clin. psychologist; b. Clinton, Iowa, July 16, 1918; s. Clarence and Harriette Sybil (Miller) J.; B.S., Coll. William and Mary, 1951; M.S. in Clin. Psychology, Richmond Profl. Inst., 1955; m. Martha Lou Mericle, Aug. 13, 1960; 1 dau., Lisa Ann. Psychologist, Mental Health Inst., Mount Pleasant, Iowa, 1952-54, East Moline (Ill.) State Hosp., 1954-56, Mich. Dept. Corrections, 1956-59, Jackson County Intermediate Sch. Dist., 1959-67, Clinton Juvenile Ct. (Iowa), 1967-69, Bi-County Spl. Edn. Coop., Morrison, Ill., 1969-78; psychologist Mich. Dept. Corrections, Jackson, 1979—; pvt. practice clin. psychology, 1957—; mem. faculty Jackson Community Coll., 1960-61; dir. Lark Enterprises, Clinton, Iowa, 1970—. Served with AUS, 1942-46. Mem. Am. Psychol. Assn., Biofeedback Soc. Am., Biofeedback Soc. Mich. Clubs: Arbor Hills Country, Elks. Home: 759 Park Rd Jackson MI 49203 Office: 509 Harris Bldg Jackson MI 49201

KLAUS, RICHARD MOORE, electromagnet co. exec.; b. Olney, Ill., Sept. 8, 1927; s. Frank Charles and Kathleen (Moore) K.; B.S. in Mech. Engring., U. Cin., 1951; M.B.A. in Mgmt., Xavier U., 1960; m. Carolyn Guelker, June 5, 1954; children—Martha, Linda, William. Founder, pres. Automatic Equipment Corp., Cin.; tchr. metallurgy Ohio Coll. Applied Sci. Pres. Westwood Town Hall Performing Arts Center; trustee Beautiful Woodlawn Bus. Assoc. (chmn. pubs. com.); bd. dirs. Cin. Sci. Center. Served with AUS. Registered profl. engr., Ohio. Recipient 3 awards nat. design competition Material in Design Engring. mag.; Disting. Service award Cin. Recreation Commn. Mem. Engring. Soc. Cin., Nat. Soc. Profl. Engrs., Cin. C. of C. (transp. com.), Cin. Hist. Soc., Cin. chap. Nat. Railway Hist. Soc. Presbyterian (vice-moderator). Club: Kiwanis, Cin. Editor: Through the Heart of Ohio. Home: 3230 Epworth Ave Cincinnati OH 45211 Office: 10005 Springfield Pike Cincinnati OH 45215

KLAUSMEYER, THOMAS HENRY, architect; b. Detroit, Oct. 19, 1921; s. Otto Henry and Lillian (Couch) K.; B.M.E., Purdue U., 1947; B.Arch., B.S. in Archtl. Engring., U. Ill., 1951; m. Doris Irene Pfaffenbach, May 30, 1947; children—John Brian, William Bruce. Pres., Creative Bldgs., Urbana, Ill., 1952-54; project designer Skidmore, Owings & Merrill, Chgo., 1955-58, project mgr., 1966-68; now cons. architect Smith, Hinchman & Grylls Assos., Detroit; project architect, sr. asso. Perkins & Will, Chgo., Washington, 1958-64; project dir., participating asso. Smith, Hinchman & Grylls, Detroit, 1964-66; cons. for hosps., indsl. research and health profession teaching facilities. Served to 1st lt. USAAF, 1942-46; CBI. Allerton Traveling scholar, 1952; Ryerson Traveling fellow, 1954. Mem. AIA, Assn. Am. Med. Colls., Am. Hosp. Assn., Tau Beta Pi, Kappa Sigma. Home: 1992 Wiltshire Berkeley MI 48072 Office: 455 W Fort St Detroit MI 48226

KLAWANS, HAROLD LEO, neurologist; b. Chgo., Nov. 1, 1937; s. Harold Leo and Blanche (Rosenberg) K.; student U. Mich., 1955-58; M.D., U. Ill., 1962; m. Paula Barkan, Aug. 23, 1959; children—Deborah, Rebecca, Jonathan. Intern, Presbyn.-St. Luke's Hosp., Chgo., 1962-63; resident in neurology U. Minn., Mpls., 1963-64, Presbyn. St. Luke's Hosp., 1966-68; practice medicine specializing in neurology, Highland Park, Ill., 1968—; instr. U. Ill. Coll. Medicine, Chgo., 1968-70; asst. prof. neurology Rush Med. Sch., Chgo., 1971-72, asso. prof., 1972-74, prof. neurol. sci. and pharmacology, 1977—, asso. chmn. Dept. Neurol. Scis., 1977—; prof. medicine U. Chgo. Pritzker Sch. Medicine, 1974-76; med. advisor Com. to Combat Huntington Disease, Midwest chpt., 1970—, Tourette Syndrome Assn., 1977—. Chmn. med. adv. bd. United Parkinson Found., 1972—; stroke com. Chgo. Heart Assn., 1972-76, chmn., 1974-75. Served with U.S. Army, 1964-66. United Parkinson Found. grantee, 1968—; Boothroyd Found. grantee, 1975—; State of Ill. Dept. Mental Health grantee, 1978-80. Fellow Am. Acad. Neurology; Mem. Am. Neurol. Assn., Am. Coll. Neuropharmacology, Internat. Coll. Neuropharmacology, Soc. Neurochemistry, Soc. Biol. Psychiatry, World Fedn. Neurology, Research Group on Huntington Chorea (sec. 1977—). Jewish. Editor, Clin. Neuropharmacology, 1974—; asso. editor: Handbook of Clin. Neurology, 1972—; contbr. numerous articles in field to med. jours. Home: 1888 McCraren St Highland Park IL 60035 Office: 1725 W Harrison Ave Chicago IL 60612

KLECHA, ALPHONSE, savs. and loan/real estate exec.; b. Chgo., Oct. 17, 1929; s. Stanley and Mary (Kubala) K.; student Loyola U., Chgo., 1947-52; grad. Pearson Real Estate Inst., Chgo., 1950; m. Geraldine Marcum, Oct. 25, 1956. Real estate appraiser Clyde Savs., 1950-51; sales mgr. George C. Powell Realty, 1951-56; v.p. Equity, Wynwood, Springwood Bldrs., Glen Ellyn, Ill., 1956-66; asst. v.p. Unity Savs. Assn., Norridge, Ill., 1966-77; pres. Highland Green, Inc., Lombard, Ill., 1978-80; asst. v.p. Unity Savs., 1980—; pvt. practice real estate appraising and consulting. Republican. Home: 3 S 177 Sequoia Dr Glen Ellyn IL 60137 Office: 4242 N Harlem Norridge IL 60634

KLECK, GAYLE DIANE, radiology adminstr.; b. Rockford, Ill., Oct. 23, 1941; d. Edward James and Virginia (Finch) K.; grad. Swedish Am. Hosp., 1959; 1 dau., Jacqueline Diane. Staff technologist St. Joseph Hosp., Elgin, Ill., 1960-61, Copley Meml. Hosp., Aurora, Ill., 1962-63; mem. staff Dwyer Clinic, Aurora, 1963-71; adminstrv. technologist dept. radiology Central Community Hosp., Chgo., 1971-81; adminstrv. technologist Glendale Heights Community Hosp., 1981—; mem. adv. bd. Moraine Valley Community

Coll.-Health Systems Agy., 1979—. Mem. Zoning Bd. Appeals, Glendale Heights, Ill., 1977-79, 81-82, mem. Planning Commn., 1977-79. Mem. Am. Hosp. Radiology Adminstrs. (pres. Midwest), Am. Registry Radiologic Technologists. Jewish. Home: 2182 Pepperwood Ln Glendale Heights IL 60137

KLECKNER, BRYAN GENE, pub. co. exec.; b. Chgo., Nov. 11, 1944; s. Harry and Evelyn (Lazar) K.; B.A., U. Wis., 1965; B.A. in Econs., No. Ill. U., 1966; postgrad. John Marshall Law Sch., 1967-68; m. Judy Solow, Sept. 12, 1971. Acctg. exec. Earle Ludgin Advt., Chgo., 1967-71; mktg. mgr. Griffith Lab., Chgo., 1971-76; pub. exec. Gorman Pub. Co., Chgo., 1976—. Mem. Internat. Assn. Food Processors, Internat. Food Processors Assn., Am. Mktg. Assn., Assn. R.R. Advt. Mgrs. Clubs: Exec., Chgo. Advt. Home: 5650 N Sheridan Rd Chicago IL 60660 Office: Gorman Publishing Co 5725 E River Rd Chicago IL 60631

KLECZKA, GERALD D., state legislator; b. Milw., Nov. 26, 1943; ed. U. Wis., Milw; married. Mem. Wis. Assembly, 1968-72, Wis. Senate, 1974—. Del., Democratic Nat. Conv. Served with Wis. Air NG, 1963-69. Mem. Polish Nat. Alliance, Wilson Park Advancement Assn., Polish Assn. Am., South Side Businessmen's Club, Milw. Soc. Address: Room 115 South State Capitol Madison WI 53702*

KLEIMAN, BERNARD, lawyer; b. Chgo., Jan. 26, 1928; s. Isadore and Pearl (Wikoff) K.; B.S., Purdue U., 1951; J.D., Northwestern U., 1954; m. Lenore Silver, Apr. 27, 1959; children—Leslie, David. Admitted to Ill. bar, 1954; practice law in assn. with Abraham W. Brussell, 1957-60; dist. counsel United Steel Workers Am., 1960-65, gen. counsel, 1965—; partner Kleiman, Cornfield & Feldman, Chgo., 1960-75, B. Kleiman, P.C., 1976-77, Kleiman & Whitney, P.C., Chgo., 1978—; mem. top industry-wide joint collective bargaining coms. in steel, aluminum, can mfg. and other industries; lectr. in field. Mem. appraiser selection com. Nat. Accelerator Lab. Site Acquisition Com. Bd. dirs., counsel CARE. Served with AUS, 1946-48. Mem. Am., Ill., Chgo., Allegheny County bar assns., Ill. Labor History Soc., Phi Alpha Delta. Contbr. articles to legal jours. Office: 1 E Wacker Dr Chicago IL 60601

KLEIN, ALICE JARVIS, civil engr.; b. Mpls., Nov. 17, 1925; d. Matthew George and Mary Margaret (Child) Jarvis; B.C.E., U. Minn., 1947, M.S. in C.E., 1951; m. Morris Jerome Klein, Aug. 24, 1952; children—Matthew Morris, Robert Joseph. Engr., Hitchcock & Estabrook, Mpls., 1947-49, Greeley & Hansen, Engrs., Chgo., 1951-55; substitute tchr. Brookfield (Ill.) Sch. Dist., 1966-72; constrn. coordinator Greeley & Hansen, Engrs., Chgo., 1972-80; supr. Consoer Townsend, Inc., Chgo., 1980—. Registered profl. engr., Ill. Mem. ASCE, Nat., Ill. socs. profl. engrs. Methodist. Home: 9417 Jackson St Brookfield IL 60513 Office: Chicago IL

KLEIN, CARL FREDERICK, elec. engr.; b. Milw., June 20, 1942; s. Paul and Rose Katherin (Ruos) K.; B.S., U. Wis., 1965, M.S. in Elec. Engring., 1967; m. Mary Jean Uschan, Nov. 23, 1969; children—Christine Jean, Mathew Frederick, John Paul. Application engr. Allis Chalmers, Milw., 1963; research and devel. technician A.O. Smith Corp., Milw., 1964; devel. engr. Louis Allis Co., Milw., 1965; research engr. Johnson Controls, Inc., Milw., 1967-72, sr. research engr., 1962-79, research scientist, 1979-80, mgr. technol. forecasting, 1980—; mem. evening div. faculty Marquette U., Milw., 1967-72. Mem. IEEE, Eta Kappa Nu. Methodist. Contbr. articles to profl. jours. Patentee in field. Home: 5740 S Lochleven Ln New Berlin WI 53151 Office: 507 E Michigan St Milwaukee WI 53202

KLEIN, CHARLES HENLE, lithographing co. exec.; b. Cin., Oct. 5, 1908; s. Benjamin Franklin and Flora (Henle) K.; student Purdue U., 1926-27, U. Cin., 1927-28; m. Ruth Becker, Sept. 23, 1938; children—Betsy (Mrs. Marvin H. Schwartz), Charles H., Carla (Mrs. George Fee III). Pres., Progress Lithographing Co., Cin., 1934-59, Novelart Mfg. Co., Cin., 1960—; dir. R.A. Taylor Corp. Founding mem. Chief Execs. Forum. Clubs: Losantiville Country, Queen City, Bankers (Cin.). Home: 6754 Fairoaks Dr Amberley Village Cincinnati OH 45237 Office: Section Rd and P-C RR Cincinnati OH 45237

KLEIN, CHARLES MOSHER, radiologist; b. Cleve., June 24, 1932; s. Matthew George and Jean Isabel (Mosher) K.; B.S., Western Res. U., 1954, M.D., 1958; m. Barbara Ann Barr, Aug. 20, 1955; children—Janet Ellen, Catherine Elizabeth, James Mosher. Rotating intern St. Luke's Hosp., Cleve., 1958-59; asst. resident radiology U. Mich. Med. Center, 1959-60, resident, 1960-61, jr. clin. instr., 1961-62, Nat. Cancer Inst. fellow, 1961-62; mem. firm Drs. Peck, Means, Straub, et al, Toledo, 1964-68; mem. Toledo Radiol. Assos., Inc., 1968—, asst. treas., 1971-73, 77-81, treas., 1973-75, pres., 1975-77. Served to lt. comdr. M.C., USNR, 1962-64. Fellow Am. Coll. Radiology (alt. councilor 1976-79, councilor 1979—); mem. Radiol. Soc. N.Am., AMA, Ohio State Med. Assn., Ohio State (sec. 1979-81, pres.-elect 1981), Northwestern Ohio (pres. 1978) radiol. socs., Acad. Medicine Toledo. Club: Torch (pres. 1971) (Toledo). Home: 5336 Northbrook Ct Sylvania OH 43560 Office: 3939 Monroe St Toledo OH 43606

KLEIN, DAVID LYNN, internist; b. Coshocton, Ohio, Dec. 8, 1948; s. Floyd Raymond and Laura Esther (Kreager) K.; B.S. summa cum laude, Ohio State U., 1970, M.D., 1973; m. Sara Elaine Wynn, Mar. 17, 1973. Intern, SUNY, Buffalo Affiliated Hosps., 1973-74, resident in internal medicine, 1974-76; practice medicine specializing in internal medicine, Zanesville, Ohio, 1976—; attending physician Bethesda Hosp., Good Samaritan Med. Center. Bd. dirs. Muskingum Valley chpt. ARC; pres. Muskingum County br. Central Ohio chpt. Arthritis Found. Mem. A.C.P., AMA, Ohio Med. Assn., Muskingum County Med. Acad., Columbus Soc. Internal Medicine, Am. Soc. Internal Medicine. Lutheran. Home: 2750 E Ray Dr Zanesville OH 43701 Office: 2447 Maple Ave Zanesville OH 43701

KLEIN, GEORGE DEVRIES, geologist; b. Den Haag, Netherlands, Jan. 21, 1933; came to U.S., 1947, naturalized, 1955; s. Alfred and Doris (deVries) K.; B.A. in Geology, Wesleyan U., 1954; M.A. in Geology, U. Kans., 1957; Ph.D. in Geology, Yale U., 1960; children—Richard L., Roger N. Research sedimentologist Sinclair Research, Inc., 1960-61; asst. prof. geology U. Pitts., 1961-63; asst. prof. to asso. prof. U. Pa., 1963-69; prof. geology U. Ill., Urbana, 1970—; vis. fellow Wolfson Coll., Oxford U., 1969; vis. prof. geology U. Calif., Berkeley, 1970; vis. prof. oceanography Oreg. State U., 1974; CIC vis. exchange prof. geophys. sci. U. Chgo., 1979-80; chief scientist Deep Sea Drilling Project Leg 58, 1977-78; continuing edn. lectr.; asso. Center Advanced Studies of U. Ill., 1974. Recipient Outstanding Paper award Jour. Sedimentary Petrology, 1970, Erasmus Haworth award in geology U. Kans., various NSF grants. Fellow AAAS, Geol. Soc. Am., Geol. Assn. Can.; mem. Am. Geophys. Union, Am. Inst. Profl. Geologists, Soc. Econ. Paleontologists and Mineralogists, Internat. Assn. Sedimentologists, Am. Assn. Petroleum Geologists, Netherlands Geol. and Mining Soc., Sigma Xi. Author: Sandstone Depositional Models for Exploration for Fossil Fuels, 1975, 2d edit., 1980; Clastic Tidal Facies, 1977; Holocene Tidal Sedimentation, 1975; asso. editor Geol. Soc. Am. Bull., 1975-81; chief cons. adv. editor CEPCO div. Burgess Pub. Co., 1979-82. Office: Dept of Geology 245 Natural History Bldg 1301 W Green St Univ of Ill Urbana IL 61801

KLEIN, GEORGE ROBERT, periodical distbn. co. exec.; b. Washington, Pa., Sept. 28, 1909; s. George Ruttman and Virginia R. (Hickey) K.; B.A., Ohio Wesleyan U., 1930; B.S., Mass. Inst. Tech., 1932; m. Mary Elizabeth Fisher, Jan. 28, 1939. Pres., George R. Klein News Co., Shaker Heights, Ohio, 1940—. Chmn. bd. trustees Ch. of the Saviour, United Methodist, 1960—; vice-chmn., trustee St. Luke's Hosp., 1965—; v.p. bd. mgrs. Central YMCA, 1946-71; trustee Christian Residences Found., 1965—, Goodwill Industries Cleve., 1967-70, Ch. of the Saviour Found., 1962—, N.E. Ohio Conf. Meth. Ch., 1965—, Cleve. Zool. Soc., 1970—; trustee, pres. Cleve. Play House Theatre; mem. Welfare Fedn. Manpower Commn., 1971-74; pres. Ohio Wesleyan U. Assos., 1960-62; trustee Mus. Arts Assn., 1973—; trustee Play House Found., 1972—, Ohio Wesleyan U., 1971—, Univ. Circle Found., 1974—. Served with USN, 1943-46. Mem. Nat. Bur. Ind. Pubs. and Periodical Distbrs. Assn. (past pres.), Mid-Am. Periodical Distbrs. Assn. (past pres.), Mag. Distributors Research Projects Group (past pres.), Nat. Council Periodical Distbrs. Assn. (past dir.), Ind. Periodical Distbrs. Great Lakes (past pres.), Cleve. Engring. Soc., Sigma Pi Sigma, Pi Mu Epsilon, Omicron Delta Kappa. Clubs: Canterbury Golf; Skating, City, Kiwanis (Cleve.); Rowfant, University, Marco Polo, Union. Home: 23699 Shaker Blvd Shaker Heights OH 44122

KLEIN, PAULA SCHWARTZ, hosp. ofcl.; b. Chgo., Oct. 16, 1941; d. Arthur A. and Rosalyn (Davidson) Schwartz; student Mich. State U., 1959-60; B.A., Governors State U., 1974, M.A., 1975; m. Sanford David Klein, Dec. 18, 1960; children—Gregory Scott, Julie Ann. Mem. editorial staff Okinawa Morning Star, Machinato, 1960-63; exec. dir. Bloom Twp. Com. on Youth, Chicago Heights, Ill., 1975-81; dir. dept. fund devel. and public relations South Chgo. Community Hosp., 1981—. Mem. Nat. Soc. Fund Raising Execs., Nat. Assn. Prevention Profls., So. Suburban Youth Service Alliance, Criminal Def. Consortium, Nat. Assn. Hosp. Devel., Twp. Ofcls. Ill., Youth Network Council, Sierra Club. Jewish. Home: 1211 Jeffery Dr Homewood IL 60430 Office: South Chgo Community Hosp 2320 E 93d St Chicago IL 60617

KLEIN, ROBERT EDWARD, pub. co. exec.; b. Cin., Dec. 27, 1926; s. Albert and Elisabeth (Muschnau) K.; A.B., Kenyon Coll., 1950; M.B.A., Cornell U., 1952; A.M., U. Chgo., 1969; now Ph.D. candidate; m. Nancy Minter, May 25, 1958; children—Robert Schuyler, Elisabeth Susan. With McGraw Hill Co., Chgo., 1969—, dist. mgr. Housing mag., 1980—; cons. to Time/Life Books, 1980. Served with U.S. Army, 1944-46. Grolier scholar, 1952. Mem. Am. Mktg. Assn., Am. Legion, Am. Hist. Assn., Beta Theta Pi. Republican. Clubs: Westmoreland Country, Cornell. Home: 633 Park Dr Kenilworth IL 60043 Office: McGraw Hill Co 645 N Michigan Ave Chicago IL 60611

KLEIN, WAYNE CARL, educator; b. Sioux Center, Iowa, Feb. 5, 1956; s. Charles and Grace (Blom) K.; B.A. in Secondary Edn., Dordt Coll., 1978; B.S. in Agrl. Edn., Iowa State U., 1980. Tchr. vocat. agr. Solon (Iowa) High Sch., 1980—. Mem. Nat. Vocat. Agr. Tchrs. Assn., Iowa Vocat. Agr. Tchrs. Assn., Am. Vocat. Assn., Iowa Vocat. Assn., NEA, Iowa State Edn. Assn., Christian Farmers Assn., Gamma Sigma Delta. Mem. Christian Reformed Ch. Home: 202 S Market St Solon IA 52333 Office: 408 S Iowa St Solon IA 52333

KLEIN, WILLIAM EDWARD, govt. ofcl.; b. Sandusky, Ohio, May 1, 1939; s. Harry Henry and Kathleen Isabelle (Dickerhoff) K.; B.M.E., Gen. Motors Inst., 1961; M.S., Case Inst. Tech., 1964; m. Nancy Mae Payne, Aug. 19, 1961; children—Charmaine, Diane, William Edward. Jr. engr. New Departure div. Gen Motors Corp., Sandusky, Ohio, 1963-64; systems engr. Lewis Research Center, NASA, Sandusky, 1964-70, project engr., 1970-74, system safety engr., auditor, Cleve., 1974-77, product assurance mgr., 1977—. Registered profl. engr., Ohio. Home: 2360 County Rd 306 Vickery OH 43464 Office: NASA Lewis Research Center 21000 Brookpark Rd Cleveland OH 44135

KLEIS, KEITH HAROLD, farmer; b. Marshalltown, Iowa, Mar. 24, 1950; s. Hans Harold and Ruth Margaret (Hayden) K.; B.S., U. Wis., Platteville, 1972; m. Judie Lynn Stamp, July 15, 1972; children—Brian Lynn, Kevin Micheal. Salesman, Ralston Purina, Fond du Lac, Wis., 1972-73; farmer, Baldwin, Iowa, 1973—; salesman Funks-G Internat., Bloomington, Ill., 1976—, tchr. Eastern Iowa Community Coll., Clinton, 1977; real estate agt. Engel Agy., Maquoketa, Iowa, 1981—; sec., dir. Baldwin Nashville Telephone Co.; dir. Baldwin Savs. Bank, Kleis Kountry Acres; agrl. adv. com. Clinton Community Coll. Mem. Lost Nation Softball Team. Mem. Jackson County Cattlemen Assn. (dir., pres. 1977, sec. 1979), Baldwin-Monmouth Jaycees (state dir. 1978, pres. 1979), Jackson County Pork Producers, Jackson County Farm Bur. Home and Office: Rural Route 1 Baldwin IA 52207

KLEIST, MELVA KATHERINE, ednl. cons.; b. Saxeville, Wis., Mar. 19, 1922; d. Otto John and Lona Marie (Handrich) Zuege; B.E., U. Wis., Stevens Point, 1939; M.S.T., U. Wis., River Falls, 1969, postgrad., 1971-73, 77; postgrad. U. Wis., Green Bay, 1980-81, U. Wis., Oshkosh, 1979-80, Mankato State Coll., 1975; m. Orin Kleist, June 10, 1946; 1 son, Thomas. Tchr., Hancock (Wis.) Elem. Sch., 1942-43, Wautoma (Wis.) Elem. Sch., 1943-46, Tri-County Sch., Plainfield, Wis., 1954-66, Coop. Ednl. Service Agy., Appleton, Wis., 1966-68; reading cons., coordinator, mem. adminstrv. staff Sch. Dist. Weyauwega-Fremont, Weyauwega, Wis., 1968—. Mem. Internat. Reading Assn., Assn. Supervision and Curriculum Devel., Wis. State Reading Assn., Central Wis. Reading Council. Lutheran. Asst. editor Wis. State Reading Jour., 1979-82. Home: Rural Route 1 Box 6 Almond WI 54909 Office: Sch Dist Weyauwega-Fremont Weyauwega WI 54983

KLEMENS, EBERHARD RUDOLF, computer software co. exec.; b. Hanover, Ger., Mar. 11, 1950; came to U.S., 1956, naturalized, 1969; s. Rudolf and Kaethe Erne (Fuchs) K.; B.S. in Engring., U. Ill., 1974; m. Cynthia Lee Woelfer, Apr. 12, 1975. Systems analyst U. Ill., Chgo., 1971-77; v.p. Schrager Klemens and Krueger, Inc., Rosemont, Ill., 1977-81; pres. Circle Software Corp., Downers Grove, Ill., 1981—, dir. Office: 1100 W 31st Downers Grove IL 60515

KLEMENS, EBERHARD RUDOLF, computer software co. exec.; b. Hannover, Germany, Mar. 11, 1950; came to U.S., 1956, naturalized, 1969; s. Rudolf and Kaethe Erna (Fuchs) K.; B.S. in Engring., U. Ill., 1974; m. Cynthia Lee Woelfer, Apr. 12, 1975. Systems analyst U. Ill., Chgo., 1971-77; v.p. Schrager Klemens and Krueger, Inc., Rosemont, Ill., 1977—, also dir. Office: 10400 W Higgins Rd Rosemont IL 60018

KLERKX, MARTIN ALAN, judicial data center exec.; b. Detroit, Dec. 1, 1942; s. Walter Martin and Sylvia Imogene (Greene) K.; B.S., Mich. State U., 1964; m. Mary Ellen Sands, Jan. 27, 1962; children—Gregory William, David Walter. Staff systems analyst Mich. Consol. Gas Co., Detroit, 1968-69; systems cons. Univ. Computing Co., Detroit, 1969-72; mgmt. cons. Ernst & Whinney, 1972-73; info. systems dir. Mich. Judicial Data Center, 1973—. Served with USN, 1964-68. Mem. Am. Mgmt. Assn., Soc. Mgmt. Info. Systems, Naval Inst. Presbyterian. Home: 37309 Charter Oaks Blvd Mount Clemens MI 48043 Office: Michigan Judicial Data Center 144 W Lafayette Blvd Detroit MI 48226

KLETSCHKA, HAROLD DALE, cardiovascular surgeon, biomedical co. exec.; b. Mpls., Aug. 26, 1924; s. Herbert Leland and Emma Elizabeth (Kopf) K.; A.S., Brainerd (Minn.) Jr. Coll., 1943; B.S., U. Minn., 1946, M.B., 1947, M.D., 1948; LL.B., Blackstone Sch. Law (Ill.), 1970; grad. Air War Coll., 1972. Intern Kings County Hosp., Bklyn., 1947-49; asst. resident surgery Univ. Hosp., Ann Arbor, Mich., 1950-51; resident gen. surgery State U. N.Y. Downstate Med. Center, 1953-54, chief resident thoracic surgery, 1952-53, 54-55; thoracic and gen. surgeon Bratrud Clinic, Thief River Falls, Minn., 1951-52; asst. chief, acting chief neurosurgery 3275th and 2349th USAF Hosps., Parks AFB, Calif., 1955-56, asst. chief thoracic surgery, 1956, chief thoracic surgery, 1956-57, founder, chief USAF Cardiovascular Research Center, 1957-58; pvt. practice thoracic and cardiovascular surgery, San Francisco and San Jose, Calif., 1958-59; thoracic surgeon VA Hosp., Syracuse, N.Y., 1959-60, chief thoracic surgery, 1960-67; asst. prof. surgery State U. N.Y. Upstate Med. Center, Syracuse, 1959-67, cons. thoracic surgery, 1959-67, USAF med. service liaison officer for surgeon gen., 1964-67; dep. comdr., chief hosp. services 102d TAC Hosp., Phalsbourg Air Base, France, 1961-62; mil. cons. to surgeon gen. USAF, surgeon Hdqrs. Command USAF, 1965-73; aerospace med. cons. to dir. Aerospace Med. Services, Malcolm Grow USAF Med. Center, 1965-73; thoracic surgeon VA Hosp., Houston, 1967-68; thoracic surgeon VA Hosp., Montgomery, Ala., 1968-72, dir. cardiopulmonary labs., 1970-72; co-founder, incorporator, chmn. bd., pres., chief exec. officer Bio-Medicus, Inc., Minnetonka, Minn., 1972—; mem. Nat. Council on U.S.-USSR Health Care, Citizen Exchange Corps, N.Y.C., 1976—; mem. exec. com. Council for U.S.-USSR Health Exchange, Boston, 1976—. Campaign mgr. Ind. Republican candidate Dist. 43B, Minn. Ho. of Reps., 1976; mem. nat. adv. bd. Am. Security Council. Named to Wisdom Hall of Fame, 1979; diplomate Am. Bd. Surgery, Am. Bd. Thoracic Surgery. Fellow A.C.S.; mem. Am. Heart Assn. (council on basic scis., council on cardiovascular surgery), AAUP, Air Force Assn., U. Minn. Alumni Assn., Am. Soc. for Artificial Internal Organs, Twin City Thoracic and Cardiovascular Surg. Soc., Am. Med. Writers Assn., Internat. Platform Assn., VFW, U. Minn. Alumni Club. Recipient Bausch & Lomb Hon. Sci. award, 1941, IR-100 award for devel. Kletschka-Rafferty artificial heart, 1972, Worldwide Symbolic grad. Air War Coll., 1973, 1st Place award Med./Analytical div. Plastics World, 1976, First prize in Med. div. 8th Bachner award competition, 1976. Club: K.C. (4 deg.) Contbr. chpt. to Progress in Surface and Membrane Science, 1973; Bd. editors, Minn. Medicine, 1960—; editor charge spl. issue Minn. Medicine 49, 1966; Contbr. articles to profl. jours.; patentee in field; pioneer Kletschka-Levowitz fracture. Home: 1925 Noble Dr Minneapolis MN 55422

KLIEWER, HENRY B., clergyman, educator, farmer; b. Henderson, Nebr., Sept. 1, 1904; s. Peter J. and Susanna (Buller) K.; A.B., York Coll., Nebr., 1931; A.M., U. Nebr., 1939; postgrad. Kans. State U., Emporia, 1953-67; m. Eva Peters, Aug. 18, 1927; children—Marion Waller, Lowell Joyce, Herald James, Ruth Elaine. Tchr. rural schs., Nebr., 1923-29; tchr. Henderson High Sch., 1931-35, prin., 1935-39; supt. Henderson Public Schs., 1939-48; prin. Hillsboro (Kans.) High Sch., 1948-55; supt. Unified Sch. Dist. 410, Hillsboro, 1955-69, Corn (Okla.) Bible Sch., 1969-72; instr. Bible, Tabor Coll., Hillsboro, 1972-75; ordained minister Mennonite Brethren Ch., 1943, pastor, Henderson, also Corn, 1969-72; sec. Mennonite Aid Plan, Dist. 25, Hillsboro, 1978—, chmn. Mennonite Brethren Bd. Publs., 1954-57. Mem. Hillsboro C. of C., Nebr. Tchrs. Assn., Kans. Tchrs. Assn., Am. Assn. Sch. Adminstrs., NEA. Club: Kiwanis (pres. Hillsboro 1976-77, lt. gov. Div. V, Kans. dist. 1979-80). Home and office: 110 N Adams St Hillsboro KS 67063

KLIGMAN, GAIL ANN, anthropologist, folklorist; b. Phila., Aug. 5, 1949; d. Albert M. and Beatrice Phyllis (Troyan) K.; B.A. in Sociology, U. Calif., Berkeley, 1971, M.A. in Folklore, 1973, Ph.D. in Sociology, 1977. Internat. Research and Exchanges Bd. postdoctoral researcher, Transylvania, Romania, 1978-79; vis. asst. prof. anthropology, U. Chgo., 1979-80, asst. prof. anthropology and the Coll., 1981—; Nat. Endowment for the Arts film project, Phila. Hummers Tradition, 1980, 81; research asso. Center for European Studies, Harvard U., 1981-82. Active Art Inst. Chgo., Chgo. Symphony. Am. Council Learned Socs. grantee, 1981-82. Mem. Am. Anthropol. Soc., Am. Folklore Soc., Am. Assn. Advancement Slavic Studies, AAUW. Club: U. Chgo. Press. Author: Calus: Symbolic Transformation in Romanian Ritual, 1981. Office: Dept Anthropology Univ Chicago 1126 E 59th St Chicago IL 60637

KLIMAS, WILLIAM CHARLES, advt. agy. exec.; b. Chgo., Jan. 5, 1941; s. Charles S. and Helen Klimas; B.A., St. Benedict's Coll., 1962. Account exec. Post-Keyes-Gardner, Chgo., 1964-67; advt. mgr. Von Schrader Mfg. Co., Racine, Wis., 1967-69; editor, writer Publishers Devel. Corp., Chgo., 1969-70; creative dir., partner Tatham-Laird-Kudner, Chgo., 1970—. Home: 2435 N Sheffield Chicago IL 60614 Office: 625 N Michigan Ave Chicago IL 60611

KLIMISCH, RICHARD LEO, chemist; b. Yankton, S.C., Jan. 1, 1938; s. Andrew R. and Opal (Haley) K.; B.S., Loras Coll., Dubuque, Iowa, 1960; Ph.D., Purdue U., 1964; m. Virginia Jenkinson, Sept. 15, 1962; children—Kurtis D., Erik R. Research chemist DuPont Co., 1964-67; research chemist Gen. Motors Co. Research Labs., Warren, Mich., 1967-70, asst. dept. head, 1970-75, head environ. sci. dept., 1975—. Mem. environ., engring. and med. adv. coms. Coordinating Research Council. Mem. AAAS, Am. Chem. Soc., Sigma Xi. Roman Catholic. Office: Environ Sci Dept Gen Motors Research Labs Warren MI 48090*

KLINCK, BRUCE DEE police officer; b. Toledo, Ohio, Nov. 24, 1940; s. Norman Earl and Minnie Mary Klinck; student U. Toledo, 1958-59, Owens Tech. Coll., 1975-78; m. Carole Faye Henson, Oct. 7, 1961; children—Bruce Allen, Lisa Michelle. Sample maker, photo specialist Owens Ill. Glass Co., Toledo, 1959-63; with Toledo Police, 1963—, with selective enforcement units, 1967-73, with planning and research unit, 1974—; cons. on constrn. and remodelling of police facilities. Recipient 1st place award Internat. Chiefs of Police Facilities Workshop, 1978. Mem. Ohio Police Planners Assn., Nat. Assn. Police Planners (charter mem.). Democrat. Lutheran. Office: 525 N Erie St Toledo OH 43624

KLINE, ANN GLORIA, occupational therapist; b. Sturgis, Mich., Oct. 30, 1954; d. Paul Richard and Gloria Alberta (Clark) K.; B.S. cum laude, Western Mich. U., 1976. Head dept. occupational therapy Restorative Services, Inc., Elkhart, Ind., 1977-79, Northside Healthcare Center, Indpls., 1979-80, Colonial Crest Nursing Center, Inc. at Rolling Hills Convalescent Center, Anderson, Ind., 1980—. Mem. Am. Occupational Therapy Assn., Ind. Occupational Therapy Assn. Methodist. Home: 5 E Plum St Apt 43 Chesterfield IN 46017 Office: Rolling Hills Convalescent Center 1821 Lindberg St Anderson IN 46012

KLINE, CHARLES EWERT, educator; b. Waukegan, Ill., Apr. 12, 1931; s. Brooks Rutherford and Anne Henrietta (Biggerstaff) K.; B.S., Ill. State U., 1953; M.S., U. Wis., 1960, Ph.D., 1968; m. Edith Margaret Williams, June 13, 1964; children—Anne, Ellen. Tchr., adminstr. Elgin (Ill.) public schs., 1956-63; mem. faculty Purdue U., 1966—, asso. prof. ednl. adminstrn., 1974—; chmn. adminstrn. and curriculum, 1978—, asso. dir. tchr. edn., 1975—; cons. in field. Mem. Am. Assn. Sch. Adminstrs., Am. Ednl. Research Assn., Assn. Supervision and Curriculum Devel., Phi Delta Kappa, Kappa Delta Pi, Gamma Theta Upsilon. Presbyterian. Author articles in field. Office: G-10 South Campus Cts Purdue U West Lafayette IN 47907

KLINE, DONALD, food co. exec.; b. Chgo., July 6, 1948; s. Ralph Waldo and Theresa (Donato) K.; A.A., Thornton Community Coll., 1969, Kishwaukee Coll., 1971; B.S., Roosevelt U., 1974, No. Ill. U., 1974; student Better Processing Control Sch., U. Wis., 1974; m. Christine Janet Kennedy, Aug. 23, 1972; children—Bethany Amber, Nathaniel Darwin Kennedy, Abraham Newton Kennedy, Seth-Andrew Brigham Kennedy. Quality control chemist Syntex Labs., Elgin, Ill., 1972-75; quality control mgr. Gt. China Food Products Co., Chgo., 1975; quality assurance mgr. TV Time Foods, Inc. subs. McCormick & Co., Inc., Bremen, Ind., 1975-80; pres. Abinadi Enterprises Internat. Corp., Nappanee, Ind., 1981—. Elder, pres. Sunday Sch., Elkhart (Ind.) Ward, Ch. of Jesus Christ of Latter-day Saints, 1979-80, project coordinator, purchasing agt. ch. fund raising projects, 1980—. Mem. Am. Soc. Quality Control, Inst. Food Technologists, Am. Chem. Soc., Am. Oil Chemists Soc., Am. Inst. Biol. Scis., AAAS. Home: PO Box 121 Nappanee IN 46550 Office: PO Box 107 Nappanee IN 46550

KLINE, JOHN NICHOLAS, ednl. adminstr.; b. Linton, Ind., Apr. 26, 1951; s. Roy Albert and Margaret Ann (Zeitler) K.; B.S. magna cum laude, Ball State U., 1973; M.S., Ind. U., 1979; m. Cindy Lynne Stohler, Aug. 25, 1973; 1 son, Jeremy David. Tchr. math., track coach Jefferson Jr. High Sch., Ft. Wayne, Ind., 1973-77; asst. to prin. Meml. Park Middle Sch., Ft. Wayne, 1979-80; tchr. math., asst. track coach R. Nelson Snider High Sch., Ft. Wayne, 1977-79, asst. to prin., 1981—. Mem. Ind. Computer Educators (past pres.), Am. Ednl. Data Systems, Ind. Middle Sch. Assn., Phi Delta Kappa, Kappa Delta Pi. Presbyterian. Clubs: Ft. Wayne Track; Summit City Track. Co-author: Computer Literacy, 1979, Computer Literacy for the Middle Sch., 1981. Home: 2410 Oakridge Rd Fort Wayne IN 46805 Office: 4600 Fairlawn Pass Fort Wayne IN 46815

KLINE, LOREN E(FFENGER), JR., psychologist; b. Phila., Feb. 16, 1917; s. Loren Effenger and Edith (Hahne) K.; B.S., Pa. State U., 1940; M.S., Tex. Coll. Arts and Industries, 1962; Ph.D., E. Tex. State U., 1966; m. Eleanor Henry Beidelman, June 3, 1945; children—Loren William, Martha Louise. Geologist, mining engr. N.J. Zinc Co., N.J., Pa., Va., 1940-45; geologist, paleontologist Humble Oil and Refining Co., Tex., Miss., 1946-52; dist. geologist Pure Oil Co., San Antonio, 1952-55; cons. geologist, mining engr., Alice, Tex., 1956-63; tchr. math and sci. Alice (Tex.) Ind. Sch. Dist., 1958-63; asso. prof. edn. Buena Vista Coll., Storm Lake, Iowa, 1966-72; pvt. practice psychology, Storm Lake, 1972—; prof. Iowa Central Community Coll., Ft. Dodge, 1975—. Mem. Am. Psychol. Assn., Iowa Psychol. Assn., Acacia. Presbyterian. Home: 211 W 3d St Storm Lake IA 50588 Office: PO Box 364 Storm Lake IA 50588

KLINE, TEX RAY, broadcaster, design engr.; b. Van Buren, Ind., Sept. 14, 1938; s. Ray Loyal and Bernice Eve (Marsh) K.; student DeVry Tech. Inst., Chgo., 1960-61; children—Troy Ray, Tracy Renee, Terri Rae. Announcer, program dir. Sta. KTUS, Istanbul, 1957-59; announcer, engr. Sta. WITE, Brazil, Ind., 1962-63, Sta. WGEE, Indpls., 1962-72, Sta. WNTS, Indpls., 1974-76; engr. WPTA-TV, Ft. Wayne, Ind., 1963-64; prodn. mgr. WTAF-TV, Marion, Ind., 1964, WTTV-TV, Indpls., 1964-75; engr., Soundstage chief engr. WRTV-TV, Indpls., 1975—; owner Kline's Music Maker Service, 1965—; co-owner, mgr. MidWestern Rec. Studio, 1968-72; dir. engring. Neon Cornfield, 1977-79; real estate broker New Leaf Realty, 1981—. Candidate for rep. Ind. Legislature, 1976. Served with USN, 1956-59. FCC 1st class radio telephone operator, gen. contractor; lic. real estate broker, securities dealer, Ind.; recipient award Citizen's Forum Beautification, 1974. Mem. Soc. Broadcast Engrs., Audio Engrs. Soc. Republican. Clubs: Indpls. Advt., Indpls. Press, Masons. Designer multi-media, audio and video equipment for custom applications. Home: 972 W Roache St Indianapolis IN 46208 Office: 1330 N Meridian St Indianapolis IN 46206

KLINENBERG, EDWARD LEE, communications co. exec.; b. Chgo., Mar. 21, 1942; s. Jerome Jacob and Muriel (Abrams) K.; B.A. in English, U. Mich., 1963; postgrad. U. Paris, 1964-65; m. Rona Lynne Talcott, May 13, 1967; children—Eric Martin, Danielle Elyse. Public info. dir. Chgo. unit Am. Cancer Soc., 1966-67; account exec. Stral Advt. Co., Chgo., 1967-69; pres. Precise Communications, Inc., Chgo., 1969—; leader seminars, speaker in field. Bd. dirs., v.p. public relations Hull House Assn., Chgo., 1977—; bd. dirs. Internat. Visitors Center Chgo., 1975-77; pres. Old Town Triangle Assn., 1975-77. Served with AUS, 1965-66. Mem. Chgo. Council Fgn. Relations (dir. 1969-76), Com. on Fgn. and Domestic Affairs (exec. com. 1978—). Club: Columbia Yacht (Chgo.). Office: 233 E Erie St Chicago IL 60611

KLING, GEORGE ALBERT, radiologist; b. Mt. Clemens, Mich., May 25, 1934; s. Albert Peter and Dorothy Mae (Elson) K.; M.D., U. Mich., 1958; m. Judith Ann Nickel, Aug. 18, 1956; children—Victoria E., Cynthia E., Jeffrey G. Intern, Harper Hosp., Detroit, 1958-59, resident, 1959-62; pres. L. Reynolds Asso., P.C., Detroit, 1975—; chief dept. radiology Harper-Grace Hosp.; mem. staff Children's Hosp.; asso. prof. radiology Wayne State U. Served with M.C., U.S. Army, 1966-68. Decorated Bronze Star; diplomate Am. Bd. Radiology. Fellow Am. Coll. Radiology; mem. AMA, Mich. State, Wayne County med. socs., Am. Roentgen Ray Soc. (mgr.), Mich. Radiol. Soc. (past sec.-treas.), Detroit Gastroent. Soc., Detroit Acad. Medicine, Bockus Internat., Profl. Conv. Mgmt. Assn. Club: Detroit Athletic. Contbr. articles in field to Am. Jour. Roentgenology. Home: 208 Moran Grosse Pointe Farms MI 48236 Office: 3990 John R St Detroit MI 48201

KLING, MERLE, political scientist, univ. ofcl.; b. Russia, June 15, 1919; came to U.S., 1921, naturalized, 1927; s. Saul and Dina (Hoffman) K.; A.B., Washington U., St. Louis, 1940, M.A., 1941, Ph.D., 1949; m. Sandra Perlman, Aug. 26, 1978; 1 son, Arnold Saul. Mem. faculty Washington U., 1946—, asst. prof. polit. sci., 1950-54, asso. prof., 1954-61, prof., 1961—, dean Faculty Arts and Scis., 1966-69, 73-76, provost, 1976—, acting chmn. dept. polit. sci., 1970-71; vis. prof. U. Ill., 1961; research asso. Center Internat. Studies, Princeton U., 1964-65. Served with AUS, 1942-45. Mem. Am. Polit. Sci. Assn. (council 1967-69), Midwest Polit. Sci. Assn. (editor jour. 1965-66, pres. 1969-70), Phi Beta Kappa, Alpha Kappa Delta, Omicron Delta Kappa. Author: The Soviet Theory of Internationalism, 1952; A Mexican Interest Group in Action, 1961; contbr. articles to profl. jours. Office: Box 1080 Washington U Lindell Blvd and Skinker Ave Saint Louis MO 63130

KLING, SIEGBERT A., agrl. irrigation equipment mfg. co. exec.; b. Gross-Friedrichsdorf, Germany, Feb. 14, 1939; came to U.S., 1956, naturalized, 1965; s. Herman and Ella Gertrude (Heldt) K.; student Suomi Coll., 1957-59; M.A., U. Munich (W.Ger.), 1966; m. Aug. 20, 1977; 1 son, Tyson Charles. Internat. advt. coordinator for central Europe, Batten, Barton, Durstine & Osborn, N.Y.C., 1963-69; dir. advt. and public relations, exec. Credit Union League, Des Moines, 1969-77; internat. ops. dir. Reinke Mfg. Co., Inc., Deshler, Nebr., 1980—; chmn., dir. World Trade Council, 1980—. Hon. bd. dirs. Iowa Ednl. Broadcast System, 1976—. Served with U.S. Army, 1959-63. Recipient various advt. awards. Mem. Midwest Internat. Trade Assn., Am. Legion, Izaak Walton League. Republican. Lutheran. Club: Lions. Home: Rural Route 1 Deshler NE 68340 Office: Reinke Mfg Co Inc PO Box 566 Deshler NE 68340

KLING, WILLIAM HUGH, broadcasting exec.; b. St. Paul, Apr. 29, 1942; s. William Conrad and Helen A. (Leonard) K.; B.A. in Econs., St. John's U., 1964; postgrad Boston U., 1964-66; m. Sarah Margaret Baldwin, Sept. 25, 1976. Dir. broadcasting St. John's U., Collegeville, Minn., 1966-70; asst. dir. radio activities Corp. Public Broadcasting, Washington, 1970-72; pres. Minn. Public Radio, Inc., St. Paul, 1972—; founding dir. Nat. Public Radio; chmn. bd. Assn. Public Radio Stas., 1973-77. Club: Minnesota. Office: 45 E 8th St Saint Paul MN 55101

KLINGEL, MARTIN ALLEN, ins. co. exec.; b. Urbana, Ill., Aug. 27, 1941; s. Allen B. and Mary Margaret O. K.; B.S. with honors, U. Ill., 1964; children—Katherine A., Martin Allen. Coll. agt. Northwestern Mut. Life Ins. Co., Milw., 1963-64, fulltime asso., 1964—; co-founder, prin. Dooley's chain, Champaign, 1970—; pres. Nat. Mini Warehouses Co., Urbana, 1973—; dir. Busey First Nat. Bank, Urbana. C.L.U. Mem. Million Dollar Round Table. Republican. Presbyterian. Home: 2003 Duncan Champaign IL 61820 Office: 811 W Springfield Ave Champaign IL 61820

KLINGER, WILLIAM RUSSELL, educator; b. Columbia City, Ind., Feb. 9, 1939; s. Russell Jennings and Marcella Mae (King) K.; student Marion Coll., 1957-59; B.S., Taylor U., 1961; M.Sc., Ohio State U., 1967, Ph.D., 1973; m. Joanne Lois Clement, July 8, 1960; 1 dau., Nancy. Tchr. math Marion (Ind.) Community Schs., 1961-68; instr. Ohio State U., 1968-73; prof. math., past dept. coordinator Marion (Ind.) Coll., 1973—; part-time lectr. Ind. U. at Kokomo, 1973—. Recipient Prof. of Year award Marion Coll. Students, 1976-77. Mem. Ind. Council Tchrs. Math., Math. Assn. Am., Nat. Council Tchrs. Math., Am. Sci. Affiliation, Phi Delta Kappa. Republican. Mem. Wesleyan Ch. Author: (with R.R. Wright) Basic Algebra, 1972. Home: 6970 Mary Ct Marion IN 46952 Office: Dept Math Marion Coll Marion IN 46952

KLINGINSMITH, CHARLES EUGENE, chiropractor; b. Trenton, Mo., Nov. 14, 1948; s. Charles Morrison and Barbara Jean (Carr) K.; B.S. in Acctg., S.W. Mo. State U., 1970; D.Chiropractic summa cum laude, Palmer Chiropractic Coll., 1977; m. Betty Sue Welch, Oct. 24, 1970; 1 son, Jeffrey Jay. Intern in technique, diagnosis and x-ray depts. Palmer Coll., 1973-74; gen. practice chiropractic medicine, Fulton, Mo., 1974-81, Crystal City, Mo., 1981—. Served to 1st lt. F.A., U.S. Army, 1970-74. Decorated Army Commendation medal. Mem. Am. Chiropractic Assn., Mo. Chiropractic Assn. (sec.), Parker Research Found., Fulton C. of C. (bd. dirs.), Fulton Jaycees (sec. 1978), Pi Tau Delta. Democrat. Mem. Christian Ch. (Disciples of Christ) (bd. dirs.). Clubs: Kiwanis (bd. dirs.), Gourmet Cooking. Home: 1204 Alexander Dr Festus MO 63019 Office: 517 Bailey Rd Crystal City MO 63019

KLINSKY, JOSEPH WESLEY, indsl. hygienist; b. Cedar Rapids, Iowa, July 17, 1921; s. Joseph and Zora Vera (Bezdek) K.; B.S. in Chem. Engring., Iowa State U., 1943; postgrad. Akron U., U. Iowa; m. Marianne Trejtnar, Sept. 3, 1943; children—J. Dennis, R. Gary, Pammela S. Chief chemist Cryovac Corp., Cedar Rapids, 1951-55; indsl. hygienist U. Iowa, Iowa City, 1955-74, 77—; coordinator occupational health Kirkwood Community Coll., Cedar Rapids, 1975-77. Mem. exec. com. Ames Patriotic Council, 1979—. Cert. Am. Bd. Indsl. Hygiene. Mem. Am. Indsl. Hygiene Assn., Am. Acad. Indsl. Hygiene, Am. Conf. Govt. Indsl. Hygienists, Am. Soc. Safety Engrs. (cert. safety profl.), Am. Inst. Chem. Engrs. Republican. Methodist. Club: Ames Lions (dir.). Home: 2207 Hayes Ave Ames IA 50010 Office: Environ Health and Safety Iowa State U Ames IA 50011

KLIPPER, STUART DAVID, artist, educator; b. Bronx, N.Y., Aug. 27, 1941; s. George J. and Raye S. Klipper; B.A., U. Mich., 1962. Instr. of photography Mpls. Coll. Art and Design, 1970, 72, 74; instr. photography studio arts dept. U. Minn., Mpls., 1974, asst. prof., summer, 1975; instr. photography Blake Sch., Mpls., 1975-76; vis. artist Colorado Coll., Colorado Springs, 1978, 79, 80; cons. Walker Art Center, 1973, Minn. State Bicentennial Com., 1976, Carlton Coll., Minn., 1974; guest curator Macalaster Coll. Gallery, 1978; guest lectr. various art centers, 1973-80 vis. artist various art schs. and colls., 1972-79. One-man shows of photographs: Mpls. Inst. Arts, 1964-70, JCC Gallery, Mpls., 1964-70, Suzanne Kohn Gallery, St. Paul, Minn., 1972-74, Peter M. David Gallery, Mpls., 1975, 76, 77, Walker Art Center, Mpls., 1978, Minn. Mus. Art, 1980, Land Mark Center, St. Paul, 1980, Douglas Kenyon Gallery, Chgo., 1981; group shows include: Nelson-Atkins Gallery, Kansas City, Mo., 1974, Walker Art Center, 1974, 81, Mpls. Inst. Arts, 1975, 76, 78, Minn. Mus. Art, St. Paul, 1976, John Michael Kohler Art Center, Sheboygan, Wis., 1978, Art Inst. Chgo., 1980, George Eastman House, 1981; represented in permanent collections: Mpls. Inst. Arts, Minn. Mus. Art, St. Paul, U. Minn. Gallery, Walker Art Center, Mpls., Art Inst. Chgo., Exchange Nat. Bank, Chgo., David and Reva Logan Found. collection, Chgo., U. Kans. Mus. Art, Chase Manhattan Art Program, Mus. Modern Art, N.Y.C., 1st Nat. Bank, St. Paul, Cray Research, Mpls., Fermi Nat. Accelerator Lab. Guggenheim Meml. Found. fellow, 1979, Nat. Endowment for the Arts Photographers fellow, 1979, Minn. Arts Bd. grantee, 1973, 75, NEA grantee, 1977; Bush Found. visual arts fellow, 1980. Contbr. photographs to various mags. and book publishers. Address: 614 W 27th St Minneapolis MN 55408

KLOBNAK, JOHN JOSEPH, media cons.; b. Alton, Ill., Jan. 4, 1951; s. Joseph and Anna (Day) K.; B.A., So. Ill. U., 1973. Dir. public affairs Ark. State U., Jonesboro, 1973-74; news reporter/producer Sta. KAIT-TV, Jonesboro, 1974-76; account mgr. Bunn Winter, Assos., Inc., St. Louis, 1976-77; media cons. Klobnak Media Cons., St. Louis, 1977—. Mem. Edwardsville (Ill.) Cable TV Commn., 1973; chmn. adv. com. Lucco for Rep. campaign, 1978. Mem. Tau Kappa Epsilon, Delta Kappa Tau. Lutheran. Club: Press of St. Louis. Contbr. to newspapers. Home and Office: 2087 Tavel Ct Saint Louis MO 63141

KLOEHN, RALPH ANTHONY, plastic surgeon; b. Milw., Dec. 18, 1932; s. Ralph Charles and Virginia Mary (Kosak) K.; B.S., Marquette U., 1954, M.D., 1958; m. Mary Theresa Landers, Nov. 4, 1961; children—Colleen, Gregory, Kristine, Patricia, Timothy, Philip, Michelle. Intern, Charity Hosp. La., New Orleans, 1958-59; resident in gen. surgery Marquette U., Milw., 1961-65; resident in plastic and maxillofacial surgery U. Tex. Med. Br., Galveston, 1965-68, fellow Shrine Burns Inst., Galveston, 1965-68; fellow in plastic and reconstructive surgery African Med. and Research Found., Nairobi, Kenya, 1968-69; practice medicine specializing in plastic surgery, Milw., 1969—; clin. instr. plastic surgery Med. Coll. Wis., Milw., 1969—. Served with M.C., USN, 1959-61. Diplomate Am. Bd. Plastic Surgery. Fellow Internat. Coll. Surgeons, A.C.S.; mem. Wis. Soc. Plastic Surgeons (v.p. 1976-78), Milw. County, Waukesha County med. socs., State Med. Soc. Wis., Am. Assn. for Hand Surgery, Am. Cleft Palate Assn., AMA, Am. Soc. Plastic and Reconstructive Surgeons, Am. Trauma Soc. (pres. Greater Milw. Area unit 1979), Midwestern Assn. Plastic Surgeons, Singleton Surg. Soc. Contbr. articles to med. jours. Home: 1305 Helene Dr Brookfield WI 53005 Office: 2323 N Mayfair Rd Suite 503 Milwaukee WI 53226

KLOPPENBORG, GERALD JOHN, data processing co. exec.; b. State Center, Iowa, Feb. 8, 1940; s. John Harlan and Clara (Celestina) K.; student Iowa State U., 1958. Draftsman, Fisher Governor Co., Marshalltown, Iowa, 1959-63, programmer, 1963-67; mgr. systems and programming Lennox Industries, Inc., Marshalltown, 1967-73; mgr. system software J.I. Case Co., Racine, Wis., 1973-74; sr. asso. PRC Pub. Mgmt. Services, Inc., San Francisco, 1974; sr. systems analyst, mgr. data processing Lockwood Corp., Gering, Nebr., 1974—; cons. in field. Democrat. Roman Catholic. Club: Eagles. Home: PO Box 222 Gering NE 69341 Office: PO Box 160 Gering NE 69341

KLOS, JEROME JOHN, lawyer; b. La Crosse, Wis., Jan. 17, 1927; s. Charles and Edna S. (Wagner) K.; B.S., U. Wis., 1948, J.D., 1950; m. Mary M. Hamilton, July 26, 1958; children—Bryant H., Geoffrey W. Admitted to Wis. bar, 1950, since practiced in La Crosse; pres. firm Steele, Klos and Flynn. Dir. Home Savs. & Loan Assn., La Crosse, Union State Bank, West Salem, Wis., La Crosse Indsl. Devel., Inc. Mem. La Crosse County Bd., 1957-74, vice chmn., 1972-74; pub. adminstr. La Crosse County, 1962-73. Bd. dirs. West Salem Area Growth, Inc., La Crosse Area Growth, Inc., LaCrosse Community Theatre; trustee Sander and McKinly Scholarship Funds of West Salem Sch. Dist. Fellow Am. Coll. Real Estate Lawyers, Am. Coll. Probate Counsel; mem. Am., Wis. bar assns. Elk, K.C. Home: 346 N Leonard St West Salem WI 54669 Office: 800 Lynne Tower Bldg La Crosse WI 54601

KLOSTER, JOHN MELDON, educator; b. Watertown, S.D., Dec. 14, 1952; s. Martin and Joy (Horne) K.; student Iowa State U., 1971-73; B.S., S.D. State U., 1975; m. Barbara Jo Albert, Dec. 28, 1974; 1 dau., Cassidy Ann. Farmer, Garden City, S.D., 1968-75; tchr. Granite Falls, Minn., 1975-79, tchr., Sleepy Eye (Minn.) Public Sch., 1981—. Served with USN, 1972. Recipient Jr. C. of C. Service award, 1978; Cystic Fibrosis and Courage Center disting. service awards, 1978, 79. Mem. Minn. Voc-Ag Instrs. Assn. (vice dist. dir. 1978-79), Sacred Heart Jr. C. of C. (pres. 1978-79), Minn. Vocat. Assn., Nat. Vocat. Agrl. Tchrs., Minn. Edn. Assn., NEA. Republican. Lutheran. Home: Rural Route 2 Fairfax MN 55332 Office: 400 4th Ave SW Sleepy Eye MN 56085

KLOTHEY, M(ICHAEL) E(DWARD), electronics mfg. co. exec.; b. Detroit, Feb. 14, 1946; s. Jackson Seymour and Marianne Patrica (Ambriose) K.; B.B.A., Columbia U., 1968; M.B.A., U. Mich., 1971. Asst. comptroller Dow Chem. Co., Midland, Mich., 1971-75; v.p. fin. Edcon Industries, Midland, 1975-81, pres., chmn. bd., 1981—; asso. prof. bus. adminstrn. Saginaw Valley State Coll., 1974—; dir. 1st Midland Bank & Trust Co. Pres., Central Mich. Arts Council, 1972—. Guggenheim fellow, 1969-70; A.P. Sloan fellow, 1970-71. Mem. Am. Mgmt. Assn., Am. Inst. Fin. Republican. Methodist. Clubs: Midland City, Masons, Kiwanis. Author: Capital and The Small Corporation, 1975. Home: Box 2258 Saginaw MI 48605 Office: PO Box 82 Midland MI 48640

KLOTZ, JOHN MELVIN, nursing asst., ednl. vol.; b. Renville, Minn., Oct. 26, 1946; s. Melvin Herman Henry and Dorothy Theresa (Benson) K.; B.A. cum laude, Luther Coll., 1968, postgrad., 1975; postgrad. Coll. Edn., U. Minn., 1968-76, Sch. Edn., U. Mo., Kansas City, 1979, St. Paul Sch. Theology, 1980-81. With VISTA, Ouachita Job Corps Conservation Center, Royal, Ark., 1967; vol. Peace Corps, Iran, summer 1968; taxicab and airport limousine driver Yellow Taxi Co., Mpls., 1968-70, 74-75; nursing asst. Children's Rehab. Center, U. Minn. Hosps., Mpls., 1970-71, Misericordia Gen. Hosp., Winnipeg, Man., Can., 1971-72; warehouseman Employers Overload, Mpls., 1972-73; nursing asst. Met. Med. Center, Mpls., 1973-74, Prospect Park Care Center, Mpls., 1976, Fair Oaks Convalescent Home, Mpls., 1976, Truman Med. Center, Kansas City, Mo., 1977-78, Kimberly Nurses, Overland Park, Kans., 1976—; crewman Mpls. Fire-Rescue Res., 1976; VISTA vol. Genesis Alternative Sch., Kansas City, 1976; with Vols. in Edn., Westport High Sch., Kansas City, 1977, Longfellow Elem. Sch., 1978; vol. disaster action team Greater Kansas City chpt. ARC, 1978—; vol. in corrections Mo. Div. Probation and Parole, 1980. Refused mil. draft, 1969; refused civilian alternative service, 1971, convicted, 1972, refused presdl. pardon, 1977. Cert. nursing asst. Mpls. Area Vocat.-Tech. Inst.; cert. in basic rescue Mpls. office CD. Mem. Am. Hist. Assn., Sons of Norway, Midwest Com. for Mil. Counseling, Central Com. for Conscientious Objectors, Phi Alpha Theta. Lutheran. Home: 901 E Linwood St Apt 24 Kansas City MO 64109

KLOTZ, ROGER STEVEN, pharmacist; b. Chgo., July 13, 1941; s. S. Joseph and Virginia (Worny) K.; student Wright Jr. Coll., Chgo., 1960-61; B.S in Pharmacy, U. Ill., 1966; m. Patricia Dietterman, July 28, 1973; children—Larissa, Stephanie, Justin. Mgr., Med. Center Pharmacy, Chgo., 1966-67; staff pharmacist Children's Meml. Hosp. of Chgo., 1967-73, dir. pharmacy services, 1973—; clin. instr. Coll. Pharmacy, U. Ill., Chgo., 1973—. Recipient Bronze award Am. Acad. Pediatrics, 1972; named One of Outstanding Young Men of Am., U.S. Jaycees, 1978. Mem. Am. Soc. Hosp. Pharmacists, Ill. Council Hosp. Pharmacists (named Pharmacist of Yr. 1973), Am. Soc. Parenteral and Enteral Nutrition, No. Ill. Soc. Hosp. Pharmacists (pres. 1975-76), AAAS. Presbyterian. Contbr. articles on hosp. pharmacy to profl. jours.; contbg. editor Hosp. Pharmacy, 1971-74. Home: 1407 Oakton St Park Ridge IL 60068 Office: Children's Meml Hosp 2300 Children's Plaza Chicago IL 60614

KLUCKMAN, REVONE W., electronics co. exec.; b. Mound City, S.D., 1929; B.S., U. S.D., 1952; married. Partner, Arthur Andersen & Co., 1952-67; with Zenith Radio Corp., Glenview, Ill., 1967—, controller, 1967-71, v.p., 1968-71, sr. v.p. mfg. and material, 1971-77, pres., chief operating officer, 1977—, also dir. Office: Zenith Radio Corp 1000 Milwaukee Ave Glenview IL 60025*

KLUCZYNSKI, THOMAS E., lawyer, former justice Ill. Supreme Ct.; b. Chgo., Sept. 29, 1903; B.A., U. Chgo., 1924, LL.B. cum laude, 1927. Admitted to Ill. bar, 1927; gen. practice law, Chgo., 1927-48; mem. Indsl. Commn. Ill., 1948-50; judge Circuit Ct. Cook County, Chgo., 1950-52, Juvenile (Family) Ct. Cook County, 1952, 53; chief justice Criminal Ct. Cook County, from 1951, Circuit Ct., 1958-63; judge Appellate Ct. Ill. 1st Dist., 1963-66, chief justice, 1964-66; justice Supreme Ct. Ill., 1966-81; mem. law firm Epton, Mullin, Segal & Druth, Chgo., 1981—. Mem. Ill. Bar Assn., Chgo. Bar Assn. Office: Epton Mullin Segal & Druth Marquette Bldg 140 S Dearborn St Chicago IL 60603*

KLUGO, RICHARD CLEMENT, surgeon; b. Blossburg, Pa., Aug. 22, 1935; s. John S. and Stella B. (Sherant) K.; B.A., U. Buffalo, 1953; M.D., Albany Med. Coll., 1962; m. Lynne Hope Miller, Aug. 10, 1962; children—Arthur, Marta-Beth, Anne, Rachael, Michael, James. Intern in surgery Albany (N.Y.) Med. Center Hosp., 1962-63; resident in surgery Roswell Park Meml. Inst., Buffalo, 1963, Beverly (Mass.) Hosp., 1965-67; NIH fellow Pondville Hosp., Mass. State Cancer

Hosp., Walpole, Mass., 1967-68, chief physician, 1968-69; resident in urol. surgery Boston VA Hosp., 1969-72; practice medicine specializing in urol. surgery Boston, 1972-73, Detroit, 1973—; clin. instr. pediatric urology Boston Floating Hosp. for Infants and Children, 1971-72; clin. instr. urology Boston U. Sch. Medicine, 1972-73, asst. urology Boston U. Hosp., 1972-73; cons. urology Brighton (Mass.) Public Health Hosp., 1972-73, Boston VA Hosp., 1972-73; mem. sr. staff Henry Ford Hosp., resident instr. urology, 1973—; clin. asst. prof. surgery U. Mich. Med. Sch., Ann Arbor, 1976—. Served with USAF, 1963-65. Diplomate Am. Bd. Urology. Fellow Am. Acad. Pediatrics, A.C.S.; mem. Am. Urol. Assn., Detroit Urol. Soc., Am. Fertility Soc., Transplantation Soc. Mich., S.W. Oncology Group (surg. exec. com. 1981—), N.Y. Acad. Scis., Royal Soc. of Medicine, Detroit Pediatric Soc. Roman Catholic. Contbr. articles on urol. surgery, to profl. jours. Home: 5746 Hobnail Circle Orchard Lake MI 48033 Office: 2799 W Grand Blvd Detroit MI 48202

KLUNZINGER, THOMAS EDWARD, communications cons.; b. Ann Arbor, Mich., Sept. 11, 1944; s. Willard Reuben and Katherine Eileen (McCurdy) K.; B.A. cum laude in Advt., Mich. State U., 1966. Copywriter, Campbell-Ewald Advt. Co., Detroit, 1966-70; travel cons. Moorman's Travel Service, Detroit, 1973-74; media dir. Taylor for Congress campaign, East Lansing, Mich., 1974; communications specialist House Republican Staff, Lansing, 1975-80; trustee Meridian Twp., Ingham County, Mich., 1980—. Chmn. orgn. com. Mich. Republican State Com., 1981—. Mem. Dramatists Guild, Am. Numismatic Soc., Mich. Numismatic Soc., Zero Population Growth, Mensa. Author: Chester!, 1981. Address: 1856 Hamilton Rd Okemos MI 48864

KLUTZNICK, PHILIP M., former sec. commerce, former ambassador; b. Kansas City, Mo., July 9, 1907; s. Morris and Minnie (Spindler) K.; student U. Kans., 1924-25, U. Nebr., 1925-26; LL.B., Creighton U., Omaha, 1929, LL.D. (hon.), 1957; D.H.L. (hon.), Dropsie Coll., 1954, Hebrew Union Coll.-Jewish Inst. Religion, 1957, Coll. Jewish Studies, 1968; LL.D. (hon.), Wilberforce (Ohio) U., 1959, Chgo. Med. Sch., 1968, Yeshiva U., 1974, Brandeis U., 1974, Roosevelt U., 1981; m. Ethel Riekes, June 8, 1930; children—Bettylu, Richard (dec.), Thomas Joseph, James Benjamin, Robert, Samuel. Admitted to bar, 1930; U.S. commr. Fed. Pub. Housing Authority, 1944-46; ltd. partner Saloman Bros.; U.S. sec. commerce, 1980-81; adv. com. Urban Investment and Devel. Co.; pres. Chgo. Bulls Basketball Team. Mem. U.S. dels. to UN, 1957, 61, 62; U.S. rep., rank of ambassador, to ECOSOC, 1961-63; mem. President's Adv. Com. on Indo-Chinese Refugees; bd. dirs. Nat. Jewish Welfare Bd.; nat. council Boy Scouts Am.; chmn. exec. com. Dearborn Park; trustee Eleanor Roosevelt Inst.; bd. dirs. Creighton U., Roosevelt U., Lyric Opera Chgo., Nat., Bur. Econ. Research vice chmn. bd. dirs., trustee Com. Econ. Devel.; pres. emeritus World Jewish Congress; Mem. UN Assn. U.S.A. (sr. dir.), Chgo. Assn. Commerce and Industry (dir.), Lambda Alpha, Phi Epsilon Pi (hon.). Mem. B'nai B'rith (hon. internat. pres.) Clubs: Cosmos (Washington); Standard, Commercial, Carlton. Home: 180 E Pearson Chicago IL 60611 Office: 875 N Michigan Ave Chicago IL 60611

KLUVER, HERMAN CHRISTOF, ophthalmologist; b. Audubon, Iowa, Feb. 25, 1902; s. Christian F. and Pauline A. (Hahn) K.; B.S. with honors, U. Chgo., 1924, M.D., 1927; m. Lois Heward Cobb, Dec. 25, 1935 (dec. 1969); 1 son, Charles Ross Hansen; m. 2d, Ruth Schroeder Carlson, 1970. Intern, Charity Hosp., New Orleans, 1928-29; asst. otolaryngologist Univ. Hosps., U. Iowa, 1929-31, asst. ophthalmologist, 1931-36; practice medicine specializing in ophthalmology and otolaryngology, Fort Dodge, Iowa, 1936—; asso. Martin, Kluver, Coughlan, 1940-50, Kluver, Coughlan & Allen, 1959-68; pres. Melville Farms, Inc., 1959-68, Kluver Land and Cattle Co., 1968-75; cons. Trinity Regional Hosp., Fort Dodge; mem. med. adv. bd. Selective Service, 1941-42. Served to comdr. USNR, 1942-46. Diplomate Am. Bd. Otolaryngology. Fellow A.M.A., A.C.S., Am. Acad. Ophthalmology and Otolaryngology; mem. Pan Am. Ophthalmology, Am. Soc. Ophthalmology and Otolaryngology Allergy, Iowa Med. Soc., Am.-Internat. Charolois Assn., Iowa Beef Improvement Assn., Am. Rifle Assn., V.F.W., Am. Legion. Mason (Shriner), Elk. Author: Cluverii Chronica, 1958, Cluver'sche Familien Archiv, 1961. Contbr. to profl. publs. in field. Home: 331 Wraywood Manor Fort Dodge IA 50501

KLUZNIK, JOHN COOKE, psychiatrist; b. Hibbing, Minn., June 24, 1941; s. John Cooke and Ruth Elizabeth (Sandberg) K.; B.A., U. Minn., 1967, M.D., 1971; 1 dau., Katherine Elizabeth. Intern, resident U. Minn. Hosps., Mpls., 1971-75; asst. prof. U. Minn., Mpls., 1974-75, 80—; staff psychiatrist St. Paul-Ramsey County Hosp., 1974-75; instr. psychiatry Harvard Med. Sch., Boston, 1975-76; asst. psychiatrist McLean Hosp., Belmont, Mass., 1975-76; dep. med. dir. Mass. Correctional Inst., Bridgewater, practice medicine specializing in psychiatry, Mpls.-St. Paul, 1977—; staff psychiatrist VA Hosp., Mpls., 1979-81; cons. St. Paul-Ramsey County Med. Center, Forensic Psychiatry Service, 1978—. Mem. Minn. Supreme Ct. Commn. on Mentally Disabled and The Cts., 1977-79. Served with USN, 1959-63. Diplomate Am. Bd. Psychiatry and Neurology. Mem. AMA, Am. Psychiatric Assn., Minn. Med. Soc., St. Paul Soc. Psychiatry and Neurology, Ramsey County Med. Soc., Minn. Psychiatric Soc., Minn. Orch. Assn., Mpls. Soc. Fine Arts, Common Cause, Union of Concerned Scientists. Democrat. Lutheran. Office: 519 Doctors Profl Bldg 280 N Smith Saint Paul MN 55102

KMIECIK, GERALD ANTHONY, electronics co. exec.; b. Chgo., Dec. 15, 1948; s. Walter Peter and Eleanor Josephine K.; B.S. in Math., DePaul U., 1971, M.B.A., 1979; m. Barbara Malocha, Nov. 10, 1979. Cons., Peat, Marwick, Mitchell & Co., Chgo., 1974-75; mgr. plan adminstrn. Mass. Mut. Life Ins. Co., Chgo., 1975-76; group ins. mgr. Internat. Minerals & Chem. Corp., Mundelein, Ill., 1977-78; field sales asst. mgr. Tex. Instruments Supply Co., Arlington Heights, Ill., 1978—; dir. Howard Thomas Drug Co. Mem. Am. Mktg. Assn. Home: 3647 N Pittsburgh St Chicago IL 60634 Office: Tex Instruments Supply Co 515 W Algonquin Rd Arlington Heights IL 60005

KNACK, THOMAS MICHAEL, psychologist; b. Saginaw, Mich., June 24, 1950; s. Francis Robert and June Rose (Bowerman) K.; A.A., Delta Coll., 1970; B.A., U. Mich., 1972, Ed.S., 1975, M.A., 1976, Ph.D., 1978; m. Susan Lynne Skalla, Aug. 22, 1980. Grad. research and teaching asst. U. Mich., 1975; sch. psychologist Birch Run (Mich.) Schs., 1975-76; clin. psychologist, dir. intensive day treatment services, supr. psychologists Norman Westlund Child Guidance Clinic, Saginaw, Mich., 1976-79; psychologist Tri-City Assessment Planning and Consultation, Inc., Saginaw, 1979-81, sec. bd. dirs., 1979-81; co-dir. Mid-Mich. Psychol. Services, P.C., 1981—; cons. Saginaw County Probate Ct., juvenile div., 1975-81, Tuscola County Probate Ct., 1979-81; instr. Saginaw Intermediate Sch. Dist., 1979-80; field instr. Central Mich. U. Grad. Sch., 1979; cons. Bay and Saginaw County Women's Centers, 1980-81. Bd. dirs. READ Assn. Saginaw County, 1976-79; adv. Saginaw County Child Devel. Centers, Inc., 1976—, Foster Parents Assn. Bay County, 1980—. Recipient Cert. of Achievement, Western Mich. Psychol. Biofeedback Inst., 1978. Mem. Am. Psychol. Assn., Nat. Register Health Services Providers in Psychology, Am. Assn. Providers Psychiat. Services for Children, Mich. Soc. Licensed Psychologists, Mich. Psychol. Assn. (mem. exec. council 1979), Mid-Mich. Psychologists, Inc. (pres. 1977-80), U. Mich. Alumni Assn. Democrat. Roman Catholic. Home: 8075 Evergreen Park Saginaw MI 48603 Office: Mid-Mich Psychol Services PC 909 S Michigan St Saginaw MI 48502

KNAKE, ELLERY LOUIS, weed scientist; b. Gibson City, Ill., Aug. 26, 1927; s. Louis Franz and Wilhelmina Dorthea (Behrens) K.; B.S., U. Ill., 1949, M.S., 1950, Ph.D., 1960; m. Colleen Mary Wilken, June 23, 1951; children—Gary Louis, Kim Paul. Tchr. vocat. agr. Barrington (Ill.) Consol. High Sch., 1950-56; mem. faculty U. Ill., Urbana, 1956—, prof. weed sci. in agronomy, 1969—. Served with AUS, 1945-46. Recipient Ciba-Geigy award, 1972, Paul A. Funk award, 1978, Educator's award Midwest Agrl. Chem. Assn., 1975; Wright fellow, 1949-50. Fellow Am. Soc. Agronomy, Weed Sci. Soc. Am. (pres. 1974); hon. mem. N. Central Weed Control Conf. (pres. 1972). Roman Catholic. Club: K.C. (3 deg.). Author numerous articles, reports in field. Editor Weeds Today mag., 1977-82. Office: 1102 S Goodwin Ave Urbana IL 61801

KNAPP, LAFAYETTE WHITMORE, JR. (PETE), educator; b. Erin, N.Y., July 19, 1925; s. Lafayette Whitmore and Jennie Jewel (Prince) K.; B.S., Cornell U., 1951, M.S., 1955; m. Jacqueline Frost, July 20, 1946; children—Deborah Louise, Christopher Whitmore. Extension agrl. engr. N.Y. State Coll. Agr., Ithaca, 1951-59; faculty dept. preventive medicine Coll. of Medicine, Inst. Agrl. Medicine, Iowa City, Iowa, 1959—, acting chief accident prevention sect., dir. internat. programs, 1974—; cons. in field. Chmn. Farm Conf., Nat. Safety Council, 1972-73. Mem. Am. Soc. Agrl. Engrs., World Safety Orgn., Am. Public Health Assn., Nat. Council for Internat. Health, Soc. for Internat. Devel., N.Y. Acad. Sci., Internat. Assn. Agrl. Medicine and Rural Health (1st v.p. 1978—), Acacia, Sigma Xi. Conglist. Clubs: Rotary, Iowa City Engrs. (pres. 1965-66). Contbr. articles to profl. jours. Home: Rural Route 6 Linder Rd Iowa City IA 52240 Office: Inst Agrl Medicine Oakdale IA 52319

KNAPP, MILDRED FLORENCE, social worker; b. Detroit, Apr. 15, 1932; d. Edwin Frederick and Florence Josephine (Antaya) K.; B.B.A., U. Mich., 1954, M.A. in Community and Adult Edn. (Mott Found. fellow 1964), 1964, M.S.W. (HEW grantee 1966), 1967. Dist. dir. Girl Scouts Met. Detroit, 1954-63; planning asst. Council Social Agencies Flint and Genessee County, 1965; sch. social worker Detroit public schs., 1967—; field instr. grad. social workers. Mem. alumnae bd. govs. U. Mich., 1972-75, scholarship chmn., 1969-70, 76-80, chmn. spl. com. women's athletics, 1972-75, class agt. fund raising Sch. Bus. Adminstrn., 1978-79; mem. Founders Soc. Detroit Inst. Art, 1969—, Friends Children's Museum Detroit, 1978—. Recipient various certs. appreciation. Mem. Nat. Assn. Social Workers, Acad. Cert. Social Workers, Nat. Community Edn. Assn. (charter), Outdoor Edn. and Camping Council (charter), Mich. Sch. Social Workers Assn. (pres. 1980-81), Detroit Sch. Social Workers Assn. (past pres.), Detroit Assn. U. Mich. Women (pres. 1980-82), Detroit Fedn. Tchrs. Methodist. Clubs: Detroit Boat, Detroit Women's City. Home: 14214 Jane St Detroit MI 48205 Office: 8401 Woodward Ave Detroit MI 48202

KNAPSTEIN, JOHN WILLIAM, rehab. psychologist; b. New London, Wis., June 20, 1937; s. John Joseph and Irene Frances (Peopke) K.; B.A., St. John's U., Collegeville, Minn., 1959; M.A., Marquette U., Milw., 1961; Ph.D., Tex. Tech U., 1970; m. Betty Ann Wilhelm, Nov. 25, 1966; children—John Karl, Susan Elise, Eric Steven. Tchr., Hortonville (Wis.) Union High Sch., 1959-60; counselor Racine (Wis.) Vocat. and Adult Sch., 1961-62; rehab. counseling psychologist John Cochran VA Hosp., St. Louis, 1970-72, Edward Hines (Ill.) VA Med. Center, 1972—; instr. U. Mo., St. Louis, 1969-70; asst. prof. So. Ill. U., Edwardsville, 1970-71. Pres. Winston Village 6 Town Home Assn., 1977-78. Served with USAF, 1962-66. Marquette U. scholar, 1960-61; Social Rehab. Adminstrn. fellow, 1966-69; recipient Spl. Service award Cochran VA Hosp., 1972. Mem. Nat. Rehab. Assn., Am. Rehab. Counseling Assn., Nat. Rehab. Counseling Assn., Am. Personnel and Guidance Assn., Nat. Vocat. Guidance Assn., Am. Psychol. Assn., Am. Congress Rehab. Medicine. Roman Catholic. Contbr. articles to profl. jours. Home: 120 Pamela Dr Bolingbrook IL 60439 Office: VA Med Center Hines IL 60141

KNEIFL, RODNEY VINCENT, chemist; b. Newcastle, Nebr., Aug. 21, 1953; s. Vincent August and Marcella Maria (Barbach) K.; B.A. in Chemistry, Mt. Marty Coll., 1975; student St. Paul Sem., 1981—. Lab. chemist Iowa Beef Processors, Inc., Dakota City, Nebr., 1976-78, asst. prodn. supr. variety meats and rendered products, 1978-79, rendering specialist, 1979-80, refinery foreman, Pasco, Wash., 1980. Mem. Am. Chem. Soc. Democrat. Roman Catholic. Clubs: Eagles, Toastmasters Internat. (sec.-treas., 1979—). Address: Rural Route 1 Box 180 Ponca NE 68770

KNELSON, NELDA LORAIN RIFE, mental health technician; b. Pierce County, N.D., June 16, 1915; d. Herbert Edward and Katie Marie (Christianson) Rife; student Sauk Valley Coll., 1968-75; m. Henry W. Knelson, Sept. 16, 1931; children—John Henry, Nelda May (Mrs. James W. Daley), James Douglas. Factory worker Brown Shoe Co., Dixon, Ill., 1937-45; waitress several locations, Dixon, 1945-47; survey worker, real estate salesperson Hurd Realtors, Dixon, 1948-50; mental health supr. and technician Dixon Developmental Center, 1964—. Pres. Lee County Home Extension, 1957-59; active Girl Scouts U.S., Boy Scouts Am., Dixon Writer Gron Community Players. Mem. Lee County, Ill. hist. socs., Clubs: Dixon Women's (pres. 1959-61), Women of Moose, CROP, Travel. Author poetry; Out of the Inkwell, 1959; Out of the Fire, 1960; Out of the Mist, 1968; (juvenile) Tiger the Autobiography of a Cat, 1975. Home: 2016 W 1st St Dixon IL 61021

KNEPPER, ELMER DALE, acct.; b. Holton, Kans., June 4, 1934; s. Elmer Owen andPearl Louella (Christian) K.; B.S. in Bus. Adminstrn. and Acctg., Kans. State U., 1962; postgrad. Mich. State U., 1972-73, Lansing (Mich.) Community Coll., 1974; m. Kathlyn Joan King, June 15, 1957; 1 son, Kevin A. Acct., Ralston Purina Co., St. Louis, 1962-64, Pataskala, Ohio, 1964; retail acct. Farm Bur. Services, Lansing, 1965-71; acct., controller Lansing Credit Exchange, 1975—. Active Boy Scouts Am., 1943-56, 72—, unit commr., 1975-81, mem. Powwow council staff, adviser Explorer Post, 1980—. Served with M.C., U.S. Army, 1957-59. Recipient Dist. Merit award, 1977. Mem. Tribe of Mic-O-Say, Kans. State U. Alumni Assn. (past pres. Mich. chpt.), Alpha Phi Omega. Republican. Mem. Christian Ch. Home: 10001 Wright Rd Eagle MI 48822 Office: Lansing Credit Exchange 520 S Washington St Lansing MI 48901

KNEPPER, EUGENE ARTHUR, realtor; b. Sioux Falls, S.D., Oct. 8, 1926; s. Arlie John and May (Crone) K.; B.S.C., Drake U., Des Moines, 1951; m. LaNel Strong, May 7, 1948; children—Kenton Todd, Kristin Rene. Accountant, G.L. Yager, pub. accountant, Estherville, Ia., 1951-52; auditor R.L. Meriwether, C.P.A., Des Moines, 1952-53; accountant govt. renegotiation dept. Collins Radio Co., Cedar Rapids, Iowa, 1953-54; head accounting dept. Hawkeye Rubber Mfg. Co., Cedar Rapids, 1954-56; asst. controller United Fire & Casualty Ins. Co., Cedar Rapids, 1956-58; sales asso. Equitable Life Assurance Soc. U.S., Cedar Rapids, 1958-59; controller Gaddis Enterprises, Inc., Cedar Rapids, 1959-61; owner Estherville Laundry Co., 1959-64; sales asso., comml. investment div. mgr. Tommy Tucker Realty Co., Cedar Rapids, 1961-74; owner Real Estate Investment Planning Assos., Cedar Rapids, 1974—; controlling partner numerous real estate syndicates; cons. in field; also fin. speaker; fin. guest lectr. Kirkwood Community Coll., Cedar Rapids, Mt. Mercy Coll., Cedar Rapids, Cornell Coll., Mt. Vernon; creative financing instr. Iowa Real Estate Commn.-Iowa Assn. Realtors. Active YMCA; patron Cedar Rapids Symphony; bd. dirs. Oak Hill-Jackson Outreach Fund, 1970—, pres., 1973-74; bd. dirs. Consumer Credit Counseling Service Cedar Rapids-Marion Area, 1974-80, pres., 1974-80. Served with USNR, 1945-46. Recipient Storm Manuscript award, 1976. Mem. Nat., Iowa (pres. comml. investment div.) assns. realtors, Nat. Assn. Accountants, Nat. Inst. Real Estate Brokers (membership chmn. Iowa 1972-73), Real Estate Securities and Syndication Inst., Cedar Rapids Bd. Realtors, Internat. Platform Assn. Methodist. Clubs: Cedar Rapids Optimist (chmn. boys work com.); Eastern Iowa Execs. (bd. dirs.). Contbr. articles to profl. jours. Home: 283 Tomahawk Trail SE Cedar Rapids IA 52403 Office: 1602 IE Tower Cedar Rapids IA 52401

KNICKEL, DEVERRE BERTRAM, adhesives co. exec.; b. Prospect, Ohio, June 18, 1937; s. Otto Bertram and Catherine Marie (Zellers) K.; student Ohio State U., 1964-65; asso. diploma Walton Sch. Commerce, Chgo., 1966; m. Karen Lenora Gritzmaker, Aug. 15, 1970; 1 son, Ben Christian. Prodn. supr. Arabol Mfg. Co., Delaware, Ohio, 1958-63; plant supr. Borden Chem. Co., Delaware, 1963-68; plant mgr. Beaver Adhesives, Inc., Hilliard, Ohio, 1968—. Pres. Hilliard Softball Assn., 1978; councilman City of Hilliard, 1979—. Served with USAF, 1960-61. Mem. Am. Chem. Soc., Central Ohio Packaging Assn., Columbus Transp. Club. Republican. Mem. United Ch. Christ. Home: 3427 Grandon Ct Hilliard OH 43026 Office: 4400 Edgewyn Ave Hilliard OH 43026

KNIERIM, VIRGIL JACOB, metallurgist; b. Adrian, Mich., Aug. 25, 1924; s. Jacob George and Cora Mae (Wood) K.; student Adrian Coll., 1946-48; B.S. in Metall. Engring., Mich. Tech. U., 1951; m. June Lorraine Hiser, June 15, 1947; children—Curtis J., Allyn. Foundry metallurgist Alcoa, Cleve., 1951-53; research metallurgist Bohn Aluminum & Brass Corp., Detroit, 1953-55; devel. engr. Bridgeport Brass Corp., Adrian, 1955-60; staff metallurgist Aeroquip Corp., Jackson, Mich., 1960—; tech. advisor Jackson Community Coll. Served with USMC, 1943-46; PTO. Registered profl. engr., Mich. Mem. Am. Soc. Metals, Nat. Assn. Corrosion Engrs., ASTM, Nat., Mich. socs. profl. engrs., Wire Assn., Alpha Sigma Mu. Methodist. Clubs: Jackson County Outdoor, Masons. Contbg. author handbooks Am. Soc. Metals. Home: 4775 Moon Lake Rd Jackson MI 49201 Office: 300 S East Ave Jackson MI 49203

KNIGHT, DAVID, actor; b. Niagara Falls, N.Y., Jan. 16, 1928; s. Eugene Grafton and Mary Letitia (Knight) Mintz; B.A., Whittier (Calif.) Coll., 1949; Fulbright scholar, Royal Acad. Dramtic Art, London, 1952; m. Wendy McClure, Nov. 25, 1963; children—Eugene Hugh, Moyra Isobel. Head theatre Putney (Vt.) Sch., 1950-52; starring actor Brit. theatre prodns. Caine Mutiny Court Martial, 1956, The Iceman Cometh, 1958; Hedda Gabler, 1960, The Tenth Man, 1962, Richard II, 1963, also films and TV, 1952-75; head theatre U. Winnipeg (Can.), 1975-76; head acting, designer new curriculum in profl. actor tng. U. Ill., Urbana, 1976—, head acting Krannert Center Performing Arts, 1976—. Mem. Am. Theatre Assn., Univ. and Coll. Theatre Assn., Brit. Actor's Equity, Screen Actor's Guild, Canadian Actor's Equity. Presbyterian. Club: Savage (London). Home: 409 Brookens Dr Urbana IL 61801 Office: 4-122 Krannert Center Univ Ill Urbana IL 61801

KNIGHT, JOHN ELLSWORTH, state ofcl.; b. Lincoln, Nebr., May 14, 1925; s. George A. and Helen E. (Gruver) K.; A.B., Nebr. Wesleyan U., 1947; postgrad. U. Nebr., 1948-49, Garrett Sch. Theology, 1950-54; m. Ruth Irene Bintz, May 25, 1946; children—Kristine Louise, Mary Jo Knight Wentz, Barbara Jean Knight Brockman, Jan Elizabeth. Ordained to ministry United Ch. of Christ, 1953; pastor Immanuel Ch. of Christ, Dubuque, Iowa, 1954-59; pastor Havelock Meth. Ch., Lincoln, 1959-63; exec. v.p. Citizens State Bank, Lincoln, 1963-75; pres. Packers Nat. Bank, Omaha, 1968-78; dir. Nebr. Dept. Welfare, Lincoln, 1979—; mgmt. and fin. cons., 1973—; mem. Nebr. Senate, 1965-71. Chmn. bd. trustees Nebr. Wesleyan U., 1973-78; active Boy Scouts Am.; life mem. PTA. Served with USN, 1943-45. Ind. Bankers Assn. fellow, 1973; John F. Kennedy Sch. Govt., Harvard U. fellow, 1980. Mem. Nebr. Bankers Assn., Am Public Welfare Assn., Lincoln C. of C. Republican. Clubs: Kiwanis, Masons. Office: State Office Bldg Lincoln NE 68509

KNIGHT, LESTER BENJAMIN, cons. engr.; b. Albany, N.Y., June 29, 1907; s. Lester B. and Louise (Vaast) K.; M.E., Cornell U., 1929; student Chgo. Kent Coll. Law, 1932-34; m. Elizabeth Anne Field, Mar. 5, 1935 (dec. 1978); children—Charles Field, Leslie Knight; m. 2d, Frances T. Edens, Mar. 22, 1980. Vice pres. Nat. Engring. Co., Chgo., 1930-43; chmn., chief exec. officer Lester B. Knight & Assos., Inc., mgmt. and cons. engrs., Chgo., 1945—; chmn. Lester B. Knight Internat. Corp., Chgo., 1952—; A.B. Knight, Karlstad, Sweden, 1962—; dir. Knight Wegenstein, Zurich, Switzerland, Knight-Wegenstein Ltd., London; spl. research foundry mgmt., operation, design, automation and mechanization. Pres., adminstrv. dir. Travelers Aid Soc. Chgo., 1958-60, pres. sponsoring bd., exec. com., 1960—; mem. pres.'s council Cornell U., U. Ill. Served to lt. comdr. USNR, 1943-45. Mem. Am. Foundrymen's Soc., ASME, Am. Mgmt. Assn., Assn. Cons. Mgmt. Engrs., Chgo. C. of C. (dir., v.p. indsl. devel. and policy com.), Ill. Engr. Council (1st v.p., dir., exec. com.), Alpha Tau Omega. Clubs: University, Mid-America, Chicago, Econ. (dir.) (Chgo.); Glenview (Ill.) Golf; Army-Navy (Washington); Country of Fla. (Golf); Quail Ridge Golf and Country (Boynton Beach, Fla.). Home: 1616 Sheridan Rd Wilmette IL 60091 Office: 549 W Randolph St Chicago IL 60606

KNIGHT, MARGARETT LEE, editor, lawyer, state ofcl.; b. Newtown, Ind., Jan. 3, 1923; d. Charles Oscar and Edna (Pace) Smith; LL.B., Ind. U. Sch. Law, 1945, J.D., 1965; A.B., Mills Coll., 1953; LL.M., Yale Law Sch., 1955; m. Robert Cook Knight, June 20, 1961. Admitted to Ind. bar, 1945; now dep. atty. gen. Home: 1318 Hoover Ln Indianapolis IN 46260

KNIGHT, RAYMOND J., mfg. co. exec.; b. East Chicago, Ind., June 15, 1939; s. Joseph W. and Jean Marie (Filasar) K.; B.S., St. Joseph's Coll., 1961; M.B.A., Purdue-St. Francis Coll., 1972; children—Danny, Mike, Joe, Jim, Sean. With Inland Steel Co., 1961-65, sales supr., 1965; sales rep., mgr. U.S. Gypsum Co., 1965-67; pres., owner Tipton Constrn. Co., 1967-68; asst. gen. order mgr. Joseph T. Ryerson & Sons Co., Chgo., 1969-76; pres. Chgo. Metal Mfg. Co., 1976—. Served with USMC, 1959-60. Home: 4314 Northcote St East Chicago IN Office: Chicago Metal Mfg Co 3724 S Rockwell St Chicago IL 60632

KNIGHT, ROBERT EDWARD, banker; b. Alliance, Nebr., Nov. 27, 1941; s. Edward McKean and Ruth (McDuffee) K.; B.A., Yale U., 1963; M.A., Harvard U., 1965, Ph.D., 1968; m. Eva Sophia Youngstrom, Aug. 12, 1966; Asst. prof. U.S. Naval Acad., Annapolis,

Md., 1966-68; lectr. U. Md., 1967-68; fin. economist Fed. Res. Bank of Kansas City (Mo.), 1968-70, research officer, economist, 1971-76, asst. v.p., sec., 1977, v.p., sec., 1978-79; pres. Alliance (Nebr.) Nat. Bank, 1979—; pres. Robert Knight Assos., banking and econ. cons., Alliance, 1979—; mem. faculty Stonier Grad. Sch. Banking, 1972— Colo. Grad. Sch. Banking, 1975—; Am. Inst. Banking, U. Mo., Kansas City, 1971-79. Trustee, Knox Presbyn. Ch., Overland Park, Kans., 1965-69; bd. regents Nat. Comml. Lending Sch., 1980—; chmn. Downtown Improvement Com., Alliance, 1981—; mem. fin. com. United Meth. Ch., Alliance, 1982—. Woodrow Wilson fellow, 1963-64. Mem. Am. Econ. Assn., Am. Fin. Assn., So. Econ. Assn., Nebr. Bankers Assn. (com. on state legislation 1980—), Am. Inst. Banking (state com. for Nebr. 1980—), Am. Bankers Assn. (econ. adv. com. 1980—), Western Econ. Assn., Econometric Soc. Clubs: Rotary, Masons. Contbr. articles to profl. jours. Home: Drawer E Alliance NE 69301 Office: Alliance Nat Bank Alliance NE 69301

KNIGHT, ROBERT MONTGOMERY, basketball coach; b. Massilon, Ohio, Oct. 25, 1940; s. Carroll and Hazel (Henthorne) K.; B.S., Ohio State U., 1962; m. Nancy Lou Knight, Apr. 17, 1963; children—Timothy Scott, Patrick Clair. Asst. coach Cuyahoga Falls (Ohio) High Sch., 1962-63; freshman coach U.S. Mil. Acad., West Point, N.Y., 1963-65, head basketball coach, 1965-71; head basketball coach Ind. U., Bloomington, 1971—. Recipient Coach of Year award Big Ten, 1973, 75, 76, 80; named Coach of Year, AP and Basketball Weekly, 1976. Mem. Nat. Assn. Basketball Coaches (dir.). Office: Indiana Univ Basketball Office Assembly Hall Bloomington IN 47405*

KNIGHT, WILLIAM D., JR., lawyer; b. Rockford, Ill., May 18, 1925; s. William D. and Lela Mae (Clark) K.; A.B., Dartmouth Coll., 1949; J.D., Northwestern U., 1952. Admitted to Ill. bar, 1953; mem. firm Knight & Knight, Rockford, 1953—. Bd. dirs., counsel Boys' Club Assn. Rockford, 1959—. Served to 1st lt., inf., AUS, 1943-46. Mem. Ill., Winnebago County bar assns., Assn. Ins. Attys., Fedn. Ins. Counsel, Internat. Assn. Ins. Counsel, Def. Research Inst., Am. Legion, Delta Upsilon, Phi Delta Phi. Republican. Methodist. Clubs: Elks, Rockford Country, Univ. (Rockford); Univ. (Chgo.); Lake Geneva Country. Home: 575 S Lake Shore Lake Geneva WI 53197 also 1205 Lundvall Ave Rockford IL 61107 Office: 708 Talcott Bldg Rockford IL 61101

KNIGHTEN, KATHERINE WELLS, educator; b. Sweetwater, Tex., Dec. 2, 1937; d. James Egbert and Katherine (Carter) Wells; B.A., North Tex. State U., 1958; postgrad. Tex. A. and M. U., 1967-72; M.E., Tex. Tech U., 1968; Ph.D., So. Ill. U., Carbondale, 1977; m. James A. Knighten, Apr. 10, 1960; children—Kathy, Jimmy. Tchr., public schs. Jefferson County, Colo., 1958-61, La Porte, Tex., 1963-64, Aldine, Tex., 1964-66, Humble, Tex., 1966-67, Calvert, Tex., 1968-69, Oakwood, Tex., 1971, College Station, Tex., 1972; reading specialist, public schs., Oakwood, 1970-71, Houston, 1974; asst. prof. edn. Ball State U., Muncie, Ind., 1977-80, asso. prof., 1980—. vis. prof. Murray (Ky.) State U., summer 1977. Mem. Nat. Council Tchrs. English, Internat. Reading Assn., AAUW, Nat. Council Social Studies, Phi Delta Kappa. Editor: Burris Briefs, 1977—; contbr. articles to profl. jours. Office: Burris Lab Sch Tchrs Coll Ball State U Muncie IN 47306

KNIGHTS, EDWIN MUNROE, pathologist; b. Providence, Dec. 25, 1924; s. Edwin Munroe and Viola Ruth (Koreb) K.; A.B., Brown U., 1948; M.D., Cornell U., 1948; m. Ruth Lindsay Currie, Sept. 23, 1961; children—Edwin B., Jessie B., Ross D., David J. Intern Bellevue Hosp., N.Y.C., 1948-49; resident in pathology R.I. Hosp., Providence, 1949-50, Henry Ford Hosp., Detroit, 1952-54; asso. pathologist Harper Hosp., Detroit, 1954; dir. labs. Hurley Hosp., Flint, Mich., 1957-62; dir. lab. Providence Hosp., Southfield, Mich., 1963-75; dir. Northland Oakland Med. Labs., Southfield, 1964—; dir. Bio Sci. Labs., Detroit, 1975—; dir. labs. Kern Hosp., Warren, Mich., 1977-81; pres. Coll. Terr. Inc., Flint, 1968—, Life Sci. Inc., 1971-72, Vet. Med. Labs., 1973-75; clin. prof. pathology Mich. State U., 1974-75; rep. Comprehensive Health Planning Council SE Mich., 1973—; mem. lab. peer rev. com. Mich. Dept. Social Services, 1979—. Served to lt. USN, 1944-46, 50-52; ETO, Korea. USPHS grantee, 1957-66. Fellow A.C.P., Coll. Am. Pathologists, Am. Soc. Clin. Pathologists (Mich. councilor 1966-68); mem. Oakland County Med. Soc. (pres. 1974), Mich. Soc. Pathologists (pres. 1970), AMA, Internat. Acad. Pathology. Club: Detroit Econ. Author: Ultramicro Methods for Clinical Laboratories, 1957, 2d edit., 1962. Patentee in a buret. Editor: Minicomputers in the Clinical Laboratory, 1970; Lifelines, 1971-75. Contbr. numerous articles to profl. jours. Home: 5153 Echo Rd Bloomfield Hills MI 48013 Office: 24469 Indoplex Circle Farmington Hills MI 48018

KNITTEL, ROBERT EDWARD, social and health programs cons.; b. St. Louis, July 22, 1923; s. George Ernest and Paula Marie (Fischer) K.; student St. Louis U., 1941-42, 45-46; B.J., U. Mo., 1948; Ph.D. in Anthropology, So. Ill. U., 1967; m. Elizabeth Rita Geers, June 5, 1948; children—George Randall, David Allen, Rita Marie. Asst. mgr. Doubleday Book Shop, St. Louis, 1948-50, mgr., New Orleans, 1950-52, Clayton, Mo., 1952-54; community relations cons. Housing Rehab. project City of St. Louis, 1954-56; community cons. Community Devel. Services So. Ill. U., 1956-57, asst. dir., 1957-59, dir., 1959-65, asst. dir. research, 1965-67, community cons. area services studies, 1967-68, research asso., 1969-74; coordinator Gulfstream Area Agy. on Aging, Palm Beach, Fla., 1974-75; asso. prof. dept. regional and community affairs U. Mo., 1975-79; pvt. practice social and health programs consulting, St. Louis, 1979—. Active Boy Scouts Am., Murphysboro, Ill., 1963-71; chmn. bd. St. Andrews Parochial Sch., Murphysboro, 1968. Served with U.S. Navy, 1943-46. Fellow Am. Anthrop. Assn., Soc. Applied Anthropology; mem. AAAS, Am. Public Health Assn., Community Devel. Soc. Am., Soc. Med. Anthropology, So. States Anthropl. Assn., Mo. Playwrights Assn. (pres. 1981). Author: Walking in Tower Grove Park, 1978. Author play: Prometheus (recipient Mo. Council for the Arts Playwrighting contest award), 1978. Editor: A Missouri Playwrights Anthology, 1981. Home and Office: 4030 Connecticut St Saint Louis MO 63116

KNOBE, RICK W., mayor; b. Barrington, Ill., Dec. 6, 1946; s. Louis C. and Nan V. K.; student Morningside Coll., Sioux City, Iowa, 1964-66, So. Ill. U., Carbondale, 1967-69; grad. Career Acad. Broadcasting, Kansas City, Mo., 1969; m. Beverly Ann Kramer, June 29, 1978; children—Brian, Meghan. With Sta. KSCJ, Sioux City, Iowa, 1970, Sta. KCHF, Sioux Falls, S.D., 1971-74; mayor Sioux Falls, 1974—. Chmn. Interagy. Water Quality Mgmt. Council, 1981; mem. Gov.'s Council Local Affairs; exec. bd. South Eastern Council Govts., Urbanized Devel. Commn. Named Disting. Citizen of Yr., Elks, Sioux Falls, 1976. Mem. S.D. Mcpl. League (pres. 1981), Nat. League Cities, Sioux Falls Jaycees (Outstanding Young Citizen 1980). Republican. Methodist. Office: 224 W 9th St Sioux Falls SD 57102*

KNOCK, CAROL ANNE, animal technician; b. Warren, Ohio, Dec. 1, 1946; d. Richard M. and Shirley R. (King) M.; grad. N. Am. Sch. Animal Scis., 1974; cert. vocat. edn. Kent State U., 1977. Dir. tng., Warren YMCA Dog Obedience Sch., 1962—; owner, operator Scratch Pad Grooming, Warren, 1962—; mail girl Ajax Magnathermic, Warren, 1964; bookkeeper 717 Credit Union Warren, 1965; all-breed groomer, salesperson Rainbow Aquarium & Pet Supplies, Warren, 1965-66; order clk. Warren City Schs., 1967-79, sec. to bus. mgr., 1969-79, sec. to personnel mgr., 1978-79; tchr. animal care Trumbull County (Ohio) Joint Vocat. Sch., 1979—; adv. to Jr. Fair Bd. for Future Farmers Am.; animal technician vet. clinic, 1975-79. Recipient award for longest running adult evening program YMCA Warren, 1979; named Adv. of Yr. in Agr., Trumbull County Joint Vocat. Sch., 1980. Mem. Nat. Dog Obedience Assn. (nat. pres. 1976-78), Nat. Groomers Assn., NEA, Ohio Edn. Assn., Ohio Registered Animal Technicians, Registered Animal Technicians (dist. dir.), Collie Club Am. Office: 528 Educational Hwy Warren OH 44482

KNODELL, ROBERT JAMES, mfg. co. exec.; b. Chgo., May 28, 1932; s. Homer Edward and Mildred Jenette (Miller) K.; student Morton Jr. Coll., 1962-65; m. Jean Marie Klean, Jan. 29, 1955; children—James, Sandra, Richard. Lab. tech. Indsl. Bio-Test Labs., Northbrook, Ill., 1962-70; service sta. dealer Standard Oil of Ind., Brookfield, Ill., 1971-77; service tech. Hobart Corp., Broadview, Ill., 1977—; also freelance writer. Bd. dirs. Library Bd., Brookfield, 1977-81; Dem. precinct capt., 1965—. Mem. Chgo. Council on Fgn. Relations, Am. Enterprise Inst. for Pub. Policy Research. Democrat. Presbyterian. Club: Kiwanis. Home: 9317 Jackson Ave Brookfield IL 60513 Office: 2747 S 25 Ave Broadview IL 60153

KNOLL, FRANKLIN JUDE, state senator; b. St. Cloud, Minn., Apr. 30, 1940; s. Franklin Oker and Agnes (Jude) K.; B.A., St. John's U., 1962; J.D., U. Minn., 1966; m. Margot Bustard, 1965; children—Elizabeth Jude, Carolin Jean, Jonathan Mandeville. Admitted to Minn. bar; patent atty. 3M Co., St. Paul, 1966-70; gen. counsel Urban Coalition Mpls., 1970-74; def. atty. Hennepin County (Minn.) Public Defender's Office, 1974—; mem. Minn. Ho. of Reps., 1973-76, Minn. Senate, 1976—. Bd. overseers St. Johns Prep. Sch. Served with USNR, 1966-73. Mem. Minn., Hennepin County bar assns., Interstate Coop. Commn., Legis. Audit Commn. Mem. Democratic-Farmer-Labor party. Roman Catholic. Office: 306 State Capitol Saint Paul MN 55155*

KNOLL, SHARON KAY, ednl. adminstr.; b. Linton, Ind., May 5, 1946; d. Claude and Alice (Robison) R.; B.S., Ind. State U., 1969, M.S., 1977, Ed.S. in Counseling and Sch. Adminstrn., 1981; children—James David and Michelle Leigh (twins), Sheri Ann. Tchr., North Knox Schs., Bruceville, Ind., 1969-70, Linton Stockton Schs., 1970-72; owner retail firm, Linton, 1972-74; secondary sch. counselor, Washington, Ind., 1977-79; elem. prin. Loogootee (Ind.) Community Schs., 1979-81; supt. schs. Greene County, Bloomfield, Ind., 1981—; personal counselor; cons. aptitude, interest and achievement testing. Cert. tchr., counselor, supt., sch. services personnel, Ind. Mem. Am. Personnel and Guidance Assn., Ind. Personnel and Guidance Assn., NEA, Ind. Tchrs. Assn., Classroom Tchrs. Assn., Ind. Assn. Elem. Prins., Ind. Assn. Curriculum and Supervision, Assn. Public Sch. Supts., Phi Delta Kappa. Mem. Ch. of God. Research on effectiveness of goal-setting in counseling, hypnosis in counseling, competency-based edn. Home: Rural Route 1 Linton IN 47441 Office: PO Box 112 Greene County Court House Bloomfield IN 47424

KNOLL, WILLIAM CARL, educator; b. Norwalk, Ohio, Nov. 19, 1943; s. Albert Jacob and Ruth Elizabeth (Heather) K.; B.S., Bowling Green (Ohio) State U., 1966, M.Ed., 1972; m. Judy Ann Suter, July 14, 1972; children—Tamara E., Kevin D., Todd G. Elem. sch. tchr. Norwalk schs., 1963-65, New London (Ohio) local schs., 1966-70; intermediate reading specialist Norwalk schs., 1970-72; reading tchr., elementary tchr. New London schs., 1972-74; life ins. agt., 1974-75; reading specialist Four County Joint Vocat. Sch., Archbold, Ohio, 1976—; cons. Reading Center, Bowling Green State U., 1969—. Mem. NEA, Ohio Edn. Assn., Right to Read Com., Four County Joint Vocat. Edn. Assn., Ohio Beekeepers Assn., Wauseon (Ohio) Community Theatre Assn. Republican. Home: 4-11291-E Wauseon OH 43567 Office: Route 1 Box 245A Archbold OH 43502

KNOOP, FLOYD C., med. microbiologist, educator; b. Troy, Ohio, Nov. 11, 1944; s. Floyd Christopher and Pearl Erna (Reiffenstein) K.; B.S., Defiance Coll., 1966; M.S., U. Dayton, 1969; Ph.D., U. Tenn. Med. Center, 1974, postdoctoral fellow, 1974-75; m. Pamela Kay Johnson, June 3, 1967; 1 dau., Tiffany Nicoll. Teaching fellow U. Dayton (Ohio), 1967-69; asst. prof. med. microbiology, Creighton U. Sch. Medicine, Omaha, 1975—. Counselor, Gt. Plains council Girl Scouts U.S.A., 1978-81. Recipient various pvt. found. grants. Mem. AAAS, Am. Soc. Microbiology, N.Y. Acad. Scis., Sigma Xi (pres. Omaha, 1981—). Republican. Presbyterian. Reviewer, Jour. of Infection and Immunity; contbr. articles to profl. jours. Home: 14335 Patrick Ave Omaha NE 68164 Office: 2500 California St Omaha NE 68178

KNOPF, ELMER AUGUST, broadcasting co. exec.; b. Holland, Mich., Oct. 13, 1913; s. Frederick William and Nella K.; grad. Flint (Mich.) Community Jr. Coll., 1933; m. Wilma Jean Climie, June 2, 1934; children—Frederick William, Richard Charles. With Sta. WFDF, Flint, Mich., 1933—, program dir., 1943-59, acting gen. mgr., 1959-61, pres., gen. mgr., 1961—. Pres., Flint Bd. Edn., Genesee (Mich.) Intermediate Sch. Dist., United Way Genesee and Lapeer Counties, Mich., United Way Mich. Mem. Mich. Assn. Broadcasters (past pres.), Broadcast Pioneers. Clubs: Flint City, Flint Civitan (past pres.). Office: 100 Phoenix Bldg Flint MI 48502

KNOPP, JAMES FRANKLIN, hosp. adminstr.; b. Morristown, Ind., Feb. 23, 1936; s. Luther Marcellus and Mary (Andis) K.; B.S. in Indsl. Engring., Gen. Motors Inst., 1959; M.B.A., Xavier U., 1971; m. Marilyn Joan Beyers, Mar. 18, 1956; children—James Mark, Denise Ann, Kathleen Sue. Student in tng. Allison div. Gen. Motors Corp., Indpls., 1954-60; indsl. engr. N.Y. Central System, Indpls., 1960-65; dir. systems mgmt. Community Hosp. of Indpls., 1965-68, asst. adminstr., 1968-75; adminstr. Westview Osteo. Med. Hosp., Indpls., 1975-77, pres., 1977—; cons. Am. Osteo. Hosp. Assn., Alliance Indpls. Hosps.; bd. dirs. United Hosp. Services, Affiliated Hosps. of Ind. Chmn. hosp. div. United Way Campaign, 1978; bd. dirs. Central Ind. Regional Blood Center, 1975—. Registered profl. engr., Ind. Mem. Am. Inst. Indsl. Engrs., Am. Coll. Hosp. Adminstrs., Am. Hosp. Assn., Nat. Soc. Profl. Engrs., Ind. Hosp. Assn., Ind. Osteo. Hosp. Assn., Hosp. Mgmt. Systems Soc. (charter mem. Ind. chpt.), Econ. Club Indpls. Baptist. Club: Rotary (Indpls.). Home: Rural Route 2 Box 84H Fountaintown IN 46130 Office: 3630 Guion Rd Indianapolis IN 46222

KNORPS, GEORGE FRANK, data processing exec.; b. Chgo., Feb. 26, 1946; s. Leo Casmir and Adeline (Stodolny) K.; B.S., U. Ill., 1968; m. Christine Dolores Perry, Oct. 25, 1969; children—Brooke Vanessa, Marc Christopher, Lindsay Allison. Systems engr. Control Data Corp., Mpls. and Los Angeles, 1968-70; corp. software devel. supr. Standard Oil (Ind.), Chgo., 1973-78; corp. mgr. support systems GATX Corp., Chgo., 1978-81; pres. Knorps Computer Cons., Inc., Chgo., 1978—. Served with USN, 1970-73. Mem. Assn. Computing Machinery, Data Processing Mgmt. Assn., Chgo. Indsl. Communications Assn., U. Ill. Alumni Assn., Chi Psi. Roman Catholic. Contbr. articles to profl. jours. Home: 1174 Ash St Winnetka IL 60093 Office: Knorps Computer Cons Inc 180 N La Salle St Suite 2901 Chicago IL 60601

KNORR, ROBERT OTTO, JR., fin. exec.; b. N.Y.C., July 15, 1940; s. Robert O. and Mary (Novhard) K.; B.S. in B.A., Rutgers U., 1962; m. Madeline Nicholes, July 29, 1967; 1 dau., Madeline Lee. Vice pres. fin. Bowmar Ali, Acton, Mass., 1973-75; v.p. fin. Fram Corp., Providence, 1975-79, v.p. mfg., 1980; v.p. fin. Auto group Bendix Corp., Southfield, Mich., 1980—, also v.p. mgmt. cons. Mem. Fin. Execs. Inst. Office: Bendix Corp Exec Offices Southfield MI 48037

KNOSPE, WILLIAM HERBERT, physician; b. Oak Park, Ill., May 26, 1929; s. Herbert Henry and Dora Isabel (Spruce) K.; B.A., U. Ill., Chgo. and Urbana, 1951, B.S., 1952, M.D., Chgo., 1954; M.S. in Radiation Biology, U. Rochester (N.Y.), 1962; m. Adris M. Nelson, June 19, 1954. Rotating intern Upstate Med. Center Hosps., SUNY, Syracuse, 1954-55; resident in medicine Ill. Central Hosp., Chgo., 1955-56, VA Research Hosp. and Northwestern U. Med. Sch., Chgo., 1956-58; investigator radiation biology Walter Reed Army Inst. Research, Washington, 1962-64, investigator hematology, asst. chief dept. hematology, 1964-66; attending physician med. service Walter Reed Gen. Hosp., Washington, 1963-64, fellow in hematology, 1964-65, asst. chief hematology service, chief hematology clinic, 1964-66; asst. attending staff physician Presbyn.-St. Luke's Hosp., Chgo., 1967-68, asst. dir. hematology Radiohematology Lab., 1967-74, asso. attending staff physician, 1968-74, sr. attending staff physician, 1974—; asst. prof. medicine Sch. Medicine, U. Ill., Chgo., 1967-69, asso. prof., 1969-72; asso. prof. medicine Rush Med. Coll., Chgo., 1971-74, prof. medicine, 1974—; dir. sect. clin. hematology Rush-Presbyn.-St. Luke's Med. Center, Chgo., 1974—. Bd. trustee Ill. chpt. Leukemia Soc. Am., 1977—, v.p., 1979-80; trustee Bishop Anderson House (Rush-Presbyn.-St. Luke's Med. Center), 1980—. Served to capt. M.C. U.S. Army, 1958-61; to lt. col. USAR, 1961-66. Diplomate Am. Bd. Internal Medicine, Sub-bd. Hematology. Fellow A.C.P.; mem. Am. Fedn. Clin. Research, AMA, Am. Soc. Hematology, Am. Soc. Clin. Oncology, Central Soc. Clin. Research, Chgo. Med. Soc., Inst. Medicine of Chgo., Internat. Soc. Exptl. Hematology, Radiation Research Soc., Acute Leukemia B Group (Walter Reed Gen. Hosp.), Southeastern Cancer Study Group, Polycythemia Vera Study Group, Eastern Coop. Oncology Group, Sigma Xi. Contbr. articles to profl. publs.; speaker profl. confs. U.S., Can., P.R., Brazil, Israel, Yugoslavia, Japan, France, Switzerland. Office: 1753 W Congress Pkwy Chicago IL 60612

KNOT, ALVAN PAUL, lawyer; b. Kalamazoo, Nov. 24, 1949; s. Bert and Adeline K.; student U. Mich., 1971-73; J.D. cum laude, Thomas M. Cooley Law Sch., 1976; m. Catherine L. Mazny, Aug. 12, 1972. Admitted to Mich. bar, 1976, 6th Circuit Ct. Appeals bar, 1980, Western Dist. Ct. bar, 1976; law clk. to judge Ingham County Circuit Ct., 1975; asso. firm Allen, Hatch, Letzring & Hill, Marshall, 1977; asst. city atty., Marshall, 1977-79, Lansing, 1979—; adj. prof. law Thomas M. Cooley Law Sch., 1979—. Scholarship chmn. Jr. Miss Pagaent of Marshall, 1978. Mem. Am. Bar Assn., Fed. Bar Assn., Mich. Bar Assn., Am. Trial Lawyers Assn., Mich. Trial Lawyers Assn., Ingham County Bar Assn., U.S. Jaycees, Marshall Jaycees (dir. 1977, treas. 1978), Phi Alpha Delta. Mem. Christian Reformed Ch. Club: Exchange. Home: 414 N Liberty St Marshall MI 49068

KNOTE, CHARLES E., lab. exec.; b. Greens Fork, Ind., Feb. 6, 1921; s. Charles E. and Eva Mae (Leisure) K.; B.S., Purdue U., 1942; m. Ruth Alice Rueseler, Oct. 7, 1950; children—Barbara Knote Vardiman, Nancy Knote Evendeh, Elizabeth, Patricia, Richard. Farm mgr. Howard Halderman Co., Wabash, Ind., 1943; salesman H.D. Hudson Mfg. Co., Chgo., 1946-48; pest control mgr. trainee Sentinel Insect Control Labs., 1948-49; owner, pres. Cape-Kem Labs., Cape Girardeau, Mo., 1949—; pest control cons. U. Ill., Purdue U., So. Ill. U., U. Mo., U. Ky., also industry; food sanitation cons. Vice pres., mem. bd. Chateau Girardeau, 1974-81; pres. Cape Girardeau Community Concert Assn., 1973-75. Served to ensign, USNR, World War II. Recipient Golden Lyre award Cape Girardeau Community Concert Assn.; registered profl. entomologist; cert. profl. food sanitarian. Mem. Mo. Pest Control Assn. (pres. 1973, profl. service award 1974), Nat. Pest Control Assn. (dir. 1963-66, 73-76, edn. com. award 1975-76), Cape Girardeau C. of C. (Friend of Agr. award 1972), Pi Chi Omega (Profl. Service award 1973). Presbyterian (elder, deacon). Clubs: Masons, Exchange. Editor: Missouri Pest Control Technician Training Manual, 1971; Missouri Pest Control Certification Manual, 1973, 74; Food Sanitation Manual, 1979. Inventor various rodent baits, bait stations and traps. Home: 2323 Brookwood St Cape Girardeau MO 63701 Office: 33 N Frederick St Cape Girardeau MO 63701

KNOTT, ALBERT PAUL, JR., physician; b. Pitts., Mar. 23, 1935; s. Albert Paul and Fannie (Scott) K.; A.B., Yale U., 1956; M.D., N.J. Coll. Medicine, 1960. Intern D.C. Gen. Hosp., 1960-61, cardiovascular research fellow Michael Reese Hosp., 1961-63; med. resident Hines VA Hosp., 1963-65; practice medicine specializing in cardiology and internal medicine, Chgo., 1967—; mem. staff Rush Presby., St. Lukes Hosp.; cons. cardiologist Daniel Hale Williams Health Center, 1967—; med. dir. Bethany Hosp., 1977-81, Statesville Correctional Instn., 1981—; dir. Inner City Industries, Inner City Devel. Co., Inc., Inner City Foods, Templeton Investment Co. Ltd., St. Johns Enterprises Ltd. Mem. Field Mus. Served with USNR, 1965-67. Mem. AMA, Am. Coll. Physicians, Sigma Pi Phi, Phi Rho Sigma. Home: 1501 N State Pkwy Chicago IL 60610 Office: 1753 Congress Pkwy Chicago IL 60607

KNOTT, THEODORE KENNETH, ins. agy. exec.; b. Niles, Mich., Apr. 8, 1935; s. Kenneth Edward and Mildred Louise K.; B.A., Kalamazoo Coll., 1957; m. Gail Kaiser, Sept. 7, 1957; children—Kimberly, Brett, Leslie, Heather, Kurt. Field rep. Aetna Life Ins. Co., 1961; ins. agt. Charles A. Boyer Inc., Manistee, Mich., 1962-67; pres. Boyer Agy., Manistee, 1967—, Gt. Lakes, Ltd., B.W.I.; dir. Security Nat. Bank, Manistee, Cayman Overseas Reins. Assn. Ltd., B.W.I., Four Point Travel, Inc. Pres., Econ. Devel. Corp.; past pres. Indsl. Devel. Corp. Served with CIC, U.S. Army, 1958-61. Recipient Boss of Yr. award Manistee Jaycees, 1970. Mem. Ind. Ins. Agts. Assn., Profl. Ins. Agts. Assn. Republican. Lutheran. Club: Rotary (past pres.). Home: 553 8th St Manistee MI 49660 Office: 300 Bank Bldg River St Manistee MI 49660

KNOTT, WILEY EUGENE, electronic engr.; b. Muncie, Ind., Mar. 18, 1938; s. Joseph Wiley and Mildred Viola (Haxton) K.; B.S. in Elec. Engring., Tri-State U., 1963; postgrad. Union Coll., 1970-73; children—Brian Evan. Asso. aircraft engr. Lockheed-Ga. Co., Marietta, 1963-65; tech. publs. engr. Gen. Electric Co., Pittsfield, Mass., 1965-77,sr. publs. engr., 1977-79, group leader, 1967-79; specialist engr. Boeing Mil. Airplane Co., Wichita, Kans., 1979-81, sr. specialist engr., 1981—; part-time bus. cons., 1972—. Active Am. Security Council, 1975—, Nat. Republican Senatorial Com., 1979—, Nat. Rep. Congressional Com., 1979—, Rep. Nat. Com., 1979—, Rep. Presdl. Task Force, 1981—; state advisor U.S. Congl. Adv. Aboard, 1981—. Served with AUS, 1956-59. Mem. Am. Def. Preparedness Assn. (life), U.S. Golf Assn., M.B.A. Assn. Methodist. Home: 9000 E Lincoln St Apt 405 Wichita KS 67207 Office: Boeing Mil Airplane Co 3801 S Oliver St Wichita KS 67210

KNOUSE, JOYCE MARIE, fin. co. exec.; b. Wheeling, W.Va., May 30, 1940; d. Russell L. and Katherine E. (Haberfield) McLaughlin; student West Liberty State Coll., 1958-60; B.A., Long Beach State U., 1962; m. Phillip K. Knouse, June 13, 1964; children—Kathryn Lynn, Linda Marie. Job and placement counselor Calif. Dept. Employment, Long Beach, 1962-66; with Community Savs. & Loan, East Moline, Ill., 1973-81; mktg. dir., agt. Quad Cities Mktg. Service, Moline, Ill., 1981—. Trustee edn. com. Christ United Methodist Ch., East Moline, i980-8i. Mem. Savs. Instn. Mktg. Soc. Am., Moline C. of C. Home: 1812 21st Ave East Moline IL 61244 Office: Quad Cities Marketing Service 3637 23rd Ave Moline IL 61265

KNOWLES, ENOCH OMER, JR., savs. and loan exec.; b. Weleetka, Okla., Feb. 7, 1920; s. Enoch and Margaret (Kelly) K.; grad. high sch.; m. Ada L. Powell, May 14, 1943; children—Betty Ann Childress, Enoch O. III, Robert O. Chief mortgage credit FHA, Tulsa and Lubbock, Tex., 1947-51, asst. mgr. Kansas City office, 1952-57; v.p., Kansas City mgr. Farm & Home Savs. Assn., 1957-60; pres., chmn. bd. People's Savs. Assn., Toledo, 1960—. Served to capt. U.S. Army, 1942-46. Mem. Savs. Instns. Mktg. Soc. Am. (pres. 1973). Democrat. Methodist. Club: Kiwanis (Toledo). Editor monthly newsletter Real Estate and the Economy. . .As I See It, 1965—; host radio show. Office: 3130 Executive Pkwy Toledo OH 43606

KNOWLES, GREGORY ADAMS, city adminstr.; b. West Point, N.Y., Jan. 9, 1947; s. Harold Ferguson and Mercedes Myrtle (Murphy) K.; B.A. in Polit. Sci., Va. Poly. Inst. and State U., 1975; M.Urban Affairs in Urban Mgmt. (HEW fellow), 1977; m. Deberah Ann Hochwalt, Sept. 9, 1972; children—Jennifer Lynn, Emily Katherine. Spl. asst. to county adminstr. County of Montgomery (Va.), 1976; asst. to village mgr. Village of Winnetka (Ill.), 1976-78; city adminstr. City of Monona (Wis.), 1978—; fin. cons. to State of Va.; curriculum adviser M.P.A. program Northwestern U. Served with USAF, 1966-73. Decorated Bronze Star with oak leaf cluster. Mem. Internat. City Mgmt. Assn. Roman Catholic. Writer, producer, dir. films on crises mgmt. Home: 914 Birch Haven Circle Monona WI 53716 Office: 5211 Schluter Rd Monona WI 53716

KNOWLES, THOMAS WILLIAM, educator; b. Chgo., June 2, 1941; s. Thomas Houlding, Jr. and Dorothy Mae (Lovell) K.; B.S. in Chem. Engring., Purdue U., 1963; M.B.A., U. Chgo., 1966, Ph.D., 1969; m. Fay Rosemary Bailey, June 18, 1966; children—Jennifer Lynn, Julie Bailey. Prodn. engr. Lever Bros. Co., Hammond, Ind., 1963-64; instr. U. Chgo. Sch. Bus., 1968-69; mem. faculty Ill. Inst. Tech., Chgo., 1970—, prof., chmn. dept. mgmt. and orgn., 1977—; cons. in field. Dep. committeeman Republican party Rich Twp. (Ill.), 1974—, pres., 1973-74; treas. Com. for Legis. Reform, 1977—; trustee Rich Twp., 1981—. Mem. Inst. Mgmt. Sci., Ops. Research Soc. Am., Am. Prodn. and Inventory Control Soc., Math. Programming Soc., Sigma Xi, Beta Gamma Sigma, Tau Beta Pi, Sigma Nu. Mem. Evangel. Covenant Ch. Author articles in field. Home: 20440 Hellenic Dr Olympia Fields IL 60461 Office: Ill Inst Tech 31st and State St Chicago IL 60616

KNOWLTON, RICHARD L., food products co. exec.; b. 1932; B.A., U. Colo., 1954; married. With Geo. A. Hormel & Co., Inc., Austin, Minn., 1948—, salesman, 1953-59, mgr. Minn. route car div., 1959-61, central mgr. Minn. and Wis. sales div., 1961-63, mgr. route car sales, 1963-67, mgr. meat products div. and route car sales, 1967-69, asst. mgr. Austin plant, then gen. mgr. Austin plant, 1969-74, group v.p. ops., 1974-79, pres., 1979—, chief exec. officer, 1981—, also dir.; dir. 1st Nat. Bank Austin. Trustee U. Minn. Found. Served to 1st lt. USAF, 1954-56. Office: Geo A Hormel & Co Inc 501 16th Ave NE Austin MN 55912

KNOX, ARTHUR LLOYD, steel co. exec.; b. Perkins, Okla., May 12, 1932; s. Myrl Frank and Margaret (Grant) K.; B.S., Okla. State U., 1955; m. Earlene Lois Luff, Feb. 19, 1955; children—Arthur Earl, Angela Marie. With Lincoln (Nebr.) Steel Corp., 1957—, exec. v.p., chief operating officer, 1979-81, pres., 1981—; v.p., dir. Lincoln/Northland, Inc.; partner 2LK Horse & Cattle Co., K&L Leasing Co., Knox Rentals; dir. Cornhusker Bank, Lincoln; adv. bd. Nebr. Dept. Econ. Devel., 1979—; del. White House Conf. Small Bus., 1974—. Chmn., Lancaster County Young Republicans, 1966-67, Nebr. Fedn. Young Reps., 1967-68, Lancaster County Rep. Com., 1972-76; asst. chmn. Nebr. Rep. Party, 1979-80; mem. Rep. Nat. Com., 1980-84; bd. dirs. Lower Platte S. Natural Resources Dist., 1974—; presdl. elector for Nebr., 1976—. Served with AUS, 1955-57. Recipient various Rep., Jaycee awards. Mem. Am. Welding Soc., Nebr. Assn. Commerce and Industry, Associated Industries Lincoln, Lincoln C. of C. (dir. 1981—), Farmhouse. Republican. Presbyterian. Clubs: Rotary (past dir. Lincoln), Elephant. Home: 920 Pine Tree Ln Lincoln NE 68521 Office: PO Box 81668 Lincoln NE 68501

KNOX, DAVID STUART, realty corp. ofcl.; b. Cedar Rapids, Iowa, June 8, 1950; s. Charles Stuart and Gloria (Lehti) K.; student Mich. Technol. U., 1968-70, U. Minn., 1970-72. Real estate sales assn. Burnet Realty Inc., Mpls., 1972-76, instr., dir. tng., 1975—, regional office sales mgr., 1977-78, founder tng. div., 1976; instr. Nat. Assn. of Realtors, Grad. Realtors Inst., 1978—; also speaker. Accredited instr. real estate edn., Minn.; cert. residential specialist. Mem. Mpls. Bd. Realtors, Realtors Nat. Mktg. Inst., Am. Soc. Tng. and Devel., Nat. Tng. Dirs. Conf., Delta Tau Delta. Republican. Presbyterian. Clubs: Toastmasters, St. Paul Athletic. Contbr. articles to Real Estate Today mag. Home: 1081 Goodrich Ave Saint Paul MN 55105 Office: Burnet Realty 1501 W 80th St Bloomington MN 55420

KNOX, ROBERT MILTON, electronics mfg. co. exec.; b. Mpls., Jan. 30, 1935; s. Donald Milton and Eugenia Irene (Turner) K.; B.S.E.E., U. Minn., 1957; M.S.E.E., U. So. Calif., 1960; m. Elfie Darlaine Anderson, June 22, 1957; children—Suzanne, Michael, Sheryl, Michele. Engr., Hughes Aircraft Co., 1959-62, Collins Radio Co., 1962-65; research engr. Ill. Inst. Tech. Research Inst., Chgo., 1965-74; co-founder, pres. Epsilon Lambda Electronics Corp., Geneva, Ill., 1974—, also dir. Served with USN, 1957-59. Hughes Masters fellow, U. So. Calif., 1959-60. Mem. IEEE (mem. nat. adv. com. microwave theory and techniques). Lutheran. Patentee in field. Home: 440 S Stone Ave LaGrange IL 60525 Office: 427 Stevens St Geneva IL 60134

KNOX, WILLIAM DAVID, publishing co. exec.; b. Sault Ste. Marie, Mich., June 9, 1920; s. Victor A. and Bertha V. (Byers) K.; B.S., Mich. State U., 1941; postgrad. Harvard U., 1943-44; LL.D. (hon.), U. Wis., 1973; m. Jane Edith Shaw, June 15, 1941; children—Georgia Knox Mode, William David, Randall S., Brian V. Youth editor Hoard's Dairyman mag., W.D. Hoard & Sons Co., Fort Atkinson, Wis., 1941-42, asso. editor, 1946-49, editor, 1949—, pres., treas., gen. mgr., 1972—; v.p. Am. Agriculturist, Inc., 1975—; pres. Nat. Brucellosis Com., 1955-66, chmn. Wis. com., 1951-60; mem. nat. agrl. adv. com., 1961-62, nat. adv. com. on trade negotiations, 1976—; dir. NN Dataforms, Inc., Wand Corp. Pres., Fort Atkinson Bd. Edn., 1948-59; bd. visitors U. Wis., 1979—; bd. dirs. Wis. Taxpayers Alliance, 1976—. Served to lt. USNR, 1942-46. Recipient Disting. Service award Nat. Brucellosis Com., 1957, Pure Milk Assn., 1966, Am. Dairy Sci. Assn., 1970, Wis. Farm Bur. Fedn., 1974, Nat. Assn. Animal Breeders, 1981; service citations Fla. Dairy Farmers Fedn., 1962, Wis. Farm Bur. Fedn., 1956, Nat. Plant Food Council, 1963, Dairy Council Central Ga., 1967; Nat. 4-H Alumni award, 1965; Mich. State U. Disting. Alumnus award, 1966; named Tri-State Man of Yr., 1966; Milw. Milk Producers Assn. Man of Yr., 1976; recipient Mid-Am. Dairymen Salute award, 1977. Mem. Agrl. Publs. Assn. (pres. 1979-81), Am. Newspaper Pubs. Assn., AVMA (hon.), Am. Jersey Cattle Club (hon.), Am. Dairy Sci. Assn., Am. Agrl. Econs. Assn., Wis. Vet. Med. Assn. (hon.), Alpha Gamma Rho, Alpha Zeta. Club: Rotary (Internat. Service citation 1956). Republican. Episcopalian. Home: 703 Robert St Fort Atkinson WI 53538 Office: 28 Milwaukee Ave W Fort Atkinson WI 53538

KNOY, ERNEST CRONE, steel tank co. exec., cons. engr.; b. Martinsville, Ind., May 19, 1936; s. Ernest Ellis and Norma Thelma (Crone) K.; B.S.M.E., Rose Poly. Inst., 1958; M.B.A., Ind. U., 1960; m. Cynthia Aileen Plymate, Mar. 17, 1978; 1 dau., Joan; children by previous marriage—Edward, Beth, Timothy, William. Project engr. Universal Tank & Iron Works, Inc., Indpls., 1960-61, purchasing agt., chief engr., 1961-64, contract adminstr., 1965-70, v.p. ops., dir., 1970-79; individual practice real estate devel., 1979—; controller Speedway Pub. Transp. Corp. (Ind.), 1975-79, pres., 1979-80; owner Tank Industry Cons., Mauxferry Farms. Nat. chmn. alumni fund Rose Hulman Inst. Tech., 1977-79. Served as 2d lt. C.E., U.S. Army, 1959. Registered profl. engr., Ind., Ohio, Minn., Ga., Ky., Mich., Pa., Miss. Mem. ASME, Am. Water Works Assn., Steel Plate Fabricators Assn., Alpha Tau Omega, Tau Beta Pi, Beta Gamma Sigma. Republican. Disciples of Christ Ch. Office: 5010 W 15th St Speedway IN 46224

KNUDSEN, SEMON EMIL, mfg. co. exec.; b. Buffalo, Oct. 2, 1912; s. William S. and Clara Elizabeth (Euler) K.; B.S. in Engring., M.I.T., 1936; m. Florence Anne McConnell, June 16, 1938. With Gen. Motors Corp., 1939-68, exec. v.p., 1966-68, also dir.; pres. Ford Motor Co., 1968-69, also dir.; chmn. Rectrans, Inc., 1970-71; chmn. bd., chief exec. officer White Motor Corp., Eastlake, Ohio, 1971-79, chmn., 1979-80, pres., 1972-75; dir. United Airlines, Mich. Nat. Bank, UAL, Inc., 1st Nat. Bank, Palm Beach, Fla., Cowles Communications Inc., Mich. Nat. Corp. Bd. dirs. Boys' Clubs Am.; mem. corp. M.I.T.; trustee Oakland (Mich.) U. Found., Cleve. Clinic Found., Internat. Oceanographic Found. Recipient Brotherhood award Detroit Round TAble, NCCJ, 1961, Man of Year award Sales and Mktg. Execs. Cleve., 1974, Mktg. Salesman of Year award Sales and Mktg. Execs. Internat., 1974. Mem. Motor Vehicle Mfrs. Assn. (sec. 1972-73, treas. 1973-74, vice chmn. 1974-76, chmn. 1977-78, treas. 1979-80), Soc. Automotive Engrs., Am. Soc. Tool Engrs., Delta Upsilon. Clubs: Detroit, Detroit Athletic, Bloomfield Hills (Mich.) Country; Union, Pepper Pike; Augusta (Ga.) Nat. Golf; Everglades, Seminole. Office: 1700 N Woodward St Suite E Bloomfield Hills MI 48013

KNUDSON, BRUCE WILLIAM, food products co. exec.; b. Mpls., Aug. 9, 1944; s. Millard Joseph and Anna Magneline (Stenberg) K.; student Augsburg Coll., 1962-64; B.S.B., U. Minn., 1967; m. Patricia Jean Kenaston, May 24, 1969; children—Derek J., Chad S. Retailing mgr. J. C. Penney Co., Mpls., 1967-79; mgmt. cons. Orgnl. Research Center, Mpls., 1979-80; mgr. mgmt. devel. The Pillsbury Co., Mpls., 1980—. Served with AUS, 1967-71. Mem. Am. Soc. for Tng. and Devel. Republican. Lutheran (chmn. steering com. 1980—). Club: Bacchus. Home: 8232 Russell Ave N Brooklyn Park MN 55444 Office: Pillsbury Co Pillsbury Center Minneapolis MN 55402

KNUTSON, HOWARD ARTHUR, state senator; b. Grand Forks, N.D., May 16, 1929; s. Arthur K. and Ella M. (Kamplin) K.; A.B., Luther Coll., Decorah, Iowa, 1951; J.D., William Mitchell Coll. Law, St. Paul, 1959; m. Jerroldine M. Sundby, Aug. 2, 1958; children—David L., Douglas A., Eric A., Annette K., Amy L. With claims dept. Federated Mut. Ins. Co., 1953-68; admitted to Minn. bar, 1959; partner firm Bergman, Knutson, Street & Ulmen, Mpls., 1968-79; individual practice law, Burnsville, Minn., 1979—; mem. Minn. Ho. of Reps. from 12th Dist., 1966-72; mem. Minn. Senate from 53d Dist., 1973—, asst. minority leader, 1975-80. Trustee Fairview Community Hosps., Ebenezer Soc. Served with AUS, 1951-53. Mem. Am., Minn., local bar assns. Republican. Lutheran. Home: 1907 Woods Ln Burnsville MN 55337 Office: 101 W Burnsville Pkwy Burnsville MN 55337

KNUTSON, NORVIN ARLYN, builder/remodeler; b. Milw., Aug. 16, 1931; s. Helmer T. and Edna A. (Hermanson) K.; B.S., U. Wis., 1953; m. Sandra J. Katzfey, Mar. 31, 1956; children—Cindy, Tamara, Julie. Sec.-treas. Knutson Bros. Builders, Inc., Milw., 1956—; cons. in field Area chmn. United Way, Milw., 1963-64. Recipient Life Spike, Hon. Order of Squires, 1979. Mem. Metro. Builders Assn. Milw. (1st v.p. 1981—), Home Improvement Council (pres. 1978-79). Republican. Lutheran. Clubs: Masons, Shriners. Office: 9330 W Lincoln Ave West Allis WI 53227

KO, BENNY SIU-PING, radiologist; b. Hong Kong, Jan. 27, 1947; s. Paddy Ping and Mary K.; came to U.S., 1965; B.S., Ind. State U., 1968, M.D., 1972; m. Vicky Jung, Nov. 19, 1971; children—Andrew Patrick, Ellen Ashley. Resident in radiology Ind. U. Med. Center, 1972-75, teaching fellow in nuclear medicine, 1975-76; dir. radiology Clay County Hosp., Brazil, Ind., 1976—, Williamsport (Ind.) Community Hosp., 1976—, Terre Haute (Ind.) Regional Hosp., 1977—; asso. faculty mem. Ind. U., Terre Haute; cons. radiologist U.S. Penitentiary Hosp., Terre Haute. Diplomate Am. Bd. Radiology, Am. Bd. Nuclear Medicine. Mem. Am. Coll. Radiology, Am. Coll. Nuclear Medicine, Radiol. Soc. N.Am., Ind. State Med. Assn. (pres. 5th dist. 1978-79, trustee 1979—), Terre Haute Acad. Medicine, Vigo County Med. Soc., Clay County Med. Soc. Home: Box 320 Rural Route 32 Terre Haute IN 47803 Office: Radiology Dept Clay County Hosp Brazil IN 47834

KO, SUNG-TAO, surgeon; b. China, June 13, 1940; M.D., Koohsiung Med. Coll., China, 1966. Intern, Mt. Sinai Hosp., Chgo., 1967-68, resident in gen. surgery, 1968-72, fellow in cardiothoracic surgery, 1973-74; clin. instr. surgery Chgo. Med. Sch., Mt. Sinai Hosp., 1974-75, asst. prof. Rush Med. Sch., Mt. Sinai Hosp., 1975—, also attending surgeon Mt. Sinai Hosp.; attending surgeon Surburban Hosp., Grant Hosp.; attending surgeon Good Samaritan Hosp., chmn. dept. surgery, 1977-79. Fellow A.C.S., Royal Coll. Surgeons (Can.); mem. AMA, Ill. Med. Soc., Chgo. Med. Soc. Office: 30 N Michigan Ave Chicago IL 60602

KOBAK, MATHEW WILLIAM, surgeon; b. Chgo., May 20, 1917; s. Disraeli William and Anna (Braudy) K.; B.S., U. Chgo.; M.D., Rush Med. Sch., 1941; m. Sharon Ann Torreano, Jan. 2, 1976; 1 dau., Caroline Beatrice. Intern, Cook County Hosp., Chgo., 1941-42; resident in pathology Billings Hosp., U. Chgo. Clinics, 1946; resident in surgery Michael Reese Hosp., Chgo., 1947, surg. preceptorship, 1949; sr. asst. resident, fellow Yale U., 1948; practice medicine specializing in surgery, Chgo. and Miami, Fla., 1949-76; chief surgeon VA Hosp., Downey, Ill., 1959; staff VA Lakeside Hosp., Chgo.; asst. clin. prof. surgery Northwestern U. Med. Sch. Served with MC, U.S. Army, 1942-46. Recipient Honors Achievement award Angiology Research Found. and Purdue Frederick Co., 1965-66; diplomate Am. Bd. Surgery. Fellow A.C.S.; mem. AMA, Ill., Chgo. (v.p., past pres. Jackson Park br., councilor Southeastern br.) med. socs. Club: Quadrangle (Chgo.). Author: Studies on the Abdominal Incision, 1965. Contbr. articles to profl. jours. Home: 916 Braemar Rd Flossmoor IL 60422 Office: 333 E Huron St Chicago IL 60611

KOBER, ARLETTA REFSHAUGE (MRS. KAY L. KOBER), ednl. adminstr.; b. Cedar Falls, Iowa, Oct. 31, 1919; d. Edward and Mary (Jensen) Refshauge; B.A., State Coll. Iowa, 1940; M.A., U. No. Iowa; m. Kay Leonard Kober, Feb. 14, 1944; children—Kay Mary, Karilyn Eve. Tchr. high schs., Soldier, Iowa, 1940-41, Montezuma, Iowa, 1941-43, Waterloo, Iowa, 1943-50, 65-67, co-ordinator Office Edn. Waterloo Community Schs., Waterloo, Iowa, 1967—; head dept. co-op. career edn. West High Sch., Waterloo, 1974—. Mem. Waterloo Sch. Health Council; nominating com. YWCA, Waterloo; Black Hawk County chmn. Tb Christmas Seals; ward chmn. ARC, Waterloo; co-chmn. Citizen's Com. for Sch. Bond Issue; pres. Waterloo PTA Council, Waterloo Vis. Nursing Assn., 1956-57, Kingsley Sch. PTA, 1959-60; v.p. Waterloo Women's Club, 1962-63, pres., 1963-64, trustee bd. clubhouse dirs., 1957—; mem. Gen. Fedn. Women's Clubs, Nat. Congress Parents and Tchrs.; Presbyterial world service chmn. Presbyn. Women's Assn.; bd. dirs. Black Hawk County Republican Women, 1952-53, United Services of Black Hawk County, Broadway Theatre League, St. Francis Hosp. Found. Mem. AAUW (v.p. Cedar Falls 1946-47), NEA, LWV (dir. Waterloo 1951-52), Black Hawk County Hist. Soc. (charter), Delta Pi Epsilon (v.p. 1966-67), Delta Kappa Gamma. Club: Town (dir.) (Waterloo). Home: 1046 Prospect Blvd Waterloo IA 50701 Office: West High Sch Waterloo IA 50702

KOBLENZ, HOWARD ROBERT, architect; b. St. Louis, Jan. 22, 1943; s. Leonard and Virginia Emily (Papin) K.; student Washington U., St. Louis, 1961-74; children—Lisa, Daniel. Draftsman S. G. Schmidt & Assos., architects, St. Louis, 1963-66, Ralph Fournier, St. Louis, 1966, Jerome Peters, architect, St. Louis, 1966-72; architect, v.p. Jerome Samuel Peters & Howard Robert Koblenz, Inc., St. Louis, 1972-75, Peters, Koblenz and Kreishman, Inc., St. Louis, 1976—. Recipient St. Louis Beautification Commn. award for Renovation Downtown St. Louis Bookstore, 1975. Registered architect Nat. Council Archtl. Registration Bds., Mo., Ill., Iowa, La., Pa., Minn., Tex. Mem. Constrn. Specifications Inst. Prin. archtl. works include The Plaza at West Port Office and Entertainment Center, Phase 1 and 2, St. Louis County, Mo., 1969—. Home: 872 Warwick St St Louis MO 63122 Office: 2025 S Brentwood Blvd St Louis MO 63144

KOBLENZ, MAXINE L., lang.-speech and hearing therapist; b. Albany, N.Y., May 23, 1935; d. Charles and Lillian (Rosen) Levy; m. Herschel Koblenz, Aug. 12, 1956; children—Marci, Brian. Speech and lang. therapist Cleve. Heights-University Heights Bd. Edn., 1977-81; originator, coordinator confirmation family learning program Park Synagogue, Cleve., 1977—; cons. Cleve. State U., 1980-81. Chairperson women's com. Jewish Community Fedn., 1975-77; mem. com. Fedn. for Community Planning, Cleve., 1974-75; chmn. outreach services for youth Jewish Family Service Assn.; mem. staff Coll. Jewish Studies, 1980—, vice-chmn. women's assn., 1980-81; chmn. United Synagogue Commn. on Jewish Edn., 1978-79. Mem. Am., Ohio speech and hearing assns. Home: 3175 Falmouth Rd Shaker Heights OH 44122

KOBYLECKY, JOSEPH JOHN, architect, interior designer; b. Chgo., Mar. 26, 1942; s. Miller and Mary Catherine (Stolarczuk/Moran) K.; B.Design in Architecture, U. Ill., 1967; m. Elizabeth M. Kenney, Dec. 21, 1963; children—Carey Lynn, Joseph Barruck. Draftsman, U. Ill., Chgo., 1964, Kantola-Mizera, Chgo., 1965; architect Hague Richards, Chgo., 1966-73; architect, asso. Warner, Brejcha, Evans & Assos., Homewood, Ill., 1973-75; pres. Joseph J. Kobylecky AIA, P.C., architect-interior design, Mokena, Ill., 1975—; specializing fin. remodeling and bldg. products; landscape artist in watercolor; dir. Capitol Fed. Savs. and Loan Assn., Evergreen Park, Ill. Recipient Nat. award Ford Motor Co., 1959. Mem. AIA (corp. mem., mem. ins. com.), Chgo. Assn. Commerce and Industry, Nat. Trust for Historic Preservation, Nat. Inst. Bldg. Scis., New Lenox Assn. Commerce. Home and Office: 184th and Virginia Ln Rural Route #1 Mokena IL 60448

KOCH, GERALD D., ednl. adminstr.; ed. Hastings Coll., U. Nebr.; postgrad. (Univ. fellow) Columbia U.; m. Joan; children—Rick, Scott. Instr., Franklin (Nebr.) Public Schs., from 1949, also coach; with Westside Community Schs., Nebr., from 1954, also dept. chmn. social scis., varsity coach basketball/baseball, dir. student activities and athletics; coordinator Omaha Suburban Area Council Schs., Bd. dirs., pres. Ralston Boys' Baseball Assn.; commr. parks and recreation Ralston City Council, also pres.; chmn. Ralston Community Improvement Council, 1968-73; pres. ch. cabinet Ralston United Ch. of Christ; mem. policy com. on effective govt. Nebr. League of Cities; mem. Nebr. State Senate, chmn. edn. com. Served with USAAF. Recipient Ralston Area C. of C. Ten Yr. award for civic leadership; C. of C. Man of Yr. award, 1972; Nebr. Council Sch. Adminstrs. Disting. Service award, 1976; Nebr. State Ednl. Assn. Disting. Service award, 1974; Nebr. Community Improvement Program Leadership award; Nat. Fedn. of Blind Service award, 1979; Am. Legion meritorious awards. Mem. Nebr. Council Sch. Adminstrs., Am. Assn. Sch. Adminstrs., Nat. Council Social Studies, Nebr. Council Social Studies, Phi Delta Kappa. Address: Ralston NE 68127*

KOCH, JOHN AMBROSE, mfg. co. exec.; b. Cleve., Dec. 9, 1939; s. Ambrose Edgar and Bernadette Carmen (Farina) K.; student U. Notre Dame, 1957-59; student bus. adminstrn. John Carroll U., 1959-61; m. Barbara Ann Gaul, Aug. 29, 1964; children—Terry, Mary Karen, John Ambrose, Thomas. Sales mgr. Columbia Metal Stamping, Cleve., 1961-69; owner John A. Koch Co., Cleve., 1969-71; gen. sales mgr. Cleve. Metal Products Co., 1971-75; pres., dir. Klaas Machine & Mfg., Inc., Cleve., 1975—, Ind. Register Co., Cleve., 1978—, Westfab & Machine, Inc., Cleve., 1979—; partner K & K Investment Co., Cleve., 1978—. Mem. adv. bd. Ursuline Coll., Pepper Pike, Ohio. Served with USAR, 1961. Mem. Am. Metal Stamping Assn., Nat. Heating and Air Conditioning Wholesalers Assn., Greater Cleve. Growth Assn., Council of Smaller Enterprises. Republican. Roman Catholic. Clubs: Downtown Cleve. Rotary, Shaker Heights Country, Mayfield Village Racquet, Cleve. Athletic. Home: 19701 Shelburne Rd Shaker Heights OH 44118 Office: 5403 E Schaaf Rd Cleveland OH 44131

KOCH, JOHN MARKUS, veterinarian; b. Van Nuys, Calif., June 20, 1946; s. Markus Edward and Doris Amelia K.; B.S., U. Mo., 1968, D.V.M., 1970; m. Judy Ann Throckmorton, June 26, 1971; children—James Markus, Jeffrey John. Staff veterinarian Skyview Animal Clinic, Cape Girardeau, Mo., 1970-74; veterinarian, owner Cape Small Animal Clinic, Cape Girardeau, 1974—. Mem. Cape Girardeau City Bicentennial Steering Com., 1975-76; chmn. Com. for Bicentennial Battle Re-enactments, 1975-76; bd. dirs. Cape County Heart Assn., 1977—; adviser Vet. Explorer Post 106, Boy Scouts Am.; bd. dirs. St. Andrew Lutheran Ch., Cape Girardeau, 1976-77. Mem. AVMA, Mo. Acad. Vet. Sci., Mo. Vet. Med. Assn., S.E. Mo. Vet. Med. Assn., Cape County Vet. Med. Assn. (pres. 1979), Cape Girardeau Jaycees (dir. 1975, sec. 1976), Cape Girardeau C. of C. (dir. 1976). Clubs: Rotary (dir. 1976—, pres. 1979) (Cape Girardeau); Beaver Bend Swamp Rangers Muzzleloading (charter mem., sec.-treas. 1975-76). Home: 1106 Hilldale Circle Cape Girardeau MO 63701 Office: Cape Small Animal Clinic 210 Christine St Cape Girardeau MO 63701

KOCH, ROBERT LOUIS, mfg. co. exec.; b. Evansville, Ind., May 6, 1913; s. Louis Joseph and Clarice (Ashburn) K.; LL.D. (hon.), Ind. State U., Evansville, 1973; m. Mary Loretta Bray, Sept. 5, 1936; children—Robert Louis, Mary Kay Koch Muehlbauer, Carolyn Koch Weigman. With George Koch Sons, Inc., Evansville, 1930—, pres., 1960—; dir. Citizens Nat. Bank, Internat. Steel Corp., Gibbs Die Casting Aluminum Co., So. Ind. Gas & Electric Co. Trustee, U. Evansville; bd. dirs. Deaconess Hosp., Deaconess Hosp. Found., Santa Claus Samaritans Inc. Found., Ind. Found. Arts and Sci.; chmn. So. Ind. Higher Edn. Mem. Met. Evansville C. of C. (dir.). Republican. Club: Kiwanis (pres. 1947). Home: 1431 Mesker Park Dr Evansville IN 47712 Office: 10 S 11th Ave Evansville IN 47712

KOCH, ROBERT LOUIS, II, coating machinery and drying ovens co. exec., city ofcl.; b. Evansville, Ind., Jan. 6, 1939; s. Robert Louis and Mary Loretta (Bray) K.; B.S., U. Notre Dame, 1960; M.B.A., U. Pitts., 1962; m. Cynthia Marian Ross, Oct. 17, 1964; children—David, Kevin, Kristen, Jennifer. Engr. Metalcraft div. George Koch Sons, Inc., Evansville, Ind., 1958-60, Thermal Products div., 1960-62, mgr. Ashdee Div., 1962-64, pres., 1964—; dir., sec., v.p. George Koch Sons, Inc., Evansville, 1973—; sec., dir. Santa Claus Land, Inc., (Ind.), 1972—; v.p., dir. Gibbs Aluminum Die Casting, Inc., Henderson, Ky., 1972—; pres., chmn. bd. Fesk, Inc., Evansville, 1964—, Water Resources Corp., 1981—; gen. partner Century Leasing, 1980—, Univ. Leasing, 1980—; dir. Union Metals, Inc., Sturgis, Ky. Mem. Sch. Bd. Screening Com., Evansville, 1971-73; controller, dep. mayor City of Evansville, 1976-80, treas., 1979-80; mem. Ind. Tax and Fin. Policy Commn., 1977—, Evansville Police Pension Bd., 1979-80; bd. dirs. Jr. Achievement Southwestern Ind., 1969-75, ARC, Evansville, 1970-74, YMCA, 1973-76, Holy Rosary Sch., 1975-76; bd. dirs. Cath. Edn. Found., treas., 1973-80, pres., 1980—. Served to 1st lt. U.S. Army, 1960-61. Registered profl. engr., Ind. Mem. Am. Plywood Assn., Screen Printing Assn., Forest Products Research Assn., TAPPI, Am. Water Works Assn., Soc. Mfg. Engrs., Nat. Soc. Profl. Engrs., Soc. Paint Tech., Nat. Kitchen Cabinet Assn., Mcpl. Fin. Officers Assn., Ind. Assn. Cities and Towns, Young Pres.'s Assn., Met. C. of C., Tau Beta Pi. Roman Catholic. Clubs: Evansville (Ind.) Country, Kennel, Central Turners, Evansville Petroleum, Tri-State Racquet, Christmas Lake Golf and Country (Evansville). Patentee in field. Contbr. articles to profl. jours. Home: 525 Martins Ln Evansville IN 47715 Office: PO Box 325 10 S 10th Ave Evansville IN 47701

KOCH, WENDELL REUBEN, physicist; b. Phillipsburg, Ohio, Aug. 12, 1909; s. Reuben and Anna Elizabeth (Musselman) K.; B.A. with distinction in Physics, Ohio State U., 1929, M.A., 1932; m. Dorotha Davis, Sept. 6, 1939; children—David Wendell (dec.), Doris Davis Koch Laurini. Physicist, Materials Lab., USAAF, 1929-39; chief physics br. Wright Field, Dayton, Ohio, 1939-51; gen. engr., dep. chief staff plans, then chief resource mgmt. Wright Air Devel. Center, 1951-61; asst. for innovations, dep. for advanced systems planning Aero. Systems div. Wright-Patterson AFB, 1961-69, cons., 1969—; tchr. mechanics Sinclair Coll., Dayton, 1937-38; tchr. advanced optics U. Dayton, 1939; bd. dirs. Honor Seminars Met. Dayton, 1962—. Elder, Dayton Westminster Presbyn. Ch.; enrollment clk. Miami Presbytery, 1974—. Registered profl. engr., Ohio. Fellow AAAS, Ohio Acad. Scis.; mem. Inst. Mgmt. Scis., Am. Inst. Aeros. and Astronautics, Optical Soc. Am., Spl. Libraries Assn., Am. Assn. State and Local History, Am. Soc. Info. Sci., World Future Soc. Club: Dayton Torch (pres. 1977). Editorial adviser Beyond The Horizon—Flight in the Atmosphere, 1975-1985, 1966. Address: 560 Monteray Ave Dayton OH 45419

KOCH, WILLIAM ERNEST, educator; b. Hecla, S.D., Oct. 11, 1910; s. Ernest Frederick and Christine (Pfutzenreuter) K.; B.A., N.D. State Tchrs. Coll., 1938; postgrad. Harvard U., 1938; M.S., Kans. State U., 1949; postgrad. Ind. U., 1952-54; m. Mary Scott Nugent (dec.), Aug. 4, 1940; children—Thomas F., Marcia J. Wheat and cattle farmer, Hecla, 1929-34; tchr. Mott (N.D.) High Sch., 1939-42; instr. English, Kans. State U., 1947-52, asst. prof., 1954-71, asso. prof., 1974—; cons. folksong and local history Great Plains; cons., performer on documentary films. Served with AUS, 1942-47; ETO. Mem. Am. Folklore Soc., Am. Dialect Soc., Am. Name Soc., Calif. Folklore Soc., Kans. Folklore Soc. (past pres.), Kans. Hist. Soc. (dir.), Riley County Hist. Soc. (dir.), Western History Assn., Phi Kappa Phi, Phi Alpha Theta, Phi Delta Kappa. Democrat. Congregationalist. Author: (with others) Kansas Folklore, 1961; Folklore from Kansas, Beliefs, Customs and Superstitions, 1980; contbr. articles in field to profl. jours. Home: 1715 Leavenworth St Manhattan KS 66502 Office: Kansas State University Manhattan KS 66502

KOCH, WILLIAM HENRY, metals co. exec.; b. Wyandotte, Mich., Aug. 12, 1934; s. Anthony Henry and Myrtle Ann (St. Amant) K.; student Internat. Corr. Schs., 1960; m. Marilyn Faye Swain, Dec. 2, 1955; children—Kerry Marie, Denise Ann, Mark William. Metallurgist McLouth Steel Corp., Trenton, Mich., 1952-62; v.p. Metall. Service & Supply, Inc., McKees Rocks, Pa., 1962—; pres. Marko Trucking Corp., New Boston, Mich., 1967—, Multiple Images, Inc., Palm Beach, Fla., 1980—, Global Import Export Corp., Wyandotte, 1969—. Served with USN, 1953-54. Mem. Assn. Iron and Steel Engrs., AIME. Roman Catholic. Club: Grosse Ile Golf and Country. Patentee in field. Home: 3301 Biddle Ave Apt 5-D Wyandotte MI 48192 Office: PO Box 398 McKees Rocks PA 15136

KOCH, WILLIAM JOSEPH, advt. and public relations agy. exec.; b. Celina, Ohio, June 6, 1949; s. George Albert and Helen Marie (McKovich) K.; B.A., U. Akron, 1974; m. Susan Margaret Griffith, June 14, 1969; children—Brian William, Dana Marie. Draftsman, Summit County Engr.'s Office, Akron, Ohio, 1968-72; public info. officer Ohio Dept. Transp., Ravenna, 1972-75; asst. dir. mktg. and public relations Metro Regional Transit Authority, Akron, 1975-78; sr. account exec. Meeker-Mayer Agy., Akron, 1978—. Adv. com. Summit County Juvenile Ct. Child Responsibility Project; mem. public relations com. Akron Regional Devel. Bd., Goodwill Industries of Akron; mem. exec. bd. mem. All-Am. Soap Box Derby, Inc., 1978—. Mem. Nat. Alliance of Bus., Public Relations Soc. Am., Advt. Club Akron, Akron Press Club. Democrat. Roman Catholic. Clubs: Jaycees (chmn. bd. Akron), K.C. Home: 1369 Hilton Dr Akron OH 44313 Office: 1862 Akron-Peninsula Rd Akron OH 44313

KOCHAN, ROBERT JOSEPH, advt. and promotion mgr.; b. Alton, Ill., Sept. 21, 1950; s. Joseph George and Emma Elizabeth (Buttle) K.; B.S., So. Ill. U., Edwardsville, 1972; m. Laura Ann Lutz, Feb. 14, 1976; 1 dau., Emily Anne. With Six Flags Over Mid-Am., St. Louis, 1972—, mgr. show ops. dept., 1972-75, mgr. public relations and publicity, 1975-77, mgr. public relations and advt., 1977-79, mgr. advt., promotions and instl. mktg., 1979—. Named Outstanding Young Alumnus, So. Ill. U., Edwardsville, 1976; 1 of 80 People to Watch in 1980, St. Louis mag. Mem. Nat. Acad. TV Arts and Scis., Advt. Club Greater St. Louis. Home: 5867 Hempline Rd Saint Louis MO 63129 Office: PO Box 60 Eureka MO 63025

KOCHAR, MAHENDR SINGH, physician, educator, researcher; b. Jabalpur, India, Nov. 30, 1943; came to U.S., 1967, naturalized, 1978; s. Harnam Singh and Chanan Kaur (Khaturia) K.; M.B., B.S., All India Inst. Med. Scis., New Delhi, 1965; M.Sc., Med. Coll. Wis., 1972; m. Arvind Kaur Khanuja, 1968; children—Baltej, Ajay. Intern, All India Inst. Med. Scis. Hosp., New Delhi, 1966, Passaic (N.J.) Gen. Hosp., 1967-68; resident in medicine Allegheny Gen. Hosp., Pitts., 1968-70; fellow in clin. pharmacology Wood VA Med. Center, Milw., 1970-71, attending physician, 1973; fellow in nephrology and hypertension Milwaukee County Gen. Hosp., 1971-73, attending physician, 1973—; attending physician St. Mary's Hosp., 1973-76; attending physician St. Michael Hosp., Milw., 1974—, dir. hemodialysis unit, 1975-80; asst. clin. prof. medicine and pharmacology and toxicology Med. Coll. Wis., Milw., 1973-75, asst. prof., 1975-78, asso. prof., 1978-82, prof., 1982—; attending physician St. Joseph's Hosp., Milw., 1975—; cons. nephrology Elmbrook Meml. Hosp., Brookfield, Wis., 1976—; chmn. medicine Northpoint Med. Group, Milw., 1974-75; chief Hypertension Clinic, St. Mary's Hosp., Milw., 1974-75; dir. Milw. Blood Pressure Program, 1975-78; dir. Hypertension Clinic, Milwaukee County Downtown Med. and Health Services, 1975-79; chief hypertension sect. Wood VA Med. Center, Milw., 1978—, asso. chief staff for edn., 1979—. Diplomate Am. Bd. Internal Medicine, Am. Bd. Family Practice. Fellow A.C.P., Am. Coll. Cardiology, Am. Acad. Family Physicians, Royal Coll. Physicians Can., Am. Coll. Clin. Pharmacology; mem. AMA, Royal Coll. Physicians (London), Internat. Soc. Nephrology, AAAS, Am. Fedn. Clin. Research, Am. Heart Assn., Am. Soc. Nephrology, Am. Soc. Internal Medicine, Am. Med. Writers Assn., Am. Diabetic Assn., Milw. Acad. Medicine. Author: Hypertension Control, 1978. Editor: Textbook of General Medicine, 1982. Home: 18630 LeChateau Dr Brookfield WI 53005 Office: 5000 W National Ave 14-A Wood WI 53193

KOCHENASH, CHRISTINA A. (CHRISTA), educator; b. Cologne, Germany, Sept. 19, 1927; came to U.S., 1961, naturalized, 1967; s. Jakob and Hedwig (Krauser) Ammann; B.S. with highest distinction, Colo. State U., 1972, cert., 1977; M.A., U. No. Colo., 1974, Ed.D., 1980; m., Apr. 30, 1959; children—Karl David, Michael Anthony. Dental asst., on-the-job trainer Drs. Mehren, Korfhagen, Gripp, Cologne, 1949-61; coordinator, tchr. health occupations edn. Minndak Vocat. Career Center, Wahpeton, N.D., 1973-75; cons., instr. career, adult and health occupations edn. Monte Vista (Colo.) Sch. Dists., 1975-76; planner, coordinator, instr. vocat. edn. and health occupations edn. Oglala Sioux Community Coll., Pine Ridge, S.D., 1977-79; cons. Indian Health Services agys., 1981. Recipient Cert. of Honor, Dental State Bd., Nord Rhein Westfalen, Cologne, 1949; Disting. Service award Boys Clubs Am., 1967; U.S. Office Edn. grad. leadership devel. fellow, 1979. Mem. Am. Vocat. Assn., Nat. Indian Ednl. Assn., Allied Health Assn., AAUW, Chadron C. of C., Colo. State U. Alumni Assn., U. No. Colo. Alumni Assn., Phi Kappa Phi, Kappa Delta Pi. Home: Box 39A Rural Route 1 Chadron NE 69337

KOCIOLKO, JOHN STEPHEN, state legislator; b. Chgo., Apr. 20, 1949; s. John Ellis and Helen Mary (Rapacz) K.; B.A. with highest honors, De Paul U., Chgo., 1970, M.A. with distinction, 1971; postgrad. Northwestern U., 1971, (Arthur J. Schmitt fellow) Loyola U., Chgo., 1972-75. With fed. research project U.S. Govt., Chgo., 1973; manpower dir. Town of Cicero (Ill.), 1975-77, trustee, 1977-81, chmn. Cicero Plan Commn., 1975—; mem. Ill. Ho. of Reps., 1981—; mem. Bd. Edn. Cicero Grade Sch. Dist., 1976-77; lectr. community groups and coll. classes, Chgo., 1972—, Cicero, 1973—; dir. Family Fed. Savs. & Loan Assn. Crusade chmn. Am. Cancer Soc., 1975-76; Cicero community rep. ARC, 1974-76; chmn. Cicero Bicentennial Commn., 1975-76; judge and registrar of election, Cicero, 1972-73; mem. Cicero Republican Orgn., 1973—; del. Ill. Rep. Conv., 1974, 76; del. county state and nat. Young Rep. convs., 1973—; commentator St. Mary of Czestochowa Parish, Cicero, 1974—. Ill. State scholar, 1966-70. Mem. Am. Hist. Assn., Hawthorne Businessmen's Assn. (treas. 1973—), Smithsonian Instn. Assos., Polish Nat. Alliance, Cicero C. of C., St. Mary of Czestochowa Holy Name Soc. (v.p. 1976-77, 79-80), Cicero Pastimes Assn., Twp. Ofcls. Ill., Am. Council Young Polit. Leaders, Am. Conservative Union, Pi Gamma Mu, Phi Eta Sigma, Delta Epsilon Sigma. Clubs: Cicero Kiwanis (sec. 1975-80, pres. 1980-81), K.C. Home: 4929 W 31st Place Cicero IL 60650 Office: 2062 Stratton Bldg Springfield IL 62706

KOCKA, FRANK EDWARD, microbiologist; b. Chgo., May 28, 1938; s. Frank James and Lucille Ella (Beck) K.; B.S., Ill. Inst. Tech., 1961, M.S., 1966; Ph.D., Kans. State U., 1969. Sr. investigator clin. microbiology Searle Diagnostic Co., Skokie, Ill., 1971-73; dir. research and devel. Biomed. div. Inolex, Glenwood, Ill., 1973; asso. dir. clin. microbiology, asst. prof. pathology U. Chgo., 1973-76; chief microbiology North Chicago VA Hosp., 1977—; asso. prof. pathology and medicine Chgo. Med. Sch., 1976—. Served with AUS, 1961-64. Mem. Am. Soc. Microbiology, Ill. Soc. Microbiology (pres. 1977-78), Ill. Acad. Sci., Acad. Clin. Lab. Physicians and Scientists, S. Central Assn. Clin. Microbiology, Sigma Xi. Lutheran. Home: 3200 N Lake Shore Dr Chicago IL 60657 Office: North Chicago VA Med Center North Chicago IL 60064

KOEBEL, THOMAS ROY, investment co. exec.; b. nr. St. Louis, June 10, 1951; s. Roy Jacob and Celeste Elizabeth (Deutschmann) K.; B.A., U. Mo., 1973; M.B.A., U. Oreg., 1977. Real estate broker Ira E. Berry, Inc., St. Louis, 1974, 78; pres., chmn. bd. dirs. Koebel International Ltd., Clayton, Mo., 1978—; pres., chmn. bd. dirs. Koebel Investment Co., Inc., Clayton, Mo., 1978—. Mem. World Future Soc., U. Mo. Columbia Alumni Assn., U. Oreg. Alumni Assn. Roman Catholic. Home: Route 3 Box 16 Hermann MO 65041 Office: Box 11786 Clayton MO 63105

KOEHN, CAROL ANN, educator; b. Bklyn., Nov. 13, 1936; d. William James and Anna Marie (Koletty) Butcher; B.A., Wellesley Coll., 1958; M.A., Columbia U., 1962; m. Enno Koehn, Nov. 25, 1967; children—William Enno, James Frederick. Tchr., MacDuffie Sch. for Girls, Springfield, Mass., 1959-61; sr. map researcher Time mag., 1961-67; tutor of disadvantaged, Lima, Ohio, 1968; lectr. geography Ohio No. U., Ada, 1968-71, lectr. history, 1974-76; lectr. geography Findlay (Ohio) Coll., 1973-74, 77; exec. dir. Ada chpt. ARC, 1975-79; exec. sec. Ada C. of C., 1975-77; feature writer Ada Herald, 1975-79; editorial researcher, writer Dean's Office, Engring. Schs., Purdue U., West Lafayette, Ind., 1979—. Sec., Hardin County Bicentennial Commn., 1975-76; del. Ohio Council Chs. assembly, 1971-78. Mem. Nat. Council Geog. Edn., Assn. Am. Geographers, AAUW (chmn. world problems 1970, edn. chmn. 1975), Wellesley Coll. Alumni Assn., Alpha Xi Delta. Republican. Lutheran. Club: Order Eastern Star. Address: 911 Sunset Ct West Lafayette IN 47906

KOENIG, ROBERT AUGUST, clergyman, educator; b. Red Wing, Minn., July 14, 1933; s. William C. and Florence E. (Tebbe) K.; B.S. cum laude, U. Wis., 1955; M.A. in Ednl. Adminstrn., U. Minn., 1965, Ph.D., 1973; M.Div. magna cum laude, San Francisco Theol. Sem., 1969; postgrad. (John Hay fellow) Bennington Coll., summer, 1965; m. Pauline Louise Olson, June 21, 1962. Supr. music Florence (Wis.) High Sch., 1955-56; dir. instrumental music Chetek (Wis.), public schs., 1958-62; tchr. instrumental music and humanities Palo Alto (Calif.) Sr. High Sch., 1962-65; asst. to minister St. John's Presbyn. Ch., San Francisco, 1964-65; student minister Bonny Doon Presbyn. Ch., Santa Cruz, Calif., 1965-69; ordained to ministry Presbyn. Ch., 1970; minister Sawyer County (Wis.) larger parish, 1969-74; tchr. gen. music Jordan Jr. High Sch., Palo Alto, 1966-69; instr., asst. to dir. Coll. Edn., U. Minn., 1969-71; adminstrv. asst. to pres. Lakewood State Community Coll., White Bear Lake, Minn., 1971-72; asst. to exec. dir. Minn. Higher Edn. Coordinating Bd., St. Paul, 1972, coordinator commn. and personnel services, 1972-74; instr. Inver Hills Community Coll., Inver Grove Heights, Minn., 1974; minister First United Presbyn. Ch. of Chippewa Falls (Wis.), 1974—; mem. study com. Presbytery of Chippewa, 1973-74, mem. ministerial relations com., 1974-77; adj. asst. prof. dept. ednl. adminstrn. U. Minn., Mpls., 1976-77; mem. faculty U. Wis. Extension, Eau Claire, 1977, chmn. 3d Ann. Bibl. Seminar, 1977, mem. faculty Communiversity, 1978—; mem. internat. coordinating com. of ch. mission Synod of Lakes and Prairies, 1978-79; mem. ministerial relations com. Presbytery of No. Waters, 1977—, chmn. ministerial relations com., 1981-82. Bd. dirs. North Central Career Devel. Center, Mpls., 1978, chmn. fin. com., 1979—. Served with U.S. Army, 1956-58; Korea. Mem. Am. Assn. for Higher Edn., Nat. Soc. for Study of Edn., Chippewa Falls C. of C. Clubs: Rotary, Elks, Masons (grand chaplain 1977-80). Contbr. articles to profl. jours. Home: 1020 W Cedar St Chippewa Falls WI 54729 Office: 130 W Central St Chippewa Falls WI 54729

KOENIG, RUTH, psychiatrist, psychoanalyst; b. Chgo., July 14, 1920; d. Nathan and Rose (Weinberg) Steinman; B.S., Lewis Inst., 1943; M.S., U. Pa., 1949; M.D., Chgo. Med. Sch., 1951; m. Harold Koenig, Feb. 11, 1945; children—Suzanne Lark, Ellen Leslie. Instr. anatomy U. Pa., 1947-49; staff physician Chgo. State Hosp., 1951-53; instr. psychiatry U. Ill., 1955-57; candidate Chgo. Inst. for Psychoanalysis, 1958-65; asso. dept. neurology and psychiatry Northwestern U. Med. Sch., Chgo., 1958-75; cons. psychiatrist Ill. State Psychiat. Inst., 1965-67; pvt. practice psychiatry, 1957—; attending in psychiatry Northwestern Meml. Hosp., 1970-75; attending Gen. Med. Research (Neurology), VA Lakeside Hosp., 1975—. Mem. Chgo. Med. Soc., AMA, Am. Psychiat. Assn., Soc. Adolescent Psychiat., Soc. Liaison and Psychosomatic Psychiat. Author: articles on neurology, psychiatry, book: Manpower Problems in Mental Hospitals (A Consultant Team Approach), 1977. Home and Office: 45 E Elm St Chicago IL 60611

KOENINGS, CHARLES PETER, social worker; b. West Bend, Wis., Oct. 16, 1953; s. Christ Peter and Elizabeth Agatha (Bahr) K.; B.S., U. Wis., Milw., 1975, M.S.W., 1977. Day camp counselor Neighborhood House Milw., summer 1975; sch. social worker Coop. Ednl. Service Agy. 9, Green Bay, Wis., 1977—; coach basketball and soccer teams. Cert. sch. social worker, Wis. Mem. Nat. Assn. Social Workers, Wis. Sch. Social Workers Assn. Club: N.E. Green Bay Kiwanis (v.p., chmn. picnic for handicapped children). Home: 1804 Western Ave Apt 3 Green Bay WI 54303 Office: 1927 Main St Green Bay WI 54301

KOEPKE, DONALD HERBERT, packaging co. exec.; b. Milw., Sept. 19, 1923; s. Herbert Hugo and Lillie (Kirchen) K.; B.A. in Bus., Valparaiso U., 1949; B.S. in M.E., Purdue U., 1951; m. Mary Ruth Brudi, June 16, 1951; children—Debora, Andrew, Thomas. Vice pres. dealer relations Valeer Industries, Inc., Mundelein, Ill., 1974-76; dir. engring. Respiratory Care, Inc., Arlington Heights, Ill., 1976-80; v.p. mfg. Custom Packaging Co., Inc., Hampshire, Ill., 1980—; pres. Liquorland Enterprises, Inc., Elgin, Ill., 1962—, also dir.; dir. S & K Advt., Inc., Elgin. Served with U.S. Army, 1943-46. Cert. mfg. engr. Mem. SAE, Soc. Mfg. Engrs., Soc. Am. Value Engrs. Republican. Lutheran. Clubs: Elgin Country, Anvil, Lions. Contbr. articles to profl. jours.; patentee in field. Home: 532 N Melrose Ave Elgin IL 60120 Office: 265 Keyes Ave Hampshire IL 60140

KOEPKE, GEORGE HENRY, physician; b. Toledo, Jan. 1, 1916; s. George Herman and Louise Florence (Kutz) K.; B.S., U. Toledo, 1945; M.D., U. Cin., 1949; m. Helen LaBoiteaux, Oct. 6, 1940; children—Susan Koepke Healy, Sandra Koepke Hitt. Intern, Toledo Hosp., 1949-50; resident Univ. Hosp., Ann Arbor, Mich., 1950-53; pvt. practice specializing phys. medicine and rehab., Toledo, 1954, Saginaw, Mich., 1976—; prof. U. Mich. Med. Sch., 1954-76, ret., 1976; mem. staff St. Mary's Hosp., Saginaw, 1976—, Community Hosp., Gen. Hosp., St. Luke's Hosp. Chmn. Am. Bd. Phys. Medicine and Rehab., 1969. Mem. AMA, Am. Acad. Phys. Medicine and Rehab., Am. Acad. Orthopedic Surgeons, Am. Congress Rehab. Medicine, Saginaw County Med Soc. Home: 377 Winthrop Ln Saginaw MI 48603 Office: St Mary's Hosp Saginaw MI 48601

KOERNER, FRED LYNN, telephone co. exec.; b. Belleville, Ill., Aug. 15, 1940; s. Fred and Dorothy Joan (Lynn) K.; B.S. in Edn., Ill. State U., 1962; M.B.A., U. Chgo., 1977; m. Karen Sue Taggart, June 4, 1967; children—Tracey Lynn, Jennifer Lynn. Tchr. math. Carl Sandburg High Sch., Orland Park, Ill., 1962-63; mgr. Ill. Bell Telephone Co., Chgo., 1963-79; gen. rate planning mgr. Central Telephone & Utilities, Chgo., 1979—. Advisor, Jr. Achievement, 1968-70; trustee Village of Shorewood, 1975-76. Served with U.S. Army, 1963-65. Home: 560 Windsor Ln Batavia IL 60510

KOERV, HENRY H., mgmt. cons.; b. Tallinn, Estonia, Oct. 26, 1932; came to U.S., 1950, naturalized, 1955; s. August and Aili K.; B.S., Northwestern U. Sch. Bus., 1956; m. Phyllis Jean George, Aug. 8, 1959; children—Hamilton, Randall. Asst. to prodn. control mgr. Shakeproof div. ITW, Elgin, Ill., 1959-60; mgr. systems and adminstrv. services ITT Kellogg, Chgo., 1960-64; mgr. systems and data processing Clow Corp., Chgo., 1964-67; sr. corp. cons. Litton Industries, Chgo., 1967-71; mgr. systems and planning No. Trust, Chgo., 1971-74; sr. prin. cons. Bendix Corp., Southfield, Mich., 1974-77; pres. H. Koerv & Assos., Birmingham, Mich., 1977—; guest lectr. at univs.; condr. profl. seminars; speaker at nat. profl. convs. Served with Adj. Gen. Corps, U.S. Army, 1957-59. Mem. Am. Mgmt. Assn., Assn. Systems Mgmt. (Service award 1958), Am. Prodn. and Inventory Control Soc. Republican. Lutheran. Contbr. articles to profl. jours.; active in privacy protection legis. activities, including research into abuses by public and pvt. sectors. Home: 2409 Partridge Ln Northbrook IL 60062

KOFMAN, SYDNEY, internist, educator; b. Toronto, Can., Dec. 7, 1926; s. Bernard and Bertha (Nachminowitz) K.; M.D., U. Toronto, 1951; m. Doris Sax, Aug. 22, 1959; children—Bonnie, Paul, Clyde, Kerri. Intern U. Ill. Coll. Medicine, 1951-52, resident in internal medicine, 1952-55; asst. prof. medicine, 1960-74, asso. Center for Ednl. Devel., 1970-72; mgr. med. info. Abbott Labs., 1968-70; asst. prof. medicine Rush Med. Coll., Chgo., 1970—; pres. SKM, Ltd., cons. in med. and health edn., Northfield, Ill., 1972—. Diplomate Am.

Bd. Internal Medicine. Fellow A.C.P.; mem. AMA, Ill., Chgo. med. socs. Home: 535 Longwood Ave Glencoe IL 60022 Office: 540 Frontage Rd Northfield IL 60093

KOGA, ROKUTARO, astro-physicist; b. Nagoya, Japan, Aug. 18, 1942; came to U.S., 1961, naturalized, 1968; s. Toyoki and Emiko (Shinra) K.; B.A., U. Calif., Berkeley, 1966; Ph.D., U. Calif., Riverside, 1974. Research fellow U. Calif., Riverside, 1974-75; research physicist Case Western Res. U., Cleve., 1975-79, asst. prof., 1979—. Mem. Am. Phys. Soc., Am. Geophys. Union, IEEE, N.Y. Acad. Scis., Sigma Xi. Condr. research gammaray astronomy and solar neutron observation; contbr. papers to profl. confs. in field. Office: Physics Dept Case Western Res U Cleveland OH 44106

KOGLIN, NORMAN ALFRED, architect; b. Chgo., May 5, 1928; s. Alfred Ernst and Elizabeth Maria (Faselt) K.; B.S. in Architecture, U. Ill., 1951. Architect Skidmore, Owings & Merrill, architects, Chgo., 1957-61; partner Tigerman & Koglin, architects, Chgo., 1961-64; asso. partner C.F. Murphy & Assos., architects, Chgo., 1965-67; pres. Norman A. Koglin Assos., Ltd., Chgo., 1967—; Served with C.E. U.S. Army, 1951-53. Mem. AIA. Clubs: Economic, Monroe, Sports Car of Am. (Chgo.). Office: 111 W Monroe St Chicago IL 60603

KOGUT, KENNETH JOSEPH, cons. engr.; b. Chgo., Dec. 3, 1947; s. Joseph Henry and Estelle Theresa (Swiercz) K.; student Lewis Coll., 1966-68; B.M.E., U. Detroit, 1971, M.E., 1972, postgrad, 1972—; m. Darlene Agnes Jedlicka, June 15, 1974. Mech. engr. Fluor Pioneer Inc., Chgo., 1972-73, cons. engr., 1973-75; project mgr. Engring. Corp. Am., Chgo., 1976-77; sr. cons. pub. utilities DeLoitte, Haskins & Sells, Chgo., 1977-79; individual practice as energy and mgmt. cons., 1979—. Registered profl. engr., Ill. Sloan fellow, 1971-73; recipient award Pres.'s Program for Energy Efficiency. Mem. Am. Nuclear Soc., Nat., Ill. socs. profl. engrs., Assn. Energy Engrs., Blue Key, Tau Beta Pi, Pi Tau Sigma, Polish Nat. Alliance. Author: Energy Management for the Community Bank. Address: 5232 W 170th Pl Oak Forest IL 60452

KOH, SEVERINO LEGARDA, mech. engr., educator; b. Manila, Philippines, Jan. 8, 1927; s. Enrique Legarda and Felisa (Un) K.; came to U.S., 1954, naturalized, 1972; student U. Philippines, Manila, 1945-47; B.S. in Meteorology, N.Y. U., 1950; B.S. in Mech. Engring., Nat. U., Manila, 1952; M.S., Pa. State U., 1957; Ph.D. in Engring. Sci., Purdue U., 1962; m. Paz L. Ongjoco, July 19, 1952; children—Amelita P. Koh-Luncsford, Bernadette Paz, Cynthia Paz, Dorothy Paz (dec.), Evangeline Paz. Meteorologist, Philippine Weather Bur., Manila, 1948-54; research asst. Johns Hopkins U., 1954-55; instr. in engring. mechs. Pa. State U., 1955-57; instr. in engring. sci. Purdue U., 1957-59, vis. research asso., 1962-64, asst. prof., 1964-66, asso. prof., 1966-72, prof., 1972—, asst. head div. interdisciplinary engring. studies, 1977—; research asso. Gen. Tech. Corp., West Lafayette, Ind., 1959-61; mech. engr. Gen. Electric Co., Louisville, 1961-62; vis. prof., research asso. Tech. U. Clausthal, Clausthal-Zellerfeld, Germany, 1968-69; vis. prof. Tech. U. Karlsruhe (Germany), 1969, U. Bonn (Germany), 1974-75; dir. Internat. Intertech., 1976—, pres., 1978-80; Balik scientist, Philippines, 1976. Recipient Outstanding Teaching award Standard Oil Found., 1967, Outstanding Prof. award Sigma Gamma Tau, 1968, Humboldt award, Germany, 1974, certificate of appreciation Soc. Engring. Sci., 1974; Purdue U. Shreve Hall faculty fellow, 1976; NSF grantee, 1971-74, 79—; U.S. Army Research Office grantee, 1972-75. Mem. Soc. Engring. Sci. (founding sec. 1963, sec. 1963-68, dir. 1970-73, 78—), ASME, Am. Soc. Engring. Edn., Am. Acad. Mechs., Soc. Rheology, Philippine Profl. Assn., Purdue Filipino Assn., Sigma Xi, Sigma Pi Sigma, Sigma Gamma Tau. Presbyterian. Contbr. numerous articles on continuum mechs., viscoelasticity, elasticity, rheology, composite materials, micormechs., geotech. engring. to tech. jours.; editor Engring. Sci. Perspective, 1976—. Home: 208 E Navajo St West Lafayette IN 47906 Office: Sch of Mech Engring Purdue U West Lafayette IN 47907

KOH-GUEVARRA, ARSENIA, physician; b. Manila, Philippines, Mar. 14, 1939; d. Eloy T. and Graciana (Saez) Koh; M.D., U. Santo Tomas, Manila, 1963; m. Nicanor M. Guevarra, Feb. 15, 1969; children—Nicanor M., Ronald Michael. Intern, Albert Einstein Med. Center, Phila., 1964; resident in internal medicine Wayne State U., Detroit, 1965-67, fellow in nephrology, 1967-69, clin. instr. Med. Sch., 1970—; physician in charge renal unit Hutzel Hosp., Detroit, 1970-72; practice medicine specializing in internal medicine, Mt. Clemens, Mich., 1972—. Diplomate Am. Bd. Internal Medicine. Mem. AMA, A.C.P., Am. Soc. Nephrology, Mich. State, Macomb County med. socs., Nat. Kidney Found. Home: Box 33 Mount Clemens MI 48043 Office: 22070 S Nunnely St Mount Clemens MI 48043

KOHL, BARBARA ANN, sociologist; b. Independence, Mo., Sept. 13, 1951; d. Alvin Alfred and Rose Marie Charlotte (Herl) K.; B.A., Ft. Hays (Kans.) State Coll., 1973; M.A. in Econs., Kans. State U., 1975; Ph.D. in Rural Sociology, Ohio State U., 1981. Teletypesetter, feature writer Hays (Kans.) Daily News, 1969-73; teaching asst. dept. econs. Kans. State U., Manhattan, 1973-75, lectr. dept. continuing edn., 1975; lectr., research project coordinator Lavras, Minas Gerais, Brazil, Escola Superior de Agricultura de Lavras, 1976-78; grad. research asso. dept. agrl. econs. and rural sociology Ohio State U., Columbus, 1978-81, lectr. dept. internat. studies, 1982—. Mem. Rural Sociol. Soc., Am. Sociol. Assn., Latin Am. Studies Assn., Midwest Sociol. Soc., Phi Beta Kappa, Gamma Sigma Delta, Phi Kappa Phi. Contbr. articles in field to profl. jours. Home: 826 S 22d St Columbus OH 43206 Office: Dept Agrl Econs and Rural Sociology 2120 Fyffe Rd Columbus OH 43210

KOHLAN, WILLIAM GEORGE, lawyer; b. Mpls., Feb. 13, 1910; s. George and Anastasia (Leschisin) K.; LL.B., Mpls. Coll. Law (William Mitchell Coll. Law), 1932; m. Helen Marie Peterson, Nov. 25, 1947. Admitted to Minn. bar, 1932; practice in Mpls., 1932—; counsel and dir. misc. groups. Mem. Hennepin County Central com. Democratic Farmer Labor party, 1948-67; ward chmn. and ward vice chmn., 1954-59, del. Dem. Farmer Labor convs., 1948-78. Served in USAF, World War II. Recipient medal of Merit, Air Force Assn., 1957; Distinguished Service award Minn. State Bar Assn., 1959, City of Mpls., 1975. Mem. Minn., Hennepin County bar assns., Air Force Assn. (past nat. v.p.), Minn. Wing (AFA) (past comdr.), Air Force Hist. Found., DAV (past judge adv. Minn. dept., past vice comdr. Mpls. chpt.), Mpls. Joint Vets. Council (past pres.). Home: 1610 5th St NE Minneapolis MN 55413 Office: Gorham Bldg Minneapolis MN 55402

KOHLI, CHANDER MOHAN, neurosurgeon; b. Mandi Baudin, India, May 14, 1940; s. Sardari and Ram Piari (Anand) K.; came to U.S., 1966, naturalized, 1975; premed. grad. Hindu Coll. (India), 1957; M.B.B.S., All India Inst. of Med. Scis., 1962; m. Karen Lee Prindle, Dec. 21, 1968; 1 child, Aneal Mohan. Neurosurgery resident Univ. Hosp., Edmonton, Alta., Can., 1968-69; intern, then resident Elyria (Ohio) Meml. Hosp., 1966-68; resident in neurosurgery Mercy Hosp., Pitts., 1969-72; practice medicine, specializing in neurosurgery, Youngstown, Ohio, 1972—; chief neurosurgery St. Elizabeth Hosp. Served with Med. Corps, Indian Armed Forces, 1962-66. Mem. AMA, Ohio Med. Assn., ACS, Am. Assn. Neurol. Surgeons, Congress of Neurol. Surgeons, Neurol. Soc. India, Soc. for Neurosci. Contbr. articles in field to med. jours. Office: 550 Parmalee Ave Youngstown OH 44510

KOHN, HENRY LOUIS, JR., travel agt.; b. Chgo., Jan. 7, 1937; s. Henry Louis and Kate (Hirschberg) K.; A.B., Harvard U., 1958; M.S., Northwestern U., 1960; M.B.A., U. Chgo., 1964; m. Carol Louise Anspach, Aug. 12, 1961; children—Henry Louis 3d, Lawrence Edgar. Adminstrv. mgr. and cons. Peat, Marwick, Caywood, Schiller & Co. (name later changed to Caywood-Schiller Assos.), Chgo., 1965-68; mgr. fin. adminstrn. Computer Tech., Inc., Skokie, Ill., 1969-70; dir. fin. planning auto group Maremont Corp., Chgo., 1970-73, asst. controller, 1973-74, v.p., asst. controller, 1974-77, v.p. adminstrn., 1978-80; pres. Anspach Travel Bur., Inc., 1980—. Mem. corp. Children's Meml. Hosp., Chgo., 1971—; personnel com. Chgo. Heart Assn., 1971-76, bd. govs., 1973-76, fin. com., 1973—. Served with U.S. Army, 1961-62. Mem. Fin. Execs. Inst., Chgo. Athletic Assn.

KOHN, JULIEANNE, travel agt.; b. Detroit, Apr. 15, 1946; d. Ralph Merwin and Jane Tacke (Meyers) K.; B.A., Heidelberg Coll., Tiffin, Ohio, 1968; postgrad. Eastern Mich. U., 1969-70; diploma Inst. Cert. Travel Agts., 1979. Travel agt. Am. Express Co., Detroit, 1970-73, Thomas Cook Inc., Detroit, 1973-75; mgr. Island Traveller, Grosse Ile, Mich., 1975-76; pres., owner Fly Suitcase, Inc., Grosse Ile, 1976—; dir. Kohn Engring. Corp., Taylor, Mich., Taylor Grinding Co. Mem. Am. Soc. Travel Agts., Pacific Area Travel Assn. Episcopalian. Club: Grosse Ile Golf and Country. Home: 27081 E River Rd Grosse Ile MI 48138 Office: 8205 Macomb St Grosse Ile MI 48138

KOHN, MARY LOUISE BEATRICE, nurse; b. Yellows Springs, Ohio, Jan. 13, 1920; d. Theophilus John and Mary Katharine (Schmitkons) Gaehr; A.B., Coll. Wooster, 1940; M.Nursing, Case Western Res. U., 1943; m. Howard D. Kohn, 1944; 1 dau., Marcia R. Nurse, Univ. Hosps., Cleve., 1943-44, Atlantic City Hosp., 1944, Thomas M. England Gen. Hosp., U.S. Army, Atlantic City, 1945-46, Peter Bent Brigham Hosp., Boston, 1947, Univ. Hosps., Cleve., 1946-48; mem. faculty Frances Payne Bolton Sch. Nursing Case Western Res. U., 1948-52; vol. nurse Blood Service, ARC, 1952-55; office nurse, Cleve., part time 1955—; free-lance writer. Bd. dirs. Aux. Acad. Medicine Cleve., 1970-72, officer, 1976—; mem. Cleve. Health Mus. Aux.; mem. women's com. Cleve. Orch., 1970; women's council WVIZ-TV. Mem. Am., Ohio nurses assns., alumni assns. Wooster Coll., Frances P. Bolton Sch. Nursing (pres. 1974-75), Assn. Operating Rm. Nurses, Antique Automobile Assn. Am., Western Res. Hist. Soc., Am. Heart Assn., Cleve. Playhouse Aux., U.S. Humane Soc., Friends of Cleve. Ballet, Smithsonian Instn., Council World Affairs, Orange Community Arts Council. Clubs: Cleve. Racquet, Women's City, Women's of Case-Western Res. U. Sch. Medicine. Author: (with Atkinson) Berry and Kohn's Introduction to Operating Room Technique, 5th edit., 1978. Asst. editor Cleve. Physician, Acad. Medicine Cleve., 1966-71. Home: 28099 Belcourt Rd Cleveland OH 44124

KOHUT, MARY POWELL, educator; b. Wampum, Pa., Feb. 11, 1952; d. Andrew James and Fannie Rose (Demaio) Powell; B.S. in Bus. Adminstrn., Youngstown State U., 1973; B.S. in Vocat. Edn., Kent State U., 1974; m. Robert Kohut, June 10, 1973. Coordinator distributive edn. J.C. Penney's, Youngstown, Ohio, 1974; sales asso. Youngstown State U., 1970-73; textile asst. mktg. dept. Athens (Ohio) High Sch., 1974-75; tchr., coordinator distributive edn. Mahoning County Joint Vocat. Sch., Canfield, Ohio, 1974-80, tchr., coordinator adult edn., 1974—. Mem. NEA, Ohio Edn. Assn., Mahoning County Joint Vocat. Edn. Assn., Am. Vocat. Assn., Ohio Vocat. Assn., Distributive Edn. Clubs Am. Roman Catholic. Club: World of Tanglewood Health Resort. Author: Junior Distributive Education In-School Teaching Manual, 1977; The Organization and Use of An Advisory Committee, 1978; Profit Isn't Always Gross, 1978. Home: 3710 Shields Rd Canfield OH 44406 Office: 7300 N Palmyra St Canfield OH 44406

KOHUTEK, KENNETH JAMES, psychologist; b. Temple, Tex., Apr. 26, 1949; s. Willie E. and Adeline Esther (Shenkir) K.; B.S., Tex. A. and M. U., 1971; M.S., N. Tex. State U., 1973, Ph.D., 1980; m. Patricia Owen, Dec. 26, 1978; 1 son, Daniel Edwin. Psychologist, Dallas Mental Health/Mental Retardation Center, 1974, Denton County (Tex.) Mental Health Unit, 1974-76; research analyst Bur. Prisons, Marion, Ill., 1976-78; clin. psychologist U.S. Penitentiary, Marion, 1978—; instr. psychology Shawnee Coll., Ullin, Ill., 1979—. Mem. Am. Psychol. Assn., Am. Assn. Correctional Psychologists. Methodist. Home: 1923 Briarwood Cape Girardeau MO 63701 Office: US Penitentiary PO Box 2000 Marion IL 62959

KOKAI, FRANK LYNN, educator; b. Fremont, Ohio, Nov. 15, 1946; s. Frank F. and Marion C. (Lindsay) K.; B.S. in Biology, Capital U., 1968; M.S. in Zoology, Ohio State U., 1976; m. Evelyn C. Riggsby, July 9, 1970; 1 son, Mitchell Lynn. Mem. sci. faculty Eastmoor High Sch., Columbus, Ohio, 1968—, head of sci. dept., 1978—; faculty Columbus Tech. Inst. Asso. Ohio State U. Mus. Zoology. Mem. AAAS, Ohio Acad. Sci., Am. Malacological Union, Ohio Hist. Soc., Sigma Xi. Republican. Lutheran. Contbr. articles to Bull. Am. Malacological Union. Home: 6960 Tanya Terr Reynoldsburg OH 43068 Office: 417 S Weyant Ave Columbus OH 43213

KOKENGE, BERNARD RUSSELL, chemist; b. Dayton, Ohio, Dec. 7, 1939; s. Bernard Hunter and Grace Russell (Lowman) K.; B.S., U. Dayton, 1961; Ph.D., Ohio U., 1965; m. Joy Camille Grooms, Nov. 28, 1959; children—Dawn Joy, Todd Russell. Grad. teaching asst. Ohio U., 1964; sr. research chemist Monsanto Research Corp., Miamisburg, Ohio, 1965-66, group leader plutonium fuels, 1966-72, plutonium processing mgr., 1972-77, mgr. nuclear tech., 1977—. Cubmaster, Farmersville Cub Scouts troop, 1973-76; pres. Valley View Band Parents Assn., 1978-79; bd. dirs. Germantown Fed. Savs. & Loan, 1978—; deacon Miamisburg Ch. of Christ, 1976—. Mem. Am. Men of Sci., Sigma Xi. Mem. Ch. of Christ. Club: Oak Creek Lions (pres. 1970). Patentee in field. Home: 5233 S Clayton Rd Farmersville OH 45325 Office: Monsanto Research Corp Mound Facility Mound Ave Miamisburg OH 45342

KOKOROPOULOS, PANOS, educator; b. Thessaloniki, Greece, Aug. 10, 1927; s. Constantine and Mary (Carvonides) K.; came to U.S., 1958, naturalized, 1965; B.S. in Chemistry, U. Thessaloniki, 1955; M.S. in Chemistry, U. Dayton, 1964; Ph.D., U. Akron, 1972; m. Carolyn A. Curran, Mar. 26, 1960; children—Mary, Constantine, George. Research chemist U. Dayton Research Inst., 1963-65; asst. prof. chem. tech. U. Akron, 1965-71, dir. Center for Info. Systems, 1965-69, mgr. academic systems and programming, 1969-71, research asso. dept. civil engring., 1971-72; prof. civil engring. So. Ill. U., Edwardsville, 1973—, pres. univ. senate, 1978-79; cons. in field; tech. reviewer Appropriate Tech. Program, Dept. Energy, 1980—. Asst. dist. commr. Greek Boy Scouts, 1945-56; mem. troup com. Cahokia Mounds council Boy Scouts Am., 1976-79. Served to 2d lt. Greek Army, 1950-52. Fullbright-Smith-Mundt grantee, 1958-59; Guggenheim grantee, 1959-60; Ford Found. grantee, 1959-60. Mem. Solar Energy Soc., Am. Chem. Soc., ASCE, ASTM, Am. Soc. Engring. Edn. (exec. bd. Ind.-Ill. sect. 1980—). Democrat. Greek Orthodox. Author: (with A. Fatemi, A. Amirie) Political Economy of the Middle East, 1970. Contbr. articles in field to profl. jours. Home: 414 W Union Edwardsville IL 62025 Office: Southern Illinois University at Edwardsville Box 65 Edwardsville IL 62026

KOLAND, DAVID JEROME, state legislator, steel bldg. co. exec.; b. Ashland, Oreg., June 28, 1942; s. Louis K. and Bessie F. (Halle) K.; B.S. in Bus. Adminstrn., U. N.D., 1972; m. Mary Ann Nelsen, Dec. 16, 1972; 1 child, Stacey. Bookmobile driver, 1961; motel night clk., 1962; acctg. clk. Northland Chem. Co., East Grand Forks, Minn., 1963-64, accounts receivable mgr., 1964-65, asst. gen. mgr., 1965-66, sec., 1966; mgr. Williston Farm Service Co. (N.D.), 1966-71; pres. Koland Inc., Minot, 1972—, Koland's of Minot, 1972—, Koland, Inc., Bottineau, N.D., 1972—; mem. Minot Vo-Ag Adv. Council, 1977—; mem. N.D. Legis. Assembly from 5th dist., 1980—, mem. appropriations com. Bd. dirs. Minot Winterfest Assn., 1974—, pres., 1976; bd. dirs. Companions for Children, 1978—, pres., 1979-81; mem. dist. steering com. Boy Scouts Am., 1979-80; vice chmn. 5th Dist. Republican Party, 1977-81. Recipient Keyman award Jaycees, 1974, Gary Helseth award, 1977, Disting. Service award, 1978; Senator, Jaycees Internat., 1978. Mem. Nat. Assn. Home Builders, U.S. C. of C., Nat. Fedn. of Ind. Bus., Minot Home Builders, Minot C. of C., N.D. Jaycees (state exec. v.p. 1977-78). Presbyterian. Clubs: Minot Country; Elks, Eagles. Home: 801 Clark Dr Minot ND 58701 Office: Koland Inc Rural Route 4 Box 1486 Minot ND 58701

KOLB, JERRY W(ILBERT), accountant; b. Chgo., Dec. 22, 1935; s. Herman and Myrtle (Richter) K.; B.S. in Accountancy with highest honors, U. Ill., Urbana, 1957; M.B.A., DePaul U., 1962; m. Marlene Joyce Tipp, Feb. 3, 1957; children—Bradley, Steven, Lisa. Acct., Deloitte Haskins & Sells, C.P.A.s, Chgo., 1957-68, partner, 1968—, partner-in-charge Chgo. office, 1976—, mem. policy com., 1979—; lectr. DePaul U., 1962-76, mem. adv. council dept. accountancy, 1981—; mem. profl. adv. bd. dept. accountancy U. Ill.; mem. adv. council Northwestern U. Sch. Acctg.; trustee Ill. C.P.A. Found. Served with U.S. Army, 1957-58. Recipient Disting. Alumni award DePaul U., 1970; C.P.A., Ill. Mem. Am. Inst. C.P.A.s (Gold Medal award 1957), Ill. C.P.A. Soc. (dir. 1973-77, v.p. 1976-77), Am. Acctg. Assn. Clubs: Chgo., Standard, Mid-Am. Office: 200 E Randolph Dr Chicago IL 60601

KOLB, JOSEPH WILBUR, state ofcl.; b. near Princeton, Ind., Jan. 5, 1902; s. Joseph and Margaret M. (Phillips) K.; A.B., Ind. U., 1926, A.M., 1931; postgrad, Evansville Coll., 1948-52, Ind. State Tchrs. Coll., 1950—, Oakland City Coll., 1952—; m. Mary Elizabeth Wolfe, June 21, 1922; children—Unalea (Mrs. Andrew Robb), Mary Lu (Mrs. Thomas Orr). Tchr., adminstr. pub. schs., Neb., Mo., Ill., Ind., 1923-68. Named Older Hoosier of Yr., Area 13 B. Mem. White House Conf. on Aging; mem. Ind. Joint Commn. on Aged and Aging, Nat., Ind., Gibson County ret. tchrs. assns. Del. Dem. Nat. Conv., 1956, 60, mem. platform com., 1972-74. Mem. NEA, Am. Assn. Ret. Persons, Wabash Valley Assn. Methodist. Mason (32deg. Shriner); mem. Order Eastern Star. Home: Box 396 Princeton IN 47670

KOLBET, KENNETH JOSEPH, ednl. adminstr.; b. New Hampton, Iowa, Nov. 10, 1940; s. Joseph John and Loraine (Burgart) K.; student Loras Coll., 1958-60; B.B.A., U. Iowa, 1962; student Northwestern U., 1963-64; M.S., No. Ill. U., 1970, C.A.S., 1973, Ed.D., 1981; m. Norma Geneva Gansen, June 30, 1962; children—Julie, Debe, Randy, Karen. Internal auditor Fed. Res. Bank of Chgo., 1962-64; internal auditor, bank officer First Nat. Bank, DeKalb, Ill., 1965-69; controller Coll. DuPage, Glen Ellyn, Ill., 1969-79, v.p. adminstrv. affairs, 1979—. Bd. dirs. Wheaton (Ill.) United Fund, 1973-76; treas., bd. dirs. Maplebrook I Home Owners Assn., 1980—. Mem. Nat. Assn. Coll. and Univ. Bus. Officers, Central Assn. Coll. and Univ. Bus. Officers, Assn. Sch. Bus. Ofcls. U.S. and Can., Ill. Assn. Sch. Bus. Ofcls., Ill. Community Coll. Bus. Adminstrs., U. Iowa Alumni Assn. Clubs: Jaycees, Rotary, Kiwanis. Home: 29 Oriole Ct Naperville IL 60540 Office: Coll DuPage Lambert Rd and 22d St Glen Ellyn IL 60137

KOLBUSZ, LINDA MARIE, educator; b. Chgo., Aug. 9, 1949; d. Robert Anthony and Marie D. (Cerone) Handley; student U. Ill., 1966-68, 70-71; B.A., No. Ill. U., 1975, M.S., 1980; postgrad. Instituto Cultural Guadalajara, Nat. Coll. of Edn.; m. Kenneth James Kolbusz, Mar. 14, 1973; children—Melisaa Renee. Cashier supr./adminstrv. asst. personnel Zayre Corp., 1966-72; bookkeeper/office mgr. Holtgren Electric, Wauconda, Ill., 1971-73; tchr. aide/migrant program Palatine (Ill.) Dist. 15, 1973-74; tchr. Schaumburg (Ill.) Sch. Dist. 54, 1976-80, coordinator bilingual program, 1980—; conductor seminars/workshop in field. Recipient Pacesetter award, Ill. State Bd. Edn., 1981; Nat. Coll. Edn. and N.W. Ednl. Coop. grantee, 1980; Title VII Grantee, No. Ill. U., 1978. Mem. Ill. Tchrs. of English to Speakers of Other Langs. (corres. sec. 1980-81), Network for Adminstrs. of Bilingual Edn. (recording sec. 1980-81), Assn. for Supervision and Curriculum Devel., Council for Exceptional Children, Nat. Assn. Bilingual Edn. Roman Catholic. Contbr. articles to profl. jours. Home: 960 Rosedale Ln Hoffman Estates IL 60195 Office: 524 E Schaumburg Rd Schaumburg IL 60194

KOLINEK, ROBERT BRETT, mktg. exec.; b. Chgo., Sept. 20, 1954; s. Jerry W. and Renee C. K.; B.S. in History, U. Chgo., 1975; postgrad. masters in econ. studies U. Wis., 1976. With Helen Brett Enterprises, Inc. and R.B.K. Enterprises, Ltd., Chgo., 1976—, exec. v.p., 1980—; pres. Petro-Tech Expos Ltd., trade show mgmt. co. oil and gas industry, Chgo., 1981—. Mem. Nat. Assn. Exhbn. Mgrs. (chmn. new memberships), Scoping 400. Office: Helen Brett Enterprises Inc 6 E Monroe St Chicago IL 60603

KOLLINS, MICHAEL JEROME, automotive engr.; b. St. Clairsville, Ohio, Mar. 20, 1912; s. Michael Arthur and Mary Ann (Peck) K.; student Coll. City Detroit, 1928-32; m. Julia Dolores Advent, Jan. 16, 1934; children—Michael Lewis, Richard, Laura. Chief sect. service engring. and tech. data Studebaker-Packard Corp., Detroit, 1945-55; mgr. tech. services Chrysler Corp., Detroit, 1955-64, mgr. warranty adminstrn., 1964-68, mgr. Highland Park Service center, 1968-75; pres. Kollins Design & Engring., Detroit, 1975—. Pres., Oakland (Mich.) U Chorus, 1969-71, Home Owners Assn. of Eastover Farms No. 1, 1981—; active Birmingham (Mich.) Chorale, Meadowbrook (Mich.) Festival Chorus; mem. adv. bd. Am. Security Council, 1972—. Served with USN, 1942-45. Mem. U.S. Auto Club (vice-chmn. tech. com. 1971—), Am. Automobile Assn. (contest bd.), Soc. Automotive Engrs., Engring. Soc. Detroit (industry ambassador 1972—). Contbr. articles to profl. publs. Designer racing cars, 1932-39, sports cars, spl. luxury vehicles, 1951—, automotive performance and safety devices, 1946—. Home: 821 Highwood Dr Bloomfield Hills MI 48013 Office: Kollins Design & Engring PO Box 214 Bloomfield Hills MI 48013

KOLMIN, KENNETH GUY, lawyer, accountant; b. N.Y.C., Oct. 22, 1951; s. Frank William and Edith (Pisk) K.; B.S. summa cum laude in Accounting, State U. N.Y., Albany, 1973; J.D. cum laude, Syracuse

U., 1975, M.S. in Acctg., 1975; m. Suzan D. Frumm. Intern, Peat, Marwick, Mitchell & Co., C.P.A.'s, Albany, N.Y., 1971-73; adj. instr. Syracuse (N.Y.) U., 1974, teaching asst., 1974-75; admitted to Ill. bar, 1976; tax cons., tax dept. Arthur Young & Co., Chgo., 1976-79, with Internat. Services Office, N.Y.C., 1978-79; asso. firm Shefsky, Saitlin & Froelich, Ltd., Chgo., 1979-81, Rooks, Pitts, Fullagar & Poust, Chgo., 1981—; speaker tax topics. C.P.A., Ill. Mem. Am., Ill., Chgo. bar assns., Justinian Law Soc., Beta Alpha Psi, Beta Gamma Sigma, Phi Alpha Delta. Contbr. articles to profl. jours. Home: 625 W Oakdale Chicago IL 60657 Office: 55 W Monroe Suite 1500 Chicago IL 60602

KOLODZIEJ, JOAN HELEN, public affairs specialist; b. Detroit, July 29, 1938; d. Joseph and Valeria (Bujak) K.; B.A., Mich. State U., 1960. Women's editor Ford Motor Co., 1964-65; promotion writer Sta. WWJ-TV, Detroit, 1961-68; public service mgr. Detroit Free Press, 1968-71; public info. dir. Mich. Cancer Found., 1971-73; exec. dir. Project HOPE, 1973-74; asst. v.p. Bank of the Commonwealth, Detroit, 1974-77; public affairs specialist Southeastern Mich. Transp. Authority, Detroit, 1977—. Mem. public relations adv. com. ARC, Detroit, 1978—. Mem. Internat. Assn. Bus. Communicators, Public Relations Soc. Am., Detroit Press Club, Econ. Club Detroit, Women's Advt. Club Detroit. Roman Catholic. Home: 27602 Parkview Blvd #104 Warren MI 48092 Office: 660 Woodward Detroit MI 48226

KOLOSKI, HELEN (LENI) SPALDING, advt. and public relations co. exec.; b. Marshfield, Wis., Sept. 19, 1927; d. Thomas Davitt and Helen (Flannigan) Spalding; B.A. magna cum laude, Lawrence U. Wis., 1949; m. Marion J. Koloski, Feb. 2, 1952; children—Paul Joseph, Mary Frances, Peter Andrew, Margaret Anne, Martha Jane. Social worker, Catholic Social Services, Columbus, Ohio, 1950-52, 55-56; dir. Marian House rest home for elder, Columbus, 1969-70, Marian House Inc. home for unwed mothers, Columbus, 1970-71; dir. pub. relations Catholic Charities/Social Concerns, Columbus, 1971-75; dir. pub. relations, info. Diocese of Columbus, 1975-77; asst. dir. devel. Ohio Dominican Coll., Columbus, 1977-78; pres. Koloski/Sidlo Assos., Inc. Columbus, 1979-80; v.p. Conway Advt. & Public Relations, Inc., Columbus, 1980—. Mem. public relations com. United Way, 1972-74, Ohio Easter Seal, 1974-80, Ohio Lung Assn.; communications com. Ohio Council Churches, 1974-77; communications dept. Cath Conf. Ohio, 1975-77. Ohio State U. scholar, 1949-50. Mem. Public Relations Soc. Am. (accredited; nat. del.), Women in Bus. (treas. 1978-80), Women in Communications, Columbus Advt. Fedn., Phi Beta Kappa. Roman Catholic. Home: 131 E North Broadway Columbus OH 43214 Office: 1490 Old W Henderson Rd Columbus OH 43220

KOLOTKIN, RICHARD ALAN, psychologist; b. Bklyn., Feb. 14, 1950; s. Kalman and Sydell (Geller) K.; B.A. magna cum laude (NIH fellow), Wesleyan U., 1972; Ph.D., U. Minn., 1978. Research asst. U. Minn., Mpls., 1973, teaching asst., 1972-76, instr. dept. psychology, 1974-76; clin. fellow dept psychiatry Harvard U. Med. Sch./Mass. Gen. Hosp., Boston, 1976-77; asst. prof. psychology Moorhead (Minn.) State U., 1977—; clin. instr. dept. neuro-sci. U. N.D., Grand Forks, 1978—; cons. Lakeland Mental Health Center, Fergus Falls, Minn., 1981—; clin. psychologist St. Lukes's Hosp./Neuropsychit. Inst., Fargo, N.D., 1980—. Moorhead State U. faculty research grantee, 1979-80. Mem. Assn. for Advancement Behavior Therapy (Merit cert. 1980), Am. Psychol. Assn., Red River Assn. for Behavior Therapy (pres. 1980), Phi Beta Kappa. Author: Coping with Stress; contbr. articles to profl. jours. Office: Dept Psychology Moorhead State U Moorhead MN 56560

KOMIE, STEPHEN MARK, lawyer; b. Chgo., Jan. 22, 1949; s. Leonard and Miriam Ruth (Wineberg) K.; B.A., U. Ariz., 1970, M.A. in Russian History, 1972; J.D., DePaul Coll., Chgo., 1976; grad. Nat. Coll. Criminal Def. Lawyers, 1978. Patrolman, Tucson Police Dept., 1972-73; intern Fed. Defender Program, Chgo., 1975-76; admitted to Ill. bar, 1976; individual practice law, Chgo. and Buffalo Grove, Ill., 1976—; mem. fed. defender panel No. Dist. Ill. Mem. Am. Bar Assn. (recipient Silver Key 1976), Chgo. Bar Assn. (sec. criminal law com. 1981-82), Lake County Bar Assn. (criminal law com.), Ill. Bar Assn., North Suburban Bar Assn. (criminal law com.), N.W. Suburban Bar Assn. (chmn. legis. subcom. of criminal law com.). Catholic Lawyers Guild, Chgo. Bar Lawyers Reference Plan, Nat. Assn. Criminal Def. Lawyers, Chgo. Council Fgn. Relations, Mid-N. Assn., English-Speaking Union, Wedgewood Soc. Home: 925 W Webster Ave Chicago IL 60614 Office: 29 S LaSalle St Chicago IL 60603 also 1 Ranch Mart Plaza Buffalo Grove IL 60090

KOMJATHY, ANTHONY TIHAMER, educator; b. Hungary, May 29, 1921; s. Oscar and Margaret K.; came to U.S., 1957, naturalized, 1963; Ph.D., Loyola U., Chgo., 1972; m. Edith Niedzielsky, Dec. 26, 1948; 1 dau., Edith. Served with Hungarian Army, 1945-51; polit. prisoner, 1951-53; various positions, 1956-67; prof. Barat Coll., Lake Forest, Ill., 1967-73, Loyola U., Chgo., 1973-76; now faculty Rosary Coll., River Forest, Ill. Nat. Endowment Humanities grantee, 1972. Mem. Am. Hist. Assn., AAUP. Roman Catholic. Author: The Crises of France's East Central European Diplomacy, 1933-38, 1976; German Minorities and the Third Reich, 1980; contbr. articles to profl. jours. Office: History Dept Rosary Coll River Forest IL 60305

KOMJATHY, NANCY CAROLYN, nurse; b. Detroit, July 27, 1942; d. George J. and Beatrice Rita (Mallock) Marsh; R.N., Providence Sch. Nursing, Detroit, 1963; B.A., U. Detroit, 1976; M.S. in Nursing Health Services, U. Mich., 1978; m. Louis A. Komjathy, II, Jan. 27, 1967; 1 son, Louis A., III. Staff nurse, Detroit Receiving Hosp., 1963-65; supr. Martin Pl. Hosp., Detroit, 1965-67; asst. dir. nurses Doctors Hosp., Detroit, 1967-71; mem. nursing staff Henry Ford Hosp., Detroit, 1973—, asst. dir. operating and recovery rooms, 1975-77, dir. med.-surg. nursing div. III, 1978-80; asso. dir. Hurley Med. Center, Flint, Mich., 1980—; mem. adj. faculty U. Detroit, U. Mich., Flint; cons., speaker in field. Mem. Am. Nurses Assn., Soc. Nursing Service Adminstrs. (asso.), Mich. Nurses Assn. Democrat. Roman Catholic. Club: Detroit Yacht. Home: 10173 Washburn Rd Columbiaville MI 48421 Office: 2799 W Grand Blvd Detroit MI 48202

KOMMER, NORMAN BUD, banker; b. Spencer, Wis., Mar. 29, 1943; s. Norman August and Erma Mary (Stargardt) K.; student Wausau Tech. Inst., 1962; grad. Grad. Sch. Banking, U. Wis., Madison, 1978; m. Virginia L. Gray, Dec. 29, 1962; children—James, Debbie, Robin, Tammi, Jonalee. Teller, auditor Central State Bank, Marshfield, Wis., 1963-68; auditor Marquette Nat. Bank, Mpls., 1968-70; asst. cashier Brooklyn Park State (Minn.), 1970-71, Central State Bank, Marshfield, 1971-74; pres. Abbotsford State Bank (Wis.), 1974—. Elder Christ Lutheran Ch. Mem. Am. Inst. Banking (dir. Wis. chpt. 1976), Abbotsford C. of C. (pres. 1978), Ind., Wis. bankers assns., Upper Midwest Agrl. Conf. Home: 205 Elm St W Abbotsford WI 54405 Office: Hwy 13 and 29 Abbotsford WI 54405

KOMUTANON, KAJORNDEJ, allergist; b. Thailand, Dec. 8, 1944; s. Jug Tiang and Peck Eng (Heng) Ko; came to U.S., 1970, naturalized, 1978; M.D., Chiangmai U., 1969; m. Rapeepan Sangthongtong, Mar. 16, 1974; children—Wina, Theda. Intern, St. Elizabeth Hosp., Chgo., 1970-71; resident, Rush Presbyn. Hosp., Michael Reese Hosp., Chgo., 1971-75; practice medicine specializing in allergy, Chgo., 1975—; cons. VA Westside Hosp. and St. Mary of Nazareth Hosp. Diplomate Am. Bd. Pediatrics, Am. Bd. Allergy and Immunology. Fellow Am. Acad. Allergy, Am. Coll. Allergists, Am. Assn. Cert. Allergists, Am. Assn. Clin. Immunology and Allergy, Ill. Soc. Allergy and Clin. Immunology; mem. Chgo. Med. Soc., Ill. Med. Soc., AMA. Buddhist. Home: 6543 W Albert Ave Morton Grove IL 60053 Office: 3218 W Lawrence Ave Chicago IL 60625

KONCELIK, JOSEPH ARTHUR, indsl. designer, educator; b. Islip, N.Y., Apr. 20, 1940; s. Arthur Adam and Marie (Anderson) K.; B. in Indsl. Design, Pratt Inst., 1962; M.A., Stanford, 1963; postgrad. (Fulbright scholar), Royal Coll. Art, London, 1965-66; m. Anastasia Hyrkiel, July 11, 1964; children—David Alban, Joseph Peter. Designer Gen. Motors Corp., Warren, Mich., 1963-65; indsl. design cons. Fairchild Hiller Corp., Bethpage, N.Y., 1966; indsl. designer William Lansing Plumb & Assos., N.Y.C., 1967; asst. prof. Coll. of Human Ecology, Cornell U., Ithaca, N.Y., 1967-73; asso. prof. Coll. of the Arts, Ohio State U., Columbus, 1973—; pres. Design & Research Services, Inc., Worthington, Ohio; adj. indsl. design R.I. Sch. of Design, Providence, 1971, 72, 73, 74. Mem. Gerontological Soc., Assn. for the Study of Man-Environ. Relations, Indsl. Design Edn. Conf. (chmn. graduate edn. and research com.). Contbr. articles on human ecology and indsl. design to profl. publs. Home: 1638 Dollivor Rd Worthington OH 43085 Office: Ohio State Univ Columbus OH 43210

KONDOROSSY, ELIZABETH DAVIS, spl. educator; b. East Canton, Ohio, Dec. 23, 1910; d. William David and Lottie Pearl (Hall) Davis; B.A., Oberlin Coll., 1934; postgrad. (Wall St. Fund Newspaper Fund fellow) U. Mich., 1962; M.Ed., Kent State U., 1968, cert. in spl. edn., 1970; student Sophia U., Tokyo; m. Leslie Kondorossy, Jan. 19, 1962. Tchr., East Canton Elementary Sch., 1934-37, Brewster (Ohio) High Sch., 1939-42, Sunbeam Sch. for Crippled Children, Cleve., 1952—; organist First Hungarian Ref. Ch., Cleve., 1948—; pvt. tchr. music, specializing in handicapped children, Cleve., 1952—; organizer, dir. handbell choirs for crippled children and geriatrics; faculty, audition judge Nat. Guild Piano Tchrs. and Nat. Assn. Organ Tchrs.; lectr. nat. workshop Am. Guild English Handbell Ringers; lectr. in field. Sec. Cleve. Council Journalism Advisors. Martha Holden Jennings grantee, 1970-71. Recipient Tchr. of Yr. citation University Heights City Council, Ohio State Council Exceptional Children, Ohio State Senate. Mem. Am. Coll. Musicians (faculty), Am. Guild Organists, Council Exceptional Children (Tchr. of Yr. Cleve. chpt. 1979), Music Educators Assn., Internat. Soc. Music Educators, Nat. Bus. Edn. Assn., Music Tchrs. Nat. Assn. Contbr. articles to profl. jours.; poet librettist for 10 1-act operas, numerous art and religious songs. Home: 14443 E Carroli Blvd University Heights OH 44118

KONIE, JOSEPH C., orthodontist; b. Chgo., Jan. 6, 1932; s. Joseph and Sophie Konieczny; B.S., U. Ill., 1955, D.D.S., 1957, M.S., 1963; 1 dau., Lisa Joy. Practice dentistry specializing in orthodontics, Oak Lawn, Ill., 1963—; instr. U. Ill. Coll. Dentistry, Chgo., 1960-61. Sec. med. field Polands Millenium of Christianity, 1966. Mem. Chgo. Soc. Orthodontists (dir. 1972), Dental Arts Club Chgo. (treas. 1966), Am. Assn. Orthodontists, Ill., Midwestern socs. orthodontists, Orthodontics Alumni Assn., ADA, Ill., Chgo. dental socs., Delta Sigma Delta. Club: Beverly Country. Served to capt. SAC, 1957-59. Home: 4 Cour St Tropez Palos Hills IL 60465 Office: 9501 S Central Ave Oak Lawn IL 60453

KONIE, ROBERT B., real estate and ins. co. exec.; b. Chgo., May 14, 1936; s. Joseph and Sophie (Malkiewicz) Konieczny; B.S., Loyola U., Chgo., 1958, postgrad., 1961. Owner, R.B. Konie & Co., Evergreen Park and Hickory Hills, Ill., 1966—; pres. Beverly Glenn Caterers, Inc., Chgo. Served with AUS, 1959-61. Mem. Nat., Ill. assns. realtors, S.W. Suburban Bd. Realtors, Chgo. Bd. Underwriters. Roman Catholic. Club: Elks. Office: 3100 W 95th St Evergreen Park IL 60642

KONIECKO, EDWARD STANLEY, biochemist; b. Poland, Mar. 24, 1913; came to U.S., 1959, naturalized, 1966; s. Alexander and Victoria (Czarniecki) K.; Food Engr., Agrl. U., Warsaw, 1957; M.S. in Food Tech., Acad. Agr., Warsaw, 1958; M.S. in Econs., Central Sch. Planning and Stats., Warsaw, 1959; Ph.D. in Biochemistry, London Coll. Applied Sci., 1961; doctoral student in nutrition, Can. U., Guelph, Ont., 1971; Ph.D. in Clin. Nutrition, NW London U., 1973. Dir. fin. and acctg., Hdqrs. of State Nutrition, Warsaw, 1950-55; asso. dir. research Warsaw Dept. Nutrition, 1956-59; chief chemist research and devel. Sugardale Foods, Inc., Canton, Ohio, 1960-76; ind. cons., writer, 1976—; books include: Handbook for Meat Chemists, 1979; Handbook for Water Analysis, 1981; Nutritional Encyclopedia for the Elderly, 1981. Mem. Am. Chem. Soc., AAAS., Assn. Ofcl. Analytical Chemists. Republican. Roman Catholic. Office: PO Box 8341 Canton OH 44711

KONIGSBERG, HARVEY ARTHUR, urologist; b. Bayonne, N.J., May 2, 1942; s. Leo L. and Frieda F. K.; B.A., Rutgers U., 1963; M.D., Tufts U., 1968; m. Marilyn Slavin, June 25, 1966; children—Eric Asher, Douglas Slavin. Intern, N.Y. Hosp.-Cornell U., N.Y.C., 1968-69, resident, 1969-75; practice medicine specializing in urology, Omaha, 1975—; asst. prof. urology Med. Sch. Creighton U. Diplomate Am. Bd. Urology. Mem. Am. Urol. Assn. Home: 8414 Hickory St Omaha NE 68124 Office: 310 Regency Pkwy Dr Omaha NE 68114

KONKEL, KURT FREDERICK, surgeon; b. Milw., Mar. 21, 1945; s. Robert J. and Elda C. (Altpeter) K.; B.S. in Biology, Marquette U., 1966; M.D., U. Wis., 1970; m. Maureen Jane Curtis, June 8, 1968; children—Theresa, Jennifer, Corine, Karen. Intern, U. Utah Med. Center, 1970-71; resident in surgery U. Wis. Med. Center, Madison, 1971-72, resident orthopaedic surgery, 1972-73; resident orthopaedic surgery Miami Valley Hosp., Dayton, Ohio, 1974-75; practice medicine specializing in orthopaedic surgery, Menomonee Falls, Wis., 1977—; mem. staff Community Meml. Hosp., 1977—, Hartford (Wis.) Meml. Hosp., 1978—; orthopaedic surgeon Falls Med. Group Service Corp., 1977—; instr. orthopaedic surgery Children's Hosp. Cerebral Palsy Clinic, 1978; clin. instr. dept. orthopaedic surgery Med. Coll. of Wis., Milw., 1978—; cons. orthopaedics Bethesda Luth. Home, Watertown, Wis., 1978—, So. Wis. Center for the Developmentally Disabled, Union Grove, Wis., 1977—. Served to lt. comdr. USN, 1975-77. Diplomate Am. Bd. Orthopaedic Surgery. Mem. Milw. Orthopaedic Soc., State Med. Soc. Wis., Waukesha County Med. Soc. (editorial bd. 1977—, chmn. 1977), AMA, Assn. of Mil. Surgeons of U.S., Wis. Med. Alumni Assn., Wis. Orthopaedic Alumni Assn., Phi Chi, Roman Catholic. Contbr. articles on orthopaedic surgery to med. jours. and sports medicine to newspapers. Home: N87 W16072 Kenwood Blvd Menomonee Falls WI 53051 Office: N84W 16889 Menomonee Ave Menomonee Falls WI 53051

KONNYU, LESLIE, ret. geographer, cartographer, author; b. Tamasi, Hungary, Feb. 28, 1914; s. Joseph and Mary (Polhamer) K.; came to U.S., 1949, naturalized, 1955; diploma Tchrs. Tng. Coll., Hungary, 1933, 44; B.Mus. Edn., St. Louis Mus. and Arts Coll., 1954, diploma cartography, 1957, M.A. in Geography, 1965; m. Elizabeth Gelencser; children—Ernest, Gabriella Konnyu Heizer, Joseph Z. Tchr. elementary sch., Hungary, 1936-42; secondary sch. tchr., Hungary, 1942-44; dir. Refugee Sch., Austria, 1944-49; ch. organist St. Peter's Ch., Jefferson City, Mo., 1949-51; lab. technician Sch. Medicine, Washington U., St. Louis, 1951-55; cartographer Def. Mapping Agy., St. Louis, 1955-73. Dir. Hungarian Radio Program, 1952-58; founder Am. Friends Hungarian Culture, 1959-64; dir. Am. Hungarian Welfare Com., 1956-64; pres. Am. Hungarian Cultural Club, 1967-68; chmn. T.S. Eliot Monument Com., 1972—; chmn. Am. Hungarian Art Hist. Com., 1979—. Recipient Distinguished Community Service award, St. Louis, 1956; certificate merit lit., London, 1972, certificate merit poetry, 1974. Mem. St. Louis Writers Guild (treas. 1968, historian 1974), St. Louis Poetry Center (pres. 1978-80), T.S. Eliot Soc. (dir. 1980), Internat. P.E.N., Mo. Writers Guild, Internat. Poetry Assn., Internat. Acad. Poets. Author 26 books in Hungarian, 1 in French, 1 in German; also author: Bond of Beauty, 1959; Against the River, 1961; A History of American Hungarian Literature, 1962; Eagles of Two Continents, 1963; Modern Magyar Literature, 1964; John Xantus, Hungarian Geographer in America, 1965. Editor: Historical Highlights of Cartography, 1965; Hungarians in the U.S.A., 1967; Collected Poems, 1968; Condensed Geography of Hungary, 1971; Hungarian Participants in the Art Exhibition of St. Louis World Fair, 1973; Acacias: Hungarians in the Mississippi Valley, 1976; Professional Hungarian Artists Outside Hungary, 1978; editor St. Louis Hungarian weekly, 1957-58; American Hungarian Rev., 1963-74. Home: 5410 Kerth Rd St Louis MO 63128

KONOPKA, MARY ANN STEPHANY, container mfg. co. exec.; b. Chgo., Jan. 30, 1933; d. Thomas Stephen and Mary Irene (Plucinski) Poltorak; student public schs., Chgo.; m. Louis Steven Konopka, Nov. 22, 1964 (dec. 1976); stepchildren—Judith Marie Konopka Orseno, Lorraine Louise Konopka Capra. With Continental Group, Inc., West Chicago, Ill., 1952—, project control supr., 1978—. Mem. Nat. Assn. Female Execs., Am. Soc. Profl. and Exec. Women, U.S. CB Radio Assn. Democrat. Roman Catholic. Club: Northwest Internat. Trade. Home: 526 E Pomeroy St West Chicago IL 60185 Office: Continental Group Inc 1700 Harvester Rd West Chicago IL 60185

KONOWITZ, SHELDON H., business exec.; b. Worcester, Mass., Sept. 16, 1923; s. Herman and Etta (Davis) K.; B.B.A., Boston U., 1950; M.B.A., Northwestern U., 1965; m. Shirley Frank, June 25, 1950; children—Judith Konowitz Berlin, Edward, Howard. Dir. mktg. research Schnadig Corp., Chgo., 1963-73, dir. data processing, 1973-77, v.p. mgmt. info. systems, 1977—. Neighborhood commr. Moraine council Boy Scouts Am., 1963-66; mem. Field Mus. Natural History. Mem. dean's council Northwestern U. Grad. Sch. Mgmt. Served with U.S. Army, World War II. Mem. Am. Mgmt. Assn., Data Processing Mgmt. Assn., Am. Mktg. Assn., Am. Statis. Assn., Alpha Phi Omega. Jewish. Club: Masons. Author: Television Industry: Its History, Demand Determinates, Multiple Regression and Analysis of Production, 1964; Role of the Computer in Marketing, 1965; Strategy Decision Making and What It Holds for the Future, 1965. Home: 555 Green Bay Rd Highland Park IL 60035 Office: 4820 W Belmont Av Chicago IL 60641

KONZELMANN, HENRY JOSEPH, pediatrician; b. Elizabeth, N.J., Aug. 11, 1935; s. Henry Joseph and Marianne Jane K.; B.S. in Biology, Holy Cross Coll., 1956; M.D., Georgetown U., 1960; married; children—Suzanne, Kathleen, Henry, Robert, Daniel, Agnes, John. Intern, Harrisburg (Pa.) Hosp., 1960-61; resident in pediatrics U. Md., Balt., 1963-66; practice medicine specializing in pediatrics, Springfield, Ill., 1966—; chmn. pediatrics dept. St. John's Hosp.; asso. clin. prof. pediatrics So. Ill. U. Med. Sch. Bd. dirs. Lake Springfield Improvement Assn. Served with USPHS, 1961-63. Diplomate Am. Bd. Pediatrics. Mem. AMA, Am. Acad. Pediatrics, Ill. Med. Soc., Sangamon County Med. Soc. Conservative Republican. Roman Catholic. Club: Edgewood Golf. Home: 1520 W Lake Dr Springfield IL 62707 Office: 2657 W Lawrence Ave Springfield IL 62704

KOO, PETER HUNG-KWAN, immuno-biochemist, educator; b. Shanghai, China; came to U.S., 1959, naturalized, 1975; s. Yung-Foo and Sun-Wa (Ko) K.; B.A., U. Wash., 1964; Ph.D., U. Md., 1970; m. Somchit Alice Hotapichayawivat, Dec. 23, 1967; children—David G., Christopher G. Research asso. Johns Hopkins U., 1970-74, asst. prof. oncology and radiology, 1975-77; staff fellow NIH, Bethesda, Md., 1974-75; asst. prof. microbiology/immunology Northeastern Ohio Univs. Coll. Medicine, Rootstown, 1977—; adj. asst. prof. chemistry and biology Kent (Ohio) State U. Deacon, 1st Christian Ch. of Kent, 1978—. Recipient Cystic Fibrosis Care Fund award 1979; NIH grantee, 1978—; Am. Caner Soc. grantee, 1979. Fellow Am. Soc. Exptl. Biology; mem. N.Y. Acad. Scis., AAAS, Sigma Xi. Research, publs. in field. Office: Northeastern Ohio Univs Coll Medicine Rootstown OH 44272

KOPAC, MILAN JAMES, microsurgery cons., cell biologist; b. Ravenna, Nebr., Mar. 12, 1905; s. James and Mary B. (Skala) K.; B.S., U. Nebr., 1927, M.S., 1929, D.Sc. (hon.), 1962; Ph.D., U. Calif., Berkeley, 1934. Research asso. biology N.Y. U., 1934-38; vis. asst. prof., 1938-43, asst. prof., 1944-46, asso. prof., 1947-49, prof. biology, 1949-73, prof. emeritus, 1973—, head all-univ. dept. biology, 1963-70, dir. Robert Chambers Lab. Microsurgery, 1968-77; specialist in microsurgery; vis. instr. U. Nebr., 1934, vis. prof. biology, 1962; mem. physiology fellowships panel NIH, 1962-66; chmn. Gordon Research Conf. Cancer, 1964. Sci. adv. com. Damon Runyon Mel. Fund Cancer Research, 1950-73, chmn., 1966-69, sci. dir., 1967-69; adv. com. instnl. grants Am. Cancer Soc., 1963-66. Served to 2d lt., inf., USAR, 1927-37. Fellow N.Y. Acad. Scis. (councilor, v.p. 1958, pres. 1960, trustee 1960-62, Gold medal award 1969); mem. Am. Soc. Cytology (founder), Harvey Soc. (life), Am. Assn. Cancer Research, Sigma Xi. Cons. editor: Mechanisms of Cell Division, 1951; Cancer Cytology and Cytochemistry, 1956; contbr. articles to tech. and sci. jours. Home: 521 Brookside Dr Lincoln NE 68528

KOPECKY, STANLEY JOHN, mfg. co. exec.; b. Berwyn, Ill., Nov. 13, 1942; s. Stanley F. and Helen C. Kopecky; B.S., U. Ill., 1964; M.S., So. Ill. U., 1969; m. Nancy A. Varco, Aug. 2, 1969. Food research scientist Armour & Co., Oak Brook, Ill., 1964-66; packaging research scientist Nat. Dairy Co., Kraftco, Glenview, Ill., 1969-79; asst. packaging mgr. Kraft Inc., Chgo., 1979-80, nat. prodn. packaging mgr. Dart & Kraft Inc., Glenview, 1980—. Mem. Packaging Inst. U.S.A. (v.p. regional activities, nat. dir., past chmn. Chgo. chpt.), Alpha Phi Omega. Club: Toastmasters. Home: 200 E Lonsdale Rd Prospect Heights IL 60070 Office: 1 Kraft Ct Glenview IL 60025

KOPKE, JERRY ELDON, county ofcl.; b. Emporia, Kans., June 7, 1948; s. Carl Eldo and Dortha Deane (Rudy) K.; B.A., Washburn U., 1972; M.P.A., Drake U., 1976. Mem. sales staff Transilwrap, Kansas City, Mo., 1973-74; asst. dir. Polk County Juvenile Home, Des Moines, 1974-76, dir., 1977—. Served with AUS, 1969-71; Vietnam. Mem. Iowa Shelter and Detention Assn. (chmn., 1978—). Democrat. Roman Catholic. Home: 1221 44th St Des Moines IA 50311 Office: 1548 Hull St Des Moines IA 50316

KOPLIK, STANLEY ZANE, state govt. ofcl.; b. N.Y.C., Apr. 29, 1944; s. Jack and Gertrude (Cooper) K.; B.A., SUNY, New Paltz, 1965; M.P.A., N.Y. U., 1971; postgrad. Johns Hopkins U., Harvard U.; m. Kathleen Solman, July 2, 1966; children—Kristen Sara, Joshua John. Prin. budget analyst State of Kans., 1971-77; dir. fiscal affairs

Mo. Dept. Higher Edn., 1977-79. dep. commr. higher edn., 1979-80, commr. higher edn., 1980—; adv. bd. United Student Aid Funds; speaker in field. Mem. Am. Council Edn., Am. Assn. Higher Edn., State Higher Edn. Exec. Officers Assn. Office: 600 Monroe St Jefferson City MO 65101

KOPP, CARL ROBERT, advt. agy. exec.; b. Detroit, Apr. 8, 1921; s. Andrew Russell and Bertha (Hecke) K.; student Ill. Inst. Tech.; grad. Advanced Mgmt. Program, Harvard U.; m. Jenna Lou Brown, Apr. 15, 1978; children—Suzie Kopp Simon, Deborah Kopp Poulin, Sally Kopp Sandberg, Jeffrey. Salesman, sales mgr., advt. mgr. Marathon Corp., Menasha, Wis., 1947-53; account exec. Needham, Louis & Brorby, Chgo., 1953-55; account exec. Leo Burnett Co., Inc., Chgo., from 1955, now chmn. bd., chief exec. officer. Mem. Chgo. Crime Commn., The Chgo. Com. Served with U.S. Army; Korea. Decorated Bronze Star, Purple Heart. Clubs: Bob O'Link Golf, Butler Nat. Golf; Tavern, Mid-Am., Racquet, Chgo. Athletic Assn. (Chgo.); Lost Tree Village; N.Y. Athletic. Leo Burnett Co Prudential Plaza Chicago IL 60601*

KOPPERUD, ROY MILTON, farmer; b. Lake Preston, S.D., Apr. 18, 1914; s. Arthur and Nellie (Knutson) K.; grad. high sch. Engaged in farming, Lake Preston, 1933—; dir. Farmers Union Oil Co., Lake Preston, 1958—, pres., 1960—; asst. sec., treas., dir. CENEX, wholesale farm supplies, South St. Paul, 1974—; partner Kopperud Bros. Farms. Served with AUS, 1941-45. Democrat. Lutheran. Address: RFD 1 Lake Preston SD 57249

KOPULSKY, MARVIN, accountant, educator; b. Chgo., Mar. 19, 1931; s. Reuben and Rose (Richter) K.; B.S., DePaul U., 1953; M.B.A., U. Chgo., 1954; Ph.D., Northwestern U., 1970; m. Barbara Jean Michaelson, June 21, 1953; 1 son, Burton Jay. Self-employed pub. accountant, Chgo.; 1960—; mem. faculty Loyola at Chgo., 1963—, instr., 1963-70, asst. prof., 1970-77, asso. prof., 1977—, also dir. univ. C.P.A. coaching program. C.P.A. Mem. Am. Inst. C.P.A.'s, Ill. Soc. C.P.A.'s, Am. Accounting Assn., Pi Gamma Mu, Beta Gamma Sigma. Home: 5523 N Christiana St Chicago IL 60625 Office: 820 N Michigan Ave Chicago IL 60611

KORDA, CAROL LYNNE, banker; b. Winona, Minn., Feb. 15, 1949; d. Lawrence Llewelyn and Annabelle Marie (Erickson) K.; student U. Nottingham (Eng.), 1970; B.A. in Econs., Lawrence U., 1971. Bond trader First Bank System, Mpls., 1971-74, investment officer, 1974-79, asst. v.p., 1980—; instr. continuing edn. for women U. Minn. Bd. dirs. YWCA, Mpls., 1979—. Mem. Nat. Assn. Bank Women (fin. chmn. 1979-80, treas. 1980-81), Fin. Analysts Fedn., Twin Cities Soc. Security Analysts, Mpls. Soc. Fine Arts. Republican. Methodist. Club: Jr. League Mpls. (dir. 1979-80). Office: 1300 First Bank Pl E Minneapolis MN 55402

KORENAK, JAMES ANTHONY, accountant; b. St. Louis, Apr. 23, 1953; s. Joseph Jacob and Pauline Helen K.; B.S. in Bus. Adminstrn., S.E. Mo. U., 1975; A.A., Jefferson Jr. Coll., 1973. Staff acct. Automobile Club Mo., St. Louis, 1975-76; acctg. supr., 1976-78; cost acct. St. Joe Lead Co., Herculaneum, Mo., 1978-80, gen. acctg. supr., 1980—. Mem. Am. Mgmt. Assn., Am. Horse Shows Assn., Mo. Horse Shows Assn. Home: 4045 W Rock Creek Rd Imperial MO 63052 Office: 881 Main St Herculaneum MO 63048

KORIN, URI, ednl. instn. exec.; b. Hadera, Israel, Sept. 20, 1938; came to U.S., 1971, naturalized, 1977; s. Jacob and Hanna K.; B.A. in Hebrew and Bible, Hebrew U., Jerusalem, 1963, M.A. in Edn., 1966; Ph.D. in Ednl. Adminstrn. and Curriculum Devel., Kent State U., 1974; m. Dolly Braude, May 16, 1961; children—Offer, Edith. High sch. tchr., Jerusalem, 1959-67, asst. prin., 1969-71; exchange tchr. high sch., Cleve., 1967-69; asso. prof. Cleve. Coll. of Jewish Studies, 1971-79; exec. dir. Bur. Jewish Edn., Indpls., 1979—; ednl. cons. Jewish Fedn., Youngstown, Ohio, 1977-79. Israeli govt. grantee, 1963-65; recipient supplementary award Kent State U., 1974. Mem. Am. Assn. Supervision and Curriculum Devel., Am. Assn. Higher Edn., Nat. Soc. for Study Edn., Council for Jewish Edn., Phi Delta Kappa. Co-author: Darkon Laivrit - A Passport to the Hebrew Language, 1975, 76, achievement tests, 1977, tchrs.' guide, 1977; contbr. articles to publs. Office: 6711 Hoover Rd Indianapolis IN 46260

KORLLOS, THOMAS STEPHEN, ednl. adminstr.; b. Homestead, Pa., Aug. 3, 1925; s. Stephen and Sophia (Lagos) K.; A.B. magna cum laude, Youngstown U., 1960; M.A. in Sociology, Kent State U., 1964; Ph.D. in Sociology, Ohio State U., 1976; m. Marion Simon, June 5, 1949; children—T. Stephen, Christopher. Tchr. social studies Howland Schs., Warren, Ohio, 1960-64; asst. prof. Kent State U., 1964-70, asst. dean coll. arts and scis., 1970-73, dean student acad. services, 1973-78, dir. grad. studies dept. sociology and anthropology, 1978—; co-dir. edn. seminar to USSR, 1971-75, dir., 1976. Served with USAAC, 1944-45. Mem. Am., N.Central sociol. assns., Comparative and Internat. Edn. Soc., AAUP, NEA, Alpha Kappa Delta, Pi Gamma Mu. Rotarian. Contbr. articles to profl. jours. Home: 1220 Lake Martin Dr Kent OH 44240

KORNDOERFER, CLAUS WOLFGANG, constrn. co. exec.; b. Racine, Wis., Aug. 28, 1925; s. Carl and Tillie (Bartels) K.; B.S. cum laude, U. Wis., 1948; m. Merll Margaret Walley, Jan. 28, 1950; children—Lee, Deborah, Carl, Wolfgang, John, Jennifer. Labor, Bell City Foundry Co., 1943; engr. Wis. Hwy. Dept., 1947; engr. Davy Engring. Co., LaCrosse, Wis., 1948-49; supt. Carl Korndoerfer, Racine, 1949-54; pres. Korndoerfer Constrn. Co., Inc., Racine, 1954—, Hotel-on-the-Cay Corp.; chmn. K.D.G. Ltd.; dir. 1st Wis. Bank Racine. Bd. dirs. YMCA, United Fund Racine, Racine A-Center. Served with USNR, 1943-45. Mem. Asso. Gen. Contractors (dir., past pres.), Racine Zool. Soc., Racine C. of C. (dir.), U. Wis. Alumni, Urban League, Racine (past pres.), Tau Beta Pi. Republican. Methodist. Home: 77 Woodfield Ct Racine WI 53402 Office: 7900 Durand Av Sturtevant WI 53177

KORNGUTH, STEVEN EDWARD, physiol. chemist; b. N.Y.C., Dec. 1, 1935; s. Eugene I. and Helen (Pardes) K.; B.A., Columbia Coll., 1957; M.S., U. Wis., 1959, Ph.D., 1961; m. Margaret Livens, Aug. 29, 1958; children—Ingrid, David. Staff, N.Y. State Psychiat. Inst., N.Y.C., 1961-63; asst. prof. neurology, physiol. chemistry U. Wis., Madison, 1963-68, asso. prof., 1968-72, prof., 1972—. NIH research, tng. grantee in neurochemistry, 1968-73. Mem. Am. Soc. Biol. Chemists, Am. Neurosci. Soc., Internat. Brain Research Orgn. Home: 5702 Hempstead Rd Madison WI 53711

KORNHABER, BERNARD R(AYMOND), diversified mfg. co. exec.; b. N.Y.C., 1924; s. A. and R. (Rothman) K.; A.B. cum laude with honors in Econs., Bklyn. Coll., 1949; A.M. in Econs., Syracuse U., 1950; children—Marda J., Peter O. Trainee. Internat. Playtex Corp., Dover, Del., 1950-55, mgr. sales stats., 1953-54, sr. economist, 1954-55; mgr. sales devel. internat. div. Allied Chem. Corp., N.Y.C., 1956-61; with Brunswick Corp., Skokie, Ill., 1962—, mktg. mgr., 1964-66, v.p. mktg., dir. corp. planning, 1975—; speaker in field; bd. dirs. Strategic Planning Inst. Served with Security Agy., U.S. Army, 1944-46. Mem. Assn. Corp. Growth (pres. Chgo. chpt. 1980, dir. chpt. 1981—), Planning Execs. Inst., Midwest Planning Soc., Am. Mktg. Assn. Clubs: Chgo. Yacht, Rotary; Skyline Country (Tucson). Home: 100 17th St Wilmette IL 60091 Office: One Brunswick Plaza Skokie IL 60077

KOROW, ELINORE MARIA VIGH, artist; b. Akron, July 31, 1934; d. Alexander and Elizabeth Helen (Doszpoly) Vigh; grad. Cleve. Inst. Art, 1957; student Siena Heights Coll., 1952-53; m. John Henry Korow, Sept. 28, 1957; children—Christopher, David, Daniel. Staff artist, designer Am. Greetings Corp., Cleve., 1957-58, 71-73; one-woman shows: Design House II, Cleve., 1968, Twinsburg (Ohio) Public Library, 1969, Cleve. Playhouse, 1973, Halle's Westgate, Fairview Park, 1971, Octogon Galleries, Patterson Library, Westfield, N.Y., 1974, Carousel Dinner Theatre, Ravenna, Ohio, 1975, Chagrin Valley Little Theatre, Chagrin Falls, Ohio, 1976; exhibited in local and nat. group shows, including nat. traveling exhbn. Am. Watercolor Soc., 1973, Kennedy Center Art Gallery, Hiram (Ohio) Coll., 1976, Am. Artists Profl. League, 1981; represented in permanent collection Cleve. Playhouse; pvt. instr. portrait painting, 1972—; instr. Orange Arts Council, Pepper Pike. Recipient Best in Oils award Cleve. Press Club, 1966; award Internat. Platform Assn. exhbn., Washington, 1980. Mem. Am. Artists Profl. League, Ohio Watercolor Soc. (charter), Internat. Platform Assn., New Orgn. for Visual Arts, Women's Art Club Cleve. (pres. 1971-72). Roman Catholic. Home: 15725 Van Aken Blvd Shaker Heights OH 44120 Studio: 3441 Lee Rd Suite 206 Shaker Heights OH 44120

KORSVIK, WILLIAM JAMES, banker, economist; b. Chgo., Sept. 9, 1917; s. Oscar J. and Anna (Shine) K.; B.S. in Bus. Adminstrn., Northwestern U., 1949; M.B.A., U. Chgo., 1955; grad. Grad. Sch. Banking, U. Wis., 1951; m. Janet Ruth Greene, Mar. 5, 1949; children—Sherry, Holly, Scott, Heather. With The First Nat. Bank of Chgo., 1935—, asst. cashier, 1949-56, asst. v.p., 1957-61, v.p. research, 1962-74, v.p. internat. banking, 1974-78, sr. v.p. worldwide banking, 1979—; asso. sec. fed. adv. council FRS, 1956—; asso. dir. Grad. Sch. Banking, U. Wis., 1953—. Trustee, treas. Norwegian Am. Hosp.; bd. dirs. Chgo. Theol. Sem. Served with AUS, 1942-45. Mem. Am. Econ. Assn., Am. Finance Assn. Democrat. Conglist. Clubs: Econ., Univ., Bankers, Nat. Economist. Contbg. columnist Chgo. Tribune, 1974-80. Home: 1738 Central Ave Wilmette IL 60091 Office: 1 First National Plaza Chicago IL 60670

KORTE, BONNIE MAE, illustrator, athlete; b. St. Louis, Dec. 9, 1949; d. Lambert R. and Irma (Reckamp) K.; B.A. cum laude, Fontbonne Coll., 1972; B.F.A., Washington U., 1973. Artist advt. agys., St. Louis, 1973-76; graphic artist instructional TV dept. St. Louis Community Coll., Forest Park, Mo., 1976-78; visual info. specialist U.S. Army Troop Support and Aviation Material Readiness Command, St. Louis, 1978—; Sr. mem. women's team U.S. Judo Assn., 1974—, team capt., 1975—; U.S. rep. in internat. judo competitions, 1974-79; nat. referee Shiai and Kata, 1976; vol. instr. sport judo, 1965—; staff Camp Olympus Nat. Judo Tng. Camp, 1975—; coach South African tour U.S. Judo Assn., 1979, 1st Olympic Women's Judo Tng. Camp, 1981. Named Ozark AAU Outstanding Female Judo Athlete, 1976-80; named in top ten list of U.S. women judo athletes Black Belt mag., 1974-77; 5-time medalist internat. judo competition; holder 4th degree Black Belt. Mem. AAU (1st athlete rep. to Judo nat. com. 1976, mem. jr. Olympic subcom. 1978-81, adv. nat. public relations subcom., chmn. girls Ozark Judo 1976-80, nat. tng. subcom., 1981, named Outstanding Female Athlete of Ozark, 1977-80), U.S. Judo Assn. (mem. bd. advisors 1975—, nat. champion Shiai and Kata 1972-78), Bon-Cal Judo Club. Contbr. articles on Judo to profl. publs.; U.S. Grand Nat. Judo champion in women's competition, 1975. Home: 7210 Howdershell Rd Hazelwood MO 63042 Office: US Army Troop Support and Aviation Material Readiness Command 4300 Goodfellow Blvd St Louis MO

KORTEBEIN, STUART ROWLAND, orthopedic surgeon; b. Evanston, Ill., Apr. 17, 1930; s. Rowland J. and Grace K.; A.A., North Park Coll., 1950; B.S., Wheaton Coll., 1952; postgrad. North Park Theol. Sem., 1952-53; M.D., Loyola U., 1957; m. Alice C. Johnson, July 10, 1954; children—William, David. Intern, Akron (Ohio) Gen. Hosp., 1957-58, resident, 1961-64; resident Hines VA Hosp., 1960, Northwestern U., 1964; practice medicine specializing in orthopedic surgery, Arlington Heights, Ill., 1965—; attending surgeon N.W. Community Hosp., Arlington Heights, 1969—, chief orthopedics, 1976; asso. surgeon Shriners Hosp., Chgo. unit, 1968; v.p. Magnetrans Research and Devel. Corp., 1972—; tech. adviser Juko-Kai Internat., 1970—; instr. emergency med. technician course Harper Coll., 1973—. Deacon, North Haven Covenant Ch., Cuyahoga Falls, Ohio, 1963; Ill. state pres. Jiu Jitsu Black Belt Fedn. Am., 1971-74, Ill. state rep., 1971-74; Sandan instr. Oikiru-Ryu Ju Jitsu, 1977—; water safety instr. ARC, 1949-54; choir dir. First Bapt. Ch., Twenty Nine Palms, Calif., 1959-60; bd. dirs. Chicagoland Drug Prevention Program, 1971—. Served to lt., M.C., USNR, 1958-60. Diplomate Nat. Bd. Med. Examiners. Fellow A.C.S., Am. Acad. Orthopaedic Surgeons; mem. Physicians Martial Arts Assn., Soc. Black Belts Am., AMA (physicians recognition award 1970—), Christian Med. Soc., Ill. State, Chgo. med. socs., Ill. Orthopaedic Soc., Hakko-Ryu Ju Jitsu Fedn. Contbr. articles to profl. jours. Office: 2010 S Arlington Heights Rd Arlington Heights IL 60005

KOSCIK, RICHARD ALLEN, mech. engr.; b. Chgo., Dec. 17, 1947; s. Edward F. and Irene R. (Kloska) K.; student Western Ill. U., 1966-69; B.S. with honors in Mech. Engring., U. Ill., Urbana, 1971; postgrad. U. Cin., 1975, U. Wis., 1976; postgrad. in bus. adminstrn. Gov.'s State U., 1976—; m. Nancy Erwin, June 26, 1971; children—Scott Michael, Kerri Ann. Project engr. Deltar Co. div. Ill. Tool Works Inc., Frankfort, Ill., 1971-77, chief engr., 1977—. Mem. Soc. Automotive Engrs., Soc. Plastics Engrs., U. Ill. Alumni Assn., Ill. Tool Works Patent Soc., Tau Beta Pi, Sigma Tau, Pi Tau Sigma. Patentee in field. Office: 21555 S Harlem Ave Frankfort IL 60423

KOSIER, MARY WILKIN, educator; b. Independence, Kans.; d. Fred Tiffany and Grace Elizabeth (McClelland) Wilkin; B.E., Washburn U.; M.Ed., Wichita State U.; m. Charles D. Kosier, Apr. 13, 1952; children—Kathryn Ann Kosier Karnaze, Mary Ann Kosier Krattli. Tchr. pub. schs., Topeka and Wichita, Kans., Kirkwood, Mo., guidance counselor Derby (Kans.) Sr. High Sch., 1967-71; dir. career devel. program Central Kans. Area Vocat. Sch. Service Area, 1971—; instr. counselor edn. Wichita State U., 1978—; cons. U.S. Office of Edn.; mem. Kans. Task Force Career Edn., 1973-74, Kans. Career Edn. Input Council, 1976—. Mem. Am. Vocat. Assn., Am. (senator 1977—), Kans. (dir. 1974-75) personnel and guidance assns., Nat. (Merit award 1974; sec. 1975-77, dir. 1975—, del assembly 1973—), Kans. (pres. 1973-74) vocat. guidance assns., Assn. Specialists in Group Work (pres. Kans. 1981-82), AAUW, LWV, Am. Sch. Counselors Assn., Phi Delta Kappa. Republican. Methodist. Home: 1115 Pinecrest Ct Newton KS 67114 Office: 218 E 7th St Newton KS 67114

KOSKELA, ALBERT AUGUST, JR., contractor; b. Schoolcraft Twp., Mich., Apr. 28, 1940; s. Albert August and Elizabeth Emily (Rengo) K.; student Henry Ford Jr. Coll., 1959, 63; m. Karen Margaret Niemi, Aug. 26, 1961; children—Jon, Molly, Kara, Lianne, David, James, Steven, Marc. Pipefitter, Ford Motor Co., Dearborn, Mich., 1959-67; plumber Paul Szoke Co., Detroit, 1963-67, Peninsula Piping Co., Hougton, Mich., 1967-68; co-owner, mgr. Valley Plumbing & Heating Inc., Dollar Bay, Wis., 1967-81, v.p., 1981—. Mem. Asso. Builders and Contractors (exec. bd.), Nat. Water Well Assn., Mich. Well Drillers Assn. Republican. Lutheran. Club: Rainbow Ravine Lodge. Home: Trap Rock Valley Calumet MI 49922 Office: Box 458 Hwy M-26 Dollar Bay MI 49913

KOSKI, PAUL GEORGE, analytical chemist; b. Oakland, Calif., May 15, 1950; s. Paul and Mae Ann (Fox) K.; B.S. in Chemistry, Calif. Poly. State U., 1973; M.S. in Analytical Chemistry, Purdue U., 1977; m. Sherry Kay Barnett, Oct. 29, 1977. Chemist, instrumental analysis group Carnation Research Labs., Los Angeles, 1977-78; sr. flavor chemist Anheuser-Busch Tech. Center, St. Louis, 1978-80, group leader, flavor chemistry, 1980, research group leader, analytical and methods devel., 1980—. Recipient Mustang award for Outstanding Service to Am. Chem. Soc., Calif. Poly. State U., 1971; Outstanding Teaching award, Dept. Chemistry, Purdue U., 1976. Mem. Am. Chem. Soc., Am. Soc. Brewing Chemists. Democrat. Lutheran. Club: Concord Tennis. Home: 1087 Anise Ln Fenton MO 63026 Office: One Busch Pl Saint Louis MO 63118

KOSTAL, OTTO ALBIN, ret. cardiologist; b. Potter County, Pa., Mar. 5, 1899; s. Albin and Marie (Bavor) K.; B.Sc., Municipal U. of Omaha, 1921; M.D., U. Nebr., 1923: m. Flo Strickland, Jan. 19, 1926; children—Betty Joan Kostal McBride, Mary Lou Kostal Hartman, Otta A., Jr. Intern, Nebr. Methodist Hosp., Omaha, 1923-24, Gorgas Meml. Hosp., C.Z., 1924; gen. practice medicine, Giltner, Nebr., 1925-36, Hastings, Nebr., 1936-46; practice medicine specializing in internal medicine and cardiology, Hastings, 1946—; past pres. staff Mary Lanning Meml. Hosp., Hastings; past chmn. bd. dirs. First Nat. Bank, Hastings. Vice chmn. bd. trustees Hastings Coll.; mem. adv. council Good Samaritan Village, Hastings. Served as comdr. USNR, 1943-46. Diplomate Am. Bd. Internal Medicine. Fellow Am. Coll. Cardiology, A.C.P., Internat. Acad. Medicine, Am. Coll. Angiology, Royal Soc. Health (Eng.); mem. Nebr. Med. Assn. (pres. 1962-63), Nebr. Heart Assn. (past pres.), Ancient and Secret Order Quiet Birdmen. Republican. Presbyterian. Clubs: Lochland Country, Mason (Shriner), Royal Order of Jesters, Navy League U.S. (past pres.). Contbr. articles in field. Home: PO Box 1004 923 N Elm Ave Hastings NE 68901

KOSTENKO, MICHAEL LEROY, purchasing agt.; b. Killdeer, N.D., Oct. 11, 1921; s. Tefon and Frances (Glovatsky) K.; B.A., Union Coll., Lincoln, Nebr., 1950; m. Mildred Verniece Martindale, Apr. 18, 1944; children—Lynda Marlene Kostenko Nelson, Victor Marshall. Cashier, bookkeeper Boulder (Colo.) Meml. Hosp., 1950-53, chief accountant, stores supt., 1953-63, purchasing agt., 1955-63, mgr. patient services, 1958-60, asst. adminstr., 1960-63; dir. purchasing Kettering (Ohio) Med. Center, 1964—; tchr. Kettering Coll. Med. Arts. Served with M.C., U.S. Army, 1942-46; ETO. Mem. Am. Soc. for Hosp. Purchasing Agts. and Materials Mgrs. Adventist. Club: Lions. Home: 6031 Marshall Rd Centerville OH 45459 Office: Kettering Med Center 3535 Southern Blvd Kettering OH 45429

KOSTYK, BARRY WILLIAM, chem. coatings industry exec.; b. Winnipeg, Man., Can., Oct. 27, 1951; s. Frederick and Elizabeth Joan (Davey) K.; B.Sc. with honors (U. Man. Alumni Assn. scholar 1969-70, Hogg scholar 1972-73), U. Man., 1973; Ph.D. in Polymers and Coatings Chemistry (NRC of Can. scholar), N.D. State U., 1977; m. Vivian Gail Sloan, July 12, 1975; children—Amanda Gail, Christopher Barry. Internat. tech. mktg. liaison, cons. U.S. govt. on industry-related toxicity regulations Thorson Chem. Corp., N.Y.C., 1977-79; mktg. liaison new bus. ventures 3M, Saint Paul, 1979-80, sr. mktg. liaison, corp. tech. planning, 1980-81, sr. market devel. coordinator Adhesives, Coatings and Sealants div., 1981—. Recipient Merit award for outstanding grad. in chemistry Soc. Chem. Industry, 1973; A.E. Rheineck Meml. award for outstanding grad. student in polymers and coatings, 1975; Roon award for article contbg. to knowledge in coatings industry, 1977. Mem. Fedn. Socs. for Coatings Tech., Am. Chem. Soc., Sigma Xi. Contbr. articles in field to sci. and tech. jours. Home: 7100 Ivystone Ave S Cottage Grove MN 55016 Office: 3M Center 223-6N AC&S Saint Paul MN 55101

KOSZEWSKI, BOHDAN JULIUS, physician; b. Warsaw, Poland, Dec. 17, 1918; s. Mikolaj and Helena (Lubienski) K.; came to U.S., 1952, naturalized, 1958; M.D., U. Zurich (Switzerland), 1946; M.S., Creighton U., 1956; children—Mikolaj Joseph, Wanda Maria, Andrzej Rohdan. Intern, St. Mary's Hosp., Hoboken, N.J., 1953; resident in pathology U. Zurich, 1944-46, resident in internal medicine, 1946-50, asso. in medicine, 1950-52; practice medicine, specializing in internal medicine, Omaha; staff mem. St. Joseph's Hosp., Luth. Med. Center, Mercy, and Meth. hosps.; instr. internal medicine Creighton U., 1956-57, asst. prof., 1957-65, asso. prof. internal medicine, 1965—; cons. in hematology Omaha VA Hosp., 1957—. Served with Polish Army, 1940-45. Recipient Honors Achievement award Angiology Research Found., 1964-65. Fellow A.C.P., Am. Coll. Angiology (gov. for Nebr.); mem. AAAS, Am. Fedn. Clin. Research, Am., Internat. socs. hematology, AMA, Polish-Am. Congress of Nebr. (pres. 1960-68). Author: Prognosis in Diabetic Coma, 1952; contbr. numerous articles to med. jours. Home: 8008 Pacific St Omaha NE 68114 Office: 4502 S 42d St Omaha NE 68107

KOTANSKY, DONALD RICHARD, mech. engr.; b. Hinsdale, Ill., July 28, 1939; s. Cyril Methodius and Catherine Marie (Mesich) K.; B. Mech. Engring., Gen. Motors Inst., 1961; M.S. (Gen. Motors Grad. fellow), Mass. Inst. Tech., 1962, M.E., 1964, D.Sc., 1966; m. Gloria Mary Copp, June 23, 1962; children—Steven, Kenneth, Keith. Asst. prof. mech. engring. Purdue U., Lafayette, Ind., 1965-68; project propulsion engr. Gen. Dynamics Corp., Ft. Worth, 1969-70; br. chief aerodynamics McDonnell Aircraft Co., McDonnell Douglas Corp., St. Louis, 1970—; cons. Allison div. Gen. Motors Corp., Indpls., 1967. Mem. AIAA, ASME, Sigma Xi, Tau Beta Pi. Home: 15400 Clover Ridge Dr Chesterfield MO 63017 Office: McDonnell Douglas Corp PO Box 516 Saint Louis MO 63166

KOTECKI, IRENE SUSAN, investment co. ofcl.; b. Rockford, Ill., Nov. 6, 1950; d. Walter Frederick and Rose Anne (King) Schultz; grad. Northeastern Ill. U., 1972; m. Richard S. Kotecki, Apr. 1, 1972. Sales communications adminstr. Merrill Lynch Pierce Fenner & Smith, Chgo., 1973-75; mktg. coordinator Marshall Internat., Skokie, Ill., 1975-78; advt./promotion mgr. Chemetron Corp., Chgo., 1978-80; nat. advt. mgr. Sealy, Inc., Chgo., 1980—. Mem. Am. Mgmt. Assn., AAUW, Advt. Club Chgo., Sigma Kappa Alumni. Home: 20646 Olympian Way Olympia Fields IL 60461 Office: 470 Merchandise Mart Chicago IL 60654

KOTEN, JOHN A., communications exec.; b. Indpls., May 21, 1929; s. Roy Y. and Margaret (Neerman) K.; B.A., North Central Coll., 1951; postgrad. Northwestern U., 1951-53; m. Catherine Hruska, Nov. 22, 1952; children—John F., Mark L., Sarah J. Field advt. supr. Montgomery Ward Co., Chgo., 1951; asst. dir. pub. relations Am. Osteopathic Assn., Chgo., 1952-53; editorial asst. Ill. Bell Telephone Co., Chgo., 1955-57, information asst., 1957-60, news service and advt. supr., Springfield, Ill., 1960-62, dist. comml. mgr., Springfield, 1962-63; customer relations supr. Am. Tel. & Tel. Co., N.Y.C., 1963-64, film project and planning supr., 1964-65; div. traffic mgr. Ill. Bell Telephone Co., Chgo., 1965-66, pub. relations mgr., 1966-67, asst. v.p., 1968-69, gen. mgr., 1970-71, asst. v.p., 1973-74; dir. state regulatory matters Am. Tel. & Tel. Co., 1971-72, pub. relations dir., N.Y.C., 1974-75; v.p. N.J. Bell Telephone Co., 1975-77; v.p. Ill. Bell Telephone Co., Chgo., 1977—. Sec. Better Schs. Com., Chgo., 1968—; dir., bus. and indsl. relations Ill. Sesquicentennial Commn., 1967-68; mem. Ill. Sch. Problems Commn., 1970-74. Trustee, vice chmn. bd. North Central Coll., 1969—; v.p. Arthritis Found., 1980—. Served with AUS, 1953-55. Mem. Pub. Relations Soc. Am., Pub. Affairs Council, Chgo. Press Club, Ill. Press Assn. Methodist (mem. bd. pensions No. Ill. conf. 1972—, chmn. 1972-76). Clubs: Chgo., Chgo. Advt. (dir. 1977—), Tavern (Chgo.); Lake Manitou Yacht (Rochester, Ind.); Economics (sec., dir. 1972—). Home: 271 Otis Rd Barrington IL 60010 Office: 225 W Randolph St Chicago IL 60606

KOTHERA, RICHARD JOHN, supt. schs.; b. Chgo., Sept. 20, 1928; s. John and Anna Kothera; B.S. in Edn., Ill. State U., 1952; M.A., U. Chgo., 1956; Ed.D., U. Kans., 1967; m. Eleanor Moeller, Aug. 19, 1950; children—James Richard, Krista Marie. Speech therapist, Skokie, Ill., 1954-56, instr., 1956-57, prin., 1957-59, asst. to supt., 1959-63; supt. schs., Shawnee Mission, Kans., 1963-69, Lombard, Ill., 1969—. Bd. dirs. Shawnee Mission Hosp.; mem. bd. advs. Assn. Retarded Children. Served with U.S. Army, 1951-53. NSF scholar, 1963; Ford Found. grantee, 1967-68. Mem. Coop. Assn. Spl. Edn. (bd. dirs.), Council Exceptional Children (chmn.), Am. Assn. Sch. Adminstrs., Spl. Edn. Assn. (bd. dirs., chmn.), Health Systems Agy., Supts. Assn. (pres.), Johnson County Mental Health Assn. (bd. dirs.). Lutheran. Home: 346 Hillcrest Ln Lombard IL 60148 Office: 21 W 364 Belden Ave Lombard IL 60148

KOTSONIS, GEORGE NICK, lawyer; b. Sheboygan, Wis., Feb. 5, 1939; s. Nick George and Viola (Spanomihos) K.; B.S., U. Wis., 1962, LL.B., 1965; m. Dianne Chaconas, Aug. 19, 1962; children—Nick, Tia, Gregory, James, Tom. Admitted to Wis. bar, 1965, Fed. Dist. Cts. bar, 1965, U.S. Supreme Ct. bar, 1972; law clk. Wis. Supreme Ct., 1965-66; mem. firm Wickham, Borgett, Skogstad & Powell, Milw., 1966-70; partner firm Niebler & Niebler, 1970-75; partner firm Chronus and Kotsonis, Milw., 1975—. Mem. Am., Wis., Milw. bar assns. Mason (Shriner). Home: 17710 Penbrook St Brookfield WI 53005 Office: 230 W Wells Milwaukee WI 53203

KOTTHA, JAGANNADHAM, biomed. engr., biomed. instrumentation co. exec.; b. Hyderabad, India, July 14, 1943; s. Pulliah and Durgamma (Koppu) K.; came to U.S., 1971; B.S. in Electronics, Osmania U., India, 1967; M.S. with honors, Case Western Res. U., 1975; M.B.A. with honors, Baldwin-Wallace Coll., 1978. Jr. tech. officer Electronics Corp. India Ltd., 1968-70; electronic engr. Def. Research & Devel. Lab., Hyderabad, India, 1967-68; biomed. engr. Case Western Res. U., Cleve., 1973-74, U. Hosps., 1973-74; dir. engring. and exec. v.p. Environ. Control of Life Systems, Inc., Cleve., 1974-79; founder, pres., chmn. bd. Gen. Systems Inc., Cleve., 1978—, Systems Gen. Corp.; instr. engring. and mgmt. Cleve. State U., 1979—; mem. consultative council Nat. Inst. Bldg. Scis., Washington; dir. Photron Instruments Co., Cleve. Mem. Instrument Soc. Am. (sr.), IEEE, Soc. Advancement of Mgmt., Assn. Advancement of Med. Instrumentation. Home: 2034 Cornell Cleveland OH 44106 Office: 18030 Brook Park Rd Cleveland OH 44135

KOUBA, FRANK HUBERT, advt. agy. exec.; b. Luzerne, Iowa, June 4, 1920; s. Frank and Frances (Zavodsky) K.; B.A., Cornell Coll., 1942; postgrad. Northwestern U., 1946-47, Harvard U. Bus. Sch., 1968-69; m. Lorraine Shirley Ross, Nov. 17, 1949; children—Christine Ann Kouba James, Kathleen Ellen. With Harris Trust & Savs. Bank, Chgo., 1945-46, Meredith Pub. Co., Des Moines, Chgo., 1946-52; v.p. Klau-Van Pietersom-Dunlap, Milw., 1952-60; v.p., advt. dir., dir. Farm Jour. Inc., Phila., 1960-71; sr. v.p., dir. Brewer Advt. div. Young & Rubicam, Kansas City, Mo., 1971-80; exec. v.p. Barickman Advt. div. Doyle Dane Bernbach, Kansas City, 1980—. Served with USAAF, 1942-45. Mem. Nat. Agrl. Mktg. Assn. Clubs: Sales and Mktg. Exec., Kansas City. Home: 2801 W 67th Terr Mission Hills KS 66208 Office: Barickman Advt Co 427 12th St Kansas City MO 64105

KOUMOULIDES, JOHN THOMAS ANASTASIOS, educator, historian; b. Greece, Aug. 23, 1938; s. Anastasios Lazaros and Sophia (Theodosiadou) K.; came to U.S., 1956, naturalized, 1969; A.B., Montclair (N.J.) State Coll., 1960, A.M., 1961; Ph.D., U. Md., 1968; student Fitzwilliam Coll., Cambridge (Eng.) U., 1965-67, vis. fellow, 1971-72. Grad. asst. U. Md., 1961-63; asst. prof. history Austin Peay State U., Clarksville, Tenn., 1963-65, Vanderbilt U., summer 1968; vis. tutor Campion Hall, Oxford (Eng.) U.; mem. faculty Ball State U., Muncie, Ind., 1968—, prof. history, 1975—. Named Archon Chartophylax of Ecumenical Patriarchate of Constantinople, 1979. Research grantee Ball State U., 1969, 70, 74, 79, Am. Philos. Soc., 1973, 80; Am. Council Learned Socs. grantee, 1969, 71, 74; Fulbright-Hays research awardee, Greece, 1977-78. Mem. Am., Brit., Cambridge U. hist. assns., Archaeol. Inst. Am., AAUP, Modern Greek Studies Assn., Soc. Promotion Hellenic Studies, Cambridge U. Philol. Assn., Phi Alpha Theta, Alpha Tau Omega. Author: Cyprus and the Greek War of Independence, 1821-1829, 2d edit., 1974; Byzantine and Post-Byzantine Monuments at Aghia in Thessaly, Greece: The Art and Architecture of the Monastery of Saint Panteleimon, 1975; (with others) Churches and Monuments of Aghia in Thessaly, Greece, 1981; also monographs, articles; editor: Greece in Transition: Essays in the History of Modern Greece 1821-1974, 1977; Greece: Past and Present, 1979; Hellenic Perspectives: Essays in the History of Greece, 1980. Home: 1210 W Wayne St Muncie IN 47303

KOVELESKI, KATHRYN DELANE, educator; b. Detroit, Aug. 12, 1925; d. Edward Albert Vogt and Delane (Bender) Vogt; B.A., Olivet (Mich.) Coll., 1947; M.A., Wayne State U., Detroit, 1955; m. Casper Koveleski, July 18, 1952; children—Martha, Ann. Tchr. schs. in Mich., 1947—; tchr. Garden City schs., 1955-56, 59—, resource and learning disabilities tchr., 1970—. Mem. PTA, Council Exceptional Children, NEA, Mich. Edn. Assn., Garden City Edn. Assn., Bus. and Profl. Women (1st v.p. Garden City 1980-81). Congregationalist. Clubs: Wayne Lit. (past pres.), Sch. Masters Bowling League, Odd Couples Bowling League. Office: 33411 Marquette St Garden City MI 48135

KOVITZ, SEYMOUR J., retail exec.; b. Chgo., Oct. 14, 1917; s. Benjamin and Minnie (Hyman) K.; student Lewis Inst.; B.S., Northwestern U., 1940; m. Elka Pincus, May 10, 1947; children—Jeffrey, Marc, Lorri, Steven. Corr., Armour & Co., Chgo., 1946-47; salesman Big Four Clothing Co., Chgo., 1947-58; pres. Style Center, Inc., Chgo. and Oak Park, Ill., 1958-75, Clothes HQ, Inc., Schaumburg, Ill., 1972-81; now pvt. retail merchandising and advt. cons. Vice pres. Beverly Farm Found., Godfrey, Ill., 1974-76. Served to 1st lt. USAAF, 1941-45. Decorated D.F.C. Mem. Nat. Assn. Men's Sportswear Buyers (dir. 1970—). Club: Masons. Co-editor Beverly Farm Reporter, 1969—. Office: PO Box 239 River Forest IL 60305

KOVLER, H. JONATHAN, basketball exec.; b. Chgo., June 22, 1946; s. Everett and Marjorie (Blum) K.; B.S.B.A., Am. U., 1968; m. Gail Epstein, Dec. 15, 1973; children—Molly Bett, Benjamin. Mng. partner Chgo. Bulls, 1974—; dir. Chgo. Profl. Sports Corp.; exec. producer film Real Life, 1979. Bd. dirs. Better Govt. Assn., Chgo.; mem. com. prints and drawing Art Inst. Chgo. Office: care Chicago Bulls 333 N Michigan Ave Chicago IL 60601

KOWAL, JAMES ALLEN, utility co. exec.; b. Joliet, Ill., Apr. 6, 1947; s. Adam Joseph and Lucille Mary (Ptaszynski) K.; B.S., No. Ill. U., 1969; M.S., Purdue U., 1976; m. Marguerite Lynn Balma, July 19, 1969; children—Kimberly Michelle, Mark Ryan, Chad Michael. Programmer analysis standards engring. and devel. Bell Labs., Naperville, Ill., 1969-72; systems analyst time sharing and data base systems, Western Electric Co., Warrenville, Ill., 1972-77, dept. chief info. systems devel., 1977-79, Lisle, Ill., 1979—; faculty Moraine Valley Community Coll., Palos Hills, Ill., 1969-77, Coll. of DuPage, Lombard, Ill., 1971-72, N. Central Coll., Naperville, 1977—, cons. in field. Pres., Naperville Country Estates Civic Orgn., 1976-78; pres. Sts. Peter and Paul Sch. Bd., Naperville, 1977—; mem. governing bd. computer sci. dept., 1981—. Cert. data processor. Mem. Math. Assn. Am., Assn. of Computer Machinery, Am. Mgmt. Assn. Home: 1100 Onwentsia Ct Naperville IL 60540 Office: 4513 Western Ave Lisle IL 60532

KOYLE, MYRON RAYMOND, bearing mfg. co. exec.; b. Massillon, Ohio, Aug. 8, 1929; s. Ernest R. and Mary Ann (Kane) K.; A.B., Kent State U., 1951; M.A., 1955; m. Adelaine Dorothea Metcalf, June 12, 1954; children—Debra Elaine, Myron Raymond, Douglas Metcalf, Barbara Anne. Indsl. engr. Timken Co., Canton, Ohio, 1955-56, supr. bearing ops., 1956-59, with internat. ops., 1959—, exec. asst. for internat. operations, 1963—. Active Boy Scouts Am. Served with U.S. Navy, 1952-53. Certified mfg. engr. Mem. Am. Mgmt. Assn., Machinery and Allied Products Inst., Soc. Mfg. Engrs., Am. Soc. Metals, Naval Res. Assn., Kent State U. Alumni Assn. (dir.), Nat. Def. Preparedness Assn., CAP (lt. col. Ohio wing). Republican. Lutheran. Club: Brookside Country. Author: (monograph) Physiological Effects of Long-Distance Travel, 1967. Analyst, 1st formulator policy for corporate use of "Jet Lag". Home: 1101 Mile Ave SW Canton OH 44710 Office: 1835 Dueber Ave SW Canton OH 44706

KOZELKA, EDWARD WILLIAM, seed and feed co. exec.; b. Monona, Iowa, July 19, 1912; s. William Frank and Elizabeth (Tayek) K.; student Loras Coll., 1929-31; m. Beulah Annette Gunderson, Feb. 24, 1941; 1 dau., Gail Kathleen. Gen. mgr. Hall Roberts' Son, Postville, Iowa, 1932-46, v.p., gen. mgr., 1946-75, treas., 1975—; salesman Dean Real Estate, Postville, 1975—; dir. Postville State Bank, Postville Telephone Co. Mem. Postville City Council, 1960-61; pres. Postville Hist. Soc., 1975-78; treas. Upper Explorerland Resource, Conservation and Devel. Com., 1969—; chmn. Upper Explorerland Regional Planning Commn., 1971-80; chmn. N.E. Iowa River Basin Com., 1976-79; mem. Iowa Policy Adv. Council on Water Quality, 1976—; mem. citizens adv. council Dept. Transp., 1977—; mem. planning and fin. com. Postville Hosp., 1959-60; chmn. bldg. com. Postville Hosp., 1960-61; co-chmn. fund raising com. Postville Good Samaritan Center, 1968; bd. dirs. Big 4 Fair, 1946-74. Recipient Distinguished Service award Jaycees, 1966; hon. future farmer FFA. Mem. Iowa Seed Dealers Assn. (pres. 1972), Iowa Grain and Feed Assn., Western Seed Dealers Assn. Republican. Roman Catholic. Clubs: Kiwanis, Postville Comml. Home: 205 Williams St W Postville IA 52162 Office: PO Box 396 Postville IA 52162

KOZLOW, RICHARD, painter; b. May 5, 1926. Graphic designer, comml. artist; instr. spl. seminars and workshops; one-man shows include Detroit Inst. Arts, 1964, Art Gallery Windsor (Ont., Can.), 1977; represented in permanent collections Detroit Inst. Arts, Art Gallery Windsor, Akron Art Mus., Butler Art Ins., Container Corp. Am. Series Great Ideas of Western Man, Archives Am. Art div. Smithsonian. Recipient Art Dirs. gold medals, 1953, 54, 55; Socrates award outstanding advt., 1956, 58; prize Mich. Artists Exhibit, 1950, 53, 58; Founder's award Detroit Inst. Arts, 1963; Alvin and Lois Spector Found. for Arts grantee, 1980. Author, illustrator: Of Man's Inhumanity to Man, 1964. Home: 176 Suffield Birmingham MI 48009 Studio: 320 Washington Sq Plaza Royal Oak MI 48067

KOZLOWICZ, THOMAS JOSEPH, credit union exec.; b. Milw., Apr. 23, 1945; s. Frank J. and Esther A. (Colwell) K.; B.A., St. Marys Coll., 1967; postgrad. U. Utah, 1967; m. Lynda J. McCook, May 30, 1969; 1 son, Frank J. Vista vol. Fort Duchesne, Utah, 1967-69; salesman K-D Mailing Service, Franklin Park, Ill., 1969-70; loan officer Paysaver Credit Union, Melrose Park, Ill., 1970-77, pres., 1977—; dir. Ill. Credit Union League. Mem. Mary Queen of Heaven Parish Bd., 1977-78. Mem. Credit Union Execs. Soc. Republican. Roman Catholic. Home: 621 W Armitage Elmhurst IL 60126 Office: 4419 W North Ave Melrose Park IL 60160

KOZUMPLIK, JOSEPH JERRY, hosp. adminstr.; b. Monroe, Mich., Apr. 8, 1940; s. Frank John and Mary Elizabeth (Popelar) K.; A.A., Washtenaw Community Coll., 1970; B.B.A., Cleary Coll., 1977; M.H.A., Ind. No. U., 1979; m. Maureen Plasters, Nov. 7, 1964; children—John, Thomas. With St. Joseph Mercy Hosp., Ann Arbor, Mich., 1968—, acctg. supr., 1973-76, dir. patient accounts, admitting and outpatient registration, 1976—. Mem. Hosp. Fin. Mgmt. Assn., Hosp. Patient Acctg. Assn. (chmn. edn. com.). Methodist. Home: 9521 Anne Dr Pinckney MI 48169 Office: 5301 E Huron River Ann Arbor MI 48106

KRAEMER, BOYD ANDRE, city ofcl.; b. N.Y.C., Jan. 29, 1947; s. Raymond Jacob and Mildred Eileen (Fetterroll) K.; student S.D. Sch. Mines and Tech., 1965-66; B.S., S.D. State U., 1970; M.P.A., U. Wis., Oshkosh, 1979; m. Kathleen Ann Thompson, Aug. 9, 1969. Landscape contractor Brookings (S.D.) Ind. Sch. Dist. 122, 1968; park caretaker, city forester City of Brookings, 1968-70; dir. parks and recreation City of Wheat Ridge (Colo.), 1970-74; landscape supt. Genesee Assos., Denver, 1974; dir. parks City of Oshkosh (Wis.), 1975—; mem. tech. adv. com. E. Central Regional Planning Commn.; mem. Fairgrounds Tech. Bd., Winnibago County, Wis.; sec., treas. Clear Creek, Inc., Wheat Ridge, 1971—. Mem. Nat. (planning com.), Mid-Continent park and recreation assns., Wis. Parks and Recreation Assn. (profl. cert. bd.), Wis. Aboretum Assn. Office: City Hall 215 Church Ave PO Box 1130 Oshkosh WI 54901

KRAFT, CHARLES WILLIAM, JR., homebuilder, real estate broker, ins. underwriter; b. Kansas City, Kans., Oct. 7, 1950; s. Charles William and Helen Virginia (Herrington) K.; B.A., Mid-Am. Nazarene Coll., 1973; postgrad. Baker U., Baldwin City, Kans., 1978-79; m. Brenda Joyce, July 31, 1976. Pres., Kraft III, Inc., Olathe, Kans.; broker Joel Pickering, Century 21 Realtors, Olathe; ins. underwriter Mut. Benefit Life Ins. Co., William E. Snooks, Jr., gen. agt. Mem. Nat. Assn. Realtors, Life Underwriters Assn. Kansas City (Mo.), Johnson County Bd. Realtors. Address: 16206 Chalet Dr Olathe KS 66062

KRAFT, GARY, athletic products co. exec.; b. Hamilton, Ohio, Apr. 24, 1949; s. Gordon Lee and Jean (Hegler) K.; student Miami U., Oxford, Ohio, 1971. Nat. sales dir. Gen. Athletic Products Co., Greenville, Ohio. Bd. dirs. Hamilton YMCA, 1977-80, Jr. Achievement, 1978-79, Hamilton United Way, 1978-79; mem. Community Forum Com., 1978-80. Mem. Hamilton Jaycees (youth, sport dir. 1976, v.p. 1977, pres. 1978-79, state dir. 1980-81), Hamilton C. of C., Fairfield C. of C. Roman Catholic. Home: 607 Harrison Ave Hamilton OH 45013 Office: 607 Riffle Ave Hamilton OH 45331

KRAFT, MICHAEL EUGENE, polit. scientist, educator; b. Los Angeles, Nov. 18, 1943; s. Louis and Pearl Kraft; A.B., U. Calif., Riverside, 1966; M.A., Yale U., 1967, Ph.D., 1973. Asso. fellow in instrn. Yale U., New Haven, 1968-70; instr. polit. sci. Vassar Coll., Poughkeepsie, N.Y., 1970-73, asst. prof., 1973-76; postdoctoral fellow in sociology U. Wis., Madison, 1976-77, asst. prof. polit. sci. and public adminstrn. U. Wis., Green Bay, 1977-79, asso. prof., 1979—, chmn. polit. sci., 1979—. Vice pres., mem. exec. com., nat. bd. dirs. Zero Population Growth, Inc., 1978—; bd. dirs. Planned Parenthood of Brown County (Wis.), 1978—. NDEA Title IV fellow, 1966-70; NIH grantee, 1976-77. Mem. Am. Polit. Sci. Assn., So. Polit. Sci. Assn., Policy Studies Orgn., Population Assn. Am., Am. Soc. Public Adminstrn., Phi Beta Kappa. Editor: Population Policy Analysis, 1978; contbr. chpts. to books. Home: 3002 Albert Dr Green Bay WI 54301 Office: Dept Polit Sci U Wis Green Bay WI 54302

KRAHL, ENZO, surgeon; b. Fiume, Italy, Apr. 22, 1924; s. Massimiliano and Camilla (Aub) K.; came to U.S., 1951, naturalized, 1955; M.D., U. Florence (Italy), 1948; m. Anne Katharine Ferbstein, June 14, 1958; children—Edward Alexander, Katharine Frances. Asst. dept. surgery U. Rome, 1948-51, Brit. Council scholar, 1949; fellow in vascular surgery Columbi Presbyn. Med. Center, N.Y.C., 1951-52, fellow in surgery, 1954-55; resident in surgery St. Vincent's Hosp., N.Y.C., 1952-54, chief resident in surgery Akron (Ohio) City Hosp., 1957-58; dir. grad. edn. Akron Gen. Hosp., 1959-60; practice medicine specializing in surgery, Akron, 1958-60, Superior, Wis., 19—; mem. staff Superior Meml. Hosp., also bd. dirs.; founder Superior Clinic, 1964. Vice pres. Duluth—Superior Symphony; mem. exec. com., bd. dirs. Health Systems Agy. Western Lake Superior; bd. dirs. Blue Cross/Blue Shield United of Wis. Served as capt. M.C., U.S. Army, 1955-57. Recipient 1st prize for thesis U. Florence (Italy), 1948; United Fund award, 1965; certificate of merit N.Y.C. CD, 1953. Diplomate Am. Bd. Surgery. Mem. Douglas County (Wis.), Wis. State (mem. peer review commn.) med. socs., AMA, U.S. Power Squadron, Am. Bridge League. Jewish. Clubs: Kiwanis, Northland Country, Duluth Indoor Tennis, Masons, Shriners. Contbr. articles to med. jours. Home: 3 White Birch Trail Superior WI 54880 Office: 3600 Tower Ave Superior WI 54880

KRAINIK, ARDIS, opera co. exec.; b. Manitowoc, Wis., Mar. 8, 1929; d. Arthur Stephen and Clara (Bracken) K.; B.S., Northwestern U., 1951; postgrad. in music, 1953-54. Tchr. drama, public speaking Horlick High Sch., Racine, Wis., 1951-53; mezzo soprano appearing with Chgo. Lyric Opera, 1955-59, Ft. Wayne (Ind.) Philharm. Orch., Tri-City Symphony, Davenport, Iowa, Cameo Opera Co., Chgo., North Shore Symphony, Winnetka, Ill., Lake Forest (Ill.) Symphony, 1954—; appeared in oratorio performances throughout Mid-West on Artists Showcase, NBC-TV, in recitals throughout area; soloist 17th Ch. Christ Scientist, Chgo., 1969-77; exec. sec., office mgr. Lyric Opera of Chgo., 1954-59, asst. mgr., 1960-76, artistic adminstr., 1976-81, gen. mgr., 1981—. Bd. dirs. Chog. br. English Speaking Union, 1963—; charter mem. Chgo. Council Fine Arts, 1976—, Northwestern U. Women's Bd., 1978—. Mem. Mortar Bd., Pi Alpha Lambda, Phi Beta, Chi Omega. Christian Scientist. Office: care Lyric Opera of Chgo 20 N Wacker Dr Chicago IL 60606*

KRAKOWER, JAMES MICHAEL, tire and wheel retail exec.; b. Poughkeepsie, N.Y., Nov. 11, 1946; s. David and Dorothy (Denzig) K.; B.S., Clarkson Coll., 1968, M.S., 1970; postgrad. Buffalo State U., 1971, U. Ill., 1972-73; m. Susan Ellen Auerbach, June 26, 1977; children—Ganyt Heather, Eleza Dawn. Pres., JMK Tire & Wheel Center, Inc., Champaign, Ill. Bd. dirs. Hillel Found., U. Ill. chpt., Champaign, 1979—; v.p. Federated Jewish Charities of Champaign Urbana, Inc., 1980-81. Served with USAF, 1969-72. Mem. Nat. Tire Dealers and Retreaders Assn. Jewish. Home: 1306 E Fairlawn St Urbana IL 61801 Office: 1510 N Neil St Champaign IL 61820

KRALL, JOSEPH I., cardiologist; b. Cleve., Apr. 9, 1938; s. Ellis H. and Margie S. (Straus) K.; A.B., U. Pa., 1960; M.D., State U. N.Y., Buffalo, 1965; m. Mary Ann Lamont, Aug. 24, 1975; children—Roy, Jennifer, Sarah. Intern, Mt. Sinai Hosp., Cleve., 1965-66; resident in cardiology Met. Gen. Hosp., Cleve., also Mt. Sinai Hosp., 1966-70; dir. cardiac catheterization lab. St. Lukes Hosp., Cleve., 1972-74; practice medicine specializing in cardiology, Cleve., 1974—; chief of medicine Shaker Med. Center Hosp., Cleve.; asst. clin. prof. medicine Case Western Res. U. Served to capt. U.S. Army, 1967-73. Diplomate Am. Bd. Internal Medicine, Am. Bd. Cardiovascular Disease. Fellow Am. Coll. Cardiology, Am. Heart Assn. (fellow Council Clin. Cardiology). Home: 2860 Attlebow Rd Shaker Heights OH 44120 Office: 11710 Shaker Blvd Cleveland OH 44120

KRAMER, CARL EDWARD, historian; b. New Albany, Ind., May 22, 1946; s. Douglas Manuel and Jane Anastacia (Markert) K.; A.B., Anderson (Ind.) Coll., 1968; M.A., Roosevelt U., 1970; M.S., U. Louisville, 1972; Ph.D., U. Toledo, 1980. Tchr., intern Urban Tchr. Corps, Chgo. Bd. Edn., 1968-70; population analyst U.S. Bur. Census, Jeffersonville, Ind., 1970-71; research planner Louisville and Jefferson County Planning Commn., Louisville, 1971-72; adj. instr. Inst. Community Devel., U. Louisville, 1976—; adj. lectr. Ind. U. S.E., 1978—; archtl. historian Historic Landmarks and Preservation Dists. Commn., Louisville, 1977-79; instr. Center for Life Long Learning, Spalding Coll., Louisville, 1977; pres. Kentuckiana Hist. Services, 1981. Mem. exec. bd. Boy Scouts Am., 1976—, v.p., 1977-78; dist. vice chmn., 1975-77, chmn. long rang planning com., 1977, dist. chmn., 1979-81; mem. by laws and auditing com. Silver Creek Hist. Museum, 1976-77; bd. dirs. Third Century, United Campus Ministry, U. Louisville, 1979-80; mem. Clark County (Ind.) Hist. Preservation Adv. Com., 1978, Jefferson County (Ky.) Judge's Task Force on Hist. Preservation, 1978-79, William Leckie Grad. scholar, 1974; recipient Nat. Disting. Service award Order Arrow, Boy Scouts Am., 1973, Dist. Merit award, 1976, Silver Beaver award, 1981; Ky. col., 1978. Mem. Am. Hist. Assn., Orgn. Am. Historian, Am. Planning Assn., Community Devel. Soc. Am., Am. Soc. Public Adminstrn., Nat. Trust Hist. Preservation, Preservation Alliance Louisville and Jefferson County, Louisville Hist. League, Commonwealth Preservation Council Ky., Louisville Central Area, Inc., Clark's Grant Hist. Soc., Am. Assn. State and Local History, Filson Club, Phi Eta Sigma, Alpha Chi, Phi Kappa Phi, Alpha Phi Gamma, Pi Gamma Mu, Phi Alpha Theta. Democrat. Mem. United Ch. of Christ. Author: Two Centuries of Urban Development in Central and Southern Louisville, 1978; A History of Eastern Louisville, 1980. Contbr. articles to Colloquim, Filson Club History Quar., Louisville Mag. Home: 506 Popp Ave Sellersburg IN 47172 Office: 4201 Grant Line Rd New Albany IN 47150

KRAMER, CECILE EDITH, librarian; b. N.Y.C., Jan. 6, 1927; d. Marcus and Henrietta (Marks) K.; B.S., CCNY, 1956; M.S. in Library Sci., Columbia U., 1960. Reference asst. Columbia U. Health Scis. Library, N.Y.C., 1957-61, asst. librarian, 1961-75; dir. Northwestern U. Med. Library, Chgo., 1975—; instr. continuing edn. Med. Library Assn., 1966-75; instr. Grad. Sch. Library Sci., Rosary Coll., Chgo., 1981—. Mem. Med. Library Assn. (chmn. Med. Schs. Libraries Group 1975-76, editor Med. Library Assn. News 1975-77), Midwest Regional Group of Med. Library Assn., Acad. Health Scis. Library

Dirs., Biomed. Communications Network (chmn. 1979-80). Home: 2626 Lakeview Ave Chicago IL 60614 Office: 303 E Chicago Ave Chicago IL 60611

KRAMER, CHARLES EUGENE, gear mfg. co. exec.; b. Hamilton, Ohio, Mar. 19, 1910; s. George and Deborah (Begley) K.; B.S. in Mech. Engring., Purdue U., 1940; m. Nelda M. Wood, Aug. 12, 1941; children—Janet Lynn, Robert Michael. Time study engr. Fairfield Mfg. Co., Inc., subs. Rexnord, Inc., Lafayette, Ind., 1940-51, chief indsl. engr., 1951-58, factory mgr., 1958-63, v.p. mfg., 1963-73, pres., chief exec. officer, 1973—; dir. Lafayette Nat. Bank, Schwab Safe Co., Inc. Bd. dirs Lafayette Purdue Research Found.; trustee Lafayette YMCA, Ind. Vocat. and Tech. Coll. Served with U.S. Army, 1944-46. Registered profl. engr., Ind. Mem. Am. Mgmt. Assn., Presidents Assn., ASME, Am. Inst. Indsl. Engrs., Am. Gear Mfrs. Assn. (dir.). Republican. Methodist. Clubs: Lafayette Country, Elks. Home: 3918 Gate Rd Lafayette IN 47905 Office: Fairfield Mfg Co Inc US 52 S Lafayette IN 47902

KRAMER, DAVID WILLIAM, univ. dean, botanist; b. Ashland, Ohio, May 19, 1938; s. William Alvin and Virginia Dinsdale (Hastings) K.; B.A. (Sohio scholar), Ohio Wesleyan U., 1960; M.A., Ind. U., Bloomington, 1963, Ph.D. (Ogg fellow), 1969; m. Gladys L. Johnson, June 10, 1961; 1 son, Kenneth Charles. Lectr., Ind. U., 1963-64, U. Mich., Flint, 1965-67; lectr., asst. to dean Ind. U. S.E., 1967-69, asst. prof., 1969, asst. dean regional campus adminstrn., asst. prof., 1969-72, asst. dean acad. affairs, 1972-73, asso. dean acad. affairs, 1973-75, asso. dean acad. adminstrn., 1975-78, asst. to v.p., adj. asst. prof. botany, univ. dir. faculty record systems, 1978-80; dean, dir. Mansfield campus, asst. prof. botany Ohio State U., 1980—. Charter mem., 1st pres. Theatre Circle, Ind. U., 1978-80; bd. trustees Mansfield Art Center, 1980—; mem. Richland County Regional Planning Commn., 1981—. Mem. AAAS, Am. Inst. Biol. Scis., Bot. Soc. Am., Mansfield/Richland Area C. of C. (dir.), Sigma Xi, Kappa Delta Pi. Democrat. Methodist. Club: Rotary (v.p. 1979-80). Contbr. articles sci. jours., book revs. Office: Ohio State University Mansfield OH 44906

KRAMER, DENNIS LEE, univ. adminstr.; b. Huntington, Ind., Nov. 6, 1942; s. Harold E. and Helen L. K.; B.S., Ball State U., Muncie, Ind., 1965, M.A.E., 1969; Ph.D., Fla. State U., 1972; m. Carolee Ann Atkinson, Dec. 22, 1962; children—Kris L., Kurt L. Dir. info. and research Ind. Dept. Public Instrn., Indpls., 1972-73; asst. prof. higher edn. Ball State U., 1976—, coordinator systems for student affairs, 1973-77, dir. univ. computing services, 1978—; cons. computer applications in edn. Charter founder Muncie Children's Mus.; div. leader, capt., treas. swim team bd. YMCA, 1975—, recipient Hustler award and Capts. award of merit; former pres. Delaware County Tchrs. Assn. v.p. Burris Lab. Sch. PTA, 1980-81, pres., 1981-82. Recipient continuing edn. cert. of merit Ball State U., 1977. Mem. Data Processing Mgmt. Assn., Assn. Computing Machinery, CAUSE. Presbyterian. Club: Kiwanis Internat. Home: Rural Route 3 Box 354 Muncie IN 47302 Office: 2000 University Ave Muncie IN 47306

KRAMER, FREDERICK CLAUDE, photographer; b. Vienna, Austria, Feb. 16, 1914; s. Joseph and Grete Kramer; grad. U. Vienna, 1938; m. Ginette Martin, June 28, 1957; children—Marion, Valerie. Photographer specializing in exec. portraits, Chgo., 1960—. Mem. Am. Humanist Assn. (past pres. Evanston chpt.). Club: Am.-Austria Soc. Midwest. Home: 446 Sandy Ln Wilmette IL 60091 Office: 6905 N Western Ave Chicago IL 60645

KRAMER, HELEN ANN TOBABEN, librarian; b. Walnut, Kans.; d. Henry J. and Amelia (Munstermann) Tobaben; A.A., Independence Community Coll., 1956; B.S., Kans. State Coll., 1964, M.S., 1976; M.S., Kans. State Tchrs. Coll., 1965; m. Sidney W. Kramer, Feb. 14, 1942 (div. May 1945); 1 son, Jim L. Cons. Roux Distbg. Co., Inc., N.Y.C., 1948-55; 57-63; librarian, asso. prof. librarianship Kans. State U., Pittsburg, 1965—; exec. dir. Nat. Library Week, 1970-72; adviser Alpha Gamma Delta, 1966—. Mem. AAUP (v.p. 1971-73), AAUW, Am., Kans. (exec. council 1969-72) library assns., Phi Theta Kappa, Kappa Delta Pi, Pi Omega Pi, Phi Alpha Theta, Delta Kappa Gamma, Phi Delta Kappa (pres. 1979-81). Lutheran. Club: Altrusa (pres. 1978-81). Home: 2001 Countryside Dr Pittsburg KS 67662

KRAMER, JOHN DAVIS, state ofcl.; b. Los Angeles, Sept. 25, 1948; s. Rex Willard and Ruth (Roseberry) K.; B.A., Stanford U., 1970; postgrad. Oxford (Eng.) U., 1970-71, Free U. W. Berlin, 1967-68; m. Susan Veronica Richards, June 19, 1972; children—Jonathan Igor Davis, Abigail Ruth Elizabeth. Exec. dir. Hwy. Action Coalition, Washington, 1971-73; dir. policy and planning Ill. Dept. Transp., 1973-77; sec. of transp. State of Ill., 1977—; project dir. U.S. adv. group transp. to Govt. Saudi Arabia, 1980-81. Asso. chmn. United Way Sangamon County, 1979. Mem. U.S. Conf. State Depts. Transp. (chmn. 1979—). Clubs: Metropolitan (Washington); Oxford and Cambridge United Univ. (London). Office: Dept Transp 2300 Dirksen Pkwy Springfield IL 62764

KRAMER, TOBA S., ednl. adminstr.; b. Chelsea, Mass., Jan. 18, 1927; s. Leo Saul and Mary (Blass) Schwartz; Mus.B., New Eng. Conservatory Music, 1948, Mus.M., 1965; m. Paul Kramer, Nov. 25, 1948; children—Judith Gale, Miriam, Jane Maxine. Faculty mem. Irene Kaufmann Music Sch., Pitts., 1958-61; piano instr. Brookline (Mass.) Music Sch., 1961-63, Malden (Mass.) Public Schs., 1963-64; music specialist Wis. Conservatory Music, Milw., 1967-68, dean, 1974-76, pres., 1976—; instr. piano and theory Wis. Coll. Conservatory, Milw., 1968-74; 1st v.p. Civic Music Assn., Milw., 1976—. Sec., treas. Arts Devel. Council, Milw. Mem. Internat. Kodaly Soc. (U.S. del.), Orgn. Am. Kodaly Educators (pres.-elect), Nat. Assn. Schs. Music (regional vice-chmn.), Music Educators Nat. Conf., Am. Assn. Higher Edn., Coll. Music Soc., Am. String Tchrs. Assn., Midwest Kodaly Educators Assn., Wis. Fedn. Music Clubs, Tempo, New Eng. Conservatory Music Alumni Assn. Office: 1584 N Prospect Ave Milwaukee WI 53202

KRAMER, WARREN READE, pharmacist; b. Akron, Ohio, Nov. 8, 1942; s. Edward Albert and Marcia Carolyn (Capoot) K.; student Kent State U., 1960-62; B.S. in Pharmacy, Ohio No. U., 1966; M.S. in Hosp. Pharmacy, N.E. La. State Coll., 1968; M.B.A., Lake Forest Sch. Mgmt., 1980; m. Linda Lou Fent, June 8, 1965; children—Vincient, Jetta, Ginger. Asst. dir. pharmacy Wyandotte (Mich.) Gen. Hosp., 1968-69; asst. dir., asst. prof. Cin. Gen. Hosp. Med. Center, 1969-71; dir. pharmacy St. Francis Hosp., Evanston, Ill., 1971-76, Wishard Meml. Hosp., Indpls., 1976-79, Am. Internat. Hosp., Zion, Ill., 1979-81; mktg. mgr. Smith Labs., Rosemont, Ill., 1981—; mem. faculty Ind. U., Purdue U., 1976-79. NSF grantee, 1963. Mem. Am. Soc. Hosp. Pharmacists, Am. Pharm. Assn., Lake County Pharmacists Assn., Ill. Soc. Hosp. Pharmacists, Phi Delta Chi, Phi Delta Theta, Rho Chi. Republican. Baptist. Contbr. articles to pharmacy jours. Home: 934 Franklin Winthrop Harbor IL 60096 Office: Smith Labs Rosemont IL 60018

KRAMSKI, ANDREW WALTER, communications engr., mfg. co. exec.; b. Ladek, Poland, May 23, 1948; came to U.S., 1960, naturalized, 1966; s. Richard and Wanda (Rychlinski) K.; B.S., U. Ill., 1971, M.S., 1972; m. Elizabeth Nowak, June 22, 1975; children—Andrew R., Eva Marie. Programmer analyst Internat. Harvester Corp., Hinsdale, Ill., 1972-78, project engr., 1978-79, sr. engr., 1979-80, product engr., 1980—; part-time coll. instr., 1980—; engring. cons. Mem. IEEE. Office: 10400 W North Ave Melrose Park IL 60160

KRANIAS, GEORGE, physician; b. Thessaloniki, Greece, Nov. 23, 1941; s. Efstratios and Evgenia (Svolakis) K.; came to U.S., 1970, naturalized, 1979; M.D., U. Thessaloniki, 1968; m. Evangelia Galani, Dec. 23, 1970; children—Efstratios, Gregory. Intern, Northwestern U. Med. Center, Chgo., 1972-73, resident in ophthalmology, 1973-76, fellow in vitreo-retinal diseases and surgery, 1976-77; asso. prof. ophthalmology U. Cin., dir. Clin. Retinal Lab., 1977—. Mem. Am. Acad. Ophthalmology, Ohio Med. Assn., Acad. Medicine Cin., Internat. Soc. Ophthalmic Ultrasound. Club: Lions. Contbr. articles to profl. jours. Home: 525 Hilltop Ln Cincinnati OH 45215 Office: 234 Goodman St Cincinnati OH 45267

KRANITZ, THEODORE MITCHELL, lawyer; b. St. Joseph, Mo., May 27, 1922; s. Louis and Miriam (Saferstein) K.; student St. Joseph Jr. Coll., 1940-41; B.S. in Fgn. Service, Georgetown U., 1948, J.D., 1950; m. Elaine Shirley Kaufman, June 11, 1944; children—Hugh David, Karen Gail and Kathy Jane (twins). Admitted to Mo. bar, 1950, U.S. Supreme Ct. bar, 1955; partner firm Kranitz & Kranitz, P.C., St. Joseph, 1950—. Active Boy Scouts; pres. St. Joseph Community Theatre, Inc., 1958-60; bd. dirs. United Jewish Fund of St. Joseph, 1957—, pres., 1958-63; sec. Boys' Baseball St. Joseph, 1964-68; trustee Temple Adath Joseph, 1970-74, 77-80; bd. dirs. B'nai Sholem Temple, 1976—, Lyric Opera Guild of Kansas City, 1980—. Served from pvt. to 1st lt. USAAF, 1942-46, ret. capt. USAF Res. Fellow Am. Acad. Matrimonial Lawyers; mem. Am. Legion, Air Force Assn., Res. Officers Assn., Am., St. Joseph (pres. 1977-78) bar assns., Mo. Bar, Am. Trial Lawyers Assn., Mo. Trial Lawyers Assn., Am. Soc. Internat. Law, Nat. Assn. Criminal Def. Lawyers. Mem. B'nai B'rith (dist. bd. govs. 1958-61). Author articles in field. Home: 2609 Gene Field Rd Saint Joseph MO 64506 Office: Boder Bldg 107 S 4th St Saint Joseph MO 64501

KRANTZ, BEATRICE V., ednl. adminstr.; b. Chgo.; d. Andrew S. and Beatrice K.; B.A., Lake Forest Coll.; M.A. in Public Law, Columbia U.; postgrad. Northwestern U., 1944-60, U. Ill., 1960-62, No. Ill. U., 1964, Ill. Inst. Tech., 1969. Formerly adminstrv. asst. to lawyer, Chgo.; tchr. social studies Deerfield (Ill.) Shields High Sch.; tchr. govt., econs. and history High Sch. Dist. 218, Blue Island, Ill., 1936-47; asst. county supt. schs., dir. tchr. personnel and placement Cook County Schs., Chgo., 1947-51, asst. supt. secondary edn., scholarships, guidance, 1967-70, asst. supt. in charge West area Ednl. Service Region, Cook County, 1970—; adminstrv. asst. to supt. Dist. 88, Du Page County, 1951-59, dean of girls, Elmhurst, Ill., 1960-66; ednl. cons., 1974—. Past mem. exec. com. Heart Assn. W. Cook Regions for County. Recipient Distinguished Alumni award Lake Forest Coll., 1976. Mem. NEA, Am. Assn. Sch. Adminstrs., No. Ill. Supts. Round Table, Pan Hellenic Assn., Delta Kappa Gamma, Alpha Xi Delta. Research in field. Office: 1032 Washington Blvd Oak Park IL 60302

KRAPF, F. DANIEL, nursing home adminstr.; b. Dayton, Ohio, May 9, 1942; s. Ordell L. and Mary Ann (Kirk) K.; B.S., U. Dayton, 1964, M.B.A., 1967; postgrad. U. Cin., 1970-71; m. Margaret Mary Dahm, Jan. 31, 1970; children—Michael, Douglas, Ryan. Surg. technician St. Elizabeth Med. Center, Dayton, 1960-66; grad. asst. U. Dayton, 1966-67; market research analyst Winters Bank, Dayton, 1967-68; adminstrv. asst. Good Samaritan Hosp., Dayton, 1968-69, asst. adminstr., 1969-70; cons., acting exec. dir. Marion (Ohio) Health Found., 1971-72; asst. adminstr. profl. services, Marion Gen. Hosp., 1971-73, asso. adminstr., 1973-74; exec. dir. Maria-Joseph Living Care Center, Dayton, 1974—. Trustee, Stillwater Health Center, 1980—; bd. dirs. Greater Miami Valley Health Systems Agy., 1975-80; mem. Ohio State-Wide Health Coordinating Council, 1975-80. Mem. Am. Coll. Hosp. Adminstrs., Ohio Hosp. Assn., Assn. Ohio Philanthropic Homes for Aging, Dayton Area Nursing Home Assn., Cath. Health Assn. Roman Catholic. Home: 298 Vintage Pl Dayton OH 45415 Office: Maria Joseph Living Care Center 4830 Salem Ave Dayton OH 45416

KRASNAPOLSKY, YURI, condr.; ed. Tanglewood, Juilliard Sch. Music; pvt. study, Vienna. Asst. condr. N.Y. Philharmonic, condr. orchs. Wolf Trap, Vancouver Internat. Festival, also orchs. of Tulsa, Okla. Miami, Fla., Omaha, Bklyn. Philarm.; now music dir., condr. Des Moines Symphony; numerous tours Europe and U.S. Ford Found. fellow. Recs. EMI Records. Address: Des Moines Symphony Orch Employers Mut Bldg Des Moines IA 50309*

KRAUS, HERBERT MYRON, public relations counsel; b. Cleve., Sept. 21, 1921; s. Joseph Emil and Eva (Meyers) K.; B.A., U. Ill., 1941; m. Catherine Eugenia Capraro, Mar. 5, 1955; 1 dau., Claudia Willa; 1 dau. by previous marriage, Gale Ann Kraus Bier. Editor, Community Papers, Chgo., 1947-48; account exec. Howard Mayer & Asso., Chgo., 1948; dir. public relations State of Israel Bonds, 1951-54; pres. Herbert M. Kraus & Co., Chgo., 1954-73; chmn. Beveridge, Kraus, Robbins & Manning, Chgo., 1973-75; pres. Manning, Selvage & Lee, Chgo., 1975-81; chmn. bd. Manning, Selvage & Lee/Mid-Am., Chgo., 1981—; instr. public relations Columbia Coll., Chgo., 1978-80. Bd. dirs. Victory Gardens Theatre, 1979—, Clarence Darrow Center, 1958; co-chmn. Clarence Darrow Commemorative Com., 1958—; del. Republican Conv., 1980. Served with U.S. Army, 1942-46. Decorated Purple Heart, Bronze Star medal. Mem. Public Relations Soc. Am. (founder, 1st pres. Chgo. chpt. counselors acad. 1968-69), Chgo. Press Vets. Assn. Republican. Clubs: Chgo. Press, Publicity of Chgo. Home: 415 Aldine St Chicago IL 60657 Office: 233 N Michigan Ave Chicago IL 60601

KRAUS, KURT DANIEL, city ofcl.; b. Massillon, Ohio, May 8, 1950; s. Clarence L. and Rita Jean K.; B.S. in Edn., Kent State U., 1973; M.S. in Recreation, Ind. U., 1974; m. Janice Nelson, Oct. 5, 1974; 1 son, Benjamin. Asst. youth dir. YMCA, Massillon, 1968-70; asst. dir. parks and recreation City of Barberton (Ohio), 1973-74; dir. parks and recreation City of Eastlake (Ohio), 1974—. Mem. Nat. Recreation and Parks Assn., Ohio Parks and Recreation Assn., Am. Parks Assn. Office: 35150 Lake Shore Blvd East Lake OH 44094

KRAUSE, ARTHUR WALTER, mfg. co. exec.; b. Milw., Jan. 2, 1919; s. Arthur R. and Selma (Kruse) K.; student U. Wis., evening div., 1947-56; m. Margaret E. Keller, June 21, 1941; 1 dau., Lynn Margaret. Asst. gen. mgr. Delta Mfg. Co., Milw., 1950-54; works mgr. Rockwell Mfg. Co., Pitts., 1954-55; chief methods engr. Controls Co. Am., 1955-59; gen. mgr. Hydraulic Machinery Co., Waukesha, Wis., 1959-62, v.p. fabricated metal products, 1962-64; pres. Hydraulic Power Equipment Corp., Milw., 1964-71; dir. br. ops. Pettibone Corp., Chgo., 1971-80, dir. corp. communications, 1980-81; pres. Pettibone Wis. Corp., Milw., 1971-81; v.p., gen. mgr. Rose Co., Milw., 1981—. Served with USMC, 1944-46. Republican. Lutheran. Home: 4532 W Fountain Ave Brown Deer WI 53223 Office: 7044 N Teutonia Ave Milwaukee WI 53209

KRAUSE, JOHN WHITNEY, crop scientist; b. Whittier, Calif., Nov. 23, 1949; s. O. John and Ruth Ellen (Nemoede) K.; B.S., Calif. Poly. State U., San Luis Obispo, 1977; M.S., Kans. State U., 1980. Asst. mgr. Kans. Crop Improvement Assn., Manhattan, 1981—. Served with USCGR, 1968-74. Mem. AAAS, Am. Genetic Assn., Crop Sci. Soc. Am., Smithsonian Instn., Am. Soc. Agronomy, Nat. Geog. Soc. Club: Lions. Office: Kans Crop Improvement Assn 205 Call Hall Kans State U Manhattan KS 66506

KRAUSE, WERNER WILLIAM, plastics co. exec.; b. Milw., Jan. 16, 1937; s. Erhard Werner and Mary T. (Kojis) K.; B.B.A., U. Wis., Milw., 1958; M.B.A., U. Chgo., 1971; m. Susan Mary Kramer, Mar. 29, 1958; children—Patricia Ann, David, Steven. Auditor, Arthur Andersen & Co., Milw., 1958-61; corporate cost mgr. Jewett & Sherman Co., Milw., 1961-63; sr. fin. analyst Miller Brewing Co., Milw., 1963-66; mgr. capital planning Allis Chalmers, Inc., West Allis, Wis., 1966-72; exec. v.p. Vinyl Plastics, Inc., Sheboygan, Wis., 1972—; instr. Mgmt. Inst., U. Wis. Extension. Bd. dirs. Milw. County Girl Scouts Am., 1970-72, Sheboygan Community Players, 1975-78. C.P.A., Wis. Mem. Wis. Soc. C.P.A.'s, Planning Execs. Inst., Asso. Industries and Mfrs. (dir., past chmn.). Clubs: Rotary, Sheboygan Yacht (officer). Office: Vinyl Plastics Inc 3123 S 9th St Sheboygan WI 53081

KRAUSEN, ANTHONY SHARNIK, physician, surgeon; b. Phila., Feb. 22, 1944; s. B. Morton and Kay S. (Hoffman) K.; A.B., Princeton U., 1965; M.D., U. Mich., 1969; m. Susan Park, Sept. 6, 1970; children—Nicole, Allison. Rotating intern Presbyn. Med. Center, Denver, 1969-70; surg. resident St. Joseph Hosp., Denver, 1970-71; resident in otolaryngology Washington U., St. Louis, 1972-76, Barnes and Affiliated Hosps., 1972-76; practice medicine specializing in otolaryngology and facial reconstructive surgery, Milw., 1976—; clin. instr. dept. otolaryngology Med. Coll. Wis., Milw., 1976-81; head and neck surgeon Milw. Med. Clinic, 1976—. Served with N.G., 1970-76. Diplomate Am. Bd. Otolaryngology. Fellow ACS; mem. Am. Acad. Otolaryngology, Am. Council Otolaryngology, Am. Acad. Facial Plastic and Reconstructive Surgery, Milw. Soc. Head and Neck Surgery, Wis. Otolaryn. Soc., Soc. Univ. Otolaryngologists. Republican. Contbr. articles to med. jours. Home: 6820 N Barnett Milwaukee WI 53217 Office: 3003 W Good Hope Rd Milwaukee WI 53209

KRAUSMAN, ARTHUR HENRY, hardware chain exec.; b. Chgo., 1913; grad. Northwestern U., 1936; m. Jean Appelgren, Sept. 21, 1945; children—Jeff, Andrea Buck. Formerly v.p., gen. mgr. Ace Hardware Corp., Chgo., now pres., chmn. bd. Past pres. Am. Field Services (Park Ridge chpt.). Mem. S. Park Ch., Park Ridge, Ill. Clubs: Park Ridge Country, Housewares of Chgo., Central States Hardware. Office: Ace Hardware Corp 2200 Kensington Ct Oak Brook IL 60521

KRAUSS, ALAN ROBERT, physicist; b. Chgo., Oct. 3, 1943; s. Paul and Shirley (Shapiro) K.; B.S., U. Chgo., 1965; postgrad. Columbia U., 1965-66; M.S., Purdue U., 1968, Ph.D., 1971; m. Julie Emelie Rosado, Aug. 28, 1965; 1 dau., Susan. Research asso. U. Chgo., 1971-74; staff physicist Argonne (Ill.) Nat. Lab., 1974—; cons. to Dept. of Energy, 1979—. Mem. Am. Phys. Soc., Am. Vacuum Soc. (publicity chmn. fusion tech. div. 1980-81), Simga Pi Sigma. Club: Downers Grove Camera (sec. 1979-81). Contbr. articles on quantum physics and surface emission to sci. jours. Office: Argonne Nat Lab 9700 S Cass Ave Argonne IL 60439

KRAVETZ, RUSSELL STUART, psychiatrist; b. Lexington, Ky., July 22, 1930; s. Louis and Florence (Byer) K.; B.S., U. Cin., 1950, M.D., 1954; m. Alberta Lee Mayer, May 7, 1959; children—Dayna Ilene, Todd Michael. Rotating intern Cin. Gen. Hosp., 1954-55, jr. resident dept. internal medicine, 1957-58, asst. resident dept. psychiatry, 1958-60, clin. fellow psychosomatic medicine dept. psychiatry, 1960-61, clinician depts. internal medicine and psychiatry, outpatient dept., 1961—, asst. attending psychiatrist, 1961—; practice medicine specializing in psychiatry, Cin., 1961—; asst. dir. psychiat. clinic City Cin. Municipal Ct., 1961-62; asst. clin. prof. dept. psychiatry U. Cin. Coll. Medicine, 1967-73, asso. clin. prof., 1973—; attending staff dept. psychiatry Jewish Hosp., Cin.; active staff dept. neuropsychiatry Christ Hosp., Cin. Trustee Central Psychiat. Clinic, 1973—, Glen Manor Home for Aged. Served as lt. M.C., USNR, 1955-57. Diplomate in psychiatry Am. Bd. Psychiatry and Neurology. Mem. Cin. Acad. Medicine, Cin. Soc., Am., Ohio psychiat. assns., AMA, Ohio Acad. Neurology and Psychiatry, Phi Beta Kappa, Alpha Omega Alpha. Home: 9000 Old Indian Hill Rd Cincinnati OH 45243 Office: 2607 Burnet Ave Cincinnati OH 45219

KRAWIEC, JOHN (JAN) FRANCIS, newspaper editor; b. Bachorzec, Poland, June 15, 1919; came to U.S., 1949; naturalized, 1957; B.S. in Polit. Sci., Loyola U., 1963. Served with Polish Army, 1939, with Polish Underground, 1939-43; interned at Auschwitz-Birkenau and Buchenwald, 1943-45; on staff Polish newspapers in Germany, 1945-49; laborer Canfield Beverage Co., Chgo., 1950-59; city editor Polish Daily News, Chgo., 1959-63; bailiff Cook County Criminal Ct., Chgo., 1963-67; social worker Cook County Jail, 1967—; editor-in-chief Polish Daily Zgoda (Dziennik Zwiazkowy), Chgo., 1968—. Address: 6100 N Cicero Ave Chicago IL 60646

KREAMER, JOHN HARRISON, lawyer; b. Downs, Kans., Sept. 12, 1922; s. John Dean and Catherine (Harrison) K.; A.B., U. Kans., 1946; J.D., Harvard U., 1949; m. Marion Jane Enggas, July 28, 1951; children—Jane Kreamer Meyer, Anne Enggas Andersen. Admitted to Mo. bar, 1949; mng. partner Gage & Tucker and predecessor firms, Kansas City, 1959—; instr. carriers U. Mo. at Kansas City Sch. Law, 1952-54; dir. Parmelee Industries, Commerce Bank, Realex Corp., Interstate Oil Co., Kansas City. Pres., bd. dirs. Mid-Am. Comprehensive Health Planning, 1973-76; bd. dirs., pres. Pub. TV 19, Inc., 1973-78; bd. dirs. Starlight Theater Assn., Mo. Arts Council, Acad. Health Scis.; trustee U. Mo. at Kansas City, Midwest Research Inst. Served to 1st lt., inf. AUS, 1942-45. Decorated Purple Heart, Bronze Star. Mem. Greater Kansas City C. of C. (dir. 1964-68, 72-75, v.p. 1964-68), U. Kans. Meml. Assn. (pres. 1965-66), Lawyers Assn. K.C. (pres. 1964-65), Internat., Am. bar assns., World Assn. Lawyers, Edn. Com. States, Beta Theta Pi, Pi Sigma Alpha. Clubs: Rotary; University (pres. 1963), Kansas City Country (dir. 1968-70), River. Home: 1246 W 59th St Kansas City MO 64113 Office: 2345 Grand Ave Kansas City MO 64106

KREBS, WILLIAM HOYT, auto co. exec.; b. Detroit, Apr. 6, 1938; s. William Thomas and Mary Louise (Hoyt) K.; B.S., U. Mich., 1960, M.P.H. in Indsl. Health, 1963, M.S., 1965, Ph.D., 1970; children—Elizabeth Louise, William Thomas II. Indsl. hygienist Kemper Ins. Group, Chgo., 1963-64; indsl. hygienist Gen. Motors Corp., Detroit, 1970-77, mgr. toxic materials control activity, 1977-81, dir. toxic materials control activity, 1981—. Mem. health and safety com. Detroit Area council Boy Scouts Am., 1980—; trustee Grosse Pointe Meml. Ch., 1978-81. USPHS grantee, 1962, 64-70. Mem. Am. Acad. Indsl. Hygiene, AAAS, Am. Indsl. Hygiene Assn., Brit. Occupational Hygiene Soc., Mich. Indsl. Hygiene Soc., N.Y. Acad. Scis., Soc. Occupational and Environ. Health. Presbyterian. Home: 529 Notre Dame Grosse Pointe MI 48230 Office: 3044 W Grand Blvd Detroit MI 48202

KREBS, WILLIAM PAUL, mgmt. cons.; b. Sioux City, July 19, 1928; s. Claude Gottlieb and Edna Louise K.; B.S.C., U. Iowa, 1952; m. Corinne Ann Brockmeier, Dec. 20, 1958; children—Leslie, Alison, Thomas. Home office rep., Group and Pension div. Aetna Life & Casualty Co., various locations, 1952-67; mgr. Life and Group Dept., Youngberg-Carlson Co., Chgo., 1967-68; cons. employee benefit plans, Chgo., 1968-70; sr. cons. Johnson & Higgins, 1970-72; mng. partner Krebs & Sisler, mgmt. cons.'s, Chgo., 1972—. Served with USN, 1946-48, USAFR, 1952-57. Mem. Planning Execs. Inst. Home: 315 Poplar St Winnetka IL 60093 Office: Krebs & Sisler 209 S LaSalle St Chicago IL 60604

KRECH, EDWARD M., JR., consumer products co. exec.; b. Paterson, N.J., June 28, 1932; s. Edward M. and Virginia (Pardee) K.; B.M.E., Cornell U., 1955, M.B.A., 1958; m. Joan Gras, Nov. 1, 1953; children—Susan, Edward, Kathleen. With internat. engring. dept. Procter & Gamble Co., 1958—, sect. head European Tech. Center, Brussels, 1966-70, mgr. design and constrn. Procter & Gamble Ltd., Newcastle, Eng., 1970-75, asso. dir. engring. for Asia and Latin Am., Cin., 1975-79, asso. dir. internat. project mgmt. and constrn., 1979—; instr. U.S. Naval Acad., Annapolis, Md., 1955-57. Active, Friends of Cin. Ballet. Served with USN, 1955-57. Mem. ASME, Cornell Soc. Engrs., Royal Yachting Assn. Partial ascent of Mt. Everest, Nepal, 1978; diving expdn. Truk Lagoon, Micronesia, 1979, 81. Office: Procter & Gamble 6060 Center Hill Rd Cincinnati OH 45224

KRECKE, CHARLES FRANCIS, radiologist; b. Detroit, Dec. 24, 1926; s. Norman W. and Frances Maria (Currie) K.; student U. Notre Dame, 1944-45; B.S., U. Mich., 1948, M.D., 1953; m. Anne Elizabeth McKamy, May 18, 1957; children—Karl Norman, Paul Raymond, Kathryn Anne. Intern, Blodgett Meml. Hosp., Grand Rapids, Mich., 1953-54; resident, Henry Ford Hosp., Detroit, 1954-57; practice medicine specializing in radiology, Birmingham, Mich., 1961-63; radiologist St. Mary's Hosp., Grand Rapids, Mich., 1963—, dir. radiology, 1968-81, vice chief of staff, 1972-78; clin. asst. prof. medicine Mich. State U., 1971-76, clin. asso. prof. radiology, 1976—; pres. Drs. Krecke, Benson, Ashby and Assos., P.C., 1968—, Kent Radiologic Inst., P.C., 1976—. Served with USNR, 1944-46; with M.C., USAF, 1954-61. Diplomate Am. Bd. Radiology. Fellow Am. Coll. Radiology; mem. AMA, Radiol. Soc. N.Am., Mich. Radiol. Soc. (pres.-elect 1980-81). Episcopalian. Clubs: Peninsular, Kent Country. Home: 936 San Lucia Dr SE East Grand Rapids MI 49506 Office: 220 Medical Arts Bldg Grand Rapids MI 49502

KREER, HENRY BLACKSTONE, mktg. and assn. exec.; b. Pitts., Sept. 2, 1923; s. George William and Fay Palmer K.; student Princeton U., 1941-42, Northwestern U., 1946; m. Irene Overman, Dec. 22, 1946; children—Laurene, Linda (Mrs. Thomas Witt). Copy writer Batten, Barton, Durstine & Osborn, Chgo., 1947-51; account supr. Campbell-Mithun Inc., Chgo., 1951-55; owner Henry B. Kreer & Co., Chgo., 1955-68; partner, pres., dir. Stevens Kirkland, Kreer Inc., Chgo., 1968-78; chmn. McKinney/Mid Am., 1978—; pres. Nat. Accounts Mktg., Inc., 1975—; exec. dir. REACT Internat., Inc., 1962-81. Chmn. radio subcom. Nat. Industry Adv. Com. FCC, 1967-73. Served to capt. USMCR, 1942-45. Decorated D.F.C., Air medal with 4 clusters. Home: 1904 Glen Oak Dr Glenview IL 60025 Office: 111 E Wacker Dr Chicago IL 60601

KREGEL, ANNA MAY, piano tchr.; b. Nebraska City, Nebr., Apr. 11, 1916; d. Robert W. and Ann (Kerrick) Kregel; B.A. cum laude, Mo. Valley Coll., 1938, Mus.B., 1939; M. Music Edn., U. Mo., Kansas City, 1976. Tchr. high sch., DeWitt, Mo., 1938-39, Kidder, Mo., 1940-42; with Kansas City Star, 1942-44; secretarial position Trans World Airlines, 1945, Thompson Hayward Chem., 1946, Johnson Sales, 1948; exec. sec. Line Material Co., 1949-51, Kansas City Philharmonic, 1951-52, City Plan Dept., Kansas City, Mo., 1952-60; tchr. Woods Studio, 1963-65, Pauline Wright Studio, 1966-70; ch. organist First Ch. rhrist Scientist, Merriam, Kans., 1954-59, 73—; pvt. tchr. piano, organ and harmony, Kansas City, Mo., 1961—; piano and organ judge Mid Am. Festival, 1966-68; free-lance organist, 1979—. Judge Spl. Olympics Music and Art Festival, 1976, 77, 78, 79, 80 organizer 1st state-wide competition, 1979. Mem. Music Tchrs. Nat. Assn., Mo., Kansas City music tchrs. assn., Federated Tchrs. of Music and Fine Arts Greater Kansas City, Nat. Secs. Assn. (editor Rainbow chapt. 1948-50), Certified Profl. Secs. Christian Scientist. Home: PO Box 4853 Kansas City MO 64109

KREHBIEL, DAVID GORDON, cons. engr.; b. Clinton, Mo., Sept. 22, 1939; s. Gordon August and Helen Louise (Smith) K.; B.S., U. Mo., Columbia, 1961, M.S., 1964; m. Dana Kay Hatcher, Aug. 25, 1962; children—Darren David, Dawn Ann. Engr., Krehbiel Constrn. Co., Columbia, Mo., 1964-65; co-founder, pres. Mo. Engring. Corp., Rolla, Camdenton, 1965-69; pres. Krehbiel Engring., Inc., Camdenton, 1969—. Surveyor, Camden County, 1977—. Served with U.S. Army, 1962-64. Rotary Club grantee, 1969. Mem. Mo. Assn. Registered Land Surveyors (pres., 1978), Am. Congress Surveying and Mapping, Nat. Soc. Profl. Engrs., Mo. Soc. Profl. Engrs. Republican. Baptist. Club: Rotary (pres., Camdenton, 1978-79). Home: 438 W Hwy 54 Camdenton MO 65020 Office: Krehbiel Engring Inc 109 Blair Ave Camdenton MO 65020

KREININ, MORDECHAI ELIAHU, economist, educator; b. Tel Aviv, Israel, Jan. 20, 1930; came to U.S., 1951, naturalized, 1960; B.A., U. Tel Aviv, 1951; M.A., U. Mich., 1952, Ph.D., 1954; m. Marlene Miller, Aug. 29, 1956; children—Tamar, Elana, Miriam. Office mgr. Efroni Advt., Israel, 1950-51; research asst. dept. econs. U. Mich., Ann Arbor, 1952-53, asst. study dir. Survey Research Center, 1954-55, study dir., 1955-56, lectr. econs., U. Mich., 1956-57; asst. prof. econs. Mich. State U., East Lansing, 1957-59, asso. prof., 1959-61, prof., 1961—; vis. prof. econs. UCLA, summer 1969, U. So. Calif., Los Angeles, summer, 1974, N.Y. U., summer, 1975, U. Hawaii, Honolulu, summer, 1977, U. Toronto (Ont., Can.), summer, 1978; vis. scholar Inst. for Internat. Econ. Studies, U. Stockholm (Sweden), 1978-80; world lectr. tours on behalf USIA, 1974-78; cons. to U.S. Dept. Commerce, 1964-66, U.S. Dept. State, 1972-74, UN, Council on Fgn. Relations, N.Y., 1965-67, Brookings Inst., 1972-75, Central Am. Common Market, 1972-75, IMF, 1976, various bus. corps, 1960-80. Recipient Disting. Faculty award Mich. State U., 1968; NSF fellow, 1964-73, Ford Found. fellow, 1960-61. Mem. Am. Econ. Assn., Midwest Econ. Assn., Western Econ. Assn., AAUP. Jewish. Author: Israel and Africa: A Study in Technical Cooperation, 1964; Alternative Commercial Policies—Their Effects on the American Economy, 1967; International Economics-A Policy Approach, 3d edit., 1979; Trade Relations of the EEC-An Empirical Investigation, 1974; (with L. Officer) The Monetary Approach to the Balance of Payments: A Survey, 1978; contbr. articles to profl. jours. Home: 1431 Sherwood St East Lansing MI 48823 Office: Econ Dept Mich State Univ East Lansing MI 48824

KREISER, FRANK DAVID, real estate exec.; b. Mpls., Sept. 20, 1930; s. Harry D. and Olive W. (Quist) K.; student U. Minn., 1950-51; m. Patricia Williams, Aug. 23, 1973; children—Sally, Frank David, Susan, Paul, Mark, Patti, Richard. Founder, owner Frank Kreiser Real Estate, Inc., Mpls., 1966—, pres., 1979—; partner, founder B & K Properties Co., Mpls., 1976—; chmn. bd., founder Transfer Location Corp., Atlanta, 1979—. Served with U.S. Army, 1948-50, Korea. Certified resdl. specialist and resdl. broker. Mem. Nat. Assn. Realtors, Mpls. Bd. Realtors (dir. 1972), St. Paul Bd. Realtors, Dakota County Bd. Realtors, Minn. Assn. Realtors, Realtors Nat. Mktg. Inst., Employers Relocation Council. Lutheran. Club: Decathlon Athletic. Address: 5036 France Ave S Minneapolis MN 55410

KREMER, MAURICE A., state legislator; b. Milford, Nebr., Aug. 31, 1907; grad. Farm Operators Coll. Agr., Lincoln, Nebr.; m. Alice M. Troyer, June 12, 1932; children—Kenneth D., Robert M., Adrys Ann Roszhart, Beth Lorraine Stucky. Farmer, stockman; partner Kremer Constrn. Co., Aurora, Nebr.; mem. Nebr. Legislature, 1964—. Former mem. and pres. Aurora Sch. Bd.; former mem. Hamilton County Extension Bd.; former chmn. Hamilton County Irrigation Assn., former Nebr. rep. High Plains Study of Ogalalla Aquifer; former mem. Nebr. Boundary Commn. Mem. Aurora C. of C., Nebr. Dairymen's Assn. (dir.), Gideons Internat. Office: 1122 13th St Aurora NE 68818*

KREMIDAS, JOHN PETER, metall. research co. exec.; b. Patras, Greece, Jan. 4, 1948; s. Peter J. and Maria J. (Milissis) K.; came to U.S., 1970, naturalized, 1981; B.Sc., Wheaton Coll., 1973; M.Sc., U. Minn., 1975; D.Sc., Nat. Tech. U., Athens, 1976; m. Irene Matsoukas, Aug. 28, 1970; children—Damaris M., Chloe C., Peter J. Sr. research engr. minerals and metals group Cities Service Research and Devel. Center, Cranbury, N.J., 1975-77; sect. head metall. dept. Armak Research and Devel. Co., McCook, Ill., 1977—; cons. on cement, extractive-nuclear metallurgy, math., 1975—. Served with Greek Army, 1968-70, NSF grantee, 1973-75. Mem. AIME, Metall. Soc., Can. Inst. Mining and Metall. Engrs., Instn. Mining and Metallurgy, Soc. Mining, Petroleum and Metallurgy Engrs. Democrat. Evang. Christian. Contbr. numerous sci. articles to profl. jours. Patentee in field. Home: 511 N Stoddard Ave Wheaton IL 60187 Office: Metall Dept Armak Research & Devel Co 8401 W 47th St McCook IL 60525

KRENZ, DEAN ALBERT, newspaper pub.; b. Wheaton, Minn., Apr. 6, 1930; s. Albert Herman and Mabel Victoria (Carlson) K.; B.A., U. Minn., 1952; m. Joan Janet Utley, Dec. 31, 1955; 1 son, Keith Allen. Asst. pub. Delaware County Daily Times, Chester, Pa., 1964-66; pub. The Trentonian, Trenton, N.J., 1966-73, Daily Jour., Elizabeth, N.J., 1973-75, Sioux City (Iowa) Newspapers, Inc., 1975—; v.p. ops. Ingersoll Newspapers, 1970-73. Bd. dirs. St. Luke's Med. Center, Sioux City, 1975-79. Served with U.S. Army, 1952-54. Decorated Army Commendation medal. Mem. Iowa Daily Press Assn. (dir.), Sioux City C. of C. (v.p. 1979). Republican. Lutheran. Office: Sioux City Newspapers Inc 515 Pavonia St Sioux City IA 51102*

KREPS, GEORGE MILTON, adminstr., educator; b. Pottstown, Pa., Dec. 30, 1931; s. John Andrew and Elizabeth (Hess) K.; student Pa. State U., 1949, U. Minn., 1951, Iowa State U., 1951-53; B.S., Manchester Coll., 1955; Th.M., Bethany Sem., 1963; M.A., Ohio State U., 1971, Ph.D., 1977; m. Martha Woolson, June 10, 1978; children—Susan Luddy, Barbara LeVora, Teresa Lightner, J. Scott LeVora, Steven M., Bradford T. LeVora, Joel A. Ordained to ministry Ch. of the Brethren, 1955; research aide U. Minn., 1950; agrl. missionary Ch. of the Brethren, 1955-57; exec. sec. United Andean Mission and Brethren in Ecuador, 1959-70; grad. instr. Ohio State U., Columbus, 1970-72, asst. prof. social scis., dept. coordinator Agrl. Tech. Inst., Wooster, 1978—; dir. vol. ser. Franklin County Children Services, 1972-78; World Neighbors rep. for Ecuador; cons. mgmt. and human relations seminars. Advisor Peace Corps tng. Ecuador; co-founder Cath./Protestant clergy group Quito, Ecuador, 1968; asst. dir. county levy renewal campaigns; bd. dirs. United Christian Center, Ohio State U., Friendship Village, Columbus; vol. counselor; condr. internat. study seminars to Ecuador, Haiti. Recipient distinguished alumni award Manchester Coll., 1975. Mem. Am. Sociol. Assn. Rural Sociol. Assn. N.Central Sociol. Assn., Wayne County Psychol. Assn., Am. Assn. Vol. Service Adminstrs., Ohio State Alumni Assn., Mid Ohio Assn. Vol. Service Adminstrs., Gamma Sigma Delta. Research on rural crime rate and environment; author study guide: Empowering Christians for Action, 1977; co-author research bulletin on rural crime, 1976. Home: 841 Buchholz Wooster OH 44691 Office: Agricultural Technical Institute Wooster OH 44691

KRESGE, STANLEY SEBASTIAN, found. exec.; b. Detroit, June 11, 1900; s. Sebastian Spering and Anna Emma (Harvey) K.; A.B., Albion (Mich.) Coll., 1923; m. Dorothy Eloise McVittie, Oct. 2, 1923; children—Walter H., Stanley Sebastian, Bruce Anderson. With S.S. Kresge Co., 1923-77, store mgr., 1927-28, various positions in main office, 1930-45, dir., 1950—; trustee Kresge Found., Troy, Mich., 1931—, pres., 1952-66, chmn. bd., 1966—. Del. Republican Nat. Conv., 1948, 52; emeritus trustee Albion Coll.; hon. dir. Detroit YMCA. Methodist. Clubs: Detroit, Detroit Athletic. Author: S.S. Kresge, 1979. Home: 1071 Lake Angelus Rd W Pontiac MI 48055 Office: 2401 W Big Beaver Rd Troy MI 48084

KRESSIN, EILEEN KAY, telephone co. sales mgr.; b. Port Washington, Wis., July 1, 1950; d. Harold Frederick and Emma Helen (Nierode) K.; B.S.B.A. in Mktg., Central Mo. State U., 1974. Directory rep. Southwestern Bell Yellow Pages, Kansas City, Mo., 1975-76, directory sales supr., 1976-78, staff mgr. directory premises tng., St. Louis, 1978-80, dist. mgr. directory telephone sales and clerical, Kansas City, 1980—; lectr. bus. Central Mo. State U. Organist, Sunday Sch. tchr. Luth. Ch. Named Miss Exec., Central Mo. State U. Bus. Sch., 1973. Mem. Am. Mktg. Assn. (v.p. St. Louis chpt. 1980). Republican. Author tng. manual. Office: 1425 Oak St Room 1505 Kansas City MO 64106

KREUL, RICHARD, state senator; b. Mt. Ida, Wis., Apr. 26, 1924; grad. high sch.; married; 5 children. Farmer; real estate broker; mem. Wis. Senate, 1978—. Mem. Fennimore Sch. Bd., 1953-78; bd. control Coop. Ednl. Services Agy., 1970-78; county jury commr., 1966-78. Mem. Farm Bur., Fennimore C. of C. Clubs: Masons, Kiwanis, Elks. Office: Room 419 South State Capitol Madison WI 53702*

KREWSON, JAMES WILLARD, architect; b. St. Louis, Aug. 21, 1929; s. Oscar and Thelma Leola (Eleam) K.; B.S. in Archtl. Engring., Washington U., St. Louis, 1951; M.Arch., Columbia Pacific U., 1979, Ph.D. in Arch., 1980; m. Marcia Jean Malone, Mar. 23, 1966; children—James W., Paul David. Architect, Bell System, St. Louis, N.Y.C. and Los Angeles, 1951-70; architect, Indio, Calif., 1971-73, Chgo., 1973-74, St. Louis, 1964-65; prin. firm Jim Krewson AIA Architect, Hannibal, Mo., 1975—. Dist. chmn., mem. exec. bd. Gt. Rivers council Boy Scouts Am., 1975—; adv. St. Louis Jr. Achievement, 1953-54; coach and adv. Hannibal YMCA, 1975-76; mem. Citizens Adv. Bd., Hannibal Bd. Edn., 1979—; adv. Hannibal Vocat. Tech. Sch., 1976-79, Hist. Hannibal, 1976-78; bd. dirs. Hannibal Arts Council. Recipient Bausch & Lomb Hon. Sci. award, 1951; Danforth Found. award, 1951, 5 nat. design awards in architecture, 1956. Mem. Internat. Platform Assn., AIA, Nat. Com. Architects for Commerce and Industry, St. Louis Engrs. Club, Nat. Council Archtl. Registration Bds. Republican. Clubs: Kiwanis, St. Louis Met. Toastmasters, Hannibal Country. Home: 838 Country Club Dr Hannibal MO 63401 Office: 2333 Palmyra Rd Hannibal MO 63401

KREY, GENEVA MARGARET, educator; b. Hazel Green, Wis., June 6, 1927; d. Thomas J. and Myra (Lenstra) Aide; diploma in elementary edn. Platteville State Tchrs. Coll., 1947; B.S. in Elementary Edn., Wis. State Coll., Platteville, 1956; M.S., U. Wis. at Superior, 1974, postgrad., 1974—; m. Robert D. Krey, June 5, 1951; 1 son, Thomas Robert. Tchr. pub. schs., Reedsburg, Wis., 1947-51, Black Earth, Wis., 1953-54, Lake Geneva, Wis., 1954-68, Superior, Wis., 1969; tchr. adult basic edn. Indianhead Tech. Inst., Superior, 1970-71; instr. reading, dir. reading clinic U. Wis., Superior, 1974-77. Chmn. decorations Douglas County Assn. Retarded Children, 1970. Mem. Internat., Wis. reading assns., Lake Superior Reading Council, Assn. U. Wis. Faculties, Assn. Supervision and Curriculum Devel., U. Wis. Alumni Assn. (life), U. Wis. Platteville Alumni Assn. (life), Phi Delta Kappa. Home: 1107 18th St N Superior WI 54880

KREY, ROBERT DEAN, educator; b. Prairie du Sac, Wis., Mar. 23, 1929; s. Oscar L. and Paula M. (Müller) K.; student Carroll Coll., 1946-47; B.S., Wis. State Coll., Platteville, 1958; M.S. (fellow), U. Wis., Madison, 1967, Ph.D. (fellow), 1968; 1 son, Thomas Robert. Rural sch. tchr., Sauk County, Wis., 1948-51; tchr. public sch., Gays Mills, Wis., 1951-53, Black Earth, Wis., 1953-54, Central Sch., 1954-58, Denison Jr. High Sch., Lake Geneva, Wis., 1958-66; project asst. dept. ednl. adminstrn. U. Wis., Madison, 1967-68; prof. ednl. adminstrn. U. Wis., Superior, 1968—, chmn. dept. ednl. adminstrn. and counseling, 1978-80, chmn. div. edn., 1981—; ednl. cons. Educators Progress Service, Inc., 1972—. Bd. dirs. Wis. Adminstrn. Found., Inc., 1969-76. Cert. tchr., Wis. Mem. Assn. Supervision and Curriculum Devel. (dir. 1973-75, chmn. nominating com. 1979), Wis. Ednl. Research Assn. (publicity com. 1968—), Wis. Assn. Sch. Dist. Adminstrs., Nat. Soc. Study of Edn., Wis. Assn. Supervision and Curriculum Devel. (pres. 1973, dir. 1972-75), Council Profs. of Instructional Supervision (chmn. nomination com. 1977, 81), Phi Delta Kappa (chpt. pres. 1975-76), U. Wis. Alumni Assn., U. Wis.-Platteville Alumni Assn. Lutheran. Author: (with others) Interdisciplinary Foundations of Supervision, 1970, Supervision of Instruction, 2d edit., 1971; contbr. articles on supervision and pedagogy to profl. jours. Home: 4007 N 21st St Superior WI 54880 Office: Div Edn U Wis Superior WI 54880

KRIEGBAUM, ROBERT EDWARD, educator; b. Springfield, Ohio, Feb. 13, 1916; s. Edward John and Margaret Dorothy (Groeber) K.; B.A., Wittenberg U., 1939; M.A., Ohio State U., 1950; m. Muriel Amelia Schmenk, July 15, 1944; children—Dennis, Roger, Caryl. Tchr. bus. edn. Glandorf (Ohio) High Sch., 1939-43, Wapakoneta (Ohio) High Sch., 1946-50; instr. U. Dayton (Ohio), Sch. Bus., 1950, asst. prof., 1951, asso. prof., 1955, acting chmn. acctg., 1964-65, asst. to chmn. sec. edn. Sch. Edn., 1968-72, acting chmn. sec. edn., 1972-74, chmn., 1974-81, asso. prof. edn.; lectr. in field. Bd. dirs. Ohio Bus. and Office Council, 1973—; career acad. adv. bd. Dayton schs., 1977-81; adv. bd. Fairview High Sch., Bus. Edn. Dept., 1977-78; others. Recipient President's Recognition, U. Dayton, 1969-70; Data Processing Mgmt. Assn. Performance award, 1977; Adminstrv. Mgmt. Soc. Diamond Merit award, 1975; Nat. Cath. Bus. Edn. Service award, 1976; Delta Sigma Pi service award, 1970. Mem. Ohio Bus. Tchrs. Assn. (pres. 1957-58), Data Processing Mgmt. Assn. (pres. 1967-68), Adminstrv. Mgmt. Soc. (pres. 1968-69), Nat. Assn. Bus. Tchr. Edn., Internat. Soc. Bus. Edn., Cath. Bus. Edn. Assn. (exec. bd. Central region 1976-81, pres. Central region 1981-83), Acctg. Careers Council (regional control chmn. 1963-68), Am. Acctg. Assn., Ohio Regional Acctg. Assn. (area rep. 1963-66), Nat. Bus. Edn. Assn., Tri State Bus. Edn. Assn., Soc. Data Educators (editor Jour. Data Edn. 1964-74), Dayton Area Bus. Soc., Miami Valley Personnel and Guidance Assn., Assn. Tchr. Edn., Southwestern Ohio Assn. for Supervision and Curriculum Devel., Ohio Bus. and Office Council (dir. 1973-81), Phi Delta Kappa (founds. rep. 1978, pres. 1980-81), Delta Pi Epsilon (newsletter reporter 1978-79). Contbr. articles to profl. jours. Home: 4363 Trails End Dr Kettering OH 45429 Office: 300 College Park Dr Dayton OH 45469

KRIER, CURTIS GENE, acctg. and fin. cons.; b. Mpls., Aug. 11, 1948; s. Curtis George and Jeanne Dale K.; B.A., U. Minn., 1970, B.S.B., 1978; M.B.A., Mankato State U., 1978; m. Nancy D. Carlson, Sept. 1980. Asst. to bank ops. officer 3d. Northwestern Nat. Bank, Mpls., 1972-75; staff acct. Robert G. Engelhart & Co., Burnsville, Minn., 1978-79, House & Nezerka, C.P.A.'s, 1979-80; controller Calc-Type, Inc., Mpls., 1980-81; pres. Curtis G. Krier & Co., acctg. and fin. cons., Edina, Minn., 1981—. Cert., Am. Inst. Banking. Mem. Nat. Assn. Accts. Home and Office: 5817 Grove St Edina MN 55436

KRIKORIAN, ROBERT V., mfg. co. exec.; b. New Haven, 1919; B.S., Yale U., 1950. With Rexnord Inc., Milw., 1950—, v.p. constrn., 1962-63, exec. v.p., 1963-67, pres., 1967-78, vice chmn., chief exec. officer, 1978-80, chmn. bd., 1980—, also dir.; dir. Parker Pen Co., Mueller Co., Black & Decker Mfg. Co., Beloit Corp. Mem. Machinery and Allied Products Inst. (exec. com.). Office: Rexnord Inc 3500 First Wisconsin Center Milwaukee WI 53201*

KRIKORIAN, THOMAS MICHAEL, radio broadcast syndication co. exec.; b. Detroit, Oct. 18, 1951; s. George and Louise Zevart (Enokian) K.; B.S.B.A., Wayne State U., 1973. With Sta. WWWW, Detroit, 1968-69; program dir. Sta. WCAR, Detroit, 1969-70; FM music/program dir. Booth Broadcasting Co., Detroit, 1967-68, 70-73; pres. Radio Programming and Mgmt., Inc., Southfield, Mich., 1973—. Adv., Armenian Community Center, Dearborn, Mich.; pres. Plum Tree Subdiv. Assn., West Bloomfield, Mich. Mem. Nat. Assn. Broadcasters, Nat. Radio Broadcasters Assn. Mem. Republican Nat. Com. Armenian Orthodox. Home: 3750 Spanish Oaks Dr West Bloomfield MI 48033 Office: 25140 Lahser Rd Suite 232 Southfield MI 48034

KRISHEN, ALOK, statistician; b. Ludhiana, India, Mar. 14, 1952; came to U.S., 1973, naturalized, 1975; s. Viapak and Nirmal K.; B.Sc. with honors, Center for Advanced Study in Math., Panjab U., 1972, M.Sc. with honors, 1973; M.S. in Stats., Fla. State U., 1976; m. Dong Trieu, Sept. 10, 1977. Statistician Dept. Environ. Regulation, State of Fla., Tallahassee, 1976-78; statistician Searle Pharms., Skokie, Ill., 1978-79, Travenol Labs., Morton Grove, Ill., 1979—. Mem. Am. Statis. Assn., Biometric Soc., AAAS. Home: 821 N Howard Ave Elmhurst IL 60126 Office: 6301 Lincoln Ave Morton Grove IL 60053

KRISHNA, GOPAL T. K., engring. corp. exec.; b. Hyderabad, India, Feb. 16, 1947; s. Srinivas Achariar T.K. and Rajammal T.G.; B.E. in Elec. Engring., Osmania U., Hyderabad, 1968; M.S. in Elec. Engring., U. Kans., 1970; M.B.A., Drake U., 1973; postgrad. in Environ. Engring., Iowa State U., 1978—; m. Rajakumari Koovappadi, July 1, 1974; children—Alvin Srinivas, Dean Venkat. Design engr. Veenstra & Kimm, Engrs. and Planners, West Des Moines, Iowa, 1970-80; pres. Krishna Engring. Consultants, Inc., West Des Moines, 1980—. Mem. Assn. Elec. and Electronic Engrs., Assn. M.B.A. Execs., Nat. Soc. Profl. Engrs., Nat. Fire Protection Assn., Water Pollution Control Fedn., Am. Water Works Assn., Iowa Engring. Soc. (John Dunlap-Sherman Woodward award 1979, named Outstanding Young

Engr., Central Iowa chpt. 1979), Iowa Water Pollution Control Assn. Author papers in field. Home: 329 35th St West Des Moines IA 50265 Office: 1200 35th St Suite 409 West Des Moines IA 50265

KRISS, MITCHEL, mktg. exec.; b. Jamaica, N.Y., Nov. 20, 1951; s. Harold and Selma (Hack) K.; B.A., SUNY, Albany, 1973; M.A., Princeton U., 1975, Ph.D., 1977; m. Toby Inez Ridzinski, Jan. 4, 1975. Sr. research analyst Quaker Oats Co., Chgo., 1977-78, research supr., 1978-79, research mgr., 1979-82, group research mgr., 1982—. Recipient Nat. Research award Psi Chi, 1973; Harold Dodds fellow Princeton U., 1976-77. Mem. Am. Mktg. Assn., Soc. Advancement Social Psychology, Sigma Xi. Home: 940 Providence Ln Buffalo Grove IL 60090 Office: Merchandise Mart Plaza Chicago IL 60645

KRIST, DONALD EUGENE, ins. assn. exec.; b. Topeka, June 26, 1926; s. George M. and Florence (McInerny) K.; B.A., Drake U., 1951; m. Marilyn McClurkin, May 29, 1948; children—Lisa Ann, James Eric. Public relations dir. U.S. Jr. C. of C., 1953-55, Meredith Co., 1955-60; exec. v.p. Iowa Consumer Fin. Assn., 1960-66, Profl. Ins. Agts. Iowa, West Des Moines, 1973—; owner, mgr. Donald Krist & Assos., Inc., public relations consultants, Des Moines, 1966-73; instr., lectr. public relations Drake U., Des Moines, 1957-70. Served with USN, 1943-46. Cert. assn. exec. Recipient Outstanding Achievement award Iowa 1752 Club, 1980. Mem. Am. Soc. Assn. Execs. (Mgmt. Achievement award 1976), Iowa Soc. Assn. Execs., Smithsonian Instn. Assos. Clubs: Statesman's, Bohemian, Des Moines Press (Pres. 1959) (Des Moines). Editor Iowa Ins. Interpreter mag., 1973—. Home: 800 52d Ct West Des Moines IA 50265 Office: Valley Plaza Bldg West Des Moines IA 50265

KRISTO, JANICE VALERIE, educator; b. Worcester, Mass., Feb. 9, 1951; d. Joseph Adam and Alice Ann (Mazeika) K.; B.A. in English, Assumption Coll., Worcester, 1973; M.A. in Edn., Columbia U., 1974; Ph.D. in Elementary Edn., U. Conn., Storrs, 1979. Tchr., Attleboro, Mass., 1974-77; grad. asst. U. Conn., 1977-79; asst. prof. early and middle childhood edn. Ohio State U., Lima, 1979—; adv. bd. Allen County Right to Read Acad., 1980; speaker in field. Grantee Martha Holden Jennings Found., 1981. Mem. Internat. Reading Assn. (pres. Allen County council 1981—; scholar Conn. council 1978), Assn. Supervision and Curriculum Devel., Nat. Council Tchrs. English, Assn. Tchr. Educators, Assn. Childhood Edn. Internat., Ohio Assn. Edn. Young Children, Kappa Delta Pi, Phi Delta Kappa. Author articles in field. Home: 3528 Georgian Ave Apt B Lima OH 45806 Office: Ohio State U 4240 Campus Dr Lima OH 45804

KRISTOF, STEVAN J., agriculturist; b. Ruma, Yugoslavia, Aug. 31, 1915; B.S., Beograd U., 1941, M.S., 1942; Ph.D., 1954; M.S., Purdue U., 1962. Tchr., high sch., Belgrad, 1945, Mech. Tech. Sch., 1946, Sch. Agr., 1947-59; instr. Purdue U., West Lafayette, Ind., 1962-67, research agronomist, Lab. for Application Remote Sensing, 1966-80, research cons., 1981—. Mem. Yugoslav Acad. Scis. and Arts, Internat. Soc. Soil Scis., Soil Sci. Soc. Am., Am. Soc. Agronomy, Ind. Acad. Scis., Purdue U. Alumni Assn. Republican. Roman Catholic. Home: 123 Waldron St West Lafayette IN 47906 Office: 1220 Potter Dr West Lafayette IN 47906

KRIT, ROBERT LEE, devel. exec.; b. Chgo., Apr. 6, 1920; s. Jacob and Tania (Etzkowitz) K.; B.S. in Commerce, DePaul U., 1946; A.B.A., N. Park Coll., 1939; children—Melissa, Margaret, Justin. Dir. Chgo. Herald Am. Mercy Fleet charity drives, 1940-41; asst. exec. dir. cancer research found. U. Chgo., 1947-48; state campaign dir. Am. Cancer Soc., Inc., Chgo., 1948-63; dir. med. devel. U. Chgo., 1963-67; v.p. devel. U. Health Scis., Chgo. Med. Sch., 1967—. Moderator TV series Tension in Modern Living, Drug Abuse, Aging and Retirement, Health and Devel. Children, Cancer, Healthy Life Style, NBC-TV: host producer TV series Med. Looking Glass, Relevant Issues in Health and Medicine, Coping; mem. adv. bd. Central States Inst. for Addiction Services; v.p. Drug Abuse Council of Ill.; bd. dirs. Lawson YMCA, Chgo.; mem. advisory council Campfire Girls Met. Chgo. Served from pvt. to 1st lt., USAAF, 1942-46. Fellow Inst. Medicine Chgo. (co-chmn. com. on pub. info., mem. editorial bd. Proceedings); mem. Chgo. Soc. Fund Raising Execs. (pres. 1964-65), Chgo. Assn. Commerce and Industry (mem. health-in-industry com.), Nat. Acad. TV Arts and Scis. Home: 1139 Deerfield Rd Apt 1-B Deerfield IL 60015 Office: 233 S Wacker Dr Suite 5330 Chicago IL 60606

KRIVOSHA, NORMAN MARVIN, chief justice Nebr. Supreme Ct.; b. Detroit, Aug. 3, 1934; s. David B. and Molly Krivosha; B.S. in Law, U. Nebr., 1956, J.D., 1958; m. Helene Miriam Sherman, July 31, 1955; children—Terri Lynn, Rhonda Ann. Admitted to Nebr. bar; partner firm Ginsburg, Rosenberg, Ginsburg & Krivosha, Lincoln, Nebr., 1958-78; chief justice Nebr. Supreme Ct., Lincoln, 1978—; city atty. City of Lincoln, 1969-70; gen. counsel Lincoln Electric System, 1969-78, Lincoln Gen. Hosp., 1969-78; mem. Uniform Law Commn., 1973—. Pres. Lincoln council Camp Fire Girls, Congregation Tifereth Israel, Lincoln, Central States Region, United Synagogue of Am., bd. dirs. YMCA, Lincoln; Nebr. chmn. Israel Bonds; chmn. fund drive Lincoln Jewish Welfare Fedn.; mem. Lincoln Charter Revision Commn.; bd. dirs. Ramah Commn., Camp Ramah, Wis. Recipient Outstanding Jewish Leader award State of Israel Bonds, 1978. Mem. Am., Nebr. (chmn. com. procedure), Lincoln bar assns., Nebr. Assn. Trial Attys. (sec. 1961-64, v.p. 1964-65), Am. Trial Lawyers Assn., Am. Soc. Hosp. Attys., Am. Public Power Assn. (chmn. legal sect.), Lincoln C. of C. (bd. dirs.), Sigma Alpha Mu (nat. v.p.). Home: 2835 O'Reilly Dr Lincoln NE 68502 Office: State Capitol Suite 2214 Lincoln NE 68509

KROCH, CARL ADOLPH, retail book bus. exec.; b. Chgo., June 21, 1914; s. Adolph Alfred and Gertrude Marie (Horn) K.; B.A., Cornell U., 1935; m. Jeanette Kennelly, Aug. 12, 1939. With Kroch's Bookstore, Inc., Chgo., 1935-54, pres., 1950-54, also dir.; pres., chief exec. officer Kroch's & Brentano's, Inc., Chgo., 1954—, also dir.; pres., chief exec. officer Booksellers Catalog Service, Inc., Chgo., 1954—; dir. Nat. Blvd. Bank Chgo. Bd. dirs. Northwestern Meml. Hosp., Chgo., Better Bus. Assn. Chgo., Ill. Humane Soc., USO, Chgo., Center for Book, Library of Congress, Washington. Served to lt. USNR, 1942-45. Mem. Ill. Retail Mchts. Assn. (dir.), Am. Booksellers Assn. Clubs: Tavern, Univ. Chgo., Chgo. Yacht, Mid-Am., North Shore Country, Pauma Valley Country. Author: So Red The Nose, 1935. Office: 29 S Wabash Ave Chicago IL 60603

KROEMER, ELDON LAWRENCE, agronomist; b. Pawnee City, Nebr., Apr. 9, 1950; s. Lawrence Henry and Malinda Frieda K.; B.S., U. Nebr., Lincoln, 1972; diploma Land O'Lakes Mgmt. Sch., 1980; m. Ginger Lee Walgren, Dec. 30, 1972; children—Ryan Michael, Jeremy Alan. Farm hand, Dwight Lyon Co., Merna, Nebr., 1973-75; cons. agronomist Inter-Am. Labs., Cozad, Nebr., 1975-77; agronomist Farmers Union Coop., Pleasanton, Nebr., 1977—. Mem. Am. Soc. Agronomy. Republican. Presbyterian. Club: Elks. Home: 350 Northview Dr Kearney NE 68847 Office: Farmers Union Coop Pleasanton NE 68866

KROENING, CARL W., state senator; B.S., M.A., U. Minn.; m. Ruth; 6 children. Prin. high sch.; mem. Minn. Ho. of Reps., 1975-80, Minn. Senate, 1980—. Chmn. dist. Democratic-Farmer-Labor party, 1970-74; mem. Minn. Higher Edn. Coordinating Commn., 1971-74, pres., 1974; mem. Jordan Action Community Council; mem. Minn. Edn. Council, 1975-78; loaned exec. United Way, 1975, 76. Mem. Am. Legion. Club: KC. Office: 235 State Capitol Saint Paul MN 55155*

KROES, CAROLYN MILLS, psychologist; b. Muskegon, Mich., July 14, 1934; d. Arthur H. and Ardyce B. (Hill) Mills; B.Ph., Grand Valley State Coll., 1975; M.A. in Feminist Therapy, Goddard Coll., 1977; Ph.D., City U. Los Angeles, 1979; m. Bill R. Kroes, Jan. 5, 1952; children—Michael, Kim, Randy. Feminist therapist Cambridge (Mass.) Women's Center, 1975-76, Every Woman's Place, Muskegon, Mich., 1976-77; pvt. practice feminist therapy, Spring Lake, Mich., 1977—; guest lectr. TV program, 1976; co-founder Wings Alternative Service Clinic, Cambridge, Mass., 1975. Bd. dirs. Women in Transition, Grand Haven, Mich., 1978. Mem. NOW (Sisterhood award 1978), Nat. Feminist Therapist Assn. (co-founder 1977), Mich. Assn. Profl. Psychologists, Am. Personnel and Guidance Assn., Assn. Women in Psychology. Address: 14955 Boom Rd Spring Lake MI 49456

KROGH, HAROLD CHRISTIAN, educator; b. Cedar Rapids, Iowa, Feb. 1, 1917; s. Hans P. and Dorathea (Meyer) K.; B.S. in Commerce, State U. Iowa, 1939, M.A., 1941, Ph.D., 1953; postgrad. Harvard Grad. Sch. Bus., 1959, N.Y. U., 1964, U. Wis., 1967, Stanford U., 1973, Northwestern U., 1974; grad. Nat. War Coll., 1967, Command and Gen. Staff Coll., Ft. Leavenworth, 1969; m. Bessie Alberta Cummins, May 31, 1942; children—Linda Marie Krogh Russell, Richard Alan, Laurie Ellen. Sales, Midland Mortgage Co., Cedar Rapids, 1939-40; instr. econs. U. Ala., Tuscaloosa, 1941-42; personnel officer VA, Des Moines 1946-47; instr., asst. prof., asso. prof. fin. Drake U., Des Moines, 1947-54; asso. prof. bus. adminstrn. U. Kans., Lawrence, 1954-60, prof., 1960—. Cons. to ins. firms, fin. instns., pension funds, 1954—; faculty exchange program U. Costa Rica, summers 1962-63; mem. research com. Internat. Ins. Seminar, Oslo, Norway, 1977, Manila, Philippines, 1978. Bd. govs., bd. electors Internat. Ins. Hall of Fame. Served with AUS, 1942-46; col. Res. ret. Mem. Am. Soc. C.L.U.'s, Am. Risk and Ins. Assn. (past pres.), Am. Fin. Assn., Midwest Fin. Assn. (past pres.), Fin. Mgmt. Assn., Soc. C.P.C.U.'s, AAUP, Soc. Fin. Analysts, Midwest Bus. Adminstrn. Assn., Midwest Econs. Assn., Kansas City Actuaries Club, Alpha Kappa Psi, Beta Gamma Sigma. Lutheran. Home: 1117 Highland Dr Lawrence KS 66044

KROLL, ROBERT JOHN, priest, sch. adminstr.; b. Michigan City, Ind., Sept. 14, 1945; s. John Stephen and Clara Marie (Widelski) K.; B.A., Marquette U., 1967; M.A., Cardinal Stritch Coll., Milw., 1973; M.Th., Aquinas Inst. Theology, Dubuque, Iowa, 1971. Ordained priest Roman Catholic Ch., 1972; dir. religious edn. So. Wis. Colony, Union Grove, Wis., 1965-68; founder, dir. St. Francis Center, Wheaton, Ill., 1968-70, cons., 1970-72; tchr. Bartlett (Ill.) Learning Center, 1972-74; founder, adminstr. St. Vincent Residential Sch., Freeport, 1974-78; exec. dir. St. Vincent-St. Joseph Campus, Freeport, 1976-81; prin. St. Bonaventure Prep. Sch., Sturtevant, Wis., 1981—. Knights of Alhambra Ednl. grantee, 1969-73. Mem. Am. Assn. Mental Deficiency, Religious Edn. Assn., Nat. Apostolate for Mentally Retarded Persons. Club: KC. Home and Office: 2017 Wisconsin St Sturtevant WI 53177

KROLL, WILLIAM JOHN, regional planner; b. Chippewa Falls, Wis., Sept. 5, 1935; s. John Frederick and Clara Mabel K.; student U. Wis., Eau Claire, 1953-54; B.S., U. Wis., Madison, 1962; m. Janice Carol Loiselle, Oct. 18, 1958; children—Mark, Michael, Brenda. Asso. city planner, Rochester, Minn., 1962-64; planning analyst State of Wis., 1964-70; regional planning dir. Miss. River Regional Planning Commn., LaCrosse, Wis., 1970—. Served with AUS, 1955-57. Mem. Am. Planning Assn., Assn. Wis. Planners. Office: 400 N 4th St LaCrosse WI 54601*

KROMM, DENNIS ROBERT, advt. art dir.; b. Balt., May 29, 1948; s. Robert Louis and Margaret Elizabeth (Miller) K.; B.F.A. in Graphic Design cum laude, Md. Inst. Coll. Art, 1970. Art asst. Gilber Sandler Advt., Balt., 1970-72; asst. art dir. Needham, Harper & Steers Advt., Inc., Chgo., 1972-73, art dir., 1973-76, art. supr., 1976-79, sr. art dir., 1979—; freelance graphic designer and cons. Recipient Clio award, 1979, 81, Internat. Broadcasting award, 1976, 78, Advt. Age Ann. award in TV, 1979. Mem. Am. Philatelic Soc., Germany Philatelic Soc. Research on lighter-than-air aero. history. Office: 303 E Wacker Dr Chicago IL 60601

KRON, LARRY LEON, nurse; b. Whiting, Iowa, Apr. 23, 1940; s. Everett Raymond and Mary Ellen (Jones) K.; R.N., Lutheran Hosp., Sioux City, Iowa, 1961; B.S., Dana Coll., Blair, Nebr., 1964; M.B.A., U. Chgo., 1978; m. Carol Louise Harvie, July 25, 1969; children—Heather Lynn, Laurel Anne, Linden Marie. Staff nurse Community Meml. Hosp., Missouri Valley, Iowa, 1961-62, dir. nurses, 1968-73; mem. faculty Mercy Hosp. Nursing Sch., Council Bluffs, Iowa, 1963-64; faculty Cottage Hosp., Galesburg, Ill., 1964-66, v.p. nursing, 1973—; mem. Central Ill. Health Systems Agy., 1978-79. Chmn. bd. Family Planning W. Central Ill., 1977-79; adv. council Luth. Welfare Service, Galesburg, 1978-79; mem. bd. W. Central Iowa Alcoholism Council, 1970-73. Served with Nurse Corps, USAR, 1966-68. Decorated Bronze Star; named Boss of Yr., Galesburg chpt. Am. Bus. Women's Assn., 1976. Mem. Am. Nurses Assn., Soc. Nursing Service Adminstrs., Ill. Nurses Assn. (dir. 1974-77). Democrat. Home: Box 85 Route 4 Galesburg IL 61401 Office: 695 N Kellogg St Galesburg IL 61401

KRONEBUSCH, PATRICIA LOUISE, state senator; b. Mpls., Mar. 17, 1927; d. James Raymond and Luella Louise (Anez) Keller; B.A., Coll. of St. Teresa, Winona, Minn., 1948; M.S., Winona State U., 1969; m. Paul Jacob Kronebusch, May 30, 1949; children—Paula Trevor, Anne, Carol, Mary Wlynczak, Barbara, James, Stephanie, Kathleen. Pvt. tchr., 1971-80; mem. Minn. Senate, 1980—. Census-taker, 1970; mem. Winona Sch. Bd., 1973-80. Address: Rollingstone MN 55969*

KRONSCHNABEL, EDWARD FRANCIS, physician; b. Appleton, Wis., Sept. 9, 1921; s. George J. and Ellen (Hardy) K.; student Coll. St. Thomas, 1938-47; M.D., Marquette U., 1951; m. Shirley Stieghorst, Dec. 30, 1953 (dec. 1981); children—Jerome, Mary Sue, Charles. Intern, Evang. Deaconess Hosp., Milw., 1951-52; individual practice medicine, Gwinn, Mich., 1952-57; resident VA Hosp., Wood, Wis., 1957-60; clin. instr. Marquette U., 1957-60; individual practice medicine, specializing in otolaryngic surgery, Marquette, Mich., 1960—; mem. staff Marquette Gen. Hosp., Bell Meml. Hosp., Ishpeming, Mich. Bd. dirs. Bay Cliff Health Camp, Marquette. Served with USNR, 1942-45. Diplomate Am. Bd. Otolaryngology. Fellow A.C.S., Am. Broncho-Esophagol. Assn., Am. Acad. Otolaryngology-Head and Neck Surgery, Am. Laryngol., Otol., and Rhinol. Soc.; mem. AMA, Mich., Marquette-Alger County med. socs., Chgo. Laryngol. and Otol. Soc., Wis. Otolaryngol. Soc. Clubs: K.C., Marquette Golf and Country. Home: 551 Forest Park Dr Marquette MI 49855 Office: 1414 W Fair Ave Marquette MI 49855

KROON, JOHN C., physicist; b. Wormer, North Holland, Netherlands, May 30, 1939; s. Gerardus and Duifje (van deNes) K.; B.Sc., U. Ottawa (Ont., Can.), 1966, M.Sc., 1968, Ph.D., 1971; m. Marian Barry, Aug. 28, 1965; children—Stephanie, Lisa. Came to U.S., 1974. Physicist, Atomic Energy Can. Ltd., Chalk River (Ont.) Nuclear Lab., 1971-72; research and devel. mgr. Reuter-Stokes Can. Ltd., Cambridge, Ont., 1972-74; v.p. applied research and devel. Reuter-Stokes, Inc., Cleve., 1974—. Mem. Am. Nuclear Soc., IEEE, Canadian Assn. Physicists. Contbr. articles to profl. jours.; patentee in field. Office: 18530 S Miles Pkwy Cleveland OH 44128

KROPAT, RENEE JEAN, occupational therapist; b. Jamestown, N.Y., Nov. 4, 1953; d. Richard Walter and Jean (Wells) K.; B.S., Ohio State U., 1975, M.A., 1979; m. Anthony Goh, Oct. 3, 1981. Occupational therapist Rehab. Services North Central Ohio, Mansfield, 1975-77; occupational therapist cons. Fairway Wacraft Sch., Bucyrus, Ohio, 1977-78; research asso. dept. indsl. design Ohio State U., Columbus, 1978-79; research cons. Design and Research Services, Worthington, Ohio, 1979; occupational therapy supr. Mount Vernon (Ohio) Devel. Center, 1979-81; day care coordinator Madison County Hosp., London, Ohio, 1981—. Mem. Am. Occupational Therapy Assn., Ohio Occupational Therapy Assn. Author: (with Joseph Koncelik) Aging and the Product Environment, 1979. Home: 398 Fenway Rd Columbus OH 43214 Office: 210 N Main St London OH 43140

KROSSNER, WILLIAM JOHN, JR., psychologist; b. Newark, Oct. 19, 1939; s. William J. and Dora (Bruder) K.; B.Chem. Engring., Cornell U., 1961; Ph.D. (NIMH fellow), Harvard U., 1965; m. Rhonda A. Parrella, Sept. 4, 1977. Asst. prof. Vassar Coll., Fordham U., N.Y.C., 1966-74; asso. prof. psychology and medicine U. Minn., Duluth, 1974-78; pres. PsyMinn Corp., Duluth, 1975—, Med. Psychometrics Inc., Duluth, 1980—; head dept. psychology St. Luke's Hosp., Duluth, 1978—. Bd. dirs. St. Louis Center for Alcohol and Drug Problems, 1978—. Center for Urban and Regional Affairs grantee, 1974-75. Mem. Am. Psychol. Assn., Minn. Psychol. Assn., Am. Statis. Assn., Minn. Biofeedback Soc. Club: Harvard. Home: 1045 Brainerd Ave Duluth MN 55811 Office: PsyMinn Corp 915 E 1st St Duluth MN 55805

KROTINE, FRANK THOMAS, mfg. co. exec.; b. Cleve., Feb. 11, 1941; s. Frank Joseph and Barbara Sara (Spehar) K.; B.S. in Metall. Engring., Case Inst. Tech., 1963, M.S. in Metallurgy, 1965; Ph. in Metallurgy (Theta Tau award 1963, Internat. Nickel Co. research fellow 1965-68), Case Western Res. U., 1968; m. Anita L. Crea, Sept. 7, 1963; children—Jennifer, Douglas. With Internat. Nickel Co., Inc., 1968-70; with Gould, Inc., 1970-80, v.p. Gould Labs., Chgo., 1976-80; sr. v.p. corp. research and devel. Sherwin-Williams Co., Cleve., 1980—; mem. research-on-research com. Indsl. Research Inst., Adv. Com. Indsl. Innovation; mem. domestic policy rev. com. Dept. Commerce, 1978-79. Chmn. alumni fund Case Western Res. Grad. Sch., 1980-81; trustee Euclid Gen. Hosp., Cleve., 1974. Mem. Soc. Automotive Engrs., Metall. Soc., AAAS, IEEE, Fedn. Socs. Coatings Tech., Sigma Xi. Author papers in field. Office: 101 Prospect Ave Cleveland OH 44115

KROTZ, EDWARD WILLIAM, supermarket exec.; b. Lincoln, Ill., Feb. 19, 1925; s. Frank C. and Dora J. K.; B.S., U. Ill., 1948, M.B.A., 1981; m. Cecilia D. Shay, July 21, 1952; children—Frank, Edward William, Mark, Sheila, Keith. Sales engr. Sparkler Mfg. Co., Mundelien, Ill., 1953-55; v.p., partner F. Krotz Food Co., Taylorville, Ill., 1955—; v.p. Bloomington Eastgate Corp., 1960—; mem. J. M. Jone Retail Adv. Bd., 1976-79. Served to lt. USN, 1943-46, 50-52. Lic. real estate broker, Ill. Mem. Ill. Retail Grocers, Food Mktg. Inst., Nat. Assn. Retail Grocers, VFW. Democrat. Roman Catholic. Clubs: K.C., Eagles, Elks. Home: 2344 Hawthorne Dr Decatur IL 62521 Office: PO Box 99 Taylorville IL 62568

KRUCKS, WILLIAM, electronics mfg. co. exec.; b. Chgo., Dec. 26, 1918; s. William and Florence (Olson) K.; B.S., Northwestern U., 1940; postgrad. Loyola U., Chgo., 1941-42; m. Lorraine C. Rauland, Oct. 23, 1947; children—William Norman, Kenneth Rauland. Auditor, Benefit Trust Life Ins. Co., Chgo., 1940-42; chief tax accountant, asst. to comptroller C.M., St.P.&P. R.R., Chgo., 1942-56; asst. comptroller, dir. taxation, asst. treas. C. & N.W. Ry., Chgo., 1956-58, treas., 1968-75; asst. treas. N.W. Industries, Inc., 1968-72; chmn. bd., chief exec. officer, pres. Rauland-Borg Corp. Bd. dirs. Civic Fedn. Chgo., North River Bus. and Indsl. Council, Chgo. Mem. Nat. Tax Assn., Tax Execs. Inst., Assn. Am. Railroads, Ill. C. of C. Republican. Methodist. Clubs: Tower; Execs., Union League, Internat. Trade (Chgo.). Home: 21 Indian Hill Rd Winnetka IL 60093 Office: 3535 W Addison St Chicago IL 60618

KRUEGER, ALAN DOUGLAS, communications co. exec.; b. Little Rock, Dec. 24, 1937; s. Herbert C. and Estelle B. K.; student U. Ill., 1956, Wright Coll., 1957-58; m. Betty J. Burns, Apr. 4, 1975; children by previous marriage—Scott Alan, Dane Keith, Kip Douglas, Bryan Lee. Project engr. Motorola, Inc., Chgo., 1956-64, service mgr., field tech. rep., 1964-67; pres. Communications Maintenance, Inc., Indpls., 1967-68, Communications Unlimited, Inc., Indpls., 1968—. Methodist. Club: Elks. Office: Communications Unlimited Inc 4032 Southeastern Ave Indianapolis IN 46203

KRUEGER, BETTY JANE, rental co. exec.; b. Indpls., Oct. 4, 1923; d. Forrest Glen and Hazel Luellen (Taylor) Burns; student Butler U., 1948-49; m. Alan Douglas Krueger, Apr. 4, 1975; 1 son by previous marriage, Michael J. Vornehm. Supr., instr. Ind. Bell Telephone Co., Indpls., 1941-54; supr. communications Jones & Laughlin Steel Co., Indpls., 1954-56, Ford Motor Co., Indpls., 1956-64, U.S. Govt., Camp Atterbury, Ind., 1964-66; dir. communications Meth. Hosp. of Ind., Indpls., 1966-79; pres., owner Rent-A-Radio, Inc. of Ind., Indpls., 1979—. Former pres. Am. Legion Aux.; chmn. for Ind., Girls State U.S.A., 1972-77; probation officer vol., 1973-74; suicide prevention counselor, 1972-73. Recipient award for outstanding community service Ford Motor Co., 1961. Mem. Am. Soc. Hosp. Engring., Am. Hosp. Assn., Nat. Assn. Bus. and Ednl. Radio, Inc., Internat. Teletypewriters for the Deaf, Asso. Public Safety Communications Officers, Inc., Am. Bus. Women. Methodist. Home: Rural Route 2 Box 119 Franklin IN 46131 Office: 4032 Southeastern Ave Indianapolis IN 46203

KRUEGER, CHARITY ANN, naturalist, educator; b. Toledo, Mar. 24, 1950; d. George Rudolph and Alice Charity (Ray) K.; B.E., U. Toledo, 1972; M.S., U. Mich., 1973; cert. Natural Resource Edn., Ohio State U., 1976. Interpretive specialist Metropark Dist. of Toledo Area, 1973-77; natural resources instr. Agr. Edn. Center, Toledo Bd. Edn., 1974—, instr. adult and continuing edn., 1977—; environ. edn. cons. Ohio State Agr. Edn. Curriculum Materials Service, 1979-81; manpower specialist, environ. edn. Youth Conservation Corps, U.S. Dept. Interior, 1977-80, program dir. U.S. Fish and Wildlife Service, Ottawa Nat. Wildlife Refuge, 1975-80; cons. environ. edn.; free lance photographer, artist, illustrator. Adv. bd. Dept. Agr. Edn. Ohio State U., 1980—; trustee Citizens for Metroparks, 1978—; pres. Ohio Audubon Council, 1980—; dir. Wildlife Rehab. Center, 1974—; co-founder, treas. Maumee Bay Coalition, 1974-77; co-founder, adv. Maumee Valley Jr. Audubon Soc. Future Farmers Am.; co-chmn. Toledo Area Environ. Awareness Weekends; program chmn. Sun Day, 1978; chmn. Wildwood Preserve Working Hist. Farm edn., 1978—; mem. Crosby Gardens. Recipient conservation award DAR, 1980. Mem. Assn. Interpretive Naturalists, Mich. Environ. Edn. Assn., Am. Fedn. Teachers, Ohio Fedn. Tchrs., Am. Vocat. Assn.,

Nat. Vocat. Agr. Tchrs. Assn., Ohio Vocat. Assn., Ohio Vocat. Agr. Tchrs. Assn. (county chmn., exec. bd. 1979—, outstanding young tchr. 1980), U. Toledo Alumnae Assn. (life), U. Mich. Alumnae Assn. (life), Peppers, Phi Kappa Phi, Kappa Delta Pi, Pi Lambda Theta. Methodist. Clubs: Maumee Valley Audubon Soc. (co-founder, pres., 1974—), Toledo Potters' Guild, Nat. Wildlife Fedn. Author slide-narrative presentations, Woodland Wildflowers, 1980, Wetlands Wildflowers, 1980, Field Wildflowers, 1981; author child's book Discovering Nature in a Metropark, 1975. Office: 5561 Elmer Dr Toledo OH 43615

KRUEGER, CLIFFORD W., state senator; b. Madison, Wis., June 24, 1918; ed. comml. coll.; married. Salesman; mem. Wis. Senate, 1947-55, 56—. Alderman, 1945-46. Mem. Farm Bur. Republican. Club: Lions. Address: Room 213 SE State Capitol Madison WI 53702*

KRUEGER, DONALD MARTIN, auditor; b. Chgo., June 16, 1936; s. Harry A. and Geneva (Eagan) K.; B.S., Roosevelt U., 1961; m. Bernadine Pater, Feb. 24, 1968; children—Diane, Renee. Controller, Theo R. Sills, Inc., Chgo., 1964-68; mng. auditor Chgo. & Northwestern R.R., 1968-70; audit mgr. Ency. Britannia, Chgo., 1970-72; EDP audit mgr. Marsh & McLennan, Chgo., 1972—; instr. EDP auditing; conf. speaker. Served with U.S. Army, 1962. Cert. internal auditor and info. systems auditor. Mem. Inst. Internal Auditors, EDP Auditors Assn. Home: 18 W 049 Holly Ave Westmont IL 60559 Office: 550 W Jackson Blvd Rm 420 Chicago IL 60606

KRUEGER, NORMAN LELAND, physician; b. Bagley, Iowa, Dec. 5, 1915; s. Charles William and Helen Young (McLellan) K.; B.A., McPherson Coll., 1941; M.D., U. Iowa, 1950; m. Alma McLamb, June 26, 1948; children—Jean, Charles. Intern, St. Francis Hosp., Wichita, Kans., 1950-51, resident in pathology, 1954-55; resident in internal medicine, VA Hosp., Wood, Wis., 1955-57; practice medicine, Casey, Iowa, 1957—; clin. instr. Marquette U., 1955-57. Served with USN, 1942-45. Mem. Iowa Med. Soc., AMA, AAAS, Am. Coll. Angiology, Am. Assn. Physicians and Surgeons, Alpha Kappa Kappa. Republican. Mem. Church of the Brethren. Office: Hayes Bldg Casey IA 50048

KRUEGER, RICHARD ARNOLD, ednl. adminstr.; b. St. Paul, Minn., Feb. 13, 1949; s. Richard Ernest and Shirley Mae (Popp) K.; B.A., Winona State U., 1971; M.A., St. Thomas U., 1973; postgrad. U. Minn.; m. Diane Susan Schiller, Apr. 14, 1973; 1 dau., Melissa Kay. Dir., Midway YMCA, St. Paul, Minn., 1971-72; tchr. social studies Stillwater (Minn.) Jr. High Sch., 1973, Lakeville (Minn.) High Sch., 1973-79; dir. Staples (Minn.) Tchrs. Center, 1979—; speaker several state, regional and nat. edn. confs. Active Democratic Party. Mem. NEA, Assn. Staff and Curriculum Devel., Nat. Council Social Studies, Phi Kappa Phi. Democrat. Lutheran. Home: 524 N 6th St Staples MN 56479 Office: 524 N 3d St Staples MN 56479

KRUEGER, ROBERT ALLEN, chem. co. exec.; b. Oak Park, Ill., Dec. 29, 1935; s. Clarence August and Edna Anne (Polke) K.; A.B. (S.C. Johnson scholar), Knox Coll., Galesburg, Ill., 1957; Ph.D., Kans. State U., Manhattan, 1965; m. Carol. I. West, June 21, 1959; children—Jeffrey, Jerald, Thomas. Chemist, Union Carbide, Chgo., 1957-58; grad. asst. Kans. State U., 1960-65; research chemist, sect. leader, tech. adminstr., dir. research and devel., v.p. research and devel., v.p. splty. chems., sr. v.p. and gen. mgr. PVC div. B.F. Goodrich, Cleve., 1957—. Served with AUS, 1958-60. Mem. Am. Chem. Soc., AAAS, Am. Inst. Chemists, Indsl. Research Inst. Jewish. Club: Cascade. Bd. editors Research Mgmt., 1979-81; contbr. articles profl. jours. Patentee in field. Office: 6100 Oak Tree Blvd Cleveland OH 44141

KRUG, EDWIN HERBERT, advt. exec.; b. South Bend, Ind., June 18, 1938; s. Solomon J. and Lillian (Joshel) K.; B.S., U. Ind., 1960; M.B.A., U. Chgo., 1973; m. Judith Fingeret, Oct. 23, 1963; children—Steven Morris, Michelle Lynn. Auditor, Altshuler, Melvoin & Glaser Co., Chgo., 1961; buyer Warshawsky & Co., Chgo., 1961-63; buyer, mdse. mgr., asst. retail sales mgr. Montgomery Ward & Co., Chgo., 1963-67; account supr. Arthur Wilk Advt. Co., Chgo., 1967-71; sr. v.p. Maxwell Sroge Co., Inc., Chgo., 1971-78; pres. Herbert Krug & Assos., Inc. and Catalog Merchandising Assos., Inc., 1978—. Served with U.S. Army, 1960-61. Mem. Am. Mktg. Assn., Direct Mail Mktg. Assn., Chgo. Assn. Direct Mktg. Co-author mail order workshop textbook. Home: 2770 Sheridan Rd Evanston IL 60201

KRUG, FRANK LEONARD, fire chief; b. Dayton, Ohio, Aug. 23, 1929; s. Frank George and Dorothy (Hunn) K.; student public schs., Dayton; numerous asso. degrees; m. Charline Hackley, May 15, 1954; children—Cynthia, Brenda, David. With Dayton Fire Dept., 1953—, lt., 1959-64, capt., 1964-67, dist. chief, 1967-78, supr. fire ops., 1978-79, dir., chief, 1979—; owner Holly Hills Golf Club, Dayton. Served with U.S. Army, 1951-53. Mem. Internat. Fire Chiefs Assn., Ohio Fire Chiefs, Montgomery County Fire Chiefs. Republican. Roman Catholic. Club: Milton Athletic. Office: 300 N Main St Dayton OH 45402*

KRUG, ROBERT JOSEPH, hosp. adminstr.; b. Ottawa, Ill., Oct. 8, 1935; s. Joseph Anthony and Mary Tucker (Thompson-Jeffries) K.; A.B., Augustana Coll., 1961; M.B.A., U. Chgo., 1965; m. Ann Louise Ek, Aug. 27, 1960; children—Robert Blair, Karen Ann. Comml. mktg. rep. Burroughs Corp., Chgo., 1961-63; mgr. Passavant Meml. Hosp., Chgo., 1965; asst. adminstr. St. George Hosp., Chgo., 1966-68; asst. dir. Louis A. Weiss Meml. Hosp., Chgo., 1968-70; asst. adminstr. Christ Hosp., Oak Lawn, Ill., 1970-73; adminstr. Milw. Psychiat. Hosp., Wauwatosa, Wis., 1973; exec. dir. Milw. San. Found., Wauwatosa, 1973; v.p. adminstrn. and fiscal services Holy Cross Hosp., Chgo., 1973—; lectr. Northwestern U. Grad. Sch. Mgmt.-Health Services Adminstrn.; clin. advisor program in health services adminstrn. U. Chgo. Grad. Sch. Bus.; trustee Chgo. Hosp. Risk Pooling Program; mem. Emergency Med. Services Commn. Met. Chgo., Southside Hosp. Forum; mem. com. on planning, subcom. on annual implementation Chgo. Hosp. Council, also com. on materials mgmt., com. on public relations; sec. SW Chgo. Area Health Planning Corp.; mem. hosp. project rev. com. Chgo. Health Systems Agy. Served with Med. Service Corps, U.S. Army, 1954-56. Mem. Am. Coll. Hosp. Adminstrs., Am. Hosp. Assn., Ill. Hosp. Assn. (Blue Cross liaison com., council on govt. affairs, chmn. annual meeting com., pres. Region II-A), Ill. Cath. Hosp. Assn. (long-range planning com.), Cath. Hosp. Assn., Hosp. Fin. Mgmt. Assn., Chgo. Area Planners Assn., U. Chgo. Alumni Assn., U. Chgo. Hosp. Adminstrn. Alumni Assn. Contbr. papers to profl. publs. and confs. Office: 2701 W 68th St Chicago IL 60629

KRUGER, ALBERT AARON, chemist; b. Bklyn., Oct. 3, 1952; s. Louis Max and Shirley Judith (Linn) K.; B.S. with honors (N.Y. State Regents scholar 1970), City U. N.Y., 1974; M.S., Syracuse U., 1975; m. Liza Lilly Markoff, June 9, 1974. Sr. tech. asso. Bell Telephone Lab., Murray Hill, N.J., 1976-78; sr. research chemist 3M, Physics and Material Research Lab., Central Research, St. Paul, 1978—. Recipient Am. Inst. Chemists Student medal, 1974; Am. Chem. Soc. Student Chpt. award, 1974; mem. honors group Westinghouse Sci. Talent Search. Fellow Am. Inst. Chemists; mem. Am. Chem. Soc., Sigma Xi. Clubs: Jaguar of Minn. (v.p.), Jaguar Drivers' Club Ltd. Contbr. articles in field to profl. jours. Home: 1559 Summit Ave Saint Paul MN 55105 Office: 3M Center Bldg 201-BE-01 Saint Paul MN 55144

KRUGER, JOHN EDWARD, optometrist; b. Fort Dodge, Iowa, Feb. 27, 1947; s. Robert Wayne and Corinne Maxine (Wierson) K.; B.A., Loras Coll., 1969; B.S.V.S., O.D., Ill. Coll. Optometry, 1976; m. Vicki Henry, June 24, 1972; children—Kristine Elizabeth, Michael John, Kimberly Ann. Pvt. practice optometry, Story City, Iowa, 1976—, also Ames, Iowa. Bd. dirs. Greater Community Congress for Story City, pres., 1979-81. Fellow in vision devel. Coll. Optometrists; mem. Am. Optometric Assn., Iowa Optometric Assn. (chmn. Central Iowa devel. group 1977-78, Young Optometrist of Yr. 1979). Republican. Lutheran. Club: Lions. Home: 1412 Riverhills Dr Story City IA 50248 Office: 216 Main St Ames IA also 605 Penn Story City IA 50248

KRUGER, WILLIAM ARNOLD, civil engr.; b. St. Louis, June 13, 1937; s. Reynold and Olinda (Siefker) K.; B.C.E., U. Mo.-Rolla, 1959; M.S., U. Ill., 1968; m. Carole Ann Hofer, Oct. 17, 1959. Civil engr. City of St. Louis, 1959; with Clark, Dietz & Assos., and predecessors, Urbana, Ill., 1961-79, sr. design engr., 1963-67, dir. transp. div., 1968-79; civil engr. div. hwys. Ill. Dept. Transp., Paris, 1979—; instr. Parkland Coll., Champaign, 1972. Served with C.E., AUS, 1959-61. Registered profl. engr., Ill., Mo., Fla., Miss., N.Y., Iowa, Del. Mem. Nat. Ill. (chpt. pres. 1974, state chmn. registration laws com. 1973, 78) socs. profl. engrs., Ill. Assn. Hwy. Engrs., ASCE, Am. Public Works Assn. (sect. dir. 1974-77, 80), Inst. Transp. Engrs., Met. Assn. Urban Designers and Environ. Planners, Ill. Registered Land Surveyors Assn., Soc. Am. Mil. Engrs., U. Mo.-Rolla Alumni Assn., Theta Tau, Tau Beta Pi, Chi Epsilon, Pi Kappa Alpha. Clubs: Urbana Sportsmans, Champaign Ski. Home: 1811 Coventry Dr Champaign IL 61820 Office: State Transp Bldg Paris IL 61944

KRUH, ROBERT F(RANK), univ. adminstr., chemist; b. St. Louis, June 15, 1925; s. Frank O. and Nelle (Dee) K.; B.A., Washington U., St. Louis, 1948, Ph. D., 1951; m. Janet Jackson, Dec. 19, 1948; children—Lindsay J., Nancy D. Asst. prof. chemistry DePauw U., 1951-52; asst. prof. U. Ark., 1952-55, asso. prof., 1956-60, prof., 1961-67; dean Coll. Arts and Scis., 1964-67; dean Grad. sch., prof. chemistry Kans. State U., 1967—; vis. prof. Washington U., 1960-61; trustee Argonne (Ill.) Univs. Assn., Argonne Nat. Lab., 1970-76; pres. Kans. State U. Research Found., 1971—; mem. Grad. Record Exams. Bd., 1978—, vice chmn., 1980-81, chmn., 1981—; chmn. policy council, Test of English as Fgn. Lang., Ednl. Testing Service, Princeton, N.J., 1978-80. Served with U.S. Army, 1943-46; ETO. Mem. Council Grad. Schs. in U.S. (bd. dirs. 1977—, chmn. 1978-79), Midwestern Assn. Grad. Schs. (pres. 1975-76, exec. sec. 1976—), Blue Key, Phi Beta Kappa, Sigma Xi, Omicron Delta Kappa. Lutheran. Research, publs. on determination of structure of crystals and liquids by means of x-ray diffraction. Office: Grad Office Kans State U Manhattan KS 66506

KRUIDENIER, DAVID, newspaper publisher; b. Des Moines, July 18, 1921; s. David S. and Florence (Cowles) K.; grad. Phillips Exeter Acad., 1940; B.A., Yale U., 1946; M.B.A., Harvard U., 1948; LL.D., Buena Vista Coll., 1960, Simpson Coll., 1963; m. Elizabeth Stuart, Dec. 29, 1948; 1 dau., Lisa. With Mpls. Star and Tribune Co., 1948-52, now vice chmn.; with Des Moines Register and Tribune, 1952—, pres., pub., 1971-78, chmn., pub., 1978—; chmn. bd. Des Moines Register and Tribune Co.; dir. Iowa-Des Moines Nat. Bank, Nat. By-Products, Inc., Register and Tribune Syndicate, Inc. Pres. Gardner and Florence Call Cowles Found.; trustee Drake U., Menninger Found., Civic Center Greater Des Moines, Am. Fedn. Arts, Midwest Research; dir., Audit Bur. Circulations. Served with USAAF, 1942-45. Mem. Sigma Delta Chi, Beta Theta Pi, Beta Gamma Sigma. Club: Des Moines. Home: 3409 Southern Hills Dr Des Moines IA 50321 Office: PO Box 957 Des Moines IA 50304

KRULL, JACOB J., state senator; b. Dec. 23, 1938; B.S., S.D. State U.; m. Phyllis Skillman, Feb. 19, 1961; 2 sons. Engaged in ins. bus.; mem. S.D. Senate, 1972—, minority leader, 1979-80. Served with U.S. Army; lt. col. S.D. NG. Mem. Watertown C. of C. (dir.). Congregationalist. Democrat. Clubs: Elks, Lions. Home: Watertown SD 57201 Office: State Capitol Pierre SD 57501*

KRUMSKE, WILLIAM FREDERICK, JR., savs. and loan exec.; b. Chgo., Dec. 17, 1952; s. William Frederick and Harriet Marie (Piwowarczyk) K.; B.S., Ill. Inst. Tech., 1974; M.S. in Bus. Adminstrn., No. Ill. U., 1978. Salesman, warehouse mgr. Lus-Ter-Oil Beauty Products, Palos Heights, Ill., 1972-74; pub. relations dir. Crouching Lion Motor Inn, Alsip, Ill., 1974; mgr. food and beverage Inn Devel. & Mgmt., Chicago Heights, Ill., 1974-75; v.p., dir. mktg. DeKalb (Ill.) Savs. and Loan Assn., 1975-81; sr. v.p. mktg. Regency Fed. Savs. and Loan Assn., St. Charles, Ill., 1981—; dir. Rock Valley Network, Inc., Rockford, Ill.; instr. Coll. Bus., No. Ill. U., 1978—; mktg. mgr. Jordan Gallagher for State's Atty. campaign, 1976; mem. Republican Nat. Com., 1978—. Recipient William J. Hendrickson award No. Ill. U. Alumnus, 1980. Mem. Ill. Inst. Tech. Alumni Admission Corps, Am. Mktg. Assn., Savs. Instn. Mktg. Soc. Am., Ill. Savs. and Loan League (mktg. com. 1977-80, chmn. 1979-80), Beta Gamma Sigma. Lutheran. Contbr. articles to profl. jours. Home: 118 Augusta Ave DeKalb IL 60115 Office: 575 S Randall Rd PO Box 775 Saint Charles IL 60174

KRUPP, STEVEN DENIS, publisher; b. Milw., Aug. 27, 1918; s. Michael J. and Holly Gene (Brooks) K.; B.S., Ripon (Wis.) Coll., 1940; m. Bonnie Beane, Apr. 29, 1938 (div. 1980); children—Sandy, David, Tyler, Leonard, Steven Denis; m. 2d, Danielle Sawall, 1980. Plant mgr. Marathon Paper Co., Neenah-Menasha, Wis., 1938-41, 45-48; pres., founder Krupp Pub. Co., Princeton, Wis., 1948—, Kitchen Sink Enterprises, 1970—; pres. Krupp Mail Order, Boulder, 1971—; v.p., co-owner Christy Smith-Aanes Dress Shop, Ripon, Wis., 1981—; dir. Farmers-Mchts. Nat. Bank. Mayor City of Princeton, 1952-54; dir. Fox Valley Theatre Group, 1974-76. Served with inf., AUS, 1941-44. Decorated Purple Heart, Bronze Star; recipient Sandra Gawronski award for civic activities LWV, 1964. Mem. Nat. Rifle Assn., Am. Legion. Republican. Roman Catholic. Clubs: Fox Valley Comic Collectors, Princeton Lions (pres. 1971-73). Author: Heart of a Midwesterner, 1968; Antique Juke Box Identification and Price Guide, 1980; contbr. articles to periodicals. Home: 2 Swamp Rd Princeton WI 54968 Office: 244 Poplaski Ave Princeton WI 54968

KRUSE, EDGAR C., hosp. ofcl.; b. Ind., June 15, 1912; s. Henry C. and Emma (Dreyer) K.; student Ind. U.; m. Mildred Kramer, May 15, 1937; children—Dale Keith, Dennis Neal, Donald Edgar. Messenger, jr. exec. Home Tel. & Tel. Co., 1928-48; gen. auditor City Utilities, Fort Wayne, Ind., 1948-52; asst. adminstr. Lutheran Hosp., Ft. Wayne, 1952-59, adminstr., 1959-71, pres., 1971-77; mem. Ind. Bd. Health Regulating and Licensing Council, 1963-67; mem. adv. bd. Sch. Practical Nursing; chmn. bd. DNK Enterprises, Inc., 1977—. Bd. dirs. Ft. Wayne chpt. ARC; bd. dirs., exec. com. No. Ind. Health System Authority, 1976—; bd. dirs. Luth. Hosp. Found., 1977—, pres., 1981—. Mem. Am. Assn. Hosp. Accountants (past pres. Ind. chpt.), Northeastern Ind. Hosp. Council (past pres.), Luth. Hosp. Assn. Am. (dir., past pres.), Tri-State Hosp. Assembly (dir., past pres.), Ft. Wayne C. of C. Clubs: Junto, Fort Wayne Executive (dir., past pres.), 100 Per Cent (dir.). Home: 6037 Ranger Trail Fort Wayne IN 46815 Office: 3024 Fairfield Ave Fort Wayne IN 46807

KRUSE, WALTER WILLIAM PETER, farmer; b. Sheldon, Iowa, May 19, 1904; s. Fred and Mary (Kersten) K.; student Iowa State U., 1923-26; m. Luella Hensch, June 14, 1927 (dec.); children—Lorna Mae, Merlyn Frederick; m. 2d, Margret Gourley, Sept. 15, 1957; stepchildren—Peggy Stagilino, John Gourley. Farmer, partner Floyd Crest Farms, Sheldon, Iowa; chmn. bd. Farmers Mut. Ins. Assn., Hartley, Iowa. Chmn. bd. Community Meml. Hosp., Sheldon; rep. Iowa Legislature, 1969-72. Served with Iowa State Guard, 1941-45. Named to Hall of Fame, Sheldon Hist. Soc., 1976. Mem. Farm Bur., Sheldon C. of C., Floyd Valley Watershed Assn. (sec., dir.), Am. Milking Shorthorn Soc. (past pres.), Tamworth Swine Assn. (past pres.), N.W. Iowa Farm Bus. Assn. (charter, past pres.), Delta Sigma Chi. Republican. Lutheran. Clubs: Kiwanis, United Comml. Travelers. Office: 91 S Central Ave Hartley IA 51346

KRUSINSKI, CLARENCE, architect; b. Chgo., Oct. 3, 1940; s. Clarence John and Evelyn A. (Anders) K.; B.Arch., Ill. Inst. Tech., 1963; m. Josette Nadine Piscitello, Sept. 1, 1962; children—Scott Michael, Brigitta Terese, Mark David, Courtney Josette. Architect, Pace Assos., Chgo., 1963-64, Schipporeit-Heinrich, Inc., Chgo., 1964-67; pres. Clarence Krusinski & Assos., Ltd., Chgo., 1967-77, Miller Krusinski Assos. Ltd., 1977-79, Krusinski Orgn., 1979—, Krusinski Gelick Foran, Ltd., 1980—; exec. v.p., chief operating officer Robert Sheridan & Partners, Chgo., 1981—. Mem. Oak Park (Ill.) Zoning Bd. Appeals. Recipient Better Homes for Living award. Registered architect, Ill., N.Y., Tex., Ky., Ind., Fla., Conn., Pa. Mem. Nat. Council Archtl. Registration Bds., AIA (past pres. Chgo. chpt.), Landmarks Preservation Council, Chgo. Sch. Architecture Found., Ill. Inst. Tech. Alumni Assn. (past pres.). Club: Arts of Chgo. Home: 526 Augusta Oak Park IL 60302 Office: 5415 N Sheridan Rd St Chicago IL 60640

KRUTEK, DONALD JOSEPH, fin. exec.; b. Oak Park, Ill., May 29, 1938; s. Joseph A. and Bernice M. (Scanlon) K.; student St. Joseph's Coll., 1956-58, De Paul U., 1960-61; m. Brigid E. Brennan, May 6, 1961; children—Paul, Mary, Joseph, Amy, Robert, Steven. With Great Am. Ins. Co., Chgo., 1959-60, Security Mutual Casualty Co., Chgo., 1960-69, Atlantic Cos., Chgo., 1969-71; v.p., corporate officer Arthur J. Gallagher & Co., Arlington Heights, Ill., 1971—; presenter risk mgmt., self ins. seminars various orgns. Fellow Ins. Inst. Am.; mem. Chartered Property and Casualty Underwriters Assn. Roman Catholic. Clubs: Rolling Green Country, Meadow. Home: 609 S Newbury Pl Arlington Heights IL 60005 Office: Gould Center Golf Rd Rolling Meadows IL 60008

KRYN, RANDALL LEE, public relations exec.; b. Chgo., Oct. 12, 1949; s. Chester N. and Beatrice K. Kryn; A.A., Morton Coll., 1970; B.S. in Journalism, No. Ill. U., 1973. Writer and researcher William M. Young & Assos., Oak Park, Ill., 1977; asst. public relations dir. Oak Park Festival, 1978; founder Oak Park Center of Creativity, 1978, pres., 1978—, public relations dir., 1978—; founder, dir. Reality Communication, Oak Park, 1976—; dir. publicity campaigns for communication related orgns., 1976—. Mem. steering com. Oak Park Heritage Assn., 1978—. Recipient Golden Trumpet award Publicity Club of Chgo., 1979; named One of 48 Outstanding Young Men of Am. from Ill., Ill. Jaycees, 1980. Mem. Public Relations Soc. Am., Ill. Soc. for Psychic Research (pres. 1980—), Mensa, Seward Gunderson Soc. (co-founder 1978). Columnist, Village Economist Newspaper, 1977-78. Home and Office: 1030 Wenonah St Oak Park IL 60304

KRYSINSKI, THOMAS FRANK, service co. exec.; b. Chgo., Nov. 6, 1945; s. Edmond Frank and Stephanie Pearl K.; A.A., Chgo. City Coll., 1968; B.S. in Indsl. Engring., Indsl. Engring. Coll., 1972; B.S. in Bus. Adminstrn., Roosevelt U., 1976; married. Purchasing agt. Union Carbide, 1963-65; indsl. engr. Hammond Organ, 1965-68; supr. indsl. engring. Nat. Video, Chgo., 1968-69; chief indsl. engr. Oak Electronics, Crystal Lake, Ill., 1969-70; indsl. engr. mgr. Gillette Co., LaGrange Park, Ill., 1970-72, prodn. mgr., 1972-74, mfg. mgr., 1974-77, plant mgr., 1977-80; owner K Car Care, Tidy Care dealer; tchr. Indsl. Engring. Coll., Chgo. Mem. Am. Inst. Indsl. Engrs., Soc. Advancement Mgmt., Indsl. Engring. Coll. Alumni Assn. (past pres.), Am. Packaging Inst., APICS, West Suburban C. of C. Roman Catholic. Club: Rotary. Patentee printing offset devices, assembly and welding equipment. Home and Office: 15 Stratford Ct Indian Head Park IL 60525

KRYSKI, HUGH ADAM, econ. forecaster, fin. analyst; b. Laufen, Germany, Aug. 21, 1948; s. Stanley Witold and Kathie (Kiessling) K.; came to U.S., 1951, naturalized, 1957; B.B.A., Eastern Mich. U., 1972, M.B.A., 1976; m. Theresa M. Kistler, Aug. 9, 1969; 1 son, Jeffery. Cost analyst Ford Motor Co., Dearborn, Mich., 1972-74; ins. sales Conn. Mut. Life Ins. Co., Boulder, Colo., 1974-75; mktg. dir. Technowatt, Inc., Troy, Mich., 1975-77; statis. analyst Gilbert Commonwealth, Jackson, Mich., from 1977, now div. adminstrv. mgr. Mem. Assn. M.B.A. Execs Inc., Am. Assn. Cost Engrs. Home: 2834 Pittsfield Blvd Ann Arbor MI 48104 Office: 209 Washington Ave Jackson MI 49201

KSHEPAKARAN, KUZHILETHU KRISHNAN, occupational therapist, educator; b. Kerala, India, Dec. 22, 1935; came to U.S., 1962, naturalized, 1976; s. Krishnan and Velumpy (Sankaran) Krishnan; B.Sc., Kerala U., 1957; student Occupational Therapy Sch., Nagpur, India, 1958-60; M.Ed., U. Puget Sound, 1975; m. Ramola Munshi, Mar. 31, 1956; 1 child, Anil. With I.P.D. Orthopaedic Center, Madras, India, 1960-62, N.J. Orthopedic Hosp., Orange, 1962-63, 69-71, Jewish Cronic Disease Hosp., Bklyn., 1963-64, BonHooghly Group of Hosps., Calcutta, India, 1964-66, Home for Handicapped Children, Patna, India, 1966-69; instr. U. Puget Sound, Tacoma, 1971-76; asst. prof. Eastern Ky. U., Richmond, 1976-77; asst. prof. occupational therapy U. Wis., Madison, 1977-80, U. Ill., Urbana, 1980—. Recipient Faculty Research award, U. Wis., 1979-80; Am. Occupational Therapy Assn. grantee, 1979-80. Mem. Am. Occupational Therapy Assn., World Fedn. Occupational Therapists, Arthritis Found. Contbr. articles to profl. jours. Home: 2109 Iris Ln Madison WI 53711 Office: 505 E Green St First Floor Champaign IL 61820

KUBIAS, FRANK OWEN, coatings co. exec.; b. Cedar Rapids, Iowa, Feb. 27, 1927; s. Frank J. and Ruth L. Kubias; B.S. in Chem. Engring., Iowa State U., 1950; m. Beverly Jean Aschinger, Dec. 28, 1950; children—Craig O., Kirk E. Process engr. Mallinckrodt Inc., St. Louis, 1950-55, mfg. supt., 1955-64, mgr. health and safety, 1964-73; mgr. safety SCM/Glidden-Durkee, Cleve., 1973-77; mgr. loss prevention SCM/Glidden Coatings & Resins, Cleve., 1977—; gen. chmn. chem. sect. Nat. Safety Council, 1976-77; bd. control Cleve. Safety Council. Served with USNR, 1945-46. Recipient Disting. Service to Safety award Nat. Safety Council, 1979; registered profl. engr., Calif.; cert. safety profl. Mem. Am. Inst. Chem. Engrs. (mem. founding com. and charter dir. safety and health div.), Am. Soc. Safety Engrs. (pres. St. Louis chpt. 1970-71), Nat. Fire Protection Assn. (chmn. com. on classification of flammables), Ohio Soc. Safety Engrs., Am. Radio Relay League, Nat. Paint and Coatings Assn. (safety com.), U.S. Power Squadron. Presbyterian (elder). Club: Masons. Office:

SCM/Glidden Coatings & Resins 900 Union Commerce Bldg Cleveland OH 44115

KUBISTA, THEODORE PAUL, gen. surgeon; b. N.Y.C., July 20, 1937; s. Theodore Anton and Antonette Helene (Balasch) K.; B.S. in Chemistry, Pa. State U., 1959; M.D., U. Pa., 1963; m. Alice Elizabeth Maris, Dec. 26, 1963; children—Theodore Stephen, Christian Gregory. Intern, Hosp. U. Pa., 1963-64; resident in gen. surgery Mayo Grad. Sch. Medicine, Rochester, Minn., 1964-69; gen. surgeon Duluth (Minn.) Clinic, Ltd., 1971—, chmn. dept. gen. surgery, 1975-76; chief of surgery St. Mary's Hosp., 1977-78, chmn. dept. inhalation therapy and resuscitation, 1974-76; adv. com. inhalation therapy Coll. St. Scholastica; asst. prof. clin. surgery U. Minn. (Duluth). Served to lt. comdr. M.C., USNR, 1969-71. Decorated Bronze Star with Combat V; recipient Dr. I.S. Ravdin prize in surgery U. Pa., 1963, Priestley prize for surg. research, 1963. Fellow A.C.S. (exec. council Minn. chpt.); mem. AMA, Minn., St. Louis County med. assns., AAAS, Assn. Mil. Surgeons U.S., Minn., Duluth (pres. 1977) surg. socs., Am. Trauma Soc., Minn. Thoracic Soc., Am. Burn Assn., Soc. Clin. Vascular Surgery. Presbyterian. Club: Kitchi Gammi (Duluth). Contbr. articles to profl. jours. Home: 216 N 33d Ave E Duluth MN 55804 Office: Duluth Clinic Ltd 400 E 3d St Duluth MN 55805

KUBISTAL, PATRICIA BERNICE, elementary sch. prin.; b. Chgo., Jan. 19, 1938; d. Edward John and Bernice Mildred (Lenz) Kubistal; A.B. cum laude, Loyola U. of Chgo., 1959, A.M., 1964, A.M., 1965, Ph.D., 1968; postgrad. Chgo. State Coll., 1962, Ill. Inst. Tech., 1963, State U. Iowa, 1963, Nat. Coll. Edn., 1974-75. With Chgo. Bd. Edn., 1959—, tchr., 1959-63, counselor, 1963-65, adminstrv. intern, 1965-66, asst. to dist. supt., 1968-69, prin. spl. edn. sch., 1969-75, prin. Simpson Sch., 1975-76, Brentano Sch., 1976—; lectr. Loyola U. Sch. Edn., Nat. Coll. Edn. Grad. Sch., Mundelein Coll.; coordinator Upper Bound Program of U. Ill. Circle Campus, 1966-68. Active Crusade of Mercy; mem. com. Ill. Constnl. Conv., 1967-69; mem. Citizens Sch. Com., 1969-71; mem. edn. com. Field Mus., 1971; ednl. advisor North Side Chgo. PTA Region, 1975; gov. Loyola U., 1961—. NDEA grantee, 1963, NSF grantee, 1965, HEW Region 5 grantee for drug edn., 1974; recipient Outstanding Intern award Nat. Assn. Secondary Sch. Prins., 1966; named Outstanding History Tchr., Chgo. Pub. Schs., 1963, Outstanding Ill. Educator, 1970, Outstanding Women of Ill., 1970; St. Luke's-Logan Sq. Community Person of Yr., 1977. Mem. Ill. Personnel and Guidance Assn., NEA, Ill., Chgo. edn. assns., Am. Acad. Polit. and Social Sci., Chgo. Prins. Club (pres. aux.), Nat. Council Adminstrv. Women, Chgo. Council Exceptional Children, Chgo. Council Fgn. Relations, Chgo. Urban League, Loyal Christian Benevolent Assn., Kappa Gamma Pi, Pi Gamma Mu, Phi Delta Kappa, Delta Kappa Gamma, (parlimentarian 1979-80), Delta Sigma Rho, Phi Sigma Tau. Book review editor of Chgo. Prins. Jour., 1970-76. Home: 5111 N Oakley Ave Chicago IL 60625 Office: 2723 N Fairfield St Chicago IL 60647

KUBLEY, JAMES DANIEL, physician; b. Indpls., Apr. 11, 1948; s. James D. and F. Katherine (Pruitt) K.; B.S., Ind. U., 1970, M.D., 1973; m. Susan M. Brown, June 6, 1970; children—Andrew J., Thomas J., Anne Elizabeth, Mary Katherine. Intern, New Hanover Meml. Hosp., Wilmington, N.C., 1973-74; pvt. practice medicine, specializing in family practice, Plymouth, Ind., 1974—; mem. med. staff Parkview Hosp., Plymouth, pres., 1975-76. Pres., Plymouth Community Sch. Bd., 1979-80, v.p., 1978-79, sec., 1977-78; mem. Plymouth Bd. Zoning Appeals, 1973-74; pres. Am. Lung Assn. North Central Ind., 1978-79. Diplomate Am. Bd. Family Practice. Mem. AMA, Ind. State Med. Assn., Marshall County Med. Assn., Am. Acad. Family Physicians, Ind. Acad. Family Physicians, Nat. Sch. Bd. Assn., Ind. Sch. Bd. Assn., Victorian Soc. Am., Hist. House Owners Assn., Plymouth Jaycees, Sigma Chi. Democrat. Episcopalian. Club: Plymouth Country. Home: 704 S Michigan Plymouth IN 46563 Office: 304 N Walnut St Plymouth IN 46563

KUBO, GARY MICHAEL, advt. agy. exec.; b. Chgo., Aug. 15, 1952; s. Robert S. and Hideko K.; B.S., Ill. State U., 1974; m. Harriet Davenport, June 14, 1975. Research project dir. Foote, Cone & Belding Communicatins, Chgo., 1974-76, account research supr., 1976-79, research mgr., 1979-80; asso. research dir. Young & Rubicam, Chgo., 1980—. Mem. Advt. Research Found., Am. Mktg. Assn. Home: 6379 Kindling Ct Lisle IL 60532 Office: 111 E Wacker Dr Chicago IL 60601

KUCERA, DANIEL WILLIAM, bishop; b. Chgo., May 7, 1923; s. Joseph F. and Lillian C. (Petrzelka) K.; B.A., St. Procopius Coll., 1945; M.A., Catholic U. Am., 1950, Ph.D., 1954. Joined Order of St. Benedict, 1944, ordained priest Roman Cath. Ch., 1949; registrar St. Procopius Coll. and Acad., Lisle, Ill., 1945-49; registrar St. Procopius Coll., Lisle, 1954-56, acad. dean, head dept. edn., 1956-59, pres., 1959-65; abbot St. Procopius Abbey, Lisle, 1964-71; pres. Ill. Benedictine Coll. (formerly St. Procopius Coll.), Lisle, 1971-76, chmn. bd. trustees, 1976-78; aux. bishop of Joliet, 1977-80; bishop of Salina (Kans.), 1980—; mem. com. human values Nat. Conf. Cath. Bishops, 1979—; mem. com. on edn. U.S. Cath. Conf., 1977—; chmn. devel. council Collegio Sant' Anselmo, Rome, 1974-77. Chaplain, Chgo. council Navy League U.S., 1974-77, Czech Cath. Union; nat. adv. bd. Holy Cross Abbey and Sch., Canon City, Ill.; trustee Cath. U. Am.; bd. dirs. Ill. Cath. Conf., weekend asst. St. Louise de Marillac Parish, 1955-64. Contbr. articles to religious publs. Club: K.C. (4 deg.). Address: Chancery Office 421 Country Club Rd Salina KS 67401

KUCERA, ROBERT FRANK, food co. ofcl.; b. Cedar Rapids, Iowa, June 22, 1923; s. Frank and Libbie (Francis) K.; ed. public schs., mil. courses; m. Dorothy Mae Heicksen, Sept. 12, 1944; children—John Robert, Carol Diane. With Collins Radio Co., 1942-70; instr. Kirkwood Community Coll., 1970-74; tng. and safety supr. Quaker Oats Co., Cedar Rapids, 1974—; indsl. edn. coms. U. Iowa, Kirkwood Community Coll.; chmn. bd. dirs. Quaker Oats Credit Union; leader seminars and work shops. Mem. Cedar Rapids Conv. Bur. Ambassadors; working com. chmn. United Way. Served with USAAF, 1943-48; ETO; mem. Res., 1948-67. Mem. Am. Soc. Tng. and Devel., Am. Legion, VFW. Methodist. Club: Masons. Home: 3322 E Ave NE Cedar Rapids IA 52402 Office: 418 2d St NE Cedar Rapids IA 52401

KUCHEL, GAYLON LYLE, educator; b. Kingsley, Iowa, June 27, 1924; s. Philip and Minnie Marie (Lage) K.; B.A., U. Iowa, 1949, M.A., 1950; m. Wanda Mae Bowden, Sept. 14, 1945; children—Wade, Kimberly. Supr., Mut. Benefit H&A Assn., Omaha, 1954-63; from asst. prof. to prof. criminal justice U. Nebr., 1963—. Mem. Nebr. Commn. Law Enforcement and Criminal Justice, 1967—, Nebr. State Bd. Parole, 1969-70, Nebr. Gov.'s Com. on Jud. and Social Reform, 1971—, Omaha City Personnel Bd., 1968-74. Served with USMCR, 1942-45, with USAF, 1951-53. Mem. Acad. Criminal Justice Scis., Am. Correctional Assn., Nebr. (pres. 1976-81), Midwest (pres. 1979) assns. criminal justice educators, Am. Assn. Wardens and Supts. Contbr. articles to profl. jours. Home: 9133 Dorcas St Omaha NE 68124 Office: U Nebr 60th and Dodge Sts Omaha NE 68182

KUCHURIS, PAUL GEORGE, JR., constrn. equipment co. exec.; b. Chgo., May 6, 1942; s. Paul George and Bess (Bageanes) K.; B.S., Ind. U., 1965; m. Priscilla Kopulos, July 5, 1975; children—Margo, Gregory Paul Brooke. With Mary Ann Baking Co., Chgo., 1955-65; with Internat. Harvester Co., Schaumburg, Ill., 1965—, product cons. crawler tractors, 1969-70, regional sales rep., 1970-71, product mgr. haulers and scrapers, 1971-74, mktg. planning mgr., mining and heavy constrn., 1974-77, mktg. tng. mgr., 1977-78, mgr. worldwide mktg. tng. and product publs., 1978—. Counselor, Jr. Achievement, 1965-69; bd. dirs. Hellenic Found. Mem. Order Am. Hellenic Ednl. Progressive Assn., Am. Soc. Tng. and Devel., Phi Delta Theta. Greek Orthodox (dir. 1969-70).

KUCINSKI, LEO, musician; b. Warsaw, Poland, June 28, 1904; s. Ludwik and Kazimira (Sokolowska) K.; came to U.S., 1914, naturalized, 1921; B. Mus., Morningside Coll., 1935, D. Mus. (hon.), 1957; postgrad. Juilliard Grad. Sch., 1930-31; m. Ethel Thompson, June 20, 1928; 1 dau., Lenore. Head string dept. Morningside Coll., Sioux City, Iowa, 1925-50; condr. Lincoln (Nebr.) Symphony Orch., 1932-42, Sioux City Symphony Orch., 1935—; dir. Municipal Band Sioux City, 1929—; guest condr. Mpls. Symphony, Omaha, El Paso (Tex.), Shreveport (La.), Guadalajara (Mexico) orchs.; v.p. Am. Symphony Orch. League, 1946-48; violin soloist; cons. in field. Served to 1st lt., AUS, 1942-45; PTO. Decorated Bronze Star. Recipient civic award medal Sioux City Kiwanis Club, 1939, Sertoma Distinguished Citizen outstanding achievement in music award Sch. Musician mag., 1973, Ia. Gov.'s Music award, 1973. Mem. Am. Bandmasters Assn., Phi Mu Alpha, Phi Beta Mu. Republican. Lutheran. Mason (Shriner), Elk. Author book on Brahms. Contbr. articles to profl. publs. Home: 219 Cook Dr Sioux City IA 51104 Office: 402 Commerce Bldg Sioux City IA 51101

KUCKEL, GARY PETER, city ofcl.; b. Hartford, Conn., June 10, 1945; s. Benjamin and Rose (Vincent) K.; B.A., U. Notre Dame, 1967; M.A. in Public Adminstrn., U. Hartford, 1972; children—Kari Beth, Sara, Michael, Daniel. Claims adjuster, supr. Liberty Mutual Ins. Co., Boston, East Hartford, Conn., 1967-71; customer services rep. Covenant Ins. Co., Hartford, 1971-72; community devel. asst. dir., adminstrv. analyst City of Jackson, Mich., 1973-74; systems and budget analyst Town of West Hartford (Conn.), 1975-76; asst. city mgr. City of Riverview (Mich.), 1976-78; city mgr. City of Coldwater (Mich.), 1978—. Bd. dirs. YMCA Camp Kimball; mem. citizens adv. com. Coldwater Regional Center for Developmental Disabilities. Mem. Mich. Mpcl. League, Internat. City Mgmt. Assn., Nat. Public Employer Labor Relations Assn., Am. Planning Assn., Public Risk Ins. Mgrs. Assn., Mich. Soc. Planning Ofcls. Republican. Presbyterian. Club: Rotary. Office: 28 W Chicago St Coldwater MI 49036

KUDART, ARTHUR RONALD, lawyer, state ofcl.; b. Mount Vernon, Iowa, July 27, 1930; s. Arthur E. and Lillian Elizabeth (Schneider) K.; student Cornell Coll., Mt. Vernon, 1948-50; B.A., U. Iowa, 1952, J.D., 1958; m. Patricia L. Brown, Dec. 12, 1954; children—Kay E., Thomas A. Admitted to Iowa bar, 1958; individual practice law, Cedar Rapids, Mt. Vernon and Mechanicsville, 1958—; mem. Iowa Senate, 1979—; field staff Congressman Fred Schwengel, 1958-60. Chmn., Republican Orgn. Linn County (Iowa); vice chmn. Young Reps. Cedar Rapids, 1960-65. Served to capt. USMC, 1952-60. Mem. Iowa Bar Assn., Linn County Bar Assn., Iowa Trial Lawyers Assn., Am. Trial Lawyers Assn. Republican. Presbyterian. Author: New Republican Politics, 1972. Office: 602 Dows Bldg Cedar Rapids IA 52401

KUDELA, GARY JOSEPH, pharmacist; b. LaSalle, Ill., May 17, 1950; s. Joseph John and Elsie May (Hutt) K.; B.S.A., Drake U., 1973; m. Sandra Battalia, Apr. 19, 1974; 1 dau., Michelle. Pharmacist, mgr. Brandner's Pharmacy, Spring Valley, Ill., 1973-75; owner Kudela's Pharmacy, Spring Valley, 1975-78; pharmacist Kunkel's Drug Store, Peru, Ill., 1978-79; pharmacist Walgreen's, Sterling, Ill., 1979—. Mem. United Sch. Dist. 91 sch. bd., Spring Valley, Ill., 1977-79; active Boy Scouts Am., Peru, Ill., 1975-78, Little League, 1973—, YMCA, 1973—. Recipient Distinguished Service award, LaSalle-Peru Jaycees, 1976. Mem. Ill. Pharm Assn., Jr. C. of C. (pres. 1976-77). Clubs: Lions, Rotary. Home: 411 Elm St Spring Valley IL 61362 Office: 15 E 3 St Sterling IL 61081

KUDRNA, FRANK LOUIS, JR., state water resources ofcl.; b. Chgo., Sept. 11, 1943; s. Frank Louis and Helen Georgiana (Malcik) K.; B.S. in Archtl. Engring., Chgo. Tech. Coll., 1963; M.S. in City and Regional Planning, Ill. Inst. Tech., 1973, Ph.D. in City and Regional Planning, 1975; m. JoAnn Helen Danca, May 2, 1964; children—Karen Ann, Matthew Frank, David Charles. Engr., div. hwys. State of Ill., Chgo., 1966-68; supervising engr. planning and flood control Met. Sanitary Dist. Chgo., 1968-76; dir. div. water resources State of Ill., Chgo., 1976—; U.S. commr. to Internat. Joint Commn. Diversion and Consumptive Use Bd.; commr. Great Lakes, Upper Miss., Ohio fed. river basin commns.; instr. dept. city and regional planning Ill. Inst. Tech., 1973-75. Registered profl. engr., Ill., Wis. Mem. Nat. Soc. Profl. Engrs., ASCE, Am. Soc. Planning Ofcls., Soil Conservation Soc. Am., Am. Public Works Assn., Am. Assn. State Hwys. and Transp. Ofcls. Contbr. numerous tech. articles to profl. publs. Office: 300 N State St Chicago IL 60610

KUDRYK, OLEG, librarian; b. Rohatyn, Ukraine, Dec. 14, 1912; s. Theodosius and Olga (Spolitakevich) K.; diploma Conservatory Music, Lviv, 1934; LL.M., U. Lviv, 1937, M.A. in Econ. Sci., 1938; postgrad., U. Vienna, 1945-46; M.A. in Library Sci., U. Mich., 1960; Ph.D. in Polit. Sci., Ukrainian Free U., Munich, 1975; m. Sophie H. Dydynski, Feb. 5, 1944. Came to U.S., 1949, naturalized, 1954. Mgr., legal advisor Coop. Agrl. Soc., Chodoriv, Ukraine, 1938-39; mgr. Import Export Corp., Cracow, Poland, 1940-44; tchr. Comml. Sch., Ulm, Germany, 1946; adminstr. UNRRA, and Internat. Refugee Orgn., Stuttgart, Germany, 1947-49; asst. treas., mgr. Self-Reliance Fed. Credit Union, Detroit, 1953-60; rep., cons. Prudential Ins., Detroit, 1955-60; catalog librarian Ind. Univ., Bloomington, 1960-63, head order librarian, 1963-70, head acquisitions librarian, 1971—; lectr. Ukrainian Free U., 1975—; guest lectr. Indiana Univ. Sch. Library and Info. Sci., 1965—. Recipient grant to survey West European book trade, Indiana Univ. Office Research and Advanced Studies Internat. Programs, 1972. Mem. Ukrainian Library Assn. Am. (v.p. 1972-75; exec. bd. mem. 1975—), AAUP (chpt. treas., mem. exec. bd. 1976—), Am. Library Assn., Assn. Coll. Research Libraries, Am. Econ. Assn., Am. Acad. Polit. and Social Scis., Shevchenko Sci. Soc. Contbr. articles to various publs. Home: 409 Clover Lane Bloomington IN 47401 Office: Indiana Univ Library Acquisitions Dept Bloomington IN 47405

KUEHL, HAL C., banker; b. Davenport, Iowa, Mar. 21, 1923; s. Donald J. and Martha A. (Sierk) K.; B.B.A., U. Wis., 1947, M.B.A., 1954, postgrad. Grad. Sch. Banking, 1953; m. Joyce M. Helms, May 20, 1950; children—Cynthia Ann, David Charles. With First Wis. Nat. Bank, Milw., 1947—, v.p., 1960-65, exec. v.p. ops., 1965-66, exec. v.p., 1966-69, pres., 1969-76, dep. chmn., 1976-77, chmn. bd., chief exec. officer, 1977—, also dir.; exec. v.p., dir. First Wis. Bankshares Corp., 1971-77, pres., chief adminstrv. officer, 1977-78, pres., chief exec. officer, 1978—, also dir.; former pres., dir. 1st Wis. Internat. Bank, now chmn. bd.; chmn., trustee First Wis. Mortgage Co.; dir. First Wis. Trust Co., others. Mem. Wis. Gov.'s Council on Econ. Devel.; bd. dirs., mem. fin. com. Milw. Blood Center; mem. exec. bd. Milw. County council Boy Scouts Am.; bd. dirs., treas. Milw. Voluntary Equal Employment Opportunity Council, Greater Milw. Com.; bd. dirs., mem. exec. com. Milw. div. Am. Cancer Soc.; trustee Citizens Govtl. Research Bur.; bd. dirs. Wis. Taxpayers Alliance, Friends of Art, United Community Services Greater Milw.; mem. corp. Columbia Hosp.; trustee Greater Wis. Found. Inc., Milw. Art Center; trustee, mem. fin. com., exec. com. Marquette U. Served with USNR, 1943-45. C.P.A., Wis. Mem. Am. Bankers Assn., Assn. Res. City Bankers, Am. Inst. Banking, Met. Milw. Assn. Commerce, Navy League U.S., Sigma Chi. Episcopalian. Clubs: Milwaukee, Milwaukee Country, University (Milw.). Office: First Wis Corp 773 E Wisconsin Ave Milwaukee WI 53202

KUEHL, RONALD JOHN, soil scientist; b. Elkader, Iowa, June 22, 1944; s. John Fred and Mildred Louise (Dahl) K.; B.S., Iowa State U., 1966, M.S., 1978. Soil scientist Soil Conservation Service, Dept. Agr., Waterloo, Iowa, 1968-71, soil scientist party leader, Elkader, 1972-78, soil specialist, Des Moines, 1979-80, asst. state soil scientist, Ames, Iowa, 1980—. Served with U.S. Army, 1966-68. Decorated Army Commendation medal. Mem. Soil Sci. Soc. Am., Am. Soc. Agronomy, Profl. Soil Classifiers Iowa. Lutheran. Home: 307 Abraham St Ames IA 50010 Office: Agronomy Lab Iowa State U Ames IA 50011

KUEKER, VIOLET LOUISE, educator; b. East St. Louis, Ill., June 27, 1929; d. Marcellus C. and Mildred M. (Meyer) Hartman; student MacMurray Coll., 1947-49; B.S. in Edn., So. Ill. U., Carbondale, 1951; M.Ed., U. Ill., 1957; m. Edmund E. Kueker, Mar. 31, 1951. Home econs. tchr. Zeigler (Ill.) High Sch., 1951-52, Waterloo (Ill.) Public High Schs., 1952—. Past mem. North Central Evaluation Team; mem. Ill. Vocat. Evaluation Team, 1981—. Mem. NEA (life), Am. Home Econs. Assn., Nat. Assn. Vocat. Home Econs. Tchrs., Am. Vocat. Assn., Am. Council Consumer Internat, Ill. Coop. Vocat. Edn. Coordinators Assn., Ill. Consumer Edn. Assn., Ill. Edn. Assn., Ill. Home Econs. Assn., (pres. dist. V 1981-82), Ill. Vocat. Home Econs. Tchrs. Assn., Ill. Vocational Assn., Monroe County Homemakers Extension Assn., Monroe County Fair Assn., Monroe County Hist. Soc., Waterloo Classroom Tchrs. Assn., Delta Kappa Gamma. Mem. Ch. of Christ. Clubs: Evening Women's Guild; Ladies Aux. Nat. Auctioneers Assn. Waterloo IL 62298 Office: Bellefontaine Dr Waterloo IL 62298

KUENSTER, JOHN JOSEPH, pub. co. exec., editor; b. Chgo., June 18, 1924; s. Roy Jacob and Kathryn Elizabeth (Holechek) K.; student Mt. Carmel Coll., Niagara Falls, Ont., Can., 1942-43, DePaul U., 1945-46; m. Mary Virginia Maher, Feb. 15, 1947; children—Kathleen Kuenster Mulcahy, James, Lois Kuenster Fitzmaurice, Virginia Kuenster Friedman, Margaret Kuenster Murphy, Kevin, Mary Frances, Robert. Sport editor New World, Chgo., 1946-48; asso. dir. publicity Cath. Youth Orgn., Chgo., 1946-48; editor The Columbian, Chgo., 1948-57; staff writer Chgo. Daily News, 1957-65; dir. devel. and public relations Mercy Hosp., Chgo., 1965-66; editor Papal Vol. mag., Chgo., 1966-68; dir. devel. and public relations The Claretian Fathers, Chgo., 1966—; v.p., advt. mgr. Columbian Pub. Co., Chgo., 1963-80; editor Baseball Digest, Evanston, Ill., 1969—. Mem. Baseball Writers Assn. Am. (chpt. pres. 1964). Club: KC. Home: 9546 S Ridgeway Ave Evergreen Park IL 60642 Office: 1020 Church St Evanston IL 60201

KUGLER, MARJORIE MEANEY, interior designer; b. Boston, Jan. 30, 1939; d. Daniel J. and Marjorie Viola (Eno) M.; student Coll. of St. Catherine's, 1956-57; B.S., U. Minn., 1961; m. John A. Kugler, Dec. 26, 1964; children—Gretchen, Teresa, Kristine. Drapery dept. Emporium, 1956-61; supr. design dept. Farnham's Office Furniture Co., 1965-67; interior designer Jacobson's Office Furniture, Mpls., 1961-65, Voight & Fourre, Architects, St. Paul, 1968-72; partner, interior designer Interspace, St. Paul, 1972—; instr. adult edn. St. Paul Schs., 1975—; lectr. in field. Constl. com. Mary Mother of the Ch. Parish Council, St. Paul, 1968-69; active Girl Scouts U.S., 1974-78; v.p., Snail Lake Parent Tchrs. Orgn., St. Paul, 1977-78, pres., 1978-79. Republican. Roman Catholic. Clubs: U. Minn. Alumni, No Name Ski, SWO Gypsies Ski, Thirty-Nine. Interior designer apt. complex, dining rooms Coll. St. Benedict's, St. Joseph, Minn., 1972-73, 1st Bank St. Paul, others. Home and office: 7 Sunset Ln North Oaks Saint Paul MN 55110

KUGLITSCH, JOHN FRANCIS, internist; b. Springfield, Mass., Dec. 27, 1942; s. Frank Gabriel and Elizabeth Mary (Frigon) K.; B.S., Marquette U., 1965, M.D., 1969; m. Maureen Rose Hall, Aug. 26, 1967; children—Paul David, Mark Patrick. Intern, St. Joseph's Hosp., Milw., 1969-70; fellow in internal medicine Mayo Clinic, Mayo Grad. Sch. Medicine, Rochester, Minn., 1970-73; practice medicine specializing in internal medicine, Fond du Lac, Wis., 1973—; mem. staff St. Agnes Hosp., 1973—, dir. med. edn., 1975-77. Diplomate Am. Bd. Internal Medicine. Mem. AMA, Am., Wis. socs. internal medicine, Fox Valley Acad. Medicine, A.C.P., Am. Geriatrics Soc., Assn. Hosp. Med. Edn., N.Y. Acad. Scis., Continuing Med. Edn. Club Wis., Wis. State, Fond du Lac County med. socs., Mayo Alumni Assn. Club: Elks. Home: 140 Fanna St Fond du Lac WI 54935 Office: Fond du Lac Clinic 80 Sheboygan St Fond du Lac WI 54935

KUHAR, JUNE CAROLYNN, fiberglass mfg. co. exec.; b. Chgo., Sept. 20, 1935; d. Kurt Ludwig and Dorothy Julia (Lewand) Stier; student William Rainey Harper Coll., Chgo.; m. G. James Kuhar, Feb. 5, 1953; children—Kathleen Lee, Debra Suzanne. Engaged in fiberglass mfg., 1970—; sec.-treas. Q-R Fiber Glass Industries Inc., Elgin, 1970—. Mem. Mt. Prospect (Ill.) Bus. and Profl. Woman's Club. Home: 2303 Meadow Dr Rolling Meadows IL 60008 Office: 701 N State St Elgin IL 60120

KUHL, MARGARET HELEN CLAYTON (MRS. ALEXIUS M. KUHL), banker; b. Louisville; d. Joseph Leonard and Maude (Mitzler) Clayton; student Loyola U. Home Study Div., Chgo., 1955—, Buena Vista Coll., Storm Lake, Iowa, summer 1964-65; m. Alexius M. Kuhl, Apr. 21, 1936; children—Carol Lynn (Mrs. Richard Benton Ford), James Michael (adopted). Sales lady, buyer Silverberg, Akron, Iowa, 1924-34; owner dress shop. Fonda, Iowa, 1934-40; librarian, Fonda, 1940-43; bookkeeper, teller First Nat. Bank, Fonda, 1943-44; tchr. librarian asst. Our Lady Good Counsel Sch., Fonda, 1963-70; dir. Pomeroy State Bank, 1959—, pres., chmn. bd., 1975—. Pres. state bd. Women in Community Service, 1970-72, state coordinator, 1973. Recipient Adult Leadership award Cath. Youth Orgn. Sioux City, Iowa, 1967; Nat. Cath. Youth Orgn. award, 1969. Mem. Cath. Daus. Am. (dist. dep. 1964-70, state del. nat. conv. 1968, 62-68, grand regent 1960-61, chmn. ecumenism 1969-71, state treas. 1969-71), Diocesan (chmn. orgn. and devel. 1964-66, pres.), Nat. (sec. diocesan bd., 1966-68, diocesan del. nat. conv. 1962, 64, 68, diocesan pres. 1968, 70, chmn. pub. relations 1962) councils Cath. women, Legion of Mary (pres. curia 1964-70, chmn. curia extension 1960-64), Internat. Biog. Assn., Internat. Platform Assn., Nat. Assn. Bank Women. Club: Fonda Country. Home: 5th and Queen Sts Fonda IA 50540

KUHL, ROBERT HENRY, surgeon; b. St. Louis, July 9, 1915; s. Robert Joseph and Carolyn B. (Waldemer) K.; A.B., Pa. State U., 1937; M.D., St. Louis U., 1941; student Washington U. Sch.

Medicine, 1947; m. Ellen Eudora Hosler, Dec. 24, 1941; children—Marilyn Lee, Katherine Ann, Robert Malcolm, Jon Gregory. Intern, St. Louis City Hosp., 1941-42; resident in surgery St. Louis County Hosp., 1946-50; since practiced medicine, specializing in surgery, Creston, Iowa; sr. surgeon, also one of founders, Creston Med. Clinic, 1953—; dir. Creston Clinic Bldg. Corp., Creston Industries, Inc. Served from 1st lt. to capt. M.C., AUS, 1942-46, 117th Gen. Hosp., Eng., 1943-44, 26th Div., ETO, 1944-45. Diplomate Am. Bd. Surgery. Fellow Internat. Coll. Surgeons; mem. AMA, Iowa, Union County med. assns., Creston C. of C. (dir.). Home: 104 S Park St Creston IA 50801 Office: 526 New York Ave Creston IA 50801

KUHLMAN, THOMAS ASHFORD, educator, writer; b. Cleve., May 24, 1939; s. Orlyn Lee and Catherine Mary (Ashford) K.; A.B. honors degree, Xavier U., 1961; A.M., Brown U., 1963, Ph.D., 1967; m. Mary Louise Haynes, Aug. 22, 1964; children—John Christopher, Katherine Mary. Teaching fellow Brown U., 1963-64; instr. English, Georgetown U., 1964-67; asst. prof. English, Creighton U., 1967-70, asso. prof., 1970—, coordinator continuing edn., 1973-74, editor jour., 1981—; vis. scholar Am. Acad. in Rome, 1981—; mem. faculty Inst. Jewish Studies, Omaha, 1974-75; regional dir. Nat. Bicentennial Youth Debates, 1975-76; dir. Copper Hollow Writers Workshop, 1977-78; regional humanist Nebr. Com. Humanities, 1976-78; project reviewer Nat. Endowment Humanities, 1979; mem. humanities curriculum com. Nebr. Ednl. TV Commn. for Higher Edn., 1979—; plays include: Each of These Landlords (Nebr. State Repertory Co. Bicentennial Playwriting Contest 1st prize), 1976; Mr. Smith Goes to the Exposition, 1978; books edited include: Creative Writing: An Experience in Publishing for Older Persons, 1979; contbr. to Riverfront: The Humanist Speaks (Harvey Leavitt, editor), 1976; contbr. articles to mags., newspapers and profl. jours. Mem. Omaha Symphony Council, 1972-79, mem. exec. com., 1974-77; Heritage chmn., bd. dirs. Omaha-Douglas County Bicentennial Commn., 1974-76; sec., bd. dirs. Met. Arts Council, 1976-78; speakers bur. chmn., bd. advisors Landmarks, Inc.; bd. dirs. Florence Arts and Humanities Council, 1979—, pres., 1980; pres. Ponca Sch. P.T.A., 1976-78. Woodrow Wilson fellow, 1961; Office of Edn. Humanities research grantee, 1968; Nebr. Arts Council grantee, 1978; Canadian Govt. Faculty Devel. Programme grantee, 1979; Creighton U. Faculty Research grantee, 1969. Mem. Popular Culture Assn., Midcontinent Am. Studies Assn. (Nebr. rep. exec. com. 1969-72), Nebr. Writers Guild, AAUP (sec. Creighton U. chpt. 1969-70), Alpha Sigma Nu. Roman Catholic. Home: 12107 N 40th St Omaha NE 68112 Office: Dept of English and Speech Creighton University Omaha NE 68178

KUHN, JOHN FRED, hosp. adminstr.; b. Ft. Myers, Fla., Jan. 13, 1950; s. Fred Albert and Margaret Katherine (Owens) K.; B.B.A., Loyola U., Chgo., 1972; M.H.A., Northwestern U., 1974; postgrad. U. Richmond, 1975-76; m. Marion Theresa Kuhn, May 23, 1976. Adminstrv. asst., chief of staff Kenner Army Hosp., Ft. Lee, Va., 1975, hosp. constrn. project officer, 1976-77; adminstr. for medicine and ambulatory care VA Med. Center, Ann Arbor, Mich., 1977-79, adminstr. for research, 1979—, quality assurance coordinator, 1981—, asst. to dir., 1981—. Active, Western Detroit Area Hosp. Council, Washtenaw County United Way, Washtenaw County Disaster Planning Council. Served with U.S. Army, 1974-77. Decorated Army Commendation medal; recipient Outstanding Scholarship award Loyola U., 1972. Mem. VA Mgmt. Tng. Program sponsored by Boston U., 1978. Mem. Am. Hosp. Assn., Am. Coll. Hosp. Adminstrs., Research Soc. Am., Am. Soc. for Hosp. Planning, Acad. of Mgmt. Home: 5226 Schooner Cove Ypsilanti MI 48197 Office: VA Med Center 2210 Fuller Rd Ann Arbor MI 48105

KUHN, KATHLEEN JO, acct.; b. Springfield, Ill., Aug. 9, 1947; d. Henry Elmer and Norma Florene (Niehaus) Burge; B.S. in Bus., Bradley U., 1969; m. Gerald L. Kuhn, June 22, 1968; 1 son, Gerald Lynn. Controller, Byerly Music Co., Peoria, Ill., 1969-70; staff acct. Clifton Gunderson & Co., Columbus, Ind., 1970-71; acct. Dept. ot Transp., State of Ill., Springfield, 1972-76; acct. Gerald L. Kuhn & Assos., C.P.A.s, Springfield, 1976-78, partner, 1979—. Recipient attendance award Continuing Profl. Edn. for Accts., 1977, 78, 79, 80; notary public, Ill.; C.P.A., Ill. Mem. Am. Inst. C.P.A.s, Ill. Soc. C.P.A.s, Am. Woman's Soc. C.P.A.s. Lutheran. Clubs: Olympic Swim, Metro. Federated Jr. Women's. Writer, editor Policy Guideline of Gerald L. Kuhn & Assos., 1979-80. Home: 2511 Westchester St Springfield IL 62704 Office: 323 S Grand Ave W Springfield IL 62704

KUHN, WILLIAM PETER, physician; b. Chgo., Sept. 27, 1932; s. Philip James and Agnes (Enright) K.; student St. Mary of Lake Sem., 1951-54, Loyola U., Chgo., 1954-56; M.D., St. Louis U., 1960; m. Mary Duchesne Marheineke, June 11, 1960; children—Joseph G., Genevieve M., William Peter II, Peter M., Kathleen A., Martin P. Intern, St. Louis U. Hosps., 1960-61; resident in pediatrics Children's Meml. Hosp., Chgo., 1961-63; practice medicine specializing in pediatrics, Arlington Heights, Ill., 1963—; mem. staff Northwest Community Hosp., Arlington Heights, Children's Meml. Hosp., Chgo.; asso., dept. pediatrics Northwestern U. Mem. Am. Acad. Pediatrics, AMA, Ill. Med. Soc., Chgo. Med. Soc., Chgo. Pediatric Soc. Roman Catholic. Home: 1106 Viator Ct Arlington Heights IL 60004 Office: 1100 W Central Rd Arlington Heights IL 60005

KUHRMEYER, CARL ALBERT, mfg. co. exec.; b. St. Paul, May 12, 1928; s. Carl and Irma Luella (Lindeke) K.; B.S. in Mech. Engring., U. Minn., 1949; m. Janet Pedersen, Oct. 31, 1953; children—Karen, John, Paul. Design engr. Magney, Tusler & Setter, 1950-51; with 3M Co., St. Paul, 1951—, div./group v.p., 1967-80, corp. v.p. adminstrn., 1980—; dir. Northwestern Nat. Bank of St. Paul. Mem. nat. adv. council Nat. Multiple Sclerosis Soc.; v.p. St. Paul Area Council Chs. Mem. United Ch. of Christ. Clubs: St. Paul Athletic, North Oaks Country, White Bear Yacht, Masons, Shriners. Patentee in field. Office: 3M Center Saint Paul MN 55144

KUKLIN, REBA MAGID, author, publisher; b. Nashville, Aug. 25, 1914; d. Victor and Becky (Frankel) Magid; B.S. in Edn. with distinction, U. Nebr., 1955, M.Ed., 1962; m. Harry H. Kuklin, Dec. 25, 1939; children—Bailey Howard, Bonnie Irene, Victor Alan. Tchr. elementary schs., Lincoln, Nebr., 1955-57; tchr. jr. high sch. English and social studies, Lincoln, 1957-77; founder, pres. Mercantine Press, Lincoln, 1979—; author: Learn to Invest and Trade on Wall Street, 1979. Mem. NEA, Assn. Women Entrepreneurs, Nebr. Edn. Assn., Lincoln Edn. Assn., Hadassah. Address: 4351 Washington St Lincoln NE 68506

KULIS, JOSEPH CHESTER, psychologist, educator; b. Chgo., Aug. 24, 1941; s. Chester J. and Rose M. Kulis; B.S. with honors, Loyola U., Chgo., 1963; M.A., Northwestern U., 1968, Ph.D., 1970; m. Diane M. Shaffer, Feb. 8, 1964; children—Joseph J., Jonathan C. Prof. psychology Chgo. City Coll., 1970—; pvt. practice psychology, Oakbrook, Ill., 1975—; cons. to fed., state, local criminal justice agys., pvt. firms, 1973—. Vol. mem. promotional evaluation bds. Chgo. Police Dept., 1975. NSF fellow, 1963-68. Mem. Am. Psychol. Assn., Midwestern Psychol. Assn., Ill. Psychol. Assn. Designer tng. techniques for devel. human relations skills. Home: 173 Gage Rd Riverside IL 60546 Office: 120 Oak Brook Center Mall Suite 321 Oak Brook IL 60521

KULPRATHIPANJA, SANTI, chemist; b. Thailand, Sept. 18, 1944; came to U.S., 1968; s. Henglee and Morsul (Gor) Lim; B.S., Chulalongkorn U., 1968; M.S., E. Tex. State U., 1970; Ph.D., Iowa State U., 1974; m. Apinya Prasertsintu, Nov. 25, 1974; children—Sathit, Ames, Ann. Research asso. M.I.T., Cambridge, 1975-78; research asso. Mass. Gen. Hosp., Boston, 1976-78; research asso. Harvard Med. Sch., 1977-78; sr. research chemist UOP, Inc., Des Plaines, Ill., 1978-81, research specialist, 1981—. Mem. Am. Chem. Soc., Soc. Nuclear Medicine, Chgo. Soc. Chromatography, Chgo. Catalysis Club, Phi Lambda Upsilon. Contbr. articles to tech. jours. Patentee in field of separations. Home: 3920 Winston Dr Hoffman Estates IL 60195 Office: Ten UOP Plaza Algonquin and Mount Prospect Rds Des Plaines IL 60016

KUMAR, ADARSH AMAR, dermatologist; b. Mianawali, India, July 15, 1944; came to U.S., 1969, naturalized, 1975; s. Lal Chand and Vidya Vati K.; M.D., All India Inst. Med. Scis., New Delhi, 1965; m. Nada, June 26, 1971; children—Ambika, Leslie, Yasmin. Intern, Cook County Hosp., Chgo., 1969-70; resident in dermatology Rush-Presbyn. St. Luke's Med. Center, Chgo., 1970-73; practice medicine specializing in dermatology, Springfield, Ill., 1973—; clin. asso. prof. medicine and dermatology So. Ill. U. Sch. Medicine, Springfield, 1973—; cons. dermatologist St. John's Hosp., Springfield Community Hosp., Meml. Med. Center; clin. asso. Barnes Hosp., Washington U. Sch. Medicine, St. Louis; cons. Dept. Public Health, Springfield, Diplomate Am. Bd. Dermatology. Fellow Royal Coll. Physicians Can., Am. Acad. Dermatology; mem. AMA, ACP, Soc. Investigative Dermatology, Am. Soc. Dermatologic Surgery, Dermatology Found., Chgo. Dermatologic Soc., St. Louis Dermatologic Soc., Mo. Dermatologic Soc., Internat. Soc. Tropical Dermatology. Clubs: Springfield Med., Am. Businessmen's. Contbr. articles to med. jours. Home: 5 Oakwood Dr Rural Route 6 Springfield IL 62707 Office: Springfield Clinic 1025 S 7th St Springfield IL 62703

KUNA, BETTE J(ANE), mcpl. ofcl.; b. East St. Louis, Ill., Apr. 4, 1936; d. William John and Catherine Josephine (von Euw) K.; B.S. in Indsl. Safety cum laude, Central Mo. State U., 1978; M.A. in Bus. Adminstrn., Webster Coll., 1980; children—John A. III, David William Schmiemeier. Substitute tchr. City of St. Louis, 1972-75; mgr., owner 2 pharmacies, St. Louis, 1970-78; safety cons., St. Louis, 1978-80; safety dir./mgr. City of St. Louis, 1980—; speaker Mo. Gov.'s Conf. on Safety, 1981. Active Girl Scouts U.S.A., 1974—; active CD. Mem. Am. Soc. Safety Engrs., Nat. Assn. Safety Mgrs., Safety Council St. Louis, Nat. Safety Council, Am. Soc. Profl. Women, Phi Kappa Phi. Roman Catholic. Home: 4832 Allemania St Saint Louis MO 63116 Office: Room 18A Municipal Courts Bldg Saint Louis MO 63103

KUNDERT, ALICE E., state ofcl.; b. Java, S.D., July 23, 1920; d. Otto J. and Maria (Rieger) Kundert; ed. North State Tchrs. Coll. Tchr. pub. schs., Campbell County, S.D., 1939-43, 49-54; from clk to mgr., buyer, dept. store and dress shop, Calif., 1943-48; dep. supt. schs. Campbell County, 1954; county clk of cts., 1955-60; county register of deeds, 1961-68; sec.-treas. Campbell County Republican party, 1962-64, finance chmn., 1962-68, vice chmn., 1964-68; presdl. elector Rep. Party of S.D., 1964; town treas., Mound City, S.D., 1965-68; state auditor S.D., 1969-79, sec. state, 1979—. Leader, project leader, 4-H; acting chmn., vice chmn. Black Hills Leaders Lab., exec. sec. citizen's responsibility com. Internat. Leaders Tng. Lab., Ireland, 1963; mem. S.D. Local Study Commn., 1967—; mem. state and local adv. coms. Office Equal Opportunity. Named Outstanding Teen Age Republican adviser, 1971-72, 76; recipient Alumni award No. State Coll. Congregationalist. Author: History of the County of Campbell, 1960. Office: State Capitol Bldg Pierre SD 57501

KUNER, CHARLES, educator; b. Chgo., July 3, 1938; s. George and Rose (Ronsky) K.; B.A. in History, Roosevelt U., 1962; M.A., Northeastern Ill. State U., 1970, M.A. in Social Sci., 1977. Tchr., Funston Elem. Sch., Chgo., 1964-65, Von Steuben Upper Grade Center, Chgo., 1963-64, Mason Upper Grade Center, Chgo., 1962-63; tchr. social sci. and social studies Farragut High Sch., Chgo., 1965—, com. chmn. to establish philosophy, objectives, renovation of curriculum, 1974, 80; mem. com. selection of textual, non-textual materials Chgo. Bd. Edn., 1972. Recipient cert. United Negro Coll. Fund, 1981; award Black Studies Workshop, Farragut High Sch., 1974; named One of Nation's Outstanding Secondary Sch. Educators, 1974. Mem. Chgo. Tchrs. Union, Nat. Council for Social Studies, Ill. Council for Social Studies, Nat. Council and Assn. for Curriculum Devel., Chgo. Art Inst., Ill. Assn. for Curriculum Devel., Field Mus., Council for Fgn. Relations. Democrat. Jewish. Contbr. articles to profl. jours. Home: 6204 N Hoyne St Chicago IL 60659 Office: 2345 S Christiana St Chicago IL 60623

KUNG, FAN HAO, educator; b. Kwangtong, China, July 7, 1935; came to U.S., 1961, naturalized, 1974; s. David Tim and Lillian S. (Lei) K.; M.F., Oreg. State U., 1962; Ph.D., Mich. State U., 1968; m. Esther L. Tan, June 11, 1966; children—Samuel, Jonathan, David. Photogrammetricist, photo-interpreter State Office, Bur. Land Mgmt., Portland, Oreg., 1962-63; research asst. dept. forestry Mich. State U., East Lansing, 1964-66, research aid dept. soil sci., 1967; inventory forester Div. Forestry, State of Wyo., Cheyenne, 1967-70; asst. prof. dept. forestry So. Ill. U., Carbondale, 1970-76, asso. prof., 1976—; chmn. N. Am. Quantitative Forest Genetics Group, 1976-77; mem. Tree Improvement Com. Walnut Council, 1973-79. Mem. Internat. Union Forest Research Orgns., Biometrics Soc., Am. Statis. Assn., Quantitative Forest Genetics Group, Western Forest Geneticists, Midwest Forest Mensurationists, Ill. State Acad. Sci., Sigma Xi, Xi Sigma Pi. Baptist. Author: A Handbook of Graphical Solutions to Forest Biometrics Problems, 1973; contbr. articles to profl. jours. Home: 204 Hewitt St Carbondale IL 62901 Office: Dept Forestry So Ill U Carbondale IL 62901

KUNKEL, LLOYD NELSON, museum curator; b. Oregon, Mo., Nov. 14, 1897; s. Bernard Nelson and Ona Bonnell (Crowell) K.; B.Sc., U. Nebr., 1929, M.D., 1931; m. Dorothy Grace Holman, Apr. 12, 1930; children—Carolyn Bonnell Kunkel Boomer, Dorothy Ann. Intern, Evang. Covenant Hosp., Omaha, 1931-32; gen. practice medicine, Weeping Water, Nebr., 1932-73; city physician, Weeping Water, 1933-73; dir. Colo. N.G. Band, 1922-23; curator Heritage House Museum, Weeping Water, 1971—; dir. various archaeol. digs, 1933—. Dir. Weeping Water Civil Def., 1965-70; bd. dirs. Weeping Water Little Symphony Orch. and Mcpl. Band, 1933-40. Served with U.S. Army, 1916-19, 40-46; A.E.F. in France. Mem. AMA, Am. Geriatric Soc., Nebr. State Med. Assn., Cass County Med. Soc. (past pres.), Internat. Violin Makers Soc., Ariz. Violin Makers Assn., Nebr. State Hist. Soc. (life). Republican. Methodist. Club: Elks. Author: Archeology of the Weeping Water Valley, 1939. Excavated 14 prehistoric Indian houses; maker of original model violins and violas. Address: 404 S Randolph St Weeping Water NE 68463

KUNTZ, EARL JEREMY, telephone communications co. exec.; b. Chgo., July 21, 1929; s. S. Emil and G. Ruth (Beitscher) K.; student Northwestern U., 1948-50; m. Mary M. Kohls, July 28, 1957; children—Karen A., Bradford G. Salesman sales display advt. Chgo. Fgn. Newspapers, Chgo., 1948-50; partner Gen. Bus. Service, Chgo., 1951-59; pres. Gen. Telephone Answering Service, Chgo., 1960—; owner Chgo. Office Forms Co., 1957—; pres. Partimers, Inc., 1970—; mktg. cons., v.p. Phone Aide Co., Inc. div. Wells Gardner Electronics, 1972-76; pres. Telephone Answering Services of Ill., Inc., 1972-74. Vice-pres. PTA, Wilmette, Ill., 1972-73; trustee Communications Research Found., Sausalito, Calif., 1976—; caucus del. Wilmette Sch. Bd., 1973-76. Mem. Assn. Telephone Answering Exchanges (dir.). Clubs: Execs., Monroe (Chgo.). Inventor telephone related devices to improve and simplify communication in telephone answering industry. Office: 30 W Washington St Chicago IL 60602

KUNZE, RALPH CARL, savs. and loan exec.; b. Buffalo, Oct. 31, 1925; s. Bruno E. and Esther (Graubman) K.; B.B.A., U. Cin., 1950; postgrad. Ind., U. 1954-56, U. Cin., 1962-63, U. So. Calif., 1973; m. Helen Hites Sutton, Apr. 29, 1978; children—Bradley, Diane Kunze Cowgill, James. With Mt. Lookout Savs. & Loan Co., Cin., 1951-63; v.p. Buckeye Fed. Savs. & Loan Assn. Columbus, Ohio, 1963, v.p., sec., 1964-67, exec. v.p., 1967-70, pres., sec., 1970-77, vice chmn. bd., 1970-77; exec. v.p. Gate City Savs. and Loan Assn., Fargo, N.D., 1977, pres., chief operating officer, dir. 1978-81; pres., chief exec. officer, dir. Home Fed. Savs. and Loan Assn., Toledo, 1981—. Pres. United Way of Franklin County, Ohio, 1977; trustee Wesley Glen Meth. Retirement Center, 1974-77; past pres. Ohio Soc. Prevention Blindness; bd. dirs. Arthritis Found. Served with USNR, 1944-45. Mem. Lambda Chi Alpha. Mason (32 deg.). Club: Rotary. Home: 2606 Emmick Dr Toledo OH 43606 Office: 629 Madison Ave Toledo OH 43604

KUO, LAWRENCE TA HSIEN, mech. engr.; b. Shanghai, China, Nov. 20, 1925; came to U.S., 1945, naturalized, 1955; s. John Y. J. and Martha M. L. K.; B.S.M.E., Chiao Tung U., Shanghai, 1944; M.S.M.E., Washington U., St. Louis, 1949; m. Shirley L. Miles, Oct. 10, 1946; children—Robin M., David L., Julie L. Research engr. Magic Chef, St. Louis, 1953; area mgr. div. climate control Singer Co., St. Louis, 1954-80; sr. project engr. div. def. systems Am. Air Filter Co., St. Louis, 1980—. Mem. Ritenour Bd. Edn., St. Louis, 1970—, pres., 1977-79; mem. Fed. Relation Network as rep. U.S. 2d Congl. Dist. for Nat. Sch. Bd. Assn. Served to maj. USAAF, 1944-46. Registered profl. engr., Mo., Wis. Mem. ASHRAE, Am. Acoustical Soc., Refrigeration Service Engrs. Soc. Presbyterian. Club: Rotary (pres. 1976-77) (Overland, Mo.). Home: 3936 Tipton Dr Saint Louis MO 63134 Office: 1270 N Price Rd Saint Louis MO 63132

KUPCINET, ESSEE SOLOMON, TV producer; b. Chgo., Dec. 7; d. Joseph David and Doris (Schoke) Solomon; Ph.B., Northwestern U., 1937; m. Irv Kupcinet, Feb. 12, 1939; children—Karyn (dec.), Jerry S. Asst. to dir. psychology dept. Michael Reese Hosp., Chgo., 1939-41; exec. producer eight Jefferson Award Shows; producer 1st Literary Arts Ball, Cultural Center, Chgo., 1979; talent coordinator Kup's Show, Chgo., 1964—; producer for spl. events, 1978—. Co-chmn. Community Arts Found.; mem. exec. bd. Free Street Theatre; mem. adv. bd. Shakespeare Festival; mem. adv. com. Chgo. Pub. Library Cultural Center, 1977; mem. adv. bd., producer 1st Annual Community Arts Found., 1978; mem. adv. bd. DePaul-Goodman Sch. Drama, Wisdom Bridge Theatre, Organic Theatre, Free St. Theatre, Stage Center at the Forum; League Chgo. Theatres, 1979. Recipient Spl. award Jefferson Com., 1976; Cliff Dwellers award, 1975; Emmy award CBS, 1977, 79; Artisan award Acad. Theatre Arts and Friends, 1977; Prime Minister's medal for service to Israel, 1974, others. Mem. Nat. Acad. TV Arts and Scis. (mem. governing bd.). Jewish. Club: Arts.

KUPCINET, IRV, columnist; b. Chgo., July 31, 1912; s. Max and Anna (Paswell) K.; m. Essee Solomon, Feb. 12, 1939; children-Karyn (dec.), Jerry; student Northwestern U., 1931; B.A., U. N.D., 1935. With Chgo. Times (now Chgo. Sun-Times), 1935—, columnist Kup's Column, 1943—, host television talk show Kup's Show, 1958—. Conducted Purple Heart Cruise, from 1945; active United Cerebral Palsy Assn., Chgo. Heart Assn., Shimer Coll., Mt. Carroll, Ill. Office: 401 N Wabash Ave Chicago IL 60611*

KURIVIAL, PATRICK FRANK, ednl. adminstr.; b. Chgo., July 17, 1946; s. Frank John and Lee K.; B.A., Monmouth Coll., 1967; M.S.Ed., No. Ill. U., 1971; m. Bobbie Lockhart, Aug. 20, 1967; 1 son, Ted. Tchr. social studies, Laraway Sch., Joliet, Ill., 1967-68; tchr. English, social studies, Dist. 109 Ill., 1968-70; chmn. social studies dept., Wilkins Jr. High Sch., Justice, Ill., 1970-79, teaching team leader, 1972-79; social studies supr. Indian Springs Dist. 109, Justice, 1979—; condr. workshops on Annehurst Curriculum Classification System, field trip planning. Active Cub Scouts Am. Mem. Assn. Supervision and Curriculum Devel., Am. Fedn. Tchrs., Annehurst Network Nat. Council Social Studies, Social Studies Supervision Assn., Ill. Assn. Curriculum and Supervision, Midwest Mil. Simulations Assn., Phi Delta Kappa. Club: Tinley Park (Ill.) Racquet Ball. Office: Indian Springs Sch 80th and 82d Ave Justice IL 60458

KUROPAS, STEPHEN, agrl. engr., real estate broker; b. Peremyshl, Ukraine, Oct. 1, 1900; came to U.S., 1927, naturalized, 1932; s. Dmytro and Marie (Pawlish) K.; Engr., Coll. Agr., Prague Czechoslovakia, 1924; m. Antoinette Mehal, Oct. 24, 1931; children—Myron, Vera. Shipping clk. Internat. Harvester Co., Chgo., 1926-27; mgr. sta. Standard Oil Co., Chgo., 1927-36, owner, operator, 1936-70, ret., 1970; real estate broker, Royal Homes Realty, Chgo., 1975—; editor Ind. Ukraine Mag., 1970-71; writer Svoboda, newspaper. Controller, Ukrainian Nat. Assn., 1938-48, v.p., 1948-70. Served with Austrian Army, 1918. Mem. Soc. Ukrainian Engrs. Republican. Byzantine Catholic. Contbr. articles to newspapers. Office: Royal Homes Realty 6841 W Belmont Chicago IL 60634

KURPIUS, RONALD THEODORE, food co. exec.; b. Elkhorn, Wis., Apr. 27, 1942; s. Theodore Wallace and Elizabeth Ann (Kappas) K.; student No. Ill. U., 1964-66; B.S., So. Ill. U., 1969; M.S., Mich. State U., 1971, M.B.A., 1971; m. Ruth Ann Campbell, Aug. 13, 1966; children—Patrick Ronald, Michael Robert, Timothy John. Food technician Armour Foods, Oakbrook, Ill., 1971; sr. food technician, Ralston Purina Co., St. Louis, 1972, project leader, 1973, mgr. tech. services, 1974, product mgr., 1975; new bus. mgr. The Park Corp., Barrington, Ill., 1975-76; with Kitchens of Sara Lee, Deerfield, Ill., 1976—, group products mgr. bakery and deli, 1981—. Served with Ordnance Corps, U.S. Army, 1961-64. Mem. Inst. Food Technologists. Office: Kitchens of Sara Lee 500 Waukegan Rd Deerfield IL 60015

KURTICH, JOHN WILLIAM, architect, film-maker, educator; b. Salinas, Calif., Oct. 18, 1935; s. John Joseph and Elizabeth (Lyons) K.; B.A. in Theatre and Cinematography, UCLA, 1957; B.Arch., U. Calif., Berkeley, 1966; M.S. in Architecture and Urban Design (William Kinne fellow, Fgn. Travelling fellow), Columbia U., 1968. Film-maker SMP, Architects, San Francisco, 1960-61; film-maker, archtl. draftsman McCue & Assos., San Francisco, 1962-66; free-lance film-maker, designer, Frieberg, N.Y., 1968; instr. Sch. of Art Inst. Chgo., 1968-70, asst. prof., 1970-74, asso. prof., 1974—, chmn. dept. design and communication, 1977—; staff architect Am. Excavations, Samothrace, Greece, 1970—; archtl. cons. Fed. Res. Bank Chgo., 1978. Served with USNR, 1957-60. Recipient Architecture medal Alpha Rho Chi, 1966; grantee NEA, 1972, Woman's Bd. Art Inst. Chgo., 1973, Union Independent Colls. Art, 1974, Fulbright-Hays (Eng.), 1976, Fulbright-Hays (Jordan), 1981. Fellow Royal Soc. Arts (London); mem. AIA (corp. mem.), Soc. Archtl. Historians, Archaeol.

Inst. Am. (asso. mem.), Oriental Inst. Multi-media productions include: Hellas, Columbia U., N.Y.C., 1968, Art Inst. Chgo., 1971, 79; Muncie: Microcosm of America (NEA grant), Muncie, Ind., 1972; Legend of the Minotaur, Art Inst. Chgo., 1973; The Seasons, Art Inst. Chgo., 1977. Home: 2054 N Humboldt Blvd Chicago IL 60647 Office: Dept Design and Communication Sch of Art Inst Chgo Columbus Dr and Jackson Blvd Chicago IL 60603

KURTIS, WILLIAM HORTON, broadcast journalist; b. Pensacola, Fla., Sept. 21, 1940; s. William A. and Wilma Mary (Horton) K.; B.S. in Journalism, U. Kans., 1962; J.D., Washburn U., 1966; m. Helen M., July 7, 1963 (dec.); children—Mary Kristin, Scott Erik. News reporter Sta. WBBM-TV, Chgo., 1966-70, anchorman, reporter, 1973—; corr. CBS News, Los Angeles, 1970-73. Served with USMCR, 1962-63. Recipient Chgo. Area Emmy for reporting Chgo. conspiracy trial, 1970, Saigon fall, 1976, Belfast investigation, 1976; Chgo. Area Emmy for individual excellence for performers who appear on camera, 1976; Overseas Press Club award for Saigon Orphans, 1975. Mem. Sigma Delta Chi. Office: 630 N McClurg Ct Chicago IL 60611*

KURTZ, MYERS RICHARD, state med. adminstr.; b. Schaefferstown, Pa., June 18, 1924; B.S., U. Md., 1958; M.B.A., Ind. U., 1963; 1 son, Ronald. Enlisted U.S. Army, 1942; commd. 2d lt., 1951; advanced through grades to lt. col.; Sta. Walter Reed Army Med. Center, U.S. Army Hosp., Wurzburg, W.Ger., Office of Surgeon Gen., Washington, ret., 1967; affiliation adminstr. N.Y. U. Med. Center, N.Y.C., 1967-69; exec. dir. Ephrata Community Hosp., Ephrata, Pa., 1969-76; supt. Longview State Hosp., Cin., 1976-79; asst. dir. Ohio Dept. Mental Health and Mental Retardation, Columbus, 1979-81, dir., 1981—; adj. asst. prof. dept. psychiatry U. Cin., 1977—. Decorated Legion of Merit. Fellow Royal Soc. Health; mem. Am. Acad. Med. Adminstrs., Am. Coll. Hosp. Adminstrs., Am. Hosp. Assn., Sigma Iota Epsilon. Home: 5007 Chuckleberry Ln Westerville OH 43081 Office: State Office Tower Suite 1182 30 E Broad St Columbus OH 43215

KURTZ, WINIFRED MARY, club woman; b. Washington, Iowa, Aug. 28, 1912; d. Charles Sanford and Gertrude Josephine (Swift) Ragan; student Washington Jr. Coll., 1949-50, St. Ambrose Coll., Davenport, Iowa, 1950; m. Robert Kurtz, Sept. 12, 1951; 1 son, Michael R. Hostess, waitress Grand Lake Lodge, Colo., 1946; desk clk. Cosmopolitan Hotel, Denver, 1946; cashier Sears Roebuck & Co., Kansas City, Mo., 1947; tchr. Pleasant Hill Sch., Washington County, Iowa, 1950-51, Riverside Sch., Brighton, Iowa, 1952-53. Pres. dist. 11, Diocesan Council Cath. Women, 1972-74, 76-78, parish rep., 1970—; Sunday sch. tchr. St. Joseph's Ch. East Pleasant Plain, Iowa, 1960-70, v.p. Altar and Rosary Soc., 1980-81; sec. Writers Round Table, 1966-80; asso. Citizens for Decency through Law, 1974—; pres. Pleasant Plain (Iowa) Sch. PTA, 1966-68; state historian Daus. Am. Colonists, 1966-68, state corr. sec., 1968-70, state 1st vice regent, 1972-74, state regent, 1974-76, chmn. nat. def., 1976-78, vice-chmn. flag U.S.A., 1976—, chmn. state nominating com. 1982; state chmn. flag of U.S.A., DAR, 1976-78, nat. vice chmn. flag U.S.A., 1976-80, chpt. regent, 1971-73, 80-83. Democrat. Home: Rt 2 Brighton IA 52540

KURTZWEIL, MARGARET JEAN, sales mgr.; b. Syracuse, N.Y., May 6, 1954; d. Terrence John and Jean Laura K.; A.A. in Liberal Arts, Lorain County Community Coll., 1974; B.A., Bowling Green State U., 1976; M.B.A., Eastern Mich. U. Sales rep., Cedar Point, Inc., Sandusky, Ohio, 1976-79, dist. sales mgr., 1979-81, regional sales mgr., 1981—; regatta chmn. Pizza Hunt, Inc., Mich., 1977, race com. chmn., 1981. Water safety instr. ARC; campaign worker Elect Reagan, 1980. Mem. Ann Arbor Bus. and Profl. Women's Club, Nat. Assn. Female Execs., Bowling Green State U. Alumni Assn., Phi Mu Alumni (sec. Ann Arbor 1981-82). Republican. Roman Catholic. Clubs: Ford Lake Sail (Ypsilanti, Mich.); Republican Women's, Civic Theatre Orgn. (Ann Arbor Mich.). Home: 2151 Lakeview Dr 31 Ypsilanti MI 48197 Office: Cedar Point Inc Mktg Dept Sandusky OH 44870

KUSAR, DANIEL DUSAN, automotive and aluminum mfg. co. exec.; b. Ljubljana, Yugoslavia, May 9, 1928; came to U.S., 1950, naturalized, 1953; s. Savo A. and Angelica Setina K.; M.B.A., U. Chgo., 1957; m. Rosanne M. Egelske, Sept. 24, 1960; children—Angelica, Jennifer. Asst. to pres. Calumet Steel div. Borg Warner Corp., 1957-61; pres. Kusar Investment Corp., 1961-67; corp. fin. asso. Hornblower-Weeks, Hemphill, Noyes, 1967-71; chmn., pres. Darfield Industries, Inc., Chgo., 1971—; chmn. All Products Co., Sun Valley Products, Inc. Served with U.S. Army, 1951-53. Republican. Roman Catholic. Clubs: Univ., Econs. Office: Darfield Industries Inc 208 S LaSalle St Chicago IL 60604

KUSEY, JULIUS, educator; b. Omer, Mich., July 1, 1931; s. Toney F. and Rose A. (Tellish) K.; B.S., Central Mich. U., 1957; M.S. in Art Edn., U. Wis., Madison, 1964. Tchr. art Rochester (Mich.) Community Sch. Dist., 1957—, kindergarten-through 12th grades art coordinator, 1975-81, art cons., 1957—; bd. dirs. Rochester Arts Commn., 1979-80. Sch. chmn. United Found., Rochester, 1959—; mem. Oakland County (Mich.) Cultural Council, 1980—. Served with M.C., U.S. Army, 1952-55. Mem. Mich. Art Edn. Assn. (Elem. Art Tchr. of Yr. award 1971, pres. 1980-82), Mich. Edn. Assn., Nat. Art Edn. Assn., Am. Crafts Council, Internat. Soc. Edn. Through Art, Am. Hort. Soc., Am. Primrose Soc. Democrat. Roman Catholic. Office: 522 W Fourth St Rochester MI 48063

KUSTOM, ROBERT LOUIS, sci. research adminstr.; b. Chgo., July 11, 1934; s. Louis W. and Mary (Henek) Kuskowski; A.A., Morton Jr. Coll., 1954; B.S. in Elec. Engring., Ill. Inst. Tech., 1956, M.S., 1958; Ph.D. in Elec. Engring., U. Wis., 1969; m. Dolores Curley, Apr. 4, 1959; children—Brittan S.L., Todd R., Jill M. Elec. engr. high voltage lab. Joslyn Mfg. & Supply Co., Chgo., 1955-58; elec. engr. high energy physics and accelerator divs. Argonne (Ill.) Nat. Lab., 1958-71, group leader ZGS synchrotron ops. group, 1971-73, asso. div. dir. accelerator research facilities div., 1973-79, div. dir., 1979—; vis. scientist Rutherford High Energy Lab., Chilton, Eng., 1970-71; vis. prof. elec. engring. U. Wis., Madison, 1978-79, 81, cons. to Superconducting Energy Storage Group, 1978, 81. Pres., St. Alexander Sch. Bd., Palos Heights, Ill., 1973-79; trustee Palos Heights Public Library, 1974-80, treas., 1976-80. Mem. IEEE, Sigma Xi. Author: Thyristor Networks for the Transfer of Energy between Superconducting Coils, 1980; contbr. articles to sci. jours. Home: 7361 Ishnala Dr Palos Heights IL 60463 Office: Argonne Nat Lab 9700 S Cass Ave Argonne IL 60439

KUTSCH, HENRY J., hosp. adminstr.; b. Tarentum, Pa., Mar. 15, 1923; B.S. in Bus. Adminstrn., Northwestern U., 1949, M.S. in Bus. Edn., 1950, M.S. in Hosp. Adminstrn., 1955; m. Patricia, Sept. 4, 1948. Personnel relations mgr. Passavant Meml. Hosp., Chgo., 1955-57; pres. Ravenswood Hosp. Med. Center, Chgo., 1957—. Served with USAAF, 1942-46. Mem. Am. Coll. Hosp. Adminstrs., Am. Hosp. Assn., Ill. Hosp. Assn., Chgo. Hosp. Council, Chgo. North Side Commn. Health Planning. Office: 4550 N Winchester St Chicago IL 60640

KUTSCHER, GORDON RALPH, educator; b. Jackson, Mo., Jan. 3, 1934; s. Richard Henry and Emilie (Kasten) K.; B.S., S.E. Mo. State Coll., 1957; M.Ed., U. Mo., 1961; student Mo. Sch. Mines, summer 1958; m. Louanna Mae Dickerson, Aug. 15, 1954; children—Richard Gordon, Randy Keith, Robert Clark. Instr. math. Sch. Dist. R-4, Benton, Mo., 1955-57, Rolla (Mo.) Sr. High Sch., 1957-59, head dept. math., 1959-61; sch. psychol. examiner, counselor, dir. guidance Rolla Jr. High Sch., 1962-67; dir. guidance Rolla Pub. Schs., 1967, supr. guidance services Mo. Dept. Edn., 1967-70, asst. dir. Research Coordinating Unit, 1970-71; exec. sec., dir. Mo. Adv. Council Vocat. Edn., 1971—; mem. State Employment and Tng. Council; co-chmn. Nat. Bicentennial Conf. on Vocat. Edn.; del. Mo. Gov.'s Conf. on Edn.; sr. research asst., Freshman orientation counselor U. Mo. at Rolla, summer 1966. Mem. Rolla Community Betterment Program, 1964; past pres. Trinity Lutheran Ch., past chmn. bd. stewardship; committeeman explorer post and scout troop Boy Scouts Am.; past bd. dirs. Cole County Conservation Commn. Mem. NEA (life), Mo. State Tchrs. Assn., Rolla Community Tchrs. Assn. (past pres.), Phelps County Mental Health Assn. (past pres.), Mo. (past pres.; editor emeritus quar. jour.), South Central (past pres.) guidance assns., Am. Personnel and Guidance Assn., Am. Sch. Counselor Assn., Nat. Vocat. Guidance Assn., Assn. Measurement and Evaluation in Guidance, Am. (life), Mo. vocat. assns., Nat. Assn. Exec. Dirs. State Vocat. Adv. Councils (past v.p.), Phi Delta Kappa (life), Council Vocat. Educators. Optimist (past pres. Jefferson City, lt. gov. Mo. dist. 1970-71, dist. boys work chmn. 1971-72, dist. community service chmn. 1972-73, dist. oratorical chmn. 1974-75, dist. sec./treas. 1975-76, 79-82, dist. gov. 1977-78, dist. candidate qualifications chmn. 1978-79, mem. internat. achievement and awards com. 1979-80, dist. fin. chmn. 1980-81). Author: 1965 Graduates Responses and Data Survey, 1968; Structure, Function and Use of Local Advisory Committees in Vocational Education, 1974; co-author: Handbook for Local Vocational Advisory Committees, 1977; contbr. articles to profl. jours. Home: 1815 Swift's Hwy Jefferson City MO 65101

KUTTER, LLOYD RAY, elec. engr.; b. Hankinson, N.D., Oct. 21, 1932; s. Bernard Martin and Hilda Sophia (Weinkauf) K.; Diploma, N.D. State Sch. of Sci., 1952; B.S. with honors in Elec. Engring., N.D. State U., 1960; m. Marjory Minnie Berner, Oct. 30, 1953; children—Bruce, Renee, Rhonda. Engr., Allis Chalmers, Milw., 1960, Am. Bosch Arma Corp., Garden City, N.Y., 1960-62, Aerojet-Gen. Corp., Sacramento, 1962-65, Sacramento Mcpl. Utility Dist., 1965-67; asso. power ops. and maintenance engr. State of Calif. Dept. Water Resources, Sacramento, 1967-75, 79-80; relay control systems engr. Basin Electric Power Coop., Bismarck, N.D., 1980—; apptd. supr. Dist. IV El Dorado County, 1975, elected supr., 1976-78, vice chmn., 1978. Mem. governing bd. Golden Empire Health Systems Agy., rural health care alternatives com.; vice chmn. Sierra-Sacramento Valley Emergency Med. Services Agy., El Dorado County Ambulance Service Area; chmn. El Dorado County Air Pollution Control Bd., El Dorado County Local Planning Council; mem. El Dorado County Drug Abuse Adv. Bd.; active Democratic party, co-chmn. 13th senatorial dist. state central com., 1974, vice chmn. El Dorado County central com., county precinct chmn. Garamendi for Assembly com., 1974, county chmn. Roth for gov. com., 1974, mem. com. Brown for gov., 1978. Served with USN, 1952-56. Registered profl. engr., Calif. Mem. IEEE, Am. Legion. Lutheran. Home: 308 2d St NW Mandan ND 58554 Office: 1717 E Interstate Ave Bismarck ND 58501

KUTZ, RALPH GEORGE, clergyman; b. St. Louis, Dec. 31, 1911; s. Joseph A. and Helen M. (Broeckelmann) K.; student St. Louis Prep. Sem., 1925-33, Kenrick Sem., 1933-37, St. Louis U., 1937-39. Ordained priest Roman Catholic Ch., 1937; chaplain Ursuline Novitiate, Festus, Mo., 1937-49; asst. pastor St. Louis Parishes, 1949-54; pastor Wellsville (Mo.), Martinsburg (Mo.) Parishes, 1954-59, Taos (Mo.) Parish, 1966-70, Argyle (Mo.) and Koeltztown (Mo.) parishes, 1970—; mem. faculty Helias High School, 1959-70, chancellor Diocese Jefferson City (Mo.), 1959-70; dir. Diocesan Cath. Charities; instr. St. Louis U., 1937-49; state chaplain Daus. of Isabella, 1968-72. K.C. Editor: Catholic Missourian, 1960-69. Address: Argyle MO 65001

KUTZA, MICHAEL JOSEPH, JR., film festival exec.; b. Chgo., Nov. 28, 1939; s. Michael Joseph and Theresa (Felicetti) K.; student Loyola U., Chgo., 1957-59; B.S., Roosevelt U., 1961; postgrad. Ill. Inst. Design, U. Chgo., 1964. Freelance motion picture cameraman pub. affairs dept. Sta. WGN-TV, Chgo., 1963-64; art dir., pub. relations exec. Milton Shufro & Assos. Chgo., 1964-66; dir. founder Chgo. Internat. Film Festival, Inc., 1964—; free-lance art dir., designer graphics for various film cos. and agys., 1965—; film and media designer Joe Hayes Prodns., N.Y.C., 1965-67; graphic designer Constl. Congress of Internat. Film and Television Students' and Graduates' Assn., Prague, Czechoslovakia, 1969; producer 1970 Spoleto (Italy) Cinema Festival; film editor for Lerner Newspapers, Chgo., 1966—; Am. film critic Il Tempo, Rome, 1976—; film instr. Lewis Coll., Lockport, Ill., 1971; mem., lectr. Chgo. Speakers Bur., div. Chgo. Adult Edn. Council. U.S. chmn. Venice Film Festival, 1971-72, recipient Silver Lion, 1971; U.S. chmn. Tehran Film Festival, 1972-73; U.S. del. Moscow Film Festival, 1971, Taormina (Italy) Film Festival, 1971; chmn. 1st Internat. Film Festival, Lima, Peru, 1973, Delhi, India, 1975; U.S. adv. Berlin (Ger.) Film Festival, 1980—. Recipient silver medal Cannes Film Festival du Amateur, 1961. Mem. Profl. Photographers Am., Chgo. Soc. Communicating Arts, Art Dirs. Club Chgo., Tau Kappa Epsilon. Home: 235 W Eugenie St Chicago IL 60614 Office: Chgo Internat Film Festival Inc 415 N Dearborn St Chicago IL 60610

KUWAYAMA, SUSUMU PAUL, physician; b. Sapporo, Japan, Nov. 8, 1932; s. Satoru and Chiyoko K.; came to U.S., 1959, naturalized, 1979; M.D., Hokkaido U., 1959; m. Barbara Ann Dresback, June 29, 1974; children—David, Steven, Jason. Intern, U.S. Naval Hosp., Yokosuka, Japan, 1959, St. Mary's Hosp., Milw., 1960; resident in pediatrics Temple U. Sch. Medicine, Phila., 1962, U. W.Va., Morgantown, 1963; fellow pediatric allergy and immunology U. Kans. Sch. Medicine, Kansas City, 1964-68; asst. clin. prof. pediatrics Med. Coll. Wis., Milw., 1971—. Fulbright scholar, 1960-63; U. Kans. Sch. Medicine dept. microbiology postdoctoral fellow, 1968-69. Diplomate Am. Bd. Pediatrics, Am. Bd. Allergy and Immunology. Mem. Am. Acad. Allergy, Am. Acad. Pediatrics, Am. Coll. Allergists, Am. Assn. Clin. Immunology and Allergy, Am. Assn. Cert. Allergists, AMA, Fulbright Scholarship Grantees Alumni Assn. Home: 15135 Woodbridge Rd Brookfield WI 53005 Office: W180 N7950 Town Hall Rd Menomonee Falls WI 53051

KUWIK, PAUL DAVID, vocat. educator; b. N.Y.C., Dec. 28, 1942; s. Paul F. and Stella Kuwik; B.S. in Edn., SUNY, Buffalo, 1962, M.S., 1964; Ph.D., Ohio State U., 1970; m. Beatrice Bucher, Aug. 17, 1967; children—Paige, Elizabeth, Sara Kathrine. Vocat. instr. and asst. dir. vocat. edn. Kemore (N.Y.) public schs., 1964-68; research fellow Ohio State U., Columbus, 1968-70; prof. indsl. edn. Coll. Tech., Eastern Mich. U., Ypsilanti, 1970—; career devel. coordinator, 1976-79, dir. bilingual vocat. instr. tng. program, 1979—; dir. bilingual vocat. edn. Mich. Dept. Edn., 1980—, dept. head interdisciplinary tech., 1981—. Bd. dirs. Humane Soc. of Huron Valley, 1974—, pres., 1976-81. Mem. Am. Vocat. Assn., Am. Indsl. Arts Assn., Epsilon Pi Tau, Phi Delta Kappa. Author various workbooks, lab. manuals and tchrs. guides for indsl. arts curriculum; contbr. articles on career edn. to profl. publs. Home: 73 Greenside Ave Ypsilanti MI 48197 Office: Eastern Mich Univ College Tech Sill Hall Ypsilanti MI 48197

KWON, SANG HAK, educator, librarian; b. Kyung-Buk, Korea, Oct. 10, 1934; s. Jung Hyung and Tae Soon (Park) K.; came to U.S., 1965, naturalized, 1975; B.A., Dan Kook U., 1957; C.A.S. in Library Sci., Yonsei U., 1964; B.A. (Joyce 7 Up scholar), Lewis U., 1968; M.L.S., Rosary Coll., 1970; m. Ella Kim, June 20, 1954; children—Peter Ji, Yu mi. Cataloger, Joliet (Ill.) Public Library, 1968-70; asst. acquisitions librarian Chgo. State U. Library, 1970-72, head acquisitions dept., 1972—, instr., 1970-75, asst. prof., 1975—, coordinator tech. processing, 1976—; book reviewer, 1972—. Mem. Ill. State U. Pres.' Adv. Bd., 1979—. Served with Korean Air Force, 1955-65. Mem. AAUP, Ill. Library Assn., ALA. Republican. Roman Catholic. Home: 15214 S 82d Ave Orland Park IL 60462 Office: 95th St at King Dr Chicago IL 60628

KYES, HELEN G. (MRS. ROGERS M. KYES), civic leader; b. Marion, Ohio; d. Benjamin and Bess (Gilmore) Jacoby; B.A., Oberlin Coll., 1926; Ph.D. (hon.), Oakland U., 1980; m. Roger M. Kyes, June 5, 1931; children—Carolyn Kyes Eggert, Frances, Katharine Kyes Leob, Anne Kyes Smith. Sec., pres. Federated Women's Club, Marion, Ohio, 1927-31; bd. dirs. Cleve. Coll. Club, 1936-41, Cleve. YWCA, 1938-41; mem. bd. Woman's Nat. Farm and Garden, 1943-56, 60—, sec., 1943-45, 54-55; dir. Children's Aid and Home Friendless, 1949—, v.p., 1961—; bd. dirs. Brookside Sch., Cranbrook, 1952-58, sec., 1957-58; bd. dirs. Kingswood Sch., Cranbrook, 1968—; charter mem. bd. trustees Oakland U. Found., 1958, v.p. exec. bd., 1960—; trustee Oakland U., 1970—; mem. Woman's Assn. Detroit Symphony; com. 100 Detroit Met. Opera; capt. spl. gifts Detroit United Fund, 1959-61; mem. Detroit Mus. Art Founders Soc.; mem. com. Detroit Foster Home Edn. and Recruitment Program, 1960—. Mem. D.A.R., AAUW (past treas., v.p. Marion). Presbyterian (vice moderator deacons). Clubs: Bloomfield Hills Country, Detroit, Village Woman's; Ocean (Delray Beach, Fla.); Gulfstream Bath and Tennis. Home: 945 Cranbrook Rd Bloomfield Hills MI 48013 also 6861 N Ocean Blvd Ocean Ridge FL 33435

KYLE, GENE MAGERL, mdse. presentation artist; b. Phila., Oct. 11, 1919; d. Elmer Langham and Muriel Helen (Magerl) K.; student Center for Creative Studies, Detroit, 1938-45. Mdse. presentation artist D. J. Healy Shops, Detroit, 1946-50, Saks Fifth Ave., Detroit, 1950-58, J.L. Hudson Co., Detroit, 1958—; tchr. workshop classes; exhibited in shows at Mich. Water Color Soc., 1944, 53, 74, Mich. Artists Exhbn., 1962, 64, Scarab Club, 1948, 49, 52, Detroit Artists Market, 1946—. Recipient various art awards. Mem. Detroit Inst. Arts Founders Soc., Mich. Water Color Soc., Windsor Art Gallery.

KYLE, MARY J., journalist; b. St. Paul; d. Ernest B. and Edith M. (Burnett) James; student U. Minn., Palmer Inst. of Writing, Croydon Inst. of Writing; m. Earle F. Kyle, Nov. 12; children—Shirley Klye Heaton, Robert C., Earlene Kyle Walker, Earle F. Editor and pub. Twin Cities Courier, Mpls., 1967—; pres. Minn. Sentinel Pub. Co., 1967—; editorial commentator Sta. KMSP-TV, 1969—; talk show host Sta. WLOL-AM-FM, 1969—; book reviewer Mpls. Sunday Tribune, 1970—; newspaper columnist, 1948-52; dir. Sta. KTCA-TV, 1973-75; lectr. on human relations, 1967—; mem. adv. bd. Northwestern Nat. Bank, 1975—. Mem. Communications Task Force, Mpls. Urban Coalition, 1972-74; mem. governing bd. YMCA, Mpls., 1970—; mem. Minn. State Bd. Law Examiners, 1977—; bd. dirs. Am. Rehab. Found. Recipient Frank Murray award St. Thomas Coll., 1971, Herman Roe Meml. award, 1967, Human Rights award Jewish Labor Com., 1967, Human Rights award Fezzan Temple Shriners, 1970, Mpls. Distingusihed Served award, 1970, Community Service award Nat. Alliance Businessmen, 1976. Mem. Nat., Minn. newspaper assns., NAACP Minn. Press Club (pres. 1975-76), Minn. Press Women (Journalism award 1976, 77, 78), AFTRA, Greater Mpls. C. of C., Mpls. Urban League (Distinguished Service award 1969), Nat. Newspaper Pubs. Assn., Minn. Council Econ. Edn. (dir. 1975—). Roman Catholic. Home: 3637 4th Ave S Minneapolis MN 55409 Office: 84 S 6th St Minneapolis MN 55402

KYNCL, JOHN JAROSLAV, pharmacologist; b. Prague, Czechoslovakia, Aug. 16, 1936; came to U.S., 1970, naturalized, 1977; s. Jan Petr and Marie Anna (Mikes) K.; Ph.D. in Pharmacology, Masaryk U., Brno, Czechoslovakia, 1959; Ph.D. in Physiology, Czechoslovak. Acad. Sci., 1967; m. Mila-Marie Tomaides, Mar. 4, 1961; children—Marketa Maria-Anna, Jan Anthony. Sr. pharmacologist Research Inst. Spofa-Pharmaceuticals, Prague, 1960-68; Alexander V. Humboldt fellow, vis. investigator pharmacology dept. U. Heidelberg (W. Ger.), 1968-70; sr. research fellow Cleve. Clinic, 1970-72; sr. investigator research and devel. Abbott Labs., North Chicago, Ill., 1972—, head antihypertensive research, 1972—; exec. officer M.M. Kyncl Corp., 1979—; farmer, 1980. Mem. Am. Soc. for Pharmacology and Exptl. Therapeutics, Am. Endocrine Soc., Internat. Soc. Hypertension, Inter-Am. Soc. Hypertension, Swiss Assn. against High Blood Pressure, Alexander V. Humboldt Soc. Contbr. articles to profl. jours.; patentee in U.S. and fgn. countries; co-inventor concept of hormonogenes, specific enzyme-activated drugs; discoverer drugs glypressin, terazosin.

KYRIAZIS, ANDREAS P., pathologist; b. Aigion, Greece, Jan. 19, 1932; s. Panayiotis and Christina (Demeli) K.; M.D., U. Athens (Greece), 1957; D.Sc. in Pathology, U. Thessaloniki, 1962; Ph.D. on Pathology, Thomas Jefferson U., 1968; m. Aikaterini Iatridou, Dec. 16, 1964; children—Joanna, Christina. Research asso. in pathology U. Chgo., 1968-70, Seymur Coman fellow in pathology, 1969-70, research asso., asst. prof. pathology, 1970-72, 74-76; asso. prof. dept. pathology U. Cin. Coll. Medicine, 1976—; vis. scientist Argonne Cancer Research Hosp., 1968-72; chmn. dept. pathology Metaxas Meml. Cancer Hosp., Piraeus, Greece, 1972-74. Served to capt. M.C., Greek Army, 1958-60. Research in tumor immunology; tumor biology; exptl. chemotherapy. Home: 508 Williamsburg Rd Cincinnati OH 45215

LAATZ, MARY JANE, med. librarian; b. Indpls., Dec. 27, 1916; d. Jacob Philip and Nell (Carey) Laatz; A.B., Butler U., 1938; B.S. in L.S., Western Res. U., 1939. Librarian, Ind. U. Extension Div., Indpls., 1939-41; cataloger Ind. U. Sch. Medicine Library, 1941-51, reference librarian, 1951, 53-57, acting librarian, 1951-53, med. librarian, 1957—, asst. prof. med. lit., 1957-72, asso. prof. med. lit., 1973—. Chmn. Council of Midwest Regional Health Scis. Library and Coop. Information Services, 1968-70; participant Conf. on Interlibrary Communication Network, A.L.A, and U.S. Office Edn., 1970; Ind. U. rep. ednl. communications network study EDUCOM, 1966; mem. Midwest Health Sci. Library Network Assembly Resource Libraries, 1973—, chmn., 1975-76; rep.-at-large faculty council Ind. U.-Purdue U. at Indpls., 1974-76. Mem. Spl. Libraries Assn. (chpt. pres. 1960-61), Med. Library Assn. (mem. scholarship com. 1972-74, chmn. 1973-74), John Shaw Billings History Medicine Soc. (sec.-treas. 1965-67), Indpls. Mus. Art, Delta Gamma. Presbyn. Contbr. articles to profl. jours. Home: 6824 Willow Rd Indianapolis IN 46220 Office: Med Sci Bldg 122 Ind U Sch Medicine Library 1100 W Michigan St Indianapolis IN 46229

LABAY, MICHAEL JAMES, educator; b. Toledo, July 9, 1942; s. James J. and Elizabeth A. (Fial) L.; B.S., Bowling Green State U., 1964; M.Ed., U. Toledo, 1967, Ph.D., 1970; m. Dorothy Jane Barut, June 13, 1964; children—Deborah, Jennifer, James, LaBay. Asst. prof. Youngstown (Ohio) State U., 1972-73; program evaluator San Diego Unified Sch. Dist., 1970-72 dir. elementary edn. Birmingham (Mich.) pub. schs., 1973—; vis. prof. Eastern Mich. U., 1975-82; pres. Oakland County (Mich.) Curriculum Council, 1981-82; mgmt. cons. Mich. State Dept. Edn., 1977-80. Mem. Mich. Assn. Supervision and Curriculum Devel. (bd. dirs.), Am. Assn. Sch. Adminstrs., Mich. Assn. Computer Users Learning, Phi Delta Kappa. Club: Lion. Home: 2601 Douglas Dr Bloomfield Hills MI 48013 Office: 550 W Merrill St Birmingham MI 48012

LABBIE, STEPHEN, clin. psychologist; b. Pitts., Apr. 18, 1944; s. Irwin and Anne (Chawenson) L.; B.A., U. Fla., 1966; M.S., Ill. Inst. Tech., 1972, Ph.D., 1974; m. Linda Fran Weinberg, Aug. 20, 1966; children—Erin Felicia, Elissa Beth. Dir. day care program for retarded children Catholic Welfare Bur., Miami, Fla., 1968-69; grad. asst., counseling center Ill. Inst. Tech., Chgo., 1971-72; clin. intern HEW grant project Health and Hosps. Governing Commn. of Cook County, Chgo., 1972-74; clin. psychologist Du Page County Health Dept., Div. Mental Health, Wheaton, Ill., 1974-75, dir. mental health div. East Satellite, 1975-81, dir. clin. and community services, 1981—; pvt. practice, Chgo., 1974—. Supr. masters level psychology students George Williams Coll., Downers Grove, Ill., 1973—. Served with AUS, 1969-71. Mem. Am. Psychol. Assn. (mem. div. counseling 1972—, mem. div. psychotherapy 1973—), Assn. for Advancement Psychology, Nat. Register Health Service Providers in Psychology, Sigma Xi. Contbr. articles to profl. jours. Home: 1133 62d Pl Downers Grove IL 60515 Office: Wendell Bldg 1121 Warren St Suite 200 Downers Grove IL 60515

LA BELLE, CHARLES EARL, mech. engr.; b. Laurium, Mich., Apr. 28, 1927; s. Charles Earl and Sigrid Aleda (Jacobson) LaB.; B.M.E., Mich. Technol. U., 1952; grad. bus. adminstrn. Alexander Hamilton Inst., 1959; m. Hilda Alvina Martin, Aug. 11, 1956; children—Charles Earl, Renee Jeanne. Exptl. engr. LeRoi Co., Milw., 1952-55, Clinton Engines Co., Maquoketa, Iowa, 1955-57; project engr. Thomas Industries, Sheboygan, Wis., 1957-63; design engr. Aro Inc., Tullahoma, Tenn., 1963-66; aircraft devel. engr. Continental Aircraft Engine, Muskegon, Mich., 1966-70; research and devel. engr. Roper Corp., Bradley, Ill., 1970-74; div. mgr. product engring. Power Air div. Thomas Industries, Sheboygan, 1974—; curriculum advisor Lakeshore Tech. Inst., Cleveland, Wis., 1974—. Served with USNR, 1945-46. Mem. ASME, Soc. Automotive Engrs., Mich. Technol. U. Alumni Assn. Club: Sheboygan Yacht. Home: Route 2 Box 290 Oostburg WI 53070 Office: 1419 Illinois Ave Sheboygan WI 53081

LABINE, PAUL, chemist; b. Nashua, N.H., June 12, 1943; s. Joseph Urgel and Jeanne Alice (Soucy) L.; B.S., U. Mass., 1964; Ph.D., Mich. State U., 1971; 1 son, Carl. Asst. prof. Purdue U., Indpls., 1969-72; chemist Nalco Chem. Co., Chgo., 1972-73; chief formulation chemist Olin Water Service, Kansas City, Kans., 1973-79; group leader cooling water research and devel. Tretolite div. Petrolite Corp., 1979—. Mem. Am. Chem. Soc. (symposium chmn. for ann. meeting 1978), Nat. Assn. of Corrosion Engrs. (symposium chmn. ann. meeting 1978, 79, 81, 82, chmn. com. corrosion inhibitors; award 1976), ASTM, Am. Inst. Chem. Engrs. Unitarian. Author tech. papers in field. Home: 7743 Keswick St Saint Louis MO 63119

LABORDE, JOYCE MARY, nurse, educator; b. Deal, Kent., Eng., Aug. 7, 1930; came to U.S., 1963, naturalized, 1967; d. Charles Frederick and Joyce Isabelle (Harrison) Lavanchy; B.S. in Nursing, Loyola U., Chgo., 1976; M.S. in Nursing, U. Ill., Chgo., 1978, Ph.D. in Nursing Sci. (grad. fellow), 1981; m. Frederick Nestor Laborde, Mar. 20, 1964. Staff nurse, asst. head nurse Grant Hosp., Chgo., 1967-73; dir. in-service edn. St. Augustine's Home, Chgo., 1974; clin. nurse Cook County Hosp., Chgo., 1976; staff nurse U. Ill. Hosp., Chgo., 1977; research coordinator Rehab. Inst., Chgo., 1980, statis. cons., scale devel. adviser nursing dept., 1980; asso. prof. nursing U. N.D., 1981—. Loyola U. scholar, 1976; Sigma Xi grantee, 1980; registered nurse, Ill., N.D. Mem. AAAS, N.Y. Acad. Scis., Midwest Nursing Research Soc., Am. Nurses Assn., Sigma Xi (asso.), Sigma Theta Tau. Contbr. articles to profl. pubs.

LABRUNE, DENNIS GENE, county ofcl.; b. Sioux City, Iowa, July 13, 1945; s. Robert E. and Jeanne Marie (Jones) LaB.; B.S., Morningside Coll., 1976; m. Nancy Louise Hoover, Dec. 3, 1977. Adminstrv. supply technician 89th USARCOM, Lincoln, Nebr., 1972-74, staff adminstrv. specialist, 1974; vets. coordinator Woodbury County, Sioux City, Iowa, 1977; exec. dir. Woodbury County Employment Tng. Center, Sioux City, 1977—. Past bd. dirs. Woodbury County Community Action Agy.; mem. nat. adv. performance mgmt. standards com. CETA; mem. bd. Gov. Iowas State Employment and Tng. Council, chmn. ednl. linkage subcom; mem. adv. com., diesel mechanics program Western Iowa Tech Community Coll. Iowa Occupational Coordinating Com. Cert., Am. Management Asso. Served with AUS, 1966-69; Vietnam. Decorated Service Medal with Bronze Star (2). Mem. DAV (past post comdr. chpt. 54), Sioux City C. of C., Am. Legion, VFW. Presbyterian. Club: Lions. Home: 2517 Lemon St S Sioux City IA 51106 Office: 808 5th St Suite 301 Sioux City IA 51102

LABSVIRS, JANIS, economist; b. Bilska, Latvia, Mar. 13, 1907; s. Karlis and Kristina L.; Mag.Oec., Latvian State U., 1930; M.S., Butler U., 1956; Ph.D., Ind. U., 1959. Tchr., Latvia, 1930-36; dir. dept. edn. Fedn. Latvian Trade Unions, 1936-37; v.p. Kr. Baron's U., Extension, Riga, Latvia, 1938-40, also exec. v.p. Filma, Inc., 1939-40; with UNRRA and Internat. Refugee Orgn., Esslinge, Ger., 1945-50; asst. prof. econs. Ind. State U., Terre Haute, 1959-62, asso. prof., 1963-68, prof., 1969-73, prof. emeritus, 1973—; head dept. public and social affairs Latvian Ministry for Social Affairs, 1938-40; dir. Sch. of Commerce and Gymnasium, Tukums, Latvia, 1941-44. Danforth grantee, 1961; Ind. State U. research grantee, 1966. Mem. Am. Latvian Assn., Am. Assn. Advancement Slavic Studies, Assn. Advancement Baltic Studies, Am. Econ. Assn., Royal Econ. Soc. Lutheran. Author: Local Government's Accounting and Management Practices, 1947; A Case Study in the Sovietization of the Baltic States: Collectivization of Latvian Agriculture 1944-1956, 1959; contbr. articles profl. jours. Home: 3313 Hovey St Indianapolis IN 46218

LA BUDDE, KENNETH JAMES, librarian; b. Sheboygan Falls, Wis., Jan. 20, 1920; s. Arno Peter and Claire (DeVoy) LaB.; A.B., U. Wis., 1941, B.L.S., 1942; student U. Chgo., 1943-44; M.A., U. Minn., 1948, Ph.D., 1954. Student asst. U. Wis. Library, 1939-42; sr. library asst. Milw. Pub. Library, 1942; librarian Sheboygan (Wis.) Press, 1944-46; instr. English, Milton (Wis.) Coll., 1946-47; dir. libraries U. Mo., Kansas City, 1950—, asst. prof. history, 1958-61, asso. prof., 1961, prof., 1962—. Served with AUS, 1942-44. Mem. ALA, Am. Studies Assn., Bibliog. Soc. Am., Mo. Library Assn. (chmn. coll. and univ. div. 1954-55), Kansas City Posse of Westerners, Joseph H. Tedrow Library Assn. (adviser), Wis. Meml. Union, Mid-Continent Am. Studies Assn. (pres. 1963-64, arts editor jour. 1959-63), Orgn. Am. Historians, Soc. Archtl. Historians, Beta Phi Mu, Phi Kappa Phi, Phi Alpha Theta. Contbr. articles to profl. jours. Office: 5100 Rockhill Rd Kansas City MO 64110

LA CAVA, CARL, mgmt. and mktg. cons., educator; b. Cleve., Mar. 20, 1932; B.B.A., Dyke Coll., 1950; cert. Inst. Public Safety, 1968, Pa. State U., 1968; M.B.A., Baldwin-Wallace Coll., 1978; M.B.A., Temple U., 1974; student Ford Mktg. Inst., 1968. Salesman, Downtown Chevrolet Motors, Inc., Cleve., 1953-55, sales exec., 1958-59, v.p., gen. mgr., 1960-62; v.p. C&G Enterprises, Emmaus, Pa., 1962-65; asst. gen. mgr. Brockway div. Mack Trucks, Inc., N.Y.C., 1965-69; spl. asst. to pres. United News and Air Freight Transp. Co., Phila., N.Y.C., 1969-70, cons., 1970-74; cons. corp. devel. and mktg. Alpo Pet Foods and Liggett Group, Allentown, Pa., 1970-75, Avis Internat., Lehigh and Berks counties, Pa., 1969-70; prof. mktg. and bus. adminstrn. and systems mgmt. Dyke Coll., Cleve., 1975-79, adj. prof., 1980—; loaned exec. in devel. manpower mgmt. info. systems study, City of Cleve., 1977-78, Jobs Council Met. Cleve., 1978-80; instr. Intex Computer Inst., Allentown, 1969-75; prof., chmn. dept. data processing and mktg., Allentown Bus. Coll., 1969-75; adj. prof. Grad. Sch. Bus., U. Notre Dame, South Bend, Ind., 1970-71. Mem. Cleve. Mayor's Econ. Adv. Com. Served with C.E., U.S. Army, 1951-52; Korea. Mem. Am. Mgmt. Assn., Sales and Mktg. Execs., Soc. Automotive Engrs., Dyke Coll. Alumni Assn. (v.p. 1979-80), Delta Mu Delta. Author numerous manuals on mktg., leasing, transp., systems mgmt. and bus. edn.; contbr. articles on bus., mgmt. and mktg. to various publs. Office: Jobs Council Met Cleve Nat Alliance of Bus 1375 Euclid Ave Cleveland OH 44115

LACH, IVAN JOHN, state ofcl.; b. Yugoslavia, Feb. 7, 1939; s. Stephen and Johanna (Kubica) L. (parents Am. citizens); B.S., So. Ill. U., 1962, M.S. in Ednl. Adminstrn., 1968; Ph.D. in Ednl. Adminstrn., U. Ill., 1973; m. Mary Ruth Hawk, Sept. 15, 1962; children—Michael, Mark, Diana, Dawn. Actuary, Trainee Country Life Ins. Co., Bloomington, Ill., 1962-63; tchr. math. Vandalia (Ill.) High Sch., 1963-67; supervising tchr. Metcalf Lab. Sch., Ill. State U., Normal, 1967-70; dir. admissions and research Lakeland Coll., Mattoon, Ill., 1970-74; asst. dir. research Ill. Community Coll. Bd., Springfield, 1974-75, asso. dir. planning, research and mgmt. info. systems, 1975—. Served with U.S. Army, 1962-68. Mem. Nat. Council Research and Planning (pres. 1979), Am. Ednl. Research Assn., Community Jr. Coll. Spl. Interest Group (chmn. 1978), Assn. Instnl. Research. Roman Catholic. Home: 4 Lamplighter Ln Springfield IL 62707 Office: 3085 Stevenson Dr Springfield IL 62703

LACHER, THOMAS FRANCIS, JR., electronic engr.; b. Kalispell, Mont., Nov. 28, 1941; s. Thomas Francis and Jane Allyn (Cockrell) L.; B.S. in Elec. Engring., B.S. in Math., Mont. State U., 1966; M.S. in Elec. Engring., Bradley U., 1969; m. Mary Elnora Beasley, May 11, 1962; children—Thomas Francis, Keri Janel. Research engr. Caterpillar Tractor Co., Peoria, Ill., 1966-73, devel. engr., 1973—. Bd. dirs. FISH of Peoria, 1972-75. Served with USN, 1959-62. Mem. IEEE, U.S. Chess Fedn. Episcopalian. Patentee engine power measuring device. Home: 7150 N Terra Vista Dr Peoria IL 61614

LACHKY, CATHY HEILMANN, advt. agy. exec.; b. Evergreen Park, Ill., Mar. 29, 1954; d. Joseph Christopher and Therese Mary (Murphy) Heilmann; B.A., U. Ill., 1976; m. Robert Charles Lachky, Aug. 29, 1980. Buyer/planner Campbell Mithun, Chgo., 1977-78, asst. media buyer, 1976; media dir. Haddon Advt., Chgo., 1978—. Vol. Five Hosp. Plan, Chgo., 1979—. Roman Catholic. Clubs: Broadcast Advt., Chgo. Advt. Home: 39 Elmwood Ct Indian Head Park IL 60525 Office: 875 N Michigan Ave Chicago IL 60611

LACHMAN, HOWARD FRANK, data processing specialist; b. St. Louis, Aug. 29, 1940; s. Max Joseph Lachman and Frances Frieda (Levin) Lachman Bly; student in math. and physics edn. U. Mo., 1959-62; diploma in electric acctg. machines equipment, second generation acctg. machines and programming Internat. Data Processing Inst., 1964; m. Rita Baum, Jan. 6, 1963. Sales, Hill Bros. Shoe Co., 1962, Wohl Shoe Co., 1963; computer operator Sigma Chem. Co., St. Louis, 1963-65, Merc. Trust Co., St. Louis, 1965-66; operator and programmer St. Louis Computer Co., 1966; sr. operator and tng. specialist McDonnell-Douglas Automation Co., St. Louis, 1966—. Pres., liaison officer Maryland Heights (Mo.) Citizens Assn.; corr. sec. men's club, treas. couples club United Hebrew Temple, St. Louis. Recipient cert. award Automobile Club Mo., 1955. Clubs: Maryland Heights Jaycees; N.W. Democratic, B'nai B'rith. Home: 2550 Wesglen Estates Dr Maryland Heights MO 63043 Office: PO Box 516 Saint Louis MO 63166

LACHTER, LEWIS ERIC, mfg. co. exec.; b. Bronx, N.Y., Jan. 17, 1929; s. Abraham and Yetta L.; B.A., CCNY; m. Muriel Olshansky, Oct. 29, 1967; 1 son, Eric; children by previous marriage—Jesse, Julia. Coll. corr., feature writer N.Y. Herald Tribune, 1948-51; editor Furniture World, 1954-56, Photog. Trade News, 1956-60; movie editor U.S. Camera, 1960-64; exec. editor Adminstrv. Mgmt., 1964-72; public relations supr. Minn. Mining & Mfg. Co., St. Paul, 1972—; lectr. profl. orgns. Served with U.S. Army, 1951-53. Mem. Internat. Micrographic Congress, Nat. Micrographic Assn. Mem. Democratic Farm Labor Party. Jewish. Home: 1870 Highland Pkwy Saint Paul MN 55116 Office: Minn Mining & Mfg Co 3M Center Saint Paul MN 55101

LACKENDER, GERALDINE SELMA, civic worker; b. Williamsburg, Iowa, Oct. 7, 1920; d. Julius J. and Anna M. (Wetjen) Buser; student public schs., Iowa; m. Glenn Lackender, Feb. 11, 1942; children—Sherry, Penny, Vicki, Cathy, Randy, Ronda. With high sch. cafeterias, Iowa City, 1970-78; bd. dirs. Am. Cancer Soc., Iowa City, 1968-72, crusade chmn., 1968, mem. state service and rehab. com., 1972-81; pres. PTA, Iowa City, 1968-72; bd. dirs. Agrl. Assn., 1978—; chmn. fair entertainment com. 4-H, 1979—, mem. county youth com., 1972-78; dist. chmn. Iowa Farm Bur. Women, 1974—, county chmn., 1967-68, public relations chmn., 1979—, mem. state resolutions com., 1979, county legis. com., 1970—; pres. Zion Lutheran Ch. Women, 1972-75, bd. dirs., 1972—; mem. County Extension Home Econs. Com., 1978—, County Extension Council, 1968-72; mem. Iowa City Community Theatre. Recipient Iowa Master Farm Homemaker award Wallaces Farmer, 1968; Outstanding Citizen award Hills Town & Country, 1979; Farm Family award Iowa City C. of C., 1980. Mem. Iowa Mothers Assn., Iowa Master Farm Homemakers Guild. Clubs: Porkettes, Cowbelles, Farm Bur. Women, U. Iowa Women's. Address: Route 3 Iowa City IA 52240

LACSINA, EMMANUEL QUIAMBAO, pathologist; b. Manila, Nov. 24, 1937; s. Nicanor Timbol and Sarah Sanchez (Quiambao) L.; came to U.S., 1963, naturalized, 1969; M.D., Far Eastern U., 1963; m. Michelle Marie Braaten, Nov. 3, 1979; children—Anita Renee, Ivetta Ann, Deanna Erin, Victor Emmanuel. Rotating intern USAF Hosp., Philippines, 1962-63, Deaconess Hosp., Milw., 1963-64; resident in anatomic and clin. pathology Akron (Ohio) City Hosp., 1964-68; asso. pathologist Mercy Hosp., Des Moines, 1972-73; dir. labs. N.W. Community Hosp., Des Moines, 1973—; dep. Polk County (Iowa) Med. Examiners Office, 1973—. Served with AUS, 1968-71. Decorated Army Commendation medal. Fellow Am. Soc. Clin. Pathologists, Coll. Am. Pathologists; mem. Polk County Med Soc. Presbyterian. Home: 5846 S Winwood Dr Des Moines IA 50324 Office: 1818 48th St Des Moines IA 50310

LACSON, GEORGE RAVELLO, architect; b. Bacolod City, Philippines, May 7, 1935; s. Pedro Aguilar and Francisca Alba (Ravello) L.; B.S. in Architecture, U. Santo Tomas, 1958; m. Leticia Arreola Dimalanta, Jan. 4, 1966; children—Frances, Kristina, George. Residential architect, indsl. designer, Manila, 1958-66; draftsman Hellmuth, Obata & Kassabaum, Inc., St. Louis, 1966-71, asso., 1971-79, v.p., 1979—. Mem. AIA. Roman Catholic. Home: 254 Penwood Ct Chesterfield MO 63017 Office: 100 N Broadway Hellmuth Obata Kassabaum Saint Louis MO 63102

LAD, PRAKASH SHRIPAD, civil engr.; b. Bombay, India, Sept. 7, 1940; s. Shripad Narayan and Sumitra (Rangnekar) L.; came to U.S., 1968, naturalized, 1977; m. Nilima Madan Pai, Apr. 17, 1972; children—Ashvin, Suneet, Shilpa. Asst. engr. S.B. Joshi & Co., Ltd., Bombay, 1964-65; sub engr. Mcpl. Corp. of Greater Bombay, 1965-68; sr. structural engr. bridge office Ill. Dept. Transp., Springfield, 1969—. Mem. ASCE. Home: 812 Rickard Rd Springfield IL 62704 Office: 2300 S Dirksen Pkwy Springfield IL 62764

LADD, GARY W(AYNE), educator; b. Buffalo, Apr. 28, 1950; s. Herbert G. and Marion V. (Johnson) L.; B.A., Grove City Coll., 1972; M.A., Alfred U., 1974; Ed.D., U. Rochester, 1978. Research asso. U. Rochester, 1978-79; asst. prof. Child devel. Purdue U., 1979—. Mem. Soc. Research in Child Devel., Am. Ednl. Research Assn., Am. Psychol. Assn. Presbyterian. Home: 2640 Willow West Lafayette IN 47907 Office: 216 CDFS Bldg Purdue U West Lafayette IN 47907

LA DU, BERT NICHOLS, JR., educator; b. Lansing, Mich., Nov. 13, 1920; s. Bert Nichols and Natalie Jessie (Kerr) La D.; B.S., Mich. State Coll., 1943; M.D., U. Mich., 1945; Ph.D., U. Calif. at Berkeley, 1950; m. Catherine Shilson, June 14, 1947; children—Elizabeth, Mary, Anne, Jane. Intern, Rochester (N.Y.) Gen. Hosp., 1945-46; research asso. N.Y. U. Research Service, Goldwater Meml. Hosp., N.Y.C., 1950-53; sr. asst. surgeon USPHS, Nat. Heart Inst., 1954-57; surgeon, sr. surgeon, med. dir. Nat. Inst. Arthritis and Metabolic Diseases, 1957-63; prof., chmn. dept. pharmacology N.Y. U. Med. Sch., N.Y.C., 1963-74; prof., chmn. dept. pharmacology U. Mich. Med. Sch., Ann Arbor, 1974-80, prof., 1980—. Mem. adv. com. Roche Inst. Molecular Biology, 1972-74; mem. toxicology adv. com. FDA, 1975-77; mem. nat. adv. com. NIH study sects., 1964-70, Nat. Inst. Arthritis and Metabolic Diseases Council, 1975-78. Served with AUS, 1943-45. Mem. AAAS, Am. Chem. Soc., Am. Soc. Biol. Chemists, Am. Soc. Pharmacology and Therapeutics, Am. Soc. Human Genetics, Biochem. Soc. (Gt. Britain), N.Y. Acad. Scis. Editor: (with others) Fundamentals of Drug Metabolism and Drug Disposition; contbr. articles to profl. jours. Home: 817 Berkshire Rd Ann Arbor MI 48104 Office: 6322 Med Sci Bldg I U Mich Med Sch Ann Arbor MI 48109

LADY, WENDELL, state legislator; b. Abilene, Kans.; B.S. in Engring., Kans. State U.; m. Mary Jean Robbins; children—Jan Lady Bean, Jill, Dave. Project mgr. Black and Veatch, Cons. Engrs.; former mem., then pres. Overland Park (Kans.) City Council; now mem. Kans. Ho. of Reps. from 19th Dist., former house minority leader, now speaker of house, chmn. interstate coop. commn., chmn. legis. budget. Mem. ASCE, Am. Water Works Assn., Johnson County Mental Health Assn., Overland Park C. of C., State-Fed. Assembly of Nat. Conf. State Legislatures, Phi Kappa Phi, Sigma Tau, Delta Tau Delta. Methodist. Home: 8732 Mackey Overland Park KS 66212

LAESSIG, RONALD HAROLD, chemist, educator, state lab. adminstr.; b. Marshfield, Wis., Apr. 4, 1940; s. Harold John and Ella Louise (Gumz) L.; B.S., U. Wis., Stevens Point, 1962; Ph.D., U. Wis., Madison, 1965; m. Joan M. Spreda, Jan. 29, 1966; 1 dau., Elizabeth. Chief clin. chemist, asst. prof. preventive medicine U. Wis., Madison, 1966-70, asso. prof., 1970-76, prof., 1971—, prof. pathology, 1972—; asst. dir. Wis. Lab. Hygiene, Madison, 1970-80, dir., 1980—; cons. in field; pres. Nat. Com. for Clin. Lab. Standards, 1980-82; chmn. invitrodiagnostic products com. FDA, 1975-76. Mem. Am. Chem. Soc., Am. Assn. Clin. Chemists, Am. Public Health Assn., Assn. State and Territorial Public Health Lab. Dirs. Contbr. articles to profl. jours. Office: 465 Henry Mall U Wis Madison WI 53711

LAFAVE, RODNEY JAY, computer service co. exec.; b. Duluth, Minn., July 5, 1935; s. Wesley Peter and Irene Marion (Round) L.; student U. Minn., Duluth, 1954; m. Kathleen Robison, Dec. 18, 1971; children—Jeffrey, Douglas, Debra, Julie. Computer operator St. Louis County, Duluth, 1958-60, data processing mgr., 1960-66; owner, mgr. Compudata Corp., Duluth, 1966—, Compudata Computer Store, Duluth, 1979—. Dir. Duluth Portorama, 1964; founder, pres. Duluth Fight Inefficient Govt. Hiking Taxes (FIGHT) Orgn., 1976; ch. fin. chmn., 1976-77. Mem. Data Processing Mgmt. Assn. (pres. Head of Lakes 1962, 71, internat. dir. 1977—, outstanding performance awards), Duluth Jaycees (hon. life mem., v.p. 1965, 66, various awards), Duluth C. of C., Duluth Conv. and Visitors Bur. Republican. Methodist. Club: Kiwanis (pres. 1972) (Duluth). Home: 202 Hawthorne St Duluth MN 55812 Office: Compudata Corp 104 W Superior St Duluth MN 55802

LAFEVERS, LARRY EDMOND, mktg. cons.; b. Kansas City, Mo., Nov. 1, 1941; s. Edmond James and Veda Elizabeth (Upton) LaF.; student Baker U., 1959-61; B.A., Kans. State Coll., Pittsburg, 1964; m. Gayle Lyn Ireland, Aug. 27, 1963; children—Brett Allen, Cole Evan. Dist. mgr. Libby, McNeill & Libby, 1964-68; partner Allied Meat Co., 1968-70; nat. sales mgr. L'Eggs Products, Inc., Winston-Salem, N.C., 1970-76; nat. sales mgr. Wilton Enterprises Inc. div. Pillsbury Co., 1976-77; dir. nat. accounts and trade relations Borden Foods Sales Co., Columbus, Ohio, 1977-80; owner Larry LaFevers and Assos., sales and mktg. cons., also mfrs. reps., Worthington, Ohio, 1980—. Mem. Nat. Account Mktg. Assn., Food Industry Assn. Execs., Heart of Am. Meat Dealers Assn. (past dir.), Internat. Platform Assn. Methodist. Clubs: Muirfield Village Golf; Worthington Hills Country; Bienville (Mobile, Ala.); Salesian Boys. Office: 1091 Circle on Green Worthington OH 43085

LAFFERRE, BRUCE ALLEN, utility co. exec.; b. Louisville, Dec. 17, 1949; s. James Allen and Mary Juanita (Thompson) L.; B.A., U. Louisville, 1971; postgrad. mgmt. U. Detroit, 1976-79; M.B.A., Mich. State U., 1981; m. Nancy Jean Ganz, June 15, 1974. Fin. and estate planner Conn. Gen. Ins. Co., Louisville, 1971; engring. systems product rep. Bruning div. AM Internat., Louisville, 1971-73, Detroit, 1973-76; microsystems product rep. Xerox Corp., Detroit, 1976-78; micrographics systems analyst Detroit Edison Co., 1978-79, residential market planner, 1979—. Recipient Olsten award excellence in records mgmt. programs; Internat. Chorus Champion, Soc. Preservation and Encouragement of Barbershop Quartet Singing in Am., 1969, 81. Mem. Engring. Soc. Detroit, Am. Mktg. Assn., Assn. M.B.A. Execs. Republican. Clubs: Detroit Athletic, Econ. Detroit. Home: 1867 Derby St Birmingham MI 48008 Office: Detroit Edison Co 2000 2d Ave Room 383 WCB Detroit MI 48226

LAFFERTY, DANIEL CHARLES, health services adminstr.; b. Detroit, July 5, 1945; s. Charles William and Elspeth Louvenia (Martin) L.; B.S., Eastern Mich. U., 1969, M.A., 1976; Asso. Degree, Washtenaw Community Coll., 1975; M.P.A., U. Mich., 1982; m. Lynda Charlene Klaus, Apr. 7, 1969; children—Erin Michelle, Matthew Brandon. Cons., Saginaw County Substance Abuse Services,

Saginaw, Mich., 1977; dir., cons. Saginaw County Central Assessment and Referral Service and Employee Assistance Programs, 1977; dir., health officer Macomb County Health Dept., Mt. Clemens, Mich., 1978-79; dep. adminstr. Macomb County Health Services, 1979—; mem. Southeastern Mich. chpt. Comprehensive Health Planning Council, also mem. sub-area adv. council; adv. Macomb County Com. for Maternal and Child Health; adv. Southeastern Mich. public health curriculum planning com. U. Mich.; mem. Regional Area Agy. on Aging of SE Mich.; mem. Project Health Care. Served with U.S. Army, 1968-74; Vietnam. Decorated Bronze Star. Cert. occupational therapist. Mem. Am. Public Health Assn., Mich. Public Health Assn., Mich. Assn. Public Health, Mich. Health Officers Assn., Mich. Assn. Local Public Health Adminstrs., Internat. Platform Assn., Phi Kappa Phi. Home: 11538 Helen St Warren MI 48093 Office: 43525 Elizabeth Rd Mount Clemens MI 48043

LAFFERTY, JOHN HENRY, food machine co. exec.; b. Huntington, W.Va., Aug. 6, 1925; s. Hugh Henry and Lulu May (Linder) L.; B.S. magna cum laude, Ohio U., 1950; m. Mary Elizabeth Crim, Dec. 27, 1951; children—David Crim, Ann Marie. Cost mgr. Hobart Corp., Troy, Ohio, 1953-61; procurement mgr., 1961-64, materials mgr., 1964-65, asst. to exec. v.p., controller, 1965-68, dir. ops. adminstrn., 1968-71, v.p. ops. adminstrn., 1971-77, v.p. adminstrn. and planning, 1977-78, v.p. logistics and materials, 1978-81, v.p. mfg. ops. services, 1981—. Pres. Troy United Fund, 1959; regional chmn. Ohio Republican Finance Com., 1970-77; chmn., participant various civic coms.; trustee Edison State Coll., 1975-79. Served to capt., Q.M.C., U.S. Army, 1943-46, 1951-52. Named Outstanding Young Man of Year, Troy Jr. C. of C., 1958; recipient Disting. Service award, Troy C. of C., 1979; Certificiate of Merit, Ohio Alumni Assn., 1968. Mem. Nat. Assn. Accts., Am. Def. Preparedness Assn. Republican. Methodist. Club: Kiwanis. Home: 157 Merry Robin Rd Troy OH 45373 Office: Hobart Corp World Headquarters Troy OH 45374

LA FOLLETTE, BRONSON CUTTING, atty. gen. Wis.; b. Washington, Feb. 2, 1936; s. Robert Marion, Jr. and Rachel Wilson (Young) LaF.; children—Robert M., Deborah C.; B.A., U. Wis., 1958, J.D., 1960. Admitted to Wis. bar, 1960, U.S. Supreme Ct., 1966. Individual practice law, Madison, Wis., 1960-62; asst. U.S. atty. Western Dist. Wis., 1962-64; atty. gen. Wis., Madison, 1964-68, 74—; Democratic nominee for Gov. Wis., 1968; lectr. Am. Specialist Abroad Program U.S. Dept. State, India, Sri Lanka, 1965. Mem. Pres.'s Consumer Adv. Council, 1966-69, chmn., 1968-69; bd. dirs. Consumers Union, Inc., 1968-76. Mem. Wis., Dane County bar assns. Office: 114 E State Capitol St Madison WI 53702

LAFONE, BARRY SHANNON, fertilizer co. exec.; b. Dunedin, Fla., Aug. 30, 1948; s. Clyde Shannon and Delores (Wilodean) L.; B.Sc. in Bus. Adminstrn., Ohio State U., 1978; m. Denise Ruth Hand, Oct. 2, 1971; children—Heather Michelle, Barry Shannon and Hilary Erika (twins). Systems scheduling coordinator Great Lakes Carbon Corp., Marion, Ohio, 1978-79; gen. mgr. Precision Post Co., Marion, 1979-81; mgr. prodn. planning and inventory control NA-Churs Plant Food Co., Marion, Ohio, 1981—. Served with USAF, 1967-71. Democrat. Baptist. Home: 2667 East Dr Marion OH 43302 Office: 421 Leader St Marion OH 43302

LAFONT, GERARDO, psychiatrist; b. Palencia, Spain, Sept. 9, 1930; s. Feliciano and Criselda L.; M.D., U. Madrid, 1958; came to U.S., 1959, naturalized, 1968; children—Marcos, Gerard, Michael. Intern, St. Johns Hosp., Cleve., 1959-60; resident Mary Mount Hosp., Cleve., 1960-61, T.M. Hosp., Warren O., 1962-63; resident N.Y. Psychiat. Inst., 1965-68; instr. psychiatry Albert Einstein Coll. Medicine, N.Y.C., 1968, asst. clin. prof., 1969; dir. Hunts Point Mental Health Center, Bronx, 1969-70, Stark County Community Mental Health Center, Canton, Ohio, 1970-71; pvt. practice psychiatry, Canton, 1971—. Served with Spanish Air Force, 1957-58. Mem. A.M.A., Am. Psychiat. Assn., Ohio Med. Assn., Stark County Med. Soc. Home: 4319 Guilford Ave NW Canton OH 44709 Office: 907 S Main St N Canton OH 44720

LAFORE, LAURENCE DAVIS, educator, author; b. Narberth, Pa., Sept. 15, 1917; s. John Armand and Anne (Shearer) L.; B.A., Swarthmore Coll., 1938; M.A., Fletcher Sch. Law and Diplomacy 1939, Ph.D., 1950. Mem. faculty Trinity Coll., Hartford, Conn., 1940-42; with State Dept., 1942-43, OWI, 1943-44; asst. press attache Am. embassy, Paris, France, 1944-46; research asso. ECA, 1948; mem. faculty Swarthmore Coll., 1946-69, prof. history, 1960-69; vis. prof. U. Iowa, 1967-68, prof. history, 1969—, chmn. dept., 1974-77. Mem. Iowa State Hist. Bd., 1979—. Mem. Am. Hist. Soc. Conf. British Studies, Phi Beta Kappa, Delta Upsilon. Author: (with Paul Beik) Modern Europe, 1958; (novel) Learner's Permit, 1962; (novel) The Devil's Chapel, 1964; The Long Fuse, 1965; (with Sarah L. Lippincott) Philadelphia, The Unexpected City, 1965; (novel) Stephen's Bridge, 1960, (novel) Nine Seven Juliet, 1969; The End of Glory, 1970; (with James Dugan) Days of Emperor and Clown, 1973; American Classic, 1975. Home: 9 Parsons St Iowa City IA 52240

LA FORGE, PAUL EDWARD, constrn. co. exec.; b. Davenport, Iowa, Nov. 18, 1947; s. Paul Francis and Ellen Berniece (Treiber) LaF.; student Labette Community Coll., 1965-67; B.S. in Civil Engring., U. Kans. at Lawrence, 1970, B.S. in Bus. Adminstrn., 1970, m. Linda Joyce Miller, Aug. 24, 1968; children—Natalie Jeanette, Valerie Lynn. Foreman, LaForge & Budd Constrn. Co., Inc., Parsons, Kans., 1962-67, project supt., 1970-72, corporate exec., 1972—; individual practice, Kansas City and Lawrence, Kans., 1968-70. Mem. Nat. Soc. Profl. Engrs., U. Kans. Alumni Assn. Roman Catholic. Home: 3009 30th Dr Parsons KS 67357 Office: 3101 Main St Parsons KS 67357

LAGES, JOHN DAVID, economist, educator; b. Denver, Jan. 25, 1936; s. Charles Richard and Ruth (Lewis) L.; A.B. cum laude, Central Meth. Coll., 1957; M.A., U. Mo., 1958; Ph.D., Iowa State U., 1967; m. Pamela Nisen, Nov. 18, 1961; children—Jane Elizabeth, Christopher Rowland. Instr. econs. Iowa State U., Ames, 1958-59; asst. prof. bus. adminstrn. Coll. of Pacific, Stockton, Calif., 1959-60; faculty S.W. Mo. State U., Springfield, 1963—, prof. econs., 1971—; vice-chmn. bd. City Utilities of Springfield, 1979-81; cons. in field. Iowa State U. Manpower Research Inst. postdoctoral fellow, 1967. Mem. Am. Econs. Assn., AAUP, Pi Gamma Mu, Phi Mu Alpha, Sigma Epsilon Pi, Omicron Delta Epsilon. Author: (with C. Ketch) Religious-Economic Survey of Springfield, Mo., 1966, Manpower Demand Survey of Selected Counties of Missouri, 1967. Office: SW Mo State U 901 S National St Springfield MO 65802

LAHNIERS, CARROLL EDWARD, clin. psychologist; b. Decatur, Ill., June 17, 1944; s. Edward Elda and Frances Maxine (Minor) L.; B.A., Miami (Ohio) U., 1965; M.A., U. Cin., 1968, Ph.D., 1971. Licensed psycholgoist, Ohio Bd. Psychology, 1973. Psychol. technician Knowle Hosp., Fareham, Hants., Eng., 1966-67; psychol. cons. Jewish Hosp., Cin., 1969—, Council of Epilepsy, Cin., 1975—, Mgmt. Design, Inc., Cin., 1974—; faculty U. Cin., 1971—, Xavier U., Cin., 1976—; dir. psychol. services Rollman Psychiat. Inst., Cin., 1971-76; psychol. cons. alcoholism care unit St. Francis Hosp., Cin., 1976—; pvt. practice clin. psychology, Cin., 1971—. Mem. Am., Cin. psychol. assns., Assn. Advancement of Psychology, Nat. Register Health Service Providers in Psychology, Alpha Delta Phi, Psy Chi, Pi Delta Phi. Contbr. articles to profl. jours. Home and office: 1247 Ida St Cincinnati OH 45202

LAHRMAN, DON EUGENE, orthodontist; b. Ft. Wayne, Ind., Mar. 12, 1932; s. Clarence F. and Orpha (Krauter) L.; B.S., Ind. U., 1954, D.D.S., 1957, M.S.D. in Orthodontics, 1965; m. Carolyn Lou Steinbacher, Aug. 29, 1953; children—Lisa Lynn, Don Eugene II. Pvt. practice dentistry, Ft. Wayne, Ind., 1959-62, practice dentistry specializing in orthodontics, Ft. Wayne, 1962—; tchr. Ind. U. at Ft. Wayne, 1966-68. Served as capt. AUS, 1957-59. Mem. Isaac Knapp Dental Soc. (del. 1967-73; pres. 1971-72), Ind., Am. dental assns., Gt. Lakes Soc. Orthodontists, Am. Assn. Orthodontists, Am. Profl. Practice Assn., Ind. Acad. Dental Practice Adminstrn., Found. Orthodontic Research, Am. Cleft Palate Assn., Fedn. Dentaire Internat., Izaak Walton League, Ft. Wayne C. of C. Republican. Lutheran. Author: Clinical Dento-Facial Biometry In Norma Frontalis, 1965. Home: 2933 Covington Lake Dr Fort Wayne IN 46804 Office: 2426 E State Blvd Fort Wayne IN 46805

LAHTI, BARBARA ANN, sch. adminstr.; b. Detroit, Mar. 17, 1941; d. Mauno S. and Eleanor C. (Frankovich) L.; B.S., Wayne State U., 1962, Ed.S., 1976, postgrad., 1977—; M.A., U. Mich., 1971. Tchr., Detroit Public Schs., 1962-63, Ferndale Public Schs., 1963-67; tchr., head dept. girls phys. edn. Southfield (Mich.) Public Schs., 1967-77, counselor, 1977-79, asst. prin., 1979—; cons. Mich. Dept. Edn. Georgia Emery scholar, 1975-76. Mem. Mich. Assn. Secondary Sch. Prins., Oakland County Assn. Secondary Prins., Southfield Assn. Sch. Adminstrs., Mich. Assn. Middle Sch. Educators, Women's Sports Found., Zonta Internat., Royal Oak Bus. and Profl. Women's Club (pres. 1973-75), Mich. Fedn. Bus. and Profl. Women's Clubs, Inc. (chmn. state program 1977-79), Wayne State U. Alumni Assn., U. Mich. Alumni Assn., Smithsonian Assos., Phi Delta Kappa, Phi Lambda Theta. Home: 1930 Massoit St Royal Oak MI 48073 Office: 24661 Lahser St Southfield MI 48034

LAHTI, LESLIE ERWIN, univ. dean; b. Floodwood, Minn., July 27, 1932; s. Frank Leon and Ester (Baaso) L.; B.S.Ch.E., Tri State U., 1954; M.S.CH.E., Mich. State U., 1958; Ph.D., Carnegie Mellon U., 1964; m. Alma L. Kelley, May 19, 1956; children—David, Mark, Paul. Glass technologist Corning Glass, Albion, Mich., 1955-57; process engr. Ren Plastics, Lansing, Mich., 1957-58; asst. prof. Tri-State U., Angola, Ind., 1958-60; asst. prof. Purdue U., Lafayette, Ind., 1963-67; asso. prof. U. Toledo (Ohio), 1967-72, prof., chmn. chem. engring., 1972-80, dean engr., prof. chem. engring., 1980—; cons. Amoco, Comml. Filters, Whirlpool, Inland Chem. Recipient Shreve prize Purdue U., 1967; Herb Thober award Am. Inst. Chem. Engrs., 1977, also named Toledo Chem. Engr. of Year, Toledo sect., 1977; Outstanding Educator of Ohio, Ohio Soc. Profl. Engrs., 1978; Ford fellow, 1960-63. Mem. Am. Inst. Chem. Engrs., Am. Chem. Soc., Am. Soc. Engring. Edn., Nat. Soc. Profl. Engrs., Ohio Soc. Profl. Engrs., Toledo Soc. Profl. Engrs. Contbr. articles to profl. jours. Home: 2460 Valleybrook Dr Toledo OH 43615 Office: 2801 W Bancroft St Toledo OH 43606

LAI, JUEY HONG, chemist; b. Taipei, Taiwan, Dec. 4, 1936; s. Kwo-Wang and Chin-Fong L.; came to U.S., 1961, naturalized, 1976; B.S. in Chem. Engring., Nat. Taiwan U., 1959; Ph.D. in Phys. Chemistry, U. Wash., 1969; m. Li-Huey Chang, June 30, 1968; children—Eric Yo-Ping, Bruce Yo-Sheng. Research specialist chemistry U. Minn., 1969-73; prin. research scientist Honeywell Tech. Center, Honeywell, Inc., Bloomington, Minn., 1973-78, sr. prin. research scientist, 1978—. Bd. dirs. Chinese Am. Assn. Minn., 1977-79. Recipient Honeywell H. W. Sweatt Tech. award, 1980. Mem. Am. Chem. Soc., Sigma Xi, Phi Lambda Upsilon. Contbr. articles on solid state chemistry, polymer chemistry and polymer materials to tech. jours. Research on polymer materials for electronics and solid state chemistry. Office: Honeywell 10701 Lyndale Ave S Bloomington MN 55420

LAIDLER, JAMES HAROLD, supt. schs.; b. Windsor, Ont., Can., May 22, 1925; s. John Alfred and Margaret (Cunningham) L.; came to U.S., 1927; naturalized, 1946; B.S., Wayne State U., 1957, M. Ed., 1963, Ed.D., 1981; postgrad. Detroit Coll. Law, 1957-59, Valparaiso U., 1961, Western Reserve U., 1962-63; m. Carolynn J. Scharrer, June 1, 1946; children—Lorraine Laidler Hughes, James B., Janet L. Laidler Beller, Catherine M. Mgmt. positions Ford Motor Co., Dearborn, Mich., 1948-58; tchr. Heintzen Schs., Southgate, Mich., 1958-65; systems analyst mgmt. services Great Lakes Steel, Ecorse, Mich., 1965-67; asst. supt. Gilbraltar Sch. Dist., Rockwood, Mich., 1967-71; supt. Morenci (Mich.) Area Schs., 1971-75; supt. Lamphere Schs., Madison Heights, Mich., 1975-78; supt. Cheboygan (Mich.) Area Schs., 1978—. Columnist, Morenci (Mich.) Observer, 1973-75. Cub Scout com. chmn. Boy Scouts Am., Gibraltar, Mich., 1961-66. Mem. Gibraltar (Mich.) Bd. Edn., 1964-67. Served with RCAF, 1943-45; USAF, 1945. Mem. Am., Mich. (mem. in-service com. 1972—, chmn. workshops 1973, 74, 75) assns. sch. adminstrs., Mich. Sch. Bus. Ofcls., Mich. Negotiators Assn., Can. Legion (pres. 1948-49). Roman Catholic (chmn. parish council 1969-71). Elk, Rotarian (pres. 1969-70, 76-77). Columnist, Cheboygan Daily Tribune, 1979—. Home: 10622 Moonlight Bay Rd PO Box 373 Cheboygan MI 49721 Office: Riverton Plaza PO Box 100 Cheboygan Area Schs Cheboygan MI 49721

LAIR, DWAYNE EUGENE, agriculturist, farmer; b. Red Oak, Iowa, Oct. 13, 1926; s. Oscar and Dorothy Irene (Carroll) L.; grad. high sch.; m. Marvella Huff, Nov. 27, 1947; children—Cheryl (Mrs. Gary Ray Carter), Dwanella (Mrs. Randall Franklin Snethern), Layne. Truck driver Huff Trucking Co., West Plains, Mo., 1947-50; farmer nr. Hocomo, Mo., 1950-53, 54—; assembly worker Gen. Motors, Kansas City, Kans., 1953; program officer, field asst. U.S. Dept. Agr., West Plains, 1964—; salesman Na-Churs Plant Food Co., 1971-77; dir. Lair Farms and Feed Co., Missouri Valley Feed Corp. Mem. Egypt Grove Sch. Bd., Hocomo, Mo., 1958-59; mem. South Fork (Mo.) Sch. Bd., 1964-65; spl. dep. sheriff, 1970-72, dep. assessor, 1960-68, 70-77, 78-79. Served with AUS, 1945-46. Mem. Am. Legion, Pork Producers Assn. (dir. 1972-73). Home: Route E Box 593 Caulfield MO 65626

LAIR, ROBERT LOUIS, aircraft co. exec.; b. Albuquerque, Aug. 13, 1921; s. Louis E. and Inez B. (Mudd) L.; student Kans. State Tchrs. Coll., Emporia, 1938-40, Kans. State Coll., Manhattan, 1940-41; m. Aug. 9, 1941; children—Christopher Louis, Catherine Ann, Cynthia Susan. Outside prodn. mgr. Boeing Co., Wichita, Kans., 1941-53; prodn. mgr. Cessna Aircraft Co., Wichita, 1953—, v.p. aircraft ops., 1966-69, sr. v.p., 1969—, also dir.; dir. Cessna Fin. Corp., Cessna Internat. Fin. Corp., Reims Aviation (France). Served with USN, 1944-46. Mem. Nat. Indsl. Conf. Bd., Nat. Aero. Assn., Army Aviation Assn. Am., Am. Mgmt. Assn., AIAA, Gen. Aviation Mfrs. Assn., Wichita C. of C. Mem. Christian Ch. Clubs: Masons; Rotary; Wichita, Wichita Country; Nat. Aviation. Home: 105 Woodlawn Ct Wichita KS 67218 Office: 5800 E Pawnee St PO Box 1521 Wichita KS 67201

LAIRD, CHARLES FRANCIS, state legislator Kans.; b. Topeka, June 4, 1941; s. Donald Leroy and Isabel Helen (Hoffman) L.; B.A., Washburn U., 1964; M.Ed., U. Md., 1970; m. Celia Sue Melton, Nov. 28, 1964; children—Tim, Dan, Mike, Patrick. Mem. Kans. Ho. of Reps., 1973—. Served to capt. USAF, 1964-70. Mem. U. Md. Alumni Assn., Am. Legion. Roman Catholic. Club: Washburn U. Alumni. Home: 3501 Shawnee Ct Topeka KS 66605 Office: St Francis Hosp and Med Center 170C W 7th St Topeka KS 66606

LAIRD, EVALYN WALSH, lawyer; b. Chgo., Feb. 6, 1902; d. Edward J. and Mae (Tarr) Walsh; J.D., DePaul Law Sch., 1926; Ph.D. (hon.), Hamilton U., 1974; m. Charles Hamilton Laird, Aug. 8, 1925 (dec. 1970); children—Lois (Mrs. Walter P. Hillmann), Betty Ann (Mrs. Donald H. Hillmann), Charles Jr. (dec.), Edward J., Jane Alice (Mrs. Daniel R. Glynn). Admitted to Ill. bar, 1926; practiced in Chgo., 1926—; mng. dir. Edward J. Walsh, ct. reporting, 1950—, owner, 1960—. Former den mother Cub Scouts; past pub. relations chmn. Rogers Park area Girl Scouts U.S.A., Chgo., del. council, mem. council personnel com., 1972-77; past pres. 7th dist. vicarate II, Chgo. Council Catholic Women; mem. Mayor Daley's Com. Women Lawyers; past co-chmn. Ill. Epilepsy League, Inc.; past pres. Glenola Club of Loyola Center; mem. exec. council real property com. Lake Michigan Fedn.; former co-chmn. Women's Campaign Com. for Esther Saperstein for Senator. Mem. Women's (past mem. speakers bur.; mem. Law Day com.), Chgo. (past house com.; real property com., contracts div., chmn. tax div., chmn. ecology div. environ. law com., sci. and tech. com., exec. council real property com.), Ill. (sr. counsellor 1976) bar assns., Chgo. and Cook County Fedn. Women's Clubs (past mem. bd.), Shell Club Field Museum, Field Museum Natural History, Okla., Texas County irrigation and water resources assns., Nat., Internat. wildlife fedns., Lake Mich. Fedn., Sierra Club, Angel Guardian Aux., Shedd Aquarium, Internat. Oceanographic Found., Ill. Right to Life Com., U.S. Figure Skating Assn., Cousteau Soc. Clubs: Skokie Valley Figure Skating; Grand Beach (Mich.) Golf and Social; Glenola (past program chmn.). Home: 19259 Pine Ave Grand Beach PO Box 75 New Buffalo MI 49117 Office: 6 N Michigan Ave Suite 1417 Chicago IL 60602

LAIRD, STEWART WILSON, med. center ofcl.; b. Anoka, Minn., May 6, 1937; s. Harry Cecil and Clementine Marie (Donais) L.; B.A., St. John's U., 1959; M.H.A., U. Minn., 1965; m. Kathleen Mary Sullivan, Nov. 25, 1961; children—Michael, Mary, Peter, Christopher, Thomas, Ann. Asst. adminstr. St. Mary's Hosp., Wausau, Wis., 1965-68, asso. adminstr., 1968-70; adminstr. Wausau (Wis.) Hosp. South, 1970-71, adminstr. Wausau Hosp., 1971-74; pres., chief exec. officer St. Francis Med. Center, LaCrosse, Wis., 1974—; dir. Blue Cross-Blue Shield United of Wis. Preceptor, U. Minn. and Xavier U.; bd. dirs. Chileda Inst. for Multi-Handicapped, Western Wis. Health Systems Agy., Shared Health Services; chmn. Wis. Health Facilities Authority. Served to capt. U.S. Army, 1959-63. Fellow Am. Coll. Hosp. Adminstrs.; mem. Cath. Health Assn. of U.S. (dir.), Cath. Hosp. Assn. Wis. (past pres.), Western Wis. Hosp. Dist. Assn. (past pres.), Wis. Public Health Assn. Republican. Roman Catholic. Clubs: Rotary, Elks, Serra. Home: 600 S 28th St LaCrosse WI 54601 Office: 700 S West Ave LaCrosse WI 54601

LAIRD, THOMAS RICHARD, physician; b. Hastings, Nebr., Feb. 2, 1938; s. Bruce and Mabel Fay (Buzzard) L.; M.D., U. Nebr., 1964. Intern, Bryan Meml. Hosp., Lincoln, Nebr., 1964-65; gen. practice medicine, Blue Hill, Nebr., 1965-70; physician emergency room services St. Elizabeth Community Health Center, Lincoln, 1970—. Owner Blue Hill Greenhouses, 1967—. Active Boy Scouts Am.; vice-chmn. Camp Kitaki com. YMCA. Mem. AMA, Nebr., Lancaster County med. socs., Am. Acad. Family Physicians, Aircraft Owners and Pilots Assn., Am. Coll. Emergency Physicians, Order of Arrow, Phi Chi. Republican. Methodist. Home: Box 126 Blue Hill NE 68930 also 2951 Park Place Dr Lincoln NE 68506 Office: 555 S 70th St Lincoln NE 68510

LAITY, RONALD LEONARD, engring. exec.; b. Hancock, Mich., July 16, 1927; s. Leonard Benjamin and Ida Sophia (Baakko) L.; B.S. in Elec. Engring., Mich. Technol. U., 1953; m. Leola Gladys Upton, Nov. 26, 1948; children—Kathryn, Teresa, Matthew. Various positions including cons., planning and design services for indsl., instl., govtl. and comml. facilities and design and system planning for utility clients Commonwealth Assos. Inc., Jackson, Mich., 1953—, staff engr. facilities and environ. div., asst. treas., 1972—. Served with USAF, 1945-47. Mem. Nat. Soc. Profl. Engrs., Mich. Soc. Profl. Engrs., IEEE, Engring. Soc. Detroit, Tau Beta Pi, Eta Kappa Nu. Presbyterian. Home: 3239 McCain Rd Jackson MI 49203 Office: Commonwealth Assos Inc 209 E Washington Ave Jackson MI 49201

LAJOIE, RICHARD JOHN, JR., fin. exec.; b. Kansas City, Mo., Apr. 10, 1947; s. Richard John and Julia Hortense (Bush) L.; B.B.A. in Fin., U. Notre Dame, 1969; M.B.A. in Accounting, Xavier U., 1972; m. Mary Alice Herod, Aug. 21, 1971; children—Richard John, Mary Eleanor. Staff accountant Peat, Marwick, Mitchell & Co., Washington, 1972-75, sr. accountant, Cin., 1975-77; mgr. internal audit Clopay Corp., Cin., 1977-80, controller plastic products div., 1980—, v.p., 1981—. Bd. dirs. Clopay Employees Fed. Credit Union, 1979—, pres., 1980, treas., 1981; vol. United Appeal, Kindervelt. Served with inf. AUS, 1969-71. Decorated Bronze Star with 3 oak leaf clusters, Army Commendation medal with oak leaf cluster, Purple Heart, Air medal; C.P.A., Ohio. Mem. Am. Inst. C.P.A.'s, Ohio Soc. C.P.A.'s, Inst. Internal Auditors (sec. Cin. chpt., bd. govs. 1980—). Roman Catholic. Clubs: Notre Dame, Queen City Racquet. Editor Cin. Internal Auditor. Home: 2122 Winchester Pl Fairfield OH 45014 Office: Clopay Sq Cincinnati OH 45214

LAKE, CHARLES WILLIAM, JR., printing co. exec.; b. LaPorte, Ind., June 21, 1918; s. Charles William and Jessie Mae (Lyon) L.; student U. Wis., 1936-37; B.S., Cornell U., 1941; M.B.A., U. Chgo., 1949; m. Louise Safford Sprague, July 4, 1946; children—Charles William III, Elizabeth Sprague. With R.R. Donnelley & Sons Co., Chgo., 1946—, successively asst. to treas., mgr. mgmt. studies, dir. indsl. engring., 1947-56, dir. engring. research and devel., 1956-58, dir. operating, 1958-59, dir. Chgo. mfg. div., 1959-63, dir. sales div., 1963-64, v.p. co., 1953-63, sr. v.p., 1963-64, pres., 1964-81, chmn. bd., 1975—, chief exec. officer, 1981—, also dir.; dir. No. Trust Co., Inland Steel Co., Am. Hosp. Supply Corp., CBI Industries, Inc. Sr. mem. The Conf. Bd.; mem. Chgo. Com.; mem. vis. com. Div. Sch., Sch. Bus., also citizens bd. U. Chgo.; emeritus trustee, mem. emeritus engring. council, univ. council Cornell U.; bd. dirs. Protestant Found. Greater Chgo., John Crerar Library; mem. Northwestern U. Assos. Served from 2d lt. to capt., ordnance, AUS, 1941-46. Mem. Am. Inst. Indsl. Engrs., Tau Beta Pi, Beta Gamma Sigma. Congregationalist. Clubs: Masons; Univ., Economic, Chgo. Sunday Evening (trustee), Comml., Chgo., Cornell (Chgo.); Hinsdale (Ill.) Golf; Old Elm Golf, Sky, Links, Hemisphere (N.Y.C.); Blind Brook (N.Y.) Golf; Lancaster (Pa.) Country; Royal Poinciana Golf, Hole in the Wall Golf (Naples, Fla.). Home: 222 E 4th St Hinsdale IL 60521 Office: 2223 Dr Martin Luther King Jr Dr Chicago IL 60616

LAKE, EDGAR RAYMOND, engr.; b. Liverpool, Eng., May 30, 1930; came to U.S., 1951, naturalized, 1959; s. Arthur Holt and Elsy Mary (Rigby) L.; B.S. in Chemistry, Liverpool Sch. Tech., 1951; children—Gina Simone, Robin Holt, Andrea Paulina. Mgr. Pyro-Chem. Labs., Unidynamics Inc., St. Louis, 1952-62; mgr. spl. projects lab. Mo. Research Labs., St. Louis, 1962-63; asst. mgr. engring. Spl. Devices Inc., Newhall, Calif., 1963; staff engr. McDonnell Aircraft Co., St. Louis, 1963—. Bd. dirs. Life Crisis

Services, Inc., St. Louis, also sec. Mem. Am. Def. Preparedness Assn., Am. Assn. Suicidology. Author in field; patentee in field. Home: 337 Greenwich Ln Apt A-4 Saint Louis MO 63108

LAKE, THOMAS PHILIP, radiologist; b. Mpls., Apr. 3, 1938; s. Philip A. and Theodora M. (Soderberg) L.; B.S. summa cum laude, Beloit Coll., 1960; M.D., U. Minn., 1964; m. Joanne R. Zimmerman, June 6, 1960; children—Paul Thomas, Gregory Thomas. Intern, St. Mary's Hosp., Duluth, Minn., 1964-65; resident in diagnostic radiology Mayo Grad. Sch. Medicine, Rochester, Minn., 1967-70; staff radiologist Meml. Med. Center, Springfield, Ill., 1970—; chmn. dept. radiology Springfield Community Hosp., 1977-80; clin. asst. prof. radiology So. Ill. Sch. Medicine, Springfield, 1973—, clin. asst. prof. diagnostic radiology, 1973—; treas. Clin. Radiologists, S.C. Served with USNR, 1965-67. Diplomate Am. Bd. Radiology. Mem. Am. Coll. Radiology, Ill. Radiol. Soc., AMA, Ill., Sangamon County med. socs., Phi Beta Kappa. Club: Illini Country (Springfield). Home: 1601 Cherry Rd Springfield IL 62704 Office: Meml Med Center Springfield IL 62781

LAKE, VICTOR HUGO, mfg. co. exec.; b. Quincy, Mass., Nov. 11, 1919; s. Victor Hugo and Edna Beatrice (Blott) L.; student Lawrence Inst. Tech., 1939-42, U. Maine, 1943; m. Jeannette Elzena Stewart, Apr. 26, 1942; children—Victor Stewart, Valerie (Mrs. John Anderson); m. 2d, Jacqueline Rose Davis, July 4, 1975. Asst. supt. Taylor Winfield Corp., Detroit, 1938-43; prodn. control mgr. Fed. Machine & Welder Co., Warren, Ohio, 1944-49; with Am. Welding & Mfg. Co., Warren, 1949—, mgr. materials, 1969—. Served with AUS, 1943-44. Mem. Am. Soc. Metals, Trumbull County Indsl. Mgmt. Assn. (pres. 1972-73). Republican. Methodist. Home: 1675 Parkman Rd NW Warren OH 44485 Office: American Welding and Mfg Co 190 Dietz Rd Warren OH 44482

LAKES, RODERIC STEPHEN, biomed. engr.; b. N.Y.C., Aug. 10, 1948; B.S. in Physics, Rensselaer Poly. Inst., 1969, Ph.D. in Physics, 1975. Research asst. U. Md., College Park, 1970-71; teaching asst. dept. physics Rensselaer Poly. Inst., Troy, N.Y., 1971-75; postdoctoral asso. engring. and applied sci. Yale U., 1975-77; asst. prof. physics Tuskegee (Ala.) Inst., 1977-78; vis. asst. prof. biomed. engring. Rensselaer Poly. Inst., 1978; asst. prof. biomed. engring. U. Iowa, Iowa City, 1978—, dir. Applied Mechanics Lab., 1980—. Mem. Am. Phys. Soc., Orthopaedic Research Soc., AAAS, ASME, Sigma Xi. Contbr. articles on biophysics to sci. jours.; reviewer Jour. Biomechs., Jour. Biomechanical Engring. and Sci.; research biophysics of bone. Home: 358 Magowan Ave Iowa City IA 52240 Office: College of Engineering Univ Iowa Iowa City IA 52242

LALLY, ANN MARIE, former ednl. adminstr.; b. Chgo., Sept. 23, 1914; d. Martin J. and Della (McDonnell) Lally; A.B., Mundelein Coll., 1935; A.M., Northwestern U., 1939, Ph.D., 1950; postgrad. Chgo. Tchrs. Coll., Chgo. Art Inst., 1935-36. Tchr., Amundsen High Sch., 1935, Lindblom and Von Steuben high schs., Chgo., 1936-38; chmn. art dept. Schurz High Sch., 1938-40; supr. art Chgo. Pub. Elementary Schs., 1940-48, dir. art Chgo. Public Schs., 1948-57; prin. John Marshall High Sch., 1957-63; supt. Dist. 16, Chgo. Pub. Schs., 1963-64, Dist. 5, 1964-80; lectr. Wright Jr. Coll., 1948; instr. creative drawing Chgo. Acad. Fine Art, 1941; instr. interior design Internat. Harvester Co., 1946-48; lectr. in edn. DePaul U., 1952-74; lectr. in edn. and art U. Chgo., 1956-59; lectr. edn. Chgo. Tchrs. Coll., 1960-62. Trustee Pub. Sch. Tchrs. Pension and Retirement Fund Chgo., 1965-71, sec.-treas., 1960-65, pres., 1965-70. Charter mem. women's bd. Loyola U.; charter mem. women's bd. Art Inst., Chgo. Mem. Am., Ill. assns. sch. adminstrs., N.E.A. (life), Ill. Edn. Assn., Dist. Supts. Assn. (pres. 1973-75), Ill. Women Adminstrs. Assn. (award 1979), Nat. Council Adminstrv. Women in Edn. (profl. relations chmn. 1958-62), Assn. Supervision and Curriculum Devel., Chgo. Area Women Adminstrs. in Edn. (award for outstanding adminstrn. 1981), Nat. Art Edn. Assn. (mem. council 1956-60), Western Arts Assn. (pres. 1956-58), Internat. Soc. Edn. in Art, Ill. Art Edn. Assn. (pres. 1955), LWV of Chgo., Chgo. Art Educators Assn. (a founder; past v.p., sec. and treas.), Ill. Club Cath. Women (dir. 1981—), Chgo. Pub. Sch. Art Soc., Chgo. Hist. Soc., Am. Assn. U. Women (Chgo. chmn. elem. and secondary edn., dir.-at-large 1962-66, 78—), Chgo. Area Reading Assn. (dir. 1963-69), Nat., Ill. assns. secondary sch. prins., Artists Equity Assn., Chgo. Council on Fgn. Relations, Mundelein Coll. Alumnae Assn. (past pres., chmn. bd., Magnificat medal 1964), Pi Lambda Theta, Delta Kappa Gamma. Contbr. articles to art and ednl. jours. Home: 1130 S Michigan Ave Chicago IL 60605

LAM, ANSELM ON-SANG, physician; b. Hong Kong, Sept. 20, 1947; came to U.S., 1962, naturalized, 1967; s. Pan-Nin and Sau-Fong (Wong) L.; B.A., Marquette U., 1969; M.D., Med. Coll. Wis., 1974. Intern, St. Michael Hosp., Milw., 1974-75, resident, 1975-77; practice medicine specializing in family practice, Mequon Wis., 1977—; instr. Med. Coll. Wis., 1979—. Diplomate Am. Bd. Family Practice. Mem. Am. Emergency Physicians. Home: 4721 W Parkview Dr Mequon WI 53092 Office: 8300 N Teutonia Dr Brown Deer WI 53209

LAM, CHARLES TAK WAI, pharm. co. exec.; b. Kwangtung, China, Dec. 22, 1942; s. Ha-On and Wan-Yee Lam; came to U.S., 1961, naturalized, 1980; B.A., Augustana Coll., Rock Island, Ill., 1965; M.S., Purdue U., 1968, Ill. Inst. Tech., 1970; m. Maria Aurora Escasa, Aug. 31, 1968; children—Prudence B., Paul A., Richard C. Asst. chemist John Deere Co., Moline, Ill., 1965; research asst. Ill. Inst. Tech., Chgo., 1968-70; asst. research scientist Research and Devel. Dept., Miles Labs. Inc., Elkhart, Ind., 1970-76, research scientist Quality Assurance Dept., 1976-79, sr. chemist-med. diagnostics Mfg. Dept., 1979—. Active, Bristol Opera House. Mem. Am. Chem. Soc., Am. Assn. Clin. Chemists, Miles Sci. Forum, Phi Lamda Upsilon. Lutheran. Contbr. articles in field to profl. jours. Patentee med. diagnostics devices field. Home: 54112 Forest Grove Ave Elkhart IN 46514 Office: Miles Labs Inc 1127 Myrtle St Elkhart IN 46515

LA MALFA, JOACHIM JACK, psychologist; b. Milw., Aug. 10, 1915; B.S., Marquette U., Milw., 1938; M.S., U. Wis., Madison, 1941; Ph.D., U. Mich., 1949; m. Constance Zarcone, Dec. 27, 1944; children—Constance Joanne, Jacquelyn Grace. Research asst. U. Mich., 1946-47; psychiat. intern and founder dept. Milwaukee County Hosp. Mental Diseases, 1947; instr. psychology Marquette U., 1947-49, asst. prof., 1951-52; founder, 1952, chmn. St. Michael's Hosp. Mental Health Clinic, 1952-73; pvt. practice, Milw., 1949—; mem. staff St. Michael's Hosp. Mem. Am. Psychol. Assn., Am. Personnel and Guidance Assn., Am. Soc. Group Psychotherapy, Nat. Register Health Service Providers in Psychology, Wis. Psychol. Assn., Milw. County Psychol. Assn., Phi Kappa Phi, Phi Delta Kappa. Republican. Roman Catholic. Club: Milw. Athletic. Home: 7821 N Lake Dr Fox Point WI 53217 Office: 115 W Silver Spring Dr Whitefish Bay WI 53217

LA MARCHE, JEAN HERTEL, artist, designer; b. Manchester, N.H., Apr. 29, 1945; s. Joseph Napolean and Carmen Marie Violet (Mailloux) La M.; student U. Houston, 1962-66, 70-72; B.S. in Architecture, Lawrence Inst. Tech., 1980, B.Arch., 1981; m. Bonita Jean Doerr, Feb. 20, 1973. Design staff Neuhaus and Taylor, 1966; designer for Richard A. Fitzgerald, architect, Houston, 1974, William E. Andrews, architect, Sarnia, Ont., Can., 1975; owner, operator La Marche Design, Detroit, 1975—; instr. design Lawrence Inst. Tech., 1979-82. Served with U.S. Army, 1966-70. Recipient 2d pl. Nat. Portland Cement Assn. Archtl. Competition, 1966, 1st pl. Landscape Design award Sarnia City C. of C., 1977, 1st pl. sch. award Reynolds Aluminum prize competition Lawrence Inst. Tech., 1978; Edward D. Stone Sr. Meml. scholar, 1979; Oscar Freimann scholar, 1979; Yamasaki scholar, 1980-81; ASCA scholar, 1980. Art and drawings exhibited in Houston, Los Angeles, St. Croix, V.I., Southfield, Mich.

LAMARTINE, BRUCE CARVELL, materials research engr.; b. Richmond, Ind., Oct. 3, 1946; s. Paul Bernard and Stella Violet (Carvell) L.; B.A., New Coll., U. South Fla., 1967; M.S., Case Western Res. U., 1970, Ph.D., 1978; m. Clare Millicent Eberhart, June 5, 1971; children—Ian, Nicole. Research fellow, lectr. dept. chemistry Case Western Res. U., Cleve., 1971-72; materials research engr. Air Force Wright Aero. Lab., Wright-Patterson AFB, Ohio, 1980—; traveling wave tube materials cons. Air Force Space div., 1976—. Mem. coaching staff Beavercreek Soccer Assn., 1980. Served with USAF, 1972-80. Decorated Air Force Commendation medal. Univ. Research fellow, U.S. Dept. Interior/Case Western Res. U., 1967-72. Mem. Am. Vacuum Soc., Am. Phys. Soc. Contbr. articles to profl. jours.; guest reviewer Jour. Applications of Surface Sci., 1980. Office: AFWAL/MLBM Wright Patterson AFB OH 45433

LAMB, DONALD DANA, govt. ofcl.; b. Warren, Ohio, Apr. 19, 1938; s. Charles Dana and Velma May (Robinson) L.; B.S., Mich. State U., 1963; M.S. in Urban and Regional Planning (Alcoa fellow), U. Pitts., 1965; m. A. Joan Balfour, Dec. 27, 1962; children—Allan Dana, Kevin Dana. Planner, Ashtabula County Plan Commn., Jefferson, Ohio, 1960-61; planner Lucas County Plan Commn., Toledo, 1963-64; planner Pitts. Regional Plan Assn., 1966-67; systems analyst, project mgr. CONSAD Research Corp., Pitts., 1967-70; mgr. environ. programs, tech. dir. S.E. Mich. Council Govts., Detroit, 1970-80; div. dir. Comprehensive Health Planning Council SE Mich., Detroit, 1980—; instr. Wayne State U.; lectr. U. Mich., Mich. State U., Harvard U., Yale U., U. Pa. Crusade chmn. Ashtabula County chpt. Am. Cancer Soc., 1961; cubmaster Boy Scouts Am., 1978, 79; treas. Fox Chase Condominium Assn., Inc., 1978—, Shadyside Civic Assn., Pitts., 1968; deacon 1st Presbyterian Ch., Mt. Clemens, 1977. Mem. Ops. Research Soc. Am., Am. Inst. Cert. Planners, Am. Planning Assn., Urban and Regional Info. Systems Assn., U.S. Power Squadron. Author: Research of Land Use Models, 1967; A Community Action Program Impact Model, 1968; An Urban-Regional Model of Area Change for Southeast Michigan, 1969. Home: 37395 Charter Oaks Mount Clemens MI 48043 Office: 800 Book Bldg Detroit MI 48226

LAMB, HOWARD ALLEN, state legislator; b. Bassett, Nebr., Oct. 8, 1924; B.S. in Agrl. Engring., U. Nebr.; m. Jo Kellenbarger, Oct. 9, 1949; children—Philip, David. Farmer, rancher; mem. Nebr. Legislature, 1976—. Pres. Custer Public Power Dist.; bd. dirs. Fed. Land Bank Assn., Broken Bow, KRVN Rural Radio Assn.; former pres. Anselmo-Merna Bd. Edn., Home: SW Star Route Anselmo NE 68813*

LAMB, POSE MAXINE, coll. educator; b. Pitts., Oct. 31, 1927. B.S. in Edn., Ohio State U., 1948, M.A. in Edn., 1952, Ph.D. in Edn., 1960. Classroom tchr. Bexley (Ohio) Pub. Schs., 1949-57; tchr. lab. sch. Ball State U., Muncie, Ind., 1957-62; coll. instr. Purdue, Lafayette, Ind., 1962—. Mem. AAUW, Internat. Reading Assn., Nat. Council Tchrs. English, Assn. Childhood Edn., Delta Kappa Gamma, Alpha Delta Kappa, Pi Lambda Theta. Author: Linguistics in Proper Perspective, 2d edit., 1977; Guiding Children's Language Learning, 1967, 72, Reading: Foundations and Instructional Strategies, 1976, 80. Certified tchr., Ind.; specialist in lang. acquisition, linguistics, lang. and reading. Home: 172 W Navajo St West Lafayette IN 47906 Office: Purdue U Dept of Edn Edn Bldg W Lafayette IN 47907

LAMB, RICHARD JOSEPH, funeral dir.; b. Evergreen Park, Ill., Sept. 7, 1940; s. Matthew J. and Margaret M. (Lawler) L.; A.B., Holy Cross Coll., 1962; Licensed Funeral Dir., Worsham Coll., 1963; postgrad. U. Chgo., 1965-68; m. Susan Palmgren, Oct. 24, 1964; children—Maureen, Christine, Jennifer, Stephen, Meghan. Corporate sec. Blake-Lamb Funer Homes, Inc., Oak Lawn, Ill., 1975—; pres. 103d St. Oak Lawn Bldg Corp., 1977—, Gold Coast Devel. Corp.; partner Mat-Rich Investments, Oak Lawn, 1963—, Lamb Flower Shop, Chgo., 1963—; sec. Lamb Auto Livery. Chmn. Lombard (Ill.) Lilac Festival, 1974-75, Lombard Blood Program, 1975-76. Mem. Nat., Ill. funeral dirs. assns., Funeral Dirs. Services Assn. (v.p.), Preferred Funeral Dirs. Internat. (pres. 1979-80, chmn. bd. 1980-81), Am. Thanatalogical Assn., Internat. Fedn. Thanatopractic Assns., Lombard C. of C. (pres. 1974). Club: Good Samaritan (chmn. 1980). Office: 4727 W 103d St Oak Lawn IL 60453

LAMB, VERNON ARTHUR, cons. chemist; b. Spencer, Iowa, Dec. 12, 1909; s. Frank Sheldon and Bertha Henrietta (Dahms) L.; student Iowa State U., 1928-29, U. Calif., Berkeley, 1930-31; B.A., State U. Iowa, 1933, M.S., 1935, Ph.D., 1937; m. Leone Shelmidine, Sept. 1, 1934; children—James D., Michael A., Donald S., John L. Instr. chemistry State U. Iowa, 1934-37, Wis. Tchrs. Coll., Platteville, 1937, U. Md., 1937-41; chemist Nat. Bur. Standards, Washington, 1941-69; asst. chief electrolysis and metal deposition, 1951-69; cons. chemist, Spencer, Iowa, 1969—. Mem. Town Council Garrett Park (Md.), 1946-50. Mem. Am. Chem. Soc., Electrochem. Soc., Am. Electroplaters Soc., Electrodepositors Tech. Soc. (London), Sigma Xi, Phi Beta Kappa. Republican. Club: Clay County Garden. Home: Rural Route 1-B Spencer IA 51301

LAMBERT, CHARLES THOMAS, real estate broker; b. Chgo., July 29, 1946; s. Roy E. and Henriette (Plew) L.; student Vincennes U. Jr. Coll., 1964-65; B.S., Ball State U., 1969; m. Pamela Elaine Flick, June 11, 1977. Sales rep. Xerox Corp., Indpls., 1969-73; asso. F.C. Tucker Co., Inc., Indpls., 1973—; cons. indsl. real estate. Mem. Indpls. Jaycees (Spark Plug award 1974, dir. human improvement 1974), Realtors Nat. Mktg. Inst., Met. Indpls. Bd. Realtors, Internat. Exchange Assn., Indpls. Mus. Art. Republican. Methodist. Clubs: Ind. Athletic, Masons, Shriners; Hillcrest Country. Home: 616 Copley Pl Indianapolis IN 46290 Office: 2500 One Indiana Sq Indianapolis IN 46204

LAMBERT, DANIEL MICHAEL, coll. adminstr.; b. Kansas City, Mo., Jan. 16, 1941; s. Paul McKinley and Della Mae (Rogers) L.; A.B., William Jewell Coll., 1963; M.A., Northwestern U., 1965; Ph.D., U. Mo., 1977; m. Carolyn Bright, Dec. 27, 1969; children—Kristian Paige, Dennis McKinley. Asst. to dean Elmhurst (Ill.) Coll., 1963-65; licensed to ministry, Baptist Ch., 1965; asso. pastor Christ Ch., Wellesley, Mass., 1965-66; dean student affairs William Jewell Coll., Liberty, Mo., 1970-76, dean student affairs, asst. to pres., 1977—, v.p., 1979—. Served with U.S. Army, 1966-70. Decorated Bronze Star. Mem. Nat. Orgn. Legal Problems in Edn., Am. Assn. Higher Edn. Home: 982 Wyckwood Dr Liberty MO 64068 Office: William Jewell Coll Liberty MO 64068

LAMBERT, LECLAIR GRIER, writer; b. Miami, Fla., Feb. 11, 1941; s. George F. and Maggie (Grier) L.; B.S., Hampton Inst., 1959; postgrad. Harvard U., 1959, U. Munich (Germany), 1965-66. Researcher, copy reader Time-Life Books, 1961-64; tchr. biology and Eng. lit., secondary level U.S. Dependent's Schs. Overseas, Tripoli, Libya, 1964-65; biology editor of high sch. textbooks Holt, Rinehart & Winston, N.Y.C., 1966-69; biology editor and writer Ency. Britannica, N.Y.C., 1969; copy editor Russian sci. monographs The Faraday Press, N.Y.C., 1970-71; writer Med. World News, N.Y.C., 1971; public relations writer Nat. Found./March of Dimes, White Plains, N.Y., 1972; lectr. community and human relations, Black cultural heritage at local schs. and colls., 1977—; radio commentator Sta. KEEY, 1975—; reporter Twin Cities Courier, Mpls., 1976—; free lance writer and designer of brochures and pamphlets, 1974—; dir. communications St. Paul Urban League, 1972-80, asst. to exec. dir., 1977-80; exec. dir. African Am. Cultural Center, 1980—; info. officer Mpls. Urban League, 1978-79. Founder, bd. dirs. Summit-University Free Press, 1974—; bd. dirs. H.E.A.R.T., 1978—; adv. bd. Concordia Coll. Minority Program, 1979—, U. Minn. Black Learning Resource Center, 1980—; mem. rev. com. Twin Cities Mayors' Public Art Awards, 1981. Served to 1st lt., Chem. Corps., U.S. Army, 1959-61. Recipient Community Martin Luther King Communications award, 1978. Mem. Public Relations Soc. Am., Twin Cities Black Journalists Assn., Minn. Press Club. Author: Reflections of Life-Poems, Prose and Essays, 1981; editor, writer: Minnesota's Black Community, 1977. Office: 2429 S 8th St Minneapolis MN 55454

LAMBERT, ROBERT DAVID, lawyer; b. Davenport, Iowa, Oct. 3, 1951; s. Robert Lansing and Margaret Irene (Philhour) L.; B.A., U. Ill., 1974; J.D., Drake U., 1977. Admitted to Iowa bar, 1977; partner firm Betty, Neuman, McMahon, Hellstrom and Bittner, Davenport, Iowa, 1977—. Mem. Am. Bar Assn., Scott County Bar Assn., Iowa State Bar Assn., Am. Assn. Trial Lawyers, Iowa Assn. Trial Lawyers, Greater Davenport C. of C. Home: 3410 Heatherton Dr Davenport IA 52804 Office: 600 Union Arcade Davenport IA 52801

LAMBRIGHT, LESLEY LOUISE, counselor; b. Pitts., Aug. 22, 1946; d. Arthur Meils and Helen Louise (Hurd) L.; B.A., Mich. State U., 1968; M.A., Wayne State U., 1974. Elem. team tchr. Jefferson County Schs., Denver, 1968-70; elem. tchr. Omaha Sch. Dist., 1970-71; group leader Continuum Center, Oakland U., Rochester, Mich., 1973-74; counselor Community Resource Center, Macomb County Community Coll., Warren, Mich., 1974—; pvt. practice counseling, 1977—. Mem. Statewide Task Force on Sexual Harassment in Work Force, 1979. Cert. social worker, 1976—, cert. transactional analyst, 1977—. Named Spirit of Detroit, City of Detroit, 1980. Mem. Internat. Transactional Analysis Assn., Am. Personnel and Guidance Assn., Assn. Specialists in Group Work, NOW (Feminist of Yr. Detroit 1980), Am. Assn. Women in Community and Jr. Colls., Mich. Orgn. Human Rights. Office: Macomb County Community Coll 14500 12 Mile Rd Warren MI 48093

LAMBRIGHT, RUTH LOUISE MILLER, hosp. food service adminstr.; b. LaGrange, Ind., Dec. 29, 1923; d. James Elmer and Rosa Ann (Yoder) Miller; student Goshen Coll., 1946-47; m. Harold Lambright, July 12, 1947; children—Birdena, Karl, Karen, Weldon, Glendon, Marcile, Marlin. Cook, Miller's Nursing Home, LaGrange, 1970-76; cook LaGrange Hosp., 1976, supr. food service, 1977—. Mem. Hosp., Instn. and Ednl. Food Service Soc. Mennonite. Office: LaGrange Hosp Route 5 LaGrange IN 46761

LAMER, LEON RAY, city ofcl.; b. Eldora, Iowa, Dec. 28, 1943; s. James Bradford and Ruth Irene (Bahr) L.; student Des Moines Area Coll., Boone, nights 1970-73, short courses U. Iowa; m. Carol Jane Fast, Feb. 7, 1965; children—Mechiele, Monte, Mark. Draftsman, Iowa Dept. Transp., Ames, 1967-73; asst. dir. public works City of Boone (Iowa), 1973-76; mgr. Keokuk (Iowa) Water Works, 1976-81, Marshalltown (Iowa) Water Works, 1981—. Mem. adminstrv. bd. Trinity United Meth. Ch., 1978—, also choir mem. Mem. Am. Water Works Assn., Iowa Water Works Assn., Am. Soc. Cert. Engring. Technicians. Club: Lions. Home: 2100 Bondeau St Keokuk IA 52632 Office: N2 23 N Center St Marshalltown IA 50158

LAMIE, EDWARD LOUIS, computer scientist; b. Kingsley, Mich., Aug. 27, 1941; s. Louis Edward and Pauline Theresa (Harrand) L.; A.B., San Diego State U., 1969; M.S., U. So. Calif., 1971; Ph.D., Mich. State U., 1974; m. Mary Ellen Bronson, Sept. 9, 1960; children—William, David, Melissa. Engring. draftsman Security Title Ins. Co., San Diego, 1962-64; computer programmer City of San Diego, 1964-69; mem. tech. staff Rockwell Internat., Downey, Calif., 1969-71; chmn., prof. computer sci. Central Mich. U., Mt. Pleasant, 1971—, mem. exptl. learning assessment team. Served with USN, 1959-62. Mem. Assn. Computing Machinery. Roman Catholic. Author, referee numerous computer sci. papers for nat. symposia and profl. jours.; author: A Concise Introduction to PL/I Programming, 1982. Home: 1120 S Elizabeth St Mount Pleasant MI 48858 Office: Computer Sci Dept Central Mich U Mount Pleasant MI 48859

LAMKIN, EUGENE HENRY, JR., state legislator Ind., physician; b. Owensboro, Ky., Feb. 23, 1935; s. Eugene Henry and Nancy Elizabeth (Davidson) L.; B.A., DePauw U., 1956; M.D., Ind. U., 1960; m. Martha Dampf, Aug. 24, 1968; children—Melinda Magness, Matthew Davidson. Intern, Phila. Gen. Hosp., 1960-61; resident internal medicine Ind. U. Med. Center, 1961-62, 64-66; practice medicine, specializing in internal medicine, Indpls., 1966—; instr. Ind. U. Med. Sch., 1966—; mem. teaching staff Methodist Hosp., Indpls.; mem. Ind. Ho. of Reps., 1967—, chmn. public safety com., independent sector study com., majority leader, 1977-80; mem. Gov.'s Traffic Safety Commn., 1967-68, chmn. Marion County ho. del., 1968-72, mem. Gov.'s Commn. on Med. Edn. and Gov.'s Traffic Safety Commn., 1969-72, chmn. affairs of Marion County com., 1967-74; chmn. Mayor's Public Transp. Task Force, 1978-79; bd. dirs. Advanced Transit Assn., 1975-78, Indpls. Conv. and Visitors Bur.; pres. Reference & Index Services, Inc. Mem. steering com. Mayor's Task Force on Drug Abuse, 1967-70; chmn. Mayor's Task Force on Met. Transp., 1969-71; project dir. Model Cities Group Practice Project, 1971; mem. Capitol City Integrated Transit Commn. adv. com. and control bd., 1980-81. Vice pres. Marion County Young Republicans, 1966-67. Bd. dirs. Kennedy Meml. Christian Home, Martinsville, Ind., 1969-75, Greater Indpls. Progress Com., 1970-81, Central Ind. council Boy Scouts Am., 1973, Meridian St. Found., Unified Funds, 1972—; mem. adv. bd. Indpls. Public Transp. Corp. Served to capt. AUS, 1962-64. Recipient Disting. Service award Indpls. Jr. C. of C., 1969; named Outstanding Young Man of Am., 1967, Outstanding Community Leader Am., 1968, One of Five Outstanding Young Men of Ind., Ind. Jr. C. of C., 1970; fellow Meth. Hosp. Found. Fellow ACP; mem. Am., Ind., Marion County med. assns., Ind. Soc. Internal Medicine (dir. 1970-71, 73-74), Indpls. Jr. C. of C. (dir. 1967-69), Phi Beta Kappa, Alpha Omega Alpha. Mem. Christian Ch. (elder). Mason (32 deg.). Club: Indianapolis Ski (past v.p.). Home: 4145 Washington Blvd Indianapolis IN 46205 Office: 1935 N Capitol Ave Indianapolis IN 46202

LAMMERT, ALBERT CHARLES, obstetrician and gynecologist; b. Pitts., June 25, 1923; s. John Harry and Hannah Mae (Barr) L.; B.S., Allegheny Coll., 1944; M.D., Case Western Res. U., 1948; m. Patricia Ann Karnosh, July 9, 1949; children—Linda Anne, Nancy Louise, Gary Karnosh, David Albert. Intern, Western Pa. Hosp., 1948-49; resident in obstetrics and gynecology Univ. Hosps., Cleve., 1950-53; staff Cleve. Clinic, 1955-66; asst. clin. prof. obstetrics and gynecology

Case Western Res. U., 1966—, also chief dept. obstetrics and gynecology Hillcrest Hosp., Mayfield Heights, Ohio, 1979—. Diplomate Am. Bd. Obstetrics and Gynecology. Mem. Am. Coll. Obstetrics and Gynecology, Central Assn. Obstetrics and Gynecology, Ohio Med. Assn., AMA, Cleve. Soc. Obstetrics and Gynecology. Mem. United Ch. of Christ. Club: Shaker Heights Country. Home: 20725 S Woodland Rd Shaker Heights OH 44122 Office: 6803 Mayfield Rd Mayfield Heights OH 44124

LAMONT, FRANCES STILES, state senator; b. Rapid City, S.D., June 10, 1914; s. Frederick Bailey and Frances (Kenney) Stiles; B.A., U. Wis., Madison, 1935, M.A., 1936; postgrad. No. State Coll., 1942-43; m. William Mather Lamont, 1937 (dec.); children—William Stiles, Nancy Brereton, Peggy Lamont Lauver, Frederick Mather. Mem. staff McCalls Mag., N.Y.C., 1936-37; mem. S.D. Senate, 1974—. Mem. S.D. Women's Commn. Civil Def., 1957-62; sec. S.D. Commn. Aging, 1959-61, govt. rep., 1961-67; mem. White House Conf. Aging, 1961; mem. S.D. Gov.'s Study Commn. Elem. and Secondary Edn., 1964-66; vice chmn. Gov.'s Commn. Status of Women, 1964-73; mem. Nat. Task Force Arts, 1968—. Named S.D. Mother of Yr., 1974; recipient nat. citation Am. Mothers Com., N.S. State Coll. Historic Preservation award, 1975, U. Wis. Disting. Alumni award, 1978. Mem. AAUW, LWV, Nat. Order Women Legislators, DAR, Mortar Bd., Phi Beta Kappa, Theta Sigma Phi. Episcopalian. Office: State Capitol Pierre SD 57501*

LA MOTHE, WILLIAM E., food mfg. co. exec.; b. Bklyn., 1926; B.S., Fordham U. With Kellogg Co., Inc., Battle Creek, Mich., 1950—, v.p. and asst. to pres., 1962-65, v.p. corp. devel., 1965-70, sr. v.p. corp. devel., 1970-72, exec. v.p. ops., 1972-73, pres., chief operating officer, 1973-80, chief exec. officer, 1979-80, chmn. bd., 1980—, also dir. Office: Kellogg Co Inc 235 Porter St Battle Creek MI 49016*

LAMOTTE, WILLIAM MITCHELL, ins. brokerage co. exec.; b. Phila., Sept. 3, 1938; s. Ferdinand and June (Mitchell) LaM.; B.A., Princeton U., 1961; m. Elizabeth Ewing, Sept. 16, 1961; children—William Mitchell, Anne Hilliard, Nicole. Underwriter, Chubb & Son, N.Y.C., 1961-62; various assignments Johnson & Higgins Pa., Inc., Phila., 1962-69, pres. Johnson & Higgins Wilmington, Del., 1969-75, pres. Johnson & Higgins Mo. Inc., St. Louis, 1975-77, Johnson & Higgins Ill. Inc., Chgo., 1977—, dir. parent firm. Vice-pres. Boys Clubs Wilmington, 1974-75; bd. dirs. St. Louis Zoo Friends Assn., 1976-77, Lincoln Park Zool. Soc., Chgo., 1981—. Clubs: Corinthian Yacht (Phila.); Chicago, Chgo. Yacht. Home: 109 Greenbay Rd Hubbard Woods IL 60093 Office: Johnson & Higgins Ill Inc 101 N Wacker Dr Chicago IL 60606

LAMOUREUX, GERARD WILLIAM, container mfg. co. exec.; b. Chgo., July 27, 1946; s. Donald Benjamin and Anna Rita (Williamson) L.; B.S. in Mech. Engring. Tech., Purdue U., 1970; m. Gloria Jean Kempa, Feb. 13, 1971; children—Gerard Joseph, Jennifer Ann, Brian Gerard. Design draftsman Whiting Corp., Harvey, Ill., 1967-69; plant engr. DeSoto, Inc., Chicago Heights, Ill., 1970-74; maintenance mgr. Panduit Corp., Tinley Park, Ill., 1974-75; plant engr., plant supt. Container Corp. Am., Dolton, Ill., 1975-79, plant engr., Anderson, Ind., 1979—. Mem. mech. adv. bd. Thornton Community Coll., South Holland, Ill., 1975-79. Mem. South Holland United Fund-Crusade of Mercy Com., 1976-78; bd. dirs. Madison County Jr. Achievement, 1980—. Mem. Am. Inst. Plant Engrs., Madison County Mgmt. Club, Anderson Jaycees, Anderson YMCA, Christian Fellowship Businessmen, Purdue U. Alumni Assn., South Holland Jaycees (pres. 1978-79, state dir. 1976-77). Roman Catholic. Home: 815 Northwood Dr Anderson IN 46011 Office: 3N Sherman St Anderson IN 46011

LAMPE, HAROLD GENE, local govt. ofcl.; b. Monett, Mo., Oct. 9, 1951; s. David and Nora Lampe; B.S. in City and Regional Planning, S.W. Mo. State U., 1973; m. Sheryl Johnston, May 25, 1974; 1 son, Byron. Planner, Lake of Ozarks Council Local Govts., Camdenton, Mo., 1975-76, exec. dir., 1976—; bd. dirs. Central Mo. Emergency Med. Services, Balance of State Planning Council; bd. dirs., pres. Mo. Small Bus. Corp. Mem. Mo. Assn. Council Govts. Exec. Dirs. Lutheran. Club: Lake Valley Country. Home: Box 35 Linn Creek MO 65052 Office: Box 786 Camdenton MO 65020

LAMPE, JOHN FRANCIS, lawyer; b. Wauwatosa, Wis., Mar. 6, 1945; s. William Otto and Catherine Rose (Campbell) Hesse-Lampe; A.B., Coll. William and Mary, 1967; J.D., U. Wis., 1970; m. Jennel Mielka, June 18, 1966; children—Jonathan Graham, Benjamin Quinn. Admitted to Ill. bar, 1975, U.S. Supreme Ct. bar, 1978; asso. firm Hinshaw, Culbertson, Moelmann, Hoban & Fuller, Chgo., 1974-76; atty. firm Joslyn & Green, P.C., Woodstock, Ill., 1977-79; individual practice law, McHenry, Ill., 1979—; spl. asst. atty. gen. Ill., 1981—; pres. CL, Ltd. Served with USMC, 1970-74. Mem. Am. Bar Assn., Ill. State Bar Assn. (mem. assembly), State Bar Wis., McHenry County Bar Assn., Chgo. Bar Assn., Ill. Trial Lawyers Def. Research Inst., McHenry Jr. C. of C. (past pres.), McHenry Area C. of C. (dir.), Wis. Law Alumni Assn. (dir. 1970-71). Republican. Roman Catholic. Editor Gen Practice Sect. Newsletter, Ill. State Bar Assn., 1976-78. Office: 3424 W Elm St McHenry IL 60050

LAMPE, WALLACE DEAN, civil and environ. engr.; b. Waverly, Iowa, July 10, 1941; s. Ernest and Louise (Dietrich) L.; B.S.C.E., U. Iowa, 1964, M.S.C.E., 1966, Ph.D., 1969; m. Susan Jean Hatten, Sept. 3, 1966; 1 son, Christopher Thomas. Successively asst. project engr., project engr., sr. project engr. Betz Environ. Engrs., Plymouth Meeting, Pa., 1969-74; prin. research engr. No. Natural Gas Co., Omaha, 1974-77, research dir., 1977—; research specialist InterNorth, Inc., 1980—. NSF trainee, 1965-66; Fed. Water Pollution Control Adminstrn. fellow, 1966-69. Mem. Water Pollution Control Fedn., Iowa Water Pollution Control Assn., Sigma Xi. Lutheran. Developer maintenance operation for improving energy efficiency of natural gas. Home: 14428 Cedar Circle Omaha NE 68144 Office: 4840 F St Omaha NE 68117

LAMPERT, WILLIAM BENTLEY, III, engring. co. exec.; b. Washington, July 30, 1944; s. William Bentley and Ada Elizabeth (North) L.; B.S. in Chem. Engring., U. Cin., 1967; M.S.E., U. Mich., 1970, postgrad. 1970-79; m. Joan Kaywood Buttrick, Aug. 20, 1966; children—Heather Elizabeth, Shannon Caryn. Chief engr. Charles E. Sech Assos., Inc., Ann Arbor, Mich., 1972-73; product engr. Wolverine Div., UOP, Inc., Dearborn Heights, Mich., 1973-77; project mgr. Zinder Engring., Inc., Ann Arbor, 1977-78; v.p. engring. Stirling Power Systems, Ann Arbor, 1978—. Bd. dirs. Pastoral Care Services of Southeastern Mich., 1980-81. Mem. Am. Inst. Chem. Engrs., Am. Chem. Soc., Am. Soc. Metals, Sigma Xi. Patentee in field. Home: 2903 Sheffield Ct Ann Arbor MI 48105 Office: 7101 Jackson Rd Ann Arbor MI 48103

LAMPL, PAUL GOTTLIEB, sales exec.; b. Circleville, Ohio, Oct. 27, 1929; s. Gottlieb J. and Selma (Weller) L.; student U. Cin., 1947-49; B.Land Arch., Ohio State U., 1954; m. Juanita Hughes, Aug. 29, 1952; 1 son, Paul Gottlieb. Landscape architect nurseries, various locations, 1954-60; free lance landscape architect, Fremont, Ohio, 1960-63; with Chemi Trol Chem. Co., Fremont, 1963—, gen. sales mgr. tank div., 1977—. Mem. ch. council St. Paul Lutheran Ch., Clyde, 1970-73, chmn., 1972-73. Mem. Nat. LP Gas Assn., Ohio LP Gas Assn. (v.p. 1981-82). Republican. Club: Green Hills Golf. Home: PO Box 84 Clyde OH 43410 Office: 2098 W State St Fremont OH 43420

LAMPPA, HERMAN ROGER, counselor; b. Embarrass, Minn., Nov. 16, 1932; s. Richard Victor and Rose Marie Lamppa; A.A., Eveleth Jr. Coll., 1952; B.S., U. Minn., Duluth, 1954; M.S., Bemidji State U., 1967; 6th yr. cert. St. Cloud State U., 1979; m. Joan Elizabeth Carlson, Mar. 7, 1953; children—Robin, Jeena, Jody, Judy, Ryan, Jaclynn. Tchr., coach Argyle (Minn.) High Sch., 1954-55, Beulah (N.D.) High Sch., 1955-58; tchr., coach, counselor Blackduck (Minn.) High Sch., 1958-67; counselor Benson (Minn.) Jr. High Sch., 1967—. Bd. dirs. Family Ed. Center, Benson, 1977-78; bd. dirs. Zion Luth. Ch., 1963-65. Hill Found. grantee, 1964; NDEA fellow, 1960, 65. Mem. Minn. Personnel and Guidance Assn., Minn. Counselors Assn., Central Minn. Counselors Assn., Benson Edn. Assn., Minn. Edn. Assn., NEA, Assn. Supervision and Curriculum Devel., Minn. Assn. Children With Learning Disabilities. Democrat. Club: Lions (Man of Yr. 1976; dir. 1970-75, pres. 1975-76, liaison 1976-81), Phi Kappa Phi. Home: 503 18th St Benson MN 56215 Office: 1400 Montana Ave Benson MN 56215

LANCE, GEORGE MILWARD, engring. adminstr., mech. engr.; b. Youngstown, Ohio, Dec. 4, 1928; s. Ray Clifford and Louisa Brigetta (Emch) L.; B.S. in Mech. Engring., Case Inst. Tech., 1952, M.S. in Instrumentation Engring., 1954; m. Phyllis Joanne Sprague, Aug. 8, 1964; children—Kathryn, Deborah, John, Rebecca, George. Instr., Case Inst. Tech., Cleve., 1952-54; research engr. TRW Inc., Cleve., 1954-56; lectr. Washington U., St. Louis, 1956-60; sr. systems engr. Moog Servocontrols Inc., East Aurora, N.Y., 1960-61; asst. prof., then prof. mech. engring. dept. U. Iowa, Iowa City, 1961—, asso. dean engring., 1974-79; cons. to McDonnell Aircraft, Boeing Airplane Co., Collins Radio Co., U.S. Army Weapons Command. Served with USN, 1946-48. Registered profl. engr., Ohio, Iowa. Mem. ASME, IEEE, Am. Soc. Engring. Edn., Sigma Xi, Tau Beta Pi, Pi Tau Sigma. Patentee in valves. Home: 609 S Summit St Iowa City IA 52240 Office: Univ Iowa College Engineering Iowa City IA 52242

LANCIONE, AMERICUS GABE, state legislator; b. Cementon, Pa., Feb. 12, 1907; s. John Batisti and Elizabeth (Del Guzzo) L.; B.A., Ohio State U., 1927, J.D., 1929; m. June Morforo, Nov. 19, 1931 (dec. Nov. 1970); children—John George, Bernard Gabe, Richard Lee; m. 2d, Madeline Hysell, Mar. 1, 1974. Admitted to Ohio bar, 1929; practiced in Bellaire, 1929—; asst. pros. atty., Belmont County, 1936-44; mem. Ohio Ho. of Reps., 1947—, speaker pro-tem, majority leader, 1949-51, minority leader, 1959, 61, 69, speaker, 1974—. Active Am. Heart Assn., Boy Scouts Am.; mem. Ohio Expositions Commn., 1979—. Served with AUS, 1944-46. Recipient Citizenship citation for meritorious ser. B'nai B'rith, 1961; named Man of Year, Ohio Democratic Com., 1973, Man of Year, Ohio Sons of Italy, 1973; Ky. col. Mem. Am., Ohio, Belmont County bar assns., Ohio Acad. Trial Lawyers, Am. Judicature Soc., Am. Trial Lawyers Assn., Bellaire C. of C., Sons of Italy, Am. Legion, Ohio Hist. Soc., Ohio State U. Alumni Assn., Buckeye Boosters. Kiwanian, Elk. Club: Dapper Dan. Home: 3800 Jefferson St Bellaire OH 43906 Office: 38th and Jefferson Sts Bellaire OH 43906

LANCIONE, BERNARD GABE, lawyer; b. Bellaire, Ohio, Feb. 3, 1939; s. A. G. and Phyllis June (Morford) L.; B.S. in Commerce, Ohio U., 1960; J.D., Capital U., 1966; m. Rosemary; children—Amy Jeanette, Caitin Mountain, Gillian Justine. Statistician, Ohio Dept. Hwys., Columbus, 1961-62; legal aide Office of Ohio Atty. Gen., Columbus, 1962-64; legal aide Nelson Lancione, Lawyer, Columbus, 1964-65; admitted to Ohio bar, 1965, since practiced in Bellaire; asso. A.G. Lancione, 1965-68; partner firm Lancione, Lancione, Lancione & Hanson, 1968-81; pres. Lancione Law Office Co., 1981—. Solicitor, City of Bellaire, 1968-72; asst. pros. atty. Belmont County (Ohio), 1969-72. Mem. Ohio Democratic exec. com. 1969-72; pres. Young Dems. of Ohio, 1970-72; mem. Belmont County Dem. Central Com., 1970-76, exec. com., 1974-76; Southeastern Ohio coordinator John Glenn for U.S. Senate, 1973-74; legal counsel Young Dems. Clubs Am., 1971-73. Mem. Am., Ohio, Belmont County (v.p. 1976-77, pres. 1977-78) bar assns., Ohio Acad. Trial Lawyers, Am. Arbitration Assn. Home: 150 Woodrow Ave Saint Clairsville OH 43950 Office: The Profl Complex 38th and Jefferson Sts Bellaire OH 43906

LAND, ROBERT DONALD, mgmt. cons.; b. Niagara Falls, Ont., Can., Feb. 16, 1926; s. Allan Reginald and Beatrice Beryl (Boyle) L.; B.A., U. Toronto, 1948; children—Brian, Diane, Susan. Securities analyst Toronto (Ont.) Gen. Trusts Corp., 1948-50; actuarial accountant Crown Life Ins. Co., Toronto, 1950-53; mgmt. cons. Profl. Mgmt. Detroit, 1953-66, mng. partner, 1964-66; pres. PM Detroit, Inc., Southfield, Mich., 1966—, also dir.; sr. v.p., dir. Black & Skaggs Assos., Inc., Battle Creek, Mich.; pres., dir. Practice Mgmt. Assos. Ltd., Toronto, Ont. Vestryman St. Joseph's Episcopal Ch., Detroit, 1956-59; coach Royal Oak Hockey Assn., Royal Oak, Mich., 1972, 74. Served with Royal Canadian Navy, 1944-46. Certified profl. bus. cons. Mem. Soc. Profl. Bus. Cons. (past dir., officer), Inst. Cert. Profl. Bus. Cons. (past trustee), Nat. Soc. Pub. Accountants, Ind. Accountants Assn. Mich., Wayne County Med. Soc., Windsor Power Squadron, Soc. for Nautical Research, Nautical Research Guild, U.S. Naval Inst., N.Am. Soc. for Oceanic History. Home: 111 Cambridge Blvd Pleasant Ridge MI 48069 Office: 17800 Northland Park Ct Southfield MI 48075

LANDEN, ERNEST WILLIAM, physicist, spectroscopist, cons.; b. Shenandoah, Iowa, Jan. 13, 1908; s. Arvid Wilhelm and Selma Alfreda (Karlson) L.; B.A., N.W. Mo. State Tchrs. Coll., 1931; M.A., U. Mo., 1933, Ph.D., 1938; m. Mary Frances Patton, Feb. 2, 1935; children—Selma Diana, Karlynn Hedwig. Lab. asst. U. Mo., 1931-38, instr., 1938-40; spectroscopist Armour Research Found., 1940-43; successively research engr., research physicist, program dir. research dept. Caterpillar Tractor Co., Peoria, Ill., 1943-73; cons., Peoria, 1973—. Vice pres. Peoria Arts and Sci. Fedn., 1958-59, pres., 1959-60; bd. dirs. Peoria Acad. Sci., 1978-80, also hon. mem.; trustee Lakeview Mus., 1978-81. Fellow AAAS; mem. Am. Phys. Soc., Optical Soc. Am., Am. Chem. Soc., Soc. Automotive Engrs., Sigma Xi, Pi Mu Epsilon. Republican. Presbyterian. Club: Masons. Contbr. articles to profl. jours. Patentee in field. Home and Office: 4111 N Hawthorne Pl Peoria IL 61614

LANDERS, FREDERICK WILLIAM, JR., mech. engr., energy cons.; b. Montclair, N.J., Feb. 16, 1942; s. Frederick William and Marie Louise L.; B.S. in Mech. Engring., U. Mich., 1965, B.S. in Sci. Engring., 1965, M.B.A., 1971; m. Rosemary Pauline Kilgus, Sept. 12, 1973; children—Christina Marie, Alexander. Field engr. Babcock & Wilcox, Barberton, Ohio, summer 1965; plant mgr. Jeske Mfg. Co., Detroit, 1965-66; chief mfg. engr. Mather Co., Milan, Mich., 1966-69; mfg. mgr. Automation Industries, Ann Arbor, Mich., 1969-70; pres. New Life Farm, Inc., Drury, Mo., 1972-79; founder, pres. Perennial Energy Inc., Dora, Mo., 1980—; tchr. solar energy S.W. Mo. State U.; pvt. cons. Music tchr. vacation bible sch. Christian Ch., 1978; bd. dirs. Douglas County Soil and Water Conservation Dist., 1977-78, Top of Ozarks Resource Conservation and Devel. Bd., 1977-78. Recipient Fed. grants, 1977-79. Mem. Assn. Energy Engrs., Internat. Solar Energy Soc. Home: West Plains MO 65775 Office: Perennial Energy Inc Dora MO 65637

LANDERS, RAY DANIEL, musician, author, composer, educator; b. Kissimmee, Fla., Nov. 17, 1942; s. John Silvey and Jewel Oline (Fain) L.; Mus.B., Sherwood Music Sch., 1964; Mus.M., Northwestern U., 1966; Mus.D., Ind. U., 1974. Asso. instr. Sch. Music, Ind. U., 1966-71; instr. dept. music Chgo. State U., 1971-75, asst. prof., 1975-79, asso. prof., 1979-80; founder, dir. Suzuki Music Acad. of Chgo., 1975—; faculty Am. Suzuki Inst., U. Wis., 1976—; participant Tchaikovsky Internat. Competition, Moscow, 1970, Vianna da Motta Competition, Lisbon, 1971, Rockefeller Competition for Excellence in Am. Music, Chgo., 1978; performed concertos with Sherwood Music Sch., Chgo. Chamber Orch., Ind. U. and Gold Coast orchs. Mem. Music Educators Nat. Conf., Music Tchrs. Nat. Assn., Am. Fedn. Tchrs., Am. Conservatory Music of Chgo., Suzuki Assn. of Americas. Composer numerous mus. compositions. Author: The Talent Education School of Shihichi Suzuki - An Analysis. Home: 1150 N Lake Shore Dr Chicago IL 60611 Office: Suzuki Music Acad Chgo Room 707 207 S Wabash Ave Chicago IL 60604

LANDERS, STUART CHARLES, dentist; b. Cleve., May 11, 1936; s. Jack M. and Rosalind (Fox) L.; student Tulane U., 1954-55, Adelbert Coll. Case Western Res. U., 1955-56, D.D.S., 1960; children—Rodger David, Aimee Beth. Practice restorative and preventive dentistry, Shaker Heights, Ohio, 1962—; mem. courtesy staff Suburban Community Hosp., Warrensville Heights, O.; supervising dental faculty U. Bridgeport, 1964; mem. faculty Case Western Res. U. Sch. Dentistry, 1971—. Vol. Free Drug Clinic. Mem. Cuyahoga County Republican Club. Served to lt. USNR, 1960-62. Fellow Royal Soc. Health; mem. Am., Ohio (dir.) acads. dental practice adminstrn., Western Res. Dental Alumni Assn., Zeta Beta Tau, Alpha Omega. Home: 3715 Warrensville Center Rd Shaker Heights OH 44122 Office: 20620 N Park Blvd Shaker Heights OH 44118

LANDES, JOE SCHUYLER, mfg. co. exec.; b. Vandalia, Ill., Aug. 19, 1942; s. Harold Joseph and Dorothy Delores (Ireland) L.; B.S., Eastern Ill. U., 1969; m. Connie Jeanne Strohl, Mar. 8, 1969; children—Jeffrey Scott, Andrea Kathleen. Account exec. Westvaco, Sandusky, Ohio and Chgo., 1970-74; asst. sales mgr. Westvaco, Sandusky, 1975-77; sales mgr. E & E Specialties, Lawrence, Kan., 1977—. Little League baseball coach, Lawrence, 1980—. Served with USN, 1963-67. Mem. C. of C., Point-of-Purchase Advt. Inst. Club: Lawrence Country. Home: 3034 Campfire Dr Lawrence KS 66044 Office: 910 E 29th St Lawrence KS 66044

LANDESS, ROBERT CHARLES, state ofcl.; b. Carroll, Iowa, Dec. 23, 1935; s. Millard Edwin and Verle (VanNordstrand) L.; B.A., U. Iowa, 1957; J.D., Drake U., Des Moines, 1962. Admitted to Iowa bar, 1962; asso. firm Whitfield, Musgrave, Selvy, Des Moines, 1962-65; asst. city atty. Urbandale, Iowa, 1963-65; dep. indsl. commr. State of Iowa, 1965-67, dep. sec. state, 1967-71, indsl. commnr., 1971—; bd. counselors Drake U. Law Sch. Vice pres. Des Moines Jaycees, 1964; legal counselor, 1968; sec. Variety Club Iowa, 1979; bd. dirs. Polk County Mental Health Assn., 1963. Served with AUS, 1957-59. Mem. Iowa Bar Assn., Polk County Bar Assn. Republican. Club: Masons. Office: 507 10th St Des Moines IA 50319

LANDGRAF, LAWRENCE EDWARD, newspaper exec.; b. Hayward, Wis., Jan. 3, 1925; s. William Hugo and Signe Teresa (Lindholm) L.; B.A. in Journalism/Advt. with honors, U. Wis., 1949; m. Edna Dolores Wells, June 7, 1947; children—James, Janet, Thomas, Terri. Advt. salesman Madison Newspapers, Inc., 1949-54, food account specialist, 1954-63, asst. retail mgr., 1963-75, retail mgr., 1975-77, advt. dir., 1977—. Served with USN, 1943-46. Mem. Advt. Fedn. Am. (chpt. Silver Medal award 1981), Madison Advt. Fedn. (past pres.), Sales and Mktg. Execs. (v.p.), Greater Madison Conv. Bur. (dir.), U. Wis. Alumni Assn. (mktg. com.), Wis. Newspaper Advt. Execs. Assn. (v.p.), Internat. Newspaper Advt. and Mktg. Execs. Assn. Mem. United Ch. of Christ. Club: Blackhawk Country. Home: 6621 Boulder Ln Middleton WI 53562 Office: PO Box 8056 1901 Fish Hatchery Rd Madison WI 53708

LANDINI, RICHARD GEORGE, educator; b. Pitts., June 4, 1929; s. George R. and Alice (Hoy) L.; A.B., U. Miami, 1954, M.A., 1956, LL.D. (hon.), 1981; Ph.D., U. Fla., 1959; m. Phyllis Lesnick, Nov. 26, 1952; children—Richard, Gregory, Matthew, Cynthia, Vincent. Asst. prof. to prof. Ariz. State U., 1959-70, asst. dean grad. coll., 1965-67, dean Litchfield Coll., 1967-70, asst. to pres., 1968-70; prof. English U. Mont., 1970-75, academic v.p., 1970-75; pres. Ind. State U., 1975—; pres. Ind. Partners of Americas, 1976-79. Served with U.S. Army, 1948-51. Mem. Am. Assn. Higher Edn., Modern Lang. Assn. Am., Nat. Council Tchrs. English, Ind. Conf. Higher Edn. Roman Catholic. Club: Rotary. Contbr. in field. Office: President's Office Ind State Univ Terre Haute IN 47809

LANDIS, C(HARLOTTE) VICTORIA, architect; b. Lansing, Mich., Nov. 10, 1951; d. Bates Henry and Charlotte Marion (Goy) L.; student Eisenhower Coll., 1969-70, Wayne County Community Coll., 1970-71; B.S. in Architecture, Lawrence Inst. Tech., 1976. Drafting cons. to Ralph J. Stephenson, P.E., Detroit, 1975-77; archtl. draftsman Wah Yee Assos., Southfield, Mich., 1977-78; jr. architect Giffels Assos. Inc., Southfield, 1978-79; with Bechtel Power Corp., Ann Arbor, Mich., 1979—, now resident architect Midland Nuclear Power Plant (Mich.). Democrat. Home: 7330 Woodview Dr Apt 1 Westland MI 48185 Office: Bechtel Power Corp 777 E Eisenhower Pkwy Ann Arbor MI 48106

LANDIS, DAVID MORRISON, state legislator; b. Lincoln, Nebr., June 10, 1948; B.A., U. Nebr., Lincoln, 1970, J.D., 1971; m. Melodee Ann McPherson, June 6, 1969; children—Matthew, Melissa. Admitted to Nebr. bar, 1972; practice law, Lincoln, 1972-74; mem. Nebr. Legislature, 1978—. Bd. dirs. Lower Platte S. Natural Resources Dist., 1977-78; officer PTA, 1979-80; adminstrv. law judge Dept. Labor, 1977-78. Home: Lincoln NE*

LANDIS, GEORGE HARVEY, psychotherapist; b. Newton, Kans., Dec. 12, 1918; s. Melvin D. and Erie Emma (Byler) L.; student Baker U., 1937-38; B.A., John Fletcher Coll., 1941; M.S.W., U. Nebr., 1948; m. Lois I. Donaldson, Sept. 26, 1943; children—Judy Carol Landis Forsman, Richard G. Caseworker, Family Service of Omaha, 1948-50; psychotherapist Midwest Clinic, Omaha, 1950—, Served with U.S. Army, 1941-46. Mem. Acad. Cert. Social Workers, Registry Clin. Social Workers. Home: 4628 Hascall St Omaha NE 68106 Office: 105 S 49th St Omaha NE 68132

LANDIS, JOHN RICHARD, biostatistician; b. Lancaster, Pa., Sept. 20, 1945; s. Sanford H. and Thelma (Neff) L.; B.S., Millersville State Coll., 1969; M.S., U. N.C., 1973, Ph.D. (fellow), 1975; m. Jean Myer, June 8, 1968; children—Nathan, Deborah. Research asst. Eastern Research Support Center, West Haven (Conn.) VA Hosp., 1969-71; asst. prof. biostatistics U. Mich., Ann Arbor, 1975-78, asso. prof., 1978-81, prof., 1981—. Fulbright sr. scholar, Australia, 1981-82. Mem. Am. Statis. Assn., Biometrics Soc., Am. Public Health Assn., Sigma Xi. Mennonite. Contbr. articles to profl. jours. Office: Dept Biostatistics Univ Mich Ann Arbor MI 48109

LANDMAN, DAVID, editor, univ. adminstr.; b. Phila., Oct. 24, 1917; s. Isaac and Beatrice (Eschner) L.; A.B. magna cum laude, Brown U., 1939; M.A., Columbia U., 1963; m. Joan Klein, Sept. 1, 1946 (div. 1963), children—Alicia, Michael Isaac; m. 2d, Hedy Backlin, Dec. 30, 1964. Reporter, Springfield (Mass.) Union, 1939; asso. editor Universal Jewish Ency., N.Y.C., 1939-40, sec. and chief exec., 1950-60; asst. dir. adult edn. Cooper Union, N.Y., 1959-61, chmn. Nuclear Age Conf., 1960, asst. to pres., 1961-63; asso. dir. devel., Princeton U., 1963-69; mem. faculty, dir. info. Harvard Bus. Sch., 1969-73; lectr. Sch. of Pub. Communication, Boston U., 1973-77; dir. pub. affairs Pathfinder Fund, 1973-77; univ. dir. pub. info. U. Ill., Chgo. and Urbana, 1977-79, editor spl. projects, editor Med. Center Alumni News, 1979—; cons. Lesley Coll., Rider Coll., Levinson Inst. Bd. dirs. Hamilton-Madison House, 1949-69, v.p., 1960-64. Served to maj. AUS, 1941-45. Decorated Bronze Star; Ford Found. fellow to Indonesia, 1955-56. Mem. Am. Soc. Journalists and Authors, Asia Soc., Am. Coll. Pub. Relations Assn., Phi Beta Kappa. Author: Look at America books, 1945-47; (with Joan Landman) Where to Ski, 1949; (with others) Prose by Professionals, 1961; co-editor, America Faces the Nuclear Age 1961; contbr. articles to mags. including Redbook, Coronet, Nation's Bus., New Republic; contbr. articles to profl. jours. and encys. Home: 40 E Cedar St Chicago IL 60611 Office: U Ill 1737 W Polk St Room 312 Chicago IL 60612

LANDMARK, AMBROSE I. (MARK), JR., assn. exec.; b. Madison, Wis., Dec. 3, 1943; s. Ambrose Imert and Julia Benoy L.; B.S., U. Wis., Madison, 1966; m. Ann Louise Thorpe, June 11, 1966; children—Eric Bruce, Rebecca Jo. Fieldman, Green Giant Co., Ripon, Wis., 1966-67; quality control staff Ralston Purina Co., Fond du Lac, Wis., 1967-72; field supr. Wis. Farm Bur., Madison, 1972-77; sec. adminstrn., legis. agt. Maine Farm Bur. Assn., Augusta, 1977-80; tng. specialist Am. Farm Bur., Park Ridge, Ill., 1980—. Served with USAF, 1966. Mem. Am. Soc. Tng. and Devel., Ill. Tng. and Devel. Assn. Republican. Methodist. Club: Toastmaster (Able toastmaster award). Office: 225 Touhy Ave Park Ridge IL 60068

LANDON, HELEN JOSEPHINE, nursing center adminstr.; b. Delaware, Ohio, May 17, 1926; d. Thomas Albert and Rachel Savilla (Wood) Sartwell; student Bliss Coll., Columbus, Ohio, 1939-40, Ohio State U., 1975-77; L.P.N., Marion Gen. Hosp., 1965; m. Roy M. Landon, Dec. 7, 1944 (dec.); children—Delores A., Danny R., Michael L., Mary R., Janice S., Patrick A., Dennis D. Adminstr., Hillside Nursing Home, 1952-70; adminstr. Maplewood Nursing Center, Marion, Ohio, 1970—, pres., 1977—; pres. Lanjor House Inc., Marion. ARC vol. County Health Dept., Delaware, 1946-50; active Booster Assn., PTA, Girl Scouts U.S.A. Recipient Single Parent of Yr. award, 1973. Mem. Ohio Licensed Practical Nurses Assn. (sec. 1974-75), Nat. Nursing Home Assn. (dist. pres. 1962-65), Am. Coll. Nursing Home Adminstrs. Republican. Methodist. Home: 1166 Greenlea Dr Marion OH 43302 Office: 218 W Center St Marion OH 43302

LANDON, JAMES VROMAN, bldg. automation systems co. exec.; b. Johnson City, N.Y., Mar. 4, 1934; s. Raymond Stewart and Erma Viola (Vroman) L.; B.S. in E.E., Milw. Sch. Engring., 1959; M.S. in E.E., Clarkson Coll. Tech., 1962; postgrad. SUNY, Buffalo, 1964-67; M.B.A., U. Dayton, 1972; m. Alma Ann Formolo, Sept. 20, 1958; 1 son, Clifford. Instr. elec. engring. Clarkson Coll. Tech., 1959-62, asst. prof., 1963-64; project engr. Gen. Electric, 1962-63; instr. SUNY, Buffalo, 1964-67; project mgr. Eastman Kodak Co., Rochester, N.Y., 1967-69; project leader NCR, Dayton, Ohio, 1969-71; pvt. practice engring. and bus. cons., Dayton, also Milw., 1971-79; program mgr. Johnson Controls, Inc., Milw., 1979—. Served with U.S. Navy, 1951-55. NSF fellow, 1966-67. Registered profl. engr., Wis. Mem. IEEE, Am. Mgmt. Assn. Republican. Roman Catholic. Club: Rosicrucian. Home: 580 S Ridge Ct Colgate WI 53017 Office: 507 E Michigan St Milwaukee WI 53201

LANDRIGAN, WILLIAM JOHN, quality assurance cons.; b. Watford, Hertfordshire, Eng., Nov. 23, 1944 (parents Am. citizens); s. William John and Vivian Peggy (Smith) L.; B.S. in Bus. Adminstrn., N.Y. U., 1977; m. 2d, Patricia Ann Misch, July 25, 1980; children—Jennifer, Laurie, Kimberly. Indsl. engr. elec. wiring and switching device mfg. Leviton Mfg. Co., Inc., Warwick, R.I., 1964-67; plant indsl. engr. Fed. Paperboard Co., Commerce, Calif., 1967-72; prodn.-inventory control mgr. A.J. Bayer Co., Torrance, Calif., 1972-75; adminstrv. asst. to v.p. Modern Dust Bag Co., Inc., West Haverstraw, N.Y., 1975-78; program dir. mfg. div. Am. Mgmt. Assns., N.Y.C., 1978-79; product assurance mgr. gen. purpose programs, def. systems div. Northrop Corp., Rollings Meadows, Ill., 1979-81; ind. quality assurance cons., Rolling Meadows, 1981—; lectr. in field. Active local Little League Baseball, Jaycees. Served with U.S. Army, 1962-64. Mem. Am. Mgmt. Assn., Am. Soc. Quality Control, Am. Inst. Indsl. Engrs., Am. Soc. Tng. and Devel. Republican. Roman Catholic. Club: K.C. Address: 3800 Eleanore Ct Rolling Meadows IL 60008

LANDRUM, THOMAS LOWELL, SR., ednl. adminstr.; b. Childress, Tex., July 24, 1935; s. Alton Virgil and Ura (Campbell) L.; B.S., Tex. A. and M. U., 1959; M.S., Purdue U., 1968, Ph.D., 1974; m. Margaret Ellen Leslie, Jan. 25, 1959; children—Leslie Christine, Holly Renee, Thomas Lowell, Jr., Timothy Lewis, James Allen. Tech. writer, supr. Pantex Plant, Amarillo, Tex., 1959-66; specifications engr. Nat. Homes, Lafayette, Ind., 1966; asst. dir. Supervisory Devel. Inst., Purdue U., West Lafayette, Ind., 1966-74, asso. dir., 1979—; cons. to bus., industry, govt., 1966—. Mem. Lafayette Sch. Bd., 1978—, pres., 1980-81; pres. Lafayette Christian Sch. Booster Club, 1972—. Mem. Am. Soc. Tng. and Devel., Nat. Sch. Bds. Assn. Methodist (chmn. bd.; fin. chmn.). Democrat. Methodist. Clubs: Lafayette Christian School Booster; Jeff Choral Booster; Jeff Athletic Booster. Home: 40 Valdez Ct Lafayette IN 47904 Office: 101 Graduate House Purdue Univ West Lafayette IN 47907

LANDSBERG, JOHN RICHARD, corp. communications ofcl.; b. Cleve., Sept. 14, 1948; s. Harry Earl and Donna Jean Landsberg; A.A., Cuyahoga Community Coll.-West, 1973; B.A. in Polit. Sci. and English, Baldwin-Wallace Coll., 1974; m. Donnamarie A. Dans, July 7, 1973; children—Todd Anthony, Jennifer. Reporter, Lorain (Ohio) Jour., 1968-69; asst. public relations dir. Northfield (Ohio) Park Raceway, 1973-74; liaison officer City of Cleve., 1974-76; tech. writer Am. Greetings Corp., Cleve., 1976-78; communications mgr. H.K. Ferguson Co., Cleve., 1978-81, United Telephone Co. of Ohio, Mansfield, 1981—; part-time sports reporter Plain Dealer, Cleve., 1971—. Served with U.S. Army, 1969-71. Mem. Public Relations Soc. Am., Internat. Assn. Bus. Communicators (Cleve. and Internat. chpts.). Roman Catholic. Club: Bay Village Jaycees (project dir., community affairs adminstr. 1978-79, Dist. Officer of Yr., Speak-Up champion, New Mem. of Year, Superstar awards). Notary public. Office: PO Box 3555 Mansfield OH 44907

LANDSMAN, SANDRA GILBERT, transactional analyst; b. Detroit, Jan. 5, 1933; d. Arthur Bernard and Ida Myra (Finkelstone) G.; B.S., Wayne State U., 1966, M.A., 1970; m. Rodney Glenn Landsman, Apr. 3, 1955; children—Victoria Louise, Jonathan Gilbert, Faith Susan, Jill Barbara. Cons., counselor Continuum Center for Women, Oakland U., Rochester, Mich., 1970-77; pvt. practice transactional analysis, Farmington Hills, Mich., 1971—; clin. cons. transactional analyst, clin. supr. North Metro & Dearborn Downriver Growth Centers, Rochester and Allen Park, Mich., 1975-78; mem. faculty Macomb County (Mich.) Community Coll., 1976-79; dir. clin. and edn. services Landsman/Foner & Assos., West Bloomfield, Mich., 1977—; distinguished lectr. Sch. Social Work, Mich. State U., 1975-78; cons. in field. Cert. social worker, Mich. Fellow Inst. Gerontology; mem. Internat. Transactional Analysis Assn. (cert. tchr.), Nat. Assn. Social Workers, Am. Personnel and Guidance Assn., Am. Coll. Personnel Assn., Assn. Specialists in Group Work, Mich. Personnel and Guidance Assn., Mich. Coll. Personnel Assn., Mich. Assn. Specialist Group Work (pres.), Mich. Assn. Women Deans, Adminstrs. and Counselors, New Directions in Edn. and Psychotherapy (charter, trustee). Contbr. articles to profl. publs. Home: 34316 Thornbrook Dr Farmington Hills MI 48018 Office: 7459 Middlebelt Rd Suite 1 West Bloomfield MI 48033

LANDSTROM, DONALD ALBERT, food broker; b. Chgo., Mar. 14, 1929; s. Harlow Albert and Loretta Sophia (Erickson) L.; B.B.A., U. Minn., 1951; m. Marilyn Jean Hicks, June 11, 1955; children—Scott, Gregg. With Fist Brokerage Co., Minnetonka, Minn., 1953—, treas., 1971—, exec. v.p., 1977—, also dir. Served as officer USN, 1951-53. Mem. Inst. Food Technologists. Episcopalian. Home: 2961 Tonkaha Dr Wayzata MN 55391 Office: 6026 Blue Circle Dr Minnetonka MN 55343

LANDTHORN, ROBERT ALLEN, electronics co. exec.; b. Columbus, Ohio, Apr. 7, 1945; s. Ernest F. and Helen F. (Benjamin) L.; B.S.E.E., Ohio State U., 1968; m. Shirley Ann Spencer, June 22, 1968; children—Tricia Lynne, Lori Michelle, Jeffrey Russel. Electronic engr. missile guidance Rockwell Internat., Columbus, Ohio, 1968-69; sales engr. Panels, Inc., Worthington, Ohio, 1971-76, sales mgr., 1976-78, v.p. sales and mktg., Westerville, Ohio, 1978-81; partner Attaboy, M.R., Inc., Worthington, 1981—; dir. Columbus Controls, Inc.; owner R.A. Landthorn & Assos., cons. engrs., Cleve. Served with U.S. Army, 1969-71. Registered profl. engr., Ohio. Mem. Am. Mgmt. Assn., Instrument Soc. Am. (past pres. Columbus sect., gen. chmn. spring symposium and exhibit Columbus 1981-82), Soc. Mfg. Engrs., Robotics Inst., Ohio State U. Alumni Assn. Republican. Methodist. Clubs: Order of Demolay. Office: 6463 Proprietors Rd Worthington OH 43085

LANDWEHR, ARTHUR JOHN, JR., clergyman; b. Highland Park, Ill., Mar. 8, 1934; s. Arthur John and Alice Eleanor (Borchardt) L.; B.A., Drake U.; B.D., Garrett Theol. Sem., 1959; grad. student U. Chgo., 1960-62; postgrad. (fellow) Contemporary Theol. Inst., Montreal, Que., Can., 1969, Stellenbosch Theol. Sem., South Africa, 1973; D.D. (hon.), North Central Coll., 1980; m. Avonna Lee Mitchell, Sept. 19, 1953; children—Arthur John III, Andrea Lea. Ordained to ministry, United Methodist Ch., 1957; pastor chs., Lyndon, Ill., 1956-59, Marseilles (Ill.) United Meth. Ch., 1959-65, Faith United Meth. Ch., Lisle, Ill., 1965-69, First United Meth. Ch., Elmhurst, Ill., 1969-75, First United Meth. Ch. of Evanston, Ill., 1975—; chmn. Commn. on Ecumenical Affairs, United Meth. Ch., 1972-76, mem. exec. com. Gen. Commn. Christian Unity and Interreligious Concerns, 1980—, mem. Gen. Council on Ministries, 1980—; faculty mem. Ecumenical Lay Acad., 1970-75; speaker Chgo. Sunday Evening Club. founder Friends of the Christian Inst. of South Africa. Bd. dirs. Ch. Fedn. Greater Chgo., John Wesley Theol. Inst.; trustee Garrett Evang. Theol. Sem., 1976—, chmn. com. academic affairs, 1977—. Mem. Am. Acad. Religion, AAAS, Am. Theol. Assn. Rotarian. Author: In the Third Place, 1972. Home: 310 Church St Evanston IL 60201

LANDWEHR, H(OWARD) MARLIN, editorial exec.; b. Northbrook, Ill., Aug. 21, 1917; s. Edward D. and Annie W. (Holste) L.; B.S. in Journalism, U. Ill., 1939; m. Carolyn D. Anderson, Apr. 30, 1942; children—James, Carl, Barbara. Reporter, Chgo. City News Bur., 1939; editor Garfieldian newspaper, Chgo., 1940-42, Garfieldian, Austin News, N.W. Jour., Chgo., 1945-67; editor Suburbanite Economist, Chgo., 1967-69; editorial dir. Economist Newspapers, including Daily Southtown Economist, Chgo., 1969—; mem. Chgo. Mayor's Adv. Com. on Press Cards. Mem. Austin Citizens Council, Chgo.; mem. Palos-Orland-Worth (Ill.) Planning Bd.,; mem. Ill. Tollway Adv. Com. Served to lt. j.g. USNR, 1942-45. Recipient Ill. Press Assn. Loomis trophy Garfieldian-Austin News, 1953, 1st Pl. Feature Writing award Ill. Press Assn., 1962, citation for service to community Ill. Gen. Assembly, 1973, City medal City of Burbank (Ill.), 1980. Mem. Sigma Delta Chi, Theta Xi. Congregationalist. Clubs: Headline; Kiwanis (pres. Austin club 1953). Office: 5959 S Harlem Ave Chicago IL 60638

LANDWEHR, WILLIAM CHARLES, mus. adminstr.; b. Milw., Sept. 19, 1941; s. Frank Albert and LaVerna Gertrude (Schumacher) L.; B.S., U. Wis., Stevens Point, 1964; M.A., U. N.D., 1968; 1 dau., Leslie Lynne. Dir. S.D. Meml. Art Center, Brookings, 1969-71, Quincy (Ill.) Art Center, 1971-73; curator exhbns. Mint Mus. Art, Charlotte, 1973-76; dir. Springfield (Mo.) Art Mus., 1976—. Mem. Am. Assn. M)useums, Midwest Mus. Conf., Mo. Mus. Assos., Western Assn. Art Museums (trustee 1978-80). Author exhbn. catalogs, including The Lithographs and Etchings of Philip Pearlstein, 1978; editor: Selections for the Permanent Collection of the Springfield Art Museum, 1980. Office: 1111 E Brookside Dr Springfield MO 65807

LANDY, AGATHA HORRIGAN (MRS. THOMAS M. LANDY), Realtor; b. Cleve.; d. Lawrence and Catherine (Day) Horrigan; student Cleve. Coll., 1931, John Carroll U., 1932-33; m. Thomas M. Landy, Jan. 23, 1943 (dec. Mar. 1955); children—Thomas M., John C., Philip F., Robert J., Kevin P. Pres., Agatha Horrigan Landy & Sons Inc., Realtors, Cleve., 1956—. Mem. Nat., Cleve. bds. realtors, Internat. Platform Assn. Club: Cleve. Skating. Office: 2647 Berkshire Rd Cleveland OH 44106 Office: 30650 Pinetree St Pepper Pike OH 44124

LANE, CONSTANCE CARMICHAEL RENICK, ednl. adminstr.; b. Rockford, Ill., Nov. 9, 1921; d. James Alexander and Nozella (Oda) Carmichael; B.S. in Edn. magna cum laude, W.Va. State Coll., 1943; M.A., Northwestern U., 1962; m. Andrew J. Lane, June 20, 1964; children—Betty Anne Renick (Mrs. Flynn Jefferson), James Renick. Tchr., Rockford Pub. Schs., 1954-62, helping tchr. elementary math., 1962-63; prin. Henrietta Primary and Intermediate Schs., Rockford, 1963-66; prin. W. Ray McIntosh Sch., Rockford, 1966—; Area IV coordinator Rockford Pub. Schs., after 1971, asst. supt. elem. edn., 1979—; part-time instr. Rockford Coll., evenings 1964-79. Mem. Tau, Inc. (pres. 1960-63, 74-78, treas. 1972-74), Ill., Rockford edn. assns., NEA, AAUW, Nat. Council Tchrs. Math., Assn. Supervision and Curriculum Devel., Rockford Prins. Assn., Nat. Elementary Prins. Assn., Delta Kappa Gamma, Phi Delta Kappa. Episcopalian. Contbr. articles to profl. jours. Home: 2224 Clover Ave Rockford IL 61102 Office: Rockford Bd Edn 201 S Madison St Rockford IL 61101

LANE, DALE WALTER, adminstr.; b. Adrian, Mich., Sept. 22, 1938; s. Floyd Lorart and Lela Belle (Vansickle) L.; B.A., Andrews U., Berrian Springs, Mich., 1970, M.A., 1971; postgrad. Leadership Devel. Program for Vocat.-Tech. Sch. Adminstrs., U. Mich., 1975; m. Carol Ann Wolf, Jan. 11, 1965; children—Christopher, Todd. With Simplex Paper Corp., Adrian, 1959-67; dir. counseling Lenawee County Vocat.-Tech. Sch., Adrian, 1971-79; mem. Mich. Career Edn. Commn., 1976-78; mem. Mich. Supts. Task Force Counseling, asst. dir. internal ops., 1979—. Sch. bd. chmn. Benedict Meml. Sch., 1970—; sec.-treas. Tecumseh's Indian Village Inc. Mem. Mich. Sch. Counselors Assn. (pres. 1976), Mich. Prins. Assn., Nat. Prins. Assn., Lenawee County Prins. Assn. (v.p.). Club: Kinawis. Home: 1575 Ives St Tecumseh MI 49286 Office: 2345 N Adrian Hwy Adrian MI 49286

LANE, JACK DALE, mech. engr.; b. Winslow, Ind., Jan. 6, 1931; s. Jim and Helen (Richardson) L.; B.S. in Metall. Engring. (Outstanding Engring. Student award 1978), Wayne State U., Detroit, 1955; M.S. in Mech. Engring., U. Detroit, 1979; m. Betty Lou Hart, July 4, 1953; 1 son, Jack L. Plant metallurgist Revere Copper and Brass Co., Detroit, 1955-57; test and devel. engr. Chrysler Missile Co., Warren, Mich., 1957-59; sr. engr. mfg. devel. Gen. Motors Corp., Warren, 1959-66, cons. co. divs., 1980—; prof. mech. engring. Gen. Motors Inst., Flint, Mich., 1966—; mem. faculty Oakland (Mich.) U., 1973. Mem. Pontiac (Mich.) Fin. Study Council, 1968; chmn. United Way drive, Flint, 1979. Cert. mfg. engr.; registered profl. engr., Mich. Mem. Soc. Mfg. Engrs., Am. Welding Soc., Robotics Internat., Computer and Systems Automation Assn., Lambda Chi Alpha. Clubs: Aquaneers, Elks. Author papers in field. Home: 16064 Silver Crest Dr Linden MI 48451 Office: 1700 W 3d Ave Flint MI 48502

LANE, JAMES A., lawyer; b. Denver, Nov. 13, 1915; student Regis Coll.; J.D., Creighton U., 1940. Admitted to Nebr. bar, 1940, practiced law, Ogallala. Pres. bd. trustees Nebr. State Colls., 1969. Served to lt. USNR, 1942-45. Fellow Am. Coll. Trial Lawyers; mem. Nebr. (pres. to 1972), Am. bar assns., Am. Trial Lawyers Assn., Am. Judicature Soc., Internat. Acad. Trial Lawyers, Servientes Ad Legem. Address: Box 119 Ogallala NE 69153

LANE, MARC JAY, lawyer; b. Chgo., Aug. 30, 1946; s. Sam and Evelyn (Light) L.; B.A., U. Ill., 1967; J.D., Northwestern U., 1971; m. Rochelle B. Nudelman, Dec. 12, 1971; children—Allison, Amanda, Jennifer. Admitted to Ill. bar, 1971, since practiced in Chgo.; pres. Law Offices of Marc J. Lane, P.C., Chgo., 1971—; pres. Medico-Legal Inst., Chgo., 1976—. Mem. Chgo. Council Lawyers (chmn. com.), Chgo. Bar Assn., Ill. State Bar Assn. Author: The Doctor's Law Guide, 1980; Legal Handbook for Nonprofit Organizations, 1980; Legal Handbook for Small Business, 1980; The Doctor's Lawyer, 1974; Taxation for the Computer Industry, 1980; Taxation for Small Business, 1980; Taxation for Engineering and Technical Consultants, 1980; Taxation for Small Manufacturers, 1980; (with others) Annual Federal Tax Course, 1978. Contbr. articles to profl. jours. Home: 6715 N Longmeadow Lincolnwood IL 60646 Office: 180 N LaSalle St Chicago IL 60601

LANE, ORRIS JOHN, JR., civil engr.; b. Sigourney, Iowa, Apr. 21, 1932; s. Orris John and Hester Hanna (Hazen) L.; B.S., Iowa State U., 1957; m. Joan Joyce Nelson, June 19, 1954; children—Jerry Paul, Beth Ann, Dona Sue, Seth Thomas. Asst. dist. materials engr. Iowa Hwy. Commn., Ames, 1957-62, spl. projects engr., 1962-64, portland cement concrete engr., 1964-73, dist. materials engr., Atlantic, 1973—. Project group adv. mem. NCHPR, Washington, 1972—. Served with AUS, 1953-55. Registered profl. engr., Iowa. Mem. Nat. Soc. Profl. Engrs., Iowa Engring. Soc., Orgn. Transp. and State Employees (bd. dirs. 1968—). Methodist. Home: Route 1 Wiota IA 50274 Office: PO Box 406 Atlantic IA 50022

LANE, ROBERT EDGAR, mfg. co. exec.; b. Kaukauna, Wis., Mar. 29, 1931; s. Herbert John and Mabel T. (Tullis) L.; B.B.A., U. Wis., 1954, M.B.A., 1957; m. Cathy Jo Talarico, Dec. 31, 1962; 1 dau., Deborah Marie. With Johnson Controls, Inc., Milw., 1954-77, mgr. ops. research, 1966-68, indsl. engring. group mgr., 1968-73, material control mgr., 1973-77, ops. mgr. Georgetown (Ky.) facilities, 1977-79; v.p. mfg. MCC Powers, Skokie, Ill., 1979—; instr. Milw. Tech. Coll., 1971-72; lectr. in field. Adv. council on curriculum Milw. Area Tech. Coll., 1972-77, Milw. Sch. Engring., 1974-77, Waukesha (Wis.) Area Tech. Coll., 1975-77. Mem. Am. Inst. Indsl. Engrs. (chpt. pres. 1976-77), Milw. Prodn. and Methods Engrs. (pres. 1958-59), Georgetown Coll. Assos., Soc. Prodn. and Methods Engrs., Inst. Mgmt. Sci., Am. Soc. Inventory and Prodn. Control. Republican. Author: Administering and Controlling Plant Operations, 1979; contbr. articles in field to profl. jours. Home: 3035 Kayjay Dr Northbrook IL 60062 Office: 3400 Oakton St Skokie IL 60076

LANE, ROBERT JOSEPH, motel exec.; b. Port Jervis, N.Y., July 1, 1922; s. Francis Aloyisius and Katherine Berta Ursula (Scarsi) L.; student Georgetown U., 1948-49, John Carroll U., 1958-60; m. Clarissa Geneva Hein, Aug. 16, 1950 (div. 1977); children—Robert, Stephen, Phillip, Eric. U.S. diplomatic courier, 1946-50; sales rep. with various firms, 1953-58; asst. mgr. Statler Hilton Corp., Cleve., 1958-60, Auditorium Hotel, Cleve., 1960-62; auditor, mgr. Howard Johnson Motor Lodges, Cleve., 1962-66; asst. mgr. Sheraton Hotel, Cleve., 1966-69; mgr. Port-O-Call Motor Inn, Brook Park, Ohio, 1969-75; gen. mgr. Exec. Inn, Fairview Park, Ohio, 1976—; developer Villa Valtellina, exec. conf. center, 1977; founder Cottage Industries, splty. items handcrafts by mail, 1980—. Served with USAAF, 1942-46; 1st lt. USAF, 1950-53. Winner Mobil Oil 4-Star award, 1973-74. Mem. U.S. Diplomatic Courier Assn. (life), Hotel Motel Sales Mgr. Assn. (v.p. 1961-62). Patentee in field. Home: 1340 Kenilworth Ave Apt 301 Lakewood OH 44107 Office: PO Box 81091 Cleveland OH 44181

LANE, RUSSELL WATSON, chemist; b. Morrison, Ill., June 18, 1911; s. Ralph Thomas and Elizabeth Loretta (Alldritt) L.; B.S., Knox Coll., 1933; M.S., Ill. Inst. Tech., 1945; m. Ione Sundberg, June 16, 1934; children—Joan Karen, Patricia Diane. Chemist, Libby McNeill & Libby, Morrison, Ill., 1933-41; research chemist Nalco Chem. Co., Chgo., 1941-45, chief phys. chemist, 1945-47, water treatment engr., 1947-49; chemist Ill. State Water Survey, Champaign, 1949-65, sr. chemist, 1965-77, head chemistry sect., 1977-80, prin. scientist, 1980—. Recipient Boss of Year award Champaign-Urbana Jr. C. of C., 1971; Edn. with Industry awards USAF, 1971-75, 79; registered profl. engr., Ill., Calif. Mem. Am. Chem. Soc., Nat. Assn. Corrosion Engrs. (citation outstanding service 1981), Am. Water Works Assn., ASME, ASTM (Max Hecht award 1978, also editorial awards 1979), Sigma Xi, Phi Lambda Upsilon. Presbyterian. Club: Lions. Contbr. articles to profl. jours. Patentee in field. Home: 1207 Devonshire Dr Champaign IL 61820 Office: 605 E Springfield Ave Champaign IL 61820

LANE, WILFRED ROGER, elec. engr.; b. Detroit, June 14, 1954; s. Eldon R. and Anna Marie (Briolat) L.; B.S.E., U. Mich., 1976. Instr. electronic tech. Delta U., University Center, Mich., 1976—; sr. prodn. engr. Dow Chem. Co., Bay City, Mich., 1976—. Sheldon engring. scholar, 1975-76. Mem. IEEE, Soc. Profl. Engrs., Intrument Soc. Am. (process measurement com. 1979—). Contbr. to profl. publs. Home: 2406 Brookfield Ln Midland MI 48640 Office: Dow Chem Co 1180 Bldg Bay City MI 48706

LANE, WILLIAM EARL, electronic engr.; b. Benham, Ky., May 10, 1936; s. Earl D. and Rosina (Bowyer) L.; student Cumberland Coll., 1954-56; B.E.E., U. Ky., 1959; m. Doris Belle Jacobs, June 12, 1960; children—William Earl, Lisa Anne. Electronic engr. Aeronaut.

Systems div. Wright-Patterson AFB, Ohio, 1954-64, electronics engr. specialist electronic warfare Avionics Lab., 1964-74, chief Ops. Analysis Group, 1974—. Mem. Am. Def. Preparedness Assn., Assn. Old Crows. Baptist (chmn. bd. fin. 1972-73, chmn. bd. deacons 1979, moderator). Home: 2751 Vickie Dr Xenia OH 45385 Office: AFWAL AAWA Wright-Patterson AFB OH 45433

LANG, ANTON, educator; b. Petersburg, Russia, Jan. 18, 1913; came to U.S., 1950, naturalized, 1956; s. George and Vera (Davidov) L.; Dr.Nat.Sci. with distinction, U. Berlin, 1939; LL.D. (hon.), U. Glasgow, 1981; m. Lydia Kamendrovsky, Apr. 24, 1946; children—Peter, Michael, Irene. Sci. asst. Kaiser-Wilhelm Inst. of Biology, Berlin/Tübingen, 1939-49; research asso. (Lady Davis Found. fellow) dept. genetics McGill U., Montreal, Que., Can., 1949; vis. prof. Tex. A&M U., College Station, 1950; Lalor Found. research fellow, sr. research fellow div. biology Calif. Inst. Tech., Pasadena, 1950-52; asst. to asso. prof. dept. botany UCLA, 1952-59; prof. div. biology Calif. Inst. Tech., Pasadena, 1959-65; dir., prof. dept. energy plant research lab. Mich. State U., East Lansing, 1965-78, prof., 1978—; mem. NSF adv. panel for developmental biology, 1959-63, adv. com. for biology and medicine, 1968-71; mem. Nat. Acad. Sci. com. on research in life sci., 1966-70, chmn. com. on effects of herbicides in Vietnam, 1971-74; adv. com. on USSR and Eastern Europe, 1964-67, 77-78; trustee Argonne U. Assn., 1965-71. NSF sr. postdoctoral fellow, 1958-59; recipient Disting. Faculty award Mich. State U., 1976; Silver medal Mass. Hort. Soc., 1981. Fellow AAAS; mem. Leopoldina German Acad. Naturalists, Nat. Acad. Sci., Am. Acad. Arts and Sci., Am. Soc. Plant Physiologists (v.p. 1962-63, pres. 1970-71, Stephen Hales prize and Charles Reid Barnes life membership award 1976), Bot. Soc. Am. (Cert. of Merit 1979), German Bot. Soc., Scandinavian Soc. Plant Physiology, Soc. for Developmental Biology (pres. 1968), Sigma Xi (Sr. Scientist award Mich. State U. chpt. 1969). Contbg. author: Ency. of Plant Physiology, editorial bd., editor vol. XV, 1950-67; editorial bd. Ann. Rev. of Plant Physiology, 1959-63, Plant Physiology, 1961-64; editorial com. Am. Jour. Botany, 1966-68; co-mng. editor Planta, 1967—; cons. editor Gt. Soviet Ency., Am. edit., 1976—. Home: 1538 Cahill Dr East Lansing MI 48823 Office: Mich State U Dept of Energy Plant Research Lab East Lansing MI 48824

LANG, DAVID STEPHEN, environ. scientist; b. Mpls., Apr. 29, 1947; s. Kenneth Elwin and Mildred (Yantzi) L.; B.S., U. Minn., 1969; M.S., 1975, Ph.D., 1978; m. Linda Lee Peterson, June 10, 1967; children—Meghan, Daniel, Kjerstin. Tchr. high sch., Boscobel, Wis., 1969-70; jr. scientist U. Minn., St. Paul, 1971-73, research asst., 1973-75, research fellow, 1976-78; sr. environ. scientist Minn. Environ. Quality Bd., 1979—. Mem. Am. Phytopathtological Soc., Am. Air Pollution Control Assn., AAAS, N.Y. Acad. Scis., Sigma Xi, Gamma Sigma Delta. Office: Minn Environ Quality Bd 550 Cedar St Saint Paul MN 55101

LANG, FRANCIS H., lawyer; b. Manchester, Ohio, June 4, 1907; s. James Walter and Mary (Harover) L.; A.B., Ohio Wesleyan U., 1929; J.D., Ohio State U., 1932; m. Rachel Boyce, Oct. 20, 1934; children—Mary Sue, Charles Boyce, James Richard. Practice of law, East Liverpool, Ohio, 1932-42, 45—; with U.S. War Dept., 1942-45; chmn., dir. First Fed. Savs. & Loan Assn.; dir. 1st Nat. Bank East Liverpool, First Nat. Bank Chester, W.Va.; dir., pres. Walter Lang Co.; dir., sec., asst. treas. Sayre Electric Contracting Inc., Electric Wholesaling, Inc.; dir. Sayre Devel., Inc. Bd. dirs. YMCA, Mary Patterson Meml., East Liverpool, Columbiana County Motor Club; mem. exec. bd. Columbiana council Boy Scouts Am., recipient Silver Beaver award, Silver Antelope award. Trustee Cope Methodist Home; trustee, pres. Candall Med. Center. Mem. Ohio State Jr. (past pres.), U.S. Jr. (nat. dir. 1941-42), East Liverpool (past pres.), chambers commerce, Ohio Bar Assn. Methodist (mem. adminstrv. bd. 1933—, del. World Meth. Conf. 1971, 76, mem. bd. dirs. global ministries 1968-76). Clubs: East Liverpool Country, Rotary (dist. gov. 1973-74), Masons (33 deg.). Home: PO Box 103 Highland Colony East Liverpool OH 43920 Office: Potters Savings and Loan Bldg East Liverpool OH 43920

LANG, GLORIA HELEN, tool engr.; b. N.Y.C., Mar. 15, 1932; d. Michael and Elizebeth (Snyder) L.; student Kent State U., 1957-61, Youngstown State U., 1977. Retail salesman, 1947-51; owner, operator tax service, Tampa, Fla., 1954-55; tool and die maker Gen. Motors Corp., Warren, Ohio, 1955—; tool and die apprentice Ohio State U., 1972-76; tooling engr., cutting tool cons., pres., chief exec. officer Lang Industries, Inc., Warren, 1977—; lectr. on females in modern machine trades. Served with U.S. Army, 1951-54. Mem. NOW, Am. Soc. Profl. and Exec. Women, Nat. Assn. Female Execs., Nat. Tool, Die and Precision Machining Assn., Nat. Small Bus. Assn., Internat. Platform Assn., Am. Legion (past comdr. post 748 Warren). Home: 4793 Ardmore Ave Youngstown OH 44505 Office: Lang Industries Inc 2026 McMyler St NW Warren OH 44485

LANG, HENRY SPENCER, food co. exec.; b. San Francisco, Feb. 13, 1947; s. Bailey McKinley and Helen Elizabeth (Lauer) L.; B.A., U. San Francisco, 1968, J.D., 1971; m. Carolyn Haddad, Sept. 18, 1971; children—Adam Spencer, David McKinley. Div. mgr. Home Juice Co., Melrose Park, Ill., 1972-74, asst. to pres., 1974-75, v.p., gen. mgr., 1975-79, pres., chief operating officer, dir., 1979—. Served to capt. U.S. Army Res., 1971-72. Office: Home Juice Co 15th and Bloomingdale Aves Melrose Park IL 60160

LANG, WALTER, chem. engr.; b. Osijek, Yugoslavia, July 21, 1932; came to U.S., 1943, naturalized, 1954; s. George and Garabella (Wishik) L.; B.A. in Chem. Engring., City Coll. N.Y., 1955; m. Judith L. Savitsky, Sept. 6, 1953; children—Brenda Joyce, Lisa Renee, Julie Eileen. Prodn. engr. B.F. Goodrich Chem. Co., Calvert City, Ky., 1955-56, process control engr., 1956-65, sr. process engr., 1965-67, sales product engr., Cleve., 1967-72, sr. product engr., 1972-74, tech. mgr., 1974-76, mktg. mgr., 1976-80, mgr. market devel., 1980—. Mem. Am. Inst. Chem. Engrs., Am. Assn. Textile Chemists and Colorists. Jewish. Club: B'nai B'rith (chpt. pres. 1963-64). Contbr. articles to profl. jours. Home: 6425 Longridge Rd Mayfield Heights OH 44124 Office: 6100 Oak Tree Blvd Cleveland OH 44131

LANGDON, DONALD EDWARD, window covering mfg. co. exec.; b. Flagler, Colo., Aug. 20, 1930; s. Charles William and Julia Irene (McMahon) L.; B.S., U. Nebr., 1956, M.P.E., 1961; m. Frances F. Fields, Oct. 31; children—Rhonda Lee, Brenda Rae. Instr., head gymnastics coach Mankato State U., 1961-65; dir. bldg. trades-employee relations No. Nat. Co., Washington, 1966-70; dist. sales mgr., dir. spl. projects AMF Am., Jefferson, Iowa, 1970-79; dir. sales Breneman Inc., Cin., 1979—; instr. U. Nebr., 1965-66. Chmn. fund raising Green County (Iowa) Republican Party, 1976. Served with USN, 1948-52. Recipient Outstanding Performance award AMF Am., 1973. Mem. Phi Delta Theta, Phi Epsilon Kappa. Republican. Methodist. Clubs: Rotary, Elks. Office: 1133 Sycamore St Cincinnati OH 45210

LANGE, ARTHUR ERNEST, tire co. exec.; b. Rhodes, Mich., Dec. 2, 1920; s. William and Emma (Cordes) L.; B.S., Bowling Green State U., 1943; student Northwestern Univ. Grad. Sch. of Commerce, 1949-50; m. Lois Lorraine Hueschen, Dec. 6, 1952; children—Debra Jean, Karen Ann. Cost accountant The Goodyear Tire & Rubber Co., Akron, Ohio, 1946-49; supervising sr. accountant Arthur Young & Co., Chgo., 1950-57; mgr. gen. accounting div. Inland Steel Corp., Chgo., 1957-62; group controller Standard Pressed Steel Corp., Cleve., 1962-68; v.p. fin., dir. Modulus Corp., Cleve., 1968-74; corporate v.p., controller The Gen. Tire & Rubber Co., Akron, Ohio, 1974—. Served to 1st lt., Q.M.C., AUS, 1943-46. Decorated Bronze Star. Mem. Financial Execs. Inst., Am. Inst. C.P.A.'s, Ill. Inst. C.P.A.'s. Home: 341 Fox Run Trail Aurora OH 44202 Office: Gen Tire and Rubber Co One General St Akron OH 44329

LANGE, C. WILLIAM, lawyer; b. St. Louis, June 15, 1946; s. Carl W. and Marion Margaret (Guenther) L.; B.A., Westminster Coll., 1968; M.B.A., St. Louis U., 1972; J.D., Oklahoma City U., 1974. With claims dept. MFA Ins. Cos., Columbia, Mo., 1968-71; admitted to Mo. bar, 1975; partner firm Lange & Lange, Cuba, Mo., 1976—; pros. atty. Crawford County, Mo., 1979-80; asso. prof. mgmt. Maryville Coll., St. Louis, 1974—; city atty., Cuba, Mo., 1978-80. Mem. Crawford County Child Welfare Adv. Com., Crawford County Child Abuse and Neglect Team. Mem. Am. Bar Assn., Mo. Bar Assn., St. Louis Met. Bar Assn., 42d Jud. Circuit Bar Assn., Am. Bus. Law Assn., Cuba C. of C. Republican. Episcopalian. Club: Optimist (Cuba). Home: Route 2 Cuba MO 65453 Office: 106 E Washington Blvd Cuba MO 65453

LANGE, FREDERICK EMIL, lawyer; b. Washington, May 24, 1908; s. Emil F. and Jane (Austin) L.; A.B., U. Nebr., 1928; LL.B., M.P.L., Washington Coll. Law, 1932; m. Leila M. Benedict, Sept. 11, 1930; children—Frederick Emil, David W., James A. Admitted to D.C. bar, 1932, Minn. bar, 1943; examiner U.S. Patent Office, 1929-35; patent lawyer Honeywell, Inc., 1935-63, mgr. Mpls. patent dept., 1954-63; partner firm Dorsey, Marquart, Windhorst, West & Halladay, Mpls., 1965-73; individual practice law, Mpls., 1973-78; pres. Kinney, Lange, Braddock, Westman & Fairbairn, P.A., Mpls., 1978—; spl. lectr. patent law U. Minn., 1949-51, Minn. Continuing Legal Edn., 1976. Bd. trustees 1st Unitarian Soc., 1970-71; chmn. Minn. br. World Federalists, 1958-60, nat. exec. com., 1958-64; bd. dirs. Group Health Plan, Inc., 1967—, 1st v.p., 1975—; bd. dirs. St. Paul Civic Symphony Assn., 1976-81, Environ. Learning Center, 1977-79. Recipient Distinguished Service award U. Nebr., 1968. Mem. Am., Minn., D.C., Hennepin County bar assns., Am., Minn. (pres. 1954-55) patent law assns., Am. Judicature Soc. Holder U.S. patents. Home: 25 Paisley Ln Minneapolis MN 55422 Office: 815 Midwest Plaza Bldg Minneapolis MN 55402

LANGE-MCGILL, KENNETH HERMAN, statistician, former govt. adminstr.; b. Tekamah, Nebr., Dec. 29, 1903; s. Herman Morse and Fidelia Luella (Oberst) McGill; A.B., U. Nebr., 1930; postgrad. U. Chgo., 1930-31; Ph.D., U. Mich., 1973; m. Mable Catherine Lange, Aug. 27, 1930; 1 son, Kenneth Herman. Tchr. public schs., Marr, Ariz. and Nebr., 1923-26, Blackbird, Riverside, 1926-29; Earhart Found. fellow, instr. U. Mich., 1931-34; analyst Pres.'s Trends Studies, Washington, 1931-34; supr. U.S. Census, Washington, 1934, FERA, Washington, 1934; dir. USPHS, Washington, 1935-41; div. chief nat. hdqrs. SSS, Washington, 1941-70, ret., 1970; mem. Am. mission to Greece and Turkey, Dept. State, 1947-48. Recipient U.S. medal for merit Fed. Govt., 1946. Mem. Am. Statis. Assn., Soc. Greek Stats. (Athens), Chinese Assn. Advancement Sci. (Taipei), Royal Soc. Health (London), Phi Beta Kappa (pres. Washington assn. 1967-68), Alpha Kappa Delta. Presbyterian. Clubs: Sertoma (pres. 1966-67, dist. gov. 1968-70) (Washington); Propeller (Athens, Greece); Masons, Shriners. Author monographs and articles. Home: Golden Spring Route 1 Box 53 Decatur NE 68020 Office: Sir John's Hill 3746 Winding Creek Ln Charlotte NC 28211

LANGENBERG, FREDERICK CHARLES, steel co. exec.; b. N.Y.C., July 1, 1927; s. Frederick C. and Margaret (McLaughlin) L.; B.S., Lehigh U., 1950, M.S., 1951; Ph.D., Pa. State U., 1955; postgrad. execs. program Carnegie-Mellon U., 1962; m. Jane Anderson Bartholomew, May 16, 1953; children—Frederick C., Susan Jane. With United States Steel Corp., 1951-53; vis. fellow M.I.T.; 1955-56; with Crucible Steel Corp., Pitts., 1956-68, v.p. research and engring., 1966-68; pres. Trent Tube div. Colt Industries, Milw., 1968-70; exec. v.p. Jessop Steel Co., Washington, Pa., 1970, pres., 1970-75, also dir.; pres., dir. Am. Iron and Steel Inst., Washington, 1975-78; pres., dir. Interlake, Inc., Oak Brook, Ill.; dir. Millcraft Industries, Inc. Active Pitts. Opera. Served with USNR, 1944-45. Alumni fellow Pa. State U., 1977. Fellow Am. Soc. Metals (trustee, David Ford McFarland award Penn State chpt. 1973, Pittsburgh Nite lectr. 1970, Andrew Carnegie lectr. 1976); mem. Am. Inst. M.E., Am. Chem. Soc., Am., Brit., Internat. iron and steel insts., Assn. Iron and Steel Engrs., Am. Ordnance Assn., U.S. C. of C. (mem. edn. and manpower devel. com. 1973), Phi Beta Kappa, Sigma Xi, Tau Beta Pi. Democrat. Clubs: Duquesne, University, St. Clair Country, Oakmont Country (Pitts.); Univ., Congressional, Burning Tree, Cosmos, Carlton (Washington); Butler Nat. Golf (Chgo.). Contbr. articles to tech. jours. Patentee in field. Home: 22 Bradford Ln Oak Brook IL 60521 Office: Commerce Plaza 2015 Spring Rd Oak Brook IL 60521

LANGER, ALVIN, physician; b. Chgo., Oct. 20, 1934; s. Joseph and Sally Bernice (Kardon) L.; B.S., U. Ill., 1956, M.D., 1958; m. Sheila Ann Herbstman, July 1, 1962; children—Betty Suzanne, Diane Marie. Intern, U. Okla. Hosps., Oklahoma City, 1958-59; resident U. Ill. Hosps., Chgo., 1959-62; practice medicine, specializing in ob-gyn Permanente Med. Group, Santa Clara, Calif., 1965-70; faculty N.J. Med. Sch., 1970-76; program dir. ob-gyn Aultman Hosp., Canton, Ohio, 1976—, Timken Mercy Med. Center, Canton, 1978-81; prof. ob-gyn Northeastern Ohio U. Sch. Medicine, 1977—; attending staff Aultman Hosp. Served to capt. USAF, 1962-64. Diplomate Am. Bd. Ob-Gyn. Mem. Am. Coll. Obstetricians and Gynecologists, A.C.S., Assn. Profs. Gynecology and Obstetrics, Central Assn. Obstetricians and Gynecologists, Cleve. Soc. Obstetricians and Gynecologists, N.J. Soc. Ob-Gyn, Stark County Med. Soc., Ohio Med. Assn., Sigma Alpha Mu, Phi Delta Epsilon. Jewish. Contbr. articles to med. jours.; editor: (with Leslie Iffy) Perinatology Case Studies by Iffy and Langer, 1978. Office: 2600 6 St SW Canton OH 44710

LANGER, GAYLE MARLENE, assn. adminstr.; b. Hancock, Wis., Sept. 15, 1937; d. Elgee and Gladys Marion (Moon) Williams; student U. Wis., Madison, 1955-58, 76—; m. Robert Edward Langer, May 17, 1958; children—Deborah Ann, David Wayne. Exec. sec. Frito-Lay Co., Madison, Wis., 1958-59; exec. sec. Wis. Alumni Assn., Madison, 1959-63, office mgr., 1963-66, asso. dir., 1967—. Mem. com. Olson for Lt. Gov. Wis., 1968; com. Hall of Fame, Pen and Mike Club, 1968—; pres., sec. women's group Lakeview Am. Lutheran Ch., 1968-69; trustee Council for Advancement and Support of Edn., Washington, 1979-81, chmn. Dist. V, 1979-80, treas. Dist. V, 1977-78. Mem. Madison Sales and Mktg. Execs. Republican. Clubs: Madison Alumni, Blackhawk Country. Home: 1005 Troy Dr Madison WI 53704 Office: 650 N Lake St Madison WI 53706

LANGER, STEVEN, cons. personnel mgmt. and indsl. psychology; b. N.Y.C., June 4, 1926; s. Israel and Anna (Glaisner) L.; B.A. in Psychology, Calif. State U., Sacramento, 1950; M.S. in Personnel Service, U. Colo., 1958; Ph.D., Walden U., 1970; m. Elaine Catherine Brewer, Dec. 29, 1979; children—Bruce, Diana, Geoffrey. Asst. to personnel dir. City and County of Denver, 1956-59; personnel dir. City of Pueblo (Colo.) 1959-60; personnel cons. J.L. Jacobs & Co., Chgo., 1961-64, adminstrv. mgr., 1966-68; sales selection mgr. Reuben H. Donnelly Corp., Chgo., 1964-66; mng. cons. Abbott, Langer & Associates, Park Forest, Ill., 1968—; vis. prof. mgmt. Loyola U., Chgo., 1969-71; community prof. behavioral scis. Purdue U., Calumet campus, Hammond, Ind., 1973-75. Registered psychologist, Ill. Mem. Midwestern Psychol. Assn., Ill. Psychol. Assn. (chmn. sect. indsl. psychologists 1971-72), Chgo. Psychol. Assn. (pres. 1974-75), Am. Soc. Personnel Adminstrn. (chmn. research award com. 1966-69), Am. Compensation Assn., Chgo. Compensation Assn. (sec. 1976-77), Mensa (pres. Chgo. chpt. 1972-74). Unitarian. Contbr. numerous reports and articles on indsl. psychology and personnel mgmt. to profl. publs. Home: 309 Herndon St Park Forest IL 60466 Office: 2710 Chicago Rd S Chicago Heights IL 60411

LANGFORD, ELIZABETH HEGGE, civic worker; b. Oslo, Norway, May 19, 1921; came to U.S., 1929, naturalized, 1934; d. Hans Thorleif and Elise (Lerche) Grüner-Hegge; B.A. in Sociology, U. Mich., 1941; m. George Robert Langford, June 14, 1941; children—Nancy Langford Hague, George Lawrence. Chmn. Washtenaw County chpt. Nat. Found.-March of Dimes, 1949-52; bd. dirs. Ann Arbor (Mich.) Vis. Nurses Assn., 1949-52; founder, 2d pres. Univ. Hosp. Vol. Services Guild, 1952-53; pres. U. Mich. Alumnae Club, 1953-54; founder, 2d pres. Ann Arbor Women's City Club, 1953-54, 69-71; vice chmn. U. Mich. Alumnae Council, 1956-58; pres. Sorosis Club Mich., 1963-65; sec. U. Mich. Alumni Fund, 1958-60, vice chmn., 1960-61; sec. Barton Hills Charter Commn., 1973; bd. dirs. Sr. Citizens Guild, 1969-75; mem. Gov.'s State Health Planning Adv. Council, 1974-78; pres. Barton Hills Village, 1973—; chmn. Motor Meals of Ann Arbor, 1975—; mem. budget com. United Way, 1974-80. Republican. Presbyterian. Home: 859 Oakdale Rd Barton Hills Ann Arbor MI 48105

LANGHAM, JAMES ROLLA, fluidpower indsl. co. exec.; b. Bedford, Ohio, Mar. 29, 1941; s. Russell and Lucille N. (Smith) L.; B.A. in Arts and Sci., B.S. in Edn., Kent State U., 1966. Med. technologist Akron (Ohio) Gen. Med. Center, 1963-67; program devel. specialist B.F. Goodrich Co., Akron, 1969-80; mgr. human resources devel. Parker Hannifin Co., Cleve., 1980—; cons. mgmt. devel. Instr., ARC, Akron. Hiram Coll. scholar, 1969-70. Mem. Nat. Soc. Performance and Instrn., Am. Soc. Tng. and Devel., Tau Kappa Epsilon (pres. chpt. 1971-72). Democrat. Episcopalian. Clubs: Teke Ednl., SAR (pres. club 1975-76). Developer numerous tng. programs. Home: 2130 Smith Rd Akron OH 44313 Office: 17325 Euclid Ave Cleveland OH 44112

LANGHORST, GERALD HENRY, city ofcl.; b. Fontanelle, Nebr., Dec. 2, 1919; s. Otto A. and Emma L.; student Midland Coll., 1938-39, Gem City Bus. Coll., 1939-41. Technician, Soil Conservation Service, Creighton, Nebr., 1947-74; mayor City of Creighton, 1974—. Ex-officio dir. Lundberg Meml. Hosp. Served with USAAF, 1942-45. Mem. Creighton C. of C. (sec., past pres.), Nebr. League Municipalities, Am. Assn. Small Cities (bd. dirs.), Am. Legion. Republican. Mem. United Ch. of Christ (bd. dirs. 1980—). Clubs: Masons, Order Eastern Star. Home: 301 State St Creighton NE 68729 Office: 708 State St Creighton NE 68729

LANGHOUT, HENRY JOHN, forest products co. exec.; b. Norwood, Ohio, July 11, 1923; s. Theodore John and Eunice (Herdtner) L.; B.A. in Bus., Miami U., Oxford, Ohio, 1947; m. Mary Virginia Schlientz, June 16, 1945; children—Bruce John, Michael Floyd, William Thomas. Salesman, Internat. Paper Co., Dallas and Cin., 1947-54, sales mgr. paperboard grades, Chgo., 1954-60; Eastern sales mgr., nat. sales mgr. Crossett div. Ga.-Pacific Corp., N.Y.C. and Chgo., 1961-65; Eastern sales mgr., nat. sales mgr. paperboard/linerboard grades Weyerhaeuser Co., Chgo., 1965-67, secondary fibre mgr., Tacoma, 1968-70, gen. mgr. shipping container div., Manitowoc, Wis., 1970-79; gen. mgr. Container div. Champion Internat. Corp., Joliet and Naperville, Ill., 1979—. Bd. dirs. Manitowoc-Two Rivers YMCA, pres., 1977-78; bd. dirs. Manitowoc County Taxpayers Assn. Served with USNR, 1943-45. Recipient Layman of Year award YMCA, 1975. Mem. Fibre Box Assn. (zone 13 chmn. 1975-76), Delta Sigma Pi. Presbyterian (elder 1974). Club: Branch River Country of Branc (Wis.) (sec., dir.). Home: 8 Fernilee Ct Aurora IL 60504 Office: Route 6 and Young Rd Joliet IL 60434

LANGSETH, KEITH L., state senator; b. Moorhead, Minn., Jan. 20, 1938; s. Norman Clifford and Ruth (Rosenquist) L.; grad. high sch.; m. Lorraine Mac Ersland, 1957; children—Danny, Gayle, Joy. Dairy farmer; mem. Minn. Ho. of Reps., 1974-78, Minn. Senate, 1980—. Chmn. dist. Democratic-Farmer-Labor party, 1973-74, chmn. Clay County com., 1975-78. Office: 328 State Capitol Saint Paul MN 55155*

LANGUIRAND, RICHARD WELDON, business exec.; b. Astoria, N.Y., Dec. 24, 1927; s. Adrien Thomas and Elsie Elizabeth (Winston) L.; Electronics Engr., RCA Inst., 1948; postgrad. Columbia U., 1954, SUNY, Albany, 1967; m. Patricia Ruth Ryan, Sept. 2, 1961; children—Cary, Shelley, Richard. Engr. ABC, N.Y.C., 1950-54; telethon producer, dir. United Cerebral Palsy Assn., N.Y.C., 1954-58; fund raiser Nat. Found., N.Y.C., 1958-60; nat. dir. fund raising Leukemia Soc., Inc., N.Y.C., 1960-61; regional dir. Greater N.Y. Muscular Dystrophy Assn. Am., N.Y.C., 1961-63; dir. corp. and found. relations Rensselaer Poly. Inst., Troy, N.Y., 1963-68; pres. Languirand Assos., Los Angeles, 1966-74; dir. devel. Loyola U., Los Angeles, 1969-72, Am. Film Inst., Beverly Hills, Calif., 1972-74; v.p. devel. Chgo. Coll. Osteo. Medicine, 1974-80; sr. mgmt. officer The Languirand Co., Homewood, Ill., 1980—. Served with N.G., 1947-54. Mem. Am. Assn. Higher Edn., Council Advancement and Support of Edn., Nat. Soc. Fundraisers, Nat. Assn. Hosp. Devel., Chgo. Soc. Fund Raising Execs., So. Calif. Soc. Fund Raisers. Democrat. Lutheran. Office: 1331 Jeffery Dr Homewood IL 60430

LANIER, BRIAN OLIVER, wire co. exec.; b. Gallipolis, Ohio, Oct. 10, 1943; s. Garland Oliver and Betty Jean (Hartinger) L.; B.S. in Math., Ohio U., 1966, M.S. in Indsl. and Systems Engring., 1969; m. Sally Lynn Dailey, Dec. 19, 1965; children—Brad, Melissa, Greta. Ops. analyst Goodyear Atomic, Piketon, Ohio, 1966-69; indsl. engr. R.R. Donnelley, Willard, Ohio, 1969-73; chief indsl. engr., plant mgr. Seneca Wire, Fostoria, Ohio, 1973-78, gen. mgr., 1979—, v.p., 1980—. Trustee, United Way, 1977—, campaign chmn., 1979; trustee YMCA, 1977-80, Betty Jane Rehab. Center, 1979—. Recipient Service award Fostoria Jaycees, 1978. Mem. Am. Mgmt. Assn., Wire Assn., Am. Inst. Indsl. Engring., Spring Mfrs. Inst. Republican. Presbyterian. Club: Fostoria Country. Contbr. article to jour. in field. Home: 575 Nickie Ln Fostoria OH 44830 Office: 319 S Vine Fostoria OH 44830

LANIER, CHARLENE HAMPTON, educator; b. Ducan, Miss., Aug. 16, 1947; d. Charles Henry and Derotha (Scott) Hampton; B.S. (Univ. System Ga. Regent's scholar 1965-66), Ft. Valley (Ga.) State Coll., 1969; M.A., U. Fla., 1974, Ed.S. (univ. scholar 1974-75), 1975; m. James Edward Lanier, July 21, 1973; 1 dau., Sanita Lynn. Tchr.'s aide Project Headstart, Warner Robins, Ga., summer 1966, 67; student asst. nursery sch. Ft. Valley State Coll., 1968; extension home econs. agt. I, Inst. Food and Agrl. Scis., U. Fla., 1970-73, counselor Project Upward Bound, 1973-75; counselor II, N. Central Fla. Community Mental Health Center, Gainesville, 1975-78;

tchr.-counselor, project team leader individualized career planning program Springfield (Ill.) Sch. Dist. 186, 1978—. Bd. dirs. Springfield-Sangamon County Youth Service Bur., 1978. Mem. Am. Personnel and Guidance Assn., Ill. Personnel and Guidance Assn., Assn. Non-White Concerns in Personnel and Guidance, Nat. Vocat. Guidance Assn., Am. Coll. Personnel Assn., Assn. Counselor Edn. and Supervision, Am. Sch. Counselor Assn., Assn. Humanistic Edn. and Devel., Ill. Personnel and Guidance Assn., Fla. Assn. Non-white Concerns in Personnel and Guidance (charter), Phi Delta Kappa, Delta Sigma Theta (life). Democrat. Baptist. Clubs: Order Eastern Star, Loyal Ladies of Golden Circle, Daus. of Isis. Contbr. articles to profl. publs. Address: 2201 Claremont Dr Springfield IL 62703

LANIER, JAMES EDWARD, educator; b. Jacksonville, Fla., Oct. 21, 1942; s. James Lee and Hortense C. (Matthews) L.; B.S., Edward Waters Coll., Jacksonville, 1969; M.A. (trainee Equal Opportunity program 1969-70), Mich. State U., 1971; Ed.S. (Fla. Dept. Rehab. Services trainee 1972-74), U. Fla., 1973, Ph.D. (grantee Fla. Ednl. Research Devel. Council 1975, Wiles Meml. award 1975-76), 1975; m. Charlene Hampton, July 21, 1973; 1 dau., Sanita Lynn. Adminstrv. asst., instr. math. Urban Adult Ednl. Inst., Detroit, 1969; grad. research asst. Mich. State U., 1970; vocat. rehab. counselor II, Fla. Div. Vocat. Rehab., Jacksonville, 1970-72; counselor, instr. Santa Fe Community Coll., Gainesville, Fla., 1974; adj. asst. prof. counselor edn. U. Fla., 1976-77; guidance counselor Alachua County Sch. Bd., Gainesville, 1974-77; asst. prof. U. S.Fla., Tampa, 1977-78; prof. human devel. counseling Sangamon State U., Springfield, Ill., 1978—, chmn. univ. black caucus, 1979-80; mem. ednl. task force Springfield Urban League, 1978—; cons. Mgmt. Research Assos. Internat. Tng. Corp. Ill., Inc., 1978—; v.p., exec. bd. dirs. Corner Drug Store, community crisis center, Gainesville, 1976-77; ednl. cons. social service dept. Springfield Housing Authority, 1978—, coach-trainer boxing club, 1978—; bd. dirs. Springfield-Sangamon County Youth Service Bd., 1978—. Vice pres. Gainesville Housing Bd., 1976-77. Served with USAF, 1960-65. Mem. Am. Personnel and Guidance Assn., Assn. Non-White Concerns in Personnel and Guidance, Nat. Vocat. Guidance Assn., Am. Coll. Personnel Assn., Assn. Counselor Edn. and Supervision, Am. Sch. Counselor Assn., Assn. Humanistic Edn. and Devel., Assn. Measurement and Evaluation, Ill. Personnel and Guidance Assn., Fla. Assn. Non-White Concerns in Personnel and Guidance (charter), Phi Delta Kappa, Phi Beta Sigma (life, pres. Gainesville grad. chpt. 1976-78, pres. Springfield grad. chpt. 1980—). Democrat. Roman Catholic. Clubs: Masons (32 deg.), Shriners. Author papers in field. Address: 2201 Claremont Dr Springfield IL 62703

LANIGAN, ROBERT JOSEPH, mfg. co. exec.; b. Bklyn., Apr. 26, 1928; s. John and Kathryn (Sheehy) L.; A.B. in Econs., St. Francis Coll., N.Y., 1950; m. Mary E. McCormick, Dec. 30, 1950; children—J. Kenneth, Betty Jean Lanigan Reed, Kathryn Ann Lanigan Armstrong, Jeanne Marie, Suzanne Marie. With Owens-Ill. Inc., Toledo, 1950—, v.p. adminstrn. and control forest products div., 1961-66, gen. mgr. primary ops. forest products div., 1966-67, v.p., dir. corp. planning, 1967-69, asst. gen. mgr. Lily Tulip div., 1969-70, mgr. div., 1970-72, gen. mgr. glass container div., 1972-75, exec. v.p. and gen. mgr. packaging group, 1975-76, pres., chief operating officer domestic ops., 1976-79, pres., chief operating officer internat. ops., 1979—; dir. Barry-Wehmiller, Dun & Bradstreet Corp., United Glass Ltd., Eng. Trustee, Cath. U. Am., Toledo Symphony Orch.; bd. dirs. Greater Toledo Community Chest; mem. president's council Toledo Mus. Art. Mem. Glass Packaging Inst., U.S. Brewers Assn. Republican. Roman Catholic. Clubs: Toledo Country, Toledo, Belmont Country (Toledo); Imperial Golf (Naples, Fla.); Muirfield Village Golf (Dublin, Ohio); Burning Tree (Bethesda, Md.); Blind Brook (Port Chester, N.Y.). Home: 6206 Valley Park Dr Toledo OH 43623 Office: Owens-Illinois Inc One Sea Gate Toledo OH 43666*

LANKER, KARL EMIL, cons. indsl. engr.; b. Absecon, N.J., Aug. 15, 1925; s. Karl Warner and Martha (Jesuncosky) L.; B.S. in Indsl. Engring., Rutgers U., 1951; M.B.A., Ohio U., 1979; m. Virginia L. Brown, Sept. 22, 1956; children—M. Kathleen, Debra A. Corporate indsl. engr., mgr. Anchor Hocking Corp., Lancaster, Ohio, 1951-56, chief plant indsl. engr., 1956-59, chief div. indsl. engr., 1959-62, corporate planning coordinator, 1962-65, acting corporate chief indsl. engr., 1965-67; facilities planning mgr. Lancaster Colony, 1967-69; cons. engr., prin. E. Ralph Sims, Jr. & Assos., Inc., Lancaster, 1969—; guest lectr. Am. Mgmt. Assn., adult edn. instr. Ohio U.; mem. Active Corps Execs., SBA. Served with USNR, 1943-46; PTO. Registered profl. engr., Ohio, N.J., Calif.; cert. mgmt. cons. Inst. Mgmt. Cons.'s. Mem. Am. Inst. Indsl. Engrs. (nat. dir. facilities planning and design div. 1975-76), Profl. Engrs. in Pvt. Practice, Internat. Material Mgmt. Soc. (cert.), Assn. Mgmt. Cons.'s (conf. dir. 1972), Assn. Cons. Mgmt. Engrs., Ohio Soc. Profl. Engrs., Rutgers Engring. Soc., Soc. Mfg. Engrs. (certified), Nat. Mgmt. Assn. (charter pres. Lancaster-Fairfield chpt.), Lancaster C. of C., Am. Legion, Chi Phi. Methodist. (dir. 1970-73). Clubs: Kiwanis, Toastmasters. Home: Route 1 1290 Wheeling Rd Lancaster OH 43130 Office: PO Box 646 Lancaster OH 43130

LANNING, JAMES WILLIAM, publishing co. exec.; b. Logan, Ohio, May 3, 1941; s. Wilbur Warren and Ruth Emily (Dill) L.; B.S., Ohio State U., 1963; M.B.A., U. Dayton, 1981; m. Ruth Eilene McGrath, Aug. 30, 1969; children—Jennifer, Christina, James. Auditor, AT&T, Columbus, Ohio, 1965-69, Alexander Grant & Co., Columbus, 1969-70; treas. Lincoln Library Encyclopedia, Columbus, 1970—. L.P.A., Ohio. Mem. Pub. Accountants Soc. Ohio, Ohio State U. Assn. (life). Club: Pinehurst Country. Home: and Office: 848 Colony Way Worthington OH 43085

LANO, CHARLES JACK, mfg. co. exec.; b. Port Clinton, Ohio, Apr. 17, 1922; s. Charles Herbin and Antoinette (Schmitt) L.; B.S. in Bus. Adminstrn. summa cum laude, Ohio State U., 1949; m. Beatrice Irene Spees, June 16, 1946; children—Douglas Cloyd, Charles Lewis. With U.S. Gypsum Co., 1941-46, Ottawa Paper Stock Co., 1946-47; accountant Arthur Young & Co., C.P.A.'s, Tulsa, 1949-51; controller Lima div. Ex-Cell-O Corp., 1951-59, electronics div. AVCO Corp., 1959-61, Servomation Corp., 1961; asst. comptroller Scovill Mfg. Co., Waterbury, Conn., 1961-62, comptroller, 1962-67; controller CF&I Steel Corp., Denver, 1967-69, v.p., controller, 1969-70; controller Pacific Lighting Corp., 1970-76; exec. v.p. Arts-Way Mfg. Co., Armstrong, Iowa, 1976—, dir., 1981—. Served with USMCR, 1942-45. C.P.A., Okla. Mem. Am. Inst. C.P.A.'s, Calif. Soc. C.P.A.'s, Iowa Soc. C.P.A.'s, Financial Execs. Inst., Nat. Assn. Accountants. Home: PO Box 198 Armstrong IA 50514 Office: Arts-Way Mfg Co Armstrong IA 50514

LANSMON, JAMES ROBERT, public utility exec.; b. Chaffee, Mo., May 4, 1926; s. George C. and Catherine Lansmon; B.S.C., St. Louis U., 1948; m. Edith Matthews, Jan. 29, 1949; children—Kathryn, Patricia, William, Theresa. Accountant, Barrow, Wade, Guthrie & Co., St. Louis, 1948-50; staff accountant Mo. Utilities Co., Cape Girardeau, Mo., 1950-57, chief accountant, 1958-60, asst. treas., 1960-62, treas., asst. sec., 1962-74, v.p., treas., 1974—. Bd. dirs. Greater Cape Devel. Corp., Cape Girardeau, pres., 1981-82; bd. dirs. St. Francis Med. Center, Cape Girardeau; v.p. exec. bd. mem. Semo council Boy Scouts Am., 1980-81; bd. mem. Otahki council Girl Scouts U.S., 1970-73. Served with USNR, 1944-46; PTO. Mem. Edison Electric Inst., Mo. Valley Electric Assn., Midwest Gas Assn. Republican. Roman Catholic. Clubs: Exchange (pres. 1966), Country, Execs. (Cape Girardeau, Mo.). Home: 2515 Allendale Dr Cape Girardeau MO 63701 Office: 400 Broadway PO Box 40 Cape Girardeau MO 63701

LANTRY, MARILYN MARTHA, state senator; b. St. Paul, Oct. 28, 1932; d. Louis Leonard and Josephine Mary (Cermak) Kunz; student public schs.; m. Jerome Horton Lantry, May 16, 1953; children—Jacqueline, Kathleen. Sec., research asst. Cons. Service Corp., St. Paul, 1968-73; legis. aide St. Paul City Council, 1973-81; mem. Minn. Senate from 67th Dist., 1981—, chmn. group health plan, 1980. Bd. dirs. Med. Edn. and Research Found., St. Paul Ramsey Hosp. Democrat. Roman Catholic. Office: State Capitol St Paul MN 55155

LANTZ, GEORGE BENJAMIN, JR., coll. pres.; b. Buckhannon, W.Va., Feb. 6, 1936; s. George Benjamin and Georgia Myrtle (Bodkin) L.; A.B., W.Va. Wesleyan Coll., 1960; S.T.B., Sch. Theology, Boston U., 1964, Ph.D., 1971; m. Mary Sue Powell, Feb. 25, 1957; children—Mary Lynne, Marsha, Kimberly, Rebecca, Todd. Mem. faculty humanities and religion, W.Va. Wesleyan Coll., 1967-75, chmn. div. humanities, 1974-75; asst. to pres. Am. Council on Edn., fellow in acad. adminstrn. Ohio Wesleyan U., 1973-74; dean Mt. Union Coll., Alliance, Ohio, 1975-80, pres., 1980—. Vice pres. Upshur County Bd. Edn., Buckhannon, W.Va., 1972-78; mem. Mayor's Commn. on Sr. Citizens, Alliance, 1978—; bd. dirs. ARC chpt., Alliance, 1980—. Served with U.S. Army, 1954-56. Mem. Am. Assn. Higher Edn., AAUP, Soc. Bibl. Lit., Omicron Delta Kappa, Psi Kappa Omega. Methodist. Contbr. articles to profl. jours. Office: 1972 Clark Alliance OH 44601

LANTZ, JUDI OVERMAN, utility exec.; b. Dayton, Ohio, Oct. 7, 1941; d. G. Robert and Jessie May (Posther) Overman; B.A. in Journalism and English, Bowling Green State U., 1964; M.A. in Mgmt. and Personnel, Central Mich. U., 1981; m. Stirling E. Lantz, Aug. 16, 1975. Dir. public relations exec. staff Girl Scouts U.S.A., Waukesha, Wis., 1965-67, dir. personnel exec. staff, Waukesha, 1968-70, asst. regional dir. nat. exec. staff, Chgo., 1970-74; account exec. Sibley-Sheehan & Assos., public relations, Atlanta, 1968; asst. dir. community relations Gas Service Co., Kansas City, Mo., 1975—. Corp. fund raiser Am. Cancer Soc., 1977-79; advisor Corp. Explorer Post, Heart of Am. council Boy Scouts Am., 1979-81; bd. dirs. Vol. Action Com., 1979-80. Recipient Leadership Kans. award, 1980. Mem. Am. Soc. Tng. and Devel., Dimensions Unltd. (dir. 1978-79), Women in Energy (chmn. exec. bd., 1981—), Women's C. of C. Republican. Methodist. Home: 6525 Burnham Dr Shawnee Mission KS 66202 Office: Gas Service Co 2460 Pershing Rd Kansas City MO 64108

LANTZSCH, HANS EDWIN, sch. supt.; b. Krogis, Germany, Aug. 7, 1923; s. Rheinhold Edwin and Louise (Ettmeier) L.; came to U.S., 1927, naturalized, 1934; B.A., Central Mich. U., 1948; M.A., U. Mich., 1950; postgrad. Wayne State U., 1952-63; m. Dora Jablinskey, June 19, 1948; children—James Edwin, Susan Elizabeth, Thomas Paul. Asst. and acting supt. Ecorse (Mich.) Pub. Schs., 1948-67; supt. Trenton (Mich.) Pub. Schs., 1967-71, Gerrish Higgins Sch., Roscommon, Mich., 1971—. Dir. Community Resources Workshop, Mich. State U., 1955-72; asst. dir. NSF Chemistry Inst., Mont. State Coll., 1958. Chmn. sch. liaison Met. Detroit Sci. Fair, 1957-68; mem. com. Wayne County Intermediate Sch. Dist. Occupational Edn., 1969-71; mem. com. for Educating New Supts. in Mich., 1973—. Trustee, Mich. Council for Econ. Edn., 1965-68. Served with AUS, 1943-46. Decorated Bronze Star. Mem. Am. Assn. Sch. Adminstrs. (life, del. assembly 1981), Mich. Edn. Assn. (life), No. Mich. Supts. Assn. (pres. 1977-78), Internat. Platform Assn., Phi Delta Kappa (life). Office: Gerrish Higgins Bd Edn Roscommon MI 48653

LAORNUAL, SAMRITH, physician; b. Chathaburee, Thailand, Dec. 9, 1941; came to U.S., 1968, naturalized, 1980; s. Santad and SangVan Laornual; M.D., Chulalongkorn U., Bangkok, 1967; m. Sujitra Chaisirikulchair, Dec. 28, 1970; children—Sandra, Samrith, Sabrena. Surg. intern Watts Hosp., Durham, N.C., 1968-69; resident in surgery Charleston (W.Va.) Gen. Hosp., 1969-70; resident in urology Charleston Area Med. Center, 1970-73; practice medicine specialising in urology, East Liverpool, Ohio, 1974—; mem. staff Liverpool City Hosp., Ohio Valley Hosp., Steubenville; pres. Samrith Laornual, M.D., Inc. Diplomate Am. Bd. Urology. Mem. Internat. Coll. Surgeons, A.C.S. Buddhist. Home: 3191 Hampton Ct PO Box 170 East Liverpool OH 43920 Office: 2232 St Clair Ave PO Box 170 East Liverpool OH 43920

LAPENSKY, M. JOSEPH, airline exec.; b. Mpls., Nov. 27, 1918; s. Frank J. and Mary (Mulkern) L.; B.A., Coll. St. Thomas, St. Paul, 1940; m. Joan M. LaCroix, Nov. 14, 1942; children—John, Stephen, Rosemary, Julianne, Michael, Joseph. With Northwest Air Lines, Inc., 1945—, comptroller, 1960-66, v.p. econ. planning, 1966-73, v.p. fin., 1973-76, pres., chief operating officer, 1976—, chief exec. officer, 1979—, also dir. Bd. dirs. St. Mary's Jr. Coll., Mpls.; chmn. bd. trustees Acad. Holy Angels; trustee St. Thomas Coll.; mem. am. adv. bd. Sogang U., Seoul, Korea. Mem. Mpls. C. of C. Clubs: Decathlon, Mpls., Minikahda (Mpls.); Minn. (St. Paul). Home: 6621 Stevens Ave Minneapolis MN 55423 Office: Northwest Air Lines Inc Mpls-St Paul Internat Airport Saint Paul MN 55111

LAPIDUS, DENNIS, computer systems exec.; b. Chgo., Oct. 21, 1942; s. Sidney and Mildred (Karlin) L.; B.S.M.E., Northwestern U., 1964; M.B.A., Roosevelt U., 1968. Dist. sales mgr. Perkin-Elmer Corp., Chgo., 1974-78; regional mgr. Basic Four, Chgo., 1978-80; pres., founder Productive Computer Systems, Chgo., 1980—; cons. litigation of computer-related cases; guest lectr. OEM Bus. Forum. Mem. ASME, Data Processors Soc. Chgo. Club: East Bank. Home: 1659 N Vine St Chicago IL 60614 Office: 233 N Michigan Ave Chicago IL 60611

LAPOINTE, FRANCIS CHARLES, ednl. adminstr.; b. Rosebud, S.D., Nov. 1, 1936; s. Elmer Clement and Neva Grace (Herman) LaP.; B.A., Rockhurst Coll., Kansas City, Mo., 1958; m. Elizabeth Randall; children—Lema, Francis Charles, Shizue, Randall, Thomasine. Editor, Rosebud Sioux Herald, 1963-71; reporter, John Hay Whitney fellow Littleton (Colo.) Ind./Arapahoe Herald, 1967; exec. dir. Sicangu Oyate Ho, Inc., St. Francis, S.D., 1971-76, comptroller, 1981—; instr. Sinte Gleska Coll., Rosebud, part-time 1972-80. Community rep. Rosebud Sioux Tribal Council, 1978—; treas. Sicangu Striders, 1981. Served with USN, 1959-63. Named Educator of Yr., S.D. Indian Edn. Assn., 1979. Mem. Am. Indian Leadership Council (charter), Am. Legion. Author: The Sioux Today, 1972; also articles. Home: Box 65 Spotted Tail Ln Rosebud SD 57570 Office: Box 155 Sicangu Oyate Ho Inc St Francis SD 57572

LA POLLA, JAMES JOSEPH, pediatrician; b. Youngstown, Ohio, Feb. 27, 1934; s. Dominic Joseph and Ann Patricia (Page) La P.; A.B., Duke U., 1956, M.D., 1960; m. Genevieve Jacobson, Oct. 20, 1962; children—Jim, Ken, Vincent, Mike. Intern, Univ. Hosp., Cleve., 1961-62; resident in pediatrics Babies and Childrens's Hosp., Cleve., 1962-64; practice medicine specializing in pediatrics, Warren, Ohio, 1966—; med. dir. Children's Rehab. Center, Youngstown Devel. Center for Retarded, Devel. Clinic. Bd. dirs. Trumbull County Mental Retardation Bd., Trumbull County Bd. Mental Health; pres. Howland Local Sch. Bd., 1977-78; exec. bd. N.E. Ohio Sch. Bds. Assns. Served to comdr., USNR, 1964-66. Named Man of Year Jaycees, 1970. Mem. Trumbull County Med. Soc. (exec. com.), Ohio Pediatric Soc. (state chmn. 1972), Ohio Med. Assn., AMA, Ohio Community Theatre Assn. (dir. award 1974), Internat. Platform Assn., Am. Acad. for Cerebral Palsy and Devel. Medicine. Clubs: Trumbull Country, Buckeye, Howland Rotary (pres.), Shriners. Contbr. articles to profl. jours., chpt. in book. Organized 1st state Olympics for mentally retarded. Home: 707 North Rd SE Warren OH 44484 Office: 8048 E Market St NE Warren OH 44484

LAPOSKY, BEN FRANCIS, comml. artist; b. Cherokee, Iowa, Sept. 30, 1914; s. Peter Paul and Leona Anastasia (Gabriel) L. Free-lance comml. artist, oscillographic designer, 1938; creator electronic abstractions, Oscillons, 1952; one-man shows include: USIA, France, 1956; group shows include: Cybernetic Serendipity, London, 1968; Computer Art, N.Y.C., 1976; Computer Art Internat., Lawrence Hall of Sci., U. Calif., Berkeley, 1979; others; contbr. articles to art jours. Recipient Gold Medal award N.Y. Art Dirs. Club, 1957. Subject of article Arts Mag., June 1980. Home and office: 301 S 6th St Cherokee IA 51012

LAPOW, LOUIS ROBERT, podiatrist; b. Newark, Mar. 16, 1947; s. Harry Aaron and Gladys L.; B.A., Rutgers U., 1968; D.P.M. cum laude, Ohio Coll. Podiatric Medicine, Cleve., 1972; m. Melanie Zaletel, Jan. 23, 1971; children—Lorence, Heather. Asso. Cleve. Foot Surgeons Inc., 1973-74; practice podiatric medicine, Milw., 1974—; dir. podiatric residency tng. Lakeview Hosp., Milw. Recipient award, podiatric staff Lakeview Hosp., 1977. Diplomate Am. Bd. Podiatric Surgery. Mem. Am. Podiatry Assn., Wis. Soc. Podiatric Medicine, Acad. Ambulatory Foot Surgeons, Assn. Hosp. Podiatrists. Jewish. Home: 5815 Glen Haven Dr Greendale WI 53129 Office: 4220 S 27th St Milwaukee WI 53221

LAPRESTA, SAMUEL JOSEPH, mfg. co. exec.; b. St. Louis, Jan. 26, 1943; s. Joseph and Mary (Valt) LaP.; B.S. in Metall. Engring., U. Mo., 1965, M.S. in Engring. Mgmt., 1971; m. Gail Ruth Loughridge, June 13, 1964; children—Erik Joseph, Gary Charles, Stacey Marie. Quality control engr. Ford Motor Co., Dearborn, Mich., 1965-68; sales engr. Climax Molybdenum Co., Chgo., 1971-72; metall. sales engr. Foote Mineral Co., Chgo., 1972-76, gen. sales mgr. foundry products, 1976—. Bd. dirs. Lake Region YMCA, 1977-81; mem. St. Thomas Sch. Bd., Crystal Lake, Ill., 1981—; v.p. St. Thomas Athletic Assn., 1980—. Mem. Ductile Iron Soc., AIME, Am. Foundrymen's Soc. Roman Catholic. Home: 7457 Foxfire Dr Crystal Lake IL 60014 Office: 25 Turner Ave Suite 202 Elk Grove Village IL 60007

LARGE, RICHARD LEROY, cons. mech. engr.; b. Wauneta, Nebr., Apr. 29, 1931; s. Everett Leroy and Jessie Mabel (Rathbun) L.; B.S., U. Nebr., 1958; m. Charlotte Mae Holl, Aug. 15, 1954; children—Jon, James, Janelle, Michael. Performance engr. Consumers Pub. Power Dist., Lincoln, Nebr., 1958-63, ops. supr., 1963-64; cons. engr. Tech. Mgmt. Inc., Lincoln, 1964-70; pres. Tech. Mgmt., 1970-71; pres. R.L. Large & Assos., Inc., cons. engrs., Lincoln, 1971—. Served with USMC, 1950-52. Registered profl. engr., Nebr., Colo. Mem. ASME (chmn. Nebr., 1969-70, sec. Region VII 1970-72), Lincoln C. of C., Am. Nuclear Soc., Nebr., Nat. socs. profl. engrs., Am. Legion. Republican. Lutheran. Patentee wheel chair devices. Home: 5111 LaSalle St Lincoln NE 68516 Office: 4740 Linden St Lincoln NE 68516

LARGENT, ALFRED JOSEPH, power co. ofcl.; b. Cadillac, Mich., June 19, 1930; s. Alfred Clay and Cecilia M. (Long) L.; ed. Traverse City (Mich.) public and parochial schs., DeForrest Radio and Electronics Sch., Internat. Corr. Schs.; m. Caroline C. Weber, June 17, 1950; children—Edward, Robert, Linda, Sherri. With Traverse City Light & Power Co., 1948—, beginning as meter reader, successively polyphase meter reader, line crew, journeyman lineman, 1948-68, supt. transmission and distbn., 1968—; mem. Grand Traverse County Bd. Commrs., 1968—. Active Boy Scouts Am., Community Chest, Walking Blood Bank. Mem. Mich. Assn. Commrs., Mich. Elec. Assn. Democrat. Roman Catholic. Club: K.C. Home: 857 Kinross St Traverse City MI 49684 Office: 400 Boardman Ave Traverse City MI 49684

LARK, JOHN DALE, architect; b. St. Louis, Jan. 27, 1947; s. Scott E. and Jane (Pearson) L.; student U. Md., 1965, Washington U., 1966, 69, Idaho State U., 1967-68; Ford Found. grantee Lab. for Computer Graphics and Spatial Analysis, Harvard U., 1968; m. Carol Vandiver, Sept. 1968; children—Jennifer Elizabeth, Jonathan Peter, Scott Jeremy. Architect, Harris Armstrong, FAIA, St. Louis, 1966-67; asst. instr. archtl. design Idaho State U., Pocatello, 1967-68; architect Layton, Layton Assos., St. Louis, 1969-71, Morgan Tovey, Jr., Pocatello, 1967-68, Donald Hudson Drayer, Washington, 1968—; founder Resource Planning and Design Group, St. Louis, 1972-77; prin. John Lark and Assos., Architects and Planners, St. Louis, 1977—; cons. City of Kirkwood (Mo.), Met. Sewer Dist., St. Louis, Neighborhood Housing Services, St. Louis; lectr. seminars assns. including AIA, Citizens for Community Devel., Housing Prodn. Inst., Am. Planning Assn., St. Louis Art Mus., Am. Forest History Soc.; bd. dirs. Double Helix Corp., 1972-76. Bd. dirs. St. Louis Open Space Council, v.p., 1977-78; bd. trustees Forest Park Preservation Trust; chmn. joint venture com. Meremec River Project, Open Space Council; mem. theme working com. SPIRIT, St. Louis. Registered architect, Mo., Ill.; recipient certificate of award St. Louis Coalition for the Environment, 1977. Mem. Soc. Archtl. Historians, Nat. Trust for Hist. Preservation, Am. Planning Assn., Design Methods Group, Met. Assn. Urban Designers and Environ. Planners, Mo. State Hist. Soc. Club: Valley Sailing Assn. Co-designer bldg. projects including Centernary Meth. Ch., Cape Girardeau, Mo., Lohman's Landing Bldg., Wetterau Office Complex, Hazelwood, Mo.; architect Master Plan for Internat. Cultural and Trade Center, Washington; restoration Pelican's Restaurant, St. Louis, Strassberger Center Arts, St. Louis; park and open space projects include Linear Park Study St. Louis County, Regional Environ. Edn. Center Weldon Spring, Meramec River Basin, Nat. Shrine of Our Lady of the Miraculous Medal, Perryville, Mo., mcpl. parks; contbr. writings in field; editor St. Louis Open Space Line, 1975-76. Home: 946 Newport Ave Saint Louis MO 63119 Office: 11 Moody Ave Saint Louis MO 63119

LARKE, GLENN RAYMOND, author; b. Sault Ste. Marie, Mich., Aug. 2, 1909; s. Richard and Hannah Melena (Becking) L.; B.A., Mich. State U., 1931; m. Helen Marguerite Tripp, Nov. 30, 1930; children—Lynn Louise Larke Hamm, Hannah Marie Larke Stuber, Thomas Arthur Tripp, Richard Glenn Tripp. Ednl. sec. Farmers and Mfrs. Beet Sugar Assn., editor Sugar Beet Jour., Saginaw, Mich., 1933-54. Served to maj. U.S. Army Res. Mem. Am. Soc. Sugar Beet Technologists, Res. Officers Assn. Republican. Presbyterian. Author: Do You Remember When — A Larke Family History and Some Memoirs, 3d edit., 1981. Address: 535 32d Ave N Apt 4 Saint Petersburg FL 33704 and 7150 N Terra Vista Dr Apt 1507 Peoria IL 61614

LARKIN, JOHN EDWARD, JR., orthopedic surgeon; b. St. Paul, Nov. 8, 1930; s. John Edward and Anna Gustava Larkin; B.S., U. Minn., 1953, M.D., 1960; m. Colles Baxter, June 16, 1981. Intern, Detroit Receiving Hosp., 1960-61; resident in surgery Harvard Service, Boston City Hosp., 1961-62; resident in orthopedic surgery Mass. Gen. Hosp., also Children's Hosp., Boston, 1962-66; teaching fellow in orthopedic surgery Harvard U., 1965-66; practice medicine specializing in orthopedic surgery, St. Paul, 1966—; mem. staff St. John's, United, Divine Redeemer, St. Joseph's hosps.; clin. instr. U. Minn. Med. Sch.; mem. Minn. Council Quality Edn., 1971-78. Trustee, benefactor Minn. Mus. Art; trustee Mpls. Soc. Fine Arts; mem. accessions com. Mpls. Inst. Art, also benefactor; bd. dirs. Minn. Opera, Irish Am. Cultural Soc. benefactor Children's Mus. of Minn.; Friend of Whitney Mus. Am. Art. Mem. New Eng. Orthopedic Soc. (hon.), Irish Orthopedic Soc. (hon.). Clubs: St. Paul Athletic; White Bear Yacht. Home: Dellwood White Bear Lake MN 55110 Office: 300 Kellogg Sq Saint Paul MN 55101

LARMER, OSCAR VANCE, artist; b. Wichita, Kans., July 11, 1924; s. Bert V. and Carrie (Yard) L.; certificate Mpls. Sch. Art, 1947; B.F.A., U. Kans., 1949, M.F.A., U. Wichita, 1955; m. Mary A. Duehring, Dec. 31, 1945; children—Mary Lynn Larmer King, Michael Vance. Asst. dir. Wichita Art Mus., 1953-55; asst. prof. Kans. State U., Manhattan, 1956-63, asso. prof., 1964-69, prof., 1970—, head dept. art, 1967-71; exhibited one-man shows Wichita, Topeka, Kansas City, Salina, Manhattan, 1950-65; exhibited in group shows Joslyn Art Mus., Omaha, Nelson Atkins Galleries, Kansas City, Mo., Wichita Art Mus., many others; represented in permanent collections: Wichita Art Assn., Kans. State U., Manhattan, Kans., U. Wichita, others. Mem. Wichita Artist Guild (past pres.), Soc. Kans. Painters, Prairie, Kans. watercolor socs., Midwest Coll. Art Assn. (bd. dirs.), Kans. Fedn. Art (past pres.), Kans. Arts Council (visual art adv. panel), Kansas City Art Coalition. Home: 2441 Hobbs Dr Manhattan KS 66502

LAROCCO, LAWRENCE, tool and die mfg. co. exec.; b. Melrose Park, Ill., Apr. 18, 1926; s. Joseph and Francis (Tuminello) LaR.; student public schs., Melrose Park; m. Jean Hummel, May 26, 1951; children—Linda, Joseph, Sandra, Tom. Tool and die maker, automated machine builder, various cos., 1941-51; tool maker aircraft missiles div. Howard Hughes Aircraft Co., Tucson, 1951-64; owner, operator job shop, Addison, Ill., 1964-68; tool and die maker D. Gottlieb Co., North Lake, Ill., 1969-74; v.p., gen. mgr. Faith Tool Co. Inc., Rockford, Ill., 1974—. Served with F.A., U.S. Army, 1944-46. Developer tools; inventor, holder two patents in field. Home and Office: 11155 Ventura Blvd Rockford IL 61111

LA ROCQUE, GERALDINE ELIZABETH, educator; b. Duluth, Minn., Feb. 28, 1926; d. Weldon A. and June LaRocque; B.S., U. Minn., 1947, M.A., 1952; Ph.D. in English Edn. (Switzer scholar, Mayr scholar), Stanford U., 1965. Tchr. English, Fergus Falls (Minn.) High Sch., 1947-49, U. Minn. High Sch., Mpls., 1949-50, Lake Forest (Ill.) High Sch., 1950-51, U. Ill. High Sch., Urbana, 1951-53; with WCTN-Radio and TV, Mpls., 1953-55; tchr. English, Evanston (Ill.) High Sch., 1955-62; acting instr. Stanford (Calif.) U., 1963-65; asst. prof. English, Tchrs. Coll., Columbia U., N.Y.C., 1965-67, asso. prof., 1967-72; vis. prof. English, U. Mo., summers, 1968-70; prof. English and English edn. U. No. Iowa, Cedar Falls, 1973—, dir. tchr. edn., 1980—; on leave to Nat. Inst. Edn., 1979-80; reading and English cons. to various public schs. and sch. dists. Mem. Nat. Council Tchrs. English, Iowa Council Tchrs. of English (pres. 1975-77, award 1977), Nat. Soc. Study Edn., Am. Ednl. Research Assn., Assn. Tchr. Educators. Contbr. articles on English edn. to profl. publs. Home: 725 Maplewood Dr Apt 203 Cedar Falls IA 50613 Office: English Dept Univ Northern Iowa Cedar Falls IA 50613

LARRABEE, GENE ROSS, health care exec.; b. Hammond, Ind., Nov. 30, 1947; s. James F. and Kathryn J. (Eggers) L.; B.A., U. Iowa and Winona (Minn.) State U., 1970; postgrad. U. Toledo, 1970-71; M.H.A., Governors State U., Park Forest South, Ill., 1972; m. Merikay L. Roth, June 27, 1970; children—Brent E.J., Kirk F.J., Aaron A.R. Unit adminstr. Elisabeth Ludeman Mental Retardation Center, Park Forest, Ill., 1972-73; adminstr. RN Convalescent Home, Berwyn, Ill., 1973-74; adminstr. Niles Manor Nursing Center, Niles, Ill., 1974; adminstr. Park Rehab. Center, Euclid, Ohio, 1974—; pres. Consultronics Corp., Euclid, 1975—; v.p. Euclid Park Nursing Center Pharmacy, Euclid, 1975—, Hermetic Chem. Labs., Inc., Euclid, 1976—; mem. seminar faculty Ohio U.; treas. St. Anthony's Continuing Care Center, Rock Island, Ill., 1978-79. Mem. Ohio Acad. Nursing Homes (bd. dirs., chmn. legal com., mem. legis. com. 1980-81, treas. 1980-81, mem. geriatric polit. action com.), Am. Coll. Nursing Home Adminstrs., Am. Health Care Assn., Ohio Health Care Assn., N.E. Ohio Nursing Home Assn., Am. Assn. Rehab. Facilities. Home: 2520 Southwood Rd Painesville OH 44077 Office: 20611 Euclid Ave Euclid OH 44117

LARSEN, AUBREY ARNOLD, pharm. co. exec.; b. Rockford, Ill., Sept. 27, 1919; s. Arnold George and Clara Emma (Baehler) L.; B.S. in Chemistry, Antioch Coll., 1943; M.S. in Chemistry, Mich. State U., 1944; Ph.D., Cornell U., 1946; m. Helen Louise Limb, Sept. 5, 1943; children—Robert, Richard, Jeanne, Donald, Barbara. Group leader chemistry Sterling Drug Co., Rensselaer, N.Y., 1946-59; asst. dept. dir. Mead Johnson Research Center, Evansville, Ind., 1960-63, dir. organic chemistry, 1963-67, v.p. phys. scis., 1967-68, v.p. research and devel., pharm. div., 1975—; v.p., sci. dir. Bristol-Myers Co., N.Y.C., 1969-75. Recipient Mead Johnson Pres.'s award, 1963; Tri-State Achievement award, 1965. Mem. AAAS, Am. Chem. Soc., N.Y. Acad. Sci., Am. Inst. Chemistry, Ind. Acad. Sci., Sigma Xi. Patentee in field. Contbr. articles to profl. jours. Home: 1240 SE 2d St Evansville IN 47713 Office: 2404 Pennsylvania St Evansville IN 47721

LARSEN, JOHN CHRISTIAN, librarian, educator; b. Menominee, Mich., Aug. 1, 1929; s. Julius Christian and Bozena Mary (Blahnik) L.; B.Design, U. Mich., 1950, M.A. in Art History, 1951, M.A.L.S., 1955, Ph.D., 1967. Reference librarian Detroit Public Library, 1954-57; head art sect. Mich. State Library, 1958-61; asso. librarian for public service Towson (Md.) State U., 1961-64; instr. U. Mich., 1965-68; asst. prof. U. Ky., 1968-71, Columbia U., 1971-77; asso. prof. library sci. No. Ill. U., DeKalb, 1977—; mem. Ill. del. White House Conf. Library and Info. Services, 1978. Mem. ALA (councilor 1970-72), Art Libraries Soc. N.Am., Assn. Am. Library Schs. (dir. 1970-72), Bibliog. Soc. No. Ill., Ill. Library Assn., Spl. Libraries Assn., Victorian Soc. in Am., Beta Phi Mu, Phi Kappa Phi. Presbyterian. Contbr. articles to profl. jours. Office: Adams Hall No Ill Univ DeKalb IL 60115

LARSEN, M. DALE, communications co. exec.; b. Red Wing, Minn., Sept. 21, 1922; s. Marshall Arnold and Marie Josephine (Hines) L.; B.S., St. Louis U., 1944; postgrad. U. Minn., 1946; m. Evelyn Ann Malmberg, Jan. 14, 1943; children—Lynne Marie, Judy Kay, Kathy Ann. With Mpls. Star and Tribune Co., 1942-56, st. sales supr., 1948-53, mem. promotion dept., 1953-56; promotion mgr. Wichita-Hutchinson Co., Inc./KTVH, Wichita, Kans., 1956-58, asst. gen. mgr., 1958-59, gen. mgr., 1959-60, v.p., gen. mgr., 1960-70, exec. v.p., gen. mgr., 1970-74, pres., 1974—; asst. v.p. Mpls. Star and Tribune Co., 1977-80, v.p., 1980-82; Bd. dirs. NCCJ, 1965—, co-chmn. bd., 1974; bd. dirs. Sedgwick County Heart Assn., 1965-71, chmn. bd., 1970-71; bd. dirs. Wichita Symphony Soc., 1963-66; co-founder Great Plains Heritage Found., 1963; bd. dirs. Wichita Hist. Mus., 1960-70, 72-76, pres., 1962, 65, 66; trustee St. Joseph Med. Center, 1975—, chmn. bd., 1981, 82; mem. U. Kans. Broadcast Adv. Council to Sch. Journalism, 1976—; bd. dirs. Wichita Med. Edn. Assn., 1976-80, Jr. Achievement, 1980—, Greater Downtown Wichita, 1980-81; chmn. campaign Kans. Am. Heart Assn., 1977; bd. dirs. Music Theatre of Wichita, 1977—. Served with AUS, 1943-45. Mem. Wichita Area C. of C. (dir. 1964-68), Kans. State C. of C. (past dir.), Wichita Better Bus. Bur. (dir. 1960-81, pres. 1963-64, chmn. bd. 1974). Home: 328 Hampton Rd Wichita KS 67206 Office: 7701 E Kellogg St Wichita KS 67207

LARSEN, MAX DEAN, educator; b. Pratt, Kans., Jan. 23, 1941; s. Harry Dean and Delores Iola (Morgan) L.; B.A., Kans. State Tchrs. Coll., Emporia, 1961; M.A., U. Kans., 1963, Ph.D., 1966; m. Lillian Matilda Grimes, Dec. 22, 1962; children—Michael Dean, Paul Joseph, Charles David. Asst. prof. math. U. Nebr., 1966-69, asso. prof., 1969-73, prof., 1973-81, dean Coll. Arts and Scis., 1974—. NSF, NEH grantee. Mem. Council Colls. of Arts and Scis. (dir. 1978-81), Internat. Council Fine Arts Deans, Am. Math. Soc., Sigma Xi. Author: Introduction to Modern Algebraic Concepts, 1969; Fundamental Concepts of Modern Mathematics, 1970; Essentials of Precalculus Mathematics, 1971; (with Paul J. McCarthy) A Multiplicative Theory of Ideals, 1971; (with Jom Fejfar) Essentials of Elementary School Mathematics, 1974; (with Monte Boisen) Understanding Basic Calculus with Applications from Management, Social and Life Sciences, 1978; contbr. articles to profl. jours. Office: College of Arts and Sciences University of Nebraska 1223 Oldfather Hall Lincoln NE 68588

LARSEN, MICHAEL JOHN, mycologist; b. London, Apr. 27, 1938; s. Gerard John and Nancy Maud (Stevens) L.; came to U.S., 1949, naturalized, 1956; B.Sc., Syracuse U., 1960, M.S., 1963; Ph.D. (NSF fellow), State U. N.Y. Coll. Forestry, 1967; children—Emily Susan, Caitlin Audrey. With Can. Forestry Service, Sault Ste. Marie, Ont., 1966-70; with Center for Forest Mycology Research, U.S. Forest Service, Madison, Wis., 1971—, research mycologist, 1971—; adj. asso. prof. U. Wis., Madison, 1974—, Mich. Technol. U., Houghton, 1978—. Mem. Mycol. Soc. Am., Can. Bot. Assn., Soc. Sigma Xi. Contbr. articles to profl. jours. Home: RFD 3 Box 262 Lodi WI 53555 Office: Center for Forest Mycology Research US Forest Service Walnut Ave Madison WI 53705

LARSEN, THEODORE EDWARD, electronics co. exec.; b. Harlowton, Mont., Oct. 23, 1927; s. Hans Albert and Anna Marie (Hansen) L.; B.S. in Mech. Engring., Mont. State Coll., 1955; m. Loraine Margaret Eide, June 28, 1952; children—Richard Harvey, Douglas Edward, Nancy Lynn. Design engr. Honeywell Inc., Mpls., 1955-62, tech. dir., Europe, Honeywell GmbH, Frankfurt, Germany, 1962-69, internat. market mgr., Mpls., 1969-73; pres., chief exec. officer Detector Electronics Corp., Mpls., 1973—. Mem. planning commn., Bloomington, Minn., 1957-62. Recipient award for Service to Scouting, 1972, others. Contbr. articles to profl. jours. Patentee in field. Home: 6216 Loch Moor Dr Edina MN 55435 Office: 6901 W 110th St Minneapolis MN 55438

LARSON, ANDREW ROBERT, lawyer; b. Pine County, Minn., Feb. 25, 1930; s. Gustaf Adolf and Mary (Mach) L.; B.A., U. Minn., 1953, B.S. Law, St. Paul Coll. Law, 1956; LL.B., William Mitchell Coll. Law, 1958; m. Evelyn Joan Johnson, Sept. 12, 1953 (div. 1980); children—Linda Suzanne, Mark Andrew. With Armour & Co., 1953-56, Minn. Dept. Taxation, 1956-58; admitted to Minn. bar, 1958; individual practice law, Duluth, Minn., 1958—. Municipal judge Village of Proctor, part-time 1961-74; dir., sec. various bus., real estate corps.; pres. firm Larson, Holmstrom, Huseby and Brodin, Ltd. Arbitrator Minn. Bur. Mediation Services; dir. Duluth Downtown Devel. Corp.; chmn. Duluth Fair Employment and Housing Commn., 1965-76; vice chmn. Mayor's Arena Auditorium Com., Duluth, 1964-65; active United Way; mem. State Bd. Human Rights, 1967-73; Midwest regional rep. nat. standing com. on legislation United Cerebral Palsy, 1967-71, bd. dirs. nat. assn., 1971-72; bd. dirs. United Day Activity Center, 1969-76, Am. Cancer Soc., 1973-75, Light House for Blind, 1975-79, 80—, Environ. Learning Center, 1978—. Recipient awards including Humanitarian Service award United Cerebral Palsy, 1965, Republican party I Care award for work in civil rights, aid to handicapped, 1964, Jr. C. of C. Distinguished Service award, 1965. Mem. Minn. Bar Assn., Minn. Jud. Council, Am. Arbitration Assn., Nat. Assn. Ind. Businessmen, Nat. Assn. Accts., Fresh Water Soc., Minn. League Municipalities, Hist. Soc., NAACP, ACLU, C. of C., U.S. C. of C., Beta Phi Kappa. Republican. Unitarian-Universalist. Kiwanian. Home: 3002 E Superior St Duluth MN 55811 Office: 333 W Superior St Duluth MN 55802

LARSON, ARVY JERALD, banker; b. Fergus Falls, Minn., June 25, 1930; s. Arthur Joe and Navy L. Larson; B.S. in Agrl. Econs., U. Minn., 1959; grad. Wis. Grad. Sch. Banking, Madison, 1975, Comml. Lending Sch., Norman, Okla., 1979; m. Mabel Laurel Engen, June 8, 1968; children—Bonnie, Mary, Susan, Ronda. Br. mgr. Prodn. Credit Assn., Grafton, N.D., 1962-66; asst. cashier, agr. rep. First Nat. Bank of East Grand Forks (Minn.), 1966-69, asst. v.p., agr. rep., 1969-72, v.p., 1972—. Pres. Valley Assn. Retarded Citizens, 1970-73, 76-79; sec., treas. Douglas Place, East Grand Forks. Served with USMC, 1950-52. Mem. Am. Inst. Banking, Robert Morris Assos., Red River Potato Growers Assn., Minn. Forage and Grassland Council, Nat. Cattlemen's Assn. Republican. Lutheran (pres. ch. council). Clubs: Toastmasters (pres. Dist. 20 1969), Rotary, Valley Country, Mason, Elks, Am. Legion. Home: 913 James Ave SE East Grand Forks MN 56721 Office: First National Bank East Grand Forks MN 56721

LARSON, CHRIS, farmer; b. Palo Alto County, Iowa, Jan. 5, 1911; s. Peter James and Theresa Marie (Jondahl) L.; student rural schs., Palo Alto County; m. Bernette A. Draman, Sept. 23, 1942; children—Gene Richard, Genice Alice, David Allan. Engaged in farming, Emmetsburg, Iowa, 1936-80; weed commr. Palo Alto County (Iowa), 1981—; mem. Graettinger Terminal Coop., Farmers Coop. Elevator, Ruthven, Dickens Coop. Elevator. Bd. dirs. Emmetsburg Twp. Sch. Bd., 1936-42; trustee Palo Alto Meml. Hosp., Emmetsburg, 1952-62, Twp. of Emmetsburg, 1953—; mem. bishop's com. Trinty Episcopal Ch., Emmetsburg, 1948-54; mem. Agr. Stblzn. Conservation Com., 1971—; guardian recipients Aid to Dependent Children, 1967—. Mem. Farm Bur. (membership capt. 1953). Democrat. Address: Emmetsburg IA 50536

LARSON, CLINTON OLIVER, electronics co. exec.; b. Mpls., Sept. 3, 1928; s. Clinton Aldrich and Lola Alberta (Pierce) L.; grad. in bus. and electronics, Dunwoody Coll., 1948; B.S., U. Minn., 1976; m. Caroline Marie Freudenberg, Sept. 22, 1950; children—Scott Paul, Craig Allen. With Honeywell, Ind., Hopkins, Minn., 1952—, production mgr. components, 1975, mgr. advanced product engring., 1976, dir. product adminstrn. and tech., 1977, dir. production, 1978-80, v.p. operations defense systems div., 1980, v.p. underseas systems operations, 1981—. Bd. dirs. N.W. Electronics Inst. Served with USN, 1946, U.S. Army, 1950-52. Registered profl. engr., Calif. Mem. Soc. Mfg. Engrs. (chmn. certification com.), Navy League, Am. Def. Preparedness Assn. Republican. Lutheran. Clubs: Masons, Shriners. Home: 16438 Argon St NW Anoka MN 55303 Office: 600 2d St NE Hopkins MN 55343

LARSON, DEAN GORDON, sch. adminstr.; b. Kewanee, Ill., Sept. 18, 1930; s. Gust G. and Esther V. (Johnson) L.; B.S., Western Ill. U., 1952, M.S., 1954; Ed.D., Ind. U., 1970. Tchr., Southeastern Community High Sch., Industry, Ill., 1952-53, Bremen Community High Sch., Midlothian, Ill., 1953-54; placement cons., research asst. U. Ill., Urbana, 1956-58; asst. supt. Libertyville (Ill.) High Sch. Dist., 1958—; mem. Sch. Facilities Planning Council. Del., Ill. White House Conf. on Library and Info. Services, 1979; v.p. Liberty-Fremont Concert Soc., 1979—; former pres., treas. and mem. council Grace Lutheran Ch. Served with AUS, 1954-56. Cert. k-12 supr., chief bus. ofcl., ltd. high sch., Ill. Mem. Am. Assn. Sch. Adminstrs., Assn. Sch. Bus. Ofcls., Assn. Supervision and Curriculum Devel., Phi Delta Kappa. Home: 620 E Rockland Rd Libertyville IL 60048 Office: 708 W Park Ave Libertyville IL 60048

LARSON, DEBORAH ANN, ednl. adminstr.; b. Oak Park, Ill., Aug. 29, 1953; d. Earl Russell and Ruth Hermine (Hajen) L.; B.A. in Edn., Concordia Tchrs. Coll., River Forest, Ill., 1975; M.A. in Edn., Lewis U., Romeoville, Ill., 1977; Ph.D. in Adminstrn. and Supervision, Loyola U., Chgo., 1981. Tchr. emotionally disturbed and behavior disordered Ray Graham Assn. for Handicapped, Elmhurst, Ill., 1975-77, program coordinator, 1976-77, curriculum specialist, 1977-79; intern, asst. dir. spl. edn. Community Unit Sch. Dist. 200, Wheaton, Ill., 1979-80; coordinator behavior disordered and autistic programs West Suburban Assn. for Spl. Edn., Oak Park, Ill., 1980—; cons., coordinator, presenter at profl. confs., 1977—; mem. humanistic edn. com. Child Welfare Consortium, 1978—. Mem. Ill. Adminstrs. Spl. Edn., Ill. Women Adminstrs. (charter), Council for Exceptional Children, Assn. for Supervision and Curriculum Devel., Phi Delta Kappa (charter). Republican. Lutheran. Home: 636 Lakeside Dr Hinsdale IL 60521 Office: 1125 S Cuyler St Oak Park IL 60304

LARSON, DON WAYNE, editor, pub.; b. Alexandria, Minn., Aug. 6, 1929; s. Jay David and Esther Marie (Chase) L.; m. Geil Maria Bundy, Mar. 27, 1949; children—Mark, Bradley, Jill, Steven. News reporter Mankato (Minn.) Free Press, 1946-49, Fort Dodge (Iowa) Messenger, 1950-58; mng. editor Mankato Free Press, 1958-61; bus. and fin. editor St. Paul Dispatch, 1961-73; editor, pub. Corporate Report Mag., Mpls., 1973—. Home: 1074 Linwood Ave Saint Paul MN 55105 Office: 7101 York Ave S Minneapolis MN 55435

LARSON, GARY THOMAS, educator; b. Kansas City, Mo., Oct. 22, 1950; s. John Thomas and Shirley Lou (Johnston) L.; B.S.E.D., Pittsburg (Kans.) State U., 1975. Staff, Eagle Pitcher Industries, Joplin, Mo., 1970-72, McNally's, Pittsburg, 1972-74; tchr. indsl. arts Everest Middle Sch., Unified Sch. Dist. 430, Everest, Kans., 1975-79; tchr.-coordinator coop. indsl. tng., coach Concordia (Kans.) Jr.-Sr. High Sch., 1979-80; football and basketball coach United Sch. Dist. 510, Powhattan, Kans., 1980—. Mem. Am. Vocat. Assn., Kans. Edn. Assn., North Cloud Edn. Assn. Kans. Assn. V.I.C.A. Advisors, Kans. Vocat. Assn., Kans. Indsl. Edn. Assn., Am. Bowling Congress, Tri-City League. Republican. Methodist. Club: Masons, Elks. Home: 1106 Pottawatomie St Hiawatha KS 66434

LARSON, GLEN GUSTAF, test pilot; b. Rawlins, Wyo., Mar. 10, 1947; s. Raymond L. and Anna M. Eaton (Hougard) L.; B.S., U. Wyo., 1970; M.B.A., U. Utah, 1977; m. Donna Rea Farthing, Nov. 22, 1976; children—Amanda Jean, Matthew Raymond. Served in USAF, 1970-79; civilian test pilot testing fighter aircraft McDonnell Douglas Corp., St. Louis, 1979—; lectr. U. Wyo., 1976. Decorated D.F.C. with 3 oak leaf clusters, Air medal with 19 oak leaf clusters, Meritorious Service medal; named Jr. Officer of Year, George AFB, Calif., 1975. Mem. Soc. Exptl. Test Pilots, Am. Inst. Aeros. and Astronautics, Sigma Chi. Republican. Author, producer film learning program for USAF; also articles. Home: 1627 Tradd Ct Chesterfield MO 63017 Office: McDonnell Douglas Corp Box 516 Dept 290 Saint Louis MO 63166

LARSON, GREG MICHAEL, mail order furniture co. exec.; b. Milw., Jan. 23, 1950; s. Leif Gunner and Carleen Ann (Swenson) L.; B.B.A., U. Wis., Whitewater, 1972; M.B.A., U. Wis., Milw., 1981; m. Margaret Julie Papia, June 16, 1973; children—Matthew Robert, Andrew. With C & H Distbrs. Inc., Milw., 1972—, mgr. pneumatics mktg., 1976; dir. indsl. sales Bus. and Instnl. Furniture Co., Milw., 1976-81, pres., 1981—. Republican. Lutheran. Office: 611 N Broadway Milwaukee WI 53202

LARSON, JERRY L., justice Iowa Supreme Ct.; b. Harlan, Iowa, May 17, 1936; s. Gerald L. and Mary Eleanor (Patterson) L.; B.A., State U. Iowa, 1958, J.D., 1960; m. Linda R. Logan; children—Rebecca, Jeffrey, Susan, David. Admitted to Iowa bar; partner firm Larson & Larson, 1961-75; dist. judge 4th Jud. Dist. Ct. Iowa, 1975-78; justice Iowa Supreme Ct., 1978—; county atty. Shelby County (Iowa), 1965-69. Mem. Iowa State Bar Assn., Iowa Judges Assn., Am. Judicature Soc. Office: State House Des Moines IA 50319

LARSON, LESLIE GORDON, constrn. co. exec.; b. Sioux Falls, S.D., Feb. 5, 1937; s. Paul S. and Ette J. L.; B.S. in Civil Engring., S.D. Sch. Mines and Tech., 1958; m. Sue Holgate, Aug. 11, 1962; children—Keiz Marie, Kip McArthur. Resident engr. Dept. Hwys., State of S.D., Sioux Falls and Chamberlin, 1959-66; constrn. engr., estimator Dave Gustafson & Co., Inc., Sioux Falls, 1966-69; v.p. Henry H. Hackett & Sons, Rapid City, S.D., 1969—. Served with C.E., U.S. Army, 1958. Mem. Nat. Soc. Profl. Engrs., S.D. State Commn. of Engring. and Archtl. Examiners (sec. 1980-81), Asso. Gen. Contractors of S.D. (pres. 1981). Republican. Episcopalian. Home: 3103 Morning View Dr Rapid City SD 57701 Office: PO Drawer 1376 Rapid City SD 57709

LARSON, LINDA LOUISE, counselor; b. Joliet, Ill., June 13, 1941; d. George Everett and Mary Louise (Wright) Flory; L.P.N., Oak Forest Sch. Practical Nursing, 1962; B.A., Sangamon State U., 1973, M.A., 1974; m. Louis Eugene Laeson, Apr. 20, 1962; 1 son, Brian. Nurse, Silver Cross Hosp., Joliet, Ill., 1962-64; spl. follow up coordinator, psychol. testing coordinator, counselor Christian County Mental Health Assn. 1974—; asso. staff mem. St. Johns Hosp., Springfield; cons. Ill. Heart Assn., 1975-76. Mem. county council PTA, 1971; bd. dirs. ARC, 1974-76, Community Concert Assn., 1973-76. Mem. AAUW, D.A.R., Ill. Assn. Retarded Citizens, Ill. Psychol. Assn., Am. Guidance and Personnel Assn. Presbyterian.

LARSON, MAURICE ALLEN, educator; b. Missouri Valley, Iowa, July 19, 1927; s. Albert Juluis and Grace Elizabeth (Chambers) L.; B.S., Iowa State U., 1951, Ph.D., 1958; m. Ruth Elizabeth Gugeler, Dec. 5, 1953; children—Richard Alan (dec.), Janet Ann, John Albert. Chem. engr. Dow Corning Corp., Midland, Mich., 1951-54; teaching asst. Iowa State U., Ames, 1954-55, instr. dept. chem. engring., 1955-58, asst. prof., 1958-61, asso. prof., 1961-64, prof., 1964—, Anson Marston Disting. prof., 1977—, chmn. dept. chem. engring., 1978—; cons. AID, Kharagpur, India, 1968; Shell vis. prof. Univ. Coll., London, 1971-72; sci. exchange visitor, Czechoslovakia and Poland, 1974; vis. prof. U. Queensland, Brisbane, Australia, 1981. Served with AUS, 1946-47. Recipient H.A. Webber Teaching award Iowa State U., 1967, Western Electric Fund award for teaching Am.

Soc. Engring. Edn., 1970, Faculty citation Iowa State U. Alumni, 1972; NSF fellow, 1965-66. Mem. Am. Inst. Chem. Engrs. (pres. Iowa 1970-71), Am. Chem. Soc. (chmn. div. fertilizer and soil chemistry 1975), Am. Soc. Engring. Edn., Sigma Xi, Tau Beta Pi, Phi Lambda Upsilon, Phi Kappa Phi, Omega Chi Epsilon. Democrat. Methodist. Club: Lions (pres. 1979-80) (Ames). Author: (with A.D. Randolph) Theory of Particulate Processes, 1971. Contbr. to profl. jours.

LARSON, OBERT LEROY, former banker; b. Worth County, Iowa, Apr. 9, 1916; s. Lauritz Nicholi and Anna Otillie (Storre) L.; student Waldorf Jr. Coll., Forest City, Iowa, 1936; B.A., Luther Coll., Decorah, Iowa, 1939; cert. banking U. Wis., 1967; m. Mary Lou McGrath, June 4, 1944; children—Mary Lynne, John Lauritz. Bookkeeper, Peterson Oil Co., Ft. Dodge, Iowa, 1939-40; retail dealer petroleum products, Eagle Grove, Iowa, 1940-41, 46-48; partner Chevrolet/Pontiac retail dealership, Eagle Grove, 1948-54, owner, 1954-56; with Security Savs. Bank, Eagle Grove, 1956-66; exec. v.p. Farmers Trust and Savs. Bank, Williamsburg, Iowa, 1966-67, pres., 1967-81, chmn. bd., 1972-81; chmn. Iowa Bankers and Ins. Services Inc., 1972-75, dir., 1971-81. Treas., corr. Rotary Ann Home sr. citizens, 1962-66; treas. Eagle Grove Community Sch. Bd., 1958-66; v.p. Wright County (Iowa) Fair Bd., 1951-66; chmn. Iowa County Cancer Crusade, 1975-76, Iowa County Am. Heart Assn., 1977; mem. Iowa County Airport Commn., 1974—, Iowa County Quality Water Study Com., 1977—. Served with USNR, 1941-45. Decorated D.F.C., Air medal with cluster. Mem. Iowa Ind. (dir. 1974-76), Iowa, Am. Ind., Am. bankers assns., Am. Inst. Banking (charter), Eagle Grove C. of C. (pres. 1950, 58), Williamsburg C. of C. (dir. 1967-69). Republican. Lutheran. Clubs: Sport Hill Golf and Country, Rotary (pres. Eagle Grove 1960), Kiwanis. Home: 24 Oak Dr Mason City IA 50401

LARSON, OSCAR EMANUEL, JR., generating co. exec.; b. Marquette, Mich., Oct. 22, 1919; s. Oscar Emanuel and Mathilda (Kappes) L.; student pub. schs., Marquette and Negaunee, Mich.; m. Lorraine Marie Babich, Mar. 28, 1950; children—Daniel R., Gary E., Dessalee A. Farmer, logger, Negaunee, 1938-44; carpenter, builder Marquette Home Improvement Co., 1947-55; maintenance supr. Upper Peninsula Generating Co., Marquette, 1955—. Served with USN, 1944-46; PTO. Mem. Marquette Range Engrs. Profl. Orgn. Episcopalian. Home: 18 Forge Rd Negaunee MI 49866 Office: PO Box 728 Marquette MI 49855

LARSON, PAUL NORDLAND, gynecologist; b. Mpls., May 8, 1906; s. Ludwig W. and Mary (Nordland) L.; M.D., U. Minn.; m. Thelma Larsen, June 23, 1932; children—P. Robert, Kent Charles, Cindy Hinkle. Intern, Hackensack (N.J.) Gen. Hosp.; fellow Mayo Clinic, 1931-34; practice medicine specializing in obstetrics and gynecology, Edina, Minn.; originator Paul Larson Obstet. and Gynecol. Clinic, Mpls. and Edina, 1962-71, ret., 1971—; instr. emeritus U. Minn.; hon. staff N.W. Abbot, Fairview, Meth. hosps.; hon. staff St. Mary's Hosp. (Mpls.); pres. N.W. Hosp., 1961-62. Fellow A.C.S., Am. Coll. Obstetrics and Gynecology (founding); mem. Am. Soc. Obstetrics and Gynecology, Internat. Coll. Surgeons, Central States Soc. Obstetrics and Gynecology. Clubs: Minikahda (Mpls.), De Anza Country, (Borrego Springs, Calif.). Contbr. articles profl. jours. Home: 5708 S Blake Rd Edina MN 55436 Office: 6517 Drew Ave S Edina MN 55435

LARSON, ROGER T., radio sta. mgr.; b. Wausa, Nebr., Oct. 28, 1925; s. Ted Olander and Alveda Cecelia (Johnson) L.; B.S. in Bus. Adminstrn., U. Nebr., 1949; m. Shirley Laflin, June 11, 1950; children—Ted, Tom, Susan. Asst. dir. U. Nebr. Student Union, 1950-53; account exec. Sta. KFOR, Lincoln, 1953-55, sales mgr., 1955-57, asst. sta. mgr., 1957-59, gen. mgr., 1959—, also v.p.; dir. Lincoln Bank South. Trustee, vice chmn. Bryan Meml. Hosp.; bd. dirs. Lancaster chpt. ARC; trustee Nat. Arbor Day Found. Served with USAAF, 1943-47. Named Ad Man of Yr.; recipient Service of Mankind award Lincoln West Sertoma Club; named to Nebr. Broadcasters Hall of Fame. Mem. Nebr. Broadcasters Assn. (past pres.), Lincoln Advt. Club, Alpha Epsilon Rho. Methodist. Clubs: Nebr. Rebounders, Masons, Shriners, Jesters. Home: 600 S 112 St Lincoln NE 68520 Office: PO Box 80209 Lincoln NE 68501*

LARSON, WAYNE HAROLD, social services adminstr.; b. Mpls., Nov. 22, 1940; s. Harold Willard and Edith Helen (Voss) L.; B.S., U. Minn., 1962; m. Carolyn Adelle Hofstrand, Mar. 28, 1961; children—Rebecca, Katherine, David, Charles. Market analyst Maytag Co., 1962-64; sales rep. Parke-Davis & Co., 1964-66; market analyst Ansul Co., Marinette, Wis., 1966-68; dir. planning and adminstrn. Medtronic, Mpls. and Holland, 1968-72; v.p. mktg. Bio-Medicus, Mpls., 1972-74; adminstr., exec. dir. Homeward Bound, Inc., New Hope and Brooklyn Park, Minn., 1974-81; mgmt. cons., 1981—. Pres., Alice Smith Sch. PTO. Mem. Assn. Residences for Retarded in Minn. (dir.), Am. Mgmt. Assn., Assn. Advancement of Edn. for Severely and Profoundly Handicapped, Am. Assn. Mental Deficiency. Lutheran. Office: 116 E Farmdale Rd Hopkins MN 55343

LARSON, WILLIAM JOHN, safety engr.; b. Benton, Ill., Mar. 8, 1923; s. Thure Alfred and Ruth Esther (Anderson) L.; student U. Nebr., 1943-44; E.E., U. Mich. and Mich. State U., 1945; B.S.M.E., Ill. Inst. Tech., 1948; m. Ruth Virginia Cannon, Mar. 17, 1945; children—Barbara Lee Larson Biskie, John Philip. Coop. student to safety engr. Hartford Accident & Indemnity Co., 1941-43, 46-57; safety engr. Argonne (Ill.) Nat. Lab., 1957-71, safety engring. supr., 1971—, supr. fire protection and safety engr., 1972—; compliance officer Dept. of Labor, 1971; safety cons. and instr. Republican precinct committeeman, 1965-71. Served with Signal Corps, AUS, 1943-46. Cert. safety profl.; registered profl. engr. Calif. Mem. Ill. Engring. Council, Am. Soc. Safety Engrs., Indsl. Conf., Nat. Safety Council (exec. com. research and devel. sect., 4 Cameron awards). Mem. Evangelical Covenant Ch. Adv. bd. Am. Soc. Safety Engrs. Jour., 1967-75, chmn., 1972-75; contbr. numerous articles to safety jours. Home: 2212 Mayfield Ave Joliet IL 60435 Office: Argonne National Laboratory 9700 S Cass Ave Argonne IL 60439

LARSON-KURZ, CHRISTINE ANN, sociologist; b. Monroe, Wis., July 25, 1953; d. August Norman and Margaret Kathleen (McDonald) Larson; B.A. in Corrections, Morehead State U., 1975, M.A. in Sociology, 1978; m. James Arthur Kurz, July 31, 1976. Social worker, supr. Ormsby Village Treatment Center, Anchorage, Ky., 1976-77, Dept. Human Services, Louisville, 1978—; adj. lectr. Morehead (Ky.) State U., 1977, Ind. U. S.E., New Albany, 1978—. Adv. bd. Louisville Urban League. Mem. Am. Sociol. Assn., Ky. Council on Crime and Delinquency, Pi Gamma Mu, Phi Kappa Phi. Roman Catholic. Home: 202 Olive Ave New Albany IN 47150 Office: Dept Human Services 216 S 5th St Louisville KY 40203

LARSSON, DOROTHY K. (MRS. KARL G.B. LARSSON), dietitian; b. Indpls., Dec. 26, 1928; d. Ralph and Anna (Klusman) King; B.S., Purdue U., 1950; m. Karl G.B. Larsson, June 9, 1961; children—Gustav Karl, Anna Karla. Dietitian residence halls State U. Iowa, 1951-52; prodn. mgr. tearoom L.S. Ayres, Indpls., 1952-53; became food service mgr. Cin. Milacron, Inc. (formerly Cin. Milling Machine Co.), 1953, now food service dir. Named Food Service Operator of Yr., recipient Silver Plate award Internat. Food Service Mfrs. Assn., 1970; Distinguished Alumni award Purdue U., 1971. Mem. Internat. Platform Assn., Am. Dietetic Assn. (dietetic internship bd. 1964-67), Soc. Food Service Mgmt. (dir.), Am. Home Econs. Assn., Ohio, Greater Cin. (v.p. 1970, pres. 1971) restaurant assns., Nat. Indsl. Cafeteria Mgrs. Assn. (pres. 1963-64), Nat. Security Indsl. Assn. (mem. food adv. com.), YWCA (Tribute to Women in Internat. Industry award 1981), Boy Scouts Am., Purdue Alumni Assn. Methodist. Club: Zonta (v.p. Cin. 1966-67). Home: 2954 Observatory Ave Cincinnati OH 45208 Office: 4701 Marburg Ave Cincinnati OH 45209

LARUE, JAMES PARKER, educator; b. Mission, Tex., Mar. 27, 1922; s. James Frank and Jessie Marie (Backer) LaR.; B.S., S.E. Mo. State U., 1947; M.A., U. No. Colo., 1952; Ed.D., Pa. State U., 1968; m. Nancy Lilian Ashton, Jan. 20, 1945; children—Linda Lee LaRue Johanningmeier, David Alan, Richard James, Kathryn Renee LaRue Gronberg. Tchr., Monett (Mo.) Jr.-Sr. High Sch./Jr. Coll., 1947-52, Perry (Iowa) Jr.-Sr. High Sch., 1952-55; faculty U. No. Iowa, Cedar Falls, 1956—, prof. indsl. tech., 1971—; cons. in field. Elder, 1st. Presbyn. Ch., Cedar Falls, 1956—. Served with A.C., USNR, 1943-45. Mem. AAUP, Am. Council for Indsl. Arts Tchrs. Edn., Am. Foundrymen's Soc. (chmn. 1978-79), Am. Indsl. Arts Assn., Iowa Higher Edn. Assn., Iowa Indsl. Edn. Assn. (recognition chmn. 1973—), Nat. Assn. Indsl. and Tech. Tchr. Educators, NEA, Waterloo Tech. Soc. (pres. 1976-77), Iowa Lambda Sigma, Phi Delta Kappa (pres. 1966-67). Club: Faculty Men's (pres. 1972-73). Home: 1015 Floral Ct Cedar Falls IA 50613

LA RUSSA, ANTHONY (TONY), profl. baseball mgr., lawyer; b. Tampa, Fla., Oct. 4, 1944; s. Tony and Oliva (Cuervo) La R.; B.A., U. South Fla., 1969; J.D. with honors, Fla. State U., 1978; m. Elaine Coker, Dec. 31, 1973; 1 dau., Bianca Tai. Profl. baseball player with Oakland A's, Atlanta Braves, Chgo. Cubs, Pitts. Pirates, St. Louis Cardinals, Chgo. White Sox, 1962-77; field mgr. White Sox AA minor league team, Knoxville, Tenn., 1978, AAA minor league team, Des Moines, 1979; 1st base coach Chgo. White Sox, 1978, mgr., 1979—; admitted to Fla. bar, 1980; asso. firm Conley & Dooley, Sarasota, Fla., 1981—. Democrat. Roman Catholic. Office: Comiskey Park Dan Ryan Expressway at 35th St Chicago IL 60616

LASEE, ALAN J., state senator, farmer; b. Rockland, Wis., July 30, 1937; grad. high sch.; married. Farmer, DePere, Wis.; 4-H leader, Brown County; mem. fiscal control bd. Sch. Dist., 1973—; town chmn. DePere, 1973—, town supr., 1971-73; mem. Wis. Assembly, 1974-77; mem. Wis. Senate, 1977—, chairperson minority caucus, mem. govtl. and vets. affairs com., others. Mem. Wis. Towns Assn., Farm Bur. (dir.). Club: Lions. Office: Room 419 SW State Capitol Madison WI 53702*

LASER, CHARLES, JR., cons. firm exec.; b. Redford Twp., Mich., July 8, 1933; s. J.C. and Gertrude L.; student Mich. Tech. U., 1952-54, Central Mich. U., 1959-60; m. Glenda Johnson, Sept. 30, 1972; 1 dau., Susan Faye. With Retail Credit Co., 1958-60; exec. dir. Saginaw County Republican Party, 1960-65; exec. dir. Republican Party of D.C., 1967; fin. dir. San Joaquin Republican Party, Stockton, Calif., 1968; owner Laser Advt., Bay City, Mich., 1969-75; exec. v.p. Vindell Petroleum, Inc., Midland, Mich., 1972-75, Geo Spectra Corp., Ann Arbor, Mich., 1977—; pres. Laser Exploration Inc., Grand Blanc, Mich., Am. Tech. Explorations, Grand Blanc. Chmn. Genesee County Republican Com., 1981-82. Served with U.S. Army, 1954-58. Mem. Mich. Diland Gas Assn. Clubs: Rotary, Elks. Office: 320 N Main Suite 301 Ann Arbor MI 48104

LASHBROOK, VELMA JANET, ednl. researcher; b. Pipestone, Minn., May 26, 1948; d. August Jacob and Lorita Belle (Swift) Wenzlaff; B.S., Iowa State U., 1970; M.S., Ill. State U., 1971; Ed.D., W.Va. U., 1976; m. William Bradshaw Lashbrook, Sept. 4, 1971; 1 dau., Nicole Maurine. Tchr., Woodruff High Sch., Peoria, Ill., 1971-73; asst. speech prof. W.Va. U., Morgantown, 1973-77; asst. prof. mktg. Auburn (Ala.) U., 1978-79; dir. research Wilson Learning Corp., Eden Prairie, Minn., 1979—; research cons., Auburn, 1977-79. Am. Forensic Assn. grantee, 1971. Mem. Internat. Communication Assn., Western Speech Communication Assn., Am. Ednl. Research Assn., Acad. Mgmt., Am. Mktg. Assn., Nat. Council Measurement in Edn., Am. Soc. Tng. and Devel., Phi Kappa Phi, Kappa Delta Pi, Chi Omicron Mu, Delta Sigma Rho-Tau Kappa Alpha. Contbr. articles to profl. jours. Home: 9566 Woodridge Dr Eden Prairie MN 55344 Office: 6950 Washington Ave S Eden Prairie MN 55344

LASHER, ESTHER LU (MRS. DONALD T. LASHER), librarian; b. Denver, June 1, 1923; d. Lindley Aubrey and Irma Jane (Rust) Pim; A.A. in Fine Arts, Colo. Women's Coll., 1943; B.A., Denver U., 1945, M.A., 1967; M.R.E., Eastern Bapt. Sem., 1948; m. Donald T. Lasher, Apr. 8, 1950; children—Patricia Sue, Donald Aubrey, Keith Alan, Jennifer Luanne. Tchr. pub. schs., Denver, 1945-46; dir. Christian edn. First Bapt. Ch., Evansville, Ind., 1948-50; asst. circulation librarian Evansville (Ind.) Pub. Library, 1950-51; tchr. music Dubois (Ind.) County Schs., 1951-52; br. librarian Jefferson County (Colo.) Pub. Library, 1962-64; acting head, reference librarian Colorado Springs Pub. Library, 1964-67; high sch. librarian Colorado Springs Dist. 2, 1967-68; head music library Butler U., Indpls., 1968-72; cataloger gen. collection Ind. State Library, 1972-77; asst. dir./reference librarian Greenwood (Ind.) Pub. Library, 1977—. Leader Hoosier Indpls. council Girl Scouts U.S.A., 1972-73; leader 4-H, Perry County, Ind., 1951-53, Denver, 1956-60; block chmn. Neighborhood Improvement Orgn., 1971-72; mem. Neighborhood Republican Com., 1970-72. Mem. Music Library Assn., Internat. Music Library Assn., Ind. Library Assn., Ind. State Library Staff Assn. (pres. 1976-77), Christian Library Assn., Internat. Platform Assn., Indpls. Mus. Art, Sigma Alpha Iota (adviser 1969-72), Phi Sigma Iota. Baptist (tchr. Sunday sch. 1968-72, 79—, supt. primary dept. 1979-80; mem. Christian edn. bd. 1969-72, Christian edn. coordinator, 1977—), Ch. and Synagogue Library Assn. Clubs: Greenwood Bus. and Profl. Women's (sec. 1979-80, pres. 1980—), Order Eastern Star. Home: 7819 S Oak Dr Indianapolis IN 46227 Office: Greenwood Pub Library 310 S Meridian St Greenwood IN 46142

LASHLEY, SYLVAN ALPHONSO, educator; b. Barbados, W.I., Jan. 3, 1952; came to U.S., 1972; s. Clarence Alexander and Veronica Gloria (Lewis) L.; B.Ed., W.I. Coll., 1972; M.A., Andrews U., 1974, Ed.D., 1981; m. Rosita Erlinda Young, June 12, 1977; 1 son, Sylvean D'nece. Prin., W.I. Coll. High Sch., Mandeville, Jamaica, 1974-77; instr. dept. edn. and history W.I. Coll., Mandeville, 1974-77; instr. Berrien Opportunities Industrialization Center, Berrien Springs, Mich., 1977-78, dep. dir., 1978-80; mem. faculty, human relations council Andrews U., Berrien Springs, 1980—, mem. master planning com., 1978-79; chmn. Humanities div. W.I. Coll., Mandeville, 1980—; ednl. cons. Sylvean Assos., Berrien Springs, 1980—; acting dean students W.I. Coll., Mandeville, Jamaica, 1981—. Mem. Assn. of Adventist Historians, Assn. Adventist Educators, Am. Ednl. Research Assn., Assn. for Supervision and Curriculum Devel., Phi Delta Kappa. Seventh-day Adventist. Contbr. articles to profl. jours. Home: Garland A 10 Berrien Springs MI 49103 Office: Dept Edn Andrews U Berrien Springs MI 49103

LASKOWSKI, LEONARD FRANCIS, JR., microbiologist, educator; b. Milw., Nov. 16, 1919; s. Leonard Francis and Frances (Cyborowski) L.; B.S., Marquette U., 1941, M.S., 1948; Ph.D., St. Louis U., 1951; m. Frances Bielinski, June 1, 1946; children—Leonard Francis III, James, Thomas. Instr. bacteriology Marquette U., 1946-48; grad. fellow St. Louis U., 1948-51, instr. bacteriology, 1951-53, sr. instr., 1953-54, asst. prof. microbiology, 1954-57, asst. prof. pathology, 1957-61, asso. prof. pathology, 1961-69, prof. pathology, 1969—, asso. prof. internal medicine, 1977—; dir. clin. microbiology sect. St. Louis U. Hosps. Labs., 1965—. Cons. clin. microbiology Firmin Desloge Hosp., St. Louis U. Group Hosps., St. Marys Group Hosps.; cons. bacteriology VA Hosp., Asst. dept. chief Pub. Health Lab., St. Louis Civil Def., 1958—; cons. St. Elizebeth's Hosp., St. Louis County Hosp. Health and tech. tng. coordinator for Latin Am. Peace Corps projects, 1962-66. Served with M.C., AUS, 1942-46. Diplomate Am. Bd. Microbiology. Fellow Am. Acad. Microbiology; mem. Soc. Am. Bacteriologists, N.Y. Acad. Scis., Am., Mo. pub. health assns., Am. Assn. U. Profs., Med. Mycol. Soc. Am., Alpha Omega Alpha. Contbr. articles in field to profl. jours. Home: Route 2 Box 440 Villa Ridge MO 63089 Office: 1402 S Grand Blvd St Louis MO 63104

LASSERS, WILLARD J., judge; b. Kankakee, Ill., Aug. 24, 1919; s. Henry and Sylvia (Oppenheim) L.; A.B., U. Chgo., 1940, J.D., 1942; m. Elisabeth Stern, June 30, 1946; 1 dau., Kippi. Admitted to D.C., bar, 1941, Ill. bar, 1942, U.S. Supreme Ct. bar, 1965; individual practice law, Chgo., 1946; practice with Alex Elson, Chgo., 1946-48, Elson and Cotton, 1948-49; atty. RFC. Chgo., 1950-51; atty. Office Price Stablzn., Chgo., 1951-53; individual practice law, Chgo., 1953-60; partner Elson, Lassers and Wolff, Chgo., 1960-78; judge Circuit Ct. of Cook County, 1978—; lectr. taxation U. Chgo., 1954-55. Mem. Gov.'s Com. to Study Consumer Credit Laws, 1962-63; chmn. Com. Ill. Govt., 1962-63. Bd. dirs. Ill. ACLU, 1965-78. Served with AUS, 1943-46. Mem. Ill., Chgo. bar assns., Am. Arbitration Assn. (mem. panel labor arbitrators 1965-78). Author: (with Alex Elson and Aaron S. Wolff) Civil Practice Forms Annotated, Illinois and Federal, 1952, 65; Scapegoat Justice: Lloyd Miller and the Failure of the Legal System, 1973. Home: 1509 E 56th St Chicago IL 60637 Office: Daley Center Chicago IL 60602

LASSWELL, TULL CRESS, inventor, chem. co. exec.; b. Springfield, Ill., May 21, 1925; s. Tull Cress and Mary Anne (Selleck) L.; student Northwestern U., 1951; m. Nancy Lee Wheeler, July 22, 1951; children—Tull Wheeler, Marsh Wheeler, Cam Wheeler, Star. Field sales engr. Fansteel Metall. Corp., 1951-53; dist. mgr. Spiegel, Inc., Chgo., 1953-56; prodn. supr. Pillsbury Mills, Springfield, Ill., 1956-58; corp. mgr. Am. Waterlock Corp., Mich., 1958-60; pres. Tri-X Corp., Oxford, Mich., 1960—. Served with Submarine Service USN, 1941-45. Mem. Internat. Brotherhood Magicians, Phi Delta Theta. Patentee in field. Home: 626 Oxford Oaks Ct Oxford MI 48051 Office: 544 Lakeville Rd Oxford MI 48051

LASTORIA, MICHAEL DONALD, coll. dean; b. Cleve., Sept. 21, 1948; s. Michael Angelo and Theresa Marie (Tirabasso) L.; B.S., Rutgers U., 1970; M.S., U. Nebr., Omaha, 1974; certificate, Grace Coll. of Bible, Omaha, 1975; postgrad. Loyola U., Chgo., 1976—; m. Cynthia Shelley Bertram, Aug. 25, 1972. Grad. asst. U. Nebr., Omaha, 1974; head resident adviser Moody Bible Inst., Chgo., 1975-77, asst. dean students, 1977—. Mem. Am. Personnel and Guidance Assn., Am. Coll. Personnel Assn. Home: 538 Germaine St Elk Grove Village IL 60007 Office: 820 N LaSalle Chicago IL 60610

LATHAM, IRIS ANNE, radio broadcaster; b. Coshocton, Ohio, Aug. 14, 1925; d. Raymond Walker and Effie Mae (Bodenheimer) Latham; grad. high sch. Continuity mgr. WGL radio, Fort Wayne, Ind., 1951-54; traffic dir. WHIZ radio, Zanesville, Ohio, 1954-57; women's dir. WANE radio, Fort Wayne, 1957-64; writer, host interview show, producer WGL radio, Fort Wayne, 1964—. Adviser, Social League Interested Women, 1969, Young Republicans Club, 1967-70, YWCA, 1968—; chmn. Judges City Council Internships, 1972; hostess Ind. U. European Tour, 1971. Bd. dirs. March of Dimes Allen County; judge Sr. Citizens Talent Contest, 1979. Recipient George Washington Honor medal Freedoms Found., 1969; Merit citations Mayor Fort Wayne, 1969-71; Sterling Cup award Sterling Mags., 1974; award Am. Bicentennial Research Inst., 1976; named Notable Woman Broadcaster Family Circle, 1969. Mem. Zonta Internat. (treas., 1971-72), Fort Wayne Press Club. Republican. Baptist. Author, producer, host radio series: They Came to America, The Woman Alcoholic, Europeans Today, Black Legacies, Marriage Today. Home: 4417 Alverado Dr Fort Wayne IN 46816 Office: 2000 Lower Huntington Rd Fort Wayne IN 46809

LATHAM, ROBERT ALLEN, veterinarian; b. Milton Junction, Wis., Nov. 20, 1922; s. Robert Allen and Lillian Gertrude (Schmidt) L.; B.S., U. Ill., 1950, D.V.M., 1952; m. LaVonne Marlys Hilmer, July 21, 1979; children—Robert Allen, Timothy John, Benjamin Walter, Katherine Diana. Gen. practice veterinary medicine, Carmi, Ill., 1952, Mt. Carroll, Ill., 1952-55, Erie, Ill., 1955—. Trustee Erie Library Dist., 1970-76; mem. Erie Elementary Sch. Bd., 1963-66. Served with USNR, 1942-46. Recipient Merit award Coll. Vet. Medicine, U. Ill. Alumni Assn., 1980. Fellow Ill. Acad. Veterinary Medicine (pres. 1971); mem. Am., Ill. State (pres. 1976), Mississippi Valley (pres. 1964) veterinary med. assns., Republican. Mem. Christian Ch. (Disciples of Christ). Club: Lions. Editor Ill. State Veterinary Med. Assn. Directory of 1977, 79. Home: 1002 6th St Erie IL 61250 Office: 810 Main St Erie IL 61250

LATHAN, SARA J. WALKER, govt. ofcl.; b. Marion, Ala., June 29, 1947; d. Jefferson Eugene, Jr. and Georgia M. (Sampson) Walker; B.S., U. D.C., 1972; postgrad. George Washington U., 1974, Lake Forest Coll., 1979; m. Leroy Lathan, Jr., July 26, 1967; 1 son, Leroy III. Employee devel. specialist Walter Reed Army Med. Center, 1973-75; tng. officer U.S. Army Recruiting Command, 1975-76; asso. dir. Supervisory Communications and Office Workforce Tng., Chgo., 1976-79, acting dir., 1979—; pres. Lathan Ltd., cons., 1978—; lectr. Chgo. Archtl. Found. Recipient cert. achievement CSC, 1977. Mem. Nat. Assn. Media Women, Chgo. Econ. Devel. Corp., Am. Soc. Tng. and Devel., Delta Sigma Theta, Phi Beta Lambda. Methodist. Home: 770 Western Ave Lake Forest IL 60045 Office: 230 S Dearborn St Chicago IL 60604

LATIMER, GEORGE, mayor; b. Poughkeepsie, N.Y., June 20, 1935; s. William Wilbur and Dorothy L.; B.S. cum laude, St. Michael's Coll., 1958; LL.B., Columbia U., 1963; m. Nancy Moore Latimer, June 20, 1959; children—Faith, George, Phillip, Kate, Tom. Practice law, St. Paul, 1963-76; mayor, St. Paul, 1976—. Chmn. Rep. Joseph Karth's campaign, 1972, 74; mem. St. Paul Sch. Bd., from 1970; regent U. Minn., 1975-76; bd. dirs. Minn. Opera Co.; bd. dirs. Minn. Orchestral Assn.; bd. trustees Guthrie Theatre. Democrat. Roman Catholic. Office: 347 City Hall Saint Paul MN 55102*

LATONDRESS, HAZEL JANET, nurse; b. Pawnee City, Nebr., Aug. 1, 1927; d. Theodore J. and Helen Mary (Martin) Schmit; R.N., Kansas City (Mo.) Gen. Hosp., 1947; B.S., Western Mich. U., 1980; m. Francis Henry Latondress, June 25, 1953; children—Nancy Ann, David Alan. Staff nurse, then head nurse Kansas City (Mo.) Gen. Hosp., 1947-49; office, pvt. duty nurse, emergency polio nurse, Kalamazoo, 1949-50; mem. nursing staff Bronson Methodist Hosp., Kalamazoo, 1950—, house supr., asst. dir., 1950-69, adminstrv. asst. patient care, 1969-71, dir. nursing services, 1971—; adv. bd.

Kalamazoo Valley Community Coll., 1976-79, Nazareth (Mich.) Coll., 1978-79. Mem. Am. Nursing Assn., Am. Soc. Hosp. Nursing, Council Nursing Educators and Nursing Adminstrs. (treas. 1978—), Mich. Nursing Assn., Mich. Nurses Assn., Kalamazoo Dist. Nurses Assn. (dir. 1981—), Southwestern Mich. Dirs. Nursing Service Council (pres.-elect 1980-81, pres. 1981—), Mich. Soc. Nurse Adminstrs., Mich. League for Nursing, Nat. League for Nursing, Council Continuing Patient Care, Council Nursing Mgmt., Council Practicing Nurses. Methodist. Club: Toastmasters (sec. 1979-80). Address: 5107 Maple Ridge Dr Kalamazoo MI 49008

LATSHAW, PATRICIA HERGET, county ofcl.; b. Lakewood, Ohio, Oct. 4, 1930; d. Walter Clyde and Helen Naomi (Jones) Herget; B.A., Principia Coll., 1951; M.A., U. Chgo., 1952; Ph.D., State U. Iowa, 1957; m. George Tarrant Latshaw, May 24, 1958; children—Christopher Herget, Michael Kevin. Instr. English, U. Nebr., 1953-55; instr. communications skills U. Iowa, 1955-57; staff writer Ill. Bell Telephone Co., Chgo., 1957-58; dir. public relations Cleve. Area YWCA, 1958-59, Ursuline Coll., Pepper Pike Ohio, 1970-73; dir. communications Univ. Services Inst., Cleve., 1973-74; dir. community relations Akron (Ohio)-Summit County Public Library System, 1974—; adj. prof. Union Grad. Sch., Yellow Springs, Ohio, 1973—. Democratic ward committeewoman, mem. Summit County Dem. Central Com., 1970-74; mem. Christian edn. dept. Episcopal Diocese Ohio, 1968-74, mem. div. ministry of laity com., 1978-79. Mem. Public Relations Soc. Am., Women in Communications, Ohio Library Assn. Club: Akron Press. Ghost writer books, articles. Home: 8005 Swallow Dr Macedonia OH 44056 Office: 55 S Main St Akron OH 44326

LATTA, DELBERT L., congressman; b. Weston, Ohio, Mar. 5, 1920; A.M., LL.B., Ohio No. U.; m. Rose Mary Kiene; children—Rose Ellen, Robert Edward. Admitted to Ohio bar, 1944; state senator, Ohio, 3 terms; mem. 86th to 97th Congresses, 5th Ohio Dist. Republican. Home: Bowling Green OH 43402 Office: 2309 Rayburn House Office Bldg Washington DC 20515*

LATTA, THOMAS JAMES, real estate co. exec.; b. Independence, Mo., Nov. 1, 1948; s. James Nelson and Emily Marie (Rheaume) L.; student Donnelly Coll., 1966-69; B.A., U. Mo., Kansas City, 1972; grad. Realtors Inst.; m. Loretta Karen Latta, May 29, 1969; children—Jeffrey Thomas, Andrew Justin, Corey Douglas. Lab. technologist Bendix Corp., Kansas City, Mo., 1968-73; asst. service mgr. Courtesy Ford Co., Lees Summit, Mo., 1973-74; sales asso., Sisson Realtors Blue Springs (Mo.), 1974-75; pres. Sunburst Real Estate Corp., Blue Springs, 1976—. Alderman ward III, City of Blue Springs, 1977-79; planning commr. City of Blue Springs, 1977-79; pres. Eastern Jackson County Bd. Realtors, 1981—. Mem. Blue Springs Jaycees (dir. 1977-78), Nat. Assn. Realtors, Mo. Assn. Realtors (dir.), Mo. Municipal League. Methodist. Clubs: Blue Springs Ski (founder), Blue Sky Investment (founder). Home: 1108 S 44th St Dr Blue Springs MO 64015 Office: 730 N 7 Hwy Blue Springs MO 64015

LAUBACH, JOHN PAUL, food co. exec.; b. Benton, Pa., Mar. 9, 1928; s. Jonathan Paul and Ethel Irene (Bray) L.; B.S., U.S. Naval Acad., 1951; m. Bobbie Lynn Gale, Nov. 5, 1966; children—Sharon, Jonathan. Constrn. exec. J. Paul Laubach Contracting Co., Benton, Pa., 1956-60; mem. tech. and mktg. staff IBM, Phila., White Plains, N.Y., 1961-67; data processing exec. Kraft Foods Co. and Kraftco., N.Y.C., Chgo., 1968-71; dir. info. services Kitchens of Sara Lee div. Consol. Foods Co., Deerfield, Ill., 1972-76; corp. dir. bus. systems Consol. Foods Corp., Chgo., 1976-78; v.p. info. services Scot Lad Foods, Inc., Lansing, Ill., 1978-81; v.p. mgmt. info. services Hollister Inc., Libertyville, Ill., 1981—. Pres., Homeowners Assn.; mem. Northbrook Caucus. Served with USN, 1951-56. Mem. ASCE, IEEE, Soc. for Mgmt. Info. Systems. Clubs: Army-Navy Country Club (Alexandria, Va.), Masons, Consistory, Shriners. Home: 3800 Charles Dr Northbrook IL 60062 Office: 1 Scot Lad Ln Lansing IL 60438

LAUBER, PETER HERMANN, marriage and family counselor; b. Glen Cove, N.Y., Feb. 26, 1944; s. Hermann and Emma Katherine (Hill) L.; A.B., Wheaton Coll., 1966; M.S.W., Wayne State U., 1968, Ph.D., 1975; m. Cheryl Anne Pump, Jan. 30, 1965; children—Deborah Susan, Steven Mark. Psychiat. social worker VA Hosp., Allen Park, Mich., 1968-73; sch. social worker, Wayne, Mich., 1973-75; prof. social sci. John Wesley Coll., 1975-79; pvt. practice social work and marriage counseling, Owosso, Mich., 1975—; psychotherapist; part-time instr. Marygrove Coll., 1974-75; field instr. U. Mich. Sch. Social Work, 1972-75. Mem. Nat. Assn. Christians in Social Work (pres. 1977-80), Nat. Assn. Social Workers, Am. Assn. Marriage and Family Therapy, Council Social Work Edn. Home: 1327 Summit St Owosso MI 48867 Office: 1060 E Main St Owosso MI 48867

LAUDA, DONALD PAUL, univ. dean; b. Leigh, Nebr., Aug. 7, 1937; s. Joe and Libbie L.; B.S., Wayne State Coll., Detroit, 1963, M.S., 1964; Ph.D., Iowa State U., 1966; m. Sheila H. Henderson, Dec. 28, 1966; children—Daren M., Tanya R. Asso. dir. Communications Center, U. Hawaii, 1966-67; asso. prof. indsl. arts St. Cloud (Minn.) State Coll., 1967-69; asst. dean Ind. State U., 1970-73; chmn. tech. edn. W.Va. U., 1973-75; dean Sch. Tech., Eastern Ill. U., Charleston, 1975—; cons. in field. Chmn., Charleston 2000, 1977—. Served with USAR, 1957-59. EPDA research fellow, 1969-70; Eastern Ill. U. Faculty research grantee, 1971. Mem. Am. Council Indsl. Arts Tchr. Edn. (Tchr. of Year award 1978, v.p.), World Future Soc., Am. Indsl. Arts Assn., Am. Vocat. Assn., Phi Delta Kappa, Epsilon Pi Tau. Author: Advancing Technology: Its Impact on Society, 1971; Technology, Change and Society, 1978; also chpts. in books, articles. Office: AAE 101 Eastern Ill Univ Charleston IL 61920

LAUDAN, JAMES ALVA, ins. co. exec.; b. Taylor, Tex., Dec. 18, 1915; s. James Verbon and Della Pearl (Barton) L.; B.B.A., U. Tex., 1939; m. Florence Claire Shannon, Sept. 22, 1940; children—Larry L., Kenneth R., Marilyn L. (Mrs. Arthur J. Frankel); m. 2d, Catherine Robbins Hamilton, May 15, 1977. Exec. v.p. Ins. Facilities Corp., Kansas City, Mo., 1957-59; asst. v.p. Holland-Am. Ins. Co., Kansas City, Mo., 1957-59; pres., chmn., Spl. Risks Underwriters Agy., Inc., Kansas City, Mo., 1959-67; exec. v.p., chmn. KLM Investment Corp., Kansas City, Mo., 1964-68; pres., chmn. Al Laudan & Co., Kansas City, Mo., 1964-67; br. mgr. Ranger Ins. Co., Kansas City, Mo., 1967-78; treas., dir. FSL Services, Inc., publishers, Overland Park, Kans., 1973-75; v.p. Am. Continental Ins. Co., 1978—; dir. Ranger Nat. Life Ins. Co., Houston, 1974-78. Vice pres., dir. Hill and Dale Montessori Sch., Overland Park, Kans., 1965-73. Coordinator, Johnson-Wyandotte Counties (Kans.) candidate Kans. ins. commr. Republican party, 1970, 72; precinct committeeman Shawnee Mission Rep. Com., 1978—; bd. dirs., sec. Kansas City chpt. City of Hope, 1965-67; mem. Greater Kansas City council People to People. Served with USNR, 1944-46. Recipient Distinguished Service award Kans. Assn. Ind. Ins. Agents, 1972. Mem. Kans. Assn. Commerce and Industry (mem. pub. affairs council 1973—), Am. Legion. Clubs: Red Coater; Kansas City Chiefs Football, Friends of Art, Masons, Elks. Home: PO Box 4311 Shawnee Mission KS 66204 Office: PO Box 19177 Kansas City MO 64141

LAUDE, RAYMOND JOSEPH, securities corp. exec.; b. Anchorville, Mich., Nov. 1, 1903; s. Edward T. and Mary (Neibeur) L.; student U. Detroit, 1920-22; m. Carol J. Henderson, July 2, 1968. Securities broker 1st of Mich. Corp., Troy, 1973—. Trustee, Alma Coll., 1955-73, emeritus, 1973—; treas. Ferndale-Pleasant Ridge Sch. Dist., 1952. Mem. Nat. Assn. Investors Brokers (past pres.), Security Traders. Republican. Presbyterian. Clubs: Bond of Detroit, Detroit Athletic, Masons; Fort Hill of Boston. Home: 5911 Orchard Bend Birmingham MI 48010 Office: 1st Mich Corp 2401 W Big Beaver St Troy MI 48084

LAUDERBACK, CLARA GERALDINE, mktg. research co. exec.; b. Cin., Apr. 7, 1917; d. Harold Thomas and Elsie Marion (Quantz) Reed; student U. Cin., 1936-38, Sin Clair Coll., 1973-74; m. Robert Donald Lauderback, Aug. 22, 1936; children—Linda Lee, Sandra Clara. Interviewer, Burke Mktg. Research Co., Dayton, Ohio, 1956-58, traveling tng. supr., 1958-64; librarian Standard Register, Dayton, 1965-69; founder, owner, operator Shiloh Research Assos. Inc., Dayton, 1970—; cons. market research Goodwill Agy., Dayton. Mem. Am. Mktg. Assn., Mktg. Research Assn., Shiloh Civic Assn. Republican. Episcopalian. Clubs: Order Eastern Star, Van-Kauvenhouven-Conover Family Assn. Home: 473 Shiloh Dr Dayton OH 45415 Office: 4215 N Main St Suite 208-210 Dayton OH 45405

LAUDICINA, PAUL FRANK, radiol. technologist; b. Chgo., Nov. 4, 1942; s. Frank P. and Ann M. (Alagna) L.; A.A., Triton Coll. of DuPage, 1973; B.A., Northeastern Ill. U., 1974, M.A. in Counselor Edn., 1977; m. Rita Lenore Lewandowski, May 21, 1966; children—Anthony, Michael. Clin. instr. dept. radiol. scis. Coll. Du Page, Glen Ellyn, Ill., 1972—, program dir./coordinator radiol. tech. program, 1977—. Active Boy Scouts Am. Served with USN, 1963-66. Mem. Am. Soc. Radiol. Technologists (edn. com. 1977-79), Ill. Soc. Radiol. Technologists (pres., dir., chmn. bd. 1976-79), Am. Registry Radiol. Technologists, Am. Personnel and Guidance Assn. Roman Catholic. Textbook cons. to pubs. of radiol. tech. textbooks; contbr. articles to profl. jours. Home: 7750 W Victoria St Chicago IL 60631 Office: Coll Du Page Glen Ellen IL 60137

LAUDICK, RICHARD EDWARD, JR., newspaper publisher; b. Ottawa, Ohio, Jan. 11, 1929; s. Richard E. and Edna C. (Gulker) L.; student Bowling Green State U., 1947-48; m. Jeanette Schmitz, Oct. 7, 1950; children—Deborah Laudick Birkemeier, Jeanne Laudick Verhoff, Kevin, Joseph, Annette. Pres., pub., editor, mgr. Putnam County (Ohio) Sentinel, Ottawa, 1974—. Pres., Putnam County Tb Health Assn., 1970-72; pres. Western Ohio Respiratory Health Assn. (now Western Ohio Lung Assn.), 1974-75, United Way of Putnam County, 1979, 80; chmn. bd. Putnam County (Ohio) Mental Health Clinic, 1974-75; mem. Ottawa Downtown Devel. Com. Mem. Ottawa C. of C. (pres. 1975). Home: 528 E 3rd St Ottawa OH 45875 Office: Box 149 Ottawa OH 45875

LAUER, HAROLD EUGENE, orthodontist; b. Waldo, Ohio, Aug. 17, 1919; s. Herbert Albert and Cloa Melinda (Lehner) L.; B.S., Ohio State U., 1941, D.D.S., 1950, postgrad., 1950-51; m. Ann Riley Nunley, 1975; children by previous marriage—H. Andrew, John Arthur, T. Herbert, Annette; stepchildren—Patricia Nunley, Julia Nunley. Gen. practice dentistry, Columbus, Ohio, 1950-51, practice dentistry specializing in orthodontics, Lima, Ohio, 1952—. Sec., H.L.P. Corp., 1957; dir. Drs. Lauer, Webb, Fowler & McFarland, Inc. Clinician, lectr. Western European Orthodontic Congress, Paris, France, 1964. Pres., Allen County Tb and Health Assn., Lima, 1956-57, Ohio State U. Orthodontic Found., 1965. Bd. dirs. Meml. Hosp. Staff. Served with F.A., AUS, 1941-46. Decorated Bronze Star. Mem. Am., Ohio, Northwestern Ohio dental assns., Am. Assn. Orthodontics, Ohio State Orthodontic Found., Lima Acad. Dentistry, Gt. Lakes Orthodontic Assn., Allen County, Ohio State Univ. Alumni Assn. (past pres.). Lutheran (chmn. devel. and property com.). Elk, Rotarian. Club: Torch (pres. Lima 1966-67). Home: 2614 Shoreline Dr Lima OH 45805 Office: 939 W Market St Lima OH 45805

LAUER, PETER HANS, employment co. exec.; b. Hamburg, Germany, May 28, 1918; s. Paul and Mathilde Lauer; came to U.S., 1938, naturalized, 1941; M.B.A., U. Chgo., 1956; m. Therese A. Paleczny; children—Steven K., Linda Lauer Deardorff. Controller, Warwick Mfg. Co., Chgo., 1955-56; controller, treas. Flexonics Corp., Chgo., 1956-61; v.p. Interstate United Co., Chgo., 1961-65; v.p. adminstrn. Dietzgen Co., Chgo., 1965-69; v.p. Cousins & Preble Co., Chgo., 1969-70; pres. Lauer, Sbarbaro Assos., Inc., Chgo., 1970—; instr. Grad. Sch. Bus. DePaul U., 1968-74, U. Chgo., 1956-59. Bd. dirs. Stein Health Services, Milw. Mem. Am. Inst. C.P.A.'s, Ill. Soc. C.P.A.'s, Fin. Execs. Inst., Am. Mgmt. Assn., Assn. Exec. Recruiting Cons., Chgo. Presidents Assn. Club: Union League (Chgo.). Home: 505 N Lake Shore Dr Chicago IL 60611 Office: 1 N LaSalle St Chicago IL 60602

LAUFENBURGER, ROGER ALLYN, former state senator Minn.; b. Winona, Minn., Sept. 5, 1921; s. Ray Morse and Rose Marie (Hoppe) L.; grad. high sch.; m. Selma Nesbit, Mar. 25, 1947; children—Carolyn (Mrs. Douglas Trainor), Bruce, Kay (Mrs. Paul Doran), Dawn. Owner-operator Laufenburger Ins. Agy., Lewiston, Minn., 1947—; mem. City Council, Lewiston, 1956-62; mem. Minn. Senate, 1962-80, chmn. Transp. Com., 1971-80, Employment and Econ. Devel. Com., 1977-80, ret., 1980. Bd. dirs. Minn. Safety Council. Named Lewiston Outstanding citizen, 1971; recipient Service to Motoring award Minn. unit Am. Automobile Assn., 1976. Democrat. Presbyn. (bd. elders 1958-64). Mason (Shriner), Elk, Lion, Eagle, Redmen. Home: 335 Main St Lewiston MN 55952

LAUGHLIN, ETHELREDA ELIZABETH ROSS, educator; b. Cleve., Nov. 13, 1922; d. Edward W. and Marie C. (Solinski) Ross; A.B., Flora Stone Mather Coll., 1942; M.S., Western Res. U., 1944, Ph.D., 1962; m. J. J. Laughlin, June 14, 1951 (div. June 1956); 1 son, J. Guy. Faculty Loyola U., Chgo., 1948-49, St. John Coll., Cleve., 1949-51, tchr. various schs., 1953-61; faculty Ferris State Coll., 1962-63; prof. chemistry Cuyahoga Community Coll., Western campus, Parma, Ohio, 1963—, dept. head scis., 1965-76; vis. prof. biochemistry Case-Western Res. U., Cleve., 1970-71. Mem. policy com. Coll. Chemistry Consultants service, 1970-76; biochemist in charge animal research Ben Venue Labs., 1947-48, Armour Research Labs., 1948, Western Res. U. Med. Sch., 1942-47; research fellow in biochemistry Cleve. Clinic Hosp. Labs., 1953. Nat. Sci. Tchrs. Assn. grantee, 1957-58, 58-59, NSF grantee, 1977-80; named Distinguished Grad., Case-Western Res. U., 1968; recipient Outstanding Regional Chemistry Tchr. award Mfg. Chemists Assn., 1973. Mem. N.E.A., Am. Chem. Soc. (chmn. com. on chemistry two-year coll. tchrs. sect. 1974, treas. 1975, chmn. teaching of chemistry com. 1976-81), Ohio Chemistry Tchrs. Assn., Ohio Jr. Coll. Tchrs. Assn., Nat. Sci. Tchrs. Assn., Ohio Edn. Assn., Audubon Soc. (pres. Western Cuyahoga chpt. 1976), Sigma Xi. Club: Sierra. Contbr. articles to publs. Home: 6486 State Rd 12 Concord Sq Village Parma OH 44134

LAUGHLIN, GEORGE M., food co. exec.; b. Chgo., June 30, 1930; s. George C. and Rosaleen E. (Montague) L.; B.A., U. Notre Dame, 1951; postgrad. Denver U., 1952, Xavier U., 1955-58; m. Mary W. Waters, Nov. 27, 1954; children—Rosaleen, Timothy, Cynthia, Thomas, Terrence, Patrick. With Kroger Co., Cin., 1957—, v.p. grocery products div., 1973—; dir. Eagle Magnetic Co. Trustee Workshop for Retarded Citizens. Served with USAF, 1951-57. Mem. Cin. Sales and Mktg. Execs. (bd. dirs.), Nat. Coffee Assn. Republican. Roman Catholic. Club: Maketewah Country. Office: 1014 Vine St Cincinnati OH 45201

LAUGHREY, J. BRUCE, pharm. pub. co. exec.; b. Zanesville, Ohio, Dec. 12, 1941; s. Joe Pardee and Margaret (Hyde) L.; B.S. in Pharmacy, S.D. State U., 1963; m. Lydia Laughrey, May 27, 1977; stepchildren—Joe, Michelle, Michael. Retail pharmacist, Macomb, Ill., 1963-67; hosp. pharmacist U. Minn. Hosps., 1968; pharmacist Haag Drug, Terre Haute, Ind., 1969; owner, mgr. four Union Prescription Centers, Indpls., 1970-77, v.p. Union Prescription Center div. Unicare, 1977-78; pres. Medi-Span, Inc., Zionsville, Ind., 1978—. Mem. Am. Pharm. Assn., Nat. Assn. Retail Druggists, Nat. Council on Prescription Drug Programs, Ind. Pharm. Assn. Clubs: Sertoma (Indpls.), Elks. Pub. Monthly Prescription Pricing Guide, OTC Pricing Guide, Medi-Span OTC Plan-o-Gram, Hospital Formulary Pricing Guide, Quar. Competetive Pricing Chart. Home: 1035 Williamsburg Ln Zionsville IN 46077 Office: PO Box 459 20 W Pine Zionsville IN 46077

LAUMAN, VONA KATHRYN (MRS. JAMES WESLEY LAUMAN), printing, pub. co. exec.; b. Strawberry Point, Iowa, Nov. 20, 1927; d. Otto Fred and Emma Katherine (Meinken) Weger; B.S.C., U. Iowa, 1950; m. James Wesley Lauman, June 28, 1950; 1 dau., Lori Ann. Sec., Owens Ill. Glass Co., Chgo., 1950-51; sec. to treas. Pacific Coast Coca-Cola Bottling Co., Los Angeles, 1951-53; office mgr. Reynolds Aluminum Co., Indpls., 1953-56; office mgr. Central Pub. Co., Indpls., 1956-59, corporate sec., 1959-65, sales mgr., 1965-69, v.p., asst. gen. mgr., 1969-78, exec. v.p., Chief operating officer, 1979—, also dir.; corporate sec. Weger Farms, Inc., Strawberry Point, Iowa, 1969—, also dir. Mem. Iowa U. Alumni Assn., Ind. Bus. Communicators, Ind. Soc. Assn. Execs. (dir.), Network of Women in Bus. Club: Toastmasters. Republican. Lutheran. Home: 8029 Burn Ct Indianapolis IN 46217 Office: 401 N College Ave Box 1652 Indianapolis IN 46206

LAUN, ARTHUR HENRY, JR., lawyer; b. Milw., May 24, 1930; s. Arthur Henry and Annette (Pfister) L.; B.B.A., U. Wis., 1954, J.D., 1954; m. Marilyn M. Johnson, Feb. 14, 1964; children—Stephen G., Cynthia T., Sharyl K., Steven C., Lisa A. Admitted to Wis. bar, 1954, since practiced in Milw.; mem. firm Quarles & Brady, 1954—, partner, 1962—. Dir. Empire Level Mfg. Corp., U-Line Corp., Unicare Services, Inc. Mem. Thiensville-Mequon Union High Sch. Dist. No. 1 Sch. Bd., 1965-70; mem. exec. bd. Y-Men's Club; adv. bd. United Fund. Recipient Meritorious Service award YMCA, 1959. Mem. Am. (past chmn. com.), Wis. (sect. dir.), Milw. (past com. chmn.) bar assns., Order of Coif, U. Wis. Found., U. Wis. Pres.'s Club, Phi Beta Kappa, Sigma Phi, Phi Delta Phi, Beta Alpha Psi, Beta Gamma Sigma, Delta Sigma Rho, Phi Eta Sigma, Phi Kappa Phi, Iron Cross, Republican. Episcopalian. Exec. editor Wis. Law Rev., 1953-54. Home: 12028 N Lake Shore Dr Mequon WI 53092 Office: 780 N Water St Milwaukee WI 53202

LAUNS, RONALD EDGAR, advt. exec.; b. Detroit, June 30, 1934; s. Arnold Dewitt and Agnes Ilene (Seurynck) L.; B.S.B.A., Bowling Green State U., 1961; M.B.A., Wayne State U., 1969; m. Judith Stanley, Aug. 15, 1959; children—Bradford Robert, Susan Lynn, Wendy Kim, Tracy Ann. Media researcher McCann Erickson, Detroit, 1961-62; media buyer Batten, Barton, Durstine & Osborn, Detroit, 1962-65; account exec. Kenyon & Eckhardt, Detroit, 1964-66; advt. dir., sales dir. Mfrs. Bank, Detroit, 1966-71; pres. R.E. Launs, Inc., Detroit, 1971—. Pres., P.T.A., 1968-69; elder Lutheran Ch., 1976-80. Served with U.S. Army, 1955-57. Recipient Clio award, 1977; Creative awards Retail Ad Conf., 1975, 76, 77, Nat. Auto Dealers Assn., 1979. Mem. Adcraft Club Detroit, Econ Club. Detroit. Republican. Lutheran. Home: 1378 Buckingham St Grosse Pointe Park MI 48230 Office: 23100 Providence Dr Suite 470 Southfield MI 48075

LAUNSTEIN, HOWARD CLEVELAND, educator; b. Flushing, Mich., Oct. 15, 1922; s. John Henry and Jennie Grace (Cleveland) L.; student Central Mich. U., 1941-43; B.A., Mich. State U., 1947, M.A., 1948; Ph.D., Ohio State U., 1956; m. Elizabeth June Snyder, May 22, 1943; children—Robert John, Howard Elmer. Grad. asst. Mich. State U., 1947-48, instr. acctg., 1948-56; asst. prof. State U. Iowa, Iowa City, 1956-58; asso. prof. Marquette U., Milw., 1958-64, prof. fin., 1964—, chmn. dept., 1959-67; ins. agt. Guarantee Mut. Life Ins. Co., Lansing, Mich., 1948-51; instr. C.P.C.U. program, 1954-55, C.L.U. programs, 1959—; ins. cons. Marquette U., 1958—; mem. edni. adv. com. Wis. Real Estate Examining Bd., 1976-78; mem. adv. com. Wis. Ins. Examining Bd., 1977-78; dir., auditor Red Cedar Coop. Assn., East Lansing, 1949-52. Asst. cub master, treas. Greendale (Wis.) cub pack Boy Scouts Am., 1960-66, committeeman Boy Scouts, 1963-66; mem. citizens com. bonding issues Greendale Sch., 1959-61. Bd. govs., dir. Nat. Inst. Consumer Credit Mgmt., 1965—; mem. bd. electors Ins. Hall of Fame, 1982—. Served with USAAF, 1942-45. Decorated Air medal. Mem. Internat. Ins. Seminars (bd. govs. 1965—, moderator 1965-71, research directorate 1979-82), Am. Fin. Assn., Midwest Econ. Assn., Am. Acctg. Assn., Am. Fin. Mgmt. Assn., Am. Risk and Ins. Assn., Beta Alpha Psi, Delta Sigma Pi, Sigma Epsilon, Beta Gamma. Methodist. Contbr. chpts. to books, articles to profl. jours. Chmn. awards com. Nat. Assn. Ind. Insurers Jour. Ins., 1962-63, 68-69, 72—. Home: 5854 Glen Flora Greendale WI 53129 Office: Marquette U Milwaukee WI 53233

LAURANCE, GEORGE EUGENE, indsl. products co. exec.; b. St. Louis, Feb. 28, 1942; s. Eugene George and Audrey Elizabeth (Gorla) L.; B.S., Rockhurst Coll., 1968; m. Carla Christen, June 27, 1970; children—Daniel Wade, Julie Ann. Sales rep. Busch Indsl. Products Corp., Appleton, Wis., 1969-73, dist. mgr., Dallas, 1973-75, asst. to dir. mktg., St. Louis, 1975-77, dist. mgr., Chgo., 1977-81, Mpls., 1981—. Served with U.S. Army, 1962-65. Mem. Am. Soc. Bakery Engrs., Allied Trades of the Baking Industry, TAPPI, Wis. Canners and Freezers Assn., Naperville C. of C. Clubs: Bakers (Chgo.), Chgo. Bakery Prodn., Chgo. Courtesy Bakers, Wis. Bakers. Home: 14511 Woodruff Rd S Wayzata MN 55391 Office: Busch Industrial Products Corp 770 Kasota Ave Minneapolis MN 55414

LAURENCE, RICHARD ROBERT, educator; b. Knoxville, Tenn., Apr. 22, 1937; s. Robert A. and Sally (Claxton) L.; B.A., U. Tenn., 1959; postgrad. Middlebury Coll., 1959; (Fulbright scholar) U. Vienna, 1959-60; M.A. (Woodrow Wilson fellow, Stanford U. fellow) Stanford U., 1962, Ph.D. (Austrian Govt. Research fellow), 1968; m. Gertraud Fuehrer, July 6, 1961; children—Daniel Robert, Sonya Christina, Alfred James. Instr. dept. humanities Mich. State U., 1966-68, asst. prof., 1968-76, asso. prof., 1976—. Nat. Endowment for Humanities grantee, 1979. Mem. Am. Hist. Assn., Conf. Peace Research in History, Popular Culture Assn. Contbr. chpt. to book. Home: 1572 Cahill Dr East Lansing MI 48823 Office: Dept Humanities Mich State U East Lansing MI 48824

LAURENSON, ROBERT MARK, mech. engr.; b. Pitts., Oct. 25, 1938; s. Robert Mark and Mildred Othelia (Frandsen) L.; student Drury Coll., 1956-58; B.S. in Mech. Engring., Mo. Sch. Mines, 1961; M.S.E. in Mech. Engring., U. Mich., 1962; Ph.D. in Mech. Engring.

(NASA tng. grantee), Ga. Inst. Tech., 1968; m. Alice Ann Scroggins, Aug. 26, 1961; children—Susan Elizabeth, Shari Lynn. Dynamics engr. McDonnell Douglas Corp., St. Louis, 1962-64, sr. dynamics engr., 1968-71, group engr., 1971-74, staff engr., 1974-75, tech. specialist, 1975-78, sr. tech. specialist, 1978-81, sect. chief, 1981—; mem. conf. organizing com., session chmn. structures Structural Dynamics and Materials Conf., 1977, chmn. tech. program, 1978, gen. co-chmn., participant, 1979, gen. chmn., 1981, adv. com., 1978-82, chmn., 1981-82; participant 14th Midwestern Mechanics Conf., 1975; lectr. engrng. mechanics St. Louis U., part-time 1969-71; adj. asso. prof. U. Mo.-Rolla Grad. Engrng. Center, 1980—; participant Symposium on Dynamics and Control of Large Flexible Spacecraft, Blacksburg, Va., 1977. Registered profl. engr., Mo. Mem. ASME (structures materials com. aerospace div. 1975—, com. chmn. 1979-81, session organizer, chmn. session ann. meeting 1975, mem. exec. com. aerospace div. 1980—, sec./treas. 1981—), AIAA (gen. chmn. dynamics specialist conf. 1981), Sigma Xi, Pi Tau Sigma, Tau Beta Pi, Phi Kappa Phi, Sigma Phi Epsilon. Episcopalian (vestryman 1972-76, sr. warden 1976, usher chmn. 1978-80, Sunday sch. tchr. 1980—). Contbr. articles to profl. jours. Home: 349 Beaver Lake Dr Saint Charles MO 63301 Office: McDonnell Douglas Corp Box 516 Saint Louis MO 63166

LAURENTS, LOUIS VINSON, JR., computer programmer; b. Lake Arthur, La., Apr. 6, 1926; s. Louis Vinson and Evelyn (Greene) L.; m. Jaunita Elizabeth Dickison, July 14, 1947; children—Eileen E., Renee E., Jennie E., Louisa E., Lounita E., Louis Vinson. Instr. tech. tng. command U.S. Air Force, 1946-55, computer programmer, analyst Data Center, Hdqrs. Air Force Logistics Command, Wright Patterson AFB, Ohio, 1955—. Librarian br. genealogy library Dayton (Ohio) stake Ch. of Jesus Christ of Latter-day Saints, instr. adult edn. program, established br. genealogy library in Cin., 1966. Served with USAF, 1946-49. Home: 227 Cash Ct Fairborn OH 45324 Office: Data Base and Interface Control Br Directorate Tech Support Wright Patterson AFB OH 45433

LAUTZENHISER, NIANN KAY, psychometrist; b. Bryan, Ohio, Jan. 29, 1945; d. Kermit Arden and Luella Marie (Keppler) L.; student Bowling Green State U., 1963, 64, 65; B.S. in Edn., Miami U., Oxford, Ohio, 1966; M.S. in Edn., St. Francis Coll., 1971, M.S., 1975; postgrad. N.W. Tech. Coll., 1976-78. Tchr. math. John F. Kennedy Jr. High Sch., Kettering, Ohio, 1966-69; tchr. math. Angola (Ind.) High Sch., 1969-70, guidance counselor, 1970-75, counseling psychometrist, 1975-77, counseling psychometrist Angola Middle Sch., 1977—. Bd. dirs. Switchboard, Inc., Angola, 1974-75; bd. dirs. Community Service, Inc., Angola, 1974-76, sec., 1976; bd. dirs. Edon (Ohio) Community Pre-Sch., 1981—. Mem. Nat. Assn. Sch. Counselors (master sch. counselor certificate 1976), Nat. Assn. Sch. Psychologists, Am., Ind., Ohio personnel and guidance assns., NEA, Ind. State Tchrs. Assn., Angola Classroom Tchrs. Assn., AAUW. Lutheran. Office: Route 4 Box 11 A Angola IN 46703

LAUX, GWENDOLYNNE, hotel exec.; b. Kansas City, Mo., May 17, 1943; d. Cletus Edward and Artie Louise (Foster) L.; grad. Draughons Coll., 1967. Supr. reservation system Hilton Hotel, Kansas City, Mo., 1970-73; asst. dir. reservations Crown Center Hotel, Kansas City, Mo., 1974-75; sales mgr. Holiday Inn, sports complex, Kansas City, 1975-76, spl. accounts mgr. City Center, 1976-77, city sales coordinator, 1977-78, dist. sales dir., St. Louis, 1978—, meeting planning coordinator, 1982—. Mem. Am. Soc. Tng. and Devel., Am. Bus. Womens Assn., Hotel Sales Mgmt. Assn. (v.p. 1977-78). Presbyterian. Home: 9630 McGee St Kansas City MO 64114 Office: 12th and Baltimore Sts Kansas City MO 64105

LAUX, PATRICIA MARIE, editor; b. Clintonville, Wis., Apr. 22, 1943; d. Joseph J. and Adeline E. (Below) Laux; B.A., Coll. of St. Teresa, Minn., 1965; postgrad. Rice U., 1965-66. Editorial asst. Prairie Farmer Mag., Chgo., 1966-67, asst. home editor, 1967-69, home editor, 1969-72; tech. editor J.J. Keller & Assos., Inc., Neenah, Wis., 1972-74, asso. editor, 1974-77, gen. editor metric publs., 1977-80, measurement project supr., 1980—; mem. Nat. Metric Speakers Bur., 1975—. Mem. allocations panel United Way of Neenah, 1977, mem. citizen agy. team, 1977; chairperson of Vicariate VIII Council, 1976-78; chairperson communications com. St. Gabriel Parish Council, 1973-78; mem. Green Bay Diocesan Pastoral Council, 1977-78; bd. dirs. Big Sisters of Neenah-Menasha, 1977—, pres. bd., 1979-81. Mem. U.S. Metric Assn., Am. Nat. Metric Council. Democrat. Roman Catholic. Home: 166 Lorraine Ave Neenah WI 54956 Office: 145 W Wisconsin Ave Neenah WI 54956

LAVER, GERALD EBY, corp. exec., mgmt. cons.; b. Elyria, Ohio, May 19, 1924; s. Edmond Ray and Edith Lucille (Eby) L.; student Baldwin Wallace U., 1943; B.B.A. in Mktg., Cleve. State U., 1947; m. Edna Frances Dumont, Apr. 25, 1948; children—Cheryl Ann, Diana Lynn Laver Bowman, Christian Eby. With Dun & Bradstreet, Inc., Cleve., 1947-53, Columbia Gas System, Elyria, Lorain and Columbus, Ohio, 1953-70; v.p. builder services Galbreath Mortgage Co., Columbus, 1970-73; pres. Marconi Bldg., Inc., 1973—, United Energies, Inc., 1975-78, United Energies of W.Va., Inc., 1976-78; partner Dumont Sales Co., Columbus, 1958—, also Dumont Bus. cons.; pres. Larry Builders, Inc., 1979—, United Mariculture, Inc., 1979—; v.p. ops. Ultimate Resources, Inc., Westerville, Ohio, 1980—, Betmar Equipment & Mfg. Co., 1980—, Ecol, Inc., 1980—; chmn. bd. United Med. Systems, Inc., 1980—. Chmn. bd. Washington Ave. Christian Ch., Elyria, 1957, N.W. Christian Ch., 1965-66; treas. 125th Anniversary Celebration of Elyria, 1958; elder N.W. Christian Ch., 1974-77, 79—, trustee Found., 1980—; pres. Friendship Village of Columbus, Inc., 1976—; trustee Friendship Village of Dayton, Inc. Served with USNR, 1943-46; PTO. Named Young Man of Yr., Elyria Jr. C. of C., 1957, One of Ohio's 10 Outstanding Young Men, Ohio Jr. C. of C., 1958. Mem. Nat. Assn. Home Builders, Home Builders Assn. Greater Columbus. Republican. Mem. Disciples of Christ Ch. Clubs: Optimist, Masons, Shriners. Home: 2158 N Parkway Dr Columbus OH 43221 Office: 3360 E Livingston Ave Columbus OH 43209

LAVIN, CARL HERSHEL, bus. exec.; b. Canton, Ohio, Apr. 11, 1924; s. Leo Benjamin and Dorothy (Weinsweig) L.; B.S., Miami U., Oxford, Ohio, 1947; grad. Advanced Mgmt. Program, Harvard Bus. Sch., 1960; m. Audrey Ann Perlman, Feb. 22, 1953; children—Maud K., Carl Hershel, Franklin L., Douglas B. With Sugardale Foods, Inc., Canton, 1947-69, pres., 1963-69; pres. Homestead Provision Co., Alliance, Ohio, Wadsworth Investment Co., Canton; chmn. Block Coal & Supply Co., Canton; dir. Intermarket Rubber Co., Cleve., Polywood Corp., Canton, Enterprise Chem. Co., Dover, Ohio. Bd. dirs., v.p. Stark Wilderness Center; chmn. Stark County Health Planning Council; past bd. dirs. Seven County Alcoholism Council, Canton Jewish Center; chmn. Jewish Welfare Dr. of Canton, 1967. Served in U.S. Army, 1943-45; ETO. Mem. Am. Meat Inst., Nat. Ind. Meat Packers Assn. (past dir.), Ohio Meat Industry Assn. (dir.), Canton C. of C. (past v.p.). Republican. Jewish. Home: 5240 Plain Center Rd NE Canton OH 44714 Office: Homestead Provision Co 6428 Union Ave PO Box 3448 Alliance OH 44601

LAVIN, LEONARD H., consumer products co. exec.; b. Chgo., Oct. 29, 1919; s. Samuel and Ella (Rissman) L.; B.A., U. Wash., 1940; D.H.L., DePaul U., 1971; m. Bernice Elizabeth Weiser, Oct. 30, 1947; children—Scott Jay, Carol Marie (Mrs. Howard Bernick), Karen Sue. With Lucien LeLong, 1940-41, 45-46; organized Leonard H. Lavin & Co., Chgo., 1953-55; pres., chief exec. officer Alberto-Culver Co., Melrose Park, Ill., 1955—; propr. Glen Hill Farm Stables and breeding farm, Ocala, Fla. Bd. dirs. Rehab. Inst. Chgo. Served with USNR, 1941-45. Mem. Young Pres. Orgn., Sales Marketing Execs. Internat. (pres. panel). Home: Glencoe IL 60022 Office: 2525 Armitage Ave Melrose Park IL 60160

LAVIN, MARGARET ELLEN, utilities co. exec.; b. Worcester, Mass., May 1, 1952; d. Walter Douglas and Ellen Margaret (Gilligan) L.; B.A. cum laude, Assumption Coll., 1974; M.B.A., Clark U., 1976. Project mgr. Central Mass. Regional Planning Commn., Worcester, 1975-76; planner and demand analyst New Eng. Telephone and Telegraph, Boston, 1978-79; sr. rate analyst Am. Electric Power Service Corp., Columbus, Ohio, 1980—. Mem. Town Meeting, Shrewsbury, Mass., 1972-76; pres., trustee Scotland Yard, Ltd. Mem. Am. Statis. Assn., Assumption Coll. Alumni Assn. Roman Catholic. Home: 5796 Hallridge Circle Columbus OH 43227 Office: 180 E Broad St Columbus OH 43215

LAVITT, BEN, photog. co. exec.; b. Chgo., July 2, 1930; s. Charles and Sara (Solovitz) L.; student U. Ill.; m. Lillian Zimbler, Aug. 2, 1952; children—Alison, Jory. Photographer Eison-Freeman Co., N.Y.C., 1948-54; founder, pres. Astra Photo Services Inc., Chgo., 1954—; pres. Gamma Photo Labs., Chgo. dir. various firms; cons. to editors, writers; judge numerous contests, speaker at schs., various groups on photo processing. Mem. Color Photo Labs. Am., Am. Soc. Mag. Photographers, Profl. Photographers Am. Editor numerous books photography, photo processing. Home: 2466 Ridge Rd Highland Park IL 60035 Office: Gamma Photo Labs 314 W Superior St Chicago IL 60611

LAW, BERNARD FRANCIS, clergyman; b. Torreon, Mexico, Nov. 4, 1931; s. Bernard A. and Helen (Stubblefield) L.; B.A., Harvard U., 1953; postgrad. St. Joseph Sem., 1953, Pontifical Coll. Josephinum, Worthington, Ohio, 1955. Ordained priest Roman Cath. Ch., 1961, bishop Diocese of Springfield-Cape Girardeau, Mo., 1973—. Office: 200 McDaniel Bldg Springfield MO 65806

LAWERENZ, MARK DAVID, engr.; b. Milw., June 10, 1949; s. Harvey Otto and Anna Elizabeth (Markowski) L.; Asso. Applied Sci., M.E., Milw. Area Tech. Coll., 1969-73; B.S. in Mech. Engrng., Marquette U., 1978; m. Susan Patricia Russell, July 17, 1971 (div. Jan. 1981); children—Matthew James, Carissa Ann, Heather Jean; m. 2d, Darlene Sharon Kolbow, July 26, 1981. Sr. draftsman Envirex Inc. Waukesha, Wis., 1972-73; draftsman Compressor div. Allis-Chalmers Corp., Milw., 1973, project coordinator, 1973-78, sr. sales engr. unit Crane and Shovel Corp., New Berlin, Wis., 1978-80; pres. M.D. Lawerenz Assos. Inc., Pewaukee, Wis., 1980; sales engr. Enreco div. The Wehr Corp., 1980-81; application engr. RTE Corp., Waukesha, Wis., 1981—. Registered profl. engr., Wis. Mem. Oconomowoc Jaycees, Phi Theta Kappa. Lutheran. Home: 2001 Dixie Dr Apt 3 Waukesha WI 53186

LAWHON, WILLIAM THOMAS, JR., lab. exec.; b. Helena, Ark., Aug. 30, 1943; s. William Thomas and Etta Flora (Inebnit) L.; B.S. in Biology, Memphis State U., 1968, M.S. in Biology, 1969; Ph.D., U. Tenn., 1973; m. Bonnie Jean Campbell, Feb. 15, 1964; children—Laurie Jean, Sara Jane, William Thomas III. Supplier, Mohawk Tire & Rubber, West Helena, Ark., 1963; lineman, Southwestern Bell Telephone, Helena, Ark., 1964; counselor, Memphis Boys Club, 1964-66; quality control, Mohawk Tire & Rubber Co., Memphis, 1967; teaching asst., Memphis State U., 1968-69; asst. prof. biology, King Coll., Bristol, Tenn., 1969-70; research asst., U. Tenn., Knoxville, 1970-73; research scientist Battelle's Columbus (Ohio) Lab., 1973-75, prin. research scientist, 1975-76, sr. ecology and ecosystems analysis sect., 1976-79, mgr. agrl. and environmental program office, 1979—; mem. Am. Soviet Working Group on Stationary Source Air Pollution Control Tech., 1977—. Active Worthington P.T.A. Served with USN, 1961-63. Named Outstanding Young Citizen of Central Ohio, Jr. C. of C., Columbus, 1977. Mem. Soc. Am. Foresters, Ecol. Soc. Am., Am. Soc. Agronomy, Soil Sci. Soc. Am., Sigma Xi. Methodist. Clubs: Ohio Hist. Soc., Masons. Contbr. articles in field to profl. jours. Home: 6565 Estel Rd Worthington OH 43085 Office: 505 King Ave Columbus OH 43201

LAWLER, JAMES WILLIAM, hosp. exec.; b. Cudahy, Wis., Mar. 13, 1921; s. Edward F. and Ida M. (Martin) L.; Ph.B., Marquette U., 1942; M.Social Adminstrn., Loyola U., Chgo., 1948; m. Rita Cecelia Tabat, Dec. 27, 1947; children—Kathleen, Mark, Margaret, Maureen, Patrick, Michael. Account supr. Blue Cross Plan for Hosp. Care, Chgo., 1948-49; personal mgr. Wallace Supplies Mfg. Co., Chgo., 1949-50; order supt. Norge div. Borg-Warner Corp., Chgo., 1950-53; asst. personnel dir. Kleinschmidt Labs., Deerfield, Ill., 1953-55; personnel mgr. George S. May Co., Chgo., 1956-60; personnel mgr. Airway Products Corp., Schiller Park, Ill., 1960-62; dir. personnel and public relations Holy Cross Hosp., Salt Lake City, 1962-65; dir. personnel and public relations Holy Cross Hosp., Jacksonville, Ill., 1965-68; v.p. devel. and human resources Holy Family Hosp., Des Plaines, Ill., 1968-81; dir. personnel Walther Meml. Hosp., Chgo., 1981—. Served with U.S. Army, 1942-45. Decorated Bronze Star. Mem. Am. Soc. for Hosp. Personnel Dirs., Am. Mgmt. Assn., Am. Hosp. Assn., Inst. Public Relations Mgmt., Chgo. Assn. Commerce and Industry. Club: Lions. Contbr. articles to profl. publs. Home: 5101 Carriage Way Dr Rolling Meadows IL 60008 Office: 1116 N Kedzie Ave Chicago IL 60651

LAWLER, WILLIAM EDWARD, JR., co. exec.; b. Chgo., June 19, 1939; s. William Edward and Elizabeth Margarette (Moisand) L.; B.S. in Mech. Engrng., Ill. Inst. Tech., 1958; m. Marian S. Drobney, Dec. 28, 1960; 1 dau., Linda Jean. Asso., Am. Engrng. & Mfg. Co., San Francisco, 1956-64; pres. Controlled Waste Inc., Chgo., 1964—. Served with AUS, 1956-59; CBI. Decorated Purple Heart; registered profl. engr., 24 states. Mem. Am. Pub. Works Assn., Am. Soc. M.E., Chgo. Builders Club. Developer automated fuel generation process from solid waste. Address: 2536 W 80th St Chicago IL 60652

LAWLOR, THOMAS JAMES, ins. co. exec.; b. Chgo., Apr. 25, 1938; s. Thomas Joseph and Catherine (O'Brien) L.; A.A., Wright Coll., 1971; m. Nancy Ann Ehrhardt, Aug. 22, 1959; children—Susan, Michael, Patricia. Div. claim mgr. Allstate Ins. Co., Northbrook, Ill., 1969-71, account exec., 1971-74; group cons. Am. Bankers Life Ins. Co., Milw., 1974-77, sr. cons., 1977-79, regional v.p., 1979—. Mem. City Council New Berlin (Wis.), 1973—, pres., 1979—. Served with USAF, 1959-62. Recipient Cert. of Appreciation, City of Chgo., 1972; Disting. Service award UN Assn. U.S., 1973. Mem. League Wis. Municipalities, League Suburban Municipalities, Am. Mgmt. Assn. Roman Catholic. Home: 3346 S El Sirroco Dr New Berlin WI 53151 Office: 401 W Michigan St Milwaukee WI 53201

LAWRENCE, CHARLES HARRIS, physician; b. Chgo., Mar. 27, 1913; s. Louis James and Hattie (Abrams) L.; B.S., U. Chgo., 1934; M.D., Rush Med. Sch., 1937; m. Elise Lieberman, Nov. 20, 1947; children—Nancy, Ann. Intern, then resident in pathology Cook County Hosp., Chgo., 1937-39; practice internal medicine, Chgo., 1946—; asso. attending physician Cook County Hosp., 1947-50, attending physician, 1953-59; mem. staff Michael Reese Hosp. and Med. Center, Chgo., 1947—, pres. med. staff, 1964-65, coordinator clin. services, 1967-69, now v.p. profl. affairs; mem. staff Ill. Research and Edn. Hosp., 1960-64. Served to maj. M.C., U.S. Army, 1940-46; PTO. Decorated Purple Heart, Combat Med. Badge; diplomate Am. Bd. Internal Medicine. Mem. A.C.P., Inst. of Medicine, Chgo. Soc. Internal Medicine, Ill. Soc. Med. Research, Am. Heart Assn., Sigma Xi, Pi Lambda Phi. Jewish. Club: Ravisloe Country. Contbr. articles to med. bulls. and profl. publs. Home: 5555 S Everett Ave Chicago IL 60637 Office: 2929 S Ellis Ave Chicago IL 60616

LAWRENCE, DAVID LONG, radiologist; b. Jamestown, Ky., July 11, 1934; s. Marshall Marvin and Opal H. (Long) L.; B.A., Centre Coll., 1955; M.S., U. Ky., 1958; M.D., U. Louisville, 1962; m. Jeanette Wesley, Jan. 30, 1954; children—Julia Long, David Wesley. Intern, Baroness Erlanger Hosp., Chattanooga, 1962-63; gen. practice medicine, Jamestown, 1963-66; resident U. Louisville Hosps., 1968-71; practice medicine specializing in radiology, 1971—; mem. staffs Mercy Meml. Hosp., Urbana, Ohio, Mercy Med. Center Community Hosp., Springfield, Ohio; instr. dept. radiology U. Louisville, 1970-71; adj. prof. radiation medicine Wittenberg U.; asst. clin. prof. dept. radiology Wright State U. Sch. Medicine. Served to lt. comdr. USN, 1966-68. USPHS summer research scholar, 1959; diplomate Am. Bd. Radiology, Nat. Bd. Med. Examiners. Mem. Am. Coll. Radiology, Am., So., Ohio State med. assns., Clark County Med. Soc., Ohio State, Miami Valley, Central Ohio radiol. socs. Methodist. Club: Masons. Home: 402 N Broadmoor Blvd Springfield OH 45504

LAWRENCE, ROGER LEE, educator; b. Boughtinville, Ohio, July 13, 1921; s. Arthur Willis and Kathleen Ada (Line) L.; B.Sc., Ohio State U., 1943; A.M., George Washington U., 1949; Ph.D., Iowa State U., 1958; m. Pauline Hilborn, Nov. 2, 1944; children—Theodore H., Janet Lee. Asso. extension agt. Ohio State U., Jefferson and Coshocton, Ohio, 1946-50; asst. state 4H Club leader, Iowa State U., Ames, 1950-55, coordinator extension personnel tng., prof. adult and extension edn., 1955—; vis. prof. Colo. State U., U. Minn., Duluth; vis. lectr. U. Helsinki, Wageningen U., The Netherlands. Bd. dirs. United Way. Served with AUS, 1943-46. Decorated Legion of Merit; Sears Roebuck scholar, 1939-42; Nat. 4H fellow, 1948-49; Iowa Adult Edn. Assn. Achievement award, 1974, Disting. Service award Iowa Assn. Lifelong Learning, 1977. Mem. Iowa Assn. Lifelong Learning, Missouri Valley Adult Edn. Assn., Adult Edn. Assn. USA, Commn. Profs. Adult Edn., AAUP, Res. Officers Assn., Phi Eta Sigma, Phi Kappa Phi, Alpha Zeta, Gamma Sigma Delta, Alpha Kappa Delta, Phi Delta Kappa, Epsilon Sigma Phi. Methodist. Clubs: Kiwanis (div. lt. gov.). Home: 2215 Kellogg St Ames IA 50010 Office: College of Education Iowa State U Ames IA 50011

LAWRENCE, ROLLIN RAY, govt. ofcl.; b. Guernsey County, Ohio, Jan. 7, 1933; s. Clarence B. and Roxie M. (Armstrong) L.; Jr. Acct. cert. Columbus Bus. U., 1951; m. Lucille Brewer, Jan. 24, 1954; children—Linda, Patricia, Debra. Dir. adminstrv. services U.S. Forest Service, Upper Darby, Pa., 1967-72; dir. adminstrv. services Region III, HEW, Phila., 1972-78; regional gen. services officer N. Central region Sci. and Edn. Adminstrn., Agrl. Research, U.S. Dept. Agr., Peoria, Ill., 1978—. Served with AUS, 1953-55. Recipient Superior Performance award HEW, 1975, 78. Republican. Club: Kiwanis (dir. Peoria North club 1980—). Office: Sci and Edn Adminstrn US Dept Agr 2000 W Pioneer Pkwy Peoria IL 61615

LAWRENCE, WILLIAM ROBERT, surgeon; b. Tunnel Hill, Ill., May 17, 1923; s. William Lloyd and Zada Belle (Choate) L.; B.E., So. Ill. Normal U., 1943; A.B., So. Ill. U., 1950; B.S., U. Ill., 1952, M.D., 1954; m. Marilyn Inez Hanna, June 15, 1957; children—Kathryn Rae, Ronald Scott, Richard Kevin. Intern, Ill. Central Hosp., Chgo., 1954-55, resident surgery, 1955-57; resident surgery pathology St. Francis Hosp., Peoria, Ill., 1957-58; chief resident surgery Ill. Central Hosp., Chgo., 1958-60, gen. surgery practice, mem. staff, 1960—; mem. staff S. Suburban Hosp., Hazelcrest, Ill., Ingalls Meml. Hosp., Harvey; spl. examiner Ill. Central R.R., 1960; clin. asso. prof. surgery U. Chgo. Med. Sch. Served to capt. USAAF, 1943-48. Diplomate Am. Bd. Surgery. Fellow A.C.S.; mem. Am. Assn. Ry. Surgeons, Pan Am. Med. Assn., AMA, Ill., Chgo. med. socs., Am. Geriatrics Soc., Midwest, Ill. surg. socs., Chgo. Inst. Medicine, Alpha Kappa Kappa, Delta Rho, Kappa Delta Pi, Kappa Phi Kappa. Republican. Presbyn. Mason (Shriner). Home: 655 Maple Ct Prestwick Frankfort IL 60423 Office: 5800 Stony Island Chicago IL 60637 also 3235 W Vollmer Rd Flossmoor IL 60422

LAWRENZ, PAUL HENRY, engineer; b. Peine, Germany, Dec. 6, 1913; s. Paul W. and Alma A. (Vahldiek) L.; came to U.S., 1927, naturalized, 1933; B.S. in Elec. Engrng., Wayne State U., 1936, M.S. in Mech. Engrng., 1943; m. Eleanor M. Thompson, Aug. 3, 1940; children—Anne, Kay. Heating engr. Mich. Consol. Gas. Co., Detroit, 1936-37; elec. engr. Kelvinator div. Nash-Kelvinator Co., Detroit, 1938-39, standards engr., 1939-44, asst. to v.p. engrng., 1944-60; adminstrv. asst. to v.p. Am. Motors Corp., Detroit, 1960-67, mgr. product reliability, 1967-68, safety engr., 1968-73, mgr. exterior lighting, automotive engrng., 1973—. Commr. planning dept. Village of Franklin, Mich., 1972—. Mem. Engrng. Soc. Detroit, Am. Soc. Heating Refrigeration and Air Conditioning Engrs., Soc. Automotive Engrs. Methodist. Home: 30405 Rosemond Dr Franklin MI 48025 Office: 1441 Maple Troy MI 48084

LAWSON, CYNTHIA JEAN, utility co. exec.; b. San Mateo, Calif., Mar. 31, 1949; d. James William and Cleo Imogene (Peters) Root; B.A., U. Mich., 1970, M.A., 1974; m. Gerald Roscoe Lawson, Dec. 10, 1980; 1 son, David William. With Indsl. Data Processing, Bloomfield Hills, Mich., 1965-70; tchr., audio visual coordinator Southfield (Mich.) Christian Sch., 1971-77; mgr. ednl. programs Detroit Edison, 1977—. Mem. Nat. Council for Social Studies, Mich. Assn. Media Educators, Mich. Assn. Ednl. Reps., Mich. Assn. Suprs. and Curriculum Developers, Mich. Aviation Edn. Assn., Mich. Council for Social Studies, Mich. C. of C. Baptist. Home: 18764 Dolores St Lathrup Village MI 48076 Office: Detroit Edison 473 WCB 2000 2d Ave Detroit MI 48226

LAWSON, DONALD ELMER, editor, writer; b. Chgo., May 20, 1917; s. Elmer Daniel and Christina (Grass) L.; B.A., Cornell Coll., Mt. Vernon, Iowa, 1939, Litt.D. (hon.), 1970; student U. Iowa Writers Workshop, 1939-40; m. Beatrice M. Yates, Mar. 30, 1945. Editor, The Advertiser, weekly newspaper, Nora Springs, Iowa, 1940-41; with Compton's Ency., Chgo., 1946-73, mng. editor, 1960-65, editor-in-chief, 1965-73, v.p., 1971-73; exec. editor United Educators, Inc., 1973-74, editor in chief, 1974—. Bd. dirs. Marcy-Newberry Assn. Settlement Houses. Served with USAAF, 1941-45; ETO. Mem. Authors Guild, Chgo. Book Clinic, Internat. Platform Assn., Chgo. Lit. Club, Soc. Midland Authors, Phi Beta Kappa. Methodist. Clubs: Cliff Dwellers, Chicago Press. Author: A Brand for the Burning, 1961; Young People in the White House, 1961, rev. edit., 1970; The United States in World War I, 1963; The United States in World War II, 1963; The United States in the Korean War, 1964; Famous American Political Families, 1965; The War of 1812, 1966; Frances Perkins: First Lady of the Cabinet, 1967; Great Air Battles: World Wars I and II, 1968; The Lion and The Rock, the Story of the Rock of Gibraltar, 1969; Youth and War: From World War I to Vietnam, 1969; Ten

Fighters for Peace, 1971; The Colonial Wars, 1972; The American Revolution, 1974; The United States in the Indian Wars, 1975; The United States in the Spanish American War, 1975; The United States in the Mexican War, 1976; The United States in the Civil War, 1977; Education Careers, 1977; Democracy, 1978; The Secret World War II, 1978; Morocco, Algeria, Tunisia and Libya, 1979; The Changing Face of the Constitution, 1979; FDR's New Deal, 1979; World War II: Homefronts, 1980; A Picture Life of Ronald Reagan, 1981; the United States in the Vietnam War, 1981; The War in Vietnam: A First Book, 1981. Home: 1122 W Lunt Ave Chicago IL 60626 Office: 801 Green Bay Rd Lake Bluff IL 60044

LAWSON, ESTHER CHANEY (MRS. ALBERT THEODORE LAWSON), sch. adminstr.; b. Chgo., July 29, 1930; d. Thomas Roosevelt and Olie Lillie (Ford) Nelson; B.S., U. Ill., 1952; M.A., U. Chgo., 1962; m. Albert Theodore Lawson, May 2, 1954; 1 dau., Laurie Lynne. Primary tchr. Chgo. Bd. Edn., 1952-65, tchr.-counselor, 1965-69; prin. Goethe Elem. Sch., 1969-72, Garrett A. Morgan Elem. Sch., Chgo., 1972-76, Thomas J. Waters Elem. Sch., Chgo., 1976-78; dir. mgmt. info. Chgo. Bd. Edn., 1978-80; prin. Hirsch High Sch., Chgo., 1980—; cons. resource Wis. Research and Devel. Center, 1973-74. Registrar, 29th dist. S.E. Community Orgn., 1965. Bd. dirs. Marynook Homeowners, 1963—, Potential Sch. for Exceptional Children, 1969-74. Recipient fellowship for outstanding tchrs. Chgo. Bd. Edn., 1964. Mem. Nat. Council Adminstrv. Women, U. Chgo. Alumni, Chgo. Prins. Assn., Samuel Stratton Soc., Individually Guided Edn. Assn., U. Ill. Alumni, Phi Delta Kappa, Delta Kappa Gamma, Delta Sigma Theta. Mem. Ch. of Christ. Pioneer in transfer of adminstrs. for integration Chgo. Pub. Schs. Home: 155 N Harbor Dr Chicago IL 60601 Office: 7740 S Ingleside Ave Chicago IL 60619

LAWSON, JAMES LEE, health services adminstr.; b. Alhambra, Calif., Jan. 7, 1949; s. Charles French and Helen Marie L.; A.A., Cypress Coll., 1970; B.A., Calif. State Coll., Fullerton, 1970; B.S., Calif. Western State U., 1974, M.B.A., 1976; m. Ilene Eleanor Sweeney, Apr. 8, 1973; children—Charles Joseph, Sara Corinne. Owner, dir. United Distbn. Systems, Inc., Garden Grove, Calif., 1968-72; emergency room charge and head nurse Pioneer Hosp., Artesia, Calif., 1974-76, La Palma Intercommunity Hosp., 1976-77; adminstrv. services asst. San Bernardino County Med. Center, San Bernardino, Calif., 1977-79; dir. nursing services Barstow (Calif.) Community Hosp., 1979-80; head nurse emergency room Meth. Hosp., Madison, Wis., 1980-81; exec. dir. So. Wis. E.M.S. Council, Inc., Madison, 1981—; mem. San Bernardino County Mobile Intensive Care Adv. Com., 1977-80; cons., lectr. Disaster Preparedness Engring. Inst., Loma Linda, Calif. Served with USNR, 1967-70, USN, 1973-74. Gloria Fisken Meml. scholar, 1969-70. Registered nurse, Calif., Fla., Ky., Ill., Wis., Ind.; nat. registered emergency med. technician. Mem. Nat. League for Nursing, Nat. Assn. Emergency Nurses (charter), Nat. Assn. Emergency Paramedics (charter), Am. Public Health Assn., Assn. Western Hosps., Am. Nurses Assn., Am. Soc. Nursing Service Adminstrs., Acad. of Polit. Sci., Alpha Gamma Sigma, Chi Gamma Iota. Democrat. Jewish. Home: 4536 Stein Ave Madison WI 53714 Office: PO Box 9806 Madison WI 53715

LAWSON, JOHN HENRY, safety products mfg. co. exec.; b. Carlsbad, N.Mex., Nov. 6, 1945; s. Richard Marion and Mattie Bee (Tidwell) L.; ed. U. Ky. Tng. officer Ky. Dept. Labor, Frankfort, 1972-75; mgr. safety Firestone Steel Products, Henderson, Ky., 1975; loss control cons. Occupational Safety Control, Inc., Lexington, Ky., 1975-76; group safety mgr. Rexnord, Inc., Danville, Ky., 1976-79; sales mgr. ITT Meyer Industries, Red Wing, Minn., 1979—. Mem. Ky. Occupational Safety and Health Standards Bd., 1976-79; pres. Fayette County Young Democrats, Lexington, 1974; pres. Boyle County Young Dems., 1978. Served with U.S. Army, 1965-68. Recipient Outstanding Service award Tau Kappa Epsilon, 1978; named Outstanding Kentucky Young Democrat, 1979. Mem. Am. Soc. Safety Engrs., Canadian Soc. Safety Engring., Nat. Fire Protection Assn., Am. Welding Soc., Nat. Safety Mgmt. Soc. Democrat. Clubs: Masons, Shriners. Home: Rural Route 1 Lake City MN 55041 Office: PO Box 114 Red Wing MN 55066

LAWSON, JOHN WALTER, public relations cons.; b. Valdosta, Ga., July 10, 1944; s. Hugh Winfield and Geraldine (New) L.; B.S., Fla. State U., 1966; M.S. in Public Relations, Boston U., 1973; m. Una Florence Bingenheimer, May 5, 1972; children—Jerry Kenneth, Kami Una. Public info. specialist Fla. Dept. Commerce, St. Petersburg, 1968-74; asst. prof. public relations U. Dayton, 1974-80; found. dir. St. Elizabeth Med. Center, Dayton, 1980-81; dir. public relations Sive/Young & Rubicam, Cin., 1981—. Am. Advt. Fedn. scholar, 1965. Mem. Public Relations Soc. Am. (dir. Dayton chpt. 1977-81, nat. faculty adv. 1979, membership com. 1978, nat. edn. com. 1979). Republican. Presbyterian. Office: 5 W 4th St Cincinnati OH 45202

LAWSON, LINDA LOU, computer planning engr.; b. Syracuse, Kans., Dec. 27, 1927; d. Frank A. and Edith Maria Christina (Sandahl) Fuller; B.A. with honors, Roosevelt U., Chgo., 1974, M.A. with honors in Polit. Sci., 1976; children—Marc F., Van E. Manual systems analyst Montgomery Ward & Co., Chgo., 1963-67; programmer/analyst R.H. Donnelly, Chgo., 1968-71; data center mgr. dept. space utilization U. Ill. Med. Center, Chgo., 1974-77; project leader Options Clearing Corp., Chgo., 1977-79; planning engr. data processing div. Chgo. Bd. of Options Exchange, 1979-81; sr. systems analyst, data processing dept. Kemper Fin. Services, 1981—; instr. computer sci. Roosevelt U., Chgo., 1977-81. Mem. Roosevelt Alumni Assn., Franklin Honor Soc. Unitarian. Author: (text) Common Business Computer Systems and Applications, External Degree Program, 1980. Home: 943 W Ainslie Chicago IL 60640 Office: 120 S LaSalle St Chicago IL 60603

LAWTON, BARBARA PERRY, public relations counselor, writer; b. Springfield, Mass., Aug. 26, 1930; d. Kenneth William and Elizabeth (McGovern) Perry; B.A., Mt. Holyoke Coll., 1952; div.; children—William C., Cynthia P., Mark R. Editor, mgr. publs. Mo. Bot. Garden, 1967-72; public relations counselor Gary Ferguson, Inc., St. Louis, 1971-81, partner, 1977-81; account exec. Wright & Manning P.R., Inc., 1981—; cons. public relations to various orgns., 1968—; contbr. articles to various publs., 1960—; columnist St. Louis Post-Dispatch, 1972—. Recipient Quill and Trowel award for garden writing, 1980, 81, Capt. Donald T. Wright award for maritime journalism, 1980. Mem. Women in Communications, Nat. Federated Press Women (1st and 2d Pl. awards 1977 Communications Contest), Landscape and Nurserymen's Assn., Garden Writers Am. Home and Office: 1430 Timberbrook Dr Kirkwood MO 63122

LAWTON, JAMES HOWARD, podiatric surgeon; b. Chgo., Dec. 25, 1945; s. James Howard and Eloise Eileen Lawton; B.S., U. Wis., Platteville, 1967; D.P.M., Ill. Coll. Podiatric Medicine, 1971; m. Cynthia Ann Osborne, Oct. 6, 1979; children—Jeffrey James, Jason Michael. Resident in podiatric surgery Franklin Blvd. Community Hosp., Chgo., 1971-73; instr. surgery Ill. Coll. Podiatric Medicine, 1973-76; asst. clin. prof. Abraham Lincoln Med. Sch., U. Ill., Chgo., 1972—; asso. prof. surgery Dr. W. Scholl Coll. Podiatric Medicine, 1981—; mem. med. staff Central Community Hosp., Chgo., 1974—; mem. faculty cons. family practice residency MacNeal Meml. Hosp., 1972—. Diplomate Am. Bd. Podiatric Surgery. Fellow Am. Coll. Foot Surgeons; mem. Am. Public Health Assn., Am. Podiatry Soc. (Ill. del. 1980-83), Ill. Podiatry Soc. (pres. 1978-79), Ill. Public Health Assn. Roman Catholic. Author research papers in field. Office: Windsor Medical Center 3722 S Harlem Ave Riverside IL 60546

LAWVER, DAVID EARL, educator; b. Joplin, Mo., Feb. 17, 1955; s. Ralph Royce and Theresa Jean (Caldwell) L.; B.S. in Agrl. Edn., U. Mo., Columbia, 1977; m. Donna Joy Bertelsen, Apr. 14, 1979. Vocat. agr. instr. East Newton High Sch., Granby, Mo., 1977-79, Bronaugh (Mo.) High Sch., 1979—. Vice-pres. Bronaugh City Park Bd., 1980—; mem. Bronaugh Community Betterment Com. Mem. Nat. Vocat. Agr. Tchrs. Assn., Am. Vocat. Assn., Mo. Vocat. Agr. Tchrs. Assn. (area sec.-treas.), Mo. Vocat. Assn., Mo. State Tchrs. Assn. Democrat. Mem. Christian Ch. Club: Booster (Bronaugh, Mo.). Home: Route 1 Bronaugh MO 64728 Office: Bronaugh High Sch Bronaugh MO 64728

LAWYER, VERNE, lawyer; b. Indianola, Iowa, May 9, 1923; s. Merrill Guy and Zella (Mills) L.; LL.B., Drake U., 1949; m. Sally Hay, Oct. 5, 1946; 1 dau., Suzanne; m. 2d, Vivian Jury, Oct. 25, 1959; children—Michael, Steven. Admitted Iowa bar, 1949, also U.S. Supreme Ct. bar; practice law, Des Moines, 1949—; mem. firm Law Offices of Verne Lawyer. Mem. Iowa Aeros. Commn., 1973-75. Trustee ATL Roscoe Pound Found., 1965-71, fellow, 1973—. Recipient Outstanding Law Alumni award Phi Alpha Delta, 1964. Fellow Internat. Acad. Trial Lawyers, Internat. Soc. Barristers, Am. Bar Found.; mem. Am. (state chmn. membership com. of ins., negligence and compensation law 1970—, com. trial techniques 1969-70), Iowa (spl. comn. on fed. practice 1971-78, spl. automobile reparations com. 1972—), Polk County bar assns., Assn. Trial Lawyers Am. (v.p. Iowa chpt. 1956-57, nat. sec. 1963-64, 67-68, bd. govs. 1962-63, chmn. for Iowa 1972-74, mem. internat. aviation com. 1973—, trial advs. scholarship soc. com. 1973—), Iowa Acad. Trial Lawyers (sec.-treas. 1962—, editor Newsbull. 1962—, editor Weekly Verdict Summary 1970—, editor Acad. Alert 1979—), Assn. Trial Lawyers Iowa, Law Sci. Acad. Am., Lawyer-Pilots Bar Assn., Am. Judicature Soc., World Assn. Lawyers (founding), World Peace Through Law Center, Trial Lawyers Assn. Des Moines, Phi Alpha Delta, Sigma Alpha Epsilon. Author: Trial by Notebook, 1964; co-author Art of Persuasion in Litigation, 1966; How to Defend a Criminal Case from Arrest to Verdict, 1967. Contbr. articles law jours. Home: 5831 N Waterbury Rd Des Moines IA 50312 Office: Fleming Bldg Des Moines IA 50309

LAY, DONALD POMEROY, U.S. judge; b. Princeton, Ill., Aug. 24, 1926; s. Hardy W. and Ruth (Cushing) L.; student U.S. Naval Acad., 1945-46; B.A., U. Iowa, 1948, J.D., 1951; m. Miariam Elaine Gustafson, Aug. 6, 1949; children—Stephen Pomeroy (dec.), Catherine Sue, Cynthia Lynn, Elizabeth Ann, Deborah Jean, Susan Elaine. Admitted to Nebr. bar, 1951, Iowa bar, 1951, Wis. bar, 1953; with firm Kennedy, Holland, DeLacy & Svoboda, Omaha, 1951-53, Quarles, Spence & Quarles, Milw., 1953-54, Eisenstatt, Lay, Higgins & Miller, 1954-66; U.S. circuit judge 8th Circuit U.S. Ct. Appeals, 1966—, chief judge, 1980—; faculty mem. on evidence Nat. Coll. Trial Judges, 1964-65. Pres., Douglas County (Nebr.) Dystrophy Assn., 1964; bd. dirs. Hattie B. Monroe Home, Omaha, 1961-67. Served with USNR, 1944-46. Recipient Hancher-Finkbine medal U. Iowa, 1980. Fellow Internat. Acad. Trial Lawyers; mem. Am., Nebr., Iowa, Wis. bar assns., Am. Judicature Soc. (dir. 1976—, exec. bd. 1979—), Jud. Conf. U.S., Law Sci. Acad. (v.p. 1960), Am. Trial Lawyers Assn. (bd. govs. 1963-65), U. Iowa Alumni Assn. (pres. Omaha-Council Bluffs chpt. 1958), Order of Coif, Delta Sigma Rho, Phi Delta Phi. Methodist (ofcl. bd. 1965-68). Mem. editorial bd. Iowa Law Rev., 1950-51. Contbr. articles to legal jours. Home: 6425 S 118 Plaza Omaha NE 68137 Office: PO Box 338 Omaha NE 68101

LAYBOURN, HALE, ins. co. exec.; b. Cedar Rapids, Iowa, July 20, 1923; s. Harold Hale and Reba S. (Strudevant) L.; B.S.B.A., U. Wyo., 1949; m. Barbara G., Dec. 21, 1947; children—Lillian Louise Laybourn Casares, Constance Grace, Deborah Hayle Laybourn Davis, Paul James, Richard Tod, Dorothy M. Asst. bus. mgr. Cheyenne (Wyo.) Newspapers, Inc., 1949-50; fiscal and personnel officer, dir. hosp. facilities Wyo. Dept. Health, 1950-60; dir. internal ops. Blue Cross and Blue Shield, Cheyenne, Wyo., 1960-65; pres. Blue Cross N.D., Fargo, 1965—; bd. dirs. Nat. Blue Cross Assn., 1973-77; chmn. Dist. X Plan Pres's., 1970-73; dir. West Fargo State Bank. Pres., Fargo-Moorhead Civic Opera Co., 1968-81; chmn. United Fund, Fargo, 1972. Served with inf. U.S. Army, 1942-45. Mem. Fargo C. of C. (pres. 1977). Republican. Episcopalian. Clubs: Elks, Kiwanis. Office: 4510 13th Ave SW Fargo ND 58121

LAYTON, JAMES RONALD, educator; b. Kings Mountain, N.C., May 1, 1936; s. James Goethal and Sara Florence (Parish) L.; B.S. in Edn., Appalachian State U., 1961, M.A., 1965; Ed.D., U. So. Miss., 1971; m. Barbara Ann Fellows, Nov. 1, 1957; 1 son, Kent. Elem. tchr. Charlotte Mecklenburg Schs., Charlotte, N.C., 1961-63, remedial reading tchr., 1963-65, reading clinician, psychol. services, 1965-66; mem. faculty, clin. dir. Appalachian State U., Boone, N.C., 1966-69; mem. adj. faculty U. So. Miss., Hattiesburg, 1969-71; prof. reading S.W. Mo. State U., Springfield, 1971—. Served with USAF, 1954-58. Mem. Internat. Reading Assn., Nat. Soc. for Study of Edn., Am. Assn. Colls. Tchr. Edn., Coll. Reading Assn., Nat. Reading Conf., Orgn. Tchr. Educators in Reading, Mo. Assn. Children with Learning Disabilities, Am. Legion. Lutheran. Club: Author: The Psychology of Learning to Read, 1979; (with others) Early Childhood Education: Theory to Research to Practice, 1980; 22 works for Media Materials, Inc., 1979-81; permanent contbg. editor for gifted in social studies sect. Social Studies Tchr.; contbr. articles to profl. jours. Home: 3340 S Danbury St Springfield MO 65807 Office: SW Mo State U Hill Hall 102 410 S National St Springfield MO 65802

LAZAR, MICHAEL HOWARD, radio sta. mgr.; b. N.Y.C., Jan. 8, 1949; s. Nat and Lita (Littman) L.; B.A., SUNY, Oswego, 1971; M.A., No. Ill. U., 1979; m. Jeanne Marie Falco, Aug. 2, 1970; children—Allison, Mark. Ops. mgr. Sta. KXCV-FM, Maryville, Mo., 1971-76; sta. mgr. Sta. WNIU-FM, DeKalb, Ill., 1976—; mem. supporting profl. staff council No. Ill. U., 1980—. Bd. dirs. DeKalb County Villages, 1978—. Recipient 1st Place investigative reporting Mo. Broadcasters Assn., 1975. Club: Lions (dir.) (DeKalb). Home: 609 Brickville Rd Sycamore IL 60178 Office: WNIU-FM No Ill Univ DeKalb IL 60115

LAZARUS, BETTY ROSS, mental health adminstr.; b. Chgo., Feb. 22, 1923; d. James Samuel and Ethel Muskogee (Jacobs) Ross; student U. Chgo., 1940-43, U. Ill., 1964-65; m. David Lazarus, Aug. 15, 1943; children—Barbara, William, Mary Ann, Richard. Parent educator U. Ill. Spl. Project Presch. Program, 1966; adminstrv. asst. Hays Sch., Urbana, Ill., 1967; coordinator Suicide Prevention Service, Champaign County Mental Health Assn., 1969-70; mental health educator Champaign County Mental Health Center, 1970-72; exec. dir. Champaign County Mental Health Bd., 1972-78; ret., 1978; cons.; mem. subcom. Ill. Dept. Mental Health, 1976-77, mental health task force East Central Ill. Health Systems Agy., 1976-78. Bd. dirs. LWV, 1958-60, 80-81, Planned Parenthood, 1955-64; mem. Council Community Integration, 1957-64. Recipient Gov.'s Voluntary Action award, 1970; Community Leadership award Assn. Mental Health, 1978. Home: 502 W Vermont Ave Urbana IL 61801

LAZARUS, RALPH, retail store chain exec.; b. Columbus, Ohio, Jan. 30, 1914; s. Fred and Meta (Marx) L.; B.A., Dartmouth Coll., 1935, LL.D., 1965; LL.D., U. Miami, 1961, Xavier U., 1965; D.C.S., Suffolk U., 1962; m. Gladys Kleeman; children—Mary (dec.), Richard (dec.), John, James. With F. & R. Lazarus & Co., Columbus, 1935-51, exec. v.p., 1950-51; exec. v.p. Federated Dept. Stores, Inc., Cin., 1951-57, pres., 1957-67, chief exec. officer, 1966-81, chmn. bd., 1967—; dir. Chase Manhattan Corp., Chase Manhattan Bank, Scott Paper Co., Gen. Electric Co. Bd. dirs. Nat. Com. on U.S.-China Relations, Inc.; trustee Dartmouth Coll. Served with War Prodn. Bd., 1941-43. Recipient Nat. Retail Mchts. Assn. Gold medal, 1974; NCCJ Brotherhood award, 1975. Mem. Cin. Bus. Com. Clubs: Comml., Commonwealth, Dartmouth, Camargo Country, Queen City, Losantiville Country (Cin.); Athletic, Winding Hollow Country, Univ. (Columbus, Ohio), Blind Brook Country, Harmonie, Sky (N.Y.C.), LaQuinta (Calif.) Country. Office: 7 W 7th St Cincinnati OH 45202

LAZURENKO, LYDIA BILINSKY, aero. engr.; b. Boryslaw, Ukraine, June 6, 1932; d. Wasyl and Maria (Swyshcz) Bilinsky; B.S., Wayne State U., 1955, M.S.M.E., 1972; m. Serhij Lazurenko, Aug. 8, 1954; children—Olha, Stephen. Analytical engr. gas turbines Continental Aviation and Engring. Corp., Detroit, 1955-63; design engr. gas turbines Chrysler Corp., Detroit, 1963-65; design and devel. engr. gas turbines Teledyne CAE, Toledo, 1965-72; devel. engr. vehicle aerodynamics Gen. Motors Corp., Warren, Mich., 1972—. Mem. Mich. Bd. Registration Profl. Engrs., Mich. Bd. Registration for Architects. Mem. Mich. Soc. Profl. Engrs., Soc. Automotive Engrs., Soc. Women Engrs. (v.p. Detroit sect. 1978—), Engring. Soc. Detroit (treas. affiliate council 1977—), Soc. Ukrainian Engrs., Mich. Assn. Professions. Club: Women of Wayne (Headliner award 1973). Office: Tech Center Gen Motors Corp Warren MI 48090

LEA, ALBERT ROBERT, mfg. exec.; b. Melrose, Mass., May 27, 1921; s. Robert Wentworth and Lillian (Ryan) L.; A.B., Amherst Coll., 1943; student Harvard Grad. Sch. Bus. Adminstrn., 1943; m. Joyce Winona Padgett, May 17, 1943 (div.); children—Patricia, Jennifer, Anne, Melissa Lea; m. 2d, Helen Clay Jones, May 12, 1961; children—Albert Robert, Robert Wentworth II. Pres. Ashcraft Inc., Kansas City, 1951—, also dir.; pres., dir. Process Plate Co., Trade Plant Inc.; pres., dir. Continental Service Industries, Inc. Served as lt. Supply Corps, USNR, 1943-46. Clubs: Mission Hills Country: University, Kansas City (Kansas City); Met. (N.Y.C.). Home: 625 W Meyer Blvd Kansas City MO 64113 Office: 816 Locust St Kansas City MO 64106

LEA, PAUL MILWARD, III, mech. engr.; b. Chgo., Sept. 19, 1942; s. Paul M. and Elda M. (Hendrickson) L.; B.S.M.E., Bradley U., 1965; m. Geri Lou Guede, Nov. 25, 1965; children—Paula Marie, Paul M. IV. Maintenance supr. U.S. Steel Co., Gary, Ind., 1965-68; project engr. Amsted Research Lab., Bensenville, Ill., 1968-71, research engr., 1971-73; chief engr. vacuum process div. John Mohr & Sons, Chgo., 1973-81, chief engr. co., 1981—. Chmn. lay council United Ch. Christ, 1973-75; chmn. pack com. Calumet council Boy Scouts Am., 1977-78, cubmaster, 1978-80, asst. scoutmaster, 1980-81, vice chmn. dist. com., 1980-81. Mem. ASME, Soc. Automotive Engrs. (pres. chpt. 1964-65), Am. Soc. Metals, Am. Vacuum Soc. Club: Internat. Order Foresters. Inventor continuous method of and apparatus for making bars from powdered metal. Home: 679 E 152d St Dolton IL 60419 Office: 3200 E 96th St Chicago IL 60617

LEACH, DAVID MASON, lawyer; b. Owatonna, Minn., Sept. 16, 1917; s. Helon E. and Mabelle (King) L.; student U. Minn., 1936-39; B.S. in Law, St. Paul Coll. Law, 1942, LL.B., 1948; m. Lucille A. Dixon, Dec. 24, 1946 (dec. Nov. 1964); 1 dau., Deborah D.; m. 2d, Mary E. Brandley, Mar. 21, 1969. Admitted to Minn. bar, 1948; individual practice law, Owatonna, 1949—; city atty., Owatonna, 1949-64; municipal judge, Owatonna, 1964-72. Bd. dirs. Owatonna Arts Council, 1974—. Served to capt. AUS, 1942-46; lt. col. Res. ret. Mem. City and Village Attys. Assn., League Minn. Municipalities (pres. 1959-60), Am., Minn., Fifth Dist. (past pres.), Steele County bar assns., Am. Judicature Soc., Am. Legion, Owatonna C. of C. (dir. 1972-75), Theta Delta Chi. Episcopalian. Elk. Club: Owatonna Exchange. Home: 424 Prospect St Owatonna MN 55060 Office: 214 S Oak St Owatonna MN 55060

LEACH, DONALD PAUL, mfg. and distbn. co. exec.; b. Mount Vernon, N.Y., Mar. 17, 1945; s. Alfred Grahame and Anne Marie (Hantz) L.; B.S., Cedarville Coll., 1968; M.B.A., U. Dayton, 1974; m. Nancy Lynne Davis, Jan. 30, 1967; children—Donald Paul, Brian, Deborah. Accountant, mem. corp. staff Top Value Enterprises, Dayton, Ohio, 1969-72; tax analyst, corp. staff Philips Industries, Inc., Dayton, 1972-73; tax mgr. Danis Industries Corp., Dayton, 1973-76, asst. v.p., 1976-78, v.p., treas. constrn. products group, 1978—; instr. acctg. Sinclair Community Coll., Dayton, 1974—. Mem. fin. com. Dayton Christian Schs., 1981—; trustee Washington Hts. Bapt. Ch., Dayton, 1981—, supt., 1977-80; treas. Alumni Council of Cedarville (Ohio) Coll., 1981—; pres. Dayton Tax Club, 1977-78. Served with U.S. Army, 1967. Mem. Nat. Assn. Accountants, Inst. Internal Auditors. Home: 7650 Bigger Rd Centerville OH 45459 Office: Danis Industries Corp 721 Richard St Miamisburg OH 45342

LEACH, JIM, Congressman; b. Davenport, Iowa, Oct. 15, 1942; s. James Albert and Lois (Hill) L.; m. Elisabeth Foxley, Dec. 6, 1975; B.A., Princeton U., 1964; M.A., Johns Hopkins U., 1966. Mem. staff Congressman Donald Rumsfeld, 1965-66; U.S. fgn. service officer, 1968-73; adminstrv. asst. to dir. OEO, 1969-70; mem. U.S. Delegation Geneva Disarmament Conf., 1971-72; mem. U.S. Delegation UN Gen. Assembly, 1972; pres. Flamegas Cos.; 1973-76; dir. Fed. Home Loan Bank, Des Moines, 1976; mem. 95th-97th Congresses from 1st Iowa Dist., 1977—, mem. com. on banking, fin. and urban affairs, com. on fgn. affairs. Mem. Nat. Fedn. Ind. Bus., C. of C., Rotary Club, Elks, Moose. Home: 2625 Wood Ln Davenport IA 52803 Office: 1406 Longworth House Office Bldg Washington DC 20515

LEACH, LARRY DEAN, cemetery exec.; b. Ky., Feb. 8, 1947; s. Alonzo and Maureen (Griffen) L.; B.A., Georgetown (Ky.) Coll., 1969; m. Cynthia Sue Stempkowski, June 24, 1972; children—Michele Renee, Kari Maureen, Larry Dean, II. Sales mgr. Chapel Lawn Meml. Gardens, Schererville, Ind., 1969-72, exec. v.p., 1979-81, owner, operator, 1981—; pres. Dean & Assos. Inc., 1981—; sales and gen. mgr. Lake St. Cemetery, Elgin, Ill., 1972-74; v.p. Sunset Burial Park, St. Louis, 1974-79; bd. dirs. Met. Chgo. Cemetery Orgn. Recipient various sales awards. Mem. Nat. Assn. Cemeteries, Pre-Arrangement Interment Assn. Am., So. Cementery Assn., Crown Point C. of C., Schererville C. of C. Republican. Clubs: Crown Point Rotary, East Chicago Elks. Home: 10625 Hendricks Pl Crown Point IN 46307 Office: PO Box 178 Schererville IN 46375

LEACH, RUSSELL, lawyer; b. Columbus, O., Aug. 1, 1922; s. Charles Albert and Hazel Kirk (Thatcher) L.; B.A., Ohio State U., 1946, J.D., 1949; m. Helen M. Sharpe, Feb. 17, 1945; children—Susan Sharpe, Terry Donnell, Ann Dunham. Admitted to Ohio bar, 1949; clk. U.S. Geol. Survey, Columbus, 1948-49; reference and teaching asst. Coll. of Law, Ohio State U., 1949-51; asst. city atty. City of Columbus, 1951-54, sr. asst. city atty., 1954-55, chief counsel, 1956, 1st asst. city atty., 1957, city atty., 1957-63, judge municipal ct., 1963-66; partner firm Bricker & Eckler, Columbus, 1966—. Commr.,

Columbus Met. Housing Authority, 1968-74; chmn. Franklin County (Ohio) Republican party, 1974-78. Served with AUS, 1942-46, 51-53. Named one of ten Outstanding Young Men of Columbus, Columbus Jaycees, 1956, 57. Mem. Am. Ohio (council of dels. 1970-75), Columbus (pres. 1973-74) bar assns., Delta Theta Phi, Chi Phi. Methodist. Home: 1232 Kenbrook Hills Dr Columbus OH 43220 Office: Bricker & Eckler 100 E Broad St Columbus OH 43215

LEACH-CLARK, MARY AGNES, therapist; b. Wichita, Kans., Aug. 5, 1931; d. Frank and May Jean (Hollow) Leach; B.S. in Edn., U. Kans., 1954; M.Ed., Wichita State U., 1978; m. Courtney Clark, June 12, 1954 (div. 1975); children—David Courtney, Bruce Colin, Anne Catherine, Jeffrey Charles. Elementary sch. tchr. gifted classroom Overland Park, Kans., 1954-56; therapist Valley Hope Treatment Referral Center and Out Patient Clinic, Wichita, 1977; activity dir. residential treatment center girls Salvation Army Hosp., Wichita, 1978; play, expressive art therapist, Wichita, from 1978; tchr. emotionally disturbed children Dist. 259, Wichita, 1979-80; founder, propr. Aidance Devel. Programs, career/retirement counseling and resume/tutoring services, 1981—; also solo pianist. Mem. AAUP, Nat. Assn. Sch. Psychologists, Am. Personnel and Guidance Assn., Kans. Assn. Sch. Psychologists, Internat. Sch. Psychologists, Internat. Platform Assn., Kans. Authors Club, Alpha Chi Omega (mem. bd. house corp. 1961-64), Delta Rho Sigma. Office: Box 825 Wichita KS 67201

LEARNED, CHARLES ALDEN, securities exec.; b. Stafford, Kans., Sept. 14, 1933; s. Wilmer Harrison and Vivian Edith (Hendershot) L.; B.S., Sterling Coll., 1955; m. Jean Starbuck, June 13, 1954; 1 son, Rodney David. Cashier mcpl. bond dept. Small-Milburn Investment, Inc., Wichita, Kans., 1956-58; mgr. mcpl. bond dept. Stockyards Nat. Bank, Wichita, 1958-64; exec. v.p., mgr. mcpl. bond dept. Mid-Continent Securities Corp., Wichita, 1964-68; v.p., mgr. mcpl. bond dept. Columbian Securities Corp., Wichita, 1968—; pres., dir. Learned Investments, Inc., Wichita, 1970—. Recipient Merit award Adminstr. Mgmt. Soc., 1971, Diamond Merit award, 1974. Mem. Adminstrv. Mgmt. Soc. (chpt. pres. 1970-72, dir. edn. div. on internat. bd. dirs. 1972-74), Wichita Ind. Bus. Assn., C. of C. Mem. Evangelical Free Ch. Mason (Shriner), Moose (life), Kiwanian. Clubs: Wichita Racquet, Wichita Shocker, Knife and Fork. Home: 6705 Magill St Wichita KS 67206 Office: 321 E William St Wichita KS 67202

LEARY, JAMES L., ednl. adminstr.; b. Barneveld, Wis., July 11, 1934; married, 5 children. B.S. in Math., U. Wis., Eau Claire, 1956; A.M. in Adminstrn., U. Mich., Ann Arbor, 1958; Ed.D. in Curriculum, Wayne State U., Detroit, 1972. Coordinator curriculum Dept. Def. Schs., Madrid, 1959-63; asst. supt. Clarenceville Sch. Dist., Farmington, Mich., 1966-74, Plymouth (Mich.) Sch. Dist., 1974-75; asso. supt. Walled Lake (Mich.) Consol. Sch. Dist., 1975—. Mem. Mich., Nat. assns. supervision and curriculum devel., Mich. Assn. Professions, Mich. Assn. Sch. Adminstrs., Assn. Childhood Edn., Oakland County Curriculum Council. Named Outstanding Tchr. of Year, 1960; recipient Citizen award, United Fund, 1974. Contbr. articles in field to profl. jours. Home: 23557 Gill Rd Farmington MI 48024 Office: 695 N Pontiac Trail Walled Lake MI 48088

LEARY, RICHARD LEE, mus. curator; b. Portsmouth, Va., Sept. 19, 1936; s. Wilbur Talmadge and Mary Katherine (Lee) L.; A.A. with honors, Old Dominion U., 1957; B.S., Va. Poly. Inst., 1959; M.S. in Geology, U. Mich., 1961; Ph.D. in Geology, U. Ill., 1980; m. Eleanor Marie Riehl, June 18, 1961; children—Seth Richard, Sara Marie. Field asst. Calif. Oil Co., summer 1959, Mobil Oil Co., summer 1960; asst. Kelsey Mus., Ann Arbor, Mich., 1960-61; mus. apprentice Newark (N.J.) Mus., 1961-62; curator geology Ill. State Mus., Springfield, 1962—; adj. asso. prof. Sangamon State U., Springfield, 1973-79. Mem. Internat. Orgn. Palaeobotany, Geol. Soc. Am., Bot. Soc. Am., Ill. State Acad. Sci. (pres. 1976-77), Sigma Xi. Presbyterian. Contbr. articles to profl. jours. Office: Ill State Mus Springfield IL 62706

LEATHEM, WILLIAM DOLARS, clin. nutritionist; b. Chgo., Jan. 6, 1931; s. Samuel Charles and Veronica (Armstrong) L.; B.S., U. Wis., 1961, M.S., 1963, Ph.D. (NIH fellow), 1965; m. Marjorie Eileen Minerick, Aug. 16, 1952; children—Janette Lynn, William Walter, Nancy Eileen. Asst. prof. Wis. State U., Whitewater, 1965-66, U. Wis., Waukesha, 1966-69; research asso. Norwich Pharmacal Co. (N.Y.), 1969-74, dir. clin. nutrition, 1974-76; mgr. marketed nutritionals, developed intravenous nutrition program Abbott Labs., North Chicago, Ill., 1976—. Served with AUS, 1948-54; Korea. Research grantee U. Wis., 1965-69, NIH, 1966-67. Mem. Am. Soc. Parenteral and Enteral Nutrition, Nutrition Today Soc., N.Y. Acad. Scis., AAAS, VFW, Sigma Xi. Episcopalian. Clubs: Masons, Moose. Contbr. articles on immune response to coccidiosis to profl. jours. Home: 541 Beck Rd Lindenhurst IL 60046 Office: Medical Dept HPD Abbott Park North Chicago IL 60064

LEBENS, JOHN CASPER, elec. cons.; b. St. Louis, July 31, 1911; s. John Casper and Katherine Gertrude (Lally) L.; B.E.E., Washington U., St. Louis, 1932, M.E.E., 1933; m. Jeannette Lewald, June 7, 1934; 1 son, Charles Alfred. Elec. engr. Bussmann Mfg. div. McGraw Edison Co., St. Louis, 1935-48, chief engr., 1948-56, v.p., 1956-64, cons., 1964-77; pres. Lebens Assos., St. Louis, 1964—, Bridge Holding Corp., St. Louis, 1974—; guest lectr. Moore Grad. Sch. Pa. U., 1950-56. Active St. Louis Regional Commerce and Growth Assn., Mo. Hist. Soc., St. Louis Art Mus., Mo. Bot. Garden, McDonnell Planetarium. Registered profl. engr., Mo. Fellow IEEE; mem. Nat. Soc. Profl. Engrs., St. Louis Elec. Bd. Trade, Soc. Automotive Engrs., Nat. Elec. Mfrs. Assn., Am. Soc. Metals, Tau Beta Pi, Sigma Xi, Pi Mu Epsilon. Republican. Roman Catholic. Clubs: St. Louis, Mo. Athletic, Engrs. Contbr. articles on elec. protection to tech. jours. Home: 4 Briarcliff Saint Louis MO 63124

LEBER, WALTER PHILIP, engring. co. exec., ret. army officer; b. St. Louis, Sept. 12, 1918; s. Walter Philip and Bonnie Vera (Blackman) L.; B.S., Mo. Sch. Mines, 1940; M.B.A., George Washington U., 1961; postgrad. Command and Gen. Staff Coll., 1955, Indsl. Coll. Armed Forces, 1958; m. Bernie Jean Palus, Sept. 9, 1950; children—Randolph Frank, Bonnie Gay, Philip Kevin (dec.). Petroleum engr. Stanolind Oil & Gas Co., 1940-41; commd. 2d lt. C.E., U.S. Army, 1941, advanced through grades to lt. gen., 1971; comdr. engring. troops 2d Inf. Div., 1941-42; faculty Engrs. Sch., Ft. Belvoir, Va., 1942; assigned Office Chief Engr. and Advanced Sect. Communications Zone, ETO, 1942-46, Manhattan Engring. Dist., Oak Ridge, 1946-47; chief tech. div. mil. liaison com. AEC, 1947-49; asst. dist. engr., exec. officer Seattle and Walla Walla dist., C.E., 1949-50; comdr. 46th Engr. Bn., Ft. Sill, Okla., 1950-51; assigned gen. staff logistics Dept. Army, 1951-55; dep. engr. 8th U.S. Army, Korea, comdr. 2d Engr. Group, Korea, 1956-57; exec. officer to chief engrs. U.S. Army, 1958-61; lt. gov. C.Z., v.p., dir. Panama Canal Co., 1961-63; div. engr. Army Engr. Div. Ohio River, 1963-66; dir. civil works Office Chief Engrs., U.S. Army, Washington, 1966-67; gov. C.Z., pres. Panama Canal Co., 1967-71; system mgr. Safeguard Anti-ballistic Missile System, 1971-74; ret., 1974; area mgr. Middle East Harza Engring. Co., Chgo., 1974-76, dir. Eastern Hemisphere mgmt., 1977—, v.p., 1978-80, area mgr. Argentina-Paraguay, 1980—. Chmn. gov. C.Z. Council Vol. Giving, 1961—; mgmt. com. Balboa YMCA; exec. bd. C.Z. council Boy Scouts Am.; trustee, exec. com. C.Z. United Fund. Decorated D.S.M. with oak leaf cluster, Legion of Merit with 2 oak leaf clusters, Bronze Star; Order Brit. Empire, L'Ordede Leopold II (Belgium); registered profl. engr., D.C., Fla. Mem. Soc. Am. Mil. Engrs., Tau Beta Pi, Phi Kappa Phi. Episcopalian. Home: 333 E Ontario Apt 4301 B Chicago IL 60611 Office: 150 S Wacker Dr Chicago IL 60606

LECH, JEROME FRANCIS, chem. co. exec.; b. Chgo., Feb. 29, 1944; s. Frank and Stephanie (Kunysz) L.; B.S., Ill. Benedictine Coll., 1966; postgrad. Roosevelt U., 1967-69; Ph.D., Mont. State U., 1973; m. Patricia Marzec, Jan. 22, 1966; children—Jeanette, Jeremy. Chemist, Argonne Nat. Lab., 1966-70; research asst. Mont. State U., 1970-73; applications chemist Vrian Assos., Palo Alto, Calif., 1974; indsl. hygiene chemist Kemper Ins. Co., Long Grove, Ill., 1975; dist. sales mgr. Applied Research Labs., LaGrange, Ill., 1976; product mgr. energy recovery group Dearborn Chem. Co., Lake Zurich, Ill., 1977-80; mgr. Analytical Labs., Econs. Labs., Inc., St. Paul, 1980—. Asst. coach Crystal Lake Soccer League, 1979; chief Indian Guides YMCA, 1978-79, nation medicine man, 1979-80; neighborhood rep. Crystal Lake Planning Commn. and Zoning Commn., 1979. Mem. Am. Chem. Soc., Soc. Applied Spectroscopy, Minn. Chromatography Forum, Sigma Xi. Contbr. articles to profl. jours.; patentee in field. Home: 3627 Willow Beach Trail Prior Lake MN 55372 Office: 840 Sibley Meml Hwy Saint Paul MN 55118

LECHNER, GEORGE WILLIAM, gen. and vascular surgeon; b. Denver, July 30, 1931; s. Frank Clifford and Hazel Mae (Elkins) L.; student U. N.Mex., 1948-49; B.A., Pacific Union Coll., 1952; M.D. summa cum laude, Loma Linda U., 1956; m. Betty Jane Baumbach, Aug. 3, 1952; children—Kathleen Ann, Elaine Marie, Carol Jean, Patricia Louise, James Richard. Instr. surgery Wayne State U., Detroit, 1963-64; intern Pontiac (Mich.) Gen. Hosp., 1956-57; resident in surgery Harper Hosp., Detroit, 1957-58, Wayne State U. Hosps., 1961-64; pvt. practice medicine specializing in surgery, Kettering, Ohio, 1964—; dir. surgery sect. 3, Kettering Med. Center, Dayton, 1967—; asso. dir. emergency medicine residency Wright State U.; mem. active staff Kettering Med. Center, Sycamore Med. Center; adj. faculty Kettering Coll. Med. Arts; pres. Kettering Emergency Room Corp.; asso. clin. prof. surgery Wright State U., 1975—. Trustee, mem. exec. com. bd. Kettering Med. Center, 1971-74; trustee Spring Valley Acad., 1973-78, pres., 1973-75. Served with AUS, 1958-61; Japan. Diplomate Am. Bd. Surgery; recipient C.V. Mosby award for acad. excellence, 1956. Fellow A.C.S.; mem. Midwest Surg. Assn., Dayton Surg. Soc., AMA, Ohio and Montgomery County med. socs., Am. Coll. Emergency Physicians, Soc. Tchrs. Emergency Medicine, Univ. Assn. Emergency Med. Service, AAAS. Seventh-day Adventist. Republican. Club: Rotary. Home: 1928 Burnham Ln Kettering OH 45429 Office: 2130 Leiter Rd Miamisburg OH 45342

LE CLAIRE, HENRI, physician; b. Lewiston, Me., Mar. 23, 1908; s. Dominique and Valada (Roy) LeC.; M.D., Loyola U. Med. Sch., 1940; m. Dorothy Maier; children—Andre, Henri Robert, Laureanne. Intern, Christ Hosp., Cin., 1940-41; resident Chgo. Tumor Inst., 1950-51; practice medicine, specializing in radiology, Cin., 1952—; cons. radiologist Highland County Hosp., Hillsboro, Ohio, 1954—; cons. radium therapist Deaconess Hosp., Cin., 1960—; raiser Thoroughbred horses. Am. Cancer Soc. fellow Barnard Skin & Cancer Hosp., St. Louis, 1951-52. Mem. AMA, Am. Radium Soc Radiol. Soc. N. Am., Am. Coll. Radiology. Republican. Clubs: Cuvier Press, Internat. Bacchus, Am. Angus Assn., Ohio Thoroughbred Horsemen's Assn., Chevalier De La Chaine Des Rotisseurs. Contbr. monographs to profl. jours. Home: Salem Hills Farm 1075 Eversole Rd Cincinnati OH 45230 Office: 19 Garfield Pl Suite 371 Cincinnati OH 45202

LEE, ALFRED PAK-HONG, fin. exec.; b. Hong Kong, Apr. 8, 1941; s. Chor Ming and Sin Ying (Chan) L.; B.A. cum laude, Kalamazoo Coll., 1966; M.S., Yale U., 1967, Ph.D. (Univ. fellow), 1970; m. Nancy Vilma Wang, June 10, 1967; children—Karen Maria, Vicki Anne, Paul Alfred. Research faculty U. Wash., Seattle, 1971-73; spl. agt. Lincoln Nat. Sales Corp. of Seattle, 1973-75, sales mgr. 1975-76, v.p., 1976-78; asst. supt. agencies Lincoln Nat. Sales Corp., Ft. Wayne, Ind., 1978-79, supt. agencies, 1979, dir. agy. devel., 1979—. Bd. dirs. Univ. Lions Found., Seattle, 1976, 77. Recipient Upjohn Chemistry award Kalamazoo Coll., 1966; NSF summer grantee, 1965. Mem. Am. Phys. Soc., Nat. Assn. Life Underwriters, Am. Soc. Chartered Life Underwriters, Phi Beta Kappa, Phi Eta Sigma. Roman Catholic. Club: Lions (3rd v.p. 1978-79). Contbr. articles to profl. jours. Home: 9217 Soaring Hill Pl Fort Wayne IN 46804 Office: 1300 S Clinton St Fort Wayne IN 46801

LEE, CHAN H., economist; b. Korea; came to U.S., 1954, naturalized, 1972; s. Seung-Nam and Sarm Nei K. L.; A.B., U. Nebr., 1957, M.A., 1959; Ph.D. in Econs., No. Ill. U., 1974; m. Soon-Ki Lee, Dec. 15, 1973; children—Charlene, Mimi, Billy. Grad. instr. No. Ill. U., 1969-74; asst. prof. econs. Valparaiso (Ind.) U., 1974-78; asso. prof. mgmt. Sangamon State U., Springfield, Ill., 1978-81; asso. prof. econs. S.W. State U., Marshall, Minn., 1981—. Chief div. research and stats. Nebr. Dept. Public Welfare, Lincoln, 1961-66. Mem. Am. Econ. Assn., Midwest Econ. Assn., Regional Sci. Assn., Midwest Fin. Assn., Midwest Bus. Adminstrn. Assn., Omicron Delta Epsilon. Founding editor Central Ill. Econ.-Bus. Rev., 1979-81. Home: 611 Van Buren St Marshall MN 56258 Office: Bus Dept SW State University Marshall MN 56258

LEE, CHUL, biochem. nutritionist; b. Taegu, Korea, Apr. 4, 1944; came to U.S., 1971, naturalized, 1976; s. Tae Young and Pun Yi Lee; B.S., Kyungpook Nat. U., 1970; M.S., Kans. State U., 1975, Ph.D., 1976; m. Un Hong Park, Oct. 10, 1969; children—David K., Marvin K. Research asso. dept. biochemistry Kans. State U., Manhattan, 1976-77, research asso. Coll. Vet. Medicine, 1980—; research nutritionist Am. Inst. Baking, Inc., Manhattan, 1977-80. Mem. Am. Coll. Nutrition, Am. Oil Chemists Soc., Inst. Food Technology, Sigma Xi. Contbr. articles in field to profl. jours. Home: 1708 Vaughn Dr Manhattan KS 66502 Office: Kans State U Dept Anatomy and Physiology Coll Vet Medicine Manhattan KS 66506

LEE, DONG SUNG, physician, anesthesiologist; b. Pyung-Buk, Korea, Jan. 1, 1933; s. Yi Bae and Soon Myong (Jie) L.; came to U.S., 1967; grad. Seoul Nat. U., 1953; M.D., Seoul (Korea) Nat. U., 1957; m. Yung Sim Kang, Feb. 1, 1959; children—Janet, Sharyl, Jill, John, David, Grace, Betty. Intern DePaul Hosp., Norfolk, Va., 1967-68; resident in anesthesiology St. Elizabeth Hosp., Youngstown, Ohio, 1968-71; partner Bel-Park Anesthesia Assos., Inc., Youngstown, 1971—. Served as med. officer to maj. Korean Air Force, 1957-67. Recipient Hon. Citizenship, State of Tex., 1963. Diplomate Am. Bd. Anesthesiology. Fellow Am. Coll. Anesthesiology; mem. Am., Ohio State med. assns., Am., Ohio socs. anesthesiologists. Home: 940 Royal Arms Dr Girard OH 44420 Office: St Elizabeth Hospital Youngstown OH 44505

LEE, E(UGENE) STANLEY, engr.; b. Hopeh, China, Sept. 7, 1930; s. Ing Yah and Lindy (Hsieng) L.; came to U.S., 1955, naturalized, 1961; M.S., N.C. State U., 1957; Ph.D., Princeton U., 1962; m. Mayanne Lee, Dec. 21, 1957; children—Linda J., Margaret H. Research engr. Phillips Petroleum Co., Bartlesville, Okla., 1960-66; asst. prof. Kans. State U., Manhattan, 1966-67, asso. prof., 1967-69, prof. Coll. Engring., 1969—; prof. U. So. Calif., Los Angeles, 1972-76. Research grantee NSF, 1971—, Office Water Resources, 1968-75, EPA, 1969-71, Dept. Def., 1967-72, U.S. Dept. Agr., 1978—, Electric Power Research Inst., 1976-78. Mem. Am. Inst. Chem. Engrs., Soc. Indsl. and Applied Math., Ops. Research Soc. Am., Sigma Xi, Tau Beta Pi, Phi Kappa Phi. Editor, Energy Sci. and Tech., 1975—; asso. editor Jour. Math. Analysis and Applications, 1974—, Computers and Math. with Applications, 1974—. Office: Durland Hall Dept Indsl Engring Kans State U Manhattan KS 66506

LEE, GARY MICHAEL, elec. engr., aircraft mfg. co. exec.; b. Chgo., Mar. 16, 1942; s. Glenard Marion and Ellen L.; B.S., Purdue U., 1964; M.S., Princeton U., 1965; Ph.D., Washington U., St. Louis, 1968; m. Karen Solima, May, 1975. With McDonnell Douglas Astronautics Co., St. Louis, 1965—, sr. tech. specialist, until 1975, program mgr., navy optical communications, 1975—; speaker in field; founder, owner Worlds Fair Houses, inner-city housing redevel., St. Louis, 1970—. Active various city, local betterment projects; trustee Twin Oaks subdiv., Ladue, Mo. NASA fellow, NSF fellow. Mem. IEEE, Sigma Xi, Tau Beta Pi, Sigma Pi Sigma, Eta Kappa Nu. Republican. Club: Elks. Contbr. over 30 articles to profl. jours. Home: 4 Twin Oaks Ln Ladue MO 63124 Office: PO Box 516 Saint Louis MO 63166

LEE, GILBERT BROOKS, research asso.; b. Cohasset, Mass., Sept. 10, 1913; s. John Alden and Charlotte Louise (Brooks) L.; B.A., Reed Coll., 1946; M.A., New Sch. Social Research, 1949; m. Marion Corrine Rapp, Mar. 7, 1943 (div. Jan. 1969); children—Thomas Stearns, Jane Stanton, Frederick Cabot, Eliot Frazar. Asst. psychologist Civil Service, Psychophysics of Vision, U.S. Naval Submarine Base, New London, Conn., 1950-53; research asso. Project Mich., Vision Research Labs., Willow Run, 1954-57; research asso. dept. ophthalmology U. Mich., Ann Arbor, 1958-72, sr. research asso., 1972-75, sr. engring. research asso. ophthalmology, 1975—. Precinct del. Democratic County Conv., Washtenaw County, 1970, 74; treas. Dem. Party Club, Ann Arbor, Mich., 1971-72, 74-79, vice chmn. nuclear arms issues, 1979; chmn. Precinct Election Inspectors, 1968-75. Served to capt. AUS, 1942-46, 61-62. Mem. Optical Soc. Am., AAAS, Fedn. Am. Scientists, N.Y. Acad. Sci., Assn. Research in Vision and Ophthalmology, Nation Assos., A.C.L.U. Contbr. articles to profl. jours. Home: 901 Edgewood Pl Ann Arbor MI 48103

LEE, JAMES CHEN-MING, chemist; b. Taipei, Taiwan, Feb. 19, 1944; s. Ben-Shin and Fan-Fung (Huang) L.; came to U.S., 1971, naturalized, 1977; B.S., Chung Yuan Christian Coll., 1968; M.S., Eastern N.Mex. U., 1973; m. Chin-Ling Wu, Nov. 16, 1970; children—Yueh Zenas, Chung Albert. Research asst. Nat. Tsing Hua U., Taiwan, 1968-69; tchr. chemistry Du Shi High Sch., Taiwan, 1969-71; teaching asst. Eastern N.Mex. U., Portales, 1971-73; chemist Thompson-Hayward Chem. Co., Kansas City, Kans., 1974-79; research scientist Farmland Industries, Inc., Kansas City, Mo., 1979—. Mem. Am. Chem. Soc., Am. Oil Chemists Soc. Home: 10805 W 95th Terr Overland Park KS 66214 Office: 103 W 26th St North Kansas City MO 64116

LEE, KENNETH DOUGLAS, mfg. co. ofcl.; b. Shreveport, La., Sept. 25, 1953; s. Isaac Douglas and Georgia Juanita (Adams) L.; B.B.A., U. Notre Dame, 1975; M.B.A., Washington U., St. Louis, 1977. Retail sales rep. Quaker Oaks Co., Chgo., 1975; jr. analyst in mktg. research Ralston Purina Co., St. Louis, 1976-77, mktg. asst., 1977-78; asso. product mgr. Swift & Co., Chgo., 1970; product mgr. Johnson Products Co., Chgo., 1980—. Mem. Nat. Mktg. Assn., Am. Mgmt. Assn., Black M.B.A. Assn., Urban League. Democrat. Mem. Christian Methodist Episcopal Ch. Home: 1626 N Sedgwick Ave Chicago IL 60614 Office: 8522 S Lafayette St Chicago IL 60620

LEE, KYO RAK, radiologist; b. Seoul, Korea, Aug. 3, 1933; s. Ke Chang and Ok Hi (Um) L.; came to U.S., 1964, naturalized, 1976; M.D., Seoul Nat. U., 1959; m. Ke Sook Oh, July 22, 1964; children—Andrew, John. Intern, Franklin Sq. Hosp., Balt., 1964-65; resident U. Mo. Med. Center, Columbia, Mo., 1965-68; instr. dept. radiology U. Mo., Columbia, 1968-69, asst. prof., 1969-71; asst. prof. dept. radiology U. Kans., Kansas City, 1971-76, asso. prof., 1976—. Served with Republic of Korea Army, 1950-52. Diplomate Am. Bd. Radiology. Recipient Richard H. Marshak award Am. Coll. Gastroenterology, 1975. Fellow Am. Coll. Radiology; mem. Radiol. Soc. N.Am., Am. Roentgen Ray Soc., Assn. Univ. Radiologists, Kans. Radiol. Soc., Greater Kansas City Radiol. Soc., Wyandotte County Med. Soc. Presbyterian. Contbr. articles to med. jours. Home: 9800 Glenwood St Overland Park KS 66212 Office: U Kans 39th St and Rainbow Blvd Kansas City KS 66103

LEE, LARRY DARNELL, mktg. exec.; b. Williamsburg, Va., May 23, 1953; s. Warren Edgar and Luheria Cornellia (Jackson) L.; B.A. cum laude, Norfolk State U., 1975; postgrad. Elmhurst Coll., 1977—. Substitute tchr. Williamsburg-James City County Pub. Sch. System, Williamsburg, Va., 1973-75; mktg. specialist Nalco Chem. Co., Oak Brook, Ill., 1975—; info. officer Colonial Williamsburg (Va.) Found., 1971-75. Mem. Soc. Automotive Engring., Nat. Tech. Assn., NAACP, Phi Beta Sigma, Order of Arrow. Home: 2811 Hobson Rd Woodridge IL 60517 Office: 2901 Butterfield Rd Oakbrook IL 60521

LEE, LARRY JAMES, city ofcl.; b. Fergus Falls, Minn., June 16, 1951; s. Raymond Harold and Arlene Sylvia (Honrud) L.; B.A., Moorhead State U., 1973; M.A., U. Minn., 1975. Teaching asst., research asst. U. Minn., Mpls., 1975-76; city planner City of Rothsay (Minn.), 1976, City of Hillsboro (N.D.), 1977-78; community devel. dir. City of Wahpeton (N.D.), 1978—. Sec., Hillsboro Community Betterment Com., 1977-78; mem. N.D. Community Betterment Adv. Council. Recipient N.D. Gov.'s Leadership award, 1978. Mem. Nat. Assn. Housing and Redevel. Ofcls., Community Devel. Soc., N.D. Planning Assn., Jr. C. of C. Clubs: Kiwanis, Toastmasters, Optimists (sec.-treas.). Home: 1307 11 St N Wahpeton ND 58075 Office: 120 N 4 St Wahpeton ND 58075

LEE, MARGARET, newspaper editor; b. Northfield, Minn., Jan. 5, 1921; d. Edward S. and Ferne Josephine (Thompson) Lee. With accounting dept. John W. Thomas Co., Mpls., 1943-44; reporter-bookkeeper Northfield News, 1944-54, news editor, 1954-56, asso. editor, 1956-62, mng. editor, 1962-67, editor, 1967—. Bd. dirs. Northfield Future, Inc. Recipient numerous writing awards Minn. Press Women, Nat. Fedn. Press Women. Mem. Minn. Press Women (editor Gopher Tidings 1959-80, past pres.), Nat. Fedn. Press Women (past regional dir.), Minn. Newspaper Assn. (past com. chmn.), Bus. and Profl. Women's Club (past pres. Northfield, dist. chmn.), Northfield Improvement assn. (past sec.), Northfield Hosp. Aux., Northfield Arts Guild, Mpls. Soc. Fine Arts, Minn. Zool. Soc., Sci. Mus. Minn., Minn. Hist. Soc., Rice County Hist. Soc. (v.p., dir.), Northfield Hist. Soc. (a founder, charter mem., sec. 1975—, tour dir. 1977—), HATPIN, Sigma Delta Chi. Club: Minnesota Press (charter mem., dir.). Home: 1012 Union St Northfield MN 55057 Office: Northfield News Northfield MN 55057

LEE, MARGARET NORMA, artist; b. Kansas City, Mo., July 7, 1928; d. James W. and Margaret W. (Farin) Lee; Ph.B., U. Chgo., 1948; M.A., Art Inst. Chgo., 1952. Lectr., U. Kansas City, 1957-61; cons. Kansas City Bd. Edn., Kansas City, Mo., 1968—; one-man shows Univ. Women's Club, Kansas City, 1966, Friends of Art, Kansas City, 1969, Fine Arts Gallery U. Mo. at Columbia, 1972; exhibited in group shows U. Kans., Lawrence, 1958, Chgo. Art Inst., 1963, Nelson Art Gallery, Kansas City, Mo., 1968, 74; represented in permanent collections Amarillo (Tex.) Art Center, Kansas City (Mo.)

Pub. Library, Park Coll., Parkville, Mo. Mem. Coll. Art Assn. Roman Catholic. Contbr. art to profl. jours.; author booklet. Home and studio: 4109 Holmes St Kansas City MO 64110

LEE, MICHAEL CHING HSUEH, mech. engr.; b. Taipei, Taiwan, China, Oct. 3, 1949; s. Yen Hsuan and Pei Chang L.; came to U.S., 1972, naturalized, 1978; Chem. Engr., Nat. Cheng Kung U., 1966, B.S., 1970; M.S. in Chem. Engring., U. Calif., Berkeley, 1974; Ph.D., in Mech. Engring., 1978; m. Amy Hsuan Yi Hsu, July 20, 1972; children—Benjamin Lee, Josephine Lee. Jr. project engr. U. Calif., Berkeley, 1977, postdoctoral chem. engr., 1978; sr. research engr. polymers dept. Gen. Motors Research Labs., Warren, Mich., 1978—. Mem. Soc. Rheology, ASME, Am. Chem. Soc., Sigma Xi. Roman Catholic. Office: Polymers Dept Gen Motors Research Labs 12 Mile and Mound Rd Warren MI 48090

LEE, MICHAEL MIN-SONG, librarian; b. Canton, China, Dec. 29, 1936; s. Si-Yee and Joan-Yee (Chu) L.; came to U.S., 1963, naturalized, 1971; M.A., Western Mich. U., 1965; B.A., Nat. Taiwan U., 1960; Ph.D., Loyola U., Chgo., 1979; m. Karen S. So, Mar. 19, 1966; children—Alice, Amy. Catalog librarian Tex. A&I U., 1965-67; head catalog dept. West Center Library, Chgo. State U., 1967-69; head librarian 1969-73, head public services Douglas Library, 1973-74, acting dir. libraries, 1974, head library ops., 1975-76, coordinator planning and devel., 1976-79; asso. prof. edn., dir. library and learning resources Saginaw Valley State Coll., University Center, Mich., 1979—. Mem. ALA, Assn. Coll. and Research Libraries, Mich. Library Assn., Library Adminstrn. and Mgmt. Assn., Library and Info. Tech. Assn., Chinese Am. Library Assn., Phi Delta Kappa. Roman Catholic. Office: Library and Learning Resources Saginaw Valley State College University Center MI 48710

LEE, NELDA KAYE, flight test engr.; b. Carrollton, Ala., Sept. 14, 1946; d. Milton Horace and Euna Faye (Johnson) Lee; B.S. in Aerospace Engring., Auburn U., 1969. Structural and mech. design engr. McDonnell Douglas Corp., St. Louis, 1969-78, sr. flight test engr., 1978—, named participant in personal devel. program, 1976. Named Accident Prevention counselor St. Louis area Dept. Transp. and FAA, 1977. Mem. AIAA (Young Profl. award 1978), Soc. Flight Test Engrs., Soc. Women Engrs., Mo. Pilots Assn., Helicopter Club Am., Ninety-Nines, Inc., Whirly-Girls, Inc. No. 247 (scholar, 1977), St. Louis N. County Tennis Assn., Delta Zeta. Baptist. Home: 1816 Exuma Dr Saint Louis MO 63136 Office: PO Box 516 Saint Louis MO 63166

LEE, ROBERT EDWIN, phys. fitness center exec.; b. East St. Louis, Ill., Nov. 26, 1948; s. Edward Paul and Cecilia Ann (Wozny) Janek (stepfather); student Belleville Area Coll., 1971-73, So. Ill. U., 1976-77. Trampoline, phys. fitness instr. Granite City (Ill.) YMCA, 1965-66; with Granite City Steel, 1967-70; mgr. Spartan Health Spa, Belleville, Ill., 1973-76; owner, mgr. Am. Fitness Center & Spa, Collinsville, Ill., 1976—; phys. fitness cons. Served with AUS, 1968-70. Mem. Internat. Phys. Fitness Assn., Collinsville C. of C., Universal Gym Assn. Club: Lions. Office: 120 E Main St Collinsville IL 62234

LEE, ROBERT ERNEST, III, clin. psychologist, marriage and family counselor; b. Los Angeles, Nov. 8, 1943; s. Robert Ernest, Jr., and Maria Agnes (Aprea) L.; A.B., Washington and Lee U., 1965; M.A., Princeton U., 1967, Ph.D., 1968; m. Patricia Ann Ball, May 18, 1973; 1 dau., Heather Ball. Intern, Merrill-Palmer Inst., Detroit, 1969-70; clin. psychologist VA Hosp., Allen Park, Mich., 1969-76; pvt. practice clin. psychology, Birmingham, Mich., 1976—; cons. Family Service of Detroit and Wayne County, Kingswood Hosp., Ferndale, Mich.; mem. adj. faculty U. Detroit, Oakland Community Coll. Pres. Mich. Psychologists Polit. Action Com., 1977, trustee, 1972-78. Recipient award of merit Detroit Inst. Tech., 1973; performance award VA, 1975; lic. psychologist, cert. marriage counselor, Mich. Fellow Am. Orthopsychiat. Assn.; mem. Am. Assn. Marriage and Family Therapy, Am. Psychol. Assn., Assn. Advancement Psychology, Mich. Assn. Marriage Counselors (pres. 1980), Mich. Interprofl. Assn. Marriage, Divorce and the Family, Mich. Psychol. Assn., Mich. Soc. Lic. Psychologists (pres.-elect), Mich. Soc. Cons. Psychologists (treas. 1977-78), Psychologists Task Force (dir.). Republican. Contbr. articles to profl. jours. Home: 6509 Alden Dr West Bloomfield MI 48033 Office: Suite 455 30200 Telegraph Rd Birmingham MI 48010

LEE, ROBERT JOHN, pharmacologist; b. Worcester, Mass., July 2, 1929; B.A., Adelphi Coll., 1958; M.S., Yeshiva U., 1959; Ph.D., SUNY, Bklyn., 1966; m. Uta M. Ophoven, Sept. 30, 1961; 1 dau., Cynthia. Tchr. sci., Union Free Sch. Dist. #4, Northport, N.Y., 1958-60; research asst. Downstate Med. Center, Bklyn., 1960-63; sr. physiologist-pharmacologist Geigy Chem. Corp., Ardsley, N.Y., 1966-69; research group leader Squibb Inst. Med. Research, Princeton, N.J., 1970-77; dir. dept. pharmacology Arnar Stone Labs., McGaw Park, Ill., 1977-78, dir. pharm. research, 1978—; adj. asst. prof. physiology Jefferson Med. Coll., Phila., 1977-79; adj. asst. prof. pharmacolgy Med. Coll. Wis., Milw., 1978—. Mem. AAAS, Am. Coll. Cardiology(program dir.), Am. Heart Assn., Soc. Toxicology, Am. Soc. Pharmacology and Exptl. Therapeutics, Soc. Explt. Biology and Medicine, Internat. Study Group for Research in Cardiac Metabolism, Alpha Epsilon Delta, Beta Beta Beta. Contbr. articles to profl. jours. Office: 1600 Waukegan Rd McGaw Park IL 60085

LEE, SHIRLEY WILLIAMS, state senator; b. Bismarck, N.D., Jan. 8, 1924; d. John E. and Maude (Edgerton) W.; student St. Olaf Coll., 1941-43; m. Warren T. Lee, 1942; children—Suzan Lee Fibelstad, John, Judy Lee Guenthner, Steven. Mem. N.D. Senate, 1973—. Vice chmn. Burleigh County Young Republicans, 1958-60; sec. Burleigh County Rep. Com., 1960-62; chmn. Burleigh County Rep. Orgn., 1962-64, N.D. Rep. Orgn., 1964-66; vice chmn. N.D. Rep. Com., 1966-68. Trustee, Mercer-McLenn Regional Library; bd. dirs. Turtle Lake Community Chest. Mem. Turtle Lake Study Club, PEO, DAR. Lutheran. Office: ND Senate State Capitol Bismarck ND 58505*

LEE, SONG PING, physician; b. Tsao-Tun, Taiwan, Dec. 2, 1934; s. Tsang-Lang and Chu-Ying C. L.; came to U.S., 1965, naturalized, 1977; B. Medicine, Nat. Taiwan U., 1961, M.D., 1961; m. Li-Ying Chen, Apr. 13, 1965; children—Donald, Edward, Andrew. Intern, Pottsville (Pa.) Hosp., 1965-66; sr. resident Univ. Hosp., Nat. Taiwan U., Taipei, 1964-65; chief resident in otorhinolaryngology Pottsville (Pa.) Hosp., 1966-68, Boston City Hosp and New Eng. Med. Center Hosp., Boston, 1969-72; teaching fellow Tufts Med. Sch., Boston, 1971-72; otolaryngologist, head neck surgeon Topeka Med. Center, 1972—, chmn. exec. com., 1975-78; practice medicine specializing in otolaryngology Topeka, 1972—; cons. in field. Diplomate Am. Bd. Otolaryngology. Fellow A.C.S., Am. Acad. Ophthalmology and Otolaryngology; mem. Shawnee County, Kans. med. socs., AMA, Am. Council Otolaryngology, Kansas City Soc. Ophthalmology and Otolaryngology, Centurian Club Deafness Research Found. Author: Otologic Assessments—Physiological Measures of the Audio-Vestibular System, 1975. Home: 210 Yorkshire Rd Topeka KS 66606 Office: 918 W 10th St Topeka KS 66604

LEE, SOO K., pediatrician; b. Korea, Mar. 1, 1940; s. Kun D. and Kae S. (Kim) L.; M.D., Kyungpook Nat. U., 1965; m. Seung Ja Seo, June 9, 1966; children—Greg, Young, Janet. Intern, resident in pediatrics Michael Reese Hosp., Chgo., 1969-72; fellow in pediatric nephrology LaRabida Hosp.- U. Chgo., 1972-74; attending pediatric physician Cook County Hosp., Chgo., 1974-76; practice medicine, specializing in pediatrics, Joliet, Ill., 1976—; instr. pediatrics U. Ill., 1974-76. Med. cons. Parent Power, 1976—. Served to capt. M.C., Korean Army, 1966-69. Mem. Am. Acad. Pediatrics, AMA. Roman Catholic. Office: 201 N Joliet Joliet IL 60431

LEE, SUNG HO, psychiatrist; b. Seoul, Korea, June 28, 1934; s. Suk K. and Chung W. (Kim) L.; came to U.S., 1964, naturalized, 1976; M.D., Yonsei U., 1959; M.Sc., Ohio State U., 1969; m. Myung Ha, Nov. 17, 1959; children—Benjamin, May. Rotating intern Seoul Red Cross Hosp., 1959-60; resident in psychiatry Yonsei U. Hosp., 1960-62, Ohio State U., 1965-67, Brentwood Hosp., Los Angeles, 1967-68; asst. prof., chmn. dept. psychiatry Ewha U. Hosp., Seoul, 1968-70; clin. dir. unit B, Broughton State Hosp., Morganton, N.C., 1970-71; chief psychiat. service Dayton (Ohio) VA Med. Center, 1970-76, sr. psychiatrist, 1976—; pvt. practice specializing in psychiatry, Dayton, 1975—; asst. clin. prof. Ohio State U. Med. Sch., Wright State U.; cons. in field. Diplomate Am. Bd. Psychiatry and Neurology. Mem. AMA, Korean, Montgomery County med. assns., Am. Psychiat. Assn. Methodist. Contbr. articles to med. jours. Home: 7706 Normandy Ln Dayton OH 45459 Office: 2801 Far Hills Ave Dayton OH 45419

LEE, TED J., ins. cons.; b. Pasco, Wash., Nov. 19, 1927; s. Bertram B. and Marie H. (Palmer) L.; B.A., U. Minn., 1945; C.L.U., 1961; children—Geoffrey B., Nancy Lee Dahl, Susan J. Bartlett, John K., Barbara A. Founder, pres. of co. specializing in retirement plans, financial and estate planning, Duluth, Minn., 1958—; co-founder Sch. Bus. and Econs., U. Minn., Duluth; speaker, cons., tchr. in field. Served with USMC, 1945-47. Mem. Am. Soc. C.L.U.'s, Minn., Arrowhead (past pres.) assns. C.L.U.'s, Life Leaders Minn., U. Minn. Alumni Assn. Republican. Conglist. Club: Kitchi Gammi (Duluth). Home: French River Duluth MN 55804 Office: 800 First Nat Bank Bldg Duluth MN 55802

LEE, WILLIAM JOHNSON, lawyer, state ofcl.; b. Oneida, Tenn., Jan. 13, 1924; s. William J. and Ara (Anderson) L.; student Akron U., 1941-43, Denison U., 1943-44, Harvard U., 1944-45; J.D., Ohio State U., 1948. Admitted to Ohio bar, 1948, Fla. bar, 1962; research asst. Ohio State U. Law Sch., 1948-49; asst. dir. Ohio Dept. Liquor Control, chief purchases, 1956-57, atty. examiner, 1951-53, asst. state permit chief, 1953-55, state permit chief, 1955-56; asst. counsel, staff Hupp Corp., 1957-58; spl. counsel City Attys. Office Ft. Lauderdale (Fla.), 1963-65; asst. atty. gen. Office Atty. Gen., State of Ohio, 1966-70; adminstr. State Med. Bd. Ohio, Columbus, 1970—; pvt. practice law, Ft. Lauderdale, 1965-66; acting municipal judge, Ravenna, Ohio, 1960; instr. Coll. Bus. Adminstrn., Kent State U., 1961-62. Mem. pastoral relations com. Epworth United Meth. Ch., 1976; chmn. legal aid com. Portage County, Ohio, 1960; troop awards chmn. Boy Scouts Am., 1965; mem. ch. bd. Melrose Park (Fla.) Meth. Ch., 1966. Mem. Am. Legion, Fla., Columbus, Akron, Broward County (Fla.) bar assns., Delta Theta Phi, Phi Kappa Tau, Pi Kappa Delta. Served with USAAF, 1942-46. Editorial bd. Ohio State Law Jour., 1947-48; also articles. Home: 4893 Brittany Ct W Columbus OH 43229 Office: Suite 510 65 S Front St Columbus OH 43215

LEE, WILLIAM WAH HING, clin. psychologist; b. N.Y.C., May 8, 1947; s. Bow and Ping (Loy) L.; B.S., Ill. Inst. Tech., 1970; M.S., Western Ill. U., 1971; Ed.D., Okla. State U., 1977; m. Melanie May Kulka, Sept. 6, 1975. Chief psychologist Spl. Edn. Dist. Lake County, Gurnee, Ill., 1974-81; adj. grad. faculty Nat. Coll. Edn., Evanston, Ill., 1976—; pvt. practice clin. psychology Gurnee, Ill., 1978—; cons. area hosps. Lic. clin. psychologist, Ill.; cert. sch. psychologist. Mem. Am. Psychol. Assn., Ill. Psychol. Assn., Am. Soc. Clin. Hypnosis, Biofeedback Soc. Am., Nat. Register Health Service Providers in Psychology. Home: 1301 N Western Ave Lake Forest IL 60045 Office: 1170 Route 41 Gurnee IL 60031

LEE, WOODROW, hosp. adminstr.; b. Chgo., Feb. 4, 1931; s. Arve and Stella Henrietta (Hanson) L.; student U. Hawaii, 1948-49; B.A., Lake Forest Coll., 1952; M.H.A., U. Minn., 1954; m. Marilyn Jean Loafman, Mar. 6, 1957; children—Mark Alan, Martha Lynne, David Arve, Daniel Glen. Adminstrv. resident St. Luke's Hosp., Milw., 1953-54; asst. dir. John D. Archbold Meml. Hosp., Thomasville, Ga., 1956-60; adminstr. McCune-Brooks Hosp., Carthage, Mo., 1960-65; adminstr., dir. St. John's Hosp., Joplin, Mo., 1965; adminstr. Audrain Med. Center, Mexico, Mo., 1966-80, Levering Hosp., Hannibal, Mo., 1980—; clin. asso. prof. grad. program in health services mgmt. U. Mo., Columbia, 1966—. Pres. Mo. Hosp. Councils, 1964, 68, 70; chmn. Permanent Blue Cross Orgn. Central Mo., 1970-72, mem. Blue Cross Hosp. Adv. Com., 1973—; adminstr. Audrain County (Mo.) Health Unit, 1966-80; vice chmn. pres.'s council Nat. Health/Welfare Mut. Life Ins. Assn., 1974—, mem. nominating com., 1977; chmn. med. adv. com. Marion County Ambulance Dist., 1980—; mem. adv. group Area II, Health Systems Agy., 1977-79; local registrar vital statistics, 1978-80; mem. Mid-Mo. Health Edn. Consortium, pres., 1979-80; treas. Mark Twain Physician Recruitment Assn., 1981—. Served with AUS, 1954-56. Mem. Am. Coll. Hosp. Adminstrs., Am. Hosp. Assn., Mo. Hosp. Assn. (trustee 1973-77, treas. 1974-76), Mexico C. of C. (dir. 1971-75). Presbyn (elder 1974-77). Rotarian (sec. 1976-78, treas. 1978, v.p. 1979, pres. 1980). Club: Hannibal Country. Home: Route 2 Woodland Acres Hannibal MO 63401 Office: 1734 Market St Hannibal MO 63401

LEEDY, EMILY L. FOSTER (MRS. WILLIAM N. LEEDY), govt. ofcl.; b. Jackson, Ohio, Sept. 24, 1921; d. Raymond S. and Grace (Garrett) Foster; B.S., Rio Grande Coll., 1949; M.Ed., Ohio U., 1957; postgrad. Ohio State U., 1956, Mich. State U., 1958-59, Case Western Res. U., 1963-65; m. William N. Leedy, Jan. 1, 1943; 1 son. Dwight A. Tchr. Frankfort (Ohio) pub. schs., 1941-46, Ross County Schs., Chillicothe, Ohio, 1948-53; elementary and supervising tchr. Chillicothe City Schs., 1953-56; dean of girls, secondary tchr. Berea City Schs., 1956-57; vis. tchr. Parma City Schs., 1957-59; counselor Homewood-Flossmoor High Sch., Flossmoor, Ill., 1959-60; teaching fellow Ohio U., 1960-62; asst. prof. edn., 1962-64; asso. prof., counselor Cuyahoga Community Coll., 1964-66; dean of women Cleve. State U., 1966-67, asso. dean student affairs, 1967-69; guidance dir. Cathedral Latin Sch., 1969-71; dir. women's service div. Ohio Bur. Employment Services, 1971—; cons. in edn. Mem. adv. com. S.W. Community Information Service, 1959-60; youth com. S.W. YWCA, 1963-70, chmn., 1964-70, bd. mgmt., 1964-70; group services council Cleve. Welfare Fedn., 1964-66; chmn. Met. YWCA Youth Program study com., 1966, bd. dirs., 1966-72, v.p., 1967-68; chmn. adv. council Ohio State U. Sch. Home Econs., 1977-80. Named Cleve. area Woman of Achievement, 1969; named to Ohio Women's Hall of Fame, 1979; recipient Cert. of Meritorious Service, Council of Home Econs., Agrl. and Natural Resources, Ohio State U., 1981. Mem. AAUW, Am., Northeastern Ohio (sec. 1958-59, exec. com. 1963-64, pub. relations chmn. 1962-64, newsletter chmn., editor 1963-64, del. nat. assembly 1959-63) personnel and guidance assns., Nat. Vocational Guidance Assn., Am., Ohio sch. counselors assns., Am. Rehab. Counseling Assn., Nat. (publs. com. 1967-69, profl. employment practices com. 1980-81), Ohio (program chmn. 1967, editor Newsletter 1968-71) assns. women deans and counselors, Cleve. Counselors Assn. (pres. 1966), N.E.A., Ohio Edn. Assn., Ohio Assn. Gifted Children, Nat. Assn. Student Personnel Adminstrs., Am. Coll. Personnel Assn., League Women Voters, Cleve. Mental Health Assn., Women's Equity Action League, Zonta Internat. (exec. bd. 1968-70, treas. 1970-72, chmn. dist. V Status of Women 1980-81), Nat. Assn. Commns. for Women (bd. dirs. 1980-81, sec. 1981-82), Rio Grande Coll. Alumni Assn. (Atwood Achievement award 1975), Bus. and Profl. Women's Club (Nike award 1973), Delta Kappa Gamma. Clubs: Columbus Met.; Women's City (Cleve.). Home: 580 Lindberg Blvd Berea OH 44017 Office: 145 S Front St Columbus OH 43216

LEEGE, DAVID CALHOUN, educator; b. Elkhart, Ind., May 18, 1937; s. Harold Martin and Nellie Josephine (Bliss) L.; B.A., Valparaiso U., 1959; postgrad. U. Chgo., 1959-60; Ph.D., Ind. U., 1965; m. Patricia Ann Schad, June 8, 1963; children—David McChesney, Lissa Maria, Kurt Johannes. Instr. social sci. Concordia Tchrs. Coll., River Forest, Ill., 1962-64; asst. prof. polit. sci., dir. public opinion survey unit U. Mo., Columbia, 1964-68; asso. prof., dir. survey research center SUNY, Buffalo, 1968-70; asso. prof. U. Ill., Chgo., 1970-72, prof., 1972-76, head dept., 1972-73; prof. govt. and internat. studies, dir. center for study of man in contemporary society U. Notre Dame, Ind., 1976—; program dir. for polit. sci. NSF, 1974-76; vis. prof. York U., Toronto, Ont., Can., 1970, U. Mich., 1971, 73, U. Leuven (Belgium), 1980. Mem. Am. Polit. Sci. Assn., AAAS, Midwest Polit. Sci. Assn. Lutheran. Author: (with Wayne Francis) Political Research, 1974. Contbr. articles to profl. jours. Home: 2014 E Jefferson Blvd South Bend IN 46617 Office: U Notre Dame Center for the Study of Man Notre Dame IN 46556

LEEMASTER, NORMAN BERNARD, mfg. co. exec.; b. Toledo, Oct. 24, 1942; s. Robert L. and Ellen L. LeeM.; student Jackson Jr. Coll., 1962, Mich. State U., 1960-63; m. Christine L. LeeMaster, July 17, 1971; children—Michelle, Mark, Nicole. Dist. sales mgr. Airco Industries, Toledo, 1963-65; sales mgr. Delta Am., Wheeling, Ill., 1965-70; regional sales mgr. E.L. Bruce, Memphis, 1970-73; gen. mgr. Bennett Industries, Peotone, Ill., 1973—. Mem. Am. Mgmt. Assn. Lutheran. Club: Olympia Fields Country. Office: Bennett Industries 515 1st St Peotone IL 60468

LEEMON, JOHN ALLEN, lawyer; b. Hoopeston, Ill., Jan. 12, 1928; s. Allen Wallace and Eva Carol (Merritt) L.; B.S., U. Ill., 1950, LL.B., 1952; m. Sally P. Pierce, July 14, 1951; children—John P., Lisa A. Admitted to Ill. bar, 1952; practiced in Savanna, Ill., 1952-54, Mt. Carroll, Ill, 1954—; mem. firms Eaton & Leemon, 1956-66, Eaton, Leemon & Rapp, 1967, Leemon & Rapp, 1968-70; dir. Mt. Carroll Fire Ins. Co. Mem. Am., Ill. (negligence council 1961-66, grievance com. inquiry div. 1967-70), Carroll County, Whiteside County bar assns. Mason (Shriner). Home: Rural Route Box 151 Mount Carroll IL 61053 Offices: National Bank Bldg Mount Carroll IL 61053 also State Bank of Shannon Bldg Shannon IL 61078

LEENHOUTS, KEITH JAMES, former judge, assn. exec.; b. Grand Rapids, Mich., Oct. 17, 1925; s. William James and Dorothy (Champion) L.; B.A., Albion Coll., 1949; J.D., Wayne State U., 1952; m. Audrey Doris Saari, June 27, 1953; children—William James, David John, Daniel S. (dec.), James Edward. Admitted to Mich. bar, 1953; practice law, Royal Oak, Mich., 1953-59; mem. firm Dell, Heber & Leenhouts, Royal Oak, 1953-59; from municipal ct. judge to Mich. Dist. ct. judge, 1959-69; pres. Vol. In Probation, Inc., Royal Oak, 1969-71; prof. dept. criminal justice U. Ala., 1976—; dir. Vols. In Probation div. Nat. Council on Crime and Delinquency, 1972—. Lectr. Nat. Coll. State Trial Judges, 1967, Nat. Coll. State Judiciary, 1972, numerous seminars; cons. Law Enforcement Assistance Adminstrn.; prin. investigator Nat. Insts. Mental Health, 1965-69. Active YMCA, Boys Club. Bd. dirs. ACTION, 1972. Served with USAAF, 1944-46. Recipient Halpern award Nat. Council on Crime and Delinquency; Distinguished Service award Jaycees; Distinguished Alumni award Albion Coll., 1967; Distinguished Service award Wayne State U., 1970. Mem. Mich. State Bar (chmn. com. on probation), Am. Judicature Soc. (dir. 1969-70), North Am. Judges Assn. (v.p. 1962-65, awards). Methodist (trustee, Sunday sch. tchr.). Lion. Author: First Offender, 1971; A Father...A Son...And a Three Mile Run, 1975, also Dutch, Portuguese, Spanish, French edits. Contbr. numerous articles to pop. mags., profl. jours. Home: 830 Normandy St Royal Oak MI 48073 Office: 200 Washington Square Plaza Royal Oak MI 48067

LEESON, JANET CAROLINE TOLLEFSON, cake specialties co. exec.; b. L'Anse, Mich., May 23, 1933; d. Harold Arnold and Sylvia Aino (Makikangas) Tollefson; student Prairie State Coll., 1970-76; master decorator degree Wilton Sch. Cake Decorating, 1974; m. Raymond Harry Leeson, May 20, 1961; 1 son, Barry Raymond; children by previous marriage—Warren Scott, Debra Delores. Mgr., Peak Service Cleaners, Chgo., 1959; co-owner Ra-Ja-Lee TV, Harvey, Ill., 1961-66; founder and head fgn. trade dept. Wilton Enterprises, Inc., Chgo., 1969-75; tchr. cake decorating J.C. Penney Co., Matteson, Ill., 1975; office mgr. Pat Carpenter Assos., Highland, Ind., 1975—; pres. Leeson's Party Cakes, Inc., cake supplies and cake sculpture, Tinley Park, Ill., 1976—; lectr. and demonstrator cake sculpture and decorating; lectr. small bus. and govt. Sec., Luth. Ch. Women; active worker Boy Scouts Am. and Girl Scouts U.S.A., 1957-63; bd. dirs. Whittier PTA, 1962-70; active Bremen Twp. Republican Party. Recipient numerous awards for cake sculpture and decorating, 1970—. Mem. Chgo. Area Retail Bakers Assn. (1st pl. in regional midwest wedding cake competition 1978, 80), Am. Bus. Women's Assn. (chpt. publicity chmn.), Ingalls Meml. Hosp. Aux. Lutheran. Home: 6713 W 163d Pl Tinley Park IL 60477 Office: Leeson's Party Cakes Inc 6713 W 163d Pl Tinley Park IL 60477 also 513 River Oaks W Calumet City IL 60409

LEFFEL, CHARLES POAGUE, appliance mfg. co. exec.; b. Evanston, Ill., May 30, 1928; s. Philip Clark and Catherine Smith (Poague) L.; A.B., Amherst Coll., 1950; m. Grace Ann (Hartnett) L.; June 2, 1962; 1 dau., Kay. Sales work Goodbody & Co., Chgo., 1950-51, Internat. Paper Co., Cleve., 1951-54; with No. Electric Co., Chgo., 1957-72, exec. v.p., 1972-74, pres., 1974-76; group v.p. Sunbeam Corp., Chgo., 1974-76, exec. v.p.,dir., 1976-77, pres., 1977—. Bd. mgrs. Robert E. Wood Boys Club, Chgo.; bd. dirs. Santa for the Very Poor; bd. dirs. summer camp Chgo. Boys Club. Served with AUS, 1954-56. Presbyterian. Clubs: Deke (N.Y.C.); Metropolitan, Racquet, Carlton (Chgo.); Glen View Golf, (Ill.). Home: 30 E Scott St Chicago IL 60610 Office: Sunbeam Corp 2001 S York Rd Oak Brook IL 60521

LEFFLER, ALLAN THEODORE, agronomist; b. Van Buren County, Iowa, Mar. 25, 1914; s. Andrew Rex and Dorothea (Steen) L.; B.S., Iowa State Coll., 1935, postgrad., 1946-49, 1968-69; m. Josephine Brown, Sept. 1, 1939; children—Allan Theodore, II, Harry R., Thomas B., Mary Ellen Leffler Hilliard. Project and area agronomist, dist. conservationist Soil Conservation Service, Falmouth, Ky., 1935—, Dayton, Ohio, 1940-41, Morocco, Ind., 1941-44; asst. extension agronomist Iowa State U., Ames, 1944-46; soil fertilizer specialist Pioneer Hi-Bred, Johnston, Iowa, 1946-49, prodn. agronomist, 1953-59, dir. tech. services, 1960-68; coordinator agriculture bus., Des Moines Area Community Coll., Ankeny, Iowa,

1968-69; agronomist Iowa Plant Food Co., Des Moines, 1949-53; product services mgr. ACCO Seed, Belmond, Iowa, 1969-79, ret., 1979; cons. agronomist to various businesses, 1980—. Mem. Am. Soc. Agronomy, Council for Agrl. Sci. and Tech., Alpha Zeta, Gamma Sigma Delta. Democrat. Congregationalist. Club: Lions. Home: 2229 Donald St Ames IA 50010

LEFFLER, JOHN SUTTON, fin. exec.; b. Cleve., July 29, 1949; s. William Bain and Marjorie Adele (Smith) L.; B.A. with high honors DePauw U., 1971; M.B.A. (Bache scholar 1972-73), Emory U., 1973; m. Leslie Dyckman McGaughey, Feb. 14, 1970; children—Lizabeth Adele, Leigh Dyckman, Laura Sutton, John William. Dir. mgmt. adv. services Arthur Young & Co., Atlanta, Portland, Cin., 1973-77; pres., chief exec. officer Leffler Industries, Inc., Marion, Ohio, 1977—; dir. various corps. Bd. dirs. Met. Econ. Devel., Portland, Oreg., 1976-77; hon. mem. bd. govs. Emanuel Found., 1977—. C.P.A., Ohio; cert. mgmt. cons. Mem. Am. Inst. C.P.A.'s, Inst. Cert. Mgmt. Cons., Ohio Soc. C.P.A.'s, Oreg. Soc. C.P.A.'s, Pres.'s Assn. of Am. Mgmt. Assn., Cum Laude Soc., Sigma Nu, Beta Gamma Sigma. Republican. Methodist. Home: 320 Reily Rd Cincinnati OH 45215

LEFTON, NORMAN BARRY, mfg. co. exec.; b. St. Louis, Apr. 25, 1934; s. Samuel Israel and Sarah (Offstein) L.; B.S. in Indsl. Engring., U. Ill., 1955; M.A. in Econs. (Woodrow Wilson fellow 1962-63), U. Chgo., 1963, Ph.D. in Econs., 1972; m. Margaret Clare Bennetto Banks, Nov. 1, 1962; children—Simon J., Sarah J. Indsl. engr. Caterpillar Tractor Co., Peoria, Ill., 1955-56; asst. prof. econs. U. Hawaii, Honolulu, 1965-70; cons. Economist Research Corp., U. Hawaii, Honolulu, 1972-74; chmn. bd. Lefton Iron & Metal Co., E. St. Louis, Ill., 1976—; adj. prof. Central Mich. U., Inst. of Personal and Career Devel., 1972—; vis. lectr. Hawaii Lao Coll., Kaneohe, 1975. Served with C.E., USN, 1956-59. U. Chgo. fellow, 1963-64. Mem. Navy League of U.S., Nat. Audubon Soc., Mil. Order World Wars, Nat. Assn. Bus. Economists, Am. Econ. Assn., Inst. Scrap Iron and Steel (exec. com. 1979—), Res. Officers Assn. U.S. Republican. Club: Media. Office: 205 S 17th St East Saint Louis IL 62207

LEGATS, KENNETH JAMES, county ofcl.; b. Akron, Jan. 23, 1942; s. Ludwig and Katherine (Hardesty) L.; B.A. in Edn., U. Akron, 1966; M.Ed. in Adminstrn., Ohio U., 1981; m. Caribeth Wallace, July 22, 1967; children—Mark, Michael. Tchr. spl. edn. Summit County Mental Retardation Program, Akron, 1965-69, also tchr. adult basic edn. Akron Bd. Edn., evenings 1966-69; supt. Muskingum County Mental Retardation Program, Zanesville, Ohio, 1969—; mem. Ohio Spl. Olympics Com., 1972-74, div. mental retardation State Fair Com., 1971-73; team leader mental retardation Ann. Physicians and Schs. Conf. Health Edn. in Ohio, 1979. Recipient Nate Milder Founders award Zanesville Jaycees, 1971, award Easter Seal Assn., 1976, award Muskingum County Mental Health Assn., 1976. Mem. Nat. Assn. Retarded Citizens, Ohio Assn. Retarded Citizens, Muskingum County Assn. Retarded Citizens, Ohio Supt. Assn. for Mental Retardation Programs, Profl. Assn. for Retarded, Ohio Sch. Bds. Assn., Ohio Assn. Children with Learning Disabilities, Muskingum County Assn. Children with Learning Disabilities, Phi Delta Kappa. Elder, dir. 1st Christian Ch., Zanesville, 1976-79. Club: Rotary. Home: 3415 Bowers Ln Zanesville OH 43701 Office: 1330 Newark Rd Zanesville OH 43701

LEGGITT, DOROTHY, educator; b. Oblong, Ill., Feb. 19, 1903; d. Clarence C. and Louise Frances (Muchmore) L.; diploma Eastern Ill. State U., 1923, D.H.L., 1977; Ph.B., U. Chgo., 1930, M.A., 1933, postgrad., intermittently, 1937-62. Tchr. rural schs., Jasper & Crawford Counties, Ill., 1920-22; tchr. high sch., Glen Ellyn, Ill., 1923-35; lectr., prof. No. Ill. State U., DeKalb, 1936-37; tchr. social studies, counselor Clayton (Mo.) pub. schs., 1937-52; tchr. Decatur (Ill.) pub. schs., 1952-54, Park Ridge (Ill.) pub. schs., 1954-61; reading specialist Joliet (Ill.) Jr. Coll., 1961-62, Niles West High Sch., Skokie, Ill., 1962-63; reading cons. Kenosha High Schs., Kenosha, Wis., 1963-65; head study skills dept. Palm Beach (Fla.) Jr. Coll., 1965-73, prof. emeritus, 1973—; summer lectr. various colls. and univs. Field rep. grad. edn. and social sci. depts. U. Chgo.; mem. found. bd. Eastern Ill. U. Recipient Walgreen Found. award in social, econ. and polit. instns., 1948, scholarship award Pi Lambda Theta, 1948, Distinguished Alumni award Eastern Ill. U., 1974. Mem. Newberry Library Assn. (asso.), Ill. Edn. Assn., AAUW. Author: Basic Study Skills and Workbook, 1942. Contbr. articles to profl. jours. Home: Windermere House 1642 E 56th St Chicago IL 60637

LEGGON, CHERYL BERNADETTE, educator; b. Cleve., Aug. 19, 1948; d. Robert Winston and Bernice (Metcalfe) L.; B.A., Columbia U., 1970; M.A., U. Chgo., 1973, Ph.D., 1975; m. Edward Wesley GraY, Jr., July 18, 1970; 1 son, Robert Raphael Leggon. Asst. prof. black studies and sociology Mt. Holyoke Coll., South Hadley, Mass., 1975-77; grad. faculty U. Mass., Amherst, 1975-77; asst. prof. sociology U. Ill., Chgo., 1977-80; postdoctoral research fellow dept. sociology U. Chgo., 1980-82. Spl. asst. to exec. dir. Chgo. Urban League, 1976; bd. dirs. Chgo. Child Care Soc. Andrew Mellon fellow, Center for Advanced Study in Behavioral Sci., Stanford U., 1977; George F. Baker Fund scholar, 1966-70; Ford Found. fellow, 1970-75; U. Ill. Chgo. Circle summer faculty fellow, 1978. Mem. Assn. Black Sociologists (sec.-treas. 1977-79), Am. Sociol. Assn., Internat. Sociol. Assn. (research com. on ethnic, race and minority relations 1979—), Sociologists for Women in Soc. Baptist. Co-editor: (with Cora B. Marrett) Jour. Research in Race and Ethnic Relations, 1977—. Author: Racism and Sexism, in press. Home: 5400 S Hyde Park Blvd Chicago IL 60615 Office: Dept Sociology U Chgo 1126 E 59th St Chicago IL 60637

LEGGON, HERMAN WESLEY, chem. co. exec.; b. Cleve., Sept. 20, 1930; s. Charles W. and Ombra Novella (Reese) L.; B.S., Case Inst. Tech., 1953; M.S., John Carroll U., 1966; m. Zara M. Kerr, Aug. 14, 1976. Head organic lab. Crobaugh Labs., Cleve., 1955-59; analytical chemist Union Carbide Corp., Cleve., 1959-67, systems analyst Parma Tech. Center, 1967—; guest lectr. Atlanta U., 1973—; instr. Dyke Coll., 1979—. Service dir. Oakwood Village, 1969-70, councilman, 1970-71, councilman-at-large, 1971-73, pres. council, 1973-75. Recipient commendation Oakwood Village, 1962. Mem. ASTM (chmn. subcom. on nomenclature), Alpha Phi Alpha. Home: 3470 Belvoir St Beachwood OH 44122 Office: PO Box 6116 Cleveland OH 44101

LE GRAND, CLAY, justice state supreme ct.; b. St. Louis, Feb. 26, 1911; s. Nic and Mary (Leifield) LeG.; student St. Ambrose Coll., 1928-30; J.D., Cath. U. Am., 1934; m. Suzanne Wilcox, Dec. 30, 1935;children—Mary Suzanne (Mrs. Thomas J. Murray), Julie, Nicholas W. Pvt. practice law, 1934-57; judge Dist. Ct., Iowa, 1957-67; justice Ia. Supreme Ct., Des Moines, 1967—. Lectr. St. Ambrose Coll., 1957-67. Recipient Alumni Achievement award Cath. U. Am., 1969; award merit St. Ambrose Coll. Alumni Assn., 1976. Mem. Am., Iowa, Scott County bar assns., Am. Judicature Soc., Inst. Jud. Adminstrn. Home: Davenport IA 52801 Office: State House Des Moines IA 50319

LEGRIS, JOEL JOSEPH, soil conservationist; b. Kankakee, Ill., Jan. 8, 1950; s. Harvey Joseph and Anna Jane (Rose) L.; student Miami U., Oxford, Ohio, 1968-70; B.S. in Agr., U. Ky., 1976; postgrad. U. Wis., 1980—; m. Sarah Wallace Kehres, July 19, 1975. Farm mgr. Schwab Farms, Inc., Oxford, 1971-75, Lancrest Farms, Lexington, Ky., 1975-76; field conservationist Wis. Dept. Natural Resources, Madison, 1976-78; soil conservationist U.S. Dept. Agr., Flemingsburg, Ky., 1980—; part time farmer, 1970—. Mem. Soil Sci. Soc. Am., Am. Soc. Agronomy, Soil Conservation Soc. Am. Home: PO Box 15 Route 2 Flemingsburg KY 41041 Office: US Dept Agr PO Box 231 Flemingsburg KY 41041

LEGWINSKI, SHARON MARIE, nursing home exec.; b. Niles, Mich., July 15, 1953; d. John Joseph and Lillian Florence (Havlik) Chervenak; B.S. in Occupational Therapy with honors, Mt. Mary Coll., Milw., 1975; m. Paul Legwinski, June 7, 1975. Staff therapist Wis. Therapy Services, Pewaukee, 1976, VA Hosp., Wood, Wis., 1976-78; dir. occupational therapy Meth. Manor Health Center, West Allis, Wis., 1978—; clin. rep. Wis. Council on Edn., 1979—; mem. cert. occupational therapy assts. adv. com. Milw. Area Tech. Coll., 1979—. Mem. Am. Occupational Therapy Assn., Wis. Occupational Therapy Assn., Pi Theta Epsilon (sec.-treas. 1974-75). Democrat. Roman Catholic. Office: Methodist Manor Health Center 8615 W Beloit St West Allis WI 53217

LEHMAN, CLYDE FREDERICK, pub. utilities adminstr.; b. Kenyon, Minn., July 16, 1917; s. Clarence F. and Olga L. (Ness) L.; student U. Wis., 1953, U. Ill., 1964; m. G. Jeanne Smith, Dec. 10, 1938; 1 dau., Roberta Jeanne (Mrs. Ronald L. Bourget). Chief engr. North Star Creamery, Kenyon, Minn., 1940-47; city engr. City of Kenyon (Minn.), 1948-52; supt., mgr. Dept. Pub. Utilities, City of Chippewa Falls (Wis.), 1952—. Pres. Wis. Waste Water Operators Conf., 1967-68, chmn. edn. com., 1974-75; instr. Dept. Natural Resources edn. program on water and wastewater, Eau Claire, Wis., 1969-75. Pres. Chippewa Found., 1971-72. Mem. Water Pollution Control Fedn. (William O. Hatfield award 1965), Am. Water Works Assn. (chmn. mgmt. edn. com. Wis. sect. 1974-76, Willing Water award 1963), Central States Water Pollution Control Assn. (chmn. pub. relations com. 1955-56, Operator of the Year award 1965), Sentral States Select Soc. of Sanitary Sludge Shovelers, Nat. Safety Council, Chippewa Falls C. of C. (dir. 1963-75), Columbus Assn. Catholic (pres. bd. 1971-73). K.C. Club: National Exchange of Chippewa Falls (dir. 1974-75). Home: 715 Water St Chippewa Falls WI 54729 Office: 30 W Central St Chippewa Falls WI 54729

LEHMAN, HYLA BEROEN, educator, performing artist; b. Story City, Iowa; d. Lewis Bernard and Helene Louise (Hagen) Beroen; student Waldorf Coll.; B.S. in Edn., Drake U., 1939; M.A., U. Iowa, 1947; postgrad. in classical theatre, Athens, Greece, 1978; m. Fredrick Bracken Lehman, Apr. 30, 1942; children—Rolfe Beroen, Rhea Helene. Tchr. theatre arts and English, LaPorte City, Iowa, Des Moines, Alexandria, Va., Los Angeles; mem. faculty dept. theatre Coe Coll., Cedar Rapids, Iowa, 1974-79; artistic cons. Dance Theatre of the Hemispheres, 1979—, performing artist, 1967—, also bd. dirs.; chairman of Board, 1981—; judge Am. Coll. Theatre Festival; performer, lectr. at various colls. and univs. Mem. Gov.'s Conf. on Edn.; mem. nat. alumni bd. Drake U.; chmn. Linn County unit Am. Cancer Soc.; mem. Public Health Nursing Bd. Recipient Disting. Alumni award Waldorf Coll., 1969. Mem. Am. Theatre Assn., AAUW (state pres. 1952-54, state arts chmn. 1950-52; fellowship named in her honor), Phi Mu Gamma (nat. alumnae dir. 1947-50, nat. pres. 1950-52), Phi Theta Kappa, Kappa Delta Pi. Lutheran. Home: 4347 Eaglemere Ct SE Cedar Rapids IA 52403

LEHMANN, M. DRUE, speech pathologist; b. Columbus, Ohio, Feb. 29, 1948; d. Selmar Lee and Clara Frances (Ketner) L.; B.S., Bowling Green State U., 1971; M.A., Ohio State U., 1973; Speech pathologist Sacred Heart Hosp., Allentown, Pa., 1973-75; asst. prof. clin. otolaryngology U. Cin. Med. Center, 1974—; clin. speech pathologist Holmes Hosp., Cin., 1974—. Mem. Am., Ohio, S.W. Ohio speech and hearing assns., Aphasiology Assn. Ohio. Roman Catholic. Home: 727 Dixmyth Apt 216 Cincinnati OH 45220 Office: Holmes Hosp Eden and Bethesda Aves Cincinnati OH 45219

LEHNER, LORENZ KARL, JR., hosp. adminstr.; b. Columbus, Ohio, July 15, 1945; s. Lorenz Karl and Mary Evelyn (Daugherty) L.; B.S. in Bus. and Mktg., Ohio State U., 1967, M.S. in Hosp. and Health Services Adminstrn., 1973; m. Diana Christine Gussett, Apr. 20, 1969; children—Troy Michael, Kristen Diane. Adminstr. asso., then asst. adminstr. Ohio State Univ. Hosps., 1973-76; adminstrv. dir. profl. services Good Samaritan Hosp. and Health Center, Dayton, Ohio, 1976-79; asso. adminstr. Flower Hosp. and Crestview Center, Toledo, 1979—; adj. instr., preceptor Ohio State U., 1976-79; trustee, treas. Dayton Community Blood Center, 1978. Asst. v.p. individual devel. Greater Dayton Jaycees, 1978-79; mem. fin. com. Englewood United Methodist Ch., Dayton, 1976-79. Served as officer U.S. Army Res., 1968-71. Mem. Am. Coll. Hosp. Adminstrs. (pres. Dayton young adminstrs. group 1978, pres. NW Ohio affiliates). Home: 6509 Marie Ln Maumee OH 43537 Office: 5200 Harroun Rd Sylvania OH 43560

LEHNER, PAUL MICHAEL, real estate mgmt. and devel. exec.; b. Mishawaka, Ind., Dec. 5, 1941; s. Paul Mathias and Margaret D. (Van Acker) L.; B.B.A. summa cum laude, U. Notre Dame, 1963; M.B.A. with distinction, Harvard U., 1969; m. Linda Suzanne Smith, Aug. 5, 1967; children—Suzanne Michelle, Paulyn Marie. Mem. cons. group Irwin Mgmt. Co., Columbus, Ind., 1969, real estate projects coordinator, 1970-76, v.p. real estate, 1977—; pres., dir. Nashville Internat. Trading Co., Inc. (Ind.), 1977-80; exec. v.p. Tipton Lakes Co., Columbus, 1981—; pres. Tipton Lakes Community Assn., Columbus, 1981—. Pres., Brown County Bd. Zoning Appeals; vice chmn. Brown County Planning Commn.; trustee Town of Nashville (Ind.); county rep. Sen. R. Lugar, Region XI Area Devel. Commn.; v.p. St. Agnes Parish Council, Nashville, 1980-81. Served with USN, 1963-67. Mem. C. of C., Internat. Council Shopping Centers, Nat. Assn. Homebuilders, Bd. Realtors. Roman Catholic. Home: 2265 W Carr Hill Rd Columbus IN 47201 Office: 235 Washington St Columbus IN 47201

LEHNER, WILLIAM EDWARD, constrn. co. exec.; b. Columbus, Ohio, June 8, 1948; s. William J. and Elizabeth J. (Gearhart) L.; A.A., Urbana Coll., 1969; B.S. in Architecture, Kent State U., 1973; m. Karen S. Fry, June 27, 1970; 1 dau., Allison R. Supt. architects and builders project Kibbey Structures, Columbus, 1973-75; mng. officer, asst. sec. Lan-Am., developers, Wooster, Ohio, 1975-77; constrn. insp. officer Wayne Savs. and Loan Assn., Wooster, 1977-79; with Holland & Assos., Architects and Engrs., Bath, Ohio, 1979—. Mem. Wooster Design Commn.; pres. Inter Club Council, Wooster. Mem. Wooster Jaycees (dir. 1976-77, v.p. 1977-78, pres. 1978-79, dist. dir. 1977-78). Home: 606 N Grant St Wooster OH 44691

LEHR, LEWIS WYLIE, mfg. co. exec.; b. Elgin, Nebr., Feb. 21, 1921; s. Louis H. and Nancy (Wylie) L.; B.S. in Chem. Engring., U. Nebr., D.S. (hon.), 1977; m. Doris Stauder, Oct. 13, 1944; children—Mary Lehr Makin, William L., Donald D., John M. With 3M Co., 1947—, v.p. tape 7 allied products group, 1974-75, pres. U.S. ops., 1975-79, vice chmn., chief exec. officer, 1979-80, chmn., chief exec. officer, 1980—; dir. First Bank Systems, Inc., Mpls. Dir. United Way St. Paul, 1977—; dir. Guthrie Theater Found.; trustee Hamline U., St. Paul, bd. overseers Harvard Coll. Vis. Com. of Med. and Dental Schs. Served with U.S. Army, 1943-46. Mem. U. Nebr. Alumni Assn. (recipient Alumni Achievement award), Am. Chem. Soc. Clubs: N. Oaks Golf, St. Paul Athletic, White Bear Yacht, Minn. Office: 3M Center Saint Paul MN 55144*

LEHRMAN, NAT, magazine editor; b. Bklyn., Aug. 5, 1929; s. Louis and Lena (Goldfarb) L.; B.A., Bklyn. Coll., 1953; M.A., N.Y. U., 1961; m. Kazuko Miyajima, Nov. 13, 1956; children—Jerome M., Cynthia H. Travel editor internat. travel dept. Am. Automobile Assn., 1955-57; editor Relax mag., 1958; editor Dude and Gent mags., 1959-63; editor, then asso. to asst. mng. editor Playboy mag., Chgo., 1963-71; editor new publs., Playboy Enterprises, 1972; editor, then asso. pub. Oui mag., 1973-75; sr. v.p., asso. pub. Playboy mag., 1976—, also dir. mag. div. (Playboy and Games), and new publ. devel.; tchr. fiction Columbia Coll., Chgo., 1967; author: Masters and Johnson Explained, 1970. Served with U.S. Army, 1953-55. Office: Playboy Enterprises Inc 919 N Michigan Ave Chicago IL 60611

LEIDER, FRANK JOHN, accountant; b. Evanston, Ill., Oct. 10, 1956; s. Frank E. and Mary M. (Bilsley) B.S. in Acctg. with honors, U. Ill., 1978; m. Laurie Ann Mauer, Oct. 20, 1979. Jr. acct. Rand McNally and Co., Skokie, Ill., 1978, staff accountant, 1979-80, mgr. gen. acctg., 1980—. C.P.A., Ill. Mem. Ill. C.P.A. Soc. Office: 8255 N Central Park Skokie IL 60076

LEIDNER, BURTON RICHARD, educator, law enforcement forensic hypnotist; b. Cleve., Nov. 28, 1928; s. Edward A. and Agnes (Zweig) L.; B.S. summa cum laude, Ohio State U., 1950; M.A., Columbia U., 1951; postgrad. U. Wis., 1954-55, Case-Western Res. U., 1958-59; Ph.D., U. Sarasota, 1973; m. June Ethel Schwartz, June 12, 1954; 1 dau., Ellen Beth. Supr. instrumental music pub. schs., Willard, Ohio, 1951-53, Xenia, Ohio, 1953-54; grad. teaching fellow U. Wis., 1954-55; asst. prof. Auburn U., 1955-56; asso. prof. Hartwick Coll., 1956-58; counseling psychologist U. Tex. at Austin, Testing and Counseling Center, 1959-60; mgmt. appraisal and devel. specialist United Air Lines, Chgo., 1961-62; mgr. employee counseling, testing and appraisal programs IBM Space-Missile Guidance Center, Owego, N.Y., 1962-65; dir. counseling services Orange County Community Coll., Middletown, N.Y., 1965-66; adult and continuing edn. specialist Zanesville br. campus Ohio U., 1966-68; counseling psychologist, asst. prof. Lorain County Community Coll., 1968-76, asso. prof., 1976—; hypnosis cons. investigator Cleve. regional office FBI, other law enforcement agys.; orgn., mgmt. devel. cons. Nat. Cash Register Co., Bendix-Westinghouse, Ohio Ferro Alloys, Romec div. Lear Siegler, Inc., Elyria Savings & Trust Nat. Bank, Elyria (Ohio) C. of C., Amherst Hosp., U.S. Steel Corp., TRW, others; lectr. forensic hypnosis Center Criminal Justice, Sch. Law, Case-Western Res. U., 1980-81; behavioral sci. cons. Ohio State Hwy. Patrol, 1981; lectr. on alcoholic problem at mgmt. level in Am. bus. and industry, also on misuse of psychol. measurement in employment and promotion process. lectr. motivation, productivity, and employee attitudes, how to be a winning you. Named One of Cleve.'s Most Interesting People, Cleve. mag., 1979; recipient Citizen Recognition Law Enforcement award City of Cleve., 1981. Cert. hypnotist Internat. Soc. Investigative and Forensic Hypnosis. Mem. Am. Personnel and Guidance Assn., Am. Coll. Personnel Assn. (mem. com. XI on student personnel programs; speaker nat. conv. 1975, 77), Phi Delta Kappa, Phi Mu Alpha, Kappa Phi Kappa, Phi Eta Sigma. Clubs: Masons, Rotary (former dir.). Contbr. articles to profl. jours. Home: 3400 Wooster Rd Suite 311 Rocky River OH 44116 Office: 1005 N Abbe Rd Elyria OH 44035

LEIF, CLAUDE (BUD) PETER, Realtor; b. Underwood, N.D., July 3, 1920; s. John J. and Frances A. (Feyen) L.; student St. Mary's Coll., 1938, Austin Jr. Coll., 1940; B.B.A., U. Minn., 1943; m. Alice Mae Ankeny, Oct. 9, 1943; children—Jerome, Georgia (Mrs. G. LaVallie), Paul, Keith, Gregory, Lawrence, Joseph, Donald, Daniel, Mary, Steven. Gen. mgr. Miller Real Estate Co., Austin, Minn., 1946-58, partner, 1954-58; gen. mgr. Miller Molde Constrn. Co., Austin, Minn., 1946-58; gen. mgr., sec. Miller Home Devel., Inc., Austin, 1946-60, 70—; prin. Bud Leif Real Estate and Ins. Co., Austin, Minn., 1958—; sec. Crestwood Home Devel., Inc., 1970—. Active Twin Valley Council Boy Scouts Am., 1952-75, chmn. Austin Council, 1962—; mem. com. United Fund, Austin, 1958—. Served with AUS, 1943-46; ETO. Recipient Silver Scout award, 1973; decorated Bronze Star (4). Mem. Austin C. of C., Austin Bd. Realtors (pres. 1962, 77, 78), Nat. Bd. Realtors, Minn. Assn. Mutual Agts., Am. Legion, V.F.W., U. Minn. Alumni Assn., St. Mary's Coll. Alumni Assn., Alpha Kappa Psi. K.C. (4 deg.), Eagles, Elks, Moose. Home: 500 17th St SW Austin MN 55912 Office: 706 W Oakland Austin MN 55912

LEIGHNINGER, DAVID SCOTT, cardiovascular surgeon; b. Youngstown, Ohio, Jan. 16, 1920; s. Jesse Harrison and Marjorie (Lightner) L.; B.A., Oberlin Coll., 1942; M.D., Case-Western Res. U., 1945; m. Margaret Jane Malony, May 24, 1942; children—David Allan, Jenny. Intern, U. Hosps. Cleve., 1945-46; research fellow cardiovascular surgery research lab. Case-Western Res. U. Sch. Medicine, Cleve., 1948-49, 51-55, 57-67; resident U. Hosps. Cleve., 1949-51, Cin. Gen. Hosp., 1955-57; pvt. practice medicine, specializing in cardiovascular surgery, Cleve., 1957-70; pvt. practice, specializing in cardiovascular and gen. surgery Edgewater Hosp., Chgo., 1970—; staff surgeon, also dir. emergency surg. services Edgewater Hosp. and Mazel Med. Center, Chgo., 1970—; instr. surgery Case-Western U. Sch. Medicine, 1951-55, sr. instr. surgery, 1957-64; asst. prof. surgery, 1964-68, asst. clin. prof. surgery, 1968-70; asst. surgeon U. Hosps. Cleve., 1951-68; asso., courtesy staff mem. or cons. staff mem. of Marymount Hosp., Cleve., Mt. Sinai Hosp., Cleve., Geauga Community Hosp., Chardon, Ohio, Bedford (Ohio) Community Hosp., 1957-70. Tchr. tng. courses in cardiopulmonary resuscitation for med. personnel, police, fire and vol. rescue workers, numerous cities, 1950-70. Served to capt. M.C., AUS, 1946-48. Recipient Chris award Columbus (Ohio) Internat. Film Festival, 1964, numerous other awards for scientific exhibits from various nat. and state med. socs., 1953-70; USPHS grantee, 1949-68. Fellow Am. Coll. Cardiology, Am. Coll. Chest Physicians; mem. AMA, Ill. State, Chgo. med. assns., U. Cin. Grad. Sch. Surg. Soc. (Cin.). Contbr. numerous articles in field to profl. jours.; contbr. numerous chpts. to med. texts. Spl. pioneer research (with Claude S. Beck) in Physiopathology of coronary artery disease and cardiopulmonary resuscitation; developed surg. treatment of coronary artery disease; achieved first successful defibrillation of human heart, first successful reversal of fatal heart attack; provided first "intensive care" of coronary patients. Home: 1124 Midway Rd Northbrook IL 60062 Office: 5700 N Ashland Ave Chicago IL 60660

LEIGHTON, GEORGE NEVES, judge; b. New Bedford, Mass., Oct. 22, 1912; s. Antonio N. and Anna Sylvia (Garcia) Leitao; A.B., Howard U., 1940; LL.B., Harvard, 1946; LL.D., Elmhurst Coll., 1964, John Marshall Law Sch., Southeastern Mass. U., 1975, New Eng. U., 1978; m. Virginia Berry Quivers, June 21, 1942; children—Virginia Anne, Barbara Elaine. Admitted to Mass. bar, 1946, Ill. bar, 1947, U.S. Supreme Ct. bar, 1958; partner Moore, Ming & Leighton, Chgo., 1951-59, McCoy, Ming & Leighton, Chgo., 1959-64; judge Circuit Ct. Cook County, Ill., 1964-69, Appellate Ct., 1st Dist., 1969-76, U.S. Dist. Ct., 1976—. Commr., as mem. character and fitness com. for 1st Appellate Dist., Supreme Ct. Ill., 1955-63, chmn. character and fitness com., 1961-62; mem. joint com. for revision jud. article Ill. and Chgo. bar assns., 1959-62, joint com. for revision Ill. Criminal Code, 1959-63; chmn. Ill. adv. com. U.S. Commn. on Civil Rights, 1964;

mem. pub. rev. bd. UAW, AFL-CIO, 1961-69. Asst. atty. gen. State of Ill., 1950-51; pres. 3d Ward Regular Democratic Orgn., Cook County, Ill., 1951-53, v.p. 21st Ward, 1964. Bd. dirs. United Ch. Bd. for Homeland Ministries, United Ch. of Christ, Grant Hosp., Chgo.; trustee Notre Dame U., 1979—. Served from 2d lt. to capt., inf. AUS, 1942-45. Decorated Bronze Star; recipient Civil Liberties award Ill. div. Am. Civil Liberties Union, 1961; named Chicagoan of Year in Law and Judiciary, Jr. Assn. Commerce and Industry, 1964. Fellow of Am. Bar Found.; mem. Howard U. Chgo. Alumni Club (chmn. bd. dirs.), John Howard Assn. (dir.), Chgo., Ill. bar assns., N.A.A.C.P. (chmn. legal redress com. Chgo. br.), Nat. Harvard Law Sch. Assn. (mem. Council), Phi Beta Kappa (hon.), Gamma of D.C. Contbr. articles to legal jours. Home: 8400 S Prairie Av Chicago IL 60619 Office: Dirksen Fed Bldg Chicago IL 60604

LEINENWEBER, HARRY DANIEL, state legislator Ill.; b. Joliet, Ill., June 3, 1937; s. Harry Dean and Emily Theresa (Lennon) L.; A.B., U. Notre Dame, 1959; J.D., U. Chgo., 1962; m. Geraldine Alicia Dunn, Sept. 9, 1961; children—Jane Dunn, John Dunn, Thomas More, Stephen Becket, Justin Lennon. Admitted to Ill. bar, 1962; city atty., Joliet, 1963-67; spl. prosecutor, Will County, 1968-70; mem. Ill. Ho. of Reps. from 42d Dist., 1972—, chmn. judiciary com., 1981—. Pres. bd. dirs. Joliet Montessori Sch., 1967. Mem. Ill., Will County bar assns., Jud. Adv. Council, Nat. Council Commrs. Uniform State Laws. Home: 613 Catherine St Joliet IL 60435 Office: 81 N Chicago St Joliet IL 60434 also Room 2018 Stratton Office Bldg Springfield IL 60706

LEINIEKS, VALDIS, educator; b. Liepaja, Latvia, Apr. 15, 1932; came to U.S., 1949, naturalized, 1954; s. Arvid Ansis and Valia Leontine (Brunaus) L.; B.A., Cornell U., 1955, M.A., 1956; Ph.D., Princeton U., 1962. Instr. classics Cornell Coll., Mount Vernon, Iowa, 1959-62, asst. prof. classics, 1962-64; asso. prof. classics, Ohio State U., 1964-66; asso. prof. classics U. Nebr., Lincoln, 1966-71, prof. classics, 1971—, chmn. dept. classics, 1967—. Mem. AAUP, Am. Comparative Lit. Assn., Am. Oriental Soc., Am. Philol. Assn., Archaeol. Inst. Am., Linguistic Soc. Am. Republican. Author: Morphosyntax of the Homeric Greek Verb, 1964; The Structure of Latin, 1975; Index Nepotianus, 1976; The Plays of Sophokles, 1982; contbr. articles to profl. jours. Home: 2505 A St Lincoln NE 68502 Office: Dept Classics U Nebr Lincoln NE 68588

LEININGER, ELMER, chemist; b. Milw., Apr. 19, 1900; s. Philip Henry and Louise (Hardtke) L.; B.S., Carroll Coll., 1923; postgrad. U. Wis., 1923-24; M.S., Mich. State U., 1931; Ph.D., U. Mich., 1941; m. Hazel Ann MacNamara, Dec. 30, 1924 (dec. June 1961); 1 dau., Mary Louise (Mrs. James Gates); m. 2d, Byrnice L. Dickinson, 1964. Instr. chem. Mich. State U., 1924-30, prof. chemistry, head analytical chemistry sect. 1930-65, prof. emeritus, 1965—; chem. cons., 1965—, Sec., dir. Geneva Lake Civic Assn., 1968-76, 79—. Mem. Am. Chem. Soc. (chmn., councilor Mich. sect.), Am. Philatelic Soc., A.A.A.S., Sigma Xi, Alpha Chi Sigma, Phi Lambda Upsilon. Republican. Clubs: Lake Geneva Country; Green Valley (Ariz.) Country. Editorial adv. bd. Analytical Chemistry. Contbr. articles to profl. jours. Address: S Lake Shore Dr Rural Route 1 Box 70 Lake Geneva WI 53147

LEIPOLD, LEE DAVID, fin. analyst; b. Norfolk, Va., July 18, 1953; s. Bob Lee and Iris D. (Mueller) L.; B.S. in Adminstrn. of Justice, U. Mo., 1976, B.S. in B.A., 1977; M.B.A., S.E. Mo. State U., 1978; 1 son, David Micheal Thomas. Grad. asst. to dean of continuing edn. S.E. Mo. State U., Cape Girardeau, 1977-78, grad. asst. staff asso. to pres., 1977-78, grad. asst. in acctg., 1978; corporate cash adminstr. Gen. Dynamics, St. Louis, 1979-80, asst. treas., voluntary polit. contbn. plan, 1979-80, mgmt. group steering com. treas., 1979-80; fin. analyst Mallinckrodt, Inc., St. Louis, 1980—. Planning council mem. United Way of Greater St. Louis, 1979—. Mem. Assn. M.B.A. Execs., Nat. Assn. Accts. Club: Lion (3d v.p. 1979-81, 1st v.p. 1981—). Home: 13261 Hobnail Dr Saint Louis MO 63141 Office: 675 McDonnell Blvd PO Box 5840 Saint Louis MO 63134

LEISER, BURTON MYRON, educator; b. Denver, Dec. 12, 1930; s. Nathan and Eva Mae (Newman) L.; B.A., U. Chgo., 1951; M.H.L., Yeshiva U., 1956; Ph.D. (Univ. fellow), Brown U., 1968; J.D., Drake U., 1981; m. Barbara Hurowitz-Tabor, June 9, 1967; children by previous marriage—Shoshana, Illana, Phillip; step children—Ellen, David, Susan. Instr. philosophy Fort Lewis Coll., Durango, Colo., 1963-65; asst. prof. philosophy N.Y. State U., Buffalo, 1965-68; asso. prof. philosophy, 1968-70; vis. asso. prof. Judaic studies Sir George Williams U., Montreal, Que., Can., 1969-71, asso. prof. philosophy, 1971-72; prof. philosophy Drake U., Des Moines, 1972—, chmn. dept., 1972—. Bd. dirs. Bur. Jewish Edn. of Des Moines, 1973-76, Polk County Mental Health Assn., 1974-76; mem. legis. com. Iowa Civil Liberties Union, 1981—. N.Y. State U. Research Found. grantee, 1967-68, Meml. Found. for Jewish Culture grantee, 1970-71, Exxon Edn. Found. grantee, 1973-74; Nat. Endowment for Humanities grantee, 1978. Mem. AAUP, Authors Guild, Am. Philos. Assn., Internat. Soc. Legal and Social Philosophy, Am. Soc. Value Inquiry (v.p.), Soc. Philos. and Public Affairs, Soc. Polit. and Legal Philosophy, Am. Profs. for Peace in Middle East (nat. exec. com.). Jewish. Author: Custom, Law, and Morality, 1969, Liberty, Justice, and Morals, 2d edit., 1979; Values in Conflict, 1981. Office: Dept of Philosophy Drake Univ Des Moines IA 50311

LEISER, DEAN, health care exec.; b. Akron, Ohio, Oct. 2, 1934; s. Charles Henry and Frances Elizabeth (Bruch) L.; B.S. cum laude, Kent (Ohio) State U., 1957; M.B.A., U. Chgo., 1959; m. Joanne Elizabeth Turrin, June 10, 1956; children—Gary Edward, Pamela Anne, Karen Alyce. Asst. adminstr. Ohio State U. Hosps., Columbus, 1960-61, Cin. Children's Hosp., 1961-66; asso. adminstr. Akron Children's Hosp., 1966-71; adminstr. Kadlec Hosp., Richland, Wash., 1971-72; asst. dir. Huron Road Hosp., Cleve., 1972-73; dir. hosp. services Damm and Assos., Cleveland Heights, Ohio, 1974-75; pres., chmn. bd. Health Care Analysis, Inc., Willoughby, Ohio, 1975—; dir. Advance Inc., Akron. Mem. Am. Coll. Hosp. Adminstrs., Health Care Adminstrs. Assn. N.E. Ohio. Republican. Presbyterian. Home: 38750 Johnnycake Ridge Rd Willoughby OH 44094 Office: 4135 Erie St Willoughby OH 44094

LEISNER, ANTHONY BAKER, publishing co. exec.; b. Evanston, Ill., Sept. 13, 1941; s. A. Paul and Ruth (Solms) L.; B.S., Northwestern U., 1964; m. Elaine Suits, Nov. 27, 1979; children—Justina, William. Salesman, Pitney Bowes Co., 1976-77; with Quality Books Inc., Northbrook, Ill., 1968—, v.p., 1972—, gen. mgr., 1979—. Pres. bd. dirs. Lake Villa (Ill.) Public Library, 1972-78; bd. dirs. No. Ill. Library Systems, 1973-78; chmn. Libertarian Party Lake County (Ill.), 1980-81; probation officer Lake County CAP, 1981. Mem. ALA, Ill. Library Assn. (Gerald L. Campbell award 1980), Am. Booksellers Assn., World Isshin Ryu Karate Assn. Methodist. Author: Official Guide to Country Dance Steps, 1980; also articles. Home: 646 Wilbur Ct Gurnee IL 60031 Office: 400 Anthony Trail Northbrook IL 60062

LEISSA, ARTHUR WILLIAM, educator; b. Wilmington, Del., Nov. 16, 1931; s. Arthur Max and Marcella E. (Smith) L.; B.M.E., Ohio State U., 1954, M.S., 1954, Ph.D., 1958; m. Gertrud E. Achenbach, Apr. 11, 1974; children—Celia Lynn, Bradley Glenn. Engr., Sperry Gyroscope Co., Great Neck, N.Y., 1954-55; research asso. Ohio State U., 1955-56, instr. engring. mechanics, 1956-58, asst. prof., 1958-61, asso. prof., 1961-64, prof., 1964—; vis. prof. Eidgenossische Technische Hochschule, Zurich, Switzerland, 1972-73; cons. in field. Performer Columbus Symphony Orch. Operas, 1971-79. Recipient Recognition plaque for Outstanding Research, Inst. de Mecanica Applicada, Argentina, 1977. Mem. ASME, Soc. Engring. Sci., AIAA; fellow Am. Acad. Mechanics. Club: Am. Alpine. Author: Vibration of Plates, 1969; Vibration of Shells, 1973; editorial bd. Jour. Sound and Vibration, 1971—, Internat. Jour. of Mech. Sci., 1972—. Contbr. articles in field to profl. jours. Home: 2978 Neil Ave Columbus OH 43202 Office: 155 W Woodruff St Columbus OH 43210

LEIST, CARL CLINTON, lawyer; b. Circleville, Ohio, Oct. 23, 1909; s. Clinton Augustus and Elizabeth F. (Crist) L.; B.A., Capital U., 1930; J.D., Ohio State U., 1933; m. Geraldine C. Merrill, Oct. 14, 1932; 1 son, Warren Carl. Admitted to Ohio bar, 1933, since practiced in Circleville; mem. firm Leist & Kitchen, 1933—, sr. mem., 1953—; city atty. Circleville, 1934-40. Dir., Atty., First Nat. Bank Circleville, 1953—; dir., mem. counsel Scioto Bldg. & Loan Co. Circleville, 1944—, treas., 1944-80. Chmn., Pickaway County chpt. ARC, 1937-45; Pickaway County appeals agt. SSS, 1950-72; mem. Circleville City Sch. Dist. Bd. Edn., 1943-61, pres., 1948-61. Chmn. Pickaway County Democratic Exec. Com., 1942-48, chmn. county Dem. central com., 1948-50. Mem. Pickaway County (past pres.), Ohio, Am. bar assns., Pickaway County Law Library Assn. (chmn. 1970—, trustee), Circleville C. of C., Delta Theta Phi. Lutheran (chmn. ch. council 1954-76, pres. congregation 1954-76). Elk, Rotarian. Home: 205 Northridge Rd Circleville OH 43113 Office: 105 W Mound St Circleville OH 43113

LEISTICO, MILDRED FAE, bank exec.; b. Hobart, Okla., July 4, 1947; d. Walter D. and Ethel Marie (Koehn) Goossen; student Wichita Bus. Coll., 1965-66; m. Melvin Allen Leistico, May 17, 1975; 1 son, Sean Duane. Sec., Farmers Ins. Group, Wichita, Kans., 1965-66; asst. cashier Nat. Life & Accident Ins., Enid, Okla., 1966; typist Dow Chem. Co., Freeport, Tex., 1967; supply clk. Kans. U. Med. Center, Kansas City, 1968; statis. sec. Columbia Union Nat. Bank, Kansas City, Mo., 1969-70, 73-79, analyst, 1979-80, word processing mgr., 1980—; sec. First Nat. Bank, Lake Jackson, Tex., 1970-71; statis. typist Arthur Andersen & Co., Kansas City, Mo., 1972. Mem. Internat. Word Processing Assn. Asst. editor Christ For Me, Inc., 1980—. Office: Columbia Union National Bank 900 Walnut St Kansas City MO 64106

LEISTLER, MYRON JOHN, police chief; b. Cin., Oct. 23, 1929; s. Myron R. and Alta M. (Streitenberger) L.; B.A., U. Cin., 1974; postgrad. M.I.T.; m. Joyce A. Budke, July 12, 1960; children—Theresa, Todd, Lisa, John. Mem. Cin. Police Dept., 1953—, chief, 1976—; occasional univ. lectr. Mem. bd. mgmt. Central Pkwy. YMCA, Cin.; adv. bd. Cin. Salvation Army. Served with USMC, 1948-52. Recipient award Cin. C. of C., 1977, Cin. City Council, 1979. Mem. Internat. Assn. Chiefs Police, Ohio Assn. Chiefs Police, Hamilton County Police Chiefs Assn., FBI Nat. Execs. Inst. (charter). Mem. Ch. of Christ. Club: Masons. Office: 310 Ezzard Charles Dr Cincinnati OH 45214

LEITNER, B. DEAN, city ofcl.; b. McDonald, Kans., June 7, 1933; s. Henery D. and Annabel N. (Rowland) L.; B.A., U. Nebr., 1974; grad. Traffic Inst., Northwestern U.; m. Rose Termine, Sept. 4, 1956; children—Gregory Dean, Debora LuAnn. With Lincoln (Nebr.) Police Dept., 1957—, sgt., 1960-68, lt., 1968-74, capt., 1974-77, asst. chief, 1977-79, chief police, 1979—; mem. Nebr. State Crime Commn., 1979—. Bd. dirs. Salvation Army, Lincoln. Served with U.S. Army, 1953-55. Mem. Internat. Assn. Chiefs Police, VFW, Police Officers Assn. Nebr., Northwestern U. Alumni Assn., U. Nebr., Alumni Assn. Republican. Lutheran. Club: Rotary. Office: 233 S 10th St Lincoln NE 68508

LEKBERG, ROBERT DAVID, chemist; b. Chgo., Feb. 2, 1920; s. Carl H. and Esther (Forsberg) L.; A.A., North Park Coll., 1940; B.S., Lewis Inst., 1943; m. Sandra Sakal, Oct. 19, 1970; children by previous marriage—Terry Lee, Jerrald Dean, Roger Daryl, Kathleen Sue, Keith Robbin. Chemist, Glidden Co., 1940-43, Wilson Packing Co., 1943-45, Libby, McNeil & Libby, 1945-47; chief chemist Dawes Labs., Chgo., 1947-50; owner, pres. Chemlek Labs. Inc., Alsip, Ill., 1950—, Chemlek Labs. Can. Ltd., Windsor, Ont., 1960-66. Exec. sec. Alsip Indsl. Dist. Assn.; violist Chgo. Civic Symphony, 1940-42, N.W. Ind. Symphony, 1976—, Chicago Heights Symphony, 1959—, Southwest Symphony, 1970—. Mem. Ill. Mfrs. Assn., Ill. Indsl. Council, Chgo. Feed Club. Republican. Club: Dolton Yacht. Editor Indsl. Dist. Assn. Newsletter, 1975—; patentee chem. processes. Home: 6624 Linden Dr Oak Forest IL 60452 Office: Chemlek Labs Inc 4040 W 123d St Alsip IL 60658

LELAK, MARY ANGELA MAURER, sch. adminstr.; b. Fort Loramie, Ohio, Dec. 29, 1945; d. Edison Allen and Bertha Melintina (Larger) Mauer; B.S., U. Dayton, 1969, M.Ed., 1972; postgrad. Ohio State U., 1979—; m. John William Lelak, Aug. 19, 1967; children—Amy Marie, Emily Dawn. Elem. sch. tchr., Dayton, Ohio, 1965-79; math. tchr. Sinclair Community Coll., Dayton, 1971-78; prin. St. Christopher Sch., Vandalia, Ohio, 1979—; cons. state edn. project 419, U. Dayton, 1979-80; panel mem. Future Prins., Archdiocese of Cin., 1981; developer, coordinator community celebration Arbor Day, Vandalia, 1980, anniversary Paul Lawrence Dunbar, Dayton, 1972; co-chmn. local state rep.'s polit. campaign, 1972. Recipient Outstanding Service award U. Dayton, 1978. Mem. NEA, Ohio Cath. Edn. Assn., Assn. for Supervision and Curriculum Devel., Greater Dayton Tchrs. Math. Assn., Dayton Urban League. Democrat. Roman Catholic. Home: 5400 Cardo Rd Fort Loramie OH 45845 Office: Saint Christopher Sch 405 E National Rd Vandalia OH 45377

LEMAÎTRE, MONIQUE JACQUELINE, educator; b. Mexico City, Mex., Mar. 31, 1935; came to U.S., 1954; d. Mariano Lemaître Arroyo and Enriqueta Léon de Lemaître; B.A. (univ. scholar), U. Pitts., 1964, M.A. (Woodrow Wilson fellow), 1966, Ph.D. (Andrew Mellon fellow), 1974; m. Hugo G. Nutini, Oct. 16, 1954 (div. 1967); children—Jean-Pierre, Francesco Gino. Mem. faculty Berlitz Sch. Langs., 1954, Marymount High Sch., 1957-62, Ecole Française Internationale, 1962; teaching asst. U. Pitts., 1965; instr. Lycée Franco Mexicain, 1968-70; instr. Boston Coll., 1970-72; asst. dir. M.A.T. Program, Experiment for Internat. Living, Brattleboro, Vt., 1972-74; asst. prof. Tufts U., Medford, Mass., 1974-79; prof. dept. fgn. lang. and lit. No. Ill. U., De Kalb, 1979—; vis. prof. Ohio Wesleyan U., 1979-80; adv. dir. Revista Iberoamericana; free lance translator. Active NOW, ACLU. French Room research fellow, 1966. Mem. MLA, Midwest MLA, Nat. Assn. Tchrs. of Spanish and Portuguese, Latin Am. Studies Assn., Midwest Latin Am. Studies Assn., Institute de Literatura, Iberoamericana. Author: Octavio Paz: Poesia y poetica, 1976; contbr. articles to profl. jours. Home: 3107 W Lincoln Hwy 7106 De Kalb IL 60115 Office: Dept Foreign Lang and Lit No Illinois U De Kalb IL 60115

LEMAN, JOHN WILLIAM, choral dir.; b. Peoria, Ill., May 1, 1940; s. Irvin William and Leona Rachel (Martin) L.; B.S., U. Ill., 1962, M.S., 1966, Ed.D., 1974; m. Sharon Ann Mattern, Aug. 16, 1964; 1 dau., Elizabeth Ann. Instr. music U. Ill., 1966-69; asst. prof. U. Cin., 1969-73, asso. prof. conducting, 1973-81, prof. choral conducting and music edn., 1981—; chorus master Cin. May Festival Chorus, 1978—. Mem. Am. Choral Dirs. Assn. Office: B-36 PCP Coll Conservatory Music U Cin Cincinnati OH 45221

LEMAR, HOMER JESS, SR., psychologist, bus. exec.; b. Pekin, Ill., Feb. 28, 1933; s. Homer John and Esther Emma LeM.; B.S., Bradley U., 1962, M.A., U. N.Mex., 1966, Ed.D. (NIMH fellow), 1969; m. Mildred Walden; children—Homer Jess, David Paul. Tchr. public schs., Ill., 1959-62, Albuquerque, 1962-66; asst. prof. Western N.Mex. U., 1969-70; asso. prof. psychology N.W. Mo. State U., 1970—; owner, operator LeMar's Originals Gifts Unusual, The Bottle Shop, Golden Spike Disco. Vol. worker Democratic Party, Albuquerque. Served from pvt. to staff sgt. USAF, 1951-59. Mem. Assn. Supervision and Curriculum Devel., Am. Legion, Phi Delta Kappa. Clubs: Masons, Shriners, Elks. Home: 1321 Parkdale St Maryville MO 64468 Office: Colden Hall 113 NW Mo State U Maryville MO 64468

LE MAR, WILLIAM BERNHARDT, civil engr., educator; b. Rapid City, S.D., Sept. 24, 1922; s. Harold Diehl and Luella (Petersen) LeM.; student Va. Mil. Inst., 1939-41; B.A. in Engring., Stanford, 1943; M.Engring. in Civil Engring., Yale, 1947; postgrad. Army War Coll., 1970; m. Mary Alma Soule, June 15, 1953 (div. 1967); 1 son, Wade H.M. Draftsman, Anaconda Copper Mining Co., N.Y.C., 1948; structural draftsman N.Y., N.H. & H. R.R., New Haven, 1948-50; dir. engring. P.F. Petersen Baking Co., Omaha, 1950-57, v.p. prodn., 1957-60; civil engr. U. S. Army Corps Engrs., Omaha, 1961; asst. prof. dept. civil engring. U. Nebr., Omaha, 1961-64, asso. prof., 1964—. Dir. Omaha Tng. Course for Sewage Treatment Plant Operators, 1963-70; mem. augmentation and cons. faculties U.S. Army Command and Gen. Staff Coll., Ft. Leavenworth, Kan., 1968-75. Served to 1st lt. AUS, 1943-46; col. Res., ret. 1975. Decorated Bronze Star medal, Meritorious Service medal. Registered profl. engr., Nebr., Iowa. Mem. ASCE, Profl. Engrs. Nebr., Profl. Surveyors Nebr., Yale Engring. Assn., Assn. U.S. Army, Navy League U.S., Res. Officers Assn., Omaha Com. on Fgn. Relations, Council Abandoned Mil. Posts, SAR, Phi Alpha Theta, Gamma Alpha. Presbyn. Clubs: Omaha Press, Omaha Engineers; Army and Navy (Washington). Home: 666 N 58th St Omaha NE 68132

LEMBCKE, THOMAS CHARLES, clin. social worker, retailer; b. Appleton, Wis., Jan. 31, 1934; s. Clarence Herman and Miriam Isebel (Lewis) L.; B.Mus., Lawrence U., Appleton, Wis., 1956; postgrad. U. Mich., 1956; M.Div., Garrett Evang. Theol. Sem., 1962; M.S. in Social Work, U. Wis., Milw., 1974; m. 2d, Grace L. Larson, June 13, 1970; children—Karen Sue, James Alan. Ordained to ministry United Methodist Ch., 1962; pastor United Meth. Ch., Bristol, Wis., 1958-61, Cudahy, Wis., 1961-66, Niagara and Goodman, Wis., 1966-68, Kenosha, Wis., 1968-69; exec. dir. Lakeview council Girl Scouts U.S.A., Waukegan, Ill., 1969-73; dir. social services unit Police Dept. Zion (Ill.), 1975-78; pvt. practice psychotherapy, marriage and family counseling, Zion, 1978—; pres. Bd. Sailing Center, Inc., 1981—; instr. Coll. of Lake County and LWV Seminar on Community Leadership; guest lectr. U. Wis., Milw. and Parkside; planning com. Nat. Conf. on Police Social Work; sec. bd. missions E. Wis. Conf. United Meth. Ch., 1962-68. Bd. dirs. Contact Teleministry Lake County, 1973-76, treas., 1974, instr. group leaders, 1977; chmn. Lake County Alcohol and Drug Abuse Planning and Coordinating Council, 1978; bd. dirs. Zion-Benton Children's Service, 1976; treas. bd. dirs. Teen Center, Niagara, Wis., 1967-68; mem. Lake County Crisis Center for Prevention and Treatment of Domestic Violence. Recipient Thanks Badge, Girl Scouts U.S.A., 1973; cert. social worker, Ill. Mem. Acad. Cert. Social Workers, Nat. Assn. Social Workers, Internat. Primal Assn. Contbr. articles to publs.; organizer, developer police social services program, Zion. Home: 1717 Hermon Ave Zion IL 60099 Office: Counseling and Psychotherapy Center Ltd also Bd Sailing Center Inc 3232 Sheridan Rd Zion IL 60099

LEMBERGER, LOUIS, pharmacologist, physician; b. Monticello, N.Y., May 8, 1937; s. Max and Ida (Seigel) L.; B.S. magna cum laude, Bklyn. Coll. Pharmacy, L.I. U., 1960; Ph.D. in Pharmacology, Albert Einstein Coll. Medicine, 1964, M.D., 1968; m. Myrna Sue Diamond, 1959; children—Harriet, Margo. Pharmacy intern VA Regional Office, Newark, summer 1960; postdoctoral fellow Albert Einstein Coll. Medicine, 1964-68; intern medicine Met. Hosp. Center, N.Y. Med. Coll., N.Y.C., 1968-69; research asso. NIH, Bethesda, Md., 1969-71; practice medicine specializing in clin. pharmacology, Bethesda, 1969-71, Indpls., 1971—; clin. pharmacologist Lilly Lab. Clin. Research, Eli Lilly & Co., Indpls., 1971-75, chief clin. pharmacology, 1975-78, dir. clin. pharmacology, 1978—; asst. prof. pharmacology Ind. U., 1972-73, asst. prof. medicine, 1972-73, asso. prof. pharmacology, 1973-77, asso. prof. medicine, 1973-77, prof. pharmacology, medicine and psychiatry, 1977—, mem. grad. faculty, 1975—; adj. prof. clin. pharmacology Ohio State U., 1975—; physician Wishard Meml. Hosp., 1976—; cons. U.S. Nat. Commn. on Marihuana and Drug Abuse, 1971-73, Can. Commn. of Inquiry into Non-Med. Use of Drugs, 1971-73; guest lectr. various univs., 1968—. Post adviser Crossroads of Am. council Boy Scouts Am., 1972-77. Served with USPHS, 1969-71. Fellow ACP, N.Y. Acad. Scis., Am. Coll. Neuropschopharmacology, Am. Coll. Clin. Pharmacology; mem. Am. Soc. Pharmacology and Exptl. Therapeutics (com. div. clin. pharmacology 1972-78, chmn. 1978—, chmn. 2d World Conf. Clin. Pharmacology; mem. council 1980—), AAAS, Am. Soc. Clin. Pharmacology and Therapeutics (chmn. neuropsychopharmacology sect. 1973-80, dir. 1975-81, chmn. fin. com. 1976—, v.p. 1981—), Am. Soc. Clin. Investigation, Collegium Internat. Neuro-Psychopharmacologicum, Am. Fedn. Clin. Research, Central Soc. Clin. Research, Soc. Neuroscis., Sigma Xi, Alpha Omega Alpha, Rho Chi. Jewish. Author: (with A. Rubin) Physiologic Disposition of Drugs of Abuse, 1976; contbr. numerous articles on biochemistry and pharmacology to sci. jours.; editorial bd. Excerpta Medica, 1972—, Clin. Pharmacology and Therapeutics, 1976—, Psychopharmacology, 1975-81, Pharmacology, Internat. Jour. Exptl. and Clin. Pharmacology, 1977—. Office: Lilly Lab Clin Research Wishard Memorial Hosp Indianapolis IN 46202

LEMBERGER, ROBERT ALOIS, cons. engr.; b. St. Louis, July 10, 1934; s. Alois A. and Marie (Stukejergen) L.; B.S. in Physics, U. Mo., Rolla, 1959, B.S. in Civil Engring., 1960; m. Beverly L. Birmingham, Feb. 14, 1959; 1 son, John Robert. Mgmt. trainee Proctor & Gamble Mfg. Co., St. Louis, 1960-63; instr. U. Mo., Rolla, 1963-66; partner Mo. Engring. Co., Rolla, 1966—; chmn. bd. dirs. Am. Planning Corp., Rolla, 1965; dir. Mo. Engring. Corp. of the Ozarks, Camdenton, Mo. Mem. Maries County (Mo.) Sch. Bd., 1975—. Served with AUS, 1953-55. Mem. Mo., Nat. socs. profl. engrs., Mo. Assn. Registered Land Surveyors, Kappa Alpha. Lion. Home: Vienna MO 65582 Office: PO Box 13 Rolla MO 65401

LEMERY, EUGENE FRANKLIN, social worker; b. Lockwood, Mo., Sept. 17, 1927; s. John Nelson and Ann (Black) L.; B.A., U. Calif., Berkeley, 1952; M.S.W., U. Utah, 1963; m. Noreen Mary Paulson, Aug. 12, 1961; children—Mary Christine, Mark Eugene. With Alaska Div. Public Welfare, 1959-63, dist. rep., Fairbanks, 1963-65; commd. corps officer Indian Hosp., USPHS, Pine Ridge, S.D., 1965-66; cons. Nev. Dept. Public Welfare, Carson City, 1966; psychiat. social worker Mo. Div. Mental Health, Springfield, 1967-75; social worker VA Med. Center Hosp., Hot Springs, S.D., 1975—. Mayor's rep. City of Hot Springs for Internat. Yr. of Child, 1979. Served with AUS, 1946-47. Recipient Letter of Commendation, Gov.

Alaska, 1979; chmn. Internat. Year of Disabled Persons com. VA Med. Center, Hot Springs, 1981. Cert. social worker, S.D. Mem. Acad. Cert. Social Workers, Nat. Assn. Social Workers, S.D. Mental Health Assn., Commd. Officers Assn. USPHS. Lutheran. Clubs: Kiwanis (v.p. 1978-79), Elks (Hot Springs); Masons. Office: VA Med Center Hosp Hot Springs SD 57747

LEMKE, LEROY WALTER, lawyer, state senator; b. Chgo., Sept. 24, 1935; s. Otto Mark and Myrtle Theresa L.; B.S.B.A., Drake U., 1959; J.D., John Marshall Law Sch., 1964; children—Lee Alan, Ronda Lee Lemke Alvarado, Kevin Keith. Admitted to Ill. bar; asso. firm Osterkamp, Jackson & Lemke, Chgo., 1964-73; individual practice law, Chgo., 1973; rep. Ill. Legislature, 1973-75; mem. Ill. State Senate, 1975—. Founder, chmn. Ill. Ethnic Heritage Commn. Named Outstanding Senator, Ill. Fedn. Pvt. Univs. and Colls.; Outstanding Legislator, Ill. Pro Life Coalition, Polish Community Council. Mem. Am. Bar Assn., Ill. Bar Assn., Chgo. Bar Assn., Bohemian Bar Assn., Casimir Pulaski Civic League, Archer Heights Civic League, West Risdon Civic League. Democrat. Lutheran. Club: Little Village Lions. Office: 4355 W 26th St Chicago IL 60623*

LEMMON, KENNETH WAYNE, psychologist; b. DuQuoin, Ill., June 21, 1938; s. Halcy Norbert and Lillie Bell (Downen) L.; B.A., U. Corpus Christi, 1966; M.A., Tex. A. and I. U., 1967; postgrad. Wayne State U., 1969-71; m. Mary Aldora Greer, Jan. 24, 1959; children—Sonya Kim, Bradley Wayne. Instr. psychology Mobile Coll., 1968-69, U. Windsor (Ont., Can.), 1969-71; lectr. Wayne County Community Coll., 1970-71; teaching fellow Wayne State U., 1969-70, instr., 1973-74; asso. prof. psychology Center for Creative Studies, Coll. Art and Design, 1971—; med. hypnotist; photographer; psychol. cons. to industry. Mem. exec. com. bd. dirs. YMCA, Royal Oak, Mich., 1975—; chmn. bd. dirs. Coastal Bend Habilitation Bd., Corpus Christi; bd. dirs. Nat. Assn. on Vols. in Criminal Justice. Served with U.S. Army, 1957-58. Whitehall fellow, 1967-68; Tex. A. and I. U. grantee, 1966-68; Nat. Bd. Ministries grantee, 1968-69. Mem. Am., Mich. psychol. assns., AAUP, Am. Sociol. Assn., Am. Art Therapy Assn., Mich. Alcohol and Addiction Assn. Episcopalian. Club: Forestors. Author: A Glossary of Statistical Terms, 1971; contbr. articles to profl. jours. Home: 923 W Eleven Mile Rd Royal Oak MI 48067 Office: 245 E Kirby St Detroit MI 48202

LEMONS, CHARLES F., banker; b. Birch Tree, Mo., Oct. 8, 1926; s. Otho C. and Wilda (King) L.; B.S., S.W. Mo. State U., 1949; postgrad. U. Wis., 1959; m. LaRue Keran, June 20, 1948; children—Keran, Renee Galer, Kelley, Deidre. Teller, Farmers State Bank, Lockwood, Mo., 1949, cashier, 1952, pres., 1969—, also dir. Pres., chmn. Dade County Mo. Republican Com., 1952-64, mem., 1952—. Served with U.S. Army, 1944-46. Mem. C. of C. (pres.), Ozark Bankers Assn. (pres.), S.W. Mo. Bank Adminstrn. Inst. (pres.), Mo. Bankers Assn. (chmn. region 7), Lockwood Indsl. Devel. Assn. Republican. Methodist. Club: Masons. Address: Lockwood MO*

LE MOYNE, NOEL JOSEPH, market analyst; b. Dayton, Ohio, Oct. 3, 1939; s. Joseph Hastings and Katherine (Cooper) LeM.; B.S., Miami U., Oxford, Ohio, 1962; M.B.A., U. Mich., 1966; m. Doris Lee Stallard. Market research analyst Standard Oil Co. of Ohio, Cleve., 1966-68; sr. market analyst R.G. Barry Co., slipper mfg., Columbus, 1968—. Marketing cons. Loaned exec. United Way, 1972; active Big Bros. Served as 1st lt. USAF, 1962-65. Mem. Am. Marketing Assn. (pres. Central Ohio chpt. 1971-73), Am. Footwear Industries Assn. (mktg. info. com.). Home: 636 Fleetrun Ave Columbus OH 43230 Office: 13405 Yarmouth Dr NW Pickerington OH 43147

LENARDSON, JAMES DUANE, cons. engr., electric co. exec.; b. Riga, Mich., June 8, 1924; s. James Wesley and Viola Martha (Becker) L.; student U. Detroit, 1941-43; B.S. in Mech. Engring., U. Ill., 1946; m. Raye Evelyn Lauderdale, Dec. 23, 1945; children—Linda Lee, Cynthia Sue, James Raymond, Richard Lee. Jr. through sr. engr. Toledo (Ohio) Edison Co., 1946-55, constrn. engr., 1955-68, plant mech. engr., 1968-70, quality assurance mgr., 1970-77, quality assurance dir., 1977—; cons. engr., 1981—. Active Boy Scouts Am. Served to comdr. USN, 1943-46. Registered profl. engr., Ohio, Calif. Mem. ASTM, Am. Concrete Inst., ASME (nat. code coms.), Am. Soc. for Quality Control (nat. standard com.), Am. Soc. for Nondestructive Testing, Nat. Rifle Assn., U. Ill. Alumni Assn., Nat. Wildlife Fedn., Am. Audubon Soc., Ducks Unltd. Republican. Lutheran. Lectr., speaker on tech. engring. Home: 14115 Potter Rd Bowling Green OH 43402

LENFERS, JACK LOUIS, appliance co. exec.; b. Evansville, Ind., June 3, 1920; s. Clayton Charles and Anna Marie (Rapp) L.; student U. Evansville, 1946-50; bus. cert. Ind. U., 1962; m. Mabelgene Witherspoon, Oct. 27, 1940. With Whirlpool Corp., Evansville, Ind., 1939—, purchasing mgr., 1952-65, product planning staff mem., 1965-67, product mgr., 1967-69, group product planning adminstr., refrigerators, freezer, air-conditioners and dehumidifiers, 1969—. Bd. dirs. United Fund, 1960-65, YMCA Bldg Fund, 1977-79. Served with C.E., U.S. Army, 1943-46, 50-52. Recipient Silver Key awards (7) Jr. C. of C. Mem. ASHRAE. Clubs: Civitan (dir. 1969-77, pres. 1973-74, gov. midwest dist. 1974-75, Outstanding Mr. Civitan award 1971, Outstanding Club Pres. award 1973, Midwest Dist. Honor Key award 1973), U. Evansville Tip-Off (dir. 1970-80), Rolling Hills Country. Home: 9888 Crestview Terr Newburgh IN 47630 Office: Whirlpool Corp Hwy 41 N Evansville IN 47727

LENGAR, JONATHAN NGAGBA ALFRED, geographer, educator; b. Yoyema, Sierra Leone, Apr. 15, 1938; s. Pasema Pelegohu and Nyaveh Kigba (Kamanda) L.; diploma in edn. U. Sierra Leone, 1972; B.A., U. Durham (Eng.), 1967; M.A., Ball State U., 1975, Ed.D., 1978; m. Jane Zenobia James, Sept. 1, 1972; children—Sarian, Joya, Tonya, Pasema. Tchr., Taiama Central and Secondary Schs., 1958-63; vice prin. designate, lectr. Freetown (Sierra Leone) Tchrs. Coll., 1968-74; asso. prof. Ind. U., Purdue U., Indpls., 1979—; curriculum devel. specialist Marion County Assn. Retarded Citizens, Indpls., 1979—. Sec., Nat. Democratic Party Sierra Leone, 1969-70. African Am. Grad. scholar, 1974-78. Mem. Sierra Leon Geog. Assn., AAUP, Assn. Tchr. Educators, Assn. for Supervision and Curriculum Devel., Phi Delta Kappa. Methodist. Author: Politics and Education in Sierra Leone, 1968-70, 1973. Home: 3244 E 38th St Apt 109 Indianapolis IN 46218 Office: Dept Geography Ind U 925 W Michigan St Indianapolis IN 46202

LENON, RICHARD ALLEN, minerals and chem. co. exec.; b. Lansing, Mich., Aug. 4, 1920; s. Theodore and Elizabeth (Amon) L.; B.A., Western Mich. Coll., 1941; postgrad Northwestern U., 1941-42; m. Helen Johnson, Sept. 13, 1941; children—Richard Allen, Pamela A., Lisa A. Mgr. fin. div. Montgomery Ward & Co., Chgo., 1947-56; v.p. fin. Westinghouse Air Brake Co., Pitts., 1963-67, treas., 1965-67; v.p., treas. Internat. Minerals & Chem. Corp., Northbrook, Ill., 1956-63, group v.p. fin. and adminstrn., 1967-68, exec. v.p., 1968-70, pres., 1970-78, chief exec. officer, 1971—, chmn. bd., 1977—, also dir.; dir. Am. Standard Inc., Bankers Trust Co., Fed. Paper Bd. Co., The Signal Cos. Served with USNR, 1942-47. Clubs: Univ. (Chgo.); Glen View (Golf, Ill.); Bankers (N.Y.C.). Office: 2315 Sanders Rd Northbrook IL 60062

LENSMITH, BETTY, wholesale co. exec.; b. Oconomowoc, Wis., Oct. 3, 1928; d. Alex F. and Vera (Zeiters) Henschel; m. Eugene A. Lensmith, Nov. 14, 1949; children—Lissa Kathleen, Larry Eugene. Receptionist, Schrader Studio, Milw., 1947; mgr. Tooley Myron Studios chain, 1948-49; owner, mgr. Country Studio, Oconomowoc, 1950—, Town and Country Studio, 1957—; founder, pres., treas. Photographers Specialized Services, Inc., Oconomowoc, 1968—; founder, pres. Golden World Products div. Ret. Persons Specialized Services, 1982; instr. Winona Sch. Photography, 1975—, Miami and Traingle Inst. (Pa.), 1977, No. Ga. Sch. Photography, 1978. Recipient awards Kodak Co. Mem. Profl. Photographers Am. (cert. photog. craftsman, recipient various awards), Am. Soc. Photographers, Am. Mgmt. Assn., Studio Suppliers Assn., Female Execs., 700 Club, Presidents Club. Author: The Guide to Lighting, Posing and Composing, 1971, rev. edit., 1980; Selling, The Name of the Game, 1976; Profitable Promotions and Merchandising Techniques, 1977; The Basic Guide to Commercial Photography, 1979, rev. edit., 1982. Home: 612 Summit Ave Oconomowoc WI 53066 Office: 650 Armour Rd Oconomowoc WI 53066

LENTZ, DANIEL MARVIN, application engr.; b. Milw., July 24, 1949; s. Frank Hugo and Arlyne Dorothy (Caspary) L.; B.S. in Engring. with honors, U. Wis., Milw., 1971, M.S., 1972. Teaching and project asst. U. Wis., Milw., 1971-73; engr. Hatco Corp., Milw., 1974; exec. dir. Wis. chpt. Am. Inst. Aero. and Astronautics, Milw., 1974-77; application engr. Vilter Mfg. Corp., Milw., 1977-80; project engr. TEC Systems, DePere, Wis., 1980—; speaker before community groups on space exploration; chmn. Dividends from Space, Wright Bros. Commemorative Council. Pres., Mission Heights Assn. Fellow Brit. Interplanetary Soc.; mem. AIAA (recipient numerous citations), Royal Aero. Soc., Dividends from Space, Am. Soc. for Aerospace Edn., Am. Soc. for Engring. Edn., ASHRAE, ASME, Am. Inst. Chem. Engrs., German Rocket Soc., The World Future Soc., Phi Kappa Phi, Tau Beta Pi. Roman Catholic. Author mgmt. guidebooks for Wis. tech. socs.; contbr. articles on space exploration to newspapers. Home: 1401 Mission Heights Rd DePere WI 54115 Office: 830 Prospect Rd DePere WI 54115

LENTZ, EDWARD ALLEN, health adminstr.; b. Superior, Wis., May 30, 1926; s. Otto Albert and Martha (Gruhel) L.; B.S. in Edn., U. Cin., 1951; M.H.A., Wayne State U., 1957; m. Margaret Ann Denier, May 30, 1952; 1 dau., Elizabeth Ann. Engaged as asst. program dir. Anti-Tb League, Cin., 1953-54; asst. dir. Pub. Health Fedn., Cin., 1954-57; dir. health planning United Community Council, 1957-62; asst. exec. dir. Columbus Hosp. Fedn., 1962-65, mem. regional planning com., 1966-78; dir. community relations and devel. Hawkes Hosp. of Mt. Carmel, Columbus, 1979—; asso. dir. Ohio Hosp. Assn., 1965-69; asst. clin. prof. preventive medicine Coll. Medicine, Ohio State U., 1957—, asso. adj. prof. hosp. and health services adminstrn., 1972—; dep. dir. med. care adminstrn. Ohio Dept. Health, 1972-75, project dir. task force on hosp. licensure and certificate of need, 1972-73; pres. Med. Advances Inst., 1975-79. Mem. bd. Citizens Research, House of Hope for Alcoholics, Franklin County unit Am. Cancer Soc.; cons. Study Community Services, Ft. Wayne, Ind., 1962. Project dir. Study Chronic Illness Services Columbus and Franklin County, 1962-64; cons. USPHS; mem. state adv. com. practical nurse edn. Ohio Dept. Edn.; mem. adv. com. community health planning div. community planning U. Cin., consultants com. health planning information Ohio Dept. Health, com. coordination of mental retardation Ohio State Dept. Mental Hygiene and Correction; exec. dir. Health Planning Assn. Central Ohio River Valley, 1969-70; chmn. Ohio med. care adv. com. Ohio Pub. Welfare Dept., 1979—. Served as seaman 1st class USNR, 1944-46, 1st lt. AUS, 1951-52. Fellow Am. Public Health Assn. (co-chmn. com. instl. planning 1972—, mem. governing council 1974—, program devel. bd. 1975-78, exec. bd. 1979—); mem. Ohio Public Health Assn. (pres. 1968-69), Royal Soc. Health, Nat. Rehab. Assn., Am. Soc. for Hosp. Planning, Ohio Soc. Hosp. Planning, Ohio Health Data Corp. (sec.), Am. Hosp. Assn. (chmn. com. long term care insts. 1966-68), Assn. Areawide Health Planning Agys. (pres. 1970), Phi Epsilon Kappa. Presbyterian. Club: Athletic (Columbus). Home: 585 Keyes Ln Worthington OH 43085 Office: Hawkes Hosp of Mt Carmel 793 W State St Columbus OH 43222

LENTZ, PATRICIA ANN, rubber mfg. mgr.; b. Jackson, Mich., Mar. 23, 1939; d. William L. and Margaret K. (Derhammer) Wragg; A.S.S., U. Akron, 1965, B.S., 1975; M.B.A., Baldwin-Wallace Coll., 1981; m. Frederick M. Lentz, May 20, 1967. Mgr. mgmt. info. systems ops. planning and control B.F. Goodrich Co., Akron, Ohio, 1976-77, mgr. mgmt. info. systems planning and orgn. devel., 1977-78, mgr. corp. edn. and tng., 1978-79, mgr. purchasing data base, 1979—. Program action council W.K. Kellogg Found. Program for Devel. of Team Leadership, U. Akron; co-chmn. task force Summit County Children's Services Bd. Mem. Assn. Systems Mgmt. (past sec.). Club: Cascade (Akron). Home: 3675 Mogadore Rd Mogadore OH 44260 Office: 500 S Main St Akron OH 44318

LENZ, MARY LOUISE, nun, coll. adminstr.; b. Carroll, Iowa, Dec. 15, 1930; d. Philip John and Hilda Louise (Wiederin) L.; B.A., Briar Cliff Coll., 1957; M.A., U. Notre Dame, 1959, Ph.D., 1962. Joined Sisters of St. Francis, Roman Catholic Ch., 1949; tchr. English, St. Mary's High Sch., Remsen, Iowa, 1952-53, St. Joseph Sch., Bode, Iowa, 1953-57, Ashton, Iowa, 1957-58; faculty Briar Cliff Coll., Sioux City, Iowa, 1962-72, dir. continuing edn., 1974-79, 81—, dir. Weekend Coll., 1979-81, dir. Center for Women, 1975-79; coordinator programming for sr. citizens St. Cecilia Cathedral, Omaha, 1972-74. Mem. Iowa Assn. Lifelong Learning, Mo. Valley Adult Educators Assn. Home: 1112 13th St Sioux City IA 51105 Office: Briar Cliff College 3303 Rebecca Sioux City IA 51104

LENZ, RALPH CHARLES, JR., adminstrv. aero. engr.; b. Beatrice, Nebr., Oct. 27, 1919; s. Ralph Carl and Lois Elsie (Sutliff) L.; B.S. in Aero. Engring., U. Cin., 1943; M.S. (Sloan fellow), Mass. Inst. Tech., 1959; m. Mary Ellen Stone, Feb. 5, 1945; children—Lois Ellen, Linda Ann. Aero. engr. Glenn L. Martin Co., Omaha, 1943-45; aero. engr. U.S. Air Force, Wright Patterson AFB, Ohio, 1947-53, chief, plans div., aero systems div., 1954-74; sr. research engr. U. Dayton (Ohio) Research Inst., 1974—; lectr., cons. tech. forecasting. Served as aero. engr. USAAF, 1945-46. Fellow AIAA (asso.); mem. Air Force Assn. (Aerospace Power award 1974), Sigma Xi, Triangle (nat. hon. mem.). Co-founder, editor Technol. Forecasting and Social Change, 1969. Home: 2899 O'Neall Rd Waynesville OH 45068 Office: Univ Dayton Dayton OH 45469

LENZO, ANTHONY SAMUEL, educator, art dealer, advt. and pub. relations cons.; b. East Chicago, Ind., Jan. 22, 1925; s. Carmelo and Antonia Lenzo; B.S., Ind. U., 1949, M.S., 1961; Ed.D., Nova U., 1975; m. Valerie Zawada, Oct. 10, 1968; children—Anthony Joseph, Julianne Marie, Holly Marie. Mgr. bus. and advt. Our Sunday Visitor, Gary, Ind., 1955-67; communications media cons. N.Y.C. and Chgo., 1954-56; radio-TV producer Kenyon & Eckhart Advt. Agy., Chgo., 1956-57; coordinator resource learning center Gary (Ind.) Pub. Schs., 1957-62; dir. instructional media East Chicago (Ind.) Pub. Schs., 1972-77; cons. vocat. resources, 1977—; pres. Crown Point Creative Interiors, Inc., Crown Point, 1977-81, T. & V. Enterprises, Inc., 1981—. Pres., East Chicago Community Council, 1973-77; sec. Riley Cultural and Arts Assn., 1972—; pres. East Chicago Hist. Soc., 1976; mem. exec. bd. Nat. Council Encouragement Patriotism; cubmaster Boy Scouts Am.; pres. Homeowners Assn., St. Michael's Sch., 1981—. Served with AUS, 1943-46, 49-52, Col. Res. Recipient Nat. Tchrs. medal Freedoms Found., 1965; Freedom award Gary Exchange Club, 1965; named Ind. Mr. Patriot, Ind. State Legislature, 1976. Mem. Gary Fedn. Tchrs. (trustee), North-West Ind. Council Tchrs. Unions (pres.), Mil. Order World Wars, Res. Officers Assn., Gary Assn. Childhood Edn. (chmn. publicity), Assn. Ednl. Communications Tech., Nat. Ednl. Broadcasters Assn., Am. Legion (awards chmn.), Phi Delta Kappa (sec.). Roman Catholic. Clubs: Elks, Lions (dir.). Home: 8425 Morse Pl Crown Point IN 46307 Office: 210 E Columbus Dr E East Chicago IN 46312

LENZO, JEFFREY JAGGER, powder co. exec.; b. Coshocton, Ohio, Dec. 2, 1947; s. Joseph M. and Audrey A. L.; A.A., Lakeland Coll., 1977; mktg. student John Carroll U., 1977-81; postgrad. in organizational devel. and analysis Case-West Res. U., m. Lois Langell Lenzo, May 5, 1967 (div. 1981); children—Joseph F., Dirk A., Alicia. Sales rep. Control Data Corp., 1969-70; programmer Austin Powder Co., Cleve., 1970-73, mgr. systems and programing, 1975-79, mgr. data processing, 1979-80; programmer/analyst Reliance Elec. Co., 1973; sr. systems rep. Burroughs Corp., 1973-75; v.p. mktg. Systems, Plus Inc., cons. co., Beachwood, Ohio, 1980-81; dir. mktg. Trend Cons. Services, Inc., Wickliffe, Ohio, 1981—; cons. Served with U.S. Army, 1966-69. Recipient awards Burroughs Corp., 1978. Mem. Data Processing Mgmt. Assn., Cleve. Jewish Community Center. Republican. Club: Mill Creek Racquet. Home: 3261 Berkshire Rd Cleveland Heights OH 44118 Office: 30432 Euclid Ave Wickliffe OH

LEON, ARTHUR SOL, research cardiologist, exercise physiologist; b. Bklyn., Apr. 26, 1931; s. Alex and Anne (Schrek) L.; B.S. with high honors in Chemistry, U. Fla., Gainsville, 1952; M.S. in Biochemistry, U. Wis., Madison, 1954, M.D., 1957; m. Gloria Rakita, Dec. 23, 1956; children—Denise, Harmon, Michelle. Intern, Henry Ford Hosp., Detroit, 1957-58; fellow internal medicine Lahey Clinic, Boston, 1958-60; fellow cardiology U. Miami (Fla.) Sch. Medicine, Jackson Meml. Hosp., Miami, 1960-61; chief gen. medicine, cardiology, dir. intern edn. 34th Gen. U.S. Army Hosp., Orleans, France, 1961-64; research cardiologist Walter Reed Army Inst. Research, Washington, 1964-67; dir. Hoffmann-La Roche Clin. Pharmacology Research Unit, Newark Beth Israel Med. Center, 1969-73; instr. dept. medicine Coll. Medicine and Dentistry N.J., Newark, 1967-69, asst. prof., 1969-72, asso. prof., 1972-73; asso. prof. medicine, physiol. hygiene, nutrition and physiology Med. Sch. and Sch. Pub. Health, U. Minn., Mpls., 1973-79, prof., 1979—; dir. grad. studies, applied research and labs., lab. physiol. hygiene U. Minn., 1973—; col., chief cardiology 5501 U.S. Army Hosp., Ft. Snelling, Minn., 1973—; mem. Med. Evaluation Team Gemini and Apollo Projects, Washington, 1964-67. Bd. dirs. Vinland Nat. Sports Health Center, 1978—. Served with M.C., U.S. Army, 1961-67. Recipient Amos Alonzo Stagg Phys. Fitness medal, 1963; Am. Heart Assn. fellow, 1960-61; William G. Anderson award AAHPER, 1981. Fellow Am. Coll. Cardiology, Am. Coll. Chest Physicians, Am. Coll. Clin. Pharm., N.Y. Acad. Sci., Am. Coll. Sports Medicine (trustee 1976-78, v.p. 1977-79, pres. Northland chpt. 1976); mem. Am. Physiol. Soc., Soc. Clin. Pharm. and Therapeutics, Am. Inst. Research, Am. Heart Assn., Am. Coll. Nutrition (v.p. Hennepin div. 1980, pres.-elect 1981), Am. Fedn. Clin. Research, Am. Soc. Biol. and Exptl. Therapeutics, Phi Beta Kappa, Phi Kappa Phi. Jewish. Contbr. articles in exercise physiology, exercise in prevention, treatment of coronary heart disease, cardiology, biochemistry, clin. pharmacology to med. jours., books. Participant White House Conf. Health and Physical Activity, 1976, 81. Home: 9701 Oak Ridge Trail Minnetonka MN 55343 Office: Lab Physiol Hygiene U Minn Stadium Gate 27 Minneapolis MN 55455

LEON, JAMES HOWARD, fin. exec.; b. Chgo., Oct. 30, 1951; s. Howard Elmer and Dolores Ruth (Kaminski) L.; B.A., Northeastern Ill. U., 1979; student Roosevelt U., 1969-71, 74-77, Triton Coll., 1971-74; m. Patricia Ann Hussey, Nov. 25, 1976. With audit dept. Prudential Ins., Chgo., also Merrillville, Ind., 1971-78, regional auditor, 1973-78; mgr. internal audit N.W. Fed. Savs. & Loan Assn., Chgo., 1979-81; internal auditor Kemper Fin. Services, Chgo., 1981—. Mem. Inst. Internal Auditors, Fin. Mgrs. Soc., Chgo. Internal Auditors (treas. 1981—). Republican. Roman Catholic. Office: 120 S La Salle St Chicago IL 60603

LEONARD, ALAN THOMAS, psychologist; b. Vermontville, Mich., Oct. 21, 1917; s. Archie George and Mable Groves (Cook) L.; B.S., Wayne State U., 1941, M.A., 1946; postgrad. Mich. State U., 1946-48; m. Anne B. Cronick, Oct. 12, 1957. Chief psychologist Grand Rapids (Mich.) Child Guidance Clinic, 1948-58; cons. psychologist, North Muskegon, Mich., 1958—. Cons. to pvt. agys., local and state govtl. agys. Host, moderator ednl. series WGRD radio sta., Grand Rapids, 1950-52; host drug abuse informational series WMKG-TV sta., Muskegon, 1968; host mental health info. series WMUS radio sta., Muskegon, 1962-64. Chmn. bd. Lincoln Found., Grand Rapids, 1950-56. Mem. Am., Mich. psychol. assns., Mich. Soc. Cons. Psychologists, Nat. Rehab. Soc., Am. Orthopsychiat. Assn., Mich. State Med. Soc. Home: 302 3rd St North Muskegon MI 49445 Office: 435 Whitehall Rd North Muskegon MI 49445

LEONARD, ANNE CHRISTINE, supt. schs.; b. N.Y.C., Dec. 22, 1936; d. Patrick A. and Mary T. (McAlpine) L.; B.S., Fordham U., 1962, M.A. in Modern European History, 1965; cert. advanced grad. studies in Ednl. Adminstrn., Boston U., 1972. Joined Sisters Congregation Notre Dame, Roman Cath. Ch., 1955; tchr., adminstr. Notre Dame Acad., S.I., N.Y., 1957-68; prin. Maternity B.V.M. Sch., Bourbonnais, Ill., 1968, St. Jude Apostle Sch., South Holland, Ill., 1969-79; supt. elem. schs. Roman Cath. Archdiocese Chgo., 1979—; pres. Archdiocesan Prins. Assn., 1974-79; mem. apostolic adv. com., provincial council Congregation Notre Dame; cons., lectr. workshop leader in field. Mem. Chief Adminstrs. Assn. Cath. Schs., Nat. Cath. Ednl. Assn., Assn. Supervision and Curriculum Devel. Author articles in field. Office: 155 E Superior St Chicago IL 60611

LEONARD, EDWARD ALLEN, communications exec., advt. agy. exec.; b. Chgo., May 1, 1949; s. James L. and Ina A. (Moscovitch) L.; B.S. in Communications, Northwestern U., 1976; postgrad. Ill. Inst. Tech., Kent State U., 1977-79; m. Carol Momi Jahn, Aug. 11, 1979. Vice pres. Britan Lighting Corp., Chgo., 1969-70; pres. Tiffiny, Inc., Chgo., 1970-73, Eat & Run, Inc., Chgo., 1978-80, E. Leonard Advt. Agy., Ltd., Evanston, Ill., 1979—, Tele-Media Communications Systems, Chgo., 1980—; personal bus. mgr. to Ernie Banks, 1980—; TV appearances on NBC Today Show, 1980, CBS News, 1981. Mem. AFTRA. Composer: (comedy song) Test Tube Baby Blues, 1980; originated Dial-A-Crazy Hotline telephone messages. Office: PO Box 867 Evanston IL 60204

LEONARD, HARRY ELVIN, indsl. relations cons.; b. Ottowa, Ill., Mar. 5, 1899; s. Andrew and Hannah (Weberg) L.; student U. Minn., 1920-21; m. Louise Anne Olson, May 13, 1940; children—Terri Lou (Mrs. Gordon Buhrer), Jacqueline Lee (Mrs. Robert Posner). With No. States Power Co., Mpls., 1923-40; asst. bus. mgr. Local 160 Internat. Brotherhood Elec. Workers, Mpls., 1940-41, union organizer, 1942-43, bus. mgr., 1944-64; maintenance supr. East Side Neighborhood Services, Mpls., 1966-67; indsl. relations cons. Minn. Nurses Assn., St. Paul, 1968-81; arbitrator for public and pvt.

employees in State of Minn., 1973-81; dir., Service Savs. and Loan Assn., St. Paul, 1956-66; instr. labor relations U. Minn. Evening Sch., 1950-51, mem. adv. council Indsl. Relations Center, 1950—. Mem. exec. com. Citizens League Greater Mpls., 1953-54; mem. staff Coummunity Chest, Mpls. 1944; commr. Mpls. Charter Commn., 1958-70, chmn., 1963-64. Chmn. 3d Ward Democratic Farmer Labor Club, 1941-46; del. Dem. Nat. Conv., 1948. Bd. dirs. Hennepin County Cancer Soc., 1959-71, hon. life mem., 1971—, 2d v.p., 1963-66. Served with U.S. Army, 1918. Named Labor Man of Year Mpls. Jr. C. of C., 1958. Mem. Amicus, Assn. for Non-Smokers Rights. Unitarian. Clubs: Masons, Shriners, Eagles (life). Home: 2939 Grand St NE Minneapolis MN 55418 Office: 1821 University Ave Saint Paul MN 55104

LEONARD, LAURIE, broadcasting sta. exec.; b. Milw., July 13, 1953; d. Richard Hart and Barbara (Klausner) L.; B.A. with honors, U. Wis., 1975; M.B.A. with Distinction, Harvard U., 1977. Reporter, Sta. WMTV, Madison, Wis., 1973-74, account exec., 1974-75; asst. regional mgr. Am. Television and Communications, San Diego, 1977-78, mgr. new market devel., Denver, 1978, dir. ops. planning, 1979; v.p., sta. mgr. Sta. WMTV, Madison, 1979-81, pres., gen. mgr., 1981—. Bd. dirs. United Way of Dane County, 1980—, also dir. public relations; bd. dirs. Madison Theatre Guild, 1981—; sec. Tempo Madison, 1981—. Mem. Nat. Assn. TV Program Execs., Madison Advt. Fedn., Wis. Broadcasters Assn. Office: 615 Forward Dr Madison WI 53711

LEONARD, ROWENA FISHER, steel co. adminstr.; b. St. Louis, Aug. 26, 1941; d. Paul Hiebert and Cordell Vesta (Overby) Fisher; A.A., Meramec Coll., 1970; B.A., St. Louis U., 1973; M.A., Webster Coll., 1980; m. Lewis Benjamin Leonard, Aug. 12, 1967. Claim rep. Firemans Fund Am. Ins. Co., St. Louis, 1960-63, 72-74; analyst Automobile Club So. Calif., Los Angeles, 1964-67; adminstrv. mgr. Aetna Ins. Co., St. Louis, 1974-77, Beth Gen. Contracting, St. Louis, 1977; personnel mgr. Tubular Steel, Inc., St. Louis, 1977—; cons. Leonard & Assos., St. Louis, 1980—. Girls week chmn. Bus. and Profl. Women, 1966-67. Served with USCG Res., 1973-76, U.S. Army Res., 1977—. Recipient Expert Pistol medal, 1974; Valley Forge Freedom Found. award for youthpower U.S.A. Conf., 1966. Mem. Am. Soc. Personnel Adminstrs., Bus. and Profl. Womens Club, Nat. Assn. Parliamentarians, Phi Theta Kappa, Pi Sigma Alpha. Republican. Presbyterian. Home: 25 Hammel Ave Webster Groves MO 63119 Office: Tubular Steel Inc PO Box 27370 St Louis MO 63141

LEONARD, W(ILLIAM) PATRICK, univ. adminstr.; b. Beech Grove, Ind., Nov. 2, 1939; s. Willard E. and Helen L. (Dixon) L.; B.S. in Edn., Ind. U., 1961, M.S. in Edn., 1962; Ph.D. in Ednl. Communications, U. Pitts., 1969; M.B.A., Loyola U., 1981. Lectr. dept. ednl. communications U. Pitts., 1966-69; dir. Instructional Materials Center, Temple U., Phila., 1969-72, asst. prof. ednl. media, 1969-72; dir. Instructional Media, Chgo. State U., 1972-74, asso. prof. library sci., 1972-78, prof., 1978—, dir. libraries, 1974-77, dean of library and learning resources, 1977—; Community prof. Govs. State U., Park Forest South, Ill., 1974, 77; mem. campus vis. teams Nat. Council Accreditation Tchr. Edn., Benedictine Coll., Kans., 1978, Oakland (Mich.) U., 1980, Okla. State U., 1981; team leader instructional design inservice workshops Chgo. Consortium of Colls. and Univs., 1976; del. Conf. on Media Applications to U. Without Walls Programs, U. Minn., Mpls., 1973. Chmn. council dirs. State U. Libraries Ill., 1979-80; mem. policy bd. Mid-Ill. Computer Coop., 1979—; sec. Chgo. Acad. Library Council, 1979; chmn. evaluation and planning com. Chgo. Met. Higher Edn. Council, 1978-79. Served to lt. Mil. Police Corps, U.S. Army, 1962-65. Mem. ALA, Ill. Library Assn., Assn. for Ednl. Communications and Tech., Nat. Soc. for Study Edn., Am. Assn. U. Adminstrs., Am. Assn. for Higher Edn., Ill. Audio Visual Assn., Am. Edn. Research Assn., Phi Delta Kappa. Roman Catholic. Contbr. articles to profl. jours. Home: 12808 Pebble Dr Palos Park IL 60464 Office: Chgo State Univ Douglas Library 9500 S King Dr Chicago IL 60628

LEONARDS, DAVID, entertainment cons.; b. Lafayette, Ind., Nov. 20, 1946; s. Gerald and Beryl Leonards; B.S., Purdue U., 1968, B.S. in Chemistry, 1970, M.S., 1973. Instr. chemistry Kankakee Valley Sch. Corp., DeMotte, Ind., 1968-69; instr. chemistry, curriculum cons. Eastern Howard Sch. Corp., Greentown, Ind., 1969-72; pres., chmn. bd. Internat. Leonards Corp., Indpls., 1973—; exec. dir. Internat. Entertainment Bur., 1973—. Republican precinct committeeman, conv. del.; mem. Marion County Lic. Rev. Bd.; bd. dirs. Mapleton-Fall Creek Neighborhood Assn. Mem. Am. Chem. Soc., Am. Fedn. Musicians, Ind. Soc. Assn. Execs., Meeting Planners Internat., Ind. C. of C., Indpls. Conv. and Visitors Bur., Indpls. C. of C., Am. Contract Bridge League. Clubs: Rotary, Columbia. Office: 3612 Washington Blvd Indianapolis IN 46205

LEONG, DAVIS, systems analyst; b. Chgo., Feb. 24, 1954; s. Linton and Sue Lin (Hong) L.; B.S., U. Ill., 1976. Systems analyst Interstate Nat. Corp., Chgo., 1976-79; lead analyst policies and procedures G.D. Searle & Co., Skokie, Ill., 1979—. Mem. Assn. for Systems Mgmt. Democrat. Home: 727 W Aldine Ave Chicago IL 60657 Office: 4901 Searle Pkwy Skokie IL 60076

LEONIDA, DOMINGO DOMINIC JOSEPH, physician; b. Honolulu, July 3, 1927; s. Fernando Gabriel and Fortunata (Ragas) L.; B.S., Marquette U., 1951; M.S., U. Cin., 1953, M.D., 1959; M.P.H., U. Mich., 1962; postgrad. (fellow) Computer Sci., U. Ill., 1978-80; m. Madelaine Ching Hua Kao, Aug. 7, 1954; children—Mark Huaming Patrick, Clara HuaCin Catherine. Intern, Mercy Hosp., Toledo, 1959-60; resident U. Mich. Hosp., Ann Arbor, 1961-62; research biochemist U.S. Indsl. Chem.-Nat. Distillers Corp., Cin., 1955-56; epidemiologist Ohio Dept. Health, Columbus, 1962-64, chief chronic diseases, 1964-65; mem. staff Physicians Alcohol Inst. Studies, Rutgers U., New Brunswick, N.J., 1964; med. dir. immunol. activities and grants, epidemiologist N.Y. Dept. Health, Albany, 1965-67; med. dir. Skokie (Ill.) Health Dept., 1967-69, Kenosha (Wis.) Health Dept., 1969-71; family practice, indsl. practice medicine, Lincoln, Ill., 1971—; instr. Coll. Medicine, Ohio State U., 1963-64, spl. edn. Ill. State U., 1973-74, Coll. Medicine, U. Ill., Peoria, 1971-77, Coll. Medicine, U. Ill., Chgo., 1980—; mem. staff Meth. Hosp., Peoria, Pekin (Ill.) Hosp., Warner Hosp., Clinton, Ill., McKinley Health Center, Urbana. Chmn. camping health safety coms. Kenosha council Boy Scouts Am., 1970-71. Served with 8th inf. U.S. Army, 1946-48; lt. M.C., USN, 1960-61; lt. col. Ill. Army Res. N.G., 1978—. Mental health profl., Hamilton, Ohio. Fellow Am. Coll. Preventive Medicine, Am. Acad. Family Practice; mem. AAAS, Ecol. Soc. Am., AMA, Ill. State, Logan County Med. Socs., Am. Heart Assn. (Chgo. br.), N.Y. Public Health Assn. Roman Catholic. Contbr. articles to med. jours. Home and Office: 42 Northbrook St Lincoln IL 62656 Office: 230 S Dearborn St Chicago IL 60604

LEPLEY, DERWARD, JR., cardiovascular surgeon; b. Viola, Wis., Jan. 10, 1924; s. Derward and Eva (Blakeley) L.; M.D., Marquette U., 1949; m. Ardis Pobanz, June 12, 1949; children—Stephen, Larry, Diane, Heide. Rotating intern Wis. Gen. Hosp., Madison, 1949-50; resident in gen. surgery Wood VA Hosp., 1952-56, resident in thoracic surgery, 1956-58; research fellow Nat. Heart Inst., U. Minn., Mpls., 1958-59; practice medicine, specializing in cardiovascular surgery; faculty Marquette U., Milw., 1956-58, 59-70, asso. prof. surgery, 1963-68, prof. surgery, 1968-70, chmn. dept. thoracic-cardiovascular surgery, 1968-74; mem. staff Milw. County Hosp., 19—, chief of cardiovascular surgery, 1962-74; attending staff Milw. Children's Hosp., VA Hosp., chief thoracic-cardiovascular surgery St. Luke's Hosp., 1962-72; clin. prof. surgery Med. Coll. Wis., Milw., 1970—. Served with USN, 1941-45, USNR, 1950-52. Named Alumnus of the Year Marquette U., 1977, Alumnus of Year Marquette U. Alumni Assn., Wisconsite of Year Am. Broadcasting Assn., Wis. Luth. Man of Yr., 1979. Diplomate Am. Bd. Surgery, Am. Bd. Thoracic Surgery. Fellow A.C.S.; mem. Am. Assn. Thoracic Surgery, Am. Coll. Cardiology, Am. Heart Assn., AMA, Am. Thoracic Soc., Central Surg. Assn., Milw. Acad. Medicine, Milw. Acad. Surgery, Milw. County (pres. 1979), Wis. med. socs., Soc. Thoracic Surgeons, Soc. Univ Surgeons, Wis. Surg. Soc., Internat. Cardiovascular Soc. Am. Coll. Chest Physicians, Wis. Heart Assn. (past pres.), Phi Beta Kappa, Alpha Omega Alpha, Alpha Sigma Nu. Contbr. numerous articles in med. jours. Home: 12600 W Stephen Pl Elm Grove WI 53122 Office: 9800 W Bluemound Rd Milwaukee WI 53226

LERCH, ROGER JAMES, labor cost analyst, time study analyst; b. Cleve., Dec. 9, 1928; s. Karl Preston and Mabel Caroline (Davis) L.; B.A., Dyke and Spencerian Bus. Coll., 1961; m. Maxine Grace Finnell, Aug. 20, 1954; children—Roger James, Linda Lee. With TRW (formerly T.A.P.C.O.), Cleve., 1947-61; in sales and inventory control Servomation, Mansfield, Ohio, 1961-64; timekeeper, prodn. clk. Dominion Electric; labor cost analyst and timestudy analyst Gorman-Rupp Co., Mansfield, Ohio, 1970—. Treas., Johnny Appleseed council Boy Scouts Am., 1963-67. Served with USNR, 1949-53. Mem. Am. Soc. Piano Technicians, Am. Mgmt. Assn., Personnel Assos., Am. Legion. Congregationalist. Club: Masons. Home: 234 S Diamond St Mansfield OH 44903

LERNER, ALBERT MARTIN, physician, educator; b. St. Louis, Sept. 3, 1929; s. Bernard and Sarah L.; m. Helen Saperstein, June 1966; children—Joshua, Emily, Joel, Elizabeth; B.A., Washington U., St. Louis, 1950, M.D., 1954; intern Barnes Hosp., St. Louis, 1954-55, sr. asst. resident, 1958-59; asst. resident Boston City Hosp., 1957-58. Diplomate Am. Bd. Internal Medicine, Pan Am. Med. Assn. (life mem. 1968). Served as med. officer USPHS, 1955-57; sr. asst. surgeon, lab. investigator Nat. Inst. Allergy and Infectious Diseases, 1955-57; research fellow medicine Thorndike Meml. Lab., Boston City Hosp. and Harvard Med. Sch., 1959-62; fellow Med. Found. Greater Boston, Inc., 1960-63; research asso., dept. biology Mass. Inst. Tech., 1962-63; chief infectious diseases Detroit Gen. Hosp., 1963-73, asso. in medicine, 1963-65, asso. in pathology, 1964-65, dir. bacteriology lab., 1964-69, clin. cons., 1969—, attending active staff in medicine, 1965-67, cons. pathology, 1965—, sr. attending staff, 1967—; cons. infectious diseases VA Hosp., Allen Park, Mich., 1963—, Sinai Hosp. of Detroit, 1964—; mem. asso. staff Harper Hosp., Detroit, 1964-67, asso. physician, mem. teaching staff, 1967-74, mem. active staff, physician dept. medicine, sect. internal medicine, 1975; chief dept. medicine Hutzel Hosp., Detroit, 1970—; mem. cons. staff, dept. pediatric medicine Children's Hosp. Mich., 1971—; mem. ad hoc adv. com. Antiviral Substances Program, Nat. Inst. Allergy and Infectious Diseases, 1971; external reviewer for research grants Med. Research Council, Ottawa, Ont., Can., 1973; cons. Nat. Inst. Dental Research, 1974; asso. prof. medicine, chief div. infectious diseases Wayne State U. Sch. Medicine, 1963-67, asso. in microbiology, 1963—, asso. in pathology, 1964—, prof. medicine, chief div. infectious diseases, 1967—, Staff award by sr. class, 1974; prof. pro-tem, dept. medicine William Beaumont Army Med. Center, El Paso, Tex., 1974; invited lectr. Johann Wolfgang Goethe U., Oberursel, Germany, 1974; vis. prof. infectious diseases Cleve. Clinic, 1974; vis. prof. dept. medicine U. Pa., 1976; test com. for medicine Nat. Bd. Med. Examiners, 1971-74; allergy and infectious diseases tng. grant com. NIH, 1971-73; adv. com. Fedn. Am. Socs. Exptl. Biology, 1975; participant 1st Ames Yissum Symposium, Hebrew U., Jerusalem, 1979—, vis. prof., 1979. Bd. dirs. Am. Soc. Health Found., 1979—. Fellow A.C.P. (govs. adv. com. Mich. 1974—, chmn. continuing edn. com. Mich. chpt. 1976—), Am. Coll. Clin. Pharmacology; mem. Am. Soc. for Microbiology, N.Y. Acad. Scis., Am. Fedn. for Clin. Research (pres. Ann Arbor-Detroit-Toledo-Lansing chpt. 1967-68), Infectious Diseases Soc. Am., Central Soc. for Clin. Research, Am. Soc. for Clin. Investigation, Am. Assn. Immunologists, Soc. for Exptl. Biology and Medicine, Am. Pub. Health Assn., Detroit Med. Club, Wayne County Med. Soc. (chmn. med. sect. 1970-72), Am. Assn. Physicians, Mich. Found. for Infectious Diseases (pres. 1976), Am. Acad. Med. Dirs., Probus Club Detroit (5th Ann. award for acad. achievement 1967), Phi Lambda Kappa (award for outstanding contbn. to research, teaching and acad. medicine 1969). Asso. sci. editor Mich. Medicine, 1968-70; contbr. articles to profl. jours. Home: 3570 Tuckahoe St Birmingham MI 48010 Office: 4707 St Antoine St Detroit MI 48201

LERNER, ALFRED, real estate investor; b. N.Y.C., May 8, 1933; s. Abraham and Clara (Abrahamson) L.; B.A., Columbia, 1965; m. Norma Wokloff, Aug. 7, 1955; children—Nancy Faith, Randolph David. Sales rep. Broyhill Furniture Factories, 1957-58, Baumritter Corp., 1958-63; distbr. Bassett Furniture Co., 1963-65; pres. Randolph Distbg. Co., 1963-65; vice-chmn., dir. Equitable Bancorp., Balt.; chmn., chief exec. officer Multi-Amp Corp., Dallas, 1970-80, Realty Refund Trust, Cleve.; pres., chief exec. officer Waybaco, Refund Advisers, Inc., Mid-Am. Mgmt. Corp., 1965-81; gen. partner Bal-Penn (Ohio Ltd. Partnership); partner Mid-Am. Cos., Cleve., 1965-81; dir. Bancohio Nat. Bank. Vice chmn. bd. visitors Columbia Coll. Served to 1st lt. USMCR, 1955-57. Mem. Young President's Orgn., Nat. Assn. Real Estate Investment Trusts. Jewish. Clubs: Beechmont, Commerce (Cleve.); Harmonie (N.Y.C.). Home: 19000 S Park Blvd Shaker Heights OH 44122 Office: 1101 Euclid Ave Cleveland OH 44115

LERNER, GERDA, historian, educator; b. Austria; B.A. (School scholar), New Sch. for Social Research, 1963; M.A. (Univ. Faculty scholar), Columbia U., 1965, Ph.D., 1966. Lectr.-instr., New Sch. for Social Research, 1963-65; asso. prof. history L.I. U., 1965-68; mem. faculty Sarah Lawrence Coll., 1968-80, ednl. dir. Summer Inst. in Women's History for High Sch. Tchrs., summer 1976, Summer Inst. in Women's History, summer 1979; dir. M.A. program in women's history, 1972-76, co-dir. program, 1978-79; Robinson-Edwards prof. history U. Wis., Madison, 1980—; resident fellow Rockefeller Found. Study and Conf. Center, Bellagio Italy, 1975; seminar participant Rockefeller fellow Aspen Summer Inst. for Humanities, 1977. Recipient honors essay prize New Sch. for Social Research, 1963; Guggenheim award, fall 1980-81; Social Sci. Research Council fellow, 1970-71; Ford Found. grantee, 1978-79. Mem. Orgn. Am. Historians (co-dir. grant for promoting black women's history 1980-83, pres. 1981-82). Author books, the most recent being: The Majority Finds Its Past: Placing Women in History, 1979; Teaching Women's History, 1981; contbr. numerous articles, revs. to profl. jours.; editor: Black Women in White America: A Documentary History, 1972. Office: Dept History U Wis 3211 Humanities Bldg 455 N Park St Madison WI 53706

LESAR, HIRAM HENRY, lawyer, educator; b. Thebes, Ill., May 8, 1912; s. Jacob L. and Missouri Mabel (Keith) L.; A.B., U. Ill., 1934; J.D., 1936; J.S.D., Yale U., 1938; m. Rosalee Berry, July 11, 1937; children—James Hiram, Albert Keith, Byron Lee. Admitted to Ill. bar, 1937, Mo. bar, 1954, U.S. Supreme Ct. bar, 1960; asst. prof. law U. Kans., 1937-40, asso. prof., 1940-42; sr., prin. atty. bd. legal examiners U.S. CSC, 1942-44; asso. prof. Law U. Mo., 1946-48, prof., 1948-57; prof. law Washington U., St. Louis, 1957-60, dean and Zumbalen prof., 1960-72; prof. So. Ill. U., Carbondale, 1972—, dean, 1972-80, interim pres., 1974, acting pres., 1979-80, disting. service prof., 1980—; vis. prof. law U. Ill., summer 1974, Ind. U., summer 1952, U. So. Calif., summer 1959, U. N.C., summer 1961, N.Y. U., summer 1965. Bd. dirs. Legal Aid Soc. St. Louis and St. Louis County, 1960-72, pres., 1966-67; bd. dirs. Land of Lincoln Legal Assistance Found., 1972—; trustee Bacon Coll., 1980—; mem. Human Relations Commn. University City, Mo., 1966-71, chmn., 1966, 67; mem. Fed. Mediation and Concilliation Service, other arbitration panels. Served from lt. (j.g.) to lt. comdr. USNR, 1944-48. Fellow Am. Bar Found.; mem. Am. Arbitration Assn., Am. Law Inst., Am. Bar Assn., Fed. Bar Assn., Mo. Bar Assn., Ill. Bar Assn., St. Louis Bar Assn., Am. Acad. Polit. and Social Sci., Am. Judicature Soc., AAUP, Phi Beta Kappa, Order of Coif, Phi Kappa Phi. Baptist. Clubs: Masons; Univ. (St. Louis); Nat. Lawyers (Washington); Yale (Chgo.); Jackson Country. Author: Landlord and Tenant, 1957. Contbr. to Am. Law of Property, 1952, supplement, 1977, also Dictionary Am. History, Ency. Brit. Office: 218 Lesar Law Bldg So Ill U Carbondale IL 62901

LESLY, PHILIP, pub. relations counsel; b. Chgo., May 29, 1918; B.S. with honors, Northwestern U., 1940; m. Ruth Edwards, Oct. 17, 1940 (div. Dec. 1971); 1 son, Craig. Copywriter advt. dept. Sears Roebuck & Co., 1940-41; asst. dir. pub. relations Northwestern U., 1941-42; account exec. Theodore R. Sills & Co., Chgo., 1942-43, v.p., 1943-45, exec. v.p., 1945; dir. pub. relations Ziff-Davis Pub. Co., 1945-46; v.p. Harry Coleman & Co., 1947-49; pres. Philip Lesly Co., Chgo., 1949—; lectr., speaker on pub. relations, pub. opinion, social dynamics. Bd. dirs. Nat. Safety Council, 1967-70. Mem. Public Relations Soc. Am. (Silver Anvil award 1946, 63, 66, Gold Anvil award 1979). Club: Mid-Am. (Chgo.). Author: (with others) Public Relations: Principles and Procedures, 1945, Everything AND the Kitchen Sink, 1955; author: The People Factor, 1974; How We Discommunicate, 1979; Selections from Managing the Human Climate, 1979; editor: Public Relations in Action, 1947; Public Relations Handbook, 1950, 62, 67; Lesly's Public Relations Handbook, 1971, 78; author bi-monthly jour. Managing the Human Climate, 1970—; contbr. articles to U.S., Brit. and Canadian mags. Home: 155 Harbor Dr Chicago IL 60601 Office: 130 E Randolph St Chicago IL 60601

LESSARD, ROBERT BERNARD, state senator; b. International Falls, Minn., May 18, 1931; s. William O. and Beatrice (Miller) L.; grad. high sch.; m. Toni Ballon; children—Wendy Jo, Kelly Jo. Owner, capt. Viking Cruises, Inc., Rainy Lake, Minn. Mem. Iron Range Resources and Rehab. Bd.; mem. Minn. State Senate, 1977—. Served with U.S. Army, 1951-54; Korea. Mem. Democratic-Farmer-Labor party. Roman Catholic. Office: 328 State Capitol Saint Paul MN 55155*

LE TARTE, CLYDE EDWARD, coll. pres.; b. Muskegon, Mich., Aug. 22, 1938; s. Harold and Ellen Lucille (Bullman) LeT.; A.B., Hope Coll., 1960; M.A., Mich. State U., 1964; Ed.D. (Mott fellow), Mich. State U., 1969; m. Kathleen Coutlette, June 18, 1967; children—Richard Michael, Rhonda Lynn. Tchr., Mt. Morris (Mich.) Jr. and Sr. High Sch., 1960-63; dir. community edn. Muskegon Pub. Schs., 1965-67; cons. Mich. Dept. Edn., Lansing, 1967-69; prof. sch. adminstrn. Eastern Mich. U., Ypsilanti, 1969-77, asso. dean Grad. Sch., 1971-77; v.p. acad. affairs Triton Coll., River Grove, Ill., 1977-81; pres. Jackson (Mich.) Community Coll., 1981—. Dir. Custom Mfg. Service, Inc. Mem. Nat. Community Edn. Assn. (pres. 1966-67, exec. sec. 1970-71), Mich. Pub. Sch. Adult Edn. Assn. (v.p. 1971), Mich. Community Sch. Edn. Assn. (dir. 1971), Mich. Council Grad. Deans (chmn. com. on post baccalaureate experiences 1974-77), Phi Delta Kappa. Presbyterian (elder). Author: (with Jack Minzey) Community Education: From Program to Process, 1972; Community Education: From Program to Process to Practice, 1979. Editorial bd. Community Edn. Jour., 1971—. Contbr. articles to profl. jours. Home: 1135 Wickwire Rd Jackson MI 49201

LETMAN, SLOAN TIMOTHY, III, lawyer, educator; b. Chgo., Aug. 4, 1947; s. Sloan Timothy and Amy Estelle (Branche) L.; B.A., Loyola U., Chgo., 1968, M.A., 1971; J.D., DePaul U., 1975; m. Clyniece L. Watson, July 7, 1973. Admitted to Ill. bar, 1977; community center asst. dir. Blessed Sacrament Parish, Chgo., 1967-68, coordinator day camp, 1968; instr. Resurrection and Santa Maria Addolorata schs., Chgo., 1969; neighborhood worker Chgo. Dept. Human Resources 1969-70; asso. editor Pilgrimage Press; lectr. Malcolm X Coll., Chgo., 1972-74; lectr. Loyola U., Chgo., 1972-74, prof. criminal justice, 1977—; lectr. citizen info. service League Women Voters, Chgo., 1972-74; supr. investigations Office Profl. Standards, Chgo., 1974-77. Bd. dirs. Hyde Park Community Conf., 1975-76; Catholic Interracial Council, 1970-74; mem. Council on Youth Ministry, Archdiocese of Chgo. Named One of Ten Outstanding Young Citizens, Chgo. Jr. Assn. Commerce and Industry, 1978. Mem. Loyola Urban Studies Assn., Acad. Criminal Justice Scis., Soc. Police and Criminal Psychology (Ill. state coordinator, chmn. standing com. minorities, pres.), Ill. Athletic Club, Blue Key, Phi Delta Kappa, Alpha Phi Alpha. Editor Jour. Crime and Justice. Contbr. articles in field to profl. jours. Home: 1461 E 56th St Chicago IL 60637 Office: 820 N Michigan Ave Chicago IL 60611

LETT, PHILIP WOOD, JR., auto co. exec.; b. Newton, Ala., May 4, 1922; s. Philip Wood and Lilly O. (Kennedy) L.; B.M.E., Auburn U., 1944; M.S. in Engring., U. Ala., 1947; Ph.D. in Mech. Engring., U. Mich, 1951; S.M. (Sloan fellow), M.I.T., 1961; m. Katy Lee Howell, June 26, 1948; children—Kathy, Warren, Lisa. With Chrysler Corp., 1954—, chief engr. def. engring., 1958-61, operating mgr., 1961-74, gen. mgr. def. div., 1974-76, gen. mgr. Sterling Def. fiv., 1976-80, v.p. engring. Chrysler Def., Inc., Center Line, Mich., 1980—; mem. faculty Coll. Engring. U. Mich., 1949-50. Bd. dirs. Friendship House, Community Center, Hamtramck, Mich.; pres. bd. dirs. Mich. Bapt. Homes; mem. engring. council Auburn (Ala.) U. Served with U.S. Army, 1943-46. Registered profl. engr., Mich. Mem. Am. Def. Preparedness Assn. (past pres. Mich. chpt., past nat. rep. Mich.), Internat. Soc. Terrain-Vehicle Systems (charter mem.), Assn. U.S. Army (mem. industry adv. com.), Sloan Fellows Soc. (past bd. govs.), Soc. Automotive Engrs., Tau Beta Pi, Pi Tau Sigma. Baptist. Contbr. articles to profl. jours. Office: 25999 Lawrence Ave Center Line MI 48015

LEUKART, RONALD JEFFREY, mfrs. rep.; b. Franklin County, Ohio, Sept. 18, 1943; s. Walter J. and Dorothy Jane Leukart; B.S., Franklin U., Columbus, Ohio, 1966; m. Vicki Susan Gill, Aug. 7, 1965; children—Kimberly Joan, Bretton J. Clk., Ohio Auditor's Office, 1963-64; purchasing agt. Dyna-Quip, Inc., Columbus, 1964-71; founder, 1971, since pres. Timron, Inc., mfrs. rep. for traffic control devices, Columbus; pres. Am. Signal Corp., Cleve., 1978—; dir. Schuler/Leukart Co., Leukart Industries, Ampsco Contracting Co. Mem. Internat. Inst. Traffic Engrs., Sales Execs. Club, Ohio State U. Alumni Assn., Franklin U. Alumni. Republican. Episcopalian. Clubs: Columbus Country, Presidents, Ohio State U. Faculty, Golf, High Twelve, Columbus Engineers, Masons, Exec. Order Ohio Commodores, Shriners, Columbus Athletic. Home: 284 S Stanwood

Rd Columbus OH 43209 Office: 30 E Columbus St Columbus OH 43206

LEUNG, MOW-WO, mech. design engr., restaurant exec.; b. Canton, China, Aug. 5, 1942; s. Yuen-Wing and Yuk-Wan (Chow) L.; came to U.S., 1969, naturalized, 1977; B.S. in Mech. Engring., Nat. Taiwan U., 1967; M.S. in Mech. Engring., U. Miss., 1973; m. Der-Ling Huah, Nov. 9, 1974; children—Eric Hao-Ming, Bonny Hsin-Yee. Programmer, U. Miss. Computer Center, 1971-73; owner Dragon House Chinese Restaurant, Oxford, Miss., 1972-75; partner King's Chop Suey, Chgo., 1976—, also mech. design engr. Cardwell Westinghouse Co., Chgo., 1974-78; mech. engr. U.S. Industries Co., Chgo., 1978-79; mech. design engr. Rockwell Internat., Chgo., 1979—. Mem. ASME. Research on alternative method of solving problem of large deflections of nonlinear viscoelastic columns. Home: 10244 S 82d Ave Palos Hills IL 60465

LEURIG, LOUIS RICHARD, coll. adminstr.; b. Rushville, Ill., Jan. 24, 1931; s. Louis F. and Lillian L. (Schiermeier) L.; B.A., U. N.Mex., 1954; m. Barbara Fye, Nov. 18, 1972; children—Karen, Margot, Kathleen, Richard, Sharlene. Coordinator computing CPC Internat., N.Y.C., 1954-62; mgr. cons. services Peat, Marwick, Mitchell & Co., N.Y.C., 1962-67; dir. data processing U. N.Mex., Albuquerque, 1967-78; asst. to pres. Systems & Computer Tech. Corp., Cleve., 1978—; exec. dir. computing Cuyahoga Community Coll., Cleve., 1978—. Mem. Internat. Platform Assn., Assn. Computing Machinery, Assn. Systems Mgmt., Data Processing Mgmt. Assn., Higher Edn. Computing Orgn. (pres. 1977-78). Republican. Club: Kiwanis. Home: 319 Timberlane Avon Lake OH 44012 Office: Cuyahoga Community Coll 2900 Community College Cleveland OH 44115

LEUSCHEN, JAMES WALTER, telephone co. exec.; b. Panama, Iowa, Aug. 20, 1940; s. Walter N. and Cornelia M. (Hoffman) L.; A.B. in Polit. Sci., Creighton U., 1962; m. M. Patricia Oppold, June 8, 1963; children—Susan, Paul, Kate, James. Adminstrv. intern Internal Revenue Service, 1962; exec. sec. U.S. Civil Service Bd. of Examiners, 1963; trainee, mgmt. devel. program Northwestern Bell Telephone Co., Omaha, 1963, advt. and news supr., 1965-71, pub. info. supr., 1971-74, Nebr. pub. relations supr., 1974-78, div. mgr., public relations, 1978-80, gen. mgr. customer relations, 1980—. Vol. pub. relations cons. Met. YMCA, Henry Doorly Zoo, United Way, Joslyn Art Mus., Old West Trail Found., Nebr. Council on Econ. Edn.; bd. dirs. Nebr. Community Improvement Program, Citizens for Quality Edn., Children's Mus., Epilepsy Council Omaha, Children's Crisis Center; bd. dirs., sec. Old West Trail Found. Co-recipient nat. award for best print advt. United Way, 1976; named Outstanding Young Omahan, Omaha Jr. C. of C., 1975. Mem. Pub. Relations Soc. Am. (accredited, sec. Nebr. chpt.), Nebr. Telephone Assn., Nebr. Press Assn., Omaha Press Club (pres.), Omaha C. of C. Roman Catholic. Home: 5210 Davenport St Omaha NE 68132 Office: 100 S 19th St Omaha NE 68102

LEVANDOWSKI, BARBARA SUE, educator; b. Chgo., Mar. 16, 1948; d. Earl F. and Ann (Klee) L.; B.A., North Park Coll., 1970; M.S., No. Ill. U., 1975, Ed.D., 1979; Tchr., Round Lake (Ill.) Sch. Dist., 1970-75; tchr., asst. prin. Schaumburg (Ill.) Sch. Dist., 1975—; curriculum cons. Spring Grove (Ill.) Sch. Dist., 1980—. Mem. staff Round Lake Park Dist., 1973—. Recipient numerous awards for excellence in teaching. Mem. Ill. Assn. Women Adminstrs., Ill. Assn. for Supervision and Curriculum Devel., Assn. Supervision and Curriculum Devel., Ill. Prins. Assn., Phi Delta Kappa. Mem. editorial bd. Ill. Sch. Research and Devel. Jour., 1981—. Home: 508 Garfield St Ingleside IL 60041 Office: 1100 Laurie Ln Hanover Park IL 60103

LEVENFELD, MILTON ARTHUR, lawyer; b. Chgo., Mar. 18, 1927; s. Mitchell A. and Florence B. (Berman) L.; Ph.B., U. Chgo., 1947, J.D., 1950; m. Iona R. Wishner, Dec. 18, 1949; children—Barry, David, Judith. Admitted to Ill. bar, 1950; asso. firm David Altman, 1951-60; partner Altman, Levenfeld & Kanter, Chgo., 1961-64, Levenfeld and Kanter, Chgo., 1964-80, Levenfeld, Eisenberg, Janger, Glassberg & Lippitz, 1980—; dir. Bank of Chgo. Bd. dirs. Spertus Coll. Judaica, Jewish Fedn. Chgo.; co-gen. chmn. Chgo. Jewish United Fund, 1977—, vice chmn. campaign, 1979. Served with USNR, 1944-45. Recipient Keter Shem Tov award Jewish Nat. Fund, 1978. Mem. Am., Ill., Chgo. bar assns., Chgo. Crime Commn. Jewish. Writer, lectr. in fed. taxation. Home: 866 Stonegate Dr Highland Park IL 60035 Office: 10 S LaSalle St Chicago IL 60603

LEVEY, SAMUEL, educator; b. Cape Town, S. Africa, July 11, 1932; came to U.S., 1949, naturalized, 1954; s. Harry and Esther (Turecka) L.; A.B., Bowdoin Coll., 1955; A.M., Columbia U., 1956; M.A., U. Iowa, 1959, Ph.D., 1961; M.S., Harvard U., 1963; m. Linda Anne Madison, Dec. 26, 1965; children—Eric B., Andrea E., Sara B. Adminstrv. asso. U. Iowa Hosps. and Clinics, Iowa City, 1958-60, instr. grad. program in hosp. and health adminstrn. Coll. Medicine, 1960-61, asst. prof., 1961-62; div. dir. Mass. Dept. Pub. Health, Boston, 1963-67; asst. dir. med. care planning Harvard Med. Sch., Boston, 1967-68, lectr. health service adminstrn. Harvard Sch. Pub. Health, 1967-69; asst. commnr. Mass. Dept. Pub. Welfare, Boston, 1968-69; prof., chmn. grad. program in health care adminstrn. City U. N.Y., 1969-77; prof., adminstr. medicine Mount Sinai Sch. Medicine, N.Y.C., 1973-77; prof., head grad. program in hosp. and health adminstrn. Coll. Medicine and Grad. Coll., U. Iowa, 1977—; hosp. and health cons.; cons. HEW, 1972—; subarea adv. council Health Systems Agy., 1978—. Named Otho Ball fellow Am. Coll. Hosp. Adminstrs., 1958-59; Faculty fellow Found. for Economic Edn., 1962; HEW post-doctoral trainee, 1962-63. Mem. Asso. Univ. Programs in Health Adminstrn. (dir. 1979—, chmn. bd. dirs. 1980-81), Am. Pub. Health Assn., Internat. Hosp. Fedn., Council on Research and Devel., AAAS, Am. Hosp. Assn., Soc. Gen. Systems Research. Author (with N. P. Loomba) Health Care Administration: A Managerial Perspective, 1973; (with N. P. Loomba) Health Care Administration: A Selected Bibliography, 1973; (with N. P. Loomba) Long Term Care Administration, Vols. I, II, 1977; (with T. McCarthy) Health Management for Tomorrow, 1980. Editor: (with H. Rosen and J. Metsch) The Consumer and the Health Care System, 1977; sr. editor: Spectrum Series on Health Systems Management, 1974—. Home: 336 MacBride Rd Iowa City IA 52240 Office: S-511 Westlawn Iowa City IA 52242

LEVI, EDWARD HIRSCH, educator, former atty. gen. U.S.; b. Chgo., June 26, 1911; s. Gerson B. and Elsa B. (Hirsch) L.; Ph.B., U. Chgo., 1932, J.D., 1935, L.H.D. (hon.); J.S.D. (Sterling fellow 1935-36), Yale U., 1938; LL.D., U. Mich., 1959, U. Calif., Santa Cruz, 1968, Jewish Theol. Sem. Am., 1968, U. Iowa, 1968, Brandeis U., 1968, Lake Forest Coll., 1968, U. Rochester, 1969, U. Toronto, 1971, Yale U., 1973, U. Notre Dame, 1974, Denison U., 1974, U. Nebr., U. Miami, Boston Coll., Yeshiva U., 1976, Columbia U., 1976, Dropsie U., 1976, U. Pa., 1976, Brigham Young U., 1979, Duke U. Law Sch., 1981, Ripon Coll., 1981; L.H.D., Hebrew Union Coll., 1968, DePaul U., 1978, Loyola U., 1970, Kenyon Coll., Bard Coll., 1975, Beloit Coll., 1976; D.C.L., N.Y. U., 1977; m. Kate Sulzberger, June 4, 1946; children—John, David, Michael. Admitted to Ill. bar, U.S. Supreme Ct. bar, 1945; asst. prof. U. Chgo. Law Sch., 1936-40, prof. law, 1945-75, 77—, dean, 1950-62, provost univ., 1962-68, univ. pres., 1968-75, pres. emeritus, 1975—, Karl Llewellyn Disting. Service prof., 1975-77, (on leave) Glen A. Lloyd Disting. Service prof., 1977—; atty. gen. U.S., 1975-77; Thomas Guest prof. U. Colo., summer 1960; Herman Phleger vis. prof. Stanford U., 1978; mem. Salzburg Seminar on Am. Studies, 1980; spl. asst. to atty. gen. U.S., Washington, 1940-45; 1st asst. war div. Dept. Justice, 1943, 1st asst. antitrust div., 1944-45; chmn. interdeptl. com. on monopolies and cartels, 1944; counsel Fedn. Atomic Scientists with respect to Atomic Energy Act, 1946; counsel subcom. on monopoly power Judicary Com., 81st Congress, 1950. Mem research adv. bd. Com. Econ. Devel., 1951-54; bd. Social Sci. Research Council, 1959-62, Council Legal Edn. and Profl. Responsibility, 1968-74; mem. Citizens Commn. Grad. Med. Edn., 1963-66, Commn. Founds. and Pvt. Philanthropy, 1969-70, Pres.'s Task Force Priorities in Higher Edn., 1969-70, Sloan Commn. Cable Communications, 1970, Nat. Commn- on Productivity, 1970-75, Nat. Council on Humanities, 1974-75. Hon. trustee U. Chgo.; trustee Internat. Legal Center, 1966-75, Woodrow Wilson Nat. Fellowship Found., 1972-75, 77-79, Inst. Psychoanalysis Chgo., 1961-75, Urban Inst., 1968-75, Mus. Sci. and Industry, 1971-75, Russell Sage Found., 1971-75, Aspen Inst. Humanistic Studies, 1970-75, 77-79, Inst. Internat. Edn. (hon.), 1969; public dir. Chgo. Bd. of Trade, 1977-80; trustee Aerospace Corp., 1978-80; bd. dirs. MacArthur Found., 1979—; bd. dirs. Nat. Humanities Center, 1978—, chmn. bd., 1979—; bd. dirs. William Benton Found., 1980—. Decorated Legion of Honor (France); recipient Disting. Citizen award Ill. St. Andrews Soc., 1975, Fed. Bar Assn. award, 1975; Herbert H. Lehman Ethics medal Jewish Theol. Sem., Miami, Fla., 1976; Learned Hand medal for excellence in fed. jurisprudence Fed. Bar Council, N.Y.C., 1976; Wallace award Am.-Scottish Found., 1976; Morris J. Kaplun Meml. prize Dropsie U., 1976; Louis Stein award Fordham U., 1977; citation of merit Yale U., 1977; Louis Dembitz Brandeis medal Brandeis U., 1978, others. Fellow Am. Acad. Arts and Scis., Am. Bar Found.; mem. Am., Ill., Chgo. (Centennial award 1975) bar assns., Am. Law Inst. (council), Am. Judicature Soc., Am. Philos. Soc., Phi Beta Kappa, Order of Coif. Clubs: Century (N.Y.C.); Chgo., Comml., Quadrangle, Mid-Am. (Chgo.); Columbia Yacht. Author: Introduction to Legal Reasoning, 1949; Four Talks on Legal Education, 1952; Point of View, 1969; The Crisis in the Nature of Law, 1969; editor: Gilbert's Collier on Bankruptcy (with J. W. Moore), 1936; Elements of the Law (with R. S. Steffen), 1950. Office: U Chgo 1116 E 59th St Chicago IL 60637

LEVI, PETER STEVEN, lawyer, assn. exec.; b. Washington, June 3, 1944; s. Kurt and Ruth (Neumann) L.; B.A. in History, Northwestern U., 1966; J.D., U. Mo., Kansas City, 1969, LL.M. in Urban Legal Affairs, 1971; postgrad. in urban transp. (Urban Mass Transit Adminstrn. fellow) Carnegie Mellon U., 1975; m. Enid Goldberg, Jan. 26, 1969; children—Joshua, Jeffrey. Admitted to Mo. bar, 1969; legal counsel Mid-Am. Regional Council, Kansas City, Mo., 1969-72, dep. dir., 1972-77, exec. dir., 1977—; adj. prof. law U. Mo., Kansas City. Pres., Kehilath Israel Synagogue, Kansas City, Mo.; bd. dirs. Council on Edn., Kansas City, Mo., Jewish Community Relations Bur., Kansas City, Mo.; mem. exec. com. Hyman Brand Hebrew Acad., Overland Park, Kans.; spl. adv. Kansas City (Mo.) Tax Commn. Recipient cert. appreciation C. of C. Greater Kansas City, 1979. Mem. Internat. City Mgmt. Assn., Am. Bar Assn., Mo. Bar, Kansas City Bar Assn., Am. Soc. Public Adminstrn., Nat. Assn. Regional Councils (vice chmn. exec. dirs. adv. com.). Author: Model Subdivision Regulations, 1975; contbr. articles to Urban Lawyer, Mo. Law Rev.; editorial bd. U. Mo.-Kansas City Law Rev., 1968-69. Home: 9316 Lee Ct Leawood KS 66206 Office: 20 W 9th St Kansas City MO 64105

LEVIN, ARNOLD MURRAY, psychotherapist; b. N.Y.C., Dec. 26, 1924; s. William and Pauline (Kramer) L.; B.A., U. Mass., Amherst, 1948; M.A., U. Chgo., 1950, Ph.D., 1976; cert. Chgo. Inst. Psychoanalysis, 1955; m. Elaine Miriam Zimmerman, Dec. 19, 1946 (dec. Aug. 1971); m. 2d, Elaine R. Bennet, Sept. 28, 1975; children—Michael S., Nancy Jo Levin-Noteman, Amy Louise. Group therapist Portal House Clinics for Alcoholism, Chgo., 1951-55; caseworker Jewish Family and Community Service, Chgo., 1950-53; exec. dir. Family Service and Mental Health Center S. Cook County, Chgo., 1953-60; pvt. practice psychotherapy, Chgo. and Homewood, Ill., 1960—; cons. Ill. Youth Commn. Diagnostic Center, Joliet, 1963-69, Scholarship and Guidance Assn., Chgo., 1968-71; lectr. U. Chgo., 1969-73, Chgo. Med. Sch., 1965; lectr., group leader, workshop leader various agencies, 1960—; ind. entrepreneur, 1948—; tech. adv. bd. Chgo. Mental Health Assn., 1975—; chmn. tech. adv. com. Juvenile Protective Assn., Chgo., 1963-68; founding mem. Alumni Assn. of Sch. Social Services Adminstrn., U. Chgo., 1955. Chmn. citizens' adv. council to dir. Ill. Dept. Mental Health and Devel. Disabilities, 1970-78; bd. dirs. S. Suburban Assn. for Retarded, 1960; pres. Condo Assn., 1977—; founder, pres. Inst. Clin. Social Work, Chgo., 1980—. Served with U.S. Army, 1943-46. NIMH fellow U. Chgo., 1972-73; recipient Dir's. award Ill. Dept. Mental Health and Devel. Disabilities, 1975; Alumnus of Yr. award Sch. Social Services Adminstrn., U. Chgo., 1979. Mem. Ill. Soc. Clin. Social Work (founder, pres., 1971-77, spl. award, 1977), Nat. Fedn. Socs. for Clin. Social Work (founder, v.p., 1971-76), Nat. Registry Health Care Providers in Clin. Social Work (founder, bd. dirs., 1975-76), Nat. Assn. Social Workers Ill. (bd. dirs., officer 1961-71), Nat. Assn. Social Workers (chmn. nat. pvt. practice study group, 1966-69, mem. cabinet of practice and knowledge, 1966-69, mem. cert. for competence bd. 1969-72 pvt. practice rev. bd.), Psychoanalytic Child Care Assn. Chgo. (pres., 1960-62), Soc. for Clin. and Exptl. Hypnosis, Sierra Club. Club: One Hundred Club of Chgo. Author: Handbook on the Private Practice of Social Work, 1967, rev. edit., 1972; contbr. articles to profl. publs. Home: 3740 N Lake Shore Dr Chicago IL 60613 Office: 30 N Michigan #1104 Chicago IL 60602

LEVIN, BARRY LIVINGSTON, educator; b. N.Y.C., May 5, 1918; s. Benjamin Bernard and Genevieve Rose (Livingston) L.; B.A., N.Y. U., 1941; M.S., Boston U., 1946; Ph.D., Columbia U., 1969; m. Ruth Kaplan, Dec. 2, 1957; 1 dau., Susan. Mental health cons. Div. Community Mental Health, Tex. Health Dept., Austin, 1953-55; acting dir., asso. dir. dept. community mental health, Erie County, Buffalo, 1958-67; asst. dir. community mental health State Fla. Dept. Mental Health and Mental Retardation, Tallahassee, 1967-69; prof. social work U. Mo., Columbia, 1969—; vis. prof. U. So. Calif. Andrus Gerontology Center, cons. Calif. Health Tng. Center, 1976-77; Gerontol. Soc. research fellow, 1979. Served with U.S. Army, 1942-46. NIMH research fellow, 1956-57; lic. psychologist, Mo. Fellow Am. Public Health Assn. (chmn. mental health sect., Challenge Fund award 1978-79); mem. Nat. Assn. Social Workers, Am. Psychol. Assn., Gerontol. Soc., Western Gerontol. Soc., Mo. Assn. Mental Health (exec. com.), Boone County Mental Health Assn. (mem. bd.), Justinian Soc., Kappa Delta Pi. Club: B'nai B'rith (v.p., treas.). Home: 1021 Duke St Columbia MO 65201 Office: 715 Clark Hall Columbia MO 65201

LEVIN, CARL, U.S. Senator; b. Detroit, June 28, 1934; s. Saul R. and Bess L. (Levinson) L.; B.A., Swarthmore Coll., 1956; LL.B., Harvard, 1959; m. Barbara Halpern, Aug. 31, 1961; children—Kate, Laura, Erica. Admitted to Mich. bar, 1959, practice in Detroit, 1959-64; asst. atty. gen., gen. counsel Mich. Civil Rights Commn., Detroit, 1964-67; chief dep. defender Detroit Defender's Office, 1968-69; mem. Detroit City Council, 1970-77, pres., 1974-77; U.S. Senator from Mich., 1979—. Instr. Wayne U. Law Sch., Detroit, 1970, U. Detroit, 1966, 68. Mem. Am., Mich., Detroit bar assns. Democrat. Office: 140 Russell Senate Office Bldg Washington DC 20510

LEVIN, CHARLES LEONARD, justice state supreme ct.; b. Detroit, Apr. 28, 1926; s. Theodore and Rhoda (Katzin) L.; B.A., U. Mich., 1946, LL.B., 1947; LL.D. (hon.), Detroit Coll. Law; m. Patricia Joyce Oppenheim, Feb. 21, 1956; children—Arthur, Amy, Fredrick. Admitted to Mich. bar, 1947, N.Y. bar, 1949, U.S. Supreme Ct. bar, 1953, D.C. bar, 1954; practiced in N.Y.C., 1948-50, Detroit, 1950-66; partner Levin, Levin, Garvett & Dill, Detroit, 1951-66; judge Mich. Ct. Appeals, Detroit, 1966-73; justice Supreme Ct. Mich., 1973—. Mem. Mich. Law Revision Commn., 1966. Trustee Marygrove Coll., Detroit, chmn., 1971-74; mem. vis. com. to Law Sch., U. Mich., U. Chgo., 1977-80, Wayne State U. Mem. Am. Law Inst. Home: 18280 Fairway Dr Detroit MI 48221 Office: 1008 Travelers Towers 26555 Evergreen Southfield MI 48076

LEVIN, JERRY WAYNE, food co. exec.; b. San Antonio, Apr. 18, 1944; s. Bernard and Marion (Bromberg) L.; B.S.E.E., U. Mich., 1966, B.S. in Math., 1966; M.B.A., U. Chgo., 1968; m. Carol Motel, Dec. 18, 1966; children—Joshua L., Abby Lee. Mgr. fin. Tex. Instruments, Dallas, 1968-72; v.p. Marsh & McLennan, Chgo., 1972-74; dir. acquisitions The Pillsbury Co., Mpls., 1974-76, v.p. mergers and acquisitions, 1976-79, v.p. corp. strategy and acquisitions, 1979-82, sr. v.p. corp. strategy and acquisitions, 1982—. Bd. dirs. St. Paul Chamber Orch. Mem. Assn. Corp. Growth (dir.). Jewish. Clubs: Minneapolis, Oak Ridge Country. Home: 7117 Fleetwood Edina MN 55435 Office: 608 2d Ave S Minneapolis MN 55402

LEVIN, MURIEL IMOGENE (MRS. SHELDON LEVIN), educator; b. Chgo., Apr. 8, 1922; d. Joseph E. Kramer and Anne (Kleinberg) Heller; B.S., Northwestern U., 1963, M.A., 1971; m. Sheldon Levin, Nov. 29, 1944; children—Carol, Diane Levin Woodley, Larry. Tchr. voice tng. Columbia Coll., Chgo., 1964-66; tchr. acting voice Goodman Theatre Sch., Chgo., 1965-68; tchr. drama Evanston (Ill.) Twp. High Sch., 1970-71; tchr. drama and English, Chgo. Pub. Schs., 1972-80; faculty English dept. Kenwood Acad. High Sch., Chgo., 1980—. chmn. performing arts dept. New Orr High Sch.; theatre coach Northwestern U., summer 1973. Television script writer; actress Country Club Theatre; dir. Hull House, Goodman Theatre, Drama Club, Evanston. Mem. Ill. Theatre Assn. (v.p.). Home: 3180 Lake Shore Dr Chicago IL 60657 Office: Kenwood Acad High Sch 5015 S Blackstone St Chicago IL 60615

LEVIN, PATRICIA OPPENHEIM, educator; b. Detroit, Apr. 5, 1932; d. Royal A. and Elsa (Freeman) Oppenheim; A.B. in History, U. Mich., 1954, Ph.D., 1981; M.Ed., Marygrove Coll., 1973; m. Charles L. Levin, Feb. 21, 1956; children—Arthur David, Amy Suzanne, Fredrick Stuart. Substitute tchr. Oak Park (Mich.) Schs., 1955-67; substitute tchr. Detroit Public Schs., 1960-67, reading and learning disabled tchr., cons., 1967-76; guest lectr. Marygrove Coll., 1974-76, coordinator spl. edn., 1976—; lectr., conf. presenter. Mem. Mich. regional bd. ORT, 1965-68; v.p. women's aux. Children's Hosp. Mich.; bd. dirs. women's com. United Community Services, 1968-73; women's com. Detroit Grand Opera Assn., 1970-75; mem. coms. Detroit Symphony Orch., Detroit Inst. Arts; torch drive area chmn. United Found., 1967-70. Mem. Friends of Detroit Public Library, NAACP (life), Internat. Reading Assn., Nat. Council Tchrs. of English, Assn. Supervision and Curriculum Devel., Nat. Assn. Edn. of Young Children, Assn. Children and Adults with Learning Disabilities, Mich. Assn. Children with Learning Disabilities (edn. v.p., exec. bd.), Council Exceptional Children, Assn. Gifted and Talented Children Mich., Mich. Assn. Emotionally Disturbed Children, Orton Soc., Nat. Soc. Study of Edn., Mich. Assn. Learning Disability Univ. Advisors (treas.), Mich. Assn. Learning Disability Educators, Assn. Emotionally Disturbed, Am. Assn. Tchr. Educators, Southeastern Mich. Reading Assn., Phi Delta Kappa, Pi Lambda Theta. Home: 18280 Fairway Dr Detroit MI 48221 Office: 8425 W McNichols St Detroit MI 48221

LEVIN, RICHARD MICHAEL, bus. exec.; b. Chgo., Apr. 16, 1925; s. Jacob and Marion (Berger) L.; B.S., U. Pa., 1947; m. Carol Ann Hoffman, June 30, 1951; children—Nancy, Michael, Ann. With Jason-Empire, Inc., Kansas City, Mo., 1949—, v.p., 1952-58, pres., chief exec. officer, 1958-80, chmn. bd., 1980—; dir. Overland Park State Bank (Kans.); mem. exec. council Thomas Hart Benton Assos. Mem. Civic Council Kansas City. Pres., Jewish Vocational Service of Kansas City, 1969-70, bd. dirs., 1960—; bd. dirs. Menorah Med. Center, v.p., 1978—; bd. dirs. United Hias Agy., N.Y.C., Kansas City Art Inst., Jewish Community Found., Kansas City; v.p. Jewish Fedn. Council, Kansas City; pres. New Reform Temple, 1979—; bd. dirs., mem. exec. com. Kansas City Area council Boy Scouts Am. Served with inf. AUS, 1943-46. Decorated Purple Heart. Mem. Am. Royal Assn. (bd. govs.). Club: Oakwood Country. Home: 835 W 64th Terr Kansas City MO 64113 Office: 9200 Cody St Overland Park KS 66214

LEVIN, STUART FRANKLIN, theatre exec.; b. Cleve., June 15, 1933; s. Samuel Allen and Cecelia (Ellerin) L.; student Cleve. Play House Sch. of Theatre, 1947-51; m. Carol Barbara Lessin, Sept. 21, 1975; children by previous marriage; Jonathan Erwin, David Allen, Deborah Ann, Jennifer Mary, Diane Elizabeth; stepchildren—Marc Alan Resnik, Deborah Joy Resnik. Dir. WJW-TV, Cleve., 1952-58; radio, tv producer, dir., writer Comstock Advt., Buffalo, 1958-60; producer Actor's Theatre, Hollywood, Calif., 1960-66; dir. Children's and Youth Theatres, Cleve. Play House, 1966-71; dir. Musicarnival Winter Theatre and Sch., also prodn. mgr. Summer Theatre, 1971-74; producer Showplace Theatre, 1975; exec. dir. Stu Levin Prodns., 1975—; pres. Cleve. Youth theatre, 1976-77; drama critic radio and TV and numerous publs., 1976—. Mem. Cleve. Play House Acting Ensemble, 1949-51, 66-71. Mem. AFTRA (mem. bd. 1975—, treas. 1976-81), Nat. Assn. Television Arts and Scis. (chmn. entertainment com. 1975-79), Actor's Equity Assn., Internat. Platform Assn. Home and office: 5129 Chickadee Ln Lyndhurst OH 44124

LEVIN, WALTER, violinist; b. Berlin, Dec. 6, 1924; postgrad. diploma Juilliard Sch. Music, 1949; m. Evi Levin, Sept. 13, 1949; children—Thomas Yaron, David Jonathan. Founder, first violinist LaSalle Quartet, 1948; mem. quartet-in-residence Colo. Coll., Colo. Springs, 1949-53; mem. quartet-in-residence U. Cin., 1953—, prof. violin and chamber music, 1953—; rec. artist Deutsche Grammophon; numerous worldwide concert tours. Recipient prix de Disque (2), Deutsche Schallplattenpreis (3), Edison prize, Tokyo prize, Italian Records prize, Grammy award nominations, dedicated string quartets to Walte Levin and premiered by LaSalle Quartet, others. Contbr. articles to mags. Home: 4208 Red Bud Pl Cincinnati OH 45229 Office: Box 29090 Cincinnati OH 45229

LEVINE, BERNARD HAROLD, Realtor, food service co. exec.; b. Eau Claire, Wis., June 29, 1925; s. Alvin A. and Eleanor (Kasper) L.p studIL.; student St. Thomas Coll., St. Paul, 1942-43, Doane Coll., 1943-44, Harvard, 1944-45, U. Wis., 1943, 47; m. Joy Shirley Baar, Apr. 22, 1948; children—Stephanie Ann, Lori Jill, Daniel Edward. With Debutante Dress Mfg. Sales, Chgo., 1947-48, Wareham-Burns, Ottowma, Iowa, 1949; owner Radio Advt., Miami, Fla., 1950-51; mgr. Fashion Store, Wausau, 1951-60; B.H. Levine Realty, Wausau, 1961—; chmn. bd. Chips Food Service, Inc., fast-food franchises, Wausau, Wis., 1966-79; pres., dir. Chips of Wausau, 1965—, Chips of Merrill, Inc., 1970-79; dir., officer No. Realty, Inc., Allied Investors Inc., Nitschke-Levine, Inc.; pres., dir. VIP Inc., 1968—, Log Cabin

Kitchen Inc., 1974-80; dir. Shops Internat., Inc., cons., Lake Geneva, Wis. Served to ensign Supply Corps, USNR, 1943-47; PTO. Recipient city beautification award, 1976; cert. rev. appraiser. Mem. Nat. Assn. Realtors, Nat. Soc. Rev. Appraisers (sr.), Wausau Area C. of C., Nat. Assn. Corp. Real Estate Execs., Am. Bonanza Soc., Aircraft Owners and Pilots Assn. Mem. B'nai B'rith. Home: 1031 Weston Ave Wausau WI 54401 Office: 114 Grand Ave Wausau WI 54401

LEVINE, BERNARD LEROY, psychologist; b. Chgo., Mar. 16, 1934; s. Joseph and Celia (Cohen) L.; student U. Ill., Navy Pier campus, Chgo., 1955-57; B.A., DePaul U., 1960, M.A., 1964; Ph.D., Ill. Inst. Tech., 1969; m. Judith F. Peurye, Dec. 24, 1961; children—David, Deborah. Sch. psychologist State of Ill., 1964; sr. psychologist Ill. State Youth Commn., Joliet, 1964-65; dir. psychol. services Rehab. Inst. Chgo., 1965-78; pvt. practice, 1978—; instr. prosthetics Northwestern U., Chgo., 1966, instr. psychiatry, 1969—; asst. prof. Chgo. City Coll., 1966—. Served with USAF, 1957-63. Registered profl. psychologist, Ill.; psychotherapist Ill. Dept. Vocat. Rehab. Specialist List. Mem. Am., Ill. psychol. assns., Ill. Assn. Psychologists in Rehab. (pres.), Psychologists in Pvt. Practice. Home: 17 Regent St Deerfield IL 60015

LEVINE, HELEN SAXON (MRS. NORMAN D. LEVINE), med. technologist; b. San Francisco; d. Ernest M. and Ann (Bello) Saxon Dippel; A.B., U. Ill., 1939; m. Norman D. Levine, Mar. 2, 1935. Supr. Lab. San Francisco Dept. Pub. Health Tb Sanatorium, 1944-46, U. Ill. Health Services, Urbana, 1952-65; research asso. immunobiology, zoology dept. U. Ill., 1965—. Mem. AAUP, AAAS, Am. Pub. Health Assn., Ill. Pub. Health Assn., Ill. Acad. Sci., Am. Soc. Med. Technologists, Am. Soc. Clin. Pathologists, Cancer Prevention Study Group, Ill. Heart Assn., Sigma Delta Epsilon. Research and publs. on devel. antigens against round worm parasites. Home: 702 LaSell Dr Champaign IL 61822 Office: Morrill Hall Urbana IL 61801

LEVINE, ISAAC JACOB, internist; b. Glasgow, Scotland, Aug. 18, 1923; s. Calman and Minnie (Bloch) L.; came to U.S., 1934, naturalized, 1941; student Cornell U., 1941-43, St. Louis U., 1944; B.S., U. Nebr., 1947, M.D., 1949; m. Dian Bernstein, Feb. 8, 1969; children—Joseph, David, Charles; step-children—William Kurtz, Michael Kurtz, Craig Kurtz. Intern, Jewish Hosp., Cin., 1949-50; resident in internal medicine Jewish Hosp., Cin., 1950-51, Univ. Hosp., Iowa City, Iowa, 1953-55; practice medicine specializing in internal medicine, Cin., 1955—; mem. McHenry (Ill.) Med. Group, 1958-60; instr. medicine U. Cin.; co-founder pulmonary unit Jewish Hosp.; sr. cons. physician Social Security Adminstrn.; life ins. examiner; FAA examiner; Am. Heart Assn. rep. for McHenry County, 1958-60. Served with M.C., USAF, 1951-53. Diplomate Am. Bd. Internal Medicine. Fellow Am. Coll. Chest Physicians; mem. Acad. Medicine Cin., Ohio Med. Assn., AMA, Am. Lung Assn., Ohio Thoracic Soc., Phi Delta Epsilon. Club: Amberley Swim. Research in pulmonary lavage, subacute bacterial endocarditis. Home: 6770 Fair Acres Dr Cincinnati OH 45213 Office: 8228 Winton Rd Cincinnati OH 45331

LEVINE, JOEL, food co. exec.; b. Bklyn., Apr. 4, 1930; s. Ben and Henrietta (Ostfeld) L.; B.A., N.Y. U., 1952; m. Iris M. Hechler, Oct. 12, 1958; children—Lawrence, Cynthia, Pamela. Statistician, Rayco Sales Co., Paramus, N.J., 1955-62; mktg. research supr. Gen. Foods Corp., White Plains, N.Y., 1962-68; mgr. mktg. research Kool Aid div., 1968-69, Maxwell House div., 1969-73, asso. dir. mktg. research, 1973-76; v.p., dir. mktg. research Pillsbury Co., Mpls., 1976—. Pres., Jewish Family and Children's Services, Mpls., 1981—. Mem. Am. Mktg. Assn. Jewish. Office: 608 2d Ave S Minneapolis MN 55402

LEVINE, JUSTIN CRAIG, psychologist, human services adminstr.; b. New Haven, Jan. 26, 1952; s. Samuel and Elinor (Goldberg) L.; B.A., Quinnipiac Coll., 1973; M.S., Ind. State U., 1979; m. Sharon Lee Ticehurst, Aug. 27, 1972; children—Jeremiah Job, Rachel Anais. Psychiat. aide Conn. Valley Hosp., Middletown, 1973-74; teaching asst. Ind. State U., Terre Haute, 1975; dir. Comprehensive Developmental Centers, Inc., Rensselaer, Ind., 1975-76; lead planner habilitation and rehab. services Central Ind. Health Systems Agy., Indpls., 1976-79; exec. dir. Damar Homes, Inc., Indpls. Mem. Ind. Statewide Genetic Disease adv. com., 1978-79; mem. early childhood edn. com. Indpls. Jewish Community Center, 1978—; mem. Central Ind. Developmental Disabilities Zone adv. bd., 1977-79; organizer, adviser Children's Coop. Daycare Center, Hamden, Conn., 1971-74, Temple St. Daycare Center, New Haven, 1970-71. Mem. Am. Assn. Mental Deficiency (chpt. 1st v.p. 1978-79, chmn. div. pvt. residential facilities 1979—), Ind. Council of Execs. for Developmentally Disabled, Nat. Assn. Pvt. Residential Facilities for Mentally Retarded. Contbr. articles to profl. jours. Home: 4515 Bonnie Brae Indianapolis IN 46208 Office: 6324 Kentucky Ave Indianapolis IN 46241

LEVINE, NATHALIE CHRISTIAN, performing arts adminstr., choreographer, ballerina; b. Las Animas, Colo., July 21, 1929; d. Fleming V. and Juanita J. (Jobe) Christian; B.A. in Polit. Sci., UCLA, 1958; student Royal Ballet Sch., London, 1959-60; student Michel Panaieff, Los Angeles, 1945-48, Mia Slavenska, Los Angeles, 1948-53, Rozelle Frey, Los Angeles, and others; m. Victor Theodore LeVine, July 19, 1958; children—Theodore Vincent, Nicole Jeanette. Tchr., Wilcoxon Sch. of Dance, Los Angeles, 1946-48, Sutro-Seyler Studio, Los Angeles, 1949-51; mem. faculty Brown Gables Conservatory of the Arts, Los Angeles, 1952-61, Ecole de Danse, Cameroun, W. Africa, 1961-62; pvt. tchr. ballet and dance, St. Louis, 1963-67; tchr. dance Dawn Quist Sch. of Dance, Accra, Ghana, W. Africa, 1969-70; mem. faculty dance div. Washington U., St. Louis, 1967-69, 70-71; prin. tchr. Le Vine Acad. of Ballet, St. Louis, 1964—; co-artistic dir. St. Louis Dance Theater, 1966-72, also choreographer, 1966-72; founder Metropolitan Ballet of St. Louis, 1974, artistic dir., 1974—; participant planning dance performances, St. Louis, 1964—; cons. to Phelps County Dance Assn., 1978-79, Rolla (Mo.) Bd. of Parks and Recreation, 1978-79; guest tchr. various dance schs. and theaters, 1964—; soloist Ballet de Los Angeles, 1948-49; soloist Radio City Music Hall, N.Y.C., 1952-53; appeared in various TV and stage prodns., Los Angeles, 1946-48, Santa Monica, Calif., 1945-50, Laguna Beach, Calif., 1946-51; appeared in Greatest Show on Earth, other motion pictures, 1950-52. Mem. Nat. Soc. Arts and Letters, Phi Beta Kappa. Office: 11607 Olive Blvd St Louis MO 63141

LEVINE, ROBERT SIDNEY, orthopaedic surgeon; b. Detroit, Aug. 1, 1942; s. Joseph and Bertha (Berkowitz) L.; B.A., U. Mich., 1963; M.D., Wayne State U., 1968; m. Faye Paula Chernikov, May 7, 1970; children—Aviva Rebecca, Rachel Anne. Intern and resident in gen. surgery St. Joseph Mercy Hosp., Pontiac, Mich., 1968-70; resident in orthopaedic surgery Wayne State U. Affiliated Hosp., Detroit, 1970-73; practice medicine specializing in orthopaedic surgery, Bloomfield Hills, Mich., 1973—; clin. asst. prof. orthopaedic surgery Wayne State U., Detroit; adj. asso. prof. bioengring. Wayne State U.; coordinator Amputee Clinic, Detroit Gen. Hosp.; cons. orthopaedic surgeon Oakland County Med. Care Facility; mem. staff St. Joseph Mercy Hosp., Pontiac Gen. Hosp., Harper Hosp., Detroit Gen. Hosp.; mem. Stapp Car Crash Conf. Adv. Com. Served to comdr. M.C., USNR. Diplomate Am. Bd. Orthopaedic Surgery. Fellow A.C.S., Am. Acad. Orthopaedic Surgeons; mem. AMA, Am. Assn. Automotive Medicine (dir. 1981—), Soc. Automotive Medicine, Wayne State U. Med. Alumni Assn. (pres. 1977-78, dir. 1978—). Jewish. Contbr. articles to profl. jours. Home: 3845 Shellmarr Ln Bloomfield Hills MI 48013 Office: 1711 N Woodward Bloomfield Hills MI 48013

LEVINE, STANLEY ROBERT, urologist; b. Bklyn., June 26, 1931; s. Max and Paula (Golub) L.; B.S., Tulane U., 1954, M.D., 1956; m. Susan Settel, July 2, 1974; children—David, Richard, Thomas (dec.), Sara, Michael, Elizabeth, Emily. Intern, Touro Infirmary, New Orleans, 1956-57, resident in gen. surgery, 1957-58; pvt. practice medicine specializing in urology, Lake Forest, Ill., 1963—; mem. staff Highland Park Hosp., Ill., Lake Forest Hosp., Ill.; cons. Hines VA Hosp., Ill., Ill. Inst. Tech. (research projects), Chgo., Mediphone, Chgo., Fertility Inst.; asso. prof. Loyola Med. Sch., Chgo., 1966-68; clin. asso. prof. urology U. Health Services Chgo. Med. Sch., 1975—; dir. clinic services Midwest Population Center, Chgo., 1970—. Served with USAF, 1958-60. Diplomate Bd. Urology. Fellow Am. Coll. Surgeons, Royal Soc. Health, London; mem. Am. Assn. Sex Educators and Counselors (certified sex therapist), Am. Urologic Assn., Chgo. Urologic Soc., Fertility Soc., Pan Am. Surgical Soc., May Clinic Alumni Assn. (fellow urology, 1960-63). Contbr. articles to Jour. Urology, Brit. Jour. Urology. Office: 800 N Westmoreland Rd Suite 101 Lake Forest IL 60045

LEVINE, WALTER ELI, chem. co. exec.; b. New Haven, Oct. 17, 1929; s. Philip Hyman and Celia (Gordon) L.; B.S.M.E., Worcester Poly. Inst., 1953; postgrad. U. Conn., 1956; m. Sharon K. MacMillan, Oct. 16, 1977; children by previous marriage—Scott E., Craig M., Cheryl A. Research engr. Worthington Corp., Holyoke, Mass., 1953-56; project engr. Edwards Co., Norwalk, Conn., 1957-62; mktg. specialist Dresser I.V.I. Div., Stratford, Conn., 1962-69; indsl. sales mgr. Consol. Controls Corp., Bethel, Conn., 1969-71; engring. mgr. Bindicator Co., Port Huron, Mich., 1972-78; mgr. spray products Acheson Colloids Co., Port Huron, Mich., 1979—. Mem. Instrument Soc. Am. (sr.), Soc. Die Casting Engrs., Forging Industry Assn. Club: Masons. Author papers and articles in field. Patentee in field. Home: 3150 Westhaven Dr Port Huron MI 48060 Office: 1600 Washington Ave Port Huron MI 48060

LEVITIN, MILTON, physician; b. N.Y.C., Nov. 5, 1918; s. Benjamin and Bessie (Rosenthal) L.; B.A., Columbia U., 1939; M.D., N.Y. U., 1943; m. Shirlie Wilson, Nov. 13, 1973; children—Lisa, Michael, Todd, Martin, Scott, Linda, Susan, Barry, Steven. Intern, Beth Israel Hosp., N.Y.C., 1944; resident Willard Parker Hosp., N.Y.C., 1945, Sea View Hosp., N.Y.C., 1947; asst. clin. prof. pediatrics Ohio State U., Coll. Medicine, Columbus, 1960—; pres. Ohio Health Care Med. Dirs., Columbus, 1978—; pres., chmn. Rocky Glenn San. and Mark Rest Center, McConnelsville, Ohio, 1955—; mem. staff Riverside, Mt. Carmel, Univ., Childrens, Grant, St. Anns hosps. (all Columbus). Served to capt. U.S. Army, 1945-47. Diplomate Am. Bd. Pediatrics. Mem. Am. Acad. Pediatrics, Am. Acad. Med. Dirs., Am. Health Care Med. Dirs. Club: Winding Hollow Country. Home: 125 S Merkle Rd Columbus OH 43209 Office: 3354 E Broad St Columbus OH 43213

LEVITT, LEROY PAUL, psychiatrist; b. Plymouth, Pa., Jan. 8, 1918; s. Samuel and Paula (Goldstein) L.; B.S., Pa. State U., 1939; M.B., Chgo. Med. Sch., 1943, M.D., 1944; m. Jane Glaim, Apr. 7, 1971; children—Steven, Susan, Jeremy, Sara. Intern, Beth David Hosp., N.Y.C., 1943-44; resident Elgin (Ill.) State Hosp., Ill. Neuropsychiat. Inst., Inst. for Juvenile Research, vet. Rehab. Center, 1947-49; practice medicine specializing in psychiatry, Chgo., 1949—; dir. psychiat. edn. Chgo. Med. Sch., 1964-66, dean, 1966-73, prof., 1966-73; dir. dept. mental health and devel. disabilities State of Ill., 1973-76; prof. psychiatry Rush Med. Coll., Chgo., 1976—; v.p. med. affairs Mt. Sinai Hosp. Med. Center, Chgo., 1976—; pres. Chgo. Bd. Health, 1979—. Served to capt. M.C., U.S. Army, 1944-46. Recipient Disting. Alumnus award Chgo. Med. Sch., 1970; named Prof. of Yr., Chgo. Med. Sch., 1964; Tchr. of the Year, Ill. State Psychiat. Inst., 1966; Gold Medal Sci. award Phi Lambda Kappa, 1974; WHO fellow in geriatrics, 1970; diplomate Am. Bd. Psychiatry and Neurology. Mem. Am. Psychiat. Assn., Am. Coll. Psychoanalysts, Ill. Psychiat. Soc., Internat. Psychoanalytic Assn., Am. Psychoanalytic Assn., Am. Coll. Psychiatrists, Midwest Profs. Psychiatry, Nat. Assn. State Mental Health Dirs., Inst. Medicine Chgo., AMA, Chgo. Psychoanalytic Soc., Council Med. Deans. Jewish. Contbr. articles and book revs. to profl. jours. Home: 1520 N Dearborn Pkwy Chicago IL 60610 Office: Mt Sinai Hosp Med Center California Ave at 15th St Chicago IL 60608

LEVITT, SEYMOUR HERBERT, physician, educator; b. Chgo., July 18, 1928; s. Nathan E. and Margaret (Chizever) L.; B.A., U. Colo., 1950, M.D., 1954; m. Phillis Jeanne Martin, Oct. 31, 1952; children—Mary Jeanne, Jennifer Gaye, Scott Hayden. Intern, Phila. Gen. Hosp., 1954-55; resident in radiology U. Calif. at San Francisco Med. Center, 1957-61; instr. radiation therapy U. Mich., Ann Arbor, 1961-62, U. Rochester (N.Y.), 1962-63; asso. prof. radiology U. Okla., Oklahoma City, 1963-66; prof. radiology, chmn. div. radiotherapy Med. Coll. Va., Richmond, 1966-70; prof., head dept. therapeutic radiology U. Minn., Mpls., 1970—; cons. in field. Exec. bd. Am. Joint Com. for End Result Reporting and Cancer Staging; com. radiation oncology studies Nat. Cancer Inst. Diplomate Am. Bd. Radiology (trustee). Served with M.C., AUS, 1955-57. Fellow Am. Coll. Radiology; mem. Am. Radium Soc. (sec. 1981—), Radiol. Soc. N. Am., Am. Assn. Cancer Research, Am. Cancer Soc. (pres. Minn. div. 1979-80), Am. Roentgen Ray Soc., Soc. Chmn. Acad. Radiation Oncology Programs (pres. 1974-76), Internat. Soc. Radiation Oncology (pres. 1981—), Soc. Nuclear Medicine, Am. Soc. Clin. Oncology, Am. Soc. Therapeutic Radiologists (exec. bd. 74-78, pres. 1978-79), Phi Beta Kappa, Sigma Xi, Alpha Omega Alpha. Home: 6413 Cherokee Trail Minneapolis MN 55435 Office: U Minn Hosp PO Box 494 Minneapolis MN 55455

LEVY, CHARLES, JR., periodical circulation co. exec.; b. Chgo., Apr. 27, 1913; s. Charles and Bertha (Friend) L.; student Wharton Sch., U. Pa.; m. Ruth Doctoroff, Oct. 15, 1939; 1 dau., Barbara. Chmn. bd. Charles Levy Circulating Co., Chgo. Bd. dirs. Jewish Fedn. Chgo., Michael Reese Hosp., Park View Home, Temple Sholom, Mt. Sinai Med. Research, Lincoln Park Zool. Soc. Served with AUS, 1942-46. Decorated Bronze Star. Mem. Periodical Inst., Mid-Am. Periodical Assn., Council Periodical Distbrs. Clubs: Standard, Bryn Mawr Country, Carleton, Mid-Am. Office: 1200 N North Branch St Chicago IL 60622

LEVY, DONALD MORRIS, plastic surgeon; b. New Orleans, May 20, 1935; s. Leo and Leontine (Capdepon) L.; M.D., La. State U., 1959. Intern, Touro Hosp., New Orleans; surg. resident Mayo Clinic, Rochester, Minn., also resident in plastic surgery; asso. prof. plastic surgery Med. Coll. Wis., Milw.; dir. hand surgery Rheumatic Disease Center, Columbia Hosp., also chmn. dept. plastic surgery; nat. lectr. in field; pres. Spanish Village Co., Phoenix. Served to maj., USAR. Named Man of Year, Milw. Cosmopolitan Club; recipient Spl. Service award Milwaukee County Civic Alliance, 1979. Mem. AMA, Med. Soc. Milw. County, Am. Soc. Aesthetic Plastic Surgery, A.C.S., Am. Burn Assn., Wis. Soc. Plastic Surgeons, Am. Soc. Plastic and Reconstructive Surgeons, Am. Cleft Palate Assn., Wis. Alumni Mayo Clinic. Contbr. articles to med. publs. Home: 3205 W County Line Rd Milwaukee WI 53217 Office: 400 W Silver Spring Dr Milwaukee WI 53217

LEVY, HOWARD BRUCE, pediatrician, educator; b. Albany, N.Y., Nov. 27, 1943; s. Ralph C. and Marion (Novik) L.; M.D., U. Ill., 1968. Intern, Cornell Cooperating Hosps., N.Y.C., 1968-69; resident U. Ill. Neuropsychiat. Hosps., Chgo., 1969, resident in pediatrics Rush-Presbyn. St. Lukes Med. Center, Chgo., 1970-72; commd. maj. M.C., U.S. Army, 1972, advanced through grades to lt. col., 1977; chief pediatrics U.S. Army Hosp., Seoul, Korea, 1972-73; officer in charge of family clinic and pediatrics, Germany, 1975-77; chief pediatrics nephrology sect. Walter Reed Army Hosp., Washington, 1977; instr. pediatrics Norwestern U., 1973-75; asst. prof. Uniformed Services Sch. Medicine, 1977; ret., 1977; asst. prof. Rush U. Med. Sch., Chgo., 1977-79, asso. prof., 1979—; chmn. pediatrics Mt. Sinai Hosp., Chgo., 1977—; chmn. Joint Program Pediatric Nephrology, Mt. Sinai Hosp.-Rush Presbyn. St. Luke's, Chgo., 1979—; pres., dir. Chgo. Pediatric Center, Ltd. USPHS fellow, 1963-64. Diplomate Am. Bd. Family Practice. Fellow Am. Acad. Pediatrics, Inst. Medicine Chgo.; mem. Am. Soc. Nephrology, Internat. Soc. Nephrology, Am. Acad. Family Practice, Ill. State Med. Soc., Chgo. Med. Soc., Soc. Adolescent Medicine, Ambulatory Pediatric Assn., Chgo. Pediatric Soc., Internat. Soc. Prevention Child Abuse and Neglect, Ill. Acad. Family Physicians, Internat. Coll. Pediatrics. Editor Pediatric Bull., Mt. Sinai Hosp. Contbr. articles to profl. jours. Office: Mt Sinai Hosp California at 15th Sts Chicago IL 60608

LEVY, MARVIN DANIEL, profl. football team coach; b. Chgo., Aug. 3, 1929; B.A., Coe Coll., Cedar Rapids, Iowa, 1950; M.A., Harvard U., 1951. High sch. coach, St. Louis, 1951-52; asst. football coach Coe Coll., 1953-55; asst. coach, then head coach U. N.Mex., 1956-59; head coach U. Calif., Berkeley, 1960-63, Coll. William and Mary, Williamsburg, Va., 1964-68; asst. coach Phila. Eagles, 1969, Los Angeles Rams, 1970, Washington Redskins, 1971-72; headcoach Montreal, Alouetts, 1973-77, Kansas City (Mo.) Chiefs, 1978—. Address: Kansas City Chiefs 1 Arrowhead Dr Kansas City MO 64129

LEVY, MARVIN JAY, retail exec.; b. LaCrosse, Wis., May 26, 1946; s. Irving E. and Dorothy (Barvin) L.; B.S., U. Wis., 1968, J.D., 1971. Admitted to Wis. bar, 1971; law clk. U.S. Dist. Ct., Memphis, 1971-72; with Ed Phillips & Sons, Madison, Wis., 1972—, exec. v.p., 1980—; dir. Security Marine Bank, Telephone & Data Systems, Inc. Pres., Greater Madison Conv. & Visitors Bur., 1975-76, dir., 1974-77. Mem. Am. Bar Assn., Wis. Bar Assn. Jewish. Clubs: Madison, Maple Bluff Country. Home: 921 Farwell Dr Madison WI 53704 Office: 2620 Royal Ave Madison WI 53713

LEVY, RONALD TRESTON, distbg. co. exec.; b. St. Louis, June 9, 1932; s. Isadore J. and Natalie (Yawitz) L.; B.J., U. Ill., 1954; m. Joyce Anne Hamburg, Aug. 15, 1954; children—Sharon Cay, Robert Jay, Mark Andrew. Research asst. Gardner Advt. Co., St. Louis, 1956-57, media research supr., 1957-59, dir. of media research, 1959-60; salesman Hamburg Distbg. Co., Champaign, Ill., 1960-62, asst. v.p., 1960-64, v.p., sec., 1964-66, pres., 1966—, dir., 1966—; adviser Champaign-Urbana Liquor Commr., 1970—, Ill. Liquor Control Commn., 1972—; wine cons. to U. Ill., 1966-76; dir. Comml. Bank, Champaign. Pres. PTA, Champaign, Ill., 1964-66; spl. bus. chmn. United Way, Champaign, 1970-71; v.p. B'nai B'rith, Champaign, 1966-68; chpt. pres. City of Hope, 1979—; bd. dirs. Playmakers, Founder, 1967, Nat. Acad. Arts, 1976—. Served to 1st lt. USAF, 1954-56; Korea. Recipient Spl. Commendation, United Way, 1970, Confraternita del Monferrato, Italian govt., 1973. Mem. Wholesale Liquor Distbrs. of Ill. (dir. 1970—, sec. 1975-76, v.p. 1977-79, pres. 1979—), Champaign-Urbana Beer Distbrs. Assn. (pres. 1968—), Wine and Spirits Wholesalers Am. (dir. 1980), Champaign C. of C., Nat. Beer Wholesalers of Am., Asso. Beer Distbrs. of Ill., Champaign-Urbana Advt. Club, U. Ill. Alumni Assn., Inter-Fraternity Alumni Assn. (pres. 1971), Zeta Beta Tau (trustee 1960-72, Nat. Service award 1972), Alpha Delta Sigma. Jewish religion. Clubs: Moose, Masons (32 deg.), Shriners, Elk, Champaign Country. Home: 5 O'Connor Court Champaign IL 61820 Office: 3104 Farber Dr PO Box 602 Interstate Research Park Champaign IL 61820

LEVY, VIRGIL LOUIS, dental cons.; b. Ligonier, Ind., Dec. 20, 1917; s. Louis L. and Ruth Ellen (Todd) L.; student Ind. U., 1935-36, Ball State U., 1936-39, Northwestern U., 1939-40; D.D.S., Loyola U., Chgo., 1948; m. Jean Ann Hughes, Sept. 5, 1941; children—Laura Ruth Levy Celarek, Todd Hughes, Lydia Ellen Levy Panyard, Lisa Ann Levy Gradeless, Thaddeus Louis. Resident surgery, anesthesiology Cook County Hosp., Chgo., 1948-50, Loyola U., Chgo., 1951; pvt. practice specializing in oral and facial surgery, Fort Wayne, Ind., 1950-73; mem. profl. attending staffs Lutheran Hosp., also St. Joseph Hosp. (both Fort Wayne), 1950-78; mem. vis. staff Parkview Meml. Hosp., Fort Wayne, 1950-75; research cons. Preventive Dentistry Research Inst. Inc., Ind. U., Fort Wayne, 1974-75; profl. cons. Aetna Life & Casualty Ins. Co., Fort Wayne, 1974-78, now dental cons.; cons. oral surgery VA Hosp., Fort Wayne, 1955-73. Pres. lay adv. bd. St. Vincent's Home, Ligonier, 1965-66; bd. dirs. St. Anne's Home, Fort Wayne, 1977—. Served to master sgt. AUS, 1942-46. Mem. Isaac Knapp Dist. Dental Soc. (pres. 1965-66), Am., Ind. dental assns., Internat., Am., Ind., Great Lakes socs. oral surgery, Am., Ind. socs. anesthesiology, Cook County Hosp. Assn. Oral Surgeons, Logan-Brophy Meml. Soc. Oral Surgeons, St. Apollonia Guild (Fort Wayne-South Bend Diocese pres. 1958-66), Fort Wayne Civil War Round Table (pres. 1965-66, 75-76), Crosier Lay Apostolate, Sigma Tau Gamma, Xi Psi Phi. Roman Catholic. K.C. (4 deg.), Elk. Address: 5121 E State St Rockford IL 61108

LEWANDOWSKI, BERNARD, hist. soc. adminstr.; b. St. Louis, Nov. 7, 1950; s. Bernard H. and Dorothy C. Lewandowski; B.A., St. Louis U., 1974, M.A., 1976. Exec. dir., asst. treas. The Hist. Soc. of St. Louis County, 1976—. Mem. Am. Hist. Assn., Orgn. Am. Historians, Mo. Hist. Soc. Roman Catholic. Club: St. Louis Univ. Home: 9455 Bluegrass St Louis MO 63136 Office: 7900 Carondelet Clayton MO 63105

LEWANDOWSKI, ERIC CHARLES, research found. adminstr.; b. Toledo, Ohio, June 19, 1954; s. Walter Lawrence and Marion Susan L.; B.A. cum laude, John Carroll U., 1976; postgrad. German Acad. Exchange Service (Fulbright fellow), U. Freiburg (Germany), 1976-77; M.A., Ohio State U., 1980; m. Gina M. Lanese, Sept. 8, 1978. Research cons. T.H. Langevin & Assos. for Battelle Meml. Inst. Found., Columbus, Ohio, 1980; sponsored program officer Ohio State U. Research Found., Columbus, 1980—. Project dir. Greater Cleve. Bicentennial Commn., 1976. Recipient Cert. of Appreciation, Am. Revolution Bicentennial Adminstrn., 1976. Mem. Am. Assn. Advancement Humanities, Am. Hist. Assn., Nat. Council Univ. Research Adminstrs. Home: 858 Kinnear Rd 212 Columbus OH 43212 Office: 200-R Ohio State U Research Found 1314 Kinnear Rd Columbus OH 43212

LEWANDOWSKI, F. R., detective; b. Chgo., June 4, 1927; s. Frank J. and Victoria B. (Chak) L.; student pub. schs., Chgo.; m. Aug. 6, 1960; children—Michael Raymond, Jeffrey Daniel. Floral designer F & J Floral Shop, 1962-73; armored guard Thillen's Checash, 1973-75; pvt. detective Ill. Counties Detective Agy., Chgo., 1979—; police block capt. 15th Dist. Chgo., 1973-75. Served with USMC, 1945-52.

Recipient Letters of Commendation, 1st Police Dist., Chgo., 1976, Am. Law Enforcement Assn., 1979, Marine Corps League, 1979. Mem. Marine Corps League (sr. comdr. 1977-78, Central div. dir. 1977-78), Am. Law Enforcement Assn., Nat. Police And Res. Officers Assn., Police Marksman Assn., Am. Law Enforcement Vol. Assn. Democrat. Roman Catholic. Club: Moose. Address: 1161 S Harvey Ave Oak Park IL 60304

LEWIS, CARY BLACKBURN, JR., educator, accountant, lawyer; b. Chgo., Sept. 13, 1921; s. Cary Blackburn and Bertha (Mosley) L.; A.B., U. Ill., 1942; M.B.A., U. Chgo., 1947; J.D., DePaul U., 1966; Advanced Mgmt. certificate Harvard, 1971; m. Eleanor Taylor, Feb. 28, 1943; 1 dau., Cheryl (Mrs. Walker Beverly IV); m. 2d, Mary Lewis, Dec., 1970; 1 son, Cary B. III. Asst. prof. accounting Ky. State Coll., Frankfort, 1947-50; asso. prof. So. U., Baton Rouge, 1950-51; sr. auditor M.T. Washington C.P.A.'s, Chgo., 1951-53; auditor Collier-Lewis Realty Co., 1953-70; auditor A.A. Rayner & Sons, 1960-72; tchr. Chgo. Pub. Schs., 1951-57; asso. prof. law, accounting Chgo. Tchrs. Coll., Chgo., 1957-65, budget coordinator, 1966-67; asso. prof. law, accounting Ill. Tchrs. Coll., 1965-67, Chgo. State Coll., Chgo., 1967-70; prof. Chgo. State U., 1970—, spl. asst. to v.p., 1976-77. C.P.A., Chgo., 1950—; lawyer, Chgo., 1966—. Budgetary cons. OEO; ednl. cons. to HEW; auditing cons. to Dept. Labor; mgmt. cons. to Black Econ. Union, 1969—; chmn. edn. adv. com. N.A.A.C.P., 1966—. Served to 2d. lt. AC, AUS, 1942-54; C.P.A., Ill. Mem. Am., Ill., Chgo. bar assns., Am. Assn. Accountants, Am. Assn. U. Profs., Am. Bus. Law Assn., Am. Judicature Soc., Am. Inst. C.P.A.'s. Club: Chgo. City. Author: How To Take an Inventory, 1948; Directory of Negro Business of Baton Rouge, La., 1950. Contbr. Bus. Men's Guide, 1971. Home: 18252 S California Ave Homewood IL 60430

LEWIS, CHARLES HENRY, educator; b. Bessmer, Ala., Nov. 22, 1930; s. Charles Montgomery and Erline (Mills) L.; B.S., Langston U., 1953; student U.S. Army Guided Missile Sch., 1955; M.A., Wayne State U., 1967; M.B.A., Mich. State U., 1974; m. Joyce Jean Hale, May 25, 1952; children—Joyce Rene, Donna Kay (dec.), Charles Michael. Recreation instr., supr. community house dept. parks and recreation City of Detroit, 1956-64; sch. community agent Detroit Public Schs., 1964-66; project dir. Commn. on Children and Youth City of Detroit, 1966-69, instr. recreation, 1969-71; dir, personnel services Blvd. Gen. Hosp., Detroit, 1971-74; asso. prof. dept. recreation and park services Wayne State U., 1974—, also chmn. dept., mem. Univ. council, 1980—; exec. sec. Detroit Joint Recreation Com. Mem. Detroit div. United Community Services, Detroit, 1974-75; mem. adv. bd. YMCA, Detroit, 1968. Served with U.S. Army, 1953-56. Mich. Council for Humanities grantee, 1975; recipient Nat. Recreation and Park Ethnic Minority Soc. Citation award, 1978; United Community Services citation, 1978. Mem. Nat. Recreation and Park Assn., Nat. Recreation and Park Ethnic Minority Soc. (pres. 1981-83), Mich. Recreation and Park Assn., World Leisure and Recreation Assn., AAHPER, World Future Soc., Nat. Indsl. Recreation Assn., Wayne State U. Alumni Assn., Mich. State U. Alumni Assn., Langston U. Alumni Assn., Alpha Phi Alpha. Lutheran. Co-host, producer Soundings, People. Home: 3202 Waverly St Detroit MI 48238 Office: Wayne State University 259 Mattheei Bldg Detroit MI 48202

LEWIS, CLEVELAND ARTHUR, indsl. engr.; b. Selma, Ala., Apr. 21, 1942; s. Levi and Elsie Rebecca L.; A.A.S., Purdue U., Indpls., 1972, B.S., 1976; m. Betty Faye Harris, Sept. 25, 1965; children—Aisha Jahmilla. Machine operator, Chrysler Corp., 1964-70, acctg. clk. 1970-71, technician 1971-72, indsl. engr., Indpls., 1972-76; project design engr. Detroit Diesel Allison div. Gen. Motors Corp., Indpls., 1976—; pres. Clevetech Work Systems, Inc., 1975-79; prof. indsl. engring. Purdue U., Indpls. Served with USAF, 1960-64. Mem. Am. Inst. Indsl. Engrs., Soc. Automotive Engrs., Inst. Certification Engring. Technicians, Human Factors Soc. Ind., Purdue U. Alumni Assn. Lutheran. Home: 5085 Knollton Rd Indianapolis IN 46208 Office: 4700 W 10th St Indianapolis IN 46206

LEWIS, DANIEL EDWIN, lawyer; b. Goshen, Ind., May 2, 1910; s. Daniel Arthur and Emma John (Williams) L.; A.B., Hanover Coll., 1932; M.S., Ind. U., 1939; J.D., Valparaiso U., 1949; m. Annette Jean Fewell, July 28, 1934; children—Daniel Edwin, Nancy Jean (Mrs. Glenn Lee Haswell). Tchr. high sch., Knox, Ind., 1932-35; tchr., athletic coach high sch., LaPorte, Ind., 1935-43; dir. indsl. relations Allis Chalmers Mfg. Co., LaPorte, 1943-55; admitted to Ind. bar, 1949, since practiced in LaPorte; partner firm Newby & Lewis, 1955-59, Newby, Lewis & Kaminski, 1959—; instr. mgmt. Purdue U., LaPorte, 1944, Ind. U., LaPorte, 1945. Pres. United Fund of Greater LaPorte, 1957, 65; chmn. LaPorte chpt. A.R.C., 1948; vice chmn. Pottawattomie council Boy Scouts Am., 1963-69; pres. Family Service Assn. LaPorte County, 1975-77; pres. LaPorte Bd. Edn., 1952-55, LaPorte County Human Relations Commn., 1967-68; chmn. LaPorte Bicentennial Plaza Meml. Com.; ambassador Asso. Colls. Ind. Bd. dirs. LaPorte YMCA, pres., 1960-62; Recipient Alumni Achievement award Hanover Coll., 1965; named Outstanding Citizen of LaPorte, LaPorte Jr. C. of C., 1955. Mem. Am., Ind., Ind. State, LaPorte County bar assns., Am. Arbitration Assn., LaPorte Athletic Club (pres. 1949), Phi Delta Kappa, Phi Alpha Delta, Phi Delta Theta. Presbyn. (Elder). Elk, Mason, Kiwanian (pres. 1954). Author: At the Crossroads (novel), 1980. Home: 207 Edgewood Lane LaPorte IN 46350 Office: 916 Lincoln Way LaPorte IN 46350

LEWIS, DAVID SLOAN, JR., aircraft co. exec.; b. North Augusta, S.C., July 6, 1917; s. David S. and Reuben (Walton) L.; student U. S.C., 1934-37; B.S. in Aero. Engring., Ga. Inst. Tech., 1939; m. Dorothy Sharpe, Dec. 20, 1941; children—Susan, David Sloan III, Robert, Andrew. Aerodynamicist, Glenn L. Martin Co., Balt., 1939-46; chief aerodynamics McDonnell Aircraft Corp., St. Louis, 1946-52, chief preliminary design, 1952-55, mgr. sales, 1955-56, mgr. projects, 1956-57, v.p. project mgmt., 1957-59, sr. v.p. ops., 1960-61, exec. v.p., 1961-62, pres., 1962-67; pres. McDonnell-Douglas Co., also chmn. Douglas Aircraft Co. div., 1967-70; chmn., chief exec. officer Gen. Dynamics Corp., 1970—; dir. Ralston Purina Co., Mead Corp., St. Louis, BankAm. Corp., San Francisco. Alderman, Ferguson, Mo., 1951-54; trustee Washington U., St. Louis. Fellow AIAA. Episcopalian. Home: 7751 Kingsbury Blvd Saint Louis MO 63105 Office: Pierre Laclede Center Saint Louis MO 63105

LEWIS, DENISE JACKSON, city ofcl.; b. Detroit, Dec. 26, 1944; d. George Edward and Bertha C. (Gomez) Jackson; B.A., Barnard Coll., 1966; M.A., Wayne State U., Detroit, 1969; m. John A. Lewis, Jan. 7, 1966; children—Andwele John, Imani Edward. Compliance supr., then asst. regional mgr. Mich. Civil Rights Commn., 1966-71; dir. human rights dept. City of Detroit, 1971-74, dir. personnel dept., 1974—; adv. bd. Sch. Labor and Indsl. Relations, Mich. State U.; adv. council Gov. Mich. Intergovtl. Personnel Act; mem. Gt. Lakes panel President's Commn. White House Fellows; tchr., cons. in field. Trustee Kirwood Gen. Hosp., Detroit; bd. dirs. Franklin Wright Settlement, Detroit; past pres. bd. dirs. Afro-Am. Museum, Detroit. Recipient Martin Luther King award SCLC, 1978; also other civic and service awards; Ford Found. fellow, 1973. Mem. Orgn. Mcpl. Personnel Officers (dir.), Internat. Personnel Mgmt. Assn. (chpt. dir.), Wayne State U. Alumni Assn. (dir.), Barnard Coll. Alumni Council (area rep.), Detroit Women's Econ. Club. Author articles in field. Office: 316 City-County Bldg Detroit MI 48226

LEWIS, EDMUND JEAN, internist; b. N.Y.C., Nov. 10, 1936; s. Herbert P. and Sylvia (Roth) L.; B.S., McGill U., 1958; M.D., U. B.C., 1962; children—Diane, Susanne. Intern, Johns Hopkins U., 1962; mem. house staff Johns Hopkins, 1962-65; research fellow Harvard, 1965-66, 68-70, asst. prof., 1970-71; asso. prof. medicine U. Chgo., 1971-73; prof. medicine, dir. sect. nephrology Rush Med. Coll., Chgo., 1973—. Chmn. med. adv. bd. Kidney Found. Ill., 1972-74, mem. exec. com., bd. dirs., 1972-77. Served with USPHS, 1966-68. Recipient Hamber Gold medal, U. B.C., 1962, Horner Gold medal, 1962. Mem. Johns Hopkins Med. and Surg. Soc., Am. Fedn. Clin. Research, Am. Soc. Nephrology, Transplantation Soc., Chgo. Med. Soc., Am. Soc. Internal Medicine, AMA, Alpha Omega Alpha. Contbr. articles to med. jours. Home: 415 W Aldine Chicago IL 60657 Office: 1753 W Congress Pkwy Chicago IL 60611

LEWIS, G(EORGE) GORDON, JR., librarian; b. Youngstown, Ohio, Jan. 1, 1945; s. George Gordon and Mary Virginia (Crooks) L.; B.A., Capital U., 1966; M.L.S., U. Pitts., 1969; M.Ed. in Ednl. Media, Temple U., 1974; postgrad. U. Mich., 1980—; m. Judith Ann Yek, Sept. 9, 1967; children—Jennifer Elaine, Stephanie Virginia, Douglas Gordon. With Pub. Library Youngstown and Mahoning County, 1967-69; with Free Library of Phila., from 1969, br. head McPherson Square Br. Library, 1971-74; dir. Farmington (Mich.) Community Library, 1974—. Served with USMCR, 1966-67. Mem. ALA (public relations services to libraries com. of library adminstrn. div. 1973-78), Library Adminstrs. and Mgrs. Assn. (architecture for public libraries com. 1978—). Mich. library assns., Assn. Ednl. Communications Tech., Detroit Suburban Librarians Roundtable (pres. 1975-76), Delta Sigma Rho, Tau Kappa Alpha, Beta Phi Mu. Lutheran. Address: 32737 W 12 Mile Rd Farmington MI 48018

LEWIS, JAMES EDWARD, chem. co. exec.; b. Ashland, Ky., July 11, 1927; s. Blaine and Hallie Maude (Heal) L.; A.B., Centre Coll. of Ky., 1950; M.S., Purdue U., 1954, Ph.D., 1956; m. Mary Ann Johnson, Feb. 23, 1952; children—Martha Ellen Lewis Innes, Glenna Ann Lewis Knox, Karen Lee. Dir. research and devel. United Carbon Co., Houston, 1965-70, Ashland Oil, Inc., Dublin, Ohio, 1970-74; v.p. research and devel. Ashland Chem. Co., Dublin, 1974-78, v.p., 1978—; dir. Radiochemistry, Inc., 1958-65. Ky. gov.'s adv. com. on Nuclear Energy and Space Sci., 1959-65; mem. Ky. Atomic Energy and Space Authority, 1961-65; exec. com. Ky. Atomic Energy Authority, 1963-65; mem. So. Interstate Nuclear Bd., 1963-65; elected Mcpl. Council Dublin, 1979. Served with U.S. Army, 1944-47. Recipient Preston Carter prize in chemistry, Centre Coll., 1950, Sally B. Warfield prize in math., 1950; apptd. Ky. Col. by gov. Ky., 1963, hon. citizen State of Tenn. by gov. Tenn., 1965. Fellow AAAS, Am. Inst. Chemists; mem. Am. Chem. Soc., Am. Phys. Soc., Soc. Chem. Industry, Licensing Execs. Soc., Indsl. Research Inst. (rep.), Sigma Xi, Phi Lambda Upsilon. Republican. Club: Muirfield Village Golf. Contbr. writings to profl. publs.; patentee. Office: 5200 Blazer Memorial Pkwy Dublin OH 43017

LEWIS, JOHN DONALD, educator; b. Paterson, N.J., Oct. 6, 1905; s. John T. and Mary (Jones) L.; A.B., Oberlin Coll., 1928; Ph.D., U. Wis., 1934; postgrad. U. Berlin, 1932-33; m. Ewart R. Kellogg, June 20, 1933 (dec. 1968); children—David K., Donalde, Ellen; m. 2d, Mary Jane Miller, Jan. 23, 1972; stepchildren—David J., Leslie. Vis. prof. Western Reserve U., 1966-67, Colo. Coll., 1972; vis. prof. (summers) U. Mich., 1949, Columbia U., 1954, U. Wis., Madison, 1951; asst. prof. govt. Oberlin (Ohio) Coll., 1935-42, asso. prof., 1942-48, prof., 1948-72, chmn. dept., 1948-50, 53-70, prof. emeritus, 1972—; Fulbright vis. lectr. Oxford (Eng.) U., 1959-60. Guggenheim fellow, 1943-44, German exchange fellow, 1932-33, resident appointee, 1933—; Social Sci. Research Council fellow, 1939-40. Mem. Am. Polit. Sci. Assn., AAUP, Am. Assn. Social, Legal and Polit. Philosophy (v.p. 1967-69), Phi Beta Kappa. Author: Genossenschaft Theory of Otto Von Gierke, 1935; Antifederalists, versus Federalists: The Study of Comparative Government, 1957; (with O. Jaszi) Against the Tyrant, 1957. Home: 255 E College St Oberlin OH 44074

LEWIS, JONATHAN JAMES, ednl. adminstr.; b. Lorain, Ohio, Mar. 31, 1939; s. Llewellyn D. and Kathryn B. (Walker) L.; B.A. in Am. Studies, Bowling Green (Ohio) State U., 1962, M.A. in Am. Studies, 1966; m. Amanda Dudas, 1973; children—Jonathan Evan, Justin Daniel. Editorial trainee Booth Newspapers, Detroit, 1966-67; news reporter Metro-East Journal, E. St. Louis, Ill., 1967-68; adminstrv. asst. Cahokia (Ill.) Sch. Dist. 187, 1968—. Mem. Cahokia Library Bd., 1976—; chmn. City-Wide Hist. Fair, 1973. Mem. Ill. Assn. Sch. Bus. Ofcls., Cahokia Adminstrs. Assn., Nat. Ill. sch. pub. relations assns. Contbr. articles in field to local newspapers. Home: 803 Joliet Cahokia IL 62206 Office: 1700 Jerome Ln Cahokia IL 62206

LEWIS, MARY CATHERINE, freelance writer; b. Chgo., Sept. 7, 1954; d. Oswald Berry and Vivian (Miller) Lewis; B.A., Oberlin Coll., 1976. Intern, research asst. Sta. WNYE-TV, Bklyn., 1975; editorial asst. Ebony Jr&I, Johnson Pub. Co., Chgo., 1977-78, mng. editor, 1978-80. Mem. Chgo. chpt. Children's Reading Round Table; bd. dirs. Chgo. chpt. Reading Is Fundamental; touring speaker merit employment youth motivation com. Chgo. Assn. Commerce and Industry, 1978-80. Recipient Youth Journalism award Internat. Black Writers Conf., 1978; Kizzy award Womanfest, 1979; cert. Chgo. Assn. Commerce and Industry, 1979; community devel. grantee Chgo. Council Fine Arts, 1981. Mem. Am. Film Inst., Smithsonian Instn., NAACP. LUtheran. Contbr. articles to Ebony Jr!. Home: 7925 S Indiana Ave Chicago IL 60619

LEWIS, MIKE, radio and TV producer; b. Chgo., May 22, 1953; student U. Ill., Chgo., 1973, Chgo. City Coll., 1972, Bi-lingual announcer WXRT-FM, Chgo., 1968-69; announcer WLAK-FM, Chgo., 1972-73, WDHF, 1970-72, WWEL-FM, 1969-70; announcer WTMJ and TV, Milw., 1973-74, WMAQ and TV, Chgo., 1974-80, FM100, Chgo., 1974-80; co-owner, writer, producer, performer Fred & Mike Prodns. Ltd., Chgo., 1979—. Named one of Ten Outstanding Young Men of Am. U.S. Jaycees, 1981. Mem. Hollywood Radio and TV Soc. Office: 21 E Chestnut St Chicago IL 60611

LEWIS, ROBERT OWEN, surgeon; b. Carmi, Ill., Oct. 13, 1927; s. Henry and Helen (Peterson) L.; B.A., DePauw U., Greencastle, Ind., 1950; B.A., U. Ill. Coll. Medicine, 1952, M.D., 1954; m. Eleanor De Vries Lewis, 1958; children—Gregory J., Robert D., John Henry. Intern, Presbyn. Hosp., Chgo., 1954-55, resident in gen. surgery, 1955-59; mem. staff Community Hosp., Ottawa, Ill., 1959—, also mem. exec. bd.; asst. prof. surgery U. Ill. Coll. Medicine. Elder Presbyterian Ch. Recipient Distinguished Service award U. Ill. Dept. Surgery, 1969. Diplomate Am. Bd. Surgery. Fellow A.C.S.; mem. AMA, Ill. State, LaSalle County med. socs., Ill. Surg. Soc. (dir. exec. bd.). Home: 325 E Pearl St Ottawa IL 61350 Office: 1703 Polaris Circle Ottawa IL 61350

LEWIS, ROY ROGERS, fast food service co. exec.; b. Dayton, Ohio, Jan. 13, 1944; s. Harold Harrell Hedges and Helen Louise (Mees); student Wilmington Coll., 1962-63, Central State U., 1965, Wittenburg U., 1970; m. Margo Ann Andersen, July 3, 1978; children by previous marriage—Roy Rogers, Andrew Cary, Jeffrey Paul, Brandi Eileen; 1 stepdau., Jennifer Marie Hansen. Various sales positions, 1963-65; mgr. Red Barn Systems, Inc., Washington, 1966-68; dept. mgr. Montgomery Ward & Co., Xenia, Ohio, 1968-69; assembly line worker Morris Bean & Co., Yellow Springs, Ohio, 1969; restaurant mgr. McDonalds Systems, Inc., Dayton, 1970-71, market tng. coordinator, 1971, field cons., Ohio, 1972-73, prof. Hamburger U., Elk Grove, Ill., 1973, nat. audio-visual prodn. tech. advisor, 1973-74, sr. prof., 1974, asst. dean, 1975—, corp. tng. materials devel. mgr., 1979-81, dir. ops. tng. devel., 1981—. Dept. advisor Sinclair Community Coll., Dayton, 1971-72; advisor Patterson Coop. High Sch., Dayton, 1971-72; v.p. Young Reps., 1971-72; mem. Zoning Bd. Appeals, Xenia, 1971-72; pres. Homeowner Assn., 1978-80, 81. Served with USNG, 1963-69. Republican. Quaker. Home: 1623 Cornell Pl Hoffman Estates IL 60194 Office: McDonald's Plaza Oak Brook IL 60154

LEWIS, RUTH MASON, counselor, educator; b. St. Louis, Mar. 29, 1938; d. Robert Henry and Artia Mae (Johnson) Mason; B.A. in Edn., Harris Tchrs. Coll., 1960; M.A., St. Louis U., 1965; m. Floyd Lewis, July 11, 1965. Elem. tchr. St. Louis Bd. Edn., 1960-66, counselor Northwest High Sch., 1966-69; counselor St. Louis Community Coll. at Forest Park, 1969—, prof. counseling, 1977—. Sec. bd. trustees First Baptist Ch., 1975—; active West County Jaycees Wives, 1970-73; bd. dirs. St. Louis Met. YWCA, 1976—, asst. sec., 1977—, chmn. personnel com., 1979—, v.p., 1980; trustee Fox Creek Estates. Named Counselor of Year, Student Govt., 1975; recipient 10 yr. Service award Jr. Coll. Dist. St. Louis; cert. for 25 yrs. service 1st Bapt. Ch., St. Louis. Mem. NEA (pres. jr. coll. dist. 1978-79, mem. Mo. minority involvement program com. 1979-80), Am. Personnel and Guidance Assn. (senator 1979—), Assn. for Non-White Concerns in Personnel and Guidance (mem. exec. council, nat. sec., past pres., mem. exec. council, charter mem. Mo. state chpt., citations for services 1978, 79, 80), Faculty Assn. St. Louis Community Coll. at Forest Park (pres.), NAACP, Mo. Personnel and Guidance Assn. (charter mem.), St. Louis Personnel and Guidance Assn., Nat. Council Negro Women, Mo. Assn. Community and Jr. Colls., Delta Sigma Theta (past pres. and exec. mem. St. Louis Alumnae chpt.). Clubs: Just We Bridge; Town and Country Bridge. Author: (with others) Peers, 1979. Contbr. chpt. to Profiles in Silhouette: Contributions of Black Women in Missouri, 1980. Home: 1045 Parkwatch Dr Ballwin MO 63011 Office: 5600 Oakland Ave Saint Louis MO 63110

LEWIS, SALLY BUTZEL (MRS. LEONARD THEODORE LEWIS), civic worker; b. Detroit, June 29, 1912; d. Leo Martin and Caroline (Heavenrich) Butzel; B.A., Vassar Coll., 1934; m. Leonard Theodore Lewis, Apr. 4, 1935; 1 son, Leonard Theodore. Mem. Women's City Club of Detroit, 1932-67, dir., 1935-38; dir., chmn. community services com. Village Woman's Club of Birmingham-Bloomfield dir. Franklin-Wright Settlement, Inc., Detroit, 1939-74, pres. 1959-60; trustee Oakland County Children's Aid Soc., 1950-64, Oakland U. Found., 1973—; mem. exec. com. Detroit Fedn. Settlements, 1961; mem. steering com., women's orgn. United Fund, 1960-61; mem. Oakland planning div. United Community Services, Met. Detroit, 1959-70; membership chmn. Bloomfield Art Assn., Birmingham, Mich.; mem. scholarship com. Meadow Brook Sch. Music, Meadow Brook Festival, Rochester, Mich.; treas. Cranbrook Music Guild, Inc., 1959, dir., 1958-63, sec., 1960-61; mem. women's com. Cranbrook Galleries Art, Bloomfield Hills; exec. com. Meadow Brook Festival, Rochester, Md., 1969-76. Mem. Nat. Council Jewish Women, Am. Jewish Com., Women's Assn. Detroit Symphony, Friends Detroit Symphony. Clubs: Women's Nat. Farm and Garden, Village, Ibex. Home: 1421 Lochridge Rd Bloomfield Hills MI 48013

LEWIS, SHIRLEY ANN, ednl. adminstr.; b. Pekin, Ill., Oct. 21, 1934; d. James Warren and Nora Mae (Sweany) Lewis; B.S., U. Ill., 1956; M.A., U. Mich., 1967. English and journalism tchr. Barrington (Ill.) Consol. High Sch., 1956-58, Carl Sandburg High Sch., Orland Park, Ill., 1958-59, USAF Dependent Schs., Eng., 1959-60, Ger., 1960-61; English and journalism tchr. Riverside-Brookfield Twp. (Ill.), 1960-66, counselor, 1967-68, adminstr., 1968—. Recipient Outstanding Tchr. award USAF Europe, 1961. Mem. Am. Personnel and Guidance Assn., Am. Sch. Counselors Assn., Ill. Women Deans and Counselors, Delta Kappa Gamma, Phi Kappa Phi. Methodist. Home: 65 Longcommon Rd Riverside IL 60546 Office: Ridgewood and Golf Rds Riverside IL 60546

LEWIS, SUGAR LEE, educator; b. Ringgold, La., May 28, 1945; d. Capus and Sugar L. (Winston) Hamptlon; A.A., Barstow Jr. Coll., Calif., 1971; B.A., U. Mo., 1973, M.A., 1977, Ed.S., 1981; m. Durrie E. Lewis, Feb. 25, 1973; children—Michell Rene, Yolanda D., Elroy. Elem. sch. tchr. and asst. to prin. Kansas City Sch. Dist., 1973-74, spl. edn. tchr., 1974—, asst. prin., 1980—. Campaign worker for gov. of Mo., Jefferson City, 1979-80; campaign worker for mayor, Kansas City, Mo., 1979-80; children's dir. Friendship Bapt. Ch., 1976—; bd. dirs. Westridge Sch. PTA, 1977-81, Raytown South Jr. High PTA, 1980-81. Recipient Internat. Sci. and Engring. Fair award 1979, Cert. of Award, Friendship Bapt. Ch., 1979, Cert. of Appreciation, Miracle Temple Ch., 1979; cert. tchr., Mo. Mem. Assn. for Supervision and Curriculum, Internat. Reading Assn., Am. Hist. Soc., Kansas City Area Assn. for Gifted and Talented, Legal Services Soc., Kansas City Tchr. Club. Home: 8124 E 74th St Kansas City MO 64133 Office: 11801 E 32nd St Independence MO 64052

LEWIS, WILLIAM FRANKLIN, marketing cons., educator; b. Jackson, Mich., Oct. 20, 1941; s. Francis Christopher and Marion Geraldine (Booth) L.; grad. A.G.S. Jackson Community Coll., 1961; B.A. in Econs., Spring Arbor Coll., 1967; M.B.A. in Marketing, Mich. State U., 1969; Ph.D. in Marketing, U. Cin., 1976; m. Dorothy Marie Schwarz, Dec. 29, 1979. Instr., Spring Arbor (Mich.) Coll., 1968-69; teaching fellow U. Cin., 1970-73, asst. prof. marketing Xavier U., Cin., 1973-76; asst. prof. of marketing Miami U., Oxford, Ohio, 1976-78; asst. prof. mktg. No. Ky. U., Highland Heights, 1979; asso. prof. U. Dayton, 1980—; guest speaker sta. WVXU-FM, 1974, 75; credit corporate treasury dept. Chrysler Corp., 1969-70; cons. in marketing to govt. agys. and various bus. firms, 1968—; pres. W.F. Lewis Associates, Inc., Cin., 1977—. Served with USNR, 1959-65. Mem. Am. (v.p. 1977-78), So. marketing assns., Acad. Mgmt., Product Devel. and Mgmt. Assn., Sales and Marketing Execs., Mu Kappa Tau (nat. pres. 1977-79), Beta Gamma Sigma, Pi Sigma Epsilon, Sigma Iota Epsilon. Baptist. Contbr. articles in field to profl. publs. Home: 7899 Christine Ave Cincinnati OH 45241 Office: Marketing Dept U Dayton Dayton OH 45469

LEYDEN, MARTHA CATHERINE, educator; b. Akron, Ohio, Apr. 3, 1932; B.S. in Elementary Edn., St. John Coll., Cleve., 1956; M.Ed. in Spl. Edn/Deaf, Kent (Ohio) State U., 1961; Ed.D. in Early Childhood Edn., Tchrs. Coll., Columbia U., 1971. Tchr. 1st grade, Akron, 1953-63; directress Our Lady of the Elms Presch., Akron, 1964-68; prof. dept. elementary edn. U. Akron, 1971—. Mem. Ohio Assn. for Edn. of Young Children (governing bd. 1972—, pres. 1977-79), Ohio Commn. for Children (2d v.p.). Cert. in elem. edn., spl. deaf edn. K-12, Ohio. Home: 1312 W Market St Akron OH 44313 Office: 302 E Buchtel Ave Akron OH 44325

LEYMAN, IRENE ANN, orthoptist; b. Flint, Mich., Mar. 27, 1948; d. Charles Stephen and Delphine Marie (Zientek) L.; B.S. in Secondary Edn., Eastern Mich. U., 1970; cert. orthoptist, Kresge Eye Inst., Wayne State U., 1973. Tchr. English and theatre Detroit Bd. Edn., 1970-71; orthoptist, Royal Oak, Mich., 1973-75; orthoptist, instr. Children's Hosp. of Mich., 1974-76: orthoptist St. Vincent Hosp. and Med. Center, Toledo, 1975-78; mem. faculty Med. Coll. of Ohio, Toledo, from 1975, instr., from 1978, orthoptist, from 1978; now mem. faculty pediatric ophthalmology sect., dept. ophthalmology U. Iowa; lectr. various community orgns. Bd. dirs. Neighborhood Improvement Found. of Toledo Inc., 1976—, chmn. funding com., 1978-79. Douglas Research Found. grantee, 1976-78; Ohio Lions Eye Research grantee, 1978-79. Mem. Internat. Orthoptic Assn., Am. Assn. Certified Orthoptists (award for outstanding service 1978-79), Canadian Orthoptic Soc., Midwestern Regional Assn. Certified Orthoptists. Republican. Clubs: Toledo Ski (dir. 1977-79), Westowne Tennis, Toledo Racquet. Editor nat. newsletter The Prism, 1976—. Home: 931 21st Ave Pl Coralville IA 52241 Office: U of Iowa Dept Ophthalmology Iowa City IA 52240

LEYMASTER, GLEN R., assn. exec.; b. Aurora, Nebr., Aug. 17, 1915; s. Leslie and Frances (Wertman) L.; m. Margaret Hendricks, June 20, 1942; children—Mark H., Mary Beth, Lynn F.; A.B., U. Nebr., 1938; M.D., Harvard U., 1942; M.P.H., Johns Hopkins, 1950; intern, asst. resident, resident Harvard Med. Service, Boston City Hosp., 1942-44. Instr. medicine Johns Hopkins Med. Sch., 1944-46, instr., asst. prof. bacteriology Sch. Pub. Health and Hygiene, 1946-48; asso. prof. pub. health, instr. medicine U. Utah Sch. Medicine, 1948-50, prof., head dept. preventive medicine, asst. prof. medicine, also dir. univ. health service, 1950-60; adviser med. edn.-preventive medicine ICA, Bangkok, Thailand, 1956-58; asso. sec. council med. edn. and hosps. AMA, Chgo., 1960-63, dir. dept. undergrad. med. edn., 1970-75; pres., dean Women's Med. Coll. Pa., 1964-70; exec. dir. Am. Bd. Med. Specialties, Evanston, Ill., 1975—. Mem. Am., Ill., Chgo. med. assns., Inst. Medicine Chgo., Phi Beta Kappa, Sigma Xi, Alpha Omega Alpha. Contbr. articles in field to profl. jours. Home: 1155 Michigan Ave Wilmette IL 60091 Office: 1603 Orrington Ave Evanston IL 60201

LEYSER, YONA, educator; b. Petha-Tikva, Israel, Sept. 24, 1937; s. Herbert and Ellen (Wolf) L.; came to U.S., 1970, permanent resident, 1977; B.A. cum laude, Tel Aviv U., 1966; Ph.D., Ind. U., 1975; m. Ayala Hammer, June 25, 1971; 1 dau., Ophra. Spl. edn. tchr., counselor, Israel, 1960-66; lectr. psychology and spl. edn. Tchrs. Coll. Israel, 1967-70; research asst. Ind. U., Bloomington, 1970-74; asst. prof. Ohio U., Athens, 1974-78; asso. prof. edn. No. Ill. U., DeKalb, 1978—. Named Outstanding Faculty in Spl. Edn., Ohio U., 1976; Bur. Edn. Handicapped grantee, 1979-82. Mem. Council Exceptional Children, Am. Assn. Mental Deficiency, Phi Delta Kappa. Home: 918 W Taylor St Dekalb IL 60115 Office: 238 Grahm Hall No Ill U Dekalb IL 60115

LI, CHARLES SHUHANG, plastic surgeon; b. Formosa, China, Aug. 1, 1930; s. Tzau and Siang (Hsu) L.; came to U.S., 1950, naturalized, 1965; B.S. magna cum laude, St. Benedict's Coll., 1954; M.D., St. Louis U., 1957; m. Marilyn Hodge, Oct. 4, 1960; children—Karen Ann, Nancy Marilyn. Intern, St. Mary's Hosp., St. Louis, 1957-58; resident in gen. surgery St. Vincent Charity Hosp., Cleve., 1958-61, sr. resident, 1961-62, resident in plastic surgery Columbia Presbyn. Med. Center, N.Y.C., 1962-64; fellow in surgery of hand Roosevelt Hosp., N.Y.C., 1964; practice medicine specializing in plastic and reconstructive surgery and surgery of hand, Parma, Ohio, 1964—; asst. clin. prof. plastic surgery Case Western Res. U., 1972—. Diplomate Am. Bd. Surgery, Am. Bd. Plastic Surgery. Mem. AMA, Ohio State Med. Assn., Cleve. Acad. Medicine, Cleve. Surg. Soc., A.C.S., Ednl. Found. of Am. Plastic and Reconstructive Surgery, Inc., Am. Soc. Plastic and Reconstructive Surgeons, Ohio Valley Plastic Surgery Soc., Webster Soc. Columbia, Am. Soc. Surgery of Hand, Pan-Pacific Surg. Assn., Presbyterian Hosp. Alumni Assn., Roosevelt Hosp. Alumni Assn. Roman Catholic. Contbr. articles in field to profl. jours. Home: 5377 W Ridgewood Dr Parma OH 44134 Office: Med Arts Center 6681 Ridge Rd Suite 303 Parma OH 44129

LI, EDDIE KA-KWAN, mfg. co. exec.; b. Canton, China, Apr. 29, 1953; s. Shu-Kan and Mo-Yin (Lo) Li; came to U.S., 1974, naturalized, 1978; student Chinese U. Hong Kong, 1972-74; B.S. in Computer Sci., U. Oreg., 1977; postgrad. U. Chgo., 1978-82; m. Iris Chiu, May 26, 1979. Research asst. U. Oreg., 1976-77; system analyst Northwestern Meml. Hosp., Chgo., 1977-78; data processing mgr. Enco Mfg. Co., Chgo., 1978-80, corp. ops. dir., 1980—; gen. mgr. Enco Data Processing Co., Chgo., 1979-80. U. Oreg. grantee, 1976-77. Mem. Assn. Computing Machinery, Data Processing Mgmt. Assn., Am. Mgmt. Assn. Home: 1213 B Central St Evanston IL 60201 Office: 5008 W Bloomingdale Ave Chicago IL 60639

LI, KAM WU, mech. engr.; b. China, Feb. 34, 1934; came to U.S., 1959; s. Yang Chung and Oy Lan L.: M.S., Colo. State U., 1961; Ph.D., Okla. State U., 1965; m. Shui Mui Chan, Aug. 30, 1956; children—Christopher, Charles. Asst. prof. mech. engring. Tex. A&I U., 1965-67; asso. prof. N.D. State U., Fargo, 1967-73, prof., 1973—; cons. Charles T. Main Inc., Boston, 1973—. Recipient cert. appreciation U.S. Navy, 1974; NSF fellow, 1966; Ford Found. fellow, 1972. Mem. ASME, N.Y. Acad. Scis., Sigma Xi, Tau Beta Pi, Pi Tau Sigma, Kappa Mu Epsilon. Contbr. numerous articles to profl. jours.; govt. engring. research, 1965—. Home: 2516 18th St S Moorhead MN 56560 Office: ND State U University Ave Fargo ND 58105

LI, NORMAN L., state ofcl.; b. Hong Kong, Mar. 11, 1947; came to U.S., 1971, naturalized, 1979; s. Po On and Lena (Lam) L.; B.A., Nat. Taiwan U., 1971; M.A., Central Mo. State U., 1974; m. Judy Cheng, May 8, 1976. Internat. mktg. dir. Tataicheong Co. Ltd., Hong Kong, 1970-72; operation mgr. New Moon of Merrillville Inc. (Ind.), 1974-79; trade specialist Ill. Dept. Commerce and Community Affairs, Chgo., 1979—; leader state trade missions to China, Hong Kong, Korea, Singapore, Taiwan; developer trade promotion agreement between Ill. and Taiwan, 1979. Mem. Internat. Bus. Council, Am. Econs. Assn. Home: 311 2d St Downers Grove IL 60515 Office: 310 S Michigan Ave Suite 1000 Chicago IL 60604

LI, THOMAS MING-TING, chemist; b. Hong Kong, Oct. 8, 1946; came to U.S., 1968, naturalized, 1981; s. Yiu-Hoi and Yuk-Chun (Cheng) L.; B.S. with honors and highest distinction in Chemistry, U. Ill., 1972, M.S., 1974, Ph.D., 1976; m. Janey O. Loh, Sept. 19, 1973; children—Diane K., Stephen Michael. Postdoctoral fellow NIH, Inst. for Cancer Research, Phila., 1976-78; research scientist Miles Labs., Inc., Elkhart, Ind., 1978-79, sr. research scientist, 1980-81; supr. Ames Immunochemistry Lab., 1981—. Edmund J. James scholar, 1969-72; Haas Found. fellow, 1972-73; USPHS fellow, 1976-78; recipient Benjamin Freund award in chemistry, 1971; Am. Inst. Chemists Outstanding award, 1972. Mem. N.Y. Acad. Sci., Am. Assn. Clin. Chemistry, Am. Chem. Soc., Biophys. Soc., Sigma Xi, Phi Kappa Phi. Contbr. articles to profl. jours.; patentee in field; contbr. to: Immunoassays Clinical Laboratory Techniques for the 1980's, 1980. Home: 2914 Brooktree Ct Elkhart IN 46514 Office: 1127 Myrtle St Elkhart IN 46514

LIAO, KUN TWU, physician; b. Yun-Lin, Taiwan, Dec. 12, 1932; s. Wan Neu and Ye How (Lee) L.; M.D., Nat. Taiwan U., 1958; m. Grace Ya-Sin Yen, Dec. 25, 1959; children—Angela, Jimmy, Margie. Resident surgery Nat. Taiwan U. Hosp., Taipei, 1960-63; intern Balt. City Hosp., 1963-64; resident surgery Del. Hosp., Wilmington, 1964-65; resident pathology Wilmington (Del.) Med. Center, 1965-69; fellow pathology Washington U., St. Louis, 1969-70; asst. pathologist Barnes Hosp., St. Louis, 1970-71; pathologist Clin. Labs. St. Louis, 1971—; dir. labs. Wood River Twp. Hosp. (Ill.), 1971; cons. pathologist Washington County Hosp., Nashville, Ill., St. Mary's Hosp., Centerville Twp. Hosp. (both East St. Louis, Ill.), Incarnate Ward Hosp., St. Louis, St. Joseph Hosp., St. Charles, Mo. Diplomate Am. Bd. Pathology. Mem. AMA, Am. Soc. Clin. Pathologists, Coll. Am. Pathologists, Mo., So. med. assns., St. Louis Med. Soc. Home: 466 Cheshire Farm Ct Creve Coeur MO 63141 Office: 11636 Adminstration Dr Creve Coeur MO 63141

LIAUTAUD, JAMES PHILIP, plastics design engr.; b. Chgo., Oct. 19, 1936; s. John Numa and Ethyl May L.; B.S.M.E., U. Ill., 1963; m. Gina, Jan. 19, 1962; children—Gregory, Jimmy John, Robbie, Lara. Pres., Univ. Publs., U. Ill., 1961-63; div. v.p. Grolier, Inc., N.Y.C., 1963-67; v.p., gen. mgr. Kingston Plastics, Chgo., 1967-68; chmn., founder Capsonic Group, Inc., Elgin, Ill., 1968—; dir. Elgin Die Mold, Inc., Fendall Co., Inc., Am. Antenna, Inc., K40 Electronics, Cecop, Inc. Served with U.S. Army, 1954-57; Korea. Mem. ASME, Soc. Plastics Engrs., Young Pres.'s Orgn., Pres. Forum, Chgo. Met. Pres. Council. Contbr. tech. articles to trade publs.; patentee in field. Home: River and Bluff Rd Cary IL 60013 Office: 1500 Executive Dr Dundee IL 60118

LIBBY, JUDITH LYNN, lawyer; b. Elgin, Ill., Oct. 20, 1948; d. Jules Leon and Virginia Marie (Marshall) L.; B.A. in English Lit., Roosevelt U., 1970; J.D. with highest distinction (Scholar), John Marshall Law Sch., 1977; m. Richard J. Coffee, II. Tchr. humanities Craigmore High Sch., Smithfield, South Australia, Australia, 1971-73; admitted to Ill. bar, 1977; asso. firm Taussig, Wexler & Shaw, Ltd., Chgo., 1977-78; chief counsel Ill. Dept. Ins., Springfield, 1978-80; partner Libby & Coffee Law Office, Springfield, 1981—. Vice pres. Evening Symphony Guild, Springfield, 1979-81; cons. Ill. Assn. for Deaf. Mem. Am. Bar Assn., Ill. State Bar Assn., Chgo. Bar Assn. Office: 522 E Monroe St Suite 703 Springfield IL 62701

LIBERTINY, GEORGE ZOLTAN, research engr.; b. Szolnok, Hungary, June 14, 1934; s. Arpad Pal and Ilona (Szendrei) L.; came to U.S., 1963, naturalized, 1974; B.Sc., U. Strathclyde, Glasgow, Scotland, 1959; Ph.D., U. Bristol (Eng.), 1964; m. Anna Vizvardi, 1956; children—Thomas, Karen. Engr., English Elec. Co., Ltd., Whetstone, 1959-60; asst. prof. mech. engring. U. Miami, Coral Gables, Fla., 1963-65, asso. prof., 1965-68; asso. prof. mechs. and aerospace engring. Ill. Inst. Tech., Chgo., 1968-71; sr. research engr. Ford Motor Co., Dearborn, Mich., 1971-73, prin. research engr. asso., 1973—; cons., expert witness design, stress and materials related to product liability cases; ad hoc visitor Accreditation Bd. Engring. and Tech. Ford Found. scholar, 1957-59, 60-63. Mem. Soc. Automotive Engrs. (R.R. Teetor award 1967), ASME, Am. Soc. Engring. Edn., Inst. Mech. Engrs. (Eng.), Soc. Exptl. Stress Analysis, Sigma Xi. Contbr. articles to profl. jours. Patentee in field. Office: Ford Motor Co American Rd Dearborn MI 48121

LIBMAN, ROBERT HERMAN, anesthesiologist; b. Chgo., Nov. 17, 1944; s. Isadore Hyman and Matilda Hannah (Glickman) L.; B.S., Northwestern U., 1965; M.D., U. Ill., 1969; postgrad. law DePaul U. Coll. Law, 1980—. Intern, then resident in anesthesia Ill. Masonic Med. Center, Chgo., 1969-72, attending psysician, 1972-80, dir. edn., dept. anesthesiology, 1974-80, dir. pain clinic, 1975-80; clin. asst. prof. U. Ill. Med. Sch., 1975—; mem. teaching faculty Cook County Grad. Sch. Medicine, Chgo., 1976—; cons. Shriners Hosp. Crippled Children, 1977—. Served to capt. M.C., U.S. Army, 1970-76. Recipient various service commendations. Diplomate Am. Bd. Anesthesiology. Mem. AMA., Am. Soc. Anesthesiologists, AAAS, Am. Cancer Soc., Am. Soc. Regional Anesthesia, Internat. Anesthesia Research Soc., Am. Dental Soc. Anesthesia, Am. Med. Writers Assn., Assn. Hosp. Med. Edn., A.C.P., Am. Coll. Anesthesiologists, Am. Coll. Chest Physicians, Am. Soc. Advancement Anesthesia in Dentistry, Ill. State Med. Soc., Ill. Soc. Anesthesialogists, Ill. Found. Med. Care, Chgo. Med. Soc., Chgo. Soc. Anesthesiologists, Chgo. Found. Med. Care, Chgo. Heart Assn., Inst. Medicine Chgo., Nat. Audubon Soc., Nat. Wildlife Fedn. Club: Executives (Chgo.). Contbr. articles to med. jours. Home: 901 S Ashland Ave Apt 1109 Chicago IL 60607

LICHTWARDT, HARRY EDWARD, physician, surgeon; b. Rio De Janeiro, Brazil, Dec. 16, 1918; s. Henry Herman and Ruth (Moyer) L.; A.B., Oberlin Coll., 1940; M.D., Washington U., 1943; m. Genevieve Isabelle Merry, July 28, 1947; children—Ronald Arthur, Gregory Edward. Intern Woman's Hosp., Detroit, 1943-44, surgery resident, 1946-47; resident surgery Dearborn VA Hosp., 1947-48; urology resident Wayne County Gen. Hosp., Eloise, Mich., 1948-51; practice medicine specializing in urology, Royal Oak, Mich., 1951—; chief urology Wm. Beaumont Hosp., Royal Oak, 1955—; vice chief urology, instr. Wayne County Gen. Hosp., 1958-65. Chmn. bd. mgmt. Birmingham (Mich.) YMCA, 1966-68. Served with M.C., AUS, 1944-46. Decorated Bronze Star. Diplomate Am. Bd. Urology. Fellow A.C.S.; mem. AMA, Mich., Oakland County med. socs., Am. Urol. Assn. (sec. North Central sect. 1971-74, pres. 1975, exec. com. 1980—). Club: Orchard Lake Country. Home: 4801 N Harsdale Bloomfield Hills MI 48013 Office: 3535 W 13 Mile Rd Royal Oak MI 48072

LICKERMAN, CAROLYN ADLER, councilwoman; b. Cleve., Dec. 21, 1929; d. Emil Herman and Frances Lucille (Reiss) Adler; student Northwestern U., 1948-50; B.S. in Bus. Adminstrn., Ind. U., 1977; m. Howard Wayne Lickerman, Aug. 12, 1950; children—David Simon, Nancy Lickerman Halik, Jo Anne. Fifth dist. rep. Columbus (Ind.) City Council, 1976—; dir. Irwin Union Bank & Trust Co.; mem. human devel. policy com. Nat. League Cities, 1979—. Founder, pres. Columbus LWV, 1961; mem. Columbus Human Rights Commn., 1967-70; pres. Columbus Redevel. Commn., 1975-76; bd. dirs. Columbus Pro Musica, 1978—; treas. Tulip Trace council Girl Scouts U.S.A., 1979—; div. chmn. United Way, 1974, campaign vice chmn., 1981; pres. Isabel Ritter chpt. Am. Field Service, 1971; mem. William R. Laws Found., 1968-76, pres., 1971; sec. nominating com. Sch. Bd. Nominating Assembly; chmn. Art in Public Places project Columbus City Hall, 1981. Mem. Columbus C. of C. (transp. com.), Beta Gamma Sigma. Democrat. Home: 3354 Woodland Pkwy Columbus IN 47201

LICKTEIG, PATRICIA ANN, artist, educator; b. Detroit, July 3, 1922; d. Marvin Allen and Erma (Nort) King; grad. Center for Creative Studies, 1960; student Wayne State U., 1959-64; children by former marriage—Sharon Gail, Edward Glenn. Instr. life drawing Macomb Community Coll., 1969-72; faculty Center for Creative Studies, Detroit, 1957—, asso. prof. fine art, 1976-80, prof., 1980—; lectr., demonstrator in field; exhibited in one-woman shows: Verve Art Gallery, 1965, Lochmoor Country Club, 1980, Macomb Theatre Gallery, 1981; group shows Detroit Artists Market, Soc. Arts and Crafts, Nat. Drawing Exhbn., Wichita, Kans. (award), West Mich. Exhbn. (Painting award), Mich. Artist Exhbn., Detroit Inst. Arts (prize), Pa. Acad., Watercolor USA, Mich. Watercolor Soc., Mich. State Fair; represented in permanent collections. Recipient painting award Internat. Platform Assn., 1981. Office: Center for Creative Studies 245 E Kirby St Detroit MI 48202

LIDDELL, LEON MORRIS, educator, librarian; b. Gainesville, Tex., July 21, 1914; s. Thomas L. and Minnie Mae (Morris) L.; B.A., U. Tex., 1937, J.D., 1937; B.L.S., U. Chgo., 1946; grad. study Internat. Law, Faculty of Polit. Sci., Columbia. Admitted to Tex. bar, 1937; claims dept. Hartford Accident and Indemnity Co., Houston, 1937-38; pvt. practice Gainesville, 1938-39; claim dept. Pacific Mutual Life Ins. Co., Kansas City, Mo., 1939-41; asst. prof. law and law librarian U. Conn., 1946-47; asst. prof. law U. Minn., 1949-50, asso. prof. law and law librarian, 1950-54, prof., 1954-60; prof. of law, law librarian U. Chgo., 1960-74, emeritus, 1974—; librarian, prof. law Northwestern U., Chgo., 1974-80. Served from 2d lt. to maj. AUS, 1941-46. Mem. Tex. State Bar, Am. Assn. Law Libraries, Spl. Libraries Assn. Home: 880 Lake Shore Dr Chicago IL 60611 Office: 357 E Chicago Ave Chicago IL 60611

LIDMAN, J(OHN) KIRBY, transp. planner; b. Dickens, Iowa, July 12, 1930; s. John Harold and Marie (Sorenson) L.; B.S., Iowa State U., 1961. Mem. Iowa Hwy. Commn., 1958-60, 61-62; wind-tunnel design engr. airframe and rotorcraft div. B & C Splty., Inc., Ames, Iowa, 1963-69; project engr. Iowa Hwy. Commn., 1969—. Registered profl. engr., Iowa. Fellow Brit. Interplanetary Soc.; mem. Am. Inst. Aeros. and Astronautics, Air Force Assn., Civil Air Patrol, Soaring Soc. Am., ASCE, Exptl. Aircraft Assn., Nat. Aeros. Assn., Nat. Soc. Profl. Engrs. Home: 607 Carroll Av Ames IA 50010 Office: Iowa Dept Transp Ames IA 50010

LIEBE, LAWRENCE ARNOLD, office supply co. exec.; b. Rosholt, Wis., Feb. 11, 1938; s. Florian P. and Delphine M. (Glischinski) L.; B.B.A., U. Wis., 1965; m. Clare Ann Blexrud, June 20, 1964; children—Susan Ellen, Jennifer Ann, Michael Lawrence, Kara Lynn. Purchasing agt. Western Products, Milw., 1964-69, prodn. control mgr., 1965-69; sr. buyer Allis Chalmers, West Allis, Wis., 1969-70; pres., owner Economy Indsl. Office Supply, Inc., New Berlin, Wis., 1970—. Pres. parish council Holy Apostle Congregation, New Berlin, 1977-80. Mem. New Berlin C. of C. (dir. 1974-77). Roman Catholic. Home: 3220 S Monterey Dr New Berlin WI 53151 Office: 14100 W Cleveland Ave New Berlin WI 53151

LIEBEN, EILEEN BROOKS, univ. adminstr.; b. N.Y.C., Jan. 23, 1916; d. Thomas and Margaret Ann (Culkin) Brooks; A.B., Manhattanville Coll., 1937; M.A., Creighton U., 1962; m. Theodore J. Lieben, Dec. 13, 1941; children—Peter, John, Thomas Geoffrey. Asst. dean of women Creighton U., Omaha, 1962-64, dean of women, asso. dean of students, 1964—, coordinator honors seminar for arts and scis. freshmen, 1977, moderator ethics and values seminars for profl. students, 1981. Recipient Mary Lucretia Creighton award for advancement of women, 1981; Disting. Adminstr. award Creighton U., 1973; Sperry Hutchinson grantee, 1971; Nebr. Arts Council grantee, 1976; Nebr. Com. for Humanities grantee, 1979. Mem. Am. Assn. Higher Edn., Nat. Assn. Women Deans, Adminstrs. and Counselors, AAUW, Nebr. Assn. Women Deans and Counselors, Joslyn Liberal Arts Soc., Friendship Force. Roman Catholic. Home: 514 S 57 St Omaha NE 68106 Office: Creighton Univ Omaha NE 68178

LIEBENOW, ROLAND RUDOLPH, ins. co. med. dir.; b. Jefferson County, Wis., Sept. 17, 1922; s. Rudolph F. and Elma L. (Loper) L.; B.S., U. Wis., Madison, 1944, M.D., 1948; m. Martha E. Anderson, May 5, 1950; children—Linda S., Ronald M., Kurt S. Intern, Colo. Gen. Hosp., Denver, 1948-49; gen. practice medicine, Stevens Point, Wis., 1949-50; practice medicine specializing in medicine and surgery, Lake Mills, Wis., 1950-67; asso. med. dir. Northwestern Met. Life Ins. Co., Milw., 1967—; teaching asst. in anatomy Med. Sch., U. Wis., 1944, research asst. in pharmacology, 1946-47; mem. med. staffs Deaconess Hosp., Milw., Watertown Meml., Ft. Atkinson Meml. hosps.; pres. exec. com. Marquardt Manor Nursing Home, Watertown, Wis., 1972-74; pres. med. staff St. Mary's Hosp., Watertown, 1959; vice chief of staff Ft. Atkinson (Wis.) Meml. Hosp., 1967; clin. asst. prof. Med. Coll. Wis., 1976—. Chmn. troop com. Sinnissippi council Boy Scouts Am., 1965-76; vice chmn. bd. elders Lake Mills Moravian Ch., 1972-75. Served to capt. M.C., U.S. Army, 1953-55. Named Alumnus of Year, Lake Mills Alumni Assn., 1972. Diplomate Am. Bd. Family Practice; cert. Bd. Life Ins. Medicine. Fellow Am. Acad. Family Practice; mem. Jefferson County Med. Assn. (pres. 1959-60), Wis. State Med. Soc. (mem. ho. of dels. from Jefferson County 1980-81, mem. Fed. legislation com. 1981), AMA, Assn. Life Ins. Med. Dirs., Aerospace Med. Assn., Soc. for Prospective Medicine, Am. Legion, Phi Kappa Phi. Republican. Clubs: Northwestern Mut. Stamp (pres. 1972-76), Wis. Fedn. Stamp Clubs, Philatelic Classics Soc., Masons. Co-author monograph on chloroform, 1951. Home: 309 Lakeview Ave Lake Mills WI 53551 Office: 720 E Wisconsin Ave Milwaukee WI 53202

LIEBERMAN, DAVID JOSEPH, physician, county Phila., Feb. 2, 1928; s. Wolf Meyer and Anne (Elman) L.; student Temple U., 1946; M.D., Jefferson Med. Coll., Phila., 1950; postgrad. U. Pa., 1952-53, 66; M.P.H., Harvard U., 1966. Rotating intern Phila. Gen. Hosp., 1950-52; camp physician Camp Pinecrest, Dingman's Ferry, Pa., 1951; ship surgeon Grace Line, N.Y.C., 1952-53; resident gen. surgery Albert Einstein Med. Center, Phila., 1953-56; tour physician Harlem Globetrotters Basketball Exhbn. World Tour, 1956; practice medicine specializing in gen. surgery Albert Einstein Med. Center, Phila., 1956-59; instr. surgery Albert Einstein Med. Center, No. Div., 1956-59, Albert Einstein Med. Center Sch. Nursing, 1956-59, Temple U. Sch. Medicine, 1956-59; asso. surgeon Rush Hosp. for Diseases of Chest, 1956-59; surgeon Home for the Jewish Aged, 1956-59; mem. courtesy surg. staff Germantown Hosp., Rolling Hill Hosp., 1956-59; ship surgeon U.S. Lines, N.Y.C., 1960; chief surg. services Warren (Pa.) State Hosp., 1960-64; physician I, Pa. Dept. Health, Bur. Field Services, 1964-65; asst. dist. health dir. Phila. Dept. Pub. Health, Bur. Dist. Health Services, 1966-67; dir. Bur. Med. Policies and Standards, Office Med. Services and Facilities, Pa. Dept. Pub. Welfare, Harrisburg, 1968-69, med. assistance adminstr. Bur. Med. Assistance, Office Family Services, 1967-68; exec. med. dir. med. assistance program N.Y.C. Dept. Health, 1969-71; dir. Dept. Ambulatory Care Services and Community Medicine, French and Polyclinic Med. Sch. and Health Center, N.Y.C., 1971-74; dir. Monroe County Health Dept., Monroe County Med. Examiner, Monroe, Mich., 1975—; non-resident lectr. dept. health planning and adminstrn. U. Mich. Sch. Public Health, 1976—; mem. tech. adv. council Mich. Cancer Found. Community Outreach Detection and Care Project, 1975-77; mem. Monroe County Substance Abuse Adv. Council, 1975—; lectr. emergency med. technicians course Monroe County Community Coll., 1977-80; bd. dirs., pres. elect Monroe Boys Club, 1976-78; bd. dirs. Monroe chpt. Mich. Soc. Mental Health, 1977-78; mem. exec. com. Monroe County Health Planning Council, 1975—, chmn., 1977-78; mem. exec. com. Monroe County Emergency Med. Services Council, 1975—, chmn., 1977-78; health services coordinator Monroe County Office Civil Preparedness, 1975—; mem. Monroe County Commn. Aging, 1975—; bd. dirs. Monroe County Opportunity Program, 1975-81; mem. environ. health adv. com. Mich. Dept. Public Health, 1976—; gen. mem. Comprehensive Health Planning

Council Southeastern Mich., 1975—; bd. dirs. Southeastern Mich. Council on Emergency Med. Services, 1977—, Monway Citizens Health Council, 1978—; trustee Monroe County unit Mich. Cancer Found., 1978-81; mem. profl. edn. com. Monroe unit Am. Cancer Soc., 1978-79; chmn. physicians subcom. United Way Monroe County, 1975, chmn. profl. div., 1976; div. co-chmn. Monroe County Health Day, Mich. Week 1979; bd. dirs. South Monroe County Citizens Health Council, 1979—. Recipient Dr. Francis W. Shain prize, Gold medal in surgery Jefferson Med. Coll., 1950, Best Resident prize Albert Einstein Med. Center Phila., 1956; USPHS traineeship grantee, 1965-66. Fellow Am. Public Health Assn. (governing council 1978), Royal Soc. Health; mem. Am. Acad. Health Adminstrn., Am. Coll. Preventive Medicine, Southeastern Mich. Health Assn. (dir. 1975—, 1st v.p. 1979-80, 2d v.p. 1981—), Mich. Public Health Assn. (dir. 1978-80, chmn. adminstrv. div. 1978-79), Alcohol and Drug Problems Assn. N.Am., Mich. Health Officers Assn. (dir. 1977-80, chmn. environ. and occupational health com. 1977-80, 81—, com. on med. examiner system 1978-80, 81—, sec. 1979-80), Mich. Alcohol and Addiction Assn. (dir. 1979-80), Nat. Assn. County Health Officers, Nat. Assn. Med. Examiners, Am. Assn. Public Health Physicians, Met. Opera Guild, Am. Hort. Soc. Jewish. Home: 3861 N Custer Rd Monroe MI 48161 Office: 650 Stewart Rd Monroe MI 48161

LIEBERMAN, STANLEY BERTRAM, real estate broker and developer; b. Trenton, N.J., Mar. 31, 1938; s. Abram Herbert and Freida (Chamowitz) L.; A.B. in Bus. Mgmt., Rutgers U., 1960; m. Jill Gustafson; children—Louis, Jonathan, Rebecca, Kimberly, Wendy, Julie. Sales mgr. Am. Photograph Corp., N.Y.C., 1960-67, Root Photographers, Chgo., 1968-71; pres. Lieberman Inc., Realtors, Buffalo Grove, Ill., 1971—, Video Homes of Am., Inc., Buffalo Grove, 1972—; instr. real estate prins. Harper Coll., Palatine, Ill. Police and fire commr. City of Buffalo Grove, 1971-75; founder, pres. Congregation Beth Judea, 1968-70; treas. United Synagogue of Am. Midwest, 1970. Served as 1st lt. U.S. Army, 1960. Mem. N.W. Suburban Bd. Realtors (pres.), Realtors Nat. Mktg. Inst. Clubs: Rotary (past treas.), B'nai B'rith. Home: Rural Route 2 Box 419 A Long Grove IL 60047 Office: 400 W Dundee Rd Buffalo Grove IL 60090

LIEBERT, LUCILLE A., psychologist; b. Coffeyville, Kans., Feb. 10, 1934; d. Albert L. and Mamie Josephine (Jordan) L.; B.M., Kans. State Coll. of Pitts., 1955; M.A., U. of Notre Dame, 1968; post-grad. U. of Mo., Kans. City, 1976—. Tchr. music Coffeyville, Kans., 1955-67; tchr. music Holy Name Jr. High Sch., Coffeyville, 1964-67; dir. counseling services Marymount Coll., Salina, Kans., 1968-71; psychologist Psychol. Services, Kansas City, Mo., 1971—; profl. cons. Cath. Diocese of Kansas City and St. Joseph, Mo., 1971—, Cath. Diocese of Jefferson City, Mo., 1975—. Mem. Mo., Kans., Am. psychological assns., Am. Personnel and Guidance Assn., Phi Kappa Phi. Roman Catholic. Home: 9100 Riggs Ln Overland Pk KS 66212 Office: 1207 Grand Ave Kansas City MO 64106

LIEBIG, APRIL MAE, moving co. exec.; b. Indpls., Feb. 26, 1955; d. Herbert George and Rosemary Ann (Doran) Liebig; student Ind. State U., 1973-75, Ind. U. Purdue U., Indpls., 1976—. Dispatcher, sec. Nora Security Inc., Indpls., 1975-79; service coordinator Carleton Transit Co., Indpls., 1979—. Leader, Girl Scouts, 1974-75. Mem. U.S. Racquetball Assn., Nat. Assn. Female Execs., Smithsonian Assos., Indpls. Mus. Art, Nat. Trust Historic Preservation, Nat. Abortion Rights Action League, Police League Ind. Presbyterian. Club: Recreational Equipment Inc. Coop. Home: 8445 Evergreen Ave Indianapolis IN 46240 Office: 1333 E 86th St Indianapolis IN 46240

LIEBLEIN, SEYMOUR, aerospace research engr.; b. N.Y.C., June 17, 1923; s. David and Rose Lieblein; B.M.E., CCNY, 1944; M.S. in Aero. Engring., Case Inst. Tech., 1952. With NASA and predecessor, 1944-76, branch chief, space power VTOL propultion, 1960-62; tech. asst. to div. chief V/STOL and noise, (all Cleve.), 1972-76; mgr., owner Tech. Report Services, Cleve., 1977—. Recipient Exceptional Service medal NACA, 1957. Asso. fellow AIAA (Goddard award 1967); mem. ASME (Gas Turbine Div. award 1961). Author papers in field. Home: 3400 Wooster Rd #320 Rocky River OH 44116 Office: PO Box 16163 Rocky River OH 44116

LIEBLER, EDWARD CHARLES, veterinarian, constrn. co. exec.; b. Brown City, Mich., Apr. 6, 1939; s. Harris D. and Golda Elfleda (Hollenbeck) L.; B.S., Mich. State U., 1962, D.V.M., 1964; student Cooley Law Sch., Lansing, Mich., 1981—; m. Carol Sue Kerrins, Sept. 10, 1960 (div. 1972); children—Juli Kristina, Edward Jae; m. 2d, Sharon D. Willis, Nov. 2, 1973. Individual practice vet. medicine, Caro, Mich., 1964-72; founder, pres. Liebler Constrn. Co., 1966—, Caro Land Devel. Corp., 1971-73; dir. Caro Devel. Corp., 1977—. Chmn. Citizens Com. to Become City, 1969-70; bd. dirs. Mich. Eye Collection Center, Inc.; mem. Tuscola County Republican exec. com., 1976—. Mem. Mich. (ethics com. 1969-70), Thumb (pres. 1967-68) vet. med. assns., Home Builders Assn. Thumb (pres. 1971), Nat. Home Builders Assn. (dir. 1974-75, 77-79). Mason, Lion (pres. 1968-69, zone chmn. 1972-73, dep. dist. gov. 1973-75). Club: Amateur Radio (Caro). Home: 645 Westchester Dr Caro MI 48723 Office: 429 N State St Caro MI 48723

LIEBLER, JOHN WILLIAM, waste water operations cons.; b. Rockville Center, L.I., Dec. 10, 1942; s. Vincent John and Bernadette Theresa (Debus) L.; grad. with highest honors, Water and Wastewater Tech. Sch., Neosho, Mo., 1975; m. Ruth P. Ellington, Feb. 7, 1964; children—Michael Gerard, Tammy Grace, Sean Christopher. With U.S. Nat. Park Service, Mt. Rainier, Grand Canyon North and South rims, 1966-74; prin., owner, founder Environ. Enterprises, Lake Ozark, Mo., 1974—. Mem. Republican Nat. Com., 1980-81. Served with USAF, 1961-65. Holder A lic. in waste water treatment, A lic. in water treatment. Mem. Am. Water Works Assn., Water Pollution Control Fedn., Nat. Wildlife Assn., Mo. Water Pollution Control, Fedn., Okla. Water Pollution Control Fedn., Mo. Water and Sewage Conf., Conservation Fedn. Mo., Nat. Audubon Soc. Roman Catholic. Home: Bagnell MO 65026 Office: PO Box 441 Lake Ozark MO 65049

LIEBMAN, MONTE HARRIS, educator, poet, songwriter, cons., psychiatrist; b. Milw., July 20, 1930; s. William and Ida (Zaichek) L.; B.S., U. Wis., 1953, M.D., 1957; 1 dau., Lori Kay. Intern, Mount Zion Hosp., San Francisco, 1958; resident psychiatry VA Hosp., Palo Alto, Calif., 1959; psychiatry fellow Marquette U., Milw., 1960-62; practice medicine, specializing in psychiatry, Milw., 1962-75; staff Mount Sinai Hosp., Milw., 1962—; asst. clin. prof. Med. Coll. Wis., Milw., 1962—; psychotherapy supr. Mount Sinai Med. Center Clinic and Clergy, Milw., 1965-74; cons. tchr. Central State Hosp., Waupun, Wis., 1974-75; cons. Pub. Health Center Waukesha (Wis.) community health aid program, 1972-73; tchr. adult non-credit sch. Marquette U., 1974-76; facilitator Free U., Milw., 1978—, Martin Luther King Center, Milw.; creative writing instr. Ind. Learning, Milw., 1980-81; counselling instr., bd. dirs. Pregnancy Aftermath Helpline, Milw., 1976—; counseling instr., bd. dirs. Birthright of Waukesha. Fellow Am. Psychoanalytic Physicians; mem. The Sayers, Internat. Soc. Psychiatric Research, Milw. Mental Health Assn., Wis. Concerned Citizens for Life, Internat. Soc. Gen. Semantics. Author: Communications from the Private World of a Psychiatrist, Counselor's Handbook on Hysteria and Schizophrenia, What Is Love and How to Find It, Introduction to Psychotherapy, Elements for Contemporary Counseling and Development (all 1977); exec. editor Med. Psych. Publs.; contbg. editor: Pasticcio, 1973 (booklet). Home: W310 N6431 N Beaver Lake Rd Hartland WI 53029 Office: 104 Hill St Hartland WI 53029

LIEBSCHER, VOLKMAR KARL CHRISTIAN, educator; b. Munich, Germany, Jan. 30, 1925; came to U.S., 1955, naturalized, 1963; s. Mathias Heinrich and Marie Minna Ida L.; B.S. in Civil Engring., Staatsbauschule Munich, 1953; M.S. in Bus., So. Ill. U., 1971, Ph.D. in Econs., 1972; m. Lotte Woellinger, Mar. 6, 1950; 1 dau., Christine. Field and design engr. Held & Franke, Munich, 1953-54; project engr. L. Moll, Munich, 1954-55; field engr. Briggs, Blitman & Posner, New Rochelle, N.Y., 1955-57; project supt. Wasson Engrs., 1957-58; resident constrn. engr. Ill. Dept. Transp., 1958-69; research and teaching asst. Bus. Research Bur., So. Ill. U., Carbondale, 1970-72; Univ. prof. econs., mgmt. and urban planning Governors State U., Park Forest South, Ill., 1972—; prin. Universal Realty Cons., 1978—. Mem. Planning Commn., also Bldg. Commn., Richton Park, Ill., 1974—. Registered profl. engr., Ill., Ind.; lic. real estate broker, Ill. Mem. AAUP, Am. Econ. Assn., Am. Real Estate and Urban Econ. Assn., Nat. Assn. Realtors, Am. Inst. Real Estate Appraisers, Realtors Nat. Mktg. Inst., Greater South Suburban Bd. Realtors, Ill. Econ. Assn., Assn. Ill. Real Estate Edn. Office: PO Box 73 4557 C W 211th St Matteson IL 60443 also Coll Bus and Public Adminstrn Governors State U Park Forest South IL 60466

LIECHTY, G(EORGE) FREDERICK, ret. hosp. service exec.; b. Monroe, Ind., Jan. 1, 1914; s. M. Simon and Rosina (Wittwer) L.; B.S., Eastern Mich. U., 1938; M.B.A., U. Mich., 1940; m. Helen Holly Van Sickle, June 23, 1945; children—Susan Liechty Hall, John, Thomas, Jane. Bus. mgr. U. Mich. Hosp., Ann Arbor, 1941-45; br. mgr. Blue Cross-Blue Shield, Chgo., 1945-47, asst. dir., 1947-63, v.p. mktg., 1963-67, sr. v.p. mktg., 1967-73, sr. v.p. corp. affairs, 1973-79; broker, sales asso. George Cyrus Co. Inc., Evanston, Ill., 1979—; lectr. Sch. Hosp. Adminstrn., Northwestern U., Evanston, 1946-50. Trustee, Meth. Student Found., Northwestern U., 1952-58; mem. Evanston High Sch. Bd. Edn., 1965-72; trustee Northwestern Meml. Hosp., Chgo., 1969-80; bd. dirs., exec. com. Chgo. Lung Assn., 1974—; bd. dirs., chmn. income devel. com. Srs. Action Services, Inc., 1980—; bd. assos., pres. Georgian Home, Evanston, 1981—. Mem. Am. Mgmt. Assn., Am. Pub. Health Assn., Ill. Hist. Soc., Ill. C. of C., Chgo. Assn. Commerce and Industry, Chgo. Athletic Assn., Field Mus. Natural History. Clubs: Execs., Rotary (Chgo. pres. 1962-63). United Methodist (del. No. Ill. Conf. 1959-80; chmn. adminstrv. bd. 1964-66, trustee 1971-77, chmn. 1973-74). Home: 2436 Central Park Ave Evanston IL 60201

LIEDERBACH, WILLIAM HERMAN, indsl. chems. co. exec.; b. Milw., May 24, 1920; s. William Philip and Meta Elsa (Kloese) L.; B.S., Iowa State U., Ames, 1948; m. Lucille Lauscher, Sept. 14, 1941; children—William Joseph, Robert Andrew. Sales engr. E.I. DuPont de Nemours & Co., Perth Amboy, N.J., 1948-56; process engr. Globe-Union, Milw., 1956-58; engring. mgr. RCA, Indpls., 1958-73; plant mgr. Brulin Co., Inc., Indpls., 1974—; a founder, v.p. sales Midwest Research Microscopy, Inc., Milw., 1971—. Committeeman Republican party, Hamilton County, Indpls., 1980—. Served with U.S. Army, 1942-46. Registered profl. engr., Ind. Fellow Am. Ceramic Soc. Republican. Methodist. Home: 820 Nantucket Dr Cicero IN 46034 Office: 2920 Martindale St Indianapolis IN 46205

LIEFER, GERALD HENRY, lawyer; b. Flint, Mich., Feb. 27, 1928; s. Henry C. and Cora Marie (Wessling) L.; B.B.A., U. Mich., 1950, M.B.A., 1951, J.D., 1954; m. Theresa Ann Bailey, Nov. 19, 1966; children—Ann, Kathryn. Admitted to Mich. bar, 1954; asst. cashier Old Kent Bank and Trust Co., 1954-63; loan officer Hartger & Williard, Inc., Grand Rapids, Mich., 1963-66; staff atty. Legal Aid Soc., Grand Rapids, 1966-73; dir. family law center Legal Aid Soc. of Western Mich., 1973-75; clk. of court U.S. Dist. Ct. for Western Dist. Mich., Grand Rapids, 1975—. Mem. Grand Rapids Bar Assn., Alpha Kappa Psi. Lutheran. Home: 2129 Chesaning Dr SE Grand Rapids MI 49506 Office: 458 Federal Bldg Grand Rapids MI 49503

LIETZEN, JOHN HERVY, railroad co. employee; b. Kansas City, Kans., July 17, 1947; s. Walter E. and Kathleen M. (Griffith) L.; B.S., Mo. Valley Coll., Marshall, 1974; M.S., U. Mo., Kansas City, 1976; m. Nora R. Massey, June 12, 1966; children—Gwendolyn Therese, Anne Gabrielle. Yard conductor Union Pacific R.R., Kansas City, Kans., 1971-77, personnel officer, Omaha, 1977-78, div. personnel, Cheyenne, Wyo., 1978-79, sr. tng. officer dept. claims, 1979—. Bd. dirs. Berkshire Village, Kansas City, Kans., 1976-77; bd. ministries Valley View Meth. Ch., Overland Park, Kans., 1976-77; pastor and staff relations com. Hanscom Park United Meth. Ch., 1980-81; asst. leader Wyo. council Girl Scouts U.S.A., Cheyenne, 1978-79, asst. leader, Omaha, 1980—; exec. bd. Nebr. affiliate Am. Diabetes Assn., 1981—. Served with U.S. Army, 1968-71. Decorated Army Commendation medal. Mem. Am. Soc. Personnel Adminstrn. (chpt. dir. 1978-79), Am. Personnel and Guidance Assn. Republican. Home: 310 S 51st St Omaha NE 68132 Office: 1416 Dodge St Omaha NE 68179

LIEU, JOHN, physician; b. Hankow, China, Aug. 15, 1904; s. Fan Hou and Sing Ten (Chen) L.; M.D., St. John's U., Shanghai, China, 1926; D.T.M., Liverpool (Eng.) U., 1939; m. Dorothy A. Irwin, Aug. 31, 1974; children—John, Gladys. Came to U.S., 1959, naturalized, 1964. Supt. Works & Mine Hosp., Tayeh, Hupeh, China, 1928; asst. med. officer, Shanghai Municipal Council, 1929-36; doctor-in-charge Municipal Hosp., Shanghai, 1936-45; chief surgeon Soochow (China) Hosp., 1945-46; pvt. practice, Soochow, 1946-49, Columbus, Ohio, 1962—; chief surg. dept. Municipal Sixth Hosp., Shanghai, 1949-57; asst. port health officer, Hongkong; dir. Emerick Hosp., Columbus State Inst., 1961-65; mem. staff Grant Hosp., Columbus. Rockerfeller scholar, 1940. Fellow Royal Soc. Health, Eng.; mem. Am., Ohio med. assns., Acad. Medicine, AAAS, Ohio Acad. Sci. Presbyn. (deacon 1968). Home: 645 Neil Ave Columbus OH 43215 Office: 370 E Town St Columbus OH 43215

LIFER, CHARLES WILLIAM, youth assn. exec., educator; b. Knox County, Ohio, Sept. 11, 1938; s. Cecil C. and Rosalie M. (Workman) L.; B.S., Ohio State U., 1961, M.S., 1966, Ph.D., 1969; postgrad. (Kellogg fellow) U. Md., 1976; m. Gwyenna Ogier, July 5, 1959; children—Jennifer, Laurie, Amy. With 4-H, 1961—, Ohio state leader extension studies and evaluation, Columbus, 1969-70, asst. dir. and state leader, Columbus, 1970—; asst. prof. agrl. edn. Ohio State U., 1969-73, asso. prof., 1973-75, prof., 1975—; grad. intern U. Md., 1976; bd. dirs. Ohio 4-H Found., Nat. 4-H Council; mem. Nat. Youth Curriculum Task Force. Served with U.S. Army, 1957-63. Recipient Hon. State Future Farmers Am. degree Ohio Future Farmers Am., disting. service award, 1977. Mem. Nat. Assn. Extension Agts., 4-H (Disting. Service award 1977), Adult Edn. Assn. U.S.A., Ohio Extension Profs. Assn., Ohio Assn. Adult Edn., Central Ohio Adult Edn., Ohio State U. Alumni Assn. (life), Epsilon Sigma Phi (Disting. Service award 1981), Gamma Sigma Delta, Phi Delta Kappa. Republican. Methodist. Clubs: Ohio State U. Pres.'s, A.B. Graham. Author 4-H publs.; editor: Extension Evaluation Handbook, 1970; Success Handbook, 1980, II, 1981. Home: 984 Lansmere Ln Columbus OH 43220 Office: 2120 Fyffe Rd Columbus OH 43210

LIFER, JEANNE MCINTURF, educator; b. Rockbridge, Ohio, Mar. 6, 1936; d. Merlyn Morgan and Hallie Elizabeth McInturf; B.S., Ashland Coll., 1963; M.Ed., Akron U., 1968; m. Gene E. Lifer, Sept. 4, 1955; children—Morgan Edward, Lise Llewellyn. Elem. tchr. West Holmes Schs., Millersburg, Ohio, 1961-62, Lucas (Ohio) Schs., 1963-68; reading tchr. Wayne County Joint Vocat. Sch., Smithville, Ohio, 1970-74, 77—. Mem. Nat. Council Tchrs. English, Internat. Reading Assn., Ohio Reading Assn., Nat. Vocat. Assn., Ohio Vocat. Assn., Mohican Area Bus. Assn., Mohican C. of C. Methodist. Home: Rural Route 2 Box 105 Loudonville OH 44842

LIFSCHULTZ, PHILLIP, cons.; b. Oak Park, Ill., Mar. 5, 1927; s. Abraham Albert and Frances (Siegel) L.; B.S., U. Ill., 1949; J.D., John Marshall Law Sch., 1956; m. Edith Louise Leavitt, June 27, 1948; children—Gregory Ross, Bonnie Gail, Jodie Ann. Tax mgr. Arthur Andersen & Co., Chgo., 1957-63; asst. controller taxes, ins. Montgomery Ward & Co., Inc., Chgo., 1963-67, divisional v.p. taxes, 1967-69, v.p. taxes, 1969-78; fin. v.p., controller Henry Crown & Co., Chgo., 1978-80; prin. Phillip Lifschultz & Assos., 1980—; v.p., dir., Randhurst Corp., Mount Prospect, Ill., 1965-77; project mgr. Exec. Services Corp. Cons. Project for Chief fin. officer Chgo. Bd. Edn. Lectr. accounting, taxation DePaul U. Evening Div., Chgo., 1957-61. Mem. adv. bd. Auditor Gen. Ill., 1965-73, chmn. adv. bd., 1972-73; chmn. Transition Task Force to Ill. Dept. Revenue, 1972-73. Mem. adv. council Coll. Commerce and Bus. Adminstrn., U. Ill. at Urbana-Champaign, 1977-78. Served with AUS, 1945-46. C.P.A., Ill. Mem. Ill. Bar Assn., Tax Execs. Inst., Nat. Retail Mchts. Assn. (chmn. taxation com. 1975-78), Am. Retail Fedn. (chmn. com. taxation and fiscal policy 1971-73), Internat. Fiscal Assn., Am. Inst. C.P.A.'s, Ill. Soc. C.P.A.'s, Nat. Assn. Tax Adminstrs., Internat. Assn. Assessing Officers, Civic Fedn. (dir. 1975—, pres. 1980), Nat. Tax Assn. Tax Inst. Am., Tau Delta Phi, Beta Alpha Psi. Clubs: City (bd. govs.), Standard, Executives (Chgo.). Home: 976 Oak Dr Glencoe IL 60022 Office: 208 S LaSalle St Chicago IL 60604

LIFSHITZ, SAMUEL, gynecologist; b. Mexico City, Mex., Sept. 24, 1944; came to U.S., 1969, naturalized, 1979; s. Ignacio and Sonia (Goldberg) L.; B.A., Nat. Prep. Sch., 1962; M.D., Nat. Autonomous U. Mex., 1968; m. Shulamith, Feb. 9, 1969; children—Ivonne, Isaac. Intern, Maimonides Med. Center, Bklyn., 1969-70, resident in ob-gyn, 1970-74; fellow in gynecologic oncology, U. Iowa, Iowa City, 1974-76, asst. prof. dept. ob-gyn, 1976-80, asso. prof., 1980-81, dir. div. gynecologic oncology, prin. investigator gynecologic oncology group; asso. prof., asso. dir. div. gynecologic oncology Southwestern Med. Sch., Dallas, 1981—. Diplomate Am. Bd. Ob-Gyn. Mem. Am. Coll. Obstetricians and Gynecologists, Soc. Gynecologic Oncologists, Central Assn. Ob-Gyn, A.C.S., N.Y. Acad. Scis., Iowa Ob-Gyn Soc. Author books; also contbr. articles to med. publs. Office: U Tex Southwestern Med Sch Dallas TX 75243

LIFTO, CLAYTON GERALD, mgmt. specialist; b. Red Wing, Minn., Sept. 27, 1946; s. James Clayton and Mattie Mae (Turner) L.; A.A., U. Md., 1977, B.S., 1977; postgrad. Bethel Theol. Sem., 1977-79, U. Wis., Stout, 1980-81; m. Ruth Ellen Anderson, June 6, 1970; children—Nickie Marie, Christopher Matthew. Gen. mgr. Red Wing Area Investment Co., 1977-79; mgmt. specialist Wis. Indianhead Tech. Inst., 1979—; founder, pres. N.Am. Mgmt. and Investment Co., New Richmond, Wis., 1980—; small bus. cons.; condr. supervisory workshops for mfg. first-line suprs. Served with U.S. Army, 1965-77; Viet Nam. Decorated Army Commendation medal, Gallantry Cross with palm. Mem. Am. Mgmt. Assn., Wis. Assn. Mgmt. Educators, Wis. Assn. Vocat. Adult Educators, St. Croix Valley Employers Assn. Republican. Baptist. Home: Route 4 Box 285A New Richmond WI 54017 Office: 1019 S Knowles Ave New Richmond WI 54017

LIGGETT, DELMAS ENOCH, chem. co. exec.; b. nr. Ravenwood, Mo., Feb. 19, 1907; s. Enoch and Lula Lenora (Coffey) L.; B.S., Northwestern Mo. State Coll., 1933; M.S., U. Mo., 1939; postgrad. U. Wyo., 1938, U. Colo., 1947. Supt. schs., Gentry County, Mo., 1935-41; dir. elementary edn. State Colo. vocational adviser VA, 1945-49; co-owner sch. training jewelers, 1949-51; with Akona Chem. Corp., Anoka, Minn., 1951-76, pres. 1953-76. Trustee Akona Chem. Corp. Employees' Profit Sharing Trust, 1970—. Served with USAAF, 1941-45. Mem. Nat. Geog. Soc., Audubon Soc., Nat. Wildlife Assn., Smithsonian Soc., Cousteau Soc., Sierra Club. Club: Mpls. Athletic. Home: 411 Dayton Rd River Manor Apt 227 Champlin MN 55316

LIGGETT, DELMORE, educator, cons.; b. Rising Sun, Ind., May 19, 1906; s. Harvey C. and Lydia Belle (Hannah) L.; B.S., Ind. U., 1941; D. Psychology in Metaphysics, D. Metaphysics, Indpls. Coll. of Divine Metaphysics, 1966, D.D., 1968. Prin. Cass-Union Sch., 1931-42; postmaster, Rising Sun, 1942-45; prin. Freedom, Ind., 1949-53; tchr. English Aurora (Ind.) High Sch., 1953-68. Cons. Ind. State Tchrs. Assn., Nat. Edn., World Field Research. Trustee BonDurant Agape Ministry, 1966—. Recipient certificate of Appreciation Nat. Police Officers Assn., 1970. Fellow World Acad.; mem. Nat. Hist. Soc. (founder), Ohio-Switzerland Counties Ret. Tchrs. Assn. (pres. 1975—), UN Assn. of U.S., Internat. Platform Assn., Memorabilia Soc. of Taylor U., Ind. U. Alumni Assn., Taylor U. Hon. Alumni Assn. OAS. Democrat. Methodist. Clubs: Pres.'s of Hanover Coll., Century, Am. Traveliares, World Traveler. Home: Box 35 RD Suite 1 Rising Sun IN 47040

LIGGETT, KENNETH RHODES, psychologist; b. Davenport, Iowa, Jan. 20, 1943; s. Kenneth Witwer and Doris (Gowan) L.; B.A., Union Coll., 1965; M.A., U. Nebr., 1975, Ph.D., 1977; m. Twila Marie Christensen, June 2, 1966. Office claims rep. State Farm Ins. Co., Lincoln, 1965-70; revenue ops. clk. Nebr. Dept. Revenue, Lincoln, 1971-73; asso. psychologist Nebr. Dept. Correctional Services, Lincoln, 1973-77, psychologist, 1977—, adminstr. programs, 1979—. Regents tuition scholar, 1972-75. Mem. Am. Psychol. Assn., Nebr. Psychol. Assn., Am. Correctional Assn., Nebr. Correctional Assn., Internat. Transactional Assn., Nebr. Soc. Profl. Psychologists. Presbyterian. Home: 3001 Kipling St Lincoln NE 68516 Office: 2800 W Van Dorn St Lincoln NE 68502

LIGGETT, THOMAS JACKSON, theol. sem. pres.; b. Nashville, May 27, 1919; s. Thomas Jackson and Lola Cleveland (Ballentine) L.; A.B., Transylvania U., Lexington, Ky., 1940, D.H.L., 1969; M.Div., Lexington Theol. Sem., 1944; LL.D. (hon.), Culver-Stockton Coll., Canton, Mo., 1959, InterAm. U., San German, P.R., 1965, Butler U., Indpls., 1975; D.D., Eureka (Ill.) Coll., 1973; m. Virginia Corrine Moore, Aug. 12, 1941; children—Thomas Milton, Margaret Ann Liggett Herod. Ordained to ministry Christian Ch. (Disciples of Christ), 1940; pastor, Danville, Ky., 1943-45; missionary to Argentina, 1946-56; prof. ch. history Facultad Evangelica de Teologia, Buenos Aires, 1949-56; pres. Seminario Evangelica de P.R., 1957-65; exec. sec. for Latin Am., Christian Ch., 1965-67; exec. chmn. World Mission, 1967-68; pres. United Christian Missionary Soc., 1968-74; pres. Christian Theol. Sem., Indpls., 1974—; mem. gen. bd. Nat. Council Chs., 1969-75; del. World Council Chs., Uppsala, Sweden, 1968. Mem. Disciple of Christ Hist. Soc., Council Christian Unity. Democrat. Author: Where Tomorrow Struggles to be Born, 1970. Office: 1000 W 42d St Indianapolis IN 46208

LIGGETT, TWILA MARIE CHRISTENSEN, instructional TV co. exec.; b. Pipestone, Minn., Mar. 25, 1944; d. Donald L. and Irene E. (Zweigle) Christensen; B.S., Union Coll., Lincoln, Nebr., 1966; M.A., U. Nebr., 1971, Ph.D., 1977; m. Kenneth R. Liggett, June 2, 1966. Dir. vocal and instrumental music Sprague (Nebr.)-Martell Public Sch., 1966-67; tchr. vocal music public schs., Syracuse, Nebr., 1967-69; tchr. Norris Public Sch., Firth, Nebr., 1969-71; cons. fed. reading project public schs., Lincoln, 1971-72; curriculum coordinator Westside Community Schs., Omaha, 1972-74; dir. State program Right-to-Read, Nebr. Dept. Edn., 1974-76; asst. dir. Nebr. Commn. on Status of Women, 1976-80; asst. dir. devel. and acquisitions Great Plains Nat. Instructional TV Library, U. Nebr., Lincoln, 1980—; cons. U.S. Dept. Edn., 1981; Far West Regional Lab., San Francisco, 1978-79. Bd. dirs. Planned Parenthood, Lincoln, 1979-81. Mem. Nat. Assn. Ednl. Broadcasters, Assn. Supervision and Curriculum Devel., Bus. and Profl. Women's Fedn., Phi Delta Kappa. Presbyterian. Home: 3001 Kipling St Lincoln NE 68516 Office: PO Box 80669 Lincoln NE 68501

LIGHT, CHRISTOPHER UPJOHN, economist, writer; b. Kalamazoo, Jan. 4, 1937; s. Richard and Rachel Mary (Upjohn) L.; A.B., Carleton Coll., 1958; M.S. (Internat. fellow 1961-62), Columbia U., 1962; M.B.A., Western Mich. U., 1967; Ph.D., Washington U., 1971; m. Lilykate Victoria Wenner, June 22, 1963; children—Victoria Mary, Christopher Upjohn. Editor, pub. The Kalamazoo Mag., 1963-66; pres. Mich. Outdoor Pub. Co., Kalamazoo, 1965-68; chmn. Fin. Dept., Roosevelt U., Chgo., 1975-78; free-lance writer, Chgo. Trustee, Harold and Grace Upjohn Found., 1967—. Recipient Mich. Welfare League ann. press award, 1967. Mem. Am. Econs. Assn., Fin. Mgmt. Assn., Midwest Fin. Assn., Soc. Profl. Journalists. Contbr. articles to profl. jours. Office: 919 N Michigan Ave Suite 3008 Chicago IL 60611

LIGHT, GARY LYLE, transp. co. exec.; b. St. Johns, Mich., July 20, 1937; s. Edward L. and Margaret N. L.; B.S. in Acctg., Ferris State Coll., 1962; m. Janet K. Henning, June 16, 1962; children—Paul, Mark, Michael. Audit mgr. Arthur Andersen & Co., Los Angeles, Indpls., 1962-69; asst. controller Stanray Corp., Chgo., 1969-71; audit mgr. Arthur Andersen & Co., Indpls., 1971-73; exec. v.p. Mayflower Corp., Indpls., 1973—. Served with USNR, 1955-58. Mem. Am. Inst. C.P.A.'s, Fin. Execs. Inst. Club: Kiwanis. Home: 3460 Briar Pl Carmel IN 46032 Office: 9998 N Michigan Rd Carmel IN 46032

LIGHTFOOT, LYLE EUGENE, architect; b. Kansas City, Kans., Feb. 7, 1921; s. Alma Lincoln and Mary Agusta (Opperman) L.; B.S., Iowa State U., 1945; m. Anna Mae Pennick, Oct. 25, 1944. Architect, asso. Gentry & Voskamp-Architects, Kansas City, Mo., 1955-63; architect Boyer & Biskup-Architects, Omaha, 1963-66; asso., chief architect Bucher & Willis, Salina, Kans., 1966-74; individual practice, Salina, 1975—; past mem. Salina Planning Commn. Recipient Design award, Stran Steel Corp., 1967. Mem. AIA. Republican. Mem. Reorganized Ch. of Jesus Christ of Latterday-Saints. Mason. Home: 1007 Scott St Salina KS 67401 Office: 1007 Scott St Salina KS 67401

LIKINS, WILLIAM HENRY, coll. adminstr., minister; b. Louisville, Feb. 7, 1931; s. William Hazel and Katherine (Horrar) L.; A.B., Asbury Coll., 1951; M.Div., Emory U., 1954; postgrad. Louisville Presbyn. Sem., 1954-56, Harvard U., 1957-58; Th.D., Boston U., 1961; Ph.D., George Peabody Coll., Vanderbilt U., 1979; m. Martha Ann Grant, June 20, 1952; children—Jeanne Marie, William Henry, David Scott. Ordained to ministry Methodist Ch., 1955; sr. minister Fisk Meml. Meth. Ch., Natick, Mass., 1962-67; dir. nat. div. higher edn. United Meth. Ch., Nashville, 1967-76; exec. dir. Area Commn. on Higher Edn., Louisville, 1976-77; v.p. for devel. Adrian (Mich.) Coll., 1979—; mem. Detroit Conf. Meth. Ch., 1979—; cons., lectr., U.S., Can., Europe. Bd. dirs. Goodwill-Lenawee Assn. Retarded Citizens, Adrian, 1980—; mem. Estate Planning Council of Lenawee County, 1980—. Orme M. Miller fellow, 1954. Mem. Council for Advancement and Support Edn., Am. Assn. for Higher Edn., World Meth. Council, Phi Delta Kappa. Club: Rotary. Author: Basic Christian Beliefs, 1978; also newspaper articles. Contbr. book revs., articles in field to profl. jours. Home: 1062 Oram Dr Adrian MI 49221 Office: Adrian Coll 110 S Madison St Adrian MI 49221

LILEY, PETER EDWARD, educator; b. Barnstaple, North Devon, Eng., Apr. 22, 1927; came to U.S., 1957; s. Stanley E. and Rosa (Ellery) L.; B.Sc., Imperial Coll., U. London, 1951, Ph.D. in Physics, 1957, D.I.C., 1957; m. Elaine Elizabeth Kull, Aug. 16, 1963; children—Elizabeth Ellen, Rebecca Ann. With British Oxygen Engring., London, 1955-57; asst. prof. mech. engring. Purdue U., West Lafayette, Ind., 1957-61, asso. prof., 1961-72, asso. sr. researcher Thermophys. Properties Research Center, 1961-72, prof. mech. engring., sr. researcher Center for Info. and Numerical Data Analysis and Synthesis, 1972—; cons. in field. Served with Royal Corps of Signals, 1945-48. Mem. ASME, Inst. of Physics (London). Lutheran. Contbr. articles to profl. jours.; author: Sect. 3, Perry's Chemical Engineers Handbook, 1963, edit. 1973; editor Internat. Jour. Thermophysics, 1980—. Home: 3608 Mulberry Dr Lafayette IN 47905 Office: Dept Mech Engring Purdue U West Lafayette IN 47907

LILLARD, JOHN STOLL, investment counselor; b. Cin., May 31, 1930; s. William Parlin and Margaret Scott (Stoll) L.; B.A., U. Va., 1952; M.B.A., Xavier U., 1961; m. Paula Polk, Sept. 12, 1953; children—Lisa, Lynn, Pamela, Angeline, Paula. Investment counselor Haydock, Peabody & Hawley, 1955-59; investment counselor Scudder, Stevens & Clark, Cin., 1959-64, gen. partner, 1964-77; pres. Scudder, Stevens & Clark, Inc. (Ill.), Chgo., 1971-77, chmn. bd., 1973-77, chmn. finance, budget and audit com. of bd. dirs., 1975-77, nat. mktg. dir., 1976-77, spl. partner, 1977-79; pres. JMB Instl. Realty Inc., Chgo., 1979—; chmn. bd. Gateway Investment Advisors, Inc., Cin., 1979—; dir. Stryker Corp., Kalamazoo, Cintas Corp., Cin., Gateway Option Income Fund, Cin., Mathers Fund. Mem. fin. com. Community Chest of Greater Cin., 1970-71; active United Appeal, United Fine Arts Funds; trustee Cin. May Festival, 1963-68, pres. bd., 1965-67; trustee Cin. Union Bethel, Hamilton County Diagnostic Clinic, Childrens Home, Boys Clubs Greater Cin., Hillsdale-Lotspeich Schs., Hull House Assn., Old Peoples Home, Chgo., Ill. Childrens Home and Aid Soc., Chgo. Orchestral Assn.; trustee Cin. Symphony Orch., 1965-71, pres., 1968-71; trustee, mem. exec. com. Ravinia Festival Assn. Served to lt. (j.g.) USN, 1952-55. Mem. Cin. Soc. Fin. Analysts (past pres.), Queen City Assn. (past pres.). Clubs: Miami of Ohio (past pres.); Racquet (past pres.), Queen City, Commercial, Commonwealth (Cin.); Camargo (past treas., mem. bd. govs.); Onwentsia (Lake Forest); Tavern (Chgo.). Home: 1300 N Waukegan Rd Lake Forest IL 60045 Office: 875 N Michigan Ave Chicago IL 60611

LILLETHORUP, GALEN KRAGH, advt. corp. exec.; b. Creighton, Nebr., Nov. 3, 193[illegible] s. Niels and Lela Magrette (Kragh) L.; student U. Nebr., Omaha, 1949-51, B.S. with distinction, 1956; student Trinity U., San Antonio, 1953-54; m. Nellie Marcene Athen, Nov. 17, 1956; children—Kerri Lynn, Timothy Scot. TV news writer, reporter, photographer, news film editor Sta. KMTV, Omaha, 1954-57, TV continuity dir., 1957-58, TV promotion mgr., 1959-63; writer, producer Bozell & Jacobs, Omaha, 1964-68, v.p., creative dir., Los Angeles, 1969-70, v.p., account supr., Omaha, 1970-80; pres. Galen & nellie, Inc., Omaha, 1980—. Served with USAF, 1951-54. Recipient Journalism Alumni Achievement award U. Nebr., Omaha, 1962; various advt. awards. Mem. Omaha Fedn. Advt. (dir. 1979), Graphic Artists Guild. Republican. Lutheran. Home: 10285 Grand Ave Omaha NE 68134 Office: Galen & Nellie Inc 1012 Douglas-on-the-Mall Omaha NE 68102

LILLIE, RICHARD HORACE, investor, real estate developer, ret. surgeon; b. Milw., Feb. 3, 1918; s. Osville Richard and Sylvia Grace (Faber) L.; B.S., Haverford Coll., 1939; M.D., Harvard U., 1943; M.S. in Surgery, U. Mich., 1950; m. Jane Louise Zwicky, Sept. 24, 1949; children—Richard Horace, Diane Louise. Intern, U. Mich. Hosp., Ann Arbor, 1943-44, resident, 1946-50; chief of surgery, Milw. Hosp., 1968-79; practice medicine specializing in surgery, Milw., 1951-81; clin. prof. emeritus Med. Coll. Wis.; pres. Lillie 18-94 Corp.; v.p. Waukesha Motor Inns.; dir. Northwestern Mut. Life Ins. Co.; investor, real estate developer, 1981—. Bd. dirs. Goodwill Industries. Served with M.C. AUS, 1944-46. Mem. Am. Bd. Surgery, A.C.S., Central Surg. Assn., AMA, Wis. Surg. Soc. Episcopalian. Clubs: Milw. Athletic, Univ. of Milw., Milw. Yacht, Town. Contbr. articles to surg. jours. Home: 6500 N Lake Dr Milwaukee WI 53217 Office: 811 E Wisconsin Ave Milwaukee WI 53202

LILLY, JAMES PETER, editor; b. Columbia City, Ind., July 6, 1926; s. DeWitt Jennings and Theresa Marie (Cates) L.; B.S. in Agr., Purdue U., 1953; m. Wilma Jean Vehling, Mar. 15, 1953; children—Cheryl Ann, Kimberly Sue, Mary Sydney. With Prairie Farmer, 1954—, editor, 1978—. Served with USAAF, 1944-46. Mem. Am. Agrl. Editors Assn. (past pres.), Am. Agrl. Econs. Assn. Presbyterian. Office: 2001 Spring Rd Oak Brook IL 60521

LIM, SUNG MAN, educator; b. Suweon, Korea, July 13, 1934; came to U.S., 1961, naturalized, 1973; s. Sun Hack and Bock Soon (Lee) L.; B.S., Seoul U., 1957, M.S., 1959; M.S., Miss. State U., 1963; Ph.D., Mich. State U., 1966; m. Ah Ok Park, Dec. 28, 1968; children—Louis Sung-Hoon, Elizabeth Chung-Min. Research asso. in plant pathology U. Ill., Urbana, 1967-71, asst. prof., 1971-77, research plant pathologist, asso. prof. U.S. Dept. Agr.-SEA-AR, Urbana, also dept. plant pathology U. Ill., 1977—; mem. Nat. Soybean Germplasm Com., 1979. Recipient Am. Soybean Assn. Research Recognition award, 1981; NIH grantee, 1967-70; U.S. Dept. Agr. grantee, 1970-74. Mem. Am. Phytopathol. Soc. (genetics com. 1978), Am. Soc. Agronomy, Crop Sci. Soc. Am. Contbr. articles to profl. jours.; asso. editor Plant Disease, 1980. Home: 2304 Shurts Circle Urbana IL 61801 Office: 1102 S Goodwin St Urbana IL 61801

LIM, TOH-WOON, dentist; b. Fukien, China, Jan. 18, 1948; s. Si-Sin and Po-Sio (Kwa) L.; came to U.S., 1971, naturalized, 1978; B. Dental Surgery, Inst. Medicine, 1971; D.M.D., Tufts U., 1973, postgrad periodontics, 1975. Staff dentist R.I. Hosp., Providence, 1974; staff periodontist Woodstock Hosp., Good Shepherd Hosp., Crystal Lake, Ill., 1976—. Mem. Chgo., McHenry County dental socs., Am., Ill. dental assns., Am. Acad. Periodontology. Methodist. Office: 111 Virginia St Crystal Lake IL 60014

LIMBACHER, JAMES LOUIS, librarian, educator; b. St. Marys, Ohio, Nov. 30, 1926; s. Fritz J. and Edith (Smith) L.; B.A., Bowling Green State U., 1949, M.A., 1954; M.S. in Edn., Ind. U., 1955; M.S. in L.S., Wayne State U., 1972. Audio-visual librarian Dearborn (Mich.) Dept. Libraries, 1955-82; instr. history and appreciation motion picture Univ. Center for Adult Edn., Detroit, 1965-72, Marygrove Coll., 1966-67, Wayne State U., 1973—. Recipient Mich. Librarian of Yr. award, 1974. Mem. Am. Fedn. Film Socs. (nat. pres. 1962-65), ALA, Ednl. Film Library Assn. (nat. pres. 1966-70), Soc. Cinema Studies, Alpha Tau Omega, Theta Alpha Phi, Omicron Delta Kappa, Beta Phi Mu. Author: Four Aspects of the Film, 1969; A Reference Guide to Audiovisual Information, 1972; Film Music: From Violins to Video, 1973; The Song List, 1973; Sexuality in World Cinema, 1982. Editor: Using Films, 1967, Feature films, annually 1968—; Haven't I Seen You Somewhere Before, 1979—, Keeping Score, 1980—. Contbr. monthly record column Previews, 1963-77, weekly column to Dearborn Press, 1956-73. Home: 21800 Morley Ave Dearborn MI 48124

LIMBERG, FRANKLIN HAROLD, pharm. co. exec.; b. Marinette, Wis., July 21, 1943; s. Franklin William and Genieve Sarah (Boivin) L.; B.S., Marquette U., 1966; M.S., Wichita State U., 1968; m. Carol Ann Wenderoth, 1944; children—Franklin C., Jason W., Neal J. Research scientist Wyeth Labs., West Chester, Pa., 1968-70; dir. quality control Badger Labs., Jackson, Wis., 1970-74; dir. quality control Marion Health and Safety div. Marion Labs., Rockford, Ill., 1974-79, v.p. quality assurance and regulatory compliance, Kansas City, Mo., 1979—. Mem. Health Industries Assn., Am. Pharm. Assn., AAAS. Home: 15907 Meadow Ln Stanley KS 66223 Office: Marion Labs 10236 Bunker Ridge Rd Kansas City MO 64137

LIMJOCO, URIEL ROMEY, surgeon; b. Philippines, May 11, 1935; s. Emilio Tinchuangco and Clara Jugo (Romey) L.; came to U.S., 1961, naturalized, 1972; A.A., M.D., U. Philippines, 1957; M.S., U. Wis., 1966; m. Carolyn Jo Olson, Aug. 22, 1964; children—Lucy, Lisa, Jeffrey, Laura, Jennifer, Victoria. Instr. anatomy U. Philippines Med. Sch., 1957-61; resident in surgery U. Wis. Hosp., 1962-67; staff surgeon VA Hosp., Madison, Wis. also instr. surgery U. Wis. Med. Sch., 1967-69; practice medicine specializing in surgery, Menomonee Falls, Wis., 1969—; mem. staff Community Meml. Hosp., Menomonee Falls, chief surgery, 1972-74, pres. med. staff, 1977-78; mem. staff Elmbrook Hosp., Brookfield, Wis. Bd. dirs., chmn. pub. edn. com. Wis. div. Am. Cancer Soc., 1974—, pres. Waukesha County unit, 1973-75. Diplomate Am. Bd. Surgery. Fellow A.C.S.; mem. Wis. Surg. Soc., Milw. Acad. Surgery, Waukesha County Med. Soc. Republican. Roman Catholic. Club: North Hills Country. Contbr. to med. jours. Home: W213 N5349 Adamdale Dr Menomonee Falls WI 53051 Office: N84 W16889 Menomonee Ave Menomonee Falls WI 53051

LIN, FU-SHAN, physician; b. Taiwan, China, Oct. 15, 1941; s. Chow-Lian and Pen (Ding) L.; came to U.S., 1971, naturalized, 1977; B.M., Taipei Med. Coll., 1967; m. Chung Chiou-Jin, Nov. 17, 1968; children—Ki-Hon, Wan-In, James Anthony, Robert John. Intern, Taipei City Hosp., Taiwan, 1966-67; resident in pediatric MacKay Meml. Hosp., Taiwan, 1968-71; rotating intern Barberton (Ohio) Citizen Hosp., 1971-72; resident in pediatrics Trumbull Meml. Hosp., Warren, Ohio, 1972-73, Akron (Ohio) Children's Hosp., 1973-74; physician The Windham (Ohio) Clinic, Inc., 1974-80, Robinson Meml. Hosp., Ravenna, Ohio, 1974—; practice medicine specializing in pediatrics and family practice, Ravenna, 1980—; instr. pediatrics Northeastern Ohio Univs. Coll. Medicine, 1980—. Served with China Air Force, 1967-68. Diplomate Am. Bd. Pediatrics, Am. Bd. Family Practice. Mem. AMA, Am. Acad. Pediatrics, Am. Acad. Family Physicians, Ohio Med. Assn., Portage County Med. Soc. Office: 6693 N Chestnut St Ravenna OH 44266

LIN, JOE JISHONG, surg. pathologist, electron microscopist; b. Yuanlin, Taiwan, Feb. 21, 1942; came to U.S., 1970, naturalized, 1976; s. True and Mee (Hwang) L.; M.D., Taipei Med. Coll., 1969; m. Sharon Cho, July 20, 1974; children—Anthony Bruce, Curtis Daniel, Evelyn Kaye. Intern U. Kans. Med. Center, 1970-71, resident in pathology, 1971-74; asso. pathologist St. Francis Hosp., Wichita, Kans., 1974—; dir. electron microscopy lab., 1977—; asso. clin. prof. pathology and surgery U. Kans. (Wichita); orthopedic researcher. Recipient best pathology paper awards U. Kans. Med. Center, 1971, 74. Mem. Internat. Acad. Pathology, Coll. Am. Pathologists, Kans. Med. Soc., Am. Soc. Clin. Pathologists, Kans. Soc. Pathologists. Contbr. to Atlas of Electron Microscopic Pathology, 1977, Year Book of Cancer, 1976. Office: 929 N Saint Francis St Wichita KS 67214

LIN, JUIYUAN WILLIAM, accountant; b. Chia-yi, Taiwan, July 8, 1937; s. Pi and Chuang (Sing) L.; came to U.S., 1969, naturalized, 1976; B.A., Nat. Chung Hsing U., 1960; M.S. (scholar 1969-70), Ill. State U., Normal, 1970; m. Meihui Su Lin, May 27, 1963; children—Eva, Karen. Tchr. acctg. Chia-yi Bus. High Sch., Taiwan, 1960-62; chief acct. Bank Communications, Taiwan, 1962-69; chief acct. Computer Service Inc., Chgo., 1970-74, Architecture Data Systems, Inc., N.Y.C., 1971-73, Bistro Restaurant Inc., Chgo., 1971-74, Astor Tower Restaurant Inc., Chgo., 1971-75; chief acct. Teng & Assos., Inc., Chgo., 1975—; tax, mgmt. cons. C.P.A., Ill. Mem. Am. Inst. C.P.A.'s, Ill. Soc. C.P.A.'s. Clubs: Tai-Chi, Tennis, Chgo. North Shore Community. Home: 1921 Washington Ave Wilmette IL 60091 Office: 220 S State St Chicago IL 60604

LIN, KUANG-MING, mech. engr.; b. Taipei, Taiwan, Mar. 10, 1932; s. Ruey-chia and Yu-twan (Hsu) L.; B.S., Nat. Taiwan U., 1956; M.S., Auburn U., 1958; Ph.D., Mich. State U., 1964; M.B.A., Bowling Green State U., 1979; m. Pi-yau Fu, Mar. 25, 1962; children—Patricia, Rhoda, Janice, Diane. Asst. instr. Mich. State U., 1958-60; asst. prof. engring. mechanics Tri-State Coll., 1961-63; asst. prof. engring. sci. Tenn. Tech. U., 1964-66, asso. prof., 1966; prin. research engr. Teledyne Brown Engring. Co., 1966-68; staff engr. tech. center Dana Corp., Toledo, Ohio, 1968-73, dep. dir. Asia-Pacific, 1973-75, mgr. internat. planning, 1975—; asso. prof. U. Ala., Huntsville, 1966-68; dir. Najico-Spicer Co., Tokyo, 1974-75. Registered profl. engr., Ohio. Mem. ASME, Soc. Automotive Engrs., ASCE, Pi Mu Epsilon, Beta Gamma Sigma. Home: 3851 Fairwood Dr Sylvania OH 43560 Office: 4500 Dorr St Toledo OH 43697

LIN, PHILIP HANS, mech. engr.; b. Fuchow, Fukien, China, Nov. 3, 1932; s. Chien Hui and Sue Inn (Chen) L.; came to U.S., 1964, naturalized, 1972; B.S., Chinese Naval Coll. Tech., Taiwan, 1955; M.S. in Mech. Engring., Tex. A. & M. U., 1965; m. Betty H. Wong, Sept. 6, 1959; children—Janet Ann, Steve M. Design engr. Comprehensive Designer, Inc., Peoria, Ill., 1965-66; devel. engr. Nat. Machinery Co., Tiffin, Ohio, 1966-79; sr. equipment engr. Hallmark Cards, Inc., Kansas City, Mo., 1979—. Fund raiser Tiffin chpt. Am. Field Service, 1974-78. Mem. Am. Soc. Mech. Engrs. United Ch. Christ. Club: Tiffin Tennis Assn. (dir., summer league chmn. 1973-78). Home: 8701 Birch Ln Prairie Village KS 66207 Office: Hallmark Cards Inc 2501 McGee St Kansas City MO 64108

LINCOLN, KENDALL T., engring. co. exec.; b. Adrian, Mo., Aug. 23, 1932; s. Howard Thomas and Frances Eddith (Timmons) L.; B.S. in Bus. Adminstrn., U. Mo., 1954; m. Patricia Lee Gratz, Apr. 6, 1957; 1 dau., Debra Lee. Auditor U.S. Army Audit Agy., Denver, 1954-55; accountant firm Peat, Marwick, Mitchell & Co., Kansas City, Mo., 1957-63; controller firm Howard, Needles, Tammen & Bergendoff, Kansas City, Mo., until 1974, finance dir., 1974-76, asso., dir. finance, 1976—. Cons. Engr., Kansas City, 1963—. Served with AUS, 1955-57. C.P.A., Mo., Kans. Mem. Am. Inst. C.P.A.'s, Mo. Soc. C.P.A.'s, Nat. Assn. Accountants, Financial Execs. Inst., Profl. Services Mgmt. Assn., Beta Gamma Sigma. Home: 6324 Dearborn Dr Mission KS 66202 Office: 1805 Grand Ave Kansas City MO 64108

LIND, CHESTER CARL, banker; b. Firesteel, S.D.,, Aug. 4, 1918; s. Carl L. and Dorothy (Kiehl) L.; student U. S.D., 1940, No. State Coll. Sch. Banking, U. Wis., 1951; m. Marie C. Decker, June 4, 1941; children—Karen (Mrs. Darrel Pederson), James, Stephen, John. With Dewey County Bank, Timber Lake, S.D., 1935, 1st Nat. Bank, Aberdeen, S.D., 1935-66, asst. v.p., 1947-50, v.p., 1950-54, exec. v.p., dir., 1954, pres., dir., 1954-66; exec. v.p. First Am. Nat. Bank, Duluth, Minn., 1966-68, pres., dir., 1968-75; exec. v.p. N.W. Bancorp., Mpls., 1975-79, pres., chief exec. officer, 1979—; tchr. bank mgmt. Minn. Sch. Banking, St. Olaf Coll. Chmn. St. Indsl. Expansion Agy., 1963-64, Nat. Alliance Businessmen, Dulugh, Superior, Wis., 1970; past v.p. bd. dirs. Upper Midwest Devel. Council. Served to maj. AUS, 1941-46. Decorated Bronze Star medal; named Outstanding Young Man, Aberdeen Jaycees, 1949, Boss of Year, 1956. Mem. Minn. Bankers Assn. (mem. council), Duluth C. of C. (past pres.). Clubs: Masons, Shriners, Elks, Mpls. Home: 8441 Irwin Rd Bloomington MN 55437 Office: 1200 NW Bank Bldg Minneapolis MN 55480

LIND, FRANK EDWIN, regional planning agy. exec.; b. New Albany, Ind., Sept. 8, 1947; s. Edwin H. and Mildred E. L.; student Ind. U. SE Campus, Jeffersonville, 1965-66, 68-69, Ball State U. Sch. Urban and Regional Planning, 1966-68, 69-70; B.S. in Sociology, U. Louisville, 1972, community devel. cert. 1980, cert. prins. and current practices urban planning, 1980, M.S. in Community Devel., 1981; 1 son. With New Albany City Plan Commn., 1964-69, 70-72, 73-74, planning technician, 1968-69, chief planner, 1970-72, exec. dir., sec., 1973-74; chief draftsman Muncie (Ind.) City Plan Commn., 1969-70; mgr. Toyz of Muncie, Inc., 1970; study dir. Madison County (Ind.) Council Govts., 1970; commr. bldg. New Albany Bd. of Public Works and Safety and City Plan Commn., 1970-72; exec. dir. River Hills Regional Planning Commn., New Albany, 1974—; mem. Rural Area Devel. Com.; mem. Ind. Transp. Adv. Group; mem. Ind. Airport Systems Plan Adv. Com.; mem. So. Ind. Transit Com.; mem. Transp. Tech. Com., Louisville; mem. Clean Air Act Subcom., Louisville; mem. indsl. devel. com. Clark County C. of C. Neighborhood vice-chmn. Metro United Way, New Albany, 1973; chmn. New Albany-Floyd County Drug Abuse Council, 1973; mem. adv. com. Prosser Vocat. Center, New Albany. Mem. Ind. Assn. Regional Councils (pres. 1978), Internat. City Mgmt. Assn. Clubs: Kiwanis (New Albany). Office: 4201 Grantline Rd New Albany IN 47150

LINDAHL, PAUL BERNARD, contract rep.; b. Ashland, Wis., Apr. 19, 1946; s. Garfield Bernard and Margaret Lorraine (Enquist) L.; B.S. with honors, Wis. State U., 1968; M.B.A., U. Wis., 1972; m. Margaret Jean Lulich, Sept. 29, 1973. Procurement analyst Def. Systems div. Sperry Univac, St. Paul, 1972-75, hardware cost estimator, 1976-77, mfg. proposal coordinator, 1977-78, cost. acctg. standard specialist, 1978-79, sr. contract rep., 1979—. Pres., Woodbury Jaycees, state bd. dirs., 1976-77, state exec. com., 1980-81. Served with U.S. Army, 1968-70. Mem. Assn. M.B.A. Execs., Nat. Contract Mgmt. Assn., Omicron Delta Epsilon, VFW, Am. Legion, Alpha Kappa Psi. Home: 7465 Paul Rd Woodbury MN 55119 Office: PO Box 3525 Saint Paul MN 55165

LINDBERG, CARL ROBERT, rehab. facility exec.; b. Chgo., July 4, 1942; s. Carl Adolf and Alma (Kinsey) L.; M.S. in Rehab. Services Adminstrn., DePaul U., 1971; m. Colleen Sue Attig, Aug. 15, 1964; children—Keith Robert, Sara Jo. Asst. dir. Opportunity House, Inc., Sycamore, Ill., 1965-65, exec. dir., 1965-68; asst. dir. Aurora (Ill.) Assn. Retarded, 1970; exec. dir. Will County Sheltered Workshop, Inc., Joliet, Ill., 1970—. Mem. Assn. Rehab. Facilities, Am. Assn. Mental Deficiency, Nat. Rehab. Assn., Ill. Assn. Rehab. Facilities (past pres.), Delta Epsilon Sigma. Presbyterian. Home: 2522 Dougall St Joliet IL 60432 Office: 455 E Cass St Joliet IL 60432

LINDBERG, CHARLES DAVID, lawyer; b. Moline, Ill., Sept. 11, 1928; s. Victor S. and Alice Christine (Johnson) L.; A.B., Augustana Coll., 1950; LL.B., Yale U., 1953; m. Marian J. Wagner, June 14, 1953; children—Christine, Breta, John, Eric. Admitted to Ohio bar, 1954—; asso. firm Taft, Stettinius and Hollister, Cin., 1953-61, partner firm, 1961—; dir. Arga Co., Bellefontaine, Ohio, 1975—, Cup Vending Co. of Ohio, Cin., 1976—, Coca-Cola Bottling Corp. of Cin., 1976—, J.J. Gillespie, Inc., N.Y.C., 1978—, Taft Broadcasting Co., Cin., 1979—, Cin. Reds, Inc., 1969-80, Cin. Bengals Profl. Football Team, 1980—, Citation-Walther Corp., 1980—; corp. sec. Taft Broadcasting Co., Cin., 1973—, Hanna-Barbera Prodns., Inc., Good Samaritan Hosp., Cin., 1975—. Chmn., Better Neighborhood Sch. Com. of Cin., 1975—; chmn. law firm div. Cin. United Appeal, 1976; chmn. policy com. Hamilton County Republican Party, 1981—; pres. City of Cin. Bd. Edn., 1971, 74; pres. Zion Luth. Ch. of Mt. Washington, Cin., 1966-69; mem. Cin. Recreation Commn., 1972-73; chief local govt. com. Cin. C. of C., 1977; bd. dirs. Augustana Coll., Rock Island, Ill., 1978—; trustee Greater Cin. Center for Econ. Edn., 1976—. Mem. Am. Bar Assn., Ohio Bar Assn., Cin. Bar Assn. Republican. Lutheran. Clubs: Queen City, Commonwealth, Queen City Optimists, Cin. Country. Editorial bd. Nat. Law Jour., 1978—. Home: 1559 Moon Valley Ln Cincinnati OH 45230 Office: 800 First National Bank Center Cincinnati OH 45202

LINDBERG, ELAYNE VERNA, art gallery ofcl.; b. Browerville, Minn., Apr. 27, 1926; d. Leslie and Velma (Breighhaupt) Averill; ed. U. Minn.; m. Russell H. Lindberg, July 26, 1941; children—Gary, Bonnie Lindberg Carlson. With Dayton's Dept. Store, Mpls., 1965-71; pres. Elayne Galleries, Inc., Mpls., 1971—; appraiser and restorer paintings. Mem. Am. Soc. Appraisers, Nat. Home Fashions League (Image Maker of Yr. 1979), World Assn. Document Examiners (charter), Internat. Soc. Appraisers, Internat. Grapho Analysis Soc. Club: Calhoun Beach (Mpls.). Co-author, composer verse, sacred music, choir arrangements. Home: 2950 Dean Blvd Minneapolis MN 55416 Office: 6111 Excelsior Blvd St Louis Park MN 55416

LINDBLOM, LAWRENCE A(NDREW), ins. co. exec.; b. Manhattan, Kans., Aug. 3, 1922; s. Lawrence Andrew and Verna (McCoin) L.; B.S., Kans. State U., 1948; m. Bonnie Howell, Sept. 14, 1946; children—David Mark, Jon Andrew. Asst. underwriter Farm Bur. Mut. Ins. Co., Inc., Manhattan, Kans., 1946-48, 64—, also mem. mgmt., investment com.; chief accountant Kans. Farm Life Ins. Co., Inc., Manhattan, 1948-51, controller, asst. treas., 1951-57, treas., asst. mgr., 1958-64, v.p., gen. mgr., 1964—, also mem. mgmt., investment com.; mem. mgmt. and investment com. KFB Ins. Co., Inc., Kans. Farm Bur., Inc.; v.p. life ins. ops. Kans. Farm Bur. Services, Inc., 1979—; dir., vice chmn. Kans. Life and Health Ins. Guaranty Assn. Vice chmn. Community Chest, Manhattan, 1952, bd. dirs., 1952-53; mem. exec. bd. dirs., v.p. Coronado area council Boy Scouts Am., mem. Nat. Council, 1963-71; mem. Manhattan City Planning Bd., 1963-69; mem. Manhattan City Commn., 1969-71; chmn. Pott County, Riley County, City of Manhattan Regional Planning Commn., 1969-72; chmn. Big Lakes Area Planning Commn., 1972-73; bd. dirs. Riley County Consol. Law Enforcement Agy., 1979—. Served with USMC, World War II. C.L.U. Mem. Kans. Life Ins. Execs. Assn. (past pres.), Actuaries Club Kansas City, Farm Bur. Accountants Nat. Association (past v.p.), Ins. Accounting and Statis. Assn. (past regional vice pres.), U.S., Kans., Manhattan (dir.) chambers commerce, Am. Council Life Ins., Inst. Life Ins., Nat. Pilots Assn., Internat. Platform Assn. Republican. Methodist. Clubs: Lions, Manhattan Country (past pres., dir.), Elks. Home: 540 Wickham Rd Manhattan KS 66502 Office: 2321 Anderson St Manhattan KS 66502

LINDESMITH, LARRY ALAN, physician; b. Amarillo, Tex., July 27, 1938; s. Lyle J. and Imogene Agnes (Young) L.; B.A., U. Colo., 1959; M.D., Bowman-Gray Sch. Medicine, Wake Forest Coll., 1963; m. Diane Joyce Bakken, Nov. 22, 1973; children—Robert James, Lisa Ann, Abigail Arleen, Nathan Lyle. Intern, U. Chgo., 1963-64; resident internal medicine U. Colo. Med. Center, 1964-66; fellow pulmonary disease U. Colo. Med. Center and Webb-Waring Inst. Med. Research, 1966-67; physician, chief sect. pulmonary physiology and occupational medicine, dept. internal medicine Gundersen Clinic, Ltd., LaCrosse, Wis., 1969—; med. dir. blood gas lab. LaCrosse Luth. Hosp., 1969—; mem. courtesy staff consultations in pulmonary disease St. Francis Hosp., LaCrosse, 1971-78; instr. clin. elective in pulmonary disease Gundersen Clinic, U. Wis. Med. Sch., 1974—. Mem. Air Pollution Control Council, State of Wis., 1978-81. Served to maj., M.C., U.S. Army, 1967-69. Diplomate Am. Bd. Internal Medicine. Fellow Am. Thoracic Soc., Am. Coll. Chest Physicians; mem. Am. Assn. Respiratory Therapy, Wis. Lung Assn. (dir. 1972—, pres. 1975-77), Wis. Respiratory Care Soc. (med. adviser 1974-75), Wis. Thoracic Soc., AMA, Wis., LaCrosse County med. socs. Republican. Lutheran. Home: W4965 Woodhaven Dr LaCrosse WI 54601 Office: 1836 South Ave LaCrosse WI 54601

LINDGREN, D(ERBIN) KENNETH, JR., lawyer; b. Mpls., Aug. 25, 1932; s. Derbin Kenneth and Margaret (Anderson) L.; B.S., U. Minn., 1954, J.D., 1958; m. Patricia Ann Ransier, Dec. 17, 1955; children—Christian Kenneth, Carol Ann, Charles Derbin. Admitted to Minn. bar, 1958, U.S. Supreme Ct. bar, 1968, U.S. Tax Ct., 1959; gen. practice law Mpls., 1958—; mem., dir. Larkin, Hoffman, Daly & Lindgren, Ltd., Mpls., 1960—; dir. Hirshfield's Inc., Moniterm Corp. Mem. Ind. Sch. Dist. 274 Bd. Edn., Hopkins, Minn., 1970-76, chmn., 1972-76; mem. Ind. Sch. Dist. 287 Bd. Edn. (Area Vocat. Tech. Schs.), 1979—. Served as lt. USAF, 1955-57. Fellow Am. Coll. Probate Counsel; mem. Am., Minn. Hennepin County bar assns. Congregationalist. Clubs: Minneapolis Athletic, Interlachen Country. Contbr. articles to profl. jours. Home: 225 Hawthorne Rd Hopkins MN 55343 Office: 1500 Northwestern Financial Center 7900 Xerxes Ave S Minneapolis MN 55431

LINDGREN, STEVEN OBED, bus. exec., state senator; b. Mpls., June 29, 1949; s. Obed Franklin and Clara Verona (Peterson) L.; B.S. with distinction, U. Minn., 1971, postgrad., 1975-77; m. Cynthia Hannah Swanson, Mar. 9, 1973. Tchr. Public Schs. Burnsville (Minn.), 1971-73; research analyst Minn. Senate, St. Paul, 1974-79, mem., 1981—; mgr. regulations Minn. Hosp. Assn., Mpls., 1980; v.p. Lindgren Bros., Inc., Bloomington, Minn., 1981—. Mem. Richfield (Minn.) Bd. Edn., 1971-74, Richfield Planning Commn., 1975-80. Recipient Eagle award Boy Scouts Am., 1965. Mem. U. Minn. Alumni Assn., Am. Swedish Inst., Citizens League, U.S. Ski Assn. Republican. Clubs: Richfield Optimists, Decathlon Athletic. Office: 9001 E Bloomington Freeway Bloomington MN 55423

LINDHART, CHARLES DAVID, agribusiness exec.; b. Humboldt, Iowa, Jan. 13, 1935; s. Nels and Maurine Annibel (Goodell) L.; B.S. in Agronomy, Iowa State U., 1962; m. Ruth Y. Garside, July 20, 1962; children—Scott, Barbara. With DeKalb AgResearch, Inc. (Ill.), 1962—, Eastern area sales mgr., 1976-77, mgr. seed ops., 1977—, corp. v.p., 1981—. Served with AUS, 1957-60. Mem. Am. Soc. Agronomy, Am. Seed Trade Assn. (past com. chmn.). Republican. Presbyterian. Club: Masons. Office: DeKalb AgResearch Inc Sycamore Rd DeKalb IL 60115

LINDLE, SAMUEL GREENE, biostatistician; b. Sturgis, Ky., Nov. 12, 1950; s. Garnett Adrian and Dorothy Louise (Greenwell) L.; B.S. (Ky. Research Found. scholar 1968-71), U. Ky., 1971, M.S. (NDEA fellow 1971-72), 1972, Ph.D. (Hagan fellow, 1972-73, Dissertation fellow 1974-75), 1976; postdoctoral student U. Iowa, 1978-79. Asst. prof. math and stats. Bowling Green (Ohio) State U., 1977-78; biostatis. postdoctoral fellow, dept. preventive medicine and environ. health Med. Center U. Iowa, Iowa City, 1978-79; biostatistician coop. studies program coordinating center VA Hosp., Hines, Ill., 1979—. Mem. Eastern N. Am. region Internat. Biometrics Soc., (regional adv. bd.), Am. Statis. Assn., Soc. Clin. Trials, Inst. Math. Stats., Ky. Acad. Sci., Phi Beta Kappa, Sigma Xi, Phi Eta Sigma. Democrat. Roman Catholic. Home: 945 Troost Ave #3 Forest Park IL 60130 Office: Coop Studies Program Coordinating Center 151K VA Hosp Hines IL 60141

LINDNER, CARL H., diversified fin. holding co. exec.; b. Dayton, 1919. Chmn. bd., pres. Am. Ins. Co., Cin.; pub. Cin. Enquirer; chmn. bd. Provident Bank, Cin., Hunter Savs. Assn., Cin., United Liberty Life Ins. Co.; partner United Dairy Farmers Investment Co., Cin.; dir. United Brands, Combined Communications, Fairmont Foods. Office: Am Fin Corp 1 E 4th St Cincinnati OH 45202

LINDOW, EDWARD SMITH, JR., civil engr.; b. Pitts., Feb. 1, 1945; s. Edward Smith and Julianna (Galvin) L.; B.S. in Civil Engring., Pa. State U., 1966, M.S. in Civil Engring., 1970, postgrad. in hwy. pavement research, 1970-75; m. Diane Cain, July 16, 1977. Project mgr. Pa. Transp. Inst., University Park, Pa., 1969-75; prin. investigator Constrn. Engring. Research Lab., Champaign, Ill., 1975-78; prin. pavement, roofing and research Soil & Materials Engrs., Inc., Detroit, 1978—; instr. in field Pa. State U.; cons. to C.E., U.S. Army. Served with U.S. Army, 1967-69. Registered profl. engr., Pa., Mich. Mem. ASCE, ASTM, Transp. Research Bd., Chi Epsilon. Contbr. numerous articles in field to tech. publs. Home: 39577 Mayville Plymouth MI 48170 Office: Soil & Materials Engrs Inc 34400 Glendale Ave Livonia MI 48150

LINDSAY, JUNE CAMPBELL MCKEE, communications exec.; b. Detroit, Nov. 14, 1920; d. Maitland Everett and Josephine Belle (Campbell) McKee; B.A. with honors in Speech (McGregor Fund Mich. grantee), U. Mich., 1943; Electronics Engring. certificate Signal Corps Ground Signal Service, 1943; postgrad. (Inst. Gen. Semantics grantee), U. Chgo., 1944-45, N.Y. U. (Armour grantee), 1945-46, Columbia U., 1946-47, Wayne State U., 1960-64, U. Mich., 1964-70, 78—; M.A., Specialist-in-Aging Cert., Inst. of Gerontology, 1982; m. Powell Lindsay, Nov. 25, 1967; 1 son, Kristi Costa-McKee. Coordinator, activator McKee Prodns., Detroit, 1943-56, Being Unltd., 1957—, InterBeing, Inc., 1979—, M.U.T.U.A.L. A.I.D., 1981—; info. dir. Suitcase Theatre, Inc., Lansing and Ann Arbor, Mich. Cons. Cornelian Corner Detroit, Inc., 1957-63, Islamic Center Found. Soc., Detroit, 1959-62, City Ann Arbor Human Relations Commn., 1966-68, Urban Adult Edn. Inst., Detroit, 1968-69, Mich. Bell Telephone Co., Detroit, 1969, African Art Gallery Founders, Detroit Inst. Arts, 1964, WKAR-TV, Mich. State U., 1971—. Bd. dirs. Mus. Youth Internat., Saline, Mich. Chaplain's asst. Univ. Hosp., Ann Arbor, 1971-72; program dir. People-to-People, Ann Arbor, 1971-72; Suitcase Theatre tour coordinator Brit. Empire's Leprosy Relief Assn., 1972—; assembly cons. Baha'i Faith, 1960—; mem. Comprehensive Health Planning Council S.E. Mich. Recipient Award for Excellence Mich. Ednl. Assn., 1971, Mich. Assn. Classroom Tchrs., 1972. Mem. Soc. for Individual Responsibility, Am. Women in Radio and TV, Broadcast Pioneers, Am. Fedn. Advt., Internat. Platform Assn., Gray Panthers, Planetary Citizens, Adult Edn. Assn. U.S., Assn. Humanistic Psychology, Assn. Holistic Health, Mental Health Assn. in Mich., Mich. Soc. Gerontology, Nat. Council Sr. Citizens, Am. Assn. Ret. Persons, ACLU, Giraffe Soc., World Future Soc., Nat. Caucus, Center for Black Aged. Home: 2339 S Circle Dr Ann Arbor MI 48103

LINDSAY, VAUGHNIE JEAN, univ. dean; b. Prague, Okla., Mar. 31, 1921; d. Irvin Frank and Cora (Kennedy) Garrette; B.S. in Edn., Central State U., Edmond, Okla., 1940; M.B.Ed. with spl. distinction, U. Okla., Norman, 1959; Ed.D. with spl. distinction (Danforth fellow 1962-64), Ind. U., Bloomington, 1966; m. Joseph D. Lindsay, III, July 21, 1947 (dec.); children—Deborah Rogers, Sandra Doreson. Tchr., Guthrie (Okla.) High Sch., 1942-43; asst. prof. edn. Southwestern State Coll., Weatherford, Okla., 1959-62; asso. prof. U. Okla., 1965-70; prof. bus. edn. Sch. Bus., So. Ill. U., Edwardsville, 1970—, dean grad. studies and research, 1973—; cons., reader in field. Recipient Teaching Excellence award So. Ill. U., Edwardsville, 1973. Mem. Nat. Assn. Bus. Tchr. Edn. (exec. bd.), Nat. Bus. Edn. Assn. (exec. bd.), Am. Assn. Higher Edn., Am. Council Edn., Am. Ednl. Research Assn., Am. Mgmt. Assn., Council Grad. Schs., Nat. Council U. Research Adminstrs., Ill. Assn. Grad. Schs. (pres. 1981-82, Ill. Bus. Edn. Assn. (exec. bd.), Delta Pi Epsilon (chpt. Outstanding Bus. Educator award 1979). Author articles in field. Editor profl. jours. Office: So Ill U Box 46 Edwardsville IL 62026

LINDSAY, WANDA PETERMAN, occupational therapist; b. Abington, Pa., Aug. 23, 1956; d. Allen Frederick and Georginia Varden Lee (Stewart) Peterman; B.S., Western Mich. U., 1978; m. Ted J. Lindsay, May 20, 1978. Receptionist, film booking clk., teaching devel. asst. Western Mich. U., 1975-78; occupational therapist Children's Inst. for Devel. Disabilities, Chgo., 1979; occupational therapist alcoholism treatment unit Mercy Hosp. and Med Center, Chgo., 1979—; occupational therapy cons. specializing in alcoholism, 1979—; mem. Ill. fetal alcohol syndrome work group Ill. Gov.'s Council on Alcoholism, 1980—. Mem. Am. Occupational Therapy Assn., Ill. Occupational Therapy Assn., Spl. Interest Group on Research. Baptist. Office: Mercy Hosp and Med Center Stevenson Expressway at King Dr Chicago IL 60616

LINDSEY, PAUL COTTRILL, social worker; b. Louisville, Apr. 25, 1924; s. Charles Conway and Eileen Loretta (Cottrill) L.; student U. Louisville, 1942, Roosevelt U., Chgo., 1947-49; M.A., U. Chgo., 1949-52; m. Ouida Hogan, Aug. 10, 1962; children—Karen and Kevin (twins). With, Ill. Dept. Public Aid, Chgo., 1956—, asst. dist. office supr. 1965—. Mem. Nat. Assn. Social Workers, NAACP, Chgo. Urban League. Democrat. Author: (with Ouida Lindsey) Breaking the Bonds of Racism, 1974. Home: 7119 S Luella St Chicago IL 60649

LINDSHIELD, JAMES HARVEY, logistics engr., res. air force officer; b. Lindsborg, Kans., June 12, 1945; s. Theodore Howard and Lois Edith Hendershott (Shores) L.; B.A., U. Kans., 1967; M.B.A., U. Utah, 1972; M.P.A., Golden Gate U., 1978; m. Ann Elizabeth Dunkley, Jan. 26, 1974; children—Christopher James, Matthew John. Commd. 2d lt., USAF, 1967; advanced through grades to capt., 1970; logistics mgr. Udorn Royal Thai AFB, 1968-69, Forbes (Kans.) AFB, 1967-68, RAF, Alconbury, Eng., 1970-72; chief supply and transp. div. USAF Aerospace Guidance and Metrology Center, Newark, Ohio, 1973-74; logistics mgr. Joint U.S. Mil. Adv. Group, Thailand, 1975-77; staff logistics officer Hdqrs. Tactical Air Command, Langley AFB, Va., 1977-79; logistics engr. Cubic Corp., San Diego, 1979—. Decorated Meritorious Service Medal. Mem. Acad. Mgmt., Am. Acad. Arts and Scis., Am. Acad. Polit. and Social Scis., Am. Econ. Assn., Am. Finance Assn., Am. Mgmt. Assn., Am. Soc. Pub. Adminstrn., Brit. Inst. Mgmt., Nat. Tax Assn., Inst. Mgmt. Sci., Royal Econ. Soc., Soc. Econ. Analysis, World Future Soc. Episcopalian. Elk. Home: 226 S Washington St Lindsborg KS 67456

LINEHAN, STEPHEN DAVID, publishing co. exec.; b. Moorhead, Minn., Apr. 14, 1950; s. John David and Florence Lorraine (Volkmann) L.; B.S.B.A., U. N.D., 1973; M.B.A., Lindenwood Coll., 1980; m. Christy Fay Zilson, June 8, 1974; 1 dau., Lisa. Med. rep. Arnar Stone Labs., 1973-74; with Aladdin Synergetics, 1975-81, dist. mgr., 1976-78, regional mgr., St. Louis, 1978-80, corp. sales mgr., 1981; dir. mktg. Concordia Pub. Co., St. Louis, 1981—. Mem. Bd. of Aldermen, City of Lake St. Louis (Mo.), 1980—. Mem. Mo. Mcpl. League, Lake St. Louis Community Assn. Lutheran. Home: 9 Rouen Ct Lake Saint Louis MO 63367 Office: 3558 S Jefferson St Saint Louis MO 63367

LING, YU-LONG, polit. scientist; b. Chungking, China, Nov. 5, 1938; came to U.S., 1965, naturalized, 1975; s. Sao-tsu and Pe-i Ling; LL.B. (scholar), Soochow U., 1963; LL.M. (Univ. scholar), Ind. U., 1967, M.A., 1968, Ph.D. in Polit. Sci. (Doctoral grantee-in-aid, fee remission scholar), 1973; m. Yuriko Tomiya, Feb. 1, 1970; 1 son, Tony Shih-yeh. Tchr. English and Chinese, Chung-Su High Sch., 1963-64; lawyer, Taipei, 1964-65; asst. prof. polit. sci. Franklin (Ind.) Coll., 1972-77, asso. prof., 1977—, dir. internat. studies, 1975—, chair polit. sci. dept., 1977—; vis. prof. Ill. Wesleyan U., 1971-72; Fulbright-Hays exchange prof. Nat. Taiwan U., 1979-80; participant Conf. European Integration and European-Am. Relations, 1973, European Integration in Europe, 1974; guest speaker Nat. Reconstrn. Conf. of Rep. of China, summer 1973. Ford Found. scholar Princeton U., 1965; recipient Pacific-Cultural Found. research grant, 1978; recipient Faculty Devel. Fund, Franklin Coll., 1977, Pacific Cultural Found. research grant, 1978, Faculty Devel. Fund, 1979-80. Mem. Am. Polit. Sci. Assn., Midwest Polit. Sci. Assn., Am. Soc. Internat. Law. Club: Rotary. Contbr. articles to periodicals. Home: 15 N Forsythe St Franklin IN 46131 Office: Franklin College Franklin IN 46131

LINGELBACH, THOMAS JACK, machinery co. exec.; b. Ft. Collins, Colo., Feb. 23, 1948; s. Jack and Dorothy Jean (Ellis) L.; B.A., U. Alaska, 1973; M.P.A., U. Nebr., 1977; m. Stephanie I. Strough, May 2, 1969. Instr. bus. adminstrn., dean evening div. Nettleton Bus. Coll., Omaha, 1973-75; instr., mgmt. cons. Met. Tech. Community Coll., Omaha, 1975-78; dir. personnel devel., sales promotion mgr. Mo. Valley Machinery Co., Omaha, 1978—; mgmt. cons.; tchr. bus. adminstrn. Exec. adv. Jr. Achievement, 1979—; vol. worker Juvenile Ct. Adv. Program, 1976—. Served with USAF, 1968-72. Named Outstanding Educator, Nettleton Bus. Coll., 1974. Mem. Am. Legion, Nat. Cattlemen's Assn., Nebr. Livestock Feeders Assn., Nebr. Motor Carriers Assn. Presbyterian. Research writer. Home: 11316 Sahler St Omaha NE 68164 Office: 401 N 12th St Omaha NE 68102

LINGREN, RONALD HAL, educator, former state legislator; b. Gowrie, Ia., June 26, 1935; s. Herbert George and Zula Melissa (Bolton) L.; B.S., Ia. State U., 1960, M.A., U. Ia., 1961, Ph.D., 1965; children—Scott Allen, Kristin Lee. Psychol. cons. Jefferson County Schs., Fairfield, Ia., 1961-62; asst. dir. Pine Sch. research project, U. Ia. Hosp., Iowa City, 1962-64, cons. child psychiatry clinic, 1963-65; faculty U. Wis., Milw., 1965-74, dir. Center for Behavioral Studies, 1965-74, on leave, 1975-80, prof., 1980—; mem. Wis. Assembly, 1975-80. Served with AUS, 1953-55. Recipient Outstanding Service awards Nat. Assn. Sch. Psychologists, 1970, 72; Outstanding Service award Wis. Assn. Sch. Psychologists, 1971; Disting. Service award Wis. Psychol. Assn., 1978, legis. citation Wis. Legislature, 1981. Mem. Nat. (dir. 1969-71), Wis. (pres. 1969-71) assns. sch. psychologists, Wis. Council of Assns. of Pupil Services (pres. 1974). Contbr. articles to profl. jours. Home: W149 N8301 Norman Dr Menomonee Falls WI 53051 Office: U Wis Milwaukee WI 53201

LINK, ARTHUR A., former gov. of N.D.; b. nr. Alexander, N.D., May 24, 1914; ed. N.D. Agrl. Coll.; m. Grace Johnson; 6 children. Farmer-rancher, Alexander; mem. 92d Congress from N.D. 2d dist.; gov. of N.D., 1973-80; dir. Bismarck State Bank (N.D.). Chmn. N.D. State Adv. Council Vocational Edn., 1969-71; past mem. McKenzie County Welfare Bd. Former mem. Randolph Twp. bd.; mem. N.D. Ho. of Reps., 1947-71, minority leader, speaker of house, 1965; active N.D. Nonpartisan League. Bd. dirs. Williston U. Center Found.; former mem. local sch. bd.; former county and state mem. Farm Security Com.; chmn. resolutions com., ann. meeting Farmers Union Grain Terminal Assn., 3 yrs.; past state co-chmn. Old West Regional Commn.; past bd. dirs. McKenzie County Hist. Soc., Lewis and Clark Trail Mus.; hon. co-chmn. Nature Conservancy-Cross Ranch Project, Great Plains Energy Center, Praire Public Radio Bismarck-Manden; bd. dirs. Young Life Voyageur Cove Camp Project; mem. solicitation com. Southwest N.D. Community Center of Salvation Army; bd. dirs. Midwest League, Am. Luth. Ch. Mem. Nat. Cowboy Hall of Fame. Mem. Nat. Gov.'s Assn. (exec. com., chmn. com. on agr.), Midwest Gov.'s Conf. (chmn. 1977-78). Lutheran (past council pres.). Club: Lions. Address: Alexander ND 58831

LINK, ROY HERBERT, mfg. co. exec.; b. Detroit, Oct. 24, 1944; s. Herbert Wolfgang and Martha Fredrica (Dieter) L.; B.S. in Mech. Engring., Mich. State U., 1966, M.B.A. in Personnel, 1968; m. Dawn Isabel Airey, July 18, 1969; children—Carrie Dawn, Matthew George. Various positions Burroughs Corp., Detroit, 1968-71, sr. systems analyst internat. systems, 1960-71; with engring., electronics, sales, adminstrv. areas Link Engring., Detroit, 1971—, v.p., 1974—. Vice pres. Homeowners Orgn., 1975, 76; active civic coms. Mem. Engring. Soc. Detroit (dir.), Soc. Automotive Engrs. (mem. com.), Soc. Mfg. Engrs. Republican. Lutheran. Home: 22847 Penton Rise Novi MI 48050 Office: 13840 Elmira Detroit MI 48227

LINKMEYER, LARRY LEE, electronic technician; b. Milan, Ind., Apr. 30, 1938; s. Denton Harry and Henrietta Amelia (Cosby) L.; student DeVry Tech. Inst., 1956-58, RCA Schs., 1958-59; m. Margaret Ann Henschen, Nov. 13, 1965; children—Jon Mark, Laurie Ann, Michael Alan. Auto mechanic Schwanholts, Aurora, Ind., 1958-60; appliance serviceman Gambles', Aurora, 1960-62; chem. technician Monsanto Co., Addyston, Ohio, 1962-66; micro electronic design technician Procter & Gamble Co., Cin., 1966—; cons. Megalogic Corp., Brookville, Ohio. Served with U.S. Army, 1958. Mem. Amateur Radio Relay League. Roman Catholic. Home: 45 Country Hills Dr Aurora IN 47001 Office: 5299 Spring Grove Ave Cincinnati OH 45217

LINKS, P. VERNON, plastics co. exec.; b. Toledo, Oct. 29, 1941; s. Thomas A. and Matilda C. (Vargo) L.; B.B.A., U. Toledo, 1970, M.B.A., 1978; m. Beverly Ann McVicker, June 26, 1965; children—Jason Scott, Stephanie Lynn. Auditor, Alexander Grant & Co., C.P.A.'s, Toledo, 1968-70; sr. auditor Arthur Young & Co., Toledo, 1970-73; treas. Capitol Plastics of Ohio, Bowling Green, 1973—; cons. in field. Served with USMC, 1960-64. C.P.A., Ohio. Mem. Am. Inst. C.P.A.'s, Am. Mgmt. Assn., Am. Prodn. and Inventory Control Soc., Ohio Soc. C.P.A.'s, Bowling Green C. of C., Beta Alpha Psi, Beta Gamma Sigma. Republican. Roman Catholic. Author manual. Home: 8384 Head-O-Lake Rd Ottawa Lake MI 49267 Office: 333 Van Camp Rd Bowling Green OH 43402

LINN, CHARLES GARY, educator; b. Verona, Ont., Can., Feb. 15, 1930; came to U.S., 1930, naturalized, 1948; s. James Oliver and Helen Thlema (Peters) L.; student U. Md., 1954; B.S., Eastern Mich. U., 1960; vocat. certification U. Mich., 1972; m. Susan Jane Schlotterbeck, May 5, 1956; children—Julia, Eric, Jenifer, Sara,

Jacquline. Tchr., Cherry Hill High Sch., Inkster, Mich., 1960-62, Wayne (Mich.) Meml. High Sch., 1962-65; vocat. automotive tchr., vocat. coordinator Dexter (Mich.) High Sch., 1965—. Com. chmn. Livingston County 4-H, 1970; asst. scoutmaster Boy Scouts Am., 1971; 4-H leader Livingston County Riding for the Handicapped, 1979. Served with USAF, 1951-55. Recipient longevity service award 4-H Clubs, 1975; service award Kiwanis Club, 1977; named vocat. hon. chpt. farmer Future Farmers Am., 1975; mechanic cert., Mich. Mem. NEA, Mich. Edn. Assn., Vocat. Edn. Assn., Dexter Edn. Assn. Republican. Home: 21010 Barton St Pinckney MI 48169 Office: Dexter High Sch 2615 Baker St Dexter MI 48130

LINN, DAVID, judge; b. Augustow, Poland, Mar. 20, 1917; s. Israel Berel and Rose (Hirschfield) L.; came to U.S., 1922, naturalized, 1935; A.B., U. Chgo., 1938, J.D., 1940; m. Doris Sandra Ellison, Jan. 2, 1948; children—James Barry, Lesley Rae. Admitted to Ill. bar, 1940, since practiced in Chicago; asso. judge Circuit Ct. of Cook County, 1971-76; justice Appellate Ct. of Ill., 1976—; instr. U.S. Judge Adv. Gen. Dept.; lectr. profl. socs. Commr., Ill. Commn. Human Relations, 1966-68. Mem. Constl. Conv., Ill., 1969-70. Served to capt. U.S. Army, 1941-45. Decorated Bronze Star medal; recipient certificates of merit Chgo. Bar Assn., Decalogue Soc. Fellow Internat. Acad. Law and Sci., Am. Acad. Matrimonial Lawyers (bd. govs.); mem. Decalogue Soc., Ill. Judges Assn. (dir.), Ill. (sect. chmn.), Chgo. (com. chmn.), S. Chgo. (pres., bd. govs.) bar assns., Judicature Soc., Law Inst., Phi Beta Delta. Clubs: Quadrangle, Covenant of Ill. (Chgo.). Mem. editorial planning bd. Ill. Family Law. Contbr. articles to profl. jours. Office: 30th Floor Daley Center Chicago IL 60602

LINNE, HENRY B(ERNARD), union exec.; b. Troy, Ind., Dec. 18, 1928; s. Francis Xavier and Anna Marie (Beckman) L.; B.A., St. Meinrad (Ind.) Coll., 1951; M.Ed., U. Detroit, 1957; m. Mary Kay Worrell, July 10, 1954; children—Stephen, Gregory, John, Nancy, Sharon. Tchr. U.S. history, world geography, civics, social studies, Latin and English, Oakwood Jr. High Sch., E. Detroit, 1955-61; pres. Mich. Fedn. Tchrs., 1961-81, sec.-treas., 1981—; mem. exec. bd. Mich. AFL-CIO, 1971-81; instr. sch. fin. U. Mich., 1975; adv. com. elementary and secondary edn. Mich. Dept. Edn., 1971-80; citizens adv. com. Thomas Sch. Fin. Study, 1966-67. Mem. Mich. Constl. Preparatory Commn., 1961. Served with AUS, 1952. Recipient Tchr.'s Day award, 1959. Mem. Am. Fedn. Tchrs., Mich. Labor History Soc. Democrat. Roman Catholic. Author articles in field. Office: 14625 Greenfield Rd Detroit MI 48227

LINNEHAN, CHRISTINE JULIANNE, mfg. co. mgr.; b. Milw., Aug. 11, 1953; s. John Joseph and Lois Florence (Rickermann) L.; B.A. cum laude, St. Norbert Coll., 1976. Head computer ops. Delta Oil Products, Milw., 1976-78; programmer, systems analyst Thiem Corp., Milw., 1978-80, mgr. ops. research and systems support, 1981—. Mem. Small Systems Users Group. Home: 3237 N Marietta Ave Milwaukee WI 53211 Office: 500 W Marquette Ave Oak Creek WI 53154

LINSENMEYER, WILLIAM STUART, educator; b. Phoenix, Aug. 26, 1937; s. Ernest Joseph and Alice Elizabeth (Moore) L.; B.S., Georgetown U., 1959; student U. Fribourg, Switzerland, 1957-58; M.A., Stanford U., 1962; Ph.D., Vanderbilt U., 1972. Teaching fellow Vanderbilt U., 1963-66; instr., asst. prof., asso. prof. U. Wis., Whitewater, 1967-81, prof. history, 1981—; vis. prof. U. Wis. Study Program in Copenhagen, 1973; Fulbright lectr., U. Perugia (Italy), 1974-76; resident dir. U. Wis./DIS Study Program in Denmark, Copenhagen, 1976-77; seminar commentator Europäische Akademie, West Berlin, 1981; lectr. Library of Congress, 1979, USIS conf. Rungsted Kyst, Denmark, 1976, Royal U. Malta, 1976, U. Turin (Italy), 1976, USIS, Milan, Italy, 1976, USIS, Trieste, Italy, 1976, U. Pro Deo, Rome, 1976, U. Rome, 1975. State of Wis. research grantee, 1971-72, 73-74, 76-77, 77-78; W. German Govt. scholarship grantee, 1981. Mem. Am. Hist. Assn., Am. Com. on History of Second World War, Fulbright Alumni Assn. Contbr. to Jour. Contemporary History. Home: 1 Langdon St Madison WI 53703 Office: Dept of History Univ Wisconsin-Whitewater Whitewater WI 53190

LINTON, CYNTHIA CARPENTER, newspaper editor; b. Bronxville, N.Y., Aug. 17, 1938; d. Ralph Emerson and Cynthia Susan (Ramsey) Carpenter; student Smith Coll., 1956-58; B.A., Boston U., 1964; m. John M. Linton, June 8, 1963; children—Terrence Marshall, Robert Carpenter. Writer, Lerner Newspapers, Highland Park, Ill., 1973-78, mng. editor, 1978-79, sr. editor Lerner Newspapers, Skokie, Ill., 1980-81, sr. editor Chgo. office, 1981—. Bd. dirs. Northbrook LWV; chmn. suburban div. Operation Breadbasket; mem. Sigma Delta Chi. Recipient hon. mention Nat. Newspaper Assn., 1976, Ill. Press Assn., 1977, Suburban Newspapers Am., 1979; 1st place award Suburban Press Club, 1980, 2d place, 1981. Clubs: Chgo. Headline, Suburban Press (Chgo.); N.W. Suburban Press. Presbyterian. Office: 7519 N Ashland Ave Chicago IL 60626

LINVILLE, KENNETH WAYNE, mfg. co. exec.; b. Kansas City, Mo., July 5, 1942; s. G.L. and Willa Mae (Lungren) L.; B.S., Central Mo. State U., 1966; M.S., U. Mo., Columbia, 1968; Ph.D., Mich. State U., 1975. Instr. agronomy U. Mo., Columbia, 1968-70; instr. soils Mich. State U., 1970-72; asst. to tech. service rep., summer 1976; field devel. specialist Kalo Labs., Kansas City, 1977-79; sr. field tech. rep. Diamond Shamrock Corp., Cleve., 1979—. Mem. Am. Soc. Agronomy, Entomol. Soc. Am., Am. Phytopathol. Soc., Mich. Pesticide Assn. Address: 2080 LaMer Ln Haslett MI 48840

LIPPERT, DAVID JAMES TRIMBORN, journalism educator; b. Milw., May 23, 1919; s. Joseph E. and Eunice (Trimborn) L.; grad. Lake Forest (Ill.) Acad., 1937; B.A. in Econs., U. Wis., 1941, M.A. in Journalism, 1947, postgrad., 1962-64; Ph.D., So. Ill. U., 1969; m. Margaret Jean Seay, June 18, 1960; children—David James, Katheryn Louise, James Seay, William Leahy. Reporter, Kenosha (Wis.) News, 1946; asso. editor Wis. State Employee mag., 1947-53; gen. assignment reporter Madison (Wis.) Capital Times, 1947-50; State Capital Bur. chief Milw. Sentinel, 1950-62; lectr. journalism U. Wis., 1962-64; head journalism program U. Wis., Oshkosh, 1966—, chmn. dept. journalism, 1968—, also mem. faculty senate. Mem. Wis. Gov.'s Com. on Employment Physically Handicapped, 1950-60; mem. Winnebago County Republican Exec. Com., 1972-77, chmn. statutory com., 1972-77; Rep. precinct committeeman, 1972—. Mem. Milw., Madison press clubs, Assn. Edn. in Journalism (exec. com. 1975-76, com. on affiliates 1977-78), Nat. Council Coll. Publs. Advisers (Disting. Campus Newspaper award 1980), Am. Soc. Journalism Sch. Adminstrs. (v.p. 1974-75, pres. 1975-76, exec. council 1974-77, chmn. convs. com. 1976-81, other coms.), Wis. State Hist. Soc., Winnebago County Hist. Soc., Wis. Journalism Sch. Council, Milwaukee County Park People, Wis. Newspaper Assn., Wingspread Conf., Oshkosh C. of C. (govtl. affairs com. 1976—), Sigma Delta Chi, Phi Gamma Delta, Kappa Tau Alpha. Club: Oshkosh Power Boat. Mem. editorial bd. Journalism Educator, 1972-77. Home: 1135 Elmwood Ave Oshkosh WI 54901

LIPPERT, DONNA RAU HARNESS, chemist; b. La Porte, Ind., May 5, 1948; d. Harry N. and Mary (Maxey) Harness; B.S., Valparaiso U., 1969; m. Gerald E. Lippert, Dec. 15, 1972. Tech. trainee main chem. lab., metall. dept. Burns Harbor plant Bethlehem Steel Corp., Chesterton, Ind., 1969-71, engr., main chem. lab., 1971-73, chief spectrographer, metall. dept., main chem. lab., 1973-75, tin plate engr., metall. dept., sheet and tin mill, 1975-76, asst. chem. supr., metall. dept., sheet and tin mill, 1976—. Democrat. Lutheran. Home: 611 Franklin St Porter IN 46304 Office: Box 248 Sheet & Tin Mill Bethlehem Steel Corp Chesterton IN 46304

LIPPNER, LEWIS ALAN, hosp. adminstr.; b. N.Y.C., Mar. 10, 1948; s. Sidney and Ruth L.; B.A. cum laude, U. Pitts., 1969; cert. internat. relations U. Oslo, 1968; M.A., George Washington U., 1972. Adminstrv. resident Kings County Hosp., Bklyn., 1971-72; asso. Block, McGibony & Assos., Inc., Silver Spring, Md., 1972-73; asst. dir., planner Bklyn. Hosp., 1973-75; asst. hosp. adminstr. John E. Runnells Hosp. of Union County, Berkeley Heights, N.J., 1975-78; adminstrv. dir. Johston R. Bowman Health Center, Rush-Presbyn.-St. Lukes Med. Center, Chgo., 1978—. Mem. Am. Coll. Hosp. Adminstrs., Am. Hosp. Assn., N.J. Asst. Hosp. Dirs. Assn., Met. Health Adminstrs. Assn., Young Adminstrs. of Chgo. Home: 3020 N Waterloo Ct Townhouse 9 Chicago IL 60657

LIPS, EVAN EDWIN, state senator, ins. co. exec.; b. Bismarck, N.D., Oct. 17, 1918; s. William E. and Margaret (Griffith) L.; B.S., U. N.D., 1941; m. Elsa M. Kavonius, 1946; children—Evan William, Deborah Jane, Erik George. Pres., Murphy Ins., Inc., Bismarck, 1952—; chmn. bd. Dakota Fire Ins. Co., Bismarck, 1957—; dir. 1st Nat. Bank, Bismarck Bldg. & Loan Assn., Provident Life Ins. Co. Republican precinct committeeman, 1950; dist. chmn. Rep. party, 1950-54; mayor of Bismarck, 1954-66; mem. N.D. Senate, 1960—; alt. del. Rep. Nat. Conv., 1976. Served to maj. USMC, 1941-46; PTO; col. Res. ret. Decorated Bronze Star, Legion of Merit; recipient Boss of Yr. award Jaycees, Disting. Service award. Mem. Am. Legion, VFW, Blue Key, Alpha Tau Omega. Lutheran. Clubs: Elks, Masons, Shriners, Eagles. Office: ND Senate State Capitol Bismarck ND 58505*

LIPSCHULTZ, M. RICHARD, accountant; b. Chgo., July 5, 1913; s. Morris David and Minnie (Moskowitz) L.; student Northwestern U., 1930-35; J.D., De Paul U., 1948; m. Evelyn Smolin, May 16, 1945 (dec. 1963); m. 2d Phyllis Siegel, July 11, 1965; children—Howard Elliott, Carl Alvin, Saul Martin. Admitted to Ill. bar, 1948; auditor State of Ill., Chgo., 1938-41; conferee Internal Revenue Service, Chgo., 1941-49; tax accountant A.I. Grade & Co., C.P.A.s, Chgo., 1949-50; sr. partner Lipschultz Bros., Levin and Gray and predecessor firms, C.P.A.s, Chgo., 1950—; financial v.p., dir. Miller Asso. Industries, Inc., Skokie, 1973-74; dir. Miller Builders, Inc.; dir., chmn. exec. com. Portable Electric Tools, Inc., Geneva, Ill., 1963-67; mem. exec. com. Midland Screw Corp., Chgo., 1958-66; faculty John Marshall Law Sch., 1951-64. Bd. dirs., sec., treas. Phil Pekow Family Found.; pres. bd. dirs. Lipschultz Bros. Family Found. Served with USAAF, 1943-46. C.P.A., Ill. Mem. Ill. Soc. C.P.A.'s, Am. Inst. C.P.A.'s, Am., Fed., Chgo., Ill. bar assns., Decalogue Soc. Lawyers, Am. Legion, Nu Beta-Epsilon. Mem. B'nai B'rith. Clubs: Standard (Chgo.); Ravinia Green Country (Deerfield, Ill.). Contbr. articles to profl. jours. Home: 1671 E Mission Hills Rd Northbrook IL 60062 Office: One Concourse Plaza Skokie IL 60076

LIPSCHULTZ, MAURICE ALLEN, machinery co. exec.; b. Chgo., Aug. 5, 1912; s. Isadore M. and Minnie (Tuchow) L.; student Crane Jr. Coll., 1928-29, U. Chgo., 1929-30; m. Sarah Goldsher, Aug. 29, 1934; children—Nathan M., Arthur H., Martin P. Pres. Malco Machinery Co., Chgo., 1939—; sec.-treas. Continental Drill Corp., Chgo., 1951-65; chmn. Viking Drill and Tool Co., St. Paul, 1965—; chmn. Reltool Corp., St. Paul, 1965—; chmn. Namco Devel. Corp., Eye Corp.; partner Namco Mgmt. Co., Namco Devel. Co.; treas. Conwell Bldg. Corp., 1960—; dir. AIM Cos., Detroit, 1969—. Mem. art vis. com. U. Chgo.; mem. art adv. bd. Spertus Mus. Bd. dirs. Gottlieb Meml. Hosp., Museum Contemporary Art, Chgo., Evanston (Ill.) Art Center, D'Arcy Galleries, Loyola U., Chgo., Ukrainian Mus. Modern Art. Jewish religion (dir. temple). Mason. Club: Covenant (Chgo.). Home: 1342 Jackson Ave River Forest IL 60305 Office: 214 S Clinton St Chicago IL 60606

LIPSCOMB, WANDA DEAN, psychologist, educator; b. Richmond, Va., Jan. 29, 1953; d. Abel and Dorothy Beatrice (Parker) Dean; B.A. cum laude, Lincoln U., 1974; M.A. in Psychology, Washington U., St. Louis, 1975; Ph.D. in Urban Counseling Psychology, Mich. State U., 1978. Research asst. Inst. Black Studies, St. Louis, 1974-75; counselor intern Halter High Sch., St. Louis, 1974-75; counselor Lynch Elementary Sch., Detroit, 1975-76; grad. asst. urban counseling Mich. State U., East Lansing, 1975-78, adminstrv. asst. student services, 1976-78, asst. prof. dept. urban and met. studies, 1978-79, asst. prof. community health scis., 1978—, admissions counselor Coll. Human Medicine, 1979-81, dir. recruitment Coll. Human Medicine, 1981—; cons. Profl. Psychol. Cons., Inc., East Lansing, 1978—; cons. in field. Active Big Bros., Big Sisters, Inc., Operation PUSH. Recipient William H. Madella award, 1974; NIMH grad. fellow, 1975-78. Mem. Am., Mich. personnel and guidance assns., Assn. Non-White Concerns in Personnel and Guidance, Mich. Assn. Non White Concerns, Assn. Black Psychologists, Mich. Alliance Black Psychologists, Nat. Alliance Black Sch. Educators, Am. Correctional Health Services Assn., NAACP, Alpha Chi, Delta Sigma Theta. Club: Order Eastern Star. Home: 3422 Penrose Dr Lansing MI 48910 Office: B106 Clin Center Mich State U East Lansing MI 48824

LIS, LAWRENCE FRANCIS, facsimile co. exec.; b. Blue Island, Ill., Jan. 27, 1941; s. Anthony C. and Ann Marion (Galazin) L.; student DeVry Inst. Tech., 1958-59; m. Barbara Jean Lisak, Oct. 19, 1963; children—Christ and Connie (twins), David S. With Telautograph Corp., Chgo., 1959-64; regional mgr. Datalog div. Litton Industries, Chgo., 1964-74; regional mgr. Rapicom Inc., Chgo., 1974-78, nat. dir. field service ops., Hillside, Ill., 1978-79, v.p. customer service div., 1979—, v.p. customer service Rapifax of Can. Ltd. subs., 1980—. Lt. col. CAP, 1957—, dep. research and devel., 1972-75, state dir. communications; dir. Emergency Services and Disaster Agy., Village of Chicago Ridge, 1977—; mem. Ill. CD Council. Mem. Assn. Field Service Mgrs., Armed Forces Communications and Electronics Assn., Suburban Amateur Radio Assn., Mendel High Sch Alumni Assn. Home: 10401 Leslie Ln Chicago Ridge IL 60415 Office: 4415 W Harrison St Hillside IL 60162

LISIO, DONALD JOHN, historian, educator; b. Oak Park, Ill., May 27, 1934; s. Anthony and Dorothy (LoCelso) L.; B.A., Knox Coll., 1956; M.A., Ohio U., 1958; Ph.D., U. Wis., 1965; m. Suzanne Marie Swanson, Apr. 22, 1958; children—Denise Anne, Stephen Anthony. Mem. faculty overseas div. U. Md., 1958-60; asst. prof. history Coe Coll., Cedar Rapids, Iowa, 1964-69, asso. prof., 1969-74, prof., 1974—, chmn. dept., 1973-81, Henrietta Arnold prof. history, 1980—; mem. exec. com. Cedar Rapids Com. Historic Preservation, 1975; William F. Vilas research fellow U. Wis., 1963-64. Served with U.S. Army, 1958-60. Recipient Outstanding Tchr. award Coe Coll., 1969; Nat. Endowment for Humanities fellow, 1969-70; Am. Council Learned Socs. fellow, 1977-78. Mem. Orgn. Am. Historians, Am. Hist. Assn., AAUP, ACLU. Episcopalian. Author: The President and Protest: Hoover, Conspiracy, and the Bonus Riot, 1974; contbr. author: The War Generation, 1975. Contbr. articles to hist. jours. Home: 4203 Twin Ridge Ct SE Cedar Rapids IA 52403 Office: Coe College Cedar Rapids IA 52401

LISMAN, WILLIAM FRANKLYN, elec. equipment mfg. co. exec.; b. Linton, Ind., Apr. 6, 1903; s. Andrew Mack and Mary Lola (Stockrahm) L.; B.E.E., Rose Poly Inst., 1924, Dr. Eng., 1967; m. Rosanne Lieser, July 24, 1937; 1 dau., Susan Ann Lisman Pence. Engring. and mktg. positions Gen. Electric Co., Ft. Wayne, Ind., also Cleve., 1924-34; chmn., pres. Leland Electric Co., Dayton, Ohio, 1934-52; v.p. Brown-Brockmeyer Co., Dayton, 1952-54; chmn., chief exec. officer Furnas Electric Co., Batavia, Ill., 1954-78, chmn. emeritus, dir., 1978—; dir. Furnas Realty Co., Furnas Electric Can. Ltd., 1st Nat. Bank Batavia, Batavia Savs. & Loan Assn. Bd. dirs. Valley Indsl. Assn., 1966-72, Furnas Found.; trustee Community Hosp. Men's Found. (pres. 1957-59). Mem. IEEE, NAM, Nat. Elec. Mfrs. Assn., Soc. Advancement Mgmt., Ill. (dir. 1966-72), Batavia (pres. 1956-58) chambers commerce, Lambda Chi Alpha. Republican. Roman Catholic. Home: 335 North Ave Batavia IL 60510 Office: 1000 McKee St Batavia IL 60510

LISSNER, ARTHUR BART, plastic surgeon; b. N.Y.C., Oct. 2, 1929; s. Arthur and Leona (Brophel) L.; B.S. cum laude, Georgetown U., 1951; M.D., Jefferson Med. Coll., 1955; m. Adrienne Hessel, June 19, 1954; children—Lee, Amy, Chris, Ken, Cindy, Jenny, Kathy, Mike. Resident gen. surgery Cornell Div. Bellevue Hosp., N.Y.C., 1958-61; resident plastic surgery Columbia U., 1961-63; asst. instr. surgery St. Louis U., 1965—; practice medicine specializing in plastic surgery, St. Louis, St. Charles, Florissant, Mo., 1963—; chief surgery Christian Northwest Hosp., Florissant, 1970-73; chief surgery St. Peters (Mo.) Community Hosp., 1980-81, bd. dirs., 1980—; pres. Plastic Surgery Consultants Ltd., 1972—. Served to lt. M.C. USNR, 1956-58. Diplomate Am. Bd. Plastic and Reconstructive Surgery. Fellow A.C.S.; mem. AMA, St. Louis County Med. Soc., Am. Soc. Plastic and Reconstructive Surgery, Am. Soc. Aesthetic Plastic Surgery. Home: 13 Royale Ct Lake Saint Louis MO 63367 Office: 6 Jungerman Circle St Peters MO 63376

LIST, CHARLES EDWARD, mfg. co. exec.; b. Chgo., May 9, 1941; s. Kermit Paul and Johanna Emma (Staat) L.; B.A., Valparaiso U., 1963; M.A., St. Marys Coll., Winona, Minn., 1980; postgrad Union Coll., Cin., 1981—; m. Susan Mary Nelson, July 20, 1968; children—Andrea Sarang, Darcy Young. Mem. personnel staff Control Data Corp., Mpls., 1965-72; mgr. human resource center Supervalu Stores, Mpls., 1973-74; dir. personnel Internat. Dairy Queen, Mpls., 1974-77; mgr. mgmt. and orgn. devel. Cardiac Pacemakers Inc., St. Paul, 1977—; instr. Met. State U., St. Paul, 1972—. Served with USMC, 1963-64. Recipient Instr. Recognition award Met. State U., 1975, 80. Mem. Am. Soc. Personnel Adminstrn., Am. Soc. Tng. and Devel. Episcopalian. Home: 4940 Winterset Dr Minnetonka MN 55343 Office: 4100 N Hamline St Saint Paul MN 55164

LIST, DAVID PATTON, lawyer; b. Belvidere, Ill., Feb. 4, 1920; s. Raymond Ford and Marguerite (Patton) L.; A.B., Dartmouth Coll., 1942; LL.B., Harvard U., 1948; m. Patricia Porter, Jan. 7, 1949 (dec. Oct. 1978); children—John, Victoria, David Patton; m. 2d, Annette M. Kohlmorgan, Nov. 16, 1979. Admitted to Ill. bar, 1948; since practiced in Chgo., partner firm Sidley & Austin, and predecessors, 1955—. Served with AUS, 1942-45. Fellow Am. Coll. Trial Lawyers; mem. Am., Ill. State, Chgo. bar assns., Legal Club Chgo., Law Club Chgo. Republican. Episcopalian. Clubs: Westmoreland Country, Univ. of Chgo. Address: 1 First National Plaza Chicago IL 60670

LISTER, COLIN HOLDEN, hockey club ofcl.; b. Perth, W. Australia, July 7, 1927; s. George Holden and Elinor (Daly) L.; student pvt. schs., Perth; came to U.S., 1958, naturalized, 1961. Teller, Commonwealth Bank of Australia, Perth/Sydney, 1942-51; clk. Lex Garages, London, 1952; asst. cashier Bank of Montreal (Que., Can.), 1953-58; partner, dir. Komet Hockey Club, Fort Wayne, Ind., 1958—, treas., 1960—, bus. mgr., 1958—. Bd. dirs. Urban Youth Ventures, Inc., Ft. Wayne, 1976-77. Mem. Ind. Amateur Baseball Congress (sec. 1969—). Mem. Calvary Temple. Club: Rotary. Home: 1025 Ridgewood Dr Fort Wayne IN 46805 Office: 4000 Parnell Ave Fort Wayne IN 46805

LISTER, LOIS MILDRED PERSCHBACHER HUMISTON, dietitian; b. Milw., Aug. 23, 1931; d. Carl John and Edna Ida (Stroessner) Perschbacher; B.S., U. Wis., 1953; m. Karl E. Humiston, Oct. 30, 1959; children—Michael, John, Matthew, Thomas, K. Frederick; m. 2d, James C. Lister, May 11, 1974; stepchildren—Jeffrey J., Mark J. Teaching dietitian Mpls. VA Hosp., 1954-56; wards teaching dietitian Stanford U. Hosps., San Francisco, 1957-59; sr. therapeutic dietitian Univ. Hosp., Seattle, 1959-60; chief dietitian Mary Bridge Children's Hosp., Tacoma, Wash., 1968-73; therapeutic dietitian Luth. Hosp., Milw., 1974-77; food service dir. Meml. Hosp., Burlington, Wis., 1977-80, Jackson Center, Milw., 1981—; nutritionist Mt. Sinai Capitol Dr. Community Health Center, Milw., 1980-81; instr. Milw. Area Tech. Coll., 1981-82. Mem. Am. Dietetic Assn., Wis. Dietetic Assn., Milw. Dietetic Assn., Am. Diabetes Assn., Am. Soc. for Hosp. Food Service Adminstrs., Phi Upsilon Omicron, Delta Zeta. Methodist. Home: 4935 S 36th St Greenfield WI 53221

LISTON, JERRY R., telephone co. exec.; b. Terre Haute, Ind., Aug. 17, 1949; s. Robert L. and Kathryn Liston; student public schs.; m. Carol R. Knipper, Nov. 16, 1968; children—Melissa Caroline, Kimberly Kathryn. Welder, A & S Steel Co., Lockport, Ill., 1971; installer Ill. Bell Telephone Co., Romeoville, Ill., 1971-79, installation foreman, 1979—. Mem. sch. bd. Taft Grade Sch. Dist. 90, Lockport, 1978—. Served with USAF, 1967-71. Mem. Lockport Jaycees (treas. 1979-80, state dir.; cert. of award 1977). Lutheran. Home: 816 South St Lockport IL 60441 Office: 1999 Aucutt Rd Montgomery IL 60538

LITKE, LARRY LAVOE, educator; b. Denver, June 1, 1949; s. Robert Milton and Mildred Pauline (White) L.; B.A., Ottawa (Kans.) U., 1971; M.S., Kans. State Tchrs. Coll., 1973; Ph.D., U. N.D., 1976; m. Roberta Jeanne Warren, Aug. 10, 1969; children—Deidre Marie, Tasha Joy. Teaching and research asst. U. N.D., Grand Forks, 1973-77; instr. anatomy Med. Coll. Ohio, Toledo, 1977-78, asst. prof., 1978—. Merit badge counselor, scoutmaster Boy Scouts Am., 1960—; pres. PTA Fellowship, Swanton (Ohio) Christian Sch., 1981—. Mem. Electron Microscopy Soc. N.W. Ohio, Ohio Acad. Sci., Electron Microscopy Soc. Am., Am. Assn. Anatomists, Sigma Xi. Club: Lions Internat. (officer 1971-73). Contbr. articles to profl. jours. Home: 108 W Garfield Ave Swanton OH 43558 Office: Med Coll Ohio CS 10008 Toledo OH 43699

LITOT, EDWARD FRANCIS, clergyman; b. Fort Wayne, Ind., June 18, 1922; s. Francis E. and Bernadette C. (Forbing) L.; student St. Joseph Coll., 1940-42; St. Meinrad Major Sem., 1942-47. Ordained priest Roman Catholic Ch., 1947; asst. pastor St. Vincent Ch., Elkhart, Ind., 1947-51; dir. Gary (Ind.) Alerding Settlement House, 1953-67; asst. pastor St. Joseph's Ch. Dyer, Ind., 1951-53; pastor, 1967—. Dir. Diocesan Info. Bur., Gary, 1957—; diocesan dir. Council Cath. Men, 1964—; chmn. Diocesan Ecumenical Commn., 1964—; diocesan dir. Confrat. Christian Doctrine, Gary Diocese, 1957-63; chaplain Gary Police, 1964-67, Ind. Guard Res., 1965—; diocesan consultor, 1969; diocesan dir. cemeteries, 1971—; pro-synodal judge, 1971. Pres., Frontiers Internat., Gary, 1967. Dir. Northwestern Ind. Council Chs., 1965—. Named Domestic prelate Pope John XXIII, 1962, monsignor,

1962. Mem. Ind. Cath. Conf. (pub. relations com. 1966—), Gary Fellowship Ministers, Gary C. of C. Editor: Gary edit. Our Sunday Visitor, 1957—. Home: 440 Joliet St Dyer IN 46311 Office: Cathedral Center 975 W 6th Ave Gary IN 46401

LITSAS, FRANK-FOTIOS K., educator; b. Messenia, Greece, Nov. 28, 1943; naturalized Am. citizen, 1971; s. Constantine J. and Georgia T. (Nickols) L.; Lic.Phil., U. Athens, 1966; M.A., Eastern Mich. U., 1974; Ph.D., U. Chgo., 1980. Teaching asst. Sch. Philosophy, U. Athens, 1965-66; tchr. Ministry of Edn., Greece, 1966-71; tchr.-dir. Greek Sch., Ann Arbor, Mich., 1971-74; instr. Northeastern Ill. U., Chgo., 1976-78; asst. prof. dept. classics U. Ill., Chgo. Circle, 1978—; cons. multi-ethnic curriculum Ann Arbor public schs., 1972-74. Bd. dirs. Greek Orthodox Seminar, Greek Diocese of Chgo., 1976—, dir.-moderator cultural radio-program, 1976—; active Hellenic Found. of Chgo., 1976—, Hellenic Voters Am., 1978—. Served to capt. Greek Army, 1969-71. Recipient 1st award for linguistic and folkloric research in region of Triphylia, Acad. Athens, Greece, 1964; Ann Arbor Dept. Edn. citation, 1974; Citizenship Council of Metro. Chgo. outstanding citizen award, 1979; named Patriarchate of Constantinople, Archon-Knight of the Order of St. Andrew, 1980. Mem. Folkloric Soc. Greece, Greek Anthrop. Assn., Am. Hist. Assn., Assn. Am. Byzantinists, Hellenic Profl. Soc. Ill. (dir. 1980—). Greek Orthodox. Author: Study of Triphylian dialect, 1968; Roots: Greek festivals and Customs, 1981; City of Coroni: An Aesthetic Prosopography, 1981; The Greek Wedding, 1981; The Babylon Manuscript: Autobiography of Alexander the Great, 1982; contbr. articles to profl. jours. Home: 5700 N Sheridan Rd Apt 1110 Chicago IL 60660 Office: Univ Ill Chicago Circle Dept Classics PO Box 4348 Chicago IL 60680

LITTEN, REGINALD KEITH, soap co. exec.; b. Phillipsburg, Ohio, Mar. 11, 1929; s. Floyd Wendell and Ruth Dawn (Goodyear) L.; grad. Dayton Art Inst. Sch., 1951; m. Marlene Ann Henry, Jan. 28, 1953; 1 dau., Yolanda Dawn Ann. Staff artist Dayton (Ohio) Jour. Herald, 1949-51; civilian illustrator USAF, Dayton, 1951-52; interior designer Rike Dept. Store, Dayton, 1953-56; asst. dir., creative services mgr. Hewitt Soap Co., Inc. Dayton, 1956—. Recipient award Nat. Paper Box Assn., 1969, 70, 72. Mem. Dayton Soc. Painters and Sculptors (pres. 1979-80), Milestone Car Soc., Ohio Assn. Artistic Publs. (state rep.), Art Center Dayton, Cin. Art Club. Club: Shriners. Home: 221 Greenmount Blvd Oakwood Dayton OH 45419 Office: 333 Linden Ave Dayton OH 45403

LITTLE, CLARENCE WILBUR, JR., educator, cons.; b. Crowley, La., Apr. 28, 1923; s. Clarence Wilbur and Adelia (Faulk) L.; student La. Poly. Inst., 1940-44; B.E.E., Johns Hopkins U., 1948, D.Eng., 1952; m. Eleanor MacWithey, June 12, 1945; children—Nancy Lee (Mrs. Glenn David Ahrens), Jonathan Avery, Christopher Mark, Peter Coffman, Martha Lee, Sarah Palmer, David Stanley, Paul Drake. Supr. physics and elec. research Allis-Chalmers Mfg. Co., West Allis, Wis., 1952-57; group leader C-Stellarator Assos. James Forrestal Research Center, Princeton, N.J., 1957-59, dir. ops., 1959-61; v.p. research and devel. Waukesha Foundry Co., Inc. (Wis.), 1961-72, exec. v.p., 1972-74, v.p., gen. mgr. manufactured products div., 1974-76, also dir.; cons., program coordinator dept. engring. and applied sci. U. Wis.-Extension, 1976—; pres., dir. Dutch Hollow Lake Property Owners Assn., LaValle, Wis., 1974-80. Active Boy Scouts Am. Served with USNR, 1944-46. Mem. Hydraulic Inst., Internat. Conf. on Standards, Sigma Xi, Lambda Chi Alpha, Tau Beta Pi, Alpha Phi Omega. Mem. Ch. Jesus Christ of Latter-day Saints. Contr. articles to tech. jours. Patentee in field. Home: 441 Summit Point Dr LaValle WI 53941 Office: 432 N Lake St Madison WI 53706

LITTLE, DONALD CAMPBELL, lawyer, former judge; b. Abilene, Kans., Jan. 29, 1901; s. Edward Campbell and Edna Margaret (Steele) L.; A.B., George Washington U., 1924; postgrad. Harvard U. Law Sch., 1924-25; LL.B., Washburn U., 1927, J.D., 1971; m. Elizabeth Copley, May 20, 1931. Admitted to Kans. bar, 1927, U.S. Supreme Ct. bar, 1942; asst. U.S. atty. for Kans., 1930-33; atty. Kans. Ho. of Reps., 1933-34; chief dep. county atty. Wyandotte County (Kans.), 1935-39; former judge U.S. Dist. Ct. 29th Kans. Dist. Republican precinctcommitteeman; chmn. Wyandotte County Rep. Com., 1956-58; mem. Kans. Civil Service Bd., 1964-65; hon. curator Ft. Leavenworth (Kans.) Mil. Mus. Served to maj. U.S. Army; NATOUSA, ETO. Decorated Bronze Star; named hon. citizen of Paola (Italy), 1944; hon. Ky. Col.; Disting. Jayhawker, Gov. Kans., 1964; Minuteman award 1965, Patriot's medal, 1964. Mem. Am. Bar Assn., Kans. Bar Assn., Wyandotte County Bar Assn., Am. Legion (past post comdr.), 40 and 8, Founders and Patriots, Soc. Colonial Wars, Mil. Order Loyal Legion, Sons Union Vets. (past state comdr.), Mil. Order World Wars, St. Andrew's Soc., SR, Soc. Colonial Clergy, Kans. Ret. Dist. Judges Assn., Phi Kappa Psi, Delta Theta Phi. Clubs: Masons (past master), Shriners. Home: Forest Lake Bonner Springs KS 66012 Office: Huron Bldg 7th Floor Kansas City KS 66101*

LITTLE, ERVIN DEWEY, JR., advt. and pub. relations co. exec.; b. Flint, Mich., Jan. 16, 1925; s. Ervin Dewey and Mary Blanche (Anderson) L.; B.A., U. Mich., 1949; M.A., U. Mo., 1951; m. Dorothy Marie Veal, Aug. 9, 1947; children—Gregory, Melinda, Randolph. Asso. editor Haywood Pub. Co., Chgo., 1951-56; asst. editor World Book Ency., Chgo., 1956-57; mgr. pub. relations Spector Freight System, Chgo., 1957-60; writer Jam Handy Orgn., Detroit, 1960-64; mgr. pub. relations Mich. Blue Shield, Detroit, 1964-67; dir. community relations Wyandotte (Mich.) Gen. Hosp., 1967-73; owner Dewey Little & Assos., Royal Oak, Mich., 1974—; editor, pub. Mich. Health Educator Mag., 1976—. Safety chmn. Starr Sch., Royal Oak, 1968-69; com. mem. Boy Scouts Am., Wyandotte, 1969-70. Served with inf. AUS, 1943-45. Decorated Purple Heart. Recipient Pub. Relations Contest First prize Am. Trucking Assn., 1958; three Internat. MacEachern Pub. Relations Contest awards Am. Acad. Hosp. Pub. Relations, 1970, 71; 2d prize New Worlds Poetry Contest, 1975. Mem. Pub. Relations Soc. Am., Am. Soc. Hosp. Pub. Relations Dirs., Mich. Hosp. Pub. Relations Assn. (state pres. 1971, pres. southeast chpt. 1974-75), Detroit Press Club, Sigma Delta Chi. Contbr. to poetry anthologies. Address: 2902 Glenview Ave Royal Oak MI 48073

LITTMAN, DOUGLAS ALAN, ins. agt.; b. Greenville, Ohio, May 9, 1949; s. Alan Verl and Janet E. (Eller) L.; B.S. in Bus. Adminstrn., Miami U., Oxford, Ohio, 1971; m. Victoria L. Harshbarger, June 12, 1971; children—Heather N., Erica L. Partner, Littman-Thomas Agy., Greenville, 1971—. Recipient numerous ins. salesmanship awards. Mem. Ind. Ins. Agts. Am., Nat. Assn. Life Underwriters, Ind. Ins. Agts. Assn. Ohio, Ind. Ins. Agts. Darke County (pres. 1978-80), Darke County Bd. Realtors, Darke County C. of C., Darke County Fish and Game Assn. (dir. 1973—, pres. 1976-77). Democrat. Club: United Ch. Christ. Clubs: Greenville Kiwanis (pres. 1978-79), Darke County Shriners. Home: 102 Redwood Dr Greenville OH 45331 Office: 515 E Main St Greenville OH 45331

LITVIN, ROBERT LOWELL, mech. contractor exec.; b. Chgo., Oct. 27, 1925; s. Thomas Henry and Theresa (Bellak) L.; B.S.C.E., U. Ill., 1946; m. K. Jean Gault, Sept. 18, 1976; children—Marilyn Beth, Michelle Ann, Robert, William. With Thomas H. Litvin Co., Chgo., 1938-46, 46— pres., 1969—; with Thoro, Inc., Chgo., 1964—, pres., 1969-76, chmn. bd., 1976—; gen. partner C.S.A. Asso. Ltd., Chgo., 1967—, 40 E. Oak St. Apts., Chgo., 1967—, Harbor House Ltd., Chgo., 1967—; partner 180 N. Michigan Ave. Bldg., Chgo., 1967-69; mech. contractor in plumbing and fire protection; chmn. No. Ill. Regional Bargaining Council Plumbing Industry. Author (with others) Chgo. Plan, 1969-70, chmn. plumbing industry operating com., 1970—. Trustee Carl Howard Litvin fellowship for Leukemia Research; bd. dirs. Mt. Sinai Med. Research Found., Mt. Sinai Hosp. Med. Center, Young Men's Jewish Council, Chgo. Youth Centers, Rest Haven Convalescent Hosp., Deborah Boys Club; founder Technion U. Israel, Hebrew U.; bd. govs. State of Israel Bonds, chmn. bldg. trades State of Israel Bonds: active Combined Jewish Appeal. Served with USNR, 1943-45. Mem. Plumbing Contractors Assn. (co-chmn. labor relations com.), Plumbing Council (dir. 1968-70), ASCE, Am. Soc. San. Engrs., Am. Soc. Plumbing Engrs., Am. Legion, Sigma Alpha Mu. Jewish (v.p. temple). Club: Standard (Chgo.). Home: 180 E Pearson St Chicago IL 60611 Office: 1355 W Washington Blvd Chicago IL 60607

LIU, C. Y., mktg. and distbn. co. exec.; b. Shanghai, China, Aug. 10, 1928; came to U.S., 1956, naturalized, 1962; B.A., Utopia U., 1949; postgrad. Columbia U., 1955, Harvard U., 1969. Corp. mgr. info. processing systems planning staff Raytheon Co., Lexington, Mass., 1968-72; asst. v.p. info. services Am. Mutual, Wakefield, Mass., 1972-73; v.p. info. processing systems Forest City Enterprises, Cleve., 1973-74; sr. v.p. planning and ops. Curtis Industries, Cleve., 1974—. Mem. Assn. Computing Machinery, Am. Mgmt. Assn., N. Am. Soc. Corp. Planning. Roman Catholic. Home: 32800 Ledgehill Dr Solon OH 44139 Office: 34999 Curtis Blvd East Lake OH 44094

LIU, CHUN NAN, engine lathe co. exec.; b. Taiwan, Mar. 29, 1942; s. Chin Chen and Chien (Lo) L.; came to U.S., 1970; M.M.E., Ill. Inst. Tech., 1973; m. Anita Sia Kee, Aug. 14, 1971; children—Christine K., Edward Quincy. Stationery engr. Oak Park (Ill.) Hosp., 1970-73; mech. engr. Sverdrup & Parcel Assos., St. Louis, 1973-74, Laramore, Douglas & Popham, Chgo., 1974-76; owner, pres. The Evenhanded Co., Skokie, Ill., 1976—; cons. to power plant industry. Registered profl. engr., Ill., Mo.; lic. marine 3d engr., China, Liberia. Mem. ASME, Am. Inst. Plant Engrs. Club: Formosan of Am. Developer computer-oriented stress analysis of orthotropic plate with 2 holes, 1973. Home and Office: 4539 W Howard St Skokie IL 60076

LIU, EDWARD CHUNG-HONG, design engr.; b. Tainan, Taiwan, Aug. 17, 1940; s. Seifu and Tsi-Fang (Chuang) L.; came to U.S., 1968, naturalized, 1976; B.S. in Chem. Engring., Chung Yuan Coll. Engring., Taiwan, 1963; M.S. in Chem. Engring., U. Mo., Rolla, 1971; m. Ingrid Yin-Guey Tzeng, Apr. 12, 1969; children—Jean Ju, Jasper Edward. Process engr. Kaohsiung Oil Refinery, Chinese Petroleum Corp., 1965-68; sr. instrument engr. Catalytic, Inc., Phila., 1973-74; design engr. Ashland Chem. Co., Dublin, Ohio, 1975-80; prin. research scientist Battelle Columbus Labs., 1980—. cons. Mem. Am. Inst. Chem. Engrs., Instrument Soc. Am., Taiwanese Assn. Am. Office: 505 King Ave Columbus OH 43201

LIU, PAUL CHI, oceanographer; b. Chefoo, China, June 18, 1935; s. Joseph Tzu-chien and Agatha I-ming (Wang) L.; came to U.S., 1959, naturalized, 1972; B.S., Nat. Taiwan U., 1956; M.S., Va. Poly. Inst., 1961; postgrad. Cornell U., Wayne State U.; Ph.D., U. Mich., 1977; m. Teresa Sheau-mei Wang, Jan. 30, 1965; 1 dau., Christina. Research phys. scientist C.E., U.S. Army, Lake Survey Dist., Detroit, 1965-71; research phys. scientist Lake Survey Center, Nat. Oceanic and Atmospheric Adminstrn., Detroit, 1971-74, phys. scientist Great Lakes Environ. Research Lab., Ann Arbor, 1974—; vis. scholar U. Mich., 1978—. NOAA fellow, 1971-72. Mem. Am. Geophys. Union, Am. Meterol. Soc., ASCE, Internat. Assn. Great Lakes Research, Sigma Xi, Phi Kappa Phi. Contbr. articles to profl. jours. Home: 2939 Renfrew St Ann Arbor MI 48105 Office: 2300 Washtenaw Ave Ann Arbor MI 48104

LIU, PHILIP KUOCHERNG, geneticist; b. Pingtung, Taiwan, Dec. 21, 1947; s. Tshun-shong and Shu-yen (Chao) L.; B.S. in Vet. Medicine, Taiwan Provincial Pingtung Inst. Agr., 1968; B.S., Westminster Coll., 1974; M.S., Mich. State U., 1974, Ph.D., 1981. Veterinarian, Taiwan Wardog Tng. Center, Taipei, Taiwan, 1968-70; research asst. dept. pediatrics and human devel. Mich. State U., East Lansing, 1978-81; research asso. dept. pathology U. Wash., Seattle, 1981—. Mem. N.Y. Acad. Sci., Environ. Mutagen Soc., Genetic Soc. Am., AAAS, Am. Chem. Soc., Sigma Xi.

LIU, RUEY-WEN, educator; b. Kiang-en, China, Mar. 18, 1930; s. Yen-sun and Wei-en (Chang) L.; came to U.S., 1951, naturalized, 1956; B.S., U. Ill., 1954, M.S., 1955, Ph.D., 1960; m. Nancy Shao-lan Lee, Aug. 18, 1957; children—Alexander, Theodore. Asst. prof. U. Notre Dame (Ind.), 1960-63, asso. prof., 1963-66, prof. elec. engring., 1966—; vis. prof. U. Calif. at Berkeley, 1965-66, Nat. Taiwan U., Taipei, China, spring 1969, Universidad de Chile, Santiago de Chile, summer 1970. Trustee Calif. Buddhism Assn., 1974-76. U. Ill. fellow, 1954; Gen. Electric fellow, 1958; NSF grantee, 1962. Fellow IEEE; mem. N.Y. Acad. Sci., Am. Math. Soc., Soc. Indsl. and Applied Maths., Sigma Xi, Tau Beta Pi, Pi Mu Epsilon. Contbr. articles to profl. jours. Home: 1929 Dorwood Dr South Bend IN 46617 Office: Dept Elec Engring Notre Dame U Notre Dame IN 46556

LIVENGOOD, RICHARD VAUGHN, hosp. adminstr.; b. Offerle, Kans., Mar. 24, 1934; s. C. Earl and Wynona M. (Block) L.; B.S. in Edn., Eastern Ill. U., 1956; M.H.A., Duke U., 1973; m. D. Joanne Desler, Aug. 11, 1962; children—Linda R., John D. Instr., Rockford (Ill.) Sch. Bus. and Engring., 1959-64; asst. adminstr. Freeport (Ill.) Meml. Hosp., 1964-68, Manatee Meml. Hosp., Bradenton, Fla., 1968-71; v.p., adminstrn. Charleston Area (W.Va.) Med. Center, 1973-75; pres. Lakeview Med. Center, Danville, Ill., 1975—, LMC Affiliated Services, Inc., 1981—. Mem. budget com. United Way Campaign, 1977—; trustee Lakeview Meml. Found., 1976—; bd. dirs. East Central Ill. Med. Edn. Found., 1976—, pres., 1979-80; bd. dirs. East Central Ill. Health Systems Agy., 1980—; bd. dirs. East Central Ill. Health Planning Orgn., 1975—, pres., 1981-82. Served with U.S. Army, 1956-58. Fellow Hosp. Fin. Mgmt. Assn., Am. Coll. Hosp. Adminstrs.; mem. Ill. Hosp. Assn. (trustee), Am. Hosp. Assn., Am. Public Health Assn., Eastern Ill. U. Alumni Assn. (dir. 1981—), Duke U. Alumni Assn., Eastern Ill. U. Found. (dir. 1980). Republican. Methodist. Clubs: Danville Country (dir. 1978-81, pres. 1980-81), Rotary (dir. 1980-82), Danville, Elks. Home: 1601 N Logan St Danville IL 61832 Office: 812 N Logan St Danville IL 61832

LIVESAY, HARLON LARRY, county ofcl.; b. Irvington, Ill., Oct. 3, 1947; s. Homer Lowell and Bessie (Cravens) L.; grad. high sch.; grad. Policy Tng. Inst., 1978; m. Janet Marie Mathus, Apr. 15, 1978. Service sta. attendant Jerry's Shell, Ashley, Ill., 1965-66; electric and radio mechanic McDonnel-Douglas Corp., Hazelwood, Mo., 1966-70; store mgr. Hill Bros. Shoe Store, St. Charles, Mo., 1971-74; boilerman Top Star Dairy, Nashville, Ill., 1974-77; patrolman Village of Okawville (Ill.), 1977; dep. sheriff Washington County (Ill.), Nashville, 1977—. Mem. Washington County Underwater Search and Recovery Rescue Team. Served with USAF, 1966. Mem. Profl. Assn. Divers and Instrs., Am. Karate Assn., Okawville Jaycees. Roman Catholic. Home: Rural Route 1 Box 18 Hoyleton IL 62803 Office: 1 Court St Louis St Nashville IL 62263

LIVINGSTON, GARY ALLEN, data processor; b. Akron, Ohio, Feb. 8, 1954; s. James A. and Nellie S. (Garl) L.; B.A. in Communication, Cleve. State U.-Ohio State U., 1976; postgrad. Mich. State U., 1978-79, Cleve. State U., 1981—; m. Denise J. Dziczkowski, May 26, 1979; 1 son, David Calvin. Profl. photographer, journalist, 1969-75; cons. on public relations, survey research, quantitative methods, 1974-79; instr. communication Mich. State U., East Lansing, 1977-78; survey researcher, data processing trainer Fed. Res. Bank, Cleve., 1978-80; data processing tng. coordinator Blue Cross N.E. Ohio, Cleve., 1980—. Pres., Cleve., Bible-Sci. Assn.; active Christian Action Council. Mem. Organizational Devel. Network, Am. Soc. for Tng. and Devel., Cleve. Profls. in Data Processing Edn. Baptist. Contbr. articles to profl. publs. Home: 15903 Clifton Blvd Lakewood OH 44107 Office: 2066 E 9th St Cleveland OH 44115

LIVINGSTON, ROBERT WAYNE, dairy co. exec.; b. Uniontown, Pa., Sept. 24, 1934; s. Harry McFee and Hannah Margret (Prinkey) L.; student Kent State U., 1956-58; m. Dorothy Ann Harford, Sept. 27, 1953; children—Deborah Ann Livingston Mowery, Robert Wayne. With Sealtest Foods Co., 1956-76, distbr. sales mgr., dist. distbn. mgr., to 1976; v.p. distbn. Reiter Foods, Inc., Akron, Ohio, 1976—. Bd. dirs. Farrax Condominiums Assn.; mem. Happy Hearts Sch. for Mentally Retarded Sch. Bd., Astabula County, Ohio, 1969-70; coach, bd. dirs. Teenage Baseball and Basketball Teams, Mentor, Ohio, 1971-78. Mem. Milk Industry Found., Pvt. Fleet Council, Internat. Assn. Ice Cream Mfrs. Republican. Baptist. Office: 1415 W Waterloo Rd Akron OH 44314*

LIVINGSTON, VON EDWARD, lawyer; b. New Boston, Ill., Dec. 10, 1903; s. Warren F. and Katherine M. (Bridger) L.; B.A. magna cum laude, Knox Coll., 1925; J.D., U. Chgo., 1928; m. Katharine True, Aug. 2, 1928; children—Katharine (Mrs. William E. Evans), Mary (Mrs. Brant R. Moore), Martha (Mrs. Don McCoy). Admitted to Ill. bar, 1928; atty. firm Cooke, Sullivan & Ricks, Chgo., 1928-39; partner Lawyer, Anderson & Livingston, Chgo., 1939-41; gen. counsel Ind. Service Corp., 1941-45, Ind. & Mich. Electric Co.; sr. partner Livingston, Dildine, Haynie & Yoder, Ft. Wayne, Ind., and predecessor firm, 1945-80, of counsel, 1980—; dir., mem. exec. com. Peoples Trust Bank & Financial, Inc.; mem. com. character and fitness Ind. Supreme Ct.; past hon. Ind. asst. atty. gen. Dir., past pres. Ft. Wayne Charity Horse Assn.; Pres. Ft. Wayne Bd. Aviation Commrs., 1950-58; former mem. Allen County Republican Com. Served to 1st lt., U.S. Army, 1925-30. Mem. Ft. Wayne C. of C. (past dir.), Ind. Soc. Chgo., Newcomen Soc., Internat. Platform Assn., Phi Beta Kappa, Sigma Delta Chi. Conglist. Clubs: Masons (Shriners, 32 deg.), Fort Wayne Rotary (past pres.), Ft. Wayne Country, Summit, Quest (past pres.) (Ft. Wayne). Home: 5219 Hickory Ln Ft Wayne IN 46825 Office: Lincoln Tower Ft Wayne IN 46802

LL, TZE-CHUNG, educator; b. China, Feb. 17, 1927; s. Ken-hsiang and Yu-hsien (Chang) L.; LL.B., Soochow U., 1948; grad. Chinese Research Inst. Land Econs., 1952; LL.M., So. Meth. U., 1957; LL.M., Harvard, 1958; M.S., Columbia, 1965; Ph.D., New Sch. for Social Research, 1963; m. Dorothy In-lan Wang, Oct. 21, 1961; children—Lily, Rose, Dist. judge, China, 1949-51; div. head dept. law Ministry Nat. Def., China, 1951-56; v.p. Atlantic Fiscal Corp., 1962-64; asst. prof. library sci., asst. librarian Ill. State U., 1965-66; asst. prof. polit. sci. and library sci. Rosary Coll., River Forest, Ill., 1966-70, asso. prof. library sci., 1970-74, prof., 1974—, dir. continuing edn., 1979—. Dir. Nat. Central Library, China, 1970-72, cons., 1974—; chmn. Grad. Inst. Library Sci., China, 1971-72; nat. vis. asso. prof. Nat. Taiwan U., 1969. Pres., Chinese-Am. Ednl. Found., Chgo., 1968-70; adviser Friends of Soochow, Los Angeles, 1974—; mem. Nat. Council Cultural Renaissance, 1971—; pres. Chinese Culture Service, 1974—. Recipient Elsie O. and Philip D. Sang Excellence in Teaching award Rosary Coll., 1971, Outstanding Educator award, 1973. Mem. Chinese Am. Librarians Assn. (pres. 1974-76, chmn. 1976—), ALA, Assn. Am. Library Schs., Chinese Library Assn. (gov. 1971-72), Internat. Assn. Orientalist Librarians (area rep. 1971-76), Phi Tau Phi (nat. treas. 1981—, pres. Mid-Am. chpt. 1981—). Asso. editor Law Digest, China, 1951-53; editor Jour. Library and Information Sci., 1974—. Author 11 books and numerous articles to profl. jours. Home: 1104 Greenfield Ave Oak Park IL 60302 Office: Roseary Coll River Forest IL 60305

LLENADO, RAMON AGUILLON, chemist; b. Manila, Philippines, Aug. 31, 1946; came to U.S., 1969, naturalized, 1974; s. Augustin A. and Marcelina (Aguillon) L.; B.S., U. Santo Tomas, 1967; Ph.D., SUNY, Buffalo, 1973. Instr., U. Santo Tomas, Manila, 1967-69; staff chemist Procter & Gamble Co., Cin., 1973-75, group leader, 1975-77, project leader, 1977-78, sect. head, 1978—. Mem. Soap and Detergent Assn., Am. Chem. Soc. (analytical chem. fellow 1972), Am. Oil Chemists Soc. Republican. Roman Catholic. Contbr. articles to profl. jours.; patentee in field. Office: Procter and Gamble Co Ivorydale Tech Center Cincinnati OH 45217

LLOYD, CORRINE AVIS, microbiologist; b. St. Louis, May 15, 1943; d. J. Howard and Pearl Elsa (Rugger) Lloyd; B.S. in Med. Tech., St. Louis U., 1965, postgrad., 1966—. Chief microbiology, infectious disease com. mem., med. technologist Cardinal Glennon Hosp. for Children, St. Louis, 1965-73; microbiologist, med. technologist, dept. community health and med. care St. Louis County Hosp., Clayton, Mo., 1973—; asst. instr. med. tech. St. Louis U., 1966—. Deacon, elder Christian educator Affton Presbyn. Ch.; active YWCA. Recipient Presdl. Sports award for swimming, 1975. Registered microbiology Am. Acad. Microbiology, 1975, registered med. technologist Am. Soc. Clin. Pathologists, 1966. Mem. Am., Mo. socs. for microbiology, Am., Mo. socs. med. tech., St. Louis U. Allied Health and Nursing Alumni Assn. (dir. 1972—, pres. 1978-80). Home: 6212 Bixby St Affton MO 63123 Office: 601 S Brentwood Blvd Clayton MO 63105

LLOYD, H. PAUL, educator; b. Oak Hill, Ohio, Mar. 18, 1935; s. Howard P. and Maridoris (Williams) L.; B.S., Rio Grande Coll., 1958; M.A., Marshall U., 1966; m. Mamie Clark, Dec. 22, 1957; children—Kevin, Karen, Alicia. Tchr., coach Pickaway County Schs., Monroe, Ohio, 1957-58; tchr. Jackson (Ohio) City Schs., 1960-65; instr. math. Rio Grande (Ohio) Coll., 1965-69, asst. prof. edn., 1969-76, asso. prof., chmn. dept. profl. edn., 1976—. Asst. chief Madison-Jefferson Fire Dept., 1970-80, trustee, 1980—. mem. central com. Republican Party, 1976—; elder Presbyn. Ch., 1972—. Recipient Outstanding Alumni award Rio Grande Coll., 1981; Ohio Dept. Edn. grantee, 1976, 80—. Mem. Assn. Tchr. Educators, Assn. for Sch. Curriculum Devel., Alpha Sigma Phi. Republican. Club: Masons. Home: Route 3 Oak Hill OH 45656 Office: Rio Grande Coll Rio Grande OH 45674

LLOYD, LARRY ALLEN, mfg. co. exec.; b. Belvidere, Ill., Nov. 19, 1947; s. Raymond L. and Darlene N. (Whitacre) L.; student Platteville (Wis.) State U., 1965-67; m. Sharon Kay Dettman, May 23, 1970; children—Brian Brenda. Shipping receiving checker Ray O Vac, Madison, Wis., 1967-68; inventory auditor Olin Corp., Baraboo, Wis., 1968-69, chief clk. property, 1969-76, chief property and traffic, 1977—. Mem. Nat. Mgmt. Assn. (bd. dirs. 1980—), Mensa. Presbyterian. Club: Olin-Badger Conservation (treas. 1979—). Home: Rural Route 3 Lodi WI 53555 Office: Badger Army Ammunition Plant Baraboo WI 53913

LLOYD, WILLIAM JOSEPH, graphic design and mktg. exec.; b. South Bend, Ind., Sept. 15, 1937; s. John Henry and Georgina (Lamy) L.; B.S., Ind. U., 1961; m. Nora M. Moore, July 29, 1972; children—W. Joseph, Melissa P. With Ind. U. Press, 1962-65; art dir., designer Robert Vogele, Inc., Chgo., 1965-66; mgr. of design Container Corp. Am., Chgo., 1966-71; with Unimark Internat., Chgo., 1971-72; self-employed graphic designer, Chgo. and Denver, 1972-74; art dir. Young & Rubicam, Chgo., 1974-75; v.p., dir. design Source, Inc., Chgo., 1975-76; pres. Lloydesign Assos., Chgo., 1976—. Bd. dirs. Youth Guidance. Served with U.S. Army, 1961-62. Mem. N.Y. Art Dirs. Club, Chgo. Art Dirs. Club, Am. Inst. Graphic Arts, Soc. Typographic Arts, Chgo. Press Club, Chgo. Ad Club. Club: Lake Shore. Home: 260 E Chestnut St Chicago IL 60611 Office: 200 E Ontario St Chicago IL 60611

LOBENTHAL, RICHARD HENRY, assn. exec.; b. N.Y.C., July 29, 1934; s. Joseph S. and Sallie (Schwartz) L.; A.B., U. Chgo., 1954, postgrad., 1955; postgrad. L.I. U., 1956, N.Y. U., 1957; children—Joshua, Adam, Lisa, Debra. Mem. treatment staff U. Chgo., 1951-53; acting dir. Boys House Community Service Soc., N.Y.C., 1956-58; with Anti-Defamation League of B'nai B'rith, Tex., Okla., N.C., Va., 1959-64, Mich. regional dir., Detroit, 1964—. Cons. N.Y. Dept. Labor, 1958-59; affiliated for spl. assignments U.S. vol. orgns. UNESCO, 1958; part-time faculty dept. sociology Wayne State U., Detroit, 1966-73; faculty adviser, founder Pub. Interest Research Group in Mich., 1971-73; cons. social sci. div. Coll. Lifelong Learning, 1974—; part time faculty dept. sociology U. Detroit, 1975—, cons., guest lectr. Urban Extension div., 1972—, field-work faculty grad. schs. social work, 1968—; guest faculty Divine Word Internat. Centre for Religious Edn., London, Ont., Can., 1971-73; field work faculty grad. schs. social work Mich. State U., James Madison Coll., 1970—; faculty U. Mich., Dearborn; adviser Nat. Center for Urban Ethnic Affairs, Detroit, 1970—; pvt. cons. civil rights; radio commentator Sta. WDET-FM; nat. cons. to police depts. Mem. bd. Narcotics Addiction Rehab. Coordinating Orgn., Detroit; chmn. coordinating council on human relations City Detroit, 1965—; mem. state bd., exec. com. Mich. Congress Parents and Tchrs., 1968-73; human relations cons. Detroit council PTA, 1966—; mem. human relations curriculum com. Mich. Dept. Edn., 1969—; mem. Detroit Mayor's Neighborhood Preservation Com., 1965; mem. community relations adv. com. New Detroit, 1971-73; mem. Interfaith Action Council Detroit, 1968—, Citizens for Advancement Pub. Edn., 1966—; mem. com. on pub. edn. Mich. Council Chs., 1968—; mem. Mich. adv. com. U.S. Commn. on Civil Rights, 1972—; mem. adv. task force Project Compact, 1973—; advisory com. Farm Worker's Edn. Fund, Archdiocese of Detroit. Bd. dirs. Urban Alliance, People Acting for Change Together, Neighborhood Service Orgn., Detroit Indsl. Mission, Health Resource Program; bd. dirs., corporate sec. Nat. Center for Resources on Instl. Oppression, Detroit, 1970—; commr. Detroit Commn. on Internat. Yr. of Children and Youth. Mem. Nat., Mich. (past pres.) assns. human rights workers, Am. Sociol. Assn., Soc. for Psychol. Study Social Issues, AAUP. Author: (with Gregory Squires) Affirmative Action: Guide to the Perplexed, 1977; (with others) Addicts Doesn't Live Here Anymore. Office: 163 Madison St Detroit MI 48226

LOCH, JOHN ROBERT, ednl. adminstr.; b. Sharon, Pa., Aug. 25, 1940; s. Robert Addison and Mary Virginia (Beck) L.; student Waynesburg Coll., 1958; A.B. Grove City Coll., 1962; postgrad Pitts. Theol. Sem., 1962; M.Ed., U. Pitts., 1966, Ph.D., 1972; m. Nov. 26, 1969 (div. 1979). Asst. to dean men U. Pitts., 1963-64, dir. student union, 1964-70, dir. student affairs research, 1970-71, dir. suburban ednl. services Sch. Gen. Studies, 1971-75; dir. continuing edn. and public service Youngstown (Ohio) State U., 1975—; research asso. Pres's Commn. on Campus Unrest, 1970. Trustee, Mahoning Shenango Health Edn. Network, 1976—, Career Devel. Center for Women, 1978-80, Youngstown Area Arts Council, 1980—, Protestant Family Services, 1981—; coordinator fund raising Nat. Unity Campagn, Mahoning County, 1980; state chmn. Young Republican Coll. council Pa., 1960. Mem. Adult Edn. Assn. U.S.A., Am. Assn. Higher Edn., Nat. U. Continuing Edn. Assn., Ohio Council Higher Continuing Edn. (pres. 1979-80), Druids, Omicron Delta Kappa, Kappa Kappa Psi, Phi Kappa Phi (pres. 1980-81), Alpha Phi Omega, Alpha Sigma Lambda. Presbyterian. Clubs: Kiwanis (dir. 1981—), Youngstown Traffic (hon. life). Home: 242 Upland Ave Youngstown OH 44504 Office: Youngstown State U Youngstown OH 44555

LOCHER, RALPH S., justice Ohio Supreme Ct.; b. Moreni, Romania, July 24, 1915; s. Ephraim and Natalie (Voigt) L.; B.A. with honors, Bluffton Coll., 1936; LL.B., Case Western Res. U., 1939; m. Eleanor Worthington, June 18, 1939; 1 dau., Virginia Lynn. Admitted to Ohio bar, 1939; former sec. to Gov. Ohio; former law dir. City of Cleve.; former mayor Cleve.; judge Ohio Ct. Common Pleas Cuyahoga County, 1969-72, Cuyahoga County Ct. Probate Div., 1973-77; justice Supreme Ct. Ohio, 1977—. Mem. Am. Bar Assn., Bar Assn. Greater Cleve., Cuyahoga County Bar Assn. Democrat. Office: State Office Tower 30 E Broad St Columbus OH 43215

LOCKE, GILES RICHARD, radiologist; b. Youngstown, Ohio, Jan. 12, 1937; s. Giles R. and Mildred (Gray) L.; B.A., DePauw U., 1958; M.D., Western Reserve U., 1962; m. Judith Blang, Aug. 2, 1958; children—Rick, Jon, Mark, Mike. Intern, Milw. County Hosp., 1962-63; resident U. Iowa, Iowa City, 1963-66; chmn. radiation oncology Decatur Meml. Hosp., Decatur, Ill., 1968-75; chmn. radiology, 1974—; pres. X-ray Service Corp., 1975—; clin. asso. prof. U. Ill.; cons. Ill. Cancer Council; regional asst. dean U. Ill., mem. exec. com. Sch. Basic Med. Scis.; clin. asso. So. Ill. U. Sch. Medicine. Served with U.S. Army, 1966-68. Recipient Distinguished Service Award, Jaycees, 1972. Mem. AMA, Am. Coll. Radiology, Am. Soc. Therapeutic Radiologists, Radiology Soc. N.Am., Am. Cancer Soc. (pres. Macon County). Presbyterian. Clubs: Decatur Country (pres.). Office: 2300 N Edward St Decatur IL 62526

LOCKWOOD, FRANK JAMES, mfg. co. exec.; b. San Bernardino, Cal., Oct. 30, 1931; s. John Ellis and Sarah Grace (Roberts) L.; student S.E. City Coll., 1955, Ill. Inst. Tech., 1963-64, Bogan Jr. Coll., 1966; m. Deborah Sue Samples, 1981; children—Fay (Mrs. Mark Huegelmann), Frank, Hedy (Mrs. Michael Machala), Jonnie, George, Katherine, Bill, Dena. Gen. foreman Hupp Aviation, Chgo., 1951-60; dept. head UARCO, Inc., Chgo., 1960-68; pres. Xact Machine & Engring. Co., Chgo., 1968—, also chmn. bd., dir.; pres. Lockwood Engring., Inc., Ill. Nat. Corp. Cons. engr. Served with USNR, 1948-50. Named Chicago Ridge (Ill.) Father of Year, 1964. Mem. Ill. Divers Assn. (pres. 1961-62). Mason (32 deg., Shriner). Club: Masons. Patentee in field. Home: Rural Route 1 Texico IL 62889 Office: 7011 W Archer Ave Chicago IL 60638

LODGE, JAMES ROBERT, educator; b. Downey, Iowa, July 1, 1925; s. Ferrel Labon and Margaret Clara (Elliott) L.; B.S., Iowa State U., 1952, M.S., 1954; Ph.D., Mich. State U., 1957; m. Jean Agnes Wessel, June 15, 1947; children—Julie Beth, James Robert. Research asst. Mich. State U., East Lansing, 1954-57; research asso. U. Ill. at Urbana, 1957-60, asst. prof. reproductive physiology, 1960-63, asso. prof. reproductive physiology, 1963-69, prof. reproductive physiology, 1969—. Participant, Internat. Cong. Reproduction, Trento, Italy, 1964, Paris, France, 1968, Krakow, Poland, 1976, Madrid, Spain, 1980. Asst. coach girls softball Babe Ruth Little League, Urbana, 1972-74. Served with AUS, 1944-46. Recipient Outstanding Instr. award Dairy Club of U. Ill., 1969; named Outstanding Instr. in Coll. of Agr., U. Ill., Alpha Zeta, 1981. NIH Research fellow, 1969. Mem. Am. Physiol. Soc., AAAS, Soc. Study Reprodn., Am. Dairy Sci. Assn., Am. Soc. Animal Sci., Soc. Cryobiology, N.Y. Acad. Sci., Sigma Xi, Phi Kappa Phi (mem. scholarship com. 1970-73, chmn. 1973), Gamma Sigma Delta. Methodist (mem. commn. edn. 1975-78). Club: Masons. Co-author: Reproductive Physiology and Artificial Insemination of Cattle, 2d edit., 1978. Contbr. articles to profl. jours. Home: 1701 S Cottage Grove St Urbana IL 61801

LODGE, RHEA EWALD (MRS. L. HARVEY LODGE), writer, editor, state ofcl.; b. Detroit; d. William Rudolph and Rhea Elizabeth (Allen) Ewald; student Wellesley Coll., 1937-39, U. Mo. Journalism Sch., 1940-42; m. Robert Brigham Ellery, Oct. 17, 1942 (dec. July 1945); 1 son, Robert Brigham (dec. 1969); m. 2d, Robert Kingsbury Vietor, Sept. 2, 1947; 1 son, Carl Frederick III; m. 3d, L. Harvey Lodge, Oct. 16, 1971 (dec. May 1976). Wire editor Pontiac (Mich.) Press, 1945-47, women's editor, 1957-60; editor Lakeland Tribune, 1960-63; account exec. A. R. Gloster Agy., Detroit, 1963-66; dir. public relations, continuing edn. Oakland U., Rochester Mich., 1965-68; free lance pub. relations cons., Birmingham, Mich., 1967-70; writer, photographer News-Tribune Publs., Inc., 1968-71; pres. Vietor-Lodge Assos., 1970-72; pub. relations specialist, former exec. asst. to dir. Mich. Dept. Labor; partner Main St. Assos. Chmn. community drives; spl. asst. Meadow Brook Music Festival, Rochester, Mich.; mem. State adv. council for bicentennial. Mem. League Women Voters (dir. 1953), Founders Soc. Detroit Inst. Arts, Nat. Fedn. Press Women, Women in Communications (sec. 1968-69, chpt. treas. 1941-42), Women in State Govt. (dir.), Alpha Phi. Clubs: Village, Nomads, Wellesley; House and Senate (past treas.) (Lansing). Address: 4113 Elizabeth Rd Lansing MI 48917

LODWICK, KATHLEEN LORRAINE, historian; b. St. Louis, Feb. 7, 1944; d. Algha Claire and Kathryn Elizabeth (Worthington) L.; B.S. with honors, Ohio U., 1964, M.A., 1965; Ph.D., U. Ariz., 1976; postgrad. U. Hawaii, 1966-67, Nat. Taiwan Normal U., 1967-68. Asst. prof. history U. No. Colo., 1976-77; asst. prof. history Ind. State U., 1977-78; research asso. John King Fairbank Center for East Asian Research, Harvard U., 1978-79; asst. prof. history S.W. Mo. State U., Springfield, 1979—; dir. index/biographical guide to Chinese Recorder and Missionary Jour. project, 1977—. Mem. AAUW, Am. Hist. Assn., Assn. Asian Studies, Nat. Assn. Fgn. Student Affairs, UN Assn., Phi Alpha Theta. Democrat. Methodist. Home: 2934 E Southeast Circle Springfield MO 65802 Office: History Dept SW Mo State U Springfield MO 65802

LOE, WILLIAM K., transp. co. exec.; b. Brooten, Minn., Oct. 27, 1940; s. Theodore Herman and Irene Rose (Schlumbohm) L.; A.A., Vermilion State Jr. Coll., 1968; B.S., St. Cloud State U., 1970; postgrad. U. Minn., 1971-72, Coll. St. Thomas, 1981; m. Alice R. Thuer, June 13, 1964; children—Mark William, Jessica Ann. Heavy equipment operator Res. Mining, Babbitt, Minn., 1960-68; personnel rep. N.W. Orient Airlines, St. Paul, 1969; employment rep. Graco, Inc., Mpls., 1970-71, supr. compensation, 1971-73, personnel mgr. U.S. ops., 1974-75, mgr. corp. compensation and benefits, internat. personnel coordinator, 1975-79; dir. personnel Murphy Motor Freight Lines, St. Paul, 1979-80, v.p. personnel, 1980—. Served with USMC, 1959-60. Mem. Am. Soc. Personnel Adminstrs., Am. Trucking Assn. (personnel practices subcom.), Soc. Advancement Mgmt., Twin City Personnel Assn., Twin City Internat. Personnel Assn. Republican. Lutheran. Home: 18400 33d Ave N Plymouth MN 55447 Office: Suite 354 Hamm Bldg St Paul MN 55164

LOEFFLER, WALTER WAYNE, JR., chem. co. exec.; b. Linn, Kans., Feb. 22, 1923; s. Walter William and Ida Belle (Knox) L.; student Pueblo Jr. Coll., 1940-42; B.A., U. Colo., 1950, M.A., 1953; m. Betty Lee Coats, July 6, 1944; children—Catherine Lee, Nancy Ann, Lawrence Wayne; m. 2d, Betty Larandon Curtis, July 22, 1978. Chemist, Sunflower Ordnance Works, Lawrence, Kans., 1953-57, biochem. sect. Chemagro Chem. Corp., 1957-64; sr. scheduler research and devel. scheduling sect. Chemagro Agrl. div. Mobay Chem. Corp., Kansas City, Mo., 1974—. Served with AUS, 1942-45. Mem. Am. Chem. Soc., K&H Systems Users Assn. (pres.). Roman Catholic. Patentee in field. Home: 9530 Windsor St Overland Park KS 66206 Office: 9600 Hawthorn Rd Kansas City MO 64120

LOEHNERT, JOHN TYLER, savs. and loan exec.; b. Cleve., June 3, 1923; s. Frank and Elizabeth (Brightman) L.; B.A. in Econs., Denison U., 1947; m. Gail Kathleen Pritchard, June 29, 1946; children—Leslie Ann, John Tyler, Gail Brooke, Todd P. Restauranteur, Granville, Ohio, 1947-51; asst. basketball coach Denison U., 1947-51, head basketball coach, 1951-53; mgmt. trainee Dollar Fed. Savs. & Loan Assn. (co. name changed to Dollar Savs. Assn. 1973), Columbus, Ohio, 1953, asst. v.p., 1957-63, v.p., 1963—. Chmn. Franklin County Cancer Soc. Crusade, 1970; mem. Bexley (Ohio) City Council, 1978—; pres. Stelios M. Stelson Found., 1976. Served with USN, 1943-46; PTO; ret. capt. Res. Recipient Meritorious Community Service award, Sec. of Navy, 1971; Distinguished Community Service award City of Bexley, 1972; Gold Wreath Recruiting award U.S. Navy, 1976. Mem. Pub. Relations Soc. Am., U.S. Savs. and Loan League, Inst. Fin. Edn., Res. Officers Assn., Am. Savs. and Loan Inst. (pres. Columbus chpt. 1962), Ohio Savs. and Loan League, Navy League U.S. (pres. Columbus counci 1966), Omicron Delta Kappa. Republican. Episcopalian. Clubs: Athletic (Columbus); Masons (Granville); Kiwanis (pres. 1957) (Columbus). Home: 120 N Cassingham St Bexley OH 43209 Office: 1 E Gay St Columbus OH 43215

LOEHR, PETER WILLIAM, supt. schs.; b. Chgo., July 25, 1945; s. Howard Clement and Audrey Josephine Loehr; M.A. in English, Youngstown (Ohio) State U., 1973; Ph.D. in Edn. Adminstrn., Kent (Ohio) State U., 1976; m. Judyth Lisabeth Connor, Feb. 6, 1981. Tchr., Tulsa Public Schs., 1966-67, Cumberland County (N.C.) Schs., 1970-71; adminstr. Hudson (Ohio) Schs., 1973-76; dir. curriculum/asst. supt. Kenton County (Ky.) Schs., 1978-79; supt. schs. Alexander Local Schs., Albany, Ohio, 1980-81; supt. schs. Newton Falls Exempted Village Newton Falls, Ohio, 1981—; cons. U. Cin., others. Mem. Tulsa Speakers Bur., 1976-78. Served with U.S. Army, 1967-70. Mem. SAR (nat. oration com.; presenter Good Citizenship awards), Buckeye Assn. Sch. Adminstrs., Nat. Orgn. Legal Problems of Edn., Assn. Supervision and Curriculum Devel., Nat. Sch. Bds. Assn., Phi Delta Kappa. Author: Decision-Making in Public Schools, 1976; editor: Child Language Development, 1974; contbr. articles to profl. jours. Home: 304 S Canal St Newton Falls OH 44444 Office: 30 N Center St Newton Falls OH 44444

LOENDORF, WILLIAM ROGER, electronic engr.; b. Racine, Wis., July 21, 1948; s. Thorwald Christian and Edna Lillian (Henriksen) L.; B.S. in Engring. Sci., U. Wis. at Parkside, 1971; M.E.E., Colo. State U., 1973. With Unico, Inc., Franksville, Wis., 1973-79, project engr., 1973-75, software devel. mgr., tchr. tech. courses, 1975-78; software specialist Digital Equipment Corp., Chgo., 1979-80; spl. project engr. Delco Electronics div. Gen. Motors Corp., Oak Creek, Wis., 1980-81; software services mgr. Nat. Control Systems, Oak Creek, 1981—; part-time lectr. in elec. engring. and computer sci. U. Wis. at Parkside, Kenosha; mem. electronic tech.-computer adv. com. Gateway Tech. Inst., Racine, 1975-79. Registered profl. engr., Wis., Colo. Mem. IEEE, Nat. Soc. Profl. Engrs., Data Processing Mgmt. Assn., U. Wis. at Parkside Alumni Assn. (vice chmn., bd. dirs. 1973-79), Eta Kappa Nu. Lutheran. Club: Unico, Inc. Employees (past v.p.). Home: 83 E Parkfield Ct Racine WI 53402

LOENSER, LARRY ELDON, county extension dir.; b. Geneseo, Ill., Mar. 18, 1944; s. Eldon William and Wilma Irene (Mohler) L.; B.S., Iowa State U., 1966, M.S., 1976; m. Eugenie Loralee Rice, June 10, 1966; children—Rebecca, Michael, Christina, Nathan. Prodn. supr. Internat. Harvester Co., E. Moline, Ill., 1966-70; county extension dir. Butler County, Allison, Iowa, 1970-72, Black Hawk County, Waterloo, Iowa, 1972—; mem. local arrangements com. World Food Conf., Iowa State U., 1976. Mem. Black Hawk County Bicentennial Commn. bd., 1974-75; exec. com. dir. N.Central Iowa Health Planning Council, 1971-72; adv. com. Area VII Dept. Social Services, 1971-72; chmn. Black Hawk County Rural Devel. Com., 1972—. Mem. Iowa State U. Extension Assn., Cedar Falls C. of C., Waterloo C. of C., Phi Kappa Phi, Epsilon Sigma Phi, Phi Delta Kappa. Lutheran. Rotarian. Home: 206 Devlin Circle Cedar Falls IA 50613 Office: 1022 W 5th St Waterloo IA 50702

LOESCH, KATHARINE TAYLOR (MRS. JOHN GEORGE LOESCH), educator; b. Berkeley, Calif., Apr. 13, 1922; d. Paul Schuster and Katharine (Whiteside) Taylor; student Swarthmore Coll., 1939-41, U. Wash., 1942; B.A., Columbia U., 1944, M.A., 1949; grad. Neighborhood Playhouse Sch. of Theatre, 1946; postgrad. Ind. U., 1953; Ph.D., Northwestern U., 1961; m. John George Loesch, Aug. 28, 1948; 1 son, William Ross. Instr. speech Wellesley (Mass.) Coll., 1949-52, Loyola U., Chgo., 1956; asst. prof. English and speech Roosevelt U., Chgo., 1957, 62-65; faculty U. Ill. at Chgo. Circle, 1968—, asso. prof. communication and theatre, 1976—. Active ERA, Ill., 1975-76. Recipient Golden Anniversary Prize award Speech Assn. Am., 1969. Am. Philos. Soc. grantee, 1970; U. Ill., Chgo., grantee, 1970. Mem. Am. Soc. Aesthetics, Linguistics Soc. Am., Speech Communication Assn. (Golden Anniversary prize award 1969, chmn. interpretation div. 1979-80), MLA, Honorable Soc. Cymmrodorion, Pi Beta Phi. Episcopalian. Contbr. writings to profl. publs. Office: Dept Communication and Theatre Box 4348 U Ill Chicago IL 60680

LOFF, WALTER PETER, businessman; b. Wilkin County, Minn., Oct. 13, 1906; s. Hans H. and Mathilda A. (Stach) L.; m. Myrtle Josephine Larson, Mar. 8, 1930; children—Wayne Ardell, Lorna M. Loff Quamme, Donavon Walter. Farmer, Richland County, N.D., 1926-57; v.p. Lillegard, Inc., 1959—, chmn. bd., 1977; mgr., dir. Farm Real Estate Partnership, 1965—; pres. Vanguard Corp., 1965—, Ponderosa Corp., 1965—; v.p. L & S Investments, 1970—; dir. Security Internat. Ins. Co., Fargo, N.D., 1963—. Mem. Galchutt Sch. Bd., 1939-51; mem. Soil Conservation Service, 1960-66; pres. Richland County Farm Bur., 1964-66; dir., mem. fin. com. Meml. Gardens, 1958—. Republican. Lutheran. Club: Elks. Address: 810 3d St N Wahpeton ND 58075

LOFGREN, CHARLES W., ink and pen mfg. co. exec.; b. Ulen, Minn., 1907; grad. Carleton Coll., Minn., 1927. Chmn. bd., dir. Sanford Corp., Bellwood, Ill.; dir. Tri-Rental Co. Office: Sanford Corp 2740 Washington Blvd Bellwood IL 60104*

LOFGREN, KARL ADOLPH, surgeon; b. Killeberg, Sweden, Apr. 1, 1915; s. Hokan Albin and Teckla Elizabeth (Carlsson) L.; student Northwestern U., 1934-37; M.D., Harvard U., 1941; M.S. in Surgery, U. Minn., 1947; m. Jean Frances Taylor, Sept. 12, 1942; children—Karl Edward, Anne Elizabeth. Intern, U. Minn. Hosps., Mpls., 1941-42, Mayo Found. fellow in surgery, 1942-44, 46-48; asst. surgeon Royal Academic Hosp., Uppsala, Sweden, 1949; asst. to surg. staff Mayo Clinic, Rochester, Minn., 1949-50, cons. sect. peripheral vein surgery, 1950—, instr. in surgery Mayo Grad. Sch. Medicine, 1951-60, asst. prof. surgery, 1960-74, comdg. officer USNR Med. Co. Mayo Clinic, 1963-67, head sect. peripheral vein surgery, dept. surgery, 1966—; asso. prof. surgery Mayo Med. Sch., Rochester, 1974-79, prof., 1979—; cons. surg. staff Rochester Meth. Hosp. and St. Mary's Hosp. Mem. adv. bd. Salvation Army of Rochester, 1959-81, pres., 1962-63. Served to capt., M.C. USNR, 1944-46. Decorated Bronze Star. Diplomate Am. Bd. Surgery. Fellow A.C.S.; mem. Soc. for Vascular Surgery, Midwestern Vascular Surgery Soc., Pan-Pacific Surg. Assn., Internat. Cardiovascular Soc., Minn., Swedish (hon.) surg. socs., Mil. Surgeons, So. Minn. Med. Assn. (pres. 1972-73), Swiss Soc. Phlebology (co-worker), Sigma Xi. Baptist. Club: Rotary of Rochester. Contbr. articles to profl. jours. and textbooks. Home: 1001 7th Ave NE Rochester MN 55901 Office: Mayo Clinic Rochester MN 55901

LOFTUS, DONALD GREGORY, hosp. adminstr.; b. St. Louis, Aug. 17, 1943; s. Charles J. and Mary A. Loftus; B.S., Ind. U., 1965; M.S., Trinity U., 1969; m. Kala Rae Gilmour, Sept. 10, 1966; children—Kelly Anne, Kyle Andrew. Adminstrv. extern Bloomington (Ind.) Hosp., 1964-65; unit mgr. dept. adminstrv. medicine Presbyn.-St. Luke's Hosp., Chgo., 1965-67; grad. asst. health resources planning unit Tex. Hosp. Assn., San Antonio, 1968; adminstrv. resident Ind. U. Med. Center, Indpls., 1968; asst. adminstr. Graham Hosp., Canton, Ill., 1969-73; adminstr. Franklin Hosp., Benton, Ill., 1973-74; exec. v.p. Holy Family Hosp., Des Plaines, Ill., 1974-76; pres., chief exec. officer Appleton (Wis.) Meml. Hosp., 1977-80; pres., chief exec. officer United Health Service Mgmt. Corp., 1980—; rep. Outagamie Community Blood Bank, 1977-79; mem. instructional workshop adv. com. Tri-State Hosp. Assembly, 1976-78; dir. Valley Bank; asso. clin. prof. U. Wis. Med. Sch., Madison. Hosp. rep. Gov.'s Prison Health Care Adv. Com., State of Wis., 1977-79; bd. dirs. Lake Winnebago Health Systems Agy., 1977—. Fellow Am. Coll. Hosp. Adminstrs.; mem. Wis. Hosp. Assn. (mem. com. on planning 1978-82), Am. Acad. Polit. and Social Sci., Sigma Iota Epsilon. Office: 229 S Morrison Appleton WI 54911

LOGAN, JEANNETTE, nursing adminstr.; b. Maywood, Ill., Mar. 1, 1933; d. Samuel and Luvena (Simmons) L.; diploma Cook County Sch. of Nursing, Chgo., 1955; B.S. in Nursing, Gov.'s State U., 1976, M. Health Sci. Adminstrn., 1978. Head nurse Cook County Hosp., Chgo., 1957-59, supr., 1959-63, adminstrv. nurse supr., 1964-69, asst. dir. med. nursing, 1969-71, dir. med. nursing, 1971-72, dir. nursing services, 1972-78, asso. adminstr. nursing and patient services, 1978—; head nurse Mt. Sinai Hosp., Chgo., 1963-64; cons., guest lectr.; mem. nursing adv. com. Malcolm X Jr. Coll., Chgo. State U., Gov.'s State U. Mem. legal task force Children's Right Council Greater Chgo. Registered nurse, Ill. Mem. Nat. League for Nursing, Am. Soc. Nursing Adminstrs. Am. Hosp. Assn., Am. Film Inst., Gov.'s State U. Alumni Assn., People United to Save Humanities. Office: Cook County Hosp 1825 W Harrison St Chicago IL 60612

LOGAN, JOHN STERLING, engr.; b. Helena, Mont., Feb. 23, 1934; s. William Ernest and Florence (Snow) L.; B.M.E., Pa. State U., 1956; m. Gwendolyn June Bickford, Nov. 7, 1959; 1 son, John Sterling. Supv. heavy vehicle chassis sect. Ford Motor Co., Dearborn, Mich., 1965-72, mgr. product engring. dept. transp. systems ops., 1972-76, mgr. transp. systems, diversified products ops., 1976-77, mgr. spl.

projects vehicle research N.Am. auto ops., 1977-78, mgr. devel. methods and services dept. N.Am. auto ops., 1978—. Served with U.S. Army, 1957. Registered profl. engr., Mich. Mem. Soc. Automotive Engrs., Mich. Engring. Soc. Patentee in automated transp. systems. Home: 24444 Emerson St Dearborn MI 48124 Office: Ford Motor Co American Rd Dearborn MI 48124

LOGAN, JOHN WESLEY, JR., civil engr.; b. Chgo., Aug. 15, 1954; s. John Wesley and Martha Elizabeth (Peterson) L.; B.C.E., Purdue U., 1975; m. Marilyn L.A. Logan. Engr., Peoples Gas Light & Coke Co., Chgo., 1973; structural engr. Eastman Kodak Co., Rochester, N.Y., 1974; staff engr. Amoco Oil Co., Chgo., 1975, 76-80, project engr., 1977-80, sr. project engr., 1980—. Mem. Nat. Soc. Profl. Engrs., ASCE, Nat. Soc. Black Engrs., Nat. Tech. Alliance. Democrat. Methodist. Home: 8602 Kingston Chicago IL 60617 Office: 200 E Randolph Dr Chicago IL 60601

LOGAN, LLOYD, pharmacist; b. Columbia, Mo., Dec. 27, 1932; s. Henry B. and Eva G. (Nelson) L.; student Purdue U., 1951-52, Belleville Jr. Coll., 1953-54; B.S. in Pharmacy, St. Louis Coll. Pharmacy, 1958; m. Lottie A. Pecot, Aug. 16, 1958; children—Terri Lynn, Connie Renee, Gerald Brian, Michael Steven, Kevin Craig. Staff pharmacist St. Louis U. Hosp., 1958-59, chief pharmacist, 1959-67, dir. pharmacy and purchasing, 1966-69; owner Mound City Pharmacy, St. Louis, 1962—, Dome Pharmacy, St. Louis, 1980—; sec. Rhodes Med. Supply, Inc., St. Louis, 1968-72; pres. Country Club Enterprise, Inc., St. Louis, 1980—. Asst. dir. purchasing services Daus. of Charity Shared Services Assn., 1970-81, acting dir., 1981—; mem. shared services adv. panel Am. Hosp. Assn.; pres. People, Inc., St. Louis, 1967-68; mem. YMCA; mem. adv. com. HELP, Inc., St. Louis; treas. Page Community Devel. Corp., St. Louis, 1971-73; trustee Lindell Hosp., St. Louis; mem. sch. bd. St. Engelbert Sch., 1969-76, pres., 1973-76; mem. St. Louis Archdiocesan Sch. Bd., 1976-79, pres., 1977—; bd. dirs. Urban League of St. Louis. Served with USAF, 1952-56. Mem. Am., Nat., Mound City (pres. 1964) pharm. assns., Am., St. Louis socs. hosp. pharmacists, Nat. Assn. Retail Druggists, Chi Delta Mu (sec. 1967-69, pres. 1973-74). Roman Catholic. Patentee. Home: 6055 Lindell Blvd Saint Louis MO 63112 Office: 2715 N Union Blvd Saint Louis MO 63113

LOGAN, SERGE EDWARD, editor, wax co. exec.; b. Chgo., Feb. 7, 1926; s. Carl and Alexandra (Honcharik) L.; student Superior (Wis.) State U., 1946-48; B.A. magna cum laude, U. Minn., 1950. Reporter, asst. city editor, Sunday editor Racine (Wis.) Jour.-Times, 1950-60; publs. mgr. S. C. Johnson & Son, Inc., Racine, 1960-65, community affairs mgr., editor, 1965-68, communications mgr., 1968-71, communications dir., 1971-81, asst. to vice chmn., 1981—, editor Johnson Mag., 1960-79. Active as scoutmaster, explorer adviser, commnr., mem. exec. bd. SE Wis. council Boy Scouts Am., 1951—, pres., 1966-68; sec. Johnson Wax Fund, Inc., 1965-68, trustee, 1978—; public relations chmn. United Fund, 1967, 70, 72, 73. Served with USNR, 1944-46; PTO. Named Outstanding Young Man of Year, Racine Jr. C. of C., 1961; recipient Silver Beaver award Boy Scouts Am., 1963, Silver Antelope, 1973. Am. Polit. Sci. Assn. Congl. fellow on Senate staff Hubert H. Humphrey, Ho. of reps. staff James Wright, 1956-57. Mem. C. of C. (publs. com. 1967—), Internat. (conf. program chmn. 1977), S.E. Wis. (officer, dir.) assns. bus. communicators, Meeting Planners Internat. (officer, dir. Wis. chpt.), Phi Beta Kappa. Methodist (steward). Home: 1737 Wisconsin Ave Racine WI 53403 Office: 1525 Howe St Racine WI 53403

LOGAN, WILLIAM, banker; b. Keokuk, Iowa, Dec. 30, 1934; s. William Archie and Carla (Huiskamp) L.; B.Sc., U. Iowa, 1956; m. Shirley Joan Tyler, Aug. 26, 1957; children—Tyler, Catherine, Laura, Archie, Daniel. Mgmt. trainee Central Bank, Denver, 1957-58; with State Central Savs. Bank, Keokuk, Iowa, 1958—, pres., 1966—; dir. Kast Metals. Bd. dirs. U. Iowa Found., 1972—; mem. City Council, Keokuk, 1966-72; treas. Lee County Republican Com., 1959-73. Mem. Iowa Ind. Bankers Assn., Ind. Bankers Assn. Am., Iowa Bankers Assn. Republican. Episcopalian. Clubs: U. Iowa Letterman's, I-Club, Rotary, Keokuk Country, Des Moines, Shriners, Masons. Office: 601 Main Keokuk IA 52632

LOGIE, JOHN HOULT, lawyer; b. Ann Arbor, Mich., Aug. 11, 1939; s. James W. and Elizabeth H. (Hoult) L.; student Williams Coll.; B.A., U. Mich., 1961, J.D., 1968; M.S., George Washington U., 1966; m. Susan G. Duerr, Aug. 15, 1964; children—John Hoult, Susannah, Margaret Elizabeth. Commd. ensign U.S. Navy, 1961, advanced through grades to lt., 1965; ops. officer U.S. Navy Destroyers-Pacific Fleet, 1962-64; instr. U.S. Naval Acad., 1964-66; resigned, 1966; admitted to Mich. bar, 1969; partner firm Warner, Norcross & Judd, Grand Rapids, 1969—; program coordinator Inst. Continuing Legal Edn., 1980—. Pres., Grand Rapids PTA Council, 1971-73, Heritage Hill Assn., 1976; chmn. Grand Rapids Urban Homesteading Commn., 1975-80, Target Area Leadership Conf., 1976-80; v.p., bd. dirs. Goodwill Industries, Am. Cancer Soc. Mem. Am. Bar Assn. (forum com. on health law 1980—), Mich. Bar Assn., Grand Rapids Bar Assn., Am. Soc. Hosp. Attys., Mich. Soc. Hosp. Attys. (pres. 1976-77). Clubs: University (dir. 1979—, pres. 1980—), Peninsular, Athletic (Grand Rapids). Home: 601 Cherry St SE Grand Rapids MI 49503 Office: 900 Old Kent Bldg Grand Rapids MI 49503

LOHMAN, KEITH DOUGLASS, ednl. adminstr.; b. Milw., Nov. 27, 1942; s. Walter Henry and Marjorie Jean (Raatz) L.; B.S., Carroll Coll., 1964; M.S., U. Wis. at Milw., 1966; Ed.D., U. No. Colo., 1971; m. Romayne Carol Beuthling, June 6, 1970. Instr. sociology U. Wis. at Whitewater, 1966-69, asso. dean student life, coordinator counseling programs, 1973—; instr. sociology U. No. Colo., 1969-70; vice prin. Mukwonago (Wis.) High Sch., 1971-72; alcohol awareness and alcohol edn. coordinator, U. Wis. Served with USAR, 1967-73. Lic. psychologist, Wis. Mem. Am., Wis. coll. personnel assns., Am. Psychol. Assn., Wis. Psychol. Assn., Am. Personnel and Guidance Assn., ACLU (mem. student rights com.), Phi Delta Kappa. Lutheran. Home: PO Box 277 Palmyra WI 53156 Office: 101 Salisbury St U Wis Whitewater WI 53190

LOHMANN, WILLIAM TOMBAUGH, architect; b. Burlington, Iowa, June 12, 1928; s. Carl John and Helen Rachel (Tombaugh) L.; student Burlington Jr. Coll., 1946-47; B.S., Iowa State U., 1950; postgrad. Ill. Inst. Tech., 1956-58; m. Evelyn Day Ward, July 15, 1951; children—Catherine Day, Melanie Ann. Draftsman Dane D. Morgan & Assos., Burlington, 1954-57; project adminstr. Robert Babbin & Assos., Chgo., 1958-62; specification writer Bertrand Goldberg Assos., Chgo., 1963-67; chief specifier Murphy/Jahn Assos., Chgo., 1968—; lectr. several Midwest campuses. Mem. Constrn. Industry Affairs Com. Chgo., 1967-69, 70—; mem. City of Chgo. Com. on Standards and Tests, 1973-80; mem. Adv. Com. on Bldg. Code Amendments, 1981—. Served with USAF, 1950-54. Recipient Constrn. Specifications Inst. Region 7 Dirs. award, 1974, others. Fellow Constrn. Specifications Inst.; mem. ASTM, AIA, Constrn. Specifications Inst. (chpt. pres. 1969-70). Methodist. Contbg. editor Progressive Architecture mag., 1975—. Home: 1232 Maple Ave Evanston IL 60202 Office: 224 S Michigan Ave Chicago IL 60604

LOHUTKO, CONRAD ANTHONY, polit. scientist; b. Detroit, Sept. 5, 1944; s. Floryan Anthony and Virginia Elizabeth (Barber) L.; A.B., Dickinson Coll., 1966; A.M., St. Louis U., 1970, Ph.D., 1978; m. Sandra Lee Moore, Apr. 17, 1967; children—Eric Conrad, Kurt Charles, Matthew Moore, Karen Virginia, Amy Davis, Janet Lynn, Sara Ellen. Dir. community relations Asso. Industries of Mo., St. Louis, 1968; spl. asst. to pres. St. Louis U., 1970-71; sr. position classification specialist U.S. Army Aviation Systems Command, 1971-80; program planning specialist U.S. Army Automated Logistics Mgmt. Systems Activity, St. Louis, 1980—. Lectr. polit. sci. St. Louis U., 1970—. Polit. strategist Independent Colls. and Univs. Mo., 1970-71. Served to 1st lt. AUS, 1968; Viet Nam. Crown Zellerbach Found. fellow, 1970-71. Mem. Am. Polit. Sci. Assn., Southwestern Polit. Sci. Assn., Alpha Chi Rho, Pi Sigma Alpha, Alpha Sigma Nu. Republican. Baptist. Author: Political Interests in Conflict: The Politics Behind the Passage and Funding of the Missouri Tuition Assistance Bill, 1978; Hydroelectric Power and the Environment: Is It Worth the Cost?, 1980. Home: 3518 Hidden Stone Ct Saint Louis MO 63129 Office: 210 N Tucker Blvd Saint Louis MO 63102

LOKE, HAROLD JAMES, golf course supt.; b. Montreal, Que., Can., Apr. 26, 1946; s. Harold Raymond and Margaret Isabel (Stevens) L.; B.S. in Agronomy, Ohio State U., 1970; m. Karen Elaine Cook, Jan. 5, 1980. Asst., Oakwood Club, Cleve., 1971-72; asst. Canterbury Golf Club, Cleve., 1973-74; supt. East Liverpool (Ohio) Country Club, 1974-75; asst. Firestone Country Club, Akron, Ohio, 1975-78, supt., 1979—. Mem. Golf Course Supts. Assn. Am., No. Ohio Golf Course Supts. Assn. Coach high sch. and youth hockey teams. Home: 2138 Glenmount Ave Akron OH 44319 Office: 452 E Warner Rd Akron OH 44319

LOLLAR, ROBERT MILLER, indsl. mgmt. exec.; b. Lebanon, Ohio, May 17, 1915; s. Harry David and Ruby (Miller) L.; Chem.E., U. Cin., 1937, M.S., 1938, Ph.D., 1940; m. Dorothy Marie Williams, Jan. 1, 1941; children—Janet Ruth (Mrs. David Schwarz), Katherine Louise (Mrs. James Punteney, Jr.). Cereal analyst Kroger Food Found., Cin., 1935-37; devel. chemist Rit Product div. Corn Products, Indpls., 1937-39, 40-41; asso. prof. U. Cin., 1941-59; tech. dir. Armour & Co., Chgo., 1959-73; mgmt. and tech. cons., pres. Lollar and Assos., 1973—; tech. dir. Tanners Council Am., Cin., 1975—. Dir. OSRD, 1942-45. Recipient Alsop award Am. Leather Chemists Assn., 1954. Mem. Am. Leather Chemists Assn. (pres., editor-in-chief), Inst. Food Technologists, Am. Chem. Soc. (nat. councillor), Am. Soc. Quality Control, World Mariculture Soc., Sigma Xi, Tau Beta Pi, Alpha Chi Sigma. Address: 5960 Donjoy Dr Cincinnati OH 45242

LOLLI, WILLIAM JAMES, ins. co. exec.; b. Highland Park, Ill., May 28, 1943; s. James and Mildred (Levanti) L.; B.S., So. Ill. U., 1966; M.B.A., U. Chgo., 1971; m. Judith Lencioni, July 3, 1965; children—Patricia, Kristin, Cynthia. With Allstate Ins. Co., Northbrook, Ill., 1966—, systems mgr., 1973-77, acctg. mgr., 1977—. Treas., City of Highwood (Ill.), 1969—. C.P.A., Ill. Mem. Am. Inst. C.P.A.'s, Soc. C.P.C.U.'s, Data Processing Mgmt. Assn., Ins. Acctg. and Statis. Assn., Ill. Soc. C.P.A.'s. Republican. Roman Catholic. Home: 224 Oakridge St Highwood IL 60040 Office: A4 Allstate Plaza Northbrook IL 60062

LOLLINI, TYRONE GUY, steel co. exec.; b. Martins Ferry, Ohio, Mar. 19, 1949; s. Marcel and Ida (Dolfi) L.; student Ohio U.; m. Patty Domyan, June 20, 1970; 1 dau., Tricia. With Wheeling-Pittsburgh Steel Corp., Wheeling, W.Va., 1969—, laborer, 1969-70, safety supr., 1971-72, supr. safety inspections, 1972-74, safety primary, 1974-75, safety supt., 1977-80, gen. mgr. corp. safety, 1980—. Active Ohio Soc. for Prevention of Blindness, Young Democrats Jefferson County (Ohio). Named Belmont County Safety Man of Year, 1974; Young Jaycee Steelworker of Year, 1980. Mem. Am. Soc. Safety Engrs., Am. Iron and Steel Inst., Belmont County Safety Council. Club: Italian-American of Martins Ferry. Home: 106 Mound Tiltonsville OH 43963 Office: 1134 Marret Wheeling WV 26003

LOLLIS, TOM ETTA HALSEY, educator; b. Chattanooga, Nov. 4, 1944; s. Thomas Mitchell and Ethel (Gates) Halsey; B.A. in History, Roosevelt U., Chgo., 1971; M.A. in Spl. Edn., Northeastern Ill. U., Chgo., 1972; div. Tchr., Chgo. Bd. Edn., 1972—. Sec., Dist. 10 Edn. Council, 1973-77, tchr. educable mentally handicapped, 1977—. Cert. in spl. edn., Ill.; specialist in educable mentally handicapped edn. Home: 8307 S Morgan Ave Chicago IL 60620 Office: John W Cook Elementary Sch 8150 S Bishop St Chicago IL 60620

LOMAX, ALLEN M., investment counselor; b. Bristow, Ind., June 19, 1902; s. William C. and Hattie (Dugan) L.; A.B., Harvard U., 1923, postgrad Bus. Sch., 1925; m. Celia Adams, Aug. 3, 1943; children—Judith, Holly. Mgr. distbn. Babson Reports Co., Wellesley Hills, Mass., 1929-40; founder, v.p., dir. David L. Babson & Co., Boston, 1950-72; investment counselor, Grosse Pointe, Mich., 1972—. Trustee, Leader Dog for the Blind. Served to comdr. USN, 1942-46. Mem. Fin. Analysts Soc. Detroit (past pres.), Harvard Club E. Mich. (past pres.), Econ. Club Detroit, Detroit Assn. Bus. Economists. Episcopalian. Clubs: Country of Detroit, Detroit, Union, Detroit Boat, Sr. Mens of Grosse Pointe, Grosse Point Skating (pres.). Home: 203 Ridge Rd Grosse Pointe MI 48236

LOMBARDI, JOHN VINCENT, educator; b. Los Angeles, Aug. 19, 1942; s. John and Janice P. L.; B.A., Pomona Coll., 1963; M.A., Columbia U., 1964, Ph.D., 1968; m. Cathryn L. Lee, Jan. 25, 1964; children—John Lee, Mary Ann. Prof. contratado Escuela de Historia Facultad de Humanidades y Educacion Universidad Central de Venezuela, Caracas, 1967; lectr. dept. history Ind. U., Southeast-Jeffersonville, 1967-68, asst. prof., 1968-69, vis. asst. prof., Bloomington, 1968-69, asst. prof., 1969-71, asso. prof., 1971-77, prof., 1977—, dir. Latin Am. Studies program, 1971-74, dean Internat. programs, 1978—. Nat. Def. Fgn. Lang. fellow, 1965; Fulbright-Hayes fellow, 1965-66, Fundacion Creole fellow, 1966-67. Mem. Latin Am. Studies Assn., Am. Hist. Assn. Author: The Political Ideology of Fray Servando Teresa de Mier: Propagandist for Independence, 1968; The Decline and Abolition of Negro Slavery in Venezuela, 1820-1854, 1971; People and Places in Colonial Venezuela, 1976; Venezuelan History: A Comprehensive Working Bibliography, 1977; contbr. articles in field. Office: International Programs Bryan Hall 205 Indiana University Bloomington IN 47405

LOMBARDO, DAVID ALBERT, educator; b. Chgo., Jan. 31, 1947; s. Ignace Palmeri and Diane Marion (Balducci) L.; B.S., U. Ill., 1974, M.Ed., 1977. Tchr., York Community High Sch., Elmhurst, Ill., 1974-75; instr. Coll. Edn., U. Ill., Urbana, 1975-77, asst. dir. career devel. and placement, 1977-79; with Accelerated Ground Schs., Urbana, 1978—, dir. nat. flight instr. refreser clinics; pres. Flying Illini, Inc., Savoy, Ill., 1972-80; pres. LEAP curriculum devel. cons., 1975-79, CFI Programs, 1979—; dir. program devel. Airmanship, Inc., Rockford, Ill., 1982—; gen. aviation cons. Lombard & Assos., Rockford, 1982—; instr. Flight Safety Internat., 1980-81; chief instr. Greater St. Louis Flight Instrs. Assn., 1980-81, bd. dirs., 1981—; accident preventor counselor FAA, 1980-81. Served with AUS, 1966-69; Vietnam. Decorated Vietnamese Gallantry Cross; recipient Flying Col. award Delta Air Lines, 1978, Ark. Traveler award Gov. Ark., 1979, Flight Instr. Proficiency award Phases I, II, III, IV, FAA, 1980, Plaque of Appreciation, Greater St. Louis Flight Instrs. Assn., 1981. Mem. Ill. Pilots Assn. (bd. dirs. 1977-79), Chi Gamma Iota, Phi Delta Kappa. Republican. Roman Catholic. Address: 1415 N Jackson Ave River Forest IL 60305

LOMBARDO, GAETANO, mfg. co. exec.; b. Salemi, Italy, Feb. 4, 1940; came to U.S., 1947; s. Salvatore and Anna Maria L.; Sc.B., Brown U., 1962; Ph.D., Cornell U., 1971; m. Nancy B. Emerson, Sept. 2, 1967; children—Nicholas Emerson, Maryanne Chilton. Sr. staff Arthur D. Little Inc., Cambridge, Mass., 1967-77; v.p. logistics Morton Salt Co., Chgo., 1977-78; dir. logistics and distbn. Gould Inc., Chgo., 1978-80; corp. dir. Bendix Corp., Southfield, Mich., 1980—; vis. prof. ops. mgmt. Boston U., 1973. Contbr. articles to profl. jours. Home: 3818 Marr Ct Bloomfield Hills MI 48013 Office: Exec Offices Bendix Center Southfield MI 48037

LOMBARDY, ROSS DAVID, food co. exec.; b. Cleve., Mar. 20, 1920; s. David Ross and Minnie (Roberto) L.; student pub. schs.; m. Louise Adelaide McMahon, Oct. 28, 1940; children—Louise, Ross David, David J., Kathleen L., Mary A., Thomas J. Pres. David Lombardy Co., Cleve., 1942-57; v.p., sec. Seaway Foods, Inc., Bedford Heights, Ohio, 1957-79, exec. v.p., 1979—. Recipient Grocery Man of Year award, 1973. Mem. Internat. Order Alhambra (Grand Comdr.). Roman Cathloic (pres. Holy Name Soc. 1955). K.C. (4 deg.). Club: K-C (trustee South Euclid, Ohio). Home: 4991 Countryside Ln Lyndhurst OH 44124 Office: 22801 Aurora Rd Bedford Heights OH 44146

LONDON, HAROLD NATHAN, educator; b. Chgo., Mar. 6, 1947; s. Al and Bernice Lilian (Pelton) L.; B.S. in Econs., U. Ill., 1969; M.A. in Math., Northeastern Ill. U., 1975; m. Sharon Brickman, Dec. 24, 1972; 1 dau., Andrea Renee. Tchr. math. Forrestville Upper Grade Center, Chgo., 1970-73; math. lab. tchr., team leader, programmer Douglass Middle Sch., Chgo., 1973-78; coordinator intensive math. improvement program Bur. Math., Chgo. Pub. Schs., 1978-80; tchr. Dett Elem. Sch., Chgo., 1980—; tchr. young adult edn. program North High Sch. Dist. 214, 1979—; editorial cons. for cassette tape program Conquering Word Problems, 1979; cons. diagnosis primary and intermediate testing program, Sci. Research Assos., 1980; cons. Cuisenaire Co. Am., 1981. Mem. Nat. Council Tchrs. Math., Assn. Supervision and Curriculum Devel., Ill. Council Tchrs. Math., Elem. Sch. Maths. Advisors Chgo. Area, Chgo. Elem. Tchrs. Math., Glenkirk Assn. for Retarded. Club: B'nai B'rith Educators. Home: 8929 Lyons St Des Plaines IL 60016 Office: 2306 W Maypole St Chicago IL 60644

LONERGAN, WALLACE GUNN, ednl. indsl. relations center exec.; b. Potlach, Idaho, Mar. 18, 1928; s. Willis Gerald and Lois (Gunn) L.; B.A., Coll. Ida., 1950; M.B.A., U. Chgo., 1955, Ph.D., 1960; m. Joan Laurie Penoyer, June 1, 1952; children—Steven Mark, Kevin James. Adminstrv. asst. U.S. Senate, Washington, 1950; research asst. Grad. Sch. Bus., U. Chgo., 1953-56, instr. indsl. relations, 1956-60, asst. prof., 1960-65, asso. dir. Indsl. Relations Center, 1965-70, dir., after 1970, now dir. Human Resources Center. dir., mem. exec. com. University Nat. Bank, Chgo., 1965. Chmn. mgmt. adv. com. Community Fund of Chgo., 1968-72. Served with AUS, 1950-53. Decorated UN medal; Internat. Scholars Exchange Program grantee to Japan, 1970. Mem. Acad. Mgmt., Indsl. Relations Research Assn., Internat. House of Japan, Internat. Indsl. Relations Research Assn. Author: Publications Management Problems and Human Behavior, 1968, Readings in Management Leadership, 1970, Critical Incidents in Leadership, 1973, Readings in Organizational Improvement and Management Development, 1974; Performance Appraisal, 1979. Home: 1404 E 55th St Chicago IL 60615 Office: 1225 E 60th St Chicago IL 60637

LONEY, RICHARD HUGH, telephone co. exec.; b. Elkhart, Ind., Dec. 5, 1931; s. Hugh Willard and June Adeline (Sands) L.; grad. pub. schs.; m. Jean Lorraine Coggan, May 31, 1953; children—Stephen Andrew, Michael Hugh, Betsy Sue. With Gen. Telephone Co. of Ind., 1950—, gen. service mgr., 1975-77, gen. retail sales mgr., 1977-78, safety dir., 1978—. Mem. youth com. Lafayette YMCA, 1964-66; scoutmaster Anthony Wayne council Boy Scouts Am., 1966-71; mem. Fort Wayne (Ind.) Fire Commn., 1978-80. Served with AUS, 1954-56. Mem. Ind. C. of C. (safety com.), Ft. Wayne C. of C. (safety com.). Republican. Episcopalian. Club: Ft Wayne Diving. Home: 6324 Holgate Dr Fort Wayne IN 46816 Office: 8001 W Jefferson Blvd PO 1201 Fort Wayne IN 46801

LONG, ALAN, psychologist; b. Logansport, Ind., Apr. 5, 1942; s. Joe D. and Ruby P. (Searer) L.; B.S., Manchester Coll., 1964; M.S., Purdue U., 1965; Ph.D., Fielding Inst., 1974. Sch. counselor, psychol. specialist Hammond (Ind.) Schs., 1965-68; sch. psychologist 3 Coops., Ind. and Ill., 1969-72; vocat. psychologist L.A.D.S.E., La Grange, Ill., 1973-75; pvt. practice psychology, Homewood, Ill., 1975—; bd. dirs. S. Suburban Council on Alcoholism, 1976—, pres., 1979. Pres. N. Manchester Civic Symphony, 1962-64. Registered psychologist, Ill.; NDEA fellow Ind. U., 1966. Diplomate Am. Acad. Behavioral Medicine. Mem. Acad. Psychologists in Marital and Family Therapy, Am., Ill. psychol. assns., Assn. Advancement Behavior Therapy, Assn. Advancement Tension Control, Soc. Personality Assessment, Biofeedback Soc. Am., Ill. (dir. 1975-76, pres. 1976-77). Club: Rotary. Author numerous papers on biofeedback. Office: 18019 Dixie Hwy Box 1277 Suite 1D Homewood IL 60430

LONG, AUDREY WILLA PETERSEN, educator; b. Humphrey, Nebr., Aug. 26, 1917; d. David William and Evelyn Lila (Anderson) Petersen; B.A., Wayne State Coll., 1963, M.S., 1967; student Kearney State Coll., summer 1969, 70, U. Colo., Greeley, summer 1971; m. Elmer George Long, May 28, 1939; children—Nadyne Audrey Long Hengen, Keith David. Tchr. rural elem. schs., Platte and Stanton Counties, 1935-40, Madison County, 1954-58; tchr. Stanton (Nebr.) public schs., 1958-61; tchr., prin. Norfolk (Nebr.) public schs., 1961-67; English instr. N.E. Tech. Community Coll., Norfolk, 1967-69; elem. prin. O'Neill Public Sch., 1969-72; tchr., elem. coordinator Northwest High Sch., Grand Island, Nebr., 1972—. Pres., Madison County Dist. 37 Sch. Bd., 1952-58; leader Madison County 4-H Club, 1956-58. Mem. Hall County Tchrs. Assn., Northwest High Tchrs. Assn., Nebr. State Edn. Assn., NEA, AAUW, Nat. Council Tchrs. English. Republican. Lutheran. Home: 2611 Koenig St Grand Island NE 68801 Office: 2710 N Road Grand Island NE 68801

LONG, CHARLES OSNER, radiologist; b. Bethlehem, Pa., Jan. 11, 1923; s. Charles Osner and Mary (Shull) L.; B.S., U. Mich., 1947; M.D., Boston U., 1951; divorced; children—Vicki Kay, Lisa Diane, Nan Claire, Lorraine. Intern Detroit Receiving Hosp.; resident in radiology Detroit Receiving and Affiliated Hosps., 1952-55; practice medicine specializing in radiology, Lansing, Mich., 1955—; established dept. radiology Howell (Mich.) McPherson Hosp., 1956, Mason (Mich.) Gen. Hosp., 1958, Eaton Rapids (Mich.) Community Hosp., 1957; established dept. radiology, 1960, since chmn. dept. Ingham Med. Center, Lansing; asso. clin. prof. radiology Mich. State U. Coll. Human Medicine; pres. Ingham Radiology Assos., P.C. Served to 1st lt. USAAF, 1942-46; PTO. Recipient Nat. Div. Tiffany award, 1970. Decorated Air medal (5). Diplomate Am. Bd. Radiology, Nat. Bd. Med. Examiners. Fellow Am. Coll. Radiology; mem. Am. Cancer Soc. (pres. Mich. div. 1972-73), AMA, Radiol. Soc. N.Am. Mich. Med. Soc., Ingham County Med. Soc. Home: PO Box

1737 East Lansing MI 48823-6737 Office: 2909 E Grand Rd Lansing MI 48912

LONG, ERNESTINE MARTHA JOULLIAN, educator; b. St. Louis, Mo., Nov. 14, 1906; d. Ernest Cameron and Alice (Joullian) Long; A.B., U. Wis., 1927; M.S., U. Chgo., 1932; Ph.D., St. Louis U., 1975; postgrad. (NSF fellow), So. Ill. U., 1969-70. Tchr. scis. Normandy High Sch., St. Louis, 1927-64; with City St. Louis Health Dept. and U.S. Maternal Child Health Div., Children's Bur., Washington, 1964; tchr. Red Bud (Ill.) High Sch., 1965-70, St. Louis pub. schs., 1971-75; asso. coordinator continuing edn. U. Mo.-St. Louis, 1976-78. Recipient Community Service award St. Louis Newspaper Guild, 1978; NSF fellow, 1967-68. Mem. Am. Personnel and Guidance Assn. (treas. St. Louis br. 1954), Am. Chem. Soc., Central Assn. Sch. Sci. and Math. Tchrs., AAAS, Am. Physics Tchrs. Assn., Am. Inst. Physics, Assn. for Supervision and Curriculum Devel., Am. Assn. for Microbiology, Nat. Sci. Tchrs. Assn., Am. Guild Organists, NEA. Composer: Organ preludes, 1945; Hymns, 1967-69; research on edn. Home: 245 N Price Rd Saint Louis MO 63124

LONG, GORDON H., podiatrist; b. Big Rapids, Mich., July 28, 1912; s. Harry P. and Mildred E. (Pullman) L.; D.P.M., Ill. Coll. Podiatric Medicine, 1932; m. Vivian E. Knepp, July 22, 1939; children—Malinda Ann. Intern, Chgo. Coll. Podiatry and Pedic Surgery, 1932-33; pvt. practice podiatric medicine and surgery, Battle Creek, Mich., 1933—; cons. in foot surgery VA Med. Center, Ft. Custer of Battle Creek, 1979—; staff Battle Creek Sanitarium Hosp., 1952—. Served with USN, 1944-45. Diplomate Am. Bd. Podiatric Surgery, Nat. Bd. Podiatry Examiners, Mich. Bd. Podiatric Medicine and Surgery (pres. 1947-53). Fellow Am. Coll. Foot Surgeons; mem. Mich. Podiatry Assn. (pres. 1943-44), Am. Podiatry Assn., Am. Hosp. Assn. Podiatrists, Mich. Foot Health Found. Home: 255 Lakeshore Dr Battle Creek MI 49015 Office: 1346 W Columbia Ave Battle Creek MI 49015

LONG, HELEN HALTER, author, publishing co. exec., educator; b. St. Louis, Nov. 19, 1906; d. Charles C. and Ida (May) Halter; A.B., Washington U., St. Louis, 1927, A.M. (grad. fellow 1927-28), 1928; Ph.D., N.Y. U., 1937; m. Forrest E. Long, June 22, 1944. Tchr. social studies, Venice, Ill., 1928-30; asst. prof. social sci. N.Y. State Coll. for Tchrs., Albany, 1930-38; head dept. social studies The Milne Sch., Albany, 1930-38; tchr. pub. schs., Mamaroneck, N.Y., 1938-42, prin. elementary and jr. high schs., 1942-54, asst. supt. schs., 1954-61; dir. curriculum studies Inst. Instructional Improvement, N.Y.C., 1962—; pres. Books of the World, Sweet Springs, Mo., 1963—; dir. Roxbury Press. Teaching fellow Sch. Edn., N.Y.U., 1936-37, div. gen. edn., 1938-39, instr. Sch. Edn., 1939-43; asso. editor The Clearing House, 1935-55; mem. N.Y. State Regents Social Studies Curriculum Com., 1935-38. Mem. Phi Beta Kappa, Pi Gamma Mu, Kappa Delta Pi, Alpha Xi Delta (Diamond Jubilee honor 1968). Author: Society in Action, 1936; National Safety Council Lesson Units, 1944-52; (with Forrest E. Long) Social Studies Skills, rev. edit., 1976. Home: 107 Medallion Dr Sweet Springs MO 65351 Office: Roxbury Bldg Sweet Springs MO 65351

LONG, JACOB JAY, ins. agt.; b. Alexandria, Ind., June 19, 1945; s. Leotas Lloyd and Norma Eileen (Wheeldon) L.; student bus. adminstrn. Ball State U., 1964-73; m. Bonnie Jean Eden, Nov. 29, 1964; children—Marnie Jo, Monica Ann. Dispatcher, maintenance supr. J. J. Long, Inc., 1964-70; accountant non-production materials Guide Lamp div. Gen. Motors Corp., Anderson, Ind., 1963-75; agt. Prudential Ins. Co., Anderson, 1975-78; ins. agt., bus. counselor Fin. Adv. Services, Anderson, Ind., 1978—. Pres. bd. dirs. Alexandria Community Center, 1978—, bd. mem., 1972—; mem. allocation com. United Way Madison County, 1975-78. Recipient Disting. Service award Alexandria Jaycees, 1972, Community Service award Prudential Ins. Co., 1978. Mem. Nat. Assn. Life Underwriters, Alexandria Jaycees (pres. 1970-72), Jaycees Internat. (senator 1977). Mem. Ch. of God. Club: Elks, Eagles. Home: Rural Route 4 Box 123 Alexandria IN 46001 Office: 1403 Ohio Ave Anderson IN 46015

LONG, JERRY WAYNE, optometrist; b. Poplar Bluff, Mo., Jan. 31, 1949; s. Walker James and Lettye Colleen (Wood) L.; student Drury Coll., 1967-68, S.E. Mo. State U., 1968-69; O.D., So. Coll. Optometry, 1973; m. Sarah Jane Price, June 9, 1972; children—Jenny Colleen, Rebecca Corey. Practice optometry, Poplar Bluff, 1973—; partner Dr. W.J. Long; state chmn. Save Your Vision Week, 1979. Chmn. stewardship drive 1st United Methodist Ch., Poplar Bluff, 1978; chmn. campaign drive United Way, 1977-78, pres. bd., 1979—. Disting. Service award, 1977-78; bd. dirs. Coe Pub. Library. Mem. Am. Optometric Assn., Mo. Optometric Assn. (trustee), S.E. Mo. Optometric Soc., Poplar Bluff Jr. C. of C. (sec. 1973-74, dir. 1974-76, pres. 1976-77, Dir. of Year 1975-76, Presdl. award for outstanding service 1975-76, Officer of Year 1976-77). Clubs: Masons, Shriners, Lions. Home: 2011 Woodhaven St Poplar Bluff MO 63901 Office: 213 N Broadway Poplar Bluff MO 63901

LONG, JOHN HAMILTON, historian; b. Brockton, Mass., Mar. 3, 1937; s. Samuel and Elizabeth Hamilton (Lewis) L.; student Princeton U., 1955-58; B.A., Northeastern U., 1966; M.A., Clark U., 1970; m. Sally Faith Tufts, Aug. 29, 1964; 1 dau., Faith Elizabeth. Asst. editor Atlas of Early Am. History project Newberry Library, Chgo., 1971-75, acting dir. H.D. Smith Center for History Cartography, 1977-78, project dir. hist. boundary data file project, 1975—; mem. Ill. Hist. Sites Adv. Council, 1980—; cons. Rand McNally Co., Office Charles and Rae Eames. Served with AUS, 1959-62. NDEA fellow, 1966-68, 69-70. Mem. Am. Hist. Assn., Orgn. Am. Historians, Assos. Inst. Early Am. History and Culture, Am. Congress Surveying and Mapping, Chgo. Map Soc. (pres. 1978-80). Office: 60 W Walton St Chicago IL 60610

LONG, LARRY RUSSELL, cons. engr.; b. Warsaw, Ind., Sept. 19, 1949; s. Russell Harry and Ester May (Shand) L.; B.C.E., Purdue U., 1972; m. Diana Kay Unruh, Aug. 22, 1969; children—Brian Larry, Benjamin David, Andrew Scott. Project engr. Clyde E. Williams & Assos., South Bend, Ind., 1976-78; pres., owner/chief engr. Larry R. Long & Assos., Warsaw, Ind., 1978—. Served with USAF, 1972-76. Registered profl. engr., Ind. Mem. ASCE, Nat. Soc. Profl. Engrs. Home: Rural Route 2 Box 114 Pierceton IN 46562 Office: 321 S High St Warsaw IN 46580

LONG, LAWRENCE LESLIE, JR., glove mfg. co. exec.; b. Chillicothe, Mo., Jan. 4, 1931; s. Lawrence Leslie and Beatrice Marie (Anderson) L.; student public schs., Chillicothe; m. Dorothy Louise Wood, June 15, 1951; children—Deborah Lynn, Linda Lou. Glove cutter Boss Mfg. Co., 1949-50; glove cutter Lambert Mfg. Co., Chillicothe, 1950-52, 54-56, asst. plant mgr., 1956-59, plant mgr., 1959-61; co-founder, v.p., plant mgr. Midwest Glove Corp., Chillicothe, 1961-69, pres., owner, 1969—. Served with U.S. Army, 1952-53; Korea. Mem. Work Glove Mfg. Assn. (dir.). Republican. Methodist. Clubs: Rotary, Masons, Shriners. Home: 906 Summit Dr Chillicothe MO 64601 Office: 835 Industrial Rd Chillicothe MO 64601

LONG, MATTIE LEE, telephone co. adminstr.; b. Collins, Miss., Jan. 12, 1948; d. Cleveland Cooper and Ruby Mae (Sullivan) Burnell; A.A., (Blain scholar), Delta Coll., 1967; B.B.A., Saginaw Valley State Coll., 1973; M.A. in Econs., Central Mich. U., 1979; postgrad. in econs. Wayne State U., 1980. Asst., fgn. lang. lab. Delta Coll., University Center, Mich., 1965-67; with Mich. Bell Telephone Co., Saginaw, 1967—, office staff supr., 1974-77, dial service supr., 1977-78, staff service supr., 1978-79, network adminstrv. supr., 1979-80, staff supr., Detroit, 1980—. Mem. NAACP, NAUW, Alpha Beta Kappa. Democrat. Mem. Pentecostal Ch. Editor jour. Women's Liberation, 1973. Home: PO Box 431 Saginaw MI 48606 Office: 1365 Cass Ave Room 710 Detroit MI 48226

LONG, MICHAEL CLARK, grocery corp. exec.; b. St. Louis, Feb. 5, 1947; s. Adrian Clark and Kathryn Jane (Walsh) L.; B.S./B.A., Washington U., 1969; postgrad. (scholar), Rolla U., 1969; M.B.A. (scholar), Washington U., 1971; m. Margaret Ann Ciarleglio, Apr. 16, 1969; 1 dau., Tricia Ann. With Schnuck Markets, Inc., St. Louis, 1967—, asst. store mgr., 1974-75, pricing coordinator, 1975-77, grocery merchandising analyst, 1977—; guest lectr. Washington U., 1977, Forest Park Community Coll., 1978, Meramec Community Coll., 1978. Mem. Am. Assn. M.B.A. Execs. Club: Allied Food. Episcopalian. Home: 1514 Kraft St Saint Louis MO 63139 Office: Schnuck Markets Inc 12921 Enterprise Way Bridgeton MO 63044

LONG, PHYLLIS JEAN, sch. prin.; b. Urbana, Ill., June 1, 1934; d. William Bryant and Nora (Innis) Long; B.S., George Peabody Coll., 1956; M.Ed., U. Ill., 1966, Ed.D., 1977; 1 son, Robert Long. Tchr., Dist. 64, Park Ridge, Ill., 1956-67, Dist. U46, Elgin, Ill., 1961; asst. prin. Dist. 64 Park Ridge, 1967-70, prin. Emerson Jr. High Sch., 1977—. Delta Kappa Gamma scholar, 1975. Mem. Ill. Prins. Assn. (dir. exhbns.), U. Ill. Alumn Assn. (dir. dept. adminstrn.), Nat. Assn. Elem. Prins., Assn. for Supervision and Curriculum Devel., Delta Kappa Gamma, Phi Delta Kappa. Office: Emerson Jr High Sch 8101 N Cumberland St Niles IL 60648

LONG, ROLAND JOHN, secondary sch. prin.; b. Chgo., Nov. 15, 1921; s. John and Lillian Catherine (Sigmund) L.; B.S., Ill. State Normal U., 1949; M.A., Northwestern U., 1951; Ed.D., Ill. State U., 1972; m. Valerie Ann Zawila, Nov. 13, 1954; children—Ronald J., Thomas E. Instr. of social sci. Ball State U., Muncie, Ind., 1951; comdt. Morgan Park Mil. Acad., Chgo., 1952-54; tchr. history Hyde Park and Amundsen high schs., Chgo., 1955-62; prin. Hubbard Elementary Sch., Chgo., 1962; founder, prin. Hubbard High Sch., Chgo., 1963—; mem. doctoral advisory com. of Ill. State U., 1973-75. Mem. Chgo. Police Dist. 8 steering com., 1974-77; bd. dirs. West Communities YMCA, Chgo., Greater Lawn Mental Health Center, Chgo. Served to 1st lt., inf., U.S. Army; ETO. Decorated Silver Star, Purple Heart, Bronze Star; Ford Found. fellow, 1973; recipient Sch. Mgmt. citation Ill. Gen. Assembly, 1972. Fellow (hon.) Harry S. Truman Library Inst.; mem. Ill. Assn. for Supervision and Curriculum Devel., Nat. Assn. of Secondary Sch. Prins., Am. Legion, Phi Delta Kappa (Educator of Yr. award 1980), Pi Gamma Mu, Kappa Delta Pi. Club: Elks. Author: Dr. Long's Old-Fashioned Basic Report Card and Parent Helper, 1977. Home: 6701 N Ionia Ave Chicago IL 60646 Office: 6200 S Hamlin Ave Chicago IL 60629

LONG, WILLIAM FREDERICK, physicist; b. Burlington, Iowa, Oct. 15, 1951; s. Leslie James and Avis Ione (Dodge) L.; B.S., Iowa State U., 1973; M.S., U. Wis., 1974. Research asst. dept. physics U. Wis., Madison, 1973—. Mem. Am. Phys. Soc., Phi Kappa Phi, Pi Mu Epsilon. Research in phenomenology of elementary particle interactions; contbr. articles to profl. jours. Home: 502 N Frances St Apt 501E Madison WI 53703 Office: Dept Physics Univ Wis Madison WI 53706

LONGMIRE, ROBERT JAMES, mfg. co. exec.; b. Tacoma, Wash., Aug. 1, 1946; s. Otis James and Dorothy Jean (Morrison) L.; B.A., Lewis U., Lockport, Ill., 1975; M.B.A., U. Cin., 1977; children—Laura Lee, Jennifer Sue, Scott Robert. With U.S. Elec. Motors div. Emerson Electric Co., Los Angeles, 1967, Dayco Corp., Los Angeles, 1968, Kearfott div. Singer/Gen. Precision, Inc., San Marcos, Calif., 1969-70, Gen. Dynamics Corp., San Diego, 1970, Deutsche Corp., Oceanside, Calif., 1970-71, Electro-Motive div. Gen. Motors Corp., La Grange, Ill., 1971-75; ops. research analyst FMC Corp., Chgo., 1977-79, applications analyst mfg. systems, 1979-80, mfg. system installation coordinator, 1980-81, mfg. edn. program mgr., 1981—; guest lectr. in field. Fellow Am. Prodn. and Inventory Control Soc. (cert.); mem. Ops. Research Soc. Am., Inst. Mgmt. Sci., Assn. M.B.A. Execs., Am. Material Mgmt. Soc. Clubs: Elks, Kiwanis. Author papers, reports in field. Office: 1700 Prudential Plaza Chicago IL 60601

LONGMOOR, BARBARA LOUISE, interior designer; b. Tulsa, Jan. 24, 1936; d. Paul Martin and Nell (Coy) Bolley; student S.W. Mo. State U., 1954-55, Kansas City Art Inst., 1967, U. Mo., Kansas City, 1967-70; B.F.A., U. Kans., 1975; m. William Volker Longmoor, Aug. 31, 1971; 1 dau. by previous marriage—Christina Lee Richey Edwards. Display designer Killingsworth's, Springfield, Mo., 1954-55, Adler's, Kansas City, Mo., 1955-56; freelance display designer, Omaha, 1956-57; interior designer Pat O'Leary Assos., Fairway, Kans., 1975-78, Jack Rees Interiors, Kansas City, 1978—; design cons., set designer Horizon Produns.; photographer prodn. stills. Vice pres. Springfield Jaycee Wives, 1963-64, bd. dirs., 1962-64. Mem. Am. Soc. Interior Designers (bd. dirs. 1979—), Friends of Art Nelson Gallery, Omaha Panhellenic Council, Greater Kansas City Panhellenic Council, Women's Aux. Research Med. Center (sec. 1979—), Nat. Assn. Parliamentarians, Alpha Sigma Alpha. Republican. Mem. Disciples of Christ. Club: Soroptimists. Home: 9703 W 96th Terr Overland Park KS 66212 Office: 4501 Belleview St Kansas City MO 64111

LONGO, FRANK JOSEPH, educator; b. St. Louis, Apr. 24, 1930; s. Frank A. and Agnes (Walbridge) L.; B.S. in Edn., Quincy Coll., 1956; m. Suzanne L. Koch, Apr. 7, 1956; children—Antoinette, Theresa, Mark, Matt, Tina. Tchr.-coach McBride High Sch., St. Louis, 1956-61, Vianney High Sch., St. Louis, 1961-64; tchr.-coach Quincy (Ill.) Coll., 1964—. Served with U.S. Navy, 1948-52. Recipient Bill Jeffrey award for outstanding contbn. to coll. soccer, 1977; named to NAIA Soccer Hall of Fame, 1974. Mem. Nat. Soccer Coaches Assn. Am., Intercoll. Soccer Assn. Am. (sec. 1978—), Nat. Assn. Intercollegiate Athletics, Soccer Coaches Assn. (pres. 1970-73). Roman Catholic. Home: 417 S 14th St Quincy IL 62301 Office: 1831 College St Quincy IL 62301

LONGO, MICHAEL ANTHONY, govt. ofcl.; b. Cicero, Ill., Nov. 7, 1914; s. Nicholas and Julia (Garippo) L.; student U. Ill., 1932-36; m. Pauline Lipps, May 14, 1944; children—Michelene (Mrs. Kenneth Smith), Gerard. Chief investigator Air Pollution Control, Cicero, 1966—; field rep. World Book Ency.; dir. Fireside Fed. Savs. and Loan Assn., Fireside Service Corp., Cicero, Michael A. Longo Ins. Spl. asst. to Congressman Henry J. Hyde, 6th Ill. Dist., 1975—. Constable, Cicero, 1960-64; chmn. Cancer Crusade, Cicero, 1971—, chmn. Cicero Unit, 1976-77. Precinct capt. Republican Orgn., Cicero, 1946—; trustee Town of Cicero, 1974—. Bd. dirs. Central Suburban unit Am. Cancer Soc., 1972—, Cicero Pub. Library, 1964—, Italian-Am. Sports Hall of Fame, Community Chest, Cicero. Served with AUS, 1942-46; ETO. Mem. Order Sons Italy Am., Holy Name Soc., St. Vincent de Paul Soc., VFW. Roman Catholic. Club: West Suburban Exec. Breakfast (charter, dir. 1976-77). Home: 1232 S 51st Ave Cicero IL 60650 Office: 5341 W Cermak Rd Cicero IL 60650

LONNING, PHILIP EUGENE, clin. psychologist; b. Thor, Iowa, July 22, 1932; s. Lennie B. and Leone B. (Hanson) L.; B.A., U. No. Iowa, 1957; M.A., U. No. Colo., 1960; Ph.D., Iowa State U., 1969; m. Carole Ann Yohn, June 4, 1960; children—Elizabeth Ann, James Brian. Tchr. bus. edn., Garner, Iowa, 1957-59; high sch. guidance dir., Garner, 1959-62; guidance cons., Humboldt and Pocahontas Counties, Iowa, 1962-75; coordinator of consultants Area V Edn. Assn., Ft. Dodge, Iowa, 1975-76; clin. psychologist, Ft. Dodge, 1970—; vis. prof. Iowa State U., 1968, Drake U., 1971, Buena Vista Coll., 1977. Pres., Zion Luth. Ch., 1975-77; active Lions Club, 1960-70, Assn. for Crippled Children and Adults, 1970—. Mem. Am. Personnel and Guidance Assn., Am. Psychol. Assn., Iowa Psychol. Assn., Soc. for Clin. and Exptl. Hypnosis, Phi Delta Kappa. Republican. Lutheran. Home: 404 11th St SW Humboldt IA 50548 Office: 320 S 12th St Fort Dodge IA 50501

LONNQUIST, JOHN HALL, agronomist, educator; b. Ashland, Wis., May 22, 1916; s. James Oscar and Ethel Selma (Hall) L.; B.S., U. Nebr., 1940, Ph.D., 1949; M.S., Kans. State Coll., 1942; postgrad. Ohio State U., 1942-43, Iowa State Coll., 1948; m. Betty Claire Hanson, July 27, 1942; children—John Hall, Ladd, George, Tom, Kathleen, Kristine, Margaret Anne, Ken. Grad. asst. Kans. State Coll., 1940-42, Ohio State U., 1942; instr. Pa. State Coll., 1943; asst. agronomist U. Nebr., 1943-49, asso. agronomist, 1949-53, prof. agronomy, 1953-61, C. Petrus Peterson prof. agronomy, 1961-67, also head corn breeding and genetics investigations; project specialist agr. Ford Found., assigned Internat. Center for Maize and Wheat Improvement as dir. internat. maize program, Mexico, 1967-70; prof. agronomy, head corn investigations U. Wis. at Madison, 1970—. Mem. agrl. panel AID; cons. vis. lectr. plant breeding, Argentina, Brazil; adviser Rockefeller Found. agrl. programs, Central and S.Am. Recipient Distinguished Service to Agr. award radio sta. KMMJ, Grand Island, Neb., 1962. Fellow Am. Soc. Agronomy (Crop Sci. award 1961); mem. Am. Genetic Assn., AAAS, Am. Inst. Biol. Scis., Sociedade Brasileira de Genetica (corr.), Sigma Xi, Gamma Sigma Delta, Alpha Zeta. Contbr. numerous sci. papers on corn breeding and genetics. Home: 7110 Donna Dr Middleton WI 53562 Office: Dept Agronomy U Wis Madison WI 53706

LOOFT, WALTER GENE, mech. engr.; b. Ottawa, Ill., Feb. 26, 1938; s. Henry Charles and Margery V. (Moss) L.; B.S. in Engring., Purdue U., 1960; m. Beverly Jean Milburn, June 7, 1959; children—Annette, Steven P., Mark A. Conveyor application engr. Chain Belt Co., Milw., 1961-63; bearing application engr. Rex Chainbelt Inc., Downers Grove, Ill., 1964-65, supr. design, 1966-68, mgr. engring., 1969-76, mgr. sales and engring., 1976—; head U.S. del. to Internat. Standards Orgn. meeting, Cologne, W.Ger., 1975, 76, mem. del., Moscow, 1977, chmn. com. airframe bearings, 1978—, chmn. U.S. Airframe Control Bearing Group on Metric Bearings, U.S. del. meeting, London, 1979; chmn. Rexword Engring. Mgrs. Council, 1972-74. Pres., Baseball Leagues, Lisle, Ill., 1973-75; sec. Lisle Sch. Bd., 1976, pres., 1977—; bd. dirs. YMCA, 1972-74. Registered profl. engr., Ill.; recipient Distinguished Vol. Service award Lisle Park Dist., 1973. Mem. Soc. Automotive Engrs., Anti-Friction Bearing Mfrs. Assn. (chmn. roller bearing engrs. com. 1982), Am. Nat. Standards Inst. Presbyterian. Home: 10411 N Greenside Ct Mequon WI 53092 Office: 4701 W Greenfield Ave West Milwaukee WI 53214

LOOKER, JACK DEVON, retail exec.; b. Richmond, Ind., June 10, 1933; s. Harold Homer and Susie Elizabeth (Carter) L.; student Ind. Tech. Coll., 1956-57; m. Bernice Ann Frey, Apr. 28, 1962; 1 son, Shane Devon. Draftsman, Stamco, Inc., New Bremem, Ohio, 1957-60; sales engr. Scott Equipment Co., Dayton, Ohio, 1960-66; regional sales mgr. Manatrol div. Perry-Fay, Inc., Elyria, Ohio, 1966-70; owner, operator Nu-Hy Co., Indpls., 1970—, also pres. Vectrol, Inc., Indpls., 1973-78; regional sales mgr. Protectaire Systems Co., Elgin, Ill., 1979—. Served with USNR, 1951-55; Korea. Mem. Fluid Power Soc., Am. Def. Preparedness Assn. Mem. Ch. of the Brethren. Home and office: 950 Birdsong Milford MI 48042

LOOMIS, HOWARD KREY, banker; b. Omaha, Apr. 9, 1927; s. Arthur L. and Genevieve (Krey) L.; A.B., Cornell U., 1949, M.B.A., 1950; m. Florence Porter, Apr. 24, 1954; children—Arthur L. II, Frederick S., Howard Krey, John Porter. Mgmt. trainee Hallmark Cards, Inc., Kansas City, Mo., 1953-56; sec., controller, dir. Mine Service Co., Inc., Ft. Smith, Ark., 1956-59; controller, dir. Electra Mfg. Co., Independence, Kans., 1959-63; v.p., dir. The Peoples Bank, Pratt, Kans., 1963-65, pres., 1966—; pres., dir. Gt. Plains Leasing, Inc., Pratt, 1966-80, Central States Inc., Pratt, 1970-76, Krey Co. Ltd., Pratt, 1978—; dir. Fed. Res. Bank, Kansas City, Mo., Garland Coal & Mining Co., Ft. Smith, All Ins., Inc., Pratt, Kans. Devel. Credit Corp., Topeka, 1974—. Past pres. Pratt County United Fund; bd. dirs., past chmn. Cannonball Trail chpt. ARC; bd. dirs., past pres. Kanza council Boy Scouts Am. Served with AUS, 1950-52. Mem. Kans. (chmn. transp. council, dir.), Pratt Area (past pres., dir.) chambers commerce, Financial Execs. Inst., Kans. Bankers Assn. (past dir.), Sigma Delta Chi, Chi Psi. Republican. Presbyterian. Elk, Rotarian. Club: Park Hills Country (past pres.). Home: 502 Welton St Pratt KS 67124 Office: The Peoples Bank 222 S Main St Pratt KS 67124

LOOMIS, SALORA DALE, psychiatrist; b. Peru, Ind., Oct. 21, 1930; s. Salora Dale and Rhea Pearl (Davis) L.; A.B. in Zoology, Ind. U., 1953, M.S. in Human Anatomy, 1955, M.D., 1958; m. Carol Marie Davis, Jan. 3, 1959; children—Stephen Dale, Patricia Marie. Intern, Cook County Hosp., Chgo., 1958-59; resident psychiatry Logansport (Ind.) State Hosp., 1959-60, Ill. State Psychiat. Inst., Chgo., 1960-62; staff psychiatrist Katharine Wright Psychiat. Clinic, Chgo., 1962-65, dir., 1965—; cons. Ill. Youth Commn., 1962-64; asst. dir. Northwestern U. Psychiat. Clinics, Chgo., 1963-65; attending psychiatrist, also vice-chmn. dept. psychiatry St. Joseph Hosp., Chgo., 1964—; psychiat. cons. Ill. Dept. Pub. Health, 1967—; attending psychiatrist, also chmn. dept. psychiatry Ill. Masonic Med. Center, Chgo., 1970—. Instr. psychiatry Northwestern U. Med. Sch., Chgo., 1962-64, asso., 1964-67; lectr. psychiatry and neurology Loyola U. Med. Sch., Chgo., 1964-65, asso., 1965, asst. prof., 1965-73; asso. prof. psychiatry U. Ill. Coll. Medicine, Chgo., 1973—. Diplomate Am. Bd. Psychiatry and Neurology. Fellow Am. Coll. Psychiatrists, Am. Psychiat. Assn., Acad. Psychosomatic Medicine; mem. A.M.A., Ill. State (chmn. council on mental health and addiction 1974-75, chmn. joint peer rev. com. 1975-78), Chgo. med. socs., Ill. Psychiat. Soc. (chmn. ethics com. 1974-75) Assn. Dirs. Ill. Gen. Hosp. Psychiat. Services (pres. 1977-79). Home: 321 Franklin St Geneva IL 60134 Office: 720 N Michigan Ave Chicago IL 60611 also 923 W Wellington Ave Chicago IL 60657

LOOS, CHARLES DELBERT, state govt. ofcl.; b. Madison, Ind., Oct. 22, 1925; s. Charles George and Ethel Ann (McDaniel) L.; diploma Lain Bus. Coll., Indpls., 1948; extension student, Purdue U., 1950; m. Martha Louise Green, Sept. 21, 1947; children—Ellen Louise Loos Gill, Philip E., Mary Kay Loos Liverett. Clk., Jefferson County, Ind., 1948-55; U.S. marshal for Ind., 1955-77; auditor State of Ind., 1978—; past v.p. Ind. County Clks. Assn. Served with AUS,

WHO'S WHO IN THE MIDWEST 422

1944-46. Named hon. Ky. col., 1979, Sagamore of Wabash, 1978. Mem. Am. Legion. Republican. Presbyterian. Clubs: Masons, Shriners. Office: Room 234 State House Indianapolis IN 46204

LOPATE, KATHLEEN MARY, writer; b. Watsonville, Calif., Sept. 13, 1948; student Loyola Marymount U., Los Angeles, 1968-69; B.A. in Journalism, Marquette U., 1975. Editor, Program mag., 1978-79, Metric News mag., 1977-78; public relations asst. Mt. Mary Coll. Theater, 1977—; free-lance writer, Brookfield, Wis., 1975-76, 77—; writer Post newspapers including Encore, 1975-77; worked toward devel. of 1st hospice in Wis., 1977—. Mem. public relations com. United Way Waukesha County, Waukesha, Wis., 1975; mem. public info. com. Kidney Found. Wis., 1973-78; public relations intern Mt. Sinai Med. Center, Milw., 1974. Mem. Am. Med. Writers Assn., Loyola Marymount U. Calif. Writers, Women in Communications, Milw. Press Club. Author: Lennie's Story, 1977. Home: 235 N Eastmoor Ave Brookfield WI 53005

LOPATER, DAVID ALLEN, indsl. psychologist; b. Chgo., Sept. 4, 1951; s. Harold Jack and Shirley Hope Lopater; B.S. (G. Huff scholar), U. Ill., 1973; M.A. in Indsl. Psychology (Levitt Found. scholar), Bowling Green State U., 1976; m. Holley Linn Cook, June 10, 1979. Teaching asst. psychology dept. U. Ill., 1972-73; research fellow Bowling Green State U., 1974-76; coordinator mgmt. devel. H.E. Butt Grocery Co., Corpus Christi, Tex., 1976-80; adj. prof. mgmt. Corpus Christi State U., 1978-80; sr. employment officer Steelcase, Grand Rapids, Mich., 1980—; speaker to local profl. assns., 1977—. Mem. Am. Soc. Personnel Adminstrs. (accredited personnel diplomate), Am. Psychol. Assn., Am. Soc. Tng. and Devel., Psi Chi. Club: U. Ill. Letterman. Rev. editor: The Personnel Adminstr., 1979-80. Office: PO Box 1967 Grand Rapids MI 49501

LO PATIN, LAWRENCE HAROLD, real estate exec.; b. Detroit, Sept. 20, 1925; s. Henry and Mary (Harelik) LoP.; LL.B., Wayne State U., 1950; m. Florence R. Grossman, Dec. 3, 1950; children—Mark, Norman. Founder, pres. L.H. LoPatin & Co., Detroit, 1959—; co-founder, chief financial officer Windsor Raceway Holdings, Inc., 1962-66; founder, pres. Capital Adv., Inc., Detroit, 1963—; founder, pres. Am. Raceways Inc. (formerly Mich. Internat. Speedway, Inc.), Detroit, 1967-70; founder, pres. Retail Site Selection Group; mem. staff Applied Mgmt. and Tech. Center, Wayne State U., 1971—; founder Surg. Centers Mich. Inc., 1976—. Chmn. City of Southfield Planning Commn., 1978. Mem. Nat. Assn. Real Estate Bds., Internat. Council Shopping Centers, Am., Mich. land devel. assns., Urban Land Inst. Home: 28545 River Crest Dr Southfield MI 48075 Office: 3000 Town Center Suite 1000 Southfield MI 48075

LOPEZ, ROBERT ANTHONY, librarian; b. Fayetteville, N.C., June 27, 1925; s. Anthony C. and Laura (Raynor) L.; student U. Fla., 1946-48; B.A. in Journalism, Emory U., 1950. Editor, New Smyrna (Fla.) Beach News, 1950-53; night supr. library Mpls. Star & Tribune Co., 1953-59; head librarian Mpls. Star & Tribune Co., 1959—. Served with USNR, 1942-46. Mem. Spl. Librarian Assn., Minn. Press Club, Sigma Delta Chi, Delta Tau Delta. Home: 7841 Zane Ave N Apt 102 Brooklyn Park MN 55433 Office: 425 Portland Ave Minneapolis MN 55415

LOPEZ B, FERNANDO, elec. appliance mfg. co. exec.; b. Mexico City, Apr. 9, 1939; s. Francisco and Clemen Lopez Barredo; C.P.A., Tech. Inst. Mexico, 1965; children—Emma, Rocio, Fernando, Juan Pablo. Vice pres., controller Sunbeam Mexicana, S.A., 1968-71; mgr. adminstrn. western hemisphere Sunbeam Corp., 1972-75, mgr. fin. planning Pan Am. group, Oak Brook, Ill., 1977—; dir. fin. Mexicana de Cobre, S.A., Mexico City, 1975-76. Mem. Mexican Inst. Fin. Execs., Nat. Assn. Accountants, Bus. Internat. Roman Catholic. Home: 236 Applewood Ln Bloomingdale IL 60108 Office: 2001 S York Rd Oak Brook IL 60521

LOPEZ-DELGADO, VALENTIN, physician; b. Tuy, Spain, June 18, 1925; s. Pablo and Jacinta (Delgado Martin) Lopez Blanco; M.D., U. Valladolid, Spain, 1953; m. Margaret Leone (Hutchinson), July 29, 1966; children—David-James, Margot-Pilar. Family physician, Badajoz, Spain, 1953-54; intern Brantford (Ont., Can.) Gen. Hosp., 1959-61; hosp. med. officer St. Joseph's Hosp., Hamilton, Ont., 1961-64; anesthesia tng., Hamilton Gen. Hosp., also Wellesley Gen. Hosp. (both Ont.), 1964-68; pvt. practice ltd. to anesthesia, Spain, 1969-71, St. Thomas-Elgin Gen. Hosp., St. Thomas, Ont., 1971—. Served as med. lt., Spanish Army, 1954-59. Roman Catholic. Club: Rotary. Home: 22 Applewood Crescent St Thomas ON N5R 1H2 Canada

L'ORANGE, FINN FAYE, dentist; b. Phila., May 20, 1911; s. Otto Henrik and Anne AMunda (Gabrielsen) L.; D.D.S., Western Reserve U., 1938; m. Margaret Elizabeth Hickson, Nov. 25, 1937; children—Mundalea L'Orange Worrell, Deborah Karen, Martha Jane, John Otto II. Intern, St. Luke's Hosp., Cleve., 1938-39; pvt. practice dentistry, Cleve., 1939—; mem. sr. dental staff surgeon St. Luke's Hosp., 1939—; clin. instr. prosthodontia Case Western Reserve U. Dental Sch., 1970—. Served to lt. col. AUS, 1942-46, 61-62. Fellow Acad. Gen. Dentistry; mem. Pierre Fauchard Acad., Acad. Gen. Dentistry, Am., Ohio dental assns., Ohio State (pres. 1956-58), Cleve. (pres. 1955-56) socs. dentistry for children, Cleve. Dental Soc., Cleve. Acad. Dental Studies, Delta Sigma Delta. Republican. Methodist. Home: 2665 Endicott Rd Shaker Heights OH 44120 Office: 11811 Shaker Blvd Cleveland OH 44120

LORANT, JOHN HERMAN, educator; b. Duesseldorf, Germany, Mar. 25, 1932; s. Hugo and Lilly Henrietta (Simon) L.; B.S., U. Wis., 1953; M.B.A., Harvard U., 1957; Ph.D. (Woytinsky scholar), Columbia U., 1966; m. Susan Margaret Haas, June 30, 1968; children—Mandy Anne, Jenny Simone. Fin. analyst Food Fair Stores, Phila., 1957-58; asst. to partners Neuberger & Berman, N.Y.C., 1959-60; fin. analyst IBM, White Plains, N.Y., 1960-61; asst. prof. econs. Douglass Coll., New Brunswick, N.J., 1966-69; research asso. AMA, Chgo., 1969-74, dir. health systems research, 1975, dir. program planning, 1976, dir. human resources div., 1976-80; prof. bus. Lake Forest (Ill.) Coll., 1980—. Served with Transp. Corps., U.S. Army, 1953-55; Korea. Mem. Am. Econ. Assn., Human Resource Planning Soc., AAUP. Club: Harvard Business School (Chgo.). Author: The Role of Capital-Improving Innovations in American Manufacturing During the 1920's, 1975. Office: Lake Forest College Lake Forest IL 60045

LORD, JAMES GREGORY, mktg. and fundraising cons.; b. Cleve., Aug. 23, 1947; s. James Nelson and Esther L.; student U. Md., Far East Campus, 1966-68, Cleve. State U., 1968-72, Antioch Coll., 1974; m. Wendy Franklin, July 10, 1977. TV news producer Far East Network, Tokyo, 1965-68; wire editor News-Herald, Willoughby, Ohio, 1968-69; public relations asso. United Way, Cleve., 1969-70; free-lance public relations person, Cleve., 1970-72; dir. public relations Ketchum, Inc., Pitts., 1972-77; cons. in public relations, in devel. philanthropic instns., Cleve., 1977—. Served with USN, 1964-68; Japan. Author: Philanthropy and Marketing, 1981; contbr. numerous articles on quality of life in Am. cities to various publs.; developed City Survey, system to compare cities; developed award winning public relations programs; one-man photography exhbns., 15 worldwide sites, 1968-72. Home: 2431 Channing Rd Cleveland OH 44118

LORD, JIM, treas. Minn.; b. Chanhassen, Minn., Nov. 26, 1948; B.A., U. Minn.; postgrad. Georgetown U., Gustavus Adolphus Coll.; J.D., William Mitchell Coll. Law. Admitted to Minn. bar, 1980; mem. staff Senator Hubert Humphrey, Senator Walter Mondale; staff asst., liaison to depts. human rights, agr. and vets affairs for Gov. Wendell Anderson; mem. Minn. Senate; treas. State of Minn.; adviser Commn. Uniform State Laws, 1980-81. Served with U.S. Mcht. Marine. Mem. Nat. Assn. Unclaimed Property Adminstrs. (pres. 1977-80). Democrat. Office: Treasurer's Office 303 Administration Bldg 50 Sherburne Ave Saint Paul MN 55155*

LORD, MARION E. MANNS, educator; b. Ft. Huachuca, Ariz., Dec. 17, 1914; d. George Wiley and Annie Pellett) Manns; student R.I. State Coll., 1932; B.S., Northwestern U., 1936; postgrad. Breadloaf Coll., summer 1936; M.Ed., Harvard, 1962; M.A., Ph.D. (F. B. Fred fellow), U. Wis., 1968; m. William Shepard Lord, Apr. 29, 1938 (div. May 1965); children—Caroline B. (Mrs. Martin L. Gross), Marion F. (Mrs. Fred W. Steadman), Jane B. N.H. State rep. Gen. Ct., Concord, N.H., 1957-62; dean of women, dir. guidance New Eng. Coll., Henniker, N.H., 1962-64; asst. to div. dir. Bur. Higher Edn. U.S. Office Edn., then dir. women's project Nat. Center Ednl. Statistics, program specialist, 1968-75; dean faculty Borough of Manhattan Community Coll., City U. N.Y., 1975-78; dean faculty Cottey Coll., Nevada, Mo., 1979—. Vice pres., dir. N.H. Council for Better Schs., 1957-64; county co-chmn. Nat. Found. Infantile Paralysis-March of Dimes, Laconia, N.H., 1958; dir. N.H. Council on World Affairs, 1957-63, Laconia Hosp. Mem. Am. Psychol. Assn., Am. Polit. Sci. Assn., D.C. Sociol. Soc. (treas., mem. com. on status of women), Nat. Council Adminstrv. women in Edn., Federally Employed Women, Order Women Legislators, N.H. State Soc. in Washington, Am. Personnel and Guidance Assn., Nat. Assn. Women Deans and Counselors, League Women Voters, AAUW, Bus. and Profl. Womens Club. Home: 929 W Cherry St Nevada MO 64772

LORD, WILLIAM HERMAN, theatre cons.; b. Providence, Feb. 28, 1931; s. Herman Maurice and Gertrude (Thompson) L.; B.A., U. Evansville (Ind.), 1953; M.A., Northwestern U., 1961; m. Catherine Lynn Ball, Sept. 14, 1957; children—Jennifer Lynn, Louise Giovanna. Lighting dir. Bosse (Ind.) High Sch., 1947-49, Evansville (Ind.) Community Players, 1947-53, also tech. dir. Evansville Coll. Theatre, 1950-53; with R.H.M. Stage Equipment Co., Indpls., 1955-57; scenic carpenter WFBM-TV, Indpls., 1957-58; tchr. speech and tech. theater, also prodn. supr. sch. theatre No. Central High Sch., Indpls., 1958—; owner, pres., dir. Theater Assos., Inc., Indpls., 1957—; owner William H. Lord theatre cons., Indpls., 1961—. Bd. dirs. Footlite Musicals Co., Indpls., 1958-60. Served with AUS, 1953-55. Decorated Am. Spirit Honor medal. Mem. Ind. State Tchrs. Assn., U.S. Inst. Theatre Tech., Ind. Speech Assn., Speech Communications Assn., Am. Theatre Assn., Illuminating Engrs. Soc. (mem. com. theatre, television and film lighting), Alpha Psi Omega, Pi Delta Epsilon, Tau Kappa Alpha, Lambda Chi Alpha. Presbyn. (elder 1971-73). Author: Installing a Theatre Lighting System, 1977; Stagecraft 1: Your Introduction to Backstage Work, 1978. Contbr. series of articles on stage lighting to Dramatics Mag., 1970-71. Home: 9210 N College Ave Indianapolis IN 46240

LORENTZSEN, NORMAN M., transp. and natural resource exec.; b. Horace, N.D., Nov. 29, 1916; s. Ivar A. and Antonette (Olson) L.; B.A., Concordia Coll., 1941; postgrad. Am. U., 1965, Harvard, 1968; m. Helen O. Broten, Sept. 20, 1943; children—Thomas, Mary, Katherine. With N.P. Ry. (name now Burlington No. Inc.), 1936—, trainmaster, asst. to gen. mgr., St. Paul, 1953-54, supt. Rocky Mountain div., 1954-57, supt. Idaho div., 1957-64, gen. mgr., Seattle, 1964-67, v.p. ops., St. Paul, 1968-70, v.p. ops. parent co., 1970-71, exec. v.p. parent co., 1971-73, pres. transp. div. parent co., 1973-76, pres., 1977-80, chief exec. officer, 1978-80, chmn. exec. com., 1980—; chmn. bd., dir. Burlington No. Air Freight, Inc.; dir. Burlington No. Inc., BN Transport Inc., Colo. & So. Ry. Co., Ft. Worth & Denver Ry. Co., Oreg. Electric Ry. Co., Twin City Fed. Savs. & Loan Assn., Mpls. trustee Oreg. Trunk Ry. Bd. dirs. N.W. Area Found., St. Paul, Luth. Brotherhood, Mpls., St. Paul Found. Served with USNR, 1941-45. Clubs: Minnesota, Town and Country, Pool and Yacht (St. Paul). Home: 675 Ivy Falls Ct St Paul MN 55118 Office: 176 E 5th St St Paul MN 55101*

LORENZ, DALE ARDEN, coll. pres.; b. St. James, Minn., Feb. 4, 1930; s. Herman August and Minnie (Olson) L.; B.S., U. Minn., 1956, M.A., 1957; m. Marilyn Ellis, Aug., 1954; children—Joni, Thomas, Michael. Dean, Willmar (Minn.) Community Coll., 1962-64, pres., 1964-66; pres. North Hennepin Community Coll., Brooklyn Park, Minn., 1966-68, Normandale Community Coll., Bloomington, Minn., 1968—; dir. Northwestern Nat. Bank Southwest. Served with USAF, 1951-54. Mem. Minn. Assn. Community and Jr. Colls. (pres. 1977-78), Minn. Assn. Post-Secondary Instns., Bloomington C. of C. (dir. 1976-79). Lutheran. Office: Normandale Community Coll 9700 France Ave S Bloomington MN 55431

LORENZ, JOHN DOUGLAS, indsl. engr.; b. Talmage, Nebr., July 2, 1942; s. Orville George and Twila Lucille (Larsen) L.; B.S. in Mech. Engring., U. Nebr., 1965, M.S., 1967, Ph.D., 1973; m. Alice Louise Hentzen, Aug. 26, 1967; 1 son, Christian Douglas. Research asst., then systems analyst U. Nebr., 1966-73; mem. faculty Gen. Motors Inst., Flint, Mich., 1973—, prof. indsl. engring., 1978—; cons. sheltered workshops, 1976—. Recipient Distinguished Teaching award Gen. Motors Inst. Alumni Assn., 1977; Danforth asso., 1979—; research grantee Am. Soc. Tool and Mfg. Engrs., 1966. Mem. Am. Inst. Indsl. Engrs. (chpt. pres. 1979-80), Soc. Automotive Engrs., Am. Soc. Engring. Edn., Sigma Xi, Alpha Pi Mu, Pi Tau Sigma, Tau Beta Pi. Republican. Presbyterian. Author papers in field. Home: 225 Oakwood Dr Flushing MI 48433 Office: 1700 W 3d Ave Flint MI 48502

LORENZEN, KRAIG ELMER, physician; b. St. Paul, Apr. 19, 1948; s. Warren Clifford and Delvina Edna (Marcotte) L.; B.S., St. John's U., 1970; Ph.D., U. N.D., 1974; B.S. in Med., Chgo. Med. Sch., 1977, M.D., 1979. Research chemist Kimberly Clark Corp., 1970; postdoctoral fellow U. N.D., Grand Forks, 1975; resident in internal medicine U. Wis., Milw., 1979—. Counselor, St. Cloud Reformatory, 1967-69; scoutmaster Boy Scouts Am., 1970, cubmaster, 1970; swimming/diving instr. YMCA, Neenah, Wis., 1970. Argonne Nat. Lab. scholar, 1968; Kimberly Clark Corp. scholar, 1969, recipient research award, 1970. Mem. AMA, A.C.P., Am. Soc. Internal Medicine. Roman Catholic. Home: 17025 Ruby Ln Brookfield WI 53005 Office: 950 N 12th St Milwaukee WI 53201

LORETTA, RICHARD DENNIS, mfg. co. exec.; b. Woodbury, N.J., Dec. 19, 1941; s. Frank Bernard and Eleanor (Butterly) L.; B.A. in Econs., Chapman Coll., 1965; M.B.A. with honors, U. So. Calif., 1967; m. Jennifer Evans, Nov. 7, 1974; children—Robert, Patrick, Andrew. Fin. analyst Ford Motor Co., Dearborn, Mich., 1965-69; fin. mgr. Clark Equipment Credit Corp., Buchanan, Mich., 1969-72, v.p., Brazil, 1972-74, sr. v.p. internat., 1974-76; v.p., gen. mgr. Clark Internat., Battle Creek, Mich., 1976—. Chmn. fin. com., local sch. bd.; chmn. Calhoun County Republican Com. Mem. C. of C. Roman Catholic. Club: Rotary. Home: 41 Hickory Ln Battle Creek MI 49015 Office: PO Box 1320 Battle Creek MI 49016

LORGE, GERALD DAVID, lawyer, state senator; b. Bear Creek, Wis., July 9, 1922; s. Joseph J. and Anna M. (Peterson) L.; J.D., Marquette U., 1952; m. Christina C. Ziegler, Apr. 15, 1958; children—Robert G., William D., Anna Marie, Julie Agnes, Christina Marie. Admitted to Wis. bar, 1952; gen. practice, Bear Creek, 1951—; mem. Wis. Gen. Assembly, 1951-54, Wis. Senate, 1954—, past chmn. com. on committees, past chmn. com. on judiciary and ins., mem. com. on interstate co-operation, past mem. com. on legislative procedure, now mem. com. on ins. and utilities. Mem. Wis. Legis. Council, Interstate Coop.; mem. Joint Survey Com. on Retirement Systems; past chmn. Justice and Law Enforcement Study com. Midwestern Council Govts., also past mem. jud. council; mem. ins. laws rev. com. Served with USMCR, 1942-45. Mem. Am., Wis., Outagamie bar assns., Nat. Conf. Ins. Legislators (dir. 1971-73, pres. 1973), Am. Legion, DAV (life). Republican. K.C. Clubs: Bear Creek, Moose, Outagame Conservative. Home: PO Box 47 Bear Creek WI 54922 Office: 204 Railroad Ave Bear Creek WI 54922 also Room 337 S State Capitol Madison WI 53702

LORMAN, BARBARA KAILIN, state senator, corp. exec.; b. Madison, Wis., July 31, 1932; d. Clarence and Edith (Choffnes) Kailin; student U. Wis., 1950-53, Whitewater, 1978-79; m. Milton Lorman, Feb. 1, 1953; children—Carol R. Lorman Weinstein, William Joseph, David B. Pres., Lorman Iron & Metal Co., Inc., Ft. Atkinson, Wis., 1979—; mem. Wis. State Senate, 1980-82. Spl. study com. Migrant Labor Council; exec. council Sinnissippi council Boy Scouts Am.; bd. dirs. Wis. Soc. Jewish Learning. Mem. Energy Com., Insurance and Utilities Com. Beth El Temple, Madison; Fort Atkinson Assn. Milw. Symphney (past co-chmn., sec.), Fort Atkinson Devel. Council (past pres.). Republican. Jewish. Office: 140 S State Capitol Madison WI 53538

LOSSE, ARLYLE MANSFIELD, librarian; b. Sheboygan, Wis., Apr. 15, 1917; d. Truman Roy and Emilie (Hildebrandt) Mansfield; B.S., Milw. State Tchrs. Coll. (now U. Wis.-Milw.), 1939; M.S. in Library Sci., U. Wis.-Madison, 1960; m. Carl H. Losse, Jan. 20, 1962. Asst. to reference librarian Mead Pub. Library, Sheboygan, 1958-59; librarian Milw. Pub. Library System, 1960—. Active mem. Sheboygan Community Players, 1957-58; leader Milw. Great Books discussion group, 1963-64. Recipient poetry sect. Lit. award Milw. State Tchrs. Coll., 1938; 1st prize modern poetry div. Nat. Fedn. State Poetry Socs., 1964. Mem. Wis. Fellowship Poets, Nat. League Am. Pen Women, Spl. Libraries Assn., ALA, Acad. Am. Poets, Inc., AAUW, Art Libraries Soc. N.Am. (com. on standards for art libraries 1973-75), Beta Phi Mu (charter mem. Beta Rho chpt. 1978). Presbyterian (deacon). Contbr. poems to jours., newspapers, anthologies. Home: 4124 W Fond du Lac Ave # 6 Milwaukee WI 53216 Office: 814 W Wisconsin Ave Milwaukee WI 53233

LOTOCKY, INNOCENT HILARION, bishop; b. Buchach, Ukraine, Nov. 3, 1915; s. Stefan and Maria (Tytyn) L.; Ph.D., U. Vienna, 1944. Ordained priest; Ukrainian Catholic Ch., 1940; superior and master of novices, Dawson, Pa., 1946-51; provincial superior Am. province Order St. Basil the Gt.; Glen Cove, N.Y., 1951-53; pastor St. George's Ch., N.Y.C.; novice master, Glen Cove, L.I., N.Y., 1958; superior St. Nicholas Ch., Chgo., 1960-61, pastor, 1961-62; pastor and superior Immaculate Conception Parish, Hamtramck, Mich., 1962-81; tchr. Immaculate Conception Ukrainian Cath. High Sch., 1962-81; mem. Provincial Council Basilian Order, 1962-81; bishop St. Nicholas Diocese for Ukrainians, Chgo., 1981—. Mem. U.S. Cath. Conf. Bishops, Cath. Conf. Eastern Rite Bishops, Assn. Eastern Rite Priests. Club: KC (hon.). Address: 2245 W Rice St Chicago IL 60622

LOTZ, HERBERT KARL, psychologist; b. Guenterod, Germany, Mar. 14, 1920; s. Karl and Maria Elisabeth (Hehl) L.; came to U.S., 1929, naturalized, 1944; student Drake U., 1938-39; B.S., Iowa State U., 1942; M.A., U. Iowa, 1947; postgrad. U. Wash., 1949-50; m. Janet Sladden Howell, May 29, 1948; children—Kathryn Ann, Steven Karl, Richard Paul, William Howell. Jr. psychologist Iowa Dept. Social Welfare, 1946-49, sr. psychologist, 1951-53; area psychologist Ill. Office Pub. Instruction, 1954-56, chief area psychologist, 1956-63; psychologist Henry County Coop. for Psychol. Services, 1963-69; chief psychologist Henry-Stark Counties Spl. Edn. Coop., Kewanee, Ill., 1969-81; pvt. practice psychology, Galesburg, Ill., 1955—; contract psychologist Ill. Div. Vocat. Rehab., 1963—; cons. Fed. Disability Program, 1964—, Positive Attitudes, Inc., 1975-76; mem. psychologist exam. com. State Ill. Dept. Registration and Edn., 1976—, chmn., 1978-81. Bd. dirs. Positive Attitudes, Inc., 1969-75. Served with U.S. Army, 1943-46. Diplomate in sch. psychology Am. Bd. Profl. Psychology; listed Nat. Register Health Providers in Psychology Mem. ACLU (treas. Western Ill. chpt. 1973—), AAAS, Am. Orthopsychiat. Assn., Am. Assn. Mental Deficiency, Council Exceptional Children, Am., Ill. (treas. 1977-80) psychol. assns. Mem. Soc. of Friends. Club: Rotary (Galesburg, Ill.). Home: 220 N Chambers St Galesburg IL 61401 Office: 216 Bondi Bldg Galesburg IL 61401

LOTZ, JANET HOWELL, psychologist; b. Springfield, Ohio, June 4, 1923; d. Folger Branson and Catherine Sladden (Tordt) Howell; student Earlham Coll., 1941-43; B.A., U. Iowa, 1945, M.A., 1948; m. Herbert Karl Lotz, May 29, 1948; children—Kathryn A., Steven K., Richard P., William H. Jr. psychologist Div. Child Welfare, State of Iowa, 1947-49; psychologist Knox-Warren Spl. Edn. Dist., Galesburg, Ill., 1964—, intern supr., 1968-70; psychologist Warren Achievement Sch., Monmouth, Ill., 1972-73; individual practice, Galesburg, 1962—; cons. psychologist Headstart Program, Galesburg. Mem. Am. (asso.), Ill. psychol. assns. Democrat. Quaker. Home: 220 N Chambers Galesburg IL 61401 Office: 1018 S Farnham Galesburg IL 61401

LOUCKS, RALPH BRUCE, JR., investment co. exec. b. St. Louis, Dec. 10, 1924; s. Ralph Bruce and Dola (Blake) L.; B.A., Lake Forest Coll., 1949; postgrad. U. Chgo., 1950-52; m. Lois Holloway, June 4, 1949; children—Elizabeth, Mary Jane. Investment fund mgr. No. Trust Co., Chgo., 1950-53, Brown Bros. Harriman & Co., Chgo., 1953-55; investment counsel, pres. Tilden, Loucks & Grannis, Chgo., 1955-80; partner Bacon, Whipple & Co., Chgo., 1981—. Bd. dirs. Ill. Epilepsy League, Epilepsy Found. Served with 11th Armored Div., AUS, 1943-45. Decorated Bronze Star medal, Purple Heart. Mem. Investment Analysts Soc., Investment Counsel Assn. Am., Huguenot Soc. Ill. (pres. 1960-61), Soc. Colonial Wars. Clubs: Economic, Racquet, University (Chgo.). Office: 134 S LaSalle St Chicago IL 60603

LOUCKS, VERNON REECE, JR., hosp. supply co. exec.; b. Kenilworth, Ill., Oct. 24, 1934; s. Vernon Reece and Sue (Burton) L.; B.A. in History, Yale U., 1957; M.B.A., Harvard U., 1963; m. Linda Kay Olson, May 12, 1972; children—Charles, Greg, Suzy, David, Kristi, Eric. Sr. mgmt. cons. George Fry & Assos., Chgo., 1963-65; with Baxter Travenol Labs., Inc., Deerfield, Ill., 1966—, exec. v.p., 1973-76, dir., 1975—, pres., chief operating officer, 1976—; dir. Continental Ill. Corp., Dun & Bradstreet Corp., Emerson Electric Co., Quaker Oats Co. Bd. dirs. Lake Forest Hosp.; chmn. Met. Crusade of Mercy, 1977; bd. dirs. John L. and Helen Kellogg Found., Protestant

Found., Econ. Club of Chgo.; trustee Rush-Presbyn.-St. Luke's Med. Center; asso. Northwestern U.; alumni trustee Yale Corp. Served to 1st lt. USMC, 1957-60. Episcopalian. Clubs: Chgo. Commonwealth, Comml. Office: One Baxter Pkwy Deerfield IL 60015

LOUDENBACK, LYNN JOSEPH, mktg. specialist; b. Wenatchee, Wash., Sept. 3, 1936; s. Everett Charles and Ida Pearl (Coons) L.; B.A., Wash. State U., 1958; M.B.A., U. Wash., 1963, Ph.D., 1969; m. Dixie Lee Rowland; children—Ross Cameron, Aaron Christian, Vallry Rae, Shawn Lee. Asst. prof. mktg. U. Nebr., Lincoln, 1967-72, asso. prof., 1972-75; prof. mktg., chmn. dept. indsl. adminstrn. Iowa State U., Ames, 1975-78; vis. prof. U. Queensland, Brisbane, Australia, summer 1973; cons. various fgn. and domestic firms. Mem. Am. Mktg. Assn. (dir. 1973-75), Sales and Mktg. Execs. Internat. Author: Anthology of Practical Marketing, 1976; contbr. articles to profl. jours. Office: Sch Bus Adminstrn Iowa State U Ames IA 50011

LOUDON, ROY VIRGIL, JR., univ. ofcl.; b. Shelby, N.C., Aug. 19, 1924; s. Roy Virgil and Nellie Veronica (Dailey) L.; B.S., U. Nebr., 1950, M.A., 1953, Ed.D., 1967; m. Elizabeth Louise Willie, Feb. 14, 1947; children—Catherine Loudon Williams, Michael Roy, John Louis, Timothy Dale, Joseph Paul, Lee Stephen. Ins. agt. Allstate Ins. Co., Lincoln, Nebr., 1953-55; ins. and retirement officer U. Nebr., Lincoln, 1955-57, dir. personnel, 1957-77, adminstr. personnel and risk mgmt., 1977—. Risk mgmt. cons. Mem. Lincoln Catholic Sch. Bd., 1969-73, pres., 1971-73; mem. Lincoln Charter Revision Com., 1968-72; mem. Gov.'s Com. Implementation State Employees Collective Bargaining Act, 1969. Served with USAAF, 1942-46. Mem. Univ. Ins. Mgrs. Assn. (dir. 1970-73), Am. Soc. Ins. Mgmt. (sec. 1973, v.p. 1974, pres. 1975), Coll. and Univ. Personnel Assn., Am. Legion. Home: 635 S 36th St Lincoln NE 68510 Office: Adminstrn Bldg U Nebr Lincoln NE 68508

LOUGHRIDGE, ROBERT FOSTER, JR., tire co. exec.; b. Fort Worth, Nov. 15, 1935; s. Robert Foster and Elizabeth (Hamlet) L.; B.A. summa cum laude, U. Tex., 1958; M.B.A., Harvard U., 1961; m. Celeste Page, June 15, 1962; children—Christopher, Mark. Various positions Exxon Corp., N.Y.C., Venezuela, Brazil, Argentina, Paraguay, Hong Kong, Spain, Houston, 1961-78; dir. econ. and strategic planning, chief economist Goodyear Tire & Rubber Co., Akron, Ohio, 1978—. Served to 1st lt. AUS, 1959. Mem. Planning Execs. Inst. (pres. Akron/Canton chpt. 1981), Am. Mktg. Assn. (dir. Akron/Canton 1981—), Internat. Bus. Council, Internat. Econ. Policy Assn., Automotive Market Research Council, Nat. Assn. Bus. Economists, Mensa (pres. E. Ohio group 1980). Republican. Club: Portage Country. Home: 201 Hampshire Rd Akron OH 44313 Office: Goodyear Tire & Rubber Co 1144 E Market St Akron OH 44316

LOUGHRIGE, ALAN CRAIG, r.r. adminstr.; b. Cumberland, Md., Dec. 24, 1946; s. Rayburn Dewey and Emma Catherine (Hershberger) L.; B.S. in Engring. Mgmt., U. Mo., Rolla, 1969; M.B.A., Drury Coll., 1976; m. Patricia Eloise Gooch, June 12, 1971; 1 son, Brian Craig. Sales engr. Columbia Laundry Machinery Co., Kansas City, Mo., 1969-70; with St. Louis-San Francisco Ry. Co., Springfield, Mo., 1970—, field engr., 1970-76, asst. engr. cost and design, 1976, gen. supr. material and stores, 1976-77, purchasing agt., 1977-81; mgr. scrap and equipment sales Burlington No. R.R., St. Paul, 1981-82, dir. scrap and equipment sales, 1982—; tchr. U.S. Med. Center for Fed. Prisoners, Springfield, 1977, Drury Coll., Springfield, 1978. Active Boy Scouts Am.; deacon Southminster Presbyterian Ch., Springfield, 1977—, stewardship chmn., 1976, 77. Exec. adviser Jr. Achievement, 1979-80. Recipient certificate of appreciation U.S. Med. Center for Fed. Prisoners, 1977; named knight St. Patrick, U. Mo., Rolla, 1969. Mem. Ry. Automotive Mgmt. Assn., Transp. Materials Mgmt. Forum, Northwest Maintenance of Way Club, Am. Soc. for Engring. Mgmt., Mensa, Tau Kappa Epsilon. Home: 2845 Icerose Ln Stillwater MN 55082 Office: 176 E 5th St St Paul MN 55101

LOUKIDIS, DIMITRIST (JIM) K(ONSTANTINE), machine tool mfg. co. exec.; b. Athens, Greece, Nov. 15, 1936; came to U.S., 1955; s. Konstantine and Evlampia L.; B.S.M.E., Ind. Inst. Tech., 1960; m. Barbara Schuppie, Nov. 26, 1960; children—Linda Lee, Deno James. Design engr. Nat. Lead Co., Chgo., 1960-62; project engr. Ladish: Tri-Clover Co., Kenosha, Wis., 1962-64; project engr. Famco Machine Co., Kenosha, 1964-69, chief engr., 1969-73; chief engr. Famco/Worden Allen Co., Kenosha, 1973-75; v.p. engring., sales Famco-Belco Industries, Inc., Kenosha, 1975—. Registered profl. engr., Wis. Mem. Soc. Mfg. Engrs. Club: Masons. Home: 3501 Indiana St Racine WI 53405 Office: 1001 31st St Kenosha WI 53140

LOURENCO, RUY VALENTIM, physician, educator; b. Lisbon, Portugal, Mar. 25, 1929; came to U.S., 1959, naturalized, 1966; s. Raul Valentim and Maria Amalia (Gomes-Rosa) L.; B.S., U. Lisbon, 1947; M.D., 1951; m. Susan Jane Lowenthal, Jan. 18, 1960; children—Peter Edward, Margaret Philippa. Intern, Lisbon U. Hosp., 1951-53, resident internal medicine, 1953-55, instr., 1955-59; fellow dept. medicine Columbia U.-Presbyn. Med. Center, N.Y.C., 1959-63, asst. prof. medicine N.J. Coll. Medicine, Jersey City, 1963-66, asso. prof., 1966-67; practice medicine specializing in pulmonary medicine, 1969—; attending physician, dir. respiratory physiology lab. Jersey City Med. Center, 1963-67; asso. prof. medicine and physiology U. Ill., Chgo., 1967-69, prof., 1969—, chmn. dept. medicine, 1977—, Foley prof. medicine, 1977—; dir. respiratory research lab. Hektoen Inst., Chgo., 1967-70; dir. pulmonary medicine Cook County Hosp., Chgo., 1969-70; attending physician U. Ill. Med. Center, Chgo., 1967—, dir. pulmonary sect. and labs 1970-77, physician-in-chief, 1977—; cons. task force on research in respiratory diseases NIH, 1972, mem. pathology study sect., 1972-76; mem. rev. bd. for Spl. Centers of Research program, 1974; cons. career devel. program VA, 1972—; mem. nat. com. Rev. Sci. Basis of Inhalation Therapy, 1973-74. Bd. dirs., mem. exec. com. Chgo. Lung Assn., 1974—; bd. dirs. Hektoen Inst. for Med. Research, 1977—. Fellow AAAS, ACP, Am. Coll. Chest Physicians (past pres. Ill. chpt.); mem. Am. Fedn. Clin. Research, Am. Heart Assn., Am. Physiol. Soc., Am. Soc. Clin. Investigation, Am. Thoracic Soc. (chmn. sci. assembly 1974-75), Assn. Am. Physicians, Assn. Profs. Medicine, Central Soc. Clin Research (councillor 1973-77), Soc. Exptl. Biology and Medicine, Central Research Club, Sigma XI, Alpha Omega Alpha (faculty). Editorial bd. Jour. Lab. and Clin. Medicine, 1973-79. Contbr. numerous articles on pulmonary diseases, respiratory physiology and biochemistry to med. jours. Home: 1000 N Lake Shore Dr Chicago IL 60611 Office: 840 S Wood St Chicago IL 60612

LOUSBERG, PETER HERMAN, lawyer; b. Des Moines, Aug. 19, 1931; s. Peter J. and Ottilia M. (Vogel) L.; A.B., Yale, 1953; J.D. cum laude, U. Notre Dame, 1956; m. JoAnn Beimer, Jan. 20, 1962; children—Macara Lynn, Mark, Stephen. Admitted to Ill. bar, 1956, Fla. bar, 1972; clk. Ill. Appellate Ct., 1956-57; asst. states atty. Rock Island County, Ill., 1959-60; partner firm Lousberg & McClean, Rock Island, Ill., 1960—; opinion commentator Sta. WHBF, 1973-74; lectr. Ill. Inst. Continuing Edn., chmn., 1981-82; lectr. Ill. Trial Lawyers seminars. Chmn. crime and juvenile delinquency Rock Island Model Cities Task Force, 1969; chmn. Rock Island Youth Guidance Council, 1964-69; adv. bd. Ill. Dept. Corrections Juvenile Div., 1976—; Ill. commr. Nat. Conf. Commrs. Uniform State Laws, 1976-78; treas. Greater Quad City Close-up Program, 1976-80. Bd. dirs. Rock Island Indsl.-Comml. Devel. Corp., 1977—; bd. govs. Rock Island Community Found., 1977—. Served to 1st lt. USMC, 1957-59. Fellow Am. Bar Found.; mem. Am., Ill. (past gov. 1969-74, chmn. spl. survey com. 1974-75, chmn. com. on mentally disabled 1979-80), Rock Island bar assns., Rock Island C. of C. (treas. 1975, pres. 1978), Am., Ill. (bd. mgrs. 1974-78) trial lawyers assns., Am. Judicature Soc., Nat. Legal Aid and Defenders Assn. (chmn. membership campaigns for Ill. 1969-71, for Midwest dist. 2 1974-75), Quad Cities Council of Chambers Commerce (1st chmn. 1979-80), U.S. Power Squadron. Roman Catholic. Rotarian. Clubs: Notre Dame, Quad Cities (Rock Island). Contbr. articles to profl. jours. Home: 2704 27th St Rock Island IL 61201 Office: 1808 3d Ave Rock Island IL 61201

LOVAN, OWEN LEE, paper co. exec.; b. Salina, Kans., Oct. 30, 1922; s. Owen L. and Myra (Rhodes) L.; B.S., U. Nebr., 1948; m. Mary Patricia Tomlinson, Dec. 27, 1957; children—Victor, Andrew. Buyer, Hall Bros., Inc., Kansas City, Mo., 1948-50; sales rep. Wertgame Paper Co., Kansas City, Mo., 1951-55, div. sales mgr., Wichita, Kans., 1955-58; partner Liberty Paper Co., Wichita, 1958-59, pres., 1959-79; owner KEY Sales Co., Wichita, 1979—; area mgr. Packaging Services Corp., Wichita, 1979—. Served with USAAF, 1942-45; lt. col. USAF Res., ret. Mem. Wichita Area C. of C., Res. Officers Assn. (past pres. dep. Kans.), Sigme Alpha Epsilon. Clubs: Wichita, Lancers, Mason, Kiwanis (past pres. North Wichita Club). Contbr. articles to trade publs. Home: 18 Ash Briar Estates 641 N Woodlawn St Wichita KS 67208 Office: KEY Sales Co Box 11534 Wichita KS 67211

LOVE, JOHN H., assn. exec., lawyer; b. Detroit, May 5, 1951; s. John William and Bernice (Robins) L.; B.S., St. Mary's Coll. of Calif., 1973; postgrad. Cath. U. Am., 1973-74; J.D., Detroit Coll. Law, 1976. Admitted to Mich. bar, 1976; mem. firm Roy, Cardamone & Love, Warren, Mich., 1976-77; mem. firm Nine and Maister, Bloomfield Hills, Mich., 1977-78; exec. dir. Am. Power Boat Assn., East Detroit, Mich., 1978—. Mem. Internat. Freedom Festival, Detroit Sportsbroadcasters Assn., Spirit Detroit Assn. (bd. dirs.). Office: 17640 E Nine Mile Rd East Detroit MI 48021

LOVE, LARRY JOHN, supt. schs.; b. Creston, Iowa, July 16, 1928; s. Harry S. and Ethel Elizabeth (McDermott) L.; B.A., Simpson Coll., Indianola, Iowa, 1949; M.S. in Edn., U. Wis., 1960; D.Pedagogy, Nat. Coll., Evanston, Ill., 1980; m. Verna Jean Herbst, Aug. 13, 1955; children—Craig J., Brian J., Kevin J. Tchr., counselor, adminstrs. schs. in Iowa, Calif. and Wis., 1949-50, 55-65; mem. adminstrv. staff Wilmette (Ill.) public schs., 1965—, supt. schs., 1974—; trustee Ill. Council Econ. Edn.; adv. bd. Mallinckrodt Coll., Wilmette, Ill. Mem. Wilmette Bd. Health, 1974—; chief examiner Wilmette Fire and Police Commn., 1967-73. Served to lt. USNR, 1950-55. Mem. Nat. Assn. Sch. Adminstrs., Assn. Supervision and Curriculum Devel., Nat. Assn. Secondary Sch. Prins., Ill. Assn. Sch. Prins., Phi Delta Kappa. Club: Wilmette Rotary (sec. 1980—). Office: 615 Locust Rd Wilmette IL 60091

LOVE, NORRIS, sch. adminstr., mktg. and research cons.; b. Chgo., Dec. 13, 1936; s. Harold Norris and Anne (Schuttler) L.; A.B., Princeton U., 1958; M.B.A., Stanford U., 1960; m. Marcena Pickett Waterman, Sept. 12, 1959; children—Kathryn, Anne, Sara. Mktg. research supr. D'Arcy Advt., Chgo., 1960-64, account exec., 1964-66; mgr. Mid Am. Research Assos., Chgo., 1966-68; mgr. mktg. research dept. D'Arcy Advt. Co., Chgo., 1967-68; asso. research dir. Campbell-Mithun Advt. Co., Chgo., 1968-72; v.p. adminstrn., dean students Lake Forest Sch. Mgmt., Lake Forest, Ill., 1972—, bd. dirs., sec., 1973—; mktg. and research cons., 1972—. Bd. dirs., trustee Chgo. Zool. Soc., mem. exec. com., 1975—; treas. Lake Mich. Fedn., Chgo., 1970-77; bd. Christian edn. Winnetka Congregational Ch. (Ill.), 1975-77, trustee, 1981—; bd. dirs., v.p. Crisis Homes, Park Ridge, 1977-81; active Shedd Aquarium, Chgo.; coach Winnetka Park Dist. Mem. Am. Mktg. Assn. Republican. Clubs: Chgo., Chgo. Golf, Skokie Country, Tawas Beach (dir. 1972-75, 81—), Swan Lake, Anglers Chgo. (pres. 1982), Halter Wildlife and Conservation (dir. 1981—); Trout Unltd. (dir. Chgo. 1976—). Home: 1175 Pelham Rd Winnetka IL 60093 Office: Lake Forest Sch Mgmt Lake Forest Coll Lake Forest IL 60045

LOVE, RICHARD HENRY, art gallery exec., art historian; b. Schneider, Ind., Dec. 27, 1939; s. Glenn and Grayce L.; art history student and degrees U. Md., Europe, 1961-63, Bloom Coll., Chicago Heights, Ill., 1963-64, U. Ill., Chicago Circle, 1964-66, Northwestern U., 1967-69; independent study Villa Schifanoia, Florence, Italy; m. E. Geraldine Olson, June 30, 1962; children—Julie Renee, Jayce Christine. Owner, pres. R.H. Love Galleries, Inc., 1967—; prof. art history Prairie State Coll., Chicago Heights, Ill., 1963-65; art critic Star Tribune Publishing Co., Chicago Heights; Art commentator Sta. WEFM, WBBM, WNIB, Chgo., Sta. WCIU, Love on American Art, Channel 26 TV, Chgo.; chmn. 19th Century Paintings Sta. WTTW Art Auction, 1979; cons. Rahr-West Mus., Manitowoc, Wis., 1978. Served with U.S. Army, 1961-64. Author: John Barber, The Man, The Artist, 1981; The Paintings of Louis Ritman 1889-1963, 1975; Theodore Earl Butler 1860-1936, 1976; Pastels By Pierre Prins, 1974; William Chadwick 1879-1962, 1977; Harriet Randall Lumis 1870-1953, 1976; Walter Clark and Eliot Clark, 1980; Cassatt: The Independent, 1980; Encyclopedia of American Impressionists, 1981. Office: 100 E Ohio St Chicago IL 60611

LOVE, RUTH B., ednl. adminstr.; b. Lawton, Okla., Apr. 22, 1932; B.A. in Elem. Edn., San Jose State U.; M.A. in Guidance and Counseling, San Francisco State U.; Ph.D. in Human Behavior, U.S. Internat. U. Tchr., Oakland (Calif.) Unified Sch. Dist., 1954-59, counselor/cons. Ford Found. Project, 1960-62, tchr. adult edn., 1961-65, supt. schs., 1975—; Fulbright exchange tchr., Cheshire, Eng., 1960; project dir. Operation Crossroads, Ghana, summer 1962; cons. Bur. Pupil Personnel Service, Calif. Dept. Edn., Sacramento, 1963-65, chief. Bur. Compensatory Edn. Program Devel., 1965-71; dir. Right to Read Effort, Office Edn., HEW, Washington, 1971-75. Recipient numerous awards and citations. Mem. Assn. Supervision and Curriculum Devel., Guidance and Counseling Assn., Assn. Childhood Edn. Internat., World Council Tchrs., Internat. Reading Assn., Am. Personnel and Guidance Assn., NEA, Calif. Tchrs. Assn., Am. Acad. Polit. and Social Sci., Women's Forum, People to People Program World Orgn. on Early Childhood Edn., Am. Assn. Sch. Adminstrs., Calif. Assn. Sch. Adminstrs., Afro-Negro Internat. Travel Club, Delta Kappa Gamma. Alpha Kappa Alpha. Author: Strengthening Counseling Services for Disadvantaged Youth, 1966; Hello World, 8 book series, 1973; contbr. articles to profl. publs. Office: Bd of Ed 228 N LaSalle Chicago IL 60601

LOVEJOY, LEONARD JAMES, public relations exec.; b. Topeka, Apr. 5, 1931; s. Leonard Mark and Margaret Mary (Zeller) L.; Ph.B., Marquette U., 1953; m. Julianne Rolla, May 29, 1954; children—Valerie, Christopher, Kimberly, Leslie, Julianne, Geoffrey. Writer Chgo. chpt. ARC, 1956-58; publicity mgr. U.S. Gypsum Co., Chgo., 1958-62; dir. public relations Holtzman-Kain Advt. Co., Chgo., 1962-64; account supr. Philip Lesly Co., Chgo., 1964-65; account supr. Burson-Marsteller Co., Chgo., 1965-68, clinent services mgr., 1968, v.p., 1969, group v.p., 1972-76, asst. gen. mgr., 1976, sr. counselor v.p., 1978—; dir. Mark Lovejoy & Assos. Public relations com. Chgo. United Way, 1978—, Drake U., 1974; chmn. fund drive ARC, Westmont, Ill., 1960; agy. chmn. fund drive Girl Scouts U.S.A., Chgo., 1972; bd. dirs. Pop Warner Little Scholars, Inc., 1975—; public relations com. Marquette U., 1970-72. Served with AUS, 1953-56. Mem. Public Relations Soc. Am. (pres. Chgo. chpt. 1981-82, Silver Anvil award, 1972, 73), Publicity Club Chgo. (dir. 1970-74, Golden Trumpet awards 1973, 74, 76, 77, 81). Roman Catholic. Clubs: Headline Chgo., Chgo. Press, Union League (Chgo.); South Haven (Mich.) Country. Home: 205 S Catherine St LaGrange IL 60525 Office: One E Wacker Dr Chicago IL 60601

LOVELL, EDWARD GEORGE, mech. engr.; b. Windsor, Ont., Can., May 25, 1939; s. George Andrew and Julia Anne (Kopacz) L.: m. Ellen Mary Tyler, Oct. 23, 1964; children—Elise Ondine, Ethan Tyler. B.S., Wayne State U., 1960, M.S., 1961; Ph.D., U. Mich., 1967. Registered profl. engr., Wis. Asst. prof. engring. mechanics U. Wis., Madison, 1968-72, asso. prof., from 1972—, now prof. engring. mechanics; structural engr. Pratt and Whitney Aircraft, E. Hartford, Conn., Boeing Co., Seattle, Ford Motor Co., Troy, Mich., Bur. Naval Weapons, Washington. Mem. ASME, Am. Acad. Mechanics. NATO sr. fellow in sci., U. Manchester (Eng.), 1973; NASA, Nat. Acad. Sci. fellow, 1967; NSF fellow, 1961. Mem. Sigma Xi, Tau Beta Pi, Phi Kappa Phi. Contbr. tech. articles to jours. ASME, ASCE, Am. Inst. Aeros. and Astronautics, Am. Nuclear Soc. Home: 7781 Cherrywood Ln Rural Route 7 Verona WI 53593 Office: 1425 Johnson Dr U Wis Madison WI 53706

LOVESTED, GARY EARL, safety engr.; b. Moline, Ill., Apr. 24, 1936; s. Earl Ivan and Bernice Estelle (Gould) L.; B.A. in Bus. Adminstrn., Augustana Coll., 1968; m. Coleen Adair Clark, June 27, 1964; 1 son, Brandon Gary. Occupational safety rep. Deere & Co., Moline, Ill., 1968-77, occupational safety specialist, 1979—; v.p. loss control Alliance of Am. Insurers, Chgo., 1977-79; dir. Devco Research & Mktg., Inc.; bd. dirs. Internat. Loss Control Mgmt. Coll. Chmn. city adv. safety com. City of Moline, 1972-73. Served with USNR, 1955-59. Recipient regional award Hartford Nat. Loss Prevention Competition, 1980; hon. Ky. Col.; cert. safety profl. and hazard control mgr. Mem. Am. Soc. Safety Engrs. (pres. Quad City chpt.), Human Factors Soc., Nat. Safety Mgmt. Soc., Nat. Safety Council (Cameron award), Indsl. Safety Assn. Quad Cities (past pres.). Republican. Clubs: Valley Sports Car, Masons. Home: 3438 53d St Moline IL 61265 Office: Deere and Co John Deere Rd Moline IL 61265

LOW, GORDON ARTHUR, utility exec.; b. Detroit, Apr. 30, 1923; s. Arthur William and Gertrude Marie (Boyd) L.; B.S.E.E., Ill. Inst. Tech., 1948; m. Eleanora R. Anthony, June 22, 1946; children—Nancy Ann, Alan Anthony, Brian Arthur. With Consumers Power Co., Jackson, Mich., 1947—, beginning as planning engr., successively div. engr., Flint, Mich., operating supt., Pontiac, Mich., mgr. constrn., exec. mgr. transmission and distbn., 1973—, exec. mgr. engring. and constrn. transmission and plant modifications, 1980—. Past pres., trustee Kiwanis Mich. Found.; pres. bd. dirs. Goodwill of Central Mich., Jackson Cath. Social Service; pres. adv. bd. Ret. Sr. Vols. Program. Served as ensign USNR, 1942-46; PTO. Registered profl. engr., Mich. Mem. IEEE, Nat. Soc. Profl. Engrs., Mich. Constrn. Users Council (founder), CIGRE Internat. Republican. Methodist. Clubs: Kiwanis, Masons. Home: 3148 Halstead St Jackson MI 49203 Office: 212 W Michigan St Jackson MI 49201

LOWE, CHALLIS MARIE, bank exec.; b. Chgo., July 21, 1945; d. Abner A. and Clotilde L. (Johnson) Waller; B.A., So. Ill. U., 1966; M. Mgmt., Northwestern U., 1978; m. John E. Lowe, Apr. 6, 1965; children—Daphne Michelle, Candice Marie. Teacher Bd. Edn., Newport News, Va., 1966-68; buyer asst. Sears Roebuck & Co., Chgo., 1968-69; employment counselor Thirty Three Personnel Center, Chgo., 1969-71; asst. sales mgr. Continental Ill. Nat. Bank and Trust Co., Chgo., 1971-73, personal banking officer, 1973-76, 2d v.p., mgr. 30 N. LaSalle banking facility, 1976-79, v.p., mgr. head office and Rookery banking facilities, 1979—. Mem. bd. mgrs. Wyler Children's Hosp., Chgo., 1975—; mem. subcom. allocations Com. United Way Met. Chgo. Mem. Nat. Assn. Bank Women (chmn. Chgo. chpt. 1978-79), Chgo. Urban League, Urban Bankers Forum (chmn. Chgo. group). Office: 231 S LaSalle St Chicago IL 60693

LOWE, CLAUDIA MARIE SANDERSON, psychiat. and med. social worker; b. Memphis, Feb. 29, 1944; d. James Calhoun and Helen (Cone) Sanderson; B.A., Huntingdon Coll., 1965; postgrad. U. Mass., 1965-66, U. Tenn., 1970-71; M.S.W., U. Ill., 1976; m. Samuel Dennis Lowe, Apr. 4, 1966; children—Victoria, Clint. Psychiat. social worker Kankakee (Ill.) State Hosp., 1966-70; psychiat. social worker Riverside Med. Center, Kankakee, 1972—, outpatient therapist, 1975-78, coordinator Riverside psychiat. day hosp. program, 1979-81, med. social worker, 1981—. Registered social worker, Ill.; cert. social worker, Ill. Mem. Am. Assn. for Partial Hospitalization, Illiana Regional Assn. for Partial Hospitalization (chmn. 1981), Nat. Assn. Social Workers, Acad. Cert. Social Workers, Kankakee County Social Workers Assn. (corr. sec. 1978-79, mem. nominating com. 1980, mem. social action com. 1981—). Home: 764 Woodstock Ln Bourbonnais IL 60914 Office: Riverside Med Center 350 N Wall St Kankakee IL 60901

LOWE, E(DWARD) JOSEPH, physician; b. Jamaica, W. Indies, July 19, 1935; s. Phillip and Irene (Wong) L.; B.A., Chico State Coll., 1962; M.D., Loma Linda U., 1967. Intern, Washington Adventist Hosp., Takoma Park, Md., 1967-68, house physician, 1968-70; resident U. Md. Hosp., Balt., 1970-72; gen. practice medicine, Piqua, Ohio, 1972—; med. dir. Shelby County (Ohio) Bd. Health, Sidney, 1973—. Diplomate Am. Bd. Family Practice. Fellow Am. Acad. Family Physicians; mem. Ohio Acad. Family Physicians, AMA, Ohio Med. Assn., Miami County Med. Soc. Adventist. Club: Sugarmill Woods Country. Home: 1303 Maplewood Dr Piqua OH 45356 Office: 113 Cassell St Piqua OH 45356

LOWE, EARL WARDLE, ret. powder metal co. exec.; b. Omaha, Dec. 11, 1898; s. John Moses and Grace (Wardle) L.; student Iowa State Coll., 1917-18; m. Ruth Marie McKeon, July 4, 1920; 1 dau., Patricia Jane (Mrs. William D. Kinsell, Jr.). Salesman various firms, 1921-32; pres. Security Analytical Service, 1932-40; exec. v.p. McAleer Mfg. Co., 1940-46; pres. Greenback Industries, Inc., 1946-72. Served with U.S. Army, 1917-19. Mem. Am. Soc. Metals, Am. Ordnance Assn., Am. Soc. Testing Materials, Bklyn. Bot. Soc., Am. Nutrition Soc., Am. Powder Metallurgy Inst., Metal Powder Producers Assn. (pres. 1961-62), Metal Powder Industries Fedn. (pres. 1963-66, Distinguished Service award 1968). Clubs: Admiral, Ambassador, Detroit Athletic, Econ. (Detroit); Marco Polo (N.Y.C.); Internat. (Chgo.). Research in microstructures powder metal compacts; developer colored photog. processes for colored transparencies for reflected light for microstructures of powdered metal specimens. Home: 915 Pilgrim Rd Birmingham MI 48009

LOWE, EDMUND WARING, photochem. co. exec.; b. Dover, Minn., July 28, 1905; s. John and Mary Alice (Chermak) L.; B.S., Hamline U., 1926; M.Sc., U. Chgo., Ph.D.; m. Elsie Traynor, Nov. 17, 1932; children—Henry A., Veronica M., Virginia Ann. Instr. in chemistry Hamline U., 1927; grad. fellow in med. chemistry U. Chgo., 1930-34; founder, pres. Edwal Labs., Chgo., 1934-50; postdoctoral research in dyes Purdue U., 1948-50; pres. Edwal Sci. Products Corp.,

Chgo., 1950-81; v.p. Edwal Sci. Products Co. div. Falcon Safety Products, Chgo., 1981—. Mem. Photog. Soc. Am., Am. Chem. Soc., Soc. Photog. Scientists and Engrs., AAAS, Sigma Xi. Republican. Mem. Brethren Ch. Author: Modern Developing Methods; What You Want to Know About Developers. Home: 160 Hemlock Park Forest IL 60466 Office: 12120 S Peoria Chicago IL 60644

LOWE, JAMES BROWNE, lawyer; b. Winfield, Kans., Jan. 24, 1935; s. John and Vera Elizabeth (Browne) L.; B.S., U. Kans., 1956, M.S., 1959, LL.B., 1962; m. Eleanor Ann Hawkinson, Aug. 20, 1961; children—Sarah Ann, Michael Browne, John Willard. Admitted to Mo. bar, 1962, since practiced in Kansas City; mem. firm Kuraner, Schwegler, Humphrey, Lowe & Fishman, Chmn. men's div. Heart of Am. United Campaign, 1973. Mem. Johnson County Republican Central Com., 1973. Bd. dirs. Family and Children's Services, Kansas City, Mo., pres., 1977-78; bd. dirs. Heart of Am. United Way, United Community Services, v.p., 1979-80, pres., 1981; mem. adv. bd. Salvation Army; bd. deacons Village United Presbyn. Ch., 1977-79, bd. elders, 1980. Served with USNR, 1956-58; capt. USCG Res. Mem. Am., Mo., Kansas City, bar assns., Kansas City Lawyers Assn. (pres. young lawyers sect. 1969-70, v.p. sr. sect. 1979-80), Delta Upsilon. Clubs: Homestead Country (Prairie Village, Kans.), Kiwanis (v.p.). Home: 3301 W 68th St Mission Hills KS 66208 Office: Commerce Bank Bldg Kansas City MO 64106

LOWE, JANET KAYE, vocat. rehab. counselor; b. Hastings, Nebr., Nov. 9, 1946; d. Francis Marion and Fern Mae (Enevoldsen) Martin; B. Music Edn., U. Nebr., 1968; M.S., St. Cloud State U., 1973; m. Douglas Sandin Lowe, Aug. 28, 1966; children—Mimi Elissa, Jessica Kirsten. Asst. dir. avocation Lincoln (Nebr.) Job Corps, 1967-68; tchr. music Omaha Schs., 1968-69; program asst. St. Cloud (Minn.) Children's Home, 1969-70; vocat. rehab. counselor Div. Vocat. Rehab., State of Minn., Mpls., 1973-77; job placement specialist Psychol. Testing Center, Mpls., 1977-78; owner, Rehab. Counselors, Mpls., 1978—; job placement specialist, cadre instr. Center for Continuing Edn., Mpls., 1977—; instr. Mankato (Minn.) U., 1978—; cons. Control Data Corp., 1979. Bd. dirs. Sister Kenny Inst., Projects With Industries. Mem. Nat. Rehab. Assn., Am. Personnel and Guidance Assn., Minn. Rehab. Assn. (dir. 1977-78), Minn. Personnel and Guidance Assn., Minn. Rehab. Counselors Assn. (pres. 1977), Delta Omicron. Methodist. Club: Order of Eastern Star. Home: 3711 Washburn Ave N Minneapolis MN 55412 Office: 1021 W Broadway Minneapolis MN 55411

LOWE, JOE FORREST, II, ins. co. exec.; b. Ft. Worth, Nov. 19, 1936; s. Hassler McFall and Irene (Stout) L.; B.B.A., North Tex. State U., 1960, M.A., 1961; m. Judith Louise Allen, Dec. 24, 1965; children—Brian Forrest, Meredith Victoria. With John Nuveen & Co., Chgo., 1965-66; regional rep. Scudder Funds, Chgo., 1966-67; v.p. mktg. Bankers Nat. Life Ins. Co., Parsippany, N.J., 1968-72; pres. Beneficial Equities, Los Angeles, 1972-73; v.p., gen. mgr. Heritage Securities, Columbus, Ohio, 1973-78; v.p., gen. mgr. Nationwide Consumer Services, Columbus, 1978—; mem. Phila.-Balt.-Washington Stock Exchange, 1969-72. Div. chmn. operating fund campaign Columbus Art Museum, 1976-77; trustee, chmn. fund campaign Ballet Met., Columbus, 1979. Served to lt. USN, 1962-65. Mem. Am. Mktg. Assn., Am. Mgmt. Assn., Am. Radio Relay League, Pension and Investment Assn. Am. (pres., dir. 1968-72). Clubs: Athletic, Brookside Golf and Country, Shriners (Columbus); Masons (Tyler, Tex.). Office: One Nationwide Plaza Columbus OH 43216

LOWE, KENNETH STEPHEN, magazine editor; b. St. Paul, July 18, 1921; B.A., U. Mich., 1948; m. Marie Elizabeth Contway, June 18, 1949; children—Stephen (dec.), Scott, Stuart. From telegraph editor to editor Daily Mining Jour., Marquette, Mich., 1948-72; engaged in public relations, 1972-75; editor monthly Mich. Out-of-Doors, 1975—; mem. Mich. Conservation Commn., 1961-63. Pres. Upper Mich. Child Guidance Clinic, 1965-66; pres. trustees Peter White Public Library, Marquette, 1965-67. Served with USNR, 1944-46. Recipient award merit Mich. United Conservation Clubs, 1958. Mem. Mich. Outdoor Writers Assn. (pres. 1969-71; citation 1952), Nat. Audubon Soc., Marquette County Hist. Soc., Ingham County Conservation League. Democrat. Author numerous articles in field. Office: Box 30235 Lansing MI 48909

LOWE, ROBERT CLINTON, steel products co. exec.; b. St. Louis, Oct. 6, 1918; s. Robert M. and Eunice (Coates) L.; B.S., U. Pitts.; m. Pauline C. Artz, Oct. 5, 1940; children—Robert Clinton, Paula Carol, Diane Louise. Asst. sec.-treas. Coates Steel Products Co., 1940-52, exec. v.p., treas., 1952-60, pres., 1960—; dir. 1st Nat. Bank. Chmn. Greenville Airport Authority. Mem. Am. Inst. Mining Metall. and Petroleum Engrs., Am. Soc. Metals, Kappa Sigma. Presbyn. Clubs: Glen Echo Country, Greenbriar Country, Sunset Hills Country, Mo. Athletic (St. Louis); Union (Cleve.); Lehigh Country (Allentown, Pa.); Burning Tree (Washington). Home: 422 E Main St Greenville IL 62246 Office: Box 100 Greenville IL 62246

LOWE, ROY GOINS, lawyer; b. Lake Worth, Fla., Apr. 8, 1926; s. Roy Sereno and May (Goins) L.; A.B., U. Kans., 1948, LL.B., 1951. Admitted to Kans. bar, 1951; gen. practice, Olathe, 1951—; mem. firm Lowe, Terry & Roberts and predecessor, 1951—. Served with USNR, 1944-46. Mem. Bar Assn. State Kans., Johnson County Bar Assn., Am. Legion, Phi Alpha Delta, Sigma Nu. Republican. Presbyn. Home: 701 W Park Olathe KS 66061 Office: Colonial Bldg Olathe KS 66061

LOWE, TERRANCE ALEXANDER, food service adminstr.; b. Detroit, July 28, 1951; s. Theodore Marian and Cecelia Pearl (Matel) L.; B.S., Mich. State U., 1973; M.B.A. Lake Forest sch. Management, 1983; m. Cathy Joyce Linville, July 27, 1974 (div. Nov. 1980). Asst. food service dir. Wishard Meml. Hosp., Indpls. 1974-77; food service dir. Altenheim Community Home, Indpls., 1977-78, Ind. Christian Retirement Park, Zionsville, 1978; food service adminstr., also project chmn. Dial-A-Dietitian, Victory Meml. Hosp., Waukegan, Ill., 1978—; lectr. Ind. U., Indpls., 1976, Purdue U., 1976. Adv. com., vice chmn. Indpls. pub. schs. Indsl. Coop. Edn. and Training, 1975-78. Recipient, Certificate of Appreciation, Purdue U. of Indpls., 1975, Indpls. Pub. Schs., 1978, Central Nine Vocational Sch. for Services, 1978; Award for outstanding contbrs. to food ser. industry. Mem. Am. Soc. for Hosp. Food Services Adminstrs., Internat. Food Service Execs. Assn., Kappa Sigma. Roman Catholic. Contbr. articles to profl. jours. Office: 1324 N Sheridan Rd Waukegan IL 60085

LOWE, WILLIAM MILNE, JR., acct.; b. Louisville, May 27, 1953; s. William Milne and Patricia Ann (Duvall) L.; B.S. in Acctg., Tri-State U., Angola, Ind., 1975; m. Margaret Mary Wagner, Sept. 1, 1973; children—Carrie Ann, Alison Kay. Agt., IRS, Detroit, 1975-76; tax specialist Alexander, Grant & Co., Toledo, 1976-78; supr. tax dept. successor firm Miller, Gardner & Co., Toledo, 1978—; v.p. Norris, Lowe, Miller, Inc., Bowling Green, Ohio, 1979—; IRS audit specialist Owens-Corning Fiberglas, 1979—. Mem. Toledo Estate Planning Council, Perrysburg (Ohio) Jaycees (dir. 1978—; Chmn. of Year award 1978). Roman Catholic. Club: Toledo. Home: 5644 Ashbrook St Toledo OH 43614 Office: Fiberglas Tower Toledo OH 43659

LOWEKE, GEORGE PAUL, educator, author; b. Detroit, Feb. 5, 1902; s. Herman Friedrich Ludwig, Jr. and Martha (Zieske) L.; student U. Chgo., 1926; A.B. with distinction, U. Mich., 1931, M.A., 1932; Ph.D., U. Berlin, 1936; M.M.E., Chrysler Inst. Engring., 1939; m. Lolamae Weians, June 22, 1937; children—Joan Virginia, Lowell Paul Weians. Head math. dept. Kans. Wesleyan U., Salina, 1936; editor Babson Statis. Orgn., Wellesley Hills, Mass., 1936-37; project engr., instr. Chrysler Inst. Engring., Highland Park, Mich., 1937-42; instr. engring. mechanics dept. Wayne State U., Detroit, 1942-45, asst. prof., 1945-51, asso. prof., 1951-68, prof. emeritus, 1968—; cons. Novamatic Products Co., 1945-52; author: The Political Plague in America, 1964; A Mathematical Development for Prime Numbers, 1968; The Lore of Prime Numbers, 1978; contbr. articles in engring., math. and astronomy to sci. publs. Pres. Rosemond Estates Assn., 1959-63; candidate for Oakland County Rep. Del., 1966. Simon Mandelbaum scholar, 1931. Mem. Math. Assn. Am., Indsl. Math. Soc., Am. Mus. Natural History. First instr. acad. space flight courses in U.S., 1957. Home and Office: 6886 W Harbor Dr Box 623 Elk Rapids MI 49629

LOWENTHAL, HENRY, card co. exec.; b. Frankfurt, Germany, Oct. 26, 1931; s. Adolf and Kella (Suss) L.; brought to U.S., 1940, naturalized, 1945; B.B.A. cum laude, Baruch Coll., 1952; M.B.A., N.Y. U., 1953, J.D., 1962; m. Miriam Katzenstein, June 29, 1958; children—Sandra, Jeffrey, Joan, Benjamin, Avi. Lectr. accountancy Baruch Coll., CUNY, N.Y.C., 1952-53; auditor Price Waterhouse & Co., N.Y.C., 1955-62; v.p., controller Am. Greetings Corp., Cleve., 1962-68; v.p. fin., treas. Tremco, Inc., Cleve., 1968-77; sr. v.p. fin. Am. Greetings Corp., Cleve., 1977—. Mem. Cleveland Heights-Citizens Adv. Com. on Community Devel., 1976-79; chmn. citizens budget rev. com. Cleveland Heights-University Heights Schs., 1972-73, mem. lay fin. com., 1974-79; v.p. Rabbinical Coll., Telshe, Inc., 1977—, chmn. bd., 1974-76; v.p. Hebrew Acad. Cleve., 1978—; pres. Cleve. chpt. Agudath Israel of Am., 1979—; mem. bd. Jewish Community Fedn. Cleve., 1979—. Mem. Fin. Exec. Inst. (chpt. sec. 1979-80), Am. Inst. C.P.A.'s, N.Y. Soc. C.P.A.'s, Ohio Soc. C.P.A.'s, Greater Cleve. Growth Assn., Beta Gamma Sigma, Beta Alpha Psi. Office: 10500 American Rd Cleveland OH 44144

LOWENTHAL, RUTH MARIE HUEFTLE (MRS. ALFRED LOWENTHAL, JR.), coll. librarian; b. Wichita, Kans., Apr. 17, 1923; d. Albert Frederick and B. Magdalene (Ebel) Hueftle; B.A., Ft. Hays (Kans.) State Coll., 1945; B.S. in L.S., U. Ill., 1946; postgrad. U. Kan., 1969; m. Alfred Lowenthal, Jr., Aug. 1, 1946; children—Deborah (Mrs. Ronald Russell Teeter), Richard Mark, David Alfred, Jeffrey Dean. Asst. librarian Fort Hays State Coll., Hays, Kans., 1946-49, cons., cataloger Oakley (Kans.) Pub. Library, 1951-53; dir. library services Colby (Kans.) Community Coll., 1966—. Editor, pub. dir. Western Plains Heritage Publs., Colby, 1970—. Neighborhood chmn. Girl Scouts U.S.A., Oakley, 1960-64, dir. Day Camp, 1962-63. Mem. Fedn. Women's Clubs, Kan. Fedn. Women's Clubs, Am., Kans., Mountain Plains, Thomas County libraries assns., Kans. Assn. Community Colls., AAUW, P.E.O., Delta Kappa Gamma. Methodist. Clubs: Shakespeare (Colby); Cameo (Oakley). Home: Route 1 Box 10K Colby KS 67701 Office: 1255 S Range St Colby KS 67701

LOWNIK, JANET THERESE, health dept. adminstr.; b. Evergreen Park, Ill., Oct. 23, 1944; d. Theodore Francis and Helen Magdeline (Novak) L.; B.A. in English, Marian Coll., Fond du Lac, Wis., 1966; M.Ed., Loyola U., Chgo., 1972; postgrad. Ill. State U., Normal; M.P.A., certificate lawyer's asst. program Roosevelt U., Chgo., 1978. Substitute tchr. Evergreen Park High Sch., 1966-67; retail saleswoman, 1967; women's resident hall asst., then women's resident hall dir. Loyola U., 1967-69; asst. dean student affairs, asso. dean women Ill. Benedictine Coll., Lisle, 1969-72; apt. mgr. Archtl. Mech. Systems Corp., Champaign, Ill., 1972-73; office receptionist, 1973-74; consumer service officer II, Chgo. Dept. Consumer Sales, Weights and Measures, 1975-79; health code enforcement inspection analyst Chgo. Dept. Health, 1979-81, acting dir. budget preparation and execution, 1981—. Mem. Ill. Public Health Assn. Author articles.

LOWRANCE, EDWARD WALTON, educator; b. Ogden, Utah, June 17, 1908; s. Samuel Franklin and Edith May (Sandusky) L.; student Utah Westminster Coll., 1926-28; A.B., U. Utah, 1930, A.M., 1932; Ph.D., Stanford U., 1937; postgrad. U. Kans., 1944-45; m. Rhoda Elizabeth Patton, June 21, 1935; children—Margaret Ann Lowrance Allman, Janet. Rockefeller research asst. in embryology Stanford U., Palo Alto, Calif., 1934-36, 37-38; instr. zoology U. Nev., Reno, 1938-39; asst. prof., 1939-43, asso. prof., 1943-49, chmn. dept. biology, 1947-49; asst. prof. anatomy U. S.D. Sch. Medicine, Vermillion, 1949-50; asso. prof. anatomy U. Mo. Sch. Medicine, Columbia, 1950-55, prof., 1955-78, emeritus prof., 1978—; acting asso. prof. anatomy Sch. Medicine, U. Kans., Lawrence, 1944-46; state sec. Mo. State Anatomical Bd., 1969-78. Rosenberg research fellow in biology, Stanford U., 1936-37. Fellow AAAS; mem. Am. Assn. Anatomists, Am. Microscopical Soc., Western Soc. Naturalists, N.Y. Acad. Scis., Mid-Mo. Camera Club, Sigma Xi, Phi Kappa Phi, Phi Beta Pi. Mem. Christian Ch. Contbr. articles to profl. jours. Home: 103 Thistledown Dr Columbia MO 65201

LOWRIE, DAVID FRANKLIN, retail electronics exec.; b. Port Huron, Mich., Apr. 27, 1951; s. Robert West and Velma Omel (Garrett) L.; student pub. schs., Port Huron; m. Mary Ellen Armstrong, Apr. 8, 1978; children by previous marriage—Thomas Franklin and Cass Jason (twins), Anjannette Elizabeth. With Main TV Radio Electronics, Inc., Port Huron, Mich., 1965—, store mgr., 1969, pres., sec., 1970—. Mem. Port Huron Businessmen's Assn. Club: Elks (Port Huron). Home: 808 Edison Blvd Port Huron MI 48060 Office: Main TV Radio Electronics Inc 1503 24th St Port Huron MI 48060

LOWRIE, RAYMOND L., govt. ofcl.; b. Alcoa, Tenn., Feb. 19, 1933; B.S. in Mining Engring., U. Tex., El Paso, 1960; M.S. in Mineral Econs., Colo. Sch. Mines, 1971. Mining engr. div. bituminous coal U.S. Bur. Mines, Washington, 1964-67, supervisory mining engr., Denver, 1967-73, chief Intermountain Field Ops. Center, 1975-78; chief div. reclamation Ohio Dept. Natural Resources, Columbus, 1973-74; regional dir. Office of Surface Mining Reclamation and Enforcement, Kansas City, Mo., 1978—. Recipient Hubert E. Risser award, 1971; registered profl. engr., Tex. Mem. AIME. Contbr. articles to profl. jours.

LOWRY, EARL CRANSTON, physician; b. Robeson County, N.C., July 20, 1907; s. Fuller and Jessie (Hatcher) L.; B.Sc., U. Chattanooga, 1927; M.D., Vanderbilt U., 1933; m. Olivia King, May 23, 1936; children—Anne King Sistrunk, Olivia Rose Odom. Intern, St. Thomas Hosp., Nashville, 1933-34, resident in surgery and urology, 1934-37; commd. 1st lt. M.C., U.S. Army, 1933, advanced through grades to col., 1944; chief profl. service div., chief cons. in surgery Office of Chief SUrgeon, U.S. Forces, ETO, 1945-46; chief dept. surgery Lawson Gen. Hosp., 1940-43, Oliver Gen. Hosp., 1946-50, Gorgas Hosp., Canal Zone, 1950-53; chief dept. urology Letterman Gen. Hosp., San Francisco, 1957; profl. dir. Office Dependents Med. Care, Dept. Def., Washington, 1957-58; prof. clin. surgery U. Ga. Med. Sch., Augusta, 1946-50; ret., 1958; pres., chief exec. officer Iowa Med. Service (Blue Shield), Des Moines, 1958-66. Diplomate Am. Bd. Urology. Decorated Legion Merit. Fellow A.C.S., Internat Coll. Surgeons, Royal Soc. Medicine (London); mem. Am. Urol. Assn., Pan Am. Med. Assn., Des Moines C. of C. (chmn. health com. 1964-65). Democrat. Methodist. Contbr. articles to profl. jours. Home and Office: 5403 Harwood Dr Des Moines IA 50312

LOWRY, JAMES HAMILTON, mgmt. cons.; b. Chgo., May 28, 1939; s. William E. and Camille C. L.; B.A., Grinnel Coll., 1961; M.P.I.A., U. Pitts., 1965; P.M.D., Harvard U., 1973; 1 child, Aisha. Asso. dir. Peace Corps, Lima, Peru, 1965-67; spl. asst. to pres., project mgr. Bedford-Stuyvesant Restoration Corp., Bklyn., 1967-68; sr. asso. McKinsey & Co., Chgo., 1968-75; pres. James H. Lowry & Assos., Chgo., 1975—. Trustee Grinnell Coll., Francis Parker Sch., Atlanta U.; bd. dirs. Chgo. Youth Centers, Michael Reese Hosp. John Hay Whitney fellow, 1963-65. Mem. Harvard Alumni Assn. (dir.). Clubs: Econ., Monroe, Univ. Home: 2020 Lincoln Park W Chicago IL 60614 Office: 303 E Wacker Dr Chicago IL 60601

LOWRY, SHELDON GAYLON, educator; b. Cardston, Alta., Can., Aug. 25, 1924; s. Marcellus Anderson and Rose Belle (Wood) L.; m. Gloria Groneman, Apr. 3, 1946; children—Pamela, Martha, Kristine, Amanda Lee. B.A., Brigham Young U., 1946; M.A., Mich. State U., 1950, Ph.D., 1954. Certified marriage counselor, 1973. Instr. Mich. State U., 1951-52; research asso. Health Info. Found., N.Y.C., 1952; asst. prof. N.C. State Coll., 1952-57; asst. prof. sociology Mich. State U., 1957-59, asso. prof., 1959-65, prof., 1965—, asso. chmn. sociology, 1966-69, dir. multidisciplinary program, 1970-78, asst. dean for grad. and undergrad. edn., 1975-79, asst. dean student affairs, 1979—; sociologist Coop. State Research Service, U.S. Dept. Agr., 1969-70. Mem. Am. Sociol. Assn., Rural Sociol. Soc. (pres. 1976-77), Nat. Council Family Relations, Am. Assn. Marriage and Family Therapists, Alpha Kappa Delta, Epsilon Sigma Phi. Editor: Rural Sociology, 1963-65; co-author: 10-Year Cumulative Index To Rural Sociology, 1965; contbr. articles to profl. jours. Office: Michigan State Univ Coll Social Science 153 Baker Hall East Lansing MI 48824

LUBAS, THADDEUS JOHN, data processing co. exec.; b. Reading, Pa., Dec. 24, 1931; s. John and Martha L.; B.B.A., U. Miami, 1954; m. Helen Irene Allan, Nov. 24, 1960; 1 dau., Tracy. Regional audit mgr. Montgomery Ward Co., Kansas City, Mo., 1957-59, catalog house controller, Balt., 1960-62, corp. systems devel. mgr., 1962-70, corp. systems planning mgr., 1971-72, data processing security, v.p., sec.-treas., 1972-73; group mgr. data processing Foster and Gallagher, Peoria, Ill., 1974-78; controller Central Pool Supply, Inc., Peoria, 1978-80, Data Processing Security, Elmhurst, Ill., 1981—. Bd. dirs. N.W Mental Health, Arlington Heights, Ill., 1970-75. Served to capt. USAF, 1954-57. Roman Catholic. Clubs: U. Miami Alumni, Peoria YMCA. Home: 309 W Eagle Nest Dunlap IL 61525 Office: 188 Industrial Dr Elmhurst IL 60126

LUBBOCK, JAMES EDWARD, writer, photographer, publicity cons.; b. St. Louis, Sept. 12, 1924; s. Winans Fowler and Hildegard Beauregard (Whittemore) L.; B.A. in English, U. Mo., 1949; m. Charlotte Frances Ferguson, Aug. 24, 1947; children—Daniel Lawrason, Brian Wade, Kathleen Harper. Asst. editor St. Louis County Observer, 1949-51; staff writer St. Louis Globe-Democrat, 1951-53, state editor, 1954-56; mng. editor Food Merchandising mag., 1956-57; free-lance indsl. writer-photographer, cons., St. Louis, 1958—; pres. James E. Lubbock, Inc., 1981—. Bd. dirs. Practical Seminar Inst. Served with Signal Corps, U.S. Army, 1943-46. Mem. Soc. Profl. Journalists, Sigma Delta Chi, St. Louis Press Club, ACLU, Common Cause. Liberal Democrat. Home and Office: 10734 Clearwater Dr Saint Louis MO 63123

LUBONOVIC, MICHAEL PETER, mktg. engr.; b. Youngstown, Ohio, Sept. 19, 1950; s. Peter A. and Mary A. (Mchar) L.; B.Engring., Youngstown State U., 1973. Application engr. Ajax Magnathermic Corp., Warren, Ohio, 1973-74; mktg. engr. Arthur H. Baier Co. & Assos., Dayton, Ohio, 1974—. Mem. Nat. Soc. Profl. Engrs., IEEE, Electronic Reps. Assn., Am. Security Council. Club: Chesterton. Home: 3161 Benchwood Rd Dayton OH 45414 Office: Arthur H Baier Co & Assos 4940 Profit Way Dayton OH 45414

LUCAS, ALFRED WINSLOW, JR., mgmt. cons. co. exec.; b. Washington, Oct. 14, 1950; s. Alfred Winslow and Mildred Elizabeth (Lawson) L.; B.A. in Sociology, Social Welfare, St. Augustine's Coll., Raleigh, N.C., 1972; M.S.W., Syracuse U., 1974; M.P.A., Roosevelt U., Chgo., 1979; m. Debra Denise DeBerry, Aug. 20, 1977; 1 son, Michael Maurice. Planner, United Way Central N.Y., 1973-74; adminstrv. asst. to dir. community devel. People's Equal Action Community Effort Inc., Syracuse, N.Y., 1972-73; research cons. Urban Inst., Washington, 1974-75; exec. dir. New Birth Community Devel., Elgin, Ill., 1975-79; pres. Raisin Mgmt. Cons., Inc., Chgo., 1979—; asso. dir. Centers for New Horizons, Chgo., 1979-80; cons. in field. Chmn. bd. dirs. Kane County (Ill.) Community Action Agy., 1976-77; bd. dirs. Kane County Overall Econ. Devel. Com., 1977-78; trustee Mildred Lawson Lucas Meml. Found., 1981—. NIMH fellow, 1972-74. Mem. Am. Mgmt. Assn., Nat. Assn. Social Workers, Acad. Cert. Social Workers, Am. Soc. Public Adminstrs., Nat. Urban League, Am. Soc. Profl. Consultants, Kappa Alpha Psi. Roman Catholic. Author: Getting Funded, Grantsmanship and Proposal Development, 1982. Home: 9447 Bay Colony Dr 1S Des Plaines IL 60016 Office: Suite 1010 664 N Michigan Ave Chicago IL 60611

LUCAS, ANDREW DANIEL, indsl. hygienist; b. Chgo., Apr. 9, 1950; s. John and Bernice (Ludwig) L.; B.S. with high honors (James scholar), U. Ill., Urbana, 1972; M.S., U. Ill. at Med. Center, Chgo., 1980. Caseworker, Ill. Dept. Public Aid, Chgo., 1975-77; co-chmn. foundry com. Chgo. Area Com. Occupational Safety and Health, 1977-80; indsl. hygienist Hazard Evaluations and Tech. Assistance br. Nat. Inst. Occupational Safety and Health, Cin., 1980—; mem. Ohio River Valley Com. for Occupational Safety and Health, 1981. Mem. Am. Conf. Govtl. Indsl. Hygienists, Am. Indsl. Hygiene Assn., AAAS, Soc. Occupational and Environ. Health, Sigma Xi, Psi Chi. Research on health hazards in arts, crafts and trades. Home: 423 Oregon St Cincinnati OH 45202 Office: Robert A Taft Laboratories 4676 Columbia Pkwy Cincinnati OH 45226

LUCAS, JAMES ROBERTS, JR., sales mgr.; b. Balt., Dec. 27, 1942; s. James Roberts and Phyllis Gwendolyn (Driver) L.; B.S.M.E., Lehigh U., 1965; M.B.A., Butler U., 1972; m. Rebecca Jane Beard, June 27, 1965; 1 dau., Erika. Gas turbine test engr. Allison Div. GMC, Mpls., 1965-67, turbine engine design engr., sr. project engr., 1967-70; transmission sr. design engr. and sr. project mgr. Detroit Diesel Allison, Indpls., 1970-76, sr. sales engr., product mgr., 1976-79, sr. staff asst., 1979-81; cons. in field. Indian Princesses adv. YWCA, Indpls., 1974-75; Sci. Fair adv., 1966, 67; bd. dirs. Woodland Springs Corp., 1975-77, treas., 1976-77. Recipient ASME Papers prize, 1965. Mem. Armor Assn., Assn. U.S. Army, Am. Def. Preparedness Assn., Tech. Mktg. Soc. Am., Smithsonian Assn., Omicron Delta Kappa. Republican. Presbyterian. Clubs: Carmel Racquet, Ambassadair. Contbr. articles to profl. jours. Office: PO Box 894-G1 Indianapolis IN 46206

LUCAS, NANCI DAI, educator; b. Los Angeles, Nov. 28, 1936; d. William Morton and Frances Augusta (Cattanach) Hindman; B.A., Colgate-Rochester (N.Y.) Div. Sch., 1958; M.Ed., U. Toledo, 1972; m. George Albert Lucas, Sept. 10, 1960; children—Bradley Scott, Traci Dai. Dir. Christian edn. Moline (Ill.) First Baptist Ch., 1958-60;

pvt. piano instr., LaPorte, Ind., 1960-62; elem. tchr. Toledo Public Schs., 1967-72; dir. Met. League Sch., Toledo, 1972-76; dir. gifted programs Toledo Bd. Edn., 1976-81; founder, 1981, since owner New Horizons Acad., Toledo; adj. prof. Bowling Green (Ohio) State U., U. Toledo, Mary Manse Coll., Toledo. Recipient Outstanding Leader in Individually Gifted Edn., U. Wis., Madison, 1978. Mem. Toledo C. of C., Phi Delta Kappa, Pi Lambda Theta, Phi Kappa Phi. Republican. Methodist. Co-author: Ideas, 1975. Contbr. articles to profl. jours. Home: 5730 Swan Creek Dr Toledo OH 43614 Office: 1716 Perrysburg-Holland Rd Holland OH 43528

LUCAS, ROBERT ELMER, soil scientist; b. Malolos, Philippines, June 27, 1916 (parents Am. citizens); s. Charles Edmond and Harriet Grace (Deardorff) L.; B.S., Purdue U., 1939, M.S., 1941; Ph.D., Mich. State U., 1947; m. Norma E. Schultz, Apr. 27, 1941; children—Raymond, Richard, Milton, Keith, Charles. Agronomist, Wm. Gehring, Inc., Rensselaer, Ind., 1946-51, 77-78; asso. prof. Mich. State U., East Lansing, 1951-57, prof., 1957-77, prof. emeritus, 1977—; vis. prof. U. Fla., Belle Glade, 1979-80; cons. vegetable growers and coops. Pres., Ottawa Dist. council Boy Scouts Am., 1965-66. Fellow Am. Soc. Agronomy, Soil Sci. Soc. Am., Internat. Peat Soc., AAAS, Council for Agrl. Sci. and Tech. Republican. Lutheran. Club: Lions. Home: 3827 Dobie Rd Okemos MI 48864 Office: Crop and Soil Scis Dept Mich State U East Lansing MI 48824

LUCAS, ROBERT ROTGER, criminal justice cons.; b. San Francisco, Mar. 26, 1925; s. Harold Andreas Lucas and Catherine Elizabeth (Fitts) Lucas Wayland; A.B., U. Calif., 1948, M.A., 1951; m. Ann Bowler, Dec. 18, 1955; children—John Gordon, Jeffrey Bowler, Andrew Robert. Dep. probation officer Santa Clara County Juvenile Probation Dept., San Jose, Calif., 1951; field probation officer Contra Costa County Probation Dept., Richmond, Calif., 1952-56; with Calif. Dept. Corrections, 1956-68, classification and parole rep. Calif. Mens Colony, San Luis Obispo, 1962-68; state dir. Ill. com. Nat. Council on Crime and Delinquency, Chgo., 1968-71, dep. dir. urban services, Homewood, Ill., 1971-73; coordinator Safer Found., Chgo., 1973—, dir. community edn., 1975—. Condr. field research HUD, Balt., Indpls., Des Moines, Richmond, Calif., 1973. Served with AUS, 1943-46. Honored by Gov. Ill. for service to Ill. Law Enforcement Commn., 1971. Mem. Am. Soc. Public Adminstrn., Chgo. Social Service Communicators, Nature Conservancy. Office: 10 S Wabash Ave 4th Floor Chicago IL 60603

LUCCA, JOSEPH SALVATORE, structural engr.; b. Sicily, Italy, June 17, 1951; s. Vincent and Teresa (Valvo) L.; came to U.S., 1954, naturalized, 1959; B.C.E., Ill. Inst. Tech., 1973; m. Mary Nolting, 1979. Structural engr. Fluor Pioneer, Chgo., 1973-75, A. G. McKee, Chgo., 1975-77; structural design group leader, project coordinator Barber Greene, Aurora, Ill., 1977-78; project structural engr., chief structural engr. Swick Assos., Chgo., 1978—, also corp. sec., treas. Ill. State scholar, 1969-73; registered structural engr., Ill.; registered profl. engr., Calif., Ky., S.C. Mem. ASCE, Cousteau Soc. Roman Catholic. Club: Alfa Romeo Owners. Home: 124 Avon Rd Elmhurst IL 60126 Office: 209 W Jackson Blvd Chicago IL 60606

LUCEK, THOMAS NOA, city ofcl.; b. Beaver Dam, Wis., Aug. 16, 1949; s. Walter Joseph and Magdalene Mary (Kazunas) L.; engring. tech. cert. U. Ill., Champaign, 1967, B.S. in Engring. with high honors, Chgo., 1972; postgrad. Northeastern U., Boston, 1979—; m. Cathryn Louise Munson, Nov. 11, 1967; children—Susan Marie, Cynthia Michelle, Jennifer Mary, Thomas Noa. Engring. technician Dept. Transp. State of Ill., Elgin and Chgo., 1967-72; civil engr. Dept. Public Works City of Rockford (Ill.), 1972-73, exec. dir., gen. mgr. Rockford Mass Transit Dist., 1973—. Bd. dirs. Winnebago County (Ill.) Paratransit System; mem. adv. bd. Inter-Governmental Consortium for Personnel Tng., Rockford, 1978-80. Registered profl. engr., Ill. Mem. Ill. Soc. Profl. Engrs. (dir. 1978-79), Nat. Soc. Profl. Engrs., Ill. Public Transit Assn. (v.p. 1975-76, pres. 1981—), Am. Public Transit Assn., Nat. Def. Exec. Res. Roman Catholic. Club: K. of C. Office: 625 S Central Ave Rockford IL 61102

LUCKER, RAYMOND ALPHONSE, clergyman; b. St. Paul, Feb. 24, 1927; s. Alphonse J. and Josephine T. (Schiltgen) L.; B.A., St. Paul Sem., 1948, M.A., 1952; S.T.L., St. Thoma U. Rome, 1965, S.T.D., 1966; Ph.D., U. Minn., 1969. Ordained to ministry Roman Catholic Ch., 1952; asst. dir. Confraternity of Christian Doctrine Archdiocese of St. Paul, 1952-57, dir., 1957-68, supt. edn., 1966-68; prof. catechetics St. Paul Sem., 1957-68; dir. dept. edn. United State Catholic Conf., Washington, 1968-71; aux. bishop Diocese of St. Paul, 1971-76; pastor St. Austin Ch., Mpls., 1971-74, Assumption Ch., St. Paul, 1974-76; bishop Diocese of New Ulm (Minn.), 1971—. Mem. Nat. Conf. Catholic Bishops, Minn. Catholic Conf., Nat. Catholic Ednl. Assn. Author: Aims of Religious Education, 1966; History of Released Time, 1969; contbr. articles in field.

LUCKERT, KARL WILHELM, educator; b. Winnenden-Hoefen, Germany, Nov. 18, 1934; came to U.S., 1953, naturalized, 1961; s. Wilhelm Gottlob and Emilie (Hilt) L.; B.A. in Philosophy, U. Kans., 1963; postgrad. Evang. Theol. Sem., Naperville, Ill., 1963-64; M.A. in History of Religions, U. Chgo., 1967, Ph.D. in History of Religions, 1969; m. Dora Maria Laemmle, July 27, 1957; children—Ursula Dorothea, Martin Karl, Heidi Marie. Painter, decorator, Germany, 1947-55, Abilene, Kans., 1955-56, 58-59; ordained elder United Meth. Ch., 1968; vis. lectr. North Central Coll., Naperville, 1968-69; asst. prof. humanities dept. No. Ariz. U., Flagstaff, 1969-79; asso. prof. history of religions S.W. Mo. State U., Springfield, 1979—. Served with U.S. Army, 1956-58. Nat. Endowment for Humanities research fellow, 1972-73; Rockefeller Found. research fellow, 1977-78. Mem. Am. Acad. Religion. Author: The Navajo Hunter Tradition, 1975; Olmec Religion: A Key to Middle America and Beyond, 1976; Navajo Mountain and Rainbow Bridge Religion, 1977; A Navajo Bringing-Home Ceremony, the Claus Chee Sonny Version of Deerway Ajilee, 1978; Coyoteway, a Navajo Holyway Healing Ceremonial, 1979; Mother Earth Once Was a Girl: A Scientific Theory on the Expansion of Planet Earth, 1979; gen. editor: American Tribal Religions (monograph series), 1977—; contbr. articles to profl. jours.; research on Am. Indian religions and history of religions. Home: 2955 E Lamonta Dr Springfield MO 65804 Office: Dept Religious Studies SW Mo State U Springfield MO 65802

LUCKINBILL, HELEN MARGARET, educator; b. Rock Rapids, Iowa, Sept. 12, 1930; d. Sam and Gladys (Spyksma) Schaafsma; B.A., Central Coll., Pella, Iowa, 1954; postgrad. Long Beach State Coll., 1961, Drake U., 1971, U. Iowa, 1981; m. Merle Ervin Luckinbill, Aug. 23, 1958 (div. 1980); children—Clinton Douglas, Cynthia Frances, Susan Maureen. Typist, First Nat. Bank, Bellflower, Calif., 1949-50; playleader dept. summer recreation Compton High Sch. Dist., Calif., 1952-54, supr. handicrafts, 1955-57; tchr. music Gilman (Iowa) Consol. Sch., 1954-55, Gladbrook (Iowa) Consol. Sch., 1955-58, Compton High Sch. Dist., 1958-59, Panora (Iowa)-Linden schs., 1968-69, 71-75, Adair (Iowa)-Casey schs., 1975-80; owner, operator Bar-L Children's Vacation Ranch, Guthrie Center, Iowa, 1967—; pvt. piano and organ tchr., 1954—. Dir. ch. choir Gilman Methodist Ch., 1954-55, Gladbrook Methodist Ch., 1955-58; organist Waterloo (Iowa) Westminster Presbyterian, 1956-58; asst. organist Paramount Calif. Reformed Ch., 1958-61, Chino (Calif.) Reformed Choir, 1962-66. Certified tchr., Iowa, Calif. Mem. Music Educators Nat. Conf., Am. Choral Dirs., Iowa Music Educators Assn., Am. Camping Assn., Ind. Camp Assn. Republican. Presbyterian. Home: Bar-L Ranch Rural Route 2 Box 263 Guthrie Center IA 50115

LUCY, DAVID CARTIER, assn. exec.; b. St. Louis, Mar. 13, 1943; s. Gregory Ramsey and Catherine Mary (Cartier) L.; student U. Mo., 1961-62, Washington U., 1963-66; B.A., U. Mo., 1969. Dir. membership Farm Equipment Mfrs. Assn., St. Louis, 1967-71; dir. membership, asso. editor Nat. Farm and Power Equipment Dealers Assn., St. Louis, 1971-73; exec. v.p. Ind. Implement Dealers Assn., Indpls., 1973—. Served with AUS, 1968-69. Mem. Am. Soc. Assn. Execs., Ind. Soc. Assn. Execs., Ind. Implement Dealers Services, Inc. (dir. 1973—), Ind. Implement Dealers Ins. Trust, Inc. (chief adminstrv. officer, trustee 1973—), Ind. Agribus. Club, Inc. (dir. 1974—), Ind. Retail Council, Ind. Better Bus. Bur., Ind. Farm Safety Council, Ind. Farmer-Retailer Com., Coalition Retail Assns., Assn. Farm and Power Equipment Mgrs. (dir. 1976—). Mason (32 deg., Shriner). Editor, pub. The Pinion, 1974—. Home: 23 Lakeshore Ct Carmel IN 46032 Office: 6112 N College Ave Indianapolis IN 46220

LUCZAK, THOMAS WILLIAM, clergyman, educator; b. Bay City, Mich., Sept. 19, 1943; s. William Frank and Myrtle Louise (Peters) L.; B.A., St. Francis Coll., Burlington, Wis., 1966; M.A., Cardinal Stritch Coll., 1973; cert. phys. edn. Sveriges Riksidrottsförbund, Stockholm, Technische Universität München Lehrstuhl für Sportpädagogik, U. Catholique de Louvain (Belgium). Catechist, So. Ill. Tng. Sch., Union Grove, Wis., 1963-66, St. Isidore Parish, Cloverdale, Ill., 1966-69; supr. spl. religious edn. Diocese of Joliet, 1970-71; tchr., chaplain Bartlett (Ill.) Learning Center, 1969-80, adminstr., 1980—. Ordained Franciscan priest Roman Catholic Ch., 1970. Mem. AAHPER, Am. Assn. Mental Deficiency. Home: 844-D Village Quarter Rd West Dundee IL 60118 Office: 801 W Bartlett Rd Bartlett IL 60103

LUDDEN, EVA OREN, ins. co. exec.; b. Black Hawk County, Iowa, Mar. 5, 1933; d. Charles J. and Grace M. (Sexton) O.; B.A., U. No. Iowa; M.B.A., U. Iowa, 1982; m. Richard L. Ludden, Aug. 28, 1951; children—L. Ruth Ludden Yarrington, Mary J. Ludden Brannon, Janet G. Ludden DeCamp. With John Deere Waterloo Tractor Works, Waterloo, 1967-73; with Lutheran Mutual Life Ins. Co., Waverly, Iowa, 1973—, v.p. personnel, 1975—; mem. state adv. council Blue Cross/Blue Shield. Mem. adv. council Hawkeye Inst. Tech. Mem. Am. Mgmt. Assn., Adminstrv. Mgmt. Soc., Am. Soc. Personnel Adminstrs. Office: Heritage Way Waverly IA 50677

LUDWICK, HARVEY L., state ofcl.; b. Wichita, Kans., May 24, 1941; s. Claude H. and Juliet C. (Green) L.; B.A., Friends U., Wichita, 1964; M.Ed., Wichita State U., 1967; Ed.D., U. Wyo., 1971; m. Phyllis Joan Sickels, June 24, 1961; children—Craig, Kurt, Matthew. High sch. prin. Albany County Sch. Dist., Laramie, Wyo., 1970-73; supt. schs. Ellsworth (Kans.), 1973-75, Hays (Kans.), 1975-80; sec. Kans. Dept. Human Resources, 1980—; grad. faculty Ft. Hays State U. Mem. adv. council Hays Art Council. Mem. Am. Assn. Sch. Adminstrs., Internat. Assn. Personnel in Employment Security. Democrat. Methodist. Office: 401 Topeka Ave Topeka KS 66603*

LUDWIG, ARNOLD FRANCIS, candy co. exec.; b. Toledo, May 30, 1934; s. Clarence J. and Helen D. (Pry) L.; B.S. (scholar), U. Wis., 1956, B.B.A., 1958; M.B.A., U. Ill., 1981; m. Betty Jean Bubolz, Dec. 31, 1958; children—Wendy Lou, Timothy Daniel. Dir. quality control Babcock Dairy Co., Toledo, 1958-60; v.p., co founder Seaway Candy Co., Toledo, 1960-69; pres., founder Ludwig Candy Co., Manteno, Ill., 1969—, also dir. Chmn. music program Manteno Bi-Centennial, 1976. Mem. U. Wis. W Club (dir.), Am. Mgmt. Assn. (pres.), U. Wis. Alumni Assn. (bd. dirs.), U. Ill. Alumni Assn., Wis. Agrl. and Life Scis. Alumni Assn. Republican. Roman Catholic. Club: Moose. Home: Rt 1 Box 45 Manteno IL 60950 Office: 395 Locust St S Manteno IL 60950

LUDWIG, FRED ALBERT, JR., mental health ofcl.; b. Waterloo, Ill., Aug. 2, 1927; s. Fred A. and Pauline (Hern) L.; A.B., U. Ill., 1949, M.A., 1971; M.S.W., Washington U., St. Louis, 1952; Ph.D., So. Ill. U., 1979; m. Virginia Goodwine, Aug. 13, 1949; children—Philip, Susan, Ann, Peter. Social worker Ill. Soldiers and Sailors Children's Sch., Normal, 1952-54; social worker Mental Health Assn. and Center, Springfield, Ill., 1954-57, exec. dir., 1957—; individual practice counseling, part-time 1958—; mem. faculty Lincoln Land Community Coll.; asso. psychiatry So. Ill. Sch. Medicine. Bd. dirs. Springfield and Sangamon County Community Action, 1965—, exec. com., 1968—; bd. dirs. Kemmerer Children's Home, 1966—, pres., 1970-73. Mem. Nat. Mental Health Assn. (membership sec. staff council 1963-65, nominating com. 1965-67), Ill. Assn. Mental Health Center Adminstrs. (pres. 1968), Am. Orthopsychiat. Assn., Nat. Assn. Social Workers (v.p. Ill. council, chmn. Springfield dist. 1980). Presbyterian (elder 1967). Contbr. articles to profl. lit. Home: 11 Linden Lane Springfield IL 62707 Office: 801 E Miller St Springfield IL 62703

LUDWIG, MARVIN JAY, coll. pres.; b. Sioux City, Iowa, Aug. 29, 1926; s. L. Harrison and Naomi K. (Strayer) L.; A.A., North Park Coll., 1948; B.A. in Phys. Edn., Ohio Wesleyan U., 1952; L.H.D. (hon.), George Williams Coll., 1975; m. Ruth Marilyn Bjorkman, June 10, 1952; children—Marshall, Robin, Rhonda. Youth dir. Marion (Ohio) YMCA, 1949-55; sec. program, devel. Ethiopian Addis Ababa, YMCA, 1955-59, nat. gen. sec., Ethiopia, 1959-67, advisor nat. bd., Ethiopia, 1967-68, dir. world service and income prodn. Internat. div. YMCA, 1969-73, dep. exec. dir., 1973-75, now mem. nat. bd. YMCAs, chmn. internat. com. Gt. Lakes Region, also mem. exec. com. Gt. Lakes Region, v.p. Gt. Lakes regional bd. YMCAs; pres. Defiance (Ohio) Coll., 1975—. Mem. Am. Council Edn., now mem. Gt. Lakes regional council; mem. corp. bd., mem. exec. com. United Ch. of Christ Bd. for World Ministries. Served as sgt. 1943-45. Recipient Haile Selassie Prize Trust award for outstanding achievements in humanitarian activities, 1964; Paul Harris fellow. Mem. Assn. Am. Colls., Assn. Ind. Colls. and Univs. (exec. com.), Ohio Coll. Assn., Ohio Found. Ind. Colls. Clubs: Rotary (found. fellowship 1955; past pres. Addis Ababa chpt.). Contbr. articles to profl. jours. Home: 705 E High St Defiance OH 43512 Office: The Defiance Coll 701 N Clinton St Defiance OH 43512

LUDWIG, PATRIC EUGENE, hosp. assn. exec.; b. Mpls., Jan. 18, 1939; s. Roy and Gertrude (Anderson) L.; B.S. in Engring., U. Mich., 1962, M.B.A., 1963; m. Carol Elizabeth Grasley, Oct. 29, 1960; children—Jana Kaye, David James, Mark Thomas. Asso. dir. Community Systems Found., Md., 1963-67, Hosp. Assn. N.Y. State, 1967-74; pres. Mich. Hosp. Assn., Lansing, 1974—; pres. Hosp. Research and Ednl. Res., 1975—, Mich. Hosp. Assn. Service Corp., 1979—; sec. Mich. Hosp. Assn. Mut. Ins. Co., 1976—; mem. Mich. Statewide Health Coordinating Council, 1976—, Mich. Health Planning Adv. Council, 1975-76, Gov. Mich. Crime Prevention Coalition, 1978-80, Mich. Council Jobs and Energy, 1978—; pres.-elect Mich. Health Council, 1981—; cons. Nat. Center Health Services Research and Devel., HEW, 1972—; chmn. trustees Community Systems Found., 1969-70, 72; mem. Placement Commn., Mich. Commn. for Blind Employer, 1980—; mem. regional adv. com. U. Mich. Health Services Research Center, 1977—; pres. Hosp. Assn. Polit. Action Com., 1976—. Trustee J. Bernard Houston Meml. Trust, 1978—. Recipient Outstanding Service award Community Systems Found., 1972. Mem. Hosp. Mgmt. Systems Soc. (Outstanding Lit. award 1971), Am. Hosp. Assn., State Hosp. Assn. Execs. Forum, Am. Soc. Assn. Execs. (cert. assn. exec.), Orgn. Execs. Mich., Am. Public Health Assn., Lansing C. of C., Hosp. Adminstrs. Study Soc. Clubs: Rotary, Capitol. Co-author: Management Engineering for Hospitals, 1970; also papers, reports. Office: 2213 E Grand River Ave Lansing MI 48912

LUDWIG, R. ARTHUR, lawyer; b. Milw., Apr. 25, 1929; s. Arthur H. and Marie (Hebien) L.; B.B.A., U. Wis., 1954, LL.B., 1955, Dr. Juris Sci., 1966; m. Evelyn L. Amacher, May 21, 1971. Admitted to Wis. bar, 1955; since practiced in Milw.; mem. firm Ludwig and Shlimovitz, S.C., 1972—. Sec., dir. Delta Printing Co., Milw., 1972—; pres., dir. Packaging Design Inc., 1971—; dir. Bea Kay Real Estate Corp., Environ. Dynamics Corp., Land Resources Corp., Navajo Land & Cattle Corp., Oak of Carmel Inc., High Chaparral Ranches Inc. Mem. Am. Bar Assn. (chmn. com. on creditors rights in estates 1979—), Wis. Bar Assn. (sec. treas. bankruptcy, insolvency and creditors rights sect. 1968—), Milw. Bar Assn. (staff Milw. lawyer, sec. bankruptcy sect. 1965), 7th Circuit Bar Assn. Editor Newsletter, 1965—. Home: 5524 N 13th St Milwaukee WI 53209 Office: 1845 N Farwell Milwaukee WI 53202

LUECKERATH, ELMER WILLIAM, reliability engr.; b. Ferguson, Mo., May 14, 1913; s. John William and Anna Elizabeth (Langenegger) L.; B.S., Washington U., St. Louis, 1936. Engr., Anheuser Busch, Inc., St. Louis, 1936-41, U.S. Corps of Engrs., St. Louis, 1941-44, Monsanto Chem. Co., St. Louis, 1946-49, Union Elec. Co., St. Louis, 1949-56, McDonnell-Douglas Corp., St. Louis, 1956-60; sr. research engr. Falstaff Brewing Co., St. Louis, 1960-68; engr. Miles Labs., Granite City, Ill., 1968-71; engr. U.S. Army Army Aviation Systems Command, St. Louis, 1971—. Mem. Ferguson Citizens Com., 1955—; treas. Ferguson Twp. Republican. Club, 1969-71, 80—. Served to lt., USNR, 1943-46. Recipient letter of commendation Am. Soc. Brewing Chemists, 1967, Pres. Falstaff Brewing Co., 1968, certificate of outstanding professionalism Hughes Helicopters, 1976, letter of appreciation Gen. Stevens U.S. Army, 1976. Mem. Nat., Mo. socs. profl. engrs., Am. Inst. Aeros. and Astronautics, Am. Def. Preparedness Assn. Baptist. Clubs: Discussion, Engrs. (St. Louis). Home: 231 Olympia Dr Ferguson MO 63135

LUECKING, RICHARD GEORGE, assn. exec.; b. St. Louis, Oct. 27, 1949; s. Ferdinand August and Armella Anne (Buescher) L.; B.A., Washington U., 1971; M.S. in Edn., U. Wis., 1978; m. Elizabeth Marie Tolbert, Sept. 2, 1977; children—Adam William and Justin Edward (twins). Rehab. counselor Ill. Div. Vocational Rehab., Benton, 1972-73; social worker Winnebago County Dept. Social Services, Oshkosh, Wis., 1974; counselor/program coordinator Winnebago County Assn. Retarded Citizens, Oshkosh, 1974-78, staff devel. dir., 1979—; adj. faculty U. Wis., Dept. Social Work, Oshkosh, 1978—; cons. in field. Mem. Nat. Assn. Retarded Citizens, Am. Assn. on Mental Deficiency (vice chmn. Wis. chpt.), Nat. Rehab. Assn. Author: (booklet) Orientation to Developmental Disabilities, 1979; author: Staff Handbook: Community Treatment Program for Disturbed Developmentally Disabled, 1979; Staff Handbook: Community Treatment Program for Autistic Children, 1979; Resource Handbook for Group Home Staff, 1981. Home: 1275 Brooks Rd Oshkosh WI 54901 Office: 1628 N Main St Oshkosh WI 54901

LUEDKE, DONALD, rehab. orgn. exec.; b. Milw., Apr. 2, 1934; s. Milton and Bernadine L.; B.B.A. in Acctg., Spencerian Coll., Milw., 1959; m. Marilyn Wendorf, June 1, 1957; 1 dau., Lynn. Gen. acct. Lakeside Labs., Milw., 1959-64; v.p. Center Fuel Co., Milw., 1964-75; v.p. fin. Goodwill Industries, Milw., 1975—. Served with U.S. Army, 1954-56. Mem. Am. Mgmt. Assn., Nat. Assn. Accts., Cedarburg C. of C. Club: Kiwanis (chmn. boys and girls com.).

LUEDTKE, ROLAND ALFRED, lawyer, state ofcl.; b. Lincoln, Nebr., Jan. 4, 1924; s. Alfred C. and Caroline (Senne) L.; B.S., U. Nebr., 1949, J.D., 1951; m. Helen Snyder, Dec. 1, 1951; children—Larry O., David A. Admitted to Nebr. bar, 1951; practiced in Lincoln, 1951—; mem. firm Kier, Cobb & Luedtke, 1961-69, Kier & Luedtke, 1969-73, Luedtke, Radcliffe & Evans and predecessor, 1973—; dep. sec. state State of Nebr., Lincoln, 1953-60; spl. legislative liaison Nebr. Dept. State, Lincoln, 1953-60; corps and elections counsel to sec. state, Lincoln, 1960-65; state senator Nebr. Unicameral Legislature, 1967-78, speaker, 1977-78; lt. gov. Nebr., 1979—. Exec. sec. Neb. Gov.'s Com. Refugee Relief, 1954-58; conferee Nat. Conf. Judiciary, Williamsburg, Va., 1971, Nat. Conf. Corrections, Williamsburg, Va., 1971; del. Nat. Conf. Criminal Justice, Washington, 1973; mem. Nat. Conf. State Cts., Williamsburg, Va., 1978; mem. exec. com. Nat. Conf. Lt. Govs.; mem. budget com. Council State Govts. Past pres. Lancaster County Cancer Soc.; dist. v.p., finance chmn. Boy Scouts Am. Treas., Nebr. Young Republicans, 1953-54; jr. pres. Founders Day Nebr. Rep. Com., 1958-59; chmn. Lancaster County Rep. Com., 1962-64. Bd. dirs. Concordia Coll. Assn., Seward, Nebr., pres., 1962-66; bd. dirs. Lincoln Luth. Sch. Assn., pres., 1964-65. Served with AUS, 1943-45; ETO. Decorated Bronze Star, Purple Heart; recipient Distinguished Service award Concordia Tchrs. Coll., 1975. Mem. Am., Nebr. (spl. com. corp. law revision), Lincoln bar assns., Am. Legion, Lincoln Jr. C. of C. (dir. 1955-57, v.p., 1956-57), Nat. Conf. State Legislators (chmn. criminal justice task force and consumers affairs com., mem. exec. com. 1977-78), Am. Judicature Soc., Delta Theta Phi. Lutheran (pres. ch. 1971-74). Club: Sertoma (pres. 1962-63, chmn. bd. 1963-64) (Lincoln). Home: 327 Park Vista Lincoln NE 68510 Office: Suite 2315 State Capitol Lincoln NE 68509

LUE-HING, CECIL, environ. and san. engr.; b. Jamaica, W.I., Nov. 3, 1930; came to U.S., 1955, naturalized, 1973; s. James and Mabel (Harris) Lue-Hing; B.C.E., Marquette U., 1961; M.S., Case Western Res. U., 1963; Sc.D., Washington U., St. Louis, 1966; children—Cecil Barrington, Robert James. Med. lab. technician U. W.I., 1949-55; supr. histopathology lab., instr. Sch. Med. Tech., Mt. Sinai Med. Center, Milw., 1956-61; asst. prof. Washington U., St. Louis, 1965-66; v.p. Ryckman, Edgerley, Tomlinson & Assos., Inc., St. Louis, 1967-71; dir. research and devel. Met. San. Dist. Greater Chgo., 1970—; prin. Peer Cons., Inc., Rockville, Md., 1978—; mem. com. U.S. EPA Sci. Adv. Bd., 1978—; chmn. engring. and tech. com., sci. adv. bd. Internat. Joint Commn., 1979—. Registered profl. engr., Ill., Mo., Md., D.C. Mem. Am. Acad. Environ. Engrs., Nat. Soc. Profl. Engrs., Water Pollution Control Fedn., ASCE, AAAS, Council Agrl. Sci. and Tech. Episcopalian. Author: Color Atlas on Sewage Organisms, 1981; contbr. articles to profl. jours. Patentee in field. Office: 100 E Erie St Chicago IL 60611

LUELOFF, JORIE ANNE PAYNE (MRS. RICHARD FRIEDMAN), journalist; b. Milw.; d. R.T. and Marjorie (Kaltenbach) Lueloff; student U. Geneva and Inst. des Hautes Etudes Internationales (Switzerland), 1961; B.A., Mills Coll., 1962; postgrad. Georgetown U. Sch. Fgn. Service, 1963; m. Richard Friedman, May 1, 1971. With CIA, Washington, 1962-63; newsfeature writer A.P., N.Y.C., 1964-65; news reporter, newscaster, commentator NBC News, Sta. WMAQ-TV, Chgo., 1965—. Mem. jr. governing bd. Chgo. Symphony; bd. dirs. Rehab. Inst. Chgo. Mem. Chgo. Acad. TV Arts and Scis. (dir.). Club: Chicago Press. Office: NBC News Merchandise Mart Chicago IL 60654

LUEMPERT, ARTHUR GEORGE, electronics co. exec.; b. Broadview Heights, Ohio, Apr. 22, 1931; s. Arthur John and Myrtle Margaret (Siebert) L.; B.S. in Elec. Engring., Ohio U., 1954; postgrad. Xavier U., 1959-60, Cin. U., 1956-59; m. Graclyn Jean Smith, Oct. 23, 1955; children—Arthur Frederick, Amy Lynne, Molly Ann. Head electronics sect. U.S. Army, Fort Belvoir, 1954-56; engr. AVCO Mfg. Corp., Cin., 1956-60; project engr. Sparton Electronics, Jackson, Mich., 1960-66, program mgr., 1968-80, v.p. dir. mktg., 1980—; asst. chief engr. Gen. Dynamics Corp., Rochester, N.Y., 1966-68. Trustee Clark Lake Sch. Bd.; chmn. Boy Scouts Am., 1968—. Served with AUS, 1954-56. Mem. IEEE, Nat. Security Indsl. Assn., Am. Ordnance Assn., U.S. Naval Inst. Clubs: Order Eastern Star, Masons; Army-Navy. Patentee in expendable timer, expendable airborne bathermograph. Home: 150 Lakeview Dr Clark Lake MI 49234 Office: 2400 E Ganson St Jackson MI 49202

LUERSSEN, FRANK WONSON, steel co. exec.; b. Reading, Pa., Aug. 14, 1927; s. George V. and Mary Ann (Swoyer) L.; B.S. in Physics, Pa. State U., 1950; M.S. in Metall. Engring., Lehigh U., 1951; m. Joan M. Schlosser, June 17, 1950; children—Thomas, Mary Ellen, Catherine, Susan, Ann. With Inland Steel Co., Chgo., 1952—, v.p. research, 1968-77, v.p. steel mfg., 1977-78, pres., 1978—, also dir.; dir. Continental Ill. Corp.; lectr. in field. Trustee, Munster (Ind.) Sch. Bd., 1957-66, sec.-treas., 1960-66; v.p., chmn. fin. com. Munster Med. Research Found.; trustee Northwestern U. Served with USNR, 1945-47. Recipient F. L. Toy award AIME, 1955, Fellow Am. Soc. Metals; mem. AIME, Engring. Found., Am. Iron and Steel Inst. (chmn. phys. chemistry of steelmaking group 1969-75, chmn. gen. research com. 1975-77), Nat. Acad. Engring. Club: Pres.'s of Loyola U. (hon.). Contbr. numerous articles to profl. jours.; patentee in field. Office: 30 W Monroe St Chicago IL 60603

LUFKIN, GEORGE THOMAS, airline co. mgr.; b. Idaho Falls, Idaho, Dec. 9, 1939; s. Thomas Eugene and Zelpha Alvina (Ellis) L.; student Idaho State U., 1959-61, Ariz. State U., 1964-65, U. Nev., 1973-76; m. Kip Cherrie Newbold, Dec. 29, 1966; children—Stacy, Ryan and Robin (twins). With Western Airlines, 1965—, mgr. reservations, Las Vegas, Nev., 1972-78, mgr. cargo sales and service, 1978-79, city mgr. of service, Mpls., 1979—; guest lectr. U. Nev., Las Vegas, 1978-79. Served with U.S. Army, 1961-64. Mem. Bloomington C. of C. Republican. Mormon. Club: Skal of Am. Home: 6009 Timberglade Dr Bloomington MN 55438 Office: Minneapolis/Saint Paul Airport Room C252 Saint Paul MN 55111

LUGAR, RICHARD GREEN, U.S. senator; b. Indpls., Apr. 4, 1932; s. Marvin and Bertha (Green) L.; B.A., Denison U., 1954; B.A., M.A. (Rhodes scholar), Oxford (Eng.) U., 1954-56; m. Charlene Smeltzer, Sept. 8, 1956; children—Mark, Robert, John, David. With Thomas L. Green & Co., Indpls., 1960—, v.p., treas., 1960-67, sec.-treas. 1967—; treas. Lugar Stock Farm Inc., Indpls., 1960—; mayor city Indpls., 1968-75; U.S. Senator from Ind., 1977—. Mem. Adv. Commn. on Intergovtl. Relations, 1968-75, vice chmn., 1970-75; mem. adv. council U.S. Conf. Mayors, 1969-75; pres. Nat. League Cities, 1970-71; mem. regional export expansion council Dept. Commerce, Indpls., 1967-73. Incorporator, 1st v.p. Community Action Against Poverty Bd., Indpls., 1965-67; mem. Indpls. Bd. Sch. Commrs., 1964-67, v.p., 1965; mem. Nat. Adv. Commn. on Criminal Justice Standards and Goals, 1971-72. Mem. adv. com. Marion County Republican Com., 1966—; keynoter Ind. Rep. Conv., 1968, del., 1970, 72; mem. platform com. Rep. Nat. Conv., 1968, 72, Keynote speaker, 1972, del., 1980; mem. exec. com. Indpls. Symphony Orch., 1964-66; trustee, vice chmn. Ind. Central U.; trustee Denison U., Indpls. Center Advanced Research, 1973-76; trustee, past mem. bldg. fund com. Westview Hosp.; mem. Nat. 4-H Service Com.; bd. visitors Joint Center for Urban Studies, Harvard-Mass. Inst. Tech. Served to lt. USNR, 1957-60. Named Outstanding Young Man, Indpls. Jr. C. of C., 1966. Mem. Washington High Sch. Men's Club (pres. 1966-68), Phi Beta Kappa, Beta Theta Pi. Methodist. Rotarian (v.p. Indpls. 1967-68). Home: 7841 Old Dominion Dr McLean VA 22102 Office: 1113 Dirksen Senate Office Bldg Washington DC 20510

LUGAR, RICHARD GREEN, U.S. senator; b. Indpls., Apr. 4, 1932; s. Marvin Leroy and Bertha (Green) L.; B.A., Denison U., 1954; B.A. (Rhodes scholar), Oxford (Eng.) U., 1956, M.A., 1956; m. Charlene Smeltzer, Sept. 8, 1956; children—Mark, Robert, John, David. Vice pres., treas. Thomas L. Green & Co., Inc., Indpls., 1960-67; treas. Lugar Stock Farm, Inc., Indpls., 1960; mayor Indpls., 1968-75; vis. prof. polit. sci. Ind. Central U., 1975-76; U.S. senator from Ind., 1977—. Mem. Adv. Commn. Intergovtl. Relations, 1969-75, vice chmn., 1970-75. Mem. Indpls. Sch. Bd., 1964-67, v.p., 1965-66; trustee Ind. Central U., Indpls., Denison U. Del., mem. resolutions com. Rep. Nat. Conv., 1968, 72, delegate and speaker, 1980. Served to lt. (j.g.) USNR, 1957-60. Mem. Nat. League Cities (pres. 1970-71), Blue Key, Phi Beta Kappa, Omicron Delta Kappa, Pi Delta Epsilon, Pi Sigma Alpha, Beta Theta Pi. Methodist. Rotarian (v.p. Indpls. 1967-68). Home: 7841 Old Dominion Dr McLean VA 22102 Office: US Senate Washington DC 20510

LUHMAN, WILLIAM SIMON, univ. adminstr.; b. Belvidere, Ill., May 15, 1934; s. Donald R. and H. Elizabeth (Rudberg) L.; A.B., Park Coll., 1956; M.A., Fla. State U., 1957. City planner, City of Moline, Ill., 1959-64; planning dir. Rock Island County, Rock Island, Ill., 1964-66; exec. dir. Bi-State Met. Planning Commn., Rock Island, 1966-71; dir. regional devel. Northeastern Ill. Planning Commn., Chgo., 1971-74, asso. dir., 1975-76, dep. dir., 1977-79, acting exec. dir., 1979-80, asst. dir., 1980-81; v.p. Public Mgmt. Info. Service, Chgo., 1981—; asst. dir. Center Govt. Studies, No. Ill. U., DeKalb, 1981—; vis. instr. Augustana Coll., Rock Island, 1967, 69. Mem. adv. council profl. devel. Center for Govt. Studies, No. Ill. U., 1976-80. Served with AUS, 1957-59. Mem. Am. Soc. Pub. Adminstrn., Am. Soc. Planning Ofcls., Internat., Ill. city mgmt. assns. Home: 1538 Fremont St Belvidere IL 61008 Office: 146 Carrol Ave DeKalb IL 60115

LUHNOW, RAYMOND BERTRAM, JR., cons. engr.; b. Kansas City, Mo., May 3, 1923; s. Raymond Bertram and Jeanette Elizabeth (McVey) L.; B.S. in Elec. Engring., U. Ill., 1944; M.B.A., U. Mo., 1964; m. Ruth E. Anderson, Sept. 6, 1947; children—Raymond Christian, Mark Frederick, Steven Kirk, Nancy Ruth. Design engr. Burns & McDonnell Engring. Co., Kansas City, 1946—, partner, 1964-74, pres., 1974—. Bd. dirs. Helping Hand of Goodwill; gov. Am. Royal Assn.; trustee Midwest Research Inst. Served with USNR, 1943-46. Registered profl. engr., Mo., Kans., N.Y., N.J., Pa., Conn., Del., Mass., D.C.; registered profl. planner, N.J. Mem. Am. Soc. Heating, Refrigerating and Air Conditioning Engrs., Kansas City C. of C., Nat. Soc. Profl. Engrs., IEEE, Soc. Fire Protection Engrs. Presbyterian (elder). Clubs: Engrs., Carriage (bd. dirs.); Mission Hills Country. Contbr. articles tech. jours. and mags. Home: 6510 Rainbow Ave Shawnee Mission KS 66208 Office: 4600 E 63d St Kansas City MO 64141

LUISI, JOHN NICHOLAS, concrete co. exec.; b. Mt. Vernon, N.Y., Apr. 12, 1946; s. Ernest M.and Anna G. (Gearity) L.; B.B.A., Iona Coll., 1968; m. Aug. 26, 1967; children—Deborah Ann, John Paul. Acct., Arthur Anderson & Co., N.Y.C., 1968-71; fin. analyst ITT Levitt & Sons, Lake Success, N.Y., 1971-74; asst. corp. controller The RichardRichards Group, N.Y.C. and Chgo., 1974-78; v.p. fin. Dominion Concrete Co., Wheeling, Ill., 1980—; pres. Dominion Enterprises, Inc. C.P.A., N.Y. State. Mem. Am. Inst. C.P.A.'s, N.Y. Soc. C.P.A.'s. Address: 707 W Colfax St Palatine IL 60067

LUKAC, GEORGE JOSEPH, hist. soc. exec.; b. Garfield, N.J., Mar. 6, 1937; s. Michael and Elizabeth (Gall) L.; B.S. in Polit. Sci., Rutgers U., 1958; student Bread Loaf Writers Conf., Middlebury (Vt.) Coll., 1971, numerous devel. continuing edn. programs; m. Alice Louise Osborn, Nov. 8, 1958; children—Mark Robert, Amy Elizabeth. Systems reviewer Prudential Ins. Co., 1958-59; asst. editor Johnson & Johnson, 1959-61; mem. staff dept. alumni relations Rutgers U., 1961-77, editor, bus. mgr. alumni monthly, 1962-68, asst. dir. alumni relations, 1967-77; pub. relations cons. and writer for polit. campaigns, 1962-77; dir. alumni affairs and devel. Sangamon State U., acting Dir. univ. relations, 1979, asst. to pres., 1980-81, also exec. officer Sangamon State U. Found., also exec. dir. Alumni Assn., 1977-80; dir. devel. and external relations, spl. asst. to soc. dir. Mo. Hist. Soc., 1981—; intern adviser, lectr., cons. fund raising, 1977—. Class corr. Rutgers U. Alumni Assn., 1958-63, class agt., 1963-68, 73-78, alumni trustee nominating com., 1968-69, regional fund campaign agt., 1961; mem. Rutgers Alumni Com. for Support Pub. Higher Edn. in N.J., 1959. Mem. arts and sci. com. Republican Nat. Com., 1967-75; publicity coordinator First Congregational Ch., Springfield, Ill. Recipient Spl. Recognition award for two-part article maj. campus controversy, also hon. mention for instl. news Am. Alumni Council, 1966; Rutgers Fund award as regional agt., 1961, Ashmead award as class agt., 1968, 76; author award N.J. Writers Conf., 1974. Mem. Council for Advancement and Support of Edn., Chi Phi, Pi Sigma Alpha. Presbyterian. Club: Rutgers Alumni Faculty (past mem. exec. com., publicity chmn.), Kiwanis (dir.) (Springfield). Author magazine articles. Editor: Aloud to Alma Mater, 1966; Copyright-The Librarian and the Law, 1972. Home: 335 Turnbury Circle Ballwin MO 63011 Office: Mo Hist Soc Jefferson Meml Bldg Forest Park Saint Louis MO 63112

LUKAS, JOSEPH, automotive engr.; b. Sausininkai, Lithuania, Jan. 27, 1942; s. Vincentas and Magdelena Victorija (Pranskevicius) Lukasevicius; came to U.S., 1949, naturalized, 1960; student Aquinas Coll., 1960-62; B.S., Western Mich. U., 1965. Engr., Gen. Motors Proving Ground, Milford, Mich., 1965, 68, sr. project engr. Diesel Equipment div. Gen. Motors Corp., Grand Rapids, Mich., 1969—. Served with AUS, 1965-68. Mem. Soc. Automotive Engrs. (vice chmn. Western Mich. sect. 1978-79), Soc. Automotive Engrs. Roman Catholic. Patentee in field. Home: 622 Tremont Ct NW Grand Rapids MI 49504 Office: 2100 Burlingame SW Grand Rapids MI 49501

LUKE, HUGH D., electronics co. exec.; b. 1911; married. With McKinsey & Co., 1948-53; with Reliance Electric Co., Cleve., 1953—, v.p., 1957-64, exec. v.p., 1964-65, pres., chief exec. officer, 1965-72, chmn. bd., chief exec. officer, 1972-76, chmn. bd., 1976—, also dir.; dir. Ameritrust Co., Parker-Hannifin Corp. Office: Reliance Electric Co 29325 Chagrin Blvd Cleveland OH 44122*

LUKE, HUGH JAY, educator; b. Kilgore, Tex., Feb. 26, 1932; s. Hugh Jay and Stella Avis (Hamon) L.; student Baylor U., 1949-50; B.A., U. Tex., Austin, 1956, M.A., 1957, Ph.D. (Univ. fellow, 1958-60), 1963; m. Virginia Carol Pavelka, Aug. 15, 1969; children—Richard Carlton, Katherine Pavelka. Instr., San Antonio Coll., 1957-58, Tex. A&M Coll., 1960-61, asst. prof., 1961-63; asst. prof. English, U. Nebr., Lincoln, 1963-66, asso. prof., 1966-71, prof., 1971—. Dir. research Dem. candidate for gov., Nebr., 1968; dir. research Nebr. for Robert Kennedy, 1968; Nebr. sgt. at arms Dem. Nat. Conv., 1968; mem. steering com. Nebr. for Edward Kennedy, 1980. Served with U.S. Army, 1951-53. Mem. AAUP, Phi Beta Kappa, Phi Kappa Phi. Unitarian. Asso. editor Prairie Schooner, 1968-79, editor, 1980—; editor: The Last Man (Mary Shelley), 1965, William Blake, A Critical Essay (A.C. Swinburne), 1971; contbr. writings to various publs. Home: 4640 Bryan Circle Lincoln NE 68506 Office: Dept English Univ Nebraska Lincoln NE 68588

LUKEN, THOMAS A., Congressman; b. Cin., July 9, 1925; A.B., Xavier U., 1947; postgrad. Bowling Green State U., 1943-44; LL.B., Salmon P. Chase Law Sch., 1950; m. Shirley Ast, 1947; 8 children. Admitted to Ohio bar, 1950; practiced in Cin.; city atty. City of Deer Park (Ohio), 1955-61; Fed. dist. atty., 1961-64; mem. Cin. City Council, 1964-67, 69-71, 73, mayor, 1971-72; mem. 93d, 95th-96th congresses from 2d Ohio Dist.; chmn. Cin. Law Observance Com. Served in USMC, 1943-45. Mem. Am. Legion, Jaycees (life). Club: K.C. Office: Room 240 Cannon House Office Bldg Washington DC 20515

LUKENS, DONALD E. BUZ, mgmt. cons., state senator, former congressman; b. Harveysburg, Ohio, Feb. 11, 1931; s. William Arthur and Edith (Greene) L.; student Ohio State U., 1950, Baylor U., 1955. Acting minority counsel house rules com. U.S. Ho. of Reps., 1961-63; nat. chmn. Young Republican Nat. Fedn., also mem. exec. com. Rep. Nat. Com., 1963-65; mgmt. cons., 1965—; owner, operator Lukens Vineyard, Harveysburg, Ohio; mem. 90th-91st Congresses 24th dist. Ohio; mem. house sci. and astronautics com., house post office and civil service com.; now mem. Ohio Senate. Nat. chmn. Am. Legis. Exchange Council, 1977-78. Mem. Middletown (Ohio) Civic Assn.; active YMCA, Boy Scouts Am., Am. Cancer Soc., Muscular Dystrophy Assn., Multiple Sclerosis Assn.; nat. polit. coordinator Reagan for Pres. Served with USAF, 1954-60; lt. col. Res. Mem. Middletown C. of C., Farm Bur., Toastmasters Internat., Res. Officers Assn. (nat. v.p.). Delta Chi, Ahepa. Clubs: Masons, Shriners, Kiwanis. Office: State Senate Columbus OH 43215

LUKENSMEYER, CAROLYN JEAN, organizational devel. cons.; b. Hampton, Iowa, May 13, 1945; d. Gerald William and Jean Rae (Swartz) L.; B.A. magna cum laude, U. Iowa, 1967; Ph.D., Case Western Res. U., 1974. Community organizer City of Yellow Knife (NW Ter., Can.), 1965; dir. English studies LaCandalabra, Bogota, Colombia, 1966; tng. dir. Goodwill Industries, Iowa City, 1966-67; asst. dean students U. Rochester (N.Y.), 1967-68; counselor for student life Cleve. State U., 1968-71, asst. prof. dept. social services, 1971-74; dir. planning and devel. Gestalt Inst. Cleve., 1978—; pres. Lukensmeyer Assos., Inc., work projects on boundary mgmt. in joint ventures between multinat. corps. and govts., Cleve., 1974—. Bd. dirs. Nat. Tng. Labs., Washington, WomenSpace, Cleve.; mem. Citizen's Action Council, Mayor's Office, Cleve., 1968-69; mem. adv. council on youth YWCA, 1968-70; mem. People's Commn. of Inquiry, Vietnam, 1970-72; mem. Internat. Assembly of Christians in Solidarity with the People of SE Asia, 1970-72. Mem. Internat. Assn. Applied Social Scientists, Am. Psychol. Assn. Address: 7 Mornington Ln Cleveland Heights OH 44106

LUM, HOMER C., JR., hotel exec.; b. DuBois, Pa., Feb. 27, 1937; s. Homer C. and Aleda Viola (Abrahamson) L.; student public sch., N. Tonawanda, N.Y.; grad. Lewis Hotel Sch., Washington, 1962; m. June Lynne Kearly, Aug. 14, 1965; children—Keith Homer, Troy Michael. Mgmt. cons. R.B.C., Rochester, N.Y., 1968-69; gen. mgr. Gotham Motor Inn, Syracuse, N.Y., 1969-70, Horizon Hotel, Utica, N.Y., 1970-71; food and beverage dir. Sheraton Inn Hopkins, Cleve., 1971-74; dir. food and beverage Motor Inn div. Hospitality Motor Inns, Cleve., 1974-77; dir. food and beverage ops. analysis, systems mgr. Harpenau Hotels, Cin.; mem. adv. panel Restaurant Bus. Mag., Cleve., 1974-76. Mem. Cleve. State Adv. Com. Continuing Edn., 1971-74. Served with USMC, 1955-58. Mem. Nat. Restaurant Assn. Presbyterian. Clubs: Elks, Masons. Home: 7444 Chinook Dr West Chester OH 45069 Office: Harpenau Enterprises 8001 Reading Rd Cincinnati OH 45237

LUMB, RAYMOND CLIFFORD, rheumatologist; b. Webster, S.D., Nov. 21, 1942; s. Elroy Raymond and Doris Geneva (Carlson) L.; B.S. with high honors, U. Md., 1964; M.D., George Washington U., 1968; m. Carol Ann Rhodes, May 22, 1971; children—Carrie, Christopher. Intern, then resident in internal medicine Barnes Hosp., St. Louis, 1968-70; resident in internal medicine, then fellow in rheumatology U. Mich. Med. Center, Ann Arbor, 1970-74; practice medicine specializing in rheumatology, Topeka, 1974—; mem. staff St. Francis, Stormont-Vail hosps.; clin. dir. internal medicine residency Topeka Affiliated Hosp.; cons. Meml., VA hosps.; asst. clin. prof. Kans. U. Med. Sch.; mem. faculty Menninger Found.; bd. govs. Kan. chpt. Arthritis Found., 1975—, chmn. med. council, mem. exec. com., 1977—; bd. dirs. Kans. Arthritis Info. and Edn. Unit, 1975-77. Served to lt. comdr. M.C., USNR, 1969-75. Grantee Regional Med. Program, 1975-77; diplomate Am. Bd. Internal Medicine (rheumatology). Mem. A.C.P., Am. Rheumatism Assn., AMA (Physicians Recognition award 1972—), Mid-Am. Rheumatism Soc., Kans. Med. Soc., Shawnee County Med. Soc., Shawnee County Med. Found. (dir.). Methodist. Home: 2210 De Sousa Ct Topeka KS 66611 Office: 901 Garfield St Topeka KS 66606

LUMICAO, BENJAMIN GUIAB, physician; b. Philippines, Mar. 15, 1936; s. Tomas B. and Josefina (Guiab) L.; came to U.S., 1962, naturalized, 1976; M.D., U. of East, Quezon City, Philippines, 1961; m. Felicitas Evangelista, May 4, 1965; children—Benjamin, Robert F. Intern, St. Peters Hosp., Albany, N.Y., 1962-63; resident in internal medicine Ill. Masonic Hosp., Chgo., 1963-64; resident in internal medicine Passavant Meml. Hosp., Chgo., 1964-66, chief resident, 1966-67; fellow in cardiology Northwestern U. Med. Sch., 1967-68, U. Ala., 1968-69; practice medicine specializing in internal medicine and cardiology, Chgo., 1969—; attending physician Northwestern Meml. Hosp., 1969—, dir. coronary care unit Passavant Pavillion, 1975—; asst. prof. medicine Northwestern U. Med. Sch. Diplomate Am. Bd. Internal Medicine. Asso. fellow Am. Coll. Cardiology; mem. A.C.P., Chgo. Soc. Internal Medicine. Home: 2629 Kingston Dr Northbrook IL 60062 Office: 707 N Fairbanks Ct Chicago IL 60611

LUMMIS, JOHN MICHAEL, funeral dir.; b. Quincy, Ill., May 1, 1949; s. John Burdeen and Dorothy Pearl (Akers) L.; student Central Mo. State Coll., 1967-68, Quincy Coll., 1971; grad. Ind. Coll. Mortuary Sci., 1972; m. Marcia Rae Leenerts, Mar. 23, 1968; children—Todd, Brett, Scott, Heather. Apprentice, Hufnagel Funeral Chapel, Mt. Sterling, Ill., 1972-73; owner, operator Ward Funeral Home, Pleasant Hill, Ill., 1973—, Gill-Lummis Funeral Home, Barry, Ill., 1979—, Lummis Funeral Home, Pittsfield, Ill., 1980. Mem. founding bd. Pike County Ambulance Service, 1976; bd. dirs. Illini Community Hosp., 1977, v.p., 1979—; treas. United Meth. Ch. Served with U.S. Army, 1969-70. Decorated Army Commendation medal; registered emergency med. technician, Ill. Dept. Pub. Health. Mem. Nat., Ill. funeral dirs. assns., Asso. Funeral Dirs., Federated Funeral Dirs. Am., Pleasant Hill Jr. C. of C. (sec.-treas. 1974, 75, external v.p. 1976). Clubs: Masons, Lions, Rotary. Home and Office: 502 S Main St Pleasant Hill IL 62366

LUMSDEN, MAGDALEN VIRGINIA, educator; b. Detroit, Oct. 3, 1921; d. Joseph Martin and Hazel Matilda (Stock) Kutz; B.S., Marygrove Coll., 1944; postgrad. Mich. Central U., 1965; m. Wilfred Lumsden, Aug. 8, 1948; children—Gregory W., Jeffrey P., Veronica A. Tchr., Whittier Jr. High Sch., Flint, Mich., 1944-45; faculty Tacoma Cath. Coll., 1945-49; tchr. St. Anne's Kindergarten, Sumter, S.C., 1958-63; tchr. homes econs. Vassar (Mich.) Pub. Schs., 1964—. Mem. Mich. Edn. Assn., NEA, Mich. Home Econs. Assn., Am. Home Econs. Assn., Thumb Area Profl. Home Economists, Mich. Ednl. Occupational Assn., Vassar Ednl. Assn. Roman Catholic. Clubs: Eagles, K.C. Aux. Home: 215 Division St Vassar MI 48768 Office: 220 Athletic St Vassar MI 48768

LUND, SISTER CANDIDA, coll. chancellor; b. Chgo.; b. Fred S. Lund and Katharine (Murray) Lund Heck; B.A., Rosary Coll., River Forest, Ill.; M.A., Cath. U. Am.; Ph.D. (LaVerne Noyes scholar 1958-60, AAUW fellow), U. Chgo., 1963; Litt.D. (hon.), Lincoln Coll., 1968; LL.D. (hon.), John Marshall Law Sch., 1979; L.H.D., Marymount Coll., 1979. Pres. Rosary Coll., 1964-81, chancellor, 1981—; commr. Ill. Commn. on Status of Women, 1977—; bd. dirs. Am. Council Edn., 1977—; trustee Carnegie Found. for Advancement Teaching, 1970-78; bd. trustees Clarke Coll., Dubuque, Iowa, 1981—. Recipient Profl. Achievement award U. Chgo. Alumni, 1975. Fellow Royal Soc. Arts, (London); mem. Am. Polit. Sci. Assn., Thomas Moore Assn. (dir. 1975—). Editor: Moments to Remember, 1980; The Days and the Nights: Prayers for Today's Woman; contbr. to The Third Branch of Government; Why Catholic. Home and Office: Rosary Coll 7900 Division St River Forest IL 60305

LUND, ROBERT CORIN, ins. co. exec.; b. Gt. Falls, Mont., May 24, 1943; s. Robert K. and Carol Joy (Bruggeman) L.; B.S., Mont. State U., 1965; m. Renate Ute Wagner, Oct. 20, 1967; children—Willard M., Heike J. Project leader Aetna Life & Casualty, Hartford, Conn., 1972-77; project mgr. Maccabees Mut. Life Ins., Southfield, Mich., 1977—. Served with U.S. Army, 1965-72, to maj., USAR, 1972—. Decorated Bronze Star, Army Commendation medal. Fellow Life Mgmt. Inst.; mem. Res. Officers Assn., Sigma Chi. Republican. Episcopalian. Home: 23360 Glencreek Farmington Hills MI 48024 Office: 25800 Northwestern Hwy Southfield MI 48037

LUND, STEWART HELMER MURPHY, lawyer; b. Webster City, Iowa, July 20, 1911; s. Frank Joel and Grace Elizabeth (Bishop) L.; student Webster City Jr. Coll., 1933; LL.B., Drake U., 1942, J.D., 1968; m. Bernice E. Sealine, Oct. 4, 1947; children—Caryl (Mrs. Roger Scheffer), Janice (Mrs. Gary Johnson). Truck driver Western Gravel Co., 1930; room clk., bookkeeper Boss Hotels, Webster City, 1931-32, Beloit, Wis., 1932-35; dist. sales and engring. positions Gen. Refrigeration Corp., Beloit, 1936-39; admitted to Ia. bar, 1942;

practiced in Webster City, 1946—, city atty., 1957-58; jud. referee, 1976—; Iowa inheritance tax appraiser Hamilton County, 1977—. Mem. adv. council Drake U. Law Sch., 1970—; county dir. Civil Def., 1947-59; mem. Iowa Gov.'s Com. Jobs for Vets., 1971—; mem. Hamilton County Hosp. Commn., 1965-75; pres. Boone River Energy Producers Inc., 1979—. Served as lt. USNR, 1942-45; PTO. Mem. Am., Hamilton County (pres. 1952, 64), 11th Jud. Dist. (sec. 1963-72), Iowa (bd. govs. 1970-73), Jud. Dist. 2-B (bd. govs. 1974—) bar assns., Am. Legion (mem. nat. Americanism commn. 1954-72, nat. exec. committeeman 1972—), Iowa Def. Counsel (pres. 1976-77). Lutheran. Kiwanian, Moose, Elk. Club: Webster City Country. Home: 728 Elm St Webster City IA 50595 Office: 623 2d St Webster City IA 50595

LUNDAHL, BETTY LEE, counselor; b. Moline, Ill., July 21, 1924; d. Leroy Walter and Sophie W. (Larson) L.; B.A., Augustana Coll., Rock Island, Ill., 1946; M.Ed., Loyola U., Chgo., 1964; postgrad. Purdue U., 1967-73. Tchr. sci. and health Columbia Jr. High Sch., Hammond, Ind., 1948-60; tchr. sci. and health Gavit Jr. Sr. High Sch., Hammond, 1960-62, counselor, 1962-64, dean girls, dir. student activities, 1964-75, acting asst. prin., 1967-68; counselor Morton Sr. High Sch., Hammond, 1975—. Mem. Ind. State, N.W. Ind. (sect. sec., div. meetings 1955; chmn. 1956), Hammond tchrs. assns., NEA, Am., Ind. personnel and guidance assns., AAHPER, Delta Kappa Gamma. Lutheran. Author numerous tchr. and student handbooks. Home: 8931 Woodward Ave Highland IN 46322 Office: 6915 Grand Ave Hammond IN 46323

LUNDBERG, DAVID GARY, utility exec.; b. Willmar, Minn., Apr. 15, 1952; s. Laurel Waldo and Inez Georgine (Lindahl) L.; A.A., Willmar Tech. Inst., 1973; acctg. cert. U.S. Dept. Agr. Grad. Sch., 1975; mgmt. cert. U. Nebr., Lincoln, 1979; m. Debara Jean DeVries, June 21, 1975. Bus. analyst Steele-Waseca Coop. Electric Co., Owatonna, Minn., 1973—, Mack Properties, Owatonna, 1974-78; mem. Minn. Adv. Com. Acctg. Occupations; mem. curriculum articulation div. Minn. Dept. Edn. Mem. Nat. Notary Assn., Minn. Rural Electric Mgmt. Assn. (pres., v.p., sec., treas., dir. office adminstrn. 1977—), Willmar Tech. Inst. Alumni Assn., Phi Eta Sigma. Lutheran. Club: Toastmasters. Home: 1104 Oakwood Ln Owatonna MN 55060 Office: 115 E Rose St PO Box 485 Owatonna MN 55060

LUNDE, HAROLD IRVING, educator; b. Austin, Minn., Apr. 18, 1929; s. Peter Oliver and Emma (Stoa) L.; B.A., St. Olaf Coll., 1952; M.A., U. Minn., 1954, Ph.D., 1966; m. Sarah Jeanette Lysne, June 25, 1955; children—Paul, James, John, Thomas. Asso. prof. econs. Macalester Coll., St. Paul, 1957-64; financial staff economist Gen. Motors Corp., N.Y.C., 1965-67; corporate sec. Dayton-Hudson Corp., Mpls., 1967-70; mgr. planning and gen. research The May Dept. Stores Co., St. Louis, 1970-72, v.p. planning and research, 1972-78; exec. v.p. adminstrn. Kobacker Stores, Inc., Columbus, Ohio, 1979; prof. mgmt. Bowling Green (Ohio) State U., 1980—. Mem. Acad. Mgmt., Am. Inst. Decision Scis., Am. Econ. Assn., Nat. Assn. Bus. Economists, Phi Beta Kappa. Club: Minneapolis. Home: 643 Wallace Ave Bowling Green OH 43402 Office: Bowling Green State U Bowling Green OH 43403

LUNDEN, JOHN PETER, broadcasting sales exec.; b. Mpls., Jan. 30, 1946; s. Laurence Raymond and Anne (Stub) L.; student Luther Coll., 1965-66; B.A. in Journalism and Advt., U. Minn., Mpls., 1972, postgrad., 1972-73. Nat. account rep. Petry TV Inc., N.Y.C., 1973-74; account exec. Sta.-KSTP, St. Paul, 1974-77, sales mgr., 1977-78, gen. sales mgr., 1978-80; account exec. United TV Inc., Sta.-KMSP-TV, Edina, Minn., 1980—; guest lectr. North Hennepin County Vocat. Tech. Inst. Mem. Minn. Advt. Fedn., Radio Advt. Bur., Nat. Assn. Broadcasters (Radio Mgmt. Seminar award 1978), TV Bur. Advt. (award 1973). Clubs: Mpls. Athletic, U. Minn. Alumni. Office: 6975 York Ave S Edina MN 55435

LUNDGREN, DENNIS DAVID, educator; b. Benton Harbor, Mich., May 9, 1950; s. Walter O. and Helen F. (Brown) L.; Mus.B., Western Mich. U., 1975; Mus.M., Andrews U., Berrien Springs, Mich., 1979; m. Colleen Bowling, Dec. 18, 1971. Vocal tchr. Lakeshore public schs., Stevensville, Mich., 1975—, musical dir., 1975—. Mem. Mich. Edn. Assn. (negotiator, del. rep. assembly), NEA, Mich. Music Educators Assn., Am. Choral Dirs. Assn., Assn. Supervision and Curriculum Devel., Mich. Edn. Assn., Music Educators Nat. Conf., Phi Delta Kappa. Lutheran. Home: 1440 Hide Away Ln Saint Joseph MI 49085 Office: Lakeshore High Sch 5771 Cleveland Ave Stevensville MI 49127

LUNDIN, RICHARD CARL, contracting co. exec.; b. Mankato, Minn., May 31, 1941; s. Hilding Ferdinand and Cora Mae (Olson) L.; student S.D. Sch. Mines and Tech., 1959-61; B.A., Mankato State U., 1964; m. Darlene Mae Balle, Aug. 19, 1962; children—Kari Mae, Richard Carl II, Lori Jo. Laborer, Lundin Constrn. Co., Mankato, foreman, summers 1957-60, supt., 1961-64, v.p., 1964-79, pres., 1979—; founder, pres. Crane Creek Asphalt Co., Owatonna, Minn., 1970—; pres., owner Central Concrete Co., also Guaranteed Sand & Gravel Co., Mankato, 1974—; sec., Riverbend Asphalt Co., Mankato, 1975—; v.p. Lundin Crane Service, Mankato, 1975—; pres. So. Minn. Asphalt Supply Co., Mankato, 1978—; dir. Northwestern Nat. Bank. Mem. Nat. Eagle Scout Assn., Twin Valley Council, Boy Scouts Am., 1976-81; bd. dirs. exec. com., Mankato YMCA. Named Boss of Yr., Mankato Jaycees, 1977. Mem. Nat. Asphalt Pavement Assn. (alt. gov. Minn. 1979-80), Minn. Asphalt Pavement Assn., Nat. Crushed Stone Assn., Minn. Limestone Producers Assn. Republican. Lutheran. Clubs: Mankato Golf, Masons, Shriners. Office: 1905 3d Ave Mankato MN 56001

LUNDQUIST, MYRTLE VERNICE, educator, author; b. Chgo.; d. Martin Luther and Anna Emily (Lorenz) Lundquist; B.A., U. Chgo., 1951, M.A., 1963. Editor, The Commentator, Fed. Res. Bank Chgo., 1942-60; tchr., Wheeling, Ill., 1960-65, Schaumburg, Ill., 1965—. Mem. Women in Communications, Internat. Assn. Bus. Communications, AAUW, NEA, Indsl. Editors Assn. Chgo., Thimble Guild, Thimble Collectors. Author: The Book of a Thousand Thimbles, 1970; Thimble Treasury, 1975; Thimble Americana, 1981. Contbr. articles to mags. Home: 630 Prairie Ave Wilmette IL 60091

LUNDQUIST, VIRGIL JOHN PERSHING, surgeon; b. Kanduyohi, Minn., Jan. 1, 1918; s. August and Olga S. (Skoglund) L.; B.A., Gustavus Adolphus Coll., St. Peter, Minn., 1938; M.D., U. Minn., 1943; m. Irma E. Olson, July 3, 1940; children—Karen, Kipton, Karna, Kada. Intern, U.S. Naval Hosp., Bremerton, Wash., 1942-43; resident U. Minn. Hosp., U.S. VA Hosp., Mpls.; practice medicine specializing in surgery, Mpls., 1950—; mem. staff Met. Med. Center, Fairview Hosp. Served with M.C., USN, 1942-47. Diplomate Am. Bd. Surgery. Fellow A.C.S.; mem. AMA, Minn., Hennepin County med. socs., Minn., Mpls. surg. socs., Mpls. Acad. Medicine. Lutheran. Clubs: Shriners. Home: 4805 Sunnyside Rd Edina MN 55424 Office: 1202 Metropolitan Med Bldg Minneapolis MN 55404

LUNDSTEDT, SVEN BERTIL, behavioral scientist, educator; b. N.Y.C., May 6, 1926; s. Sven David and Edith Maria Lundstedt; A.B., U. Chgo., 1952, Ph.D., 1955; S.M. (fellow), Harvard U., 1960; m. Jean Elizabeth Sanford, June 16, 1951; children—Margaret, Peter, Janet. Asst. dir. Found. for Research on Human Behavior, 1960-62; asst. prof. Case-Western Res. U., Cleve., 1962-64, asso. prof., 1964-68; asso. prof. adminstrn. sci. Ohio State U., 1968-69, prof. public adminstrn., 1969—, chmn. Battelle endowment program for tech. and human affairs, 1976-80; dir. project on edn. of chief exec. officer Aspen Inst., 1978-80; cons. E.I. du Pont de Nemours & Co., B.F. Goodrich Co., Bell Telephone Labs., Battelle Meml. Inst. Pres., Cleve. Mental Health Assn., 1966-68; mem. Ohio Citizen's Task Force on Corrections, 1971-72. Served with U.S. Army, 1944-46. Lic. in psychology, N.Y. State, Ohio; cert. Council for Nat. Register of Health Services; Bell Telephone Labs. grantee, 1964-65; NSF grantee, 1965-67; Kettering Found. grantee, 1978-80; Atlantic Richfield Found. grantee, 1980-82. Mem. Am. Psychol. Assn., Am. Econ. Assn., AAAS, Am. Soc. for Public Adminstrn. (pres. Central Ohio chpt. 1975-77), AAUP. Unitarian. Author: Higher Education in Social Psychology, 1968; co-author: Managing Innovation, 1982; contbr. articles to profl. jours. Home: 197 Riverview Park Dr Columbus OH 43214 Office: Sch Public Adminstrn Ohio State U 1775 College Rd Columbus OH 43210

LUNDY, BARBARA JEAN, public relations exec.; b. Frankfurt, Germany, Aug. 1, 1953; d. Roger J. and Helen E. (Branch) L.; B.A. in Journalism, Ohio State U., 1974. Edn. specialist Ohio Hist. Soc., Columbus, 1975-76; asst. chief communications Ohio Youth Commn., Columbus, 1976-79; public info. coordinator Central Ohio Transit Authority, Columbus, 1979-81; owner B.J. Lundy Enterprises, Columbus, 1981—; communications cons. Fedn. of Community Orgns., 1980, Driving Park Area Commn., 1980, Driving Park Civic Assn., 1980. Chairwoman membership com. Leadership Columbus, 1980-81; mem. Central Ohio Young Republicans Nominating Com., 1981. Mem. Public Relations Soc. Am. (public service com. 1980-81), Internat. Assn. Bus. Communicators (chairwoman accreditation exam com. 1981). Baptist. Club: Columbus Metropolitan. Contbr. articles to newspapers. Office: 1600 McKinley Ave Columbus OH 43222

LUNDY, LLOYD P., motel exec.; b. Vinita, Okla., Dec. 28, 1920; s. William Edward and Matilda May (Herod) L.; student pub. schs., Vinita; m. Ida M. Simms, Dec. 25, 1947; children—Connie Jean Lundy Norris, Jane Ann Lundy Matlock. Mgr. lessee Sands Best Western Motel, Salina, Kans., 1961-66; mgr. co-owner Vagabond Best Western, Hays, Kans., 1966—; gen. mgr. co-owner Continental Inn Best Western, Manhattan, Kans., 1967—; co-owner Budget Inn Vagabond II, Salina, Kans., Best Western Jayhawk Third, Junction City, Kans., Budget Inn Villa, Hays; owner Best Western La Fonda Motel, Liberal, Kans. Bd. dirs., past pres. Homer B. Reed Tng. and Adjustment Center, Hays. Served with USAAF, 1942-46. Mem. Kans. Lodging Assn. (dir. 1968—, pres. 1971-72, Man of Yr. 1974), Nat. Innkeeping Assn., Kans. Hotel/Motel Assn. (dir. 1980-81), Hays C. of C. (dir. 1968-72, 78—, pres. 1981-82), Am. Legion (past comdr.). Methodist. Clubs: Rotary, Masons, Shriners. Home: 205 Skyline Ct Hays KS 67601 Office: PO Box 822 Hays KS 67601

LUNN, JOSEPH KENNETH, ins. co. exec.; b. Chgo., Apr. 16, 1946; s. Joseph H. and Evelyn Marie (Migon) L.; B.A. in Psychology, North Park Coll., 1973; M.A. in Clin. Psychology, Roosevelt U., 1980. With Kemper Ins. Cos., 1969—, comml. underwriting analyst, Chgo., 1973-74, underwriting supr., Chgo., 1974-76, ins. mktg. specialist, Chgo., 1976—, mem. spl. task force to develop agy. computer interface, 1981—. Bd. dirs. Chgo. Urban Devel. Corp., 1973-74, PUSH, Chgo., 1978-79; mem. Citizens Com. on Battered Children, Chgo., 1973-75; chmn. Ill. Jaycees Govtl. Affairs Commn., 1975; chmn. events com., co-op edn. program Chgo. City Colls., 1976-78; pres. Chgo. Jaycee Found., 1977-78; vice chmn. bus. impact com. Citywide Advisory Com. Desegregation, Chgo., 1978-79; pres. Joint Orgn. to Promote Equality, Chgo., 1978-80; pres. Sch. for Treatment Emotional Problems in Children, Chgo., 1980-81; mem. computer tng. adv. com., edn. chair sickle cell com. Chgo. Urban League, 1977-78; mem. community affairs com. N.W. Community Mental Health Center, Chgo. Recipient numerous awards, including William D. Saltiel award Chgo. Jaycees, 1974, Disting. Service award, 1975, Community Service award, Sch. for Treatment Emotional Problems in Children, 1978; Beautiful People award Chgo. Urban League, 1980; named Vol. of Yr., Mental Health Assn., 1974; One of Chgo.'s Ten Outstanding Young Citizens, 1980. Mem. Chgo. Assn. Commerce and Industry (ex-officio dir. 1977-78), Chgo. Jr. Assn. Commerce and Industry (pres. 1977-78), World Trade Council, Ill. Psychol. Assn., M.W. Psychol. Assn., Cousteau Soc., Jazz Gallery. Democrat. Author: (study) Business Views the Public School Graduate, 1978; research on coping and def. in sickle cell patients, 1979; leader nat. fight for women's membership and withdrawal of Chgo. Jaycees from U.S. Jaycees, 1971-78. Home: 4124 N Central Park Ave Chicago IL 60618 Office: Kemper Group 330 E Main St Lake Zurich IL 60047

LUNTZ, HARRY ADAM, fin. exec.; b. Pitts., July 19, 1946; s. Henry Adam and Dorothy Marie (Hallstein) L.; B.B.A. cum laude, Drake Coll. of Fla., 1969; grad. Duff's Bus. Inst., 1966-67; m. Diana A. Conicella, July 19, 1969; children—Eileen Marie, Erica Ann, John Michael. Internal auditor H.K. Porter Co., Inc., Pitts., 1969; chief acct. Banks-Miller Supply Co., Huntington, W.Va., 1970-77; acctg. mgr. Tidewater Supply Co., Huntington, 1977—; mem. credit com. West vasamco Fed. Credit Union. Mem. Huntington Area Postal Customers Council, 1980-81. Mem. Am. Mgmt. Assn. Republican. Lutheran. Home: Route 2 PO Box 584 South Point OH 45680 Office: PO Box 1358 Huntington WV 25715

LUQUIRE, WILSON, univ. dean; b. Greenwood, S.C., July 28, 1942; s. William and Elizabeth (Styron) L.; B.A., Furman U., 1960; M.Mus., Ind. U., M.L.S., 1970, D.Mus., 1973, Ph.D., 1976. Librarian, Ind. U., 1969-76; mem. Council Library Resource Mgmt. Internship, 1976-77; asso. dir. library services, asso. prof. library services East Carolina U., 1977-80; dean library services, prof. Eastern Ill. U., 1980—. Served as officer USAR, 1963-65. Office: Eastern Ill U Charleston IL 61920

LURA, MICHAEL RAYMOND, state senator; b. Eldora, Iowa, Aug. 24, 1948; s. Geahard Raymond and Opal Mae (Fredrickson) L.; B.S. in Bus. cum laude, Columbus (Ga.) Coll., 1974; m. Susan Lee Revell, Sept. 15, 1967; children—Jason Robert, Jessica Leigh, Jillian Lee, Jacob Michael. Auditor, Def. Dept., Denver, 1974-75; mem. Iowa Ho. of Reps., 1979-80, Iowa Senate, 1981—. Exec. dir. Iowa Reagan-Bush Campaign, 1980; legis. campaign dir. Iowa Republican Com., 1981. Served with U.S. Army, 1968-72. Mem. Farm Bur., Am. Legion. Methodist. Club: Kiwanis. Office: State Capitol Des Moines IA 50319

LURIE, MAX LEONARD, psychiatrist; b. Cin., Aug. 5, 1920; s. Louis A. and Osna (Bernstein) L.; B.S., U. Cin., 1941, M.D., 1943; m. Miriam Rudnick, Apr. 23, 1944; children—Ona R., Ellen S. Intern, Cin. Gen. Hosp., 1944; resident psychiatry Ill. Neuropsychiat. Inst., Chgo., 1945, Psychopathic Hosp., Iowa City, Iowa, 1946; pvt. practice medicine, specializing in psychiatry, Cin., 1948—; sr. active staff Jewish Hosp., Cin.; mem. staff Christ Hosp., Cin. Gen. Hosp., Emerson North Hosp. (all Cin.); asso. clin. prof. psychiatry U. Cin., Coll. Medicine, 1973—. Bd. dirs. Children's Protective Service, 1963—. Served to capt. M.C., AUS, 1946-48. Fellow Am. Psychiat. Assn.; mem. A.M.A., Ohio Med. Assn., Ohio Psychiat. Assn., Cin. Psychiat. Soc., Central Neuropsychiat. Assn. (pres. 1981—), Acad. Medicine Cin. Contbr. articles to profl. jours. Home: 7402 Willowbrook Ln Cincinnati OH 45237 Office: 3120 Burnet Ave Apt 301 Cincinnati OH 45202

LUSCH, LAWRENCE JOSEPH, ednl. adminstr.; b. Centralia, Ill., Mar. 24, 1950; s. Bernard Lee and Betty Ruth (Rostance) L.; A.A. cum laude, Kaskaskia Coll., 1970; B.S. cum laude in Biology, So. Ill. U., Carbondale, 1972; M.Ed., U. Mo., St. Louis, 1980; m. Suzanne F. Beauchamp, Nov. 27, 1971; 1 dau., Chauntelle S. Tchr. sci., Ft. Zumwalt Sch. Dist., O'Fallon, Mo., 1972-75, sci. curriculum coordinator, 1975-79, tchr. sci., 1979-81, asst. prin. Ft. Zumwalt Central Jr. High Sch., 1981—; chmn. St. Charles-Lincoln County Regional Sci. and Engring. Fair, 1978-81. Mem. Assn. Supervision and Curriculum Devel., NEA, Am. Ednl. Research Assn., St. Louis Area Sci. Suprs., Nat. Sci. Tchrs. Assn., Phi Kappa Phi. Club: K.C. (O'Fallon). Home: 411 Imperial Ct O'Fallon MO 63366 Office: 210 Virgil St O'Fallon MO 63366

LUSCOMB, ROBERT CHARLES, JR., automobile mfg. corp. exec.; b. Lansing, Mich., Apr. 29, 1936; s. Robert Charles and Gertrude Ann Luscomb; B.S. in Mech. Engring., Gen. Motors Inst., 1958; S.M. in Mgmt. (Sloan fellow), Mass. Inst. Tech., 1970; m. Patricia L. Storkamp, Aug. 31, 1957; children—Mark C., Roberta D., Philip Z., James D. Supt. press plants Oldsmobile div. Gen. Motors Corp., Lansing, 1970-73, dir. prodn. engring., 1973-76, mgr. mfg. plants Cadillac div., 1976—. Active Boy Scouts Am., 1945—. Registered profl. engr., Mich. Mem. Soc. Automotive Engrs., Soc. Mfg. Engrs. Office: Cadillace Motor Car Div Gen Motors Corp 2860 Clark St Detroit MI 48232

LUSK, JEANNETTE CRAWFORD, ret. publisher; b. Huron, S.D., Aug. 1, 1905; d. Coe I. and Lavinia (Robinson) Crawford; student Coe Coll., 1923; student Huron Coll., 1924-26, L.H.D. (hon.), 1976; Hum.D. (hon.), S.D. State U., 1981; m. Robert Davies Lusk, Jan. 5, 1927 (dec. Dec. 1962); 1 dau., Victoria Coe. Pres., Huron Pub. Co., 1963-80; pub. Daily Plainsman, Huron, 1963-80; pres. Dakota West Corp., 1963-80. Mem. S.D. State Bldg. Authority, 1967-68; charter mem. S.D. Fine Arts Council, 1966-70. Bd. dirs. Huron United Fund, 1966, chmn. fund dr., 1967; charter mem. bd. S.D. Meml. Fine Arts Center, pres., 1969-75; trustee Huron Coll., 1967-73. Recipient Woman of Yr. award Huron Bus. and Profl. Women, 1972, S.D. Gov.'s award for outstanding support of arts, 1973; Distinguished Pub. Service award S.D. State U. Alumni Assn., 1976; Disting. Civic Service award Huron C. of C., 1979. Mem. P.E.O., Kappa Tau Alpha (hon.), Delta Kappa Gamma (hon.). Episcopalian. Home: 265 5th St SE Huron SD 57350

LUSK, RAYMOND FRANCIS, natural gas distbn. co. exec.; b. Lima, Ohio, Sept. 9, 1917; s. Raymond F. and Martha Frances (Vancleave) L.; student public schs., Columbus Grove, Ohio; m. Betty Jane McAdams, Oct. 29, 1944; children—Linda, Nancy, Cindy. Office mgr., gen. supr. Equity Dairy Stores, Inc., Lima, 1947-58; with West Ohio Gas Co., Lima, 1958—, mdse. salesman, 1958-60, bus. promotion, 1960-72, mgr. contracts and claims, 1972-74, utilization, conservation and public affairs mgr., 1972-77, adminstrv. asst., 1977—. Mem. Ohio Ho. of Reps., 1963-67; pres. Putnam County Regional Planning Commn., 1970-77; sec. Putnam County Bd. Mental Retardation, 1972-77; precinct committeeman Republican party, 1961—, chmn. Putnam County central and exec. coms., 1981; mem. Columbus Grove Bd. Edn., 1968-72, 74-78. Served with USMC, 1941-45. Mem. Am. Gas Assn., Nat. Mgmt. Assn., Lima Area C. of C. Republican. Mem. Ch. of Christ. Clubs: Elks, Lions (dist. gov. 1978-79). Home: 620 W Sycamore St Columbus Grove OH 45830 Office: 319 W Market St Lima OH 45802

LUTES, BILLY LOUIS, metalworking mfg. co. exec.; b. Blytheville, Ark., July 29, 1936; s. Harry Louis and Gertrude Lucille (Voss) L.; student U. Ark., 1954-57; B.S., Ark. State U., 1961; postgrad. Loyola U., Chgo., 1972-73. With Randall Co. div. Textron Inc., Cin., 1957-68, indsl. engr., 1967-68; controller Pyramid div. Indian Head Co., Chgo., 1968—, treas. Pyramid Employees Credit Union, 1971-81. Music dir. Calvary Bapt. Ch., Elgin, Ill. Mem. Am. Mgmt. Assn., Ill. Mfrs. Assn. Democrat.

LUTES, MARYBELLE PEARSON, mfrs. rep.; b. Chgo., Apr. 12, 1921; d. Carlo Arnold and Annie Laura (Fasten) Pearson; student U. Wis., 1937; m. John R. Lutes, June 20, 1941 (dec. July 1980); children—Jacqueline Karen, John. Sec., Ind. Rating Bur., South Bend, 1949-52; legal sec. to atty., Dowagiac, Mich., 1952-64; corp. officer John R. Lutes Co., Niles, Mich., 1952—, now sec.-treas. Mem. Election Canvas Bd., Niles, Mich., 1963-70. Republican. Home: 1205 Sassafras Ln Niles MI 49120 Office: 1400 Chicago Rd Niles MI 49120

LUTHAR, RAJINDAR SINGH, mathematician; b. Sialkot, Pakistan, Jan. 26, 1926; naturalized Am. Citizen; s. Hari Ram and Ved Kaur L.; B.A., Murray Coll., Pakistan, 1945; M.A., U. Ill., 1964; m. Raj Sehgal, Dec. 14, 1955; children—Harsh, Navneet, Vipan. Tech. asst. in-charge Govt. India, New Delhi, 1948-62; grad. teaching asst. U. Ill., Urbana, 1962-64; math. instr. Cheshire Acad., Cheshire, Conn., 1964-65; math. instr. Colby Coll., 1965-67; asst. prof. math. U. Wis. Center System, Janesville, 1967—. Mem. Waukesha Math. Soc. (founding mem.), Am. Math. Soc. Democrat. Hindu. Asso. editor Mathematics mag., 1979-80; founder math. jour. DELTA. Contbr. articles to profl. publs. Home: 1741 S Oakhill Janesville WI 53545 Office: U Wis Center Janesville WI 53545

LUTHER, ANDREW CHARLES, JR., playing card co. exec.; b. Kansas City, Mo., Dec. 17, 1942; s. Andrew C. and Virginia B. (Liscomb) L.; ed. Harvard U. and U. Cin.; m. Jane T. Stine, Mar. 9, 1972; children—Matthew Madison, Luke Robert. Asst. plant mgr. U.S. Playing Card Co., Cin., 1970-72, dir. indsl. relations, 1972-74, sales mgr., 1974-75, v.p. sales, 1975-76, pres., 1976—, also dir.; dir. Internat. Playing Card Co., Can. Playing Card Co. Clubs: Maketewah Country, Las Vegas Country, Queen City. Office: Beech and Park Sts Cincinnati OH 45212

LUTHER, DON PRESTON, assn. exec.; b. Flint, Mich., Dec. 8, 1920; s. Clarence Dar and Hazel Rhea (Crandall) L.; student U. Mich., 1952; B.A., Wayne State U., 1976; m. Frances Almeda Denton, June 3, 1943; children—Darleen R. Luther Hatt, Norma O. Luther Acton. Asst. ct. reporter St. Clair County, Port Huron, Mich., 1942; sec. San Diego Employers Assn., 1946-49; exec. sec. The Economic Club Detroit, 1949-64, asst. to pres., 1964-68, exec. dir., 1968—, sr. v.p., 1980—. Co-chmn. Mich. Rendezvous at EXPO 70, 1969-70; pres. Los Buenos Vecinos de Detroit, Spanish good neighbors club, 1958-59; bd. dirs. Lula Belle Stewart Center, 1976—. Served with USNR, 1942-45. Mem. Pub. Relations Soc. Am. (chpt. chmn. pub. service com. 1975-78), English-Speaking Union. Clubs: Circumnavigators (sec.-treas. Mich. chpt. 1980—), Renaissance, Detroit Press. Episcopalian. Home: 2211 Lafayette Towers E Detroit MI 48207 Office: 920 Free Press Bldg Detroit MI 48226

LUTHER, ROBERT ALAN, musician; b. Sibley, Iowa, Sept. 22, 1942; s. August A. and Carrie K. Luther; B.Mus., Drake U., Des Moines, 1964, M.Mus., 1966; postgrad. U. Mich., Eastman Sch. Music, Rochester, N.Y. Instr. piano organ in prep. dept. Drake U., 1964-66; instr. music theory Grand View Jr. Coll., Des Moines, 1964-66; asst. prof. music U. Evansville (Ind.), 1967-75, Carleton

Coll., Northfield, Minn., 1975—, also coll. organist, accompanist for coll. choir; recitalist throughout Midwest, concerts tours in Europe, also radio broadcasts; rep. by Phyllis Stringham Concert Mgmt. Mem. Am. Guild Organists (recitalist regional conv. Milw. 1981), Music Tchrs. Nat. Assn., Internat. Tchrs. Music Assn., Phi Mu Alpha Sinfonia, Pi Kappa Lambda. Lutheran. Home: 1190 Cannon Valley Dr Northfield MN 55057 Office: Carleton Coll Northfield MN 55057

LUTHER, WILLIAM PAUL, state senator; b. Fergus Falls, Minn., June 27, 1945; s. Leonard Henry and Eleanor (Suenneby) L.; B.S., U. Minn., 1967, J.D., 1970; m. Darlene Joyce Dunphy, 1967; 1 son, Alex. Admitted to Minn. bar; jud. clk. U.S. Ct. Appeals, 1970-71; practice law; mem. Minn. Ho. of Reps., from 1974, Minn. Senate, 1976—. Mem. Minn. Gov.'s Council Consumer Affairs, 1974—. Mem. Mpls. Citizens League, Hennepin County Legal Advice Clinics, Tau Beta Pi, Phi Delta Phi, Alpha Delta Phi. Roman Catholic. Office: 203 State Capitol Saint Paul MN 55155*

LUTZ, CARLENE, educator; b. Chgo., Feb. 4, 1946; d. John Calvin and Helen (Kwast) L.; student Chgo. Tchrs. Coll., 1964-65; B.S. in Edn., No. Ill. U., 1967; M.A. in Edn., U. Conn., 1971. Tchr., Chgo. Public Schs., 1967-69, adjustment tchr., 1969-70, reading resource tchr., 1971—; EPDA fellow U. Conn., 1970-71. Ill. State scholar, 1964-65, 65-67. Mem. Kindergarten Primary Assn. (pres. 1971-75), Chgo. Tchrs. Union (del.), Chgo. Assn. for Supervision and Curriculum Devel. (treas.), Delta Kappa Gamma. Home: 5400 S Walnut Pl Downers Grove IL 60515 Office: Hearst Sch 4640 S Lamon Ave Chicago IL 60638

LUTZ, GAIL LAVERNE MCGRADY, univ. adminstr.; b. Jackson, Miss., Oct. 12, 1941; d. Henry C. and Maude W. Skinner; B.A., DePaul U.; m. Craig Lutz; 1 son, Steven. Office mgr. Quartet Mfg. Co., Lincolnwood, Ill., 1960-66; internat. banking specialist Am. Express Co., Mannheim, Germany, 1967-69; sr. acct. Bland Lincoln Mercury, Chgo., 1969-70; exec. adminstr., office of pres. Johnson Products Co., Inc., Chgo., 1970-81; dir. univ. relations Sangamon State U., Springfield, Ill., 1981. Recipient cert. of leadership YMCA of Met. Chgo., 1975. Mem. Chgo. Urban League (recipient Beautiful Black People award 1976), People United to Save Humanity, Toastmasters Internat. Roman Catholic. Office: Sangamon State U Shepherd Rd PAC 570 Springfield IL 62708

LUTZ, RICHARD WILLIAM, biologist, educator, photographer; b. New Orleans, Mar. 10, 1938; s. William Ferdinand and Catherine May (Lumley) L.; B.S., Coe Coll., 1968; M.S., U. Iowa, 1970, Ph.D., 1975; m. Ruth Louise Wilmsmeyer, Aug. 1, 1965; 1 son, Michael Eugene. Field engr., IBM, Cedar Rapids, Iowa, 1961-65; grad. student dept. Botany, U. Iowa, Iowa City, 1968-75; propr. R.W. Lutz Photography, Iowa City, 1972—; postdoctoral asso. dept. pharmacology U. Iowa, Iowa City, 1975—: vis. asst. prof. dept. biology Augustana Coll., Rock Island, Ill., 1979-80. Served with USAAF, 1956-60. NDEA Title III fellow, 1968-70. Mem. AAAS, Electron Microscopy Soc. Am., Iowa Acad. Sci., Biol. Photographers, Profl. Photographers Am. Contbr. articles to profl. publs. Home: 1310 Esther St Iowa City IA 52240 Office: RW Lutz Photography 1700 1st Ave Eastdale Village Iowa City IA 52240

LUUS, GEORGE AARNE, physician; b. Estonia, Apr. 23, 1937; s. Edgar and Aili (Poldmaa) L.; M.D., U. Toronto (Ont., Can.), 1962; m. Margit Jaanusson, Sept. 14, 1962; children—Caroline Anna Elizabeth, Clyde Gregory Edgar, Lia Esther Isabelle. Intern Toronto East Gen. and Orthopaedic Hosp.; practice medicine specializing in family medicine, Sault Ste Marie, Ont., 1963—; mem. Algoma Dist. Med. Group, 1966—; sec. med. staff Gen. Hosp., 1972—, v.p., bd. dirs., 1973. Adv. bd. Can. Scholarship Trust Found., 1976-77. Mem. Algoma West Med. Acad., Acad. Medicine Toronto. Club: Rotary. Home: 42 Linstedt St Sault Ste Marie ON Canada Office: 240 McNabb St Sault Ste Marie ON P6B 1Y5 Canada

LUXENBERG, LEON, advt. firm exec.; b. N.Y.C., May 9, 1926; s. Morris and Beatrice (Jaffe) L.; B.B.A., CCNY, 1948; m. Gloria Knox, Aug. 28, 1948; children—Mitchell, Steven, Ellen. With Daniel Starch & Staff, N.Y.C., 1948-50, Am. Weekly mag., N.Y.C., 1950-55; dir. sales devel. CBS Radio Network, N.Y.C., 1955-70, CBS-TV, Chgo., 1970-76; sr. v.p., dir. network relations J. Walter Thompson Co., Chgo., 1976—. Served with USAAC, 1944-45. Home: 3126 Palm Ln Northbrook IL 60062 Office: J Walter Thompson Co 875 N Michigan Ave Chicago IL 60611

LUZADRE, JOHN HINKLE, obstetrician, gynecologist; b. Logansport, Ind., Dec. 4, 1921; s. John Franklin and Mary Gladys (Hinkle) L.; B.S., U. Pitts., 1942, D.D.S., 1945; M.D., Duke U., 1951; m. Barbara Louise Cary, Sept. 24, 1949; children—John Cary, Jo Ann, Robert Allan, David James, Timothy Hart. Instr., U. Pitts., Sch. Dentistry, 1947; intern Henry Ford Hosp., Detroit, 1951-52, resident in obstetrics and gynecology, 1952-55; practice medicine specializing in obstetrics and gynecology, Grosse Pointe Farms, Mich., 1955—; mem. staffs St. John Hosp., Detroit, Cottage Hosp., Grosse Pointe Farms. Served as capt. Dental Corps U.S. Army, 1945-47; ETO. Diplomate Am. Bd. Obstetrics and Gynecology. Fellow A.C.S., Am. Coll. Obstetrics, Gynecology; mem. Continental Gynecologic Soc., Alpha Omega Alpha. Republican. Presbyterian. Clubs: Country of Detroit; Hillsboro (Fla.); Tennis House (Grosse Pointe Farms). Home: 1311 Devonshire Rd Grosse Pointe Park MI 48230 Office: 25250 Kelly Rd Roseville MI 48066

LUZE, RICHARD JAMES, coll. adminstr.; b. Vinton, Iowa, Dec. 22, 1942; B.A., Drake U., Des Moines, 1965; postgrad. Boston U., 1965-66; m. Margaret Diane Mosimann; 1 son, David. Asst. to adminstrv. v.p. Garland Jr. Coll., Boston, 1966; mem. adminstrv. staff North Central Coll., Naperville, 1966—, asst. dir. admissions, 1968-69, dir. admissions, 1969—, also v.p. continuing edn. Mem. Nat. Assn. Coll. Admissions Counselors, Phi Delta Theta. Methodist. Office: North Central Coll Naperville IL 60540*

LYBERG, MATTHEW LOUIS, floor covering co. exec.; b. Howell, Mich., Aug. 3, 1947; s. John King and Phyllis Jane (Long) L.; B.A., Capital U., 1969; postgrad. Evang. Luth. Theol. Sem., 1969, U. Mich., 1970; m. Mary Anne Kennedy, June 17, 1972; children—Elizabeth Jane, Sarah Anne, Basil John, Matthew Peter. Asst., Rickett Sch. for Mentally Handicapped, 1962-64; Head Start tchr. Livingston County Intermediate Sch. Dist., Howell, summers, 1962-71; tchr., dir. phys. edn. St. Joseph Sch., Howell, 1971-72; tchr., Mich. Dept. Corrections, Camp Brighton, Pinckney, 1970-75; tchr. Livingston County (Mich.) Sheriff's Dept., 1972-73; pres. Hamburg Warehouse, Inc., Hamburg, Mich., 1972—; trustee dir. Workskills Corp., Brighton, Mich., 1975—, pres., 1980—; sports announcer Sta. WHMI, 1975—. Mem. fin. and stewardship bd. Zion Luth. Ch., Ann Arbor, Mich., 1979. Mem. Am. Assn. Mental Deficiency, Retail Floor Covering Inst., Jaycees, Fellowship of Christian Athletes. Clubs: Optimist, Kiwanis. Home: 524 W Sibley St Howell MI 48843 Office: 10588 Hamburg Rd Hamburg MI 48139

LYDIC, FRANK AYLSWORTH, ret. riverman, poet; b. Farnam, Nebr., Jan. 22, 1909; s. Robert Johnston and Lula Ethel (Aylsworth) L.; B.F.A., Kearney (Nebr.) State Coll., 1931; m. Florence Faye Meadows, July 2, 1934; children—Marcelle, Bernice Joy (dec.), Robert Norman. Tchr. schs., Calif., 1931-56; riverman various vessels Mississippi River, 1961—; del. Nat. Maritime Union Conv., 1966, 69, 72, 76, named union poet laureate, nat. conv., 1980. Served in U.S. Mcht. Marine, 1943-48, 56-61. Mem. Am. Acad. Poets, Western Writers Am. (asso.), Nebr. Writers Guild, Nebr. Poets Assn. (asso.), Ill. State Poetry Assn., Chgo. Poets and Patrons, Little Big Horn Assos. Democrat. Author: Desert Lure, 1971; Rhymes of a Riverman, 1973; When My Stretch on the River is Done, 1974; Nebraska! Oh Nebraska, 1975; San Francisco Revisited, 1976; At the Little Bighorn, 1976; The Far West's Race with Death, 1979; Rhymed Lines from the River, 1980. Home: PO Box 36 Joliet IL 60434

LYDON, DANIEL PATRICK, assn. exec.; b. Chgo., Mar. 19, 1924; s. John Joseph and Delia Theresa (Geraghty) L.; student DePaul U., 1946-49; m. Mary Louise Genette, Oct. 20, 1951; children—Daniel John, Patricia Delia, John Joseph, Stephen Michael. Reporter, editor Garfieldian Publs., Chgo., 1952-57; dir. pub. info. City of Chgo., 1957-68; exec. dir. Plumbing Council Chicagoland, 1968—; v.p. Plumbing Heating Cooling Info. Bur., 1979; sec.-treas. San Jose Cable TV Corp., 1968-79. Chmn., Chgo.'s St. Patrick's Day Parade, 1955-57, coordinator, 1958—; mem. adv. com. Sec. State Ill. Communications, 1972-76. Served with U.S. Army, 1943-45; ETO. Recipient Journalism award Ill. Press Assn., 1954, 55, 56. Mem. Am. Soc. San. Engring. (sec. Ill. chpt. 1971-75), Chgo. Hist. Soc., Chgo. Press Vets. Assn., Am. Soc. Assn. Execs. Clubs: Variety, Publicity, Irish Fellowship (chmn.), Execs., Chgo. Press (Chgo.). Editor: Pan-American Games, 1959 Yearbook; Comprehensive Plan of Chicago, 1966. Home: 11 Evergreen St Elk Grove Village IL 60007 Office: 1400 W Washington St Chicago IL 60607

LYDON, JEFFREY STANLEY, archtl. designer; b. St. Louis, Jan. 3, 1953; s. Thomas H. and Alicia (Kircher) L.; student Sch. Architecture, Washington U., 1971-76. Chief operating officer Renaissance Design Group, St. Louis, 1975-76; pres. Encore, Inc., St. Louis, 1976-77; ind. archtl. designer, St. Louis, 1977-78; project mgr. Union Center Venture, St. Louis, 1978; project mgr., partner St. Louis Sta., 1979—. Bd. dirs. Lafayette Sq. Restoration Com., 1976, 77-78; mem. preservation task force East-West Gateway Coordinating Council, 1976, housing task force Skinker-Debaliver Community Council, 1974. Mem. Assn. Preservation Technology, Am. Soc. Interior Designers, Mo. Mo. Bot. Garden. Office: 1820 Market St St Louis MO 63103

LYKOUDIS, PAUL S., educator; b. Preveza, Greece, Dec. 3, 1926; s. Savvas Paul and Loukia (Miliaressis) L.; came to U.S., 1953, naturalized, 1964; Mech. and Elec. Engring. degree, Nat. Tech. U. Athens (Greece), 1950; M.S. in Mech. Engring., Purdue U., 1954, Ph.D., 1956; m. Maria Komis, Nov. 26, 1953; 1 son, Michael. Mem. faculty Purdue U., 1956—, prof. aeros., astronautics and engring. scis., 1960-73, prof., head sch. nuclear engring., 1973—, dir. Aerospace Scis. Lab., 1968-73, Vis. prof. aero. engring. Cornell U., 1960-61; cons. RAND Corp., 1960—. NSF grantee, 1960—. Asso. fellow AIAA (former asso. editor jour.); mem. Am. Phys. Soc., Am. Astron. Soc., Am. Nuclear Soc., Sigma Xi. Contbr. numerous papers on fluid mechanics, magneto-fluid-mechanics, astrophysics, and fluid mechanics of physiol. systems. Office: Dept Nuclear Engring Purdue U Lafayette IN 47907

LYLE, WILLIS EDWIN, veterinarian; b. St. Clairsville, Ohio, Apr. 30, 1922; s. Edwin Ray and Lena Agnes (Boyd) L.; D.V.M., Ohio State U., 1944; M.S., U. Wis., 1951; m. Mildred Ellen Todd, Mar. 18, 1944; children—Robert, Thomas, Ted, Janet. Veterinarian, Edgerton, Wis., 1944-50; extension veterinarian U. Wis., Madison, 1950-51; veterinarian, Deerfield, Wis., 1952-62; dir. Wis. Animal Health Labs., Madison, 1962-77; adminstr. animal health div. Wis. Dept. Agr., Madison, 1977—; lectr. in field. Mem. Deerfield Sch. Bd., 1962-68; dir. Coop. Ednl. Service Area, 1966-68. Served with U.S. Army, 1943-44. Mem. Am. Assn. Veterinary Lab. Diagnosticians (pres. 1970), AVMA, Wis. Veterinary Med. Assn. (pres. 1963), North Central Animal Health Assn. (pres. 1979-81), U.S. Animal Health Assn. Club: Lions. Home: 29 Hannerville Rd Edgerton WI 53534 Office: 801 W Badger Rd Madison WI 53708

LYMAN, HOWARD B(URBECK), psychologist; b. Athol, Mass., Feb. 12, 1920; s. Stanley B(urbeck) and Ruth Mary (Gray) L.; A.B., Brown U., 1942; M.A., U. Minn., 1948; Ph.D., U. Ky., 1951; m. Patricia Malone Taylor, May 4, 1966; children—David S., Nancy M., D. Jane Lyman Paraskevopoulos; stepchildren—Richard P. Taylor, Martha C. Kitsinis, Robert M. Taylor, David P. Taylor. Acting dir. student personnel E. Tex. State Tchrs. Coll., Commerce, 1948-49; counselor, research asst. univ. personnel office U. Ky., Lexington, 1949-51; research psychologist tests and measurements U.S. Naval Exam. Center, Norfolk, Va. and Gt. Lakes, Ill., 1951-52; asst. prof. psychology U. Cin., 1952-62, asso. prof., 1962—; dir. Acad. Edn. and Research in Profl. Psychology Ohio 1975—. Served with AUS, 1942-46. Licensed psychologist, Ohio. Fellow Am. Psychol. Assn.; mem. Ohio (dir. 1960—, Distinguished Service award 1974), Midwestern, Cin. psychol. assns., Assn. Measurement and Evaluation in Guidance, Nat. Council Measurement in Edn., Psi Chi. Author: Single Again, 1971; Test Scores and What They Mean, 3d edit., 1978; editor Ohio Psychologist, 1967-79. Home: 3422 Whitfield Ave Cincinnati OH 45220

LYMAN, JANICE KAY, psychologist, psychiat. social worker; b. Macon, Mo., Jan. 3, 1945; s. John Thomas and Lorene (Nisbeth) L.; student Culver Stockton Coll., 1963-66; A.B., North East Mo. State U., 1971, M.A., 1977. Social worker Div. Family Services, Macon, 1966-69, dept. mental health Kirksville (Mo.) Regional Center for the Developmentally Disabled, 1970—. Religious edn. scholar Culver Stockton Coll. Mem. Am. Personnel and Guidance Assn. Mem. Christian Ch. Disciples of Christ. Home: 210 Jackson St Macon MO 63552 Office: 1702 E Laharpe St Kirksville MO 63501

LYMAN, LANCE LARM, elec. engr.; b. Ft. Wayne, Ind., Nov. 7, 1942; s. Richard Crowell and Mary Ann (Larm) L.; student U. Md.; m. Angelita Esmao; 1 son, Lawrence. Vol., Peace Corps, Malaysia, 1964-71, dir. communication Malaysian Ministry Interior, 1965-71; dir. for Asia and Pacific, Canadian Marconi Co., Manila, Philippines, 1977-80; v.p. systems Shefford Electronics Corp., Montreal, Que., Can., 1980—; cons. on high-tech. systems to Harris Corp., Melbourne, Fla. Served with USAF, 1959-63. Decorated by King of Malaysia, by Sultan of Selangor (Malaysia). Mem. IEEE, Armed Forces Communication and Electronics Assn., Am. Def. Preparedness Assn., Am. Cryptogram Assn., Am. Radio Relay League. Republican. Methodist. Home: 8759 Usher Rd Olmsted Falls OH 44138 Office: PO Box 1255 Melbourne FL 32901

LYNAGH, PETER MICHAEL, educator; b. Washington, June 3, 1935; s. James Joseph and Catherine Selina (Greene) L.; B.S., U. Md., 1960; M.B.A., U. Okla., 1964; Ph.D., Mich. State U., 1970; m. Patricia Butler, Oct. 28, 1961; children—Nancy Ellen, Michael James. Transp. specialist Western Electric Co., N.Y.C., 1960-61, Oklahoma City, 1961-64, Denver, 1964-65; instr. Mich. State U., East Lansing, 1965-68; asst. prof. U. Md., College Park, 1968-75; asso. prof. Concordia U., Montreal, Que., Can., 1975-78; asso. prof. mktg./transp. Kent (Ohio) State U., 1978—. Served with U.S. Army, 1954-56. Mem. Am. Advt. Fedn., Am. Mktg. Assn., Am. Soc. Traffic and Transp., Nat. Council of Phys. Distbn. Mgmt., So. Mktg. Assn., Assn. ICC Practitioners, Beta Gamma Sigma, Delta Sigma Pi, Delta Nu Alpha. Democrat. Roman Catholic. Contbr. articles to profl. jours. Home: 1121 Hawthorne Circle Sagamore Hills OH 44067 Office: Dept Mktg and Transp Kent State U Kent OH 44242

LYNCH, CHARLES THEODORE, scientist, adminstr.; b. Lima, Ohio, May 17, 1932; s. John Richard and Helen (Dunn) L.; A.A., George Washington U., 1953, B.S. in Chemistry, 1955; M.S., U. Ill., 1957, Ph.D. in analytical chemistry, 1960; m. Betty Ann Korkolis, Feb. 3, 1956; children—Karen Elaine, Charles Theodore, Richard Anthony, Thomas Edward. Grad. teaching asst. U. Ill., 1955-60; research materials engr. and lead scientist, USAF Materials Lab., Wright-Patterson AFB, Ohio, 1962-66; chief advanced metall. studies br., USAF-AFML, Ohio, 1966-72, sr. scientist, 1969-76, sr. scientist environ. effects, 1976-81; dir. materials div. Office Naval Research, Arlington, Va., 1981—; lectr. chemistry Wright State Campus, Miami (Ohio) State U., Dayton, 1964-66; Air Force liaison mem. Materials adv. bd. panel on solid processing Ad Hoc Com. on ceramic Process; mem. AIME-IMD Composites Com, 1968-75; mem. DoD Interagy. Panel on Stress Corrosion; mem. AFML Post-doctoral Com.; co-chmn. Dayton Conf. Composite Materials 1970; mem. adv. bd. Sci. and Engring. Inst. Dayton, 1969-71. Mem. Fairborn (Ohio) Pub. Sch. Parent Tchrs. Orgn., pres. 1967-69; choir dir. Univ. Bapt. Ch., Champaign, Ill., 1957-60, Wright-Patterson AFB Chapel II, 1960-64; mem. George Washington U., Traveling Troubadours, 1950-55; choir dir. Trinity United Ch. Christ, Fairborn, 1968-81; mem. Dayton Opera Chorus, 1979-81. Served to 1st lt. USAF, 1960-62, capt. Res. NSF fellow, summer 1959. Recipient numerous USAF patent awards; Award for Scientific Achievement, 1968. Mem. Am. Chem. Soc. (treas. Dayton sect. 1966), AIME (corrosion and environ effects com. 1974—, sec. 1980—, mem. composite materials com. 1968-75), Sci. Research Soc. Am., Alpha Chi Sigma, Omicron Delta Kappa, Phi Lambda Upsilon, Delta Sigma Rho. Baptist (choir dir.). Patentee in field. Contbr. articles to profl. jours.; editor Handbook of Materials Sci. series, 1974—; author: Book on Composites, 1970. Home: 387 Cherrywood Dr Fairborn OH 45324 Office: Materials Div Office Naval Research Arlington VA 22217

LYNCH, FREDERICK, JR., banker; b. N.Y.C., Sept. 24, 1914; s. Frederick Henry and Maude (Dutton) L.; grad. Lincoln Sch. of Tchrs. Coll., N.Y.C., 1932; Colgate U., 1936; m. Janet W. Spurrier, Nov. 30, 1936; children—Frederick III, Holly Reid (Mrs. Hilborn). Mgr. personnel Western Union Telegraph Co., N.Y.C., 1936-42; dir. indsl. relations ABC, N.Y.C., 1942-50; with Central Nat. Bank Cleve., 1950—, v.p. personnel, 1955-57, sr. v.p. personnel and gen. services, 1957-67, sr. v.p. staff and community relations, 1967-73, sr. v.p. corporate relations and pub. affairs, 1973-79; exec. v.p. George S. Voinovich Inc., Cleve., 1979—. Former mem. faculty N.Y. U., Stonier Grad. Sch. Banking, Rutgers U. Bd. dirs., chmn. finance com. Regional Transit Authority, 1975—; past mem. bd., mem. exec. com. Greater Cleve. chpt. A.R.C., past chmn. Cleve. chpt.; past trustee United Appeal Greater Cleve.; bd. dirs. WVIZ Ednl. TV Assn. Mem. Greater Cleve. Growth Assn., Am. Inst. Banking, Am. Mgmt. Assn., Newcomen Soc. N.Am., Phi Kappa Psi. Clubs: Country, Clevelander. Home: 12000 Edgewater Dr Lakewood OH 44107 Office: 1224 Huron Rd Cleveland OH 44115

LYNCH, GEORGE ARTHUR, physicist; b. Titusville, Pa., May 4, 1938; s. Harvey Thomas and Georgianna Beatrice (Porter) L.; B.S. in Engring. Physics, Wright State U., 1974; m. Lucille Joyce Rocco, May 9, 1959; children—Kim R., Tammy A., Terri J. Research devel. specialist USAF, Dayton, Ohio, 1964-74, physicist acoustics, 1974, physicist electro-optics, 1974—. Commr., Boy Scouts Am., 1973; chmn. Mad River Sch. Bd. Adv. Com.. 1974. Served with USAF, 1956-64. Decorated AF Commendation medal, Order of Engr. Mem. Ohio Soc. Profl. Engrs., Am. Legion, DAV, Nat. Rifle Assn., Ohio Congress Parents and Tchrs. (hon. life), League Ohio Sportsmen (dist. v.p.), Ohio Wildlife Fedn. (dist. v.p., trustee), Wright State U. Alumni Assn. (life). Clubs: Eagles; Wright Patterson AFB Rod and Gun (past pres.). Home: 5649 Hunters Ridge Dayton OH 45431 Office: FTD SQS Wright Patterson AFB OH 45433

LYNCH, JACK CHARLES, broadcasting exec.; b. Lidgerwood, N.D., Mar. 29, 1921; s. Jack Francis and Alice (Mapes) L.; student St. Thomas Coll., 1939-40, Wis. State Coll. at LaCrosse, 1945-46; m. Mayme Qvale, Jan. 30, 1942; children—Jack, Michael, Kathleen, Shannon. Announcer radio sta. WMIN, Mpls. St. Paul, 1939-40, radio sta. WKBH, LaCrosse, 1942-46; announcer radio sta. KWLM, Willmar, Minn., 1940-42, sales mgr., 1946-68, mgr., 1968—. Mem. Minn. Higher Edn. Coordinating Commn., 1965—, pres., 1973; mem. Willmar Sch. Bd., 1960-69, pres., 1966-68; mem. New Ulm (Minn.) Diocesan Sch. Bd., 1969-72; mem. Karishon Dist. exec. bd. Viking council Boy Scouts Am., 1956—, chmn., 1956-61; mem. Kandiyohi County (Minn.) Fair Bd., 1956—; mem. Willmar United Fund Bd., 1955—, pres., 1955-56; state chmn. Brotherhood Week NCCJ, 1960; bd. dirs. Rice Meml. Hosp., Willmar, 1981—; mayor of Willmar, 1973-76. Served with USAAF, 1942-45. Recipient Silver Beaver award Boy Scouts Am., 1962. Roman Catholic. Lion, K.C. Home: 618 W 10th St Willmar MN 56201 Office: Station KWLM Willmar MN 56201

LYNCH, JAMES FRANCIS, mfg. exec.; b. Cohoes, N.Y., May 30, 1921; s. Frederick J. and Anne (Byrnes) L.; B.S., Siena Coll., 1952; M.B.A., U. Buffalo, 1955; postgrad. N.Y. U., 1952-53, Siena Coll., 1953-54, Xavier U., 1967-68; m. Catherine E. Dolon, June 1, 1946; children—James Francis, Mary J., Edward J., Robert P., Catherine A. Chief indsl. engr. Watervliet Arsenal, 1947-52; plant mgr. Am. Locomotive Co., Schenectady, 1952-58; dist. mgr., nat. sales mgr. Ladish Co., Milw., 1958-68; plant mgr. W. J. Baker Co., Newport, Ky., 1968-77, spl. asst. to pres., 1978-80; contract adminstr. Western Stress Inc., 1980—; tchr. adult edn. State N.Y., 1948-52. Rector, founder Curcillo de Christianity, Cin., Louisville, Memphis, Columbus, Ohio, Kansas City, Mo., Covington, Ky. Served with U.S. Army, 1942-45; ETO. Decorated D.F.C. with one cluster, Air medal with six clusters, Purple Heart (3). Mem. Am. Mktg. Assn., Am. Mgmt. Assn., Assn. Tool and Mfg. Engrs. Democrat. Roman Catholic. Clubs: Nat. Rifle Assn., Ohio Gun Collectors, Cin. Revolver, Village Indian Hill Gun. Home: 1282 Aldrich Ave Cincinnati OH 45231 Office: PO Box 1177 Newport KY 41071

LYNCH, JAMES VICTOR, educator; b. New Tazewell, Tenn., Dec. 4, 1919; s. Charles G. and Martha M. Lynch; B.S. in Agr., U. Tenn., 1950; postgrad. Purdue U., 1955-56; m. Gwen Malone Lynch, Feb. 11, 1941; children—Brenda, Vickie. Tchr., Prairie Twp. High Sch., Sharpsville, Ind., 1951-63; tchr. vocat. agr. No. Community, Tipton County, Ind., 1964—, Tri-Central High Sch., Sharpsville, Ind., 1964-70; adv. Future Farmers Am., 1950-81. Served with USN, 1940-46. NSF grantee, River Falls State Coll., 1963. Mem. Nat. Vocat. Agr. Tchrs. Assn., Nat. Vocat. Tchrs. Assn., Ind. Vocat. Agr. Tchrs. Assn., Ind. Vocat. Tchrs. Assn. Republican. Club: Masons.

LYNCH, JERRY LEE, mag. sales exec.; b. Cleve., Jan. 25, 1936; s. John Joseph and Margaret Evelyn (Abbey) L.; student John Carroll U., 1955-56, 60-61; m. Martha L. Loges, Apr. 16, 1966; children—Daniel, Michael, Timothy, Sean, Colleen, Katherine. Sales rep. IBM, 1960-65; advt. account exec. Fox & Assos., 1965-68; v.p., regional mgr. De/Jour. mag., Cleve., 1968-75; dist. mgr. Newsweek mag., Cleve., 1975-78, Detroit, 1978-79; Detroit br. mgr. advt. sales Inside Sports mag., 1979-81; Detroit mgr. Nat. Geographic, 1981—; public speaker. Served with USN, 1955-60. Named Media Salesman of Yr., Cleve., 1975. Mem. Detroit Advt. Assn., Indsl. Marketers Assn., Indsl. Marketers of Detroit. Republican. Roman Catholic. Clubs: Oakland Hills Country, Bloomfield Open Hunt (Birmingham, Mich.); Shaker Heights (Ohio) Country; Hermit, TF (Cleve. pres. 1974), (Cleve.); Pitts. Press; Fairlane (Detroit); Optimist (charter pres. Mentor 1975). Home: 5569 Cromwell Ct West Bloomfield MI 48035 Office: 3000 Town Center 720 Southfield MI 48075

LYNCH, JOHN JAMES, judge; b. Chgo., June 28, 1915; s. John Joseph and Mary C. (Duffin) L.; B.A., Ohio State U., 1938, J.D., 1940; m. Vernie Rogan, Sept. 13, 1947 (dec. May 1968); children—John, Arlene, Dennis; m. 2d, Emma Gentile Bartholomew, Aug. 9, 1975. Admitted to Ohio bar, 1940; spl. agt. FBI, 1940-43; practice law, Youngstown, 1946-65; asst. atty. gen., 1959-63, judge Ct. of Appeals, 7th appellate dist. Ohio, 1965—, chief justice, 1977—. Mem. Ohio Ho. Reps., 1949-58, chmn. Democrat mems. policy com., 1957; chmn. Mahoning County com. Bus. and Profl. Men and Women for Kennedy-Johnson, 1960. Served with AUS, 1943-46. Mem. Am., Ohio, Mahoning County bar assns., Ohio State Alumni Assn., Amvets, Am. Legion, Nat. Counter Intelligence Corps Assn. Democrat. Roman Catholic. K.C. Home: 2718 Normandy Dr Youngstown OH 44511 Office: Ct House Youngstown OH 44503

LYNCH, JOHN JOSEPH, JR., banker; b. Chgo., Feb. 7, 1947; s. John J. and Erma E. (Staman) L.; B.A., St. Benedict's Coll., 1969; m. Stephanie Loftin, Sept. 27, 1980. Loan officer Palatine (Ill.) Nat. Bank, 1970-73; asst. v.p. Deerfield (Ill.) State Bank, 1973-74; v.p., div. head comml. loans LaSalle Nat. Bank, Chgo., 1974—. Served with U.S. Army, 1969-70. Mem. Am. Bankers Assn., Ill. Mfrs. Assn., Robert Morris Assos. Clubs: K.C., Inverness Golf, Univ. Address: 135 S LaSalle St Chicago IL 60690

LYNCH, LARRY LEE, mfg. co. exec.; b. Liberal, Kans., June 28, 1949; s. Laurel L. and Maurine A. (Hunter) L.; A.A., Hutchinson Jr. Coll., 1969; postgrad. Kans. State U., 1969-70; B.S., Central Mo. State U., 1975, M.B.A., 1978; m. Denise C. Richmond, Oct. 17, 1970; children—Kelly Patrick, Casey Scott, Courtney Ryan. Grad. asst. fin. aids and collections Central Mo. State U., 1977; adminstrv. asst. H. Lynn White, Inc., Lenexa, Kans., 1979; prodn. planner Bendix Corp., Kansas City, 1979-80; mfg. supr., 1980—. Served with USAF, 1970-77. Cert. tchr., Mo. Mem. Am. Businessmen's Communications Assn. Methodist. Club: Bendix Corp. Mgmt. Home: 1404 Tomahawk Ln Olathe KS 66062 Office: 2000 E Bannister St Kansas City MO 64131

LYNCH, MARTIN JOSEPH, systems analyst; b. Youngstown, Ohio, Sept. 2, 1950; s. Martin Joseph and Agnes Marie (Slavin) L.; B.S., Marquette U., Milw., 1972; M.S., U. Wis., Milw., 1977; m. Mary Jean Bjork, July 13, 1974. Sr. systems analyst data processing-ops. support Northwestern Mut. Life Ins. Co., Milw., 1972—; lectr. U. Wis., Milw.; 1978—. Cert. data processor. Mem. Assn. Computing Machinery. Roman Catholic. Home: 5925 N Santa Monica Blvd Whitefish Bay WI 53217 Office: 720 E Wisconsin Ave Milwaukee WI 53202

LYNCH, REGINALD SHELDON, fast food exec.; b. Charleston, W.Va., Dec. 13, 1937; s. Bernard Grey and Eileene Louise (Burks) L.; B.S., Hampden-Sydney Coll., 1959; m. Doris Ann Davis, Sept. 27, 1966; children—Reginald Sheldon, Deborah, Lisa, Pamela. Vice pres. Four Flags Internat., Inc., Mpls., 1964-66, Sveden House Internat., Mpls., 1966-69; pres., chief exec. officer The White House, Mpls., 1969-70; div. mgr. Church's Fried Chicken, Inc., St. Louis, 1970-78; pres. Reggie's Fried Chicken, Inc., St. Louis, 1978—; guest lectr. St. Louis Community Coll. at Forest Park, 1980—. Bd. dirs. Martin Luther King Jr. Meml. Fund. Mem. Minn. Restaurant Assn. (past dir.), Mo. Restaurant Assn. (pres. St. Louis chpt. 1981—, state bd. dirs.), Nat. Restaurant Assn. (exec. mem.), Foodservice Execs. Assn., NAACP, Congress of Racial Equality (patron). Democrat. Baptist. Contbr. articles to profl. jours. Home: 1405 Schulte Rd Saint Louis MO 63141 Office: 1340 S 7th St Saint Louis MO 63104

LYNG, ANNA L., home economist; b. Thendara, N.Y., Aug. 1, 1920; d. William Scott and Mary Elizabeth (Stoeber) L.; diploma in hosp. dietetics Rochester Inst. Tech., 1940; B.S., Syracuse U., 1943. Dietitian, Iola Sanatorium, Rochester, N.Y., 1940-41, Auburn (N.Y.) City Hosp., 1943-44, Univ. Hosp., Syracuse, N.Y., 1944-45; home service rep. Rochester Gas & Electric Co., 1947-53; with laundry/home care products Procter & Gamble Co., Cin., 1953—, dir. home econs. 1963—. Served with U.S. Army, 1945-47. Mem. Am. Home Econs. Assn., Am. Apparel Mfrs. Assn., Am. Assn. Textile Chemists and Colorists, ASTM, Ohio Home Econs. Assn., Home Economists in Bus., Elec. Women's Round Table (past nat. pres.), Assn. Home Appliance Mfrs., Soap and Detergent Assn. Republican. Presbyterian. Club: Order Eastern Star. Contbr. articles in field to profl. jours. Home: 7901 Burgundy Ln Cincinnati OH 45224 Office: Procter & Gamble Co Ivorydale Technical Center 5299 Spring Grove Ave Cincinnati OH 45217

LYNN, ARTHUR DELLERT, JR., educator, economist; b. Portsmouth, Ohio, Nov. 12, 1921; s. Arthur Dellert and Helen B. (Willis) L.; student Va. Mil. Inst., 1938-39, U.S. Naval Acad., 1939; B.A., Ohio State U., 1941, M.A. in Econs., 1943, J.D., 1948, Ph.D. in Econs., 1951; postgrad. Law Sch., U. Mich., 1968-70; m. Pauline Judith Wardlow, Dec. 29, 1943; children—Pamela Wardlow, Constance Karen, Deborah Joanne, Patricia Diane. Mem. faculty Ohio State U., 1941—, prof. econs., 1961—, asso. dean Coll. Commerce and Adminstrn., 1962-65, asso. dean faculties, 1965-70, lectr. Coll. Law, 1961-67, adj. prof. law, 1967—, prof. public adminstrn., 1969—, lectr. exec. devel. program, 1958-71, acting dir. div. public adminstrn., summers 1973, 74, acting dir. Sch. Public Adminstrn., summer 1975; vis. prof. econs. Ohio Wesleyan U., 1958-59, U. Calif.-Berkeley, summer 1972; admitted to Ohio bar, 1948, U.S. Supreme Ct., 1966; mem. firm Lynn & Lynn, Portsmouth, 1949-50; mem. Ohio Gov.'s Econ. Research Council, 1966-70. Trustee Griffith Meml. Found. Ins. Edn.; chmn. external econs. adv. com. Marietta Coll., 1975-79. Served to 1st lt. F.A., AUS, 1942-46. Mem. Am. (chmn. com. state and local taxes sect. taxation 1961-63), Ohio, Columbus bar assns., Am., Midwest, Royal econs. assns., AAUP, Nat. Tax Assn. (chmn. com. model property tax assessment and equalization methods and procedures 1961-65, mem. exec. com. 1965-73, v.p., pres. 1969-70), Tax Inst. (adv. council 1960-63), Nat. Tax Assn.-Tax Inst. Am. (sec. 1975—), Am. Arbitration Assn. (nat. panel), AAAS, Acad. Mgmt., Ohio Council Econ. Edn. (dir. 1964-74), Com. on Taxation, Resources, and Econ. Devel. (chmn. 1979—), Internat. Fiscal Assn., Inst. Internat. des Finances Publiques, Internat. Assn. Assessing Officers (edn. adv. com.), Omicron Delta Epsilon, Beta Theta Pi, Phi Delta Phi, Beta Gamma Sigma, Pi Sigma Alpha. Episcopalian. Clubs: Rotary; Faculty, Athletic, Torch (Columbus). Editor: The Property Tax and Its Administration, 1970; Property Taxation, Land Use and Public Policy, 1976. Editorial adv. bd. Tax Bramble Bush, 1959-70, Am. Jour. Econs. and Sociology, 1980—; asso. editor Nat. Tax Jour., 1971—. Office: 1775 S College Rd Columbus OH 43210

LYNN, ELIZABETH MEAGHER, mgmt. tng. cons.; b. Oshkosh, Wis.; d. Joseph E. and Gertrude J. (DeYoung) Meagher; B.A., Marygrove Coll., Detroit, 1960; M.A., Villanova U., 1962; M.Ed., Columbia U., 1971; Ph.D., Ind. U., 1974; m. Lowell A. Lynn (dec.). Chem. sales corr. Westvaco, 1963-65; tchr. English, Phila. Bd. Edn., 1965-66; film production coordinator Marathon Internat. Productions, 1966; broadcast editor Nat. Assn. Broadcasters, Code Authority, 1966-67; writer CBS-TV's 21st Century, Nat. Citizens Com. Public Broadcasting, 1967-68; lectr. City Coll. N.Y., 1968-71; asso. instr. Ind. U., 1971-74; instr. Cuyahoga Community Coll., Cleve., 1974-75; sr. research asso. Case Western Res. U., Cleve., 1975-76; communications cons., profl. lectr., Cleve., 1976-77; staff asso.-tng. Standard Oil Co. (Ohio), Cleve., 1977; speaker, cons. corps., univ. schs. mgmt., profl. assns.; speech writer, lectr.; editorial reviewer profl. manuscripts ERIC, Wadsworth and Addison-Wesley publishing orgns. Grantee, Nat. Inst. Edn., Ind. U., Pi Lambda Theta, Hunter Coll. (CUNY), Villanova U.; fellow Columbia U. Mem. Am. Arbitration Assn., Am. Soc. Tng. and Devel., Speech Communication Assn., Am. Bus. Communication Assn., Alpha Psi Omega (hon.), Lambda Iota Tau (hon.), Pi Lambda Theta (hon.). Author: Improving Classroom Communication, 1976; co-author U.S. govt. HEW report: The Role of the Professional Nurse in Primary Health Care; contbr. articles to profl. jours., ERIC system. Office: Standard Oil Co (Ohio) 1517 Midland Bldg Cleveland OH 44115

LYNN, MARY ANN, educator; b. Cleve., Nov. 22, 1936; d. Willard J. and Leava A. (Woodward) Frederick; B.S. in Edn., Miami U., Oxford, Ohio, 1958; M.S. in Edn., Kent State U., 1960; Ed.D. (Edn. Profl. Devel. Act fellow), Ill. State U., 1974; m. Richard M. Lynn, July 11, 1959; 1 dau., Kelly Elizabeth. Instr. bus. edn. Youngstown (Ohio) U., 1960-64; instr. Ill. State U., 1966-68, asso. prof. ednl. adminstrn. and founds., 1977—; tchr. Univ. High Sch., Normal, Ill., 1968-73, dept. chmn., 1970-73, adminstrv. asst., 1972-73, prin., 1973-77; mem. profl. evaluation teams. Mem. Nat. Assn. Secondary Sch. Prins, Ill. Bus. Edn. Assn. (pres. 1973-74), Nat. Bus. Edn. Assn., Ill. Vocat. Assn., Am. Vocat. Assn., Am. Assn. Sch. Adminstrs., Ill. Assn. Sch. Adminstrs., Ill. Prins. Assn., Phi Delta Kappa, Delta Kappa Gamma. Editor Planning & Changing, 1980—. Office: 331 De Garmo Hall Ill State U Normal IL 61761

LYNN, MICHAEL EDWARD, III, profl. football team exec.; b. Scranton, Pa., May 18, 1936; s. Robert Norman and Gertrude (Smith) L.; student Pace U.; m. Jorja Swaney, July 12, 1967; children—Louisa, Robert, Michael Edward, Lucia. Mgr., Dixiemar-Corondolet, Inc., Memphis, 1965-67; pres. Mid South Sports, Inc., Memphis, 1967-74; v.p., gen. mgr. Minn. Vikings, 1974—; founder East-West All Am. Basketball Game, 1968, Mid South Prodn. Co., 1970; chief exec. officer Memphis Am. Basketball Team, 1970. Founder Morris County Theatre League and Highstown Little Theatre Group, 1961. Served with U.S. Army, 1955-58. Roman Catholic. Office: Minnesota Vikings 9520 Viking Dr Eden Prairie MN 55344

LYNN, ROBERT ATHAN, coll. dean; b. Oak Park, Ill., Nov. 11, 1930; s. Harvey L. and Mabel (Brian) L.; B.S., Maryville (Tenn.) Coll., 1951; M.S., U. Tenn., 1955; Ph.D. (Ford Found. fellow), U. Ill., Urbana, 1958; m. Naomi Burgos, Aug. 28, 1954; children—Mary Lou, Nancy, Judy, JoAn. Mem. faculty Maryville Coll., 1955-64, prof., 1962-64; asso. prof. bus. adminstrn. Whiteman AFB program U. Mo., Columbia, 1964-66, prof., dir. program, 1966-68; dean Coll. Bus. Adminstrn., prof. Kans. State U., Manhattan, 1968—. Served with AUS, 1952-53. Mem. Am. Mktg. Assn., Midwest Mktg. Assn., Am. Econ. Assn., Midwest Econ. Assn., So. Econ. Assn. Democrat. Club: Rotary. Author: Basic Economic Principles, 1965, 70, 74, 80; (with James P. O'Grady) Elements of Business, 1978.

LYON, EDWARD ELLSWORTH, geographer; b. Paxton, Ill., Dec. 14, 1930; s. Ellsworth Douglas and Dorothy (Cooper) L.; B.S. in Edn., Ill. State U., 1958, M.S. in Edn., 1959; Ph.D. in Sci. Edn., Ohio State U., 1972; m. Carol Jeanne Roth, Aug. 21, 1954; children—Wesley, Teresa, Thomas, Tamara, Timothy. Tchr., Danvers (Ill.) High Sch., 1958-59; mem. faculty Ball State U., Muncie, Ind., 1959—, prof., 1976—, chmn. dept. geography and geology, 1973-80; sci. cons., public schs. Served with USAF, 1951-55. NSF grantee, 1962-63. Mem. Assn. Am. Geographers, Nat. Council Geog. Edn., Am. Meteorol. Soc., Hoosier Assn. Sci. Tchrs., Ind. Acad. Social Scientists. Mem. Soc. Friends. Sr. author: Earth Science: A Programmed Text, 1965; Earth Science Manual, 4th edit., 1975; Physical Geography and Earth Science: A Programmed Text Review Manual, 1978. Sr. editor: Indiana: Crossroads of America, 1978. Home: 921 Riley Rd Muncie IN 47304 Office: Dept Geography and Geology Ball State U Muncie IN 47306

LYON, JAMES ROBERT, utility co. exec.; b. Otterville, Mo., Nov. 30, 1927; s. William H. and Laura Virginia (Eubank) L.; student Missouri Valley Coll., 1945-46; B.S. in E.E., U. Mo., 1951; m. Janet Drescher, Sept. 1, 1951; children—Sally Beth, Suzanne. Substa. engr. Bonneville Power Adminstrn., Portland, Oreg., 1951-53; with Iowa Power and Light Co., Des Moines, v.p. ops., 1966-71, sr. v.p., 1971-73, exec. v.p., 1973-79, pres., 1979—. Active United Way, Des Moines; bd. dirs. Mercy Hosp., Des Moines; bd. dirs. Des Moines Area Community Coll. Found. Served with U.S. Army, 1945-47. Mem. IEEE, Nat. Soc. Profl. Engrs., Iowa Engring. Soc., Iowa Mfg. Assn. Office: Iowa Power and Light Co 666 Grand Ave Des Moines IA 50303

LYON, STERLING, premier Man. (Can.); b. Windsor, Ont., Can., Jan. 30, 1927; s. David Rufus and Ella Mae (Cuthbert) L.; B.A., U. Winnipeg, 1948; LL.B., U. Man., 1953; m. Barbara Jean Mayers, Sept. 26, 1953; children—Peter, Jonathan, Nancy, Andrea, Jennifer. Admitted to Man. bar, 1953; crown atty., dep. atty. gen. Man., 1953-57; mem. Man. Legis. Assembly, 1958-69; atty. gen. Man., 1958-63, minister of municipal affairs, 1960-61, of public utilities, 1961-63, 66-69, of mines and natural resources, 1963-66, of tourism and recreation, 1966-68, commr. No. affairs, 1966-68; corp. counsel, 1969-74; leader of opposition; mem. Man. Legis. Assembly, 1976-77; Premier of Man., 1977—; pres. Can. Council Resource Ministers, 1965-66. Chmn., 1st Can. Conf. on Pollution, Montreal, 1966; del. Hague Conf. on Pvt. Internat. Law, 1968; past trustee Wildlife Found. Man., N.Am. Wildlife Found.; bd. regents U. Winnipeg. Served in RCAF Res., 1950-53. Recipient U. Winnipeg Alumni Assn. Jubilee award, 1973; created Queen's Counsel, 1960. Mem. Law Soc. Man., Can., Man. bar assns. Progressive Conservative. Mem. United Ch. Club: Winnipeg Trap and Skeet. Office: Office of Premier 204 Legislative Bldg Winnipeg MB R3C 0V8 Canada

LYONS, BERNARD ANTHONY, publisher; b. Peoria, Ill., Apr. 23, 1932; s. Edward Joseph and Mary Ellen (Brettner) L.; student Loyola U., Chgo., 1958-61; m. Louise Marie Caron, Sept. 15, 1962; children—Benedict, Edward, Martin, Therese, Michael, Mary Ellen. News editor Peoria Register, 1955-57; editor, bus. mgr. AIM newspaper, Chgo., 1957-59; supr. public relations Old Equity Life Ins. Co., Evanston, Ill., 1959-60; publisher, editor Voice Publs., pub. newsletters on direct mktg./mail order, including Key, Mail Order Counselor, Mail Order Product, Mail Order Info. Seller, Goreville, Ill., 1960—; cons. U.S. direct mail order firms. Served with USAF, 1951-55. Author: Parish Councils: Renewing the Christian Community, 1967; Programs for Parish Councils, 1968; Voices from the Back Pew, 1970; Leaders for Parish Councils, 1971. Office: Voice Publs Goreville IL 62939

LYONS, J. ROLLAND, civil engr.; b. Cedar Rapids, Iowa, Apr. 27, 1909; s. Neen T. and Goldie N. (Hill) L.; B.S., U. Iowa, 1933; m. Mary Jane Doht, June 10, 1924; children—Marlene Lyons Sparks, Sharon Lyons Hutson, Lynn Lyons Panichi. Jr. hwy. engr. Works Projects Adminstrn. field engr. Dept. Transp., State Ill., Peoria, 1930-31, civil engr. I-IV Central Office, Springfield, 1934-53, civil engr. V, 1953-66, municipal sect. chief, civil engr. VI, 1966-72. Civil Def. radio officer Springfield and Sangamon County (Ill.) Civil Def. Agy., 1952—. Recipient Meritorious Service award, Am. Assn. State Hwy. Ofcls., 1968; 25 Yr. Career Service award, State Ill., 1966; Certificate Appreciation, Ill. Municipal League, 1971. Registered profl. engr., Ill.; registered land surveyor, Ill. Mem. Ill. Assn. State Hwy. Engrs., State Ill. Employees Assn., Am. Pub. Works Assn., Am. Assn. State Hwy. Ofcls., Amateur Trapshooters Assn. Clubs: K.C., Sangamon Valley Radio; Lakewood Golf and Country. Address: 3642 Lancaster Rd Springfield IL 62703

LYONS, JERRY LEE, engr.; b. St. Louis, Apr. 2, 1939; M.E., Okla. Inst. Tech., 1964. Project engr. Harris Mfg. Co., St. Louis, 1964-70; project engr. Essex Cryogenics Industries, Inc., St. Louis, 1970-73, also v.p.; mgr. engring. research Fluid Controls div. Chemtron Corp., St. Louis, 1973—; pres. Yankee Ingenuity Inc., St. Louis, 1974—; adj. prof. Bradley U., 1977—; chmn. exec. com. Mo. U. Continuing Engring. Edn., St. Louis, 1980-81. Chmn. exec. adv. bd. continuing edn. Mo. U., Columbia, 1980-81; mem. U.S. Congressional Adv. Bd., 1981—. Registered profl. engr., Calif.; cert. mfg. engr. in product design. Mem. St. Louis Soc. Mfg. Engrs. (chmn. 1979-80) Soc. Mfg. Engrs. for Registration in Mo. (chmn. 1976), Nat. Fluid Power Assn. (mem. com. 1974-76), ASME (chmn. valve com. of ops., applications and components div. 1975—), Am. Security Council (mem. nat. advisory bd. 1975—), Nat. Soc. Profl. Engrs., Mo. Soc. Profl. Engrs., Soc. Mfg. Engrs., Instrument Soc. Am., St. Louis Engrs. Club (award of merit 1977), Computer and Automated Systems Assn. (chmn. 1980). Author: Lyons Encyclopedia of Valves, 1975; ISA Handbook Control Valves (with J.W. Hutchinson), 1976; ISA Control Valve Study Series on Acuators and Accessories, 1981; Lyons' Valve Designers Handbook, 1980; The Designers Handbook of Pressure Sensing Devices, 1979. contbr. articles, papers to profl. jours. Home: 7535 Harlan Walk Saint Louis MO 63123 Office:

LYONS, THOMAS HARSHMAN, librarian; b. Detroit, Apr. 15, 1923; s. Ward Irving and Margaret Smith (Peters) L.; student Olivet Coll., 1940-43; B.A., Wayne State U., 1947, M.S. in Edn., 1949, Edn. Specialist in Instructional Tech., 1977; A.M. in L.S., U. Mich., 1964; m. Harriet Ann Hamilton, July 8, 1944; children—Norman Hamilton, David John, Thomas Michael. Tchr., librarian West Bloomfield Schs., Orchard Lake, Mich., 1949-67; librarian, audio-visual dir. Northwood Inst., Midland, Mich., 1967-74; asso. prof., dir. audio visual services Oakland U., Rochester, Mich., 1974-78; dir. media center Mid-Mich. Community Coll., Harrison, 1978—. Active Inst. Sch. Library Personnel Western Mich. U., 1965, Media Inst. Mich. State U., 1968-69. Served with AUS, 1943-46. Mem. Mich. Library Assn., Assn. for Ednl. Communications and Tech., Mich. Assn. for Media in Edn., Mich. Soc. Instructional Tech. Home: 2315 Cheltingham Sylvan Lake MI 48053 Office: Mid Mich Community Coll Harrison MI 48625

MA, ALEX, surgeon; b. Toronto, Ont., Can., June 6, 1930; s. Timothy K. Wou and Anna (Lee) M.; M.A. in Physiology and Biochemistry, U. Toronto, 1954, M.D., 1958; m. Grace Ling, June 20, 1959 (dec. 1981); children—Brian Andrew, Enid Ann, Alison Celeste, Charles Edward, Peter Timothy. Intern Toronto Gen. Hosp., 1958-59; resident Toronto East Gen. Hosp., 1959-61, U. Hosp., Saskatoon, Sask., 1961-63; fellow surgery U. Sask., 1963-64; mem. staff Mississauga (Ont.) Hosp., 1965-69, 70—, Oasis Hosp., Abu Dhabi, Arabian Gulf, 1969-70, 72, 75. Chmn. bd. Young Men's Christian Inst., Toronto, 1972—. Fellow Royal Coll. Physicians and Surgeons Can. Presbyn. (elder). Address: 687 Sir Richards Rd Mississauga ON Canada

MA, DAVID CHIA-CHIUN, civil engr.; b. China, Aug. 10, 1948; came to U.S., 1971; s. Chou-Chi and Fong-Ming Ma; M.S. in Civil Engring., Ill. Inst. Tech., 1974, Ph.D., 1976; m. Linda Hsia, Sept. 2, 1978. Civil engr. Reactor Analysis and Safety Div., Argonne (Ill.) Nat. Lab., 1976—. Mem. ASCE, Sigma Xi. Home: 5534 W Lawrence Ave Chicago IL 60630 Office: 9700 S Cass Ave Argonne IL 60439

MAACK, H. DENNIS, mgmt. cons.; b. Wichita, Kans., Oct. 22, 1942; s. Harold C. and Oretta (Jones) M.; B.A., Southwestern Coll., 1964; B.D., So. Meth. U., 1967; M.A., U. Kans., 1973, Ph.D., 1976; m. Nova A. Kilgore, Jan. 21, 1965; 1 son, Steven K. Ordained to ministry, United Meth. Ch., Kans. Conf., 1967; minister Kans. Conf., 1967-72; asst. instr. communications and group dynamics U. Kans., 1972-75; pres. Communications Consulting, Lawrence, Kans., 1972-77; mgr. orgn. devel. B.F. Goodrich Co., Akron, 1977-80; dir. personnel Nordson Corp., Amherst, Ohio, 1980—; orgn. cons. Democratic precinct committeeman, Wichita, 1968. Mem. Am. Psychol. Assn., Orgn. Devel. Network, Internat. Assn. Applied Social Sci., Consultant/Trainers S.W. Office: 555 Jackson St Amherst OH 44001

MAAG, ALLEN WAYNE, electronics co. exec.; b. Chgo., June 12, 1949; s. Edward J. and Genieve (Citrano) M.; B.A. in Communication, U. Ill., 1971; m. Michaelle Rotman, June 15, 1974. With Magnecraft Electric Co., Chgo., 1971-74, advt. mgr., 1973-74; dir. advt. and communications Molex Inc., Lisle, Ill., 1974—. Mem. Meeting Planners Internat. Assn., Nat. Trade Show Assn. Republican. Roman Catholic. Club: Fox Valley Ad. Office: Molex Inc 2222 Wellington Ct Lisle IL 60532

MAAHS, WERNER H., foods co. exec.; b. Milw., Jan. 15, 1927; s. William H. and Marie (Mueller) M.; grad. high sch.; m. Gladys M. Anderson, June 24, 1950; children—Sandra Marie, Nancy Jean, Christine Lynn, David Werner, Judy Annette. Patrolman, White Fish Bay (Wis.) Police Dept., 1950-54; pres. Alto Shaam, Inc., Milw., 1955-59; v.p. Chicken Delight, Inc., Rock Island, Ill., 1956-64; pres. Chicken Delight of Calif., Los Angeles, 1959-64; pres., dir. Franchise Devel. Corp., Los Angeles, 1962-64; chmn. bd. Chicken Delight Eastern, Inc., Paterson, N.J., 1962-64; partner Linkletter, Maahs, Bolte & Assos., Inc., 1965—; pres. Buffalo Bill's Steak Village, Inc., 1965-70, Buffalo Bill's Wild West, Inc., Los Angeles, 1967-70, Buffalo Bill's Properties Inc., 1968-70; v.p. Fitzgerald, Maahs & Miller Assos., 1965-70; v.p. Alto Shaam Inc.; pres. M & M Enterprises, Inc.; regional dir. Chicken Delight, Inc., Los Angeles; dir., producer Adventure Prodns., Inc., 1969; sales mgr. Hanna Industries, Inc., 1970-71; gen. mgr. franchise sales TraveLodge Internat., Inc., 1971-73; v.p. Energy Savs. Appliances Corp., 1977-80, A.W. Huss Co., 1980, Alto Shaam Internat.; pres. Natural Lite Food Products Corp., 1979; dir. Computoreturn Tax Preparation Service, Captain Tim's Seafood Galley, Chicken Delight Southwestern, Inc., Dallas, Rewdco Distbg. Co. Mem. ethics com. Internat. Franchise Assn., 1959-64; del. White House Conf. on Small Bus., 1980. Mem. Creative Mktg. Assos., Nat. Assn. Food Equipment Mfrs. Lutheran (pres. council). Home: N63 W

33959 Lakeview Dr Oconomowoc WI 53066 Office: 6040 Flint Rd Milwaukee WI 53209

MAAS, MAX EDWARDS, mfg. co. exec.; b. Massena, Iowa, Nov. 27, 1931; s. Glenn D. and Ruth M. (Edwards) M.; B.A., U. Ala., 1957; m. Judy Prehn, May 27, 1978; children—Todd, Scott, John. Gen. mgr. Atlantic Bottling Co., Atlantic, Iowa, 1958-63; regional mgr. Seven-Up Co., St. Louis, 1963-64; gen. mgr. Creston (Iowa) Bottling Co., 1964-67; with Cornelius Co., Anoka, Minn., 1967—, v.p. sales and mktg. 1979—. Served with USAF, 1952-56. Decorated Purple Heart. Mem. Sales and Mktg. Execs. Mpls., Anoka C. of C. (dir. 1979—), Am. Legion, V.F.W. Republican. Lutheran. Club: Elks. Home: 15861 NW Dolomite St Anoka MN 55303 Office: Cornelius Co One Cornelius Place Hwy 10W Anoka MN 55303

MAASS, ARTHUR EDWARD, mfg. co. exec.; b. Rochester, Minn., Sept. 8, 1937; s. Arthur Herbert and Mary Elizabeth (Clark) M.; A.A., Rochester Jr. Coll., 1957; B.B.A., U. Minn., 1959; m. Diane Beverly Duncanson, Sept. 13, 1958; children—Deborah Jean, John Edward, Thomas Lester. Sales staff Gen. Mills Inc., Mpls., 1959-77, product sales mgr., 1971-77; pres. Magne Corp., Inc., Mpls., 1977—, also dir., London. Mem. Detroit Jaycees (past dir.). Patentee shelf mgmt. device. Home: 2405 Xylon Ave N Minneapolis MN 55427 Office: MagneCorp Shelard Tower Minneapolis MN 55426

MAASS, VERA SONJA, psychologist; b. Berlin, Germany, July 6, 1931; d. Willy Ernst and Walli Elisabeth (Reinke) Keck; came to U.S., 1958, naturalized, 1970; B.A., Monmouth Coll., 1971; M.A., Lehigh U., 1974; Ph.D., U. Mo., 1978; m. Joachim A. Maass, Dec. 24, 1954. Teaching asst. Lehigh U., Bethlehem, Pa., 1971-72; tutor in adult basic edn. Teaching Assistance Orgn., Kansas City, Mo., 1973-74; grad. research asst. U. Mo., Kansas City, 1974-76; intern U. Ky. Med. Sch., Lexington, 1975-76; psychologist-therapist Dunn Mental Health Center, Richmond, Ind., 1976-80, psychologist; br. dir., Winchester, Ind., 1980—; developer, conductor workshops in rational behavior therapy, Lexington, 1975-76, Richmond, 1976-77; v.p. Vitatronics, Inc., Wall, N.J., 1969—. Recipient Cert. of Appreciation, Ky. Coll. Medicine, 1978; cert. sex counselor. Mem. Am. Personnel and Guidance Assn., Nat. Council Family Relations, Internat. Assn. Applied Psychology, Am. Psychol. Assn., Internat. Platform Assn., Psi Chi. Contbr. articles to profl. jours. Home: 221 N Meridian St Winchester IN 47394

MAAZEL, LORIN, conductor, violinist; b. Paris, France, Mar. 6, 1930 (parents U.S. citizens); s. Lincoln and Marie (Varencove) M.; Mus.D. (hon.), U. Pitts., 1965; H.H.D., Beaver Coll., 1973; m. Israela Margalit; children—Anjali, Daria, Fiona, Ilann. Debut as conductor, 1938, condr. major orchs. U.S. 1938—, festivals in Edinburgh (Scotland), Bayreuth (Germany) and Salzburg (Germany), Orange (France), Lucerne (Switzerland); world tours include Japan, Latin Am., Australia, USSR; dir. Deutsche Oper Berlin and Radiosymphonic Orch., Berlin, 1964-75; prin. guest condr. Philharm. London; music dir. Radio France; condr., dir. Cleve. Orch.; recs. for London Records, Columbia Records, Philharmonia. Office: Cleveland Orch 11001 Euclid Ave Cleveland OH 44106

MABEL, THOMAS ARTHUR, physician; b. Hammond, Ind., Dec. 4, 1941; s. Arthur A. and Wilma L. (Shrock) M.; A.B., Ind. U., 1964, M.D., 1970; m. Nancy L. Barnes, June 17, 1967; children—Andrew Joseph, Leann Kristin. Intern, Meth. Hosp., Indpls., 1970-71, resident in family practice, 1973-74; practice family medicine, Noblesville, Ind., 1975—. Served with USAF, 1971-73. Diplomate Am. Bd. Family Practice. Mem. Am. Acad. Family Physicians, Sigma Alpha Epsilon. Home: 1222 Willow Way Noblesville IN 46060 Office: 110 Lakeview Dr Noblesville IN 46060

MACAROL, MARY ELVIRA, village ofcl.; b. Chgo., May 30, 1923; d. Fred and Josephine (Karlovich) Kulich; student bus. Fox Coll., 1970-71, Morraine Valley Jr. Coll., 1971-72; m. Anthony Macarol, May 4, 1946; children—Joseph Anthony, Marc Anthony. Clk. Village of Chicago Ridge (Ill.), 1965—, lectr. in field. Mem. Mcpl. Finance Officers Assn., Mcpl. Treas.'s Assn. (asso.), Mcpl. Clks. Ill., Mcpl. Clks. Assn. S. and W. Suburbs (pres.), Internat. Inst. Municipal Clks., St. Mary's Alumnae (pres. 1943-44), Our Lady of the Ridge Altary and Rosary (pres. 1960-61). Democrat. Roman Catholic. Club: Brother Rice Mother's (pres. 1964-65). Home: 5843 W 108th Pl Chicago Ridge IL 60415 Office: 10655 S Oak St Chicago Ridge IL 60415

MAC CAUGHELTY, THOMAS CAMERON, physician; b. Glen Ridge, N.J., July 16, 1944; s. Thomas and Naomi Elizabeth (Ferguson) MacC.; A.B. (William Neal Reynolds scholar), Duke U., 1965; postgrad. Emory U. Sch. Medicine, 1965-66; M.D., U. N.C., 1969; m. Bennie Jo (Jody) Riley; children—Adela Elizabeth, Michael Cameron, Marissa Lynn, Ashley Knight. Intern, U. Calif. Med. Center, San Francisco, 1969-70; resident in anesthesiology U. N.C., 1972-74, resident in anesthesiology in intensive care, 1974-75; pvt. practice medicine specializing in anesthesiology and critical care medicine, Lynchburg, Va., 1975-76; attending anesthesiologist Washington U. Med. Center, St. Louis, 1976-77; anesthesiologist, specialist in critical care medicine St. Joseph's Hosp., St. Louis, 1977—, also chmn. intensive care com.; instr. anesthesiology U. N.C., 1975, Washington U., 1976. Served with USAF, 1970-72. Diplomate Am. Bd. Anesthesiology. Fellow Am. Coll. Anesthesiologists; mem. Am. Soc. Anesthesiologists, Internat. Anesthesia Research Soc., Soc. Critical Care Medicine, St. Louis Soc. Critical Care Medicine, Soc. Neurosurg. Anesthesia and Neurol. Supportive Care, AMA, Mo. State Med. Soc., St. Louis Med. Soc. (councillor), Am. Soc. Clin. Hypnosis, So. Med. Assn., Alpha Omega Alpha, Pi Sigma Alpha. Presbyterian. Club: Kirkwood (Mo.) Optimist. Home: 12764 Spruce Pond Rd Town and Country MO 63131 Office: St Joseph Hosp 325 Couch St Kirkwood MO 63122

MACCHIA, DONALD DEAN, physiologist, pharmacologist; b. Gary, Ind., May 17, 1948; s. Michael D. and Elizabeth (Pilla) M.; A.B., Ind. U., 1971; M.S., U. Ill., 1974, Ph.D. in Physiology and Biophysics, 1977; m. Gloria Jean Sicuro, Jan. 25, 1969; children—Anthony Phillip, Marianne Michelle. Chemist, U.S. Steel Corp., 1970-71; grad. teaching asst. dept. physiology and biophysics U. Ill., Urbana, 1972-74; instr. physiology Columbia U. Faculty of Medicine, N.Y.C., 1974-75; research asso. medicine cardiology sect. U. Chgo., 1976-77, research asst. prof. physiology and pharmacology, 1977-79; asst. prof. physiology and pharmacology Ind. U. Sch. Medicine, Gary, 1979—, mem. grad. faculty, 1980—. Sunday sch. tchr. Trinity Gospel Ch., 1978-80; bd. dirs. Christian Assembly Ch., 1980—. Nat. Heart, Lung and Blood fellow, 1977-79; NIH research award, 1980. Mem. Am. Physiol. Soc., Am. Heart Assn., Biophys. Soc., AAAS, Internat. Soc. for Heart Research, Soc. Gen. Physiologists, Sigma Xi. Republican. Contbr. articles to sci. jours. Office: Indiana Univ School of Medicine Northwest Center for Education 3400 Broadway Gary IN 46408

MAC CREADY, INGRID MARIA, instrument mfg. co. exec.; b. La Paz, Bolivia, Nov. 21, 1940; came to U.S., 1961, naturalized, 1963; d. Albert and Ilse S. (Wienmannn) Samter; B.A., Am. Inst., La Paz, 1959; M.Langs., U. Munich (W. Ger.), 1961; divorced; children—Paul Barclay, Howard V. Export clk. Packard Internat. Co., Downers Grove, Ill., 1971-74; internat. ops. mgr. Portec Inc., Oakbrook, Ill., 1974-76, Sargent Welch Sci. Co., Skokie, Ill., 1976-78; mgr. internat. div. Continental Can Co., 1978—, also supr. internat. distbn.; pres. Westwind Maritime, 1981—. Mem. exec. bd. Darien Youth Club. Mem. N.W. Internat. Trade Club (sec. Ill. 1979-80), Nat. Assn. Female Execs. Republican. Christian Scientist. Home: 7333-3 Winthrop Way Downers Grove IL 60515 Office: 1700 Harvester Rd West Chicago IL 60185

MACDONALD, ELMER, concrete co. exec., state legislator; b. Cin., Mar. 24; s. Eugene and Dora (Mueller) MacD.; B.S. in Bus., Ind. U., 1952; m. Hyrlene Alice Ivy, Aug. 26, 1950; children—Gregory E., Suzanne. Electrician, Westinghouse Electric Corp., Cin., 1946-49; machinist Zollner Piston Corp., Ft. Wayne, Ind., 1949-53; gen. mgr. Erie Materials, Inc., Ft. Wayne, 1953-57; with W&W Concrete Inc., Roanoke, Ind., 1957—, v.p., gen. mgr., 1957-61, pres., gen. mgr., 1961—; mem. Ind. Ho. of Reps., 1965-66, 71-78, Ind. Senate, 1979—; dir. Home Loan & Savs. Assn., Advance Mixers, Inc. Mem. Allen County (Ind.) Council, 1969-70. Served to capt. U.S. Army, 1942-46; ETO. Decorated Bronze Star, Purple Heart; Ky. col.; named Sagamore of the Wabash, Ind. Mem. Nat. Ready Mixed Concrete Assn., Midwest Ready Mixed Concrete Assn., Am. Concrete Inst., Nat. Home Builders Assn., Associated Gen. Contractors Assn., Ft. Wayne C. of C., Res. Officers Assn., VFW (comdr. local post 1969-70). Republican. Presbyterian. Clubs: Rotary, 100 Percent, Elks (exalted ruler Lodge 155, 1968-69), Shriners (potentate 1976—, v.p. Gt. Lakes Shrine Assn.). Office: care State Legislature Indianapolis IN 46204*

MACDONALD, LESLIE WALDROP, coll. adminstr.; b. Chgo., Mar. 15, 1948; d. Roy Eugene and Shirley Ann (Keitz) Waldrop; B.A. in Spanish, Northeastern Ill. U., Chgo., 1970; M.Ed., Loyola U., Chgo., 1975; m. J. Fred MacDonald, Oct. 16, 1971. Grad. placement officer, then coordinator alumni affairs Northeastern Ill. U., 1971-75; dir. career services Truman Coll., Chgo., 1975-79; dir. ednl. services for bus., industry and govt. Oakton Community Coll., Des Plaines, Ill., 1979—. Mem. Am. Soc. Tng. and Devel., Adult Edn. Assn., Nat. Assn. Women Deans, Adminstrs. and Counselors, Northbrook C. of C. (trustee), Civil War Roundtable, Sierra Club, Nat. Wildlife Found. Author book revs. Home: 2744 W Rascher St Chicago IL 60625 Office: 1600 E Golf Rd Des Plaines IL 60016

MACDONALD, REYNOLD COLEMAN, steel co. exec.; b. Billings, Mont., Oct. 7, 1918; s. Donald and Claudia (Reynolds) MacD.; student Los Angeles City Coll., 1936-37; m. Mary Helen Smith, Mar. 27, 1938; children—Glory, Darcy. Asst. gen. supt. Kaiser Steel Corp., Fontana, Calif., 1946-63; v.p. ops. Lone Star Steel Co. (Tex.), 1963-67; pres., dir. Interlake Steel Corp., Chgo., 1967-69, pres., chief exec. officer, 1969-81, chmn., chief exec. officer, 1981—; dir. Central Nat. Bank, ARA Services, Inc., Parker Hannifin Corp. Pres., Cucomonga (Calif.) Sch. Bd., 1961-63. Mem. Am. Iron and Steel Inst. (dir.), Assn. Iron and Steel Engrs. (pres. 1972, dir.), Chgo. Assn. Commerce and Industry (dir.), U.S. Auto Club (dir.). Club: Masons. Office: Interlake Steel Corp 2015 Spring Rd Oak Brook IL 60521*

MACDONOUGH, JOHN NEWMAN, mktg. exec.; b. Detroit, Dec. 7, 1943; s. William A. and Elizabeth (Newman) MacD.; m. Kathleen M. Sullivan, Jan. 11, 1981. Product mgr. Gen. Mills, Inc., Mpls., 1968-77; Natural Light mktg. mgr. Anheuser-Busch, Inc., St. Louis, 1977-78, Budweiser mktg. mgr., 1978-79, group mktg. mgr., 1979-80, v.p. brand mgmt., 1980—; dir. Anheuser-Busch Internat., St. Louis, Black Sports Network, Washington. Club: Racquet. Office: 1 Busch Pl Saint Louis MO 63118

MAC DOUGALL, BRUCE BARTON, public health adminstr.; b. Pontiac, Mich., Sept. 8, 1933; s. Alfred Putnum and Irene Majorie (Moss) MacD.; R.N., Harper Hosp., 1960; B.S., Drury Coll., 1971; M.A., U. Detroit, 1976; div.; children—Douglas, Curtis. Supr. Rehab. Inst. Detroit, 1960-68; asst. dir. nursing Pontiac (Mich.) Osteo. Hosp., 1968-72; dir. nursing Genesee Meml. Hosp., Flint, Mich., 1972-78; acting dir. nursing, dir. edn. Riverbend Nursing Home, Grand Blanc, Mich., 1978-79. Mem. Mich. Public Health Assn., ARC. Republican.

MAC DOUGALL, GENEVIEVE ROCKWOOD, journalist, educator; b. Springfield, Ill., Nov. 29, 1914; d. Grover Cleveland and Flora Maurine (Fowler) Rockwood; B.S., Northwestern U., 1936, M.A., 1956, postgrad., 1963—; m. Curtis D. MacDougall, June 20, 1942; children—Priscilla Ruth, Bonnie MacDougall Cottrell. Reporter, Evanston (Ill.) Daily News Index, 1936-37; asso. editor Nat. Almanac & Yearbook, Chgo., 1937-38, News Map of Week, Chgo., 1938-39; editor Springfield (Ill.) Citizens' Tribune, also area supr. Ill. Writers Project, 1940-41; reporter Chgo. City News Bur., 1942; tchr. English-social studies Skokie Jr. High Sch., Winnetka, Ill., 1956-68, coordinator TV, 1964-68; tchr. English Washburne Sch., Winnetka, 1968-81; editor Winnetka Public Schs. Jour., Winnetka Public Schs. Newsletter, 1981—; dir. Winnetka Jr. High Archeology Field Sch., 1971—; cons., lectr. in field. Winnetka Tchrs. Centennial Fund scholar, 1964, 68. Named Tchr. of Year, Winnetka, 1976; Educator of Decade, Northwestern U. and Found. for Ill. Archeology, 1981. Mem. Winnetka Tchrs. Council (pres. 1971-72), Nat., Ill. edn. assns., Ill. Assn. Advancement Archeology, Women in Communications (pres. N. Shore alumni chpt. 1949-53), Pi Lambda Theta. Author: Grammar Book VII, 1963, 68; (with others) 7th Grade Language Usage, 1963, rev. 1968. Contbr. articles to profl. publs. Home: 537 Judson Ave Evanston IL 60202 Office: 515 Hibbard Rd Winnetka IL 60093

MACDOUGALL, PRISCILLA RUTH, lawyer; b. Evanston, Ill., Jan. 20, 1944; d. Curtis Daniel and Genevieve Maurine (Rockwood) MacD.; B.A., Barnard Coll., 1965; grad. degree with honors U. Paris, 1967; J.D., U. Mich., 1970. Admitted to Wis. bar, 1970, Ill. bar, 1970; asst. atty. gen. State of Wis., 1970-74; lectr. law U. Wis. Law Sch. and System, 1973-75; staff counsel Wis. Edn. Assn. Council, 1975—; speaker, cons., organizer on women's rights, names, labor and edn. issues. Mem. Wis. State Bar (founder and chairperson sect. on individual rights and responsibilities 1974-76, 78-79), Am. Bar Assn., Dane County Bar Assn., Legal Assn. For Women (founding steering com.), Nat. Women and Law, ACLU, NOW. Contbr. articles to legal jours. Home: 346 Kent Ln Madison WI 53713 Office: 101 W Beltline Hwy Madison WI 53708

MAC GIBBON, JAMES DUNCAN, radiologist; b. Mpls., Feb. 13, 1935; s. Everett Elsworth and Lucinda (Hedding) Mac G.; B.A., U. Minn., 1956, M.D., B.S., 1960; m. Janice Roberta Booker, Aug. 22, 1959; children—Susan Anne, Bruce Everett, Nancy Lynn. Intern, Mpls. Gen. Hosp., 1960-61; resident in radiology VA Hosp., Mpls., 1964-67, U. Minn., Mpls., 1964-67; practice medicine specializing in radiology, Edina, Minn., 1968—; mem. staffs Suburban Radiologic Cons. Ltd., Fairview Hosp., Mpls., Fairview Southdale Hosp., Edina. Served with M.C. USAF, 1962-63. Mem. AMA, Minn. State Med. Assn., Hennepin County (Minn.) Med. Soc., Minn. State Radiol. Soc., Am. Coll. Radiology, Radiol. Soc. N.Am. Roman Catholic. Clubs: Decathlon Athletic, Olympic Hills Golf. Home: 6601 Iroquois Trail Edina MN 55435 Office: 471 Southdale Med Bldg Edina MN 55435

MAC GREGOR, DONALD MAX, electronic engr.; b. U.K., Oct. 2, 1949; B.A. in Math., Cambridge (Eng.) U., 1970; Ph.D. in Electronic Engring., Univ. Coll. North Wales, 1973. Lead engr. Electrocon Internat., Inc., Ann Arbor, Mich., 1973—. Quaker. Office: Electrocon Internat Inc 611 Church St Ann Arbor MI 48104

MACHINIS, PETER ALEXANDER, civil engr.; b. Chgo., Mar. 12, 1912; s. Alexander and Catherine (Lessares) M.; B.S., Ill. Inst. Tech., 1934; m. Fay Mezilson, Aug. 5, 1945; children—Cathy, Alexander. Civil engr. Ill. Hwy. Dept., 1935-36 engr., estimator Harvey Co., Chgo., 1937; project engr. PWA, Chgo., 1938-40; supervisory civil engr. C.E., Dept. Army, Chgo., 1941-78; asst. to project mgr. Chgo. Urban Transp. Dist., 1978—; partner MSL Engring. Consultants, Park Ridge, Ill., 1952—. Mem. Civil Def. Adv. Council Ill., 1967—. Served with USAF, also C.E., U.S. Army, 1943-45; ETO; lt. col. Res. ret. Registered profl. engr., Ill. Fellow Soc. Am. Mil. Engrs.; mem. ASCE (life), Nat. Soc. Profl. Engrs. (life), Am. Congress Surveying and Mapping, Assn. U.S. Army, Greek Orthodox (ch. trustee). Home: 10247 S Oakley Ave Chicago IL 60643 Office: 123 W Madison St Chicago IL 60602

MACIAS, DONA MAE, nurse; b. Walcott, Iowa, Sept. 21, 1927; d. Walter and Lillian Bertha (Sinksen) Dietz; R.N., U. Iowa, 1949; children—Pamela Ann, David Lee. Staff nurse neurology dept. U. Iowa, Iowa City, 1949-50; head nurse psychiat. unit Immanuel Hosp., Mankato, Minn., 1950-51, St. Peter (Minn.) State Hosp., 1951-56; dir. nurses Minn. Security Hosp., St. Peter, 1963—. Democrat. Roman Catholic. Home: 145 Shadywood Ave Mankato MN 56001 Office: 2000 Minnesota Ave St Peter MN 56082

MAC INTOSH, JAMES FRANCIS, IV, ins. co. exec.; b. Gary, Ind., Nov. 27, 1946; s. James Francis and Emiliee Viola (Padol) MacI.; student U. Notre Dame, 1964-67; B.S., Ind. U., 1970; m. Barbara Stone, Dec. 28, 1968; children—Mitsi M., James Francis. Retail advt. rep. Gary (Ind.) Post Tribune, 1968-70; sales asst. Mut. of N.Y., Hinsdale, Ill., 1970-74, gen. sales mgr., 1974-80; gen. sales mgr. Hinsdale Assos., 1980—. Pres. Ardmore Assn., Libertyville, Ill., 1978—. Served with U.S. Army, 1970. C.L.U., cert. bus. planning specialist, cert. estate planning specialist. Mem. Nat. Assn. Life Underwriters (chmn. sales conf.), Notre Dame Alumni Assn., Ind. U. Alumni Assn., Vincennes Alumni Assn., Scottish Tartan Soc. Roman Catholic. Home: 1343 Old Dominion Naperville IL 60540 Office: 119 E Ogden Ave Hinsdale IL 60521

MAC INTYRE, PATRICIA NELLE, speech-lang. pathologist; b. E. Cleveland, Ohio, July 2, 1923; d. Robert Isadore and Blanche Esther (Schlesinger) Grossman; B.A., Western Reserve U., 1945; M.A., Case Western Reserve U., 1968; m. William James MacIntyre, Sept. 16, 1947; children—Kathleen Suzanne, Steven James. Staff mem. dept. speech pathology Soc. Crippled Children, Cleve., 1968-75, clin. dir., 1975-79; coordinator outside center services Cleve. Hearing and Speech Center, 1979—; clin. instr. dept. speech communication Case Western Res. U., 1973—; adj. asst. prof. dept. communication Cleve. State U., 1973-79; active in teaching presch. children, Head Start speech-lang. services. Bd. dirs. Flora Stone Mather Coll., 1957-61. Certificate clin. competence speech pathology; Receptive-Expressive Lang. Tng. Program grantee, 1976-79. Mem. Am., Ohio, Northeastern Ohio (v.p. 1973) speech and hearing assns., Internat. Assn. Logopedics and Phoniatrics. Home: 3108 Huntington Rd Shaker Heights OH 44120 Office: 11206 Euclid Ave Cleveland OH 44106

MACIUSZKO, JERZY JANUSZ, educator; b. Warsaw, Poland, July 15, 1913; s. Bonifacy and Aleksandra (Lipman) M.; M.A., U. Warsaw, 1936; M.S. in L.S., Western Res. U., 1953; Ph.D., Case Western Res. U., 1962; m. Kathleen Lynn Post, Dec. 11, 1976. Came to U.S., 1951, naturalized, 1957. Insp. Brit. Ministry of Edn. Polish Secondary Schs., Eng., 1946-51; head John G. White dept., Cleve. Pub. Library, 1963-69; chmn. dept. Slavic Studies Alliance Coll., Cambridge Springs, Pa., 1969-73, chmn. div. Slavic and modern langs., 1973-74; prof., library dir. Baldwin-Wallace Coll., Berea, Ohio, 1974-78, prof. emeritus, 1978—. Lectr. in Polish language, lit. Case Western Res. U., Cleve., 1964-69. Dir. Alliance Coll. Year Abroad program at Jagellonian U., Cracow, Poland, 1969-74. Served with AUS, 1945-46. Recipient Doctoral Dissertation award Kosciuszko Found., 1967, Hilbert T. Ficken award, 1973. Mem. Am. Assn. of Tchrs. of Slavic and East European Langs. (chpt. pres. 1965-66), ALA (chmn. slavic subsect. assn. of coll. and research libraries 1968-69), Am. Assn. Advancement of Slavic Studies, Modern Lang. Assn., Polish Inst. Arts. and Scis., Polish Am. Hist. Assn., Case Western Res. U. Library Sch. Alumni Assn. (pres. 1970-71), Slavic Honor Soc. Clubs: Rowfant (Cleve.). Home: 133 Sunset Dr Berea OH 44017

MACK, FAITE ROYJIER-PONCEFONTE, sch. psychologist, educator; b. Chgo., Feb. 23, 1944; s. F. Lafaite and Katie (Von Brun-Rothchild) M.; B.S., Ind. U., 1966; M.A., Roosevelt U., 1967; Ph.D. (Office Edn. fellow 1969, Ill. Gov.'s fellow 1970), U. Ill., 1972; Ed.Spec., Mich. State U., 1981. Tchr., Chgo. Public Schs., 1966-69; chief research evaluator U. Ill., 1971-72; chief evaluator compensatory edn. Mich. Dept. Edn., 1972; asst. prof. edn. Grand Valley State Colls., Grand Rapids, Mich., 1972-74, asso. prof., 1974-79, prof., 1979—, sch. psychologist, 1979—; mem. Mich. Compensatory Edn. Adv. Com.; mem. Mil. Acad. Selection Com. local congressional dist. Mem. long range planning bd. United Fund, Grand Rapids; bd. dirs. Latin Am. Council Mich. Mem. Am. Psychol. Assn., Nat. Assn. Sch. Psychologists, Mich. Assn. Sch. Psychologists, Mich. Psychol. Assn., Am. Ednl. Research Assn., Mich. Ednl. Research Assn., MENSA, Grand Valley State Colls. Faculty Assn., Assn. Urban Edn. (dir. 1976), Phi Delta Kappa. Mem. Fountain St. Non-Denominational Ch. Author: Reading Skills and Activities for the Adult, 1977; Learning Games, 1981; contbr. articles to profl. jours. Home: 61 College Ave NE Grand Rapids MI 49503 Office: State of Mich Bldg Suite 5-B 350 Ottawa Ave NW Grand Rapids MI 49503

MACK, IRVING, physician; b. Vilna, Poland, Apr. 15, 1919; s. Meilach and Rebecca (Zelcer) M.; came to U.S., 1921, naturalized, 1927; B.S., U. Chgo., 1939, M.D., 1942; m. Jean Charlotte Tarrant, Nov. 8, 1959 (dec. Nov. 1969); children—Melissa, Susan. Intern Cook County Hosp., Chgo., 1942-43; sr. resident medicine Michael Reese Hosp., Chgo., 1944-45, sr. fellow dept. cardiovascular research, 1945-46, research asso. Cardiovascular Inst. of hosp., 1946-59, roentgenologic cons. of inst., 1950-55, chest cons. Psychosomatic and Psychiat. Inst. of hosp., 1950—, chief Thursday chest clinic of hosp., 1952-73, attending physician dept. thoracic medicine of hosp., 1947-73, sr. attending physician, 1973—; practice medicine, specializing in internal medicine, Chgo., 1946—; clin. asso. prof. medicine Chgo. Med. Sch., 1949-73; clin. prof. medicine Pritzker Sch. Medicine, U. Chgo., 1973—; cons. Herrick House for Rheumatic Fever, 1948-54. Mem. exec. com. Michael Reese Hosp., 1962-66; trustee Michael Reese Hosp. and Med. Center. Recipient Freer medal, dept. medicine U. Chgo. Coll. Medicine, 1942. Diplomate Am. Bd. Internal Medicine, Nat. Bd. Med. Examiners. Fellow A.C.P., Am. Coll. Chest Physicians (chmn. sect. on electrocardiography 1953-59, mem. com. on postgrad. courses 1955-66), Am. Coll. Cardiology; mem. Am. Fedn. for Clin. Research, Am. Thoracic Soc., Am. Heart Assn., Am. Psychosomatic Soc., Am. Soc. Internal Medicine, AMA, Am. Acad. Tb Physicians, Chgo. Soc. Internal Medicine, Chgo. Inst.

of Medicine, Phi Beta Kappa, Sigma Xi, Alpha Omega Alpha. Author numerous articles in med. jours. on cardiac arrythmias, rheumatic heart disease, electrocardiography, pulmonary physiology, emphysema, Tb and related fields. Mem. editorial bd. Cardiology, 1958-67. Home: 5490 S Shore Dr Chicago IL 60615 Office: 104 S Michigan Ave Chicago IL 60603

MACK, JAMES EDGAR, mfg. co. exec.; b. South Bend, Ind., Sept. 18, 1934; s. John Grant and Kathleen Lorraine (Martin) M.; B.B.A., U. Notre Dame, 1956; m. Jane Huguenard, Oct. 21, 1961; children—Kathleen A., Michael J., Timothy A., Gregory G. Sales trainee U.S. Rubber Co., 1958-60; with Clark Equipment Co., various locations, 1961-76, mng. dir. sales, Michigan City, Ind., 1971-75, v.p. mktg. refrigeration, Niles, Mich., 1975-76; founder, v.p. mktg. Tyler Refrigeration Corp., Niles, 1976-80, exec. v.p., 1980, pres., 1981—, also dir.; dir. Pacesetter Bank S.W., Niles. Served with USN, 1956-58. Roman Catholic. Home: 3335 LaSalle Trail Michigan City IN 46360 Office: 1329 Lake St Niles MI 49120

MACK, PAUL, ednl. counselor; b. Pitts., Sept. 17, 1945; s. Joseph Michael and Rosalie Valerie M.; student Sch. Fgn. Service, Georgetown U., 1963-66; B.A., U. Wis., 1968, M.S. with high honors, 1975; m. Nancy Anne Nollau, 1971; children—Kristopher Nollau, Katharine Valerie. Peace Corps vol., Brazil, 1969-70, Midwest rep. Peace Corps Sch. Partnership Program, Chgo., 1970-71; adminstrv. asst. Food and Nutrition Service, U.S. Dept. Agr. Chgo., 1971-72; jr. high sch. guidance counselor, Dodgeville, Wis., 1975-79; middle sch. guidance counselor, Platteville, Wis., 1979—. Bd. dirs. Mineral Point Hist. Soc., 1979-80; chmn. Iowa County Dem. Party, 1979-81. Cert. profl. counselor Wis. Dept. Public Instrn. Mem. Wis. Personnel and Guidance Assn. (exec. bd. 1976-77), Wis. Sch. Counselors Assn., Phi Delta Kappa. Home: 250 Shake Rag St Mineral Point WI 53565

MACK, RICHARD ARTHUR, edn. co. exec.; b. Bagley, Minn., Dec. 24, 1941; s. Lloyd Benton and Rose Delia (Belland) M.; B.S., U. Wis., 1968, M.S., 1974, Ph.D., 1980; postgrad. U. Wis., 1971, U. Hawaii, 1971, U. Utah, 1976; m. Gloria Jean Gooding, Oct. 6, 1965; children—John, Christopher, Elizabeth, Jennifer, Nicholas, Mary. Tech. writer McGraw-Edison, Milw., 1962-65; writer Marrow Pub., Berkeley, Calif., 1968-70; curriculum cons. Milw. public schs., 1970-72; dir. research and devel. Ramco Cons. Services, Aurora, Ill., 1972-75; gen. mgr. Nevada Mgmt. & Tng. Co., Carson City, 1975-79, now dir.; chief exec. officer Edn. Systems Co., Garfield, Minn., 1979—; dir. Ramco Cons. Services, Edn. Systems Co. Served to lt. comdr. U.S. Army, 1959-62. Mem. Communications Assn. Am., Am. Correctional Assn., Tech. Edn. Assn., Christian Family Movement. Roman Catholic. Clubs: K.C., Eagles. Home: 502 Marion St Alexandria MN 56308 Office: Douglas County 82 PO Box 38 Garfield MN 56332

MACKAY, JOHN RICHARDSON, lawyer; b. Chgo., Oct. 7, 1917; s. John Miller and Isabel (Mackay) M.; student Loyola U., Chgo., 1945; J.D., John Marshall Law Sch., Chgo., 1949; children—John Richardson, James D. Admitted to Ill. bar, 1950; underwriter, claims atty. Hartford Accident & Indemnity Co., Chgo., 1940-51; practice law, Wheaton, Ill., 1951—; spl. asst. atty. gen. Ill., 1956-59; chmn. Senator Percy's com. to study fed. jud. dists. in Ill.; mem. Gov.'s Task Force on Law and Edn. Mem. Ill. (pres. 1974-75, bd. govs. 1967—), DuPage County (pres. 1965-66) bar assns., Ill. Bar Officers Conf. (pres. 1966-67), 7th Dist. Fedn. Local Bar Assns. (pres. 1957-58). Club: Masons. Office: 422 W Wesley Wheaton IL 60187

MACKENZIE, KENNETH DONALD, mgmt. cons.; b. Salem, Oreg., Dec. 20, 1937; s. Kenneth Victor and Dorothy Vernon (Miniker) M.; A.B. in Math., U. Calif., Berkeley, 1960, Ph.D. in Bus. Adminstrn., 1964; m. Sally Jane McHenry, June 16, 1957; children—Dorothy Jane, Carolyn Beta, Susan Gamma, Nancy Delta. Asst. prof. indsl. adminstrn. Carnegie-Mellon U., 1964-67; asso. prof. industry Wharton Sch., U. Pa., 1967-71; prof. mgmt. scis. U. Waterloo (Ont.), 1969-72; Edmund P. Learned disting. prof. Sch. Bus., U. Kans., Lawrence, 1971—; pres. Organizational Systems, Inc., Lawrence, 1976—. Served with USMCR, 1957. Mem. Am. Mgmt. Assn., Am. Psychol. Assn., Internat. Communications Assn., Ops. Research Soc., Inst. Mgmt. Scis., AAAS, Human Systems Mgmt. Assn. Republican. Author: An Introduction to Continuous Probability Theory, 1969; A Theory of Structures, 2 vols., 1976; Organizational Structures, 1978; mem. editorial bds. profl. jours.; editor Organizational Behavior Series. Home: 502 Millstone Dr Lawrence KS 66044 Office: 311 Summerfield Hall Sch Bus Univ Kans Lawrence KS 66045 also Organizational Systems Inc PO Box 1118 Lawrence KS 66044

MACKEY, DIANA PARSONS, recruiter; b. Columbus, Ohio, Mar. 26, 1946; d. Reid Ivan and Charleen Lois (Krieg) Parsons; B.A. in Edn., Miami U., Oxford, Ohio, 1968; children—Michelle, Jon. Asst. librarian Columbus Pub. Library, 1968-70; sales and adminstrv. placement counselor Snelling & Snelling, Columbus, 1976-80; recruiter Am. Electric Power Service Corp., Columbus, 1980—. Co-founder, S.E. Civic Assn., Columbus, 1974, pres., 1976—; Democratic candidate for county commr., 1976. Soroptimist scholar, 1964. Mem. Franklin County Women's Polit. Caucus, Miami U. Alumni, Kappa Delta Alumnae. Home: 1340 Wilson Ave Columbus OH 43206 Office: 180 E Broad St Columbus OH 43215

MACKEY, FRANCES THERESA, educator, artist, mfrs. rep.; b. Highland Park, Mich., Jan. 2, 1932; d. Frank C. and Elizabeth (Fleming) M.; Ph.B., Siena Heights Coll., Adrian, Mich., 1954; M.A., Wayne State U., 1966; M.A.T. in Spl. Edn. and Learning Disabilities, Oakland U., 1974. Tchr., Dearborn (Mich.) Public Schs., 1968—; mfrs. rep. Kazari div. Cronar Ltd., Japanese Bunka Embroidery Co., Inc., 1976—, Clarke's Osewez Needle Co., 1979—; owner Carriage House div. Heritage Crafts; designer; cons.; tchr. workshops and demonstrations. Rhodes scholar nominee, 1965. Mem. Dearborn Fedn. Tchrs., Mich. Assn. Children with Learning Disabilities, Bus. and Profl. Women, Founders Soc. Detroit Inst. Arts. Home and Office: 26440 Westphal Dr 212 Dearborn Heights MI 48127

MACKEY, JOHN EUGENE, food co. exec.; b. St. Louis, Nov. 8, 1946; s. Eugene Joseph and Mary (Curtin) M.; B.A. in Russian and Brit. History, Yale U., 1969; m. Jane Howard Shapleigh, Sept. 19, 1970; children—Alexander McKinney, John Wells. With Pet Inc., St. Louis, 1972—, product mgr. frozen foods div., 1975-76, v.p. mktg. Whitman's Chocolates div., Phila., 1976-78, v.p. mktg. frozen foods div., splty. group, St. Louis, 1978-82, corp. v.p. venture mgmt., 1982—. Mem. devel. bd. St. Louis Children's Hosp., 1975-76; bd. dirs. Bi-State chpt. ARC, 1979—, vice chmn., 1981—; vice-chmn. Mo.-Ill. Blood Services, 1980-81, chmn., 1981—; bd. dirs. Theatre Project Co. Served to lt. (j.g.) USN, 1969-72. Clubs: Yale (dir. 1979—), St. Louis Country, Noonday (St. Louis). Office: Pet Inc PO Box 392 Saint Louis MO 63166

MACKEY, ROBERT BENJAMIN, psychologist; b. Niobrara, Nebr., Aug. 11, 1920; s. John B. and Rachel W. (Frazier) M.; student Nebr. State Coll., 1940-42; B.S., U. So. Calif., 1952; m. Virginia Florine Sharp, Feb. 23, 1947; children—Robert II, Sharon Kay, Richard. With Goodwill Industries Am., Sioux City, Iowa, 1947-49, 57-59, 67-68; with Gen. Electric Co., Sioux City and Clinton, Iowa, Chandler, Ariz., 1968-70; exec. dir., psychol. clinician Community Mental Health Center N.W. Alaska, Kotzebue, 1977—. Served with USMCR, 1942-45, Korea, 1950-52. Decorated Purple Heart; recipient Order of Silver Star, Am. Legion, 1945. Mem. Nat. Assn. Native Am. Social Workers, Am. Personnel and Guidance Assn., Am. Psychol. Assn. Republican. Presbyterian. Clubs: Masons, Order of Eastern Star. Home: c/o Dan Frazier Rt 2 Niobrara NE 68760

MACKINNEY, ARTHUR CLINTON, JR., psychologist, educator, univ. ofcl.; b. Kansas City, Mo., Oct. 16, 1928; s. Arthur Clinton and Doris (Long) Mac.; B.A., William Jewell Coll., 1951; M.A., U. Minn., 1953, Ph.D., 1955; m. Lois Elizabeth Lineberry, Sept. 5, 1953; children—Arthur Clinton III, Gordon L., Nada L. Instr. U. Minn., 1953-55, Macalester Coll., 1955; cons. psychologist R.N. McMurry & Co., Chgo., 1953; research psychologist Gen. Motors Corp., 1955-57; asst. prof. to prof., head dept. psychology Iowa State U., 1957-70; dean Coll. Sci. and Soc. of U. Wis.-Parkside at Kenosha, 1970-71; dean grad. studies and research Wright State U., Dayton, Ohio, 1971-76; vice chancellor acad. affairs U. Mo., St. Louis, 1976—, prof. psychology, 1976—; vis. prof. U. Minn., 1960, U. Calif., 1962-63, 66; cons. to industry. Served with AUS, 1946-47, 51. Lic. psychologist, Mo., Ohio. Fellow Am. Psychol. Assn. (Cattell research design award 1968, pres.-elect div. indsl.-organizational psychology 1980-81, pres. 1981-82); mem. Midwestern, Iowa (pres. 1966), Wis., Ohio, Mo. (sec. 1981-82) psychol. assns., Psychonomic Soc., Psychometric Soc., Am. Assn. Higher Edn., Acad. of Mgmt., Nat. Council Univ. Research Adminstrs., Council of Grad. Schs. of U.S., Sigma Xi, Kappa Alpha. Unitarian. Contbr. articles to profl. jours. Research on long-term development complex human performance. Office: 8001 Natural Bridge Rd Saint Louis MO 63121

MACKINTOSH, REBECCA ANN, gourmet food co. exec.; b. Bismark, N.D., Mar. 23, 1950; d. Christian Henry and Oral Lorraine (Geisler) Koch; A.A., Spencerian Bus. Coll., 1970; m. Michael Townsend Mackintosh, May 21, 1975. Asst. to Donald Miller, Milw. Co., 1972-74, Smith Barney Co., Milw., 1974-75; pres. Deliciously Different, Milw., 1975—. Mem. Tempo. Club: Milw. Athletic. Home: 2219 N Lake Dr Milwaukee WI 53202 Office: Deliciously Different Century Bldg 230 W Wells St Suite 406 Milwaukee WI 53203

MACKIW, THEODORE, educator; b. Strutyn, Ukraine, May 30, 1918; s. Ivan and Maria (Jankiw) M.; came to U.S., 1950, naturalized, 1956; Ph.D., Frankfurt (Germany) U., 1950; postgrad. Seton Hall U., 1951-54; m. Ellen Kraus; 1 son, Stephen. Instr., Seton Hall U., 1950-54; tchr. Blue Ridge Country Day Sch., Milwood, Va., 1954-55, Cushing Acad., Ashburnham, Mass., 1955-56; vis. prof. history Schwyz (Switzerland) Coll., 1956-57; prof. Lane Coll., 1957-58; tchr. Hamden Hall Country Day Sch., Hamden, Conn., 1958-60; asst. prof. U. R.I., 1960-62; prof. Slavic studies, dir. Soviet area studies U. Akron, 1962—; head search sect. documents intelligence UNRRA; postdoctoral research fellow Yale U., 1959-60; NDEA grad. fellow Ind. U., 1967. Mem. AAUP, AAAS, Am. Assn. Tchrs. of Slavic and E. European Langs., Am. Hist. Assn., Shevchenko Sci. Soc. Author: Mazepa im Lichte der zeitgonoessischen deutschen Quellen (1639-1709), 1963; Prince Mazepa: Hetman of Ukraine, 1687-1709, 1967. Office: U Akron Akron OH 44325

MAC LAREN, DAVID SARGEANT, pollution control equipment co. exec.; b. Cleve., Jan. 4, 1931; s. Albert Sargeant and Theadora Beidler (Potter) MacL.; A.B., Miami U., Oxford, Ohio, 1955. Mgr. Jet, Inc., Cleve., 1958-60, chmn. bd., pres., 1961—; founder, chmn. bd., pres. Air Injector Corp., Cleve., 1958-78; founder, chmn. bd., pres. Sargeant Realty, Inc., Cleve., 1979—; founder, pres. Fluid Equipment, Inc., Cleve., 1962-72, chmn. bd., 1962-72; founder, pres. T&M Co., Cleve., 1963-71, chmn. bd., 1964-71; founder, pres. Alison Realty Co., Cleve., 1965—, chmn. bd., 1967—; founder, pres. Mold Leasing, Inc., Cleve., 1968-71; dir. MWL Systems. Mem. tech. com. Nat. Sanitation Found., Ann Arbor, Mich., 1967—. Mem. Republican State Central Com., 1968-72, Cuyahoga County Republican Central Com., 1968-72; registered legislative agt. 110th Ohio Gen. Assembly, 1973-74. Served with arty. AUS, 1955-58. Fellow Royal Soc. Health (London); mem. Nat., Ohio environ. health assns., Nat. Precast Concrete Assn., Am. Pub. Health Assn., Nat. Water Pollution Control Fedn., Ohio Water Pollution Control Fedn., Am. Mgmt. Assn., Ohio Gun Collectors Assn., Defenders Wildlife, Friends of Animals, Central Tackwondo Assn., Mercedes Benz Club N.Am. (pres. 1968), U.S. Martial Arts Assn. (black belt, instr.), Jiu-Jitsu/Karati Black Belt Fedn., Scottish Tartans Soc., Clan MacLaren Soc., Vintage Sports Car Club, Nat. Audubon Soc., Ferrari Club Am., Cleve. Animal Protective League, Highland Heights Citizens League, SAR, Fraternal Order Police, Delta Kappa Epsilon (nat. dir. 1974—; dir. Kappa chpt. alumni assn. 1969—). Clubs: Light of Yoga Soc. (life), Mentor Harbor Yachting, Cleveland Skating, Cleveland Racquet, Country (Cleve.); Union League, Yale, Deke (N.Y.C.). Patentee in field. Home: West Hill Dr Gates Mills OH 44040 Office: 750 Alpha Dr Cleveland OH 44143

MACLAREN, LINDA LISBETH, spark plug mfg. co. exec.; b. Detroit, July 29, 1941; student Miami U., Oxford, Ohio, 1959-62; postgrad. U. Toledo, 1962-64, Lourdes Coll., 1976-78; children—Tamara Ann, Margaret K., Kenneth C. Tchr., Sylvania (Ohio) Bd. Edn., 1962-64; placement counselor Imperial Placement Service, Toledo, 1976-77; interviewer Champion Spark Plug Co., Toledo, 1977-78, personnel adminstr., 1978—. Bd. dirs. United Central Services. Mem. Internat. Assn. Personnel Women (chpt. pres. 1981—), Am. Soc. Personnel Adminstrn., Toledo Personnel Mgrs. Assn., Employers Assn. Toledo. Office: Champion Spark Plug Co PO Box 910 Toledo OH 43661

MACLAUCHLAN, DONALD JOHN, JR., real estate co. exec.; b. S.I., N.Y., Mar. 2, 1935; s. Donald John and Alice Lucy (Macklin) MacL.; B.A. magna cum laude, Harvard U., 1957; m. Mary Eleanor Manor, Oct. 14, 1967; children—Douglas Laird, Phyllis Ann, Donald John III. Mortgage analyst Conn. Gen. Life Ins. Co., Hartford, 1957-60; mortgage broker James W. Rouse & Co., Balt., 1960-62; devel. mgr. Devel. & Constrn. Co., Inc., Balt., 1962-66; v.p. Nat. Homes Corp., Lafayette, Ind., 1966-75; pres., dir. The Criterion Group, Lafayette, 1975—. Elder, Central Presbyn. Ch., Lafayette, 1971—; mem. gen. council Presbytery of Wabash Valley, 1976-78. Mem. Lafayette Bd. Realtors, Greater Lafayette C. of C., Ind. Apt. Assn. (dir. 1980—), Tippecanoe County Apt. Assn. (dir. 1977—, pres. 1980). Republican. Clubs: Lafayette Country, Romwell Foxhounds (joint master). Office: PO Box 275 Lafayette IN 47905

MACLAUGHLIN, CHARLES ANDREWS, indsl. machinery co. exec.; b. Fort Lewis, Wash., June 5, 1931; s. John Andrews and Ruth Charshee (Hill) MacL.; grad. Balt. Poly. Inst., 1949; student Johns Hopkins U., 1949-51; B.S. in Civil Engring. (Dresser scholar 1955), Tri-State U., 1956; postgrad. Cornell U., 1981; m. Myrle Stewart Gorgas, July 12, 1958; children—Susan Andrews, Anne Stewart, Elizabeth Hill. Civil engr. Howard, Needles, Tammen & Bergendoff, 1956-59; Eastern sales mgr., advt. mgr. Hilti, Inc., 1960-66; v.p. James A. Ford Advt., Stamford, Conn., 1966-67; mktg. services mgr. Ramset div. Olin Corp., New Haven, 1967-72; Eastern regional mgr. Sweco, Inc., subs. Emerson Electric, Florence, Ky., 1972-75, nat. sales mgr., 1975-76, div. mgr. finishing equipment div., 1976-79, v.p., gen. mgr. finishing equipment div., 1979—, also dir. Vestryman, Episcopal Ch., 1971-72; active various community drives. Served to 1st lt. U.S. Army, 1952-54; Korea. Decorated Bronze Star; recipient Distinguished Alumnus award Tri-State U., 1971, Merit award State of R.I., 1964. Mem. Soc. Mfg. Engrs., Nat. Machine Tool Builders Assn., Phi Gamma Delta. Republican. Episcopalian. Clubs: Amateur Fencers League Am., Queen City Racquet. Home: 15 Dorino Pl Wyoming OH 45215 Office: 8040 US Hwy 25 Florence KY 41042

MACLAUGHLIN, HARRY HUNTER, Judge; b. Breckenridge, Minn., Aug. 9, 1927; s. Harry Hunter and Grace (Swank) MacL.; B.B.A. with distinction, U. Minn., 1949, LL.B., J.D., 1956; m. Mary Jean Shaffer, June 25, 1958; children—David, Douglas. With Gen. Motors Corp., Mpls., 1949-52, Minn. Mining Co., St. Paul, 1952-54; law clk. to Justice Frank Gallagher Minn. Supreme Ct., 1955-56; admitted to Minn. bar, 1956; practice law, Mpls., 1956-72; partner firm MacLaughlin & Harstad, 1960-72; asso. justice Minn. Supreme Ct., 1972-77; U.S. dist. judge Dist. of Minn., 1977—; lectr. U. Minn. Law Sch., 1973—; part-time instr. William Mitchell Coll. Law, St. Paul, 1958-63. Mem. Mpls. Charter Commn., 1966-72, Minn. State Coll. Bd., 1971-72, Minn. Jud. Council, 1972; nat. adv. council Small Bus. Adminstrn., 1968-70. Served with USNR, 1945-46. Mem. Am., Minn., Hennepin County bar assns., Am. Trial Lawyers Assn., Beta Gamma Sigma, Phi Delta Phi. Methodist. Bd. editors Minn. Law Rev., 1954-55. Home: 2301 Oliver Ave S Minneapolis MN 55405 Office: US Court House Minneapolis MN 55401

MAC LEAN, LOWE (SANDY), univ. adminstr.; b. Laurium, Mich., June 24, 1934; s. Angus Lowe and Marion (Stannard) MacL.; B.A., No. Mich. U., 1956; M.A., Mich. State U., 1960; postgrad. U. No. Iowa, 1960-63; Ed.D., Ind. U., 1967; m. Judith Ellen Rea, July 12, 1969; children—Kent Allen, Brian Lowe. Tchr., coach Crystal (Mich.) Community Schs., 1958-59; grad. adviser Mich. State U., 1959-60; dir. men's halls U. No. Iowa, 1960-63; head counsellor Ind. U., 1963-66; asst. dean students, prof. edn. U. Mo., Columbia, 1966-70; dean students Eastern Mich. U., 1970-76, asso. v.p. student affairs, 1976-81; dean student affairs U. Mo., St. Louis, 1981—. Chmn., Ypsilanti Summer Festival Commn., 1975; chmn. adv. council Ypsilanti Sch. Dist., Title VII, 1976-80; bd. govs. Washtenaw United Way, 1974-80; bd. dirs. Ypsilanti Area Futures, Inc.; past pres. Estrabrook Parent Tchr. Orgn. chmn. for Washtenaw and Livington County, Tel-Med Com., 1978-81; active Boy Scouts Am. Served with AUS, 1956-58. Mem. Am. Coll. Personnel Assn. (coordinator govt. relations 1976-79, exec. council), Am. Assn. Higher Edn., Am. Mgmt. Assn., Am. Personnel and Guidance Assn. (govtl. relations com.), Mich. Personnel and Guidance Assn., Nat. Assn. Student Personnel Admnstrs., Mo. Coll. Personnel Assn., Tau Kappa Epsilon (dir. Ednl. Found., mem. president's adv. council), Phi Delta Kappa. Home: 8520 Roanoke Dr Saint Louis MO 63121

MAC MAHON, HAROLD BERNARD, mfg. co. exec.; b. Newton, Mass., Nov. 15, 1917; s. Harold A. and Alma A. (McCabe) MacM.; B.S. in Edn., Boston U., 1940; m. Mary M. Savage, Jan. 1, 1942; 1 dau., Karen D. MacMahon Levisay. Plant mgr. Bassick div. Stewart-Warner Corp., Spring Valley, Ill., 1958-66, controller Alemite and Instrument div., Chgo., 1966-73, asst. gen. mgr., 1973-74, gen. mgr. Hobbs div., Springfield, Ill., 1974—, v.p., 1976—; dir. Springfield Marine Bank. Bd. dirs. Greater Springfield C. of C., 1978-81; mem. adv. council St. John's Hosp.; mem. Sangamon County Pvt. Industry Council. Served with U.S. Army, 1943-45. Mem. Soc. Automotive Engrs., Newcomen Soc. N.Am., Ill. C. of C., Kappa Delta Phi. Club: Sangamo (Springfield). Home: 1525 W Ash Springfield IL 62704 also 260 E Chestnut St Chicago IL 60611 Office: Yale Blvd and Ash St Springfield IL 62705

MAC MILLAN, VELMA JEANNE, educator; b. Chgo., 1926; d. Ernest Wilfred and Velma Jennie (Paramore) B.M., Coe Coll., 1948, 1949; M.S. in Music Edn., U. Ill., 1959; Ph.D. (NDEA Title IV fellow), U. Wis., 1969. Instr. vocal music Buffalo Center (Iowa) Consol. Schs., 1948-49; music supr. Manchester (Iowa) Public Sch., 1949-52; music instr. Kenosha (Wis.) Public Schs., 1952-67; critic tchr., 1963-66; asso. prof. ednl. adminstrn. U. Wis., Superior, 1969—, coordinator ednl. adminstrn. programs, 1978—. Named Outstanding Educator, 1975. Mem. Gov.'s Commn. on Edn. Seminar, 1966; chmn. Regional Public Hearing Kellett Commn. Gov.'s Commn. on Edn., 1970. Mem. Assn. for Supervision and Curriculum Devel., Nat. (dir. 1965-67), Wis. fedns. bus. and profl. women's clubs (pres. 1965-67), Assn. Wis. Sch. Adminstrs., Assn. U. Wis. Faculty, Mu Phi Epsilon, Pi Kappa Lambda, Pi Lambda Theta, Phi Delta Kappa. Lutheran. Home: 2909 John Ave Superior WI 54880 Office: Coll Edn U Wis Superior WI 54880

MAC MULLAN, MARCIA WELLMAN, social worker; b. Columbus, Ohio, Jan. 27, 1925; d. Burton Singley and Blanche (Gardner) Wellman; A.B., U. Mich., 1947, M.S.W., 1967; m. Harry L. Fitch, May 7, 1948; children—Marcia L. Fitch Meyer, Sarah, Peter; m. 2d, Donald D. MacMullan, May 16, 1967. Intelligence analyst Dept. Def., 1947-49; artist, art tchr., Key West, Fla., 1958-63; caseworker Fla. Dept. Welfare, 1963-65; coordinator intake and community services Washtenaw County (Mich.) Juvenile Ct., 1967—; exec. sec. Center Occupational and Personalized Edn., Inc., Ann Arbor, Mich., 1980; v.p. Washtenaw County Coordinating Council Children at Risk, 1980; instr. U. Mich. Symposia, 1976-77, Eastern Mich. U., 1977-78; chmn. drug crime task force Ann Arbor Citizens Council, 1975-76; mem. children and youth com. Mich. League Human Services, 1976-77. Mem. Nat. Assn. Social Workers (chmn. juvenile justice com. Mich. chpt. 1975-80; Social Worker of Year, Huron Valley chpt. 1975, Huron Valley unit 1980), ACLU, NOW, Law and Soc. Assn., Mich. Assn. Ednl. Options (legis. chmn. 1980), Phi Beta Kappa, Phi Kappa Phi, Delta Gamma. Author papers, reports in field. Home: 2020 Chalmers St Ann Arbor MI 48104 Office: 2270 Platt St Ann Arbor MI 48104

MACNEARY, JOY SALLY, savs. and loan exec.; b. Milw., May 11, 1950; d. Ludwig L. and Selma (Monhardt) MacNeary; student Milton Coll., 1968-71. Sec. property tax dept. Great Midwest Savs. and Loan Assn., Milw., 1971-72, loan sec. tng., 1972, loan sec., Brookfield, Wis., 1972-77, br. mgr., Hartland, Wis., 1978—. Mem. Hartbrook Mchts. Assn. (treas. 1979—), Women in Asso. Real Estate Mgmt. (treas. 1979-80, sec. 1980-81), Hartland C. of C. (sec. 1980-81, dir.). Office: 600 Hartbrook Dr Hartland WI 53029

MACOMB, J. DE NAVARRE, JR., former steel co. exec., nature/travelogue lectr.; b. Bay Head, N.J., July 30, 1913; s. John de Navarre and Leonie (Lentilhon) M.; M.E., Princeton U., 1935; Ferrous Metall. Engr., Armour Inst. Tech., 1937; m. Marjorie Robidoux Street, Oct. 13, 1951. With Inland Steel Co., 1934-77, successively mill apprentice, various sales positions, public relations dept., 1951-77; asst. to dir. corp. communications, 1957-77. Mem. Chgo. Public Relations Clinic, Citizenship Council Met. Chgo., Lawrence Hall Sch. for Boys, Chgo. Served in U.S. Army, 1941-46; now lt. col. ret. Decorated Silver Star, Bronze Star (2), Purple Heart (U.S.); Croix de Guerre with gold star (France); Order of Red Star (USSR). Mem. Chgo. Audubon Soc., Am. Mus. Natural History, Art. Inst. Chgo., Field Mus., Soc. Colonial Wars, Colonial Lords of Manors, Descs. Signers of Declaration of Independence, Nat. Audubon Soc., Am. Ornithol. Union, Cooper Ornithol. Soc., Wilson Ornithol. Soc., St. Nicholas Soc., Chgo. Acad. Scis., Smithsonian Instn., Nature Conservancy, Ill. St. Andrew Soc., Mil. Order Loyal

Legion, Republican. Episcopalian. Clubs: Univ., Adventurers (Chgo.); Princeton (Chgo., N.Y.C.); Sea Pines (Hilton Head, S.C.); Intrepids (N.Y.C.); Indian Hill (Winnetka, Ill.). Home: 588 Arbor Vitae Rd Winnetka IL 60093

MACRAE, DONALD ALEXANDER, educator; b. Eldora, Iowa, Dec. 3, 1916; s. William and Mary (Stewart) MacR.; B.A., U. No. Iowa, 1943; M.A., U. Iowa, 1950, Ph.D., 1962; m. Adeline Taylor, July 8, 1943 (dec. Jan. 1963); children—Margaret Ann, Pamela, Patricia; m. 2d, Joyce M. Spooner McCrea, June 1, 1968. Prin., Solon (Iowa) High Sch., 1943-44, Riverton (Iowa) High Sch., 1944-45, 47-48; instr. U. Iowa, 1949-54; prof. bus. adminstrn. Mankato (Minn.) State U., 1954—. Bd. dirs. United Fund, 1971-76. Served with AUS, 1946-47. Mem. Am. Bus. Writing Assn., Nat. Bus. Edn. Assn., Internat. Soc. Bus. Edn., Adminstrv. Mgmt. Soc., St. Andrew's Soc. Minn., Sigma Tau Delta, Kappa Delta Pi, Pi Omega Pi, Delta Pi Epsilon, Phi Delta Kappa. Presbyterian. Home: 211 Woodshire Dr Mankato MN 56001 Office: College of Business Mankato State University Mankato MN 56001

MACUMBER, JOHN PAUL, ins. co. exec.; b. Macon, Mo., Jan. 21, 1940; s. Rolland Deardorf and Althea Villa (Cason) M.; B.A., Central Meth. Coll., Fayette, Mo., 1962; Asso. in Risk Mgmt., Ins. Inst. Am., 1978; m. Marilyn Sue Ashe, Nov. 10, 1962; children—Leanne, Cheryl. Casualty underwriter U.S. Fidelity & Guaranty Co., St. Louis, 1962-66; automobile underwriter Am. Indemnity Co., Galveston, Tex., 1966-69; auto casualty underwriter St. Paul Cos., New Orleans, 1969-73; sr. comml. casualty underwriter Chubb/Pacific Indemnity, Portland, Oreg., 1973-75; casualty underwriter Interstate Nat. Corp., Los Angeles, 1975-76, underwriting supr., 1976-78, v.p., br. mgr., Mpls., 1978—. Served with USAF, 1962-68. Nat. Methodist scholar, 1958. Mem. Minn. Assn. Spl. Risk Underwriters. Republican. Mem. Unity Ch. (sec. bd. dirs. 1979). Clubs: Optimists (charter pres. 1968) (Friendswood, Tex.); Kiwanis (pres. 1979, dir. 1981-82), Ins. of Mpls., Blue Goose (Mpls.). Home: 3716 Canterbury Dr Bloomington MN 55431 Office: 5001 W 80th St Minneapolis MN 55437

MACY, JANET KUSKA, broadcaster, educator; b. Omaha, Nov. 9, 1935; d. Val and Marie (Letovsky) Kuska; B.S., U. Nebr., 1957; M.S., Kans. State U., 1961; M.Ed., S.D. State U., 1970; postgrad. Iowa State U., 1965-67, Colo. State U., 1965, U. Minn., 1975, U. Ariz., 1979, 80; div. Broadcaster Sta. KSAC, Kans. State U., Manhattan, 1957-61; extension home econs. editor U. Nebr., Lincoln, 1961-62; TV specialist Iowa State U. Sta. WOI-TV, 1962-67; asst. prof. Coll. Home Econs., TV specialist Sta. KESD-TV, S.D. State U., Brookings, 1967-71; field editor Better Homes and Gardens Book div. Meredith Pub. Co., 1972-73; media cons. U.S. Consumer Product Safety Commn., Minn., 1977-79; asso. prof. Coll. Agr., extension info. specialist, broadcaster Sta. KUOM, U. Minn., St. Paul, 1971—; public relations cons. Rational Emotive Edn. Center. Recipient Nutrition Communication award Am. Women in Radio and TV, 1977; Alumni Recognition award U. Nebr., 1973; Agrl. Coll. Editors Blue Ribbon awards, 1967, 68, 69, 79 Sch. Bell award Minn. Edn. Assn., 1980, 81. Mem. Internat. TV Assn., Women in Internat. Devel., Am. Soc. for Tng. and Devel., Am. Home Econs. Assn., Council for Univ. Women's Progress, AAUP, Nat. Assn. Farm Broadcasters, Agrl. Communicators in Edn. (superior awards 1979, 81), Nat. Agrl. Mktg. Assn., Gamma Sigma Delta, Phi Delta Gamma, Theta Sigma Phi, Delta Gamma. Club: Ski. Home: 1570 Vincent St Saint Paul MN 55108 Office: 433 Coffey Hall 1420 Eckles Ave Saint Paul MN 55108

MADDEN, JOHN FRANCIS, pub. accountant, editor, pub.; b. Evansville, Ind., Apr. 22, 1902; s. William Martin and Veronica (Keller) M.; student parochial and pub. schs., Indpls.; m. Geneva Louise Stalcup, July 24, 1924; children—John William, Charles Edward, Francis Joseph. Asso. W.M. Madden & Co., C.P.A.'s, Indpls., 1921—, sole owner, 1954—; publisher Ind. Cath. and Record, 1933-56; editor, pub. Marion County Mail; pres. Shield Press, Inc., Mail Printing & Pub. Corp. C.P.A., Ind. Mem. Newcomen Soc. N.Am., Ind., Marion County hist. socs., Indpls. Art Assn. Republican. Roman Catholic. Home: 10770 Crooked Stick Ln Carmel IN 46032 also 1545 Moonridge Rd Tucson AZ 85718

MADDEN, THOMAS JOSEPH, JR., electronic engr.; b. Chgo., Feb. 26, 1931; s. Thomas Joseph and Doris Amanda (Oksnee) M.; B.S. in Elec. Engring., U. Ill., 1953; m. Marjorie June Forbes, Jan. 31, 1953; children—John, James, Jeffery. Electronic engr. Ralph M. Parsons, Pasadena, Calif., 1953-54, Farnsworth Electronics, Ft. Wayne, Ind., 1956-57; project engr. Cook Electric Co., Morton Grove, Ill., 1957-65; mgr. office automation product devel. A. B. Dick Co., Chgo., 1967—. Served with U.S. Army, 1954-56. Mem. League Am. Wheelmen. Lutheran. Patentee in field. Home: 428 Lilac Ln Elk Grove IL 60007 Office: 5700 W Touhy Chicago IL 60648

MADDOX, ARNOLD WAYNE, engr.; b. Kansas City, Mo., Mar. 28, 1933; s. Hugh Maxwell and Anna Allene (Cobb) M.; B.S. in Mech. Engring., U. Mo., Rolla, 1955, Profl. Aerospace Engr., 1977; M.S. in Mgmt. Sci., U. So. Calif., 1972; m. Carolyn Marie Daniels, Sept. 4, 1955; 1 dau., Lisa Marie. Dep. chief engr. aerothermodynamics McDonnell Douglas Astronautics Co.-West Santa Monica, Calif., 1965-68, program mgr., 1968-70; corp. dir. tech. planning McDonnell Douglas Corp., St. Louis, 1972—; v.p., treas. Instacomp Inc., 1968-72; adj. faculty Webster Coll., Webster Groves, Mo. Served with U.S. Army, 1957. Registered profl. engr., Mo. Mem. AAAS, Inst. Mgmt. Sci. Home: 13346 Amiot Ct Saint Louis MO 63141

MADDOX, LUCY JANE, librarian, educator; b. Port, Okla., Apr. 6, 1922; d. Robert T. and Tollie (Pierce) Maddox; A.A., Central Coll., 1942; A.B., Seattle Pacific Coll., 1944; M.A., Colo. State Coll., 1948; M.A.L.S., U. Mich., 1956, Ph.D., 1958. Instr. speech and English, Eaton (Colo.) Pub. High Sch., 1945-48; dean women, asst. prof. speech and English, Spring Arbor (Mich.) Coll., 1948-51, 52-53; asso. prof. speech and English, Seattle Pacific Coll., 1951-52; librarian, prof. English, Owosso (Mich.) Coll., 1953-55, chmn. div. lit., langs. and fine arts, 1958-59; asst. dept. library sci. U. Mich., Ann Arbor, 1957-58; dir., instr. library technician program Ferris State Coll., Big Rapids, Mich., 1959-62; library curriculum coordinator Spring Arbor (Mich.) Coll., 1962-63; dir. library, prof. English, 1963—. Lectr. library sci. U. Mich., Ann Arbor, part-time, 1957-65; vis. instr. library sci. Colo. State Coll., Greeley, summers 1958-61, 65. Mem. Assn. Christian Librarians, Conf. Christianity and Lit., ALA, Mich. Acad., Beta Phi Mu. Free Methodist. Home: 174 E Harmony Rd Spring Arbor MI 49283

MADDOX, TERRY LADD, elec. engr.; b. Fulton, Mo., Dec. 12, 1956; s. Wayne Ladd and Frances Edith (Mosley) M.; B.S.E.E., U. Mo., 1978. Computer programmer Mo. Dept. Conservation, Columbia, 1976-78; elec. engr. data processing dept. Ill. Power Co., Decatur, 1978—; instr. electronics Richland Coll., Decatur, 1980-81. Registered engr.-in-tng., Mo., Ill. Mem. IEEE, Central Ill. Soc. Profl. Engrs. (membership and steering chmn. 1980-81), Power Engring. Soc., Order of Arrow. Republican. Presbyterian. Club: Commodore Toastmasters (v.p. adminstrn. 1979, v.p. edn. 1980, pres. 1981, asst. gov. for adminstrn. Decatur, Mattoon, Charleston and Effingham 1981 Commodore award 1980, competent Toastmaster award 1981). Developer computer programs for power system planning and analysis. Home: 21 Madison Dr Decatur IL 62521 Office: 500 S 27th St Decatur IL 62525

MADDOX, WILLIAM CLARENCE, ret. pedodontist, photographer; b. Dayton, Ohio, June 30, 1927; s. Clarence William and Olive Myrtle (Althouse) M.; B.S. in Edn., Ohio State U., 1950, D.D.S., 1954, pedodontic certificate, 1956, M.Sc., 1967; m. Roberta Lee Clark, Aug. 16, 1952; children—Rickey William, Marjorie Lee, Winifred Ann. Practice pedodontics, from 1954, now ret.; instr. pedodontics Ohio State U., 1956-66, asst. prof., 1966-67; asso. staff Children's Hosp., Columbus, from 1956; pres. bd. Riverglen Profl. Bldg., Inc., Worthington, Ohio, 1964-66, 73-76. Asst. dist. commr. Central Ohio council Boy Scouts Am., 1960-66, dist. chmn., 1966-67. Mem. bd. edn. Worthington Christian Schs., 1972; mem. missionary commn. Grace Brethren Ch., 1978—. Served with USNR, 1945-46. Fellow Am. Acad. Pedodontics, Pierre Fauchard Acad.; mem. Ohio Soc. Pedodontists (pres. 1968-69), Ohio Soc. Dentistry Children, (pres. 1957-58), Columbus Soc. Dentistry Children (pres. 1956-57), Photog. Soc. Am., Profl. Photographers Am., Profl. Photographers Ohio, Phi Delta Theta, Psi Omega, Alpha Phi Omega. Club: Ohio State University Faculty. Home: 267 Highgate Ave Worthington OH 43085 Office: 3722 J Olentangy River Rd Columbus OH 43214

MADDURI, SIVAPRASAD DAYANANDA, urologist; b. Narsapur, A.P., India, Aug. 8, 1943; came to U.S., 1970, naturalized, 1973; s. Pullaiah and Malathi (Vastadu) M.; B.Sc., Loyola Coll. (India), 1960; M.B., B.S., Med. Coll. Kurnool (India), 1965; M.S. in Gen. Surgery, Med. Coll. (India), 1969; married. Rotating intern Kingsbrook Jewish Med. Center, Bklyn., 1970-71; resident in gen. surgery Polyclinic Hosp., N.Y.C., 1971-73, Columbia Presbyn. Med. Center and the Squier Clinic, N.Y.C., 1972-73; resident in urology Coll. Medicine and Dentistry N.J.-N.J. Med. Sch. and Affiliated Hosps., Newark, 1973-76; practice medicine specializing in urology, Poplar Bluff, Mo., 1977—; cons. in urology Martland Hosp., Newark, 1976-77, St. Michael's Med. Center, Newark, 1976; urologist Doctors Hosp. and Kneibert Clinic, Poplar Bluff, 1977—; instr. surgery Coll. Medicine and Dentistry N.J.-N.J. Med. Sch., 1976-77; cons. in urology Lucy Lee Hosp., Poplar Bluff, 1978—, VA Hosp., Poplar Bluff, 1979-80. Recipient Gold medal in surgery, Seshagiri Rao Meml. prize Venkateswara Univ., 1965; F.C. Valentine fellow, 1976-77; lic. physician, N.J., Mo. Mem. AMA, Mo. Med. Assn., Butler Wayne Ripley County Med. Assn. Contbr. articles to profl. jours. Office: 666 Lester St Poplar Bluff MO 63901

MADEY, RICHARD, educator; b. Bklyn., Feb. 23, 1922; s. Elia Doher and Dorothy Ann (Diab) M.; B.E.E. (Conn. Alumni scholar), Rensselaer Poly. Inst., 1942; Ph.D. in Physics, U. Calif. at Berkely, 1952; m. Mary Lou Kirch, Sept. 8, 1951; children—Doren Louise, Diane Claire, Daryl Jane, Richard Kirk, Ronald Eliot, Randall Clarke. Elec. engr. Allen B. Dumont Labs., Passaic, N.J., 1934-44; physicist Lawrence Radiation Lab., Berkeley, 1947-53, guest scientist, 1971, 73, 77-79, 81; asso. physicist Brookhaven Nat. Lab., Upton, L.I., N.Y., 1953-56, guest scientist, 1961, 74; scientist Republic Aviation Corp., Farmingdale, N.Y., 1956-58, sr. scientist, 1958-61, chief staff scientist modern physics, 1961-62, chief applied physics research, 1964; prof. physics Clarkson Coll. Tech., Potsdam, N.Y., 1965-71, chmn. dept., 1965; prof. physics, chmn. dept. Kent (Ohio) State U., 1971—. Cons. Ross Radio Corp., Berkeley, 1952-53, West Coast Electronics Lab., Willys Motors Co., Oakland, Calif., 1953-55, Kaiser Aircraft & Electronics Corp., Palo Alto, Calif., 1955-56, Health and Safety Lab., U.S. AEC, N.Y.C., 1965-75, ERDA, 1975-77, Environ. Measurements Lab., Dept. of Energy, 1977—, Lawrence Berkeley Lab., 1978, Ecol. Energy Systems, 1979-80, Life Systems, Inc., 1981—; guest scientist Nevis Cyclotron Lab., Columbia U., Irvington-on-the-Hudson, N.Y., 1955, 76, 77, Foster Radiation Lab., McGill U., Montreal, Que., Can., 1967, 68, NRC, Ottawa, Ont., Can., 1968, 69, 70, Nuclear Structure Lab., U. Rochester (N.Y.), 1970, Lawrence Berkeley Lab., 1971, 72, 77-79, 81—, Ind. U. Cyclotron Facility, Bloomington, 1975—, Cyclotron Lab., U. Md. at College Park, 1973, 74, 75, 78; prin. investigator U.S. Air Force, 1963-75, AEC, 1967-75, ERDA, 1975-77, Dept. Energy, 1977—, NSF, 1971—, Nat. Cancer Inst., NIH, 1973-80, NASA, 1974—; radiation biology adv. panel to NASA Office Life Scis., Am. Inst. Biol. Scis., 1979—; mem. rev. panel and site visit team Nat. Cancer Inst., 1979. Served from ensign to lt. (j.g.), USNR, 1944-46. Decorated Naval Ordnance Devel. award (U.S.); Letter Commendation (Brit. Admiralty); recipient Army-Navy "E" award, 1943. Registered profl. elec. engr., Calif. Fellow N.Y. Acad. Scis., AAAS; mem. Inst. Colloid and Surface Sci., IEEE, Ohio Acad. Scis., AAUP, Am. Geophys. Union, Am. Phys. Soc., Am. Nuclear Soc. (membership com. 1962-63; membership com. shielding, dosimetry div. 1964-65, nominating com. 1965-66, exec. com. 1966-68; chmn. membership com. aerospace div. 1962-63, exec. com. 1963-65, treas. 1964-65; dir. N.Y. met. sect. 1960-61, spl. program chmn. 1960-62, sec. 1962-63, vice chmn. 1963, chmn. 1964, award 1965), Sigma Xi, Sigma Pi Sigma, Eta Kappa Nu, Pi Delta Epsilon. Author: (with Robert M. Winter) Modern Physics, 1971. Contbr. numerous articles tech. lit. Patentee in field.

MADEYSKI, WOJCIECH MARIA ANDREW PORAY, architect; b. Warsaw, Poland, Apr. 6, 1937; came to U.S., 1966, naturalized, 1974; s. Julian Feliks and Anna Helena (Krasuska) M.; M.Arch., Warsaw U., 1962; m. Danuta Bartnik, Nov. 23, 1963; children—Ursula, Mark. Designer, Guillaume Gillet, Paris, 1963-66, Fitch, Laroca, Chgo., 1966-68; sr. asso. C.F. Murphy Assos., Chgo., 1976-81; v.p., prin. designer Perkins Will, Chgo., 1981—; prin. archtl. works include 2 N. LaSalle Office Bldg., Chgo., 1979, 101 N. Wacker Dr. Office Bldg., Chgo., 1980, U. Chgo. Med. Center Replacement Hosp., 1981, Fed. Plaza Office Bldg., Milw., 1981, Lake County Public Library, Merrillville, Ind., 1981. French Govt. grantee, 1960. Mem. AIA. Roman Catholic. Office: 2 N LaSalle St Chicago IL 60602

MADIGAN, EDWARD R., congressman; b. Lincoln, Ill., Jan. 13, 1936; s. Earl T. and Theresa (Loobey) M.; grad. bus. Lincoln Coll., 1957; L.H.D. (hon.), Lincoln Coll., 1975, Millikin U., 1976, Ill. Wesleyan, 1978; m. Evelyn George, Sept. 1, 1954; children—Kim, Kellie, Mary. Mem. 93-97th Congresses from Ill. 21st dist., chmn. House Republican research com., mem. energy and commerce com., ranking minority mem. subcom. on health and the environment. Mem. Ill. Ho. of Reps., 1966-72; del. European Parliamentary Exchange, Russian Parliamentary Exchange. Recipient Outstanding Legislator award Ill. Assn. Sch. Supts., Outstanding Achievement award Lincoln Coll. Alumni Assn. Named Outstanding Freshman Congressman Nat. R.R. Unions. Home: 404 5th St Lincoln IL 62656 Office: 2457 Rayburn Bldg Washington DC 20515

MADISON, LESLIE P., coll. pres.; b. Pierre, S.D., Aug. 14, 1927; s. Walter Leon and Marguerite (McFarling) M.; cert. Moody Bible Inst., 1950; B.A., Rockmont Coll., 1954; Th.M., Dallas Theol. Sem., 1960; Th.D., Dallas Sem., 1963; m. Florence Ross, Dec. 21, 1945; children—Joanne, Ruth. Ordained minister Ind. Fundamental Chs. Am., 1950; pastor Kendrick (Colo.) Bible Ch., 1950-56; asst. pastor Prairie Creek Bapt. Ch., Dallas, 1956-62; pastor N.W. Bible Ch., Ft. Worth, 1962-74; pres. Calvary Bible Coll., Kansas City, Mo., 1974—; v.p. Ind. Fundamental Chs. Am., 1968-70, 75-77. Author: Abraham's Tests of Faith, 1972; Redemption in Ruth, 1974; Jonah, God's Disobedient Prophet, 1978. Office: Calvary Bible Coll Kansas City MO 64147

MADSEN, RUSSELL DUWANE, educator; b. Mpls., Oct. 5, 1926; s. LeRoy Burns and Elvira (Pearson) M.; B.S., U. Minn., 1950, M.A., 1958, Ph.D., 1969; m. Jean M. Judson, June 30, 1951; children—Janet, John. Supr., Minn. State Dept. Edn., St. Paul, 1951; bus. tchr. public schs., Kensington, Minn., 1951-53, Starbuck, Minn., 1953-57; instr. Moorhead (Minn.) State Coll., 1958-59; faculty St. Cloud (Minn.) State U., 1960—, prof. bus. edn. and office adminstrn., 1975—. Bd. dirs. Central Minn. council Boy Scouts Am., 1976—; treas. United Meth. Ch., St. Cloud, 1972—; treas. local orgn. Republican Party, 1979—. Served with U.S. Army, 1945-46. Mem. NEA, Nat. Bus. Edn. Assn., Assn. Records Mgrs. and Adminstrs., Delta Pi Epsilon. Club: Kiwanis. Contbr. articles in field to profl. jours. Home: 902 8th Ave S St Cloud MN 56301 Office: St Cloud State Univ Coll of Business St Cloud MN 56301

MADSON, CARLISLE, land surveyor; b. Wichita Falls, Tex., Apr. 3, 1920; s. Carlisle and Merlon Mae (Dennison) M.; student U. Minn., 1938-40, 50-56; m. S. Arleen Severson, May 22, 1948; children—Peggy Annette, John Carlisle, James Arby. Draftsman, Minn. Hwy. Dept., 1941; engring. aid, spl. engring. div. Third Locks Project, C.Z., 1942-43; draftsman, party chief A.C. Smith Co., 1946-50; sr. engring. aide, party chief City of St. Louis Park (Minn.), 1950-56; prin. land surveyor, exec. v.p. Schoell & Madson, Inc. cons. engrs. and land surveyors, Hopkins, Minn., 1956—; surveyor Carver County, 1970—; partner Carben Surveying Reprints. Served with AUS, 1943-46; CBI. Mem. Am. Congress Surveying and Mapping (life; Surveying Excellence award Land Survey div. 1978), Minn. Land Surveyors Assn. (Ann. Achievement awar 1971; historian, past pres.), Hennepin County Surveyors Assn., Minn. Surveyors and Engrs. Soc., Wis., Iowa, N.D. socs. profl. land surveyors, Mont. Assn. Registered Land Surveyors, Tex. Surveyors Assn., VFW, Am. Legion, Confederate Air Force, Minn. Hist. Soc., Danish Am. Inst. Republican. Congregationalist. Club: Interlachen. Home: 209 Shady Oak Rd Hopkins MN 55343 Office: 50 9th Ave S Hopkins MN 55343

MADURA, JAMES ANTHONY, physician; b. Campbell, Ohio, June 10, 1938; s. Anthony Peter and Margaret Ethel (Sebest) M.; A.B., Colgate U., 1959; M.D., Western Res. U., 1963; m. Loretta Jayne Sovak, Aug. 8, 1959; children—Debra Jean, James Anthony II, VikkiSue. Intern, Ohio State U., Columbus, 1963-64; resident in surgery, 1966-71; practice surgery, Indpls., 1971—; mem. staff Ind. U. Hosp., 1971—, Indpls. VA Hosp., 1971—, Wishard Meml. Hosp., Indpls., 1971—; asst. prof. surgery Ind. U. Med. Sch. Indpls., 1971-75, asso. prof., 1976-81, prof., 1981—. Dir. safety and health Indpls. Youth Hockey League, 1975-77. Served with AUS, 1964-66: Vietnam. NIH surg. trainee, 1967-71. Diplomate Am. Bd. Surgery. Fellow ACS (sec.-treas. Ind. chpt. 1978-81, pres. 1982); mem. Assn. Acad. Surgeons, Soc. Surgery Alimentary Tract, Ind. Med. Assn., Marion County Med. Soc., Central Surg. Assn., ASTM, Midwest Surg. Soc. Sigma Xi. Roman Catholic. Clubs: Columbia, Elks. Contbr. articles to profl. jours. Home: 9525 Copley Dr Indianapolis IN 46260 Office: 1100 W Michigan St Indianapolis IN 46260

MADUZIA, EDWARD M., lawyer; b. Chgo., Apr. 5, 1941; s. Wells H. and Dorothy (Voss) M.; B.S., Northwestern U., 1963; J.D., U. Chgo., 1966; m. Sandra J. Brantlay, May 23, 1970; children—Amber Monite, Donald Kendrick. Admitted to Ill. bar, 1966, U.S. Supreme Ct. bar, 1970; asso. mem. firm Thomas, Blass, Simpson & Tyler, Chgo., 1966-70, mem. firm, 1970-76; individual oractice law, Chgo., 1976—; lectr., Coll. DuPage, 1974—. Vol. fireman Lombard (Ill.) Fire Dept., 1966-79; active Lombard chpt. ARC, 1969-79, chmn., 1976-77; mem. Lombard Library Renovation Com., 1977-79. Recipient Outstanding Alumnus award Northwestern U., 1977. Mem. Am., Ill. bar assns., Judicature Soc., Am. Assn. Vol. Firefighters. Democrat. Clubs: Rotary, Elks, Masons. Home: 4505 N Manor Chicago IL 60625

MAESEN, WILLIAM AUGUST, social worker; b. Albertson, N.Y., May 18, 1939; s. August and Wilhelmina (Gaska) M.; B.A., Oklahoma City U., 1961, B.S. in Bus., 1961; M.A., Ind. State U., 1968; D. Social Work, U. Ill., Chgo., 1979; postgrad. Mich. State U., 1980-81; m. Sherry Lee Jaeger, Aug. 13, 1971; children—Ryan and Betsy (twins), Steven. Instr. sociology Aquinas Coll., Grand Rapids, Mich., 1967-70; asso. prof. behavioral sci. Coll. St. Francis, Joliet, Ill., 1970-78; lectr. U. Ill., Chgo., 1974-78; asso. prof. Grand Valley State Coll., Allendale, Mich., 1978-82; pres. Chgo. Inst. for Advanced Studies, 1982—; dir. residential treatment Cathedral Shelter of Chgo., 1982—. Chmn., Christian social relations dept. Episcopal Diocese Western Mich., 1979-80, mem. Bishops Council, 1979-80. Served with USAFR, 1962-68. Mem. Nat. Assn. Social Workers, Am. Sociol. Assn., Clin. Sociology Assn. (exec. bd.), Community Devel. Soc., Soc. Psychol. Study Social Issues, Gerontol. Soc., Beta Gamma, Alpha Kappa Delta. Editor, Clin. Sociology Rev., 1980-81; contbr. articles to profl. jours. Home: PO Box 4380 Chicago IL 60680

MAGDALENO, JULIAN MELQUIADES, JR., mgmt. cons.; b. Buenos Aires, Argentina; s. Julian M. and Maria Nelly (Orono) M.; came to U.S., 1956, naturalized, 1963; B.S. in Biomed. Engring., Rensselaer Poly. Inst., 1976, M.S. in Health Systems Engring., 1977; m. Jeannette Marie Siel, Feb. 17, 1979. Coordinator, Swine Flu Vaccination Program, Troy, N.Y., 1976; mgmt. cons., health systems engr. Ernst & Ernst, Chgo., 1977—. Active local Police Boys Club, Boy Scouts Am.; chmn. Rensselaer Med. Adv. Com., 1975-77. Recipient Phalynx award Rensselaer Poly. Inst., 1977. Mem. Am. Hosp. Assn., Am. Inst. Indsl. Engrs., Am. Public Health Assn., Assn. Am. Med. Colls., Health Mgmt. Systems Soc. Office: 150 S Wacker Dr Chicago IL 60606

MAGDOVITZ, BENJAMIN I., newspaper exec.; b. New Bethlehem, Pa., May 28, 1924; s. Sam and Esther (Tucker) M.; student Bethany Coll., 1941-43; B. Journalism, U. Mo., 1948, M.A., 1949; m. Sylvia Kornblet, Sept. 5, 1949; children—Beth Magdovitz Timen, Sam, Alan. Lectr. retail advt. Univ. Coll., Washington U., St. Louis, 1956-63; asst. retail advt. mgr. St. Louis Globe-Democrat, 1958, retail advt. mgr., 1958, advt. mgr., 1959, advt. dir., 1963-79; dir. advt. Toledo Blade Co., 1979—, v.p., 1980—. Bd. dirs. Greater Toledo Community Chest, 1980—, Downtown Toledo Assos., 1979, Temple B'Nai Israel, Jewish Family Service; co.-chmn. United Way, 1980; trustee Toledo Better Bus. Bur., 1980—, bd. dirs., 1979; pres. Central States region United Synagogue Am., also nat. v.p. United Synagogue Am. Served with U.S. Army, 1943-46. Mem. Advt. Club Toledo, Internat. Newspaper Advt. Mktg. Execs. (met. Sunday newspapers sales adv. com.). Club: Kiwanis (Downtown Toledo). Office: 541 Superior St Toledo OH 43660

MAGEE, LAURA JEAN, arts edn. cons.; b. Lake Cormorant, Miss., May 10, 1938; d. Julius E. and Ottomece (Price) M.; B.F.A., Newcomb Coll. Tulane U., 1959; M.A., La. State U., 1970; Ed.D., Ariz. State U., 1973. Instr. art Delgado Coll., New Orleans, 1964-68; grad. teaching asst., art, La. State U., Baton Rouge, 1968-70, Ariz. State U., Tempe, 1971-73; asst. prof. art Drake U., Des Moines, 1973-76; cons. arts edn. Iowa Dept. Pub. Instrn., Des Moines, 1976—; TV cons. IPBN, Des Moines, 1974—; media cons. Phoenix Coll.,

1972; TV cons. Sta KAET, Tempe, 1971-72. Mem. Nat. Art Edn. Assn. (co-chmn. documentation evaluation 1977). Author publs. in field. Home: 2838 Forest Dr Des Moines IA 50312 Office: Iowa Dept Public Instruction Grimes State Office Bldg Des Moines IA 50319

MAGGART, THOMAS ALLEN, accountant; b. Hamilton, Ohio, Jan. 12, 1946; s. Clarence Cecil and Rhomilda Catherine (Fischer) M.; B.S. in Bus. Adminstrn. (Charles Dodd scholar, Jr. Achievement scholar), Miami U., 1966; M.B.A., U. Cin., 1967; postgrad. Xavier U., 1976—; m. Theo Ann Wells, Mar. 8, 1969; children—Timothy Allen, Todd Andrew. Grad. teaching asst. U. Cin., 1966-67; sr. cost analyst MacGregor div. Brunswick Corp., Cin., 1967-68; internal auditor, fin. analyst Procter & Gamble Co., Cin., 1971-73; controller Pat & Joe's, Inc., Cin., 1973-74; mgr. internal auditing Bethesda Hosp. and Deaconess Assn., Cin., 1974-79, controller, 1979-81, asst. v.p. fin./controller, 1981—; acting operation mgr. Bethesda Scarlet Oaks, 1975, acting gen. mgr., 1977; instr. U. Md. in Vietnam, 1970; lectr. Raymond Walters Coll., U. Cin., 1977—; dir. Bethesda Hosp. Fed. Credit Union, 1974—, v.p., 1979-80, pres., 1980—. Served to capt. M.S.C., AUS, 1968-71. Decorated Bronze Star (2), Army Commendation medal. C.P.A., Ohio. Fellow Hosp. Fin. Mgmt. Assn.; mem. Am. Hosp. Assn., Hosp. Fin. Mgmt. Assn., Am. Inst. C.P.A.'s, Ohio Soc. C.P.A.'s, Current Health Care Users of MSA (dir. 1980—), Beta Alpha Psi. Roman Catholic. Home: 10445 Walkingfern Dr Harrison OH 45030 Office: Bethesda Hospital and Deaconess Assn 619 Oak St Cincinnati OH 45206

MAGNES, G(ERALD) DONALD, dentist; b. Chgo., Sept. 27, 1933; s. Herman S. and Fae (Ray) M.; B.S., U. Ill., 1956, D.D.S., 1958; m. Loretta Bass, Aug. 5, 1956; children—Scott A., Craig N. Individual practice dentistry, Chgo., 1958—. Cons., Warner-Chilcott Labs., Morris Plains, N.J., 1964—; instr. U. Ill. Coll. Dentistry. Recipient certificate recognition Am. Dental Assn., 1967; award winning exhibit Nat. Am. Dental Assn., 1967; donor sci. exhibit U. Ill. Med. Sch., 1968. Fellow Royal Soc. Health; mem. Am. Dental Assn., Chgo. Dental Soc., Am. Cancer Soc. (speaker 1969-70), Internat. Assn. Dental Research, Am. Assn. Dental Research, U. Ill. Alumni Assn., Alpha Omega. Contbr. articles to profl. jours. Home: 4625 West Grove Skokie IL 60076 Office: 2601 W Peterson Ave Chicago IL 60659

MAGNUSON, CAROLYN SUE, educator; b. Topeka, Sept. 5, 1939; d. Carl McClelland Magnuson and Rebecca J. Magnuson Jackson; stepdau. Roy C. Jackson; B.A., Coll. Emporia (Kans.), 1961; M.A., George Peabody Coll., Nashville, 1964; M.Ed., U. Mo., 1972, Ed.S., 1973, Ph.D., 1981. Tchr., Wichita (Kans.) Public Schs., 1961-63; tchr. Shawnee Mission (Kans.) Schs., 1963-67, reading specialist, 1967-73; asst. dir. career edn. curriculum project U. Mo., 1973-75, asst. dir. career edn. inservice project, 1975-76, counselor, 1976-77, instr. career edn., 1973-81, grad. teaching asst., 1977-81; asst. prof. counselor edn. Lincoln U., Jefferson City, Mo., 1981—; cons. in field. Mem. Values Realization Assos., Nat. Assn. Career Edn., Am. Personnel and Guidance Assn., Am. Sch. Counselors Assn., Assn. Counselor Edn. and Supervision, Nat. Vocat. Guidance Assn., Assn. Humanistic Edn. and Devel., Am. Vocat. Assn., Mo. Guidance Assn., Mo. Personnel and Guidance Assn., Mo. Vocat. Assn., NEA, Kappa Delta Pi, Delta Kappa Gamma (Jenny Watson award 1970, Tessie Agan award 1972, Mayme Hamilton award 1978), Pi Lambda Theta, Phi Delta Rappa. Presbyterian. Author: (with others) Missouri Career Education, 1975, rev., 1976, 77, Mainstreaming Handicapped Students in Vocational Education, 1978; You & Others —???, 1974; You & ???—Friendship, 1974; You & ???—Communication, 1975; (with Marilyn H. White) Career Education Methods and Processes, 1974. Home: 1005 Queen Ann #14 Columbia MO 65201 Office: 112 Martin Luther King Lincoln Univ Jefferson City MO 65101

MAGOSKY, PATRICIA ANN, pvt. investigator; b. Chgo., Aug. 17, 1942; d. Walter A. and Bertha (Topp) Troy; student U. Wis., Parkside, 1979—; widow; children—Jodi Ann, Heather Leigh. Clk., E.J. Brach & Sons, Chgo., 1960-65; mgr. Lake-of-the-Woods Lodge, Nestor Falls, Ont., Can., 1966-67; tech. coordinator Joliet (Ill.) Wrought Washer, 1971-72; office mgr. dental office, Elkhorn, Wis., 1972-73; communications officer Lake Geneva (Wis.) Police Dept., 1973-81, part-time police matron; pvt. investigator Braden & Olson law firm, Lake Geneva, 1977—. Founding, past pres. Assn. Prevention of Family Violence, 1978-79. Recipient Walworth County Mental Health award, 1979. Mem. Lake Geneva Profl. Policemen's Protective Assn. (past pres., chmn. contract negotiations team, 1974—), Lake Geneva Bus. and Profl. Women's Club (legis. chmn., 1st v.p.), Lake Como Beach Property Owners Assn. (treas.). Republican. Roman Catholic. Home: Rt 2 Box 402 Lake Geneva WI 53147 Office: 626 Geneva St Lake Geneva WI 53147

MAGRATH, C(LAUDE) PETER, univ. pres.; b. N.Y.C., Apr. 23, 1933; s. Laurence Wilfrid and Guilia Maria (Dentice) M.; m. 2d, Diane Skomars, Mar. 25, 1978; 1 stepdau., Monette Fay; 1 dau. by previous marriage, Valerie Ruth; B.A., U. N.H., 1955; Ph.D., Cornell U., 1962. Faculty, Brown U., 1961-68, prof. polit. sci., 1967-68, asso. dean Grad. Sch., 1965-66; dean Coll. Arts and Sci., U. Nebr., 1968-69, dean of faculties, 1969, interim chancellor, 1969, interim v.p. U. Nebr. System, 1971-72, prof. polit. sci., 1968, vice chancellor for acad. affairs, 1972; prof. polit. sci. State U. N.Y. at Binghamton, 1972-74; pres. U. Minn., Mpls., 1974—. Mem. exec. com. Nat. Assn. State Univs. and Land Grant Colls.; mem. U.S. Bd. Internat. Food and Agrl. Devel. Mem. Am., Midwest polit. sci. assns., Orgn. Am. Historians, Phi Beta Kappa, Phi Kappa Phi, Pi Gamma Mu, Pi Sigma Alpha. Author: The Triumph of Character, 1963; Yazoo: Law and Politics in the New Republic, The Case of Fletcher v. Peck, 1966; Constitutionalism and Politics: Conflict and Consensus, 1968; The American Democracy, 1973. Home: 176 N Mississippi River Blvd Saint Paul MN 55104 Office: Morrill Hall U Minn Minneapolis MN 55455

MAGRO, LAURA FRANCIS, educator; b. Cap, Va., June 20, 1924; d. Loyd P. and Margie (Hampton) Gardner; B.S., Radford Women's div. Va. Poly. Inst., 1946; m. Frank Joseph Magro, June 18, 1949; children—Frank Lee, John David. Tchr., Big Island, Va., 1946-47, New Buffalo, Mich., 1947-58, Buchanan, Mich., 1958-61, Three Oaks, Mich., 1961-63; tchr. vocat. clothing Michigan City (Ind.) Elston High Sch., 1963—; mem. home econs. curriculum com. State of Ind., 1980—, mem. vocat. evaluation team, 1980-81. Mem. NEA, Michigan City Edn. Assn., Am. Home Econs. Assn., Am. Vocat. Assn., Ind. State Tchrs. Assn., Ind. Vocat. Home Econs. Assn., Nat. Vocat. Home Econs. Assn., Ind. Vocat. Assn. Club: Eastern Star. Home: 529 Buffalo St New Buffalo MI 49117 Office: Elston High School Michigan City IN 46360

MAGRUDER, WILLIAM ROGER, pharmacist; b. Aurora, Ill., May 5, 1947; s. Stanley Edward and Ruth E. (Ekstrom) M.; B.S. in Pharmacy, U. Ill., 1970; M.B.A., Rosary Coll., 1980; m. Barbara T. Zmudka, Nov. 28, 1970; children—Michael William, Christopher Ryan. Pharmacist supr. Grimms Drug Inc., St. Charles, Ill., 1970-71; dir. pharmacy services Westlake Community Hosp., Melrose Park, Ill., 1971-80; asst. dir. pharmacy for spl. projects Michael Reese Hosp. and Med. Center, Chgo., 1980—; asso. clin. instr. U. Ill. Coll. Pharmacy, 1979—. Chmn. pharmacy group purchasing subcom. Chgo. Hosp. Council, 1979—. Recipient Service award Westlake Community Hosp., 1976. Mem. Am. Soc. Hosp. Pharmacists, Ill. Council Hosp. Pharmacists, U. Ill. Coll. Pharmacy Alumni Assn. Roman Catholic. Office: 29th and Ellis Ave Chicago IL

MAGSIG, DANNY JOHN, mfg. co. exec.; b. Toledo, Apr. 19, 1943; s. Manly Albert and Mary Elizibeth (Garn) M.; B.S. in Engring., Mich. State U., 1965; m. Janet Elaine Kelley, Sept. 14, 1963; children—Heath, Trent, Quinn. Supr. indsl. engring. Allis Chalmers, Springfield, Ill., 1969-71; mgr. material handling ops. Internat. Harvester Co., Melrose Park, Ill., 1971-75; pres. Systems Unlimited, Inc., Coldwater, Mich., 1975—. Mem. Soc. Mfg. Engrs., Am. Mgmt. Assn. Republican. Methodist. Club: Rotary. Home: 263 Almary Dr Coldwater MI 49036 Office: 505 Race St Coldwater MI 49036

MAHAN, EUGENE ROBERT, state senator, farmer; b. Union County, S.D., Aug. 14, 1933; s. Michael Frances and Helen (McCarthy) M.; B.S., S.D. State U., 1963; m. Mary Louise Swedean, 1959; children—Michael Eugene, Brian Patrick, Timothy James, Michelle Mary. Farmer, Union County, S.D., 1955—; salesman Equitable Life Assurance Co., Calif., 1964-67; mem. S.D. Ho. of Reps., 1971-73; mem. S.D. Senate, 1973—, asst. majority leader, 1975-76, minority leader, 1977—. Served with U.S. Army, 1953-55; Korea. Roman Catholic. Office: State Capitol Pierre SD 57501

MAHAN, GENEVIEVE ELLIS, sociologist; b. Canton, Ohio, Aug. 1, 1909; d. William and Lillian (Ellis) Mahan; A.B., Western Res. U., 1931, A.M., 1941; postgrad. (Ford Found. fellow) Yale, 1952, Akademie fur Politische Bildung, Tutzing, Germany, 1963. Tchr. high schs., Canton, 1937-52; research asst. dept. sociology Yale, 1953-55; lectr. sociology Walsh Coll., Canton, 1970. Participant Instns. Atlantic and European Cooperation Seminar, Coimbra, Portugal, 1970; participant World Congress of Sociology, Evian, France, 1966. Trustee, Stark County Psychiat. Found., 1961-68. Fellow Am. Sociol. Assn.; mem. Internat. Sociol. Assn., Eastern Sociol. Soc., Am. Acad. Polit. and Social Sci., Nat., Ohio (exec. bd. 1962-69, pres. 1965) councils for social studies, A.A.A.S., Am. Assn. U. Women (mem. exec. bd. Canton 1966-67), Ohio Acad. Sci., Ohio Soc. N.Y. Clubs: Canton Womans, Canton College. Research in polit. caricature, 1955—. Home: 804 5th St NW Canton OH 44703

MAHAN, HAROLD DEAN, museum exec.; b. Ferndale, Mich., June 11, 1931; s. Elbert Verl and Jo Ann Magdeline (Upton) M.; m. Mary Jane Gardiner, June 9, 1954; children—Michael, Eric, David, Christopher, Thomas; B.A., Wayne U., 1954; M.S., U. Mich., 1957; Ph.D., Mich. State U., 1964. Prof. biology Central Mich. U., 1957-73, dir. Center for Cultural and Natural History, 1970-72; pres. Environ. Enterprises, Inc., Mt. Pleasant, Mich., 1970-73; dir. Cleve. Mus. Natural History, 1973—; adj. prof. Case-Western Res. U., 1973—; resident scientist Museo de Historia Natural, Cali, Colombia, 1968; v.p. Midwest Museums Conf., 1974-76, pres., 1976-80. Mem. Airport Commn. Mt. Pleasant, 1965-68; pres. Mich. Audubon Soc., 1972-73; mem. Ohio Natural Areas Council, 1974-80; trustee Inst. for Environ. Edn., Shaker Lakes Regional Nature Center, Holden Arboretum (corporate bd.), Greater Cleve. Garden Center, Univ. Circle, Inc., Rapid Recovery, Inc. Mem. Ohio Museums Assn. (pres. 1976-80), Assn. Sci. Mus. Dirs. (pres. 1980—), Assn. Systematic Collections (v.p. 1979—), Sigma Xi, Phi Kappa Phi, Phi Sigma, Beta Beta Beta, NSF faculty fellow Mich. State U., 1965. Clubs: Cleve. Playhouse, Rowfant; Explorers (N.Y.C.). Author: (with George J. Wallace) An Introduction to Ornithology, 1975; editor: The Jack Pine Warbler, 1965-72; Nature columnist Cleve. Press, 1973-74; book rev. editor Explorer mag., 1974—; contbr. articles to profl. jours. Home: 28050 Gates Mills Blvd Pepper Pike OH 44124 Office: Mus Natural History Wade Oval University Circle Cleveland OH 44106

MAHANNA, SIMON ALBERT, construction mgmt. co. exec.; b. St. Louis, Sept. 14, 1948; s. Simon Albert and Patricia Ruth (Swift) M.; B.S., U. Mo., 1970, M.S., 1975; m. Debra Ann Brady, July 24, 1971. Civil engr. City of St. Louis, 1970-72; sr. planning engr. Bechtel Power Corp., 1973-76; project engr. McCarthy Bros. Co., St. Louis, 1976-77; sr. v.p. Escrow Mgmt., Inc., Crestwood, Mo., 1977—; pres. Profl. Devel. and Mgmt. Services, 1977—, also dir.; pres. Profl. Builders of St. Louis, Inc., 1979—; gen. partner Profl. Realty Assos. Served with U.S. Army, 1969-77. Registered profl. engr., Mo., Calif., Ill. Mem. ASCE, Nat. Soc. Profl. Engrs., Am. Fedn. Scientists. Maronite Catholic. Office: PO Box 56 Chesterfield MO 63017

MAHAPATRA, AMRITA, occupational therapist; b. India, May 31, 1951; came to U.S., 1977; d. Baldev Singh and Bimla (Sethi) Bedi; grad. Physio-Occupational Therapy Coll., New Delhi, India, 1971; m. Sabyasachi Mahapatra, July 12, 1974; 1 dau., Sujata Mahapatra. Hon. lectr. Physio-Occupational Therapy Inst., New Delhi, 1971-72; occupational therapist, hosps. in India, 1972-77; occupational therapist Rehab. Inst., Detroit, 1978—, asst. dir., occupational therapy clinic, 1978—. Mem. Am. Occupational Therapy Assn. Hindu Sikh. Home: 17320 Whitcomb 229 Detroit MI 48235 Office: 261 Mack Ave Detroit MI 48201

MAHAR, WILLIAM F., state senator; b. nr. Belleville, Wis., Jan. 1, 1919; B.S., U. Wis.; m. Alice Lauter; 2 sons. Owner, operator coin operated laundry co.; pres. investment co.; former mem. Ill. Ho. of Reps.; mem. Ill. Senate. Trustee, Homewood, Ill., from 1961, pres., 1965; mem. exec. bd. Cook County (Ill.) Council Govt.; mem. Chgo. Area Transp. Study Council of Mayors; chmn. chpt. Salvation Army. Mem. Am. Legion. Clubs: Moose. Office: State Capitol Springfield IL 62706*

MAHEDY, THOMAS BRIAN, truck leasing co. exec.; b. San Diego, Nov. 26, 1946; s. William Peter and Loretta Marie (Engler) M.; B.A., San Diego State Coll., 1970; m. Susan Marie Smith, May 10, 1968; children—Thomas Brian, Steven William. Patrolman, San Diego Police Dept., 1968-69; city mgr. Ruan Leasing Co., Des Moines, 1973-75, dist. mgr., 1975-77, sales mgr., 1977-79, dir. ops., 1980—. Bd. mgrs. South Suburban YMCA, Des Moines, 1978—, chmn., 1981—; mem. futures com. Greater Des Moines YMCA, 1980—, co-chmn. capital fund drive, 1979. Served with USMC, 1970-73. Mem. Nat. Assn. Furniture Mfrs., Nat. Council Phys. Distbn. Mgmt. Republican. Roman Catholic. Club: Echo Valley Country. Office: 666 Grand Ave Des Moines IA 50309

MAHER, DAVID WILLARD, lawyer; b. Chgo., Aug. 14, 1934; s. Chauncey Carter and Martha (Peppers) M.; A.B., Harvard, 1955, LL.B., 1959; m. Jill Waid Armagnac, Dec. 20, 1954; children—Philip Armagnac, Julia Armagnac. Admitted to N.Y. bar, 1960, Ill. bar, 1961; practiced in Chgo., 1961—; asso. Kirkland & Ellis, and predecessor firm, 1960-65, partner, 1966-78; partner firm Reuben & Proctor, 1978—; lectr. Loyola U. Sch. Law., Chgo. Bd. dirs. Chgo. Better Bus. Bur. Served to 2d lt. USAF, 1955-56. Mem. Am., Ill., Chgo. bar assns. Roman Catholic. Clubs: Bull Valley Hunt, Chicago Literary, Tavern. Home: 311 Belden Ave Chicago IL 60614 Office: 19 S LaSalle St Chicago IL 60603

MAHER, MERICI, educator; b. Chgo., July 27, 1926; d. Edward Byron and Lillian Martha (Maddock) M.; B.S., Coll. St. Teresa, 1953; M.S.P.H., U. Mo., Columbia, 1970; postgrad. U. Ill., Urbana. Joined Sisters of Franciscan Congregation, Roman Catholic Ch., 1945; head nurse, supr. St. Mary's Hosp., Rochester, Minn., 1950-69; team leader Mile Sq. Neighborhood Health Center, Chgo., 1970-72; team leader Vis. Nurse Assn., Chgo., 1972-74; instr. community nursing DePaul U., Chgo., 1974-77, asst. prof., 1977—. Mem., Ill. Prolife Com., 1976-79; mem. Coalition of Polit. Honesty, 1974-76. Mem. Am. Nurses Assn., Nat. League Nursing, Am. PUblic Health Assn. Democrat. Roman Catholic. Co-author: Community Health Nursing Continuing Education Review. Home: 7011 Addison St Chicago IL 60634 Office: 2323 N Seminary St Chicago IL 60614

MAHMOOD, KHALID, physician; b. Gujranwala, Pakistan, Feb. 15, 1938; s. Mohammad Saied and Mumtaz Begum (Ata Mohammad) Mazharie; came to U.S., 1971, naturalized, 1977; F.Sc., Govt. Coll., Abbottabad, Pakistan, 1956; B.Sc., U. Punjab, Lahore, Pakistan, 1960; M.B., B.S., King Edward Med. Coll., Lahore, 1962; m. Patricia Hope Ashleman, June 15, 1975; children—Farrah Renee, Tarik Adam. Intern, Danbury (Conn.) Hosp., 1963-64, Lewis Gale Hosp., Roanoke, Va., 1964-65; resident otolaryngology Albert Einstein Coll. Medicine, N.Y.C., 1965-69; research fellow otolaryngology U. Toronto (Ont., Can.), 1969-70; practice medicine, specializing in otolaryngology, Toronto, 1971, Sandusky, Ohio, 1972—; mem. staff, cons. Providence Hosp., chief div. otolaryngology, 1974—; mem. cons. staff, chief otolaryngology Good Samaritan Hosp., 1972—. Bd. dirs. Erie County (Ohio) unit Am. Cancer Soc. Fellow A.C.S., Am. Acad. Otolaryngology and Head and Neck Surgery; mem. AMA, Erie County Med. Soc., Ohio State Med. Assn. Research on tritiated thymidine study of irradiated cancer larynx, 1968-69. Home: Sandusky OH Office: 1221 Hayes Ave Sandusky OH 44870

MAHNIC, FRANK, JR., state legislator; b. Garfield Heights, Ohio, July 10, 1946; s. Frank and Mary (Kuznik) M.; student Cuyahoga Community Coll., 1975; B.A., Case Western Res. U., 1977; m. Elsa Busetto, Feb. 24, 1968; children—Lisa, Jennifer. Mem. Ohio Ho. of Reps., 1978—, mem. edn., utilities, fin. instns., health and retirement, ins. coms. Mem. Garfield Heights Boys Baseball League, Human Relations Council, Recreation Bd., 1976-77; Democratic precinct committeeman, Garfield Heights, 1972-82; mem. Cuyahoga County Dem. exec. bd. dirs., 1974-82. Served with U.S. Army, 1966-68. Decorated Purple Heart; recipient Slovene Man of Yr. award, 1979; Man of Yr. award Cuyahoga Community Coll., 1975. Mem. Cath. War Vets., Am. Legion, Alliance of Poles, Slovenian Dem. League (co-chmn. 1976), Ohio Sch. Bds. Assn., Nat. Sch. Bds. Assn. Roman Catholic. Clubs: Elmwood PTA, KC, Dad's Booster. Home: 11019 Plymouth Ave Garfield Heights OH 44125 Office: Statehouse Columbus OH 43215

MAHONEY, RICHARD JOHN, diversified mfg. co. exec.; b. Springfield, Mass., Jan. 30, 1934; s. Maurice E. and Marion L. (Kennedy) M.; B.S. in Chemistry, U. Mass., 1955; m. Barbara M. Barnett, Jan. 26, 1957; children—Stephen, William, Robert. Sales trainee chem. div. U.S. Rubber Co., Naugatuck, Conn., 1955-56; field sales Alco Chem. Corp., New Eng., 1959-62; successively product devel. specialist various sales and tech. service positions, market mgr. new products div. Monsanto Co., 1962-67, div. sales dir. plastic products, Kenilworth, N.J., 1967-71, sales dir. agrl. div., St. Louis, 1971-72, dir. sales, 1972-74, dir. ops. internat. Monsanto Agrl. Products Co., 1974, gen. mgr. overseas div., 1975, corp. v.p. and mng. dir., 1976, group v.p. and mng. dir. Monsanto Plastics & Resins Co., 1976-77, exec. v.p., 1977—, dir., 1979—; dir. First Nat. Bank St. Louis, Met. Life Ins. Co.; mem. Internat. Trade Adv. Council, Japan-U.S. Trade Council. Mem. adv. bd. St. John's Mercy Med. Center, 1979; mem. chancellor's council U. Mo., St. Louis, 1979. Served to 1st lt. USAF, 1956-59. Mem. Chem. Mfrs. Assn., U.S. C. of C. Club: Bellerive Country. Office: 800 N Lindbergh Blvd Saint Louis MO 63166

MAHR, ALLAN DAVID, poet; b. Belleville, Ill., Jan. 7, 1910; s. Allan D. and Sadie Lee (Duffy) M.; student St. Louis U. Extension, 1953, Mo. U. Extension, 1963; m. Cora Belle Sanders, Dec. 14, 1940; children—Cosandra Lee, Allan David, Michael Anthony, Noel Kriston (dec.), Jan Corlus, Dale Brian, Coraminita Elizabeth, Coralicia Dawnisse. Author over 2000 poems, 1936—: Eye of the Heart, 1973; tapes of 88 poems donated to Tape Talk for the Blind, Webster Groves, Mo.; contbr. poetry to various lit. publs. and anthologies; poems displayed in collections of Winston Churchill Meml. Library, Kennedy Meml. Library, L.B. Johnson Meml. Library, The Truman and Tom Dooley Room at Notre Dame, Forest Park Community Coll., Florissant Valley Community Coll., St. Louis Public Library System, others; guest of Midwest Lit., Mich. State U., 1979. Sec., treas. Holy Ghost council Boy Scouts Am., 1960-65; poet, composer for Zeta Sigma chpt. Sigma Gamma Rho. Recipient various awards including Hon. Mention, St. Louis Poetry Center, 1965, Dag Hammarskjold award Poems of Decade Anthologies, Eng.; diploma of honor Centro Studi E Scambi Internazionali-Accademia Leonardo Da Vinci, 1982; Cultural Litt.D. award World Univ. Roundtable, Tucson, 1981. Mem. Acad. Am. Poets of N.Y., Ariz. Poetry Soc., Avalonian Writers of San Angelo (Tex.), McKendree Writers, Centro Studi Escambi of Rome. Roman Catholic. Address: 4838 Cote Brilliante Saint Louis MO 63113

MAHRT, DELMAR HERMANN, radiologist; b. Colon, Nebr., Jan. 9, 1936; s. Herman Jurgens Frederick and Kathleen Mercedes (Hoffstetter) M.; M.D., U. Nebr., 1960; m. Dorothea Ann Wetzel, Dec. 19, 1975; children—David Delmar, Kristian Hunter, Nikolaus Justin. Intern, Immanuel Hosp., Omaha, 1960-61; resident in radiology Washington U., St. Louis, 1961-64; attending radiologist Reid Meml. Hosp., Richmond, Ind., 1964-65; attending therapeutic radiologist Wm. Beaumont Hosp., Royal Oak, Mich., 1965—, dir. dept. radiation oncology, 1981—. Pres. Oakland County (Mich.) unit Am. Cancer Soc., 1974-76; bd. dirs. Mich. div. Am. Cancer Soc., 1972—, pres., 1979-80; bd. govs. Comprehensive Cancer Center Detroit; bd. dirs. Comprehensive Health Planning Council of Southeastern Mich., 1982—. Mem. Mich. Soc. Therapeutic Radiologists (pres., chmn. bd.), Oakland County Med. Soc. (sec.). Lutheran. Home: 855 N Pemberton Rd Bloomfield Hills MI 48013 Office: 3601 W Thirteen Mile Rd Royal Oak MI 48072

MAIANU, ALEXANDRU, educator, researcher; b. Moldoveni, Romania, Jan. 8, 1931; came to U.S., 1977; s. Nedelcu and Voica (Burtea) M.; B.S., U. Bucharest (Romania), 1953, M.S., 1954, Ph.D., 1962. Research soil scientist Romanian Agr. Research Inst., 1954-63; sr. research soil scientist, head Soil Reclamation Lab., Romania, 1963-77; asst. prof. soil sci. U. Bucharest, 1963-66; asso. prof. soil sci., head Soil Characterization Lab., N.D. State U., Fargo, 1980—; nat. supr. Romanian research programs in soil reclamation, 1969-74. Head, Romanian dept. Emmanuel Christian Ministry, Taking Christ to Millions, Internat., Inc. Recipient Ion Ionescu de la Brad award Romanian Acad. Scis., 1966, Emil Racovitza award, 1972; award Romanian Dept. Edn., 1968. Mem. Am. Soc. Agronomy, Soil Sci. Soc. Am., Internat. Soc. Soil Sci. Author: Secondary Soil Salinization, 1964; (with A. Ghidia) Improving Soil Fertility in Greenhouses, 1974; (with G. Obrejanu) Limnology of the Romanian Sector of the Danube River, 1967, Soil Study on the Experimental Stations of Romanian Agriculture, 1958. Home: 2599 Villa Dr 215 Fargo ND 58103 Office: ND State U Soils Dept Waldron Hall 202 PO Box 5575 Fargo ND 58105

MAIER, BETTY, educator; b. Plainview, Tex., Feb. 8, 1927; d. Arthur Leonard and Thelma Ruth (Amberg) Mangum; student Tex. Tech. U., 1944-45; B.S., Ft. Hays (Kans.) State U., 1962, M.S., 1966; postgrad. Kans. U., 1967, Kans. State U., 1969, U. Nebr., 1977; m. Sam Maier, Sept. 24, 1947; children—Judith Ladine, Robert Glenn. Tchr. rural schs., Barton County, Kans., 1957-65; tchr. math., sci. Hoisington (Kans.) United Sch. Dist. #431, 1965-66, founder, dir. speech therapy program, 1966-69, tchr. hearing impaired, deaf-hearing cons., 1969—. Mem. Kans. Speech-Lang.-Hearing Assn., Am. Speech and Hearing Assn., Alexander Graham Bell Assn. of

Deaf, Gt. Bend Bus. and Profl. Women (named Woman of Yr. 1973). Republican. Lutheran. Home: 5304 Broadway Great Bend KS 67530 Office: 516 N Pine Hoisington KS 67544

MAIER, DEL RALPH, vending co. exec.; b. Bismarck, N.D., July 20, 1929; s. Emil and Emma E. (Bickel) M.; grad. Bismarck Jr. Coll., 1951; m. Marilyn M. Otis, June 5, 1955; children—Robert D., David R., Lyn M. Partner, S & M Vending, 1955-57; pres. Del-Mar Vending & Wholesale, Bismarck, 1957—. Served with USAF, 1948-50. Mem. N.D. Candy and Tobacco Assn. (pres. 1979-80), Am. Legion. Republican. Presbyterian. Clubs: Eagles, Elks. Home: 1004 W Highland Acres Rd Bismarck ND 58501 Office: 1840 Revere Dr Bismarck ND 58501

MAIER, HENRY W., mayor; b. Dayton, Ohio, Feb. 7, 1918; s. Charles Jr. and Marie L. (Knisley) M.; B.A., U. Wis., 1940; M.A., U. Wis.-Milw., 1964; m. Karen Lamb, May 8, 1976; children by previous marriage—Melinda Ann Maier Carlisle, Melanie Marie. Mem. Wis. Legislature, 1950-60, minority floor leader for Senate, 1953, 55, 57, 59; mayor of Milw., 1960—. Served as lt. USNR, World War II; PTO. Named 1 of 60 most influential men in Am., U.S. News and World Report, 1975, 76; Disting. Urban Mayor, Nat. Urban Coalition, 1979. Mem. U.S. Conf. Mayors (pres., 1971-72, now mem. exec. com.), Nat. Conf. Dem. Mayors (past pres.), Nat. League of Cities (dir., past pres.). Democrat. Author: Challenge to the Cities, 1966. Home: 1324 W Birch St Milwaukee WI 53209 Office: City Hall Milwaukee WI 53202

MAIER, HOWARD ROBERT, city planner; b. Cleve., Oct. 10, 1944; s. Ernest and Florence Blanche (Newman) M.; B.A., Ohio State U., 1966, M.City Planning, 1972; M.Public Mgmt. Sci., Case Western Res. U., 1974; m. Sue Ann Salomon, Feb. 4, 1973; children—Matthew Aaron, Abigail Faye. Asso. planner Met. Health Planning Corp., Cleve., 1970-71; planner, prin. planner Regional Planning Commn., Cleve., 1971-75; community planner, asst. planning dir. City of Cleveland Heights (Ohio), 1975-78, dir. dept. planning and devel., 1978—; adj. asso. prof. dept. urban studies Cleve. State U. Mem. adv. com. dept. city and regional planning Ohio State U. Mem. Am. Planning Assn. (treas. Ohio chpt. 1980-82), Am. Inst. Cert. Planners, Am. Soc. Public Adminstrn., Ohio Planning Conf. Office: 2953 Mayfield Rd Cleveland Heights OH 44118

MAIER, PAUL LUTHER, author, clergyman, educator; b. St. Louis, May 31, 1930; s. Walter A. and Hulda (Eickhoff) M.; A.B., Concordia Sem., 1952, B.D., 1955; student Harvard U., 1948-50, M.A., 1954; postgrad. Heidelberg U. (Germany), 1955; Ph.D. summa cum laude, U. Basel (Switzerland), 1957; m. Joan M. Ludtke, June 17, 1967; children—Laura Ann, Julie Joan, Krista Lynn. Ordained to ministry Lutheran Ch., 1958; Luth. campus chaplain Western Mich. U., Kalamazoo, 1958—, prof. history, 1959—. Recipient Harvard Detur award, 1950, Alumni award for teaching excellence Western Mich. U., 1974, Disting. Faculty Scholar award, 1981. Mem. Am. Hist. Assn., Bach Soc. Kalamazoo. Author: Caspar Schwenckfeld, 1959; A Man Spoke, A World Listened, 1963; Pontius Pilate, 1968; First Christmas, The True and Unfamiliar Story, 1971; First Easter, The True and Unfamiliar Story, 1973; First Christians, Pentecost and the Spread of Christianity, 1976; The Flames of Rome, 1981; editor: The Improvement of College and University Courses in the History of Civilization, 1965; The Best of Walter A. Maier, 1980; contbr. articles in field to gen. and profl. jours. Home: 8383 W Main St Kalamazoo MI 49009

MAIER, SAMMI, advt. exec.; b. Geneva, Ill., June 24, 1950; d. George and LaVerne Harriett (Kiefer) M.; B.A. in Polit. Sci., Knox Coll., 1972. Sales promotion ofcl. Auto Tech, Inc., St. Charles, Ill., 1973-74; mktg. services mgr. Audio-Visual div. Dukane Corp., St. Charles, 1974-80, mktg. services mgr. A-V and Communications Systems div., 1980-81; corp. mgr. advt., 1981—. Active Community Theatre, Fox Valley Playmakers; former bd. dirs. Aurora Stage Co.; precinct committeewoman Kane County Democratic Orgn., 1976-78. Mem. Execs. Club Chgo., Valley Ad Club (past dir.), Delta Delta Delta. Lutheran. Address: care 2900 Dukane Dr Saint Charles IL 60174

MAIKOWSKI, THOMAS ROBERT, supt. schs.; b. Milw., Oct. 20, 1947; s. Thomas Robert and Eugenia A. (Rogowski) M.; B.A., St. Francis Coll., Milw., 1970, Notre Dame Coll., St. Louis, 1976; M.S. in Edn., St. Francis U., Ft. Wayne, Ind., 1972; M.A., Cardinal Stritch Coll., Milw., 1974; M.Ed., Marquette U., Milw., 1977; M.Div., Kenrick Sem., St. Louis, 1976; Ph.D., St. Louis U., 1980. Elem. sch. tchr., 1967-70; secondary sch. tchr., 1970—; coll. instr., 1973—; secondary adminstr. and tchr., 1976—; supt. schs. Roman Cath. Diocese of Gallup, 1978—; ordained priest Roman Cath. Ch., 1976. Mem. Nat. Cath. Ednl. Assn., Assn. Supervision and Curriculum Devel., Assn. Tchr. Educators, Am. Assn. Mental Deficiency. Author articles in field. Office: PO Box 214 Farmington NM 87401

MAIN, D(ERWOOD) GREGORY, planner; b. Belding, Mich., Nov. 1, 1942; s. Western Clinton and Barbara Jean (Halpin) M.; student Lansing Community Coll., 1962-65; B.S. with honors, Mich. State U., 1970; m. Barbara Jean Clark, Aug. 24, 1963; children—Todd, Jennifer, Adam, Katharine, Elizabeth. Planner, City of Lansing (Mich.), 1965-70; chief planner Central Upper Peninsula Planning and Devel. Regional Commn., Escanaba, Mich., 1970-76, exec. dir., 1976—. Chmn. Mich. Gov.'s Task Force on Small and Rural Communities, Mich. Gov.'s Wood Resources Devel. Task Force; pres. Escanaba Area Cath. Bd. Edn. Mem. Mich. Soc. Planning Ofcls. (pres.). Roman Catholic. Club: Escanaba Lions. Office: 2415 14th Ave S Escanaba MI 49829

MAINES, DAVID RUSSELL, sociologist; b. Anderson, Ind., May 6, 1940; s. Gerald W. and Ellen (Ward) M.; B.S., Ball State U., 1967; M.A., U. Mo., 1970, Ph.D., 1973; NIMH postdoctoral fellow Columbia U., 1973-74; m. Mahin Dokht Rowshan; children—David Edward, Monda Monique. Instr., U. Minn., 1972-73; lectr. Columbia U., 1973-74; asst. prof. Hunter Coll., N.Y.C., 1974-76; vis. asst. prof. Upsala Coll., E. Orange, N.J., 1976-77; research fellow Yale U., New Haven, 1977-78; vis. asst. prof. Northwestern U., Evanston, Ill., 1978-79, research asso., asst. prof., 1979—; research sociologist U. Chgo., 1979. Recipient award Nat. Research Services, 1977-78; grantee Nat. Inst. Edn., 1979—. Mem. Am. Sociol. Assn., Midwest Sociol. Soc., Soc. Study Symbolic Interaction, Soc. Study Social Problems, Eastern Sociol. Soc. Co-editor: Research in the Inter Weave of Social Roles, 1980; contbr. articles to profl. jours. Home: 1112 Edmer Ave Oak Park IL 60302 Office: Sch Edn Northwestern U Evanston IL 60201

MAISEL, JACK HOWARD, ins. co. exec.; b. Cin., Aug. 24, 1937; s. Howard Charles and Anne Louise (Welch) M.; B.S. in Psychology, Xavier U., 1959, M.B.A., 1976; postgrad. Chase Law Sch., 1962-63; m. Mary Ella Royston, Sept. 1, 1962; children—Maria, John, Michael. Dept. mgr. Allied Dept. Stores, Cn., 1959-61; sales rep. Hosp. Care Corp., Cin., 1961-63, employee relations mgr., 1963-66, mgr. prospective accounts, 1966-68, dist. sales mgr., 1968-71, market devel. mgr., 1971-74, dir. mktg., 1974-77, regional v.p.-mktg., 1978—. Councilman, City of Greenhills (Ohio), 1961-66, chmn. Recreation Commn., 1963-66. Served in USAR, 1960-64. Mem. Sales and Mktg. Execs. Club Cin. (dir. 1979—). Club: Optimists (pres. Cin. 1975). Contbr. articles to profl. jours. Home: 10193 Lochcrest Dr Cincinnati OH 45231 Office: 1351 Taft Rd Cincinnati OH 45206

MAITLAND, JOHN W., JR., state senator; b. Normal, Ill., July 29, 1936; s. John and Elsa M.; ed. Ill. State U.; m. Joanne Sieg; children—Jodi Ann, Johnny, Jay. Farmer; mem. Ill. Senate. Mem. McLean County (Ill.) Regional Planning Commn. Mem. Farm Bur. (pres. 1974-77), Covell Farmers Grain. Republican. Lutheran. Club: Kiwanis. Office: State Capitol Springfield IL 62706*

MAJCHEREK, CAROL ANN, advt. agy. ofcl.; b. Detroit, July 17, 1951; d. Chester and Lottie Francis (Maleski) M.; B.F.A. in Advt. (scholar), Center for Creative Studies, Detroit, 1974; postgrad. Wayne State U., 1974. Layout artist, advt. dept. J.L. Hudson's Detroit, 1970-72; art dir. J. Walter Thompson Co., Detroit, 1974-78, Campbell-Ewald, Detroit, 1978-79, Kenyon & Eckhardt, Detroit, 1979—; guest speaker Center for Creative Studies, Detroit. Mem. Creative Advt. Club of Detroit, Smithsonian Inst., Detroit Inst. of Arts. Office: 30700 Telegraph Birmingham WI 48010

MAJHER, EDWARD ALLEN, ednl. adminstr.; b. Cleve., Apr. 5, 1940; s. Edward and Verna (Lang) M.; B.S. in Bus. Adminstrn., Dyke Coll., 1962; student Baldwin-Wallace Coll., 1958-59; m. Judith Turner, Aug. 25, 1962; children—Cynthia, Matthew. Asst. supr., bank examiner Fed. Res. Bank, Cleve., 1963-68; sr. auditor Ernst & Ernst, Cleve., 1968-71; asst. controller Central Security Nat. Bank, Lorain, Ohio, 1971; controller Lakeland Community Coll., Mentor, Ohio, 1971—. Councilman, City of Mentor on the Lake, Ohio, 1976-77. Registered pub. accountant, Ohio. Mem. Nat. Assn. Accountants (dir. Cleve. E. chpt. 1976-79, v.p. 1979—), Assn. Sch. Bus. Ofcls., Mcpl. Fin. Officers Assn. Club: Masons. Home: 5606 Marine Pkwy Mentor on the Lake OH 44060 Office: I-90 and State Route 306 Mentor OH 44060

MAKINS, DONALD REGIS, JR., engring., contracting co. exec.; b. Naperville, Ill., Mar. 14, 1950; s.Donald Regis and Ruth Louise (Schwartz) M.; student Marquette U., 1968-70. Pres., Sencon Engring Inc., Elgin, Ill., 1976—. Served with USMCR, 1970-73. Mem. Naperville Jaycees. Roman Catholic. Inventor in passive solar energy systems.

MAKKAI, ADAM, linguist, lexicographer, poet; b. Budapest, Hungary, Dec. 16, 1935; s. John D. and Rózsa (Ignácz) M.; came to U.S., 1957, naturalized, 1963; student U. Budapest, 1954-56; B.A. cum laude in Slavic Langs., Harvard U., 1958; M.A. (Ford Found. fellow, Wilson fellow) in Gen. Linguistics, Yale U., 1962, Ph.D. (Jr. Sterling fellow) in Gen. Linguistics, 1965; m. Valerie June Becker, June 5, 1966; children—Sylvia, Rebecca Rose. Tchr. of Latin, German, Russian and French, Iolani Coll. Prep. Acad., Honolulu, 1958-60; lectr. in Russian, U. Hawaii, Honolulu, 1958-60; instr. in Russian, Yale U., New Haven, 1962-63; vis. asst. prof. linguistics U. Malaya, 1963-64; asst. prof. linguistics and Russian, Occidental Coll., Los Angeles and asst. prof. English, Calif. State U., Long Beach, 1966-67; asst. prof. linguistics U. Ill. at Chgo. Circle campus, 1967-69, asso. prof., 1969-74, prof., 1974—: researcher in computational linguistics Rand Corp., Santa Monica, Calif., 1965-66; founder Zoltán Kodály Hungarian Cultural Soc. Chgo., 1968, pres., 1968—; Found. exec. dir. of Lacus, Inc., 1974—, dir. publs., 1974—, chmn. bd., 1974—; author: Idiom Structure in English, 1973; Readings in Stratificational Linguistics, 1973; A Dictionary of Space English, 1973; maj. contbr. The Living Webster's Encyclopedic Dictionary of the English Language, 1971; A Dictionary of American Idioms, 1975; Szomj és ecet (collected poems in Hungarian), 1966; co-editor The Poetry of Hungary; contbr. poetry to English and Hungarian anthologies; contbr. numerous articles on linguistics and semantics to linguistic jours.; editor Forum Linguisticum, 1976—; editorial bd. Indian Jour. Linguistics, 1975—, Studi Italiani della Linguistica Teorica ed Applicata, 1975, Őtágú Síp, 1973-76. NSF grantee, 1965-66, Paderewski Found. and Internat. Devel. Found. Travel grantee, 1963-64. Mem. Linguistic Soc. Am., Modern Lang. Assn. (chmn. spl. interest group on gen. linguistics 1977-78), Internat. Linguistic Assn. (mng. editor jour. 1973-74). Home: 360 MacLaren Ln Lake Bluff IL 60044 Office: Dept Linguistics U Ill Chicago Circle PO Box 4348 Chicago IL 60680

MAKKAI, VALERIE JUNE BECKER, educator; b. Vinton, Iowa, July 29, 1936; d. Edwin Shaw and Lydia Myrtle (Pocock) Becker; B.A. summa cum laude, Mo. Valley Coll., 1957; postgrad. U. Besancon, France, 1957-58; M.A., Yale, 1962, Ph.D., 1964; m. Adam Makkai, June 5, 1966; children—Sylvia, Rebecca Rose. Instr. French and Spanish, MacMurray Coll., Jacksonville, Ill., 1958-60; research asst. dept. Indic and Far Eastern langs. Yale U., 1961-62; asst. prof. linguistics Purdue U., Lafayette, Ind., 1965-66; postdoctoral research fellow Rand Corp., Santa Monica, Calif., 1966-67; asst. prof. linguistics U. Ill., Chgo., 1967-70, asso. prof., 1970—; dir., pres. Jupiter Press. Fulbright scholar, 1957-58; NSF fellow, 1966-67. Mem. Linguistic Assn. Can. and U.S. (dir., sec.-treas., coordinating editor 1974—), Linguistic Soc. Am., Modern Lang. Assn., Am. Fedn. Astrologers, Delta Zeta, Beta Gamma Phi. Author Phonological Theory: Evolution and Current Practice, 1972. Editor: (with Adam Makkai) First Lacus Forum, 1975; (with Adam Makkai and Luigi Heilmann) Linguistics at the Crossroads, 1977. Contbr. articles to profl. jours. Mng. editor Forum Linguisticum, 1976—; asso. editor Studies in Language Learning, 1975—. Home: 360 MacLaren Ln Lake Bluff IL 60044 Office: Linguistics Dept U of Ill Chicago Circle Chicago IL 60680

MAKKER, SUDESH PAUL, physician; b. Naushehra, India, June 8, 1941; came to U.S., 1966, naturalized, 1975; s. Manohar L. and Daya W. (Kharbanda) M.; F.Sc., Panjab U. (India), 1959; M.D., All India Inst. Med. Scis., 1964; m. Donna Mae Stohs, Feb. 15, 1969; children—Vishal James, Kirin Joya. Internal medicine intern All India Inst. Med. Scis., New Delhi, 1965, resident in internal medicine, 1966; rotating intern Queens Gen. Hosp., N.Y.C., 1966-67; resident in pediatrics U. Chgo. Hosps., 1967-69; research fellow in pediatric nephrology Case Western Res. U., Cleve., 1969-71; fellow in pediatric nephrology U. Calif., San Francisco, 1971; Univ. Hosp., Cleve., 1969—; instr. dept. pediatrics Sch. Medicine, Case Western Res. U., Cleve., 1971-72, sr. instr., 1972-73, asst. prof., 1973-76, asso. prof., 1976—, head div. pediatric nephrology, 1974-79; vis. prof. pediatric nephrology Akron (Ohio) Gen. Hosp., 1977, 80. Diplomate Am. Bd. Pediatrics, Am. Bd. Pediatric Nephrology. Mem. Am. Soc. Pediatric Nephrology, Internat. Soc. Pediatric Nephrology, Soc. Pediatric Research, Am. Heart Assn. Sci. Council, Am. Soc. Nephrology, Northeast Ohio Pediatric Soc., Transplantation Soc. Northeast Ohio, Soc. for Exptl. Biology and Medicine, Sigma Xi. Contbr. articles to profl. jours. Home: 2368 Queenston Rd Cleveland Heights OH 44118 Office: 2101 Adelbert Rd Cleveland OH 44106

MAKUPSON, AMYRE ANN PORTER, television exec.; b. River Rouge, Mich., Sept. 30, 1947; d. Rudolph Hannibal and Amyre Ann (Porche) P.; B.A., Fisk U., 1970; M.A., Am. U., Washington, 1972; m. Walter H. Makupson, Nov. 1, 1975; 1 son, Rudolph Porter. Public relations dir. Mich. HMO Plans, Detroit, 1973-75; asst. news dir. WGPR TV, Detroit, 1975-76; public relations dir. Kirwood Hosp., Detroit, 1977; news and public affairs mgr. WKBD TV, Southfield, Mich., 1977—. Recipient Outstanding Public Service awards Arthritis Found. Mich., 1979, Mich. Mechanics Assn., 1980, Service Appreciation award Salvation Army, 1980, Humanitarian Service award DAV, 1981, Community Service award Jr. Achievement, Service award Cystic Fibrosis Found., 1981; named Outstanding Woman of Year, Prince Matchabelli, 1980. Mem. Women in Communications, Am. Women in Radio and TV (award for Outstanding Achievement 1981), Public Relations Soc. Am., Detroit Press Club, Adcraft. Roman Catholic. Office: 26955 W 11 Mile Rd Southfield MI 48037

MALANY, LE GRAND LYNN, lawyer, state ofcl.; b. Chgo., May 14, 1941; s. LeGrand Franklin and Marion (Jaynes) M.; B.S. in Engring. Physics, U. Ill., 1964, J.D., 1970; m. Barbara Bumgarner, June 26, 1965; children—LeGrand Karl, Siobhan, Carleen. Asst. astronomer Adler Planetarium, Chgo., 1960-63; research asst. Portland Cement Research Assn., Skokie, Ill., 1964; instr. dept. gen. engring. U. Ill., 1965-70, instr. Office Instrn. Resources, 1967-68, instr. Hwy Traffic Safety Center, 1968-69; lectr. Police Tng. Inst., Urbana, Ill., 1969-70; project dir. driver control program U.S. Dept. Transp., 1971-73, project dir., author driver license examiner tng. curriculum, 1973; asso. drivers license adminstr. State of Ill., Springfield, 1973-74, asst. auditor gen., 1977—; expert U.S. Fed. Energy Adminstrn., 1974; counsel juvenile div. Circuit Ct., Sangamon County, Ill., 1973-75; chief counsel Ill. Dept. Motor Vehicles, Springfield, 1974. Trustee Meret Center, Inc., 1973-75; Dem. candidate for States Atty., Sangamon County, Ill., 1980. Registered profl. engr., Ill.; lic. real estate brokers. Mem. Am. Phys. Soc., Nat., Ill. socs. profl. engrs., Am. Bar Assn. Developer statewide motorcycle driver licensing program. Home: 600 S Rosehill St Springfield IL 62704 Office: 524 S 2d St Springfield IL 62706

MALAS, CORNELIA, employee relations specialist; b. Cin.; d. John C. and Katherine (Farres) Malas; student U. Cin., 1940-42; bus. certificate Littleford Nelson Bus. Coll., 1943; student Schuster Martin Sch. Drama, 1943; certificate Patricia Stevens Modeling Sch., 1944; student Campbell Bus. Coll., 1956. Head central filing dept. Gruen Watch Co., Cin., 1945-50; expediter purchasing dept. MacGregor Sport Products, Cin., 1950-57; employee relations Eagle-Picher Industries, Inc., Cin., 1957—. Chmn. Rosie Reds Night at Crosley Field, Rooters Organized to Stimulate Interest and Enthusiasm in Cin. Reds Baseball Team, 1967, v.p., 1972, pres., 1975-76, trustee, 1971-79; mem. women's com. Nat. Gov.'s. Conf., 1968; mem. ticket com. Cin. Symphony Orch., 1968; publicity chmn. May Festival, 1969, mem. women's com., 1971-73; solicitor Fine Arts Fund, 1974-75; judge Jr., Achievement, 1965, 67. Mem. Nat. Secs. Assn. (pres. Ohio div. 1969-70), Internat. Assn. for Personnel Women-Cin. (treas. 1978—), Adminstrv. Mgmt. Soc., Am. Soc. for Personnel Adminstrn., Internat. Platform Assn., Cin. Opera Guild (trustee 1980—, v.p. ticket sales 1980), Alpha Delta Pi. Clubs: Hyde Park Golf and Country, Cincinnati, Internat. Toastmistress, Williams (pres. 1966-67). Home: 715 McMakin St Cincinnati OH 45232 Office: 580 Bldg Cincinnati OH 45202

MALCOLM, ROSA WALLS, educator; b. Charleston, Miss., Dec. 5, 1943; d. Fred and Ida Virginia (Short) Walls; B.S., Miss. Valley State Coll., 1965; M.A., Governors State U., 1974; m. ElDevon Malcolm, Aug. 8, 1970; 1 son, ElDevon Dushea. Stenographer, N.Y. Life Ins. Co., Los Angeles, 1965; clk. typist U.S. Dept. Agr., Clarksdale, Miss., 1965-66; exec. sec., office mgr. Early Childhood Devel. program, Clarksdale, 1966-68; tchr. Coahoma County schs., Clarksdale, 1968-69; clk. typist Chgo. Housing Authority, 1969; tchr. Sch. Dist. 169, East Chicago Heights, Ill., 1969-72; instr. bus. Chgo. City Colls., 1973—. Mem. Nat. Bus. Edn. Assn., Am. Bus. Communication Assn., Chgo. Bus. Edn. Assn., Phi Beta Lambda. Democrat. Methodist. Proofreader: Nostrand Publishing Co., N.Y.C. Address: 57 W 124th St Chicago IL 60628

MALCOLM, RUSSELL LAING, JR., pathologist; b. Ann Arbor, Mich., Dec. 21, 1929; s. Russell Laing and Bernice Francis (Staebler) M.; A.B., Earlham Coll., 1951; M.A., Ind. U., 1960, M.D., 1960; m. Ann Elizabeth Wissler, Aug. 15, 1956; children—Christine Laing, Albert Staebler, Melissa Ann. Intern Marion County Gen. Hosp., Indpls., 1960-61; resident in pathology Ind. U. Med. Center, 1961-65, chief resident-instr. pathology, 1964-65; asso. pathologist Middletown (Ohio) Hosp. Assn., 1965—; instr. U. Cin. Med. Sch., 1965-72, Wright State Med. Sch., 1981—. Served with USN, 1951-55. Clin. fellow Am. Cancer Soc., 1964-65. Diplomate Am. Bd. Pathology. Fellow Coll. Am. Pathologists; mem. AMA, Am. Soc. Clin. Pathologists, Internat. Acad. Pathology, AAAS, S.W. Ohio Heart Assn. (pres. 1973-75). Republican. Quaker. Home: 8000 W Alexandria Rd Middletown OH 45042 Office: 105 McKnight Dr Middletown OH 45092

MALEC, JAMES FRANCIS, clin. psychologist; b. East St. Louis, Ill., Jan. 7, 1950; s. Z. John and Lorraine (Bihss) M.; student Augustana Coll., 1968-70; B.A., So. Ill. U., Edwardsville, 1972; M.A., U.S.D., 1975, Ph.D., 1977; m. Linda Stinson, Feb. 6, 1971. Fellow in neuropsychology U. Wis., Madison, 1977-78, clin. asst. prof. dept. rehab. medicine and chief psychologist, 1978—. Mem. Am. Psychol. Assn., Am. Congress Rehab. Medicine, Am. Soc. Clin. Hypnosis, Assn. Advancement Psychology, Assn. Advancement Behavior Therapy. Contbr. articles in field to profl. jours. Office: U Wis E3/350 Clin Sci Center 600 Highland Ave Madison WI 53793

MALEK, REZA SAID, urol. surgeon; b. Teheran, Iran, Aug. 22, 1940; s. Said and Banoo (Rais) M.; M.B., B.S., U. London (Eng.), 1964; M.S. in Urology, U. Minn., 1971; m. Haleh F. Rassa, Feb. 9, 1980. Intern, St. Marys Hosp., Eastbourne, Eng. and Lister Hosp., Hitchin, Eng., 1964-65; resident, sr. house officer St. Thomas's Hosp., U. London, 1965-66, Mayo Grad. Sch. Medicine, Rochester, Minn., 1967-71; research fellow in calculous disease or urinary tract, vis. clin. surgeon Bowman-Gray Sch. Medicine, Winston-Salem, N.C., 1971-72; cons. urology Mayo Clinic, Rochester, Minn., 1972—, cons. pediatric urology, 1974—, instr. urology, 1972-74, asst. prof., 1974-76, asso. prof., 1976—; adviser to regional dir. WHO, 1972. Diplomate Am. Bd. Urology (chmn. task force, exam. com. 1980); specialist certificate Royal Coll. Surgeons of Can. Fellow Am. Acad. Pediatrics, Royal Coll. Physicians and Surgeons of Can., A.C.S.; mem. Minn. Urol. Soc. Royal Soc. Medicine (London), Brit. Assn. Urol. Surgeons, Canadian Urol. Assn., Am. Urol. Assn., N.Central Sect. Am. Urol. Assn., Northwestern Pediatrics Soc., Société Internationale de Chirurgie, Sigma Xi. Clubs: Univ., Minn. Alumni Mpls.). Contbr. 60 articles to profl. jours. and textbooks. Office: Mayo Clinic Rochester MN 55901

MALEY, CHARLES DAVID, lawyer; b. Highland Park, Ill., Aug. 18, 1924; s. Lyle West and Irene (Davis) M.; A.B., State U. Iowa, 1948; J.D., De Paul U., 1952; m. Mildred J. Tobin, Apr. 27, 1957; 1 dau., Annabel Irene. Admitted to Ill. bar, 1952, U.S. Supreme Ct. bar, 1956; asso. firm Friedlund, Levin & Friedlund, Chgo., 1952-58; pvt. practice law, Chgo., 1958-68, Lake Bluff, Ill., 1966-72, Lake Forest, Ill., 1972—; pub. adminstr. Lake County, 1971-74. Asst. dist. commr. Boy Scouts Am., 1963-65; trustee Lake County Mus. Assn., 1978-79, Lake Forest-Lake Bluff Hist. Soc., 1979—; bd. dirs. Petite Ballet, 1975-80. Mem. Lake County Republican Central Com., 1967-72, 76—, Rep. State Com., 1971-74. Served with AUS, 1943-46, Decorated Purple Heart with oak leaf cluster, Bronze Star. Mem. Am., Seventh Circuit,

Ill., Chgo., Lake County bar assns., Am. Judicature Soc., Assn. Trial Lawyers Am., Chgo. Law Inst., S.A.R., Am. Legion (post comdr. 1967-68, 74-81, service officer 1968-69, adj. 1982—), Am. Arbitration Assn. (mem. panel 1965-67), Lake Forest C. of C., Phi Gamma Delta, Phi Alpha Delta. Republican. Presbyn. Kiwanian (bd. govs. 1976-80). Clubs: Capitol Hill (Washington); Tower (Chgo.). Home: 241 W Washington St Lake Bluff IL 60044 Office: 711 McKinley Rd Lake Forest IL 60045

MALICK, AHMAD WASEEM, pharm. research scientist; b. Karachi, Pakistan, Nov. 15, 1947; came to U.S., 1969, naturalized, 1972; s. Muhammad Akram and Nusrat (Akram) M.; B.Sc., Govt. Coll., Lahore, 1964; B.Pharm., Panjab U., 1967, M.Pharm., 1969; M.S., Columbia U., 1972; Ph.D. (univ. fellow 1973-75), U. Mich., 1976; m. Aneeza Aslam Mufti, Mar. 2, 1979. Teaching asst. Columbia U. Coll. Pharm. Scis., 1969-72, U. Mich. Coll. Pharmacy, 1972-75; asst. prof. Wayne State U. Coll. Pharmacy, Detroit, 1975-78; sr. research investigator Am. Critical Care Co., McGaw Park, Ill., 1978—. Recipient award contbn. pharmacy edn. Wayne State U., 1978, named Outstanding Instr., 1978 (2). Mem. Am. Pharm. Assn., Acad. Pharm. Scis., Parenteral Drug Assn., Am. Chem. Soc., Am. Assn. Colls. Pharmacy, Am. Inst. of History Pharmacy, Midwest Acad. Pharm. Scis. Author papers in field, chpts. in books. Home: 111 Deerpath Dr Vernon Hills IL 60061 Office: 1600 Waukegan Rd McGaw Park IL 60085

MALIK, RAYMOND HOWARD, scientist, economist, corp. exec., inventor; b. Lebanon, Feb. 4, 1933; s. John Z. and Clarice R. (Malik) M.; came to U.S., 1948, naturalized, 1963; B.A. in Bus. Adminstrn., Valparaiso U., 1950; B.S. in Bus. Adminstrn. and Econs., Simpson Coll., 1951; M.S. in Bus. Adminstrn., So. Ill. U., 1956, Ph.D. in Electronics and Econs., 1959. Supr., Arabian Am. Oil Co., Beirut, Lebanon, 1952-54; prof., head world trade programs Central YMCA Community Coll., Chgo., 1966-74; pres. Malik Internat. Enterprises, Ltd., Chgo., 1959—. Fulbright scholar, 1948-50; Methodist Ch. scholar, 1950-51; So. Ill. U. fellow 1954-59). Mem. Am. Mgmt. Assn. (treas.), Am. Econ. Assn. (v.p.), Am. Mktg. Assn. (sec.), Import Clubs U.S. (v.p.), Internat. Bus. Council (pres.), IEEE, Internat. Platform Assn., Phi Beta Kappa, Sigma Xi, Delta Rho, Beta Gamma Sigma, Alpha Phi Omega. Pioneer developer interplanetary communication system, 1961; inventor selectric typing mechanism, 1959, circle of sound concept of sound propogation, 1967, auto-ignition instant hot water heater, 1981, gamma ray breast cancer detector, 1976, heater humidifier-dehumidifier, 1963; introduced modular concept in color TV, 1973. Author: The Roadguide to Youth, Health and Longevity, 1980. Home: PO Box 70-100 Antelias Lebanon Office: PO Box 3194 Chicago IL 60654

MALIN, CHESTER J., retail exec.; b. Chgo., Jan. 18, 1914; s. John A. and Sophia M.; B.S.Ch.E., Ill. Inst. Tech., 1936; M.A. in Personnel Adminstrn., Northwestern U., 1942; m. Janina D., Sept. 12, 1938; children—Constance Elaine, Holly Pamela. With Goldblatt Bros., Inc., Chgo., 1942-80, v.p., dir. personnel and labor relations; pvt. mgmt. cons., Northbrook, Ill., 1980—. Co. gen. chmn. Crusade of Mercy, Chgo., 1953—; solicitor Chgo. Boys Club, 1976. Recipient award for fair employment Met. C. of C.; Crusade of Mercy award. Mem. Execs. Club Chgo. Roman Catholic. Office: 40 The Ct of Greenway Northbrook IL 60062

MALIN, JOYCE ELAINE, med. librarian; b. Campbell, Mo., Apr. 8, 1936; d. John Arthur and Vergie Marie (Polsgrove) Malin; A.B., Eastern Mich. U., 1958; A.M. L.S., U. Mich., 1963. Faculty-tchr. Birmingham (Mich.) Bd. Edn., 1958-64; faculty-asst. to librarian Macomb County (Mich.) Community Coll., 1964-65; librarian Detroit Osteo. Hosp. Corp., 1965-67; dir. med. library Henry Ford Hosp., Detroit, 1967-78; librarian William Beaumont Hosp., Royal Oak, Mich., 1978—. Mem. alumni bd. Eastern Mich. U., 1963-66. Mem. Med. Library Assn., U. Mich. (life), Eastern Mich. U. (life) alumni assns., Pi Kappa Delta. Home: 1022 E 6th St Royal Oak MI 48067 Office: William Beaumont Hosp 3601 W 13 Mile Rd Royal Oak MI 48072

MALLEN, GARY PATRICK, newspaper creative dir.; b. Kansas City, Mo., Feb. 19, 1949; s. Arthur Louis and Annebell (Putney) M.; student U. Mo., Kansas City, 1967-69; B.F.A., Kansas City Art Inst., 1973; m. Vicki Ellen Schulz, Sept. 24, 1976. Art dir. Travis/Walz/Lane Advt., Overland Park, Kans., 1973-74; v.p. Mid-Continent Advt. and Public Relations, Kansas City, Mo., 1975-76; pres. Gary Mallen Design Cons., Kansas City, Mo., 1975—; creative dir. Galvin/Farris/Ross Advt., Kansas City, Mo., 1976-78; mgr. creative services Kansas City (Mo.) Times and Star (Kansas City Star Co.), 1978—; instr. typography, Johnson County Community Coll., 1977. Bd. dirs. Bishop Hogan High Sch., 1978-79, chmn. public relations com., 1979. Winner Kimberly Clark Bi-Centennial Design Competition, 1977; recipient 28 local Addy awards, 5 regional Addy awards, N.Y. Art Dirs. Club award, Dallas Soc. Visual Communications award. Mem. Kansas City Art Dirs. Club (8 awards), Ad Club of Kansas City (chmn. Addy awards com., 1981). Mem. Christian Church. Clubs: Country, Kansas City. Designer books: Historic Kansas City Architecture, 1974, The Star: The First 100 Years, 1980; Folly Theatre Commemorative Book, 1981. Office: 1729 Grand Ave Kansas City MO 64108

MALLONE, SUSAN MARIE CHRISTNER, nursing adminstr.; b. Ashtabula, Ohio, Oct. 23, 1943; d. Ralph E. and V. Marion (Maki) Christner; diploma Fairview Park Hosp. Sch. Nursing, 1964; B.S. in Applied Sci., Youngstown State U., 1978. Charge nurse Fairview Park Hosp., Cleve., 1964-65; staff nurse Northeastern Ohio Gen. Hosp., Madison, 1965, asst. dir. nursing service, 1972-77, dir., 1977—; charge nurse George Washington U. Hosp., Washington, 1965-66; staff nurse Lake County Meml. Hosp., Painesville, Ohio, 1966-67; cons. Applied Nursing Consultation and Ednl. Resources. Mem. Am. Assn. Critical Care Nurses, Am. Heart Assn. (mem. council cardiovascular disease), Northeastern Ohio Heart Assn., Northeastern Ohio Hosp Assn., Nat. League Nursing, Ohio League Nursing, Cleve. League Nursing, Am. Hosp. Assn.-Nursing Dirs. Republican. Lutheran. Contbr. articles on critical care nursing to profl. jours. Home: 488 Eastwood St Geneva OH 44041 Office: Northeastern Gen Ohio Hosp 2041 Hubbard Rd North Madison OH 44057

MALLORY, ARTHUR LEE, state ofcl.; b. Springfield, Mo., Dec. 26, 1932; s. Dillard A. and Ferrell (Claxton) M.; B.S. in Edn., S.W. Mo. State Coll., 1954; M.Ed., U. Mo. at Columbia, 1957, Ed.D., 1959; L.H.D., S.W. Bapt. Coll., 1972; m. Joann Peters, June 6, 1954; children—Dennis Arthur (dec.), Christopher Lee, Stephanie Ann, Jennifer Lyn. History supr. U. Mo. Lab. Sch., Columbia, 1956-57; asst. to supt. schs. Columbia Pub. Schs., 1957-59; asst. supt. schs. Pkwy. Sch. Dist., St. Louis County, Mo., 1959-64; dean evening div. U. Mo. at St. Louis, 1964; pres. S.W. Mo. State Coll., Springfield, 1964-70; commr. edn. Dept. Elem. and Secondary Edn., Jefferson City, Mo., 1971—. Pres., Great Rivers council Boy Scouts Am., 1971-73. Mem. bd. A.R.C. Cole County; mem. adv. com. Mo. 4-H Found., 1974; mem. Gov.'s Council on the Arts, 1965-66; mem. St. Louis Ednl. TV Comm. Bd.'s Adv. Council KETC-TV, Mo. Law Enforcement Assistance Council, Juvenile Delinquency Task Force, Edn. Commn. States; chmn. bd. dirs. Mo. Council on Econ. Edn.; chmn. com. bds. So. Bapt. Conv., 1973, mem. exec. bd. Mo. Bapt. Conv., 1972-75, 77-80. Bd. dirs. Mid-Continent Regional Ednl. Lab., Midwestern Bapt. Theol. Sem., 1968-72, Internat. House, U. Mo., 1956-59, trustee Meml. Hosp., Jefferson City; bd. regents William Jewell Coll., 1972-74. Mem. Am., Mo., S.W. Mo. assns. sch. adminstrs., NEA, Mo. State Tchrs. Assn., Mo. Congress Parents and Tchrs. (hon. life). Baptist (deacon). Mason (33 deg.), Rotarian. Home: 3261 S Ten Mile Dr Jefferson City MO 65101 Office: 100 E Capitol Ave Jefferson City MO 65101

MALLORY, JAMES DONALD, mfg. co. exec.; b. Toledo, Mar. 7, 1923; B.S. in Mech. Engring., Marquette U., 1944; M.S., U. Mich., 1950. With Owens-Ill. Inc., 1950-52, 57—, sect. chief process machine devel., Toledo, 1978—; sr. project engr. Electric Auto-Lite Co., 1952-57; cons. in field. Served with USNR, 1942-55. Registered profl. engr., Ohio, Fla., S.C. Mem. Nat. Soc. Profl. Engrs., Soc. Am. Value Engrs., Ohio Soc. Profl. Engrs., Toledo Soc. Profl. Engrs. Roman Catholic. Patentee in field. Home: 626 Valley Dr Maumee OH 43537 Office: 1 Seagate Toledo OH 43666

MALLORY, RACHEL ASHBURN, occupational therapist; b. Los Angeles, July 15, 1953; d. Jacob Julian and Helen (Bemse) Ashburn; B.S. in Allied Medicine, Ohio State U., 1977; m. Marvin S. Mallory, Dec. 23, 1973; 1 son, Adam Christopher. Occupational therapist gen. medicine and surgery Mt. Carmel East Hosp., Columbus, Ohio, 1977; staff therapist Columbus Devel. Center Mental Retardation, 1978-79, 80—; dir. occupational therapy dept. geriatric rehab. St. Luke Convalescent Center, Columbus, 1979-80; mem. adv. bd. Sch. Allied Med. Professions Ohio State U., 1979-80; mem. clin. council for suprs. of occupational therapy students Ohio State U. Organist, missionary worker Oakley Bapt. Ch. Qualified mental retardation profl., Ohio. Mem. Am. Occupational Therapy Assn., Ohio Occupational Therapy Assn. (chmn. geriatric speciality group Columbus Dist.), Alpha Kappa Alpha (grad. adv. Ohio State U. chpt.). Office: 1601 W Broad St Columbus OH 43223

MALLORY, REX DARWIN, electronics engr.; b. Des Moines, June 27, 1923; s. Charles E. and Winifred F. (Peterman) M.; B.S. in Engring., Iowa State U., 1949; M.B.A., Creighton U., 1965; m. Phyllis G. Young, Feb. 18, 1944; children—Becky, Linda. With Western Electric Co., Omaha, 1957—, supr. cable engring., 1969—; vis. lectr. Creighton U., Omaha, 1967-69. Served with U.S. Army, 1943-46. Clubs: Masons; Shriners (Omaha).

MALLORY, TROY L., accountant; b. Sesser, Ill., July 30, 1923; s. Theodore E. and Alice (Mitchell) M.; student So. Ill. U., 1941-43, Washington and Jefferson Coll., 1943-44; B.S., U. Ill., 1947, M.S., 1948; m. Magdalene Richter, Jan. 26, 1963. Staff sr., supr. Scovell, Wellington & Co., C.P.A.'s, Chgo., 1948-58; mgr. Gray Hunter Stenn, C.P.A.'s, Quincy, 1959-62, partner, 1962—. Mem. finance com. United Fund, Adams County, 1961-64. Bd. dirs. Woodland Home for Orphans and Friendless, 1970—, v.p., 1978-81, pres., 1981—. Served with 84th Inf. Div. AUS, 1942-45. Decorated Purple Heart, Bronze Star. Mem. Quincy C. of C. (dir. 1970-76), Am. Inst. C.P.A.'s, Ill. Soc. C.P.A.'s. Rotarian (dir. Quincy 1967-70, pres. 1978-79). Home: 51 Wilmar Dr Quincy IL 62301 Office: 200 Quincy Peoples Bldg PO Box 32 Quincy IL 62306

MALLOY, JAMES DENNIS, telephone co. exec.; b. Gary, Ind., June 7, 1947; s. James Dennis and Margaret Edith M.; B.A. in Psychology, Ind. U., 1972, M.S. in Edn., 1974, M.S. in Bus., 1980; m. Mona McLellen, Sept. 16, 1972; 1 son, Evan Michael. Underwriter, Am. States Ins. Co., Indpls., 1972-73; traffic mgr. Central Soya, Harrisburg, Pa., 1973-75; various positions in mgmt. GTE, 1975-79, service adminstr. No. region, Westfield Ind., 1981—; dist. mgr. Gen. Telephone of Ind., Pendleton, 1979-81; Counselor Ft. Wayne Jr. Ahicevement, 1978-79; adv. bd. Pendleton Heights High Sch., 1980—; vol. United Way, 1979—. Served with AUS, 1978-80; Vietnam. Decorated Army Commendation medal with V, Air medal. Mem. Cicero Civic League, Westfield Bus. Assn., Noblesville C. of C., Ind. U. Alumni Assn. Club: Pendleton Lions. Home: Rural Route 4 Box 415K Anderson IN 46011

MALLOY, WILLIAM W., public sch. adminstr.; b. Harrisburg, Pa., July 20, 1940; s. Henry and Ruth M. (Summers) M.; B.A. (Senatorial scholar), Lincoln U., 1963; Ed.M., Temple U., 1965; Ed.D., Ind. U., 1975; m. Carol Flynn, Aug. 18, 1943; 1 son, Michael. Tchr. educable mentally handicapped, Phila., 1963-65, Harrisburg, 1965-67, Gary, Ind., 1967-68; spl. edn. adminstr. Gary Public Schs., 1968-73; supr. spl. edn. student tchrs. Ind. U., Bloomington, 1973-74; dir. exceptional child edn. Dade County, Fla., 1975-77; asst. supt. div. exceptional edn. Milw. Public Schs., 1977—; mem. devel. disabilities com. Mental Health Planning Council, 1979—. Mem. adv. com. Milw. County Guardianship Program, 1980—; bd. dirs. North Suburban YMCA, 1980—. Recipient Service award South Fla. Soc. Autistic Children, 1977, Richard Allen Anvil award, Milw., 1979, Sarah Scott Adminstrv. Leadership award, Milw., 1980. Mem. Am. Assn. Mental Deficiency, Soc. Applied Anthropology, Council for Exceptional Children, Black Adminstrs. and Suprs. Council, Omega Psi Phi (Outstanding Educator award 1978). Presbyterian. Contbr. articles on ednl. adminstrn. to profl. pubs. Home: 3609 N 41st St Milwaukee WI 53216 Office: 5225 W Vliet St Milwaukee WI 53208

MALLOZZI, PHILIP JAMES, physicist; b. Norwalk, Conn., Feb. 12, 1937; s. Philip and Jennie (Saltarelli) M.; B.A., Harvard, 1960; M.S., Yale, 1962, Ph.D., 1964; m. Judy Ju-Yuan Wang, July 29, 1961; children—Stephen Alexander, Lisa Valerie, Richard Philip, Julie Marie. Instr. physics Yale, New Haven, 1964-66; sr. scientist Battelle Meml. Inst., Columbus, Ohio, 1966-70, head laser applications center, 1970-81; ind. cons. in laser applications, 1981—; owner, operator Olentangy Indian Caverns, 1977—. Recipient IR-100 award, 1980. Mem. Am. Phys. Soc., Nat. Caves Assn., Sigma Xi. Inventor in field. Contbr. articles to profl. jours. Home: 1783 Home Rd Delaware OH 43015 Office: 1779 Home Rd Delaware OH 43015

MALMAD, DANIEL F., broadcasting co. exec.; b. Bklyn., Mar. 19, 1941; s. George and Rachel Malmad; B.A., Fairleigh Dickinson U., 1965; M.A., Adelphi U., 1967; m. Betty Krevsky, Nov. 22, 1967; children—Mindy, Jeffrey, Kimberly. Buyer, planner Dancer-Fitzgerald-Sample, N.Y.C., 1968-71; account exec. HR TV, N.Y.C., 1971-75, Blair TV, N.Y.C., 1975-77; v.p. Blair TV, Cleve., 1977—. Mem. Ohio Assn. Broadcasters, Cleve. Advt. Club, Cleve. Assn. Broadcasters. Home: 25467 Halburton Rd Beachwood OH 44122 Office: Nat City Center 1900 E 9th St Cleveland OH 44114

MALNAK, ALLEN BERT, internist; b. Du Quoin, Ill., Oct. 12, 1928; s. Nathan Hyman and Rae (Cornick) M.; B.S., Roosevelt U., Chgo., 1950; B.S., U. Ill. Coll. Medicine, 1952, M.D., 1954; m. Tillie Shaewitz, Aug. 14, 1955; children—Nancy, Scott, Wendy, Peter. Intern, Cook County Hosp., Chgo., 1954-55; resident in internal medicine U. Ill. Hosps. and West Side VA Hosp., Chgo., 1955-58; chief resident in internal medicine Mt. Sinai Hosp., Chgo., 1960-61; sr. attending physician Gottlieb Meml. Hosp., Melrose Park, Ill., 1962—, chmn. dept. internal medicine, 1969-70, 72-74, pres. med. staff, 1974-75; clin. asst. prof. Stritch Sch. Medicine, Loyola U., Maywood, Ill., 1969—. Served as capt. USAR, 1958-60. William J. Cook scholar, 1946-50. Diplomate Am. Bd. Internal Medicine. Mem. AMA, Ill., Chgo. med. assns., Am. Heart Assn., Chgo. Backgammon Club. Clubs: Whitehall (Chgo.); Friends of Acapulco. Contbr. articles to med. jours. Home: 2215 Whiteoak Dr Northbrook IL 60062 Office: Gottlieb Hosp 8720 W North Ave Melrose Park IL 60160

MALOLA, MARY E., educator; b. Evansville, Ind., May 25, 1923; d. John M. and Irene Christine M. (Heinlin) Work; A.B., Ind. State U., 1945, M.A., 1959, 6th Yr. degree, 1968; m. John C. Tranbarger, Jan. 10, 1945 (dec. 1968); 1 dau., Ann Irene Phillips; m. 2d, Mousa Asaaf Malola, Nov. 24, 1976; 1 son, Hane M. Classified advt. supr. Tribune-Star Pub. Co., Terre Haute, Ind., 1945-58; tchr. English and journalism, public relations chmn. Gerstmeyer High Sch.. Terre Haute, 1959-72, Terre Haute N. Vigo High Sch., 1972-80, Terre Haute S. Vigo High Sch., 1980—; founder 1st chpt. Quill and Scroll in local public schs., 1959. Sunday sch. supt. St. George Orthodox Ch., 1979—, sec. parish council, 1978-79, pres. ladies soc., 1978-79. AAUW fellowship grant named in her honor, 1977. Mem. NEA, Ind. State Tchrs. Assn., Vigo County Tchrs. Assn., Assn. Tchr. Educators, Nat. Assn. Journalism Dirs., Ind. Council Tchrs. English, Nat. Council Tchrs. English, Ind. High Sch. Press Assn., AAUW (dir. Terre Haute br. 1969-76, sec. 1969-70, 1st v.p. 1971-72, pres. 1973-74), Delta Kappa Gamma. Republican. Club: Ind. State U. Wives. Contbr. to Nat. Poetry Anthology, 1960—; newsletter editor Vigo County Sch. Corp.; 1961-65, ARC, 1961-66. Home: 4422 S 10th Ave Terre Haute IN 47802 Office: 3737 S 7th St Terre Haute IN 47802

MALONE, ALICE DEMBY, nurse; b. Republic, Ala., June 29, 1926; d. James and Beulah May (Naylor) Demby; diploma Cleve. City Hosp. Sch. Nursing, 1948; student Sch. Nursing, Western Res. U., 1954-58; B.A., Cleve. State U., 1976, postgrad. bus. adminstrn., 1977—; m. Jerry H. Malone, Sept. 26, 1947. Nurse, Cleve. City Hosp., 1948-53; with Planned Parenthood of Cleve., 1953—, coordinator infertility research, asst. nursing supr., 1953-70, dir. edn. and tng., 1970-77, dir. program, 1977-80, exec. dir., 1980—. Chmn. steering com. Coalition for Teenage Reprodn. and Health, 1978, mem. exec. com., 1979; chmn. subcom. health allocations panel United Way Services; 2d v.p. Adult Edn. Council, 1974-75; trustee Family Health Assn., pres. bd. trustees, 1980-81. Recipient Alan Guttmacher award Planned Parenthood, 1978. Mem. Am. Public Health Assn., Am. Soc. Tng. and Devel., Cleve. Area Council Nursing, Alpha Kappa Alpha. Episcopalian. Home: 1801 E 12th St Cleveland OH 44114 Office: 2027 Cornell Rd Cleveland OH 44106

MALONE, CHARLES ALLEN, sales exec.; b. Jamestown, Tenn., Aug. 23, 1935; s. John Matthew and Alice M. M.; grad. York Agrl. Inst., 1956, Weaver Airline Tech. Sch., 1959; m. Shirley Ann DuVall, Aug. 13, 1960; children—Charles Allen, Jeffrey Scott, Melissa Ann. Pvt. detective, Dayton, Ohio, 1958-59; dist. sales mgr. Hertz Rent-A-Car, 1959-60; sta. agt. Lake Central Airlines, Dayton, 1960-67, lead sta. agt., 1967-68, sta. mgr., Zanesville, Ohio, 1968-70, regional sales mgr., Columbus and Dayton, 1970-77, dist. sales mgr., 1979—. Mem. Sales and Mktg. Execs. Internat., Columbus Sales Execs. Club, Columbus Aviation Com., Gideons Internat., Bon Vivants. Republican. Baptist. Office: 4393 E 17th St Columbus OH 43219

MALONE, GERALDINE SCOTT, hosp. ofcl.: b. Campbell, Ohio, June 3, 1931; d. David and Nellie (Elmore) Scott; diploma Youngstown (Ohio) Hosp. Assn. Sch. Med. Tech., 1956; B.S. in Secondary Edn., Rockford (Ill.) Coll., 1973, M.A., 1980; m. Wilfort Gentry Malone, Apr. 2, 1965; children—Sharon, Melanie. Hematology technologist Youngstown Hosp. Assn., 1957-58; from chemistry technologist to spl. chem. supr. St. Anthony Hosp., Rockford, 1958-72; edn. coordinator med. tech. pro gram Freeport (Ill.) Meml. Hosp., 1972-80, dir. med.-tech. program, 1980—; adj. faculty No. Ill. U., 1978-82, also mem. med.-tech. com.; adj. faculty Ill. State U., 1978-82; accreditation surveyor Nat. Accrediting Agy. for Clin. Lab. Scis., 1980-81; mem. health occupations adv. com. Stephenson Area Career Center; resource person Speakers Bur., Regional Office of Edn. Chmn., S.W. Area Heart Fund, Rockford, 1978, Nat. Diabetes Week, Freeport Meml. Hosp., 1976-78. Recipient Disting. Ser. award St. Anthony Hosp., 1968, Freeport Meml. Hosp., 1977. Mem. Am. Soc. Med. Tech., Am. Soc. Clin. Pathologists (asso.), Ill. Med. Tech. Assn. (dir.), Central Mich. U. Alumni Assn., Delta Sigma Theta, Omicron Sigma. Democrat. Baptist. Clubs: Rockford Coll. Alumni, Order Calanthe. Home: 1254 Rose Ave Rockford IL 61102 Office: Pathology Dept Freeport Meml Hosp 1045 W Stephenson St Freeport IL 61032

MALONE, JAMES WILLIAM, bishop; b. Youngstown, Ohio, Mar. 8, 1920; s. James Patrick and Katherine V. (McGuire) M.; A.B., St. Mary Sem., Cleve., 1945; M.A., Cath. U. Am., 1952, Ph.D., 1957. Ordained priest Roman Catholic Ch., 1945; asst. pastor, Youngstown, 1945-50; supt. schs. Diocese of Youngstown, 1950-65; instr. ednl. adminstrn. St. John's Coll., Cleve., 1953; aux. bishop of Youngstown, 1960-68, bishop, 1968—; apostolic adminstr. Diocese Youngstown, 1966-68; adv. Bishops' Com. Ecumenical and Interreligious Affairs Nat. Conf. Cath. Bishops, co-chmn. Cath./United Meth. Nat. Dialogue, Internat. Commn. English in The Liturgy, rep., 1st vice chmn. bd. dirs., mem. Episcopal Bd., consultor bishops' com. liturgy. Office: 144 W Wood St Youngstown OH 44503

MALONE, JEAN ARDELL, retail store exec.; b. Wisconsin Dells, Wis., Mar. 13, 1930; d. Hans Arnold and Isla Marie (Stafford) Kneubuhler; B.S., U. Wis.-Madison, 1964; m. Francis William Malone, June 10, 1971; 1 dau., Tara. Tchr. home econs. West Bend (Wis.) Sch. Dist., 1964-65; owner, pres. Elsie's Inc., Burlington, Wis., 1965—; dir. Bank of Burlington. Bd. dirs. Human Resource Center, chmn., 1978-79. Mem. Burlington C. of C. (pres. 1973), Nat. Retail Mchts. Assn., Wis. Mchts. Fedn. Congregationalist. Office: Burlington WI

MALONE, JOHN (HENRY), ednl. adminstr., psychologist; b. St. Louis, Mar. 21, 1928; s. Alfred and Minerva (Blanche) M.; B.S.M., St. Louis Coll. Mortuary Sci., 1954; B.A., Philander Smith Coll., 1956; M.A., U. Detroit, 1964; Ph.D., U. Mich., 1973. Mil. adjustment clk. Army Fin. Center, St. Louis, 1959-54; embalmer Miller Funeral Home, Little Rock, 1954-56; tchr., St. Louis Bd. Edn., 1956-61, Detroit Bd. Edn., 1961-66; pvt. practice psychology, Detroit, 1966—; instr. Wayne Community Coll., 1966-68, U. Mich., 1966-70; prin. Fairbanks Elem. Sch., Detroit, 1970—; therapy group trainee Ball State U., 1964, U.S. Office Edn., 1964; cons. in field. Bd. dirs. Urban Program in Edn., U. Mich., 1970-73; mem. City-Wide Coms. to Select Asst. Prins. and Staff Coordinators, Detroit, 1973; mem. Region I Curriculum Com., 1975; mem. project adv. bd. Wayne State U., 1975; mem. New Center Adv. Council, Detroit, 1979; bd. dirs., chmn. personnel Fedn. Girl's Homes, Detroit, 1980; lay reader, mem. vestry St. Timothy Episcopal Ch., Detroit. Served with Signal Corps, U.S. Army, 1950-52. Mem. Mich. Assn. Supervision and Curriculum Devel., Assn. Supervision and Curriculum Devel., Am. Assn. Spl. Educators, Council Exceptional Children, Black Psychologists, Am. Ednl. Research Assn., Mich. Ednl. Research Assn., Internat. Reading Assn., Orgn. Sch. Adminstrs. and Suprs., Nat. Assn. Elem. Sch. Prins., Nat. Assn. Black Sch. Educators, Mich. Reading Assn., Phi Delta Kappa, Phi Beta Sigma. Author: Implications For Better Identification Of The Socially Maladjusted and Emotionally Disturbed Placement

In The Detroit Public Schools, 1966. Home: 20205 Appoline St Detroit MI 48235 Office: 8000 John Lodge St Detroit MI 48202

MALONE, OLIVIA BANKS, elem. sch. prin.; b. St. Louis, July 24, 1924; d. Charles J. and Gladys I. (Reeves) Banks; B.A. in English and Edn., Stowe Tchrs. Coll., 1946; M.A. in Edn., U. Ill., 1950; postgrad. St. Louis U., 1981; m. William H. Malone, Nov. 14, 1969; 1 son, William J. With St. Louis Bd. Edn., 1946—; tchr. O'Fallon Sch., St. Louis, 1946-54; tchr., sch. coordinator various reading programs Franklin Sch., St. Louis, 1954-59; supr. tchr. in charge Turner Reading Clinic, St. Louis, 1959-64; supr. primary edn. Enright Dist., 1964-68; prin. Hamilton Sch., St. Louis, 1968-69, Waring Sch., St. Louis, 1969-74, Clinton Br. Sch., St. Louis, 1974-77, Chouteau Sch., St. Louis, 1977, Shenandoah Sch., St. Louis, 1977-80, Carver Sch., St. Louis, 1980—. Bd. dirs. Wheatley Br. YWCA, 1965-68, Jr. Kindergarten of Jr. League, 1967-69; sec. adv. bd. Head Start, St. Louis, 1968-69; mem. St. Louis City Planning Commn., 1970-74; vice chmn. Sumner High Sch. Centennial Celebration, 1975. Recipient Mayors Citizens award, 1974. Mem. NEA, Assn. Supervision and Curriculum Devel., Internat. Reading Assn., Mo. State Tchrs. Assn., Am. Fedn. Adminstrn. Roman Catholic. Club: Tallies Bridge. Home: 9430 Laguna Dr Saint Louis MO 63132 Office: Carver Sch 3325 Bell Ave Saint Louis MO 63104

MALONE, OLLIE, JR., educator; b. St. Louis, Oct. 18, 1953; s. Ollie and Evelyn (Bandy) M.; B.A. in Communication, William Jewell Coll., 1975; M.S. in Edn., U. Kans., 1976; doctoral candidate U. Mo., Kansas City; m. Christal Ann Smith, Aug. 15, 1975; 1 son, Nathan Everett. Cons., program adminstr. vocat. rehab., Kansas City, Kans., 1973-76; tchr., coach Kans. Sch. for Deaf, Olathe, 1976-78; edn. supr. AT&T, 1978—. Sponsor, Explorer Post, Boy Scouts Am., Wesport High Sch.; dir. ch. choir; past pres. Registry of Interpreters for Deaf. Comprehensive cert. interpreter Registry of Interpreters for Deaf. Recipient Bron Baker award, Alexander Doniphan award; award SCLC, 1982. Mem. Am. Soc. Tng. and Devel., Nat. Assn. Tchrs. of Singing, Alpha Psi Omega, Phi Mu Alpha Sinfonia. Mem. Full Faith Church of Love. Music editor, singer, pianist, arranger. Guest soloist radio, TV, personal appearances. Home: 1304 E 123rd St Olathe KS 66061 Office: 811 Main St Rm 880 PO Box 1418 Kansas City MO 64141

MALONE, RONALD LEE, hosp. adminstr., city ofcl.; b. Marion, Ohio, Jan. 21, 1947; s. John Raymond and Ella (Large) M.; B.A., Ohio State U., 1975; m. Jill Marie Fetter, Jan. 23, 1971; children—Megan Beth, Kate Marie. Laborer, Internat. Harvester Co., Springfield, Ohio; lab. technician Mercy Med. Center, Springfield; asso. lab. dir. Grady Meml. Hosp., Delaware, Ohio, now asst. adminstr; mayor Marion (Ohio), 1980—. Chmn. bd. Homemakers Health Aide Service, 1977; bd. govs. Marion Gen. Hosp., 1980—; chmn. Marion Bd. Health, 1980—; bd. dirs. Marion Jr. Achievement, 1980—; adv. bd. Marion Jr. Achievement, ARC; mem. Democratic Precinct Com., Marion; 1st v.p. Marion County Dem. Club, Young Dem. Club. Served with USAF, 1967-71. Mem. Am. Med. Technologists Assn., Ohio State U. Alumni Assn., Am. Legion. Club: Lions (Marion). Office: City Hall Marion OH 43302

MALONE, THOMAS FRANCIS, research inst. adminstr.; b. Sioux City, Iowa, May 3, 1917; s. John and Mary (Hourigan) M.; B.S., S.D. Sch. Mines and Tech., 1940; Sc.D., M.I.T., 1946; L.H.D., St. Joseph Coll., West Hartford, Conn., 1965; D.Eng., S.D. State Sch. Mines and Tech., 1962; m. Rosalie Ann Doran, Dec. 30, 1942; children—John H., Thomas F., Mary E., James K., Richard K., Dennis P. Instr., M.I.T., 1942-43, asst. prof., 1943-51, asso. prof., 1951-56; dir. Travelers Research Center, Travelers Ins. Co., Hartford, Conn., 1955-56, dir. research, 1956-69, sr. v.p., 1968-70, chmn. bd. Travelers Research Center, Inc., 1961-70; dean Grad. Sch. U. Conn., Storrs, 1970-73; dir. Holcomb Research Inst., Butler U., Indpls., 1973—; chmn. bd. Univ. Corp. for Atmospheric Research; mem. Nat. Adv. Com. on Oceans and Atmosphere, 1972-75; chmn. Nat. Motor Vehicle Safety Adv. Council, 1967-70, U.S. Nat. Commn. for UNESCO, 1963-66; mem. Conn. Research Commn., 1965-71; treas. Internat. Council Sci. Unions, 1978—; pres. Inst. Ecology, 1978—. Mem. Am. Meteorol. Soc. (pres. 1960-62), Am. Geophys. Union (pres. 1961-64), Nat. Acad. Scis. (fgn. sec. 1978—), Am. Acad. Arts and Scis., AAAS. Roman Catholic. Clubs: Cosmos (Washington); Hartford (Conn.); Columbia (Indpls.). Editor: Compendium of Meteorology, 1951. Office: 4600 Sunset Ave Indianapolis IN 46208

MALONE, WILLIAM FRANCIS, dentist; b. Chgo., Sept. 18, 1930; s. Francis J. and Ruth I. (Lingen) M.; student John Carroll U., 1948-51; D.D.S., Northwestern U., 1955, Ph.D., 1973; cert. U. Ill. Coll. of Dentistry, 1963; M.S., U. Ill., 1964; m. Mary Ellen Wrenn, Aug. 8, 1953; children—William, Patrick, Timothy, Robert, Mary Ruth, Maureen, Christine. Practice dentistry, Chgo., 1958-75, Palos Heights, Ill., 1975—; instr. dept. operative dentistry Dental Sch., Northwestern U., Chgo., 1957-58, now prof. advanced prosthodontics; asst. prof. dept. fixed partial prosthodontics U. Ill., Chgo., 1963-65, chmn. dept. operative dentistry, 1966-69; chmn. dept. fixed prosthodontics Loyola U., Maywood, Ill., 1969-76, dir. grad. prosthodontics, 1976-80; lectr. radio and TV programs, 1967-68. Served to maj. U.S. Army, 1955-62. Recipient Nell Snow Talbot All Sch. award, 1965-68. Mem. Am. Dental Assn., Ill. Dental Soc., Chgo. Dental Soc., Am. Acad. Crown and Bridge Prosthodontics, Am. Prosthodontic Soc., Am. Coll. Dentists, Sigma Xi, Omicron Kappa Upsilon. Contbr. articles on prosthodontics to profl. jours.; author: (with T.K. Barber, Howard Redmann) Teenage Dentistry, 1969; Electrosurgery, 1973; co-author: Tylman's Fixed Prosthodontics, 1978; sect. editor Jour. Prosthetic Dentistry, 1980—. Home: 13009 S 83d Ct Palos Park IL 60464

MALONEY, DAVID MONAS, bishop; b. Littleton, Colo., Mar. 15, 1912; s. James Edward and Margaret (Flynn) M.; student U. Colo., 1929-30; A.B., St. Thomas Sem., Denver, 1933; S.T.L., Gregorian U., Rome, 1937; J.C.D., Apollinaire U., Rome, 1940. Ordained priest Roman Catholic Ch., 1936, consecrated bishop, 1961; curate St. Philomena Ch., Denver, 1940-43; asst. chancellor Archdiocese of Denver, 1943-54, chancellor, 1954-60; domestic prelate, 1949; titular bishop Ruspae, aux. bishop Diocese of Denver, 1960-67; bishop Diocese of Wichita (Kans.), 1967—. Home: 424 N Broadway Wichita KS 67202*

MALONEY, DENNIS MICHAEL, psychologist; b. Portland, Oreg., Dec. 19, 1947; s. Bernard A. and Margaret (Stickel) M.; A.B. with honors, Gonzaga U., 1969; M.A. in Psychology (Univ. fellow), U. Kans., 1972, Ph.D., 1973; 1 son, Kevin Michael. Dir. research and evaluation BIABH Study Center, Morganton, N.C., 1973-75; research fellow Center for Study Youth Devel., Boys Town, Nebr., 1975-78, dir. program dissemination Youth Care Dept., 1978—; faculty fellow U. Nebr. Grad. Sch., Omaha, 1976—. Research grantee, 1971-76. Mem. Am. Psychol. Assn., Assn. Advancement Behavior Therapy, Nat. Teaching-Family Assn. Contbr. articles, book revs., short stories to misc. publs. Office: Youth Care Dept Boys Town NE 68010

MALONEY, JOHN CLEMENT, mktg. cons.; b. Laurel, Nebr., Aug. 19, 1929; s. Clement Mathew and Annette (McCabe) M.; B.A., U. Nebr., 1951; M.S., Purdue U., 1953, Ph.D., 1954; m. Maybelle Margaret Reinsch, Aug., 1950; children—Connie (Mrs. Leland Robinson), Sheila, Barbara, Jane, Lynn. Mgr. personnel testing Mpls. Honeywell Co., 1954-55; dir. market research Omar, Inc., Omaha, 1955-58; mgr. research and devel. Leo Burnett Co., Chgo., 1958-66; research dir. Urban Journalism Center, asso. prof. advtg. and journalism Northwestern U., 1966-72; v.p. research Arthur Meyerhoff Assos., Inc., Chgo., 1972-78; pres. John C. Maloney & Assos., Inc., Chgo., 1978—. Cons. various ednl. and research founds., corps., govt. agys. Ford Found. grantee, 1968-69. Mem. Am. Psychol. Assn. (dir. consumer psychology div. 1964-65), AAUP (pres. Northwestern U. chpt. 1970), Am. Mktg. Assn., AAAS. Contbr. articles to profl. jours. Home: 147 Plumtree Rd Deerfield IL 60015 Office: John C Maloney & Assos Inc 620 N Michigan Ave Chicago IL 60611

MALONEY, VINCENT JOHN, social worker; b. Bryn Mawr, Pa., June 21, 1949; s. Vincent John and Mary Margaret (Lavelle) M.; B.A., U. Mich., 1971, M.S.W., 1976; m. Katherine M. Brown. Teaching aide Wastenaw Assn. Retarded Children, Ann Arbor, Mich., 1971-72; child care worker U. Mich. Hosp., Ann Arbor, 1972-74; summer camp dir. Hemophilia of Mich., Ann Arbor, 1976-77; clin. supr. Down River Guidance Clinic, Lincoln Park, Mich., 1976-78, Cornerstone Counseling, Sumpter, Mich., 1978—; field instr. U. Mich., Ann Arbor, 1978—; cons. Consultation and Learning Center, Ypsilanti, Mich. Cert. social worker, Mich. Mem. Nat. Assn. Social Workers (cert.), Am. Camping Assn. Democrat. Home: 1018 S Congress Ypsilanti MI 48197 Office: 23501 Sumpter Rd Belleville MI 48111

MALOON, JERRY LEE, physician, lawyer, medicolegal cons.; b. Union City, Ind., June 23, 1938; s. Charles Elias and Bertha Lucille (Creviston) M.; B.S., Ohio State U., 1960, M.D., 1964; J.D., Capital U. Law Sch., 1974; children—Jeffrey Lee, Jerry Lee II. Intern, Santa Monica (Calif.) Hosp., 1964-65; tng. psychiatry Central Ohio Psychiat. Hosp., 1969, Menninger Clinic, Topeka, Kans., 1970; clin. dir. Orient (Ohio) Developmental Center, 1967-69, med. dir., 1971-81; asso. med. dir. Western Electric, Inc., Columbus, 1969-71; pvt. practice law with Michael F. Colley & Assos., Columbus, 1978—. Guest lectr. law and medicine Orient Developmental Center, also Columbus Developmental Center, 1969-71; dep. coroner Franklin County (Ohio), 1978—. Served to capt. M.C., AUS, 1965-67. Fellow Am. Coll. Legal Medicine; mem. AMA, Columbus and Franklin County Acad. Medicine, Ohio State Med. Assn., Am., Ohio, Columbus bar assns., Am., Ohio, Columbus trial lawyers assns., Ohio State U. Alumni Assn., U.S. Trotting Assn., Am. Profl. Practice Assn. Club: Ohio State U. Pres.'s. Home: 1439 Lake Shore Dr Columbus OH 43204 Office: 536 S High St Columbus OH 43215

MALOTT, R. H., mfg. co. exec.; b. Boston, Oct. 6, 1926; s. Deane W. and Eleanor (Thrum) M.; A.B., Kans. U., 1948; M.B.A., Harvard, 1950; student N.Y. U. Law Sch., evenings 1953-55; m. Elizabeth Harwood Hubert, June 4, 1960; children—Elizabeth Hubert, Barbara Holden, Robert Deane. Asst. to dean Harvard Grad. Sch. Bus. Adminstrn., 1950-52; with FMC Corp., 1952—, v.p., mgr. film ops. div. Am. Viscose div., 1966-67; exec. v.p., mem. pres.'s office, 1967-70, mgr. machinery divs., 1970-72, pres., chief exec. officer corp., 1972—, chmn. bd., 1973—; dir. FMC Corp., Chgo., Continental Ill. Bank, Chgo., Continental Ill. Corp., Standard Oil Ind., Bell & Howell, United Technologies Corp. Trustee Kans. Endowment Assn., U. Kans. Served with USNR, 1944-46. Mem. Machinery and Allied Products Inst. (exec. com.), Bus. Council, Phi Beta Kappa, Beta Theta Pi, Alpha Chi Sigma. Clubs: Indian Hill (Kenilworth, Ill.); Links, Explores (N.Y.C.); Econ., Mid-Am. (Chgo.). Office: 200 E Randolph Dr Chicago IL 60601

MALPASS, LESLIE FREDERICK, univ. pres.; b. Hartford, Conn., May 16, 1922; s. Fred J. and Lilly (Elmslie) M.; B.A., Syracuse U., 1947, M.A., 1949, Ph.D., 1952; m. Winona Helen Cassin, May 17, 1946; children—Susan Heather (Mrs. Poulton), Peter Gordon, Jennifer Joy, Michael Andrew. Psychologist, Onondaga County (N.Y.) Child Guidance Center Syracuse, 1948-52; lectr. Syracuse U., also U. Buffalo, 1949-52; asst. prof., then asso. prof. So. Ill. U., 1952-60; vis. prof. U. Fla., 1959-60; prof. psychology, chmn. div. behavioral scis. U. So. Fla., 1960-65; dean Coll. Arts and Scis., Va. Poly Inst., Blacksburg, 1965-68, v.p., 1968-74; pres. Western Ill. U., Macomb, 1974—. cons. in field. Dir. First Nat. Exchange Bank Va., 1965-74. Served with M.C., AUS, 1945-46. Diplomate Am. Bd. Examiners Profl. Psychology. Fellow Am. Psychol. Assn.; mem. AAAS, AAUP, Assn. Higher Edn., Sigma Xi, Psi Chi, Theta Chi Beta, Omicron Delta Kappa, Beta Gamma Sigma. Club: Rotary. Author books and articles in field. Home: 2001 Wigwam Hollow Rd Macomb IL 61455

MALTER, ROSALIE, occupational therapist; b. Chgo., Feb. 26, 1940; d. Sam and Annabelle (Zeid) Moss; B.S. cum laude, U. Ill., 1961; postgrad. Roosevelt U., 1980—; m. Richard F. Malter, June 18, 1961; children—Adina, Alan, Naomi, Judith. Occupational therapist Emory U. Hosp., Atlanta, 1961-62, Out-Patient Clinic, Ill. Mental Health Center, Chgo., 1962-63, Mercy Hosp., Urbana, Ill., 1963-64; teaching asst. Child Devel. Center, U. Ill., Urbana, 1964-65; chief occupational therapy dept. N.W. Community Hosp., Arlington Heights, Ill., 1974-78; adminstr., therapist N.W. Suburban Child Devel. Clinic, Arlington Heights, Chgo., 1979—; condr. workshops, seminars for occupational therapists. Sec., Schaumburg Twp. Mental Health Bd., 1980—; mem. Woodfield Jewish Day Sch. bd., 1975-79. Recipient Guardian of Torah award Woodfield Jewish Day Sch., 1977. Mem. Ill. Occupational Therapy Assn., Am. Occupational Therapy Assn., La Leche League, Center for Study of Sensory Integrative Dysfunction, NOW. Jewish. Office: 15 S Dryden Pl Arlington Heights IL 60004

MALTZ, ROBERT, surgeon; b. Cin., July 21, 1935; s. William and Sarah (Goldberg) M.; B.S., U. Cin., 1958, M.D., 1962; m. Sylvia Moskowitz, Aug. 24, 1958; children—Mark Edward, Deborah Lynn, Steven Alan, David Stuart. Intern, Cin. Gen. Hosp., 1962-63; resident Barnes Hosp., St. Louis, 1965-69; asst. prof. surgery Stanford U. Med. Center, Palo Alto, Calif., 1969-71; asso. prof. otolaryngology U. Cin. Med. Center, 1971—. Mem. brotherhood bd. Rockdale Temple, Cin., 1975—. Served in USAF, 1963-65. USPHS fellow, 1968-69; Eli Lilly Co. research grantee, 1971, 76; Burroughs Wellcome Co. research grantee, 1972; diplomate Am. Bd. Otolaryngology. Fellow Am. Coll. Surgeons; mem. Am. Acad. Otolaryngology-Head and Neck Surgery, Am. Acad. Facial Plastic and Reconstructive Surgery (chmn. constn. and by-laws com., No. chmn. credentials com.), Am. Assn. Cosmetic Surgeons (sec.-treas.), Royal Soc. Health (Eng.), Am. Council Otolaryngology, Pan Am. Assn. Otorhinolaryngology and Bronchoesophagology, Internat. Acad. Cosmetic Surgery, Cin. Acad. Medicine (chmn. public relations com.). Clubs: Amerley Village Swim and Tennis, Queen City Racquet, Losantiville Country, B'nai B'ith. Home: 2601 Willowbrook Dr Cincinnati OH 45237 Office: 10496 Montgomery Rd Cincinnati OH 45242

MAMOLEN, MARK CLASTER, lawyer, fin. exec.; b. Cumberland, Md., Jan. 4, 1946; s. Benjamin Edward and Sarah (Claster) M.; B.A., George Washington U., 1968, M.B.A., 1974; J.D., U. Chgo., 1977. Admitted to Ill. bar, 1977; in systems engring. IBM, Washington, 1968-70, in sales, 1970-71; chmn. NAPCO, Washington, 1971-74; chmn. Brazil Imports, Chgo., 1974-77; cons. Boston Cons. Group, 1977-78; atty. firm Pritzker & Pritzker, Chgo., 1978—. Served with U.S. Army, 1968-74. Mem. Am., Ill.. Chgo. bar assns. Democrat. Club: East Bank. Mem. Georgetown Law Rev., 1972-73. Home: 155 W Burton Pl Chicago IL 60610 Office: 2 First National Plaza Chicago IL 60603

MANATT, RICHARD, educator; b. Odebolt, Iowa, Dec. 13, 1931; s. William Price and Lucille (Taylor) M.; B.Sc., Iowa State U., 1953, M.S., 1956; Ph.D., U. Iowa, 1964; m. Sally Jo Johnson, Aug. 20, 1952; children—Tamra Jo, Ann Lea, Joel Price; m. 2d, Jacquelyn M. Nesset, Feb. 25, 1970; 1 dau., Megan Sue. Prin. Oskaloosa (Iowa) Schs. 1959-62; research asso. U. Iowa Iowa City, 1962-64; asst. prof. Iowa State U., Ames, 1964-67, asso. prof. ednl. adminstrn., 1967-72, prof., sect. leader ednl. adminstrn., 1972-81; disting. vis. prof. Calif. State U., Los Angeles, 1977-78; cons. performance evaluation for com. colls. and pub. schs. Served with AUS, 1953-55. Named Disting. Prof., Nat. Acad. Sch. Execs., 1979, Outstanding Cons., Assn. for Supervision and Curriculum Devel., 1981. Mem. NEA, Nat. Assn. Secondary Sch. Prins., Am. Assn. Sch. Adminstrs., Phi Kappa Phi, Phi Delta Kappa, Delta Chi. Democrat. Methodist. Author: Educator's Guide to the New Design. Home: 2926 Monroe Dr Ames IA 50010

MANCINI, ROBERT ANTHONY, advt. exec.; b. Detroit, Sept. 28, 1945; s. Widdy and Emma Marie M.; B.A., Wayne State U., 1967, M.A., 1973, postgrad, 1973-74; m. Judith Ann Montgomery, Nov. 22, 1969; children—Eric Robert. Copywriter, producer A.D. Kahn Advt., Detroit, 1967-68; mem. staff classified dept. Detroit News, 1970; media planner D'Arcy-MacManus & Masius, Bloomfield Hills, Mich., 1971-73; v.p. group media supr. Campbell Ewald Co., Warren, Mich., 1973-81; v.p., dep. dir. media services J. Walter Thompson, Dearborn, Mich., 1981—; instr. Walsh Coll., 1978; guest lectr. Wayne State U., Central Mich. U. Served with AUS, 1968-70. Decorated Bronze Star. Mem. Adcraft Club Detroit. Clubs: Troy Swim, Bald Mountain Gun. Lyricist, composer (with Steven Moore) Tell It Like It Is, 1972. Office: 17000 Executive Plaza Dearborn MI 48126

MANCUSI-UNGARO, MARIO FRANCESCO-LODOVICO, import/export mktg. exec.; b. Newark, N.J., Feb. 6, 1936; s. Lodovico Giuseppe and Frances Groves (Chambers) M-U.; B.S., Rutgers U., 1959; M.B.A., Harvard U., 1964. Dir. mktg. Comml. Trading Imports div. Control Data Inc., Mpls., 1977—; pvt. practice import/export trader, Chgo., 1973-77. Served with U.S. Army, 1960-63. Recipient Ackerman award Rutgers U., 1959. Mem. Minn. World Trade Assn. Club: Harvard U. Bus. of Chgo., Mpls. Roman Catholic. Home: 7330 Gallagher Dr Edina MN 55435 Office: Commercial Trading Imports Inc 474 Concordia Ave St Paul MN 55105

MANCUSO, GEORGE P(HILIP), hosp. adminstr.; b. Chgo., Nov. 11, 1931; s. George A. and Josephine P. (Pizzuto) M.; B.B.A., Loyola U., Los Angeles, 1955; M.S. in Hosp. Adminstrn., Northwestern U., 1959; postgrad. in mgmt. St. Louis U., 1965-68; m. Patricia A. Leone, Sept. 12, 1955; children—George, Gary, Mark, Paul, Anne, Tricia, John. Adminstrv. asst. GrandHosp., Chgo., 1957-58, adminstrv. resident, 1958-59; asso. adminstr. St. Mary's Hosp., Marquette, Mich., 1959-64; instr. in hosp. and health care adminstrn., cons. hosp. adminstr., dir. div. assn. services Catholic Hosp. Assn., 1964-69; dir. bus. services Regional Urban Devel. Studies Services, Edwardsville, Ill., 1969-70; asst. prof., asst. to dean, coordinator health care services So. Ill. U. Sch. Dental Medicine, 1970-71; dir. phys. health planning div. Alliance Regional Commn. Health, St. Louis, 1971-72; mgmt. cons. to health care facilities So. Ill. U., 1972-76; exec. dir. St. Joseph Riverside Hosp., Warren, Ohio, 1976—; cons. health care; lectr. in numerous mgmt. devel. programs for hosps. and nursing homes; condr. numerous seminars for Catholic religious communities; TV appearances for health care related programs. Mem. exec. com. Trumbull County (Ohio) Council on Alcoholism, 1979-81; mem. adv. bd. Rape Crisis Team, Warren, Ohio, 1978-79; trustee Health Systems Agy. Eastern Ohio, 1978-81. Served to 1st lt. Med. Service Corps, USAF, 1955-57. Hill Burton grantee, 1963; So. Ill. U. Med. Dept. grantee, 1971; So. Ill. U. grantee, 1975. Mem. Am. Coll. Hosp. Adminstr., Am. Hosp. Assn., East Ohio Hosp. Assn., Cath. Conf. Ohio (chmn. com. mission statement 1979 legislation com. 1980-81), Cath. Health Assn. (communications services com. 1980-81), Warren Area C. of C. Roman Catholic. Contbr. articles to profl. jours. Office: 1400 Tod Ave NW Warren OH 44485

MANCUSO, ROBERT POPE, automobile dealership exec.; b. Chgo., Feb. 2, 1951; s. James Vincent and Clarissa Rosary (Pope) M.; A.B. in Psychology, Princeton U., 1973. Vice pres. Mancuso Chevrolet, Inc., Skokie, Ill., 1969—; pres. Mancuso Cadillac Honda Inc., Barrington, Ill., 1974—, also RPM Systems, Inc., Consumer Concepts, Ltd. Career advisor Barrington Bd. Edn. Recipient Nat. Auto Dealers Edn. award, 1977. Mem. Nat., Barrington (past pres.) auto dealers assns., Chicagoland Cadillac Dealers Assn. (exec. com. 1979—, chmn. advt. com.), Chicagoland Honda Dealers Assn. (exec. com. 1979—, pres. 1981-82), Barrington C. of C. (treas. 1976-77, v.p. 1977-79, pres. 1979—), Chgo. Auto Trade Assn. Roman Catholic. Club: Rotary (chpt. dir., pres. 1981-82). Office: 1445 S Barrington Rd Barrington IL 60010

MANCY, GEORGE K., restaurant exec.; b. Toledo, June 26, 1937; s. Gus J. and Margaret (Kostopolous) M.; B.A. in Bus., Ohio State U., 1959; m. Sarah A. Rahal, June 23, 1963; children—Mike, Dena, Nick. Mgr. Holiday Inn, Gladieux Corp., Muncie, Ind., 1961-64; owner, operator Mancy's Restaurant, Toledo, 1964—. Chmn. Greek-Am. Festival, Toledo, 1977-79. Served with U.S. Army, 1959-61. Recipient plaques for services Greek Orthodox Ch., 1979. Mem. Northwestern Ohio Restaurant Assn. (pres. 1977-78, Service award 1978), Ohio Restaurant Assn. (Pro award 1977, dir. 1978—), Nat. Restaurant Assn., Toledo C. of C., Toledo Conv. Bur. (chmn. 1979-80), Better Bus. Bur. Republican. Clubs: Toastmasters (service plaque 1979), Press Club Toledo, Ahepa, Optimists. Home: 5228 Carling Fort St Toledo OH 43623 Office: 953 Phillips Toledo OH 43612

MANDEL, DOUGLAS ALLAN, podiatrist; b. Cleve., June 13, 1952; s. Harold and Harriet Mandel; B.A., Ohio State U., 1974; D.P.M., Ohio Coll. Podiatric Medicine, 1979; m. Iris Ruth Mendlowitz, Sept. 1, 1974; 1 dau., Jill Shana. Practice podiatric medicine, Northfield, Ohio, 1979—; clinician Fraternity Podiatric Clinic, Cleve., 1979—. Fellow Acad. Ambulatory Foot Surgery; mem. Am. Podiatry Assn., Ohio Podiatry Assn.

MANDEL, SHELDON LLOYD, dermatologist; b. Mpls., Dec. 6, 1922; s. Maurice and Stelle N. M.; B.A., U. Minn., 1943, B.S., 1944, M.B., 1946, M.D., 1946; m. Patricia E. Mandel; 1 dau. by previous marriage, Melissa Ann. Intern U. Okla. Hosp., 1946-47; trainee Valley Forge Hosp., 1947-49; fellow Grad. Sch. U. Minn., 1949-53; resident (preceptee Dr. H.E. Michelson) VA Hosp., 1949-53; practice medicine specializing in dermatology, Mpls., 1953—; clin. prof. dermatitus U. Minn., 1970—, course dir. resident-staff seminars in dermatology, 1972—; mem. staffs Northwestern Hosp., Abbott Hosp., Mpls. Served to capt. M.C. AUS, 1947-49. Diplomate Am. Bd. Dermatology. Fellow Am. Acad. Dermatology; mem. AMA, Minn., Hennepin County med. socs., Mpls. Acad. Medicine, AAUP, Noah Worcester, Minn. (past pres.) dermatol. socs., Pan Am. Med. Assn. Clubs: Mpls. Athletic, Mpls. Golf. Contbr. articles to med. jours. Home: 2828 Burnham Blvd Minneapolis MN 55416 Office: 715 Med Arts Bldg Minneapolis MN 55402

MANDELL, STEVEN LESLIE, educator; b. Newark, Aug. 10, 1944; s. Herbert and Gail Pearl (Lavich) M.; B.A., Lehigh U., 1966, B.S. in Chem. Engring., 1967; M.B.A., U. Pa., 1969; D. Bus. Adminstrn., George Washington U., 1975; m. Colleen Jane Bailik, July 12, 1969; children—Hollis Elizabeth, Zachary Jonathan, Bradford Allen. Systems engr. IBM, Fairfax, Va., 1969-70; asso. dir., computer specialist U.S. Civil Service Commn., Washington, 1972-75; asso. prof. information systems Bowling Green (O.) State U., 1975—, dir. Mgmt. Information Inst., 1977—; cons. Bur. Land Mgmt., AID. Served to capt. U.S. Army, 1970-72. Decorated Army Commendation medal. IBM fellow, 1968-69; Am. Metal Climax scholar, 1966-67. Club: Bowling Green Tennis. Author: The Management Information System is Going to Pieces, 1975; Multinational Corporate Computer Systems, 1975; Organizational Intelligence Networks, 1977; Principles of Data Processing, 2d edit., 1981; PLI/PLC: A Short Course, 1977; Computers and Data Processing, 1979, Introduction to Business, 1981. Home: 463 Truman Bowling Green OH 43402 Office: Acctg and MIS Bowling Green State U Bowling Green OH 43402

MANDERS, KARL LEE, neurol. surgeon; b. Rochester, N.Y., Jan. 21, 1927; s. David Bert and Frances Edna (Cohan) Mendelson; student Cornell U., 1946; M.D., U. Buffalo, 1950; m. Ann Laprell, July 28, 1969; children—Karlanna, Maidena; children by previous marriage—Karl, Kerry, Kristine. Intern, U. Va. Hosp., Charlottesville, 1950-51, resident in neurol. surgery, 1951-52; resident in neurol. surgery Henry Ford Hosp., Detroit, 1954-56; practice medicine specializing in neurol. surgery, Indpls., 1956—; med. dir. Community Hosp. Rehab. Center for Pain, 1973—; chief hosp. med. and surg. neurology Community Hosp., 1977, chmn. sect. baromedicine, 1979—; coroner Marion County (Ind.), 1977; pres. Manders-Marks, Inc.; pres. Bioscan Inc. Served with USN, 1952-54; Korea. Recipient cert. achievement Dept. Army, 1969. Diplomate Am. Bd. Neurol. Surgery, Nat. Bd. Med. Examiners, Am. Bd. Clin. Biofeedback. Fellow A.C.S.; mem. AMA, Am. Assn. Neurol. Surgery, Congress Neurol. Surgery, Internat. Assn. Study of Pain, Am. Assn. Study of Headache, N.Y. Acad. Sci., Am. Coll. Angiology, Am. Soc. Contemporary Medicine and Surgery, Am. Holistic Med. Assn. (a founder), Undersea Med. Soc., Am. Acad. Forensic Sci., Am. Assn. Biofeedback Clinicians, Soc. for Cryosurgery, Pan Pacific Surg. Assn., Biofeedback Soc. Am., Acad. Psychosomatic Medicine, Pan Am. Med. Assn., Am. Soc. for Stereotaxic and Functional Neurosurgery, Soc. for Computerized Tomography and Neuroimaging, Ind. Coroners Assn. (pres. 1979). Home: 5845 Highfall St Indianapolis IN 46226 Office: 5506 E 16th St Indianapolis IN 46218

MANDERSCHEID, LESTER VINCENT, agrl. economist, educator; b. Iowa, Oct. 9, 1930; s. Vincent John and Alma (Sprank) M.; B.S., Iowa State U., 1951, M.S., 1952; Ph.D., Stanford U., 1961; m. Dorothy Helen Varnum, Aug. 29, 1953; children—David, Paul, Laura, Jane. Research asst. Iowa State U., 1951-52, Stanford U., 1952-56; faculty Mich. State U., East Lansing, 1956—, prof. agrl. econs., 1970—, asso. dept. chmn., 1973—, chmn. steering com. Univ. Acad. Governance System, 1978-80; cons. Tex. A&M U., 1970, Pfizer Co., 1971-72, AID, 1976-80. Pres., Bedford Hills Home Owners Assn., 1957-59; extraordinary minister St. Thomas Aquinas Roman Catholic Ch., 1975—. Travel grantee Internat. Conf. Agr. Economists, Minsk, USSR, 1970; recipient Disting. Faculty award Mich. State U., 1977. Mem. Am. Agrl. Econs. Assn. (Outstanding Undergrad. Teaching award 1974), Internat. Assn. Agrl. Economists, Am. Econs. Assn., Am. Statis. Assn., AAAS, Am. Assn. for Advancement Humanities, Mich. Acad. Sci. Arts and Letters, NAACP, Phi Kappa Phi (pres. Mich. State U. chpt. 1979-80). Club: University. Co-author: Improving Undergraduate Education-Report of the Committee on Undergraduate Education, 1967, Economics and Management in Agriculture, 1962. Office: Dept Agrl Econs 202 Agr Hall Mich State U East Lansing MI 48824

MANDICH, DONALD R., banker; b. 1925; B.B.A., U. Mich., 1946, M.B.A., 1950; married. With Detroit Bank & Trust Co., 1950—, asst. cashier, 1957-61, asst. v.p., 1961-63, v.p., 1963-69, sr. v.p., 1969-74, exec. v.p., 1974-77, pres., 1977—, also chmn. bd., chief exec. officer Detroitbank Corp. Office: Detroit Bank & Trust Co Fort and Washington Blvd Detroit MI 48231*

MANDLE, EARL ROGER, mus. adminstr.; b. N.J., May 13, 1941; s. Earl and Phyllis Key (O'Berg) M.; B.A. cum laude, Williams Coll., 1963; M.A., N.Y. U., 1967, also postgrad.; m. Gayle Wells Jenkins, July 11, 1964; children—Luke Harrison, Julia Barnes. Intern, Met. Mus. Art, N.Y.C., Victoria and Albert Mus., London, 1966-67; asso. dir. Mpls. Inst. Arts, 1967-74; asso. dir. Toledo Mus. Art, 1974-76, dir., 1977—. Chmn. youth comm. ARC, 1967; chmn. internat. service com. Rotary, 1978-79; trustee Toledo Arts Commn., Art Interests, Toledo Hosp.; mem. Toledo Econ. Planning Council; mem. exec. com. Intermuseum Conservation. Andover Teaching fellow, 1963, Ford Found. fellow, 1966, Nat. Endowment for the Arts fellow, 1974. Mem. Am. Assn. Mus., Am. Assn. Art Mus. Dirs., Coll. Art Assn., Internat. Council Mus., Ohio Found. for Arts, Ohio Art Council, Young Pres.'s Orgn. Clubs: Toledo, Carranor Hunt & Polo, Tile. Contbr. articles to profl. jours. Office: 2445 Monroe St Toledo OH 43697

MANELLI, DONALD DEAN, writer, producer motion pictures; b. Burlington, Iowa, Oct. 20, 1936; s. Daniel Anthony and Mignon Marie M.; B.A., U. Notre Dame, 1959; children by former marriage—Daniel, Lisa. Communications specialist Jewel Cos., 1959; script writer Coronet Films, Chgo., 1960-62; freelance writer, 1962-63; creative dir. Fred A. Niles Communications Centers, Chgo., 1963-67; sr. writer Wild Kingdom, NBC-TV network, also freelance film writer, 1967-70; pres. Donald Manelli & Assos., Inc., Chgo., 1970—. Recipient internat. film festival and TV awards. Mem. Writers Guild Am., Nat. Acad. TV Arts and Scis., Outdoor Writers Assn. Am. Office: 307 N Michigan Ave Chicago IL 60601

MANEWAL, WILTON LOUIS, JR., investments co. exec.; b. St. Louis, July 15, 1918; s. Wilton Louis and Celeste (Grimm) M.; A.B. in Econs., St. Louis U., 1940; postgrad. Harvard U., 1966; m. Helen Joanne Taylor, June 14, 1947; children—Richard Taylor, Lucia Ellen, Mary Ann Manewal West, Susan Manewal Bluhm. Vice pres. gen. merchandising mgr. Ely & Walker, Inc. div. Burlington Industries, St. Louis, 1945-66; v.p. Midvale Coal Co., St. Louis, 1960-70; v.p. Drexel Burnham Lambert Inc., St. Louis, 1978—; dir. Pecan Shoppe of Ga. Bd. dirs. St. Louis Priory, 1960—, Maryville Coll., 1963-70; del. Republican Nat. Conv., 1976. Served with U.S. Navy, 1940-45. Republican. Roman Catholic. Home: 38 Lake Forest St Saint Louis MO 63117 Office: 7701 Forsyth St Saint Louis MO 63105

MANFORD, BARBARA ANN, mezzo-soprano; b. St. Augustine, Fla., Nov. 13, 1929; d. William Floyd and Margaret (Kemper) Manford; Mus.B. in Voice, Fla. State U., 1951, Mus.M., 1970; studied with L. Palazzini, A. Strano, Japelli, E. Nikolaid, E. Joseph. Appearances in Europe, performing major roles in 12 leading opera houses, 1951-68, with condrs. including Alfred Strano, Felice Cilario, Robert Shaw, Arnold Gamson, Guiseppe Patané, Ottavio Ziino, also numerous concerts and recitals in Paris and throughout Italy; performed in world premiere Fugitives (C. Floyd), Fla. State U., Tallahassee, 1950; chosen by Gian Carlo Menotti for leading role in world premiere The Leper, Fla. State U., 1970; numerous radio, TV, and concert appearances, U.S., 1968—; artist-in-residence, asso. prof. voice Ball State U., Muncie, Ind., 1970—; numerous recs. Semi-finalist vocal contest, Parma, Italy, 1964; winner contest, Lonigo, Italy, 1965. Mem. Nat. Assn. Tchrs. Singing, Sigma Alpha Iota, Pi Kappa Lambda. Christian Scientist. Home: 104 Colonial Crest Apts Muncie IN 47304 Office: Ball State Univ Muncie IN 47306

MANFRO, PATRICK JAMES (PATRICK JAMES HOLIDAY), radio artist; b. Kingston, N.Y., Dec. 30, 1947; s. Charles Vincent and Anna Agnes (Albany) Manfro; Asso. Sci. in Accounting, Ulster Coll., 1968; diploma Radio Electronics Inst., 1969; student St. Clair Coll., 1974—; m. Janice Lynn Truscott, July 5, 1975; 1 son, Wesley Patrick. Program dir., radio artist WKNY, Kingston, 1966-70; radio artist WPTR, Albany, N.Y., 1970, WPOP, Hartford, Conn., 1970, CKLW, Detroit, 1970-71, WOR-FM, N.Y.C., 1971-72; radio artist CKLW Radio, Detroit, 1972—, asst. program dir., 1978-80, program dir., 1980—; pres. Pat Holiday Prodns., Detroit. Radio Cons.; pres., chief exec. officer Internat. Data Corp., Wilmington, Del.; adviser New Contemporary Sch. Announcing, Albany, 1973—; comml. announcer radio, television, 1970—. Judge, Miss Mich. Universe Pageant, 1970. Mem. N.Y. State N.G., 1968-74. Recipient 5 Year Service ribbon N.Y. State, 1973; named Runner-up Billboard Air Personality awards, 1971. Mem. AFTRA, Screen Actors Guild, Smithsonian Assos., BMI Songwriters Guild. Club: Dominion Golf and Country. Home: 1637 Goyeau St Windsor ON Canada Office: 1640 Ouellette Windsor ON N8X 1L1 Canada

MANGIN, JOSEPH JOHN, cert. public acct.; b. Waterloo, Iowa, Feb. 18, 1928; s. John Michael and Effie May (O'Brien) M.; student Iowa State Tchrs. Coll., 1948-49; B.S., U. Iowa, 1951; m. Marilyn Alvina Farmer, Aug. 18, 1951; children—Deborah S., David J. Sr. acct. Calmenson, Abramson & Co., 1953-58; comptroller, dir. Capitol Acceptance Corp., 1958—. partner Mangin & Van Wychen, C.P.A.'s, St. Paul, 1963—; pres., dir. Sudden Service, Inc., 1978—; comptroller Hillcrest Devel., 1958—; pres., dir. Mr. X Inc., 1970—; sec.-treas., dir. Condo, Inc., 1979—; pres., dir. Wyoming, Inc. Treas. bd. dirs. Insight Inc., Minn. State Prison. Served with USN, 1946-47. C.P.A. Mem. Am. Inst. C.P.A.'s, Minn. Soc. C.P.A.'s. Home: Route 3 Glenmont Rd River Falls WI 54022 Office: 796 E 7th St Saint Paul MN 55106

MANGUM, RONALD SCOTT, lawyer; b. Chgo., Nov. 14, 1944; s. Roy Oliver and Marjorie Wilma (Etchason) M.; B.A., Northwestern U., 1965, J.D., 1968; m. Kay Lynn Booton, July 14, 1973; children—Scott Arthur, Katherine Marie. Admitted to Ill. bar, 1968; asst. univ. atty. Northwestern U., 1968-73; asso. firm Lord, Bissell & Brook, Chgo., 1974-76; partner firm Liss, Mangum & Beeler, Chgo., 1976-80, Mangum, Beeler, Schad & Diamond, Chgo., 1980—; lectr. Northwestern U., 1972-74; pres. Planned Giving, Inc., 1978—, 1426 Chicago Ave Bldg. Corp., 1975-76, Parkinson Research Corp., 1970-74. Chmn. Am. Hearing Research Found., 1977-79, v.p., 1972-77; bd. dirs. Episcopal Charities, 1978—; trustee Evanston Art Center, 1977-78; mem. health care subcom. Nat. Fire Protection Assn., 1980—. Recipient cert. of appreciation Ill. Inst. Continuing Legal Edn., 1972. Mem. Chgo. Bar Assn., Ill. Bar Assn., Am. Bar Assn., Nat. Assn. Coll. and Univ. Attys., Am. Soc. Hosp. Attys., Ill. Assn. Hosp. Attys., Chgo. Estate Planning Council, Art Inst. Chgo. (life), Nat. Rifle Assn. (life), Nat. Soc. Fund Raising Execs. Psi Upsilon. Clubs: Union League (Chgo.), John Evans (dir.). Author: (with R.M. Hendrickson) Governing Board and Administrator Liability, 1977; Tax Aspects of Charitable Giving, 1976. Contbr. articles to legal jours. Home: 1326 Asbury St Evanston IL 60201 Office: 208 S LaSalle St Chicago IL 60604

MANGUS, THOMAS EUGENE, found. exec.; b. Oklahoma City, Jan. 3, 1936; s. Virgil H. and Ophelia C. M.; student U. Okla., 1954-56, Lincoln U., 1973-74; grad. Program for Health Systems Mgmt., Harvard U., 1978; m. Mary Elizabeth Jaques, Feb. 14, 1969; children—Karlene Diane, James Douglas. Mgr., Crown Drug Co., Jefferson City, Mo., 1965-70; asst. drug claims supr. div. welfare State of Mo., Jefferson City, 1970-72, supr. in div. welfare, 1972-74; exec. dir. S.E. Mo. PSRO, also S.E. Mo. Found. for Med. Care, Cape Girardeau, 1974-75; exec. dir. Mid-Mo. PSRO Found., Jefferson City, 1975—; bd. dirs. Peer Rev. Network. Bd. dirs. Meml. Hosp., Jefferson City. Mem. Mo. Soc. Assn. Execs., Am. Assn. Profl. Standards Review Orgns. (exec. com. exec. dirs. sect. 1980-82), Mo. Hosp. Assn. (asso.). Clubs: Mid-Mo Old Car, Masons. Home: 3235 S 10 Mile Dr Jefferson City MO 65101 Office: 1025 Southwest Blvd Jefferson City MO 65102

MANIJAK, WILLIAM, historian, former educator; b. Holyoke, Mass., July 4, 1913; s. Stanley and Catherine (Padlo) M.; B.A. in English, Am. Internat. Coll., 1949; M.A. in Journalism, U. Wis., 1952, postgrad., 1949-59; Ph.D. (fellow), Ball State U., 1975; m. Phyllis Mae Hatch, Aug. 13, 1949; children—William Stafford, Catherine Anne. Copy chief Kulzick Advt. Agy., Madison, Wis., 1952-55; continuity dir. sta. WISC, Madison, 1956-67; public relations, editor house organ Gardner Baking Co., Madison, 1957-58; editor Americana Press, Madison, 1958; asst. coordinator Internat. Tchr. Devel. Program, U. Wis., Madison, 1959; dir. public relations, instr. in history, chmn. div. social scis. St. Francis Coll., Ft. Wayne, Ind., 1959-66, chmn. dept. social studies, 1960-78, v.p. coll. relations, 1966-71, coll. grad. council, exec. com., 1960-68, prof. emeritus history and govt., 1978—; resource person, lectr. Negro history sta. WANE-TV, Ft. Wayne, 1977; lectr. on coll., fgn. relations, community relations Ft. Wayne area. Vice pres. Community Betterment Assn., Ft. Wayne, 1966; mem. mayor's subcom. on neighborhoods, 1970; coordinator Fourth Congressional Dist. History Day, 1978. Served with USAF, 1940-45. Recipient award Collier's mag., 1948; All-Am. Selections Panel, football, 1948, others. Mem. Am. Hist. Assn., Assn. Am. Historians, Ind. Hist. Soc., Ind. Acad. Social Scis., Am. Cath. Hist. Assn., Polish-Am. Hist. Assn., Polish-Am. Mus., Kosciuszko Found., Ft. Wayne-Allen County Hist. Soc., Ft. Wayne-Allen County C. of C. (edn. and state policies coms., 1962-70), Sigma Delta Chi. Democrat. Roman Catholic. Clubs: K.C., Elks. Winner short story competition, Criterion, Am. Internat. Coll., 1948; contbr. articles to profl. jours. Home: 1719 Edenton Dr Fort Wayne IN 46804

MANILLA, JOHN ALLAN, office furniture co. exec., elevator co. exec.; b. Sharon, Pa., July 17, 1941; s. Vito John and Helen Elizabeth (Papai) M.; B.S., Youngstown State U., 1966; postgrad. Duquesne U., 1967-68, Aquinas Coll., 1979—; m. Paula Gale Jurko, Nov. 26, 1960; children—Jacqueline Lee, John Paul, Paul Allan, Bradley James. Sr. staff asst. Elevator Co., Westinghouse Electric Corp., Pitts., 1966-68, salesman I, 1968-70, salesman II, Union, N.J., 1971, Miami, Fla., 1971-72, dist. mgr., Indpls., 1973-77, regional mgr. archtl. systems div., Grand Rapids, Mich., 1977-79, splty. sales mgr., 1979—; v.p. Yankee Lake Amusement Co., Yankee Lake Village, Ohio, 1961-66, 70-71; elevator cons. architects, engrs., bldg. mgr., contractors. Chief, YMCA Indian Guides, Allison Park, Pa., 1970; asst. scoutmaster Boy Scouts Am., Dania, Fla., 1971-72; asst. to Boys Scouts Am., Ind. Sch. for Blind, Indpls., 1973; jr. high sch. prin., instr. Christian Doctrine, St. Ursula Ch., Allison Park, 1968-70, St. Sabastion Ch., Masury, Ohio, 1970-71; pres. bd. edn. Our Lady of Mt. Carmel Sch., Carmel, Ind., 1973-76; mem. Carmel Dad's Club, 1973-74. Recipient First in Performance award Westinghouse Electric Corp., 1972, 120 Club Honor Roll, 1968, 69, 70, 71, 72. Mem. Bldg. Owners and Mgrs. Assn., Constrn. Specification Inst., Assn. Gen. Contractors Ind., Am. Water Ski Assn., West Mich. Water Ski Assn. Clubs: Rotary, Indpls. Athletic; Yankee Lake (Ohio) Water Ski (pres.); Renaissance (Detroit). Home: 1924 Lockmere SE Kentwood MI 49508 Office: 4300 36th St SE PO Box 8367 Grand Rapids MI 49508

MANION, DANIEL A., lawyer, state legislator; b. South Bend, Ind., Feb. 1, 1942; s. Clarence E. and Virginia (O'Brien) M.; student in polit. sci. Notre Dame U., 1964; J.D., Ind. U., 1973. Salesman, Mountain Valley Spring Co., 1967-68; dir. indsl. devel. Ind. Dept. Commerce, 1969-73; dep. atty. gen. State of Ind., 1973-74; asso. firm Doran, Manion, Boynton, Kamm, and Esmont, South Bend, from 1974, now partner; mem. Ind. Senate, 1978—; del. Republican Nat. Conv., 1976; dir. St. Joseph Bank & Trust Co., South Bend. Bd. dirs. Jr. Achievement Michiana, Inc. Served to 1st lt. U.S. Army, 1965-66; Vietnam. Mem. Ind. Bar Assn., St. Joseph's County (Ind.) Bar Assn., Am. Legis. Exchange Council, Am. Legion, VFW. Roman Catholic. Office: Suite 725 Saint Joseph Bank Bldg South Bend IN 46601

MANKA, MATTHEW JAMES, JR., counselor, cons.; b. Chgo., Aug. 27, 1948; s. Matthew James and Wanda Victoria M.; B.S. in Edn., So. Ill. U., 1971; M.A. in Human Relations Services, Governors State U., 1976; m. Gayle Eleanore Wishba, June 26, 1971. Tchr. high sch. Sch. Dist. 228, Tinley Park, Ill., 1971-72; juvenile and family counselor Calumet City (Ill.) Youth and Family Services, 1973-75, exec. dir., 1975-78; exec. dir. The Place, Park Forest South, Ill., 1978-80; pvt. practice counselor and cons., Crestwood, Ill., 1980—; guest lectr. Purdue U.; community prof. Gov.'s State U.; sr. cons. Let-A-Kid, Calumet City, 1978—. Mem. adv. bd. community services dept. Thornton Community Coll., 1978-79; mem. adv. bd. Communications Lab., 1977, 78. Recipient certificate of achievement Calumet Adult Edn. Center, Thornton Community Coll., 1976; certificate of appreciation Communications Lab., 1977, The Place, 1980; Outstanding Young Man of Am. award U.S. Jaycees, 1978. Mem. Am. Personnel and Guidance Assn., Am. Mental Health Counselors Assn. Author: Even Rich People Have Ugly Kids (poetry), 1975. Office: Community Counseling Assos 4744 W 135th St Crestwood IL 60445

MANKOFF, PHILLIP, psychologist; b. Chgo., Mar. 1, 1924; s. Abraham and Sarah (Spivack) M.; B.S., Roosevelt U., 1961, M.A., 1963; M.A., U. Chgo., 1965; m. Lillian L. Aronovitz, July 14, 1946; children—Charles, Bruce, Brad, Paul. Probation officer Juvenile Ct., Skokie, Ill., 1962-63, staff psychologist, 1963-64, chief psychologist, 1964-66; psychologist Niles Twp. High Sch., Skokie, Ill., 1966—; pvt. practice clin. psychology specializing in learning disabilities. Served with U.S. Army, 1942-46. Registered and cert. clin. psychologist, Ill.; cert. sch. psychologist, Ill. Mem. Am. Psychol. Assn. (asso.), Nat. Council on Crime and Delinquency, Midwestern Psychol. Assn., Ill. Acad. Criminology, Ill. Psychol. Assn. Republican. Jewish. Home: 9300 N Kenneth Ave Skokie IL 60076 Office: Niles North High School Old Orchard and Lawler Ave Skokie IL 60077

MANLEY, EUGENE BENEDICT, tech. inst. adminstr.; b. Adrian, Minn., Mar. 15, 1939; s. Bernard Benedict and Therese Marie (DeBates) M.; B.S., Mankato State U., 1969, M.S., 1973; m. Kathleen Ann Johanneck, June 8, 1968; children—Linda Marie, Laura Jean. Salesman, Great Plains Gas Co., Mpls., 1965-69; tchr. Morgan (Minn.) Public Schs., 1969-75; dir. optometric asst. program Granite Falls (Minn.) Area Vocat. Tech. Inst., 1975—, coach basketball, 1969—. Sec. Granite Falls Utility Commn., 1976-80. Served with U.S. Army, 1957-58. Mem. Am. Vocat. Assn., NEA, Minn. Edn. Assn., Granite Falls Edn. Assn., Minn. Bus. Educators Inc., Am. Optometric Assn. Roman Catholic. Home: 1600 8th Ave Granite Falls MN 56241 Office: Hwy 212 Granite Falls MN 56241

MANLEY, ROBERT EDWARD, lawyer, economist; b. Cin., Nov. 24, 1935; s. John M. and Helen (McCarthy) M.; B.S., Xavier U., 1956; M.A., U. Cin., 1957; J.D., Harvard U., 1960; student London Sch. Econs. and Polit. Sci., 1960; m. Roberta Anzinger, 1972. Taft teaching fellow econs. U. Cin., 1956-57; admitted to Ohio bar, 1960; since practiced in Cin. partner firm Manley, Jordan & Fischer; adj. prof. econs. Xavier U., 1962-73; lectr. law Salmon P. Chase Law Sch., 1965-73; vis. lectr. community planning U. Cin., 1967-73, adj. asso. prof. urban planning, 1973—, lectr. law, 1977-80, adj. prof. law, 1980—. Chmn. environ. adv. council City of Cin., 1975-76. Trustee Hope Cincinnati, Albert J. Ryan Found., Cin. Legal Aid Soc.; mem. Pub. Defender Commn. Hamilton County (Ohio), 1976-80. Served to capt. AUS. 1961. Fellow Cin. Coll. Philosophers; mem. Am., Ohio, Cin. bar assns., Am. Judicature Soc., Law and Society Assn., Am. Econ. Assn., Am. Acad. Polit. and Social Scis., Am. Coll. Real Estate Lawyers, Xavier, Cin. alumni assns., Harvard U. Law Sch. Assn., Alpha Sigma Nu (nat. dir. 1966-76), Tau Kappa Alpha, Omicron Delta Epsilon, Phi Alpha Delta. Republican. Roman Catholic. Clubs: Queen City, Harvard; Explorers (N.Y.C.); S. Am. Explorers (Lima, Peru). Contbr. articles to profl. jours. Home: Dexter and Wold Cincinnati OH 45206 Office: Carew Tower Cincinnati OH 45202

MANLOVE, DONALD CULLEN, educator; b. Milton, Ind., Mar. 28, 1918; s. Harry Robert and Maude (Pritchard) M.; B.S., Purdue U., 1939, M.S., 1949; Ed.D., Ind. U., 1959; m. Reba J. Hunt, July 1, 1939; children—Larry, Judith, Kim, Sherrie, Lissa. Tchr. English, public schs., Wallace, Ind., 1938-44, Salem, Ind., 1945-47, Richmond, Ind., 1947-51; asst. prin. Richmond Sr. High Sch., 1951-53, prin., 1953-59; asso. prof. edn. Ind. U., Bloomington, 1959-64, prof., 1964—, exec. dir. Nat. Study Sch. Evaluation, 1970—; mem. nat. adv. council nurses tng. HEW, 1973-77; vis. prof. U. Colo., SUNY, Plattsburgh; sr. Fulbright lectr., USSR, 1978; cons. schs., U.S., Europe, Latin Am. Served to capt. USAAF, 1941-45. Decorated Air medal (3); recipient Pres.'s award for disting. teaching Ind. U., 1980. Mem. Nat. Assn. Sch. Prins. (dir. 1967-71), North Central Assn. Edn., Am. Assn. Sch. Adminstrs., Nat. Assn. Secondary Sch. Prins., Assn. Supervision and Curriculum Devel., Ind. Secondary Sch. Adminstrs., Phi Delta Kappa. Republican. Methodist. Clubs: Rotary (past pres.), Lions (past pres.), Y's Men's (past pres.), Masons. Author: (with David Beggs) Flexible Scheduling, 1965; contbr. articles to profl. jours. Home: 2109 Covenanter Dr Bloomington IN 47401 Office: Sch Edn Ind U Bloomington IN 47405

MANN, HORST N., editor; b. Ulzen, W. Ger., July 8, 1950; came to U.S., 1956; s. Oskar and Hulda Mann; student Wayne State U., 1968-71. Producer, Sta. WXON-TV, Inc., Detroit, 1971; asso. editor, pub. The Partisan, Detroit, 1972; editor Detroit Monitor/Metro Monitor, Detroit, 1972—; ed., dir. Liberty News Internat., 1971—. Bd. dirs., publicist Inst. for Econ. Studies, Detroit, 1971-75; bd. dirs. Public Forum, Detroit, 1980-81. Mem. Detroit Press Club. Lutheran. Office: 33490 Groesbeck Fraser MI 48026

MANN, JAMES RICHARD, city ofcl.; b. Chgo., Nov. 14, 1944; s. James Charles and Alexandria Maria M.; B.A., So. Ill. U., 1971, M.A., 1973; m. Trudy S. DeRousse, Mar. 18, 1972; 1 son, James Richard. Dir. planning City of Crystal Lake (Ill.), 1973-78; exec. dir. Coles County Planning Commn., Charleston, Ill., 1978-80; devel. cons., Charleston, 1980-82; village mgr. Village of Brookfield (Ill.), 1982—; treas. Southeastern McHenry County Council, 1973-78; commr. McHenry County Planning Commn., 1976-78; com. adv. Charleston Area C. of C., 1979-81. Served with Security Agy., U.S. Army, 1965-69. Recipient Community Service award Crystal Lake Kiwanis,

1978; Ill. State scholar, 1962. Mem. Internat. City Mgmt. Assn., Am. Planning Assn., Community Devel. Soc. Office: 8820 Brookfield Ave Brookfield IL 60513*

MANN, JOHN C., lawyer; b. Latham, Ill., Oct. 12, 1898; s. Frank and Josephine (Canary) M.; student James Millikin U., 1917-19; J.D., U. Ill., 1922; m. Irene Watkins, Mar. 26, 1927; 1 dau., Linda. Admitted to Ill. bar, 1922; practiced law in Decatur, Ill., 1923-34; law dept. Chgo. Title & Trust Co., Chgo., 1934-63, asso. gen. counsel, 1960-63. Served pvt. U.S. Army, World War I. Mem. Ill., Chgo. bar assns., Order of Coif. Sigma Alpha Epsilon, Phi Delta Phi. Club: Glen Oak Country. Author: Title Examinations Involving Chancery Proceedings, 1948; Illinois Chancery Procedure and Forms, 1969; Escrows; Their Use and Value, 1949, 75; Joint Tenancies Today, 1956; Is Joint Tenancy the Answer, 1953; Joint Tenancy and Survivorship Problems in Estate Planning, 1975. Editor: (with John Norton Pomeroy, Jr.) Pomeroy's Specific Performance of Contracts, 3d edit., 1926. Contbr. various articles to legal publs. Home: 515 N Main St Apt 3CS Glen Ellyn IL 60137 Office: 111 W Washington St Chicago IL 60602

MANN, JOHN JOSEPH, lawyer; b. Chgo., Dec. 25, 1951; s. John Clarence and Loretta Ruth Mann; A.B. in English, Loyola U., Chgo., 1973, M.B.A. in Acctg., 1976; J.D., De Paul U., 1979. Admitted to Ill. bar, 1979, U.S. Dist. Ct. bar, 1979; tax atty. specializing in internat. tax Sunbeam Corp., Chgo., 1979—; substitute prof. bus. law Triton Coll. Mem. Am. Bar Assn., Ill. State Bar Assn., Chgo. Bar Assn. Club: Chicagoland Assn. of S Gaugers (pres.). Asst. editor "S" Gaugian Mag., 1977—.

MANN, JOHN PARIS, mining machinery co. exec.; b. Shawano, Wis., May 22, 1925; s. John Paris and Margaret Marie (Cattau) M.; B.S., U. Wis., 1949, J.D., 1951; M.S., Bradley U., 1968; m. Elizabeth Jane Ebert, Aug. 21, 1948; children—John Paris, Gail Elizabeth, Thomas Arnold, Robert Charles. Engr., FWD Corp., Clintonville, Wis., 1951-56, 59-63; mgr. research and devel. Westinghouse Air Brake Co., Peoria, Ill., 1963-68; v.p. engring. Lima div. Clark Equipment Co., Lima, Ohio, 1968-74; v.p. engring. Jeffrey Machinery div. Dresser Industries, Columbus, Ohio, 1975—. Mem. Clintonville Bd. Edn., 1960-63; chmn. troop com. Boy Scouts Am., 1959-72, scoutmaster, 1972-75, council exec. com., 1975—. Served with AUS, 1943-46. Mem. Soc. Automotive Engrs., Am. Mining Congress. Registered profl. engr., Wis. Club: Masons. Patentee in field. Home: 6380 Plesenton Dr Worthington OH 43085 Office: Jeffrey Machinery div Dresser Industries 274 E 1st Ave Columbus OH 43201

MANN, SUSIE HAIRE, ednl. counselor; b. Scooba, Miss., Apr. 28, 1929; d. Thomas and Deseree (Birch) Haire; B.S., Tuskegee Inst., 1951, M.S., 1952; M.A., St. Louis U., 1971, also postgrad.; m. George L. Mann, July 6, 1961; children—Doris Elise, Lucia Carol. Instr., dietitian Jackson (Miss.) Coll., 1952-54; tchr. East St. Louis, Ill., 1954-70, counselor high sch., 1970—; chmn. sabbatical leave East St. Louis Sch. Dist.; human relations and career edn. cons. Active PTA, Assn. Retarded Children; vice chmn. adminstrv. bd. Samaritan Meth. Ch., also sec. bd. trustees. Carnegie Found fellow, 1950-51; James Fund grantee, 1952. Mem. Mo. Assn. Social Welfare (pres. St. Louis Bridge unit 1976—), Am. Bridge Assn. (sr. life master), Am. Fedn. Tchrs. (exec. bd. Local 1220), Am., Mo., Ill. personnel and guidance assns., St. Clair County Tchrs. Planning Inst.-County Mental Health Bd., NAACP (life), League Women Voters, Tuskegee Alumni Assn. (life), Alpha Kappa Alpha, Beta Kappa Chi. Democrat. Methodist. Home: 8303 Amherst St St Louis MO 63132 Office: 910 Summit St East St Louis IL 62201

MANNARINO, ANTONIO DOMENICO, physician; b. Crotone, Italy, Nov. 20, 1927; s. Antonio G. and Eugenia (Borrelli) M.; came to U.S., 1952, naturalized, 1957; M.D., U. Bari (Italy), 1951; m. Catherine Colosimo, Dec. 31, 1952; children—Maria, Eugenia, Antonio Domenico, Francesco. Intern, St. Elizabeth Hosp., 1953-55; resident VA Hosp., Dayton, Ohio, 1958-61, Ohio State U., Columbus, 1961-63; dir. clin. labs. Greene Meml. Hosp., Xenia, Ohio, 1963—, Clinton Meml. Hosp., Wilmington, Ohio, 1967—; asso. clin. prof. pathology Wright State U., Dayton, 1976—; clin. instr. pathology Ohio State U. Med. Sch., Columbus, 1963—. Bd. dirs. Dayton chpt. ARC, 1972. Fellow Coll. Am. Pathologists, Am. Soc. Clin. Pathologists; mem. Ordine Dei Medici of Italy, Ohio Med. Assn., Ohio Soc. Pathologists, Greene County Med. Soc. (past pres., del.). Roman Catholic. Club: Xenia Rotary. Home: 2970 Cathy Ln Dayton OH 45429 Office: Greene Meml Hosp Xenia OH 45385

MANNING, JAMES HALLISSEY, JR., music pub. co. exec., fiber broker; b. Cornell, Ill., May 2, 1934; s. James H. and Lucille Myrtle (Robertson) M.; grad. high sch.; children—James Hallissey III, Ken Neal, Raymond James, Monica Frances. Sales rep. Lissner Paper Grading Co., Chgo., 1960-66, Royal Typewriter Co., Chgo., 1966-69, Curtis 1,000, Inc., Rolling Meadows, Ill., 1969—; co-owner, v.p. GiGi-Dor Music Co., Chgo., 1969—; account exec. Consol. Fibres, 1972—; pres., owner Chgo. Global Fibres Co., 1975—. Instr., cons. graphoanalysis, 1964—. Served with USAF, 1952-56. Recipient Hon. graphoanlysis degree St. Dominics, St. Charles, Ill., 1964. Mem. Internat. Platform Assn. Club: Western Irish Setter. Author adult and juvenile fiction. Home and Office: 2332 W Superior St Chicago IL 60612

MANNING, TYRA LYNN, ednl. adminstr.; b. Brownfield, Tex., June 4, 1947; d. Clifton Henry and Dorothy Faye (Sexton) Decker; B.Ed., Washburn U., 1972; M.Ed., U. Kans., 1977, Ed.D., 1979; div.; 1 dau., Laura Elizabeth Hull. Med. records clk. Meth. Hosp., Lubbock, Tex., 1966-68; tchr. social studies East Topeka Jr. High Sch., 1972-74; dist. middle sch. coordinator Topeka Schs., 1974-76; prin. Boswell Jr. High Sch., Topeka, 1977-79; prin. Robinson Middle Sch., Topeka, 1979—; middle sch. cons. Mem. United Sch. Adminstrs., Assn. for Curriculum Devel., Nat. Middle Sch. Assn., Kans. Assn. Middle Level Edn. Democrat. Home: 2809 SW Prarie Rd Topeka KS 66614 Office: 1125 W 14th St Topeka KS 66604

MANNINO, THOMAS ANTHONY, physicist; b. Bridgeport, Conn., Nov. 17, 1945; s. Thomas P. and Mary E. Mannino; B.S. in Physics, U. New Haven, 1972; M.S., Drexel U., 1974; m. Donna Lee Keller, Mar. 22, 1974; children—Michele, Thomas. Instrumentation flight test engr. Sikorsky Aircraft, Stratford, Conn., 1974-76; prin. engr. Sperry Flight Systems, Phoenix, 1976-81, Rosemount, Inc., Eden Prairie, Minn., 1981—; instr. physics Phoenix Coll. Research in pressure sensing.

MANNIX, JOHN ROBERT, health services cons.; b. Cleve., June 4, 1902; s. Harry P. and Cecelia (O'Malley) M.; student private schs.; children—J. Frank, Rose Ann Mannix Post, John Robert. Exec. 3 hosps., Cleve. and Elyria, Ohio, 1921-39; pres. Blue Cross, Detroit, Chgo., 1939-48; pres. Blue Cross N.E. Ohio, Cleve., 1949-65, cons. health services, 1965—; lectr. on health financing U. Minn., 1947-67. Recipient Honor cert. Ohio Public Health Assn., 1971, Disting. Service award Greater Cleve. Hosp. Assn., 1976, Service award AMA, 1978, Disting. Service award Acad. Medicine Cleve., 1979; Disting. fellow Cleve. Clinic, 1972. Charter fellow Am. Coll. Hosp. Adminstrs.; mem. Am. Hosp. Assn. (Trustees award 1964, Justin Ford Kimball award 1972), Ohio Hosp. Assn. (hon., pres. 1933-34, Disting. Service award 1978), Am. Assn. Health Data Systems (hon. life). Roman Catholic. Contbr. numerous articles in health field to profl. jours. Home: 12540 Edgewater Dr Lakewood OH 44107 Office: Blue Cross N E Ohio Suite 200 1021 Euclid Ave Cleveland OH 44115

MANNON, JAMES MONROE, educator; b. Oak Park, Ill., Feb. 16, 1942; s. James Monroe and Lucille (Evans) M.; B.A., So. Ill. U., 1966, M.A., 1968, Ph.D., 1975; m. Molly Huber, Aug. 8, 1969; children—Sarah, Susan. Instr. sociology Monmouth (Ill.) Coll., 1968-71; asst. prof. sociology Millikin U., Decatur, Ill., 1973-75, DePauw U., Greencastle, Ind., 1975—; cons. Wishard Meml. Hosp., Indpls., 1978-80, Mental Health Assn. Ind., 1980-81. Bd. dirs. United Episcopal Charities, 1979-81, Putnam County Health Services Clinic, 1981. Mem. Am. Public Health Assn., North Central Sociol. Assn., Assn. for Humanistic Sociology, Ind. Public Health Assn. Democrat. Episcopalian. Author: Emergency Encounters, 1981; contbr. articles to profl. jours. Home: 506 Maple St Apt 5 Greencastle IN 46135 Office: Dept Sociology DePauw Univ Greencastle IN 46135

MANOGURA, BEN JALON, ins. agt.; b. Philippines, Dec. 29, 1936; came to U.S., 1970, naturalized, 1977; s. Domingo D. and Epifania J. M.; B.S.C. in Bus. Adminstrn., Lincoln Coll., Iloilo, P.I., 1960; m. Rosie Parcon, June 28, 1967; children—Shirley, Napoleon, Matthew and Emmanuel (twins). Supr., Connell Bros., Philippines, 1964-70; sales rep. Nedlog Co., Chgo., 1971-73; divisional sales mgr. U.S. Fin. Consultants, Inc., Chgo., 1973-75; pres. Midwest Fin. Consultants, Inc., Chgo., 1975—; gen. ins. agt. All Am. Life, a U.S. Life Co. Pres. Kahirup of the Midwest, Inc., 1978—, founder Kahirup scholarship program. Served to capt. Philippine Army, 1961-64. Recipient Pres.'s award All Am. Life Ins. Co., 1975-81. Mem. Filipino Am. Council, Philippine Pro Golfers. Home: 8944 N Lincolnwood Dr Skokie IL 60076 Office: 5875 N Lincoln Ave Chicago IL 60659

MANOOGIAN, RICHARD A., mfg. co. exec.; b. Long Branch, N.J., July 30, 1936; s. Alex and Marie (Tatian) M.; M.; B.A. in Econs., Yale, 1958. Asst. to pres. Masco Corp., Taylor, Mich., 1958-62, exec. v.p., 1962-68, pres., 1968—, also dir.; dir. Emco Ltd., London, Ont., Flint & Walling, Livonia, Mich., R.P. Scherer, Troy, Mich., Nat. Bank of Detroit. Bd. dirs. Henry Ford Hosp., Detroit. Mem. Young Pres.'s Orgn. Clubs: Country of Detroit, Grosse Pointe Yacht, Grosse Pointe Hunt; Detroit Athletic. Home: 204 Provencal Rd Grosse Pointe Farms MI 48236 Office: 21001 Van Born Rd Taylor MI 48180

MANOS, STEVEN S., assn. exec.; b. Mpls., Feb. 2, 1940; s. Theodore and Ruth M.; B.A., U. Minn., 1962; J.D., N.Y. U., 1968, M.P.A., 1974. Admitted to N.Y. bar, 1969; asso. mem. firm Abbott & Morgan, N.Y.C., 1968-70; chief exec. officer Manhattan Bowery Corp., N.Y.C., 1971-75; dir. mgmt. systems, asst. dist. atty. New York County, 1975-77; sr. adminstr. N.Y. Hosp.-Cornell Med. Center, N.Y.C., 1977-79; asst. exec. dir. adminstrn. and fin. Am. Bar Assn., Chgo., 1979—. Chgo. dir. Fund for Justice, 1980—; mem. N.Y. State Adv. Council on Alcoholism, 1978-79; bd. dirs., 1st v.p. Coalition of Mental Health, Mental Retardation and Alcoholism Services, N.Y.C., 1972-79. Served with USN, 1962-65. Mem. Am. Bar Assn., Am. Mgmt. Assn. Office: 1155 E 60th St Chicago IL 60637

MANSDORF, SEYMOUR ZACK, indsl., environ. health scientist; b. Akron, Ohio, Jan. 6, 1947; s. William and Dorothy M.; B.A., U. Akron, 1969; M.S., U. Mich., 1972; postgrad. Drexel U., 1974-75; M.S., Central Mich. State U., 1980; m. Marsha Bennington, Dec. 3, 1968; children—Brett Edward, Bart Allen. Group leader biomed. research U. Akron, 1968-69, ops. mgr., 1969-71; programmer U. Mich., Ann Arbor, 1972-73; scientist, trustee Creative Biology Lab., Barberton, Ohio, 1976-79; prin. scientist Midwest Research Inst., Kansas City, Mo., 1979-81; owner, mgr. S.Z. Mansdorf & Assos., occupational and environ. health cons., Akron, 1981—; lectr., cons. in field. Trustee Forest Hills Co-op., 1972. Served to capt., Med. Service Corps., U.S. Army, 1973-76. USPHS grantee, 1972; cert. indsl. hygienist; registered sanitarian. Mem. Am. Inst. Biol. Scis., Controlled Release Soc. (sec.), Am. Pub. Health Assn., Nat. Environ. Health Assn., AAAS, Am. Indsl. Hygiene Assn. (editorial adv.), Am. Acad. Indsl. Hygiene, ASTM, Phi Sigma, Lambda Chi Alpha. Lutheran. Research in slow-release, especially to control aquatic weeds, also indsl. hygiene. Patentee in field. Office: 2455 Deepridge Circle Akron OH 44313

MANSER, GEORGE ROBERT, ins. co. exec.; b. Mpls., May 7, 1931; s. George Louis and Helen Blanche (Krusemark) M.; A.A., B.S., U. Minn., 1958; M.B.A., Capitol U., 1974; m. Jeanne De Wolf Seebe, June 21, 1952; children—Richard Louis, Ronald Alan, Pamela Ann, Michael Wayne. Youth dir. Union Congl. Ch., Mpls., 1955-58; exec. dir. Minn. Republican Party, 1958-61; adminstrv. asst. Gov. Minn., 1961-63; ins. salesman, sales mgr. N.Am. Equitable Life Assurance Co., Columbus, Ohio, 1964-68, pres., 1969—; pres. Brookings Internat. Life Ins. Co. (S.D.), 1968—; pres., chief exec. officer, dir. N.Am. Nat. Corp.; dir. N.Am. Equitable Life Assurance Co., Brookings Internat. Life Ins. Co., Asset Data Systems, Inc., Cardinal Foods, Inc., Pan Western Life Ins. Co., Redding Inc. Extradition referee State of Minn., 1961-63; mem. Met. Airports Commn., 1966-67. Bd. regents Augustana Coll, Sioux Falls, S.D.; former chmn. Found. N. Congl. Ch. Columbus; bd. dirs. Parkview Nursing Home. Served with USAF, 1951-55. Mem. Nat. Assn. Life Cos. (treas., dir.), Nat. Assn. Life Underwriters, Newcomen Soc. Mem. United Ch. of Christ. Mason. Club: Worthington Hills Country. Home: 756 Highland Dr Columbus OH 43214 Office: 1015 E Broad St Columbus OH 43205

MANSFIELD, NANCY, psychologist, business exec.; b. Milw.; d. John and Melanie Szeremeta; Ph.D., U. Chgo., 1971; children—Alison, John. Staff psychologist Vernon Psychol. Lab., Chgo., 1954-70; founder, prin. Hume Mansfield Silber, Chgo., 1970-77; founder, pres. Mansfield Human Resources, Chgo., 1977—; lectr., indsl./orgnl. cons. Mem. Am. Psychol. Assn., Midwest Psychol. Assn., Ill. Psychol. Assn., Indsl. Orgn. Psychologists of Ill. (pres. 1976-79), Acad. Health Care Educators (adv. bd.), Nat. Orgn. Women Bus. Owners. Researcher, developer honesty-theft questionnaire. Office: 520 N Michigan Suite 516 Chicago IL 60611 also 811 E Wisconsin Ave Suite 231 Milwaukee WI 53202

MANTEY, PHILIP MICHAEL, fin., investment banking and brokerage exec.; b. Fort Morgan, Colo., Aug. 24, 1943; s. Paul John and Alma Jean (Quackenbush) M.; B.S. in Elec. Engring. cum laude, U. Notre Dame, 1965, M.S. (Douglas Aircraft scholar, Walsh-Hudson-Cavanaugh scholar), 1967; M.B.A. (GTE fellow), Harvard U., 1973; m. Katherine Krandall, Apr. 11, 1970; children—Joseph Paul, Ingrid Ann. Security analyst Fidelity Mgmt. & Research Co., Boston, 1973-74; fin. analyst product devel. Controller's Office, Ford Motor Co., 1974-75; coal project asst. to group v.p. Pickands Mather & Co., Cleve., 1975-79; corp. fin. asso. McDonald & Co., Cleve., 1979—. Mem. St. Raphael Sch. Bd. Served to lt. USNR, 1967-71. Mem. Tau Beta Pi. Roman Catholic. Home: 26814 Bruce Rd Bay Village OH 44140 Office: 2100 Central Nat Bank Bldg Cleveland OH 44114

MANTLO, SHIRLEY JEANNINE SMITH, educator; b. Champaign County, Ill., June 8, 1930; d. Charles Russell and Lillian Mildred (Daniels) Smith; B.A., U. Ill., 1952; M.S. in Edn., No. Ill. U., 1978. Tchr. pub. schs., Rantoul, Ill., 1953-54, Henrico County, Va., 1956-58, 59-60, Zion, Ill., 1958-59, Thornton, Ill., 1960-62; tchr. Chgo. Public Schs., 1962-81, faculty integration adviser, 1979—; instr. DePaul U., 1978-79; cooperating cons. Ill. Office of Edn., 1977-79. Mem. Nat. Council for Social Studies (past chmn. Econ. and Consumer Edn. Spl. Interest Group), Ill. Council for Social Studies (past pres.), Chgo. Council for Social Studies (past pres.), Chgo. Hist. Soc., Ill. Hist. Soc., Ill. Assn. for Supervision and Curriculum Devel., Assn. for Supervision and Curriculum Devel., Ill. Consultation for Ethnicity in Edn., Ill. Consumer Edn. Assn., Environ. Assn. Ill., Beta Sigma Phi. Republican. Presbyterian. Author: (with Ruth B. Smith) World of Work Economic Education, 1974; How a Business Operates, 1978; Consumer Education Resource Guide, 1980; adv. bd. Social Edn., 1979-81. Address: 1825 N Lincoln Plaza Chicago IL 60614

MAPLES, EVELYN LUCILLE (MRS. WILLIAM EUGENE MAPLES), ret. editor, author; b. Ponce de Leon, Mo., Feb. 7, 1919; d. Thomas Sherman and Bertie Josephine (Dalby) Palmer; ed. S.W. Mo. State U.; m. William Eugene Maples, Dec. 23, 1938; children—Norman Francis, Billi Jo, Matthew McBride. Tchr. rural sch., Greene County, Mo., 1937-38; proofreader Herald Pub. House, Independence, Mo., 1953-63, editor, 1963-81; author Monthly Poetry Corner, Saints Herald, 1978-80; lectr. N.W. Mo. State U., 1978, 79; tchr. writing various workshops. Mem. Community Assn. for the Arts, Mo. Writers Guild. Mem. Reorganized Ch. Jesus Christ of Latter Day Saints (congregation publicity dir. 1964-68, ch. sch. tchr. 1960-70, campus ministry cons. 1964-71). Republican. Author: What Saith the Scriptures, 1961; Norman Learns About the Sacraments, 1961; Jomo the Missionary Monkey, 1966; That Ye Love, 1971; The Brass Plates Adventure, 1972; Lehi, Man of God, 1972; Norman Learns About the Scriptures, 1972; The Many Selves of Ann-Elizabeth, 1973. Home: Route 1 Niangua MO 65713

MAPPES, CARL RICHARD, zoologist, sci. info. specialist; b. St. Louis, Feb. 17, 1935; s. Theodore Roosevelt and Elsie Clark (Day) M.; B.A. in Zoology, U. Mont., 1965; postgrad. U. Mo., 1972-74; Ph.D. in Biol. Scis., 1979; 1 dau., Tanya Lizette. Public relations rep. Assn. of Am. R.R.'s, Washington, 1953-54; design engr. William H. Singleton Co., Springfield, Va., Kendrick & Redinger, Arlington, Va., A. Dee Counts & Lawrence, Washington, 1954-56, 58-59; asso. sci. researcher Ellesmere Island-Greenland expdn., 1956; customer services rep. Eastern Air Lines, Inc., Washington, 1960-61; resource mgr. U.S. Forest Service, Mont., 1966, Nat. Park Service, Wyo. and Ariz., 1966; cons. to numerous industries and govt. agys., Mont., N.Mex. and Europe, 1966-69; info. specialist Office of Info., U.S. Dept. Agr., Washington, 1969; sci. researcher and info. specialist Nat. Park Service, U.S. Dept. Interior, So. Fla., 1969; info. specialist to numerous industries and govt. agys., Albuquerque, 1969-70, Walton, N.Y., 1970-71, Kimberling City, Mo., 1971-80; social scientist Bur. Census, U.S. Dept. Commerce, 1980—. Served with USN, 1956-58. Fellow Am. Geog. Soc., Royal Geog. Soc., Royal Photog. Soc.; mem. Am. Soc. Mammalogists, Am. Soc. of Ichthyologists and Herpetologists, Am. Soc. Limnology and Oceanography, Ecol. Soc. Am., Entomol. Soc. Am., Entomol. Soc. Can., Royal Entomol. Soc., Brit. Ornithologists Union, Freshwater Biol. Assn., Wilson Ornithol. Soc., Am. Ornithologists Union, Arctic Inst. N.Am., Herpetologists League, Brit. Ecol. Soc., Royal Australasian Ornithologists Union, Malacological Soc. London. Contbr. numerous articles on research in oceanography, zoology and ecology to profl. publs. Home: Star Route 5 Box 223 Kimberling City MO 65686

MAPSTONE, TIMOTHY BOYD, neurol. surgeon; b. Cleve., June 23, 1950; s. Boyd E. and Adelle C. (Hajostek) M.; B.S. in Math., B.S. in Mgmt., M.I.T., 1973; M.D., Case Western Res. U., 1977; m. Barbara J. Talian, Oct. 12, 1979. Fellow in neurol. surgery Univ. Hosp., Cleve., 1977—. Am. Cancer Soc. fellow, 1974-75. Mem. AAAS, Sigma Xi. Home: 2959 Coleridge Cleveland Heights OH 44118 Office: Univ Hosp DN Neurosurgery Adelbert Ave Cleveland OH 44106

MARABLE, JUNE MOREHEAD, educator; b. Columbus, Ohio; d. J. W. and Minnie J. Morehead; B.S. in Secondary Edn., Central State U., Wilberforce, Ohio, 1948; M.S. in Guidance, U. Dayton (Ohio), 1965; Ph.D. in Edn. Adminstrn. and Reading, Miami U., Oxford, Ohio, 1975; m. James Palmer Marable; children—James Palmer, Manning, Madonna. Tchr. elementary Dayton Bd. Edn., 1954-68, reading supr. elementary, 1968-70; grad. asst. Miami U., 1970-72; asst. prof. edn. Wright State U., Dayton, 1972-77; Tchrs. Corps asso. vis. prof. Miami U., 1978-80; v.p. Black Research Assos., Inc.; state commr. Right to Read. Past pres. Dayton chpt. Jack and Jill of Am., Inc.; nat. coordinator Alpha Kappa Alpha Reading Program for Minorities; ednl. dir., co-owner Marable Early Childhood Edn. Center, Dayton. Mem. NEA, Internat. Reading Assn., Nat. Assn. Edn. Young Children, Assn. Elementary Tchrs. English, Assn. Childhood Edn. Internat., Central State U. Alumni Assn., Phi Delta Kappa, Delta Kappa Gamma, Alpha Kappa Alpha, Alpha Kappa Mu, Sen Mer Rek. Authored articles and audio media devel. materials. Specialist in reading. Home: 5145 Dayton Liberty Rd Dayton OH 45418

MARAGOS, NICOLAS ERNEST, otorhinolaryngologist; b. Waukesha, Wis., Apr. 23, 1946; s. Ernest Nicholas and Mary (Voorlas) M.; B.S., U. Wis., 1968, M.D., 1972; m. Constance G. Zahhos, Aug. 31, 1969; children—Anastasia, John. Intern, Mayo Grad. Sch., Rochester, Minn., 1972-73, resident in otolaryngology, 1973-77, instr., 1977—; otorhinolaryngologist Mayo Clinic, 1977—. Bd. dirs. Rochester Civic Theater, Minn. Soc. Prevention of Blindness. Diplomate Am. Bd. Otolaryngology. Mem. Am. Acad. Otolaryngology, Minn. Acad. Ophthalmology and Otolaryngology, Greek Orthodox Midwestern Choir Fedn. (dir., past pres.), Nat. Forum Greek Orthodox Ch. Musicians (founding). Home: 3625 Lakeview Ct NE Rochester MN 55901 Office: Dept Otolaryngology Mayo Clinic Rochester MN 55901

MARCH, JACQUELINE FRONT, chemist; b. Wheeling, W.Va., July 10, 1914; d. Jacques Johann and Antoinette (Orenstein) Front; B.S., Case Western Res. U., 1937, M.A., 1939; Wyeth fellow med. research U. Chgo., 1940-42; postgrad. U. Pitts., 1945, Ohio State U., 1967, Wright State U., 1970-76; m. Abraham W. Marcovich, Oct. 7, 1945 (dec. 1969); children—Wayne Front, Gail Ann. Chemist, Mt. Sinai Hosp., Cleve., 1934-40; med. research chemist U. Chgo., 1940-42; research analyst Koppers Co., also info. scientist Union Carbide Corp., Mellon Inst., Pitts., 1942-45; propr. March. Med. Research Lab., etiology of diabetes, Dayton, Ohio, 1950-79; guest scientist Kettering Found., Yellow Springs, Ohio, 1953; Dayton Found. fellow Miami Valley Hosp. Research Inst., 1956. mem. chemistry faculty U. Dayton, 1959-69, info. scientist Research Inst., 1968-79; prin. investigator Air Force Wright Aero. Labs., Wright-Patterson AFB Tech. Info. Center, 1970-79; tech. info. specialist, div. tech. services Nat. Inst. Occupational Safety and Health, Health and Human Services, Cin., 1979—; designer info. systems, speaker in field. Recipient Recognition cert. U. Dayton, 1980. Mem. Am. Soc. Info. Sci. (treas. South Ohio 1973-75), Am. Chem. Soc. (pres. Dayton 1977, selection com. Patterson-Crane award 1981), Soc. Advancement Materials and Process Engring. (pres. Midwest chpt. 1977-78, nat. dir. for Midwest 1979), Affiliated Tech. Socs. (Outstanding Scientist and Engr. award 1979), AAUP (exec. bd.), Sigma Xi (treas. Dayton 1976-79). Club: Royal Oak Country (Cin.). Contbr. articles to profl. publs. Office: 4676 Columbia Pkwy Cincinnati OH 45226

MARCHETTI, RODNEY DAVID, mfg. engr.; b. Meriden, Conn., July 28, 1920; s. Rodney D. and Elena Marie (Magnano) M.; student mech. engring., U. Conn., 1946-49; m. Theresa M. Maniscalco, Apr. 22, 1946; children—Cheryl Marie Bia, Patricia Ann Munn. Process analyst Am. Cynamid, 1947-52; plastics engr. Am. Standard, 1952-59; molding supr. Waterbury Cos. (Conn.), 1959-63; machinery sales and service rep. Bipel Internat., 1963-69; mgr. thermosets Perry Plastics, 1969-72; asst. to pres. LaPorte Plastics, 1972-75; cons., 1975-78; mgr. mfg. engring. Ideal Industries, Inc., Petersburg, Ill., 1978—; instr. Elgin U., Bowling Green U., U. Pa. Served with USAAF, World War II. Decorated D.F.C. with oak leaf cluster, Air Medal with 2 oak leaf clusters. Mem. Soc. Plastics Engrs. (dir. edn.), VFW (comdr. post). Roman Catholic. Author several courses in plastics tech. Home: Rural Route 2 Box 151 Athens IL 62613 Office: 1120 N 4th St Petersburg IL 62675

MARCHMAN, WATT P(EARSON), ret. librarian, historian; b. Eatonton, Ga., Sept. 1, 1911; s. Watt Pearson and Mary (Hudson) M.; A.B., Rollins Coll., 1933, A.M., 1937; student Duke, 1936; L.H.D. (hon.), Findlay Coll., 1980; m. Virginia Orebaugh, Oct. 16, 1937 (dec. June 1960); 1 son, David; m. 2d, Martha J. Dawson McGrain, Nov. 27, 1963. Instr., Ga. Mil. Acad., 1934; sec. Rollins Press, Inc., Winter Park, Fla., 1934-40; archivist Rollins Coll., 1935-40, dir. alumni placement service, 1937-40; librarian, corr. sec. Fla. Hist. Soc., 1939-42; sec., dir. research Rutherford B. Hayes & Lucy Webb Hayes Found.; dir. Rutherford B. Hayes Library, Fremont, Ohio, 1946-80; mgr. Rutherford B. Hayes State Meml., 1950-80. Trustee, sec. St. Augustine (Fla.) Pub. Library, 1942, Birchard Pub. Library of Sandusky County, 1968—. Served in Signal Corps, AUS, 1943-46; ETO. Recipient merit citation Martha Kinney Cooper Ohioana Library Assn., 1971. Mem. Ohio (exec. bd. 1952-53), Martha Kinney Cooper Ohioana (trustee 1970-79), Birchard (sec. 1959—, trustee) library assns., Ohio, Fla. hist. socs., Ohio Acad. History (award of Merit 1969), Manuscript Soc. (v.p. 1950-64), Phi Delta Theta. Clubs: Rotary (local pres. 1963-64) (Fremont, Ohio). Author monographs on historical subjects; exec. editor: Hayes Hist. Jour., 1976-80; contbr. to periodicals. Home: 534 Crestwood Ave Fremont OH 43420

MARCINKOSKI, ANNETTE MARIE, educator; b. Akron, Ohio, Aug. 2, 1933; d. Frank J. and Barbara (Popielarczyk) Marcinkoski; B.S., U. Akron, 1955; M.A., U. Mich., 1959. Tchr. Flint (Mich.) Pub. Schs., 1955-63, tng. tchr. Coop. Tchr. Edn. Program, 1963-69, elementary tchr., 1969—. Active Big Sister program; sponsor Jr. Red Cross, 1959-63; tchr. Confraternity of Christian Doctrine. Mem. United Tchrs. of Flint (del. rep. assembly), Mich. Edn. Assn. (bd. dirs. 1978—, pres. Region X, 1976-77), NEA (regional dir. 1973-78), Elementary, Kindergarten and Nursery Educators, Mich. (treas. 1970-72, pres. 1973-75), Flint (sec. 1959-62) assns. childhood edn., Assn. Childhood Edn. Internat., AAUW (v.p. 1967-69, area rep. in edn. 1969-72), Theta Phi Alpha (adviser Gen. Motors Inst. chpt. 1973—, chmn. bd. dirs. 1973-79, sec. Founders Found. 1978—, nat. treas. 1980—), Cath. Bus. Women (sec. 1970-72, del. council state orgns. 1974-76), Flint Area Reading Council, Mich. Reading Assn., Delta Kappa Gamma, Phi Delta Kappa. Home: 1911 Laurel Oak Dr Flint MI 48507 Office: 1402 W Dayton St Flint MI 48504

MARCUS, DONALD HOWARD, advt. agy. exec.; b. Cleve., May 16, 1916; s. Joseph and Sarah (Schmitman) M.; student Fenn Coll., 1934-35; m. Helen Olen Weiss, Feb. 12, 1959; children—Laurel Kathy Marcus Heifetz, Carol Susan, James Randall (dec.), Jonathan Anthony. Mem. publicity dept. Warner Bros. Pictures, Cleve., 1935-37; mem. advt. dept. RKO Pictures, Cleve., 1937-40; mem. sales dept. Monogram Pictures, Cleve., 1940-42; pres. Marcus Advt. Inc., Cleve., 1946—, Marcus Advt. Art Inc., Cleve., 1978—; partner Cleve. Baseball Co., 1974—, Budget Inns Am., Cleve., 1973—; dir. Women's Fed. Savs., Cleve., 1978—. Guarantor, N.E. Ohio Opera Assn., 1965—; mem. Ohio Democratic exec. com., 1969-70, del. nat. conv., 1968; vice-chmn. communication div. Jewish Welfare Fund Appeal Cleve., 1964-70, chmn., 1971-72; trustee Jewish Community Fedn., 1973-74, Better Housing Inc., 1968-72, Cleve. Israel Bond Com., 1964-73, Cleve. Jewish News, 1974—; bd. dirs. Cuyahoga County unit Am. Cancer Soc., Ohio Soc. Prevention of Blindness. Served to 1st lt. USAAF, 1942-46. Mem. Ohio Commodores, Cleve. Brandeis U. Club (trustee 1964—), Mid-Day Club, Commerce Club Cleve., Cleve. Advt. Club, Cleve. Growth Assn., Mensa. Jewish (trustee temple). Club: Beechmont Country (pres. 1973-74). Home: 22449 Shelburne Rd Shaker Heights OH 44122 Office: Marcus Advt Inc 29001 Cedar Ave Lyndhurst OH 44124

MARCUS, LARRY DAVID, TV sta. exec.; b. N.Y.C., Jan. 27, 1949; s. Oscar Moses and Sylvia (Ackerman) M.; B.B.A., City U. N.Y., 1970, postgrad., 1970-73; m. Noreen M. Vermeal, Dec. 24, 1975. Computer systems analyst Johnson & Johnson, New Brunswick, N.J., 1970-72; mgmt. services cons. Coopers & Lybrand, N.Y.C., 1972-73; acctg. mgr. Sta. WPLG-TV, Miami, 1974-75; v.p. adminstrn. and planning Sta. KPLR-TV, St. Louis, 1976—. Mem. Mo. Assn. Broadcasters, Broadcasters Fin. Mgmt. Assn., Nat. Acad. TV Arts and Scis., Internat. Found. Employee Benefit Plans, Am. Women in Radio and TV. Jewish. Office: 4935 Lindell Blvd Saint Louis MO 63108

MARCUS, STEPHEN HOWARD, hotel co. exec.; b. Mpls., May 31, 1935; s. Ben D. and Ceil M.; B.B.A., U. Wis., Madison, 1957; LL.B., U. Mich., 1960; m. Joan Glasspiegel, Nov. 3, 1962; children—Greg, David, Andrew. Pres., treas., dir. Marcus Corp., Milw.; exec. v.p. The Marc Plaza Corp.; dir. Heritage Bank of Milw.; chmn. Preferred Hotels Assn. Bd. dirs. Multiple Sclerosis Soc. Milw., 1965-67, Milw. Jewish Fedn., 1970-76, Milw. Jewish Chronicle, 1973-77; United Performing Art Fund, 1973—, Friends of Art, 1973-74, Jr. Achievement, 1976—; trustee Mt. Sinai Hosp., 1978—; chmn. bus. div. United Fund, 1971; pres. Summerfest, Milw., 1975. Served with U.S. Army, 1961-62. Mem. Am. Hotel and Motel Assn. (dir. 1976-79), Greater Milw. Hotel and Motel Assn. (pres. 1967-68), Wis. Innkeepers Assn. (pres. 1972-73), Milw. Conv. and Visitors Bur. (pres. 1970-71), Wis. Assn. Mfrs. and Commerce (dir. 1979—), Downtown Assn., Milw. Expn. Conv. Center and Arena (dir. 1975—). Office: Marcus Corp 212 W Wisconsin Ave Milwaukee WI 53203

MARCY, PAT JOHN, JR., pub. co. exec.; b. Chgo., Dec. 11, 1958; s. Pat and Katherine Margaret (Delvechio) M.; student U. Ill., 1976-78; B.A. summa cum laude, Columbia Coll., 1980. Researcher D'arcy, MacManis, Masius Advt., Chgo., 1976-78; account exec. Faces, Chgo., 1978—, also advt. dir., pub. Chgl. Faces Publs., Inc., 1978—, pres., 1980—; pres. Pat Marcy Jr. and Assos., Ltd. Multi-Media Advt., Chgo., 1978—. Dep. sheriff Cook County Sheriff's Police, 1981—; com. exec. dir. State of Ill. joint legis. condominium study. Recipient Appreciation award Maryville Acad., 1977, 78, 79, Bronze award for TV comml. Mem. Chgo. Conv. and Tourism Bur., Chgo. Press Club. Clubs: Faces; Freddies; K.C. Office: 65 E S Water St Chicago IL 60601

MARDELL-CZUDNOWSKI, CAROL DOLORES, psychologist; b. Chgo., Nov. 30, 1935; d. Albert and Lee (Mandel) Goldstein; children—Benjamin, Dina, Ruth. B.S., U. Ill., 1956; M.A., U. Chgo., 1958; Ph.D., Northwestern U., 1972. Elementary teaching certificate, 1956; supervisory certificate, 1969; learning disabilities certificate, 1970; adminstrv. certificate, 1970; sch. psychologist certificate, 1973; adminstrv. certificate with supt. endorsement, 1974; registered psychologist, Ill. Classroom tchr., Skokie, Ill., 1956-59, sch. psychometrist, 1959-60; pvt. practice psychology, Skokie, 1962-65; tutor, Skokie, 1965-68; learning disabilities tchr., Highland Park, Ill., 1969-70, learning disabilities cons., 1970-71; research project dir. Ill. Office Edn., Chgo., 1971-73; asst. prof. Northwestern U., Evanston, Ill., 1973-74; asso. prof. Northeastern Ill. U., Chgo., 1974-78, co-dir. Spl. Edn. for Presch. Children Project, 1976-78; asso. prof. No. Ill. U., De Kalb, 1978—; mem. Ill. Early Childhood Task Force, 1972-73; bd. mem. Fund for Perceptually Handicapped Children, 1973-78; mem. State Task Force for Child Care Tng., 1973-75; editorial bd. Jour. Learning Disabilities, 1976—; asso. editor Exceptional Children, 1977-79. Mem. Am. Psychol. Assn., Council for Exceptional Children, Assn. Children with Learning Disabilities, Nat. Assn. for Edn. Young Children, Alpha Lambda Delta, Kappa Delta Pi (No. Ill. U. sponsor), Pi Lambda Theta, Phi Kappa Phi, Phi Delta Kappa. Author: (with Dorothea S. Goldenberg) Developmental Indicators for the Assessment of Learning, 1973; (with Janet Lerner and Dorothea S. Goldenberg) Special Education for the Early Childhood Years; contbr. articles to profl. jours. Home: 6 Jennifer Ln De Kalb IL 60115 Office: Dept Learning Devel and Spl Edn No Ill U De Kalb IL 60115

MARDEN, MICHAEL RICHARD, social worker; b. Lead, S.D., Apr. 18, 1951; s. Richard M. and Gertrude Anita Marden; B.A. cum laude, Coll. St. Scholastica, 1976; m. Sandra Peterson, Aug. 28, 1976; children—Alyssa Joy, Heather Lynn. Med. social worker Nat G. Polinsky Meml. Rehab. Center, Duluth, Minn., from 1977; now social worker, initial intervention unit St. Louis County Social Services Dept., Duluth. Vol. Am. Heart Assn., 1977-79. Mem. Nat. Assn. Social Workers, Am. Personnel and Guidance Assn., Minn. Personnel and Guidance Assn., Pi Gamma Mu. Home: 25 Boland Dr Duluth MN 55804 Office: 211 W 2d St Duluth MN 55805

MARDIGIAN, EDWARD STEPHAN, machine tool co. exec.; b. Stambul, Turkey, Oct. 25, 1909; s. Stephan and Agavine (Hagopian) M.; came to U.S., 1914, naturalized, 1929; student Wayne U., 1932-34; m. Helen Alexander, June 5, 1938; children—Marilyn, Edward, Robert. Asst. tool engr. Briggs Mfg. Co., Detroit, 1935-37, chief tool engr., Eng., 1937-45, chief project engr., 1945; owner, operator Mardigian Corp., Warren, Mich., 1948-69, Marco Corp., Warren, 1954, bought Buckeye Aluminum Co., Wooster, Ohio, 1956, Mardigian Car Corp., Warren, 1966—; pres. Hercules Machine Tool & Die Co., Warren, 1973—; chmn. bd. Central States Mfg. Co., Warren, 1973—. Pres. Armenian Gen. Benevolent Union Am., 1972—; chmn. Chief Exec. Forum, Warren, 1974. Decorated medal St. Gregory by Vasken 1st Supreme Patriarch of All Armenians, 1966; named Man of Year Diocese Armenian Ch. N.Am., 1977. Home: 1525 Tottenham Rd Birmingham MI 48009 Office: Hercules Machine Tool & Die Co 13920 E Ten Mile Rd Warren MI 48089

MARECEK, GREGORY JOHN, sports commentator, producer; b. St. Louis, Feb. 9, 1949; s. John and Mae Laverne M.; student U. Mo., Columbia, 1967-68, William Jewell Coll., 1968; B.A., Washington U., St. Louis, 1971; m. Helen Patricia Boscia, Apr. 5, 1975; 1 son, John Gregory. Sports editor St. Louis Suburban Newspapers, Inc., 1971-75; exec. sports editor, 1975—; exec. v.p. SNI Sports Network, St. Louis, 1975—; sports commentator TV, St. Louis Stars Pro Soccer, 1973; radio play-by-play St. Louis U. Coll. Hockey, 1973-75; TV commentator U. Mo. football and basketball, 1979-81; TV play-by-play Voice of St. Louis Blues Hockey, 1980—. Mem. AFTRA. Lutheran. Club: Algonquin Golf (St. Louis). Office: 7014 Chippewa St Saint Louis MO 63119

MARECEK, LYNN MARIE, educator; b. Chgo., May 11, 1951; d. Hugh H. and Martha E. (Kalchbrenner) Brown; B.S. (Pres. scholar), Valparaiso U., 1973; M.S., Purdue U., 1976; m. Gerald Marecek, June 16, 1973. Tchr. high sch. math. Sch. Town of Highland (Ind.), 1973—; guest lectr. math. Purdue U. Calumet Campus, Hammond, Ind., 1977—. Recipient S. C. Johnson Outstanding Chemistry Student award Valparaiso U., 1970. Mem. Nat. Council Tchrs. Math. Lutheran. Home: 17786 Arlington Dr Country Club Hills IL 60477 Office: 9135 Erie St Highland IN 46322

MARESH, RICHARD, state ofcl.; b. Milligan, Nebr., Sept. 8, 1917; s. Joseph F. and Anna M.; student U. Nebr., evenings; m. Ruth Sweney, May 24, 1942; children—Dixie Maresh Placek, Janet Maresh DeFlyer, Chere Maresh Uldrich. Farmer, Milligan, Nebr.; chmn. Agrl. Stblzn. and Conservation Com., Fillmore County, Nebr., 1960-70; mem. Nebr. Senate, 1970-81, chmn. bus. and labor com., 1973-81; dep. dir. agr. State of Nebr., Lincoln, 1981—. Served with USAF, 1942-45. Decorated Air medal with 4 oak leaf clusters, D.F.C. Mem. Nebr. Soybean Assn., Nat. Cattlemen's Assn., Grange, VFW, Am. Legion, Nebr. State Fair Bd. Republican. Methodist. Address: Dept Agr 301 Centennial Mall S Lincoln NE 68509

MARI, REGINALD R., JR., civil engr., city ofcl.; b. Springfield, Ill., June 18, 1931; s. Reginald and Rose (Colantino) M.; B.S., U. Ill., 1955. Foreman, pipe mill Youngstown Sheet & Tube Co., Indiana Harbor, Ind., 1955-57; field supr. constrn. elevated hwys., sewers, sts., tunnels, dock walls and airport facilities City of Chgo., 1957-76, head constrn. subsect. airport programs Bur. Engring., 1976—. Registered profl. engr., Ill. Mem. ASCE, Internat. Platform Assn. Home: 5241 NE River Rd Chicago IL 60656 Office: City of Chgo Bur Engring 320 N Clark St Chicago IL 60610

MARIGOLD, LAWRENCE LEE, malt beverage mfg. co. exec.; b. Tehachapi, Calif., Oct. 14, 1940; s. George Austin and Pauline Marie (Vukich) M.; A.A., Contra Costa Coll., 1960; B.S., U. San Francisco, 1964; M.B.A., Golden Gate U., 1967; m. Julie Ann Chohon, Sept. 9, 1978; children—Eric, Michelle. Exchange analyst Standard Oil (Calif.), San Francisco, 1960-64; div. mgr. Unigas Inc. subs. Union Oil Co., Denver, 1964-69, corp. mgr. residual products Union Oil Calif., Chgo., 1969-74; corp. mgr. energy planning and devel. Anheuser-Busch Inc., St. Louis, 1974—; energy cons. food industry; mem. Coal Industry Adv. Com. to U.S. Dept. Energy, 1978—. Active Boy Scouts Am.; solicitor bldg. fund St. Louis YMCA, 1979. Mem. Soc. Automotive Engrs., Assn. Energy Engrs., Greater St. Louis indsl. Energy Conservation Group, Porsche Club Am. Republican. Roman Catholic. Club: Elks. Home: 172 Green Trails Dr Chesterfield MO 63017 Office: Anheuser-Busch Inc 2800 S 9th St Saint Louis MO 63118

MARIN, VIRGINIA PARKER, data processor; b. Huntsville, Ala., Dec. 27, 1937; d. Lawrence Goldsmith and Hester W. Parker; A.A., West Valley Coll., Saratoga, Calif., 1976; m. Richard P. Marin, Jan. 26, 1974. Sr. sec. specialist IBM Corp., 1962-73; sr. sec. specialist, tech. writer Service Bur. Co., Campbell, Calif., 1973-74, sr. installation specialist data processing, 1976—. Mem. Internat. Platform Assn., Nat. Assn. Female Execs. Republican. Club: Still Waters Golf and Country (Dadeville, Ala.). Home: 3159 Creekside Dr Westlake OH 44145 Office: 700 W Hamilton Ave Campbell CA 95008

MARINE, CLYDE LOCKWOOD, grain co. exec.; b. Knoxville, Tenn., Dec. 25, 1936; s. Harry H. and Idelle (Larue) M.; B.S. in Agr., U. Tenn., 1958; M.S. in Agrl. Econs., U. Ill., 1959; Ph.D. in Agrl. Econs., Mich. State U., 1963; m. Eleanor Harb, Aug. 9, 1958; children—Cathleen, Sharon. Sr. market analyst Pet Milk Co., St. Louis, 1963-64; mgr. market planning, agr. chems. div. Mobil Chem. Co., Richmond, Va., 1964-67; mgr. ingredient purchasing Central Soya Co., Ft. Wayne, Ind., 1970-73, corporate economist, 1967-70, v.p. ingredient purchasing, 1973-75, group v.p., 1975—. Bd. dirs. Ft. Wayne Fine Arts Found., 1976-80, Ft. Wayne Public Transp. Corp., 1975-80; v.p. Ft. Wayne Philharmonic, 1974-76. Served with U.S. Army, 1959-60. Mem. Nat. Soybean Processors Assn. (chmn.), U.S. C. of C., Am. Agrl. Econs. Assn., Am. Feed Mfrs. Assn. (chmn. purchasing council), Chgo. Bd. Trade, Chgo. Merc. Exchange. Episcopalian. Club: Ft. Wayne Country. Office: 1300 Fort Wayne Bank Bldg Fort Wayne IN 46802

MARINICS, CARL DENNIS, civil engr.; b. Akron, Ohio, Apr. 4, 1945; s. Charles Steven and Susan (Goffee) M.; B.S. in Civil Engring., U. Akron, 1968; m. Sandra Baer, Oct. 1, 1966; children—Dennis Todd, Keith Eric. Urban renewal engr., then dep. service dir. City of Akron, 1968-77; city engr., dir. pub. works City of Richfield (Minn.), 1977-79; project mgr. Stanley Cons. Inc., Muscatine, Iowa, 1979-81; prin. engr. Woolpert Cons.'s, Dayton, Ohio, 1981—; mem. tech. adv. com. Minn. Met. Council, 1978-79; mem. Mayor Akron Cabinet, 1973-77; mem. North East Four County Planning Orgn., Nat. Urban Tech. Transfer System, 1974-77. Recipient Distinguished Service award City of Akron, 1977; registered profl. engr., Ohio, Minn. Mem. Am. Public Works Assn., Ohio Water Pollution Control Conf., Am. Water Works Assn., Water Mgmt. Assn. Ohio (trustee). Office: Woolpert Cons's 2324 Stanley Ave Dayton OH 45404

MARISH, VICKI LYNN, nurse, educator; b. Lancaster, Wis., May 9, 1950; d. Raymond Donald and Marcella Geraldine (Rossing) Stenner; B.S. in Nursing, U. Wis., Eau Claire, 1972; M.S. in Edn., Guidance and Counseling, U. Wis., Platteville, 1979; m. Donald Henry Marish, June 26, 1971; children—Jason, Brian. Charge nurse Good Samaritan Center, Fennimore, Wis., 1972-75; nursing asst., instr. practical nursing SW Wis. Vocat.-Tech. Inst., Fennimore, 1975-78, health occupations coordinator, 1980—; nursing instr. Upper Iowa U., Fayette, 1978-80; active continuing edn. workshops for nursing assts. and lic. practical nurses. Treas., Mother Hubbard Nursery Sch., 1979-81; chmn. Blood Pressure Screening Program, 1979-81. Recipient award Sudden Infant Death Syndrome Program for Public Info., 1980. Mem. Am. Nurses Assn., Wis. Nurses Assn., Wis. Assn. Vocat. Adult Edn. Lutheran. Club: Jaycettes. Home: 1470 11th St Fennimore WI 53809 Office: Bronson Blvd Fennimore WI 43809

MARK, BETSY YVONNE, educator; b. Ironwood, Mich., Aug. 25, 1947; B.S. in Spl. Edn., U. Mich., Ann Arbor, 1973, M.A. in Edn., 1978. Tchr./cons. Hawthorn Center for Emotionally Impaired, Northville, Mich., 1975; tchr./cons. for physically and otherwise health-impaired Jackson (Mich.) Public Schs., 1973—; lectr. on non-vocal communication, 1979—. Adminstrv. asst. Temple Beth Emeth Religious Sch., Ann Arbor, 1978-80, mem. religious edn. com., 1977—; mem. Jackson County Communication Enhancement Team, 1978—; vol. Mich. Community Theatre Found., 1980—. Mem. Council Exceptional Children, NEA, Mich., Jackson County edn. assns., Mich. Assn. Affective Edn., S. Quadrangle Quadrants Hon. Soc. Club: Huron Valley Corvette (dir. 1975—). Developed techniques of affective-humanistic edn. Home: 1471 Gregory St 19 Ypsilanti MI 48197 Office: 1226 S Wisner St Jackson MI 49203

MARK, FLORINE, weight control orgn. exec.; b. Detroit, Feb. 21, 1936; d. Charles Issac and Ruth (Heidt) Grossberg; student Wayne State U., 1954; children—David, Sheri, Jeffrey, Richard, Lisa. Pres., area dir. Weight Watchers, Southfield, Mich., 1966—, also pres. Weight Watchers Greater Detroit, Greater Cin., Greater Boston, R.I., Mex. Mem. exec. bd. Detroit Area council Boy Scouts Am., 1966—; mem. exec. bd. March of Dimes, 1971—, vice chmn. mothers march, 1971—; treas. Detroits Fashion Group, 1968—; chpt. chmn. Alyn Orthopedic Hosp. and Rehab. Center, 1968—. Recipient various awards. Mem. Womens Guild of Sinai Hosp. Clubs: Womens Econ., B'nai B'rith, Haddassah. Author: (with others) Happy Dieter, 1977. Office: Weight Watchers PO Box 125 LV Southfield MI 48076

MARK, JACK CHARLES, gas co. exec.; b. Mpls., Aug. 10, 1930; s. Abraham and Betty (Herzbach) M.; B.A., U. Minn., 1952, M.A., 1956; m. Marjorie Ellen Robinson, Dec. 19, 1965; children—Jonathan David, Brian Alan. With Minn. Gas Co., 1956—, advt. supr., 1959-62, asst. mgr. mdse. sales, 1962-63, mgr. advt. and sales promotion, 1965-73, mgr. consumer communications, 1973—, dir. consumer communications, 1974, dir. communications services, 1980—; instr. Sch. Journalism and Mass Communications, U. Minn., 1968—. Chmn. public relations com., mem. exec. com. Minn. Heart Assn., 1979. Mem. Am. (mem. mktg. research, communications residential advt. com. 1966—), Midwest (chmn. advt. sect. 1966-72) gas assns., Advt. Club Minn. (dir. 1965, pres. 1969), Am. Mktg. Assn., Pub. Utilities Commn. Assn. (pres. 1974, sec. 1976), Sigma Alpha Mu, Sigma Delta Chi. Mason (Shriner). Home: 3735 Glenhurst Ave Minneapolis MN 55416 Office: 733 Marquette Ave Minneapolis MN 55402

MARK, NORMAN BARRY, journalist, talk show host; b. Chgo., Sept. 6, 1939; s. Arthur I. and Belle (Harman) M.; B.S., Northwestern U., 1961; m. Rhoda Kravets, Feb. 2, 1963; children—Geoffrey Wayne, Joel Richard. With Chgo. Daily News, 1966-78, daily radio-TV columnist, 1969-75; critic at large for CBS, Chgo., 1973-78; host Today in Chgo., 1978-80, Chgo. '82, The Baxters; host WIND-AM, 1978—, WFLD-TV, Chgo., 1977—. Instr. Roosevelt U., Chgo., 1975-79. Media cons. Regional Transit Authority Election Campaign, Chgo., 1974. Served with Ill. N.G., 1963-69. Recipient AP News-feature writing award, 1968; Public Service award Sigma Delta Chi, 1980. Mem. Newspaper Guild, A.F.T.R.A., S.A.G., Writers Guild West. Author: Norman Mark's Chicago, 1977; The CR Century, 1978; Mayors, Madames and Madmen, 1979; (with others) The San Francisco Weight Loss Method, 1975, also various television scripts and plays produced in regional theaters; contbr. articles to profl. jours. Office: 401 N Wabash St Chicago IL 60611

MARKEN, CLINTON CRAY, mfrs. sales rep.; b. Hampton, Iowa, Aug. 2, 1945; s. Gideon A. and Cleone M.; student Area 10 Community Coll., 1967-69; B.S., Iowa State U., 1971; m. Diane; children—Melanie Anne, Brandi Christen. Seedman, Com. Agrl. Devel., Iowa State U., Ames, 1971-72; field man Arco Chem. Co., Grafton and Rockwell, Iowa, 1972-73; plant mgr., 1973; sales rep. FMC Corp., Hampton, Iowa, 1973—. Served with USAF, 1963-67. Mem. Iowa Cattle Assn., Am. Quarter Horse Assn., Iowa State U. Alumni Assn. Home: Rural Route 2 Box 50 Hampton IA 50441

MARKER, DAVID GEORGE, physicist, coll. adminstr.; b. Atlantic, Iowa, Mar. 20, 1937; s. Calburt David and Vera Susan (Smith) M.; B.A., Grinnell Coll., 1959; M.S., Pa. State U., 1962, Ph.D., 1966; m. Cynthia Headlee, Jan. 28, 1966; children—Paul Calburt, Elizabeth Anne. Asst. prof. Hope Coll., Holland, Mich., 1965-68, asso. prof., 1969-71, prof., 1972—, chmn. computer sci. dept., 1973-74, asso.

dean acad. affairs, 1973, dir. computer center, 1965-76, provost Hope Coll., 1974—. Mem. standing com. Commn. on Ministry, Diocese of Western Mich., Episcopal Ch., 1976-80. NSF grantee, 1971-72. Mem. Am. Phys. Soc., Am. Conf. Acad. Deans, Am. Assn. Higher Edn., Phi Beta Kappa, Sigma Xi, Pi Mu Epsilon. Contbr. articles to profl. jours. Office: Hope Coll Holland MI 49423

MARKHAM, CLARENCE MATTHEW, JR., publishing co. exec.; b. San Antonio, June 20, 1911; s. Clarence Matthew and Lena (Dillwood) M.; student Wittenberg Coll., 1933-35; m. Olga Hughes, July 23, 1935; children—Clarence Matthew III, Melvin, Olga, Pierre, Leslie. Founder Bellmen Porters Assn., Springfield, O., 1933; operator porter and news butcher service Cin. and Lake Erie R.R. Co., Toledo, 1933-37; supt. dining car service Ann Arbor R.R. Co., Toledo, 1937-38; founder Travelers Research Pub. Co. Inc., Chgo., 1942, editor, pub., 1942—. Democrat. Roman Catholic. Home: 8034 S Prairie Ave Chicago IL 60619 Office: 11717 S Vincennes Ave Chicago IL 60643

MARKI, PAUL PATRICK, JR., hosp. exec.; b. Milw., Nov. 21, 1944; s. Paul Peter and Shirley L. (Young) M.; A.D.S. in Hotel-Restaurant Cookery, Milw. Inst. Tech., 1965; B.S. in Hotel-Restaurant Mgmt., Cornell U., 1967; M.B.A., U. Iowa, 1977; postgrad. Ind. U., 1976—; m. Lee K. Steffen, May 4, 1968; 1 son, David Paul. Chef, Wis. Sportservice, Milw., 1967-71; supr., mgr. Nino's Inc., Milw., 1971-73; dir. food service Elmbrook Meml. Hosp., Brookfield, Wis., 1973-76; dir. food service St. Joseph's Hosp., Ft. Wayne, Ind., 1976—; cons. group purchasing programs; instr. Ivy Tech., Fort Wayne, 1977—. Mem. Am. Mgmt. Soc., Am. Soc. for Hosp. Food Service Adminstrs., Northeastern Ind. Chef's Guild. Republican. Lutheran. Club: Rotary. Contbr. articles to profl. jours. Home: 4105 Reed Rd Fort Wayne IN 46815 Office: 700 Broadway Fort Wayne IN 46802

MARKING, T(HEODORE) JOSEPH, JR., transp. and urban planner; b. Shelbyville, Ind., June 28, 1945; s. Theodore Joseph and Alvena Cecelia (Thieman) M.; B.A., So. Ill. U., 1967, M. City and Regional Planning, 1972; m. Kathy K. Hagerman, Nov. 25, 1969. Intelligence research specialist Def. Intelligence Agy., Washington, 1967-68; planner 1, St. Louis City Plan Commn., 1970; transp. planner Alan M. Voorhees & Asso., St. Louis, 1970-74, sr. transp. planner, 1974-78, asso., 1978; sr. transp. planner Booker Assos., Inc., St. Louis, 1978-80, chief traffic and transp. sect., 1980—; guest lectr. St. Louis Community Coll. Dist. Mem. Am. Inst. Cert. Planners, Am. Planning Assn. (past pres. St. Louis sect.), Inst. Transp. Engrs., Traffic Engrs. Assn. Met. St. Louis. Office: 1139 Olive St Saint Louis MO 63101

MARKL, EDWARD MARTIN, III, automobile dealer; b. Kansas City, Kans., Dec. 28, 1954; s. Edward Martin, Jr. and Pamela Sue (Newkirk) M.; student Tex. Christian U., 1976, Gen. Motors Inst., 1975. With Markl Motors Inc., Overland Park, Kans., 1971—, sales mgr., 1973-76, exec. v.p., gen. mgr., 1976—; dir. Wrenn Ins. Agy.; mem. Rolls Royce Regional Dealer Council, 1978-80. Dir. natural sci. soc. Kansas City (Mo.) Museum Sci. and History. Mem. Mercedes-Benz Star Sales Guild, Tex. Christian U. Alumni Assn., Jr. League Kansas City (Kans.), Am. Trap Assn., Bacchus Found., Ducks Unltd. (state com.), Tuileries Assn. (dir.), Kappa Sigma. Clubs: Prospectors Breakfast (past pres.), Safari Internat.

MARKLE, ALLAN, psychologist; b. Chgo., Feb. 4, 1941; s. Louis H. and Elaine M.; B.S., U. Ill., 1962; M.A., Ga. State U., 1971, Ph.D., 1972; children—Ronald, Richard. Asst. prof. psychology Lake Forest (Ill.) Coll., 1972-75; coordinator outpatient program Huntsville-Madison County Mental Health Center, Huntsville, Ala., 1975-78; pvt. practice psychology, Northbrook, Ill., 1972—; coordinator Behavior Dysfunction Clinic VA Med. Center, North Chgo., 1978—; adj. asst. prof. Chgo. Med. Sch., 1979—; cons. in field. Mem. Am. Psychol. Assn., Southeastern Psychol. Assn., Ill. Psychol. Assn., Profl. Bowlers Assn., Assn. Advancement of Behavior Therapy. Jewish. Author: (with Roger C. Rinn) Positive Parenting, 1977; Author's Guide To Journals in Psychology, Psychiatry & Social Work, 1977; contbr. in field. Home: 3819 Medford Circle Northbrook IL 60062 Office: VA Med Center North Chicago IL 60064

MARKLEY, HERBERT EMERSON, mfg. co. exec.; b. Elmore, Ohio, Oct. 5, 1914; s. Henry J. and Amelia (Wilde) M.; B.A. in Bus. Adminstrn., Miami U., Oxford, Ohio, 1934, LL.D. (hon.), 1972; J.D., William McKinley Law Sch., Canton, Ohio, 1939; grad. Advanced Mgmt. Program, Harvard U., 1951, U. Pa., 1956; LL.D. (hon.), Tri-State Coll., 1976, Malone Coll., 1979; D.B.A. (hon.), Limestone Coll., 1974; m. Nancy Mulligan, June 22, 1946; children—Sheila, Herbert James, Maura, Noreen. With Timken Co., Canton, Ohio, 1938—, exec. v.p., 1959-68, pres., 1968-79, chmn. exec. com., 1979—, dir., 1959—; dir. Fire Tire & Rubber Co., Am. Electric Power Corp. Trustee, Case Western Res. U.; mem. Ohio Devel. Adv. Council. Served with AUS, 1943-46. Recipient Excellence in Mgmt. award Industry Week mag., 1979. Sr. mem. Conf. Bd.; mem. NAM (chmn. 1979). Republican. Methodist. Clubs: Canton, Brookside Country (Canton); Union (Cleve.); Internat. (Washington), Downtown Athletic (N.Y.C.); Ocean Reef (Key Largo, Fla.). Office: 1835 Dueber Ave SW Canton OH 44706

MARKLEY, ROGER BRUCE, accountant; b. Bluffton, Ind., Feb. 25, 1921; s. Herman Roderick and Beulah May (Harmon) M.; B.A., Internat. Coll., 1940; postgrad. Ball. State U., Oxford (Eng.) U., others; m. Betty June Sheffer, Feb. 14, 1942; children—Jeffrey Bruce, Patrice Faye, Rodney Lee. Commd. pvt. USAAF, 1941, advanced through grades to maj. U.S. Air Force, 1961, ret., 1964; controller Rockledge Products, Inc., Portland, Ind., 1964-69, Jay Petroleum, Inc., Portland, 1970-74; treas. Puterbaugh's Inc., Wehrly Motor Sales Inc. (both Portland) auditor OEO, 1964-74; pvt. practice as accountant, auditor, tax cons., Portland, 1964—; mgr. Wabash Village Apts., also Salt Creek Shopping Park, Nashville, Ind. Tchr. accounting and bookkeeping Purdue U. Farm Schs., 1968-74. Leader Jay County 4-H Club, 1964-69; area camping dir. Boy Scouts Am., Portland, 1938-42. City councilman City of Portland, 1958-62. Bd. dirs. Jay County Fair Assn., 1968-74. Decorated Purple Heart, Air medal; recipient award Am. Legion, 1962, State of Ind., 1962. Mem. Nat., Ind. (chpt. pres. 1968-69) assns. pub. accountants, Am. Legion (treas. 1964-70), Res. Officers Assn. U.S., V.F.W., Jay County Horse Club (pres. 1967-69). Methodist (treas. 1966-71). Mason; mem. Order Eastern Star. Home: Rural Route 3 Artist Dr Nashville IN 47448 Office: Wabash Village Rural Route 5 Nashville IN 47448

MARKMAN, MICHAEL DON, state ofcl.; b. Worthington, Minn., July 11, 1950; s. Donald Lee and Doris Louise (Zierke) M.; B.A. magna cum laude, U. Minn., 1972; M.Public Policy, U. Mich., 1974, cert. Inst. Gerontology; m. Ann Marie Groebuer, Aug. 26, 1972; 1 son, Jacob. Policy analyst Mich. Dept. Commerce, Lansing, 1973-75; asst. commr. Mich. Ins. Bur., Lansing, 1976-79; commr. ins. Minn. Ins. Div., St. Paul, 1979—. Mem. Nat. Assn. Ins. Commrs. Office: 500 Metro Sq Saint Paul MN 55101*

MARKOVITZ, MICHAEL CHAIM, ednl. adminstr.; b. N.Y.C., Apr. 24, 1950; s. Jacob and Cornelia (Solomon) N.; B.S., CCNY, 1968; M.A. (USPHS fellow), U. Chgo., 1973, Ph.D., 1975. Exec. dir. Family Counseling Agy. Will County (Ill.), 1973-75; columnist Copley Newspapers, 1974-76; lectr. mgmt. Northwestern U., 1975—; founder, 1975, since pres., dir. Ill. Sch. Profl. Psychology, Chgo.; publisher, dir. New Jewish Times News mag., 1979—. Mem. AAAS, Am. Psychol. Assn., Assn. Advancement Behavior Therapy, Ill. Psychol. Assn., N.Y. Acad. Scis. Republican. Jewish. Author: Filial Behavior in Japanese Quail, 1975; Tracking the Psychological D: A Report On The Illinois School, 1977; Practical Management for Results, 1980; Study Guide for the Psychology Licensure Examination, 1980. Office: 14 E Jackson Blvd Suite 1722 Chicago IL 60604

MARKOWITZ, THOMAS, pharm. co. exec.; b. Ungvar, Hungary, July 27, 1931; came to U.S., 1938, naturalized, 1945; s. Jacob and Helen Markowitz; B.S., Columbia U., 1954; m. Barbara Plotnik, Apr. 5, 1959; children—Linda, Jay. With Eli Lilly & Co., 1963—, mktg. plans asso., 1973-74, med. info. coordinator, Indpls., 1974—. Served to capt. USAF, 1955-58. Mem. Drug Info. Assn., Am. Soc. Info. Scis., Ind. Pharm. Assn., Columbia U. Alumni Assn. Club: Old Oakland Golf. Home: 8710 Staghorn Rd Indianapolis IN 46260 Office: 307 E McCarty St Indianapolis IN 46206

MARKS, BERT HENRY, elec. engr.; b. Chgo., Dec. 23, 1918; s. Charles William and Elva Bertha (Jahnke) M.; B.S., U. Wis., 1942; m. Mary Margaret Melhuse, Dec. 5, 1942; children—Richard Paul, Judith Ann. Mgr. capacitor engring. Centralab div. Glore-Union Inc., Milw., 1944-64; mgr. engring. and quality control Solar Mfg. Corp., Los Angeles, 1964-66; mgr. integrated circuit ops. Sprague Electric Co., Grafton, Wis., 1966-70; mgr. applications engring. Radio Materials Corp., Chgo., 1974—. Mem. Electronic Industries Assn. (dir.). Republican. Lutheran. Author, patentee in field. Office: 4242 W Bryn Mawr Ave Chicago IL 60646

MARKS, CLIFFORD DUNHAM, aero. engr.; b. Chgo., Jan. 5, 1925; s. John and Elizabeth M.; B.S. cum laude, U. Notre Dame, 1945; m. Virginia Kronner, Aug. 3, 1946; children—Michael John, Patrick James, Mary Elizabeth, Carol Irene. Stress engr. Boeing Aircraft Corp., 1946; with McDonnell Aircraft Corp., St. Louis, 1947-65; with McDonnell Douglas Astronautics Co., St. Louis, 1966—, v.p., program mgr. Harpoon, 1976—. Bd. dirs. St. Peters (Mo.) Community Hosp., 1980—. Served with U.S. Navy, 1943-46. Fellow AIAA (asso.). Roman Catholic. Office: PO Box 516 St Louis MO 63166

MARKS, JEROME, city ofcl.; b. St. Louis, Aug. 10, 1922; s. Harry Ely and Frieda (Meyer) M.; B.J., U. Mo., 1948; m. Helen Z. Patek, Dec. 9, 1948; children—Gail Ellen, Joy Arlene. Newspaper reporter in Minn., Tex., Kans. and Iowa and editor Chgo. bur. Internat. News Service, 1948-68; asst. to exec. dir. N.E. Minn. Devel. Assn., 1969-71; account exec. J.F.P. and Assos., Duluth, 1971-72; dir. indsl. devel. Seaway Port Authority, Duluth, Minn., 1972—; pres. Metro Duluth Econ. Devel. Assn., 1972—; mem. Mayor Duluth Com. Econ. Devel. Served with Signal Intelligence, AUS, World War II. Recipient Journalism award Sigma Delta Chi. Mem. Minn. Indsl. Devel. Assn., Kappa Tau Alpha. Home: 1201 Brainerd Ave Duluth MN 55811 Office: 1200 Port Terminal Dr Duluth MN 55806

MARKS, KENNETH EDWARD, orthopaedic surgeon; b. Cleve., Mar. 8, 1942; s. Henry Thomas and Mary Marcelle (Snedecor) M.; A.B., Baldwin-Wallace Coll., 1965; M.D., Case-Western Res. U., 1970; m. Hilda Constance Knusli, July 1, 1967; children—Caroline Louisa, Kristin Noel. Intern, Cleve. Clinic, 1970-71; resident U. Va., Charlottesville, 1971-72, Cleve. Clinic, 1972-75; practice medicine, specializing in orthopaedic surgery, Cleve., 1975—; head sect. orthopaedic oncology, Cleve. Clinic Cancer Center, 1977—, chmn. task force on musculoskeletal oncology, 1979—. Lord Nuffield scholar in orthopaedic surgery, Oxford (Eng.) U., 1975-76; diplomate Am. Bd. Orthopaedic Surgery. Mem. Am. Acad. Orthopaedic Surgeons, Orthopaedic Research Soc., Girdlestone Soc. of Oxford, Nat. Med. Soc., AMA, Ohio Med. Soc. Republican. Mem. United Ch. of Christ. Club: Chagrin Valley Country. Contbr. articles to med. jours.; editor med. text book. Home: 32781 Meadowlark Way Pepper Pike OH 44124 Office: 9500 Euclid Ave Cleveland OH 44106

MARKS, LEONARD BENJAMIN, ednl. adminstr.; b. Phila., Feb. 8, 1934; s. Charles and Anna Marks; B.A., N.J. State Tchrs. Coll., Glassboro, 1960; M.Ed., U. N.D., 1970; m. Stefanie Lisa Ballin, Feb. 24, 1956; children—Audrey Arlene, Michael Jeffrey. Tchr. elem. sch., Quinton, N.J., 1956-62; tchr. elem. sch. Mt. Pleasant Spl. Sch. Dist., Wilmington, Del., 1962-67; sci. cons. McGraw Hill Co., Manchester, Mo., 1967-74; asst. prof. sci. edn. U. N.D., Grand Forks, 1969-74; dir. The New City Sch., St. Louis, 1974-81; curriculum coordinator Wellston Sch. Dist., St. Louis, 1981—; cons. elem. sci. study. Bd. dirs. Nursery Found.; mem. citizen adv. com. St. Louis Public Schs., 1975—. Recipient grants NSF, 1972, 74, HEW, 1976, 78, Office Edn., 1980. Mem. Assn. Supervision and Curriculum Devel., Ednl. Confedn., Child Day Care Assn., Conf. on Edn., Ind. Schs. Assn. Club: Triple A Golf and Tennis. Home: 1122 Olivaire Ln Olivette MO 63132 Office: 6574 St Louis Ave Saint Louis MO 63121

MARKS, RENEE LEE, educator; b. Chgo., Nov. 20, 1936; d. Sol and Celia (Freund) Kaplan; B.S.J., Northwestern U., 1958, postgrad. (Chgo. Bd. Edn. scholar), summer 1978; B.J.S., Spertus Coll., 1972; M.A., Mundelein Coll., 1975; M.Ed. with distinction, De Paul U., 1981; postgrad. in ednl. adminstrn. Northeastern Ill. U., 1980-81, Nat. Coll. Edn., Evanston, Ill., 1981—; postgrad. in edn. U. Chgo., 1981—; m. Donald Norman Marks, June 22, 1958; children—Robin Debra Marks Dombeck, Steven Michael, Jody Ilene. Tchr., Beth Emet Synagogue, Evanston, Ill., 1967-81, North Shore Congregation Israel, Glencoe, Ill., 1981—; tchr. Collins High Sch., Chgo. Bd. Edn., 1976—; lectr. on Holocaust. Mem. Nat. Council for Social Studies, Chgo. Council for Social Studies, Assn. for Supervision and Curriculum Devel. Jewish. Author, Holocaust curriculum for Chgo. Bd. Edn., 1980. Office: 1313 S Sacramento Chicago IL 60623

MARKSTROM, PAUL RAGNVALD, clergyman; b. Skanninge, Sweden, May 30, 1921; came to U.S., 1922, naturalized, 1970; s. Gustaf Eric and Elsa Marie (Markstrom) Karlson; student Zion Bible Inst., 1940-41, Central Bible Coll. and Sem., Springfield, Mo., 1941-44, So. Methodist U., 1948, Southwestern State Coll., 1961-62, Am. Clin. Pastoral Assn., 1962-63; m. Berniece Elva Hoehn, June 1, 1944; children—Paul Eugene, Sondra Kay Markstrom Todd. Ordained to ministry Assemblies of God Ch., 1947; pastor Assembly of God Ch., Ely, Nev., 1944-46, Newburgh, N.Y., 1946-49, Bucklin, Kans., 1950-57, Coldwater, Kans., 1958-63; instr. Central Bible Coll. and Sem., 1966-72; dir. Instl. Chaplaincies of Assemblies of God, Springfield, Mo., 1963—, dir. spl. ministries, 1974-80; dir. Am. Indian Bible Inst., Phoenix, 1974-80. Mem. Nat. Assn. Evangelicals (chmn. spl. ministries com. 1967-80), Am. Protestant Correctional Chaplains Assn. (dir. 1963, pres. central region 1974), Ministerial Assn. (pres. 1953-60). Republican. Club: Lions. Author: Bible Basics, 1964; The Book of Acts, 1965; The Five Books of Moses, 1965; The Four Gospels, 1966; Outstanding Bible Profiles, 1967; Summary of The Old Testament, 1966. Volunteers in Corrections, 1977; Chaplains Manual, 1973. Contbr. articles in field to prof. jours. Home: 1520 Devon St Springfield MO 65804 Office: 1445 Boonville St Springfield MO 65802

MARKUSEN, RICHARD JOSEPH, EDP exec.; b. Racine, Wis., Nov. 22, 1944; s. Earl Joseph and Marie Agnes (Nielsen) M.; B.S. in Applied Math. and Engring. Physics, U. Wis., Milw., 1968. Systems specialist Gettys Mfg., Racine, 1975-77, ops. coordinator, 1977-78, chief programmer, 1978—; owner DonMar Container Co., Racine, 1978—; programming cons. Info. Mgmt. Software Specialists, Racine, 1978—. Served with USAF, 1968-72. Decorated Air Force Commendation medal. Mem. EDP Mgrs. Assn., Am. Mgmt. Assn., Assn. Small Computer Users, Library Computer and Info. Scis., Internat. Platform Assn., Smithsonian Inst., Nat. Geog. Soc. (life). Office: 2700 Golf Ave Racine WI 53404

MARKWARDT, L(ORRAINE) J(OSEPH), cons. engr.; b. Lansing, Iowa, Nov. 26, 1889; s. Joseph F. and Louisa (Besch) M.; B.S., U. Wis., 1912, C.E., 1922; m. Lula May Starks, June 21, 1917. Asst. city engr., Madison, Wis., 1912; instr. drawing, descriptive geometry, engring. coll. U. Wis., 1915-17; research engr. U.S. Forest Products Lab., Madison, 1912-14, asst. chief div. timber mechanics, 1917-39, chief, 1939-43, asst. dir., 1943-59, cons. engr., 1959—. Del. timber research conf. Internat. Union Forest Research Orgns., Princes Risborough, Eng., 1937, 39; U.S. del. internat. confs. mech. wood tech. FAO, UN, Geneva, Switzerland, 1948, 49, Igls, Austria, 1951, Paris, France, 1954, Madrid, Spain, 1958; chmn. program com. Forest Products sect. 5th World Forestry Congress, 1958-59; mem. subcom. wood and plastics for aircraft NACA, 1944-47, aircraft structural materials, 1947-49. Dep. mem. materials com. Resources and Devel. Bd., Dept. Def., 1952-53; mem. materials adv. bd. and bldg. research adv. bd. Nat. Acad. Scis., NRC, 1954-59. Recipient hon. citation for engring. achievement U. Wis., 1950, Superior Service award USDA 1957; Hitchcock award for outstanding research accomplishments in wood industry Hitchcock Pub. Co. and Forest Products Research Soc., 1963; Ann. L.J. Markwardt Wood Engring. Research award established by ASTM and Forest Products Research Soc. Fellow ASTM (Edgar Marburg lectr. award 1943; bd. dir. 1944-54, v.p. 1948-50, pres. 1950-51, chmn. com. methods testing bldg. constrns. 1946-48, chmn. com. wood 1948-64 hon. mem.; recipient Walter C. Voss award in bldg. tech. 1965); mem. Am. Standards Assn. (chmn. sect. com. methods testing wood, 1922—, sect. com. safety code constrn., care, use of ladders 1950—, mem. constrn. standards bd., 1943—, sect. com. specifications wood poles, 1946—), Am. Wood Preservers Assn., Am. Ry. Engring. Assn. (com. wood bridges and trestles 1944-48), ASCE (hon. life), Nat. Soc. Profl. Engrs. (life), Soc. Am. Foresters, AAAS, Forest Products Research Soc., Internat. Wood Research Soc. (v.p.), Am. Inst. Timber Constrn. (chmn. tech. rev. bd. 1960-75, profl. life mem.), Sigma Xi, Tau Beta Pi, Chi Epsilon. Presbyterian. Clubs: Masons, Rotary (pres. Madison 1950-51), Black Hawk Country (hon. pres. 1973, Madison). Co-author: Descriptive Geometry (with Millar and Maclin), 1919, also subsequent revisions; Autobiography of the Spirit Oak, 1975; Blackhawk Indian Mounds on National Register of Historic Places, 1979; The Blackhawk Country Club and its Historic Indian Heritage, 1976; also sects. on timber several engring. handbooks; govt. bulls., tech., sci. papers. Address: 12 Lathrop St Madison WI 53705

MARLOW, FRANK WESLEY, statistician; b. Ft. Worth, Dec. 6, 1918; s. Frank W. and Josephine Gay (Bullard) M.; m. Helen Louise Hellerud, June 12, 1942; children—Terence, Joan; B.A., U. Iowa, 1940. Sr. statis. analyst, sr. methods accountant, staff statistician, survey statistician Southwestern Bell Telephone Co., St. Louis, 1941—. Bd. dirs. Salem Meth. Ch., 1970—; treas. St. Louis hdqrs. Telephone Credit Union, 1954-75; dir. Mo. Credit Union League, 1969—; pres. Gateway Chpt. Credit Unions, 1975. Mem. Am. Mktg. Assn. (dir. St. Louis chpt. 1970—, v.p. 1974, treas. 1975-81), Pi Kappa Phi. Club: Hacienda Bath and Tennis. Home: 12017 Villa Dorado Dr Saint Louis MO 63141 Office: 1010 Pine St Saint Louis MO 63101

MARLOW, HAROLD JAMES, bus. exec.; b. Redfield, S.D., July 11, 1934; s. Harold LeRoy and Gladys Irene (Larson) M.; B.S., S.D. Sch. Mines and Tech., 1961; m. Marlys Frances Smith, Sept. 1, 1957; children—Harold James, Michael Francis, Deborah Kay. Prodn. engr. Remington Rand Univac, St. Paul, 1961-63; package engr. 3M Co., St. Paul, 1963; contract hardware mgr. Midwest Builders Supply, Rapid City, S.D., 1963-65; div. mgr. archtl. products div. R & S Lumber Co., Rapid City, 1965-67; pres., gen. mgr., dir. Engring. Spltys., Inc., Rapid City, 1967-81; partner R & E Enterprises, Rapid City, 1975—, JM Properties, 1981, J Mar Acres, 1981, Heritage Liquors, 1981, PMI Real Estate, 1981; pres. Marlow Entities, 1981—; treas. Waterbeds West, 1981. Served with USAF, 1952-56. Mem. Rapid City C. of C. (diplomats com., wholesale and mfg. com., environ. com.), Nat. Soc. Profl. Engrs., Constrn. Specifications Inst. (asso.), Nat. Assn. Wholesalers, Asso. Gen. Contractors. Republican. Presbyterian. Clubs: Arrowhead Country, Optimist. Home: 6003 Pioneer Circle Rapid City SD 57701 Office: Box 9277 429 Kansas City Suite 4 Rapid City SD 57709

MARLOWE, DAVID RONALD, civil engr.; b. Bay Shore, N.Y., Oct. 11, 1944; s. Frank Oscar and Barbara Irene (Spence) M.; B.S., U. Md., 1966; M.S., Syracuse U., 1971; m. Loretta Irene Tollefson, Dec. 24, 1965; 1 son, Owen Shawn. San. engr. N.Y. State Health Dept., Albany, 1971-74; sr. project engr. Alyeska Pipeline Service Co., Fairbanks, 1974-77; chief ops. engr., chmn. ops. dept. Robert E. Meyer Cons.'s, Beaverton, Oreg., 1977-79; mgr. environ. affairs Lorin Industries, Muskegon, Mich., 1980—; tchr. Portland (Oreg.) State U., 1977-79. Chmn. City Engring. Commn. Manchester (Oreg.), 1972-74. Mem. Water Pollution Control Fedn., Am. Water Works Assn. Republican. Presbyterian. Club: Lions. Home: 1729 Lee Ave Muskegon MI 49444 Office: 1960 S Roberts Muskegon MI 49442

MARON, HENRY EDWIN, mech. engr.; b. Cloquet, Minn., June 7, 1918; s. Richard N. and Stephanie P. M.; B.S. Mech. Engring., U. Minn., 1940; postgrad. Tex. Christian U., 1952, U. Colo., 1958; m. Claire Schurger, Nov. 4, 1940; children—Richard H., J. Michael. Mfg. engr. Manhattan Project, Oak Ridge, Tenn., 1944-46; plant mgr. Munsingwear, Barron, Wis., 1946-51; indsl. engr. Gen. Dynamics, Fort Worth, 1951-58; mgmt. engr. Martin Marietta, Denver, 1958-64, sr. cons. engr. George Williams Assos., Mpls., 1964-73; dir. mgmt. engring. Health Central, Inc., Mpls., 1973—. Registered profl. engr., Colo. Mem. Am. Inst. Indsl. Engrs. (dir. Colo. 1959-63), Hosp. Mgmt. Systems Soc. (nat. com. chmn. 1981). Roman Catholic. Home: 8111 Fairmont Circle Fridley MN 55432 Office: 550 Osborne Rd Fridley MN 55432

MAROSKY, JOHN EDWIN, endodontist; b. Indpls., July 3, 1941; s. Clarence H. and Wilma J. Marosky; A.B., Ind. U., 1963, D.D.S., 1967, M.S.D., 1975; m. Janet Sue Adams, Dec. 26, 1965; children—Julie Kay, Jill Suzanne. Practice dentistry, Indpls., 1969—. Instr., Ind. U. Sch. Dentistry, 1969-73, asst. prof., 1975—. Co-chmn., tech. coordinator Ice Skating Nat. Championships, Indpls., 1982; bd. dirs. Alexander Christian Found. Served to capt. AUS, 1967-69. Decorated Bronze Star Medal. Mem. Am., Ind., Indpls. dental assns., Harry J. Healey Endodontic Study Club (sec.-treas.), Hamilton Study Club, Am., Ind. assns. endodontists, Alpha Tau Omega. Mem. Christian Ch. (pres. Ind. Men's Fellowship 1974). Contbr. articles to profl. jours. Home: 5959 Cape Cod Ct Indianapolis IN 46250 Office: 1010 E 86th St Winterton Indianapolis IN 46240

MAROTTO, THOMAS CARL, business machine mfg. co. exec.; b. Omaha, Aug. 27, 1936; s. Samuel M. and Mollie E. (Palladino) M.; B.S. in Mktg., U. Nebr.. 1959; m. Carole Ann Hemstreet, June 4, 1960; children—Christine, Karen, Dianne, Thomas Carl, Terri. With advt. and sales promotion dept. Safeway Food Chain, 1959-62; with Xerox Corp., 1962—, br. mgr., Cin., 1974-78, v.p. mktg., 1978-80, v.p. ops., Mundelein, Ill., 1980, pres., gen. mgr., 1980—. Office: 404 Washington Blvd Mundelein IL 60060

MAROVITZ, WILLIAM A., state senator, lawyer; b. Chgo., Sept. 29, 1944; s. Sydney Robert and Jane (Chulock) M.; B.A., U. Ill., 1966; J.D., DePaul U., 1969. Admitted to Ill. bar, 1970; tchr. Chgo. Bd. Edn., 1969-70; partner firm Marovitz, Powell, Pizer & Edelstein, Chgo., 1970-82; asst. corp. counsel City of Chgo., 1973-74; mem. Ill. State House, 1975-80; mem. Ill. State Senate, 1981—. Mem. Young Men's Jewish Council; chmn. Spanish Speaking Peoples' Study Commn. in Ill., 1976—. Mem. Ill. Bar Assn., Chgo. Bar Assn., Decalogue Soc. Lawyers. Named Best Freshman Legislator, Ill. Young Democrats, 1975; Outstanding Young Legislator, 1981, Chgo. Jaycees, 1976 (Young Citizens award). Jewish. Office: Marovitz Powell Pizer & Edelstein 134 N LaSalle St Chicago IL 60602

MARQUIS, GERALDINE MAE HILDRETH (MRS. FORREST W. MARQUIS), educator; b. Ankeny, Iowa, Aug. 8; d. Vernon Otto and Alma Leona (Woods) Hildreth; student U. No. Iowa; M.A., Drake U., 1972; m. Forrest William Marquis; 1 son, Robert William. Elementary tchr., Ankeny and Ft. Dodge, Iowa, 1944-49, 56—; organizer Ft. Dodge Coop. Nursery Sch. Mem. NEA, Iowa, Ft. Dodge edn. assns., Assn. Childhood Edn. Internat. (Ia. pres. 1974-77), Nat. Assn. Edn. Young Children, Civic Music Assn., TTT Nat. Soc. (pres. chpt.), Delta Kappa Gamma (local pres. 1974-77), Phi Sigma Alpha. Republican. Methodist. Home: 2602 Williams Dr Fort Dodge IA 50501 Office: 615 N 16th St Fort Dodge IA 50501

MARR, THOMAS JOHN, physician; b. Chgo., Aug. 19, 1942; s. Joseph and Catherine (Marano) M.; M.D., Loyola U., Chgo., 1967; m. Rita Beleckis, Sept. 16, 1967; children—Claudia Marie, Felicia Eve. Pediatric intern Cook County Children's Hosp., Chgo., 1967-68; resident in pediatrics Children's Meml. Hosp. of Chgo., 1970-72, fellow in pediatric nephrology, 1972-73; practice medicine specializing in pediatrics Evanston, Ill., 1973—, Chgo., 1973—; active attending pediatrician, pediatric nephrologist Children's Meml. Hosp.; asso. attending pediatrician Northwestern Meml. Hosp., Chgo.; adj. attending pediatrician Evanston Hosp.; asst. prof. clin. pediatrics Northwestern U., Chgo., 1977—; guest lectr. various hosps. and med. and health care orgns., 1973—. Served to capt. M.C., U.S. Army, 1968-70. Diplomate Am. Bd. Pediatrics. Fellow Am. Acad. of Pediatrics, Inst. of Medicine of Chgo., Am. Soc. Pediatric Nephrology; mem. Internat. Soc. Nephrology, Internat. Pediatric Nephrology Assn., Chgo. Med. Soc., Am. Diabetes Assn., Ill. Med. Soc., AMA, Chgo. Pediatric Soc., Children's Meml. Hosp. Corp. Contbr. articles to med. jours.

MARREN, MARY ELIZABETH, retail co. exec.; b. Balt., Feb. 23, 1952; d. Thomas J. and Rosemary (Lopez) M.; B.S. in Bus., U. Colo., 1974; m. Bill Heideman, Sept. 15, 1979. With Midwest div. R. H. Macy & Co. Inc., Kansas City, Mo., 1974—, asst. buyer, 1974, sales mgr., 1975, exec. tng. coordinator, 1976-78, exec. recruiting mgr., 1979—. Mem. Am. Mktg. Assn. (nat. guest speaker), Midwest Coll. Placement Assn., Nelson Art Gallery Friends of the Arts, U. Nebr. Mktg. Club, Mu Kappa Tau, Gamma Phi Beta (pres. Beta Rho chpt. 1973-74; alumni mem.). Office: 1034 Main Kansas City MO 64105

MARRERO, PAUL STEVEN, food co. mgr.; b.. Bronx, N.Y., Aug. 1, 1952; s. Robert and Elaine Sandra (Pollack) G.; B.B.A., Pace U., 1974. With Del Monte Sales Co., 1974—, bus. trainee, Hartsdale, N.Y., 1974-75; order supr. Del Monte Corp., San Francisco, 1975, staff asst., 1975-76, sales accountant, Detroit, 1976—, mgr., Oak Park, Mich., 1976—. Internal dir. Rochester Jr. C. of C., 1978-79, internal v.p., 1979-80, chpt. mgmt. v.p., 1980, chmn. mgmt. v.p., 1981-82. Mem. Am. Mgmt. Assn. Pub., editor Jr. C. of C. Heartbeat Monthly News Letter, 1979-82. Home: 29766 Wagner Warren MI 48093 Office: 25900 Greenfield Rd 106 Oak Park MI 48237

MARRINER, NEVILLE, orchestral dir.; b. Lincoln, Eng., Apr. 15, 1924; s. Herbert Henry and Ethel May (Roberts) M.; ed. Royal Coll. Music, Paris Conservatory; m. Diana Margaret Corbutt, May 10, 1949 (div. 1957); m. 2d, Elizabeth Sims, Dec. 20, 1957; children—Susan Frances, Andrew Stephen. Prof., Eton Coll., 1947, Royal Coll. Music, 1952; violinist Martin String Quartet, 1946-53, Virtuoso String Trio, 1950, Jacobean Ensemble, 1952, London, Philharmonia, 1952-56, London Symphony Orch., from 1956; condr. Los Angeles Chamber Orch., 1969-77; music dir., condr. Minn. Orch., 1979—; guest condr. Gulbenkian Orch., Lisbon, Spain, Israel Chamber Orch., Australian Chamber Orch., N.Y. Chamber Orch., N.Y. Philharm. Orch., Orchestre de Paris, others; dir. South Bank Festival of Music, 1975-78, Meadowbrook Festival, Detroit, 1979—. Bd. dirs., founder Acad. of St. Martin-in-the Fields, 1959—. Recipient Grand Prix du Disque, Edison award, Mozart Gemeinde prize, Tagore prize, others. Office: care Columbia Artists Mgmt 165 W 57th St New York NY 10019 also Minn Orch 1111 Nicollet Mall Minneapolis MN 55403

MARRON, MICHAEL THOMAS, educator; b. Buffalo, Jan. 31, 1943; s. Thomas Urban and Anna Alberta (Bloom) M.; B.S., U. Portland, 1964; M.A., Johns Hopkins U., 1965, Ph.D. (NIH fellow), 1969; m. Mary Elizabeth O'Brien, July 2, 1966. Research asso. Theoretical Chemistry Inst., Madison, Wis., 1969-70; asst. prof. U. Wis., Parkside, Kenosha, 1970-73, asso. prof. chemistry, 1973-80, prof., 1980—, chmn. dept., 1976-78, chmn. div. sci., 1978—. Mem. Racine (Wis.) Air Pollution Control Appeals Bd., 1971-76. Mem. AAAS, Wis. Acad. Sci., Arts and Letters, Am. Chem. Soc., Sigma Xi, Phi Lambda Upsilon. Contbr. articles to profl. jours. Home: 1307 Main St Racine WI 53403 Office: U Wis-Parkside PO Box 2000 Kenosha WI 53141

MARSCHALL, VERNELL LEE, mineral exploration co. exec.; b. Fargo, N.D., June 24, 1946; s. Albert David and Delores Esther (Marquardt) M.; student Columbia Basin Coll., 1964, Eastern Wash. State Coll., 1965-69; m. Susan Frances Carrington, May 11, 1974; 1 son, Nathan. Field foreman Bear Creek Mining Co., western Mont., 1967-68; head surveyor Kenneth L. Preston Mining Engring. Co., No. Idaho, 1969; asst. geophys. technician, Noranda Exploration Inc., Reno, 1970; chief geophys. technician, Rhinelander, Wis., 1971-79; owner Marschall, Preston & Assos., Coeur d'Alene, Idaho, 1979—; co-owner Marschall-Sweet Geophysics, Denver and Coeur d'Alene. Mem. Soc. Exploration Geophysicists, Prospectors and Developers Assn., Am. Congress on Surveying and Mapping, Idaho Assn. Land Surveyors, N.W. Mining Assn., Trout Unlimited (pres. N. Woods chpt. 1976-77), Ducks Unlimited, Coeur d'Alene Retreiver Club, Sierra Club. Mem. United Ch. Christ. Geophys. discoverer Pelican River ore deposit Oneida County, Wis., 1973. Home: 12245 Kelley Rae Dr Hayden Lake ID 83835 Office: PO Box 514 Coeur d'Alene ID 83814

MARSH, DON ERMAL, supermarket exec.; b. Muncie, Ind., Feb. 2, 1938; s. Ermal W. and Garnet M. (Gibson) M.; B.A., Mich. State U.; m. Marilyn Faust, Mar. 28, 1959; children—Don Ermal, Arthur Andrew, David Alan, Anne Elizabeth, Alexander Elliott. Pres., chief exec. officer Marsh Supermarkets, Inc., Yorktown, Ind.; dir. Kokomo Land, Inc., Mchts. Nat. Bank of Muncie, Mundy Realty, North Portland, Inc., Northwest Kokomo, Inc., Universal Tank & Iron Works, Inc., Village Pantry, Inc. Bd. dirs., nat. chmn. Ball State U. Found.; bd. dirs. Crossroads of Am. council Boys Scouts Am. Mem. Am. Mgmt. Assn. (dir.), Grocery Mfrs. Am., Inc., Internat. Assn. Food Chains, Ind. Retail Grocers Assn., Ind. State C. of C., Lambda Chi Alpha, Pi Sigma Epsilon. Presbyterian. Clubs: Am. Bus., Burnham Park Yacht, Crecket, Delaware Country, Elks, Masons, Rotary. Home: 1250 Warwick Rd Muncie IN 47304 Office: PO Box 155 Yorktown IN 47396

MARSH, FRANK, govt. ofcl.; b. Norfolk, Nebr., Apr. 27, 1924; s. Frank and Delia (Andrews) M.; B.S. in Edn., U. Nebr., 1950; hon. degree Lincoln Sch. Commerce; m. Shirley Mac McVicker, Mar. 5, 1943; children—Sherry Anne Marsh Tupper, Dory Michael, Stephen Alan, Corwin Frank, Mitchell Edward, Melissa Lou Fisher. Builder, tchr., businessman, 1946-52; sec. state Nebr., 1953-71, lt. gov., 1971-75, state treas., 1975-81; state dir. Farmers Home Adminstrn., 1981—; partner Lincoln Landscaping, Inc. Govt. liaison adviser Mayor's Com. Internat. Friendship; past pres. Nat. Council Internat. Visitors; past internat. trustee Am. Field Service/Intercultural Programs, U. Nebr. Fgn. Student Host Program; past pres., mem. exec. com. Am. Youth Hostels, Inc.; mem. Nebr. Plant 2 Trees State Com.; pres. Nebr. Chamber Orch. Mem. Combined Orgn. Police Services, Am., Nebr. correctional assns., Central States Corrections Assn. (past pres.), Capitol City Footprinters, Nebraskaland Found., Nat. Assn. State Treasurers (past pres.), Midwest Internat. Trade Assn., Orgn. Profl. Employees of U.S. Dept. Agr., Lincoln Agri-Bus. Orgn., VFW, DAV, Am. Legion, Scottish Soc. Nebr., Nebr. Hist. Soc., U. Nebr. Alumni Assn. (life), Am. Kitefliers Assn., Alpha Phi Omega (life). Republican. Methodist (bd. trustees). Clubs: Lincoln Gem and Mineral, Lincoln Stamp, Polemic, Univ. Home: 2701 S 34th St Lincoln NE 68506 Office: 308 Fed Bldg 100 Centennial Mall N Lincoln NE 68508

MARSH, JAYNE ELIZABETH, info. coordinator; b. Detroit, May 11, 1954; d. Guy Rendell and Jean Beulah (Render) M.; B.A., Mich. State U., 1976, M.A., 1978. Freelance communications work, East Lansing, Mich., 1974—; prodn. and research asst. Sta. WKAR-TV, East Lansing, 1974-75; legis. reporter Mich. Senate Info. Office, Lansing, 1975-76; with Sta. WCER-AM-FM, Charlotte, Mich., 1976-77; editorial asst. Mich. State U. Info. Services-4-H Youth, 1976-77, info. specialist, 1977-79, info. coordinator, 1979—. Mem. Nat. Assn. Ext. 4-H Agts. (public relations and promotional chmn. nat. conv. 1980), Nat. Agrl. Communicators in Edn. (steering com. chmn. nat. conv. for 1981), Women in Communications, Inc., (nat. student chpt. adv. task force 1980-81, nat. profl. chpt. adv. task force 1981-82, chpt. pres. 1979-81), Am. Women in Radio and TV, Public Relations Assn. Mich. Office: 10 Agriculture Hall Mich State U East Lansing MI 48824

MARSH, JEREMIAH, lawyer; b. Freeborn County, Minn., June 5, 1933; s. Howard E. and Mildred (Larson) M.; A.B. magna cum laude, Harvard U., 1955, J.D., 1958; m. Marietta Cashen, June 16, 1956. Practice law, Chgo., 1958-62; legis. asst. to Sen. Edward M. Kennedy, Washington, 1963-64; mem. firm Hackbert, Rooks, Pitts., Fullagar & Poust, Chgo., 1964-68; spl. counsel to Gov. Ogilvie, Chgo., Springfield, Ill., 1969-72; mem. firm. Hopkins & Sutter, Chgo., 1973—; mem. faculty John Marshall Law Sch., 1959-68, 75—; mem. Nat. Conf. Commrs. Uniform State Laws, 1969-73, 77—; chmn. Ill. Adminstrv. Rules Commn., 1977—. Treas., bd. dirs. Gateway House Found.; mem. adv. council Misericordia Home; mem. Com. on Resources, Harvard U. Med. Sch.; mem. Mayor's Airport Adv. Com. Mem. Am., Ill., Chgo., 7th Circuit, Fed. bar assns., Selden Soc., Am. Judicature Soc., Supreme Ct. Hist. Soc., Law Club, Chgo. Assn. Commerce and Industry. Home: 456 Elder Ln Winnetka IL 60093 Office: 3 First Nat Plaza Chicago IL 60602

MARSH, R. BRUCE, advt. agy. exec.; b. Milw., Aug. 31, 1929; s. Lester B. and Margaret (Hermsen) M.; B.A. in Econs., State U. Iowa, 1951; m. Margaret Ross, Oct. 11, 1952; children—Marilyn Elaine, Robert Ross, Gregory Bruce; m. 2d, Gayle Johnson, June 14, 1981. Profl. baseball pitcher, 1951-52; indsl. sales rep. 3M Co., 1952-55; advt. sales rep. Curtis Publishing Co., 1955-56; advt. sales rep., then nat. sporting goods sales mgr. Sports Illus. mag., Chgo., 1956-64; v.p., account supr. Campbell Mithun Inc., Chgo., 1964-67; pres. R. Bruce Marsh, Inc., pubs. reps., Chgo., 1967-70, R. Bruce Marsh, Inc., real estate, Chgo., 1970-71; v.p. mktg. Johnson & Quin, Inc., printers, Chgo., 1971-72; Midwest mktg. mgr. Project Health div. G.D. Searle & Co., Chgo., 1972-73; v.p., account supr. Fuller, Smith & Ross Advt., Chgo., 1974-75; sr. v.p. Frank C. Nahser, Inc./Advt., Chgo., 1975—. Coach, Northfield (Ill.) Boys Baseball Assn., 1968-78, pres., 1972-76, bd. dirs., 1970—; chmn. North Suburban chpt. Fellowship Christian Athletes, 1980-82; area chmn. United Fund Northfield, 1963-65. Recipient spl. recognition award contbn. to youth Community of Northfield. Mem. Bible Ch. Clubs: Sunset Ridge Country (Northbrook, Ill.); University (Chgo.). Address: 346 Crooked Creek Ln Northfield IL 60093

MARSH, ROBERT CHARLES, writer, music critic; b. Columbus, Ohio, Aug. 5, 1924; s. Charles L. and Jane A. (Beckett) M.; B.S., Northwestern U., 1945, A.M., 1946; Sage fellow Cornell U., 1946-47; postgrad. U. Chgo., 1948; Ed.D., Harvard, 1951; postgrad. U. Oxford, 1952-53, U. Cambridge, 1953-56; m. Kathleen C. Moscrop, July 4, 1956. Instr. social sci. U. Ill., 1947-49; lectr. humanities Chgo. City Jr. Coll., 1950-51; asst. prof. edn. U. Kansas City, 1951-52; vis. prof. edn. State U. N.Y., 1953-54; humanities staff U. Chgo., 1956-58, lectr. social thought, 1976; music critic Chgo. Sun-Times, 1956—. Nat. adv. com., project for tng. music critics U. So. Calif., 1964-72. Recipient Peabody award. Ford Found. fellow, 1965-66. Episcopalian. Club: Press (Chgo.). Author: Toscanini and the Art of Orchestral Performance, 1956, revised edit., 1962; The Cleveland Orchestra, 1967. Editor: Logic and Knowledge, 1956; contbg. editor High Fidelity, 1955-66, 71. Home: 1825 N Lincoln Plaza Chicago IL 60614 Office: Chgo Sun-Times 401 N Wabash Ave Chicago IL 60611

MARSH, SHIRLEY MAC, state senator; b. Benton, Ill., June 22, 1925; d. Dwight McVicker; B.A., Social Welfare, U. Nebr., Lincoln, 1972; M.B.A., 1978; m. Frank Irving Marsh, Mar. 5, 1943; children—Sherry, Stephen, Dory, Corwin, Mitchell, Melissa. Asst. Red Cross Field dir. Naval Diesel Tng. Sch., Richmond, Va., 1944; sec. to chief inspector Elgin Watch Co., Lincoln, Nebr., 1948-49; placement asst. U. Nebr., 1966-70; casework practicum dept. welfare County of Lancaster, Lincoln, 1971-72; mem. Nebr. Legislature, 1972—, chmn. com. on coms., 1979-82. Mem. adminstrv. bd. United Methodist Ch., Lincoln, del. Meth. Gen. Conf., 1980; Chairperson Nebr. adv. com. U.S. Commn. Civil Rights. Named One of 10 Outstanding Legislators, 1978. Mem. Order Women Legislators, Capitol Bus. & Profl Women's Club (named Woman of the Year 1976), Nat. Conf. State Legislatures (exec. bd. 1980-81), Nat. Assn. Social Workers (recipient Nebr. Public Citizen of the Year award 1978), PEO, Delta Kappa Gamma. Republican. Office: State Capitol Lincoln NE 68509

MARSH, THOMAS BRADFORD, electronics m:g. co. exec.; b. Oak Park, Ill., Dec. 30, 1953; s. Richard Eugene and Ruth French (Thompson) M.; student Williams Coll., 1972-73, 76; m. Marcie Ann Mosley, June 18, 1976; 1 dau., Marissa Ann. With Marsh Products Inc., Batavia, Ill., 1974—, exec. v.p., j975-80, pres., 1980—, also dir. Republican. Mem. United Ch. of Christ. Home: 344 McKee Batavia IL 60510 Office: 336 McKee Batavia IL 60510

MARSHALL, CHARLES, utility co. exec.; b. Vandalia, Ill., Apr. 21, 1929; s. William F. and Ruth C. M.; B.S. in Agr., U. Ill., 1951; m. Millicent Bruner, Jan. 2, 1953; children—Ruth Ann, Marcia Kay, William Forman, Charles Tedrick. With Ill. Bell Telephone Co., 1953-59, 61-64, 65-70, 71-72, 77—, pres., chief exec. officer, Chgo., 1977—; with AT&T, 1959-61, 64-65, 70-71, v.p., treas., N.Y.C., 1976-77; v.p. Tex. ops. Southwestern Bell Telephone Co., Dallas, 1975-76; mem. bus. advisory council Chgo. Urban League; mem. Econ. Devel. Commn. of Chgo.; mem. governing bd. Ill. Council Econ. Edn.; dir. Harris Bankcorp., Inc. and subs. Harris Trust & Savs. Bank, GATX Corp., Inland Steel Corp. Bd. dirs. Chgo. Central Area Com., Protestant Found. Greater Chgo., United Way of Met. Chgo.; trustee Adler Planetarium, Chgo., Chgo. Symphony Orch., U. Chgo., Garrett-Evang. Theol. Sem., Museum Sci., Industry, Chgo., Rush-Presbyn.-St. Luke's Med. Center, Chgo.; mem. adv. council Northwestern U. Grad. Sch. Mgmt.; trustee Lakefront Garden; mem. Gov.'s Council on Jobs and the Economy; mem. MERIT Employment Steering Com. Served to 1st lt. USAF, 1951-53. Mem. Chgo. Council Fgn. Relations (dir.), Nat. Alliance Businessmen (advisory council), Econ. Club Chgo. (dir.), Northwestern U. Assos., U. Ill. Found. Clubs: Chgo., Comml., Econ., Mid-Am. (bd. govs.) (Chgo.); Barrington Hills Country. Office: Ill Bell Telephone Co 225 W Randolph St Chicago IL 60606

MARSHALL, DALE EARNEST, agrl. engr, researcher; b. Pinckney, Mich., Aug. 13, 1934; s. Clarence E. and Irene Loina (Hoffman) M.; B.S. in Agrl. Engring., Mich. State U., 1960, M.S., 1975; m. Patricia Jean Cochran, Apr. 9, 1955; children—Brenda Joy, Todd Edson, Tricia Ann. Jr. project engr. Farmhand, Inc., Hopkins, Minn., 1961-63; project engr. Chore-Time Equipment, Inc., Milford, Ind., 1963-66; agrl. engr. Agrl. Research Service, U.S. Dept. Agr., Lake Alfred, Fla., 1966-69, Mich. State U., East Lansing, 1969—. Recipient award for creative research in agrl. engring. Pickle Packers Internat., Inc. and Gt. Lakes Vegetable Growers Conf., 1980. Mem. Am. Soc. Agrl. Engrs. (Engring. Concept of Yr. award 1978), Am. Soc. Hort. Sci., Phi Lambda Tau, Alpha Epsilon (nat. pres. 1976). Research in fruit and vegetable harvesting; patentee in field; designer 1st mech. rhubarb harvester to be manufactured commercially, 1976, developer mech. pepper harvester. Home: 5411 Marsh Rd Haslett MI 48840 Office: Dept Agricultural Engineering Michigan State U East Lansing MI 48824

MARSHALL, DORIS BINKLEY (MRS. FRED TAYLOR MARSHALL), info. sci. cons.; b. Troy, Ohio, June 27, 1918; d. Charles Gordon and Onda Marie (Quinn) Binkley; B.A. in Chemistry, Ohio State U., 1940; postgrad. U. Chgo., 1940-41; M.A. in Library and Info. Sci., U. Mo., 1975; m. Fred Taylor Marshall, Mar. 28, 1942; children—Karen Louise (Mrs. Stephen Paul Booth), Carol Anne (Mrs. Paul Edward Derrickson), Fred Gordon. Asst. tech. librarian Universal Oil Products Co., Chgo., 1940-41; tech. librarian Monsanto Co., Dayton, Ohio, 1941-44; librarian Am. Zinc, Lead & Smelting Co., Kirkwood, Mo., 1956-60; owner pvt. bus., Kirkwood, 1960-64; librarian mgmt. info. center Ralston Purina Co., St. Louis, 1966-72, info. scientist, 1972-80, ret., 1980; cons., 1981—; trainer data base Nat. Agrl. Library, Kans. State U., 1977; workshop leader in field. Mem. Spl. Libraries Assn. (pres. St. Louis chpt. 1972-73, mem. internat. adv. council 1971-73, mem. div. cabinet 1976-78, chpt. employment chmn. 1976-78, editor chpt. bull. 1968-70; mem. nominating com. documentation div. 1975; mem. nominating com. food and nutrition div. 1973, 81, nominating com. chmn. 1974, div. sec. 1975-76, chmn. 1977-78, internat. nominating com. 1974-75, internat. standards com. 1978-82), Greater St. Louis Library Club (mem. nominating com. 1976), ALA, Inst. Info. Scientists (Eng.), Am. Soc. for Info. Sci. (chmn. nominating com. Mo. chpt. 1974-75), St. Louis Online Users Group (hon.), Am. Chem. Soc., Nat. Geneal. Soc. Am., Soc. Mayflower Descs. (Mo. bd. assts. 1975—, corr. sec. Mo. chpt. 1976, membership chmn. 1977-80, jr. membership chmn. 1981—), Luth. Laymen's Movement, Ch. Women United (chmn. nominating com. St. Louis area 1964, auditor 1965-68), Luth. Ch. Women (del. nat. conv. 1970). Lutheran. Contbr. articles to profl. jours. Home: 477 Burns Ave Kirkwood MO 63122

MARSHALL, EDWIN COCHRAN, optometrist; b. Albany, Ga., Mar. 31, 1946; s. John and Hazel (Cochran) Hairston; B.A., Ind. U., 1968, B.S., 1970, O.D., 1971, M.S., 1979; m. Robin Anderson Howlette, Dec. 30, 1978; children—Erin and Erika (twins). Lectr. optometry Ind. U., 1971-73, asst. prof., 1973-77, asso. prof., 1977—, adminstrv. intern Office of Vice Pres., 1976-77; dir. Community Care Optometry Center, 1973-77; dir. Ind. U. Summer Inst. in Health Related Professions, 1973-81; lectr.; adv. bd. Monroe County Health Services Bur., 1975—; mem. med. adv. com. Monroe County Head Start, 1975-78; dir. Public Health Nursing Assn. of S. Central Ind., 1976—; mem. Health Brain Trust, U.S. Congl. Black Caucus, 1977—; cons. Nat. Vision Care Centers, Inc., Chgo., 1977-78, Office of Health Resources Opportunity, HEW, 1978-80; mem. tech. rev. com. Health Career Opportunity Grants, HEW, 1978-79. MUCIA internat. travel grantee, 1977, 78; Spl. Health Career Opportunity Grants grantee HEW, 1974-78, Health Career Opportunity Grants grantee, 1978-81; Overseas Conf. Fund grantee Ind. U., 1977, 78. Mem. Nat. Optometric Assn. (pres. 1979-81, Optometrist of Year 1976), Nat. Optometric Found. (vice chmn. 1977-79), Am. Acad. Optometry, Am. Public Health Assn. (vision care sect. council 1979-83), AAAS, Am. Optometric Assn., Ind. Optometric Assn., Nat. Assn. Community Health Centers, Sigma Xi, Kappa Alpha Psi. Methodist. Clubs: Mogul Mongrels Ski. Contbr. to Public Health and Community Optometry, 1980. Research on health manpower availability and accessibility. Home: 4426 Cambridge Ct Bloomington IN 47401 Office: School of Optometry Indiana University Bloomington IN 47405

MARSHALL, GRAYSON WILLIAM, JR., biomaterials scientist; b. Balt., Feb. 12, 1943; s. Grayson William and Muriel Mare M.; B.S. in Metall. Engring., Va. Poly. Inst., 1965; Ph.D. in Materials Sci., Northwestern U., 1972; m. Sally Jean Rimkus, July 4, 1970. Research asso., design and devel. center Northwestern U., Evanston, Ill., 1972-73, NIH fellow, 1973, instr. Dental and Med. schs., Chgo., 1973-74, asst. prof. Dental Sch., 1974-78, asso. prof. Dental Sch. and Grad. Sch., 1978—; cons. Greenmark, Inc. Fellow AAAS; mem. Am. Assn. Dental Schs. (sect. officer 1981—), Soc. Biomaterials, Internat. Assn. Dental Research (Chgo. sect. officer 1978-80), Am. Coll. Sports Med., Am. Soc. Metals, Electron Microscopy Soc. Am., AIME, AAUP, Midwest Biolaser Inst. (trustee), Navy League U.S., U.S. Power Squadrons, Alpha Sigma Mu, Sigma Xi, Sigma Gamma Epsilon, Omicron Kappa Upsilon. Contbr. articles to profl. jours. Office: 311 E Chicago Ave Chicago IL 60611

MARSHALL, HERBERT DEE, mus. dir., farmer; b. Blackwell, Okla., July 6, 1936; s. Herbert S. and Goldie Ernestine (Corn) M.; student Okmulgee A&M Tech. Coll., 1955-56, Wichita State U.,

1956-57; B.A., Friends U., Wichita, 1961; postgrad. Kans. State Tchrs. Coll., Friends U., Kans. State U., Mather Tng. Center of Nat. Park Service; children—Shaun Michael, Peter Kent. Instr., Denver Public Schs., 1961, Joplin (Mo.) Public Schs., 1961-64, Arkansas City (Kans.) Public Schs., 1964-77; curator, dir. Cherokee Strip Living Mus., Arkansas City, 1965—, also farmer, 1977—; coordinator, mgr. Marshall Heritage Tours, Blackwell, Okla., 1981—; painter, designer, writer, speaker; author: The History of the Cherokee Strip and the Cherokee Strip Museum, 1967; designer plate for 100th Anniversary of South Haven Methodist Ch.; designer Kans. Bicentennial Quilt. Bd. dirs. Cher-o-Kan Gateway Assn., 1969—, pres., 1969-75. Recipient Community Service award Arkansas City, 1977. Mem. Kans. Mus. Assn., Kans. Hist. Soc., Mountain Plains Mus. Assn., Okla. Hist. Assn., Cherokee Strip Heritage Assn. (founder 1980, pres. 1981), 101 Ranch Old Timers Assn., Nat. Ret. Tchrs. Assn. Republican. Methodist. Home: Box 35 South Haven KS 67140 Office: Cherokee Strip Living Museum S Summit Rd Arkansas City KS 67005

MARSHALL, IRL HOUSTON, JR., co. exec.; b. Evanston, Ill., Feb. 28, 1929; s. Irl H. and Marjorie (Greenleaf) M.; A.B., Dartmouth, 1949; M.B.A., U. Chgo., 1968; m. Barbara Favill, Nov. 5, 1949; children—Alice Louise Vogler, Irl Houston, Barbara Carol, Susan Jean. Gen. mgr. Duraclean Internat., Deerfield, Ill., 1949-61, pres., gen. mgr., 1977—; pres. Houston Advt. Agency, Skokie, Ill., 1959-61; mgmt. Montgomery Ward, Chgo., 1961-77; dir. 1st Nat. (Deerfield) Bank. Trustee Highland Park (Ill.) Hosp., 1971-81, exec. com., 1974-81, treas., 1977-81; bd. dirs. Chgo. Suburban Chamber Music Soc., 1972-80. Mem. Internat. Franchise Assn. (dir. 1960-61, 82—). Clubs: Exmoor, Univ., Cliff Dwellers (dir. 1975-77, treas. 1976, pres. 1977). Home: 1248 Ridgewood Dr Northbrook IL 60062 Office: Duraclean Internat 2151 Waukegan Rd Deerfield IL 60015

MARSHALL, MARY ELLEN, power and light co. exec.; b. Washington, Apr. 17, 1946; d. George John and Evangelia Mantzuranis; B.S., Fla. State U., 1969; M.A. in Counseling, Chapman Coll., Calif., 1976; M.A. in Bus. Mgmt., Central Mich. U., 1981; m. Bruce Lambert Marshall, Dec. 28, 1969; children—Chrisopher George, Robert Ambler. Counselor, instr. Merced (Calif.) Coll., 1974-75; mgr. office services Federated Dept. Stores, Cin., 1975-78; mgr. bldgs., office services Dayton Power & Light Co. (Ohio), 1978—; cons. in field office automation, part-time 1978—. Co-chmn. United Way campaign, 1979, chmn. campaign Dayton Power & Light Co., 1980. Recipient Spl. Recognition award YWCA Salute to Career Women, 1980. Mem. Am. Mgmt. Assn., Adminstrv. Mgmt. Soc., Southwestern Ohio Word Processing Assn., Sigma Iota Epsilon. Republican. Mem. Eastern Orthodox Ch. Home: 891 Watkins Glen Dr Spring Valley OH 45370 Office: Dayton Power & Light Co Courthouse Plaza SW PO Box 1247 Dayton OH 45401

MARSHALL, PAUL RICHARD, mfg. co. mgr.; b. Koppel, Pa., Apr. 10, 1933; s. Harold Coulter and Anna Lillian Marshall; B.S., Pa. State U., 1955; m. Anita Louise Hazlewood, Apr. 18, 1959; children—Carrie, Peter, Christine, Gregory. With Westinghouse Electric Corp., 1955—, with elevator div., 1965—, dist. mgr., Cin., 1974-79, regional mgr., 1979—. Republican. Home: 7946 Hunters Knoll Montgomery OH 45242 Office: 2210 Reading Rd Cincinnati OH 45202

MARSHALL, SALLY JEAN, biomaterials scientist, swimming coach; b. Racine, Wis., Jan. 8, 1949; d. Charles and Adele Ruth Rimkus; B.S. with distinction in sci. engring., Northwestern U., 1970, Ph.D. in Materials Sci. and Engring., 1975; m. Grayson William Marshall, Jr., July 4, 1970. Instr. biol. materials Northwestern U., Chgo., 1974-75, asst. prof., 1975-80, asso. prof., 1980—; varsity swimming coach Northwestern U., Evanston, Ill., 1970—. Recipient spl. dental research award Nat. Inst. Dental Research, 1977. Mem. Am. Soc. Metals, AIME, Soc. Women Engrs., Am. Swimming Coaches Assn., Ill. Swimming Assn. (Women's Collegiate Coach of Year 1978-79), Nat. Collegiate Women's Swimming Coaches Assn., Internat. Assn. Dental Research, Am. Assn.' Dental Research (1st place research award Chgo. sect.), N.Y. Acad. Scis., Am. Coll. Sports Medicine, Soc. Biomaterials, AAHPER, Sigma Xi. Contbr. articles sci. jours. Home: 116 Maple Ave Wilmette IL 60091 Office: 311 E Chicago Ave Chicago IL 60611

MARSHALL, SIMEON CURTIS, photographer; b. Portsmouth, N.H., Feb. 5, 1942; s. Charles H. and Mary J. Marshall; B.F.A. cum laude, Pratt Inst., 1968; m. Janice Thompson, Nov. 8, 1980. Exec. art dir. Campbell-Ewald Co., Chgo., 1970-71, Leo Burnett Co., Chgo., 1971-73; creative dir., v.p. Don Tennant Co., Chgo., 1973-80; pres., dir. photography Simeon Marshall Studios Inc., Chgo., 1980—. Served with USAR, 1961-64. Home: 1938 N Sedgwick St Chicago IL 60614 Office: 617 W Fulton St Chicago IL 60606

MARSHALL, STEPHANIE ANNE, ednl. adminstr.; b. N.Y.C., July 19, 1945; s. Dominick Martin and Anne (Price) Pace; B.A., Queens Coll., 1967; M.A., U. Chgo., 1971; postgrad. Loyola U., Chgo.; m. Robert Marshall, Dec. 23, 1977. Tchr., Public Schs. Alsip (Ill.), 1967-74, gifted coordinator, 1971-74; nat. social studies cons., 1973-76; asst. curriculum dir. Public Schs. Naperville (Ill.), 1974-76; asst. supt. schs. Batavia (Ill.), 1976—; adj. prof. Nat. Coll. Edn.; mem. Ill. Textbook Adv. Com., Ill. Adv. Com. Gifted Edn.; cons. Mem. Assn. Supervision and Curriculum Devel., Am. Assn. Sch. Adminstrs., Ill. Assn. Supervision and Curriculum Devel., Nat. Assn. Gifted Children, Nat. Council Exceptional Children, Nat. Council Social Studies, AAUW, Phi Delta Kappa, Pi Lambda Theta. Home: 1145 Wheaton Oaks Dr Wheaton IL 60187 Office: 12 W Wilson St Batavia IL 60510

MARTA, JOHN B., JR., radiologist; b. Laurium, Mich., July 29, 1932; s. John B. and Mary T. (Silva) M.; student Mich. Tech. U., 1950-52; M.D., Marquette U., 1957; M.S., U. Minn., 1963; m. Louise P. Koopikka, June 8, 1957; children—Michael, Michele, Lisa, David. Intern Receiving Hosp., Detroit, 1957-58; fellow in radiology Mayo Clinic, Rochester, Minn., 1960-63; practice medicine specializing in radiology, Lansing, Mich., 1963-67, St. Paul, 1967—; instr. anatomy Mich. State U., 1965-67; instr. dept. radiology and nuclear medicine U. Minn., 1967—; mem. staffs United Hosps., Childrens Hosp., St. Joseph Hosp., St. John's Hosp. Pres. Mounds View Sch. Dist. PTO, 1971-72. Served with MC USAF, 1958-60. Joseph Collins scholar 1956-57; recipient Russell Carman award Mayo Clinic Dept. Roentgenology, 1963. Mem. AMA, Ramsey County, Minn. State med. socs., Am. Coll. Radiology, Radiol. Soc. N.Am., Am. Roentgen Ray Soc., Soc. Nuclear Medicine. Roman Catholic. Club: Elks. Contbr. articles to med. jours. Home: 11 Ridge Rd Saint Paul MN 55110 Office: S-6 Doctors Profl Bldg Saint Paul MN 55102

MARTELL, CHARLES GETMAN, advt. agy. exec.; b. Watertown, N.Y., Feb. 5, 1936; s. Gerald and Ruth Elizabeth (Getman) M.; B.A. magna cum laude, St. Lawrence U., 1958; postgrad. Sorbonne, Paris, 1958-59; M.A., Duke U., 1960; postgrad. Northwestern U., 1960-62; m. Linda Radley Willner, May 11, 1972. With J. Walter Thompson Co., Chgo., 1962-75, 79—, sr. v.p., creative dir., 1972-75, sr. v.p., group creative dir., creative bd. chmn., 1979—; sr. v.p., creative dir. McCann-Erickson, San Francisco, 1975-79. Fulbright fellow, 1958-59. Mem. Phi Beta Kappa. Office: 875 N Michigan Ave Chicago IL 60611

MARTEN, GORDON CORNELIUS, educator; b. Wittenberg, Wis., Sept. 14, 1935; s. Clarence George and Cora Levina (Verpoorten) M.; B.S., U. Wis., 1957; M.S., U. Minn., 1959, Ph.D., 1961; postgrad. Purdue U., 1962; m. Lynette Joy Hanson, Sept. 9, 1961; 1 dau., Kimberly Joy. Research agronomist U.S. Dept. Agr., U. Minn., St. Paul, 1961-72, research supervisory agronomist, research leader, 1972—; prof. agronomy U. Minn., St. Paul, 1971—. NSF grad. fellow, 1959-61; Am. Forage and Grassland Council merit award, 1976; Civil Servant of the Yr. award Twin Cities (Minn.), 1976. Fellow Am. Soc. Agronomy; mem. Crop Sci. Soc. Am. (bd. dirs. 1975-77), Am. Forage and Grassland Council (bd. dirs. 1977-80), Council Agr. Sci. and Tech., Biol. Club, Sigma Xi, Gamma Sigma Delta, Alpha Zeta, Delta Theta Sigma. Lutheran. Club: St. Paul Torch. Contbr. numerous articles to profl. jours.; asso. editor Crop Sci., 1972-74. Office: 1509 Gortner Ave Saint Paul MN 55108

MARTIN, A. JOHN, ednl. adminstr.; b. Grafton, N.D., Sept. 24, 1939; s. August G. and Helen M. (Fischer) M.; B.A., Westmar Coll., 1961; M.S. in Edn., Moorhead State Coll., 1963; Ed.S., U. No. Iowa, 1968; m. Marilyn Ruth Yackel, June, 1963; children—Lisa Michelle, August Timothy. Tchr., West Sioux (Iowa) Community Sch., 1960-61; tchr., Sheldon, Iowa, 1961-63, prin. schs., 1963-66; asst. prof. Buena Vista Coll., 1966-67; student teaching coordinator U. No. Iowa, 1967-69; dir. internship Drake U., Des Moines, 1969-70; with Iowa Dept. Public Instrn., Des Moines, 1970—, dir. instrn. and curriculum, 1974—; cons. Charles Kettering Found. Del., Iowa State Republican Conv., 1976; chairperson Crawford Twp. Republicans, 1977-80. Mem. Assn. Supervision and Curriculum Devel., Assn. Individually Guided Edn., Phi Delta Kappa. Methodist. Club: Rotary (pres. Winterset 1979-80). Office: Grimes State Office Bldg Des Moines IA 50319

MARTIN, CHARLES ALLEN, aero.-mech. engr.; b. Detroit, Apr. 3, 1938; s. Joseph Allen and Anna Lorretta (Piontkowski) M.; B.S. in Aero. Engring., Wayne State U., 1961, M.S. in Engring. Mechs., 1963, M.M.E., 1975; m. Jeanette Bienko, Aug. 31, 1963; children—Jacqueline Marie, Christopher Charles. Product design engr. Ford Motor Co. Engring. & Research Center, Dearborn, Mich., 1962-63; instr. in engring. mechs. U. Detroit, 1964-65; asso. prof. mech. engring. Gen. Motors Inst., Flint, Mich., 1965-75; vis. scientist NASA Johnson Space Center, Houston, 1975; product research mgr. Ex-Cell-O Aerospace Devel. Center, Walled Lake, Mich., 1975—. Mem. Soc. Automotive Engrs., ASME, ASTM, Engring. Soc. Detroit, AIAA (chmn. Mich. sect. 1977-79, treas. 1979—). Roman Catholic. Home: 16884 Renwick St Livonia MI 48154 Office: 850 Ladd Rd Walled Lake MI 48088

MARTIN, CLAUDE RAYMOND, JR., marketing cons., educator; b. Harrisburg, Pa., May 11, 1932; s. Claude R. and Marie Teresa (Stapf) M.; B.S., U. Scranton, 1954, M.B.A., 1963; Ph.D., Columbia U., 1969; m. Marie Frances Culkin, Nov. 16, 1957; children—Elizabeth Ann, David Jude, Nancy Marie, William Jude, Patrick Jude, Cecelia Marie. Newsman, sta. WILK-TV, Wilkes-Barre, Pa., 1953-55; news dir. sta. WNEP-TV, Scranton, Pa., 1955-60; dir. systems Blue Cross & Blue Shield Ins., Wilkes-Barre, 1960-63; lectr. in mktg. St. Francis Coll., Bklyn., 1964; lectr. in mktg. U. Mich., Ann Arbor, 1965-68, asst. prof., 1968-73, asso. prof., 1973-77, prof., 1977—, Isadore and Leon Winkelman prof. retail mktg., 1980—; dir. Huron Valley Bank, Ann Arbor, 1977—; cons. in mktg. to various fin. instns., 1966—. Served with USN, 1955-57. Mem. Acad. of Mktg. Sci., Am., Southwest mktg. assns., Bank Mktg. Assn., Assn. for Consumer Research, Am. Collegiate Retailing Assn. Roman Catholic. Contbr. articles on mktg. analysis and consumer research to profl. jours. Home: 1116 Aberdeen Dr Ann Arbor MI 48104 Office: Graduate School of Business Administration Univ of Michigan Ann Arbor MI 48109

MARTIN, CLYDE VERNE, psychiatrist; b. Coffeyville, Kans., Apr. 7, 1933; s. Howard Verne and Elfrieda Louise (Moehn) M.; student Coffeyville Coll., 1951-52; A.B., U. Kans., 1955, M.D., 1958; M.A., Webster Coll., St. Louis, 1977; m. Barbara Jean McNeilly, June 24, 1956; children—Kent Clyde, Kristin Claire, Kerry Constance, Kyle Curtis. Intern, Lewis Gale Hosp., Roanoke, Va., 1958-59; resident psychiatry U. Kans. Med. Center, Kansas City, 1959-62, Fresno br. U. Calif., San Francisco, 1978; staff psychiatrist Neurological Hosp., Kansas City, 1962; pvt. practice psychiatry, Kansas City, Mo., 1964—; founder, med. dir., pres. bd. dirs. Mid-Continent Psychiat. Hosp., Olathe, Kans., 1972—; adj. prof. psychology Baker U., Baldwin City, Kans., 1969—; pres., editor Corrective and Social Psychiatry, Olathe, 1970—. Bd. dirs. Meth. Youthville, Newton, Kans., 1965-75, Spofford Home, Kansas City, 1974-78. Served to capt. USAF, 1962-64. Fellow Royal Soc. Health; mem. AMA, Am., Mid-Continent psychiat. assns., Assn. for Advancement Psychotherapy, N.Y. Acad. Sci., Aerospace Med. Assn., Phi Beta Pi, Pi Kappa Alpha. Methodist (del. Kans. E. Conf. 1972-80, bd. global ministries 1974-80). Clubs: Carriage; Kansas City. Mason. Contbr. articles to profl. jours. Home: 5531 E Mission Dr Mission Hills KS 66208 Office: 800 W 47th St Suite 318 Kansas City MO 64110 also 400 E Red Bridge Rd Suite 321 Kansas City MO 64131

MARTIN, DENISE RENEE, educator; b. Chgo., July 25, 1951; d. Charles Grady and Ernestine (Marion) Guillebeaux; B.A., Northwestern U., 1973, M.A.T., 1974; m. Joseph L. Martin, Dec. 23, 1978; children—Kristian, Joseph L. With Bramsons, Evanston, Ill., 1967-73; recreation leader City of Evanston (Ill.), 1972-73; lab. asst. G.D. Searles, Skokie, Ill., summer 1969; tchr. social studies Evanston Twp. High Sch., 1973-78, dean students, 1978-80, asst. prin., 1980—. Mem. Nat. Assn. Secondary Sch. Prins., Nat. Assn. for Curriculum and Devel., Nat. Assn. Social Studies, Alpha Kappa Alpha. Baptist. Office: 1600 Dodge St Evanston IL 60201

MARTIN, DENNIS RAY, mfr. control systems; b. Saginaw, Mich., Mar. 10, 1949; s. Glenn Ray and Alice Rosealla (Spencer) M.; B.S., U. Mich., 1972; grad. Mich. Police Acad., 1976; m. Jacquelyn Ann Terlewski, Mar. 9, 1968; children—Denise Raygina, Jennifer Marie. Dep. sheriff Saginaw County, Mich., 1975—; pres., owner Denmar Engring. and Control Systems Inc., Saginaw, 1977—; dir. Community Emergency Patrol Systems Inc., 1975—; legis. agt. State of Mich., 1972-79; mem. Police Community Relations Commn., 1976—; mem. United Community Action Com. Prevention Crime, 1975—. Mem. parent council adv. bd. Saginaw Public Schs., 1977-79. Recipient Luther Christman award Nat. Male Nurse Assn., 1976; Health and Services award Mich. State U., 1976; Officer of Year award Exchange Club Saginaw, 1977; Liberty Bell award Saginaw County Bar Assn., 1979. Mem. Am. Assn. Correctional Facility Officers (pres. 1977), Dep. Sheriff Assn. (pres. 1977), Nat. Male Nurse Assn. (pres. 1971-79), Am. Assn. Trauma Specialists (dir.), Mich. Health Council (dir.), Saginaw C. of C. Republican. Baptist. Clubs: Tri-City Ski, Bridgeport Country, Saginaw Health. Author articles in field. Home: 6562 E Curtis Rd Bridgeport MI 48772 Office: 2309 State St North Office Saginaw MI 48602

MARTIN, DONALD RAY, mfg. co. exec.; b. Humphrey, Ark., Sept. 9, 1951; s. Clarence and Bobbie (Pointer) M.; A.A., Vincennes U., 1972; student Purdue U., 1981—; m. Dewitt Delores Harmon, Aug. 17, 1974. With Joy Mfg. Co., Michigan City, Ind., 1974—, prodn. planner, 1980, supr. tech. pub., 1980—. Mem. Michigan City Human Rights Commn., Michigan City Youth Service Bur., 1978-80, Ind. Black Expo Pageant, 1976-80; precinct vice committeeman Democratic Party, 1975-76. Recipient Community Service cert. Elks Club, 1976. Mem. Am. Mgmt. Assn., Nat. Mgmt. Assn., Michigan City Jaycees, Omega Psi Phi. Baptist. Clubs: Joy Management, Michiana Advertising. Home: 233 N Ridgeland Ave Michigan City IN 46360 Office: Joy Mfg Co 900 Woodland Ave Michigan City IN 46360

MARTIN, EDWIN DONALD, banker; b. Topeka, Kans.; s. William Donald and Leota Fay (Becker) M.; m. Brenda Joyce Medeiros, Nov. 26, 1977; children—Joshua William, Phillip Robert. Exec. v.p., dir. Kaw Valley State Bank & Trust Co., Wamego, Kans., 1979—. Mem. Am. Bankers Assn., Kans. Bankers Assn., Pottawatomie County Bankers Assn. (Agrl. Key Banker 1978, 79, 80), Kans. Livestock Assn., Wamego Jaycees (pres., chmn. bd.). Methodist. Home: Rural Route 2 Box 202 Wamego KS 66547 Office: Kaw Valley State Bank & Trust Co Lincoln St Wamego KS 66547

MARTIN, ERIC WILLIAM, univ. ofcl., hosp. adminstr.; b. Monette, Mo., May 28, 1953; s. Uylan Allen and Clara Dee (Nichols) M.; B.A., Creighton U., 1975, M.S., 1982; m. Karen Ann Kelly, Jan. 30, 1981. Admissions counselor Midland Luth. Coll., Fremont, Nebr., 1976-77; asst. dir. devel. Creighton U., Omaha, 1977—; acting dir. devel. St. Joseph Hosp., Omaha, 1978-81. Mem. Presidents Club of Omaha C. of C., Nat. Assn. Hosp. Devel. Republican. Baptist. Home: 4216 Shirley St Omaha NE 68105 Office: 2500 California St Omaha NE 68178

MARTIN, GARY LEE, educator; b. Clarinda, Iowa, Jan. 2, 1942; s. Mildred H. (Downing) M.; B.S., U. Iowa, 1967; M.S., U. S.D., 1969, Ph.D., 1970; m. Shirley Hoffman, Dec. 29, 1964; children—Catherene, Darcie. Epidemiologist, Univ. Health Center, U. Nebr., Lincoln, 1970—, asst. dir. Univ. Health Center, 1972-74, asso. dir., 1974-76, asst. prof. epidemiology, 1970—; sec.-treas. Health Edn., Inc., Lincoln, 1977-81. Vice pres. NW Community Center Bd., Lincoln, 1974-76; v.p. Belmont Community Center Bd., Lincoln, 1979—. Served with U.S. Army, 1960-63. Mem. Am. Psychol. Assn., Human Factors Soc., Sigma Xi. Contbr. articles in field to profl. jours. Home: 4442 Grandview Blvd Lincoln NE 68521 Office: 211 Coliseum U Nebr Lincoln NE 68508

MARTIN, JAMES DAVID, railroad, constrn. and indsl. equipment co. exec.; b. Madison, Wis., May 7, 1943; s. Ruscal Wendel and Phyllis (Edwards) M.; B.S. in Sociology, U. Wis., 1968; postgrad. Northeastern U., Chgo., 1970-72; m. Melinda Robinson, July 17, 1968; children—James Richard Lawrence, Geoffrey Michael. Freelance writer, 1971—; staff writer, editorial asst. Chicogan mag., 1973-74; staff writer Ill. Div. Tourism, 1974-75, also owner of public relations firm; speechwriter for gov. Ill., 1975-77; speechwriter, staff writer Gould, Inc., Rolling Meadows, Ill., 1977-79; editor Chicagoland mag., 1977-79; dir. communications Portec Inc., Oak Brook, Ill., 1979—; author: The Gould Charge Coloring Book, 1977; co-author feature film The Last Affair, 1975; writer, co-producer film Where Total Systems Responsibilities Means Everything (Silver award N.Y. Internat. Film Festival), 1979; vis. prof. film Columbia Coll., Chgo., 1973; bd. dirs. Chgo. Internat. Film Festival, 1972-77. Mem. Am. Film Inst., Assn. R.R. Advt. Mgrs., R.R. Public Relations Assn., Internat. Assn. Bus. Communicators, Ry. Progress Inst. (chmn. public relations com. 1981-82). Club: Chgo. Press. Home: 2623 Prairie Ave Evanston IL 60201 Office: 300 Windsor Dr Oak Brook IL 60521

MARTIN, JAN C, hosp. adminstr.; b. St. Paul, May 4, 1936; s. Cyrus Albert and Geraldean Maude (Clinkenbeard) M.; B.S. in B.A., U. Md., 1965; children—Barbara Ann Martin Centeno, Virginia. Personnel dir. Washington Hosp. Center, 1965-69; v.p. human resources St. Lawrence Hosp., Lansing, Mich., 1969—. Mem. retirement com. Sisters of Mercy Health Corp., Farmington, Mich., 1972—. Served with USN, 1954-62. Mem. Am. Hosp. Assn., Mid-Mich. Personnel Assn. (pres. 1972-73, dir. 1970-76). Clubs: Elks, Comdrs. of Mich. (bd. dirs. 1977-79). Office: 1210 W Saginaw St Lansing MI 48914

MARTIN, JOHN EDWARD, physician; b. Rockford, Ill., Dec. 28, 1937; s. Charles Edward and Marion (Hoffman) M.; B.S., Drake U., 1959; M.D., U. Ill., 1964; m. Jeanette Walters, Feb. 27, 1960; children—Paul, David, Steven, Anne, Karen. Intern, Cook County Hosp., Chgo., 1965-66; resident West Side VA and Univ. Ill. hosps., Chgo., 1968-71; fellow in pulmonary disease Presbyn.-St. Lukes Hosp., Chgo., 1971-72, dir. pulmonary lab., 1972-74; instr. Rush Med. Coll., Chgo., 1972-77, asst. prof. medicine, 1977—; dir. pulmonary medicine Grant Hosp., Chgo., 1974-81, chmn. dept. medicine, 1974—; dir. pulmonary function lab. respiratory therapy Holy Cross Hosp. Chgo., 1972-78; dir. pulmonary physiology lab. and respiratory therapy West Suburban Hosp., Oak Park, Ill., 1978-81; asst. attending Presbyn.-St. Luke's Hosp., Chgo., 1971-80, asso. attending, 1980—. Diplomate Am. Bd. Internal Medicine. Fellow Am. Coll. Chest Physicians, A.C.P., Inst. of Medicine; mem. AAAS, AMA, Am., Ill. thoracic socs., Ill., Chgo. med. socs., Chgo. Soc. Internal Medicine, N.Y. Acad. Sci. Contbr. articles to profl. jours. Home: 4318 Grand St Western Springs IL 60558 Office: 550 W Webster Chicago IL 60614

MARTIN, JOHN EDWARD, JR., chem. co. exec.; b. Wheeling, W.Va., July 5, 1947; s. John Edward and Nancy (Ayres) M.; B.S., Temple U., 1971; m. Nina Claire Smith, Aug. 30, 1968; children—Derek, Ross. Mktg. communications specialist Betz Labs., Trevose, Pa., 1971-74; v.p. mktg. Martin Planning, Inc., Phila., 1974-76; mktg. communications supr. Gas Group, Air Products & Chems., Inc., Allentown, Pa., 1976-79; dir. mktg. communications Dow Corning Corp., Midland, Mich., 1979—; mem. Dow Corning Polit. Action Com.; communications cons. Expando Seal. Inc., Spring House, Pa. Bd. dirs., com. chmn. IVB Phila. nolG Classic, 1974—. Served to capt. U.S. Army, 1969-7i. Recipient Objectives and Results award Am. Bus. Press, 1980; Effie award Am. Mktg. Assn., 1980. Mem. Assn. Nat. Advertisers, Bus. Profl. Advt. Assn. (Gold and Silver Pro-Communications awards), Bus. Publs. Audit, Inc.. Am. Advt. Fedn., Mich. Advt. Alliance. Republican. Roman Catholic. Club: Midland Country. Office: Box 1767 Midland MI 48640

MARTIN, LUTHER WASHBURN, broadcasting co. exec.; b. Wichita, Kan., July 31, 1919; s. Luther and Mabel St. Clair (Washburn) M.; grad. high sch.; m. Jeanne Frances Reynolds, Dec. 24, 1939; children—Lynn, Judy (Mrs. Robert L. Miers), Tara (Mrs. George W. Calhoun), Kurt, Marta (Mrs. Bob Ward). Ordained to Ministry Ch. of Christ, 1941; staff engr. sta. KWTO, Springfield, Mo., 1938-45; dir. engring. stas. WGAA, WRLD, Cedartown, West Point, Ga., 1945-47; owner, gen. mgr. sta. KTTR, Rolla, Mo., 1947-68; v.p. sta. KALV, Martin Broadcasting Corp., Alva, Okla., 1968—, sta. KVLH, Garvin County Broadcasting, Inc., Pauls Valley, Okla., 1973—. Vice pres. Triad Printing Corp., Rolla, 1960-70, chmn. bd., 1970-77; sec.-treas. Show-Me Electronics, Inc., Rolla. Radio cons. engr. FCC, Washington, 1945-47. Mem. nat. council Fla. Coll. at Temple Terrace. County chmn. Phelps County Republican Party, 1966-70, 76—; mem. Phelps County Rep. Central Com., 1966—. Recipient Boss of Year award Rolla Jr. C. of C., 1967; also numerous pub. service honors, Rolla. Mem. Soc. Broadcast Engrs. (sr.), Phelps County Hist. Soc. (life). Club: Optimists. Staff writer Searching the

Scriptures, 1965—; contbr. numerous articles religious jours. Home: 707 Salem Ave Rolla MO 65401 Office: 1006 Pine St Rolla MO 65401

MARTIN, LYNN MORLEY, congresswoman; b. Chgo., Dec. 26, 1939; d. Lawrence William and Helen (Hall) Morley; B.A., U. Ill., 1960. Tchr. public schs., DuPage-Winnebago County, 1963-69; mem. Winnebago County Bd., 1972-76; mem. Ill. Ho. of Reps., 1976-78, Ill. Senate, 1978-80; mem. 97th Congress from Ill. Mem. Phi Beta Kappa. Republican. Office: 1318 E State St Rockford IL 61108

MARTIN, MARVIN, editor; b. South Bend, Ind., June 19, 1926; s. Herbert and Esther (Zhiss) M.; B.A. in English, Roosevelt U., 1951; m. Gloria Loden, Sept. 9, 1967; children—Michael, Andrea, Joshua, Jessica. Asst. advt. mgr. W.D. Allen Co., Chgo., 1951; advt. account salesman Chgo. Daily News, 1951-56; advt. copywriter Bastian-Blessing Co., Chgo., 1956-60; editor World Book Ency., Chgo., 1960-62; with Ency. Brit., Inc., Chgo., 1962—, asst. editor, 1962-68, editor Brit. Jr. Ency., 1968—; free-lance writer, editorial cons. Pres. Oscar Mayer Sch. Edn. Council, Chgo., 1980-81. Served with Ordnance Corps, U.S. Army, 1944-46; PTO. Mem. Assn. Supervision and Curriculum Devel., Nat. Council Social Studies. Home: 2113 N Dayton St Chicago IL 60614 Office: 425 N Michigan Ave Chicago IL 60611

MARTIN, MAXINE GLASGOW, ednl. adminstr.; b. Hodges, Ala., May 1, 1916; d. Kemper Talmadge and Lela Ross (Tompkins) Glasgow; B.S., Florence State U., 1951; cert. teaching U. Ala., 1968; M.A., U. Ala., 1968; m. Richard William Martin, Aug. 8, 1973. Tchr. 1st grade, public schs., Red Bay, Ala., 1936-39, 4th grade, public schs., Bear Creek, Ala., 1939-65; reading supr. Phillips High Sch., Bear Creek, 1965-73; reading dir. Keeneyville Sch. Dist. 20, Hanover Park, Ill., 1974—. Mem. Internat. Reading Assn., Ill. Reading Assn., Parent-Tchr. Orgn., Ill. Ednl. Assn., Keeneyville Ednl. Assn., NEA, Delta Kappa Gamma. Mem. Ch. of Christ. Home: 1348 Beverly Ln Streamwood IL 60103 Office: 5208 Arlington Circle Hanover Park IL 60103

MARTIN, REX, bus. exec.; b. Elkhart, Ind., Oct. 4, 1951; s. Lee and Geraldine Faith Martin; student Albion Coll., 1970-72; B.A. in English, Ind. U., 1974. Field salesman NIBCO S.W., Houston, 1975-76; prodn. supr. NIBCO Inc., La Junta, Colo., 1977, sales mgr. plumbing products, Elkhart, 1978, dir.; pres. PVF Mktg., Inc., Columbus, Ohio, 1979—, chmn. bd., 1978—; plant mgr. Middlebury div. Nibco, Inc. (Ind.), 1981—, also dir.; dir. PVF Mktg., Inc. Mem. Ind. U. Alumni Assn., Wellhouse Soc., Culver Legion. Club: Elks. Home: 131 Burrell Dr Elkhart IN 46516 Office: PO Box 1218 Middlebury IN 46540

MARTIN, ROBERT ALFRED, iron co. exec.; b. West Orang, N.J., Aug. 28, 1931; s. Arthur Dona and Tilsey Celia (Cornish) M.; B.A., Upsala Coll., 1962; m. I. Margaref Caruso, Oct. 19, 1952; children—Jo Ellen, Patrice, Mary Jane, Guy Louis, Susan. Service rep. Public Service E & G, East Orange, N.J., 1950-62; mgmt. cons. Proudfoot, Inc., Chgo., Naus & Newlyn, Paoli, Pa., 1962-66; dir. performance audit Republic Indsl. Corp., N.Y.C., 1966-69; v.p. ops. Kaynar, Inc., Fullerton, Calif., 1969-72; exec. v.p. Cold Forming Specialities, Fullerton, 1972-73; v.p., gen. mgr. Valley Mould & Iron, Chgo., 1973—. Chmn. fin. com., mem. exec. com. South Chicago Community Hosp., 1978—; bd. dirs. YMCA, 1975-79. Served with U.S. Army, 1952-54. Mem. Am. Iron and Steel Inst., Am. Mgmt. Assn., Soc. Aerospace Process Engrs., Rubber Plastics Group, Battelle Cold Forming Group, Ill. Mfg. Assn., East Side C. of C. (adv. com. 1976—), South Chicago C. of C. (indsl. com. 1978-79). Republican. Roman Catholic. Clubs: Exec. (Chgo.); Republican Nat. Com.; Nat. Travel. Office: 108th St and Calumet River Chicago IL 60617

MARTIN, ROBERT EDWARD, architect; b. Dodge City, Kan., Mar. 17, 1928; s. Emry and Alice Jane (Boyce) M.; student McPherson Coll., 1947-48, U. Cin., 1948-54; children—Lynn, Amy, Blaine. Mem. firm Samborn, Steketee, Otis & Evans, Inc., 1957; partner firm Schauder & Martin Architects, Toledo, 1958-73; prin. Collaborative, Inc., architects, engrs., landscape architects, 1973—. Mem. Planning Commn. City of Toledo, 1971-74, mem. Bd. Bldg. Standards City of Toledo, 1967—; mem. Citizens Adv. Fire Commn., Toledo, 1974—; mem. Urban Area Citizens Adv. Com. Toledo Met. Area Council Govts., 1977-80; mem. Toledo Bd. Zoning Appeals. Served with USAF, 1954-56. Mem. Architects Soc. Ohio (treas. 1970-71, pres. 1975), AIA (treas. Toledo chpt. 1966), Toledo Artists Club, NW Ohio Watercolor Soc. (treas. 1978-80). Mem. Ch. of Brethren. Elk. Club: Sylvania Country. Home: 5119 Regency Dr Toledo OH 43615 Office: 1647 S Cove Blvd Toledo OH 43606

MARTIN, SANDY JEAN, advt. agy. exec.; b. St. Louis, Jan. 29, 1949; d. Frank John and Vivian Florine (Rathbone) M.; B.S., U. Mo., 1969; postgrad. Meramac Coll., 1969-70. Music dir., program dir., producer Sta.-KMOX, St. Louis, 1965-70; sta. mgr. Sta. KGRV/KKSS, St. Louis, 1970-75; gen. mgr., dir. ops. Sta.-KUDL-AM-FM, Kansas City, Mo., 1975-77; partner, v.p. Pasternak-Higbee Advt., Kansas City, Mo., 1977—. Bd. dirs. Theatre League Assn., Kansas City, Lyric Opera, Kansas City, Cystic Fibrosis, Kansas City. Recipient Outstanding Achievement award Cystic Fibrosis Found., 1980, Heart Assn., 1981; Service award Cystic Fibrosis, 1980, 81; Alsac Hnor award St. Jude Hosp., 1971. Mem. Am. Women in Radio and TV (dir. 1977-80, Account Exec. of Yr. 1980), Kansas City Advt. Club, St. Louis Advt. Club, Media Exchange, Am. Mktg. Assn., Am. Notary Assn., Internat. Platform Assn., Am. Bus. Women Assn., Fashion Group, Am. Soc. Notaries, Mo. Broadcasters Assn., Kansas City C. of C. Jewish. Office: 7720 Ward Pkwy Kansas City MO 64114

MARTIN, SHIRLEY WHITCHURCH, home economist; b. Centralia, Ill., Sept. 29, 1936; d. Harry Robert and Lula Ann (King) Whitchurch; A.A., Centralia Jr. Coll., 1956; B.S., So. Ill. U., 1958, M.S., 1969; m. Bob J. Martin, Oct. 29, 1977. Home adv. Randolph County Extension Service, Sparta, Ill., 1958-63; home adv. Franklin County Extension Service, Benton, Ill., 1963-65, area resource devel. adv., 1965-74; program specialist in home econs. U. Ill. State Staff, Benton, 1974—. Chmn., Sparta Beautification, 1962-68; tchr., music dir. Zion Hill Baptist Ch., 1954-76. Recipient Job Corps award, 1968, Rural Service award OEO, 1969; honored by Shirley Whitchurch Day, Sta. WHCO, Sparta, 1963. Nat. Assn. Extension Home Economists (conv. chmn. 1969), Am. Home Econs. Assn., Ill. Home Econs. Assn., Adult Edn. Assn., Epsilon Sigma Phi (sec.-treas., Disting. Service award 1972, Leadership award 1979), Gamma Sigma Delta. Home: 1605 E Main St Benton IL 62812 Office: 901 W Washington St Benton IL 62812

MARTIN, THOMAS LYLE, JR., univ. pres.; b. Memphis, Sept. 26, 1921; s. Thomas Lyle and Malvina (Rucks) M.; B.E.E., Rensselaer Poly. Inst., 1942, M.E.E., 1948, Dr. Engring., 1967; Ph.D., Stanford, 1951; m. Helene Hartley, June 12, 1943; children—Michele Marie, Thomas Lyle III. Prof. elec. engring. U. N.Mex., 1948-53; prof. engring. U. Ariz., 1953-63, dean engring., 1958-63; dean engring. U. Fla., Gainesville, 1963-66, So. Meth. U., Dallas, 1966-74; pres. Ill. Inst. Tech., Chgo., 1974—; dir. Stewart-Warner Co., Inland Steel Co., Cherry Elec. Products Corp., Hyatt Internat., Amsted Industries, Commonwealth Edison Co., Sundstrand Corp., Kemper Mut. Funds. Mem. Dallas-Fort Worth Regional Airport Bd., 1970-74. Bd. dirs. Museum Sci. and Industry, 1975—, Inst. Gas Tech. Served to capt. Signal Corps, AUS, 1943-46. Decorated Bronze Star medal. Fellow IEEE; mem. Nat. Acad. Engring., Sigma Xi, Tau Beta Pi, Eta Kappa Nu, Sigma Tau. Author: UHF Engineering, 1950; Electronic Circuits, 1955; Physical Basis for Electrical Engineering, 1957; Strategy for Survival, 1963; Electrons And Crystals, 1970; Malice in Blunderland, 1973. Home: 990 Lake Shore Dr Apt 19C Chicago IL 60611

MARTIN, WALTER TRAVIS, JR., health products mfg. co. exec.; b. Corpus Christi, Tex., Jan. 3, 1933; s. Walter Travis and Lucille (Lawrence) M.; B.S., E. Carolina Coll., 1955, M.A., 1961; Ed.D., Duke U., 1966; m. Yvonne Etter, June 13, 1959; children—Cyndie, Mimi, Laura Lynn. Public sch. tchr., 1958-66; pres. Hawkeye Inst. Tech., Waterloo, Iowa, 1966-75, Rend Lake Coll., Ina, Ill., 1975-78; registered rep. Investors Diversified Services, Mpls., 1978-79; CETA adminstr. Kankakee (Ill.) Community Coll., 1979-80; gen. mgr. Forever Living Products, Inc. of Tempe (Ariz.), Columbus, Ohio, 1980—. Mem. Am. Personnel and Guidance Assn., Coll. Personnel Assn., Am. Assn. Community and Jr. Colls., Am. Vocat. Assn., Phi Delta Kappa, Kappa Delta Pi. Presbyterian (elder). Club: Rotary. Address: Forever Living Products So Ohio 1438 Brenthaven Dr Columbus OH 43228

MARTIN, WAYNE MALLOTT, lawyer, real estate co. exec.; b. Chgo., Jan. 9, 1950; B.A., Drake U., 1972; J.D., De Paul U., 1977; m. JoAnn Giordano, Mar. 1978. Admitted to Ill. bar, 1978; sales dir., atty., financing Inland Real Estate Corp., Chgo., Oak Brook, then Palatine, Ill., 1977—; loan officer Clyde Savs. & Loan Assn., Chgo., 1972-75, Am. Nat. Bank, Chgo., 1976-77. Mem. Am., Ill., Chgo. bar assns. Home: 219 Golfview Terr Palatine IL 60067 Office: Inland Real Estate Corp 829 E Dundee Rd Palatine IL 60067

MARTIN, WILFRED SAMUEL, mgmt. cons.; b. Adamsville, Pa., June 11, 1910; s. Albert W. and Elizabeth (Porter) M.; B.S., Iowa State U., 1930; M.S., U. Cin., 1938; m. Elizabeth Myers, July 9, 1938; children—Peter, Judith (Mrs. Peter Kleinman), Nancy (Mrs. Richard Foss), Paula. Chem. engr. process devel. dept. Procter & Gamble Co., Cin., 1930-50, mgr. drug products mfg., 1950-51, asso. dir. chem. div., 1952-53, dir. product devel., soap products div., 1953-63, mgr. mfg. and products devel. Food Products div., 1963-71, sr. dir. research and devel., 1971-75; mgmt. cons., 1975—. Mem. Wyoming (Ohio) Bd. Edn., 1961-69, pres., 1965-68. Bd. dirs. Indsl. Research Inst., 1964-68, v.p., 1968-69, pres., 1970-71; chmn. trustee Ohio Presbyn. Homes, Columbus, Ohio, 1959-69, 73-77; vice chmn. bd. trustees Pikeville (Ky.) Coll., 1973-76, 80—, chmn. bd. trustees, 1976-78, mem., 1980—. Adv. council Clarkson Coll., Potsdam, N.Y., 1975—. Fellow AAAS; mem. Am. Chem. Soc., Am. Inst. Chem. Engrs., Soc. Chem. Industry, Am. Oil Chemist Soc., Engring. Soc. Cin. (dir. 1972-75), N.Y. Acad. Scis., Am. Mgmt. Assn. (research devel. council 1974—), Soc. Research Adminstrs. Club: Wyoming Golf (Cin.). Home: 504 Hickory Hill Ln Cincinnati OH 45215

MARTINDALE, DOUGLAS J, banker; b. Dayton, Ohio, Aug. 11, 1953; s. Charles Allyn and Joan Rosalynn (Trumpler) M.; B.B.A., U. Cin., 1976; m. Leondia Mary Edsall, May 20, 1978. With Gem Savs. Assn., Dayton, 1974—, 76—, project mgr. corp. planning, research and devel. dept., 1977—; speaker in field. Office: Gem Savs Assn Gem Plaza Dayton OH 45402

MARTINELLI, DAVID FORTUNATO, mfg. co. exec.; b. Chgo., Apr. 4, 1943; s. David Innocente and Inez Joan (Frigo) M.; B.S. in Polit. Sci., Loyola U., Chgo., 1966; m. Sandra L. Wiencek, Aug. 8, 1968. Mem. contract adminstrn. staff Hallicrafters Corp., Rolling Meadows, Ill., 1968-69, Gen. Time Corp., Rolling Meadows, 1969-70; adminstr. U. Chgo., 1971-74; sr. contract adminstr., nuclear contract adminstrn. Graver Tank & Mfg. Co., East Chicago, Ind., 1974-75; sr. coordinator Inst. Gas Tech., Chgo., 1975; mgr. contracts and def. contracts Blaw-Knox Foundry & Mill Machinery, East Chicago, 1976-79; contract mgr. U.S. Gypsum Co., Chgo., 1979; contract mgr. Tiger Equipment & Services Ltd., Chgo., 1980; mgr. contract adminstrn. Am. Pouch Food Co. Inc., Willowbrook, Ill., 1980; cons., sr. contract adminstr. Sonicraft, Inc., Chgo., 1980-81; v.p. govt. relations Land O' Frost, Lansing, Ill., 1981; cons. grant and contract adminstrn. and negotiations. Cert. profl. contracts mgr. Home and Office: 10153 S 87th Ave Palos Hills IL 60465

MARTINEZ, BETTY ELNORA, chem. co. exec.; b. Oklahoma City, Jan. 7, 1937; d. Jim and Jewell Frances Smith; B.S., Oklahoma City U., 1974, M.B.A., 1975; m. June 29, 1956 (div. July 1968). Pvt. booking agt. and bus. mgr., rock and roll bands, Okla., Colo., 1960-67; with Kerr McGee Corp., Oklahoma City, 1965—, accountant, 1974-76, solvent sales rep., from 1975, asso. sales rep. to 1981; in petrochem. sales No. Petrochem. Co., Des Plaines, Ill., 1981—. Del. Okla. Democratic Conv., 1972. Mem. M.B.A. Club Oklahoma City U. (pres. 1975), ACLU. Home: 529 Verde St Schaumburg IL 60194 Office: No Petrochem Co 2350 E Devon Ave Des Plaines IL

MARTINEZ, ELENA, psychiat. social worker; b. Havana, Cuba, Jan. 4, 1947; came to U.S., 1961, naturalized, 1974; d. Manuela (Duarte) M.; B.A., Mundelein Coll., Chgo., 1969; M.S.W., U. Ill., Chgo. Circle, 1974. Team leader I, Catholic Charities Chgo., 1970-76; psychiat. social worker children's div. Katharine Wright Clinic, Chgo., 1976-79, part-time 1979—; dir., planner Evanston (Ill.) Latinam. Assn., 1979-81; exec. dir. Transitional Living Programs, Inc., Chgo., 1981—; part-time psychiat. social worker St. Francis Hosp., Evanston, 1979; cons. in field, condr. workshops. Mem. Pres.'s Adv. Com. Women, 1980—; bd. dirs. Am. Spanish Inst., 1981—, Campfire, Inc., 1981—; del. Democratic Nat. Conv., 1980; chmn. Latinos for Jane Byrne for Mayor Com., 1978-79. Cath. Charities Chgo. scholar, 1972. Mem. Acad. Cert. Social Workers, Nat. Assn. Social Workers (chpt. del.), Progressive Assn. Latino Americans (dir. 1976—), Nat. Coalition Cuban Americans (dir. 1978—), Mental Health Assn. Greater Chgo. (dir. ednl. com. 1979—), Ill. Women's Polit. Caucus, Nat. Fedn. Dem. Women. Mem. Christian Ch. (Disciples of Christ). Home: 3925 N Claremont Ave Chicago IL 60618 Office: 1920 N Lincoln Ave Chicago IL 60614

MARTIN-REYNOLDS, JOANNE JANE, educator; b. Marshalltown, Iowa, Dec. 1, 1940; d. Ralph E. and Helen L. (Buschbom) Dougherty; B.A., U. No. Iowa, 1963; M.A., U. Kans., 1969; Ph.D., Bowling Green (Ohio) State U., 1977; m. Bill J. Reynolds, June 10, 1978; children—Dustin, Kevin. Tchr. French, Dist. 102 Schs., LaGrange Park, Ill., 1963-65, Lyons Twp. High Sch., LaGrange, 1965-67; grad. asst. dept. French, U. Kans., 1967; clin. supr. Bowling Green State U., 1973-77, asst. prof. edn., 1977-79, asso. prof. edn., 1980—; coordinator elem. student teaching program Bowling Green City Schs., 1976—; dir. Newbury Student Teaching Center, Toledo, 1974-76. Mem. ch. council St. Mark's Luth. Ch., 1980. Mem. Assn. for Supervision and Curriculum Devel., Assn. for Tchr. Edn., Ohio Assn. Supervision and Curriculum Devel. (v.p. 1979-80), Modern Lang. Tchrs. Assn., Kappa Delta Pi, Delta Kappa Gamma, Phi Delta Kappa. Democrat. Contbr. articles on edn. to profl. publs. Home: 471 Truman St Bowling Green OH 43402 Office: 529 Education Bldg Bowling Green State Univ Bowling Green OH 43403

MARTOCCIA, JOYCE SGRO, ednl. adminstr.; b. Cleve., Aug. 24, 1939; d. Santo M. and Johanna Mathilda (Lienerth) Sgro; B.A. in Bus. Edn. and German, Baldwin-Wallace Coll., 1959; M.A. in Guidance and Counseling, Case Western Res. U., 1967; M.A., John Carroll U., 1974; m. William R. Martoccia, Mar. 28, 1968; 1 son, Marc William. Legal sec. Van Aken, Arnold, Bond and Withers, Cleve., 1959-62; bus. tchr. Cleve. Pub. Schs., 1963-66, guidance and placement counselor high schs., 1966-73; adminstr., asst. prin., unit prin. Audubon Jr. High Sch., Cleve., 1973—; mem. accrediting team N. Central Assn. High Schs. and Colls. Fine arts chmn. Cleve. Ballet, 1976—; co-chmn. vols. Shaker Lakes Regional Nature Center, 1975—; mem. Cleve. Mus. Art; women's com. Cleve. Orch.; hon. v.p. Lincoln Jr. High Sch. PTA; adv. bd. John Carroll U.; vol. St. Luke's Hosp., 1980; vol. fundraising Am. Cancer Soc., Muscular Dystrophy Assn. Honored for best tutorial program in City of Cleve., 1975-78). Mem. Am., Ohio, N.E. Ohio (pres. 1976-77) personnel and guidance assns., Cleve. Council Adminstrs. and Suprs., Ohio, Nat. (commn. on profl. employment practices, co-author handbook 1977) assns. women deans, adminstrs. and counselors, Ohio Sch. Counselors Assn., Ohio Assn. Secondary Sch. Adminstrs., Indsl. Edn. Club of Cleve., Greater Cleve. Prins. Discussion Group (pres.), John Carroll U. Educators Alumni Assn. (pres., educators cons.), Delta Phi Alpha, Phi Delta Kappa, Alpha Delta Kappa. Republican. Roman Catholic. Home: 16125 Van Aken Blvd Shaker Heights OH 44120 Office: 1380 E 6th St Cleveland OH 44114

MARTZ, GEORGE E., lawyer; b. Indpls., Apr. 26, 1926; s. Joseph Arthur and Addie May (Hoss) M.; B.S., Ind. U., 1949, J.D., 1957; m. Patricia Lee Terry, Dec. 29, 1973; children by previous marriage—George E., Linda, Steven, Dennis, Christopher, Kimberly. Admitted to Ind. bar, U.S. Supreme Ct. bar, Ct. of Mil. Appeals bar, U.S. Dist. Ct. bar, Circuit Ct. of Appeals bar; practice law, Indpls., 1957—; chief pub. defender Marion County Criminal Ct., 1959-62; spl. trial dep. Marion County prosecutor's office, 1975-78. Served with USAAF, 1943-44, USAF, 1949-53. Mem. Am., Ind., Indpls. bar assns., Am., Ind. Trial Lawyers Assns., Am. Judicature Soc., Smithsonian Inst., Frat. Order Police (asso.), Phi Alpha Delta. Democrat. Presbyterian (elder). Mason (Shriner). Home: 9060 Stonegate Rd Indianapolis IN 46227 Office: 915 First Federal Bldg Indianapolis IN 46204

MARUSIN, STELLA LUCIE, chem. engr.; b. Prague, Czechoslovakia, Feb. 15, 1936; d. Jaroslav Karel and Bozena Anna (Reich) Vinduska; came to U.S., 1977; M.S. in Chem. Engring., Chem. Tech. U. Prague, 1960, M.S. in Ceramic Engring., 1971, Ph.D. in Silicate Scis., 1974; m. Alex David Marusin, Dec. 7, 1957; children—Stela Ellen, Lucie Diane. Head lab. PREFA, Prague, 1960-69; research scientist, head dept. bldg. materials Research and Devel. Inst. Bldg. Industries, Prague, 1969-76; sr. chemist Wiss, Janney, Elstner & Assos., Inc., Northbrook, Ill., 1978—. Mem. Am. Ceramic Soc., Nat. Inst. Ceramic Engrs., Am. Concrete Inst. (mem. coms.), Transp. Research Bd. (mem. coms.). Roman Catholic. Contbr. articles to profl. jours. Office: 330 Pfingsten Rd Northbrook IL 60062

MARUYAMA, HENRY HATSUO, product devel. engr.; b. Rocky Ford, Colo., Oct. 20, 1923; s. Zengoro and Koto (Awa) M.; student Santa Rosa (Calif.) Jr. Coll., 1942; B.S. in Physics, U. Mich., Ann Arbor, 1947; m. Haruko Okuda, June 23, 1957. Chemist, Pontiac Motor Car div. Gen. Motors Corp., 1958; tech. specialist engr. Engring. and Research Office, Chrysler Corp., Highland Park, Mich., 1958—. Served with inf. AUS, 1944-45. Decorated Bronze Star, Purple Heart. Mem. Soc. Automotive Engrs., Nat. Inventors Council, Oreg. Inventors Council, Internat. Platform Assn., VFW, Disabled Am. Vets. Democrat. Methodist. Inventor mech. devices, 1944—. Home: 5137 Buckingham Pl Troy MI 48098 Office: 12800 Lynn Townsend Dr Highland Park MI 48231

MARUYAMA, MAGOROH, anthropologist; b. 1929; B.A. in Math., U. Calif., Berkeley, 1951; postgrad. U. Munich, 1954-55, U. Heidelberg, 1955; Am.-Scandinavian Found. fellow, U. Copenhagen, 1955-57; Ph.D. (Swedish State fellow), U. Lund, 1959. Jr. research psychologist Inst. Human Devel., U. Calif., Berkeley, 1960-62; research asso. Inst. for Study Human Problems, Stanford U., 1962-64; community devel. specialist in Aleut villages in Alaska destroyed by tidal wave, 1964; sr. counselor Parks Job Corps Center, OEO, Pleasanton, Calif., 1965; asso. prof. psychology San Francisco State U., 1965-67; research asso. Lemberg Center for Study Violence, Brandeis U., 1967-69; vis. research fellow Culture and Mental Health Program, Social Sci. Research Inst., U. Hawaii, 1970-71; vis. prof. computer sci. and communication studies Antioch Coll., Yellow Springs, Ohio, 1971-72; prof. systems sci. Portland (Oreg.) State U., 1973-76; vis. prof. anthropology U. Ill., Urbana, 1976—; cons. Calif. Dept. Pub. Health, 1960-62, Calif. Dept. Mental Hygiene, 1963-64, Dept. Interior, 1964, OEO, 1966-67, Nat. Bur. Standards, 1971, U.S. C.E. Inst. for Water Resources, 1972-75, Canadian Fed. Ministry State for Urban Affairs, 1974-75, NASA, 1975. Fellow Am. Anthrop. Assn., AAAS; mem. Am. Planning Assn., Am. Psychol. Assn., Am. Sociol. Assn. Recipient Distinguished Article of Year award Am. Scientist, 1963; contbr. sci. articles to profl. jours. Home: PO Box 233 Champaign IL 61820 Office: Dept Anthropology U Ill Urbana IL 61801

MARVEL, RICHARD D., state legislator; b. Hastings, Nebr., Dec. 8, 1917; student U. Leipzig, (Germany); A.B., Hastings Coll., 1940; M.A., U. Nebr., 1960, Ph.D., 1966; m. Oline Ida Lindermann, May 17, 1941; 2 children. Prof. polit. sci. Nebr. Wesleyan U., also chmn. dept.; mem. Nebr. Legislature, 1950—, speaker, 1979-81. Served with U.S. Army, World War II; PTO. Mem. Am. Legion, VFW. Club: Masons. Address: 1240 N Lexington Hastings NE 68901*

MARVIN, DANIEL E., JR., univ. pres.; b. East Stroudsburg, Pa., Apr. 25, 1938; s. Daniel E. and Hazel E. M.; student Susquehanna U., 1956-58; B.S. in Edn., East Stroudsburg State Coll., 1960; M.S., Ohio U., 1962; Ph.D., Va. Poly. Inst., 1966; m. Maxine James, June 15, 1958; children—Brian, Laurie, Amy. Grad. asst. Ohio U., 1960-61, instr. in biology, 1961-62; asst. prof. biology Radford Coll., 1962-67, prof., dean div. natural scis., 1967-68, v.p. acad. affairs, 1968-70, acting pres., 1968-69; asso. dir. Va. State Council Higher Edn., 1970-72, dir., 1972-77; pres. Eastern Ill. U., 1977—; mem. Nat. Adv. Council on Extension and Continuing Edn.; mem. Resource Center for Planned Change; mem. Am. Council on Edn. Commn. on Acad. Affairs. Contbr. articles on biology, higher edn. in Va. to profl. jours.; author Va. Plan for Higher Edn. Office: Eastern Ill U Charleston IL 61920*

MARVIN, PHILIP, fin. analyst, indsl. engr., author; b. Troy, N.Y., May 1, 1916; s. George G. and Marjorie C. Marvin; B.Indsl. Engring., Rensselaer Poly. Inst., 1937; M.B.A., Ind. U., 1951, D.B.A., 1951; LL.B., LaSalle Extension U., 1954; Sc.D. (hon.) Inst. Applied Research, 1974; cert. Inst. Chartered Fin. Analysts, 1963; m. Grace Ernestine Meerbach, Aug. 22, 1942. Dir. chem. metall. engring. Bendix Aviation Corp., 1943-44; dir. research and devel. Baso, Inc., 1945-51; cons. Booz, Allen & Hamilton, 1952; dir. Basic Research, Inc., 1952-54; v.p. Commonwealth Engring. Co., Dayton, Ohio, 1952-54, dir., 1952-54; dir. mgr. Am. Mgmt. Assn., N.Y.C., 1956-64; sr. v.p. and dir. Dunlap & Assos., Inc., Greenwich, Conn., 1964-65; pres., dir. Clark, Cooper, Field, and Wohl, Inc., N.Y.C., 1964-65; prof.

profl. devel. and bus. adminstrn. U. Cin., 1965-79, dean profl. devel., 1965-73, prof. mgmt., 1979—. Fellow Fin. Analysts Fedn., Inst. Dir. of London; mem. N.Y. Soc. Security Analysts, Nat. Acad. TV Arts and Scis., IEEE, Am. Def. Preparedness Assn., Fin. Mgmt. Assn., Newcomen Soc. N.Am. Author books on mgmt., latest being: Fundamentals of Effective R and D Development, 1973; Managing Your Career, 1974; Managing Your Successful Career, 1978; Executive Time Management, 1980; patentee elec. control devices and gas plating process. Home: 2750 Weston Ridge Dr Cincinnati OH 45239 Office: U Cincinnati Cincinnati OH 45221

MARX, GERALD VINCENT, mfg. co. exec.; b. Westbury, N.Y., July 23, 1926; s. Francis John and Mildred (Keller) M.; B.A., U. Buffalo, 1948; m. Mildred Rieman, Sept. 11, 1948; children—Barbara M., Gerald Vincent, Diane R. Field sales rep. William Wrigley Jr. Co., Buffalo, 1948-52, regional sales mgr., St. Louis, 1956-68, nat. mktg. mgr., Toronto, Ont., Can., 1968-72, Midwest area sales mgr., Chgo., 1972-79, dir. sales tng., Schaumburg, Ill., 1979—. Served with USN, 1944. Mem. Am. Soc. for Tng. and Devel. (regional v.p. sales tng. div. 1980-81). Roman Catholic. Clubs: Lions, Rotary, Toastmasters (v.p. adminstrn. 1980-81). Office: 1827 Walden Office Sq Suite 304 Schaumburg IL 60195

MARX, THOMAS GEORGE, economist; b. Trenton, N.J., Oct. 25, 1943; s. George Thomas and Ann (Szymanski) M.; B.S. summa cum laude, Rider Coll., 1969; Ph.D., Wharton Sch., U. Pa., 1973; m. Arlene May Varga, Aug. 23, 1969; children—Melissa Ann, Thomas Jeffrey. Fin. analyst Am. Cyanamid Co., Trenton, N.J., 1968-68; economist FTC, Washington, 1973; econ. cons. Foster Assos., Inc., Washington, 1974-77; sr. economist Gen. Motors, Detroit, 1977-79, mgr. indsl. econs., 1980—, dir. econ. policy studies, 1981—; mem. faculty Temple U., U. Pa., 1972-73; adj. prof. Wayne State U., 1981. Served with USAF, 1961-65. Mem. Nat. Econs. Club, Am. Econ. Assn., Nat. Assn. Bus. Economists, Detroit Area Bus. Economists, Econ. Soc. Mich., So. Econ. Assn., Western Econ. Assn. Roman Catholic. Asso. editor Bus. Econs., 1980-81; editorial bd. Akron Jour. Bus. and Econs., 1981—; contbr. articles to profl. jours. Home: 4100 Shore Crest Dr West Bloomfield MI 48033 Office: 3044 W Grand Blvd Detroit MI 48202

MASCHO, GEORGE LEROY, educator; b. Warsaw, N.Y., Feb. 5, 1925; s. Clayton Leroy and Dorothy Emma (Bailey) M.; B.Ed., SUNY-Geneseo, 1948; M.A., Stanford U., 1950; Ed.D., Ind. U., 1961. Tchr., Ontario (N.Y.) Jr. High Sch., 1948-49, Burris Lab. Sch., Muncie, Ind., 1950-61; faculty Ball State U., Muncie, 1961—, prof. edn., 1967—. Bd. dirs., treas. United Day Care Center, 1977—; mem. nat. com. developing Head Start program, 1965-66. Served with inf. U.S. Army, 1943-46. Mem. Nat. Assn. for Edn. Young Children, Ind. Assn. for Edn. Young Children (chmn. legis. com. 1968-70), Assn. for Childhood Edn., Ind. Arabian Horse Assn. (dir. 1968-73), Phi Delta Kappa. Republican. Contbr. articles to profl. jours. Reviewer: Curriculum Adv. Service in Elem. Math., 1964-66. Home: Apt 2-211 4501 Wheeling St Muncie IN 47304 Office: Dept Edn TC 816 Ball State U Muncie IN 47306

MASCHOFF, JANET BRANDT, sch. adminstr.; b. St. Louis, Aug. 24, 1937; d. Oliver William and Esther Rose (Koehler) Brandt; B.S. in Edn., Concordia Tchrs. Coll., River Forest, Ill., 1959, M.A. in Edn., 1967; Edn. Specialist, So. Ill. U., 1981; m. Karl Edgar Maschoff, June 10, 1967. Tchr., prin. Lutheran Schs., N.J. and Mo., 1959-66; with Hazelwood Sch. Dist., St. Louis County, 1967—, instructional specialist, 1971-78, prin., 1981—. Mem. Assn. Supervision and Curriculum Devel., Internat. Reading Assn., Nat. Council Tchrs. Math., Am. Ednl. Research Assn., Nat. Assn. Elem. Sch. Prins., Delta Kappa Gamma, Phi Delta Kappa, Kappa Delta Pi. Lutheran. Contbr. to ednl. materials. Home: 2280 Derhake Rd Florissant MO 63033 Office: 2324 Redman Ave Saint Louis MO 63136

MASEK, RAYMOND JOHN, lawyer; b. Cleve., Sept. 1, 1946; s. Raymond Clement and Rita Ann (Kalous) M.; B.B.A., Cleve. State U., 1969, J.D., 1975. Internal auditor, asst. to acctg. mgr. Procter & Gamble Co., Balt. and Cin., 1969-71; cost/fin. analyst Ford Motor Co., Toledo and Cleve., 1971-75; corp. auditor Harris Corp., Cleve., 1975-77; sr. corp. auditor Midland-Ross Corp., Cleve., 1977-78; mgr. internat. audits, corp. counsel Reliance Electric Co., Cleve., 1978—; admitted to Ohio bar, 1977. Named Outstanding Coop. Edn. Student in Sch. Bus., Cleve. State U., 1969. Mem. Cleve. State U. Bus. Alumni Assn. (dir. 1979-82), Bar Assn. of Greater Cleve., Ohio Bar Assn., Inst. Internal Auditors. Home: 2250 Par Ln Willoughby Hills OH 44094 Office: 29325 Chagrin Blvd Pepper Pike OH 44122

MASEK, TERRENCE JAMES, personnel exec.; b. Joliet, Ill., June 24, 1950; s. Glenn James and Helen Margaret (Gleason) M.; B.A. with honors, U. Ill., 1972, M.Ed., 1974. Psychiat. asst. St. Joseph's Hosp., Joliet, Ill., 1973; personal lines underwriter Kemper Ins. Co., Chgo., 1974-75; vocat. counselor Skills, Inc., Moline, Ill., 1975-76, job placement specialist, 1976-78, dir. job placement/dir. pub. relations, 1978-79; dir. personnel and public relations Illini Hosp., Silvis, Ill., 1979—. Publicity asst. local Boy Scouts Am., 1977-79. Ill. State scholar, 1968. Mem. Ill. Rehab. Assn. (treas. Spoon River chpt. 1977-78, pres. job placement div. 1979-80), Rock Island Jaycees, Nat. Rehab. Assn., Am. Soc. Personnel Adminstrn., Nat. Assn. Student Personnel Adminstrs., Am. Soc. Hosp. Public Relations, Am. Soc. Hosp. Personnel Adminstrn., Mensa, Psi Chi. Home: 4503 12th Ave Apt 5 Moline IL 61265 Office: 801 13th Ave Silvis IL 61282

MASICA, CHARLOTTE ELIZABETH, fin. exec.; b. Mpls., Nov. 28, 1926; d. Joseph John and Agnes Viola (Smykal) Mangen; diploma Am. Savs. and Loan Inst., 1948; m. Michael Donald Masica, Oct. 2, 1948; children—Stephen, Lisa, Michael, Christina. Asst. treas. new accounts Midwest Fed. Savs., Mpls., 1966-69, asst. v.p. new accounts, 1969-71, 1st v.p. service corps., 1978-79, exec. v.p., sec., mng. officer, 1979—, also dir.; v.p., sec./controller Green Tree Corp., Mpls., 1971-79. Named Top Ten Bus. Woman of 1980, Am. Bus. Women's Assn. Mem. Nat. Forum for Exec. Women, Am. Bus. Women's Assn. (v.p. dist. V, 1981-82), Nat. Assn. Female Execs. Roman Catholic. Home: 21 Balsam Ln Plymouth MN 55441 Office: 801 Nicollet Mall Minneapolis MN 55402

MASKREY, JOYCE ELOISE, real estate co. exec.; b. Des Moines, Apr. 11, 1944; d. Earl Raymond and Bernice Elizabeth (Taylor) Wagner; B.A. in Journalism, Drake U., 1967; M.S.T., Drake U., 1970; m. Richard Maskrey, Apr. 11, 1970; children—Chris, Chad, Natalie Jo. Advt. copywriter Sta. KCBC, Des Moines, 1967-68; writer Iowa Credit Union League, Des Moines, 1968; tchr. Fed. Tchr. Corps Program, 1968-69; tng. officer, manpower coordinator, employee counselor Greater Opportunities, 1969-73; pharm. sales rep. Lederle Labs., Des Moines, 1973-75; pharm. salesman Rachelle Labs., Des Moines, 1975-81; pres., broker So. Realty, Des Moines, 1977—; owner, pres. R & J Enterprises, R & J Trucking, R & J Snow Removal, R & J Lawn Aid (all Des Moines). Active local PTA, Des Moines; Mem. Drug Travelers Assn., Homebuilders Assn., Iowa Assn. Realtors, South Des Moines C. of C. Office: 1123 SW Army Post Rd Des Moines IA 50315

MASON, EARL JAMES, JR., physician; b. Marion, Ind., Aug. 26, 1923; s. Earl James and Grace A. (Leer) M.; student Marion Coll., 1940-41; B.S. in Medicine, Ind. U., 1944, A.B. in Chemistry, 1947, M.A. in Bacteriology, 1947; Ph.D. in Microbiology, Ohio State U., 1950; M.D., Western Res. U., 1954; m. Eileen Gursansky, Dec. 2, 1967. Teaching asst. dept. bacteriology Ind. U., 1945-47; research fellow depts. ophthalmology and bacteriology Ohio State U., Columbus, 1947-48, teaching asst. dept. bacteriology, 1948-50; Crile research scholar Western Res. U., Cleve., 1951-53; Damon Runyon cancer research fellow dept. pathology Western Res. U.-Cleve. City Hosp., 1951-56; dept. chief dept. pathology USPHS Hosp., San Francisco, 1956-58; fellow pathology U. Tex. Postgrad. Sch. Medicine, M.D. Anderson Hosp. and Tumor Inst., Houston, 1958-59; asst. prof. dept. pathology Baylor U. Coll. Medicine, 1959-60; asst. pathologist Jefferson Davis Hosp., 1959-60; asst. pathologist Michael Reese Hosp. and Med. Center, Chgo., 1960-61; asso. dir. dept. pathology, dir. dept. biol. scis. Mercy Hosp., 1960-65; dir. labs. St. Mary Med. Center, Gary and Hobart, Ind., 1965—; asso. prof. pathology Chgo. Med. Sch., 1966—; clin. prof. pathology Ind. U. Med. Sch., 1976—. Diplomate Am. Bd. Pathology, Am. Bd. Nuclear Medicine. Mem. Coll. Am. Pathologists, Am. Assn. Pathologists and Bacteriologists, Am. Soc. Clin. Pathologists, Internat. Acad. Pathologists, Am. Soc. Exptl. Pathology, Am. Assn. Cancer Research, Am. Assn. Blood Banks, Am. Soc. Hematology, Am. Acad. Dermatology, Soc. Nuclear Medicine, Lake County Med. Soc., Am. Soc. Cytology, Sigma Xi. Research on cellular origin of antibodies and virus-cell interactions. Home: PO Box 485 7 Summit Rd Ogden Dunes Portage IN 46368 Office: 540 Tyler St Gary IN 46402

MASON, GARY MAC, photojournalist; b. Coffeyville, Kans. June 17, 1936; s. Albert P. and Mildred E.M.; B.S., Emporia State Tchrs. Coll., 1958; M.S., 1967; m. Sarah Price, Aug. 17, 1963; children—Samuel A., Heather A. Tchr., dir. photog. services Emporia State Tchrs. Coll., 1958-63; vol. tchr. Navajo Nation, 1963-64; spl. collections librarian Emporia State Tchrs. Coll., 1964-68; asst. prof. photojournalism U. Kans., Lawrence, 1968-75, dir. photojournalism, 1975—, asso. prof., 1979—. Cubmaster, Boy Scouts. Served with USAR, 1956-62. Mem. Nat. Press Photographers Am., Sigma Delta Chi. Democrat. Episcopalian. Author: A Bibliography of William Allen White, 2 vols., 1968; Lyric Images (photographs), 1963. Home: Rural Route 3 Baldwin KS 66006 Office: Flint Hall Lawrence KS 66045

MASON, HAROLD MANFRED, ins. broker; b. Vienna, Austria, Oct. 15, 1946; came to U.S., 1946, naturalized, 1964; s. Harold Floyd and Margarete Katherine (Moslinger) M.; student Rockhurst Coll., Kansas City, Mo., 1973-74; m. Donna Sue Paulsell, Feb. 8, 1969; children—Heath Michael, Brian Daniel. Various positions in sales, 1968-69; ins. salesman, 1969—; pres. A.P.P.S., Inc., Raytown, Mo., 1975—; tchr. ins. classes. Pres. St. Stephen Lutheran Ch., Liberty, Mo., 1978-80. Served with USAF, 1965-68; Vietnam. Mem. Nat. Assn. Life Underwriters, Profl. Ins. Agts. Assn., Nat. Assn. Realtors, Clay-Platte Life Underwriters Assn. (past pres.), Jounson County Bd. Realtors, Raytown C. of C., Liberty Jaycees (pres. 1978; numerous awards 1974—), Raytown Jaycees. Home: 121 N Fairview St Liberty MO 64068 Office: PO Box 16598 6530 Raytown Rd Suite B Raytown MO 64133

MASON, RICHARD LEE, coll. pres.; b. Wayne County, Ill., Apr. 25, 1937; s. Ross and Mildred M.; B.S., Eastern Ill. U., 1959; M.S., 1966, Specialist in Edn., 1969; m. Shirley Fitch, June 23, 1962; children—Lisa, Leslie. Tchr., coach Cisne Elementary Sch., 1959-67; prin. Stillman Valley Sch., Stillman Valley, Ill., 1967-68; occupational counselor Olney (Ill.) Central Coll., 1969-70; pres. Frontier Community Coll., Fairfield, Ill., 1970—; research specialist Eastern Ill. U., 1968-69. Commr., Fairfield Little League, 1974—; mem. Energy Conservation Commn. Study, 1978. Recipient Disting. Service citation Dept. Def., 1973, Dedicated Service award Ill. Eastern Community Colls., 1980. Mem. U.S.A. Adult Edn. Assn., Public Adult and Continuing Educators, Ill. Adult Edn. Assn., Phi Delta Kappa. Baptist. Clubs: Rotary, Kiwanis. Contbr. articles to profl. jours. Home: Rural Route 3 Fairfield IL 62837 Office: Rural Route 1 Fairfield IL 62837

MASOTTI, LOUIS HENRY, educator; b. N.Y.C., May 16, 1934; s. Henry and Angela Catherine (Turi) M.; A.B., Princeton U., 1956; M.A., Northwestern U., 1961, Ph.D., 1964; m. Iris Patricia Leonard, Aug. 28, 1958 (div. May 1981); children—Laura Lynn, Andrea Anne. Fellow, Nat. Center for Edn. in Politics, 1962; asst. prof. polit. sci. Case Western Res. U., Cleve., 1963-67, asso. prof., 1967-69, dir. Civil Violence Research Center, 1968-69; sr. Fulbright lectr. Johns Hopkins U. Center for Advanced Internat. Studies, Bologna, Italy, 1969-70; asso. prof. Northwestern U., Evanston, Ill., 1970-72, prof. polit. sci., urban affairs and policy research, 1972—, dir. Center for Urban Affairs, 1971-80, Program in Public and Not-For-Profit Mgmt., Kellogg Sch. Mgmt., 1979-80. Cons. to numerous publs. and govtl. agys.; vis. asso. prof. U. Wash., summer 1969; exec. dir. Mayor Jane Byrne Transition Com., Chgo., 1979. Research dir. Carl Stokes for Mayor of Cleve., 1967; mem. Cleveland Heights Bd. Edn., 1967-69; adviser to various congl. and gubinatorial campaigns, Ohio, Ill., N.J. Served to lt. USNR, 1956-59. Recipient Distinguished Service award Cleve. Jaycees, 1967; numerous fed. and found. research grants, 1963—. Mem. Am. Polit. Sci. Assn., Midwest Polit. Sci. Assn. (v.p. 1976-77). Author: Education and Politics in Suburbia, 1967; Shootout in Cleveland, 1969; A Time to Burn?, 1969; Suburbia in Transition, 1973; The New Urban Politics, 1976; The City in Comparative Perspective, 1976; co-editor: Metropolis in Crisis, 1968, 2d edit., 1971; Riots and Rebellion, 1968; The Urbanization of the Suburbs, 1973; After Daley: Chicago Politics in Transition, 1981; editor Edn. and Urban Soc., 1968-71, Urban Affairs Quar., 1973-80. Home: 200 E Delaware Pl Chicago IL 60611

MASSEY, CURTIS LEE, ins. co. exec.; b. Huntsville, Tenn., Oct. 30, 1939; s. Oscar L. and Julia M. (Brown) M.; extension student U. Md., 1958-59; M.S. in Mgmt., M.I.T., 1974; m. Linda L. Frizzell, Feb. 18, 1961; children—Lori Lynn, Jason Todd. Asst. sales and office mgr. N. Am. Van Lines, Terre Haute, Ind., 1961-63; br. mgr. Gen. Fin. Corp., Terre Haute, 1964-65; with Blue Cross and Blue Shield Ind., 1966—, sr. v.p. ins. services, Indpls., 1975-79, sr. v.p. govt. bus., 1979—; past bd. dirs. Marion County Mental Health Assn. Active local United Fund, Jr. Achievement. Served with USAF, 1956-60. Recipient various appreciation and service awards. Mem. Soc. Sloan Fellows, M.I.T. Alumni Assn., Ind. C. of C., Indpls. C. of C. Club: Columbia (Indpls.). Home: 7133 Moorgate Rd Indianapolis IN 46250 Office: 120 W Market St Indianapolis IN 46204

MASSEY, JAMES EARL, clergyman; b. Ferndale, Mich., Jan. 4, 1930; s. George Wilson and Elizabeth (Shelton) M.; student U. Detroit, 1949-50, 55-57; B.Th., B.R.E., Detroit Bible Coll., 1961; A.M., Oberlin Grad. Sch. Theology, 1964; postgrad. U. Mich., 1967-69; D.D., Asbury Theol. Sem., 1972; postgrad. Pacific Sch. Religion, 1972; m. Gwendolyn Inez Kilpatrick, Aug. 4, 1951. Ordained to ministry Church of God, 1951; asso. minister Ch. of God of Detroit, 1951-53; sr. pastor Met. Church of God, Detroit, 1954-76, pastor-at-large, 1976; speaker Christian Brotherhood Hour, 1977—. Prin. Jamaica Sch. Theology, Kingston, Jamaica, 1963-66; campus minister Anderson (Ind.) Coll., 1969-77, asst. prof. religious studies, 1969-75, asso. prof., 1975-80, prof. N.T. and homiletics, 1981—; chmn. Commn. on Higher Edn. in the Church of God, 1968-71; vice-chmn. Bd. Publs. Church of God, 1968—. Dir. Warner Press, Inc. Mem. Corp. Inter-Varsity Christian Fellowship. Served with AUS, 1951-53. Mem. Nat. Assn. Coll. and Univ. Chaplains, Nat. Com. Black Churchmen, Nat. Negro Evang. Assn. (bd. dirs. 1969—). Author: When Thou Prayest, 1960; The Worshipping Church, 1961; Raymond S. Jackson, A Portrait, 1967; The Soul Under Siege, 1970; The Church of God and the Negro, 1971; The Hidden Disciplines, 1972; The Responsible Pulpit, 1973; Temples of the Spirit, 1974; The Sermon in Perspective, 1976; Concerning Christian Unity, 1979; gen. editor: Christian Brotherhood Hour Study Bible, 1979; Designing the Sermon, 1980; editorial bd. The Christian Scholar's Rev. Home: 1138 Kingsmill Rd Anderson IN 46012

MASSEY, JAMES EDWARD, elec. contracting co. exec.; b. Olney, Ill., Sept. 23, 1923; s. William Iraand Jean S. (Higgins) M.; B.S., U. Detroit, 1950; m. Patricia A. Curry, Jan. 28, 1950; children—James P., Thomas M., Daniel B., Mary Beth, Maureen Ann. Vice pres. mktg. and sales Pulte-Strang Inc., Ft. Myers, Fla. and Detroit, 1960-63; pres. Cullen-Massey Inc., Detroit, 1963-76, Hall Engring. Co., Detroit, 1976—. Chmn. U. Detroit Alumni Fund, 1960-61. Served with U.S. Army, 1943-45. Mem. Nat. Assn. Elec. Contractors (Southeastern chpt.), Iron and Steel Assn., Plant Engring. Soc. Detroit. Republican. Roman Catholic. Clubs: Detroit Athletic, Western Golf and Country, Errol Estates Country. Office: 12644 Marion Detroit MI 48239

MASSEY, WALTER EUGENE, physicist; b. Hattiesburg, Miss., Apr. 5, 1938; s. Almar Cleveland and Essie (Nelson) M.; B.S., Morehouse Coll., 1958; M.A., Washington U., St. Louis, 1966; Ph.D., 1966; m. Shirley Streeter, Oct. 25, 1969; children—Keith Anthony, Eric Eugene. Physicist, Argonne (Ill.) Nat. Lab., 1966-68; asst. prof. physics U. Ill., Urbana, 1968-70; asso. prof. Brown U., Providence, 1970-75, prof., dean Coll., 1975-79; cons. Argonne Nat. Lab., dir., 1979—; NSF, cons. Nat. Acad. Scis., NRC. Mem. Human Relations Commn., Urbana, 1967-68; bd. dirs. Urban League R.I., 1972-74. NSF fellow, 1962; NDEA fellow, 1959-60. Mem. Am. Phys. Soc., Am. Assn. Physics Tchrs. (Distinguished Service award 1975), AAAS, Sigma Xi. Contbr. articles on sci. edn. in secondary schs. and in theory of quantum fluids to profl. jours. Home: 5811 S Dorchester Ave Chicago IL 60637 Office: Argonne Nat Lab Argonne IL 60439*

MASSMAN, VIRGIL F., library adminstr.; B.A. in English, St. John's U.; M.A. in English, U. Minn.; M.A. in L.S.; Ph.D. in L.S., U. Mich., 3 children. Head reference librarian Bemidji (Minn.) State Coll., 1960-65; asso. prof. English U. of S.D., 1965-66; dir. libraries, 1966-71; exec. dir. James J. Hill Reference Library, St. Paul, 1971—; cons. in field, pres. S.D. Library Assn., 1970-71. Mem. AAUP, Am., Minn. (mem. state library adv. council 1971-75; chairperson academic div. 1974) library assns., Assn. Coll. and Research Libraries (chmn. conf.-planning com. 1981), Minn., S.D. hist. socs. Mem. editorial bd. Jour. Acad. Librarianship, 1978-81; contbr. articles to profl. jours. Home: 3411 Vivian Ave Saint Paul MN 55112

MASTALERZ, BEVERLY MCKEE, banker; b. Nevada, Mo., Jan. 1, 1933; d. Marion Newton and Cela Lila (Fisher) McKee; student Morton Coll., 1968-70; cert. nurses asst. McHenry County Coll., 1976; m. Gregory H. Mastalerz, July 7, 1977; 1 son by previous marriage—Gregory A. Slad. Adminstrv. services officer Madison Bank, Chgo., 1967—. Pres. women's aux. St. Procopius Coll., 1960-61. Democrat. Roman Catholic. Home: 1400 N Lake Shore Dr Chicago IL 60610 Office: 400 W Madison St Chicago IL 60606

MASTERS, DAVID LAWRENCE, diagnostic co. exec.; b. Downers Grove, Ill., Jan. 24, 1941; s. Lawrence Eugene and Audrey (Rose) M.; student U. Ill., Champaign, 1959-61; B.S. in Chemistry, Elmhurst Coll., 1966; m. Apr. 1, 1967; children—Diane, Monica. Research chemist Argonne (Ill.) Nat. Lab., 1966-68; salesman Sherwood Med. Industries, St. Louis, 1968-70; salesman Calbiochem, LaJolla, Calif., 1970-74, sales mgr., 1974-75; sales mgrs. midwest and Can., Worthington Diagnostics div. Millipore Corp., Elk Grove, Ill., 1975-80. Mayor of Prairie Grove (Ill.), 1977-81, chmn. police com., 1977—. Clara Shaw Scholar, 1959-61. Mem. McHenry County Mcpl. Assn. Republican. Club: Moose. Home: 3120 S Barreville Rd Prairie Grove IL 60014

MASTERSON, WILLIAM LLOYD, race track exec.; b. Chgo., Aug. 19, 1949; s. Lawrence and Lorraine Mae (Shaw) M.; student public schs., Chgo. Organiser, United Farm Workers, various locations, 1968-72; innkeeper Holiday Inns, Skokie, Ill., 1973-74; sec. Ill. Racing Bd., Chgo., 1974-79; gen. mgr. Maywood Park (Ill.) Race Track, 1979—. Mem. exec. bd. Com. on Ill. Govt., 1975—. Recipient Outstanding Achievement award Chgo. div. Horsemens Benevolent and Protective Assn. Mem. Nat. Assn. State Racing Commrs. (hon. life), Amnesty Internat., Bus. and Profl. People for the Public Interest, Egyptian Trotting Assn. (dir.), Harness Tracks of Am. (dir.), Harness Publicists Assn., Art Inst. Chgo. Democrat. Lutheran. Club: Lakeshore Racquet. Home: 4024 Clarendon St Chicago IL 60613 Office: 8600 W North Ave Maywood IL 60153

MASUR, ERNEST FRANK, engring. educator; b. Berlin, Germany, July 15, 1919; s. Martin M. and Else (Brukstein) M.; came to U.S., 1939, naturalized, 1944; B.S., U. Pitts., 1941; M.S., Ill. Inst. Tech., 1948, Ph.D., 1952; m. Eva Henriette Magnus, Dec. 16, 1944; children—Robert Edward, Howard Alan, Sandra. Instr., asst. prof., then asso. prof. civil engring. Ill. Inst. Tech., 1948-55; asso. prof., prof. engring. mechanics U. Mich., 1955-64; prof. engring., head dept. materials engring. U. Ill., Chgo., 1964—; cons. structural, aerospace engring., 1948—; cons. NSF, 1962—, dir. div. civil and mech. engring., 1979-80; Nat. Acad. Scis. exchange scientist with Bulgaria, 1972, Poland, 1977. Served with AUS, 1943-46. Recipient Laurie award ASCE, 1960. Fellow ASCE (past chmn. engring. mechanics div.), Am. Acad. Mechanics; mem. ASME, AAUP, Sigma Xi, Chi Epsilon. Editor: Jour. Structural Mechanics. Contbr. articles to profl. jours. Home: 510 Elmwood Ave Evanston IL 60202 Office: U Ill Chicago Circle Box 4348 Chicago IL 60680

MATA, RAMON ALBERTO, educator; b. San Joaquin, Venezuela, Aug. 31, 1949; came to U.S., 1976; s. Miguel Jesus and Nina D. M.; B.Math., Instituto Pedagogico de Caracas, 1972; M. Computer Sci. and Bus. Adminstrn., Fla. Inst. Tech., 1978; m. Anahis Ramos, Aug. 13, 1976; children—Yamileth, Harold, Lys Alejandra. Math. tchr. high sch., Caracas, Venezuela, 1970-75; head dept. math. Fco de Miranda Coll., Caracas, 1975-76; prof. computer sci. Kans. State U., Manhattan, 1980—. Venezuelan Govt. grantee, 1976. Mem. Colegio de Profesores de Venezuela, IEEE, Assn. Computing Machinery.

MATANKY, ARNIE, city ofcl.; b. Oak Park, Ill., June 25, 1930; s. Harry and Mary (Jakobowsky) M.; A.A., Wright Coll., 1950; postgrad. U. Chgo., 1954-55. City desk asst. Chgo. Sun, 1947; with Chgo. Jour. of Commerce, 1948; radio news editor Community News Service, Chgo., 1948-51; news editor CBS News, Chgo., 1953-59; owner, operator Info. Cons., Chgo., 1959-71, 79—; dir. pub. info. Chgo. Park Dist., 1971-79; pub. Near North News, Chgo., 1956—. Pres., Lincoln Park Villas Condominium Assn., Chgo., 1978—; Am. Legion chmn. Pan Am. Games, 1959; chmn. del. Dept. of France, Am. Legion, 1974-80; pres. Sandburg Village Council, Chgo., 1970-72; chmn. 18th Dist. Community Police Council, Chgo., 1969-71; pres.

Park Synagogue of Chgo., 1970-72; bd. dirs. Internat. Visitors Center, 1972—. Served with Signal Corps, U.S. Army, 1951-53. Mem. Am. Legion (comdr. 1958-59), Nat. Am. Vets Press Assn. (pres. 1977-79), Chgo. Council on Fgn. Relations, Library of Internat. Relations, Psywar Soc. (U.K.), Chgo. Assn. Commerce and Industry, Jewish War Vets. Democrat. Jewish. Clubs: Chgo. Press, Adventurers, Gaslight, B'nai B'rith (pres. 1965-67). Contbg. editor Public Relations, 1970. Home: 1920 N Clark St Chicago IL 60614 Office: 26 E Huron St Chicago IL 60611

MATASOVIC, STELLA, mech. products co. exec., ranch exec.; b. Lovington, Ill., July 19, 1916; d. Charles K. and Agnes (Nickus) Butkauskas; B.E., Ill. State Normal U., 1935; m. John L. Matasovic, Feb. 26, 1938; children—Linda Swiercinsky, Marilyn. Tchr. elementary sch., Pana, Ill., 1935-37; partner OXO Welding Equipment Co., New Lenox, Ill., 1944—; partner Universal Welding Supply Co., New Lenox, Ill., 1944—; mgr. Oxo Hereford ranches, Mokena, Ill., 1952—. Mem. Nat. Welding Supply Assn., New Lenox C. of C. (sec. 1969), Am. Nat. Cattlemen's Assn., Ill., Colo. hereford assns., Am. Hereford Aux. (pres. 1969-70), Ill. Beef Aux. Home: Rural Route 1 Mokena IL 60448 Office: Cedar and Oak Sts New Lenox IL 60451

MATCHETT, HUGH MOORE, lawyer; b. Chgo., Apr. 24, 1912; s. David Fleming and Jennie E. (Moore) M.; A.B., Monmouth (Ill.) Coll., 1934; J.D., U. Chgo., 1937; m. Ilo Venona Wolff, May 12, 1956. Admitted to Ill. bar, 1937, since practiced in Chgo. Served with USNR, 1942-46; MTO, PTO; lt. comdr. JAGC, USNR. Mem. Fed. (chmn. mil. law com. Chgo. chpt. 1954-55, mem. com. 1960-61), Am., Ill. (mem. assembly 1980—), Chgo. bar assns., Judge Advs. Assn., Tau Kappa Epsilon, Phi Alpha Delta. Republican. Presbyterian. Counsel in litigation establishing rule that charitable instns. are liable in tort to extent of their non-trust funds. Home: 5834 S Stony Island Ave Chicago IL 60637 Office: 10 S La Salle St Chicago IL 60603

MATCZYNSKI, AVALON NOLEN, sch. counselor; b. Kansas City, Mo., Nov. 18, 1932; d. Thomas J. and Estella (Banks) Nolen; B.S., Lincoln U., Jefferson City, Mo., 1953; postgrad. Central State U., Wilberforce, Ohio, 1958-59; M.S., Miami U., Oxford, Ohio, 1968; certificate adminstrn., Wright State U., Dayton, Ohio, 1975, M.S. in Supervision and Curriculum and Adminstrn.; 1 son, Mark Damian. Tchr. comml. edn. Sedalia, Mo., 1953-54; elementary tchr., Dayton, Ohio, 1959-68, elementary counselor, 1968-69, 71-73; counselor Patterson Vocat. Coop. High Sch., Dayton, 1968-71, Stivers-Patterson Vocat. High Sch., Dayton, 1973—; cons. in field. Adviser Del-Teen Club, Dayton, 1966—. Martha Jennings Holden scholar, 1968-69. Mem. Am. Personnel and Guidance Assn., Ohio Personnel and Guidance Assn., Miami Valley Personnel and Guidance Assn., Am., Ohio sch. counselors assns., NEA, Ohio Edn. Assn., Dayton Edn. Assn., Phi Delta Kappa, Delta Sigma Theta. Democrat. Roman Catholic. Home: 1752 Burroughs Dr Dayton OH 45406 Office: Patterson Coop High Sch 1313 E 5th St Dayton OH 45403

MATEK, ORD, psychotherapist, educator; b. Kamenetzpadolsk, Russia, May 10, 1922; s. Samson and Sonia (Torgow) M.; came to U.S., 1923, naturalized, 1929; B.S., Roosevelt U., 1949; M.A., U. Chgo., 1951; m. Betsy Stein, July 11, 1948; children—Beth Weinstein, Deborah, Joel, Michael. Caseworker, Jewish Children's Bur. of Chgo., 1951-56; adminstr. Eisenberg unit Marks Nathan Hall, Chgo., 1956-69; pvt. practice psychotherapy, Chgo., 1959—; asso. prof. Jane Addams Coll. Social Work, U. Ill., Chgo., 1969—; cons. to social work agys., psychiat. facilities, schs.; mem.faculty Ill. Sch. Profl. Psychology. Served with U.S. Army, 1943-46. Mem. Nat. Assn. Social Workers, Acad. Cert. Social Workers, Am. Assn. Children's Residential Centers, Nat. Assn. Temple Educators (curriculum award 1965), Am. Assn. Sex Educators, Counselors and Therapists, Union Am. Hebrew Congregations, Ill. Soc. for Clin. Social Work, Ill. Group Psychotherapy Soc., Am. Art Therapy Assn. Jewish. Author: The Bible Through Stamps, 1974. Editor: Jour. Residential Group Care and Treatment; cons. editor Jour. Social Work and Human Sexuality. Home: 9000 Ewing St Evanston IL 60203 Office: U Ill Box 4348 Chicago IL 60680 also 67 Old Orchard St Skokie IL 60077

MATESA, LAWRENCE GEORGE, mergers and acquisitions co. exec.; b. Dearborn, Mich., Feb. 26, 1931; s. George G. and Caroline (Krusac) M.; student Henry Ford Community Coll., 1950-54, Wayne State U. and Wayne State Law Sch., 1956; m. Lois Watkins Gregor, Nov. 17, 1978; children—Kelly, Michelle. Vice pres. F. J. Winckler Co., Detroit, 1956-64; salesman Manley Bennett McDonald, N.Y. Stock Exchange, Detroit, 1964-66; v.p. First Detroit Securities Corp., stock brokers and underwriters, Detroit, 1966-74; pres. Mich. Eagle Corp., Detroit, 1974—; dir. Ind. Liberty Life Ins. Co., Grand Rapids, Mich., 1963—, mem. audit com., 1979—; guest speaker Focus Radio Show, WJR, Detroit, 1966-71. Republican. Clubs: Detroit Yacht; Great Oaks Country (Rochester, Mich.); University (Flint, Mich.). Home: 447 Antoinette Dr Rochester MI 48063 Office: 859 Forest St Suite 16 Birmingham MI 48008

MATHEIN, JAMES DANIEL, health promotion co. exec.; b. Evanston, Ill., Jan. 31, 1943; s. Edward Lawrence and Isabel (Wynn) M.; B.S., U. Ill., 1968; postgrad. Forest Inst. Profl. Psychology, 1979-80; m. Veronica G. Beutler, Aug. 27, 1966; children—Adam Scott, Jason Daniel. Lab. automation cons. Am. Hosp. Supply, Chgo., 1969-71, support service supr., Dallas, 1971, ops. mgr., Mpls., 1971-73, dir. tech. support, Chgo., 1974-78; area ops. mgr. Can. Lab. Supply Ltd., Toronto, Ont., 1973-74; v.p. community relations, exec. dir. personal mgmt. systems Forest Hosp. and Found., Des Plaines, Ill., 1978—. Mem. Am. Soc. Tng. and Devel., Am. Soc. Health Manpower Edn. and Tng., Nutrition for Optimal Health Assn. Author: The Personal Management System, 1979; contbr. articles to profl. jours. Home: 2945 Landwehr Rd Northbrook IL 60062 Office: 555 Wilson Ln Des Plaines IL 60016

MATHER, BETTY BANG, musician, educator; b. Emporia, Kans., Aug. 7, 1927; d. Read Robinson and Shirley (Smith) Bang; B.Mus., Oberlin Conservatory, 1949; M.A., Columbia U., 1951; m. Roger Mather, Aug. 3, 1973. Mem. faculty U. Iowa, Iowa City, 1952—, prof. music, 1973—; editor Romney Press; leader workshop Baroque Interpretation for Woodwinds, Coe Coll., 1975-80; condr. workshops, demonstrations, master classes, lectr. Carleton Coll., 1978, Idaho State U., 1978, U. Calif., San Diego, 1978, Nat. Flute Conv., 1978, 79, Wash. Flute Soc., 1978, St. Louis Flute Club, 1979, Cedar Rapids Flute Club, 1977, 78, 79, 80. Author: Interpretation of French Music from 1675-1775, 1973; (with David Lasocki) Free Ornamentation for Woodwind Instruments from 1700-1775, 1976, The Classical Woodwind Cadenza, 1978; editor: 30 Virtuosic Selections in the Gallant Style for Unaccompanied Flute, 1975; Opera Duets Arranged for Two Flutes by Berbiguier, 1976; 60 Favorite Airs in the Gallant Style for Unaccompanied Flute, 1978; contbr. articles to profl. publs. Home: 308 4th Ave Iowa City IA 52240 Office: Sch Music U Iowa Iowa City IA 52242

MATHER, ROGER FREDERICK, musician, educator; b. London, May 27, 1917; s. Richard and Marie Louise (Schultze) M.; came to U.S., 1938, naturalized, 1948; B.A. with honors, Cambridge (Eng.) U., 1938, M.A. (hon.), 1941; M.Sc., Mass. Inst. Tech., 1940; m. Betty Louise Bang, Aug. 3, 1973; children by previous marriage—Arielle Diane, Christopher Richard. Research metallurgist Inland Steel Co., East Chicago, Ind., 1940-42; chief metallurgist Willys-Overland Motors Co., Toledo, 1942-46, Kaiser-Frazer Corp., Willow Run, Mich., 1946-50; project mgr. U.S. Steel Corp., Pitts., 1950-61; dir. research and engring. Mine Safety Appliances Co., Pitts., 1961-62; mem. staff research div. E. I. DuPont de Nemours & Co., Wilmington, Del., 1962-63; br. chief nuclear power tech. NASA, Cleve., 1963-73; pub., exec. editor Romney Press; adj. prof. Sch. Music, U. Iowa, Iowa City, 1973—; condr. flute clinics workshops. Registered profl. engr., Ohio, Mich., Pa. Mem. Am. Musical Inst. Soc., Am. Recorder Soc., Nat. Flute Soc., Nat. Assn. Mus. Inst. Technicians, Galpin Soc., Am. Inst. Mining, Metall., Petroleum Engrs., Am. Soc. Metals, Am. Inst. Aeros., Astronautics, ASME, ASTM, Soc. Automotive Engrs., Mensa, Pennsylvania Soc. Author: The Art of Playing the Flute; contbr. articles on engring., flute to profl. jours. Home: 308 Fourth Ave Iowa City IA 52240 Office: Sch Music U Iowa Iowa City IA 52242

MATHESON, WILLIAM ANGUS, JR., farm machinery co. exec.; b. Oregon City, Oreg., Dec. 6, 1919; s. William Angus and Maude (Moore) M.; B.S. in Bus. Adminstrn., Lehigh U., 1941; m. Jeanne Elyse Manley, Feb. 14, 1942; children—Jeanne Sandra, Susan Manley, Bonnie Ann. Procurement engr. Office Chief of Ordnance, 1942-43; mgr. contract sales Eureka-Williams Corp., Bloomington, Ill., 1946-49; dist. sales mgr. Perfex Corp., Milw., 1949-51; v.p. sales Internat. Heater Co., Utica, N.Y., 1951-53; sales mgr. heating div. Heil Co., Milw., 1953-55; v.p. sales, dir. Portable Elevator Mfg. Co., Bloomington, 1955-70; exec. v.p. portable elevator div. Dynamics Corp. Am., 1971-75, pres., 1975—, dir., 1971—. Bd. dirs. Jr. Achievement Central Ill., 1959-71, pres. Bloomington dist., 1964. Served from pvt. to 1st lt. AUS, 1943-46. Mem. Farm Equipment Mfrs. Assn. (dir. 1961-80, pres. 1969, treas. 1970-80), Ill. C. of C. (dir. 1978—), McLean County Assn. Commerce and Industry (pres. 1974), Truck Equipment and Body Distbrs. Assn. (co-founder 1963), Am. Legion, Flying Farmers, Nat. Pilots Assn., Chi Phi. Republican. Presbyterian. Clubs: Rotary, Bloomington Country, Masons, Shriners, Elks. Home: 1404 E Washington St Bloomington IL 61701 Office: PO Box 2847 920 E Grove St Bloomington IL 61701

MATHEWS, JOHN ANDREW, optometrist; b. Montmorency County, Mich., Oct. 8, 1922; s. James Wilbert and Lena Lois (McCoy) M.; D.Optometry, No. Ill. Coll. Optometry, 1948; m. Shirley Ruth Langton, Oct. 26, 1951; children—James, Mary, Julie, Lois, Kent, Douglas, Lori. Pvt. practice optometry, Three Rivers, Mich., 1949—. Dir. Three Rivers (Mich.) Savs. & Loan Assn. Mem. St. Joseph County Bd. Election Canvassars, 1966-70. Served with USAAF, 1942-46; lt. col. Res., ret. 1969. Decorated Air medals. Mem. Am., Mich. optometric assns., Southwestern Mich. Optometric Soc. (pres. 1968-71), Three Rivers C. of C., Am. Legion, V.F.W., Res. Officers Assn. U.S. (life), Nat. Rifle Assn., Ret. Officers Assn., Am. Assn. Ret. Persons, Farm Bur. Home: 55188 Buckhorn Rd Three Rivers MI 49093 Office: 3 1/2 N Main St Three Rivers MI 49093

MATHEWS, YVONNE EVADNEY, city ofcl.; b. Georgetown, Guyana, July 30, 1941; d. Nora Victoria Stock; grad. Nebr. Coll. Bus., Omaha, 1973, Bellevue (Nebr.) Coll.; children—Chanelle S., Lloyd W. III. Secretarial position Oldsmobile div. Gen. Motors Corp., Omaha, 1973-74; employment interviewer Nebr. Job Service, Omaha, 1975-76; employee relations officer City of Omaha Comprehensive Employment and Tng. Agy. Program, 1976—; mem. EEO Task Force, Washington; mem. planning com. Women's Employment Opportunities Nebr. Mem. Am. Bus. Women's Assn. (program chmn.), Personnel Assn. Midlands (hosp. chmn.), Jack and Jill of Am. Inc. (pres.), Selected Leadership Omaha, 1980-81. Democrat. Presbyterian. Home: 11814 S 34th St Omaha NE 68123 Office: City of Omaha CETA 5002 S 33d St Omaha NE 68107

MATHEWSON, HUGH SPALDING, physician, educator; b. Washington, Sept. 20, 1921; s. Walter Eldridge and Jennie Lind (Jones) M.; student Washburn U., 1938-39; A.B., U. Kans., 1942, M.D., 1944; children—Jane (Mrs. Gary Holcombe), Geoffrey K., Brian E., Catherine E., Jennifer A. Intern, Wesley Hosp., Wichita, Kans., 1944-45; resident U. Kans. Med. Center, Kansas City, 1946-48; practice medicine specializing in anesthesiology, Kansas City, Mo., 1948-69; chief anesthesiologist St. Luke's Hosp., 1948-69; med. dir., sect. respiratory therapy U. Kans. Med. Center, Kansas City, Kans., 1969—, asso. prof., 1969-75, prof., 1975—; examiner schs. respiratory therapy, 1975—; oral examiner Nat. Bd. Respiratory Therapy; mem. Council Nurse Anesthesia Practice, 1974—. Trustee Kansas City Mus., 1960-70. Served to lt. comdr. USNR, 1956. Recipient Bird Lit. prize Am. Assn. Respiratory Therapists, 1976. Mem. Mo. (pres. 1963), Kans. (pres. 1974-77) socs. anesthesiologists, Sigma Xi, Phi Beta Kappa. Author: Structural Forms of Anesthetic Compounds, 1961; Respiratory Therapy in Critical Care, 1976; Pharmacology for Respiratory Therapists, 1977, 2d edit., 1981; contbr. numerous articles to profl. jours.; editorial bd. Anesthesia Staff News, 1975—; asst. editor Respiratory Care, 1980—. Home: 6523 Overbrook Rd Shawnee Mission KS 66208 Office: 39th and Rainbow Sts Kansas City KS 66103

MATHEWSON, JAMES L., state senator; b. Warsaw, Mo., Mar. 16, 1938; student Redding Jr. Coll., Calif. State U., Chico; m. Doris Angel, Dec. 1964; 3 children. Real estate appraiser; mem. Mo. Ho. of Reps., 1974-80, Mo. Senate, 1980—. Served with U.S. Army. Mem. Am. Legion, C. of C. Democrat. Baptist. Clubs: Masons, Scottish Rite, Shriners, Elks, Moose. Office: State Capitol Jefferson City MO 65101*

MATHIPRAKASAM, B., energy engr.; b. Virudhunagar, India, Jan. 3, 1942; s. G. Balakrishnan and B. Rajammal; L.M.E., Virudhunagar Poly., India, 1961; M.E., Mysore U., 1976; Ph.D., Ill. Inst. Tech., 1980; m. M. Pavalamani, Sept. 11, 1972; 1 child, Murthy. Lectr., Virudhunagar Poly., 1961-68, workshop supt., 1968-74; research asst. Ill. Inst. Tech., Chgo., 1976-79; asso. energy engr. Midwest Research Inst., Kansas City, 1980-81, sr. energy engr., 1981—. Mem. ASME, Sigma Xi. Home: 6709 W 87th St 201 Overland Park KS 66212 Office: 425 Volker Blvd Kansas City MO 64110

MATHIS, JACK DAVID, advt. exec.; b. La Porte, Ind. Nov. 27, 1931; s. George Anthony and Bernice (Bennethum) M.; student U. Mo., 1950-52; B.S., Fla. State U., 1955; m. Phyllis Dene Hoffman, Dec. 24, 1971; childern—Kane Cameron, Jana Dene. With Benton & Bowles, Inc., 1955-56; owner Jack Mathis Advt., 1956—; creative cons. film That's Action!, 1977. Mem. U.S. Olympic Basketball Com. Recipient citation Marketing Research Council N.Y. Mem. Alpha Delta Sigma. Author: Valley of the Cliffhangers; creative cons. motion picture That's Action, 1977. Home: Libertyville IL 60048 Office: Forum Sq 1117 S Milwaukee Ave Libertyville IL 60048

MATHIS, TERRY DON, tranducer research engr.; b. Shawnee, Okla., May 11, 1943; s. Willard Johnson and Tollye Rae (Brown) M.; A.A., Northeastern Okla. A&M Coll., 1963; B.S., Okla. State U., 1966, M.S., 1967; Ph.D., U. Houston, 1971; postdoctoral research fellow U. Birmingham, Eng., 1971-72; m. Jamey Gayle Dayton, June 1, 1968; children—Lindsey Dawn, Stacy Erin. Summer engr. Armco Steel Co., Houston, 1964, 65; summer intern NASA Manned Spacecraft Center, Houston, 1967, grad. intern, 1968; mem. tech. staff Underwater Acoustics Group, Bell Telephone Labs., Whippany, N.J., 1972-74, mem. tech. staff Fiber Optics Group, Atlanta, 1974-78; transducer research engr. Koss Corp., Milw., 1978—; tchr. engring. U. Houston, U. Birmingham, DeKalb Coll. (Atlanta); designer. Exec. advisor Jr. Achievement, 1980-81. Mem. Acoustical Soc. Am. Baptist. Ad hoc reviewer acoustics, physiology and perception NSF, 1981-82. Research onparticle velocity of underwater horns, prediction of far-field acoustic array patterns from near-field data; patentee optical feber splicing method. Home: 7626 W Willowbrook Dr Mequon WI 53092 Office: 4129 N Port Washington Ave Milwaukee WI 53212

MATHISON, IAN WILLIAM, coll. dean; b. Liverpool, Eng., Apr. 17, 1938; s. William and Grace (Almond) M.; B.Pharm., U. London, 1960, Ph.D., 1963, D.Sc., 1976; came to U.S., 1963; m. Mary Ann Gordon, July 20, 1968; children—Mark W., Lisa A. Research asso. U. Tenn. Center Health Scis., Memphis, 1963-65, asst. prof., 1965-68, asso. prof., 1968-72, prof., 1972-76; dean, prof. medicinal chemistry Sch. Pharmacy, Ferris State Coll., Big Rapids, Mich., 1977—; mem. State Mich. Dept. Mental Health Drug Quality Assurance Commn., 1979—. Pharm. Industry research grantee, 1965—. Mem. Chem. Soc. London, Pharm. Soc. Gt. Britain, Am. Pharm. Assn., Acad. Pharm. Scis., Am. Chem. Soc., Royal Inst. Chemistry, Am. Assn. Colls. Pharmacy, Am. Soc. Hosp. Pharmacists, Mich. Pharm. Assn. Episcopalian. Mem. editorial adv. bd. Jour. Pharm. Scis., 1981-84; contbr. articles to profl. jours.; patentee in field. Home: 820 Osburn Circle Big Rapids MI 49307 Office: 901 S State St Big Rapids MI 49307

MATHUR, PRACHEESHWAR SWAROOP, metallurgist; b. Shahjahanpur, India, Dec. 19, 1945; came to U.S., 1967; s. Parmeshwar and Gopal Rani M.; B.Sc., Agra Coll. (India), 1962; B.Tech., Indian Inst. Tech., Kanpur, 1967; S.M., M.I.T., 1968, Sc.D., 1972; m. Meena Mathur, Dec. 27, 1976. Metall. cons., 1969-71; research asst. M.I.T., Cambridge, 1969-72, research asso., 1968-69; mech. metalworking engr. aircraft engine group Gen. Electric Co., Lynn, Mass., 1972-78, mgr. metals processing, Cin., 1978-80, mgr. customer support, 1980—. Recipient numerous awards Gen. Electric Co. Mem. Am. Soc. Metals, AIME, ASM, Metals Soc. Eng. Contbg. author: Superalloys—Processing, 1981. Patentee in field (5).

MATIA, PAUL RAMON, lawyer, state senator; b. Cleveland, Oct. 2, 1937; s. Leo Clemens and Irene Elizabeth (Linkert) M.; B.A. cum laude, Western Res. U., 1959; J.D., Harvard U., 1962. Admitted to Ohio bar, 1962; law clk. Cuyahoga County (Ohio) Common Pleas Ct., Cleve., 1963-66; asst. atty. gen. State of Ohio, 1966-69; adminstrv. asst. Ohio Atty. Gen., Columbus, 1969-70; mem. Ohio Senate, 1971-75, 79—, chmn. elections, fin. instns. and ins. com.; partner firm Hadley, Matia, Mills & MacLean Co., L.P.A., Cleve., 1975—; instr. bus. law Ashland (Ohio) Coll., 1976. Vice chmn. Cuyahoga County Republican Exec. Com. Recipient Outstanding Public Service award, Ohio Public Transit Assn., 1974; Outstanding Service award, Ohio Assn. Retarded Citizens, 1974. Mem. Ohio League of Young Republican Clubs (state chmn. 1968, recipient Robert A. Taft Distinguished Service award, 1967). Mem. Bar Assn. Greater Cleve., Citizens League of Greater Cleve. Republican. Office: 1800 E Ohio Bldg Cleveland OH 44114

MATIASKA, ERNEST ALLAN, instruments and controls engring. co. exec.; b. Cleve., Nov. 20, 1930; s. Charles A. and Emma (Hanzlik) M.; B.M.E., Cleve. State U., 1963; m. Barbara Ann Yonchak, Sept. 23, 1967; children—Douglas, Carla. Devel. project engr. Bailey Meter Co. div. Babcock & Wilcox (name now Bailey Controls Co.), Wickliffe, Ohio, 1959-63, mgr. engring. test lab., 1963-66, mgr. product reliability and testing, 1966-69, mgr. product engring., 1969-80, mgr. internat. tech., 1980—; U.S.A. expert to Internat. Electrotech. Commn., 1976—. Served with USAF, 1951-55; Korea. Mem. ASME, Instrument Soc. Am., Am. Nat. Standards Inst., Sci. Apparatus Makers Assn. Home: 21990 Roberts Ave Euclid OH 44123 Office: 29801 Euclid Ave Wickliffe OH 44092

MATRE, RICHARD ANTHONY, univ. adminstr.; b. Chgo., Feb. 27, 1922; s. Richard Joseph and Gertrude (O'Rourke) M.; Litt.B., Xavier U., Cin., 1945; A.M., Loyola U., Chgo., 1949; Ph.D., Northwestern U., 1961; m. Marilu Flanagan, Aug. 9, 1947; children—Patrick, Michael, Margaret Hartley, Elizabeth, Jeanne, Teresa Baldwin, Richard, Loretta, John. Instr. history and polit. sci. Loyola U. Chgo., 1947-53, asst. prof. history, 1953, asst. dean Coll. Arts and Scis., 1951, dean Univ. Coll., 1952-65, dir. summer session, 1954-64, asso. prof., 1965-69, prof., 1969—, dean Grad. Sch., 1965-69, v.p., dean faculties, 1969-79, provost med. center, 1979—. Adv. council Chgo. Building Commr., 1954-56. Mem. Holy Name Soc. Union (officer Archdiocese of Chgo. 1955-56), Am. Hist. Soc., Nat. Cath. Edn. Assn. (sec. coll. and univ. dept., 1962-68, v.p. coll. and univ. dept. 1968- 70, pres. 1970—), Assn. for Continuing Higher Edn. (chmn. research and study com. 1955-58, pres. 1960-61), North Central Assn. (cons.-examiner 1969—), Am. Assn. Univ. Adminstrs. (dir.), Pi Gamma Mu, Blue Key. Home: 4030 Fairway Dr Wilmette IL 60091 Office: 2160 S First Ave Maywood IL 60153

MATSESHE, JOHN WANYAMA, gastroenterologist; b. Kakamega, Kenya, June 5, 1941; s. James K. and Anyachi S. (Nyikuli) M.; came to U.S., 1970; M.D., Makerere U., Kampala, Uganda, 1969; m. Rebecca Z. Wazome, Mar. 14, 1970; children—Lily, Carolyn, Lynn, Andrew. Intern, Stamford (Conn.) Hosp., 1971-72; resident in medicine Northwestern U. Hosps., 1972-74; fellow in gastroenterology Mayo Clinic, Rochester, Minn., 1974-77, cons. in medicine and gastroenterology, 1977-78; instr. medicine Mayo Med. Sch., 1976-78, asst. prof., 1978; practice medicine specializing in gastroenterology, Libertyville, Ill., 1978—; asst. prof., Chgo. Med. Sch., U. of Health Scis., 1981; cons. Condell Meml. Hosp., St. Therese Hosp., Waukegan, VA Hosp., North Chicago. Diplomate Am. Bd. Internal Medicine (gastroenterology). Mem. AMA, A.C.P., Am. Gastroent. Assn., Am. Soc. Gastrointestinal Endoscopy, Sigma Xi. Address: 890 Garfield St No 210 Libertyville IL 60048

MATSON, VIRGINIA MAE FREEBERG (MRS. EDWARD J. MATSON), educator, author; b. Chgo., Aug. 25, 1914; d. Axel George and Mae (Dalrymple) Freeberg; B.A., U. Ky., 1934; M.A., Northwestern U., 1941; m. Edward John Matson, Oct. 18, 1941; children—Karin (Mrs. Rudolf A. Renfer, Jr.), Sara M. (Mrs. Carl B. Drake III), Edward Robert, Laurence D., David O. Tchr. high schs., Chgo., 1934-42, Ridge Farm, 1944-45, Lake County Pub. Schs., 1956-59; founder Grove Sch., 1958—. Mem. Ill. Council on Exceptional Children; mem. woman's council Brain Research Found., U. Chgo., 1966—. Recipient Humanitarian award Ill. Med. Soc. Women's Aux. Mem. Friends Lit. Democrat. Author: Shadow on the Lost Rock, 1958; Saul, the King, 1968; Abba, Father (Friends Lit. Fiction award 1972), 1970; Buried Alive, 1970; A School for Peter, 1974. Home: 950 N Saint Mary's Rd Libertyville IL 60048 Office: 40 E Old Mill Rd Lake Forest IL 60045

MATSUMOTO, GEORGE MASARU, dentist; b. San Francisco, Nov. 3, 1916; s. Ben Toyomatsu and Teruko (Taniguchi) M.; A.B., U. Calif. at Berkeley, 1940; D.D.S., Loyola U., Chgo., 1949; m. Masako Ishii, Jan. 8, 1946; 1 son, Gregory Yutaka. Pvt. practice dentistry, Chgo., 1950-68; asst. prof. anatomy and histology Loyola U. Dental

Sch., 1950-58; clin. investigator NIH, 1968-72; staff dentist Ill. Dept. Mental Health, 1968-76; chief hosp. dental service Lincoln (Ill.) Developmental Center, 1976—; guest lectr. oral medicine Parkland Coll., Champaign, Ill., 1968—; mgmt. cons. Served with AUS, World War II. Fellow Royal Soc. Health; mem. Am., Ill., Chgo. dental assns., Am. Soc. Geriatric Dentistry (sec. 1969-72). Home: 2724 N Mildred Ave Chicago IL 60614

MATSUSHIMA, AKIRA PAUL, internat. co. exec.; b. Tokyo, July 7, 1937; s. Hiromasa and Tomiko (Watanabe) M.; came to U.S., 1970; B.S., Waseda U., Tokyo, 1961, M.S. in Mech. Engring., 1964; M.Mgmt., Northwestern U., 1981; m. Kathleen Sue Rowland, Aug. 18, 1968; children—John Hikaru, Karen Emi, Amy Kathryn. Asst. mgr. research and devel. Nippon Oil Seal Industry, Tokyo, 1965-67, mgr. research planning, 1968-70; dir. engring. NOK, Inc., Los Angeles, 1970-72, v.p., 1973-74, exec. v.p., Chgo., 1975—, sec., 1979—, dir., 1971—; Japanese Govt. del. to Internat. Standardization Orgn., 1973—. Adv. bd. Christopher House, Chgo., 1977-80; ch. officer, 1972-74, 77—. Registered profl. engr., Calif. Mem. Am. Mgmt. Assn., Soc. Automotive Engrs. (adv. bd. seals com., chmn. various subcoms.), Am., Japan socs. lubrication engrs., Nat. Soc. Profl. Engrs., Japan Soc. M.E., N.W. Suburban YMCA. Presbyterian. Contbr. articles to tech. jours. Patentee sealing device; holder numerous Japanese patents in field. Home: 633 S Bristol Ln Arlington Heights IL 60005 Office: 631 N Busse Rd Bensenville IL 60106

MATTA, RAM KUMAR, aero., acoustic engr.; b. Karachi, India, May 9, 1946; s. Madhavdas Lalchand and Damyanti (Ahuja) M.; came to U.S., 1967, naturalized, 1976; B. Tech., Indian Inst. Tech., New Delhi, 1967; M.S., U. Minn., Mpls., 1969, Ph.D., 1973; m. Linda Carole Russell, July 1, 1972. Engring. trainee Automobile Products Co. India, Bombay, summer 1965, MAN Industries, Jaipur, India, summer 1966; grad. asst. mechanics U. Minn., Mpls., 1967-68, research asst., 1968, teaching asso., 1968-69, research asso., 1969, research fellow, 1969-73; acoustics engr. advanced engring. and tech. program dept., engring. div. Aircraft Engine Group, Gen. Electric Co., Evendale, Ohio, 1973-75, mgr. turbomachinery acoustics, 1975-76, mgr. component acoustic tech., 1976-77, sr. engr. cycle systems analysis, 1977-78, sr. engr. aero-thermo systems, comml. engring. operation dept., 1979-80, mgr. new engine design support, 1980—. Exec. mem., vol. Minn. Internat. Center, Mpls., 1970-72; chmn. Citizens Com. for Community Devel., Forest Park, Ohio, 1975-76. Recipient Profl. Performance award, 1975, Mgmt. award, 1979. Merit scholar, also Dir.'s Gold Medal, Indian Inst. Tech., 1967; grad. tuition scholar U. Minn., 1968. Mem. Am. Inst. Aeros. and Astronautics, Sigma Gamma Tau. Contbr. articles to profl. publs. Patentee in field. Home: 823 Carpenter Rd Loveland OH 45140 Office: G40 Gen Electric Co Cincinnati OH 45215

MATTA, RONALD JOHN, mfrs. rep.; b. Cleve., Nov. 5, 1929; s. John Charles and Ann LaVerne (Pankuch) M.; student Baldwin-Wallace Coll., 1949-51; M.A., Mich. State U., 1963; postgrad. U. Wis., 1966; m. Betty Jean Crook, Sept. 30, 1950; children—James R., Sherrill J., John G., Jeffrey R. Sales rep. Lamson & Sessions Co., Cleve., 1951-60; sales mgr. Ferry Cap & Set Screw Co., 1960-68; owner, pres. Selpro Co., Inc., Deerfield, Ill., 1968—; fastener applications cons. Co-chmn. Greater Cleve. Indsl. div. United Fund, 1962; co-chmn. Neighborhood Watch Program, Green Oaks, Ill., 1980—. Mem. Mfrs. Agts. Nat. Assn., Chgo. Bolt, Nut and Screw Assn. Republican. Lutheran. Club: Boca Del Mar Country. Office: 747 Lake Cook Rd Deerfield IL 60015

MATTER, MICHAEL CARL, pharmacist; b. Williamsport, Pa., Sept. 25, 1945; s. Paul H. and Mary L. (Gladewitz) M.; B.Sc. in Pharmacy, Temple U., Phila., 1968; m. Pamela Sue Gault, Feb. 9, 1974; 1 son, Drew Michael-Paul. Resident in hosp. pharmacy Bethesda Hosp., Zanesville, Ohio, 1968-69, spl. project pharmacist, 1969; dir. pharmacy services Med. Center Hosp., Chillicothe, Ohio, 1970—; evening instr. pharmacology Hocking Tech. Coll., Chillicothe, 1977—. Mem. Am. Soc. Hosp. Pharmacists (preceptor; accredited residency in hosp. pharmacy), Ohio Soc. Hosp. Pharmacists (treas. 1979-82), Central Ohio Soc. Hosp. Pharmacists, Nat. Order Symposiarchs (past pres. Zeta chpt.). Home: 204 Vine St Chillicothe OH 45601 Office: Med Center Hosp PO Box 708-A Chillicothe OH 45601

MATTESON, RICHARD ARTHUR, JR., public affairs profl.; b. Lock Haven, Pa., Dec. 26, 1950; s. Richard Arthur and Jeanne (Keeler) M.; B.S. with high honors, U. Fla., 1973; postgrad. Central Mich. U., 1973-75; m. Sue A. Cornell, Aug. 12, 1972; children—Sandra Rene, Jonathon Richard. Copy editor Midland (Mich.) Daily News, 1973-74, city editor, 1975-76; copy editor Oakland Press, Pontiac, Mich., 1976-77, copy desk chief, 1977-78, city editor, 1978; mng. editor Cadillac (Mich.) Evening News, 1978-79, exec. editor, 1979-81; communication projects coordinator Consumers Power Co., Jackson, Mich., 1981—. Mem. bd. edn. St. Ann's Parish, 1980-81. Mem. Mich. Press Assn., Inland Daily Press Assn., Cadillac Area C. of C., Sigma Delta Chi, Kappa Tau Alpha, Phi Kappa Phi. Roman Catholic. Home: 1020 Maple Grove Rd Jackson MI 49201 Office: 212 W Michigan Ave Jackson MI 49201

MATTHEIS, DUANE JOHN, ednl. assn. exec.; b. Ellendale, N.D., Oct. 20, 1927; s. John and Katherine (Ammon) M.; B.S. in Sci., N.D. State Normal and Indsl. Coll., Ellendale, 1950; M.S. in Sch. Adminstrn., Colo. State Coll. Edn., 1954; M.Ednl. Adminstrn., Stanford U., 1971; m. Beverly Jane Tiosvold, June 26, 1955; children—Peter, Erik. Tchr., coach Granite Falls (Minn.) Public Schs., 1950-53, prin. jr.-sr. high sch., 1954-56; prin., tchr., coach LeRoy (Minn.) Public Schs., 1953-54; asst. prin. jr.-sr. high sch., Owatonna (Minn.) Public Schs., 1956-58, supt. schs., 1958-64; commr. edn. State of Minn., St. Paul, 1964-69; dep. commr. sch. systems U.S. Office Edn., Washington, 1971-74, exec. dep. commr., 1974-76; asso. dir. Ednl. Research Council Am., Cleve., 1976—. Served with U.S. Army, 1946-48. Recipient Outstanding Alumni award N.D. State Normal and Indsl. Coll., 1967. Mem. Am. Assn. Sch. Adminstrs. (life), NEA (life), Ohio Assn. Sch. Adminstrs., Assn. Supervision and Curriculum Devel., Phi Delta Kappa (life). Republican. Lutheran. Clubs: Rotary, Masons, Shriners. Home: 20756 Parkcliff Dr Fairview Park OH 44126 Office: 614 W Superior Ave Cleveland OH 44113

MATTHEW, NEIL EDWARD, artist, educator; b. Anderson, Ind., Jan. 19, 1925; s. Mark N. and Mary B. (Clifford) M.; B.A. in Edn., Ariz. State U., 1949; M.F.A., Ind. U., 1955; postgrad. Acad. Fine Arts, Stuttgart, Germany, 1959-60, U. Iowa, 1957-58; m. Jeannette Morrow, Dec. 22, 1963. Tchr. art Covington (Ind.) Jr. High Sch., 1949-50, Clay High Sch., South Bend, Inc., 1955-57; mem. faculty dept. art Ind. U., Kokomo campus, 1960-64, Indpls., 1964—, asso. prof. Herron Sch. Art, Ind. U.-Purdue U., Indpls., 1974—; one-man shows of paintings and prints include: Lieber's Gallery, Indpls., 1962, 68, Purdue U., West Lafayette, Ind., 1962; group shows include: Butler Art Inst., Youngstown, Ohio, 1954, John Herron Art Mus., Indpls., 1954-59, 61, Ball State U., Muncie, Ind., 1955, 59, 62, Bradley U., Peoria, Ill., 1955, Cin. Art Mus., 1955, 67, Boston Mus. Fine Arts, 1955, Seattle Mus. Art, 1956, 62, Library of Congress, Washington, 1956, 58, 59, Depauw U., Greencastle, Ind., 1964, Ohio U., Athens, 1965, Purdue U., West LaFayette, 1966, 69, Lafayette (Ind.) Art Center, 1967, 68; represented in permanent collections: South Bend (Ind.) Art Center, Ariz. State U., Tempe, U. Iowa, Iowa City, Evansville (Ind.) Mus. Arts and Scis., also pvt. collections; one-man photog. shows: Herron Gallery, Indpls., 1977, Archtl. Center, Indpls., 1978. Group photog. shows include: Bergman Gallery, U. Chgo., 1970, Ball State U., Muncie, Ind., 1971, Lafayette (Ind.) Art Center, 1976, Ft. Wayne Mus. Art, 1977. Served with U.S. Army, 1950-52. Fulbright grantee, 1959-60. Mem. Coll. Art Assn., Soc. Ind. Pioneers, AAUP. Republican. Presbyterian. Home: 212 E 49th St Indianapolis IN 46205 Office: Cavanaugh Hall Ind U-Purdue U Indpls 925 W Michigan St Indianapolis IN 46202

MATTHEWS, FRANK THOMAS, JR., retail co. exec.; b. Astoria, N.Y., Dec. 19, 1930; s. Frank Thomas and Elizabeth Mary (Murray) M.; student Queens Coll., N.Y.C., 1949-51; m. Ann Alfano, June 5, 1954; children—Frank Thomas III, Patrick Thomas, Darren Thomas. Display designer John H. Beyer, N.Y.C., 1953-55; with Montgomery Ward & Co., N.Y.C., 1955-65, region store planning mgr. North Central Chgo., 1965-73; corp. v.p. advt. and sales promotion, display and store design constrn., real estate dir. Gamble-Skogmo Inc., Mpls., 1973-80; corp. dir. real estate and distbn. Wickes Cos., 1980—; pres. Gamble Devel. Co.; dir. Amor Bldg. Corp., Buse Bldg. Corp., Bluff House, Green Turtle Cay, Bahamas. Served with U.S. Army, 1951-53. Mem. Minn. Advt. Rev. Council, Minn. Boys Club. Republican. Roman Catholic. Home: 309 Brampton Ln Lincolnshire IL 60045 Office: 2215 Sanders Rd Northbrook IL 60062

MATTHEWS, GERTRUDE ANN URCH, librarian, writer; b. Jackson, Mich., July 16, 1921; d. Charles P.A. and Amy (Granville) Urch; student Albion Coll., 1940-41; A.A., Jackson Jr. Coll., 1941; B.S., M.S. in Library Arts, U. Mich., 1959; m. Geoffrey Matthews, June 30, 1942 (dec.). Adult services librarian Jackson, Mich., 1959-63; asst. dir., librarian Franklin Sylvester Library, Medina, Ohio, 1963-81. Pres., Hist. Soc., 1966-67; active Dollars for Scholars Com., 1966—; mem. Bicentennial Com.; officer diocesean leval Episcopal Ch.; mem. vestry St. Paul's Ch., Medina. Mem. Am. Library Assn., Ohio Library Assn., Ch. Library Assn. Republican. Clubs: AAUW (dir.), LWV (dir.). Contbr. articles to profl. and popular publs.; weekly newspaper columnist. Home: 750 Weymouth Medina OH 44256

MATTHEWS, KENNETH C., cons.; b. Cin., Aug. 18, 1924; s. William Earle and Mosella (Cragg) M.; B.S. in Chem. Engring., Purdue U., 1945; m. Sandra Virda Marcum, Dec. 24, 1970; children—Bruce, Mark, Scott, Eric, Britt. Ret. chmn. bd. Henry P. Thompson Co., Cin.; pres. Rep-Aid Corp., M&I Corp., Unifilt Corp.; v.p. Gray Engring. Group, E&I Corp., Air Water Systems; dir. Katydyne USA. Served with USN, 1942-45. Office: PO Box 42272 Cincinnati OH 45242*

MATTHIAS, RUSSELL HOWARD, lawyer; b. Milw., Aug. 7, 1906; s. Charles G. and Lena (Martin) M.; A.B., Northwestern U., 1930, J.D., 1932; m. Helene Seibold, Dec. 28, 1932; children—Russell Howard, William Warrens, Robert Charles. Admitted to Ill. bar, 1933, D.C. bar, 1947, Okla. bar, 1947, Fla. bar, 1979; spl. asst. to atty. gen. U.S. R.R. Retirement Act, 1934-35; sec. Ill. Fraternal Congress, 1935-40, 45-60; partner firm Meyers & Matthias, Chgo., 1951-78; pres., treas. Meyers & Matthias, P.C., 1978—; chmn. bd., dir. Old Orchard Bank & Trust Co.; dir. Georgetown Life Ins. Co.; exec. v.p., dir., gen. counsel Bankers Mut. Life Ins. Co.; dir., gen. counsel United Founders Life Ins. Co. of Ill., United Founders Life Ins. Co. of Okla.; dir., gen. counsel Wesco Inc.; gen. counsel Nat. Ind. Statis. Service. Drafting com. Ill. Ins. Code, 1938, annotating com., 1940; mem. drafting com. La. Ins. Code, 1948, also 12 other states; chmn., mem. code revision com. Nat. Fraternal Code, 1980. Trustee Valparaiso U. Law Sch.; sec., treas., dir. Technology Fund, Inc. Served capt. to lt. col., AUS, 1942-46. Recipient Alumni award Northwestern U., 1973, also merit award, 1981. Mem. Luth. Brotherhood (dir., gen. counsel), Assn. Life Ins. Counsel, Internat. Assn. Life Ins. Counsel, Phi Delta Theta. Republican. Lutheran. Clubs: Indian Hill Country; Mid-Day, University (Chgo.); Kenilworth; Minneapolis; Citrus, Country (Orlando, Fla.). Home: 1500 Sheridan Rd Wilmette IL 60091 Office: 230 W Monroe St Room 2220 Chicago IL 60606

MATTHIES, FRED JOHN, archtl.-engring. co. exec.; b. Omaha, Oct. 4, 1925; s. Fred J. and Charlotte Leota (Metz) M.; B.S.C.E., Cornell U., 1947; postgrad. U. Nebr., 1952-53; m. Carol Mae Dean, Sept. 14, 1947; children—John Frederick, Jane Carolyn. Civil engr. Henningson, Durham & Richardson, cons. engrs., Omaha, 1947-50, 52-54; sr. v.p. for devel. Leo A. Daly Co., architects, engrs., planners, Omaha, 1954—; mem. Dist. Export Council, 1981-83; lectr. on doing bus. with fed. govt. presented paper on alternative energies Internat. Seminar on Engring. in Cold Regions, 1978. Mem. central com. Douglas County (Nebr.) Republican Party, 1968-72; regent Augustana Coll., Sioux Falls, S.D., 1976—; bd. dirs. Orange County Lutheran Hosp. Assn., Anaheim, Calif., 1961-62; bd. dirs. Lutheran Hosp., Omaha, 1978—. Served to 1st lt. USMCR, 1943-46, 50-52. Registered profl. engr., Iowa, Nebr., Wash., Calif., Fla. Fellow ASCE, Instn. Civil Engrs. (London); mem. Air Force Assn., Am. Acad. Environ. Engrs. (diplomate), Am. Waterworks Assn., Nat. Soc. Profl. Engrs. Am. Legion. Republican. Lutheran. Clubs: Happy Hollow Country, Rotary. Contbr. articles to Proc. ASCE, Cons. Engr. Mag. Home: 337 S 127th St Omaha NE 68154 Office: 8600 Indian Hills Dr Omaha NE 68114

MATTIX, STEWART WAYNE, ednl. adminstr.; b. Chgo., Oct. 29, 1931; s. Stewart Leroy and Lillian Florence (King) M.; B.S., Ball State U., 1954, M.S., 1960; postgrad. Purdue U., 1967, Ind. U., 1968-69; m. Connie Irene Day, Aug. 7, 1954; children—Richard Bruce, Lori Jo, Beth Ann. Tchr. public schs., Hobart, Ind., 1954—, prin. George Earle Sch., 1962—. Mem. Hobart Park Dept., 1963-75, pres., 1965, 68, 74; mem. Hobart Plan Commn., 1975—, v.p., 1978, 81. Served with USNR, 1950-52, U.S. Army, 1955-57. Recipient Disting. Service award Hobart Jr. C. of C., 1959; Dist. One Prin. of Yr., 1976; Ind. Prin. of the Yr., 1976; Outstanding Alumni, Ball State U., 1979. Mem. Hobart Classroom Tchrs. (pres. 1958-59), Ind. Assn. Elem. Sch. Prins. (dist. rep. 1967-71, state pres. 1972), Nat. Assn. Elem. Sch. Prins. (state rep. 1977-79, dir. 1979—), Assn. for Supervision and Curriculum Devel. Episcopalian. Club: Rotary. Contbr. articles to profl. jours. Office: 400 N Wilson St Hobart IN 46342

MATTOX, MARK EDWARD, architect; b. Kewanna, Ind., Mar. 5, 1946; s. Arthur Taber and Audrey Veronica Enyart; B.Arch., Ball State U., 1971. In hist. documentation Ind. Covered Bridge Soc., 1971-72; project architect John S. Kane, Architect, Anderson, Ind., 1972-78; project architect, Interior Design, Gooden Assos., Muncie, Ind., 1978; architect Johnson & Richhardt, Anderson, 1978-79; project architect James Assos., Lafayette, Ind., 1979—. Mem. AIA (corp.), Wabash Valley Trust for Hist. Preservation. Club: Ind. Covered Bridge Soc. (hist. documentation of eight bridges for consideration of nat. register status, 1971-72). Home: 709 S Tenth St Lafayette IN 47905 Office: Suite 300 Rivercity Market Lafayette IN 47901

MATTSON, WILLIAM JOHN, surgeon; b. Chgo., Nov. 1, 1938; s. William J. and Mary Florence (Hardman) M.; A.B., Dartmouth Coll., 1960, B.M.S., 1961; M.D., Harvard U., 1963; m. Janet Marie Harvey, July 15, 1965; children—Jon Eric, James Harvey. Intern, U. Ill. Research and Ednl. Hosps., 1963-64; resident in surgery Univ. Hosp., Ann Arbor, Mich., 1964-69; staff surgeon Rapid City (S.D.) Regional Hosp., 1971—; practice medicine specializing in surgery, Rapid City, 1971—; instr. surgery U. S.D. Sch. Medicine, 1976-78, asso. clin. prof. surgery, 1978—. Served with USNR, 1969-71. Diplomate Am. Bd. Surgery. Fellow A.C.S.; mem. AMA, Soc. Clin. Vascular Surgery. Republican. Lutheran. Home: 228 Pinedale Dr Rapid City SD 57701 Office: 725 Meade St PO Box 2623 Rapid City SD 57709

MATUSCHKA, ERNEST PAUL, clin. psychologist; b. Omaha, Nov. 22, 1929; s. Milton Paul and Edna Frieda (Petermann) M.; B.A., Kearney State Coll., 1951; M.A., No. Colo. U., 1955; Ph.D., U. N.D., 1968; m. Verla Lee Smith, Sept. 16, 1951; children—Paul Richard, Diane Lyn, Mark Dolan, Laurie Lee. Prof. psychology Kearney (Nebr.) State Coll., 1970—; pvt. practice clin. psychology, Kerney, 1970—. Served with USAF, 1951-53. Mem. Am. Psychol. Assn., Nebr. Psychol. Assn. Contbr. articles to profl. jours.

MATUSZEWSKI, STANLEY, clergyman; b. Morris Run, Pa., May 4, 1915; s. Andrew and Mary (Czekalski) M.; grad. St. Andrew's Prep. Sem., Rochester, N.Y.; student La Salette Coll., Hartford, Conn., Scholastic Sem., Altamont, N.Y. Ordained priest Roman Catholic Ch., 1942; disciplinarian, prof. classics, La Salette Sem., Olivet, 1942-46, dir., 1948—; superior Midwest province LaSalette Fathers; founding editor Our Lady's Digest, 1946—; exec. bd. Nat. Catholic Decency in Reading Program; faculty adv. Midwest Conf. of Internat. Relations Clubs sponsored 1944 in Chgo. by Carnegie Endowment for Internat. Peace. Trustee Nat. Shrine of Immaculate Conception, Washington. Honored by Rochester, N.Y. Centennial Com. 1934 as Monroe County (N.Y.) orator. Mem. Mariological Soc. Am. (1954 award), Missionaries of Our Lady of La Salette, Catholic Press Assn., Canon Law Soc., Catholic Broadcasters' Assn., Religious Edn. Assn., Polish-Hungarian World Fedn. (trustee). K.C. Author: Rochester Centennial Oration; Youth Marches On. Home: Box 777 Twin Lakes WI 53181

MATZ, MILTON, clin. psychologist, rabbi; b. N.Y.C., June 30, 1927; s. Joshua E. and Sonja (Kiat) Matz; m. Anne L. Jaburg, June 20, 1952; children—Deborah, David. B.A., Yeshiva U., 1947; M.H.L., rabbinic ordination, Hebrew Union Coll., 1952, D.D. (hon.), 1977; Ph.D., U. Chgo., 1966. Certification Ohio Psychol. Assn. Bd. Examiners Psychologists, 1966; Licensed, Ohio Bd. Psychology, 1973. First lt. USAF, 1952-54; asst. rabbi Kehilath Anshei Maariv Temple, Chgo., 1954-57; rabbi Congregation B'nai Jehoshua, Chgo., 1957-59; dir. pastoral psychology, asso. rabbi The Temple, Cleve., 1959-66; sr. staff psychologist Fairhill Psychiat. Hosp., Cleve., 1966-69; adj. prof. Cleve. State U., 1966-70; clin. instr. Case-Western Res. Sch. Medicine, 1966-73, asst. clin. prof., 1973—, dir. Pastoral Psychology Service Inst., 1973—, clin. dir. bereavement project, 1978—; pvt. practice in clin. psychology, Beachwood, Ohio, 1966—; cons. dir. Erie Pastoral Psychology Inst., 1977—; cons. dir. pastoral tng. project Central Conf. Am. Rabbis, 1978-79. Sec., v.p. Greater Cleve. Bd. Rabbis, 1964-66; bd. mem. Jewish Children's Bur. and Bellefaire Jewish Community Center, Cleve., 1952-64; advisory bd. Div. Child Welfare, Cuyahoga County, Ohio, 1962-66; founding mem. Cuyahoga County Community Mental Health and Retardation Bd., Cleve., 1967-71, chmn., 1972-73; chmn. Central Conf. Am. Rabbis Com. on Judaism and Health, N.Y.C., 1975—. Diplomate Am. Assn. Pastoral Counselors; mem. Am., Ohio psychol. assns., Am. Assn. Pastoral Counselors. Author numerous papers and articles on treatment of marital conflict and grief, primary prevention of mental illness, psychology and religion, and pastoral tng.; recipient commendation for outstanding leadership in mental health Bd. Commrs. of Cuyahoga County, 1973. Home: 3346 Stockholm Rd Cleveland OH 44120 Office: 3609 Park East Beachwood OH 44122

MATZKO, MICHAEL NEWTON, personnel adminstr.; b. Butler, Pa., Nov. 17, 1940; s. Michael Frank and Elizabeth Ann (Palace) M.; B.A., Washington and Jefferson Coll., 1962; postgrad. Krannert Sch. Mgmt., Purdue U.; m. Pamela Dunning Zelt, Mar. 4, 1967; 1 son, David Michael. Loss prevention and loss prevention account rep. Liberty Mut. Ins. Co., Boston, 1969-72; corp. safety dir. Nat. Homes Corp., Lafayette, Ind., 1972-74, mgr. corp. safety and security, 1974-75, mgr. corp. safety, security and benefits, 1975-79, mgr. corp. personnel services, 1979—; lectr. to profl. groups on safety. Mem. Tippecanoe County (Ind.) CD Advisory Council, 1974—. Served to capt. U.S. Army, 1962-68; Vietnam. Decorated Air medal with 12 oak leaf clusters. Mem. Am. Soc. Safety Engrs., Am. Soc. Indsl. Security, Nat. Safety Council (exec. com. wood products and constrn. sect.), Nat. Fire Protection Assn., Am. Soc. Personnel Adminstrn., Phi Alpha Theta, Delta Tau Delta. Republican. Presbyterian. Club: Elks. Home: 2790 Linda Ln West Lafayette IN 47906 Office: PO Box 680 401 S Earl Ave Lafayette IN 47903

MAUGANS, JOHN CONRAD, lawyer; b. Miami County, Ind., May 10, 1938; s. Willis William and Evelyn Jeannette (Mills) M.; A.B., Manchester Coll., 1960; LL.B. with distinction (Krannert scholar), Ind. U., 1962, J.D., 1970; m. Judith M. Gallagher, Jan. 24, 1960; children—Lisa Denise, Stacy Erin, Kristen Cherie. Admitted to Ind. bar, 1962; with firm Barnes, Hickam, Pantzer & Boyd, Indpls., 1962-63; practice in Kokomo, 1966—; partner firm Bayliff, Harrigan, Cord & Maugans, 1969—; guest lectr. Coll. Bus., Manchester Coll. Chmn. Howard County fund dr. Manchester Coll., 1971; bd. dirs. Tribal Trials council Girl Scouts U.S.A., 1977—, Vols. in Community Service, 1978—. Served to capt. AUS, 1963-66. Mem. Am., Ind., Howard County bar assns., Am., Ind. trial lawyers assns., Manchester Coll. Alumni Assn. (chmn. area chpt. 1970), Manchester Coll. M. Alumni Assn. (pres. 1972), Order of Coif, Phi Delta Phi. Lutheran. Contbr. articles to legal jours. Home: 2013 S Malfalfa Rd Kokomo IN 46901 Office: Box 2249 123 N Buckeye Kokomo IN 46901

MAUL, WARREN EARL, publisher; b. Mpls., Jan. 7, 1923; s. Earl C. and Corinne Elizabeth (Hutchins) M.; student Army Coll. Program, Washington and Jefferson Coll., 1943-44; B.A., U. Minn., 1949; children by previous marriage—Daniel E., Peter W., Gordon R.; m. 2d Naomi A. Segal, Jan. 10, 1982. Reporter, adminstv. asst. Fin. and Commerce daily newspaper and Daily Market Record newspaper, Mpls., 1947-52, bus. news and market news editor, 1952-63, asst. pub., 1963-73, pres., pub., 1973—. Bd. dirs., pres. Legal Aid Soc. Mpls., Inc., 1980, Central Minn. Legal Services, 1981; bd. dirs., treas. Automobile Club Mpls.; moderator Trinity Community Ch., Mpls., 1967; trustee Colonial Ch., Edina, Minn., 1969-71, deacon, 1978-81. Served with inf. U.S. Army, 1942-45. Mem. Nat. Newspaper Assn., Am. Ct. and Comml. Newspaper Assn. (pres. 1955, 67, dir. 1977-78), Minn. Newspaper Assn. (Outstanding Service to Journalism award 1967, pres. 1970, 1970, dir. 1964-71), Sigma Delta Chi (treas. Minn. chpt.). Clubs: Mpls. Athletic (dir. 1970-73), Rotary (dir. 1973), Minn. Press (dir. 1971-75). Office: 615 S 7th St Minneapolis MN 55415

MAULDIN, WILLIAM H., cartoonist; b. Mountain Park, N.Mex., Oct. 29, 1921; s. Sidney Albert and Edith Katrina (Bemis) M.; ed. pub. schs., N.Mex. and Ariz.; student art Chgo. Acad. Fine Arts; M.A. (hon.), Conn. Wesleyan U., 1946; L.H.D. (hon.), Lincoln Coll., 1970; Litt.D. (hon.), Albion Coll., 1970, N.Mex. State U. at Las Cruces, 1972; m. Norma Jean Humphries, Feb. 28, 1942 (div. 1946); children—Bruce Patrick, Timothy; m. 2d, Natalie Sarah Evans, June 27, 1947 (dec. Aug. 1971); children—Andrew, David, John,

Nathaniel; m. 3d, Christine Ruth Lund, July 29, 1972; 1 dau., Kaja Lisa. Cartoonist, St. Louis Post-Dispatch, until 1962, Chgo. Sun-Times, 1962—; tech. adviser, actor in movie Teresa, 1950; actor The Red Badge of Courage, 1950. Served with AUS, 1940-45; with 45th Div. (worked part time on div. newspaper); transferred to Mediterranean edit. Stars and Stripes, 1943; participated in campaigns, Sicily, Italy, France, Germany. Decorated Purple Heart, Legion of Merit; recipient Pulitzer prize for cartoons, 1944, Pulitzer prize for satiric comment on plight of Boris Pasternak, 1958; Sigma Delta Chi journalism award for cartoons, 1964, 70, 72, Distinguished Service award, 1969; Prix Charles Huard de dessin de presse Found. Pour L'Art et la Recherche, 1974. Fellow Sigma Delta Chi. Author, cartoonist: Up Front (Book of the Month Club selection), 1945; Back Home (Book of the Month selection), 1947; cartoonist: Star Spangled Banter, 1941; Sicily Sketch Book, 1943; Star Spangled Banter (separate collection of cartoons), 1944; Mud, Mules and Mountains (Italy), 1944; This Damn Tree Leaks (Italy) 1945; A Sort of a Saga, 1949: Bill Mauldin's Army, 1951; Bill Mauldin in Korea, 1952; What's Got Your Back Up?, 1961; I've Decided I Want My Seat Back, 1965; The Brass Ring, 1972 (Book of Month Club selection); Mud and Guts, 1978. Address: care Chgo Sun-Times Chicago IL 60611

MAURER, JOHN J., state senator; b. Kenosha, Wis., July 11, 1922; student Marquette U., 1945-49; married; 2 children. Comml. airline pilot; mem. Wis. Senate, 1975—. Mem. Wis. Council Aeros.; town supr., Pleasant Prairie, Wis., 1961-63, town chmn., 1969-75. Served with USAAF, 1942-45. Mem. Air Line Pilots Assn. Internat. (chmn.), Air Force Assn., VFW, Kenosha County Assn. Retarded Citizens. Democrat. Address: Room 134 South State Capitol Madison WI 53702*

MAURER, RALPH RUDOLF, research physiologist; b. Monroe, Wis., Feb. 28, 1941; s. Fredrick Nicholas and Freida Marie (Wegmueller) M.; B.S., U. Wis., 1963; M.S., Cornell U., 1966, Ph.D., 1969; postgrad. (fellow) U. Goettingen (W. Ger.), 1969-71; m. Janet Emily Brew, June 16, 1963; children—Pamela Ann, Serena Beth, Melissa Dawn. Research asst., research asso. Cornell U., Ithaca, N.Y., 1963-69; sr. staff fellow Nat. Inst. Environ. Health Sci., Research Triangle Park, N.C., 1971-76; research physiologist Roman L. Hruska U.S. Meat Animal Research Center, Clay Center, Nebr., 1976—. Vice pres. bd. dirs. Hastings (Nebr.) Family Planning Clinic, 1980-81; fin. chmn. Community United Ch. of Christ, Raleigh, N.C., 1975-76; mem. bd. diaconate 1st Congl. United Ch. of Christ, Hastings, 1979, sec.-treas., 1980-81. Lalor fellow, 1969-70; Alexander von Humbolt fellow, 1969-71. Mem. Soc. for Study Reprodn., Soc. for Study Fertility, Am. Soc. Animal Sci., Am. Inst. Biol. Scis., Teratology Soc., Soc. for Cryobiology, Internat. Embryo Transfer Soc., Am. Tissue Bank Assn., AAAS, Sigma Xi. Contbr. articles to profl. jours., also chpts. to books. Home: 806 N 2d Ave Hastings NE 68901 Office: PO Box 166 Clay Center NE 68933

MAURICE, S. JOSEPH, physician; b. Chgo., Sept. 3, 1935; s. Samuel J. and Jennie (Colletti) M.; B.S., Loyola U., Chgo., 1956, M.D., 1960; m. Nancy L. Larkin, June 29, 1963; children—Samuel, Joseph, Gregory. Intern Cook County Hosp., Chgo., 1960-61; resident in surgery West Side VA Hosp., Chgo., 1963-67; practice medicine specializing in surgery, Chgo., 1967—; mem. staff Loretto Hosp., Oak Park Hosp. Served as flight surgeon USAF, 1961-63. Fellow A.C.S.; mem. Ill. Surg. Soc., Internat. Coll. Surgeons, AMA. Office: 5428 W Addison St Chicago IL 60651

MAURIEL, JOHN JOSEPH, JR., educator; b. Schenectady, May 4, 1932; s. John J. and Rosemary (Araneo) M.; A.B., U. Mich., 1953; M.B.A., Harvard U., 1961, D.B.A., 1964; m. Maryanne Kennedy, Aug. 25, 1962; 1 son, Michael. Sales rep IBM Corp., Schenectady, 1956-59; research asst. Harvard U., Cambridge, Mass., 1961-62, lectr. in econs., 1963-64, lectr. bus. adminstrn., 1964-65; asst. prof. U. Minn., Mpls., 1965-69, asst. prof., 1969-71, asso. prof., 1971—, dir. exec. program, 1971—, dir. exec. devel. center, 1979—; vis. prof. N. European Mgmt. Inst., 1975; dir. H.B. Fuller Co., Cowin Steel Co., Honeywell Aerospace & Def. Group Mgmt. Devel. Center, Midwest Group Relations CTR. Bd. dirs. Ind. Sch. Dist. 275, Golden Valley, Minn., 1977—. Served with U.S. Navy, 1953-56. Recipient Nat. Accountants Assn.-Twin Cities article of the Yr. award, 1969; Bush Found. Pub. Sch. Exec. fellow program co-dir. and grantee, 1976-80, others. Mem. Am. Acctg. Assn., Acad. Mgmt. Roman Catholic. Contbr. articles to profl. jours. Home: 4521 Westwood Ln Minneapolis MN 55416 Office: 324 BA 271 19th Ave Minneapolis MN 55455

MAUSBACH, MAURICE JAMES, research soil scientist; b. Viborg, S.D., Dec. 16, 1945; s. William Ernest and Mildred Ardell (Austin) M.; B.S., S.D. State U., 1967; M.S., Iowa State U., 1969, Ph.D., 1973; m. Connie Lynne McFarland, Aug. 6, 1966; children—Suzanne Renee, Heidi Erin. Research asst. Iowa State U., Ames, 1967-69, research asso., 1971-73; soil scientist U.S. Dept. Agr., Soil Conservation Service, Mitchell, S.D., 1969-71, Salem, S.D., 1973-76, research soil scientist Nat. Soil Survey Lab., Soil Conservation Service, Lincoln, Nebr., 1976—. Mem. Am. Soc. Agronomy, Soil Sci. Soc. Am., Soil Conservation Soc. Am., AAAS, Nebr. Soc. Profl. Scientists, Gamma Sigma Delta. Mem. United Ch. of Christ. Contbr. articles to profl. jours. Home: 2120 S 61st St Lincoln NE 68506 Office: Box 82503 100 Centennial Mall N Lincoln NE 68501

MAUZEY, ARMAND JEAN, physician; b. Findlay, Ill., Apr. 18, 1905; s. George Washington and Catherine E. (Cloos) M.; B.S., Eureka (Ill.) Coll., 1928; B.S., U. Ill., 1931, M.D., 1932; postgrad. U. Pa., 1937-38, M.Sc., 1940, D.Sc., 1948; m. Virginia E. Tompkins, May 25, 1945; children—Katherine E., John M., Suzanne R. Surveyman, U.S. C.E., East St. Louis, Ill., Coal Creek, Tenn. and Fairfax County, Va., summers 1925-30; intern St. Luke's Hosp., Chgo., 1932-33; gen. practice medicine, Shelbyville, Ill., 1934-37; resident in ob-gyn U. Ill. Coll. Medicine, Chgo., 1938-40, to clin. asso. prof.; practice medicine specializing in ob-gyn, Elmhurst, Ill.; cons. gynecologist Cook County Hosp., Chgo., 1946-49, Elgin (Ill.) State Hosp., 1949-52, Booth Meml. Hosp., Chgo., 1952-58; chmn. dept. ob-gyn Elmhurst Meml. Hosp., 1954-58, 66-67; pres. med. staff Meml. Hosp., DuPage County, Elmhurst, 1968-69. Bd. dirs. Elmhurst YMCA. Recipient 25 Year Teaching award U. Ill. Coll. Medicine, 1963; Achievement Citation award Eureka Coll., 1968; named to Athletic Hall of Fame, Eureka Coll., 1970. Served from 1st lt. to maj. M.C., AUS, 1941-46; ETO. Recipient Asso. Prof. Emeritus citation U. Ill. Coll. Med., 1976; diplomate Am. Bd. Obstetrics and Gynecology. Fellow A.C.S.; mem. A.M.A., Ill. (chmn. sect. obstetrics and gynecology 1951-52), Du Page County med. socs., Am. Coll. Obstetrics and Gynecology, Internat. Coll. Surgeons, Chgo. Gynecol. Soc., N.Y. Acad. Scis., Huguenot Soc. S.C., Nat. Huguenot Soc., Va. Hist. Soc., S.C. Hist. Soc., SAR, Huguenot Soc. London, Lambda Chi Alpha, Alpha Kappa Kappa. Republican. Episcopalian. Mason (50 Yr. Membership citation Findlay 1979). Author: The Mauzey-Mauzy Family-From the Crusades to Colonial America. Contbr. articles to med. jours. and hist. mags. Home: 21 Spinning Wheel Rd Apt 6A Hinsdale IL 60521

MAVIS, FREDERIC THEODORE, cons. engr.; b. Crocketts Bluff, Ark., Feb. 7, 1901; s. Martin John and Hinda (Cassens) Mewes; B.S. in C.E., U. Ill., 1922, M.S., 1926, C.E., 1932, Ph.D., 1935; postgrad. Technische Hochschule Karlsruhe, 1927-28; m. Edith Frances Foley, June 7, 1930. Office engr. charge of design Kelker, DeLeuw & Co., Cons. Engrs., Chgo., 1922-27; Freeman fellow ASCE, 1927-28; asst. prof. to dept. head U. Iowa, also cons. engr. Iowa Inst. Hydraulic Research, 1928-39; prof., head dept. civil engring. Pa. State Coll., 1939-44, Carnegie Inst. Tech., 1944-57; dean engring., prof. U. Md., 1957-67; ret., 1967; cons. engr., Macomb, Ill., 1967—; rep. Nat. Acad. Scis.-NSF, 1955-63. Recipient Wason medal for research Am. Concrete Inst., 1958; registered profl. engr., registered structural engr., Ill. Fellow ASCE; mem. ASME, Am. Waterworks Assn., Soc. Am. Mil. Engrs., Am. Soc. Engring. Edn., Sigma Xi, Tau Beta Pi, Phi Kappa Phi, Chi Epsilon, Pi Tau Sigma, Pi Kappa Phi. Republican. Club: Rotary (Paul Harris fellow). Author: (with Edith F. Mavis) Four Hundred Wildflowers in McDonough County, 1972; Construction of Nomographic Charts, 1939. Cons. editor Civil Engring. Series, 1948-54. Contbr. articles to profl. jours. Home: 215 W Piper St Macomb IL 61455

MAVRELIS, WILLIAM PETER, physician, surgeon; b. Waterloo, Iowa, Jan. 12, 1912; s. Peter L. and Amelia (Commandros) M.; student Iowa State Tchrs. Coll., 1930-32; B.S., U. Minn., 1934, M.D., 1937; m. Cornelia MacDonald, Mar. 1, 1938; children—Penelope, Amy, Peter. Intern, St. Francis Hosp., Peoria, Ill., 1936-37, resident, 1937-38; jr. pathology resident Cook County Hosp., Chgo., 1938-42, sr. pathology resident, 1942, sr. pathologist, 1946-50; pathologist, clin. pathologist Ill. Central Community Hosp., 1950-77; asst. prof. Northwestern Med. Sch., 1946-81; police surgeon, Chgo., 1957-81. Sec. bd. dirs. Ill. Central Community Hosp., 1974—. Served to lt. col. U.S. Army, 1942-46. Diplomate Am. Bd. Path. Anatomy. Mem. AMA, Am. Assn. Rwy. Surgeons, Assn. Practitioners and Infection Control, Am., Ill. assns. blood banks, Ill., Chgo. med. assns., Chgo. Path. Soc., Chgo. Gas Chromotography, Chgo. Mycol. Soc. Greek Orthodox. Clubs: Beverly Hills Tennis; Chgo. Athletic Assn. Home: 614 S Lombard Ave Oak Park IL 60304 Office: 5800 Stony Island Ave Chicago IL 60637

MAXFIELD, DONALD VINCENT, ins. exec.; b. Centralia, Ill., Apr. 19, 1914; s. Hurem Allen and Blanche (Copple) M.; B.S. in Accounting, U. Ill., 1936; grad. Sch. Banking, U. Wis., 1957; m. Elizabeth A. Hartz, May 19, 1945; children—James Allen, Susan Mary. Sr. accountant Grey, Hunter, Stenn, C.P.A.'s, Marion, Ill., 1936-39; asst. to controller Ill. Agrl. Assn., Chgo., 1939-41; asst. controller Clinton Foods (Iowa), 1945-50; systems analyst Hotpoint, Inc., Chgo., 1950-51; contoller Peter Fox Brewing Co., Chgo., 1951-53; asst. auditor Northern Trust Co., Chgo., 1953-57; asst. v.p., asst. controller Continental Casualty Co., Chgo., 1957-58, controller, 1958-60, v.p., 1960-62; v.p., treas. Canteen Corp., Chgo., 1962-64, fin. v.p., 1964-68, adminstrv. v.p., 1968, also dir. sub.'s; fin. v.p. Ky. Fried Chicken Corp., Nashville, 1968-70, pres. chief exec. officer, treas. Satellite 3 in 1 Corp., Atlanta, 1970-71; v.p. fin. Equity Nat. Industries, Atlanta, 1971-73; controller Central States S.E. and S.W. areas Health Welfare and Pension Funds, Chgo., 1973-79; cons., 1980—; dir. Mdse. Nat. Bank Chgo. Served to maj. AUS, 1941-45. Decorated Purple Heart. Mem. Fin. Execs. Inst., Am. Mgmt. Assn., Nat. Rifle Assn. Home: 1207 Inverleith Rd Lake Forest IL 60045 Office: 8550 W Bryn Mawr Chicago IL 60631

MAXMEN, HAROLD AARON, endodontist; b. Detroit, Jan. 26, 1909; s. Samuel Joseph and Anna (Galison) M.; Ph.C., Wayne U., 1931, B.S., in Pharmacy, 1932; D.D.S., U. Detroit, 1936; m. Ethel Tucker, July 3, 1941; children—Jerrold Samuel, Robert Leslie. Sr. dentist in charge Oakland County, Children's Fund Mich., 1936-37; supervising asso. dentist, Detroit Dept. Health Dental Clinics, 1937-45; individual practice endodontics, Detroit, 1939-63, Southfield, Mich., 1963—; cons. Sinai Hosp., Detroit, 1976—, ednl. commn. Detroit Dental Soc. Bd. dirs. Mich. chpt. Am. Cancer Soc., trustee, 1974-76; pres. Detroit Dist. Dental Soc. Found., 1973-74. Recipient merit award Detroit Dist. Dental Soc., Sinai Hosp. of Detroit, Certificate of Merit R.A. Sommer Endodontic Study Club U. Mich., 1976. Diplomate fellow Am. Bd. Endodontics. Fellow Acad. Internat. Dentistry, Internat. Coll. Dentists (recipient Brother's Keeper award 1971), Am. Coll. Dentists, Am. Coll. Stomatology; mem. Am. Assn. Endodontics, Detroit Dental Clinic Club, Am., Mich. (pres. 1950) socs. dentistry for children, Mich. Assn. Endodontists (founding pres. 1962-63), Mich. State (com. edn. and specialties), Detroit Dist. (chmn. health edn., trustee Found.), dental socs., U. Detroit Dental Alumni Assn. (pres.), ORT (founder Detroit chpt.), AAAS, Detroit Clinic Club (hon. life), Alpha Omega (internat. merit award, Maimonides award). Contbr. articles to dental jours. Home: 23087 Riverside Dr Southfield MI 48035 Office: 26789 Woodward Suite 201 Huntington Woods MI 48070

MAXON, HARRY RUSSELL, internist; b. Muncie, Ind., Aug. 28, 1941; s. Harry Russell and Mary Evelyn (Fox) M.; B.A., Stanford, 1963; M.D. with honors, Tulane U., 1967; m. Mary Isabelle Moss, June 17, 1967; children—Harry Russell, IV, Mary Evelyn, Ashley Layden. Intern, Naval Hosp., Portsmouth, Va., 1967-68, resident in internal medicine, 1968-71; spl. research fellow in nuclear medicine Cin. Gen. Hosp., 1973-74; practice medicine specializing in thyroidology, Cin., 1974—; asst. prof. radiology (nuclear medicine) U. Cin. Coll. Medicine, 1974-79, asso. prof., 1979—, asst. prof. medicine (endocrinology), 1974-79, asso. prof., 1979—; mem. staff Holmes Hosp., Cin., 1974—, chmn. med. records com., 1976-79; mem. staff Jewish Hosp., Cin., 1974—, Middletown Hosp., 1979—; spl. cons. thyroid effects of ionizing radiation to Brookhaven Nat. Lab., Nuclear Regulatory Commn., Nat. Council Radiation Protection; cons. MEDCO Peer Review, Inc.; dir. Maxon Corp., Muncie; v.p., dir. Assos. in Nuclear Medicine, Inc., Cin. Served with USN, 1967-73. Diplomate Am. Bd. Internal Medicine, Am. Bd. Nuclear Medicine; decorated Navy Commendation Medal. Fellow A.C.P.; mem. AMA, Am. Thyroid Assn. (environ. hazards com.), Ohio Med. Assn., Am. Soc. Nuclear Medicine, Soc. Internal Medicine Cin., Cin. Acad. Medicine. Republican. Episcopalian. Contbr. numerous articles to med. jours. Office: Cin Gen Hosp Cincinnati OH 45267

MAXWELL, FLORENCE HINSHAW (MRS. JOHN WILLIAMSON MAXWELL), civic worker; Nora, Ind., July 14, 1914; d. Asa Benton and Gertrude (Randall) Hinshaw; B.A. cum laude, Butler U., 1935; m. John Williamson Maxwell, June 5, 1936; children—Marilyn, William Douglas. Coordinate, bd. dirs. Sight Conservation and Aid to Blind, 1962-73, nat. chmn., 1969-73; active various fund drives; chmn. jamboree, hostess coms. North Central High Sch., 1959, 64; Girl Scouts U.S.A., 1937-38, 54-56; mus. chmn. Sr. Girl Scout Regional Council, 1956-57; scorekeeper Little League, 1955-57; bd. dirs. Nora Sch. Parents' Club, 1958-59, Eastwood Jr. High Sch. Triangle Club, 1959-62, Ind. State Symphony Soc. Women's Com., 1965-67, 76-79, Symphoguide chmn., 1976-79; vision screening Indpls. innercity pub. sch. kindergartens, pre-schs., 1962—, also Headstart, 1967—; asst. Glaucoma screening clinics Gen. Hosp., Glendale Shopping Center, City County Bldg., Am. Legion Nat. Hdqrs., Ind. Health Assn. Conf., 1962—; chmn. sight conservation and aid to blind Nat. Delta Gamma Found., Indpls., Columbus, Ohio, 1969-73; mem. telethon team Butler U. Fund, 1964; symphoguide hostess Internat. Conf. on Cities, 1971, Nat. League of Cities, 1972; mem. health adv. com. Headstart, 1976—, assessment team of compliance steering com., 1978-79; founder People of Vision Aux., 1981. Recipient Cable award Delta Gamma, 1969, Outstanding Alumna award, 1973, scholarship honoree, 1981; Key to City of Indpls., 1972, those Spl. People award Women in Communication, 1980. Mem. Nat., Ind. (dir. 1962—, exec. com. 1971—, sec., Sight Saving Award 1974) socs. to prevent blindness, Delta Gamma (chpt. golden anniversary celebration decade and communication chmn. 1975, treas. Alpha Tau house corp. 1975-78, nat. chmn. Parent Club Study Com. 1976-77; Service Recognition award 1977, Shield award 1981). Republican. Address: 1502 E 80th St Indianapolis IN 46240

MAXWELL, GORDON EARL, physician; b. Quinter, Kans., Nov. 30, 1929; s. George Earl and Mary (Hargitt) M.; student Fort Hays State Coll., 1948-49; B.A., U. Kans., 1951, M.D., 1955; m. Evelyn Mae Westhoff, May 31, 1952; children—Gregory Earl, Mary Evelyn, Cynthia Elaine, Stephanie Louise. Intern, Milw. County Gen. Hosp., 1955-56; resident in ob-gyn Confederate Meml. Med. Center, Shreveport, La., 1958-61; practice medicine specializing in ob-gyn Salina (Kans.) Clinic, 1961—; clin. instr. U. Kans. Med. Sch., Wichita br., 1979—; mem. Kans. State Bd. Healing Arts, 1979—. Trustee, Kans. Wesleyan U., Salina, 1979—; bd. dirs. Land Inst., 1976—. Served with USPHS, 1956-58. Diplomate Am. Bd. Ob-Gyn. Mem. Salina County Med. Soc., Kans. Med. Soc., Christian Med. Soc., Am. Coll. Ob-Gyn. Democrat. Mem. 1st Covenant Ch. Club: Presidents Assos. Marymount Coll. Contbr. articles to profl. jours. Home: 414 Wayne St Salina KS 67401 Office: 135 E Claflin St Salina KS 67401

MAXWELL, MADALYN, lawyer; b. Nashville, Ill., Jan. 9, 1926; d. Judge Ralph L. and Beulah (House) Maxwell; student Whitworth Coll., 1943-45; B.S., U. Ill., 1947, M.A., 1949; m. Thomas H. McGary, 1968. Admitted to Ill. bar, 1951; practiced in Nashville, Ill., 1951-53; with inheritance tax div. Ill. Atty. Gen. Office, Springfield, 1953-55, asst. atty. gen. in charge pub. assistance claims enforcement div., 1956—; asst. to treas. Sangamo Electric Co., Springfield, Ill., 1955-56. Vol. worker Springfield Meml. Hosp.; bd. dirs. Springfield Symphony, Sojourn Women's Center. Mem. Am., Ill., Sangamon County bar assns., Ill., Washington County, Sangamon County hist. socs. Episcopalian. Club: Pilot (Springfield). Home: 1100 Orendorff Pkwy Springfield IL 62704 Office: 524 S 2d St Springfield IL 62706

MAXWELL, PATRICIA JOY, assn. exec.; b. Belle Plaine, Iowa, Feb. 7, 1937; d. Verne Edwin and Julia Inez (Beem) M.; student Pepperdine Coll., 1954-55; B.S., Iowa State Tchrs. Coll., 1958; m. Davis H. Wright, Aug. 28, 1971 (div.). Dir. resource devel. Boys Clubs Am., Chgo., 1978-80; dir. mktg. and public affairs St. Francis Hosp., Wichita, Kans., 1980—; dir. profl. services Ency. Britannica Ednl. Corp.; cons. Prentice Hall Inc.; dir. VIP activities U.S. State Dept., 1958. Mem. Am. Mktg. Assn., Nat. Assn. Hosp. Devel., Public Relations Soc. Am., Nat. Soc. Fund Raising Execs. Republican. Methodist. Clubs: Eastern Star, Rebekah, Order White Shrine. Office: 1130 S Michigan Ave Chicago IL 60605

MAY, DIANNA LEE, home economist; b. Winfield, Kans., Dec. 11, 1943; d. Elbert Lewis and Helen Ruth (Limpp) Callison; student Cowley County Community Coll., 1970-72; B.S., Southwestern Coll., 1975; M.S. (Kans. Home Econs. Assn. Biennial scholar, 1975-76) Kans. State U., 1976; postgrad., 1979-81; children—Misti, Kelly, Randy. Tchr. home econs., jr. high sch., Independence, Kans., 1976-78; home econs. coordinator Cloud County Community Coll., 1978—; condr. human sexuality seminars for sr. high youth and parents United Meth. Ch. Mem. NEA, Kans. Edn. Assn., Am. Home Econs. Assn., Kans. Home Econs. Assn., Am. Vocat. Assn., Kans. Vocat. Assn., Kans. Assn. Vocat. Home Econs. Tchrs., Order of Mound, Kappa Omicron Phi, Omicron Nu, Phi Upsilon Omicron. Methodist. Club: Concordia Music (pres.), Concordia Tennis, Community Players, Community Band. Founder, devel. curriculum and design lab. facility for home econs. dept. Cloud County Community Coll., 1978-80. Home: 707 1/2 W Fifth Concordia KS 66901 Office: 2221 Campus Dr Concordia KS 66901

MAY, DOROTHY GRACE, biologist, musician; b. Kansas City, Mo., Oct. 5, 1942; d. Ralph Harold and Adelaida Gertrude (Elbe) Kelly; B.A., U. Kans., Lawrence, 1964, B.S. in Edn., 1965; Ph.D. in Entomology (AAUW predoctoral fellow), 1970; m. J. Russell May, Jr., Aug. 10, 1963; children—Charles Nephi, Ruth Frances. Instr., Longview Community Coll., Lees Summit, Mo., 1971-78; lectr. in biology Avila Coll., Kansas City, Mo., 1979—; vis. asst. prof. biology Rockhurst Coll., Kansas City, 1977-78; cellist Med. Arts Symphony, Kansas City (Kans.) Symphony; dulcimer player. Leader, Girl Scouts U.S.A. Mem. Sigma Xi, Sigma Delta Epsilon. Mem. Reorganized Ch. of Jesus Christ of Latter Day Saints. Club: Prairie Dulcimer. Author: Dulcimer Songbag, a Book for Beginners, 1978; Dulcimer Songbag for Christmas, 1978; Dulcimer Classicks, 1980; contbr. articles to sci. jours. Home: 7324 Canterbury St Prairie Village KS 66208 Office: Dept Biology Avila Coll 11901 Wornall St Kansas City MO 64145

MAY, EUGENE PINKNEY, psychologist; b. Louisville, May 1, 1931; s. Eugene Pinkney and Amanda Miller (Baskette) M.; B.A., George Peabody Coll., Nashville, 1953, M.A., 1966; Ph.D., U. Ill., Urbana, 1971. Tchr., Dade County, Fla., 1962-66; counselor Dade County schs., 1966-71; head resident, supervising counselor Hendrick House, Urbana, 1970-71; grad. counselor, research asst. U. Ill., 1969-71; psychologist VA Med. Center, Cleve., 1971—; pvt. practice, Cleve., 1973—; cons. psychologist, mem. adj. med. staff dept. psychiatry Evening Mental Health Clinic, Cleve. Met. Gen. Hosp., 1974—; adj. clin. asst. prof. dept. psychology Case-Western Res. U., 1978—; adj. prof. Ursuline Coll., 1980—; counselor Peace Corps advanced tng. project for Korea, summer 1966. Mem. Am., Ohio, Cleve. psychol. assns., Assn. Humanistic Psychology, Am. Personnel and Guidance Assn., Assn. Counselor Edn. and Supervision, Cleve. Acad. Cons. Psychologists, U. Ill. Alumni Assn., Phi Delta Kappa, Kappa Delta Pi. Author articles in field. Home: 2641 Euclid Heights Blvd Cleveland Heights OH 44106 Office: 10701 E Boulevard Cleveland OH 44106

MAY, JOHN LAWRENCE, archbishop; b. Evanston, Ill., Mar. 31, 1922; S.T.L., St. Mary of Lake Sem., Mundelein, Ill., 1947. Ordained priest Roman Cath. Ch., 1947; gen. sec., v.p. Cath. Ch. Extension Soc., 1959-67; titular bishop of Tagarbala, aux. bishop of Chgo., 1967-69; bishop of Mobile, 1969-80; archbishop of St. Louis, 1980—. Address: Chancery Office 4445 Lindell Blvd Saint Louis MO 63108

MAY, LINDA KAREN CARDIFF, plastic products mfg. co. exec.; b. San Mateo, Calif., Oct. 26, 1948; d. Leon Davis and Jane Vivian (Gallow) Cardiff; student Parkland Coll., 1976, U. Ill., 1976-78; m. Donald William May, Dec. 7, 1969; children—Charles David, Andrew William. Indsl. nurse C.S. Johnson Co., Champaign, Ill., 1978-79; safety dir. Solo Cup Co., Urbana, Ill., 1979—. Mem. Champaign County Crime Prevention Council, 1978-82, dir., 1980-82; mem. Champaign County Task Force on Arson, 1981—, Mercy Hosp. Aux. Mem. Nat. Registry Emergency Med. Technicians, Ill. Emergency Med. Technicians Assn., East Central Ill. Health Systems Agy., Am. Soc. Safety Engrs., Eta Sigma Gamma. Methodist. Home: 2703 Trafalgar Sq Champaign IL 61820

MAY, MARGRETHE, allied health educator; b. Tucson, Oct. 6, 1943; d. Robert A. and Margrethe (Holm) M.; student in nursing U. Mich., 1961-65, B.S. in Human Biology, 1970. Mem. operating room staff Hartford (Conn.) Hosp., 1965-68, U. Mich. Hosp., Ann Arbor,

1968-70; asst. operating room supr. U. Ariz. Hosp., Tucson, 1971-72; coordinator operating room tech. Pima Community Coll., Tucson, 1971-76; asst. prof., coordinator surg. tech. program Delta Coll., University Center, Mich., 1978—; cons. in surg. tech.; mem. Health Care Team Project; mem. Nat. Certifying Exam. Writing Com., 1974-76, 80—, chmn., 1981; co-chmn. Liaison Council on Cert., 1977, chmn., 1978, sec.-treas., 1979; mem. Visitation Team for Surg. Tech. Program Accreditation, 1974—; workshop presenter. Cert. surg. technologist, emergency med. technologist. Mem. Assn. Surg. Technologists, Am. Soc. Allied Health Professions. Home: 2616 Abbott Rd Apt I3 Midland MI 48640 Office: Delta College University Center MI 48710

MAY, ROBERT PORTER, electronics co. exec.; b. Mohawk, N.Y., Jan. 28, 1934; s. Calvin Andrew and Lila Marie (Porter) M.; B.S., Syracuse U., 1956; postgrad. Marshall-Wythe Sch. Law, Coll. William and Mary, 1970, George Washington U., 1973; m. Mary Ann Sullivan, Sept. 3, 1967; children—Susan Michele, Kelly Ann. Auditor, U.S. Air Force Auditor Gen., Utica, N.Y., 1957-60; price analyst U.S. Air Force, Griffiss AFB, Rome, N.Y., 1960-63; mgr. purchasing Page Communications Engrs., Washington, 1963-65; mgr. contracts Litcom div. Litton Industries, New Rochelle, N.Y., 1965-69; dir. contract mgmt. Cin. Electronics Corp., 1969—. Pres. Cin-Tronics Fed Credit Union. Certified profl. contracts mgr. Mem. Nat. Def. Preparedness Assn., Nat. Contract Mgmt. Assn. (past pres., dir. Cin. chpt.), Assn. Old Crows, Nat. Security Indsl. Assn. (mem. com.), Cin. Electronics Mgmt. Club (past pres., dir.). Republican. Clubs: Masons, Shriners. Home: 8825 Tammy Dr West Chester OH 45069 Office: 2630 Glendale-Milford Rd Cincinnati OH 45241

MAY, RONALD CHARLES, mfg. co. exec.; b. Corpus Christi, Oct. 4, 1945; s. Warren Charles and Kathryn Marie (Mange) M.; B.S., U. Mo., 1973; M.B.A., So. Ill. U., 1978; m. Lynda D. Sylvester, Jan. 5, 1973. Draftsman, Sterling div. Fed. Mogul Corp., St. Louis, 1964-67; buyer Wagner div. McGraw Edison Co., St. Louis, 1973-74, asst. purchasing agt., 1974-75, purchasing agt., 1975-76, mgr. purchases, brake products, 1976-80, mgr. corp. purchases, automotive parts, 1980-81; dir. purchasing Hussmann Refrigerator div. IC Industries, St. Louis, 1981—. Served with USAF, 1967-71. Mem. Nat. Assn. Purchasing Mgmt., Am. Foundrymens Soc., Assn. M.B.A. Execs., Soc. Automotive Engrs. Home: 709 Paschon Ct Florissant MO 63034 Office: 12999 St Charles Rock Rd Bridgeton MO 63044

MAY, TIMOTHY JON, mfg. co. exec.; b. Garrett, Ind., May 19, 1952; s. Norbert John and Cordelia Leora (Diederich) M.; B.S., Ball State U., 1974; M.B.A., Butler U., 1979; m. Doris Adele Nelson, Aug. 23, 1975; children—Lauren Elizabeth, Andrea Nicole. Computer operator Warner Gear div. Borg Warner Corp., Muncie, Ind., 1974-75, prodn. planner, 1975-79, buyer, 1980-81; materials mgr. Chgo. Gear ops. Ex-Cell-O Corp., Chgo., 1981—; tchr. Ind. Vocat. Tech. Inst. Mem. Nat. Assn. Purchasing Mgrs., Am. Prodn. and Inventory Control Soc., Am. Soc. M.B.A.'s. Home: 650 Willow Rd Naperville IL 60540 Office: 2823 W Fulton St Chicago IL 60625

MAYBERG, DONALD MAC MILLAN, psychiatrist; b. Mpls., Oct. 31, 1924; s. Marc Norman and Grace Margaret (Challman) M.; B.A., U. Minn., 1948, M.D., 1952; m. Betty Lou Davis, Oct. 29, 1971; children—Stephen, Susan, Marc, Nancy, Barbara. Intern, Madigan Army Gen. Hosp., Tacoma, 1952-53; resident in psychiatry U. Minn. Hosps., Mpls., 1954-57; instr. psychiatry U. Minn., 1957-58; practice medicine specializing in psychiatry, Mpls., 1958—; clin. prof. psychiatry U. Minn.; dir. psychiat. edn. and tng. Abbott-Northwestern Hosp.; med. dir. Med. Psychiat. Assos.; cons. Dept. Def., FAA, McGraw-Hill Publs. Served to capt., USAF, 1942-46, 52- 54. Fellow Am. Psychiat. Assn.; mem. Am., Minn. (pres.) psychiat. assns., AMA, Family and Children's Assn. (bd. dirs.), Hennepin County Psychiat. Soc., Hennepin County Med. Assn., Alpha Delta Phi, Nu Sigma Nu. Presbyterian. Contbr. to Modern Medicine, 1954-59. Office: 2545 Chicago Ave Minneapolis MN 55404

MAYBERRY, WILLIAM EUGENE, physician; b. Cookeville, Tenn., Aug. 22, 1929; s. Henry Eugene and Beatrice Lucille (Maynard) M.; student Tenn. Technol. U., 1947-49; M.D., U. Tenn., 1953; M.S. in Medicine, U. Minn., 1959; intern U.S. Naval Hosp., Phila., 1953-54; resident Mayo Grad. Sch. Medicine, Rochester, Minn., 1956-59; m. Jane G. Foster, Dec. 29, 1953; children—Ann Graves, Paul Foster. Mem. staff New Eng. Med. Center, Boston, 1959-61, Nat. Inst. Arthritis and Metabolic Diseases, 1962-64; staff Mayo Clinic, Rochester, 1960-62, 64—, cons. internal medicine, endocrine research and lab. medicine, chmn. dept. lab. medicine, 1971-75, bd. govs., 1971—, vice chmn., 1974-75, chmn., 1976—, chief exec. officer, 1977—; asst. in medicine Tufts U. Med. Sch., 1959-60; faculty Mayo Grad. Sch. Medicine and Mayo Med. Sch., 1960—, now prof. lab. medicine. Trustee, Mayo Found., 1971—, vice chmn., 1974—. Diplomate Am. Bd. Internal Medicine. Fellow A.C.P.; mem. Am. Thyroid Assn., Am. Chem. Soc., Am. Fedn. for Clin. Research, Endocrine Soc., Central Research Club, Central Soc. for Clin. Research, Am. Clin. and Climatol. Assn., Sigma Xi. Clubs: Rochester Golf and Country, Mpls. Recipient Distinguished Alumni award Tenn. Technol. U., 1976; NIH research fellow, 1959-60, Am. Cancer Soc. research fellow, 1962-64; NIH research grantee, 1965-71; mem. editorial bd. Jour. of Clin. Endocrinology and Metabolism, 1971-73; contbr. articles to profl. jours. Home: 705 SW 8th Ave Rochester MN 55901 Office: 200 SW 1st St Rochester MN 55901

MAYE, RICHARD, clergyman; b. Uniontown, Ala., Oct. 25, 1933; s. Johnny and Frances (May) Boykin; B.A., Sangamon State U., Springfield, Ill., 1972, M.A., 1972; m. Rose Owens, June 24, 1978; children—Darryl Kermit, Byron Keith. Juvenile parole agt. Ill. Dept. Corrections, Chgo., 1967-70, adminstrv. asst., Springfield, 1970-72; lectr. polit. sci. Ill. State U., Normal, 1973-77; ordained to ministry Baptist Ch., 1960; pastor Pleasant Grove Bapt. Ch., Springfield, 1970—; mem. faculty Chgo. Bapt. Inst., 1968-70. Mem. Springfield Civil Service Commn., 1979—; mem. sch. integration commn., Springfield, 1977-79; bd. dirs. Morgan-Washington Home Girls, Springfield, 1977, Lincoln Library, Springfield, 1975-76; mem. grad. council So. Ill. U., 1975-76; mem. citizen's adv. com. Ill. Dept. Children and Family Services, Springfield, 1980-81; chmn. bd. dirs. Access to Housing, Springfield, 1981-83. Served with AUS, 1954-56. Grad. fellow U. Iowa, 1977-78, 79-80; grad. dean fellow So. Ill. U., 1975-76; recipient Citizen of Year award Springfield NAACP, 1976, Public Service award U.S. Dist. Ct., Springfield, 1978. Mem. Nat. Polit. Sci. Assn., Greater Springfield Interfaith Assn. (v.p.).

MAYER, CHARLOTTE MARIE, counselor; b. Hutsonville, Ill., Nov. 5, 1914; d. Ralph Monroe and Beulah May (Lionberger) Young; B.S., Butler U., 1937; M.S., U. Ill., 1939; M.A., Syracuse U., 1955; specialist cert. in counseling, Northwestern U., 1964; postgrad No. Ill. U., 1968-70; Ph.D., Walden U., 1978; m. Merl G. Mayer, Dec. 25, 1961 (dec.); children—Michael, Mark, Marshall, Judith, Mary Lynn. Sci. tchr., Ill., Ohio, N.C., 1942-52; counselor Central High Sch., Charlotte, N.C., 1952-55; sci. tchr. Charlotte Country Day Sch., 1955-61; sci. editor Laidlaw Pub. Co., River Forest, Ill., 1968-70; counselor, com. Sch. Dist. 21, Wheeling, Ill., 1962-68, 70-80; cons. in field. Leader, Girl Scouts U.S.A., Dover, Ohio, 1945-47. Ford fellow, 1954-55; recipient Star Tchr. award Nat. Sci. Tchrs. Assn., 1960. Mem. AAUW (chairperson Ohio State arts 1947), Ill. Edn. Assn., NEA, Ill. Guidance And Personnel Assn., Am. Ednl. Research Assn., Ill. Sch. Counselors Assn., Am. Personnel and Guidance Assn., Nat. Soc. Arts and Letters (art chairperson 1976-77). Congregationalist. Home: 49 Waverly Clarendon Hills IL 60514

MAYER, FOSTER LEE, JR., biologist; b. Fletcher, Okla., Nov. 17, 1942; s. Foster Lee and Annis Lucille (Edwards) M.; student U. Okla., 1960-61; B.S. in Biology and Chemistry, Southwestern State U., Weatherford, Okla., 1965; M.S. in Wildlife Biology, Utah State U., 1967, Ph.D. in Toxicology, 1970; m. Anita June Poarch, Aug. 31, 1962; children—Sunie Kaye, Carolyn Elizabeth. Instr. Utah State U., 1969; research sect. leader Columbia (Mo.) Nat. Fisheries Research Lab., 1970-72, asst. chief biologist, 1973-74, chief biologist, 1974-81, research scientist, 1981—; research asso. U. Mo., 1972—; mem. U.S.-USSR Sci. Exchange, 1978-79, 81. Project leader 4-H, Columbia, 1968—. Federal Water Quality and Pollution Control Adminstr. fellow, 1967-70; NSF grantee, 1964; recipient U.S. Fish and Wildlife Service Spl. Achievement award, 1973, 81, citation for outstanding performance, 1977, Quality Performance award, 1977. Mem. Am. Chem. Soc., Am. Fisheries Soc. (v.p. water quality sect. 1977-78, pres. 1978-79), ASTM, N. Am. Benthological Soc., Soc. Toxicology, Am. Inst. Fishery Research Biologists. Democrat. Baptist. Club: Columbia Green Valley Rifle and Pistol. Mem. editorial bd. Jour. of Environ. Sci. and Health, 1978—. Contbr. articles to profl. jours. Home: 7440 Sunnyvale Dr Columbia MO 65201 Office: Columbia Nat Fisheries Lab Route 1 Columbia MO 65201

MAYER, FREDERICK WILLIAM, city planner; b. Bloomfield, N.J., Sept. 18, 1937; s. Frederick William and Frances Marie (Smithley) M.; student Pratt Inst., 1955-58; A.B. (Henry Rutgers scholar), Rutgers U., 1961; M.R.P. (Sears fellow in city and regional planning), Cornell U., 1963; m. Carole Jean Miller, Aug. 6, 1966; children—William, Robert. Asso. Marcou-O'Leary & Assos., Washington, 1963-65; asst. univ. planner U. Mich., Ann Arbor, 1966-68, univ. planner, 1968-74, asst. dir. capitalpplanning and univ. planner, 1974—, also guest lectr. higher edn. program. Bd. dirs. Ann Arbor Library, 1976—, chmn., 1978—. Registered profl. community planner, Mich. Mem. Am. Planning Assn., Am. Inst. Cert. Planners, Soc. Coll. and Univ. Planning, Mich. Soc. Planners, Phi Beta Kappa. Roman Catholic. Club: Huron Portage Yacht. Author: Campus Planning-1967, 1967; contbr. articles in field to profl. jours.; editor: Contrasting Concepts in Campus Planning, 1966; author master plans for Frostburg, Maryland and Greencastle, Pa.; co-author master plans for Waynesboro, Pa., Wyoming County, W.Va., key growth areas of Chesapeake City, Va. Editor: Planning for Higher Education, 1980—. Home: 1731 Waltham Ann Arbor MI 48103 Office: 326 E Hoover Ann Arbor MI 48109

MAYER, GEORGE RICHARD, banker; b. Sandusky, Ohio, June 22, 1934; s. Eugene M.; B.S.B.A., Kent State U., 1957; postgrad. Grad. Sch. Banking, U. Wis., 1970; m. Barbara Ann Maurer, June 4, 1960; 1 dau., Lisa Michele. With Western Security Bank (now BancOhio Nat. Bank), Sandusky, Ohio, 1960; br. mgr. Erie County Bank, Vermilion, Ohio, 1960-65, cashier, 1965-70, sr. v.p., 1970-72, exec. v.p., 1972-73, pres., 1973—, chmn. bd., 1974—; instr. Ohio Sch. Banking at Ohio U., Grad. Sch. Banking, U. Wis.; mem. Ohio State Banking Bd., 1977—. Bd. dirs. Bowling Green State U., Firelands Coll., Sandusky Concert Assn.; mem. Erie County Health Planning Bd.; mem. N.E. affiliate Am. Heart Assn. Served in U.S. Army, 1958-60. Mem. Am. Bankers Assn. (exec. com. community bankers div. 1973-76), Ohio Bankers Assn. (past dir., past group chmn.). Episcopalian. Club: Rotary. Office: 4700 Liberty Ave Vermilion OH 44089

MAYER, HAROLD MAX, former meat packing co. exec.; b. Chgo., Mar. 18, 1917; s. Oscar G. and Elsa (Stieglitz) M.; B.S., Cornell U., 1939; m. June Sirotek, Nov. 16, 1963; children—Harold F., Richard A., Robert O. With Oscar Mayer & Co., 1939-81, trainee Madison (Wis.) plant, 1939-41, plant mgr., Chgo., 1953-61, v.p., 1948-66, sec., 1962-81, dir., 1951-81, exec. v.p., 1966-81, vice chmn. bd., 1973-77, chmn. exec. com., 1977-81; pres. Kartridg Pak Co., 1953-73, chmn. bd., 1973-77; past v.p., dir. Chgo. Profl. Basketball Team; past dir. Gen. Life Ins. Co., Milw., Williams Bros. Paper Box Co., St. Joseph, Mich. Mem. Chgo. Com. Alcoholism, 1957—, v.p., 1959, exec. v.p., 1960, vice chmn., 1972. Bd. dirs. Skokie Valley Community Hosp., St. Francis Hosp., Evanston, Ill.; past trustee U. Chgo. Cancer Found., Ill. Children's Home Aid Soc., Elmhurst (Ill.) Coll. Served to maj. AUS, 1942-46. Mem. Chgo. Assn. Commerce and Industry (dir.), Young Pres.'s Orgn. (past chpt. chmn.), Ill. C. of C., Chgo. Pres.'s Orgn. (pres. 1967-68), Cornell Alumni Assn., Cornell Soc. Hotelmen. Mason (Shriner). Clubs: Executives, Economic, Mid-Am., Metropolitan, Chgo. Yacht, Chgo. Athletic Assn. (Chgo.); Meadow (Rolling Meadows, Ill.); Imperial Golf (Naples, Fla.); North Shore Country (Glenview, Ill.). Home: 1420 Sheridan Rd #4-E Wilmette IL 60091 Office: One Northfield Plaza Suite 330 Northfield IL 60093

MAYER, HERBERT CARLETON, JR., computer scientist; b. Newton, Mass., Aug. 2, 1922; s. Herbert Carleton and Elsie Marie (Hauser) M.; B.S., Parsons Coll., 1943; M.S., U. Iowa, 1947; Ph.D., U. So. Calif., 1975; m. Maryetta Brodkord, Aug. 21, 1948; children—Judith Marie, Christine Louise. Instr. math. U. Idaho, Moscow, 1947-48, U. Utah, Salt Lake City, 1949-51; edn. adminstr. Gen. Electric Co., Richland, Wash., 1951-59; adj. prof. mgmt. U. Tex., El Paso, 1976-78; univ. industry specialist IBM Corp., Chgo., 1959-81. Pres., Tri-City Heights Assn., Kennewick, Wash., 1956-58; pres. PTA, Kennewick, 1957-58; v.p. Kennewick Sch. Bd., 1958, pres., 1959. Mem. Math. Assn. Am., Assn. Ednl. Data Systems, Am. Soc. Engring. Edn., Phi Delta Kappa. Office: 1 IBM Plaza Chicago IL 60611

MAYER, JEAN LOIS, health edn. program cons.; b. Cleve., May 12, 1931; d. Lewis Everett and Irene Marguerite (Warren) Yost; B.A., Denison U., Granville, Ohio, 1953; M.A., Mich. State U., 1975; m. Endre Agoston Mayer, June 17, 1956; children—Susan Jean, Sandra Jane, Warren Endre. Service rep. Ohio Bell Telephone Co., 1953-57; field dir., camp coordinator Camp Fire Girls, Pontiac, Mich., 1968-72; asst. to producer Sta. WXYZ-TV, Southfield, Mich., 1972-73; Christian edn. resource person 1st Baptist Ch., Mt. Clemens, Mich., 1975—; sr. health educator Am. Cancer Soc., Southfield, 1976-78; program cons. stroke, hypertension and heart disease in the young Mich. Heart Assn., 1978—; owner, operator Jean'Store, Wolverine, Mich., 1981—. Chmn. Birmingham (Mich.) Dial-a-Ride Study Com., 1976—. Mem. AAUW, Am., Mich. personnel and guidance assns., Mich. Assn. Group Workers, Mich. High Blood Pressure Council, Mich. Assn. Rehab. counselors. Baptist. Club: Altrusa (pres. 1981-82). Author articles. Home: 945 Poppleton St Birmingham MI 48008 Office: PO Box 160LV Lathrup Village MI 48076

MAYER, MICHAEL JOHN, psychologist; b. Columbia, Mo., July 7, 1941; s. Dennis Thomas and Virginia Louise (Miller) M.; B.A., Cardinal Glennon Coll., 1963; M.Ed., U. Mo., 1966; Ed.D., U. No. Colo., 1973. Dir. guidance and counseling Quincy (Ill.) Public Schs., 1966-78; psychologist Mark Twain Mental Health Center, Hannibal, Mo., 1978—; instr. adolescent psychology Quincy (Ill.) Coll. Chmn. Mayor's Adv. Commn., Quincy, 1979—; pres. Family Service Agy. Bd., Quincy, 1977; v.p. bd. dirs. Quincy Soc. Fine Arts, 1977. Registered psychologist, Ill. Mem. Ill. Parent Tchr. Assn., Am. Personnel and Guidance Assn., Am. Psychol. Assn., Group for Interagy. Devel., Phi Delta Kappa. Democrat. Roman Catholic. Author: How to Love, Understand and Cope with Teenagers, 1979. Home: 3100 Lantern Ln Quincy IL 62301 Office: 109 Virginia St Hannibal MO 63401

MAYER, RAYMOND RICHARD, educator; b. Chgo., Aug. 31, 1924; s. Adam and Mary (Bogdala) M.; B.S., Ill. Inst. Tech., 1948, M.S., 1954, Ph.D., 1957; m. Helen Lakowski, Jan. 30, 1954; children—Mark, John, Mary, Jane. Indsl. engr. Standard Oil Co., Whiting, Ind., 1948-51; organizational analyst Ford Motor Co., Chgo., 1951-53; instr. Ill. Inst. Tech., Chgo., 1953-56, asso. prof., 1958-60; asst. prof. U. Chgo., 1956-58; Walter F. Mullady prof. bus. adminstrn. Loyola U., Chgo., 1960—. Served with USNR, 1944-46. Ingersoll Found. fellow, 1955-56; Machinery and Allied Products Inst. fellow, 1954-55; Ford Found. fellow, 1962. Mem. Acad. of Mgmt., Am. Econ. Assn., Am. Statis. Assn., Am. Inst. for Decision Scis., Nat. Assn. Purchasing Mgmt., Polish Inst. Arts and Scis. in Am., Alpha Iota Delta, Alpha Kappa Psi, Beta Gamma Sigma. Author: Financial Analysis of Investment Alternatives, 1966; Production Management, 1962, rev. edit., 1968; Production and Operations Management, 1975, rev. edit., 1982; Capital Expenditure Analysis, 1978. Home: 1705 Ridge Ave Evanston IL 60201 Office: 820 N Michigan Ave Chicago IL 60611

MAYER, RICHARD, JR., newspaper editor; b. Sioux City, Iowa, May 26, 1923; s. Richard P. and Laura Wilma (Rouse) M.; B.S., Washburn U., 1949; postgrad. Kans. U., 1951-52; m. Anna Marie Simons, Oct. 29, 1950; children—Deborah, Bryce, Jill, Mike, Amy. Mem. staff Clay County (Nebr.) News, 1952-53; editor North Vernon (Ind.) Plain Dealer and Sun, 1954—. Sec. North Vernon Park Bds., 1959—. Mem. Hoosier State Press Assn. (dir.), North Vernon C. of C. (dir., pres.). Home: 12 Hare Ln North Vernon IN 47265 Office: 528 E O & M Ave North Vernon IN 47265

MAYERSAK, JEROME STEPHEN, urologist; b. Superior, Wis., July 4, 1938; s. Joseph Walter and Libby Jean (Conroy) M.; B.A., Johns Hopkins, 1960; M.D., George Washington U., 1964; m. Priscilla M. Kurtzweil, Mar. 27, 1976; children—Kathlyne Mary, Priscilla Kathlyne. Intern dept. surgery George Washington U. Hosp., Washington, 1964-65, resident in urology, 1966, chief resident, 1968; resident in surgery D.C. Gen. Hosp., 1965-66, resident in urology, 1966-67, sr. resident, 1967; resident in urology George Washington U. Sch. Medicine, 1966-69; sr. resident VA Hosp., 1968, chief resident, Washington, 1969; practice medicine specializing in urology, Wisconsin Rapids, Wis., 1969-71, Merrill, Wis., 1971—; urologist Med. Arts Group, Wisconsin Rapids, 1969-71; mem. staff Taylor County Meml. Hosp., Medford, Wis., 1970—; mem. staff Holy Cross Hosp., Merrill, Wis., 1971—, Tri-County Meml. Hosp., Whitehall, Wis., 1971—; mem. cons. staff Riverview Hosp., Wisconsin Rapids, 1969-73, Sacred Heart Hosp., Tomahawk, Wis., 1971—, Wild Rose (Wis.) Community Meml. Hosp., 1970—, Neillsville (Wis.) Meml. Hosp., 1969-73; jr. cons. to St. Elizabeth's Hosp., Washington, 1968-69; urologist J.S. Mayersak Service Corp., Merrill, 1971—; cons. urologist Langlade County Meml. Hosp., Antigo, Wis., Eagle River (Wis.) Hosp., Park Falls (Wis.) Hosp. Chmn. adv. airport com. to Airport Commn., Merrill, Wis., 1970-75; bd. dirs. Tri-County Meml. Hosp. Fellow William Beaumont Hon. Research Soc., St. George Cancer Soc.; mem. AMA, State Med. Soc. Wis., Am. Assn. Physicians and Surgeons, Am., Internat. socs. nephrology, Minn., Twin Cities urol. socs., Flying Physicians Assn., Wis., Lincoln County (pres. 1974-78), Aerospace med. socs., Am. Soc. Microbiology, A.C.S., Va. Acad. Scis., Pan Am. Med. Assn., Renal Physicians Assn., Royal Soc. London, Asociacion Medica Panamericana, Sociedad Ecuatoriana de Urologia (hon.), Am. Fertility Soc., Internat. Platform Assn., Wis. Physicians Union, AAAS, Mensa, Sigma Xi, Nu Sigma Nu. Club: Elks. Home and Office: 717 Tee Lane Dr Merrill WI 54452

MAYERSDORF, ASSA, physician; b. Israel, Sept. 21, 1937; M.D., Hebrew U.-Hadassah Med. Sch., Jerusalem, 1963; m. Nira Mayersdorf, 1965, 2 children. Intern, Hadassah-Hebrew Univ. Hosp., Jerusalem, 1962-63, resident in medicine, 1963; house officer neurosurgery Tel-Hashomer Govtl. Hosp., Israel, 1964-66; asst. resident dept. neurology Balt. City Hosp., 1966-68; asst. resident in neurology Johns Hopkins Hosp., Balt., 1968-69, chief resident, 1969; fellow Johns Hopkins Univ. Sch. Medicine, 1966-69; instr. div. neurology U. Fla. Coll. Medicine, Gainesville, 1970, asso. mem. Center for Neurobiol. Scis., 1970; chief sect. neurology Soroka Med. Center, Univ. Center for Health Scis., Ben-Gurion Univ., Beer-Sheva, Israel, 1971-74, guest lectr. Faculty Scis., 1971-74; asst. prof. dept. neurology U. Minn. Sch. Medicine, Mpls., 1974-80; asso. prof. neurology Med. Coll. Wis., 1980—; dir. Epilepsy Treatment Center VA Hosp., Mpls., 1974-80; chief neurology service Wood VA Med. Center, 1980—. Bd. dirs. Minn. Epilepsy League, 1975-78, sec., 1977-78. Served with Israel Def. Armed Forces, 1963-66. Diplomate Am. Bd. Neurology and Psychiatry. Mem. Am. Acad. Neurology, Am. Epilepsy Soc., Epilepsy Found. Am., Am. Med. EEG Assn., Central EEG Assn., Israel Med. Assn., Israel Neurol. Soc. Israel Soc. Electroencephalography.

MAYESKI, FRAN ELIZABETH, ednl. devel. adminstr.; b. Rolla, Mo., Nov. 6, 1941; d. Charles Emil and Katherine Dorothy (Parker) Gelven; B.S. in English, St. Louis U., 1964; postgrad. in edn. U. Wash., 1974; M.B.A., City Coll. Seattle, 1980; m. John Kent Mayeski, May 21, 1966; 1 son, Mark Edward. Publs. asst. St. Louis U., 1965-66; tchr. English, social studies, University City, Mo., 1964-65, Spokane, Wash., 1967-68, Colorado Springs, Colo., 1969, Bellevue, Wash., 1971-74; tchr. social studies Interlake High Sch., Bellevue, 1974-76, area chairperson for social studies, 1976-77, tchr., project leader in social studies, 1977-79; trainer Profl. Devel. Center, 1979-80; dir. staff devel. Ednl. Service Unit 10, Kearney, Nebr., 1980—; instr. Seattle Pacific U., 1979-80, Kearney State Coll., 1980—; pres. Puget Sound Council for Social Studies, 1974-75, Wash. State Council for Social Studies, 1976-77. Pres. sch. bd. Holy Family Sch., Kirkland, Wash., 1976-77. Mem. Assn. Supervision and Curriculum Devel., Nebr. Assn. Supervision and Curriculum Devel., Women in Mgmt. Assn., Ednl. Service Unit Assn. for Staff and Inservice Devel. Roman Catholic. Clubs: Kearney State Coll. Faculty Wives, Order Does. Editor monthly faculty newspaper St. Louis U. (Am. Coll. Public Relations Assn. 2 nat. certs. spl. merit 1966), 1965-66. Office: Ednl Service Unit 10 PO Box 2007 Kearney NE 68847

MAYFIELD, DARRELL GEORGE, hosp. adminstr.; b. Chgo., July 22, 1952; s. Lawrence and Helen M.; student Dartmouth Coll., 1969-72; B.A., Chgo. State U., 1975; M.Mgmt., Northwestern U., 1977; m. Jan Elaine Irwin, Oct. 21, 1978. Adminstrv. intern Michael Reese Hosp. and Med. Center, Chgo., 1974, Am. Hosp. Assn., Chgo., 1975, U. Minn. Hosps., Mpls., 1977; staff cons. Arthur Andersen & Co., Chgo., 1977-79; asst. adminstr. Provident Hosp. and Tng. Sch. Assn., Chgo., 1979—. Mem. Am. Coll. Hosp. Adminstrs., Am. Mgmt. Assn., Hosp. Fin. Mgmt. Assn., Nat. Assn. Health Services Execs., Nat. Black M.B.A. Assn., Young Adminstrs. Chgo. Office: 426 E 51st St Chicago IL 60615*

MAYHEW, SHARON CALDWELL, educator; b. Marshalltown, Iowa, June 4, 1939; d. Daniel Maurice and Louise Jean (Lawson) Caldwell; B.S., Bob Jones U., 1960; M.A., Mich. State U., 1975, now postgrad.; children—Mark Robert, Peter Robert. Asst. dietition and social sec. Student Center, Bob Jones U., 1960-62; tchr. home econs. Miami (Fla.) schs., 1962-66; tchr. home econs. Bowie (Md.) schs., 1966-68; tchr. home econs. Lindenhurst (N.Y.) schs., 1968; tchr. home econs., bus. edn. Owosso (Mich.) schs., 1968-73, tchr. foods and nutrition, chmn. dept., 1974—; designer pre-sch. program Cherry Hills Preschool, Springfield, Ill., 1973-74. NSF fellow, 1966. Mem. Am. Home Econs. Assn., Mich. Home Econs. Assn., Mich. Occupational Ednl. Assn., Am. Vocat. Assn., Owosso Edn. Assn., Mich. Ednl. Assn., NEA, Soc. Profs. Edn., AAUW, Delta Kappa Gamma. Baptist. Home: 1015 Krust Dr Owosso MI 48867 Office: 765 E North St Owosso MI 48867

MAYHUE, BERTHA EVELYN, dietitician; b. Muskogee, Okla., Apr. 8, 1936; d. Samuel and Alma M.; B.A., Wichita State U., 1958; M.S., Kans. State U., Manhattan, 1976. Intern, Kans. U. Med. Center, 1958-59; clin. dietitian St. Francis Hosp., Wichita, 1959-67, clinic dietitian, 1967-72, instr. nutrition, 1972-80; now cons. dietitian nursing homes; advisor Wichita Food Service Suprs. Assn. Former bd. dirs. Diabetes Assn. Kans. Mem. Wichita Dietetic Assn. (past pres.), Black Nurses Assn. (past dir.), Am. Dietetic Assn. Methodist. Home and Office: 2319 E 20th St Wichita KS 67214

MAYL, JACK JOSEPH, lawyer; b. Dayton, Ohio, June 21, 1930; s. Eugene Aloysius and Helen Irene (Cooper) M.; B.S. cum laude, U. Notre Dame, 1952; J.D., Georgetown U., 1958; m. Gay Reddig, Apr. 8, 1972. Admitted to Ohio bar, 1960; partner firm Murphy & Mayl, Dayton, 1960—; dir. Central Pharmacal Co., Seymour, Ind., R.L. Consol. Inc., Canton, Ohio. Served to lt. USNR, 1953-56. Mem. Internat., Inter-Am., Am., Ohio, Dayton bar assns., Antique Automobile Club Am., Rolls Royce Owners Club, Packards Internat., Classic Car Club Am., Phi Alpha Delta. Clubs: Lawyers, Dayton Country, Dayton Racquet; Union (Cleve.). Home: Plantation Ln Kettering OH 45419 Office: 2660 Winters Bank Tower Dayton OH 45423

MAYLATH, DONALD OLIVER, food ingredient supply co. co. exec.; b. Granite City, Ill., Dec. 9, 1933; s. Aladar and Mary Margaret (Petesh) M.; B.S., U. Ill., 1955; postgrad. St. Louis U., 1959-62, U. Minn., 1963-68; children—Pamela, Mark, Carol. Reporter, St. Louis Globe-Democrat, 1955-56; asst. advt. mgr. Bemis Co., Inc., St. Louis, 1958-63, market research analyst, Mpls., 1963-67, asst. pricing mgr., 1967-68; mgr. mktg. research Union div. Miles Labs., Inc., Granite City, Ill., 1968-71, mgr. mktg. research Marschall div., Elkhart, Ind., 1971-75, mgr. mktg. services, 1976—. Served with U.S. Army, 1956-58. Mem. Am. Mktg. Assn., Inst. Food Technologists, European Chem. Mktg. Research Assn., European Assn. Indsl. Mktg. Research, European Mktg. Assn., Internat. Market Research Assn., Assn. M.B.A. Execs., Acad. Mktg. Sci., Nat. Assn. Bus. Economists, Mktg. Communication Execs., Am. Statis. Assn., Midwest Planning Assn., Midwest Chem. Mktg. Assn., Sigma Delta Chi. Roman Catholic. Club: Elks. Home: 51068 Shady Ln Elkhart IN 46514 Office: PO Box 932 1127 Myrtle St Elkhart IN 46515

MAYMAN, MARTIN, educator; b. N.Y.C., Apr. 2, 1924; s. Abraham and Anna (Mann) M.; B.S., Coll. City N.Y., 1943; M.S., N.Y. U., 1947; Ph.D., U. Kans., 1953; m. Rosemary Walker, Oct. 12, 1960 (div.); children—Sara, Stephen, Daniel. Clin. psychologist Menninger Found., Topeka, Kans., 1944-46; clin. instr. U. Kans. and Winter VA Hosp., Topeka, 1946-51; dir. psychol. training Menninger Found., Topeka, 1951-65; vis. prof. U. Colo., Denver; 1965-66, U. Calif. at Berkeley, summer 1966; prof. psychology U. Mich., Ann Arbor, 1966—, also dir. Psychol. Clinic; faculty Topeka Psychoanalytic Inst., 1960—, Mich. Psychoanalytic Inst., Detroit, 1967—. Participant Nat. Conf. on Profl. Tng. in Clin. Psychology, 1960. Fellow Am. Psychol. Assn., Am. Bd. Examiners Profl. Psychology; mem. Mich. Psychoanalytic Assn., Topeka Psychoanalytic Assn., Soc. for Personality Assessment (pres. 1967-68). Author: Psychoanalytic Research: Three Approaches to the Experimental Study of Subliminal Processes, 1973; (with K. A. Menninger and P. Pruyser) The Vital Balance, 1963; (with K. A. Menninger and P. Pruyser) A Manual for Psychiatric Case Study, 2d edit., 1963; editor: Psychoanalytic Inquiry, 1980—; adv. editor jour. Consulting Psychology, 1965-70, Psychotherapy, 1975—. Home: 3969 Penberton Ann Arbor MI 48105

MAYO, FRANCIS THOMAS, research lab. adminstr.; b. Bklyn., June 16, 1924; s. Francis Joseph and Katherine (Keevan) M.; B.S. with honors in Civil Engring., U. Utah, 1950; m. Margaret Betts, Mar. 22, 1947; children—Katherine, Maureen, Kevin, Patrick, Franette, Michael. Hydrological engr. U.S. Geol. Survey, Salt Lake City, 1950-52; chief water resources div. Utah State Engr.'s Office, Salt Lake City, 1952-66; regional enforcement rep. San Francisco regional office Fed. Water Pollution Control Adminstrn., 1966-68; dir. div. of planning and interagy. program Fed. Water Control Adminstrn., Washington, 1968-70; regional adminstr. region V,EPA, Chgo., 1970-76; dir. mcpl. environ. research lab. EPA, Cin., 1976—; alt. commr. Great Lakes Basin Commn., 1970, commr., 1971-76; U.S. co-chmn. Great Lakes Water Quality Adv. Bd., Internat. Joint Commn., 1971-76; commr. Ohio River Basin Commn., 1971-76; commr. Upper Mississippi River Basin Commn., 1972-75; commr. Ohio River Valley Water Sanitation Commn., 1972-76. Chmn. bd. dirs. South Davis County (Utah) Sewer Improvement Dist., 1960-65; mem. Utah Public Employees Retirement Bd., 1965-66; pres. Utah State Employees Assn., 1964-65. Served with U.S. Army, 1943-46. Registered profl. engr., Utah. Recipient Disting. Alumnus award dept. civil engring. U. Utah, 1977; Bronze medal EPA, 1980. Mem. Am. Water Works Assn., Water Pollution Control Fedn., Chi Epsilon, Tau Beta Pi. Mormon. Club: Lions. Office: 26 W St Clair Cincinnati OH 45268

MAYRON, BART RICHARD, cardiologist; b. Chgo., Apr. 29, 1939; s. Max and Florence Minette M.; M.D., U. Ill., 1963; m. Myrna J. Roth, Sept. 10, 1958; children—Joel, Sheri, Amy. Intern, Presbyn.-St. Luke's Hosp., Chgo., 1963-64; resident in cardiology Westside VA Hosp., Chgo., 1967-69; practice medicine specializing in cardiology, Chgo., 1969—; asst. prof. medicine U. Ill. Diplomate Am. Bd. Internal Medicine. Fellow Am. Coll. Cardiology, Soc. Cardiac Angiography, Council on Clin. Cardiology, Am. Heart Assn.; mem. AMA, A.C.P. Jewish. Contbr. article in field to profl. publ. Office: 25 E Washington St Chicago IL 60602

MAYS, MAJOR DEWAYNE, soil scientist; b. Lexa, Ark., Nov. 22, 1946; s. Prince Albert and Almeta (Howse) M.; B.A., Ark. Agrl., Mech. and Normal Coll., 1968; M.S., Kans. State U., 1971; postgrad. U. Nebr., 1978—; m. Jareldine Bonds, Jan. 29, 1968; 1 son, Brian Dewayne. Teaching and research asst. Ark. AM&N Coll., Pine Bluff, 1966-68; soil scientist student trainee Soil Conservation Service, Nacogdoches, Tex., summers 1966-67, soil scientist, 1972-73, Athens, Tex., 1973-77, Nat. Soil Survey Lab., Lincoln, Nebr., 1977—; grad. research asst. Kans. State U., 1968-69; vol. conservation tchr. Lincoln Public Elem. Schs. Served with U.S. Army, 1969-70. Recipient Outstanding Group Performance award Soil Conservation Service, 1973, Superior Service Group Performance award, 1981. Mem. Soil Sci. Soc. Am., Soil Conservation Soc. Am., Internat. Soil Sci. Soc., NAACP, Coalition of Black Men, Alpha Phi Alpha. Baptist (deacon). Clubs: Toastmasters (treas.), Kiwanis (dir. club 1976-77). Home: 5001 Goldenrod Ln Lincoln NE 68512 Office: Soil Conservation Service Fed Bldg and US Courthouse Lincoln NE 68502

MAYS, RICHARD ANDREW, city ofcl.; b. Hempstead, N.Y., Aug. 10, 1950; s. William Ernest and Lucinda Sue (LaBella) M.; B.S., Western Ill. U., 1973; M.A. in Public Affairs, No. Ill. U., 1977; m. Anne Walters, Oct. 1, 1977. Supt. recreation Carol Stream (Ill.) Park Dist., 1973-75; supt. recreation Batavia (Ill.) Park Dist., 1975-78, exec. dir., 1978-81; dir. mgmt. services Village of Homewood (Ill.), 1981—; chmn. Batavia July 4th Fireworks Com., 1978, 79, 80, Batavia Arbor Day Com., 1981. Mem. Ill. Parks and Recreation Assn. (chmn. standing coms.), Suburban Parks and Recreation Assn., Nat. Parks and Recreation Assn., Ill. Community Edn. Assn., Alpha Tau Omega. Club: Kiwanis (Batavia). Home: 837 N 3d Ave Geneva IL 60134 Office: PO Box 433 Batavia IL 60510

MAZU, MICHAEL JOHN, statistician; b. Akron, Ohio, Jan. 27, 1943; s. Mike and Mildred Julia Mazu; B.S. in Math., U. Akron, 1971, M.S. in Stats., 1977; m. Patricia Baldwin, May 13, 1967; children—Christine, Gregory. With B.F. Goodrich Co., Akron, 1968—, sr. quality devel. engr., 1976-78, statistician tire group, 1978—; cons., tchr. in field. Served with USAR, 1965-67. Mem. Math. Assn. Am., Am. Statis. Assn., ASTM, Am. Soc. Quality Control, Akron Rubber Group, Akron Council Engring. and Sci. Socs., Am. Legion. Author papers in field. Home: 1025 Emma Ave Akron OH 44302 Office: 500 S Main St Akron OH 44318

MAZZUCA, LOIS CAMILLE, coll. cons.; b. Chgo., May 10, 1941; d. Lewis D. and Camille Carol (Parrillo) Mazzuca; B.A., Marycrest Coll., 1963; M.A., Northeastern Ill. State U., 1970. Tchr., counselor Notre Dame High Sch., Chgo., 1963-68; asso. dir. admissions Marycrest Coll., Davenport, Ia., 1968-70; counselor Prospect High Sch., Mt. Prospect, Ill., 1970-71; coll. cons. High Sch. Dist. 214, Rolling Meadows, Ill., 1971—. Vice chmn. Wood Dale Planning Bd., 1972-77; chmn. Wood Dale Bicentennial Commn., 1976; trustee, Addison Twp., 1977—; mem. Wood Dale Youth Commn., 1973; alderman City of Wood Dale, 1980; trustee DuPage County Regional Sch. Bd. Recipient Youth Achievement award, Chgo. Daily News, 1959; Vol. Service award, Dept. Mental Health, State of Ill., 1965-68; Distinguished Service award Ill. Bicentennial Commn., 1976. Mem. Nat. (pres. elect 1981), Ill. (pres. 1979) assns. coll. admissions counselors, Am., Ill. personnel and guidance assns. Republican. Roman Catholic. Club: Chgo. Council on Fgn. Relations. Contbr. articles to profl. jours. Home: 288 Charmille Ln Wood Dale IL 60191 Office: 2901 Central Rd Rolling Meadows IL 60008

MAZZULLA, RICHARD ANTHONY, govt. ofcl.; b. Chgo., July 16, 1941; s. Frank John and Angelina (Perri) M.; B.S. in History, Loyola U., 1963; m. Louise Ann Medor, Oct. 5, 1963; children—Laura Ann, Richard Anthony. Asst. adjudication VA, Chgo., 1966—. Pres., South Elm Baseball, 1978-79; mem. Dist. 401 Bd. Edn., Elmwood Park, Ill. Served to 1st lt. U.S. Army, 1964-66; maj. Res. Mem. Italian Am. Vets. (comdr. 1979-80), Sigma Pi Alpha (pres. 1977-79). Roman Catholic. Office: 536 S Clark Chicago IL 60608

MC ADAMS, PHILIPPINA DOHRMANN, educator; b. St. Louis, July 26, 1933; d. Frank Martin and Philippina Augusta (Maschmeier) Dohrmann; A.A., Harris Jr. Coll., 1952; R.N., Deaconess Hosp. Sch. Nursing, 1955; B.S. in Nursing, Washington U., 1957; M.Ed., U. Mo., 1977; m. Robert McAdams, June 29, 1957; children—James Robert, Paul Philip. Staff nurse Vis. Nurse Assn. Greater St. Louis, 1955-58; clin. instr., supr. outpatient clinic Deaconess Hosp., St. Louis, 1958-63, part-time staff nurse, 1963-66, part-time faculty Sch. of Nursing, 1966-69; clin. instr. nursing The Jewish Hosp. of St. Louis, 1970—, part-time counselor Sch. Nursing, 1977—. Vis. Nurse Assn. scholar, 1956; Jewish Hosp. scholar, 1976. Mem. Nat. League for Nursing, Am. Personnel and Guidance Assn., U. Mo. at St. Louis Alumni Assn. United Ch. of Christ. Office: 216 S Kingshighway Saint Louis MO 63110

MC ALEECE, DONALD JOHN, educator; b. Detroit, May 26, 1918; s. Joseph Patrick and Kathryn (DeLeeuw) McA.; B.S., Purdue U., 1952; M.A., Ball State U., 1968; m. Margaret Ann Mull, Nov. 25, 1954; children—Stephen Donald, Michele Denise. With Gen. Electric Co., Ft. Wayne, Ind., 1936-66; faculty Purdue U., Ft. Wayne Campus, 1966—, prof. dept. mech. engring. tech., 1966—; design engr. advanced safety research Ford Motor Co., Dearborn, Mich., 1972. Job placement cons. Outreach Office, Nat. Alliance of Businessmen, Ft. Wayne, 1968; indsl. engr. cons. Am. Hoist & Derrick Co., Ft. Wayne, 1969; mech. and indsl. engr. cons. Franklin Electric Co., Ft. Wayne, Ind., 1970; cons. vehicle dynamics Internat. Harvester Co., 1977; mem. tech. accreditation commn. Accreditation Bd. Engring. and Tech., 1979-81; indsl. engring. cons. Scott & Fetzer's WHECo. div., 1979. Served with AUS, 1946-47. Recipient Ralph R. Teetor award Soc. Automotive Engrs., 1972. Ednl. Profl. Devel. Act Afro-Am. Studies grantee, 1971. Mem. Am. Soc. Engring. Edn., Am. Tech. Edn. Assn., Soc. Automotive Engrs. (Outstanding Faculty Advisor Service award 1974, mem. nat. electric vehicle com. 1976-81, nat. student activity com. 1976-80), Soc. Am. Mil. Engrs., ASME (chmn. program com. 1971-75), Am. Soc. Heating, Refrigeration and Air Conditioning Engrs. (mem. nat. engring. council profl. devel. accreditation team), United Comml. Travelers, Pi Tau Sigma. Baptist (deacon 1968-72). Mason (Shriner). Home: 4426 Dicke Rd Fort Wayne IN 46804

MC ALINDON, JAMES DANIEL, surgeon, hosp. adminstr., educator; b. Bay County, Mich., May 19, 1926; s. James Peter and Anna Mary (Potla) McA.; B.S., U. Detroit, 1950; M.D., Loyola U., Chgo., 1954; m. Mary Naomi Solomon, Nov. 25, 1961; children—Robert, Donald, James, Peter, Mary. Resident in surgery Georgetown U. Hosp., Washington, 1955-59; dir. med. edn. St. Joseph Hosp., Flint, Mich., 1963-67; chmn. dept. surgery McLaren Gen. Hosp., Flint, 1969—; clin. asst. prof. surgery Mich. State Med. Sch., East Lansing, 1970 and after, subsequently asso. clin. prof. surgery. Served with USN, 1944-46. Diplomate Am. Bd. Surgery. Fellow A.C.S. Contbr. article to med. jours. Home: 1423 Oxyoke Dr Flint MI 48504

MC ANDREWS, JAMES PATRICK, lawyer; b. Carbondale, Pa., May 11, 1929; s. James Patrick and Mary Agnes (Walsh) McA.; B.S. in Accounting, U. Scranton, 1949; LL.B., Fordham U., 1952; grad. Real Estate Inst., N.Y. U., 1972; m. Mona Marie Steinke, Sept. 4, 1954; children—James P., George A., Catherine M., Joseph M., Michael P., Anne Marie, Edward R., Daniel P. Admitted to N.Y. State bar, 1953, Ohio bar, 1974; asso. James F. McManus, Levittown, N.Y., 1955; atty. Emigrant Savs. Bank, N.Y.C., 1955-68; counsel Tchrs. Ins. and Annuity Assn., N.Y.C., 1968-73; asso. firm Thompson, Hine & Flory, Cleve., 1973-74, partner, 1974—; mem. law faculty Am. Inst. Banking, 1968-69. Served with JAGC, USAF, 1952-54. Fellow Am. Bar Found., Am. Coll. Real Estate Lawyers; mem. Am., Ohio, Cleve. bar assns., Am. Land Title Assn., Ohio Land Title Assn., Nat. Assn. Corp. Real Estate Execs., Urban Land Inst., Mortgage Bankers Assn., Internat. Council Shopping Centers, Am. Legion, Delta Theta Phi. Roman Catholic. Club: Rotary. Contbr. articles to profl. publs. Home: 2971 Litchfield Rd Shaker Heights OH 44120 Office: 1100 Nat City Bank Bldg Cleveland OH 44114

MCAREAVY, JOHN FRANCIS, govt. ofcl.; b. Coggon, Iowa, Sept. 22, 1927; s. John B. and Kathryn C. (McMeel) McA.; B.A., U. Iowa, 1951, M.S., 1955, Ph.D., 1969; m. Joan M. Nilles, Sept. 8, 1949; children—Susan McAreavy Potthoff, Kathryn McAreavy McLaughlin, Mary McAreavy Eggenburg, Martha McAreavy Freemole, Brian, John L., Joseph, Thomas, Julie, Amy, Douglas, Molly. Tchr., coach Muscatine (Iowa) High Sch. and Community Coll., 1952-56; mathematician U.S. Army Mgmt. Engring. Tng. Agy., Rock Island, Ill., 1956—, dept. head, asso. dir., 1956-80, dir., 1980—; mgmt. cons. Served with U.S. Army, 1946-48. Mem. Am. Psychol. Assn., Acad. Mgmt. Clubs: Elks, K.C. Office: US Army Mgmt Engring Tng Agy Rock Island IL 61299

MCARTHUR, JOAN DEDERICH, state ofcl.; b. Sauk County, Wis., Sept. 27, 1933; d. Lawrence A. and Grace (Thering) Dederich; B.S., U. Wis., Madison, 1957, M.S., 1959; m. John F. McArthur, Nov. 16, 1957; children—Morgan J., Laura Grace. Developer communication disorders program Columbia County (Wis.), 1959-61; pvt. practice communicative disorders, Baraboo, Wis., 1961-78; chief flight/instrument instr., charter pilot Chaplain Aviation Inc., Baraboo, 1976-79; commr. Wis. Transp. Commn., 1979—, chmn., 1981—; responsible for Wis. trucking deregulation, 1982; mem. com. motor and air carriers Nat. Assn. Regulatory Utility Commns., 1980—; cons. communicative disorders dept. St. Clare Hosp., Baraboo, 1977-79. Mem. Barbaboo Bd. Edn., 1965-79. Mem. Am. Speech and Hearing Assn., Am. Assn. Sch. Bds., Am. Acad. Pvt. Practitioners in Speech Pathology and Audiology, Wis. Speech and Hearing Assn., Wis. Sch. Bd. Assn.

MCARTHUR, STEVEN FRANCIS, psychologist; b. Grand Rapids, Mich., Aug. 12, 1954; s. George Harold and Evelyn Therese McA.; B.A., Aquinas Coll., 1975; M.A., Eastern Ill. U., 1978; m. Barbara Louise Duch, Oct. 18, 1975; 1 son, Ryan Anthony. Counselor, The Bridge for Runaways, Inc., Grand Rapids, Mich., 1977-80; staff psychologist Grand Rapids (Mich.) Osteo. Hosp., 1980—; mem. Gov's. Task Force on Violence and Vandalism in Schs., 1978-79. Mem. Am. Psychol. Assn. (asso.), Mich. Psychol. Assn., Grand Rapids Area Psychol. Assn. Office: 1919 Boston St SE Grand Rapids MI 49506

MCAULIFFE, MICHAEL F., bishop; b. Kansas City, Mo., Nov. 22, 1920; student St. Louis Preparatory Seminary and Cath. U. Ordained priest Roman Cath. Ch., 1945; consecrated bishop, 1969; bishop diocese of Jefferson City (Mo.), 1969—. Address: Bishops House 605 Clark Ave PO Box 417 Jefferson City MO 65101*

MCAVOY, WILLIAM LEE, podiatrist; b. Chgo., Dec. 16, 1947; s. George LeGrande and Claudia (Anthony) McA.; student U. Iowa, 1966-69; D.P.M., Ill. Coll. Podiatric Medicine, 1973; m. Jane Marie Schmidt, July 30, 1969; children—Amy Christine, Erin LeAnne, Lisa Marie. Lab. technician Evanston (Ill.) Hosp., 1970-73; chief podiatry Midlands Community Hosp. Med. Center, Papillion, Nebr., 1978—; pvt. practice podiatry, Papillion, 1979—. Bd. dirs. Midlands Community Hosp. Found., 1979—. Served with U.S. Army, 1973-75, USAF, 1975-78. Mem. Am. Podiatry Assn., Acad. Sports Medicine, Am. Acad. Podiatric Sports Medicine, Nebr. Podiatry Assn., Papillion C. of C. Diplomate Am. Bd. Foot Orthopedists and Foot Surgery. Republican. Clubs: Omaha Baseball Collectors Assn., Plains Track (editor 1978-80). Author: Foot Care for Runners, 1974; Practice Mgmt. in Podiatric Sports Medicine, 1979. Home: 825 Donegal Dr Papillion NE 68046 Office: 401 E Gold Coast Rd Suite 326 Papillion NE 68128

MC BETH, NADINE LEE REITER, ins. underwriter; b. Chgo., Sept. 13, 1939; d. Richard Charles and Eleanor Catherine (Oaks) Reiter; B.A., U. Dubuque (Iowa), 1961; M.A., Northeastern Ill. U., Chgo., 1978; divorced; 1 son, Derek John. Engaged in ins., 1967—; with Protection Mut. Ins. Co., Park Ridge, Ill., 1978—. Sec. Des Plaines, Mt. Prospect, Arlington Heights and Palatine Water Commn., 1964-75. Mem. Am. Personnel and Guidance Assn., AAUW, Mensa. Presbyterian. Home: 1444 S Busse St Mount Prospect IL 60056

MC BRAYER, JAMES DONALD, univ. adminstr.; b. Pueblo, Colo., July 7, 1936; s. Benjamin Edgar and Helene Eva McB.; B.S., St. Louis U., 1957, M.S., 1962; diploma Von Karman Inst. Fluid Dynamics, 1963; D.Sc., Washington U., 1967; m. June Ann Reiss, Aug. 2, 1958; children—Kenneth Edgar, Timothy James, Theresa Ann. Sr. engring. specialist Emerson Electric Co., St. Louis, 1957-62, 63-67; asso. prof. mech. engring. U. Mo.-Rolla, St. Louis Grad. Engring. Center, 1967-70; asso. dean of coll. Parks Coll. of St. Louis U., Cahokia, Ill., 1970-74; dean of coll. Central Meth. Coll., Fayette, Mo., 1974-77; v.p. acad. affairs and provost Franklin U., Columbus, Ohio, 1977—. NSF trainee, 1964-65, 66-67; NASA trainee, 1965-66. Mem. AIAA (asso. fellow), Am. Soc. Engring. Edn., ASME, Sigma Xi. Methodist. Club: Rotary. Home: 202 Greenglade Ave Worthington OH 43085 Office: 201 S Grant Ave Columbus OH 43215

MC BRIDE, LLOYD MERRILL, lawyer; b. Corydon, Iowa, July 20, 1908; s. Ernest Eugene and Jeannie (Randolph) McB.; A.B. cum laude, Carleton Coll., Northfield, Minn., 1930, LL.D. (hon.), 1979; student Harvard U., 1931-32; J.D., Northwestern U., 1934; m. Alice Rowland, June 8, 1935; children—Patricia Ann, Barbara Jean. Admitted to Ill. bar, 1934, since practiced in Chgo.; with firm Stearns & Jones, 1934-41, partner in successor firm Stearns & McBride, 1941-43, McBride & Baker, 1943-58, 81—, McBride, Baker, Wienke & Schlosser, 1958-81; sec., dir. SMI Investment Co., Bayou Corp., Vermilion Corp.; chmn. exec. com. Wallace Computer Services, Inc.; dir. FRC Investment Corp., Stenning Industries, Inc., Wallace Bus. Forms, Inc.; pres., dir. 1550 State Pkwy. Condominium Assn. Trustee, Carleton Coll.; sec., trustee Morton Arboretum. Mem. Phi Beta Kappa. Republican. Clubs: Tower, Mid-Am., Mid-Day, Racquet (Chgo.). Home: 1550 N State Pkwy Chicago IL 60610 Office: Three 1st Nat Plaza Chicago IL 60602

MC BRIDE, VICKIE DARLENE BURCH, nurse; b. Tampa, Fla., Jan. 17, 1944; d. Harold Victor and Dorothy June (Higley) Burch Keen; B.S. in Nursing, Marycrest Coll., 1966; postgrad. U. Guam, 1967-68, Ohio State U., 1976-77; postgrad. in health care adminstrn. U. Cin., 1980—. Staff nurse Mercy Hosp., Davenport, Iowa, 1966, St. Elizabeth Hosp., Youngstown, Ohio, 1969; staff devel. instr. med., coronary and surg. ICU, Cleve. Clinic, 1969-73; dir. Free Clinic West, Cleve., 1973-74; inservice coordinator Green Cross Gen. Hosp., Cuyahoga Falls, Ohio, 1974-75, dir. nursing, 1975-76; dir. nursing service Kaiser Cleve. Med. Center, 1976-79; regional coordinator staff devel. Kaiser Permanente Med. Care Program of Ohio, 1979—; course coordinator, instr. critical care nursing Cleve. State U., 1973-75. Mem. adv. bd. div. of health Cuyahoga Falls Vocat. Sch., 1975-76; mem. nursing adv. com. Summitt County Vis. Nurses Assn., 1975; trustee Free Clinics of Cleve., 1972-73. Served with Nurse Corps, USNR, 1966-69. Named outstanding CPR instr. in health care facility Akron Heart Assn., 1976. Mem. Am. Assn. Critical Care Nurses (founder and pres. Greater Cleve. chpt. 1972-73), Nat. League for Nursing, Cleve. Area League for Nursing, Am. Heart Assn. (certified in basic life support, certified CPR instr., certified CPR instr. trainer). Republican. Roman Catholic. Home: 3101 Granger Rd Medina OH 44256 Office: Kaiser Cleve Med Center 11203 Fairhill Cleveland OH 44104

MCBRIDE-KIRKLAND, PAULA JEAN, accountant; b. Highland Park, Mich., Apr. 26, 1941; d. Paul Thomas and Hazel (Stith) Mihalick; student Columbia U., 1959-61; A.Acctg., Western Piedmont Community Coll., 1976; m. William Kirkland, June 20, 1980; children by previous marriages, Christine Blanchard, Polly Dugger, Elizabeth Dugger. With Pontiac Motor div. GMC, Pontiac, Mich., 1963-70; asst. to controller Hendredon Furniture, Morganton, N.C., 1971-78; mill accountant James River Rochester (Mich.), 1978-79; mem. staff Jenkins, Eshman & Magnus, Bloomfield Hills, Mich., 1979-80; pres. Kirkland & Co., Mgmt. Cons., Troy, Mich., 1981—; bd. dirs. Henredon Employee Credit Union, 1977-78. Mem. Nat. Assn. Accts., Nat. Bus. and Profl. Women, NOW. Republican. Club: Toastmistress. Author: Ego Flights, 1978; Poetry, 1981. Address: 1200 Villa Park Troy MI 48098

MC BURNEY, GEORGE WILLIAM, lawyer; b. Ames, Iowa, Feb. 17, 1926; s. James William and Elfie Hazel (Jones) McB.; B.A., State U. Iowa, 1950; J.D., 1953; m. Georgianna Edwards, Aug. 28, 1949; children—Hollis Lynn, Jana Lee, John Edwards. Admitted to Iowa bar, 1953, Ill. bar, 1954; practiced in Chgo., 1953—; with firm Sidley & Austin and predecessor firm, 1953—, partner, 1964—. Mem. Chgo. Crime Commn., 1966—. Trustee, pres. Old Peoples Home City Chgo.; trustee, v.p., counsel The Georgian, Evanston, Ill. Served with inf., AUS, 1944-46. Fellow Am. Coll. Trial Lawyers; mem. Am. Judicature Soc., Am., Ill., Chgo. bar assns., Law Club Chgo., Legal Club Chgo., Bar Assn. 7th Fed. Circuit, Am. Arbitration Assn. (panel), Nat. Coll. Edn. (bd. assos.), U.S. C. of C. (govt. and regulatory affairs com., council on antitrust policy), Phi Kappa Psi. Omicron Delta Kappa, Delta Sigma Rho, Phi Delta Phi. Republican. Presbyterian. Clubs: Union League, Mid-Day (Chgo.); Westmoreland Country (Wilmette). Editor: Iowa Law Rev., 1952-53. Home: 1110 13th St Wilmette IL 60091 Office: One First Nat Plaza Chicago IL 60603

MCBURNEY, WENDELL FARIS, univ. adminstr., educator; b. Spring Valley, N.Y., Feb. 2, 1933; s. Edwin H. and Marian (Faris) McB.; B.S., Geneva Coll., 1955; M.A.T., Ind. U., 1966, Ed.D., 1967; m. E. Jean Willson, June 8, 1956; children—Cynthia Jean, Willson Stuart, Laurie Kay. Sci. tchr. Beaver (Pa.) Area Schs., 1956-63; coordinator sch. sci., asst. prof. sci. edn. Ind. U., 1967-73, asso. prof., 1974—, asst. dean research, 1973-76, asso. dean research, 1976-78, dean research, 1979—. Served with U.S. Army, 1956-58. Recipient numerous NSF grants. Mem. Assn. Midwestern Coll. Biology Tchrs., Hoosier Assn. Sci. Tchrs., Ind. Acad. Sci., Nat. Assn. Biology Tchrs., Nat. Council Univ. Research Adminstrs., Nat. Sci. Tchrs. Assn., Sigma Xi, Phi Delta Kappa. Author numerous works in field; contbr. articles to profl. jours. Office: 355 Lansing St Ind U Indianapolis IN 46202

MC BURROWS, EARNEST, artist; b. Moultrie, Ga., Sept. 3, 1947; s. John Wesley and Mina Bell (Burke) McB., B.S. in Art Edn. with high honors, Hampton (Va.) Inst., 1969; M.A., U. Wis., 1970, M.F.A. in Painting, 1971. Mem. faculty U. Ill., Chgo. Circle, 1972—, asst. prof. art, 1975—, also tchr., dir. univ. students in art program Cook County Jail, 1975—; lectr. Chgo. area schs.; mem. art faculty Kankakee (Ill.) Community Coll., 1981—; cons. Pace Inst.; mem. visitation com. to evaluation high schs. North Central Assn.; mem. tech. planning task force on edn. Pace/Cook County Dept. Corrections; exhibited in group shows U. Ill. Faculty Exhibits, 1974, 77, 78, Mus. Performing Arts, Milw., 1976, Truman Coll., Chgo., 1978, N.A.M.E. Gallery, Chgo., 1978, Montgomery Ward Gallery, 1978, 79, 80, U. Ill. Med. Center, Chgo., 1979, South Side Community Art Center, Chgo., 1981, Meadowview Bank, Kankakee, 1981; one-man shows include U. Wis. Gallery, 1970, U. Wis. Art Gallery, 1971, Rosenstone Gallery, Chgo., 1975, Sheraton Inn, Homewood, Ill., 1978, Hull House Gallery, Chgo., 1980; two-man shows N.A.M.E. Gallery, 1977; two-man show South Side Community Art Center, 1977, now art cons., exhbn. and edn. coordinator; curator various exhbns. Danforth fellow, 1969-70; Southern fellow, 1969-71; grantee Links, Inc., 1978. Mem. Black Emergency Cultural Coalition (citation 1976), Nat. Conf. Artists, Soc. for Black Cultural Arts (dir.). Author: A Prison Art Program, 1976. Home: 1155 E Maple St Apt 1 Kankakee IL 60901 Office: PO Box 888 River Rd Kankakee IL 60901

MC CABE, ARTHUR LEE, chemist; b. Otsego, Mich., Dec. 18, 1937; s. Arthur Lee and Florence Gertrude (Mollison) McC.; student Kalamazoo Coll., 1956-58, Western Mich. U., 1958-59; m. Nancy Lee Smith, June 26, 1959; children—Janet Lee, William Arthur, Sherry Linn, Arthur Lee, Elizabeth Ann, Susan Faye. Asst. mgr. D & C Stores, Kalamazoo, 1959-60; asst. fleet supt. McNamara Motor Express Co., Kalamazoo, 1960-61; with Upjohn Co., Kalamazoo, 1961-63; chemistry technician Consumers Power Co., Kalamazoo, 1963-66, sr. chemistry technician, 1966-73, sr. radiation protection technician Palisades plant, Covert, Mich., 1973-74, chemistry supr., Palisades Nuclear Plant, 1974-78, fossil fuels specialist, Jackson, Mich., 1978-79, fuel transp. adminstr., 1979—. Dist. commr. Southwestern Mich. council Boy Scouts Am., 1973-74. Republican. Inventor in field. Home: PO Box 84 215 Hanover St Concord MI 49237 Office: 1945 Parnall Rd Jackson MI 49201

MCCABE, MILO FRANCIS, economist; b. Oconomowoc, Wis., Apr. 5, 1931; s. Milo John and Mary Catherine (Anglesberg) McC.; B.S. in Sociology, Marquette U., 1956; M.A. in Econ. Edn., Ohio U., 1968; M.S. in Econs., U. Ill., 1968; m. Jeanne E. Schraa, Aug. 25, 1956; children—James, Jeanne Marie, Timothy, Margaret. High sch. tchr. in Wis. and Ill., 1956-70; supervising tchr. sociology for practice tchrs. Alverno Coll., Milw., 1963-64; supervising tchr. Am. history Carthage Coll., Kenosha, Wis., 1966-69; mem. faculty U. S.D., Vermillion, 1970—, asso. prof. econs., dir. Henry T. Quinn Center Econ. Edn., 1975—; exec. dir. S.D. Council Econ. Edn., 1978—. Served with AUS, 1951-53; Korea. Summer fellow Gen. Electric Co., NSF, NDEA, Libby Found., others. Mem. Am. Econ. Assn., Am. Acad. Polit. and Social Scis., Nat. Assn. Bus. Economists, Nat. Council Social Studies, Nat. Bus. Edn. Assn., Midwest Econ. Assn., S.D. Council Social Studies, S.D. Bus. Edn. Tchrs. Assn., Beta Gamma Sigma, Omicron Delta Epsilon. Clubs: K.C., Lions (treas. 1976—). Author curriculum materials, articles in field. Home: 933 Eastgate Dr Vermillion SD 57069 Office: 218 Patterson Hall Sch Bus Vermillion SD 57069

MC CABE, WILLIAM PETER, plastic surgeon; b. Pawtucket, R.I., Oct. 19, 1939; s. William Edward and Mary Josephine (Farrell) McC.; A.B. cum laude, Harvard U., 1961; M.D., Cornell U., 1965; m. Maureen Virginia Crowley, June 12, 1965; children—P. Christopher, Michelle E. Inter, Boston City Hosp., 1965-66, resident, 1966-67; resident Henry Ford Hosp., Detroit, 1969-72; Commonwealth fellow St. George's Hosp., London, 1972-73; practice medicine specializing in plastic surgery, Grosse Pointe Woods, Mich., 1973—; mem. staffs St. John, Harper, Children's, Bon Secours hosps.; clin. asst. prof. plastic surgery Wayne State U., 1974—; vice chmn. bd. Physicians Ins. Co. of Mich.; corp. dir. Blue Cross/Blue Shield of Mich. Co-chmn. Detroit Physicians Crisis Com., 1976—. Served with U.S. Army, 1967-69. Decorated Commendation medal. Fellow A.C.S.; mem. AMA, Mich. Med. Soc., Wayne State Med. Soc., Mich. Acad. Plastic Surgeons (sec., treas. 1978-80, pres. 1980—). Roman Catholic. Clubs: Dunes, (Narragansett, R.I.); Grosse Pointe Yacht, Harvard (dir. 1978—), Harvard of Eastern Mich. (sec. 1979-80, v.p. 1980—). Contbr. articles in field to profl. jours. Office: 20361 Mack Ave Grosse Pointe Woods MI 48236

MCCAFFREY, THOMAS JOSEPH, U.S. postal service ofcl.; b. St. Louis, May 12, 1926; s. Thomas Eugene and Frances Hedwig (Dickhaus) McC.; student in commerce, fin., law St. Louis U., 1946-53; m. Rita F. Beyert, June 14, 1952; children—Michael T., Thomas Joseph, Timothy A. Treasury agt. U.S. Dept. Treasury, St. Louis, 1950-56; chief acct. Metal Fabricator, St. Louis, 1957-60; internal auditor U.S. Postal Inspection Service, St. Louis, 1961-68; gen. mgr. St. Louis Postal Data Center, 1969—; tax cons. Served with U.S. Army, 1944-46. Enrolled agt. U.S. Dept. Treasury. Mem. Am. Mgmt. Assn. Club: Am. Legion (comdr., St. Louis, 1962-63). Office: 1720 Market St Saint Louis MO 63180

MC CAIN, WINFIELD REYNOLDS, accountant; b. New Underwood, S.D., June 5, 1912; s. Merle A. and Mary Eliza (Reynolds) McC.; student S.D. Sch. Mines, 1930-31; m. Dorothy Agnes Read, July 4, 1936 (dec. Dec. 1961); children—John B., Charles E., Janet R. McCain Greer, Anne A. McCain Raga; m. 2d, Gratia Jones Engberg, Apr. 25, 1968. Asst. cashier First Nat. Bank Black Hills, Rapid City, S.D., 1933-47; acting sec. Rapid City (S.D.) C. of C., 1947-48; sales rep., traveling auditor Buckingham Transp. Co., Rapid City, 1948-60; pvt. practice as accountant, Rapid City, also Hill City, S.D., 1960—; owner, operator Circle S Motel, Hill City, 1970-76; credit mgr. Ray Dental Group, Rapid City, 1977—. Organizer, Rapid City Youth Center, 1943-47, Rapid City YMCA, 1948-51, Rapid City Community Chest, 1945-47; pres. S.D. Jr. C. of C., 1946-47. Recipient Distinguished Service award Rapid City Jr. C. of C., 1945. Mem. Hill City Motel Assn. (dir. 1971-75), Rapid City, Hill City (pres. 1972-74, dir. 1972-77) chambers commerce, Black Hills Assn. Chambers Commerce (v.p. 1973—), Minnilusa Hist. Assn. (pres. 1981—). Republican. Episcopalian. Clubs: Masons (master 1977-78), Shriners, Order Eastern Star (worthy patron 1981), Elks, Rotary (pres. 1975-77). Address: Hill City SD 57745

MCCALL, CHERYL ANN, bus. service co. exec.; b. South Bend, Ind., Mar. 21, 1939; d. Claude McRae and Blanche Mae (Selle) Storey; student Mt. Mary Coll., Milw., 1957-58, Rock Valley Coll., Rockford, Ill., 1968-69, 73-74; m. Terry Neil McCall, Oct. 7, 1961. Service rep. Ill. Bell Telephone Co., 1958-65; receptionist Rockford div. Borg Warner Corp., 1965-72, acctg. clk., 1972-73, cost acctg. analyst, 1973-77; sec.-treas. Wash. Calibration Midwest, Inc., Rockford, 1977-79, pres., dir., 1979—; guest speaker Am. Soc. Quality Control. Roman Catholic. Club: Rockford Lady Elks (pres. 1980-82). Home: 7502 Kishwaukee Rd Stillman Valley IL 61084

MCCALL, DAVID DEAN, educator; b. Seaman, Ohio, June 28, 1936; s. John Robert and Mary Elizabeth (McClelland) McC.; B.S., U. Cin., 1977, M.Ed., 1980; m. Deloris Jean Hull, Apr. 9, 1955; children—Veronica Deanne, Claudia Suzanne. Lithographer, Reynolds & Reynolds Co., Dayton, Ohio, 1952-74; tchr. graphic arts Dayton Adult Night Sch., 1975-78, Wilbur Wright High Sch., 1976-77; tchr. graphic communications Patterson Coop. High Sch., Dayton, 1977—. Mem. Internat. Assn. Printing House Craftsmen, Am. Vocat. Assn., Ohio Vocat. Assn., Dayton Edn. Assn., Kappa Delta Pi. Republican. Mem. Christian Ch. Club: Masons. Home: 343 Beverly Place Oakwood OH 45419 Office: Patterson Coop High School 118 E First St Dayton OH 45402

MC CALL, DON CHARLES, elec. engr.; b. Amarillo, Tex., Apr. 7, 1953; s. Embrey and Willie Jewell (Capps) McC.; B.S. in E.E., So. Meth. U., 1975; m. Carol Jean Armitage, Aug. 31, 1979. Coop. engr. Collins Radio, Microwave Engring. Dept., Dallas, 1974; field engr. Schlumberger Well Services, Tyler, Tex., 1975-77, engr.-in-charge Carthage (Texas) Depot, Schlumberger, 1978, Houston sales engr. Schlumberger Well Services, 1979, dist. mgr. Schlumberger, Traverse City, Mich., 1979-81, div. sales mgr., Lansing, Mich., 1981—. Del., Tex. Republican State Conv., 1972; adminstrv. bd. Marvin United Meth. Ch., Tyler, 1977. Mem. IEEE, Soc. Profl. Well Log Analysts, Soc. Petroleum Engrs. (chmn. No. Mich. sect. 1980-81). Methodist. Home: 3721 Colchester Lansing MI 48906 Office: 3721 W Michigan Ave Lansing MI 48917

MC CALL, MAURICE HENDERSON, univ. ofcl.; b. Hampton, Va., Mar. 8, 1943; s. Morris O. and Bennie E. (Staton) McC.; B.F.A., Carnegie Inst. Tech., 1966, M.F.A., 1967; D.Mus. Arts (So. Edn. fellow), U. Cin., 1975; m. Ernestine Foreman, Aug. 28, 1976. Instr. music Hampton (Va.) Inst., 1967-70; lectr. Afro-Am. musical history U. Cin., 1971-75, acting asst. to dean, 1974-75, exec. asst. to dean, 1975-76; registrar Clermont Coll., Batavia, Ohio, 1976—; univ. adv. Hanarobi Contemporary Gospel Ensemble, U. Cin. Dir. minority affairs radio sta. WGUC-FM, Cin., 1973-74; cons. on minority broadcasting Corp. for Pub. Broadcasting, Washington, 1974-75; guest lectr. Afro-Am. music St. Joseph's Coll., Rensselaer, Ind., summers 1974, 75, 76. Mem. adv. council Beamon-Hough Arts Fund, Cin., 1975—. Bd. dirs. Jewish Community Center Concert Series, Newport News, Va., 1969-70; bd. dirs. Clermont County Community Mental Health Center, 1978—, pres., 1980—; bd. dirs. Pro Musica, Cin., 1979-80; bd. dirs. North Central region Council on Black Am. Affairs, 1978—, v.p., 1979-81, treas., 1981—. Recipient Ganzel award for Music Composition Cin. Lit. and Mus. Soc., 1973. Mem. Assn. of Black Electronic Communicators (sec. 1974-75), Am. Assn. Collegiate Registrars and Admissions Officers, Nat. Assn. Coll. Deans, Registrars and Admissions Officers. Home: PO Box 20108 Cincinnati OH 45220 Office: 105 Clermont Coll Batavia OH 45103

MC CALLEN, PEGGY, retail store exec.; b. Terre Haute, Ind., Jan. 6, 1929; d. Bernard Theodore and Jessie Rose (Connett) Van Borssum; student Ind. State U., 1946-47, Eastern Ill. U., 1947-48; m. Robert Ray McCallen, Jr., June 20, 1948; children—Peggy, Page, Bryan, Paula, Robert III. Asst. to exec. sec. Meth. Bd. Edn., Bloomington, Ind., 1953-56; owner-retailer The Village Annex, Wabash, Inc., 1976-82; pres., founder Maid-in-Wabash, Inc., 1979—; owner Antiques Anonymous, 1979—. bridal cons. Chmn. Wabash County Roush for Congress Com., 1962; mem. Wabash County Centennial Com., 1966; newsletter editor Friendly Nursing Homes, 1968-70; aux. sec., newsletter editor Wabash County Hosp. Aux., 1971-77. Vice pres. bd. trustees Wabash City Sch. Bd., 1978, pres., 1979, sec., 1981; mem. City Parks Bd., 1978, v.p., 1981; precinct committeeperson, 1980. Lic. real estate salesperson. Mem. Nat. Fedn. Ind. Bus. Democrat. Presbyterian. Home: PO Box 546 Crestwood Dr Wabash IN 46992 Office: 1209 N Cass St Wabash IN 46992

MC CALLUM, CHARLES EDWARD, lawyer; b. Memphis, Mar. 13, 1939; s. Edward Payson and India Raimelle (Musick) McC.; B.S., M.I.T., 1960; Fulbright scholar U. Manchester (Eng.), 1960-61; J.D., Vanderbilt U., 1964; m. JoAnn Hepinstall, Sept. 21, 1974; children—Florence Andrea, Printha Kyle, Chandler Ward Payson. Admitted to Mich. bar, 1964; asso. firm Warner, Norcross & Judd, Grand Rapids, Mich., 1964-69, partner, 1969—; rep. assemblyman State Bar Mich., 1973-78; lectr. continuing legal edn. programs. Chmn. Grand Rapids Area Transit Authority, 1976-79, mem., 1972-79; regional v.p. Nat. Municipal League, 1978—, mem. council, 1971-78; pres. Grand Rapids Art Mus., 1979-81, trustee, 1976—; chmn. Butterworth Hosp., 1979—, trustee, 1977—; mem. Citizens Com. Consolidation of Govt. Services, 1981—; ednl. counselor M.I.T., 1974—; nat. chmn. Vanderbilt Law Sch. Devel. Com., 1977-78; trustee Kent Med. Found., 1979—. Woodrow Wilson fellow, 1960-61. Mem. Am., Tenn., Mich., Grand Rapids bar assns., Grand Rapids C. of C. (pres. 1975, dir. 1970-76), Order of Coif, Sigma Xi. Clubs: Kent Country, Grand Rapids Athletic, Peninsular. Home: 656 Manhattan Rd SE Grand Rapids MI 49506 Office: 900 Old Kent Bldg 1 Vandenberg Center Grand Rapids MI 49503

MC CALLUM, JAMES SCOTT, state ofcl.; b. Fond du Lac, Wis., May 2, 1950; s. George Duncan and Marilyn Joy (Libke) McC.; B.A., Macalester Coll., 1972; M.A., Johns Hopkins U., 1974. Legis. aide U.S. Ho. of Reps., Washington, 1972-74; Republican caucus analyst Wis. Senate, Madison, 1974-75, mem., 1976—; program dir. YMCA, Fond du Lac, 1975-76. State chairperson Youth in Govt., YMCA, 1978-79. Mem. Fond du Lac Jaycees (dir. 1974-76). Republican. Office: 323 S State Capitol Madison WI 53702

MCCAMEY, DELENER S., ednl. cons.; b. Kingsland, Ark., Aug. 3, 1946; d. Odell and Alberta McC.; B.S., U. Ark., 1968; M.A., Oakland U., 1970; Ph.D., U. Mich., 1976; postdoctoral in Resource Devel., George Washington U., 1977-78. Tchr., sci. cons. Detroit Bd. Edn., 1968-73, ednl. cons., 1973—; process cons. dept. governmental relations Howard U., Washington, 1977-78; cons. minorities and women's div. Nat. Inst. Edn., Washington, 1979; research cons. Future Studies Conf., 1980; cons. dept. resource devel. Tuskegee (Ala.) Inst., 1981—. Mem. Women's Conf. Concerns Polit. Task Force, vice chmn. ednl. task force, 1975; mem. Mayor's Human Rights Com., 1977. Ednl. Policy Seminar fellow, 1978-79. Mem. Ednl. Research Assn., Nat. Black Child Achievement Assn., AAUW, Am. Assn. Sch. Adminstrs., Assn. for Supervision and Curriculum Devel., Nat. Alliance for Women in Edn., Nat. Council Negro Women, Am. Sociol. Assn., Delta Sigma Theta. Roman Catholic. Contbr. articles to profl. jours. Address: Suite 2 4326 St Antoine Detroit MI 48201

MC CAMLEY, PETER JOHN, chemist; b. Wisconsin Rapids, Wis., Sept. 20, 1932; s. Howard J. and Jennie A. (Minta) M.; B.S., U. Wis., 1960; m. Theresa Sopa, Sept. 16, 1961; children—Maureen, Patrick, Mary. Research chemist Fiberite Corp., Winona, Minn., 1960- 72, mgr. research and devel., 1973-74, product mgr., 1975—. Served with U.S. Army, 1954-56. Mem. Am. Chem. Soc., Soc. Plastic Engrs. Roman Catholic. Clubs: Lions (past pres.), VFW, YMCA. Home: 1212 Birch Fountain City WI 54629 Office: 515 W 3d St Winona MN 55987

MC CANDLESS, BARBARA J., cons.; b. Cottonwood Falls, Kans., Oct. 25, 1931; d. Arch G. and Grace (Kittle) McC.; B.S., Kans. State U., 1953; M.S., Cornell U., 1959; postgrad. U. Minn., 1962-66, U. Calif. at Berkeley, 1971-72; m. Allyn O. Lockner, 1969. Home demonstration agt. Kans. State U., 1953-57; teaching asst. Cornell U., 1957-58, asst. extension home economist in mktg., 1958-59; consumer mkgt. specialist, asst. prof. Oreg. State U., 1959-62; instr. home econs. U. Minn., St. Paul, 1962-63, research asst. agrl. econs., 1963-66; asst. prof. Coll. Home Econs., U. R.I., Kingston, 1966-67; asso. prof. family econs., head mgmt., housing equipment dept. Coll. Home Econs., S.D. State U., Brookings, 1967-73; asst. to sec. S.D. Dept. Commerce and Consumer Affairs, Pierre, 1973-79; cons., Kansas City, Mo., 1979—. Mem. Nat. Council Occupational Licensing, dir., 1974-75, v.p., 1975-79. Mem. Am. Mktg. Assn., Am. Council on Consumer Interests, League of Women Voters, Nat. Council Family Relations, Am. Agrl. Econs. Assn., Am. Home Econs. Assn., Kans. State U. Alumni Assn., Pi Gamma Mu. Club: Brookings Country. Research on profl. and occupational licensing bds. Address: 722 Walnut St Kansas City MO 64106

MC CANN, CLAUDE, health care exec.; b. Detroit, Apr. 7, 1934; s. Sing and Blanche McC.; B.S., U. Detroit, 1962; M.A., U. Mich., Ann Arbor, 1966, M.P.H., 1975; postgrad. Wayne State U., Detroit, 1972; m. Clara Jackson, Oct. 4, 1961; children—Jennifer Alyn, Claude Allen. Tchr. math. Detroit public schs., 1962-65; sales rep. Mich. Blue Cross and Blue Shield, 1965-66, asst. actuary, 1965-68; dir. health care service plans div. Mich. Dept. Commerce Ins. Bur., 1968-75; cost containment cons. Mich. Dept. Public Health, 1975-76; v.p. mktg. Blue Cross of N.E. Ohio, Cleve., 1976—. Mem. policy com. on homemakers home health services NAACP; del. assembly, mem. allocation com. United Way; bd. dirs. Am. Sickle Cell Anemia Assn. Recipient resolution for contbns. in health care Mich. Legislature, 1976. Mem. Sales and Mktg. Execs. Cleve., U. Detroit Alumni Assn., U. Mich. Alumni Assn., Am. Public Health Assn., Ohio Public Health Assn., Case Western Res. U. Genetics Adv. Com., Harvard U. Bus. Sch. Club: Cleve. Contbr. articles on health care to profl. jours. Home: 25161 S Woodland St Beechwood OH 44122 Office: 2066 E 9th St Cleveland OH 44115

MCCANN, GARRY MICHAEL, graphic artist; b. Detroit, Feb. 12, 1956; s. William Thomas and Louise Geneveve (Shook) McC.; B.F.A. in Graphic Design, Kent State U., 1978; postgrad. in bus. adminstrn., Cleve. State U. Display cons. Halles Dept. Store, Cleveland Heights, Ohio, 1974-78; prodn. artist Gordon Advt., Lyndhurst, Ohio, 1978; sr. graphic artist in-house art dept. Systems div. Allen-Bradley Co., Highland Heights, Ohio, 1978—. Mem. Cleve. Soc. Communicating Arts, Kent State U Alumni Assn. (chmn. public relations Cleve. chpt.). Club: Toastmasters (charter). Home: 1199 Haselton Rd Cleveland Heights OH 44121 Office: 747 Alpha Dr Highland Heights OH 44143

MCCANN, JACK ARLAND, constrn. and mining equipment co. exec.; b. Chestnut, Ill., Apr. 16, 1926; s. Keith Ogden and Miriam Imogene McC.; A.B., Bradley U., 1950; m. Marian Adele Gordon, Mar. 31, 1956; 1 son, Christopher John. Mgr., Washington office R.G. LeTourneau Inc., 1950-53; mgr. def. and spl. products Westinghouse Air Brake Co., 1956-64, mgr. nat. accounts, 1964-67, mng. dir. Belgian plant and European mktg., 1967-70; gen. sales mgr. WABCO div. Am. Standard Inc., Peoria, Ill., 1970-73, v.p. mktg., 1973-80, v.p. staff, 1980—. Served with USNR, 1944-46. Decorated chevalier Ordre de la Couronne (Belgium). Mem. Nat. Def. Transp. Assn. (life), U.S. C. of C., Am. Legion. Clubs: Bradley Chiefs; Creve Coeur, Shriners (Peoria); Union League (Chgo.); Masons. Office: WABCO Div Am Standard Inc 2301 N Adams St Peoria IL 61639

MC CANN, MARY KATHLEEN, lawyer; b. Milw., Dec. 4, 1944; d. Ray Thomas and Annetta Mary (O'Connor) McC.; B.A. in Psychology cum laude, U. Wis., Madison, 1967, M.S. in Counseling and Guidance, 1970; J.D., Marquette U., 1981. With United Calif. Bank, 1967-68; social worker Milwaukee County Dept. Public Welfare, 1971-79; asso. Leonard L. Loeb, S.C., Milw., 1981—. Active Milw. Jr. League. Mem. Am. Personnel and Guidance Assn., Wis. Bar Assn., Phi Kappa Phi. Home: 2733 N Cramer St Milwaukee WI 53211 Office: 111 E Wisconsin Ave Milwaukee WI 53205

MC CANN, WILLIAM ALBERT, real estate co. exec.; b. Chgo., Oct. 7, 1937; s. William Ambrose and Louise (Shover) McC.; student Thornton Jr. Coll., 1955-56; Asso. Bus. Adminstrn., Central Jr. Coll., 1958-64; m. Louise M. Stahmer, Sept. 17, 1966; children—Brian, Kathleen, Michael, Charmaine, William. Loan officer, appraiser Central Fed. Savs. & Loan, Cicero, Ill., 1958-60; field supr., appraiser Mid Am. Appraisal Co., Chgo., 1960-62; owner, pres. William A. McCann & Assos., Inc., Chgo., 1962—. Chmn. Ill. Savs. & Loan Commn., 1972-75. Mem. Am. Inst. Real Estate Appraisers, Soc. Real Estate Appraisers, Ill. Assn. Certified Real Estate Appraisers, Am. Right of Way Assn., Chgo. Real Estate Bd., Nat. Assn. Real Estate Bds., Mich. Ave. Club, Lambda Alpha (hon.). Office: 180 N LaSalle St Chicago IL 60601

MCCANTS, GARY, state ofcl.; b. Cin., July 22, 1948; s. James Wesley and Willa Mae (Tinsley) McC.; B.S., Central State U., Wilberforce, Ohio, 1971; M.B.A., Atlanta U., 1973; m. Galda I. Garnett, Feb. 22, 1975; 1 dau., Khalilah Renee. Youth worker Cin. Union Bethel Neighborhood Sers. Orgn., summer 1971—; salesman Birds Eye div. Gen. Foods Corp., Syracuse, N.Y., 1972—; mktg. research staff analyst A.B. Dick Co., Niles, Ill., 1973-75; sr. legis. staff analyst, speaker of house, Ill. Ho. of Reps., Springfield, 1975-81, supr. staff intern program, 1979-81; staff analyst issues devel. unit, house minority leader's staff, 1981—. Mem. exec. council Citizens for Effective Voter Participation and Communication; Springfield rep. 16th Ward Regular Democratic Orgn., Chgo., 1975—; mem. Sangamon State U. Found., 1980—; bd. dirs. Springfield Urban League, 1980—. Recipient Cert. achievement Nat. Exec. High Sch. Internships, 1979. First Nat. City Corp. scholar, 1971-72: Sloan Found. scholar, 1972-73. Mem. Am. Mktg. Assn., Central State U. Alumni Assn., NAACP, Urban League, Atlanta U. Alumni Assn., Black Assn. MBA Execs., Basileus, Omega Psi Phi (Omega Man of Yr. 1980), Omega Nu. African Methodist Episcopalian. Club: The Group (chmn. bd.). Home: 2105 S 4th St Ct Springfield IL 62703 Office: Room 540 State House Springfield IL 62706

MC CARDELL, ARCHIE RICHARD, mfg. co. exec.; b. Hazel Park, Mich., Aug. 29, 1926; s. Archie and Josephine (Gauthier) McC.; B.B.A., U. Mich., 1948. M.B.A., 1949; m. Margaret Edith Martin, June 17, 1950; children—Sandra Beth, Laurie Wynne, Clay Vincent. With Ford Motor Co., 1949-60, finance exec., Dearborn, Mich., 1960; sec.-treas. Ford of Australia, 1960-63; dir. finance Ford of Germany, 1963-66; group v.p. for corporate service Xerox Corp., Rochester, N.Y., 1966-68, exec. v.p., 1968-71, pres., 1971-77, also chief operating officer, dir.; chmn., chief exec. officer Internat. Harvester Co., 1979—; dir. Am. Express Co., Am. Express Internat. Banking Corp., Gen. Foods Corp., Harris Trust & Savs. Bank, Harris Bankcorp, Inc., Honeywell, In.; former chmn. nat. adv. com. Blue Cross Assn. Formerly mem. adv. council Stanford U. Grad. Sch. Bus.; bd. dirs. Children's Meml. Hosp.; trustee U. Chgo. Served with USAAF, 1943-45. Office: International Harvester Co 401 N Michigan Ave Chicago IL 60611

MCCARREN, CARROL, theater co. adminstr.; b. Ft. Knox, Ky., Dec. 9, 1947; d. Edwin J. and Mary Otilia (Perry) McCarren; B.F.A., U. R.I., 1969; postgrad. Loyola U.; 1 dau., Kathryn S. Hoch. Gen. mgr. Free Street Theater, Chgo., 1978—. Mem. Am. Council on Arts, Theater Communications Group, Found. for Extension and Devel. of Am. Profl. Theater. Home: 3051 N Leavitt Chicago IL 60618 Office: 59 Hubbard St Chicago IL 60610

MC CARTEN, JOHN JAMES, lawyer; b. Marshalltown, Iowa, May 18, 1916; s. Frank T. and Agnes (Coulton) McC.; B.S.C., Creighton U., 1938, J.D., 1940; m. Maureen Riley, June 16, 1947; children—Jean McCarten Kerr, Paul, Mary, Riley. Admitted to Iowa bar, 1940, Minn. bar, 1940; practiced Sioux City, Iowa, 1940-41; mem. firm Dell & McCarten now firm McCarten & Tillitt, Alexandria, Minn., 1946—; pres. Alexandria Telephone Co., 1955-71; sec.-treas. Central Minn. TV Co. (KCMT-TV-FM, Alexandria, KNMT-TV, Waker, Minn., KXJB-TV, Fargo, N.D.), 1955—; county atty. Douglas County, Minn., 1951-66; pres. E.F.I. Co. (lakeshore devel.), Alexandria, 1958—, Tentelino Enterprises (theatres), Alexandria, Riley Co. (grain) S.D., 1948—, Alexandria Interurban Telephone Co., 1955-71, Alexandria Telephone Cable Co., 1965-71; v.p., sec. Bellanca Aircraft Co., Alexandria; sec. Minn. All-Channel Cable Vision, Inc., Arrowwood Lodge Inc., Alexandria, Minn. Chmn. lay adv. bd. Mercy Hosp., 1950-69; pres. bd. trustees Douglas County Hosps., 1969-73; advisor to dean Sch. Law, Creighton U., 1974—. Served as lt. USAAF, 1941-46. Designated knight Order St. Gregory the Great. Decorated D.F.C., Air medal; recipient Alumni Merit award Creighton U., 1974. Mem. Am., Minn. (bd. govs.), Iowa, 7th Jud. Dist. Minn. (pres. 1964-65), Fed. bar assns., Am. Legion (past comdr.), Am. Judicature Soc., Nat. Dist. Attys. Assn., Soc. Hosp. Attys., AIM (pres.'s council), Am. Mgmt. Assn., VFW, Gamma Eta Gamma. Roman Catholic. Clubs: K.C. (4 deg.), Elks, Eagles, Kiwanis; Mpls. Athletic; Alexandria Country. Home: Blakes by the Lakes Alexandria MN 56308 Office: McCarten & Tillitt Bldg Alexandria MN 56308

MCCARTER, WILLIAM J., JR., broadcasting exec.; b. Phila., June 10, 1929; s. William J. and Julia R. (Miller) McC.; McC.; B.A., Lafayette Coll., 1951; postgrad. Temple U. Sch. Communication, 1957-58; m. Emma Linda Warner, Jan. 19, 1952; children—Julianne, William J. II, Amy, James Andrew. Dir., WFIL-TV, Phila., 1953-57; program dir. WHYY-TV, Phila., 1957-62; program devel. officer Nat. Ednl. Television, N.Y.C., 1962-64; pres., gen. mgr. WETA-TV/FM, Washington, 1964-71; pres., gen. mgr. WTTW-TV, Chgp., 1971—; lectr. U. Pa., Am. U., Northwestern U.; TV cons. Govt. V.I.; pres. Eastern Ednl. TV Network, 1968-71. Mem. Pres.'s Commn. on Human Rights, 1968; telecommunications adviser to mayor of Washington. Trustee, St. John's Coll., Washington; bd. mgrs. Pub. Broadcasting Service, mem. Chgo. com. bd. dirs. Served to 1st lt. AUS, 1951-53. Decorated Bronze Star medal, Purple Heart. Recipient Bd. Govs.' award Washington Acad. Television Arts and Scis., 1971. Mem. Nat. (v.p. 1967-69), Washington (pres. 1966-68) acads. television arts and scis., Public TV Mgrs. Council, Nat. Assn. Ednl. Broadcastors (dir. 1970-72, vice chmn. 1970-72), Radio and TV Corrs. Assn., Chgo., Council Fgn. Relations (dir.). Clubs: National Press, International (Washington); Mid-Am., Union League (Chgo.). Office: WTTW-TV 5400 N Saint Louis Ave Chicago IL 60625*

MC CARTHY, DONALD RUSSELL, credit union ofcl.; b. Elliott, Iowa, Apr. 20, 1906; s. Emmet C. and Clara E. (Hartman) McC.; A.B., Simpson Coll., 1927; M.A., U. Iowa, 1938; m. Irja W. Hasu, June 25, 1948; children by previous marriage—Duane R., Darlagene. Tchr., coach Toledo (Iowa) High Sch., 1927-28, Indianola, Iowa, 1929-41, William Penn Coll., 1941-42, Lyons High Sch., Clinton, Iowa, 1942-45, Hinsdale Twp. High Sch., 1945-69; treas. South Dupage Schs. Credit Union, Downers Grove, Ill., 1955—. Recipient Alumni Achievement award Simpson Coll., 1979. Mem. Ill. Credit Union League (past pres. Aurora chpt.), Ill. Council Credit Union Execs. (treas. 1977-80, mgr. of year 1975), Downers Grove C. of C., Simpson Coll. Alumni Assn., Edn. Credit Union Council U.S., N.E.A. (life), Am. Council Consumer Interests, U.S. Track Coaches Assn., Nat. Ret. Tchrs. Assn., Phi Delta Kappa, Lambda Chi Alpha. Republican. Club: Hinsdale Kiwanis (treas. 1965-80). Home: 436 Norfolk Ave Clarendon Hills IL 60514 Office: 5202 Washington St Downers Grove IL 60515

MC CARTHY, DONALD WANS, utility exec.; b. Mpls., Feb. 11, 1922; s. Donald and Carolyn (Beach) McC.; B.S., U.S. Naval Acad., 1943; m. Anne Leslie, Jan. 2, 1947; children—Donald, Peter, Thomas, Jill. Commd. ensign U.S. Navy, 1940, advanced through grades to lt., 1943; active duty, 1943-48, 52-53; resigned, 1953; with No. States Power Co., Mpls., v.p., mgr. Mpls. div., 1969-72, 1972-73, exec. v.p., 1973-76, pres., dir., 1976—, chmn. bd., 1978—, also chief exec. officer; dir. Northwestern Nat. Bank, Mpls. Decorated Bronze Star. Mem. Mpls. Engrs. Club. Clubs: Mpls., Woodhill Country, Minn. Address: No States Power Corp 414 Nicollet Mall Minneapolis MN 55401

MC CARTHY, JOHN FRANCIS, civil engr.; b. St. Louis, May 5, 1920; s. John William and Helen Mary (McGinnis) McC.; B.S. in Civil Engring., U. Mo., 1948, M.S. in Civil Engring., 1950; m. Mariclare Ann Mohan, June 30, 1956; children—John, Ann, Thomas, Kathi, Maureen. Instr. civil engring. U. Mo., 1948-51; chief structural engr. Fruin-Colnon Co., 1951-52; chief structural engr. W.R. Bendy Co., 1953-54; asst. prof. St. Louis U., 1955-58, asso. prof., 1958-60, prof., 1961-69, chmn. dept. civil engring., 1956-69; supt. Met. St. Louis Sewer Dist., 1969—, tech. coordinator, 1975—. Chmn. St. Louis County Bldg. Code Review Com., 1961—. Served with AUS, 1941-45. Recipient Award of Merit, Engrs. Club St. Louis, 1971. Fellow ASCE; mem. Nat., Mo. socs. profl. engrs., Fed., Mo. water pollution control assns., Soc. Am. Value Engrs. Roman Catholic. Author: Fluid Mechanics Handbook, 1968. Home: 11756 Long Leaf Circle St Louis MO 63141 Office: 9200 S Broadway St St Louis MO 63125

MCCARTHY, JOHN FRANCIS, JR., aero. engr., govt. research adminstr.; b. Boston, Aug. 28, 1925; s. John Francis and Margaret Josephine (Bartwood) McC.; S.B., M.I.T., 1950, S.M. in Aero. Engring., 1951; Ph.D. in Aeros. and Physics, Calif. Inst. Tech., 1962; m. Camille Dian Martinez, May 4, 1968; children—Margaret I., Megan, Jamie M., Nicole E., John F. Supr. air/ground communications TWA, Rome, 1946-47; project mgr. aeroelastic and structures research lab. M.I.T., 1951-55, prof. aeros. and astronautics, 1971-78; ops. analyst Hdqrs. SAC, Offutt AFB, Nebr., 1955-59; dir., asst. chief engr. Apollo Space div., N. Am. Aviation, Inc., Downey, Calif., 1961-66; v.p. Los Angeles div./Space div., Rockwell Internat. Corp., 1966-71; dir. and prof. M.I.T. Center for Space Research, 1974-78; dir. NASA Lewis Research Center, Cleve., 1978—; mem. Internat. Council Aero. Scis., Koln, Germany, 1978—; mem. USAF Sci. Adv. Bd., Washington, 1970—; mem. sci. adv. group Joint Chiefs of Staff, Joint Strategic Target Planning Staff, Offutt AFB, 1976-81; com. mem. Energy Engring. Bd., Assembly Engring., NRC, 1979; mem. Nat. Acad. of Engring., Am. Mgmt. Assn., Rensselaer Poly technic Inst. dept. advisory bd., bd. of gov. Cleve. Airshow; cons. in field. Campaign chmn. Downey Community Hosp., 1968-69; bd. govs. Nat. Space Club, Washington, 1978—; chmn. Fed. Exec. Bd., Cleve., 1979-80. Served with USAAF, 1944-46. Recipient Apollo Achievement award NASA, 1969, Meritorious Civilian Service medal USAF, 1973, Exceptional Civilian Service medal, 1978. Fellow AIAA (dir. 1975-76), AAS; asso. fellow Royal Aero. Soc. (London); mem. Am. Soc. Engring. Edn. (exec. com. aerospace div. 1969-72), Sigma Xi, Sigma Gamma Tau. Unitarian. Clubs: Cosmos, Cleve. 50. Author numerous tech. reports; patentee impact landing system. Home: 18819 Canyon Rd Fairview Park OH 44126 Office: NASA Lewis Research Center Cleveland OH 44135

MCCARTHY, LENORE BISKUP, coll. dean; b. Phila., Oct. 1, 1942; d. John and Eleanor (Fay) Biskup; B.S., Wheelock Coll., 1964; M.Ed., Boston U., 1970; Ph.D., Northwestern U., 1977; m. Paul McCarthy, July 3, 1965; children—Elizabeth Desta, Sarah Fay. Tchr., Quincy, Mass., 1964-65, Brussels, Belgium, 1965-66, Addis Ababa, Ethiopia, 1966-68; cons. Ednl. Services, Chgo., 1972-73; faculty Nat. Coll. Edn., Chgo., 1973-79, dean, 1979—; dir. Baker Demonstration Sch., 1979—; cons. in field. Bd. dirs. Park West Community Assn., 1979—. Ill. Office Edn. grantee, 1978-79. Mem. Internat. Reading Assn., Nat. Council Tchrs. of English, Chgo. Area Reading Assn., Nat. Assn. Lab. Schs., Phi Delta Kappa. Contbr. articles to profl. jours. Home: 2434 N Orchard St Chicago IL 60614 Office: 2840 Sheridan Rd Evanston IL 60201

MCCARTHY, WALTER JOHN, JR., electric utility co. exec.; b. N.Y.C., Apr. 20, 1925; s. Walter J. and Irene (Trumbland) McC.; B.M.E., Cornell U., 1949; postgrad. Oak Ridge Sch. Reactor Tech., 1951-52; D.Eng. (hon.), Lawrence Inst. Tech., 1981; m. Alice Anna Ross, Sept. 3, 1947; children—Walter, David, Sharon, James, William. Engr., Public Service Electric & Gas Co., Newark, 1949-56; sect. head Atomic Power Devel. Assos., Detroit, 1956-61; gen. mgr. Power Reactor Devel. Co., Detroit, 1961-68; project mgr. Detroit Edison Co., 1968-71, mgr. engring., 1971-73, mgr. ops., 1973-74, v.p. ops., 1974-75, exec. v.p. ops., 1975-77, exec. v.p. divs., 1977-79, pres., 1979-81, chief operating officer, 1979—, chmn. bd., 1981—, also dir.; dir. DETROITBANK Corp., Wolverine Aluminum Corp., Electric Vehicle Council. Bd. dirs. Cranbrook Inst. Sci., Detroit Econ. Growth Corp., Detroit Symphony Orch., Met. Affairs Corp., United Found.; trustee New Detroit, Harper-Grace Hosps.; bd. visitors Sch. Econs. and Mgmt., Oakland U. Named One of 5 Outstanding Young Men in Mich., Mich. Jr. C. of C., 1958. Fellow Am. Nuclear Soc., Engring. Soc. Detroit; mem. ASME. Methodist. Clubs: Detroit Athletic, Detroit, Renaissance (Detroit). Contbr. numerous articles on nuclear engring. to profl. jours. Office: 2000 2d Ave Detroit MI 48226

MC CARTNEY, RALPH FARNHAM, lawyer, dist. judge; b. Charles City, Iowa, Dec. 11, 1924; s. Ralph C. and Helen (Farnham) McC.; J.D., U. Mich., 1950; B. Sci., Iowa State U., 1972; m. Rhoda Mae Huxsol, June 30, 1950; children—Ralph, Julia, David. Admitted to Iowa bar, 1950; mem. firm Miller, Heuber & Miller, Des Moines, 1950-52, Frye & McCartney, Charles City, 1952-73, McCartney & Erb, Charles City, 1973-78; judge Dist. Ct. Iowa, Charles City, 1978—; mem. jud. coordinating com. Iowa Supreme Ct. Chmn., Iowa Republican Conv., 1972, 74; mem. Iowa Ho. of Reps., 1967-70, majority floor leader, 1969-70; mem. Iowa Senate, 1973-74. Bd. regents U. Iowa, Iowa State U., U. No. Iowa, Iowa Sch. for Deaf, Iowa Braille and Sight Saving Sch. Served with AUS, 1942-45. Mem. Am., Iowa bar assns., Am. Judicature Soc., Iowa Judges Assn. (chmn. legis. com.). Home: RFD 1 Charles City IA 50616 Office: Ct Chambers Courthouse Charles City IA 50616

MC CARTY, LORRAINE CHAMBERS, painter; b. Detroit; d. Allan and Louise Heinrika (Swift) Chambers; student Stephens Coll., Wayne State U.; m. Howard J. McCarty; children—Allan Grant, Jean Louise, Jill McCarty Hartley, Read Swift. Exec. designer Internat. Women's Air and Space Mus., Oklahoma City, 1970-73; instr. Flint (Mich.) Inst. Arts, 1971—; mem. Oakland County (Mich.) Cultural Council, 1975—; aircraft pilot, 1960—, appt. ofcl. air force artist, 1980—; one-woman shows: Central Mich. U., 1976, Habatat Gallery, Dearborn, Mich., 1976, Midland (Mich.) Center Arts., 1976, Dayton Inst. Arts, 1978, Dept. Transp., Washington, 1978, Hackley Art Mus., Muskegon, Mich., 1979, Battle Creek (Mich.) Civic Art Center, 1979; group shows include: Butler Mus. Am. Art, Youngstown, Ohio, 1967, 69, 71, 75, Detroit Inst. Arts., 1967, 69, Flint Inst. Arts, 1972, 75, 77, 79, 81, Bowling Green (Ohio) U., 1981, Battle Creek Art Mus., 1974, Grand Rapids Art Mus., 1973, Smithsonian Air and Space Mus., 1981, Am. Acad. Arts and Letters; represented in permanent collections: Fed. Aviation Agency, Bede Aircraft, Butler Mus. Am. Art, Detroit Inst. Art, No. Ill. U., Muskegon (Mich.) Mus. Art, K Mart Internat. Hdqrs., Dow. Chem. Co. Recipient various awards for paintings. Mem. Mich., Associated arts councils, Mich. Acad. Arts, Scis. and Letters, Archives Am. Art, Mich. Water Color Soc., Detroit Soc. Women Painters and Sculptors, Artists Equity, Internat. Orgn. Women Pilots, Mich. Pilots, Am. Aviation Hist. Soc. Club: Scarab (Detroit). Murals: Mich. Dept. Aviation, Internat. Women's Air and Space Mus. Home and Office: 1112 Pinehurst St Royal Oak MI 48073

MC CASLAND, MICHAEL, aircraft engine mfg. co. exec.; b. Big Spring, Tex., Dec. 15, 1944; s. Ardis and Fannie Douglas (Cain) McC.; B.S. in Aerospace Engring., U. Tex., Austin, 1968; M.B.A. in Mktg., Xavier U., Cin., 1977; m. Elise McCree, Dec. 27, 1966; 1 dau., Erin Elizabeth. With aircraft engine div. Gen. Electric Co., Evendale, Ohio, 1968—, drives and pneumatics evaluation engr., 1976-78, tech. mktg. program mgr., 1978-80, mgr. variable cycle engine programs, 1980—. Fin. sec. Friendship United Methodist Ch., Wyoming, Ohio, 1976-78, mem. pastor-parish relations com., nominating com., 1979—. Served with USAR, 1969-71. Mem. Am. Inst. Aeros. and Astronautics, Tech. Mktg. Soc. Am. Republican. Home: 50 Vermont Ave Wyoming OH 45215 Office: 1 Neumann Way Mail Drop H-9 Evendale OH 45215

MCCATHRIN, EDWINA ZOE BARGDILL, banker; b. Columbus, Ohio, Aug. 23, 1936; d. Edwin L. and Nora F. Bargdill; student Ohio U., 1954-56; B.A. with honors in English, Otterbein Coll., 1974; m. John E. McCathrin, Apr. 12, 1969; 1 son, Lee Edwin. Dir. communications BancOhio/Ohio Nat. Bank, Columbus, 1974-75, public relations officer, 1976-77; dir. public relations, public relations officer BancOhio Corp., Columbus, 1977, asst. v.p., dir. public relations, 1977-79; v.p., dir. public relations BancOhio Nat. Bank, Columbus, 1979—. Del. gov.'s com. Ohio Commn. on Status of Women, 1970. Recipient Fiction Writer of Yr. award Quill and Scroll, Otterbein Coll., 1971. Mem. Public Relations Soc. Am. (pres. Central Ohio chpt., public relations award 1979, 80), Internat. Assn. Bus. Communicators (spl. event awards Central Ohio), Am. Inst. Banking, Women in Communication, Ohio Hist. Soc., Westerville Hist. Soc., Urban League. Clubs: Columbus Met., Central Ohio Press. Office: BancOhio Nat Bank Plaza 155 E Broad St Columbus OH 43265

MC CAULEY, HUGO WAYNE, indsl. designer; b. Flagstaff, Ariz., Apr. 24, 1935; s. Shelby Samuel and Agnes Ione (Anderson) McC.; B.S., U.S. Naval Acad., 1957, Dipl. Navy Postgrad. Sch., 1964; M.S., Ill. Inst. Tech., 1974; m. Lois Cook, Oct. 20, 1962; 1 dau., Meghan Cybele. Commd. ensign, U.S. Navy, 1957, advanced through grades to lt. comdr., 1966-68, comdg. officer adminstrv. unit, 1966-68, now capt. Res.; owner, mgr. Designtext (and predecessor co.), Chgo., 1971—; mem. faculty Sch. Art and Design, U. Ill., Chgo. Circle, 1971—, asst. prof., 1974—; asso. Dahl Kemper Assos., Evanston, Ill., 1978-79. Mem. Design Methods Group, Environ. Design Research Assn., Assn. Man-Environment Relations, Am. Booksellers Assn., World Future Soc., Human Factors Soc., Internat. Ergonomics Assn., Naval Reserve Assn., Naval Acad. Alumni Assn., Mensa. Lodge: Ind. Order Odd Fellows. Home: 802 Forest Ave Evanston IL 60202 Office: PO Box 2622 Chicago IL 60690

MC CAULEY, MICHAEL FREDERICK, editor; b. Chgo., Apr. 12, 1947; s. George Lawrence and Virginia Marie (Johnson) McC.; A.B. in English, Loyola U., 1969; m. Gabrielle Mary Goder, May 29, 1971; children—Megan Colleen, Maura Eileen, Timothy Edward. Tchr. of English, Woodlands Acad., Lake Forest, Ill., 1969-70; asst. editor Critic mag., Thomas More Assn., Chgo., 1970-73, book reviewer, 1971—, exec. editor newsletters including Overview, 1973-81; mng. editor Cross-Reference, Am. Hosp. Assn., 1981—; book reviewer Commonweal mag., 1974—; author: A Contemporary Meditation on Doubting, 1976; editor: On the Run: Spirituality for the Seventies, 1974; The Jesus Book, 1978. Roman Catholic. Home: 146 N Taylor Ave Oak Park IL 60302 Office: 840 N Lake Shore Dr Chicago IL 60611

MC CHESNEY, KATHRYN MARIE (MRS. THOMAS DAVID MCCHESNEY), educator; b. Curwensville, Pa., Jan. 14, 1936; d. Orland William and Lillian Irene (Morrison) Spencer; B.A., U. Akron, 1962; M.L.S., Kent State U., 1965, postgrad., 1971—; m. Thomas David McChesney, June 12, 1954; 1 son, Eric Spencer. Tchr. English, Springfield Local High Sch., Akron, Ohio, 1962-63, librarian, 1963-64, head librarian, 1965-68; asst. to dean, instr. Kent (Ohio) State U. Sch. Library Sci., 1968-69, asst. dean, 1969-77, asst. prof., 1969—. Rep. Uniontown Community Council, 1964-66. Mem. Am., Ohio (chmn. Library Edn. Roundtable 1971-72, exec. council Div. VI Library Edn. 1972—) library assns., AAUP, Am., Ohio assns. sch. librarians, Beta Phi Mu, Phi Sigma Alpha, Phi Alpha Theta, Sigma Phi Epsilon. Club: Uniontown Jr. Womans (pres. 1965-66). Contbr. articles, book revs. to profl. periodicals. Home: 3611 Edison St NW Uniontown OH 44685 Office: Kent State U Kent OH 44242

MCCLAIN, MARION PETERING, health care evaluator; b. Kalamazoo, Sept. 22, 1947; d. Harold George and Eva Catherine (Petersen) Petering; Presser scholar, Earlham Coll., 1965-68; A.B. in Zoology, Miami U., 1969; M.S. in Biostatistics (Dean's Office scholar, Faculty and Staff scholar), U. Pitts., 1975; m. Craig J. McClain, June 27, 1970. Research asst. biochemistry and immunochemistry U. Cin. Children's Hosp. Research Found., 1969-70, biochemistry St. Jude Children's Research Hosp., 1970-72, rheumatology U. Pitts., 1972-75; biostatistician, coordinator St. Louis Park (Minn.) Med. Center, 1975-79, asst. clin. prof. Center Health Services Research U. Minn., 1979, sr. biostatistician, coordinator, 1979-80; prin. health care evaluator U. Minn. Hosps. and Clinics, Mpls., 1980—. Merit fellow Minn. Health Services Research, 1979-80; named outstanding woman employee St. Louis Park Med. Center, 1979. Mem. Am. Statis. Assn., Biometric Soc., N.Y. Acad. Scis., AAAS, Assn. Women in Sci. Contbr. articles profl. jours. Home: 3926 Zenith Ave S Minneapolis MN 55410 Office: Box 725 Mayo University of Minnesota Hospitals Minneapolis MN 55455

MC CLAIN, MICHAEL FRANCIS, lawyer, state legislator; b. Quincy, Ill., Aug. 31, 1947; s. Elmo and Margaret (McIntire) McC.; B.S., St. Benedict's Coll., 1969; postgrad. Western Ill. U., 1969-71; J.D., St. Louis U., 1975; m. Cathleen M. Cannon, June 14, 1969; children—Patrick Elmo, Colleen Erin, Daniel Michael. Tchr., Quincy Jr. High Sch., 1969-71; admitted to Ill. bar, 1977; legal asst. Adams County Pub. Defenders Office, 1972; asso. firm Scholz & Staff, Quincy, 1972-75, Goehl, Adams & Schuering, Quincy, 1975-78; partner firm Awerkamp & McClain, Quincy, 1978—; mem. Ill. Ho. of Reps., 1973—, asst. minority leader, 1981—. Served as 2d lt. Ill. N.G., 1972. Recipient Appreciation award Ill. State Chaplains, 1974; A award Ill. Edn. Assn., 1976; cert. of commendation Ill. Office Edn. and Ill. Assn. Regional Supts., 1976; Outstanding Legislator award Ill. Edn. Assn., Ill. Fedn. Ind. Colls. and Univs.; cert. of appreciation Am. Legion Post 37, others; named Outstanding Freshman Legislator, 1974, Outstanding Legislator, Young Democrats of Ill., 1976. Mem. Am. Bar Assn., Ill. Bar Assn., Adams County Bar Assn., Quincy Jaycees. Democrat. Roman Catholic. Clubs: K.C. (4 deg.); Mart

Heinen; Killen-McClain. Home: 2311 Hampshire St Quincy IL 62301 Office: 701 Broadway Quincy IL 62301*

MCCLELLAN, PATRICIA DONLEY, occupational therapist; b. Norfolk, Va., Feb. 19, 1930; d. David Edward and Cordella (Weaver) Donley; student Cornell U., 1947-49; B.S., Western Mich. U., 1952, M.A. in Occupational Therapy, 1966; m. George A. McClellan, July 26, 1953 (div. Jan. 1980); children—Diane Linn, David Charles, James Ray. Therapist, Red Feather Agy., Dayton, Ohio, 1952-53; head occupational therapy dept. Eastern Orthopedic Sch., Grand Rapids, Mich., 1960-66, therapist, 1969-72; head occupational therapy dept. Parkview Sch., 1966-67; dir. occupational therapy dept. Ottawa High Sch., Grand Rapids, Mich., 1972-79; dir. occupational therapy assisting program Grand Rapids Jr. Coll., 1979—. Nat. dir. Disaster Assistance Team program Nat. Campers and Hikers Assn., 1976-78, recipient awards for service; pres. Muscular Dystrophy Assn., 1956-58. Mem. Western Mich. Dist. Occupational Therapy Assn. (Therapist of Yr. 1980), Am. Occupational Therapy Assn., Mich. Occupational Therapy Assn., Physically Impaired Assn. Mich. Home: 8665 28th St Ada MI 49301 Office: 143 Bostwick St NE Grand Rapids MI 49503

MCCLELLAN, RAYMOND PATRICK, communications co. exec.; b. Bklyn., Oct. 9, 1929; s. William Thomas and Catherine Agnes (McGrath) McC.; B.B.A., CCNY, 1962; m. Mary Andrea Schneider, Aug. 31, 1963; children—Amy Catherine, David. Trust dept. Mfrs.-Hanover Trust Co., N.Y.C., 1953-58; asst. controller Roosevelt Hosp., N.Y.C., 1958-67, Beekman Downtown Hosp., N.Y.C., 1967-68; systems analyst State Bond Cos., New Ulm, Minn., 1968-70; v.p. fin. Mickelson Media, Inc., New Ulm, 1970—; guest lectr. Columbia U., WHO, 1961-63. Bd. dirs., sec. Sioux Valley Hosp., 1969-80; v.p., dir. Highland Manor Nursing Home, 1975—; bd. dirs. Brown County Head Start Program, Mankato, Minn., 1970-75. Served with Signal Corps, AUS, 1951-53; Korea. Recipient Presdl. award Toastmasters Club, 1972; named Exec. of Yr., New Ulm, 1980. Mem. Am. Mgmt. Assn., Newspaper Controllers and Fin. Officers Assn., Nat. Cable TV Assn. Democrat. Mem. United Ch. of Christ. Clubs: New Ulm Country, Turner of New Ulm. Home: 3 Sunrise Dr New Ulm MN 56073 Office: 200 1/2 N Minnesota St New Ulm MN 56073

MC CLELLAND, JAMES CRAIG, III, educator; b. Berea, Ohio, Apr. 29, 1938; s. James Craig and Eleanor May (Hamilton) McC.; B.A., Amherst Coll., 1960; M.A., Yale U., 1963; Ph.D., Princeton U., 1970; m. Virginia Ann Wikstrom, Aug. 24, 1963; children—Jeffrey Craig, James Scott. Instr. history Stanford U., 1967-71; asst. prof. U. Calif., Santa Barbara, 1971-79; asso. prof. history U. Nebr., 1979—; participant in U.S.-USSR Acad. Exchange, 1965-66. Fulbright-Hays grantee, 1965-66; Ford fellow, 1966-67; Am. Council Learned Socs. and Social Sci. Research Council grantee, 1974-75. Mem. Am. Assn. Advancement of Slavic Studies, Am. Hist. Assn., AAUP, Sierra Club, Friends of Earth. Author: Autocrats and Academics, 1979; contbr. articles to profl. jours. Home: 2906 Summit Blvd Lincoln NE 68502 Office: Dept History U Nebr Lincoln NE 68588

MC CLELLAND, JAMES MORRIS, rehab. facility exec.; b. New Smyrna Beach, Fla., Nov. 24, 1943; s. Ernest James and Gwendolyn Byrd (Reid) McC.; B.I.E., Ga. Inst. Tech., 1966; m. Jane Marie Pengelly; 1 son, James Scott. Exec. intern Goodwill Industries, Houston, 1970-72, exec. v.p., Beaumont, Tex., 1972-73; v.p. ops. Goodwill Industries of Central Ind., Inc., Indpls., 1973-74, pres., 1974—; pres. Goodwill Industries Internat. Council, 1980—; exec. v.p. Goodwill Industries Found. of Central Ind., Inc., 1974—; bd. dirs. Goodwill Industries Am., 1980—. Mem. Greater Indpls. Progress Com., 1978—; pres. Ind. Partners of the Ams., 1979—. Served with U.S. Environtl. Sci. Services Adminstrn., 1967-70. Mem. Goodwill Industries Conf. of Execs. (vice chmn. 1976-77), Nat. Rehab. Assn., Ind. Commn. for Handicapped. Club: Rotary (dir. 1977-79). Home: 2028 Mystic Bay Ct Indianapolis IN 46240 Office: 1635 W Michigan St Indianapolis IN 46222

MC CLENAHAN, ANN CATHERINE, psychologist; b. Sioux City, Iowa, Apr. 17, 1932; d. Harold L. and Beatrice A. (Wilbur) McC.; B.A., U. S.D., 1953, Ed.D., 1974; M.Ed., S.D. State U., 1969. Tchr., Sioux Falls (S.D.) Pub. Schs., 1955-60; counselor/psychometrist Brandon Valley (S.D.) Schs., 1969-71; asst. prof. edn., psychology Dakota Wesleyan U., Mitchell, S.D., 1974-75; child psychologist Intercommunity Human Service Center, Mitchell, 1975-76; child psychologist Area Edn. Agy., Sioux Center, Iowa, 1976—; part-time pvt. practice psychology, Sioux Falls, 1977—. Mem. Am., S.D. psychol. assns., Iowa Sch. Psychologists Assn., Am. Personnel and Guidance Assn., Pi Beta Phi. Home: 2202 Pendar Ln Sioux Falls SD 57105 Office: 102 S Main Sioux Center IA 51250 also 801 N Elmwood Burnside Plaza Sioux Falls SD 57105

MCCLENDON, EDWIN JAMES, educator; b. Troy, Okla., Dec. 3, 1921; s. Charles Wesley and Mattie (Reed) McC.; B.S., Okla. East Central State U., 1946; M.Ed., U. Okla., 1954; Ed.D., Wayne State U., Detroit, 1964; m. Ruby Wynona Scott, May 5, 1950; children—Edwin J. Jr., Melody Jan, Joy Renee. Instr., U. Okla., Norman, 1946-47; head speech dept., tchr. Wewoka (Okla.) High Sch., 1947-49; asso. dir. TB Control, Oklahoma City, 1949-51; dir. sch. health project State Dept. Health and Edn., Oklahoma City, 1951-54; asso. dir. TB Control, Wayne County, Mich., 1954-56; dir. sch. health, Wayne County, 1956-63; dir. secondary edn. Wayne County Intermediate Sch., Detroit, 1963-67; supt. schs. Highland Pk., Mich., 1967-68; v.p. Highland Park (Mich.) Coll., 1968-69; asst. supt. health Mich. Dept. Edn., Lansing, 1969-71; prof., chmn. health edn. U. Mich., Ann Arbor, 1971—, prof. health behavior and public health, 1971—; cons. WHO, 1978—, dir. field study for Western Pacific, 1981; health field study of Arabic states, 1979-80. Chmn. bd. dirs. Am. Cancer Soc., Detroit, 1977-78, mem. nat. public edn. com., 1969—, hon. life mem., 1980—; mem. nat. adv. council Alcohol Abuse, 1976-80; pres. Plymouth-Canton Sch. Bd., 1974-78; mem. Tax Review bd., Plymouth, Mich., 1980—; chmn. Jr. Red Cross S.E. Mich., 1969-73. Served with USN, 1942-46. Decorated Bronze Star. Recipient William A. Howe award Am. Sch. Health Assn., 1976, Disting. Service award Am. Sch. Health Assn., 1962, Disting. Service award Mich. Sch. Health Assn., 1967, Disting. Health Edn. award Central Mich. U., 1978. Fellow Am. Public Health Assn., Am. Sch. Health Assn. (pres. 1970-71), Royal Soc. Health; mem. NEA, AAUP, Am. Social Health Assn. (dir.), Nat. Assn. Curriculum and Devel., Am. VD Assn., Alliance Advancement Health Edn., Soc. Public Health Edn., Soc. Sex Educators and Counselors, Phi Delta Kappa. Democrat. Methodist. Clubs: Rotary Internat., Soc. Native Am. Indians. Author: Maxi Minds in Mini Cages, The Gifted, 1972, Healthful Living for Today and Tomorrow, 1981, Drug Education A Teacher's Guide, 1969; contbr. articles to profl. publs. Home: 40742 Crabtree Ln Plymouth MI 48170 Office: 1017 Sch Edn Bldg Univ Mich Ann Arbor MI 48109

MC CLORY, ROBERT, congressman; b. Riverside, Ill., Jan. 31, 1908; s. Frederick Stephens and Catherine (Reilly) McC.; student L'Institut Sillig, Vevey, Switzerland, 1925-26, Dartmouth Coll., 1926-28; LL.B., Chgo.-Kent Coll., 1932; m. Audrey Vasey (dec. Sept. 1967); children—Beatrice (Mrs. Donald Etienne), Michael, Oliver; m. 2d, Doris S. Hibbard, Mar. 1969. Admitted to Ill. bar, 1932; practiced in Chgo. and Waukegan, Ill., 1932-62; mem. Ill. Ho. of Reps., 1951-52, Ill. Senate, 1952-62; mem. 88th-97th congresses from 13th Dist. Ill., mem. select com. on intelligence, ranking Republican House Judiciary Com.; participant Ditchley Conf., London, 1966, mem. congl. del. Interparliamentary Union, 1964—, Environ. Conf., Stockholm, 1972. Mem. Am., Ill., Lake County bar assns., Navy League, Waukegan-North Chgo. C. of C., Psi Upsilon, Phi Delta Phi. Christian Scientist. Clubs: Chicago Law; Bath and Tennis (Lake Forest, Ill.); Capitol Hill (Washington). Home: 321 Constitution Ave NE Washington DC 20002 also 340 Prospect Ave Lake Bluff IL 60044 Office: Rayburn House Office Bldg Washington DC 20515 also Lake County Bldg Waukegan IL 60085 also 1200 Meadowdale St Carpentersville IL 60110 also 56 N Williams St Crystal Lake IL 60014

MCCLOSKEY, JACK, profl. basketball team exec.; m. Anita McCloskey. Basketball coach U. Pa., 1956-66, Wake Forest Coll., 1966-72; head coach Portland (Oreg.) Trail Blazers, 1972-80; gen. mgr. Detroit Pistons, 1980—. Address: Detroit Pistons Pontiac Silverdome 1200 Featherstone St Pontiac MI 48057*

MC CLOSKEY, KEITH RICHARD, physician; b. Lock Haven, Pa., Apr. 10, 1939; s. Richard K. and Gwendolyn I. (Stringfellow) McC.; B.S. with highest distinction in Chemistry, U. Ill., 1960; M.D., Johns Hopkins U., 1964; m. Apr. 20, 1963; children—Patricia, Gordon. Research asso. life scis. dept. Martin-Marietta Corp., Balt., 1962; intern pediatrics Johns Hopkins Hosp., Balt., 1964-65, asst. resident pediatrics, 1968-69; chief resident pediatrics Sinai Hosp., Balt., 1968, Balt. City Hosps., 1969; fellow child psychiatry Johns Hopkins Hosp. and U., 1969-70; practice medicine specializing in pediatrics, Arlington Heights, Ill., 1970-73; practice medicine specializing in behavior and learning disorders in children, adolescents and adults, Arlington Heights, 1973—; psychiatry resident U. Chgo., 1976-78; vis. physician pediatric out-patient services Balt. City Hosps., 1969-70; mem. courtesy staff Northwest Community Hosp., Arlington Heights, 1970-73; attending physician Children's Meml. Hosp., Northwestern U., Chgo., 1970-73; mem. med. adv. bd. Samuel A. Kirk Devel. Tng. Center, Palatine, Ill., 1971-74; vis. lectr. dept. spl. edn. No. Ill. U., 1976, So. Ill. U., Carbondale, 1978; research asso. dept. psychiatry U. Chgo., 1973—; cons. and mem. faculty minimal brain dysfunction Abbott Labs., 1975—; mem. faculty Speakers Bur., CIBA, 1976—, Nat. Coll. Juvenile Justice Inst., 1976; mem. cons. med. staff dept. pediatrics Northwest Community Hosp., 1973—. Mem. adv. council pre-sch. program for handicapped children Sch. Dist. 57, Mt. Prospect, Ill., 1972-74; mem. bd. govs. Northwest Suburban Council of Understanding Learning Disabilities, 1972-74. Served to capt., M.C., U.S. Army, 1965-67. Diplomate Am. Bd. Pediatrics. Fellow Am. Acad. Pediatrics, Am. Acad. Cerebral Palsy; mem. N.Y. Acad. Scis., Assn. for Children with Learning Disabilities, AAAS, Johns Hopkins Med. Soc., Northwest Suburban Council on Understanding Learning Disabilities (chmn. advisory bd.), Sigma Xi, Phi Beta Kappa, Phi Alpha Mu (pres. 1959-60), Phi Eta Sigma, Phi Kappa Phi, Omega Beta Pi (pres. 1959-60). Contbr. articles to med. and psychiat. jours. Office: 1011 S Evergreen Ave Arlington Heights IL 60005

MCCLOW, THOMAS ALAN, lawyer; b. Detroit, Apr. 25, 1944; s. Kenneth Ray and Rita Beatrice (Periard) McC.; B.S., Mich. State U., 1966; J.D., Loyola U., 1969; children—Amy Christine, Adam Andrew. Admitted to Ill. bar, 1969, U.S. Supreme Ct. bar, 1973; asso. mem. firm Douglas F. Comstock, Geneva, Ill., 1970-73, John L. Nickels, Elburn, Ill., 1973-78; partner firm Nickels & McClow, Elburn, 1978—; public conservator, guardian, adminstr. Kane County, 1975-78. Bd. dirs. Kane County Council Econ. Opportunity, 1st vice chmn., 1971-73; bd. dirs. Tri City Youth Project, 1972-73; faculty dean Parent Edn. Center, 1974-76. Mem. Am. Bar Assn., Ill. Bar Assn., Chgo. Bar Assn., Kane County Bar Assn. (chmn. membership and admissions com. 1979—), Am. Judicature Soc., Fox Valley Estate Planning Council, Mensa. Democrat. Home: 106 Briar Ln Geneva IL 60134 Office: 130 N Main St Elburn IL 60119

MC CLUNEY, GREGORY DAY, advt. and pub. relations exec., publisher; b. Kansas City, Mo., Dec. 27, 1946; s. Glenn G. and Dorothy N. Boone McC.; B.S. in Journalism, U. Kans., Lawrence, 1970; postgrad. U. Mo.-Rolla, 1974; m. Anita L. Barnes, June 1, 1968. Advt. writer, TV producer Fremerman-Papin Advt., Kansas City, Mo., 1970-71; account exec. Valentine-Radford Advt., Kansas City, 1971—; founder, exec. v.p. McCluney/Brewer Inc., Pub. Relations Inc., Overland Park, Kans. and Atlanta, Dallas, 1973—; partner, exec. v.p. Am. Auto Systems, Inc., Overland Park; exec. v.p., dir. Hudco Inc., Kansas City, 1973-76, also dir.; v.p., treas. NAS Mktg. Inc., Overland Park, 1975-77, also dir. Corp. chmn. spl. gifts Greater Kansas City chpt. Cancer Soc., 1969-70; promotional chmn. Greater Kansas City Vol. Action Center, 1971-72; co. chmn. Publicity Greater Kansas City United Fund, 1972-73; active Friends of Art Nelson Gallery and Mus. Hon. fellow Truman Library Inst., Independence, Mo., 1974-75. Promotional bd. Jr. Women's Philharmonic Assn. Kansas City, Mo., 1974—; hon. dir. Rockhurst Coll., Kansas City, 1977—; publicity chmn. Women's Internat. Jazz Festival, 1978-79; public relations chmn. Gemini Sch. for Spl. Edn., Kansas City, 1978-79. Mem. Am. Advt. Fedn. (Addy award 9th Dist. 1972, 73, 75), Aviation and Space Writers Assn., Am. Bus. Writers Assn. (founding), Internat. Platform Assn., Assn. Indsl. Advertisers, Am. Mgmt. Assn., Public Relations Soc. Am., Advt. and Sales Execs. Club. Clubs: Kansas City, Leawood Country; Lakewood Country; Nat. Press (Washington). Home: 8518 Ensley Pl Leawood KS 66204 Office: 300 Fox Hill Office Center 4550 W 109th St Overland Park KS 66211

MCCLURE, CHARLES RICHARD, advt. agy. exec.; b. Dayton, Ohio, June 3, 1947; s. Richard Allison and Mary Lois McC.; B.A., Ohio State U., 1969; m. Patricia Ann Stridsberg, Apr. 4, 1969; children—Lisa Marie, Richard Ryan. News reporter Sta. WBNS-TV-Radio, Columbus, Ohio, 1967-70; asst. dir. public relations Ohio State U., Columbus, 1970-73; communications dir. Columbus Devel. Dept., 1973-75; account exec. Paul Werth Assos., 1975-78; account exec., public relations mgr. Howard Swink Advt., 1978—. Served to 1st lt. Army N.G., 1969-73. Mem. Am. Mktg. Assn., Public Relations Soc. Am., Columbus Advt. Fedn., Ohio Press Club. Episcopalian. Club: Athletic. Office: Howard Swink Advt 1383 Dublin Rd Columbus OH 43216

MC CLURE, FLORENCE HELEN, savs. and loan assn. exec.; b. Chgo., July 21, 1930; d. George and Minnie (LaBarbara) Torre; student Ind. U., 1948-50, Kent State U., 1967-68, Lake Erie Coll., 1969-70; m. Richard D. McClure, Feb. 16, 1952; children—Kimbert, Brian, Douglas, Ronald. Tchr. elementary grades Assumption Sch., Geneva, Ohio, 1966-71; coordinator traffic dept. True Temper Corp., Saybrook, Ohio, 1971-72; dir. mktg., public relations Peoples Savs. and Loan Assn., Ashtabula, Ohio, 1973—. Co-chmn. Right-to-Read Com., Geneva Area Schs., 1969-71; panel chairperson mgmt. standards and allocations com. United Way of Ashtabula County, Ohio, 1976-78; chmn. membership Ashtabula council Girl Scouts U.S.; coordinator Northeastern Ohio Scholastic Art Awards, 1973-78; bd. dirs. Salvation Army Ashtabula Center; trustee Northeastern Ohio Scholastic Art Awards and Scholarships Fund. Mem. Savs. Instns. Mktg. Soc. Am., Sales and Mktg. Execs. Cleve., Ashtabula Advt. Club (pres. 1978-79), Savs. and Loan Marketers Ohio (dir.). Republican. Roman Catholic. Clubs: Zonta, Geneva Study (pres. 1966-67). Home: 214 Greenridge Dr Geneva OH 44041 Office: 4438 Main Ave Ashtabula OH 44004

MCCLURE, GEORGE WILLIAM, III, newspaper pub. co. exec.; b. Cin., May 10, 1950; s. G. William and Ellen C. McClure; B.A., Ohio Wesleyan U., 1972; postgrad. Candler Sch. Theology, Emory U., 1972-75; M.B.A., Harvard U., 1975; m. Amy Carol Anderson, Dec. 27, 1973. Asst. to pres. Agawam Assos., Rowley, Mass., 1974; mktg. cons. Exec. Jet Aviation, Columbus, Ohio, 1975-76; exec. v.p. Brown Pub. Co., Urbana, Ohio, 1977-79, pres., chief exec. officer, 1979—. Mem. Young Presidents Orgn. (sec.), Ohio Newspaper Assn. (dir.), Inland Daily Press Assn. (group newspaper com.). Methodist. Club: Harvard Business School (Columbus). Home: 8751 Craigston Ct Dublin OH 43017 Office: Brown Pub Co 310 Patrick Ave Urbana OH 43078

MC CLURE, JON EARL, cons. engr.; b. Des Moines, June 8, 1929; s. Earl E. and Sylvia (Wetteland) McC.; B.S., Iowa State U., 1951; m. Carla Bixler, Aug. 20, 1950; children—Martha, Melissa, Mary Beth, Jon P. With Getheman Constrn. Co., 1954; city engr. City of Jefferson (Iowa), 1955; founder, owner McClure Engring. Co., 1955-59; pres. McClure & Culver, Engrs., Jefferson, Iowa, 1959-63; pres. McClure Engring Co., Ft. Dodge, Iowa, 1964—; dir. First Nat. Bank. Mem. Air Pollution Control Commn., 1972, Jud. Nominating Com., 1975; trustee First Methodist Ch., Trinity Regional Hosp.; bd. dirs. Blanden Art Gallery. Served with C.E., U.S. Army, 1951-53; Korea. Mem. Nat. Soc. Profl. Engrs., Am. Water Works Assn., Water Pollution Control Fedn., Soc. Land Surveyors Iowa, Am. Cons. Engrs. Council. Republican. Methodist. Clubs: Rotary, Elks, Masons. Office: McClure Engring Co 705 1st Ave N Fort Dodge IA 50501

MC CLURE, MARILYN EUNICE, social worker, state govt. ofcl.; b. Embudo, N.Mex., Jan. 11, 1943; d. Eloy G. and Evangeline (Garcia) Vigil; B.A., Macalester Coll., 1964; M.A. in Social Work, U. Chgo., 1969; m. Michael A. McClure, Aug. 21, 1964; 1 dau., Miquela Nicole. Sch. social worker St. Paul Public Schs., 1970-76; clin. social worker Latino program Ramsey County Mental Health Dept., St. Paul, 1976-78; instr., coordinator U. Minn. Sch. Social Work, 1978-79; commr. Minn. Dept. Human Rights, St. Paul, 1979—; cons. Human Resource Assos., 1972-75. Chair, Minn. Chicano Fedn.; vice-chair Minn. Spanish Speaking Affairs Council, 1978; bd. dirs. Family Service Greater St. Paul, People, Inc., 1981—. Cert. Acad. Cert. Social Workers. Mem. Nat. Assn. Social Workers (dir. Minn. 1982). Democrat. Presbyterian. Contbr.: Social Work Processes (Beulah Compton and Burt Galoway), 1979. Office: Minn Dept Human Rights 500 Bremer Tower 7th Pl and Minnesota St Saint Paul MN 55101

MC CLURE, MARY ANNE, state senator S.D.; b. Milbank, S.D., Apr. 21, 1939; d. Charles Cornelius and Mary Lucille (Whittom) Burges; B.A., U. S.D., 1961; postgrad. U. Manchester (Eng.), 1961-62; M.P.A., Syracuse U., 1980; m. D.J. McClure, Nov. 17, 1963; 1 dau., Kelly Joanne. Various secretarial positions, 1959-64; with budget div. Office Gov. S.D., Pierre, 1964-65; clk. appropriations com. S.D. Legislature, 1965; tchr. schs. in Pierre and Redfield, S.D., 1964-70; registrar, counselor S.D. Girls State, 1971-79; mem. sch. bd. Redfield Ind. Sch. Dist., 1970-75, vice chmn., 1972-74; mem. S.D. Senate from 5th Dist., 1975—, pres. protem, 1979—. Bd. dirs. Asso. Sch. Bds. S.D., 1972-74, central v.p., 1973-74; sec. Western region Nat. Sch. Bds. Assn., 1973-75. Fulbright scholar, 1961-62; govt. exchange rep. to Venezuela, Am. Council Young Polit. Leaders. Mem. Phi Beta Kappa. Republican. Congregationalist. Address: 910 E 2d St Redfield SD 57469

MC CLURE, MICHAEL DESTEWART, profl. baseball team exec.; b. Chgo., Jan. 23, 1942; s. Charles F. and Janette L. (Lawler) McC.; B.A., DePauw U., 1964; m. Brenda G. Jones, Oct. 24, 1964; children—Michael C., Matthew D. Reporter, City News Bur., Chgo., 1964-65, Chgo. Tribune, 1965-66; public relations cons. Peoples Gas Co., Chgo., 1966-69; sports dir. Sta. WLFI-TV, Lafayette, Ind., 1969-70; service bur. dir. Big Ten Conf., 1970-73; dir. public relations and mktg. Chgo. Bulls, 1973-78; v.p. public relations and mktg. Houston Oilers, 1978-81; v.p. mktg. Chgo. White Sox, 1981—; v.p. Houston Oilers Publs., Inc., Houston Oilers Dancers, Inc.; dir. NFL Properties; founder Luv Ya Blue!, lic. program. Recipient Best in Nation awards Cosida, 1972, 73; Matrix award Houston chpt. Women in Communication, 1981; named One of 10 Outstanding Young Citizens, Chgo. Jaycees, 1974. Mem. Houston Advt. Fedn., Houston Sportswriters and Sportscasters Assn., DePauw U. Alumni Assn., Am. Mktg. Assn., Am. Legion, Purdue Coaches Club, Sigma Delta Chi, Sigma Chi. Presbyterian. Editor Big Ten Records Book, 1970-73; editor Houston Oilers Pro mag., 1979. Home: IN 455 Indian Knoll West Chicago IL 60185

MC CLURG, JAMES EDWARD, biochemist; b. Bassett, Nebr., Mar. 23, 1945; s. Warren James and Delia Emma (Allyn) McC.; B.S., Nebr. Wesleyan U., 1967; Ph.D., U. Nebr., 1973. Mem. faculty U. Nebr. Med. Center, Omaha, 1973-76; gen. mgr. Streck Labs., Inc., Omaha, 1974-76; v.p., tech. dir. Harris Labs., Inc., Lincoln, Nebr., 1976—, also dir.; dir. Streck Labs., Inc. Chmn. class alumni fund drive Nebr. Wesleyan U., 1979-81. Recipient Ann. Research award Central Assn. Ob-Gyn, 1976; NIH fellow, 1970-73. Mem. Am. Pharm. Assn., Acad. Pharm. Scis., AAAS, Am. Chem. Soc., Am. Soc. Microbiology, Am. Assn. Clin. Chemists, Am. Fertility Soc., Soc. Cosmetic Chemists, Assn. Clin. Pharmacology, Am. Soc. Clin. Pharmacology and Therapeutics, N.Y. Acad. Scis., Sigma Xi. Club: Lincoln University. Patentee in field. Office: 624 Peach St Lincoln NE 68502

MCCLUSKEY, TED DANIEL, mfg. co. exec.; b. St. Louis, Aug. 1, 1938; s. Ted and Ethel May (Weeks) McC.; student Washington U., St. Louis, 1956-57, U. Mo., 1957-59, Meramec Jr. Coll., 1980-81; m. Sandra S. Smith, June 1, 1979; children—Ted Daniel, Cynthia Mae. Vice pres. Tallman-McCluskey Fabrics Co., St. Louis, 1957-67, Tallman Conduit Co., Louisiana, Mo., 1965-68; elec. engr. Monsanto Co. CED, St. Louis, 1967-72; pres. Mech-Tronics Co., St. Louis, 1962—; exec. v.p. Gen. Gasket Corp., St. Louis, 1972—. Served with U.S. Army, 1957-65. Registered profl. engr., Mo. Mem. Engrs. Club of St. Louis. Methodist. Clubs: Masons, Shriners. Home: 9572 General Lee Dr Sappington MO 63126 Office: 2322 S 7th St Saint Louis MO 63104

MCCLUSKEY, WILLIAM JAMES, mfg. plant mgr.; b. Wilkensburg, Pa., Oct. 6, 1917; s. Norman James and Lou Ella Mae (Fisher) McC.; B.S. in Gen. Edn., U. Nebr., Omaha, 1965; m. Iris Irene Ahearn, Nov. 18, 1943; children—Darlene I., Sandra Y., Rick W., Twila L., Jeri J., James L., Kim K., Dennis N., Michael P., Marla M. Student mining engr. Harmarville Coal Co., U.S. Steel Co., Harmarville, Pa., 1936-40; commd. 2d lt., U.S. Air Force, 1941, advanced through grades to lt. col., 1963; test and fighter pilot; chief of maintenance engring. worldwide, 1943-59; ret., 1963; plant mgr. Walker Mfg. Co. div. Tenneco, Inc., Jackson, Mich., 1963—; dir. aircraft and missile maintenance mgmt. Chanute AFB, Ill., 1959-63. Chmn. Racine and Jackson United Fund drives, 1963-70, 75-80. Decorated Air Medal. Mem. Am. Soc. Safety Engrs., Area Mfg. Assn., Ret. Officers Assn., World War II Night Fighter Assn., VFW. Republican. Methodist. Home: 2920 Emmertsen Rd Racine WI 53406 Office: 1201 Michigan Blvd Racine WI 53402

MC COIN, JOHN MACK, social worker; b. Sparta, N.C., Jan. 21, 1931; s. Robert Avery and Ollie (Osborne) McC.; B.S., Appalachian State Tchrs. Coll., Boone, N.C., 1957; M.S. in Social Work, Richmond (Va.) Profl. Inst., 1962; Ph.D., U. Minn., 1977. Social service worker Broughton State Hosp., Morganton, N.C., 1958-59, John Unstead State Hosp., Butner, N.C., 1960-61; clin. social worker Dorothea Dix State Hosp., Raleigh, N.C., 1962-63; child welfare case worker Wake County Welfare Dept., Raleigh, 1963-64; psychiat. social worker Toledo Mental Hygiene Clinic, 1964-66; sr. psychiat. social worker N.Y. Hosp.-Cornell U. Med. Center, 1966-68; social worker VA Hosp., Montrose, N.Y., 1968-73, also vol. mental health worker Westchester County Mental Health Assn. and Mental Health Bd., White Plains, N.Y.; seminar instr. Grad. Sch. Social Work, U. Minn., Mpls., 1973-74; social worker F.D.R. VA Health Care Facility, Montrose, 1975-77; asst. prof. social work U. Wis., Oshkosh, 1977-79, chmn. dept. community liaison com., 1978-79; asso. prof. social work Grand Valley State Colls., Allendale, Mich., 1979-81; social worker VA Med. Center, Battle Creek, Mich., 1981—; cons. 44th Gen. Hosp., USAR, Menasha, Wis., 1978-79, 5540th Support Command, USAR, Grand Rapids, Mich., 1979—; cons. in field. Served with USMC, 1948-52; USMCR, 1957-72; maj. USAR, 1972—. Recipient Outstanding Performance award VA, 1971; grantee NIMH, 1974; cert. social worker, Mich., N.Y. Mem. Nat. Assn. Social Workers (social action com. W. Mich. br. 1980—), Acad. Cert. Social Workers, Council Social Work Edn., Res. Officers Assn. U.S., Am. Soc. Pub. Adminstrn., Alpha Delta Mu. Democrat. Baptist. Home: 4231 W Dickman Rd 1-D Springfield MI 49015

MC COLLEM, DONALD EARL, guidance counselor; b. Streator, Ill., Jan. 23, 1923; s. Richard Cray and Stella Athalina (Kosinske) McC.; B.S. in Edn., Ill. State U., Normal, 1961; M.S. in Edn. (NDEA Inst. grantee), U. Ill., 1963; m. Mary C. Watson, Sept. 10, 1960; children by previous marriage—Donald Earl, Sean David; 1 dau., Kathleen; stepchildren—Mark, John and Bill Caplinger. Tchr. English, Crete-Monee, Ill., 1959-60, Oblong (Ill.) High Sch., 1961-62; counselor, tchr. English, Macon (Ill.) High Sch., 1963-64; guidance counselor Armstrong (Ill.) High Sch., 1964—, tchr. English, 1978—. Served with USMC, 1943-45; PTO. Mem. Ill. Edn. Assn., NEA, Vermillion, North Vermillion (pres. 1968-69) tchrs. assns., Am. Sch. Counselors Assn., Vermillion County Counselors Assn. (pres. 1975-76), Am., Ill. guidance and personnel assns. Home: Rural Route 1 Armstrong IL 61862 Office: Armstrong High Sch Armstrong IL 61812

MC COLLEM, MARY CAROLYN WATSON, sch. counselor; b. McLean County, Bloomington, Ill., Nov. 10, 1925; d. William Francis and Estella B. (Kellogg) Watson; student Ill. Wesleyan U., 1944-47; B.S., Ill. State U., 1959; M.S., Purdue U., 1966; m. Donald McCollem, Sept. 10, 1960; children by previous marriage—Mark, John, Bill Caplinger; 1 dau., Kathleen McCollem; stepchildren—Don, Sean. Tchr. English, El Paso (Ill) High Sch., 1958-61, Oblong (Ill.) High Sch., 1961-62, Blue Mound (Ill.) High Sch., 1963-64, Mt. Pulaski (Ill.) High Sch., 1964-65; guidance counselor Normal (Ill.) Community High Sch., 1966-67; tchr. English, Univ. High Sch., Ill. State U., Normal, 1969-71; guidance counselor Potomac (Ill.) High Sch., 1973-77, guidance counselor, tchr. English, 1977-79, guidance counselor, tchr. art, 1979—. NDEA grantee, 1965-66. Mem. NEA, Ill. Edn. Assn., Am. Personnel and Guidance Assn., Ill. Guidance and Personnel Assn., Am. Sch. Counselors Assn., Vermilion County Counselors Assn. (v.p. 1975-76), DAR, Kappa Kappa Gamma. Democrat. Roman Catholic. Home: Rural Route 1 Box 14 Armstrong IL 61812 Office: Route 136 Potomac High Sch Potomac IL 61865

MC COLLISTER, HOWARD RICHARD, oil co. exec.; b. Iowa City, Dec. 29, 1924; s. John Milton and Thelma Ruth (Yetter) McC.; B.A., U. Iowa, 1947; m. Marilyn Browning McCollister, Dec. 6, 1947 (dec. Aug. 1975); children—Howard M., Diane, Christine; m. 2d, Shirlee Lee Wallace Rushton, Feb. 14, 1976; stepchildren—Terri Rushton, Robin Rushton, John Rushton. Sales rep. IBM, Milw., 1947-54; v.p. McCollister Grease & Oil Corp., Omaha, 1954-65, Empak Industries, Omaha, 1965-72; pres. SW Grease & Oil Co. (Omaha), Inc., 1972—; v.p., SW Petro-Chem. Inc., Omaha, 1972—, also dir. Served with USNR, 1943-46. Mem. Ind. Oil Compounders Assn. (pres. 1964-66), Nebr. Amateur Golf Assn. (dir. 1964-67). Republican. Club: Happy Hollow (pres. 1975). Home: 1030 S 111th Plaza Omaha NE 68154 Office: 6200 N 16th St Omaha NE 68110

MC COLLISTER, JOHN YETTER, lubricants mfg. exec.; b. Iowa City, Iowa, June 10, 1921; s. John M. and Ruth (Yetter) McC.; B.S. in Commerce, State U. Iowa, 1943; m. Nanette Stokes, Aug. 22, 1943; children—John S., Stephen J., Bruce C. With IBM Corp., 1946-53; pres. McCollister & Co., Omaha, 1953—; mem. 92d-94th congresses from 2d Dist. Nebr. Pres. Mid-Am. council Boy Scouts Am., 1963-66, regional chmn., 1969-70, mem. nat. exec. bd., 1969-70; bd. dirs. Greater Omaha Community Action, 1967-70. County commr. Douglas County (Neb.), 1965-70; chmn. 2d Congl. Dist. Republican Com. Neb., 1960-64; del. Rep. Nat. Conv., 1968. Served to lt. (j.g.) USNR, 1943-46. Presbyn. (chmn. bd. trustees 1965-66, ruling elder 1967-70). Kiwanian (pres. 1961). Home: 3003 Paddock Plaza Omaha NE 68124 Office: 2200 South Ave Council Bluffs IA 51502

MC COLLUM, WILLIAM BALLEW, surgeon; b. Leavenworth, Kans., Jan. 25, 1941; s. Orville Eugene and Lou Ann Mildred (Ballew) McC.; A.B., U. Kans., 1962, M.D., 1966; Ph.D., Baylor U., 1971; m. Mary Louise Baumgartner, Aug. 23, 1964; children—Margaret Louise, Walter Ballew. Intern in surgery Baylor Coll. Medicine, Houston, 1966-67, resident in gen. surgery, 1970-74, resident in thoracic surgery, 1974-76, instr. cellular biophysics, 1971-76, instr. surgery, 1971-76; practice medicine specializing in cardiovascular, thoracic and gen. surgery, Leavenworth, 1976—; mem. staff Cushing Hosp., 1976—, pres. med. staff, 1979-80; mem. staff St. John's Hosp., 1976—, v.p. med. staff, 1979-80; cons. VA Hosp., Munson Army Hosp. Mem. council bd. St. Mary's Coll., Leavenworth. Served with USAF, 1967-69. Lic. physician, Kans., Tex., Mo.; diplomate Am. Bd. Surgery, Am. Bd. Thoracic Surgery, Nat. Bd. Med. Examiners. Fellow Am. Coll. Cardiology, A.C.S., Am. Coll. Angiology, Am. Coll. Chest Physicians; mem. AAAS, Am. Heart Assn. (unit. chmn. 1978), Am. Fedn. Clin. Research, Am. Trauma Soc., Asso. Acad. Surgeons, Internat. Coll. Angiology, Southwestern Surg. Congress, Denton Cooley Cardiovascular Surg. Soc., Michael DeBakey Cardiovascular Surgeons, Assn. Advancement of Med. Instrumentation, Leavenworth County Med. Soc. (pres. 1979-80), Leavenworth C. of C. Club: Rotary. Contbr. articles on clin. surgery and myocardiobiology to med. and basic sci. jours. Home: 3601 S 4th St Leavenworth KS 66048 Office: Plaza Profl Center 3601 S 4th St Trafficway Leavenworth KS 66048 also 8919 Parallel Pkwy Kansas City KS

MCCOMBS, HOWARD LEWIS, JR., mfg. co. exec.; b. Mishawaka, Ind., July 19, 1920; s. Howard Lewis and Mabel Elizabeth (Heick) McC.; student public schs., South Bend, Ind.; m. June E. Grubbs, May 14, 1944; 1 dau., Linda Sue. Flight and ground sch. instr. Stockert Flying Service, South Bend, 1941-42, 46-48; with Bendix Corp., South Bend, 1948—, sr. staff engr. energy controls div., 1978—; air sci. instr. Ind. U., South Bend, 1960-65. Served with USAF, 1943-46. Decorated Air medal with oak leaf cluster; recipient Innovation Profitability award Bendix Corp., 1948. Republican. Clubs: Bendix Mgmt.; St. Joseph Valley Engrs., Res. Officers Assn. Patentee in field. Office: 717 N Bendix Dr South Bend IN 46620

MC COMBS, SHERWIN, oil and gas co. exec.; b. Sterling, Ill., Jan. 27, 1934; s. C. Vernon and Helen (Jennings) McC.; grad. Palmer Chiropractic Coll., 1956-60; m. Rita J. Page, Feb. 8, 1957; children—Kim, Kelly, Jeff, Terry. Owner McCombs Chiropractic Clinic, Sterling, Ill., 1960—, McCombs Petroleum Prodns., Sterling, 1966—; v.p., dir. Coyote Oil & Gas Corp., Casper Wyo., 1968-75, exec. v.p., dir., 1975—; v.p., dir. Coyote Assos., Inc., Ankeny, Iowa, 1970-72; pres., dir. Coyote Oil & Gas Programs, Inc., Ankeny, 1970-72; with McCombs-Conrad & Barrett Oil & Gas Properties, Sterling, Ill., 1972—. Served with USNR, 1952-54. Mem. Internat., Prairie, Whiteside County chiropractic assns., Internat. Chiropractic Honor Soc. Home: 1808 Thome Dr Sterling IL 61081 Office: 507 W 3d St Sterling IL 61081

MC CONNAUGHEY, GEORGE CARLTON, JR., lawyer; b. Hillsboro, Ohio, Aug. 9, 1925; s. George Carlton and Nelle (Morse) McC.; B.A., Denison U., 1949; J.D., Ohio State U., 1951; m. Carolyn Schlieper, June 16, 1951; children—Elizabeth, Susan, Nancy. Admitted to Ohio bar, 1951; asst. atty. gen. Ohio, 1951-54; partner firm McConnaughey & McConnaughey, Columbus, Ohio, 1954-57, McConnaughey, McConnaughey & Stradley, 1957-62, Laylin, McConnaughey & Stradley, 1962-67, George, Greek King, McMahon & McConnaughey, Columbus, 1967-79, McConnaughey, Stradley, Mone & Moul, Columbus, 1979-81, Thompson, Hine & Flory, Columbus, 1981—; sec., dir. Mid-Continent Telephone Corp.; dir. N.Am. Broadcasting Co. (WMNI Radio, Columbus), Newark Telephone Co. (Ohio), Mem. Upper Arlington (Ohio) Bd. Ed., 1962-70, pres., 1967-69; Presdl. elector, 1956; chmn. Ohio Young Republicans, 1956. Former trustee Buckeye Boys Ranch, Columbus. Served with AUS, 1943-45; ETO. Mem. Am., Ohio, Columbus bar assns., Columbus Town Meeting Assn. (pres. 1974-76), Sigma Chi, Phi Delta Phi. Presbyterian (elder). Mason. Clubs: Columbus, Columbus Athletic; Scioto Country (Columbus). Home: 1969 Andover Rd Upper Arlington OH 43212 Office: 100 E Broad St Columbus OH 43215

MC CONNELL, DAVID HOLTON, consumer goods mfg. co. exec.; b. Ft. Worth, Sept. 7, 1926; s. David Franklin Bruce and Hattie Laura (Holton) McC.; B.S., Davidson Coll., 1949; postgrad. U. Ky., 1949-50; m. Lois Anne Crowe, May 21, 1960; children—Anne Crowe, Juliet Holton, David Franklin Bruce II. Various personnel positions Procter & Gamble Co., Cin., 1950—, mgr. human resource devel., research and devel., 1978—. Active Greater Cin. Fedn. Settlements and Neighborhood Houses; United Appeal; pres. bd. trustees Springer Ednl. Found., 1977-78; chmn. Guilford Sch. Com., 1976-80; bd. dirs. Charter Com. Greater 1979-80, Personnel Accreditation Inst., 1980—. Served to comdr. USNR, 1944-46. Mem. Am. Soc. Personnel Adminstrn. (accredited personnel diplomate; dist. dir. 1970-71, mem. accreditation com. 1978-80) Navy League of U.S. (pres. Cin. council 1978-79), Cincinnatus Assn. (treas. 1972-73), Cin. Personnel Assn. (pres. 1969-70), Wine Tasters (sec.-treas. 1970-74), Pewter Collectors Club Am., Mt. Lookout Swim Club, Cin. Tennis Club, Beta Theta Pi. Republican. Presbyterian. Wine editor Cincinnati Celebrates, 1974. Home: 27 Elmhurst Pl Cincinnati OH 45208 Office: Procter & Gamble Co Hillcrest Tower 7162 Reading Rd Cincinnati OH 45222

MCCONNELL, E. HOY, II, advt. agy. exec.; b. Syracuse, N.Y., May 14, 1941; s. E. Hoy and Dorothy R. (Schmitt) McC.; B.A. magna cum laude, Yale U., 1963; M.B.A., Harvard U., 1965; m. Patricia Irwin, June 26, 1965; children—E. Hoy III, Courtney. Pres., D'Arcy-MacManus & Masius, Inc., Chgo. Dir., Evanston United Way, 1980; pres. Evanston Boys Hockey Assn., 1980. Served to lt. USNR, 1966-74. Mem. Better Bus. Bur. Chgo., Chgo. Advt. Club. Democrat. Unitarian. Clubs: University, East Bank. Office: 200 E Randolph Chicago IL 60601

MC CONNELL, JOHN HENDERSON, steel co. exec.; b. New Manchester, W.Va., May 10, 1923; s. Paul A. and Mary Louise (Mayhew) McC.; B.A., Mich. State U., 1949; m. Margaret Jane Rardin, Feb. 8, 1946; children—Margaret Louise, John Porter. With blooming mill Weirton Steel Co. (W.Va.), 1941-43, with sales dept., 1950-52; with sales dept. Shenango Steel Co., Farrell, Pa., 1953-55; founder, chief exec. officer Worthington Steel Co. (Ohio) (name changed to Worthington Industries, 1971), 1955—; dir. Liebert Corp., Worthington, Exec. Jet Aviation, Bank One of Columbus, Wendy's Internat., Columbus. Mem. Ohio State U. Zoning Commn.; mem. Ohio Gov.'s Devel. Advisory Council, also chmn. legis. sub-com. Bd. dirs. Pilot Dogs Inc., Columbus, Ohio; trustee Children's Hosp., Columbus, Ashland (Ohio) Coll. Served with USNR, 1943-46. Recipient Gov.'s award State of Ohio, 1980; named Central Ohio Mktg. Man of Year, 1975. Mem. Columbus C. of C. (dir., chmn. aviation com., vice chmn. 1977, chmn. 1978), Columbus Indsl. Assn. (dir.), Mich. State U. Bus. Alumni Assn. (dir.). Republican. Presbyn. (past trustee). Mason (Shriner, 32 deg.). Clubs: Columbus Athletic, Columbus; The Golf (New Albany, Ohio); Brookside Country (Worthington); Muirfield Village Golf (Dublin, Ohio); Bob O' Link Golf (Chgo.); Sea Pines (Hilton Head, S.C.); Waialae Country (Honolulu); Keenland (Lexington, Ky.). Home: 244 Tucker Dr Worthington OH 43085 Office: 1205 Dearborn Dr Columbus OH 43085

MC CONNER, DOROTHY, mfg. co. exec.; b. Birmingham, Ala., May 15, 1929; d. Charles Oscar and Mattie Lee (Conner) Hamilton; student Hampton Inst., Cortez Peters Bus. Coll.; B.S. in Bus. Adminstrn., Chgo. State U.; m. Stanley J. McConner, Apr. 5, 1974. Sec., Fuller Products Co., Chgo., 1950-60; with Johnson Products Co., Chgo., 1960—, corp. sec., 1962—, adminstrv. v.p., 1972—, also dir. Bd. dirs. Rehab. Inst. Chgo., Chgo. Econ. Devel. Corp.; bd. dirs. Chgo. Urban League, chairwoman ann. Golden Fellowship dinners, 1974, 75; trustee DePaul U.; mem. Black Women's Agenda, Ancillary Group of Chgo. State U. Found., Chgo. Community Trust Assos., Operation PUSH. Recipient Beautiful People award Chgo. Urban League, 1971, Salute to Women in Bus., Operation PUSH, 1975, Humanitarian award St. Matthew's A.M.E. Ch., 1977; named Urban Leaguer of Year, Chgo., 1975, Bus. Woman of Year, Cosmopolitan C. of C., 1974, Blackbook, 1975; award Southtown YMCA, 1979. Mem. Am. Soc. Corp. Secs., League of Black Women, Northwestern U. Assos., Alpha Gamma Pi. Clubs: Chgo. State U. Women, Zonta, Chgo. City, Chgo. Network, Toastmasters. Office: 8522 S Lafayette Ave Chicago IL 60620

MC CORD, JOHN HARRISON, educator, lawyer; b. Oceanside, N.Y., Dec. 22, 1934; s. John Francis and Elsie (Powers) M.; A.B., Fordham Coll., 1957; J.D. (St. Thomas More fellow), St. John's U., 1960; LL.M., U. Ill., 1965; m. Maureen Ursula MacLean, Dec. 30, 1961; children—John F.X., Paul V., David G., Maureen E. Admitted to N.Y. bar, 1960, Ill. bar, 1964; atty. U.S. Dept. Justice, Washington, 1960-61; mem. faculty U. Ill. Coll. of Law, Champaign, 1964—, prof. law, 1965—. Acad. cons. Ill. Inst. on Continuing Legal Edn., 1968-72; vis. prof. law U. N.C., 1975, U. Hawaii, 1976. Mem. adv. council U. Miami Inst. on Estate Planning. Served to capt. USAF, 1961-64. Mem. Am. (mem. com. on continuing legal edn. and chief reporter for study outline on buying, selling and merging businesses sect. fed. tax 1969-73; mem. com. estate and gift taxes 1973—, Ill. (mem. exec. council fed. tax sect. 1966-73, chmn. sect. 1971-72), Chgo. Bar Assn., Am. Judicature Soc., AAUP, Am. Arbitration Assn. (mem. nat. panel arbitrators 1969—), Eastern Ill. Estate Planning Council (pres. 1970-71), Assn. Am. Law Schs. (mem. fed. taxation roundtable council 1969-72), Order of Coif. Club: U-C Serra. Author: (with Keeton and O'Connell) Crisis in Car Insurance, 1967; Buying and Selling Small Businesses, 1969; (with O'Byrne) Deskbook for Illinois Estate Planners, 1969; Closely Held Corporations, 1971; (with O'Neill, Pearlman and Stroud) Buying, Selling and Merging Businesses, 1975; (with Lowndes and Kramer) Estate and Gift Taxes, 3d edit., 1974; (with McKee) Federal Income Taxation-A Summary Analysis, 1975; (with Kramer) Problems for Federal Estate and Gift Taxes, 1976; 1976 Estate and Gift Tax Reform, 1977; Estate and Gift Taxes-A Summary Analysis, 1980; editor: Dimensions of Academic Freedom, 1969; With All Deliberate Speed: Civil Rights Theory and Reality, 1969. Editor: Ill. Law Forum, 1965-69. Contbr. articles in field to profl. jours. Office: University Illinois College of Law Champaign IL 61820

MCCORMACK, JOHN TIMOTHY, state senator; b. Cleve., Aug. 28, 1944; s. Earl Patrick and June (Whitcomb) McC.; B.A., Miami U., Oxford, Ohio; J.D., Cleve. Marshall Law Sch. Practice, law, 1972—; mem. Euclid (Ohio) City Council, 1970-72, Ohio Ho. of Reps., 1973-74, Ohio Senate, 1975—. Roman Catholic. Office: State Senate Columbus OH 43215*

MC CORMACK, LAWRENCE JOHN, pathologist; b. Kansas City, Mo., July 13, 1921; s. Lawrence Ralph and Mildred (Hungate) McC.; B.S., Northwestern U., 1942, M.D., 1945, M.S., 1950; M.S. in Pathology, U. Minn., 1951; m. Dorothy Rice; children—Lawrence R., Kathleen Ann, Thomas A., James R. Intern, Cook County Hosp., Chgo., 1945; head dept. surgery Sch. Aviation Medicine, Randolph Field, Tex., 1946-48; fellow in pathology, asso. staff mem. Mayo Clinic, Rochester, Minn., 1948-51; mem. staff Cleve. Clinic Found., 1952—, dir. labs.; clin. prof. biochemistry Cleve. State U. Served with AUS, 1943-47. Diplomate Am. Bd. Pathology. Fellow Am. Coll. Chest Physicians; mem. Coll. Am. Pathologists (pres. elect 1978-79, pres. 1979-81), AMA, Am. Soc. Clin. Pathologists, Am. Assn. Pathologists, Ohio Med. Assn. Club: Pasteur (Cleve.). Contbr. chpts. to books, articles to profl. jours. Home: 4983 Countryside Ln Lyndhurst OH 44124 Office: 9500 Euclid Ave Cleveland OH 44106*

MC CORMACK, SHIRLEY MARIE, govt. auditor; b. Arcadia, Kans., Mar. 21, 1930; d. Frank Lee Wheeler and Stella Marie (Garrett) Brinkle; B.S. in Bus. Edn., Kans. State U., Pittsburg, 1957, M.S. in Bus. Edn., 1970; postgrad. Washburn U., 1964-65, U. Okla., 1973-74; M.A. in Bus., Central Mich. U., 1979; m. Joseph Marion McCormack, Apr. 29, 1949 (dec.); children—Johnny Joe, Joseph Marion. Tchr. public high schs., Kans., 1957-65, 66-72; clk. Emporia (Kans.) Bd. Edn., 1965-66; instr. Dakota State Coll., 1972-73, Southwestern State Coll., 1973-74, Coffeyville Community Jr. Coll., 1974-75; auditor Region VII, HUD, 1975—. Recipient spl. award HUD Disaster Field Office, 1979, letter of commendation HUD, 1979; C.P.A., Mo.; cert. internal auditor. Mem. Am. Women's Soc. C.P.A.'s, Inst. Mgmt. Accts., Nat. Assn. Female Execs., Internat. Platform Assn., Delta Pi Epsilon. Democrat. Methodist. Home: 2910 S 51 Terr Kansas City KS 66106 Office: HUD Office Insp Gen 13th Floor 1103 Grand Kansas City MO 64106

MC CORMICK, BROOKS, former mfg. exec.; b. Chgo., Feb. 23, 1917; s. Chauncey and Marion (Deering) McC.; grad. Groton Sch., 1936; B.A., Yale U., 1940; m. Hope Baldwin, 1940. With Internat. Harvester Co., 1940-80, mfg. sales positions various locations U.S. and Gt. Britain, 1940-54, dir. mfg., 1954-57, exec. v.p., 1957-68, pres., 1968-77, chief exec. officer, 1971-78, chmn., 1977-79, chmn. exec. com., 1979-80, also dir.; ret., 1980; dir. 1st Nat. Bank, Chgo., Commonwealth Edison Co., 1964-81. Gen. chmn. Crusade of Mercy, 1961; bd. dirs. Community Fund of Chgo., 1960-77, pres., 1973-75; chmn. Nat. Safety Council, 1965-67. Life trustee Rush Presbyn. St. Luke's Med. Center; trustee Art Inst. Chgo., 1954—, Ill. Inst. Tech., 1962-75, Motor Vehicle Mfrs. Assn. (chmn. 1973-74), Chgo. Urban League (chmn. bus. adv. council 1967-76); pres. United Way Met. Chgo., 1976-77; chmn. Polish-U.S. Econ. Council, 1974-77; dir. U.S.-USSR Trade and Econ. Council, Inc., 1975-80; mem. Adv. Com. for Trade Negotiations, 1978-80. Episcopalian. Clubs: Chicago, Commercial. Office: 410 N Michigan Ave Chicago IL 60611

MCCORMICK, KEITH C., state senator, real estate broker; Real estate broker; mem. Ind. Senate, 1963—. Fin. chmn. Boone County Republican Com.; del. Rep. State Conv.; chmn. Ind. Real Estate Commn. Served with USAF. Mem. Ind. Real Estate Assn. (v.p.), Am. Legion, Lebanon C. of C. Clubs: Masons, Elks, Kiwanis. Presbyterian. Office: State Capitol Indianapolis IN 46204*

MCCORMICK, MARK, state justice Iowa; b. Ft. Dodge, Iowa, Apr. 13, 1933; s. Elmo Eugene and Virgilla (Lawler) McC.; A.B., Villanova U., 1955; LL.B., Georgetown U., 1960; m. Marla Rae McKinney, June 11, 1966; children—Marcia, Michael, Paul. Admitted to Iowa bar, 1960; law clk. to judge U.S. Ct. Appeals, 1960-61; practice law, Ft. Dodge, 1961-68; asst. county atty. Webster County, 1963-67; judge 11th and 2d jud. dists., 1968-72; justice Iowa Supreme Ct., Des Moines, 1972—. Served with USN, 1955-58. Mem. Am., Iowa bar assns., Am. Judicature Soc. Office: Capitol Bldg Des Moines IA 50319*

MC CORMICK, SANDRA JEAN CLEMENTS, hosp. adminstr.; b. La Crosse, Wis., Feb. 28, 1937; d. LaMont F. and Josephine (Hundt) C.; student U. Wis., La Crosse, 1955-57; B.S., U. Wis., Oshkosh, 1964; M.S. in Social Work, U. Wis., Madison, 1972; m. Richard D. McCormick, Jan. 12, 1963; children—Patricia Ann, Michael John. Social worker Fond du Lac County Dept. Social Services, 1964-66; social worker, acting social work supr. La Crosse County (Wis.) Dept. Social Service, La Corsse 1966-73; dir. med. social services Gundersen Clinic, Ltd., La Crosse, 1973-78; asst. adminstr. community services La Crosse Luth. Hosp., 1978—; cons. on social service to various hosps. Bd. dirs. Medary Sch. and Workshop for Retarded Persons, 1974—, treas., 1975-76, chmn., 1977-78; bd. dirs. Nat. Found. March of Dimes, 1978—, Western Wis. Health Systems Agy., 1981—; sec. New Horizons Women's Center, 1978-79; bd. dirs. Community Care Orgn. of La Crosse, 1977-78. Mem. Nat. Assn. Social Workers (treas. 1980—), AAUW, Soc. Hosp. Social Work Dirs. of Am. Hosp. Assn., Wis. Social Service Assn., W. Central Social Service Assn. (pres. 1972), Wis. Council on Human Concerns, Nat. Kidney Assn., Gt. Plains Orgn. for Perinatal Health Care. Home: 313 Olivet St La Crosse WI 54601 Office: La Crosse Luth Hosp 1910 South Ave La Crosse WI 54601

MC CORMICK, THOMAS FULLER, ret. metallurgist, civic worker; b. Gallipolis, Ohio, May 13, 1904; s. Earl Leander and Ruth Emily (Fuller) McC.; B.Met.Engr., Ohio State U., 1927; postgrad. in metallurgy U. Pitts., 1939-40, Carnegie Mellon Inst. Tech., 1940-41; m. Dorothy Marie Garr, Aug. 12, 1932; 1 dau., Patricia Jane. With Alcoa Co., 1927-69, asst. chief metallurgist Pitts. office, 1956-63, chief product metallurgist, 1963-69, ret., 1969; mem. faculty Purdue U., 1942-43, Carnegie Mellon U., 1959-62; vol. exec. Jr. Achievement, 1970-77; mem. bldg. com., chmn. bd. trustees Baldwin

Community Methodist Ch., Pitts. Recipient recognition for service to country Internat. Exec. Service Corps, 1972, 77. Mem. AIME (Legion of Honor 1977), Am. Soc. Metals, N.Y. Acad. Scis., Sigma Xi, Tau Beta Pi, Pi Mu Epsilon, Sigma Gamma Epsilon. Republican. Club: Univ. (Pitts.). Contbr. articles to profl. jours.; inventor extrusion press. Home: Guid Haddon II Box 130 Route 3 Gallipolis OH 45631

MC CORMICK, WILLIAM EDWARD, assn. exec.; b. Potters Mills, Pa., Feb. 9, 1912; s. George H. and Nellie (Mingle) McC.; B.S., Pa. State U., 1933, M.S., 1934; m. Goldie Stover, June 6, 1935; children—John F. (dec.), Kirk W. Tchr., Centre Hall (Pa.) High Sch., 1934-37; chemist Willson Products, Inc., Reading, Pa., 1937-43; indsl. hygienist Ga. Dept. Pub. Health, Atlanta, 1946; mgr. indsl. hygiene and toxicology B.F. Goodrich Co., Akron, Ohio, 1946-70, mgr. environ. control, 1970-73; mng. dir. Am. Indsl. Hygiene Assn., Akron, 1973—; exec. sec. Soc. Toxicology, 1976—. Mem. exec. com., rubber sect. Nat. Safety Council, 1955-73; mem. environ. health com. Chlorine Inst., 1968-73; mem. food, drug and cosmetic chems. com. Mfg. Chemists Assn., 1960-73, chmn., 1967-69, also mem. occupational health com., 1965-73; mem. adv. com. on heat stress U.S. Dept. Labor, 1973. Served to capt. USPHS, 1943-46. Mem. Am. Chem. Soc., Soc. Toxicology, AAAS, Am. Indsl. Hygiene Assn. (pres. 1964), Indsl. Hygiene Roundtable, Am. Acad. Indsl. Hygiene. Republican. Episcopalian. Clubs: Akron City, Masons (32 deg.), Shriners. Contbr. articles to profl. jours. Home: 419 Dorchester Rd Akron OH 44320 Office: Am Indsl Hygiene Assn 475 Wolf Ledges Pkwy Akron OH 44311

MCCOWN, HALE, justice state supreme ct.; b. Kansas, Ill., Jan. 19, 1914; s. Ross S. and Pauline (Collins) McC.; A.B., Hastings Coll., 1935; LL.B., Duke U., 1937; m. Helen Lanier, July 15, 1938; children—Robert B., William L., Mary Lynn. Admitted to Oreg. bar, 1937, Nebr. bar, 1942; with firm Carey, Hart, Spencer & McCulloch, Portland, Oreg., 1937-42; individual practice law, Beatrice, Nebr., 1942-65; mem. firm McCown, Baumfalk & Dalke; asso. justice Nebr. Supreme Ct., Lincoln, 1965—. Served to lt., USNR, 1943-45. Fellow Am. Coll. Trial Lawyers, Am. Coll. Probate Counsel; mem. Am. Bar Assn., Nebr. Bar Assn. (chmn. ho. dels. 1955-56, pres. 1960-61), Am. Law Inst. (mem. council 1969—), Am. Judicature Soc. Presbyterian. Contbr. articles to legal jours. Office: State Capitol Bldg Lincoln NE 68509

MC COY, DONALD EDWARD, mgmt. cons.; b. Stanberry, Mo., Nov. 7, 1923; s. William Arthur and Gretchen Beulah (Frederick) McC.; B.A., U. Kansas City, 1946, M.A., 1948; AST fgn. area studies U. Calif. at Los Angeles, 1944; postgrad. U. Kans., 1947-49; Ph.D., U. Ill, 1952; m. Mary Sue Kearny, Aug. 31, 1946 (dec. 1967); children—Janet Sue, William Kearny, Barbara Anne; m. 2d, Ann Marie Barnes, Dec. 13, 1967; 1 dau., Tina Marie. Mem. faculty U. Kansas City, 1946-47, U. Kans., 1947-49, U. Ill., 49-52, 1956-61, U. Minn., 1952-56; prof. English, dir. summer sessions Principia Coll., Elsah, Ill., 1961-68; vis. prof. English U. Mo. at St. Louis, 1968-70; partner Higginbotham & McCoy, mgmt. cons., St. Louis, 1968-71; prin. D.E. McCoy Assos., ednl. and mgmt. cons., St. Louis, 1971—. Vice pres. Sales Dynamic Supply Inc. and Dynamic Prodns., St. Louis, 1971-75; pres. McCoy & Ross, Inc., communication resources assos., St. Louis, 1975—; pres. Communication Centers Am., St. Louis, 1977-78. Served with AUS, 1943-46; ETO; capt. USAF Res., ret. Fellow Internat. Inst. Arts and Letters (Geneva); mem. Am. Soc. Tng. and Devel., Internat. Platform Assn., Sigma Tau Delta. Clubs: Cadillac LaSalle, Rotary. Author: Keys to Good Instruction, 1956, 58, 67; (with T.J. Kallsen) Rhetoric and Reading: Order and Idea, 1962. Editor Word Study, quarterly, 1958-70. Home: 1138 Westmoor Pl Saint Louis MO 63131 Office: 11901 Olive Blvd Saint Louis MO 63141

MC COY, E. JASON, JR., wholesale distbg. co. exec.; b. Canton, Ohio, July 5, 1923; s. Edgar Jason and Irene May (Stahl) McC.; B.A. magna cum laude, Kenyon Coll., 1944; M.B.A., Harvard U., 1947; m. Janet Ann Lynn, Mar. 3, 1945; children—Marjorie McCoy Mapes, Eric, Bradley. Sec., J.B. McCoy & Son Inc., Canton, Ohio, 1947-62, pres., 1962—. Bd. trustees YMCA, 1963—, internat. pres. Internat. Assn. of Y's, 1964; v.p. Buckeye Council Boy Scouts Am., 1976—; pres. Jr. Achievement, 1977-78; elder, former deacon Calvary Presbyn. Ch.; trustee Central Stark County United Way, 1977. Served to lt. comdr. USNR, 1943-46. Named Man of the Yr., Eastern Ohio Restaurant Assn., 1969. Mem. C. of C. (trustee 1972-76), Canton Wholesalers Assn. (past pres.), Nat. Candy Wholesalers Assn. (past dir.), Jr. Candy Execs. (past pres.), Phi Beta Kappa. Clubs: Rotary (pres. Canton chpt. 1974), Beta Theta Pi. Contbr. articles to trade mags. Home: 2923 Acacia Dr NW Canton OH 44718 Office: 1310 5th St NE Canton OH 44704

MC COY, EVA LEAH ROBINSON, social worker; b. Marion, Ill., Feb. 2, 1930; d. James Harry and Della (McGough) Robinson; B.A., Bapt. Mission Tng. Sch., 1953; m. William E. McCoy, Dec. 16, 1953; children—Paula Christine and Patricia Kathleen (twins). Program dir. Emmanuel Christian Center, Bklyn., 1954-55; caseworker Gallia County Child Welfare, 1966-67; acting dir. social services Gallipolis (Ohio) Devel. Center, 1967-74, admissions worker, 1974—, now unit social worker. Pres. elem. P.T.A., Rio Grande, Ohio, 1967-68. Mem. Nat. Assn. Social Workers, Ohio State Social Workers (so. region mental retardation coordinator), Am. Assn. Mental Deficiency, Gallia Assn. Chs. (charter bd. mem. 1965), Am. Bapt. Women, Rio Grande Bapt. Women's Assn. (v.p. for communications). Baptist (pres. bd. Christian edn. 1961-62, 72—, deacon). Club: Writers. Home: Box 182 Route 2 Bidwell OH 45614 Office: Gallipolis Developmental Center Gallipolis OH 45631

MC COY, FREDERICK JOHN, physician, surgeon; b. McPherson, Kans., Jan. 17, 1916; s. Merle D. and Mae (Tennis) McC.; B.S., U. Kans., 1938, M.D., 1942; m. Mary Bock, May 17, 1972; children—Judith, Frederick John, Patricia, Melissa, Steven. Intern Lucas County (Ohio) Hosp., Toledo, 1942-43; resident in plastic surgery U. Tex. Sch. of Medicine, Galveston, 1946; preceptorship in surgery, Grand Rapids, Mich., 1947-50; practice medicine specializing in plastic and reconstructive surgery, Kansas City, Mo., 1950—; mem. staff, chief plastic surgery Kansas City Gen. Hosp. and Med. Center, 1952—, Children's Mercy Hosp., 1954—, Research Hosp., 1950—, St. Luke's Hosp., 1951—, Baptist Hosp., 1958—, Meml. Hosp., 1950—; chmn. maxillo-facial surgery U. Kansas City Sch. of Dentistry, 1950-57; asso. prof. surgery Sch. of Medicine, U. Mo., Kansas City, 1964-69, clin. prof. surgery, 1969—. Bd. govs. Kansas City Mus., 1959—, pres., 1973-74. Served to maj. M.C., U.S. Army, 1943-46. Diplomate Am. Bd. Plastic Surgery (dir. 1973—, chmn. 1979). Mem. Am. Soc. of Plastic and Reconstructive Surgeons (sec. 1969-72, dir. 1973-76, pres. 1976, chmn. bd. 1977), Pan-Pacific, Singleton (v.p. 1965) surg. socs., Am. Assn. of Plastic Surgeons, Am., Internat. socs. for aesthetic plastic surgery, Jackson County Med. Soc. (pres. 1964-65), Kansas City Southwest Clin. Soc. (pres. 1971), Mo. State Med. Assn. (v.p. 1975), AMA, A.C.S., Internat. Coll. Surgeons (v.p. 1969), Kansas City C. of C., Explorers Club, Conservation Fedn. of Mo., Natural Sci. Soc. (founder, chmn. 1973), Citizen's Assn. of Kansas City, Phi Delta Theta, Nu Sigma Nu. Republican. Mem. Christian Ch. Clubs: Mission Hills Country. Contbr. articles in field to profl. jours. and books; editor Year Book of Plastic and Reconstructive Surgery, 1971—. Home: 5814 Mission Dr Shawnee Mission KS 66208 Office: 4177 Broadway Kansas City MO 64111

MCCOY, JEANIE SHEARER, chemist; b. Mancelona, Mich., May 27, 1921; d. Theophilus R. and Goldie Margaret (Halladay) Schroeder; A.A., North Park Coll., 1941; B.S., Northwestern U., 1944; M.S., No. Ill. U., 1970; m. Theodore R. Shearer, June 14, 1958 (div. 1964); 1 son, Blair B.; m. 2d, George A. McCoy, July 23, 1966. Jr. analytical chemist Buick Motor div. Gen. Motors, Melrose Park, Ill., 1944-45; asst. research chemist Hodson Corp., Chgo., 1945-47; asst. analytical chemist Internat. Harvester Co., 1947-49, analytical chemist, 1949-63, prin. chemist, 1963-75, supr. metall. process control, testing labs., 1975-78, supr. metal process devel., 1978—. Mem. Am. Chem. Soc., Am. Soc. Lubrication Engrs., Soc. Applied Spectroscopy, Soc. Automotive Engrs. Editor: Lubrication Engring. mag., 1976—. Home: 654 West Rd Lombard IL 60148 Office: International Harvester Co Melrose Park IL 60160

MC COY, JOHN DAVID, fin. co. exec.; b. Bainbridge, Ohio, Dec. 1, 1935; s. Frank Branson and Louise (Campbell) McC.; student Ohio U., 1953-55, U. Dayton, 1959; m. Mary Ann Sharp, Oct. 20, 1956; children—Christine, Lori, Susan, John David. Prodn. control specialist Wood Shovel & Tool, Piqua, Ohio, 1956; sales mgr. U.S. Credit Corp., Ohio, 1956; collection mgr., mgr. adminstrn. Hobart Corp., Troy, Ohio, 1970-76, mgr., br./agency accounts, customer fin., 1976-79, gen. credit mgr., 1979—. Served with USAF, 1961-62. Recipient Wilder Edn. award, 1973. Mem. Nat. Assn. Credit Mgmt. (dir. Dayton chpt.), Am. Mgmt. Assn., Dayton Assn. Credit Mgmt., Credit Research Found. Republican. Roman Catholic. Clubs: K.C., Esquire. Home: 1106 Scudder St Piqua OH 45356 Office: Hobart Corp Grant St S Troy OH 45373

MC COY, L(ELAND) DEAN, mech. engr.; b. Kokomo, Ind., Feb. 13, 1902; s. Charles Evington and Blanche Gertrude (Griffith) McC.; B.S.M.E., Purdue U., 1926, postgrad., 1934-35; postgrad. Morris Harvey Coll., Charleston, W. Va., 1940, Washington U., St. Louis, 1943; m. Ruth V. Borden, June 12, 1927; children—Patricia Arlene Gerry, James Alan. Design engr., project engr., city and state liaison, asst. supt. phys. plant-campus devel. Purdue U., Lafayette, Ind., 1926-36; project engr., liaison fed. govt., asst. supt. maintenance and constrn., positions adminstrn., plant acquisitions Monsanto Co., St. Louis, 1936-38, Nitro, W.Va., 1938-42, Sauget, Ill., 1942-67; staff various engring., archtl. firms Given and Assos., St. Louis, 1967-69, Murphy, Downey, Wofford & Richman, St. Louis, 1969-71, Tyrrell Co., St. Louis, 1972-76, L.D. McCoy, Cons., St. Louis, 1976-77, Lopinot & Weber, St. Louis, 1978, Horner and Shifrin Co., St. Louis, 1979—; cons in field. Active youth work, YMCA, 1948-50, Boy Scouts Am., 1951; mem. U. Mo. Extension Council, St. Louis County, 1966-70, 76—, pres., 1969-70; pres. Webster Groves (Mo.) Community Garden Project, 1978; bd. dirs. St. Louis Urban Gardening Program, 1978—. Fellow Royal Hort. Soc. (Gt. Britain); mem. Engrs. Club St. Louis, Am. Hort. Soc. Am. Magnolia Soc. (charter; dir. 1979—), Am. Assn. Bot. Gardens and Arboreta, Men's Garden Club Webster Groves (pres. 1967-68, 80-81), Men's Garden Club Am. (pres. Midwest region 1976-77, nat. dir. 1979—, accredited hort. judge), Pi Tau Sigma. Club: Masons. Home: 215 McDonald Pl Webster Groves MO 63119

MC COY, ROBIN, ednl. adminstr.; b. Oklahoma City, Okla., Feb. 14, 1914; s. Frank Thomas and Virginia (Hightower) McCoy; A.B., Harvard U., 1935, A.M., 1940; B.A., Cambridge (Eng.) U., 1937, M.A., 1941; postgrad. U. Colo., 1937, U. Pitts., 1943-44. Tchr. Shattuck Sch., Faribault, Minn., 1937-39; instr. Okla. Agrl. and Mech. Coll., Stillwater, 1940-41; tchr. Milw. Country Day Sch., 1941-42, Phillips Exeter Acad., Exeter, N.H., 1942, 45, Milton (Mass.) Acad., 1944-46; founding head master, tchr. Thomas Jefferson Sch., St. Louis, 1946-80, headmaster emeritus, 1980—. Served with USAAF, 1942-44. Mem. Soc. Italian Studies (Eng.), Classical Assn. New Eng. (hon.), Harvard Clubs Boston, N.Y.C., St. Louis. Contbr. articles to profl. publs. Address: 7750 Ravensridge Rd Saint Louis MO 63119

MC CRACKEN, HAROLD MACKENZIE, business exec.; b. Farmington, Mich., Feb. 3, 1904; s. Harry Norton and Isabella Florence (MacKenzie) McC.; A.B., Albion Coll., 1926; m. Helene Charlotte Sooy, June 10, 1933. Teller, 1st Nat. Bank of Commerce, Detroit, 1926-28; tax clk. Oakland County (Mich.), 1928-29; treas. Gray Marine Motor Co., 1930-47; sec., treas., co-founder MP Pumps, Inc., Detroit, 1942-69, dir., 1942-75; past chmn. bd., co-founder, dir. Am. Community Mut. Ins. Co., 1938—; partner McBee Investors, 1943-76. Mem. Ins. Inst. Am., Nat. Assn. Accountants, S.A.R., U.S. Power Squadron, Tau Kappa Epsilon. Presbyterian. Clubs: Masons, K.T., Rotary; Round Table (Plymouth, Mich.); Detroit Yacht, Economic (Detroit). Home: 295 Stephens Rd Grosse Pointe Farms MI 48236

MC CRACKEN, WILLIAM LAURIN, architect; b. Meridian, Miss., Nov. 12, 1942; s. William R. and Ellouise (McLaurin) McC.; student Auburn U., 1961-65; B.Arch., Rice U., 1967, B.A., 1967; M.Arch. and Urban Planning, Princeton U., 1972; m. Mary Lou Oswalt, Aug. 13, 1965; children—Mary Leslie, Laura Elizabeth. Draftsman, R.B. Clopton, architect, Meridian, Miss., part-time 1960-65, S.I. Morris Associate Architects. Houston, Tex., 1966-67; designer with Michael Graves, architect, Princeton, N.J., 1970-72; asso. partner, designer Caudill Rowlett Scott Architects Planners, N.Y.C., 1972-76; dir. design services Fitch/Larocca Associates, architects, Chgo., 1976-79; asso., v.p. devel. Fujikawa, Conterato Lohan and Assos., Architects, Chgo., 1979—; adj. faculty architecture Triton Coll., River Grove, Ill., 1979; major works include: phys. edn. complex Northeastern Ill. U., Chgo., 1976, Fed. City Coll., Washington, 1975, Sheridan Correctional Center, Sheridan, Ill., 1977, Jensen Sound Lab., Schiller Park, Ill., 1977, South Side Bank, Chgo., 1978. Bd. dirs. Oak Park-River Forest Village Art Fair, 1978—. Served to capt. C.E., U.S. Army, 1967-70. Internat. Research and Exchange Commn. grantee, 1971; registered architect, N.J., Ill., Tex. Mem. AIA, Soc. for Mktg. Profl. Services, Nat. Assn. Corp. Real Estate Execs. Home: 207 N Elmwood Oak Park IL 60302 Office: One Illinois Center 111 E Wacker Dr Chicago IL 60601

MC CRARY, W(ARREN) ASHTON, physician; b. Lake City, Iowa, Feb. 29, 1924; s. Warren Encell and Lilah Mary (Ashton) McC.; B.S., Northwestern U., 1945, B.M., 1947, M.D., 1948; m. Marilyn Maree Fountain, Dec. 25, 1950; children—Toni Maree, Warren Ray, Stuart Ashton, Brian Fountain. Intern, Gorgas Meml. Hosp., Ancon, C.Z., 1947-49; gen. practice medicine, Lake City, 1949—; partner McCrary-Rost Clinic, Lake City and Rockwell City, Iowa, 1949—; state surgeon Iowa N.G., 1968-80; mem. med. adv. bd. Omaha Regional Midwest Blood Bank, 1967—; bd. dirs. Lake City Home for Aged. Served with U.S. Army, 1942-45, 50-52; Korea. Diplomate Am. Bd. Family Practice. Mem. Am. Acad. Dermatology, Assn. Mil. Surgeons, AMA, Iowa Med. Soc., Am. Acad. Allergy, Kansas City S.W. Clin. Soc., Calhoun County Med. Soc. (pres. 1972-81), Am. Contract Bridge League (life master), Am. Legion. Club: Masons. Home: 819 W Madison St Lake City IA 51449 Office: 300 E Main St Lake City IA 51449

MC CRAY, BILLY QUINCY, state senator, real estate broker; b. Geary, Okla., Oct. 29, 1927; s. John Joel and Ivory Beatrice (Jessie) McC.; m. Wyvette M. Williams, Oct. 12, 1952; children—Frankie Leen Conley, Anthony, Melody McCray Miller, Kent. Mem. Kans. Ho. of Reps., Wichita, 1967-72, Kans. Senate, 1973—; real estate broker. Mem. Human Relations Comm., 1961-63; mem. Mayor's Adv. Com., 1964—. Served with USAF, 1947-51. Mem. African Methodist Episcopal Ch. Democrat. Mason. Home: 1532 N Ash St Wichita KS 67214 Office: Kans State Senate Topeka KS 66612

MC CREARY, PATT ROSELINE, artist, photographer; b. Fremont, Nebr., Feb. 6, 1931; d. Harry Lyle Tong and Joan Marie (Pensick) Lyman; student pub. schs. Fremont; children—Jalae A'Dayle, Kyle Lou. With advt. dept. Fremont Guide Tribune, 1950-53; with Am. Photograph Corp., N.Y.C., 1953-63; mgr. portrait photography studios Kilpatrick's Dept. Store, Omaha, 1953-60, Brandeis Store, Omaha, 1960-63; 21 dealer Harrah's Club, Reno, Nev., 1963-65; co-owner, photographer Patt Cylae Studio (1st profl. color protrait studio in Omaha), 1965-67, Gem Color Studio, Omaha, 1967-69; pvt. practice portrait photography, Omaha, 1965-78; owner, artist, photographer Art House, Inc., Omaha, 1974-75; co-owner, artist, photographer Impressions Photography Art, Omaha, 1978—; tchr. photography and photography mgmt., 1960—; photographer sales, advt., fashion, animal, Santa promotions, polit. and theatrical personalities, mus. album covers, high sch. and coll. students; decorating cons.; framing specialist; artist in oils. Named Miss Fremont, 1951; recipient twelve top ten portrait photography nat. awards, 1956-63. Mem. Nat. League Am. Pen Women, Nebr. Photographers Assn., Internat. Platform Assn. Clubs: Astara, Triangles, Spiritual Frontiers Am. Author pvt. sales and procedure manuals in portrait photography Calandra Camera Co., Omaha; composer music. Home: 726 N 91 Plaza Embassy Park Omaha NE 68114 Office: Impressions Photography Art 280 NE Parking Area Westroads Omaha NE 68114

MC CREERY, GENE SHARP, internat. relations adminstr.; b. Gaston, Ind., May 14, 1912; s. Harry Delbert and Dora Hazel (Sharp) McC.; A.B., Ball State U., 1934; M.A., Colubia U., 1940; Ed.D., Ind. U., 1953; m. Mary Jane Robbins, Feb. 21, 1942; children—Richard Allen, John Thomas. Tchr. math. and sci. Washington Twp. Consol. Schs., Gaston, 1935-40, prin., 1940-42; instr. to asso. prof. math., sci. and edn. Ball State U., Muncie, Ind., also Burris Lab. Sch., 1944-49, 51-54, 56-57; dir. profl. lab experiences, placement and research Newark State Coll., 1957-62; staff programs U.S. Dept. State in Egypt, 1954-56, Thailand, 1962-64, South Vietnam, 1964-65, 67-70, Ethiopia, 1965-67; tchr. edn. advisor Ill. State U., Normal, 1970-72; prof. edn. Quincy (Ill.) Coll., 1974-78; state dir. student Ambassador program Ind. People-to-People Program, Gaston, 1978—; lectr., cons. in field. Pres., Miss. chpt. and chmn. Miss. Valley council People to People Internat., 1975-77; chmn. missions Union United Meth. Ch., Quincy, Ill., 1975-77; chmn. adminstrn. bd. Gaston United Meth. Ch., 1979—; chmn. Sister Cities Com. of City of Quincy, 1978—; bd. dirs. Chaddick Boys Sch., 1975-78. Served with USAF, 1942-44. Decorated Medal of Honor (Vietnam). Mem. Assn. Superivision and Curriculum Devel., N.J. Student Tchrs. Assn. (pres.), Assn. Coll. Tchrs., Internat. Tchr. Edn., Sigma Zeta, Phi Delta Kappa. Republican. Clubs: Rotary (sec. Quincy East 1976-78), Masons, Shriners. Home and Office: Route 1 Box 97 Gaston IN 47342

MC CREERY, LYNN ZIMMERMAN, banker, cons.; b. Chgo., Apr. 13, 1945; d. George John and Jane Topping (Zimmerman); B.S., Northwestern U., 1967, M.A., 1969; m. David G. McCreery, Apr. 10, 1976; 1 dau., Susan. Asst. dir. admissions Northwestern U., 1967, teaching asst., univ. fellow, 1968-72; asst. mgr. Student Book Exchange, 1968-74; public affairs officer Glenview (Ill.) State Bank, 1974-75, personnel devel. officer, 1975-79, asst. v.p., dir. tng. and cons. services, 1979-81; pres. LZM Enterprises, 1981—. Bd. dirs. Glenkirk Assn. Retarded, 1971-77, 79-82, v.p. bd., 1971-73, 80-82; aux. minister, mem. coms. Our Lady of Perpetual Help Ch., 1980—; mem. Glenkirk Sch. Bd., 1970-73, pres., 1971-73; mem. fund raising com. Girl Scouts Am., 1978; mem. exec. com. Evanston Infant Welfare, 1971-73; mem. bd. Glenview United Way, 1979-81. Mem. Nat. Assn. Bank Women (vice-chmn., co-founder North Suburban chpt.), Am. Soc. Tng. Dirs., Bank Mktg. Assn. Profl. Devel. Council. Roman Catholic. Co-author: How to Make Successful Business Development Calls, 1980. Home: 1934 Central Rd Glenview IL 60025 Office: 800 Waukegan Rd Glenview IL 60025

MC CREERY, ROBERT HERMAN, metall. engr.; b. Muncie, Ind., Sept. 11, 1925; s. Herman and Margaret Allena (McKinley) McC.; student U. Ky., 1943, Ball State U., 1944-45; B.S. in Metall. Engring., Purdue U., 1948; m. Helen Brown, Dec. 21, 1947; children—Ann, Sarah. Metallurgist Internat. Harvester Corp., Evansville, Ind., 1948-51, prin. metallurgist, 1951-55; plant metallurgist Warner Gear div. Borg Warner Corp., Muncie, 1955-60; chief metallurgist Teledyne Portland Forge (Ind.), 1960-76; v.p. metall. engring. and raw materials Teledyne, Portland Forge, 1976—. Mem. Portland City Council, 1980—. Fellow Am. Soc. Metals (nat. trustee 1969-71); mem. Nat. Soc. Profl. Engrs. Presbyterian (deacon, elder). Mason (32 deg.), Elk, Rotarian (pres. Portland 1964-65). Home: 321 E High St Portland IN 47371 Office: Teledyne Portland Forge PO Box 905 Portland IN 47371

MC CROWEY, GEORGE ANTHONY, rehab. psychologist; b. Athens, Ga., Feb. 7, 1936; s. Scott and Mary Frances (Elder) McC.; B.A., Roosevelt U., 1967; M.S., Ill. Inst. Tech., 1973; m. Sherby Jean Harrell, Jan. 3, 1959; 1 son, George Christopher. Rehab. counselor, casework supr. Ill. Div. Vocat. Rehab., Chgo., 1967, rehab. facilities coordinator, service supr., 1972-74; asst. dir. Univ. Without Walls Chgo. State U., 1974-75; rehab. services program specialist HEW Rehab. Services Adminstrn., Chgo., 1975—. Pres. sch. bd. Holy Angels Catholic Sch., 1960-70; pres. Men's Club Holy Angels Catholic Ch., 1968-69; coordinator ARC Blood Drive for Cook County Region of Ill. Div. Vocat. Rehab., 1973. Served with U.S. Army, 1959-61. Research fellow rehab. psychology Ill. Inst. Tech., 1974-75; certified rehab. counselor Commn. Rehab. Counselor Certification, 1975. Mem. Nat. Rehab. Assn. (dir. 1980—), Nat. Rehab. Counseling Assn. (bd. dir. 1975-77), Am. Personnel and Guidance Assn., Am. Rehab. Counseling Assn., Am. Mgmt. Assn., Ill. Rehab. Assn. (pres. 1974), Ill. Rehab. Counselors Assn. (pres. 1975). Clubs: K.C. Editor Ill. Rehab. Counseling Assn. Quarterly, 1972. Office: 300 S Wacker Room 1500 Chicago IL 60606

MC CUBBIN, HAMILTON II, sociologist; b. Honolulu, July 20, 1941; s. Jonathan Kuihe and Betsy Chisayo (Yamamoto) McC.; B.S., U. Wis., Madison, 1964, M.S., 1966, Ph.D., 1970; postdoctoral tng., Yale U., 1970-71; m. Marilyn Ann Behrens, Nov. 1, 1963; children—Todd Jonathan, Wendy Ann, Laurie Dawn. Dir. research U.S. Army Retng. Program, Ft. Riley, Kans., 1969-71; dir. drug and alcohol treatment program Presidio of San Francisco, 1971-72; dir. family studies Naval Health Research Center, San Diego, 1972-76; asso. prof. Family Study Center and social work U. Minn., 1976-78, prof., chmn. dept., 1978—. Bd. dirs. Swimming Assn., LaMesa, Calif., 1975-76. Served to maj. AUS, 1969-76. Decorated Meritorious Service Medal; U.S. Children's Bur. fellow, 1968-69; grantee Gillette Med. Center, 1979, Dept. Navy, 1974, Office Naval Research, 1975. Mem. Nat. Assn. Social Workers (dir.), Am. Public Health Assn., Am.

Sociol. Assn., Nat. Council Family Relations, Am. Assn. Correctional Psychologists. Author: Family Separation and Reunion, 1974; Families in the Military System, 1976; Family Stress Coping and Social Support, in press; asso. editor Jour. Marriage and the Family, 1977-80, Jour. Family Issues, 1980—; spl. editor Jour. Family Relations, 1979-80; contbr. articles to profl. jours., chpts. to books. Home: 3001 Flag Ave N New Hope MN 55427 Office: 290 McNeal Hall U Minn Saint Paul MN 55108

MC CUBBREY, DAVID RAYMOND, surgeon; b. Canada, Dec. 15, 1928; s. David Dunlop and Ann (Zayots) McC.; came to U.S., 1929, naturalized, 1937; M.D., U. Mich., 1953; m. Claire Ward Lambert, Mar. 25, 1950; children—David, Douglas, Doris. Intern, Albany (N.Y.) Hosp., 1953-54; resident St. Joseph Hosp., Ann Arbor, Mich., 1957-61; practice medicine specializing in surgery, Plymouth, Mich., 1961—; mem. staff St. Joseph Hosp., Ann Arbor, St. Mary Hosp., Livonia, Mich. Served with AUS, 1955-57. Mem. A.C.S. Home: 505 McKinley St Plymouth MI 48170 Office: 221 Sheldon St Plymouth MI 48170

MC CUE, JAMES JOSEPH, credit union exec.; b. Springfield, Ill., July 20. 1918; s. Peter W. and Mary (Brown) C.; B.S., DePaul U., 1941; m. Louise C. Wiesner, Oct. 21, 1944; children—Monica M., Michael J. Mgr., Am. Motors Credit Union, Milw., 1950-55; mgr. Collins Employees Credit Union, Cedar Rapids, Iowa, 1955-75, exec. v.p., 1975—; mem. Gov.'s Task Force Guaranteed Student Loans (Iowa), 1977—, Iowa Credit Union Rev. Bd., 1979—. Treas., Family Service Agy., 1975-76. Mem. Credit Union Execs. Soc. (dir., sec.-treas.), Iowa Credit Union League (dir.), Iowa League Corp. Central Credit Union (chmn. bd.), Nat. Accountants Assn. Club: K.C. Home: 3018 Leonard Terr NE Cedar Rapids IA 52402 Office: 1150 42d St NE Cedar Rapids IA 52402

MCCUEN, HUBER MASON, dentist; b. Butler, Ohio, Sept. 20, 1917; s. Orvil Henry and Treva Estelle (Long) McC.; B.A. in Edn., Ashland Coll., 1941, B.S. in Edn., 1947; D.D.S., Ohio State U., 1952; postgrad. U. Pa., 1977-80; m. Joanna Hess, June 7, 1942; children—Michael Hess (dec.), Joel Mason. Tchr., coach Ashland (Ohio) County Sch. System, 1941; golf coach Ashland Coll., 1946-47; instr. Ohio State U., Columbus, 1952; gen. practice dentistry, Ashland, 1952-81; mem. staff Samaritan Hosp., Ashland, 1953-81; dir. Parkwest Lanes Bowling Corp., 1966-81. Mem. Ashland Bd. Health, 1960-64, pres., 1964. Served to lt. comdr. USNR, 1941-46. Mem. ADA, Ohio Dental Assn., Am. Orthodontic Soc., Ohio State U. Assn. (life), Young Men's Bus. Club (pres. 1964-65), Am. Forestry Assn., Delta Sigma Delta (life), Alpha Psi Omega. Elk. Club: Country of Ashland. Home: 1643 Edgewood Ct Ashland OH 44805 Office: 58 W 2d St Ashland OH 44805 Died Sept. 19, 1981.

MCCULLOUGH, DONALD RAY, mfg. co. exec.; b. Pennsboro, W.Va., Dec. 10, 1931; s. Alva Seckman and Dortha Elizabeth (Williamson) McC.; student Marietta Coll., 1968, Wittenburg U., 1964, Ohio U., 1980—; m. Helen B. Kelly, May 16, 1951; children—Steven R., Penny Lee, Janis K. With Weirton Steel Co. (W.Va.), 1950-51, Union Carbide Corp., Sistersville, W.Va., 1956-61; sr. asst. health, safety and environment Shell Chem. Co., Belpre, Ohio, 1978—; mem. faculty Parkersburg (W.Va.) Community Coll., 1980-81. First aid chmn. ARC, Parkersburg, 1974-76. Served with USN, 1951-56. Cert. safety profl. Mem. Am. Soc. Safety Engrs. (chpt. pres. 1971-72), Internat. Soc. Fire Service Instrs. Republican. Home: 710 4th St Belpre OH 45714 Office: PO Box 235 Belpre OH 45714

MC CULLOUGH, DOROTHEA GERBRACHT, editor; b. Hettinger, N.D.; d. John H. and Pearl (Rossiter) Gerbracht; student Dickinson State Coll., 1934-35; B.A., U. N.D., 1937; M.A., N.D. State U., 1962; m. S. K. McCullough, 1945 (dec. 1958); children—Paul K., Amoret C., Donald S. With various newspapers, 1933-42; grad. asst. dept. botany N.D. State U., Fargo, 1939, asst. agrl. editor, 1943-46, asso. agrl. editor, asst. prof. communications, 1957-73, asso. prof. communications, agrl. editor, 1973-81, mem. Univ. senate, 1974-77; owner (with husband) drug store, Casselton, N.D., 1946-53. Mem. forestry com. City of Fargo, 1981. Mem. N.D., S.D., Cass County hist. socs., N.D., Minn. hort. socs., N.D. Acad. Sci. (editor 1975-77), Fargo-Moorhead Unitarian Fellowship (dir., sec. 1964-65, 67-68, pres. 1975-76), Fargo-Moorhead Audubon Soc. (corr. sec., editor), N.D. Natural History Soc., Minn. Ornithol. Union, LWV, Fargo-Moorhead Garden Soc. (v.p. 1962-63), Federated Womens Clubs (dist. and state history chmn. 1958-59), Epsilon Sigma Phi (annalist 1970-78), N.D. Press Women, Toastmasters Internat. (sec. 1979-81). Republican. Mem. United Ch. of Christ. Club: Order Eastern Star. Editor N.D. Farm Research, 1958-81, N.D. Extension Rev., 1957-74. Home: Route 5 Box 365 Detroit Lakes MN 56501

MC CULLOUGH, JAYNE ELIZABETH ANDREWS, data processing cons.; b. Norfolk, Va., Jan. 20, 1945; d. Reginald Harry and Clara B. (Hager) Andrews; grad. Meml. Mission Hosp. Sch. X-Ray, 1962; B.S. in Gen. Edn., Northwestern U., 1979; m. John W. McCullough, July 1, 1979. Programmer, Blue Cross/Blue Shield, Chgo., 1969-71; systems analyst City of Gary (Ind.), 1971-74, AMA, Chgo., 1974-76, United Ins. Co., Chgo., 1976-78; cons. Systems and Programming Resources, Oak Brook, Ill., 1978-80, asst. mgr., 1980—; tchr. data processing Ind. Vocat. Tech. Inst., Gary, 1972-74. Mem. Systems Programming Soc., Nat. Assn. Ret. Tchrs. Democrat. Home: 1020 Dodge St Evanston IL 60202 Office: 1211 W 22d St Suite 600 Oak Brook IL 60521

MC CULLOUGH, JOHN JEFFREY, physician, med. center adminstr., educator; b. Boston, Apr. 29, 1938; s. Joe Thompson and Mary Elizabeth (Brunner) McC.; B.A., Northwestern U., 1959; M.D., Ohio State U., 1963. Intern Vanderbilt U. Hosp., Nashville, 1963-64, resident in medicine, 1969-70; fellow dept. lab. medicine U. Minn. Hosps., Mpls., chief resident lab. medicine, 1967-69, dir. blood bank, 1970—; prof. dept. lab. medicine and pathology U. Minn., 1978—; med. dir. St. Paul Regional ARC Blood Center, 1970-74, dir., 1974—; practice medicine specializing in clin. pathology and blood transfusion; mem. blood program adv. com. to pres. ARC, 1976-78. Served with USPHS, 1964-67. Grantee ARC, 1972—, Nat. Heart Lung and Blood Inst., 1971—, Nat. Cancer Inst., 1975—. Recipient award Am. Cancer Soc., 1967. Mem. Am., Minn. (past pres.) assns. blood banks, AAAS, Minn. State Med. Assn. (com. on blood banks and labs. 1973—, Ramsey County Med. Soc. (chmn. com. on blood and blood banks 1972-76), Minn., Am. (council on immunohematology 1975—) socs. clin. pathologists, Central Soc. Clin. Research, Am. Soc. Hematology, Am. Fedn. for Clin. Research, Am. Assn. Pathologists, Am. Assn. for Clin. Histocompatibility Testing, Central Soc. for Clin. Research. Contbr. chpts. to med. books, articles to profl. jours. Home: 9 Greenway Gables Minneapolis MN 55403 Office: Box 198 Mayo U Minnesota Minneapolis MN 55455

MC CULLOUGH, JOSEPH, artist, inst. of art ofcl.; b. Pitts., July 6, 1922; s. Joseph Phillip and Margaret (List) McC.; diploma in painting, Cleve. Inst. Art, 1948; B.F.A., Yale, 1950, M.F.A., 1951; m. Florence Elizabeth Cramer, Mar. 31, 1945; children—Marjorie, Warren. Instr. art San Jose State Coll., 1948-49; asst. instr. Yale, 1949-51; asst. dir. Cleve. Inst. Art, 1952-55, dir., 1955-74, pres., 1974—; exhibited Cleve. Mus. Art, Butler Inst. Am. Art, Carnegie Mus. (Pitts.), Stanford, Oberlin Coll., Corcoran Gallery, Springfield (Mass.) Mus., U. Del., Akron Art Inst., U. Ill. Biennial. Addison Gallery Am. Art, Andover, Mass. Chmn. fine arts adv. com. City Planning Commn. Recipient prizes in painting, Pitts. Playhouse, Cleve. Mus. Art, Canton Art Inst., Ohio U., Asso. Artists Pitts., Butler Inst. Am. Art. Fellow Nat. Assn. Schs. Art (past pres.); mem. Cleve. Mus. Art (adv. bd.), Coll. Art Assn., Cleve. Art Assn. (sec.). Home: 2637 Wellington Rd Cleveland Heights OH 44118 Office: 11141 East Blvd Cleveland OH 44106

MC CULLOUGH, ROSE VERNIE, editor, author; b. Charleston, S.C.; d. David Augustus and Rose Eunice (Paille) Rodgers; student parochial schs.; m. John Hudson McCullough (dec. May 1974); 1 son, Alan David. Editorial sec. Rough Notes Co., Inc., Indpls., 1948-52, editorial asst., 1955-57, asst. editor, 1957-78, asso. editor, 1978—; editor Bulls. on Effective Agy. Mgmt., 1975—, Reports on Agy. Mgmt., 1975—, Insights for the Ins. Woman, 1979—. Speaker on communications, career and personal devel. Mem. Adminstrv. Mgmt. Soc. (dir.), Indpls. Assn. Ins. Women (exec. bd.), Ins. Co. Edn. Dirs. Soc., Soc. Ins. Research, Women in Communications, Nat. Assn. Ins. Women, Nat. Assn. Female Execs. Democrat. Presbyterian. Home: 5263 Crestview Indianapolis IN 46220 Office: 1200 N Meridian St Indianapolis IN 46204

MC CULLY, WILLIAM CRAIG, JR., library adminstr.; b. Richmond Heights, Mo., Sept. 15, 1947; s. William Craig and Amelia Agnes (Kearns) McC.; B.A., U. Notre Dame, 1969, M.A., 1970, Ph.D., 1973; M.S., U. Ill., 1975; m. Nancy Louise Buddenbaum, June 19, 1976; 1 dau., Claire Louise. Dir., Everett M. Dirksen Congl. Leadership Research Center, Pekin, Ill., 1976-78; dir. Pekin Public Library (Ill.), 1975—, Ill. Valley Library System, Pekin, 1980—. Served with U.S. Army, 1973-74. NDEA fellow, 1969-71; U.S. Steel Found. fellow, 1971-73. Mem. ALA, Am. Hist. Assn., Ill. Library Assn. Roman Catholic. Club: Kiwanis. Contbr. articles to profl. jours. Home: 705 McLean St Pekin IL 61554 Office: 301 S 4th St Pekin IL 61554

MCCUNE, EMMETT LEE, vet. microbiologist; b. Cuba, Mo., Jan. 2, 1927; s. Roy Earl and Rhoda Angeletta (Housewright) McC.; B.S., U. Mo., 1956, D.V.M., 1956, M.S., 1961, Ph.D., 1968; m. Mable June Rector, June 8, 1952; children—Martha Grace, Roy Allen, Gordon Norman. Instr., U. Mo., Columbia, 1956-61, asst. prof., 1962-68, asso. prof., 1969-78, prof. microbiology and avian pathology, 1978—. Cubmaster, Boy Scouts Am., Columbia, 1968-72; pres. High St. Neighborhood Assn., 1972. Served with U.S. Army, 1945-46; ETO. NIH fellow, 1963-64. Mem. Am. Coll. Vet. Microbiologists, AVMA, Am. Soc. Microbiology, Am. Assn. Avian Pathologists, N.Y. Acad. Sci., Sigma Xi. Contbr. articles to profl. jours. editor: Avian Diseases, 1977. Home: 506 High St Columbia MO 65201 Office: Vet Med Diagnostics Lab U Mo Columbia MO 65211

MC CURDY, LARRY WAYNE, automotive parts mfg. co. exec.; b. Commerce, Tex., July 1, 1935; s. Weldon Lee and Eula Bell (Quinn) McC.; B.B.A., Tex. A. and M. U., 1957; m. Anna Jean Ogle, June 2, 1956; children—Michael, Kimberly, Laurie. Jr. accountant Tenneco Inc., Houston, 1957-60, sr. accountant Tenneco Oil Co., Houston, 1960-64, accounting supr. Tenneco Chems., Houston, 1964-69, div. controller, Saddle Brook, N.J., 1970-72, corp. controller, 1972-74, v.p. fin., 1974-78, sr. v.p. fin. Tenneco Automotive, 1978-79; pres. Walker Mfg. Co., Racine, Wis., 1980-81, exec. v.p., Deerfield, Ill., 1981—. Trustee, Somerset County Coll., Somerville, N.J., 1974-78; elder Liberty Corner Presbyn. Ch., N.J., 1973-78; dist. chmn. Lake County Jr. Achievement, 1979-80. Served to capt. Air Def., USAR, 1958-66. Mem. Nat. Assn. Accountants, Fin. Execs. Inst.

MC CURRY, DONALD REID, mktg. research exec.; b. Nashville, July 21, 1928; s. Ray Reid and Victoria Wanda (Stranz) McC.; B.A., Cornell U., 1950; m. Flora McKenzie, July 21, 1950; children—Diane, Kathryn, Laura. Research statistician A.C. Nielsen Co., Northbrook, Ill., 1955-56, asst. to pres., 1956-62, client service exec., 1962-67, v.p., 1967-74, exec. v.p., 1974—, also dir.; chmn. bd. Compumark, Inc., Coordinated Mgmt. Systems. Served with USAF, 1951-53. Mem. Am. Mktg. Assn., Phi Beta Kappa. Club: Knollwood (Lake Forest, Ill.). Home: 600 W Westleigh Rd Lake Forest IL 60045 Office: Nielsen Plaza Northbrook IL 60062

MCCUTCHAN, JEAN ANNALEE, educator; b. Cleve., Aug. 20, 1952; d. H. Robert and Myrna Jean (Flory) Gemmer; B.A., Manchester Coll., North Manchester, Ind., 1974; M.A., Ball State U., Muncie, Ind., 1975; postgrad. Ind. U., South Bend, Andrews U., Berrien Springs, Mich.; cert. Human Devel. Tng. Inst., 1979, Effectiveness Tng. Inst., 1979; m. Larry J. McCutchan, Dec. 24, 1973; 1 son, Eric Daniel. Sch. psychologist Baugo-Concord-Wa-Nee Spl. Edn. Coop., Wakarusa, Ind., 1975-80, dir. spl. edn., 1980—; lectr. Andrews U., Berrien Springs, Mich., 1977, 80; vis. instr. Ind. U., South Bend, 1979; coordinator Elkhart (Ind.) County Pediatric/Ednl. Survey, 1978-79. Bd. dirs. H.C. Gemmer Family Christian Found., 1977—, Family Counseling Service, Elkhart County, 1980—; mem. Elkhart County Adv. Council Children and Youth, 1979—. United Christian Missionary Soc. scholar 1970. Mem. Assn. Supervision and Curriculum Devel., Nat. Assn. Sch. Psychologists, Council Exceptional Children, Assn. Children with Learning Disabilities, Nat. Com. Prevention Child Abuse, Ind. Council Adminstrs. Spl. Edn., Am. Orthopsychiat. Assn. Home: 60324 Missouri Ave Goshen IN 46526 Office: 204 N Elkhart St Wakarusa IN 46573

MCDANIEL, BRUCE ALAN, economist, educator; b. Warsaw, Ind., June 12, 1946; s. Maurice M. and Hatti M. (Stidham) McD.; B.S., Manchester Coll., N. Manchester, Ind., 1968; M.A., Ball State U., Muncie, Ind., 1972; Ph.D., Colo. State U., 1979; m. Darcy L. Stouder, Dec. 29, 1972; children—Rachel Lynn, Nathan Alan. Asst. prof. econs. Anderson (Ind.) Coll., 1971-72, Genesee Community Coll., Batavia N.Y., 1972-75, Colo. State U., 1975-79, Ind. U., Indpls., 1979-81, Marquette U., Milw., 1981—. Mem. Am. Econs. Assn., Assn. Evolutionary Econs., Assn. Social Econs., Midwest Econs. Assn., Omicron Delta Kappa, Phi Kappa Phi. Author articles in field. Office: Dept Econs Marquette U Milwaukee WI 53233

MC DANIEL, CHARLES WAYNE, chiropractor; b. Spencer, S.D., June 13, 1927; s. Wayne and Bertha (Duxbury) McD.; B.S., S.D. State U., 1950; D. Chiropractic, Nat. Coll. Chiropractice, Lombard, Ill., 1970; m. Florence Claussen, Mar. 21, 1949; children—David (dec.), James, Sharon McDaniel Zoellner, Susan. High sch. instr., Canova, S.D., 1950-52; with Soil Conservation Service, U.S. Dept. Agr., Milbank, Leola, Wessington Springs, S.D., 1952-65; chiropractic physician, Brookings, S.D., 1970—. Scoutmaster, mem. troup com. Boy Scouts Am., 1954-65. Served with Signal Corps, U.S. Army, 1945-46. Club: Kiwanis, Elks. Home: 1442 LeGeros Dr Brookings SD 57006 Office: 611 6th St Brookings SD 57006

MC DANIEL, JAMES AUSTIN, assn. exec.; b. St. Louis, Apr. 5, 1915; s. Joseph Cleveland and Harriet Lunar (Hastings) McD.; student Southeast Mo. U., 1933-36; m. Helen Estelle Buscher, June 4, 1938; children—Fredrick Olin, John Paul, Philip Buscher. With Bonne Terre Farming & Cattle Co. (Mo.), 1936-46; accountant St. Joseph Lead Co., 1946-58; auditor, Mo., 1958-61; out supt. adminstrn. Mo. Div. Mental Health, 1961-71; adminstr. Perry County Meml. Hosp., Perryville, Mo., 1971-81; hosp. surveyor Mo. Profl. Liability Ins. Assn., Jefferson City, 1981—. Mem. Perry County ARC Blood Program; mem. adv. council St. Francis Mental Health Center; past pres. Southeast Mo. Council; mem. Vocat. Adv. Bd., State Health Coordinating Council. Leader Boy Scouts Am., 1938-58; Active local musical groups. Councilman, Bonne Terre, 1952-54. Served with USNR, 1944-46. Mem. Mo. Mental Health Assn., Assn. Mental Health Adminstrs., Am. Acad. Med. Adminstrs., Mo. Hosp. Assn. (past treas., trustee), Perryville C. of C., Am. Legion, Soc. Preservation and Encouragement Barber Shop Quartet Singing in Am. (v.p.). Methodist (chmn. adminstrv. bd., choir dir.). Mason (Shriner), Lion, Rotarian. Clubs: Perryville Country. Home: 113 E School St Bonne Terre MO 65102 Office: Mo Profl Liability Ins Assn Jefferson City MO 65102

MC DANIEL, JAMES EDWIN, lawyer; b. Dexter, Mo., Nov. 22, 1931; s. William H. and Gertie M. (Woods) McD.; A.B., Washington U., St. Louis, 1957, LL.B., 1959; m. Mary Jane Crawford, Jan. 22, 1955; children—John William, Barbara Anne. Admitted to Mo. bar, 1959; partner firm Barnard and Baer, St. Louis; pros. atty. City of Glendale (Mo.), 1970—. Served with USAF, 1951-55. Mem. Am. Bar Assn. (ho. of dels. 1976-80, chmn. com. student loan fund), Bar Assn. Met. St. Louis (pres. 1972-73), Mo. Bar (gov. 1974—, pres. 1981—), Assn. Def. Counsel (pres. 1968), Legal Aid Soc. (treas., bd. dirs., 1965—), Mo. Savs. and Loan League (pres. attys. com. 1977-78), Phi Delta Phi. Congregationalist. (past moderator, chmn. bd. trustees). Home: 767 Elmwood Ave Glendale MO 63122 Office: 818 Olive St Saint Louis MO 63101

MCDANIEL, MARLIN K., state senator, lawyer; B.S., Purdue U.; LL.B. (scholar), George Washington U.; postgrad. U. Oslo. Admitted to Ind. bar, 19—; practice law; mem. Ind. Senate. Chmn., Republican Nat. Com.; mem. Rep. State Platform Com., 1964; chmn. Wayne County Rep. Com. Served as officer Ind. NG. Mem. Wayne County Bar Assn. Presbyterian. Clubs: Elks, Eagles, Masons, Shriners. Office: State Capitol State Senate Indianapolis IN 46204*

MCDANIEL, MARY ELSIEBETH, pub. co. exec., author; b. Evanston, Ill.; d. Moses Slaughter and Amy Louise (Schults) McDaniel; B.A., Wheaton Coll., 1939, M.A., 1971. Copy controller editorial dept. Ency. Britannica, 1943-48; editor Woodworking Digest Hitchcock Pub. Co., Wheaton, Ill., 1948-60; dir. Early Childhood Publs., Scripture Press, Wheaton, 1960—; tchr. Moody Bible Inst., Chgo., part-time, 1963-70. Author: You and Children, 1973; You and Preschoolers, 1974; You Can Reach Families Through Their Babies, 1981; You Can Teach Primaries, 1981; Early Heroes of the Bible, Stories of Jesus. Home: 812 E Liberty Dr Wheaton IL 60187

MC DERMOTT, DENNIS MICHAEL, assn. exec.; b. Akron, Ohio, Jan. 9, 1947; s. Gerard Joseph and Irene Cathryn (Lenz) McD.; B.S. in Journalism, Kent (Ohio) State U., 1969; postgrad., 1973-76; postgrad. Chapman Coll., Calif., 1971-72; m. Margaret Mary Hayden, Dec. 14, 1968; children—Martin Jerome, Kathleen Marie. Reporter, Akron Beacon Jour., 1967-69; cons. mgr. Am. Sch. Health Assn., Kent, 1973-74, asst. exec. dir., 1974-77; exec. dir. Emergency Dept. Nurses Assn., Chgo., 1977—; guest lectr. Kent State U.; cons. in field. Served with USAF, 1969-72. Knight Found. scholar, 1965-69. Mem. Am. Soc. Assn. Execs., Public Relations Soc. Am., Sigma Delta Chi. Office: 666 N Lake Shore Dr Chicago IL 60611*

MC DERMOTT, WILLIAM STEPHEN, librarian; b. Omaha, Feb. 24, 1930; s. Philip Charles and Edna Frances (Smith) McD.; B.S. in Bus. Adminstrn., Creighton U., 1963, B.A., 1965; M.L.S., Kans. State Tchrs. Coll., 1968; m. Carol Ann Wiegand, June 13, 1964; children—Philip Charles, Michael Stephen, Matthew William. Machinist apprentice, Union Pacific R. R., Omaha, 1948-51, machinist, 1951-66; acting head librarian Fremont (Neb.) Pub. Library, 1968-69, head librarian, 1969-71; library dir. Keene Meml. Library, Fremont, 1971—. Served with AUS, 1953-55. Mem. Nebr. Library Assn. (treas. 1972-73). Optimist (pres. 1970-71). Home: 1700 Mayfair Ave Fremont NE 68025 Office: 1030 N Broad St Fremont NE 68025

MC DEVITT, MICHAEL ROBERT, credit union adminstr.; b. Columbus, Ohio, July 18, 1942; s. John Edward and Esther Linda (Manhulter) McD.; student Ohio State U., 1960-61, Rio Grande Coll., 1962-64, Stark Tech. Coll., 1975-81; children—Richard, Barbara, Michele. Lab technician Ohio State U. Hosp., Columbus, 1960-65; mgmt. trainee Nat. City Bank, Cleve., 1966; mgr. ITT Aetna Fin. Co., Cuyahoga Falls, Ohio, 1966-71; gen. mgr. Summit Fed. Credit Union, Akron, Ohio, 1971—; instr. Akron Bd. Vocat. Edn., 1973-76; lectr. in field. Mem. Credit Union Exec. Soc., Edn. Council Credit Unions, Credit Union Soc., Ohio Credit Union League. Office: 100 Wheeler St Akron OH 44311

MC DONALD, DONALD JOHN, mech. engr.; b. Lynch, Ky., Dec. 4, 1927; s. Thomas Charles and Ethel May (Casey) McD.; student U. Ky., U. Louisville, 1943-47; m. Betty Jean Prewitt, Nov. 22, 1949; children—Donald John, Michael, Jeanette, Bonnie. Constrn. supt. Babcock & Wilcox, Paducah, Ky., 1953-58; chief insp. Ky. Dept. Pub. Safety, 1962-70; dir. Nat. Bd. Boiler and Pressure Vessel Insps., Columbus, Ohio, 1970—; engrng. cons. Served with USMC, 1950-53. Mem. ASME, Am. Welding Soc. Republican. Mormon. Club: Masons. Office: 1055 Crupper St Columbus OH 43229

MC DONALD, DOUGLASS WAYNE, clergyman; b. Marshalltown, Iowa, July 22, 1953; s. Wayne Eldon and Miriam Gertrude (Thurber) McD.; B.A., William Penn Coll., 1974; postgrad. Christian Theol. Sem., 1974—; m. Kay Louise Stangeland, Sept. 14, 1974. Minister to youth Carmel (Ind.) Friends Ch., 1974-77; fellow counselor Buchanan Counseling Center, Meth. Hosp., Indpls., 1977-79; pastoral minister First Friends Ch., Noblesville, Ind., 1977—; vice-chmn. Quaker Haven Found., 1979-81; chmn. Friends Ch. Western Yearly Meeting Bd. Christian Edn., 1980—; mem. Friends United Meeting Ministries Commn., 1978-81, chmn. spiritual life com., 1981—; program com. chmn. Quaker Hill Found., Inc., Richmond, Ind., 1978—; Charles Vincent lectr., Jamaica, 1979. Mem. Noblesville City Council, 1980-84; Noblesville (Ind.) area chmn., pres. bd. dirs. Citizens Against Pari-Mutuel in Hamilton County. Recipient Community Service award Seventh Day Adventist Ch., 1979. Mem. Am. Assn. Pastoral Counselors, Am. Assn. Marriage and Family Therapists, Am. Assn. Christian Counselors. Republican. Club: Kiwanis (sec. 1978-80) (Noblesville). Office: 1055 Division St PO Box 375 Noblesville IN 46060

MCDONALD, ELLIOTT RAYMOND, JR., lawyer; b. Peoria, Ill., Feb. 10, 1929; s. Elliott Raymond and Florence Valera (Cobb) McD.; B.A., U. Iowa, 1950, J.D., 1952; m. Mary Julienne Jensen, May 6, 1952; children—Beth, Elliott Raymond III. Admitted to Iowa bar, 1952, Ill. bar, 1954; practiced in Davenport, 1954—; mem. firm McDonald, Stonebraker & Cepican. Trustee, Davenport Pub. Library, 1972—, chmn. Served with USAF, 1952-54. Mem. Scott County Bar Assn. (pres. 1975-76). Home: 2800 E Locust St Davenport IA 52803 Office: 301 Northwest Tower Davenport IA 52806

MC DONALD, JOHN DAVID, bus. exec.; b. Centralia, Ill., Mar. 25, 1929; s. Jefferson Faulkner and Ella Annette (Johnson) McD.; B.S., U. Ill., 1951; student Centralia Jr. Coll., 1947-48; m. Gloria Jean

(Edwards) Rhinehart, June 25, 1967; 1 step-dau., Sherylyn Rhinehart; 1 dau., Catherine. Ins. agt. Chgo. Met. Mut. Assurance Co., Centralia, 1952-59; asst. mgr. McDonald's Paint & Wallpaper Store, Centralia, 1959-64; mgr. mech. store dept. Murray Center, Centralia, 1964-67, personnel technician, 1967-68, asst. personnel dir., 1968-74, bus. mgr., 1974—; dir. Murray Employees Credit Union, 1967—, chmn. supervisory com., 1967-76, membership com., 1976—. Mem. adv. com. Kaskaskia Coll. Bus. Learning Center, 1978—, chmn., 1980-81; pres. Field Sch. Dads Club, 1975; chmn. groundbreaking com. 2d Bapt. Ch. Ednl. Bldg., 1980. Served with AUS, 1946-47. Named One of 50 Top State Employees, Gov. Ill., 1972. Mem. Ill. State Employees Assn. (del. 1978), U. Ill. Alumni Assn. (alumni rep. homecoming discussion panel 1971), NAACP (treas. Centralia br. 1979), Alpha Phi Alpha. Baptist. Club: Masons. Home: 727 S Locust St Centralia IL 62801

MC DONALD, JOSEPH DOUGLAS, civil engr.; b. Holloday, Utah, Oct. 26, 1931; s. Joseph Stevenson and Evelyn May (Douglas) McD.; B.S. in C.E., U. Utah, 1959; M.S. in Civil Engring., U. Mo., 1974; m. Nanette Carpenter, Sept. 14, 1956; children—Blair Jay, Sidney, Rachel, Carmen, Loril Joseph. Structural engr. Utah Hwy. Dept., Salt Lake City, 1959-61; design engr. Kennecott Copper Corp., Salt Lake City, 1961-64; design engr. FMC Corp., Green River, Wyo., 1964-67; prin. engr. City of Everett (Wash.), 1967-71; asst. city engr. City of Kansas City (Mo.), 1971—; instr. Everett Community Coll., 1968-71. Served with U.S. Army, 1953-55. Mem. Nat. Soc. Profl. Engrs., Mo. Land Surveyors Assn., Am. Soc. Testing and Materials, Am. Congress Surveying and Mapping, Kansas City Engrs. Club. Home: 7607 E 118th Terr Kansas City MO 64134 Office: 414 E 12th St Kansas City MO 64106

MCDONALD, LEE SANFORD, rubber co. exec.; b. Peoria, Ill., Aug. 3, 1925; s. Howard Martin and Blanch M. (MacDonald) McD.; B.A., Knox Coll., 1948; M.B.A., Miami U., Oxford, Ohio, 1950; postgrad. State U. Iowa, 1955-56; m. Jeanne Berlin, Mar. 21, 1953; children—Vicki, Scott, Mark, Nancy, David. Asst. prof. mktg. Miami U., Oxford, Ohio, 1950-55, exec.-in-residence, 1978, mem. bus. council Sch. Bus., 1977-79; with Goodyear Tire & Rubber Co., Akron, 1956—, mktg. mgr. auto, recreational and cycle tires, 1977-79, mgr. stategric planning, tires, 1980—. Chmn., United Fund, 1975, YMCA div., 1976. Served with USAAF, 1943-46. Mem. Am. Mktg. Assn., Am. Statis. Assn., Sales Mktg. Assn., Am. Mgmt. Assn., Assn. Nat. Advertisers. Republican. Methodist. Clubs: Fairlawn Country. Home: 776 Hampton Ridge Rd Akron OH 44313 Office: 1144 E Market St Akron OH 44316

MCDONALD, LORRAINE COLEMAN, health services cons. co. exec.; b. Chgo., Jan. 9, 1931; d. Thomas Samuel and Willa Mae (Turner) Coleman; grad. Cook County Sch. of Nursing, 1967; A.A. with honors, Central Community Coll., Chgo., 1973; B.S. in Personnel Mgmt., Ill. Inst. Tech., 1975, M.B.A., 1977; student DePaul U. Coll. Law, 1980—; m. John Spence McDonald, June 1, 1965; children—Thomasina, Mary Alana, Andre. Indsl. nurse R.R. Donnelley & Sons, Chgo., 1968-72; charge nurse Cook County Hosp., Chgo., 1967-68; nursing dir., asst. adminstr. Regent Plaza Nursing Center, Chgo., 1973-75; nursing dir. Albany Gardens, Inc.; supr. psychiatry Jackson Park Hosp., Chgo., 1975-77; preceptor Chgo. State Univ. Without Walls program, 1979—, Rush-Presbyn.-St. Lukes Grad. Nursing Program, Chgo., 1980; pres. McDonald & Assos., Inc., Chgo., 1979—; asst. adminstr. Jackson Park Hosp. and Med. Center, Chgo., 1977-80, dir. community relations, 1980—. Mem. planning com. Family Focus, Inc., 1979-80; chairperson Family Focus, Woodlawn Advisory Council, 1979—; mem. exec. bd. Ill. Assn. Community Mental Health Agencies, 1979—. Mem. Am. Nurses Assn., Am. Mgmt. Assn., Am. Hosp. Assn., Cook County Sch. of Nursing Alumni Assn., Ill. Inst. Tech. Alumni Assn., Phi Alpha Delta, Lambda Phi Alpha. Republican. Home: 400 W 96th St Chicago IL 60628 Office: 7531 Stony Island Chicago IL 60649

MCDONALD, MARY JANE, univ. adminstr.; b. Akron, Ohio, May 24, 1937; d. Paul Warren and Evelyn Marie (Conrad) Jagger; B.A., Denison U., 1959; children—Steven Jagger, Anne Cooper, Nancy Kendall. Polit. cons., Ohio, 1970-75; spl. asst. to pres. Denison U., Granville, Ohio, 1975-77, exec. dir. univ. resources and public affairs, 1977-80, v.p., 1980—. Mem. U.S. Circuit Judge Nominating Commn., 6th Circuit Panel, 1977—; mem. Nat. Democratic Platform Com., 1976; mem. Ohio Rhodes Scholar Selection Com., 1976—; mem. state policy bd. Ohio Citizens' Council, 1974-77; mem. Gov's. Task Force on Higher Edn., 1973-75; bd. dirs. Licking County United Way, 1973-79; mem. Ohio Gov.'s Jud. Selection Commn., 1973-74; mem. Ohio State Dem. Exec. Com., 1971-73; mem. bd. Licking County Health Camp, 1968-71; chmn. Ohio Elections Commn., 1979—; mem. bd. Family Service Assn., 1980—, Licking Meml. Hosp., 1981—. Mem. League Women Voters (past bd. mem.), Council Advancement and Support Edn., Nat. Soc. Fundraising Execs., Phi Beta Kappa, Kappa Delta Pi, Tau Kappa Alpha. Democrat. Presbyterian. Home: 695 Snowdon Dr Newark OH 43055 Office: Denison U Drawer A Granville OH 43023

MCDONALD, MARY JOYCE, sch. psychologist; b. Boston, Dec. 20, 1939; d. James Joseph and Harriet Marie (Fougere) Kiley; B.S. in Edn., Boston State Coll., 1961; M.Ed., R.I. Coll., 1967; M.A., Mich. State U., 1969; postgrad. No. Ill. U., 1979; m. Edward McDonald, Aug. 24, 1960 (div. Mar. 1977); children—Catherine, Maureen, Edward. Tchr., Silver Lake Regional High Sch., Kingston, Mass., 1962; tchr. Easton (Mass.) Jr. High Sch., 1962-63, Meml. High Sch., Middleboro, Mass., 1963-64, Hope High Sch., Providence, 1965-66; guidance counselor Grand Ledge (Mich.) Jr. High Sch., 1977-79; psychometrist, Hammond (Ind.) city schs., 1969-70; diagnostician Eaton County Intermediate Sch. Dist., Charlotte, Mich., 1968-69; coordinator programs for emotionally disturbed and learning disabled, psychometrist N.W. Ind. Spl. Edn. Cooperative, Highland, 1970-72; instr. Ind. U., Northwest Campus, Gary, 1970-72; program dir. Trade Winds Rehab. Center for Children, Gary, 1972; supervising sch. psychologist Thornton Fractional Township High Sch., Calumet City, Ill., 1973—. Vice pres. Wilbur Wright Middle Sch. P.T.A., 1975-76; mem. planning bd. Lake Area United Way, 1973—; 1st v.p. Greater Hammond Community Council, 1976. Recipient Hammond Community Council award, 1974-76; NDEA fellow, 1967-68. Mem. Nat. Assn. Sch. Psychologists, Council Exceptional Children, Am. Fedn. Tchrs., Ill. Psychol. Assn., Ill. Sch. Psychol. Assn., Assn. Supervision and Curriculum Devel., Phi Delta Kappa. Unitarian. Home: 863 Greenbriar Ln Park Forest South IL 60466 Office: 1601 Wentworth Ave Calumet City IL 60409

MCDONALD, RALPH EARL, ednl. adminstr.; b. Indpls., May 12, 1920; s. Earl Samuel and Addie Elizabeth (Cottom) McD.; B.S., Ind. U., 1942, D.D.S., 1944, M.S., 1951; m. Sarah Jane Wyatt, Aug. 23, 1942; children—John S., Scott W., Barbara L. Instr. pedodontics Ind. Univ. Sch. Dentistry, Indpls., 1946-49, asst. prof. pedodontics, 1949-50, chmn. pedodontics, 1952, 53-63, asso. prof., prof., chmn. dept. pedodontics, 1963-69; dir. Riley Hosp. Dental Clinic, Indpls., 1969—; sec. Grad. Dental Edn., Ind. U. Sch. Dentistry, 1963-69; asst. dean Ind. Univ. Sch. Dentistry, Indpls., 1964-68, acting dean, 1968-69, dean, 1969—. Served with Dental Corps, USNR, 1944-46. Mem. Assn. Pedodontic Diplomates (pres. 1973-74), Ind. Univ. Sch. Dentistry Alumni Assn. (pres. 1969-70), Ind. Soc. Pedodontics, Ind. Soc. Dentistry for Children (pres. 1955), Am. Dental Assn., Indpls. Dental Soc. (chmn. bd. censors 1968-69), Internat. Assn. Dental Research, Am. Acad. Pedondontics (pres. 1966-67), Am. Soc. Dentistry for Children (pres. 1962-63), Sigma Xi, Omicron Kappa Upsilon. Methodist. Club: Mason. Author: Pedodontics, 1963; Dentistry for Child and Adolescent Education, 1969, 3d edit., 78. Contbr. articles to various publs. Home: 5040 Potters Pike Indianapolis IN 46234 Office: Indiana Univ Sch of Dentistry 1121 W Michigan St Indianapolis IN 46202

MCDONALD, RUTH HELEN BADER, nursery and garden center exec.; b. Saginaw, Mich., Mar. 30, 1929; d. William S. and Helen M. (Schultz) Bader; student Mercy Coll., 1948, Delta Coll., 1959-63; B.B.A. with honors in Mktg., Northwood Inst., Midland, Mich., 1979; m. Thomas W. McDonald, Mar. 31, 1951; children—Thomas W., Kathleen, Diane, Joanne, William. With McDonald Nursery, Inc., Saginaw, 1963—, gen. mgr., pres., 1980. Active ARC. Mem. Am. Mgmt. Assn., Better Bus. Assn., Saginaw C. of C., Hobby Industry Am., Am. Assn. Nurserymen. Roman Catholic. Home: 1520 S Thomas Rd Saginaw MI 48603 Office: 1019 N Center Rd Saginaw MI 48603

MC DONALD, SHARON JOY, educator; b. Farmington, Mo., Jan. 15, 1948; B.S. in Edn., U. Mo., 1969; M.S. in Edn., Kans. State U., 1973; m. Gayle McDonald; 1 son, Leslie. Tchr. educable mentally retarded Ottumwa (Iowa) schs., 1969, Washington (Iowa) schs., 1969-71, Holton (Kans.) Unified Sch. Dist. 336, 1971-73; tchr. educable mentally retarded Holton Spl: Edn. Coop., 1973-76. Pres. Jackson County Assn. Retarded Citizens. Mem. NEA. Kans., Holton (negotiations com. 1974—) edn. assns. Club: Pilot (pres.) (Holton). Cert. as tchr., Kans., Iowa, Mo.; specialist in educable mentally retarded. Office: Holton Jr Middle Sch Spl Edn Holton KS 66436

MC DONALD, SHIRLEY PETERSON, social worker; b. Indpls., July 7, 1934; d. Harry and Marcella Iona (Kober) Peterson; B.A., Denison U., 1956; teaching credentials Chgo. State U., Nat. Coll. Edn., Prairie State U.; M.S.W., U. Ill., 1976; m. Stanford Laurel McDonald, Apr. 26, 1964; children—Stacia Elizabeth Virginia, Jeffrey Jared Stern, Kathleen Shirley, Patricia Marie. Tchr., Chgo. Public Schs., 1962-64, Flossmoor, Ill., 1972-74; communication devel. program social worker S. Met. Assn., Harvey, Ill., 1976-79; sch. social worker S.W. Cook County Coop. Spl. Edn., Oak Forest, Ill., 1979—. Religious edn. dir. All Souls Unitarian Ch., 1968-71; religious edn. dir. Unitarian Community Ch., Park Forest, 1975-79, bd. dirs., 1978-81, chmn. bldg. feasibility com., 1981, chmn. bldg. com., 1981—, also adv. to bd. Mem. Acad. Cert. Social Workers, Nat. Assn. Social Workers, Ill. Assn. Sch. Social Workers (area rep.; mem. com. consultation service, program com. state conf. 1981, adv. 1981-83), Kappa Kappa Gamma, Women's Internat. League Peace and Freedom (past chpt. pres.), Pi Sigma Alpha. Home: 255 Rich Rd Park Forest IL 60466

MC DONALD, STANFORD LAUREL, clin. psychologist, educator; b. Lincoln, Nebr., Mar. 14, 1929; s. Laurel C. and Irene V. (Frey) McD.; A.B., Nebr. Wesleyan U., 1956; M.A., U. Nebr., 1959; Ph.D., Fielding Inst., 1974; m. Shirley P. Peterson, Apr. 26, 1964; children—Stacia E.V., Jeffrey J.S., Kathleen S., Patricia M. Intern, Nebr. Psychiatric Inst., Omaha, 1957-58; staff psychologist Presbyn. St. Luke's Hosp., Chgo., 1960-61; psychologist Chgo. Bd. Edn., 1961-65; supr. psychol. services SPEED, Chicago Heights, Ill., 1965-79; clin. psychologist, pres. Stanford L. McDonald, Ph.D., Olympia Fields, Ill., 1980—; mem. faculty Chgo. Sch. Profl. Psychology, 1978—, Nat. Coll. Edn., Evanston, Ill., 1969—; lectr. Ind. U., 1968-71. Bd. dirs. South Suburban Epilepsy Soc., 1978—. Served with USMC, 1950-52. Fellow Am. Orthopsychiat. Assn.; mem. Am., Midwestern, Ill. psychol. assns., Acad. Psychologists in Marital, Sex and Family Therapy, Biofeedback Soc. Am., Biofeedback Soc. Ill. (past pres.), Soc. Behavioral Medicine, N.Y. Acad. Scis., Zeta Psi, Phi Delta Kappa, Psi Chi. Home: 255 Rich Rd Park Forest IL 60466 Office: 2555 W Lincoln Hwy Olympia Fields IL 60461

MC DONALD, STANLEIGH BUELL, mfg. co. exec.; b. St. Louis, Feb. 3, 1924; s. Buell Barger and Ruth Matilda (Pearson) McD.; B.S. in Bus. Adminstrn., Butler U., 1948; postgrad. Law Sch. Ind. U., 1948-51; m. Mary Ann Culhan, May 17, 1947; children—Kathryn Ann, Scott Andrew, Bruce David. Chief research project adminstrn. Gen. Motors Corp., Indpls., 1952-62; mgr. tng. and devel. Burroughs Corp., Detroit, 1962-67; mgr. mgmt. devel. div. J.C. Penney Co., N.Y.C., 1967-69; sr. compensation cons. A.S. Hansen, Inc., Chgo., 1970-74; dir. compensation and personnel cons. Coopers & Lybrand, Chgo., 1974-76; v.p. personnel Schnadig Corp., Chgo., 1976-80; mng. dir. Buell Assos., exec. recruitment, 1981—; lectr. Wayne State U., 1962-67, Eastern Mich. U., 1966, N.Y. U., 1967-68. Mem. City Council, Lake Forest, Ill., 1979-82. Served with AUS, 1943-45; ETO. Mem. Am. Compensation Assn., Am. Soc. Tng. and Devel. Presbyterian. Club: Lake Forest (pres. 1974-75). Author: Ten Weeks to A Better Job, 1972. Home: 434 Linden Ave Lake Forest IL 60045 Office: 434 Linden Ave Lake Forest IL 60045

MC DONALD, WILLIAM R., employee-benefits cons.; b. Mt. Vernon, Ill., Nov. 1, 1929; s. Archie R. and Vernadean Pearl (Bailey) McD.; B.S., Ind. State U., 1953; m. Dec. 26, 1953 (div. 1967). Pres., Youth, Inc., Terre Haute, Ind., 1947; dist. mgr. New Eng. Life Ins. Co., Sacramento, 1958-62; v.p. Sutter Sq., Inc., Sacramento, 1960-62; v.p. Southland Trust Co., Tucson, 1963-65; v.p. Am. Equity Group, Inc., Indpls., 1966-68; sr. partner Ins.-Investors' Guidance Systems, Mt. Vernon, 1972—; pres. Interstate Investors & Growers Syndicate, Inc., Indpls., 1975—; mng. partner Halia Crest Land Trust, Mt. Vernon, 1977-79; pres. Intermed. Self-Ins. Group, Mt. Vernon, 1979—; sr. gen. partner Interstate Investors Golf and Garden Solar Lodges, 1980—; dir. Southland Trust Life Ins. Co., Phoenix, 1964; cons. So. Ill. U., Carbondale, 1973. Chmn. United Crusade, Sacramento, 1960; pres. Civitan Internat., Sacramento, 1961; chmn. bd. dirs. Salvation Army, Sacramento, 1961; bd. dirs. USO, 1962. Served with USAF, 1951-57. Recipient Outstanding Flight Officer Achievement cert. USAF, 1957; named Disting. Grad., Aviation Cadets, 1953; U.S. Rookie of Year, New Eng. Life Ins. Co., 1959. Mem. Mt. Vernon C. of C. Republican. Office: PO Box 946 Mount Vernon IL 62864 also Suite 1012 130 E Washington St Indianapolis IN 46204

MC DONNELL, GERALD M., engring. co. exec.; B.S. in Civil Engring., U. Ill.; M.S. in Bus. and Pub. Adminstrn., U. Chgo. Engr. plant design and pollution control, project mgr., sr. civil engr., asso. and asst. civil engr. Met. San. Dist. of Greater Chgo., 1959-69; project mgr. design and constrn. mgmt. div. Roy F. Weston, Inc., 1969-76; v.p., dir. Snell Environ. Group, Indpls., 1976—. Diplomate Am. Acad. Environ. Engrs. Mem. ASCE (chmn. program com. Phila. sect., dir.), Water Pollution Control Fedn., Am. Pub. Works Assn. Contbr. tech. articles to profl. jours. Office: Snell Environmental Group 4930 N Pennsylvania St Indianapolis IN 46205

MC DONNELL, SANFORD NOYES, aircraft co. exec.; b. Litte Rock, Oct. 12, 1922; s. William Archie and Carolyn (Cherry) McD.; B.A. in Econs., Princeton U., 1945; B.S. in Mech. Engring., U. Colo., 1948; M.S. in Applied Mechanics, Washington U., St. Louis, 1954; m. Priscilla Robb, Sept. 3, 1946; children—Robbin McDonnell MacVittie, William Randall. With McDonnell Douglas Corp. (formerly McDonnell Aircraft Corp.), St. Louis, 1948—, v.p., 1959-66, pres. McDonnell Aircraft div., 1966-71, corp. exec. v.p., 1971, corp. pres., 1971-80, corp. chmn., 1980—, chief exec. officer, 1972—, also dir.; dir. First Union, Inc., St. Louis. Active St. Louis United Way; exec. bd. St. Louis council Boy Scouts. Fellow AIAA; mem. Aerospace Industries Assn. (gov.), Navy League U.S. (life), Am. Helicopter Soc., Assn. U.S. Army, Air Force Assn., C. of C. U.S., Armed Forces Mgmt. Assn., Nat. Def. Transp. Assn., Am. Ordnance Assn., Am. Security Council, Nat. Aero. Assn., Tau Beta Pi. Presbyterian (trustee, elder). Office: McDonnell Douglas Corp PO Box 516 Saint Louis MO 63166

MCDONOUGH, JAMES JOSEPH, JR., clin. psychologist; b. Mpls., June 9, 1947; s. James Joseph and Mary Josephine (Gangl) McD.; B.A. in Psychology, Coll. of St. Thomas, St. Paul, 1969; Ph.D., U. Minn., 1975; m. Jean Catherine Hewitt, Aug. 22, 1981. Psychologist, Mt. Sinai Hosp., Mpls., 1972-73; instr., project dir. Center for Youth Devel. and Research, U. Minn., St. Paul, 1974-76; psychol. cons. Abbott-Northwestern Hosp., Mpls., 1977-81; exec. dir. McDonough & Assos., Mpls. and St. Paul, 1977—; adj. asso. prof. St. Mary's Coll., Winona, Minn., 1977—, Coll. of St. Thomas, 1978—. Bd. dirs. Urban Coalition Mpls., 1976-77; mem. St. Louis Park (Minn.) Human Rights Commn., 1978—, St. Louis Park Chem. Dependency Task Force, 1979—. NIMH grantee, 1970-74. Mem. N. Am. Soc. Adlerian Psychology, Am. Psychol. Assn., Can. Psychol. Assn., Minn. Psychol. Assn., Nat. Com. Prevention of Child Abuse, U. Minn. Alumni Assn., Planetary Soc., Minn. Sci. Mus. Author: The Self-Evaluation Method for Hotlines and Youth Crisis Centers, 1976; also articles. Home: 2840 Cavell Ave S Saint Louis Park MN 55426 Office: 3015 Utah Ave S Saint Louis Park MN 55426

MCDOWELL, ALMA SUE, fin. exec.; b. Bedford, Ind., Oct. 16, 1942; d. Claude Edward and Lydia Helen McD.; B.S., Ind. U., 1978, also postgrad. Calculating clk., assigned risk examiner Grain Dealers Mut. Ins. Co., Indpls., 1960-62; with Keach & Grove Ins. Agy., Inc., Bedford, 1962-65; account clk., acctg. mgr. Purdue U., Indpls., 1965-71; fin. asst. to dean adminstrv. affairs Ind.-Purdue U., Indpls., 1971-75; asst. bus. mgr. Ind. U.-Purdue U., Indpls. Center Advanced Research, Inc., from 1975, now controller, dir. central adminstrv. services. Asst. treas. E. 38th St. Christian Ch., mem. exec. com. planning 5-state singles seminar; vol. VA Hosp. Mem. Nat. Assn. Accountants. Republican. Home: 5402 E 20th Pl Indianapolis IN 46218 Office: 1219 W Michigan St Indianapolis IN 46202

MC DOWELL, DANIEL QUINCE, JR., airline agt.; b. Bklyn., Dec. 6, 1949; s. Daniel Quince and Amelia (DeFreese) McD.; A.S., Ill. Central Coll., 1977; B.S., Bradley U., 1980; m. Lesa Belle Wurmnest, July 5, 1980. Sr. rep. ground services Overseas Nat. Airways, N.Y.C., 1967-70; sta. agt. Ozark Airlines, Peoria, Ill., 1971-81, Mpls., 1981-82; freelance photographer; pvt. pilot. Dep. comdr. CAP, search and rescue pilot, 1977-80, comdr., 1980—, Air N.G. liaison officer. Served with USAF, 1970-71; Vietnam. Decorated Nat. Def. medal, others. Mem. Asso. Photographers Internat., Air Force Assn., Aircraft Owners and Pilots Assn., Am. Soc. Aerospace Edn., Midstate Air Inc., U.S. Air Force Mus., Am. Def. Preparedness Assn. Roman Catholic. Patentee in field. Office: Ozark Airlines Greater Peoria Airport Peoria IL 61607

MC DOWELL, JAMES, chem. products mfg. co. exec., mech. engr.; b. Belfast, N. Ireland, Sept. 16, 1929; s. Robert and Margaret (Kernaghan) McD.; came to U.S., 1957, naturalized, 1964; student Lurgan Tech. Jr. Coll., Ireland, 1948-49; B.S. in Mech. Engring., Belfast Coll., 1950-56; postgrad. Ill. Inst. Tech., 1958-59; m. Mildred Isabel McShane, July 17, 1954; children—Colwyn James, Craig Jay. Research engr., Scully Jones & Co., Chgo., 1957-59; dir. equipment research/devel. Diversey Corp., Chgo., 1959-65; dir. equipment mfg. ops. DuBois Chems., Cin., 1965—; tchr. math. and engring. tech. Lurgan Jr. Coll., Ireland, 1956-57. Commr. of youth soccer in Ohio, 1974-76; head soccer coach U. Cin., 1975—; chmn. of fin. and bldg. Methodist Ch., 1958-65. Recipient citation Materials in Design Engring. mag., 1962. Mem. ASME. Club: Golf. Author: ABC's of Soccer, 1975; contbr. articles on splty. chems. and equipment applications to profl. jours.; patentee in field. Home: 1620 Collinsdale Ave Cincinnati OH 45230 Office: DuBois Tower Cincinnati OH 45202

MC ELENEY, DONALD ARTHUR, dermatologist; b. Clinton, Iowa, Dec. 28, 1924; s. Leo Patrick and Elsie Helen (Bonnemann) McE.; B.A., U. Iowa, 1948, M.D., 1951. Intern, Highland-Alameda County Hosp., Oakland, Calif., 1951-52; resident in dermatology U. Iowa Hosp., 1952-55; practice medicine specializing in dermatology, Cedar Rapids, Iowa, 1958—; preceptor family practice residency program Mercy and St. Luke's Hosps., Cedar Rapids. Served with U.S. Army, 1943-46. Fellow Am. Acad. Dermatology; mem. AMA, Iowa State, Linn County med. socs., Iowa Dermatol. Soc., N. Am. Clin. Dermatol. Soc., Internat. Soc. Tropical Dermatology. Roman Catholic. Club: Cedar Rapids Rotary. Home: 1718 Applewood Pl NE Cedar Rapids IA 52402 Office: 2720 1st Ave NE Cedar Rapids IA 52402

MC ELROY, RICHARD LEE, magazine editor, educator; b. Smithfield, Ohio, Jan. 16, 1947; s. Lee Montgomery and Virginia (Cooper) McE.; B.S., Kent State U., 1969, M.Ed., 1975; postgrad. U. Akron, 1976-77; m. Pamela Harris, June 17, 1967; children—Matthew, Rachael, Luke. Tchr., Stow (Ohio) High Sch., 1970-72; social studies tchr. N. Canton (Ohio) Portage Sch., 1972—; editor Ohio Cues Mag., 1974—; editor, pub. Buckeye Flyer, 1977-80, Plainly Speaking; sports coach, 1969—. Officer Christ United Presbyn. Ch.; pres. Canton Recreation Leagues, 1975-76; active Philomatheon Soc. for the Blind, Muscular Dystrophy Assn., YMCA, Canton Urban League; mem. bicentennial com. Kent State U., 1976-77; co-chmn., county coordinator Anderson for Pres., 1980. Mem. Ohio Hist. Soc., Stark County Hist. Soc., Ohio High Sch. Coaches Assn., Ohioana Library Assn., Ohio Edn. Assn., N. Canton Heritage Soc., Ohio Council Social Studies, North Canton and Plain Twp. Jaycees (numerous awards; chpt. pres., state dir.), U.S. Hang Gliding Assn., Cleve. Indians Wahoo Club. Republican. Author: The Best of Baseball Trivia. Contbr. articles to publs. including Western Res. Mag., Ohioana Monthly, Ohio Cues, Buckeye Flyer, local newspapers, 1974—. Home: 3751 Shanabruck NW Canton OH 44709 Office: Portage School 239 Portage St North Canton OH 44720

MC ELWAIN, JOHN ALLEN, printing co. exec.; b. Chgo., July 7, 1901; s. Frank and Bertha (Thompson) McE.; student Dartmouth Coll., 1920-22, Northwestern U., 1923; m. Jane Catherine McKenna, Apr. 3, 1926; children—Edward Frank, Phyllis Jane (Mrs. Richard Forward), John Allen IV. Tool draftsman Miehle Printing Press Corp., Chgo., 1923-24; rodman Chgo. North Shore & Milw. R.R., Chgo., 1924; circulation mgr. Toys and Novelties, Am. Artisan, Chgo., N.Y.C., 1925-27; sales engr. U.S. Gypsum Co., Chgo., 1927-33; pres. John A. McElwain & Co., Chgo., 1933—. Trustee Hinsdale (Ill.) San. Dist., 1949—, pres., 1957—; chmn. DuPage County Drainage Com., 1955-56; precinct committman DuPage County Republican Com., 1940-60. John A. McElwain Water Reclamation Facility named in his honor. Mem. Ill. Assn. San. Dist. Trustees (pres. 1960-61, 79-80, Ill. award 1979), Chgo. Tennis Assn. (dir. 1942-52, pres. 1949), Kappa Sigma. Club: Hinsdale (Ill.) Golf. Home: 714 S Washington St Hinsdale IL 60521 Office: 231 S Green St Chicago IL 60607

MCELYEA, LOU ANN, automated systems cons. co. exec.; b. Poplar Bluff, Mo., Sept. 10, 1946; d. Arthur Eugene and Hazel Irene (Trosper) McE.; B.S., Washington U., St. Louis, 1975; postgrad. Lindenwood Coll., 1979—. Dir. adminstrv. services Washington U., 1972-77; account exec. Bache, Halsey-Stuart Shields, Inc., St. Louis, 1977-78; project mgr. office systems dept. Mallinckrodt, Inc., St. Louis, 1978-80; pres., founder Info. Systems, Inc., St. Louis, 1980—.

Mem. Internat. Word Processing Assn. (dir. 1980-81, v.p. 1980-81, nat. cons. council), Adminstrv. Mgmt. Soc., Womens Commerce Assn. St. Louis, Alpha Sigma Lambda. Baptist. Office: Information Systems Inc 909 Feefee Rd Maryland Heights MO 63043

MC ENANY, PATRICK GERALD, assn. exec.; b. Davenport, Iowa, Nov. 2, 1942; s. Leonard Dale and Mary Eileen (O'Hare) McE.; B.A. in Polit. Sci., U. Iowa, 1967; M.A. in Guidance and Counseling, Roosevelt U., 1975. Admissions officer Cornell Coll., Mt. Vernon, Iowa, 1969-70; tchr. social scis. Oak Park (Ill.) Elem. Sch. Dist., 1971-78; research and devel. specialist Inst. of Fin. Edn., Chgo., 1978—. Served with U.S. Army, 1967-69. Mem. Am. Soc. for Tng. and Devel., Am. Polit. Sci. Assn. Editor: Personal Awareness in Business: Reading, Problems and Activities, 1979; Political Action, 1979. Office: Inst Fin Edn 111 E Wacker Dr Chicago IL 60601

MC ENROE, PATRICIA SOLON, land mgmt. investor; b. Algona, Iowa, Nov. 19, 1922; d. John Edward and Kathryn Leone (Solon) McE.; student Briar Cliff Coll., 1942-44; B.M.E., M.Mus., Northwestern U., 1948. With Iowa Sch. for Braille and Sight Saving, Vinton, 1948-51, Chgo. Day Sch., 1951-52, Chgo. Bd. Edn., 1952-54; tchr. music and sci. Dover (Minn.) Consol. Schs., 1954-55; music supr. Fountain (Colo.) Pub. Schs.; rep. Chgo. Archdiocese, Chgo. Pub. Schs., 1965-70; investor land in Iowa, Ariz., Calif. and Fla., also investor oil explorations. Recreational dir., Evanston, Ill., 1948, Algona, 1951; founder Kossuth County Democratic Women's Club, 1962; participant Iowa Women's Polit. Caucus. Mem. AAUW, Kossuth County Hist. Soc., Themis Soc., Delphian Soc., NOW, Dorian Soc., Rochester Civic Music Guild. Roman Catholic. Clubs: Ill. Cath. for Women, Sheil. Composer: Rhapsody Ragtime Blues, 1973. Home: 408 N Thorington St Algona IA 50511

MC EVERS, ROBERT DARWIN, banker; b. Washington, May 18, 1930; s. John Henry and Beatrice (Holton) McE.; B.S. with distinction, U.S. Naval Acad., 1952; M.B.A. with distinction, Harvard U., 1958; m. Joan Manning, Mar. 29, 1954; children—Robert Darwin, Allison Holton. With First Nat. Bank of Chgo., 1958-61; spl. asst., exec. offices Trans Union Corp. (formerly Union Tank Car Co.), Chgo., 1961-64, gen. mgr. Canadian subsidiary, Toronto, Ont., 1964, asst. to pres., Chgo., 1964-65, v.p., gen. mgr. Tank Car div., 1965-70, pres., 1970-73; v.p. Trans Union Corp., 1965-73, dir., 1966-73; sr. v.p. 1st Nat. Bank, Chgo., 1973-75, head trust dept., 1974-77, exec. v.p., 1975—, head exec. dept., 1977-81, head bldg./security dept., 1981—; pres. Ft. Dearborn Income Securities, Inc., 1973-77; dir. Marquette Co., Reading Industries, Inc. Bd. dirs. Central YMCA Community Coll., AMFUND. Served to 1st lt. USAF, 1952-56. Mem. Am. Mgmt. Assn., Chgo. Council Fgn. Relations, Newcomen Soc. N.Am., Beta Theta Pi. Clubs: Economic, Mid-Am., University, Mid-Day (Chgo.); Army-Navy Country (Arlington, Va.); Kenilworth (Ill.); Indian Hill (Winnetka, Ill.). Office: One First Nat Plaza Chicago IL 60670

MCEWEN, BOB, congressman; b. Hillsboro, Ohio, Jan. 12, 1950; B.B.A. in Econs., U. Miami, 1972; m. Liz McEwen, 1976. Vice pres. Boebinger, Inc.; mem. 97th Congress from 6th Ohio Dist.; mem. Ohio Ho. of Reps., 1974-80. Mem. Farm Bur., Gideons, Grange, Jaycees, Sigma Chi. Republican. Clubs: Optimist, Rotary. Address: Room 507 Cannon House Office Bldg Washington DC 20515*

MC FADDEN, DANIEL, mining contractor; b. Evansville, Ind., Sept. 3, 1940; s. John Hanie and Agnes Edith (Notter) McF.; E.M., Colo. Sch. Mines, 1963; m. Sandra McGowen, Feb. 6, 1964; children—Kimberly Ann, Shane Michael. Engr., Patrick Harrison, Inc., Denver, 1963-64; asst. supt. F.H. Linneman, Inc., Denver, 1964-65; pres. Frontier Constructors, Inc., Evergreen, Colo., 1965-79; partner, constrn. mgr. Frontier-Kemper Constructors, Evansville, Ind., 1974—. Mem. AIME. Clubs: Oak Meadow Country, Petroleum, Kennel, Elks. Home: Route 7 Box 342F Evansville IN 47712

MCFADDEN, MARILYN JOYCE, educator; b. Otterbein, Ind., July 10, 1937; d. Dale Arley and Wanda Imogene (Simons) Bowers; B.S. in Elem. Edn., Ball State U., 1959; postgrad. U. Hawaii, summer, 1960; M.S. in Edn., Purdue U., 1974; m. Robert D. McFadden, July 31, 1963; children—Beth Ellen, Diane Carol, Jill Elaine. Tchr., Crown Point (Ind.) Community Sch. Corp., 1959—, tchr. Dwight D. Eisenhower Elem. Sch., 1972—, also career edn. cons.; state reviewer for reading textbook adoptions, 1977-78, Career Edn. Grant Proposals, 1979. Mem. Ind. Career Edn. State adv. council, 1979—; mem. Ind. Educators for Reagan-Bush Com., 1980, Educators for Harold Negley, 1980. Named Ind. Tchr. of Yr., Ind. Dept. Public Instrn., 1976; Outstanding Tchr.'s Coll. Alumni, Ball State U., 1976; Ind. Career Edn. State Adv. Council service award, 1981. Mem. Young Authors Conf. (chmn. 1978), Internat. Reading Assn., Ind. Internat. Reading Assn. (rec. sec., state council 1979-80), Kankakee Valley Reading Council (corr. sec. 1974-75, pres. 1976-77), Assn. for Supervision and Curriculum Devel., Ind. Assn. for Supervision and Curriculum, Nat. State Tchrs. of Yr. (v.p. 1980-81, pres. 1981-82), NEA, Ind. Edn. Assn. Republican. Methodist. Home: 508 Mary Ln Crown Point IN 46307 Office: 1450 S Main St Crown Point IN 46307

MC FADDEN, MARY FRASER, personnel specialist; b. Victoria, Tex., Nov. 7, 1944; d. Edward S. and Elsie M. (Thomas) F.; B.A., No. Ill. U., 1967, M.A., 1976; children—Todd Fraser Morey, Thomas Harold Morey. Asst. dir., coordinator Admission Publ. No. Ill. U., DeKalb, Ill., 1971-73; mgr. corporate pub. relations DEKALB AgResearch, Inc., 1974-77; dir. personnel GTE Automatic Electric, Genoa, Ill., 1977-80, EEO adminstr., Northlake, Ill., 1981—. Sec.-treas. DeKalb County Personnel Assn., 1976-77, 2d v.p., 1977, 1st v.p., 1978, pres., 1979; mem. mktg.-mgmt. adv. bd. Kishwaukee Community Coll., 1976—, mem. career guidance adv. bd., 1978—; mem. Kishwaukee Secretarial and Office Adv. Com., 1978—; mem. vocat. edn. adv. council Genoa-Kingston High Sch., 1978—. Mem. Am. Soc. for Personnel Adminstrn. Office: 400 N Wolf Northlake IL 60164

MC FADDEN, WILLIAM PATRICK, banker; b. Chgo., Apr. 17, 1945; s. William Paul and Sara Margaret McF.; B.S. in Indsl. Engring., Purdue U., 1967; M.B.A., Loyola U., Chgo., 1970; m. Nancy J. Gottschalk, Nov. 17, 1973. Engr., Grumman Aerospace Corp., Bethpage, N.Y.; v.p. institutional banking Am. Nat. Bank of Chgo., 1971—. Mem. adv. bd. Chgo. Civic Fedn.; dir. Camp Fire, Inc., Chgo. Met. Council. Mem. Am. Bankers Assn., Am. Mgmt. Assn. Republican. Club: Lion. Office: American National Bank 33 N LaSalle Chicago IL 60532

MC FARLAND, CHARLES WARREN, chemist; b. Schenectady, N.Y., Jan. 24, 1942; s. George Leonard Jr. and Rosalind Kenway (Lewis) M.; A.B., Oberlin Coll., 1964; postgrad. N.Mex. State U., 1964-66; Ph.D., Case Western Res. U., 1971; m. Anne Southworth, June 9, 1964; 1 son, Michael Edward. Sr. research asst. biology dept. Case Western Res. U., Cleve., 1971-72, research asso., chemistry dept., 1972-73; postdoctoral research asso. Cuyahoga County Coroner's Office, Cleve., 1972-73; research chemist R.O. Hull & Co., Cleve., 1973-75, research mgr., 1975-77, tech. asst. to research dir., 1977—; cons. in field. NASA trainee, 1965-66; NIH predoctoral research fellow, 1968-70. Mem. Am. Chem. Soc., Am. Electroplaters Soc., Am. Inst. Chemists, AAAS, Ohio Acad. Sci., Am. Soc. for Info. Sci., Soc. for Applied Spectroscopy, Sigma Xi. Contbr. articles to profl. jours. Patentee in field. Home: 2905 Scarborough Rd Cleveland Heights OH 44118 Office: 3203 W 71st St Cleveland OH 44102

MCFARLAND, CLAUDETTE, corp. exec., lawyer, sociologist, minister; b. St. Louis, Dec. 8, 1935; B.A., Roosevelt U., 1958; LL.B., N.C. Central U., 1965, J.D., 1970; M.S.W., U. Ill., 1971, M.A. in Bus. Adminstrn., 1973, Ph.D. in Sociology, 1977; m. Vernon A. Winstead, 1964; children—Claudette, Vernon A. Automobile saleswoman, 1956; social worker, 1957; real estate broker, 1959; probation officer Cook County Juvenile Ct., Chgo., 1961; pres. McFarland Enterprises, Inc., real estate mgmt. and investments, Chgo., 1962—; v.p. V.A.W. Industries, Inc., indsl. janitorial and maintenance contractors, Chgo., 1971—; pres. Multi-Media Services, public relations and advt. firm; atty. Chgo. Dwellings of Chgo. Housing Authority, 1972; ordained minister Universal Life Ch., 1978; co-founder, co-pastor Holy Family United in God 1st Ch. and Soc.; cons. Chgo. Dept. Housing, 1980—. Exec. bd. Girl Scouts U.S.A.; dir. Provident Hosp. Women's Aux.; exec. bd. Chgo. Beautiful Com.; trustee DuSable Mus. African Am. History; exec. bd. LWV; White House cons. Women and Minority Affairs and Status of ERA, 1979; cons., participant White House Conf. on Minority Human Experimentation, 1975; co-founder, dir. South Shore Sr. Citizens Center, sponsor, participant youth and sr. citizens programs, 1975—; mem. consumer adv. bd. Chgo. Defender newspaper; mem. exec. bd. South Shore Commn. Recipient numerous awards and citations for civic work including outstanding achievement award Nat. Council Negro Women, 1972, 73, 75, public service award Sta. WAUT, Nat. Council Jewish Women, outstanding woman award Tau Gamma Delta, 1975, Outstanding Women of Yr. award Girl Scouts of Chgo., 1975. Mem. Nat. Council Negro Women (pres. Chgo. chpt.), South Shore Ministerial Assn. (v.p. 1980-82), Nat. Assn. Women in Ministry (asst. nat. dir.), NAACP (life), PUSH, Chgo. Urban League, Chgo. Restaurant Assn., Ill. Restaurant Assn., Nat. Bar Assn., Am. Bar Assn., Nat. Council Jewish Women, Women's Internat. League for Peace and Freedom, Chgo. Council Fgn. Relations, Ch. Women United, Nat. Links, Inc., Women in Community Service Assn., Jack and Jill Am. (chmn. Chgo.), Citizens of Greater Chgo. Council, Tau Gamma Delta (life), Alpha Kappa Alpha (life). Office: Suite 925 7426 S Constance Ave Chicago IL 60649 also 407 S Deaborn St Chicago IL 60605 *

MCFARLAND, KAY ELEANOR, state justice Kans.; b. Coffeyville, Kans., July 20, 1935; d. Kenneth W. and Margaret E. (Thrall) McF.; B.A. magna cum laude, Washburn U., Topeka, 1957, J.D., 1964. Admitted to Kans. bar, 1964; pvt. practice, Topeka, 1964-71; probate and juvenile judge Shawnee County, Topeka, 1971-73; dist. judge, Topeka, 1973-77; justice Kans. Supreme Ct., 1977—; owner, operator Quilts by Kay McFarland, Topeka, 1961-64. Mem. Am., Kans., Topeka bar assns., Dist. Judges Assn., Nat. Assn. Juvenile Judges, Nat. Assn. Probate Judges. Home: 4401 W 10th St Topeka KS 66604 Office: Supreme Ct Kansas State House Topeka KS 66612*

MCFARLAND, SUZANNE LOUISE, educator; b. Harrisburg, Pa., Aug. 27, 1942; d. John David and Dorothy Louise (Lauer) Dickson; B.S., Millersville State Coll., 1964; M.Ed., Temple U., 1967; D.Ed., Ind. U., 1976; m. Bruce Ludwig, Mar. 13, 1965; children—Matthew, Jonathan. Tchr., Penn Manor Sch. Dist., Millersville, Pa., 1964-65; tchr., counselor Coatesville (Pa.) Sch. Dist., 1965-72; tchr., intern, instr. Ind. U., Bloomington, 1972-75; asst. prof. edn. Miami U., Oxford, Ohio, 1975-76; asso. prof. U. Toledo, 1976—. Vice pres. Toledo YWCA, 1971-73, chmn. day care adv. com., 1979—. Recipient grants U. Toledo, Ind. U., Phi Lambda Theta. Mem. Ohio Assn. Edn. Young Children (pres. 1981-83), Toledo Assn. Edn. Young Children (pres. 1978-80), Advocates for Young Children for Spl. Needs (founding), World Future Soc., Ohio Assn. Gifted, Assn. Supervision and Curriculum Devel., Assn. Gifted. Home: 3441 Deepwood Dr Lambertville MI 48144 Office: U Toledo Sch Edn Toledo OH 43606

MC FARLAND, TERRY LYNN, constrn. co. exec.; b. Knoxville, Tenn., July 8, 1947; s. Jacob E. and Virginia Kay (Allen) McF.; student Ind. U., 1969-70; m. Hazel C. Davis, Nov. 1, 1975. Prodn. control staff R.R. Donnelley & Sons, Warsaw, Ind., 1965-68; insp. Bendix Corp., South Bend, Ind., 1968-69; mgr. Wickes Bldgs. div. Wickes Corp., Argos, Inc., 1970-71, Crawfordsville, Ind., 1971-73, Macon, Ga., 1973-76, dist. mgr. Ill., Ind., Mich., Wis., 1976-79, mgr. Wickes bdgs. ops. in S.C., 1979-80; v.p., gen. mgr. Douglass Bldg. Service, Inc., Columbia, S.C., 1980-81; ter. mgr. Butler Mfg. Co., Kansas City, Mo., 1981—. Served with U.S. Army, 1966-68; Korea. Mem. Am. Legion, Nat. Geog. Soc. Democrat. Clubs: Moose, Masons, Scottish Rite, Shriners. Office: 7400 E 13th St Kansas City MO 64126

MCFARREN, ANN ELISABETH, health agy. exec.; b. Detroit, July 6, 1937; d. Paul Stevens and Grace Bigby; B.S. in Nursing, U. Mich., 1959; divorced; children—Stanley William Larmee, Jr., Kimberly Ann Larmee. Staff nurse for doctors, Ann Arbor, Mich., 1959-61; nurse Washtenaw County League Planned Parenthood, Ann Arbor, 1959-62; exec. dir. Planned Parenthood Assn. N.W. Ind., Merrillville, 1964—; project developer Planned Parenthood Fedn. Am., N.Y.C., 1967; cons. in field. Bd. dirs. N.W. Ind. Symphony Soc. Mem. Am. Assn. Sex Educators, Counselors and Therapists, Am. Public Health Assn., ACLU. Club: Columbia (Indpls.). Author articles in field. Home: 8253 Howard Ave Munster IN 46321 Office: 8645 Connecticut Ave Merrillville IN 46410

MCFATRICH, CHARLES MICHAEL, agronomist; b. Sedalia, Mo., Dec. 12, 1952; s. Charles Herbert and Dorothy Elizabeth McFatrich; student U. Tex., Arlington, 1970-71; B.A., U. Mo., 1974; M.S., Oreg. State U., 1977. Seed technology researcher U. Mo., Columbia, 1977-78; soybean researcher, plant breeder McCurdy Seed Corp., Fremont, Iowa, 1978-81, soybean ops. mgr., 1978-81; dir. tech. services and research Schettler Seed, Inc., Carroll, Iowa, 1981—; vis. lectr. genetics Indian Hills Coll., Ottumwa, Iowa, 1978-81. Mem. Am. Soc. Agronomy, Crop Sci. Soc. Am., Council for Agrl. Sci. and Tech., Nat. Audubon Soc., Whale Protection League, Smithsonian Instn. (asso.), NOW. Contbr. articles on crop mgmt. to profl. publs. Home: 1820 Randall Rd Carroll IA 51401 Office: 626 North Ct Carroll IA 51401

MC GADY, DONALD LAWRENCE, elec. engr.; b. Chgo., July 22, 1947; s. David Lawrence and Irene Veronica (O'Connor) McG.; B.S. in Elec. Engring., Chgo. Tech. Coll., 1974; m. Joan May Bachman, Sept. 5, 1970; children—Jody Katherine, Donald Lawrence Carlson, Noel Veronica-Clare, Ryan David. Elec. supr. Mercy Hosp. and Med. Center, Chgo., 1969-73, mng. elec. engr., 1973-76, asst. dir. engring., 1976-78; asst. dir. engring. Ill. Masonic Med. Center, Chgo., 1978-80, dir. engring., 1980—. Mem. IEEE, Bio-med. Engring. Group, Industry Application Soc., Elec. Maint. Engrs., Ill. Fire Chiefs Assn., Internat. Assn. Elec. Inspectors, Am. Soc. for Hosp. Engring. of Am. Hosp. Assn., Kappa Sigma Kappa. Roman Catholic. Inventor in field of computerized monitoring, data logging and control system for hosp. sterilization equipment. Home: 7827 Pine Pkwy Darien IL 60559 Office: 836 W Wellington Chicago IL 60657

MCGANN-GILLILAND, MARLENE, nurse; b. Hartford, S.D., Dec. 19, 1928; d. William Fred and Frieda Goldie (Lueth) Reuter; B.S., Augustana Coll., 1950; M.S., George Washington U., 1958; M.S.N., Vanderbilt U., 1974; postgrad. U. N.Mex., 1971-73; m. Robert F. Gilliland, May 29, 1976; children by previous marriage—Paul McGann, Kevin McGann. Asst. prof. Augustana Coll., Sioux Falls, S.D., 1967-70; asst. prof. to asso. prof. U. N.Mex., Albuquerque, 1970-73; clin. specialist Sioux Valley Hosp., Sioux Falls, 1975-78, dir. health edn., dir. Hypertension Clinic, 1978—; asso. prof. S.D. State U.; cons. to nursing homes; speaker in field; med. adv. bd. Juvenile Diabetic Assn., 1975-80; mem. categorization com. S.D. Dept. Health, 1975-80, v.p. hypertension adv. council, 1980-81. health projects chmn. Med. Aux., 1978-80. Mem. Encore; bd. dirs. Center for Women, 1981; mem. edn. com. Am. Cancer Soc., 1981. Served with Nurses Corps, U.S. Army, 1951-52. Mem. Am. Nurses Assn. (cert. adult nurse practitioner), Am. Hosp. Assn. (pres. Minnehaha unit 1979—), Sigma Xi, Sigma Theta Tau. Republican. Lutheran. Clubs: Westward Ho Country, Elks Aux. Contbr. articles profl. jours. Home: 1510 S Center Ave Sioux Falls SD 57105 Office: 1100 S Euclid Ave Sioux Falls SD 57105

MCGANNON, JOHN BARRY, univ. adminstr.; b. Humboldt, Kans., Apr. 18, 1924; s. Patrick J. and Jane Clare (Barry) McG.; B.A., St. Louis U., 1947, M.A., 1952, S.T.L., 1957, Ph.D., 1963. Dean Coll. Arts and Scis., St. Louis U., 1963-73, v.p. for devel., 1977—; v.p. Rockhurst Coll., Kansas City, Mo., 1973-77, prof. ednl. adminstrn. St. Louis U., 1970—; cons. examiner North Central Assn., 1960—. Trustee Regis Coll., 1976—. Mem. Independent Colls. and Univs. Mo., Nat. Assn. Independent Colls. and Univs., Phi Beta Kappa. Roman Catholic. Office: 221 N Grand Blvd St Louis MO 63103

MC GARY, THOMAS HUGH, lawyer; b. Milburn, Ky., Mar. 6, 1938; s. Ollie James and Pauline Elizabeth (Tackett) McG.; A.B., Elmhurst Coll., 1961; J.D., U. Chgo., 1964; m. Madalyn Maxwell, July 4, 1968. Admitted to Ill. bar, 1964; asst. atty. gen. State of Ill., 1965-67, supr. consumer credit, 1967-71; ind. practice law, Springfield, Ill., 1971—; v.p., dir. Citizens Bank of Edinburg (Ill.), 1971—, Bank of Kenney (Ill.), 1977—; instr. Lincolnland Coll., 1970-73; asso. prof. med. humanities So. Ill. U. Sch. Medicine. Mem. Ill. Spl. Com. on Uniform Credit Code, Springfield Art Assn., Springfield Symphony Assn.; mem. Springfield Election Commn.; mem. Ill. Adv. Commn. on Group Ins. Mem. Am., Ill., Sangamon County bar assns., Am. Judicature Soc., 3d House, Sangamon County Hist. Assn., Chgo. Council on Fgn. Relations. Democrat. Episcopalian. Club: Sangamo (Springfield). Home: 1100 Orendorff Pkwy Springfield IL 62704 Office: 600 S 4th St Springfield IL 62703

MCGAUGH, JACK DARWIN, clin. psychologist; b. Holdenville, Okla., Oct. 2, 1939; s. Lonnie Lester and Jalean Leona (Crow) McG.; B.A., U. Okla., 1961, M.S., 1964; student Gestalt Inst. Cleve., 1972-73; Ph.D., U.S. Internat. U., 1974; m. Della LeaAnn Coggins, May 26, 1963; children—Stacy, Eric. Staff psychologist Decatur Mental Health Center, 1964-68; exec. dir. Moultrie County Mental Health Dept., Sullivan, Ill., 1968-72; clin. dir. Shelby County Mental Health Center, Shelbyville, Ill., 1974-76; treatment supr. Genesee County Mental Health Center, Flint, Mich., 1976-77; instr. Millikin U., 1965-70; pvt. practice psychology, Flint, 1977—; cons. Gen. Motors Inst., 1976-77. Mem. Council Community Services, Decatur, Ill., 1964-68. Bd. dirs. Concordia Youth Soccer Club. Mem. Am. Psychol. Assn., Mich. Psychol. Assn., Mich. Soc. Lic. Psychologists, Am. Assn. Biofeedback Clinicians. Home: 414 Chalmers St Flint MI 48503 Office: 400 N Saginaw Suite 300 Flint MI 48502

MCGAW, ROBERT WALTER, city ofcl.; b. Rockford, Ill., Apr. 9, 1923; s. James Lincoln and Loren (Lynch) McG.; B.S., No. Ill. U., 1950, M.S., 1966; m. Margaret Arlene Schindler, June 21, 1946; children—Marlis Jean McGaw Young, Roberta Sue, Raymond William. With Shabhona Pub. Sch., 1950-52; tchr. Harlem Consol. Schs., 1952-72, tchr., 1952-68, adminstr. Rock Cut Sch., Rockford, Ill., 1968-72; mayor of Rockford, 1972—. Chmn. bd. Park Tours, Inc., Rock Cut State Park, Ill., Alderman, City of Rockford, Ill., 1955-63; pres. Ill. Mcpl. League, 1979-80; del. Democratic Conv. 1968, 72, county chmn., 1962-64, candidate lt. gov., 1960. Served with U.S. Army, 1942-46. Mem. Nat., Ill. edn. assn., V.F.W. Clubs: Masons (32 deg.), Shriners, Moose. Home: 2016 E State St Rockford IL 61108 Office: City Hall Bldg 425 E State St Rockford IL 61104

MC GEE, ALETHA KENDRICK, club woman; b. Page County, Iowa, May 12, 1910; d. Miles Thornton and Ora Orieanna (Orme) Kendrick; student public schs., Page County and Villisca, Iowa; m. Lester M. Christensen, Apr. 15, 1934; 1 dau., Janet Lee; m. 2d, Harry F. McGee, Dec. 14, 1947. With May Seed & Nursery, Shenandoah, Iowa, 1927-29; advt. mgr., editor Tyler Echoes, Tyler Bros., Villisca, Iowa, 1929-30; office mgr., bookkeeper Beatrice Foods Co., Villisca, 1930-35; asst. to head voucher dept. Carpenter Paper Co., Omaha, 1940-42; office mgr., cashier bookkeeper Tyler Coca-Cola Co., Villisca, 1942-47; sch. bd. sec. Villisca Community Sch. Dist., 1952-58; statis. typist, asst. to auditor Robert R. Wade, C.P.A., Omaha, 1959-62; sec., bookkeeper Van Horne Investments, Inc., Omaha, 1963-75. Sec. Omaha Republican Woman's Club, 1966-68; precinct chmn. Rep. Party, 1968-72; regent Maj. Isaac Sadler chpt. DAR, 1975-78, charter chaplain of chpt., 1980-82, state chmn. motion picture-TV com., 1976-78, state chmn. Americanism and DAR manuals for citizenship com., 1978-80, nat. vice chmn. motion picture-TV com. N.W. Central div. 1977-80, state chmn. insignia com., 1980-82; mem. Freedoms Found. Valley Forge, Am. Security Council. Methodist. Home: 9103 Susan Circle Omaha NE 68124

MCGEE, DAMOUS EMANUEL, clergyman; b. Fleming, Ky., Sept. 2, 1930; s. Sebastian and Callie (Evans) McG., Jr.; diploma Bible Tng. Inst., 1968; M.S., Old Dominion U., 1970; Th.M., Bible Bapt. Sem., 1952; postgrad. U. Wis., 1971-72, Union Theol. Sem., Va., 1965-66; m. Shirlene Powell, June 14, 1952; 1 dau., Karen Renae. Tchr. public schs., Norfolk and Virginia Beach, Va., 1956-59; internat. dir. Youth for Christ, Greenville, S.C., Ft. Worth, 1950-52; material releaseman Convair-Vultee Air Craft Co., Ft. Worth, 1950-52; ordained to ministry Ch. of God of Prophecy, 1952; pastor Ch. of God of Prophecy, Richmond, Va., 1952-56, Norfolk, 1956-61, Newport News, Va., 1962-70, overseer of Wis., 1970-72, of Calif., 1972-76; pres. Calif. Holding Assn., 1972-76; v.p. West Coast Bible Tng. Inst., Fresno, Calif., 1972-76; overseer Ill. Ch. of God for Propechy, Bartonville, 1976—. Trustee, Tomlinson Coll., 1968-74. Mem. Soc. of Pentecostals. Author: Marriage Booklet, 1968.

MC GEE, JAMES HOWELL, lawyer, mayor; b. Berryburg, W.Va., Nov. 8, 1918; s. Spanish and Perrie (Dalton) McG.; B.S., Wilberforce U., 1941; LL.B., Ohio State U., 1948; m. Elizabeth McCracken, Jan. 23, 1948; children—Annette, Frances. Admitted to Ohio bar, 1949, since practiced in Dayton. Past pres., bd. dirs. Dayton br. NAACP; pres., bd. dirs. Dayton Urban League; commr. City of Dayton, 1967-70, mayor, 1970—. Served with AUS, 1942-45; ETO. Mem. Alpha Phi Alpha. Home: 1518 Benson Dr Dayton OH 45406 Office: 1526 W 3d St Dayton OH 45407

MCGEE, RICHARD BLAINE, ednl. pub. co. exec.; b. Oklahoma City, Apr. 14, 1944; s. William Arthur and Jessie Lulu (Anderson) McG.; student U. Ariz., 1962-63, U. Okla., 1964-65; m. Judith Inez Nix, Dec. 27, 1963; children—Richard Darin, Rhonda Lynn, Jennifer Dawn. With Economy Co., 1963—, plant mgr., dir. traffic, warehousing and distbn., Indpls., 1976—. Mem. Jamestown (Ind.) Bd. Trustees, 1979—; emergency med. technician Jamestown Vol. Fire Dept., 1978—. Democrat. Methodist. Home: 237 W Elm St Jamestown IN 46147 Office: Economy Co 5455 W 84th St Indianapolis IN 46268

MCGEE, WILLIAM HENRY, III, polit. scientist; b. Springfield, Mass., Sept. 4, 1951; s. William H. and Doris M. (Dubie) McG.; B.A., George Washington U., 1973; M.A., U. Mich., 1980, postgrad., 1980—; m. Susan G. Schlobin, Oct. 27, 1974. Research asst. Center

Polit. Studies, Inst. Social Research, U. Mich., Ann Arbor, 1976—; research cons. Brookings Instn., Washington, 1980—; teaching fellow U. Mich., 1976—. Mem. Washtenaw County Domestic Violence Project, 1979—. Mem. Am. Polit. Sci. Assn., Midwest Polit. Sci. Assn. Democrat. Club: AMAZON. Author: (with P.E. Converse, J.D. Dotson and W.J. Hoab) The American Social Attitudes Data Sourcebook, 1947-78, 1980. Home: 511B Longshore St Ann Arbor MI 48105 Office: 4023 Inst Social Research U Mich 426 Thompson St Ann Arbor MI 48109

MC GEEVER, PATRICK JOHN, polit. scientist; b. Johnstown, Pa., May 7, 1938; s. James Joseph and Kathleen Theresa (Hughes) McG.; A.B., St. Louis U., 1963, M.A., 1964, Ph.L., 1964; Ph.D., U. Pa., 1971; m. Mary Rachel Maloney, July 25, 1970; children—Kathleen, Timothy, Brendan. Instr., Scranton Prep. Sch., 1964-67; legislative asst. Phila. City Council, 1969; asst. prof. polit. sci. Ind. U., Indpls., 1971-75, asso. prof., 1975-81, prof., 1981—, dir. overseas study, Dijon, France, 1981—; vis. lectr. polit. sci. Nat. U. Ireland, Galway, 1978; cons. WISH-TV, Indpls., 1975—. Recipient Best Paper award Mo. Acad. Sci. Conv., 1964; Am. Polit. Sci. Assn. fellow, 1968, Ind. Com. Humanities grantee, 1973. Mem. Am. Fedn. Tchrs., Am. Polit. Sci. Assn., AAUP, Common Cause, Caucus for a New Polit. Sci., Midwest Polit. Sci. Assn., Ind. Acad. Social Scis. Author: The United States Governmental System, 1978; Why Government Fails, 1980. Home: 4440 N Central St Indianapolis IN 46205 Office: 925 W Michigan St Indianapolis IN 46202

MC GETTIGAN, BRIAN JEROME, Realtor; b. Darlington, Wis., May 10, 1937; s. William J. and Beryl (Mead) McG.; grad. Wis. Realtors Inst.; m. Josephine A. Palzkill, Sept. 27, 1958; 1 son, Kevin J. Br. mgr. Household Finance Corp., Madison, Wis., 1957-72; realtor Pyramid Realty Inc., Madison, 1971, v.p., gen. mgr., 1972-76, pres., 1976—, also dir.; dir. various cos. Group chmn. United Givers, 1963-66; pres. Cursillo Movement Diocese Madison, 1970; mem. council Parish, 1973-75, chmn. edn. commn., 1974-75, instr. religious edn. High Sch., 1968-75, Immaculate Heart of Mary Cath. Ch., Madison, also pres. Men's Club, 1969. Mem. Realtors Nat. Mktg. Inst. (cert. residential specialist; state pres. 1980, co-chmn. membership Wis. 1976—), Wis. 1976—), Greater Madison Bd. Realtors (dir. 1976, v.p. 1978), Wis. Realtors Assn. (dir. 1978—, state chmn. public relations communications 1981, vice-chmn. state communication public relations com.; mem. Honor Soc. 1979, 80), Madison Builders Assn., Ws. Builders Assn., Nat. Assn. Home Builders, Nat. Assn. Realtors (vice chmn. chpt. growth 1981). Home: 3710 Valley Ridge Rd Middleton WI 53562 Office: 4200 University Ave Suite 2030 Madison WI 53705

MC GETTRICK, WILLIAM JOHN, plastics corp. exec.; b. Chgo., Mar. 14, 1937; s. William Henry and Margaret Mary McGettrick; B.S., Notre Dame U., 1958; postgrad. Northwestern U. Bus. Sch., 1965-66; m. Patricia Loftus, Oct. 6, 1964; children—Brian, Colleen, Leslie. Dist. mgr. indsl. div. Uniroyal, Chgo., 1961-63; sales mgr. comml. div. Powers Regulator Corp., Chgo., 1963-65; v.p. sales Structural Fibers Corp., Chardon, Ohio, 1965-77; pres. Middlefield Corp. (Ohio), 1977—; dir. D. Frank Co., 1978—, Gilliland & Assos., 1978—. Served to 1st lt. USMCR, 1959-61. Mem. Am. Mgmt. Assn., Retail Assn. Am., Water Quality Assn., Am. Hardware Assn., Plastic Pipe Inst. Republican. Roman Catholic. Clubs: Sales and Mktg. Execs. of Cleve.; Madison Country, Grandview Country, Barclay, Exec. of Cleve., Elks. Home: 38105 Dodd's Hill Dr Willoughby Hills OH 44094 Office: Middlefield Corp 15650 Madison Rd Middlefield OH 44062

MC GHEE, JOHN EDWARD, biochemist; b. Gary, Ind., May 29, 1931; s. Willie Wesley and Margarett Eleanor (Dawson) McG.; B.S., Millikin U., Decatur, Ill., 1957; postgrad. Bradley U., Peoria, Ill., Ill. State U., Normal, U.S. Agrl. Research Grad. Sch., Peoria; m. Geraldine Augusta Winfrey, Jan. 30, 1960; children—Laurie Anne, John Wesley, Marcia Lynn, Steven Edward. Analytical chemist Agrl. Research Service No. Regional Research Center, Dept. Agr., Peoria, 1957-60, research biochemist, leader biochem. engring. project, 1960—; cons. to industry and govt. Counselor Boys Clubs of Peoria, Inc., 1965-70, Boy Scouts Am., 1971-77; Peoria area design for leadership officer Millikin U., 1976-77; mem. Peoria Area Air Pollution Adv. and Appeals Bd., 1974-77; judge Nat. Sci. and Engring. Sci. Fair, 1958-77. Recipient Internat. Sci. Competition award, 1974. Mem. Am. Oil Chemists Soc., Am. Assn. Cereal Chemists, Am. Translators Assn., Les Amis de la France (sec.-treas.), Mid-Am. Classical Guitar Soc. Contbr. articles to profl. jours., chpts. in books. French and German interpreter and translator in communication with fgn. scientists. Home: 2224 W Westport Rd Peoria IL 61614 Office: 1815 N University St Peoria IL 61604

MC GHEE, PATRICIA LOUISE OHLSEN, educator; b. Monticello, Wis., Sept. 14, 1934; d. Michael Peter and Alicia Alma (Ellefson) Ohlsen; B.A., U. Ariz., 1956; M.A., Marquette U., 1958; postgrad. U. Wis-Madison, 1972-74; m. John Ferdinan; 2 children. Tchr. social studies pub. schs., Milw., 1960-62, Fox Point-Bayside (Wis.), 1963-67, Shorewood, Wis., 1971-72, Waukesha, Wis., 1974—; tchr. social studies Milw. Area Tech. Coll., 1968-74; participant NEH-Carnegie-Mellon project on social history, summer 1981. Sec. Ozaukee County Democratic party, 1973; participant Wis. Conf. on Arms Control, Wingspread, 1978. Taft fellow, 1975; Newspaper in Edn. scholar, 1980. Mem. Am. Hist. Assn., Hist. Assn., Historians Film Com., Soc. History Edn., Internat. Assn. for Audio-Visual Media in Hist. Research and Edn., U.S. Tennis Assn., Gamma Phi Beta, Pi Gamma Mu. Home: 2802 Buckingham Waukesha WI 53186 Office: 401 E Roberta Ave Waukesha WI 53186

MC GIBBON, EDMUND LEAVENWORTH, lawyer, rancher; b. Grand Rapids, Mich., May 27, 1908; s. William and Franc (Leavenworth) McG.; A.B., Dartmouth Coll., 1929; J.D., Northwestern U., 1933; m. Catherine Jean Klink, Aug. 29, 1941; children—William, Catherine, Bonnie Laurie. Admitted to Ill. bar, 1934, since practiced in Chgo; asso. firm Robertson, Crowe & Spence, 1934-38; partner Robertson & McGibbon, 1947-53, Williston, McGibbon & Stastny, 1953-66, Williston & McGibbon, 1966-71, Williston, McGibbon & Kuehn, 1971—. Chmn. bd. Santa Rita Ranch, Inc. Mem. hon. bd. govs. Scottish Old Peoples Home. Served from lt. to comdr. USNR, 1940-45, comdg. officer destroyer escort; capt. USNR. Mem. Am. Mgmt. Assn. (pres.'s council), Am., Ill., Chgo. bar assns., Nat. Rifle Assn. (life), Aircraft Owners and Pilots Assn., Ill. St. Andrew Soc. (past pres.), Phi Kappa Psi, Phi Alpha Delta. Republican. Episcopalian. Clubs: University, Chicago (Chgo.); Barrington Hills (Ill.) Country; Tucson Country, Old Pueblo (Tucson); Guadalajara (Mexico) Country. Home: Ridge Rd Barrington IL 60010 Office: 20 N Wacker Dr Chicago IL 60606 also 102 N Cook St Barrington IL 60010 also Santa Rita Ranch Box 647 Green Valley AZ 85614

MCGILL, ANDREW RALPH, newspaper exec.; b. Detroit, Sept. 2, 1947; s. Ralph Henry and Dolores Ann (Barto) McG.; student Loyola U., 1968-71; cert. Columbia U. exec. program in bus. adminstrn., 1977; m. Katherine Louise Wunderlich, Aug. 11, 1979; 1 dau., Katherine Louise. News editor UPI, Detroit and Chgo., 1966-72; bus.-fin. editor Miami Hearld, 1973-76; Walter Bagehot fellow in bus. and econs. journalism Columbia U., N.Y.C., 1976-77; asst. to mng. editor The Detroit News, 1977—; guest lectr. U. Mich., 1978—, U. So. Calif., 1979-80, U. N.C., 1981; cons. urban revitalization City of Camden (N.J.), 1981—. Served with USAF, 1966. Recipient Public Service award AP, 1979; W. Averill Harriman scholar Am. Assemblies, 1976-77. Mem. Exec. Assn. of Columbia U. Grad. Sch. Bus., Columbia Alumni Assns. of Detroit and N.Y. Home: 26099 York Rd Huntington Woods MI 48070 Office: 615 W Lafayette St Detroit MI 48231

MCGILL, LARRY DAVID, clergyman; b. Vancouver, B.C., Can., May 19, 1951; s. Kenneth James and Irene Thelma (Bickner) McG.; B.A. in Theology, Pacific Union Coll., 1973; M.A. in Counseling, Loma Linda U., 1975; m. Joanne E. Klopfenstein, June 27, 1976; children—Jeremy David, Michael Seth. Ordained to ministry Seventh-day Adventist Ch., 1977; asso. pastor, dir. youth activities Seventh Day Adventist Ch., Hayward, Calif., 1973; marriage and family counselor, Loma Linda, Calif., 1976; campus pastor, sch. counselor Mt. Ellis Acad., Bozeman, Mont., 1976-78; campus chaplain, counselor Union Coll., Lincoln, Nebr., 1978—; mem. Edn. for Successful Pairing, 1974-76; condr. workshops. Spl. dep. sherriff, Nappa Valley, Calif., 1973; bd. dirs. Lincoln Police Dept., 1979—, police chaplain, 1979—. Mem. Am. Assn. Marriage and Family Counselors, Nat. Council Family Relations, Am. Assn. Pastoral Counselors, Western Interstate Commn. Higher Edn. Home: 5808 NW Gary Lincoln NE 68506 Office: 3800 S 48th St Lincoln NE 68506

MC GILL, SHIRLEY STEFFEN (MRS. JAMES PATRICK MCGILL), antiques dealer; b. St. Louis, Sept. 1, 1925; d. Edward Charles and Claire Marie (Miller) Steffen; student U. Ariz., 1943-45; m. James Patrick McGill, July 14, 1961; children—Dianne (Mrs. Gerald Thomas Gibbons), Claire Miller Codding. Owner, Shirley McGill Antiques, Geneva, Ill., 1962—; exhibitor, mgr. antiques shows, 1962—. Mem. Nat., No. Ill. (dir. 1971-72) assns. dealers in antiques, Chgo. Suburban Antiques Dealers Assn. (pres. 1963-65, dir. 1965-76), Chi Omega. Mem. Order Eastern Star. Home: 323 E Washington St West Chicago IL 60185 Office: 717 E State St Geneva IL 60134

MC GILLEY, SISTER MARY JANET, coll. pres.; b. Kansas City, Mo., Dec. 4, 1924; d. James P. and Peg (Ryan) McG.; B.A., St. Mary Coll., 1945; M.A., Boston Coll., 1951; Ph.D., Fordham U., 1956; postgrad. U. Notre Dame, 1960, Columbia U., 1964. Joined Sisters of Charity of Leavenworth, Roman Catholic Ch., 1946; social worker Catholic Welfare Bur., Kansas City, Mo., 1945-46; tchr. Billings (Mont.) Central High Sch., 1951-53; tchr. Hayden High Sch., Topeka, 1948-50; faculty English dept. St. Mary Coll., Leavenworth, Kans., 1956-64, pres., 1964—; mem. Study Tour Group to People's Republic of China, 1978. Mem. Mayor's Adv. Council, Leavenworth, 1967-72; bd. dirs. United Leavenworth Fund. Mem. Kans. City Regional Council for Higher Edn. (dir.), Kans. Found. for Pvt. Colls. (dir.), Asso. Ind. Colls. Kans. (dir.), Nat. Council Tchrs. English, Assn. Am. Colls. (mem. commn. on liberal learning 1970-73, commn. on curriculum and faculty devel. 1979—), Am. Assn. Higher Edn., Am. Council on Edn. (mem. commn. on women in higher edn. 1980—), Delta Epsilon Sigma. Contbr. poetry, articles, short stores, addresses to nat. jours., lit. mags. Home and Office: Saint Mary Coll Leavenworth KS 66048

MC GINLEY, PATRICK MICHAEL, educator; b. Chgo., June 20, 1949; s. Andrew John and Alice Marie McG.; B.S. in Edn., Quincy Coll., 1971; M.S. in Elem. Edn., Western Ill. U., 1973, Ed.S., 1975. With Turn-Style Family Centers, Chgo., 1965-70, phys. inventory mgr., 1967-70; tchr. Madison Elem. Sch., Quincy, Ill., 1971—. Scoutmaster, Boy Scouts Am., 1972—, camp dir., 1977, 78, 80, 81, cubmaster, 1974-76, mem. scout leader devel. staff, 1978. Recipient award of merit Blackhawk dist. Boy Scouts Am., 1978, Scouter's Key, 1978, Scouter's Tng. award, 1978. Mem. Miss. Valley Reading Council, Quincy Edn. Assn. (pres. 1974-77), Nat. Rifle Assn. Democrat. Roman Catholic. Club: Optimist (v.p. 1978-80). Home: 204 N 25th St Quincy IL 62301 Office: Madison Elem Sch 2435 Maine St Quincy IL 62301

MC GINN, PETER VINCENT, psychologist; b. N.Y.C., July 15, 1948; s. Vincent Edward and Alice Bolton (Mundorff) McG.; B.A., Johns Hopkins U., 1970, M.A., 1975, Ph.D., 1976; M.S., Pa. State U., 1971; m. Marilyn Clare Ricchiuti, Aug. 22, 1970; children—Kathryn Clare, Kerry Elizabeth. USPHS trainee Pa. State U., 1970-71; sch. psychologist Balt. City Public Schs., 1971-73; legis. research fellow Senator Bill Brock, U.S. Senate, 1976; dir./psychologist Alcoholism Center, Bixby Hosp., Adrian, Mich., 1977-80; cons. psychologist Rohrer, Hibler & Replogle, Southfield, Mich., 1980—; cons. Sienna Heights Coll. Counseling Center, Adrian, 1979-80. Chmn. curriculum com. Adrian Bd. Edn., 1979-81; v.p. Assn. Retarded Citizens Lenawee County, 1978; bd. dirs. Mental Health Assn. Met. Balt., 1975-76. Named Outstanding Young Man, U.S. Jr. C. of C., 1979; Boss of Yr., Lenawee County chpt. Am. Bus. Women's Assn., 1979. Mem. Am. Psychol. Assn., Mich. Psychol. Assn., Mich. Assn. Indsl. Organizational Psychologists. Roman Catholic. Club: Civitan. Home: 3260 Bluett St Ann Arbor MI 48105 Office: 200 Mark Plaza 21411 Civic Center Dr Southfield MI 48076

MC GINNIS, JAMES EDWARD, accountant; b. Oxford, Mass., July 31, 1917; s. John James and Jennie Catherine (Fenner) McG.; A.B., Youngstown (Ohio) Coll., 1950; m. Catherine Irene Cronk, July 12, 1941; children—Barbara McGinnis Cash II, Kathleen (Sister Jude McGinnis), Patricia McGinnis Vavrinak, James Brian, John Edward, Robert Michael. Accountant, W.L. Reali, Pub. Accountant, Youngstown, 1945-50; pvt. practice pub. accounting, Youngstown, 1950-80; office mgr. Patterson Buckeye, Inc., North Lima, Ohio, 1950-80, also dir.; exec. v.p., treas. Patterson Buckeye, Inc., 1980—; dir., gen. mgr., exec. v.p., treas. Wolf Food Distbrs., 1980—; income tax preparer; cons. state, county and local taxes. Chmn. Vets. Day Parade, Youngstown, 1970—, chmn. Meml. Day parade, 1971—; chmn. Mahoning County (Ohio) Grave Decorating Com., 1969-81, mem. Civic Day Com., 1970—; Ohio Bicentennial Com., 1974-75, Mahoning County Soldiers and Sailors Relief Commn., 1980-81. Served to sgt. AUS, 1940-45; PTO. C.P.A., Ohio Mem. Amvets (past comdr.), V.F.W., 37th Div. Vets. Assn., D.A.V., United Vets. Council of Mahoning County (comdr. 1972), Nat. Soc. Pub. Accts., Public Accountants Soc. Ohio, Mahoning Valley Gaelic Soc., Irish Nat. Caucus, Irish Am. Cultural Inst., Youngstown U. Alumni Assn., Sigma Kappa Phi. Roman Catholic. K.C. (3 deg.). Home: 3821 Frederick St Youngstown OH 44515 Office: 550 W Pine Lake Rd North Lima OH 44452

MC GIVERIN, ARTHUR A., justice Supreme Ct. Iowa; b. Iowa City, Nov. 10, 1928; s. Joseph J. and Mary B. McG.; B.S.C. with high honors, U. Iowa, 1951, J.D., 1956; m. Mary Joan McGiverin, Apr. 20, 1951; children—Teresa, Thomas, Bruce, Nancy. Admitted to Iowa bar, 1956; practice law, Ottumwa, Iowa, 1956; alt. mcpl. judge, Ottumwa, 1960-65; judge Iowa Dist. Ct. 8th Jud. Dist., 1965-78; asso. justice Iowa Supreme Ct., Des Moines, 1978—. Mem. Iowa Supreme Ct. Commn. on Continuing Legal Edn., 1975. Served to 1st lt. U.S. Army, 1946-48, 51-53. Mem. Iowa Bar Assn. Roman Catholic. Office: Supreme Ct of Iowa Capitol Bldg 10th and Grand Des Moines IA 50319

MC GLADE, KEITH LYNN, publishing co. exec.; b. Zanesville, Ohio, Dec. 8, 1937; s. Kenneth Edward and Dorothy Louise McG.; student Ohio U., 1955-57; B.S. in Econs., U. Pa., 1959; M.B.A., U. Mich., 1967; m. Linn Gale, Aug. 22, 1964; 1 dau., Kimberly Ann. With Chevrolet div. Gen. Motors Corp., Detroit, 1959-67; with Ernst & Ernst, C.P.A.'s, Detroit, 1967-71; controller Detroit Free Press, 1971-73, treas., controller, 1973-77, bus. mgr., treas., 1977; v.p., gen. mgr. Beacon Jour. Pub. Co., Akron, Ohio, 1977—. Vice chmn. Akron Action Com., 1979; hon. chmn. Am. Diabetes Assn., 1979; asst. treas., bd. dirs. Akron Art Inst.; bd. dirs. Akron Gen. Med. Center, United Way of Summit County; bd. dirs., mem. exec. com. Akron Regional Devel. Bd., Downtown Akron Assn.; trustee Beacon Jour. Fund, Inc. Served with U.S. Army Res., 1961. Mem. Financial Execs. Inst., Nat. Assn. Accountants; Am. Inst. C.P.A.'s, Mich. Assn. C.P.A.'s, Am. Mgmt. Assn., Inst. Newspaper Controllers and Financial Officers, Ohio Newspaper Assn. (trustee). Presbyterian. Club: Cascade; Portage Country. Home: 2390 Stockbridge Rd Akron OH 44313 Office: 44 E Exchange St Akron OH 44328*

MC GLINN, JOSEPH FRANCIS, realtor; b. Phila., Aug. 19, 1918; s. Michael Joseph and Marion Ann (Sweeney) McG.; student Villanova Coll., 1940; M.B.A., U. Dayton, 1967; m. Marjorie Kidnocker, June 21, 1947; children—Joan, Kathleen, Michael. Pres., Monarch Die Engring. Co., Dayton, Ohio, 1965-69; pvt. practice security analysis, Dayton, 1969-75; asso. Long Realty, Dayton, Ohio, 1976—; asso. S. Park Land Livestock Co., Inc.; bd. dirs. Monarch Die and Engring. Co.; cons. to bus. Chmn. bd. dirs. Catholic Charities, Dayton, 1960-65. Mem. Am. Mktg. Assn. (charter, Dayton chpt.), Dayton Tool and Die Assn. Roman Catholic. Clubs: Dayton Country, K.C. Home: 842 Revere Village Ct Centerville OH 45459 Office: 2090 Hewitt Ave Dayton OH 45440

MC GONIGAL, EDGAR RAY, accountant; b. Indpls., June 2, 1953; s. William E. and Katherine (White) McG.; B.S. in Acctg., Ind. U.-Purdue U., 1974; postgrad. Ind. U., 1975-77; m. Judith A. Money, July 15, 1977. Clk., Lind, Deckard, O'Brien and Lawson, Attys., Danville, Ind., 1973; asst. plant acct. Fed.-Mogul Corp., Mooresville, Ind., 1973-74, corporate internal auditor, Southfield, Mich., 1974-75; partner Bailey-Williams and Co., Indpls., 1975—. Mem. Ind. Assn. C.P.A.'s, Am. Inst. C.P.A.'s, Beta Gamma Sigma. Methodist. Clubs: Masons, Shriners, Columbia. Home: 5721 Bluespruce Dr Indianapolis IN 46227 Office: 1 Virginia Ave Suite 222 Indianapolis IN 46204

MC GOVERN, CASSANDRA JANE, librarian; b. Chgo., Oct. 8, 1942; d. Terrence E. and Agnes Jane (Cruden) McG.; B.A., Knox Coll., Galesburg, Ill., 1964; M.A. in L.S., Rosary Coll., River Forest, Ill., 1967; M.A., Northwestern U., 1974, Ph.D. in Counselor Edn., 1976; 1 son, Terrence Joseph Talbot. Library technician Chgo. Public Library, 1965-66; asst. circulation librarian Harper Library, U. Chgo., 1966-67, part-time asst. circulation librarian, 1967-68; reference librarian Coll. of Lake County, Grayslake, Ill., 1970—, tchr. library sci., 1971-74, 75—, tchr. counseling dept., 1974-75, continuing edn. dept., 1975—, psychology dept., 1981—; cons. in field, 1976—. Mem. Am. Fedn. Tchrs., ALA, Assn. Humanistic Psychology, Am. Personnel and Guidance Assn., Nat. Assn. Female Execs., Assn. Specialists in Group Work. Home: 186 Blueberry Rd Libertyville IL 60048 Office: Coll Lake County Grayslake IL 60030

MCGOVERN, EUGENIA GAYE, sch. supt.; b. Boston, Oct. 21, 1943; d. Louis Harry Jr. and Mary Eugenia (Coleman) Roddis; B.S., U. Pitts., 1963; M.A., U. Redlands, 1965; Ed.D., UCLA, 1970; m. William Lloyd McGovern, June 29, 1963; 1 dau., Elizabeth Amy. Tchr. public schs., Beaumont, Calif., 1964-66, summer sch., 1964-68, adult edn. sch., 1966-68, counselor, 1965-66, acting asst. prin., 1967, dean girls, 1966-68; counselor Santa Maria Unified Sch. Dist., Calif., Righetti High Sch., 1968-69, dean girls, 1969-70, prin. Santa Maria Summer Sch., 1970; asst./acting prin. Syracuse City Sch. Dist., Nottingham High Sch., 1970-71, dir. sec. edn., 1971-72; dir. to the dep. supt. for program implementation Harrisburg (Pa.) City Sch. Dist., 1972-73, dir. curriculum and supervisory services, 1973-74; program specialist Capital Area Intermediate Unit, Pa., 1974-76; dir. pupil services Wilmington (Ohio) City Sch. Dist., 1976, dir. curriculum/pupil services, 1976-79; supt. Miami East Sch. Dist., Ohio, 1979-81; supt. East Palestine (Ohio) City Sch. Dist., 1981—; adj. prof. edn. Wright State U., Dayton, 1978, U. Dayton, 1976-77; asst. prof. edn. Lebanon Valley Coll., 1974-75; instr. U. Calif., Santa Barbara, 1969-70, U. Calif., Riverside, 1966-68; cons. in field. Mem. adv. bd. Miami County Juvenile Ct., 1979-81; vestry, Trinity Episcopal Ch., 1980-81, St. James, 1981—; bd. dirs. Clinton County United Way, 1977-79, v.p., 1979; mem. Clinton County Health Planning Council, 1976-79; mem. Clinton County Adv. Com. on Alcohol Counseling, 1976-79; bd. dirs. Clinton County Vol. Action Center, 1976-77; v.p. Clinton County Human Services Assn., 1977-78, others. Recipient Outstanding Young Woman of the Yr. award, Wilmington Jr. C. of C., 1979, others. Mem. Buckeye Assn. Sch. Adminstrs., Am. Assn. Sch. Adminstrs., Assn. for Supervision and Curriculum Devel. (nat. bd. dirs. 1979-80), Ohio Soc. for Supervision and Curriculum Devel., Ohio Assn. Sch. Bus. Ofcls., Dayton Area Supts. Assn. (v.p. 1980-81), Phi Delta Kappa, Pi Lambda Theta. Republican. Contbr. articles to profl. jours. Office: 360 W Grant St East Palestine OH 44413

MC GOVERN, GEORGE STANLEY, former senator; b. Avon, S.D., July 19, 1922; s. Joseph C. and Frances (McLean) McG.; B.A., Dakota Wesleyan U., 1945; M.A., Northwestern U., 1949, Ph.D., 1953; m. Eleanor Stegeberg, Oct. 31, 1943; children—Ann, Susan, Teresa, Steven, Mary. Prof. history and polit. sci. Dakota Wesleyan U., 1949-53; exec. sec. S.D. Democratic Party, 1953-56; mem. U.S. Ho. of Reps. from 1st dist. S.D., 85th-86th congresses, 1956-60; food-for-peace dir. Kennedy Adminstrn., 1960-62; mem. U.S. Senate from S.D., 1963-80; lectr. Northwestern U. Democratic candidate for Pres. U.S., 1972. Served as pilot USAAF, World War II. Decorated D.F.C. Mem. Am. Hist. Assn. Methodist. Mason (33 deg., Shriner), Elk, Kiwanian. Author: The Colorado Coal Strike, 1913-14, 1953; War Against Want, 1964; Agricultural Thought in the 20th Century, 1967; A Time of War A Time of Peace, 1968; (with Leonard Guttridge) The Great Coalfield War, 1972; An American Journey, 1974. Home: Mitchell SD 57301*

MCGOVERN, JOHN EDWARD, JR., lawyer; b. Chgo., Mar. 25, 1931; s. John Edward and Marion A. (McMahon) McG.; B.S. cum laude in Engring., Princeton U., 1953; J.D., Harvard U., 1959; m. Karen Armour Osborne, Feb. 19, 1966; children—John Edward, III, Courtney Osborne. Admitted to Ill. bar, 1959; asso. firm Wilson & McIlvaine, Chgo., 1959-66, partner, 1967—. Trustee, Nat. Council Crime and Delinquency, 1968-70, Lake Forest (Ill.) Coll., 1972—, Ravinia Festival Assn., 1980—; bd. dirs. Lake Forest Hosp., 1971-80; bd. govs. Chgo. Heart Assn., 1966—; alderman City of Lake Forest, 1978—. Served with USNR, 1953-56. Mem. Am. Bar Assn., Ill. Bar Assn., Chgo. Bar Assn. (chmn. securities law com. 1979-80), Law Club Chgo. Clubs: Chgo., Old Elm, Onwentsia, Racquet, Mid-Day; Princeton (N.Y.C.). Home: 79 N Mayflower Rd Lake Forest IL 60045 Office: 135 S LaSalle St Chicago IL 60603

MCGOWEN, BONNIE CAROLYN, educator; b. Hillsboro, Ill., Dec. 10, 1944; d. Eldon Ellis and Laura Isabell (Stogsdill) Bethard; B.Ed., S.E. Mo. State U., 1966, M.A. in Edn., 1972; m. Sam

McGowen, Apr. 16, 1966; children—James Brian, Sarah Christine, Nanetta Carol. Tchr., Cape Girardeau (Mo.) public schs., 1966-67; tchr. Bonne Terre Elem. Schs., 1967-68; tchr. sci., elem. counselor Farmington (Mo.) public schs., 1969-79; learning disabilities tchr., remedial reading tchr. Fredericktown (Mo.) schs., remedial reading tchr., 1979—. Mem. Assn. for Supervision and Curriculum Devel., Mo. State Tchrs. Assn. Baptist. Home: Route 4 Box 136 Dexter MO 63841

MC GRANE, MARTIN EDWARD, editor; b. Des Moines, Apr. 6, 1943; s. L.B. and Veronica K. (Rhody) McG.; B.A., Drake U., 1966; M.S., Iowa State U., 1972; m. Sandra Johnson, Aug. 22, 1977; children—Kelly, Maura, Mark, Daniel. With Miller Pub. Co., Mpls., 1966-69; mem. faculty U. Idaho, 1972-73, U. S.D., 1973-78; editor S.D. Rural Electric Assn., Pierre, S.D., 1978—; owner Caleb Perkins Press. Mem. Coop. Editorial Assn., Western Rural Editorial Exchange (pres.), Nat. Rural Electric Editors Assn. Roman Catholic. Author: Forty Years of History at the James Farm; contbr. articles on Midwest Civil War history to periodicals. Office: 222 W Pleasant Dr Pierre SD 57501*

MCGRATH, JOHN FRANCIS, power and light co. exec.; b. Freeport, N.Y., May 4, 1925; s. John Francis and Catherine Frances (Maune) McG.; B.S., U.S. Merchant Marine Acad., 1943; A.B., Muhlenberg Coll., 1948; J.D., St. John's U., 1952; postgrad. U. Minn., 1973; m. Catherine Elizabeth Zainor, June 22, 1946; children—Joseph R., Susan M., Martha J., Thomas J. Admitted to N.Y. State bar, 1952, Minn. bar, 1958; atty. Casey, Lane & Mittendorf, N.Y.C., 1953-58; jud. inquiry asst. counsel N.Y. Supreme Ct., N.Y.C., 1957-58; atty. U.S. Steel Corp., Duluth, Minn., 1958-64; adminstrv. asst. Minn. Power & Light Co., Duluth, from 1964, sr. v.p., gen. counsel, sec., 1979—; dir., Utility Services Ins. Co. Ltd., Hamilton, Bermuda; adj. prof. Coll. St. Scholastica, 1979—. Bd. dirs. Duluth Cathedral High Sch., St. Ann's. Served with U.S. Mcht. Marine, 1943-46, USNR, 1943-68. Mem. Am. Bar Assn., Minn. Bar Assn., St. Louis County Bar Assn., Minn. Bar Assn., Edison Electric Inst. Democrat. Roman Catholic. Clubs: Northland Country, Kitchi Gammi, K.C. Office: 30 W Superior St Duluth MN 55802

MCGRATH, KRISTIN SERUM, newspaper co. exec.; b. Mpls., May 19, 1942; d. Edwin and Dorothy Marie (Evensta) Serum; B.A., Carleton Coll., 1962; M.A., Stanford U., 1965; Ph.D., U. Minn., 1977; m. William Mayo, Dec. 29, 1967; children—Margit Ann, William Edwin. Reporter Mpls. Star, 1966-69; instr. U. Minn., Mpls., 1972-73; asst. prof. Medill Sch. Journalism, Northwestern U., Evanston, Ill., 1973-75; asst. news editor Minneapolis Star, 1975-76; news research mgr. Mpls. Star and Tribune, Mpls., 1976-77, research dir., 1977—. Mem. bd. Jr. League Mpls., 1980-81, chmn. pub. affairs, 1980-81; sec., treas. State Pub. Affairs Com., 1980-81, chmn., 1981—; mem. bd. Urban Coalition Mpls., 1977-79. Recipient Fulbright fellowship in India, 1965-66; Pub. Affairs Reporting award, Am. Polit. Sci. Assn., 1967. Mem. Newspaper Research Council (mem. bd.), Am. Mktg. Assn., Am. Assn. Public Opinion Research, Internat. Newspaper Promotion Assn. Presbyn. Home: 6212 Braeburn Circle Edina MN 55435 Office: 425 Portland Ave Minneapolis MN 55488

MCGRATH, WILLIAM MAYO, JR., food processing exec.; b. Grand Island, Nebr., May 3, 1937; s. William Mayo and Mildred Edith (Castell) McG.; B.A., Harvard, 1959; M.B.A., Stanford, 1964; m. Harriet Kristin Serum, Dec. 29, 1967; children—Margit Ann, William Edwin. Product mgr. Gen. Mills, Inc., Mpls., 1964-70; v.p. prepared foods and new products Green Giant Co., Mpls., 1970-80; v.p. bus. devel. Pillsbury Co., Mpls., 1980—. Dir. St. Paul Chamber Orch., 1980—; pres. Stanford Grad. Sch. Bus. Club Minn., 1967-68; Mpls. major gifts chmn. KTCA Action Auction, 1979-80. Served with U.S. Navy, 1959-62. Home: 6212 Braeburn Circle Edina MN 55435 Office: 608 2d Ave S Minneapolis MN 55402

MC GREGOR, DOUGLAS JOHN, mfg. co. exec.; b. Detroit, Jan. 4, 1941; s. Buell William and Elizabeth Jane (Alber) McG.; B.B.A., U. Mich., 1964; M.B.A., Eastern Mich. U., 1969; m. Charlotte Aupperle, Dec. 19, 1970; children—Erica Elise, Craig Douglas. Fin. supr. Ford Motor Co., Plymouth, Mich., 1970-73; with Rockwell Internat., Troy, Mich., 1973--, dir. mktg. and bus. planning, 1976-78, v.p., gen. mgr., 1978—. Chmn. no. sect. sustaining membership Detroit Area council Boy Scouts Am.; deacon Cana Lutheran Ch., Berkley, Mich. Mem. Soc. Automotive Engrs., Engring. Soc. Detroit. Club: Birmingham (Mich.) Country. Office: 2135 W Maple Rd Troy MI 48084

MC GUIRE, GLEN JOE, pharmacist; b. Anadarko, Okla., Sept. 5, 1947; s. Loyd George and Betty LaWanna (Ikard) McG.; B.S. in Pharmacy, Southwestern Sch. Pharmacy, Weatherford, Okla., 1970; m. Jo Anna Janousek, May 25, 1968; children—Dayna Dyan, Erin Suzan, Adria Anne. Asst. mgr. Mays Drugs, Ottumwa, Iowa, 1970-72; pharmacist, mgr. Mid-west Pharmacies, Inc., Dodge City, Kans., 1972-75; pharmacist, owner Prescription Center, Ulysses, Kans., 1975—; pharmacist Bob Wilson Meml. Hosp., Ulysses, 1976—; pres. McGuire, Inc., Ulysses, 1975—; lab. instr. Southwestern Sch. Pharmacy, Weatherford, 1969-70. Mem. Am. Pharm. Assn., Kans. Pharm. Assn., Kans. Soc. Hosp. Pharmacists. Mem. Ch. of Christ. Clubs: Elks, Rotary. Home: 843 N Cheyenne St Ulysses KS 67880 Office: 111 E Kansas St Ulysses KS 67880

MCGUIRE, JACK JOHN, communications cons. firm exec.; b. Chgo., Feb. 7, 1925; s. Martin John and Kathryn McGuire; student Monmouth Coll., 1946-49; B.S., Northwestern U., 1951. With Jack McGuire Public Relations, 1951-61, Peitscher/Janda Advt. Agy., 1961-65, Jack McGuire & Assos, Inc., Chgo., 1965-77; owner, communications cons. McGuire Communications, Inc., Glen Ellyn, Ill., 1977—; instr. Am. Mgmt. Assn., 1979—. Served with AUS, 1943-46. Mem. Public Relations Soc. Am., Counselors Acad. Club: Publicity of Chgo. (pres. 1980-81). Contbg. editor Meeting News, 1980—. Contbr. articles in field to profl. jours.

MCGUIRE, JAMES THOMAS, co. exec.; b. Medford, Mass., Sept. 3, 1918; s. Thomas J. and Teresa McAvaney McG.; A.B., Boston Coll., 1939; m. Audrey M. Costello McGuire, Sept. 24, 1944; children—Carol Ann, James T. With Canteen Corp., Chgo., 1940—, sr. v.p., 1972-76, exec. v.p., 1976—. Served to 1st lt. U.S. Army, 1943-46. Mem. Nat. Automatic Merchandising Assn. (dir. emeritus), Nat. Restaurant Assn., Chgo. Restaurant Assn., Ill. Restaurant Assn., Ill. State C. of C. Clubs: Evanston Golf (past pres.), Merchants and Mfrs. (bd. govs.), Chgo. Athletic Assn., Executives, KC. Office: Canteen Corp 1430 Merchandise Mart Chicago IL 60654

MCGUIRE, JOHN PATRICK, ins. co. exec.; b. Chgo., Mar. 31, 1944; s. James Thomas and Adelaide (Peters) McG.; B.A. in Psychology, Parsons Coll., 1967; m. Margaret Lorreta Scanlan, Sept. 11, 1965; children—Kathy, Brian, Maureen. Mgr. sales tng. CNA Ins. Co., Chgo., 1967-80; dir. tng. United Ins. Co. Am., Chgo., 1980—. Bd. dirs. N.E. Civil Def. Council, 1973-74, 81—, v.p., 1974—; bd. dirs. Hanover Park (Ill.) Emergency Services, 1974—; commr. human relations bd. Village of Hanover Park, 1971-72. Named Outstanding Young Man, Village of Hanover Park, 1975, Citizen of Yr., Mayor of Hanover Park, 1976. Mem. Nat. Honor Soc. for Psychology Students. Office: United Ins Co Am 1 E Wacker Dr Chicago IL 60601

MC GUIRE, RICK MICHAEL, broadcasting co. exec.; b. Pueblo, Colo., Aug. 12, 1953; s. Orville Thomas and Patricia Rayona (Nelson) McG.; B.A., Augustana Coll., 1975. Staff announcer WVIK-FM, Rock Island, Ill., 1971, news dir., gen. mgr., 1972-75; morning announcer, dir. spls. Sta. KIIK, Davenport, Iowa, 1976—; daily show on WOC-TV; free-lance writer for nat. mags. and newspapers. Methodist (pres. youth fellowship 1970-71). Home: 11719 1st St Milan IL 61264 Office: KIIK 805 Brady St Davenport IA 52808

MC GUIRE, SANDRA LYNN, nurse; b. Flint, Mich., Jan. 28, 1947; d. Donald Armstrong and Mary Lue (Harvey) Johnson; B.S.N., U. Mich., 1969, M.P.H. (USPHS fellow), 1973; m. Joseph L. McGuire, Mar. 6, 1976; children—Matthew, Kelly, Kerry. Staff nurse Univ. Hosp., Ann Arbor, Mich., 1969; public health nurse Wayne County Health Dept., Eloise, Mich., 1969-72; instr. community health nursing Madonna Coll., Livonia, Mich., 1973; public health coordinator Plymouth Center Human Devel., Northville, Mich., 1974-75; early intervention cons. Wyandotte (Mich.) Child Appraisal Center, 1974; asst. prof. community health nursing U. Mich., 1975—; vol. camp nurse Archdiocese of Detroit Ministry to Handicapped, 1976, 78, 79, 80; resource person Mich. Gov.'s Commn. on Unification of Mental Health Services, 1979-80. USPHS fellow, 1972-73. Mem. Am. Public Health Assn., Mich. Public Health Assn., Mich. League Nurses, Nat. League Nursing, Mich. Assn. Retarded Citizens (residential services chmn. 1976-79, health services chmn. 1980—, dir. 1980—), Assn. Retarded Citizens Nat., Assn. Retarded Citizens Plymouth, Sigma Theta Tau. Author: (with Clemen and Eigsti) Comprehensive Family and Community Health Nursing, 1981; also articles. Home: 9347 Silver Maple Whitmore Lake MI 48189 Office: 400 N Ingalls Ann Arbor MI 48109

MC GURK, JAMES HENRY, mfg. exec.; b. Phila., July 24, 1936; s. James Henry and Ednah Mae (Kleinsmith) McG.; B.S., Pa. State U., 1957; postgrad. in Econs., Temple U., 1960-62; m. LaVerne M. Kraynek, 1960; children—Heather, Melanye. Cons. mfg., various states, 1968-72; ops. chief mfg. cons. Manatech Internat., Westmont, N.J., 1970-72, A.T. Oxford Inc., N.Y.C., 1972-74; mem. corporate staff mfg. cons. Aspro Inc., Westport, Conn., 1974-77; pres., dir. LHM, Inc., cons., Rochester, Mich., 1977—; exec. v.p. Morse Hemco Inc., Holland, Mich., also dir. Served with USAF, 1957-59. Mem. Am. Mgmt. Assn. Nat. Rifle Assn. (life). Republican. Home: 39 Forest Hills Dr Holland MI 49423 Office: 455 Douglas Ave Holland MI 49423

MC HARGUE, WAYNE ORVAL, ins. agt.; b. Brazil, Ind., Feb. 17, 1937; s. Raymond D. and Cathern L. (Maxwell) McH.; student Ind. U., 1955-59; B.S. in Bus. Adminstrn., Ind. State U., 1961; m. Edwina; 1 dau., Kristi Ellen. Asst. to dean of men Ind. State U., 1960-61; mgmt. trainee Ind. Nat. Bank, Indpls., 1962-65; sales rep. Am. United Life, Indpls., 1965—; estate and fin. planner. Mem. exec. council Indpls. Mus. Art, 1971-73, spl. gifts div. chmn., 1971-72; div. chmn. United Way of Greater Indpls., Inc., 1966, pres. Loaned Exec. Club, 1967. Recipient Nat. Sales Achievement award Nat. Assn. Life Underwriters, 1970, Nat. Quality award, 1967; Health Ins. Quality award Nat. Assn. Health Urnderwriters, 1975. Registered health underwriter. Mem. Estate Planning Council Indpls., Indpls., Am. socs. C.L.U., C.L.U. Found., Am. United Life Presidents Club, Indpls. Assn. Life Underwriters (dir.), Life Underwriter Polit. Action Council Century Club, Indpls. Jaycees (dir.; Key Man award 1967; Outstanding Service award 1962), Delta Sigma Pi Alumni Club (pres. 1961-62), Phi Kappa Psi Alumni Club (pres. 1966-67). Republican. Methodist. Club: Sertoma (pres. 1974-75, chmn. bd. 1975-76) (Indpls.). Home: 8201 Castleton Blvd Indianapolis IN 46256 Office: 6535 E 82d St Suite 106 PO Box 50189 Indianapolis IN 46250

MCHENRY, KEITH WELLES, JR., oil co. exec.; b. Champaign, Ill., Apr. 6, 1928; s. Keith and Jayne McH.; B.S. in Chem. Engring., U. Ill., 1951; Ph.D., Princeton U., 1958; m. Lou Petry, Aug. 23, 1952; children—John, William. With Standard Oil Co. (Ind.) and affiliates, 1955—, research asso., 1967-68, asst. dir. fuels research, 1968-70, dir. process and analytical research, 1970-74, mgr. process research, Naperville, Ill., 1974-75, v.p. research and devel., Naperville, Ill., 1975—; Charles D. Hurd lectr. Northwestern U., 1981; mem. U.S. nat. com. World Petroleum Congress. Mem. adv. council Catalysis Center, U. Del., Princeton U. Sch. Engring. and Applied Sci., U. Ill. Coll. Engring., Chgo.; trustee North Central Coll.; elder Presbyterian Ch. Served in U.S. Army, 1946-47. Mem. Am. Inst. Chem. Engrs., Am. Chem. Soc., AAAS, Am. Petroleum Inst., Sigma Xi, Tau Beta Pi. Editorial bd. Am. Inst. Chem. Engrs. Jour., 1975-78; contbr. articles to profl. jours. Patentee in field (4). Office: PO Box 400 Naperville IL 60566

MC HENRY, MARION ELINOR, educator; b. Kenosha, Wis., Feb. 4, 1929; d. Leo and Olga (Schultz) Ratshinske; student U. Wis. Extension System, 1947-49; B.Ed., U. Wis., Whitewater, 1963, M.S. in Reading, 1976, reading specialist, 1977; m. James Willems McHenry, Jan. 11, 1951 (dec. 1979); 1 dau., Ellen Ann McHenry Amaya. Tchr. English, Racine (Wis.) Tech. Inst., 1963-64; tchr. English and social studies, counselor Racine Unified Schs., 1964-66; tchr. English and reading Union High Sch., Union Grove, Wis., 1966—, reading specialist, reading and writing tchr., 1977—, reading coordinator, 1978—. Troop leader Racine council Girl Scouts U.S.A., 1960-65; catechist, minister of eucharist, lector, mem. Parish Council edn. com. St. Edward's Ch., Racine. Recipient cert. of appreciation Racine County Sch. Office, Div. Spl. Edn., 1977-81. Mem. Internat. Reading Assn., Wis. State Reading Assn., Assn. Supervision and Curriculum Devel., Wis. Council Tchrs. of English, NEA, Wis. Edn. Assn., Union High/Union Grove Edn. Assn. Club: Elks (complimentary). Home: 1515 Cleveland Ave Racine WI 53405 Office: 3433 S Colony Ave PO Box 36 Union Grove WI 53182

MC HENRY, MARTIN CHRISTOPHER, physician; b. San Francisco, Feb. 9, 1932; s. Merl and Marcella (Bricca) McH.; student U. Santa Clara (Calif.), 1950-53; M.D., U. Cin., 1957; M.S. in Medicine, U. Minn., Mpls., 1966; m. Patricia Grace Hughes, Apr. 27, 1957; children—Michael, Christopher, Timothy, Mary Ann, Jeffrey, Paul, Kevin, William, Monica, Martin Christopher. Intern, Highland Alameda County (Calif.) Hosp., Oakland, 1957-58; resident, internal medicine fellow Mayo Clinic, Rochester, Minn., 1958-61, spl. appointee in infectious diseases, 1963-64; staff physician infectious diseases Henry Ford Hosp., Detroit, 1964-67; staff physician Cleve. Clinic, 1967-72, head dept. infectious diseases, 1972—. Asst. clin. prof. Case Western Res. U., 1970-77, asso. clin. prof. medicine, 1977—; asso. vis. physician Cleve. Met. Gen. Hosp., 1970—; cons. VA Hosp., Cleve., 1973—. Chmn. manpower com. Swine Influenza Program, Cleve., 1976. Served with USNR, 1961-63. Named Distinguished Tchr. in Medicine Cleve. Clinic, 1972. Diplomate Am. Bd. Internal Medicine. Fellow A.C.P., Am. Coll. Chest Physicians (chmn. com. cardiopulmonary infections 1975-77); mem. Am. Soc. Clin. Pharmacology and Therapeutics (chmn. sect. infectious diseases and antimicrobial agts., 1970-77, 80—, dir.), Am. Soc. Clin. Pathologists, Royal Soc. Medicine of Great Britain (asso.), Infectious Diseases Soc. Am., Am. Fedn. Clin. Research, Am. Soc. Microbiology, N.Y. Acad. Scis. Contbr. 75 articles to profl. jours., also chpts. to books. Home: 2779 Belgrave Rd Pepper Pike OH 44124 Office: 9500 Euclid Ave Cleveland OH 44106

MC HUGH, CHARLES THOMAS, physician, surgeon; b. Passaic, N.J., Dec. 5, 1937; s. Charles Patrick and Mary Gertrude (Kelly) McH.; A.B., Wesleyan U., Middletown, Conn., 1960; M.D., Albany (N.Y.) Med. Coll., 1964; m. Anne Ewing Jones, Sept. 7, 1974; children—David Charles, Kelly Jean. Intern in surgery U. Chgo. Hosps., 1964-65; sr. asst. surgeon USPHS-Peace Corps, Tanzania, 1965-67; resident in surgery Northwestern U. Hosps., 1967-71; chief resident in surgery Columbus Hosp., Chgo., 1971-72; practice medicine specializing in family practice and surgery, Chgo., 1972—; v.p. med. edn. Columbus-Cuneo-Cabrini Med. Center, 1972-79, staff Family Practice Center, 1980—, trustee, 1980—; asso. surgery Northwestern U. Med. Sch., 1972—; med. coordinator Med. Disciplinary Bd. Ill., 1979—; cons. continuing med. edn. Ill. Council Continuing Med. Edn.; mem. council on state legis. Ill. Hosp. Assn., 1978—; physician adv. Ill. Acad. Physician Assts., 1978-80. Bd. mgrs. Lathrop Chgo. Boys Club, 1973—; bd. dirs. Edn. Resource Center, Chgo., 1976-77; mem. alumni council Wesleyan U., 1978-79. Diplomate Nat. Bd. Med. Examiners, Am. Bd. Surgery, Am. Bd. Family Practice. Fellow ACS; mem. Am. Acad. Family Physicians, AMA, Ill. (mem. council edn. and manpower 1976-79, chmn. 1978-79, chmn. com. physician's assts. 1976-78), Chgo. med. socs., Soc. Tchrs. Family Medicine, Inst. Medicine Chgo. Club: Wesleyan (pres. 1979—) (Chgo.). Home: 3162 N Pine Grove Ave Chicago IL 60657 Office: 2520 N Lakeview Ave Chicago IL 60614

MC ILRATH, DAN M., steel co. exec.; b. Carroll County, Ind., May 18, 1928; s. L. L. and Mabel P. (Patty) McI.; B.S., Purdue U., 1952; m. Martha Agnes McCord, Dec. 27, 1948; children—Marie, David, Elinor, James, Beth, Robert, Rebecca. With Continental Steel Co. (now Penn-Dixie), Kokomo, Ind., 1952-74; resident mgr. Midstates Steel & Wire div. Keystone Consol. Industries, Inc., Greenville, Miss., 1974, mgr. ops., Greenville and Jacksonville, Fla., 1975-76, v.p. operations, Greenville, Jacksonville, Sherman, Tex. and Crawfordsville, Ind., 1976-78, dir. wire ops. Keystone Group, 1978-79, plant mgr., 1979—. Served with USN, 1946-48. Named Wireman of Yr., Wire Tech., 1976. Mem. Wire Assn., Ind. Mfrs. Assn., Miss. Mfrs. Assn., Am. Inst. Steel Engrs., Crawfordsville C. of C. Republican. Roman Catholic. Clubs: Country, Rotary, Elks. Home: Rural Route 5 Crawfordsville IN 47933 Office: PO Box 392 Crawfordsville IN 47933

MC ILVAINE, CLIFFORD JAMES, mfg. exec.; b. St. Charles, Ill., Oct. 16, 1941; s. Oran T. and Nettie (Root) McI.; student Waubonsee Coll., 1969. Tech. engr. Energy Kontrols, Inc., Geneva, Ill., 1960-61; gen. mgr. Photo-Crystals Co., St. Charles, 1961-65, pres., 1965—; partner Electronic Products Co., 1964—; partner Mid-Valley Service Co., 1968—; owner, founder McIlvaine Electronic Security Systems, Inc., 1972—, McIlvaine Constrn. Co., 1975—. Radio officer St. Charles Civil Def. Corps, 1965-69. Home: 605 Prarie St St Charles IL 60174

MCINTIRE, DOROTHY LOUISE, banker; b. Cambridge, Ohio, Apr. 25, 1924; d. Edwin and Elma (Kelly) Morgan; student Am. Inst. Banking, 1970-72, U. Toledo, 1977-79; m. A.M. McIntire, Sept. 23, 1972; children by previous marriage—Daniel J. Desmond, Dennis R. and Lawrence S. Todak. With United Savs. & Loan Assn., 1967-69; asst. v.p., coordinator spl. orgnl. services Ohio Citizens Bank, Toledo, 1969—; public speaker, seminar designer. Honoree Tribute to Women and Industry, 1980-81. Mem. Am. Inst. Banking, Am. Bus. Women's Assn., Nat. Assn. Bank Women. Office: Ohio Citizens Bank SOS PO Box 1688 Toledo OH 43603

MC INTIRE, LARRY DOUGLAS, otolaryngologist; b. Curtis, Nebr., Oct. 29, 1941; s. Victor Vernon and Flora Lois (Maust) McI.; B.A., Adams State Coll., Alamosa, Colo., 1963; D.O., Kirksville Coll. Osteo. Medicine, 1971; m. Donna Louise Stucky, Aug. 26, 1961; children—Kent, Susan. Intern, Rocky Mountain Osteo. Hosp., Denver, 1971-72; resident Kirksville (Mo.) Osteo. Hosp., 1972-75; ear, nose and throat surgeon, head of service Osteo. Hosp. of Maine, Portland, 1975-80; chmn. ear, nose and throat dept. Kirksville Coll. Osteo. Medicine, 1980—. Trustee, South Portland Ch. of Nazarene, 1976-80, Osteo. Hosp. of Maine, 1977-80, Eastern Nazarene Coll., 1978-80; dist. adv. bd. Maine Ch. of Nazarene, 1979-80. Mem. Am. Osteo. Assn., Osteo. Coll. Ophthalmology and Otolaryngology. Home: Box 191 Rt 3 Kirksville MO 63501 Office: 902 E LaHarpe Kirksville MO 63501

MC INTIRE, MURIEL ELAINE, dietitian; b. Saskatoon, Sask., Can.; d. Stafford Lenox and Nellie Susan (Whitehead) Osborne; came to U.S., 1915, naturalized, 1922; B.S., Lewis Inst. Tech., 1938; m. Claude Vernon McIntire, Nov. 23, 1941; children—Patricia Anne McIntire Maker, Susan Elaine McIntire Beranek. Intern, Walter Reed Hosp., Washington, 1940; head dietitian Sta. Hosp., Ft. Sheridan, Ill., 1939-40, Regional Hosp., Scott Field, Ill., 1940-43; therapeutic dietitian Barnes Hosp., St. Louis, 1948; head dietitian Hines (Ill.) Hosp., 1956-57; staff dietitian Ohio State U. Hosp. and Health Center, 1957-59; staff dietitian Oak Forest (Ill.) Hosp., 1960-61, exec. dietitian, 1961-69; chief dietitian Little Company of Mary Hosp., Evergreen Park, Ill., 1980. 1971-77, therapeutic dietitian, 1977—. Served to 1st lt. USAAF, 1943-45. Named Employee of Yr., Little Company of Mary Hosp., 1980. Mem. Am. Dietetic Assn., Am. Home Econs. Assn., Soc. for Nutrition Edn., Chgo. Nutrition Assn. Co-author: Manual of Clinical Dietetics, 1975. Home: 7144 S Fair Elms Ave La Grange IL 60525 Office: Little Company of Mary Hosp 2800 95th St Evergreen Park IL 60642

MC INTOSH, MARY FRANCES, interior decorator; b. Wesco, Mo., Sept. 21, 1927; d. William Austin and Ava Frances (Roberts) Gravatt; student St. Louis Inst. Music, 1945-46, Chgo. Sch. Interior Decoration, 1963-64; m. Calvin Eugene McIntosh, Nov. 30, 1947; children—Dennis Eugene, Gail Sue McIntosh Stanfast. Music and theory tchr., St. James, Mo., 1946-47; receptionist, sec. White Rodgers Elec. Co., St. Louis, 1947-48; clk. GAO, St. Louis, 1948-50; receptionist, sec. VA Social Service Div., 1950-51; sec. John F. Hodge Grade Sch., St. James, 1960-62; co-owner, operator, interior decorator McIntosh Furniture, Salem, Mo., 1962—. Cons., bd. dirs. HUD. Club: Cosmopolitan Federated. Office: McIntosh Furniture Co 3d and Henderson Sts Salem MO 65560

MC INTURF, FAITH MARY, thoroughbred harness racing exec., presch. edn. field exec.; b. Grand Ridge, Ill., Aug. 22, 1917; d. Lynne E. and Margaret (Garver) McInturf; grad. high sch. With The J.E. Porter Corp., Chgo., 1963-65, v.p., 1951-65, sec., 1951-65, also dir.; v.p., sec. Potomac Engring. Corp., 1941—; sec.-treas., dir. Chgo. Harness Racing Inc., also Balmoral Jockey Club, Inc., 1967-72, sec., dir., 1974-78; sec., treas., dir. Balmoral Park Trot, Inc., 1969-72; sec., dir. Horse Racing Promotions, Inc., 1974-77. Roman Catholic. Home: 1360 Lake Shore Dr Chicago IL 60610 Office: 720 N Michigan Ave Chicago IL 60611

MC INTYRE, FRANK JOSEPH, water and chem. treating lab. exec.; b. Columbus, Ohio, June 30, 1907; s. Edward Brown and Ula (Davis) McI.; grad. Ohio State U., 1930; m. Rebecca Jane Clark, Aug. 9, 1933; children—Daniel Allison, Louanne McIntyre Byrd. Chemist, Columbus, 1927-31; established Columbus Water and Chem. Testing Lab., 1931—; mem. Am. Council Ind. Labs. Councilman, Village of Riverlea, 1957-69. Registered profl. engr., Ohio. Mem. Am. Inst.

Chemists, Am. Water Works Assn. (life), Water Pollution Control Fedn. (life), Nat., Franklin County socs. profl. engrs. Clubs: Masons, Shriners. Office: 4628 Indianola Ave Columbus OH 43214

MC INTYRE, JOYCE WILEY, civic worker; b. Auburn, Ind., Nov. 11, 1926; d. Robert Sheldon and Lois Katherine (Dolan) Wiley; student Ind. U., 1944-46; m. James McIntyre, Sept. 14, 1946; children—Shelley McIntyre Draper, James, William. Mem. Auburn Bd. Zoning Appeals, 1973—; mgr. bookstore, 1970—; v.p. Auburn Cord-Duesenburg Mus., 1973-74, sec., 1974—; treas. Auburn Automeals, Inc., 1972-77; pres. Auburn Improvement Assn., Inc., 1974—; leader Boy Scouts Am., 1959-72, YMCA, 1962-67, bd. dirs. Northeastern Ind. Regional Coordinating Council. Mem. Nat. Trust for Hist. Preservation, Common Cause. Democrat. Presbyterian (choir dir. 1962-66). Clubs: Ladies Lit., Greenhurst Country. Home: 730 N Main St Auburn IN 46706

MC INTYRE, THOMAS GEORGE, banker; b. Toledo, Ohio, May 24, 1947; s. William Davis and Prudence Adlaide (Harrington) McI.; B.S., John Carroll U., 1970; M.B.A., Eastern Mich. U., 1972; m. Sheila Mary Wingerter, Mar. 1, 1975; children—Kathleen Elizabeth, Patrick Kernan, Maureen Mary, William Davis II. With Monroe Auto Equipment Co., 1964-73; internat. account officer Mfrs. Hanover Trust Co., N.Y.C., 1973-76; comml. lending officer, v.p. Empire Nat. Bank, Traverse City, Mich., 1976-80; chmn. Passageways Travel Service, Inc.; dir. Empire Nat. Bank. Bd. dirs. YMCA; mem. adminstrv. council St. Francis Parish. Republican. Roman Catholic. Clubs: Rotary; Hidden Valley (Gaylord, Mich.); University (N.Y.C.); Golf and Country, Economic (Traverse City). Home: 515 N Elmwood Ave Traverse City MI 49684 Office: 116 Cass St Traverse City MI 49684

MC KAY, BARBARA JOAN, psychologist, clergyperson; b. Chgo., Nov. 23, 1931; d. Benjamin Mark and Margaret June (Regan) Squires; B.S., Northwestern U., 1953, Ph.D., 1974; M.A., Garrett Theol. Sem., 1970; m. Lewis Anton Musil, May 3, 1973; children—James Robert, Deborah Lynn, Thomas Michael. Ordained to ministry United Methodist Ch., 1970; counseling minister Glenview (Ill.) Community Ch., 1971-76, dir. adult ministries, 1977-78; pastor The New Ch.: A Caring Community, 1979—; pvt. practice psychologist, Winnetka, Ill., 1974—; psychologist Asso. Psychotherapists of Chgo., 1974-76, Asso. Mental Health Services of Chgo., 1976—; cons. Inst. for Christian Living, Winnetka, Ill., 1976—; also lectr. Bd. dirs. LINKS North Shore Mental Health Services, Northfield, Ill., 1976-77; adv. bd. Wilmette Family Service. Mem. Am., Ill., psychol. assns., Chgo. Met. Assn. United Ch. Christ (mem. exec. council), Pi Lambda Theta, Gamma Phi Beta Alumna. Composer 3 musical comedies, 1 opera, 1 revue, 3 religious works, 6 piano suites, 1964-72. Author: The Unabridged Woman: A Guide to Growing up Female, 1979; also articles. Home: 1639 Elmwood Ave Wilmette IL 60091 Office: 525 Lincoln Ave Winnetka IL 60093

MC KAY, CONSTANCE GADOW, hotel exec.; b. Aurora, Ill., Mar. 7, 1928; d. William H. and Esther E. (Olson) Gadow; student U. Ill., U. Wis., Madison, U. Wis., Milw.; widow; children—Richard A., Scott A., Mark G. Dir. catering Arlington Park (Ill.) Race Track, 1966-68, Arlington Park Hilton Hotel, Arlington Heights, Ill., 1969—. Commr., Arlington Heights Bd. Local Improvements, 1979—, Arlington Heights Relocation of Post Office Com., 1958-59, Arlington Heights Zoning Bd., 1959-60; youth commr. Village of Arlington Heights, 1981—. Named Outstanding Bus. Woman, Paddock Publs., Arlington Heights, 1977. Mem. Catering Execs. Club Am., Women in Mgmt. Republican. Home: 604 S Waterman Ave Arlington Heights IL 60004 Office: Arlington Park Hilton Hotel Euclid Ave and Rohlwing Rd Arlington Heights IL 60006

MCKAY, JOHN PATRICK, metallurgist; b. Ironwood, Mich., Mar. 12, 1931; s. Belmont Martin and Victoria Agnes (Deitz) McK.; B.S. in Metall. Engring., Mich. Tech. U., 1960, M.S. in Metall. Engring. (Am. Soc. for Metals scholar, Am. Iron and Steel Inst. fellow), 1961; m. Dora L. Cartwright, Jan. 15, 1954; children—Michael P., Michele P., Charles A., Teresa K. Devel. engr. semicondr. products Gen. Electric Co., Clyde, N.Y., 1961-64, rectifier devel. engr., Auburn, N.Y., 1965-66, metall. devel. engr., Magnetic Materials Group, Edmore, Mich., 1966-69; devel. engr. Arnold Engring. Co., Marengo, Ill., 1969-73, product metallurgist, 1973—. Served with USN, 1951-55; Korea. Mem. Am. Soc. for Metals (officer), Am. Powder Metallurgy Inst., AIME (officer), Am. Foundrymen's Soc. (chmn. No. Ill.-So. Wis. chpt.), Golf Digest Hole-in-One Club, Alpha Sigma Mu, Sigma Gamma Epsilon. Democrat. Roman Catholic. Club: Moose (Harvard, Ill.). Patentee in field; inventor vacuum beveling device for silicon pellets, 1963, improvements on magnetic alloys, directional grain growth devel., 1970-80. Home: Route 1 Box 97 Walworth WI 53184 Office: PO Box G Marengo IL 60152

MC KEAGUE, ROGER JAMES, architect; b. Chgo., Aug. 5, 1927; s. John Patrick and Alice Mary (Rodgers) McK.; B.S. in Architecture, U. Ill., 1951; m. Mary Theresa Gross, June 20, 1953; children—Roger James, Kevin J., Arthur J. With Holabird & Root, architects, Chgo., 1951-53, Ekroth, Martorano, Ekroth, architects, Chgo., 1953-56, Roger J. McKeague, architect, Chgo., 1956-58; architect Chgo. Bd. Edn., 1958-68, 79—; architect City of Chgo. Dept. Pub. Works, 1969-79. Served with U.S. Army, 1945-47. Mem. AIA, Ill. Soc. Architects. Roman Catholic. Home: 400 E Randolph Dr Chicago IL 60601 Office: City of Chgo Bd Edn Chicago IL 60601

MCKEAN, KEITH, polit. scientist; b. Logan, Iowa, Aug. 31, 1934; s. Harry Hazen and Kathleen Alice (Witt) McK.; student U. Iowa, 1952-55; Ph.B., U. N.D., 1956; postgrad. St. Vladimir's Sem., 1956-59; M.A., Fordham U., 1964; M.A., Case Western Res. U., 1968; Th.D., Geneva Theol. Coll., 1972; m. Susan Joy Rafa, June 27, 1976; children—Ronald Anthony, Eric John, Vincent Joseph, Michael Hazen. Asst. librarian Fordham U., 1961-63; mem. faculty dept. polit. and social sci. Youngstown State U., 1963—; lectr. philosophy and religion Cleve. State U., 1970-71. Pres., Republican Assos. of Mahoning Valley, 1976-80; pres. Fish-Samaritan House, 1976-79; pres. Youngstown Pastoral Counseling Service, 1976—; pres. Orthodox Book Soc., 1960-61; trustee Soc. of St. Basil, 1964-77. Mem. Am. Polit. Sci. Assn., Univ. Profs. for Acad. Order (dir. Ohio), Am. Acad. Polit. and Social Sci., Assn. for Clin. Pastoral Edn., Nat. Assn. Christian Edn. Eastern Orthodox. Home: 285 Redondo Rd Youngstown OH 44504 Office: 410 Wick Ave Youngstown OH 44503

MC KEE, DALE, promotions, premiums and incentives co. exec.; b. Ironton, Ohio, May 24, 1938; s. Frank and Eloise McK.; B.S., U. Dayton, 1966; student Sinclair Community Coll., 1975; m. Barbara Jean Robinson, June 15, 1957; children—Dale, Jeffery Scott. Pres., McKee & Parrish Bldg. Contractors, Miamisburg, Ohio, 1968-72; pres. McKee & McKee Bldg. Contractors, Miamisburg, Ohio, 1972-79; pres., treas. World Wide Crusade, Inc., Miamisburg, 1971-79; pres. Del Diablo Recording, Miamisburg, 1978-79; pres. Del Diablo Pub. Co., Miamisburg, 1978-79; asso. realtor Joe McNabb Realtor, Miamisburg, 1978-79; announcer WCXL & WQRP Radio F.M., 1978-79; v.p., dir. Bar Del, Inc., Miamisburg, 1974—; supr. Frigidaire div. Gen. Motors Corp., Dayton, 1956—. Mem. Am. Ind. Party Central Com., 1973-74; scoutmaster Sequoia council, Boy Scouts Am., 1971-73. Mem. IEEE, Dayton Area Bd. Realtors, Ohio Bd. Realtors, Internat. Platform Assn., Country Music Assn., Nashville Songwriters Assn., Am. Fedn. Musicians. Democrat. Roman Catholic. Clubs: Foremans' Club of Dayton, Moose. Composer: Ten Days I'll Be Getting Out of Prison, 1978; The Bottle Almost Empty, 1978. Home: 1232 Holly Hill Dr Miamisburg OH 45342 Office: Kettering Blvd Dayton OH 45439

MC KEE, DONALD DARRELL, real estate broker; b. Highland, Ill., July 20, 1932; s. Earl Michael and Leta Evelyn (Dresch) McK.; grad. high sch.; m. Emma A. Becker, Aug. 28, 1956; children—Dale Michael, Gail Ann. Sales clk. C. Kinne & Co., Highland, 1952-63; salesman Lowenstein Agy., Inc., Highland, 1963-69; owner Don McKee Ins., 1970-77; owner Don McKee Realty, Highland, 1969-73; owner Century 21-McKee Realty, Highland; owner Key Antiques, Key Sales Co. Tchr. real estate So. Ill. U., Edwardsville, 1974-81, Lewis and Clark Community Coll., Godfrey, Ill., Belleville (Ill.) Area Coll.; pres. Real Estate Inst., 1973-79; exec. officer Edwardsville-Collinsville Bd. Realtors, 1975-76. Mem. So. Ill. Tourism Council, 1969-79. Mem. So. Ill. Independent Ins. Agts. (pres. 1974-75), Edwardsville-Collinsville Bd. Realtors (pres. 1974), Nat., Ill. (v.p. dist. 1977) assns. Realtors, Highland C. of C., Highland Hist. Soc. (dir.), Helvetia Sharpshooters Soc., St. Louis Art Mus. Club: Highland Country. Contbr. articles to profl. jours. Home: 1403 Pine St Highland IL 62249 Office: 825 Main St Highland IL 62249

MCKEE, DONNA JEAN, educator; b. Seneca, Mo., Aug. 29, 1945; d. Leroy and Mary McKee; B.S. in Edn., Central Mo. State U., 1969; M.S. in Edn., So. Ill. U., 1973; Ph.D., St. Louis U., 1981. Tchr. social studies McCluer High Sch., Florissant, Mo., 1969-76; resource coordinator Title VI, Florissant Jr. High Sch., 1976-77; program coordinator Title VI, Ferguson-Florissant Sch. Dist., St. Louis County, 1977-78, coordinator various ednl. programs Title IV-C, 1978-81, ednl. cons.-staff and curriculum devel., innovative programs, 1977—, program reviewer, 1977-79, mem. dist. adminstrv. inservice adv. bd., 1980-81; facilitator IDEA prin.'S inservice program. Recipient Outstanding Young Woman of Yr. award, 1976; cert. tchr., secondary prin., supt., Mo. Mem. Assn. for Supervision and Curriculum Devel., Greater St. Louis Assn. for Supervision and Curriculum Devel. (sec.-treas. 1979-81), Assn. for Individually Guided Edn., Nat. Assn. Supervision and Curriculum Devel., Kappa Delta Pi. Office: 1248 N Florissant Rd Ferguson MO 63135

MC KEE, GEORGE MOFFITT, JR., cons. civil engr.; b. Valparaiso, Nebr., Mar. 27, 1924; s. George Moffitt and Iva (Santrock) McK.; student Kans. State Coll. Agr. and Applied Sci., 1942-43, Bowling Green State U., 1943; B.S. in Civil Engring., U. Mich., 1947; m. Mary Lee Taylor, Aug. 11, 1945; children—Michael Craig, Thomas Lee, Mary Kathleen, Marsha Coleen, Charlotte Anne. Draftsman, Jackson Constrn. Co., Colby, Kans., 1945-46; asst. engr. Thomas County, Colby, 1946; engr. Sherman County, Goodland, Kans., 1947-51; salesman Oehlert Tractor & Equipment Co., Colby, 1951-52; owner, operator George M. McKee, Jr., cons. engrs., Colby, 1952-72; sr. v.p. engring. Contract Surety Consultants, Wichita, Kans., 1974—. Adv. rep. Kans. State U., Manhattan, 1957-62; mem. adv. com. N.W. Kans. Area Vocat. Tech. Sch., Goodland, 1967-71. Served with USMCR, 1942-45. Registered profl. civil engr., Kans., Okla. Mem. Kans. Engring. Soc. (pres. N.W. profl. engrs. chpt. 1962-63, treas. cons. engrs. sect. 1961-63), Kansas County Engr's. Assn. (dist. v.p. 1950-51), Northwest Kans. Hwy. Ofcls. Assn. (sec. 1948-49), Nat. Soc. Profl. Engrs., Kans. State U. Alumni Assn. (pres. Thomas County 1956-57), Am. Legion (Goodland 1st vice comdr. 1948-49), Colby C. of C. (v.p. 1963-64), Goodland Jr. C. of C. (pres. 1951-52). Methodist (chmn. ofcl. bd. 1966-67). Mason (32 deg., Shriner); Order Eastern Star. Club: Kansas State University Wildcat. Home: 34 Lakeview Circle Route 1 Towanda KS 67144 Office: 6500 W Kellogg Wichita KS 67209

MC KEE, JAMES ARDEN, physicist; b. Hays, Kans., May 29, 1925; s. Cecil William and Zita (Bissing) McK.; student U. Ga., 1943, Ft. Hays (Kans.) State Coll., 1954; B.S. in Physics, U. Wash., 1957, postgrad., 1958-60; postgrad. U. Ill., 1957-58. Owner Midway Enterprises, Hays, 1945-54; owner Mdse. Mart, Hays, 1945-50, pres., 1950-54; sec.-treas. central div. Nat. Credit Card, Inc., Hays, 1951-53; physicist applied physics lab. U. Wash., 1955-60; operations analyst ops. evaluation group Mass. Inst. Tech., 1960-61; sr. operations analyst Nat. Cash Register Co. (now NCR Corp.), Dayton, Ohio, 1961-62, sect. head ops. research, 1962-63, dept. head ops. evaluation, 1963-64, mgr. ops. evaluation, 1964-71, dir. ops. evaluations, 1971-74, cons. engring. and mfg., 1974-79, dir. strategic planning, engring. and mfg. group, 1979-80, dir. ops. planning, devel. and prodn. group, 1980—. Cons. physics, ops. research, mgmt. scis., behavioral sci. Served with AUS, 1943-45, 50-51. Mem. Am. Phys. Soc., Ops. Research Soc. Am., Inst. Mgmt. Scis., Am. Mgmt. Assn., Phi Beta Kappa. Lion. Contbr. tech. papers to tech. jours. Home: 1300 W Rahn Rd Dayton OH 45459 Office: NCR World Hdqrs Devel and Prodn Group Dayton OH 45479

MC KELVEY, JOHN CLIFFORD, research inst. exec.; b. Decatur, Ill., Jan. 25, 1934; s. Clifford Venice and Pauline (Lytton) McK.; B.A. in Social Sci., Stanford, 1956, M.B.A., 1958; m. Carolyn Tenney, May 23, 1980; children—Sean, Kerry, Tara, Aaron, Evelyn. Research analyst Stanford Research Inst., Palo Alto, Calif., 1959-60, indsl. economist, 1960-64; sr. economist Midwest Research Inst., Kansas City, Mo., 1964-66, asst. div. dir., econs. and mgmt. sci. div., 1966-69, dir., 1969-70, v.p. econ. and mgmt. sci., 1970-73, exec. v.p., 1973-75, pres., chief exec. officer, 1975—. Active Civic Council Greater Kansas City; parliamentarian 7th Ward Republican Club, 1964—; bd. dirs. NCCJ; mem. external adv. com. Ga. Inst. Tech.; pres. Kansas City Council on Edn.; trustee Rockhurst Coll., Livestock Merchandising Inst., Oxford Park Acad., Avila Coll., Menninger Found. (exec. com.), Yellow Freight System, Inc. Mem. Nat. Assn. Bus. Economists, Hammer and Coffin Soc., Alpha Kappa Lambda. Clubs: Stanford, Carriage, Mission Hills Country. Home: 912 W 121st Terr Kansas City MO 64145 Office: 425 Volker Blvd Kansas City MO 64110

MC KEMY, STEVEN WAYNE, mfg. co. ofcl.; b. Kansas City, Mo., Jan. 25, 1954; s. Robert Bruce, Jr., and Alberta Louise (Young) McK.; B.B.A. (Curator's scholar), U. Mo., Kansas City, 1975, M.B.A., 1978; m. Karen Sue Kennedy, Mar. 7, 1975; 1 dau., Sara Janel. Asst. product controller Hallmark Cards, Inc., Kansas City, Mo., 1975-76, product controller, 1976-77, compensation analyst, 1977-79, sr. compensation analyst, 1979-80; personnel mgr. Osage Products, Osage City, Kans., 1980—. Mem. Phi Kappa Phi, Beta Gamma Sigma, Omicron Delta Epsilon. Methodist. Office: PO Box 17 Osage City KS 66523

MC KENNA, RICHARD HENRY, hosp. exec.; b. Covington, Ky., Dec. 19, 1927; s. Charles Joseph and Mary Florence (Wieck) McK.; B.S. in Commerce, U. Cin., 1959; M.B.A., Xavier U., 1963; m. Patricia Ann Macdonald, Jan. 6, 1979; children—Linda Ann, Theresa K., Joan Marie. Accountant, Andrew Jergens Co., Cin., 1947-55; treas., dir. Ramsey Bus. Equipment, Inc., Cin., 1955-59; with Oakley Die & Mfg. Co., also Electro-Jet Tool Co., Cin., 1959-60; pvt. practice accounting, No. Ky. and Cin., 1960-62; bus. mgr. St. Joseph Hosp., Lexington, Ky., 1962-66; asst. adminstr. fin. U. Ky. Hosp., Lexington, 1966-70; v.p. fin. St. Lawrence Hosp., Lansing, Mich., 1970—; part-time lectr. Aquinas Coll., Grand Rapids, Mich., 1980—. Former mem. adv. com. to commr. of finance State of Ky.; chmn. cath. div. Oak Hills Bus. Com.; mem. speakers com. Oak Hill Sch. Dist. Served with U.S. Mcht. Marine, 1945-47, U.S. Army, 1948-51. C.P.A., Ohio, Ky. Mem. Hosp. Fin. Mgmt. Assn. (Follmer award, past dir. Ky. chpt.), Am. Mgmt. Assn., Am. Inst. C.P.A.s, Ky. Soc. C.P.A.s, Mich. Hosp. Assn. (former mem. com. on reimbursement), Delta Mu Delta, Alpha Sigma Lambda. Home: 1444 Cambridge Rd Lansing MI 48910 Office: 1210 W Saginaw St Lansing MI 48914

MC KENNA, RONALD FRANCIS, tech. co. exec.; b. Hoboken, N.J., Sept. 6, 1940; s. Arthur Joseph and Virginia Eleanor (McBride) McK.; B.S.M.E., Fairleigh Dickinson U., 1962; M.S., U. So. Calif., 1966; M.B.A., No. Ill. U., 1974; m. Mary E. Extine, Apr. 24, 1965; children—Cathy, Rhonda, Cliff. Engr. spacecraft & missile systems Rocketdyne div. Rockwell Internat. Co., Canoga Park, Calif., 1962-65; prin. engr. rocket propulsion Bell Aerosystems div. Textron, Buffalo, 1966-69; mgr. advanced systems, energy systems div. Sundstrand Corp., Rockford, Ill., 1970—; asso. prof. mech. engring. Erie County Tech. Inst., Amherst, N.Y., 1967-69. Mem. Bus.-Indsl. Polit. Action Com., 1978-79; mem. fin. Com. Rockford Republican Com., 1978-79, mem. nat. senatorial com., 1979. Mem. Assn. M.B.A. Execs., ASME, AIAA, Am. Security Council (adv. bd.), Figure Skating Club Rockford, Rockford Hockey Club. Roman Catholic. Inventor rocketry, developer propulsion/power plants for spacecrafts, satellites and terrestrial applications. Home: 3156 Spring Lake Dr Rockford IL 61111 Office: Sundstrand Corp 4751 Harrison Ave Rockford IL 61108

MCKENNEY, HENRY FIELDS, energy cons.; b. Morgantown, W.Va., Aug. 1, 1918; s. Henry Fields and Marian Josephine (McKinley) McK.; E.E., U. Cin., 1942; postgrad. Poly. Inst. Bklyn., 1946; m. Eileen Geneva O'Connell, June 12, 1956; children—Eloise, Nancy, Elizabeth, Carolyn, Kathleen, Geneva, Patrice, Melissa. Chief engr. Ford Instrument div. Sperry Rand, Long Island City, N.Y., 1946-53, head engring. div., 1953-56; v.p. engring. Missile div. Electronics Corp. Am., Cambridge, Mass., 1956-57; exec. engr. Chrysler Corp., Sterling Heights, Mich., 1957-62, div. gen. mgr., 1962-71, dir. advanced devel., 1971-74; cons. Environ. Research Inst. Mich., Ann Arbor, 1974-78, mgr. tactical programs, 1978—; cons. Mich. Energy Resource Research Assn., Mich. Solar Energy Research Corp. Mem. Mich. Transp. Research Com., 1977—. Recipient cert. of appreciation Australian Weapons Research Establishment, 1967. Fellow AIAA (asso.); mem. AAAS, Am. Rhododendron Soc., IEEE. Patentee in field. Home: 3701 Franklin Rd Bloomfield Hills MI 48013 Office: PO Box 8618 Ann Arbor MI 48107

MC KENZIE, JOSEPH ARTHUR, mfg. co. exec.; b. Princeton, W.Va., Dec. 27, 1934; s. Arthur Modoc and Lily Catherine (Mandeville) McK.; B.S. in Aero. Engring., Va. Poly. Inst., 1957; M.B.A., Xavier U., 1971; m. Wilma Jean Teel, June 9, 1956; children—Deborah Lynn, Jeffrey Arthur, Jennifer Jean. Project engr. United Aircraft Co., East Hartford, Conn., 1957-61; major test project engr Gen. Electric Co., Evendale, Ohio, 1961-63, advanced project engr., 1963-67, mgr. test engring., 1967-74, sr. engr., data systems program, 1974-77, sr. engr. evaluation analysis, 1977-79, program mgr. advanced tech. mktg., 1979—. Mem. Warren County Regional Planning Commn.; chmn. City Planning Commn.; elder Lebanon United Presbyn. Ch. Mem. AIAA, Elfun Soc. Club: Optimists. Office: H9 Cincinnati OH 45215

MCKEOWN, JAMES EDWARD, sociologist, educator; b. Detroit, Sept. 3, 1919; s. Francis Joseph and Grace Margaret (Ruddon) McK.; B.A., Wayne U., 1941, M.A., 1945; Ph.D., U. Chgo., 1949; m. Mary Elizabeth McNamara, Aug. 6, 1955. Instr. social sci. St. Xavier Coll., Chgo., 1945-48; asst. prof. sociology N.Mex. Highlands U., Las Vegas, 1948-52; asst. prof. sociology DePaul U., Chgo., 1952-55, asso. prof., 1955-57, prof. sociology, 1957-70, chmn. dept., 1962-70; prof. sociology U. Wis.: Parkside, Kenosha, Wis., 1970—; vis. prof. sociology Emory U., summer 1952, Escuela Nacional de Asistencia Publica, La Paz, Bolivia, 1958, Northwestern U., 1965, Concordia Tchrs. Coll., River Forest, Ill., 1965, 66, Universidad Catolica, Santiago, Chile, 1968; fellow Fund Advancement Edn., summer 1954; Smith-Mundt lectr., Bolivia, 1958; Fulbright Hays lectr., Chile, 1968. Social Sci. Research Council travel grantee, 1958. Mem. Am. Sociol. Soc., AAAS, Am. Acad. Polit. and Social Sci., AAUP, Pi Gamma Mu, Psi Chi, Phi Sigma Iota. Club: Quadrangle. Author: Sociology, 1981. Co-editor: The Changing Metropolis, 1964, 2d edit., 1971. Contbr. articles to profl. jours., also to Britannica Book of Year, 1968-72. Home: 1469 N Sheridan Rd Kenosha WI 53140

MC KEOWN, MARY ELIZABETH, educator; b. Chgo.; d. Raymond Edmund and Alice (Fitzgerald) McNamara; B.S., U. Chgo., 1946; M.S., DePaul U., 1953; m. James Edward McKeown, Aug. 6, 1955. Supr. high sch. dept. American Sch., Chgo., 1948-68, high sch. prin., 1968—, mem. corp., 1972—, mem. exec. com., 1974—, trustee, v.p., 1979—. Mem. Nat. Council Tchrs. Math., Central States Assn. Sci. and Math. Tchrs., Adult Edn. Assn., LWV, Nat. Assn. Secondary Sch. Prins., Assn. for Supervision and Curriculum Devel. (v.p.). Home: 1469 N Sheridan Rd Kenosha WI 53140 Office: 850 E 58th St Chicago IL 60637

MCKIBBEN, PATRICK SCOTT, newspaper exec.; b. Mpls., Apr. 4, 1953; s. B. Dean and Patricia Lou (Loehr) McK.; student (scholar) U. Wis., Superior, 1971-72; B.S., U. Wis., River Falls, 1975; m. Brenda Sue Fisher, July 26, 1975; children—Jamie, Ashley. Retail salesman Green Bay (Wis.) Press Gazette, 1975-77; dir. sales Oshkosh (Wis.) Northwestern, 1977-80; advt. dir. Rapid City (S.D.) Jour., 1980-81, v.p. ops., 1981—. Fund raising chmn. YMCA, Rapid City, 1980, bd. dirs., 1981—; chmn. United Way, Oshkosh, 1979; mem. council St. Josephat's Parish. Recipient various advt. awards. Mem. Internat. Newspaper Advt. Execs. Assn., Am. Newspaper Pubs. Assn., S.D. Press Assn., Rapid City C. of C., Black Hills Ad Club. Republican. Clubs: Arrowhead Country, Elks. Home: 3116 Flint Dr Rapid City SD 57701 Office: 507 Main St Rapid City SD 57701

MC KILLIP, WILLIAM JOHN, data processing supply co. exec.; b. Chgo., Sept. 24, 1942; s. Hugh Anthony and Helen Jane (Graham) McK.; B.S.A., Walton Sch. Commerce, Chgo., 1962; m. Antonette Marie Wyrwicki, Nov. 12, 1966; children—Gwen, Sandra, Melissa, Vanessa, William Anton. Sr. accountant Harry B. Bernfield and Co., C.P.A.'s, Chgo., 1962-67; corporate controller Pryor Corp. (formerly Info. Supplies Corp.), Chgo., 1967-77, corporate treas., 1977—. Mem. Am. Acctg. Assn., Am. Inst. Corp. Controllers. Office: 400 N Michigan Ave Chicago IL 60611

MC KIM, JERRY MICHAEL, educator; b. Tell City, Ind., Apr. 7, 1950; s. John Odowl and Loretta Irene (Clark) McK.; A.S., Vincennes Jr. Coll., 1970; B.S., St. Joseph Coll., 1972; postgrad. Ariz. State U., 1973-74, No. Ariz. U., 1976-77; M.A.L.S., Valpariaso U., 1982; m. Georgia Ann Nagel, Aug. 11, 1973; children—Sean, Paul, Anne. With Ariz. Boys Ranch, 1973-74; tchr. Crown King (Ariz.) Elem. Sch., 1974-76, Williams (Ariz.) High Sch., 1976-78; tchr. spl. edn. resource, vocat. work program coordinator, coach football/basketball Rensselaer (Ind.) Central High Sch., 1978—. Youth dir. St. Augustine Parish, Rensselaer, 1979-80. PTA grantee. Republican. Roman Catholic. Club: K.C. Home: 531 N McKinley St Rensselaer IN 47978 Office: 1204 E Grace St Rensselaer IN 47978

MC KIMMY, DOYLE LYNN, hosp. ofcl.; b. Midland, Mich., June 3, 1947; s. Hurley Edwin and Frances Magdelene (Link) McK.; B.S. in Bus. Adminstrn., Greenville (Ill.) Coll., 1970; Asso. Hosp. Mgmt., Northwood Inst., Midland, Mich., 1971; M.Health Care Adminstrn. candidate Trinity U., San Antonio, 1981—; m. Nancy Weeden, June 12, 1976; 1 son, Jason. Payroll auditor Fisher Body div. Gen. Motors Corp., Flint, Mich., 1971-72; adminstrv. asst. Ingham Med. Center, Lansing, Mich., 1972-73; mgmt. analyst Genessee County, Flint, 1973-75; field cons. Am. Hosp. Assn., Chgo., 1975-76; dir. human resources Halstead (Kans.) Hosp., 1976-79; asst. dir. personnel St. Joseph Med. Center, Wichita, Kans., 1979—; chmn. personnel com. S. Central Hosp. Council, 1979—; dir. Employee Assistance Consultants, Wichita. Mem. Am. Soc. Hosp. Personnel Adminstrn., Am. Soc. Personnel Adminstrn., Kans. Hosp. Personnel Mgmt. Assn. (treas. 1977-78, sec. 1981). Home: 9020 Funston Ct Wichita KS 67207 Office: 3600 E Harry St Wichita KS 67218

MCKINLAY, ROBERT TODD, ophthalmic surgeon; b. Chgo., Dec. 11, 1938; s. Robert Todd and Helen Elizabeth (Eaton) McK.; B.A., Yale U., 1960; M.D., U. Pa., 1964; m. Helen Elizabeth Ann Griffin, June 17, 1961; children—Kathleen, Lisa, Allyson, Elizabeth, Stephen. Commd. ensign U.S. Navy, 1963, advanced through ranks to comdr., 1973; gen. med. officer in ophthalmology Sta. Hosp., Danang, Vietnam, 1968-69; resident ophthalmology Nat. Naval Med. Center, Bethesda, Md., 1968-72; chief of ophthalmology Naval Hosp. Boston, Chelsea, Mass., 1972-74; pres. Robert T. McKinlay, M.D., Inc., Columbus, Ohio, 1975—; vice chmn. dept. surgery Marion Gen. Hosp., 1976—; Clin. asst. prof. ophthalmology Ohio State U. Coll. Medicine, 1974-79, clin. asso. prof., 1979—; ophthalmology cons. VA Center Hosp., Dayton, Ohio, 1979—. Decorated Navy Commendation medal with Combat V. Diplomate Am. Bd. Ophthalmology. Fellow Am. Acad. Ophthalmology; mem. Ohio Ophthalmologic Soc. (gov. 10th dist. 1981—), Columbus EENT Soc., AMA, Ohio State Med. Assn., Columbus and Franklin County Acad. Medicine. Republican. Roman Catholic. Clubs: Yale; Westerville Rotary. Home: 1303 Goldsmith Dr Westerville OH 43081 Office: 2700 E Dublin-Granville Rd Columbus OH 43229

MC KINLEY, MARY CHERYL, counseling psychologist; b. Evergreen Park, Ill., Sept. 12, 1946; d. James Michael and Dorothy Grace (Shean) McK.; B.A., Loyola U. Chgo., 1968, M.Ed., 1974, Ph.D., 1978. Tchr. history Prosser Vocat. High Sch., Chgo., 1968-70; asst. dean students, also dir. activities Loyola U. Chgo., 1971-75, research asst. counseling, 1975-76, counselor, 1977-78, co-therapist Sci. Anxiety Clinic; asst. prof. psychology, counselor Oakton Community Coll., Chgo., 1978—; cons. in field. Univ. dissertation fellow, 1977-78. Mem. Am. Personnel and Guidance Assn., Ill. Group Psychotherapy Assn., Internat. Transactional Analysis Assn., Nat. Assn. Women Deans, Adminstrs. and Counselors. Home: 5056 N Marine Dr Chicago IL 60640 Office: Oakton Community Coll 1600 E Golf Rd Des Plaines IL 60616

MC KINNEY, BRYAN LEE, electrochemist; b. San Antonio, Jan. 2, 1946; s. Oscar Bryan and Mamye Maxine (Faubion) McK.; B.S., U. Tex. ar Arlington, 1968; Ph.D., U. Oreg., 1972; m. Joan Diane Miller; children—Samuel Bryan, Jennifer Rachel, Joel Aron. Research electrochemist Battelle Meml. Inst., Columbus, 1973-77; staff electrochemist Gould Inc., Rolling Meadows, Ill., 1977-79, group leader, 1980-81; sr. electrochemist Johnson Controls, Inc., Milw., 1982—. Robert A. Welch postdoctoral fellow, Baylor U., 1972-73. Mem. Electrochem. Soc. (sec.-treas. Columbus sect. 1976, chmn. Chgo. sect. 1980), Am. Chem. Soc. Democrat. Baptist. Home: N 84 W 15979 Menomonee Ave Menomonee Falls WI 53051 Office: 5757 N Green Bay Ave Milwaukee WI 53201

MC KINNEY, DALTON CLAY, hotel chain exec.; b. Greensburg, Ky., Apr. 9, 1937; s. William T. and Carrie E. (Kidd) M.; B.S. in Accounting, Bradley U., 1960; m. L. Edith Kneebone, Apr. 21, 1973; 1 dau., Heather Susanne. Accountant Klingbeil Accounting Services, Peoria, Ill., 1960-66; comptroller Tazewell Publishing Co., Morton, Ill., 1966-71; Jumer's Castle Lodge, Inc., Peoria, 1971—, also corp. sec., dir. Fin. dir. Mid-East Bluff Neighborhood Assn., 1976, 77; past bus. edn. advisor Morton Twp. High Sch. Mem. Assn. Accountancy, Peoria C. of C. Republican. Mormon. Home: 1912 W Riviera Dr Peoria IL 61614 Office: 3126 SW Adams St Peoria IL 61605

MC KINNEY, DONALD LEE, author, clergyman, educator; b. Centerville, Ind., May 31, 1909; s. Andrew and Ida (Ebersole) McK.; M.A., Ball State U., 1949; m. Jan. 11, 1935; 1 dau., Carolyn. Ordained minister Religious Soc. Friends, 1933, minister Interfaith Apts., Richmond, Inc., 1970—; feature wrtier Richmond Palladium Item, 1933—; tchr. Wayne County (Ind.) Schs., 1945-65, prin., 1965-70; faculty Earlham Coll. extension Ind. U., 1970-74; tchr. adult edn. Richmond High Sch., 1947—; asst. prin. Williamsburg (Ind.) High Sch., 1945-52; prin. Boston High Sch., 1965-70. Chmn. Centerville Bicentennial Commn., 1976—. Rector scholar DePauw U., 1928-32; named outstanding citizen Centerville Jaycees, 1970. Pres. Greater Centerville Inc., 1977—. Mem. Authors Guild, Soc. Children's Book Writers, Authors League Am. Club: Queen City Writers (pres. Cin. 1976—). Author: A Crooked Tree, 1973; Joy Begins with You, 1975; Living With Joy, 1976; To Follow a Dream, 1979; Builders of History, 1980. Home: 6017 Nolansfork Rd Richmond IN 47374 Office: Box 91 Centerville IN 47330

MCKINNEY, JOHN PAUL (JACK), profl. basketball coach; b. Chester, Pa., July 13, 1935; grad. St. Joseph's Coll., Philadelphia, Pa., 1957; coach St. James High Sch., Chester, Pa., 1960-65 asst. coach St. Joseph's U., 1965-66, coach, 1974-76; coach Phila. Textile Coll., 1966-74, asst. coach Milwaukee Bucks, 1976-79, asst. coach Portland Trail Blazers, 1979-80; coach Los Angeles Lakers, 1980—; Ind. Pacers. Served U.S. Army, 1957-60. Address: 151 N Delaware St Suite 60 Indianapolis IN 46204

MCKINNEY, MELVIN, safety mgr.; b. Forrest City, Ark., June 16, 1953; s. John and Daisy (Templeton) McK.; B.S. in Biology, U. Ark., Pine Bluff, 1976; postgrad. Central Mo. State U., 1976-77; m. Minnie V. Brooks, Dec. 24, 1977; 1 son, Melvin Douglas. Sci. tchr. King Upper Grade Center, Kankakee, Ill., 1975-76; loss control rep. Allstate Ins. Co., Rolling Meadows, Ill., 1978; safety engr. Aetna Ins. Co., Chgo., 1978-80; loss control rep. Continental Ins. Co., Chgo., 1980—. Mem. Am. Soc. Safety Engrs., Am. Soc. Casualty Engrs., Phi Beta Sigma. Mem. Ch. of God in Christ. Home: 1679 E Williamsburg Ct Wheaton IL 60187 Office: 200 S Wacker Dr Chicago IL 60606

MC KINNEY, ROBERT LESTER, psychologist, clergyman; b. Bolivar, Mo., Feb. 22, 1930; s. J. Albert and Katie Lucille (Cable) McK.; A.B., William Jewell Coll., 1952; M.Div., So. Baptist Theol. Sem., 1958; postgrad. Washington U., 1959-62, 69-70; m. Lavona Meekee Williams, June 7, 1951; children—Constance, Kathryn, Carrie, Kelly. Ordained to ministry Baptist Ch., 1951; minister, Lone Jack, Mo., St. Louis, Mo., Frankfort, Ky., 1951-59; prof. Mo. Baptist Coll., St. Louis, Mo., 1959-62; asso. prof. psychology William Jewell Coll., Liberty, Mo., 1962-79, chmn. dept., 1962-73; sr. minister Birmingham Baptist Ch., Kansas City, Mo., 1967-71; pres. Residential Redevel. Co.; partner McKinney-Philpot Assos.; exec. dir. Counselors and Behavior Specialists; dir. Yokefellows of Mid-Am. Minister of music South Liberty Bapt. Ch., 1972-75; asso. minister Independence Ave. Bapt. Ch., 1975-78; pastor Tryst Falls Bapt. Ch., Kearney, Mo., 1978—. Mayor, Village of Glenaire, Mo., 1974-76. Bd. dirs. United Community Services Clay and Platte Counties, United Community Services Met. Kansas City, Mental Health Assn. Clay, Platte and Ray Counties, Midcontinent Psychiat. Hosp. Grantee J.McK. Cattell Fund, 1963, Kansas City Regional Council on Higher Edn., 1966, Am. Psychol. Assn., 1967. Mem. Am., Greater Kansas City psychol. assns. Baptist. Club: Sertoma (charter pres. 1968, chmn. bd. 1969) (Liberty). Home: 401 Smiley Rd Route 4 Liberty MO 64068 Office: Yokefellows Mid-Am 315 Smiley Rd Route 4 Liberty MO 64068

MCKINNEY, ROBERT NELSON, personnel exec.; b. Glendale, Ohio, Feb. 19, 1942; s. Nelson and Goldie McKinney; B.A., Miami U., Oxford, Ohio, 1964; M.B.A., Mich. State U., 1971; m. Peggy A. Kear, Oct. 17, 1964; children—Robby, Jennifer. Claims supr. CNA Ins., 1964-65; personnel rep. R.R. Donnelley & Sons, 1965-67; personnel mgr. Whirlpool Corp., 1967-72; personnel dir. Percy Wilson Mortgage Co., Chgo., 1972-73; employee relations mgr. R.J. Frisby Mfg. Co., Elk Grove Village, Ill., 1973-74; dir. human resources Tech. Pub., Barrington, Ill., 1975—. Active Boy Scouts Am., Little League, United Fund. Mem. Am. Mgmt. Assn., Am. Soc. for Tng. and Devel., Am. Soc. Personnel Adminstrs., Am. Compensation Assn., C. of C. Republican. Methodist. Office: Tech Pub 1301 S Grove Ave Barrington IL 60010

MCKINNON, BAIN LAUGHLIN, ret. plastics molding exec.; b. Lethbridge, Alta., Can., Sept. 30, 1908 (parents Am. citizens); s. John William and Winnifred Eunice (Bain) McK.; B.S. in Chem. Engring., Oreg- State Coll., 1932, M.Sc., 1933; postgrad. U. Mich., 1934; m. Gladys Muriel Thompson, Sept. 7, 1942. Plant chemist exptl. sodium sulfate plant, Sask., Can., 1935; chemist B.C. Pulp & Paper Co., Can., 1937-42; research chemist Puget Sound Pulp & Timber Co., Bellingham, Wash., 1942-47; mfg. chemist Paschall Labs., Seattle, 1947-50; owner, operator McKinnon, Bain & Co., Detroit, 1951-80, ret., 1980. Pioneer in automatic injection molding of plastics; patentee plastic spray device for treatment of asthma; research on ethyl alcohol.

MC KINNON, DONALD WILLIAM, dentist; b. Oconomowoc, Wis., Dec. 19, 1930; s. Joseph J. and Irene G. (Knuth) McK.; student U. Wis., 1949-50; D.D.S., Marquette U., 1956; postgrad. U. Calif. at Los Angeles, 1958; m. Kathleen Ann McKevitt, June 29, 1957; children—Michael McKevitt, James Shawn, Daniel William, John Donald. Individual practice dentistry, Appleton, Wis., 1959—; mem. staff Appleton Meml., St. Elizabeth's hosps., Appleton, Theda-Clark Hosp., Neenah, Wis. Chmn., Outagamie County (Wis.) dental div. United Fund, 1968. Mem. Appleton area bd. Catholic Edn., 1974-76. Served to lt. comdr. USNR, 1956-59. Mem. Am. Dental Assn., Madison Soc. Clin. Hypnosis, Am. Soc. Clin. Hypnosis, Am. Soc. Geriatric Dentistry, Can.-Am. Dental Soc., Wis., Outagamie County (pres. 1969—) dental socs., Appleton C. of C., Marquette U. Alumni Assn. Roman Catholic. Home: 1603 Orchard Dr Appleton WI 54911 Office: 819 W Wisconsin Ave Appleton WI 54911

MCKINNON, ROBERT HAROLD, ins. co. exec.; b. Holtville, Calif., Apr. 4, 1927; s. Harold Arthur and Gladys Irene (Blanchar) McK.; B.S., Armstrong Coll., 1950, M.B.A., 1952; m. Marian Lois Hayes, Dec. 18, 1948; children—Steven Robert, Laurie Ellen, David Martin. Regional sales mgr. Farmers Ins. Group, Austin, Tex., 1961-66, Aurora, Ill., 1966-68; dir. life sales Farmers New World Life, Los Angeles, 1966-75; v.p. mktg. Warner Ins. Group, Chgo., 1975—; mem. Conners Exchange Dairy Adv. Com., 1977-81. Scoutmaster Boy Scouts Am., 1971-72. Served with U.S. Army, 1944-45. C.L.U. Mem. Soc. C.P.C.U.'s, Internat. Ins. Seminars, Am. Soc. Profl. Cons.'s. Episcopalian. Club: Anvil (East Dundee, Ill.). Home: 974 Williamsburg Park Barrington IL 60010 Office: 4300 Peterson St Chicago IL 60646

MC KNELLY, WILLIAM VON, JR., educator, psychiatrist; b. St. Louis, Aug. 23, 1929; s. William Von and Jennie (Todd) McK.; B.A., Westminster Coll., 1951; B.S., U. Mo., 1953; M.D., St. Louis U., 1955; m. Joyce Preis, June 13, 1954; children—Maureen, Michele, William Von III, Jennifer. Intern, St. Louis City Hosp., 1955-56; resident Barnes-Renard Hosps., St. Louis, 1956-57, 59-61; asst. psychiatry Washington U. Sch. Medicine, St. Louis, 1956-57, 59-61; instr. psychiatry Kans. U. Sch. Medicine, Kansas City, 1961-62, asst. prof., 1963-66, asso. prof., 1966—, dir. Univ. Affective Diseases Clinic, 1965—, dir. Univ. Methadone Clinic, 1966, dir. postgrad. psychiat. tng., dir. psychiat. cons. service U. Med. Center, 1961-68; psychiatrist VA Hosp., Kansas City, Mo., 1961—. Served to lt. USNR, 1957-59. Mem. AMA, Am. (pres. Western Mo. dist. br. 1972), Mo. (pres. 1973) psychiat. assns., Am. Coll. Psychiatrists, Jackson County Med. Soc., Phi Beta Pi, Phi Gamma Delta. Methodist. Office: Dept Psychiatry Univ Kansas Med Center 3900 Rainbow Blvd Kansas City KS 66103

MCKNIGHT, RICHARD LEE, aero. engr.; b. Ironton, Ohio, Dec. 7, 1936; s. Russell Henry and Marie McK.; B.S. in Mech. Engring., U. Cin., 1959, M.S. in Mech. Engring., 1966, Ph.D. in Aero. Engring., 1975; m. Marilyn Sue Rupp, Nov. 7, 1964; 1 dau., Carol Jean. Mech. engr. Dayton Malleable Iron Co., Ironton, Ohio, 1959-60; sr. engr. Westinghouse Plant Apparatus div., Pitts., 1965-69; sr. engr. preliminary design and advanced engring. Aircraft Engine Bus. group Gen. Electric Co., Cin., 1969-77, mgr. nonlinear analysis methods, 1977—. Served with AUS, 1960-62. Recipient Perry T. Egbert award Aircraft Engine Group, 1977. Mem. Elfun Soc., Evendale Gen. Electric Mgmt. Assn., Sigma Xi. Republican. Methodist. Home: 11817 Cedarcreek Dr Cincinnati OH 45240 Office: 1 Neumann Way Aircraft Engine Bus Group Mail Drop K71 General Electric Co Cincinnati OH 45215

MC KNIGHT, VAL BUNDY, engring. cons.; b. Budapest, Hungary, Sept. 14, 1926; s. Valentine B. and Maria E. (Heray) Mariahegyi; came to U.S., 1966, naturalized, 1971; student Inst. Tech., Budapest; M.E.E., Tech. U. Budapest, 1954; postgrad. Bradley U., 1966-68; m. Ruby P. Fulop, Aug. 3, 1947; children—Bela, Suzy. Mgr. engring. Ministry of Constrn. Industry, Budapest, 1955-57; supervising engr. Canadian Brit. Aluminum Co., Baie Comeau, Que., 1958-66; utilities cons. Caterpillar Tractor Co., Peoria, Ill., 1966—. Mem. Republican Nat. Com.; radio communication advisor Civil Def. System, 1969-76; nat. adv. bd. Am. Security Council, 1975-77; deacon Westminster Presbyterian Ch. Served to lt., Budapest Mil. Acad., 1954-55. Named Innovator of Yr., 1955; knighted, Order of Knights, 1942; cert. plant engr.; registered profl. engr., Que. Mem. Am. Inst. Plant Engrs. (plant engr. of year 1976-77, pres. chpt. 93, 1979-80, del. dir. 1981—), Nat., Ill. (govt. relations and public affairs com. 1977-80) socs. profl. engrs., Corp. of Profl. Engrs. of Que., IEEE, Illuminating Engring. Soc., Nat. Assn. Bus. Ednl. Radio, NAM (policy com.), Engring. Inst. Can., Mfrs. Radio Frequency Adv. Council (dir. 1978—, v.p.), Assn. Energy Engrs., Nat. Machine Tool Builders Assn. (joint indsl. council), Am. Assn. Engring. Socs. (internat. affairs council). Clubs: Masons, Shriners. Home: 6831 N Michele Ln Peoria IL 61614 Office: 100 NE Adams St Peoria IL 61629

MCKONE, DON T., business exec.; b. Jackson, Mich., 1921; grad. U. Mich., 1947. Chmn. bd., chief exec. officer, dir. Libbey-Owens-Ford Co., Toledo, Ohio; dir. Hayes-Albion Corp., Consumers Power Co., Ohio Citizens Bancorp, Inc. Nat. Bank Detroit. Office: Libbey-Owens-Ford Co 811 Madison Ave Toledo OH 43695

MCKOWN, RICHARD DALE, bus. exec.; b. Columbia City, Ind., Apr. 2, 1947; s. Ralph and Itha McK.; student Ball State U.; B.S., Ind. U., 1971; M.B.A., St. Francis Coll., 1976; 1 dau., Kelley L. From personnel mgr. to sales coordinator Sun Metal Products, Warsaw, Ind., 1971-76; gen. mgr. Hamelin Industries, Warsaw, 1971-76; exec. v.p. Lyall Internat., Inc., Kendallville, Ind., 1980—; dir. FEM Leaing, Inc., Hamelin Industries, Inc. Chmn. ch. council, supt. ch. sch. program. Served in U.S. Army, 1966-68; Vietnam. Mem. Soc. Plastics Engrs., Ft. Wayne Rubber and Plastics Group, Am. Mktg. Assn., Am. Mgmt. Assn., Am. Legion, Beta Gamma Sigma. Republican. Address: Route 6 Columbia City IN 46725*

MC KOY, JENNIE UMBEL, nursing adminstr.; b. Connellsville, Pa., Dec. 4, 1923; d. Charles J. and Jennie M. (MacMaster) Umbel; student Bethany Coll., 1940-42; B.S. in Nursing, U. Pitts., 1957, M. in Nursing Edn., 1964; children—Pamela Johnsen, Lida O'Neill Mulligan. Staff nurse VA Hosp., Canandaigua, N.Y., 1957-58, head nurse, 1958-62; asst. dir. nursing service Presbyn.-U. Hosp. Pitts., 1964-65; supr. St. Elizabeth's Hosp., Washington, 1965-67; asso. dir. nursing service Freedmen's Hosp., Washington, 1967-70; chief nursing service VA Hosp., San Fernando, Calif., 1970-71, VA Hosp., Hampton, Va., 1971-74, VA Hosp., Buffalo, N.Y., 1974-77; clin. asso. prof. Sch. Nursing, Niagara U., Niagara Falls, N.Y., 1975-77; chief nursing service VA Hosp., Hines, Ill., 1977—; asst. prof. nursing service adminstrn. U. Ill. Med. Center, Chgo., 1978—, Rush-Presbyn. U., Chgo., 1977—; guest speaker various ednl. and profl. confs., 1965—; cons. to New Careers Sch. Practical Nursing, Newport News, Va., 1972-74. Bd. dirs. Heart Assn., Hampton, Va., 1972-74. Mem. Am. Nurses Assn. (cert. in nursing adminstrn., advanced), Nat. League for Nursing, Ill. League for Nursing, Am. Hosp. Assn., Am. Soc. Hosp. Nursing Service Adminstrs., Council Nursing Service Facilitators, Assn. Mil. Surgeons of U.S., Sigma Theta Tau. Home: PO Box 515 Hines IL 60141 Office: Chief Nursing Service VA Medical Center Hines IL 60141

MC LAIN, DAVID JOHN, JR., choreographer, educator, adminstr.; b. Brighton, Tenn., Dec. 29, 1931; s. John David and Elsie (Burt) McL.; B.S. in Edn., U. Ark., 1953; M.A., Wayne State U., 1962. Tchr., Am. Ballet Center, N.Y.C., 1962-63, Severo Ballet Sch., Detroit, 1957-62, Schwarz Sch. Dance, Dayton, Ohio, 1963-66; chmn. dance div., asso. prof. dance Conservatory Music U. Cin., 1966-71, prof., 1972—; asst. to artistic dir. Severo Ballet, Detroit, 1957-62; asst. to dir. Robert Joffrey Ballet Co., N.Y.C., 1962; ballet master Dayton Civic Ballet Co., 1963-66; artistic dir. Columbus (Ohio) Civic Ballet Co., 1965-66; exec. artistic dir. Cin. Ballet Co., 1966—; founder, dir. David McLain Dance Theatre, Cin., 1969-70; guest artist, tchr. Chgo. Nat. Assn. Dance Masters, 1968-70; guest tchr. So. Assn. Dance Masters, Memphis, 1968-69, Ohio Dance Masters, Inc., Cleve., 1969; guest lectr. Wayne State U., 1962, Colo. State U., 1968; artist-in-residence Utah State U., summer 1970, Louisville Sch. Music, 1973-74. Named Outstanding Alumnus in Fine Arts U. Ark. Alumni Assn., 1962; recipient Cohen award for excellence in teaching U. Cin., 1971; Rosa F. and Samuel Sachs award Cin. Inst. Fine Arts, 1975; Ohiana Library Assn. award, 1980; ofcl. Ark. Traveler, Ky. col. Mem. Am. Assn. Dance Cos. (dir. 1970-72), Phi Mu Alpha Sinfonia, Kappa Kappa Psi, Phi Delta Theta. Choreographer: Songs of Silence, commnd. for centennial dedication Conservatory Music U. Cin., 1967; The Nutcracker for premiere Cleve. Orch., Dayton Civic Ballet, 1963; Concerto and Romanza for premiere Cin. Symphony Orch., Cin. Ballet Co., 1969, Winter's Traces; Dilemmas Moderne Guitar Concerto, 1970; Clouds, 1971. Home: 854 Rue de la Paix Cincinnati OH 45220

MC LAIN, JAMES MARION, educator; b. Atlanta, May 16, 1913; s. Elisha Alexander and Jessie (Starnes) McL.; B.A., U. Akron, 1940; M.A., Western Res. U., 1942; Ph.D., Ohio State U., 1959; m. Lela E. Howse, Feb. 27, 1940; children—James Thaden, Lela Elizabeth. Undergrad. asst. U. Akron, 1938-40; grad. asst. Western Res. U., 1941; instr. econs. U. Akron, 1946-53, asst. prof., 1953-69, asso. prof., 1969-77, prof., 1977—; asst. instr. Ohio State U., Columbus, 1950-52, lectr., 1968. Served to capt., inf. AUS, 1942-46. Decorated Bronze Star medal, Purple Heart. Mem. Am. Econ. Assn., Indsl. Relations Research Assn., AAUP. Contbr. to publs. in field. Home: 2192 Coon Rd Copley OH 44321 Office: U Akron Akron OH 44304

MC LAIN, MYRTLE SUNDBERG, physician; b. Ensign, Mich., Dec. 24, 1930; d. Ferdinand Isaac and Marie Ingeborg (Hagglad) Sundberg; B.S. in Chemistry, U. Mich., 1952, M.D., 1966; m. Ernest Linton McLain, Sept. 1, 1951; children—Alice L., Jan M., Dawn C., Carol P., Kenneth W., Ross A. Intern, St. Mary's Hosp., Grand Rapids, Mich., 1966-67, emergency physician, 1967—, also med. dir. Emergency Care Center, chmn. dept. emergency medicine; mem. staff Butterworth Hosp.; asst. clin. prof. Coll. Human Med., Mich. State U.; pres. Mich. Emergency Health Services Council, 1977. Recipient Moses Gomberg prize chemistry, 1951; diplomate Am. Bd. Emergency Medicine. Mem. Am. Coll. Emergency Physicians (charter), AMA, Mich., Kent County med. socs., Am. Women's Med. Assn., Univ. Assn. Emergency Medicine, Alpha Epsilon Iota. Home: 645 Oakleigh Rd NW Grand Rapids MI 49504

MC LANE, EARL LEE, hosp. adminstr.; b. Alexandria, Va., Apr. 25, 1938; s. Earl Russell and Elizabeth Parkingson (Ballanger) McL.; B.S., Va. Poly. Inst., 1962; M.A., Central Mich. U., 1975; m. Betsy Jean Creasy, Apr. 7, 1962; 1 son, Michael James. Asst. dir. personnel Riverside Methodist Hosp., Columbus, Ohio, 1970-72, dir. personnel, 1972-80, v.p. for human resources, 1981—. Served to maj. AUS, 1963-70. Decorated Bronze Star medal. Mem. Health Careers of Ohio (mem. exec. bd.), Personnel Soc. Columbus, Ohio Hosp. Assn. (mem. state personnel com. 1978-80), Am. Soc. Personnel Adminstrn., Am. Soc. Hosp. Personnel Adminstrn., Central Ohio Personnel Assn. Republican. Lutheran. Clubs: Central Ohio Pony (dist. commr. 1976-79), U.S. Pony. Home: 9420 E State Route 37 Sunbury OH 43074 Office: 3535 Olentangy River Rd Columbus OH 43214

MC LANE, HELEN J., exec. search cons.; b. Indpls.; d. Alvin R. and Ethel (Ranck) McLane; B.S. with distinction, Northwestern U., 1951; M.B.A., 1965. Pub. relations writer Chgo. Assn. Commerce and Industry, 1952-53; press dir. Community Fund, Chgo., 1953-56; asso. Beveridge Orgn., Inc., Chgo., 1956-61, v.p., 1961-66; pub. relations cons. Internat. Harvester Co., Chgo., 1966-69, asst. to dir. pub. relations. 1969-70; asso. Heidrick & Struggles, Chgo., 1970-74, v.p., 1974—. Mem. Nat. Assn. Investment Clubs (dir. 1957-69, trustee 1969-72, adviser 1972—). Clubs: Economic, Metropolitan (Chgo.).

Author: (with Patricia Hutar) The Investment Club Way to Stock Market Success, 1963; Selecting, Developing and Retaining Women Executives, 1980. Home: 124 Robsart Rd Kenilworth IL 60043 Office: 125 S Wacker Dr Chicago IL 60606

MCLAREN, CHARLES MIKE, pension fund exec.; b. Bloomington, Ill., July 30, 1947; s. James L. and Mary L. McL.; A.A., Springfield (Ill.) Jr. Coll., 1967; B.S. in Fin., U. Ill., 1973; C.L.U., Am. Coll. Life Underwriters, 1975; m. Colleen Beth Bergstrom, June 28, 1980. Sales and mgmt. positions Mut. of Omaha, 1971-75; asso. dir. Ill. State Univ. Retirement System, 1975-79; exec. dir. Public Employees Retirement Assn., St. Paul, 1979—; adv. council Minn. State Bd. Investment. Active Boy Scouts Am., Big Brother Assn., Youth for Christ; mem. Campus Crusade for Christ, Champaign and St. Paul. Served with AUS, 1968-71; Vietnam. Decorated Army Commendation medal, Bronze Star, Silver Star. Recipient numerous sales and mgmt. awards. Mem. Am. Soc. C.L.U.'s, Am. Mgmt. Assn., U. Ill. Alumni Assn. Club: St. Paul Athletic. Author: Estate Planning Procedure Manual for Salesmen; Retirement System Administration Manual. Office: 203 Capitol Sq Bldg 550 Cedar St Saint Paul MN 55101

MC LAUGHLIN, EUGENE RAY, pharm. co. exec.; b. Aberdeen, S.D., Sept. 20, 1921; s. George Alfred and Marguerite (Lesh) McL.; student U. Minn., 1940-42, The Citadel, 1942, Rugers U., 1942-43, U. Manchester, Eng., 1945; B.S. in Pharmacy, N.D. State U., 1949; m. Marion Joan McCulloch, 1946; children—Joan M., Janet R., Julie A. Pharmacist, Schwankl Drug, Sauk Rapids, Minn., 1949-50, Hopkins (Minn.) Drug, 1950-51, Dunn Drug, Brainerd, Minn., 1951-54; gen. mgr. Service Drug Inc., Brainerd, 1954—; founder McLaughlin Enterprises, Brainerd, 1960, pres. bd., 1960—, dir. Marion Prodns., 1960—; profl. cinematographer Sta. KSTP-TV, Mpls., 1955-59. Served with U.S. Army, 1942-46. Mem. Minn., Ariz. pharm. assns., Internat. Platform Assn., Am. Def. Preparedness Assn., Nat. Writers Club, Associated Locksmiths of Am., Vets. Assn. Am. Legion, DAV, Nat. Rifle Assn. Republican. Presbyterian. Producer films: Helping Hands, 1961, 3 documentary movies, 1963-67, also TV news stories, 1963-69. Home: 310 3d Ave NE Brainerd MN Office: McLaughlin Enterprises PO Box 564 Brainerd MN 56401

MC LAUGHLIN, HARRY ROLL, architect; b. Indpls., Nov. 29, 1922; s. William T. and Ruth E. (Roll) McL.; student John Herron Art Sch., Indpls., 1936, 40, 41; m. Linda Hamilton, Oct. 23, 1954; 1 son, Harry Roll. Partner charge pub. relations, pres. James Assos., Architects and Engrs., Inc., Indpls., 1956—; sec., dir. James and Berger, Architects, Engrs., Planners, Economists, Inc., specializing in restoration of historic bldgs.; advisory bd. Pompeiiana Inc., Indpls. Mem. Mayor's Indpls. Progress Com., Arts and Culture Com., 1965—. Dir., Historic Landmarks Found., 1964—, pres., 1964-74, chmn. bd., 1974-79, chmn. emeritus, 1979—; dir., past v.p. Marion County Hist. Soc.; past dir. Carmel Clay Ednl. Found.; nat. dir. Preservation Action; mem. archtl. adviser Historic Madison, Inc.; mem. adv. council Historic Am. Bldgs. survey Nat. Park Service, 1967-73; past adv. bd. Conner Prairie Mus., Pattrick Henry Sullivan Found.; past adviser Indpls. Historic Preservation Commn., New Harmony Historic Dist.; past mem. preservation com. Ind. U.; architect mem. state profl. adv. com. Nat. Register Nominations and State Inventory; architect mem. Indpls.-Meridian St. Preservation Commn., 1971—. Bd. dirs. Park Tudor Sch.; bd. dirs., hon. mem. Ind. Bicentennial Commn.; trustee Indpls. Mus. Art. Served with USNR, 1943-45. Recipient Town Crier award Zionsville C. of C., 1967; City of Indpls. Mayor's Citation for Outstanding Services to Community in Preservation, 1972; citations for design and environment in historic preservation Lockerbie Sq. Historic Dist., Indpls. Union Sta.; award for excellence in devel. City of Indpls., 1980; registered architect, Ind., Ohio, Ill., Va., Md., D.C., Alaska, Nat. Council Archtl. Bds. Fellow AIA (nat. com. historic bldgs., chmn. nat. historic resources com. 1970, state preservation coordinator); mem. Ind. Soc. Architects (preservation officer 1960—, 1st Design award 1972, Merit award 1972), Constrn. League Indpls. (dir. 1969-71), Nat. Trust Historic Preservation (past trustee, adv. bd., com. property mgmt. programs 1975-79), Soc. Archtl. Historians (past dir.), Am. Assn. State and Local History, Zionsville C. of C. (past dir.), U.S. Capitol Hist. Soc. (hon. mem. and hon. trustee), Victorian Soc. Am. (adviser), Ohio Valley Victorian Soc. (dir.), Smithsonian Assos., East African Wildlife Soc., Conservation Council, Ind., Zionsville hist. socs., Navy League U.S. (life), Ind. State Museum Soc. (charter), Athenaeum Turners, Nat. Audubon Soc., English-Speaking Union (dir. Indpls. br.), Ind. Acad. Clubs: Portfolio, Amateur Movie, Athletic, Indpls. Literary, Woodstock (Indpls.); Masons (33 deg.). Restorations include: Old State Bank State Meml., Vincennes, Old Opera House State Meml., New Harmony, Old Morris-Butler House, Indpls., Market St. Restoration and Maria Creek Baptist Ch., Vincennes, Ind., Restoration of Present Benjamin Harrison House, Old James Ball Residence, Lafayette, Ind., Lockerbie Sq. Master Plan and Park Sch., Indpls., Knox County Court House, Vincennes, J.K. Lilly House, Indpls. Waiting Station Crown Hill Cemetery, Indpls., Crown Hill Cemetery Chapel, Glenn A. Black Mus. Archaeology at Ind. U., Angel Mounds Archeol. Site and Interpretative Center, Morgan County Courthouse, Martinsville, Ind., Indpls. City Market, Scofield House, Madison, Ind., Foster Hall, Indpls., Old Indpls. Water Co. Whiteriver Pumping Station. contbr. articles to jours. Illustrator; Harmonist Construction. Home: 950 W 116th St Carmel IN 46032 Office: 2828 E 45th St Indianapolis IN 46205

MC LAUGHLIN, WILLIAM GAYLORD, metal products mfg. co. exec.; b. Marietta, Ohio, Sept. 28, 1936; s. William Russell and Edna Martha (Hiatt) McL.; B.S. in Mech. Engring., U. Cin., 1959; M.B.A., Ball State U., 1967; children—Debora, Cynthia, Leslie, Teresa, Kristin, Jennifer. Plant engr. Kroger Co., Marion, Ind., 1959-62; with Honeywell, Inc., Wabash, Ind., 1962-75, mgr. metal products ops., 1971-72, gen. mgr. ops., 1972-75; pres. MarkHon Industries Inc., Wabash, 1975—; dir. Frances Slocum Bank & Trust Co., Wabash. Pres. Wabash Assn. for Retarded Children, 1974-75; gen. chmn. United Fund Drive, 1971; mem. Wabash County Arts Council; bd. dirs. Wabash Valley Dance Theater. Treas., Young Republicans., Wabash, 1968-70. Bd. dirs. Youth Service Bur., Sr. Citizens, Jr. Achievement. Recipient Ind. Jefferson award for public service, 1981; Disting. Citizen award Wabash, 1981; named Outstanding Young Man of Year, Wabash Jr. C. of C., 1972. Mem. Indsl. (pres. 1973-74), Wabash Area (pres. 1976) chambers commerce, Am. Metal Stamping Assn. (chmn. Ind. dist. 1978), Young Presidents Orgn. (dir.), Cincinnatus Soc. Rotarian (pres. 1970-71, dist. youth exchange officer 1974-77, dist. gov. 1979-80). Methodist (mem. ofcl. bd. 1966-71, pres. Methodist Men 1975-77). Clubs: Wabash Country (v.p. 1972-76), Masons. Patentee design electronic relay rack cabinet. Home: 141 W Maple St Wabash IN 46992 Office: 200 Bond St Wabash IN 46992

MCLAUGHLIN, WILLIAM HARRIS, chem. engr.; b. San Antonio, June 21, 1927; s. Harris M. and Viola (Essen) McL.; B.S. in Chem. Engring., Northwestern U., 1949; m. Jean Trangmar, Aug. 21, 1954; children—Thomas H., Karen J. Process engr. Abbott Labs., North Chicago, Ill., 1949-60; mgmt. sci. mgr. Monsanto Co., St. Louis, 1960-76, gen. engr., 1977—; gen. mgr. The Hugo Essen Farms, St. Louis County, 1968—. Trustee, gen. mgr. Hiram Cemetery, Creve Coeur, Mo., 1964—; pres. Graeler Park Assn., St. Louis County, 1966-68. Served with U.S. Army, 1945-46. Mem. Nat. Assn. Cemeteries, Asso. Cemeteries of Mo., Asso. Cemeteries of St. Louis (bd. dirs. 1979-80), Sigma Xi, Triangle. Clubs: Masons, Shriners. Patentee in field. Home: 7 Gandy Dr Creve Coeur MO 63141 Office: 800 N Lindbergh Blvd Saint Louis MO 63166

MC LEAN, ARTHUR FREDERICK, mech. engr.; b. Bristol, Eng., Apr. 16, 1929; s. Frederick Robert and Edith (Hawkins) McL.; came to U.S., 1959; naturalized, 1966; Nat. and Higher Nat. degrees in Mech. Engring., Bristol Coll. of Tech., 1952; m. Oriole R. Robinson, Aug. 30, 1952; children—Mark F., Peter A. Sr. engr. aircraft control systems Bristol Aero (Eng.), Orenda Engines Can., 1954-59; sr. engr. power systems research Bendix Corp., Southfield, Mich., 1959-61; supervisor turbine systems sect. Ford Motor Co., Dearborn, Mich., 1961-66, mgr. turbine research and devel., 1967-78, mgr. ceramic materials research, 1979—. Served as engring. officer RAF, 1951-54. Mem. ASME (past chmn. vehicular com. and ceramics com.), Soc. Automotive Engrs. (past mem. turbine com.), Am. Ceramic Soc., Inst. Mech. Engrs. Patentee in field. Contbr. articles to profl. jours. Address: 860 Arlington Blvd Ann Arbor MI 48104

MCLEAN, MARQUITA SHEILA MCLARTY, univ. adminstr.; b. Richmond, Va., Aug. 5, 1933; d. William Charles and Daisey (Dabney) McLarty; B.A. with distinction, Va. State Coll., 1953; M.A., Ohio State U., 1956; postgrad. U. Cin., 1957-69; m. Cecil P. McLean, July 25, 1958. Tchr. girls' sch., Delaware, Ohio, 1954-57, Robert A. Taft Sr. High Sch., Cin., 1957-62; counselor Sawyer Jr. High Sch., Cin., 1962-65, Withrow High Sch., Cin., 1965-67; asso. Guidance Services div. Cin. Public Schs., 1968-73; dir. office univ. commitment to human resources U. Cin., 1973-77, asso. sr. v.p. univ. personnel services, 1977—. Active Pres.'s Youth Campaign, Cin., 1968—; mem. Sch.-Community Guidance Task Force, 1970—, Mayor's Com. Youth Program, 1970—, Cin. Manpower Commn., 1970-71, Pres.'s Council Youth Opportunity, 1968—; mem. alumni adv. council Ohio State U., 1971—; mem. steering com. Leadership Cin., 1978-81; trustee Camp Joy, Traveler's Aid; past trustee Cin. Tech. Coll. Mem. Ohio Edn. Assn., Am. Personnel and Guidance Assn., Cin. Personnel and Guidance Assn. (pres. 1967-68), Am. Sch. Counselors Assn. (nat. task force counselor negotiations 1969—, v.p. middle sch. 1970-71), Ohio Sch. Counselors Assn. (southwestern rep. 1969), Assn. Counselor Edn. and Supervision (co-chairperson commn. non-white concerns), Nat. Assn. Sch. Counselors (nat. dep. chmn.-v.p. 1972), Delta Sigma Theta (pres. 1963), Ohio State U. Alumni Assn. (scholarship chairperson Cin. 1969-72). Home: 5324 Kenwood Rd Cincinnati OH 45227 Office: U Cin Cincinnati OH 45221

MCLEAN, WALTER ROBERT, educator, adminstr.; b. Fayetteville, N.C., Mar. 12, 1946; s. Walter Watson and Annie Bell (Smith) McL.; B.A., N.C. Central U., 1968; M.S., Wayne State U., 1974, Ed.D., 1978. Tchr. public schs., Fayetteville, N.C., 1968-73, Detroit, 1973-81; adminstr. Guest Middle Sch., Detroit, 1978-81; instr. Wayne State U., Detroit, part-time, 1978-81; cons. alternative edn., vocal music, curriculum-supervision of instrn. Mich. Assn. Middle Schs., 1978-80, Detroit public schs., 1979-80. Bd. govs. Wayne State U., 1980—; dir. music Hope Presbyn. Ch., Detroit, 1976-80. Recipient Leadership award Phi Delta Kappa, 1980, 81, N.C. Central U., 1980, 81; Service award Phi Delta Kappa, 1980. Mem. World Educators Fellowship, Assn. Supervision and Curriculum Devel., Music Educators Nat. Conf., Assn. Middle Sch. Educators. Baptist. Author: A Study of Afro-American Folksongs, 1974; A Study of the Perceptions of Administrators in Alternative Education in Selected Cities Within the United States and the Province of Ontario, Canada, 1978. Home: 14187 Archdale St Detroit MI 48227 Office: 17525 Wyoming Ave Detroit MI 48227

MC LELLAND, MALCOLM JOHN, state ofcl. Ind.; b. Buffalo, Dec. 25, 1912; s. Ronald Joseph and Mary Margaret (Baker) McL.; B.S., U. No. Ia., 1937; M.S., 1941; m. Mary Evadine Rhamy, Aug. 6, 1949; children—Steven A., Richard J., Susan M., Malcolm John. High sch. tchr. and coach, Farmersburg, Ia., 1937-41; asst. prof., adminstrv. asst. to head Sch. Health, Phys. Edn. and Recreation, Ind. U., 1946-52; health edn. cons. Ind. Bd. Health, Indpls., 1952-57, dir. Bur. Adminstrn. and Devel., 1967—; lectr. pub. health Ind. U., 1964—. Bd. dirs. Ind. div. Am. Heart Assn., Ind. Health Careers; bd. dirs., treas. Ind. Pub. Health Found. Served to capt. USAAF, 1942-46. Fellow Am. Pub. Health Assn., Am. Sch. Health Assn.; mem. Ind. Assn. Health, Phys. Edn. and Recreation (pres. 1962-63), Ind. Pub. Health Assn. (pres. 1964-65), Phi Delta Kappa, Phi Epsilon Kappa. Contbr. to textbook. Author film strip Health and Safety for Elementary Schools, 1964. Home: 310 S Union St Bloomington IN 47401 Office: Ind Bd Health 1330 W Michigan St Indianapolis IN 46202

MC LENDON, HENRY LEWELLYNN, real estate broker; b. Valdosta, Ga., Feb. 16, 1908; s. Henry Kirk and Lila (Sharp) McL.; student U. Miami, 1927, U. Ky., 1928-29; m. Mary Louise Plummer, May 27, 1938; children—Vicky Lu, Judy, James Clifford. Sec., treas. Zanesville Devel. Co., 1947—. Mem. Zanesville Exchange Club. Home: 3058 Lookout Dr Zanesville OH 43701 Winter: 615 Rabbit Rd Sanibel Island FL Office: 330 Main St Zanesville OH 43701

MCLENDON, JAMES ANDREW, state senator, lawyer; b. Washington, Ga., May 7, 1906; s. Toombs and Fannie (Willis) McL.; A.B., Fisk U., 1928; J.D., Northwestern U., 1932; m. Elnora Davis, 1943. Admitted to Ill. bar, 1933; practiced in Chgo., 1933—; master in chancery, Chgo., 1948; mem. Ill. State Senate, 1979—. Served to maj., Judge Adv. Gen. Corps, U.S. Army, 1941-46; lt. col. Res. ret. Decorated Army Commendation medal. Mem. Am. Bar Assn., Ill. Bar Assn., Cook County Bar Assn., Chgo. Bar Assn. Office: One N LaSalle St Chicago IL 60602

MCLENNAN, RODERICK COLIN, ednl. adminstr.; b. Des Moines, Nov. 30, 1924; s. Donald McKenzie and Leola Bell (Peterson) McL.; B.A., U. No. Iowa, 1949; M.A., Northwestern U., 1953; Ph.D., 1967; m. Marilyn Joyce Leithardt, Aug. 21, 1948; children—Karen Lynn Schuster, Bonnie Ann Gates, Diane Louise McLennan. Math./sci. tchr. Arlington High Sch., Arlington Heights, Ill., 1949-53; math. tchr. New Trier High Sch., Winnetka, Ill., 1953-54; chmn. math. dept. Arlington and Prospect High Sch., Arlington Heights, 1954-61; dist. instructional coordinator Twp. High Sch. Dist. 214, Mt. Prospect, Ill., 1961-66; asso. supt. instrn., 1966—; grad. sch. instr. Schs. Edn., Northwestern U., Evanston, Ill., 1958-59, 60, Nat. Coll., Wilmette, Ill., 1970, Roosevelt U., Chgo., 1979—. Chmn., Cook County Council Govts., Com. on Career Opportunities for Youth, 1968, 69; pres. N.W. Cook County Vol. Services Bur., 1971, 72. Served with USAAF, 1943-46. Mem. Am. Assn. Sch. Adminstrs., Assn. Supervision and Curriculum Devel., Nat. Assn. Secondary Sch. Prins. Clubs: Mount Prospect Country; Hot Springs Village Country. Author: Plane Geometry, 1957; Brief Units in Solid Geometry, 1958; Elementary Concepts of Sets, 1959; Contemporary Geometry, 1962. Home: 323 S Rammer St Arlington Heights IL 60004 Office: 799 W Kensington Rd Mount Prospect IL 60056

MC LEROY, THOMAS STANDIFER, educator; b. Freeport, Ill., Apr. 23, 1929; s. Mark Burton (dec.) and Harriet Proctor (Clarke) McL.; B.S., Bob Jones U., 1952; M.S., No. Ill. U., 1955, Ed.D., 1968; m. Marion Joyce Busjahn, Aug. 9, 1957; children—Thomas Franklin, Laurie Jo, Jeffrey Mark. Salesman circulation and display advt. Freeport Jour.-Standard, 1943-51; tchr., adminstr. East Leyden High Sch., Franklin Park, Ill., 1955-66; mem. faculty U. Wis., Whitewater, 1966—, prof. bus. edn., 1969—, dean continuing edn. and outreach, 1970—. Pres. bd. Christian League for Handicapped, 1980—; v.p. bd. Fairhaven Corp., 1980—; mem. City Council, 1970-75, 78—, pres., 1971-75. Served with U.S. Army, 1952-54. Recipient Lyle Maxwell award No. Ill. U., 1973. Mem. Nat. Bus. Edn. Assn., Bob Jones U. Alumni Assn., Assn. U. Wis. Faculties, Nat. Univ. Continuing Edn. Assn., North Central Bus. Edn. Assn., Nat. Educators Fellowship, Wis. Bus. Edn. Assn., Milw. Area Bus. Edn. Assn., N.Am. Assn. Summer Sessions. Club: Kiwanis (pres.). Home: 1215 W Melrose St Whitewater WI 53190 Office: 800 W Main St Whitewater WI 53190

MC LOCHLIN, JAMES FRANCIS, ednl. adminstr.; b. Logansport, Ind., Jan. 6, 1947; s. Francis James and Martha May (Hoffman) McL.; B.S., Ball State U., 1969, M.A., 1971; postgrad. Ind.-Purdue U., Indpls., 1972-76, U. Calif., Riverside, 1978; m. Karen Sue Judd, July 17, 1971. Spl. edn. tchr. Marion (Ind.) Community Schs., 1969-71; psychol. cons. Indpls. public schs., 1971-78; supr. psychol. services Warren Twp. Schs., Indpls., 1978-80, asst. dir. spl. edn., 1980—. Mem. adv. com. Gallahue Mental Health Center; bd. dirs. Marion County Assn. Retarded Citizens. Mem. Am. Psychol. Assn., Nat. Assn. Sch. Psychologists, Ind. Psychol. Assn., Ind. Council Adminstrs. Spl. Edn., Sigma Chi. Home: Rural Route 2 Box 280 New Palestine IN 46163 Office: 9039 E 10th St Indianapolis IN 46229

MC LUCAS, GRACE B., pub. relations exec.; b. Oak Park, Ill., Oct. 10, 1911; d. Charles Franklin and Leah (Van Blarcom) Beezley; B.A., Wellesley Coll., 1933; postgrad. Northwestern U., intermittently, 1939—, Moser Bus. Coll., 1933-34; m. Don Hamlin McLucas, Feb. 29, 1936 (div. 1961); children—Don Hamlin, Bruce Beezley, William Stoddard (dec.). Sec., research asst. to dir. econ. research Internat. Harvester Co., Chgo., 1934-36; office mgr. office of counselors Northwestern U., 1936-37, sec. grad. div. Sch. Commerce 1937-38; ofcl. rep. in Chgo. area Wellesley Coll., 1953-57; copy editor sch. map and book dept. Rand McNally & Co., Skokie, Ill., 1961; asst. editor Jour. Assn. Coll. Admissions Counselors, Evanston, 1962, Jour. Med. Edn., Assn. Am. Med. Colls., 1962; dir. pub. relations Vis. Nurses Assn. Chgo., 1963-66; nat. program coordinator Council on Religion and Internat. Affairs, Evanston, Ill., 1967-68; dir. pub. relations YWCA Met. Chgo., 1969-74; v.p. Rathje and Assos., Chgo., 1975-77; dir. pub. relations Am. Assn. Med. Assts., 1977-79; cons. in communications, 1979—. Bd. dirs. North Shore Sr. Center. Mem. Newberry Library Assos., Northwestern U. Library Assos., Kenilworth Hist. Soc. (bd. dirs.), Wellesley Alumnae Assn. Home: 314 Oxford Rd Kenilworth IL 60043 Office: One E Wacker Dr Chicago IL 60601

MCLUEN, WILLIAM DOUGLAS, radio sta. exec.; b. Omaha, Dec. 15, 1940; s. William Benjamin and Bette Elaine (Lathen) McL.; student U. Iowa, 1959-62; B.S. in Journalism, Iowa State U., 1965; m. Mary Ann Issendorf, Apr. 30, 1971; 1 dau., Kari Elizabeth. News reporter, photographer WOI-AM-FM-TV, Ames, Iowa, 1962-66; news reporter, photographer KRNT Radio and TV, Des Moines, 1966-69; broadcast specialist, sr. div. publicist 3M Co., St. Paul, Minn., 1969-74; gen. mgr., exec. Twin Lakes Broadcasting, Inc., Monticello, Ind., 1974—; group mgr. Lee Buck Enterprises, Franklin, Tenn., 1976—; judge radio-TV news award contests Assos. Press and Northwest Broadcast News Assn., 1969-73. Dir. Monticello C. of C., 1975-79, pres., 1977; dir. White County United Way, 1977—. Served with Army N.G., 1965-71. Recipient Community Service award Monticello C. of C., 1974; Outstanding Young Man award Jr. C. of C., 1975; Radio Documentary award A.P., 1975. Mem. Ind. Broadcasters Assn. Club: Rotary (Monticello, Ind.). Address: PO Box 570 Monticello IN 47960

MCMAHON, EDWARD ANTHONY, mech. engr.; b. Oak Park, Ill., Jan. 11, 1946; s. Edward and Gladys McM.; B.M.E., Christian Bros. Coll., Memphis, 1968; postgrad. Ill. Benedictine Coll., evenings 1971-75, Keller Grad. Sch. Mgmt., 1980—; m. Suan M. Hempel, Aug. 8, 1970. With McMahon Bros. Machine Works, Inc., Cicero, Ill., part-time 1960-68; gen. mgr. Arkon Mfg., Inc., Chgo., 1968; indsl. engr. Spraying Systems Co., Wheaton, Ill., 1970-75, plant and indsl. engring. supr., 1976-78, mfg. engring. supr., 1979—; cons. in field. Served with U.S. Army, 1968-70; Vietnam. Decorated Bronze Star, Purple Heart, others. Mem. VFW (chpt. dir. 1977—), Soc. Mfg. Engrs. (sr.), Am. Inst. Indsl. Engrs. (sr.). Roman Catholic. Club: Radar. Contbr. articles to profl. jours. Home: 1811 Grey Willow Rd Wheaton IL 60187 Office: North Ave at Schmale Rd Wheaton IL 60187

MC MAHON, JOHN JOSEPH, cons. surveyor and community planner; b. Chgo., Oct. 6, 1910; s. James Joseph and Marie (Albert) McM.; student U. Detroit, 1929-32, U. Fla., 1954, Wayne State U., 1943-44; m. Janet Ruth Moffat, Apr. 3, 1937; children—Margaret B., Susan J., John Jeffrey, John Joseph. Engr. surveyor James McMahon cons., Detroit, 1938-53; surveyor, civil engr., community planner, sec., chmn. bd. McMahon Engring. Co., Detroit, 1953—; v.p., Mich. Engrs., Inc., 1960—; v.p. Lehner & Son cons. engrs., planners, Mt. Clemens, Mich., 1970—. Fellow Am. Congress Surveying and Mapping, Guild Surveyors London; mem. Mich. Soc. Registered Land Surveyors (life; surveyor of year state, 1970), Cons. Engrs. Council Mich., Engring. Soc. Detroit, Mich. Engrs. Soc., Nat. Council Engring. Examiners (chmn. uniform land surveying exam. com. 1980), Cons. Engrs. Council U.S. (recipient Excellence award). Mem. adv. bd. Mich. Hwy. Dept., 1958-62; meme., chmn. Mich. Bd. Registration for Land Surveyors, 1970-79; mem., chmn. Mich. Bd. Registration for Architects, 1970-79. Editor, publisher Mich. Surveyor Newsletter, 1965-71. Home: 20314 Webber Dr Harper Woods MI 48225 Office: 16058 E Eight Mile Rd Detroit MI 48205

MCMAHON, MARIBETH LOVETTE, physicist; b. Bradford, Pa., June 8, 1949; d. James Harry and Josephine Rose (Sylvester) Lovette; B.S. in Math., Pa. State U., 1971, B.S. in Physics, 1971, M.S. in Physics, 1974, Ph.D. in Physics, 1976; m. Frank Joseph McMahon, Nov. 19, 1976. Research asst. Pa. State U., 1971-76; advanced research and devel. engr. GTE Sylvania, 1976-78; sr. physicist 3M Co., St. Paul, 1978-79, market devel. supr., 1979—. Recipient Cert. in Appreciation of Service, Pa. State U., 1971. Mem. Optical Soc. Am., Assn. Women in Sci., Assn. Physicists in Medicine, Sigma Pi. Sigma, Sigma Chi. Home: 504 E Arlington Ave Saint Paul MN 55101 Office: 3 M Co Bldg 223-2Sw Saint Paul MN 55101

MC MAKEN, HARRY VOLNEY, social worker; b. Piqua, Ohio, June 25, 1916; s. Harvey Nolan and Bessie Mae (Killian) McM.; B.A., U. Miami (Fla.), 1938; B.S. in Edn., Ohio U., 1939; M.A. in Social Work, Ohio State U., 1947; m. Jean Alice McCartney, Feb. 15, 1942; children—Jack Douglas, Jill Ann. Exec. dir. United Way and Council of Community Services, Sioux City, Iowa, 1951-55, United Way and Community Welfare Council of Springfield and Clark County, Ohio, 1955-62; asso. exec. dir. allocations Community Chest and Council of Cin., 1962-71, dir. allocations United Way, Inc. of Dayton (Ohio), 1971—. Mem. allocations adv. com. United Way of Am., Alexandria, Va., 1975-78; mem. Dayton Metro. Area Council on Camping, 1976-80, Montgomery County Council on Aging, 1977-80, adj. instr. Ohio State U., Columbus, 1977-78. Served with U.S. Army, 1942-45. Mem. Nat. Assn. Social Workers, Acad. Cert. Social Workers, Phi Mu Alpha Sinfonia. Democrat. Presbyterian. Clubs: Rotary, Elks. Home:

187 Cheltenham Dr Dayton OH 45459 Office: 184 Salem Ave Dayton OH 45406

MCMANNIS, CYNTHIA ANN, dietitian; b. Canton, Ohio, Mar. 3, 1942; d. Georgia Alberta McM.; B.S. in Home Econs., Ohio U., 1964; dietitian cert. Drexel U., 1965. Therapeutic dietitian Lankenau Hosp., Phila., 1965-68; chief therapeutic dietitian Whelan Food Service at St. Mary Hosp., Phila., 1969-72; patient service dietitian Inst. Pa., Phila., 1972-75; patient service dietitian St. Vincent Hosp. and Med. Center, Toledo, 1975—; adv. N.W. Ohio Hosp., Institutional, Ednl. Food Service Soc. Committee woman Republican Party, Phila., 1972-74. Cert. food service mgr., vocat. tchr., Ohio. Mem. Am. Dietetic Assn. (registered dietitian), Ohio Dietetic Assn., Am. Mgmt. Assn. Republican. Methodist. Club: Pilot. Home: 1805 Brownstone Toledo OH 43614 Office: 2213 Cherry St Toledo OH 43608

MC MANUS, EDWARD JOSEPH, fed. judge; b. Keokuk, Iowa, Feb. 9, 1920; s. Edward W. and Kathleen (O'Connor) McM.; student St. Ambrose Coll., 1936-38; B.A., U. Iowa, 1940, J.D., 1942; m. Sally A. Hassett, June 30, 1948; children—David P., Edward W., John N., Thomas J., Dennis Q. Admitted to Iowa bar, 1942; gen. practice law, Keokuk, 1946-62; city atty. Keokuk, 1946-55; mem. Iowa Senate, 1955-59; lt. gov. Iowa, 1959-62; chief U.S. judge No. Dist. Iowa, 1962—. Mem. Iowa Devel. Commn., 1957-59. Del., Democratic Nat. Conv., 1956, 60. Served as lt., AC, USNR, 1942-46. Office PO Box 4815 Cedar Rapids IA 52407

MC MANUS, MARGARET ANN, educator; b. DeWitt, Iowa, Aug. 6, 1912; s. Edward J. and Hazel Mae (Butterfield) McM.; B.S., Coll. St. Teresa, 1939; M.S., St. Louis U., 1945, Ph.D., 1958. Joined Sisters of Mercy, Roman Cath. Ch., 1932; dir. Schs. of Med. Tech. and Radiol. Tech., Mercy Hosp., Cedar Rapids, Iowa, 1939-44; supr. depts. clin. pathology and radiology Kalispell (Mont.) Gen. Hosp., 1951-54; chairperson div. natural sci. and maths. Mt. Mercy Coll., Cedar Rapids, 1958-68, chairperson, prof. dept. biology, 1969-79; genetic counselor Mercy Hosp., Cedar Rapids, 1980—. Mem. Gov.'s Adv. Com. on Biomedical Ethics, Iowa. Mem. AAAS, Am. Soc. Med. Technologists, Am. Soc. Radiologic Technologists Iowa Acad. Sci., Albertus Magnus Guild, Sigma Xi. Republican. Contbr. articles to profl. jours. Office: 701 10th St SE Cedar Rapids IA 52403

MC MANUS, ROBERT LEE, mktg. profl. services co. exec.; b. Carmi, Ill., Dec. 3, 1922; s. Merle LeRoy and Laura Marie (Dissman) McM.; B.A., U. Ill., 1950; children—Laurie Ann McManus Kammerer, Katharine Sue, Bridgit Kathleen. Sales engr. James L. Lyon Co., Chgo., 1951-56; pres., R.L. McManus & Co., Peoria, Ill., 1956-65; dir. project devel. John Hackler & Co., architects, Peoria, Ill., 1966-80; specifications mgr. Beling Consultants Inc., 1980—; treas. Prairie State Legal Services Corp., 1977-79, v.p., 1979-80, pres., 1980-81. Pres., Greater Peoria (Ill.) Legal Aid Soc., 1972-74, Central Ill. Agy. on Aging, 1972-75; chmn. Comprehensive Geriatric Treatment Service, 1972-75; chmn. Mayor's Commn. on Aging, 1975—; pres., Sr. Citizens Found., Inc., 1972-78. Served with USAAF, 1941-43. Fellow Constrn. Specifications Inst. (pres. Central Ill. chpt. 1973-75, chmn. inst. tech. documents com., Tech. Excellence in Specification Writing award 1973, Honor award 1978); mem. U. Ill. Alumni Assn. Club: Creve Coeur (Peoria, Ill.). Home: 7133 N Terra Vista #202 Peoria IL 61614 Office: 7620 N University Suite 2200 Peoria IL 61614

MCMANUS, WILLIAM EDWARD, clergyman; b. Chgo., Jan. 27, 1914; s. Bernard Aloysius and Marie Therese (Kennedy) McM.; S.T.L., St. Mary of Lake Sem.; M.A., Cath. U. Am. Ordained to ministry, Roman Cath. Ch.; supt. Cath. schs., Archdiocese of Chgo., 1957-67, aux. bishop, 1967-76; bishop, Diocese of Fort Wayne-South Bend, 1976—. Vice-chmn. Ill. State Scholarship Commn., 1958-76. Mem. Nat. Cath. Edn. Assn. Club: Quest (Fort Wayne). Office: PO Box 390 Fort Wayne IN 46801

MCMILLAN, JAMES ALBERT, electronics engr., educator; b. Lewellen, Nebr., Feb. 6, 1926; s. William H. and Mina H. (Taylor) McM.; B.S. in Elec. Engring., U. Wash., 1951; M.S. in Mgmt., Rensselaer Poly. Inst., 1965; m. Mary Virginia Garrett, Aug. 12, 1950; children—Michael, James, Yvette, Ramelle, Robert. Commd. 2d lt. U.S. Air Force, 1950, advanced through grades to lt. col., 1970; jet fighter pilot Columbus AFB, Miss., Webb AFB, Tex., 1951-52, Nellis AFB, Nev., 1953, McChord AFB., Wash., 1953-54; electronic maintenance supr. Lowry AFB, Colo., 1954, Forbes AFB, Kans., 1954-56, also in U.K., 1956-59; electronic engr., program dir. Wright-Patterson AFB, Ohio, 1959-64; facilities dir. Air Force Aero Propulsion Lab., Wright-Patterson AFB, 1965-70, ret., 1970; instr. div. chmn. Chesterfield-Marlboro Tech. Coll., S.C., 1971-75; asso. prof., chmn. indsl. programs Maysville (Ky.) Community Coll., 1976—; cons. mgmt. and electronic maintenance, 1970—. Served with U.S. Army, 1943-45. Mem. IEEE (sr.), Soc. Mfg. Engrs., Nat. Rifle Assn., Sigma Xi. Republican. Presbyterian. Clubs: Rotary, Masons (32 deg.), Shriners. Author: A Management Survey, 1965. Home: 6945 Scoffield Rd Ripley OH 45167 Office: Maysville Community College Maysville KY 41056

MC MILLAN, KENNETH G., state senator; b. Macomb, Ill., Sept. 7, 1942; s. Keith Edward and Opal Leone (Dimmitt) McM.; B.S. in Agr., U. Ill., 1967, M.S. in Agrl. Econs., 1969; Nat. pres. Future Farmers of Am., 1962-63; asst. dir. legislation, asst. to pres. Ill. Farm Bur., 1968-72; spl. asst. U.S. Sec. Agr.,Washington, 1972; asst. Congressman Leslie C. Arends of Ill., 1973; confidential asst., chief speechwriter to Earl L. Butz, Sec. Agr., 1973-74; mem. Ill. Senate, 1976—. Mem. exec. com. Agr. Com., Ill. Econ. and Fiscal Commn. Registered Suffolk sheep producer. Mem. Am. Agrl. Econs. Assn., Nat. Suffolk Sheep Assn. (dir. 1979-81). Republican. Methodist. Club: Rotary. Office: 1040 Stratton Bldg Springfield IL 62706

MCMILLAN, LEON, investment co. exec.; b. Detroit, Mar. 28, 1937; s. Lyle and Grace I. (Gardner) McM.; B.S., Wayne State U., Detroit, 1960; M.B.A., N.Y. U., 1961; m. Phyllis A. Nevitt, July 3, 1961. Trainee, Thomson & McKinnon Co., N.Y.C., 1961-63; investment analyst Nat. Bank Detroit, 1963-65, First Mich. Corp., 1965-66, Robert W. Baird Co., Milw., 1966-67; sr. investment analyst Supervised Investors Services, Chgo., 1967-71, Lincoln Nat. Investment Mgmt. Co., Chgo., 1971-81, Continental Ill., 1981—. Mem. Investment Analysis Soc. Chgo., Electro-Sci. Analysts N.Y., Chgo. Sci. Analysts (past pres.), Chicagoland Old English Sheepdog Club (past pres.). Home: 480 Lee Rd Northbrook IL 60062 Office: 30 N LaSalle St Chicago IL 60693

MCMILLAN, LILIA MINEVA, city ofcl.; b. Sofia, Bulgaria, Apr. 9, 1923; came to U.S., 1950, naturalized, 1955; d. Christo and Penca (Turlakova) Minev; M.M.S., U. Climent (Bulgaria); M.S., U. Vienna, 1949; m. Wilfred McMillan, Feb. 17, 1953; 1 son, Christopher. Researcher in biochemistry dept. Northwestern U., Chgo., 1953-61; sr. electron microscopist City of Chgo. Water Dept., 1961—. Mem. Am. Water Works Assn., Electron Microscipy Soc. Am., Ill. Microscopy Soc., Standard Methods for Am. Public Health Assn., Sigma Xi. Democrat. Contbr. articles to profl. jours. Office: City of Chicago Water Dept 1000 E Ohio St Chicago IL 60611

MC MILLAN, MARGARET LANGSTAFF, librarian; b. Eaglegroove, Iowa; d. Harry C. and Elizabeth Louise (Tryon) McM.; B.S., Central Mo. State U., 1921; M.S., U. Mo., 1923; postgrad. U. Neuchatel (Switzerland), 1947. Dir. library Columbia (Mo.) Coll., 1926-59; librarian Mo. State Hist. Soc. Library, Columbia, 1959-60; reference librarian Mid Continent Library Service, Independence, Mo., 1961-76; faculty summer sessions Central Mo. State U., Warrensburg, Northwest Mo. State Coll., Maryville, U. Mo., Columbia; speaker various local groups. Active, Med. Center, Independence, also mem. aux. Mem. AAUW, State Hist. Soc., Jackson County Hist. Soc., Pi Lambda Theta, Delta Kappa Gamma. Republican. Methodist. Clubs: Women's City (Kansas City); Mary Paxton Study. Home: 2525 Lees Summit Rd Independence MO 64055

MCMILLAN, R(OBERT) BRUCE, mus. exec., archaeologist; b. Springfield, Mo., Dec. 3, 1937; s. George Glassey and Winnie Mae (Booth) McM.; B.S. in Edn., S.W. Mo. State U., 1960; M.A. in Anthropology, U. Mo., Columbia, 1963; Ph.D. in Anthropology (NSF fellow), U. Colo., Boulder, 1971; m. Virginia Kay Moore, Sept. 30, 1961; children—Robert Gregory, Michael David, Lynn Kathryn. Research asso. in archaeology U. Mo., 1963-65, 68-69; asso. curator anthropology Ill. State Mus., Springfield, 1969-72, curator anthropology, 1972-73, asst. mus. dir., 1973-76, mus. dir., 1977—; exec. sec. Ill. State Mus. Soc., 1977—; lectr. in anthropology Northwestern U., 1973; bd. dirs. Found. Ill. Archaeology, 1978—. Mem. Ill. Spl. Events Commn., 1977—, program chmn., 1977-78. NSF grantee, 1971, 72, 79; Nat. Endowment Humanities grantee, 1978. Fellow AAAS, Am. Anthrop. Assn.; mem. Am. Assn. Museums (council), Midwest Museums Conf. (pres.), Soc. Am. Archaeology, Cureent Anthropology (asso.); Am. Quaternary Assn., Sigma Xi. Editor: (with W. Raymond Wood) Prehistoric Man and His Environments, 1976. Office: Ill State Mus Spring and Edwards Sts Springfield IL 62706

MC MILLAN, ROBERT LAWRENCE, ednl. adminstr.; b. Xenia, Ohio, Dec. 18, 1934; s. James C. and Ruth (Collins) McM.; B.S. in Edn. and Music Supervision, Wittenberg U., 1957; M.Ed. in Supervision and Curriculum, Wright State U., Dayton, Ohio, 1970; m. Helene L. Von Steuben; children—Robert Lawrence, Scott Von Steuben, David Cameron, Daniel Gavin. Supr. music Fairborn (Ohio) City Schs., 1967—; music asso. Wright State U., 1968—. Bd. dirs. Fairborn Arts Council, 1970—; sr. organist Shiloh Ch., Dayton. Mem. Ohio Music Edn. Assn. (exec. sec., state treas. 1980—, contest adjudicator), Am. Guild Organists (past treas.), Am. Choral Dirs. Assn. (pres.-elect Ohio div. 1981—). Recipient Distinguished Service award Fairborn Jaycees, 1970. Certified in music edn. and supervision, Ohio. Home: 1319 Kevin Dr Fairborn OH 45324 Office: 200 Lincoln Dr Fairborn OH 45324

MCMILLION, JOHN MACON, newspaper pub.; b. Coffeyville, Kans., Dec. 25, 1929; s. John Dibrell and Mattie Anna (Macon) McM.; student Vanderbilt U., 1947-49; B.S. in Journalism, U. Kans., Lawrence, 1956; m. Virginia Johanna Stumbaugh, Feb. 12, 1956; children—John Thomas, Johanna, Jennifer. With Amarillo (Tex.) Globe-News, 1956-57, Grand Junction (Colo.) Daily Sentinel, 1957-59, Alliance (Nebr.) Times-Herald, 1959, Clovis (N.Mex.) Jour., 1959-63, Pasadena (Tex.) Citizen, 1963, U.P.I., Albuquerque, 1963-67, Albuquerque Jour., 1967-70, Albuquerque Pub. Co., 1972-75; with Duluth (Minn.) Herald and News-Tribune subs. Knight-Ridder Newspapers Inc., 1975—, pub., 1976—. Served with USN, 1950-54; Korea. Office: Duluth Herald and News-Tribune 424 W 1st St Duluth MN 55801

MC MILLON, FLOYD ALLEN, fin. exec.; b. Poplar Bluff, Mo., Oct. 20, 1946; s. Paul J. and Thelma K. (Transue) McM.; B.A., Mid-Am. Nazarene Coll., 1975; student Washington U., 1973; postgrad. U. Pa., 1976. With Mercantile Mortgage Co. and First Nat. Bank of Clayton (Mo.), 1966-70; acct. Washington U., St. Louis, 1973; exec. v.p., founder Nat. Inst. Cert. Tax Accts., 1975—; corporate pres., chmn. bd. F.A. McMillon & Co., Olathe, Kans., 1975—; exec. dir. Taxpayer's Success Inst.; guest speaker various bus., tax, fin. seminars, schs.; cons. in field. Served with USAF, 1966. Cert. tax acct., Kans. Mem. Nat. Inst. Cert. Tax Accts., Polit. Action Group, Nat. Assn. Accts., Nat. Soc. Public Accts., Assn. Tax Cons., Olathe Area C. of C. Republican. Mem. Christian Ch. Home: 1001 S Lindenwood Olathe KS 66062 Office: 1620 E Rogers Rd Olathe KS 66061

MC MORDIE, WILLIAM ROBERT, clin. psychologist, neuropsychologist; b. Phila., Apr. 3, 1946; s. John and Edna Elmira (Shepley) McM.; B.A., Glassboro (N.J.) State Coll., 1968; M.S., Western Ill. U., 1972; postgrad. Iowa State U., 1973; Ph.D., U. Ottawa (Can.), 1978; m. Sherilyn Kay Lanham, July 3, 1971; 1 son, Corey Scott. Tchr. algebra, Pennsauken, N.J., 1968; psychology technician VA Med. Center, Knoxville, Iowa, 1972-75; instr. psychology Des Moines Area Community Coll., 1975; clin. psychologist VA Med. Center, Knoxville, Iowa, 1977—, also pvt. practice clin. psychology and neuropsychology, Indianola, Iowa, 1981—; dir. Neuropsychology Behavioral Lab., VA Med. Center, 1978—; cons. Juvenile Care Facility, 1979-81, Contemporary Compliments, 1979—. Recipient Superior Performance award VA, 1975, 81; lic. psychologist, Iowa. Mem. Am. Psychol. Assn., Internat. Neuropsychol. Soc., Nat. Acad. Neuropsychologists, Behavioral Neuropsychology Spl. Interest Group, Iowa Psychol. Assn., Central Iowa Psychol. Assn. Democrat. Presbyterian. Research and publs. on neuropsychology, gerontology, hypnosis, forensic psychology, death and dying, profl. issues; editorial bd. Behavioral Neuropsychology Newsletter, 1979-80. Home: 1204 Stephen Ct Indianola IA 50125 Office: VA Medical Center Knoxville IA 50138

MCMORRIS, DONALD LESTER, trucking co. exec.; b. Weldon, Iowa, Apr. 28, 1919; s. Wm. Fred and Eliza (Bunch) McM.; grad. Chillicothe Bus. Coll., 1941; B.S., Kans. U., 1948; m. Asenath Breece Evans, Dec. 4, 1944; children—Asenath Marie, Sandra Jane, Linda Kay. With H.R. McMorris, C.P.A., 1946-48; auditor, controller, treas. Riss & Co., Inc., Kansas City, 1948-54; controller Yellow Freight System, Inc., Kansas City, Mo., 1954-57, v.p., 1957-63, exec. v.p., dir., 1963-68, pres., 1968—; dir. Leawood Nat. Bank. Served to 1st lt. AUS, 1942-46. Methodist. Club: Mission Hills (Kans.) Country; Kansas City (Mo.). Office: Yellow Freight System Inc 10990 Roe Ave Shawnee Mission KS 66207

MC MURRIN, LEE RAY, supt. schs.; b. Ind., June 29, 1930; s. Albert R. and Mrytle E. (Brickley) McM.; m. Frances McMurrin, Aug. 19, 1956; children—Michelle, Marianne, Marshall; B.S. in Secondary Edn., Olivet Coll., Kankakee, Ill., 1952; M.Ed., U. Cin., 1955; postgrad. Miami U., Oxford, Ohio, 1955, Kent (Ohio) State U., 1957, Ohio State U., 1958-65; Ph.D., U. Toledo, 1971. Elementary tchr. Sharonville (Ohio) Local Schs., 1952-55; prin. elementary supr. Leetonia (Ohio) Exempted Village Schs., 1955-58; asst. supt. Dover (Ohio) City Schs., 1958-60, South-Western Ohio City Schs., 1960-65; asst. supt. Toledo Pub. Schs., 1965-71, dep. supt., 1971-75; supt. schs. Milw. Pub. Schs., 1975—. Pres., mem. exec. com. Council of Gt. City Schs., Univ. Council on Ednl. Adminstrn. Bd. dirs. Jr. Achievement of Southeastern Wis.; corporate bd. mem. Milw. Symphony Orch., Milw. Children's Hosp. Mem. Am. Assn. Sch. Adminstrs., Wis. Assn. Sch. Dist. Adminstrs., Assn. Supervision and Curriculum Devel., NAACP, Phi Delta Kappa. Clubs: Rotary (dir.), Kiwanis. Home: 3435 N Lake Dr Milwaukee WI 53211 Office: 5225 W Vliet St PO Drawer 10K Milwaukee WI 53201

MCNALLY, ANDREW, III, printer, publisher; b. Chgo., Aug. 17, 1909; s. Andrew and Eleanor (Vilas) McN.; A.B., Yale U., 1931; m. Margaret Clark MacMillin, Nov. 20, 1936; children—Betty Jane, Andrew, Edward Clark. With Chgo. factory Rand McNally & Co., 1931, N.Y. sales office v.p., dir., 1933, pres., 1948-74, chmn. bd., 1974—; dir. Nat. Ry. Publ. Co., N.Y.C., Harvey Hubbell Inc. Past pres. Graphic Arts Tech. Found., now bd. dirs. Served as capt., C.E. Army Map Service, 1942-45. Mem. Chgo. Hist. Soc. (past pres., trustee). Office: Rand McNally & Co 8255 N Central Park Skokie IL 60076

MC NALLY, FRANCIS MICHAEL, mfg. co. exec.; b. Chgo., Dec. 17, 1943; s. Francis Patrick and Rita (Fitzgerald) McN.; B.S., Marquette U., 1967; m. Nancy Norton, Aug. 12, 1967; children—Colleen, Kathleen. Foreman, prodn. mgr., systems analyst Grede Foundries, Inc., Milw., 1967-72; dist. sales mgr., asst. sales mgr. Acme Resin Corp., Forest Park, Ill., 1972-78, regional sales mgr., 1978-81, mktg. mgr., 1981, mgr. market planning and analysis, 1981—. Served with USMC, 1967-69. Mem. Am. Foundrymen's Soc. Roman Catholic. Club: K.C. Home: 1526 Applegate Dr Naperville IL 60565 Office: 1401 S Circle Ave Forest Park IL 60130

MCNAMARA, JOHN FRANCIS, profl. baseball team mgr.; b. Sacramento, June 4, 1932; student Sacramento State Coll. Profl. baseball player minor leagues, 1951-67; mgr. minor league baseball teams, 1959-67; coach Oakland (Calif.) Athletics, 1968-69, mgr., 1970; coach San Francisco Giants, 1971-73; mgr. San Diego Padres, 1974-77; coach Calif. Angels, 1978; mgr. Cin. Reds, 1979—. Address: Cin Reds 100 Riverfront Stadium Cincinnati OH 45202*

MCNAMARA, KEITH, lawyer; b. Upper Sandusky, Ohio, Oct. 12, 1928; s. James B. and Gertrude (Saylors) McN.; B.A., Amherst Coll., 1950; J.D., Ohio State U., 1953; m. Adelaide Sayre, Sept. 13, 1952 (dec.); children—Robert K., Jean S., Bruce S., Elizabeth W. Admitted to Ohio bar, 1953; atty., of counsel law firm McNamara & McNamara, Columbus; mem. Ohio Bar Examiners, 1980—. Mem. Ohio Bd. Regents, 1980—; mem. Ohio Gen. Assembly, 1961-72; past trustee Columbus Acad., Six Pence Sch., Wesleyan U. Parents Assn., Franklin County Children's Mental Health Center. Mem. Ohio Bar Assn., Columbus Bar Assn., Client Security Fund, Am. Bar Assn. Republican. Presbyterian. Clubs: Rocky Fork Hunt and Country; Capitol Hill; University. Home: 225 S Drexel St Columbus OH 43209 Office: 88 E Broad St Columbus OH 43215

MC NAMARA, LAWRENCE J., bishop; b. Chgo., Aug. 5, 1928; s. Lawrence and Margaret (Knusman) McN.; B.A., St. Paul Sem., 1949; S.T.L., Catholic U. Am., 1953. Ordained priest Roman Catholic Ch., 1953; parish priest, tchr. Kansas City-St. Joseph Diocese, 1953-57; dir. diocesan Refugee Resettlement, 1957-60; chaplain Jackson County Jail, 1957-64; exec. dir. Campaign for Human Devel., 1973-77; bishop of Grand Island (Nebr.), 1978—. Recipient award Cath. Relief Services. Address: 804 W Division St Box 1531 Grand Island NE 68801*

MC NAY, CURTIS EUGENE, II, archtl. designer; b. Des Moines, Nov. 30, 1948; s. Curtis Eugene and Betty Jane (Lutz) McN.; B.A., Wichita State U., 1971; m. Debra Lynn Scogin, Mar. 25, 1978. Archtl designer project mgmt. Comml. Builders Kans. Inc., Wichita, 1968-79; pres. Caber Assos., Inc., design bldg. and engring., Wichita, 1978—. Mem. Profl. Assn. Diving Instrs., Wichita State U. Karate Club, Alpha Kappa Psi. Republican. Home: 2428 Rivera St Wichita KS 67211 Office: PO Box 16336 Wichita KS 67216

MC NEAL, HARLEY JOHN, lawyer; b. Birmingham, Ala.; s. John Harley and Alfretta (Frederick) McN.; A.B., U. Mich., 1932, student Law Sch., 1934, student Med. Sch., 1936; LL.B., J.D., Western Res. U., 1936, LL.M., 1966, student Case Sch. Applied Sci., 1938-39, student Med. Sch., 1940; student U. Wis. Law Sch., 1935, Cleve. Coll., 1938; m. Virginia Marie Hutzel, Feb. 8, 1936; children—Virginia Marie (Mrs. Thomas Woodard), Sandra Jean (Mrs. Thomas Highley). Admitted to Ohio bar, 1935; mem. firm John H. McNeal and Harley J. McNeal, Cleve., 1935-45; partner firm Burgess, Fulton & Fullmer, Cleve., 1945-50; partner firm McNeal & Schick, Cleve., 1950-81, sr. partner, 1969—; lectr. Western Res. U. Med. Sch., also Dental Sch., 1945-62, Cleve. Marshall Law Sch., 1958-60, Western Res. U. Law Sch., 1958-62; trustee Am. Bd. Profl. Liability Attys. Mem. council Bay Village, Ohio, 1950-52; mem. center com. on law and environment World Peace Through Law Center, Belgrade, Yugoslavia, 1971. Mem. adminstrn. justice adv. com. Greater Cleve. Asso. Found.; mem. com. for justice Greater Cleve. Growth Assn.; bd. dirs. Def. Research Inst. Served to capt. JAG Dept., USAAF, 1942-45; ETO. Fellow Am. Coll. Trial Lawyers (chmn. com. on procedures and preservation oral argument), Internat. Acad. Trial Lawyers, Am. Acad. Forensic Scis., Am., Ohio bar founds.; mem. Am. Bd. Profl. Attys. (trustee), Internat. Assn. Ins. Counsel (pres. 1966-67), Fedn. Ins. Counsel Assn., Am. Bar Assn. (chmn. rules and procedure and trial technique coms. ins. sect., co-chmn. profl. liability com. litigation sect., mem. council litigation sect. 1978—), Internat. Bar Assn., Fed. Bar Assn., Inter-Am. Bar Assn., Ohio Bar Assn. (chmn. individual rights and responsibilities com.), Greater Cleve. Bar Assn. (chmn. modern jud. system com., trustee 1980-81), Cyahoga County Bar Assn., World Peace Through Law (maritime com., chmn. litigation sect.), Seldon Soc. (Eng.), Am. Judicature Soc., Ohio Jud. Conf. (rules adv. com.), Maritime Law Assn. U.S., Nat. Assn. R.R. Trial Lawyers, Am. Soc. Internat. Law, Internat. Acad. Law and Sci., Greater Cleve. Growth Assn., Phi Delta Phi, Sigma Alpha Epsilon, Druids. Republican. Presbyn. Mason (32, K.T.). Clubs: Clifton, Westwood Country (Rocky River, Ohio); Union, Nisi Prius, Hermit, Mid Day (Cleve.); Coquille (Lantana, Fla.); Lotos (N.Y.C.). Author numerous articles profl. jours. Co-author: Personal Injury Litigation in Ohio. Asso. editor The Forum, 1965-69. Home: 26828 W Lake Rd Bay Village OH 44140 Office: Williamson Bldg Cleveland OH 44114

MCNEAL, JAMES HECTOR, JR., mfg. co. exec.; b. Dover, Del., Nov. 22, 1927; s. James Hector and Elizabeth Vickers (Hodgson) McN.; B.S., U. Del., 1951; m. Lucy Cooper Finn, June 16, 1951; children—James Hector, Edwin Howell, Sarah Elizabeth. With Budd Co., 1951—, v.p. mfg. services, Troy, Mich., 1972-73, group v.p. automotive products, 1973-74, pres., chief operating officer, 1974—, also dir.; dir. Automotive Co. of Can. Ltd. Bd. dirs. Detroit Area council Boy Scouts Am. Served with USNR, 1945-46. Mem. Newcomen Soc. N.Am., Econ. Club Detroit. Clubs: Bloomfield Hills Country; Oakland Hills Country; Detroit Athletic. Office: Budd Co 3155 W Big Beaver Rd Troy MI 48084*

MC NEAL, MARY JANE, dietitian; b. Estherville, Iowa, Jan. 27, 1925; d. Roy Sutton and Kathryn Ellen (Howe) McN.; B.S. in Foods and Nutrition, Mundelein Coll., Chgo., 1947. Instr. home econs. Crosby (N.D.) High Sch., 1948-50; clin. dietitian Parkview Episc. Hosp., Pueblo, Colo., 1950-57, Trinity Hosp., Minot, N.D., 1957-62; dir. dietetics St. Luke's Hosp., Fargo, N.D., 1962—; state del. Am. Dietetic Assn., 1971-74; by-laws com. State Nutrition Council,

1978—. Mem. Fargo Health Adv. Com.; bd. dirs. Minn.-Dakota Health Systems Agy. Mem. Am. Dietetic Assn., N.D. Dietetic Assn. (past pres.), Fargo-Moorhead Dietetic Assn. (past pres.), Am. Soc. Hosp. Food Ser. Adminstrs. Roman Catholic. Club: Quota. Office: Saint Lukes Hospital 5th St and Mills Ave Fargo ND 58122

MC NEAL, R(ALPH) RICHARD, ins. cons.; b. Oakville, Iowa, Aug. 19, 1925; s. Ralph Vincient and Zella Barr (Wright) McN.; student U. Minn., 1943, Coll. St. Thomas, 1943-44; B.C.S., Drake U., 1948; m. Ruth Lucille Morgan, Aug. 31, 1947; children—Michael, Deborah McNeal Wood, Nancy McNeal Burtch. Mktg. rep. Aetna Life & Casualty Co., St. Louis, 1948-54; operator Kennew Land & Ins. Co., Atlanta, 1954-59; operator W. Lyman Case & Co., Columbus, Ohio, 1959-64; pres. R. Richard McNeal Assos., Co., Columbus, 1964—; speaker to various mgmt. groups. Served with USNR, 1943-45. Recipient Young Man of Yr. award, Jr. C. of C., Cobb County, Ohio, 1958; Salesman of Yr. award Upper Arlington Civic Assn., 1972. Mem. Soc. Ins. Research, Am. Assn. Risk Analysts (trustee 1969—), Am. Mgmt. Assn. Young Bus. Men's Club. Lion. Clubs: Scioto Country, Athletic, Ohio State U. Faculty (Columbus); Arlington (Upper Arlington, Ohio); Optimist (Atlanta). Contbr. articles to profl. jours. Home: 2171 Pinebrook Rd Columbus OH 43220 Office: 1880 Mackenzie Dr Columbus OH 43220

MC NEELY, E. L., merchandising co. exec.; b. Pattonsburg, Mo., Oct. 5, 1918; s. Ralph H. and Viola (Vogel) McN.; student Central Bus. Coll., Kansas City, Mo., 1935-36, U. Mo., 1936-37; A.B., No. Mo. State U., Kirksville, 1940; student Rockhurst Coll., Kansas City, Mo., 1942; m. Alice Elaine Hall, Sept. 18, 1948; children—Sandra (Mrs. Ronald Gessl), Gregory, Mark, Kevin. With Montgomery Ward & Co., 1940-64, divisional mdse. mgr., 1961-64; dir. marketing Wickes Corp., Saginaw, Mich., 1964-65, sr. v.p., 1965-69, pres., 1969-74, chief exec. officer, chmn., 1974—, also dir. chmn.; chief exec. officer Gamble-Skogmo, Inc subs.; dir. Dayco Corp., Fed. Mogul Corp., Mich. Nat. Corp., Mich. Nat. Bank Detroit, Transam. Corp. Bd. dirs. YMCA, City of Hope; trustee Scripps Clinic and Research Found., Boys Clubs Am. Served as officer USNR, 1942-46; PTO. Mem. Beta Gamma Sigma, Alpha Phi Omega. Republican. Presbyterian. Clubs: Saginaw; Union League, Metropolitan (Chgo.); La Jolla Country; Cuyamaca (San Diego). Home: 1020 La Jolla Rancho Rd La Jolla CA 92037 Office: 1010 2d Ave San Diego CA 92101 also Gamble-Skogmo Inc 5100 Gamble Dr Minneapolis MN 55481

MC NEESE, WILMA WALLACE, social worker; b. Chgo., Apr. 30, 1946; d. Nettie Fletcher Wallace; student Wilson City Coll., 1964-66; B.A., So. Ill. U., 1969; M.S.W., Loyola U., Chgo., 1976; m. Mose D. McNeese, Dec. 27, 1969; children—Derrick, Christina. Program coordinator Intensive Tng. and Employment Program, East St. Louis, Ill., 1970-71; methods and procedures adviser Ill. Dept. Pub. Aid, Chgo., 1972-73; social work intern Robbins (Ill.) Presch. Center, 1974; with U.S. Probation Office, Chgo., 1975; officer U.S. Pretrial Services Agy., Chgo., 1976—. Recipient Community Service award Village of Robbins, 1975; advanced tng. cert. Fed. Jud. Center.; cert. social worker, Ill. Mem. Nat. Assn. Social Workers, Acad. Cert. Social Workers, Fedn. Probation Officers Assn. Baptist. Home: 209 Todd St Park Forest IL 60466 Office: 219 S Dearborn St Room 1100 Chicago IL 60604

MC NELLY, FREDERICK WRIGHT, JR., psychologist; b. Bangor, Maine, Apr. 14, 1947; s. Frederick and E. Frances (Cutter) McN.; foster children—Joseph, Ronald, Michael; 1 adopted son, Roger; B.A. magna cum laude, U. Minn., 1969; M.A., U. Mich., 1971, Ph.D., 1973. USPHS trainee, 1969-70, 72. Research coordinator NSF project U. Minn., Morris, 1968-69, lab. instructor, 1969; teaching fellow psychology U. Mich., 1970-72; ednl. examiner Ann Arbor (Mich.) Public Schs., 1971; dir. psychol. services Childrens Devel. Center, Rockford, Ill., 1972—; lectr. Rock Valley Coll., Rockford, 1974-75; part-time pvt. practice psychology, Rockford and Belvidere, Ill., 1980—. Active Boy Scouts Am.; chmn. spl. edn. regional advisory com. Bi-County Office of Edn., Rockford, 1976-78; mem. Nat. and Ill. Com. on Child Abuse; co-chmn. Winnebago County Child Protection Assn., 1980; elder Willow Creek United Presbyn. Ch., Rockford. Registered clin. psychologist Ill.; named U.S. Jaycees Outstanding Young Man of 1977. Mem. Am., Midwestern, Ill. No. Ill. (chmn. 1976-77) psychol. assns., Soc. Research in Child Devel., Nat., Ill. assns. retarded citizens, Am. Humane Assn. (children's div.), Nat. Register Health Service Providers in Psychology, Nat., Ill. Foster parents assns. Contbr. articles to profl. jours. Home: 11591 Beverly Ln Belvidere IL 61008 Office: Childrens Devel Center 650 N Main St Rockford IL 61103

MC NERNEY, WALTER JAMES, assn. exec.; b. New Haven, June 8, 1925; s. Robert Francis and Anna Gertrude (Shanley) McN.; B.S., Yale U., 1947; M.H.A., U. Minn., 1950; m. Shirley Ann Hamilton, June 26, 1948; children—Walter James, Peter Hamilton, Jennifer Allison, Daniel Martin, Richard Hamilton. Research asst. Labor-Mgmt. Center, Yale U., 1947; instr. advanced math. Hopkins Prep. Sch., New Haven, 1947-48; adminstrv. resident R.I. Hosp., Providence, 1949-50; asst. to coordinator Hosp. and Clinics Med. Center, U. Pitts., 1950-53, instr., then asst. prof. hosp. adminstrn., 1953-55; asso. prof., dir. program hosp. adminstrn. Sch. Bus. Adminstrn., U. Mich., 1955-58, prof., dir. Bur. Hosp. Adminstrn., 1958-61; pres. Blue Cross Assn., Chgo., 1961-77; pres., chief exec. officer Blue Cross and Blue Shield Assns., Chgo., 1977—. Pres., Nat. Health Council, 1972-73; bd. dirs., Nat. Center for Health Edn.; Independent Sector; HHS; dir. Group Health Assn. Am., The Stanley Works; chmn. task force on medicaid and related programs HEW, 1969-70; mem. council mgmt. Internat. Fedn. Voluntary Health Service Funds, pres., 1970-72, 1980-82; Nat. Council on Health Planning and Devel.; Nat. Commn. on Nursing; charter mem. Inst. Medicine, Nat. Acad. Scis.; trustee Hosp. Research and Edn. Trust; Nat. Exec. Com. on Public Policy, U. Chgo.; chmn. com. on devel. Yale U. Served to lt. (j.g.), USNR, 1943-46. Named 1 of 100 most important young men and women in U.S., Life Mag., 1962; recipient Justin Ford Kimball award, 1967; Outstanding Achievement award U. Minn., 1970; Sec.'s Unit Citation (HEW), 1970; Silver Medal Award, Am. Coll. Hosp. Adminstrs. 1978; Yale medal, 1979; Special Award for Meritorious Ser., Am. Med. Assn., 1981; Award of Honor Am. Hosp. Assn., 1982; Nuffield Provincial Hosps. Trust-King's Fund fellow, Eng., 1970. Fellow Am. Pub. Health Assn., Am. Coll. Hosp. Adminstrs., mem. Royal Soc. Health, Am. Hosp. Assn., Internat. Hosp. Fedn., Am. Mgmt. Assns. (trustee), Assn. Yale Alumni, Sigma Xi, Delta Sigma Pi. Clubs: Mid-Am., Whitehall, Chgo. (Chgo.); Yale (N.Y.C.); Cosmos (Washington). Author: Hospital and Medical Economics, 1962; Regionalization and Rural Health Care, 1962; editor: Working for a Healthier America, 1980; contbr. articles to profl. jours.

MC NICHOLAS, JOSEPH ALPHONSUS, bishop; b. St. Louis, Jan. 13, 1923; s. Joseph Alphonsus and Mary Blanche (Tallon) McN.; ed. Cardinal Glennon Coll., St. Louis, Kenrick Theol. Sem., St. Louis, M.S.W., St. Louis U., 1957. Ordained priest Roman Catholic Ch., now bishop; asst. pastor St. Louis Cathedral, 1949-55, Holy Name Parish, 1955-66; Cath. chaplain St. Louis City Juvenile Ct., 1957-71; mem. Secretariat Roman Cath. Ch., Orphan Bd., 1959-75; pastor Old Cathedral of St. Louis, 1969-75; asst. dir. Cath. Charities St. Louis, 1957-70; aux. bishop Archdiocese of St. Louis, 1969-75; bishop Diocese of Springfield (Ill.), 1975—. Trustee, Cath. U. Am., 1977—; v.p. Child Welfare League Am., 1971-79. Named Mo. Social Worker of Yr., Mo. Assn. Social Welfare, 1968. Mem. Nat. Conf. Cath. Bishops (adminstrv. bd. 1974-77, 78-81), Ill. Cath. Conf., U.S. Cath. Conf., Nat. Assn. Social Workers. Club: KC. Author: Adoptions—Happiness or Tragedy?; contbr. articles profl. jours. Home and Office: 524 E Lawrence St Springfield IL 62705*

MCNIER, ROBERT MICHAEL, physician; b. Saginaw, Mich., Apr. 29, 1946; s. Robert Leroy and Betty Virginia (Simkins) McN.; student Central Mich. U., 1965-67; B.A., U. Mich., 1971; M.D., Wayne State U., 1975; m. Linda Kay Bonjour, May 15, 1970; children—Melissa Lynne, David Bonjour. Resident in internal medicine William Beaumont Hosp., Royal Oak, Mich., 1975-78, fellow in gastroenterology, 1978-80; pvt. practice gastroenterology, Saginaw, 1980—; asst. clin. prof. Mich. State U. Diplomate Am. Bd. Internal Medicine. Mem. AMA, A.C.P. (asso.). Address: 1080 River Forest Dr Saginaw MI 48603

MCNITT, KAY GENE, educator; b. Lansing, Mich., Mar. 20, 1938; d. Ralph Raymond and Gene(Galvin) McN.; B.S. in Math., Mich. State U., 1959; M.A. in Math., Ball State U., 1971, Ed.D., 1975; m. John Mogush, Nov. 19, 1977children—Robert, Anna, Douglas, Patrick, Christopher. Statistician, computer programmer Mich. State U., 1959; tutor, substitute tchr. public schs., New Castle, Ind., 1968-70; instr. Ball State U., 1971-73, sr. analyst computer center, 1974-76, coordinator of systems for student affairs, 1977—. Bd. dirs. LWV, 1967-69. Mem. Ind. Assn. Women Deans, Adminstrs. and Counselors, Nat. Assn. Women Deans, Adminstrs. and Counselors, Phi Delta Kappa. Home: 290 Lone Beech Dr Muncie IN 47302 Office: Ball State Univ Muncie IN 47306

MC NURLAN, GLEN ARTHUR, law firm exec.; b. Harris, Minn., July 7, 1919; student Northwestern U., 1936-40; m. Iva Jean Thresher, Sept. 21, 1947; children—Raymond, Robert, Ronald and Donald (twins). Condr., Chgo. and Northwestern Ry., Fond du Lac, Wis., 1946-56; owner, operator Fond du Lac Sales (Wis.), 1946-55; legal staff Brotherhood R.R. Trainmen, Kansas City, Mo., 1956-60; chief investigator Rerat Law Firm, Mpls., 1960-70, bus. adminstr., 1970-72, gen. mgr., 1972—; lectr. in field. Served with A.C., U.S. Army, 1940-45. Mem. United Transp. Union. Democrat. Lutheran. Club: Mpls. Athletic. Home: 1770 Sandy Beach Rd MR 26 Fond du Lac WI 54935 Office: Rerat Law Firm 330 2d Ave S Suite 790 Minneapolis MN 55401

MCPEAK, MICHAEL DON, metal products mfg. corp. exec.; b. Bay City, Mich., July 13, 1942; s. Bion Don and Faith Cecelia (Anderson) McP.; B.S. in Mech. Engring., Mich. State U., 1966; m. Mary Ann Congdon, Aug. 29, 1964; children—Kristine Sue, Kerry Lynn. With Modern Metalcraft Inc., Midland, Mich., 1966—, v.p., mgr., 1969—. Pres. bd. dirs. Unitarian-Universalist Fellowship of Midland, 1972-73, v.p. Mich. ch. bd., 1977-80; treas. local blood bank, 1976-78, sec., 1978-80, v.p., 1980-81. Recipient Disting. Service award Midland Jaycees, 1975. Mem. Soc. Mfg. Engrs., Instrument Soc. Am., TAPPI, Tau Beta Pi. Club: Sunrise Optimist (Midland). Home: 4309 Sherwood Ct Midland MI 48640 Office: Modern Metalcraft Inc Route 3 Midland MI 48640

MCPHAIL, ELIZABETH CLAY, educator; b. Dayton, Ky., Feb. 6, 1948; d. Glenn Washington and Margaret Elizabeth (Randle) Clay; B.S., U. Ky., 1970; M.S., Kans. State U., 1977; m. James Dupont McPhail, Aug. 16, 1970. Home econs. tchr., Bourbon County Jr. High Sch., Paris, Ky., 1970-71, Manhattan (Kans.) Jr. High Sch., 1975-76; home econs. tchr. Manhattan High Sch., 1976-77, occupational home econs. tchr., coordinator, 1978—. Sec. adv. com. Kans. State U., 1980—; mem. State of Kans. Adv. Council for Vocat. Edn., 1981—. Mem. NEA, Am. Vocat. Assn., Nat. Assn. Female Execs., Manhattan Unified Edn. Assn., Kans. Nat. Edn. Assn., Kans Assn. Vocat. Home Econs. Tchrs., Kans. Vocat. Assn., Phi Upsilon Omicron, Omicron Nu, Alpha Xi Delta. Presbyterian. Home: 3040 Tamarak Dr Manhattan KS 66502 Office: Manhattan High School Sunset and Poyntz Manhattan KS 66502

MC PHEETERS, JAMES WALTER, III, hosp. adminstr.; b. Poplar Bluff, Mo., May 4, 1938; s. James Walter and Emma Louise (Ringo) McP.; B.S., U. Mo., 1961; M.H.A., Washington U., St. Louis, 1967; m. Sandra Kay Worley, Aug. 26, 1961; children—Elizebeth Louise, James Walter IV, Jonathan Wright. Adminstrv. resident Muskogee (Okla.) Gen. Hosp., 1966-67, asst. adminstr., 1967-69; asst. dir. exchange of med. info. program Okla. U. Med. Sch., Oklahoma City, 1969-71; adminstr. McCune-Brooks Hosp., Carthage, Mo., 1972—; instr. Okla. U. Sch. Medicine, 1969-71. Sponsor, Boy Scouts Am., 1975; chmn. Area Multiple Sclerosis, 1973; chmn. Ozark Gateway Home Health Care Task Force, 1974; bd. dirs. S.W. Mo. Health Systems Agy., Inc., 1976—, S.W. Mo. Emergency Med. Services, Carthage Area Sheltered Workshop, 1972-75; dir. Carthage Area United Fund, 1977; county chmn. Heart Fund. Served to lt. USN, 1962-65. Named Outstanding Citizen of Yr., 1976; VA grantee, exchange of med. info. program, 1969-71. Mem. Am. Coll. Hosp. Adminstrs., Am., Mo. (mem. finance com., planning com. 1975, trustee 1978—, treas. 1980—) hosp. assns., S.W. Mo. Hosp. Council (pres. 1975), Ozark Gateway Health Planning Council, Washington U. Alumni Assn., Carthage C. of C. (dir. 1977—). Roman Catholic. Clubs: Rotary; Broadview Country (dir. 1973-76) (Carthage, Mo.). Home: 1823 Wynnwood St Carthage MO 64836 Office: 627 W Centennial St Carthage MO 64836

MC QUIGGAN, MARK CORBEILLE, physician; b. Detroit, May 15, 1933; s. Mark Ronald and Catherine Charlotte (Corbeille) McQ.; B.S., U. Mich., 1954, M.D., 1958; m. Carolyn Ann Brunk, Mar. 25, 1961. Intern, Univ. Med. Center, Ann Arbor, Mich., 1958-59, resident in urology, 1961-64; jr. clin. instr. U. Mich., Ann Arbor, 1959-64; asso. practice urology, Detroit, 1964-67; dir. med. edn. Providence Hosp., Southfield, Mich., 1967-69; practice medicine specializing in urology, Southfield, 1969—; sec. staff North Detroit Gen. Hosp., 1975-79. Mem. A.C.S., Am. Urol. Assn., Oakland County Med. Soc., Detroit Surg. Assn., Alliance Francaise. Republican. Methodist. Club: Detroit Gun. Home: 29653 Club House Ln Farmington MI 48018 Office: 22250 Providence Dr Southfield MI 48075

MC QUISTON, JAMES STUART, internist; b. Pitts., May 27, 1904; s. Edward Curtis and Sophia B. (Irwin) McQ.; B.S., Allegheny Coll., 1926; M.D., U. Pa., 1929; M.S. in Medicine, U. Minn., 1934; m. Jean Dollman Kriz, Jan. 24, 1976; 1 son by previous marriage, Edward Conner. Intern, Western Pa. Hosp., Pitts., 1929-30; resident in internal medicine, Mayo Clinic, Rochester, Minn., 1930-34; practice medicine specializing in internal medicine, Cedar Rapids, Iowa, 1934—, sr. partner five internists, 1974—; attending staff St. Luke's Meth. Hosp., Cedar Rapids, Mercy Hosp., Cedar Rapids; cons. in internal medicine. Served to lt. col. M.C., AUS, 1942-46. Recipient Founders award St. Lukes Health Care Found. Fellow A.C.P.; mem. AMA, Linn County (pres., 1950), Iowa State Med. Socs., Iowa Clin. Soc. (pres. 1940), Am. Heart Assn. Republican. Methodist. Clubs: Cedar Rapids Country, Rotary (pres. Cedar Rapids 1938), Masons. Contbr. articles to med. jours. Home: 2222 1st Ave NE Cedar Rapids IA 52402 Office: 1328 2d Ave SE Cedar Rapids IA 52403

MC QUISTON, RICHARD LANNING, med. social service exec.; b. Pitts., May 22, 1949; s. Roy Lincoln and Jean Lois (Reynolds) McQ.; B.S., Mo. Valley Coll., 1972; M.S.W., George Warren Brown Sch. Social Work, 1974; m. Gail Sue King, Jan. 8, 1972; children—Michelle Renee, Cara Lynn. Social caseworker Christian Hosp. Northwest, St. Louis, 1974-75, asst. dir. med. social service, 1975-77, dir. med social service, 1977—; social service cons. extended care facilities. Mem. exec. com. bd. dirs., chairperson service and rehab, com., co-chairperson transp. com. Met. St. Louis chpt. Am. Cancer Soc., 1978—. Nominee Jefferson award, 1979. Mem. Nat. Assn. Social Workers, Soc. Hosp. Social Work Dirs. Greater St. Louis Area, Mo. Assn. Hosp. Social Work Dirs. Methodist. Home: 1606 Watson St Saint Charles MO 63301 Office: 11133 Dunn Rd Saint Louis MO 63136

MC REE, EDWARD BARXDALE, hosp. adminstr.; b. Pauls Valley, Okla., Oct. 20, 1931; s. Henry Barxdale and Mary (Shumate) McR.; B.A., Okla. City U., 1953; student U. Okla., 1953; student Central State Coll., 1954-55; m. Jan Bryant, Aug. 23, 1953; children—Scott, Kent, Chad. Adminstr. Eaton Rapids (Mich.) Community Hosp., 1957-61; pres. Ingham Med. Center, Lansing, Mich., 1961—; dir. Grad. Med. Edn., Inc., 1970—, treas., 1978-79, pres., 1979; pres. Mid-Mich. Emergency Services Council, 1978—; dir. Pacesetter Bank-Lansing, N.A. Mem. Eaton Rapids (Mich.) Bd. Edn., 1964-71, treas., 1968-71. Pres., Tri-County Emergency Med. Services Council, 1974—, also mem. bd. dirs.; bd. dirs. Blue Cross Mich., 1974-75; bd. dirs. Hosp. Purchasing Service Mich., 1973—, pres., 1976-77; bd. dirs. Mid-Mich. chpt. ARC, 1979—, treas., 1980—. Served with AUS, 1955-57. Mem. Mich. (v.p. 1965-68), Southwestern Mich. (pres. 1968) hosp. assns., Am. Coll. Hosp. Adminstrs., Am. Hosp. Assn., Lambda Chi Alpha. Beta Beta Beta. Methodist (mem. West Mich. Conf. Bd. Finance 1972—). Club: Rotary. Contbr. articles to profl. jours. Home: 201 S Center St Eaton Rapids MI 48827 Office: 401 W Greenlawn Ave Lansing MI 48910

MC ROY, PAUL FURGESON, broadcasting co. exec.; b. Carbondale, Ill., June 25, 1912; s. Robert D. and Ann Elizabeth (Furgeson) McR.; B.Ed., So. Ill. U., 1934; M.Philosophy, U. Wis., 1939; m. Mary Eleanor Helm, June 12, 1937; children—Paul, Ann (Mrs. Larry E. Meyer). Tchr., dir. audio-visual edn. Houston Sch. System, 1934-43; instr. U. Houston, 1940-43; owner, mgr. radio sta. WCIL-WCIL-FM, Carbondale, 1946—; developer Bonnie Brae Subdiv., 1964—, builder, owner Southgate Shopping Center, 1964— (both Carbondale); dir. Carbondale Savs. & Loan, 1947—, pres., 1962—; dir. Carbondale Indsl. Corp., 1967-73, pres., 1968-73. Dir. Holden Hosp., 1949-55, So. Ill. U. Alumni Found., 1959-65; chmn. United Fund, 1952; mem. Carbondale Grade Sch. Bd., 1949-55; scoutmaster Boy Scouts Am., 1952-53, adviser Explorer troop, 1953-54. Served to lt. comdr. USNR, 1943-46. U. So. Ill. Found. cum laude fellow, 1974. Recipient We All Made It award Boy Scout Philmont Sky Ranch, 1954. Mem. So. Ill. U. Alumni Assn. (pres. 1958), Flying Scot Sailing Assn. (gov. Midwest dist. 1967), Carbondale C. of C. (pres. 1956, Man of Year award 1973), So. Ill. Golf Assn., U.S. Golf Assn., N.Am. Yachting Union. Methodist (trustee 1950-56, chmn. 1956). Shriner, Rotarian (pres. Carbondale 1950, Paul Harris fellow 1979). Clubs: Crab Orchard Lake Sailing (commodore 1957), Jackson Country. Home: 25 Bonnie Brae Carbondale IL 62901 Office: 211 W Main St Carbondale IL 62901

MCSHANE, DAMIAN ANTHONY, psychologist; b. Spooner, Wis., May 19, 1950; B.A., Mankato State Coll., 1973; M.A. in Psychology, George Peabody Coll., 1976; Ph.D., Vanderbilt U., 1980; m. Anne Marie Herring, Apr. 30, 1974; children—Clear Brook, Damian Peter. Recreational park supr. City of Cloquet, Minn., summer, 1967, 68; asst. instr. Minn. Outward Bound., Ely, summer, 1969; Tb. control health worker Peace Corps, Hilo, Hawaii, 1971, Seoul, Korea, 1971; phys. tng. instr. and dormitory supr. Tenn. Law Enforcement Agy., Donelson, 1974; psychology intern MPS Psychol. Services Center, Mpls., 1976-77; asst. to dir. dept. Indian edn. Mpls. public schs., Mpls., 1977-78; dir. mental health unit Indian Health Bd. Clinic, Mpls., 1978-79; psychologist and spl. edn. coordinator Lac Courte Oreilles Indian Reservation Ojibwa Schs., Hayward, Wis., 1979-81; dir. epidemiology of emotional disturbance research project Oreg. Health Scis. U., Portland, 1982; mem. Mpls. Spl. Edn. Adv. Com., 1978—; cons. to Indian mental health workshops, 1979-81. Bd. dirs. South Minneapolis Day Care Activity Center, Inc., 1977—. Child Study Center grantee, 1975. Mem. Am. Psychol. Assn. Home and office: PO Box 296 Route 1 Springbrook WI 54875

MC SHANE, WILLIAM LEO, mental health exec.; b. Wayne, Mich., Feb. 22, 1942; s. Leo Bernard and Helen Blanch (Harleton) McS.; B.S., Eastern Mich. U., 1965; M.S.W., Wayne State U., 1972; m. Patricia Joyce Joens; children—Molly, Jennifer, Diana, Joseph, Sean, Ryan. Supr. Office Drug Abuse Macomb County (Mich.) Community Mental Health, 1971-74; regional coordinator Southeastern Mich.-Mich. Dept. Public Health, Detroit, 1974-75, asst. dir., 1975-78; exec. dir. St. Clair County (Mich.) Community Mental Health, Port Huron, 1978—; tchr. Oakland U., St. Clair County Community Coll.; mem. Gov.'s Task Force on Substance Abuse, 1972; mem. Gov.'s Com. Public Mental Health Unification, 1979. Cert. social worker, Mich. Mem. Acad. Cert. Social Workers, Comprehensive Health Planning Council Southeastern Mich., Blue Water Psychol. Assn. (pres. 1976-77), Nat. Assn. Social Workers (chairperson St. Clair chpt. 1978), Mich. Assn. Community Mental Health Dirs. (treas. 1978-79, pres. 1981-82). Club: Rotary. Home: 4589 Lake Shore Port Huron MI 48060 Office: 627 Fort St Port Huron MI 48060

MCSHERRY, MAUREEN THERESA, educator; b. Evergreen Park, Ill., Jan. 7, 1948; d. John Thomas and Catherine Marie (Mullarkey) Diggins; B.A. in English, St. Xavier Coll., 1969; M.A. in English, Loyola U., Chgo., 1975; M.Ed. in Adminstrn., U. Ill., 1979; m. Donald Thomas McSherry, Oct. 6, 1979. Tchr. English, H.H. Conrady Jr. High Sch., Hickory Hills, Ill., 1969-70, Thornton Twp. High Sch., Dist. 205, Harvey, Ill. 1970-79; chmn. Thornridge High Sch., Dolton, Ill. 1979—. Mem. NEA (conv. del. 1980-81), Ill. Edn. Assn. (conv. del. 1979, 80, 81), Faculty Assn. Dist. 205 (v.p. 1978-80), Nat. Council Tchrs. English, Assn. for Supervision and Curriculum Devel., St. Xavier Alumni Assn., Loyola Alumni Assn., U. Ill. Alumni Assn. Roman Catholic. Home: 153 Hemlock St Park Forest IL 60466 Office: Thornridge High Sch Sibley and Cottage Grove Aves Dolton IL 60419

MCSWANE, DAVID ZACHARY, educator; b. Clinton, Ind., July 19, 1948; s. Paul Eugene and Katherine Amogene (Bair) McS.; A.B., Wabash Coll., 1970; M.P.H., Ind. U., 1972, H.S.D., 1980; m. Linda Marie Speth, Aug. 23, 1969; children—Christopher Paul, Kelli Lynn, Jonathan David, Ryan Michael. Asst. prof. pub. and environ. affairs Ind. U., Indpls., 1975—; public health sanitarian Ind. State Bd. Health, Indpls., 1970-71; adminstr. Monroe County Health Dept., Bloomington, Ind., 1971-75. Coordinator, Am. Cancer Soc.'s Smoking Cessation Program, State of Ind., 1979—. Named Outstanding Sanitarian of Central Dist. of Ind. Assn. Sanitarians, 1980. Diplomate Am. Bd. Acad. Sanitarians. Mem. Am. Public

Health Assn., Nat. Environ. Health Assn. (cert. of merit 1980), Internat. Assn. Milk, Food and Environ. Sanitarians, Ind. Public Health Assn., Ind. Assn. Sanitarians, Ind. Assn. Health Educators, Phi Delta Kappa. Clubs: Elks, K.C. Contbr. articles to profl. jours.; pub. The Hoosier Sanitarian, 1978-81. Home: 540 Bailliere Dr Martinsville IN 46151 Office: 801 W Michigan St Indianapolis IN 46202

MCSWEENEY, WILLIAM LINCOLN, JR., corp. tng. specialist; b. Boston, Nov. 9, 1930; s. William Lincoln and Ruth Patricia (Desmond) McS.; B.S., Boston Coll., 1953; M.L.A., So. Meth. U., 1980; m. Anne Cornelia Bulman, Aug. 18, 1956; children—Anne C., William L., Siobhan K., Arthur J., Sean B. Tchr. English, Killingly (Conn.) High Sch., 1956-57; with Hallmark Cards, Inc., Kansas City, Mo., 1957—, area personnel mgr., 1968, sales tng. mgr., 1969-70, dir. corp. tng. and devel., 1970—. Bd. dirs. Cath. Social Services, Kansas City Archdiocese, 1975—, pres., 1980-81; bd. dirs. United Community Services Kansas City, 1978—, mem. exec. com., 1978—; bd. dirs. Kansas City Amigos De Las Americas, 1977-80, pres., 1979; bd. dirs. Johnson County YMCA, 1978-79; bd. dirs. Pan Ednl. Inst., 1979—, pres., 1980-81; mem. Boston Coll. Alumni Admissions Council, 1976—; mem. Chancellor's Adv. Bd. Met. Community Colls., 1979-80; mem. Democratic Com., Johnson County, Kans., 1980—. Served with U.S. Army, 1953-56. Mem. Am. Soc. Personnel Adminstrn., Am. Soc. Tng. and Devel., Boston Coll. Alumni Assn. (past dir.). Roman Catholic. Clubs: Boston Coll. (Kansas City), Ancient Order Hibernians. Office: 2501 McGee Kansas City MO 64108

MC SWEENY, AUSTIN JOHN, physician; b. N.Y.C., Sept. 30, 1924; s. Austin John and Madelene (Jasmagy) McS.; student Queen's Coll., 1943, U. Ill., 1944; M.D., Loyola U., Chgo., 1949; m. Erna Eleanor DeSollar, June 10, 1945; children—Austin John, III, James Dennis, Catherine Lynn, Christopher Shawn, Terence Shane. Intern, E.J. Meyer Meml. Hosp., Buffalo, 1949-50; resident Buffalo (N.Y.) VA Hosp., 1950-51; fellow Mayo Clinic, Rochester, Minn., 1953-55; practice medicine specializing in psychiatry, Danville, Ill., 1955-57, Janesville, Wis., 1957—; clin. dir. Academy Assos. at Psychiatry, Janesville, 1973-81; mem. staffs Meml. Community Hosp., Edgerton, Mercy Hosp., Janesville. Served with U.S. Army, 1943-46, USAF, 1951-53. Recipient medal Acad. Psychosomatic Medicine, 1976. Mem. Am. Psychiat. Assn., Wis. Psychiat. Assn., AMA, Internat. Soc. Hypnosis, Am. Soc. Clin. Hypnosis, Internat. Coll. Psychosomatic Medicine, Acad. Psychosomatic Medicine, A.C.P., Am. Med. Soc. of Vienna, Rock County Med. Soc. Contbr. articles to profl. jours. Home: 1311 Camden Sq Janesville WI 53545 Office: 415 Dodge St Janesville WI 53547

MC SWEENY, AUSTIN JOHN, physician; b. N.Y.C., Sept. 30, 1924; s. Austin John and Madelene (Jasmagy) McS.; student Queen's Coll., 1943, U. Ill., 1944; M.D., Loyola U., Chgo., 1949; m. Erna Eleanor DeSollar, June 10, 1945; children—Austin John, III, James Dennis, Catherine Lynn, Christopher Shawn, Terence Shane. Intern, E.J. Meyer Meml. Hosp., Buffalo, 1949-50; resident Buffalo (N.Y.) VA Hosp., 1950-51; fellow Mayo Clinic, Rochester, Minn., 1953-55; practice medicine specializing in psychiatry, Danville, Ill., 1955-57, Janesville, Wis., 1957—; clin. dir. Asso. Psychiat. Cons., Janesville, 1973-77; mem. staffs Meml. Community Hosp., Edgerton, Mercy Hosp., Janesville. Served with U.S. Army, 1943-46, USAF, 1951-53. Recipient medal Acad. Psychosomatic Medicine, 1976. Mem. Am. Psychiat. Assn., Wis. Psychiat. Assn., AMA, Internat. Soc. Hypnosis, Am. Soc. Clin. Hypnosis, Internat. Coll. Psychosomatic Medicine, Acad. Psychosomatic Medicine, A.C.P., Am. Med. Soc. of Vienna, Rock County Med. Soc. Contbr. articles to profl. jours. Home: 1311 Camden Sq Janesville WI 53545 Office: 415 Dodge St Janesville WI 53545

MC SWINEY, CHARLES RONALD, lawyer; b. Nashville, Apr. 23, 1943; s. James Wilmer and Jewell Allen (Bellar) McS.; A.B., Kenyon Coll., 1965; J.D., U. Cin., 1968; m. Jane Detrick, Jan. 2, 1970. Admitted to Ohio bar, 1968; partner firm Smith & Schnacke, Columbus, Ohio, 1968—. Presdl. interchange exec. Pres.'s Commn. on Personnel Interchange, 1972; program adviser EPA, 1972-73, recipient Bronze medal, 1973. Mem. Am., Ohio, Columbus bar assns. Presbyterian. Clubs: Moraine Country, Scioto Country, Athletic. Home: 2696 Sandover Rd Columbus OH 43220 Office: 100 E Broad St Suite 700 Columbus OH 43215

MC SWINEY, JAMES WILMER, pulp and paper mfg. co. exec.; b. McEwen, Tenn., Nov. 13, 1915; s. James S. and Delia (Conroy) McS.; grad. Harvard U. Advanced Mgmt. Program, 1954; m. Jewel Bellar, 1940; children—Charles Ronald, Margaret Ann. Lab. technician, shipping clk. Nashville div. The Mead Corp., 1934-39, asst. office mgr. Harriman div., 1939, plant mgr., Rockport, Ind., 1940, asst. office mgr. Kingsport (Tenn.) div., 1941-44, exec. asst. to pres., Dayton, Ohio, 1954-57, v.p. devel., 1957-59, adminstrv v.p., 1959, group v.p., gen. mgr. Mead div., 1961-63, exec. v.p. corp., 1963-67, pres., chief exec. officer, 1968-71, chmn. bd., chief exec. officer, 1971-81, chmn. bd., 1981—, also dir.; acct., office mgr., asst. sec.-treas. Brunswick Pulp & Paper Co. (Ga.), 1944-54, now dir.; dir. Ga. Kraft Co., Gem City Savs. Assn., Dayton, Northwood Pulp Ltd., Prince George, B.C., Vulcan Materials Co., Birmingham, Phillips Industries. Trustee, Sinclair Coll., Dayton. Served as aviation cadet USAAF, 1942-44. Home: 2300 Ridgeway Rd Dayton OH 45419 Office: Mead World Hdqrs Dayton OH 45463

MC TEE, LYLE PATRICK, coll. adminstr; b. North Platte, Nebr., May 26, 1951; s. Lyle Junior and Teresa Arlene (Lannin) M.; B.S., U. Nebr., 1974, M.S., 1979. Tchr. Lincoln (Nebr.) Pub. Schs., 1974-75; asst. coordinator for fraternities, sororities and cooperatives student affairs dept. U. Nebr., Lincoln, 1975-77; asst. dir. residential life Morningside Coll., Sioux City, Iowa, 1977-79, dir. programs and activities, 1979-80, dir. housing, 1980—. Recipient Outstanding Service award Acacia Nat. Frat., 1972. Mem. Am. Personnel and Guidance Assn., Am. Coll. Personnel Assn., Nat. Assn. Student Personnel Adminstrs., Assn. Fraternity Advisors, U. Nebr. Alumni Assn., Acacia (nat. counselor). Republican. Roman Catholic. Home: 3600 Peters Ave Sioux City IA 51106 Office: Student Services Center Morningside Coll Sioux City IA 51106

MC VEY, FRANCIS DANIEL, aero. engr.; b. St. Louis, Jan. 19, 1929; s. Martin P. and Marguy J. (Boeckler) McV.; B.S. in Mech. Engring., Washington U., St. Louis, 1952, M.S., 1954; postgrad. Princeton U., 1955; m. Anna Elizabeth Moss, Nov. 26, 1958; children—Mark Andrew, Marguy Denise, Michael Sean. Instr. mech. engring. Washington U., St. Louis, 1954-55; group project engr. missiles engring. div. McDonnell Aircraft Co., St. Louis, 1955-58, asso. scientist research div., 1961-64, br. mgr. engring. tech. div., 1964-74, prin. staff engr., 1974—; chief aerodynamicist Cleve. Pneumatic Co., Washington, 1959-61. Lectr., St. Louis U., 1964-70, U. Mo., St. Louis/Rolla Extension, 1971. Panel mem. Navy Bur. Weapons Adv. Com. on Aeroballistics, 1957-72; mem. air breathing propulsion com. Joint Army, Navy, NASA, Air Force Propulsion Information Agy., 1970-73. Served with AUS, 1946-48. Recipient Lloyd R. Koenig prize in engring. Washington U., 1952. Asso. fellow Am. Inst. Aeros. and Astronautics (St. Louis sect. chmn. 1964-65, Service award 1967); mem. Am. Rocket Soc. (v.p. St. Louis chpt. 1962-63), Sigma Xi. Home: 7030 Delmar Blvd University City MO 63130 Office: PO Box 516 Saint Louis MO 63166

MC VEY, LOLA WINIFRED CLAAR, speech pathologist; b. Lakin, Kans., Feb. 21, 1923; d. Leonard Thomas and Anna Katrina (Kieft) C.; B.A., Wichita State U., 1964; m. Raymond Ernest McVey, June 1, 1947 (dec. Feb. 1981); children—Marlyn Roann, Lyndon Eugene, Raymond Lee. Tchr. public schs. Seward and Reno counties, Kans., 1943-48; speech pathologist Great Bend, Kans., 1964-66, Kismet Plains Unified Sch. Dist., Kismet, Kans., 1966-79; pvt. practice speech pathology, Kismet, 1979—; tchr. lang. devel. class public sch., Liberal, Kans., 1980—. Mem. Kans. Speech and Hearing Assn. (sec.), Am. Speech and Hearing Assn., Kans. Nat. Edn. Assn. Methodist. Corr., S.W. Daily Times, 1970-73. Home: 813 Main St Kismet KS 67859

MC VICAR, JOHN FRANKLIN, cemetery exec.; b. Mansfield, Ohio, Sept. 2, 1930; s. Chester D. and Gladys B. McV.; student in bus. adminstrn. Tri-State Coll., Angola, Ind., 1948-51; m. Jean Arlene Dalzell, May 6, 1951; children—Robert L., Richard L., Jon Malcolm. Supr. data processing Mansfield Telephone Co., 1956-58, Gen. Telephone of Marion, Ohio, 1958-59; supr. and computer programmer Fulfillment Corp. Am., Marion, 1959-67; office mgr. Central Ohio Breeding Assn., Columbus, Ohio, 1967-68; gen. mgr. Mansfield Meml. Park, 1968—. Committeeman troop 106 Johnny Appleseed council Boy Scouts Am., 1974-76, United Appeal, Mansfield, 1974-75; capt. fund raising team Salvation Army, Mansfield, 1978; deacon First Christian Ch., Mansfield. Served to sgt. USAF, 1951-56. Recipient Americanism award plaque VFW, 1978. Mem. Ohio Assn. Cemeteries (trustee 1973-79, sec. 1978-79, pres. 1980-81), Nat. Assn. Cemeteries, Richland Area C. of C., V.F.W. Clubs: Kiwanis (committeeman Youth Key Club 1974-79, trustee local club 1976—), Elks (Mansfield). Office: 2507 Park Ave W Mansfield OH 44906

MEACHAM, WILLIAM WARREN, sales co. exec.; b. San Francisco, Mar. 23, 1938; s. William Almer and Wilma Gale (Taylor) M.; B.A., Elmhurst Coll., 1976; M.B.A., DePaul U., 1979; m. Margo Ransom, Dec. 14, 1971; 1 son, Jim; children by previous marriage—Cindy, Sandy, Julie. Mgr., Meachams Food Center, Topeka, 1960-63; dist. sales mgr. Purex Corp. Ltd., Kansas City, Mo., 1963-66, bd. mgr., 1966-70; gen. mgr. Midwest region Hanes DSD Co., Villa Park, Ill., 1970—; instr. Elmhurst Coll., Ill. Benedictine Coll. Served with USN, 1956-60. Mem. Am. Mgmt. Assn. Republican. Home: 864 Woodland Dr Glen Ellyn IL 60137 Office: 1199 N Ellsworth St Villa Park IL 60181

MEAD, JAMES H(AROLD), coll. adminstr.; b. Red Oak, Iowa, Feb. 17, 1929; s. Harold Dudley and N(elly) Ruth (Bryant) M.; A.B., Olympic Coll., 1957; postgrad. M.I.T., 1957; m. Joy Christine Pollatz, Oct. 10, 1975; 1 son, Christopher James. Sec., gen. mgr. Nibco New Eng., Hartford, Conn., 1971-72; sr. analyst mfg. systems Tally Industries, Thomaston, Conn., 1972-74, Insilco, Middleton, Conn., 1974; dir. computer services St. Marys Coll., Notre Dame, Ind., 1974—. Mem. Cass County (Mich.) Spl. Edn. Sch. Bd., 1969-70. Served with U.S. Army, 1949-51. Mem. Assn. for Computing Machinery, Data Processing Mgmt. Assn., Spl. Interest Group Computer Sci. Edn., Assn. Systems Mgmt. Lutheran. Office: St Mary's Coll Lemans Hall Notre Dame IN 46556

MEADOR, CAROL LYNN VAN BAALE, occupational therapist; b. Newton, Iowa, Oct. 18, 1946; d. Howard and Ida Mae (Buckingham) Van Baale; B.S. in Occupational Therapy, Washington U., St. Louis, 1972; m. Lloyd Edward Meador, Aug. 18, 1967; 1 son, Colyn Blake. Staff occupational therapist Christian Welfare Hosp., East St. Louis, Ill., 1972-73; chief occupational therapy St. Joseph Hosp., St. Charles, Mo., 1973-74, Washington U.-I.W.J. Inst. Rehab., 1974-76; staff occupational therapist Christian Hosp. N.W., Florissant, Mo., 1980, supr. occupational therapy, 1980—; clin. instr. occupational therapy and neurology, 1974-76. Religious edn. instr. First Unitarian Ch., St. Louis, 1980-81. Mem. Am. Occupational Therapy Assn., Mo. Occupational Therapy Assn. (treas. 1974-76), AAUW. Office: 1225 Graham Rd Florissant MO 63031

MEADOR, JIMMY CLAY, computer cons.; b. Lafayette, Tenn., Dec. 11, 1948; s. C.J. and Mabel Louise (Hawkins) M.; B.S., Miami U., 1970; m. Charlotte M. Galloway, Aug. 15, 1970; children—Michelle C., Jennifer L. Computer systems analyst Ohio Edison Co., Akron, 1970-73, sr. programmer analyst, 1973-75, sr. tech. systems analyst, 1977-78; cons. Computer Dynamics, Inc., Southfield, Mich., 1978; adv. software analyst Republic Steel Corp., Cleve., 1978-79; coordinator sci. and spl. projects Ohio Edison Co., 1979—; instr. Akron U. Home: 1105 Mt Vernon St Akron OH 44310 Office: 76 S Main St Akron OH 44308

MEANS, ARTHUR CHANDOS, oil co. ofcl.; b. Indpls., July 15, 1948; s. Raymond Curtis and Mabel Gertrude (Carter) M.; B.A. in Edn., Concordia Tchrs. Coll., 1970; M.A. in L.S., No. Ill. U., 1974. Br. mgr. Rockford (Ill.) Public Library, 1974-75; reference librarian Mt. Prospect (Ill.) Public Library, 1975-78; serials/govt. documents librarian Fed. Res. Bank Chgo., 1978; records mgr. Material Service Corp. subs. Gen. Dynamics Corp., Chgo., 1979-81; records specialist Standard Oil Co. (Ind.), Chgo., 1981—. Mem. West End Revitalization Council, Rockford, 1974-75; mem. West End Bus. Assn., Rockford, 1974-75, treas., 1974-75. Mem. Assn. Records Mgrs. and Adminstrs. (editor, librarian local chpt. 1979—, nat. standards bd., records retention com. 1981), Asso. Info. Mgrs., Nat. Micrographic Assn., Friend Royal Sch. Ch. Music. Episcopalian. Home: 1130 N Dearborn Pkwy Chicago IL 60610 Office: Material Service Corp 300 W Washington St Chicago IL 60606

MEANS, CHARLES LEE, univ. adminstr.; b. Holly Springs, Miss., Sept. 6, 1942; s. Charles Elias and Odessa Louise (Ruff) M.; B.S. in Polit. Sci., So. Ill. U., 1967; M.S. in Social Sci., Webster Coll., 1969; Ph.D. in Urban Edn., St. Louis U., 1973; m. Robin Williams; 1 son, Chuck Means III; 1 dau. by previous marriage, J. Markelle. Community relations specialist Job Corps, 1966; dir. relocation City of East St. Louis (Ill.), 1967, exec. dir. Urban renewal, 1968-72; exec. dir. community devel., 1972-74; vice provost for minority affairs Bowling Green State U., 1974, vice provost for acad. services, 1975-78, vice provost for ednl. devel., 1978—. Mem. exec. bd. Toledo Area council Boy Scouts Am.; mem. Bowling Green (Ohio) City Housing Commn., 1978—. Recipient award for effort in completion, Mary E. Brown Community Center, Ill. Ho. of Reps., 1976. Mem. Am. Assn. Univ. Adminstrs., Am. Assn. Higher Edn., Am. Assn. State Colls. and Univs., Ohio Assn. Ednl. Opportunity Program Personnel, Mid-Am. Assn. Ednl. Opportunity Program Personnel, Soc. Coll. and Univ. Planning, Internat. Reading Assn., Phi Delta Kappa. Democrat. Baptist. Editor conf. procs. 4th Ann. Ohio Devel. Edn. Conf., Bowling Green, 1976. Office: Room 238 Adminstrn Bldg Bowling Green State U Bowling Green OH 43403

MEARS, DARLENE WANDA HIND (MRS. DAVID EDMUND MEARS), lawyer; b. Oceanside, N.Y., July 19, 1946; d. Ira Flint and Wanda Mary (Terry) Hind; student El Camino Jr. Coll., 1965; B.A., Valparaiso U., 1968, J.D., 1971; m. David Edmund Mears, Jan. 25, 1969; 1 son, Dax Evan. Admitted to Ind. bar, 1971; nat. exam. and closing atty. Chgo. Title & Trust Co., 1971-72; pvt. practice law, Hammond, Ind., 1971-76; dep. prosecutor Lake County (Ind.) Juvenile Div., Hammond, 1972-76; referee juvenile div. Lake Superior Ct., 1976-78, sr. judge, 1978—. First v.p. Calumet Area Humane Soc., Inc., Hammond, 1971-72, atty., 1971-74, pres., 1977-78; bd. dirs. Hammond YWCA, v.p., 1977-78; v.p. Christ Lutheran Ch. Women, Hammond, 1976. Recipient Disting. Alumni award Luth. High Sch. Assn. So. Calif., 1975; Lake County Outstanding Woman award, 1978. Mem. Am. Bar Assn., Ind. Bar Assn. (treas. family and juvenile law sect., chmn. 1976-77, dir. 1977—), Hammond Bar Assn., Nat. Council Family and Juvenile Ct. Judges, Ind. Council Family and Juvenile Ct. Judges (treas. 1979—), Am. Judges Assn., Ind. Judges Assn., Valparaiso U. Sch. Law Alumni Assn. (treas. 1973-74, v.p. 1974-75, pres. 1975-76, dir.), Phi Alpha Delta, Kappa Tau Zeta (sec. alumni 1972, treas. 1975-76). Home: 7303 88th Pl Crown Point IN 46307 Office: 400 Broadway Gary IN

MEATES, SUSAN CLAIRE, computer scientist; b. Bronx, N.Y., Apr. 10, 1950; d. Richard Frederick and Vera Elois (Schumacher) M.; A.B.T., U. Toledo, 1970, B.B.A. cum laude, 1971; postgrad. Ohio State U., 1974—. Programmer/analyst Med. Coll. Ohio, Toledo, 1971; applications analyst Compu-Serv Network, Inc., Columbus, Ohio, 1971-72, corp. tech. support supr., 1972-73, nat. accounts service rep., 1974-75, mgr. corp. systems services, 1975-76; system project leader Borden, Inc., Columbus, 1976-77, mgr. quality assurance chem. div., 1977-78; mgr. corp. info. systems Compu-Serve Inc., Columbus, 1978-80; exec. v.p. Diacon Systems Corp., Columbus, 1980-81; chief fin. officer Software Results Corp., Columbus, 1981—, also dir.; mem. part-time faculty Ohio State U., 1977-79; dir. O.S.P., Inc. Mem. Data Processing Mgmt. Assn., Assn. M.B.A. Execs., Am. Bus. Womens Assn., Beta Gamma Sigma, Phi Kappa Alpha. Home: 3649 Kilkenny Dr Columbus OH 43220 Office: 1229 W 3d Ave Columbus OH 43215

MEBUST, WINSTON KEITH, surgeon, educator; b. Malta, Mont., July 2, 1933; s. Hans G. and Anna C. (Leiseth) M.; student U. Wash., 1951-54; M.D., 1958; m. Lora June Peterson, Sept. 15, 1955; children—Leanne, Kevin, Kreg, Kari. Intern, King County Hosp., Seattle, 1958-59; resident Virginia Mason Hosp., Seattle, 1959-63; Kans. U. Med. Center, 1963-66; practice medicine specializing in urology, 1966—; instr. surgery and urology U. Kans. Med. Center, Kansas City, 1966-69, asst. prof., 1969-72, asso. prof., 1972-76, chmn. urology sect., 1974—, prof., 1977—; chief urology service VA Hosp., Kansas City, Mo., 1966-74. Served with U.S. Army, 1961-63. Diplomate Am. Bd. Urology (co-chmn. exam. com.), Mem. Am. Cancer Soc., Am. Bd. Surgery, Kansas City Urol. Soc., Assn. for Acad. Surgery, Am. Urol. Assn. (treas. South Central sect.), Wyandotte Med. Soc., Kans. State Med. Assn., Am. Coll. Surgeons, Soc. Univ. Urologists, Am. Assn. Genitourinary Surgeons, Sigma Xi, Alpha Omega Alpha. Republican. Contbr. articles, chpts. to med. jours. and texts. Home: 309 Apache Trail W Lake Quivira KS 66106 Office: 39th and Rainbow Blvd Kansas City KS 66103

MECKE, THEODORE HART, JR., assn. exec.; b. Phila., Mar. 6, 1923; s. Theodore Hart and Genevieve (Loughney) M.; student La Salle Coll., Phila., 1941; m. Mary E. Flaherty, July 14, 1956; children—William, Theodore Hart III, John, Stephen. Mng. editor Germantown (Pa.) Courier, 1942-43, 46-49; with Ford Motor Co., 1949-80, exec. asst. to v.p. pub. relations, 1955-57, gen. pub. relations mgr., 1957-63, v.p. pub. relations, 1963-69, v.p. pub. affairs, 1969-80; pres. Economic Club of Detroit, 1980—; dir. Detroitbank Corp., Detroit Bank & Trust Co., Ex-Cell-O Corp., Troy, Mich., Detroit Legal News Co. Bd. dirs. United Found. of Detroit. Served with AUS, 1943-45; ETO. Mem. Pub. Relations Soc. Am., Greater Detroit C. of C. Roman Catholic. Clubs: Detroit Athletic, Detroit, Country Detroit, Witenagemote, Yondotega (Detroit). Home: 296 Cloverly Rd Grosse Pointe Farms MI 48236 Office: 920 Free Press Bldg Detroit MI 48226

MECKLENBURG, ROY A., horticulturist, hort. soc. exec.; b. Elmhurst, Ill., Feb. 10, 1933; s. John and Emma M.; B.S. in Horticulture, Mich. State U., 1958; M.S., Cornell U., 1961, Ph.D., 1964; m. Eleanor Phillips, June 25, 1960; children—John, Mark, Jane. Asst. prof. horticulture Mich. State U., East Lansing, 1964-70, asso. prof., 1970-77, prof., 1977; pres. Chgo. Hort. Soc. and dir. Botanic Garden, Gencoe, Ill., 1977—. Served with U.S. Army, 1951-53. Mem. Mich. Assn. Nurserymen (hon.), Am. Assn. Mus., Am. Soc. Hort. Sci., Am. Assn. Botanical Gardens and Arboreta. Lutheran. Co-author: Nursery Management: Administration and Culture, 1981. Home: 1675 Dartmouth Ct Deerfield IL 60015 Office: PO Box 400 Glencoe IL 60022

MEDEIROS, KENNETH HENRY, police chief; b. Worcester, Mass., Aug. 24, 1940; s. Manuel and Helen Sarah (Scott) M.; B.S. in Criminal Justice, U. Nebr., Omaha, 1975; m. Jeanne Ann Liaknickas, Aug. 15, 1960; children—Toni Linn, Russell Scott. Commd. U.S. Marine Corps, 1958, advanced through grades to capt.; investigative and law enforcement adminstrn. positions, 1962-78; ret., 1978; chief of police City of Bismarck (N.D.), 1978—; mem. Commn. on Accreditation for Law Enforcement Agys. Mem. Internat. Assn. Chiefs of Police (legis. com. 1977-78, 82-83), N.D. League of Cities (legis. com. 1979—), N.D. Peace Officers Assn. (legis. com. 1979—), N.D. Chiefs Assn. (legis. com. 1980—), FBI Nat. Acad. Assos. Clubs: Kiwanis, Elks, Eagles (Bismarck). Office: 700 S 9th St Bismarck ND 58501

MEDVED, JOSEPH BRUNO, environ. engr.; b. Milw., Nov. 11, 1945; s. Frank Frank and Evelyn Frances (Poplawski) M.; B.S. in Mec. Engring., Gen. Motors Inst., 1969; M.S. in Occupational and Environ. Health and Indsl. Hygiene, Wayne State U., 1976; m. Georgeann Marie Wade, June 4, 1966. With Gen. Motors Corp., Flint, Mich., 1964—, mech. engr., Buick motor div., 1968-71, ventilation engr. Buick motor div., 1971-73, environ. engr. Buick motor div., 1973-76, divisional environ. coordinator Central Foundry div., 1976-81; adminstr. environ. activities Central Foundry div., 1981—. Mem. res. unit Flint (Mich.) Police Dept., 1967-72; active Saginaw United Way Campaign, 1979—. Recipient mayor's cert. of appreciation, Flint, 1967; registered profl. engr., Mich. Mem. Am. Indsl. Hygiene Assn. (chmn. air pollution com.), Am. Acad. Indsl. Hygiene (diplomate), Am. Foundryman's Soc., Motor Vehicle Mfrs. Assn., Nat. Soc. Profl. Engrs., Mich. Assn. Environ. Profls. (charter), Mich. Soc. Profl. Engrs. (Young Engr. of Yr. award Flint chpt. 1976), Mich. Indsl. Hygiene Soc. Roman Catholic. Club: K.C. Office: Central Foundry Div Gen Motors Corp Divisional Office Box 1629 77 W Center St Saginaw MI 48605

MEDZIHRADSKY, FEDOR, biochemist; b. Kikinda, Yugoslavia, Feb. 4, 1932; s. Miklos and Melanie (Gettmann) M.; M.S., Technische Hochschule Munich, Germany, 1961; Ph.D., 1965; m. Mechthild Westmeyer, Sept. 13, 1967; children—Sofia, Oliver. Instr. biochemistry U. Munich, 1965-66; asst. prof. biochemistry U. Mich. Med. Sch., Ann Arbor, 1969-73, asso. prof., 1973-81, prof., 1981—, research asso. pharmacology, 1971-74, asso. prof., 1975-81, prof., 1981—. Vis. asso. prof. pharmacology Stanford Med. Center, 1975-76. Postdoctoral fellow NIH, U. Wis., Madison, 1966-67, Nat. Inst. Neurol. Diseases and Blindness, Washington U., St. Louis, 1967-69; Nat. Research Service grantee, 1975-76. Mem. Soc. German Chemists, Soc. Biol. Chemistry (Germany), Am. Soc. Neurochemistry, Am. Chem. Soc., Am. Soc. Biol. Chemists, Am. Soc.

Pharmacology and Exptl. Therapeutics. Research neurochemistry, biochem. pharmacology. Home: 1615 E Stadium Blvd Ann Arbor MI 48104 Office: Dept Biological Chemistry Univ Michigan Medical School Ann Arbor MI 48109

MEECE, RICHARD CHARLES, sales exec.; b. Chgo., Sept. 13, 1940; s. Brown Louis and Jessie (Harden) M.; B.B.A., U. Notre Dame, 1962. Sr. mcpl. examiner Auditor of State of Ohio, Columbus, 1970-71; adminstrv. officer Ohio River Basin Commn., Cin., 1971-73; dep. fin. dir. City of Columbus, 1973-75; health care mktg. rep. Bus. Telephone Systems, Inc., Columbus, 1975-80; sales exec. Systel Corp., Grand Rapids, Mich., 1981—; permanent group leader Dale Carnegie Sales Course. Mem. labor relations com. Ohio Mun. League, 1974-75; exec. com. Columbus Zool. Assn., 1975; exec. com. Franklin County (Ohio) Rep. Party, 1978-79; fin. chmn. Young Rep. Nat. Fedn., 1975-76. Served with U.S. Army to capt., 1963-69. Decorated Bronze Star medal with oak leaf cluster, Army Commendation medal with 2 oak leaf clusters, Air medal; recipient awards Freedoms Found., 1965, 67, James A. Rhodes award, Ohio League of Young Reps., 1977; winner, Young Rep. Nat. Fedn. nat. speech contest, 1975; nat. sales contest winner No. Telecom, Inc., 1977, 78. Mem. Am. Hosp. Assn., Am. Mgmt. Assn., U. Notre Dame Alumni Assn. Roman Catholic. Clubs: Toastmasters Internat.; No. Telecom Pres.'s. Office: Systel Corp 2450 Buchanan St SW Grand Rapids MI 49508

MEEDER, JEANNE ELIZABETH, food technologist; b. Erie, Pa., Mar. 5, 1950; d. Theodore Roosevelt and Linnie Loretta (Drury) M.; B.A., Houghton Coll., 1972; M.B.A., Kent State U., 1982. Product devel. technician Welch Foods Inc., Westfield, N.Y., 1972-73, tech. asst., 1973, asso. tech. asst., 1973-76, sr. tech. asst., 1976; research asst. Stouffer Foods Corp., Solon, Ohio, 1976-77, entree team leader research and devel., 1977-80, entree team leader product devel., 1980—; also mem. flavor profile panel. Active West County Hist. Assn. Operation, Hazel Kibler Meml. Mus. Mem. Home Economists in Bus., Inst. Food Technologists, Am. Home Economists Assn., Assn. MBA Execs, Daughters Am. Revolution, West County Hist. Assn. Republican. Presbyterian. Mem. Order Eastern Star. Office: 5750 Harper Rd Solon OH 44139

MEEKS, LOUIS WALTER, orthopedic surgeon; b. Ann Arbor, Mich., July 4, 1937; s. A. James and Leona Frances (Gale) M.; B.A., Albion Coll., 1959; M.D., U. Mich., 1963; m. Berneda Slavik, May 21, 1970; children—Michelle, Louis, Jonathan, Laura, James. Intern, St. Joseph Mercy Hosp., Ann Arbor, 1963-64, asst. resident in gen. surgery, 1964-65; resident in orthopedic surgery U. Mich., 1965-66, 68-70; practice medicine specializing in orthopedic surgery, Ann Arbor, 1970—; mem. staff, past chief dept. surgery Beyer Meml. Hosp., Ipsilanti, Mich.; vice chief dept. orthopedics St. Joseph Mercy Hosp.; clin. instr. in surgery U. Mich. Med. Center; cons. Wayne County (Mich.) Gen. Hosp., Wayne; orthopedic cons. Dept. State, 1979. Served as capt. M.C., U.S. Army, 1966-68. Diplomate Am. Bd. Orthopedic Surgery. Fellow AAUP, Internat. Coll. Surgeons, Am. Coll. Sports Medicine, A.C.S., Am. Acad. Orthopedic Surgeons; mem. Washtenaw County (Mich.), Mich. State med. socs., AMA, Am. Acad. Sports Medicine, Am. Soc. for Sports Medicine, Mich. Orthopedic Soc., Beta Beta Beta. Contbr. articles to textbooks and profl. jours.; author sound slide program: Low Back Pain, 1976. Home: 180 Riverview Ct Ann Arbor MI 48104 Office: 5305 E Huron River Dr Suite 3B100 Ypsilanti MI 48197

MEERSON, MARY LOU JANICE, ednl. adminstr.; b. Flint, Mich.; d. Kenneth A. and Violet Katherine Quigley; B.A., Mich. State U., 1965, M.A., 1969; m. Irving Joseph Meerson, July 28, 1956; children—David, Deborah. Tchr., grade sch., Westwood Heights, Mich., 1963-64; tchr. Speech and English, Longfellow Jr. High Sch., Flint, 1965-74, cons. reading and English, 1974-78, acting coordinator humanities, 1978-79, coordintor alternative programs, 1979—; ednl. cons., 1979—. Chmn., Mayors Adv. Com. on Cable TV, 1974-79. Mich. State Acad. scholar, 1953-56. Mem. Mich. Council Women in Ednl. Adminstrs. (pres.), Flint Congress Sch. Adminstrs. (v.p.), Am. Assn. Sch. Adminstrs., Assn. for Supervision and Curriculum Devel., Phi Delta Kappa, Phi Kappa Phi. Democrat. Jewish. Co-author: Speech Communication in the High School, 1972; Good English 7, 1980; Good English 8, 1980. Office: 923 E Kearsley St Flint MI 48502

MEESE, ERNEST HAROLD, surgeon; b. Bradford, Pa., June 23, 1929; s. Ernest D. and Blanche (Raub) M.; B.A., U. Buffalo, 1950, M.D., 1954; m. Margaret Eugenia McHenry, Oct. 4, 1952; children—Constance Ann, Roderick Bryan, Gregory James. Resident in gen. surgery Millard Fillmore Hosp., Buffalo, 1955-59; resident in thoracic surgery U.S. Naval Hosp., St. Albans L.I., N.Y., 1961-63; group practice thoracic and cardiovascular surgery, Cin., 1965—; asst. clin. prof. surgery Cin. Med. Center, 1972—; head sect. thoracic and cardiovascular surgery St. Francis Hosp., Deaconess Hosp.; mem. staff Good Samaritan, St. George, Bethesda, Christ, Providence, Childrens, Epp Meml. and St. Luke hosps., Cin. Pres. bd. dirs., chmn. service com. Cin.-Hamilton County unit Am. Cancer Soc., trustee Ohio div.; trustee, exec. bd. Southwestern Ohio chpt. Am. Heart Assn. Served to comdr. M.C., USN, 1959-65. Diplomate Am. Bd. Surgery, Am. Bd. Thoracic Surgery. Fellow A.C.S., Soc. Thoracic Surgeons, Am. Coll. Chest Physicians, Am. Coll. Angiology, Cin. Surg. Soc., Am. Coll. Cardiology; mem. Gibson Anat. Hon. Soc., A.M.A., Am. Thoracic Soc., Assn. Mil. Surgeons U.S., Acad. Medicine Cin., Phi Beta Kappa, Phi Chi. Clubs: Bankers, Western Hills Country, Queen City (Cin.). Contbr. articles to profl. jours. and textbooks. Home: 174 Pedretti Rd Cincinnati OH 45238 Office: 311 Howell Ave Cincinnati OH 45220 also 3502 Boudinot Cincinnati OH 45211

MEESE, WILLIAM GILES, utility co. exec.; b. Rugby, N.D., Aug. 27, 1916; s. William Gottlieb and Emma (LaPierre) M.; B.S., Purdue U., 1941, D.Eng. (hon.), 1972; m. Mary Edith Monk, Apr. 4, 1942; children—Elizabeth, Stephen, Richard. With Detroit Edison Co., 1941—, asst. v.p. constrn. and engring., 1967, v.p., 1967-69, exec. v.p. prodn., 1969-70, pres., 1970-75, chief exec. officer, 1971—, chmn. bd., 1975—, also dir.; dir. Mfrs. Nat. Bank, Mfrs. Nat. Corp., Eaton Corp., Ex-Cello Corp. Trustee Detroit Renaissance, Rackham Engring. Found.; bd. dirs. United Found. Served to maj., F.A., AUS, 1941-45. Decorated Bronze Star medal; recipient Distinguished Alumnus award Purdue U., 1969; Internat. B'nai B'rith Humanitarian award, 1977; registered profl. engr., Mich. Fellow Engring. Soc. Detroit; mem. IEEE, Conf. Internationale des Grands Reseaux Electriques, Newcomen Soc. N.Am., Tau Beta Pi, Eta Kappa Nu. Clubs: Detroit, Detroit Athletic, Economic of Detroit (dir.). Home: 570 Rudgate Rd Bloomfield Hills MI 48013 Office: 2000 2d Ave Detroit MI 48226

MEFFERD, THOMAS OWEN, ednl. cons. co. exec.; b. Chgo., Oct. 7, 1951; s. Richard C. and Edith R. M.; ed. high sch. Communications dispatcher Ill. State Police, Joliet, 1969-73; service mgr. Alarm Detection Systems Ill. Inc., Aurora, 1973-77; ambulance attendance Overman Funeral Chapel, Plainfield, Ill., 1971-78; dir. emergency services, ambulance mgr. Village of Plainfield Emergency Services and Disaster Agy., 1978-81; ednl. specialist Gt. Lakes Ednl. Consultants Inc., Battle Creek, Mich., 1981—; lectr. in field. Pres. N.E. Ill. CD Council, 1979—, regional v.p. Ill. CD Council, 1979—. Recipient Lifesaving award Village of Plainfield, 1978, 1st place Audio-visual competition U.S. CD Council, 1978. Mem. Nat. Assn. Emergency Med. Technicians, Ill. Assn. Emergency Med. Technicians, U.S. CD Council. Office: Great Lakes Ednl Consultants Inc Federal Center Battle Creek MI 49016

MEGGERS, JOHN FRED, univ. adminstr.; b. Sheboygan, Wis., Mar. 11, 1927; s. John W. and Clara M. (Heinemann) M.; Teaching cert. Sheboygan County Normal, Sheboygan Falls, Wis., 1949; B.S., Wis. State U., Oshkosh, 1956; M.S., U. Wis., Madison, 1958, Ph.D., 1966; m. Donna Wattawa, May 30, 1953; children—Roxanne Meggers Terrien, Jill. Dir. elementary edn. Oshkosh (Wis.) schs., 1959-62; supt. schs. West Sales (Wis.) schs., 1962-64; asst. to dean Sch. Edn. U. Wis., Madison, 1964-66; dean U. Wis. Center, Barron County, Rice Lake, 1966—. Served with U.S. Army, 1950-52. Mem. NEA, Am. Assn. Sch. Adminstrs., Wis. Assn. Sch. Dist. Adminstrs., Rice Lake C. of C. (dir. 1980—). Lutheran. Clubs: Rotary, Elks. Office: 1800 College Dr Rice Lake WI 54868

MEHBOD, HASSAN, nephrologist; b. Shiraz, Iran, Sept. 10, 1933; s. Mehdi and Homa (Anvar) M.; came to U.S., 1959, naturalized, 1969; M.D., Tehran U., 1958; m. Darlene Van Putten, June 6, 1964; children—William M., Diane H., Susan L. Intern, Bergen Pines County Hosp., Paramus, N.J., resident in internal medicine, 1960-61, 63-64; chief resident Goldwater Meml. Hosp., 1961-62; fellow Hahnemann Med. Coll. and Hosp., Phila., 1962-63, 64-65; pvt. practice medicine and nephrology, Dayton, Ohio; asso. clin. prof. medicine Wright State U.; coordinator internal medicine, mem. attending staff Good Samaritan, St. Elizabeth hosps. Diplomate Am. Bd. Internal Medicine. Fellow A.C.P.; mem. AMA, Ohio Med. Assn., Montgomery County Med. Soc. (trustee), Am., Internat. socs. nephrology. Contbr. articles to profl. jours. Office: 2716 W Hillcrest Ave Dayton OH 45406

MEHLENBACHER, DOHN HARLOW, ednl. adminstr.; b. Huntington Park, Calif., Nov. 18, 1931; s. Virgil Claude and Helga (Sigfridson) M.; B.S. in Civil Engring., U. Ill., 1953; M.S. in City and Regional Planning, Ill. Inst. Tech., 1961; M.B.A., U. Chgo., 1972; m. Barbara Ruth Stinson, Dec. 30, 1953; children—Dohn Scott, Kimberly Ruth, Mark James, Matthew Lincoln. Structural engr., draftsman Swift & Co., Chgo., 1953-54, 56-57, DeLeuw-Cather Co., Chgo., 1957-59; project engr. Quaker Oats Co., Chgo., 1959-61, mgr. constrn., 1964-70, mgr. real property, 1970-71, mgr. engring. and maintenance, Los Angeles, 1961-64; chief facilities engr. Bell & Howell Co., Chgo., 1972-73; v.p. design Globe Engring. Co., Chgo., 1973-76; project mgr. I.C. Harbour Constrn. Co., Oak Brook, Ill., 1976-78; dir. estimating George A. Fuller Co., Chgo., 1978; pres. Food-Tech Co., Willowbrook, Ill., 1979-80; dir. phys. resources Ill. Inst. Tech., 1980—. Served with USAF, 1954-56. Registered profl. engr., Ill., N.Y., Calif. Mem. Nat. Soc. Profl. Engrs., Am. Mgmt. Assn., ASCE, Constrn. Specifications Inst., Am. Arbitration Assn. Home: 3101 S Wabash Ave #302 Chicago IL 60616 Office: IIT Center Chicago IL 60616

MEHLHAF, MILTON T., banker; b. Menno, S.D., May 7, 1926; s. Theodore and Emelia (Reiser) M.; B.S., U. S.D., 1949; m. Jacqueline Jean Waltner, Aug. 22, 1948; children—Mark S., Jan K. Coach basketball, baseball and track Lake Norden (S.D.) High Sch., 1949-53; v.p., dir. First Nat. Bank, Freeman, S.D., to 1981, pres., dir., 1981—. Counselor S.D. Boys State, 1952-57; treas. S.D. Amateur Baseball Assn., 1974—. Mem. Freeman Sch. Bd. Vice pres. bd. dirs. Freeman Jr. Coll.; trustee S.D. Fellowship Christian Athletes. Served with USNR, 1944-46. Mem. S.D. Bankers Assn. (chmn. edn. com. 1972), C. of C. (pres. 1962, sec.-treas. 1966), Am. Legion. Republican. Mem. Mennonite Ch. (chmn., tchr.). Home: 728 S Cherry St Freeman SD 57029

MEHN, W. HARRISON, surgeon; b. Monroe, Wis., Nov. 25, 1918; s. William Herman and Hedwig Gertrude (Butenhoff) M.; B.A., North Central Coll., Naperville, Ill., 1940; B.S., Northwestern U. Med. Sch., 1944, M.D., 1944, M.S. in Pathology, 1944; m. Jean Belle Dorr, Sept. 23, 1945; children—Mary Ann, Judith Susan. Intern, Passavant Meml. Hosp., Chgo., 1944, resident in surgery, 1947-50; resident in pathology Children's Meml. Hosp., Chgo., 1945, Alexian Bros. Hosp., Chgo., 1946-47, resident in surgery Cook County Hosp., Chgo., 1949-53; clin. asst. dept. surgery Northwestern U., 1948-52, instr. in surgery, 1952-53, asso. in surgery, 1953-58, asst. prof. surgery, 1958-73, asso. prof., 1973-74, prof. clin. surgery, 1974—; practice medicine specializing in surgery, Chgo.; mem. staffs Passavant Meml. Hosp., VA Lakeside Hosp.; med. dir. Commonwealth Edison Co., Chgo., 1955—; mem. accident prevention com. Edison Electric Inst., N.Y.C., 1960—; participant profl. research task forces Electric Power Research Inst., Palo Alto, Calif., 1973—; mem. U.S.-USSR Coop. Agreement on UHV, 1977—, U.S.-USSR Coop. Agreement on Biologic Effects of Electric Fields, 1977—. Bd. dirs. NCCJ, 1968—; mem. bd. ruling elders Presbyn. Ch., Evanston, Ill., 1971—, bd. dirs. Presbyn. Home, Evanston. Served to lt. M.C. USN, 1945-46, to lt. comdr., 1953-55. Diplomate Am. Bd. Surgery. Mem. A.C.S. (mem. Chgo. com. on trauma 1970—), Chgo. Heart Assn., Chgo., Western surg. socs., Soc. Surgery Alimentary Tract, Collegium Internationale Chirurgiae Digestivae, Inst. Medicine, Chgo., Ill. State med. socs., AMA, Indsl. Med. Assn., Am. Trauma Soc., McGraw Wildlife Found., Sigma Xi, Pi Kappa Epsilon, Phi Beta Pi. Clubs: Westmoreland Country (Wilmette, Ill.) (pres.); Internationale, Anglers, Campfire (Chgo.). Contbr. articles to profl. publs. Home: 3033 Normandy Pl Evanston IL 60201 Office: 707 N Fairbanks Ct Chicago IL 60611

MEHR, JOSEPH JOHN, psychologist; b. Chgo., June 23, 1941; s. Peter Joseph and Elizabeth Alma (Gartner) M.; B.A., Bradley U., 1963, M.A., 1964; Ph.D., Ill. Inst. Tech., 1971; m. Nancy Claire Harrison, Apr. 4, 1970; 1 son, Ian Jason. Psychology intern Chgo. State Hosp., 1964-65; dir. family therapy program Elgin (Ill.) State Hosp., 1965-68, dir. fed. mental health tng. project, 1968-70, asst. dir. extended care program, 1970-74, dir. spl. programs, 1974-77, chief psychologist, dir. intensive behavior therapy program, 1977—; prof. psychology Northeastern Ill. U., 1971-74; adj. prof. No. Ill. U., 1973—, Elmhurst (Ill.) Coll., 1977—; v.p., dir. Center for Human Potential, Inc., Elgin, Ill., 1974—. Registered Psychologist, Ill.; Certified Service Provider in Psychology, Council for Nat. Register of Health Service Providers in Psychology. Mem. Am., Ill. psychol. assns., Assn. Mental Health Adminstr. Author: Human Services: Concepts and Intervention Strategies, 1980; (with W. Fisher, P. Truckenbrod) Power, Greed and Stupidity in the Mental Health Racket, 1973; (with W. Fisher, P. Truckenbrod) Human Services: The Third Revolution in Mental Health, 1974; co-editor (with R. Agranoff, W. Fisher, P. Truckenbrod) Explorations in Competency Module Development: Relinking Higher Education and the Human Services, 1975. Contbr. articles to profl. jours. Home: 1028 N Spring St Elgin IL 60120 Office: 750 S State St Elgin IL 60120

MEHRENS, WILLIAM ARTHUR, educator; b. Lordsburg, N.Mex., Sept. 20, 1937; s. Arthur W. and Gertrude (Spatz) M.; B.S., U. Nebr., 1958, M.Ed., 1959; Ph.D., U. Minn., 1965; m. Bethel J. Wulf, Mar. 22, 1959; children—Lori, Machell. Tchr. Mpls. schs., 1959-61, counselor, 1962-63; prof. ednl. measurement Mich. State U., East Lansing, 1965—. Mem. Am. Personnel and Guidance Assn., Am. Psychol. Assn., Am. Ednl. Research Assn., Nat. Council Measurement in Edn. Republican. Lutheran. Author 12 books including Measurement and Evaluation in Education and Psychology, 1978. Home: 2193 Butternut Okemos MI 48864 Office: 462 Erickson Michigan State U East Lansing MI 48824

MEHTA, DEV V., polymer scientist; b. India, Dec. 28, 1938; came to U.S., 1962, naturalized, 1971; B.S. in Chemistry, U. Bombay, 1959; M.S. in Chemistry, LL.B., U. Gujarat, 1961; B.S. in Chem. Engring., U. Mo., Rolla, 1964; M.S., 1965; Ph.D. in Polymer Sci. (fellow Dept. Interior 1965-71), U. Akron (Ohio), 1971. Postdoctoral fellow Inst. Polymer Sci., U. Akron, 1970-71; sr. research scientist Ames Co., div. Miles Labs., Elkhart, Ind., 1971-76; dir. research and devel. Gelman Sci. Inc., Ann Arbor, Mich., 1976-80, dir. div. electronics, 1980—. Active local Big Bros. Am., 1971-76. Recipient Midwest regional conf. award Am. Inst. Chem. Engrs., 1964. Mem. Am. Mgmt. Assn., Am. Chem. Soc., Am. Electrochem. Soc., Japanese Electrochem. Soc., TAPPI. Patentee polymer membranes, film tech. Home: 9747 Queens Dr Manchester MI 48158 Office: 600 S Wagner Rd Ann Arbor MI 48106

MEIER, BEN, sec. of state N.D.; b. Napoleon, N.D., Aug. 1, 1918; s. Bernhardt and Theresia (Helzenderger) M.; diploma Dakota Bus. Coll., Fargo, N.D.; student U. Wis. Sch. Banking; m. Clara Kacyznski, Dec. 30, 1944; 1 son, Bernie. With Stock Growers Bank, Napoleon, 1943-45, Bank of Gackle (N.D.), 1945-47; v.p. Bank of Hazelton (N.D.), 1947-50; oil broker, real estate exec., ins. salesman, Bismarck, N.D., 1950-54; pres., owner Mandan Security Bank (N.D.), 1957-74; pres. Bismarck State Bank, 1977-81; sec. of state State of N.D., 1955—. Mem. Nat. Assn. Secs. State (past pres.), Nat. Assn. State Contractor Lic. Registars (past pres.). Republican. Roman Catholic. Clubs: Elks, Moose. Office: Capitol Bldg Bismarck ND 58501

MEIER, CRAIG A., clin. social worker; b. Freeport, Ill., Sept. 16, 1947; s. Harry P. and Lois M. M.; A.B., Wheaton Coll., 1969; M.S.W., Loyola U., Chgo., 1975. Mental health worker Luth. Gen. Hosp., Park Ridge, Ill., 1971-73, staff social worker, 1976-78, clin. social worker supervisory level, 1978-80; asst. mgr. social services MacNeal Meml. Hosp., Berwyn, Ill., 1980-81; field instr. George Williams Coll., Downers Grove, Ill., 1978-81; pvt. practice counseling, psychotherapy, Niles, Ill., 1978—. Mem. Nat. Assn. Social Workers, Am. Orthopsychiat. Assn., Acad. Cert. Social Workers, Register of Clin. Social Workers, Ill. Soc. Clin. Social Workers, Ill. Small Businessmen's Assn., Assn. Labor-Mgmt. Adminstrs. and Consultants on Alcoholism, Psi Chi. Office: Suite 708 Golf Mill Profl Bldg Niles IL 60648

MEIER, KAREN LORENE, educator; b. Davenport, Iowa, Aug. 17, 1942; d. Charles Frank and Minnie Louise (Arp) Meier; B.A., U. Iowa, 1963, M.A., 1974. Tchr., librarian Plano (Ill.) High Sch., 1963-67; tchr. social studies Moline (Ill.) High Sch., 1967—, also Secondary Social Studies Coordinator. Bd. dirs. Quad-City World Affairs Council; active League Women Voters. Mem. Nat., Ill. (sec. 1973-74, v.p. 1974-75), Iowa councils social studies, NEA, Ill. (sec.-treas. regional council 1975-79), Moline (pres. 1977-78) edn. assns., Am. Soc. Profl. and Exec. Women, Social Studies Suprs. Assn., Assn. Supervision and Curriculum Devel., AAUW, Alpha Delta Kappa. Home: 2230 1/2 Ripley Davenport IA 52803 Office: 3600 23d Ave Moline IL 61265

MEIER, WILBUR LEROY, JR., educator; b. Elgin, Tex., Jan. 3, 1939; s. Wilbur Leroy and Ruby (Hall) M.; B.S., U. Tex. at Austin, 1962, M.S., 1964, Ph.D., 1967; m. Judy Lee Longbotham, Aug. 30, 1958; children—Melynn, Marla, Melissa. Planning engr. Tex. Water Devel. Bd., Austin, 1962-66; research engr. U. Tex. at Austin, 1966-67; asst. prof. Tex. A and M U., College Station, 1967-68, asso. prof., 1968-70, prof. indsl. engring., 1970-72; prof., asst. head dept., 1972-73; prof., chmn. dept. indsl. engring. Iowa State U., 1973-74; prof., head sch. indsl. engring. Purdue U., 1974—; cons. Computer Graphics Internat. Inc., Bryan, Tex., Tex. Water Devel. Bd., Austin, Tex. Gov.'s Office, Austin, Water Resources Engrs., Inc., Walnut Creek, Calif., Environments for Tomorrow, Inc., Washington, Kaiser Engrs., Inc., Oakland, Calif. Named Outstanding Young Engr. of Year, Travis chpt. Tex. Soc. Profl. Engrs., 1966. Mem. Am. Inst. Indsl. Engrs. (past editor newsletter, regional chmn., program chmn., div. dir., chpt. pres., regional v.p., exec. v.p.), Operations Research Soc. Am., Inst. Mgmt. Scis. (past v.p. sect.), ASCE (past br. sec.-treas., com. chmn.), Tex. Soc. Profl. Engrs. (past chpt. dir.), Am. Soc. Engring. Edn. (past pres. chpt., chmn. div.), Sigma Xi, Tau Beta Pi, Alpha Pi Mu (regional dir., exec. v.p., pres.), Chi Epsilon, Phi Kappa Phi. Rotarian. Contbr. articles to profl. jours. Home: 368 Overlook Dr West Lafayette IN 47906

MEIER, WILLARD CHARLES, lawyer; b. Chgo., Sept. 22, 1914; s. Edward and Florence (Kindt) M.; B.A., Denison U., 1936; J.D., DePaul U., 1940; m. Judith H. Howes, June 10, 1947; children—Barbara Meier Gatten, Willard Charles. Admitted to Ill. bar, 1940; mem. firm Scott, MacLeish & Falk, Chgo., 1945-51; atty. Bachmann Uxbridge Worsted Corp., Uxbridge, Mass., 1951-55; mem. firm Nisen, Elliott & Meier, Chgo., 1955—; dir. Johnson Bros. Metal Forming Co., Berkeley, Ill., NASH Industries, Inc., Chgo., Jack Denst Designs, Inc., Chgo., Woodbridge Ornamental Iron Co., Chgo. Mem. Wilmette (Ill.) Harmony Conv. Served with USNR, 1941-45. Mem. Am., Ill., Chgo., Fed. bar assns., Am. Judicature Soc. (mem. antitrust com. 1970—). Clubs: Sheridan Shore Yacht (dir. 1965) (Wilmette); The Attic (Chgo.); Kenilworth (Ill.); Valley Lo. Home: 1809 F Tanglewood Dr Glenview IL 60025 Office: 1 N LaSalle St Chicago IL 60602

MEIERHENRY, MARK V., state atty. gen.; b. Gregory, S.D., Oct. 29, 1944; s. Vernon Meierhenry and Mary (Casey) Meierhenry O'Neill; B.A., U. S.D., 1966, J.D., 1970; m. Judith Knittel, May 14, 1961; children—Todd, Mary. Partner firm Camerer, Meierhenry, and Tabor, Scottsbluff, Nebr., 1970-71, Meierhenry, DeVany & Krueger, Vermillion, S.D., 1974-78; dir. S.D. Legal Services, Mission, 1971-74; atty. gen. State of S.D., Pierre, 1978—. Mem. Vermillion Sch. Bd., 1976-78; mem. S.D. Bd. Fin., 1979—; mem. S.D. Crime Commn., 1979—. Mem. State Bar Assn. S.D., S.D. Trial Lawyers Assn. Republican. Office: State Capitol Pierre SD 57501

MEIERS, HAROLD NORMAN, ins. agt.; b. Appleton, Wis., Apr. 18, 1943; s. Harold Paul and Lucille (Beschta) M.; B.S., U. Wis., Madison, 1967; m. Karen A. Thomson, June 27, 1980. With Union Mutual Ins. Co., Madison, Wis., 1967—, v.p. James F. McMichael & Assos., 1980—. Merit badge counselor Boy Scouts Am. Recipient Man of Yr. award Union Mut. Life Ins. Co., 1968, Disting. Sales award, 1969, 80; Nat. Quality award Nat. Assn. Life Underwriters, 1975-80, Nat. Sales Achievement award, 1975, 79; C.L.U. Mem. Nat. Assn. Life Underwriters, Madison Assn. Life Underwriters, Madison Jaycees (dir.). Lutheran. Office: Union Mutual Ins Co 6314 Odana Rd Suite 12 Madison WI 53719

MEISEL, JEROME, educator; b. Cleve., Aug. 9, 1934; s. David and Anne Irene (Meisel) Marmorstein; B.S.E.E., Case Inst., 1956, Ph.D., 1961; M.S.E.E., Mass. Inst. Tech., 1957; children—Denise Lauren, David Marc. Asst. prof. elec. engring. Case Inst., 1960-65; mem. tech. staff Bell Telephone Labs., Holmdel, N.J., 1965-66; asso. prof. elec. engring. Wayne State U., 1966-70, prof., 1970—; cons. in field. Union Carbide fellow; Mpls. Honeywell fellow. Mem. IEEE. Author: Principles of Electromechanical Energy Conversion, 1966. Contbr.

articles to profl. jours. Home: 2190 W Lincoln Birmingham MI 48009 Office: Department of Electrical Engineering Wayne State University Detroit MI 48202

MEISNER, EDWARD CHARLES, mfg. exec.; b. Dayton, Ohio, Mar. 12, 1913; s. Charles Philip and Louisa (Schoettinger) M.; student Ohio State U., 1931-32; B.S. in Mech. Engring., U. Dayton, 1936; m. Martha Eileen Cull, June 13, 1945; children—Michael E., Patricia A., Geoffrey C. Head phys. testing lab., asst. metallurgist, head tool planning and processing Nat. Cash Register Co., 1936-46; chief indsl. engr., plant mgr., gen. mgr. Plant 7, Crosley div. Avco Mfg. Corp., 1946-55; gen. mgr. insulation div. Philip Carey Mfg. Co., 1955-59, div. v.p., 1959-63, co. v.p., 1963-68; mgr. mfg. engring. Nat. Cash Register Co., Cambridge, Ohio, 1968-71, mfg. devel. engr., Dayton, 1971-77; ret., 1977. Registered profl. engr., Ohio. Mason (Shriner). Home: 10088 Tanager Ln Cincinnati OH 45215

MEISTER, BERNARD JOHN, chem. engr.; b. Maynard, Mass., Feb. 27, 1941; s. Benjamin C. and Gertrude M. M.; B.S. in Chem. Engring., Worcester Poly. Inst., 1962; Ph.D. in Chem. Engring., Cornell U., 1966; m. Janet M. White, Dec. 31, 1971; children—Mark, Martin, Kay Ellen. Engring. researcher Dow Chem. Co., Midland, Mich., 1966—, sr. research specialist, 1978—. Mem. Am. Inst. Chem. Engrs., Soc. Rheology, Sigma Xi. Mem. Ch. of Nazarene. Contbr. articles to profl. jours. Home: 3875 S Carter Rd Auburn MI 48611 Office: 438 Bldg Dow Chem Co Midland MI 48640

MEISTER, JAMES WALTER, med. center exec.; b. Gladwin, Mich., Apr. 6, 1948; s. Walter Harold and Florance L. (Rumminger) M.; student Delta Coll., 1966-68; B.B.A., Saginaw Valley State Coll., 1980; m. Diana Kaye Dubay, Feb. 1, 1969; children—Bryan James, Marc Alan. Lab. asst. Dow Chem. Co., Midland, Mich., 1968; bus. office mgr. Gladwin (Mich.) Area Hosp., 1968-75; mgr. systems dept. Bay Med. Center, Bay City, Mich., 1975—; cons. in field. Coordinator Gladwin County blood program ARC, 1971-72; chmn. Gladwin br. Aid Assn. for Lutherans, 1972; hosp. coordinator fund drive United Way of Bay County, 1975. Mem. Hosp. Fin. Mgmt. Assn. (advanced), Hosp. Info. Systems Sharing Group, Soc. Mgmt. Info. Systems. Republican. Home: 2161 S Nine Mile Rd Kawkawlin MI 48631 Office: 1900 Columbus Ave Bay City MI 48706

MEISTER, RICHARD THOMAS, editor, pub.; b. Cleve., Feb. 11, 1919; s. Edward George and Elsie (Giesen) M.; B.S., Cornell U., 1940; M.B.A., Harvard U., 1943; m. Lila Elizabeth Janes, Jan. 28, 1943; children—Cathy E., Linda S., Deborah D. Editor, Am. Fruit Grower Pub. Co., 1946-54; editorial dir., gen. mgr. Meister Pub. Co., Willoughby, Ohio, 1954-79, pres., editorial dir., 1979—; dir. Lake County Nat. Bank, 1970—. Councilman, Village of Waite Hill, 1970-78. Served to capt. U.S. Army, 1943-46. Mem. Am. Soc. Hort. Sci., Ohio State Hort. Soc., Am. Agrl. Editors Assn., Chi Psi. Episcopalian. Club: Kirtland Country. Home: Hobart Rd RD 3 Willoughby OH 44094 Office: 37841 Euclid Ave Willoughby OH 44094

MELAMED, LEO, lawyer, investment co. exec.; b. Bialystok, Poland, Mar. 20, 1932; s. Isaac M. and Fygla (Barakin) M.; came to U.S., 1941, naturalized, 1955; student U. Ill., 1950-52; LL.D., John Marshall Law Sch., 1955; m. Betty Sattler, Dec. 26, 1953; children—Idelle Sharon, Jordan Norman, David Jeffery. Admitted to Ill. bar, 1955; sr. partner firm Melamed, Kravitz & Verson, Chgo., 1956-66; chmn. Dellsher Investment Co. Inc., Chgo., 1965—. Mem. Chgo. Merc. Exchange, 1953—, gov., 1967—, sec. bd., 1967-69, 71-75, chmn. bd., 1969-71, 75-77; chmn. bd. Internat. Monetary Market, 1972-75, spl. counsel, 1976—; mem. Chgo. Bd. Trade, 1969—; mem. Chgo. Mayor's Council Manpower and Econ. Advisers, 1972—. Named Man of Year, Israel Bonds, 1975. Mem. Am., Ill., Chgo. bar assns., Am. Judicature Soc., Nat. Futures Assn. (chmn. 1976—), Am. Contract Bridge League (life master). Office: 222 S Riverside Plaza Chicago IL 60606

MELAND, BERNARD EUGENE, educator, theologian; b. Chgo., June 28, 1899; s. Erick Bernhard and Elizabeth (Hansen) M.; A.B., Park Coll., 1923, D.D., 1956; student U. Ill., 1918, 23-24, McCormick Theol. Sem., 1924-25; B.D., U. Chgo., 1928. Ph.D., 1929; postgrad. U. Marburg, Germany, 1928-29; m. Margaret Evans McClusky, Aug. 6, 1926 (dec.); children—Bernard Eugene (dec.), Richard Dennis. Ordained to ministry Presbyn. Ch., 1928; prof. religion and philosophy Central Coll., Fayette, Mo., 1929-36; asso. prof. religion, head dept. Pomona Coll., Claremont, Calif., 1936-43, prof. religion, 1943-45, Clark lectr., 1947; prof. constructive theology U. Chgo., 1945-64, prof. emeritus Div. Sch., 1964, vis. prof. theology, 1965-68, pastors inst. lectr. Div. Sch., 1945; vis. prof. philosophy of religion Union Theol. Sem., N.Y.C., 1968-69; Hewitt vis. prof. humanities Ottawa U. (Kans.), 1971; Barrows lectr., Calcutta and Bangalore, India, Rangoon, Burma; vis. lectr. Serampore Coll. (India), 1957-58; Barrows lectr. U. Calcutta, Poona, 1964-65. Served with U.S. Army, 1918. Mem. Am. Theol. Soc. (v.p. 1951-52, pres. Midwest div. 1960-61). Author: Modern Man's Worship, 1934; (with H.N. Wieman) American Philosophies of Religion, 1936; Write Your own Ten Commandments, 1938; The Church and Adult Education, 1939; Seeds of Redemption, 1947; America's Spiritual Culture, 1948; The Reawakening of Christian Faith, 1949; Higher Education and the Human Spirit, 1953; Faith and Culture, 1953; The Realities of Faith: The Revolution in Cultural Forms, 1962; The Secularization of Modern Cultures, 1966; Fallible Forms and Symbols, 1976; co-editor: Jour. Religion, 1946-64; editor, contbr. The Future of Empirical Theology, 1969. Home: 5842 Stony Island Ave Chicago IL 60637

MELBERG, WILLIAM FREDERICK, JR., econometrician; b. Buffalo, Sept. 13, 1948; s. William Frederick and Pearl Melberg; B.S. in Indsl. Engring., SUNY, Buffalo, 1970, M.B.A., 1972; Ph.D., Ill. Inst. Tech., 1981. Asst. prof. econs. North Park Coll., Chgo., 1973-78, asso. prof., 1978—; lectr. Northwestern U., 1979—. Mem. Am. Econ. Assn., Am. Statis. Assn., Assn. Computing Machinery. Author: Stability of Parameters and Variables of Equity Valuation Models Over Time, 1981. Home: 1522 Lincoln St Evanston IL 60201 Office: 5125 N Spaulding Ave Chicago IL 60625

MELCHERT, LENORA JEAN, bus. exec.; b. Detroit, Feb. 14, 1928; d. William Allan and Elizabeth Lillian (Miller) Currie; student U. Mich. Grad. Sch. Bus. Adminstrn., 1968; m. Kenneth Karl Melchert, July 10, 1948; children—Bruce Allen, Linda Christine Melchert Lenehan. With Automotive Parts, Inc., Detroit, 1946-48; payroll clk. Wettlaufer Mfg. Co., Southfield, Mich., 1948-49; with Genito Urinary Surgeons Ltd., P.C., Detroit, 1961—, mgr., 1965—, dir. pension and profit sharing funds, 1969—. Office: 952 Fisher Bldg Detroit MI 48202

MELDMAN, ROBERT EDWARD, lawyer; b. Milw. Aug. 5; s. Louis Leo and Lillian (Gollusch) M.; B.S., U. Wis., 1959; LL.B., Marquette U., 1962; LL.M. in Taxation, N.Y. U., 1963; m. Sandra Jane Setlick, July 24, 1960; children—Saree Beth, Richard Samuel. Admitted to Wis. bar, 1962, U.S. Tax Ct., 1963, U.S. Supreme Ct. bar, 1970, U.S. Ct. Claims, 1971; practice tax law, Milw., 1963—; adj. prof. taxation U. Wis., Milw. Mem. Am., Fed. (pres. Milw. 1966-67), Milw. (chmn. tax sect. 1970-71), bar assns., Wis. State Bar (dir. tax sect. 1964—, chmn. 1973-74), Marquette Law Alumni (dir. 1972-77), Phi Delta Phi, Tau Epsilon Rho (chancellor Milw. 1969-71, supreme nat. chancellor 1975-76). Jewish (trustee congregation 1972-77). Mem. B'nai B'rith (Ralph Harris meml. award Century Lodge, 1969-70; trustee). Author: (with Mountin) Federal Taxation Practice and Procedure, 1981; co-editor: Federal Tax Procedure—Supplemental Materials, 1980-81; contbr. articles to legal jours. Home: 9015 N King Rd Milwaukee WI 53217 Office: 788 N Jefferson St Milwaukee WI 53202

MELICHAR, ERNEST ALOIS, newspaper pub.; b. Hamilton, Ont., Can., May 24, 1936; s. Alois and Blanche Kristina (Sustek) M.; came to U.S., 1946, naturalized, 1955; A.A., Morton Jr. Coll., 1955; B.S., Northwestern U., 1957, M.S., 1958; m. Phyllis A. Dorociak, June 6, 1964; children—Joseph E., Frances Mary, Ann Louise. Co-publisher, Independent Newspapers, Wheeling, Ill., 1959-63; asst. editor Skyscraper Mgmt. Mag., Chgo., 1963-65; editor Chicagoland's Real Estate Advt., Chgo., 1965-68, pub., editor, 1968-70, pub. 1971—; dir. Clyde Fed. Savs. & Loan Assn., North Riverside, Ill., Nat. Baking Co., Inc., Chgo., N.W. Investment Co., Northbrook, Ill. Vice-pres. Riverside Community Fund, 1968-69, Riverside Twp. Regular Republican Orgn., 1977—; pres. Riverside Twp. Gold and Blue Commn., 1977—. Mem. Nat. Guard Assn. Ill., Moravian Cultural Soc. (founding pres. 1965-66), Chgo. Real Estate Bd., Lambda Alpha. Clubs: Chgo. Press, Monroe, Plaza. Rotary. Home: 235 Maplewood Rd Riverside IL 60546 Office: 415 N State St Chicago IL 60611

MELICK, GAIL, banker; b. Waterloo, Iowa, Jan. 11, 1928; s. Roy Elza and Mary Elizabeth (Quinn) M.; B.A., Carleton Coll., Northfield, Minn., 1952; M.B.A., U. Chgo., 1962; m. Nancy Eaton, Aug. 29, 1953; children—Daniel, Mary, Matthew. With Continental Ill. Bank, Chgo., 1952—, sr. v.p., from 1966, cashier, from 1970, exec. v.p. ops. and mgmt. services dept., to 1981, exec. v.p. Continental Ill. Corp., 1981—; dir. Tower Products Inc.; bd. dirs. Northwestern U. Banking Research Center. Trustee Lutheran Gen. Hosp.; bd. dirs. Chgo. Crime Commn. Served with USNR, 1946-48. Unitarian. Clubs: Chgo. Econs., Chgo. Bankers, Meadow, Metropolitan. Office: 231 S LaSalle St Chicago IL 60693*

MELL, DOROTHY MAY, educator; b. Elvins, Mo., May 10, 1928; d. Leslie Lee and Della Mae (Rosenstengel) West; B.S. in Edn., S.E. State U., 1971, M.Ed., 1976; m. Donald Richard Mell, June 7, 1953; children—Edward Lee, Paul Henry. Tchr., Desloge (Mo.) Public Sch., 1947-49, Elvins (Mo.) Public Sch., 1949-51, Leadwood (Mo.) Public Sch., 1951-53; art instr., counselor Farmington (Mo.) Middle Sch., 1964—. Den mother Cub Scouts, 1964-70. Recipient Den Mother's award Cub Scouts. Mem. Am. Personnel and Guidance Assn., Mo. State Tchrs. Assn., Mo. Guidance Assn. Lutheran. Club: 25 Gardeners Garden. Home: 336 W 6th St Farmington MO 63640

MELL, RONALD EDGAR, mfg. co. exec.; b. Detroit, Nov. 12, 1933; s. Edgar Emil and Helen (Cleary) M.; student parochial schs. Fort Wayne; m. Lorena Ann Bakalar, Dec. 15, 1950; children—Sheryl Ann, Sandra Marie, Thomas Edgar, Rick Lee. Retail sales Baker Bros. Shoe Store, Fort Wayne, 1951-53, also C&H Shoe Store; mgr. shoe stores, Anderon,Peru, Ind., 1954-57; mgr. advt. sales WSTR-AM, Sturgis, Mich., 1958-59; mgr. sales, program dir. WELL-AM, Battle Creek, Mich., 1960-65; with Marshall Brass Co. (Mich.), 1965—, dir. sales and mktg., 1972-78, v.p. sales and mktg., 1978—. Mem. Nat. Liquid Propane Gas Assn. (nat. dir.), Warehouse Distbrs. Assn., Recreational Vehicle Industry Assn., Manufactured Housing Inst., SPEBSQSA. Lutheran (elder). Club: Optimist (lt. gov. Mich. 1965-66). Home: 167 Maplehurst Blvd Battle Creek MI 49017 Office: 450 Leggitt Rd Marshall MI 49068

MELLAND, ROBERT BRUCE, automotive retail co. exec., state legislator; b. Fargo, N.D., Aug. 7, 1929; s. Russell Orville and Gunvor Alfedd (Wichmann) M.; student Jamestown Coll., 1947-48, Concordia Coll., Moorhead, Minn., 1948-49; m. Sept. 1, 1949 (dec. 1975) children—James, Deborah; m. 2d, Angeline C. Stein, May 1, 1976. With Melland Inc., Jamestown, N.D., 1950—, salesman, sales mgr., 1950-71, pres., gen. mgr., 1971—; mem. N.D. Senate, 1967—. Republican. Lutheran. Clubs: Lions, Elks, Eagles, Masons. Office: 802 17th St SW Jamestown ND 58401

MELLEROWICZ, MARY THERESE SARPOLUS, computer programmer; b. Detroit, Dec. 5, 1954; d. Victor Sam and Dolores Theresa (Schnaubelt) Sarpolus; Assoc. Computer Sci., Marygrove Coll., 1975; grad. Control Data Inst., 1974; B.S. in Vocat. Edn., U. Mich., Flint, 1981; 1 dau., Kathleen Marie. Clk., computer operator DAB Industries, Troy, Mich., 1975; computer accounting analyst Clintondale Community Schs., Mount Clemens, Mich., 1975, head data processing dept., analyst, 1976—, systems mgr., 1977—, vocat. instr., 1977—; jr. programmer analyst Chrysler Corp., Highland Park, Mich., 1978; computer programmer Pontiac div. Gen. Motors, Pontiac, Mich., 1979—. Home: 2396 Atlas Dr Troy MI 48084 Office: Pontiac Motor Div Gen Motors Corp Pontiac MI 48053

MELLINGER, JOHN JAMES, coll. adminstr.; b. Menominee, Mich., Dec. 8, 1945; s. John Charles and Margaret Ida (Meintz) M.; B.S., No. Mich. U., 1968, postgrad., 1979—; M.A., Mich. State U., 1974; m. Sharon A. Lemieux, June 13, 1970; children—Christine K., Sarah E., John James III. Electronics tchr./co-op. edn. coordinator St. John's (Mich.) High Sch., 1972-76; partner M-N Constrn., St. John's, 1973-76; placement dir. Bay de Noc Community Coll., Escanaba, Mich., 1976—; pres., owner Crown Distbrs., Escanaba, 1977—, dir., 1977-79; cons. several ednl. instns., 1978-80. Bd. dirs. Big Bros./Big Sisters, 1980-81; vol. United Way, 1978—. Served with AUS, 1969-71. Decorated D.S.M. Mem. Coll. Placement Council, Nat. Assn. for Co-op. Edn., Personnel and Guidance Assn., Midwest Coll. Assn., Blue Key. Republican. Roman Catholic. Club: Kiwanis (pres. local group 1980, Outstanding Leadership award 1980). Contbr. articles to profl. jours. Home: 1701 5th Ave S Escanaba MI 49829 Office: Bay de Noc Community Coll College Ave Escanaba MI 49829

MELNICOFF, IRA LEE, rheumatologist, physician; b. Washington, Sept. 8, 1941; s. Ben Ivan and Iola Bernice (Elstein) M.; B.A., U. Va., 1963; M.S. in Cellular Physiology and Cell Biochemistry, W.Va. U., 1966; D.O., Chgo. Coll. Osteo. Medicine, 1970; m. Lorraine Janet Billowitz, June 19, 1965; children—Shara Bryne, Jared Benjamin. Intern Nassau County Med. Center, East Meadow, N.Y., 1970-71; resident in medicine Brown U.-R.I. Hosp., Providence, 1971-72; fellow in rheumatology and clin. immunology Roger Williams Gen. Hosp., Providence, 1972-74; research fellow bio-med. scis. Brown U., Providence, 1972-73, teaching fellow, 1973-74, research asso., 1973-74, instr. medicine, 1974; practice medicine specializing in rheumatology, Chgo., 1974—; chief rheumatology-clin. immunology Chgo. Osteo. Hosp., 1974-80; asso. prof. medicine Chgo. Coll. Osteo. Medicine, 1978-80; attending staff, cons. rheumatic diseases Holy Family Hosp., Des Plaines, Ill., 1980—; clin. asso. in medicine (rheumatology) U. Ill. Sch. Medicine, 1980—; attending rheumatologist Luth. Gen. Hosp. Diplomate Nat. Bd. Med. Examiners, Am. Bd. Internal Medicine. Mem. R.I. Arthritis Found., New. Eng. Rheumatism Soc., A.C.P., Am. Rheumatism Assn., Chgo. Arthritis Found., Chgo. Rheumatism Soc., Chgo. Found. for Med. Care, Am. Soc. Internal Medicine, Chgo., Ill. med. socs., Chgo. Soc. Internal Medicine. Contbr. articles to med. jours. Home: 4855 Lindenwood Ln Northbrook IL 60642 Office: 9101 Greenwood Niles IL 60648

MELNYKOVICH, GEORGE OREST, coll. adminstr.; b. Sudatenland, Germany, Nov. 27, 1943; came to U.S., 1949, naturalized, 1954; s. William and Eva M.; B.A., Hiram Coll., 1965; M.A., U. Pitts., 1969, Ph.D., 1973; m. Caroline Thomas, June 18, 1966; children—Kristen, William, Rachel. Mem. faculty dept. Spanish Hiram (Ohio) Coll., 1969-75, prof., 1975-77, dir. admissions, 1975-77; asso. dean continuing edn. Kent State U., 1977-79, dean Coll. Spl. Programs, 1979—. Bd. dirs. Portage County Heart Assn. Mem. Am. Soc. Tng. Dirs., Am. Council Higher Continuing Edn., Ohio Council Higher Continuing Edn. Club: Rotary. Author: Reality and Expression in the Poetry of Carlos Pellicer, 1979. Contbr. articles to profl. jours. Office: 327 Rockwell Hall Kent State U Kent OH 44242

MELONAS, PETER CONSTANTINE, corp. recruitment exec.; b. Chgo., Apr. 12, 1941; s. Gust Peter and Maryanthy (Athens) M.; B.A. in Psychology, Drake U. and DePaul U., 1964; student U. Mich., 1964, DePaul U. Law Sch., 1968. Coordinator recruitment, tng. and minority affairs Atlantic Richfield Co., N.Y.C., 1969-72; personnel mgr. The Interpublic Group of Cos., N.Y.C., 1972-75, dir. mktg. recruitment, 1975-78; v.p., dir. personnel Kenyon & Eckhardt, Inc., N.Y.C., 1978-79; exec. dir. Kenyon & Eckhardt Found., 1978-79; v.p., dir. worldwide recruitment KMG Internat., Inc., Chgo., 1979-81; pres. Peter Melonas & Assos., Inc., 1981—. Served with Peace Corps, Iran, 1964-66. Mem. Am. Assn. Advt. Agencies. Eastern Orthodox. Club: Masons. Office: Suite 4150 1290 Ave of Americas New York NY 10010

MELOON, ROBERT A., newspaper editor; b. Davenport, Iowa, July 13, 1928; s. John and Evelyn Mae (Ede) Case; student public schs., Davenport; m. Leslee Zermuhlen, July 31, 1967; children—Mark Robert, Brian Alfred. Reporter, The Capital Times, 1957-71, asso. editor, 1971-72, mng. editor, 1972-78, exec. editor, 1978—, gen. mgr., 1981—. Mem. Am. Newspaper Pubs. Assn., Inland Daily Press Assn., Wis. AP Assn., Wis. Newspaper Assn. Unitarian. Home: 6602 Piping Rock Rd Madison WI 53711 Office: 1901 Fish Hatchery Rd Madison WI 53708

MELOY, HAROLD H., lawyer; b. Waldron, Ind., Nov. 29, 1913; s. James Henry and Pearl (Haymond) M.; LL.B., Ind. U., 1939; m. Loretta Marie Schrader, Sept. 9, 1951. Admitted to Ind. bar, 1939; practice law, Shelbyville, Ind., 1939—; historian Mammoth Cave, 1960—; lectr. on history, legends and folklore of Mammoth Cave. Pros. atty. for 16th Jud. Circuit Ct. of Ind., 1945-50; city judge, Shelbyville, 1956. Bd. dirs. Maj. Hosp. Found., Shelbyville, pres., 1976—; mem. adv. bd. Shelbyville Salvation Army, chmn., 1971-72; Served with AUS, 1941-43. Fellow Nat. Speleol. Soc.; mem. Am. Spelean History Assn. (dir. 1968—), Shelby County Bar Assn. (pres. 1958), Cave Research Found., Mammoth Cave Nat. Park Assn. (dir. 1974—). Democrat. Methodist. Mason (Shriner). Elk. Author: Mummies of Mammoth Cave, 1968, 7th edit., 1980. Contbr. numerous articles on history of Mammoth Cave to various jours. Home: PO Box 454 Shelbyville IN 46176 Office: 302 Methodist Bldg PO Box 454 Shelbyville IN 46176

MELOY, LORETTA MARIE SCHRADER, lawyer; b. Shelbyville, Ind., Apr. 26, 1924; d. Conrad and Anna Elisabeth (Kranz) Schrader; B.S., Ind. U., 1946, J.D. (Wendell Willkie law scholar), 1968; m. Harold Meloy, Sept. 9, 1951. Admitted to Ind. bar, 1969; individual practice law, Shelbyville, 1969—; judge City Ct. Shelbyville, 1972-76. Mem. Shelby County Bar Assn. (pres. 1981). Address: PO Box 454 Shelbyville IN 46176

MELOY, SYBIL PISKUR, lawyer; b. Chgo., Dec. 1, 1939; d. Michael M. and Laura (Stevenson) Piskur; B.S., U. Ill., 1961; J.D., Ill. Inst. Tech., 1965; postgrad. John Marshall Law Sch., 1966-72, Harvard U., 1979; children—William, Brad. Admitted to Ill. bar, 1965; patent chemist G.D. Searle & Co., Skokie, Ill., 1961-65, patent atty., 1965-67, sr. atty., 1967-71, internat. counsel, 1971-72; regional counsel Abbott Labs., North Chicago, Ill., 1972-77; assoc. firm J.P. Biestek & Assos., Arlington Heights, Ill., 1979; asst. gen. counsel Alberto Culver Co., Melrose Park, Ill., 1979—, also of counsel firm Palmer, Blackman, Mancini & Riebandt P.C.; dir. Inst. Advanced Ednl. Resources. Recipient BNA prize, 1965. Mem. Am. Bar Assn., Chgo. Bar Assn., Am. Patent Law Assn., Am. Chem. Soc., Women's Bar Assn. Ill., N.W. Suburban Bar Assn., Lic. Execs. Soc., Phi Beta Kappa, Phi Kappa Phi, Iota Sigma Pi. Home: 431 N Northwest Hwy Park Ridge IL 60068 Office: 2525 Armitage St Melrose Park IL 60160 also 950 N Northwest Hwy Park Ridge IL 60068

MELOY, WILBUR ROBERT, assn. exec.; b. Bloomington, Ind., Sept. 19, 1929; s. John Wilson and Lulu (Buchanan) M.; B.A., Monmouth Coll., 1951; postgrad. U. Toledo, 1953-54. Program dir., residence dir. Central Br. Toledo YMCA, 1954-58; membership dir., program dir., residence dir. Honolulu Central YMCA, 1959-63; asso. program dir. Vanderbilt YMCA, N.Y.C., 1963-64, asso. exec. dir., dir. pub. relations, residence dir., 1964-78; exec. dir. Aberdeen (S.D.) YMCA, 1978—. Served with U.S. Army, 1951-53. Mem. Assn. Profl. Dirs. YMCA, Tau Kappa Epsilon. Republican. Methodist. Club: Toastmasters (pres.) (Aberdeen). Home: 616 23d St NE Aberdeen SD 57401 Office: 420 S Lincoln St Aberdeen SD 57401

MELTON, ALTON RAY, mech. engr.; b. Lee County, Va., Oct. 10, 1931; s. Willie and Gladys (Lively) M.; B.S.M.E., U. Ky., 1954; m. Elizabeth Jean Richards, Jan. 29, 1950; children—Cynthia Rae, Tommy Ray. Plant mgr. Logan Long Co., Franklin, Ohio, 1958-65; asst. plant mgr. Philip Carey Mfg. Co., Lockland, Ohio, 1965-66; chief engr. Beckett Paper Co., Hamilton, Ohio, 1966-79, gen. supt., 1979—. Deacon, Victory Bapt. Ch., Trenton, Ohio. Mem. Paper Industry Mgmt. Assn., TAPPI. Home: 402 N Miami St Trenton OH 45067 Office: 400 Dayton St Hamilton OH 45011

MELTON, EMORY LEON, lawyer, publisher, state legislator; b. McDowell, Mo. June 20, 1923; s. Columbus Right and Pearly Susan (Wise) M.; student Monett Jr. Coll., 1940-41, S.W. Mo. State U., 1941-42; LL.B., U. Mo., 1945; m. Jean Sanders, June 19, 1949; children—Stanley Emory, John Russell. Admitted to Mo. bar, 1944; individual practice law, Cassville, Mo., 1947—; pres. Melton Publs.,

Inc., pub. 4 newpapers, 1959—; pros. atty. Barry county (Mo.), 1947-51; mem. Mo. Senate, 1973—. Chmn., Barry County Republican Com., 1964-68. Served with AUS, 1945-46. Recipient award for meritorious public service St. Louis Globe-Democrat., 1976. Mem. Mo. Bar Assn. Baptist. Clubs: Lions, Masons. Office: 201 W 9th St Cassville MO 65625

MELTON, LUCILLE ELIZABETH, nurse; b. Keswick, Iowa, May 28, 1914; d. Joseph and Lillian (Conn) Galbraith; R.N., St. Lukes Hosp., Davenport, Iowa, 1937; m. Walter Charles Melton, Sept. 23, 1946; children—Christena Melton Walter, Elaine Melton Johannees. Surg. floor, night supr. St. Lukes Hosp., Davenport, 1937-40; pvt. duty nurse, 1946-52; nursing asst., aide instr. Salina (Kans.) Vocat. Tech. Sch., 1963—. Served to capt. Nurse Corps, U.S. Army, 1940-46. Mem. Am. Nurses Assn., Kans. State 5th Dist. Nurses Assn., Am. Vocat. Assn., Kans. Vocat. Assn. (life), Salinas Vocat. Edn. Assn., Am. Assn. Ret. Persons. Republican. Presbyterian. Home: 614 W Republic St Salina KS 67401

MELUCCI, RICHARD ALLEN, printing co. exec.; b. Detroit, Nov. 23, 1949; s. Evo Joseph and Doreen Hilda (Woodcock) M.; student Macomb County Community Coll., 1977; m. Roberta Eve Bevan, May 6, 1972; children—Scott Allen, Amy Lynn, Wendy Michelle. With Atom Print Shop Inc., Warren, Mich., 1968—, supt., 1972-73, v.p., 1973—. Served with USN, 1969-75. Mem. Tri County Printers Council (founder), Printing Industries Am., Printing Industries Mich., Detroit Sportsmens Congress, S.E. Mich. Amateur Radio Assn. (cert. appreciation), Amateur Radio Relay League (cert. merit). Lutheran. Office: 23045 Ryan St Warren MI 48091

MEMON, ABDUL MAJEED, physician; b. Dhoraji, India, June 3, 1946; s. Haji Qasim and Hanifa Hajiyani (Lashkerwala) M.; M.B., B.S., Liaquat Med. Coll., Pakistan, 1971; married; children—Saima, Mohammed Faisal. Intern, Rutgers Med. Sch., 1973-74; resident, N.J. Coll. Medicine, Newark, 1974-76; pulmonary fellowship N.J. Med. Sch., 1976-78; pvt. practice medicine, Warrenton, Mo., 1978—; clin. instr. N.J. Coll. Medicine, 1974-78; mem. staff St. Francis Mercy Hosp., Washington, Mo., St. Peters (Mo.) Community Hosp. Diplomate Am. Bd. Internal Medicine. Mem. Warren Franklin Gasconade County Med. Soc., Am. Thoracic Soc., Mo. Thoracic Soc. Club: Rotary. Home: 624 Hidden Lake Dr Saint Peters MO 63376 Office: 213 E Main St Warrenton MO 63383

MENCHIN, ROBERT STANLEY, board of trade exec.; b. Kingston, N.Y., Oct. 31, 1923; s. Abraham H. and Gertrude (Gorlin) M.; B.A., N.Y. U., 1948; m. Marylin Barsky, Dec. 26, 1949; children—Jonathan, Scott. Account exec. DKG Advt., N.Y.C., 1949-51; dir. spl. projects Am. Visuals Corp., N.Y.C., 1952-59; dir. advt. and public relations Arthur Wiesenberger & Co., N.Y.C., 1959-65; pres. Wall St. Mktg. Communications, Inc., N.Y.C., 1967-77; dir. mktg. communications Chgo. Bd. Trade, 1977—. Served with AUS, 1942-45. Mem. Public Relations Soc. Am., Fin. Planners Assn. Author: The Last Caprice, 1964; Where There's a Will, 1977; editor: The Financial Futures Professional, 1977—. Home: 1313 Ritchie Ct Chicago IL 60610 Office: Chgo Bd Trade LaSalle and Jackson Sts Chicago IL 60604

MENDELSOHN, AVRUM JOSEPH, psychologist; b. Chgo., June 22, 1940; s. Jack and Lena (Applebaum) M.; B.S., U. Ill., 1964; M.S., Ill. Inst. Tech., 1968; Ph.D., Heed U., 1977; children—Debra, Susan. Sr. psychologist Chgo. Police Dept., 1965-68; resident psychologist Ridgeway Hosp., Chgo., 1968-72; cons. psychologist Chgo. Bd. Health, 1969-72; chief psychologist Bur. Testing Services, Chgo., 1974-77; partner Police Cons., Hillside, Ill., 1969—, v.p. 1974—. Mem. Am. Psychol. Assn., Ill. Psychol. Assn., Advancement for Ethical Hypnosis. Office: Police Consultants 4415 Harrison St Hillside IL 60162

MENDELSOHN, ROBERT SAUL, physician; b. Chgo., July 13, 1926; s. Herman Martin and Rosamond (Kanter) M.; Ph.B., U. Chgo., 1947, B.S., 1949; M.D., 1951; m. Rita Remer, Mar. 29, 1952; children—Ruth Mendelsohn Lockshin, Sally Mendelsohn Lowenfeld. Intern, Cook Country Hosp., Chgo., 1951-52; resident in pediatrics Michael Reese Hosp., Chgo., 1952-55; practice medicine specializing in pediatrics and family medicine, Chgo., 1955—; asso. prof. dept. preventive medicine and community health U. Ill. Coll. Medicine, Chgo., 1969-80. Served with USNR, 1944-45. Diplomate Am. Bd. Pediatrics. Jewish. Author: Confessions of a Medical Heretic, 1979; MalePractice, 1981. Syndicated newspaper column: The People's Doctor, 1976—. Office: 1210 Lake St Evanston IL 60201

MENDELSON, DAVID FREY, neurologist; b. St. Louis, Mo., Feb. 25, 1925; s. Harry and Lorine Esther (Korngold) M.; A.B., U. Cal., 1946; M.D., Ind. U., 1948; m. Mary Ann Lavis, June 21, 1956 (div. 1978); children—Lori, David, Elizabeth, Jonathan. Intern, Ind. U. Med. Center, Indpls.; resident Children's Meml. Hosp., Chgo., 1950, Barnes Hosp., 1950-51; practice medicine specializing in neurology, St. Louis, 1958—; clin. fellow neurology U. Minn., Mpls., 1953-56; instr. U. Minn., 1956-58; clin. asst. prof. neurology St. Louis U., 1958—; clin. prof. neurology Maryville Coll., 1972—. Bd. dirs. Mo. Med. Service, 1964-72; trustee Mo. Blue Shield, 1972—. Served with AUS, 1943-46, USAF, 1951-53. Fellow Am. Acad. Neurology, St. Louis Soc. Neurological Scis., A.M.A., St. Louis County Med. Soc. Home: 575 Stratford St St Louis MO 63130 Office: 141 N Meramec St Clayton MO 63105

MENDHEIM, JOHN MURRAY, mgmt. cons. co. exec.; b. Berlin, May 24, 1926; s. Salli M. and Feodora (Weisshaus) M.; came to U.S., 1940, naturalized, 1943; B.A. in Psychology, Northwestern U., 1949, M.B.A., 1953; m. Stephanie LaCroix, May 3, 1976; 1 son, Justin; children by previous marriage—Kim, Michael. Corporate personnel dir. Solo Cup Corp., 1958-60, Griffith Labs., 1960-64; v.p. personnel Kitchens of Sara Lee div. Consol. Foods, Deerfield, Ill., 1964-68; v.p. employee relations Hardwicke Corp., N.Y.C., 1968-71; pres., chief exec. officer Mendheim Co., Chgo., 1968—, chmn. Post Mil. Career subs., 1969-73, also pres. Informa div., Lincolnwood, Ill. Served with U.S. Army, 1942-45. Decorated Bronze Star, 5 battle stars. Mem. Am. Mgmt. Assn., Northwestern U. Alumni Assn., Urban League. Office: Mendheim Co 6055 N Lincoln Ave Chicago IL 60659

MENDUS, WILLIAM EDWARD, accountant; b. Kansas City, Mo., Aug. 4, 1948; s. Fred A. and Mary Ruth (Klein) M.; B.A. in History (Nat. Merit scholar), Rockhurst Coll., Kansas City, 1970, B.S. in Acctg., 1977; M.B.A., U. Okla., 1975; m. Nancy Marie Vandergriff, June 2, 1970; m. 2d, Sharon Lee Schulz, July 1, 1979. Partner, Mendus & Keech, Kansas City, Mo., 1980—; tchr. Rockhurst Coll., Kansas City, 1977—. Treas. Hist. Kansas City Found., 1978-79. Mem. Am. Inst. C.P.A.'s, Mo. Soc. C.P.A.'s. Roman Catholic. Home: 435 E 62d St Kansas City MO 64110 Office: 4510 Belleview 100 Kansas City MO 64111

MENEFEE, FREDERICK LEWIS, advt. agy. exec.; b. Arkansas City, Kan., Oct. 22, 1932; s. Arthur LeeRoy and Vera Mae (Rather) M.; student Arkansas City Jr. Coll., 1952; B.A., U. Wichita, 1958; m. Margot Leuze, Sept. 16, 1955; children—Gregory Shawn, Christina Dawn. Vice-pres., account exec. Asso. Advt. Agy., 1958-64; with McCormick-Armstrong Co., advt. agy., Wichita, 1964—, agy. mgr., 1964—, account supr., 1965—, gen. mgr., 1972—; pres., chief exec. officer McCormick-Armstrong Advt. Agy., Inc., 1979—. Served with AUS, 1953-55. Named Advt. Man of the Year, Advt. Club of Wichita, 1964, Advt. Man of the Year, 9th Dist. Am. Advt. Fedn., 1965. Mem. Am. Advt. Fedn. (dist. gov. 1968-69, chmn. nat. council govs. 1969-70, Wichita Wagonmasters (capt. 1974-75, dir.; charter), Wichita Area C. of C., Western Kans. Mfrs. Inc., Wichita Advt. Club (pres. 1963-64), Alpha Delta Sigma. Home: 2235 Redbud Lane Wichita KS 67204 Office: 1501 E Douglas St Wichita KS 67201

MENIER, VINCENT JOSEPH, coffee equipment mfg. co. exec.; b. Lakeside, Ohio, May 20, 1929; s. Vito James and Catherine Ida (Ruffa) M.; B.S. in Mech. Engring., U. Okla., 1953; m. Joan Sawyer, July 7, 1953; children—Mark, John, Patricia. Product mgr. Westinshouse Co., Dallas, 1955-65; mgr. mktg. GTE-Sylvania, Detroit, 1965-73; exec. v.p. Mr. Coffee, Bedford Heights, Ohio, 1973—. Mem. Bd. Health San Antonio, 1955-57. Served as pilot USAF, 1953-55. Mem. Am. Inst. Aeros. and Astronautics, Cleve. Engring. Soc., Air Force Assn., Res. Officers Assn., Aircraft Owners and Pilots Assn., Soc. Auto. Engrs., IEEE, Warbirds of Am., Exptl. Aircraft Assn. Am., Confederate Air Force (col.). Republican. Roman Catholic. Club: K.C. Home: 2 Pepper Creek Pepper Pike OH 44124 Office: 5433 Perkins Rd Bedford Heights OH 44146

MENIKHEIM, MARIE-LOUISE LOLAND, educator, nurse; b. St. Charles, Ill., Mar. 30, 1939; d. Harold John and Inger Astrid (Petersen) Loland; B.S., Case Western Res. U., 1963; M.S., Cath. U. Am., 1968; postgrad. U. Minn., 1975—; m. Douglas Karl Menikheim, Nov. 2, 1963; children—Maureen, Mary-Katherine, Molly. Instr., Southwestern Coll., San Diego, 1969-71, Sch. Nursing, U. Hawaii, Honolulu, 1971-72; lectr. Sch. Nursing U. Minn., Mpls., 1976-78; instr. Met. Comml. Coll., 1973-75; coordinator upper div. nursing curriculum Met. State U., St. Paul, 1978-81, asso. dean, 1981—. Bd. dirs. Neighborhood InvolVement Program, Mpls., 1974-77; mem. adv. bd. Normandale Community Coll., Edina, Minn., 1976—; bd. dirs. Contact Twin Cities, 1979—, chmn.-elect, 1981; bd. dirs. 1st Call For Help United Way, 1981. Mem. AAUW, AAUP, Am. Nurses Assn., Minn. Nurses Assn. (dir. 1981—), Nat. League Nursing, NOW. Episcopalian. Club: Woman's (Mpls.). Home: 2901 Benton Blvd Minneapolis MN 55416 Office: Metropolitan State Univ 121 Metropolitan Sq Bldg Saint Paul MN 55101

MENKE, WILLIAM CHARLES, lawyer; b. Cin., Aug. 30, 1939; s. William Gerhardt and Margaret Philomena (Mercurio) M.; B.S., U. Detroit, 1961, J.D., 1976; M.B.A., Ind. U., 1974; m. Mary Lou Lapan, Jan. 7, 1967; children—William Leo, Lorelei Louise. Sr. engr. Gen. Electric Co., Cin., 1964-67; v.p., gen. mgr. Preventicare Systems, Inc., Dearborn, Mich., 1967-71; dir. Comshare, Inc., Ann Arbor, Mich., 1971-76; admitted to Ohio bar, 1976; individual practice law, New Richmond, Ohio, 1976—. Served with USN, 1961-64. Fellow Lawyers in Mensa; mem. Am. Bar Assn., Am. Trial Lawyers Assn., Ohio Bar Assn., Mensa. Home: 1432 Indian Ridge Trail New Richmond OH 45157 Office: William Charles Menke-Lawyer New Richmond National Bank Bldg PO Box 10 New Richmond OH 45157

MENNE, MARY BARBARA, ednl. adminstr.; b. St. Louis, July 20, 1946; d. Leo Lawrence and Marguerite Ellen (Wiesemeyer) M.; B.A. in Elem. and Spl. Edn., Fontbonne Coll., 1968; M.A. in Spl. Edn., St. Louis U., 1972, Ph.D. in Ednl. Adminstrn., 1977. Tchr. educable mentally retarded Spl. Sch. Dist., St. Louis County, Mo., 1968-75; elem. prin. Valley Park (Mo.) Sch. Dist., 1975—; asst. prof. edn. U. Mo., St. Louis, summer 1980. Active, Webster Groves Theater Guild. Mem. Assn. for Supervision and Curriculum Devel., Prins. Assn. (nat., state, local levels, officer local chpt., 1980—), Phi Delta Kappa (pres. St. Louis chpt. 1977-78). Roman Catholic. Contbr. articles to publs. including Mo. Schs., Nat. Elem. Prin. Office: 356 Meremec Station Rd Valley Park MO 63088

MENNING, ARNOLD J., coll. dean; b. Alton, Iowa, Dec. 20, 1930; s. Bert and Nell M.; B.A., U. No. Iowa, 1952, M.A., 1956; Ph.D., S.D. State U., 1973; m. Thelma M. Intveld, June 10, 1952; children—Jeri, Darrell, Dale, Carla. High sch. tchr., Hull and Estherville, Iowa, 1954-64; dir. student personnel Iowa Lakes Community Coll., Estherville, 1964-69; dir. spl. services S.D. State U., Brookings, 1969-74, dean Coll. Gen. Registration, 1974—, dir. Career Acad. Planning Center, 1975—; cons. Elder, Presbyterian Ch., 1967-69, 71-74; mem. County Republican Workers, 1974-80. Served in U.S. Army, 1952-54. Recipient Outstanding Educator award Iowa Lakes Community Coll., 1969. Mem. Am. Assn. Higher Edn., Acad. Affairs Adminstrs., Nat. Orientation Dirs. Assn., Am. Personnel and Guidance Assn., Kappa Delta Phi, Phi Kappa Phi, Gamma Sigma Delta. Club: Jackrabbit. Contbr. articles to profl. jours. Home: 1920 3d St Brookings SD 57006 Office: SD State U Brookings SD 57007

MENSCER, DARRELL VANCE, electric utility exec.; b. Statesville, N.C., May 13, 1934; s. Clinton Marvin and Myrtle (Cline) M.; B.S.E.E., N.C. State U., 1960; m. Carolyn Westmoreland, Dec. 21, 1952; 1 dau., Darlyne. Various positions to sr. v.p. Carolina Power & Light Co., Raleigh, N.C., 1960-80; pres., chief operating officer Public Service Co. Ind., Inc., Plainfield, 1980—; dir. Mchts. Nat. Corp., Mchts. Nat. Bank & Trust Co.; exec. bd. East Central Area Reliability Coordination. Bd. dirs. N.C. State U. Found., Inc.; exec. bd. Crossroads of Am. council Boy Scouts Am. Served with USAF, 1952-56. Registered profl. engr., N.C., S.C. Mem. Ind. Mfrs. Assn. (dir.), Phi Kappa Phi, Eta Kappa Nu. Democrat. Presbyterian. Clubs: Indpls. Athletic, Columbia, Meridian Hills Country, Capital City (Raleigh). Office: 1000 E Main St Plainfield IN 46168

MENSENDIKE, RAY ARNOLD, ednl. adminstr.; b. Camp Point, Ill., Mar. 27, 1926; s. C.O. and Della Beatrice (Dutton) M.; B.S., Bradley U., 1950, M.A., 1953; advanced certificate in Edn., U. Ill., 1957; m. Edith Ann Schmiedeskamp, July 9, 1950; children—Alice Ann, Ray Richard, Jane Louise, Willa Jean, John Orland. Maintenance dept. Caterpillar Tractor Co., Peoria, Ill., 1947-50, 51-52; tchr. public schs., N. Pekin, Ill., 1952-56; elementary prin. Lanark, Ill., 1956-58, Pecatonica, Ill., 1958-68; supt. schs., Hanover, Ill., 1968-71; dir. Jo Daviess-Carroll Vocat. Center, Elizabeth, Ill., 1971-75; supt. schs., Orangeville, Ill., 1975—; income tax cons. Mem. Hanover Village Bd., 1970-75, Jo Daviess County Health Bd., 1974-75; sec. long range planning commn. No. Ill. Conf. United Meth. Ch.; tchr. ch. sch.; bd. dirs. Stephenson Area Career Center. Served with U.S. Army, 1944-46, 50-51. Recipient awards Gifted Seminar, Rockford Coll., 1964, Jo Daviess-Carroll Area Vocat. Center, 1973; I.D.E.A. fellow, 1981. Mem. Ill. Assn. Sch. Adminstrs. Republican. Clubs: Lions, Odd Fellows. Home: PO Box 261 Orangeville IL 61060 Office: PO Box 218 Orangeville IL 61060

MENSON, ELIZABETH C., educator; b. N.Y.C.; d. John Thomas and Elizabeth H. (McSorley) Carroll; B.S., Columbia U., 1940; M.Ed., Ohio U., 1970, Ph.D., 1978; m. John Menson, Sept., 1939; children—John, Robert, Richard, Thomas, James, Betsy, Susan. Chief examiner for testing services Ohio U., Lancaster, 1971-72, dir. student services, 1972-74, dir. admissions and student services, 1974-76; coordinator experiential learning program Ohio U., Athens, 1977-80, dir. adult learning services, 1980—; regional mgr. E. Central States CAEL, chmn. Experiential Learning Com., gen. mgr. Kellogg grant. Founder LWV, Lancaster, mem. regional planning commn.; pres. Women's Assn., Presbyn. Ch.; bd. dirs. Waldon House mem. 648 bd. Fairfield Mental Health Clinic. Mem. Am. Personnel and Guidance Assn., Am. Coll. Personnel Assn. (commns. XIV, VII), Nat. Assn. Women Deans, Nat. Assn. Women Adminstrs., Adult Edn. Assn., Am. Counselor Educators, Nat. Vocat. Guidance Assn., AAUW, Phi Delta Kappa. Club: Bus. and Profl. Women. Home: 133 Honor Ct Lancaster OH 43130 Office: 309 Tupper Hall Ohio Univ Athens OH 45701

MENZ, WILLIAM WOLFGANG, research exec.; b. Zweibruecken, Germany, Mar. 2, 1917; s. Michael Rudolf and Rosel (Putzel) M.; B.S., U. Munich, 1937, M.S., 1939; postgrad. Ohio State U., 1949-50; m. Gertrude Weissman, May 17, 1941; children—Roberta (Mrs. John J. Suhrbier), Paul Fred. Came to U.S., 1939, naturalized, 1944. Br. chief intelligence dept. USAAF, Dayton, Ohio, 1946-50; editor USPHS, Cin., 1950-51; tech. info. analyst Gen. Aniline & Film Corp., Easton, Pa., 1951-52, Ethyl Corp., Detroit, 1952-57; sect. chief R.J. Reynolds Industries, Winston-Salem, N.C., 1957-70; v.p. research, exec. sec. Dairy Research Inc., Rosemont, Ill., 1970—. Served with USAAF, 1941-45. Mem. Am. Chem. Soc. (sect. chmn. 1962, nat. awards com. 1962-64), Soc. Tech. Writers and Editors (pres. 1960), Am. Dairy Sci. Assn., Inst. Aero. Scis., Sigma Xi. Home: 111 S Baybrook Dr Apt 603 Palatine IL 60067 Office: 6300 N River Rd Rosemont IL 60018

MERCER, ROBERT E., rubber co. exec.; b. Elizabeth, N.J., 1924; grad. Yale U.; married. With Goodyear Tire & Rubber Co., Akron, Ohio, 1947—, mgr. indsl. products ops., 1963-66, div. gen. sales mgr., 1966-68, div. gen. mgr., 1968-73, asst. to pres., 1973-74, pres. Kelly-Springfield Tire Co. subs., 1974-76, exec. v.p. parent co., 1976-78, pres., chief operating officer, 1978—, also dir. Office: Goodyear Tire & Rubber Co 1144 E Market St Akron OH 44316*

MERCEREAU, MAE DOLORES, nurse; b. Chgo., Feb. 17, 1932; d. Clarence Wetherell and Frances Dolores (Bender) M.; R.N., Ravenswood Hosp., Chgo., 1962; flight nurse, Sch. Aerospace Medicine, Brooks AFB, Tex., 1967. Operating room nurse Ravenswood Hosp., 1962-64; 1st aid nurse Chgo. Dept. Aviation, 1964-65; labor and delivery room nurse Gottlieb Hosp., Melrose Park, Ill., 1965; office staff and nurse Northwest Airlines, Chgo., 1966-71; surg. asst. Dr. Dooley Found., Ban Houei Sai, Laos, 1967-68; operating room staff nurse Copley Hosp., Aurora, Ill., 1971-73; hosp. and med. center rep. Pennwalt Pharm. Co., Chgo., 1974; nurse Northlake (Ill.) Sr. Citizens Residence, 1975-78, Vital Measurements, Inc., 1975—, Red Cross Blood Service, 1979—; nurse cons. Northlake Hosp., 1978-79; mng. dir. Trav-A-Nurse Service, Chgo., 1969—. Served with USAF Res., 1967-71; maj. Ill. N.G., 1971—. Named Nurse of Year, Air N.G., 1975. Mem. Aerospace Med. Assn. (life), Assn. Mil. Surgeons U.S. (life mem.; bd. dirs. flight nurse sect. 1976—), N.G. Assn. U.S. (life), N.G. Assn. Ill. (life), Air Force Assn. (life), Res. Officers Assn. (life; past chpt. pres.), Emergency Dept. Nurses Assn., Dooley Overseas Vols. (pres.). Lutheran. Club: Marine Meml. Office: PO Box 66318 AMF OHIAP Chicago IL 60666

MERCHANT, FREDERICK TAYLOR, surgeon; b. Marion, Ohio, July 19, 1911; s. Harry J. and Hazel L. (Taylor) M.; A.B., Ohio Wesleyan U., 1933; M.D., Johns Hopkins U., 1937; m. Ethyl Irene Rush, June 29, 1940; 2 daus., Joan, Cathy. Intern in surgery Johns Hopkins Hosp., Balt., 1937-38; intern pathology Royal Victoria Hosp., Montreal, Que., Can., 1938-39, resident in surgery, 1940-42; instr. pathology McGill U., 1938-39, surgery, 1940-42; sr. intern in surgery Lakeside Hosp., Cleve., 1939-40; practice of surgery, Marion, Ohio, 1946-78; attending surgeon Marion Gen. Hosp., 1946-78, chief of staff, 1949-59, former chief of surgery, mem. bd. govs., 1959-65, 1968-78; former attending surgeon at the Wyandot Meml. Hosp., Morrow Co. Hosp., Mt. Gilead, Ohio, Community Med. Center Hosp., Marion; dist. surgeon Penn Central R.R., 1947-71. Dir. Bank One of Marion. Mem. State Med. Bd. Ohio, 1957-72, pres., 1963, 69; mem. Nat. Bd. Med. Examiners, 1965-75, vice chmn., mem. exec. com.; mem. exec. com. Fdn. State Med. Bds. U.S., pres., 1970-71; gen. chmn. Fedn. Licensing Exam. Program, 1968-78, now permanent sec.; mem. test com. Ednl. Commn. for Fgn. Med. Grads.; med. dir. Marion Health Found., Inc., 1978-81. Mem. exec. com. Rice Found. Premed. Edn., Ohio Wesleyan U. Gen. chmn. 1955 United Appeals. Served with AUS, 1942-45, chief surgeon thoracic surg. team, 1st aux. surg. group; disch. as lt. col.; recalled for spl. service as asst. chief, surg. cons. div. Office Surgeon Gen Army, Washington, 1950-51. Diplomate Am. Bd. Surgery. Fellow A.M.A., A.C.S.; mem. Ohio Med. Assn. (com. hosp. relations 1957-60, mem. profl. and jud. com. 1960-65, council 1964-68), Pan-Pacific Surg. Assn., C. of C. (dir. 1948-55, pres. 1950), Res. Officers Assn. (surgeon Ohio dept., pres. Marion area), Ohio Surg. Assn., Am. Legion, Assn. Mil. Surgeons U.S., Phi Gamma Delta, Nu Sigma Nu, Symposiarchs. Episcopalian. Contbr. articles to profl. jours. Home: 800 King Ave Marion OH 43302

MERCIER, RAYMOND GEORGE, psychiatrist; b. Dearborn, Mich., June 29, 1940; s. Joseph Gerard and Cecile Marie (Maurais) M.; B.A., U. Mich., 1962; M.D., Wayne State U., Detroit, 1966; m. Miriam Edith Koski, Nov. 6, 1971; children—Claire Marie, Daniel James. Intern, Los Angeles County Gen. Hosp., 1966-67; resident in psychiatry Lafayette Clinic, Detroit, 1969-72; mem. faculty Wayne State U. Med. Sch., 1972—, asst. prof. psychiatry, 1974—; med. dir. Franklin Center Behavior Change, Southfield, Mich., 1974—; psychiat. cons. Armed Forces Examining and Entrance Sta.; med. expert HEW. Served with USNR, 1967-69; Vietnam. Decorated Bronze Star. Mem. Am. Psychiat. Assn., Assn. Advancement Behavior Therapy, Mich. Psychiat. Soc. Lutheran. Home: 3730 Balfour St Troy MI 48084 Office: 3990 John R St Detroit MI 48201

MEREDITH, CHARLES PETTIGREW, psychologist; b. Idabel, Okla., July 1, 1938; s. Charles and Gladys (Ford) M.; B.A., Phillips U., 1960; B.D., Grad. Sem., Enid, Okla., 1963; M.Th., Tex. Christian U., 1965; Ph.D., Fla. State U., 1970; m. Betty Lou Hall, Aug. 31, 1960; children—Charles Toland, Susan Elaine. Ordained to ministry Christian Ch. (Disciples of Christ), 1965; pastor First Christian Ch., Canyon, Tex., 1965-68; psychotherapist Met. Guidance Center, Southfield, Mich., 1970-73; adj. instr. Wayne State U., Detroit, 1971-73; pres., dir. Charles P. Meredith, Ph.D., P.C., Farmington Hills, Mich., 1973—. Mem. Am. Psychol. Assn., Am. Assn. Marriage and Family Therapy, Assn. Advancement of Psychology, Mich. Psychol. Assn., Mich. Marriage Counselors Assn. Democrat. Home: 46850 Timberlane Northville MI 48167 Office: 29226 Orchard Lake Rd Farmington Hills MI 48018

MEREDITH, JAMES HARGROVE, judge; b. Wederburn, Oreg., Aug. 25, 1914; s. Willis H. and Ollie (Hargrove) M.; A.B., Mo. U., 1935, LL.B., 1937; m. Dorothy Doke, Sept. 7, 1937 (dec. Feb. 1972); 1 son, James Doke; m. 2d, Susan B. Fitzgibbon, 1977. Admitted to Mo. bar, 1937; practice law, New Madrid County, Mo., 1937-42, 46-49; spl. agt. FBI, 1942-44; partner firm Stolar, Kuhlman & Meredith, St. Louis, 1952-61, Cook, Meredith, Murphy and English, 1961-62, Stuart and Meredith, Washington, 1961-62; chief counsel Mo. Ins. Dept., Jefferson City, 1949-52; U.S. dist. judge Eastern Dist. Mo., 1962—, chief judge, 1971-79; mem. U.S. Fgn. Intelligence Surveillance Ct., 1979-81. Mem. Mental Health Commn. Mo., 1961-62; active Friend Mo. U. Library Assn. Served with USNR,

1944-46. Recipient Patriots award S.R., 1974. Mem. Mo. Acad. Squires, Jud. Conf. U.S. (subcom. improvement judiciary 1971-81), U.S. Jud. Conf. (exec. com. 1976-79), Am. Bar Assn., Mo. Bar Assn., D.C. Bar Assn., St. Louis Bar Assn., Lawyers Assn. St. Louis, Order Coif, Phi Delta Phi (Disting. Alumni award), Sigma Chi (Significant Sig award). Presbyterian. Mason (Shriner). Clubs: Mo. Athletic, Old Warson Country (St. Louis). Home: 108 Runnymede Dr Saint Louis MO 63141 Office: US Dist Court 1114 Market St Saint Louis MO 63101

MERGLER, DON HARMON, oil co. exec.; b. Pennington Gap, Va., Apr, 15, 1924; s. Robert Wayne and Myrtle Lorena (Tilson) M.; student Lynchburg Coll., 1942, Norwich U., 1943; B.S. in Civil Engring., Va. Poly. Inst., 1951; postgrad. Loyola U. Law Sch., 1962; M.B.A., U. Chgo., 1964; m. Martha Elise Watkins, June 14, 1947; children—Deborah Ellen, Don Harmon. Project mgr., purchasing agt. Leonard Constrn. Co., Chgo., 1952-64; partner Plant Location Cons., Chgo., 1964-65; staff engr. Standard Oil Co., Chgo., 1966—; owner, operator Leesville Beef Farm, 1972—. Pres., Rich Twp. Republicans, 1970-72; pres. bd. Sch. Trustees, Park Forest, Ill., 1956—. Served with USAAF, 1943-47. Decorated Air medal. Registered profl. engr., Ill., Va. Mem. ASCE, Soc. Am. Mil. Engrs., Nat. Soc. Profl. Engrs., Res. Officers Assn., Nat. Wildlife Assn., Nat. Congress Parents and Tchrs. Episcopalian. Club: Decatur Country. Home: 25 E Rocket Circle Park Forest IL 60466 Office: 200 E Randolph Chicago IL 60680

MERILLAT, CALVIN LEE, educator; b. Hudson, Mich.; s. Norman and Rosetta Belle Merillat; B.S., Mich. State U., 1973, M.S., 1978. Vocat. agr. tchr. Benzie Central Schs., Benzonia, Mich., 1972-76, Adams Central Sch., Monroe, Ind., 1977—; advisor Future Farmers Am.; football coach. Mem. Am. Vocat. Assn., Ind. Vocat. Assn., Nat. Vocat. Agr. Tchrs. Assn., Ind. Vocat. Agr. Tchrs. Assn., NEA, Ind. State Teachers Assn. Address: Box 43 Monroe IN 46772

MERISALO, CARL B., aluminum co. exec.; b. Worcester, Mass., Jan. 6, 1924; s. Toivo B. and Anna E. (Helin) M.; student U. Wis., Superior, 1941-43, 46; B.S., U. Wis., Madison, 1948; M.B.A., U. Chgo., 1952; m. Jean Anna Kratt, June 17, 1955; children—Carl B., Anita E., Laura J., Emily A. Personnel trainee Am. Steel & Wire Co., Duluth, Minn., 1948-50; safety and tng. mgr. Kraft Foods Co., Chgo., 1952-53, personnel mgr., Hillside, N.J., 1953-55; staff mem. NAM, N.Y.C., 1955; asst. personnel dir. Rheem Mfg. Co., Sparrows Point, Md., 1955-59; indsl. relations mgr. Wm. Kratt Co., Union, N.J., 1959-72; dir. human resources Quality Aluminum Casting Co., Waukesha, Wis., 1973—. Served with USAAF, 1943-45; PTO. Decorated Air medal with 2 oak leaf clusters. Mem. Nat. Foundry Assn., Am. Foundrymen's Assn., Indsl. Relations Research Assn., Wis. Alumni Assn., U. Chgo. Sch. of Bus. Alumni Assn., C. of C. Waukesha. Clubs: Lions, Masons. Home: 34860 Shangri-la Dr Dousman WI 53118 Office: PO Box 148 Waukesha WI 53187

MERKEL, JAYNE SILVERSTEIN, art historian and writer; b. Cin., Sept. 28, 1942; d. Elmore Herman and Ruth Dell (Feiler) Silverstein; B.S., Simmons Coll., 1964; M.A., Smith Coll., 1968; postgrad. U. Mich., 1966-68, U. Cin., 1978—; m. Edward Wagner Merkel, Jr., Aug. 7, 1965; children—Mary Feiler, Jane Scranton. Curatorial asst. U. Mich. Mus. Art, Ann Arbor, 1965-68; curator Contemporary Arts Center, Cin., 1968-69; dir. edn. and public relations Taft Mus., Cin., 1969-74; instr. art history Art Acad. Cin., 1973-78; vis. instr. art history Miami U., Oxford, Ohio, 1978-79; architecture critic Cin. Enquirer, 1977—; teaching fellow dept. architecture U. Cin., 1978-80. Mem. panel Ohio Arts Council, 1979-80. Mem. AIA (juror for awards 1975, 77, 80, recipient Spl. award for archtl. writing 1973), Coll. Art Assn. Club: Cin. Tennis. Contbr. articles to profl. jours. Office: Cin Enquirer 617 Vine St Cincinnati OH 45201

MERKEL, NICHOLAS BART, steel co. exec.; b. Cleve., Aug. 19, 1947; s. Wilbur Wilson and Ann (Auburn) M.; B.A., Nasson Coll., Springvale, Maine, 1969. Sales mgr. Merrymaid Plastics Corp., Cleve., 1972, pres., 1973; controller Metal Blast Inc., Cleve., 1974-78, v.p., 1978-79, pres., 1979—. Served with USMC, 1969-72. Mem. Euclid C. of C. (trustee). Republican. Episcopalian. Home: Woodstock Rd Gates Mills OH 44040 Office: 871 E 67th St Clgveland OH 44103

MERKELO, HENRI, scientist, educator; b. Borky, Ukraine, June 12, 1939; came to U.S., 1956, naturalized, 1961; s. Alexander and Natalia (Niushko) M.; C.A.P., Coll. Moderne et Tech., Reims, France, 1956; M.S., U. Ill., 1962, Ph.D., 1966. Research scientist physics and thermodynamics Douglas Aircraft Co., Santa Monica, Calif., 1962; mem. faculty U. Ill., Urbana, 1966—, asso. prof. 1972—, dir. Quantum Electronics Research Lab., 1973—; cons. in field. Ford Found. fellow, 1960-62, IBM fellow, 1963; Kodak fellow, 1964; grantee in field. Mem. Am. Inst. Physics, Am. Phys. Soc., IEEE, AAAS, Sigma Xi. Contbr. articles in field to profl. jours.; patentee in field. Home: 7 Pine Circle Urbana IL 61801 Office: U Ill 155EEB Quantum Electronics Research Lab Urbana IL 61801

MERRELL, NORMAN L., state senator; b. nr. Williamstown, Mo., Apr. 12, 1924; B.S. in Bus. Adminstrn., Culver-Stockton Coll.; M.Bus. Edn., U. Colo.; 1 child. Former tchr., prin., supt. schs.; owner, operator farms, Lewis County, Mo.; mem. Mo. Senate, 1970—, pres. pro tem. Served with USAAF, World War II. Recipient numerous awards for civic activities. Mem. Am. Legion, Mo. Assn. Sch. Adminstrs., Mo. Sch. Tchrs. Assn., NE Mo. Sch. Adminstrs. Democrat. Mem. Christian Ch. Clubs: Masons, K.T., Shriners. Office: State Capitol Jefferson City MO 65101*

MERRIAM, GENE, state senator; b. Mpls., Nov. 1, 1944; s. George C. and Frances (Couillard) M.; B.S.B.A., U. Minn., 1967; m. Maureen Elizabeth Brown, 1965; children—Jeffrey Vincent, Brian Patrick, Kathryn Jean. Acct., 1970—; councilman-at-large, Coon Rapids, Minn., 1973-74; mem. Minn. Senate, 1975—. Served with USMCR, 1962-70. C.P.A., Minn. Mem. Beta Alpha Psi. Mem. Democratic-Farmer-Labor party. Roman Catholic. Office: 24F State Capitol St Paul MN 55155*

MERRIAM, GREGORY JAY, ins. co. exec.; b. Chgo., Nov. 2, 1945; s. Jack G. and Georgia C. (Grow) M.; B.S. in Bus. Mgmt., Fairleigh Dickinson U., 1968; m. Gertrude Elizabeth Guttenburger, Nov. 24, 1974; 1 dau., Karen Lynn. Loss control engr. Sentry Ins. Co., Morristown, N.J., 1970-73, loss control mgr., Cedar Knolls, N.J., 1973-77, loss control mgr., Chgo., 1977—. Scoutmaster Morris County council Boys Scouts Am., 1967-68. Served with U.S. Army, 1969-70. Cert. safety profl., cert. hazard control mgr. Mem. Am. Soc. Safety Engrs., Nat. Fire Protection Assn., Assn. Mut. Ins. Engrs., Alliance of Am. Insurers (mem. loss control com. 1977—, chmn. comml. vehicle safety com. 1980—), Fairleigh Dickinson U. Alumni Assn. Republican. Home: 348 Green Valley Dr Naperville IL 60540 Office: 10 S Riverside Plaza Chicago IL 60606

MERRICKS, JAMES WESLEY, JR., urologist; b. Charleston, W.Va., Apr. 28, 1908; s. James Wesley and Nannie Lincoln M.; B.A., W.Va. U., 1930, B.S., 1931; M.D., Rush Med. Coll., 1934; m. Virginia A. White, May 3, 1935. Intern, Harper Hosp., Detroit, 1933-34; resident in urology Rush-Presbyn. Hosp., Chgo., 1934-35; fellow urology Mayo Clinic, 1935-37; instr. urology Rush Med. Coll., Chgo., 1937-42; asst. prof. U. Ill. Coll. Medicine, Chgo., 1943-45, asso. prof., 1945-70; prof. emeritus dept. urology Rush Med. Coll., Chgo., 1970—; urologist Presbyn.-St. Luke's Hosp., Chgo., 1937-70; head sect. urology Highland Park (Ill.) Hosp., 1976—; cons. urology Lake Forest Hosp. (Ill.), 1975—. Diplomate Am. Bd. Urology. Mem. Am. Urol. Assn. (gold and silver awards, membership and pathology coms. 1952-72, gold award Brussels World Fair 1958), A.C.S. (gold and silver awards), A.M.A., Am. Med. Writers Assn., Am. Geriatric Assn., Western Surg. Assn., Ill. Med. Soc. (gold and silver awards), Chgo. Med. Soc. (sec.-treas. Northside br. 1940-42), Chgo. Urol. Soc. (gold and silver awards, sec., pres. 1944-48), Rush Med. Alumni Assn. (sec., pres. 1960-70), Sigma Xi, Phi Beta Kappa, Alpha Omega Alpha, Phi Lambda Tau, Sigma Chi, Alpha Kappa Kappa, Pi Kappa Epsilon. Contbr. articles in field to profl. jours. Home: 30 Riparian Rd Highland Park IL 60035 Office: 480 Elm Pl Highland Park IL 60035

MERRILL, FRANK EDWARD, stage equipment co. exec.; b. Indpls., Feb. 4, 1948; s. Robert H. and Helen Marie (Billeter) M.; B.A. in Speech and Theatre, Brigham Young U., Laie, Hawaii, 1972; m. Alexa Keala Thoene, June 6, 1970; children—Chryssa Kealaokamaile, Robert Alexander, Erin Kamakanaokapuanani. Stage mgr. Polynesian Cultural Center, Laie, Hawaii, 1970-71, tech. dir., 1977-79; regional sales mgr. Electro Controls, Inc., Salt Lake City, 1974-77; owner, operator Merrill Stage Equipment, Indpls., 1979—. Search mission pilot CAP; missionary Mormon Ch., 1967-69. Mem. U.S. Inst. for Theatre Tech., Am. Nat. Standards Inst., Am. Theatre Assn., Ind. Theatre Assn. Office: Merrill Stage Equipment 6520 Westfield Blvd Indianapolis IN 46220

MERRILL, WILLIAM H., JR., lawyer; b. Indpls., Apr. 11, 1942; s. William H. and Jane (Robinson) M.; B.S., Butler U., 1965; J.D., Ind. U., 1967; m. Winifred Jane Baur, July 25, 1964; children—Michele Jane, Betsy Diane. Admitted to Ind. bar, 1967; trust officer Merchants Nat. Bank, 1965-69; gen. counsel Everett I. Brown Co., Indpls., 1969—; v.p., gen. counsel Landeco, Inc., 1970—; pres. Baumer, Inc., 1973—; pres. Bash Seed Co., 1975—. Mem. Carmel (Ind.) City Plan Commn., 1975—. Mem. Am., Ind., Indpls. bar assns., Am. Judicature Soc. Clubs: Crooked Stick Golf, Columbia. Home: Rural Route 2 Box 339A Carmel IN 46203 Office: 5406 W Bradbury Ave Indianapolis IN 46241

MERRITT, DONALD BERT, JR., indsl. engr.; b. Kirksville, Mo., Aug. 18, 1952; s. Donald Bert and Vera Gene (Bowen) M.; B.S., U. Mo., Rolla, 1974; student N.E. Mo. State U., 1971-72; m. Pamela Sue Buttler, Dec. 17, 1977; 1 son, Michael. Indsl. engr. Midwest div. Lennox Industries, Inc., Marshalltown, Iowa, 1975—. Mem. Am. Inst. Indsl. Engrs., Nat. Mgmt. Assn. Republican. Baptist. Home: 503 New Castle Rd Marshalltown IA 50158 Office: 200 S 12th Ave Marshalltown IA 50158

MERRITT, JEANNINE CHARLOTTE, state ofcl.; b. Indpls., Dec. 18, 1928; d. Ralph E. and Charlotte M. (Mount) Updike; B.S., Ind. U., 1950; M.S., Butler U., Indpls., 1968; postgrad. Purdue U., Ind. U.; m. John W. Merritt, Nov. 17, 1960; children—Karen, Kelly, Kevin, John W., Jackie. Tchr. English, drama coach, chmn. dept. drama Decatur Central High Sch., Indpls., 1953-56; producer, host children's TV show, Indpls., 1956-57; chief copywriter Bobbs-Merrill Publishing Co., Indpls., 1957-60; tchr. world lit. North Central High Sch., Indpls., 1962-73; asso. supt. public instrn. State of Ind., 1973-78; exec. dir. Ind. Community Services Adminstrn., 1973—, Ind. Commn. Aging, 1981—; pres. Washington Twp. (Ind.) Classroom Tchrs. Assn., 1970-72; sec. Nat. Assn. State EEO Dirs., 1978-80; speaker in field. Vice pres. Mayor Indpls. Task Force Women, 1971; chmn. adv. council Met. Office Women's Programs Marion County (Ind.), 1971; trustee William Woods Coll., Liberty, Mo., 1979-81; bd. dirs. Booth Tarkington Civic Theatre, Indpls., 1979; mem. Commn. Downtown Indpls., Gov. Ind. Com. Youth Employment, Ind. Employment and Tng. Council; mem. energy task force Greater Indpls. Progress Com. Recipient Spl. Recognition award Ind. Bd. Vocat. and Tech. Edn., 1976, Outstanding Service award, 1976; Outstanding Service award Vocat. Indsl. Clubs Am., 1976; named Sagamore of Wabash, Gov. Ind., 1979; also numerous civic and service awards. Mem. Alumni Assn. William Woods Coll. (pres. 1978-80), Ind. U. Alumni Assn., Phi Delta Kappa, Phi Beta. Republican. Club: Indpls. Press. Author articles in field. Office: 115 N Pennsylvania St Indianapolis IN 46204

MERRITT, TOM, state senator Ill.; b. Rossville, Ill., Oct. 20, 1911; s. Guy W. and Florence E. (Elliott) M.; student DePauw U., 1930-32, Purdue U., 1945-48; m. Martha Ann Sandusky, Sept. 6, 1952; children—Tom B., Judith Ann (Mrs. Henry T. Garvey). Asst. cashier Wellington State Bank (Ill.), 1932-37; owner Tom Merritt & Co. Real Estate, Hoopeston, Ill., 1937—; dir. Wellington State Bank, 1950—, vice chmn. bd., 1968-75, chmn. bd., 1975—; treas. City of Hoopeston, 1937-43; mem. Ill. Senate, 1964—, chmn. ins. and financial instns. com., 1973—, mem. agr. and conservation com., 1965—, exec. com., 1967-74, transp. and pub. utilities com., 1973-74. Ill. del. White House Conf. on Children and Youth, 1960; chmn. Ill. Commn. Econ. Devel., 1968—. Mem. Vermilion County Bd. Suprs., 1947-64; county chmn. Vermilion County Republican Party, 1962-64. Mem. Am., Ill. socs. profl. farm mgrs. and rural appraisers, Ill., Vermilion County assns. ins. agts., Vermilion County Farm Bur. Methodist (adminstrv. bd. 1968—). Rotarian (pres. Hoopeston 1942—), Mason (Shriner), Moose. Home: 858 E Lincoln St Hoopeston IL 60942 Office: 202 S Market St Hoopeston IL 60942

MERRITT, WALTER DAVIS, JR., newspaper editor; b. Roanoke Rapids, N.C., Oct. 29, 1936; s. Walter Davis and Elizabeth Byrd (Suiter) M.; A.B. in Journalism (Morehead scholar 1954-58), U. N.C., 1958; m. Elizabeth Ann Little, June 5, 1958; children—Walter Davis, III, Robert Charles, Anna Elizabeth. With Knight Newspapers, 1958-75, news editor Washington bur., 1972-75; exec. editor Wichita (Kans.) Eagle and Beacon, Knight-Ridder Newspapers, 1975—; vis. editor Kans. U. Mem. Morehead Award Com., 1963-69. Mem. Am. Soc. Newspaper Editors, Kans. Press Assn. Home: 21 Cypress St Wichita KS 67206 Office: 825 E Douglas St Wichita KS 67201*

MERRY, CARROLL EUGENE, mfg. co. exec.; b. Richland Center, Wis., Jan. 8, 1948; s. Elmo Carroll and Helen Evelyn (Peaslee) M.; B.S. in Journalism, U. Wis., Oshkosh, 1973; m. Amy Jo Sweet, Oct. 21, 1967; children—JaNelle Paulette, Jennifer Erin. Bur. chief Oshkosh Daily Northwestern, Berlin, Wis., 1973-74; advt. coordinator J I Case Outdoor Power Div., Winneconne, Wis., 1974-76; advt. mgr. Gehl Co., West Bend, Wis., 1976-78, mktg. communications mgr., 1978—. Chmn. communications com. St. Joseph's Community Hosp., West Bend, 1980-81; v.p. Washington County 4-H Leaders Assn., 1981. Served with USAF, 1968-72. Mem. Nat. Agri-Mktg. Assn. (dir., sec. Badger chpt.). Office: 143 Water St West Bend WI 53095

MERRYMAN, GEORGANNE LATHOM, lab. adminstr.; b. Chgo., Feb. 12, 1943; d. George Norman and Dorothy Elizabeth Lathom; B.S., Rockford Coll., 1965; m. Wesley Merryman, May 7, 1966. Med. tech. intern Swedish Am. Hosp., Rockford, Ill., 1964-65, staff technologist, instr., 1965-66; staff technologist Dr. Earl Malone, Roswell, N.Mex., 1966-67, Jackson County Meml. Hosp., Altus, Okla., 1967-68; with Riverside Meth. Hosp., Columbus, 1968—, chief med. technologist, 1975—. Mem. Am. Soc. Clin. Pathologists, Am. Soc. Med. Technologists, Ohio Soc. Med. Technologists. Home: 606 Fairholme Rd Gahanna OH 43230 Office: Riverside Methodist Hospital 3535 Olentancy River Rd Columbus OH 43214

MERSBERGER, JAMES JOHN, assn. exec.; b. Sheboygan, Wis., Aug. 27, 1924; s. Jake John and Mary Gertrude (Trimberger) M.; student U. So. Ill., 1948-50, Purdue U., 1950-51; m. Ruth Ruby Ertel, Aug. 16, 1947; children—Virginia Jorenby, Mary Armstrong, James R. Foreman, Roth Bldg. Supply, Sheboygan, 1946-47; orgn. dir. Sheboygan Farm Bur., 1948-50; dir. orgn. Wis. Farm Bur., Madison, 1953-68, mgr. spl. programs, 1975-79; dir. Young Farmers and Ranchers activities Am. Farm Bur. Fedn., 1979—; mgr. pub. relations Rural Ins. Cos., Madison, Wis., 1969-75. Mem. Wis. Gov.'s Com. on Youth, 1954-55; mem. exec. com. U. Wis., Stevens Point, 1964-75; polit. edn. chmn. Wis. Congl. Dist. III, 1966-67; mem. Nat. 4-H Sponsors Council. Recipient Am. Freedom award Harding Coll., 1958. Mem. Pub. Relations Soc. Am., Internat. Assn. Health Underwriters, Nat. Assn. Agrl. Instrs. (exec. com.), Am. Automobile Assn., Nat. Travel Club, Madison East (chmn. 1973-75), Monona Grove (membership chmn. 1965) businessmens assns. Home: 1340 Fortune Bay Ct Hoffman Estates IL 60195 Office: 225 Touhy Ave Park Ridge IL 60068

MESEK, JEANIE MAY, therapist; b. Omaha, May 18, 1926; d. Archie Mason and Lela May (Lanning) Schreiber; B.S., George Williams Coll., 1976; postgrad. No. Bapt. Theol. Sem., 1976; M.S. in Social Work, U. Louisville, 1978; m. Fred Mesek, Nov. 18, 1944 (div. 1975); children—Fred, Randelyn, Gary. Advocate, Ill. Status Offenders Services, DuPage County, 1975-77; social worker Riveredge Hosp., Forest Park, Ill., 1978; child care worker Fox Hill Home for Girls, Batavia, Ill., 1979; clin. therapist Guardian Angel Home, Joliet, Ill., 1979—; dir. social service Westmont (Ill.) Health Centre, 1978—; prin. May Cons. Service, Downers Grove, Ill., 1978-80. Leader Camp Fire Girls, 1947; program dir. Cub Scouts, 1956-57; vol. Hinsdale Hosp., 1965-72; v.p. Clyde Estates Property Owners, 1967. Cert. tchr., Ill.; cert. social worker, Ill. Mem. Acad. Cert. Social Workers, Nat. Assn. Social Workers, Ill. Health Improvement Assn. Republican. Club: West Suburban Christian Women's.

MESENBRINK, PHILIP EDWARD, cons. engr.; b. Lincoln, Nebr., Aug. 6, 1937; s. William Gregory and Dolores Elizabeth (Quinn) M.; B.S. in Civil Engring., U. Colo., 1962; M.S. in Civil Engring., Wayne State U., 1965; m. Joan Evelyn Erbecker, July 3, 1973; children—Thomas, Michael, Margaret; stepchildren—Christopher, Anne, Lisa. Designer, Colo. Dept. Hwys., Denver, 1957-58; sales engr. Internat. Pipe & Ceramics Corp., Denver, 1958-61, plant engr., Ada, Okla., 1961-62, prodn. control supt., Detroit, 1962-65; supr., maintenance and plant engr. LTV Aerospace Corp., Warren, Mich., 1965-68; asst. indsl. dept. head Giffels Assos., Detroit, 1968-73; mfg. div. dir. Smith, Hinchman & Grylls Assos., Detroit, 1973-77; pres. Mfg. Tech. Assos., Inc., Southfield, Mich., 1977—. Mem. bd. Com. to Incorporate Farmington Hills (Mich.), 1971. Registered profl. engr., Mich., Ohio, Ill. Mem. Nat. Soc. Profl. Engrs., Am. Inst. Indsl. Engrs., ASCE, Internat. Materials Mgmt. Soc., Chi Epsilon. Republican. Roman Catholic. Club: Oakland Hills Country. Home: 290 Chesterfield Rd Bloomfield Hills MI 48013 Office: 26011 Evergreen Rd Southfield MI 48076

MESERVE, WALTER JOSEPH, JR., ednl. adminstr., educator; b. Portland, Maine, Mar. 10, 1923; s. Walter Joseph and Bessie Adelia (Bailey) M.; A.B., Bates Coll., 1947; M.A., Boston U., 1948; Ph.D., U. Wash., 1952; m. Mollie Ann Lacey, June 18, 1981; children—Gayle Ellen, Peter Haynes, Jo Alison, David Bryan. Instr., U. Kans., 1951-53, asst. prof. English, 1953-58, asso. prof., 1958-63, prof., 1963-68; prof. theatre and drama Ind. U., Bloomington, 1968—, asso. dean arts and humanities Office Research and Grad. Devel., 1980—; vis. lectr. Victoria U., Manchester, Eng., 1959-60; vis. prof. U. Calif., Santa Barbara, 1967-68; Rockefeller scholar, Bellagio, Italy, 1979. Served with AC, U.S. Army, 1943-46. Nat. Endowment for Humanities fellow, 1974-75. Mem. Am. Soc. Theatre Research (exec. com.), Am. Theatre Assn., Author's Guild, Assn. Asian Studies, Asia Soc., Popular Culture Assn., Am. Studies Assn. Club: Cosmos. Author five books, including: An Emerging Entertainment: The Drama of the American People to 1828, 1977; American Drama to 1900, 1980; editor seven books, including: The Complete Plays of W.D. Howells, 1960; mem. editorial bd. Modern Drama, 1960—. Office: Dept Theatre and Drama Ind U Bloomington IN 47405

MESHEL, HARRY, state senator; b. Youngstown, Ohio, June 13, 1924; s. Angelo and Ruby (Markakis) M.; B.S. in Bus. Adminstrn., Youngstown State U., 1949; M.S. in Urban Land Econs., Columbia U., 1950; postgrad. U. Wis., 1968; m. Judy Lazich, July 25, 1948; children—Barry, Melanie. Div. mgr. Waddell & Reed, Inc., Kansas City, Mo., 1962; exec. asst. to mayor of Youngstown, 1964-68; urban renewal dir., Youngstown, 1969; mem. faculty Youngstown State U., 1950-70; real estate broker, Youngstown, 1972—; mem. Ohio Senate, 1971—. Mem. Ohio Commn. Local Govt., Gov.'s Commn. Employment Handicapped, Supervisory Commn. Criminal Justice; vice chmn. exec. com., chmn. precinct com. Democratic Party, 1960-74; mem. N. Central Columbiana County Men's Dem. Club, 1973; bd. dirs. Ohio Rehab. Assn., Heart Assn. Mahoning County, Mahoning Valley Health and Welfare Council. Served with USNR, 1943-46. Mem. N. Side Community Action Council, AAUP, Mahoning Valley Comprehensive Plan Assn., NAACP, Columbia U. Alumni Assn., Youngstown U. Alumni Assn., VFW, Phi Sigma Kappa. Greek Orthodox. Club: Elks. Office: State Senate Columbus OH 43215*

MESSANA, JOSEPH, ednl. adminstr.; b. Detroit, July 31, 1928; s. Frank Richard and Eleanor (Scaglione) M.; B.S., Wayne State U., 1951, M.Ed., 1957, Ed.D., 1968; m. Mary Jane Sasala, Sept. 18, 1954; children—Frank Stephen, Janet Lynn. Tchr., Clawson Pub. Schs., 1955-57; tchr. music and social studies Detroit Pub. Schs., 1957-63, counselor, work tng. coordinator, 1963-66, jr. adminstrv. asst. guidance and counseling, 1966-69; asst. dir. measurements and guidance Oakland Schs., Pontiac, Mich., 1969-72, dir., 1972-79, dir. div. gen. edn., 1979—. Served with USAF, 1951-55. Recipient Certificate of Dedicated Service, Wayne State U. Edn. Alumni Assn., 1973. Mem. Assn. for Supervision and Curriculum Devel., Am. (past senator, recipient Disting. Service award 1968), Mich. (past pres., recipient Outstanding Service award 1973) personnel and guidance assn., Am. Sch. Counselors Assn., Assn. Counselor Edn. and Supervision, Nat. Vocat. Guidance Assn., Assn. Measurement and Evaluation in Guidance, Guidance Assn. Met. Detroit (past pres.), Oakland Area Counselors Assn., Phi Delta Kappa, Phi Mu Alpha. Contbr. articles in field to profl. jours. Home: 14432 Lakeshore Dr Sterling Heights MI 48078 Office: 2100 Pontiac Lake Rd Pontiac MI 48054

MESSER, ANTHONY DAVID, steel co. exec.; b. Lima, Ohio, Jan. 2, 1952; s. Hiram and Nora (Handshoe) M.; B.S.B.A. in Ops. Mgmt., Ohio State U., 1975; m. Linda D. Schooler, July 3, 1976; 1 dau., Andrea R. Prodn. clk., iron foundry Teledyne Ohio Steel Co., Lima, 1975-78, prodn. supr. dept. heat treat, 1978-79, asst. mgr. prodn. control, 1979—. Mem. Nat. Mgmt. Assn. Club: Masons. Home: 901 Western Ohio Lima OH 45805

MESSERLY, JAMES WILLIAM, chemist; b. Martins Ferry, Ohio, May 30, 1940; s. Warren William and Lillie Ora (Duff) M.; B.S. in Chemistry, Kent State U., 1962; m. Mary Lou Kinsey, Sept. 9, 1961; children—Sharon, Steven, Mark, Michael. With B.F. Goodrich, 1962—, sect. mgr. materials research and devel. engineered systems, Brecksville, Ohio, 1974-78, mgr. materials research and devel., 1978-79, mgr. materials sci., 1979—. Mem. Redistricting Adv. Com., Stow City Schs., 1978; mem. Stow City Organized Youth Activities, 1973—. Mem. Am. Chem. Soc., Akron Rubber Group. Republican. Patentee in field. Office: 9921 Brecksville Rd Brecksville OH 44141

MESSERSCHMIDT, NANCIE KARYN SUE, TV sta. account exec.; b. Ft. Wayne, Ind., Feb. 27, 1952; d. Herbert Herman L. and Ruth W. Messerschmidt; B.A. in Liberal Arts, Graphic Design, and Advt., Ind. U., Bloomington, 1974; postgrad. in bus. adminstrn. Ind. U., Ft. Wayne. Pool mgr. Canterbury Green Country Club, Ft. Wayne, 1971-76; announcer radio comml. Sta.-WGL, Ft. Wayne, 1974-76; sports writer Jour. Gazette, Ft. Wayne, 1976-77; graphic designer DEK/Electro, Ft. Wayne, 1976-77; graphic arts coordinator Majestic Co./Am. Standard, Huntington, Ind., 1977-79; advt. mgr. Wayne Hardware, Inc., Ft. Wayne, 1979-81; account exec. WANE-TV, CBS affiliate, Ft. Wayne, 1981—; free-lance artist, Ft. Wayne, 1975—. Free-lance and tournament racquetball player, including mem. playing staff Omega Sportinggood, Oakland Park, Kansas City, Mo., 1981—. State racquetball doubles champion, 1980; various athletic competition awards YMCA, 1979, 80. Mem. Advt. Club Ft. Wayne, Greater Ft. Wayne Racquetball Assn. (v.p.). Lutheran. Home: 5538-8 OID Dover Blvd Fort Wayne IN 46815 Office: 2915 W State Blvd Fort Wayne IN 46806

MESSERSMITH, KENNETH GERALD, educator; b. Alliance, Nebr., Aug. 3, 1948; s. Kenneth Max and Verna Luella (Glenn) M.; B.S., U. Nebr., 1971, M.S., 1978; m. Donaleen Fay Stricker, Aug. 12, 1973; children—Jake, Glenn. Vocat. agr. tchr., Future Farmers Am. adv. St. Paul Public Schs., 1971-78; asst. prof. prodn. agr. tech. U. Nebr., Curtis, 1978—; v.p. Universal Investments. Bd. dirs. Nebr. Vocat. Agr. Found., 1976-78. Mem. Nat. Vocat. Agr. Tchrs. Assn., Am. Vocat. Assn., Nebr. Vocat. Assn., Nebr. Vocat. Agr. Assn. Republican. Methodist. Home: 226 Crook Ave Curtis NE 69025 Office: U Nebr Curtis NE 69025

MESSINEO, ANTHONY ONOFRIO, JR., restaurant exec.; b. Lincoln, Nebr., Jan. 24, 1941; s. Anthony Onofrio and Josephine M.; B.S., U. Nebr., Lincoln, 1965; m. Carmen Monaco, Apr. 20, 1963; children—Deborah, Michael, Anthony Onofrio III. Mgr., Tony and Luigi's Restaurant, Lincoln, 1965-71, chmn. bd., 1978—, pres., 1978—; owner, chmn. bd., pres. Valentino's Pizza, Lincoln, 1971—, Valentino's of Am., Lincoln, 1978—. Mem. Young Pres. Orgn. Republican. Roman Catholic. Clubs: Sertoma, Rotary. Home: 7535 S Hampton St Lincoln NE 68506 Office: 825 Terminal Bldg Lincoln NE 68508

MESTMAN, IRV BENJAMIN, govt. ofcl.; b. St. Louis, Dec. 10, 1939; s. Herman and Dorothy Mestman; B.S. in Public Adminstrn., U. Mo., 1962; LL.B., LaSalle U., 1965; M.A. in Public Adminstrn. and Mgmt., Webster Coll., 1976; Ps.D. in Psychology, Coll. Divine Metaphysics, 1967; div.; 1 son, Irv Benjamin. Pres., Mo. Cons., St. Louis, 1962-66; pres. Vocat. Careers Corp., St. Louis, 1966-70; auditor State of Mo., St. Louis, 1970-74; pres. Courtesy Merchandising Inc., St. Louis, 1974—; EEO officer U.S. Govt., St. Louis, 1974—; mgmt. and mktg. cons. Served with U.S. Army, 1962. Jewish. Club: Kerpans Health. Home: 9472 Olive St F Saint Louis MO 63132 Office: 625 N Euclid St Saint Louis MO 63103

METANOMSKI, WLADYSLAW VAL, chem. engr.; b. Vienna, Austria, Oct. 3, 1923; came to U.S., 1964; naturalized, 1971; s. Justyn and Amalia (Bloch) M.; student U. Bologna (Italy), 1945-46; B.Sc., U. London, 1952; M.Sc., U. Toronto (Ont., Can.), 1960, Ph.D., 1964; m. Helena K. M. Felsztyn, Mar. 23, 1966; 1 dau., Marianne. Chemist, Dearborn Chem. Co., Toronto, 1952-56, service engr., 1956-58; chem. engring. demonstrator U. Toronto, 1958-64; asst. editor Am. Chem. Soc.'s Chem. Abstracts Service, Columbus, Ohio, 1964-66, group leader, 1966-71, asst. to editor, 1971-72, mgr. editorial devel., 1972—. Served with Polish Army, 1942-46. Decorated Polish Cross Valor. Brit. Govt. grantee, 1947-52; Ont. Research Found. grantee, 1961-64. Mem. Am. Chem. Soc., Assn. Profl. Engrs. Province Ont. Contbr. articles to sci. jours. Home: 1670 Ardwick Rd Columbus OH 43220 Office: 2540 Olentangy River Rd Columbus OH 43210

METCALF, HAROLD ROBINSON, mgmt. cons.; b. Waco, Tex., Aug. 10, 1922; s. Eliab Wight and Clara Belle (Woodin) M.; student Oberlin Coll., 1940-41, U. So. Calif., 1943, Stanford U., 1946-47; M.A. in History, U. Chgo., 1953; m. Karlyn Adele Anderson, Sept. 2, 1960. Asst. to dean U. Chgo. Grad. Sch. Bus., 1954-55, asst. dean of students, 1955-56, dean of students, 1956-75, dean student and alumni affairs, 1975-76, dir. athletics, dept. phys. edn. and athletics, 1976—. Served with USMC, 1942-46.

METTERT, DORIS STEPHENS, educator; b. Eaton, Ohio, 1925; d. Harry M. and Mary Stephens; B.S., U. Cin., 1946; m. Robert L. Mettert, Sept. 7, 1946; 1 dau., Susan Mettert Wenk. Public health staff nurse, Montgomery County, Ohio, 1946-48; instr. Reid Meml. Hosp. Sch. Profl. Nursing, Richmond, Ind., 1948-58, coordinator in-service edn., 1958-74, founder, dir. Richmond Sch. Practical Nursing, 1964-72, dir. hosp.-wide dept. staff devel., 1974—. Mem. Am. Nurses Assn., Nat. League Nursing, Am. Soc. Health Manpower Edn. and Tng. Home: 100 S 27th St Richmond IN 47374 Office: Dept Staff Devel Reid Meml Hosp Richmond IN 47374

METTERT, WESLEY KENNETH, soil scientist; b. Crestline, Ohio, Feb. 14, 1924; s. John Wesley and Christine Florence (Nebro) M.; B.S., Ohio State U., 1946; M.S., Mich. State U., 1962; m. Dorothea Marie Rodenfels, Mar. 22, 1947; children—Barbara, Robert, Patricia, Becky Jean, Diane. Vocat.-agr. tchr., public schs., Burgoon, Ohio, 1946, Chesterfield High Sch., Morenci, Mich., 1947-50; with Soil Conservation Service, U.S. Dept. Agr., 1951—, soil survey party leader, various counties, Mich., 1957-70, soil scientist, area staff, Flint, Mich., 1970-78, soil survey party leader Tuscola County, Mich., 1978—. Recipient cert. merit Soil Conservation Service, 1971, 73, 76, 78, Outstanding Performance award U.S. Dept. Agr., 1975. Mem. Soil Sci. Soc. Am., Agronomy Soc. Am., Soil Conservation Soc. Am., Soil Classifiers Assn. Mich. Episcopalian. Clubs: Masons, Shriners. Conducted crop yield, soil and mgmt. studies, Osceola County, 1961; author Osceola County (Mich.) Soil Survey, 1969, Gladwin County (Mich.) Soil Survey, 1972. Home: 6278 Elro St Davison MI 48423 Office: 142 W Burnside St Caro MI 48723

METTLER, RUBEN FREDERICK, electronics and engring. co. exec.; b. Shafter, Calif., Feb. 23, 1924; s. Henry Frederick and Lydia M.; student Stanford U., 1941-43; B.S. in Elec. Engring., Calif. Inst. Tech., 1944, M.S., 1947, Ph.D. in Elec. and Aero. Engring, 1949; L.H.D. (hon.), Baldwin-Wallace Coll., 1980; m. Donna Jean Smith, May 1, 1955; children—Matthew Frederick, Daniel Frederick. Asso. div. dir. systems research and devel. Hughes Aircraft Co., 1949-54; spl. cons. to asst. sec. def., 1954-55; asst. gen. mgr. guided missile research div. Ramo-Wooldridge Corp., 1955-58, pres., dir. Space Tech. Labs., Inc., Los Angeles, 1962-68; exec. v.p., dir. TRW Inc. (formerly Thompson Ramo Wooldridge, Inc.), 1965, asst. pres., 1968-69, pres., 1969-77, chmn. bd., chief exec. officer, 1977—; dir. Bank Am. Corp., Goodyear Tire & Rubber Co., Merck & Co.; past vice-chmn. Ind. adv. council Dept. Def. Adv. com. United Negro Coll. Fund, nat. campaign chmn., 1980; mem. bd. advisers Council for Fin. Aid to Edn., Case Western Res. U.; chmn. Pres.'s Sci. Policy Task Force, 1969; mem. Emergency Com. for Am. Trade; nat. chmn. Nat. Alliance Businessmen, 1978-79; bd. dirs. Greater Los Angeles Urban Coalition; trustee Calif. Inst. Tech., 1969—, mem. Caltech Assos., 1963—; mem. council Rockefeller U.; trustee, research policy com. Com. Economic Devel.; trustee Nat. Safety Council, Cleve. Clinic Found., Nat. Fund Minority Engring. Students; aerospace chmn. U.S. Ind. Payroll Savs. Commn.; mem. bd. Smithsonian Nat. Assos. Served with USNR, 1943-46. Registered profl. engr., Calif. Named 1 of ten Outstanding Young Men of Am., U.S. Jr. C. of C., 1955; recipient Meritorious Civilian Service award Dept. Def., 1969. named Engr. of Yr., Engring. Socs. So. Calif., 1964; Alumni Disting. Service award Calif. Inst. Tech., 1966; Nat. Human Relations award NCCJ, 1979; Excellence in Mgmt. award Industry Week mag., 1979. Fellow IEEE, AIAA; mem. Sci. Research Soc. Am., Calif. Inst. Tech. Alumni Assn. (dir.), Nat. Acad. Engring., James Smithson Soc., Sigma Xi, Eta Kappa Nu (named nation's outstanding young elec. engr. 1954), Tau Beta Pi, Theta Xi. Clubs: Cosmos (Washington); Union, 50 (Cleve.). Author reports airborne electronic systems. Patentee interceptor fire control systems. Office: 1 Space Park Redondo Beach CA 90278 also 23555 Euclid Ave Cleveland OH 44117

METZ, CONRAD ROBERT, investment analyst; b. Boston, July 21, 1953; s. David Emerson and Judith Winifred (Arnold) M.; A.B. (Calif. State scholar), U. Calif., Berkeley, 1975, M.B.A., 1978; m. Anne Elizabeth Marsh, Mar. 12, 1979. Asst. editor Jour. Inorganic Chemistry, UCLA, 1975-76; investment analyst Nat. Bank Detroit, 1978-81, sr. investment analyst, 1981—; lectr. internat. econs., monetary policy. Mem. Assn. M.B.A. Execs., Internat. Bus. Assn., Fin. Analysts Fedn., Fin. Analysts Soc. Detroit, M.B.A. Assos. U. Calif. (Berkeley). Democrat. Home: 557 Neff Rd Grosse Pointe MI 48230 Office: Nat Bank Detroit 611 Woodward Ave Detroit MI 48232

METZ, PAUL ALOYSIUS, city ofcl.; b. Okeene, Okla., Feb. 26, 1923; s. William Henry and Anna Mary M.; B.S. in Bus. Adminstrn., Central State U., Edmond, Okla., 1950; postgrad. U. Okla., 1951-52; m. Jo Dean Pyle, Oct. 20, 1956; 1 son, Raymond Paul. Mgr. systems and procedures dept. Farmland Industries, Kansas City, Mo., 1952-66; adminstrv. officer, systems City of Kansas City, 1966-68, city treas., 1968—. Pack chmn. Cub Scouts; troop treas. Boy Scouts Am.; bd. dirs. Dismas House; bd. dirs., budget dir., treas. St. Pius X High Sch.; bd. dirs., past pres. bd., past budget dir. St. Charles Ch. Served with USAAF, 1942-45; served with USAF, 1950-51. Mem. Assn. for Systems Mgmt. (past pres. Kansas City chpt., Outstanding Dir. award Kansas City chpt. 1963, Nat. Merit award for Outstanding Service 1968), Municipal Fin. Officers Assn., Mo. City Clks. and Fin. Officers Assn. (past pres.), Western Mo. City Clks. and Fin. Officers Assn (past pres.), Mo. Municipal League, Kansas City Urban League (dir.). Democrat. Roman Catholic. Club: K.C. Office: City of Kansas City 414 E 12th St Kansas City MO 64106

METZENBAUM, HOWARD MORTON, Senator of Ohio; b. Cleve., June 4, 1917; s. Charles I. and Anna (Klafger) M.; B.A., Ohio State U., 1939, L.L.D., 1941; m. Shirley Turoff, Aug. 8, 1946; children—Barbara Jo, Susan Lynn, Shelley Hope, Amy Beth. Chmn. bd. Airport Parking Co. Am., 1958-66, ITT Consumer Services Corp., 1966-68; chmn. bd. Com Corp., 1969-74, after 1975; U.S. senator from Ohio, 1974, 77—. Mem. War Labor Bd., 1942-45, Ohio Bur. Code Rev., 1949-50, Cleve. Met. Housing Authority, 1968-70, Lake Erie Regional Transit Authority, 1972-73. Mem. Ohio Ho. of Reps., 1943-46, Ohio Senate, 1947-50; now mem. U.S. Senate from Ohio; mem. Ohio Democratic Exec. Com., 1966; mem. Ohio Dem. Finance Com., 1969—. Trustee Mt. Sinai Hosp., Cleve., 1961-73, treas., 1966-73; bd. dirs. Council Human Relations, United Cerebral Palsy Assn., Nat. Council Hunger and Malnutrition, Karamu House, St. Vincent Charity Hosp., Cleve., St. Jude Research Hosp., Memphis; nat. co-chmn. Nat. Citizens' Com. Conquest Cancer; vice-chmn. fellows Brandeis U. Mem. Am. Bar Assn., Ohio Bar Assn., Cuyahoga Bar Assn., Cleve. Bar Assn., Am. Assn. Trial Lawyers, Order of Coif, Phi Eta Sigma, Tau Epsilon Rho. Office: 347 Russell Senate Office Bldg Washington DC 20510*

METZGER, FREDERICK LAMB, mfg. co. exec.; b. Toledo, Ohio, July 17, 1920; s. Frederick William and Alice (Lamb) M.; A.B., U. Mich., 1943, postgrad., 1952-54; m. Ann Maloney, Oct. 26, 1943; children—Judith Ann, Nancy Graham. Factory budget analyst Libbey Owens Ford Co., Toledo, 1946-48, indsl. engr., 1948-68, mgr. distbr. packaging dept., 1968—. Served to lt. (j.g.) USN, 1943-46. Mem. Am. Inst. Indsl. Engrs., Soc. Packaging and Handling Engrs., Tech. Soc. Toledo. Republican. Mem. United Ch. of Christ. Club: Toledo Sailing. Home: 3515 Wesleyan St Toledo OH 43614 Office: 1705 E Broadway Toledo OH 43605

METZGER, JOHN DAVID, found. exec.; b. Columbus, Ohio, Feb. 28, 1924; s. Albert Columbus Delano and Anna (Huston) M.; USAAF trainee Eau Claire State Tchrs. Coll., 1942-43; B.F.A., Ohio U., 1947; m. Doris Jean Fahrbach, Sept. 14, 1946; children—John David, Daniel Virgil, Karla Ann, Marytha Jane. Founder, mgr. Sta. WOUB, Athens, Ohio, 1943, 46-47; announcer, writer, producer Sta. WCOL, Columbus, Ohio, 1947-49, Sta. WLW-C-TV, Columbus, Ohio, 1949-51; radio-TV dir. Byer & Bowman Advt. Agy., Columbus, 1951-64; sec., account exec. Joe Hill & Assos., Columbus, Ohio, 1965-66; exec. dir. Central Ohio Ednl. TV Found., Inc., Columbus, 1967—. Served with USAAF, 1943-46. Mem. Nat. Acad. TV Arts Scis. (Founder Columbus Cin. Dayton chpt. 1962), Nat. Assn. Ednl. Broadcasters. Presbyterian. Home: 718 Grandon Ave Bexley OH 43209 Office: 2400 Olentangy River Rd Columbus OH 43210

METZLER, DWIGHT FOX, state ofcl.; b. Carbondale, Kans., Mar. 25, 1916; s. Ross R. and Grace (Fox) M.; B.S. in Civil Engring., U. Kans., 1940, C.E., 1947; S.M., Harvard U., 1948; m. Lela I. Ross, June 20, 1941; children—Linda Diane, Brenda Lee, Marilyn Anne, Martha Jeanne. Asst. engr. Kans. Bd. Health, Lawrence, 1940-42, san. engr., 1946-48, chief engr., 1948-62; commd. health service officer USPHS, 1942-46; advisor Govt. of India, 1960, USSR, 1962, WHO, 1964—; exec. sec. Kans. Water Resources Bd., Topeka, 1962-66; dep. commr. N.Y. State Dept. Health, Albany, 1966-70; dep. commr. N.Y. State Dept. Environ. Conservation, Albany, 1970-74; sec. Kans. Dept. Health and Environment, Topeka, 1974-79, dir. water supply devel., 1979—; prof. dept. civil engring. U. Kans., 1948-66; mem. Nat. Acad. Engring.; mem. Assembly of Engring., NRC; cons. WHO. Chmn. bd. elders Westside Christian Ch. Recipient Outstanding Alumni citation U. Kans., 1970; diplomate Am. Acad. Environ. Engrs. Fellow Royal Soc. Health (hon.), ASCE (sec. 1959-61, chmn. san. engring. div. 1963, pres. Kans. sect.), Am. Public Health Assn. (past pres., past mem. exec. bd., past chmn. action bd., mem. governing council, Centennial award 1972, Sedgewick medal 1981), Nat. Acad. Engring., Am. Water Works Assn. (George Warren Fuller award 1954, Purification Div. award 1957), Water Pollution Control Fedn. (Bedell award 1963), Kans. Public Health Assn. (Crumbine award 1965), Kans. Engring. Soc., Sigma Xi, Tau Beta Pi. Club: Shawnee Country. Co-author: (with Irving Sax) Dangerous Properties of Industrial Materials, 1968; (with Morris Cohn) Pollution Fighters, 1973; contbr. chpt. to Chicago/Cook County Health Survey, 1949; contbr. articles to profl. jours. Home: 3219 MacVicar Ave Topeka KS 66611 Office: Dept Health and Environment Topeka KS 66620

MEXICOTTE, BERNARD GEORGE, banker; b. Detroit, Feb. 1, 1944; s. Bernard and Anna Marie M.; student Mott Community Coll., 1967; m. Judith Kay Gildner, Aug. 22, 1964; children—Michelle, Christina. Asst. mgr. Nobil Shoe Co., Flint, Mich., 1962-64; mgr. comml. loans and discounts Genesee Mchts. Bank and Trust Co., Flint, 1964-70, credit analyst, 1970-71, br. adminstr., 1971-72, v.p. in charge of trust ops., 1972—. Active United Way of Genesee County, 1978-80, 81, United Way of Mich., 1981. Mem. Am. Inst. Banking. Roman Catholic. Home: 9144 Pine Bluff Dr Flushing MI 48433 Office: 1 E 1st Flint MI 48502

MEYDELL, STEPHAN BARCLAY, JR., equipment mfg. corp. exec.; b. Bklyn., Dec. 21, 1928; s. Stephan Barclay and Else (Bredal) M.; B.S., N.Y. U., 1952; m. Dorothy J. Muller, June 21, 1951; 1 son, Stephan Barclay III. Dir. purchasing Gray Co., Mpls., 1962-68, Cornelius Co., Mpls., 1968-70; mgr. mfg., distbn. Brown & Bigelow, St. Paul, 1970-73; dir. corp. purchasing Am. Hoist & Derrick Co., St. Paul, 1973—; lectr., seminar leader Am. Mgmt. Assn., U. Minn. Pres. Local home owners assn. Served with USNR, 1946-47. Mem. Am. Foundrymen's Soc. (purchasing council), Machinery and Allied Products Inst., Twin City Purchasing Mgmt. Assn. Republican. Lutheran. Club: Mason. Home: 14409 Lake St Extension Minnetonka MN 55343 Office: Am Hoist & Derrick Co 63 S Robert St Saint Paul MN 55107

MEYER, A. DAVID, lawyer; b. Batesville, Ind., May 1, 1945; s. Charles Albert and Florence Elizabeth (Walke) M.; A.B. in Polit. Sci. and Econs., Ind. U., 1967, Certificate in Urban Studies, 1967, J.D., 1970, M.B.A., 1979; m. Pamela C. Gibson, Aug. 20, 1966; 1 dau., Natalie Lynn. Admitted to Ind. bar, 1970; partner firm Buschmann, Carr & Meyer and predecessors, Indpls., 1975—; officer, dir. Third Century Venture Corp. Bd. dirs. State Mus. Found. of Ind., Inc., 1978—. Mem. Am. Bar Assn., Fed. Bar Assn., Ind. State Bar Assn., Indpls. Bar Assn., Bar Assn. 7th Fed. Circuit, Comml. Law League Am., St. Thomas More Soc. Indpls. (pres. 1982), Nat. Assn. Accts., Assn. Trial Lawyers Am., Ind. U. Alumni Assn., Beta Gamma Sigma. Roman Catholic. Home: 3139 Albright Ct Indianapolis IN 46268 Office: 1015 Merchants Plaza East Tower Indianapolis IN 46204

MEYER, AUGUST CHRISTOPHER, lawyer, television exec.; b. Brookport, Ill., Oct. 28, 1900; s. Gus and Ida (Pierce) M.; grad. So. Ill. U., 1922; J.D., U. Ill., Urbana, 1928; m. Clara Rocke, Feb. 2, 1929; 1 son, August Christopher. Banker, Brookport, 1917-28; admitted to Ill. bar, 1928; practice law, Champaign, 1928—; mem. firm Leonard & Meyer, 1928-34, Meyer & Franklin, 1934-54, Meyer & Capel, 1954-65; atty. Ill. Press Assn., 1946-54; organizer Midwest Television, Inc., 1952, pres., 1952-76, chmn. bd., 1976—; chmn. bd. Bank of Ill. (formerly Trevett-Mattis Banking Co.), Champaign, 1962—. Mem. CBS-TV affiliates adv. bd., 1960-63, 66-69. State of Ill. rep. in negotiations for procurement airport for U. Ill., 1943-45; mem. com. to study future devel. Sch. of Aeros. and devel. of aviation, U. Ill. Past pres., bd. dirs. Burnham City Hosp., Champaign; trustee Lincoln Acad. Ill. Mem. Def. Orientation Conf. Assn., Nat. Assn. Broadcasters, Assn. of Maximum Service Telecasters (dir.), Ill., Champaign County bar assns., Phi Alpha Delta, Alpha Kappa Psi. Republican. Presbyn. Clubs: President's (U. Ill.); Burning Tree (Bethesda, Md.); Cuyamaca (San Diego); Champaign Country. Assisted in procuring publ. Dyess Story, which told of Bataan Death March. Home: 1208 Waverly Dr Champaign IL 61820 Office: 509 S Neil St Champaign IL 61820

MEYER, AUGUST CHRISTOPHER, JR., lawyer, broadcasting co. exec.; b. Champaign, Ill., Aug. 14, 1937; s. August C. and Clara (Rocke) M.; A.B. cum laude, Harvard U., 1959, LL.B., 1962; m. Karen Haugh Hassett, Dec. 28, 1960; children—August Christopher F., Elisabeth Hassett. Admitted to Ill. bar, 1962; partner firm Meyer, Capel, Hirschfeld, Muncy, Jahn and Aldeen, Champaign, 1962—; pres. Midwest TV Inc., Champaign; owner Sta. KFMB-TV-AM-FM, San Diego, Sta. WCIA-TV, Champaign, Sta. WMBD-AM-TV, Sta. WKZW-FM, Peoria, Ill., 1976—; spl. asst. atty. gen. Ill., 1968-76; dir. Bank of Ill. Vice chmn. bd. trustees Carle Found. (Hosp.), Urbana, Ill. Mem. Champaign County Bar Assn., Ill. Bar Assn., Seventh Fed. Circuit Bar Assn. Club: Champaign Country. Office: 509 S Neil St Champaign IL 61820

MEYER, BETTY ANNE (MRS. JOHN ROLAND BASKIN), lawyer; b. Cleve.; d. William Henry and Monica (McSherry) Meyer; student Denison U., 1941-43; A.B., Flora Stone Mather Coll., Western Res. U., 1946, LL.B., 1947; m. John Roland Baskin, May 12, 1967. Admitted to Ohio bar, 1947; asst. to dean Adelbert Coll., Western Res. U., 1948-49; asso. firm Kiefer, Waterworth, Hunter & Knecht, Cleve., 1965-74; mem. firm Knecht, Rees, Meyer, Mekedis & Shumaker, Cleve., 1974—. Mem. Alpha Phi. Home: 2679 Ashley Rd Shaker Heights OH 44122 also Key Largo FL also East Chop Martha's Vineyard MA Office: Terminal Tower Cleveland OH 44113

MEYER, CAROLYN ANNE, mfg. co. exec.; b. Abilene, Kans., Jan. 30, 1945; d. Bernard Francis and Mary Edith (Carroll) M; student Marymount Coll., 1963-65; B.A., Wichita State U., 1969. Copywriter, Crown Drug Co., Kansas City, Mo., 1969-71; traffic supr., copywriter Ray Advt. Co., Kansas City, Mo., 1971-74; advt. mgr. Adlers, Shawnee Mission, Kans., 1974-77; advt. and promotion mgr. Lily div. Owens-Ill., Inc., Toledo, 1977-79; communications coordinator The Fuller Brush Co., Kansas City, Mo., 1979—. Recipient Merit award 5th Dist. Am. Advt. Fedn., 1978, award Communications Annual, 1978. Mem. Women's Advt. Club Toledo (dir. 1978—), Women in Communications, Advt. Club Toledo (Silver award 1978, Gold award 1978, Bronze award 1979). Democrat. Roman Catholic. Home: 2031 NE Russell Rd Apt 15 Kansas City MO 64116 Office: The Fuller Brush Co 2800 Rockcreek Pkwy Suite 400 North Kansas City MO 64117

MEYER, FRANK HENRY, educator; b. N.Y.C., July 11, 1915; s. Frank X. and Anna Helen (Wenzinger) M.; B.S., City Coll. N.Y., 1936; postgrad. Newark Coll. Engring., 1945-48; M.S., Poly. Inst. Bklyn., 1951; postgrad. Okla. State U., 1955-60, U. Wash., 1961-63; M.A., U. Minn., 1968; m. Winifred Josephine Duffy, Aug. 5, 1946; children—Frank, Vivian. X-ray crystallographer Textile Research Inst., Princeton, N.J., 1951-53; research physicist Continental Oil Co., Ponca City, Okla., 1954-60; research engr., project leader Kaiser Aluminum Co. Chem. Corp., Spokane, Wash., 1960-63; sr. research engr. Univac, Sperry Rand, St. Paul, 1963-65; asst. prof. physics and philosophy U. Wis., Superior, 1966—. Referee Am. Jour. Physics, 1972—. Dir. New Sci. Advocates, Inc. Dir. Lake Superior Spirit of '76 Forum, 1972-76. Am. Cancer Soc. grantee, 1948-51; U. Wis. grantee, 1970-75. Mem. Am. Phys. Soc., Am. Crystallographic Assn., Am. Assn. Physics Tchrs., A.A.U.P., Fedn. Am. Scientists, Minn. Acad. Sci., Common Cause, Soc. Physics Students, Sigma Pi Sigma. Unitarian Universalist. Editor: Reciprocity, 1971—. Patentee in field. Contbr. articles to profl. jours. Home: 1103 15 Ave SE Minneapolis MN 55414 Office: U Wis Physics Dept Superior WI 54880

MEYER, FRED ALBERT, JR., polit. scientist; b. Milw., Oct. 7, 1942; s. Fred Albert and Rose H. (Hafemann) M.; B.A., U. Wis., 1964; M.A., U. Wis., Milw., 1966; Ph.D., Wayne State U., 1974. Legis. fellow Mich. Senate, 1965-66; grad. asst. Wayne State U., 1966-70, instr., 1969-70; instr. Carroll Coll., Waukesha, Wis., 1970-71; asso. prof. dept. polit. sci. Ball State U., Muncie, Ind., 1971—. Nat. Endowment for Humanities grantee, 1977. Mem. Am. Polit. Sci. Assn., Policy Studies Orgn., Assn. Voluntary Action Scholars, So. Polit. Sci. Assn., Western Polit. Sci. Assn., Midwest Polit. Sci. Assn., Ind. Polit. Sci. Assn. (pres. 1976-79), Audubon Soc. Club: Sierra. Author: (with Ralph Baker) The Criminal Justice Game, 1980; editor: (with Ralph Baker) Evaluating Alternative Law Enforcement Policies, 1979, Determinants of Law Enforcement Policies, 1979; editorial bd. Policy Studies Jour., 1979—. Office: Polit Sci Dept Ball State U Muncie IN 47306

MEYER, FRED WILLIAM, JR., meml. parks exec.; b. Fair Haven, Mich., Jan. 7, 1924; s. Fred W. and Gladys (Marshall) M.; A.B., Mich. State Coll., 1946; m. Jean Hope, Aug. 5, 1946; children—Frederick, Thomas, James, Nancy. Salesman Chapel Hill Meml. Gardens, Lansing, Mich., 1946-47; mgr. Roselawn Meml. Gardens, Saginaw, Mich., 1947-49; dist. mgr. Sunset Meml. Gardens, Evansville, Ind., 1949-53; pres., dir. Memory Gardens Mgmt. Corp., Indpls., Hamilton Meml. Gardens, Chattanooga, Covington Meml. Gardens, Ft. Wayne, Ind., Chapel Hill Meml. Gardens, Grand Rapids, Mich., White Chapel Meml. Gardens, Huntington, W.Va., Forest Lawn Memory Gardens, Indpls., Lincoln Memory Gardens, Indpls., Sherwood Meml. Gardens, Knoxville, Tenn., Chapel Hill Meml. Gardens, South Bend, Ind., Tri-Cities Meml. Gardens, Florence, Ala., Woodlawn Meml. Gardens, Paducah, Ky., White Chapel Meml. Gardens, Springfield, Mo., Floral Hills Meml. Gardens, Clarksburg, W.Va., Beverly Hills Meml. Gardens, Morgantown, W.Va., Mercury Devel. Corp., Indpls., Quality Marble Imports, Indpls., Quality Printers, Indpls., Am. Bronze Craft, Inc., Judsonia, Ark., Blakley Granite Co., Indpls. Mem. C. of C., A.I.M., Nat. Assn. Cemeteries, Am. Cemetery Assn., Sigma Chi, Phi Kappa Delta. Elk. Clubs: Nat. Sales Executives, Athenaem Turners, Columbia, Meridian Hills Country. Home: 110 E 111th St Indianapolis IN 46280 Office: 3733 N Meridian St Indianapolis IN 46208

MEYER, H. JOHN, metall. engr.; b. Jonesboro, Ark., Aug. 13, 1935; s. H. John and Ursula (Walsh) M.; B.S. in Metall. Engring., Mo. Sch. Mines, 1960; m. Judith Ann Herman, June 4, 1960; children—Margaret, Phillip, Paul, Peter. Gen. foreman N.J. Zinc Co., DePue, Ill., 1960-63; research engr. Gen. Dynamics Co., Ft. Worth, Tex., 1963-65; application engr. Air Reduction Co., Birmingham, Ala., 1965-69; asst. mgr. Ala. Oxygen Co., Birmingham, 1969-70; supt. beryllium prodn. Brush Wellman, Elmore, Ohio, 1970—. Served with USN, 1955-57. Office: Brush Wellman South River Rd Elmore OH 43416

MEYER, HERBERT ALTON, III, editor, publisher; b. Kansas City, Mo., June 15, 1947; s. Herbert Alton, Jr. and Mary Janet (McDonald) M. B.S. in Bus. Adminstrn., U. Kans., 1969; m. Dorothy Dianne Eddins, June 3, 1969; children—Herbert Alton IV, Scott William. Courthouse reporter Lawrence (Kans.) Daily Jour.-World, 1969-71; editor, pub. Independence (Kans.) Daily Reporter, 1971—. Mem. Governmental Ethics Commn. State Kans., 1974-78. Trustee William Allen White Found., U. Kans.; bd. dirs. Mercy Hosp., chmn., 1977; bd. dirs. Mid-Am., Inc.; v.p. Jr. Achievement of Mid-Am., Inc., 1979-81. Served with AUS, 1969-70. Mem. Kans. Press Assn. (bd. dirs.), Independence C. of C., Sigma Chi. Republican. Episcopalian. Elk, Rotarian. Home: 912 Birdie Dr Independence KS 67301 Office: 320 N 6th St Independence KS 67301

MEYER, JEANETTE R. (JAN), ins. co. exec.; b. Manitowoc, Wis., Dec. 10, 1928; d. Ervin L. and Margaret Meyer; B.S., U. Wis., Oshkosh, 1956; M.S., U. Wis., Madison, 1959. Head speech dept. Washington Park High Sch., Racine, Wis.; edn. dir. Career Inst., Mundelein, Ill.; mgr. program research and devel. and corp. tng. Bankers Life & Casualty Co., Chgo.; participant mgmt. seminars. Mem. Am. Soc. Tng. and Devel., Ill. Tng. and Devel. Assn., Internat. Orgn. Women Execs. (chmn. program com. 1979-80), Women in Mgmt. Author interior design home study course; editor photography and dress design courses, programs for mgmt. tng. and devel. and on-the-job tng. Home: 9515-C Gross Point Rd Skokie IL 60076 Office: 4444 W Lawrence Ave Chicago IL 60630

MEYER, LEE DELBERT, chem. engr.; b. Fremont, Nebr., Jan. 26, 1949; s. Delbert John and Frances Clara (Maas) M.; B.S., U. Nebr., Lincoln, 1971, M.B.A., 1979; m. Trudy Ann Lamberty, Apr. 1971; children—Benjamin Tyson, Sarah Anne. Chem. engr., Quaker Oats Co., Omaha, 1971-72, prodn. asst., 1972-74, furfural and unloading mgr., 1974-78, adminstrn. mgr., 1978-79, mfg. mgr., 1979—. Deacon, dir. bd. evang. St. Mark Luth. Ch. Mo. Synod, 1979—. Registered profl. engr., Nebr., notary public Nebr. Mem. Am. Inst. Chem. Engrs., Nebr. Soc. Profl. Engrs., Am. Inst. Plant Engrs. Home: 1636 N 106th St Omaha NE 68114 Office: 302 Pierce St Omaha NE 68102

MEYER, LEON JACOB, wholesale co. exec.; b. Chgo., Nov. 12, 1923; s. Joseph and Minnie (Lebovitz) M.; student Lake Forest Coll., 1941-43; B.S., U. Calif., Los Angeles, 1948; m. Barbara Gene Bothman, Oct. 17, 1948; children—Charles Scott, John Mark, Ellen Renee. Owner, operator Christopher Distbg. Co., Santa Monica, Calif., 1951-53; pres. J. Meyer & Co., Waukegan, Ill., 1953-80, Western Candy & Tobacco Co., Carpentersville, Ill., 1970-78, Ill. Briar Pipe & Sundry Co., Waukegan, 1963-78; chmn. bd. Phillips Bros. Co., Kenosha, Wis., 1975—, Ill. Wholesale Co., 1976—. Served with U.S. Army, 1943-46; PTO. Named Sundry Man of Year, 1976, Candy Distbr. of Yr., 1976; recipient Alex Schwartz Meml. award, 1978. Mem. Nat. Assn. Tobacco Distbrs. (trustee), Ill. Assn. Candy-Tobacco Distbrs. (past chmn. bd.), Federated Merchandising Corp. (past pres.), Internat. Tobacco Wholesaler Alliance (past chmn. bd.), Nat. Automatic Merchandisers Assn., Nat. Candy Wholesalers Assn., UCLA Alumni Club, Waukegan/Lake County C. of C. Clubs: Elks, Eagles. Home: 3444 University Ave Highland Park IL 60035 Office: 3055 Washington St Waukegan IL 60085

MEYER, MARTY, lit. tng. cons.; b. Little Falls, Minn., Feb. 15, 1948; d. Alex Michael and Joanna Magdalina (Grigaitis) M.; B.A., Mary Manse Coll., 1974; cert. in liturgy Inst. Pastoral Liturgical Ministries, Detroit, 1978; M.A., St. John U., Minn., 1979. Tchr. elem. schs. Garden City, Mich., 1970-72, Bowling Green, Ohio, 1972-73, Sandusky, Ohio, 1973-74; parish liturgy coordinator, St. Monica Parish, Detroit, 1974-76; staff mem. dept. Christian worship Detroit Archdiocese, 1976-77; cons. on liturgy, Detroit, 1977-78; program coordinator Office Divine Worship, Chgo. Archdiocese, 1979-80, lit. tng. cons., 1980—; bd. dirs., tchr. Lay Ministry Tng. Program Chgo. Mem. Am. Soc. for Tng. and Devel., Learning Exchange, Sacred Dance Guild. Roman Catholic. Club: Toastmasters. Author: A Liturgical Education Sourcebook, 1977; At Home with the Word, 1980; (with Stephanie Certain) Goal Setting for Liturgy Committees, 1981. Office: 155 E Superior St Chicago IL 60611

MEYER, MARY COELI, mgmt. cons.; b. Brighton, Mass., Mar. 16, 1943; d. Herbert Walter and Eleanor Beecher M.; B.A., Nat. Coll. Edn., 1965; postgrad. Ind. U., 1968-69, Case Western Res. U., 1972-73, Calif Western Coll., 1977-79. Prin. cons. Coeli Designs, Boston, 1967-72; mgr. human resource devel. Addressograph Multigraph, Cleve., 1972-77; instr. Harper Coll. Sch. Bus., Palatine, Ill., 1976—; prin. cons. human resource systems Cheshire Ltd., Wheeling, Ill., 1977—. Kent State U. music scholar, 1958-60; Eva Grace Long scholar, 1964-65. Mem. Creative Edn. Found., Nat. Tng. Labs., Am. Soc. Tng. and Devel., Ill. Tng. and Devel. Assn., Soc. Personnel Adminstrs., Am. Soc. Personnel Adminstrs. Midwest O.D. Network. Author: Sexual Harassment; contbr. articles to profl. jours.; research in demotivation. Office: PO Box 682 Wheeling IL 60090

MEYER, MAVIS NADINE, vol. services adminstr.; b. Albert Lea, Minn., Feb. 10, 1917; d. James William and Elizabeth Beatrice (Smith) Elliott; B.S., U. Wis., Milw., 1939; student Prospect Hall, 1941, Layton Sch. Art, 1940-41, Marquette U., 1959; m. Roman Theodore Meyer, May 25, 1968; stepchildren—Ted, Timothy, Barbara. Sec., Allis-Chalmers, West Allis, Wis., 1942-52; sec. Seefurth & McGiveran, Milw., 1952-61; adminstrv. sec. West Allis Meml. Hosp., 1961-66, dir. public relations and vol. services, 1966-73, dir. vol. services, 1966—. Mem. Milw. Mayor's Beautification Com., 1965-66, chmn. fin. com., 1965-66. Cert. profl. sec., 1960. Mem. Am. Soc. Dirs. Vol. Services (mem. ednl. conf. faculty 1975), Wis. Assn. Dirs. Vol. Services, Milw. Assn. Dirs. Hosp. Vol. Services, Nat. Secs. Assn. Office: 8901 W Lincoln Ave West Allis WI 53227

MEYER, PAUL EMMETT, restaurant and motel mgmt. co. exec.; b. Detroit, Aug. 24, 1931; s. Herbert M. and Agnes E. Meyer; B.A., Mich. State U., 1954. Multi-unit motel supr., 1957-70; mgr. Magic Pan Restaurant, Chgo., Aspen, Colo., 1970-71, Sundog Restaurant, Detroit, 1971-72; dir. food service, hosp. div. ARA Services, Indpls. and Richmond, Ind., 1972-75; supr. motor inn, Detroit, 1975-77; Haymarket mgr. Hilton Hotels, Detroit, 1977-78; mgr. restaurants Sheraton Hotel, Detroit, 1978-81; gen. mgr. Bill Panek's L.C. Restaurant, Detroit, 1980—; owner P Emmett Meyer Corp., 1981—; instr. Whitcomb Hotel-Motel, 1962-64; real estate broker, 1960—. Mem. Detroit Mayor's Com. on Safety and Security, 1967-68, Mayor's Com. Polish Day Festival Hamtramck, 1981. Mem. Greater Detroit Motel Assn. (pres. 1959-67), Food Service Exec. Assn., Am. Entrepreneurs Assn., Nat. Restaurant Assn. Contbg. staff editor food sect. Reporter Publs., 1975—. Home: 19427 Warrington Detroit MI 48221 Office: 11620 Jos Campau Hamtramck MI 48212

MEYER, PAUL REIMS, orthopaedic surgeon; b. Port Arthur, Tex., Nov. 2, 1931; s. Paul Reims and Evelyn Meyer; B.A., Va. Mil. Inst., 1954; M.D., Tulane U., 1958; m. Eileen Carroll, 1937; children—Kristin Lynn, Holly Dee, Paul Reims, III, Stewart Blair. Prof. orthopaedic surgery Northwestern U. Med. Sch., 1981—, dir. acute spinal cord injury, 1972—; co-dir. Midwest Regional Spinal Cord Injury Care System, McGaw Med. Center, 1972—; mem. President's Council Spinal Cord Injury; cons. HEW. Served as officer M.C., USAR, 1963-65. Decorated Commendation medal. Mem. AMA, Am. Acad. Orthopaedic Surgeons, A.C.S., Am. Spinal Injury Assn. (pres. 1979-81), Am. Trauma Soc. (Curtis P. Artz award 1979), 20th Century Orthopaedic Assn., Internat. Med. Soc. Paraplegia, Ill. Orthopaedic Soc., Chgo. Orthopaedic Soc. Author articles in chief, chpts. in books. Office: 707 N Fairbanks Ct Suite 511 Chicago IL 60611

MEYER, RAYMOND JOSEPH, basketball coach; b. Chgo., Dec. 18, 1913; s. Joseph E. and Barbara (Hummel) M.; B.A., U. Notre Dame, 1938; m. Margaret Mary Delaney, May 27, 1939; children—Barbara Meyer Starzyk, Raymond Thomas, Patricia Meyer Butterfield, Meriann Meyer McGowan, Joseph, Robert. Asst. coach U. Notre Dame, 1941-42; basketball coach DePaul U., Chgo., 1942—. Named Coach of Year, Chgo. Basketball Writers, 1943, 44, 48, 52, Mem. Nat. Basketball Writers Assn., 1978, 79; named to Basketball Hall of Fame, 1979. Mem. Nat. Basketball Coaches Assn. Roman Catholic. Author: How to Play Winning Basketball, 1960; Basketball as Coached by Ray Meyer, 1967. Office: 1011 W Belden Ave Chicago IL 60614

MEYER, ROBERT WILLIAM, mech. engr.; b. Bonne Terre, Mo., Aug. 12, 1944; s. William Herman and Lois Alma (Jones) M.; B.S., U. Mo., Rolla, 1966, M.S., 1969, Ph.D., 1971; m. Sandra Lee Piltz, Mar. 15, 1975. Product test engr. Ford Motor Co., Livonia, Mich., 1973-75; sr. researcher Holcroft Co., Livonia, 1975-79, mgr. technology devel., 1979—. Served with U.S. Army, 1972. St. Joe Minerals Corp. scholar, 1962-66. Mem. Am. Soc. Metals, Instrument Soc. Am., Phi Eta Sigma, Pi Tau Sigma, Tau Beta Pi. Patentee heat exchanger. Home: 24347 Hampton Hill Novi MI 48050 Office: 12068 Market St Livonia MI 48150

MEYER, ROGER FREDERICK, physician; b. Napoleon, Ohio, Jan. 11, 1939; s. William D. and La Vina L. (Baden) M.; M.D., Ohio State U., 1965; M.S. in Ophthalmology, U. Mich., 1971. Intern, Milw. County (Wis.) Gen. Hosp., 1965-66; resident in ophthalmology U. Mich., 1968-71; fellow Francis I. Proctor Found. for Research in Ophthalmology, San Francisco, 1973-74; fellow U. Fla., Coll. Medicine, Gainesville, 1974-75; practice medicine specializing in ophthalmology, Ann Arbor, Mich., 1975—; asso. prof. dept. ophthalmology U. Mich. Med. Center, 1975—, dir. of corneal and external ocular disease service, 1975—; med. dir. Michigan Eye Bank, Ann Arbor, 1975—; cons. VA Hosp., Ann Arbor, 1971—, Wayne County (Mich.) Gen. Hosp., Eloise, 1971—. Served to capt. USAF, 1966-68. Diplomate Am. Bd. Ophthalmology. Fellow Am. Acad. Ophthalmology; mem. Assn. for Research in Vision and Ophthalmology, Mich. Ophthal. Soc., Soc. of Heed Fellows, Castroviejo Soc. of Corneal Surgeons, Assn. of Proctor Fellows, Phi Chi, Sigma Nu. Lutheran. Contbr. chpts. to books, articles to sci. jours. Home: 3012 Brockman Ann Arbor MI 48104 Office: Univ of Michigan Medical Center Dept of Ophthalmology Ann Arbor MI 48109

MEYER, THOMAS ERNEST, cemetery co. exec.; b. Evansville, Ind., Feb. 23, 1950; s. Fred W. and Jean Hope Meyer; B.S., Ball State U.; m. Judy L. Weaver, Aug. 25, 1973; children—Thomas Bradley, Wendy Jean. Salesman, Forest Lawn Memory Gardens, Indpls., 1973-74; gen. mgr. Lincoln Memory Gardens, Indpls., 1974-77; v.p. public relations Am. Bronze Craft, Indpls., 1977; v.p. cemetery ops. Memory Gardens Mgmt. Corp., Indpls., 1978—. Mem. Am. Cemetery Assn., Nat. Assn. Cemeteries, So. Cemetery Assn., Ind. Cemetery Assn. (pres.), Pre-Arrangement Interment Assn. Am., Cemetery Supply Assn., Zionsville Jaycees, Sigma Chi. Lutheran. Home: 510 E 111th St Indianapolis IN 46280 Office: 3733 N Meridian St Indianapolis IN 46208

MEYERHOFF, ARTHUR EDWARD, advt. agy. exec.; b. Chgo., Mar. 12, 1895; s. Emanuel and Jennie (Lewin) M.; student pub. schs., Chgo.; m. Madelaine H. Goldman, 1921; m. 2d, Elaine Clemens, Jan. 27, 1945; children—Jane, Arthur E., Joanne, William, Judith Lynn. With Hood Rubber Co., 1914-22; classified advt., circulation mgr. Wis. News, Milw., 1922-29; with Neisser & Meyerhoff, Chgo., advt. and merchandising, 1929-41; pres. Arthur Meyerhoff Assos., Inc. (formerly Arthur Meyerhoff & Co.), Chgo., 1941-65, chmn. bd., 1965-80, chmn. bd. BBDO Chgo. (formerly Arthur Meyerhoff Assos., Inc.), 1980—; organizer Gibraltar Industries, Inc., 1958; pioneered comic page advt.; dir. Santa Catalina Island Co., Chgo. Nat. League Ball Club, Inc.; developer Myzon products; Myzon, Inc. organized, 1951; mem. adv. bd. KBIG-KBRT, Los Angeles. Served with AEF, World I. Received 1st prize Marshall Field candid div., 6th ann., 3d internat. competition and salon, 1939; George Washington Honor Medal award Freedoms Found. at Valley Forge, 1967. Mem. Am. Assn. Advt. Agys., C. of C. Author: Strategy of Persuasion, 1965. Office: 410 N Michigan Av Chicago IL 60611

MEYERHOFF, DONALD FREDERICK, sch. adminstr.; b. Readlyn, Iowa, Jan. 8, 1939; s. William Edward and Leona (Orth) M.; B.A., U. Iowa, 1962; M.A. Drake U., 1969, Edn. Specialist, 1974; postgrad. Clarke Coll., 1971, Western Ill. U., 1972-74, 76; m. Marilyn Rose Menke, July 27, 1974; children—Javon Scott, Brian Michael. Tchr., Lost Nation (Iowa) schs., 1962-64; tchr., coach Ringsted (Iowa) schs., 1964-66; tchr. Harlem schs., Rockford, Ill., 1966-67; tchr. West Central Sch., Maynard, Iowa, 1967-68; tchr. Central High Sch., Davenport, Iowa, 1968-76; cons. math. Mississippi Bend Area Edn. Agy., Davenport, 1976-80; dir. curriculum South Tama County Schs., Tama, Iowa, 1980—. NSF grantee, 1964, 65, 69, 71. Mem. Iowa Council Tchr. Math., Ill. Council Tchrs. Math., Nat. Council Tchrs. Math., Assn. Supervision and Curriculum Devel., Iowa Assn. Elem. Middle Sch. Prins., Sch. Sci. Math. Assn., Phi Delta Kappa. Roman Catholic. Clubs: Tama-Toledo Country, Moose. Home: 208 W 14th St Tama IA 52339 Office: 1702 Harding St Tama IA 52339

MEYERS, ARTHUR RALPH, machine tools mfg. co. exec.; b. Chgo., Sept. 7, 1921; s. Nathan and Jennie M.; B.S., Met. State Coll., 1973; postgrad. Colo. State Coll., Ft. Collins, 1974; m. Gertrude Selig, Dec. 20, 1946; 1 son, Michael Jeffry. Apprentice, tool and die maker Internat. Harvester Co., Chgo., 1940-48; tool and die maker Quadriga Mfg. Co., Chgo., 1948-55; sales engr. DoAll Co., Des Plaines, Ill., 1955-66, dir. tng., 1974—; vocat. tchr. Denver Public Schs., 1966-74. Served with USAAF, 1942-45. Decorated Air Medal with 3 oak leaf clusters. Mem. Soc. Mfg. Engrs., Soc. Carbide Engrs., Am. Soc. Metals. Clubs: Lions, Civitan, Elks. Home: 1517 Winnetka Rd Glenview IL 60025 Office: 254 N Laurel Ave Des Plaines IL 60016

MEYERS, DONALD WILLIAM, mfg. co. exec.; b. Chgo., Jan. 30, 1929; s. Robert Francis and Alberta Mae (McMahon) M.; B.Sc., Loyola U., Chgo., 1954; M.B.A., U. Chgo., 1967; m. Sandra Jean Young, May 28, 1971. Personnel asst. Allstate, Skokie, Ill., 1954-64; mgr. personnel Ohmite Mfg. Co., Skokie, Ill., 1964-68; mgr. indsl. relations Warner Electric, South Beloit, Ill., 1968-70; employee relations mgr. Clark Equipment, Buchanen, Mich., 1970-73; dir. employee relations, engine components Wallace Murray Corp., Indpls., 1973—; corp. v.p. adminstrn. Maul Tech. Corp., 1981—. Mem. salary compensation com. City of Carmel, Ind., 1977-78; mem. workmans compensation com. State of Ind., 1977-79. Served with USN, 1946-48, 50-52. Mem. Am. Soc. Personnel Adminstrs., Ind. Personnel Assn., Indpls. Personnel Assn. Home: 10549 LaSalle Rd Carmel IN 46032 Office: Wallace Murray Corp 1025 Brookside Indianapolis IN 46206

MEYERS, GERALD CARL, mfg. co. exec.; b. Buffalo, Dec. 5, 1928; s. Meyer and Berenice M.; B.S., Carnegie Inst. Tech., (now Carnegie-Mellon U.), 1950; M.S. summa cum laude, 1954; m. Barbara Jacob, Nov. 2, 1958. With Ford Motor Co., Detroit, 1950-51, Chrysler Corp., Detroit and Geneva, 1954-62; with Am. Motors Corp., Detroit, 1962—, exec. v.p., 1975-77, pres., 1977, chief operating officer, 1977, chmn., chief exec. officer, 1978—. Bd. trustees Carnegie-Mellon U., 1976—; bd. dirs. Detroit Renaissance, Inc., 1978—; mem. adv. bd. Jr. Achievement of S.E. Mich., 1979—; bd. dirs. Detroit Symphony Orch., 1979—, Detroit Renaissance, Inc., United Found. Met. Detroit; trustee Citizens Research Council Mich. Served with USAF, 1951-53. Decorated chevalier Legion of Honor. Mem. Conf. Bd., Traffic Safety Assn. Detroit (trustee 1979), Hwy. Users Fedn. (dir. 1977—), Motor Vehicle Mfrs. Assn. (dir. 1977—, chmn. 1980-81), Soc. Automotive Engrs., Automotive Orgn. Team, Inc., Greater Detroit C. of C., U.S. Council of Internat. C. of C. (trustee 1978—). Club: Economic (dir. 1979-81) (Detroit). Office: 27777 Franklin Rd Southfield MI 48034

MEYERS, MARSHA LYNN, hosp. social worker; b. Springfield, Ohio, Dec. 3, 1948; d. Dennis Wathan and Juanita (Ratliff) Easterling; B.A. in Sociology, Olivet Nazarene Coll., Kankakee, Ill., 1971; m. Wade Trent Meyers, Oct. 5, 1974; 1 dau., Lindsay Dionne. Asst. aide Kankakee County Tng. Center for Disabled, Bourbonnais, Ill., 1971; coordinator social service Mercy Meml. Hosp., Urbana, Ohio, 1972—, also mem. home health care adv. bd.; coordinator social service Urbana Care Center, Inc., 1972—. Mem. Champaign County (Ohio) Welfare Adv. Bd., 1977—; bd. dirs. Champaign County unit Am. Cancer Soc., 1972-78; mem. Champaign County planning com. White House Conf. on Handicapped, 1976. Mem. Nat. Assn. Social Workers, Soc. Hosp. Social Work Dirs., Nat. Assn. Christians in Social Work (v.p. Ohio chpt. 1978-79). Republican. Nazarene. Club: Welcome Wagon. Home: 223 College St Urbana OH 43078 Office: 904 Scioto St Urbana OH 43078 or 741 E Water St Urbana OH 43078

MEYOCKS, RICHARD DEAN, advt. agy. exec.; b. Urbana, Iowa, Oct. 23, 1931; s. Raymond Francis and Charlotte Iantha (Martin) M.; B.S., Iowa State U., 1956; m. Donna Lee Floyd, Oct. 12, 1951; children—Mark Ray, Craig Lee, Brad Lynn, Marci Jo. With Morrell Co., Ottumwa, Iowa, 1956-67, regional sales mgr., 1966, corp. sales promotion mgr., 1967; with Creswell Munsell Schubert Advt. Agy., Cedar Rapids, Iowa, 1967—, v.p. dir. client mgmt. services, 1977, sr. v.p., dir. client mgmt. services, 1979—. Chmn. fin. com. Republican County Com., 1963; dist. commr. Boy Scouts Am., 1965. Mem. Am. Advt. Fedn. (pres. chpt. 1971-72), Nat. Agri-Mktg. Assn. (Work Horse of Yr. award 1974, nat. chmn. Agr. Day 1974, chpt. pres. 1976-77, pres. Ag Day Found. 1978-79). Presbyterian. Club: Elmcrest Country. Home: Rural Route 1 500 Fairfax Rd Fairfax IA 52228 Office: 4211 Signal Ridge Rd NE Cedar Rapids IA 52406

MICHAEL, CAROL MUSSELMAN, educator; b. Dayton, July 20, 1949; d. Orville Glen and Evelyn Charlotte Musselman; student Manchester Coll., 1967-69; B.S. magna cum laude, Ohio State U., 1971, M.S. in Home Econs., 1973; m. James L. Michael, Sept. 16, 1972. Instr. food service Bur. Vocat. Rehab., Trotwood, Ohio, 1973; tchr. Hamilton City (Ohio) Schs., 1973; instr. home econs. Miami U., Oxford, Ohio, 1974-78, asst. prof., 1978—; tech. cons. Major Appliance Consumer Action Panel. Chairperson world hunger task force So. Ohio Dist. Ch. of the Brethren, 1977. Mem. Am. Home Econs. Assn., Ohio Home Econs. Assn., Coll. Educators in Home Equipment, Phi Upsilon Omicron, Omicron Nu, Phi Kappa Phi. Contbr. articles to profl. jours. Home: 409 E Chestnut St Oxford OH 45056 Office: 189 McGuffey Hall Miami University Oxford OH 45056

MICHAELS, ARTHUR EDWARD, III, steel co. exec.; b. Cleve., Mar. 8, 1945; s. Arthur Edward and Florence Keturah (Winner) M.; B.S. in Metallurgy, Case Inst. Tech., 1967; postgrad. in Indsl. Mgmt., U. Akron, 1967-73; m. Diane Kay Bechtel, July 10, 1971; children—Kara Lynn, Todd Alan, Emily Elizabeth. Metall. trainee Timken Co., Canton, Ohio, 1967-69, applications metallurgist, 1969-73, asso. sales engr., 1973, sales engr., Cleve., 1973-81, mgr. sales devel. and adminstrn., steel div., 1981—. Active United Fund, 1967-70. Timken Co. scholar, 1963. Mem. Am. Soc. Metals, Beta

Gamma Sigma. Republican. Evang. Protestant. Office: 3645 Warrensville Center Rd Shaker Heights OH 44122

MICHAK, HELEN BARBARA, educator, nurse; b. Cleve., July 31; d. Andrew and Mary (Patrick) Michak; Diploma Cleve. City Hosp. Sch. Nursing, 1947; B.A., Miami U., Oxford, Ohio, 1951; M.A., Case Western Res. U., 1960. Staff nurse Cleve. City Hosp., 1947-48; pub. health nurse Cleve. Div. Health, 1951-52; instr. Cleve. City Hosp. Sch. Nursing, 1952-56; supr. nursing Cuyahoga County Hosp., Cleve., 1956-58; pub. information dir. N.E. Ohio Am. Heart Assn., Cleve., 1960-64; dir. spl. events Higbee Co., Cleve., 1964-66; exec. dir. Cleve. Area League for Nursing, 1966-72; dir. continuing edn. nurses, adj. asso. prof. Cleve. State U., 1972—. Trustee N.E. Ohio Regional Med. Program, 1970-73; mem. adv. com. Dept. Nursing Cuyahoga Community Coll., 1967—; mem. long term care com. Met. Health Planning Corp., 1974-76, plan devel. com. 1977—; mem. policy bd. Center Health Data N.E. Ohio, 1972-73; mem. Rep. Assembly and Health Planning and Devel. Commn., Welfare Fedn. Cleve., 1967-72; mem. Cleve. Community Health Network, 1972-73; mem. United Appeal Films and Speakers Bur., 1967-73; mem. adv. com. Ohio Fedn. Licensed Practical Nurses, 1970-73; mem. tech. adv. com. TB and Respiratory Disease Assn. Cuyahoga County, 1967-74; mem. Ohio Commn. on Nursing, 1971-74; mem. Citizens com. nursing homes Fedn. Community Planning, 1973-77; mem. com. on home health services Met. Health Planning Corp., 1973—. Mem. Nat. League Nursing (mem. com. 1970-72), Am. (accreditation visitor 1977-78), Ohio (com. continuing edn. 1974-79), Greater Cleve. (joint practice com. 1973-74, trustee 1975-76) nurses assns., Cleve. Area Citizens League for Nursing (trustee 1976-79), Zeta Tau Alpha. Home: 4686 Oakridge Dr North Royalton OH 44133 Office: Cleve State Univ 2344 Euclid Av Cleveland OH 44115

MICHALETZ, JAMES ERNEST, clergyman, ednl. adminstr.; b. Chgo., Aug. 9, 1931; s. Ernest S. and Philomena K. (Schafer) M.; B.A., St. Ambrose Coll., 1955; M.S., Loyola U., Chgo., 1957, Ph.D., 1974. Joined Clerics of St. Viator, Roman Catholic Ch., 1952, ordained priest, 1960; prin. St. Viator High Sch., Arlington Heights, Ill., 1969-72; asst. supt. Archdiocese of Chgo., 1973-75, dir. planning, 1975-77; dir. edn. Clerics of St. Viator, Arlington Heights, 1977—; cons. in ednl. planning, mgmt.; vis. prof. U. Notre Dame, South Bend, Ind. Mem. Nat. Cath. Edn. Assn., Chief Adminstrs. Cath. Edn., Nat. Assn. Secondary Sch. Prins., Assn. Supervision and Curriculum Devel., World Future Soc., Phi Delta Kappa. Research, publs. in ednl., innovation and religious leadership. Home and Office: 1212 E Euclid St Arlington Heights IL 60004

MICHALSKI, HELEN MARYANNE, acct.; b. Cleve., Aug. 31, 1924; d. Anthony Frank and Sophia Mary (Kozlowski) M.; B.B.A., Case Western Res. U., 1966. With engine parts div. Imperial Clevite Inc., Cleve., 1942—, systems analyst, 1968-73, systems analyst-acct., 1973-74, salary payroll adminstrn., 1974—. Solicitor Heart Fund, 1958; fin. adviser Jr. Achievement. Mem. Assn. for Systems Mgmt., Am. Soc. Women Accts., Polish Nat. Alliance. Republican. Roman Catholic. Club: Cath. Alumni. Home: 4903 Autumn Ln Brooklyn OH 44144 Office: Imperial Clevite Inc 17000 St Clair Ave Cleveland OH 44110

MICHAS, NICHOLAS ATHANASIOS, fin. economist; b. Moose Jaw, Sask., Can., July 25, 1940; s. Athanasios and Eftychia (Mercou) M.; B.A., U. Alta., 1963; M.S., U. Ill., 1964, Ph.D., 1967; m. Kathryn Ann Schoen, Aug. 16, 1969; children—Koren Elise, Paul Nicholas. Asso. prof. econs. No. Ill. U., DeKalb, 1973-75; statis. research dir. Heinold, O'Connor & Cloonan, Chgo., 1975-77; asso. prof. fin. U. Ill., Chgo., 1977-79; cons. A.S. Hansen, Inc., Chgo., 1979—; vis. prof. Athens (Greece) Grad. Sch. Econs. and Bus. Scis., 1972-73. No. Ill. U. research grantee, 1974. Mem. Am. Econs. Assn., Am. Fin. Assn., Fin. Mgmt. Assn., Investment Analysts Soc. Chgo. Author: (with Lloyd G. Reynolds) Principles of Economics: Macro and Principles of Economics: Micro, Plaid Series, 1971, 73, 79, A Guide to Economics, 1981; contbr. articles to profl. publs. Home: 304 S Pine Mount Prospect IL 60056 Office: 3 First National Plaza Chicago IL 60602

MICHEL, CARYLE LEON, fertilizer co. exec.; b. Farina, Ill., Dec. 11, 1922; s. Adolph and Marie Myrtle (Holzhausn) M.; B.A., So. Ill. U., 1948; m. Catherine Wilson, Dec. 27, 1949; children—Starr, Teri, Kay, Christopher. Former tchr. Greenfield, Mo.; former salesman E.F. McDonald; v.p. super market chain, Buffalo; owner fertilizer co. (acquired by Farmland Industries), 1967-77; owner, operator Michel Fertilizer Co., Mt. Vernon, Ill., 1977—. Served to lt. USN, 1942-46. Mem. Jefferson County C. of C., Ill. Fertilizer and Chem. Assn., Ill. Oil and Gas Assn. Baptist. Club: Elks. Home: 22 Wildwood Mount Vernon IL 62864 Office: 1313 Shawnee St Mount Vernon IL 62864

MICHEL, RICHARD EDWIN, physicist, educator; b. Saginaw, Mich., Oct. 31, 1928; s. Jacob and Laura May (Lacey) M.; B.S., Mich. State U., 1950, M.S., 1953, Ph.D., 1956; m. Martha Lou Stephens, June 29, 1951; children—Jane, Carol, Paul. Mem. gen. research group RCA Labs., Princeton, N.J., 1956-62; sr. research physicist Gen. Motors Research Labs., Warren, Mich., 1962-73; dean Sch. for Asso. Studies, chmn. physics dept. Lawrence Inst. Tech., Southfield, Mich., 1973—. Served with U.S. Army, 1951-52. Decorated Purple Heart. Mem. Am. Phys. Soc., Am. Assn. Physics Tchrs., Sigma Xi. Home: 453 Kimberly Birmingham MI 48009 Office: 21000 W Ten Mile Southfield MI 48075

MICHEL, ROBERT HENRY, congressman; b. Peoria, Ill., Mar. 2, 1923; s. Charles and Anna (Baer) M.; B.S., Bradley U., 1948; L.H.D. (hon.), Lincoln Coll.; m. Corinne Woodruff, Dec. 26, 1948; children—Scott, Bruce, Laurie, Robin. Adminstrv. asst. Congressman Harold Velde, 1949-56; mem. 85th-97th Congresses, 18th Dist. Ill., house minority whip 94th-96th Congresses, minority leader 97th Congress. Vice pres. Towne House Inn, Inc. Del. Republican Conv., 1964, 68, 72, 76, 80. Served with inf. AUS, World War II; ETO. Decorated Bronze Star Medal, Purple Heart; recipient Distinguished Alumnus award Bradley U., 1961. Mem. Am. Legion, V.F.W., D.A.V., Amvets, Cosmopolitan Internat. Home: 1029 N Glenwood St Peoria IL 61606 Office: Rayburn Office Bldg Washington DC 20515

MICHELS, LOUISE ANN, guidance counselor; b. Toledo, June 21, 1947; d. Leo Joseph and Margaret Mary (Kreuz) Michels; B.A., Mary Manse Coll., 1969; M.Edn., Bowling Green (Ohio) State U., 1976. Tchr., Our Lady of Perpetual Help Sch., Toledo, 1969-76; elementary guidance counselor Ashtabula (Ohio) Area City Schs., 1976-77; high sch. guidance counselor Tecumseh High Sch., New Carlisle-Bethel schs., New Carlisle, Ohio, 1977—. Sec., Maumee (Ohio) Civic Theatre, 1973-76, bd. dirs., 1976-77. Mem. Am. Personnel and Guidance Assn., Am. Sch. Counselor Assn., Ohio School Counselor Assn., Nat., Ohio, New Carlisle-Bethel edn. assns., Ohio Personnel and Guidance Assn., Central Ohio Tchrs. Assn., Ohio Tennis Coaches Assn., Nat. Hist. Soc. Roman Catholic. Club: Dayton Cath. Alumni. Home: 842 Woodview Ct Vandalia OH 45377 Office: Tecumseh High Sch 9830 W National Rd New Carlisle OH 45344

MICHNO, DOROTHY ANTONIA, counselor, editor; b. Chgo., July 31, 1945; s. Stanley Peter and Clara Ann (Rogusz) M.; B.S.Ed., Loyola U., Chgo., 1969, M.Ed., 1971. Auditor, Bankers Life & Casualty Co., Chgo., 1967-72; dir. guidance Queen of Peace High Sch., Burbank, Ill., 1972-74; counselor Sch. Dist. 59, Elk Grove Village, Ill., 1974-78; coll. and career counselor Warren Twp. High Sch., Gurnee, Ill., 1978—; editor Polish Museum of Am. Quaterly, 1974—. Program chmn. Community Services Orgn., Elk Grove Village. Grantee, Jagiellonian U., Krakow, Poland, summer 1974. Mem. Am. Personnel and Guidance Assn., Am. Sch. Counselors Assn., Nat. Vocat. Guidance Assn., Ill. Sch. Counselors Assn., Ill., Chgo. guidance and personnel assns., Nat. Cath. Guidance Conf., Polish Am. Educators Assn., Ladies Aux. Polish Mus. Am., Phi Delta Kappa. Democrat. Roman Catholic. Club: Polish Arts. Home: 725 Shepard Ct Gurnee IL 60031 Office: 500 N O'Plaine Rd Gurnee IL 60031

MICK, DAVID LEE, entomologist; b. Newton, Iowa, Oct. 25, 1937; s. Clifford Merlyn and Errisje (Kolfschoten) M.; B.S., Iowa State U., 1960, M.S., 1961, Ph.D., 1969; m. Phyllis Lorraine Monsma, June 2, 1959; children—Todd, Krista, Kayla. Extension agronomist Iowa State U., Ames, 1962-65, extension entomologist, 1965-69; asso. prof. Coll. Medicine, U. Iowa, Iowa City, 1969-74; dir. Land Quality Div., Dept. Environ. Quality, Des Moines, Iowa, 1974; entomologist Laverty Sprayers, Inc., Indianola, Iowa, 1974—; cons. in field. Mem. budget com. United Fund, 1971-72; mem. Park and Recreation Commn., Indianola, 1977-79). Mem. Entomol. Soc. Am., Aircraft Owners and Pilots Assn., Iowa Agrl. Chem. Adv. Com., Sigma Xi, Gamma Sigma Delta. Presbyterian. Club: Lion. Patentee in log burning support, fireplace grate device; contbr. articles in field to profl. jours. Home: 409 Madison Pl Indianola IA 50125 Office: PO Box 198 Indianola IA 50125

MICKELSON, JOHN CHESTER, educator; b. Winter, Wis., Nov. 16, 1920; s. Axel Leonard and Alice Michelson; A.B., Augustana Coll., Rock Island, Ill., 1941; M.S., U. Iowa, 1948, Ph.D., 1949; m. Grace M. Erdahl, July 26, 1947; children—Judith Kay, John Chester, Barbara Jo, Becky Sue. Asst. prof. Wash. State U., 1949-54; staff geologist Sohio Petroleum Co., Billings, Mont., 1954-60; sr. geologist Sunray DX Oil Co., Tulsa, 1961; asso. prof. S.D. Sch. Mines, Rapid City, 1961-66, dept. head, 1968-78, prof. geology and geol. engring., 1966—. Mem. Rapid City Planning Commn., 1962-69; mem. S.D. Water Rights Commn., 1975-79, chmn., 1976-77. Served with U.S. Army, 1943-46. Decorated Bronze Star medal; recipient Lowden award U. Iowa, 1947. Fellow Geol. Soc. Am.; mem. Am. Assn. Petroleum Geologists, Am. Inst. Profl. Geologists, VFW, Sigma Xi. Home: 133 E St Charles St Rapid City SD 57701 Office: 500 E St Joseph St Rapid City SD 57701

MICKELSON, ROBERT EVERETT, ins. co. exec.; b. Vermillion, S.D., May 22, 1932; s. Edward A. and Mabel Elizabeth Mickelson; B.S., U. Wis., Eau Claire, 1959; postgrad. edn. U. Wis., 1959; m. Judith Alice Aschebrook, Dec. 29, 1957; children—Robert Edward, David Norman. With Cadott (Wis.) Sentinel, 1950-51; with Aid Assn. for Lutherans, Appleton, Wis., 1959—, public activities adminstr., 1968-72, mgr., 1972-77, dir. public activities and publs., 1977-78, asst. v.p. public activities and publs., 1978-80, asst. v.p. communication services, 1980—. Served with USAF, 1951-55. Mem. Public Relations Soc. Am., Life Ins. Advertisers Assn., Ins. Conf. Planners Assn., Nat. Fraternal Congress Am. (exec. bd. press and public relations sect. 1978—, mem. public relations com. 1977—, chmn. 1979-80), Internat. Luth. Laymen's League, Wis. Ins. Club, Pi Delta Epsilon. Home: 41 S Meadows Dr Appleton WI 54911 Office: Aid Assn for Lutherans 4321 N Ballard Rd Appleton WI 54919

MICUN, RICHARD PETER, lawyer, educator; b. Chgo., Nov. 14, 1927; s. John Peter and Tekla (Marozas) M.; B.S., De Paul U., 1948, J.D., 1950, M.S. in Taxation, 1973; M.B.A., U. Chgo., 1958; m. Maureen M. Haggerty, Nov. 17, 1962; children—Thomas, Timothy, Terrence. Admitted to Ill. bar, 1950, U.S. Supreme Ct. bar, 1965; corp. atty. Brunswick Corp., Chgo., 1955-62; atty. Internat. Minerals & Chem. Corp., 1962-65; lectr. Chgo. City Jr. Colls., 1961-64, asst. prof., 1965-68, asso. prof., 1968-75, prof., 1975—. Served from 1st lt. to capt. AUS, 1950-55; col. J.A.G. Res. Decorated Bronze Star medal. Mem. Am., Fed., Chgo. bar assns. Home: 2647 W 94th Pl Evergreen Park IL 60642

MIDDLETON, DAN FRANK, ins. agy. exec.; b. Pitts., Sept. 15, 1930; s. Frank Riordon and Florence Anna Marie (Gross) M.; student Miami U., Oxford, Ohio, 1948-49, Ohio State U., 1951-54; m. Marilyn Joyce Calentine, Apr. 5, 1958; children—Timothy Irwin, Suzanne Marie. With Atkinson-Dauksch Agys., Columbus, Ohio, 1955—, asst. v.p., 1969-70, v.p., 1970—, dir., 1973—, mem. exec. com., 1974—, chmn. profit sharing plan adminstrn. com., 1970—. Served with USAF, 1951-52. C.P.C.U. (chpt. dir. 1967-68); asso. in risk mgmt. Mem. Ins. Bd. Columbus, Columbus Power Squadron, Jaguar Assn. Central Ohio (pres. 1978-79, del. to nat. conv. Jaguar Clubs N. Am. 1979), Nat. Trust for Hist. Preservation, Columbus Landmarks Found. Methodist. Clubs: Columbus Maennerchor, Executive, V.I.P. (Columbus); Scioto Country; Jaguar Drivers (U.K.). Home: 2410 Cambridge Blvd Upper Arlington OH 43221 Office: 50 W Broad St Columbus OH 43215

MIDDLETON, JAMES WEATHERS, diagnostic co. exec.; b. Lexington, Ky., Dec. 21, 1950; s. James and Josephine Washington M.; B.A., Eastern Ky. U., 1974; M.B.A., U. Ky., 1978; m. Barbara Gray, Nov. 11, 1978; 1 son, James Weathers III. Sales rep. Ortho Diagnostics, Inc., Pitts., 1974-76; ter. mgr. Corning Med., Charleston, W.Va., 1978—. Mem. Am. Mktg. Assn., Assn. Bus. Mgmt., Kappa Alpha Psi. Baptist.

MIDDLETON, MARC EDWIN, mfg. co. exec.; b. Henderson, Ky., Sept. 20, 1952; s. Carl Louis and Elizabeth May (Mahoney) M.; student Western Mich. U. m. 2d, Jacqueline A. Boltz, Aug. 22, 1981. Supr., Duffy Mott's Inc., Hartford, Mich., 1973-75, ITT Continental Baking Co., Schiller Park, Ill., 1976-77; process mgr. Schulze & Burch Biscuit Co., Chgo., 1977-80; co-owner, v.p. sales and mktg., gen. mgr. Middleton's, The Spindle Railing Co., Bronson, Mich., 1980—; cons. in field. Roman Catholic. Office: 303 Southern Rd Rural Route 4 Box 138 Bronson MI 49028

MIDDLETON, PHILLIP EDWARD, surg. oncologist; b. Balt., May 23, 1941; s. Carlisle Anthony and Mary Bernadette Middleton; B.S. in Biology, Loyola Coll., Balt., 1963; postgrad. Johns Hopkins U., 1962-67; M.D., U. Md., 1970; m. Ruth E. Lawrence, June 19, 1971; children—Matthew, Luke, Rebecca, James Ivan, Phillip Carlisle. Asso. engr. Westinghouse Electric Corp., Glen Burnie, Md., 1965-67; rotating med. intern Kansas U. Med. Center, 1970-71; resident in gen. surgery U. Md. Hosp., 1971-72; resident in gen. surgery Washington Hosp. Center, 1972-76, chief resident, 1975-76; resident in surg. oncology and endoscopy Roswell Park Meml. Inst., 1976-78; emergency room physician South Haven (Mich.) Community Hosp., 1978; practice medicine, specializing in gen. surgery, endoscopy and surg. oncology, Beatrice, Nebr., 1978—; mem. attending staff Luth. Hosp., Beatrice Community Hosp., 1978—. Served to capt. Army N.G., 1971-77. Am. Cancer Soc. surg. fellow, 1978; diplomate Am. Bd. Surgery. Fellow Am. Soc. Gastrointestinal Endoscopy; mem. Am. Coll. Emergency Physicians, AMA. Roman Catholic. Club: Library of Science. Office: 1216 S 8th St Beatrice NE 68310

MIDDOUGH, WILLIAM VANCE, engring. exec.; b. Cleve., July 30, 1917; s. LeRoy Case and Cecilia (Loop) M.; B.S., Case Sch. Applied Sci., 1939; postgrad. Case Inst. Tech., 1941-42; m. Elisabeth June Heick, Sept. 5, 1942; children—Beverly Timothy, Daniel. Elec. supr. Arthur G. McKee & Co., 1940-47; head steel mill. elec. div. Osborn Engring. Co., Cleve., 1947-50; elec. cons. Lake Shore Electric Corp., Bedford, Ohio, 1950-51; chmn. bd. W. Vance Middough & Assos., Cleve., 1951—; v.p. Umbrella Heater Co.; dir. Technical Facilities Corp., Internat. Ventures Mgmt. Mem. Am. Inst. E.E., Soc. Naval Architects and Marine Engrs., Assn. Iron and Steel Engrs., Ohio Soc. Profl. Engrs., Eta Kappa Nu. Clubs: Propeller of U.S., Cleve. Athletic (Cleve.). Home: 3179 Ludlow Rd Shaker Heights OH 44120 Office: 1367 E 6th St Cleveland OH 44114

MIDGLEY, WESLEY RONALD, civil engr.; b. Endicott, N.Y., Sept. 9, 1923; s. Cecil Wilmer and Laura May M.; B.S., Rensselaer Poly. Inst., 1951, M.S., 1952; m. Cecile C. Walker, June 18, 1948; children—Cynthia, John, Ronald. Head structural testing sect. U.S. Steel Corp., Monroeville, Pa., 1960-63; staff engr. Avco Space Systems Co., Lowell, Mass., 1963-69; mgr. engring. Republic Steel Corp., Youngstown, Ohio, 1969-78; prin. Midgley-Clauer Assos., Youngstown, 1978—; mem. faculty Carnegie Inst., 1958-60, Youngstown State U., 1978—. Sec., Northernpike Civic Assn., Monroeville, 1959-63. Served with U.S. Army, 1943-46; CBI. Mem. ASCE, Rack Mfrs. Assn. (chmn. specification com. 1974-78). Republican. Lutheran. Club: Kiwanis. Office: 860 Boardman Canfield Rd Youngstown OH 44512

MIDHA, DEEPAK, surgeon; b. Jamshedpur, India, Oct. 10, 1939; came to U.S., 1969, naturalized, 1976; s. Soshil Chander and Kaushalya M.; M.B., B.S., Prince of Wales Med. Coll., 1963; M.S., Patna U., India, 1967; m. Gillian A. Baxter, Feb. 27, 1971; children—Sonita, Kiran, Anil. Rotating intern Orange (N.J.) Meml. Hosp., 1969-70, resident in surgery, 1970-73; sr. resident in surgery Huron Rd. Hosp., Cleve., 1973-74; practice medicine specializing in surgery, Creston, Iowa; mem. staffs Greater Community Hosp. Fellow Royal Coll. Surgeons (Can.), Internat. Coll. Surgeons, A.C.S., Am. Soc. Abdominal Surgeons; mem. AMA, Iowa Med. Assn., Union County Med. Assn. Democrat. Hindu. Club: Rotary. Home: Rural Route 4 Creston IA 50801 Office: Creston Medical Clinic Creston IA 50801

MIECHUR, THOMAS FRANK, union ofcl.; b. Martins Creek, Pa., Jan. 25, 1923; s. Adam and Sophia (Buczek) M.; student Princeton, 1943-44; m. Lorraine Wesolowski, Oct. 19, 1957. Dist. rep. United Cement, Lime and Gypsum Workers Internat. Union, Easton, Pa., 1957-59, asst. to pres., Chgo., 1959-71, pres., 1971—; mem. gen. bd. AFL-CIO, exec. bd. indsl. union dept., maritime trades dept., v.p. union label and service trades dept. Served with AUS, 1943-45. Mem. Indsl. Relations Research Assn., Chgo. Council Fgn. Relations, Smithsonian Assos., Acad. Polit. Sci. Democrat. Roman Catholic. K.C. Club: Moose. Home: 141 S Iroquois Trail Wood Dale IL 60191 Office: 7830 W Lawrence Ave Norridge IL 60656

MIESS, MARTIN MICHAEL, educator; b. Bistritz, Romania, Oct. 16, 1926; came to U.S., 1952, naturalized, 1957; s. Johann and Maria (Gross) M.; Ph.D., U. Innsbruck (Austria), 1952. Instr. German, Berlitz Lang. Sch., Chgo., 1952-54; instr. German, Army Lang. Sch., Monterey, Calif., 1955-56; prof. German, Eastern Ill. U., Charleston, 1956—, chmn. dept. fgn. langs., 1962-76. Mem. Am. Assn. Tchrs. German, Internat. Linguistic Soc., Internat. Dialictology Soc., Pedagogical Seminar for Germanic Philology, Arbeitskreis fur Siebenburgische Landeskunde, Heidelberg. Author: Die Jot-Gemeinden im mittleren Siebenburgen, 1952; Dialektgeographische Studien in Siebenburgen, 1954; Wortmachen in Rode, 1969; Im Regenbogen, 1975. Home: 2750 Whippoorwill Dr Charleston IL 61920 Office: Eastern Ill U Charleston IL 61920

MIFSUD, PAUL CHARLES, banker; b. N.Y.C., Jan. 25, 1947; s. Charles John and Florence Evelyn (Verity) M.; B.B.A. in Mgmt., Angelo State U., 1970; postgrad. Pace U., 1971-72; M.B.A. with honors in Organizational Behavior, Case Western Res. U., 1975; m. Brenda Kay Blasingame, Oct. 5, 1968; children—Paula, Charles, Anthony. Office asst., counselor, recreation worker Boy's Athletic League, N.Y.C., 1960-65; tax cons., numismatic dealer, San Angelo, Tex., 1968-72; with Irving Trust Co., N.Y.C., 1970-72, mgr. brokers loans dept., 1972; asst. cashier Union Commerce Bank, Cleve., 1972-73, asst. v.p., 1973-77, v.p. adminstrn., 1977-81; exec. v.p. G.S. Voinovich Inc., 1981—; co-owner Mifsud & Assos., ops. and fin. cons., 1975—. Co-chmn. Berea (Ohio) Citizens Civic Center Com., 1975; chmn. bd. trustees Woodvale Union Cemetery, 1978—; mem. exec. bd. Berea Republican Orgn., 1972—; mem. exec. com. Cuyahoga County Rep. Orgn., 1978—; mem. city council City of Berea, 1977—. Served with USAF, 1966-70. Named Outstanding Young Man of Am., U.S. Jaycees, 1978, 80. Mem. Am. Bankers Assn., Am. Mgmt. Assn., Bank Adminstrn. Inst., Am. Inst. Banking, Adminstrv. Mgmt. Soc., Greater Cleve. Growth Assn., Berea Hist. Soc., Citizens League, Nat. Arbor Day Found., Pvt. Industry Council, Beta Gamma Sigma. Roman Catholic. Club: Rotary (Berea). Office: Union Commerce Bank 917 Euclid Ave Cleveland OH 44115

MIGALA, LUCYNA, radio sta. exec.; b. Krakow, Poland, May 22, 1944; d. Joseph and Estelle (Suwala) M.; came to U.S., 1947, naturalized, 1955; student Loyola U., Chgo., 1962-63, Chicago Conservatory of Music, 1963-70; B.S. in Journalism, Northwestern U., 1966; m. Kazimierz Wieclaw, Nov. 27, 1971 (div. Jan. 1978). Radio announcer, producer sta. WOPA, Oak Park, Ill., 1963-66; writer, reporter, producer NBC news, Chgo., 1966-69, 1969-71, producer NBC local news, Washington, 1969; producer, coordinator NBC network news, Cleve., 1971-78, field producer, Chgo., 1978-79; v.p. Migala Communications Corp., 1979—; program dir., on-air personality Sta. WCEV, Cicero, Ill., 1979—; lectr. City Colls. Chgo., 1981. Soloist, mgr. Lira Singers, Chgo., 1965—; mem., chmn. various cultural coms. Polish Am. Congress, 1970—; bd. dirs. Nationalities Services Center, Cleve., 1973-78; bd. dirs., v.p. Cicero-Berwyn Fine Arts Council, Cicero, Ill. Washington Journalism Center fellow, spring 1969. Office: Sta WCEV 5356 W Belmont Ave Chicago IL 60641

MIHALCIK, ALBERT JAMES, hosp. supply co. exec.; b. Perth Amboy, N.J., Oct. 21, 1943; s. Michael and Anna (Rybnicky) M.; m. Wendy Lou Aaroe, Feb. 14, 1980; children—James John, Lisa Ann. Sr. x-ray technician, head cardiovascular evaluation lab Perth Amboy (N.J.) Gen. Hosp., 1962-69; office mgr., physician's asst. Drs. Harris, Markman and Grubman, Perth Amboy, 1969-78; mgr. A.C.M.I. Endoscopy div. Am. Hosp. Supply Co., Des Plaines, Ill., 1978—. Cert. x-ray technician; cert. urology technician. Mem. Am. Urology Assn. Allied. Roman Catholic. Home: 51 Stanton Ct Schaumburg IL 60194 Office: 2360 E Devon Suite 1013 Des Plaines IL 60018

MIHALIK, EMIL JOHN, bishop; b. Pitts., Feb. 7, 1920; s. William and Mary (Jubic) M.; student Catholic Inst. Pitts., 1938-40, St. Procopius Sem., 1940-45. Ordained priest Roman Catholic Ch., 1945, bishop, 1969; pastor Sts. Peter and Paul Chs., Struthers, Ohio, 1945-55, Endicot, N.Y., 1955-61, St. Thomas Ch., Rahway, N.J., 1961-69; dir. vocations Diocese of Passaic, mem. Diocesan Tribunal, chancellor of Diocese, 1968; mem. Diocesan Bd. Consultors, 1968;

bishop of Parma, Ohio, 1969—. Mem. Nat. Ohio confs. Cath. bishops. Home: 1900 Carlton Rd Parma OH 44134*

MIHALO, ROBERT MATTHEW, anesthesiologist; b. Stamford, Conn., July 9, 1940; s. John Joseph and Elizabeth Mary (Laszlo) M.; B.S., Poly. Inst. Bklyn., 1962; M.D., Wayne State U., 1972; m. May 21, 1972. Intern, Providence Hosp., Southfield, Mich., 1972-73, resident in anesthesia, 1973-75, staff anesthesiologist, 1975—. Served with U.S. Army, 1962-65, USAFR, 1975—. Decorated Air Force Commendation medal. Diplomate Am. Bd. Anesthesiology. Fellow Am. Coll. Anesthesiologists; mem. Aerospace Med. Soc., Soc. U.S. Air Force Flight Surgeons, AMA, Mich. Med. Soc., Am. Legion. Republican. Roman Catholic. Contbr. articles to profl. jours. Home: 4210 W Newland St West Bloomfield MI 48033 Office: 16001 W Nine Mile Rd Southfield MI 48075

MIILLER, VICTOR LEROY, ins. co. exec.; b. Laurel, Iowa, Apr. 26, 1919; s. Henry F. and Lydia H. (Sash) M.; A.A., Marshalltown (Iowa) Community Coll., 1939; m. Carol Alice Smeltzer, Apr. 19, 1941; children—Carolyn S. Stidwell, Mary F. Orcutt, Victor L., Jane Elizabeth. Mgmt. trainee Swift & Co., Marshalltown, 1940-41; in retail and wholesale bus., Laurel, Gladbrook, and Marshalltown, 1946-57; agt. Penn Mut. Life Ins. Co., Marshalltown, 1957, dist. mgr., 1958, gen. agt., Davenport, Iowa, 1959-70; dir. field devel. Equitable of Iowa, Des Moines, 1970—; career counselor, guest tchr. Grand View Coll., Des Moines, 1976-77. Active ARC, United Fund. Served with U.S. Army, 1942-46. Mem. Des Moines Life Underwriters Assn., Des Moines Gen. Agts. and Mgrs. Assn., Nat. Assn. Life Underwriters (past committeeman), Iowa Gen. Agts. and Mgrs. Assn. (past pres.). Republican. Methodist. Clubs: Masons, Elks. Writer, pub. mgmt. and agt. tng. programs. Home: 1847 NW 80th Pl Des Moines IA 50322 Office: 604 Locust St Des Moines IA 50306

MIKALONIS, STANLEY JOHN, JR., mktg. exec.; b. Wilkes-Barre, Pa., Jan. 1, 1940; s. Stanley John and Leona Ann (Arsavage) M.; B.B.A., Temple U., 1961, M.B.A., 1962; m. Jane Ann Zelinsky, Nov. 9, 1963; children—Karen Maria, Lori Ann, Stanley John III. Regional sales mgr. N.E. region Hertz Corp., truck div., 1966-74; dir. transp. Potomac Electric Power Co., Washington, 1974-78; mktg. ops. mgr. Itel Corp., Balt., 1978-79; mktg. mgr. Midwest region Saunders Leasing System, Inc., Columbus, Ohio, 1979—. Served with U.S. Army, 1962. Mem. Edison Electric Inst. (co-chmn. subcom.), Southeastern Electric Exchange (sec. transp. com.), Soc. Automotive Engrs., Electric Utility Fleet Mgrs. Conf., Sales and Mktg. Execs. Republican. Roman Catholic. Clubs: K.C., Optimist (dep. lt. gov., v.p. 1961, life). Home: 5336 Aryshire Dr Dublin OH 43017 Office: 1865 Fountain Square Ct Columbus OH 43224

MIKESELL, SHARELL LEE, research and product devel. co. exec.; b. Coshocton, Ohio, Nov. 24, 1943; s. Forrest and Wilma Madeline (Axline) M.; A.B., Olivet Nazarene Coll., Kankakee, Ill., 1965; M.S., Ohio State U., 1968; Ph.D. (NDEA fellow), U. Akron, 1971. Chemist, Edmont-Wilson Co., Coshocton, Ohio, 1965; polymer chemist Gen. Electric Co., Coshocton, 1971-72, project mgr. polyester glass, 1972-74, mgr. market devel., 1974, mgr. indsl. product devel., 1975; lab. mgr. textile systems Owens-Corning Fiberglas, Granville, Ohio, 1976-78, research dir. Textile Operating div./fabric structures, 1978—. Mem. Am. Chem. Soc., Am. Assn. Textile Chemists and Colorists. Office: Owens-Corning Fiberglas Corp Technical Center Granville OH 43023

MIKHAIL, GEORGE RIZK, dermatologist, clin. adminstr.; b. Cairo, Egypt, Dec. 6, 1914; s. Rizk and Chafikah (Girgis) M.; M.B., B.Ch., Cairo U., 1939; M.S. in Pathology (Univ. research fellow), Wayne State U., 1963; m. Elizabeth Noemie Duranti, May 19, 1955; children—Michael, Marianne. Practice medicine specializing in dermatology, Cairo, 1939-43; dermatologist, Ministry Pub. Health, Port Said, Egypt, 1943-61; dermatologist Henry Ford Hosp., Detroit, 1963—, head, chemosurgery sect., 1969—, mem. teaching cons. staff, dept. dermatology, 1963—; clin. asso. prof. dermatology U. Mich. Sch. Medicine, 1978—. Diplomate Am. Bd. Dermatology, also Sub-board Dermatopathology. Fellow Am. Acad. Dermatology, Am. Soc. Dermatopathology, Am. Coll. Chemosurgery (sec.-treas. 1975-77, pres. 1978-79); mem. Am. Dermatol. Assn., Mich. Dermatol. Soc. (pres. 1981—). Republican. Coptic Orthodox. Contbr. articles to med. jours. and chpts. to books. Office: Henry Ford Hosp 2799 W Grand Blvd Detroit MI 48202

MIKHAIL, RAMZY NAGUIB, surgeon; b. Cairo, Egypt, Mar. 19, 1933; s. Naguib Nicolas and Angele (Youssef) M.; came to U.S., 1959, naturalized, 1972; Baccalaureate in Scis., Coll. Ste. Famille, Cairo, 1950; M.B., Ch.B., Ain-Shams U., Cairo, 1957; m. Maryse Doss, Apr. 14, 1957; children—Francis, Nagwa, Laila, John. Sr. staff surgeon Am. Mission Hosp., Tanta, Egypt, 1965-67; surgeon Grant (Mich.) Community Hosp., 1968-70; practice medicine specializing in colon rectal surgery with spl. interest in colonscopic techniques, Toledo, Ohio, 1970—; chief, sect. colon rectal surgery, St. Vincents Hosp. Med. Center, Toledo, 1973-80; vice-chief sect. colon and rectal surgery St. Luke's Hosp., Maumee, Ohio, 1975—; active staff Toledo Hosp.; asso. staff Flower Hosp., Sylvania, Ohio; clin. asso. surgery, Med. Coll. Ohio, Toledo, 1971—. Diplomate Am. Bd. Surgery, Am. Bd. Colon Rectal Surgery. Fellow A.C.S., Internat. Coll. Surgeons, Am. Soc. Colon Rectal Surgeons, Am. Soc. Gastrointestinal Endoscopy; AMA, Ohio Med. Assn., Toledo and Lucas County Acad. Medicine.

MIKRUT, JOHN JOSEPH, JR., labor arbitrator, educator; b. Erie, Pa., Mar. 23, 1944; s. John Joseph and Helen Frances (Dorobiala) M.; B.S., Edinboro Coll., 1966; postgrad. U. Mass., 1966-68; Ed.D., U. Mo., Columbia, 1976; m. Lois Ann Leonard, Aug. 26, 1968. Intern edn. dept. United Steelworkers Am., Pitts., 1967-68; instr. labor studies Pa. State U., 1968-69; labor specialist, asso. prof. labor edn. U. Mo., Columbia, 1969—; labor arbitrator Nat. Ry. Adjustment Bd.; mem. labor arbitration panels Fed. Mediation Conciliation Service, Nat. Mediation Bd., Am. Arbitration Assn. Chmn., City of Columbia Personnel Adv. Bd., 1976—; chmn. Columbia Mayor's Spl. Labor Negotiations Rev. Com. Mem. Soc. Profls. Dispute Resolution, Iowa Pub. Employee Relations Bd., Univ. and Coll. Labor Edn. Assn., Indsl. Relations and Research Assn. Contbr. articles to profl. jours. Home: 2236 Country Ln Columbia MO 65201 Office: Dept Labor Edn Univ MO Columbia MO 65211

MIKSCH, RICHARD ALAN, sales exec.; b. Bellefontaine, Ohio, Dec. 2, 1952; s. Donald Eugene and Betti Jo M.; E.E., Wittenberg U., 1975; m. Therese Jean Ingram, June 5, 1970; children—David, Gayle. Supr. ITE, Bellefontaine, 1971-74; mgr. Cassano's Pizza & Seafood, Russells Point, Ohio, 1974-77; sales mgr. Zettler Software, Inc., Columbus, Ohio, 1977—. Recipient 15 awards of excellence Zettler Software, Inc., 1977—. Mem. Am. Mgmt. Assn., Profl. Selling, Inst. Ins. Research, Sales Mgrs. Bull., Selling Knacks. Clubs: Masons, Order Eastern Star. Home: 2490 Nottingham Rd Columbus OH 43221 Office: 300 E Wilson Bridge Rd Columbus OH 43085

MIKULKA, THOMAS JOHN, food services adminstr.; b. Lansford, Pa., Dec. 9, 1923; A.B., Washburn U., 1954; children—Thomas Paul, Phyllis Nickelson. Mem. dept. food service St. Lukes Hosp., N.Y.C., 1941-46; chef Hotel Jayhawk, Topeka, 1946; asst. dir. food services Menninger Found., Topeka, 1946-62, dir., 1962—. Bd. dirs. Topeka and N.E. Kans. Assn. Better Bus. Bur. Served with USAAF, 1942-45. Recipient City of Topeka Mayor's Commendation, 1971. Fellow Health Care Food Service Adminstrs.; mem. Topeka Restaurant and Purveyors Assn. (pres. 1969, dir. 1970—), Am. Soc. Hosp. Food Service Adminstrs. Democrat. Roman Catholic. Club: Moose. Home: 2940 Gage St Topeka KS 66614 Office: PO Box 829 Topeka KS 66601

MIKUTA, CHARLES F., banker; b. Chgo., Jan. 18, 1926; s. Charles F. and Augusta (Hess) M.; student U. Ill., 1943, Elmhurst Coll., 1947-48; B.S., Northwestern U., 1950; m. Rita M. Smith, Apr. 28, 1951; children—Thomas C., Jane C., Beth A., Laura E. Asst. advt. mgr. Ekco Products Co., Chgo., 1950-52; nat. sales promotion mgr. Borg-Warner Corp., Chgo., 1952-55; account supr. Russell M. Seeds Agy., Chgo., 1955-57; v.p., account supr. Kenyon & Eckhardt, Inc., Chgo., 1957-60; sr. v.p., gen. mgr. Chgo. office, dir. Compton Advt., Inc., Chgo., 1960-71; v.p., mgmt. supr. Clinton E. Frank, Inc., Chgo., 1971-74; v.p., head corp. communications dept. No. Trust Co., Chgo., 1975—. Served with AUS, 1944-46. Mem. Public Relations Soc. Am., Am. Mgmt. Assn., Am. Mktg. Assn., Am. Bankers Assn., Conf. Bd., Bank Mktg. Assn. Clubs: Inverness Golf, Chgo. Athletic Assn. Office: 50 S La Salle St Chicago IL 60675

MIKVA, ABNER JOSEPH, judge, former congressman, educator; b. Milw., Jan. 21, 1926; s. Henry Abraham and Ida (Fishman) M.; J.D. cum laude, U. Chgo., 1951; LL.D., Chgo. Coll. Osteo. Medicine, 1971, U. Ill., 1980; m. Zoe Wise, Sept. 19, 1948; children—Mary, Laurie, Rachel. Admitted to Ill. bar, 1951; law clk. to U.S. Supreme Ct. Justice Sherman Minton, 1951; partner firm Devoe, Shadur, Mikva & Plotkin, Chgo., 1952-68, D'Ancona, Pflaum, Wyatt & Riskind, 1973-74; faculty Northwestern U. Law Sch., Chgo., 1973-75; mem. Ill. Gen. Assembly from 23d Dist., 1956-66; mem. 91st-92d congresses, 2d Dist. Ill. 94th-96th congresses from 10th Dist. Ill. circuit judge U.S. Ct. of Appeals, Washington, 1979—. Chmn. Ill. Bd. Ethics, 1973. Served with USAAF, World War II. Recipient Page One award Chgo. Newspaper Guild, 1964; Best Legislator award Ind. Voters Ill., 1956-66; Clarence Darrow Humanitarian award for public service in Darrow tradition, 1963; Excellence in Politics award Com. on Ill. Govt., 1973; Congressman of Yr. award Ill. Speech and Hearing Assn., 1978; spl. award Nat. Fedn. Ind. Bus., 1978; award of merit Nat. Council Sr. Citizens, 1978; named One of Ten Outstanding Young Men in Chgo., Jr. Assn. Commerce and Industry, 1961. Mem. Am. (council sect. individual rights and responsibilities 1973-77, council sect. litigation 1975-76), Chgo. (bd. mgrs. 1962-64) bar assns., ACLU, Phi Beta Kappa, Order of Coif. Democrat. Home: 442 New Jersey Ave SE Washington DC 20003 Office: US Courthouse 3d and Constitution Washington DC 20001

MILAM, EVELYN LOUISE, coll. pres.; b. Memphis, Tex., Feb. 12, 1921; d. John K. and Bessie Lee (Harper) M.; B.A., W. Tex. State U., 1942; M.A., Tex. Tech. U., 1951; Ph.D., U. Wyo., 1968. Censor, bus. mail Civil Service, San Antonio, Tex., 1942-43; high sch. tchr. Hereford (Tex.) and Perryton (Tex.) ind. sch. dists., 1943-47; jr. high registrar-counselor Pampa (Tex.) ind. Sch. Dist., 1947-50; high sch. counselor, coordinator guidance, 1951-62; admissions counselor, dir. admissions and fin. aid Austin Coll., Sherman, Tex., 1962-68, asso. prof., 1968-74, prof. edn. and psychology, 1974; pres. Cottey Coll., Nevada, Mo., 1974—. Pres., Top 'O Tex. Credit Unions, 1960-61. Recipient Distinguished Alumnus award W. Tex. State U., 1979-80, U. Wyo., 1981. Mem. Nat. Assn. Ind. Colls. and Univs., Am. Psychol. Assn., Am. Personnel and Guidance Assn., AAUW, Nevada-Vernon County C. of C. (bd. dirs. 1975-78), Delta Kappa Gamma (M. Margaret Stroh internat. scholarship 1967-68), Phi Kappa Phi. Home: PO Box 252 Nevada MO 64772 Office: Cottey Coll Office Pres Nevada MO 64772

MILANO, NICHOLAS PHILLIP, metallurgist; b. Milw., July 31, 1922; s. Lucas and Sarah (LaPorte) M.; student Ohio U., 1943-44; B.S. in Mech. Engring., Marquette U., 1950; M.S. in Metallurgy, U. Wis., 1954; m. Maxine R. Kulas, May 28, 1949; children—Dean, Paul, Mark, Steven, Phillip. Tool making apprentice Durant Mfg. Co., Milw., 1940-42; accounting clerk Internat. Harvester Co., Milw., 1942-43, cost accountant, 1946-48, asst. chief metallurgist, 1951-61, chief metallurgist, 1961-64, metals engr., Hinsdale, Ill., 1964-68, chief engr. metals, 1968-71; dir. mfg. Ill. Gear-Wallace Murray Corp., Chgo., 1971-73, dir. metallurgy, 1974—; cons. gear heat treat problems, Eng., France, Germany, 1965, 69. Water safety instr., disaster training instr., first aid instr. Am. Red Cross, 1946-75. Served with U.S. Army, 1943-46. Recipient Engring. Disting. Service citation U. Wis., 1979. Fellow Am. Soc. Metals (pres. 1977-78), Soc. Automotive Engrs. (certificate appreciation 1972), ASTM, Am. Welding Soc., Soc. Mfg. Engrs. Roman Catholic. Club: K.C. Contbr. articles on carburizing and carbonitriding to profl. jours. Home: 292 Oak St Glen Ellyn IL 60137 Office: 2108 N Natchez Ave Chicago IL 60635

MILES, FRANCES JANE LYON, interior designer; b. Cleve., July 4, 1919; d. Albert Harvey and Bertha Alma (Phillips) Lyon; student U. Ill., 1937-39; B.S., Ind. State U., 1944; postgrad. U. Ill., 1963; m. Harold Wayne Miles, Dec. 6, 1941; children—Karin Miles Ariens, Eric Lyon, Gregory Foster. Free-lance color cons., 1954-65; founder interior design firm, 1965, inc., 1969, owner, pres. Jane Miles, Inc., Beverly Shores, Ind., 1969—; art supt., tchr., jr. and sr. high schs., Chesterton, Ind., 1962; adj. prof. jr./sr. design Ind. State U., Terre Haute; v.p. Miles, Inc., Hammond, Ind., Studio Arts, Inc., Indpls. Vice pres. bd. Nagoille Sch. of Sculpture, Lewis U., Glen Ellyn, Ill., 1977-80. Mem. Kappa Pi, Kappa Delta Pi, Alpha Chi Omega. Home: 21 Ridge Dr Dune Acres Chesterton IN 46304 Office: Jane Miles Inc US Hwy 12 Beverly Shores IN 46301

MILES, LARRY DEWAYNE, fin. broker; b. Evansville, Ind., Dec. 12, 1947; s. O. Ray and Bonnie Mae Miles; student U. Evansville, 1965-66, Ind. U., 1967-69, Ball State U., Muncie, Ind., 1969-71; m. Barbara Ann Baumeister, June 26, 1976; children—Ryan Michael, Meredith Ann. Ins. agt., 1972-75; v.p. Am. Mktg. Assos., Indpls., 1975-78; pres., chmn. bd. Fin. Brokers Exchange, Inc., Indpls., 1978—; pres. FBE Fin. Corp., Indpls., 1980—. Mem. Internat. Assn. Fin. Planners, Internat. Entrepreneurs Assn., Nat. Assn. Fin. Cons., Nat. Alliance Bus. Brokers. Republican. Home: 5220 Ladywood Dr Indianapolis IN 46226 Office: 1111 E 54th St Indianapolis IN 46220

MILES, RICHARD ALFRED, II, controller; b. Bethesda, Md., Feb. 7, 1949; s. Richard Alfred and Ann Susan (Lindsay) M.; student Old Dominion Coll., 1966-68; B.B.A. in Acctg., Augusta Coll., 1974; m. Linda Gail Matthews, Feb. 14, 1970; children—Douglas Wayne, Lori Jean. Sr. auditor Arthur Andersen & Co., Atlanta, 1974-77; sr. internal auditor Fuqua Industries, Inc., Atlanta, 1977-78; corp. controller Fuqua Metals subs. Fuqua Industries, Chgo., 1978-80; controller Trans Union Leasing Corp., Chgo., 1980—, v.p., controller, 1981—. Vice pres. Buffalo Grove Recreation Assn., 1979—. Served to 1st lt., AUS, 1968-71. C.P.A., Ga., Ill. Mem. Am. Assn. Equipment Lessors, Am. Inst. C.P.A.s, Ill. Soc. C.P.A.s. Presbyterian. Home: 1419 Mill Creek Dr Buffalo Grove IL 60090 Office: 111 W Jackson Blvd Chicago IL 60604

MILES, WENDELL A., fed. judge; b. Holland, Mich., Apr. 17, 1916; s. Fred T. and Dena Del (Alverson) M.; A.B., Hope Coll., 1938; M.A., U. Wyo., 1939; J.D., U. Mich., 1942; m. Mariette Bruckert, June 8, 1946; children—Lorraine Miles Rector, Michelle Miles Kopinski, Thomas Paul. Admitted to Mich. bar; partner firm Miles & Miles, Holland, 1948-53, Miles, Mika, Meyers, Beckett & Jones, Grand Rapids, Mich., 1961-70; pros. atty. County of Ottawa (Mich.), 1949-53; U.S. dist. atty. Western Dist. Mich., 1953-60, U.S. dist. judge, 1974—, chief judge, 1979—; circuit judge 20th Jud. Circuit Ct. Mich., 1970-74; instr. Hope Coll., 1948-53, adj. prof., 1981—; instr. Am. Inst. Banking, 1953-60; mem. Mich. Higher Edn. Commn., 1978—. Pres., Holland Bd. Edn., 1952-63. Served to capt. U.S. Army, 1942-47. Fellow Am. Bar Assn.; mem. Mich., Fed., Ottawa County bar assns., Am. Judicature Soc. Clubs: Rotary, Torch, Masons. Office: US Dist Ct 482 Fed Bldg 110 Michigan St NW Grand Rapids MI 49503

MILESTONE, WAYNE DONALD, mech. engr.; b. Darlington, Wis., Apr. 27, 1935; s. Arthur E. and Opal M.; B.M.E., Ohio State U., 1959, M.S., 1960, Ph.D., 1966; m. Mary V. Hughes, Dec. 28, 1970; children—Sarah, David. Research asso. mech. engring. Ohio State U., Columbus, 1960-66; asst. prof. mech. engring. U. Wis.-Madison, 1966-71, asso. prof., 1971—; engring. specialist Pratt & Whitney Aircraft, West Palm Beach, Fla.; cons. in field. Mem. Spl. Com. on Product Liability, Wis. Legis. Council, 1977-80; adv. com. amusement rides and devices Wis. Dept. Industry, Labor and Human Relations, 1976—. Recipient Excellence in Teaching award U. Wis., 1971, named Outstanding Mech. Engring. Prof., 1976, 81; registered profl. engr., Ohio. Mem. ASME (Centennial medal 1980), ASTM, Am. Soc. Engring. Edn., Sigma Xi, Tau Beta Pi, Pi Tau Sigma. Lutheran. Contbr. articles to tech. publs. Home: 4147 Iroquois Dr Madison WI 53711 Office: U Wis 1513 University Ave Madison WI 53706

MILETICH, IVO, library scientist, bibliographer; b. Pucisca, Yugoslavia, Apr. 18, 1936; came to U.S., 1966, naturalized, 1972; s. Josip and Mandina (Bagic) M.; A.B., Acad. Edn., Split, Yugoslavia, 1960; A.M. in History, U. Skopje, Macedonia, Yugoslavia, 1966; cert. English Inst., 1969; M.A. in Library Sci., Rosary Coll., River Forest, Ill., 1971; m. Mira Pilja, Mar. 11, 1967; children—George-Edward, Marina. Tchr., Yugoslavia, 1959-65; asst. to bibliographer Slavic lang., lit. Harper and Regenstein Library, U. Chgo., 1967-71; bibliographer Old Dominion U., Norfolk, Va., 1971-74; tchr. Croatian lang. co-edn. div. YMCA, Chgo., 1969-71, 74—; asst. prof. library sci., bibliographer, dept. head Chgo. State U., 1974—; tchr. Croatian lang. Berlitz Sch. Langs., Chgo., 1980—; translator English, Croatian, Serbian, Macedonian, Bulgarian, Slovene, lit., sci. and legal documents, interpreter, 1974—; lectr. S. Slavonic langs., hist., culture Balkan states, transl. techniques. Mem. Am. Translators Assn., Am. Assn. Linguists, Beta Phi Mu. Contbr. articles to profl. jours. Home: 618 Exchange Ave Calumet City IL 60409 Office: Room E-203F Chgo State U 95th St at King Dr Chicago IL 60628

MILICH, RICHARD SAMUEL, psychologist; b. N.Y.C., June 26, 1949; s. Lester Julien and Helen (Strauss) M.; B.A., Columbia U., 1971; Ph.D., Washington U., 1976. Post-doctoral research asst. dept. psychiatry U. Iowa, Iowa City, 1976-77, research asst., 1977-79, research scientist, 1979—. Set cons. Iowa City Community Theater, 1977—. NIMH grantee, 1979-84. Mem. Am. Psychol. Assn., Soc. Pediatric Psychology. Club: U. Iowa Soccer (treas. 1977-79). Home: 1019 Rider St Iowa City IA 52240 Office: Dept Psychiatry U Iowa Iowa City IA 52242

MILLAR, GORDON HALSTEAD, farm equipment co. exec.; b. Newark, Nov. 28, 1923; s. George Halstead and Dill E. (McMullen) M.; B.M.E., U. Detroit, 1949, D.Sc. (hon.), 1977; Ph.D., U. Wis., 1952; m. Virginia M. Jedryczka, Aug. 24, 1957; children—George B., Kathryn M., Juliett S., John, James. With Ford Motor Co., Dearborn, Mich., 1952-57; engring. mgr. Meriam Instrument Co., Cleve., 1957-59; dir. new products McCulloch Corp., Los Angeles, 1959-63; dir. research Deere & Co., Moline, Ill., 1963-69; asst. gen. mgr. John Deere Waterloo (Iowa) Tractor Works, 1969-71; with Deere & Co., Moline, 1971-72, v.p. engring., 1972—. Gen. chmn. United Way of Rock Island and Scott Counties, Ill., 1975; gen. indsl. adv. bd. U. Detroit, 1976—; chmn. bd. regents Ill. State Colls. and Univs., 1965-69; bd. dirs. Boy Scouts Am., Moline, 1973-77. Served with U.S. Army, 1942-46. Decorated Purple Heart; recipient Alumnus of Year award U. Detroit, 1976. Fellow Soc. Automotive Engrs.; mem. Nat. Acad. Engring., ASME, Am. Soc. Agrl. Engrs., N.Y. Acad. Sci., Engrs. Joint Council, Indsl. Research Inst., Engring. Soc. Detroit (mem. coll. of fellows), Ill. Soc. Profl. Engrs., Ill. Better Govt. Assn., Am. Nat. Metric Council, Sigma Xi. Club: Quiet Birdmen. Contbr. articles to profl. jours.; patentee in field. Office: John Deere Rd Moline IL 61265

MILLARD, JOSEPH NESTER, SR., banker; b. St. Louis, May 18, 1937; s. Francis Earl and Dorothy (Nester) M.; B.S., Ill. Coll., 1959; m. Doris Donna, Oct. 21, 1961; children—Joseph Nester, Elizabeth Ann. Supt., Obear Nester Glass Co., East St. Louis, Ill., 1960-70; chmn. Bankers Trust Co. Belleville, Ill., 1970—; dir. Bankers Trust Co. Treas., Okaw Valley council Boy Scouts Am., 1971—; merit commr. St. Clair County, Ill., 1972—; trustee Blessed Sacrament Roman Catholic Ch., Belleville, 1971-81. Served with C.E., AUS, 1959-60. Mem. Assn. Modern Banking, Am. Inst. Banking, Belleville C. of C. Club: St. Clair Country (past pres.). Home: 76 Country Club Pl Belleville IL 62223 Office: 6400 W Main St Belleville IL 62223

MILLARD, KEN MARTIN, automotive parts co. exec.; b. Omaha, May 1, 1928; s. Martin V. and Louisa L. Millard; student U. Nebr., Omaha, 1948, Alexander Hamilton Inst., 1964; m. Shirley Meth, Aug. 18, 1928; children—Deborah, Scott. Sales rep. B.F. Goodrich Co., 1950-54; v.p. Hook-Millard Tire Co., Omaha, 1954-59; dist. mgr. Dunlop Tire Co., Omaha, 1959-63; exec. v.p. Carl A. Anderson Co., Omaha, 1963-77; owner Art's Auto Supply, Omaha, 1977—; pres., owner Millard's Inc., Omaha, 1977—; partner Slutsky Auto Parts Co., Omaha, 1977—; mem. Auto Exhaust Adv. Council, 1972, 74, 78, Automotive-Rubber Adv. Council, 1978—. Deacon, Jaynes St. Community Ch., 1954—, chmn. ch. bd., 1980. Served with AUS, 1945-47. Named to Auto Service Hall of Fame, 1974. Mem. Omaha C. of C., Automotive Service Industry Am., Automotive Warehouse Dist. Am., Nebr. Automotive Assn. Republican. Clubs: Shriners, Optimists. Home: 712 Leawood Dr Omaha NE 68154 Office: 1011 Mason St Omaha NE 68108

MILLER, ALVIN V., state senator; b. Clear Lake, Iowa, Feb. 2, 1921; s. Claude O. and Cora M.; grad. high sch.; m. Frances Elizabeth Sorensen, 1943; children—Marlene, Marcia, Danny. Former retail chem. firm exec.; ins. agt., farmer, Ventura, Iowa; now mem. Iowa Senate; dir. Cerro Gordo Mut. Ins. Assn. Mem. Clear Lake C. of C., Farm Bur. Clubs: Lions, Odd Fellows. Office: State Senate State Capitol Des Moines IA 50319*

MILLER, ANN PATRICIA, social worker; b. Ft. Worth, July 24, 1944; d. John Coleman and Ann Miriam (Storm) Radcliffe; A.B., Webster Coll., St. Louis, 1966; M.Ed. in Counseling Edn., U. Mo., St. Louis, 1971; m. Harold James Miller, Jr., Feb. 14, 1981. Social worker St. Louis div. Children's Services, 1966-68, Jewish Center Aged, St. Louis, 1968-71; clin. caseworker St. Louis State Hosp., 1971-72; dir.

social service St. Joseph Hosp., Kirkwood, Mo., 1972—; cons. social worker Clayton House, St. Louis, 1973—; social work cons. St. Sophia Geriatric Center, 1974-75; grad. practicum instr. George Warren Brown Sch. Social Work, Washington U., St. Louis, 1972—, Sch. Social Service, St. Louis U., 1978—, Sch. Social Service, U. Mo., St. Louis, 1980—. Mem. Nat. Assn. Social Workers, Am. Personnel and Guidance Assn., Am. Hosp. Assn. Soc. Hosp. Social Work Dirs. (sec. 1975-77, treas. 1977), Soc. Hosp. Social Work Dirs. Greater St. Louis, Mo. Assn. Social Welfare. Republican. Roman Catholic. Home: 7190 Kingsbury Saint Louis MO 63130 Office: 525 Couch Ave Kirkwood MO 63122

MILLER, BERNARD JOSEPH, JR., advt. exec.; b. Louisville, July 31, 1925; s. Bernard Joseph and Myrtle (Herrington) M.; B.S. in Mktg., Ind. U., 1949; m. Jayne F. Hughes, Aug. 7, 1948 (div. 1970); children—Bernard Joseph III, Jeffrey, Janet, Brian; m. 2d, Brita Naujok, Nov. 24, 1970. Merchandising mgr. Brown-Forman Distilleries Corp., Louisville, 1949-52; advt. dir. Medley Distilling Co., Owensboro, Ky., 1952-55; v.p. Phelps Mfg. Co., Terre Haute, Ind., 1955-60; with Columbian Advt. Inc., Chgo., 1960—, chmn. bd., pres., 1961—; dir. Point-of-Purchase Advt. Inst., N.Y.C. Served with USAF, 1943-46; PTO. Mem. Kappa Sigma. Club: Saddle and Cycle (Chgo.). Home: 1300 N Lake Shore Dr Chicago IL 60610 Office: 155 E Superior St Chicago IL 60611

MILLER, BERT M., public relations exec.; b. Cin., Jan. 26, 1926; s. Hubert W. and Kathryn M. (Mansfield) M.; B.S., U. Cin., 1948; m. Leona Van Houten, May 17, 1962; 1 dau., Lisa. Partner, Lorens and Miller Assos., Cin., 1950-59; co. mgr. Cin. Playhouse in the Park, 1959-61; with Boy Scouts Am., 1961—, with public relations dept., Cin., 1970, dir. public relations, Cleve., 1977—; conf. public relations instr.; stage mgr., producer, various community theaters and summer stock. Bd. dirs. United Way of Greater Cleve.; v.p. Shaker Heights (Ohio) Dance Club, 1980, pres., 1981. Mem. Public Relations Soc. Am., Ad Club, Lambda Chi Alpha. Republican. Episcopalian. Clubs: Communicators, Mid-Day, Chagrin Falls Sq. Dance. Editor The Scouter, 1970-77, The Informer, 1977—. Home: 2512 Kingston Rd Cleveland Heights OH 44118 Office: Boy Scouts Am Scoutway Corner Cleveland OH 44115

MILLER, BETTY LOUISE LEE, nurse; b. Kansas City, Kans., Aug. 9, 1929; d. Gerald Wesley and Elizabeth Louise (Miller) Lee; R.N., Research Hosp. Sch. Nursing, Kansas City, Mo., 1950; student Emporia U., 1978-79; B.A., Ottawa U., 1980; m. Marvin Dale Miller, Oct. 30, 1950; children—Dale Wesley, Cathy Louise, Christine Ann, Lee Marvin. Emergency room nurse, various hosps., Kansas City, Mo., intermittently, 1950-64; public health nurse Kansas City-Wyandotte County (Kans.) Health Dept., 1969-73; nurse Sch. Dist. #500, Kansas City, Kans., 1973—; tchr., cons. in field. Sec. PTA, Welborn Sch., Kansas City, Kans., 1956-58, chaplain, 1957-59, mem. exec. bd., 1973-75; active Boy Scouts Am., 1956-66, Girl Scouts U.S.A., 1957-68. Recipient Den Mothers Tng. award Boy Scouts Am., 1961, Den Mother Nat. Key award, 1963; R.N., Mo., Kans. Mem. Public Health Assn., Bus. and Profl. Women, Research Hosp. Alumni, NEA, Kans. Edn. Assn., Democrat. Lutheran. Clubs: Order Eastern Star, Shriners. Home: 5312 Yecker Kansas City KS 66104 Office: 625 Minnesota Kansas City KS 66101

MILLER, BRUCE EDWARD, clergyman, coll. pres.; b. Mankato, Minn., Oct. 20, 1924; s. Cecil Edward and Ruth Marie (Churchyard) M.; B.A., Minn. Bible Coll., 1946; M.A., Butler U., 1956; M.Div., Christian Theol. Sem., 1951, D.Min., 1974; m. Thelma VanEst, Aug. 29, 1948 (dec. 1978); children—Martin, David, Laura, Karen. Ordained to ministry, Ch. of Christ, 1945; pastor chs., Marion, Minn., 1945-46, Columbus, Ind., 1946-48, Noblesville, Ind., 1948-51; minister North Tacoma Christian Ch., Indpls., 1951-73; pres. Minn. Bible Coll., Rochester, Minn., 1973—. Bd. dirs. Christian Hour Radio Broadcast, Sr. Citizens, Inc. Mem. Christian Theol. Sem. Alumni Assn. (past v.p.). Club: Exchange (past pres.). Office: Minn Bible Coll 920 Mayowood Rd SW Rochester MN 55901

MILLER, BRUCE WALLACE, advt. agy. exec.; b. Evanston, Ill., Sept. 5, 1947; s. George Warren and Elizabeth Ann (Wallace) M.; B.A. in Advt., Mich. State U., 1970; A.A. in Bus. Adminstrn., Oakland Community Coll., 1968; m. Terri L. Gremel, Dec. 28, 1978; 1 dau. by previous marriage, Amanda Elizabeth. Media planner J. Walter Thompson Co., Detroit, 1970-71, mgr. traffic and prodn. dept., Atlanta, 1972-73, account rep., New Orleans, 1973-75, Detroit, 1976-78, v.p., account supr., 1979—. Mem. Am. Fedn. TV and Radio Artists. Republican. Presbyterian. Club: Detroit Advt. Football League (commr. 1976-81). Office: 17000 Executive Plaza Dr Dearborn MI 48126

MILLER, CHARLES PETER, state senator Iowa; b. Harbor Beach, Mich., Apr. 29, 1918; s. William H. and Anna (Eppenbrock) M.; student Burlington (Iowa) Community Coll., 1947-48; grad. Palmer Coll. Chiropractic, Davenport, Iowa, 1952; m. Virginia Mae Ferrington, Aug. 3, 1946; children—Charles, David, Steven, Dennis, Evelyn, Scot. Practice chiropractic, Burlington, 1952—; mem. Iowa Ho. of Reps. from Des Moines County, 1962-68, speaker pro-tem, 1965-66; mem. Iowa Senate from 42d Dist., 1969—. Mem. exec. bd. S.E. Iowa council Boy Scouts Am., 1956—. Served with USNR, 1940-46. Recipient Fellow award Palmer Acad. Chiropractic, 1966; Silver Beaver award Boy Scouts Am., 1958. Mem. Internat. Chiropractors Assn. (1st v.p. 1965; Fellowship award 1969), Chiropractic Soc. Iowa (pres. 1956-60, mem. bd. 1960-76), Am. Legion, VFW. Democrat. Lion, Eagle, Elk, K.C. Home: 801 High St Burlington IA 52601 Office: 701 Jefferson St Burlington IA 52601

MILLER, CHELSEY CALVIN, fed. land bank exec.; b. Berne, Ind., Oct. 4, 1925; s. Benjamin Harrison and Alma Florence (Halberstadt) M.; B.S. in Agr., Purdue U., 1951; m. Helen Mae Rinehart, Feb. 7, 1953; children—Janet Jeanine, Debra Louise. With Coop. Extension Service, New Castle, Ind., 1951-53; part-time announcer Sta. WCTW, New Castle, 1952-53; salesman Davison Chem. Co., Columbus, Ohio and Lansing Mich., 1953-57; soil scientist Soil Conservation Service, U.S. Dept. Agr., Warsaw, Columbia City and Bluffton, Ind., 1957-64; with Fed. Land Bank of Louisville, 1964—, asst. v.p., 1977-80, asso. regional v.p., Monroe, Ind., 1980—. Sunday Sch. tchr., Sunday Sch. supt., mem. coms. Ch. of Brethren. Served with USAAF, 1943-45. Decorated Purple Heart, Air medal with one oak leaf cluster. Mem. Am. Soc. Farm Mgrs. and Rural Appraisers, Soc. Ind. Pioneers. Home and office: Route 1 Box 66A Monroe IN 46772

MILLER, CLARENCE E., congressman; b. Lancaster, Ohio, Nov. 1, 1917; hon. degree Rio Grande Coll.; m. Helen M. Brown; children—Ronald, Jacqueline (Mrs. Thomas Williams). Mem. City Council, Lancaster, 1957-63; mayor, Lancaster, 1963-65; mem. 90th to 97th congresses from 10th Ohio Dist. Bd. dirs. Fairfield County chpt. A.R.C., YMCA. Hon. mem. Ohio Valley Health Services Found.; hon. alumnus Ohio U. mem. coms. on appropriations. Republican. Methodist. Club: Elks. Address: 2208 Rayburn House Office Bldg Washington DC 20215*

MILLER, DANE ALAN, surg. implant mfg. co. exec.; b. Bellefountaine, Ohio, Feb. 7, 1946; s. Ersie E. and Ruth E. Miller; B.S. in Mech. and Materials Sci. Engring., Gen. Motors Inst., 1969; M.S. in Biomed. Engring., U. Cin., 1971, Ph.D. in Biomed. Engring., 1974; m. Mary Louise Schilke, Feb. 26, 1965; children—Kimberly Ruth, Stephany Marie. Research and teaching asst. depts. orthopedic surgery and metall. engring. U. Cin., 1969-72; dir. devel. engring. and custom products Zimmer div. Bristol Meyers Corp., Warsaw, Ind., 1972-75; dir. biomed. engring. Cutter Biomed. div. Cutter Labs., San Diego, 1975-78; pres. Biomet Inc., Warsaw, 1978—; cons. to various legal firms, 1975-78. Mem. Soc. for Plastic Engrs. (pres. student chpt. 1966-68), Orthopedic Research Soc. Presbyterian. Contbr. articles on biomech. devices to profl. jours. Home: Route 9 Box 16 Warsaw IN 46580 Office: PO Box 587 Airport Indsl Park Warsaw IN 46580

MILLER, DANIEL JOSEPH, editor; b. St. Paul, May 16, 1945; s. Ralph Daniel and Mary B. (Brick) M.; B.A., U. Minn.; m. Michelle Marie Miller, Sept. 17, 1966; children—Nicole Marie, Jennifer Judith, Rebecca Ruth. Editorial writer, asst. fin. editor Chgo. Daily news, 1969-78; editor Crain's Chgo. Bus., 1978—. Office: 740 N Rush St Chicago IL 60611

MILLER, DAVID HERBERT, info. processing cons.; b. Breckenridge, Minn., May 2, 1937; s. Herbert Hamlin and Berieth Cughan (Johnson) M.; Ph.B., U. N.D., 1960; m. Lorraine M. Siegel, Oct. 20, 1962; children—Paul David, John Herbert. With Dept. Hwys., State of Minn., St. Paul, 1960, Blue Cross of Minn., St. Paul, 1960-68, Health Mgmt. Services, Chgo., 1968-70, Blue Cross of N.D., Fargo, 1970-72; owner, pres. David Miller & Assos., Fargo, 1973—; mem. faculty Moorhead State U., 1978; lectr. in field. Publicity chmn. Communitywide Evang. Crusade, Fargo, 1979; mem. adv. com. Spl. Edn.-Gifted Children, Fargo, 1976-77. Mem. Red River Valley Info. Processing Assn. (pres. 1973-74, dir. 1971-75), System/34 Users Group. Methodist. Club: Kiwanis (bd. dirs. 1978-80). Home: 172 Westwood Rt 3 Fargo ND 58103 Office: 122 1/2 Broadway Fargo ND 58102

MILLER, DAVID JAMES, chemist; b. Bismarck, N.D., Nov. 7, 1948; s. Herbert Christ and Mona (Hoffman) M.; B.A. in Chemistry, Dickinson State Coll., 1974; postgrad. N.D. State U., Frago, 1974-75; m. Elizabeth Brunella Walsh, Aug. 25, 1973; children—Johnathan David, Michol Herbert. Lab. technician, project lignite U. N.D., Grand Forks, 1975-76; research chemist Dept. Energy, Grand Forks, 1976—. Served with USN, 1966-70. Recipient Spl. Achievement award ERDA, 1977. Mem. Am. Chem. Soc., Am. Soc. Mass Spectroscopy, N.D. Acad. Sci., Sigma Xi. Lutheran. Home: 2118 24th Ave S Grand Forks ND 58201 Office: Dept Energy 15 N 23d St Grand Forks ND 58202

MILLER, DIANE HARDIN, nurse; b. Ft. Yuma, Calif., June 9, 1943; d. Harry Arthur and Frances (Miller) Hardin; R.N., Methodist Hosp., Indpls., 1964; B.S., Governor's State U., Park Forest South, Ill., 1978, M.H.S., 1980; m. Robert G. Miller; 1 dau., Kimberly D. Mem. nursing staff Riverside Hosp., Kankakee, Ill., 1964-76, dir. nursing, 1976; supr. St. James Hosp., Chicago Heights, Ill., 1976-77, asso. dir. nursing, 1977—. Mem. Soc. Nursing Service Adminstrs., Nat. League Nursing. Presbyterian. Home: 10 Cambridge Ct Bourbonnais IL 60914 Office: 1423 Chicago Rd Chicago Heights IL 60411

MILLER, DONALD CALVIN, banker; b. Geneseo, Ill., Mar. 31, 1920; s. Otto H. and Mary (Erdman) M.; A.B., U. Ill., 1942, A.M., 1943, Ph.D., 1948; m. Marjorie Grace Morgan, Dec. 18, 1943; children—Barbara Grace, Donald Calvin, Douglas Morgan. Asst. prof. econs. UCLA, 1949-51; economist, chief govt. fin. sect. Bd. Govs. FRS, 1951-58; 2d v.p. Continental Ill. Nat. Bank & Trust Co., Chgo., 1958-59, v.p., 1959-68, sr. v.p., 1968-72, exec. v.p., 1972-81, vice chmn. bd. dirs., 1976-81, vice-chmn., chief fin. officer, 1981—; public gov. Chgo. Merc. Exchange, 1979—; dir. Royal Globe Ins. Co., A.E. Staley Mfg. Co.; mem. faculty adminstrv. com., asso. dir. Grad. Sch. Banking, U. Wis., Madison. Bd. dirs. U. Ill. Found. Served with AUS, 1943-46. Mem. Am. Bankers Assn. (govt. borrowing com.), Assn. Res. City Bankers, Nat. Tax Assn. (treas. 1961—), U.S. C. of C. (dir. 1979—), Phi Beta Kappa, Beta Theta Pi. Author: Taxes, The Public Debt and Transfers of Income, 1950. Office: 231 S LaSalle St Chicago IL 60693*

MILLER, DONALD EDGAR, chemist; b. Oak Park, Ill., Dec. 3, 1933; s. Frank Charles and O. Lillian (Samuel) M.; B.S., U. Ill., 1950, M.S., 1951. Asst. plant mgr. Carnation Co., Houston, 1951-54; with Durkee Famous Foods, Chgo., 1954-66; with Durkee Foods div. SCM Corp., Strongsville, Ohio, 1967—, sect. head research and devel., 1968—. Mem. Inst. Food Technologists, Sigma Xi, Alpha Zeta. Patentee in field. Home: 17260 Akita Ct Strongsville OH 44136 Office: 16651 Sprague Rd Strongsville OH 44136

MILLER, DONALD VINCENT, newspaper pub.; b. Chgo., July 29, 1937; s. Vincent Francis and Marie Harriet (Wills) M.; student So. Ill. U., 1970; grad. PMD program Harvard U., 1973; m. Shirley Gene Inman, July 29, 1967; children—Claudine, Laurel. Foreman, Dow Jones, 1969; supr. Copley Newspapers, 1970; v.p. prodn. Harte Hanks Newspapers, San Antonio, 1971; pub. Dear Newspaper & Radio, Inc., Washington, 1977; pres., pub. The Sedalia (Mo.) Democrat Co., 1977—. Bd. dirs. Jr. Achievement, United Way; pres. Sacred Heart Sch. Found. Served with U.S. Army, 1960-62. Mem. Am. Newspaper Pubs. Assn., Mo. Newspaper Pubs. Assn., Sedalia Area C. of C. (pres.). Republican. Roman Catholic. Club: Rotary (dir.) (Sedalia, Mo.). Office: Sedalia Democrat 700 S Massachusetts St Sedalia MO 65301

MILLER, DUANE ALLEN, sheet metal co. exec.; b. Sioux Falls, S.D., Mar. 5, 1935; s. Louis A. and Myrtle K. (Bergstrom) M.; B.S., S.D. State U., 1958; m. Phyllis J. Weber, July 3, 1961; children—Paul A., Michelle A., Scott M. Engr. in tng. The Spitznagel Partners, Sioux Falls, 1958-63; mech. engr. Tessier Sheet Metal Works, Inc., Sioux Falls, 1963-81, v.p., 1974—. Trustee Our Saviors Lutheran Ch., Sioux Falls. Served with USAF, 1958. Mem. ASHRAE, Profl. Engring. Soc. Republican. Club: Elks. Home: 1300 S Jefferson Ave Sioux Falls SD 57105 Office: 700 W Cherokee St Sioux Falls SD 57104

MILLER, EARLE GEORGE, JR., pub. co. exec.; b. Chgo., Aug. 22, 1946; s. Earle George and Betty Elizabeth (Emmons) M.; A.B., Johns Hopkins U., 1968; M.B.A., U. Chgo., 1976; m. Francine P. Beyer, June 15, 1974; children—Katherine Anne, Elizabeth Patti. Account exec. Dean Witter Reynolds, Inc., Chgo., 1970-74; investment portfolio mgr. First Nat. Bank of Chgo., 1974-76; sr. analyst fin. planning Playboy Enterprises, Inc., Chgo., 1976-77; v.p. fin., treas. Devel. Systems Corp., Chgo., 1978—, also dir. C.P.A., Ill. Mem. Nat. Assn. Bus. Economists, Planning Execs. Inst., Am. Inst. C.P.A.'s. Home: 5329 Florence St Downers Grove IL 60515 Office: 500 N Dearborn St Chicago IL 60610

MILLER, EDWARD PERCIVAL, librarian, univ. adminstr.; b. St. Catharines, Ont., Can., May 10, 1924; s. Percival Charles and Anne Elizabeth (Swayze) M.; B.Applied Sci., U. Toronto, 1946; B.Div. cum laude, Kenyon Coll., 1953; M.L.S., U. Okla., 1965, Ph.D. in Indsl. Engring., 1972; children—Mark Stephen, Martha Anne, Andrew Gordon, Matthew Edward. Research engr. Kellett Aircraft, 1947, Cornell Aero Lab., 1948-50; ordained to ministry Episcopal Ch., 1953; minister chs., Niagara Falls, N.Y., Riverside, Calif., Oklahoma City, Amarillo, Tex., 1953-63; librarian Tulsa City-County Library, 1965-70; asst. prof. info. sci. U. Mo., Columbia, 1972-74, dean Sch. of Library and Info. Sci., prof., 1974—; partner EGM Assos., Cons. Served with Can. Navy, 1944-46. Mem. Am. Soc. Info. Sci., AAAS, ALA, Spl. Libraries Assn. (chmn. by laws com. 1970-72, pres. chpt. 1981—), Mo. Library Assn. Contbr. articles to profl. jours. Office: 104 Stewart Hall U of Mo Columbia MO 65211

MILLER, ERIC ARNOLD, music educator; b. Knoxville, Tenn., Mar. 5, 1943; s. Arthur A. and Florence J. (Gattis) M.; B.S. in Music Edn., N.E. Mo. State U., 1965, M.A. in Music, 1966. Dir. vocal music Beecher Jr. High Sch., Hazel Park, Mich., 1965-68, Wilfred Webb Jr. High Sch., Ferndale, Mich., 1968-72, Hazel Park (Mich.) High Sch., 1972-77, United Oaks and Lee O. Clark Elem. Schs., Hazel Park, 1978—. Named Outstanding Young Educator, Hazel Park Jaycees, 1975. Mem. Assn. for Supervision and Curriculum Devel., Mich. Edn. Assn., Hazel Park Edn. Assn. (mem. exec. bd. 1979—), Mich. Music Edn. Assn., Mich. Vocal Dirs. Assn., NEA. Presbyterian. Composer: (choral) Our Time Will Come, 1975. Home: 23465 Reynolds Hazel Park MI 48030 Office: 23126 Hughes St Hazel Park MI 48030

MILLER, ERIC RUDOLPH, retail store exec.; b. Columbus, Ohio, Sept. 8, 1949; s. Milburn E. and Georgia E. (Wylie) M.; B.S., Ohio U., 1968-72; m. Sharon Lynn Edison, Aug. 4, 1974; children—Kyle Christopher, Kevin Edison. With C & O R.R., Columbus, Ohio, 1968-71; mgr. Susie's Casual's, Columbus, 1972-75; mgr. Madison's Inc. of Columbus, 1975-80; regional sales mgr. Internat. Import, Columbus, 1980—. Mem. promotion com. Eastland Mall, Columbus, 1974-75; bd. dirs. Northland Mall, 1977-78. Mem. Gahanna Jr. C. of C. (pres. 1978-79), Ohio U. Alumni Assn. Republican. Evangelical Ch. Home: 644 Moss Oak St Columbus OH 43219

MILLER, ERVIN FRANK, mfg. co. exec.; b. Appleton, Wis., Jan. 5, 1920; s. Frank John and Lillian Rose (Behrens) M.; student Houston U., 1943; B.S.M.E., Marquette U., 1947; M.S.M.E., U. Wis., 1959; m. Elizabeth Kurnat, May 26, 1945; children—Lillian May, Peggy Ann, Sharon Kay, Lorraine Gretchen. Machinist, Kearney & Trecker, Milw., 1939-43; standards supr. Cutler Hammer, Milw., 1947-61, mgr. quality assurance, 1961-78; mgr. quality assurance Eaton, Milw., 1978—; instr. Marquette U., Milw., 1957-64, Engring. Evening Sch., 1980. Served with USNR, 1943-45. Mem. Engrs. Soc. Milw., Am. Inst. Indsl. Engrs., Am. Soc. Quality Control, Milw. Council Engring. and Sci. Socs. Congregationalist. Mem. adv. bd. Am. Soc. Quality Control Mag., 1975-77; author: Plans and Training Manual, 1957; Capital Equipment Replacement Policy, 1959. Home: 1858 N 84th St Wauwatosa WI 53226 Office: 4201 N 27th St Milwaukee WI 53216

MILLER, EUGENE, financial co. exec.; b. Chgo., Oct. 6, 1925; s. Harry and Fannie (Prosterman) M.; B.S., Ga. Inst. Tech., 1945; A.B. magna cum laude, Bethany Coll., 1947, LL.D., 1969; diploma Oxford (Eng.) U., 1947; M.S. in Journalism, Columbia, 1948; M.B.A., N.Y. U., 1959; m. Edith Sutker, Sept. 23, 1951 (div. Sept. 1965); children—Ross, Scott, June; m. 2d, Thelma Gottlieb, Dec. 22, 1965; stepchildren—Paul Gottlieb, Alan Gottlieb. Reporter, then city editor Greensboro (N.C.) Daily News, 1948-52; S.W. bur. chief Bus. Week mag., Houston, 1952-54, asso. mng. editor, N.Y.C., 1954-60; dir. pub. affairs and communications McGraw-Hill, Inc., 1960-63, v.p., 1963-68; v.p. pub. relations and investor relations, exec. com. N.Y. Stock Exchange, N.Y.C., 1968-70; sr. v.p., 1970-73; sr. v.p. CNA Fin. Corp., Chgo., 1973-75; v.p. U.S. Gypsum Co., 1977—; adj. prof. mgmt. Grad. Sch. Bus. Adminstrn., N.Y. U., 1963—; prof. bus. adminstrn. Fordham U. Grad. Sch. Bus. Adminstrn., 1969—; chmn., prof. finance Northeastern Ill. U., 1975—. lectr. econs. pub. relations to bus. and sch. groups; author syndicated bus. column, 1964—. Dir. Tabb, Inc., Ann Arbor, Mich. Cons. to sec. commerce, 1961-66. Alumni dir., trustee Bethany Coll.; mem. alumni bd. Columbia Sch. Journalism. Served to ensign USNR, World War II; comdr. Res. Mem. Am. Econs. Assn., Am. Finance Assn., Nat. Assn. Bus. Economists, Soc. Am. Bus. Writers, Pub. Relations Soc. Am., Newcomen Soc., Fin. Analyst Soc., Sigma Delta Chi, Alpha Sigma Phi. Clubs: Mid-Am. (Chgo.); Green Acres Country, N.Y.U. (N.Y.C.). Author: Your Future in the Securities Business, 1974; Barron's Guide to Graduate Business Schs., 1977. Contbg. editor: Public Relations Handbook, 1971. Home: 376 Sunrise Circle Glencoe IL 60022 Office: 101 S Wacker Dr Chicago IL 60606

MILLER, EVELYN LOUISE, banker; b. Conception Junction, Mo.; d. Charles E. and Lucy Jane (Stackhouse) Martin; B.A., Tarkio Coll., 1941; m. John R. DeVore, Apr. 22, 1943; 1 son, Ted R.; m. Robert M. Miller, Nov. 22, 1956. Head commerce dept. Watson (Mo.) High Sch., 1945-51; editor Watson Ind., 1951-52; exec. sec. S. Riekes & Sons, Omaha, 1952-54; editor Bellevue (Nebr.) Press, 1954-55; with Peoples State Bank, Ellinwood, Kans., 1955—, v.p., cashier, 1976-80, sr. v.p., cashier, 1980—, dir., 1981—, sec. bd., 1955—. Chmn., Centennial Com., 1972; co-chmn. Bicentennial Com., 1976; bd. dirs. Salvation Army, 1956—; pres. Library Bd., 1979—. Recipient Disting. Servant award Ellinwood Rotary Internat., 1979. Mem. Bank Adminstrn. Inst. (pres. Golden Belt chpt.), Am. Inst. Banking, Nat. Assn. Bank Women, Kans. Bankers Assn. Republican. Methodist. Clubs: Modern Literature (pres. 1971, 75, 81); Great Bend Petroleum. Home: 200 W 5th St Ellinwood KS 67526 Office: 13 N Main St Ellinwood KS 67526

MILLER, FRANCIS PETER, psychopharmacologist; b. Bklyn., Sept. 5, 1941; s. Milton Peter and Florence Dorothea (Gattavara) M.; B.S., Manhattan Coll., 1963; M.S., George Washington U., 1965; Ph.D., Ind. U., 1968; m. Marie Suzanne Gaspar, Dec. 24, 1962; children—Marie Suzanne, Francis Peter, Eric Alan, Kristin Elizabeth; m. 2nd Jacquelin Joyce McKee, Feb. 25, 1978. Chemist, NIH, Bethesda, Md., 1963-65; research asst. dept. psychology Ind. U., Bloomington, 1965-68; pharmacologist Lakeside Labs., Milw., 1968-75; sr. research pharmacologist Merrell Research Center, Cin., 1975—. Mem. Sigma Xi. Roman Catholic. Contbr. articles in field to profl. jours. Home: 336 Broadway Loveland OH 45140 Office: 2110 E Galbraith Rd Cincinnati OH 45215

MILLER, FREDERICK GENE, educator; b. Greentown, Ind., Jan. 1, 1936; s. Floyd Dennis and Ruth Helena (Knote) M.; B.A., Butler U., 1958; M.A., Ball State Tchrs. Coll., 1964, Ph.D., 1969; m. Linda Lou Walker, June 15, 1958; children—Douglas Alan, Deanna Jean, Melinda Kay. Tchr., Kokomo (Ind.) Center Twp. Schs., 1961-66; teaching fellow Ball State U., Muncie, Ind., 1966-68; prof., dir. Curriculum Publs. Clearinghouse, Western Ill. U., Macomb, 1968—. Mem. McDonough County Planning Commn., 1978—. Served with USAF, 1958-61. Ill. State Bd. Edn./Dept. Adult Vocat. Tech. Edn. grantee, 1978-81. Mem. Nat. Council for Social Studies (Outstanding Service award 1980), Ill. Council for Social Studies, Assn. Supervision and Curriculum Devel., Assn. Childhood Edn. Internat., Internat. Council Edn. for Teaching. Presbyterian. Author: The 1920's and 1930's, 1976; co-author: Leadership, 1976; co-editor: Internat. Social Studies Directory, 1979; Procs: Second Ann. Practioner's Conf. on Energy Edn., 1980; mem. editorial adv. bd. Jour. Geography, 1974—. Office: Horrabin Hall 46 Western Ill U Macomb IL 61455

MILLER, FREDERICK HOWARD, podiatrist; b. Chgo., Oct. 8, 1947; s. Samuel I. and Sylvia (Ekter) M.; B.S., Loyola U., 1969; D.P.M. summa cum laude, Ill. Coll. Podiatric Medicine, 1975; m. Carole Pamala Schwab, June 27, 1971; children—David, Ryan.

Resident in podiatric surgery Northlake Community Hosp., 1976-77; practice podiatry, Mt. Prospect, Ill., 1976—; mem. staff Thorek Hosp. and Med. Center, Chgo., Northlake (Ill.) Community Hosp., Northwest Surg. Center, Arlington Heights, Ill. Mem. Am. Podiatry Assn., Ill. Podiatry Soc., Acad. Ambulatory Foot Surgery, Am. Coll. Podopediatrics. Club: Mt. Prospect Lions. Office: 530 W Northwest Hwy Mt Prospect IL 60056

MILLER, GEORGE AVERY, III, accountant; b. Lancaster, Pa., Jan. 2, 1941; s. George Avery and Ruth Mae (Freeman) M.; B.S., Ferris State Coll., 1972; m. Gladys Laverne Stoltzfus, Oct. 31, 1964; children—Gregory Lynn, Gina Louise. With Sperry New Holland, New Holland, Pa., 1961-70, gen. acct., 1969-70; staff acct. Touche Ross & Co., C.P.A.'s, Grand Rapids, Mich., 1973; corp. acct. Dentsply Internat., Inc., York, Pa., 1973-75, gen. acctg. supr., 1975, asst. acctg. mgr., 1975-77, div. acctg. mgr., Cin., 1977—. Served with U.S. Army, 1959-61. Mem. Nat. Assn. Accts. Home: 137 Brushwood Dr Loveland OH 45140 Office: 96 Caldwell Dr Cincinnati OH 45216

MILLER, GERALD ALLEN, contractor, real estate developer; b. Evanston, Ill., July 21, 1947; s. Robert John and Louise (Keckley) M.; B.S., Miami U., Oxford, Ohio, 1969; m. Gail Christine Benedict, Aug. 17, 1974; children—Stuart Holbrook, Christina Benedict. Tchr., Chgo. Bd. Edn., 1969-72; founder, pres. Gerald A. Miller Co., Chgo., 1971—, A-1 Am. Constrn. Co., Chgo., 1973—, Great Lakes Constrn., Chgo., 1974—, Abbot & Stuart, Chgo., 1980—. Pres. Bd. Youth Guidance, Chgo., 1974-76; exec. v.p. aux. bd. Henrotin Hosp., 1975—, bd. govs., 1979—; pres., asso. bd. Grant Hosp., Chgo., 1976—. Mem. Am. Subcontractors Assn. Republican. Episcopalian. Clubs: Racquet, Saddle and Cycle. Office: 1769 W Armitage St Chicago IL 60622

MILLER, HARRY GEORGE, educator; b. Waukesha, Wis., Feb. 15, 1941; s. Harry Fricke and Ethel Ruth (D'Amato) M.; B.A., Carroll Coll., 1963; M.Ed., U. Neb., 1967, Ed.D., 1970; m. Mary Frances Shugrue, June 20, 1964; children—Alicia, Michael, Anne, Deirdre, Courtney. Tchr., Westside Community Schs., Omaha, 1964-68; demonstration tchr. East Edn. Complex, Lincoln (Nebr.) Pub. Schs., 1967-68; instr. curriculum research Tchrs. Coll., U. Nebr., Lincoln, 1968-70; faculty So. Ill. U., Carbondale, 1970—, asso. prof. edn., dept. secondary edn., 1972-75, chmn. dept. secondard edn., 1973-75, prof., chmn. dept. ednl. leadership, 1975—, asso. dean Sch. Tech. Careers, 1980—. Cons. to various orgns. and instns., 1969-74. Mem. Ill. Migrant Council, 1974; mem. adv. bd. Evaluation and Devel. Center, Rehab. Inst., Carbondale, 1974-75; mem. Ill. State CETA Adv. Bd., 1979—. Mem. Pub. Adult and Continuing Edn. Assn., Rural Edn. Assn., Ill. Council for Social Studies (hon.), Greater Cleve. Council for Social Studies (hon.), Phi Delta Kappa, Kappa Delta Pi. Democrat. Roman Catholic. K.C. Author: Strong Confrontation as an Educational Technique, 1973; Drill Re-examined: A Taxonomy for Drill Exercises, 1975; Beyond Facts: Objective Ways to Measure Thinking, 1976; Adults Teaching Adults, 1978; The Adult Educator, 1979; Adult Education in Thailand, 1979; The Education of Adults, 1981; editorial bd. Tng., 1976; asso. editor Jour. Tech. Careers, 1980—. Home: 2908 W Kent Dr Carbondale IL 62901

MILLER, HARRY JOHNSON, internist, hematologist; b. Miles City, Mont., Feb. 19, 1926; s. Harry Garfield and Harriet Ruth (Wildish) M.; student U. Wis., 1946-48; B.S., Northwestern U., 1952, M.D., 1952; m. Lucia Fairchild Taylor, Dec. 31, 1947; children—Sally, Elizabeth, Katherine, Patricia, Blair. Intern, White Cross Hosp., Columbus, Ohio, 1952-53; resident in internal medicine Northwestern U., Chgo., 1955-58, fellow in hematology, 1958-59; practice medicine specializing in internal medicine and hematology, Evanston, Ill., 1959—; mem. staff Evanston Hosp., pres. staff, 1974-75; instr. medicine Northwestern U. Med. Sch., 1959-61, asso., 1961-70, asst. prof., 1970-76, asso. prof. clin. medicine, 1976—. Served with USAAF, 1944-46. Diplomate Am. Bd. Internal Medicine. Fellow A.C.P.; mem. AMA, AAAS, Ill., Chgo. med. socs., Am. Soc. Hematology, Am. Soc. Clin. Oncology, Am. Fedn. Clin. Research, Chgo. Soc. Internal Medicine. Unitarian. Home: 136 Maple St Wilmette IL 60091 Office: 2500 Ridge St Evanston IL 60201

MILLER, HOWARD C., food co. exec.; b. Erie, Pa., 1926; s. Howard C. and Elsie M. (Hays) M.; B.S., U. Pa., 1950; m. JoAnne D. DeGraw, Sept. 8, 1948. Instr. U. Pa., Phila., 1950-51; sales engr. E.F. Houghton & Co., 1951-58; tech. sales div. mgr. Lubrizol Corp., Euclid, Ohio, 1958; asst. to pres. Dairy Pak Butler Inc., Cleve., 1958-61; cons. Robert Heller & Assos., Cleve., 1961-63; mgr. organizational devel. ITT, N.Y.C., 1963, mgr. indsl. products, 1964, product line mgr. consumer services, 1965-67, v.p., group exec. consumer services, 1967-72; pres., chief exec. officer Canteen Corp., Chgo., 1972—; dir. TWC, Lake Shore Nat. Bank. Mem. exec. bd. U.S. Olympic Com. Served to 1st lt. USAAF, 1945-46. Office: 1430 Merchandise Mart Chicago IL 60654*

MILLER, IRVING MORTON, pediatrician; b. Detroit, Dec. 30, 1932; s. Jacob and Rose (Steinberg) M.; B.S. in Chemistry with distinction, Wayne State U., 1954, M.D., 1958; m. Marcia Ellen Morris, Aug. 24, 1961; children—Laurie Beth, Stephen Mark, Susan Rachel. Intern, Mt. Zion Hosp., San Francisco, 1958-59; resident Children's Hosp. of Mich., Detroit, 1959-62, now mem. staff; practice medicine, specializing in pediatrics, Farmington, Mich., 1962—; mem. staff Pediatric Assos., Farmington, 1962—, pres., 1971—; mem. staff Sinai Hosp., Detroit, St. Mary's Hosp., Livonia, Mich.; adj. clin. asst. prof. pediatrics Wayne State U. Trustee, Birmingham Temple, Farmington, 1971-74, mem. exec. bd., 1975-77, pres. temple, 1977-78. USPHS fellow, summer 1956. Diplomate Am. Bd. Pediatrics. Fellow Am. Acad. Pediatrics; mem. Detroit Pediatric Soc., Oakland County Med. Soc., Mich. State Med. Soc. Home: 29652 Pond Ridge Farmington Hills MI 48018 Office: 23133 Orchard Lake Rd Farmington MI 48024

MILLER, JAMES ALAN, chemist; b. Akron, Ohio, Oct. 27, 1939; s. Roy E. and Marie W. (Robinett) M.; m. Nancy L. Scott, June 25, 1965; children—Scott E., Mary L., Carol A. B.S. in Chemistry, U. Akron, 1964. Lab. technician Morgan Adhesives Co., Stow, Ohio, 1961-64, jr. chemist, 1964-68, plant chemist, 1968-70, research dir. graphic arts div., 1970-73, mgr. tech. service and devel., 1973-81, mgr. advanced tech., 1981—. Emergency coordinator Summit-Portage Counties (Ohio), 1972-79; pres. Community Amateur Radio Service, Akron, 1972-74; disaster communications officer Summit County chpt. ARC, 1972—; trustee Community Amateur Radio Service, 1974-78; elder Trinity United Ch. of Christ, Akron, 1976-79; vol. communications cons. N.E. Ohio div. ARC, 1978—; Webelos den leader Cub pack 3153, Cub Scouts Am., 1978-79. Mem. Cuyahoga Falls Amateur Radio Club, Am. Radio Relay League, Am. Chem. Soc., Akron Rubber Group, Cleve. Soc. Coatings Tech. Patentee in field. Home: 3057 Kent Rd Silver Lake Village Cuyahoga Falls OH 44224 Office: 4560 Darrow Rd Stow OH 44224

MILLER, JAMES IRWIN, mfg. co. ofcl.; b. Toledo, June 29, 1956; s. William Irving and Doris Mae (Schwellinger) M.; B.B.A. in Mktg. (Tagmar scholar, Curtin & Pease mktg. scholar), U. Toledo, 1978. Internat. sales coordinator Robinair Mfg. Corp., Montpelier, Ohio, 1978-79, asst. sales mgr., 1979-80, nat. advt. mgr., 1980—. Republican. Lutheran. Club: Moose (Montpelier). Home: 501 E Washington St Montpelier OH 43543 Office: Robinair Mfg Corp Robinair Way Montpelier OH 43543

MILLER, JAMES WILLIAM, cons. co. exec.; b. Oak Park, Ill., Mar. 22, 1926; s. Walter Arthur and Marie (Romanowski) M.; student U. Ill., 1946-48; m. Gertrude M. Simonis, July 5, 1947; children—Patricia, Barbara, Gloria, James William, Cathleen, Carol, Mary. Draftsman, Nat. Biscuit Co., Evanston, Ill., 1949-51; plant engr. Keebler Co., Melrose Park, Ill., 1951-67; plant engr. GAF Corp., Joliet, Ill., 1967-71; pres. Preventive Maintenance Co., Schiller Park, Ill., 1971—, also dir. Sec. Cook County Dist. 81 Sch. Bd., 1966-75, pres., 1975. Served with USMCR, 1943-45. Decorated Purple Heart medal. Mem. St. Vincent De Paul Soc. (pres. 1964-79, pres. Vicarate IV 1976-79), Am. Soc. Bus. Mgmt. Consultants, Soc. Plant Engrs., VFW, DAV. Republican. Roman Catholic. Club: K.C. Home: 4132 Prairie Ave Schiller Park IL 60176 Office: 3808 W North Ave Melrose Park IL 60165

MILLER, JOHN RANDELL, army officer; b. Clifton Forge, Va., Aug. 14, 1945; s. John Preston and Dorothy Irene (Vess) M.; B.A. in Am. History, Washington and Lee U., 1967; M.A. in Am. Diplomatic History, U. Ga., 1974; M.S., Command and Gen. Staff Coll., 1981; m. Brenda Gale Dingledine, Oct. 14, 1967; children—Lara, Sara. Commd. 2d lt., U.S. Army, 1967, advanced through grades to maj., 1977; platoon leader 6th Armored Cavalry Regt., 1967-68; adj. div. combat assistance team, Vietnam, 1968-69; instr., Adj. Gen.'s Sch., 1970-72; asst. prof. mil. sci. Washington and Lee U., 1974-77; dir. personnel and community affairs, Fulda, West Germany, 1977-78; comdr. Regional Personnel Center, Bad Kreuznach, W. Ger., 1978-79, chief personnel services 8th Inf. Div., 1979-80; assigned to Def. Lang. Inst., 1981—. Decorated Bronze Star with oak leaf cluster, Meritorious Service medal, Army Commendation medal with 2 oak leaf clusters, Air medal. Mem. Am. Hist. Assn., Assn. U.S. Army, Phi Kappa Phi, Phi Alpha Theta. Editor: The Citizen-Soldier: A Washington and Lee Tradition, 1977. Home: Box 94 Natural Bridge VA 24578 Office: DLIFLC GM Presidio of Monterey CA 93940

MILLER, JOHN ROBERT, petroleum co. exec.; b. Lima, Ohio, Dec. 28, 1937; s. John O. and Mary (Zicafoose) M.; B.S. in Chem. Engring., U. Cin., 1960; m. Karen A. Miller, Dec. 30, 1961; children—Robert A., Lisa A., James E. With Standard Oil Co. (Ohio), 1960—, dir. fin., 1974, v.p. fin., 1975, v.p. transp., 1978, sr. v.p. tech. and chems., 1979, pres., chief operating officer, 1980—, also dir.; dir. Nat. City Bank, Nat. City Corp., White Consol. Industries, Inc., Gt. Lakes Constrn. Co., Am. Petroleum Inst. Trustee Ohio No. U., U. Young Ams., Cleve. Playhouse, Univ. Hosps. Cleve., Greater Cleve. Growth Assn. Mem. Tau Beta Pi. Clubs: Pepper Pile, Union. Office: Standard Oil Co Midland Bldg 101 Prospect Ave Cleveland OH 44115

MILLER, JOSEPH IRWIN, mfr.; b. Columbus, Ind., May 26, 1909; s. Hugh Thomas and Nettie Irwin (Sweeney) M.; A.B., Yale, 1931, M.A. (hon.), 1959, L.H.D. (hon.), 1979; M.A., Oxford (Eng.) U., 1933; LL.D., Bethany Coll., 1956, Tex. Christian U., 1958, Ind. U., 1958, Oberlin Coll., 1962, Princeton U., 1962, Hamilton Coll., 1964, Case Inst. Tech., 1966, Columbia U., 1968, Mich. State U. 1968, Dartmouth Coll., 1971, U. Notre Dame, 1972, Ball State U., 1972; Hum.D. (hon.), Manchester U., 1973, Moravian Coll., 1976; L.H.D., U. Dubuque, 1977; m. Xenia Ruth Simons, Feb. 5, 1943; children—Margaret Irwin, Catherine Gibbs, Elizabeth Ann Garr, Hugh Thomas II, William Irwin. With Cummins Engine Co., Inc., Columbus, Ind., 1934—, v.p., gen. mgr., 1934-42, exec. v.p., 1944-47, pres. 1945-51, chmn. bd. 1951-77, chmn. exec. and fin. com., 1977—; pres. Irwin-Union Bank & Trust Co., 1947-54, dir., 1937—, chmn., 1954-75, chmn. exec. com., 1976—. Chmn., Pres.'s Spl. Com. East-West Trade Relations, 1965; mem. Pres.'s Commn. Postal Orgn., 1967-68, Com. Urban Housing, 1967-68; mem. Commn. Money and Credit, 1958-61, also Bus. Council; chmn. Nat. Adv. Commn. for Health Manpower, 1966-67; vice chmn. UN Com. Multinat. Corps., 1973-74; mem. advisory council Dept. Commerce, 1976-77. Pres. Nat. Council Chs. Christ in U.S.A., 1960-63; mem. U.S. Study Com. on So. Africa. Mem. Nat. Indsl. Conf. Bd.; trustee Mayo Found., Yale Corp., 1959-77, Nat. Humanities Center. Fellow Branford Coll., Balliol Coll., Oxford. Served lt. USNR, aboard U.S.S. Langley, 1942-44. Recipient Rosenberger medal U. Chgo., 1977. Fellow Am. Acad. Arts and Scis.; mem. Am. Philos. Soc., AIA (hon.), Phi Beta Kappa, Beta Gamma Sigma. Mem. Christian Ch. (elder). Clubs: Yale, Century, Links (N.Y.C.); Chicago; Indianapolis Athletic, Columbia (Indpls.). Home: 2760 Highland Way Columbus IN 47201 Office: 301 Washington St Columbus IN 47201

MILLER, LARRY FRANK, ins. co. ofcl.; b. Biloxi, Miss., Mar. 1, 1952; s. Frank W. and Roberta Jean M.; student public schs.; m. Kathy Denise Hess, Sept. 17, 1970; children—Todd Alan, Nathan Ray. Concrete finisher Crees' Enterprises, Ankeny, Iowa, 1970-72; agt. Farm Bur. Ins. Cos. Iowa, 1972-78, agy. supr., Des Moines, 1978-79, div. mgr., 1980—; registered rep. F.B. Growth Fund, West Des Moines, 1974—. Mem. Iowa Assn. Life Underwriters, Saylorville Jaycees (v.p. 1979-80), Iowa Farm Bur. Republican. Methodist. Clubs: Variety of Iowa, Highland Park Businessmen's. Home: 6905 NW 6th Dr Ankeny IA 50021 Office: 5400 University St West Des Moines IA 50265

MILLER, LARRY LEE, ins. co. exec.; b. Galesburg, Ill., Feb. 2, 1948; s. Robert Eugene and Frances Eleanor (Burke) M.; B.Bus. in Fin., Western Ill. U., 1972; m. Brenda Elaine Seaman, Aug. 25, 1973. Owner, Larry L. Miller Ins. Agy., also Edgar T. Wenstrom Agy., Galesburg, 1972—, Everingham-Miller Ins. Agy., Rock Island, Ill., 1980—. Pres., Cultural Council of Galesburg, 1975-76; treas. Western Ill. Big Bros.-Big Sisters, 1973-75; pres. Galesburg Exchange Club, 1977-78, v.p., 1976-77, bd. dirs., 1976—. Served with U.S. Army, 1968. Mem. Galesburg Jaycees (Gold Key award 1976), Am. Bus. Clubs, Nat. Assn. Ind. Agts., Ill. Assn. Ind. Agts, Nat. Assn. Securities Dealers (lic.). Republican. Roman Catholic. Home: Route 1 Box 83 Wataga IL 61488 Office: Box 1385 36 Park Plaza Galesburg IL 61401

MILLER, LAVERNE GERTRUDE, nurse; b. Monroe, Wis., May 4, 1922; d. Frederick Helmuth and Ida Marie (Brand) Flueckiger; R.N., Presbyn.-St. Luke's Hosp., Chgo., 1966; B.S. in Health Arts, Coll. St. Francis, now postgrad.; m. Edward J. Miller, Jr., Nov. 16, 1946; 1 son, Gary E. Charge nurse surg. unit Presbyn.-St. Luke's Hosp., 1966-69; head nurse supr. Oak Park (Ill.) Hosp., 1969-77, now inservice coordinator. Vol. ARC blood donor drives. Recipient Presbyn.-St. Luke's Med. Staff award for outstanding patient care, citizenship and scholastic achievement. Mem. Am. Assn. Critical Care Nurses, Chgo. Council Cath. Nurses Assn. (dir.), Am. Nurses Assn., Nat. League Nursing, Women's Tabernacle Guild, Oak Park Hosp. Women's Aux., Fenwick High Sch. Mother's Club (life), Am. Cancer Soc., Swiss Benevolent Soc., Swiss Ladies Benefit Soc., Internat. Platform Assn. Republican. Roman Catholic. Home: 525 W Jackson Blvd Oak Park IL 60304

MILLER, LOUISE CHRISTINE, ret. electric co. exec.; b. Junction City, Wis., Aug. 2, 1913; d. Martin and Anna (Nelson) Miller; grad. pub. schs., Chgo., 1932. With Miller Electric Mfg. Co., Appleton, Wis., 1935-78, office mgr., 1935-50, chief accountant, 1935-64, v.p., 1964-75, fin. officer, 1963-78; office mgr., chief acct. Miller Welding Supply Co., Appleton, 1947-64, asst. sec.-treas., 1963-77. Mem. Assn. for Systems Mgmt. (profl.), Internat. Platform Assn., Altrusa Club (dir. Appleton 1969-72, sec. 1961-62, 68—, chmn. internat. relations and vocat. services com. 1966-71, mem. auditing com., by-laws, classification and membership com. 1971-72). Republican. Christian Scientist (dir., clk., treas., sec., Sunday Sch. tchr., supt., 1st reader, fin. adviser, mem. bldg. com.). Home: 926 E Windfield Pl Appleton WI 54911

MILLER, LYNNE TOMER, ednl. cons.; b. Chgo., Oct. 15, 1947; d. William Ralph and Dorothy (Skorupa) Tomer; B.S. in Edn., Northwestern U., 1969; M.Ed., Loyola U., Chgo., 1976; m. Neal P. Miller, May 7, 1977; 1 son, Brandon Allen. Tchr. public schs., Arlington Heights, Ill., 1969-70; ednl. program dir. Gateway House, Chgo., 1970-73; counselor Northeastern Ill. U., 1973-74; cons. Region V Drug and Alcohol Abuse Prevention Tng. Center, U.S. Office of Edn., Chgo., 1974-77; curriculum writer Nat. Dairy Council, Chgo., 1977; pres., dir. L.T. Miller & Assos., Inc., Chgo., 1977—. Mem. Am. Ednl. Research Assn., Assn. Supervision and Curriculum Devel. Co-author: From Groping to Gripping with Groups, videotape series. Address: 3909 N Hoyne Chicago IL 60618

MILLER, MARC EDWARD, psychologist; b. Lancaster, Ohio, Oct. 2, 1942; s. Walter F. and Elizabeth M. (Mowry) M.; B.A., Ohio U., 1967, M.Ed., 1969; postgrad. Nordenfjord U. (Denmark), Wright State U., 1970-72; Ed.D., Western Colo. U., 1976; m. Frances Lucille Levacy, Nov. 26, 1964; children—Kristina E., Marcy F. Tchr. developmentally disabled children pub. schs., 1964-69; therapist Ednl. Clinic, Inc., 1970-71; psychol. intern Wright State U., 1971-72; psychologist, coordinator programs Ednl. Clinic, Inc., Columbus, Ohio, 1972-75, asst. dir., psychologist, 1975—; instr. Capital U., 1973-74; cons. Columbus State Inst., Ohio Disability Determination Commn.; pvt. practice med. evaluation. Pres. St. Mary's Sch. Bd., Lancaster, 1977; v.p. Fairfield County Health Systems Council, 1976-77. Mem. Am., Ohio psychol. assns., Central Ohio Psychologists (pres.), Biofeedback Soc. Ohio (pres. 1977-78), World Edn. Assn. Republican. Roman Catholic. Contbr. articles to profl. jours. Home: 3702 Stringtown Rd Lancaster OH 43130 Office: 3400 N High St Columbus OH 43202

MILLER, MARY SUE MONSEES, educator; b. Pettis County, Mo., Dec. 30, 1928; d. Seltzer Gilbert and Waneta (Allcorn) Monsees; student U. Mo., Columbia, 1946-50; B. B.S., Eastern Conn. State Coll., 1964, M.S., 1967; Ph.D., U. Mo., Kansas City, 1974; m. Eldridge L. Miller, Dec. 24, 1950; children—Vonda Sue, Myra Lou, Gilbert Lee, Lesley Ann. Tchr., prin. pub. schs., Pettis County, Mo., 1947-51; tchr. pub. schs., Macomb County, Mich., 1957-59, Montville, Conn., 1960-62, Colchester, Conn., 1962-66; instr., supr. Eastern Conn. State Coll. Lab. Sch., Willimantic, 1966-67; asst. prof. edn. William Jewell Coll., Liberty, Mo., 1967-76, asso. prof. edn., 1976-80; dir. secondary edn. Stephens Coll., Columbia, Mo., 1980—. Recipient Achievement award U. Mo.-Kansas City Women Alumni, 1974. Mem. Council of Mo. Orgns. for Tchr. Edn. (organizer, pres.), Assn. of Tchr. Educators (mini-clinic coordinator, mem. conv. planning com. 1980, coordinator specialized topics seminars 1976, exec. bd. 1980—, past pres., exec. sec. Mo. unit), Assn. Supervision and Curriculum Devel., Nat. Council Social Studies, Nat. Council Tchrs. Math., Mo. Council Geog. Edn., Mo. Council Social Studies, Mo. Assn. Colls. Tchr. Edn. (coll. rep.), AAUW, Kappa Delta Pi, Phi Delta Kappa, Pi Lambda Theta. Baptist.

MILLER, MASON FERRELL, elec. engr.; b. Rockford, Nebr., Nov. 5, 1919; s. Martin Robertson and Bertha Luella (Story) M.; B.S., U. Nebr., 1940; M.S., Mass. Inst. Tech., 1941; m. Irene Elizabeth Westerman, Sept. 25, 1942; children—Paul Martin, James Mason, Marianne. Student engr. AT&T, N.Y.C., 1941; jr. engr. U.S. Navy, Bath, Maine, 1941; with NASA, Langley AFB, Va., 1941-51, aero. research scientist, 1948-51, Cleve., 1951-55; engr. specialist AiResearch Mfg. Co., Phoenix, 1955-57; preliminary design engr. Allison div. Gen. Motors Co., Indpls., 1957-61; sr. engring. specialist, supr. N. Am. Rockwell, Columbus, Ohio, 1961-69; performance engr. Gen. Electric Co., Aircraft Engine Group, Evendale, Ohio, 1969—; teaching advisor Gen. Motors Inst., 1960. Mem. Washington Twp. Sch. Planning Com., Indpls., 1961; asst. scoutmaster Boy Scouts Am., Berea, Ohio, 1954-55, pack treas., Phoenix, 1956-57, cubmaster, com. chmn., Indpls., 1959-61. U. Nebr. Regent's scholar, 1936; Mass. Inst. Tech. scholar, 1940; recipient NASA Merit Service award, 1948; Cleve. City and Plain Dealer award ARC program, 1953. Mem. Am. Def. Preparedness Assn., AIAA, Pi Mu Epsilon, Sigma Tau. Presbyterian (deacon). Club: Order of DeMolay. Contbr. articles in field to profl. jours. Home: 10572 Hadley Rd Cincinnati OH 45218 Office: Gen Electric Co Cincinnati OH 45215

MILLER, MICHAEL RALPH, hosp. adminstr.; b. Hastings, Nebr., Sept. 13, 1936; s. Ralph Arthur and Florence Adeline (Kealy) M.; B.A. in Bus., Hastings Coll., 1959; M.H.A., U. Minn., Mpls.,1966; m. Helen Louise Langemo, Aug. 5, 1967; children—Eric Michael, Cynthia Louise. Bus. mgr. Mesa (Ariz.) Lutheran Hosp., 1964; adminstr. Stevens County Meml. Hosp., Morris, Minn., 1966-67; Marinette (Wis.) Gen. Hosp., 1967-73, Meml. Hosp. Dodge County, Fremont, Nebr., 1973-77; pres. St. John's Regional Med. Center, Joplin, Mo., 1978—, mem. bd. dirs.; mem. various profl. coms. and dist. offices. Mem. exec. bd. Mo-Kan area council Boy Scouts Am. Served to lt. (j.g.) USN, 1960-63. Fellow Am. Coll. Hosp. Adminstrs.; mem. Am. Hosp. Assn., Mo. Hosp. Assn., Catholic Hosp. Assn., Joplin C. of C. (dir.). Roman Catholic. Clubs: Rotary, Elks. Office: Saint Johns Regional Med Center 2727 McClelland Blvd Joplin MO 64801

MILLER, MILFORD MORTIMER, lawyer; b. Evansville, Ind., Mar. 20, 1937; s. Milford Mortimer and Dorothy (Welborn) M.; A.B., Dartmouth Coll., 1959; J.D. with distinction, Ind. U., 1962; m. Mary Elizabeth Patterson, Aug. 17, 1963; children—Milford Mortimer III, John Patterson, Calvert Sterling, Rebecca Welborn. Admitted to Ind. bar, 1962, U.S. Supreme Ct.; asso. law firm Livingston, Dildine, Haynie & Yoder, Ft. Wayne, Ind., 1962-67, partner, 1967-79, mng. partner, 1979—; mem. com. on character and fitness Ind. Supreme Ct. Bd. Law Examiners, 1980—. Bldg. chmn. Center of Performing Arts, Ft. Wayne, 1967-73. Pres., bd. dirs. Ft. Wayne Civic Theatre, 1963-79; bd. dirs., mem. exec. com. Ft. Wayne Fine Arts Found.; pres. bd. dirs. Legal Aid of Ft. Wayne. Mem. Allen County (chmn. grievance com. 1970-72, mem. jud. selection and tenure com. 1968-74, trustee 1974-76, law med. rev. panel 1977—, chmn. jud. liaison com. 1978-80), Ind., Am., 7th Circuit bar assns., Am. Judicature Soc., Assn. Am. Trial Lawyers, Ind. Trial Lawyers Assn., Def. Research Inst., Order of the Coif, Sigma Nu. Democrat. Presbyterian. Clubs: Dartmouth Alumni Club of Ft. Wayne, Ft. Wayne Country. Bd. editors Ind. Law Rev. Jour. Home: 4220 Old Mill Rd Fort Wayne IN 46807 Office: One Summit Sq Fort Wayne IN 46802

MILLER, NORMAN JOHN, bacteriologist; b. Evansville, Ind., Apr. 14, 1905; s. I. and Carrie (Blount) M.; B.S., Iowa State Coll., 1930; Sc.D., Evansville Coll., 1959; m. Jeanne Thomas, Feb. 25, 1938; 1 dau., Marcia Ellen Miller Holland. Bacteriologist, Mead Johnson & Co., 1930-35, asst. chief bacteriologist, 1935-51, dir. bacteriology control, 1951-60, cons., 1960-64. Mem. Soc. Am. Bacteriology (Ind.

br. pres., 1944-45, nat. councilor 1946, 47, emeritus), Am. Dairy Sci. Assn. (hon.), Am. Dairy Assn. (life), Am. Soc. for Microbiology (emeritus), Iowa State U. Alumni Assn. (life), Purdue U. Alumni Assn. (life), U. Evansville Alumni Assn. Contbr. articles to sci. jours. Home: 850 Covert St Evansville IN 47713

MILLER, OTIS LOUIS, historian; b. Belleville, Ill., Aug. 8, 1933; s. Otis Louis and Viola (Neubarth) M.; B.A., So. Ill. U., 1956, M.S., 1963; Ph.D., St. Louis U., 1972; m. Sandra Jo Schilling, June 16, 1962; children—Deborah, Stacy. Tchr. Belleville Twp. (Ill.) High Sch., 1958-65; instr. history, polit. sci. Belleville Area Coll., 1965—, chmn. dept. social sci., 1967-73; owner, operator Belleville Coin Shop; instr. history, sociology McKendree Coll., Lebanon, Ill., part-time 1975—; cons. in field. Mem. Ill. Ho. of Reps., 1961-62; alderman 7th ward City of Belleville, 1963-81, acting mayor, 1978-79; mem. Belleville Pub. Library Bd., 1963-77, pres., 2 years; mem. SW Regional Planning Commn. Ill., 1976-81; pres. Douglas Sch. PTA, 1975-77. Mem. Orgn. Am. Historians, Am. Hist. Assn., Ill., Ark., Mo. hist. socs., Am., St. Louis, Mo. numis. socs., Nat. Council Social Sci. Republican. Mem. United Ch. Christ. Clubs: Masons, Elks, Eagles, Moose. Home: 413 S Virginia St Belleville IL 62221 Office: 2500 Carlyle Ave Belleville IL 62221

MILLER, PATRICIA MARIA, real estate broker; b. Detroit, Feb. 10, 1933; d. John and Fannie (Pulkanin) Carberry; student U. Akron, 1968-70; m. William Farquar Miller, Sept. 8, 1950; children—William S., Lisa B., Robert J. Interviewer, Nat. Opinion Research Center, U. Chgo., 1965-66; mgr. classified advt. Falls News, Cuyahoga Falls, Ohio, 1966-67; sales asso. Frank Krause Realty, Akron, Ohio, 1967-74; sales mgr. Trail Realty, Cuyahoga Falls, 1974-75; broker, owner Century 21, PMA Realty, Inc., Cuyahoga Falls, 1975—. Sec., League Women Voters Cuyahoga Falls, 1961-63, pres., 1963-65; mem. Cuyahoga Falls Charter Rev. Commn., 1965; mem. Mayor's Adv. Commn. on Urban Renewal, 1966-67; precinct committeewoman, also sec. Cuyahoga Falls Republican Central Com., 1967-68; mem. Cuyahoga Falls Planning Commn., 1966-71; mem. Summit County Planning Commn., 1976-79; mem. Akron Regional Devel. Bd., 1979—, trustee, 1981—. Mem. Akron Area Bd. Realtors, Realtors Nat. Mktg. Inst., Cuyahoga Falls C. of C. (pres. 1981). Methodist. Home: 345 Marian Lake Blvd Cuyahoga Falls OH 44223 Office: 2427 State Rd Cuyahoga Falls OH 44223

MILLER, PATRICIA SUSAN KREILING, journalist, photographer; b. Pitts., Mar. 21, 1943; d. Herbert John Jr. and Ann (Jackson) Kreiling; student Culver-Stockton Coll., 1961; children—John Scott, Kurt Lawrence, Doug Andrew. Model, sales Bonwit Teller, Oak Brook, Ill., 1962-63; market research Leo Burnett Advt., Chgo., 1967-68; reporter, columnist, photographer Suburban Life Newspapers, La Grange, Ill., 1974-77; public relations dir. Community Meml. Gen. Hosp., La Grange, 1977—; free-lance writer, photographer, 1962—, cons. public relations, speaker, researcher, 1961—. Vice pres. La Grange Highlands Civic Assn., 1973; v.p. Dist. 106 PTA, 1974; chmn. La Grange Highlands Safety Com., 1975. Recipient Golden Trumpet award Publicity Club of Chgo., 1980. Mem. Ill. Women's Press Assn. (Mate E. Palmer awards 1977-79), Nat. Fedn. Press Women, Chgo. Hosp. Public Relations Soc. (program chmn. 1978-79), Nat. Assn. Future Women (chmn. bd. public relations com.), Am. Soc. Hosp. Public Relations, Ill. Hosp. Public Relations Soc. (conv. speaker 1978-79, ann. state meeting gen. chairperson 1979, sec.-treas. 1979-80, pres.-elect 1980, pres. 1981), Women in Mgmt., Alpha Xi Delta Alumnae. Roman Catholic. Contbr. numerous articles, photographs to books, mags., newspapers, jours. Home: 1002 Coronet Ln La Grange IL 60525 Office: Community Meml Gen Hosp 5101 Willow Springs Rd La Grange IL 60525

MILLER, RAYMOND LEE, supt. schs.; b. Chandlerville, Ill., Jan. 23, 1922; s. Abraham and Rachel (Masten) M.; B.S., Western Ill. State U., 1945; M.S., U. Ill., 1947, advanced certificate, 1961; Ed.D., No. Ill. U., DeKalb, 1973; m. Mavis Yvonne Remsburg, Apr. 4, 1946; children—Douglas Kent, Merridee Beth, Todd Randall. Tchr., coach Manito (Ill.) Grade Sch., 1942-44; tchr. Mason City (Ill.) High Sch., 1945-46; prin. Balyki High Sch., Bath, Ill., 1947-51; unit. supt. Delavan (Ill.) Com. Unit Schs., 1951-62; supt. schs. Lisle, Ill., 1962—. Bd. dirs. Spl. Edn. Coop. Mem. NEA, Ill. Edn. Assn. (dir., past pres. Peoria div.), Am., Ill. (legis. com.) assns. sch. adminstrs., West Suburban Supts. Assn. (pres.), Supts. Round Table No. Ill. (membership chmn.), County of DuPage Supts. (pres.), N. Central Assn. (chmn. evaluation team), Phi Delta Kappa. Methodist. Kiwanian (past pres.). Home: 5601 Westview Ln Lisle IL 60532 Office: 5211 Center Ave Lisle IL 60532

MILLER, RICHARD G., JR., indsl. mfg., engring. and constrn. co. exec.; b. Chgo., 1918; grad. Marshall U., 1942. Pres., Roberts & Schaefer Co., 1963—; v.p. Elgin Nat. Industries, Inc., Chgo., 1968-72, pres., chief exec. officer, 1977—, also dir. Office: 120 S Riverside Plaza Chicago IL 60606

MILLER, RICHARD VEITUS, mktg. rep.; b. Elkhart, Ind., Jan. 25, 1926; s. Henry Bernard and Thelma Irene (Stanley) M.; student Marine Corps Inst., 1951-52, Rochester Inst. Tech., 1952-55; m. Dorothy Edna Ellison, May 24, 1947; 1 son, David Paul. Sales clk. Requa Electric Co., Rochester, N.Y., 1947-51; electrician Taylor Instrument Co., Rochester, 1952-55; service engr. Taylor Instrument Co., Rochester, 1955-67; sr. mktg. rep. Bendix HVSG, Elyria, Ohio, 1967—. Served with U.S. Navy, 1943-45, USMC, 1951-52. Mem. Am. Def. Preparedness Assn., VFW. Club: Elks. Home: 1440 6 Prospect St Elyria OH 44035 Office: 901 Cleveland St Elyria OH 44036

MILLER, ROBERT ALLEN, hosp. adminstr.; b. Ottumwa, Iowa, Dec. 15, 1949; s. Carl Robert and Margaret Irene (Allen) M.; A.S., Indian Hills Community Coll., 1970; student U. Minn., 1977-80; m. Connie Lynn Lindsey, Sept. 2, 1969; children—Destin Robert, Kiley Allen. Asst. produce mgr. Hy-Vee Food Stores, Ottumwa, Iowa, 1967-70; bus. mgr. Henry County Meml. Hosp., Mt. Pleasant, Iowa, 1970-72, asst. adminstr., 1972-75; adminstr., chief exec. officer Henry County Health Center, Mt. Pleasant, 1975—. Pres., S.E. Iowa Blood Center; chmn. Henry County Bd. Health; chmn. March of Dimes, 1975-77; dir. local chpt. Am. Cancer Soc., 1975—. Mem. Iowa Hosp Assn., Am. Hosp. Assn., Hosp. Fin. Mgmt. Assn. Republican. Baptist. Club: Rotary (dir.). Home: Rural Route 3 Box 37 Mount Pleasant IA 52641

MILLER, ROBERT CARL, physicist; b. Chgo., Oct. 26, 1938; s. Carl and Violet (Nelson) M.; B.S. in Physics, Ill. Inst. Tech., 1961; M.S. in Physics, No. Ill. U., 1965, Certificate Advanced Study in Physics, 1972; m. Mary Kay Ball, Sept. 3, 1969. Researcher particle accelerator div. Argonne (Ill.) Nat. Lab., 1961-66, researcher high energy physics div., 1966—. Registered profl. engr., Ill. Mem. Am. Phys. Soc., Am. Nuclear Soc., IEEE, Nat. Soc. Profl. Engrs., Soc. Certified Data Processors, Instrument Soc. Am., Am. Inst. Aero. and Astronautics, Mensa, Internat. Soc. for Philos. Enquiry, Sigma Xi, Sigma Pi Sigma. Contbr. articles to profl. jours. Home: 1105 Elizabeth Ave Naperville IL 60540 Office: High Energy Physics Div Argonne Nat Lab Bldg 362 Room G-216 9700 S Cass Ave Argonne IL 60439

MILLER, ROBERT EDWARD, public speaker, mgmt. devel. cons.; b. Engelwood, N.J., June 22, 1947; s. Wilfred Russell and Christine Ida (Ross) M.; Asso. Degree, DeVry Inst. Tech., Chgo., 1969; B.A., Augustana Coll., Rock Island, Ill., 1975; M.S., Western Ill. U., 1979. Responsible for mgmt. devel. and sales tng. Johnson Controls, Inc., Milw., 1976-79; mgmt. devel. cons., public speaker, Milw., 1979—. Mem. Am. Soc. for Tng. and Devel., Nat. Speakers Assn., Wis. Profl. Speakers Assn. (dir.). Club: Toastmasters. Home and Office: PO Box 1079 Milwaukee WI 53201

MILLER, ROBERT FREDERICK, ednl. adminstr.; b. Richmond, Va., Mar. 10, 1947; s. Elmer T. and Ruth G. (Vick) M.; A.B., Coll. of William and Mary, 1969; Mus.M., East Carolina U., 1973; Ph.D., U. Ill., 1979. Tchr. instrumental music Fairfax County (Va.) Public Schs., 1969-72; teaching fellow dept. music edn. East Carolina U., Greenville, N.C., 1972-73; instr. music edn. Oberlin (Ohio) Coll. Conservatory Music, 1974-77; lectr. music edn. U. Md., 1977-78; vis. lectr. music edn. Sch. Music, U. Ill., Urbana, 1978-79; dir. aesthetic edn. program CEMREL, Inc., St. Louis, 1979—; cons. to various sch. systems, 1972—, Am. Research Inst. for Arts; free-lance photographer, 1971—. Named Outstanding Young Educator, No. Va. Jaycees, 1972; cert. tchr., Va. Mem. Council for Research in Music Edn., Sinfonia, Nat. Rifle Assn., St. Louis Practical Pistol Club. Mem. United Ch. Christ. Contbr. articles on music edn. to profl. publs. Office: CEMREL Inc 3120 59th St Saint Louis MO 63139

MILLER, ROBERT GEORGE, hosp. adminstr.; b. Chariton, Iowa, July 18, 1927; s. Elton M. and Lola M.; B.A., U. Iowa, 1951, M.A. in Hosp. Adminstrn., 1954; m. Diane A. Hardin; children—Stephen, Stuart. Adminstrv. asst. Sheboygan (Wis.) Clinic, 1953-54; asst. adminstr. St. Lukes Hosp., Marquette, Mich., 1954-56; adminstr. F.A. Bell Meml. Hosp., Ishpeming, Mich., 1956-63; pres. Riverside Med. Center, Kankakee, Ill., 1963—. Bd. dirs. Community Services Council. Served with M.C., USN, 1945-47. Mem. Am. Coll. Hosp. Adminstrs., Am. Hosp. Assn., Ill. Hosp. Assn. (trustee), Kankakee C. of C. (dir.). Presbyterian. Club: Kankakee Rotary. Office: 350 N Wall St Kankakee IL 60901

MILLER, ROBERT HASKINS, state supreme ct. justice; b. Columbus, Ohio, Mar. 3, 1919; s. George L. and Marian Alice (Haskins) M.; student Ohio State U., 1936-37; A.B., Kans. U., 1940; LL.B., 1943; grad. Nat. Coll. State Trial Judges, Phila., 1967; m. Audene Fausett, Mar. 14, 1943; children—Stephen F., Thomas G., David W., Stacey Ann. Admitted to Kans. bar, 1943; practiced law, Paola, Kans., 1946-60; judge 6th Jud. Dist., Paola, 1961-69, U.S. Magistrate Dist. Kans., Kansas City, 1969-75; justice Kans. Supreme Ct., 1975—. Served with U.S. Army, 1942-46. Mem. Kans., Shawnee County bar assns., Am. Judicature Soc., Am. Legion, Phi Gamma Delta, Phi Delta Phi. Presbyterian. Club: Masons. Author: (with others) Pattern (Civil Jury) Instructions for Kansas, 1966, 69. Office: Kans Judicial Center Topeka KS 66612

MILLER, ROBERT SLADE, accountant; b. Chgo., Jan. 3, 1949; s. James G. and Dagmar Marie (Anderson) M.; A.A., Chgo. City Coll., 1967; B.S., Roosevelt U., 1969, M.S., 1971; m. Sharon Anne Wallace, Aug. 30, 1969; children—Brian Slade, James Geoffery, Sheila Renee, Melinda Anne. Sr. tax acct. S. D. Leidesdorf & Co., Chgo., 1970-74; dir. tax dept. Alberto-Culver Co. & Subs.'s, Melrose Park, Ill., 1974-75; tax partner Favorite, Perry & Miller, C.P.A.'s, South Holland, Ill., 1975—; treas., dir. Modern Life and Accident Ins. Co., Am. Family Life Ins. Assn., Chgo., 1981—; chmn. acctg. dept. Northwestern U. Sch. Continuing Edn., 1973—. Bd. dirs. United Way, South Holland, 1978—. C.P.A., Ill. Mem. Am. Inst. C.P.A.'s, Ill. C.P.A. Soc. (pres. Chgo. S. chpt. 1976-77, dir. 1979—), Am. Acctg. Assn. Republican. Mem. Ch. Jesus Christ of Latter-day Saints. Office: 705 E 162d St South Holland IL 60473

MILLER, ROBERT STERLING, mfg. co. exec.; b. Millersburg, Ohio, Oct. 20, 1926; s. Roscoe C. and Evelyn M. Miller; B.Sc. in Bus. Adminstrn., Ohio State U., 1951; M.B.A., Ohio U., 1981; m. Norma Jean Bird, June 12, 1948; children—Lee H., Sallie Jane. Indsl. sales mgr. Miracle Adhesives Corp., New Philadelphia, Ohio, 1953-58; sales mgr. Buehler Bros. Co., Dover, Ohio, 1958-68; gen. mgr. consumer div. Franklin Chem. Industries, Columbus, Ohio, 1968—. Served with USAAF, 1945. Recipient Outstanding Citizen award, Dover, 1968. Methodist. Author: Adhesives and Glues-How to Choose and Use Them, 1980. Home: 4208 Greensview Dr Upper Arlington OH 43220 Office: 2020 Bruck St Columbus OH 43207

MILLER, ROGER ALAN, interior design exec.; b. Wichita, Kans., Aug. 25, 1946; s. Wilbur Bryant and Mary (Bozarth) M.; A.A., Butler County Community Jr. Coll., 1973; B.B.A., Wichita State U., 1975. Owner, mgr. Miller's, Inc., Wichita, 1971—. Chairperson Remodeling Council Wichita. Served with USNR, 1968-72. Mem. Wichita C. of C., Wichita Area Builders Assn. (dir.). Republican. Methodist. Office: 2803 E Central St Wichita KS 67214

MILLER, RONALD LEE, mfg. and entertainment co. exec.; b. Columbus, Ohio, Aug. 17, 1940; s. Bruce Eugene and Opal Maxine (Boss) M.; B.S. in Mech. Engring., Ohio State U., 1966; M.B.A., U. Beverly Hills, 1977, Ph.D., 1979; children—Kellie Ann, Christina Lynn, Erin Nichole. Corp. engr. chems. civ. U.S. Steel Corp., Circleville, Ohio, Pitts., 1970-72; owner Quality Mold, Grand Rapids, Mich., 1972-73; v.p. Nika Plastics, Grand Rapids, 1973-75; pres. Internat. Prototypes, Grand Rapids, 1975-79; founder, chief exec. Nat. Prototypes, Grand Rapids, 1977-79; pres. Hilco Plastics, Grand Rapids, 1977—; pres., founder Position Inc., Grand Rapids, 1980—, RLM Prodns., Hollywood, 1980—; cons. product devel. Mem. ednl. adv. com. Grand Rapids Area Colls.; mem. U.S. Senatorial Adv. Com. Served with USMCR, 1957-58. Mem. Soc. Plastics Engrs., N.Y. Acad. Scis. Republican. Roman Catholic. Author texts in field. Office: 6505 S Division Grand Rapids MI 49508 also 4498 Woodman St Suite A122 Sherman Oaks CA 91423

MILLER, RUTH MARIE, data processor; b. San Mateo, Calif., Nov. 3, 1949; d. Thomas Luckett and Charlotte O. Miller; diploma programming and electronics, Brown Inst., Mpls., 1976; divorced; 1 dau., Jennifer Brady. Data processor U.S. Dept. Agr., Mpls., 1976-78; v.p. data processing Minn. Mut. Fire & Casualty Co., Mpls., 1978—. Mem. Data Processing mgmt. Assn. Home: 14508 County Rd 6 Plymouth MN 55441 Office: 1200 Shelard Tower Minneapolis MN 55426

MILLER, SHARON MONAHAN, educator; b. Oak Park, Ill., Jan. 1, 1942; d. Douglas and Elaine Iva (Markuson) Monahan; B.A. in Biology, Northwestern U., 1963, M.S. in Biology, 1965; postgrad. Stanford U., 1968; Ph.D. in Biol. Scis., U. Calif., Santa Cruz, 1972; m. Thomas Raymond Miller, May 29, 1965. Asst. prof. biology and chemistry, dir. allied health programs Coll. St. Francis, Joliet, Ill., 1969-75; med. technologist Silver Cross Hosp., Joliet, 1974-75; asso. prof., dir. med. tech. program, acting asst. chmn. Sch. Allied Health Professions, No. Ill. U., Coll. Profl. Studies, DeKalb, 1977—. Bd. dirs. Comprehensive Health Planning of N.W. Ill., 1980-82; mem. program survey teams State of Ill. Bd. Edn., Dept. Adult and Vocat. and Tech. Edn., 1980—; mem. adv. bd. career-vocat. edn. programs, regional Office of Edn. Boone-Winnebago Counties, 1978—. Lt. comdr. USNR. NSF grantee, 1971-72. Mem. Am. Soc. Med. Tech. (trustee edn. and research fund 1980—, chmn. regional biochemistry sci. assembly 1981), Ill. Med. Tech. Assn. (chmn. biochemistry sci. assembly 1979-81, dir. 1979—), Ill. Acad. Scis., Am. Soc. Clin. Pathologists, AAAS, Phi Beta Kappa. Republican. Episcopalian. Club: Forest City Dog Tng., Order Eastern Star. Contbr. articles to profl. jours. Office: Sch Allied Health Professions Northern Ill U DeKalb IL 60115

MILLER, SOL, research microbiologist, indsl. hygienist; b. Akron, Ohio, June 3, 1914; s. Phillip and Mollie (Drutz) M.; B.A., Akron U., 1936; M.S., Ohio State U., 1939; Ph.D., Sussex (Eng.) U., 1975; m. Rosalyn Raful, Dec. 28, 1937; children—Barbara Claire Miller Olschwang, Kenneth Arnold. Bacteriologist, Ohio Dept. Health, 1939-42; chief chemist Q.O. Ordnance Corp., Grand Island, Nebr., 1942-43; research asso. Children's Fund of Mich., Detroit, 1944-54; bacteriologist James Labs., Chgo., 1954-55; group leader, research bacteriologist IIT Research Inst., Chgo., 1955-72; corp. biohazard control Abbott Labs., North Chicago, Ill., 1972—; adj. instr. Chgo. Med. Sch., 1973—; mem. exec. com., tng. chmn. research and devel. sect. Nat. Safety Council, 1974—. Cert. specialist Nat. Registry Microbiologists; cert. hazard control mgr.; cert. profl. chemist. Fellow Am. Inst. Chemists, Am. Acad. Microbiology; mem. Am. Inst. Biol. Scis., Am. Chem. Soc., Am. Soc. for Microbiology, Am. Soc. Indsl. Microbiology, Ill. Soc. for Microbiology, Am. Assn. Clin. Chemists, Am. Indsl. Hygiene Assn., Sigma Xi. Mem. B'nai B'rith (past pres. Lodge 1455). Contbr. articles to profl. jours. Home: 706 Waukegan Rd Glenview IL 60025 Office: 1400 Sheridan Rd North Chicago IL 60064

MILLER, STEPHEN JOHN, univ. ofcl., social scientist; b. Secaucus, N.J., Sept. 11, 1936; s. George W. and Constance (Adamowicz) M.; B.S. in Sociology, St. Peter's Coll., Jersey City, 1958; Ph.D., St. Louis U., 1963; m. Roberta M. Brahm, Sept. 17, 1960; children—Andrew S., Rodney J., Jessica A. Resident sociologist, research projects dir. Community Studies, Inc., Kansas City, Mo., 1962-64; asst. prof. social research Brandeis U., 1964-67, asso. prof. sociology Florence Heller Grad. Sch. for Advanced Studies in Social Welfare, 1967-72; asst. dir. Center for Community Health and Med. Care Med. Sch. and Sch. Pub. Health, Harvard, 1968-69, asso. dean for urban affairs Med. Sch., 1969-72, mem. pres.'s adv. com. on community relations, 1970-71, asso. dean admissions, 1970-74, asso. prof. preventive and social medicine, 1973-76; v.p. Affiliated Hosps. Center, Boston, 1972-76; asso. provost Northwestern U., 1976—, prof. community medicine Med. Sch., 1976—, mem. bd. McGaw Med. Center, 1976—, exec. com., 1977—; cons. River City Project, Chgo., 1976—, Assn. Am. Med. Colls., 1966-67, R.I. Dept. Pub. Assistance, 1967-69. Fellow Am. Sociol. Assn.; mem. Soc. for Study Social Problems, Midwest, Eastern sociol. socs. Author: A Division of Nursing Labor, 1965; Prescription for Leadership: Training for the Medical Elite, 1970; dep. editor Jour. Health and Social Behavior, 1969-71; contbr. articles to profl. jours. Address: Northwestern U Evanston IL 60201

MILLER, THEODORE ROBERT, clin. psychologist; b. Glen Ridge, N.J., June 29, 1949; s. Edward Rodgers and Ellen (Bowman) M.; B.A., Rutgers U., 1971; M.A., Fairleigh Dickinson U., 1973; Ph.D., U. S.D., 1977; m. Bente Birgitte Blidt, Aug. 21, 1976; 1 dau., Jennifer Kristen. Sr. clinician Northwestern Community Mental Health Center, Shenandoah Office, Woodstock, Va., 1977-79; psychologist Center for Mental Health, Elwood, Ind., 1979—. Mem. Am. Psychol. Assn. Presbyterian. Home: Rural Route 1 Box 442-C Alexandria IN 46001 Office: Center for Mental Health PO Box 304 Elwood IN 46036

MILLER, THOMAS J., atty. gen. Iowa; b. Dubuque, Iowa, Aug. 11, 1944; s. Elmer John and Betty Maude (Kross) M.; B.A., Loras Coll., Dubuque, 1966; J.D., Harvard U., 1969. Admitted to Iowa bar, 1969; with VISTA, 1969-70; legis. asst. to U.S. congressman, 1970-71; legal edn. dir. Balt. Legal Aid Bur., also mem. part-time faculty U. Md. Sch. Law, 1971-73; pvt. practice, McGregor, Iowa, 1973-78; city atty., McGregor, 1975-78; atty. gen. of Iowa, 1978—. Pres. 2d Dist. New Democratic Club, Balt., 1972. Mem. Am., Iowa bar assns., Common Cause. Roman Catholic. Office: Hoover Bldg 2d Floor Des Moines IA 50319

MILLER, VERNON RICHARD, state senator, nursing home exec.; b. Des Moines, July 27, 1939; s. Wallace Thomas and Enid Lillian (Conklin) M.; B.S., Purdue U., 1963; M.S. in Bus. Adminstrn., Ind. U., South Bend, 1973; m. Jane Kay Rothrock, Aug. 19, 1961; children—Vernon Richard, Pamela Sue. Dept. foreman Jomac North Ltd., Warsaw, Ind., 1959-61; lab. technician Purdue U., 1963-64; microbiologist Pabst Brewing Co., Peoria Heights, Ill., 1964-65; dept. mgr. Ocean Spray Cranberries, North Chicago, Ill., 1965-67; exec. Miller's Merry Manor, Inc., Plymouth, Ind., 1967—; mem. State of Ind. Senate, 1976—. Chmn. Marshall County Ind. March of Dimes, 1973-76; blood chmn. Marshall County Red Cross, 1970-74. Mem. Am. Coll. Nursing Home Adminstrs. Republican. Methodist. Clubs: Plymouth Country, Kiwanis (pres. 1972, lt. gov. 1975), Mason, Shriner, Order Eastern Star. Office: PO Box 498 Plymouth IN 46563

MILLER, W. GORDON, water conditioning co. exec.; b. Havre, Mont., July 6, 1932; s. Walter Wesley and Vivian (Vagg) M.; B.A., Carleton Coll., 1954; M.S., Syracuse U., 1955; m. Gayle I. Highberg, Dec. 29, 1954; children—Peggy, Debby, David. Pres. Culligan Water Conditioning Co., Marlette, Mich., 1958—, Port Huron, Mich., 1979—, Clean Water Corp., La Crosse, Wis., 1974—; dir. Wolverine State Bank, WQA Nat. Ins. Trust, U.S. Water Co., Mpls. Chmn. Sanilac County Mental Health Bd., 1971-76; v.p. Marlette Community Hosp., 1971—; sec. Sanilac County Bldg. Authority, 1972—. Recipient Key Man award, Internat. Water Quality Assn., 1976. Mem. Mich. Water Conditioning Assn. (founder, past pres.), Internat. Water Quality Assn. (past pres.), Mich. Culligan Assn. (past pres.), Marlette C. of C. (past pres.). Republican. Presbyterian. Clubs: Masons, Shriners. Home: 6623 Cooper Rd Marlette MI 48453 Office: 3099 Main St Marlette MI 48453

MILLER, WALTER MAURICE, mfg. co. exec.; b. Yonkers, N.Y., July 12, 1938; s. Maurice and Margaret (Cawley) M.; B.S. in Elec. Engring., Union Coll., 1960; M.B.A., Baldwin-Wallace Coll., 1979; m. Geraldine Herricks, Nov. 24, 1965; children—Kathryn Ann, Carolyn Faye. Engring. mgr. Lorain Products subs. Reliance Electric Co., Cleve., 1975-80, gen. mgr., 1980—. Chmn. Internat. Energy Conf., 1971; active Jr. Achievement. Served with USAF, 1960-63. Registered profl. engr., Tex. Mem. IEEE, U.S. Power Squadron. Presbyterian. Club: Toastmasters. Patentee in med. field. Office: 1122 F St Lorain OH 44052

MILLER, WILLIAM DEVANNY, state ofcl.; b. Chgo., Mar. 27, 1944; s. Richard Haywood and Helen Mary (Devanny) M.; student St. Joseph's Coll., Ind., 1962-63, Conception Sem., Mo., 1963-64, U. Ill., 1964; B.S. with high honors in Police Adminstrn., Mich. State U., 1966, M.S. in Criminal Justice, 1971; m. Carol Ann Klaas, June 18, 1966; children—Mary Christine, William Devanny, Mary Carol. Public safety officer Mich. State U. Police, 1966-70; police specialist Wis. Council Criminal Justice, 1970-71; adminstrv. asst. div. criminal investigation Wis. Dept. Justice, 1971-74, chief budget and mgmt., 1974-80; commr. public safety State of Iowa, Des Moines, 1980—;

mem. Iowa Crime Commn.; bd. dirs. Iowa Crime Prevention Coalition. Mem. Diocese of Madison Bd. Edn., 1978-80, pres., 1980. Recipient award of bravery Mich. State U. Dept. Public Safety, 1970. Mem. Internat. Assn. Chiefs of Police, Iowa Chiefs of Police and Peace Officers Assn., Am. Soc. Public Adminstrn., YMCA. Roman Catholic. Club: Serra. Office: Wallace State Office Bldg Des Moines IA 50319

MILLETT, ESTHER LEE, educator; b. Nevada, Iowa, Aug. 28, 1937; d. Leo Merle and Esther Veronica (Telfer) Dayhuff; student Mt. Mercy Coll., 1956-61; B.S., Drake U., 1967, M.S., 1970; postgrad. Iowa State U., 1971-73; m. Merlin Lyle Millett, Aug. 21, 1970. Elem. tchr. All Saints Sch., Cedar Rapids, Iowa, 1960-63, Jefferson (Iowa) Community Schs., 1963-67, Ames (Iowa) Community Sch., 1967-75, Rockwood Community Sch. Dist., Fenton Mo., 1975-79, Wichita (Kans.) Public Schs., 1979—; leader ednl. in-service workshops; bldg. rep. for curriculum devels. Mem. Kappa Delta Pi. Author: What? Four Little Surprises!, 1977; Togetherness Is Love, 1977. Home: 8240 Brookhollow Ln Wichita KS 67206

MILLETT, MERLIN LYLE, JR., aero. engr.; b. East Moline, Ill., Dec. 29, 1923; s. Merlin L. and Erie L. (Hyland) M.; B.S. in Aero. Engring., Iowa State Coll., 1945, M.S., 1948, Ph.D. in Theoretical and Applied Mechanics, 1957; m. Esther Lee Dayhuff, Aug. 21, 1970; 1 dau., Debra Sue Lynn. Draftsman, Am. Machine and Metals Co., 1941; flight testing engr. Douglas Aircraft Co., Santa Monica, Calif., 1948-52; asst. prof. aero. engring. Iowa State Coll., Ames, 1952-57, asso. prof., 1957-61, prof., 1961-75; prof. aerospace engring. Parks Coll., St. Louis U., 1975-78, also dean of faculty; sr. specialist engr. Boeing Wichita Co. (now Boeing Mil. Airplane Co.), Wichita, Kans., 1978-81; adj. prof. mech. and aerospace engring. Okla. State U., 1979, 82; adj. prof. aero. engring. Wichita State U., 1980; engring. supr. Boeing Military Airplane Co., Wichita, 1981—; aero. cons., 1955-78. Treas., First Christian Ch., Ames, 1955-70, chmn. ofcl. bd., 1965-68. Served with USN, 1941-46. Registered profl. engr., Iowa. Mem. AIAA, Am. Soc. Engring. Edn., Aircraft Owners and Pilots Assn., Sigma Xi, Tau Beta Pi, Phi Kappa Phi, Pi Mu Epsilon, Phi Mu Alpha (pres. 1943-44, student dir. of band 1943-45), Knights of St. Patrick. Club: Rotary (sec.-treas. 1968-75). Home: 8240 Brookhollow Ln Wichita KS 67206 Office: Boeing Military Airplane Co 3801 S Oliver Wichita KS 67210

MILLETT, STEPHEN MALCOLM, historian; b. N.Y.C., Feb. 22, 1947; s. John David and Catherine (Letsinger) M.; A.B., Miami U., Oxford, Ohio, 1969; M.A., Ohio State U., 1970, Ph.D., 1972; m. Patricia McBurney, Aug. 1, 1970; children—Jennifer Jane, Ann Elizabeth. Commd. 2d lt. USAF, 1971, advanced through grades to capt., 1976; asst. prof. humanities Air Force Inst. Tech., 1973-77; adj. asst. prof. U. Dayton, 1974-77; area mgr. Ohio Valley area Air Force Jr. ROTC, Columbus, Ohio, 1977-79; research scientist Battelle Meml. Inst., Columbus, 1979—. Mem. Orgn. Am. Historians, Soc. Historians Am. Fgn. Relations. Author: Selected Bibliography of American Constitutional History, 1975; American Diplomacy Before the Courts, 1977. Office: Battelle Meml Inst 505 King Ave Columbus OH 43201

MILLIGAN, EVAN JANE, retail co. exec.; b. Carbondale, Ill., Nov. 16, 1919; d. James W. and Alma E. (Cruse) M.; B.Ed. magna cum laude, So. Ill. U., 1941. High sch. tchr., Benton, Ill., 1941-44; mng. partner Town & Country, Benton, 1944-52; with Marshall Field & Co., Chgo., 1952—, mgr. induction and systems tng., 1952-55, tng. dir., 1955-74, v.p., gen. personnel mgr., 1974-78, sr. v.p. gen. personnel mgr., 1978—; dir. First Fed. of Chgo., Ill. Power Co. Chmn. adv. council Sch. Bus., U. Ill.; adv. council NCCJ, Double E; bd. dirs. Jr. Achievement; trustee Fourth Presbyn. Ch. Recipient leadership award for outstanding achievement in bus. YWCA, 1979. Mem. Indsl. Relations Assn., Chgo. Network. Club: Women's Athletic. Office: 111 N State St Chicago IL 60690

MILLIGAN, FREDERICK JAMES, lawyer; b. Upper Sandusky, Ohio, Nov. 14, 1906; s. William G. and Grace (Kuenzli) M.; B.A., Ohio State U., 1928; LL.B., Franklin U., 1933; J.D., Capitol U., 1966; m. Virginia Stone, June 30, 1934; children—Frederick James, David Timothy. Asst. nat. sec. Phi Delta Theta, 1928; asst. dean of men Ohio State U., 1929-33; admitted to Ohio bar, 1933; asst. atty. gen. State of Ohio, 1933-36; pvt. practice, Columbus, Ohio, 1937—; exec. sec. Adminstrv. La. Commn. of Ohio, 1940-42; exec. sec. to Gov. of Ohio, 1947; dir. commerce State of Ohio, 1948; sec. Louis Bromfield Malabar Farm Found., 1958-60. Pres. Central Ohio council Boy Scouts Am.; trustee Columbus Town Meeting; asst. dir. Pres.'s Commn. on Inter-govt. Relations, 1953; pres. Ohio Information Com., Inc., 1966—; chmn. Blendon Twp. Bicentennial Commn., 1974-77. Mem. athletic council Ohio State U., 1958-64; trustee Blendon Twp., 1971-78. Served from 1st lt. to maj. USAAF, 1942-45. Decorated Legion of Merit; recipient Silver Beaver award Boy Scouts Am., 1949; Ann. History award Franklin County Hist. Soc., 1957; D.A.R. Citizenship award, 1958; Distinguished Service citation Ohioana Library Assn., 1970. Mem. Am., Ohio, Columbus bar assns., Columbus Jr. C. of C. (hon. life mem.; pres. 1934), Ohio (trustee 1952-77, pres. 1963-65, Franklin County (pres. 1954-56) hist. socs., Ohio State U. Assn. (trustee 1952-55), Amvets (state comdr. 1949). Am. Legion, S.A.R., League of Young Republican Clubs of Ohio (pres. 1941-42). Presbyn. Clubs: University (trustee 1956-58), Ohio State U. Faculty (Columbus). Home: 3785 Dempsey Rd Westerville OH 43081 Office: 3791 Dempsey Rd Westerville OH 43081

MILLIGAN, ROBERT GEORGE, SR., psychologist; b. St. Paul, June 30, 1920; s. George and Clara Ida (Gottwald) M.; B.A., Coll. of St. Thomas, 1947; M.A., Fordham U., 1949; Ph.D., Loyola U. Chgo., 1958; m. Anna Birgit von Malmborg, July 4, 1952; children—Robert George, Stephen Mark. Chief psychology service Black Hawk County Mental Health Center, Waterloo, Iowa, 1958-60; asst. prof. psychology, dir. testing and counseling center U. San Francisco, 1960-67; cons. psychologist in pvt. practice, San Francisco, 1964-71; chief psychology service Dept. Justice, Fed. Prison Service, Fed. Correctional Inst., Sandstone, Minn., 1971—; cons. Cath. Social Service, Oakland, Calif., 1964-66, Luth. Charities, Oakland, 1968-70, Marianists, Cupertino, Calif., 1963-79, Lakewood Coll., White Bear, Minn., 1971-75. Served with C.E., U.S. Army, 1941-46. Recipient Outstanding Prof. award U. San Francisco, 1964; lic. psychologist, Minn.; lic. cons. psychologist, Calif.; lic. family and marriage counselor, Calif. Mem. Am. Psychol. Assn., Am. Correctional Assn., Psi Chi. Clubs: Employees Fed. Correctional Inst. Office: Fed Correctional Inst Sandstone MN 55072

MILLIGAN, ROBERT LEE, JR., computer co. exec.; b. Evanston, Ill., Apr. 4, 1934; s. Robert L. and Alice (Connell) M.; B.S., Northwestern U., 1958; m. Susan A. Woodrow, Mar. 23, 1957; children—William, Bonnie, Thomas, Robert III. Account rep. IBM, Chgo., 1957-66; sr. cons. L.B. Knight & Assos., Chgo., 1966-68; v.p. mktg. Trans Union Systems Corp., Chgo., 1968-73; sr. v.p. sales and mktg. Systems Mgmt. Inc., Des Plaines, Ill., 1973—, also dir.; chmn. bd., treas. SMI-Service Corp., Des Plaines, 1981—; dir. Nanofast, Inc., Chgo., 1968—. Div. mgr. N. Suburban YMCA Bldg., 1967. Area chmn., Northfield Twp. Republican Party, 1965-71. Bd. dirs. United Fund, Glenview, Ill., 1967-69, Robert R. McCormick Chgo. Boys Club, 1974—; pres. bd. mgrs. Glenview Amateur Hockey Assn., 1974-79, gen. mgr. Glenbrook South High Sch. Hockey Club, 1973-78; bd. dirs. Chgo. Boys Clubs, 1974—. Served with AUS, 1953-55. Mem. Data Processing Mgmt. Assn., Consumer Credit Assn. (bd. dirs., sec. 1969-70), Info. Systems Software Internat. (charter, dir.), Phi Kappa Psi. Presbyn. Clubs: Northwestern (dir. 1973-75) (Chgo.); Glen View (Ill.). Home: 702 Glendale Dr Glenview IL 60025 Office: 10400 W Higgins Rd Des Plaines IL 60018

MILLIKEN, WILLIAM GRAWN, gov. Mich.; b. Traverse City, Mich., Mar. 26, 1922; s. James Thacker and Hildegarde (Grawn) M.; A.B., Yale U., 1944; m. Helen Wallbank, Oct. 5, 1945; children—Elaine, William Grawn. Pres., J. W. Milliken, Inc., dept. store, Traverse City, 1952-69; mem. Mich. Senate from 27th Dist., 1960-64, majority floor leader, 1963-64; lt. gov. Mich., 1965-68, gov., 1969—. Mem. Mich. Waterways Commn., 1947-55; pres. Scenic Trails council Boy Scouts Am., 1956; visited W. Ger. on intercultural exchange program Dept. State, 1953; chmn. Grand Traverse County Republican Com., 1948-54; trustee Northwestern Mich. Coll., 1957-60; chmn. Edn. Commn. of the States, 1979-80. Served with USAAF, World War II; ETO. Decorated Purple Heart. Mem. Nat. Governors Assn. (chmn. 1977-78), Council of State Govts. (pres. 1977-78), Traverse City C. of C. (past pres.). Club: Rotary. Office: State Capitol Bldg Lansing MI 48909

MILLIMET, STANLEY, armament mfg. co. exec.; b. Weehawken, N.J., Mar. 27, 1928; s. Peter and Bertha Lenore Millimet; B.S., Va. Mil. Inst., 1948; M.S. with distinction, Air Force Inst. Tech., 1967; M.S. in Mgmt., Am. Technol. U., 1976; m. Sonia Comora, Sept. 3, 1948; children—Kathi, Beth, Scott. Commd. 2d lt. U.S. Army, 1949, advanced through grades to col., 1971; comdr. tank bn., 1970-71, corps logistician, Vietnam, 1972-73, sr. advisor to Thai army, 1973-74, comptroller research and devel. activity Combined Arms Test Agy., Ft. Hood, Tex., 1975-76, dep. comdr. logistics, Korea, 1976-78, dir. logistics materiel systems Army Logistics Center, Ft. Lee, Va., 1978-79, ret., 1979; program mgr. integrated logistics support Abrams tank Chrysler Def., Inc., Center Line, Mich., 1979—; prof. mgmt. Am. Technol. U., Killeen, Tex., 1974-76. Pres., Little League Baseball, U.S. Forces Japan, 1964-66; active PTA, 1958-69; mem. Republican Nat. Com., 1980. Decorated Legion of Merit with oak leaf cluster; named Key Logistician, Dept. Army, 1970. Mem. Soc. Logistics Engrs., Am. Def. Preparedness Assn., Assn. U.S. Army. Jewish. Club: Chrysler Management. Home: 2667 Pearl Dr Troy MI 48098 Office: Chrysler Defense Inc 25999 Lawrence Ave Center Line MI 48015

MILLMAN, CARL, vending food service co. exec.; b. Wausau, Wis., Aug. 5, 1921; s. Louis I. and Sylvia (Kaplan) M.; B.A., U. Wis., 1943; m. Phyllis J. Rabin, Nov. 7, 1943; children—Nancy Dee, Robert Frederick. Owner, Millman's Dept. Store, 1945-50; pres. Automatic Merchandising Corp., Milw., 1951-81; dir. BVA Coop, Inc.; lectr. on sales, food service and merchandising. Pres., Wis. Jewish Publs. Found.; bd. dirs. Milw. Jewish Fedn.; mem. Wis. exec. com. NCCJ; past pres. Milw. bd. Jewish Edn., Zionist Orgn. Am., Beth El Ner Tamid. Served with ordnance AUS, 1943-46. Recipient Leadership award Israel Bonds, 1972, John S. Mill award for Outstanding Industry Salesman, Vending Food Service Industry, 1957. Mem. Nat. Automatic Mdse. Assn. (past pres.), Wis. Automatic Merchandising Council (past pres.), Food Service Execs. Assn., Sales Execs. Assn., Indsl. Relations Assn. Clubs: Brynwood Country, Masons. Home: 9255 N Pelham Pkwy Milwaukee WI 53217 Office: 16500 W Cleveland Ave New Berlin WI 53151

MILLOY, FRANK JOSEPH, JR., physician; b. Phoenix, June 26, 1924; s. Frank Joseph and Ola (McCabe) M.; student Notre Dame U., 1942-43; M.S., Northwestern U., 1949, M.D., 1947. Intern, Cook County Hosp., Chgo., 1947-49, resident, 1953-57; practice medicine, specializing in surgery, Chgo., 1958—; asso. attending staff Presbyn.—St. Lukes Hosp.; mem. staff U. Ill. Research Hosp.; clin. asso. prof. surgery, U. Ill. Med. Sch.; asso. prof. surgery Rush Med. Sch. Cons. West Side Vet. Hosp. Served as apprentice seaman USNR, 1943-45; lt. M.C., USNR, 1950-52; PTO. Diplomate Am. Bd. Surgery and Thoracic Surgery. Mem. A.C.S., Chgo. Surg. Soc., Am. Coll. Chest Physicians, Soc. Thoracic Surgeons, Phi Beta Pi. Clubs: Metropolitan, University (Chgo.). Home: 574 Jackson Ave Glencoe IL 60022 Office: 800 Westmoreland Lake Forest IL 60045

MILLS, ADRIENNE BRAM, artist; b. Chgo., Feb. 12, 1936; d. Aaron D. and Irene (Oringel) Bram; student U. Wis., 1954-56, Art Inst. Chgo., 1958-60, Nat. Tchrs. Coll., 1956-57; B.A., Barat Coll., Lake Forest, Ill., 1977; pvt. art studies with Jacob Burck, Kaye Hoffman Schwartz, Bill Wichlenski; children—Robin, Wendy. Sculptor; works represented in pvt. collections Chgo. area; works exhibited Festival of Arts (Highland Park, Ill.), Riverwoods, Barat Coll., Highland Park Library, Suburban Fine Arts Center, Gallery Elizabeth; commns. include archtl. sculpture for North Shore Bank; art dir. David Scott Industries, Inc. Home: Highland Park IL 60035

MILLS, JOSEPH ALFRED, ednl. cons., media specialist; b. Portsmouth, Va., Nov. 29, 1946; s. Joseph Alfred and Ethel Virginia (Copeland) M.; B.S., Hampton Inst., 1968; M.Ed., Wayne State U., 1971, M.L.S., 1978. Tchr., Detroit Public Schs., 1968-76, media specialist, 1979-80; ednl. cons. Wayne State Univ., Detroit, 1976-78, research asst., 1979, research, adminstrv. asst., 1980-81; learning resources coordinator Wayne County Community Coll., Belleville, Mich., 1981—; profl. musician Mariners Episcopal Ch., Detroit, 1977-81. Pres., Detroit-Hampton Alumni Assn., 1973-75, Brazeal Dennard Chorale, 1973-76. Mem. Phylon Soc., ALA, NAACP, Phi Delta Kappa. Mem. United Ch. of Christ. Author: Like Waves...A Collection of Poetry and Philosophical Writings, 1980; Goin' Off. Home: 9083 Evergreen St Detroit MI 48228 Office: 9555 Haggerty Rd Belleville MI 48111

MILLS, MORRIS HADLEY, state senator: b. West Newton, Ind., Sept. 25, 1927; s. Howard Samuel and Bernice Christie (Hadley) M.; A.B., Earlham Coll., 1950; M.B.A., Harvard. U., 1952; m. Mary Ann Sellars, Aug. 8, 1954; children—Douglas, Frederic, Gordon. Partner, Mills Bros. Farms, 1962—; dir. Maplehurst Farms, Inc.; mem. Ind. Ho. of Reps. from Marion County Dist., 1969-72, Ind. Senate from 35th Dist., 1973—. Bd. dirs. Marion County Farm Bur. Coop., Inc.; trustee Earlham Coll. Found. Served with U.S. Army, 1946-47. Republican. Quaker. Club: Lions. Home: 7148 W Thompson Rd Indianapolis IN 46241*

MILLS, OSCAR PHILIP, JR., regional farm coop. editor; b. Auxvasse, Mo., July 4, 1949; s. Oscar Philip and Virginia Fay (Martin) M.; B.A., Westminster Coll., 1971; m. Linda Sue Ann Wake, Dec. 16, 1972; children—Amy Marie, Rebecca Ann. Editor, Fulton (Mo.) Daily Sun-Gazette, 1972-73; dir. info. Mo. Dept. Agr., Jefferson City, 1973-75; asst. editor Today's Farmer, MFA Inc., Columbia, Mo., 1975-79, editor Today's Farmer, 1979-81, publs. editor, 1981—; asso. editor Implement & Tractor mag., Overland Park, Kans., 1979. Second ward committeeman Callaway County (Mo.) Republican Central Com., 1972-73, treas., 1971-73. Recipient Photo award Nat. Council Farmer Coops., 1977. Mem. Coop. Editorial Assn. (chmn. writing com. 1981—, award for editorial writing 1981), Am. Agrl. Editors Assn., Am. Soc. Bus. Press Editors. Presbyterian. Office: 201 S 7th St Columbia MO 65201

MILLS, RANDY KEITH, educator; b. Mt. Vernon, Ill., Nov. 2, 1951; s. Keith L. and Mary Alice (Newell) M.; B.A. in Social Studies (Jefferson scholar, President's scholar), Oakland City Coll., 1973; postgrad. U. Evansville, 1981; M.A. in History, Ind. U., 1976; m. Marsha F. Monroe, June 17, 1972; 1 son, Ryan Keith. Tchr. social studies Loogootee (Ind.) Sch. Corp., 1973—, chmn. social studies dept., 1975—; part-time instr. Vincennes U., 1980—. Mem. Ind. Polit. Action Com., 1976-78; mem. Christian bd. edn. Salem United Ch. of Christ. Mem. Nat. Council for Social Studies, Ind. Council for Social Studies (acad. freedom com. 1980), Nat. Assn. for Supervision and Curriculum Devel., NEA, Loogootee Tchrs. Assn. (v.p. 1976, pres. 1977). Home: 512 E 15th St Jasper IN 47546 Office: 201 Brooks Ave Loogootee IN 47553

MILLS, REBECCA ANN, advt. agy. exec.; b. Storm Lake, Iowa, May 11, 1950; d. Omer H. and Awanda Lucille (Mathison) Roth; student Northwestern U., summers 1968, 70; B.S. in Journalism with honors, Drake U., 1972; m. Timothy Lemar Mills, Dec. 22, 1973; 1 dau., Sarah Rebecca. Editor house organ Des Moines Register & Tribune, 1972-73; coordinator Mktg. Services Corp. of Iowa Credit Union League, Des Moines, 1973-74; account exec. Prescott Co., Denver, 1974-75; co-owner, pres. Mills Agy., Storm Lake, 1975—; guest lectr. Buena Vista Coll.; featured speaker Iowa Bank Mktg. Conf., 1979, 82, Internat. Telephone Credit Union Assn. conv., Dallas, 1978. Parents adv. bd. Day Care Center. Recipient numerous ADDY awards for excellence in advt. Mem. Am. Soc. Profl. and Exec. Women, Women in Communications, Advt. Club Sioux Cities, Nat. Fedn. Ind. Bus., Des Moines Advt. Club (past chmn. edn. com.), Storm Lake C. of C. (dir.), DAR (regent Buena Vista chpt.). Republican. Presbyterian. Clubs: Keystone (sec.), Eastern Star (past officer). Home: 131 N Emerald St Storm Lake IA 50588 Office: 612 Seneca St Storm Lake IA 50588

MILLS, ROBERT WINTON, telephone co. exec.; b. Lincoln, Nebr., May 22, 1927; s. Robert Wendell and Ann S. (Keiber) M.; B.S., U. Nebr., 1952; m. Rosella Helen Pankratz, Oct. 23, 1948; children—Steven Robert, Wendell Paul, Lori Rosann. With Central Telephone & Utilities Corp., 1952—, asst. to dir. labor relations, Lincoln, 1953-56, asst. to v.p., asst. to dir. personnel, 1956-74, v.p. personnel, Chgo., 1974-77, v.p. labor relations and tng., 1977—; dir. Suburban Realty, Inc., Lincoln, 1962—. Trustee Fairview Baptist Home, Downers Grove, Ill. Served with arty. U.S. Army, 1945-47. Mem. Am. Soc. Personnel Adminstrn. (accredited exec. in personnel), Ind. Telephone Pioneer Assn., 312 Pioneer Assn., Alpha Phi Omega. Republican. Baptist. Home: 1605 Barberry Ln Mount Prospect IL 60056 Office: Central Telephone & Utilities Corp 5725 E River Rd Chicago IL 60631

MILLS, ROYCE JOHNSON, automotive co. exec.; b. Rush City, Minn., Dec. 18, 1925; s. Roy J. and Myrtle B. (Johnson) M.; ed. pub. sch. Cresco, Iowa, 1937-39, Harmony, Minn., 1939-43; m. Erlene K. Strauser, Dec. 6, 1950; children—Deborah, Pamela, Tina. With Goodyear Tire & Rubber Co., 1950-70, dist. mgr., Peoria, Ill., 1966-68, Indpls., 1968-70; exec. v.p. Ameron Automotive Centers, St. Louis, Mo., 1970-75, pres., 1975-78; pres., gen. mgr. Triangle Bandag Tire Co., Inc., Cedar Rapids, Iowa, 1978—. Served with USMC, 1945-46, 50-51. Republican. Clubs: Masons (32 deg.), Shriners. Home: 2021 Sandalwood Dr NE Cedar Rapids IA 52402 Office: 1251 2d Ave Marion IA 52302

MILLSTEAD, IVAN EDWARD, hosp. personnel dir.; b. Springfield, Mo., Apr. 4, 1936; s. Paul Edward and Susie Priscilla M.; A.B., Drury Coll., 1958, M.B.A., 1969, cert. in hosp. mgmt., 1969; m. Sandra A. Millstead, Sept. 29, 1973; children—Bart, Robert, Suzanne, Michael. Asst. credit mgr. Heer's Dept. Store, Springfield, 1957-60; asst. personnel dir. Reynold's Mfg. Co., Springfield, 1960-65; dir. personnel Lester E. Cox Med. Center, Springfield, 1965—; mem. Gov.'s Adv. Council on Comprehensive Health Planning; pres., owner Millstead's Photography, Ltd. Vol. Council on Public Higher Edn. State of Mo.; budget chmn. United Way; active dist. council, dist. adminstr., leader Med. Explorer Post, Boy Scouts Am.; mem. adv. com. R-12 Sch. Dist.; deacon 1st and Calvary Presbyterian Ch. Served with USNR, 1958-66. Mem. Springfield Personnel Assn. (pres.), Am. Soc. Hosp. Personnel Dirs., Mo. Hosp. Personnel Assn., Am. Hosp. Assn., S.W. Mo. Hosp. Assn., Am. Soc. Hosp. Security Dirs., Profl. Photographers of Am., Kappa Alpha. Clubs: Elks, Masons, Shriners. Home: 5327 S Holland St Springfield MO 65807 Office: 1423 N Jefferson St Springfield MO 65802

MILNER, HAROLD WILLIAM, real estate trust and hotel exec.; b. Salt Lake City, Nov. 11, 1934; s. Kenneth W. and Olive (Schoettlin) M.; B.S., U. Utah, 1960; M.B.A., Harvard U., 1962; m. Susan Emmett, June 19, 1959 (div. 1976); children—John Kenneth, Mary Sue; m. 2d, Lois Friemuth, Aug. 14, 1977; 1 dau., Jennifer Rebecca. Instr., Brigham Young U., Provo, Utah, 1962-64; v.p. Gen. Paper Corp., Mpls., 1964-65; dir. finance Amalgamated Sugar Co., Ogden, Utah, 1965-67; corp. treas. Marriott Corp., Washington, 1967-70; pres., chief exec. officer, trustee Hotel Investors, Kensington, Md., 1970-75; pres., chief exec. officer Americana Hotels Corp., Chgo., 1975—. Served as lt. AUS, 1960. Mem. Greater Chgo. Hotel Assn. (dir. 1977—), Young Pres.'s Orgn., Am. Hotel and Motel Assn. (industry adv. council). Mem. Ch. Jesus Christ Latter-day Saints. Author: A Special Report on Contract Maintenance, 1963. Home: 474 Butler Dr Lake Forest IL 60045 Office: 532 S Michigan Ave Chicago IL 60605

MILNER, NEIL, banking assn. exec.; b. Hillsboro, Ohio, Aug. 14, 1936; s. Arthur H. and Helen Lockwood (Pettyjohn) M.; B.S. in Agrl. Econs., Ohio State U., 1958; m. Jeannette Callies, July 6, 1974; children—Monica, Marcie, Matt, Lesley. Public relations dir. Ohio Bankers Assn., 1962-66, dep. mgr., 1966-68; exec. mgr. S.D. Bankers Assn., 1968-72; exec. v.p. Iowa Bankers Assn., Des Moines, 1972—. Sec., Huron Airport Bd., 1971; pres. Greater Huron Devel. Corp., 1972; pres. Ohio State Jr. Fair Bd., 1954-55; pres. Pheasant council Boy Scouts Am., 1972. Cert. assn. exec. Mem. Iowa Soc. Assn. Execs. (sec.-treas. 1978-79, v.p. 1979-80, pres. 1980-81, past pres. 1981-82), Am. Bankers Assn. (chmn. state assn. div. 1978-79, bd. dirs.), Am. Soc. Assn. Execs. (Key award 1981), Greater Des Moines C. of C. (dir. 1979-80). Presbyterian. Clubs: Masons, Shriners. Home: 1505 Park Ave Des Moines IA 50315 Office: 430 Liberty Bldg Des Moines IA 50308

MILROY, LARRY F., mfg. co. exec.; b. Mason City, Iowa, Feb. 7, 1948; s. Lynn E. and Frances A. (Wagner) M.; A.A., North Iowa Area Community Coll., 1968; B.A., Coe Coll., 1970; m. Marsha L. White, Sept. 25, 1971; children—Lori L., Christopher M. Supr. benefit dept. Life Investors, Inc., Cedar Rapids, Iowa, 1971-73, asst. mgr. benefit dept., 1973-75, mgr. benefit dept., 1975-77, v.p. ops. NN Investors Life Ins. Co. and Investors Fidelity Life Ins. Co. div., Birmingham, Ala., 1977-78, mgr. ind. life and health claims, mgr. policy values and rewrites, mgr. health premium renewals, Cedar Rapids, 1978; mgr. employee benefits Rockwell-Collins, Cedar Rapids, 1978-79, mgr. employee benefits and nursing services, 1979—, mgr. employee prescription center, 1980—. Mem. Internat. Claims Assn. (diplomate). Office: 400 Collins Rd NE Mail Station 126-201 Cedar Rapids IA 52406

MILTON, JAMES LLOYD, mech. engr.; b. Quincy, Fla., Nov. 10, 1941; student Fla. A&M U., 1960-62; B.S. in Mech. Engring., Howard U., 1967; M.S. in Mech. Engring., U. Mass., Amherst, 1970, Ph.D., 1973; m. Martha Ann Sailor, Dec. 23, 1967; 1 son, Frederick Lloyd. Engring. trainee Pratt & Whitney Aircraft Co., East Hartford, Conn., summer 1967; research engr. Wyman Gordon Co., Worcester, Mass., summer 1969, Norton Co., Worcester, summer 1970; research asst., teaching asst. U. Mass., Amherst, 1967-70; mem. tech. staff Computer Application and Phys. Design Dept., Bell Telephone Labs., Columbus, 1972-77, supr. connector evaluation and reliability group, Interconnection Components Lab., 1977—; cons. in field. Gadsden County Fla. A&M U. Alumni scholar, 1960-61, Olin scholar, 1966-67, U. Mass. Univ. fellow, 1970-72. Mem. ASME (chmn. Columbus sect. 1979-80). Author articles on food processing engring., numerical analysis and heat transfer, phys. design, heat transfer and electronic packaging. Office: Bell Telephone Labs 6200 E Broad St Columbus OH 43213

MILTON, JOHN RONALD, educator, author; b. Anoka, Minn., May 24, 1924; s. John Peterson and Euphamia Alvera (Swanson) M.; B.A., U. Minn., 1948, M.A., 1951; Ph.D., U. Denver, 1961; m. Leonharda Allison Hinderlie, Aug. 3, 1946; 1 dau., Nanci Lynn. Instr. English, philosophy, Augsburg Coll., Mnpls., 1949-57; asso. prof. English Jamestown (N.D.) Coll., 1957-60, also acting chmn., 1957-60, prof., 1961-63, chmn. English dept., 1961-63; prof. English U. S.D., Vermillion, 1963—, also editor S.D. Rev., 1963—, dir. writing program, 1965—, chmn. dept. English, 1963-65. Vis. prof. N.D. State U., summer, 1966, Ind. State U., Summer, 1966, Bemidji (Minn.) State Coll., 1969; chmn. Dakota Press, U. S.D., 1968—. Served with AUS, 1943-46; PTO. Recipient Gov.'s Award for Achievement in Arts, 1978. Wurlitzer Found. fellow, 1965; Hill Found. grantee, 1966, 69, 70, Whitney Found. grantee, 1970, 72, S.D. Arts Council grantee, 1969, 70, 74, 74, U. S.D. grantee, 1963, 64; Nat. Endowment for Arts writing fellow, 1976-77. Mem. Am. Studies Assn. (regional bd. 1957-59), Western Lit. Assn. (pres. 1971, editorial bd. 1966—), Western History Assn. Author: (poetry) The Loving Hawk, 1962, Western Plains, 1964, The Tree of Bones, 1965, This Lonely House, 1968, The Tree of Bones and Other Poems, 1973, The Blue Belly of the World, 1974; (novel) Notes to a Bald Buffalo, 1976; (biography) Oscar Howe, 1972, Crazy Horse, 1974; (interviews) Three West, 1970, Conversations with Frank Waters, 1971, Conversations with Frederick Manfred, 1974; (history) South Dakota: A Bicentennial History, 1977; The Novel of the American West (criticism), 1980. Editor: The American Indian Speaks, 1969; American Indian II, 1971; The Literature of South Dakota, 1976. Conbr. numerous essays, stories and revs. to lit. publs. Home: 630 Thomas Vermillion SD 57069 Office: Box 111 University Exchange Vermillion SD 57069

MIMS, ALBERT, safety cons. exec., educator; b. Keyser, Ky., Feb. 28, 1924; s. Albert and Lelia F. M.; A.B., U. N.C., 1953, M.S., 1954; postgrad. U. Cin., 1962, Ph.D., 1973; m. Laura Fern Hensley, Dec. 26, 1946; children—John Albert, Rebecca Fern. Safety engr. Procter & Gamble, Cin., 1957-72; asso. prof. indsl. safety U. Wis. System, 1973—; safety cons., pres. A. Mims Assos., Madison, Wis., 1972—; expert witness in field. Active United Appeal/Way, Little League baseball, football, basketball, Dan Beard council Boy Scouts Am., 1962-67. Served with USN, 1942-46. Profl. safety engr.; cert. safety profl., hazard control mgr. Mem. Am. Soc. Safety Engrs., Am. Indsl. Hygiene Assn., Nat. Safety Mgmt. Soc., Human Factors Soc., System Safety Soc., World Safety Orgn., Nat. Safety Council (exec. com., gen. chmn. chem. sect., 1979-80). Republican. Editorial bd. Profl. Safety, 1979—; active hazardous materials tng. program for compliance officers U.S. Dept. Labor USHA Tng. Inst., 1973-74; contbr. articles to profl. jours. Office: PO Box 8151 Madison WI 53708

MINARD, THOMAS MICHAEL, r.r. products co. exec.; b. St. Charles, Ill., Dec. 31, 1944; s. Clarence Scott and Ruth L. (Larson) M.; grad. Coll. Advanced Traffic, 1964. Gen. mgr. Iowa Terminal R.R. Co., Mason City, 1968-70; mgr. quality control C.&N.W. Ry. Co., Chgo., 1970-73; pres., gen. mgr. Great Plains Ry. Co., Seward, Nebr., 1973-76; rail product mgr. L.B. Foster Co., Des Plaines, Ill., 1976-80, mgr. r.r. sales and procurement, 1980—. Mem. Nat. Ry. Hist. Soc., Elec. Railroaders Assn., Coll. Advanced Traffic Alumni Assn., Delta Nu Alpha. Home: 1211 N LaSalle Dr Chicago IL 60610 Office: L B Foster Co 1111 E Touhy Ave Des Plaines IL 60018

MINDELL, MARK GREGORY, mfg. co. exec.; b. Moline, Ill., Nov. 21, 1951; s. Stan H. and Dale S. (Badner) M.; B.A., No. Ill. U., 1973; M.A., Central Mich. U., 1974; Ph.D., Kent State U., 1977; m. Lynette Sue Mindell, July 29, 1973. Mgr. corp. orgn. research and devel. B.F. Goodrich, Akron, Ohio, 1976-80, corp. cons. Abbott Labs., North Chicago, Ill., 1980-81; dir. orgn. planning and devel. Herman Miller, Inc., Zeeland, Mich., 1981—. Mem. Am. Psychol. Assn., Internat. Communication Assn., Acad. Mgmt., Speech Communication Assn., Nat. Orgn. Devel. Network, Internat. Communication Auditor. Author: Employee Values in a Changing Society, 1981; contbr. articles to profl. jours. Home: 996 Kenwood Holland MI 49423 Office: Herman Miller Inc 8500 Byron Rd Zeeland MI 49464

MINDES, GAYLE DEAN, educator; b. Kansas City, Mo., Feb. 11, 1942; d. Elton Burnett and Juanita Maxine (Mangold) Taylor; B.S., U. Kans., 1964; M.S., U. Wis., 1965; Ed.D., Loyola U., Chgo., 1979; m. Marvin William Mindes, June 20, 1969; 1 son, Jonathan Seth. Tchr. public schs., Newburgh, N.Y., 1965-67; spl. educator Ill. Dept. Mental Health, Chgo., 1967-69; spl. edn. supr. Evanston (Ill.) Dist. 65 Schs., 1969-74; lectr. Northeastern Ill. U., Chgo., 1974, Loyola U., Chgo., 1974-76, Coll. St. Francis, Joliet, Ill., 1976-79, North Park Coll., Chgo., 1978; cons. Chgo. Head Start, 1978-79; asst. prof. edn. Oklahoma City U., 1979-80; vis. asst. prof., research asso. Roosevelt U. Coll. Edn., Chgo., 1980—; cons. Arts Council Okalhoma City, Okla. Indian Affairs Commn., 1979-80; bd. dirs. North Side Family Day Care, 1981; mem. edn. adv. com. Okla. Dept. Edn., 1979-80; mem. planning com. Lake View Citizens Council Day Care Center, 1978-79. Cerebral Palsy Assn. scholar, 1965; U. Wis. fellow in mental retardation, 1964-65; U. Kans. scholar, 1960. Mem. Assn. Supervision and Curriculum Devel., Assn. Children with Learning Disabilities, Nat. Assn. Edn. Young Children, Am. Ednl. Research Assn., Council for Exceptional Chidren, Ill. Council for Exceptional Children, Council for Adminstrs. Spl. Edn., Council on Children with Behavioral Disorders, Am. Orthopsychiat. Assn., Alpha Sigma Nu, Phi Delta Kappa, Pi Lambda Theta. Contbr. articles to profl. jours. Office: Coll Edn Roosevelt U Chicago IL 60605

MINER, DORIS P., state senator; b. Mar. 13, 1936; ed. public schs.; m. Kenneth Miner; 4 children. Rancher-homemaker, Gregory, S.D.; mem. S.D. Ho. of Reps., 1976—. Former mem. Common Sch. Bd.; state dir. Multiple Sclerosis. Mem. Farmers Union. Democrat. Roman Catholic. Office: State Capitol Pierre SD 57501*

MINER, THOMAS HAWLEY, internat. cons.; b. Shelbyville, Ill., June 19, 1927; s. Lester Ward and Thirza (Hawley) M.; student U.S. Mil. Acad., 1946-47; B.A., Knox Coll., 1950; J.D., U. Ill., 1953. Admitted to Ill. bar, 1954; atty. Continental Ill. Nat. Bank & Trust Co., Chgo., 1953-55; pres. Harper-Wyman Internat. S.A., Venezuela and Mexico, 1955-58, Hudson Internat. S.A., Can. and Switzerland, 1958-60, Thomas H. Miner & Assos., Inc., Chgo., 1960—; pres., dir. Lakeside Travel; dir. Lakeside Bank; chmn. Ill. dist. export council U.S. Dept. Commerce, 1971-76. Bd. dirs. Sch. Art Inst. Chgo., 1977-81; former chmn. UN Assn. Chgo.; pres., founder Mid-Am. Com.; former bd. dirs. UNICEF; trustee 4th Presbyterian Ch., Chgo.; governing life mem., sustaining fellow Art Inst. Chgo. Served with USNR, 1945-46; served to capt. AUS, 1946-47. Named One of Chgo.'s 10 Outstanding Young Men, 1962, Chicagoan of Year, Chgo. Assn. Commerce and Industry, 1968; hon. consul Republic of Senegal. Mem. Am. Mgmt. Assn., Chgo. Assn. Commerce and Industry, MidAm.-Arab C. of C. (past dir.), Chgo. Bar Assn., Chgo. Com., Chgo. Council Fgn. Relations (past dir.), Council of Ams., Internat. Bus. Council (past dir., past pres.), Japan-Am. Soc., Nat. Council U.S.-China Trade, English Speaking Union (chmn.), U.S.-USSR Trade and Econ. Council, Mus. Contemporary Art, Newcomen Soc. N.Am., Thomas Minor Soc., Phi Delta Phi, Phi Gamma Delta. Clubs: Chicago, Economic, Mid-Am., Rotary; Tryall Golf and Beach (Jamaica); Internat. (Washington); University (Milw.). Home: 1350 Lake Shore Dr Chicago IL 60610 also Shelbyville IL Office: 135 S LaSalle St Chicago IL 60603

MINGLE, MARY MAXINE, hosp. exec.; b. Brevard, N.C., Mar. 17, 1919; d. James Everett and Mary Ethel Thomas; student Butler U., 1955, Purdue U., 1955, Ind. U., 1956-57, 70—, Mich. State U., 1958, Columbia U., 1967; m. H. Bryan Mingle, Nov. 15, 1941. Mgr. dept. Hook Drug Co., 1943-49, credit mgr., 1949-55; dir. adult program YWCA, Indpls., 1956-63; office mgr., personnel counselor Stand By Office Service, Indpls., 1963-65; dir. vol. services Ind. U. Hosps., Indpls., 1965—; mem. volunteerism adv. council Ind. Central U.; lectr. hosp. and nursing home adminstrn. Ind. U. Founding chmn. Indpls. Pre Sch. Assn., 1958; clk. Southwood Friends Ch., 1974. Recipient Public Service award Office Mayor Indpls., 1967, Gov. Ind., 1976. Mem. Am. Bus. Womens Assn. (pres. Indpls. charter chpt. 1967, Woman of Year award Indpls. chpt. 1968, Lucky 13 chpt. 1980), Ind. Soc. Dirs. of Vol. Services (founding pres.), Am. Soc. Dirs. Vol. Services, Am. Hosp. Assn., Ind. Hosp. Assn., Indpls. Dirs. of Vol. Services. Republican. Club: Order Eastern Star. Office: 1100 W Michigan St Indianapolis IN 46223

MINHAS, JASJIT SINGH, ednl. adminstrn., instructional technologist; b. India, Mar. 22, 1933; came to U.S., 1965, naturalized, 1975; s. Charan S. and Chanan K. M.; B.A., Punjab (India) U., Chandigarth, 1955, B.E.D., 1957; M.A., Catholic U. Am., 1971, Ph.D., 1975; m. Surjit K., June 19, 1960; children—Jasdip S., Sandip S. Edn. specialist Embassy of India, Washington, 1965-72; program specialist Applied Sci. Co., McLean, Va., 1970-73; program dir. Dickinson (N.D.) Public Schs., 1974-78; asst. acad. dean United Tribes Edn. Tech. Center, Bismarck, N.D., 1978—; condr. workshops on instructional tech. to nat., state, local profl. orgns. Mem. Assn. Ednl. Tech. and Communications, Am. Vocat. Assn., Nat. Assn. Curriculum Devel., Nat. Assn. Sch. Execs. Democrat. Sinh. Clubs: Lions, Elks. Author numerous self instructional teaching manuals for retarded students in vocat. edn. Home: 400 Augusburg Ave Bismarck ND 58501 Office: 3315 S Airport Rd Bismarck ND 58501

MINION, DALE REUBEN, constrn. co. exec.; b. Mountain Lake Minn., Aug. 17, 1941; s. Reuben and Lily Grace (Redding) M.; student public schs., Windom, Minn.; m. LaVonne Ann Sogge, Apr. 27, 1963; children—Daren Dale, Karen Ann. With Reuben Minion & Son, Inc., Bingham Lake, Minn., 1953—, partner, 1969, v.p., 1979—. Mem. Bingham Lake Council, 1966-79, 81—, also acting mayor; fireman Bingham Lake, 1964—. Mem. Land Improvement Contractors Am. Republican. Lutheran. Club: Masons. Address: PO Box 338 Bingham Lake MN 56118

MINKOWYCZ, WOLODYMYR J., educator; b. Libokhora, Ukraine, Oct. 21, 1937; came to U.S., 1949, naturalized, 1956; s. Alexander and Anna Minkowycz; B.S. in Mech. Engring., U. Minn., 1958, M.S., 1961, Ph.D., 1965; m. Diana Szandra, May 12, 1973; 1 dau., Liliana. Instr., U. Minn., Mpls., 1961-66; asst. prof. dept. energy engring. U. Ill., Chgo., 1966-68, asso. prof., 1968-79, prof., 1979—. Pres. Ukrainian Scouts, Ukrainian Choir Surma, Ukrainian Dance Groups Cheremosh and Verkhovyna. Recipient Silver Circle award for excellence in teaching, 1975, 76, 81. Mem. ASME. Ukrainian Greek Catholic. Editor series textbooks: A Series in Computational Methods in Mechanics and Thermal Science, 1978—; asso. editor Internat. Jour. Heat and Mass Transfer, 1967—, Letters in Heat and Mass Transfer jour., 1974—; founding editor Numerical Heat Transfer jour., 1978—; editor two books; contbr. tech. papers to profl. jours. Office: Univ Illinois Chicago Circle PO Box 4348 Chicago IL 60680

MINKUS, RAYMOND DAVID, communications cons.; b. Chgo., Aug. 8, 1953; s. Fred and Roslyn Minkus; B.S. in Journalism, U. Mo., Columbia, 1975; m. Sara Anthony, June 26, 1977; 1 dau., Stephanie Raye. Reporter, asst. sect. editor Fairchild Publs., N.Y.C., 1975, Chgo.-Midwest editor, 1976; fin. news columnist Milw. Sentinel, 1976-78; sr. communications specialist, mgr. media relations Miller Brewing Co., Milw., 1978-81; v.p. Michael Weiser & Assos., Ltd., Chgo., 1981—. Bd. dirs. Future Milw., 1980-81; mem. mktg. com. United Performing Arts Fund, 1980-81; legis. asst. Mo. Ho. of Reps., 1974-75. Recipient Outstanding Corp. Publ. award Bus. and Profl. Adv. Assn. Milw., 1979-80. Mem. Public Relations Soc. Am., Milw. Advt. Club, Milw. Press Club. Contbr. articles to Common Stock Reporter, Women's Wear Daily, Chgo. Tribune, others. Home: 1304 Lincoln Ave Highland Park IL 60035 Office: 20 N Clark St Chicago IL 60602

MINNESTE, VIKTOR, JR., electronic co. exec.; b. Haapsalu, Estonia, Jan. 15, 1932; s. Viktor and Alice (Lembra) M.; B.S. in Elec. Engring., U. Ill., 1960. Electronic engr. Bell & Howell Co., 1960-69, microstatics div. SCM Co., 1969-71, Multigraphics div. A-M Co., 1972-73; electronic engr. bus. products group Victor Comptometer Co. (merged with Walter Kidde Corp. 1977), Chgo., 1973-74, service mgr. internat. group, 1974-75, now with research group; pub. Motteid/Thoughts, 1962-68; chmn., Estonian-Ams. Polit. Action Com., 1968-72; supr. electronics design group Victor Bus. Products. Served with AUS, 1952-54. Home: 3134 N Kimball Ave Chicago IL 60618 Office: 3900 N Rockwell Chicago IL 60618

MINNEY, R. BRENT, lawyer; b. Parkersburg, W.Va., Oct. 7, 1953; s. Ronzel D. and Lura Maude M.; B.A., Ohio No. U., 1975; J.D., U. Dayton, 1978. Admitted to Ohio bar, 1978; asst. pros. atty. County of Muskingum, Ohio, 1978-81; individual practice law, Zanesville, Ohio, 1978-81; with firm McDowall & Whalen, Cuyahoga Falls, Ohio, 1981—. Mem. Am. Bar. Assn., Ohio Council Sch. Bd. Attys., Am. Bar Assn., Ohio State Bar Assn., Akron Bar Assn., NSBA Council Sch. Attys. Republican. Methodist. Club: Elks. Author: (with Ronzel D. Minney) Student Rights: A Handbook for Parents & Students, 1977. Home: 210 N Main St Apt B1D Munro Falls OH 44262 Office: 135 Portage Trail PO Box 8 Cuyahoga Falls OH 44222

MINNICH, JOSEPH EDWARD, ry. cons.; b. Swanton, Ohio, Sept. 13, 1932; s. Charles Vincent and Leila Elizabeth (Gaiman) M.; student Gonzaga U., 1952, Eastern Wash. Coll. Edn., 1953, U. Toledo, 1956-58; m. Frances K. Minnich; children—Christopher, Susan, Teresa. With Toledo (Ohio) Trust Co., 1956-62, ops. mgr., 1961-62; ins. agt. Allstate Ins. Co., Toledo, 1962-63; ins. agt., asst. office mgr., partner Wright, Russell & Bay Co., Toledo, 1963-67; pres., gen. mgr. Toledo Lake Erie & Western Ry., 1977—; editor Trainline, dir. Tourist Ry. Assn., 1978—; sr. partner Heritage Ry. Services, 1980—; ch. adminstr. St. Paul's Luth. Ch., Toledo, 1968-80. Ch. mgmt. cons.; cons. on chapel mgmt. U.S. Air Force, 1974-76; exec. dir. St. Pauls Camp, Hillsdale, Mich., 1963-69; sec.-treas. Covenant House Inc., Toledo, 1969-75; v.p. 8404 Corp., 1974—; Mich. dist. treas., mem. exec. com. Am. Luth. Ch., 1969-73; Toledo Conf. treas., mem. exec. com., 1968-72. Served with USAF, 1951-55. Fellow Nat. Assn. Ch. Bus. Adminstrs. (chpt. pres. 1973-77, nat. sec. 1975-76), Soc. for Religious Organizational Management (dir. 1980—); mem. Am. Camping Assn. Home and Office: 200 Birchdale Dr Perrysburg OH 43551

MINNICK, COLE WESLEY, banker; b. Bainbridge, Ga., Aug. 21, 1944; s. Cole W. and Evelyn M. (McLeod) M.; student Grinnell Coll., 1962-63; B.S., U.S. Mil. Acad., 1967; M.B.A., Northwestern U., 1974; m. Ann Marie Fenley, June 29, 1968. Mem. ops. staff Continental Ill. Nat. Bank, Chgo., 1971-72; 2d v.p. Am. Nat. Bank, Chgo., 1972-79; v.p., cashier First Nat. Bank of Mt. Prospect (Ill.), 1979; sr. v.p. Exchange Nat. Bank of Chgo., 1979—. Served with U.S. Army, 1967-71. Mem. Midwest Automated Clearing House Assn. (pres. 1980), Chgo. Council Fgn. Relations, West Point Soc. Chgo. Republican. Presbyterian. Office: 130 S LaSalle St Chicago IL 60603

MINNING, ROBERT CHARLES, hydrogeologist; b. Indpls., Sept. 23, 1942; s. Richard Harry and Blanche Ella (Glass) M.; B.A., Wittenberg U., 1965; M.A.T., Ind. U., 1968; M.S. (NSF trainee), U. Toledo, 1970; 1 dau., Laura Lyn. Instr. geology Wittenberg U., Springfield, Ohio, 1966-68; asst. in geology U. Toledo, 1968-70; instr. natural sci. Lansing (Mich.) Community Coll., 1970-73; pres. W.G. Keck & Assos., Inc., Lansing. 1971—; pres., cons. hydrogeologist Keck Cons. Services, Inc., 1973—; dir. Richlyn Industries; cons. to UN in Haiti and Guyana, 1973-76. Pres. Skyline Hills Homeowners Assn., 1977-78; v.p. Donley Sch. PTO, 1978-79. Mem. Am. Water Works Assn., Nat. Water Well Assn. (Sci. award 1974, v.p., bd. dirs. 1976-78), Mich. Basin Geol. Soc., Am. Geophys. Union, Assn. Profl. Geol. Scientists (cert. geologist; pres. Mich. sect. 1978-79), Sigma Gamma Epsilon. Mem. editorial bd. Jour. Ground Water, 1976—; contbr. articles to profl. jours. Alt. U.S. Men's Olympic Volleyball Team, 1968, 72. Home: 6089 Skyline Dr East Lansing MI 48823 Office: 1099 W Grand River Ave Williamston MI 48895

MINOR, ALBERTA MAE, ednl. adminstr.; b. Asheville, N.C.; d. John J. and Eliza Annabel Haynes; B.S., Miami U., Oxford, Ohio, 1959-64; M.Ed., Wright State U., 1971; m. Maurice J. Minor, Dec. 23, 1940; children—Barbara O., Raymond A., Marlon J. Exec. sec. dist. 7 Internat. Union Elec., Radio and Machine Workers, AFL-CIO, Dayton, Ohio, 1952-64; tchr. bus. edn. Dayton Sch. System, 1964-72, vocat. counselor, 1972-77, project coordinator, 1977—; adj. prof. bus. edn. Wright State U., Dayton, 1972—. Mem. NAACP, Nat. Assn. Vocat. Edn. Spl. Needs Personnel, Am. Vocat. Assn., Ohio Vocat. Assn., Ohio Bus. Tchrs. Assn., Ohio Assn. Vocat. Edn., Dayton Sch. Mgmt. Assn., Southwestern Ohio Assn. Supervision and Curriculum Devel., Iota Phi Lambda. Democrat. Club: Internat. Toastmistress. Home: 2747 Soldiers Home West Carrollton Rd Dayton OH 45418

MINTON, DAVID KENNETH, podiatric surgeon, physician; b. Washington, Nov. 18, 1946; s. George and Doris Evelyn (Geltzner) M.; B.S., U. Tenn., 1969; D.Podiatric medicine cum laude, Ohio Coll. Podiatric Medicine, 1973; m. Diana Elizabeth McWhorter, June 27, 1968; children—Aimee Elizabeth, Neeley Kate. Intern, Monsignor Clement Kern Hosp., Warren, Mich., 1973-75, resident in surgery, 1973-74; pvt. practice medicine, specializing in podiatric medicine and surgery, Southgate, Mich., 1975-81, Troy, Mich., 1977—; mem. staff Dearborn Med. Hosp., Monsignor Clement Kern Hosp. for Spl. Surgery; med. and legal cons. to various orgns., 1980—. Served with USMC, 1967-68. Diplomate Am. Bd. Podiatric Surgery. Fellow Am. Coll. Foot Surgeons; mem. Am. Assn. Hosp. Podiatrists, Mich. State Podiatry Assn., Am. Podiatry Assn. Home: 915 Harmon St Birmingham MI 48009 Office: 12885 Northline Rd Southgate MI 48195

MINTON, JOHN PETER, surgeon; b. Columbus, Ohio, Nov. 29, 1934; s. Harvey Allen and Elsie (Steiger) M.; B.Sc., Ohio State U., 1956, M.D., 1960, M.Med. Sci., 1966, Ph.D. in Microbiology, 1969; m. Janice Arlene Gurney, Aug. 29, 1958; children—Cathryn Anne, Elizabeth Ellen, Cynthia Jane, Christina Lynn. Intern Ohio State U., 1960-61; clin. asso. surgery Nat. Cancer Inst., Bethesda, Md., 1962-65; resident in surgery Univ. Hosp., Ohio State U., Columbus; asst. prof. surgery Ohio State U., Columbus, 1969-73, asso. prof., 1973-77, prof., 1977—, Am. Cancer Soc. prof. clin. oncology, 1979—; mem. grant rev. com. Nat. Cancer Inst., Am. Cancer Soc. Served with USPHS, 1962-65. Mem. ACS (Ohio State U. field liaison chmn.), Ohio State Med. Soc., Columbus Surg. Soc., Soc. Univ. Surgeons, Am. Assn. Acad. Surgeons, Am. Assn. Cancer Edn., Am. Soc. Clin. Oncology, Internat. Fedn. Surgeons. Republican. Presbyterian. Clubs: Columbus Rose (pres. 1979), Central Ohio Rose Soc., Am. Rose Soc., Lido Soc. Contbr. articles to med. jours. Office: 410 W 10th Ave Columbus OH 43210

MINTZER, OLIN WESLEY, III, civil engr.; b. Spokane, Wash., June 6, 1916; s. Olin W. and Ruth (Sugg) M.; B.C.E., U. Tenn., 1942; M.C.E., Purdue U., 1949; m. Marion Elizabeth Head, June 11, 1941; children—Elizabeth Wesley Mintzer Herron, Michael Olin, Patricia Ruthellen Mintzer Hopkins. Engring. aide TVA, Chattanooga, 1938-39, Paris, Tenn., 1940; instr. civil engring. Purdue U., Lafayette, Ind., 1947-49, asst. prof. hwy. engring., 1949-52, research engr., 1947-49; asst. prof. Case Inst. Tech., Cleve., 1952-56; prof. AID project in India, Punjab Engring. Coll., Chandigarh, India, 1956-58; asso. prof. civil engring. Ohio State U., Columbus, 1958-74, prof., 1974—; vis. prof. Escola Superior De Agricultura, U. Sao Paulo, Brazil, summer 1973. Asst. scoutmaster Central Ohio area council Boy Scouts Am., 1961-68; mem. bd. Trinity Meth. Ch., Columbus, Ohio, 1965-66. Served with C.E., U.S. Army, 1940-46. Decorated Legion of Merit; Deutscher Akademischer Austauschdienst fellow, 1970; registered profl. engr., Ohio, Ind.; registered profl. surveyor, Ohio. Mem. ASCE, Am. Soc. Engring. Edn., Nat. Soc. Profl. Engrs., Transp. Research Bd. of NRC, Res. Officers Assn., Am. Soc. Photogrammetry (citation 1972, 73), Sigma Xi, Chi Epsilon. Author: Manual of Highway Engineering Applications of Photogrammetry, 1959; (with others) Airphoto Interpretation of Soils and Rocks for Engineering Purposes, 1953; contbr. chpt. to Manual of Remote Sensing; contbr. numerous articles on applications of aerial photography to civil engring. practice to profl. jours.; developed various terrain analysis techniques. Office: 2070 Neil Mall Columbus OH 43210

MINTZES, BARRY, prison warden; b. N.Y.C., Mar. 28, 1943; s. Nathan and Rose Adele (Weltman) M.; B.B.A., CCNY, 1964; M.A., Kent State U., 1967; Ph.D., Mich. State U., 1970; m. Sheryl Lynn Dahlke, Aug. 23, 1975. Chief psychologist, Jackson Prison, Mich. Dept. Corrections, 1970-74, dir. programs, 1974-75, asst. to dir. corrections dept., 1975-77, supt. Kinross Correctional Facility, 1977-80, warden Jackson prison, 1980—. Mem. adv. bd. criminal justice tng. Mich. State U., East Lansing, 1980—; mem. criminal justice adv. council, Jackson, Hillsdale, Lenawee counties, 1980—; mem. Community Mental Health Bd., Lansing, Mich., 1976-77. Lic.

psychologist, Mich. Mem. Am. Psychol. Assn., Am. Correctional Assn., N. Am. Assn. Wardens and Supts., Am. Assn. Correctional Psycologists, Am. Law Enforcement Officers Assn. Office: 4000 Cooper St Jackson MI 49201

MIOTKE, THOMAS OLIVER, constrn. and devel. co. exec.; b. Milw., Apr. 6, 1946; s. Huber August and Dorothy Elizabeth (Keller) M.; B.S.C.E. cum laude, Marquette U., 1969; m. Dona Marie Schmidt, Mar. 11, 1972; children—Oliver, Anna. Laborer, supt., project engr. Jansen Co., Milw., 1966-72, sales engr., head estimator, 1973-77; v.p. Joseph P. Jansen Co., Milw., 1980-81; v.p., dir. Jansen Devel., Inc., Milw., 1978—. Bd. dirs. Hartford Community Day Care Assn. Registered profl. engr., Wis. Mem. Mason Contractors Assn. (dir.), Am. Soc. Cost Engrs., Nat. Soc. Profl. Engrs., Allied Contractors Assn., Associated Gen. Contractors. Clubs: KC, Lions. Home: Box 27B Route 1 Rubicon WI 53078 Office: 6333 W Douglas Ave Milwaukee WI 53218

MISCH, HERBERT LOUIS, auto co. exec.; b. Sandusky, Ohio, Dec. 7, 1917; s. William Albert and Ethel Alice (Haller) M.; student Miami U., Oxford, Ohio, 1935-38; B.S. in Mech. Engring., U. Mich., 1941; m. Caroline Jane Brinkerhoff, Oct. 7, 1939; children—Suzanne L. Misch Wells, Thomas A. With Packard Motor Co., 1941-56, chief engr. 1954-56; dir. advanced planning Cadillac div. Gen. Motors Corp., 1956-57; asst. chief engr. Lincoln-Mercury div. Ford Motor Co., Dearborn, Mich., 1957-59, exec. engr. Ford div., 1959-60, chief body engr., 1960-61, exec. dir. engring. staff, 1961-62, v.p. engring. and research staff, 1962-70, v.p. engring. and mfg., 1970-72, v.p. environ. and safety engring., 1972—. Fellow Engring. Soc. Detroit, Soc. Automotive Engrs. (dir. 1965-68); mem. Coordinating Research Council (dir., pres.), Am. Soc. Body Engrs., Nat. Acad. Engring., Tau Beta Pi, Phi Kappa Phi. Clubs: Grosse Pointe Yacht, Detroit Athletic. Home: 1411 Lochridge Rd Bloomfield Hills MI 48013 Office: Ford Motor Co The American Rd Dearborn MI 48121

MISCHLEY, WALTER ANTHONY, hosp. adminstr.; b. Alpena, Mich., Feb. 28, 1920; s. Anthony V. and Veronica M. M.; student Purdue U., 1943; B.S., Mich. State U., 1947; m. Ann F. Mischley, Jan. 17, 1948; children—Walter A., Sally Jo. City mgr., Hart, Mich., 1948-49, Manistee, Mich., 1950-51; chief mcpl. br. AEC, Richland, Wash., 1952-56; hosp. adminstr. Middletown (Ohio) Hosp., 1957—; pres. Cin. Hosp. Council; faculty Xavier U., Ohio State U.; bd. dirs. Ohio Hosp. Ins. Co.; chmn. adv. com. Blue Cross; life mem. bd. dirs. Butler County unit Am. Cancer Soc. Chmn. bd. govs. Middletown Fine Arts Center. Served with U.S. Army, 1942-46. Decorated Bronze Star. Fellow Am. Coll. Hosp. Adminstrs.; mem. Am. Hosp. Assn. (del. regional adv. bd.), Internat. Hosp. Assn., Ohio Hosp. Mgmt. Systems (pres.), Ohio Hosp. Assn. (chmn. bd. dirs.). Roman Catholic. Clubs: Rotary, Torch, Browns Run Country. Contbr. articles to profl. publs.; speaker in field Mexico, P.R., Brussels. Home: 1629 Croydon Ln Middletown OH 45042 Office: 105 McKnight Dr Middletown OH 45042

MISHOE, KENNETH LEROY, III, pub. co. exec.; b. Conway, S.C., Apr. 14, 1948; s. Kenneth L. and Mers W. (Bass) M.; B.S. in Econs., U. SW La., 1971; M.B.A., U. West Fla., 1972, M.A. in Psychology, 1973; m. Norma Zeiger, Dec. 22, 1968; children—Kenneth L., Joshua Z. Cons. personnel U.S. Navy, Pensacola, Fla., 1972, Monsanto Chem. Co., Pensacola, 1973; dir. edn. and devel. Day Cos., Atlanta, 1973-74; corporate mgr. inst. for personnel devel. B.F. Goodrich Co., Akron, Ohio, 1974-76; corporate dir. organizational devel. Meredith Corp., Des Moines, 1976—; cons. Hickman Mental Health Center, Broadlawns Hosp. Certified jr. coll. instr., Fla. Mem. Am. Mgmt. Assn., Am. Soc. Tng. and Devel., Adminstrv. Mgmt. Soc. Republican. Baptist. Author: Client Behavior Analysis, 1976. Home: Rt 1 Van Meter IA 50261 Office: Meredith Corp Locust at 17th St Des Moines IA 50336

MISHRA, VISHWA MOHAN, educator; b. Hilsa, Patna, India, Nov. 12, 1937; s. Pandit Sheo Nath and Pandita Nitya (Rani) M.; came to U.S., 1956, naturalized, 1964; B.A. with honors, Patna U., 1954, M.A., 1956; M.A., U. Ga., 1958; Ph.D., U. Minn., 1968; m. Sally Schroeder, June 18, 1977; children—Aneil Kumar, Allan Kumar, Anand Kumar, Jennifer Kumari. Staff reporter, Hindusthan Samachar, Ltd., Patna, India, 1950-56; exec. dir. India for Christ, Inc., Mpls., 1960-64; research fellow, instr. Sch. Journalism and Mass Communication, U. Minn., 1964-68; asst. prof. U. Okla., 1968-69; asso. prof. Mich. State U., East Lansing, 1969—; dir. market and communication research Panax Corp., East Lansing, 1975-76; adminstrv. asst., research cons. to pres. Lansing (Mich.) Community Coll., 1976—. Vice chmn. Eaton-Ingham Substance Abuse Commn. Recipient NSF award, 1969; Bihar Rastrabhasha Parishad Lit. award, 1st prize, 1954. Mem. Am. Mgmt. Assn., Am. Statis. Assn., Am. Pub. Opinion Research Council, Newspaper Research Council, Radio and TV News Dir.'s Assn., Assn. for Edn. in Journalism, Internat. Communication Assn., Am. Platform Assn., Smithsonian Instn. Assos., Kappa Tau Alpha, Sigma Delta Chi. Clubs: East Lansing Rotary, University. Author: Communication and Modernization in Urban Slums, 1972; The Basic News Media and Techniques, 1972; Law and Disorder; also monographs. Contbr. articles to scholastic jours. Home: 2176 Donovan Pl Okemos MI 48864 Office: Sch Journalism Mich State Univ East Lansing MI 48824

MISKUS, MICHAEL ANTHONY, elec. engr., cons.; b. East Chicago, Ind., Dec. 10, 1950; s. Paul and Josephine M.; B.S., Purdue U., 1972; A.A.S. in Elec. Engring. Tech., Purdue U., Indpls., 1972; cert. mgmt. Ind. U., 1972, Ind. Central Coll., 1974; m. Jeannie Ellen Dolmanni, Nov. 4, 1972. Service engr. Reliance Electric & Engring. Co., Hammond, Ind., 1972-73; maintenance supr., maintenance mgr. Diamond Chain Co./AMSTED Industries, Indpls., 1973-76; primary and facilities elec. engr. Johnson & Johnson Baby Products Co., Park Forest South, Ill., 1976—; prin. Miskus Cons., indsl./comml. elec. cons., 1979—; plant and facilities engring. mgr. Sherwin Williams Co., Chgo. Emulsion Plant, Chgo., 1981—; instr., lectr. EET program Moraine Valley Community Coll., Palos Hills, Ill., 1979, Prairie State Coll., Chicago Heights, Ill., 1980—; mem. Elec. Industry Evaluation Panel. Mem. faculty adv. bd. Moraine Valley Community Coll., 1980—. Mem. IEEE, Assn. Energy Engrs., Illuminating Engring. Soc. N.Am., Internat. Platform Assn. Club: Purdue of Chgo. Address: PO Box 292 Olympia Fields IL 60461

MITCHELL, BARBARA JEAN ELLIS DONEGAN, elem. sch. prin.; b. Chgo., Mar. 22, 1933; d. C.B. and Hilda (Davis) Ellis; B.E., Chgo. Tchrs. Coll., 1952; M.A., Roosevelt U., 1955; postgrad. U. Chgo., 1955, Chgo. State U., 1959, 68-69; m. Leon A. Donegan, Nov. 25, 1960 (div. 1963); 1 son, Leon Ellis; m. 2d, Ivory D. Mitchell, Apr. 16, 1966 (div. 1969); 1 son, Brian DeWitt, Tchr., Betsy Ross Sch., Chgo., 1952-57, Andrew Carnegie Sch., Chgo., 1957-62; tchr. 61st and University Sch., Chgo., 1962-63, asst. prin., 1963-68; asst. prin. Robert A. Black Mini-Magnet Sch., Chgo., 1968-71; prin. Charles S. Brownell Sch., Chgo., 1971-77, Henry Clay Sch., Chgo., 1977-80, Edward F. Dunne Sch., Chgo., 1980—; adult edn. tchr., 1964-66; adjustment counselor, 1964-68; sch. librarian, 1964-68; curriculum coordinator, 1970. Recipient merit certificate Carnegie Sch. PTA, 1959, Disting. Service recognition Ill. Congress Parents and Tchrs., 1961, recognition award for outstanding community service, Park Manor Neighbors Community Council, 1975. Mem. Chgo. Prins. Assn., Nat. Council Adminstrv. Women, Phi Delta Kappa. Episcopalian. Author: A Comparative Study of Faculty Meeting Procedures, 1955. Home: 2231 E 67th St Chicago IL 60649 Office: 10845 S Union Ave Chicago IL 60628

MITCHELL, DEAN ALAN, consumer goods co. exec.; b. Brazil, Ind., Mar. 28, 1927; s. M. Frank and Josephine Louise (Tucker) M.; A.B., DePauw U., 1951; m. Martha J. Dunlavy, Oct. 25, 1952; children—Leslie, Katherine, Elizabeth. With Procter & Gamble Co., Cin., 1951—, mgr. merchandising div., 1960-65, advt. mgr., 1965-66, v.p., gen. mgr. P&G Italia, 1966-71, v.p., gen. mgr. P&G Venezuela, 1971-72, gen. mgr. P&G Latin Am., 1972-73, gen. mgr. indsl. cleaning products world-wide, 1973—; dir. Hewitt Soap Co., Dayton, Ohio, Mavesa, S.A., Caracas, Venezuela. Bd. dirs. Temple U., 1968-75, St. Christopher's Sch., 1969-72. Served with USMCR, 1944-46. Mem. U.S. Navy League (dir.), Am. C. of C. (dir. 1966-71), U.S. C. of C., Soap and Detergent Assn., Assn. Nat. Advertisers, Sigma Delta Chi, Sigma Alpha Epsilon. Clubs: Cin. Country, Tippecanoe Country, Queen City. Home: 6700 Wyman Ln Cincinnati OH 45243 Office: 301 E 6th St Cincinnati OH 45202

MITCHELL, ELAYNE SUDAK, investment advisor co. exec.; b. Cleve., Sept. 8, 1929; d. Sol and Leona (Simms) Sudak; B.A., Miami U., Oxford, Ohio, 1951; cert. fin. planner Coll. for Fin. Planning, Denver, 1975; children—Marcy, Ross, Dale Jonathon. Sales mgr., fin. planner Normali-Woodworth, Cleve., 1971-77; registered prin. Will S. Halle Co., Cleve., 1975-77; partner Mitchell-Katzbach Planning Agy., Inc., Beachwood, Ohio, 1977-78; pres. Elayne Mitchell Agy., Inc., Beachwood, 1978—; mem. teaching faculty Coll. for Fin. Planning. Mem. Internat. Assn. Fin. Planners (v.p. edn. N.E. Ohio chpt.), Inst. Cert. Fin. Planners (dir.). Home: 4597 Mayfield Rd South Euclid OH 44121 Office: 3401 Richmond Rd Beachwood OH 44122

MITCHELL, EVELYN WELCH, nursing educator; b. La Fayette, N.Y., Mar. 9, 1918; d. Harry J. and Freida E. (Siler) Welch; diploma in Nursing, New Eng. Sanitarium and Hosp. Sch. Nursing, 1939; B.S. in Nursing, Pacific Union Coll., 1943; postgrad. Catholic U., 1952-54; M.S., Boston Coll., 1973; m. Erie Edward Mitchell, June 16, 1954; children—Clifton, Myrle Ann, Sheralie, RoLayne, Michele. Dir. nurses Kendu Bay Hosp., Kenya, 1944-47; dir. nursing and nursing edn. Dar es Salaam, Baghdad, Iraq, 1948-50; staff nurse Washington Sanitarium and Hosp., Takoma Park, Md., 1950-52; public health nurse D.C. Health Dept., Washington, 1952-54; staff nurse Mimbres Meml. Hosp., Deming, N.Mex., 1954-55; public health nurse Luna County (N.Mex.) Health Dept., 1955-56; staff nurse Meml. Hosp., Las Cruces, N.Mex., 1957-61; staff nurse and relief supr. Gerald Champion Meml. Hosp. Alamogordo, N.Mex., 1965-67, Ardmore (Okla.) Adventist Hosp., 1967-69; charge nurse Edgewood Lodge Nursing Home, Ardmore, 1969; head nurse New Eng. Meml. Hosp., Stoneham, Mass., 1970-71; clin. instr. Atlantic Union Coll., Lancaster, Mass., 1971-72; supr. surg. floor New Eng. Meml. Hosp., 1974; asst. prof. nursing Andrews U., Berrien Springs, Mich., 1974—. Mem. Am. Public Health Assn., Assn. of Seventh-day Adventist Nurses, AAUP. Mem. Seventh-day Adventist Ch. Home: 421 W Ferry St Berrien Springs MI 49103 Office: Andrews Univ Dept of Nursing Berrien Springs MI 49104

MITCHELL, FREDERICK EDWARD, educator; b. Ashland, Wis., Apr. 15, 1945; s. Edward L. and Mary M.; student Mid-State Tech. Inst., 1963-64; B.S., U. Wis., 1971, M.S., 1972; postgrad. Marquette U., 1979—; m. Bobbie J. Marsh, Sept. 25, 1965; children—Theresa J., Christine M. Constrn. welder Wis. Bridge & Iron, Wisconsin Rapids, 1967-68; maintenance welder Dana Machine Co., Wisconsin Rapids, 1968-69; tchr. 916 Vo-Tech. Inst., White Bear Lake, Minn., 1972-75; faculty Waukesha County Tech. Inst., Pewaukee, Wis., 1975—, chmn. indsl. occupations div. 1978—. Served with U.S. Army, 1965-67. Mem. Am. Vocat. Assn., Am. Soc. Tng. and Devel., Am. Tech. Edn. Assn., Wis. Am. Vocat. Assn., Midwest Assn. Individualized Instrn. Republican. Roman Cahtolic. Club: Kiwanis. Home: 532 Greenland Ave Oconomowoc WI 53066 Office: 800 Main St Pewaukee WI 53072

MITCHELL, FREDERICK JAYNES, business exec.; b. Grand Rapids, Mich., Feb. 13, 1926; s. William David and Myrva Ruth (Mellons) M.; grad. Grand Rapids Jr. Coll., 1950; m. Mary M. Rinkus, Jan. 17, 1948; children—Lynn, Michele, Karen, Chris. Mgr., Am. Investment Co., 1950-58; sales rep. Scott & Fetzer Co., Grand Rapids, 1958; pres. Fred J. Mitchell Inc., 1959-73; owner Belmont's Restaurant, Custom Aluminum Products, 1959-73; exec. v.p. sales Health-Mor, Inc., Chgo., 1973—. Served with USNR, 1944-46. Republican. Office: 35 E Wacker Dr Chicago IL 60601

MITCHELL, GEORGE TRICE, physician; b. Marshall, Ill., Jan. 20, 1914; s. Roscoe Addison and Alma (Trice) M.; B.S., Purdue U., 1935, postgrad., 1935-36; M.D., George Washington U., 1940; m. Mildred Aletha Miller, June 21, 1941; children—Linda Sue, Mary Kathryn. Intern Meth. Hosp., Indpls., 1940-41; practice medicine, Marshall, 1946—; mem. courtesy staff Union, Regional hosps., Terre Haute, Ind.; clin. asso. Sch. Basic Med. Sci. U. Ill. Chmn. bd., dir. First Nat. Bank, Marshall. Mem., pres. Marshall Community Unit Sch. Bd., 1955-67; coroners physician, Clark County, Ill., 1958—; mem. Bd. Health, 1946—; mem. City Planning Commn., 1953—; chmn. county med. adv. com. Ill. Dept. Public Aid, 1947-63, mem. state med. adv. com., 1965—. Mem. adv. council premedicine Eastern Ill. U., 1965-69. Alt. del. Republican Conv., 1968, del., 1972; trustee Lakeland Jr. Coll. Served from 1st lt. to lt. col., USAAF, 1941-45. Fellow Am. Acad. Family Physicians; mem. Clark County, Ill. med. socs., AMA, Aesculapian Soc. of Wabash Valley (pres. 1965), Clark County Hist. Soc. (pres. 1968-70). Republican. Methodist. Mason (32 deg., Shriner). Home: RFD 2 Marshall IL 62441 Office: 410 N 2d St Marshall IL 62441

MITCHELL, GERALD B., mfg. co. exec.; b. 1927; married. With Dana Corp., Toledo, 1939—, v.p. mfg. Hayes Dana Ltd. subs., Thorold, Ont., Can., 1958-63, pres., 1963-67, pres. parent co., from 1973, now chmn. bd., chief exec. officer, dir. Office: Dana Corp 4500 Dorr St Box 1000 Toledo OH 43697*

MITCHELL, GORDON LYNN, elec. engr.; b. Spokane, Wash., Dec. 20, 1942; s. Frank Leonard and Vesta Dorothy (Shaw) M.; B.S., U. Wash., 1964, Ph.D., 1974; m. Skaidrite Liesma Iesalnieks, July 17, 1966; children—Douglas, Adele, Vicki. Mem. research faculty U. Wash., Seattle, 1974-78; prin. research scientist, fiber optics group leader Honeywell Inc., Mpls., 1978—; comml. arbitrator. Served as aviator USN, 1964-69. NSF research grantee, 1974-78; Technicon grantee, 1975; registered profl. engr., Wash., Oreg., Calif., Minn. Mem. IEEE (sr.), Optical Soc. Am., U.S. Strategic Inst. Contbr. articles to profl. jours. Office: Systems and Research Center Honeywell Inc 2600 Ridgway Pkwy Minneapolis MN 55413

MITCHELL, JOHN F., electronics co. exec.; b. 1928; B.S., Ill. Inst. Tech., 1950; married. With Motorola, Inc., Schaumburg, Ill., 1953—, v.p., 1968-72, v.p. and gen. mgr. communications div., 1972-75, exec. v.p. and asst. chief operating officer, 1975-80, pres., asst. chief operating officer, 1980—, also dir. Served with USN, 1950-53. Office: Motorola Inc 1303 E Algonquin Rd Schaumburg IL 60196*

MITCHELL, KEVIN ROBERT, leasing and fin. services co. exec.; b. Quincy, Mass., Oct. 23, 1948; s. Peter James and Gertrude E. (Robertson) M.; B.S. in Bus. Adminstrn., Suffolk U., 1970; M.B.A., U. Detroit, 1975; postgrad. U. Minn., 1979-80; m. Elizabeth O'Keefe, Nov. 15, 1969; children—Jennifer, Renee, Joshua, Faith. Audit rev. specialist Herbert F. French & Co. C.P.A.'s, Boston, 1968-70; mgr. planning and mgmt. reporting Ford Motor Credit, Detroit, 1970-74; asst. v.p., mgr. mktg. services FBS Fin., Mpls., 1974-75; v.p., controller Gelcofleet & Mgmt. Services Co., Eden Prairie, Minn., 1975-80; v.p. sales fin. div. Citicorp Consumer Services Group, St. Louis, 1980-81; v.p. adminstrn. Gelco Corp., Eden Prairie, Minn., 1981—. Mem. Nat. Assn. Accts., Am. Mgmt. Assn., Beta Gamma Sigma. Home: 4102 Blueberry Ln Ln Eagan MN 55123 Office: 1 Gelco Dr Eden Prairie MN 55123

MITCHELL, MICHAEL JOSEPH, mfg. co. exec.; b. South Bend, Ind., Feb. 1, 1924; s. Michael Albert and Alfreda Dorothy (Sygler) M.; B.S., Butler U., 1950; cert. indsl. tech., Purdue U., 1959; M.B.A., U. No. Iowa, 1972; m. Lorraine M. Wilson, Oct. 2, 1948; children—Michael Bruce, Dawn Marie. Indsl. engr. Bendix Aviation Corp., South Bend, 1950-52; project engr. Acme Steel Co., Riverdale, Ill., 1952-54; chief indsl. engr. Anderson Co., Gary, Ind., 1954-64; gen. mgr. Des Moines div. Lennox Industries, Inc., 1964—. Served to capt. AUS, 1943-46; ETO. Mem. Soc. Mfg. Engrs. (cert.), Am. Mgmt. Assn., Des Moines C. of C., Indsl. Mgmt. Soc. Republican. Roman Catholic. Club: New Pioneer Gun. Contbr. articles to profl. jours. Home: Rural Route 2 Box 21S Waukee IA 50263 Office: 1665 Madison St Des Moines IA 50316

MITCHELL, MICHAEL STAMM, marketing exec.; b. Flint, Mich., Sept. 8, 1941; s. Sam A. and Margaret Edith (Stephens) M.; B.S. in Econs., Western Mich. U., 1968. Account exec. J. Walter Thompson Advt., 1970-73; regional advt. mgr. Mid-East region Campbell Ewald Advt., Cin., 1973-76; advt. and corp. sponsor, Carowinds Theme Park, Charlotte, N.C., 1976-77; dir. mktg. Space World, Inc., New Boston, Mich., 1978-81; account mgr. Robert Landau Assos., Inc., 1981—; founder, dir. Air Mich. Airlines, Kalamazoo. Bd. dirs. Nashville Music Consortium, S.E. Mich. Travel and Tourist Assn., Carolinas Carousel, Charlotte; advt. cons. Spaulding for Children, Ann Arbor, Mich; fin. chmn. Care and Health, Inc. Served with Signal Corps, U.S. Army, 1962-64. Mem. Yesteryears Mus. Assns., Adcraft Club Detroit, Detroit Bus. Forum, Econs. Club Detroit. Republican. Episcopalian. Home: Detroit MI Office: 23400 Michigan Ave Dearborn MI 48124

MITCHELL, MICHAEL WESLEY, hosp. sterile processing mgr.; b. Mansfield, Ohio, May 7, 1955; s. Wesley Acey and Ethyl Maria (Strong) M.; operating room technician cert. Naval Regional Med. Center, Portsmouth, Va., 1977, emergency med. technician cert., 1979; A.S., Tidewater Community Coll., 1979; B.S., Ohio State U., 1982; m. Mary Theresa Siurano, Nov. 18; children—Karen, Moses, Tina. Enlisted in U.S. Navy, 1973; asst. supr. surg. ward NavaNaval Regional Med. Center, Roosevelt Rds., P.R., 1973-74, supr. pediatrics ward, 1974-75; physician asst. 3d Bn. 6th Marines, 1975-76, supr. physician assts., 1976-77; operating room technician Naval Regional Med. Center, Portsmouth, 1977-78, asst. supr. central supply room, 1978-81; sterile processing mgr. Shelby (Ohio) Meml. Hosp., 1981—; cons. Va. Assn. Hosp. Central Service Practitioners. Mem. Am. Soc. Hosp. Central Service Personnel, Internat. Assn. Hosp. Central Service Personnel (registered central supply technician), Assn. Practitioners in Infection Control, Va. Assn. Central Service Practitioners, Ohio Soc. Central Service Practitioners, Hosp. Fin. Mgmt. Assn., Nat. Assn. Nurse Edn. and Service. Roman Catholic. Research on hazards of ethylene oxide. Home: 1741 E Evergreen Ave Mansfield OH 44905 Office: Shelby Meml Hosp PO Box 608 Shelby OH 44875

MITCHELL, OTIS CLINTON, JR., educator; b. Spearville, Kans., Jan. 10, 1935; s. Otis Clinton and Joeanna Esther (Woodring) M.; A.B., Wichita U., 1957; M.A., Kans. State Coll., 1960; Ph.D., U. Kans., 1964; m. Darlene Foley, Aug. 20, 1966. Instr., Wichita State U. (Kans.), 1963-64; asst. prof. U. Cin., 1964-69, asso. prof., 1969-75, prof. history, 1975—. Dir. civic com., Hidden Valley Lake, Ind., 1975, bd. dirs., 1978-79. Served with CIC, AUS, 1957-59. Taft fellowship fund grantee, 1969-74, 81. Mem. Am. Hist. Assn., A.A.U.P., Phi Alpha Theta. Author: (with Walter Langsam) The World Since 1919, 1971; Two Totalitarians, 1965; The Western Cultural Way, 1965; A Concise History of Western Civilization, 2d edit., 1976. Editor, contbr. Nazism and the Common Man, 2d edit., 1981; Fascism: An Introductory Perspective, 1978; Turning Points in History: The Great European Revolutionary Era of 1789-1815, 1979; A Concise History of Brandenburg-Prussia to 1786, 1980. Home: 1520 Lowgiver St Hidden Valley Lake Lawrenceburg IN 47025 Office: Dept History U Cin Cinnati OH 45221

MITCHELL, PHILIP JAMES, bank exec.; b. Manchester, Eng., May 23, 1930; came to U.S., 1954, naturalized, 1965; s. David Ernest and Marie (Dilbeck) M.; grad. U. Wis. Sch. for Bank Adminstrn., 1973; m. Charlotte Studer, Aug. 10, 1957 (dec. 1979); 1 son, Mark Philip. Theatre mgr. J. Arthur Rank Orgn., London, 1952-54; chief acct. Whitehall Labs. Inc., Elkhart, Ind., 1955-66; asst. controller/cashier St. Joseph Valley Bank subs. SJV Corp., Elkhart, 1966—, asst. treas. parent co., 1976—. Bd. dirs. Elkhart County Mental Health Assn., 1967-78, pres., 1973-75; bd. dirs. Mental Health Assn. Ind., 1975-77, Michiana Ballet, 1981—; treas. Elkhart Concert Club, 1973—. Served with Royal Corps of Signals, Brit. Army, 1948-52. Recipient Service award Elkhart County Mental Health Assn., 1975. Mem. Nat. Assn. Accts., Bank Adminstrn. Inst. No. Ind. Episcopalian. Club: Lions (Charter Treas. award 1970, treas. 1970-76). Home: 2100 E Bristol St Apt A204 Elkhart IN 46514 Office: St Joseph Valley Bank 121 W Franklin St Elkhart IN 46516

MITCHELL, ROBERT EUGENE, psychologist; b. Omaha, Mar. 2, 1945; s. Robert Monroe and Ollie Marie (Sidener) M.; B.A., Creighton U., 1967; M.A., Ohio State U., 1969, Ph.D., 1971. Cons., Clarinda (Iowa) Mental Health Inst., 1973-75, Christian Home, Council Bluffs, Iowa, 1974-76; chief psychologist Douglas County Hosp., Omaha, 1975-80; asst. prof. psychology Creighton U. Med. Sch., Omaha, 1972—, dir. div. behavioral scis., 1974—. Mem. Am. Psychol. Assn., Neb. Psychol. Assn. (pres. 1981-82), Nebr. Soc. Profl.

Psychologists (pres. 1977-78). Office: 314 Criss II Creighton Med Sch Omaha NE 68178

MITCHELL, ROBERT JAMES, petroleum co. exec.; b. Montour Falls, N.Y., Mar. 16, 1925; s. Robert Bowlby and Helen (Bates) M.; student Ga. Inst. Tech., 1944, U. Richmond, 1945, Sampson Coll., 1947-48; student Valparaiso U., 1948, J.D., 1953; m. Pearl Kohnken, Aug. 30, 1947; children—Susan E., LuAnne, Robert James II. Adjuster, State Farm Mut. Auto Ins., Valparaiso, 1953-54; dist. rep. life ins. Aid Assn. for Lutherans, Hoffman, Ill., 1954-57; with dept. of devel. Valparaiso (Ind.) U., 1957-58; oil producer, Hoffman, 1958-64; founder Ego Oil Co., Inc., 1964, pres., 1964—, also dir. Bd. dirs. Law Sch. Alumni Bd., 1970-73. Served with USNR, 1941-46, 50-52. Mem. Ind. Petroleum Assn. Am. (dir. 1976—), Delta Theta Phi. Rotarian. Home: PO Box 87 Hoffman IL 62250 Office: 123 S Locust St PO Box 787 Centralia IL 62801

MITCHELL, STEPHEN CONNALLY, engr.; b. Albuquerque, Sept. 27, 1943; s. Claude Stephen and Alma Nelle (Cashion) M.; B.C.E., U. N.Mex., 1966, M.C.E., 1968; M.B.A., U. Chgo., 1974; m. Cynthia Eugenia McDonell, June 8, 1968; 1 son, Graham. Research asst. Civil Engring. Research Facility, N.Mex., 1964-68; engr. Inland Steel Co., East Chicago, Ind., 1968; sr. soils engr. Westenhoff & Novick, Cons. Engrs., Chgo., 1968; project mgr. Bauer Engring., Chgo., 1972-74, asst. dir. planning, 1974-75; sr. v.p. and long range planning Lester B. Knight & Assos., Inc., 1975—. Served to 1st lt., C.E., U.S. Army, 1969-72. Mem. ASCE (pres. Ill. sect. 1979-80), Soc. Am. Mil. Engrs., Sigma Tau. Home: 208 W St Paul St Chicago IL 60614 Office: 549 W Randolph St Chicago IL 60606

MITCHELL, WILLIAM HENRY, ret. state ofcl.; b. Macon, Ga., Mar. 18, 1913; s. Charles J. and Anna Mae (Smith) M.; B.A., Fisk U., 1941; m. Marion M. McWilliams, Jan. 11, 1941. Library asst. Chgo. Pub. Library, 1937-43; lab. asst. for atomic bomb Manhattan Dist. Project of Metall. Lab., U. Chgo., 1943-44, 46; supr. female record section Chgo. Health Dept., 1946; dep. Ill. Dept. Labor, Div. Unemployment Compensation, Chgo., 1946-54, dep. reviewer, 1954-55, adjudication supr., 1955-63, office mgr., Evanston, 1963-64, Elgin, Ill., 1964-69, Harvey, Ill., 1969-75. Served with USN, 1944-46. Mem. Ill. Unemployment Compensation Assn. Assn. (chpt. chmn. 1963-64), Internat. Assn. Personnel Employment Security (state treas. 1973-75), Ill. State Employees Assn., Assn. Ret. State Employees (dir.), Am. Legion (comdr. 1974-75), Kappa Alpha Psi. Home: 7552 S Wabash Ave Chicago IL 60619

MITCHLER, ROBERT WALTER, former state senator; b. Aurora, Ill., June 4, 1920; s. John L. and Clara L. Mitchler; B.S., Aurora Coll., 1953; m. Helen Drew Mitchler, June 16, 1950; children—John Drew, Kurt David, Heidi Louise. With Chgo. Burlington & Quincy R.R., 1937-54; sales and packaging engr. Better Boxes, 1954-58; sales and public relations positions No. Ill. Gas Co., 1958-75; mem. Ill. State Senate, 1965-81; with Ill. Dept. Vet. Affairs, 1981—. Served with USNR, 1941-53. Mem. Am. Legion, V.F.W., AMVETS, Navy League U.S. Republican. Methodist. Clubs: Masons, Scottish Rite, Shriners, Moose.

MITCHUSSON, GENE ALLEN, advt. agy. exec., priest; b. Cin., June 16, 1931; s. Charles Marion and Annie Corrine (Williams) M.; B.S. in Bus. Adminstrn., U. Cin., 1958; licentiate theology St. Albans Sem., 1979; m. Edythe E. Rimmer, July 3, 1965; 1 son, James Harry. With Allis Chalmers, Norwood, Ohio, 1950-69; account exec. Lohre & Assos., Inc., Cin., 1970-73, v.p., 1973-81; v.p. Robert Acomb Inc., 1981—; ordained to ministry Am. Episcopal Ch. as deacon, 1974, priest, 1975, apptd. archdeacon, 1980, dean No. Deanery, 1980, ch. gen. sec., 1976-79. Served to lt. AUS, 1951-54. Decorated Bronze Star medal. Mem. Cin. Indsl. Advertisers (dir. 1971-74). Home: 1197 Herschel St Cincinnati OH 45208 Office: 420 E McMillan St Cincinnati OH 45206

MITRA, SMARAJIT, chemist; b. Calcutta, India, June 29, 1949; s. Sourindra Krishna and Uma (Ghosh) M.; B.Sc., Calcutta U., 1969, M.Sc., 1971; Ph.D., U. Mich., 1977; m. Sumita Basu, July 15, 1974. Research asso. Case Western Res. U., Cleve., 1977-78; sr. research chemist 3M Co., St. Paul, 1978—. Govt. India scholar, 1966, 66-72; Sherwin Williams research fellow, 1974-77. Mem. AAAS, N.Y. Acad. Sci., Am. Chem. Soc. (co-chmn. membership com. div. polymer chemistry 1981—), Sigma Xi. Mem. editorial bd. Jour. Applied Photog. Engring., 1980—; contbr. articles to profl jours. Home: 7180 Aberdeen Curve Woodbury MN 55125

MITROFANOV, MICHOLAS, nuclear physicist; b. Russia, Feb. 5, 1918; came to U.S., 1968, naturalized, 1970; s. Michael and Anastasia (Shirokov) M.; M.S., U. Moscow, 1940, Ph.D. in Physics, 1943; widower. Redactor jour. Columbus, Russian weekly in Austria, 1945-48; mem. faculty U. Chile, Santiago, 1950-62; research prof. U. Md., 1962-64; with Harshaw Chem. Co., Cleve., 1965—, sr. research scientist, 1962—; cons. in field. Author: Textbook of Physics, 1946; (poetry) Caravels, 1980; also articles. Patentee in field.

MITROVIC, MILAN, psychologist; b. Gelsenkirchen, Germany, May 31, 1949; s. Pantelija Theodore and Amanda Maria (Podvalej) M.; B.S., U. Ill., Chgo., 1971; M.A., DePaul U., 1973, Ph.D., 1977. Psychology intern Chgo. Read Mental Health Center, 1974-75; clin. psychologist Northwest Community Mental Health Center, Lima, Ohio, 1977, Naval Regional Med. Center, Great Lakes, Ill., 1977—; mem. part-time faculty De Paul U., Chgo., 1976-77, Trinity Coll., Deerfield, Ill., 1980-81. Arthur J. Schmitt fellow, 1971-74. Mem. Am. Psychol. Assn., Midwest Psychol. Assn., Ill. Psychol. Assn., Nat. Register Health Service Providers, Biofeedback Soc. Am. Office: Psychiatry Service Naval Regional Med Center Great Lakes IL 60088

MITTELMANN, EUGENE, cons. electronics engr.; b. Bratislava, Czechoslovakia, May 29, 1903; s. Ludwig and Louise (Perlblum) M.; came to U.S., 1938, naturalized, 1942; E.E., Vienna Inst. Tech., 1927; Ph.D., U. Vienna, 1931; m. Gusta Davidsohn, Nov. 21, 1939. Dir. labs. Austrian br. ITT, 1931-36; ind. cons., Europe and U.S., 1936-41; biophys. researcher Rush Med. Coll., Chgo., 1939, Northwestern U., 1940-42; dir. electronic research Ill. Tool Works, 1942-46; cons. indsl. electronics, Chgo., 1946-81; cons. to industry, Argonne Nat. Lab., Oak Ridge Labs. Recipient spl. award Am. Congress Phys. Therapy, 1938; Outstanding Achievement award IEEE-IECI, 1975, Disting. Achievement award, 1979. Fellow IEEE, Instrument Soc. Am., AAAS; mem. N.Y. Acad. Scis., Sigma Xi. Editorial bd. Spectrum, 1973-80; contbr. articles tech. and sci. jours. Holder more than 100 U.S. and fgn. patents. Died Apr. 6, 1981. Home: 1368 E Madison Park Chicago IL 60615

MITTLER, JAMES EMMETT, mgmt. cons.; b. St. Louis, Feb. 8, 1943; s. Emmet J. and Frances K. (Ketler) M.; B.S. in Bus. Adminstrn., Drury Coll., Springfield, Mo., 1969; M.B.A., So. Ill. U., 1978; m. Francene E. Duepner, Oct. 10, 1964; children—James Emmett, Lynn Ann. Personnel asst. Kroger Co., St. Louis, 1969-72; personnel mgr. Sealtest Foods Co., Memphis, 1972-73; pres. Mittler Realty Co. and Exigency Service, personnel cons. firm, Washington, Mo., 1973-76; dir. employment and compensation Banquet Foods Co., St. Louis, 1976-80; sr. asso. Hay Assos., St. Louis, 1981—; pres. Franklin County Bd. Realtors, 1975-76. Served with USAR, 1966-69. Recipient Human Relations award Dale Carnegie Inst., 1970. Mem. Urban League Career Edn. Council, Personnel Mgrs. Assn. Mo. Republican. Roman Catholic. Clubs: Elks, Optimists (past pres. Washington). Home: 823 Westwood St Ballwin MO 63011 Office: 222 S Central Saint Louis MO 63105

MITZE, CLARK H., arts adminstr.; b. Cedar Falls, Iowa, Mar. 28, 1918; s. George H. and Alace C. (Brown) M.; B.A., U. No. Iowa, 1939; M.A., U. Iowa, 1947; m. Verla Marie Diekman, May 20, 1942; children—Thomas, Michael Terry, Robert. Mem. faculty Washington U., St. Louis, 1950-67; music critic St. Louis Globe Democrat. 1960-67; dir. fed.-state programs Nat. Endowment Arts, 1968-76; dir. Calif. Arts Council, Sacramento, 1976-78; dir. Ill. Arts Council, Chgo., 1978—. Served to lt. col. USAF, 1941-46. Office: 111 N Wabash Chicago IL 60602

MIYARES, MARCELINO, research and advt. exec.; b. Havana, Cuba, Mar. 23, 1937; s. Marcelino and Adela (Sotolongo) M.; came to U.S., 1962, naturalized, 1976; J.D., Villanova U., Havana, 1960; M.A., Georgetown U., 1966; Ph.D., Northwestern U., Evanston, Ill., 1974; m. Marta Clemente, Apr. 20, 1963; children—Marcelino Jose, Juan Antonio, Maria Isabel, Anne Marie. Chmn. polit. sci. dept., asso. prof. polit. sci. Ill. Benedictine Coll., Lisle, 1964-72; pres. Ops., Market, Advt. Research, Inc., Chgo., 1969—. Campaign dir., finance dir. Hispanic-Am. Com. for Re-election of Pres., 1972; bd. mem. Non-Partisan Com. Re-election Mayor Daley, 1974; mem. Ill. Bd. Edn., 1976—, parent's bd. Schs. Sacred Heart; bd. dirs. Chgo. Community Renewal Soc., 1976—; mem. Mayor Jane Byrne's transition team, 1979; bd. govs. State Colls. and Univs. Ill., 1981—; mem. at-large exec. com. Chgo. United. Named Pan-Am. Man of Year, Spanish TV Guide, 1974, Social Sci. Tchr. of Year, Ill. Benedictine Coll., 1967. Mem. Am. Polit. Sci. Assn., Am. Marketing Assn., Am. Research Found., Bus.-Profl. Advt. Assn., Am. Assn. Advt. Agys., Blue Key. Roman Catholic. Club: Internat. (Chgo.). Author: Models of Political Participation of Hispanic-Americans, 1974; Hispanic-American's Strategy for the Future, 1975; polit. sci. editor Cath. Book List, 1966-69. Office: 5525 Broadway Chicago IL 60640

MIZEL, GERALD M., loan co. exec.; b. Mitchell, S.D., Nov. 18, 1933; s. Philip and Esther (Martinsky) M.; B.B.A., U. Miami, 1957; postgrad. Law Sch., DePaul U.; m. Liora Katzengold, Nov. 1, 1966; children—Michelle, Elliana. With Midland Fin. Co., Chgo., 1957—, now exec. v.p., sec., treas., dir.; exec. v.p., sec.-treas., dir. U.S. Auto Sales Inc., Chgo. Participant, 3d Econ. Conf., Jerusalem, 1973. Office: Midland Finance Co 7541 N Western Ave Chicago IL 60645

MIZRAHI, ABSHALOM, mathematician, educator; b. Tel Aviv, Israel, Jan. 21, 1935; s. Jacob and Georgia (Yitzhak) M.; B.A., So. Ill. U., 1959; M.S., Ill. Inst. Tech., 1962, Ph.D., 1965; m. Caryl Polansky, Dec. 21, 1964; children—Tamar, Laura. Mem. faculty dept. math. Ind. U. NW, Gary, 1965—, chmn. dept. math., 1967-69. Mem. Gary Council Econ. Advisors; mem. Gary Legis. and Fin. subcom.; mem. Gary City Wide Devel. Corp. Served with Israeli Army, 1954-56. NSF grantee, 1969-72. Mem. Am. Math. Soc., Am. Profs. for Peace in Mid-East, Israeli Students Orgn. in U.S. and Can. Author: (with Michael Sullivan) Calculus with Applications, 1976; Mathematical Models with Applications in the Social Sciences Business, 1979; Topics in Elementary Mathematics, 1971; Finite Mathematics with Application, 1973; Calculus and Analytic Geometry, 1982.

MLSNA, KATHRYN KIMURA, lawyer; b. Yonkers, N.Y., Apr. 23, 1952; d. Eugene T. and Grace W. (Watanabe) Kimura; B.A., Northwestern U., 1974, J.D., 1977; m. Timothy Mlsna, Oct. 4, 1975. Admitted to Ill. bar, 1977; atty., McDonald's Corp., Oak Brook, Ill., 1977—. Mem. Am. Bar Assn., Ill. Bar Assn., Chgo. Bar Assn. Methodist. Office: 1 McDonald's Plaza Oak Brook IL 60521

MOAYAD, CYRUS, otolaryngologist; b. Iran, June 27, 1928; s. Dr. Mir and Mahbooba (Forouzan) M.; came to U.S., 1958; M.D., Geneva Med. Sch., 1957. Intern, Kingston-Gen. Hosp., Queens U., Can.; resident in otolaryngology Cleve. Clinic Found.; asst. prof. surgery Case-Western Res. U., to 1968; practice medicine specializing in otolaryngology, facial plastic and cosmetic surgery, Valparaiso, Ind., 1968—; staff Valparaiso, LaPorte hosps.; pres. Moayad E.N.T., Inc. Diplomate Am. Bd. Otolaryngology, Am. Bd. Cosmetic Surgery. Fellow A.C.S.; mem. AMA, Ind. Med. Assn., Am. Acad. Otolaryngology, Am. Acad. Facial Plastic Surgery, Am. Soc. Ophthalmology and Otolaryngology Allergy, Am. Soc. Study of Headache, Internat. Coll. Surgeons, Internat. Acad. Cosmetic Surgery, Chgo. Laryngo-otological Club. Author studies and articles about lost cities of the world; contbr. articles to profl. jours. Home: 90 W County Rd 550 N Valparaiso IN 46383 Office: Moayad Clinic 1105 Glendale Blvd Valparaiso IN 46383

MOBERLY, RICHARD C., savs. and loan exec.; b. Florence, Kans., Jan. 31, 1926; s. Socrates Evans and Lillie Ethel (Simmons) M.; student Salt City Bus. Coll., 1946-47; m. Betty A. Houtz, June 23, 1946; children—Cheri J., Diane K., Gloria L. Vice-pres. R.R. Savs. & Loan, Newton, Kans., 1947-55, controller, 1955-68, v.p., sec., 1968-77, exec. v.p., sec., 1977-81, pres., mgr., 1981—, also dir. Dir. United Way; vice-chmn. Zoning Bd. Appeals. Served with U.S. Army, 1944-46. Mem. V.F.W., C. of C. (bd. dirs. 1979-82). Republican. Clubs: Lions (dist. sec.-treas. 1975-76), Wichita, Elks, Newton Country. Home: 304 Lakeshore Dr Newton KS 67114 Office: 129 E Broadway Newton KS 67114

MOBLEY, GORDON ORVAL, retail exec.; b. Ottumwa, Iowa, Nov. 9, 1934; s. Orval S. and Loraine (Jessen) M.; student Drake U., 1953-57; m. JoAnn B. Baker, July 12, 1960; children—Christy, Cindy, Colleen. Store mgr., Spurgeon Mercantile Co., Centerville, Fort Madison, Iowa, 1960-67; owner, pres. The Villa Inc., Charles City, Iowa, 1967—, also dir. Mem. Planning Zoning Commn. City of Ft. Madison, 1966-67; treas. Lutheran Ch., 1966-67. Served with AUS, 1957-59. Mem. Charles City C. of C. (dir.), Iowa Retail Assn., Cedar Mall Assn. Republican. Club: Elks. Home: 120 Cedar Circle Charles City IA 50616 Office: 130 Cedar Mall Charles City IA 50616

MOBLEY, TONY ALLEN, univ. dean, educator; b. Harrodsburg, Ky., May 19, 1938; s. Cecil and Beatrice (Bailey) M.; B.S. in Physics and Phys. Edn. cum laude, Georgetown (Ky.) Coll., 1960; M.S. in Recreation, Ind. U., 1962, Re.D., 1965; M.R.E., So. Theol. Sem., Louisville, 1963; m. Betty Weaver, June 10, 1961; 1 son, Derek Lloyd. Tchr., coach, camp dir., to 1965; mem. faculty Western Ill. U., Macomb, 1965-72, asso. prof., 1969-72, chmn. dept. recreation and park adminstrn., 1967-72; asso. prof. Pa. State U., 1972-75, prof., 1975-76, chmn. recreation and parks, 1972-76; prof. recreation and park adminstrn., dean Sch. Health, Phys. Edn. and Recreation, Ind. U., Bloomington, 1976—; cons., speaker. Recipient Disting. Fellow award Soc. Park and Recreation Educators, 1978; Spl. Service citation Nat. Recreation and Park Assn., 1978; Garrett G. Eppley Alumni Recognition award Ind. U., 1975; Am. Council on Edn. fellow, 1971. Fellow Soc. Park and Recreation Educators (pres. 1975); mem. Nat. Recreation and Park Assn. (pres. 1979), AAHPER, Phi Delta Kappa. Author: (with others) Educating for Leisure-Centered Living, 1977. Editor: An Integrative Review of Research in Church Recreation and Related Areas, 1975; also articles. Office: Ind U Bloomington IN 47405

MOCHA, FRANK, educator; b. Babice, Silesia, Poland, Feb. 18, 1921; s. Paul and Anna (Mandel) M.; came to U.S., 1951, naturalized, 1956; student U. London, 1946-48; B.Sc. magna cum laude, Columbia U., 1961, M.A. (Nat. Def. Fgn. Lang. fellow), 1963, Ph.D., 1970; m. Doreen Constance Hampson, Sept. 21, 1951; children—Paul Alexander, Jane Helena, Mark Henry. Proofreader, Retnak Press, N.Y.C., 1952-62; instr. U. Pitts., 1966-68, asst. prof., 1968-71; asso. editor Polish Rev., Polish Inst. Arts and Scis. in Am., 1972-75, chmn. lit. sect., 1974-77, dir., 1974-77; asso. prof. slavic langs. and lits. U. Ill., Chgo. Circle, 1976-78; mem. faculty Loyola U., Chgo., 1979—; lectr. on lang. Kosciuszko Found., 1963-64, on lit., 1975-76; adj. asst. prof. N.Y. U. Sch. Continuing Edn., 1974-76. Pres. Polish Arts Club of Chgo., 1977-79; bd. dirs. Polish Am. Congress Ill. Div., 1977-78. Served with inf. Polish Army, 1939-45. Internat. Research and Exchanges Bd. grantee, 1971-72; Kosciuszko Found. grantee, 1973, 74, 75. Mem. MLA, Polish Am. Educators Assn. (pres. 1981—), Am. Assn. Advancement Slavic Studies, Am. Assn. Tchrs. Slavic, East European Langs., Phi Beta Kappa. Author: Poles in America: Bicentennial Essays, 1977; contbr. articles to profl. jours. Home: 1112 W North Shore Ave Apt 11 Chicago IL 60626 Office: Loyola U Lewis Towers 820 N Michigan Ave Chicago IL 60611

MOCHON, MARION JOHNSON, anthropologist, educator, univ. adminstr.; b. Saratoga Springs, N.Y., June 6, 1929; d. James Moylan and Marion (Elliott) Johnson; B.A., U. Tex., 1950; M.A., U. Wis., 1966, Ph.D., 1972; children—Michael Scott, Barbara, John. Faculty, U. Wis., Parkside, Kenosha, 1966-76, chmn. Div. Social Scis., 1973-74; ACE fellow, U. Calif., Irvine, 1974-75; asst. to vice chancellor U. Wis. - Parkside, 1975-76; dean acad. affairs Ind. U. N.W., Gary, 1976—; cons. VISTA, Indian Affairs. Mem. Ind. Com. for the Humanities, 1979-82; v.p. Friends of Art, Milw. Art Center, 1961-62, sec., 1962-63; mem. nat. adv. council Nat. Commn. on Higher Edn. Issues, 1981—. Am. Council on Edn. fellow, 1974-75; Am. Philos. Soc. grantee, 1965; Wis. Alumni Research Fund grantee, 1973. Fellow Am. Anthropol. Assn., AAAS, Am. Council on Edn., Soc. Applied Anthropology; mem. Soc. Am. Archaeology, Central States Anthropol. Soc. Contbr. articles to profl. jours. Office: 3400 Broadway Gary IN 46408

MODELL, ARTHUR B., profl. football team exec.; b. Bklyn., June 23, 1925; m. Patricia Breslin, July 25, 1969; stepchildren—John, David. Owner, pres. Cleve. Browns football team, 1961—; pres. Nat. Football League, 1967-70. Office: Cleveland Stadium Cleveland OH 44114*

MODIC, JAMES PAUL, retail and rental co. exec.; b. Cleve., Nov. 9, 1936; s. James Vincent and Pauline Mary (Tabor) M.; ed. DePaul U., 1966-70, Am. Inst. Banking, 1967-70; m. Jeanette Marie Kraus, June 14, 1958; children—John, Janis, Jennifer. Methods analyst Chgo. Police Dept., 1957-58, sr. methods analyst, 1959-61, prin. methods analyst, 1961-66; supr. methods div. Continental Bank, Chgo., 1966-72, mgr. trust dept., 1970-72; pres., owner 6 stores Gingiss Formalwear Inc., Kansas City area, 1972—; regional adv., mem. chmns. club Gingiss Internat.; owner 3 retail food stores, Kansas City area; pres. J. J. Advt., Lenexa, Kans. Dir., Kansas City Chiefs Football Club, mem. coach club, 1980, 81, chmn. ticket drive, 1978, 81. Served with USMC, 1954-57. Recipient award for job placement program Kansas City (Kans.) Sch. System, 1978; award of excellence Gingiss Internat., 1979. Mem. Am. Mgmt. Assn. (lectr. 1967-69), Am. Formalwear Assn. (charter), Menswear Retailers Am., Overland Park C. of C., Kansas City C. of C., Nat. Alliance Businessmen (v.p. Chgo. chpt., cert. of merit). Roman Catholic. Clubs: Improved Order Red Men Lenexa Tribe #5, Masons (32 deg.), Shriners, Red Coat (exec. com.), Porsche of Am., Com. 101. Home: 8426 Rosehill Rd Lenexa KS 66215 Office: 11555 W 95th St Overland Park KS 66214

MODLY, ZOLTAN MARIA, research chemist; b. Budapest, Hungary, Sept. 21, 1928; s. Bela and Margit (Tahy) M.; came to U.S., 1950, naturalized, 1953; B.A., Coll. of St. Imre, Budapest, 1947; postgrad. U. Sci., Budapest, 1948; postgrad. Fenn Coll., Cleve., 1955-60; m. Doris Matherny, June 15, 1957; children—Charlotte, Thomas, Dora, Suzanne, Mira. Sr. lab. technician Ferro Corp. Color Research and Devel. Lab., Cleve., 1953-58; project leader research and devel. dept. Brookpark, Inc., Cleve., 1958-60; mgr. Plastic Pigment div. The O. Hommel Co., Pitts., 1961-62; sr. chemist pigment research central research and devel. dept. Harshaw Chem. Co., Cleve., 1962-76, group leader color dept., 1976—. Served with AUS, 1951-53. Mem. Fedn. Socs. for Coatings Tech. Patentee in field. Home: 3350 Chalfant Rd Shaker Heights OH 44120 Office: 1945 E 97th St Cleveland OH 44106

MOE, DONALD M., state senator; b. Dec. 24, 1942; B.S., U. Minn. Mem. Minn. Ho. of Reps., 1970-80, Minn. Senate, 1980—. Mem. Legis. Audit Commn., 1979-80. Served with U.S. Army, 1964-66. Mem. Democratic-Farmer-Labor party. Office: 323 State Capitol St Paul MN 55155*

MOE, JOHN FREDERICK, historian, folklorist, educator; b. Grand Forks, N.D., Mar. 18, 1944; s. Ralph H. and Mildred M. (Dahl) M.; student Grinnell Coll., 1962-64; B.A., U. Iowa, 1966; M.A. in History, 1969, M.A. in Folklore, 1972, Ph.D. in History and Am. Studies, Ind. U., 1978; postgrad. Case Western Res. U. Sch. Law, 1979-81. Asso. instr. dept. history Ind. U., Bloomington, 1967-70, 73, dept. Afro-Am. studies, 1970-72; asst. prof. dept. Am. studies Heidelberg Coll., Tiffin, Ohio, 1973-75; asso. instr. Poynter Center for Study Public Instns., Ind. U., 1976-77; vis. faculty depts. history and speech communication Manchester Coll., North Manchester, Ind., 1976-77; vis. asst. prof. dept. history Central Mich. U., Mt. Pleasant, 1978-79; vis. asst. prof. Am. studies U. Iowa, summer 1979; asst. prof. Am. studies Case Western Res. U., Cleve., 1979-81, dir. Center for Regional and Community Studies, 1980—; asso. dir. continuing edn., adj. prof. history Ohio State U., Columbus, 1981—; cons. Am. folklore and community studies, 1973—; guest lectr. Am. studies to various colls. and univs., 1977—; mem. George Polk Awards Nat. Com., 1979—. Nat. judge History Day, Washington, 1980. Recipient Russell B. Nye Prize award Popular Culture Assn., 1979. Mem. Orgn. Am. Historians, Am. Historians, Am. Hist. Assn., So. Hist. Assn., Ohio Folklore Soc. (pres. 1980—), Am. Folklore Soc., Phi Alpha Theta. Lutheran. Contbr. articles to scholarly jours.; mem. editorial bd. Folklore Forum, 1975-76; editor: Jour. Ohio Folklore Soc. Newsletter, 1981—. Home: 310 N Galena Rd Sunbury OH 43074 Office: Office of Continuing Edn 2400 Olentangy River Rd Ohio State U Columbus OH 43210

MOE, ROGER DEANE, state senator; b. Crookston, Minn., June 2, 1944; s. Melvin Truman and Metheldia (Njus) M.; B.S. in Edn., Mayville State Coll., 1966; postgrad. Moorhead State Coll., summer 1969, N.D. State U., summer 1970; m. Nancy Lee Westaard, 1964; children—Dean Karl, Amy Lee. Tchr., Ada (Minn.) High Sch., 1966—; mem. Minn. Senate, 1971—. Del. Democratic-Farmer-Labor state conv., 1970. Mem. NEA, Minn. Edn. Assn., Ada Edn. Assn. Lutheran. Office: 208 State Capitol St Paul MN 55155*

MOE, THOMAS MELVIN, heavy constrn. mfg. co. exec.; b. Aurora, Ill., Jan. 30, 1935; s. Melvin Bernard and Cathrine (Albert) M.; student Aurora Coll., 1953-55, Ill. Inst. Tech., 1955-61; m. Carol Jean Wegman, Mar. 2, 1957; children—Cathrine Ann, Sarah Marie. With Barber Greene Co., Aurora, 1955-71, promotion mgr., 1970-71, dir. sales, 1975—; gen. sales mgr. Trico Equipment Co., Atlanta, 1971-75; seminar participant on drum mix asphalt plant prins. Served with C.E. U.S. Army, 1957-58. Mem. Nat. Asphalt Paving Assn., Asso. Gen. Contractors Am., Constrn. Industry Mfrs. Assn. (chmn. asphalt plant mixing com.). Home: 806 Kehoe Dr Saint Charles IL 60174 Office: 400 N Highland Ave Aurora IL 60507

MOE, WALTER WILLIAM, metal co. exec.; b. Milan, Minn., Jan. 28, 1913; s. Anton John and Sophie (Christopherson) M.; student St. Paul Vocat. Sch., 1934; m. Hazel Margaret Streed, Nov. 8, 1936; children—Arlene Jean (Mrs. Maurice Freeman), Gary. Farmer, Milan, 1934-43, Montevideo, Minn., 1943-47; owner Montevideo Mfg. & Metal Co., 1948—. Active Boy Scouts of Am. Treas. country sch. dist., 1944-46. Recipient Grand prize for hydraulic loader, Minn. Inventors Congress, 1969, grand prize for combination trailer and sled, 1970. Mem. C. of C. Eagle. Inventor: power driven post hole digger, 1942, corn stalk shredder, 1948. Patentee bolt gauge novelty, 1959, automotive air cleaner, hydraulic loader, truck hoist. Home: 502 S 12th St Montevideo MN 56265 Office: Wilking St Montevideo MN 56265

MOECKEL, BILL REID, univ. dean; b. Pekin, Ill., Sept. 2, 1925; s. Willis E. and Daisy M. (Hess) M.; B.S., U. Ill., 1948, M.S., 1949, Ph.D., 1953; m. Pauline C. Fox, Sept. 1, 1946; children—Steven, Cindy, Nancy. Instr. U. Mo., Columbia, 1949-51; asst. prof. George State U., Atlanta, 1953-54; asso. dean Ohio State U., Columbus, Ohio, 1954-67; dir. USAF Sch. Logistics, Wright-Patterson AFB, Ohio, 1958-65; dean Sch. Bus. Miami U., Oxford, Ohio, 1967—. Vice pres. Am. Assembly Collegiate Schs. Bus., 1980-81, pres., 1981-82. Served with U.S. Army, 1943-46; ETO. Mem. Air Force Inst. Tech. Assn. Grads., Ky. Colonels, Beta Gamma Sigma (nat. pres. 1976-78), Alpha Delta Sigma, Omicron Delta Kappa, Alpha Kappa Psi, Pi Sigma Epsilon, Mu Kappa Tau, Beta Alpha Psi. Home: 1026 S Locust St Oxford OH 45056 Office: Miami Univ Oxford OH 45056

MOEHRING, ROBERT LEO, hosp. exec.; b. Cin., Nov. 6, 1938; s. Elmer Robert and Clara Marie (Spitzmiller) M.; B.S., U. Cin., 1964; m. Suzanne Marie Hays, May 7, 1960; children—Jennifer, Robert, Michael, Joseph, James, Mark. With Service Bur. Corp., 1958-61, Automatic Data Processing Co., 1961-64; systems analyst Good Samaritan Hosp., Cin., 1964-68, dir. EDP, 1975-79, dir. data processing, 1979—; dir. EDP Sisters of Charity Religious Order, Cin., 1968-75; instr. Mt. St. Joseph Coll.; cons. Occam Inc., 1977-79; head football coach Our Lady Victory Grade Sch., 1975-79, mem. bd. PTA and Parish Council, 1976-77. Served with U.S. Army, 1956-58. Mem. Assn. Systems Mgrs., Hosp. Fin. Mgrs. assn., Electronic Health Orgn., Patient Care Systems Devel., Am. Mgmt. Assn. Clubs: Overhill Swim and Tennis, Western Hills Tennis and Racquet. Home: 5504 Alomar Ct Cincinnati OH 45238 Office: 3219 Clifton Ave Cincinnati OH 45220

MOEINIAN, BIJAN, economist; b. Tehran, Iran, May 30, 1949; came to U.S., 1978; s. Aliakbar and Azam (Mahvash) M.; B.S. in Econs. and Public Adminstrn., Pahlavi U. (Iran), 1971; M.S., U. Lille (France), 1974; Ph.D., U. Sorbonne, Paris, 1977; m. Anna Rae Holland, Feb. 14, 1980. Asst. prof. Tehran Bus. Sch., 1977; asst. prof. faculty econs. and polit. sci. Nat. U. Iran, 1977-79; asst. prof. dept. econs. U. Md., College Park, 1979; asst. prof. Prince George's Coll., Largo, Md., 1980; asso. prof. dept. bus. and econs. Lakeland Coll., Sheboygan, Wis., 1980—; owner, dir. IEC-Internat. Econ. Cons., Milw., 1981—. Served with Peace Corps, 1971-73. French Govt. scholar 1973-77; French Petroleum Co. scholar, 1978. Mem. Am. Econ. Assn., Iranian Econ. Assn., French Econ. Assn. Islam. Home: 1009 N Jackson St Milwaukee WI 53202 Office: IEC 1321 N Franklin Pl Milwaukee WI 53202

MOEN, DONALD ALBERT, mech. engr.; b. Mayville N.D., Mar. 25, 1940; s. Marcus Ingvald and Margaret Emmeline (Klessig) M.; B.S. in Mech. Engring., U. N.D., 1963, M.S., 1966; Ph.D. in Nuclear Engring. (AEC spl. fellow 1968-70), Iowa State U., 1971; m. Juneal Marie Lind, June 9, 1978. From grad. teaching asst. to asst. prof. U. N.D., occasionaly 1964-71; evaluation engr. Honeywell, Inc., Mpls., 1966-67; reactor and plant performance engr. Iowa Electric Light & Power Co., Cedar Rapids, 1971-75; mgr. plant engring. and constrn. Coop. Power Assn., Mpls., 1975—. Registered profl. engr., Minn., N.D. Mem. ASME, Am. Nuclear Soc., Sigma Xi, Phi Eta Sigma, Phi Kappa Phi, Sigma Tau. Co-author papers in field. Home: 2159 W Neilson Ave Long Lake MN 55356 Office: 8020 Mitchell Rd Eden Prairie MN 55344

MOEN, ROGER ORIN, indsl. engr.; b. Champaign, Ill., Dec. 21, 1924; s. Reuben Olaf and Grace (Zimmerman) M.; A.B., Duke U., 1945; M.A., State U. Iowa, 1948; postgrad. U. N.C., Charlotte, 1964; m. Mittie Isabell Boggan, July 24, 1948; children—Karen Elizabeth, Janice Lynn, Roger Eric, John Michael. Crop reporter Agr. Adjustment Adminstrn., Raleigh, summer 1942; with Erwin Cotton Mills, Durham, N.C., summer 1947; indsl. engr. Erwin Mills, Inc., Durham and Cooleemee, N.C., 1948-50, 53-55; dept. head, program coordinator Change Control, Douglas Aircraft Co., Inc., Charlotte, N.C. and Santa Monica, Calif., 1955-66; personnel dir. Allen Overall Co., Monroe, N.C., 1966-67; staff asst. to mgr. prodn. Beech Aircraft Corp., Wichita, Kans., 1967-68; dir. indsl. engring. St. Joseph Med. Center, Wichita, 1969—; founder, co-owner Catawba Motors, Belmont, N.C., 1965; founder, sec.-treas. Spectrum Enterprises, Inc., Wichita, 1968; founder, owner Crown Printing Co., Wichita, 1970; part-time lectr. indsl. mgmt., bus. adminstrn. Wichita State U., 1968-70; part-time instr. mgmt. and systems analysis Webster Coll., St. Louis, 1977-78. Served to lt. comdr. USNR, 1943-46, 50-53. Mem. Am. Inst. Indsl. Engrs. (chpt. treas. 1977-78), Hosp. Mgmt. Systems Soc., Am. Hosp. Assn. Club: Moose. Contbr. articles in field to profl. jours. Home: 2928 Amidon St Wichita KS 67204 Office: 3600 E Harry St Wichita KS 67218

MOFFAT, ALEC WEIR, non-profit co. exec.; b. Manistique, Mich., Oct. 3, 1947; s. John Weir and Mary Margaret Moffat; B.S. in Bus. Adminstrn., Ferris State Coll., 1973; m. Jill Ann Kampmann, Nov. 30, 1968; children—Kim, Tamara, Trista, Tiffany. Fiscal mgr. Kent County Substance Abuse Agy., Grand Rapids, Mich., 1974-76; acct. C. Reiss Coal Co., Sheboygan, Wis., 1976-79; dir. fiscal ops. R.C.S., Inc., Sheboygan, 1979--; instr. Lakeshore Tech. Inst.; cons. in data processing. Served with USN, 1967-71. Mem. Nat. Assn. Accts. (chpt. sec. 1977-79), Rehab. Facilities of Wis. Inc., Wis. Assn. Community Human Service Programs, Chi Gamma Iota, Mich. Assn. Collegiate Vets. (v.p. 1972, pres. 1973). Republican. Lutheran. Home: 1719 Grams Ct Sheboygan WI 53081 Office: 1305 Saint Clair St Sheboygan WI 53081

MOFFIT, WILLIAM C., musician, educator; b. New Philadelphia, Ohio; B.A. cum laude, Baldwin-Wallace Coll.; Masters Degree, U. Mich.; Mus.D. (hon.), Otterbein Coll. Tchr. pub. schs. in Mich. and Ohio, 10 years; mem. faculty Mich. State U., East Lansing; mem. faculty, dir. marching band U. Houston; now mem. faculty, dir. All-American marching band Purdue U. condr. Patterns of Motion Workshops at numerous colls. and univs.; adjudicator music festivals; guest condr. at major band events. Nat. Program Dir., Nat./Internat. Music Festivals. Recipient George Washington medal Freedoms Found. at Valley Forge, 1978; Distinguished Service to Music medal, Alumni Award Baldwin-Wallace Coll.; named Top Prof., U. Houston Mortar Board. Mem. Am., Tex. (pres., condr. Dirs. Band) bandmasters assns., Nat. Band Assn. (bd. dirs.), ASCAP, Kappa Kappa Psi (dist. gov.). Sponsor 12 ann. nat. band scholarship awards. Author: Patterns of Motion. Arranger: Soundpower Series; published works include numerous arrangements of patriotic music; first published version of all five U.S. Service Songs (Armed Forces Salute). Office: Hall of Music Purdue U West Lafayette IN 47907

MOGDIS, FRANZ JOSEPH, developer, bus. mgmt. co. exec.; b. Hastings, Mich., Jan. 12, 1941; s. Joseph and Frances Lucille (Maurer) M.; student Northwestern U., 1959-60; B.A., U. Mich., 1970; m. Diane L. Fuller, July 16, 1977. Linguist, Nat. Security Agy., Ft. Meade, Md., 1962-64; dept. mgr. applied social sci. research Bendix Aerospace Systems div., Ann Arbor, Mich., 1964-74, gen. mgr. applied sci. and tech. div., 1974-75, gen. mgr. Energy, Environment and Tech. Office, 1975-76; pres. Chase-Mogdis Inc., 1976—; pres. T/Drill Inc., Ann Arbor, 1978-80. Lectr. Fgn. Service Inst., 1970-74. Mem. Mayor's Policy Com. on Circulation, 1973-75; mem. Ann Arbor Planning Commn., 1971-75; pres. Ann Arbor Tomorrow, 1974-77, bd. dirs., 1972-79. Served with AUS, 1961-64. Mem. Am. Soc. Planning Ofcls., Am. Polit. Sci. Assn., Am. Mgmt. Assn., Am. Statis. Soc., AAAS. Home: 1220 Ferdom St Ann Arbor MI 48104 Office: 204 E Washington St Ann Arbor MI 48104

MOHAN, NARASIMHAIYENGAR, oil co. exec.; b. Bangalore, India, Jan. 20, 1951; s. V.N. and Pushpa N.; B.E.E., Bangalore U., 1971; M.Ops. Research, Case Inst. Tech., 1973; m. Usha Ramaiyengar, Dec. 13, 1973; 1 child, Anitha Mohan. With Standard Oil Co. (Ohio), Cleve., 1974—, mgmt. application specialist, 1980—; mem. part time faculty Cleve. State U., 1974-80. Mem. Inst. Mgmt. Scis., Ops. Research Soc. Am., Am. Inst. Indsl. Engrs. Home: 25089 Arlington Ln North Olmsted OH 44070 Office: 101 Prospect Ave Cleveland OH 44115

MOHLER, EDWARD FRANCIS, JR., environ. engr.; b. Toledo, Ohio, Aug. 26, 1920; s. Edward Francis and Gertrude Dorothy (Aylward) M.; B.S., U. Toledo, 1943, M.S., 1959; student Columbia U., 1944, Balliol Coll. Oxford U. (Eng.), 1945, Drexel U., 1964; m. Dorothy Catherine Downey, June 21, 1947; children—Martin E., Carolyn M., Joan T., Claire P., Elizabeth A., Edward T., Margaret C., Steven F. With Sun Co., Inc., Toledo, Ohio, 1943—, chemist, 1943-46, jr. analytical chemist, 1946-51, sr. analytical chemist, 1951-57, chem. foreman, 1957-66, asst. supt. operations, 1966-68, sr. staff asso., 1968-71, sr. environmental engr., 1971-77, environmental mgr., 1977—. Served with USNR, 1944-46. Registered corrosion engr.; cert. mgr. Mem. Ohio Petroleum Council (vice-chmn. air and water research com. 1973—), Nat. Mgmt. Assn. (nat. dir. 1976—, Midwest Area gov. 1977, 78), Am. Chem. Soc. (chmn. Toledo sect. 1957-58), Nat. Assn. Corrosion Engrs., ASTM, Tech. Soc. Toledo, Sun Oil Tech. Soc., Sun Supervisory Assn., Am. Petroleum Inst., Am. Inst. Chem. Engrs., Air Pollution Control Assn., Water Pollution Control Assn. (Quarter Century award 1979), Ohio Water Pollution Control Conf. (F.H. Waring award 1971, J.W. Ellms award 1977, v.p. 1977-78, pres. 1979-80), Toledo Mus. Art, Maumee Valley Hist. Soc., Nat. Geographic Soc., Toledo Area C. of C. (environ. studies com.), Ohio C. of C. (environ. and energy policy com.). Roman Catholic. Clubs: Rosary Cathedral Holy Name Soc. (pres. 1965-66), Council Catholic Men. Contbr. articles to tech. jours. Patentee improvement in water treatment. Home: 315 Boston Pl Toledo OH 43610 Office: Sun Co PO Box 920 Toledo OH 43693

MOHLER, EDWARD ROY, systems cons.; b. Streator, Ill., July 3, 1926; s. Harvey Dell and Margaret Mary (Corrigan) M.; student Rockford Sch. Bus., 1947-48; m. Elinor Maryann Shoudy, Jan. 14, 1950; children—Wendy, Michael, Diane, John, Suzanne, Nanette. Asst. supt. statis. dept. Am. Ins. Co., Rockford, Ill., 1948-57; asst. controller CNA, Chgo., 1958-76, sr. systems cons., 1979—; asst. v.p. corp. systems Am. Res. Corp., Chgo., 1976-79. Mem. Nat. Tax Limitation Com., Center for Def. of Free Enterprise, Am. Tax Reduction Movement. Served with USAAF, 1945-46. Mem. Ins. Acctg. and Statis. Assn., Mensa. Roman Catholic. Home: 729 E Highland Ave Naperville IL 60540 Office: Continental Plaza Chicago IL 60685

MOHLER, TERENCE JOHN, psychologist; b. Toledo, July 8, 1929; s. Edward F. and Gertrude A. (Aylward) M.; B.S. in Edn., Toledo U., 1955, M.Ed., 1966, Ed.S. in Psychology and Counseling, 1975; Ph.D., Walden U., 1979; m. Carol B. Kulczak, Oct. 1, 1955; children—Renee, John, Timothy. Psychologist, Toledo Bd. Edn., 1969—; sr. partner Psychol. Assos., Maumee, Ohio, 1970—; asso. fellow Inst. for Advanced Study in Rational Psychotherapy, N.Y.C., Alfred Adler Inst., Chgo. Served with AUS, 1951-53; Korea. Licensed psychologist, Ohio. Mem. Am., Ohio, Northwestern Ohio, Maumee Valley psychol. assns., Soc. Behavioists, Nat. Registry Mental Health Providers, Council for Exceptional Children, Kappa Delta Phi. Club: Rotary. Home: 1113 Winghaven Rd Maumee OH 43537 Office: 5757 Monclova Rd Maumee OH 43537

MOHR, ALBERT CARL, banker; b. Branch County, Mich., Aug. 11, 1921; s. Albert E. and Ruth L. (Hemenway) M.; student Western Mich. U., 1946-48; B.S. with honors in Agrl. Econs., Mich. State U., 1950, postgrad. (Fellow), 1950; m. Viola G. Fritz, Dec. 22, 1947; children—Robert L., Nancy L., Susan L. Asst. mgr. Fed. Land Bank Assn., St. Johns, Mich., 1950-54, mgr., Charlotte, Mich., 1954-66, regional v.p., asst. sec., Saint Paul, 1966-72, v.p., sec., 1972-73, pres., 1973—. Chmn. Cub Scout troop Boy Scouts Am., Charlotte, 1959-60; pres. PTA Southridge Sch., Charlotte, 1960-61; pres. Eaton County (Mich.) Agrl. Council, 1960-61, Mich. Assn. Farm Mgrs. and Rural Appraisers, 1958-59. Served with U.S. Army, 1942-45; ETO. Club: Masons. Office: 375 Jackson St Saint Paul MN 55101

MOHR, KENT EDWARD, counseling psychologist; b. Peoria, Ill., Dec. 21, 1935; s. Edward Dale and Gladys E. (Meeker) M.; B.S., Bradley U., 1957, M.A., 1964; Ed. D., Ind. U., 1970; m. Gloria Ann van Steyn, Aug. 14, 1971; 1 son, Kent Edward. Tchr., Peoria public schs., 1960-63; tchr., counselor public schs., LaGrange, Ill., 1963-64; psychology intern Peoria State Hosp., East Peoria Schs., 1964-66; sch. psychologist Peoria County Spl. Edn., 1966-67; dir. spl. edn. public schs., Robinson, Ill., 1967-68; psychologist Dist. 88 public schs., Elmhurst, Ill., 1969-75; pvt. practice clin. psychology, Carol Stream, Ill., 1975—. Mem. Peoria Mental Health Adv. Bd., 1965-66; bd. dirs. Youth Community Resource Center, Elmhurst, 1969-73. Served with U.S. Army, 1957-59. Mem. Central Ill. Sch. Psychologists Assn. (pres. 1965-66), West Surburban Sch. Psychologists Assn. (pres. 1971-72), Am. Psychol. Assn., Am. Assn. Biofeedback Clinicians, Ill. Psychol. Assn., DuPage County Psychologists in Pvt. Practice. Republican. Roman Catholic. Clubs: Rotary, Midland Soc. Geneaology. Home: 606 Saddle Rd Wheaton IL 60187 Office: 373 S Schmale Rd Carol Stream IL 60187

MOHR, ROBERT, mktg. cons.; b. Detroit, Jan. 3, 1943; s. Raymond and Dorothy M.; student Macomb Community Coll., 1962-65, Wayne State U., 1965-67; m. Elizabeth G. Lombardo, May 31, 1969; 1 dau., Rebecca Cecelia. With Am. Salesmasters, Inc., Denver, 1968-71; pres., chief exec. officer Master Mktg. Corp., Troy, Mich., 1971—. Mem. Nat. Speakers Assn., Am. Soc. Tng. Dirs., Greater Detroit C. of C. Roman Catholic. Columnist, Somerset Gazette, 1980—. Address: 2180 Grenadier St Troy MI 48098

MOHR, ROBERT C., corp. exec.; b. Chgo., 1927; grad. U. Ill., 1949; postgrad. Harvard U. Grad. Sch. Bus. Adminstrn. Pres., dir. Universal Power Piping, Inc., Chgo., John Mohr & Sons, J. Mohr Electric Corp.; dir. S. Chgo. Savs. Bank. Office: 3200 E 9th St Chicago IL 60617*

MOISIO, ELMER WILLIAM, nurse, educator; b. Newberry, Mich., May 20, 1946; s. Elmer Donald and Anna Marie (Mattson) M.; R.N., St. Luke's Hosp. Sch. Nursing, 1967; B.S. in Nursing, No. Mich. U., 1971; M.S. in Nursing, No. Ill. U., 1974; m. Marie Ann Gervais, May 20, 1972; 1 dau., Sara Marie. Nursing services supr. Newberry (Mich.) State Hosp., 1968-73; staff nurse Helen Newberry Joy Hosp., 1968-70; instr. Coll. St. Scholastica, Duluth, Minn., 1974-77; mental retardation program dir. Newberry Regional Mental Health Center, 1977-80; asso. prof. No. Mich. U., Marquette, 1980—; clin. instr. Lake Superior State Coll., Sault Ste. Marie, Mich., 1971-72. Officer, Zone IV Comprehensive Health Planning for Upper Mich., 1971-73; vol. Duluth (Minn.) Free Clinic, 1974-76; mem. health adv. council Duluth W. End Community Center, 1974-77. Named Mich. Student Nurse of Year, Mich. Student Nurses Assn., 1966; Outstanding Sr. award Marquette County Med. Aux., 1967. Mem. Mich. Nurses Assn. (dir. 1968-70), Newberry Dist. Nurses Assn. (pres. 1968-72), Am. Assn. Mental Deficiency (vice chmn. 1979—), Am. Nurses Assn. Lutheran. Home: 418 W Ridge St Marquette MI 49855 Office: Northern Mich Univ Marquette MI 49855

MOKMA, ARNOLD LEE, educator; b. Hamilton, Mich., Oct. 20, 1940; s. Lewis T. and Jeannette (Joostberns) M.; student Hope Coll., 1958-59, 60-61; B.S., Mich. State U., 1963, M.S., 1967, Ph.D., 1975; m. Marilyn J. Boeve, June 13, 1961; children—Craig Alan, Mary Beth, Timothy Lee. Tchr. vocat. agr. Big Rapids (Mich.) Public Schs., 1963-67, Sparta (Mich.) Area schs., 1967-72; tchr. educator Inst. Agrl. Tech., Mich. State U., 1972-77, coordinator, 1977-78; faculty devel. coordinator Agrl. Tech. Inst., Ohio State U., Wooster, 1978-79, asst. dir. acad. affairs, 1979—; cons. in field. Pres., coach Haslett (Mich.) Youth Recreation Assn.; coach Triway Recreation, Inc., Wooster. Mem. Ohio Vocat. Agr. Tchrs. Assn., Am. Vocat. Assn., Nat. Vocat. Assn., Nat. Assn. Colls. and Tchrs. Agr., Am. Assn. Tchr. Educators in Agr., Phi Delta Kappa. Home: 2572 Jane St Wooster OH 44691 Office: US Route 250 Wooster OH 44691

MOLDAUER, HAL PERRY, corp. ofcl.; b. Bklyn., July 24, 1947; s. David and Eileen Belle Moldauer; B.Arch., Kans. State U., 1970, M.S. in Computer Sci., 1978; m. Nora Catherine Dickerson, June 8, 1973. Project mgr. Synectics, Inc., Kansas City, Mo., 1973—; pres. The Strocker Project, Overland Park, Kans., 1978—; temporary instr. Kans. State U., 1976—. Profl. mem. Nat. Entertainment and Campus Activities Assn. Owner, exhibitor collection of original Calif. citrus-crate label art. Home: 7733 Colonial Dr Prairie Village KS 66208 Office: 5612 Brighton Terr Kansas City MO 64130

MOLDENHAUER, JAMES G., engr.; b. Kenosha, Wis., May 20, 1930; s. Rufus H. and Hulda C. (Klingman) M.; B. in Physics, U. Wis., 1952, M. in Physics, 1954; m. Marjorie A. Gilbert, Sept. 14, 1952; children—Kari Y., Viki Y. Chief scientist Applied Sci. Corp., Santa Paula, Calif., 1961-63; mgr. fundamental research div. Naval Missile Center, Point Mugu, Calif., 1963-66; v.p. systems devel. group Raven Industries, Sioux Falls, S.D., 1966-70; mgr. systems engring. dept. Ares, Inc., Port Clinton, Ohio. Served with USAF, 1956-59. Mem. Am. Phys. Soc., Am. Inst. Physics, Am. Def. Preparedness Assn., Assn. U.S. Army. Contbr. articles to profl. jours.; patentee edreobenthic manned observatory for undersea research, 1970. Home: 5236 Opperman Rd Bellevue OH 44811 Office: Bldg 818 Front St Erie Industrial Park Port Clinton OH 43452

MOLDENHAUER, WILLIAM CALVIN, soil scientist; b. New Underwood, S.D., Oct. 27, 1923; s. Calvin Fred and Ida (Killam) M.; B.S., S.D. State U., 1949; M.S., U. Wis., 1951, Ph.D., 1956; m. Catherine Ann Maher, Nov. 26, 1947; children—Jean Ann, Patricia, Barbara, James, Thomas. Soil surveyor S.D. State U., Brookings, 1948-54; soil scientist U.S. Dept. Agr., Big Spring, Tex., 1954-57, Ames, Iowa, 1957-72, Morris, Minn., 1972-75, research leader Nat. Soil Erosion Lab., Agrl. Research Service, 1975—; prof. dept. agronomy Purdue U., West Lafayette, Ind., 1975—. Served with U.S. Army, 1943-46. Fellow Am. Soc. Agronomy, Soil Sci. Soc. Am., Soil Conservation Soc. Am. (pres. 1979). Contbr. articles to profl. jours. Office: Nat Soil Erosion Lab West Lafayette IN 47907

MOLENDA, CHARLES ANTHONY, mktg. exec.; b. Cin., Dec. 23, 1939; s. Leonard Joseph and Wilma Ruth (Blackmore) M.; B.B.A., U. Tex., 1970; m. Petra Marina Deavours, Dec. 4, 1965; 1 son, David Christopher. Salesman, Dun & Bradstreet, Fort Worth, Tex., 1970-71; dist. sales mgr. Phila., 1971-72, regional mgr., St. Louis, 1972-75, regional v.p., Chgo., 1975—; regional mgr. Qwip systems Exxon Enterprises, 1977-79; v.p. Alves-Hill and Assos., mgmt. consultants, 1979-81; prin. Molenda & Assos., 1981—. Active Boy Scouts Am. Served with U.S. Army, 1960-68. Decorated D.F.C., Bronze Star, Air medal. Republican. Methodist. Club: Naperville Country. Home: 1933 Hansom Ct Naperville IL 60540 Office: Suite 12 65235 Steeple Run Naperville IL 60540

MOLER, DONALD LEWIS, educator; b. Wilsey, Kans., Jan. 12, 1918; s. Ralph Lee and Bessie Myrtle (Berry) M.; B.S., Kans. State Tchrs. Coll., Emporia, 1939; M.S., U. Kans., Lawrence, 1949, Ph.D., 1951; m. Alta Margaret Ansdell, Nov. 6, 1942; 1 son, Donald Lewis Jr. Tchr., Centralia (Kans.) High Sch., 1939-42, Carthage (Mo.) High Sch., 1946-48; asst. dir. Reading Clinic, U. Kans., 1948-51; dir. reading program Eastern Ill. U., 1951-70, prof. dept. ednl. psychology and guidance, 1963—, chmn. dept., 1963—, dean Sch. Edn., 1980; vis. scholar U. Fla., 1965. Served with Signal Corps, U.S. Army, 1942-46. Recipient C.A. Michelman award, 1974. Mem. Ill. Guidance and Personnel Assn. (pres. 1968-69), Ill. Counselor Educators and Suprs., Ill. Coll. Personnel Assn., Am. Personnel and Guidance Assn. (senator 1970-71), Assn. Counselor Edn. and Supervision, Assn. Humanistic Edn. and Devel., Phi Delta Kappa, Xi Phi, Pi Omega Pi, Pi Kappa Delta, Sigma Tau Gamma. Methodist. Asso. editor Ill. Guidance and Personnel Assn. Quar., 1970—. Home: 407 W Hayes St Charleston IL 61920 Office: Department of Ednl Psychology and Guidance Eastern Illinois University Charleston IL 61920

MOLITOR, JOHN R., ins. co. exec.; b. Chgo., Apr. 24, 1941; s. John A. and Arlene M. (Nicolaisen) M.; B.S. in Mktg., No. Ill. U., 1964; M.S. in Mktg. Communications with honors, Roosevelt U., 1977, M.B.A., 1979; m. Maureen Sadler, Jan. 27, 1968; children—John, Michele, Victoria. Adminstrv. mgr. Tower Life & Accident Ins. Co., Chgo., 1970-71, dir. mktg., 1971—, asst. sec., 1975-77, dir. claims, 1977—, dir. ops., 1977—, dir. sales, 1977—, asst. v.p., 1975-77, exec. v.p., 1977—, dir. corp. tng., 1977—. Served to lt. USNR, 1964-70. Mem. Chgo. Assn. Direct Mktg., Chgo. Policyholders Service Assn.

(v.p. 1971-72), Direct Mail Mktg. Assn., Life Office Mgmt. Assn., Windy City Ins. Advertisers Assn. (pres. 1977-80), Beta Gamma Sigma. Home: 216 Tomahawk Ln Barrington IL 60016 Office: Tower Life and Accident Ins Co 435 N Michigan Ave Chicago IL 60611

MOLITOR, ROGER JOHN, retail sales co. exec.; b. Sibley, Iowa, May 25, 1949; s. John B. and Eileen (Kenyon) M.; B.S. in Agr. Bus., Iowa State U., 1971. Asst. county supt. FHA-U.S. Dept. Agr., Fairfield, Iowa, 1971-72; loan officer Prodn. Credit Assn., Algona, Iowa, 1972-74; owner mgr. Farmagra, Inc., Ruthven, Iowa, 1974—; part-time instr. Iowa Lakes Community Coll. 1974-77. Recipient Golden Dealer award Chevron Chem. div. Standard Oil, 1979. Mem. Ruthven C. of C. (pres. 1975), Iowa Fertilizer and Chem. Dealers Assn., Iowa Assn. Realtors, Nat. Farm and Land Inst., Aircraft Owners and Pilots Assn., Iowa Farm Equipment Dealers. Contbr. articles to profl. jours. Address: PO Box 100 Ruthven IA 51358

MOLL, EDWIN ALLAN, business exec.; b. Chgo., July 16, 1934; s. Maurice and Lillian (Lederman) M.; B.S., Loyola U., 1956; Ed.M., Northwestern U., 1960, Asso. in Police Sci., 1962; m. Natalie Kepner, Mar. 11, 1962; children—Kelli Lee, Dean Allan. Vice pres. Linnea Perfumes, Inc., 1950; owner, operator three restaurants, Chgo., 1952-56; producer, moderator radio shows This is Chgo., Grant Part Concert Rev., Fort Dearborn Concert, Chgo., 1957-65; bus. mgr. Chgo. Adler Planetarium, 1958-59; adminstrv. aide to mayor Chgo., 1959-63; pres. Edwin A. Moll Pub. Relations, Chgo., from 1963; pres. Profl. Adminstrv. Services Inc., 1975-78, Profl. Service System, Inc., 1975-78; chief ranger Cook County (Ill.) Forest Preserve, 1975-76; exec. Lee Optical Co., 1976-78; chmn. bd. Profl. Med. Guidance Corp.; dir. Glenwood State Bank; chmn. bd. Am. Travel Bur., Ltd., 1979, Edwin A. Moll and Assos.; mgmt. cons. to professions; lectr. pub. relations and practice mgmt. Commr., Youth Welfare, Skokie, Ill., 1963-66. Exec. bd. mem. 40th ward Democratic Orgn., Chgo., 1948-68. Bd. dirs. Ill. Vision Services Corp., Nate Gross Found., Asthmacade. Recipient citation Red Cross, 1957. Mem. Am. Soc. Assn. Execs., Soc. Optometric Assn. Execs., Optometric Council for Polit. Edn. (exec. dir. 1968-69), Ill. Optometric Assn. (exec. sec. 1963-69, Optometric Layman of Year award 1967), Ill. Pub. Health Assn., Internat., Ill., West Suburban, South Suburban, North Suburban assns. chiefs of police, Ill. Police Assn., Internat. Platform Assn., Chgo. Forum Execs., Tau Delta Phi. Clubs: Illinois Athletic (Chgo.); President's (Washington). Author: Sell Yourself Big, 1966.

MOLTER, HAROLD MARTIN, psychologist; b. New Brighton, Pa., June 29, 1935; s. Elmer Byron and Esther Mae (Bowman) M.; B.S., U. Pitts., 1968; M.A., Mich. State U., 1972, postgrad. 1972; m. Leticia Santiago Ramirez, May 28, 1966. Rehab. counselor State of Mich., Saginaw, 1968-72; psychologist State of Mich., Caro, 1972-75; sch. psychologist Tuscola Intermediate Sch. Dist., Caro, 1975-77; pvt. practice psychol. cons., Saginaw, 1977-78; sch. psychologist Bridgeport-Spaulding Community Schs., Mich., 1978—; vocat. cons. Served with U.S. Army, 1956-58. Certified rehab. counselor. Mem. Am. Psychol. Assn., Nat. Assn. Sch. Psychologists, Am. Personnel and Guidance Assn., Mich. Assn. Profl. Psychologists, Am. Rehab. Counselors Assn., Mich. Assn. Sch. Psychologists. Address: 185 W Pineview Dr Saginaw MI 48603

MOLUMBY, ROBERT EUGENE, architect, city planner; b. Willow Lake, S.D., May 22, 1936; s. Joseph A. and Irma Marian (Wilkinson) M.; B.Arch., U. Notre Dame, 1959; M.A. in City and Regional Planning, U. Calif., Berkeley, 1961; m. Edith Nina Taylor, Oct. 11, 1969; children—Katherine Hall, Nina Elizabeth. Architect-planner Perkins & Will Partnership, Chgo., 1965-71; sr. planner Village of Skokie, Ill., 1971-73, acting dir. planning, 1973, dir. planning, 1973—. Asso. mem. Evanston (Ill.) Plan Commn., 1977-78, mem., 1978—; sr. warden St. Mark's Episcopal Ch., Evanston, 1980—. Served with USN, 1961-65. Mem. Am. Planning Assn., Nat. Trust for Historic Preservation, Chgo. Archtl. Found., Chgo. Landmarks Preservation Council. Office: 5127 Oakton St Skokie IL 60077

MONACO, JOSEPH THOMAS, orthopedic surgeon; b. Chgo., Mar. 10, 1946; s. Joseph Thomas and Dorothy Jane (Daley) M.; B.S., Boston Coll., 1968; M.D., U. Ill., 1972; m. JoAnn Theresa Markey, June 19, 1970; children—Meredith Ann, Dana Michelle. Intern, Evanston (Ill.) Hosp., 1972-73; resident in orthopedic surgery Northwestern U. Med. Sch., Chgo., 1973-77; practice medicine specializing in orthopedic surgery, Chicago Heights, Ill.; mem. staff St. James Hosp., Suburban Heights Med. Center. Diplomate Am. Bd. Orthopedic Surgery. Fellow Am. Acad. Orthopedic Surgeons; mem. AMA, Ill. Med. Soc., Chgo. Med. Soc. Home: 3715 Poplar Rd Flossmoor IL 60422 Office: 333 Dixie Hwy Chicago Heights IL 60411

MONAGHAN, ROBERT JOSEPH, health care co. exec.; b. Scranton, Pa., June 18, 1946; s. Robert Henry and Mary Jane (Murphy) M.; student Keystone Jr. Coll., 1965-67; B.S. in Bus. Adminstrn., Ariz. State U., 1974; M.B.A. in Mktg., Calif. State Coll., 1978; m. Linda Ann Wilson, July 21, 1973; children—Patrick Steven, Sally Ann. Asso. salesman The Arrow Co., Phoenix, 1974-75; indsl. sales rep. Am. Sci. Products Co., Riverside, Calif., 1975-78, region mgr. biomed., Los Angeles, Hawaii, 1978-79, mktg. mgr. biomed div., Chgo., 1979—. Served with U.S. Army, 1967-73. Decorated Purple Heart, Bronze Star (5), Combat Infantryman's badge. Mem. Am. Mgmt. Assn., Biomed. Mktg. Assn., Tissue Culture Assn., Sales and Mktg. Execs. Assn. Republican. Roman Catholic. Home: 667 Sedgwick Dr Libertyville IL 60048 Office: 1430 Waukegan Rd McGaw Park IL 60085

MONAHAN, TIMOTHY IRWIN, assn. exec.; b. Chgo., Aug. 10, 1946; s. Michael I. and Marion P. (Deering) M.; B.A., DePaul U., 1968; M.A., Northeastern Ill. U., 1973; m. Kathleen M. Prebil, Mar. 20, 1970; children—Sean, Timothy, Daniel, Ryan. Tchr., Chgo. Bd. Edn., 1968-69, Sch. Dist. 83, Franklin Park, Ill., 1969-72; prin. Chgo. Assn. for Retarded Citizens, 1972-75, dir. children's services, 1975—; faculty U. Ill., Chgo. Circle, 1978—. Mem. St. Francis de Sales Sch. Bd., 1977—, pres., 1978-79. Mem. Am. Assn. on Mental Deficiency (chmn. Ill. chpt. 1979-81), Am. Assn. for Edn. Severely and Profoundly Handicapped. Roman Catholic. Office: 8 S Michigan Ave Chicago IL 60603

MONAT, WILLIAM ROBERT, educator; b. Biwabik, Minn., Oct. 9, 1924; s. William Stephen and Milda Aleta (Sundby) M.; A.A., Virginia (Minn.) Jr. Coll., 1947; B.A. magna cum laude, U. Minn., 1949, Ph.D., 1956; postgrad. Wayne U., 1949-50; m. Josephine Ann Sclafani, Sept. 9, 1951; children—Lise Ann, Kathryn, Margaret, William Michael, Eric. Asst. prof. Wayne U., 1954-57; exec. asst. to Gov. Mich., 1957-60; asso. prof. Pa. State U., 1960-65, prof. polit. sci., 1965-69, asso. dir. Inst. Pub. Adminstrn., 1962-69; majority budget dir. Pa. Ho. of Reps., 1968-69; prof., chmn. dept. polit. sci. No. Ill. U., DeKalb, 1969-71, provost, 1976-78, pres., 1978—; prof., dean faculties Baruch Coll., City U. N.Y., 1971-74, v.p. acad. affairs, 1974-76; cons. USPHS, 1956, Office of Sec. Dept. Labor, 1963-64, Bur. Labor Standards, 1966, Office of Gov. Pa., 1968. Mem. social justice adv. council Ill. Bd. Higher Edn., 1970-71. Served with AUS, 1943-46. Decorated Bronze Star medal. Mem. Am. Polit. Sci. Assn., Am. Soc. Pub. Adminstrn., AAUP, Am. Assn. for Higher Edn., Phi Beta Kappa. Author: Labor Goes to War, 1965; The Public Library and its Community, 1967; Politics, Poverty and Education, 1968. Editor: Public Adminstration in Era of Change, 1962. Contbr. articles profl. jours. Home: 901 Woodlawn Ave DeKalb IL 60115 Office: Northern Il U DeKalb IL 60115*

MONGO, CELESTINE, ednl. adminstr.; b. Oakwood, Tex., Nov. 27, 1929; d. Henry and Bertha (Turner) Lacey; B.S., U. Calif., Berkeley, 1949; M.Ed., Wayne State U., 1962, Ed.D., 1979; m. George Mongo, June 19, 1949; 1 dau., Carol. Fin. resource investigator City of Detroit, 1951; bus. edn. tchr. Detroit public schs., 1957-67, dept. chairperson, 1967-79, supr. spl. projects in bus. edn., 1971-72, supr. bus. edn., 1979—; asso. prof. bus. edn. Colo. State U., Ft. Collins, 1974-75; participant projects; chairperson Nat. Policies Commn. for Bus. and Econ. Edn., 1977-78; mem. Nat. Bus. Edn. Task Force for Career Edn. Named Woman of Yr., Iota Phi Lambda, 1970; recipient Leadership award Mich. Occupational Edn. Assn., 1971; Disting. Service award Mich. Bus. Edn. Assn., 1971. Mem. Assn. Sch. Adminstrs. and Suprs., Bus. Tchrs. Assn. Met. Detroit, Mich. Bus. Edn. Assn., Nat. Bus. Edn. Assn., Iota Phi Lambda, Dlta Pi Epsilon. Mem. Presentation Ch. Author: (with others) Occupational Orientation, 1967; Business Preparation, 1968. Home: 18313 Marlowe St Detroit MI 48235 Office: 5057 Woodward Ave Detroit MI 48202

MONICATTI, LAWRENCE ANGELO, aerospace co. exec.; b. Detroit, Nov. 18, 1934; s. Michael and Linda (Poli) M.; B.S. in Physics, Western Mich. U., 1957; B.S. in Aero. Engring., U. Mich., 1958; M.S. in Aerospace Engring., U. So. Calif., 1963; m. Kathleen Mary Maroney, Jan. 16, 1965; children—Kathryn, Matthew, Christian. Missile checkout technician Chrysler Missile Corp., Warren, Mich., 1957; structures engr. N.Am. Aviation, Los Angeles, 1958-63; program mgr. Vought Corp., Sterling Heights, Mich., 1963-77; program mgr. Honeywell Corp., Mpls., 1977—; past pres., treas., bd. dirs. Vought Mich. Fed. Credit Union, Ferndale North Homeowners Assn., 1979; active YMCA; past chmn. Christian service commn. Roman Catholic Ch. Mem. Am. Inst. Aeros. and Astronautics, Aircraft Owners and Pilots Assn., Smithsonian Assos. Club: Elks. Home: 660 Brockton Ln Plymouth MN 55447 Office: Honeywell Corp Defense Systems Div Minneapolis MN 55400

MONK, JOHN THOMAS, cons.; b. Balt., Apr. 12, 1946; s. Galloway and Margaret (Fannan) M.; B.A., U. Okla., 1968; M.B.A., Ohio State U., 1975; M.D.P., Washington U., 1977; m. Susan Ann Sitorius, June 7, 1969; 1 son, Justin. Commd. 2d lt. U.S. Army, 1968; advanced through grades to maj., 1979; project mgr. Monsanto Co., St. Louis, 1979-81; cons. Peat, Marwick, Mitchell & Co., St. Louis, 1981—; various command and staff positions in Europe and U.S., 1968-71; served combat tour with Spl. Forces in Kontum, Vietnam, 1971-72; project mgr. U.S. Army Automated Logistics Mgmt. Agy., St. Louis, 1975-79. Chmn., Eureka Economic Devel. com.; pres. Eureka Khoury League Assn.; chmn., vice-chmn. Hilltop Villages Community Assn.; chmn. Eureka Town Meeting. Decorated Bronze Star medal, Cross of Gallantry with palm, Army Commendation medal with oak leaf cluster; named Eureka Outstanding First Yr. Jaycee, 1976; U.S. Army grad. fellow, 1973-75. Mem. Data Processing Mgmt. Assn., IEEE Computer Soc., Nat. Assn. Accountants, Assn. U.S. Army, Delta Upsilon, Gamma Gamma, Jaycees. Home: 15996 Quiet Oak Rd Chesterfield MO 63017 Office: 720 Olive St Saint Louis MO 63101

MONNINGER, ROBERT HAROLD GEORGE, ophthalmologist, educator; b. Chgo., Nov. 5, 1918; s. Louis Robert and Katherine (Lechner) M.; A.A., North Park Coll., 1939; B.S., Northwestern U., 1941, M.A., 1945; M.D., Stritch Sch. Medicine, 1953; Sc.D. (hon.), 1968; m. Anna Evelyn Turunen, Sept. 1, 1944; children—Carl John William, Peter Louis Philip. Intern St. Francis Hosp., Evanston, Ill., 1953-54; resident Presbyn.-St. Luke's, U. Ill. Research and Eye, VA hosps., 1954-57; mem. leadership council Ravenswood Hosp. Med. Center; instr. chemistry Lake Forest (Ill.) Coll., 1946-47; instr. biochemistry, physiology Loyola Dental Sch., 1948-49; clin. asso. prof. ophthalmology Stritch Sch. Medicine, Maywood, Ill., 1957-72; practice medicine specializing in ophthalmology, Lake Forest, 1957—; guest lectr. numerous univs. med. centers U.S., Can., Europe, Central and S.Am., Orient; resident lectr. Klinikum der Goethe-Universität, W. Ger., 1981; mem. panel Nat. Disease and Therapeutic Index; cons. Draize eye toxicity test revision HEW, cons. research pharm. cos. Nat. asso. Smithsonian Instn.; bd. dirs. Eye Rehab. and Research Found.; postgrad. faculty Internat. Glaucoma Congress; lectr. Hopital Dieu, Paris; lectr. postgrad. courses for developing nations physicians WHO; life mem. Postgrad. Sch. Medicine, U. Vienna; cons. Nat. Acad. Sci.; adv. bd. Madera Del Rio Found. Served with USMCR, 1941-44. Recipient citation Gov. Bahamas, 1960, Ophthalmic Found. award, 1963, Sci. Exhibit award Ill. State Med. Soc., 1966, Franco-Am. Meritorious citation, 1967, Paris Post No. 1 Am. Legion award, 1967, citation Pres. Mexico, 1968, Sightsaving award Bausch & Lomb, 1968, exhibit award Western Hemisphere Congress Internat. Surgeons, 1968, Research citation Japanese Soc. Opthalmology, 1969; Barraquer Gold Medallion; Physician's Recognition award AMA; Bicentennial citation Library of Congress Registration Book; meritorious citation Gov. of Ill.; citation and medal Lord Mayor of Rome, also Pres. of Italy, 1981; Catherine White Scholarship fellow, 1945-46. Diplomate Am. Bd. Cosmetic Plastic Surgery. Fellow Internat. Coll. Surgeons (postgrad. faculty continuing edn.), Am. Coll. Angiology, Oxford Ophthal. Congress and Soc. (lectr. 1960-61), Royal Soc. Health, Internat. Acad. Cosmetic Surgery (editorial bd.), Sociedad Mexicana Ortopedia (hon.), C. Puestow Surg. Soc.; mem. AAAS, Internat. Soc. Geog. Ophthalmology (program course coordinator, lectr. ocular electrophysiology VI Internat. Congress, Rio de Janeiro), Pan Am. Assn. Ophthalmology, Assn. for Research Ophthalmology, Am. Assn. Ophthalmology, Am. Soc. Contemporary Ophthalmology, Internat. Glaucoma Soc., Ill. Soc. for Med. Research, Ill. Assn. Ophthalmology, Internat. Soc. Clin. Electrophysiology of Vision (hon., lectr. 1978), Brazilian Soc. Ophthalmology (hon. corr.), German Ophthal. Soc., Internat. Fedn. Clin. Chemists (lectr.), Primum Forum Ophthalmologicum (lectr.), European Ophthal. Soc. (lectr.), Internat. Congress Anatomists (lectr.), Association des Diabetologues Francaise (lectr.), German Soc. for Internal Medicine (lectr.), Met. Opera Guild, Fedn. Am. Scientists, N.Y., Ill. acads. sci., AAUP, Nat. Soc. Lit. and Arts, Nat. Hist. Soc., Rush Med. Sch.-Presbyn. St. Luke's Alumni Assn., Internat. Platform Assn., Cousteau Soc., Sigma Xi, Sigma Alpha Epsilon, Phi Beta Pi, Theta Kappa Psi. Cons. author Textbook of Endocrinology. Editorial bd. Clin. Medicine, 1958—, EENT Digest, 1958—, Internat. Surgery, 1972—, Internat. Bull., 1976—, Cosmetic Surgery, 1980—; contbr. articles to profl. jours. Home: 734 S Oak Knoll Dr Lake Forest IL 60045 Office: 320 E Vine St Lake Forest IL 60045

MONOPOLI, DANIEL MARCO, mktg. exec.; b. Cranston, R.I., Sept. 15, 1939; s. Donato and Santa (Tedeschi) M.; student R.I. Coll., 1961-62, U. R.I., 1962-68; m. Susan Adkins, Apr. 13, 1973; 1 dau., Jennifer Marie. Service technician Voicewriter div. McGraw Edison, Cranston, 1962-63; non-destructive testing specialist Gen. Dynamics/Electric Boat, Groton, Conn., 1963-64; mgr. employee relations ITT Hammel-Dahl, Warwick, R.I., 1964-66; personnel mgr. Clifton div. Litton Industries, Fall River, Mass., 1966-68, dir. indsl. relations Revenue Control Systems div., N.Y.C., 1968-70; v.p. ops. Symphonic Electronic, Lowell, Mass., 1970-73; pres. Marc Enterprises, Wheeling, Ill., 1973-77; v.p. mktg./adminstrv. services ECM Motor Co., Schaumburg, Ill., 1977—. Served with USNR, 1958-61. Home: 6315 Giant Oaks Rd Wonder Lake IL 60097 Office: 1301 E Tower Rd Schaumburg IL 60196

MONROE, LOREN EUGENE, state ofcl.; b. Thomasville, Ga., Apr. 5, 1932; s. Eugene and Leona Lucile (Shepard) M.; B.S. in Acctg., Wayne State U., 1958, J.D., 1970; m. Lei Wan Newby, July 12, 1975; children—Dawn, Claire, John, Michael. Field auditor Mich. Dept. of Treasury, 1959-70; admitted to Mich. bar, 1970; tax mgr. Coopers & Lybrand, Detroit, 1970-76; partner firm Mosley & Monroe, P.C., Detroit, 1976-78; treas. State of Mich., Lansing, 1978—; mem. Mcpl. Fin. Commn., State Adminstrv. Bd., Mich. Housing Devel. Authority, Mackinac Bridge Authority, State Hosp. Fin. Authority, Task Force on Hosp. Capacity, Mcpl. Employees Retirement System, Probate Judges Retirement Bd., Judges Retirement System, Mich. Public Sch. Employees' Retirement Bd., State Employees Retirement Bd., Resource Recovery Commn., Mich. EEO Council, Mich. Gov.'s Community Devel. Cabinet; trustee Environ. Research Inst. Mich.; bd. dirs. Brown-McNeely Med. Malpractice Ins. Fund. Bd. dirs. Inner City Bus. Improvement Forum, Detroit, 1977—; mem. taxation adv. com. Walsh Coll., 1979. Served with U.S. Army, 1953-55. C.P.A., Mich. Mem. Detroit Bar Assn., Mich. Bar Assn., Mich. Assn. C.P.A.s, Am. Inst. C.P.A.s, Nat. Assn. Black Accts. Baptist. Club: Masons. Office: PO Box 15128 Lansing MI 48901

MONROE, ROGER GEORGE, med. center exec.; b. Peoria, Ill., Mar. 28, 1934; s. Zack Oral and Frieda M.; B.S., Bradley U., 1955, M.A., 1956; m. Nancy Jane Hanson, May 22, 1960; children—Roger Daniel, Zackie Scott. Staff announcer WSIV-AM, Pekin, Ill., 1959-60; news dir. WPEO-AM, Peoria, 1960-61; sta. mgr. WJIL-AM, Jacksonville, Ill., 1961-62; dir. tng. and public relations Nathan Hale Ins. Cos., Springfield, Ill., 1962-65; dir. tng. and public relations Georgetown Life Ins. Co., Peoria, 1965-68; dir. community relations Meth. Med. Center Ill., Peoria, 1968—. mem. faculty Ill. Central Coll. Pres., Tri County Arthritis Found., 1970-72; chmn. Housing Bd. Appeals Peoria, 1976; coordinator baseball program Peoria Christian Center 1974-77; chmn Peoria County Cancer Crusade, 1978, 81; mem. Zoning Bd. Appeals, Peoria, 1978—; mem. Peoria County Bd. Suprs., 1980—; bd. dirs. St. Jude Midwest Affiliate, 1975—; mem. Republican Precinct Com., 1970—; charter mem. Peoria chpt. Vols. in Action, Heart of Ill. Epilepsy League; mem. Am. Cancer Soc. Served with AUS, 1956-58. Recipient Nat. Vol. Service citation Arthritis Found., 1972; award of merit St. Jude Midwest affiliate St. Jude Children's Research Hosp., 1972. Mem. Ill. Hosp. Public Relations Soc. (pres. 1977-78), Ill. Press Assn., Am. Soc. Hosp. Public Relations, Public Relations Assn. Greater Peoria. Methodist. Club: Am. Bus. (pres. Peoria 1978). Home: 2708 W Overbrook Dr Peoria IL 61604 Office: 221 NE Glen Oak St Peoria IL 61636

MONSMA, STEPHEN VOS, state senator; b. Pella, Iowa, Sept. 22, 1936; s. Martin and Marie (Vos) M.; A.B., Calvin Coll., 1958; M.A., Georgetown U., 1961; Ph.D., Mich. State U., 1965; m. Mary A. Carlisle, Dec. 19, 1964; children—Martin Stephen, Kristin Joy. Asst. prof. State U. Coll., Plattsburgh, N.Y., 1964-67; asst. prof. dept. polit. sci. Calvin Coll., Grand Rapids, Mich., 1967-69, asso. prof., 1969-73, prof., 1973-74, chmn. dept. polit. sci., 1969-74; mem. Mich. Ho. Reps., 1975-78; mem. Mich. Senate, 1979—. Mem. Kent County Democratic Exec. Com., 1969—; chmn. 5th Dist. Kennedy for Pres. Com., 1968; bd. dirs. Center for Theology and Pub. Policy, 1976—, Evangs. for Social Action, 1978—. Served with AUS, 1960. Mem. Midwest Polit. Sci. Assn. (exec. council 1972-75), Grand Rapids Urban League (v.p. 1972-75). Mem. Christian Ref. Ch. Author: American Politics: A Systems Approach, 1969, 73, 76; The Unraveling of America, 1974; co-author: The Dynamics of the American Political System, 1972; co-editor: American Politics: Research and Readings, 1970; editorial bd. Am. Jour. Polit. Sci., 1973-75; contbr. articles to profl. jours. Home: 829 N Kent View Dr NE Grand Rapids MI 49505*

MONTAGUE, ROBERT JAMES, accountant; b. Momence, Ill., Aug. 28, 1932; s. Robert James and Mary (Kovacich) M.; B.S. in Acctg., So. Ill. U., 1957; postgrad. Northwestern U., 1959; m. Janice Loraine O'Connor, July 23, 1960; children—Diana Marie, Brian Walter, Bruce Robert, Mary Kathryn, Ellen Marie, Megan Lynn. Statis. analyst, dept. microbiology So. Ill. U., Carbondale, 1954-57; auditor Price Waterhouse & Co., Chgo., 1957-61, Joseph C. Gianotti, C.P.A., Kankakee, Ill., 1961-68; controller Paramount Textile Machines Co., Paramount So. Co., Pope Brace Co., Metalcut Mfg. Co., 1968-74; pvt. practice acctg., Bradley, Ill., 1968—. Chmn., State of Ill. Audit Adv. Bd., 1977-81; pres. Broadway Council, 1980; mem. bd. edn. Bishop McNamara High Sch., 1980—; mem. St. Joseph Parish council, 1974-77; bd. dirs. United Parents for Exceptional Children, 1971-75. Served with U.S. Army, 1952-54. C.P.A., Ill. Mem. Am. Inst. C.P.A.'s, Ill. Soc. C.P.A.'s, Acctg. Research Assn., Twp. Ofcls. of Ill., Momence C. of C., Kankakee Area C. of C., V.F.W., Am. Legion. Roman Catholic. Clubs: The 100, Rotary Internat. (bd. dirs. 1981-82), Lions, Kankakee Sportsmen's, Moose, K.C. (4 deg.). Home: 196 N Grand Ave Bradley IL 60915 Office: 253 W Broadway Bradley IL 60915 also 119 N Dixie Hwy Momence IL 60954

MONTAYRE, MAXIMO ESCORIAL, accountant; b. Cebu City, Philippines, Nov. 18, 1936; s. Saturnino T. and Candelaria A. (Escorial) M.; B.S., U. San Carlos (Philippines), 1958; m. Concepcion Lamb Pacana, May 6, 1962; children—Arne, Joffre, Nelson, Bernard. Staff accountant Colgate-Palmolive Philippines, Inc., 1960-66, Gen. Motors Dealer, Philippines, 1967-69; cost accountant Stewart Warner Electronics, Chgo., 1969-70; corporate sr. tax accountant A.B. Dick Co., Niles, Ill., 1970—. C.P.A., Philippines; lic. real estate broker, Ill. Mem. Inst. Property Taxation, Internat. Assn. Assessing Officers, Bisaya Circle Am. (pres. 1979-80), Chgo. Philippine C.P.A. Assn. (chmn. reciprocity com. 1975-76). Roman Catholic. Clubs: Chgo. Tax, Toastmasters (pres. 1976-77). Home: 5519 N St Louis Ave Chicago IL 60625 Office: 6310 N Lincoln Ave Chicago IL 60659

MONTES, PEGGY ANN, counselor; b. Chgo., Oct. 17, 1938; d. Thomas and Myrtle (Thomas) Booker; student Howard U., 1956-58; B.Ed., Chgo. State U., 1960; postgrad. Gov.'s State U., Chgo., 1973-74; m. Paul Joseph Montes, Dec. 17, 1960; children—Paul, Pia. Elementary tchr. Chgo. Bd. Edn., 1960-71, adjustment tchr.-counselor, 1971-74, coordinator counseling services dept. Percy Julian High Sch., 1975—; cons. in field. Pres. Profl. Aux. Provident Hosp., 1973—; bd. dirs. Harriet Harris YWCA, 1972—, Chgo. Area Planned Parenthood Assn., 1974-76. Named Woman of Year, Civic Aux. Planned Parenthood Assn., 1975. Mem. Am. Personnel and Guidance Assn., Council for Exceptional Children, Am. Assn. Supervision and Curriculum, League Black Women, Nat. Council Negro Women, Phi Delta Kappa, Phi Delta Kappa.

MONTESI, ALBERT JOSEPH, educator; b. Memphis, Jan. 10, 1921; s. Alexander and Amelia (Boldreghini) M.; B.S., Northwestern U., 1949; M.A., U. Mich., 1950; Ph.D., Pa. State U., 1955. Instr. Pa. State U., 1952-55; asst. prof. The Citadel, Charleston, S.C., 1955-57; asst. prof. St. Louis U., 1957-63, asso. prof. English, 1963-71, prof., 1971—. Vis. prof. Wesleyan U., Middletown, Conn., 1963, U. Buffalo, 1968, U. on Ruhr, Bochum, Ger., 1974-75. Served with USAAF,

1942-46. A.J. Montesi Achievement awards established in his honor by alumni St. Louis U., 1980. Mem. Modern Lang. Assn. Am., Am. Assn. U. Profs., Coll. Tchrs. of English. Author: (poetry) Micrograms, 1970; Micrograms, 1970; Windows and Mirrors, 1977; (with Richard Hill) Five Dinners to Quick Lunch, 1980. Asso. editor Talisman, 1957-62, Twentieth Century Lit., 1965-66, Two Rivers, Deep Channel Packet, 1961-62; faculty adviser Fleur de Lis, 1960-68. Contbr. poems and articles tech. lit. Home: 22 Benton Pl St Louis MO 63104

MONTGOMERY, FRANCIS EUGENE, chemist; b. Loogootee, Ind., Sept. 26, 1946; s. Eugene Vernis and Mary Margaret (Ryan) M.; student Marian Coll., Indpls., 1964-67; B.S. in Chemistry, Purdue U., 1969; m. Cynthia Marie Hoagland, Jan. 1, 1973; children—Sonya Michele, Laura Anne, Maria Christine, Debra Francine. Chemist, In-Service Engring. div. Naval Ammunition Depot, Crane, Ind., 1971-75; chemist Mfg. Tech. div. Applied Scis. dept. Naval Weapons Support Center, Crane, 1975-78; platoon leader Co. B, Engring. Bn., Lawrenceville, Ill., 1978—. Served to 1st lt. F.A., AUS, 1969-71. Mem. Am. Def. Preparedness Assn., Nat. Rifle Assn., Am. Legion. Roman Catholic. Club: K.C. Contbr. articles tech. jours. Patentee in field. Office: Naval Weapons Support Center Code 505 Crane IN 47522

MONTGOMERY, JOHN OSBORN, public relations exec.; b. Detroit, Mar. 21, 1921; s. Henry Arthur and Bessie Ellen (Henderson) M.; B.S. in Agr., Mich. State U., 1950; m. Joy Evelyn Dunlop, Mar. 2, 1946 (dec.); children—John Henry Earl, James Lawrence, Jeffrey Michael; m. 2d, Kathryn M. Vogel, Mar. 12, 1978. Mem. editorial staff Detroit Times, 1937-40, columnist state capitol bur., 1946-49; owner, operator dairy farm, Howell, Mich., 1949-52; mem. pub. relations staff Chrysler Corp., Detroit, 1952-55, dir. pub. relations Chrysler div., 1955-60, corp. mgr. news relations, 1960-74, mgr. indsl. pub. relations, 1974-79; sr. v.p. P/R Assos., Detroit, 1980—. Chmn. pub. relations com., bd. dirs. ARC, Detroit, 1971—; bd. dirs., chmn. pub. relations com. Wayne County unit Am. Cancer Soc., 1974-79; chmn. pub. relations com. Boy Scouts Am., 1970-79. Trustee Greater Detroit Council on Alcoholism, 1970-74. Served with AUS, 1940-46, PTO. Mem. Pub. Relations Soc. Am. (chpt. dir. 1962-64, pres. 1970, dir. 1971, Silver Anvil award, 1957). Mich. Press Assn., Detroit Press Club (dir. 1978—), Detroit Bd. Commerce, Detroit Hist. Soc., Founders Soc., Detroit Inst. Arts, Soc. Mayflower Desc., St. Andrews Soc. Clubs: Detroit Boat, Players, Crisis (Detroit). Home: 745 University Place Grosse Pointe MI 48230 Office: 1800 City Nat Bank Bldg Detroit MI 48226

MONTGOMERY, REX, biochemist; b. Halesowen, Eng., Sept. 4, 1923; s. Fred and Jane (Holloway) M.; came to U.S., 1948, naturalized, 1963; B.Sc., U. Birmingham (Eng.), 1943, Ph.D., 1946, D.Sc., 1963; m. Barbara Winifred Price, Aug. 9, 1948; children—Ian, David, Jennifer, Christopher. Research asso. U. Minn., 1951-55; mem. faculty U. Iowa, Iowa City, 1955—, prof. biochemistry, 1963—, asso. dean Coll. Medicine, 1974—; cons. Gen. Mills, Inc., 1964-69, NRC Can., 1973; mem. study sect NIH, 1968-72, mem. drug devel. contract rev. com., 1975-77, mem. devel. therapy com. Nat. Cancer Inst., 1977-79; chmn. com. biol. chemistry Nat. Acad. Scis., 1961-64; vis. prof. Nat. Australian U., 1969-70. Postdoctoral fellow Ohio State U., 1948-49; Sugar Research Found. fellow, U.S. Dept. Agr., 1949-51. Author: Chemical Production of Lactic Acid, 1949; Chemistry of Plant Gums and Mucilages, 1959; Quantitative Problems in the Biochemical Sciences, 1969, 2d edit., 1976; Biochemistry-A Case-Oriented Approach, 1974, 3d edit., 1980; editorial adv. bd. Carbohydrate Research, 1968-79; contbr. articles to profl. jours. Home: 5 Princeton Ct Iowa City IA 52240 Office: Office Dean Coll Medicine U Iowa Iowa City IA 52242

MONTGOMERY, ROBERT LEW, educator; b. Grayson, Ky., July 2, 1941; s. Everett DeForest and Ruth Agnes (Glass) M.; B.A., Bethany Coll., 1964; M.S., Okla. State U., 1967, Ph.D., 1968; m. Frances Marie Maemmerlie, June 16, 1979; children—Melissa, John. Instr., research asst. Okla. State U., 1964-68; asst. prof. psychology U. Mo., Rolla, 1968-73, prof., 1975—, head dept. psychology, 1975—; vis. prof. psychology U. Fla., 1974-75. Nat. Campbell scholar, 1963-64; NIMH fellow, 1964-67; NDEA fellow, 1967; recipient Phi Kappa Phi Disting. Service award, 1975. Mem. Am. Psychol. Assn., Psychonomic Soc., Midwestern Psychol. Assn., Southwestern Psychol. Assn., Mo. Acad. Sci. Democrat. Episcopalian. Club: Kiwanis. Contbr. articles to profl. jours. Home: Route 4 Box 223 Rolla MO 65401 Office: University of Missouri Rolla MO 65401

MONTGOMERY, ROBERT MAX, dentist; b. Topeka, Nov. 27, 1918; s. Simpson K. and Ella Mae (Roberts) M.; Asso. Sci., Kemper Mil. Sch., 1938; B.S., U. Mo. at Kansas City, 1943, D.D.S., 1943; m. Nola K. Sannaman, May 28, 1958; children—Mindy Sue, Tammy Kay. Dentist, Clay Center, Kans., 1946—. Mem. U.S. Assay Commn., 1971. Served to lt. (s.g.), USNR, 1943-46. Mem. Am. Numis. Assn. (life), Clay Center C. of C., Kans., Am. dental assns. Republican. Elk. Home: 1801 6th St Clay Center KS 67432 Office: 712 6th St Clay Center KS 67432

MONTI, GREGORY L., mktg. exec.; b. Bklyn., Oct. 28, 1946; s. LeRoy John and Mary Alice (Foley) M.; B.S., St. Joseph's Coll., 1968; M.S., Roosevelt U., 1981. With Continental Ill. Nat. Bank, Chgo., 1970-71; with Monti & Assos., Inc., Arlington Heights, Ill., 1971—, v.p. sales and mktg., 1976—. Served with U.S. Army, 1968-70. Decorated Army Commendation medal. Mem. Air Conditioning and Refrigeration Wholesalers (asso.), Refrigeration Service Engrs. Soc., Refrigeration Machinery Assn. Home: 808 Park Plaine Park Ridge IL 60068 Office: 1050 E Addison Ct Arlington Heights IL 60005

MONYAK, WENDELL PETER, pharmacist; b. Chgo., Sept. 14, 1931; s. Wendell and Mary Elizabeth M.; B.S. in Chemistry, Roosevelt U., 1957; B.S. in Pharmacy, St. Louis Coll. Pharmacy, 1961; m. Lorraine Mostek, Aug. 29, 1964. Asst. chief pharmacist Little Co. of Mary Hosp., Chgo., 1961-66; chief pharmacist MacNeal Meml. Hosp., Berwyn, Ill., 1966-72; dir. pharmacy Ill. Masonic Med. Center, Chgo., 1972, dir. pharm. services, 1972—; teaching asso. U. Ill. Bd. dirs. Bohemian Home for Aged, 1980. Served with M.C., AUS, 1955-57. Mem. Am. Pharm. Assn., Am. Soc. Hosp. Pharmacists, Ill. Pharm. Assn. (Spl. Recognition award), No. Ill. Soc. Hosp. Pharmacists, Chgo. Hosp. Council. Club: Exec. (Chgo.). Author: Hospital Formulary and Therapeutic Guide for Residents and Interns, 1974. Home: 19 W 059 Chateau N Oak Brook IL 60521 Office: 836 W Wellington St Chicago IL 60657

MOODY, BLAIR, JR., state supreme ct. justice; b. Detroit, Feb. 27, 1928; s. Blair and Mary (Williamson) M.; B.A., U. Mich., 1949, LL.B., 1952; m. Mary Lou Kennedy, Aug. 18, 1951; children—Diane Marie, Blair III, Susan Beth, Brian Thornton, Peter Kennedy. Reporter, Detroit News, summers 1949-50; reporter Washington Post, 1952; admitted to Mich. bar, 1952; practiced in Detroit, 1953-65; mem. firm Sullivan, Eames Moody & Petrillo, 1953-65; judge Circuit Ct. Wayne County, Detroit, 1966-76; justice Mich. Supreme Ct., 1977—. Democratic precinct del., 1954-62; chmn. Citizens for Kennedy Wayne County, 1960. Served with USAF, 1952-53. Mem. Phi Delta Theta, Phi Delta Phi. Presbyterian. Clubs: Detroit Press, Lawyers, Economic. Office: 1425 Lafayette Bldg Detroit MI 48226

MOODY, G. WILLIAM, aerospace mfg. co. exec.; b. Cleveland Heights, Ohio, Nov. 6, 1928; s. John Walter and Anna Barbara (Keck) M.; student Ohio U., 1948-49; B.S. in Civil Engring., Mich. State U., 1952; m. Loisjean Kanouse, Sept. 17, 1955; children—Elizabeth Jean, Cynthia Ann, G. William. Sales engr. Rich Mfg. Corp., Battle Creek, Mich., 1952-55; chief engr. Air Lift Co., Lansing, Mich., 1955-61; product engr. Aeroquip Corp., Jackson, Mich., 1961-62, chief engr. Barco div., 1962-68, v.p., gen. mgr., 1968-72, v.p., ops. mgr. AMB div., 1972-74, v.p., gen. mgr. aerospace div., 1974-81, group v.p. gen. products, 1981—; dir. Aeroquip S.A., Nu-Matic Grinders, Inc.; sr. design engr. Clark Floor Machine Co., Muskegon, Mich., 1962. Gen. campaign chmn. Jackson County United Way, 1976, pres., 1980; mem. planning commn. North Barrington, Ill., 1967-72; chmn. Joint Com. for an Area Hosp., Barrington, 1969-72; trustee Foote Hosp., 1980—; bd. dirs. United Way of Mich., 1977—. Served with U.S. Army, 1946-48. Mem. Soc. Automotive Engrs., ASME, Am. Mgmt. Assn., Jackson C. of C. Lutheran. Clubs: Jackson Country, Jackson County Sportsman's, Jackson Town (dir. 1981). Patentee in field. Home: 612 S Bowen Jackson MI 49203 Office: 300 S East Ave Jackson MI 49203

MOODY, JAMES D., state senator; b. Sept. 2, 1935; B.A., Haverford Coll.; M.P.A., Harvard U.; Ph.D. in Econs., U. Calif., Berkeley. Former CARE rep., Yugoslavia and Iran; former Peace Corp rep., Pakistan; former AID loan officer; former econ. analyst Dept. Transp.; asst. prof. econs. U. Wis.-Milw.; mem. Wis. Assembly, 1976-78, Wis. Senate, 1978—. Mem. Am. Econs. Assn., Nat. Tax Assn., Transp. Research Bd. Democrat. Office: 310 South State Capitol Madison WI 53702*

MOODY, TOM, mayor; b. Columbus, Ohio, Nov. 26, 1929; B.S. summa cum laude, Ohio State U., 1954; J.D., Franklin U., 1956; m. Jean Watson, Sept. 9, 1949; children—Todd, Trent, Paula Jean. Admitted to Ohio bar, 1956; pvt. practice law, Columbus, 1956-63; judge Franklin County (Ohio) Municipal Ct., 1963-67; judge Common Pleas Ct. Franklin County, 1969-71; mayor, Columbus, Ohio, 1971—; counsel firm Crabbe, Newlon, Potts, Schmidt, Brown & Jones, Columbus, 1971—. Lectr. in torts Law Sch., Franklin U., 1958-60; lectr. in evidence Captial U., Franklin Law Sch., 1968-70. Mem. city council, Columbus, 1961-63; mem. 28th Ward Republican Com., 1958-63. Past pres., bd. dirs. Franklin County chpt. Muscular Dystrophy Assn. Am.; chmn. membership drive South Side YMCA; mem. legal div. United Appeals; mem. exec. bd. Central YMCA. Mem. Am., Ohio State, Columbus bar assns., Ohio Jud. Conf., Ohio Municipal Judges Assn. (past v.p.), Am. Legion, Kappa Sigma. Lutheran. Clubs: Barristers, Lawyers, Masons, Shriners. Office: City Hall 90 W Broad St Columbus OH 43215*

MOOG, FLORENCE EMMA, biologist, educator; b. Bklyn., Jan. 24, 1915; d. George Alfred and Freda (Ott) M.; A.B., N.Y. U., 1936; Ph.D., Columbia U., 1944; Sc.D. (hon.), LaSalle Coll., Phila., 1974. Med. records clk. U.S. Dept. Labor, 1937-38; instr. biology U. Del., 1940; instr. biology Washington U., St. Louis, 1945-48, research asso., 1942-45, asst. prof. 1948-52, asso. prof., 1952-58, prof., 1958—, Charles Rebstock prof. biology, 1976—; Walker-Ames prof. U. Wash., Seattle, 1973; mem. study sect. on human embryology and devel. NIH, 1966-70; Merck postdoctoral fellow Cambridge U., 1954-55. Mem. Soc. Devel. Biology, Am. Soc. Cell Biology, Am. Soc. Zoologists, Soc. Gen. Physiology, AAAS, Union Concerned Scientists, ACLU, NAACP, Phi Beta Kappa, Sigma Xi. Author: Structure and Development of Vertebrates, 1949; (with T.S. Hall) Life Science, 1955. Office: Dept Biology Washington Univ Saint Louis MO 63130

MOOK, AMY WOLF, sch. prin.; b. Rochester, Pa., Mar. 9, 1944; d. Arthur Lee and Harriet Louise (White) Wolf; B.S., Slippery Rock State Coll., 1966; M.A., U. Iowa, 1977, Ph.D., 1981; 1 dau., Cathleen. Tchr. health and phys. edn., Pa. and Conn., 1962-72; cons. environ. studies Nat. Field Research Center, Iowa City, 1978; prin. Olin (Iowa) High Sch., 1978-79, Minnetonka (Minn.) High Sch., 1979—. Mem. AAUW, Administrv. Women in Edn., Oreg. Women in Edn., Minnetonka Assn. Prins., Minn. Assn. Secondary Sch. Prins. Home: 6269 Saint Johns Dr Eden Prairie MN 55344 Office: 18301 Hwy 7 Minnetonka MN 55343

MOON, CHARLES REDMAN, lawyer; b. St. Anthony, Idaho, Nov. 21, 1913; s. C. Redman and Elsa (Haass) M.; student Dartmouth, 1931-33; A.B., U. Mich., 1935, J.D., 1937; m. Miriam G. Robertson, Oct. 14, 1939 (dec. 1967); children—Charles R., William R.; m. 2d, Janet Faden Crow, Feb. 8, 1969; stepchildren—Allen F., Stephen L., Jeffrey L. Admitted to Mich. bar, 1937, since practiced in Detroit; asso. Dickinson, Wright, Moon, Van Dusen & Freeman, 1937-48, partner, 1948—; dir. Douglas & Lomason Co.; justice of peace, Pleasant Ridge, Mich., 1949-60. Served as lt., USNR, 1942-46; PTO. Mem. Am., Mich., Detroit bar assns., Am. Judicature Soc., Order of Coif, Mil. Order World Wars, Kappa Sigma, Phi Delta Phi. Clubs: Barristers, Detroit Athletic (dir. 1977—, sec. 1979—), Bond, Country of Detroit, Detroit (Detroit). Presbyterian. Home: 302 Touraine Rd Grosse Pointe Farms MI 48236 Office: First National Bldg Detroit MI 48226

MOON, WILLIAM ISHAM, truckstop services co. exec.; b. Cook County, Ill., Dec. 13, 1932; s. William Isham and Nellie Ethyl (Carrol) M.; B.S., S.W. Mo. Coll., 1958; grad. Harvard Bus. Sch., 1977; m. Carolyn Blanch Cusac, Nov. 5, 1961; children—William Isham, Delia Ann, Carolyn Jill. Sales engr. Standard Oil Co., Wichita, Kans., 1958-60; mgr. Truckstop Standard Oil Co., Kansas City region, 1960-65; pres. Iowa 80 Truckstop Inc., Walcott, 1965—. Served with inf. AUS, 1952-54; Korea. Mem. Nat. Truckstop Operators Assn. (J.L. Schaffer award outstanding truckstop operator 1974), Am. Truck Hist. Soc. (dir. 1974-77, pres. 1980). Methodist. Home: 403 Main St N Walcott IA 52773 Office: Interstate 80 & 40 Walcott IA 52773

MOONEY, JOHN ALLEN, bus. exec.; b. Amery, Wis., May 17, 1918; s. Harry Edmon and Maybelle (Johnson) M.; student U. Wis., River Falls; m. Nettie O. Hayes, Aug. 29, 1940; children—John Allen, Suzanne, Jean, Nancy. Salesman, Reid Murdock & Co., Chgo., 1940-45, Consol. Foods Corp., Chgo., 1945-69; nat. sales mgr., v.p. M & R Sales Corp., Oak Park, Ill., 1969-78, pres., chief exec. officer, dir., 1978—; nat. sales mgr., v.p. Western Dressing, Inc., Oak Park, 1970-78, pres., chief exec. officer, dir., 1978—; dir. 1st Nat. Bank of LaGrange (Ill.), Waunakee Alloy Casting Corp. Bd. govs. Shrine Hosp. for Crippled Children, Chgo., Mpls., St. Paul; asso. bd. govs. LaGrange Meml. Hosp. Club: Masons (past potentate Zor Shrine Temple, Madison, Wis., hon. past potentate Medinah Shrine Temple, Chgo.). Office: 1515 N Harlem Ave Oak Park IL 60302

MOORE, CARL EDWARD, chemist; b. Frankfort, Ky., Sept. 25, 1915; s. Leslie and Effie Hudson (Goins) M.; B.S., East Ky. State U., 1939; M.S., U. Louisville, 1947; Ph.D., Ohio State U., 1952; m. Mary Agnes Bohn, Dec. 27, 1940; children—Carl Edward, Mary Ann, Martha Vivian, Paul Douglas. With Nat. Distillers, 1939-41, E.I. duPont de Nemours & Co., Inc., 1941-45; cons. Am. Air Filter Corp., 1948-50; faculty U. Louisville, 1947-50; faculty Loyola U., Chgo., 1952—, formerly chmn., now prof. dept. chemistry; cons. to chem. industry. Chmn., Morton Grove (Ill.) Air Pollution Control Commn. Mem. Soc. for Applied Spectroscopy (Spectroscopist of Year 1976), Am. Chem. Soc. (sci. adv. Ill. Dist. 10), AAAS. Contbr. articles to profl. jours. Patentee in field. Home: 9535 Oriole St Morton Grove IL 60053 Office: Dept Chemistry Loyola U 6525 N Sheridan Rd Chicago IL 60626

MOORE, DAN TYLER, writer; b. Washington, Feb. 1, 1908; s. Dan T. and Luvean Jones (Butler) M.; B.S., Yale U., 1931; m. Elizabeth Valley Oakes, Mar. 12, 1932; children—Luvean O. Moore Owens, Elizabeth Oakes Moore Thornton, Harriet Moore Ballard, Dan Tyler. Asst. to pres. Intercontinental Hotels Corp., Istanbul, Turkey, 1948-50; pres. Middle East Co., Cleve., China Co., Cleve., 1946-48; former nat. fgn. corr. in Middle East, N.Am. Newspaper Alliance. Pres. Greater Cleve. Muscular Dystrophy Assn., 1952-65. Mem. exec. com. Cuyahoga County Democratic Party, 1951-70, mem. state exec. com., 1962-65; commr. Ohio Fed. Jury, 1961-68. Trustee Cleve. Museum Natural History; bd. dirs. Near East Rehab. Center, Near East Coll. Assn., Karamu Theatre, Cleve., Cleve. Mus. Natural History. Served with AUS as chief counterintelligence for OSS in Cairo, 1942-44. Mem. Internat. Platform Assn. (chmn. bd., dir. gen). Author: Cloak and Cipher, 1962, The Terrible Game, 1957; Wolves Widows and Orphans, 1966; Lecturing For Profit, 1967. Contbr. articles to popular mags. in U.S. and fgn. countries.

MOORE, DENNIS FREDERIC, hematologist, oncologist; b. Kansas City, Mo., Apr. 10, 1936; s. Frederic D. and Rhetta L. (Dowling) M.; B.A., Westminster Coll., 1958; M.D., Tulane U., 1962; m. Mary Jane O'Malley, Sept. 3, 1960; children—Dennis Frederic, Thomas Allen, Timothy Joseph, Michael Christopher. Intern, St. Francis Hosp., Wichita, Kans., 1962-63; resident VA Hosp., Wichita, 1963-66; chief out-patient services USPHS Hosp., Galveston, Tex., 1966-67, dep. chief med. service, 1967-68, advanced sr. fellow M.D. Anderson Hosp., Houston, 1968-69; practice medicine specializing in hematology and oncology, 1969—; clin. instr. medicine U. Tex., Galveston, 1968; clin. asso. Kans. U., Wichita State Branch, 1973-76, clin. asso. prof. medicine and pediatrics, 1977—; mem. staffs. St. Joseph Med. Center, Wesley Med. Center, St. Francis Hosp., Osteopathic Hosp., VA Hosp., Wichita; Central Kans. Med. Center, Great Bend, Kans., Hadley Regional Med. Center, Hays, Kans.; clin. investigator SW Oncology Group., Wichita, 1971—. Active ARC, Wichita, 1975—; cubmaster Quivira council Boy Scouts Am., Wichita, 1972-80; trustee Leukemia Soc. Am., 1974—. Served with USPHS, 1966-68. Diplomate Am. Bd. Internal Medicine. Fellow Am. Coll. Physicians; mem. Am. Med. Assn., Internat. Cancer Congress, Am. Soc. Hematology, Am. Fedn. Clin. Research, Am. Soc. Clin. Oncology, N.Y. Acad. Sci., Kans., Sedgwick County med. socs., Nat. Pilots Assn. Republican. Club: Wichita Country. Contbr. articles to med. jours. Home: 7439 Tanglewood Ln Wichita KS 67206 Office: Suite 265 1035 N Emporia Wichita KS 67204

MOORE, GARY ELWOOD, educator; b. Lempasas, Tex., Feb. 24, 1947; s. Wendell McGee and Eulalia (Priest) M.; B.S., Tarleton State U., 1969; M.S., Ohio State U., 1973, Ph.D., 1975; m. Barbara Allen Bonar, June 16, 1973; 1 son, Micah Matthew. Vocat. agr. instr. Medicine Lodge (Kans.) High Sch., 1969-70, Fort Frye High Sch., Beverly, Ohio, 1970-73; grad. teaching asso. Ohio State U., Columbus, 1973-75; asst. prof. Ala. A&M U., Huntsville, 1975-76; asso. prof. vocat. agr. Purdue U., West Lafayette, Ind., 1976—; book field reviewer McGraw-Hill Book Co., 1979-81. Sunday sch. tchr., associational youth dir. Baptist Ch., 1970-80; scout master Boy Scouts Am., 1969-70; adv. bd. Washington County Vocat. Sch., 1970-73. Recipient Humanities, Social Scis. and Edn. Teaching award Purdue U., 1979, Ind. Vocat. Assn. Outstanding Service award, 1980. Mem. Am. Vocat. Edn. Research Assn., Am. Assn. Tchr. Educators in Agr. (regional editor Jour. 1976-79), Am. Vocat. Assn., Nat. Vocat. Agr. Tchrs. Assn., Am. Ednl. Research Assn., Phi Kappa Phi, Phi Delta Kappa (Outstanding Teaching award 1974), Gamma Sigma Delta. Author: (with William B. Richardson) Working in Horticulture, 1980; contbr. articles in field to profl. jours. Home: 5251 Moore's Bay Rd West Lafayette IN 47906 Office: Dept Vocat-Agr F-15 South Campus Courts Purdue U West Lafayette IN 47907

MOORE, HERBERT ROYAL, physician; b. Providence, Sept. 16, 1916; s. Royal Tolman and Alta Gladys (Jenkin) M.; B.S., U. Ill., 1940, M.D., 1942; m. Frances Ruth Metcalf, Sept. 12, 1940; children—William, Richard Herbert, Robert James. Intern, U. Ill. Research and Ednl. Hosps., Chgo., 1942-43, resident, 1946-48; resident Chgo. Contagious Disease Hosp., 1946-48; pvt. practice medicine specializing in pediatrics, Dayton, Ohio, 1948—; mem. staffs Kettering Meml., St. Elizabeth, Miami Valley, Good Samaritan hosps., Children's Med. Center. Served to maj., M.C., AUS, 1943-46. Mem. Montgomery County Med. Soc., Western Ohio Pediat. Soc., Ohio Pediatric Soc., Am. Acad. Pediatrics, AMA, Am. Coll. Allergists. Methodist. Home: 5425 Mad River Rd Dayton OH 45459 Office: 533 E Stroop Rd Dayton OH 45429

MOORE, HOWARD DENIS, editor, publisher; b. St. Louis, July 22, 1939; s. Howard Stanley and Dorothy Ola (Woltjen) M.; student U. Mo., 1957-60, Nikon Sch. Photography, 1971, 73; m. Mary Jean Brauch, June 1, 1963; children—Michael Anthony, Mark Denis. Newsboy, St. Louis Globe Democrat, 1948-52; with St. Clair Chronicle, 1953-57; advt. editor Tri County News, Sullivan, Mo., 1960-63, editor, 1963-81, pub., 1970-81; v.p. sec. Moore Enterprises, Inc., Sullivan, Mo., 1966-79, pres., treas., 1979—, also dir. Founding pres. Sullivan Indsl. Devel. Corp., 1973-74; v.p. Sullivan Community Betterment, 1963-72, pres., 1972-78; police commr. Sullivan, 1974-76; treas. Crawford County Citizens and Friends for Meramec Park Lake, 1977-78; pres. Sullivan United Republican Club, 1972-73; bd. dirs. Meramec Basin Assn., 1977—, vice-chmn., 1979—. Recipient Leadership award Mo. Gov., 1972. Mem. Nat. Newspaper Assn., Mo. Press Assn., C. of C. (pres. 1973), Sigma Tau Gamma. Republican. Roman Catholic. Rotarian (pres. 1972-73). Home: 650 Crestview Dr Sullivan MO 63080

MOORE, JACK FAY, labor union ofcl.; b. Springfield, Mo., Feb. 19, 1927; s. Elba Fay and Stella (Inmon) M.; student Drury Coll., 1959; m. Betty Lou Johnston, Dec. 29, 1950; children—Thomas Joseph, Deborah Moore Mills, Marilyn Faye Moore Simpson. Electrician, Aton-Luce Electric Co., Springfield, 1946-58; bus. mgr. Local 453 Internat. Brotherhood Elec. Workers, Springfield, 1958-76, mem. exec. council, 1966-76, internat. v.p., 1976—. Labor mem. Mo. Bd. Mediation, 1971-75; pres. Springfield Labor Council, 1958-76; mem. exec. bd. State Com. on Polit. Edn., 1964-76. Mem. Springfield Park Bd., 1962-68. Served with USNR, 1944-46, 50-51. Mem. Mo. Elec. Workers (pres. 1960—). Democrat. Mem. Ch. of Christ. Home: 1300 Cozy St Springfield MO 65804 Office: 300 S Jefferson Ave Springfield MO 65806

MOORE, JAMES OTIS, chem. co. exec.; b. Fayetteville, Tenn., Aug. 29, 1935; s. Harry Freeman and Nell (Commons) M.; B.S., Middle Tenn. State U., 1957, M.A., 1967; m. Sara Pauline Powel, Aug. 8, 1959; children—Christopher, Lauren. Tchr., coach Madison High Sch., Nashville, 1960-66; with E.I. DuPont, 1966—, safety and protection supt., Chattanooga, 1980—. Bd. dirs. Iowa Safety Council, Chattanooga YMCA. Served to capt. AUS, 1957-59. Mem. Am. Soc. Safety Engrs., Nat. Fire Protection Assn. Republican. Presbyterian. Office: PO Box 451 Clinton IA 52732

MOORE, JAMES STUART, JR., radiologist; b. Mpls., Oct. 7, 1941; s. James Stuart and Evangeline Pauline (VanHoose) M.; A.B., U. Minn., 1963, M.D., 1967; m. Sally Ruth Brown, Aug. 6, 1966; children—Anne Elizabeth, James Stuart III, John Alexander. Intern in internal medicine U. Ill., Chgo., 1968; resident in radiology U. Minn., Mpls., 1971-73, fellow in neuroradiology, 1973-74, instr. dept. radiology, 1974-75; dir. neuroradiology Mpls. VA Hosp., 1974; practice medicine specializing in radiology, St. Paul, 1974—; mem. staffs St. Jospeh's Hosp., United Hosps., St. John's Hosp.; clin. asst. prof. radiology U. Minn. Served as sr. asst. surgeon USPHS, 1969-71. Diplomate Am. Bd. Radiology. Mem. AMA, Am. Soc. Neuroradiology, Am. Coll. Radiology, Radiol. Soc. N.Am., Minn. Med. Assn., Ramsey County Med. Soc., Minn. Soc. Neurol. Scis., Minn. Radiol. Soc., Clin. Club St. Paul (sec.-treas.), St. Paul Med. Assembly (past pres.), Am. Inst. Ultrasound in Medicine, Twin Cities Soc. Neuroradiology, AAUP, Chi Psi. Club: Town and Country (St. Paul). Contbr. numerous papers to confs. and publs. Home: 645 Montcalm Pl Saint Paul MN 55116 Office: 69 W Exchange St Saint Paul MN 55102

MOORE, JOHN CURTIS, transp. co. exec.; b. Cleve., Mar. 31, 1952; s. Jack S. and Mary B. Moore; B.A., Miami U., Oxford, Ohio; M.Theol. Studies, Trinity Luth. Sem., 1979; m. Jane Marie Visocan, Apr. 12, 1978. Transp. planner Mid-Ohio Regional Planning Commn., Columbus, 1979-80; exec. dir. Transp. Resources, Inc., Columbus, 1979—; cons. paratransit system design, 1980—. Mem. Am. Planning Assn., C.G. Jung Found. Democrat. Home: 741 Mohawk St Columbus OH 43206 Office: 1965 E Main St Columbus OH 43205

MOORE, KATHLEEN ELAINE, hosp. adminstr.; b. Van Wert, Ohio, Oct. 5, 1936; d. Francis Harold and Nora Lehoma (Mumy) M.; R.N., Toledo Hosp. Sch. Nursing, 1957; student Wittenberg U., 1958-60; B.S.N., Mary Manse Coll., 1966; M.Ed., U. Toledo, 1982. Staff nurse, head nurse Toledo (Ohio) Hosp., 1960-69; staff nurse Vis. Nurse Service, Toledo, 1969-71; instr. staff end. Riverside Hosp., Toledo, 1971—; mem. adv. com. diversified health occupations programs Whitmer High Sch., 1977-80. Membership chmn. Toledo Choral Soc., 1965-67, sec., 1968; sec. Monroe St. United Meth. Ch. Wesleyan Chorus, 1974, treas., 1975-76, pres., 1977, adminstrv. bd. mem., 1976—, lay del. annual W. Ohio Conf., 1977, 78, 79, 80, 81; instr.-trainer Basic Cardiac Life Support, 1976—; instr. multimedia first aid ARC, 1975—. Mem. Am. Nurses Assn., Nat. League Nursing, Ohio Nurses Assn. (mem. continuing edn. com. 1978-80), N.W. Ohio League Nursing (chmn. nominating com. 1979-81), Joint Council Continuing Edn. (chmn. 1973-74), Am. Hosp. Assn., Am. Heart Assn. (mem. nursing edn. com. 1977-80), Toledo Area Staff Devel. Council (pres. 1976), Mental Health Assn. Greater Toledo, Toledo Hosp. Alumnae Assn. Republican. Methodist. Home: 5468 Bentbrook St Sylvania OH 43560 Office: 1600 Superior St Toledo OH 43604

MOORE, KENNETH E., anthropologist, educator; b. Niagara Falls, N.Y., Sept. 19, 1930; s. Gordon Winfield and Marie Frances (Sinclair) M.; B.A., Mich. State U., 1953; M.A., U. Ill., 1968, Ph.D. (NIMH fellow and grantee), 1970. Vice pres., account exec. Wimble, Lane & Assos., Flint, Mich., 1954-58; editor McGraw Hill Pub. Co., N.Y.C., 1958-59, Am. Soc. Planning Ofcls., Chgo., 1962-64; asso. prof. anthropology U. Notre Dame (Ind.), 1970—; cons. on urban anthropology. Recipient numerous grants. Mem. Am. Anthrop. Assn., Central States Anthrop. Assn., Soc. Urban Anthropology, Soc. Study Symbolic Interaction. Roman Catholic. Author: Those of the Street, the Catholic-Jews of Mallorca, 1976; editor (with Anthony Kerrigan and Saul Bellow) trans. Rebellion of the Masses (Ortega Y. Gasset), 1981; editor (with James Clemens) Planning, 1964. Address: Dept Sociology and Anthropology U Notre Dame Notre Dame IN 46556

MOORE, KITTY PIERSE, editor; b. Spencer, Ind., July 2, 1935; d. Jewell N. and Bliss L. (Franklin) McKee; ed. Laney Coll.; m. Francis R. Moore, Dec. 3, 1971; children—Scott W. Pierse, Keith E. Pierse; stepchildren—Scott Moore, Kimberly Moore, Tucker Moore. Communications mgr. Firstmark Corp., Indpls., 1969-77; communications specialist Stokely-Van Camp, Indsp., 1977-78; public relations dir. Internat. Center, Indpls., 1978-79; editor Nat. News Am. Legion Aux., Indpl., 1979—. Adviser Marion County Teen Guide Counsel, 1969-71. Mem. Ind. Bus. Communicators, Internat. Assn. Bus. Communicators (award; named Editor of Year, 1979, others). Address: 777 N Meridan Indianapolis IN 46204

MOORE, KURT RICHARD, anthropologist, art historian; b. Scott AFB, Ill., Oct. 9, 1955; s. Richard Vernal and Irmgard Ludwiga (Bennewitz) M.; A.B., U. Ill., 1976, B.F.A., 1976; M.A., So. Ill. U., 1981, postgrad., 1981—. Grad. teaching asst. So. Ill. U. Field Sch. Archaeology, Carbondale, 1977, Center Continuing Edn., 1978, archaeol. field/lab. asst. Center Archaeol. Investigations, 1978-79, grad. research asst., 1979-80; archaeologist Ill. State Mus. Soc., Springfield, Ill., 1980—. Edmund J. James scholar U. Ill., Urbana, 1972-73, John T. Rusher Meml. scholar, 1975-76; So. Ill. U. scholar, 1981-82. Mem. African Studies Assn., Am. Anthrop. Assn., Am. Com. to Advance Study Petroglyphs and Pictographs, Artist Blacksmith Assn. N. Am., Assn. Field Archaeology, Current Anthropology (asso.), Soc. Am. Archaeology, Soc. Archaeol. Scis., Soc. Humanistic Anthropology, Central States Anthrop. Soc., Phi Kappa Phi. Author monographs; contbr. articles to profl. jours. and sci. meetings. Home: 590 S Park St Paxton IL 60957 Office: Ill State Mus Archaeol Research Program Spring and Edwards Sts Springfield IL 62706

MOORE, LYNN, bus. cons.; b. East Chicago Heights, Ill., Sept. 13, 1957; d. Clyde J. Moore and Irene S. (Dalian) Moore Kojder; student Princeton U., 1977-78, So. Ill. U., 1973-74, Joliet Jr. Coll., 1975-78, Loop Coll. Chgo.; B.S., B.A. in Mktg./Advt., Loyola U., 1981. Office clk. Ralph M. Parsons Constrn., Lemont, Ill., 1975-76; project office mgr. Dart Industries, Joliet, Ill., 1976-77; mktg. orgn. Western Electric, Lisle, Ill., 1977-79; pres., chief exec. officer Moore Efficiency Bus. Cons.'s, Chgo., 1980—; tchr. voice, piano, guitar, 1971-78; freelance singer, songwriter, 1971—; actress as Mary Magdalene in Jesus Christ Superstar, 1974; cast mem. Godspell, 1975; tchr. high sch., dir. musicals Godspell, 1975-76, Winnie the Pooh, 1974-75. Mem. staff Reagan for Pres. Campaign, 1976. Mem. Word Processing Mgmt. Assn. Chgo., Internat. Orgn. Women Execs. (planning com.). Contbr. poems to various publs.; contbg. bus. editor Transport Fleet News. Home: 123 Acacia Dr #611 Indian Head Park IL 60525 Office: 180 N Michigan Ave #707 Chicago IL 60601

MOORE, MARECE ELIZABETH GIBBS, librarian; b. Boston; d. Warmoth Thomas and Marece Allen (Jones) Gibbs; B.S., N.C., Agrl. and Tech. State U., 1940; B.L.S., U. Chgo., 1945, postgrad., 1947-48; m. Herman M. Moore, Jr.; Dec. 26, 1953 (div. Feb. 1965). Instr. French and English, N.C. Agrl. and Tech. State U., Greensboro, 1940-43, asst. librarian, 1943-44; cataloger Fisk U., Nashville, 1945-48; cataloger Detroit Pub. Library, 1949-53, reference librarian, 1953-54, supr. reference services cataloging, 1955-67; Detroit area librarian Burroughs Corp., 1967-71, mgr. corp. library, 1971-79; head librarian Mich. Bell Corp., 1979—; instr. library sci. Fisk U., 1945-46, Wayne State U., 1970. Bd. dirs. Friends Detroit Pub. Library; bd. dirs., rec. sec., co-chmn. Delta Home For Girls; bd. dirs. Your Heritage House; mem. allocation and rev. com. United Community Services, 1976—; Mich. del. White House Conf. on Libraries and Info. Services, 1979. Recipient Alumni award for outstanding service Midwest region N.C. Agrl. and Tech. Alumni Assn., 1969, Nat. Alumni award, 1973. Mem. NAACP (life), Am. Library Assn. (life), Spl. Libraries Assn. (dir. 1981—), Am. Soc. Info. Sci., Women's Nat. Book Assn. (2d v.p. Detroit chpt. 1971-73), N.C. Agrl. and Tech. State U. Alumni Assn., Delta Sigma Theta (life). Episcopalian. Club: Women's Economic (dir. archivist 1971-72) (Detroit). Home: 1008 Trevor Pl Detroit MI 48207 Office: 1365 Cass Ave Detroit MI 48226

MOORE, PAUL BERNARD, mfg. co. exec.; b. Monmouth, Ill., Mar. 23, 1946; s. Byron Calvert and Mary Sarah (Dunbar) M.; student U. Ariz., 1964-66, U. Mo., 1966-67; m. Nancy Lee Richardson, July 10, 1976; children—Anne Bernadette Wilkerson, Nicholas Byron. Test engr. Deutsch Co., Los Angeles, 1969-72; planner Certified Alloy Products, Long Beach, Calif., 1972-77; prodn. control mgr. NL Industries, Hightstown, N.J., 1977-79; mgr. planning, control and advt. Taracorp. Industries, Granite City, Ill., 1979—. Served with USN, 1963-66. Mem. Nat. Rifle Assn., Am. Press Assn. Republican. Roman Catholic. Inventor Lawrence Brand Magnum Bullet Alloy, 1980. Home: 6000 La Chateau Ct Saint Louis MO 63129 Office: 16th and Cleveland Sts Granite City IL 62040

MOORE, RICHARD ALAN, mfg. co. exec.; b. Lebanon, Ind., Oct. 24, 1949; s. Max and Dorothy Jean Moore; B.S., Ind. U., 1977; postgrad. Butler U.; diploma horology Bowmen Tech. Sch., 1970; m. Mary B. Saxon. Retail cons. Wolfe's, Terre Haute, Ind., 1972-73; retail salesman F.R. Lazarus, Indpls., 1973, 74-75, L.S. Ayres, Indpls., 1976-77; mktg. research analyst Hyster Co., Danville, Ill., 1977-79; mgr. mktg. devel. Stewart-Warner Co., Indpls., 1979—. Mem. Am. Mgmt. Assn., Ind. Watchmakers Assn., Ind. U. Alumni Assn., Sigma Pi Alpha. Republican. Home: 9507 San Miguel Dr Indianapolis IN 46250 Office: Stewart-Warner Co 1514 Drover St Indianapolis IN 46221

MOORE, ROBERT DUANE, fund raiser, public relations cons.; b. Wayne City, Ill., Mar. 1, 1927; s. William Komer and Alta Louise (Wolfe) M.; B.S., George Williams Coll., 1949, M.S. in Organizational Adminstrn. cum laude, 1968; m. Anne W. Giauque, Apr. 28, 1950; children—Susan Lynn, Sandra Kay, Nancy Anne. Community dir. Chgo. YMCA, 1945-50, br. exec., Washington, 1950-52; pres. Moore & Palmer, Inc., 1952-54; exec. dir. Grand Rapids (Mich.) YMCA, 1954-62; v.p. devel. George Williams Coll., 1962-76; v.p. devel. Evang. Hosp. Assn., Oak Brook, Ill., 1976—; fund raising cons. to hosps., chs. and schs.; chmn. Internat. Conf. Philanthropy. Elder, Christ Ch., Oak Brook. Served with AUS, 1954-56. Cert. social worker. Mem. Nat. Soc. Fund Raising Execs. (pres. Chgo.), Exec. Club Oak Brook (pres.), Nat. Assn. Hosp. Devel., Public Relations Soc. Am. Club: Lake Barrington Shores Golf. Home: 4814 Bryan Pl Downers Grove IL 60515 Office: 2025 Windsor Dr Oak Brook IL 60521

MOORE, ROBERT LEE, utility co. exec.; b. Boulder, Colo., Nov. 20, 1934; s. Alden Montgomery and Vera Mae (Smith) M.; B.A., U. Colo., 1961; children—Pamela, Shauna. Advt. rep. Sterling (Colo.) Jour.-Advocate, 1961-65; advt. asst. Kans. Gas & Electric Co., Wichita, 1965, communications specialist, 1973-78, consumer news coordinator, 1978—. Served with USAF, 1953-57. Mem. Public Utilities Communicators Assn., Advt. Club Wichita (dir. 1969-72, 2d v.p. 1972). Home: 2715 Exchange Pl Wichita KS 67217 Office: PO Box 208 Wichita KS 67201

MOORE, THOMAS ALEXANDER, II, mfg. co. exec.; b. Glendale, W.Va., Dec. 11, 1951; s. Thomas Alexander and Dorothy Louise (Brock) M.; B.A. cum laude, W.Va. U., 1973. Tech. sales rep. Richardson Co., Des Plaines, Ill., 1976-78, Dallas, 1978-79; product mgr. Surfactants, Des Plaines, 1979—. Served with USNR, 1974-76. Mem. Soc. Cosmetic Chemists, Chgo. Drug and Chem. Assn. Home: 110 E George St #616 Bensenville IL 60106 Office: 2400 E Devon Ave Suite 184 Des Plaines IL 60018

MOORE, THOMAS HUGH, assn. exec.; b. Morrilton, Ark., Jan. 13, 1929; s. James Thomas and Annie (Van Marion) M.; student Hendrix Coll., 1947-48; B.A., Ark. State Tchrs. Coll., 1951; m. Clara Jean Jackson, Nov. 18, 1950; children—Melanie Anne, Stephanie Suzanne, James Van. Dir. pub. relations Ark. State Electric Coop., Inc., North Little Rock, 1957-61; exec. v.p. Assn. Ill. Electric Coops., Springfield, 1961—. Pres. Ill. Farm Electrification Council; bd. dirs. Farm Electrification Council, 1962-64. Bd. dirs. Ill. 4-H Club Found. Served to lt. USNR, 1951-57. Mem. Rural Electric Statewide Mgrs. Assn. (pres.), Ill. Fedn. Consumers (pres.), Springfield Assn. Execs. Methodist. Mason (Shriner). Home: 2117 Kenwood Dr Springfield IL 62704 Office: PO Box 3787 Vice 1180 Springfield IL 62708

MOORE, THOMAS ORVILLE, county ofcl.; b. Rochester, Minn., Oct. 19, 1927; s. William Robert and Norma (Strom) M.; B.S. in Civil Engring., U. Minn., 1952; m. Doris Ann Reilly, June 3, 1948; children—Thomas W., Katherine A. Constrn. Engr. City of Rochester (Minn.) Engr.'s Office, 1953-56; planning dir. City of Rochester Planning Dept., 1956-75; operational supr. consol. planning dept. Olmsted County (Minn.), Rochester, 1975-77, planning dir., 1977—. Pres. Holmes Sch. PTA, Rochester. Served with AUS, 1946-47, 52-53. Registered profl. engr., Minn. Mem. Am. Inst. Cert. Planners, Minn. Soc. Profl. Engrs. (past chpt. pres.). Lutheran. Club: Lions. Home: 1409 Berkman Ct SE Rochester MN 55901 Office: 1421 3d Ave SE Rochester MN 55901

MOORE, VERNON EDWARD, business exec.; b. Summerfield, Ohio, Sept. 10, 1927; s. Elwell C. and Lillie L. (Cunningham) M.; ed. public schs.; m. Norma Jean Mann, June 5, 1948; children—Carol Jean, Judy Kay, Joyce Lynn, Janet Marie. Bookkeeper, Farm Bur. Coop., Caldwell, Ohio, 1946-47; farmer, substitute mail carrier, sch. bus. driver, 1947-53; timekeeper, mgr. shipping Cleve. Graphite-Bronze, Caldwell, Ohio, 1953-55; time study and prodn. foreman Remington Rand, Marietta, Ohio, 1955-57; stores mgr., prodn. supt., maintenance equipment inspector, mgr. quality control, mgr. shipping, mgr. maintenance, mgr. environ. control, mgr. prodn. and plant services, asst. plant mgr. Ohio Ferro Alloys Corp., Philo, 1957-80, plant mgr., 1980—. Pres. Noble local sch. bd., 1966-70; pres. ch. bd. Summerfield United Meth. Ch.; v.p. Vol. Fire Dept.; treas. Boosters Club. Mem. Nat. Mgmt. Assn. (pres. 1978-79, outstanding service award 1979), Am. Soc. Metals. Republican. Clubs: Lehigh Country, Order Eastern Star Ipatron 1958), Masons. Home: 1295 Kevrob Dr Zanesville OH 43701 Office: Main St Philo OH 43771

MOORE, VERNON LEE, utility co. exec.; b. Kansas City, Kans., Mar. 26, 1923; s. Robert Sanford and Velma Margaret (Parker) M.; student Internat. Corr. Schs., 1963-65; m. Mary Bernice Janssens, Nov. 25, 1950; children—Russell Parker, Dana Margaret. With Kansas City Power & Light Co., Kansas City, Mo., 1948—, tng. coordinator, 1979—. Served with U.S. Navy, 1941-47. Mem. Am. Soc. Tng. and Devel. Presbyterian. Home: 5832 W 87th Terr Overland Park KS 66207 Office: 8700 Hawthorn Rd Kansas City MO 64120

MOORE, WOODVALL RAY, librarian; b. Flatwoods, Ky., May 19, 1942; s. Clyde Raymond and Erma (Gallion) M.; A.A., So. Bible Coll., Houston, 1963, B.S., 1965; M.S. in L.S., U. Ky., 1972; m. Sarah Ellen Markham, Dec. 14, 1963; children—Tamra Sheri, Woodvall Allen. Dir. library So. Bible Coll., 1968-76; dir. library services Evangel Coll., Springfield, Mo., 1976—; ordained minister Assemblies of God Ch., 1969. Precint chmn. Republican Party, Houston, 1972-76. Mem. ALA, Mo. Library Assn., Assn. Christian Librarians (dir. 1979—), Springfield Librarians Assn. Republican. Office: 1111 N Glenstone St Springfield MO 65802

MOORHEAD, ROBERT GRANT, printing co. exec.; b. Orleans, Ind., Sept. 4, 1921; s. Robert L. and Roxie (Sanders) M.; A.B., Ind. U., 1942; postgrad. Carnegie Inst. Tech., 1948; m. Margaret Bachelder, Feb. 21, 1948; children—James R., Richard B., Barbara J., Margaret S., Janet A. With Central Pub. Co., Indpls., 1947—, sales mgr., 1951-53, plant mgr., 1954-61, gen. mgr., 1961-63, pres., gen. mgr., 1963—; v.p. Sta. WFYI, 1979—; dir. Arsenal Savs. Assn. Mem., v.p. Indpls. Police Merit Bd., 1973-79; pres. Ind. State Armory Bd., 1972—; mem. Indpls. Bd. Public Safety, 1980-81; mem. adv. bd. Salvation Army, 1980—; bd. dirs. Crossroads council Boy Scouts Am., pres. 500 Festival, 1963, v.p., 1976-78; bd. dirs. Veterans Day Council, 1965—, U.S. Auto Club; bd. dirs. Am. Cancer Soc., chmn., 1978-80. Served to capt., U.S. Army, 1942-46; served to maj. gen. N.G., 1948-78. Decorated Legion of Merit with oak leaf cluster, D.S.M., Bronze Star with oak leaf cluster; recipient Sagamore of the Wabash award Govs. Ind., 1972, 76. Mem. Printing Industries of Ind. (v.p. 1980—), Res. Officers Assn., Indpls. C. of C. (dir. 1975—), Am. Legion, Nat. Guard Assn. U.S. (exec. council 1980—, Meritorious Service award 1975), Ind. N.G. Assn. (pres. 1954-55), Assn. U.S. Army (pres. Ind. chpt. 1966-67, regional pres. and trustee 1980—), Phi Delta Theta. Republican. Presbyterian. Clubs: Kiwanis (Civic award 1971), Athletic, Columbia, Service of Indpls., Army-Navy, Masons; Meridian Hills Country; Tippecanoe Lake Country. Home: 5349 Whisperwood Ln Indianapolis IN 46226 Office: 401 N College Ave Indianapolis IN 46206

MOORHEAD, THOMAS EDWARD, lawyer; b. Owosso, Mich., Aug. 27, 1946; s. Kenneth Edward and Lillian Jane (Becker) M.; B.A. in Communication Arts, Mich. State U., 1970; J.D., Detroit Coll. Law, 1973; m. Marjorie E. Semans, Sept. 9, 1967; children—Robert Scott, Kristine Elizabeth. Admitted to Mich. bar, 1973; legal counsel Legis. Service Bur., State of Mich., Lansing, 1973-74; partner firm Des Jardins, Des Jardins & Moorhead, Owosso, 1974—. Pres., Bentley Sch. PTO, Owosso; mem. adminstrv. bd. 1st United Meth. Ch., Owosso; bd. dirs. Shiawassee Arts Council; treas. Cub Scout Pack 67 Boy Scouts Am. Mem. Am. Bar Assn., Shiawassee County Bar Assn. (pres.-elect), State Bar of Mich., Owosso Jaycees (pres.; named Outstanding Local Pres. by state assn. 1977). Republican. Home: 800 Riverlane Owosso MI 48867 Office: 312 W Main St Owosso MI 48867

MOORHEAD, THOMAS JAMES, pub. co. exec.; b. Evanston, Ill., Apr. 7, 1930; s. Robert Emmet and Madeline (McGrath) M.; B.S., Loyola U., Chgo., 1953; M.B.A., Northwestern U., 1955; m. Jill Atwood, June 25, 1960; children—Julie, Michael, James, Thomas, Steven. Asst. to pres. City Products Corp. div. HFC, 1958-60; sales mgr. Fawcett Publs., 1960-68; partner Grant, Howlett & Moorhead, N.Y.C., 1968-80; pres. Moorhead Communications, Inc., Northbrook, Ill., 1980—, No. Properties, Inc., Lake Forest, Ill., 1972-80. Co-chmn. fin. campaign State Ill., Ronald Reagan, 1976. Served with USNR, 1953. Mem. Pharm. Mfrs. Assn., Midwest Pharm. Advt. Club (pres. 1975). Republican. Roman Catholic. Clubs: Knollwood, Winter (Lake Forest, Ill.); North Star. Home: 401 Ahwahnee Lake Forest IL 60045 Office: 899 Skokie Blvd Northbrook IL 60062

MOORMAN, RUTH HELM, ednl. adminstr.; b. Franklin County, Va., Jan. 30, 1929; d. Herbert G. and Willie (Bond) Helm; B.S., Va. State U., 1952; M.A., Eastern Mich. U., 1960; Ph.D. (Univ. fellow), U. Mich., 1973; m. Golden Turner Moorman; 1 dau., Tanya Vedette. Tchr., Franklin County public schs., Rocky Mount, Va., 1952-56, Edmonson Jr. High Sch., Ypsilanti, Mich., 1956-60; tchr. Willow Run Community Schs., Ypsilanti, 1960-64, reading cons., 1964-70, adult edn. tchr., 1968-70; counselor emotionally disturbed boys U. Mich., Ann Arbor, 1970, research asst., 1971-73, co-dir. community agt. tng., 1973-76; asst. prof. Wayne State U., Detroit, 1973-75; dir. personnel and instrn. Willow Run Community Schs., Ypsilanti, Mich., 1975-77, asst. supt. schs., 1977—; cons. edn., bus. and profl. agys. and orgns., 1970—; guest lectr. various univs., 1972—; chmn. bd. Specialty Enterprises, Inc., 1981—. Bd. dirs. Willow Run Council for Arts, 1976—. U. Mich. Inst. Social Research grantee, 1971-73. Mem. Am. Assn. Sch. Adminstrs., Assn. Curriculum Devel., Mich. Assn. Sch. Age Parents, Nat. Council Negro Women, Ypsilanti Bus. and Profl. League, NAACP, Internat. Reading Assn., Phi Delta Kappa, Delta Kappa Gamma, Alpha Kappa Alpha. Baptist. Home: 46 E Forest St Ypsilanti MI 48197 Office: 2171 E Michigan Ave Ypsilanti MI 48197

MOOSBRUGGER, MARY COULTRIP, mktg. exec.; b. Urbana, Ill., Sept. 1, 1947; d. Donald Lyle and Charlotte Carol (Barber) Coultrip; B.A., U. Ill., 1969; postgrad. in bus. adminstrn. U. Chgo.; m. John Robert Moosbrugger, Apr. 24, 1971; children—Peter John, Kathryn Rose. Research analyst Leo Burnett Co., Chgo., 1969-72; research cons., study dir. Booz Allen & Hamilton, Chgo., 1972-73; research supr. Quaker Oats Co., Chgo., 1974-75; mgr. mktg. research Kitchens of Sara Lee, Deerfield, Ill., 1975-77; pres. Moosbrugger Mktg. Research, LaGrange Park, Ill., 1977—. Mem. Am. Mktg. Assn. (guest speaker Midwest research conf. 1975). Roman Catholic. Address: 934 N Brainard Ave LaGrange Park IL 60525

MORACZEWSKI, ROBERT LEO, magazine editor; b. St. Paul, Nebr., May 13, 1942; s. Leo J. and Florence (Wadas) M.; B.S., U. Nebr., 1964; m. Virginia Rohman, Aug. 12, 1960; children—Mark, Matt, Monica, Mike. Asso. editor The Farmer, St. Paul, Minn., 1964-72; mng. editor Farm Industry News, St. Paul, Minn., 1972-74; editor Big Farmer, Frankfort, Ill., 1974-75; editorial dir. Webb Ag Services, St. Paul, 1975-76; editor/gen. mgr. Farm Industry News, St. Paul, 1976—. Recipient Writing award Chgo. Bd. Trade, 1969; Pfizer Nat. Writing award, 1971. Mem. Am. Agrl. Editors Assn., Nat. Agrl. Marketers Assn. Roman Catholic. Contbr. numerous articles to mags. Office: 1999 Shepard Rd Saint Paul MN 55116

MORAIN, FREDERICK GARVER, editor, pub.; b. Jefferson, Iowa, June 1, 1941; s. Frederick Elwyn and Lois Irene (Garver) M.; A.A., Graceland Coll., 1961; B.A., U. Iowa, 1963; M.A., Yale U., 1965, Ph.D., 1970; m. Kathleen Anne Boyle Murray, Feb. 2, 1980; 1 son David; stepchildren—Daniel Murray, Molly Murray. News editor, asst. pub. Bee & Herald Pub. Co., Jefferson, 1967-76, editor, pub., 1976—. Mem. Iowa Republican State Central Com., 1975-79; chmn. Greene County Rep. Central Com., 1972-75. Mem. Iowa Press Assn., Nat. Newspaper Assn., Jefferson C. of C. (pres. 1979), Phi Beta Kappa. Club: Rotary (pres. 1973-74). Home: 105 S Maple St Jefferson IA 50129 Office: 214 N Wilson St Jefferson IA 50129

MORAN, CHARLES FRANCIS, union ofcl.; b. Holyoke, Mass., Nov. 16, 1917; s. Charles Henry Edward and Laura (Horrigan) M.; m. Marie Ahern, Sept. 12, 1964. Sec. Lodge 621, Internat. Brotherhood of Boilermakers, Iron Shipbuilders and Helpers Am., 1942-46, sec. Holyoke Central Labor Union, 1944-47, dist. rep., 1946-59, internat. v.p., 1959-73; sec.-treas. Internat. Brotherhood of

Boilermakers, Iron Ship Builders, Blacksmiths, Forgers and Helpers, Kansas City, Kans., 1973—. Office: 565 New Brotherhood Bldg Kansas City KS 66101

MORAN, DONALD RICHARD, coll. adminstr.; b. Thomasboro, Ill., Mar. 5, 1933; s. Patrick Phillip and Margaret F. (Benting) M.; student Western Ill. Tchrs. Coll., 1950; B.S., Eastern Ill. U., 1957; M.Ed., U. Ill., 1966; B.M., U. Ky., 1977; m. Judyth Ann Tenenholtz, July 31, 1978; children—Lisa Ann Moran Busboom, Lori Jean, Lynda Kay. Tchr., Rantoul (Ill.) High Sch., 1957-67; faculty Parkland Coll., Champaign, Ill., 1967—, div. chmn. bus., 1968-73, asst. bus. mgr., 1973-75, bus. mgr., 1975—; sec. bd. dirs. Rantoul Motor Sales Inc., 1961-72, Kingman Datsun Inc., Champaign, 1973-76. Mem. Ch. Bd., Am. Luth. Ch., Champaign, 1965-68, chmn. deacons, 1968; bd. edn. Rantoul High Sch. Dist. 137, 1970-73. Served with U.S. Army, 1951-54. Mem. Champaign C. of C. (dir. 1979, treas. 1981), Ill. Community Coll. Assn. Bus. Ofcls. (dir. 1978—, chmn. 1980), Ill. Assn. Sch. Bus. Ofcls., Nat. Assn. Sch. Bus. Ofcls. (registered sch. bus. ofcl., sch. bus. adminstr.), Chi Gamma Iota, Delta Pi Epsilon. Republican. Clubs: Kiwanis, Rotary, Moose. Home: 203 W Elmore Dr Thomasboro IL 61878 Office: 2400 W Bradley Ave Champaign IL 61820

MORAN, JOHN FRANCIS, devel. center exec.; b. Chgo., Nov. 3, 1946; s. John James and Edith Evelyn (Weaver) M.; A.B., St. Louis U., 1969; M.S. Ed., So. Ill. U., Edwardsville, 1971; Ph.D., St. Louis U., 1978; m. Barbara JoAnne Maisonneuve, June 6, 1970; children—Amy Christine, Kate Elizabeth. Tchr. severely retarded high sch. students, Kankakee, Ill., 1969-70; tchr. mildly retarded high sch. students Wood River (Ill.) High Sch., 1970-73; dir. deaf blind program, dir. staff devel. Kiel Sch., St. Louis State Sch. and Hosp., 1973-75; coordinator staff devel., dir. media and TV prodn. Gov. Samuel Shapiro Devel. Center, Kankakee, 1975—; pres. Video Inventory Systems, Bradley, Ill., 1978—; cons. Mo. Dept. Mental Health, 1978—; instr. St. Louis U., 1972-74, So. Ill. U., 1973—, Kankakee Community Coll., 1976-79. Maj., tng. officer Aux. Police, Bourbonnais, Ill., 1976—. Mem. Am. Soc. Tng. and Devel., Am. Assn. Law Enforcement Officers, St. Jude Police League. Roman Catholic. Editor, Healthcare Protection Mgmt. Jour., 1981—. Home: 291 Coyne St Bourbonnais IL 60914 Office: Shapiro Devel Center 100 E Jeffery St Kankakee IL 60901

MORAN, JOHN VINCENT, lawyer; b. Detroit, Oct. 8, 1913; s. Edward J. and Margaret (Quigley) M.; A.B., U. Detroit, 1935; LL.B., U. Mich., 1938; m. Ellen Thompson, July 5, 1943; children—John T., Edward T. Legal research asst. Mich. Supreme Court, 1938-39; transp. bus., Detroit, 1939-40; practice in Detroit, 1940-43, 46—; dir. McCormick Industries, Inc. Served from pvt. to capt. AUS, 1943-46. Mem. Cath. Lawyers' Soc. (dir., past pres.), Mich. State Bar Assn. (dist. chmn. character and fitness com.), Alpha Sigma Nu. Author articles in field. Home: 292 Merriweather Rd Grosse Pointe Farms MI 48236 Office: 3263 City National Bank Bldg Detroit MI 48226

MORAN, THOMAS JOSEPH, justice Supreme Ct. Ill.; b. Waukegan, Ill., July 17, 1920; s. Cornelius Patrick and Avis Rose (Tyrrell) M.; B.A., Lake Forest Coll., 1947, J.D. (hon.), 1977; J.D., Ill. Inst. Tech.-Chgo. Kent Law Sch., 1950; m. Mary Jane Wasniewski, Oct. 4, 1941; children—Avis Marie, Kathleen, Mary Jane, Thomas G. Admitted to Ill. bar; individual practice law, 1950-56; state's atty., Lake County, Ill., 1956-58; judge Probate Ct. 19th Circuit, 1961-64; judge Appellate Ct. 2d Dist., 1964-76; justice Ill. Supreme Ct., 1976—; mem. faculty Appellate Judges seminars N.Y. U., Continuing Legal Edn. seminars La. State U. Served with USCG. Mem. Inst. Jud. Adminstrn., Am. Judicature Soc., Am. Bar Assn., Ill. Bar Assn., Lake County Bar Assn. Office: 215 N Utica St Waukegan IL 60085

MORANKAR, SUDHAKAR DATTATRAY, machine devel. engr.; b. India, Oct. 10, 1944; s. Dattatray V. and Sulochana (Dattatray) M.; came to U.S., 1968; M.S. in Indsl. Engring., Okla. State U., 1969, M.S. in Mech. Engring., 1971; M.B.A., Northwestern U., 1981; m. Vijaya Mahadeo Shukla, Oct. 8, 1971; children—Anand, Madhavi. Tool designer Crane Packing Co., Morton Grove, Ill., 1971-72, machine devel. engr., 1972—. Co-chmn. Smithsonian on Tour-India, India League Am., Chgo., 1976. Mem. ASME (chmn. Skokie Valley subsect. 1980-81), Maharashtra Mandal of Chgo. (sec. 1975-76, v.p. 1977-78, pres. 1978-79). Home: 1418 Redbud Ln Glenview IL 60025 Office: 6400 W Oakton St Morton Grove IL 60053

MORARAS, THEERAGUL, physician; b. Sakolnakorn, Thailand, Sept. 8, 1942; came to U.S., 1966, naturalized, 1978; s. Chantr and Tonglaud M.; M.D., Chiengmai Med. Sch., 1965; Intern, Youngstown (Ohio) Hosp. Assn., 1966-67; resident in medicine St. Francis Hosp., Evanston, Ill., 1967-70, fellow in cardiology, 1970-72; practice medicine specializing in internal medicine and cardiovascular disease, Evanston, 1972—; mem. staff St. Francis Hosp., 1972—, dir. coronary care unit, 1974—; clin. asst. prof. medicine Loyola U., Chgo., 1977. Diplomate Am. Bd. Internal Medicine. Fellow Am. Coll. Cardiology; mem. AMA, Ill. State Med. Soc., Chgo. Med. Soc., Am. Soc. Echocardiography, Am. Heart Assn. Buddhist. Home: 3633 W Grove St Skokie IL 60076 Office: 800 Austin St Suite 504 Evanston IL 60202

MORASON, ROBERT HENRY, dentist; b. Toledo, Jan. 30, 1938; s. Henry and Jenniveve M.; A.B., Miami U., Oxford, Ohio, 1960; D.D.S., Ohio State U., 1964; m. Peggy Jean Kappelman, May 3, 1963; children—Cathrine, Robert Todd. Individual practice dentistry, Toledo, 1964—. Mem. N.W. Ohio Cancer Planning Network; adviser diversified health occupations. dept. Sylvania (Ohio) Schs. Served with USAF, 1966; now maj. USAF Res. Decorated Air Force Commendation medal. Mem. ADA, Ohio Dental Assn., Toledo Dental Soc. (chmn. peer rev. com. 1977—, pres. 1981—), Acad. Gen. Dentistry (dir. dist. 3 Ohio chpt. 1979), Mil. Surgeons Assn. U.S., Res. Officers Assn. U.S., Pierre Fauchard Acad., Sigma Alpha Epsilon. Editor Family Dentist, newsletter Ohio Acad. Gen. Dentistry. Home: 4835 Rudgate Blvd Toledo OH 43623 Office: 3030 Sylvania Ave Toledo OH 43613

MORAVEC, DANIEL FRANCIS, pharmacist, hosp. pharm. adminstr.; b. St. Paul, Nebr., May 16, 1919; s. Louis E. and Emily M. (Bartle) M.; A.B., U. Nebr., 1946, B.S. in Pharmacy, 1949, M.S., 1950, postgrad., 1950-51; m. Marion Elizabeth Dredla, Feb. 4, 1944; 1 son, Daniel Francis. Pharmacist, Wagey Drug Co., Lincoln, 1950-51; dir. pharmacy Lincoln Gen. Hosp., 1951—; mem. faculty dept. pharmacy U. Nebr., 1955-60; guest lectr. hosp. pharmacy U. Tex., 1958; cons. hosp. pharmacy Letourneau & Assos., Chgo., 1960-68. Served to 1st lt., arty. U.S. Army, 1941-46; ETO. Recipient Feinberg award N.Y. Pharm. Assn., 1954. Mem. Am. Soc. Hosp. Pharmacists, Nebr. Soc. Hosp. Pharmacists (pres. 1952-55), Am. Pharm. Assn., Nebr. Pharmacists Assn., Sigma Xi, Rho Chi, Phi Kappa Psi. Co-author: Intravenous Therapy, 1967; contbr. articles to profl. jours.; feature editor Pharm. Salesman, 1974-78; pharmacy editor Hosp. Mgmt. Mag., 1954-74, Today's Nursing Home, 1981—. Home: 5105 Washington St Lincoln NE 68506 Office: 2300 S 16th St Lincoln NE 68506

MORAVY, GERALD JAY, transp. services co. exec.; b. Mt. Pleasant, Mich., Aug. 15, 1937; s. Herbert Lee and Ida Blanche (Ankrom) M.; student pub. schs., Mt. Pleasant; m. Evelyn Joyce Tyler, May 8, 1964; children—Steven James, Michael Wayne, Sherry Lynn, Kimberly Yvonne (dec.), Jeremy Jay. Truck driver Gordon Drilling Co., Mt. Pleasant, 1954-59; driller McClure Drilling Corp., Mt. Pleasant, 1959-61; toolpusher N.Am. Drilling Co., Mt. Pleasant, 1961-64, Moco Drilling Co., Mt. Pleasant, 1964-67) pres. Moravy Trucking Co., Mt. Pleasant, 1967—, also Midwest Pollution Control; sec.-treas. Aviation Services, Inc., Mt. Pleasant. Mem. Mich. Oil and Gas Assn., Mich. Trucking Assn., Mich. Ltd. Carriers Assn., Independent Petroleum Assn., Liquid Indsl. Control Assn. (dir. 1977—). Baptist. Clubs: Kiwanis, Moose, Elks. Home: 2051 S Lincoln Rd Mount Pleasant MI 48858 Office: 1934 Commercial Dr Mount Pleasant MI 48858

MORDECAI, BENJAMIN, theatre dir.; b. N.Y.C., Dec. 10, 1944; s. Allen Lewis and Florence (Goldman) M.; B.A., Buena Vista Coll., 1967; M.A., Eastern Mich. U., 1968; postgrad. Ind. U., 1968-70; m. Sherry Lynn Morley, July 20, 1974; 1 dau., Rachel Elizabeth. Costumer; co-founder, producing dir. Ind. Repertory Theatre, Indpls., 1972—. Cons. Found. for Extension and Devel. Am. Profl. Theatre, from 1974. Bd. dirs. Hosp. Audiences, Inc., Indpls., from 1974, pres., 1975; pres. Profl. Cultural Alliance, Indpls., from 1976. Mem. Am. Theatre Assn., League Resident Theatres (chmn. children's theatre com. from 1974, exec. com. from 1976). Producer, dir. Am. premiere: Bird in the Hand, 1975. Home: 5255 N New Jersey St Indianapolis IN 46220 Office: 140 W Washington Indianapolis IN 46204

MOREHEAD, ROGER WARREN, editor; b. Los Angeles, Apr. 9, 1944; s. Warren Oliver and Irene Edna M.; B.A., Ft. Wayne Bible Coll., 1967; M.A. cum laude, Wheaton Coll., 1971; m. Elizabeth Ann Ellis, June 6, 1966; children—David, Cynthia, Daniel. Phys. distbn. mgr. Tyndale House Pubs., Wheaton, Ill., 1970-71, asst. prodn. mgr., 1971-78; mng. editor David C. Cook Pub. Co., Elgin, Ill., 1978—. Office: 850 N Grove Ave Elgin IL 60120

MOREHOUSE, RICHARD EDWARD, coll. adminstr.; b. LaCrosse, Wis., May 21, 1941; s. Ervin Lenard and Anna (Weiland) M.; B.S., U. Wis., LaCrosse, 1971, M.S.T., 1973; Ph.D. in Program Design and Implementation, Union Grad. Sch., 1979; m. Rita May Spangler, Aug. 20, 1966; 1 dau., Lyda Ann. Tchr. history Aquinas High Sch., 1966-67; faculty asst. div. tchr. edn. U. Wis., LaCrosse, 1971-72, lectr., 1973-80; ednl. cons., fed. program coordinator Coop. Ednl. Services Agy., LaCrosse, 1971-80; dir. coop. edn., lectr. psychology Viterbo Coll., LaCrosse, 1980—; instr. workshops Western Wis. Tech. Sch., 1977-79. Mem. exec. bd. LaCrosse County Democratic Party, 1977; mem. adv. bd. Western Dist. Employment and Tng., 1980—. Mem. Am. Ednl. Research Assn., Midwestern Ednl. Research Assn., Wis. Ednl. Research Assn., Phi Delta Kappa. Unitarian. Author: Is Drug Education Effective: An Evaluation of Two Methods of Instruction, 1975. Home: 1131 Charles St LaCrosse WI 54601 Office: Viterbo College 815 S 9th St LaCrosse WI 54601

MORELAND, WILLIAM JOHN, real estate broker; b. Chgo., Feb. 21, 1916; s. James C. and Izora M. (McCabe) M.; A.B., U. Ill., 1938; student Northwestern U., 1937. With James C. Moreland & Son, Inc., real estate and home building, Chgo., 1938—, pres., 1952—; pres. Moreland Realty, Inc., Chgo., 1952-72. Builder, operator Howard Johnson Motor Lodge, Chgo., 1960-72. Helped develop model housing community, El Salvador, Central Am., 1960's. Presidential appointment to commerce com. for Alliance for Progress, 1962-64. Served to lt. USNR, 1941-46. Mem. Home Bldrs. Assn. Chicagoland (pres. 1961-62), Chgo. Assn. Commerce and Industry, Chgo., N.W. real estate bds., N.W. Bldrs. Assn., Nat. Assn. Home Bldrs. (hon. life dir. 1972—), Chi Psi. Republican. Roman Catholic. Office: 5717 Milwaukee Ave Chicago IL 60646

MORETSKY, LEWIS ROBERT, telecommunication cons. co. exec.; b. Bklyn., Aug. 25, 1940; s. Samuel and Shirley (Wexelbaum) M.; B.S. in Public Accounting, N.Y. U., 1963; M.A. with honors in Bus., Central Mo. State U., 1971; m. Rhoda L. Weisler; children—Susan Faye, David Michael, Michele Amy Weisler, Brett Alan Weisler. Treas., United System Supply, Inc., Westwood, Kans., North Electric Co., Lenexa, Kans.; mgr. sales Original Equipment Mfg., 1971-73, eastern regional mktg. mgr., 1973-75, nat. accounts sales rep., 1975-77; mgr. consumer products North Supply Co., Lenexa, 1977-79; treas., chief operating officer Suma Corp., Lenexa, 1979—. Served to capt. USAF, 1963-68. Home: 9015 High Dr Leawood KS 66206

MORGAN, BETTY JEAN SCHIERLOH, counselor; b. St. Louis, July 12, 1946; d. Arthur Frederick and Erna Margaret Elizabeth (Dempewolf) Schierloh; student Meramec Community Coll., 1964-66; B.S. in Elem. Edn., S.E. Mo. State U., 1968; scholar Eden Theol. Sem., 1975; M.Ed. in Gen. Counseling, U. Mo., St. Louis, 1977; m. John Stephen Morgan, May 27, 1967; 1 dau., Jennifer Marie. Tchr., Mehlville Sch. Dist., St. Louis, 1968-69, South San Antonio Sch. Dist., 1969-70, Normandy Sch. Dist., St. Louis, 1971-75; elem. guidance counselor Windsor Sch. Dist., Imperial, Mo., 1978—; pvt. practice guidance counseling, Imperial. Co-chair peace action com. Calvary United Ch. of Christ, 1972-73; active civil rights movement. Mem. Am. Personnel and Guidance Assn., Assn. Humanistic Edn. and Devel., Am. Sch. Counselor Assn., Mo. Guidance Assn., Jefferson County Guidance Assn. (v.p. 1980-81). Home: 2201 Meadow Dr Barnhart MO 63012

MORGAN, CLAUDE D'VAL, III, mktg. firm exec.; b. Carthage, Mo., Dec. 17, 1947; s. Claude D'Val and Margaret (Speer) M.; B.S. in Bus. Adminstrn., Mo. So. State U., 1970; m. Kathryn Morrow, Jan. 6, 1973; children—Claude D'Val IV, Thomas Michael, Amelia Morrow. News dir. KDMO-AM, Carthage, 1965-67; news dir., regional sales mgr., gen. sales mgr., asst. sta. mgr. KTVJ-TV (CBS), Joplin, Mo., 1967-74; pres. Morgan & Assos., Inc., Joplin, 1974—. Bd. dirs. Mo-kan council Boy Scouts Am., 1979—, Spiva Art Center, 1979—; mem. Jasper County Republican Com., 1968—; mem. blue ribbon adv. council U. Mo. Sch. Journalism, 1975, Mo. Council for Higher Edn., 1978. Mem. Am. Assn. Advt. Agys., Public Utility Communicators Assn., Mo. Asso. Press Broadcasters Assn., Mo. Radio/TV News Dirs. Assn., Aircraft Pilots and Owners Assn., Joplin C. of C. (dir. 1978-80). Roman Catholic. Home: 1905 Southwood Ln Carthage MO 64836 Office: Morgan & Assos Inc 3d and Main Sts Joplin MO 64801 also 207 W Center Fayetteville AR 72701

MORGAN, GEORGE ERNEST, newspaper exec.; b. Wichita, Kans., Oct. 7, 1933; s. Guy Wesley and Mildred Martha (Mahlandt) M.; m. Ellen Nannie Copeland, July 15, 1954; children—Catherine Marie, Cheryl Lynn. With Enquirer and News, Battle Creek, Mich., 1950—, pressroom foreman, 1965-73, prodn. mgr., 1973-78, prodn. dir., 1978—. Served with U.S. Army, 1953-55. Mem. Nat. Mgmt. Assn. (pres. Wolverine council 1972), Battle Creek Mgmt. Club (pres. 1970). Baptist. Home: 10638 Verona Rd Battle Creek MI 49017 Office: 155 W Van Buren St Battle Creek MI 49016

MORGAN, GLEN MICHAEL, ednl. adminstr.; b. Marquette, Mich., Oct. 28, 1946; s. Glen Frank and Margaret Ann (Rozum) M.; B.S., No. Mich. U., 1970; M.S. in Teaching, U. Wis., Oshkosh, 1973, M.S. in Supervision and Curriculum, 1979; m. Connie Jean Engman, Sept. 23, 1967; children—Michelle, Kristin. Supr. gen. edn. Lakeshore Tech. Inst., Cleveland, Wis., 1970—; cons. in listening/communications, 1970—. Chmn. Mayors Ad Hoc Refugee Resettlement Com., 1979—; mem. Wis. Council on Aging. Mem. Am. Vocat. Assn., Wis. Vocat. Assn., Kappa Delta Pi. Contbr. articles to profl. jours. Home: 1611 George St Manitowoc WI 54220

MORGAN, GRAHAM JAMES, mfg. exec.; b. Aurora, Ill., Sept. 19, 1917; s. Caradoc James and Nina Hermana (Herbrandson) M.; B.A., Carleton Coll., 1938; m. Nancy Loraine Meeker, June 15, 1940 (dec. Oct. 1948); 1 dau., Heather Lynn; m. 2d, Vernile Ann Murrin, 1952. With U.S. Gypsum Co., 1939—, successively in sales, dist. mgr., Omaha, div. mgr. Western div., Midwest div., mdse. mgr. insulation products, gen. mdse. mgr., v.p. merchandising, 1939-54, v.p., asst. to chmn. bd., 1954-59, exec. v.p., 1959-61, pres., 1960-71, chmn., chief exec. officer, 1971—, dir., 1958—, chief exec. officer, 1965-71; dir. BPB Industries, Ltd., London, Eng., Am. Hosp. Supply Co., Evanston, Ill., IC Industries, Ill. Central Gulf R.R., Ill. Bell Telephone Co., Internat. Harvester Co., Trans Union Corp.; adv. bd. Kemper Ins. Co. Mem. nat. adv. com. Housing Center; past vice chmn. Pres.'s Com. on Urban Housing. Bd. dirs. Chgo. Boys Clubs, Chgo. Central Area Com., Northwestern Meml. Hosp., Nat. Park Found.; trustee Orchestral Assn., Northwestern U., Mus. Sci. and Industry; mem. Council Medicine and Biology of U. Chgo. Recipient Housing and Urban Devel. Pioneer medal U.S. Dept. Health, Edn. and welfare; (past v.p., dir.), Hardboard Assn. (past dir.), Bldg. Research Inst. (dir.). Office: 101 S Wacker Dr Chicago IL 60606

MORGAN, J. P., state supreme ct. justice; b. Silex, Mo., June 12, 1917; s. John P. and Pearl J. (Bagbey) M.; B.S., N.W. Mo. State U., 1940; J.D., U. Mo., 1947; m. Emma Lee Vance, May 3, 1941; children—Bill, Betty Morgan Osborne, John. Admitted to Mo. bar; city atty. City of Chillicothe (Mo.), 4 years; pros. atty. Livingston County, Mo., 6 years; circuit judge 43d Jud. Circuit, 6 years; judge Ct. Appeals, Kansas City (Mo.) Dist., 2 years; now justice Mo. Supreme Ct., Jefferson City. Served with USAAF, World War II; CBI. Mem. Am. Bar Assn., Mo. Bar, Am. Judicature Soc. Lion (Mo. chmn. 1954). Office: Supreme Court Bldg Jefferson City MO 65101

MORGAN, JAMES EDWIN, roofing-sheet metal co. exec.; b. Evansville, Ind., Feb. 13, 1928; s. James W. and Ruth M.; grad. Solar Tng. Inst., 1980; m. Ruby E. Letterman, Oct. 22, 1949; children—James R., Dennis D. Draftsman, Mesker Steel, Evansville, 1946-50; sheet metal worker Tri State Sheet Metal Co., Evansville, 1950-52; with Midwest Roofing-Sheet Metal Co., 1952—, pres., 1976—. Bd. dirs. Boy Scout Council, 1974—, v.p., 1978—; pres. Evansville Lutheran Found., 1979—; bd. dirs. Evansville Protestant Home, 1978—, Evansville Lutheran Community Action, 1980—, Solar Tng. Inst., 1980—. Served with N.G., 1949-74. Republican. Home: 2009 N Heidelbach Ave Evansville IN 47711 Office: Midwest Roofing-Sheet Metal Co 1208 N Harlan Ave Evansville IN 47711

MORGAN, JANE HALE, library adminstr.; b. Dines, Wyo., May 11, 1926; d. Arthur Hale and Billie (Wood) Hale; B.A., Howard U., 1947; M.A., U. Denver, 1954; m. Joseph Charles Morgan, Aug. 12, 1955; children—Joseph Hale, Jane Frances, Ann Michele. Mem. staff Detroit Public Library, 1954—, exec. asst. dir., 1973-75, dep. dir., 1975-78, dir., 1978—. Mem. Mich. Library Consortium Bd., exec. bd. Southeastern Mich. Regional Film Library; mem. Mich. State Library Adv. Council. Trustee New Detroit, Inc.; v.p. United Found.; pres. Univ.-Cultural Center Assn.; bd. dirs. Rehab. Inst., YWCA. Mem. ALA, Mich. Library Assn., Urban League, NAACP, Women's Econ. Club, Women's Nat. Book Assn., Assn. Mcpl. Profl. Women, Alpha Kappa Alpha. Democrat. Episcopalian. Home: 19358 Lauder St Detroit MI 48235 Office: Detroit Public Library 5201 Woodward Ave Detroit MI 48202

MORGAN, JANET RAE, counselor; b. Fargo, N.D., Apr. 4, 1933; d. Russell C. and Sylvia L. (Gustafson) M.; B.A., Macalester Coll., 1955; M.A. in Ednl. Psychology, U. Minn., 1960; postgrad. St. Cloud State U., 1977. Dir. religious edn. St. Paul's United Ch., St. Paul, 1955-58; guidance counselor S. St. Paul High Sch., 1959—, chairperson guidance dept., 1969—; mem. Nat. Adv. Council Edns. Profl. Devel. Act, 1972-74, Human Services Occupational Adv. Council, 1979-81. Mem. tchr. adv. com. State Bd. Edn., Minn., 1967-69; mem. Minn. Gov.'s Human Services Occupational Adv. Bd., 1979—; scholarship coordinator Ind. Republican Com., 1976; chairperson secondary edn. sect. Republican Task Force on Edn., 1968. Mem. Am. Personnel and Guidance Assn., Am. Sch. Counselors Assn. (Secondary Sch. Counselor of Year award 1979, chair govt. relations com. 1981), Nat. Vocat. Guidance Assn., NEA (del. to convs. 1961-70), Minn. Edn. Assn. (commr. legis. commn. 1971-75, 76-79), Minn. Vocat. Guidance Assn., Minn. Sch. Counselors Assn. (Sch. Counselor of Year award 1978), St. Paul Suburban Counselors Assn., AAUW (mem. scholarship trust com. 1963-68), Delta Kappa Gamma (past chpt. pres.). Home: 1945 Oakdale Ave W Saint Paul MN 55118 Office: 700 N 2d St S Saint Paul MN 55075

MORGAN, JEROLD LYNN, bus. machines co. exec.; b. Marshalltown, Iowa, Sept. 20, 1951; s. Mervin Rolland M.; B.A., S.W. Bapt. Coll., 1973; M.B.A., S.W. Mo. State U., 1977. Asst. mgr. Thrifty Drug & Discount, Los Angeles, 1974; sales rep. Amco Wholesale Inc., Springfield, Mo., 1975-76; account mgr., fin. systems NCR Corp., Springfield, 1978—. Republican. Methodist. Home: 2020 E Bennett Apt C11 Springfield MO 65804 Office: NCR Corp 1315 E Battlefield St Springfield MO 65802

MORGAN, JOHN DERALD, educator; b. Hays, Kans., Mar. 15, 1939; s. John Baber and Avis Ruth (Wolf) M.; B.S. in Elec. Engring., La. Tech. U., 1962; M.S. in Elec. Engring., U. Mo., Rolla, 1965; Ph.D., Ariz. State U., 1968; m. Elizabeth June McKneely, June 23, 1962; children—Laura Elizabeth, Kimberly Ann, Rebecca Ruth, John Derald. Elec. engr. Tex. Eastman div. Eastman Kodak, 1962-63; instr. elec. engring. U. Mo., Rolla, 1963-65; instr. Ariz. State U., 1965-68; asso. prof. elec. engring. U. Mo., Rolla, 1968-72, Alcoa Found. prof. elec. engring., 1972-75, chmn. dept., 1978—, asso. dir. Center for Internat. Programs, 1974-78, Emerson Electric prof. elec. engring., 1976—; cons. Ariz. Pub. Service, Westinghouse, Electric Power Research Inst., Union Electric Co., A. B. Chance Co., Black & Veatch, Emerson Electric, Mobil. Pres. bd. trustees First Meth. Ch., 1973-75; v.p. bd. adminstrn. People to People, 1976; bd. dirs., cubmaster Ozarks dist. Boy Scouts Am., 1968-79, asst. dist. commr., 1972-73, dist. chmn. Meramec dist., 1979-81; bd. dirs. Partners of the Americas. Recipient Scouters Key award Ozarks council Boy Scouts Am., 1971; T. H. Harris scholar, 1959-61, John H. Horton scholar, 1961-62; registered profl. engr., Mo. Mem. IEEE (sec. power system engring. com. 1979-81, vice chmn. 1981—, award of honor St. Louis sect. 1979), Am. Soc. Engring. Edn., Nat., Mo. socs. profl. engrs., Engrs. Club St. Louis (awards and recognition com. 1971-75, edn. com. 1970-74), Sigma Xi, Tau Beta Pi, Eta Kappa Nu, Omicron Delta Kappa, Phi Kappa Phi. Author: Power Apparatus Testing Techniques, 1969; Computer Monitoring and Control of Electric Utility Systems, 1972; Control and Distribution of Megawatta Through Man-Machine Interaction, 1973; contbr. articles to profl. jours. Home: Route 4 Box 112 Rolla MO 65401 Office: 123 Elec Engring U Missouri Rolla MO 65401

MORGAN, JUNE P., state supreme ct. justice; b. Silex, Mo., June 12, 1917; s. John and Pearl Jane (Bagbey) M.; B.S., N.W. Mo. State U., 1940; J.D., U. Mo., Columbia, 1947; m. Emma Lee Vance, May 3, 1941; children—William V., Betty Ann Morgan Osborne, John Lee. Admitted to Mo. bar, practice law, Chillicothe, Mo.; former pros. atty. Livingston County (Mo.); judge 43d Jud. Circuit, 1961-67, Kansas City (Mo.) Ct. Appeals, 1967-69; justice Mo. Supreme Ct., 1969—, chief justice, 1977-79. Bd. regents N.W. Mo. State U. Served in USAF, 1941-46. Recipient Disting. Grad. award N.W. Mo. State U., U. Mo. Law Sch., 1978. Mem. Conf. Chief Justices (dir.), Am. Bar Assn., Mo. Bar Assn., Am. Judicature Soc., Am. Legion. Mem. Christian Ch. Club: Lions (past dist. gov., state chmn.). Home: 2631 Schellridge Jefferson City MO 65101 Office: Supreme Ct Bldg Jefferson City MO 65101

MORGAN, LEE LAVERNE, tractor co. exec.; b. Aledo, Ill., Jan. 4, 1920; s. L. Laverne and Gladys (Hamilton) M.; B.S., U. Ill., 1941; m. Mary Harrington, Feb. 14, 1942. With Caterpillar Tractor Co., Peoria, Ill., 1946—, mgr. sales devel., 1954-61, v.p. charge engine div., 1961-65, exec. v.p., 1965-72, pres., 1972-77, chmn. bd., 1977—, also chief exec. officer, dir.; dir. 3M Co., Comml. Nat. Bank, Mobil Corp.; vice chmn. European Community-U.S. Businessmen's Council, Adv. Council on Japan-U.S. Econ. Relations. Bd. dirs. Monmouth Coll., Proctor Community Hosp.; trustee Conf. Bd., Com. for Econ. Devel. Served to maj. AUS, 1941-46. Mem. Soc. Automotive Engrs., Bus. Roundtable, Council Fgn. Relations. Presbyterian. Clubs: Masons, Peoria Country, Creve Coeur; Chicago, Union League (Chgo.); Tucson Nat. Golf; Augusta Nat. Office: Caterpillar Tractor Co 100 NE Adams St Peoria IL 61629

MORGAN, LEWIS V., JR., judge; b. Elmhurst, Ill., Dec. 17, 1929; s. Lewis V. and Meta (Schmidt) M.; B.A., DePauw U., 1951; J.D., U. Chgo., 1954; m. Marilyn F. Sherman, Nov. 17, 1950; children—Barbara Anne Morgan Oshlo, Lewis V. III, Diane Marie Reilly; m. 2d, Alice E. Phillips, May 8, 1971; m. 3d, Linda L. Holmes, Mar. 31, 1978; 1 dau., Laura Lynne. Admitted to Ill. bar, 1954; mem. law firm Locke & Locke, Glen Ellyn, Ill., 1956-59; practice law, Wheaton, Ill., 1959-75; partner law firm Redmond, Morgan, Mraz & Bennorth, 1965-70, Morgan & Wilkinson, 1972-74, Morgan & Van Duzer, 1974-75; asso. circuit judge 18th dist., DuPage County, Ill., 1975-81, circuit judge, 1981—; asst. state's atty., DuPage County, Ill., 1958-61; mem. Ill. Ho. Reps., 1963-71, chmn. elections com., 1967, 69, majority leader, 1969-71. Chmn. Milton Twp. Republican orgn., DuPage County, 1961; precinct committeeman Rep. party, 1957-66, 69-73. Chmn. Ill. Commn. on Atomic Energy, 1966-71; mem. County Bd. Sch. Trustees, DuPage County, 1973-75; trustee Wheaton Pub. Library, 1966-78; bd. dirs. DuPage County Family Service Assn., United Way of Wheaton, Inc. Served with AUS, 1954-56. Recipient Outstanding Legislator award Eagleton Inst. Politics, Rutgers U., 1965. Mem. Acad. Matrimonial Lawyers (bd. mgrs. Ill. chpt.), Ill., DuPage County bar assns., Ill. Trial Lawyers Assn. (former dir.), Ill. Judges Assn. (dir. 1978—), Sigma Nu. Methodist. Club: DuPage Writers. Contbg. author: DuPage Discovery, 1776-1976. Home: 1622 Coloma Pl Wheaton IL 60187 Office: DuPage County Courthouse Wheaton IL 60187

MORGAN, MELANIE MC KENZIE, advt. co. exec.; b. Chgo., Apr. 1, 1950; d. Robert H. and Olive (McKenzie) Satkowski; B.S.J., Northwestern U., 1972, M.S.J., 1973. With Internat. Harvester Corp., Chgo., 1973-80, project coordinator, 1974-76, planning coordinator export advt., 1976-77, agrl. program coordinator N.Am. ops., supr. comml. prodn. and scheduling U.S. Farm Report weekly TV program, 1977-78, supr. mktg. communications media programs and agrl. equipment N.Am. ops., 1978-80; account exec. copy/contact work Marsteller, Inc., Chgo., 1980—. Mem. Am. Mktg. Assn., Am. Soc. Profl. and Exec. Women. Club: Seafans Scuba Diving. Home: Wilmette IL 60091 Office: 401 N Michigan Ave N Chicago IL 60611

MORGAN, MICHAEL ALLEN, wholesale co. exec.; b. Gallipolis, Ohio, June 12, 1948; s. John Willard and Naomi Elizabeth (Long) M.; B.S., Eastern Ky. U., 1970; postgrad. Wright State U., 1972; m. Melody Lynn Lambert, July 31, 1971; children—Michael C., Amanda J. Tchr. scis., coach football Public Schs. Reedsville, Ohio, 1970-73; office mgr., sales mgr. Oak Hill Parts Inc. (Ohio), 1973-79; songwriter Green Pastures Music Inc., also Sugar Plum Music, Nashville, 1980—. Mem. Nashville Songwriters Assn., Eastern Ky. U. Alumni Assn., Country Music Assn., Nat. Acad. Rec. Arts and Scis. Methodist. Club: Masons. Composer songs: The Feel of Being Gone, 1979, I Was on My Way Before the Dawn, 1975, Let's Just Pretend, 1971, Washed in the Blood, 1980. Office: 134 Broadway St Jackson OH 45640

MORGAN, ROBERT DALE, judge; b. Peoria, Ill., May 27, 1912; s. Harry Dale and Eleanor (Ellis) M.; A.B., Bradley U., 1934; J.D., U. Chgo., 1937; m. Betty Louise Harbers, Oct. 14, 1939; children—Thomas Dale, James Robert. Admitted to Ill. bar, 1937; practiced in Peoria, 1937-42, 46-67, Chgo., 1946-50; partner firm Morgan, Pendarvis & Morgan, Peoria, 1946-57, Davis, Morgan & Witherell, Peoria, 1957-67; U.S. judge Central Dist. Ill., Peoria, 1967—, now chief judge. Mayor, Peoria, 1953-57; bd. dirs. YMCA Peoria, 1940-72, pres., 1947-53. Trustee Bradley U. Served from 1st lt. to maj., AUS, 1942-46. Mem. Am., Ill., Peoria County bar assns., Am. Judicature Soc. Presbyterian. Clubs: Rotary (pres. 1962-63), Creve Couer, Country (Peoria). Contbr. articles to law revs. Office: Room 216 Federal Bldg 100 NE Monroe St Peoria IL 61602

MORGAN, ROBERT EDWARD, state justice; b. Mitchell, S.D., Aug. 13, 1924; s. Chester Lawrence and Phyllis Mae (Saterlie) M.; student Creighton U., 1942, 46-47, 48; J.D., U. S.D., 1950; m. Mary Doyle, Oct. 28, 1950; children—Mary Alice, Michael Chester, Thomas Wayne, Margaret Jane; m. 2d, Mary Ann Ver Meulen, June 1, 1974; 1 son, Daniel James. Admitted to S.D. bar, 1950; mem. firm Mitchell & Chamberlain, S.D., 1950-76; justice S.D. Supreme Ct., Pierre, 1977—. Served with USAAF, 1943-45. Mem. S.D. Bar Assn. Club: Elks. Office: care U SD Sch Law Vermillion SD 57069

MORGAN, RONNIE GLEN, agrl. engr.; b. Waurika, Okla., Nov. 17, 1952; s. Glen Dale and Helen Lucille M.; B.S., Okla. State U., 1975, M.S., 1976; Ph.D., Tex. A&M U., 1979; m. Sharon Sue Lemons, May 25, 1974. Research asso. Tex. A&M U., College Station, 1976-77, instr. agrl. engring., 1977-79; project leader Ralston Purina Co., St. Louis, 1979-80, sr. project leader, 1980-81, dir. research and devel. info. systems, 1981—, mem. corp. devel. bd. Chmn. deacons Manchester Heights Baptist Ch., 1979-80. Mem. Am. Soc. Agrl. Engrs. (editor newsletter), Nat. Soc. Profl. Engrs., Inst. Food Technologists, Phi Kappa Phi, Tau Beta Pi, Alpha Zeta. Author articles in field. Home: 722 Wildview Manchester MO 63011 Office: 4RN Checkerboard Sq Saint Louis MO 63188

MORGAN, RUTH MILDRED, med. technologist; b. Indpls., Mar. 8, 1917; d. James Franklin and Lula Floy (Heiny) M.; B.S. in Allied Health Edn., Ind. U.-Purdue U., Indpls., 1976; student Ind. U., 1954-57, 76-77, Butler U., 1958. Dental asst., med. asst. and med. technologist, Indpls., 1953—; tchr. hematology Med. Lab., 1970-79, supr. hematology, 1960-79, gen. supr., 1980—. Fin. chmn. 8th precinct 20th Ward of Indpls., 1977-79. Recipient citation Mayor Richard Lugar, 1976; registered med. technologist, lic. health facility adminstr. Mem. Am. Soc. Clin. Pathologists (affiliate), Am. Soc. Profl. and Exec. Women, Marion County Council Republican Women, Nat. Fedn. Republican Women, Am. Coll. Nursing Home Adminstrs. (asso., asso. Ind. chpt.), Brown County Art Gallery Assn., Ind. Soc. Med. Technologists. Club: Eastern Star (matron 1950). Inventor, patentee cabinets for indsl. use. Office: 5940 W Raymond St Indianapolis IN 46241

MORGAN, WILLIAM FRANK, ednl. adminstr.; b. Robertsdale, Pa., Apr. 7, 1945; s. Jesse O. and Dorothy Catherine (Corrie) M.; B.A., Malone Coll., 1968; B.S., U. Akron, 1972, M.A., 1974; m. Patricia A. Alleshouse, May 22, 1977; children—Timothy William, Todd Jesse. Tchr., Brown Local Schs., Malvern, Ohio, 1968-69; account-clk. tchr. Plain Local Schs., Canton, Ohio, 1969-72, occupational coordinator Canton City Schs., 1972-75; adminstrv. asst. Marlington Local Schs., Alliance, Ohio, 1975—; guest lectr. U. Akron. Mem. budget com. United Fund; auditor Vol. Fire Dept. R.P.A., Ohio. Mem. Am. Assn. Sch. Adminstrs., Assn. Supervision and Curriculum Devel., Ohio Assn. Sch. Bus. Ofcls., Buckeye Assn. Sch. Adminstrs., Phi Delta Kappa. Home: 3310 Beechwood Ave Alliance OH 44601 Office: 10320 Moulin Ave NE Alliance OH 44601

MORGAN, WILLIAM RICHARD, plastic surgeon; b. Oahu, Hawaii, July 21, 1934; s. William Richard and Margaret (Eckhout) M.; B.S., U. Okla., 1955, M.D., 1958; m. Janice J. Kelly, Aug. 6, 1960; children—Amy Marie, Michael Christopher, Patrick Brian, Leigh Kathleen, Katherine Kelly, Mollie Kristin. Intern, Cin. Gen. Hosp., 1958-59; gen. surgery resident, U. Okla., Oklahoma City, 1959-63; practice medicine specializing in gen. surgery, Yuma, Ariz., 1965-71; resident in plastic surgery Kans. U., Kansas City, 1971-73; practice medicine specializing in plastic surgery, Kansas City, Mo., 1973—; pres. med. staff St. Joseph Hosp., Kansas City, 1981—. Served with USN, 1963-65. Diplomate Am. Bd. Surgery, Am. Bd. Plastic Surgery. Fellow A.C.S.; mem. AMA, Mo. State Med. Assn., Jackson County Med. Soc., Am. Soc. Plastic and Reconstructive Surgeons. Roman Catholic. Home: 10216 Oakridge Dr Overland Park KS 66212 Office: 1010 Carondelet Dr #440 Kansas City MO 64114

MORGANSTERN, RAMON JEROME, lawyer; b. St. Louis, Dec. 14, 1932; s. David Martin and Elsie (Merkadeau) M.; A.B., Washington U., 1955, J.D., 1957; m. Lois Elaine Levin, July 25, 1965; children—Denise Holly, Julie Faith. Admitted to Mo. bar, 1957; asso. atty. Husch, Eppenberger, Donohue, Elson & Cornfeld, St. Louis, 1959-65; pvt. practice, St. Louis, 1965-69; partner Schramm & Morganstern, Clayton, 1970-76, Gallop, Johnson, Godiner, Morganstern & Crebs, 1976-80, Morganstern, Drumm, Soragnan, Stockenberg & Kitrick, 1981—. Pres., Good Shepherd Sch. for Spl. Children Parents Assn., 1972-73; pres., rep. Wash. U. dept. neurology to St. Louis Met. Council Developmental Disabilities, 1971—. Bd. dirs. St. Louis Assn. for Retarded Children, 1975—. Served to 1st lt. AUS, 1957-59. Mem. Am., Mo., St. Louis County, St. Louis bar assns., Jewish Fedn. St. Louis (mem. leadership devel. council 1971-74), Phi Beta Kappa, Pi Sigma Alpha, Phi Delta Phi, Sigma Alpha Mu. Democrat. Mason. Home: 1328 Benbush Dr St Louis MO 63141 Office: 7733 Forsyth Blvd Clayton MO 63105

MORGISON, F. EDWARD, investment broker, govt. ofcl.; b. Clay Center, Kans., Oct. 4, 1940; s. Fred and Lena Edna (Chaput) M.; B.A. in Math., Emporia State U., 1963; M.S. in Bus. Adminstrn., U. Mo., Columbia, 1964; M.S. in Acctg. candidate U. Mo., Kansas City, 1981—; m. Karen Lorene Herdman, Nov. 21, 1964; 1 dau., Diana Michelle. Computer programmer U. Mo. Med. Center, Columbia, 1964-65; adminstrv. and budget analyst Urban Renewal Project, Independence, Mo., 1965-66; account exec., bank broker Stifel Nicolaus & Co., Kansas City, Mo., 1966-73; pres., chief exec. officer Will-Mor Investment Systems, Kansas City, Mo., 1973-75; br. mgr. Edward Jones & Co., 1975; editorial and exec. asst. to Morgan Maxfield, candidate for U.S. Congress, Kansas City, 1976; sr. account exec., merger and acquisitions specialist R. Rowland & Co., Kansas City, Mo., 1976-77; chmn. bd., pres., chief exec. officer Mo. Securities Inc., Kansas City, 1977-78; v.p., regional mgr. Charles Schwab & Co., Kansas City, 1978-79; v.p. Profl. Assistance, 1979-81; registered agt. Offerman & Co., Kansas City, 1979-81; chief exec. officer Morgison & Assos., Kansas City, 1979-81; fiscal dir. Housing Authority of Kansas City, 1980-81; account exec. charge acctg. and banking placements Sales Recruiters of Kansas City, 1981—; diamond counselor Internat. Diamond Corp., Kansas City, 1980—; sec., treas., dir. several Kansas City corps. Recipient Bausch and Lomb Sci. award, 1959; Sci. award Lambda Delta Lambda, 1962; registered account exec. N.Y. Stock Exchange, Am. Exchange, registered securities agt., Mo., Kans., Ill. Mem. U. Mo. (life), Emporia State U. (life) alumni assns., Nat. Rifle Assn. (life), U.S. Chess Fedn. (life), Mensa (life). Home: 1000 NE 96th Terr Kansas City MO 64155 Office: 1125 Grand Ave Suite 2002 St Kansas City MO 64106

MORIARTY, MARY KAY, occupational therapist; b. Canton, Ohio, July 22, 1952; d. Michael Lawrence and Mary Catherine (Sauers) M.; B.S. in Occupational Therapy, U. Kans., 1974; m. Doug E. Wallace, Apr. 1, 1978. Occupational therapist Fergus Falls (Minn.) schs., 1975-76, Infant Stimulation Program, Waterloo, Iowa, 1977—; mem. Marshalltown Project Adv. Bd., 1980. Mem. Am. Occupational Therapy Assn. Roman Catholic. Home: 1625 A Baltimore Terr Waterloo IA 50702 Office: 3421 W 9th St Waterloo IA 50702

MORIARTY, ROBERT VINCENT, coll. pres.; b. Chgo., Feb. 5, 1941; s. Thomas C. and Bridget M. (Flaherty) M.; B.A., St. Mary's Coll., 1963; M.S., No. Ill. U., 1967, Ed.D., 1970; m. Karen Meier, Oct. 18, 1975; children—Robert A., Bridget M., Seat T. Instr. Marmion Mil. Acad., Aurora, Ill., 1963-66; counselor Commn. Unit Dist. 300, Carpentersville, Ill., 1966-67; counselor William Rainey Harper Coll., Palatine, Ill., 1969-75; dean student affairs Morton Coll., Cicero, Ill., 1975-80, pres., 1981—; pres. Alpha Assos., Inc., 1971-74; vis. prof. Northwestern Univ., 1975. Mem. adv. com. to Sec. of State Ill., 1974-76; pres. St. Mary's Coll. Nat. Alumni Assn., 1976. Ill. Bd. Regents fellow, 1969; recipient award Ill. Sec. of State, 1976. Mem. Am. Assn. Higher Edn., Nat. Assn. Student Personnel Adminstrs., Am. Assn. Community Jr. Colls., Ill. Assn. Community Coll. Adminstrs., Am. Assn. Coll. Registrars and Admissions Officers, Phi Delta Kappa. Home: 309 Cove Rd Wildwood IL 60030 Office: 3801 S Central Ave Cicero IL 60650

MORING, KATHY ANNETTE, systems analyst; b. Freeport, Ill., Dec. 7, 1949; d. Carl Wesley and Jean (Dornink) Cahoon; B.S. in Math., U. Wis., Platteville, 1972; m. Ronald Laverne Moring, Sept. 1, 1973. Programmer trainee Interstate Power Co., Dubuque, Iowa, 1972-73; programmer analyst, project leader Ingersoll Milling Machine Co., Rockford, Ill., 1973-78; software specialist, corp. sec., gen. partner Custom Computer Software Services, Ltd., Rockford, 1978—. Mem. Assn. for Systems Mgmt., Zeta Tau Omega. Methodist. Club: Ski. Home: 115 Douglas St Rock City IL 61070 Office: 3101 11th St Rockford IL 61109

MORITZ, KAREN LYNNE, psychiatrist, psychoanalyst; b. La Grande, Oreg., May 9, 1940; d. Eugene Clinton and Marcella Rae (Gardner) Shultz; B.A. in English with distinction magna cum laude (Angier B. Duke scholar), Duke, 1962; postgrad. U. Calif., Berkeley, 1964-65; M.D. cum laude (Thosteson Meml. fellow), St. Louis U., 1970; postgrad. St. Louis Psychoanalytic Inst., 1974—; m. Gerald William Moritz, Aug. 26, 1961 (div. Apr. 1976); children—Jason Rande, Judd Hunter. Editor, Stanford Research Inst., 1962-66; intern St. Louis Children's Hosp., 1970; resident dept. psychiatry St. Louis U., 1970-73, instr. psychiatry, 1973—; adj. asso. prof. George Warren Brown Sch. Social Work, Washington U., St. Louis, 1978—; practice medicine specializing in psychiatry, and psychoanalysis, Clayton, Mo., 1973—; mem. staff St. Louis VA Hosps., 1970-77; cons., trainer vols. CONTACT, St. Louis. Mem. Am. Psychoanalytic Assn., Eastern Mo. Psychiat. Assn., St. Louis Psychoanalytic Soc., Council for Advancement Psychoanalytic Edn., Phi Beta Kappa, Alpha Omega Alpha, Gamma Pi Epsilon. Author: (with Willard D. Tiffany) Amateur Radio: An International Resource for Technological, Economic, and Sociological Development, 1966. Home: 31 Salem Estates Saint Louis MO 63124 Office: 141 N Meramec Ave Suite 108 Clayton MO 63105

MORITZ, TIMOTHY BOVIE, physician; b. Portsmouth, Ohio, July 26, 1936; s. Charles Raymond and Elisabeth Bovie (Morgan) M.; B.A., Ohio State U., 1959; M.D., Cornell U., 1963; m. Joyce Elizabeth Rasmussen, Oct. 13, 1962 (div.); children—Elizabeth Wynne, Laura Morgan. Resident in psychiatry Cornell U. Med. Center, N.Y.C., 1964-67; spl. asst. to dir. NIMH, Bethesda, Md., 1967-69; dir. Rockland County Community Mental Health Center, Pomona, N.Y., 1970-74; dir. Ohio Dept. Mental Health and Mental Retardation, Columbus, 1975-81; asst. prof. psychiatry Cornell U., 1970-73; cons. HEW, 1973—; dir. psychiatry Miami Valley Hosp., Dayton, Ohio, 1981—; clin. prof. psychiatry Wright State U., 1981—. Mem. cabinet Gov. James A. Rhodes of Ohio, 1975-81; bd. dirs. Rockland County Health and Social Services Bd., 1970-73. Served with USPHS, 1967-69. Diplomate Am. Bd. Psychiatry and Neurology. Fellow Am. Psychiat. Assn.; mem. AMA, Am. Pub. Health Assn., Assn. Mental Health Adminstrs., N.Y. Acad. Scis., Phi Gamma Delta. Republican. Contbr. chpts. to books, articles to profl. jours. Home: 210 Jackson St Dayton OH 45402

MORK, GORDON ROBERT, historian; b. St. Cloud, Minn., May 6, 1938; s. Gordon Matthew and Agnes (Gibb) M.; B.A., Yale U., 1960, M.A., U. Minn., 1963, Ph.D., 1966; m. Dianne Jeannette Muetzel, Aug. 11, 1963; children—Robert, Kristiana, Elizabeth. Instr. history U. Minn., 1966; lectr., asst. prof. history U. Calif., Davis, 1966-70; mem. faculty dept. history Purdue U., West Lafayette, Ind., 1970—, asso. prof., 1973—, resident dir. Purdue-Ind. U. Program, Hamburg, W. Ger., 1975-76; research fellow in humanities U. Wis., Madison, 1969-70. Mem. citizens task force Lafayette Sch. Corp., 1978-79; bd. dirs. Murdock-Sunnyside Bldg. Corp., 1980—, sec., 1980—. Social Sci. Research Council fellow, 1964-65. Mem. Am. Hist. Assn., Conf. Group on Central European History, Soc. History Edn., Leo Baeck Inst., Conf. Group on German Politics, Phi Beta Kappa. Presbyterian. Author: Modern Western Civilization: A Concise History, 2d edit., 1981. Mem. editorial bd. Societas: A Rev. of Social History, 1971—. Contbr. articles to profl. jours. Home: 1521 Cason St Lafayette IN 47904 Office: Dept History Purdue U West Lafayette IN 47907

MORKOC, HADIS, elec. engr.; b. Turkey, Oct. 2, 1947; came to U.S., 1971; s. Mustafa and Saadet M.; B.S., Istanbul Tech. U., 1968, M.S., 1969; postgrad. Mich. State U., 1971-73; Ph.D., Cornell U., 1976; m. July 24, 1976. Instr., Istanbul Tech. U., 1969-71; research asso. Cornell U., Ithaca, N.Y., 1975-76; mem. tech. staff Varian Research Labs., Palo Alto, Calif., 1976-78; asst. prof. elec. engring. U. Ill., Urbana, 1978—; resident visitor Bell Labs. (Murray Hill, N.J.). Recipient award for best paper Inst. Elec. Engring. Gt. Britain, 1978; NATO fellow, 1971-74; OECD fellow, 1971-72; Ministry of Edn. scholar, 1964-69. Mem. IEEE (sr.), Electrochem. Soc., AAAS, Sigma Xi, Eta Kappa Nu, Phi Kappa Phi. Research on III-V compound semicondrs.; contbr. articles profl. jours. Office: Dept Elec Enging Coordinated Science Lab U Ill Urbana IL 61801

MORLEY, FRANKLIN PERSHING, ednl. adminstr.; b. Elmira, N.Y., Feb. 16, 1920; s. Mack Bud and Eugertha Ruth (Everitt) M.; A.B., Alfred U., 1942; diploma, U.S. Army Advanced Sch. Tng. Program, W.Va. U., 1944; M.A., Syracuse U., 1950; Ed.D., Columbia U., 1958; postgrad. Eden Theol. Sem., 1980-81; m. Muriel Frances Strong, Oct. 5, 1943; children—William L., Gayle E., Cynthia A., John F. Tchr., Warwick (N.Y.) Jr.-Sr. High Sch., 1946-47, Middletown (N.Y.) High Sch., 1948-51, James Madison Sch., Arlington (Va.) County Dist., 1952-53; asst. supt. DeKalb (Ill.) Sch. Dist., 1953-58; curriculum dir. Parma (Ohio) Sch. Dist., 1958-61; with Ladue (Mo.) Sch. Dist., St. Louis, 1961—, asst. supt. for instrn. 1972—. Pres. bd. dirs. Citizenship Edn. Clearing House, St. Louis, 1980—; pres. bd. mgrs. Webster Groves (Mo.) YMCA, 1979—; mem. bd. mgrs. Met. St. Louis YMCA, 1979—. Served with U.S. Army, 1942-46. Mem. NEA, Nat. Soc. Study Edn., Nat. Assn. Secondary Sch. Prins., Nat. Council for Social Studies, Assn. for Supervision and Curriculum Devel. (dir. 1980—), Mo. Assn. for Supervision and Curriculum Devel., Mo. Tchrs. Assn., Phi Delta Kappa. Congregationalist. Author: Modern Guide to Effective K-12 Curriculum Planning, 1973. Home: 101 Arthur Ave Webster Groves MO 63119 Office: Ladue School District 9703 Conway Rd St Louis MO 63124

MORNEAULT, A. JOEL, bus. exec.; b. St. Agatha, Maine, Aug. 15, 1936; s. Leo and Catherine (Plourde) M.; B.S. in Engring., UCLA, 1967; m. Sally Street, July 29, 1961; children—Monique, A. Joel. Process engr. TFI, Los Angeles, 1967-69; devel. engr. RCA, Indpls., 1969-71; sr. tech. service rep. ICI Am., Wilmington, Del., 1971-73; dir. engring. Wabash Tape Corp., Huntley, Ill., 1973-75; founder, pres. TRI, Cary, Ill., 1975—; tech. cons. Kuwaiti Co., Kuwait. Served with USAF, 1956-60. Mem. IEEE, Dundee Bus. and Profl. Assn. (membership chmn. 1978-79). Republican. Roman Catholic. Office: 150 Chicago St Cary IL 60013

MORREALE, ROLAND ANTHONY, coll. adminstr.; b. N.Y.C., Mar. 19, 1934; s. Peter and Martha (Moore) M.; B.A., U. Utah, 1955; M.S., Boston U., 1958; m. Janet L. McCroskey, July 6, 1963; 1 son, Craig. Asst. dir. Menorah Med. Center, Kansas City, Mo., 1960-65; mgmt. cons. Cresap, McCormack & Paget, N.Y.C., 1965-66; owner, cons. Roland A. Morreale & Assos., Overland Park, Kans., 1966-67; corp. tng. dir. Nat. Bellas Hess Co., Kansas City, Mo., 1967-69; asst. sales mgr. Funeral Security Plans Co., Kansas City, 1969-72; asst. dir. tng. Human Resources Corp., Kansas City, 1973; corp. dir. tng. Whitaker Cable Corp., North Kansas City, Mo., 1973-74; with Met. Community Colls., Kansas City, Mo., 1974—, placement counselor Project Outreach, Met. Inst., Community Services, 1974-75, program coordinator Pioneer Community Coll., 1975—; co-founder, Career Crossroads for Women, 1975—; creator Met. Computerized Vocat.

Counseling Network, 1979; pres. Occupational Guidance Assos., 1980—. Founding bd. dirs. Kansas City chpt. Amigos de las Americas; bd. dirs. Johnson County Vol. Action Center, Mission, Kans. Served with AUS, 1955-57. Mem. Personnel Mgmt. Assn. Greater Kansas City Mo. (Outstanding Achievement awards), Am. Soc. Tng. and Devel., Am. Soc. Personnel Adminstrn. Presbyterian. Club: Johnson County Leisure-Aires. Writer, producer 1st human relations tng. program for animal control officers, 1979. Home: 8437 Woodson Dr Overland Park KS 66207 Office: PO Box 4062 Overland Park KS 66204

MORRILL, VAUGHAN, III, educator, real estate asso.; b. St. Louis, Feb. 6, 1944; s. Vaughan and Elizabeth Angele (Lane) M.; student Harvard U., 1962-65; A.B. in Biology, Washington U., 1969; M.S. in Biology, U. Mo., 1977; m. Linda Christine Dvorak, Mar. 17, 1978. Tchr. secondary sch. sci. St. Louis Bd. Edn., 1971—; real estate asso. Realty World, G. Angleitner Realty Co., St. Louis, 1978—. Mem. Real Estate Bd. Met. St. Louis, Mo. Assn. Realtors, Nat. Assn. Realtors. Home: 520 West Dr Saint Louis MO 63130 Office: 1512 S Brentwood Blvd Saint Louis MO 63144

MORRILL, WALTER DUNLAP, coll. librarian; b. Pitts., Jan. 11, 1936; s. Allen Conrad and Eleanor (Dunlap) M.; A.B., Monmouth Coll., 1957; M.S., U. Ill., 1960; m. Marcia Lou Simpson, Aug. 18, 1957; children—Allen Simpson, Matthew Richard, Stephen Conrad. Rhetoric instr. U. Ill., 1957-59, asst. catalog librarian, 1959-60, binding librarian, 1960-61; coll. librarian Muskingum Coll., 1961-65; asst. dir. libraries Kent State U., 1965-66; dir. libraries Hanover (Ind.) Coll., 1966—. Adminstrv. cons. Library Service Center of Eastern Ohio, 1965-66; mem., also chmn. adv. council Ind. Library and Hist. Bd. Mem. ALA, AAUP, Ind. Library Assn. (pres. 1974-75), Assn. Coll. and Research Libraries, Beta Phi Mu, Sigma Omicron Mu, Pi Delta Kappa, Theta Chi. Republican. Presbyn. (elder). Rotarian. Contbr. articles to profl. jours. Home: Box 53 Hanover IN 47243

MORRIS, CHARLES EMMET, banker; b. Chgo., Sept. 28, 1935; s. Hugh G. and Ann M. (Connolly) M.; student Sch. of Banking, U. Va., 1968, Stonier Grad. Sch. Banking, Rutgers U., Am. Inst. Banking, 1964; m. Micki Bruno, May 5, 1962; children—Charles E., Nancy C., Jon C. With Mercantile Nat. Bank of Chgo., 1960-74, sr. v.p. comml. lending, 1968-74; sr. v.p. lending Oak Brook Bank (Ill.), 1974-76, pres., 1976—; formerly instr. Am. Inst. Banking. Mem. Bd. Edn., Dist. 44, Lombard, Ill., 1970-75, pres., 1974-75. Mem. Robert Morris Assos. Clubs: Bankers; Exec. (Chgo.); Glen Oak Country. Office: Oak Brook Bank 2021 Spring Rd Oak Brook IL 60521

MORRIS, DAVID ALEXANDER NATHANIEL, chemist; b. Jamaica, West Indies, May 13, 1944; came to U.S., 1963, naturalized, 1981; s. Richard Gustavus Adolphus and Edna Lucille (Campbell) M.; B.S. summa cum laude, Interam. U., 1966; M.S., U. Wis., Milw., 1971; Ph.D., U. Notre Dame, 1977; m. Barbara Jean Brown; children—David, Melinda. Asst. research scientist Miles Labs., Elkhart, Ind., 1970-73, asso. research scientist, 1973-76, research scientist, 1976-79, supr. phys. chemistry group, Ames Co. Research Labs., 1979—. Mem. Elkhart County Juvenile Planning Com., 1979-80; bd. dirs. Elkhart County Big Bros., Big Sisters Agy., 1978-80. Mem. Am. Chem. Soc., Am. Assn. Clin. Chemistry. Patentee in field. Home: 56660 Pinecrest Dr Elkhart IN 46516 Office: PO Box 70 Ames Div Miles Labs Elkhart IN 46515

MORRIS, DAVID BURTON, chem. co. exec.; b. Grand Forks, N.D., Feb. 20, 1922; s. David B. and Jessie M. (Evans) M.; B.S. in Bus. Adminstrn., U. Kans., Lawrence, 1947; m. Margaret Hardie, Dec. 28, 1945; children—David III, Margaret. Merchandising supr. Montgomery Ward & Co., Kansas City, Mo., 1947-48; with Lyon Chems., Inc. (merged with Van Waters and Rogers div. Univar Corp.), St. Paul, 1948-73, v.p., 1969-73, also dir.; area sales mgr. Van Waters and Rogers div. Univar Corp., 1973-78, sales coordinator, 1978—. Served with U.S. Army, 1942-46. Mem. Am. Water Works Assn. (life, George Warren Fuller award 1979), Water Pollution Control Fedn. Ducks Unltd., Wildlife Fedn., Smithsonian Assos., Ramsey County Hist. Soc., Minn. Hist. Soc., Minn. Zool. Soc., Sci. Mus. of Minn., Internat. Assn. for Med. Assistance, Walker Art Center, Nat. Audubon Soc., Sierra Club. Republican. Episcopalian. Clubs: Town & Country, St. Paul Athletic, Pool & Yacht, Elks, Izaak Walton League. Home: 740 River Dr Saint Paul MN 55116 Office: 845 Terrace Ct Saint Paul MN 55101

MORRIS, EDWIN WALTER, data processing co. exec.; b. Chgo., July 25, 1939; s. Charles T. and Muriel A. (Kummelehne) M.; student Ill. Wesleyan U., 1958, DePaul U., 1968; m. Romona M. Lesko, Mar. 17, 1962; 1 dau., Michelle E. Programmer trainee Household Fin. Corp., Chgo., 1962-63; systems analyst LaSalle Extension U. Chgo., 1964-67; with N. Am. Car Corp., Chgo., 1965, Assn. Am. R.R.'s, Washington, 1968-74, Chgo. Transit Authority, 1974-77; pres. Meta Trans, Inc., Lansing, Ill., 1978—; lectr. in field. Republican precinct capt., City of Chgo., 1960-61. Served with USN, 1958-60. Mem. Mensa. Republican. Clubs: Masons, Shriners. Home:

MORRIS, EUGENE, ins. co. exec.; b. Promise City, Iowa, Sept. 27, 1918; s. William Harley and Ethel (Enright) M.; student pub. schs., Promise City; m. Helen Eloise McCart, Sept. 27, 1938; 1 son, Elgin Eugene. Farmer nr. Corydon, Iowa, 1938-47; ins. insp. Grinnell Mut. Re-Ins. Co. (Iowa), 1947-49; parts man Forest City Motor Co. (Iowa), 1949-50; owner, real estate broker Eugene Morris Ins. and Realty, Forest City, 1950—. Dir. Forest City Devel. Inc., 1960—. Mem. city council Forest City, 1964-76, mayor, 1976—; gen. chmn., local pageant dir. Miss Forest City Pageant, 1975—. Mem. Ind. Ins. Agts. Assn., Nat., Iowa real estate assns., Forest City C. of C. (past pres.), Iowa Numis. Assn. (pres. 1975-76), Winnebago Hist. Soc. (pres. 1981-82). Clubs: Lions (dist. gov. 1959-60, 63-64, Key of Nations award 1967, local Mr. Lion award 1970, also 4 dist. awards), Odd Fellows (past local noblegrand). Home: 234 Riverview Dr PO Box 467 Forest City IA 50436 Office: 234 N Clark St Forest City IA 50436

MORRIS, EUGENE DAVIS, hosp. exec.; b. Drew, Miss., Jan. 11, 1919; s. John Patrick and Ethel (Davis) M.; student pub. schs., Chgo.; m. Dorothy Miriam Fast, Oct. 13, 1945; children—Eugene Leigh, Joan Ann. Sales rep. Economy Printers Products, Chgo., 1936-42, 46-50, Western Newspaper Union, Chgo., 1950-59; adminstr. Edward Hosp., Naperville, Ill., 1959—; dir., sec. Naperville Savs. & Loan Assn., 1965—. Mem. group purchasing com. Chgo. Hosp. Council, 1972-80, chmn., 1980—. Served with U.S. Army, 1942-46. Mem. Am. Coll. Hosp. Adminstrs., Am. Soc. Hosp. Public Relations, Ill. Hosp. Assn. (dist. pres. 1979—), Naperville C. of C. (chmn. edn. com. 1968—), Phi Delta Kappa, VFW. Roman Catholic. Home: 8S600 River Dr Naperville IL 60565 Office: Edward Hospital S Washington St Naperville IL 60566

MORRIS, MARILYN ANN, psychiat. social worker; b. Chgo., Feb. 18, 1945; d. Jack Sidney and Melba Lea (Hakan) M.; B.A. in Sociology, Roosevelt U., Chgo., 1967; M.A. in Social Work, U. Chgo., 1969. Psychotherapist, Ill. Dept. Mental Health, Chgo., 1968-74; coordinator intake Roscoe House, Chgo., 1974-75; psychiat. social worker Chgo.-Read Mental Health Center, 1976—; pvt. practice psychotherapy, Chgo., 1973—; field work instr. Jane Addams Sch. Social Work, 1970-74. Certified social worker, Ill. Mem. Nat. Assn. Social Workers, Acad. Certified Social Workers. Home: 1240 Park Ave W Highland Park IL 60035

MORRIS, MARK ARTHUR, direct mktg. communications exec.; b. Mpls., Mar. 20, 1950; s. Arthur M. and Virginia M.; student Ariz. State U., 1968-69; B.S. in Bus. Adminstrn., U. Minn., 1972; m. Cheryl Sinning, June 17, 1977. Salesman, Can. Life Assurance Co., 1972-73; mgr. mktg. communications Med. Gen., 1973-74; founder, chief exec. officer Mark Morris & Co., Inc., Mpls., 1975—; partner Nomark Properties, 1980—; dir. Photo Offset Plate Co. Mem. Direct Mail/Mktg. Assn., Orono Jaycees. Home: 2610 Maple Ridge Ln Orono MN 55331 Office: 1825 Chicago Ave S Minneapolis MN 55404

MORRIS, ROBERT ALAN, mfg. co. exec.; b. N. Platte, Nebr., Sept. 9, 1934; s. Robert Allen and Frieda Annabelle Morris; B.S. in Journalism, Northwestern U., 1956, M.S., 1957; m. Joyce Darlene Rigg, Dec. 5, 1959; children—Linda Kathleen, Laura Darlene, Robert Alexander. Reporter, editor Chgo. Tribune, 1958-60; public relations dir. central states Brit. Overseas Airways, Chgo., 1960-64; with IBM Corp., 1964-77, dir. communications IBM Americas/Far East Corp., 1974-77; v.p. communications Borg-Warner Corp., Chgo., 1977—. Served with U.S. Army, 1956-57. Mem. Chgo. Public Relations Clinic, Public Relations Seminar, SDX Headline Club, Conf. Board (co. rep.). Republican. Clubs: Chgo. Press, University (Chgo.); Lake Forest. Office: 200 S Michigan Ave Chicago IL 60604

MORRIS, TIMOTHY LESTER, educator, farmer; b. Kenmare, N.D., Oct. 24, 1953; s. Truman Lester and Marian Janet (Pederson) M.; Asso. Sci. in Math., N.D. State U., Bottineau, 1973; B.S. in Biology, Minot State Coll., 1977. Farm foreman Watne Realty, Minot, N.D., 1973-75; tchr. sci., head sci. dept. asst. basketball coach Lansford (N.D.) High Sch., 1977-79; tchr. math. and drivers edn., asst. basketball coach Sherwood (N.D.) High Sch., 1979—; farmer, Tolley, N.D. Mem. Sherwood Vol. Fire and Ambulance Crew. Mem. NEA, Nat. Sci. Tchrs. Assn., N.D. Edn. Assn., Lansford Edn. Assn. (pres. 1979), Jr. C. of C., Sherwood Progressive Assn. (sec./treas.). Methodist. Club: Sherwood Gun. Home: Rural Route 1 Tolley ND 58787 Office: Sherwood High Sch Sherwood ND 58782

MORRIS, WILLIAM BURKE, mayor, cons.; b. Hawarden, Iowa, Aug. 18, 1945; s. Rog and Bea (Burke) M.; B.S. in Journalism, No. Ill. Univ., 1967; student Coll. Lake County, 19—; postgrad. Webster Coll., 1981—; m. Mary Suzanne Entress, June 3, 1966; children—Patrick, Tina. Sports dir., reporter, announcer WGSB Radio, St. Charles, Ill., 1962-68; reporter, newscaster WKRS Radio, Waukegan, Ill., 1969-73; editor Kane County Herald, Batavia, Ill., 1968-69; Mem. Ill. Senate, 1975-77; owner MOR Communication, Waukegan, 1973—; mayor City Waukegan, 1977—. Recipient Disting. Service award Waukegan North Chgo. Jr. C. of C., 1973; named Best Fresham Senator, Ill. Edn. Assn., 1975, 76, Best Legislator, Ind. Voters Ill., 1975, 76. Office: City of Waukegan 106 N Utica St Waukegan IL 60085

MORRISEY, EDWARD LEE, research co. exec.; b. Lima, Ohio, Nov. 28, 1944; s. Walter John and Mary Lenore (Meyers) M.; B.S., Ohio State U., 1968; M.B.A., Xavier U., 1978; m. Sarah Lou Davis, Jan. 15, 1972; 1 son, William Arthur. Corp. auditor Battelle Meml. Inst., Columbus, Ohio, 1973-75, sr. acctg., 1975-78, supr. acctg., project mgmt. div., 1978-80, fin. advis., div., 1980—. Treas., Cub Scouts Pack, Columbus, 1980—. Served with AUS, 1969-71. Mem. Nat. R.R. Model Assn., Am. Legion, U.S. Power Squadron. Roman Catholic. Club: K.C. Office: 505 King Ave Columbus OH 43201

MORRISH, WILLIAM RICHARD, newspaper editor and publisher; b. Chgo., Feb. 23, 1920; s. Charles Howard and Mary Amaryllis (Robison) M.; B.A., DePauw U., Greencastle, Ind., 1942; m. Marcella June Hillis, Mar. 16, 1954; 1 dau., Marcella Shackleford Sites. Asst. to exec. sec. N.Y. State Pubs. Assn., 1946-47, asso. exec. sec., 1953-54; asst. to chmn. labor relations com. Am. Newspaper Pubs. Assn., 1947-53; asst. to pub. The Oregonian, Portland, 1954-65; pub. Jersey Jour., Jersey City, 1965-66; bus. adminstr. Wichita (Kans.) Eagle and Beacon, 1966-69; editor, pub. LaPorte (Ind.) Herald-Argus, 1969—. Pres. LaPorte United Fund, 1975; mem. LaPorte Econ. Devel. Commn., 1972—; adv. com. Ind. Exec. Council State Planning, 1974—. Served with USNR, 1942-46; PTO. Decorated Purple Heart. Mem. Am. Soc. Newspaper Editors, Am. Newspaper Pubs. Assn., Inland Daily Press Assn., Hoosier State Press Assn., Ind. Republican Editorial Assn. (pres. 1981-82), LaPorte C. of C. (v.p. 1975). Republican. Presbyterian. Clubs: Rotary, Elks. Office: 701 State St LaPorte IN 46350

MORRISON, DAVID LEE, chemist, research inst. exec.; b. Butler, Pa., Jan. 25, 1933; s. Charles R. and Mildred (McFadden) M.; B.S., Grove City Coll., 1954; M.S., Carnegie Mellon U., 1960, Ph.D., 1961; m. Carole J. White, July 31, 1954; children—Scott, Karyn. Chemist, Callery Chem. Co. (Pa.), 1954; with Battelle Meml. Inst., Columbus, Ohio, 1961-77, mgr. environ. systems and processes sect., 1970-74, mgr. energy and environ. programs office, 1974-75, asso. dir., 1975-77; exec. v.p., dir. IIT Research Inst., Chgo., 1977—; mem. industry adv. com. AEC, cons. adv. com. on reactor safeguards; chmn. indsl. energy conservation com. NRC. Mem. exec. staff Ohio Citizens Environ. Task Force. Served with USAF, 1954-57. Mem. Am. Nuclear Soc., Am. Chem. Soc., Internat. Solar Energy Soc., AAAS, Ohio Acad. Sci., Sigma Xi, Omicron Delta Kappa. Contbr. articles to profl. jours. Office: IIT Research Inst 10 W 35th St Chicago IL 60616

MORRISON, DOUGLAS HARRY, mental health cons.; b. Jersey City, Mar. 5, 1915; s. Francis Adelbert and Emily (Sidman) M.; A.A., St. Helena Ext., Coll. William and Mary, 1948; A.B., Union Coll., 1949; M.S.W., Howard U., 1951. Med. social worker Governeur Hosp., N.Y.C., 1951-53; program dir. North End Community Center, Hartford, Conn., 1953-54; program dir. Social Settlement, Omaha, 1954-55; social group worker Essex County Youth House, Newark, N.J., 1956-60; dir. social services Ohio State Reformatory, Mansfield, 1960-62; dir. Alcohol Treatment Center, Newark, 1962-65; dir. Floyd County Community Action Program, Prestonsburg, Ky., 1966-70; community mental health cons. Madison (Ind.) State Hosp., 1970-79; field work cons. human relations CCNY, 1956-60; fieldwork cons. social work Ohio State U., 1960-62. City dir. John Longo Assn., 1962-65; nat. adv. bd. Am. Security Council, 1976—; Ind. State adv. bd. Crane for President Com., 1978—; bd. dirs. Am. Cancer Soc., Jefferson County Chpt. Served with AUS, 1934-40, 42-45. Named Ky. Col., 1967. Mem. Nat. Assn. Social Workers, Am. Acad. Polit. and Social Scis., AAAS, Nat. Conf. on Social Welfare, Nat. Council on Crime and Delinquency. Republican. United Methodist. Clubs: Masons, Lions (pres. Madison). Home: 1926 Maple St Madison IN 47250

MORRISON, ESTHER EILEEN, hosp. adminstr.; b. Wooster, Ohio, Mar. 28, 1926; d. Sylvester Theobald and Mable May (Faulkner) Fath; C.S. Tech., U. Chgo., 1970; student Akron U., 1978; m. Bazle Eugene Franks, Dec. 22, 1944 (dec. 1966); children—Joe Eugene, Clifford Allen, Edward Lemoine; m. 2d, Harry Albert Morrison, July 31, 1970. With Wooster (Ohio) Community Hosp., 1957-59, 60—, central service supr., 1963—. Mem. Internat. Assn. Hosp. Central Service Mgmt. (pres. 1977-79), Ohio Assn. Hosp. Central Service Mgmt. (pres., founder 1978—). Democrat. Mem. Ch. of God. Club: Wooster Bus. and Profl. Women (pres. 1970-71). Inventor of instantaneous pneumatothorax, 1968. Home: 5108 Lehr Rd Wooster OH 44691 Office: 1761 Beall St Wooster OH 44691

MORRISON, HELEN LOUISE, forensic, adult, and child psychiatrist; b. Greensburg, Pa., July 9, 1942; student Franklin Sch. Sci. and Arts, Phila., 1960-61, Community Coll. Phila., 1967-68, Temple U., 1968-69; M.D., Med. Coll. Pa., 1972; postgrad. Chgo. Inst. Psychoanalysis, 1975—; m. George J. Dohrmann, III, Dec. 22, 1979. Research asso. Johnson & Johnson Research Found., 1962-65; lab. personnel dir. AME Assos., Princeton, N.J., 1965-67; asso. dir. Biosearch, Inc., 1967-70; intern U. Wis. Hosp., 1972-73, resident in psychiatry, 1972-75, fellow in child psychiatry, 1975-76; research asso. Wis. Psychiat. Research Inst., 1976-77; dir. child psychiatry Stritch Sch. Medicine, Loyola U., Chgo., 1978-80; dir. The Evaluation Center, Chgo., 1980—; mem. exec. bd. U. Wis. Hosps.-Madison Center Health Scis., also pres. house staff assn., 1975-76. Diplomate Am. Bd. Psychiatry and Neurology, Am. Bd. Forensic Psychiatry. Mem. Am., Chgo. psychoanalytic socs., Am., Ill. psychiat. assns., AMA, State Med. Soc. Ill., Am. Acad. Child Psychiatry, Am. Acad. Psychiatry and Law, Am. Acad. Forensic Scis., Candidates Assn. of Inst. for Psychoanalysis (pres. 1980-81). Co-author: Contemporary Issues in the Treatment of Psychotic and Neurologically Impaired Children: A Systems Approach; editor: Children of Depressed Parents: A Comprehensive Study in Research and Treatment; contbr. articles to profl. jours. Office: 919 N Michigan Ave Chicago IL 60611

MORRISON, JAMES FRANK, optometrist; b. Colby, Kans., Apr. 11, 1942; s. Lloyd Wayne and Catherine Louise M.; student U. Kans., 1960-64, then postgrad.; B.S., then O.D., So. Coll. Optometry, 1964-67; m. Karen Jean Carr, Aug. 25, 1963; children—Mike, Jeffrey, Scott. Partner optometric practice, Garden City, Kans., 1967-69; individual practice, Colby, 1969—; founder, chief staff N.W. Kans. Ednl. Diagnostic and Referral Center for Children, Inc., Colby; asst. chief engr. Sta. KXXX AM-FM, 1977—; satellite systems communications engr., 1978—; prof. vision dept. Colby Community Coll., 1979—; compter systems design and software cons. to Colby Public Schs., 1980—; broadcast engring. cons. various radio Stas.; lectr. in field. Cub master Cub Scout pack, Colby, 1970-80, committeeman troop Boy Scouts Am., 1971-79, dist. chmn., 1977-79; mem. adv. bd. Colby Good Samaritan Home, 1971—. Fellow Am. Acad. Optometry, Coll. Optometrists in Vision Devel (asso); mem. Kans. Optometric Assn. (dir. extension program, com. grad. edn.), Am. Soc. Broadcast Engrs., Kans. (founder, pres. 1970-71), N.W. Kans. (v.p. 1970-72) Assns. children learning disabilities, Thomas County Assn. Retarded Children. Methodist (mem. bd.). Clubs: Lions (chmn. signt com. 1970-72; chmn. com. children and youth 1971—), Kiwanis (pres. 1971-72), Masons, Shriners. Office: 180 W 6th St Colby KS 67701

MORRISON, JEAN ANN, human resources exec.; b. Cedar Falls, Iowa, Sept. 19, 1952; d. Dewey Raymond and Wava Helene (Trunnell) Breisch; certificat d'etudes (Rotary scholar) L'Institut de Touraine, Tours, France, 1970; B.A. summa cum laude, Concordia Coll., Moorhead, Minn., 1973; postgrad., U. Minn., 1977—; student Am. Inst. Banking, Mpls., 1974-78; m. John Edward Morrison, Dec. 15, 1973. Fgn. exchange asst. Northwestern Nat. Bank, Mpls., 1974-75, gen. devel. trainee, 1975-76, compensation specialist, 1976-77, ops. tng. and devel. coordinator, 1977-78; personnel dir. St. Joseph Bank, South Bend, Ind., 1978, Mich. Nat. Bank, Cassopolis, 1978-79; personnel mgr. Pillsbury Co., Mpls., 1979-80, personnel mgr. Green Giant Co. div., Chaska, Minn., 1980-81, dir. human resources research and devel., 1981—; tutor French, U. Minn. Coordinator, Jr. Achievement. Mem. Am. Soc. Tng. and Devel., Soc. Am. Mgmt., Twin Cities Personnel Assn., Am. Soc. Personnel Adminstrn., Am. Bus. Women's Assn., Edina Newcomers, YWCA, U. Minn. Alumni Assn., Rotex, LWV. Republican. Lutheran. Club: Jr. League (Mpls.). Home: 4524 Drexel Ave S Edina MN 55424 Office: Research and Devel Dept Pillsbury Co 311 2d St SE Minneapolis MN 55414

MORRISON, JOHN WILLIAM, fin. exec.; b. Hamilton, Ohio, Aug. 23, 1932; s. Michael M. and Alice L. (Board) M.; student Miami U. Oxford, 1951-52; grad. Ohio Sch. Banking, 1961; grad. Sch. Banking U. Wis., 1965; m. Antoinette Massarelli, Oct. 17, 1953; children—John J., Ann M. Comml. loan officer Second Nat. Bank, Hamilton, Ohio, asst. v.p., 1954-77; treas., fin. advisor, partner Hamilton Merchandising Co., 1955—, JMJ Realty Co., 1979—. Past treas. Butler County March of Dimes; past trustee Greater Cinn. March of Dimes; past treas. Arthritis Found.; fin. com. St. Peter in Chains Ch., Hamilton; trustee Butler County Cath. Social Services. Served with U.S. Army, 1952-54. Mem. Ohio (trustee 1966-68), Butler County bankers assns. Republican. Roman Catholic. Clubs: New London Hills, Moose, Elks; Hamilton City. Home: 1308 Cleveland Ave Hamilton OH 45013 Office: 844 East Ave Hamilton OH 45011

MORRISON, MONA STEPHAINE, retail co. exec.; b. Phila., May 19, 1947; d. Joseph and Ruth (Rosoff) Morrison; certificate Charles Morris Price Sch. Advt. and Journalism, 1966. Advt. prodn. mgr. Sale Meeting Mag., Phila., 1966-68; asst. advt. mgr. Phila. Mag., 1968-69; traffic mgr. Weightman Advt. Agency, Phila., 1969-70; advt. mgr. K Mart Corp., Steven Point, Wis., 1973-75, Duluth, Minn., 1975-78, advt. coordinator, 1978—. Mem. Charles Morris Price Sch. Alumni. Clubs: Duluth Playhouse-Community Theatre, Lake Superior Advt. Office: 1734 Mall Dr Duluth MN 55811

MORRISON, NORMA TURNAU, stock broker; b. Cin., Aug. 6, 1907; d. Louis William and Dora (Wiehe) Turnau; student YMCA Bus. Sch., Cin., 1924; m. Franklin D. Morrison, Aug. 3, 1931; children—Henry Clay Morrison, Thomas Lyle Morrison. With cost dept. Flintkote Co., Cin., 1931; stock broker Hayden Miller & Co., Cleve., 1966-69, Stone & Webster, Cleve., 1969-72, Joseph, Mellen & Miller, Inc., Cleve., 1972, merged into Joseph, Miller & Russel, Inc., which merged with Prescott, Ball & Turben, Inc., 1978—. Chmn. Affiliation Women's Clubs in Japan, 1949-50, Japanese Brides Sch., Tokyo, 1951; chmn. fin. com. West Side Community House, Ridgewood United Meth. Ch., Cleve., 1959—. Recipient Gov.'s award, Tokyo, 1950, 51. Mem. Michi Kawai Christian Fellowship (chmn.), Ikebana Internat. Republican. Club: Garden (Cleve.). Office: 1331 Euclid Ave Cleveland OH 44115

MORRISON, PETER GIFFORD, fin. cons.; b. Washington, Iowa, Sept. 2, 1948; s. G. Gifford and Sara Lu M.; student Robert Morris Coll., 1967-69; A.B., U. Iowa, 1972, postgrad., 1972. Tax cons. Morrison, Morrison & Morrison, 1966-78; fin. and investment cons. N.W. Bank & Trust Co., Davenport, Iowa, 1974-79; trust officer and affiliate mgr. Iowa-Des Moines Nat. Bank, 1979; specialist in probate and taxation Morrison Law Office, Washington, Iowa, 1980—; lectr. estate and fin. planning. Mem. Kappa Sigma. Republican. Presbyterian. Home: 215 1/2 S Iowa Ave Washington IA 52352 Office: 213 S Marion Washington IA 52353

MORROW, SISTER JEAN ANN, ednl. adminstr.; b. Omaha, June 4, 1940; d. Clarence Edwin Jr. and Frances Jeanette (Olry) M.; B.A., Duchesne Coll., 1967; M.A. T.M., U. Detroit, 1969; M.S. in Secondary Adminstrn., Creighton U., 1974. Joined Order of Servants of Mary, Roman Catholic Ch., 1958; tchr. elem. schs., including: St. Pius X, Omaha, 1961-62, Immaculate Conception, Sioux City, Iowa, 1962-63, St. Juliana, Detroit, 1963-64, St. Joseph, Salix, Iowa, 1964-65, St. John Berchman, Detroit, 1965-68; secondary tchr. Servite High Sch., Detroit, 1968-69, 71-73, Immaculate Conception, Cherokee, Iowa, 1969-71; tchr. Marian High Sch., Omaha, 1973-74, secondary adminstr., 1974-75; secondary adminstr. Holy Name High Sch., Omaha, 1975-78; curriculum dir., asst. prin. Roncalli High Sch., Omaha, 1978—. Recipient Tchr. of Yr. award Detroit News, 1968, Coach of Yr. award Roncalli High Sch., 1978, 79. Mem. Nat. Council Tchrs. Math., Assn. Supervision and Curriculum Devel., Nebr. Coaches Assn.

MORROW, RICHARD M., oil co. exec.; b. Wheeling, W.Va., 1926; B.M.E., Ohio State U.; married. With Standard Oil Co. (Ind.), Chgo., 1948—, v.p. Amoco Internat. Oil Co. subs., 1965-66, exec. v.p. subs., 1966-70, exec. v.p. Amoco Chem. Corp., 1970-74, pres., 1974-78, pres. parent co., 1978—; dir. First Chgo. Corp. Bd. dirs. Am. Petroleum Inst., NAM. Office: Standard Oil Co (Ind) 200 E Randolph Dr Box 5910 A Chicago IL 60601

MORSE, C. DWAYNE, state ofcl., pub. health adminstr.; b. Kewanee, Ill., Nov. 26, 1939; s. Carl C. and Anna M. (Cole) M.; B.S. in Microbiology, Ariz. State U., 1966; M.P.H., U. of N.C., 1973, Dr. P.H., 1975; m. Susan Virginia Simon, Apr. 30, 1966; children—Matthew Carl, Jeremy Dwayne, Bridget Kathryn, Alan Anton. Microbiologist Maricopa County Health Dept., Phoenix, 1966-72; br. lab. dir. Ariz. State Dept. of Health, Tucson, 1972; research asst. U. of N.C., Chapel Hill, 1972-74, Center for Disease Control, Atlanta, 1974-75; dep. dir. Office of Labs. and Research, Kans. Dept. of Health and Environment, Topeka, 1975-76, dir., 1976-78; dir. Div. Pub. Health Labs. Minn. Dept. Health, Mpls., 1978—; adj. asst. prof. of microbiology U. Kans., 1977-78. Served with USN, 1957-60. USPHS grantee, 1972. Mem. Am. Soc. for Microbiology, Am. Pub. Health Assn., Minn. Pub. Health Assn., Conf. Pub. Health Lab. Dirs., AAAS, Assn. State and Territorial Pub. Health Lab Dirs., Sigma Xi. Roman Catholic. Contbr. articles to profl. jours. Home: 4650 Morris Circle Bloomington MN 55437 Office: Minn Dept Health 717 Delaware St SE Minneapolis MN 55440

MORSE, ELSIE LOUISE, educator; b. Laingsburg, Mich., Feb. 20, 1933; d. Carl Alonzo and Neva Ernestine Morse; B.S., Olivet Nazarene Coll., 1955; M.B.Ed., Ga. State U., 1973. Sec., Dow Chem. Co., Mich. and Calif., 1955-64; asst. personnel dir. Alexander Hamilton Life Ins. Co., Farmington Hills, Mich., 1964-68; tchr. Grand Rapids (Mich.) public schs., 1968-70, Marietta (Ga.) public schs., 1973-74; asst. prof. Delta Coll. U. Center, Mich., 1974—. Mem. Nat. Bus. Edn. Assn., Am. Bus. Communication Assn., AAUP, Mich. Bus. Edn. Assn., Delta Pi Epsilon. Republican. Methodist. Home: 4686 Colonial Dr Saginaw MI 48603 Office: Delta College University Center MI 48710

MORSE, H. CLIFTON, IV, publishing co. exec., indsl. engr.; b. Chgo., Sept. 3, 1924; s. Henry Clifton III, and Augusta (Metz) M.; B.A., Glendale Coll., 1946; M.F.A., Brown U., 1950. Mem. planning staff Howard Hughes, Culver City, Calif., 1958-60; asst. to gen. mgr. Aircraft Engine div. Ford Motor Co., Chgo., 1952-58; pres. Wyatt & Morse, Inc., mgmt. cons., Chgo., 1960-66; pres. Morse Mktg. Ltd., indoor advt., Chgo., 1966—. Pres., Chgo. Chamber Orch. Assn., 1960-62; chmn. Better State and Local Govt. Bus. Practices Bur., Chgo., 1960-66. Bd. dirs. Wesley Found., 1961-62. Served with USNR, 1942-45. Recipient TV Author's award TV Acad. Arts and Scis., 1949. Mem. Inst. Mgmt. Scis. (pres. Chgo chpt. 1959-61, nat. chmn. 1962), Operations Research Soc. (charter mem.), Am. Mgmt. Assn., Nat. Assn. Advancement Sci., Chgo. Urban League. Club: Union League (Chgo.). Author: Machinery Replacement Analysis, 1955; Operations Research for Nontechnical Management, 1956; Organization-Function Guide for Manufacturers, 1957; Numerically Controlled Machine Tools, 2d edit., 1971; Cost Reduction Guide for Manufacturing Management, 2d edit., 1978; Autofacturing, 1965. Editor: Profit Improvement and Cost Reduction Newsletter, 1960-80; Book of Mistakes, 1982; Cost Reduction and Profit Improvement Guide (CEBA advt. award), 1980; patentee 1-piece printed slidechart constrn. Home: 345 Fullerton Pkwy Chicago IL 60614 Office: 2530 N Lincoln Ave Chicago IL 60614

MORSE, JAMES LEONARD, data corp. exec.; b. Evanston, Ill., Feb. 16, 1942; s. Gerald Griffin and Elizabeth Lavinia (Dimmick) M.; B.S. in Elec. Engring., Purdue U., 1965; M.B.A., U. Pa., 1971; m. Veronica Kay, June 30, 1973; children—James Leonard, Kimberly Irene, Shannon Elizabeth, Jonathan Joseph. Mktg. rep. Leasco Response, Chgo., 1971-73; sr. mktg. rep. On Line Systems, Chgo., 1973-75; pres. Morse Data Corp., Chgo., 1975—. Served to lt., USNR, 1965-69. Office: Morse Data Corp 189 W Madison Ave Chicago IL 60602

MORSE, RUSSELL LAVERNE, evangelist, educator; b. Los Angeles, Jan. 4, 1929; s. Justin Russell and Gertrude Erma (Howe) M.; student Minn. Bible Coll., 1947-49; B.A., Cin. Bible Sem., 1954, B.Th., 1960; student Summer Inst. Linguistics, U. Okla., 1954, Wheaton (Ill.) Coll., 1970-75; m. Lois Carol Elliott, Mar. 27, 1953; children—Marcia, Mark, Cynthia, Beth, Shirley. Missionary, Yunnan-Tibetan Christian Mission, S.W. China, 1949-50; educator North Burma Christian Mission, 1950-64; asst. prof. Cin. Bible Sem., 1965—; founder, coordinator S.E. Asia Evangelizing Mission, Cin., 1966—; vice chmn. Internat. Disaster Emergency Services, Marion, Ind.; mem. gen. council Gospel Satellite, Joplin, Mo.; dir. Christian Video Corp. Mem. Nat. Assn. Fgn. Student Affairs, Delta Alpha Tau. Mem. Ch. of Christ. Editor S.E. Asia Challenge, 1967-79. Office: 2700 Glenway Ave Cincinnati OH 45204

MORTENSEN, ARVID LEGRANDE, bus. services co. mktg. exec.; b. Bremerton, Wash., July 11, 1941; s. George Andrew and Mary Louise (Myers) M.; B.S. in English and Psychology, Brigham Young U., 1965, M.B.A. in Mktg. and Fin., 1967; diploma in life ins. mktg. Life Underwriters Tng. Council, 1974; J.D. cum laude, Ind. U., 1980; m. Elaine Marie Mains, Aug. 2, 1968; children—Marie Louise, Anne Catherine. Agt., Connecticut Mut. Life Ins. Co., Salt Lake City, 1967-68, agt. and br. mgr., Idaho Falls, Idaho, 1968-74; with Research and Rev. Service Am., Inc./Newkirk Assos., Inc., Indpls., 1974—, sr. editor, 1975-79, mgr. advanced products and seminars, 1979-80, dir. mktg., 1980—; also tchr., lectr.; admitted to Ind. bar, 1980. Missionary, Ch. of Jesus Christ of Latter-day Saints, 1960-62, bishop, 11th ward, Idaho Falls, Idaho, 1969-74, mem. High Council, Indpls. North Stake, 1975—. Recipient award for outstanding legal scholarship in ins. law Am. United Life, 1980, award for service to Ind. Law Rev., Am. Fletcher Nat. Bank, 1978, award for demonstrated legal excellence Lawyers Coop., 1978, 80; C.L.U. Mem. Assn. Advanced Life Underwriting, Estate Planning Council Indpls., Am. Bar Assn. Ind. Bar Assn., Indpls. Bar Assn., Am. Soc. C.L.U.'s (Indpls. chpt.), Nat. Assn. Life Underwriters, Ind. Assn. Life Underwriters, Indpls. Assn. Life Underwriters. Author: Employee Stock Ownership Plans, 1975; Fundamentals of Corporate Qualified Retirement Plans, 1975, 78, 80; (with Norman H. Tarver) The IRA Manual, 1975, 76, 76, 78, 79, 80, 81 edits.; (with Norman H. Tarver) The Keogh Manual, 1975, 77, 78, 80 edits.; (with Norman H. Tarver) The Section 403 (b) Manual, 1975, 77, 78, 80 edits.; (with Leo C. Hodges) The Life Insurance Trust Handbook, 1980; contbr. articles to profl. jours., mags.; editor-in-chief Business Insurance Course, 1974-80, The Estate Protection Course, 1974-80, The Pensions and Profit-Sharing Course, 1974-80; Estate Planner's Service, 1979-80; In Sound, 1979-80; bd. editors Ind. Law Rev., 1977-78. Home: 715 Sugarbush Dr Zionsville IN 46077 Office: 6213 LaPas Trail PO Box 1727 Indianapolis IN 46206

MORTENSEN, ROBERT HENRY, landscape architect; b. Jackson, Mich., June 9, 1939; s. Henry and Charlotte Marie (Brown) M.; B.Landscape Arch., Ohio State U., 1961; M.Landscape Arch., U. Mich., 1965; div. Sept. 1974; children—Phillip, Paul, Susan, Julia; m. 2d, Meta Jane Hearne Blakely, Nov. 1975; stepchildren—Laura Cotner and Kathryn Blakely. Landscape architect Miller Wihry & Lantz, Landscape Architects, Engrs., Louisville, 1960, 61-63, State of Ohio Div. Parks, Columbus, 1960-61, Arthur Hills & Assos., Landscape Architects, Toledo, 1963, 65-67; pvt. practice landscape architecture, Ann Arbor, Mich., 1963-65; partner Mortensen, Meyers & Assos., 1967-69, prin. Mortensen, Meyers, Squire & Smith, Inc., 1969-73, Collaborative, Inc., Architects, Engrs., Landscape Architects, 1973-78 (all Toledo); pres. Harvey Jones and Assos., Clearwater, Fla., 1979—; owner Mortensen Assos., Toledo and Falls Church, Va., 1979—; asso. prof. U. Mich. Am. Grad. Sch., 1973; vis. lectr. Ohio State U., 1965—, Bowling Green (Ohio) State U., 1969—, U. Mich., Purdue U., 1971—, Mich. State U., 1973—; lectr. civic, social, pvt. groups, 1966—. Mem. Ohio Bd. Unreclaimed Strip Mined Lands, 1973-76; mem. Lucas County facilities rev. com. Health Planning Assn. N.W. Ohio, 1972-76, chmn. maternal and child health subcom., 1972-74, recipient Distinguished Service award 1973; mem. archtl., environ. rev. com. Ohio Arts Council, 1974-78; mem. adv. com. Toledo Econ. Planning Com., 1980—; co-founder, bd. dirs. Bicycle Council, 1980—. Fellow Am. Soc. Landscape Architects (registration com. 1962-63, chmn. pvt. practice com. 1970-72, 76-77, council profl. practice 1973-74, nat. pub. relations com. 1974-75, officer Ohio chpt. 1968-74, pres. 1972-74, trustee 1977—); Ohio Soc. Landscape Architects (pres. 1969-71), Am. Soc. Planning Ofcls., Toledo C. of C. (chmn. sts. hwys. transit com. 1972-73), Sigma Phi Epsilon. Roman Catholic. Clubs: Toledo, Washington Golf and Country Editor: Handbook Professional Practice, 1972. Home: 1920 Collingwood Blvd Toledo OH 43624 also 6843 Churchill Rd McLean VA 22101 Office: 1920 Collingwood Blvd Toledo OH 43624 also 210 Little Falls Rd Falls Church VA 22046

MORTL, FRANK LEE, trade assn. exec.; b. Kingsford, Mich., July 22, 1943; s. Frank and Betty Jane (Farley) M.; B.S. in Bus. Adminstrn., No. Mich. U., 1967; M.B.A., Central Mich. U., 1970; m. Anne Elizabeth Quinn, Dec. 30, 1967; children—Frank Lee, Theresa Anne. Mfg. mgr. Buick div. Gen. Motors Corp., Flint, Mich., 1967-70; exec. v.p. Mich. Oil and Gas Assn., Lansing, 1971—. Served with USN, 1961-64. Mem. Am. Soc. Assn. Execs., Mich. Soc. Assn. Execs., Am. Petroleum Inst., Ind. Petroleum Assn. Am., Acad. Mgmt., Soc. Petroleum Engrs., Petroleum Accts. Soc. Mich., Mich. Assn. Petroleum Landmen. Roman Catholic. Clubs: Commanders, Capitol, KC. Home: 3851 W Howe Rd Dewitt MI 48820 Office: PO Box 15069 Lansing MI 48901

MORTON, MARGARET KIRCHER, advt. co. exec.; b. Chgo., Jan. 19, 1924; d. Albert and Mame Elizabeth (Murray) Kircher; B.S., Drake U., 1946, M.A., 1947; postgrad. Northwestern U., 1949; m. Richard G. Morton, Nov. 27, 1947 (div. 1963); children—Margaret, Richard G. Pres., M.K. Morton C., advt., 1962—. Trustee, Lake Forest Acad., Ferry Hall, 1964—; sec.-treas. bd. dirs. Am. Hearing Research Found., 1963—, pres. women's bd., 1975—; bd. dirs., asst. sec. Evang. Hosp. Assn., 1975—, sec. bd., 1977—, also 75th anniversary chmn.; founding dir. Nat. Hearing Assn., 1977; bd. dirs. Door County Property Owners Assn., 1970—, Good Samaritan Hosp., Downers Grove, Ill., 1977—; trustee First Congregational Ch., Western Springs, Ill., 1972-76; mem. governing council Christ Hosp., Oak Lawn, Ill. Mem. Nat. League Am. Pen Women, Allied Arts Club, Kappa Kappa Gamma. Republican. Clubs: Woman's Athletic of Chgo., Rotary Women. Home: Locust Point Farm Box 263 Downers Grove IL 60515

MORTON, STEPHEN DANA, chemist; b. Madison, Wis., Sept. 7, 1932; s. Walter Albert and Rosalie (Amlie) M.; B.S., U. Wis., 1954, Ph.D., 1962. Asst. prof. chemistry Otterbein Coll., Westerville, Ohio, 1962-66; postdoctoral fellow water chemistry, pollution control U. Wis., Madison, 1966-67; water pollution research chemist WARF Inst., Madison, 1967-73; head environ. quality dept., 1973-76; mgr. quality assurance Raltech Sci. Services, 1977—. Served to 1st lt. Chem. Corps, AUS, 1954-56. Mem. Am. Chem. Soc., Am. Water Works Assn., Am. Soc. Limnology and Oceanography, Water Pollution Control Fedn., AAAS. Author: Water Pollution—Causes and Cures, 1976. Home: 1126 Sherman Ave Madison WI 53703 Office: PO Box 7545 Madison WI 53707

MORVIS, GEORGE MICHAEL, mgmt. and mktg. corp. exec.; b. Chgo., Dec. 27, 1940; s. George and Sadie (Kosanovich) M.; B.S. in Journalism, U. Ill., 1963; M.S. in Bus., George Washington U., 1966; m. Carolynne K. McDevitt, Oct. 16, 1965; children—Mary, George Michael, Christopher, Jamie. Dir. public relations Ill. Bankers Assn., Chgo., 1966-68, exec. sec., 1968-74; pres., chief exec. officer Financial Shares Corp., Chgo., 1974—; dir. Market Shares Corp., Chgo.; faculty mem. Iowa Banking Sch., Tenn. Banking Sch. Pres. Chgo. Fin. Advisers Club, 1972; bd. dirs. Ill. Council on Econ. Edn., 1968—, 1st v.p., 1980—. Served with Intelligence Corps, U.S. Army, 1963-65. Mem. Bank Mktg. Assn. (Service Mem. Council, chmn., 1979-80), Savs. Instns. Mktg. Soc. Am., Public Relations Soc. Am., Serbian Nat. Fedn. Serbian Eastern Orthodox. Clubs: Chgo. Press; Ruth Lake Country (Hinsdale, Ill.); Ocean Reef (Key Largo, Fla.). Home: 718 S Lincoln St Hinsdale IL 60521 Office: 62 W Huron St Chicago IL 60610

MOSBY, DORIS VIRGINIA PERRY, clin. psychologist, educator; b. Starkville, Miss., Mar. 11, 1940; d. Martin James and Maydella (Watson) Perry; A.B., Washington U., St. Louis, 1960, Ph.D. (Univ. fellow), 1965; m. Wilbert Lee Mosby, Sept. 29, 1962; children—Krista Joi, Jay Jourard. Clin. psychologist Jewish Hosp. of St. Louis, 1964-65, 66-68, St. Louis Bd. Edn., 1965-66; asst. prof. psychology, clin. psychologist U. Mo., St. Louis, 1968-71; asso. prof. Ga. State U., 1971-72, Webster Coll., 1972-74, Washington U., 1974-77; coordinator psychology St. Louis State Sch. and Hosp., 1977—; cons. Mich. State U., 1977-78; pvt. practice clin. psychology, St. Louis, 1974—; cons. in field; v.p. home health care advisory bd. St. Louis Comprehensive Health Center, 1973-75. Recipient award of appreciation for vol. services King-Fanon Mental Health Center of St. Louis Assn. Black Psychologists, Inc., 1976; USPHS trainee, 1960-64. Mem. Am. (vis. psychologists program 1974-75), Mo. psychol. assns., Assn. Black Psychologists Nat., St. Louis Assn. Black Psychologists (co-chmn. 1969-70, sec. 1974-75), Phi Beta Kappa, Alpha Lambda Delta, Sigma Gamma Rho. Lutheran. Contbr. articles to profl. publs. Home: 6328 Emma Ave Saint Louis MO 63136 Office: 10695 Bellefontaine Rd Saint Louis MO 63137

MOSBY, WILBERT LEE, educator; b. St. Louis, Jan. 13, 1936; s. Paul and Stella Mae (Patton) M.; A.A., Tex. So. U., 1959; B.A., U. Mo., 1970; M.A., Webster Coll., 1974; M.S., So. Ill. U., 1976; m. Doris Perry, Oct. 29, 1962; children—Krista Joi, Jay Jourard. Police officer, St. Louis, 1963-68; tchr. St. Louis public schs., 1968-70; instr. St. Louis Jr. Coll., 1976—; coordinator spl. service program U. Mo., St. Louis, 1977—; cons. div. family services State Mo. Jr. Coll., part-time, 1972-78. Served with U.S. Army, 1959-61. Recipient Notable Am. award Am. Biol. Inst., 1980. Mem. Am. Polit. Sci. Assn. Lutheran. Home: 6328 Emma St St Louis MO 63136 Office: 8001 Natural Bridge Normandy MO 63121

MOSELY, RUSSELL CHARLES, educator; b. Omro, Wis., July 31, 1914; s. Harley Ralph and Agnes Ethel (Smith) M.; Ed.B., U. Wis., 1936, postgrad. 1949-52; M.A., Lawrence U., 1943; m. Irene M. O'Connell, Aug. 5, 1937; children—Gail Ann Mosely Much, Mary Ellen Mosely Thomas, Patrick Russell. Tchr. elem. and secondary schs., Omro public schs., 1936-45, adminstr., 1945-49; vis. lectr. U. Wis., Madison, 1963, U. Wis., Platteville, 1966, U. Wis., Eau Claire, 1967, U. Wis., Superior, 1968; supr. secondary edn. Dept. Public Instrn., State of Wis., 1949-65, coordinator curriculum devel. and implementation, 1949-65, dep. adminstr. instructional services, 1975-81; leader instructional devel. team to Nicaragua, 1974; mem. study-travel seminar to India, 1969; staff mem. Ind. Consortium for Internat. Programs Workshop, 1975; cons. ednl. measurement projects, 1953-63. Mem. Gov.'s Commn. on UN, State of Wis., 1976—; mem. Wis. Ednl. Communications Bd., 1972-81. Fulbright fellow, 1969-76. Mem. Assn. for Supervision and Curriculum Devel., Wis. Assn. for Supervision and Curriculum Devel., Nat. Council for Social Studies, Wis. Council for Social Studies (exec. bd. 1949-65), World Council for Curriculum and Instrn. Author: The College Preparatory Function in Wisconsin High Schools, 1958; The Social Sciences Through Understanding, 1940; Scope and Sequence for Social Studies in Wisconsin Schools, 1968; India-A Look Across Cultures, 1975; Nicaragua-A Look Across Cultures, 1975; Toward Excellence in Education, 1975; contbr. articles to jours. in edn. Home: 3209 Lake Mendota Dr Madison WI 53705

MOSER, DANIEL HYDE, cons. mech. engr.; b. Warren, Ohio, July 10, 1932; s. George W. and Rea Bertine (Boyd) M.; B.Engring., Youngstown U., 1955, postgrad. in mech. engring., 1970-71; m. Holyn Ruth Fusselman Masters, June 28, 1980; 1 stepson, James L. Masters. Engr. detailer Taylor Winfield Co., Warren, 1957-58; design engr. Nat. Gypsum Co., Miles, Ohio, 1958-60; design engr. Valentz, Inc., Warren, 1961-65; design sect. leader Consol. Comstock Co., Warren, 1966-71; project mgr. Venetta, Inc., Warren, 1971-75; pres., chmn. bd. RARE Corp., Warren, 1976—; mgmt. cons., 1976—. Served to lt. AUS, 1955-57. Registered profl. engr., Ohio. Mem. ASME, Nat. Soc. Profl. Engrs., Assn. Iron and Steel Engrs., Standards Engring. Soc., Res. Officers Assn. U.S. (life). Republican. Methodist. Home and Office: 189 Ohio Ave NW Warren OH 44485

MOSER, GERALD EUGENE, music co. exec.; b. Wells County, Ind., Feb. 27, 1945; s. Eugene Carl and Mabeline Elizabeth (Smith) M.; B.A., Ft. Wayne Bible Coll., 1968; M.A., St. Francis Grad. Coll., Ft. Wayne, 1970; m. Rosalyn Jean Mertz, Aug. 9, 1969; children—Tamara Lynn, Michelle Renee. Tchr., N. Side High Sch., Ft. Wayne, 1968-70, Carroll High Sch., Flora, Ind., 1970-71, Tri-Central High Sch., Kokomo, Ind., 1971-72; operator Mygrant Music Store, Kokomo, 1972—; owner, operator Musik Stunde, music studios, Kokomo, 1973—; landlord single and duplex homes; instr. band pvt. schs.; dir. ch. music various chs. Ind., 1963—. Mem. Haynes-Apperson Festival Com., 1975—. Democrat. Baptist. Club: Kiwanis (charter pres. SunRisers, Kokomo, 1975, sec. 1978-80, lt. gov. 1980-81), Elks. Home: 3606 S Webster St Kokomo IN 46901 Office: 107 W Mulberry St Kokomo IN 46901

MOSER, HANNAH SCHLESINGER, audiologist; b. Vienna, Austria, Apr. 22, 1921; d. Isidor and Emilie (Wirz) Schlesinger; came to U.S., 1949, naturalized, 1955; B.A., Hunter Coll., 1954; M.A., Northwestern U., 1956; m. John B. Moser, Mar. 6, 1954; 1 dau., Barbara Elizabeth. Teaching asst. audiology Northwestern U., Evanston, Ill., 1955-56; tchr., supr. edn. for deaf, dir. auditory tng. Chgo. Pub. Schs., 1956-75; audiologist Whitney Young Magnet High Sch., Chgo., 1975—; lectr. No. Ill. U., 1970, Northwestern U., 1970, 73; audiologist Centro para la Salud del Pueblo, Chgo., 1972. Mem. Am. Speech and Hearing Assn., (cert. in audiology), Ill. Speech and Hearing Assn., Chgo. Speech and Hearing Assn., Chgo. Tchrs. of Hearing Impaired (pres. 1972-74), Zeta Phi Eta. Home: 415 Audubon Rd Riverside IL 60546 Office: 211 S Laflin St Chicago IL 60607

MOSER, ROBERT LEE, civil engr.; b. Bern, Kans., Apr. 15, 1933; s. Aaron and Hulda (Giesel) M.; B.S., Finlay Engring. Coll., Kansas City, Mo., 1960; m. Norma Jean Williams, Dec. 15, 1957; children—Bradley Scott, Leslie Ann. Land surveyor Kans. Hwy. Commn., 1955-57; civil engr. Ill. Hwy. Dept., Dixon, 1960-64; civil engr., mgr. Kans. Engrs., Newton, 1964-67; civil engr., owner Moser & Assos., Engrs. & Planners, Newton, Kans., 1967—; owner, pub. City Power; owner Project Funding Service, Inc. Cons. Northview Opportunity Center for Retarded Children, 1968; mem. Southcentral Kans. Health Planning Council, 1968, Newton Housing Authority; chmn. County United Fund, 1971. Bd. dirs. Community Chest, 1971. Served with USAF, 1951-55. Registered profl. engr., Kans., Mo., Okla., Iowa, Nebr., Ark., Colo., Ill. Mem. Am. Cons. Engrs. Council, Nat. Soc. Profl. Engrs., Kans. Engring. Soc., Kans. Cons. Engrs. (v.p.), Newton C. of C., Am. Legion, VFW. Methodist. Elk. Club: Toastmasters International (past v.p. Newton). Home: 1401 Terrace Newton KS 67114 Office: 500 1/2 Main St Newton KS 67114

MOSES, HAROLD ALTON, educator; b. Flippin, Ark., Dec. 20, 1926; s. William J. and Mae (Hampton) M.; B.S., S.E. Mo. State U., 1955; M.A., U. Mich., 1960; Ed.D. (Rehab. Services Adminstrn. fellow), U. Mo., 1965; m. Martha L. Hopkins, Mar. 3, 1950; children—Randall H., Joe M. Tchr., counselor Hazelwood (Mo.) Sch. Dist., 1955-65; asst. prof. edn. U. Ill., Urbana, 1965-70, asso. prof., 1970—; pvt. practice psychotherapy, Champaign, Ill., 1965—. Served with U.S. Army, 1943-45. NDEA fellow, 1959-60. Mem. Am. Psychol. Assn., Nat. Rehab. Assn., Nat. Register Health Service Providers in Psychology, NEA, Am. Personnel and Guidance Assn., Phi Theta Kappa, Phi Alpha Theta, Kappa Delta Pi, Phi Delta Kappa. Democrat. Baptist. Club: Masons. Author: (with J.S. Zaccaria) Facilitating Human Development through Reading, 1968; (with Zaccaria and J.S. Hollowell) Bibliotherapy in Rehabilitation, Educational, and Mental Health Settings, 1978; sr. editor: Readings in Rehabilitation Counseling, 1971; Research Readings in

Rehabilitation, 1973; Student Personnel Work in General Education, 1974; contbr. articles to profl. jours. Home: 804 Stratford Dr Champaign IL 61820 Office: Dept Edn Univ Ill Urbana IL 61801

MOSES, IRVING BYRON, architect; b. Chgo., Aug. 5, 1925; s. Morris Lester and Dorothy (Berns) M.; B.S. in Architecture, U. Ill., 1950, B.S. in Naval Sci., 1946, B.S. in Liberal Arts, 1946; m. Toby Kornfeld, June 29, 1947; children—Barbara Susan, Jack Robert, Carol Lynn. With Small Homes Council of Ill., Urbana, 1947-48; design draftsman Holsman, Holsman Klekamp & Taylor & Mies Van der Rohe, Chgo., 1950-51; partner Comm, Comm & Moses, AIA, Chgo., 1951-62; prin. I. Moses & Assos., AIA, Chgo., 1962—; adj. prof. architecture Central YMCA Community Coll., 1970-78. Appearance rev. commr. City of Highland Park, 1977—. Served with USNR, 1943-46. Recipient scroll of honor State of Israel, 1973. Mem. AIA (honor awards), Nat. Council Archtl. Registration Bds., Ill. Soc. Architects, Am. Arbitration Assn. (judge-arbitrator). Jewish. Home: 145 Blackhawk Rd Highland Park IL 60035 Office: I Moses & Assos AIA 53 W Jackson Blvd Chicago IL 60604

MOSHER, GREGORY DEAN, theatre dir.; b. N.Y.C., Jan. 15, 1949; s. Thomas Edward and Florence Christine M.; student Oberlin Coll., 1967-69; B.F.A., Ithaca Coll., 1971; postgrad. Juilliard Sch., 1971-74. Dir., Stage 2, Goodman Theatre, Chgo., 1974-77, artistic dir., 1978—; producer new works by Tennessee Williams, Studs Terkel, David Mamet, John Guare, Michael Weller, Wole Soyinka; producer Samuel Beckett's first directing work in U.S., Krapp's Last Tape, 1979, Endgame, 1980. Office: Goodman Theatre Chicago IL 60603*

MOSHER, RONALD FRANCIS, state comptroller; b. Fort Dodge, Iowa, July 8, 1943; s. Clarence Melvin and Grace Elva (Fisher) M.; B.S., U. Denver, 1966; M.B.A., Cornell U., 1971; m. Patricia Ann Chapman, June 1, 1963; children—Christopher Ronald, Jonathan Clark. Mem. audit staff Price Waterhouse & Co., C.P.A.'s, Denver, 1966-69; with Scott Paper Co., 1971-77, gen. mgr. recreation subs., Dover, Del., 1972-74, mgr. fin. and logistics, 1974-77; budget dir., State of Del., 1977-79; state comptroller, chief fin. officer, fin. adv. to Gov., State of Iowa, Des Moines, 1979—. Bd. dirs. Central Iowa Health Assn., 1980--. Served with USAF, 1963-67. Mem. Nat. Assn. State Budget Officers (mem. exec. council), Am. Soc. Public Adminstrn. (exec. council Iowa chpt.), Am. Inst. C.P.A.'s. Republican. Episcopalian. Office: State Capitol Des Moines IA 50319

MOSIER, C. FRED, constrn. co. exec.; b. Muncie, Ind., Apr. 16, 1930; s. Claude F. and Ethel (Tussey) M.; student Chgo. Tech., 1949-50; m. Natalie Joan Milhollin, June 4, 1950; children—Linda Kay Thrope, Daniel R., Robert J. Owner, C. Fred Mosier, bldg. contractor, Muncie, 1950-65; pres. Mosier Constrn., Inc., Muncie, 1965—. Cub scoutmaster Boy Scouts Am., 1965-67. Pres. bd. dirs. Muncie Mission, 1969-70, trustee, 1970—; bd. dirs. Ind. Masonic Home & Hosp., 1965-67; div. chmn. United Way, 1979. Mem. Nat. Home Builders Assn., Asso. Gen. Contractors Am., Muncie Contractors Assn. (pres. 1973-78). Clubs: Masons, Order Eastern Star, Kiwanis Internat. Home: Rural Route 2 Box 42 Ridgeville IN 47380 Office: 4309 S Madison St Muncie IN 47302

MOSIER, FRANK ALAN, govt. ofcl.; b. Hoxie, Kans., Dec. 27, 1929; s. Decker and Lela Frances (Mowry) M.; B.S. in Bus. Adminstrn. and Acctg., Kans. State U., 1951, M.A. in Agrl. Econs., 1958; m. C. Joan Mahanna, Aug. 28, 1949; children—Rebecca, Derek, Craig (dec.). Asst. bus. mgr. dept. intercollegiate athletics Kans. State U., Manhattan, 1951-61; asso. dir. research Kans. Farm Bur., Manhattan, 1961-66; bus. mgr., dir. public relations Schilling Inst. Tech., Salina, Kans., 1966-67; asst. v.p. 1st Nat. Bank of Manhattan, 1967-69; Kans. liaison for U.S. Sen. Bob Dole, 1969-70; state exec. dir Agrl. Stblzn. and Conservation Service, Dept. Agr., Manhattan, 1970-77, 81—; exec. dir. Big Lakes Regional Council Local Govts., Manhattan, 1977-81. Former chmn. Kans. Farm-City Council; chmn. State Emergency Bd.; bd. dirs. Unified Sch. Dist., 1973-77, Kans. Assn. Sch. Bds., 1974-77. Mem. Manhattan C. of C., Alpha Kappa Psi, Phi Delta Kappa. Republican. Methodist. Club: Manhattan Solar Kiwanis (past pres., past lt. gov. div.). Office: 2601 Anderson Ave Manhattan KS 66502*

MOSIER, JOHN ADELBERT, plastics co. exec.; b. East Cleveland, Ohio, May 20, 1938; s. Clifford Charles and Virginia Mae (Belville) M.; student Ohio State U., 1957-60, Cleve. State U., 1960-66, Western Res. U., 1966; m. Margaret Sabol, Nov. 12, 1960; children—Tammy, Gretchen, Wendy, John Adelbert. Field sales engr. Glastic Corp., Cleve., 1961-66, asst. sales mgr., advt. mgr., 1968-70; field sales engr. Ward Leonard, Mt. Vernon, N.Y., 1966-67; Taylor Corp., Valley Forge, Pa., 1967-68; account mgr. Rockwell Internat., Detroit, 1970-76; sales and mktg. mgr. Zehrco Plastics, Inc., Ashtabula, Ohio, 1976-79; v.p. mktg. Roller Plastics, Inc., Ashtabula, 1979-81; bus. mgr. railroad products Gen. Tire and Rubber Co., Southfield, Mich., 1981—. Mem. Soc. Plastics Inc., U.S. C. of C., Ducks Unltd. Contbr. articles to profl. jours. Office: 21700 Telegraph Rd Southfield MI

MOSIMANN, GARY FRED, sch. prin.; b. Greenville, Ill., Aug. 31, 1938; s. Fred August and Ruth Caroline (Wade) M.; B.S., So. Ill. U., 1966, M.S. in Adminstrn., 1969, specialist ednl. adminstrn. cert., 1974, postgrad., 1979—; m. Joyce Ann Eaves, Dec. 17, 1960; children—Kimberly Ann, Laura Lynn. Tchr., Cahokia (Ill.) Unit Sch. 187, 1966-75, prin. Chenot Middle Sch., 1980—; cons. Area Service Center, Lebanon, Ill., 1972-76; site coordinator Tchr. Corps, 1979, So. Ill. U., Edwardsville/Cahokia, 1979-80, also mem. adv. com. ednl. adminstrn. Supt. Sunday Sch., Bethany United Meth. Ch., Columia, Ill., 1981, lay leader, 1980. Served with M.I., AUS, 1962-65. Mem. Ill. Assn. Supervision and Curriculum Devel., Nat. Assn. Supervision and Curriculum Devel., Cahokia Admintrv. Assn., So. Ill. U. Alumni Assn., Phi Delta Kappa. Club: Columbia Bath and Tennis. Home: Route 1 Box 232b Columbia IL 62236 Office: 5721 Church Ln Cahokia IL 62297

MOSKAL, STEPHEN LEE, librarian; b. Winterhaven, Fla., Mar. 16, 1946; s. Leonard Raymond and Donna Lee (Bagley) M.; B.A. in History, Lewis U., Lockport, Ill., 1967, M.B.A., 1980; M.A. in L.S., Rosary Coll., River Forest, Ill., 1971; m. Fredereike Anne Maleski, July 1, 1967; children—Anatasia, Stephen Lee. Asst. circulation librarian U. Chgo. Law Library, 1970-71; audio visual cons. Bur Oak Library System, Joliet, Ill., 1971-74; dir. LaGrange (Ill.) Public Library, 1974—; del. White House Conf. Libraries, 1978. Mem. Assn. Info. Mgrs., Ill. Library Assn., Library Administrs. Conf. No. Ill. Roman Catholic. Producer cable TV programs, 1973. Office: 10 W Cossitt St LaGrange IL 60525

MOSKAL, WILLIAM FREDERICK, hosp. ofcl.; b. Detroit, Aug. 22, 1946; s. Wasyl and Mary (Husak) M.; B.A., Wayne State U., 1969, Ed.S., 1976; Ed.D., 1978; M.Ed., Marygrove Coll., 1971; m. Diane Evangelista, Oct. 14, 1977; 1 son, Christian. Tchr. various schs., 1967-75; psychologist Ednl. Resource Group, Detroit, 1975—; asst. prof. Oakland U., 1978-79; orgn. devel. cons. Henry Ford Hosp., Detroit, 1979—. Mem. Am. Soc. for Tng. and Devel., Am. Soc. Health, Edn. and Tng., Orgn. Devel. Inst., Am. Mgmt. Assn., Ukrainian Democratic Club. Home: 12839 Klinger St Detroit MI 48212 Office: Henry Ford Hosp 2799 W Grand Blvd Detroit MI 48202

MOSLER, JACOB EUGENE, educator; b. Hoxie, Kans., Feb. 5, 1924; s. Decker and Lela (Mowry) M.; D.V.M., Kans. State U., 1945, M.S., 1948; m. Betty Jean Willey, Sept. 16, 1945; children—Steven, Michael, Kelly, Susan. Instr., Kans. State U., 1945-48, asst. prof., 1948-49, asso. prof., 1951-54, prof., 1954—, head dept. surgery and medicine, 1961-81; asst. prof. U. Ill., 1949-50; cons. in field. Mem. Manhattan Planning Commn., 1966-70, chmn., 1969-70; bd. dirs. Manhattan YMCA. Recipient award Am. Animal Hosp., 1974, Intermountain Vet. Med. Assn., 1977, FDA Commr.'s spl. citation, 1977. Mem. World (v.p. 1977-80), Am. (exec. bd. 1971-76, chmn. 1974-75), Kans. (pres. 1971) vet. med. assns., Am. Animal Hosp. Assn., Am. Assn. Lab. Animal Sci., N.Y. Acad. Scis., Am. Assn. Vet. Clinicians (past pres.), Manhattan C. of C. (past dir.), Sigma Xi, Phi Kappa Phi, Gamma Sigma Delta. Clubs: Lions, Rotary. Contbr.: Current Therapy in Veterinary Medicine, 1971, 73, 76; Merck Veterinary Manual, 1967, 73, 79; Intervetebral Disc Protrusion in the Dog, 1966; Veterinary Clinics of North America, 1971, 77-78; Canine Medicine, 1979; Veterinary Theriogenology, 1980; The Great Dane, 1981. Office: Veterinary Medicine Center Kansas State U Manhattan KS 66502*

MOSLEY, DUSHUN HOMER, computer scientist; b. Chicago Heights, Ill., June 8, 1948; s. Walter Lee and Mary Riehley (Johnson) M.; A.A., Ferris State Coll., 1968; M.S. in Computer Sci., Mich. State U., 1975. Computer operator, programmer, programmer analyst Auto Owners Ins. Co., Lansing, Mich., 1969-73; programmer analyst, systems analyst State of Mich., Lansing, 1973-76; systems analyst trainer Blue Cross, Blue Shield, Chgo., 1976-77; mgr. Boeing Computer Service, Chgo., 1977-78; founder, pres. Eduteach, Inc., Chgo., 1978—; cons. and instr. data processing. Named Outstanding Instr., Boeing Computer Service, 1978. Mem. Assn. Computing Machinery, Ind. Computer Cons. Assn., Systems Programmers Soc., Data Processing Mgmt. Assn. Developer structure temp, 1977; creator systematic software devel. courses, 1978. Home: 908 W Agatite Chicago IL 60640 Office: Eduteach Inc Suite 907 162 N State St Chicago IL 60601

MOSS, ANITA NOREEN FRANKEL, occupational therapist; b. Cleve., May 18, 1954; d. Leon H. and Nina (Zwerdling) Frankel; B.S. in Allied Health Professions, Ohio State U., 1976; m. Kenneth S. Moss, Nov. 19, 1978. Acting chief therapist Luth. Med. Center, Cleve., 1976-77; therapist Univ. Hosps. of Cleve., 1977-78; adminstrv. chief therapist St. Louis County Hosp., Clayton, Mo., 1978—; cons. in field Mid-Am. Rehab., Warrenburg, Mo., 1979—. Lic. occupational therapist, Ohio. Mem. Am. Occupational Therapy Assn. (nat. registration), Ohio Occupational Therapy Assn., Mo. Occupational Therapy Assn., Cleve. Dist. Occupational Therapy Assn. (edn. chmn., 1977-78, treas., 1978), Alpha Lambda Delta, Delta Phi Epsilon. Club: Orgn. Rehab. Tng. Home: 1226 Traverton Dr Chesterfield MO 63017 Office: 601 S Brentwood Blvd Clayton MO 63105

MOSS, CRUSE WATSON, automobile co. exec.; b. Kent, Ohio, Apr. 7, 1926; s. Cruse Watson and Lucille M. (Shafer) M.; B.S. in Indsl. Engring., Ohio U., Athens, 1948; m. Virginia Ann Patton, Dec. 22, 1949; children—Stephen, Carol Susan, Michael. Pres., Kaiser Jeep Automotive div., also exec. v.p. Kaiser Jeep Corp., 1960-70; group v.p. Am. Motors Corp., 1970; pres., dir. AM Gen. Corp., Detroit, 1970-79; pres., chief exec. officer, dir. White Motor Corp., Farmington Hills, Mich., 1979-81; chmn., chief exec. officer Gen. Automotive Corp., Ann Arbor, Mich., 1979—. Adv. council Internat. Eye Found.; mem. founders soc. Detroit Inst. Arts. Served with USNR, 1944-46. Mem. Assn. U.S. Army (chmn. council trustees), Soc. Automotive Engrs., Confrerie des Chevaliers du Tastevin, Chief Execs. Forum, Beta Theta Pi. Presbyterian. Clubs: Circumnavigators, Detroit Athletic. Home: 2205 Melrose St Ann Arbor MI 48104 Office: 1900 Manchester Rd Ann Arbor MI 48104

MOSS, JAMES BURKE, ins. co. exec.; b. Clarksburg, W.Va., Apr. 29, 1933; s. Hayward B. and Edith E. (Reeder) M.; student Defience Coll., 1951-52, Ohio State U., 1953; m. Carol M. Kuck, July 26, 1952; children—Robert, Steven, Rebecca, Kathy, Donald, Mark. Agt., Nat. Life and Accident Ins. Co., Lima, Ohio, 1953-54, staff mgr., Springfield, Ohio, 1954-57; prin. James B. Moss Ins. Agy., Lima, Springfield, Ohio, South Bend, Ind., Huntington, Ind., 1957-76; v.p. mortgage banking/savs. and loan bus. Am. Bankers Life Assurance Co., Miami, Fla., 1976-78, v.p. fin. manpower devel., 1978-80; v.p. Med. Life Ins. Co., Cleveland, Ohio, 1980-81; Dir. Money Concepts Internat. of N. Central U.S. Inc.; pres. Investment Diamond Assests LTD. Dist. chmn., bd. dirs. council Anthony Wayne Area council Boy Scouts Am., 1973-74, dist. fin. chmn. South Fla. council, 1976, dist. chmn., 1978, council tng. dir., exec. bd., 1979. Recipient numerous sales awards. Office: 225 S Detroit St Kenton OH 43326

MOSS, JOHN ALLEN, automobile accessories mfg. co. exec.; b. Lima, Ohio, Oct. 6, 1949; s. Hayward B. and Edith Moss; A.A., Tri-State Coll., Angola, Ind., 1972; m. Barbara Ann Keller, Aug. 12, 1972; children—John Allen, Kristi Anne, James Adam. Design draftsman Vulcraft Corp., St. Joseph, Ind., 1972; injection mold designer Sheller Globe Corp., Grabill, Ind., 1972-74; sr. project designer Bowmar Instruments, Ft. Wayne, Ind., 1974; sr. tool designer Magnavox Corp., G & I, Ft. Wayne, 1974-75; pres. Moss Mfg. Co., Lima, Ohio, 1975—, also dir. Bd. dirs. Trinity council Boy Scouts Am., 1980—, Lima (Ohio) Salvation Army. Methodist (bd. dirs. ch.). Home: 1809 W Spring St Lima OH 45805 Office: 895 Shawnee Rd Lima OH 45805

MOSS, LEONARD W(ALLACE), anthropologist, educator; b. Detroit, Sept. 7, 1923; s. Adolph and Minnie (Moskowitz) M.; B.Sc., Wayne State U., 1947, M.A., 1950; Ph.D., U. Mich., 1955; m. Beebe Gottesman, Dec. 2, 1945; 1 dau., Amelia Moss Simms. Instr. Wayne State U., Detroit, 1952-57, asst. prof., 1957-61, asso. prof., 1961-65, chmn. dept. sociology and anthropology, 1962-68, prof. anthropology, 1965—, dir. social sci. program, 1967-68; Fulbright research scholar U. Rome, 1955-56, Fulbright sr. lectr., 1961-62, sr. research scholar, 1968-69; vis. lectr. Scuola Italiana per Servizio Sociale, 1956, Universita Internazionale degli Scienzi, Italy, 1962; vis. prof. Trinity Coll., Barbieri Center, Rome, 1970-76; cons. to various univs., govt. agys., publishers and broadcasting stations, 1956—. Vice chmn. Citizens Adv. Com. to Oak Park (Mich.) Bd. Edn., 1960-61; mem. regional adv. bd. Anti-Defamation League, 1961-63, 64-69, 71-74. Served to sgt. Intelligence Corps, USAAF, 1942-45. Decorated Order of Merit (Italy); recipient Faculty Service award Wayne State U., 1976, 77, 80. Fellow Am. Anthrop. Assn., AAAS, Royal Anthrop. Assn.; mem. Mich. Sociol. Soc. (pres. 1963-64), Central States Anthrop. Soc. (pres. 1969-70, Disting. Lectr. award 1980), Mich. Acad. Sci. Arts and Letters (mem. exec. council 1963-64), Am. Italian Hist. Assn. (founder 1966, mem. exec. bd. 1966-73, 80—), Italian Assn. of Social Scis., Italian Am. Cultural Soc., Sigma Xi. Contbr. articles to scholarly jours. in U.S., Israel, USSR, Eng. and Italy; contbr. chpts. to books on anthropology. Home: 12950 Northfield Blvd Oak Park MI 48237 Office: Dept Anthropology 137 Manoogian Hall Wayne State U Detroit MI 48202

MOSSBAUER, LOUIS, optometrist; b. Bavaria, Germany, Mar. 1, 1902; s. Karl and Margaret (Meister) Mossbauer; student Fortbildungsschule and Musikschule, Bavaria; postgrad. Hosp. and Med. Sch., Chgo., 1945; O.D., Monroe Coll. Optometry, 1946; m. Alice Harkness, Nov. 15, 1947; 1 son, Louis Carl. Came to U.S., 1927, naturalized, 1937. Dir. United Artists Conservatories Music, Balt., 1928-40; owner Berman Optical Co., Washington, 1940-47; practice optometry, Chgo. and Elmhurst, Ill., 1946—; pres. Midwestern Sch. Optics, 1946-52; pres. German-Am. Contact Lens Mfg. Co., Elmhurst; founder Internat. Contact Lens Specialists. Mem. Am. (hon. life mem.), Ill. (trustee 1959-61) optometric assns., N.E. Ill. Optometric Soc. (rec. sec. 1953-56, 59-63, pres. 1957-58, 64-65), Ednl. Council Optometry (past sec.), Am. Pub. Health Assn. (vision com.), Med. Research Assos. Adv. Panel, Ill. Soc. for Prevention Blindness, AAAS, Ill. Coll. Optometry Alumni Assn., Tomb and Key, Kappa Phi Delta. Rotarian (past dir. Elmhurst). Research in fitting and mfg. latest types corneal contact lenses. Home: Elmhurst IL 60126 Office: 191 Addison Ave Elmhurst IL 60126

MOSSER, DONALD ALLAN, insurance agy. exec.; b. Rockford, Ill., Oct. 29, 1933; s. Glenn Arthur and Mary Anna (Stotler) M.; B.A. cum laude in Econs., Beloit Coll., 1955; m. Doris C. Clausius, July 28, 1962; children—David Glenn, Michael Donald, Susan Marie. With Camlin Ins. Agy., Rockford, 1957—, now exec. v.p. Vice pres. Rockford Area Council Chs., 1968; chmn. of congregation Our Saviors Lutheran Ch., 1975; mem. Rockford Human Relations Commn., 1966-68; pres. Rockford Y's Mens Club, 1962, dist. gov., 1963; mem. Beloit Coll. Alumni Council, 1971-74; treas. Rockford Area Council for Arts and Scis., 1978-80; pres. Winnebago County Opportunities Industrialization Center, 1973, Booker T. Washington Community Center, 1974; chmn. long range planning com. United Way, 1978-80; bd. dirs. Rockford YMCA. Served with USN, 1956-57. C.L.U.; C.P.C.U. Mem. Assn. Ind. Ins. Agts. of Rockford (pres. 1957). Home: 411 N Prospect St Rockford IL 61107 Office: 318 N 1st St Rockford IL 61110

MOSTAD, DAVID LOREN, mcpl. engr.; b. Kelliher, Minn., Nov. 4, 1942; s. Edwin Wilfred and Elna Marie (Nelson) M.; ed. public, service and vocat. schs.; m. Judith Kay Wallin Aug. 20, 1976; children by previous marriage—Dulci Lynn, Bonnie Michelle, Matthew Todd, Christian Michael. Maintenance engr. Mt. Sinai Hosp., Mpls., 1970-77; city engr. City of Kelliher, 1977-80; ind. plumbing and heating contractor, Kelliher, 1980—. Supr., chmn. bd. dirs. Twp. of Kelliher, 1979—. Served with USN, 1962-70. Cert. mcpl. water operator, cert. wastewater operator, Minn. Mem. Am. Water Works Assn., Water Assn. Northeastern Minn., Am. Legion. Club: Kelliher Community. Home and Office: Box 79A Star Route N Kelliher MN 56650

MOTE, W. NEWTON, educator; b. Cin., Aug. 20, 1927; s. Ralph Irvin and Cora (Griffing) M.; B.S., Ohio State U., 1951; M.S., Kent State U., 1978; m. Mary Leland Lord, June 10, 1950 (div. 1970); children—Susan Diane, Leslie Jane, W. Ralph; m. 2d, Patricia Ann McDonald, Aug. 10, 1974. Dist. salesman Ralston Purina Co., St. Louis, 1952-61; dist. mgr., regional mgr. Cargill, Inc., Mpls., 1961-75; tchr., coordinator agr. bus. Polaris Vocat. Center, Middleburg Heights, Ohio, 1975-77; instr. farm bus. planning analysis Lorain County Vocat. Center, Oberlin, Ohio, 1977—; cons. farm tax acctg., 1977—. Mem. Lorain County Soil Conservation Dist. Adv. Bd., 1980—, Lorain County Agrl. Council, 1979—; mem. adv. bd. Lorain County Extension Dept., 1978—. Mem. Lorain County Farm Bur., Am. Vocat. Assn., Ohio Vocat. Assn., Nat. Vocat. Agr. Tchrs. Assn., Ohio Vocat. Agr. Tchrs. Assn., Ohio State U. Alumni Assn. (life), Alumni Assn. Ohio State U. Marching Band, Alpha Gamma Rho. Republican. Presbyterian. Clubs: Masons, Kiwanis. Home: 209 Best St Berea OH 44017 Office: 15181 State Route 58 Oberlin OH 44074

MOTES, MARVIN EUGENE, cleaning co. exec.; b. Chillicothe, Ohio, Oct. 25, 1935; s. John Griffith and Lorraine Louise (Litter) M.; B.S. in Bus. Adminstrn., Ohio State U., 1961; m. Loretta Lee Maughmer, Feb. 2, 1957; children—Kelly Lee, Julia Ann, Lisa Joan. Office mgr. Research div. Mead Corp., Chillicothe, 1956-66; pres., gen. mgr. AA Cleaning Co., Inc., Chillicothe, 1963—, AA Cleaning Supply Co., Inc., Chillicothe, 1965—, Pickaway Indsl. Packaging Co., Inc., Circleville, Ohio, 1979—. Bd. dirs. Med. Center Hosp., Chillicothe, 1977-80, chmn. fin. com., 1979-80, treas., 1979-80; active Small Bus. Adminstrn. Mem. Bldg. Services Contractors Assn. Democrat. Methodist. Club: Elks. Home: 1 Applewood Dr Chillicothe OH 45601 Office: 28155 River Rd Circleville OH 43113

MOTLEY, ROBERT JOSEPH, educator; b. New Hartford, Mo., Nov. 26, 1932; s. Ernest Cleveland and Ethel (Pritchett) M.; B.S. in Edn., N.E. Mo. State U., 1953, M.A. in Bus. Edn., 1958; Ed.D., U. Colo., 1967. Tchr., Osceola (Mo.) High Sch., 1955-61; mem. faculty Kansas City (Kans.) Jr. Coll., 1961-62, So. Ill. U., Edwardsville, 1962-64, U. Wyo., Laramie, 1965-66, Morehead (Ky.) State U., 1966-67, Utah State U., Logan, 1967-68; mem. faculty Western Ill. U., Macomb, 1968—, prof. bus. edn. and adminstrv. office mgmt., 1980—. Served with U.S. Army, 1953-55. Mem. Nat. Bus. Edn. Assn., Ill. Bus. Edn. Assn., Ill. Vocat. Assn., North Central Bus. Edn. Assn., Western Ill. Bus. Edn. Assn., Adminstrv. Mgmt. Soc., Am. Bus. Communications Assn., Central Ill. Word Processing Assn., Soc. for Preservation and Encouragement of Barber Shop Quartet Singing in Am. (pres. Macomb chpt. 1976, 79). Presbyterian. Author: (with Marj P. Leaming) Administrative Office Management, 1979, Cases in Administrative Office Management, 1979. Home: 1130 Stacy Ln Macomb IL 61455 Office: Stipes Hall Western Ill U Macomb IL 61455

MOTLEY, VIRGIL LORENZO, city ofcl.; b. Gary, Ind., Dec. 12, 1936; s. William and Bessie Motley; cert. in law enforcement Calumet Coll., 1974; cert. Law Enforcement Officers Tng. Sch., 1965; grad. Mortuary Sci. Coll., Chgo.; m. Elaine Horton; children—Veronica, Virgil, Erica, Cydnei. Elec. and insulin shock therapist VA Hosp., Battle Creek, Mich.; relief foreman U.S. Steel Corp., Gary; embalmer, funeral dir. Guy and Allen Funeral Home, Gary; hwy. insp. Ind. Hwy. Commn.; with Gary Police Dept., 1965—, detective, 1971-73, exec. asst. to chief police, 1973-77, sgt., from 1977, now dep. chief police with assigned duties acting chief police; mem. Region I, Ind. Criminal Justice Planning Agy.; mem. state-wide task force Ind. Criminal Justice Planning and Law Enforcement; mem. Lake County Law Enforcement Council. Mem. Lake County Coordinating Council. Served with USAF, 1954-58. Recipient citation Am. Legion, 1968; merit award Am. Fedn. Police, 1968, 70, Latin Am. Orgn. Gary, also Mayor of Gary; commendation award Frontiers Internat. Service

Club, Gary; award of honor City of Gary, 1975, also numerous letters of appreciation; cert. Ind. Dept. Public Instrn. Mem. Nat. Assn. Chiefs of Police, Ind. Assn. Chiefs of Police, Internat. Assn. Chiefs of Police, Nat. Orgn. Black Law Enforcement Execs., NAACP, VFW (hon.). Office: 1301 Broadway Gary IN 46407

MOTTL, RONALD MILTON, congressman; b. Cleve., Feb. 6, 1934; s. Milton and Anna (Hummel) M.; B.S., U. Notre Dame, 1956, LL.B., 1957; m. Debra Mary Budan; children—Ronald Milton, Ronda Ann, Ronald Michael, Amanda Leigh. Admitted to Ohio bar, 1957; gen. practice law; asst. dir. law City of Cleve., 1958-60; councilman from 2d Ward, Parma City Council, 1960-61, pres. council, 1961-67; mem. Ohio Ho of Reps. from 51st Dist., 1967-69, Ohio Senate from 24th Dist., 1969-75; mem. 94th-97th Congresses from 23d Ohio dist., chmn. Spl. Investigating Subcom. of House Vet. Affairs Com., mem. interstate and fgn. commerce com., vet. affairs com., oversight and investigations communications subcom.; founder, co-chmn. Suburban Caucus. Served with U.S. Army, 1957-58. Democrat. Home: 7713 Wake Robin Dr Parma OH 44130 Office: 2459 Rayburn House Office Bldg Washington DC 20515*

MOUDGIL, VIRINDER KUMAR, biochem. endocrinologist; b. Ludhiana, India, July 25, 1945; came to U.S., 1973; s. Harbhagwan and Lajwanti (Devi) M.; B.Sc., Panjab U., India, 1967; M.Sc., Banaras Hindu U., 1969, Ph.D. in Zoology, 1972; m. Parviz S. Gandhi, Aug. 29, 1973; children—Sapna, Rishi. Research fellow Banaras Hindu U., 1969-71, asst. research officer, 1971-73, sr. research fellow, 1973; research asst. Mayo Clinic, Rochester, Minn., 1973-76; asst. prof. biol. scis. Oakland U., Rochester, Mich., 1976—. NIH grantee, 1978—. Mem. Endocrine Soc., Am. Physiol. Soc., Am. Chem. Soc., Biophys. Soc., AAUP, AAAS, People to People Internat., Sigma Xi. Author: Progesterone Receptors, 1982. Home: 159 Nesbit Ln Rochester MI 48063 Office: Oakland University Rochester MI 48063

MOULDER, EARLINE, organist; b. Buffalo, Mo., Oct. 11, 1934; d. Earl Young and Ruby Moulder; Mus.B. magna cum laude, Drury Coll., 1956, B.A. magna cum laude in French and Biology, 1973; Mus.M., Ind. U., 1963; postgrad. U. Mo., Amsterdam Conservatory of Music; m. David Plank, Dec. 21, 1980; children by previous marriage—Cherie Jeannine, Jon Michael, Timothy Allen Stanton. Exec. editor Drury Mirror, 1971-73; organist Linwood Methodist Ch., Kansas City, Mo., 1956-60; organist St. Paul Methodist Ch., Springfield, Mo., 1961—; prof., chmn. organ dept. Drury Coll., Springfield, 1968—; concert organist U.S., Europe, Middle East; journalist USNR, 1975-77. Mem. Mo. Pilots Assn., Mortar Board, Appaloosa , Assn., Sigma Alpha Iota, Alpha Lambda Delta, Beta Beta Beta, Pi Delta Phi. Methodist. Composer Psalm 150, 1971, performed at U.S. Air Force Acad., 1971; Crucifixion, 1972. Author articles on Middle East. Home: PO Box 522 Buffalo MO 65622 Office: Drury Coll Springfield MO 65602

MOULDER, JAMES EDWIN, civil engr.; b. Roach, Mo., Aug. 29, 1926; s. Cyrus B. and Lela (Morgan) M.; B.S. in Civil Engring., U. Mo., 1953, M.S., 1955; m. Eldora Rhodes, Dec. 19, 1954; children—Robin Edwin, Bradley James. Structural engr. Boeing Airplane Co., Wichita, Kans., 1953; research engr. U. Mo., Columbia, 1953-56; cons. engr. Smith & Gillespie, Engrs., Jacksonville, Fla., 1956-60; cons. engr. Booker Assos., Inc., St. Louis, 1961—, dir., v.p., 1963-66, sec., dir., v.p., 1966-68, exec. v.p., dir., 1968-73, pres., 1973-77, chmn. bd., pres., dir., 1977-80, chmn. bd., chief exec. officer, 1980—; dir. Merc. Commerce Trust Co., St. Louis. Mem. adv. council Coll. Engring., U. Mo., Columbia; bd. dirs. Downtown St. Louis Inc., 1981—; mem. Mo. Coordinating Bd. for Higher Edn. Served with USMC, 1945-46; with AUS, 1950-52. Recipient Mo. Honor award, 1977; Faculty/Alumni award U. Mo., Columbia, 1979; award of merit St. Louis Engrs. Club, 1981. Fellow Am. Cons. Engrs. Council; mem. ASCE, Nat. Assn. Housing Redevel. Ofcls., Nat. Soc. Profl. Engrs., Mo. Soc. Profl. Engrs. (treas. 1981-82), Mo. Planning Assn., Cons. Engrs. Council Mo. (pres. 1975-76), Nat., Mo. parks and recreation assns., Hwy. Engrs. Assn. Mo., Alliance of Alumni Assns., U. Mo. at Columbia Alumni Assn. (pres. engring. div. 1977-78). Club: Rotary. Home: 93 Rue Grand Lake Saint Louis MO 63367 Office: 1139 Olive St Saint Louis MO 63101

MOULTRIE, GEORGE WILLIS, safety engr.; b. May 6, 1933; s. George Lonza and Lula Mae (Calhoun) M.; cert. U. Denver, 1952; student Joliet Jr. Coll., 1975-78; m. Sonia Perez, Mar. 11, 1978; 1 son, Jacque Marcel. Environ. health insp. City of Saginaw (Mich.), 1954, police officer, 1954-55; clk., carrier U.S. Post Office, Chgo., 1960-63; treater-coater operator 3M Co., Chgo., 1963-67; operator Dow Chem. Co., Midland, Mich., 1968-71; safety insp. No. Petrochem. Co., 1971-78; safety engr. No. Natural Gas Co., 1978-81; dir. safety compliance No. Plains Natural Gas Co., Omaha, 1981—. Served with USAF, 1951-53. Mem. Am. Soc. Safety Engrs., Am. Indsl. Hygiene Assn., Am. Legion. Club: Lions. Home: 3000 Farnam St Omaha NE 68131 Office: 224 S 108th St Omaha NE 68154

MOULTRIE, JOHN WESLEY, JR., state ofcl.; b. Marion, S.C., May 23, 1904; s. John Wesley and Missouri (Crockett) M.; A.B., Allegheny Coll., Meadville, Pa., 1927; postgrad. Harvard Law Sch., 1927-28, U. Mich. Law Sch., 1929-30, U. Minn., 1935-36, 38-39; M.A., Roosevelt U., 1967; m. Alice Gibson, Oct. 1, 1939 (dec. Nov. 1962); children—John Wesley III, Stanton Randolph. Prin. rural sch., Jacksonville, Fla., 1932-33; editor-in-chief The Spotlight, Chgo., 1934-35; dir. Consumer Center, Phyllis Wheatley House, Mpls., 1941-42; interviewer, unit supr. Minn. State Employment Service, Mpls., 1942-54; interviewer, counselor Gen. Indsl. Office, Ill. State Employment Service, Chgo., 1959-65, counseling supr., 1965-69, program coordinator, 1969-81, asst. mgr. local office, 1981—; real estate broker, Chgo., 1955—, ins. broker, Chgo., 1956—. Mem. Internat. Assn. Personnel in Employment Security. Methodist (pres. ch. credit union). Home: 4354 S Martin Luther King Dr Chicago IL 60653 Office: Ill State Employment Service 506 S Wabash Ave Chicago IL 60605

MOUNKES, WILLIAM LEE, publishing co. exec.; b. Allen, Kans., June 9, 1934; s. Vernon Richard and Alice Amelia (Schlesener) M.; student public schs., Emporia, Kans.; m. Kay Young, June 13, 1954; children—Dale Lynn, Lawrence Lee, Sherman Ray. Salesman, Imperial Book Co., Phila., 1957-60, Children's Press, Chgo., 1960-61, Kansas City News Distbrs. (Mo.), 1961-62, E. M. Hale Co., Eau Claire, Wis., 1962-66, Ace Books, N.Y.C., 1966-70, Pocket Books Distbg. Co., N.Y.C., 1970-75; regional coordinator Harlequin Books, Inc., Hackensack, N.J., 1975—; regional sales mgr. Harlequin Sales Corp., 1979—. Served with U.S. Army, 1955-57. Mem. Airline Passengers Assn., Am. Mgmt. Assn., Mo.-Kans. Mktg. Assn. (pres. 1973-75), 25 Yr. Club. Lutheran. Club: Masons. Home: PO Box 495 Gardner KS 66030 Office: Harlequin Sales Corp 580 White Plains Rd Tarrytown NY 10591

MOUNTZ, LOUISE CARSON SMITH (MRS. GEORGE EDWARD MOUNTZ), b. Fond Du Lac, Wis., Oct. 20, 1911; d. Roy Carson and Charlotte Louise (Scheurs) Smith; student Western Coll., Oxford, Ohio, 1929-31; A.B., Ohio State U., 1933; M.A., Ball State U., 1962; postgrad. Manchester Coll., 1954, Ind. U., 1960-61; m. George Edward Mountz, May 4, 1935 (dec. Oct. 3, 1951); children—Peter Carson, Pamela Teeters (Mrs. George Edmund McDonald). Tchr. high sch., Monroeville, Ind., 1953-54, Riverdale High Sch., St. Joseph, Ind., 1954-55; tchr., librarian high sch., Avilla, Ind., 1955-58; head librarian Penn High Sch., Mishawaka, Ind., 1958-67, Northwood Jr. High Sch., Fort Wayne, 1967-69, McIntosh Jr. High Sch., Auburn, Ind., 1969-74; dir. Media Center DeKalb Jr. High Sch., Auburn, 1974-78; ret., 1978; cons. media center planning Penn Harris Madison Sch. Corp., Mishawaka, 1966—. Bd. dirs. DeKalb County chpt. ARC, 1938-42, 51-53, DeKalb County Heart Assn., 1946-52, DeKalb County Community Concert Assn., 1946-58, Am. Field Service chpt., Mishawaka, 1960-67. Mem. AAUW, ALA, World Confedn. Orgns. Teaching Professions, Nat. Council Tchrs. English, NEA, Ind. Sch. Librarians Assn. (dir. 1963-67), Internat. Assn. Sch. Librarianship, Fort Wayne Art Mus., Ind. Assn. Ednl. Communication and Tech., Assn. Ind. Media Educators, Ind. Tchrs. Assn., Ind., Garrett, DeKalb County, Allen County, Ft. Wayne hist. socs., DeKalb County, Ind., Nat. ret. tchrs. assns., Fort Wayne YWCA, Nat. Trust for Historic Preservation, Delta Kappa Gamma (charter mem., v.p. Beta Beta chpt. 1960-62), Kappa Kappa Kappa (state officer 1941-45, pres. Alpha Chi chpt. 1938-40, Garrett asso. chpt. 1971-73), Delta Delta Delta (house pres.), Epsilon Sigma Omicron. DeKalb Meml. Hosp. Women's Aux. (life). Methodist. Mem. Order Eastern Star. Clubs: Greenhurst Country, Fort Wayne Women's, Athena Lit. (hon. mem.), Auburn Ladies Lit. Author: Biographies for Junior High Schools. Contbr. articles to profl. jours. Home: Auburn IN 46706

MOUREK, ANTON PETER, building contractor, indsl. land developer; b. Chgo., Oct. 19, 1908; s. Anton and Anna Josefa (Prucha) M.; student Northwestern U., 1926-27; m. Margaret J. Walsh, Sept. 7, 1935; children—Anthony John, James Otto, Michael Thomas. Partner, A. Mourek & Son, Elmhurst, Ill., 1929-46, pres., 1946-78, chmn. bd., 1946—; dir. J.A.M. Inc., Amtex Inc., Lincoln Fed. Savings and Loan, 1948—, founder, dir. Bank of Elmhurst, 1970-76; trustee, Ill. Benedictine Coll., 1967—. Sec., Cicero Library Bd., 1936-42. Served with U.S. Army, 1943-46. Recipient hon. Sc.D., Ill. Benedictine Coll., 1977. Roman Catholic. Clubs: Riverside Country, Key Biscayne Yacht, Knights of Columbus, Elks. Address: 970 N Oaklawn Ave Elmhurst IL 60126

MOURNING-STEWART, JEAN FAYE, retailer; b. Springfield, Ohio, July 23, 1917; d. George H. and Clada E. Shank; student Springfield Bus. Coll., 1935-36; m. Donald E. Mourning, May 18, 1937 (dec. Jan. 1959); 1 son, Donald E.; m. Alfred B. Stewart, Aug. 13, 1969. Stenographer, Ins. Exchange Bldg., Chgo., 1937-43; owner, mgr. Mourning's Office Equipment & Supply, Jackson, Ohio, 1949-73, pres., treas., 1974—; dir. State Ohio Distributive Edn. State Adv. Com., 1975-76; mem. adv. com. distributive edn. program Gallia-Jackson-Vinton Joint Vocat. Sch., Rio Grande, Ohio, 1975-77. Mem. Nat. Office Products Assn., Nat. Office Machine Dealers Assn., Jackson C. of C. (dir. 1975-77). Republican. Methodist. Clubs: Woman's Literary (Jackson, Ohio); Order Eastern Star. Office: Mournings Inc 427 E Main St Jackson OH 45640

MOUZAKEOTIS, THEODORE CONSTANTINE, surgeon; b. Chgo., July 13, 1906; s. Constantine John and Catherine (Kozialis) M.; B.S., U. Ill., 1930, M.D., 1933; m. Helen Karedes, Jan. 28, 1940; children—Kathy (Mrs. Clayton E. Whiting, Jr.), Teddy (Mrs. Plato Foufas), Sonia (Mrs. Stuart Leventhal), Theodore Constantine. Intern Cook County Hosp., Chgo., 1933-34; instr. surgery and cardiology Rush Med. Sch., U. Chgo., 1934-39; instr. phys. diagnosis U. Ill. Coll. Medicine, 1939-43, instr. obstetrics and gynecology, 1943-46, clin. instr. obstetrics and gynecology 1946-62; practice medicine specializing in surgery, Chgo., 1935—; asso. in obstetrics and gynecology Chgo. State Hosp., 1947-49; mem. staff Columbus, Ill. Masonic, Cuneo hosps., Chgo; mem. att. staff Research and Edn. Hosp., Chgo., 1943-61, Weiss Meml. Hosp., Chgo., 1954-57. Dir. Howard Savs. & Loan, Evanston, Ill. Former explorer troop chmn. Boy Scouts Am. Trustee Roycemore Sch., Evanston, Ill., 1951-53, exec. com., 1951-53. Mem. AMA, Ill. Med. Soc. (key mem. 1980—), Chgo. Med. Soc. (practice com. 1978—, continuing med. edn. com. 1980—; alt. councillor N. Suburban br. 1978—), AHEPA, Phi Sigma Epsilon (founder, hon. pres.). Clubs: Saddle and Cycle (Chgo.); Point Of Woods Country (Benton Harbor, Mich.). Contbr. articles profl. jours. Home: 7 Woodley Rd Winnetka IL 60093 Office: 55 E Washington St Chicago IL 60602

MOVCHAN, JULIAN GEORGE, physician, journalist; b. Zorokiv, Ukraine, Feb. 19, 1913; s. George John and Olga O. (Kolomijec) M.; student Ukrainian Inst. Journalism, 1932-35; M.D., Kharkiv and Iviv Med. Colls., 1943; m. Helen Skibicka, Sept. 3, 1949; children—Ola Movchan Ivanicki, Lida. Came to U.S., 1949, naturalized, 1956. Corr. staff several Ukrainian newspapers, 1932-37; intern Alexian Bros. and Elizabeth hosps., N.J., 1949-53; practice medicine specializing in internal and gen. medicine, Malinta, Oakwood and Macedonia, Ohio, mem. staff Bedford (O.) Municipal Hosp., 1960—. Vice pres. Paulding County (Ohio) Bd. Health, 1957-60. Mem. Ohio Med. Assn., Summit County Med. Soc. (award 1964). Author: How to Cure Oneself and Others in Emergency Cases, 1946; Things Worth Knowing, 1966; Doctor's Notes, 1970. Contbr. articles to med. lit. Home and office: 10115 Valley View Rd Macedonia OH 44056

MOWERY, JOHN HENRY, psychologist; b. Cin., Jan. 22, 1920; s. John Henry and Minna Henrietta (Hageman) M.; B.A., Bowling Green State U., 1950; M.A., Kent State U., 1951; m. Carolyn Rubel, June 4, 1960. Clin. psychologist Ind. Mental Health Div., Indpls., 1952; personnel psychologist Aero Mayflower Transit Co., Indpls., 1952-55; personnel adminstr. Am. Legion Nat. Hdqrs., Indpls., 1955-56; psychologist Am. Legion State Hdqrs., Indpls., 1956; asst. personnel dir. Hook Drugs Inc., Indpls., 1956-60; staff psychologist Psychol. Service Center, Toronto, Ont., Can., 1960-62; pvt. practice clin. psychologist, Mpls., 1963—; cons. psychologist Lutheran Social Service Minn., 1970—. Served with USAAF, 1942-46. Lic. and cert. psychologist, Minn., Ont. Mem. AAAS, N.Y. Acad. Scis., Am., Minn., Internat. psychol. assns., Nat. Register Health Services Providers in Psychology, Psi Chi, Theta Chi. Methodist. Clubs: Mason, Statesman's, Regency. Home: 3101 E Calhoun Pkwy Minneapolis MN 55408

MOWREY, DENNIS D., chem. mfrs. co. exec.; b. Lincoln, Nebr., Nov. 18, 1941; s. Louis and LaVerne Mowrey; student public schs., Lincoln, Nebr.; m. Celesta Criswell, July 29, 1961; children—Danette, Darren. Supr., Paramount Linen, Lincoln, Nebr., 1958-66; tech. rep. H. Kohnstamm & Co., Omaha, 1966-72, sales rep., Detroit, 1972-80, eastern sales mgr., Chgo., 1980—. Bd. dirs. Oakland-Livingston Human Services Agy., 1978—; bd. dirs. Livingston County Community Mental Health Agy., 1979—; mem. exec. com. Livingston County Republican Party, 1978—; bus. mgr., mem. exec. com. Howell Bicentennial Commn., 1975-76; bus. mgr., mem. exec. com. Howell Archives Bd., 1977-80. Recipient outstanding state chmn. award Mich. Jaycees, 1974, outstanding local pres. award Mich. Jaycees, 1975, Giessenbier award Mich. Jaycees, 1975, outstanding exec. com. mem. award, 1977, outstanding chaplain award, 1979, citation and cert. for contbn. in Mich. Bicentennial, 1976. Mem. Mich. Assn. Instl. Laundry Mgrs., Laundry and Cleaners Allied Trades Assn., Internat. Fabricare Inst., Inst. Indsl. Launderers, Nat. Assn. Instl. Laundry Mgrs., Nat. Automatic Laundry and Cleaners Council, Textile Rental Services Assn., Nat. Inst. Infant Services, Howell Jaycees (pres. 1975), Mich. Jaycees (state chmn. 1974, presdl. asst. 1977), Internat. Jaycees (senator), U.S. Jaycees. Republican. Club: Howell Elks. Co-chmn., bus. mgr. Howell History, 1976, Howell History Pictorial Addition, 1976. Office: 11 E Illinois St Chicago IL 60611

MOWRY, DAVID DEE, educator; b. Fairfield County, Ohio, Oct. 21, 1936; s. David William and Betty Madge (Mericle) M.; B.Sc. in Bus. Adminstrn. Ohio State U., 1958, B.Sc. in Edn., 1960; M.Ed., Ohio U., 1969; m. Kathy Suzanne Beavers, Sept. 7, 1975. Tchr. Lancaster (Ohio) City Schs., 1960-63, sci. supr., 1963-69; asst. prin. Lancaster High Sch., 1969-70; asst. prof. zoology Ohio U., Lancaster, 1970—. Bd. dirs. Fairfield County Heart Assn., Fairfield County unit Am. Cancer Soc. ruling elder Bremen United Presbyterian Ch., Bremen, Ohio, 1974—. Inducted into Ohio Jr. Sci. and Humanities Hall of Fame. Fellow Ohio Acad. Sci.; mem. AAUP, AAAS, Ohio Edn. Assn., World Population Soc., Ohio Coll. Biology Tchrs. Assn., Population Reference Bur., Phi Delta Kappa. Republican. Clubs: Masons, Shriners (past pres. med. unit Aladdin Temple), Kiwanian, Jesters. Home: 129 Strayer Ave Bremen OH 43107 Office: 1570 Granville Rd Lancaster OH 43130

MOWRY, JOHN L., lawyer; b. Baxter, Iowa, Dec. 15, 1905; s. William and Grace (Conn) M.; B.A., U. Iowa, 1929, J.D., 1930; student Ohio State U., 1926-27; m. Irene E. Lounsberry, Oct. 9, 1941; 1 dau., Madelyn E. (Mrs. Stephen R. Irvine). Admitted to Ia. bar, 1930, N.Y. bar, 1945; spl. agt. F.B.I., 1930-34; mem. staff firm Thomas E. Dewey, N.Y.C., 1935-36; mem. exec. dept. N.Y. State, 1946; pvt. practice law, Marshalltown, Iowa, 1936-41, 1947—; owner Evans Abstract Co., also G.M.K. Inc., Marshalltown, 1950—. County atty. Marshall County (Iowa), 1939-41; mayor City of Marshalltown, 1950-55; rep. Iowa Gen. Assembly, 1956-68, majority floor leader, 1963-65; senator Iowa Gen. Assembly, 1968-72; del. Republican Nat. Conv., Miami, Fla., 1972. Served with USAAF, 1941-45. Mem. Soc. Former Spl. Agts. FBI (nat. pres. 1945), Marshall County, Iowa bar assns., Iowa Pioneer Lawmakers Soc., Marshall County Hist. Soc., SAR. Republican. Presbyn. Mason (Shriner), Elk. Home: 503 W Main St Marshalltown IA 50158 Office: 25 N Center St Marshalltown IA 50158

MOY, CARYL TOWSLEY, therapist, educator; b. Aurora, Ill., Sept. 10, 1932; d. Myron Hallam and Genevieve(Brayton) Towsley; B.S., U. Ill., 1954; M.S.W., U. Chgo., 1969; Ph.D., So. Ill. U., 1980; m. Richard Henry Moy, Aug. 21, 1954; children—Phlip, Eric. Home econs. dept. chairperson Evergreen Park (Ill.) High Sch., 1954-58, 61-67; children's services cons. Ill. Commn. on Children, summer 1970; counselor/instr. Lincolnland Community Coll., Springfield, Ill., 1970-72; asso. prof. child, family and community services Sangamon State U., Springfield, 1972—; marital and sex therapist So. Ill. U. Sch. Medicine. Founding pres. Springfield Planned Parenthood, 1970-75; bd. dirs. Ill. Family Planning Council, 1973-79, 80-81, pres., 1976-78; elder Westminster Presbyn. Ch., 1976-79; mem. Ill. Licensing Adv. Bd. Outpatient Surg. Centers, 1976—. Certified sex therapist and educator; cert. Acad. Cert. Social Workers. Mem. Nat. Council Family Relations, Ill. Council Family Relations, Am. Assn. Marriage and Family Therapy, Am. Assn. Sex Edn., Counseling and Therapy, AAHPER, Nat. Assn. Social Workers, Phi Beta Kappa. Contbr. chpt.: Communicating Sexuality, 1980. Home: 25 Wildwood Rd Springfield IL 62704 Office: Sangamon State U Shepherd Rd Springfield IL 62708

MUCCIOLI, ANNA MARIA, artist; b. Detroit, Apr. 23, 1922; d. Anthony and Josephine (Coccardi) Di Pascale; student Soc. Arts Crafts, 1970-75; m. Joseph E. Muccioli, Dec. 26, 1942; children—Ronald, Nathan, Edward, James. One-woman shows of water color paintings include: Verve Gallery, Detroit, 1965, Left Bank Gallery, Flint, Mich., 1969, Univ. Liggett Sch., Grosse Pointe Farms, Mich., 1974; group shows include: Ford Motor Co., Dearborn, Mich., 1961-65, 68-69, 74, 76-78, Scarab Club, Detroit, 1965, 69, 70, 71, 73, 76-79, Ann Arbor (Mich.) Street Art Fair, 1966, 67, Birmingham Art Festival, 1966, Waterfront Fair, Charlevoix, Mich., 1967, 68, Oakland (Mich.) Community Coll., 1967, Detroit-Windsor Internat. Freedom Festival, 1967-69, Lafayette Park Community Assn., 1967-69, Mich. State Fair, 1968-69, 71, 73, 76, 78, Butler Inst. Am. Art, Youngstown, Ohio, 1969, Detroit Artists Market, 1970, Birmingham (Ala.) Mus. Arts, 1972, Gallery North, Mt. Clemens, Mich. Watercolor Soc., Detroit, 1969-70, 76, Am. Water Color Soc., N.Y.C., 1971, Nat. Art Club, N.Y.C., 1971, Birmingham (Ala.) Mus. Arts, 1971, Detroit Inst. Arts, 1976, Battle Creek (Mich.) Civic Art Center, 1974, Carrol Reece Mus., Johnson City, Tenn., 1974, Gallery One, Petoskey, Mich., 1970; traveling exhbn. Nat. Small Painting Exhbn., 1973, 74, 76, 78; group show exhibit of sculpture includes: Scarab Club, 1971, 73, 76, 78, 79; represented in permanent collection: rental galleries Detroit Inst. Art, Bloomfield Art Assn.; propr., dir. Muccioli Studio Gallery, Detroit, 1973—. Recipient numerous awards Ford Motor Co., 1961-79, Watercolor award Lafayette Park Community Assn., 1967, numerous others. Mem. Mich. Watercolor Soc. Roman Catholic. Home: 16194 Sprenger East Detroit MI 48021 Gallery: 511 Beaubien Detroit MI 48226

MUCHISKY, THOMAS PETER, corp. exec.; b. Dercy, Conn., 1934; s. Pete and Tess Muchisky; B.S. in Engring., U. Conn., 1956; M.B.A., Harvard U., 1960; m. Nancy Jensen, Aug. 1981; 5 children. Mech. engr. IBM Corp., Kingston, N.Y., 1956-58; mgmt. cons. Booz, Allen & Hamilton Inc., Cleve., 1960-62; div. mgr. Hexcel Corp., Dublin, Calif., 1962-66; gen. mgr. Boise Cascade Corp., St. Louis, 1966-68; div. gen. mgr. Litton Industries, Des Plaines, Ill., 1968-70; corp. pres. Gen. Medventures Internat., Inc., 1970—, Gen. Physiotherapy, Inc., 1970—, Gen. Theraphysical Inc., 1970—, Gen. X-Ray Inc., 1970—, Gen. Imex Mfg. Co. Inc., 1970—, Gen. Respiratory Inc., 1970—, La Compagnie d'Equipment de Physiotherapie du Can. Ltee, 1970—, Fischer Industries, Inc., 1980—. Served with USMCR, 1957-65. Mem. Mensa, Ethical Soc. St. Louis. Unitarian. Patentee in field. Address: 784 Hawthicket Ln Des Peres MO 63131

MUCZYK, JAN PIOTR, educator; b. Sahryn, Poland, Feb. 12, 1939; s. John and Anastasia (Rarata) M. (parents Am. citizens); B.S., U. Md., 1964, M.B.A., 1966, D.B.A., 1972; m. Jennie Dianne Councilman, Apr. 4, 1964; children—Mark, Michael, Lisa, David. Systems analyst Vitro Labs., Silver Springs, Md., 1965-67; instr. U. Md., College Park, 1967-71; asso. prof. bus. adminstrn. and econs. Shippensburg (Pa.) State Coll., 1971-73; prof., chmn. dept. mgmt. and labor relations Coll. Bus. Adminstrn., Cleve. State U., 1973—. Served with USAF, 1958-62. Mem. Acad. Mgmt., Am. Psychol. Assn. (div. 14 organizational and indsl. psychology), Acad. Mktg. Sci., Am. Soc. for Personnel Adminstrs., Phi Kappa Phi, Beta Gamma Sigma. Democrat. Roman Catholic. Author: Principles of First and Second Level Supervision, 1979, 81; Readings in Personnel Administration, 1980. Contbr. articles to profl. jours. Home: 2572 Fenwick Rd University Heights OH 44118 Office: 1983 E 24th St Cleveland OH 44115

MUDGE, JOY JEAN NORTH (MRS. GLEN R. MUDGE), librarian; b. Cleve., Mar. 14, 1929; d. John Edward and Doris Eileen (McKinnon) North; A.B., Beaver Coll., 1951; postgrad. Kent State U., 1955; M.S., Wayne State U., 1962; m. Glen R. Mudge, Dec. 27, 1955 (dec. Aug. 1977). Tchr., Glenmoor Sch., East Liverpool, Ohio,

1951-55; librarian Wayne State U., Detroit, 1955-58; librarian Oak Park, Clinton Jr. high schs., Oak Park, Mich., 1958-68; dir. sch. librarian Charlevoix (Mich.) Schs., 1968—. Named Girl Scout Career Woman of Year, East Liverpool, 1963. Mem. ALA, Mich. Sch. Librarians Assn., Alpha Delta Kappa, Pi Lambda Theta. Home: Box 96A Ellsworth MI 49729 Office: Charlevoix Pub Schs Garfield St Charlevoix MI 49720

MUDGE, WILLIAM ALBERT, JR., physician; b. Mpls., Nov. 23, 1917; s. Dr. William Albert and Elizabeth (Martins) M.; B.S., Northwestern U., 1940; M.D., Med. Coll. Wis., 1944; m. Faith MacDade, Sept. 6, 1956; children—Jane, Mary, Ann, Susan, William Albert III. Resident, Hines (Ill.) VA Hosp., 1949-53; pres., dir. Physicians Park, Inc., 1959-63; asso. clin. prof. medicine Marquette U., Milw., 1959-72; adj. prof. clin. medicine No. Mich. U., 1975—; staff Milwaukee County Gen. Hosp., 1959-72. Mem. cancer study group Wis. Regional Med. Program, 1969-72; mem. Wis. Gov.'s Task Force on Edn., 1970-71; mem. exec. com. and bd. United Migrant Opportunity Service, Inc., 1964-68; mem. north central regional adv. com. Upper Peninsula Health Systems Agy., Inc., 1977-81; mem. health resources com. Health Systems Agy., 1976-81; mem. Marquette City Commn. on Aging, 1977-78; bd. dirs. Marquette-Alger Planned Parenthood, Inc., 1979—, Superior Hospice Assn., 1981—. Served as capt. M.C., USAAF, 1945-47. Mem. Wis. Heart Assn., Kenosha Anti Tb Assn. (v.p. 1958-60, dir. 1957-62), AMA, Mich., Marquette-Alger County (pres. 1980) med. socs., Upper Peninsula Areawide Comprehensive Health Planning Assn. (dir. 1975), Am. Soc. Internal Medicine, A.C.P. Episcopalian (vestryman 1963-66, 74-77). Rotarian (pres. 1958-59). Home: 419 E Arch St Marquette MI 49855

MUELLER, ALLAN GEORGE, state senator; b. St. Louis, Dec. 16, 1942; s. Aaron Barney and Theresa Maries (Schaffler) M.; B.B.A., St. Mary's U., 1965; m. Carol Coleman, 1973. Vice pres. Land Systems, Inc.; mem. Mo. Ho. of Reps., 1970-77, Mo. Senate, 1977—. Served to capt. USMC, 1966-68; Vietnam. Democrat. Roman Catholic. Office: State Capitol Jefferson City MO 65101*

MUELLER, BARBARA, artist, educator; b. Summit, N.J., July 24, 1937; d. Albert P. and Mildred A. (Meekings) M.; B.A. in Art, Maryville Coll., 1959; M.A. in Painting, U. Iowa, 1961; m. William Gary Crist, Mar. 18, 1978. Instr., Maryville (Tenn.) Coll., 1961-65, asst. prof., 1965-66; instr. dept. art U. Mo., Kansas City, 1966-68, asst. prof., 1968-77, asso. prof., 1977—; vis. scholar Center for South Asian Studies, U. Wash., Seattle, 1972-73, Hamline U., St. Paul, Minn., summer, 1975; one-woman shows of paintings include: Ward-Nasse Gallery, N.Y.C., 1977, Unitarian Gallery, Kansas City, Mo., 1977; group shows include: Avila Coll., Kansas City, Mo., 1977, Del Mar Coll., Corpus Christi, Tex., 1977, Albrecht Mus., St. Joseph, Mo., 1977, Fine Arts Gallery, U. Mo., Kansas City, 1977, Nelson Gallery, Kansas City, Mo., 1974. Fulbright summer seminar grantee, 1971, U. Mo. research grantee, 1972, 76, 77, 80. Mem. Coll. Art Assn., Mid-Am. Coll. Art Assn. (dir. 1975-76), Women's Caucus for Art, Kansas City Artists Coalition, AAUP. Presbyterian. Office: Dept Art and Art History Univ Missouri Kansas City MO 64110

MUELLER, DON SHERIDAN, sch. adminstr.; b. Cleve., Nov. 4, 1927; s. Don P. and Selma Christina (Ungericht) M.; B.S., Mt. Union Coll., 1948; M.A., U. Mich., 1952; Ed.S., Mich. State U., 1968; Ph.D., Am. Internat. U., 1977; m. Vivian Jean Santrock, Aug. 27, 1947; children—Carl Frederick, Cathy Ann. Tchr., Benton-Harbor Fair Plain (Mich.) Schs., 1947-52; dir. music edn. Okemos (Mich.) Pub. Schs., 1952-64; jr-sr. high prin. Dansville (Mich.) Schs., 1964-68; prin. DeWitt (Mich.) High Sch., 1968-73; supt. Carsonville-Port Sanilac Schs., Carsonville, Mich., 1973—. Recipient Community Leader of Am. award, 1968, 72, 73-74; Acad. Am. Educators award, 1973-74. Mem. Am., Mich. assns. sch. adminstrs., Mich. Assn. Sch. Bds., NEA, Assn. Supervision and Curriculum Devel., Clinton Prins. Assn. (pres. 1972-73), Ingham Prins. Assn. (pres. 1967-70), Mich. Sch. Band/Orch. Assn. (sec. 1962-63, pres. dist. 5 1958-60), Okemos Edn. Assn. (pres. 1962-63), River Area Supts. Assn. (pres. 1979-80). Home: 188 S High St Box 2577 Carsonville MI 48419 Office: 100 N Goetze Carsonville MI 48419

MUELLER, HAROLD, flutist, conductor, educator; b. Austin, Tex., Jan. 28, 1920; s. Robert and Leona (Mayer) M.; Mus.B., U. Mich., 1941, Mus.M., 1946; Ph.D., Eastman Sch. Music, U. Rochester, 1956; postgrad. Juilliard Sch. Music, 1947, L'Ecole Monteux, summers, 1948-51; m. Beatrice J. Baldinger, June 26, 1959; children—Harold Edward, Robert Baldinger. Instr., Corpus Christi (Tex.) High Sch., 1941; flutist Columbus (Ohio) Philharm. Orch., 1946-48; flutist New Orleans Symphony Orch., 1948-53; instr. Eastman Sch. Music, Rochester, N.Y., 1953-56; asst. prof. U. Minn., 1956-57; asso. prof. Austin Coll., Sherman, Tex., 1958-61, prof., 1961-67, chmn. music dept., 1958-66, chmn. fine arts area, 1960-66; prof. Marietta (Ohio) Coll., 1967—, head Edward E. MacTaggart dept. music, 1967-75, condr. Marietta Coll. Civic Symphonette, Marietta Oratorio Chorus, 1967—; music commentator Sta. WMRT-FM, 1976—. Bd. dirs. Orgn. Ohio Orchs. Served with USAAF, 1941-46. Mem. AAUP, Am. Musicology Soc. (past chpt. chmn.), Coll. Music Soc., Music Library Assn., Am. Symphony Orch. League, Pi Kappa Lambda, Phi Mu Alpha-Sinfonia, Phi Delta Kappa, Kappa Kappa Psi. Lutheran. Editor, pub. compositions of Andreas Hammerschmidt. Contbr. articles to profl. jours. Home: 518 4th St Marietta OH 45750

MUELLER, RICHARD ALLAN, mktg. agy. exec.; b. Toledo, July 22, 1926; s. Valentine Richard and Madeline Frances (Sutton) M.; student U. Toledo, 1946-50; m. Janice Ann Boden, June 7, 1952; children—Sharon, Shirley, Richard Allan, Linda, Anne. Editor, West Toledo Herald, 1956-59; account exec. Solon Assos., Toledo, 1959-62; v.p. advt., public relations Ohio Citizens Bank, Toledo, 1962-77; v.p., dir. public relations Communications Concepts, Toledo, 1977—. Mem. Bedford Twp. (Mich.) Planning Commn., 1974—; bd. dirs. United Way of Monroe County, 1976—, Monroe County chpt. ARC, 1980—; mem. public relations com. Toledo chpt. ARC, 1978—. Named One of Toledo's Outstanding Young Men, 1958, 59, 60, 61, 62; recipient Mich. Minuteman citation, 1979. Mem. Public Relations Soc. Am. (pres. N.W. Ohio chpt. 1977-78), Downtown Coaches Assn. (pres. 1974-75), Pi Kappa Phi. Episcopalian. Clubs: Advt. of Toledo (Silver medal 1974, pres. 1970-71), U. Toledo Rocket, Press of Toledo (treas. 1975-78), Sertoma, Jr. Chamber Internat. (senator 1964—); Bedford (Mich.) Athletic Boosters. Home: 2661 Torrey Hill Ct Lambestville MI 48144 Office: Communications Concepts 316 N Michigan St Toledo OH 43624

MUELLER, ROLAND FREDERICK, surgeon; b. St. Joseph, Mo., Aug. 29, 1905; s. Charles Frederick and Elizabeth (Krebs) M.; A.A., Kansas City (Mo.) U., 1925; student Kans. U., 1926; M.D. cum laude, Washington U., 1929; m. children—Nancy (Mrs. Robert H. Pecha), Judith (Mrs. Roger W. Hall), Kathryn Lucile (Mrs. Rex Logemann). Resident in surgery Barnes Hosp., St. Louis, 1929-33; instr. surgery Washington U., 1930-33; practice surgery, Canton, Mo., 1933-37; chief surgeon Two Harbors (Minn.) Hosp., 1937-46, also asso. chief surgeon Duluth, Mesabi & Iron Range R.R., 1937-46; practice surgery, Lincoln, Nebr., 1949—; attending surgeon St. Elizabeth's Hosp., Bryan Meml. Hosp.; prof. surgery Creighton U.; cons. VA Hosp., Lincoln; pres. Lincoln Community Blood Bank, 1976, 78, States Oil Royalty Co. U.S. del. 7th Inter-Am. Congress Surgery, Peru, 1950. Recipient 25 Year Faculty award Creighton U., Outstanding Prof. in Surgery award, 1978. Fellow A.C.S.; mem. Central Surg. Assn., Southwestern Surg. Congress, Internat. Soc. Surgery, Peruvian Acad. Surgery (hon.), Am. Thyroid Assn., AMA, Nebr. State, Lancaster County (pres. 1977) med. assns., Phi Beta Pi, Alpha Omega Alpha. Clubs: University (Lincoln); Washington University (St. Louis). Contbr. articles to profl jours. Home: 1000 Fall Creek Rd Lincoln NE 68510 Office: 1000 Fall Creek Rd Lincoln NE 68510

MUELLER, SAMUEL ALVIN, sociologist, educator; b. Peoria, Ill., May 4, 1939; s. Alvin August and Agnes Emma (Loesch) M.; B.A., Valparaiso U., 1961; M.A., Roosevelt U., 1965; Ph.D. (fellow 1966-67), Northwestern U., 1970. Instr. sociology Loyola U., Chgo., 1967-68; asst. prof. sociology Ind. U., Bloomington, 1968-73; asso. prof. sociology, U. Akron, Ohio, 1973—. Data processing adv. com. Summit County United Way, 1976—. U. Akron research grantee, 1976; Fulbright summer fellow 1978. Mem. Am. Sociol. Assn., N. Central Sociol. Assn. (council 1974-79), Soc. for Sci. Study of Religion, Religious Research Assn. (bd. dirs., 1974-78), Assn. for Sociology of Religion, Internat. Conf. for Sociology of Religion, Sigma Xi. Lutheran. Club: University (Akron). Co-editor Sociological Focus, 1974-79; contbr. articles to profl. jours. Office: Department of Sociology University of Akron Akron OH 44325

MUELLER, WILLIAM ALBERT, JR., lawyer; b. Watseka, Ill., Nov., 5, 1945; s. William Albert and Marjorie Alice (Parcell) M.; B.A., U. Ill., 1969, J.D., 1972; m. Constance Geiger, Dec. 28, 1968; children—Anne Elizabeth, Katherine Ann, Emily Christine. Admitted to Ill. bar, 1972; asst. states atty. McLean County, Ill., 1972-73; asso. firm Markowitz, Lawrence, Lenz, Jennings, Naylor, Bloomington, Ill., 1973-75; partner firm Markowitz, Lawrence, Lenz, Jennings, Naylor & Mueller, Bloomington, 1975-78, Naylor, Mueller & Freese, Bloomington, 1978—. Bd. dirs., sec. McLean County Alcohol & Drug Assistance Unit, 1972—; bd. dirs. McLean County Planned Parenthood, 1973-75, sec., 1974-75; bd. dirs. McLean County Assn. Retarded Children, 1974, McLean County Center for Human Services, 1981; co-chmn. McLean County Heart Assn., 1978. Served with Army ROTC, 1965-69. States Atty. Assn. scholar, 1972. Mem. Am. Bar Assn., Ill. Bar Assn., McLean County Bar Assn. (bd. govs. 1974-77), McLean County Trial Lawyers Assn., Am. Judicature Soc., Workmen's Compensation Lawyers Assn., Jr. C. of C. (sec. 1974-75). Roman Catholic. Home: 1118 E Monroe St Bloomington IL 61701 Office: PO Box 3155 412 Unity Bldg Bloomington IL 61701

MUELLER, WILLYS FRANCIS, JR., pathologist; b. Detroit, July 15, 1934; s. Willys Francis and Antoinette Frances (Stimac) M.; M.D., U. Mich., 1959; m. Dolores Mae Vella, Aug. 25, 1956; children—Renee Ann, Willys Francis, Paul E., Mark A., Maria D., Beth M., Matthew P. Intern, Providence Hosp., Detroit, 1959-60, resident, 1960-62; resident Wayne County Gen. Hosp., Eloise, Mich., 1962-64; asst. pathologist Grace Hosp., Detroit, 1964; asso. pathologist Hurley Hosp., Flint, Mich., 1964-66; asso. pathologist Hurley Med. Center, Flint, 1968—, dir. lab., 1981—; chief dep. med. examiner Genesee County, Mich., 1971—; pres. Pathology Assos. Inc.; asso. clin. prof. Coll. Human Medicine, Mich. State U.; exec. head blood services Flint region ARC, 1981—. Served with M.C., U.S. Army, 1966-68. Fellow Am. Soc. Clin. Pathologists, Coll. Am. Pathologists, Am. Acad. Forensic Scis.; mem. AMA (Physician's Recognition award 1974-77, 78-81), Genesee County, Mich. State med. socs., Mich. Soc. Pathologists (sec.-treas.), Nat. Assn. Med. Examiners. Republican. Roman Catholic. Club: K.C. Editor: Bull. of Genesee County Med. Soc. Home: 13335 Pomona Dr Fenton MI 48430 Office: Dept Pathology Hurley Med Center Flint MI 48502

MUHLENBRUCH, CARL WILLIAM, mgmt. cons.; b. Decatur, Ill., Nov. 21, 1915; s. Carl W. and Clara Agnes (Theobald) M.; B.C.E., U. Ill., 1937; M.C.E., Carnegie Inst. Tech., 1943; m. Agnes M. Kringel, Nov. 22, 1939; children—Phyllis Elaine Muhlenbruch Wallace, Joan Carol Muhlenbruch Wenk. Research engr. Aluminum Research Labs., Pitts., 1937-39; cons. civil engr., 1939-50; mem. faculty Carnegie Inst. Tech., 1939-48; asso. prof. civil engring. Northwestern U., 1948-54; pres. Tec-Search, Inc., Wilmette, Ill., 1954-67, chmn. bd. dirs., 1967—; pres. Profl. Centers Bldg. Corp., 1961-76. Bd. dirs. Aid Assn. for Lutherans, 1964-76; mem. Bd. Local Improvements Wilmette, 1972—. Registered profl. engr., Ill., Pa. Mem. Am. Indsl. Devel. Council, ASTM (Sanford Thompson award 1945), Am. Planning Assn., ASCE, Am. Soc. Engring. Edn., Nat. Soc. Profl. Engrs., Sigma Xi, Tau Beta Phi. Republican. Lutheran-Mo. Synod (dir., mem. exec. com., vice chmn. 1965-79). Club: Rotary Internat. (dist. gov. 1980-81). Author: Experimental Mechanics and Properties of Materials, 1955; contbr. articles to engring. jours. Home: 4071 Fairway Dr Wilmette IL 60091 Office: 3330 Old Glenview Rd Wilmette IL 60091

MUHLER, JOSEPH CHARLES, educator; b. Ft. Wayne, Ind., Dec. 22, 1923; s. Howard and Lauretta (Zurabach) M.; B.S., Ind. U., 1945, D.D.S., 1948, Ph.D. in Chemistry, 1951; m. Majetta Jean Stewart, Feb. 2, 1949; children—Joseph Charles, James Patrick. Teaching fellow Ind. U., 1948-49, asst. prof., 1951-55, asso. prof., 1955-59, prof., 1959-61, research prof. basic scis., 1961—, chmn. dept. preventive dentistry, 1958—, dir. Preventive Dentistry Research Inst., Indpls., 1968-72, Ft. Wayne, 1972—; cons. in field. USPHS fellow, 1948-51. Fellow Am. Coll. Dentists, AAAS, Am. Inst. Chemists; mem. Am. Chem. Soc., Am. Dental Assn., Internat. Assn. Dental Research (sec.-treas. 1961-64, councilor 1959-61), Soc. Exptl. Biology and Medicine, Ind. Acad. Sci., AAUP, Am. Soc. Dentistry for Children, Indpls. Dist. Dental Soc., Am. Public Health Assn., Ind. Dental Assn., Am. Med. Writers Assn., Phi Beta Kappa, Sigma Xi, Omicron Kappa Upsilon, Phi Lambda Upsilon. Democrat. Roman Catholic. Developer toothpaste; editor: Jour. Ind. Dental Assn., 1958—. Home: 70883 Klinger Lake Rd Sturgis MI 49091 Office: 2101 Coliseum Blvd E Fort Wayne IN 46805

MUHRER, MERLE EDWARD, biochemist, educator; b. Clark County, Mo., Aug. 5, 1913; s. Henry Victor and Elizabeth Belle (McLaughlin) M.; B.S., N.E. Mo. State U., 1935; M.A., U. Mo.-Columbia, 1940, Ph.D., 1944; m. Madaline Acklie, Feb. 4, 1939; children—Verle, Darryl, Merlin, Henry. Tchr. high sch. sci., Kahoka, Mo., 1935-39; asso. prof. chemistry N.W. Mo. State U., Kirksville, 1941-43; mem. faculty U. Mo.-Columbia, 1943—, prof. biochemistry, 1950—, chmn. dept., 1954-67, cons. to univ. dir. research, 1967—. Pres. Columbia Community Improvement Assn., 1969-72. Friends of Rocheport Hist. Soc., 1972-73; 4-H Club project leader, 1950-65. Mem. Strawn Bd. Edn., 1946-68; pres. Boone County Sch. Bd., 1956-68. Bd. dirs. Pachyderms, Columbia YMCA, Nat. Thrombosis Council. Recipient Grim award N.E. Mo. State Coll., 1935. Curators scholar, 1936; Markle grantee, 1944. Mem. Am. Chem. Soc. (past pres. Mo. div.), Gamma Sigma Delta (past pres.). Mem. United Ch. of Christ (pres. men's club 1970). Kiwanian. Club: U. Mo.-Columbia Faculty. Contbr. articles to profl. jours. Co-author: Zinc Metabolism, 1966. Patentee in field. Home: 3009 I-70 Dr NW Columbia MO 65201

MUIR, DOROTHY LUELLA, constrn. co. exec.; b. Parkersburg, Iowa, July 15, 1916; d. Axel William and Gertrude Mae (Hersey) Jochumsen; student Gates Bus. Coll., Waterloo, Iowa; m. Harry Rex Muir, Sept. 26, 1937. Bookkeeper, Hughes Dry Goods Co., Cedar Falls, Iowa, 1937-43; office mgr., bookkeeper Cedar Crest Hatchery, Cedar Falls, 1943-68; asst. sec., acct. Wendell Lockard Constrn., Inc., Waterloo, 1968—. Pres., Waterloo-Cedar Falls women's aux. Shriners Crippled Children's Hosp., 1972. Mem. Nat. Assn. Women in Constrn. (treas. chpt. 1972-74, 75-76), Nat. Assn. Accts., Nat. Notary Assn. Republican. Methodist. Clubs: Eastern Star, White Shrine, Daus. of Nile. Home: 1804 Birch St PO Box 23 Cedar Falls IA 50613 Office: 901 Black Hawk Rd PO Box 2220 Waterloo IA 50704

MUKERJEE, PASUPATI, educator; b. Calcutta, India, Feb. 13, 1932; s. Nani Gopal and Probhabati (Ghosal) M.; B.Sc., Calcutta U., 1957, M.Sc., 1951; Ph.D., U. So. Calif., 1957; m. Lalita Sarkar, Feb. 29, 1964. Lectr., vis. asst. prof. U. So. Calif., 1956-57; research asso. Brookhaven Nat. Lab., L.I., 1957-59; reader in phys. chemistry Indian Assn. Cultivation of Sci., Calcutta, 1959-64; guest scientist U. Urecht (Holland), 1964; sr. scientist chemistry dept. U. So. Calif., 1964-66; vis. asso. prof. U. Wis., Madison, 1966-67, prof. Sch. Pharmacy, 1967—; vis. prof. Indian Inst. Tech., Kharagpur, 1971-72. Mem. commn. on colloid and surface chemistry Internat. Union Pure and Applied Chemistry; grantee USPHS, NSF, Nat. Bur. Standards, Petroleum Research Fund. Fellow AAAS, Am. Inst. Chemistry; mem- Chem. Soc. Gt. Britain, Am. Chem. Soc., Fedn. Am. Scientists, Am. Pharm- Assn., Acad. Pharm. Scis., Am. Assn. Colls. Pharmacy, Rho Chi. Contbr. articles to profl. jours.; editorial bd. Jour. Colloid and Interface Sci., 1978-80, Asian Jour. Pharm. Scis., 1978—, Colloids and Surfaces, 1980—. Home: 5526 Varsity Hill Madison WI 53705 Office: 425 N Charter St Madison WI 53706

MUKHERJEE, MUKUNDA DEV, physician; b. Calcutta, India, July 5, 1942; came to U.S., 1968; s. Nritya Gopal and Basanti (Chatterjee) M.; M.B., B.S., King's Coll., Newcastle-upon-Tyne, Eng., 1966; m. Sarah Ann Wheeler, Nov. 24, 1973; children—Michelle, Matthew, Monica. Intern in surgery Cumberland (Eng.) Infirmary, 1966; intern in internal medicine Leeds (Eng.) Gen. Infirmary, 1967; resident in pediatrics Sheffield (Eng.) Children's Hosp., 1967, Boston Children's Hosp., 1968-69, Mass. Gen. Hosp., Boston, 1969-70; resident in obstetrics Sheffield (Eng.) Hosp. for Women, 1968; nutrition research asso. M.I.T., 1970; instr. Albert Einstein Coll., Bronx, N.Y., 1971-73; asst. clin. prof. pediatrics, Boston U., 1973-76; instr. community medicine Tufts U., Medford, Mass., 1975; dir. health services Columbia Point Health Center and South Boston Satelite Clinic, 1973-76; asso. dir. family practice residency program, asso. prof. U. N.D. Med. Sch., Minot, 1976-78; asso. prof. depts. family practice and pediatrics Wright State U. Sch. Medicine, Dayton, Ohio, 1978—, dir. research, dept. family practice, 1978—; practice medicine specializing in family practice and pediatrics, Dayton, 1978—; mem. staff Miami Valley, Children's, St. Elizabeth hosps. Past pres. Methodist Internat. House, Newcastle, Eng. Served with 2d Bengal Air Squadron, India, 1955-58. Fellow Am. Acad. Pediatrics, Am. Acad. Family Practice; mem. AMA (Physicians Recognition award), Ohio Acad. Family Physicians, Am. Public Health Assn., Am. Cancer Soc., Am. Lung Assn. Episcopalian. Home: 3643 Knollwood Dr Beavercreek OH 45432 Office: 601 Miami Blvd W Dayton OH 45408

MUKKAMALA, APPARAO, radiologist; b. Budhavaram, India, July 14, 1945; came to U.S., 1970, naturalized, 1978; s. Bhaskara Rao and Hymavathi (Kakarala) M.; M.B., B.S., Guntur (India) Med. Coll., 1970; m. Sumathi Anne, May 30, 1970; children—Srinivasa-Bhaskar, Aparna. Intern, St. Margaret Hosp., Pitts., 1970-71; resident in surgery Mt. Carmel Hosp., Detroit, 1971-72; resident in radiology Hurley Med. Center, Flint, Mich., 1972-75, radiologist, 1975—; asst. prof. Mich. State U., 1976—; v.p. Seva, Inc. Treas., Telugu Found.; sec. Bharatiya Temple, Flint; bd. dirs. Chinmaya Mission West. Diplomate Am. Bd. Radiology. Mem. Am. Coll. Radiologists, Mich. Radiol. Soc., Mich. Soc Therapeutic Radiologists, Genesee County Med. Soc., Mich. State Med. Soc. Clubs: India of Greater Flint, Telugu Assn. N. Am. (treas. 1978-79). Home: 6548 Kingspointe Rd Grand Blanc MI 48439 Office: Hurley Medical Center 6th and Begole Sts Flint MI 48502

MUKOYAMA, HELEN KIYOKO, social worker; b. Paia, Maui, Hawaii, Nov. 13, 1914; d. Ginichi and Shio (Takahashi) Takehara; B.A., Simpson Coll., 1937; student summer session U. Denver, 1936; M.A., U. Chgo., 1943; m. Teruo Mukoyama, June 11, 1936 (div. 1956); children—Marshall H., Howard T., Wesley K. Caseworker, Chgo. Welfare Adminstrn., 1938-41, Cook County Dept. Welfare, Chgo., 1945-46; cons. to Japanese Ams. relocating to Chgo., Ill. Public Aid Commn., 1945-46, welfare adminstrv. aid supr., 1949-69; caseworker Travelers Aid Soc.-Immigrants Service, Chgo., 1951-65; intake worker Homemaker Service, Salvation Army Family Service, Chgo., 1957-65; social work supr. of intake Ill. Dept. Children and Family Services, 1965-67; caseworker III, Salvation Army Family Service, Chgo., 1967-72; casework supr. Jewish Family and Community Services, Chgo., 1972-73; supr. intake Council for Jewish Elderly, Chgo., 1973-77, supr. community aides, welfare adminstrv. coordinator, 1977-79; coordinator elderly housing Japanese Am. Service Com., mgr. Heiwa Ter. Japanese Am. Elderly Housing, Chgo, 1980—. Mem. Council of Ministries, Welfare Div. of United Meth. Ch., 1963-69. Recipient award Japanese Am. Service Com., 1963. Mem. Acad. Cert. Social Workers, Nat. Assn. Social Workers, Ill. Cert. Social Workers, Chgo. Human Relations Commn., Japanese Am. Citizens League, Japanese-Am. Soc., Art Inst. Chgo., Epsilon Sigma, Pi Gamma Mu. Methodist. Contbr. articles to profl. jours. Home: 912 S Mason Ave Chicago IL 60644 Office: 920 W Lawrence St Chicago IL 60640

MULARZ, STANLEY LEON, credit info. services exec.; b. Chgo., Apr. 11, 1923; s. Stanley A. and Frances (Baycar) M.; A.B., St. Louis U., 1944; M.A., De Paul U., 1956; M.B.A., U. Chgo., 1960; Ph.D., Loyola U., Chgo., 1971; m. Lillian M. Kammerer, Apr. 10, 1948 (dec.); children—James P., Thomas E., Geraldine E., Joanne F., John F., Paul S., Donna M. Tchr., Benedictine Jr. Coll., Savannah, Ga., 1945-46, Grant Community High Sch., Fox Lake, Ill., 1946-47; fgn. corr. Continental Ill. Nat. Bank, 1947-48; tchr., adminstr. Morgan Park Mil. Acad. and Jr. Coll., 1948-51; mgr. Spiegel, Inc., 1951-52; regional credit mgr. Aldens, Inc., Chgo., 1952-54, ops. mgr., 1954-67, mgr. indsl. relations, 1967-68, credit div. group mgr., 1968-69; pres. Credit Info. Corp., 1969-79, Trans Union Credit Info. Co., Chgo., 1979—; v.p. Trans Union Systems Corp., Chgo., 1972—; mem. consumer adv. council Fed. Res. Bd., 1981—; lectr., adv. consumer edn. Mem. Gov.'s Commn. Schs./Bus. Mgmt. Task Force; chmn. State Info. Systems Com., 1974-77. Trustee, Felician Coll. Mem. Internat. Consumer Credit Assn. (pres. Dist. V 1975-77), Mchts. Research Council (dir., treas. 1975—), Associated Credit Burs. (dir. 1978—), Soc. Cert. Consumer Credit Execs. (pres. 1980-81), Am. Statis. Assn., U. Chgo. Exec. Program Club, Phi Delta Kappa (pres. chpt. 1970-71). Office: 111 W Jackson Blvd Chicago IL 60604

MULDARY, THOMAS WILLIAM, psychologist; b. Lackawanna, N.Y., Apr. 20, 1949; s. Charles Gallagher and Winifred Ann (Ebbitt) M.; B.S., Eastern Mich. U., 1971, M.S., 1973; Ph.D., U.S. Internat. U., 1979; m. Patricia Mary Spezeski, Sept. 20, 1980. Instr. psychology Jackson (Mich.) Community Coll. at State Prison of So. Mich.,

1973-76; chmn. dept. psychology Siena Heights Coll., Adrian, Mich., 1974-76; clin. intern U.S. Navy Alcoholism Rehab. Center, San Diego, 1978-80; prof. psychology and human behavior Nat. U., San Diego, 1978-80; instr. psychology U. Calif. Extension, San Diego, 1980; psychologist Robert L. Meyer and Assos., Ann Arbor, Mich., 1980—; lectr. dept. psychology Eastern Mich. U., Ypsilanti, 1980—; cons. Jackson Police Dept., 1981—, Dept. Vocat. Rehab., Ann Arbor. Lic. marriage, family and child therapist, Calif; lic. psychologist, Mich. Mem. Am. Psychol. Assn., Am. Personnel and Guidance Assn., Calif. Psychol. Assn., Calif. Assn. Marriage and Family Therapists. Contbr. articles to profl. jours. Home: 212 Stratford Ave Adrian MI 49221 Office: 2311 E Stadium Blvd Suite 109 Ann Arbor MI 48104

MULDER, GERARD WILLIAM, electronics co. exec.; b. Muskegon, Mich., Feb. 6, 1913; s. Henry J. and Swaney J. (Van Keppel) M.; A.B., Calvin Coll., 1933; B.S., U. Mich., 1935, M.S., 1936, Ph.D., 1939; m. Alyda D. Dykstra, Dec. 19, 1936; children—Judith Marie, Gerard William, Susan Jeanne. Vice pres., gen. mgr. Cleve. Container Co., 1945-55; pres. Gibbs Mfg. & Research Corp., Janesville, Wis., 1956-68; pres. O.C. Electronics, Inc., Milton, Wis., 1969—; dir. Rock County Nat. Bank, Rock Savs. & Trust, Rock Bancorp, N.W. Telephone Co., Gazette Printing Co. Trustee, Milton Coll., 1968—; chmn. bd. Rock County Health Care Center, 1972-75. Served to lt. col. U.S. Army, 1940-45; to col., 1950-52. Mem. Sigma Xi, Phi Kappa Phi. Republican. Presbyterian. Author: The Van Keppel Dynasty, 1977. Patentee in field. Address: Route 2 Milton WI 53563

MULDER-EDMONDSON, ANNE ENGLAND, educator; b. Bowling Green, Ky., June 18, 1935; d. Courtney Clark England and Frances (Page) England Chilton; A.B., Transylvania Coll., 1957; M.A., U. Mich., 1967, postgrad., 1977—; postgrad. Mich. State U., 1975, Western Mich. U., 1972, Am. U., 1956; m. Don Edmondson; children—Emily, Amy. Tchr. high sch., 1957-61; dir. student activities Grand Rapids (Mich.) Jr. Coll., 1961-63; instr. in English, 1959-72, coordinator women's programs, 1972-75, dir. community services, 1975-76, asst. dean of continuing edn., 1976—, dean acad. services, 1981—, also asst. to pres.; Marshall lectr. Transylvania U., 1977; cons. in women's programming and in continuing edn. Pres. Grand Rapids Arts Council; bds. dirs. Women's Resource Center, YWCA, Civic Theatre; mem. Festival of the Arts Com., chmn. 1972; actress local theatre; active arts activities; women's advocate; arts cons. Mem. Mich. Community Colls. Community Services Assn. (pres.), State Adv. Council Adult and Continuing Edn. (chmn. community relations com.), Am. Assn. Women in Community and Jr. Colls. (nat. chmn. profl. devel. 1976), Delta Kappa Gamma, Phi Beta, Delta Delta Delta. Democrat. Writer for mags., 1963-72; contbr. articles to profl. jours. Home: 8200 Vergennes NE Ada MI 49301 Office: Grand Rapids Junior College 143 Bostwick NE Grand Rapids MI 49503

MULÉ, LOUIS PETER, environ. biologist; b. Chgo., Aug. 30, 1946; s. Joseph Anthony and Mary Antoinette (Ciaccio) M.; B.S. in Biology, St. Louis U., 1968; M.S., Chgo. State U., 1972. Tchr. sci. Argo (Ill.) Community High Sch., 1968-77; asso. instr. Nat. Coll. Edn., Evanston, Ill., 1974-77; asso. instr. Moraine Valley Community Coll., Palos Hills, Ill., 1974-81; prof. environ. sci. and coop. edn., div. sci. Coll. Arts and Scis., Governors State U., Park Forest South, Ill., 1977—. Bd. advisors Citizens for a Better Environment, Chgo., 1973-74; founder Save Our Resources and Environment, Summit, Ill., 1970; co-founder, dir. Heritage Lands, Inc., Chicago Ridge, Ill., 1976-79. Recipient Environ. quality award EPA, 1974. Mem. AAAS, Nat. Assn. Biology Tchrs., Environ. Assn. Ill., Ill. State Acad. Sci., Moraine Valley Oral History Assn. (founder). Roman Catholic. Home: 9311 W 135th St Orland Park IL 60462 Office: Div Sci Governors State U Park Forest South IL 60466

MULLALLY, PIERCE HARRY, steel co. exec.; b. Cleve., Oct. 6, 1918; s. Pierce Harry and Laura (Lynch) M.; student U. Western Ont., 1935; B.S., John Carroll U., 1939; M.D., St. Louis U., 1943; m. Mary Eileen Murphy, Feb. 22, 1943; children—Mary Kathleen, Pierce Harry. Intern, St. Vincent Charity Hosp., Cleve., 1943, resident in surgery, 1944, 47-50, staff surgeon, 1951-62, head peripheral vascular surgery, 1963-76, dir. med. edn., 1967-73, dir. dept. surgery, 1968-75, trustee, 1977—; plant physician Republic Steel Corp., Cleve., 1952-68, med. dir., 1968-76, corp. dir. occupational medicine, 1976—. Vice-chmn. Cleve. Clinic-Charity Hosp. Com. Surg. Residency Tng., 1970-78; health com. Bituminous Coal Operators Assn. Served to capt. U.S. Army, 1944-46; PTO. Diplomate Am. Bd. Surgery. Fellow ACS, Am. Coll. Angiology; mem. Am. Iron and Steel Inst. (chmn. health com. 1977—), Am. Acad. Occupational Medicine, Am., Ohio occupational med. assns., Acad. Medicine, Cleve. (dir. 1969-72), Cleve. Surg. Soc., Western Res. Med. Dirs., Soc. Clin. Vascular Surgery. Roman Catholic. Clubs: Cleve. Skating, Cleve. Playhouse, Serra. Home: 2285 Harcourt Dr Cleveland Heights OH 44106 Office: Republic Steel Corp PO Box 6778 Cleveland OH 44101

MULLEN, PATRICK WILLIAM, diversified grocery exec.; b. Hamilton, Ohio, June 22, 1948; s. Jack Edward and Elaine Marie (Reese) M.; B.A. with honors, Tulane U., 1970; postgrad. U. Hamburg (W. Ger.), Goethe Inst., Munich, W. Ger., Am. Edn. Inst.; postgrad. in bus. adminstrn. Coll. of St. Thomas, St. Paul; m. Jacqueline Marie Daw, Aug. 11, 1973; children—Bridget Colleen, Erin Maureen. With Peace Corps, Katmandu, Nepal, 1971-72; high sch. tchr. Colegio Pan Americano Bucaramanga, Colombia, 1973-74; chef's apprentice Royal Sonesta Hotel, New Orleans, 1974-77; claims rep. Travelers Ins. Co., 1977-79; dir. loss prevention and security Lewis Grocer Co., Indianola, Miss., 1979-81; corp. loss prevention specialist Super Valu Stores, Inc., Mpls., 1981—; lectr. Delta State U., Cleveland, Miss.; causalty claim law asso. Pres. men's club Immaculate Conception Roman Cath. Ch., Indianola, 1980—. Mem. Am. Soc. Safety Engrs., Nat. Safety Mgmt. Soc., Nat. Safety Council, Delta Phi Alpha, Sigma Chi. Republican. Club: Indianola Lions (officer 1979—). Home: 4601 Portland Ave S Minneapolis MN 55407 Office: PO Box 990 Minneapolis MN 55440

MULLEN, RICHARD ALLEN, mfg. co. exec.; b. Dayton, Ohio, Feb. 13, 1942; s. Howard Allen and Mary Jane (Ellis) M.; B.B.A., U. Cin., 1965; m. Donna May Allread, June 19, 1965; children—Christine Lee, Scott Allen, Elizabeth Ann. With Mobil Oil, Milw., Detroit, 1965-68; mgr. budgets and financial analysis Philips Industries, Dayton, Ohio, 1968-70, asst. treas., 1970-72, controller mfg. housing and recreation vehicle div., 1972-73, div. v.p. fin., 1973-74, corp. v.p. fin., treas., 1974-78, pres. Lau Industries Div., 1978—. Mem. Sigma Phi Epsilon. Methodist. Club: AMBUCS. Home: 1976 Spring Tree Ct Dayton OH 45459 Office: 2027 Home Ave Dayton OH 45407

MULLER, ADELYN CAMERON, ret. educator; b. Greenville, Tex., Mar. 5, 1913; d. Frank Clifton and Hortense (White) Cameron; B.A., B.A. in English and Math., E. Tex. State U., Commerce, 1934; M.A. in Math. Edn., U. Mo., Kansas City, 1968; Ph.D. in Math. Edn., Kans. State U., Manhattan, 1975; m. John G. Muller; children—Ken Cameron, Jon Tackaberry. Tchr., Greenville (Tex.) Pub. Schs., 1936-40; aero. liasion engr. Ft. Worth Consol.-Vultee, 1943-46; coordinator math. Valley View Sch. Dist., Overland Park, Kans., 1960-69, Shawnee Mission (Kans.) Pub. Schs., 1969-79; adj. prof. Kans. State U., U. Mo., Kansas City. Mem. AAUW, Shawnee Mission Pub. Sch. Adminstrs. Assn., Nat. Council Tchrs. Math., Phi Delta Kappa, Delta Kappa Gamma. Recipient Nat. Edn. Assn. Pacemaker award, 1969. Participant in HEW 3-month tour of India; Nat. Sch. Assn. people-to-people tour Russia, Switzerland, France, Eng. Contbr. articles in field to profl. jours. Home: 370 Terrace Trail W Lake Quivira KS 66106

MULLER, EMMA FLEER, ret. educator; b. Brillion, Wis., July 11, 1896; d. E. John and Emma (Collatz) Fleer; Mus. B., Marquette U., 1918; B.S. (Honor Entrance scholar 1921, Marie Mergeler scholar, 1922-23, 23, 24), U. Chgo., 1923, postgrad., 1924-32, 50-53; m. Frederick H. Muller, Aug. 2, 1930 (dec. Nov. 1954); 1 son, Carl H. Instr. music Marquette U., 1915-21; organist and choir dir. Milw. and Chgo.; research asst. dept. physiology U. Chgo., 1924-25; tchr. physiology Chgo. Tchrs. Coll. (now Chgo. State U.), 1924-28, dean, 1928-38, dir. personnel, 1938-61, ret.; dean women Woodrow Wilson Jr. Coll., 1934-37. Vol. worker Chgo. Wesley Meml. Hosp., 1961-72, Northwestern Meml. Hosp., 1972—. Recipient citation Marquette U., 1965. Mem. Nat. (citation 1961), Ill. (citation 1953) assns. women deans and counselors, Ill. Assn. Deans Women (pres. 1940-42), Am. Personnel and Guidance Assn., Ill. Guidance and Personnel Assn., Student Personnel Assn. for Tchr. Edn., Am., Ill. assns. Collegiate Registrars and Admissions Officers, Chgo. Conf. Collegiate Registrars and Admissions Officers (pres. 1953-54), Nat., Ill. edn. assns., Am. Assn. Sch. Adminstrs., Art Inst. Chgo., Lyric Opera Guild, Chgo. Symphony Soc., Chgo. Ednl. TV Assn., Field Mus. Natural History, Phi Beta Delta, Sigma Xi, Pi Lambda Theta, Delta Kappa Gamma (chpt. pres. 1953-54), Sigma Delta Epsilon (nat. treas. 1926-27, chpt. pres. 1929-30). Contbr. articles to profl. jours. Home: 1360 N Lake Shore Dr Chicago IL 60610

MULLER, JOHN BARTLETT, educator; b. Port Jefferson, N.Y., Nov. 8, 1940; s. Frederick Henry and Estelle May (Reeve) M.; A.B., U. Rochester, 1962; student Westminster Sem., 1962-63; M.S., Purdue U., 1968, Ph.D., 1975; m. Barbara Ann Schmidt, May 30, 1964 (dec. Sept. 1971). Asst. prof. psychology, dir. research, div. chmn. Roberts Wesleyan Coll., Rochester, N.Y., 1964-65, 67-70; vis. asst. prof. Wabash Coll., Crawfordsville, Ind., 1970-71; research asso. Ind.-Purdue U., Indpls., 1971-72; prof. psychology Hillsdale (Mich.) Coll., 1972—, div. chmn., dir. instl. research, 1972-80, v.p. for acad. affairs, 1976—. NIMH fellow, 1963-64; Townsend fellow, 1962. Mem. AAAS, Am. Psychol. Assn., Assn. Instl. Research, Am. Sci. Assn., Am. Assn. Higher Edn., Phi Beta Kappa, Phi Kappa Phi. Contbr. articles to profl. jours. Home: 133 Lake Pleasant Rd Osseo MI 49266 Office: Hillsdale Coll Hillsdale MI 49242

MULLER, JULIA KING, banker; b. Salina, Kans., Nov. 14, 1941; d. Richard Weldon and Julia (Koester) K.; A.A., Stephens Coll., 1961; B.S., U. Kans., 1963; M.S., So. Ill. U., Carbondale, 1967, Ph.D., 1976. Tchr., Stoneham (Mass.) High Sch., 1963-65; instr. So. Ill. U., Carbondale, 1963-68, acad. adv., 1967-70, coordinator, 1970-78; asst. dean student affairs U. Mo., St. Louis, 1978-79, acting dean student affairs, 1979, dean student affairs, asst. prof. behavioral studies, 1979-81; v.p. United Mo. Bancshares, St. Louis, 1981—. Bd. dirs. Girls Clubs Am.; bd. dirs. Carbondale United Way, 1978, mem. budget com., 1978; mem. Carbondale Bi-Centennial Commn., 1975-76; sec. Friends of Carbondale Library, 1976-78; mem. capital improvements bond issue citizens com., University City, Mo., 1978-79. Mem. AAUW, Am. Coll. Personnel Assn., Am. Personnel and Guidance Assn., Am. Assn. Higher Edn., Nat. Assn. Women Deans, Adminstrs. and Counselors, U. Mo. St. Louis Faculty Women (pres. 1980-81), Phi Theta Kappa, Pi Lambda Delta, Phi Delta Kappa, Phi Kappa Phi. Club: So. Ill. U. Women's (retiring pres., adv. 1978-79, mem. bd. 1970-72, 77-79). Home: 7476 Ahern Ct Saint Louis MO 63130 Office: United Mo Bancshares Box 1126 Saint Louis MO 63188

MULLER, SIGFRID AUGUSTINE, dermatologist; b. Panama City, Panama, Feb. 20, 1930; s. Luis and Marciana (Espino) M.; came to U.S., 1932, naturalized, 1967; A.B., Pepperdine U., 1949; M.D., St. Louis U., 1953; M.S., Mayo Grad. Sch. Medicine, 1958; m. Jane Barbara Zierden, Dec. 28, 1964; children—Sigfrid Augustine, Stephen, Scott, Maria. Intern, Gorgas Hosp., Canal Zone, 1953-54; resident Indpls. Hosp., 1954-55, Mayo Grad. Sch. Medicine, 1955-58; practice medicine, specializing dermatology, Rochester, Minn., 1961—; cons. dermatology Mayo Clinic, Rochester, Minn., 1961—; asst. prof. dermatology U. Panama, 1958-60; prof. dermatology Mayo Clinic Med. Sch., Rochester, Minn., 1972—. Bd. dirs., treas. Found. for Internat. Dermatologic Edn., 1976—. Recipient Pres.'s award, Pepperdine U., 1973. Fellow A.C.P.; mem. Am. Dermatological Assn, Am. Acad. Dermatology, Soc. of Investigative Dermatology, Am. Soc. Human Genetics, Am. Soc. Dermatopathology, AAAS, AMA, Am. Fedn. Clin. Research, Minn. Dermatological Soc. (pres. 1972-73), Soc. Dermatologic Genetics (pres. 1972-73), Noah Worcester Dermatologic Soc. (pres. 1972-73), Internat. Soc. Tropical Dermatology (v.p. 1974-79; sec. gen. 1979—). Contbr. articles to profl. jours. Asst. chief editor Archives of Dermatology, 1972-74. Editorial bd. Archives of Dermatology, 1974—; Medicina Cutanea, 1968—; Internat. Bull. Psoriasis, 1973—. Home: 24 Skyline Dr Rochester MN 55901 Office: 200 1st St SW Rochester MN 55901

MULLIGAN, BARBARA E., coll. adminstr.; b. Grand Rapids, Mich., June 25, 1927; d. Raymond Christopher and Gertrude (Moran) Mulligan; B.A., Marquette U., 1962, M.A., 1964. Instr. polit. sci., asst. dir. continuing edn. Alverno Coll., Milw., 1966-68, dir. continuing edn., 1968-71, asst. dean, 1971-72, co-dir. Research Center on Women, 1970-72; asst. dir. Div. Continuing Edn., Marquette U., 1972-74, asso. dir. Div. Continuing Edn. and Summer Sessions, 1974—, acting dir., 1979. Mem. Gov.'s Commn. Status of Women, 1967-71; gov.'s appointee Wis. Ednl. Approval Bd., 1968-71. First vice chmn. Wis. Women's Republican Club, 1964-68. Bd. dirs. Greater Milw. chpt. ARC, 1973-74, also personnel com., community services programs com. Mem. Adult Edn. Assn. U.S.A., Adult Edn. Assn. Wis. (dir. 1969-71, 75-77), Wis. Polit. Sci. Assn. (treas. 1970-72), Milw. Council Adult Learning, Wis. Soc. Health and Tng., Nat. Univ. Extension Assn., Marquette U. Alumni Assn., AAUW, Am. Assn. Univ. Adminstrs. (dir. Delta chpt. 1975-76), Nat. Council Adminstrv. Women in Edn. (council on continuing edn. unit), Am. Assn. Higher Edn., Nat. Trust Historic Preservation, Smithsonian Assos. Home: 2703 N Hackett Ave Milwaukee WI 53211

MULLIKEN, ROBERT SANDERSON, educator; b. Newburyport, Mass., June 7, 1896; s. Samuel Parsons and Katherine (Mulliken) M.; B.S., Mass. Inst. Tech., 1917; Ph.D., U. Chgo., 1921; Sc.D. (hon.), Columbia, 1939, Marquette U., Cambridge U., 1967, Gustavus Adolphus Coll., 1975; Ph.D. (hon.), Stockholm U., 1960; m. Mary Helen von Noé, Dec. 24, 1929 (dec. Mar. 1975); children—Lucia Maria (Mrs. John P. Heard), Valerie Noé. Research on war gases, Washington, 1917-18; tech. research with N.J. Zinc Co., 1919; research on separation isotopes, 1920-22; researches on molecular spectra and molecular structure, 1923—. Nat. research fellow U. Chgo., 1921-23, Harvard, 1923-25; asst. prof. physics Washington Sq. Coll. (N.Y. U.), 1926-28; asso. prof. physics U. Chgo., 1928-31, prof. physics, 1931-61, Ernest DeWitt Burton Distinguished Service prof., 1956-61, Distinguished Service prof. physics and chemistry, 1961—; Distinguished Research prof. chem. physics Fla. State U., 1965-71. Baker lectr. Cornell U. 1960; vis. prof. Bombay, 1962, Indian Inst. Tech., Kanpur, 1962; Silliman lectr. Yale, 1965; Jan Van Geuns vis. prof. Amsterdam U., 1965. J.S. Guggenheim fellow for European study, 1930, 32; leave of absence, 1942-45, as dir. information div. Plutonium Project at Chgo.; editor Plutonium Project Record in Nat. Nuclear Energy Series. Fulbright research fellow for research at Oxford, 1952-53; vis. fellow St. John's Coll., Oxford, 1952-53; sci. attaché Am. embassy, London, 1955. Served with C.W.S., U.S. Army, 1918. Recipient medal U. Liege, 1948; Gilbert N. Lewis medal Calif. sect. Am. Chem. Soc., 1960, Theodore W. Richards medal Northeastern sect., 1960, Peter Debye award Am. Chem. Soc., 1963, J.G. Kirkwood award New Haven sect., 1964, Willard Gibbs medal Chgo. sect., 1965; Nobel prize for chemistry, 1966. Fellow Am. Phys. Soc. (chmn. div. chem. physics 1951-52), A.A.A.S.; hon. fellow Indian Nat. Acad. Sci., London Chem. Soc.; mem. Nat. Acad. Scis., Am. Philos. Soc., Am. Chem. Soc., Internat. Acad. Quantum Molecular Sci., Am. Acad. Arts and Scis., Royal Soc. (fgn. mem.), Soc. de Chimie Physique (hon.), Royal Soc. Sci. of Liège (corr.), Royal Irish Acad. (hon.), Chem. Soc. Japan (hon.), Gamma Alpha. Clubs: Quadrangle; Cosmos (Washington). Home: 5825 S Dorchester Ave Chicago IL 60637

MULLINS, BARBARA JEANNE, petroleum mktg. exec.; b. Day, Fla., Aug. 29, 1938; d. James Eli and Bessie Geraldine (Johnson) Grantham; cert. acctg. Longview Community Coll., Mo., 1977; m. Mikel Burton Mullins, Dec. 20, 1956; children—Ronald Lee, Richard Bryan, Mikel Duane. Fin. asst. J. M. Fields, Melbourne, Fla., 1962-63; acctg. clk. Radiation, Inc., Melbourne, 1963-64; bookkeeper/sec. Sam Hammonds, C.P.A., Oklahoma City, 1964-65; with Bride Co., Leawood, Kans., 1970—, bookkeeper, 1970-74, chief acct., 1974-75, controller, 1975-79, v.p. adminstrn., 1979—, corp. sec., 1973—, registered agt., 1973-80; corp. sec. Data Freight, Inc., 1980—. Recipient 1st Pl. award Distributive Edn. Clubs Am. Mo. Competition, 1976. Mem. Am. Petroleum Inst., Nat. Assn. Accts. (dir. Kansas City chpt. 1978—, treas. Heartland regional council 1981-82). Democrat. Baptist. Home: 24303 W 86th Terr Olathe KS 66061 Office: 4701 College Blvd Suite 202 Leawood KS 66211

MULLINS, JAMES BOLL, ins. co. exec.; b. Dallas, June 19, 1934; s. Frank Morris and Alice Ophelia (Holland) M.; B.A. N. Tex. State U., Denton, 1956; postgrad. So. Methodist U. Law Sch., 1959-60; m. Joann Barnett, Aug. 6, 1954; children—Kiann, Kala-Joy. With Allstate Ins. Co., 1956-77, regional claim mgr., Valley Forge, Pa., 1973-76, zone claim mgr. East zone, N.J., 1976-77; v.p. claims CNA/Ins., Chgo., 1977—; bd. govs. Ins. Crime Prevention Inst., 1979. Author: Management Digest Series, 1975. Office: CNA Plaza Chicago IL 60685

MULLINS, RICHARD AUSTIN, chem. engr.; b. Seelyville, Ind., Apr. 22, 1918; s. Fred A. and Ethel (Zenor) M.; B.S. in Chem. Engring., Rose Poly. Inst., 1940; postgrad. Yale, 1942-43; m. Margaret Ann Dellacca, Nov. 27, 1946; children—Scott Alan, Mark Earl. Chemist, Ayrshire Collieries Corp., Brazil, Ind., 1940-49; chief chemist Fairview Collieries Corp., Danville, Ill., 1949-54; preparations mgr. Enos Coal Mining Co., Oakland City, Ind., 1954-72, Enoco Collieries, Inc., Bruceville, Ind., 1954-62; mining engr. Kings Station Coal Corp.; mgr. analytical procedures Old Ben Coal Corp., 1973—. Am. Mining Congress cons. to Am. Standards Assn. and Internat. Orgn. for Standards, 1960-74; mem. indsl. cons. com. Ind. Geol. Survey, 1958-72; mem. organizing com. 5th Internat. Coal Preparation Congress, Pittsburgh, 1966. Mem. exec. bd. Buffalo Trace council Boy Scouts Am., also mem. speakers bur. Bd. dirs. Princeton Boys Club. Served with AUS, 1942-46; ETO. Decorated Medaille de la France Liberee (France); recipient Eagle Scout award, Boy Scouts Am., 1935, Silver Beaver award, 1962, Wood Badge Beads award, 1960; Outstanding Community Service award Princeton Civitan Club, 1964; Engr. of Year award S.W. chpt. Ind. Soc. Profl. Engrs., 1965; Prince of Princeton award Princeton C. of C., 1981. Registered profl. engr., Ind., Ill. Mem. AIME, ASTM, Am. Chem. Soc., Nat. Soc. Profl. Engrs., Ind., Ill. mining insts., Ind. Coal Soc. (pres. 1958-59), Am. Mining Congress (chmn. com. coal preparation 1964-68), Am. Legion, 40 and 8, Ind. Soc. Profl. Land Surveyors, Rose Tech. Alumni Assn. (pres. 1976-77, Honor Alumnus 1980), Order of Ring, Sigma Nu. Methodist (lay speaker). Mason, Elk. Contbr. articles to profl. jours. Home: 8 Circle Dr Princeton IN 47670 Office: Old Ben Coal Co div Sohio 2425 Bldg Hwy 41 N Evansville IN 47711

MULLIN-TRAYNOR, VI ANNE, market research exec.; b. St. Paul, July 2, 1944; d. Vi Anne Sattre Christensen; B.S., Mankato (Minn.) State U., 1967; M.A., Old Dominion U., Richmond, Va., 1971; M.S., Sloan Sch. Mgmt., M.I.T., 1981; m. George F. Traynor, June 31, 1979; 1 son, Mark. Tchr. English, Norfolk (Va.) schs., 1968-70; instr. English, Old Dominion U., 1970-72; with Control Data Corp., Mpls., 1973—, market developer acad. edn., computer-bases edn., 1978-79, mgr. mktg. programs U.S. mktg. and sales, 1979-81, mgr. market research and strategy planning, 1981—. Bush Leadership fellow, 1979; Sloan fellow M.I.T., 1980-81. Mem. Soc. Applied Learning Tech., Assn. Devel. Computer-Bases Instn. Systems, Internat. Reading Assn., Common Cause, Am. Mktg. Assn., World Future Soc. Democrat. Lutheran. Home: 1489 Fairmount Ave Saint Paul MN 55105 Office: 8100 34th Ave S Bloomington MN 55440

MULVANEY, DALLAS EDWARD, psychologist; b. Lawrence, Kan., June 15, 1946; s. Albert Edward and Bettye Baker (Besemann) M.; B.A., Ind. U./Purdue U., 1970; Ph.D., Ind. U., 1974; children—Ari F., Faye N. Post-doctoral research fellow Ind. U. Sch. Medicine, Indpls., 1974-75; asst. prof. Ind. Central U., Indpls., 1975-76; dir. research New Castle (Ind.) State Hosp., 1976—; dir. edn. and research Diversified Human Resources, Indpls., 1979—; cons. Columbus (Ind.) Women's Center, 1979-80; instr. Ind. U., 1979-. Residents' advocate in nursing home industry, State of Ind., 1979—. U.S. Office of Edn. fellow, 1970-73, 1974-75. Mem. Am. Psychol. Assn., AAAS, Canadian Psychol. Assn. Contbr. articles to profl. jours. Home: 4201 E 146th St Carmel IN 46032 Office: PO Box 34 New Castle IN 47362

MULVANEY, RONALD, bank assn. exec.; b. Bklyn., July 26, 1933; s. Martin Vincent and Jean Catherine (Zabinski) M.; B.A., Marquette U., 1960; m. Joan M. Helget, June 7, 1958; children—Therese, Sharon, Janet, Daniel, David, Susan. Asso. editor Mid-Western Banker Mag., Milw., 1960-65; asst. cashier Midland Nat. Bank, Milw., 1965-66; exec. dir. Engrs. & Scientists of Milw., Inc., 1966-71; asso. dir. Wis. Bankers Assn., Madison, 1971—, also editor Bank Notes; organizer Midtown State Bank, Milw., 1967. Pres. Coop. West Side, Inc., 1964; chmn. 10th Dist. Wis. Democratic Com., 1965; treas. 5th Congl. Dist. Wis. Dem. Com., 1966; Congl. candidate in primary, 1978. Served with USMC, 1953-56. Mem. Wis. Profl. Speakers' Assn. Roman Catholic. Club: Toastmasters. Home: 17540 Sierra Ln Brookfield WI 53005 Office: 16 N Carroll St Madison WI 53703

MULVANEY, WILLIAM PETER, urologist, clin. dir.; b. Cin., Mar. 28, 1921; s. William Peter and Elsie Marie (Heil) M.; B.S., Xavier U., Cin., 1943; M.D., Loyola U., Chgo., 1946; postgrad. U. Minn., 1949-52; m. Pauline Dwenger, 1970; children—Mary Kathleen, Sharon, William P., James Foley, Terence M. Practice medicine specializing in urology, Cin., 1952—; asst. prof. urology U. Cin., 1953-68, laser researcher, 1970-74; dir. urology Good Samaritan Hosp., 1952-72, dir. urol. research, 1974—; dir. Camargo Manor Nursing Home. Trustee Chatfield Coll., St. Martins, Ohio. Recipient

Sci. Exhibits awards Am. Urol. Soc., 1973-75; diplomate Am. Bd. Urology. Fellow ACS; mem. Internat. Soc. Laser Surgeons, Am. Soc. Laser Medicine and Surgery. Inventor first topical solvent for kidney bladder stones; oral drug for preventing and dissolving cystine kidney stones. Home: 687 N Meadowcrest Cr Cincinnati OH 45231

MUMA, JACK WESLEY, ins. exec.; b. Villa Grove, Ill., Jan. 5, 1927; s. Wilbert W. and Maxine L. (Wood) M.; B.S.C.E. in Structural Engrng., Wayne State U., 1950; m. Dolores M. Power, June 24, 1950; children—Michael W., Lindsay A., Margaret E., Andrew J., David P. Fire protection engr. Homer Warren & Co., Detroit, 1950-54; adminstrv. asst., jr. partner Grow, Sumner, Englebert, Detroit, 1954-58; v.p. Hudson & Muma, Inc., Southfield, Mich., 1958-66, pres., 1966-70; pres., chief exec. officer Guardian Nat. Corp., Royal Oak, Mich., 1970-73; pres., chief operating officer, mem. exec. com., dir. Fin. Guardian Group, Inc., Kansas City, Mo., 1973-79; sr. v.p. Reed Shaw Stenhouse, Inc. Pres. Detroit Homeowners Assn., 1962-64. Served with USNR, 1945-71; PTO, CBI; comdr. Res. ret. Mem. Nat. Assn. Casualty and Surety Agts., Mo. Assn. Ind. Ins. Agts., Nat. C. of C., Alpha Sigma Phi (treas. alumni 1951-59). Home: 11815 Pennsylvania Ave Kansas City MO 64114 Office: 1270 Ave of Americas New York NY 10020

MUMA, RICHARD ALLEN, fin. exec.; b. Warren, Mich., Dec. 29, 1940; s. Forest Amber and Elizabeth Maude (Troyer) M.; B.S. in Edn., No. Mich. U., 1972; m. Dagmar Ann Brock, June 12, 1965; children—Jeffrey Michael, Cheryl Lynn, David Richard. Dir. phys. edn. Pinconning (Mich.) Area Schs., 1972-73; with Schater Chevrolet, Pinconning, Mich., 1974-76; agt. Prudential Ins. Co., Grand Rapids, Mich., 1976—, new manpower devel. mgr., 1977—. Served with USN, 1959-67. Recipient No. Star award, Prudential Ins. Co. Am., 1978, 79. Mem. Nat. Assn. Life Underwriters (life underwriters polit. action com.). Reformed Ch. of Am. Clubs: Ch. Golf League. Home: 7788 Emberly St Jenison MI 49428 Office: 161 Ottawa NW 4115 Waters Bldg Grand Rapids MI 49503

MUMMERT, THOMAS ALLEN, mfg. co. exec.; b. Toledo, Ohio, Dec. 24, 1946; s. James Allen and Betty Alice (Thomas) M.; student U. Toledo, 1965-66; m. Icia Linda Shearer, Dec. 17, 1966; children—Sherry Lynn, Robert Thomas, Michael Allen. Pres., Mummert Electric & Mfg. Co., Inc., Toledo, 1969-70; research engr. Am. Lincoln Corp., Bowling Green, Ohio, 1970-73; test engr. Dura div. Dura Corp., Toledo, 1973-74; research dept. head Jobst Inst., Inc., Toledo, 1975—. Served with USN, 1968-69. Mem. AAAS, Ohio Acad. Sci., N.Y. Acad. Sci., Am. Soc. for Quality Control, Am. Soc. Engrng. Edn., Nat. Mgmt. Assn., Assn. for Advancement of Med. Instrumentation. Baptist. Inventor sequential dual window operating mechanism, 1974, therapeutic appliance for flexing joints, 1980; patentee in field. Office: 653 Miami St Toledo OH 43694

MUNKACHY, LOIS DEUTSCH, educator; b. Detroit, Sept. 16, 1929; d. Louis and Ethel (Nagy) D.; B.Music Edn., Baldwin Wallace Coll., 1951; M.A., U. Mich., 1969, Ph.D., 1974; m. Ernest Frederick Munkachy, Mar. 29, 1950; 1 son, Richard Lee David. Tchr. elem. music Dearborn (Mich.) public schs., 1952-54, high sch. tchr. English and music, Westwood, Mich., 1954-68; jr. high sch. tchr. English and social studies, Woodhaven, Mich., 1968-69; tchr. elem. music Romulus (Mich.) Community Schs., 1969-72; tchr. drama, English and choir Romulus High Sch., 1972—; dir. Universal Self-Help Center, 1981. Mem. Assn. Supervision and Curriculum Devel., NEA, Mich. Edn. Assn., Mich. Sch. Vocal Assn., Nat. Writers Club, Assn. Advance Ethical Hypnosis, Phi Delta Kappa. Clubs: Huron Valley Gun Collectors, Rosicrucians. Office: 960 Newburgh Rd Westland MI 48185

MUNNS, WILLIAM LAWRENCE, univ. dean; b. Quincy, Ill., Nov. 8, 1929; s. William Kenneth and Wilma C. (Stone) M.; B.A., Colo. State U., 1951; M.S., U. Colo., 1956; Ed.D., U. No. Colo., 1962; m. Constance Eileen Boeyink, July 20, 1957; children—William Lawrence, Jeffrey Scott. Tchr., Logan County High Sch., Sterling, Colo., 1956-58; adminstrv. asst. to supt. Gill (Colo.) public schs., 1958-59; dist. guidance dir. Twin Falls (Idaho) public schs., 1959-60; coordinator psychol. services, Barrington, Ill., 1960-62; dir. Univ. Counseling Center, coordinator grad. guidance program Wis. State U., Oshkosh, 1962-65; asso. dean, prof. psychology Ariz. State Coll., Flagstaff, 1965-67; v.p. student affairs, asst. chancellor, dean students, prof. edn. U. Wis., River Falls, 1967—; personnel cons. Oshkosh Law Enforcement candidates; cons. D.A.T.A., Inc. Student Admissions Center, Tri-County Mental Health Assn., Supplementary Edn. Center-Inst. for Culturally Disadvantaged, Flagstaff. Active, River Falls Twp. Planning Commn. Served with USAF, 1951-54. Mem. Am. Personnel and Guidance Assn., Am. Coll. Personnel Assn., Assn. for Counselor Edn. and Supervision, Nat. Assn. Student Personnel Adminstrs., Am. Mental Health Counselors Assn., Wis. Personnel and Guidance Assn., Tau Kappa Epsilon, Psi Chi, Phi Delta Kappa. Republican. Clubs: Masons; Lions; German Shepherd Dog of Am. Contbr. articles to profl. jours. Home: Route 5 232 Edgewater Ln River Falls WI 54022 Office: 124 Hathorn U Wis River Falls WI 54022

MUNOZ, MARIO ALEJANDRO, city ofcl.; b. Havana, Cuba, Feb. 27, 1928; s. Ramon and Concepcion (Bermudo) M.; came to U.S., 1961, naturalized, 1968; M.Arch., U. Havana, 1954; postgrad. City Colls. Chgo., 1974, 1970. m. Julia Josephine Garrofe, Jan. 17, 1970. Owner, Munoz Bermudo-Construcciones, Havana, 1954-61; designer various cos., Chgo., 1961-65; designer Chgo. Transit Authority, Mdse. Mart, Chgo., 1965-69; civil engr. Dept. Water and Sewers, City of Chgo., 1969-79, supervising engr. Dept. of Sewers, 1979—; mem. central area subway system utilities com. City of Chgo., 1974—, mem. computer graphics com., 1977-78. Mem. Am. Pub. Works Assn., Western Soc. Engrs., Chgo. Architecture Found., Chgo. Council Fgn. Relations, Internat. Platform Assn. Roman Catholic. Clubs: Ground Hog, Execs. (speaker's table com.) (Chgo.). Home: 5455 N Sheridan Rd Apt 1912 Chicago IL 60640 Office: 121 N LaSalle St Chicago IL 60602

MUNOZ, ROMEO SOLANO, educator; b. Philippines, July 2, 1933; s. Maximo Marcaida and Fe (Solano) M.; A.B., Colegio de San Juan de Letran, 1964; M.S.Ed., Eastern Ill. U., 1968; postgrad. (fellow), So. Ill. U., 1968-70, Govs. State U., 1980—; m. Soledad Roselada, Jan. 2, 1964; children—Francis-Vincent, Theresa Lourdes, Romualdo-Romeo, Cecilia, Anafe, Stephen. Dir. audiovisual center Ateneo de Manila (Philippines) U., 1962-67; dir. audiovisual service, chmn. learning resource center Olive Harvey Coll., Chgo., 1969—, asso. prof. instructional media, 1969—. Mem. Philippine Educators in Am. (v.p. internal affairs 1972-76), Assn. Ednl. Communication and Technology, ALA, Assn. Supervision and Curriculum Devel., Ill. Assn. Ednl. Communication and Technology. Republican. Roman Catholic (permanent deacon Chgo.). Club: Lions. Home: 573 Harrison St Calumet City IL 60409 Office: Sch Edn Olive Harvey Coll 10001 S Woodlawn Ave Chicago IL 60628

MUNSON, STEPHAN DENNIS, pharmacist; b. Mendota, Ill., Sept. 4, 1952; s. Francis Gail and Edith Marion (Barth) M.; B.S., U. Ill., 1975. Apprentice pharmacist Goslin Drug Store, Mendota, intermittently 1972-74, E. Von Hermann Pharmacy, Chgo., 1973-75, Karad Drugs, Chgo., fall 1974; dir. pharmacy Mendota Community Hosp., 1975—; teaching asso. U. Ill. Coll. Pharmacy. Mem. Am. Pharm. Assn., Am. Soc. Hosp. Pharmacists, Ill. Pharm. Assn., Ill. Valley Pharm. Assn., U. Ill. Alumni Assn. (life), Soc. Barbershop Quartet Singers Am. Republican. Methodist. Club: Elks. Home: 706 2d Ave Mendota IL 61342 Office: Mendota Community Hosp Route 51 and Memorial Dr Mendota IL 61342

MURAWSKI, PHILLIP EDMUND, mfg. co. exec.; b. Chgo., Mar. 16, 1948; s. Edmund Anthony and Virginia Mary M.; B.A., U. Ill., 1970; m. Elaine A. Kowalczyk, June 19, 1971; 1 son, David Phillip. Indsl. designer Creative Displays, 1970-72; with Alkco Mfg. Co., Franklin Park, Ill., 1972—, advt. mgr., project estimator mgr., indsl. graphic designer, 1972—. Charter mem. Greenpeace Found., 1978—. Mem. Illuminating Engrng. Soc. (dir. Chgo. sect.), Nat. Wildlife Fedn. Roman Catholic. Office: Alkco Mfg Co 11500 Melrose Ave Franklin Park IL 60131

MURDOCK, MARY JEAN, educator; b. Portland, Oreg., Apr. 4, 1943; d. Orison Carlos and Louise Marie Murdock; B.A., Graceland Coll., 1965; M.Ed. in Curriculum and Instrn., U. Mo., 1972; postgrad. No. Ill. U., Boston U., Washington U., St. Louis, U. No. Iowa, others. Classroom tchr. Kansas City (Mo.) public schs., 1965-66, Independence (Mo.) public schs., 1966-71; reading specialist, Mehlville, Mo., 1972-75; asst. prof. edn. Graceland Coll., Lamoni, Iowa, 1975—; ednl. cons. Mem. Iowa Small Coll. Human Relations Com., 1978-79; dean of women Camp Personality Summer Camps, 1974; chmn. program for tutoring disadvantaged children, Independence, 1967-69. Recipient several scholarships, citations. Mem. Internat. Reading Assn., Assn. for Children with Learning Disabilities, Disabled Reader Group, Iowa Conservation Edn. Council, Puppeteers of Am., Am. Assn. Coll. Tchr. Educators, NOW (Iowa state bd.). Republican. Mem. Reorganized Ch. of Jesus Christ of Latter Day Saints. Clubs: Iowa Puppet Guild, Rainbow Girls (life). Editor The Image, 1978-79; contbr. articles to profl. jours. Office: Graceland Coll Lamoni IA 50140

MURDOCK, PHELPS DUBOIS, JR., mktg. and advt. agy. exec.; b. Kansas City, Mo., May 5, 1944; s. Phelps Dubois and Betty Jane Murdock; student U. Mo., Kansas City, 1962-66; m. Nancy Jane Winfrey, June 7, 1977; children—Susan, Kathleen, Mark, Brooks, Phelps DuBois III, Molly. Sales service mgr. Sta.-KCMO-TV, Kansas City, Mo., 1965-66; account exec. Fremerman-Papin Advt., Kansas City, Mo., 1966-71, TV prodn. mgr., 1966-70, v.p., 1970-71; mng. partner New Slant Prodns., Kansas City, Mo., 1971-73; v.p., creative dir. Travis-Walz-Lane Advt., Kansas City, Mo., and Mission, Kans., 1973-76; pres. Phelps Murdock Mktg. Assos., Kansas City, Mo., 1976-77; pres., chief exec. officer Phelps-Meyer Mktg. Assos., Kansas City, Mo., 1977—; guest lectr. colls., univs. Active Heart of Am. United Way, 1966-80, mem. exec. bd., 1976, bd. dirs., 1976-80; active Help Educate Emotionally Disturbed, Inc., Kansas City, Mo., 1968-80, pres. bd. dirs. HEED Found., 1979-80; mem. communications com. Heart of Am. council Boy Scouts Am., 1971-72; bd. govs. Bacchus Ednl. and Cultural Found., Kansas City, Mo., 1973-76, found. chmn., 1975; mem. promotion com. Kansas City Bicentennial Commn., 1975-76; vol. coach, local youth leagues, 1975-81; cons. Com. for County Progress Campaigns, Charter Campaign, Jackson County, Mo. Recipient various awards including United Way Nat. Communications award, 1975; Effie citation N.Y. Mktg. Assn., 1975; 1st Place Print Ad award and 1st Place Poster award 9th Dist. Addy Awards, 1975, 1st Place Regional-Nat. TV Campaign award, 1976; Omni award, 1980; 1st Place TV Campaign award KCAF Big One Show, 1976; Best-of-Show award Dallas Soc. Visual Communications, 1976, Gold Medal award, 1976. Mem. Advt. and Sales Execs. Club (found. 1966-81), Am. Advt. Fed., Nat. Agri-Mktg. Assn. Democrat. Author numerous TV, radio commls., film, TV and radio musical compositions; film and television direction; creator "Modulatin' With McCall" NBC, 1976-77. Home: 609 W 113th St Kansas City MO 64114 Office: 421 Seville Sq 500 Nichols Rd Kansas City MO 64112

MURDOCK, RICHARD JAMES, acct., educator; b. Akron, Ohio, May 26, 1946; B.S.B.A. cum laude, Ohio State U., 1970; M.S. in Acctg., Cornell U., 1973, Ph.D. in Acctg., 1977; m. Kathleen Marie Stitz, July 24, 1971; children—Stephen, Erin. Intern, staff acct. Peat, Marwick, Mitchell & Co., Columbus, Ohio, 1969; lectr. Ithaca Coll., 1972-73; lectr. Ohio State U., Columbus, 1974-76, asst. prof. acctg., 1976-81, asso. prof., 1981—; tchr. continuing edn. courses. Recipient Richard S. Claire award Arthur Andersen & Co., 1978; C.P.A., Ohio. Mem. Am. Acctg. Assn. (chmn. current acctg. research session Midwest regional meeting 1976, chmn. empirical research in acctg. Midwest, region 1977, program chmn. Ohio regional meetings 1981 prog. advisory com., 1982), Am. Inst. Decision Scis. (chmn. sect. regulation research Midwest region 1977), Midwest Bus. Adminstrn. Assn., Nat. Regulatory Research Inst. (inst. asso.), Beta Alpha Psi (outstanding faculty v.p. 1978, nat. councilor 1981—), Ohio Soc. C.P.A.'s (editorial adv. bd. book review ed.), Beta Gamma Sigma. Author: (with others) Assessing the Economic Impact of FASB8, 1979; editor: Published Earnings Forecasts, 1977; Profile of Public Accounting Firm Careers, 1979; contbr. articles to profl. pubis. Office: 1775 College Rd Columbus OH 43210

MURFIN, ALLEN EUGENE, assn. exec.; b. Kirksville, Mo., Sept. 29, 1938; s. John Larkin and Lois Pauline (Epperson) M.; grad. high sch.; m. Evelyn Marie Rottinghaus, May 25, 1963; children—Christina Marie, Jo Ann Renee, Marcie Lynn. With Davis Paint Co., Kansas City, Mo., 1956-58; various positions Massey Ferguson, Inc., Kansas City, Kans., 1962-68; office mgr. real estate co., 1968-70; pres. Mo. Jr. C. of C., Sedalia, 1970-71; v.p. U.S. Jr. C. of C., Tulsa, 1971-72, dir. regional office, Marlboro, Mass., 1972-74; tng. officer U.S. Jaycees, Tulsa, 1974-76; exec. v.p. Columbia (Mo.) C. of C., 1975-81; asso. mgr. Food and Energy Council, Inc., 1981—. Mem. City Planning Commn., Gladstone, Mo., 1966-70; mem. City Zoning Bd. of Adjustments, Gladstone, 1970-72; bd. dirs. Wonder Land Camp Found., 1969-71, Spl. Bus. Dist., Columbia, 1979-81, Columbia Conv. and Visitors Bur., 1979-81; bd. dirs., pres. Anderson Hayes Child Care Center, 1975-78, Voluntary Action Center, 1981—; bd. dirs., v.p. Show-Me Community Devel. Credit Union, 1980—; mem. Boon County Indsl. Revenue Bond Authority, 1981—; dist. commr. Boy Scouts Am. Served with USAR, 1956, USMC, 1958-62. Clubs: Elks, Cosmopolitan, Kiwanis. Home: Route 1 Box 268 Rocheport MO 65279 Office: 409 Vandiver W Suite 202 Columbia MO 65201

MURGAS, WILLIAM JOSEPH, mfg. co. exec.; b. Plainfield, N.J., Mar. 12, 1931; s. William Joseph and Caroline Josephine M.; B.S.M.E., Lafayette Coll., 1953; M.S.M.E., U. Wis., 1961. Sr. engr. steam turbine dept. Allis-Chalmers, 1953-63; with Velvac, Inc., New Berlin, Wis., 1963—, pres., 1965—. Bd. dirs. ARC; dist. vice chmn Waukesha County council Boy Scouts Am., active nat. Boy Scouts Am. Served with U.S. Army, 1954-56. Mem. ASME, Council Ind. Mgrs. (dir.), Engrs. Soc. Milw., Am. Mgmt. Assn., Ind. Bus. Assn. Wis., Nat. Assn. Emergency Med. Technicians, Wis. Emergency Med. Technicians Assn., Phi Beta Kappa, Tau Beta Pi. Club: Masons. Patentee in field. Home: 180 Stockton Ct Brookfield WI 53005 Office: 2900 S 160th St New Berlin WI 53151

MURLEY, MARION F., ednl. adminstr.; b. St. Louis, Dec. 27, 1924; B.S. in Indsl. Arts and Scis., Central Mo. State U., Warrensburg, 1951, M.S. in Adminstrn., 1954; m. Virginia; children—James, Patricia, Peggy. High sch. prin. Fayette (Mo.) pub. schs., 1954-60; high sch. counselor St. Charles (Mo.) pub. schs., 1960-64, elementary prin., 1964-73, dir. personnel, 1973-78, asst. supt. personnel, 1978—. Home: 10 Ashland St Saint Charles MO 63301 Office: 1916 Elm St Saint Charles MO 63301

MURNANE, GEORGE THOMAS, II, life ins. broker; b. El Paso, Tex., June 5, 1921; s. George Thomas and Willie W. (Watts) M.; student U. Minn., 1951-55; m. Frances Ann Rusciano, Feb. 14, 1969; children—G. Thomas, Kathleen C. Life ins. salesman, 1946-48; asst. to pres. Union Nat. Life Ins. Co., Lincoln, Nebr., 1948-50; recruiting and tng. supr. Provident Mut. Life Ins. Co., Mpls., 1950-67; life ins. broker, Mpls., 1967—; instr. Life Underwriters Tng. Council. Mem. layman's guild Jesuit Retreat House; former gen. chmn., now bd. dirs. Mpls. Aquatennial. Served with M.C., U.S. Army, 1940-44. Named to Provident Mut. Sr. Agt. Hall of Fame. Mem. Million Dollar Round Table (qualifying life), Mpls. Assn. Life Underwriters (dir.), Am. Coll. C.L.U.'s (pres. Mpls. chpt.), Navy League, Republican. Roman Catholic. Clubs: Kiwanis, Hams and Eggs (co-founder, charter mem., past pres.). Home: 2812 Benton Blvd Minneapolis MN 55416 Office: 2201 Nicollet Ave Minneapolis MN 55404

MURNANE, MICHAEL JOHN, rehab. center exec.; b. Indpls., Nov. 19, 1944; s. Russell E. and Sonya A. (Schlee) Westfall; B.S., Ind. U., 1968; M.S., So. Ill. U., 1973, postgrad., 1973-74; m. Yvonne Marie Janik, Aug. 24, 1968; 1 son, R. MacShane. Research asso. Sch. Medicine, So. Ill. U., 1972-74; planner Comprehensive Health Planning Agy., Milw., 1974-75; with Curative Rehab. Center, Milw., 1976—, mgr. edn. and tng.; cons. in field. Served with U.S. Army, 1970-72. Mem. Am. Soc. Tng. and Devel., Am. Hosp. Assn., Soc. Public Health Educators, Am. Soc. Health Manpower Edn. and Tng., Sigma Phi Epsilon, Phi Epsilon Kappa. Republican. Roman Catholic. Office: 9001 W Watertown Plank Rd Milwaukee WI 53226

MURPHY, ALAN CHARLES, accountant; b. Frederic, Wis., July 20, 1937; s. Edward Lester and Irene Margaret (Rogers) M.; B.B.A., U. Wis., 1959. Timekeeper, Stokely-VanCamp, Inc., Milltown, Wis., 1955-59; partner Touche Ross & Co., Mpls. and St. Paul, also Dayton, Ohio, 1960—. Served with AUS, 1959-60. C.P.A., Wis., Minn., Ohio, S.D., La., N.C. Mem. Am. Inst. C.P.A.'s, Minn., Wis., Ohio socs. C.P.A.'s, Inst. Internal Auditors, Nat. Assn. Accountants for Co-ops. Clubs: Sycamore Creek Country (Springboro, Ohio); Racquet (Dayton); Mpls. Athletic, Greenway Athletic (Mpls). Home: 1200 on the Mall Apt 502 Minneapolis MN 55403 Office: 900 Pillsbury Center Minneapolis MN 55402

MURPHY, AMANDA LUCKETT, psychologist; b. Huntsville, Ala., Feb. 27, 1936; d. Erise and Willie Beatrice (Glover) Daniel; B.S. in Nursing, Washington U., St. Louis, 1969; M.A., St. Louis U., 1971, Ph.D., 1973; diploma in nursing Homer G. Phillips Hosp., 1955; m. George Earl Murphy, Mar. 24, 1976; 1 son, Marc Andrew Luckett. Nurse, VA Research Hosp., Chgo., 1959-61, Michael Reese Hosp., Chgo., 1961-62, Jewish Hosp., St. Louis, 1962-64; head nurse Barnes Hosp., St. Louis, 1964-70; coordination Mental Health Center, East St. Louis, Ill., 1971-76, adminstrv. asst. clin. services, 1976-77; adminstr. Comprehensive Mental Health Center St. Clair County, Inc., 1977-80; project dir. Yeatman Union Sarah Mental Health Center, St. Louis, 1980—; pvt. practice psychology, St. Louis; cons. to various community orgns. and agys. Recipient community services award Top Ladies of Distinction Inc., 1976. Mem. Am. Psychol. Assn., Nat. Assn. Black Psychologists, Internat. Transactional Analysis Assn., NAACP, Phi Lambda Theta, Iota Phi Lambda. Home: 6211 McPherson St Saint Louis MO 63130 Office: Yeatman Union Sarah Mental Health Center 4731 Delmar Saint Louis MO 63108

MURPHY, CHARLES FRANCIS, JR., architect; b. Chgo., Dec. 17, 1928; s. Charles F. and Josephine (Christiani) M.; B.Arch., U. Notre Dame, 1951; m. Patricia Winston; 1 son, Luke Lawson; children by previous marriage—Elita, Charles III, Marisa Alexandra. Pres., Murphy/Jahn, Inc., Chgo. Past pres. Graham Found. for Advanced Studies in Fine Arts, Chgo.; trustee Field Mus. Chgo. Fellow AIA. Clubs: Chicago, Saddle and Cycle, Economic, Athletic, Racquet (all Chgo.). Maj. archtl. works include: O'Hare Internat. Airport, First Nat. Bank New McCormick Pl., Civic Center, Rustoleum Hdgrs., Xerox Center (all Chgo.); FBI Bldg., Washington. Office: 224 S Michigan Ave Chicago IL 60604

MURPHY, CHRISTOPHER JOSEPH, III, banker; b. Washington, Apr. 24, 1946; s. Christopher Joseph and Jean Olive (Connelly) M.; B.A. in Govt. and Internat. Relations, U. Notre Dame, 1968; J.D., U. Va., 1971; M.B.A. with distinction in Mgmt. and Fin., Harvard U., 1973; m. Carmen Morris Carmichael, Feb. 1, 1969; children—Christopher, Sean, Kelly, Kevin, Conor, Dillon. Admitted to Va. bar, 1971, U.S. Dist. Ct. bar for D.C., 1971; v.p. Citicorp. Mgmt. Services and Nationwide Fin. Services, St. Louis, 1974-76; sr. v.p. First Bank & Trust Co., South Bend, Ind., 1976-77, pres., chief exec. officer, 1977—; pres. FBT Bancorp, Inc., South Bend, 1979—, dir., 1972—. Bd. dirs. South Bend Symphony, 1977, No. Ind. Med. Edn. Found., 1978; pres. Michiana Econ. Devel. Found., 1980; mem. exec. com., mem. bd. dirs. United Way St. Joseph County, 1980, gen. chmn. campaign, 1980; mem. adv. com. John F. Kennedy Center for Performing Arts, Washington; adv. council Coll. Arts and Letters, U. Notre Dame, 1981. Nat. Endowment for Arts grantee, 1968. Mem. Am. Bar Assn., Ind. Bar Assn., Young Pres.'s Orgn., Robert Morris Assos. Roman Catholic. Home: 1237 E Jefferson Blvd South Bend IN 46617 Office: PO Box 1602 133 S Main St South Bend IN 46634

MURPHY, GORDON DONALD, mfg. co. exec.; b. Bklyn., Jan. 26, 1947; s. Robert Donald and Sue (Wolf) M.; B.S. in Indsl. Engring., Purdue U., 1969; M.S. in Bus. Adminstrn., Ind. U., 1978; m. Maureen Kay Monney, July 11, 1970; 1 dau., Kristin Leigh. Mfg. engr. South Bend Lathe (Ind.), 1969-73; corp. mgr. indsl. engrng. Starcraft Corp., Goshen, Ind., 1973-74; mgr. indsl. engrng. Bendix Corp., South Bend, 1974-77, dir. bus. devel., 1978—; cons. in field. Area capt. United Way, South Bend, 1979-80. Mem. Ind. Soc. Profl. Engrs. Republican. Presbyterian. Clubs: Four Lakes Country, Elks (treas. 1980—). Home: 16875 Edinburg St South Bend IN 46635 Office: 401 N Bendix St South Bend IN 46634

MURPHY, GRETA WERWATH, educator; b. Milw., Aug. 24, 1910; d. Oscar and Johanna (Seelhorst) Werwath; student U. Wis., summer, 1929, Ohio State U., 1943-45; m. John Heery Murphy, Sept. 18, 1941. With Milw. Sch. Engring., 1928-79, v.p. public relations and devel., 1966-79, regent, 1974—. Mem. Milwaukee County Planning Commn., 1966, vice chmn., 1974-75, chmn., 1976-77. Mem. Public Relations Soc. Am. (chpt. pres. 1957, dir. 1952-53; Spl. Service citation 1960, Presdl. citation 1955), Am. Coll. Public Relations Assn. (dir. 1953-55, trustee, 1960-61), Council for Advancement of Edn. Relations. Lutheran. Clubs: Woman's of Wis., Zonta Internat. (dir. regional govt. 1961-62, pres. 1959-60). Home: 5562 S Cedar Beach Rd Belgium WI 53004 also 1032 Malaga Ave Coral Gables FL 33134

MURPHY, HAROLD JOSEPH, savs. and loan assn. exec.; b. Evergreen Park, Ill., May 31, 1933; s. Harold Joseph and Mary Ruth (Tanko) M.; student Xavier U., 1951-54; B.Sc., Loyola U., 1959; m. Maureen L. O'Connor, May 11, 1974. Asst. v.p., auditor Home Fed. Savs., Chgo., 1959-75; product mgr. U.S. League of Savs. Assns.,

Chgo., 1975—. Served with U.S. Army, 1957-59. Mem. Inst. Internal Auditors. Roman Catholic. Club: K.C. Home: 9750 Albany Evergreen Park IL 60642 Office: 111 E Wacker Dr Chicago IL 60601

MURPHY, JAMES EDWARD, food co. exec.; b. East St. Louis, Ill., Sept. 6, 1936; s. John J. and Margaret V. (Powers) M.; B.J., U. Ill., 1958; m. Patricia M. Galus, Sept. 29, 1962; children—Jason, Sean, Courtney. Reporter, Buffalo Evening News, 1958-59; asst. dir. public relations Nat. Gypsum Co., Buffalo, 1959-62; mgr. public relations Owens-Corning-Fiberglas, Toledo, 1962-68, dir. public relations and merchandising, 1968-72, gen. mgr. decorative and home furnishings div., 1972-76, gen. mgr. Weaver Products div., 1976-78; v.p. public affairs Beatrice Foods Co., Chgo., 1978-80, sr. v.p., dir. corp. relations, 1980—. Former v.p., treas. Greater Toledo Public TV Found.; mem. bus. adv. com. U. Ill.; former trustee Maumee Valley Country Day Sch.; trustee, treas. North Shore Country Day Sch. Served with C.I.C., AUS, 1959-61. Named Outstanding Young Man of Yr., Toledo, 1968. Mem. Public Relations Soc. Am. (accredited; 2 Silver Anvil awards, past pres. N.W. Ohio). Clubs: Union League (Chgo.); Atrium (N.Y.C.); Palmetto Golf (Aiken, S.C.). Office: 2 N LaSalle St Chicago IL 60602

MURPHY, JAMES WILLIAM, state senator, ins. co. exec.; b. St. Louis, July 2, 1936; s. William John and Evelyn Margaret (Hirbe) M.; student St. Louis U., 1957-58; m. Marilyn R. Ban, July 4, 1958; children—Timothy, James, Robert, Barbara, Margaret. With Western Electric Co., 1958-69; with Northwestern Nat. Life Ins., St. Louis, 1969-72, Am. Family Life Ins., St. Louis, 1972-73, Gen. Am. Life Ins., St. Louis, 1973-74; v.p. Futures Cons., Inc., St. Louis, from 1974. Democratic committeeman 12th Ward, St. Louis, from 1972; constable 6th dist., St. Louis, from 1975; mem. Mo. Senate, 1976—. Served with AUS, 1958-59. Mem. Hiberians, Haven Club, Judge Dowd Soccer League (pres. 1960-63). Roman Catholic. Lion, Elk. Club: Carondelet Sunday Morning. Home: 3942 Upton St St Louis MO 63116 Office: 3742 Opton St Saint Louis MO 63116*

MURPHY, JEANETTE CAROL, supt. schs.; b. Hot Springs, S.D., June 6, 1931; d. George W. and Jessie S. (Whetstone) M.; A.B., U. S.D., 1960; M.S. in Edn., Chadron State Coll., 1978, Ed.S., 1979. Mgr. central supply and operating rooms Luth. Hosp., Hot Springs, S.D., 1957-58, 60-61; tchr. Spanish and French, Sidney (Nebr.) High Sch., 1962-64; reservations clk. Peninsula Hosp., Burlingame, Calif., 1964-65; tchr. San Lorenzo Valley Unified Schs., Felton, Calif., 1965-67; propr. Masters Career Inst., Salinas, Calif., 1969-70; tchr. Oglala Community High Sch., Pine Ridge, S.D., 1970-72, Hot Springs High Sch., 1971-73; clk. Fall River County (S.D.) Treasurers Office, 1973-74; Title I tchr. Loneman Day Sch., Ogala, S.D., 1974-75, adminstr., 1975-77; contract dir. and exec. officer bd. Unified Sch. Bd. Found., Inc., Pine Ridge, 1977-78; grad. asst. div. edn. and psychology Chadron (Nebr.) State Coll., 1978-79; supt. schs. Lyman (Nebr.) public schs., 1979-80, Kadoka (S.D.) Sch. Dist., 1981—. Chairperson Heart Fund Drive, Hot Springs, 1974-76; Bible sch. tchr. United Presbyn. Women, 1976-77; mem. choir Presbyn. Ch., 1970-76. Served with WAC, 1954-57. Mem. Am. Assn. Sch. Adminstrs., Nebr. Council Sch. Adminstrs., Nebr. Assn. Women Adminstrs., Assn. Sch. Bus. Ofcls., Assn. Sch. Curriculum Devel., Assn. of Sch., Coll. and U. Staffing, Nebr. Coalition for Women, AAUW, Delta Kappa Gamma, Phi Delta Kappa. Democrat. Clubs: Order Eastern Star, Daus. of Nile. Home: 6 Bayberry St PO Box 218 Kadoka SD 57543 Office: 1 Bayberry St Kadoka SD 57543

MURPHY, JEROME EUGENE, telecommunications co. exec.; b. Libertyville, Ill., June 16, 1935; s. William Dennis and Violet (Hitchings) M.; student Lewis Coll., 1953-54, Elmhurst Coll., 1957, Western Ill. U., 1977; B.S. in Mgmt., Calif. Western U., 1981; m. Donna M. DuBois, Sept. 5, 1959; children—Mary Jeanne, Jean Marie, Michael Thomas, James Patrick. Div. mgr. equip. engring. GTE Automatic Electric, Northlake, Ill., 1971-76, supt. engring., 1976-79, dir. systems engring., 1979-80, dir. spl. products, 1980—, jr. staff pres., 1971. Sustaining mem. Rep. Nat. Com., 1979-81. Served with U.S. Army, 1955-57. Mem. Am. Mgmt. Assn., Greater Chgo. C. of C., Am. Inst. Design and Drafting, Ind. Telephone Pioneers Assn. Republican. Roman Catholic. Club: U.S. Senatorial. Office: 400 N Wolf Rd Northlake IL 60164

MURPHY, JOHN LAWRENCE, psychologist; b. Racine, Wis., Sept. 7, 1924; s. Edward Charles and Mabel Grace (Stuebe) M.; B.A. in Philosophy, St. Francis Sem., 1946; M.A. in Philosophy, Catholic U. Am., 1961; S.T.D. (State of Italy nat. scholar in music) Gregorian U., Rome, 1957; Ph.D. in Psychology (LaVerne Noyes fellow), U. Chgo., 1974. Ordained priest Roman Catholic Ch., 1949; asst. pastor St. Thomas Parish, Milw., 1949-54, St. Gall's Parish, Milw., 1957-58; asst. prof. religious edn. Catholic U. Am., 1958-62; prof. dogma St. Francis Sem., 1962-67; psychology intern, staff psychologist Chgo.-Read Mental Health Center, 1970-74, service chief, 1974-79; staff psychologist Green Bay (Wis.) Correctional Instn., 1979--. Mem. Am. Psychol. Assn., Wis. Psychol. Assn., Cath. Theol. Assn., Cath. Bibl. Soc. Am., Am. Guild Organists, Sigma Xi. Author books, the most recent being: With the Eyes of Faith, 1965; asso. editor Am. Ecclesiastical Rev., 1958-62. Home: 985 N Broadway De Pere WI 54115 Office: PO Box W-R Green Bay WI 54305

MURPHY, MARY KATHRYN, indsl. hygienist; b. Kansas City, Mo., Apr. 16, 1941; d. Arthur Charles and Mary Agnes (Fitzgerald) Wahlstedt; B.A., Avila Coll., Kansas City, 1962; M.S., Central Mo. State U., 1975; m. Thomas E. Murphy, Jr., Aug. 26, 1963; children—Thomas E., III, David W. Indsl. hygienist Kansas City area office Occupational Safety and Health Adminstrn., 1975-78, regional indsl. hygienist, 1979—; asst. dir. safety office U. Kans. Med. Center, 1978-79. Summer talent fellow Kaw Valley Heart Assn., 1961; cert. in comprehensive practice of indsl. hygiene. Mem. Am. Indsl. Hygiene Assn. (sec.-treas. Mid-Am. sect. 1978-79, dir. 1981—), Am. Chem. Soc., Am. Conf. Govt. Indsl. Hygienists, Am. Acad. Indsl. Hygiene, N.Y. Acad. Scis., AAAS. Home: 1019 E 109th Terr Kansas City MO 64131 Office: 911 Walnut St Suite 3000 Kansas City MO 64106

MURPHY, MAX RAY, lawyer; b. Goshen, Ind., July 18, 1934; s. Loren A. and Lois (Mink) M.; B.A., DePauw U., 1956; J.D., Yale Law Sch., 1959; student Mich. State U., 1960; m. Ruth Leslie Henricson, June 10, 1978; children—Michael Lee, Chad Woodrow. Admitted to Mich. bar, 1960; legal asso. Glassen, Parr, Rhead & McLean, Lansing, Mich., 1960-67; instr. Lansing Bus. U., 1963-67; partner firm Dalman, Murphy, Bidol, & Bouwens, P.C., Holland, Mich., 1967—. Democratic candidate for Ingham County (Mich.) Pros. Atty., 1962, 1964; asst. pros. atty. Ottawa County, Mich., 1967-70. Mem. Ottawa County, Ingham County, Am. bar assns. Clubs: Holland Country, Michigan Jaycees. Home: 4941 Rosabelle Beach Holland MI 49423 Office: 272 E 8th St Holland MI 49423

MURPHY, PAUL KERNS, advt. exec.; b. Phila., Feb. 7, 1938; s. John Joseph and Anna (Reigart) M.; A.B., Harvard U., 1960; m. Patricia Ann Petrus, Jan. 22, 1966; children—Scott Kerns, Brooke Calder. Account exec. Gallup & Robinson, Inc., Princeton, N.J., 1963-66; research account supr. Compton Advt., Inc., N.Y.C., 1966-69; v.p., research dir. TV Testing Co., N.Y.C., 1969-71, pres., 1971-76; asso. research dir. Young & Rubicam, Inc., N.Y.C., 1976-79, v.p., research dir., Chgo., 1979—. Served with USMC, 1960. Columbia U. research grantee, 1962-63. Mem. Am. Mktg. Assn. Republican. Episcopalian. Club: Harvard (N.Y.C.). Home: 165 N Green Bay Rd Lake Forest IL 60045 Office: 111 E Wacker Dr Chicago IL 60601

MURPHY, ROMALLUS OLGA, coll. pres.; b. Oakdale, La., Dec. 18, 1928; d. James and Mary (Jackson) M.; B.A., Howard U., 1951; J.D., U. N.C., 1956; m. Norma Carter Murphy; children—Natalie, Kim, Romallus, Lisa. Admitted to N.C. bar, 1956, U.S. Supreme Ct., 1960; asso. Robert D. Glass, New Bern, N.C., 1956-57; individual practice law, Elizabeth City, N.C., 1957-58, Wilson, N.C., 1958-62; exec. dir. Erie (Pa.) Human Relation- Commn., 1962-65; patner firm Mitchell & Murphy, Raleigh, N.C., 1965—; spl. asst. to pres., dir. fed. relations Shaw U., Raleigh, N.C., 1968-69, exec. asst. to pres., 1969, v.p. devel. and univ. relations, 1970; pres. Shaw Coll. at Detroit, 1970—; mem. panel of arbitrators Am. Arbitration Assn., 1968—; intermittent cons. conciliator EEOC, Washington, 1966-69. Bd. dirs. New Bern Ave. Day Care Center, Boys' Clubs Am., Raleigh Community Services Council, Inc., N.C. Council Human Rights, Household Assistance, Inc.; trustee St. Paul A.M.E. Ch.; pres. local chpt. NAACP; mem. edn. task force Detroit Urban League; pres. Positive Futures, Inc.; mem. central governing bd. Model Neighborhood Area, Detroit, also mem. edn. com.; bd. dirs. Met. Fund, Inc.; charger mem. Regional Citizens, Inc. Served to capt. USAF, 1951-53. Recipient Rotary award, 1947; Outstanding Service award Detroit Howard U. Alumni Assn., 1974; key to city New Orleans, 1974; Citizen of Year award Omega Psi Phi, 1977. Mem. Am. Council Edn., Am. Assn. Higher Edn., Am. Bar Assn., Am. Trial Lawyers Assn., Am. Mgmt. Assn., Assn. Ind. Colls. and Univs. Mich. (dir.), Center for Study of Presidency, Council for Advancement of Small Colls. (dir.), Internat. Council Shopping Centers, Nat. Assn. Coll. and Univ. Attys., Nat. Assn. Equal Opportunity in Higher Edn. (dir.), Nat. Alliance Bus., Nat. Assn. Human Rights Workers, Nat. Bar Assn., Soc. Coll. and Univ. Planning, Southeastern Lawyers Assn., others. Baptist. Office: 7351 Woodward Ave Detroit MI 48202

MURPHY, RUBY SIMMS, nursing adminstr.; b. Tucker, Ark., Apr. 10, 1940; d. Lasto and Augusta (Wilkins) Simms; R.N., Fordham Sch. Nursing, 1960; student Wayne State U., 1967-69; m. Oliver Murphy, May 24, 1969; children—Connie, Oliver III. Staff nurse Fordham Hosp., Bronx, N.Y., 1960-61, Providence Hosp., Detroit, 1962, VA Hosp., 1963-66, Vis. Nurses Assn., Detroit, 1963-69; nursing supr. Kirwood Hosp., Detroit, 1969-75; afternoon nursing supr. Grace Northwest Hosp., Detroit, 1975—. Served to 1st lt. USAF, 1961-63. Recipient Best Bedside Nursing award Fordham Hosp., 1960. Mem. Am. Assn. Evening and Night Suprs. Democrat. Baptist. Office: Grace NW Hosp 18700 Meyers Rd Detroit MI 48235

MURPHY, STEPHANIE CHOUTEAU, market analyst; b. St. Louis, Dec. 18, 1946; d. Edwynne Paul and Jeanne Cerre (Chouteau) Murphy; B.A., St. Louis U., 1968. Mem. pub. relations research staff Hellmuth Obata Kassabaum Inc., St. Louis, 1968-69; mgmt. asst. Scdtt Thompson, Architects, St. Louis, 1969-71; mem. research info. service staff Sta. KPLR-TV, St. Louis, 1971-73; v.p. market research O'Connor Lurie Ltd., N.Y.C., 1973-77; commodity research coordinator Maduff & Sons, c., Chgo., 1977—, also exec. asst. to chmn. bd.; dir. Murco Inc., Renters Reference Inc., United Buying Service. Mem. City of St. Louis Bicentennial Commn., 1964; jr. nat. chmn. Nat. Hemophilia Found., 1968. Recipient citations for civic work St. Louis mayors, 1971, 73, Mo. Gov., 1972, Ill. Gov., 1977. Mem. Nat. Soc. Colonial Dames Am., UDC, D.A.R., Chgo. Art Inst. Republican. Roman Catholic. Club: English Speaking Union (Chgo.). Home: 55 W Chestnut St Chicago IL 60610 Office: 222 S Riverside Plaza Chicago IL 60606

MURPHY, THOMAS AQUINAS, ret. automotive co. exec.; b. Hornell, N.Y., 1915; B.S., U. Ill., 1938. With Gen. Motors Corp., 1938-80, v.p. and exec.-car and truck group, 1970-72, vice chmn. bd., 1972-74, chmn., chief exec. officer, 1974-80, now dir.; dir. NBD Bankcorp, Inc., PepsiCo, Inc. Mem. Morgan Guaranty Internat. Council; mem. policy com. Bus. Roundtable; exec. com. Bus. Council; trustee Alfred P. Sloan Found.; bd. dirs. U. Ill. Found.; chmn. Detroit Econ. Growth Corp. Office: Gen Motors Bldg 3044 W Grand Blvd Detroit MI 48202

MURPHY, THOMAS JOE, fin. co. exec.; b. Mt. Vernon, Mo., Nov. 25, 1942; s. Champ Clark and Opal Francis (Roller) M.; student S.W. Mo. State U., 1960-63; m. Janet Carol Jensen, June 16, 1973; children—Tammy Jill, Stacy Michele, Sean Thomas Joseph. With Borg Warner Acceptance Corp., various locations, 1967—, now v.p., gen. mgr. marine div.; dir. Alkota Inc., Alcester, S.D., CEDCO Capital Corp. Served with U.S. Army, 1964-66. Mem. Research Inst. Am., Am. Mgmt. Assn., Jaycees. Republican. Home: 700 Twisted Oak Ln Buffalo Grove IL 60090 Office: 1355 E Remington Rd Schaumburg IL 60195

MURPHY, THOMAS VINCENT, mgmt. cons.; b. Phila., Oct. 12, 1928; s. James Frances and Mary Magdeline (McLaughlin) M.; bus. certificate Columbia Bus. Coll., 1948; student Temple U., 1948-49, 49-50, Alexander Hamilton Bus. Mgmt., 1954-59; children—Thomas Vincent, John M., Richard G., David G. With Nat. Cash Register Co., Phila., 1949-50, Stewart Equipment Co., Phila., 1950-60; with Bell Equipment Corp., leasing engineered equipment to petroleum industry, Los Angeles, 1960-78, exec. v.p., 1968-78, dir., 1972-78; pres. Bell Worldwide, Inc. (now Tiger Equipment & Services Ltd.), Chgo., 1973-78; individual practice as mgmt. cons., 1978—; dir. Bell Worldwide Ltd., Bell Caribbean N.V., Soon Douglas (Pte.) Ltd. Singapore, Cons. Quebec Iron & Titanium, Tin and Asso. Minerals, Royal Dutch Shell, Colvac Internat., Pacific Tin. Alyeska Pipeline Service Co., others; cons. Pettibone Corp., Chgo. Judge of elections State of Pa., Springfield, 1953-54. Served with AUS, 1944-46. Decorated Purple Heart. Mem. Am. Mgmt. Assn., Am. Material Handling So. Inc., Franklin Inst. Mech. Arts, Smithsonian Instn., Mid-Am.-Arab C. of C. Clubs: Sleepy Hollow Country (Scarsborough, N.Y.); 21 Club Soc. (London, Eng.); World Trade Center. Contbr. to profl. pubs. Patentee in field. Address: O Hara Bldg 9501 Devon Rosemont IL 60018

MURPHY, WILLIAM A., personnel exec.; b. Chgo., May 25, 1924; s. Richard A. and Grace M. M.; student Loyola U., Chgo., 1942, 45-46; children—Kathleen M., Brian D., Christopher J., William A. II, Kevin P., Matthew S. Founder, owner, pres. Murphy Employment Service, Inc., Oak Brook, Ill., 1957—, also operator 19 suburban offices; pres., chief exec. officer Murphy Temporary Service; speaker internat. confs.; del. Internat. Confedn. of Pvt. Employment Agencies Assns. Mem. Pres.'s Jobs for Vets. Com. Served to 1st lt. USAAF, 1942-45. Cert. placement cons. Mem. Nat. Assn. Personnel Consultants (Nelson award, nat. pres.), Ill. Assn. Personnel Consultants (Lincoln award), U.S. C. of C. Roman Catholic. Office: 1301 W 22d St Oak Brook IL 60521

MURPHY, WILLIAM VALENTINE, cable TV exec.; b. Bronx, N.Y., Feb. 14, 1937; s. William Francis and Bridget Josephine (Morahan) M.; B.E.E., Manhattan Coll., 1959; M.S., Adelphi U., 1964; M.B.A., N.Y. U., 1970; m. Roberta Jean Ritter, Apr. 19, 1969. Design engr. Def. Contractors, 1959-64; mgr. airborne computer systems Grumman Aircraft Co., 1964-69; a founder, sr. v.p. systems ops. Telemed Corp., Hoffman Estates, Ill., 1969-77; pres. Nat. Gen. Corp., Chgo., 1978—. Mem. Am. Mgmt. Assn., IEEE, Assn. Computing Machinery, Soc. Consumer Electronics, Soc. Broadcasting, Soc. Cable TV Engrs. Author articles on application of computers to medicine. Home: 1580 Lake Shore Dr S Barrington IL 60010 Office: 336 Post Office Rd Waldorf MD 20601

MURRAY, CHARLES JOHN, bldg. and constrn. exec.; b. Oak Park, Ill., July 25, 1934; s. Harold James and Evelyn (Stephens) M.; student Tex. Mil. Inst., 1951-53; B. in Bus. Adminstrn., So. Meth. U., 1958; m. Christl Reitinger, May 16, 1960; children—Mark F., Linda M., Katherine A. Field projects engr. Mellish & Murray Co., Chgo., 1960-62, projects capt., 1962-63, projects coordinator, 1963-65, constrn. mgr., 1965-68, treas., 1968-71, sec., treas., 1971—, also dir. Instr. Dale Carnegie courses Mid-West Inst., Chgo., 1969—. Mem. exec. bd. Horace Mann Sch. P.T.A., Oak Park, Ill., 1968—; pres. Near Northwest Civic Com., Inc., Chgo., 1969—. Trustee Granco Trust, Chgo., Pension Fund Local 73 Sheet Metal Worker Internat. Assn. Served with AUS, 1958-60. Mem. Am. Soc. Heating, Refrigerating and Air-Conditioning Engrs. (chmn. scholarship and edn. com. Ill. chpt. 1972), Ventilating and Air Conditioning Contractors Assn. Chgo. (mem. air test and balance com. 1970), U.S. Power Squadron, Chgo. Assn. Commerce and Industry. Home: 931 Forest Ave Oak Park IL 60302 Office: 1720 Fulton St Chicago IL 60612

MURRAY, DANIEL GARDNER, marketing exec.; b. Troy, N.Y., Apr. 13, 1934; s. Daniel George and Theressa Eleanor (Riley) M.; A.A. Sci., State U., N.Y., 1953; B.S., U. Ga., 1962, M.S., 1963; m. Patricia ann Hollis, Nov. 24, 1956; children—Timothy F., Daniel Steven. Supr., Nat. Starch and Chem., Plainfield, N.J., 1963-67; mgr. product devel. Grain Processing Corp., Muscatine, Ia., 1967-69, mgr. food tech. services, 1969-73; marketing dir. Pure Culture Products, Inc., Chgo., 1973—. Chmn. low rent housing commn., Muscatine, Ia., 1971-73; Republican committeeman, county central com. Muscatine, 1970-73. Served with USAF, 1954-59. U. Ga. grad. fellow, 1962; recipient Distinguished Service award for community service, C. of C., 1972. Mem. Research and Devel. Assn. (bd. dirs. 1975-77, exec. v.p. 1980-81, pres. 1981-82), Inst. Food Technologists (exec. com. 1977-79), Am. Marketing Assn., Am. Assn. Cereal Chemists, Am. Meat Inst., Food and Drug Law Inst. (dir. 1981), U.S. Air Force Acad. Republican. Episcopalian. Patentee in field. Home: 1205 Clyde Dr Naperville IL 60540 Office: 200 E Randolph Dr Chicago IL 60601

MURRAY, DANIEL RAY, farmer-rancher, real estate co. exec.; b. Scottsbluff, Nebr., Aug. 16, 1945; s. Donald Myles and Alice Edith Viola (Johnson) M.; B.A., U. Nebr., 1968; M.A., U. Okla., 1972; m. Jeanne Carole Woten, June 21, 1970; children—Anita Jeanne, Bryan Daniel. Commd. 2d lt. U.S. Air Force, 1968, advanced through grades to maj., 1980; now mem. USAFR; farmer-rancher, Banner County, Nebr.; Gateway Realty of Scottsbluff, Inc. Mem. ch. council Calvary Lutheran Ch., Scottsbluff, 1981—. Decorated Joint Service Commendation medal. Mem. Air Force Assn., Nat. Assn. Realtors, U. Nebr. Alumni Assn. Democrat. Home: 724 Rosedale Dr Scottsbluff NE 69361

MURRAY, GEORGE ELMER, JR., state senator; b. St. Louis, Aug. 9, 1923; s. George Elmer and Marie Caroline (Straub) M.; B.S. in Bus. Adminstrn., LL.B., J.D., Washington U., St. Louis, 1948; m. Elizabeth Russell Cooper, Nov. 20, 1948; children—Elizabeth, George Elmer, III, Peggy, Mary Kathleen. Admitted to Mo. bar, 1948, since practiced in St. Louis; city atty., Fenton, 1955-66; mem. Mo. Ho. of Reps. from 38th Dist., 1966-74, Mo. Senate from 26th Dist., 1974—. Mem. Gov. Mo. Commn. Dental Care of Handicapped, 1963—; exec. dir. Mo. Elks Benevolent Trust, 1965—; pres. George Khoury Assn. Baseball Leagues, 1972—. Served with AUS, 1942-44. Mem. Am., Mo., Met. St. Louis, bar assns. Republican. Roman Catholic. Home: 3 Williamsburg Rd Creve Coeur MO 63141 Office: 763 S New Ballas St Creve Coeur MO 63141

MURRAY, JOHN RICHARD, cons. scientist; b. Chgo., Oct. 6, 1921; s. William G. and Olive M. (Kimmet) M.; B.S., U. Mich., 1947; J.D., DePaul U., 1950; m. Grace M. Gast, June 7, 1944; children—John Terrence, Mary Jill, Kathleen, Nancy, Carolyn, William G. Pres., cons. meteorologist Murray & Trettel, Northfield, Ill., 1947—; cons. in meteorology Commonwealth Edison Co., No. Ill. Gas Co., U.S. Steel Corp., Res. Mining Co., others; councilman City of Lake Forest (Ill.), 1965-67. Served with USAAF, 1943-46. Cert. cons. meteorologist. Fellow Am. Meteorol. Soc.; mem. AAAS, Am. Public Works Assn. Roman Catholic. Clubs: Knollwood, Sky Harbor. Home: 240 Buckminster Ct Lake Bluff IL 60044 Office: 414 W Frontage Rd Northfield IL 60093

MURRAY, JOHN STEVENSON, lawyer, state legislator; b. Ames, Iowa, Mar. 22, 1939; s. William Gordon and Mildred Caroline (Furniss) M.; A.B., Cornell U., 1961; M.A. in Public Law and Govt., Columbia U., 1962; J.D., U. Iowa, 1968; m. Robin Ruhe, Mar. 24, 1973; children—David Crighton, Peter McCall. Admitted to Iowa bar, 1968, N.Y. bar, 1968; asso. firm Cleary, Gottlieb, Steen & Hamilton, N.Y.C., 1968-70; exec. asst. to Gov. Robert D. Ray of Iowa, 1970-72; partner firm Murray, Curtis & Finn, Ames, 1972—; mem. Iowa Senate, 1973—. Served with USMC, 1962-65. Mem. Order of Coif, Phi Beta Kappa, Phi Kappa Phi. Republican. Unitarian. Editor-in-chief Iowa Law Rev., 1967-68. Office: 2330 Lincoln Ave Ames IA 50010 also State Senate Office State Capitol Des Moines IA 50319

MURRAY, LAURA LEE FOSDICK, ednl. adminstr.; b. Columbus, Ohio, Sept. 29, 1950; d. Lee Beach and Florence Moore (Urmston) Fosdick; B.S., Purdue U., 1972; M.S., No. Ill. U., 1976; m. William R. Murray, Jan. 28, 1972; 1 son, Daniel Howard. Tchr. math, Glenbard South High Sch., Glen Ellyn, Ill., 1972-78, guidance counselor, adminstrv. asst., 1978-80, dean students, 1980—. Mem. Glenbard South Edn. Assn. (pres. 1976-77), Ill. Assn. Math. Tchrs., Nat. Assn. Math. Tchrs., Ill. Guidance and Personnel Assn., Am. Guidance and Personnel Assn., Ill. Deans Assn., Chgo. Suburban Deans Assn., Nat. Assn. Secondary Sch. Prins., Assn. Supervision and Curriculum Devel., Nat. Assn. Student Activity Advisors, Delta Kappa Gamma, Kappa Alpha Theta. Republican. Presbyterian. Home: 215 Bryn Mawr Itasca IL 60143 Office: Glenbard South High Sch Park Blvd Glen Ellyn IL 60137

MURRAY, LEONARD HUGH, r.r. exec.; b. Evanston, Ill., Sept. 26, 1913; s. Albert L. and Estella A. (Matthews) M.; J.D., U. Minn., 1938; m. Virginia P. Dutcher, Aug. 23, 1940; children—Carole J., Linda P., John L. Admitted to Minn. bar, 1938; legal sec. to asso. justice Minn. Supreme Ct., 1938-40; pvt. practice law, Mpls., 1940-42; chief price atty. dist. office OPA, Minn., 1942-44; pvt. practice law, specializing r.r. re-orgn., Mpls., 1944-54; asst. to pres. Duluth, S. Shore & Atlantic R.R., 1949-52, v.p., 1952-58, pres., dir., 1958-60; v.p., dir. Wis. Central R.R., 1954-60, v.p., gen. counsel, dir., 1958-60; counsel C.P. Ry. Co., 1958-60; pres., chief exec. officer, dir. Soo Line R.R. Co., 1961-78, chmn. bd., chief exec. officer, 1978-79, chmn. exec. com., 1980—; dir. First Bank System, 1978-80, Gt. No. Ins. Co. Former trustee Jr. Achievement of Mpls., pres., 1964-66; former trustee Dunwoody Indsl. Inst., pres., 1966-67; bd. dirs. Correctional Service of Minn. Recipient Outstanding Achievement award U. Minn., 1971.

Mem. Greater Mpls. C. of C. (pres. 1977-78), Beta Gamma Sigma. Republican. Episcopalian. Club: Mpls.

MURRAY, MERRILL R., ednl. adminstr.; b. New Castle, Ind., Aug. 3, 1917; s. Arthur Gray and Mary (Dixon) M.; student Hanover Coll., 1935-36, Kent State U., 1943; B.S., Ball State U., 1949, M.S., 1951; Ed.D., Ind. U., 1960; m. Eva Jean Yergin, Mar. 30, 1940; 1 son, Michael Russell. Math. tchr. high sch., New Castle, Ind., 1949-51, 53-54; dir. USAF Dependents Schs., Burtonwood, Eng., 1952-53; prin. high sch., Ridgeville, Ind., 1954-56; research asso. Ind. U., Bloomington, 1956-58; dean of students Tri-State U., Angola, 1958-59; dean specialized edn. div. Ferris State Coll., Big Rapids, Mich., 1959-65, asst. dean Sch. Gen. Edn., 1965-69, asso. dean, 1969—, asso. dean Coll. Optometry, 1977—; dir. Central Mich. Bank & Trust. Bd. dir. Area Crippled Childrens Soc. Served with USAAF, 1943-47; col. USAF Res. (ret.). Mem. Nat. U. Continuing Edn. Assn. (div. chmn.), Mich. Coordinating Council Continuing Higher Edn. (pres.), Am. Soc. for Tng. and Devel., Am. Personnel and Guidance Assn., Am. Optometric Assn. (asso.), Mich. Optometric Assn. (asso.), Air Force Assn., Mich. Assn. Schs. and Colls., Res. Officers Assn., Am. Assn. Higher Edn., Mecosta Pilots Assn. (pres.), Phi Delta Kappa, Kappa Delta Phi, Sigma Mu Sigma. Presbyn. (elder). Mason, Rotarian (pres. 1964-65). Home: 14851 Chula Vista Dr Big Rapids MI 49307 Office: Ferris State Coll Optometry Big Rapids MI 49307

MURRAY, MICHAEL RUSSELL, personnel adminstr.; b. New Castle, Ind., Oct. 20, 1953; s. Merrill Russell and EvaJean (Yergin) M.; B.S. in Bus. Adminstrn., Central Mich. U., 1975; M.B.A., Ball State U., 1976; m. Debra Ann Brinkman, Jan. 24, 1981. Grad. asst. Ball State U., Muncie, Ind., 1975-76; personnel officer Central Mich. Bank & Trust, Big Rapids, Mich., 1976-78, asst. v.p., 1978-79; personnel officer Mfrs. Nat. Bank Detroit, 1979—; mem. faculty dept. mgmt. Ferris State Coll., Big Rapids, 1977-79. Mem. Am. Mgmt. Assn., Mich. Bankers Assn. (personnel com. 1977-80). Democrat. Clubs: Order of DeMolay, Rotary. Home: 24727 Verdant Sq Farmington Hills MI 48018 Office: 411 W Lafayette St Detroit MI 48226

MURRAY, MICHAEL WILLIAM, theatre dir.; b. Washington, Mar. 31, 1932; s. William M. and Sally N. (Stock) M.; B.A., Cath. U. Am., 1954; M.F.A., Boston U., 1955; m. Jane Campbell (div.); children—Caitlin, Nathanael; m. 2d, Lynn Ritchie, 1980. Artistic dir. Charles Playhouse, Boston, 1957-68; free-lance dir. and writer, 1968-75; producing dir. Cin. Playhouse in the Park, 1975—. Author: The Videotape Book, 1974; contbr. articles to N.Y. Times, Commonweal. Office: Cin Playhouse in the Park PO Box 6537 Cincinnati OH 45206

MURRAY, RICHARD DEIBEL, physician; b. Youngstown, Ohio, Dec. 25, 1921; s. Thomas Henry and Olive (Deibel) M.; B.S., U. Notre Dame, 1942; M.D., Georgetown U., 1946; M.S., U. Pa., 1953. Intern, Youngstown Hosp. Assn., 1946-47, mem. attending staff, chief of plastic surgery service; resident in plastic surgery Kings County Hosp. Bklyn., 1952-54; practice medicine specializing in plastic surgery, Youngstown, 1955—; mem. courtesy staff St. Elizabeth Hosp.; mem. cons. staff Salem City Hosp.; plastic surgery cons. Hosp. of Our Lady of Maryknoll, Kowloon, Hong Kong, Louis Guerrera Meml. lectr. Santo Tomas U., Manila, Philippines, 1964. Served to lt. (j.g.), M.C., USNR, 1947-49. Recipient Frank Purnell award for outstanding contributions to the Youngstown Community; Physician of Yr. award and citation City of Youngstown, 1979. Executed marble Orpheus fountain, Youngstown, other sculptures. Exhibited in group shows at Am. Physicians Art Assn., Butler Art Inst., Am. Soc. Cleft Palate Rehab. Pres. Youngstown Symphony Soc. Decorated Order St. John of Jerusalem. Mem. Am. Soc. Plastic and Reconstructive Surgery, Robert Ivy Soc. Phila., Ohio Valley Plastic Soc., Kings County Soc., A.M.A., Ohio, Mahoning County med. socs. Elk. Clubs: Youngstown Country, Rotary (Youngstown); N.Y. Athletic. Author: The Rise and Fall of the State, 1967; The Key to Nostradamus, 1975; Signs and Wonders, 1979; contbr. articles to sci. jours. Home: 171 Newport Dr Youngstown OH 44512 Office: 2125 Glenwood Ave Youngstown OH 44511

MURRAY, ROBERT EUGENE, coal co. exec.; b. Martins Ferry, Ohio, Jan. 13, 1940; s. Albert Edward and Mildred Etheline (Shepherd) M.; B.Engring., Ohio State U., 1962; postgrad. Case Western Res. U., 1968-70; m. Brenda Lou Moore, Aug. 26, 1962; children—Sherri Sue (dec.), Robert Edward, Jonathan Robert, Ryan Michael. Asst. to mgr. indsl. engring. and coal preparation N.Am. Coal Corp., 1961-63, sect. foreman, plant foreman, gen. mine foreman, Ohio div., 1963-64, asst. supt., 1964-66, supt. 1966-68, asst. to pres., Cleve., 1968-69, v.p. operations, v.p. eastern div., 1969-74, pres. Western div., 1974—; pres. Coteau Properties Co., Falkirk Mining Co., Western Plains Mining Co., Missouri Valley Properties Co.; mining engring. departmental asst. Ohio State U., 1960-62; past pres., chmn. bd. N.D. Lignite Council. Mem. exec. bd., past v.p. dist. ops. No. Lights council Boy Scouts Am.; past pres., bd. dirs. United Way of Bismarck; bd. regents Mary Coll. Registered profl. engr., Ohio. Mem. Am. Mining Congress, Mining Electro-Mech. Assn. (pres. Ohio Valley br. 1967-68), Pitts. Coal Mining Inst. Am., AIME (chmn.-elect, past program chmn. coal div., exec. com. coal div.), Rocky Mountain Coal Mining Inst. (past pres., program chmn.), Ohio (pres. east Ohio chpt. 1966-67), Nat. socs. profl. engrs., Ohio Engrs. in Industry (mem. bd. govs. 1966-67), Ill. Mining Inst., N.D. Water Users Assn. Republican. Methodist (trustee, mem. adminstrv. bd. 1968-69, lay speaker, tchr.). Mason (32 deg., Shriner). Home: 1230 W Highland Acres Rd Bismarck ND 58501 Office: Kirkwood Office Tower Bismarck ND 58501

MURRAY, ROBERT WALLACE, chemist; b. Brockton, Mass., June 20, 1928; s. Wallace James and Rose Elizabeth (Harper) M.; A.B., Brown U., 1951; M.A., Wesleyan U., 1956; Ph.D., Yale U., 1960; m. Claire K. Murphy, June 10, 1951; children—Kathleen A., Lynn E., Robert Wallace, Elizabeth A., Daniel J., William M., Padraic O'D. Mem. tech. staff Bell Labs., Murray Hill, N.J., 1959-68; prof. chemistry U. Mo., St. Louis, 1968-81, Curators prof., 1981—, chmn. dept., 1975-80; cons. industry and govt. Mem. Warren (N.J.) Twp. Com., 1962, 63, mayor, 1963, mem. planning com. and Bd. Health, 1962-64, mem. Bd. Edn., 1966-68. Served with USN, 1951-54. Recipient grants EPA, NSF, NIH. Fellow AAAS, N.Y. Acad. Sci., Am. Inst. Chemists; mem. Am. Soc. Photobiology, Am. Chem. Soc., Chem. Soc. London, Sigma Xi, Internat. Ozone Assn. Editor: (with H.H. Wasserman) Singlet Oxygen, 1979; contbr. articles to profl. jours. Home: 1810 Walnutway Dr Saint Louis MO 63141 Office: Dept Chemistry U Mo Saint Louis MO 63121

MURRAY, WALTER ALLAN, JR., lawyer; b. Washington, Mo., May 6, 1942; s. Walter Allan and Ruth Estora Sullivan M.; A.B., Central Methodist Coll., 1964; J.D., Washington U., St. Louis, 1967; m. Monica Louise Klekamp, Aug. 5, 1972; children—Walter Allan III, Andrew Todd, Laura Louise. Admitted to Mo. bar, 1967; legal clk. Strubinger, Wion & Burke, St. Louis, 1966-67; asso. firm Wion, Burke & Boll, Clayton, Mo., 1968-69; pvt. practice law Union, Mo., 1969—; asst. pros. atty. Franklin County (Mo.), 1970-79, pros. atty., 1981—; city atty. City of Union, 1973—. Adv. bd. Profl. Counseling Center, New Haven, Mo., 1972—. Treas. Franklin County Republican Central Com., 1970—. Mem. Franklin County Youth Fair Bd., 1969-72, treas., 1971; bd. dirs. Profl. Health Services, Inc., New Haven. Mem. Union Jaycees (Region legal council 1971-72, presl. award 1970), Mo. Bar Assn., 20th Jud. Dist. Bar Assn., Union C. of C., Mo. Municipal Attys. Assn., Sigma Alpha Chi, Phi Delta Phi. Presbyn. (clk. session). Rotarian (pres. Union 1972). Home: 12 Valley Dr Union MO 63084 Office: 316 E Locust St Union MO 63084

MURRY, CHARLES EMERSON, adj. gen. N.D.; b. Hope, N.D., June 23, 1924; s. Raymond Henry and Estelle Margarete (Skeim) M.; m. Donna Deane Kleve, June 20, 1948; children—Barbara, Karla, Susan, Bruce, Charles; B.S., U. N.D., 1950, J.D., 1950. Admitted to N.D. bar, mem. firm Nelson & Heringer, Rugby, 1950-51; dir. N.D. Legis. Council, 1951-75; adj. gen. N.D., Bismarck, 1975—; cons. Council State Govts.; mem. res. forces policy bd. for sec. def. Vice pres. Missouri Slope Lutheran Home, Bismarck. Mem. Am., N.D. bar assns., NG Assn., Nat. Legis. Conf. (past chmn.), Adjs. Gen. Assn. (exec. com.), Commrs. on Uniform State Laws. Clubs: Masons; Elks; Exchange of Bismark (past pres.). Recipient Sioux award U. N.D., Gov.'s Nat. Leadership award. Contbr. articles to profl. jours. Home and office: PO Box 1817 Bismarck ND 58505

MURTON, WILLIAM NORMAN, II, mgmt. systems cons.; b. Lakewood, Ohio, Sept. 12, 1944; s. William Norman and Marcia Lydia (Elkins) M.; student Syracuse U., 1962-64; B.S. in Bus. Adminstrn., Ohio State U., 1977; m. Margaret Ann Cavan, Sept. 9, 1967; children—Margaret Sibley, Amy Elkins, Joshua William, Nathan Douglas. Programmer, SCOA Industries, Columbus, Ohio, 1969; mgr. systems programming Ohio State U. Hosps., Columbus, 1969-73; sr. systems planner/programmer Mgmt. Horizons Data Systems, Columbus, 1973-77; mgr. Arthur Andersen & Co., Columbus, 1977—. Trustee, asst. treas. Riverside Bible Ch., Worthington, Ohio. Mem. Central Ohio Assn. Systems Mgmt. (chmn. seminar com.), Central Ohio EDP Auditors Assn., Ohio State U. Assn. Computing Machinery (past pres., founder student chpt.). Office: 100 E Broad St Columbus OH 43215

MURTONEN, DONALD JOHN, optometrist; b. Laurium, Mich., Jan. 28, 1939; s. David John and Florence Tyne (Liimatta) M.; student U. Mich., 1956-58; B.S., O.D., Ill. Coll. Optometry, 1961; m. Helen Marlene Hartje, Apr. 18, 1968; children—Jason David, Aaron Henry, Heidi Erika. Practice optometry, Calumet, Mich., 1966—, Hancock, Mich., 1970—; pres. Redjacket, Inc., devel. co., 1978—, Peninsula Travel Service, Ltd., Houghton, Mich., 1978—. Served to capt. USAF, 1961-66. Pres. Coppertown USA Devel. Corp., 1974-76, Coppertown Fund, 1975-78, v.p. Calumet Theatre Bd., 1974-76; mem. Copper Country Council for Arts, 1976-79. Mem. Am., Mich. (pres. local soc. 1968-70) optometric assns., Am. Optometric Found., North Central States Optometric Conf. (cabinet mem. 1970-72), Calumet C. of C. (pres. 1972-74, chmn. exec. bd. 1972-75), Copper Country Chorale (pres. 1968). Elk, Lion (pres. 1970-71). Clubs: University of Michigan (pres. 1970-76), Investment (pres. 1970-72), Calumet Rotary. Home: 1167 Calumet Ave Calumet MI 49913 Office: Box 468 Calumet MI 49913 also Box 639 Hancock MI 49930

MURVIHILL, JANE LYNN, concrete products mfg. co. exec.; b. Michigan City, Ind., July 29, 1942; d. Willard Roy and Beatrice Marie (Lidke) Fausch; A.S., Purdue U., 1979; m. Charles Richard Murvihill, Sept. 10, 1966. Mktg. asst. ITT Phillips Drill Div., Michigan City, 1966-74; asst. advt. mgr. Sullair Corp., Michigan City, 1974-76; advt. mgr. ITT Phillips Drill Div., Michigan City, 1976-81, editor Redheadliner mag., 1979—, mgr. mktg. services, 1981—; owner Dick-N-Janes Fin Inn, tropical fish store, Michigan City, 1971—. Mem. publicity com. United Way, Michigan City, 1979. Mem. Michiana Advt. Club (dir. 1980-81), Nat. Assn. Female Execs., Purdue Alumni Assn. Lutheran. Clubs: LaPorte Amateur Radio, Michigan City Amateur Radio. Writer, pub., Dick-N-Jane's Newsletter, 1978—. Office: US 12 and Liberty Trail Michigan City IN 46360

MUSINSKI, DONALD LOUIS, physicist; b. Winsted, Conn., Mar. 29, 1946; s. Louis Edward and Dorothy Elisabeth (Shaw) M.; B.S., Trinity Coll., 1968; M.A., U. Rochester, 1970, Ph.D., 1973; m. Jean Elisabeth Abramson, June 12, 1971. Research asso. Cornell U., Ithaca, N.Y., 1973-75; research scientist KMS Fusion, Inc., Ann Arbor, Mich., 1975-79, sr. tech. mgr., 1979—. Mem. Am. Phys. Soc., Am. Vacuum Soc. Office: S Industrial Hwy Ann Arbor MI 48104

MUSSER, ROBERT DANIEL, JR., hotel exec.; b. Circleville, Ohio, Apr. 29, 1932; s. Robert Daniel and Elizabeth (Woodfill) M.; B.A., Dartmouth, 1955; m. Amelia Epler, Nov. 30, 1957; children—Robin Epler, Margaret Stewart, Robert Daniel, III. Asst. mgr. Grand Hotel, Mackinac Island, Mich., 1957-61, pres., gen. mgr., 1961—, owner, 1979—. Mem. Mich. Travel Commn., 1976—, vice-chmn., 1979-81, chmn., 1981—. Served with AUS, 1956-57. Mem. Mich. C. of C. (dir.), Mackinac Island C. of C. (v.p. 1963—), Am. Hotel and Motel Assn., Hotel Sales Mgmt. Assn., Alpha Delta Phi. Republican. Episcopalian. Clubs: Mackinac Island Yacht, Lansing Country. Home: 13855 Peacock Rd Laingsburg MI 48848 Office: 116 W Ottawa Lansing MI 48901 summer Grand Hotel Mackinac Island MI 49757

MUSSMAN, JOHN FRANKLYN, steel co. exec.; b. Chgo., Aug. 11, 1940; s. Fredrick Edward and Isora Albertina (Kullbom) M.; B.A., Dartmouth Coll., 1962; M.B.A., U. Chgo., 1970; m. Judith Townsend, Aug. 17, 1963; children—Lisa, John Franklyn, Susan. Asst. dist. sales mgr. U.S. Steel Corp., Memphis, 1973-75, asst. dist. sales mgr., Chgo., 1975-76, dist. sales mgr., Kansas City, Kans., 1976-78, regional mgr. sales, Chgo., 1978-80, gen. mgr. sales, Central Area, 1981—. Served with U.S. Army, 1962-63. Mem. Farm and Indsl. Equipment Inst., Steel Service Center Inst., Chgo. C. of C. Republican. Clubs: Union League (Chgo.); LaGrange Country. Office: 208 S LaSalle St Chicago IL 60690

MUSTAIN, DOUGLAS DEE, lawyer; b. Shreveport, La., Nov. 2, 1945; s. Reginald K. and Dorothy J. M.; student Knox Coll., 1963-64, Murray State Coll., 1964-66; B.S., U. Ill., 1971; J.D., U. Iowa, 1974; m. Sharon L. Tegarden, Aug. 19, 1967; children—Kristi Kaye, Kari Dee, Kenton Douglas. Admitted to Iowa bar, 1974, Ill. bar, 1974; law clk. firm Schulman, Phelan, Tucker, Boyle & Mullen, Iowa City, 1972-74; asso. firm Stuart, Neagle & West, Galesburg, Ill., 1974-76; partner firm West, Neagle & Williamson, Galesburg, 1977—; instr. real estate law Carl Sandburg Jr. Coll., Galesburg, 1977—. Served with U.S. Army, 1966-69. Decorated Army Commendation medal with oak leaf cluster. Mem. Am. Bar Assn., Knox County Bar Assn. (v.p. 1978-79, pres. 1980-81), Am. Trial Lawyers Assn. Home: 1234 N Prairie St Galesburg IL 61401 Office: West Neagle & Williamson 58 S Cherry St Galesburg IL 61401

MUSTION, ALAN LEE, pharmacist; b. Oklahoma City, Feb. 6, 1947; s. Granville E. and Iris E. (Graham) M.; B.S. in Pharmacy, Southwestern Okla. State U., 1970; m. Bonne Chere Bryant, June 19, 1970; children—Jeffrey Alan, Jennifer Chere. Staff pharmacist VA Med. Center, Oklahoma City, 1970-74; dir. pharmacy VA Med. Center, Saginaw, Mich., 1974-76; asst. dir. pharmacy VA Med. Center, Richmond, Va., 1976-77; dir. pharmacy VA Med. Center, Iowa City, Iowa, 1977—; asst. prof. clin./hosp. div. U. Iowa, 1977—. Capt. U.S. Army Res. Recipient VA Spl. Achievement awards, 1973, 77. Mem. Am. Soc. Hosp. Pharmacists, Iowa Soc. Hosp. Pharmacists, Assn. Mil. Surgeons of U.S., Res. Officers Assn., Kappa Psi. Methodist. Home: 208 6th St Apt A-2 Coralville IA 52241 Office: VA Med Center Hwy 6 West Iowa City IA 52240

MUTTALIB, KALAM, lawyer; b. Cleve., Apr. 21, 1943; s. Roy and Ruby (Pitts) Mathis; B.A., Cleve. State U., 1971; J.D., Case Western Res. U., 1974; children—Khabir, Rasool. Admitted to Ohio bar, 1974; mem. firm Carl J. Character Co., Cleve., 1975-78; individual practice law, Cleve., 1978—. Served with USAF, 1961-64. Mem. Am. Bar Assn., Am. Trial Lawyers Assn., Nat. Bar Assn., Greater Cleve. Bar Assn., Ohio Bar Assn., Cuyahoga County Bar Assn., John Harlan Law Club, World Assn. Lawyers. Muslim. Home: 3347 East Blvd Cleveland OH 44104 Office: 1460 E 9th St Room 1 Cleveland OH 44114

MUTZ, JOHN MASSIE, state lt. gov.; b. Indpls., Nov. 5, 1935; s. John Loughery and Mary Helen (Massie) M.; B.S. in Advt. and Bus. Mgmt., Northwestern U., 1957, M.S., 1958; m. Carolyn Hawthorne, June 21, 1958; children—Mark, Diana. Copy editor Indpls. News, summer, 1953, 54; dir. public relations for residential bldg. products Aluminum Co. Am., Pitts., 1958-60; dir. advt. and public relations, sec., asst. to pres. Perine Devel. Corp., Indpls., 1960-61; instr. dept. public and environ. affairs Ind. U., Indpls., 1976-79; v.p. Circle Fin. Corp., Indpls., 1962-79; v.p. Circle Leasing Corp., Indpls., 1962-79; v.p. Fast Fodd Mgmt. Corp., 1978-79; mem. Ind. Ho. of Reps., 1967-71, chmn. interim sch. fin. com., 1962-69, chmn. taxation subcom. of ways and means com., 1969-70; Republican candidate state treas. Ind., 1970, mem. Ind. State Senate, 1972-80, chmn. budget subcom. of fin. com., chmn. affairs of Marion County com., chmn. met. affairs com.; lt. gov. Ind., 1980—; Mem. Sch. Property Tax Control Bd. Indpls., 1975-76; bd. govs. United Way Indpls., 1978-79; mem. bd. missions United Meth. Ch., Indpls., 1976-78; bd. dirs. Suemma Coleman Agy., 1975-79, Community Services Council Indpls., 1976-77; trustee Christian Theol. Sem., 1976-79. Mem. Nat. Restaurant Assn. (dir. 1978-79), Ind. Restaurant Assn. (dir. 1977-79), Marion County Mental Health Assn., Northwestern U. Alumni Assn., Pi Alpha Mu, Deru (pres. 1956-57), Beta Theta Pi (v.p. 1956-57). Home: 5940 E 79th St Indianapolis IN 46250 Office: Room 333 State House Indianapolis IN 46204

MUTZ, RICHARD ELWOOD, civil engr.; b. Sandusky, Ohio, Feb. 21, 1928; s. Edwin R. and Ina (Wagner) M.; B.S. in Civil Engring., Ohio No. U., 1953; 1 dau., Justina Danielle. Designer firm Granville E. Scott, Architect & Engr., Norwalk, O., 1953-54; partner firm Archer, Mutz & Starkey, Cons. Engrs., Norwalk, 1954-55, Mutz & Starkey, Norwalk, 1955-60; owner Richard E. Mutz & Assos., Cons. Engrs., Norwalk, 1960—, REM COM Contract Mgmt., 1970—. Served with AUS, 1946-48. Registered profl. engr., Ohio, N.Y., N.J., Fla., Mass., Ky., Mich., Wis. Fellow Am. Soc. C.E., Ohio Soc. Profl. Engrs.; mem. Nat. Soc. Profl. Engrs., Profl. Engrs. in Pvt. Practice, Cons. Engrs. of Ohio, Am. Soc. for Testing and Materials, Am. Water Resources Assn., Nat. Fedn. Ind. Bus. Mason (32 deg.). Elk. Home: 911 Meadow Ln Norwalk OH 44857 Office: One Town Sq Milan OH 44846

MUTZABAUGH, JAMES CHARLES, project engr.; b. Perth Amboy, N.J., May 5, 1950; s. Benjamin Charles and Florentine Barbara (Lakomski) M.; B.S. in Elec. Engring., Northwestern U., 1973; m. Mary Ann Domzalski, Apr. 30, 1977. Design engr. Riley Co., Skokie, Ill., 1973-76, sr. project engr., 1976, 77—; project engr., instrumentation supr. Alnor Instrument Co., Niles, Ill., 1976-77; cons. in field. Mem. Hoffman Estates Aux. Policy. Served with U.S. Army, 1968-70. Registered Emergency Med. Technician, Ill. Mem. Instrument Soc. Am. Roman Catholic. Home: 1936 Hidden Creek Circle Palatine IL 60067 Office: 7401 N Hamlin Skokie IL 60076

MYATT, SAMUEL JOSEPH, educator; b. Memphis, Apr. 25, 1951; s. William Joseph and Jane (Phelan) M.; B.S., Lambuth Coll., 1975; M.Ed., Memphis State U., 1977; m. Dorothy Woodard, Aug. 27, 1972; children—Bill, Lili, Janie. Mgr., Myatt Oil Co., Brownsville, Tenn., 1972-75; tchr. Haywood County High Sch., Brownsville, 1975-77; grad. teaching asst. Memphis State U., 1977-80; asst. prof. office adminstrn. and bus. edn. dept. SW Mo. State U., Springfield, 1980—; mem. adv. bd. Brownsville Bank, 1974-76. Mem. Adminstrv. Mgmt. Soc., Nat. Bus. Edn. Assn., N.-Central Bus. Edn. Assn., Mo. Bus. Edn. Assn., Internat. Info./Word Processing Assn., Soc. Data Educators, Delta Pi Epsilon (pres. 1978-79), Kappa Delta Pi, Phi Kappa Phi. Baptist. Home: 3427 S Newton St Springfield MO 65807 Office: 901 S National St Springfield MO 65804

MYEROWITZ, P. DAVID, cardiac surgeon; b. Balt., Jan. 18, 1947; s. Joseph Robert and Merry (Brown) M.; B.S., U. Md., 1966, M.D., 1970; M.S., U. Minn., 1977; m. Susan Karen Macks, June 18, 1967; children—Morris Brown, Elissa Suzanne, Ian Matthew. Intern in surgery U. Minn., Mpls., 1970-71, resident in surgery, 1971-72, 74-77; resident in cardiothoracic surgery U. Chgo., 1977-79; practice medicine, specializing in cardiovascular surgery, Madison, Wis., 1979—; asst. prof. thoracic and cardiovascular surgery U. Wis., Madison, 1979—. Served with USPHS, 1972-74. Mem. A.C.S., Am. Coll. Cardiology, Assn. for Acad. Surgery. Jewish. Contbr. articles to profl. jours. Office: 600 Highland Aye Madison WI 53792

MYERS, DEAN WESLEY, ret. livestock products co. exec.; b. Benedict, Nebr., May 19, 1897; s. John Wesley and Nettie Ann (Grobe) M.; grad. York Bus. Coll., 1922; m. Clara Snitzen, Oct. 15, 1922 (div. 1929); 1 son, James Dean; m. 2d, Charlotte Cramer, July 12, 1932 (dec. 1948); 1 adopted son, Richard Dale; m. 3d, Margaret Taylor, Oct. 15, 1952. Livestock dealer, York and Stanton, Nebr., 1919-25; rep. J.M. Opper Co., 1927-30; zone mgr. Walnut Grove Mineral Co., 1931-43; organizer M. & M. Livestock Products Co., Clarion, Iowa, 1943, pres., gen. mgr., 1943-70, pres., 1968-71, chmn. bd., 1971-76. Mem. pres.'s council Sch. of the Ozarks, 1974—, bd. dirs., curator commemorative arms Ralph Foster Mus., 1977—. Served with U.S. Navy, 1918. Mem. Nat. Rifle Assn. (life), DAV (life), Nat. Feed Ingredient Assn. (past dir.), Eagle Grove C. of C. (pres. 1961). Republican. Clubs: Masons, Elks. Contbr. articles and stories to livestock publs. Home: Sch of Ozarks PO Box 548 Point Lookout MO 65726

MYERS, HAL HANAUER, mfg. co. exec.; b. Karlsruhe, Ger., Aug. 9, 1930; s. David Nathan and Inez Marcella (Pink) M.; came to U.S., 1941, naturalized, 1951; B.S. in Chem. Engring., Case Inst. Tech., 1953; children—Robert, Andrew. Engr., Byerlyte Corp., Cleve., 1957-62; mgr. Cook United Co., Syracuse, N.Y., 1962-66; plant mgr., Cleve. area mgr., Koppers Co., 1966-72; gen. mgr. Lake Erie Asphalt Co., Cleve., 1972-74; v.p. mfg. Mameco Internat., Cleve., 1974—. Trustee Bur. Jewish Edn.; trustee, treas. Montefiore Home, Sch. on Magnolia; treas. Jewish Welfare Fedn. Served to capt. USAF, 1953-57. Mem. ASTM, Am. Chem. Soc., Am. Inst. Chem. Engrs., Am. Assn. Asphalt Paving Technologists. Democrat. Home: 3565 Daleford Rd Shaker Heights OH 44120 Office: 4470 E 175th St Cleveland OH 44128

MYERS, JACK FREDRICK, artist; b. Lima, Ohio, Feb. 17, 1927; s. Harold Frank and Lesta Arvilla (Ross) M.; student Cleve. Inst. Art, 1947-49; M.F.A., Kent State U., 1980; m. Frances Dydek, Apr. 30,

1949; children—Steven, David, Kevin. With Birch Portrait Studio, photographers, Cleve., 1948; staff artist Bur. Office Services, Cleve., 1949-51; free lance artist, 1952-56, 70—; staff artist Bill Ripley and Assos., Cleve., 1951-56; with Premier Indsl. Corp., Cleve., 1956-70, art dir., 1959-70; instr. graphics and painting Cooper Sch. Arts, Cleve., 1970-80; joint exhbns. with wife Baldwin-Wallace Coll., Berea, 1966, 68, 72, 76, Freedson Gallery, Lakewood, Ohio, 1969; group exhbns. include Cleve. Mus. Art, 1949-54, 76—, Jay Show, Cleve., 1949-53, Cleve. Invitational, 1973, Lima Art Assn., 1974, Butler Inst. Am. Art, Youngstown, Ohio, 1976, 78, 79, Nat. Print Competition, San Diego State U., 1980, Bonfoey Gallery, Cleve., 1981, Marshall U., Huntington, W.Va., 1981. Served with USNR, 1945-46. Recipient 1st prize art category Documentary Film competition, 1969; 1st prize ASIFA-East Animation award, 1974; Purchase prize Butler Inst. Am. Art, 1979. Mem. New Orgn. Visual Arts, Coll. Art Assn. Address: 187 Kraft St Berea OH 44017

MYERS, JOHN THOMAS, congressman; b. Covington, Ind., Feb. 8, 1927; s. Warren E. and Myra (Wisher) M.; B.S., Ind. State U., 1951; m. Carol Carruthers, May 30, 1953; children—Carol Ann, Lori Jan. Farmer Covington, 1951—; with Fountain Trust Co., Covington, from 1952; mem. 90th-97th Congresses from Ind. 7th Dist. Served with AUS, 1944-46; ETO. Mem. Am. Legion, VFW, Wabash Valley Assn., Res. Officers Assn., Sigma Pi. Republican. Clubs: Masons, Elks, Lions. Office: 2301 Rayburn House Office Bldg Washington DC 20515

MYERS, LAWRENCE RADCLIFFE, state ofcl.; b. Jamaica, B.W.I., Apr. 16, 1944; s. Egbert and Ruby Sylvia (Townsend) M.; came to U.S., 1952, naturalized, 1957; B.A., Tarkio (Mo.) Coll., 1967; M.A., U. Nebr., 1972. Asso. dir. Nebr. Urban League, Omaha, 1968-69; sales trainee Internat. Harvester, Omaha, 1969; field rep. Omaha Human Relations Dept., 1969-71, sr. field rep., 1971-74; exec. dir. Nebr. Equal Opportunity Commn., Lincoln, 1974—. Mem. adv. com. Operation Pride, 1968-70; mem. Omaha Ins. Liaison Council, 1972—, Com. for Equal Opportunity in Ins. Industry, 1972-74. Bd. dirs. NAACP, 1st v.p., 1970-73; bd. dirs. Comprehensive Health Assn., Greater Omaha Community Action, Inc., chmn., 1972-73; bd. dirs. Nebr. Urban League, 1970-75, v.p., 1974-75; bd. dirs Lincoln Action Program, 1974—. Mem. Am. Sociol. Assn., Midwest Sociol. Soc., Nat. (dir. 1973—), Nebr.-Iowa (pres. 1973—) assns. human rights workers, Internat. Assn. Ofcl. Human Rights Agys. (dir., Midwest regional rep. 1976—), Mid-City Businessmen's Assn., Lincoln Opportunities Indsl. Center, Nebr. Civil Liberties Union, Phi Beta Sigma. Home: 5836 Oto E Lincoln NE 68506 Office: 301 Centennial Mall Lincoln NE 68509

MYERS, MICHAEL LEE, background music co. exec.; b. Cin., July 22, 1940; s. Lester Meyer and Fannie (Blickstein) M.; B.F.A., Cin. Coll. Conservatory of Music; m. Karen Marie Rider, May 1, 1976; children—Lester, Carrie, James. Announcer, salesman WPFB Radio and Musiplex Background Music Co., Middletown, Ohio, 1958-62; pres. Kaufman Bargain Store, Inc., Hillsboro, Ohio, 1962-75; with Musiplex Co., Middletown, Ohio, 1975—, gen. mgr., to 1979; dir. nat. account sales Audio Environments, Inc., Seattle, 1979—. Chmn. adv. bd. Highland County Sr. Citizens Center, 1970-75; pres. 48ers, Vol. Action Group of WCET-TV Pub. Television, Cin., 1978-79; deacon Trinity United Ch. of Christ, Cin., 1981-84. Mem. Greater Cin. Restaurant Assn., Ind. Background Music Assn. Rotarian. Home: 257 Compton Rd Wyoming OH 45215 Office: 230 Northland Blvd Cincinnati OH 45246

MYERS, MONTAGUE (MONTE) KAY, interior designer; b. Rockford, Ill., Sept. 29, 1928; s. Sam F. and Wanda B. M.; student Mich. State U., 1946-47, Meinzinger Design Sch., Detroit 1948-51, Schunour Sch. Design, Calif., 1951-53. Apprentice to interior designer, Kalamazoo, Mich., 1953-55; freelance interior designer Kalamazoo, 1955-61, 79—; interior designer Wolf & Dessauer Dept. Store, Ft. Wayne, Ind., 1961-65; owner, operator Monte K. Myers Studio, Ft. Wayne, 1965—; lectr. in field. Mem. Am. Soc. Interior Designers, Nat. Soc. Interior Designers. Home and Office: 4024 Oakland Dr Kalamazoo MI 49008

MYERS, RAY F., banker; b. Council Bluffs, Iowa, Aug. 22, 1920; s. Ray F. and Birdie Mae (Burgess) M.; A.B., DePauw U., 1941; LL.B., 1948; postgrad. Stanford, 1966; m. Mary Elizabeth Mounts; children—John Randolph, Thomas Edward, David Scott. With Continental Ill. Nat. Bank and Trust Co., 1948—, 2d v.p., 1956—, v.p. corp. div., 1959, head trust corp., 1960, v.p. CICorp, 1969, sr. v.p., 1969-71, exec. v.p. bank, 1971, exec. v.p., corp. counsel CICorp, 1974, exec. v.p., corp. counsel, sec. bd. CICorp and parent co., 1974, chmn. trust exec. com., 1975, corp. counsel, 1975, gen. counsel, 1980—. Trustee, LaRabida Children's Hosp. and Research Center, Chgo., 1964—; mem. Northwestern U. Assos. Served to lt. (j.g.) USNR, 1942-46. Clubs: Chgo., Comml. Office: 231 S LaSalle St Chicago IL 60693*

MYERS, RAY FRANKLIN, banker; b. Council Bluffs, Iowa, Aug. 22, 1920; s. Ray F. and Birdie Mae (Burgess) M.; A.B., De Pauw U., 1941; LL.B., Harvard Law Sch., 1948; grad. Sch. Bus. Exec. Program, Stanford, 1966; m. Mary Elizabeth Mounts, Sept. 12, 1942; children—John Randolph, Thomas Edward, David Scott. With Continental Ill. Nat. Bank & Trust Co., Chgo., 1948—, asst. sec., 1951, 2d v.p., 1956, v.p., 1959, sr. v.p., 1969-70, exec. v.p., 1970-81, exec. v.p., gen. counsel, 1981—, sec. bd. dirs., 1974—; dir. Nat.-Ben Franklin Ins. Co. Ill. Trustee La Rabida Children's Hosp. Research Center, 1954—, pres., 1965-73; sec.-treas. Home for Destitute Crippled Children, 1956—; v.p. Methodist Found., 1965-66, pres. 1966-68; mem. Northwestern U. Assos., Am. Bankers Assn., Am., Chgo. (treas. 1967-70) bar assns., Chgo. Assn. Commerce and Industry, Corp. Fiduciaries Assn. Chgo. (sec.-treas. 1968, v.p. 1969, pres. 1970), Economic Club. Club: Chicago. Office: 231 S LaSalle St Chicago IL 60693*

MYERS, ROBERT G., printing co. exec.; b. Denison, Tex., Nov. 30, 1932; s. Gilbert G. and Jeannette (Richeson) M.; B.S., Iowa State U., 1954; M.B.A., M.I.T., 1971; m. Karyl Yates, Sept. 11, 1954; children—Gregory, Karyn, Richard. Sales mgr. Glaser Crandell Co., Chgo., 1957-62; sales mgr. R.R. Donnelley, Chgo., 1963-70, mgr. operating group, 1972-73, sr. v.p., 1974, sr. v.p. mag. div., 1974—. Bd. dirs. Pritzer Sch. Medicine, U. Chgo. Clubs: Shoreacres (Lake Bluff, Ill.); Butler Nat. (Oak Brook, Ill.); sky (N.Y.C.). Office: 2223 S King Dr Chicago IL 60616

MYERS, RODMAN NATHANIEL, lawyer; b. Detroit, Oct. 27, 1920; s. Isaac Rodman and Fredericka Hirschman M.; B.A., Wayne State U., 1941; LL.B., U. Mich., 1943; m. Jeanette Polisei, Mar. 19, 1957; children—Jennifer Sue, Rodman Jay. Agt., IRS, Detroit, 1943; mem. firm Butzel, Keidan, Simon, Myers and Graham, Detroit, 1943—; dir. Mich. Nat. Bank, Farmington. Bd. dirs. United Community Services of Met. Detroit, 1978—, v.p., 1981—; bd. dirs. Children's Center of Wayne County, 1963—, pres., 1969-72; founding mem. Detroit Sci. Center; commr. Detroit Mcpl. Parking Authority, 1963-71; trustee Temple Beth El; former trustee Jewish Vocat. Service and Community Workshop. Mem. Am. Bar Assn., State Bar Mich., Detroit Bar Assn. Club: Renaissance. Home: 3833 Lakeland Ln Bloomfield Hills MI 48013 Office: 1990 1st National Bldg Detroit MI 48226

MYERS, ROGER HAROLD, assn. ofcl.; b. Columbus, Ohio, Apr. 27, 1920; s. Roger Harold and Mildred Leona M.; B.B.A., Sinclair Coll., 1956; m. Marjorie Louise Krimmel, Dec. 2, 1942; children—Roger Frederick, Patrica Ellen, Paula Kaye, Jeannie Carol. Baker, sales supr. White Baking Co., Dayton, Ohio, 1946-57; office mgr. Ed Bolin and Sons Painting Contractor, Columbus, Ohio, 1957-62; fin. officer Am. Legion Dept. of Ohio, Inc., Columbus, 1962—. Pres. Kar Mel Civic Assn., 1959-60; founding pres. Sinclair Coll. Alumni Assn., 1956-57; active Central Ohio council Boy Scouts Am., 1932-46, Stilios Stelson Found. Served with U.S. Army, 1942-46. Named Student of Yr., Sinclair Coll., 1954; Eagle Scout. Mem. Ohio Hist. Soc., Am. Legion, Am. Assn. Retired Persons. Forty and Eight. Republican. Methodist. Office: 4060 Indianola Ave Columbus OH 43214

MYERS, THOMAS ALDEN, diversified co. exec.; b. Akron, Ohio, Dec. 1, 1945; s. Minor and Ruth (Libby) M.; B.S. in Bus. Adminstrn., Ohio State U., 1968; M.B.A., U. Cin., 1970; postgrad. U. Akron, 1974, 75; m. Lynn Dee Ann Locke, Aug. 24, 1969; children—Emily Michelle, Timothy Alden. Fin. analyst Mid-Continent Telephone Corp., Hudson, Ohio, 1973-77, supr. fin. results, 1977-78; public relations account exec. Edward Howard & Co., Cleve., 1978-79; mgr. investor relations TRW Inc., Cleve., 1979—. Co. photographer Ohio Ballet, Akron, 1976—, trustee, 1979—. Served with U.S. Army, 1970-73. Mem. Ohio State U. Alumni Assn. Club: Ohio State U. Marching Band Alumni. Home: 156 N Highland Ave Akron OH 44303 Office: TRW Inc 23555 Euclid Ave Cleveland OH 44117

MYERS, WILLIAM OSGOOD, thoracic and cardiovascular surgeon; b. Hastings, Nebr., Aug. 19, 1929; s. Joy Uberto and Lena C. (Osgood) M.; B.A., Hastings Coll., 1951; M.D., Northwestern U., 1955; m. Lois Mae Payne, Dec. 26, 1952; children—Jessica, Wendell, Inez, John, Michael. Intern, City Detroit Receiving Hosp., 1955-56, resident in anesthesiology, 1956-57; gen. practice medicine, Blue Hill, Nebr., 1959-62; cons. in anesthesia, anesthesiologist, Mary Lanning Meml. Hosp., Hastings, Nebr., Webster County Hosp., Red Cloud, Nebr., and Smith County Hosp., Smith Center, Kans., 1959-62; surg. resident Sacred Heart Hosp., Yankton, S.D., 1962-65; instr. anatomy U. S.D. Med. Sch., Vermillion, S.D., 1963-65; resident in gen. surgery U. Kans. Med. Center, Kans. City, 1965-66; fellow thoracic and cardiovascular surgery U. Kans. Med. Center, 1966-68; cardiovascular surgeon Marshfield Clinic, Marshfield, Wis. and St. Joseph's Hosp., Marshfield, 1968—, chmn. sect. thoracic and cardiovascular surgery, 1972-76, chmn. dept surgery, 1974-79, asst. chmn. surg. services, 1981—; clin. asso. prof. surgery U. Wis., 1981—; bd. dirs. Marshfield Med. Found., 1978—. Active Boy Scouts Am.; mem. respiratory therapy adv. com. Midstate Tech. Inst., Marshfield, 1975—; elder 1st Presbyn. Ch., Marshfield, 1974—. Served with USAF, 1957-59. Diplomate Am. Bd. Surgery, Am. Bd. Thoracic Surgery. Mem. Wis., Wood County med. socs, AMA, Wis. Surg. Soc., A.C.S., Am. Coll. Cardiology, Am. Thoracic Soc., Am. Assn. Thoracic Surgery, Frederick A. Coller Surg. Soc., Central Surg. Assn., Western Surg. Assn. Contbr. articles to profl. jours. Home: 1110 Balsam Ave Marshfield WI 54449 Office: 1000 N Oak Ave Marshfield WI 54449

MYERS, WILLIAM RICHARD, SR., seminary pres.; b. Council Bluffs, Iowa, Feb. 1, 1926; s. Walter Lemuel and Velna Fern (Huffaker) M.; B.A., U. Cin., 1951; B.D., So. Bapt. Theol. Seminary, 1954; D.D., No. Bapt. Theol. Seminary, 1964; L.H.D., Sioux Empire Coll., 1966; Ed.D. (hon.), Judson Coll., 1977; m. Geraldyne M. Brown, July 15, 1949; children—Christine, Richard, Beth, Bruce. Ordained to ministry Bapt. Ch., 1953; pastor Ridgeview Bapt. Ch., Danville, Ill., 1954-58, Irving Park Bapt. Ch., Chgo., 1958-63, North Shore Bapt. Ch., Chgo., 1963-75; 7th pres. No. Bapt. Theol. Sem. Oak Brook, Ill., 1975—; pres., mem. common Council, Chgo. Cluster Theol. Schs., 1975—; dir. Halley's Bible Handbook, Inc., 1980—; mem. Minister's Council, Chgo. Bapt. Assn., 1958—. Mem. Chgo.-Uptown Commn., 1965-70; bd. dirs. Urban Progress Center, Chgo., 1970-75; mem. bd. Edgewater-Uptown Consortium Religious Instns., 1971-75, Irving Park YMCA, 1959-62; chmn. exec. com. Billy Graham 1971 Greater Chgo. Crusade, 1969-72; mem. adv. com. Chgo. Sunday Evening Club, 1974—. Served with U.S. Navy, 1943-46. Recipient John Mason Peck award, Chgo. Bapt. Layman-Clergy, 1963, award So. Bapt. Theol. Sem., 1972. Mem. Am. Bapt. Assn. Sem. Adminstrs., Fellowship Evangelical Sem. Presidents, Ministers Council Am. Bapt. Chs., Midwest Commn. on Ministry ABC. Home: 256 Winthrop St Elmhurst IL 60126 Office: 660 E Butterfield Rd Lombard IL 60148

NABAKOWSKI, RONALD L., state senator; b. Lorain, Ohio, Feb. 15, 1942; student Ohio Sch. Banking, Ohio U., Baldwin-Wallace Coll., John Carroll U., Kent State U.; m. Dorothea Jurinec, 1961; children—Pamela, Deanne, Michael, Ronald, Robert. Br. mgr. Century Security Nat. Bank, 1970-72; city auditor, Lorain, 1972-76; mem. Ohio Senate, 1977—. Mem. Lorain County Community Action Agy., Lorain County Council Alcoholism. Named Disting. Man of Yr., Lorain Jaycees, 1968. Roman Catholic. Office: State Senate Columbus OH 43216*

NABER, EDWARD CARL, nutritionist, educator; b. Fond du Lac, Wis., Sept. 12, 1926; s. Alfred F. and Edna (Kluenner) N.; B.S., U. Wis., 1950, M.S., 1952, Ph.D., 1954; m. Marie Anne Peterson, June 20, 1953; children—Thomas E., Diane M. Asst. nutritionist Clemson U., 1954-56; asst. prof. Ohio State U., Columbus, 1956-59, asso. prof., 1959-63, prof., 1963-69, prof., chmn. dept., 1969—; vis. prof. U. Wis., Madison, 1964-65. Mem. poultry nutrition subcom. NRC, 1966-71, 74-77, mem. animal nutrition com., 1973-77. Served with USNR, 1944-46. Mem. Am. Inst. Nutrition, Am. Chem. Soc., Poultry Sci. Assn. (exec. com. 1970-72, 74-78, pres. 1976-77), Am. Inst. Biol. Scis. (governing bd.), AAAS, World's Poultry Sci. Assn., Sigma Xi, Gamma Alpha, Phi Kappa Phi, Phi Sigma, Gamma Sigma Delta, Alpha Zeta, Alpha Gamma Rho. Lutheran (deacon 1968-74). Club: Faculty. Contbr. articles to profl. jours. Editor: (asso.) Poultry Sci., 1963-69. Home: 3600 Clearview Ave Columbus OH 43220

NACHT, FERN GAIL, hosp. adminstr.; b. Mpls., June 9, 1952; s. Nathan and Miriam Nacht; student U. Minn., 1978. Personnel rep. Fairview Hosp., Mpls., 1974-79; asst. dir. personnel, 1979—. Mem. Health Care Personnel Assn. Minn., Twin City Personnel Assn., Twin City Health Care Personnel Assn., Twin City Diabetes Assn. Office: 2312 S 6th St Minneapolis MN 55454

NADELBERG, STEPHEN, distillery exec.; b. N.Y.C., June 8, 1941; B.A., Hunter Coll., 1962; M.B.A., Columbia U., 1964. Various sales and mktg. positions Standard Brands Co., N.Y.C., 1964-67, Canada Dry Corp., N.Y.C., 1969-74, Thomas J. Lipton, Inc., Englewood Cliffs, N.J., 1967-69; v.p., dir. mktg. Hiram Walker Inc., Detroit, 1974—. Office: PO Box 33006 Detroit MI 48232

NADER, ROBERT ALEXANDER, state legislator; b. Warren, Ohio, Mar. 31, 1928; s. Nassif Joseph and Emily Marie (Nader) N.; student Ohio State U., 1946; B.A., Adelbert Coll., 1950; LL.B., Western Res. U., 1953; m. Nancy Veauthier. Admitted to Ohio bar, 1953; practiced in Warren, 1953—; mem. Ohio Ho. of Reps. from 55th Dist., 1971—, vice-chmn. jud. com., 1973-76, chmn. reference com., 1979-80, chmn. judiciary and criminal justice com., 1981—. Pres., Trumbull New Theatre, Inc., 1958; councilman City of Warren, 1960-66. Bd. dirs. Family Service Assn.; trustee City Golf League. Served with AUS, 1946-48. Recipient Community Action award Warren Area Bd. Realtors, 1967; Outstanding Service award Kent State U., 1978, Children's Rehab. Center, 1980. Mem. Trumbull County Bar Assn. (pres. 1967), Trumbull County Law Library Assn. (trustee 1958-72), Warren C. of C., Football Ofcls. Assn., Lambda Chi Alpha. Roman Catholic. Clubs: Elks, K.C. Home: 798 Wildwood Dr NE Warren OH 44483 Office: 280 N Park Ave Warren OH 44481

NAGAR, ARVIND KUMAR, mech. engr.; b. Achheja (Ghaziabad), India, July 4, 1939; s. Kaley Singh and Risalo (Bhati) N.; came to U.S., 1960, B.S. in Mech. Engring., Okla. State U., 1969; M.M.E., Midwest Coll. Engring., Lombard, Ill., 1978; Postgrad. in engring. Ohio State U., 1981—; m. Sampat Dhabhai, June 5, 1971; children—Anil, Sunil, Jayesh. Mech. engr. Xerox Corp., Webster, N.Y., 1969-71; mech. designer Multigraphics div. A.M. Corp., Mt. Prospect, Ill., 1972-73; mech. engr. All Steel, Inc., Aurora, Ill., 1973-78; research scientist fatigue and fractures projects Battelle Columbus Labs., Battelle Meml. Inst. (Ohio), 1978-80; spl. lectr. Coll. Engring., Ohio State U., Columbus, 1980. Registered profl. engr., Ill., Ohio. Mem. Nat., Ill. socs. profl. engrs., ASME, Altrusa Salutes, Toastmasters Internat. (certificate of merit), Pi Tau Sigma, Sigma Pi Sigma. Club: Flying Aviation. Asst. editor, bus. mgr., contbr. Engring. Coll. mag., 1960-63. Home: 3045 Rightmire Blvd Columbus OH 43221 Office: 155 W Woodruff Ave Columbus OH 43210

NAGARAJ, HOLAVANAHALLY SESHACHAR, research chemist; b. Markonahally, Karnataka, India, Sept. 14, 1949; s. Holavanahally Krishnachar Seshachar and Holavanahally Sechachar Subhadramma; B.E. (Nat. Merit scholar), Bangalore U., 1970; M.E. (scholar), Indian Inst. Sci., 1972; Ph.D., Ga. Inst. Tech., 1977; m. Vimala Devi Nagaraj. Teaching asst. Ga. Inst. Tech., Atlanta, 1973, research asst., 1973-76, State U. N.Y., Stony Brook, 1972; research analyst Mech. Tech. Inc., Latham, N.Y., 1977—. Mem. ASME, Am. Soc. Lubrication Engrs. Hindu. Contbr. articles on numerical control of machine tools, elastohydrodynamic lubrication to sci. jours. Home: 2107 Lovington Ave Apt 204 Troy MI 48084

NAGATA, EIICHI, trade assn. exec.; b. Kyoto-city, Japan, Apr. 5, 1947; s. Kiyoshi and Shigeko (Murai) N.; B.A. in Econs., Ritsumeikan U., 1970; m. Etsuko Shirahata, June 9, 1973; children—Akiko, Hiroko. Mem. dept. fin. Japan External Trade Orgn., Tokyo, 1970-72, mem. dept. planning, 1973-75, mem. dept. publications, 1975-76, mem. dept. agr., 1977-79; trainee Internat. Devel. Center of Japan, Tokyo, 1976-77; dir. agr. dept. Japan Trade Center, Chgo., 1980—. Office: 230 N Michigan Ave Chicago IL 60601

NAGATA, YOSUKE, trading co. exec.; b. Kobe, Japan, Feb. 25, 1949; came to U.S., 1976; s. Mitsuro and Setsuko Nagata; law degree Keio U., 1970; m. Keiko Marui, Nov. 20, 1976. Vice pres. Nagata Am. Corp., Elk Grove, Ill., 1979—. Shinto. Office: 1420 Landmeier Rd Elk Grove IL 60007

NAGEL, JON ALAN, mgmt. cons.; b. Cin., Nov. 8, 1950; s. Arthur R. and Marie Ann (Vollmer) N.; B.A., U. Cin., 1972, M.A., 1975; M.B.A., Columbia U., 1973; postgrad. Emory U. Law Sch., Harvard U., Oxford (Eng.) U.; m. Susan Ellen Horowitz, Apr. 28, 1979. Mgmt. cons., Cin. and N.Y.C., 1975—; dir. ARNCO, Inc., 1972—; Mem. pres.'s council Vis. Nurse Service of N.Y. Mem. Am. Econ. Assn., Am. Fin. Assn., Young Men's Merc. Library Assn. Cin., Phi Alpha Delta. Clubs: Doubles, Met., Met. Opera, St. Bartholomew's (N.Y.C.). Author: World Trade, 1973; Multinational Corporations in World Politics: Ecopolitics and Nation-State Responses, 1975. Home: 2875 Montana Ave Cincinnati OH 45211 also One E 60th St New York NY 10022 Office: PO Box 11336 Cincinnati OH 45211 also 425 E 63d St New York NY 10021

NAGIN, IRA, hosp. mgmt. engr.; b. Los Angeles, Jan. 10, 1936; s. Eugene and Helen (Yohalem) N.; student Occidental Coll., 1954-56; B.S. in Mech. Engring., U. Calif., Berkeley, 1958; postgrad. M.I.T., 1963-64. Sr. engr. Aerojet-Gen. Corp., Sacramento, 1958-69; mgmt. engr. cons. staff Drake, Sheahan, Stewart, Dougall, N.Y.C., 1970; mgmt. engr. trainee Johns Hopkins Hosp., Balt., 1971; hosp. mgmt. engr. Mary Washington Hosp., Fredericksburg, Va., 1972-74; hosp. mgmt. engr. Potomac Hosp., Woodbridge, Va., 1974-76; hosp. indsl. engr. Walter Reed Army Med. Center, Washington, 1976-77; hosp. mgmt. engr. Cleve. Clinic Hosp., 1977-80; dir. mgmt. engring. St. Vincent Hosp., Green Bay, Wis., 1980-81; sr. mgmt. engr. St. Joseph Mercy Hosp., Ann Arbor, Mich., 1981—; cons. Sheraton-Fredericksburg Motor Inn, 1974-76. Served with USAF, 1958-62. Mem. Hosp. Mgmt. Systems Soc., Am. Inst. Indsl. Engrs., Soc. for Advancement of Mgmt., Am. Mgmt. Assn. Contbg. author: Am. Hosp. Assn. Guide to Selection and Employment of Management Counsultants for Health Care, 1978. Home: 2520 Bittersweet Ave Green Bay WI 54301 Office: St Joseph Mercy Hosp PO Box 995 Ann Arbor MI 48106

NAGLE, BARRY JOSEPH, geneticist; b. Newton, Mass., May 22, 1953; s. William Richard and Constance (Keefe) N.; B.A., Hobart Coll., Geneva, N.Y., 1975; M.S., Ph.D. (research asst. 1976-81; John Longwell Plant Breeding award 1979, Devin Miller Meml. Plant Breeding award 1978), N.D. State U., 1981; plant breeder, sta. mgr. Pfizer Genetics Inc., Mason City, Ill., 1981—. Mem. Am. Soc. Agronomy, Am. Seed Trade Assn. Republican. Presbyterian. Home: Rural Route 2 Box 177 New Holland IL 62671 Office: Pfizer Genetics PO Box 33 Mason City IL 62664

NAGY, DENES, cons. engr.; b. Budapest, Hungary, Oct. 19, 1929; s. Denes and Margit (Lukacs) N.; came to U.S., 1957, naturalized, 1962; student Hungarian Comml. Inst. of Pest, 1950; B.A., Tech. U. Budapest, 1954, B.S. in Mech. Engring., 1954, M.S. in Mech. Engring., 1954; m. Margarita Penaherrera, Jan. 13, 1968. Design engr. Gebr. Van Swaay, Mij., engrs. and constructors, The Hague, Holland, 1956-57; project engr., design engr. Walter Scholar & Assos., Inc., architects and engrs., Lafayette, Ind., 1957-65; project engr. Dalton-Dalton Assos., Inc., architects and engrs., Cleve., 1965-67; pres., dir., chief engr. Environ. Engring. Corp., Chgo., 1967-72; pres., dir. Martin-Nagy-Tonella Assos., Inc., cons. engrs., Chgo., 1972-76; partner, dir. MNT Internat., Quito, Ecuador, 1975—; owner, pres. Denes Nagy Assos., Ltd., Chgo. Registered profl. engr., Ind., Ill., Wash., Wis., Mass., N.Y., Calif., W.Va. Mem. ASME, ASHRAE, Internat. Dist. Heating Assn., Nat. Soc. Profl. Engrs., Ill. Soc. Profl. Engrs., Nat. Fire Protection Assn., Constrn. Specifications Inst., Air Pollution Control Assn., Automated Procedures for Engring. Cons. (trustee 1968-71), Soc. Am. Value Engrs., Am. Cons. Engrs. Council, Cons. Engrs. Council Ill., Ill. Architect-Engr. Council (pres. 1979, mem. exec. com.), U.S. Power Squadron, U.S. Coast Guard Aux., Internat. Visitors Center, Chgo. Council on Fgn. Relations. Home: 505 N Lake Shore Dr Apt 2604 Chicago IL 60611 Office: 65 W Division St Chicago IL 60610

NAGY, LOU, broker, investment banker; b. Warfield, Ky., Oct. 27, 1922; s. Louis and Fannie (Vizy) N.; student U. Chgo., 1941-42; B.S.E.E., U. Toledo, 1949; m. Dorothy Ellen Fallowes, June 23, 1943; children—Joel Gordon, Lora Lynn, Russell Eric. Communications engr.-mktg. Motorola Communications and Electronics, Inc., Toledo, also Ft. Lee, N.J., 1949-59; broker J.N. Russell, Cleve., 1959-65; partner Ball, Burge & Kraus/Prescott, Ball & Turbin, Stockbroker, Cleve., 1965-73; v.p. Fulton, Reid & Staples, Cleve., 1973-76; sr. v.p. Dean Witter Reynolds, Cleve., 1976-78; sr. v.p., partner Fulton, Reid & Staples div. William C. Roney, Cleve., 1978—; chmn. bd. Unitec Corp., Cleve.; dir. TSI, Inc., Phila. Bd. dirs. Kiwanis Found., Cleve., 1974-81; trustee Ohio Synod, Luth. Ch. Am., 1973-74, Luth. Home for Aged, Westlake, Ohio, 1974-81, Luther House, 1974-79; chmn. bd. Tetelestai, Inc., 1978-81. Served with USAF, 1942-46. Republican. Lutheran. Clubs: Cleve. Athletic, Clevelander, Westwood Country, Kiwanis (lt. gov. 1976) (Cleve.); Lutheran Businessmen's, Torch. Home: 22475 Spencer Ln Fairview Park OH 44126 Office: Bond Court Bldg 1300 E 9th St Cleveland OH 44114

NAGY, MARGARITA EUGENIA, nutritionist; b. Quito, Ecuador, Oct. 18, 1938; d. Gonzalo A. and Eugenia (Mateus) Penaherrera; came to U.S., 1958; B.S. in Home Econs. (Internat. scholar), Purdue U., 1962; M.S. in Nutrition, State U. Iowa, 1964; m. Denes Nagy, Jan. 13, 1968. Nutrition intern State U. Iowa Hosps., 1962-63, therapeutic dietitian, 1963; cons. to two Vozandes hosps. and to physicians in Ecuador, 1964-65; dietitian Maternidad Isidro AYORA, Quito, 1964; research asst. dept. foods and nutrition Purdue U., 1965-66; research nutritionist Highland View Hosp., Cleve., 1966-68; research asso. sect. food sci., dept. foods and nutrition AMA, Chgo., 1968-71, research asso. clin. nutrition, 1971-80, sec. nutrition adv. group, 1971-80; v.p., sec. Denes Nagy Assos., Ltd., Chgo., 1977-81; coordinator sci. and tech. Stokely Van Camp, Inc., Indpls., 1981—; participant nat. and internat. confs. on nutrition. Active, Internat. Visitors Center, Chgo. Council on Fgn. Relations, U.S. Power Squadron, U.S. Coast Guard Aux. Recipient Stanley Louise Latin Am. award Am. Home Econs. Assn., 1961. Mem. Am. Dietetic Assn., Am. Soc. for Parenteral and Enteral Nutrition (sec., mem. exec. council), Inst. Food Technologists, Critical Care Dietitians. Club: Toastmasters Internat. Author: (with C.J. Geiger and P.L. White) Nutritional Assessment of Hospitalized Patients, 1979; editor: (with P.L. White) Total Parenteral Nutrition, 1974; (with J.L. Breeling) Symposium on Newer Food Processing Technology: Safety and Quality Assurance, 1973. Office: 941 N Meridian St Indianapolis IN 46206

NAIL, WILLIAM ALDEN, public relations exec.; b. Crawford, Tex., Apr. 26, 1926; s. Benjamin Miles and Avie Maria (Harrison) N.; student Baylor U., 1943-45; B.A., U. Tex., 1946, M.A., 1948; m. Betty Young, Feb. 16, 1952; children—John Joseph, James Douglas. Instr. broadcasting Oreg. State U., Corvallis, 1948-49; program dir. broadcasting service U. Ala., University, 1949-51; program devel. officer USIA, Voice of Am., N.Y.C., 1951-53; asst. prof. English, McNeese State Coll., Lake Charles, La., 1953-54; asst. to dir. public relations Zenith Radio Corp., Chgo., 1954-64, asst. dir. pub., 1964-65, corp. dir. public relations, 1965—; mem. Consumer Electronics Group, EIA, 1960—, public relations chmn., 1974-75. Mem. Council of Better Bus. Burs., 1971—; mem. devel. council Williams Coll. 1978, charter mem. parents council, 1975-78; mem. public relations com. United Way/Crusade of Mercy, 1972—, vice chmn., 1978, chmn., 1979; mem. Mayor of Chgo. Jobs for Youth Com., 1972-76; active Boy Scouts Am., Chgo., 1972—. Mem. Internat. Public Relations Assn., Public Relations Soc. Am., Public Relations Clinic (v.p. 1979—), Public Relations Seminar. Democrat. Episcopalian. Clubs: Chgo. Press, Nat. Press, Ill. St. Andrews Soc., Clan Douglas Soc. (vice regent Midwest 1978—). Author: What Did You Say, 1971; contbr. articles to profl. jours. Office: 1000 Milwaukee Ave Glenview IL 60091

NAIMARK, ARNOLD, univ. pres., physiologist, internist; b. Winnipeg, Man., Can., Aug. 24, 1933; s. Harvey and Lisa N.; M.D., U. Man., Winnipeg, 1957, B.Sc.Med., 1957, M.Sc., 1960; postgrad. U. London, 1962-63, U. Calif., 1960-62; m. Barbara Jean Alder, Feb. 28, 1960; children—David, Mila. Registrar in medicine Hammersmith Hosp., London, 1962-63; asst. prof. physiology U. Man., 1963-64, asso. prof., 1965-66, prof., 1967-71, acting head dept. physiology, 1966-67, head dept., 1967-71, dean Faculty of Medicine, 1971, now pres. univ., mem. bd. govs. U. Man., 1972—; bd. govs. St. Boniface Gen. Hosp., Health Scis. Centre; cons. to govts. agys., founds. Served to lt. Royal Can. Arty., 1950-53. Recipient Queen Elizabeth Silver Jubilee medal; medal in physiology U. Man., 1955, Stefansson Meml. prize, 1957, Prowse prize in clin. research, 1959; Isbister scholar, 1950-53, 54-56. Fellow Royal Coll. Physicians, AAAS; mem. Can. Med. Assn., Can. Physiol. Soc., Am. Physiol. Soc., Can. Soc. Clin. Investigation, Med. Research Soc. Gt. Brit., Assn. Chairmen Depts. Physiology, Can. Tb and Respiratory Disease Assn., Can. Assn. Univ. Tchrs., Council on Respiratory Disease, Am. Heart Assn. Contbr. numerous articles to profl. jours. Home: 205 Girton Blvd Winnipeg MB R3P 0A6 Canada Office: 753 McDermot Ave Winnipeg MB R3E 0W3 Canada

NAIR, B. RAMACHANDRAN, pediatrician; b. Trivandrum, India, July 31, 1940; came to U.S., 1969, naturalized, 1978; s. Bhaskara and Bharathi (Amma) Panicker; student Kerala U. (India), 1958-59, M.D., 1964; m. Geeta Nair, Sept. 2, 1965; children—Meera, Uuni, Asha. Tutor pharmacology and therapeutics Med. Coll., Trivandrum, India, 1965-66; intern Mercy Hosp., Toledo, Ohio, 1970-71; resident pediatrics Milw. Children's Hosp., 1972-73, pediatric endocrinology fellow, 1973-74, pediatric pathology fellow, 1975-76; pvt. practice medicine specializing in pediatrics, Milw., 1976—; mem. staff Milw. Children's Hosp., Mt. Sinai Med. Center, St. Joseph's Hosp., Milw.; clin. asst. prof. pediatrics Med. Coll. Wis., Milw., 1973—. Served as capt. M.C., Indian Army, 1966-69. Diplomate Am. Bd. Pediatrics. Fellow Am. Acad. Pediatrics, Internat. Coll. Pediatrics; mem. A.C.P. Home: 14620 Mesa Ct Brookfield WI 53005 Office: 3070 N 51st St Milwaukee WI 53210

NAITO, HERBERT KUNIO, physiologist; b. Honolulu, Nov. 25, 1942; s. Yukio and Elsie T. Naito; B.A. in Biol. Sci., U. No. Colo., 1963, M.A. in Zoology, 1965; Ph.D. in Physiology, Iowa State U. Sci. and Tech., 1971. Postdoctoral fellow in exptl. pathology Cleve. Clinic Found., 1973, mem. sr. staff dept. atherosclerosis and thrombosis research, 1973—, head lipid and lipoprotein labs., div. lab. medicine, 1973—, mem. com. on clin. nutrition, 1975-79; adj. asst. prof. dept. chemistry Cleve. State U., 1973-75, clin. asst. prof., 1975-77, clin. asso. prof., 1977-80, Clin. prof., 1980; Fellow Nat. Acad. Clin. Biochemistry (chmn. sci. com. 1977—), Am. Coll. Nutrition, Council on Cardiovascular Disease (chmn.), Council on Arteriosclerosis; mem. AAAS, Am. Inst. Nutrition, Am. Assn. for Clin. Chemistry (pres.-elect N.E. Ohio sect. 1978-79, Young Investigator award 1977), Endocrine Soc., Soc. for Exptl. Biology and Medicine, N.Y. Acad. Scis., Am. Chem. Soc., Am. Oil Chemists Soc., Am. Assn. Exptl. Pathologists, Am. Heart Assn., Council on Arteriosclerosis, Am. Soc. Clin. Pathologists, Sigma Xi, Phi Delta Kappa, Phi Kappa Phi, Lambda Sigma Tau. Contbr. numerous articles on exptl. studies on lipoproteins and cholesterol metabolism to sci. jours. Home: 3335 S Green Rd Beechwood OH 44122 Office: Cleveland Clinic Foundation 9500 Euclid Ave Cleveland OH 44106

NAKATO, TATSUAKI, hydraulic engr.; b. Okayama, Japan, Jan. 17, 1942; s. Masaru and Yukie N.; B.S. in Civil Engring., Nagoya (Japan) U., 1966, M.S. in Civil Engring., 1968; Ph.D. in Mechanics and Hydraulics, U. Iowa, 1974; m. Sharon Esther Garbarsky, Mar. 25, 1979; 1 dau., Misa Dawn. Research asst. Inst. Hydraulic Research, U. Iowa, Iowa City, 1971-74, postdoctoral research engr., 1975, asst. research scientist, 1975-78, research scientist, 1978—, adj. asst. prof., 1977—. Mem. Japan Soc. Civil Engrs., ASCE, Sigma Xi. Home: 806 9th Ave Coralville IA 52241 Office: Inst Hydraulic Research U Iowa Iowa City IA 52242

NAM, SANG BOO, physicist; b. Kyung Nam, Korea, Jan. 30, 1936; came to U.S., 1959, naturalized, 1978; s. Sae Hi and Boon Hi (Kim) N.; B.S., Seoul (Korea) Nat. U., 1958; M.S. (Univ. fellow), U. Ill., 1961, Ph.D., 1966; m. Wonki Kim, June 1, 1969; children—Sae Woo, Jean Ok. Research asso. U. Ill., Urbana, 1966; research fellow Rutgers U., New Brunswick, N.J., 1966-68; asst. prof. physics U. Va., Charlottesville, 1968-71; vis. prof. physics Seoul Nat. U., 1970, Belfer Grad. Sch., Yeshiva U., N.Y.C., 1971-74; sr. research fellow in physics Nat. Acad. Sci.-NRC, Washington, 1974-76; research prof. physics U. Dayton (Ohio), 1976-80; sr. research physicist Grad. Research Center, Wright State U., Dayton, 1980—. Served with Korean Army, 1958-59. Fellow Am. Phys. Soc., Korean Phys. Soc.; mem. AAAS, N.Y. Acad. Sci., Sigma Xi. Contbr. articles to profl. jours. Home: 7735 Peters Pike Dayton OH 45414

NAMDARI, BAHRAM, surgeon: b. Iran, Oct. 26, 1939; s. Rostam and Sarvar (Bondarian) N.; M.D., U. Tehran, 1966; came to U.S., 1968; m. Kathleen Diane Wilmore, Jan. 5, 1976; children—Mondona, Mietra. Intern, Deaconess Hosp., St. Louis, 1968-69; resident in gen. surgery, St. John's Mercy Med. Center, St. Louis, 1969-73; fellow in cardiovascular surgery with Michael DeBakey, Baylor Med. Coll., Houston, 1974-75; practice medicine specializing in gen. and vascular surgery, Milw., 1976—; mem. staff St. Mary's Hosp., Milw. Diplomate Am. Bd. Surgery. Fellow A.C.S., Internat. Coll. Surgeons; mem. Med. Soc. Milwaukee County, Milw. Acad. Surgery, Wis. Med. Soc., Wis. Surg. Soc. Royal Soc Medicine Eng. (affiliate), Wis. Med. Soc., AMA, Michael DeBakey Internat. Cardiovascular Soc. Patentee med. instruments. Office: 2388 N Lake Dr Milwaukee WI 53211

NANDA, DAVE KUMAR, geneticist; b. Mandibahuddin, India, Mar. 15, 1938; s. Chaman Lal and Ganga Devi (Sehgal) N.; B.Sc., Delhi U., 1958; M.S., Indian Agrl. Research Inst., 1960; Ph.D. in Agronomy and Genetics, U. Wis., 1964; m. Connie Kalra, Sept. 17, 1966; children—Arvin Kumar, Paul Kalra. Internat. trainee DeKalb Ag Research (Ill.), 1964-65; dir. research Edward J. Funk & Sons, Inc., Kentland, Ind., 1965-68; Eastern area research dir. Pfizer Genetics, Inc., Windfall, Ind., 1968-80; dir. research O's Gold Seed Co., Parkersburg, Iowa, 1980—. Mem. Am. Soc. Agronomy, Crop Sci. Soc. Am., Soil Sci. Soc. Am., Am. Seed Trade Assn., Ind. Seed Producers Assn. Ind. (past pres.), Sigma Xi. Contbr. articles to profl. jours. Home: 2717 Minnetonka Dr Cedar Falls IA 50613 Office: PO Box 460 Parkersburg IA 50665

NANNE, LOUIS VINCENT, hockey club exec.; b. Sault Ste. Marie, Ont., Can., June 2, 1941; s. Michael and Evelyn N.; B.S. in Mktg., U. Minn., 1963; m. Francine Yvette Potvin, Aug. 22, 1962; children—Michelle, Michael, Marc, Marty. Player, Minn. North Stars, 1967-78, gen. mgr., 1978—. Roman Catholic. Office: 7901 Cedar Ave S Bloomington MN 55420*

NAPHIN, FRANCIS JOSEPH, lawyer; b. Chgo., Jan. 17, 1907; s. Patrick Henry and Margaret Agnes (Brennan) N.; A.B., Loyola U., Chgo., 1927; J.D., Northwestern U., 1930; m. Isabel Mary Byrne, Feb. 22, 1938; children—Isabel Mary, Francis Joseph, Martha Ann (Mrs. John J. O'Toole), Mary M. (Mrs. Allan J. Frenzel), Rosemary B., Catherine E. (Mrs. James Huntress). Admitted to Ill. bar, 1930; asso. firm Alden, Latham & Young, Chgo., 1930-39, Pruitt & Grealis, Chgo., 1939-55; partner firm Grealis & Naphin, Chgo., 1955-60, Grealis, Naphin, Sullivan & Banta, 1960-61; sr. partner firm Naphin, Sullivan & Banta, Chgo., 1961-69, Naphin, Banta & Cox, 1969—. Mem. Am., Ill., Chgo. bar assns. Roman Catholic. Home: 210 Broadway Wilmette IL 60091 Office: Xerox Centre 55 W Monroe St Chicago IL 60603

NAPIER, GEORGE HUELON, microbiologist; b. Tulsa, Apr. 28, 1929; s. George H. and Edna Napier; B.S., Detroit Inst. Tech., 1954; postgrad. Wayne State U., 1955-61; m. Bertina M. Guillory, Sept. 11, 1951; children—George Huelon III, Diana Lynn, Denise, Charles. Chief microbiologist Detroit Osteo. Hosp., 1961—. Mem. Am. Soc. Clin. Pathologists, Am. Soc. Microbiology, Am. Soc. Med. Tech., S. Central Assn. Clin. Microbiology, Omega Psi Phi, NAACP (life). Roman Catholic. Home: 19467 Snowden St Detroit MI 48235

NAPP, MICHAEL CHRISTY, ednl. adminstr.; b. Alton, Ill., Mar. 21, 1941; s. Gerhardt William and Mary Luker N.; married; children—Sarah, Adam. Tchr. elementary sch., Wood River, Ill., 1964-68, prin. elem. sch., 1968-70; prin. elem. schs., Belvidere, Ill., 1970-78; supt. schs., Smithton, Ill., 1978—. Mem. Am. Assn. Sch. Adminstrs., Ill. Assn. Sch. Adminstrs., Am. Assn. Curriculum Devel., Phi Delta Kappa. Club: Lions. Home: 220 W Fischer St PO Box 16 Smithton IL 62285 Office: Franklin and Hickory Sts PO Box 218 Smithton IL 62285

NARDONE, PRISCO DOMINIC, JR., automotive parts mfg. co. ofcl.; b. Detroit, May 24, 1942; s. Prisco Dominic and Catherine Marie (Marasco) N.; A.A., Macomb Community Coll., Warren, Mich., 1972; children—Joseph, Michael, John, Robert. Sr. design engr. Essex Internat. Co., Detroit, 1972-74; owner Nardone & Assos., mfrs. rep., Roseville, Mich., 1974-78; sales mgr. Elicon div. Microdot Inc., Troy, Mich., 1978-80; v.p. sales McCord Winn div. Ex-Cell-O Corp., Detroit, 1980—. Mem. Soc. Automotive Engrs. Democrat. Roman Catholic. Clubs: Hillcrest Country (Mt. Clemens); Fairlane (Dearborn, Mich.); Eagles. Home: 38592 Wingate St Mount Clemens MI 48044 Office: 2850 W Grand Blvd Detroit MI 48202

NASATIR, STEVEN BARRY, orgn. exec.; b. Oak Park, Ill., Mar. 27, 1945; s. Bernard and Alyce M. (Galinsky) N.; B.S., U. Ill., 1967; M.A., Roosevelt U., Chgo., 1969; Ph.D., Northwestern U., 1979; m. Natalie A. Levey, Dec. 17, 1966; children—Lonnie, Randy, Scott. Instr., Coll. Edn., U. Ill., Chgo., 1967-71; mem. staff Jewish Fedn. Met. Chgo., 1971—, exec. dir., 1979—; vis. prof. edn. George Williams Coll., Chgo., 1972-74, Spertus Coll. Judaica, Chgo., spring 1980; bd. dirs. United Way Met. Chgo., 1980—; bd. dirs. Chgo. Alliance Collaborative Effort, 1980—. Mem. Nat. Conf. Jewish Communcal Service, Assn. Jewish Community Orgn. Personnel, Assn. Sociol. Study Jewry. Club: Standard (Chgo.). Author: The Existential Notion of Authenticity and its Utility as a Viable Construct of Administrative Theory, 1979; also articles. Office: 1 S Franklin St Chicago IL 60606

NASE, VIOLETA CO, dietitian, food services adminstr.; b. Manila, May 3, 1940; d. Santos and Virginia (Gan) Co; came to U.S., 1965, naturalized, 1976; B.S. in Food and Nutrition, U. Santo Thomas, Philippines, 1965; M.A., Kent State U., 1969; m. Michael Nase, Dec. 30, 1972. Grad. asst. home econs. Kent (Ohio) State U., 1967-68; staff therapeutic dietitian St. Luke's Hosp., Cleve., 1968-71; asst. head dietitian Johnston Willis Hosp., Richmond, Va., 1971-72; staff dietitian Norfolk (Va.) Gen. Hosp., 1973; asst. dir. food ser. dept. Luth. Med. Center, Cleve., 1974-75; dir. food ser. dept. Health Hill Hosp. for Children, Cleve., 1976—; cons. dietitian Bolton Nursing Home, Cleve., United Cerebral Palsy Ind. Living. Mem. Cleve. Dietetic Assn., Am. Dietetic Assn. (cons. dietitian spl. interest group). Home: 2699 Warrensville Center Rd Shaker Heights OH 44122 Office: 2801 E Boulevard Cleveland OH 44104

NASH, JAY ROBERT, III, author, playwright, columnist; b. Indpls., Nov. 26, 1937; s. Jay Robert and Jerrie Lynne (Cosur) N.; B.A. in Lit., U. Paris (France), 1958; m. Janice Patricia Schwartz, Sept. 15, 1962 (div.); children—Lee Travis, Andrea Lynne. Editor, Milw. Lit. Times, 1961; editor Antioch (Ill.) News, 1962; mng. editor Am. Trade Mags., Chgo., 1962-66; editorial dir. PRM Corp., Chgo., 1967; editor-in-chief Chgo. Land Mag., 1967-70; freelance writer, Chgo., 1970—; editor, pub. Lit. Times, jour. of fine arts, Chgo., 1961-70. Served with Intelligence Service, AUS, 1956-58. Mem. Authors Guild Inc., Midland Authors Assn. Author: Lost Natives & Expatriates, 1965; Dillinger: Dead or Alive?, 1970; Citizen Hoover, 1972; Bloodletters and Badmen, A Narrative Encyclopedia of American Criminals from the Pilgrims to the Present, 1973; On All Fronts, 1974; Hustlers and Con Men, 1976; Darkest Hours, 1976; Among the Missing, 1978; Murder America, A Social History of Homicide in the United States from the Revolution to the Present, 1980; Jay Robert Nash's Crime Almanac, 1981; A Crime Story, 1981; Look for the Woman, 1981; People To See, 1981; (play) Last Rites for the Boys, 1979. Office: Box 4327 Chicago IL 60680

NASH, JOHN PRITCHARD, lawyer; b. Manitowoc, Wis., Dec. 29, 1908; s. Archie Lyman and Mary (Pritchard) N.; student Lake Forest Acad., 1925; grad. Lawrenceville Sch., 1927; B.A., Princeton, 1931; LL.B., Harvard, 1934; m. Ruth Chapelle, Nov. 3, 1951; children—Barbara Pritchard, James Lyman. Admitted to Wis. bar, 1934, Fed. Dist. Ct., Eastern Dist. Wis., Western Dist. Wis., 7th U.S. Ct. Appeals bars; practice law Manitowoc, 1934—, with Nash & Nash, 1934-36, partner Nash & Nash (now Nash, Spindler, Dean & Grimstad), 1936—; dir. A.M. Richter Sons Co., The Manitowoc Co., Inc., Manitowoc Indsl. Devel., Inc., Richter Vinegar Corp. Chmn. fund raising Manitowoc County unit Am. Cancer Soc., 1954-56; active Manitowoc Community Fund, 1940-60; mem. adv. council Boy Scouts Am., 1972—. Chmn. Manitowoc County com. Higher Edn., 1960-64; chmn., Wis. Commn. Higher Ednl. Aids, 1967-69; mem. state adv. council Fed. Higher Edn. Act., 1965—, vice chmn., 1966-68, chmn., 1968—; mem. citizens adv. council U. Wis.-Green Bay, 1969—; mem. Gov.'s Commn. Edn., 1969-71. Bd. dirs. Holiday House, Rahr-West Fund Bd.; pres. Manitowoc Meml. Hosp., 1980—; bd. dirs. Manitowoc Day Care Center, YMCA; bd. advisers Salvation Army. Served to major, AUS, 1942-46. Decorated Bronze Star medal. Recipient Certificate Merit Manitowoc, 1967, award of merit U. Wis., 1972. Mem. Am., Wis., Manitowoc County (pres. 1958-59) bar assns. Manitowoc C. of C. Presbyn. (trustee 1957-60, elder 1965-68; trustee Wis. Synod 1969-72). Rotarian (pres. 1959-60). Clubs: B and B, Branch River Country (Manitowoc); University (Milw.). Home: 819 N 14th St Manitowoc WI 54220 Office: 201 E Waldo Blvd Manitowoc WI 54220

NASH, KATHERINE ELIZABETH, artist, educator; b. Mpls., May 20, 1910; d. Carl W. and Elizabeth M. (Peterson) Flink; B.S., U. Minn., 1932; D.F.A. (hon.), Doane Coll., 1964; m. Robert Cyrus Nash, Mar. 21, 1934. Tchr., Northrop Collegiate Sch., 1946; mem. faculty dept. art U. Nebr., Lincoln, 1947-52, U. Nebr., Omaha, Joselyn Art Mus., 1952-57, San Jose State Coll., 1959-61; prof. dept. art U. Minn., 1961—; exhbns. include: Brussels World's Fair, Whitney Mus., Denver Mus., San Francisco Mus. Art; represented in permanent collections: Walker Art Center, U. Minn., Denver Mus. Gallery named in her honor U. Minn., 1979. Mem. Artists Equity Assn., Soc. Minn. Sculptors, Sculptors Guild, Internat. Computer Arts Soc. Episcopalian. Office: Studio Art Dept Univ Minn Minneapolis MN 55454

NASH, RUSSELL WILLIAM, sociologist, educator; b. Mpls., Feb. 25, 1921; s. Maurice William and Elsie Emily (Nordehn) N.; A.B., U. Minn., 1943; M.A., Columbia U., 1948; m. Ruth L. Cole, Feb. 1, 1944; children—Andrew, Pamela. Instr. English and sociology Pratt Inst., N.Y.C., 1947-51; asst. prof. sociology and psychology, Whitman Coll., Walla Walla, 1952-56; asst. prof. sociology Coe Coll., Cedar Rapids, Iowa, 1957-65; asso. prof. sociology, head dept. sociology and social work U. Dubuque (Iowa), 1965—. Pres., Iowa Conf. of NAACP Brs., 1963-64; chmn. Dubuque County com. to elect McCarthy, 1968, com. for George McGovern, 1972; pres. Dubuque Fine Arts Soc., 1976; past pres. Dubuque Citizens Council on Community Relations; past pres. West 11th St. Neighborhood Assn.; mem. citizens adv. com. Dubuque Met. Area Trans. Service; mem. Dubuque County Dem. Com., 1980—. Served to lt. (j.g.) USNR, 1944-46. NSF fellow, 1977; Inst. on Africa fellow Hamline U., 1978. Mem. Am. Sociol. Assn., Midwest Sociol. Assn., Iowa Sociol. Soc. (pres., 1977-78), Soc. Study of Social Problems, Nat. Council Family Relations. Democrat. Author: (with Ruth C. Nash) Iowa Art Cooperatives, 1976; art editor: (with Ruth C. Nash) Julien's Jour., 1976—. Home: 596 W 11th St Dubuque IA 52001 Office: Sociology and Social Work Dept U Dubuque IA 52001

NASH, STEVEN G., state senator; b. Chgo.; grad. Chgo. City Coll.; postgrad. Chgo. Tchrs. Coll., Columbia Coll., John Marshall Law Sch. Active hotel and real estate mgmt. bus.; now mem. Ill. Senate. Active numerous charitable orgns. including New Horizon Center for Retarded Children, Ill Central Community Hosp., United Hellenic-Am. Council Am., Chgo. Area council Boys Scouts Am.; chmn. exec. com. 30th Ward Regular Democratic Orgn.; del. Dem. Nat. Conv., 1976. Mem. Old Timers Baseball Assn., Polish Nat. Alliance, Polish Roman Cath. Union, Am. Hellenic Dem. Council Ill. Clubs: Moose, Lions. Office: State Capitol Springfield IL 62706*

NASON, HOWARD KING, research exec., cons.; b. Kansas City, Mo., July 12, 1913; s. Eber James and Florence (King) N.; student Kansas City Jr. Coll., 1929-32; A.B., U. Kans., 1934; postgrad. Washington U., St. Louis, 1937, Harvard Grad. Sch. Bus. Adminstrn., 1950; m. Phyllis Maddock. Chief chemist Anderson-Stolz Corp., Kansas City, 1935-36; research chemist, asst. dir. research plastics div., asso. dir., dir. central research dept., asst. to v.p., research dir.

organic chems. div. Monsanto Chem. Co., St. Louis, 1936-56, gen. mgr. research and engring. div., v.p., 1956-60, pres. Monsanto Research Corp., 1960-77; pres. Indsl. Research Inst. Research Corp., St. Louis, 1976-80, Howard K. Nason Assos., 1976—; dir. Carboline Co. mem. adv. com. isotopes and radiation devel. AEC, 1964-68; mem. Atomic-Energy, Labor-Mgmt. Adv. Com.; mem. Pres.'s Commn. on Patent System, 1965-68; mem. Planetarium Commn., St. Louis; mem. patent adv. com. U.S. Patent Office, 1968-72; v.p. mem. exec. com. Atomic Indsl. Forum, 1971-73; mem. Aerospace Safety Adv. Panel, 1972-80, nat. materials adv. bd. Ad Hoc Com. on Materials Sci. Application and Coordination, 1972-74; nat. materials adv. bd. Nat. Acad. Engring., 1973-78; mem. task force demonstration projects ERDA, 1975; spl. cons. to acting dir. industry relations NSF, 1976—. Chmn. bd. St. Louis Research Council, 1971-73; dir., mem. exec. com. St. Louis Regional Commerce and Growth Assn., 1971-74. Trustee-at-large Univs. Research Assn., 1971-78; trustee Charles F. Kettering Found., 1973—; trustee C. of C. U.S., 1968-70, also mem. com. on sci. and tech. Exec. fellow Rensselaer Inst., 1977-80. Mem. Soc. Chem. Industry, Am. Inst. Chem. Engrs., Am. Chem. Soc., AAAS, ASTM (dir. 1948-54), Nat. Rifle Assn., AIAA, Am. Inst. Chemists, Sci. Research Soc. Am., Mfg. Chemists Assn. (trustee, nuclear com.), Washington U. Faculty Conf. Center Assn. Clubs: St. Louis, Quiet Birdmen (St. Louis); Cosmos (Washington). Contbr. articles to profl. jours. Holder one fgn., 10 U.S. patents. Office: 7800 Bonhomme Ave Saint Louis MO 63105

NASR, SHERIF MAHMOUD, computer cons. co. exec.; b. Gizeh, Egypt, Apr. 2, 1942; came to U.S., 1966; s. Mahmoud and Ismat (Kamel) N.; B.Sc., U. Alexandria (Egypt), 1962; postgrad. U. London, 1964-66; M.S., U. Ill., 1976; 1 son, Ahmed Sherif. Instr. U. Alexandria, 1962-64; research asst. Purdue U., West Lafayette, Ind., 1966-67; project leader R.R. Donnelley, Chgo., 1968-72; pres. Production Scheduling, Chgo., 1972—. Mem. Ops. Research Soc. Am., IEEE, Assn. Arab-Am. U. Grads. Muslim. Club: Egyptian-Am. Author: (with others) Digital Control of the Stream Propulsion System of a Naval Vessel; contbr. articles to profl. jours. Home: 1656 Farragut St Chicago IL 60640 Office: Production Scheduling 135 S LaSalle St Chicago IL 60603

NASSI, SAMUEL, profl. basketball team exec.; b. N.Y.C., Dec. 17, 1921; s. Albert and Leona (Quain) N.; student CCNY, U. So. Calif.; m. Anka Timova Miller, May 29, 1948; children—Albert, Lisa, Kim. With White Front Stores div. Interstate Dept. Stores, 1954-69, v.p., merchandising and sales promotion mgr., 1954-69; propr. Sam Nassi Co., 1970—; pres., owner, dir. Ind. Pacers Basketball Team, Indpls., 1979—. Served as navigator USAAF, World War II. Decorated Air medal with 3 oak leaf clusters. Mem. Nat. Basketball Assn. (gov.). Clubs: La Costa Country and Spa, El Caballero Country. Office: 9100 Wilshire Blvd Suite 404 Beverly Hills CA 90212 also 151 N Delaware Suite 60 Indianapolis IN 46205

NASSIRPOUR, FARROKH, mech. engr.; b. Iran, Mar. 15, 1947; came to U.S., 1971; s. Hedayat and Heshmat (Lighvani) N.; B.S., Tehran Poly. U., 1968, M.S., 1968; M.S.M.E., U. Wis., 1974, Ph.D.M.E., 1976; m. Golrokh Homayoun-Farrokh, June 28, 1979. Teaching and research asst. U. Wis., Madison, 1973-76; sr. cons. IDRO, Tehran, 1977-79; vis. asst. prof. mech. engring. U. Wis., 1979-80; asst. prof. mech. engring. U. Detroit, 1980—, dir. CAD/CAM Center, 1980—. Mem. ASME, Soc. Mfg. Engrs., Sigma Xi. Islam. Contbr. articles profl. jours. Office: Mechanical Engineering Dept University of Detroit Detroit MI 48221

NATANI, KIRMACH, psychologist; b. Milw., June 5, 1935; s. Whit Baer and Natachia (Rucoss) Naabane; student U. Nev., Reno, 1953-57, U. Calif., Berkeley, 1959-61, U. Hawaii, 1963-64, Oklahoma City U., 1966; M.S., U. Okla., 1971; Ph.D., U. Okla. Health Sci. Center, 1977; m. Anna M. Scorsone, Oct. 8, 1976; 1 son, Oshkie Ure. Nuclear physics research technician Lawrence Berkeley Lab., 1959-60, computer programmer, 1960-63; vol. Peace Corps, Thailand, 1963-66; research asst. Okla. Med. Research Found., Oklahoma City, 1966-71, research asso., 1972-74; research psychologist Oklahoma City VA Hosp., 1975-77; NRC research asso. in neuropsychology U.S. Air Force Sch. Aerospace Medicine, 1978-79; human factors engr., engring. psychology dept. McDonnell Douglas Astronautics Co., St. Louis, 1979—; instr. Oscar Rose Jr. Coll., 1975; asst. prof. Okla. U. Sch. Medicine, 1977-79; cons. aviation, computer software devel. NSF travel grantee, 1970, 72; Nat. Acad. Scis. sci. exchange visitor to USSR, 1974. Mem. AAAS, Am. Psychol. Assn., Soc. Neurosci., Soc. Psychophysiol. Research, Internat. Soc. Chronobiology, Aircraft Owners and Pilots Assn. Contbr. articles to profl. jours. Office: Dept E422 Bldg 101 Level 2 Mail Stop 10 McDonnell Douglas Astronautics PO Box 516 Saint Louis MO 63166

NAU, JAMES MICHAEL, mech. engr.; b. Hickory, N.C., Dec. 26, 1951; s. Walter Theodore and Elizabeth Ann (Esch) N.; B.S. in Mech. Engring., N.C. State U., Raleigh, 1974, M.S. in Mech. Engring., 1977; m. Mary Benjamin Hester, July 31, 1977. Research asst. in acoustics dept. mech. engring. N.C. State U., Raleigh, 1972-73, grad. teaching asst., 1974-76; mech. engr. Corporate Cons. and Devel. Co., Ltd., Raleigh, 1974-76, sr. engr., 1976-77; grad. research and teaching asst. dept. civil engring. U. Ill., Urbana, 1977—. Recipient Outstanding Engring. Sr. award Sch. Engring., N.C. State U., 1974; U. Ill. fellow, 1977-79. Mem. ASME, ASCE, N.C. State U. Alumni Assn., Sigma Xi, Tau Beta Pi, Phi Kappa Phi, Pi Tau Sigma. Lutheran. Home: 318 Fairlawn Dr Urbana IL 61801 Office: 3204 Newmark Civil Engring Lab Dept Civil Engring 208 N Romine St U Ill Urbana IL 61801

NAUERT, ROGER CHARLES, mgmt. cons.; b. St. Louis, Jan. 6, 1943; s. Charles Henry and Vilma Amelia (Schneider) N.; B.S., Mich. State U., 1965; J.D., Northwestern U., 1969; M.B.A., U. Chgo., 1979; m. Elaine Louise Harrison, Feb. 18, 1967; children—Paul, Christina. Admitted to Ill. bar, 1969; asst. atty. gen. State of Ill., 1969-71; chief counsel Ill. Legis. Investigating Commn., 1971-73; asst. state comptroller State of Ill., 1973-77; dir. adminstrn. and fin. Health and Hosps. Governing Commn. Cook County, Chgo., 1977-79; nat. dir. health care services Alexander Grant & Co., Chgo., 1979—; vis. lectr. public regulation and health adminstrn. U. Chgo., 1978—; cons. govt. affairs Am. Mgmt. Assn., 1977—. Commr. capital improvements City of Bloomingdale (Ill.). Ford Found. grantee, 1968-69. Mem. Am. Hosp. Assn., Am. Public Health Assn., Am. Coll. Hosp. Adminstrs., State Bar Ill., Hosp. Fin. Mgmt. Assn. (faculty mem.), Alpha Phi Sigma, Phi Delta Phi, Delta Upsilon. Club: Nordic Hills Raquet. Author: The Comptroller—Illinois' Chief Fiscal Control Officer, 1976; The Demography of Illness, 1978; Proposal for a National Health Policy, 1979; Health Care Feasibility Studies, 1980; Health Care Planning Guide, 1981. Home: 310 Hempstead Ln Bloomingdale IL 60108 Office: 6th Floor Prudential Plaza Chicago IL 60601

NAUMAN, DELBERT ARNOLD, chemist; b. Frankfort, Kans., Nov. 22, 1932; s. Irving Agustus and Hazel (Arnold) N.; B.S. in Chemistry, Kans. State U., 1955; postgrad. U. Wichita, 1957, U. Ala., 1964, Purdue U., 1969-72; m. Joanne Alberta Lindeen, May 29, 1952; children—Jo Deaun, Mark Arnold. Chemist, Dowell, Inc., Tulsa, 1955-56; engr. Boeing Co., Wichita, Kans., 1956-62; sr. engr. Chrysler Corp., Huntsville, Ala. and Cape Canaveral, Fla., 1962-69, Western Elec. Co., Indpls., 1969—, chief chemist, 1972—. Elder, Trinity Luth. Ch., Indpls. Mem. Soc. Applied Spectroscopy, Microbeam Analysis Soc., Am. Chem. Soc., Mensa. Republican. Clubs: Moose, Gideons Internat. Contbr. articles to tech. jours. Home: 2434 Constellation St Indianapolis IN 46229 Office: 2525 Shadeland Ave Indianapolis IN 46206

NAUMANN, WILLIAM HENRY, educator; b. Green Springs, Ohio, Dec. 16, 1930; s. Lewis Henry and Mary Ethel (Knipp) N.; B.A., Asbury Coll., 1951; M.A., Kent State U., 1954; B.D., Oberlin Coll., 1957; M.A. (Monroe fellow), Yale U., 1959, Ph.D., 1966; postgrad. Inst. of Islamic Studies, McGill U., Can., 1968-69; m. Helen Claire Gamertsfelder, Aug. 10, 1968; children—Gary Barrett, Rex Barrett, William Henry, D. Scott Barrett, Terence, Teri Barrett, Nancy, Jeffrey. Tchr. elem. schs. Bath-Richfield Sch. Dist., Ohio, 1952-53; tchr. jr. high sch. Manchester Sch. Dist., Clinton, Ohio, 1953-54; instr. North Central Coll., Naperville, Ill., 1960-63, asst. prof., 1963-67, asso. prof., 1967-75, prof. humanities and religious studies, 1975—. Pres. Naperville Y's Men's Club, YMCA, 1972-73. Recipient Dissinger Faculty award for disting. teaching North Central Coll., 1979. Mem. Am. Acad. Religion, Am. Soc. Ch. History, Am. Research Inst. of Egypt, Middle East Inst. Contbr. articles on religion to profl. publs. Office: North Central College Naperville IL 60540

NAVARRETE, ANTONIO MARTINEZ, physician; b. Naga City, Philippines, Oct. 16, 1944; s. Constancio Chavez and Tomasa Sapugay (Martinez) N.; came to U.S., 1974; B.S., U. Philippines, Quezon City, 1965, M.D., 1972; m. Priscila Alejos, Feb. 13, 1972; children—Angelina, Marie Antoinette, Anne Kristine. Surg. resident Vets. Meml. Hosp., Quezon City, Philippines, 1972-73; rotating intern Little Co. of Mary Hosp., Evergreen Park, Ill., 1974; practice medicine specializing in family practice, Chgo., 1975—; mem. staff S. Shore Hosp., Chgo., Little Co. of Mary Hosp. Diplomate Am. Bd. Family Practice. Fellow Am. Acad. Family Practice; mem. AMA, Ill. Med. Soc., Chgo. Med. Soc., Ill. Acad. Family Practice, Am. Coll. Emergency Physicians. Roman Catholic. Home: 12715 86th Ave Palos Park IL 60464 Office: 9654 S Ewing St Chicago IL 60617

NAVRAT, DENNIS EDWARD, artist; b. Marion, Kans., May 15, 1942; s. Edward William and Veva Lucille (Howell) N.; B.A., Kans. State U., Manhattan, 1964; M.F.A., Wichita (Kans.) State U., 1966; postgrad. U. Iowa, 1969; m. Sue Ellen Summervill, Aug. 18, 1962; children—Ryan Wesley, Kristin Kay, Neal Edward. Mem. faculty Inst. Logopedics, Wichita, 1965-66; mem. faculty Dickinson (N.D.) State Coll., 1966—, asso. prof. art, 1971-79, prof., 1979—, chmn. dept., 1971-79, also gallery dir., exhbns. organizer; Fulbright-Hays exchange scholar-tchr. Southport (Merseyside, Eng.) Coll. Art, 1976-77; mem. N.D. Council Arts, 1971-80; mem. fine arts adv. com. Dickinson C. of C., 1973-76; dir. 1st-5th Biennial Internat. Matmedia Exhbns., 1967-75; works include: Sexist Serigraph Series, 1973-76, England and Friends Series, 1977—, New Light Insight traveling exhbn. of photographs, 1979; dir. Images on Exchange, group traveling exhbn., 1978-80; r research in Cibachrome color solarization. Del. N.D. Democratic Conv., 1968. Mem. NEA, Mid-Am. Coll. Art Assn., Graphic Soc., N.D. Edn. Assn., N.D. Higher Edn. Assn. Home: 258 E 12th St Dickinson ND 58601 Office: Dept Art Dickinson State Coll Dickinson ND 58601

NAWN, TIMOTHY JOSEPH, social service assn. adminstr.; b. Boston, Sept. 20, 1940; s. John Albert and Arlene (Horgan) N.; A.B., Stonehill Coll., 1963; M.S.W., Cath. U. Am., 1968; m. Paula F. Peppler, May 24, 1969; children—Andrea F., Jeffrey V. Asso. exec. dir. United Way, York, Pa., 1968-72; exec. dir. United Way of Holyoke, Mass., 1972-76, United Way of Aurora, Ill., 1976—. Mem. Nat. Assn. Social Workers. Club: Rotary (Aurora). Home: 659 S Gladstone St Aurora IL 60505 Office: 31 W Downer St Aurora IL 60506

NAWROCKI, JOHN EDWARD, retail corp. exec.; b. Chattanooga, Jan. 30, 1944; s. Felix Anthony and Mary June (Shelford) N.; student U. Cin., 1962-64; m. Sherry Lynn, July 31, 1976. Various positions R.L. Polk Co., Cin., 1966-74, Singer Bus. Machines, Utica, N.Y., 1974-77; mgr. retail data processing Federated Dept. Stores, Cin., 1977—; mem. adv. com. SE Ind. Vocat. Tng. Program, 1978—. Served with U.S. Army, 1968-69. Mem. Cin. Hist. Soc., College Hill Hist. Soc., Data Processing Mgmt. Assn. (student club coordinator 1978-82, v.p. edn. 1981-82). Contbr. papers to profl. lit. Home: 5434 Hamilton Ave Cincinnati OH 45224 Office: Federated Dept Stores 222 W 7th St Cincinnati OH 45202

NAWROCKI, RONALD JOHN, educator, credit union ofcl.; b. Chgo., Nov. 22, 1935; s. John and Camille Julia (Kazirod) N.; A.A., Wilson Jr. Coll., 1956; Ed.B., Chgo. Tchrs. Coll., 1958; Ed.M., U. Ill., 1969; m. Diana M. Borst, May 4, 1963; children—Deborah Anne, Marcia Joi. Tchr. acctg. Kelly High Sch., Chgo., 1958-69, asst. prin., 1969-71; tchr. acctg. Curie High Sch., Chgo., 1971—, chmn. dept. bus., 1973-80; dir. Union Tchrs. Credit Union, 1964—, treas., 1965-67, pres., chmn. bd., 1971-82. Recipient Outstanding Key Club award, 1968, Service to Community award, 1967, New City Lions Tchrs. award, 1971, Outstanding Tchrs. award Archer Rd. Kiwanis, 1982. Mem. Chgo. Bus. Tchrs. Assn., Distributive Edn. Clubs Ill. (service award 1968), Chgo. Tchrs. Union, Nat. Assn. Credit Union Pres.'s. Roman Catholic. Clubs: Archer Rd. Kiwanis (pres.'s award 1968, fund raising award 1971), Archer Brighton Community Conservation Council, Immaculate Heart of Mary Father's, Polish Nat. Alliance. Home: 10320 Cambridge St Westchester IL 60153 Office: 201 N Wells St Chicago IL 60606

NAYDEN, JOHN MICHAEL, radiologist; b. Canton, Ill., Mar. 25, 1938; s. John Joseph and Frances Lucille (Champlin) N.; B.S., U. Ill., 1960, M.D., 1964; m. Carol Jean Siegfried, Dec. 28, 1963; children—John Michael, Mark Howard, Max Edward, Catherine Lynn. Intern, Ill. Central Hosp., Chgo., 1964-65; resident in radiology U. Ill. Hosp., Chgo., 1968-71, instr. Abraham Lincoln Sch. Medicine, U. Ill., 1968-73, asst. prof., 1973—; radiologist, S. Suburban Hosp., Hazelcrest, Ill., 1971—, pres. med. staff, 1975-77, bd. dirs., 1977-81. Served as flight surgeon M.C. USAF, 1965-68. Diplomate Am. Bd. Radiology, Am. Bd. Nuclear Medicine. Republican. Home: 684 Brookwood Dr Olympia Fields IL 60461

NAYLOR, GEORGE LEROY, lawyer, r.r. exec.; b. Bountiful, Utah, May 11, 1915; s. Joseph Francis and Josephine Chase (Wood) N.; student U. Utah, 1934-36; student George Washington U., 1937; J.D. (Bancroft Whitney scholar, 1950-51, 52), U. San Francisco, 1953; m. Maxine Elizabeth Lewis, Jan. 18, 1941; children—Georgia (Mrs. Ralph E. Price), RoseMaree (Mrs. Glenn B. Hammer), George LeRoy II. Admitted to Calif. bar, 1954, Ill. bar, 1968; v.p., sec., legis. rep. Internat. Union of Mine, Mill & Smelter Workers, CIO, Dist. Union 2, Utah-Nevada, 1942-44; examiner So. Pacific Co., San Francisco, 1949-54, chief examiner, 1955, asst. mgr., 1956-61; carrier mem. Nat. R.R. Adjustment Bd., Chgo., 1961-71, chmn., 1970-77; atty. Village of Fox River Valley Gardens, Ill., 1974-77; practice law, legal cons., Barrington, Ill., 1977—; gen. counsel for Can-Veyor, Inc., Mountain View, Calif., 1959-64. Served with AUS, World War II. Mem. Am. Bar Assn. Mem. Ch. of Jesus Christ of Latter Day Saints. Author: Defending Carriers Before the NRAB and Public Law Boards, 1969, Choice Morsels in Tax and Property Law, 1966, Underground at Bingham Canyon, 1944; National Railroad Adjustment Board Practice Manual, 1978. Home: 8417 Klondike Rd Pensacola FL 32506 Office: 128 Center St Barrington IL 60010

NAZETTE, RICHARD FOLLETT, lawyer; b. Eldora, Iowa, July 27, 1919; s. Hilmer H. and Genevieve A. (Follett) N.; B.A., U. Iowa, 1942, J.D. with distinction, 1946; m. M. Joan Chehak, June 20, 1942; children—Ronald D., Randall A. Admitted to Iowa bar, 1946; practice law Cedar Rapids, Iowa, 1946—; asst. atty. Linn County, Iowa, 1951-56, county atty., 1957-63; dir. United State Bank, Cedar Rapids, Iowa, 1968—; dir. State Surety Company, Des Moines, 1966-78. Bd. dirs. Linn County Health Center, 1968-73, chmn., 1968-69; mem. Iowa Bd. Parole, 1981—. Served with AUS, 1942-44. Fellow Am. Bar Found.; mem. Iowa (bd. govs. 1972-76), Linn County (pres. 1963) bar assns., Iowa County Attys. Assn. (pres. 1959), Cedar Rapids Law Club (pres. 1954), Iowa Acad. Trial Lawyers (pres. 1964), Sigma Phi Epsilon. Republican. Presbyterian. Clubs: Elks, Masons, Shriners, Jesters, Optimist (internat. v.p. 1955), Cedar Rapids Country (pres. 1975). Home: 2224 Country Club Pkwy SE Cedar Rapids IA 52403 Office: 200 1st St SW Cedar Rapids IA 52404

NAZZARO, JOHN JOSEPH, chemist; b. Rochester, N.Y., Mar. 27, 1950; s. Frank Richard and Assunta Ann (Simotti) N.; B.S., Butler U., 1972, postgrad., 1972-74; m. Leslie Anne Ten Eyck, Oct. 11, 1975; children—Katherine Elizabeth, John Patrick. Chemist, Jardine Water Purification Plant, Chgo., from 1975; now supr. labs. South Water Filtration Plant, Chgo. Mem. Am. Water Works Assn. (water dept. corrosion com., research com.). Home: 10957 S Fairfield Ave Chicago IL 60655 Office: South Water Filtration Plant 3300 E Cheltenham Pl Chicago IL 60649

NEAL, CHARLOTTE ANNE, ednl. adminstr.; b. Hampton, Iowa, May 8, 1937; d. Sebo and Marion Bradford (Boutin-Clock) Reysack; B.A., U. No. Iowa, 1958; M.Ed., DePaul U. (Chgo.), 1966; postgrad. No. Ill. U.; m. Paul Gordon Neal, Mar. 29, 1969; children—Rachel Elizabeth, Kory Bradford. Tchr., 4th grade, Des Moines Ind. Sch. Dist., 1958-59; tchr., 3d grade Glenview (Ill.) Pub. Schs., 1959-61, tchr. 3d grade, psychol. ednl. diagnostic Schaumburg Dist. Schs., Hoffman Estates, Ill., 1961-69; supr. learning disabilities and behavior disorders Springfield (Ill.) Pub. Schs., 1969-73; psycho-ednl. diagnostician Barrington (Ill.) Sch. Dist. 220, 1973-77; ednl. strategist Area Edn. Agy. 7, Cedar Falls, Iowa, 1978—; ednl. cons. Spl. Edn. Dist. Lake County, Gurnee, Ill., summer, 1968. Certified K-14 teaching and supervising in guidance, counseling, elementary supervisory K-9, elementary K-9 teaching, spl. K-12 learning disabilities. Mem. NEA, Ill. Edn. Assn. Author: Handbook for Learning Disabilities Tchrs., 1971. Home: 1102 Sunset Dr Parkersburg IA 50665 Office: 3712 Cedar Hts Dr Cedar Falls IA 50613

NEAL, DANIEL EUGENE, health care adminstr.; b. Dexter, Maine, June 22, 1954; s. Clayton E. and Beverly A. (Hinton) N.; A.S., U. Maine, 1976. Health care adminstr. Vitreo Retinal Consultants and Surgeons, P.A., Wichita, Kans., 1977—. Mem. Wichita Area C. of C., Wichita Area Med. Group Mgmt. Assn., Kans. Med. Group Mgmt. Assn., Med. Group Mgmt. Assn. Republican. Home: 2239 Aloma St Wichita KS 67211 Office: 3333 E Central St Wichita KS 67208

NEAL, DENNIS EUGENE, mfg. co. exec.; b. Taylorville, Ill., Aug. 9, 1940; s. Lawrence Learned and Bonnie Iola (Cairel) N.; B.S. in Bus. Adminstrn., Millikin U., Decatur, Ill., 1962; postgrad. DePaul U., Chgo., 1963-64; m. Sharon Kay Peterson, Mar. 16, 1963; children—Joan Elaine, Adam Paul, Heather Adele. Internal auditor Continental Casualty Co., Chgo., 1962-64; audit mgr. Murphey, Jenne & Jones, C.P.A.'s, Taylorville, 1964-72; bus. adminstr. Taylorville Hosp. Clinic, 1972-74; pvt. practice acctg., Taylorville, 1974-76; pres. Neal & Ford, Ltd., C.P.A.'s, Taylorville, 1976-81; sec.-treas., controller MFC Enterprises, Inc., Taylorville, 1981—, also dir.; dir. Rabco Builders Supply, MFC Devel. Co., MFC Constrn. Co., MFC Realty Co., Taylorville Trucking. Treas., bd. dirs. Christian County Mental Health Assn.; bd. dirs., lay adv. bd. St. Vincent's Meml. Hosp.; founding mem. Christian County YMCA. Recipient Disting. Service award Taylorville Jaycees, 1974; C.P.A., Ill. Mem. Am. Inst. C.P.A.'s, Ill. Soc. C.P.A.'s, Taylorville Assn. Commerce and Industry (dir.). Club: Taylorville Optimist (pres.). Roman Catholic. Home: 220 E Adams St Taylorville IL 62568 Office: 1st Trust Bank Bldg Taylorville IL 62568

NEARY, DENNIS PATRICK, state senator; b. La Porte, Ind., Feb. 11, 1944; s. Charles Joseph and Loretta (Vollrath) N.; B.S., Murray (Ky.) State Coll., 1967; M.A., Ind. U., 1973; m. Mary Beth Holloway, Nov. 29, 1969; children—Robert, Ryan, Abigail. Tchr., Michigan City (Ind.) schs., 1968—; mem. Ind. Senate from 8th Dist., 1976—, caucus chmn. Democratic precinctman, 1968—. Roman Catholic. Address: 2316 Hazeltine Dr Michigan City IN 46360

NEBEL, LARRY HARMAN, sales exec.; b. Jefferson City, Mo., July 6, 1942; s. Emil Harman and Dixie Dean (Cutler) N.; B.S. in Elec. Engring., U. Mo., Columbia, 1965; m. Helen Noreen, June 6, 1964; children—Andrew Harman, Larra Noreen. Applications analyst Control Data Corp., Houston, 1965-66; mem. tech. staff Sci. Data Systems, Santa Monica, Calif., 1966-67; area mgr. Remote Computing Corp., Los Angeles, 1967-75; regional mgr. Tymnet, Inc., Houston, 1975-79; v.p. sales Uninet, Inc., Kansas City, Mo., 1979—. Chmn., Uninet United Way campaign, 1980; arbitrator Better Bus. Bur., 1980—; mem. Com. 88, Emmanuel Bapt. Ch., 1980, usher, 1980, usher chmn., 1981; mem. exec. bd. Nottingham Forest Homes Assn., 1981—. Clubs: Memorial West Community (pres. 1979, dir.). Home: 12002 Goddard St Overland Park KS 66213 Office: 2525 Washington St Kansas City MO 64108

NEBENZAHL, KENNETH, rare book and map dealer; b. Far Rockaway, N.Y., Sept. 16, 1927; s. Meyer and Ethel (Levin) N.; student Columbia U., 1947-48; m. Jocelyn Hart Spitz, Feb. 7, 1953; children—Kenneth (dec.), Patricia Suzanne (Mrs. William J. Frish), Margaret Spitz (Mrs. Constantino Quintong, Jr.), Suzanne Spitz. Solicitor new bus. United Factors Corp., N.Y.C., 1947-50; sales rep. Eromm & Sichel, Inc., N.Y.C., 1950-52; v.p. Cricketeer, Inc., Chgo., 1953-58; pres. Kenneth Nebenzahl, Inc., Chgo., 1957—; mem. Lloyds of London, 1978—; dir. Imago Mundi, Ltd., London, 1976—. Sponsor, Kenneth Nebenzahl, Jr. Lectures history cartography Newberry Library, Chgo., 1965—; trustee Glencoe Public Library, 1963-69, pres., 1966-69; bd. dirs. N. Suburban Library System, 1966-69; mem. exec. com. Northwestern U. Library Council, 1973-75; assos. bd. govs. Newberry Library, 1965-78, chmn., 1976-78, trustee, 1978—; mem. assos. council John Crerar Library, Chgo., 1972—, trustee, 1976—; bd. dirs. Beverly Farm Found., Godfrey, Ill., 1961-67; trustee Adler Planetarium, Chgo., 1969—, v.p., 1974-77, chmn., 1977-81; bd. dirs. Evanston Hosp. Corp., 1978—, Nature Conservancy of Ill., 1980—; mem. vis. com. to library U. Chgo., 1978—; mem. Am. Geog. Soc. Collection adv. com. U. Wis.-Milw., 1979—. Served with USMCR, 1945-46. Fellow Royal Geog. Soc., Am. Geog. Soc.; mem. Manuscript Soc. (dir. 1965-71), Am. Library Trustees Assn. (nat. chmn. com. intellectual freedom 1967-68), Antiquarian Booksellers Assn. Am. (bd. govs. 1965-67, v.p. 1975-77), Am. Antiquarian Soc. (bd. govs. 1981—), Soc. History of Discoveries (dir. 1974-76), Chgo. Map Soc. (dir. 1980—), Bibliog. Soc. Am. Republican. Jewish. Clubs: Caxton (bd. govs. 1961-68, 74—, pres.

1964-66), Arts, Tavern (bd. govs. 1979—), Wayfarers' (Chgo.); Lake Shore Country (Glencoe, Ill.); Century (N.Y.C.). Author: Atlas of the American Revolution, 1974; Bibliography of Printed Battle Plans of the American Revolution, 1975; contbr. articles to profl. jours. Home: 135 Crescent Dr Glencoe IL 60022 Office: 333 N Michigan Ave Chicago IL 60601

NEBERGALL, DONALD CHARLES, bank exec.; b. Davenport, Iowa, Aug. 12, 1928; s. Ellis W. and Hilda (Bruhn) N.; B.S., Iowa State U., 1951; m. Shirley Elaine Williams, Apr. 12, 1952; children—Robert W., Nancy L. Nebergall Bosma. With Poweschiek County Nat. Bank, 1958-72, sr. v.p., to 1972; pres., dir. Brenton Bank and Trust Co., Cedar Rapids, Iowa, 1972—; dir. Brenton Banks, Inc.; dir. Telephone & Data Services Inc. Vice-pres., dir. Iowa 4-H Fedn., 1972-76; div. campaign chmn. United Way; bd. dirs. ARC, Boy Scouts Am., Meth-Wick Manor Retirement Home. Served with AUS, 1946-48. Mem. Cedar Rapids Greater Downtown Assn. (pres., dir.), Alpha Zeta, Gamma Sigma Delta, Delta Upsilon. Republican. Methodist. Club: Rotary Internat. Office: Brenton Bank & Trust Co 150 1st Ave NE Cedar Rapids IA 52401

NEBERGALL, ROGER ELLIS, educator; b. Davenport, Iowa, July 3, 1926; s. Ellis William and Hilda (Bruhn) N.; A.B., Augustana Coll., 1949; M.A., Bradley U., 1951; Ph.D., U. Ill., 1956; m. Nelda Lee Smith, Apr. 10, 1958; 1 dau., Madelon. Instr., asst. prof. speech Bradley U., 1951-54, 54-55; asst. prof. U. Okla., Norman, 1955-60, asso. prof., 1960-65, prof. speech, 1965-69, chmn. dept. speech, 1959-69; prof. speech communication U. Ill., Urbana, 1969—, head dept., 1969-78; exec. sec. Missouri Valley Forensic League, 1959-69. Served with AUS, 1946-47; PTO. Recipient Golden Ann. Prize Fund award Speech Assn. Am., 1966. Mem. Speech Commn. Assn. (group chmn.), Central States, Ill. speech assns., Internat. Communication Assn., Pi Kappa Delta, Pi Kappa Alpha, Gamma Alpha Beta. Republican. Lutheran. Author: (with W.R. Carmack) Communication and Supervision, 1960; (with others) Attitude and Attitude Change: The Social Judgment Involvement Approach, 1965. Editor: Dimensions of Rhetorical Scholarship, 1963; Central States Speech Jour., 1967-70; Speech Monographs-Communication Monographs, 1974-77. Contbr. articles to profl. jours. Home: 2105 Plymouth Dr Champaign IL 61820

NEBLETT, THOMAS RANDOLPH, clin. microbiologist; b. Lexington, Ky., June 4, 1928; s. Thomas Walter and Deborah Jewell (Eades) N.; B.A., Mich. State Coll., 1951; postgrad. U. Louisville, 1951-52; M.S., Wayne U., 1955; Ph.D., Mich. State U., 1957; m. Nancy Ellen Glunz, Feb. 27, 1960. Asso. in charge Serology Lab., Dept. Pathology, Henry Ford Hosp., Detroit, 1957-66, head Bacteriology-Serology div., 1966—, chief microbiologist, 1976-79; chief microbiologist Flint Clin. Pathologists, P.C., also McClaren Gen. Hosp., St. Joseph Hosp. (both Flint, Mich.), 1979—; adj. asst. prof. microbiology Wayne State U., 1975—, Mich. State U., 1974-75. NIH research grantee antinuclear factors, 1968-69. Mem. U.S. Power Squadron (Dist. 9 chmn. advanced grades 1972-77), Am. Soc. Microbiology (continuing edn. com. 1973-77, pres. Mich. br. 1978-79), South Central Assn. Clin. Microbiology (area dir. 1973-75, dir. at large 1980—), Mich. Abraham Lincoln Civil War Round Table, Sigma Xi, Phi Kappa Tau. Clubs: Rotary, Detroit Yacht, Detroit Navigators. Researcher fluorescent antibody detection of antinuclear factors, serum complement, serological tests syphilis, urinary tract bacteriology, anaerobic bacteriology, Legionnaire's Disease bacterium. Home: 22455 Walsingham Dr Farmington Hills MI 48024 Office: 401 S Ballenger Hwy Flint MI 48502

NECHIN, HERBERT BENJAMIN, lawyer; b. Chgo., Oct. 25, 1935; s. Abraham and Zelda (Benjamin) N.; B.A. with distinction and honors in History, Northwestern U., 1956; LL.B., Harvard U., 1959; m. Susan Zimmerman (div.); 1 dau., Jill Rebecca; m. 2d, Roberta F. Aronfeld, Oct. 24, 1976; 1 son, Stefan E. Aronfeld. Admitted to Ill. bar, 1960; prin. Holleb & Coff Ltd. Bd. dirs. Jewish Vocational Service, Chgo., 1970—, sec., 1974-75, treas., 1975-76; trustee Harris Sch., Chgo., 1972-75; pres. young peoples div. Jewish Fedn. Met. Chgo., 1967-68. Served with AUS, 1960-66. Mem. Am., Ill., Chgo. bar assns., Phi Beta Kappa. Home: 399 Fullerton Pkwy Chicago IL 60614 Office: Suite 4040 One IBM Plaza Chicago IL 60611

NEDERLANDER, ROBERT ELLIOTT, lawyer; b. Detroit, Apr. 10, 1933; s. David T. and Sarah (Applebaum) N.; B.A., U. Mich., 1955, J.D., 1958; m. Caren Elaine Berman, June 17, 1962; children—Robert Elliott, Eric Arthur. Admitted to Mich. bar, 1958; since practiced in Detroit; pres. Nederlander, Dodge & McCauley, P.C., Detroit, 1960—; pres. Nederlander Worldwide, Inc.; exec. v.p. Nederlander Theatrical Corp., 1960—; partner N.Y. Yankees, Baseball Club, 1973—; dir. Mich. Nat. Bank of Detroit. Regent, U. Mich., 1969—; V.P. Muscular Dystrophy Assn. Am.; v.p. Muscular Dystrophy Assn. SE Mich. Home: 4616 Private Lake Dr Birmingham MI 48010 Office: 1930 Buhl Bldg Detroit MI 48226

NEDERVELD, TERRILL LEE, mktg. exec.; b. Hudsonville, Mich., Jan. 26, 1934; s. Fred and Clara (DeGroot) N.; student Purdue U. 1952, U. Mich. 1976, in profl. sales mgmt. W.Mich. U. 1975; m. Ruth E. Schut, June 6, 1952; children—Courtland Lee, Valerie Lynn Nederveld Heisey, Darwin Frederic. Design mgr. Packaging Corp. of Am., Lancaster, Pa. 1959-67, mkt. coordinator 1967-73, mgr. mkt. coordination Grand Rapids, Mich. 1973-74, mktg. mgr. 1974-76, corp. mktg. mgr. 1976-80, dir. corp. mktg. services, 1980—; owner, chief exec. officer Night Surf Waterbed Co., Grand Rapids, Mich.; lectr. Mich. State U. Sch. of Packaging, East Lansing, 1977-78, now adv. bd. Recipient silver award for outstanding package development Fibre Box Assns. 1966. Mem. Sales Mktg. Execs. (1st v.p. 1976-77, pres. 1978-79, bd. dirs. 1980-81), U.S. Power Squadron, Soc. of Packaging and Handling Engrs., Pi Sigma Epsilon. Mem. Presbyterian Ch. (deacon). Clubs: Nat. Campers and Hikers, Caravan Shrine, Mason, Shriner. Inventor in field of packaging; holder 6 U.S. patents in field. Office: 470 Market St SW Grand Rapids MI 49502

NEDRICH, JOHN LAWRENCE, transp. co. exec.; b. Nanty-Glo, Pa., Mar. 16, 1940; s. John and Ann (Demchak) N.; B.B.A., Cleve. State U., 1970; M.B.A., Lehigh U., 1975; m. Elaine Ann Bell, Oct. 20, 1962; children—Christal Fern, Shawn Lawrence, Kelly Elaine. With, Air Products & Chems., Allentown, Pa., 1963-79, fleet adminstr., 1979-80; fleet mgr. AGA Burdox, Cleve., 1980; gen. mgr. Contract Transp. Systems subs. Sherwin Williams, Cleve., 1981—. Scoutmaster, Boy Scouts Am., 1978-79. Served with USCG, 1959-61. Mem. Pvt. Carrier Conf. (dir.), Pa. Motor Truck Assn., Contract Carrier Assn., Am. Transp. Assn. (pvt. truck council), Nat. Council Phys. Distbn. Mgrs., Am. Soc. Traffic and Transp., ICC Practioners Assn. Roman Catholic. Office: Sherwin Williams PO Box 5856 Cleveland OH 44101

NEDZA, EDWARD A., state senator; b. Chgo., July 26, 1927; ed. U. Calif.; m. Tina Pretzer; children—James, Kathleen Ann. Former resident engr. Chgo. Dept. Public Works; now 1st dep. commr. Dept. Aviation, Chgo.; now mem. Ill. Senate. Comitteeman 31st Ward Democratic party, 1976—. Served with USMC, World War II. Mem. Chgo. Assn. Commerce and Industry, Am. Soc. Cert. Engring. Technicians, Inst. Engring., Am. Assn. Airport Execs., Airport Operators Council Internat., Ill. Public Airport Assn., VFW, Polish Am. Congress, Great N. Pulaski Devel. Corp. Office: State Capitol Springfield IL 62706*

NEDZI, LUCIEN NORBERT, former congressman; b. Hamtramck, Mich., May 28, 1925; s. Alexander and Estelle (Wojszko) N.; A.B. in Econs., U. Mich., 1948, J.D., 1951; postgrad. U. Detroit, 1949; m. Margaret Kathleen Garvey, Jan. 28, 1952; children—Lucien Alexander, Bridget Kathleen, Brendan Thomas, Gretchen Teresa, Eric Francis. Admitted to Mich. bar, D.C. bar; practiced in Hamtramck, Mich., 1952—, Washington, 1981—; pub. adminstr., Wayne County, Mich., 1955—; mem. 87th-88th Congresses, 1st Dist. Mich.; mem. 89th-96th Congresses from 14th Dist. Mich., acting chmn. house adminstrn. com.; chmn. installations and facilities subcom., personnel subcom. armed services com.; chmn., vice chmn. joint com. on library; chmn. select com. on intelligence. Served with AUS, 1944-46, 51. Decorated Bronze Star. Mem. numerous legal, fraternal and veterans orgns. Roman Catholic.

NEE, KAY BONNER, advt. exec.; b. Plummer, Minn., Oct. 26; d. David Thomas and Helena Mary (Franken) Bonner; B.A. in English and Speech, Coll. St. Catherine, St. Paul; postgrad. U. Minn.; m. William Joseph Nee, Apr. 19, 1947; children—Christopher, Nicole, Lisa, Rachel. Program dir. radio sta. KATE, Albert Lea, Minn., 1941-43; with Spl. Service Forces, ETO, 1943-45; mgr. radio sta. Armed Forces Network, Pilsen, Czechoslovakia, 1945; actress radio sta. WTCN, Mpls., 1945-50; free-lance radio and TV actress, 1950-52; radio/TV dir. Manson-Gold-Miller, Mpls., 1952-54; dir. sta. WCCO-TV, Mpls., 1954-56; pres. North State Advt. Co., Mpls., 1956-70; radio writer and producer Target Stores, Inc., also writer-producer sta. KTCA-TV, St. Paul, 1970-72; exec. dir. Minn. Assn. Vol. Social Service Agys., St. Paul, 1972-81; pres. North State Advt. Co., Mpls., 1981—; cons. in field. Mem. Gov. Minn. Commn. Status Women, 1965-67. Mem.-at-large Minn. Democratic-Farm-Labour Exec. Com., 1963-65, chmn. Anoka County Com., mem. Central Com. 3d Dist., 1962-65; del. Dem. Nat. Conv., 1964; TV dir. McCarthy for Pres. campaign, 1968. Decorated Bronze Star; recipient Best Actress award Fridley Theatre, 1960, 65. Mem. A.F.T.R.A., League Women Voters, Delta Phi Lambda. Author: Powhatan, 1971; co-author: Eugene J. McCarthy, U.S. Senator, 1964. Home: 219 Logan Park Way Fridley MN 55432 Office: Midland Bank Bldg Minneapolis MN 55401

NEEDHAM, THOMAS MICHAEL, ret. airline exec.; b. Homestead, Pa., Sept. 17, 1914; s. Michael Thomas and Margaret (Bosch) N.; student Normandale State Coll., 1972; m. Mary Elizabeth Harris, Apr. 10, 1937; children—Sue (Mrs. Daryl J. Sauer), Dennis P., Thomas Michael, Mark K., Mary Beth. Transp. agt. Trans World Airlines, Pitts. and Washington, 1935-43, asst. sta. mgr., 1943-45, sta. mgr., 1945-47; supt. stations North Central Airlines, Mpls., 1947-59, dir. ground ops., 1959-65, v.p. ground ops., 1965-79, sr. v.p. ground ops., 1979; ret., 1979. Home: 7200 York Ave S Apt 208 Beard Rd Minneapolis MN 55435

NEEL, VERNON L., mktg. exec.; b. Kokomo, Ind., Jan. 31, 1940; s. Frederick V. and Virginia L. (Raber) N.; m. Theda F. Miller, Feb. 12, 1961; children—Brian W., Jeffery S., Kimberly A. Prodn. mgr. Our Sun. Visitor, Inc., Huntington, Ind., 1960-71; v.p. Curtin Promotions, Inc., N.Y.C., 1971-77; pres. Triplex Mktg., Inc., Huntington, 1977—. Recipient Cert. of Merit, Huntington County Retarded Children's Assn., 1973; Key Man awards Huntington Jaycees, 1970; named Boss of the Yr., Am. Bus. Women's Assn., 1974. Mem. Promotional Mktg. Assn. Am. Methodist. Club: Kiwanis. Home: Rural Route 1 PO Box 78 Huntington IN 46750 Office: 232 E Washington St Huntington IN 46750

NEELY, EDGAR SAMUEL, civil engr.; b. Phila., Dec. 30, 1942; s. Edgar Samuel and Helen Lilian (Hunter) N.; B.S. (Phila. Contractors Assn. scholar 1961-63), Pa. State U., 1964; M.S., Carnegie-Mellon U., 1964, Ph.D., 1971; m. Leta Ann Whittington, May 14, 1966. Project field engr. Frank H. Wilson Co., Phila., 1962-63; design engr. Bethlehem (Pa.) Steel Corp., 1964; design engr. Blaw Knox, Chem. Plants, Pitts., 1965-68; prin. investigator Constrn. Engring. Lab., Champaign, Ill., 1971—; cons. CSI Edn. Com., Program Adv. Com., Parkland Coll., Engring. & Constrn. Tech., 1980-83. Recipeint Award of Excellence, Assn. of Record Mgmt. & Adminstrs., 1980; Research and Devel. award of yr. Dept. Army, 1981, Meritorious Performance award, 1981; Spl. Act award Corps of Engrs., 1981; Ford Found. fellow, 1964-65; NDEA fellow, 1968-70; NSF trainee, 1970-71; registered profl. engr., Ill. Mem. Constrn. Specifications Inst., ASCE, Nat. Soc. Profl. Engrs., Ill. Soc. Profl. Engrs., Sigma Xi, Chi Epsilon. Club: Cosmopolitan (pres. 1975-76, dir. 1973—, pres. bd. 1977). Office: PO Box 4005 Champaign IL 61820

NEELY, JAMES HAROLD, research psychologist; b. Chillicothe, Mo., Sept. 18, 1949; s. Carl Chester and Patricia Marie (Raney) N.; B.A., U. Mo., Kansas City, 1971; Ph.D., Yale U., 1975; m. Lydia Josephine Wilson, July 8, 1978. Asst. prof. U. S.C., 1976-78; asst. prof. psychology Purdue U., West Lafayette, Ind., 1978—. NSF fellow, 1971-74; Nat. Inst. Child Health and Human Devel. grantee, 1980-82. Mem. Am. Psychol. Assn., AAUP. Contbr. articles to profl. jours. Home: 426 Waldron St West Lafayette IN 47906 Office: Dept Psychology Purdue U West Lafayette IN 47907

NEELY, JAMES ROBERT, chem. co. exec.; b. Nashville, Jan. 3, 1939; s. James Orris and Rubye (Simmons) N.; B.Engring. in Chem. Engring., Vanderbilt U., 1961; postgrad. George Washington U., 1962-63; m. Carolyn Chevallier, May 2, 1964; children—Margaret, Richard. Chem. engr. Naval Ordnance Sta., Indian Head, Md., 1961-66, program mgr., 1966-67; devel. engr. Celanese Co., Cumberland, Md., 1967-68, mfg. supr., 1968-71, project engring. supt., Rock Hill, S.C., 1971-73, mfg. supt., 1973-74; dir. corp. engring. Sun Chem. Corp., Ft. Lee, N.J., 1974-77, gen. mgr. group mfg. and engring., Northlake, Ill., 1977-80, br. mgr., Chgo., 1980—. Active Boy Scouts Am. Named Boss of Yr., Nat. Secs. Assn., Rock Hill, 1974. Republican. Patentee gyratory solids feeder. Office: Sun Chem Corp 135 N Lake St Northlake IL 60164

NEETZEL, RAYMOND JOHN, transp. analyst; b. St. Paul, Apr. 2, 1937; s. John R. and Alyce I. (Berge) N.; m. Marlene F. Jezerski, 1974; children—John, Michael, Thomas. B.A., U. Wis., Green Bay, 1973; cert. urban transp. planning, 1976; postgrad. St. Thomas Coll., 1968. Free-lance photographer, St. Paul, 1955-72; planning cons. City of Green Bay (Wis.), 1972-73; transit analyst Met. Transit Commn., St. Paul, 1973-76, sr. transit analyst, 1977-79, mgmt. trainer, 1979—; owner Neetzel's Wood Works, Inc., 1979—; lectr., U. Aston, Birmingham, Eng., 1972, U. Wis., Green Bay, 1973; panelist Nat. Transp. Research Bd., 1977. Sec. Neenah (Wis.) Planning Commn., 1967-69. Mem. Nat. Inst. Transp. Engrs., Norwegian Am. Mus. (life), Boundary Waters Conservation Alliance, Alpha Phi Omega. Author: Winter Survival Techniques, 1980. Contbr. research papers in field. Office: Metropolitan Transit Commission American Center Bldg St Paul MN 55101

NEFF, KENNETH D., realtor; b. Montpelier, Ind., Oct. 19, 1929; s. Clyde A. and Cora I. (Neff) N.; B.S., Ball State U., 1953; postgrad. Purdue U. Extension, 1974; student Ford Motor Marketing Inst., 1965, Indsl. Coll. of the Armed Forces, 1972; m. Nancy Sue Stiffler, Dec. 26, 1951; children—David K., Susan L. Neff Edwards, Julie A. Neff-Woodward, K. Bradley. Propr., mgr. C.D. Neff & Son Ford Agy., Montpelier, Ind., 1956-75; v.p. Brookside Cemetary Assn., Montpelier, 1965—; propr. Thunderbird Rental Mgmt., Montpelier, 1968—; propr. Kenneth D. Neff Realty & Ins., Montpelier, 1976—, Spring-Wayne Apts., 1977—; partner Fairlane Fin. Co., Montpelier, 1966-72. Regional vice chmn. Ind. Criminal Justice Planning Agy., 1969-80; asst. dir. Sagamore council Boy Scouts Am., 1977-80; projects chmn. Montpelier Bicentennial Com., 1975-77; chmn. Montpelier Planning and Zoning Bd., 1964-70; mem. Sheriff Merit Bd., 1979—. Served with USAF, 1953-55, 61-62; served to base commdr. Ind. Air N.G., 1974-77, Res. ret. Recipient Montpelier Jaycee Pub. and Civic award, 1965; Ford Dealer's Distinguished Achievement award, 1965; Indiana Beautiful award, 1966; Auto Dealer's Traffic Safety Council award, 1965; Auto Dealers Nat. and State Assn. awards; Ind. Commendation awards (2), Ind. Disting. Service medal, 1981. Mem. Soc. Real Estate Appraisers (asso.), Montpelier C. of C. (pres. 1959, 60-66, Citizen of Year award 1963), N.G. Assn. of Ind., N.G. Assn. of U.S., Am. Legion, Res. Officers Assn. (chpt. 12 v.p.), State Res. Officer's Assn. (v.p. air 1981—), Methodist. Clubs: Kiwanis (pres. 1964-68, lt. gov. 1965), Masons. Author: Indiana Air National Guard History Book, 1969. Home: 129 S Washington St Montpelier IN 47359 Office: 109 W Huntington St Montpelier IN 47359

NEFF, RAY ALLEN, educator; b. Bristow, Va., Jan. 23, 1924; s. Charles Edward and Mary Elizabeth (Runion) N.; B.A., Bridgewater Coll., 1950; postgrad. Med. Coll. Va., 1954; M.S., Jefferson Med. Coll., 1960; Ed.D., Ball State U., 1975; m. Augusta Mae Kossman, Dec. 19, 1948; children—Charles Frederick, Robert Allen. Food cons. Commonwealth Va. Dept. Health, Richmond, 1950-54; analyst FDA, U.S. Dept. Health, Edn. and Welfare, 1955; sr. analyst Smith, Kline & French Labs., Phila., 1956-58; Walter G. Karr research fellow Jefferson Med. Coll., Phila., 1958-60; health officer Cape May County (N.J.) Dept. Health, 1960-67; asst. prof. dept. health and safety Ind. State U., Terre Haute, 1967-75, asso. prof., 1975—. Vice pres., dir. research and devel. Visu-Phonics, Inc., Terre Haute, 1968-79, also dir.; dir., chmn. bd., pres. Ray A. Neff Assos., Inc., cons., Terre Haute, 1979—; cons. Sunn Classics Prodns., Salt Lake City, 1976-78. Served with USNR, 1944-45. Fellow Soc. Mil. Historians. Am. Pub. Health Assn.; mem. Ind. Pub. Health Assn., N.J. Health Officers Assn., Royal Soc. Health (Gt. Britain). Pub., Abraham Lincoln Lithographs, 1968; Pawn of Traitors, 1969. Patentee solvent extractor, aircraft proximity device. Home: 514 N 8th St Marshall IL 62441 Office: Ind State U Parsons Hall Terre Haute IN 49809 also 1547 S 7th St Terre Haute IN 47802

NEFF, ROBERT MARSHALL, mfg. co. exec.; b. New Orleans, June 28, 1941; s. Marshall Snow and Viola Ruth (Hall) N.; B.S., Fla. State U., 1963; postgrad. Stetson U., 1968, U. No. Colo., 1970; children—Robert Marshall, Richard Roy. With Gen. Electric Co., Phoenix, 1964-69, supr. cost accounting, 1968-69; internal auditor Samsonite Corp., Denver, 1969-70; controller Buehner Schokbeton Co., Denver, 1970-71; corporate controller North Star Concrete Co., Mankato, Minn., 1971-72, divisional v.p., gen. mgr., 1972-73; mgmt. cons. Gulf & Western, Southfield, Mich., 1973-74, div. controller, Danville, Ill., 1974-79, group controller, 1979-81; mgr. acctg. systems TRW, Cleve., 1981—. Scout master Boy Scouts Am., Phoenix, 1968-69. Mem. Nat. Assn. Accts., Am. Inst. Corporate Controllers, Fin. Mgmt. Assn., Beta Alpha Psi. Republican. Baptist. Home: 4800 Dalebridge Rd Apt 601 Warrensville Heights OH 44128 Office: 20600 Chagrin Blvd Cleveland OH 44122

NEGA, WALTER JOHN, state senator; b. Chgo., July 23, 1917; s. Frank Michael and Teresa (Wilk) N.; A.B., DePaul U., 1940, student law, 1946-48; m. Harriet Evelyn Kendzierski, Jan. 15, 1955; children—Marya, Joseph, Teresa. Adminstrv. asst. to Congressman Dan Rostenkowski, 1959-79; mem. Ill. State Senate, 1979—. Served with AUS, 1942-46. Decorated Bronze Star, Purple Heart with 2 oak leaf clusters. Mem. Am. Legion, VFW, Polish Nat. Alliance, Polish Roman Catholic Union, Purple Heart Vets. Democrat. Roman Catholic. Clubs: Moose, K.C. Office: 2150 N Damen Ave Chicago IL 60647

NEGLEY, HAROLD HOOVER, educator; b. Indpls., Dec. 13, 1921; s. Arthur O. and Alma (Hoover) N.; A.B., DePauw U., 1944, LL.D. (hon.), 1975; M.A., Butler U., 1947; Ed.D., Ind. U., 1962; m. Barbara Pashos, Sept. 22, 1978; children—Susan, Janet, Jeffrey. History tchr., 1947-58; dir. econ. edn. Indpls. Public Schs., 1958-60, supr. in-service edn., 1960-67; dir. curriculum Ind. Dept. Public Instrn., Indpls., 1967, asst. supt. public instrn., 1967-70, supt. public instrn., 1973—, also chmn. Ind. State Bd. Edn., Ind. State Bd. Vocat. and Tech. Edn.; dir. Ball State U. Program at Grissom AFB, Ind., 1971-72; dir. Cemrel, Inc. Served to lt. (j.g.) USNR, 1943-46. Recipient Cert. of Recognition for work in disaster assistance U.S. Dept. Agr., 1974; named Educator of Yr., Ind. Council, Internat. Reading Assn., 1975; recipient Nat. Vocat. Agr. Citation, Future Farmers Am., 1977. Mem. Adult Edn. Assn., Ind. Assn. Public Sch. Supts., Council of Chief State Sch. Officers, Joint Council on Econ. Edn., Nat. Council Social Studies, Ind. Hist. Soc., Phi Kappa Phi, Phi Delta Kappa. Republican. Club: Masons. Author: (with Leonard Ralston) United States History, 1973; editor: Indiana Government, 1968. Office: Ind Dept Public Instrn 229 State House Indianapolis IN 46204

NEGRI, ROBERT MICHAEL, banker; b. Dayton, Ohio, July 11, 1947; s. Ralph G. and Virginia N. N.; B.A., Denison U., 1969; M.S., Miami U., Oxford, Ohio, 1972; m. Susan Wenger, June 16, 1973; children—Melissa, Laura. Vice-pres. retail planning and devel. Bancohio Nat. Bank, Columbus, 1978-79, v.p. tng. and devel., 1979-80, v.p. productivity improvement div., 1980—; mem. adj. faculty Franklin U., Columbus, 1978-79. Bd. mem. Rosemont Sch., Jr. Achievement Central Ohio, United Negro Coll. Fund, Options. Served with U.S. Army, 1969-70. Mem. Am. Mgmt. Assn., Human Resource Planning Soc., Am. Bankers Assn. Republican. Episcopalian. Clubs: Columbus Athletic, Columbus Maennechor, Brookside Country. Home: 1042 Loch Ness Ave Worthington OH 43085 Office: 155 E Broad St Columbus OH 43265

NEHER, BOBIJEAN CESNIK, TV producer; b. Indpls., Dec. 28, 1948; d. Rudy L. and Iris V. (Norton) Cesnik; student Ind. U.-Purdue U., Indpls., 1970-77, Butler U., 1979-80; 1 son, Eric Simon. Sec.-treas. Heat-Cool Sales & Service, Inc., Danville, Ind., 1971-76; travel dept. coordinator Ambassadair, Inc., Indpls., 1976-78; asst. community affairs dir. WISH-TV, Indpls., producer Indy Today, also host producer Community, 1978-80; producer PM Mag., WTHI-TV, Terre Haute, Ind., 1980—. Lic. 3d class radiotelephone operator with broadcast endorsement FCC. Mem. Nat. Assn. Female Execs. Mem. Christian Ch. Office: 918 Ohio St Terre Haute IN 47808

NEHER, WILLIAM WALTER, univ. adminstr.; b. Lafayette, Ind., June 22, 1944; s. Loyal Prentice and Edith Zelma N.; B.A., Butler U., 1966; M.A., Northwestern U., 1967, Ph.D. (Intersocietal Studies Council fellow), 1970; m. Nancy Ann Davis, Aug. 21, 1966. Asst. prof. speech Butler U., 1970-74, asso. prof., 1975—, dean Univ. Coll.,1974—, dir. univ. honors program, 1974—; cons. in speech. Mem. appropriations com. United Way of Greater Indpls., 1974-79, mem. Speakers Bur., 1978. Named Outstanding Young Hoosier, Ind. Jaycees, 1978. Mem. Speech Communication Assn., Internat. Communication Assn., Central States Speech Assn., African Studies Assn., AAUP, Nat. Honors Assn., Nat. Orientation Dirs. Assn., Indpls. Jaycees, Indpls. Sigma Chi Alumni Club. Clubs: Kiwanis (treas.), Indpls. Lit. (Indpls.). Author: (with David H. Waite) Nuts and Bolts: A Manual of Effective Professional Communications, 1977; contbr. articles on communication in Africa, parliamentary procedure to profl. jours.; research on polit. campaigns in Kenya. Office: 4600 Sunset Ave Indianapolis IN 46208

NEHRING, EARL WILFRED, food mfg. co. ofcl.; b. Marion, Wis., Mar. 27, 1926; s. Rinehart Robert and Ophelia Holdina (Zigenhagen) N.; B.S. in Chemistry, U. Wis., Oshkosh, 1948; m. Donna Marie Baumann, Oct. 1, 1955; 1 dau., Melanie Ann. Tchr. high sch. chemistry and sci., Elcho and Westfield, Wis., 1948-51; chemist, supr. U.S. Rubber Co., Joliet (Ill.) Arsenal, 1951-57; sr. analytical chemist Quaker Oats Co., Barrington, Ill., 1957-62, coordinator product standards, 1962-68, mgr. product standards, 1968-70, asso. dir. quality assurance standards, 1970-76, asso. dir. quality assurance product safety, 1976—. Fund drive chmn. Lake Region YMCA, 1962, bd. dirs., 1962-63, chmn. bd., 1964-65; mem. ch. bd. United Ch. of Christ, Crystal Lake, Ill., 1973-75. Mem. Grocery Mfrs. Am., Am. Corn Millers Fedn., Am. Soc. Quality Control, Assn. Food and Drug Ofcls., Coblenz Soc., Inst. Food Technologists, Am. Chem. Soc., Nat. Wildlife Fedn., Nat. Rifle Assn., Smithsonian Assos. Club: Masons. Home: 6118 Robin Ln Crystal Lake IL 60014 Office: 617 W Main St Barrington IL 60010

NEIBEL, OLIVER JOSEPH, JR., med. services exec.; b. Kansas City, Mo., Apr. 17, 1927; s. Oliver Joseph and Eula Lee (Durham) N.; J.D., U. Va., 1952; B.S., U. Ariz., 1949; m. Patricia Helen O'Keefe, June 24, 1950 (div. 1971); children—Oliver Joseph III, Deborah Sue; m. 2d, Diane Bachus Nelson, Apr. 11, 1981. Instr., U. Washington, 1952-53; admitted to Wash. bar, 1952, Ill. bar, 1961, Nebr. bar, 1973; practiced in Seattle, 1953-57; asst. atty. gen. State of Wash., 1957-61; legislative atty. AMA, Chgo., 1961-63; exec. dir., gen. counsel Coll. Am. Pathologists, Chgo., 1963-72; v.p., gen. mgr. Physicians Lab., Omaha, 1973—. Justice of peace, Mountlake Terrace, Wash., 1955-57. Served with USNR, 1945. Mem. Am. Wash., Nebr., Ill. bar assns., Med. Group Mgmt. Assn., Phi Kappa Psi (chpt. pres. 1948-49), Delta Theta Phi, Alpha Kappa Psi, Delta Sigma Rho. Mason, Elk, Rotarian. Clubs: Wash. Athletic (Seattle); Tavern (Chgo.); Omaha Press, University (Nebr.). Home: 7918 Potter Plaza Omaha NE 68122 Office: 105 N 37th St Omaha NE 68131

NEIBERG, ALAN DAVID, physician; b. Pitts., July 22, 1942; s. Morris J. and Ethel (Zerelstein) N.; B.S., U. Pitts., 1962; M.A. in Psychology, U. Cin., 1963, Ph.D., 1967; M.D., Mich. State U., 1973; m. Vicki B. Evans, Mar. 1, 1964; children—Maurine, Forrest. Intern Mich. State U. Hosps., Lansing, 1973-74, resident in internal medicine, 1973-76; rotating resident Yale-New Haven (Conn.) Hosp., 1974, resident in gastroenterology, 1975, resident in med. oncology, 1976; practice medicine specializing in internal medicine, Lansing, 1976—; asst. prof. psychology U. Mich., 1968-70, vis. lectr., 1970-75; clin. instr. medicine Mich. State U., Lansing, 1973—; mem. staff E.W. Sparrow, St. Lawrence hosps., Ingham Med. Center. Diplomate Am. Bd. Internal Medicine. Mem. A.C.P., Am. Coll. Emergency Physicians, AAAS, N.Y. Acad. Scis., Sigma Xi. Contbr. articles on exptl. psychology, ednl. psychology and emergency medicine to profl. jours. Home: 1615 Roseland East Lansing MI 48823 Office: 2909 E Grand River Lansing MI 48912

NEIL, RANDOLPH LANING, assns. exec.; b. Kansas City, Mo., Dec. 16, 1941; s. Randolph Steele and Elizabeth Floyd (Laning) N.; B.S. in Journalism, U. Kans., 1966; 1 dau., Merritt Angeline. Founder, exec. dir. Internat. Cheerleading Found., Inc., Shawnee-Mission, Kans., 1964—, exec. dir., chmn., 1976—, editor Cheerleading, 1973—; founder, pres. Nat. Film Soc., Shawnee-Mission, 1975-80, pub. Am. Classic Screen mag., 1976-80. Mem. exec. com. Muscular Dystrophy Assn. of Hawaii; vice chmn. Johnson County (Kans.) Democratic Party; mem. Mayor's Corps for Progress, Kansas City, Mo.; founder Pi Epsilon Pi, nat. honor soc. for cheerleaders, 1981. Named Good Will Ambassador, U.S. Savs. Bonds div. Treasury Dept., 1967; honored for guiding preservation of heritage of industry of motion pictures Women of Motion Picture Industry, 1977. Mem. Am. Soc. Assn. Execs., Nat. Trust Hist. Preservation, So. Poverty Law Center, Nat. Collegiate Athletic Assn., Am. Film Inst., Colonial Williamsburg Found., Greater Kansas City C. of C., Kansas City Philharmonic Assos., Decorative Arts Trust, Soc. Colonial Am. (founder 1980), Bibliog. Soc. Am. Episcopalian. Club: Rockhill Tennis (Kansas City, Mo.). Author books on cheerleading, including: You Can Become A Cheerleader, 1974; The Encyclopedia of Cheerleading, 1975; Official Cheerleader's Handbook, 1979; The Official Pep and Spirit Handbook, 1981. Home: 5100 W 111th Terr Leawood KS 66211 Office: The Neil Bldg 4425 Indian Creek Pkwy Shawnee-Mission KS 66207

NEILL, MICHAEL CLAIR, agrl. supplies and service co. exec.; b. Galesburg, Ill., Dec. 1, 1954; s. Clair Hugh and Roberta Fern (Phillips) N.; B.S. in Agrl., Western Ill. U., 1976, postgrad, 1977-78; m. Sharon Lynn Neill, July 22, 1973; children—Gregory Michael, David Clair. Asst. mgr. Augusta (Ill.) Farmer's Co-op, 1976-77; plant mgr. Schuyler-Brown F.S., Rushville, Ill., 1977—. Chmn. 4-H Youth Council, Rushville, 1978-79. Mem. Alpha Zeta, Alpha Gamma Sigma. Republican. Lutheran. Home: Rural Route 3 Rushville IL 62681 Office: Rural Route 1 Camden IL 62319

NEIMAN, LIONEL JOSEPH, educator, sociologist; b. Cleve., May 23, 1921; s. Lionel and Essie (Nyman) N.; A.B., Ind. State U., 1943; M.A., 1946; postgrad. Ind. U., 1947-52; m. Edith Blanche Grossman, Dec. 26, 1943. High sch. tchr., 1943-46; dir. Monroe County Welfare Dept., Bloomington, Ind., 1952-60; parole officer Ind., 1952-56; faculty Ball State U., Muncie, Ind., 1962—, prof. sociology, 1975—, coordinator criminal justice and corrections, 1973-76, chmn. dept. criminal justice and corrections, 1976-81. Lectr., Ind. U., 1972—; cons. in field. Grantee Ind. Criminal Justice Planning Agy., 1970-73, Law Enforcement Assistance Adminstrn., 1970—, Lilly Endowment, 1974. Mem. Am., Ind. (Distinguished Service award 1974, pres. 1978) correctional assns., Am. Sociol. Assn., AAUP, Ind. Conf. Social Welfare, Am. Judicature Soc., Nat. Council Crime and Delinquency, Acad. Criminal Justice Scis., Am. Soc. Criminology, ACLU.

NEIMAN, ROBERT LEROY, mgmt. cons.; b. Chgo., Feb. 9, 1930; s. Maurice and Shirley (Albin) N.; B.S. in Communications with honors, U. Ill., 1951, M.A. in Social and Behavioral Scis., 1952; m. Barbara Milkes; 1 dau., Debra Bea. Asst. to pres. Utility Plastic Packaging Co., Chgo., 1953-54; from dept. mgr. to v.p. Castle and Assos., Chgo., 1954-73; v.p. Mendheim Co., Chgo., 1973-77, sr. v.p., 1977—. Chmn. M.K. Neiman Meml. Found. of Am. Cancer Soc., 1972-75. Served as 1st lt. USAF, 1951-53. Mem. Am. Personnel and Guidance Assn., Am. Inst. Indsl. Engrs., Soc. Mfg. Engrs., Am. Mgmt. Assn., Sigma Delta Chi, Sigma Delta Pi. Club: Skokie Valley Kiwanis (program chmn.). Author articles in field. Home: 9401 Natchez Ave Morton Grove IL 60053 Office: 6055 N Lincoln Ave Chicago IL 60659

NEIMARK, PHILIP JOHN, editor, fin. cons.; b. Chgo., Sept. 13, 1939; s. Mortimer William and Hortense Adrienne (Peters) N.; student U. Chgo., 1956-58, Northwestern U., 1958-59; D. Bus. Mgmt. (hon.), Ricker Coll., Houlton, Maine, 1976; children—Tanya Lee, Joshua Daniel. Mem. Chgo. Mercantile Exchange, 1968-74; owner Josephson Neimark Trading Co., Chgo., 1972-73; partner Rosenthal & Co., Chgo., 1973-77; owner, prin. Philip J. Neimark Investments, Miami, Fla., 1977-79, Chgo., 1979—; editor, pub. Philip J. Neimark Viewpoint, N.Y.C., 1976—; fin. editor Money Maker mag., 1979—; mem. Internat. Monetary Market, 1971-74, N.Y. Mercantile Exchange, 1973-74, Chgo. Bd. of Options Exchange, 1973-75. Mem. Fla. Exec. Planning Assn., South Fla. Fin. Planners Assn. Author: How to Be Lucky, 1975; contbg. editor Consumers Digest mag., 1977—. Office: 5705 N Lincoln Ave Chicago IL 60659

NEINFELDT, GERALD OTTO, ednl. adminstr.; b. Janesville, Wis., Dec. 1, 1937; s. Otto E. and Freda C. (Gackstaetter) N.; B.E., U. Wis., Whitewater, 1959; M.S. in Bus. Edn., U. Wis., Madison, 1967; m. Judith A. Kehl, Nov. 8, 1958; children—Laurie, Timothy, Jennifer. Instr. bus. edn. Pittsville (Wis.) Pub. Schs., 1959-60, Wisconsin Rapids (Wis.) Vocat. Sch., 1959-60; instr. bus. edn. Elkhorn (Wis.) Sch. Dist., 1960-67, bus. mgr., 1967—; adult evening supr. Gateway Tech. Inst., Elkhorn, Wis., 1979-81. Registered sch. bus. adminstr.; cert. tchr., sch. bus. ofcl., Wis. Mem. Am. Assn. Sch. Adminstrs., Assn. Sch. Bus. Ofcls., Am. Mgmt. Assn., Wis. Assn. Sch. Bus. Ofcls., Delta Kappa, Phi Pi Epsilon. Lutheran. Home: 519 N Edgewood Ave Elkhorn WI 53121 Office: Adminstrv Service Center 1887 Bldg Elkhorn WI 53121

NELLESSEN, ALFRED HENRY, cons. chem. engr.; b. St. Paul, June 13, 1918; s. Peter Henry and Elizabeth Willomena (Wolking) N.; B.Chem.Engring., U. Minn., 1949; m. Ruth V. Nimlos, Aug. 13, 1955; children—James Edward, Jeanne Marie, Marita Lee. Product devel. supr. reflective products 3M Co., St. Paul, 1954-68, chem. engring. specialist recreation and athletic products, 1968-75, sr. research specialist Comml. Tape div., 1975-79, sr. product devel. specialist spl. enterprises, 1979—. Served to cpl. AUS, 1943-46. Mem. Am. Inst. Chem. Engrs., Am. Chem. Soc., Fedn. Socs. for Paint Tech. Club: K.C. Patentee on reflection and absorption of light and energy. Home: 411 S Owasso Blvd Saint Paul MN 55113 Office: 3M Co 3M Center Saint Paul MN 55101

NELSEN, DAVID HALL, aerospace co. exec.; b. Aurelia, Iowa, Sept. 1, 1942; s. Andrew Skosen and Marjorie May (Hall) N.; B.S., Morningside Coll., Sioux City, Iowa, 1965; m. Carol Deanne Johnson, Aug. 4, 1973; children—Wayne, Jodi. Coop. advt. asst. Amana Refrigeration, Inc. (Iowa), 1965-68; sr. cost accountant Owens Co., Iowa City, Iowa, 1968-71; advt. asst. Barber-Colman Co., Rockford, Ill., 1971-72; energy systems contract and budget adminstr. Sundstrand Corp., Rockford, 1972—; advisor Sundstrand Jr. Achievement, 1972-75. Vol., Contact Teleministries Rockford, 1972—, facilitator trainer, 1974. Served with USAR, 1966-71. Mem. Am. Mgmt. Assn., Nat. Assn. Accountants, Sigma Tau Delta, Alpha Phi Gamma, Phi Beta Mu, Tau Kappa Epsilon. Republican. Lutheran. Club: Masons (32 degrees). Home: 707 Parkside Dr Rockford IL 61108 Office: 4747 Harrison Ave Rockford IL 61101

NELSON, AMERICA ELIZABETH, pediatrician; b. Chgo., Apr. 9, 1932; d. Lorenzo Raymond and Blanche Juanita (Crawford) Nelson; A.B. in English, U. Mich., Ann Arbor, 1952, M.S. in Zoology, 1954; postgrad. Tenn. State U., 1952-53, U. Chgo., 1955-56; M.D., Howard U., 1961; M.P.H., U. Ill., 1973. Intern, Hahnemann Med. Sch. and Hosps., Phila., 1961-62; resident pediatrics Michael Reese Hosp., Chgo., 1962-63, U. Mich., Ann Arbor, 1964; practice medicine specializing in pediatric cardiology, Detroit, 1963; with father, practice medicine specializing in pediatrics, Baldwin, Mich., 1964-71, 75—; pediatrician Tice Clinic, U. Ill., Cook County Hosp., 1965, 66; pediatrician Mile's Sq. Health Center, Chgo., 1967; pediatrician Infant Welfare Soc., Chgo., 1968; cons. pediatrician, child devel. Kalamazoo Child Guidance Clinic, 1969-70, coordinator drug abuse program, 1969-70; med. dir. Chgo. Residential Manpower Center, 1971-72; pediatrician, child devel. Dyslexia Meml. Inst., Chgo., 1972—; founder, project dir., med. dir. Deerwood Developmental Center, Inc., Cherry Valley Twp., Lake County, Mich.; lectr. U. Ill. at Chgo. Circle, 1972-73; clin. instr. U. Ill.-Presbyn.-St. Luke's Hosp.; asst. prof. Mental Retardation Inst., N.Y. Med. Coll., 1974; cons. in field. Mem. AAAS, Pi Lambda Theta. Contbr. articles to profl. jours. Home: PO Box 768 Baldwin MI 49304

NELSON, BONNIE EILEEN, sch. adminstr.; b. De Kalb, Ill., Sept. 29, 1946; d. Gunnard T. and Violet L. (Hall) Johnson; A.B., (Ill. State scholar), Augustana Coll., 1968; M.S. in Edn., Western Ill. U., 1977; postgrad., Blackhawk Coll., 1970, U. Ill., 1972; extension courses Nat. Coll. Edn., 1969, 70-71; m. Richard L. Nelson, Aug. 3, 1968; 1 dau., Signe. Tchr. elem. schs., 1968-75; Title I reading tchr. and coordinator Apollo Elementary Sch., Carbon Cliff, Ill., 1975—, prin., 1977—. Mem. NEA, Ill. Edn. Assn., Ill. Prins. Assn., Ill. Women Adminstrs., Ill. Assn. Supervision and Curriculum Devel., Nat. Assn. Supervision and Curriculum Devel., Phi Kappa Phi, Nat. Button Soc., Ill. Button Soc., Button Buffs. Home: 2905 27th Ave Rock Island IL 61201 Office: Apollo Elementary Sch Box 10A Carbon Cliff IL 61239

NELSON, C. HJALMAR, retired newspaper editor; b. nr. Escanaba, Mich., Apr. 28, 1905; s. Edward and Esther (Swanson) N.; student U. Wis., 1926-29; m. Isadora Haight, July 24, 1937. Reporter, Escanaba Daily Press, 1923-26, Wis. State Jour., 1928-29, Rockford (Ill.) Republic, 1929-30; reporter Rockford Morning Star, 1930-44, city editor, 1944-51, mng. editor, 1951-58, asso. editor, 1958-69; asso. editor Rockford Register-Republic, 1961-69; editor Rockford Morning Star and Register-Republic, 1969-70; lectr. politics Rock Valley Coll., 1971-72. Vice pres. bd. trustees Rockford Pub. Library, 1977-81; mem. bd. trustees No. Ill. Library System, 1977—. Recipient Freedoms Found. George Washington medals, 1964, 65. Mem. Am. Hort. Soc., Garden Writers Assn. Am., Rockford C. of C., Am. Soc. Newspaper Editors, Men's Garden Clubs Am. (nat. pres. 1973), Sigma Delta Chi, Theta Chi. Mason (Shriner). Author: Sinnissippi Saga, A History of Rockford and Winnebago County, Illinois, 1968; We, the People. . ., 1975; Rockford College: A Retrospective Look, 1980. Editor: The Gardener, 1960-72. Home: 806 Overlook Rd Rockford IL 61107. *During my years as a newspaper editor, whenever anger overwhelmed me, when temptation became too enticing, when decisions appeared impossibly difficult—my escape valve was to go home, put on my oldest clothes, and dig in the garden, seeking closeness to nature.*

NELSON, CHARLES RICHARD, mental health adminstr.; b. Kansas City, Mo., June 6, 1943; s. Roy and Lynne (Burkhart) N.; Certificate of Grad. with honors, Moody Bible Inst., 1964; B.A., No. Ill. U., 1967, M.A. in Public Affairs, Mental Health Adminstrn., 1974; m. Nancy Marie Johnson, Oct. 2, 1971. Vocational rehab. counselor Elgin (Ill.) State Hosp., 1967-69; asst. subregion dir. Elgin Mental Health Center, 1969-74, dir. acute treatment services, 1974-78, dir. adult treatment services, 1979—; prof. supervision and adminstr. Ill. Sch. Profl. Psychology, Chgo., 1978. Bd. dirs., pres. Tyler Bluff Homeowners Assn., Elgin, 1974-76, treas., 1979-81. Mem. Am. Soc for Public Adminstrn., Assn. Mental Health Adminstrs., Ill. Soc. Mental Health and Law, Delta Epsilon Chi, Psi Chi. Home: 1145 Florimond Elgin IL 60120 Office: 750 S State St Elgin IL 60120

NELSON, DALE ALLEN, architect; b. Kansas City, Mo., Sept. 14, 1926; s. Robert Wayne and Ester (Koch) N.; Asso. Sci., Kansas City Jr. Coll., 1947; B.S., U. Kans., 1950; m. Lorraine E. Hennigin, Feb. 28, 1952; 1 dau., Mary Elizabeth. Chief draftsman Tanner-Mitchell, Inc., Sunflower, Kans., 1950-56; project architect, mgr. drafting room E.W. Tanner & Asso., Kansas City, Mo., 1956-60; in-house architect Bennett Constrn. Co., Inc., Kansas City, 1956-60, Vick-Lintecum Gen. Contractors, Inc., North Kansas City, Mo., 1968; staff architect Herbert E. Duncan Architect, Inc., Kansas City, 1969-71; staff architect Marshall & Brown, Inc., Kansas City, 1972; mgr. engring. and constrn. dept., corporate architect Western Auto Supply Co., Kansas City, 1972-79; archtl. dept. mgr. spl. project div. Burns and McDonnell, engrs., architects, planners, Kansas City, Mo., 1980—. Served with AUS, 1945-46. Mem. AIA (corp. mem., del. Heart of Am. Architects and Engrs. Legis. Council 1980, chmn. tours com. 1974—), Constrn. Specifications Inst. (2d v.p. 1980, pres.-elect 1981), Mo. Council Architects, Midwest Concrete Industry Bd. (co-founder 1958, pres. 1969, chmn. edn. com. 1980-81, Constrn. Industry Affairs Council (co-founder 1970, dir. 1970-72), Greater Kansas City C. of C., Am. Arbitration Assn. (regional comml. panel 1977), U. Kans. Alumni Assn. Mem. Christian Ch. Mason. Clubs: Woodside Racquet, Jacomo Sailing, Perry Yacht. Home: 5109 Cambridge St Kansas City MO 64129 Office: Burns & McDonnell PO Box 173 Kansas City MO 64141

NELSON, DAVID ALBERT, electric utility co. exec.; b. Kingston, Pa., May 6, 1940; s. Albert Edward and Irene May (Brozka) N.; B.S., U.S. Naval Acad., 1963; M.S. in Bus., San Diego State U., 1971; m. Sandra Sue Disse, Dec. 22, 1965; children—Geoffrey, Kristen, Scott. Mgr. market research Gen. Atomic, San Diego, 1971-75; mgr. market planning TRW Controls, Houston, 1976-77; economist Gulf Oil, Houston, 1977-78; v.p. Toledo (Ohio) Edison, 1978—; lectr. mktg. San Diego State U., 1970-75. Bd. dirs. Jr. Achievement, Toledo, 1978—; dist. commr. Boy Scouts Am., 1980—. Served with U.S. Navy, 1963-69. Decorated Viet Nam Service medal. Mem. Am. Mktg. Assn., Am. Mgmt. Assn., U.S. Naval Acad. Alumni Assn. Home: 4809 Carskaddon St Toledo OH 43615 Office: 300 Madison Ave Toledo OH 43652

NELSON, DAVID LEONARD, mfg. co. exec.; b. Omaha, May 8, 1930; s. Leonard A. and Cecelia (Steinert) N.; B.S. in Gen. Engring., Iowa State U., Ames, 1952; m. Jacqueline J. Zerbe, Dec. 26, 1952; 1 dau., Nancy Jo. With Ingersoll Rand, Chgo., 1954-56; with AccuRay Corp., Columbus, Ohio, 1956—, exec. v.p., gen. mgr., 1967, pres., 1967—, chief exec. officer, 1970—, dir., 1967—; dir. Herman Miller, Inc., Beverage Mgmt., Inc., Cardinal Fund, Cardinal Govt. Securities Trust. Served to capt. USMCR, 1952-54. Mem. Newcomen Soc., Polish U.S. Econ. Council, Instrument Soc. Am., Tau Beta Pi, Phi Kappa Phi, Phi Eta Sigma, Delta Upsilon. Patentee in field. Office: 650 Ackerman Rd PO Box 02248 Columbus OH 43202

NELSON, DONALD A., profl. basketball coach; b. Muskegon, Mich., May 15, 1940; student U. Iowa. Player profl. basketball team, Chgo., 1962-63, Los Angeles Lakers, 1963-65; with Boston Celtics, 1965-76; head coach Milw. Bucks, 1976—. Address: Milw Bucks 901 N 4th St Milwaukee WI 53203*

NELSON, DONALD OLIVER, hosp. adminstr.; b. Horton, Kans., Mar. 1, 1930; s. Oliver James and Edna Mae Nelson; B.A., Washburn U., 1956; M.S. in Indsl. Psychology, Kans. State U., 1957; m. Sevie Esther Johnson, Nov. 27, 1963; children—Donna Marie, James Eric. Prodn. welder and machinist Nelson Machine Works, Whiting, Kans., 1946-51; prodn. schedule planner Boeing Airplane Co., Wichita, Kans., 1957; personnel mgr. W.Va. Pulp & Paper Co., Kansas City, Kans., 1958-62; asst. dir. Research Med. Center, Kansas City, Mo., 1962-73; asso. dir. Providence-St.Margaret Health Center, Kansas City, Kans., 1974—; pres. Hosp. Linen Services, Inc., 1978-80; mem. faculty continuing edn. U. Mo., Columbia and Kansas City, 1966-72; mgmt. cons., 1966-77. First aid instr. ARC, 1960-62; chmn. United Way, Kansas City, Kans., 1962; bd. dirs. Wyandotte County (Kans.) Mental Health Assn., 1961-62. Fellow Am. Coll. Hosp. Adminstrs.; mem. Am. Hosp. Assn., Kans. Hosp. Assn., Am. Hosp. Assn. Planning Soc., Am. Mgmt. Assn., Kansas City Area Hosp. Assn., Phi Kappa Phi. Mem. United Chs. of Christ. Club: Homestead Country. Contbr. articles on hosp. adminstrn. to profl. publs. Home: 3110 Tomahawk Rd Mission Hills KS 66208 Office: Providence St Margaret Health Center 8929 Parallel Pkwy Kansas City KS 66112

NELSON, GERALDINE BERNICE, community relations exec.; b. Mpls., Oct. 11, 1932; d. Roy and Bernice Irene (Dubay) Simonson; student Miami U., Piqua, Ohio, 1964, Wright State U., 1972; children—Valerie, Christopher, Leslie, LuAnn, Martina, Abby Maria. Editor, Arcanum (Ohio) Times, 1967-69; mem. editorial staff Greenville (Ohio) Daily Advocate, 1970-71; dir. community relations Tri County Bd. Mental Health, Troy, Ohio, 1971—. Bd. dirs. Public TV Communications Center, Troy, 1979-80; mem. Arcanum Village Council, 1965-69; Lay reader Episcopal Ch., Greenville, Ohio. Recipient Nat. Bell award Nat. Assn. Mental Health, 1974. Mem. Public Relations Soc. Am., Miami County Mental Health Assn., Brukner Nature Center Vols., Darke County Oratorio Soc. Office: 3130 N Dixie Hwy Troy OH 45373

NELSON, GORDON LEON, educator; b. Chippewa County, Minn., Dec. 28, 1919; s. John Anton and Hilda (Weberg) N.; B.Agrl. Engring., U. Minn., 1942; certificate naval engring. design, U.S. Naval Acad. Postgrad. Sch., 1945; M.Sc., Okla. State U., 1951; Ph.D., Iowa State U., 1957; m. Florence Jeanne Wise, June 7, 1942; children—Gordon Leon, Carol (Mrs. James Earl), Linda (Mrs. Arthur Ochsner), Janet (dec.), David, Barbara. Sr. agrl. engr. Portland Cement Assn., Chgo., 1946-47; asso. prof. to prof. agrl. engring. Okla. State U., 1947-69; prof., chmn. dept. agrl. engring. Ohio State U., also Ohio Agrl. Research and Devel. Center, 1969—; dir. Ohio State U.-Ford Found. project Coll. Agrl. Engring., Punjab (India) Agr. Univ., 1969-72; cons. in field. Mem. 7 engring. edn. and accreditation ad hoc visitation teams to evaluate agrl. engring. curricula Engrs. Council Profl. Devel. Chmn. bd. dirs. Stillwater (Okla.) Municipal Hosp., 1956-60; mem. grad. council Ohio State U., 1970-74; bd. dirs. Council for Agrl. Sci. and Tech., 1975-79. Served to comdr. USNR, 1942-68. NSF Sr. Postdoctoral fellow U. Calif., Berkeley and Davis, 1964, 65-66. Fellow Am. Soc. Agrl. Engrs. (dir. awards, bd. dirs. 1979-81, dir. edn. and research 1979; Metal Bldg. Mfg. award 1960, 7 outstanding Paper awards); mem. Am. Soc. Engring. Edn., Sigma Xi, Tau Beta Pi, Sigma Tau, Alpha Epsilon, Phi Kappa Phi, Phi Tau Sigma, Gamma Sigma Delta. Republican. Baptist (chmn. deacons 1971). Contbr. numerous articles to profl. jours. Office: 2073 Neil Ave Columbus OH 43210

NELSON, GWENDEL ADAIR, ednl. adminstr.; b. Wewoka, Okla., Aug. 29, 1925; s. Walter Allison and Mary N.; B.S., Pittsburg (Kans.) State U., 1951, M.S., 1953; Ed.D., Kans. U., Lawrence, 1959; m. Luella Smith, May 17, 1946; children—Marsha Lynn, Michael Adair. Tchr., prin. Greenwood County (Kans.) Public Schs., 1947-50; dir. guidance Columbus (Kans.) Public Schs., 1950-54; dir. curriculum Lawrence Public Schs., 1954-56; cons. Sci. Research Assos., Chgo., 1956-59; asst. supt. Wichita (Kans.) Public Schs., 1959-66; exec. dir. S. Central Regional Lab., Little Rock, 1966-68; pres. Cowley County Community Coll., Arkansas City, Kans., 1968—; cons. U.S. Office of Edn., numerous sch. dists. Pres., Human Relations Commn., Arkansas City, 1969-71, United Way, Arkansas City, 1971-72. Served with USNR, 1943-46. Decorated Bronze Star (2); recipient Ark. Traveler award, 1968; Disting. Alumnus award Pittsburg State U., 1977; Harry Long award Kans. Salvation Army, 1977. Mem. Am. Personnel and Guidance Assn., Assn. Counselor Edn. and Supervision, Am. Assn. Community and Jr. Colls., Kans. Assn. Community Colls. (dir. 1972-74), Kans. Council of Pres.'s (pres. 1972-75), Arkansas City C. of C. (dir. 1969-81), Phi Delta Kappa, Kappa Delta Pi. Republican. Clubs: Rotary (hon.), Kiwanis, Am. Legion, VFW, Eagles. Contbr. numerous articles, spl. features, weekly edn. columns to newspapers, numerous scholarly articles to profl. publs.; editor, contbr. Research Bull., jour. Wichita Public Schs., 1959-66. Home: 211 N 3d St Arkansas City KS 67005 Office: Cowley County Community Coll 125 S 2d St Arkansas City KS 67005

NELSON, JANIE MAE, psychologist; b. Clarks, La., Nov. 23, 1935; d. Ermon and Helen (Stewart) N.; B.Ed., Chgo. Tchrs. Coll., 1956; M.A., Roosevelt U., 1968, 77; Ph.D., Kent State U., 1981. Tchr. elementary sch., psychologist Chgo. Public Schs., 1956—. Pres., v.p. Holy Angel's Blessed Sacrament Soc., 1975-77; bd. dirs. Nat. Alliance Black Feminists, 1979-81. Mem. Operation PUSH, Am. Psychol. Assn., Assn. Black Psychologists, Woman's Orgn. for Minority Affairs and Needs (co-founder, dir.), NOW, Phi Delta Kappa. Home: 7659 S Normal Blvd Chicago IL 60620 Office: Nat Alliance Black Feminists 202 S State St Chicago IL 60604

NELSON, JOHN RICHARD, acct.; b. Barberton, Ohio, Dec. 5, 1946; s. Floyd Kenneth and Hilda Marguerite (Buccigrossi) N.; B.S. in Acctg., U. Akron, 1974; m. Janice Katherine Kuntzleman, Sept. 13, 1969; children—Tennille Dawn, Erica Marie. Systems operator PPG Industries, Barberton, 1970; supr. fin. systems and records Gen. Tire & Rubber Co., Akron, Ohio, 1971-72; sr. EDP auditor B.F. Goodrich Co., Akron, 1973-75, sr. internal auditor, 1976-78, chem. plant controller, 1978, mgr. chem. comml. acctg., Independence, Ohio, 1978-79, dir. auditing, Akron, 1979-80, dir. EPG acctg. and reporting, 1980—; internal auditor BancSystems Assn., Cleve., 1975-76; lectr., instr. Inst. of Internal Auditors; guest speaker local univs. Pres. Scenic Recreation Assn. Jackson Twp., 1975. Served with Security Agy., U.S. Army, 1965-68. Mem. Nat. Assn. Accts., Inst. Internal Auditors (gov., past v.p.), Akron Bd. Realtors, Postal Commemorative Soc. Republican. Lutheran. Home: 463 Forest Ln Wadsworth OH 44281 Office: B F Goodrich Co 25-B D0714 Akron OH 44318

NELSON, JOHN WILTON, symphony condr.; b. San Jose, Costa Rica, Dec. 6, 1941; came to U.S., 1953; s. Wilton Mons and Thelma (Agnew) N.; B.Mus., Wheaton Coll., 1963; M.Mus. (teaching fellow), Julliard Sch., 1965, postgrad. diploma (teaching fellow), 1967; m. Anita Christine Johnson, Sept. 4, 1964; children—Kirsten, Kari. Music dir. Pro Arte Chorale, Ridgewood, N.J., 1965-74; condr. N.Y. Mozart Festival, 1967, Julliard Opera Theatre, N.Y.C., 1968; music dir. Greenwich Philharm. Orch., N.Y.C., 1966-74; condr. N.Y.C. Opera, 1973-75, Santa Fe Opera, 1973, Geneva (Switzerland) Grand Theatre, 1974, Met. Opera, N.Y.C., 1974—; condr., music dir. Indpls. Symphony Orch., 1977—; music adv. Nashville (Tenn.) Symphony Orch., Cin. Orch., London Royal Philharm., Swiss Romade and others; conducting faculty Julliard Sch., N.Y.C., 1968-72; dir. Aspen Choral Inst., 1968-73. Recipient Irving Berlin Conducting award, 1967. Office: care Indianapolis Symphony Orchestra 4600 Sunset Ave Indianapolis IN 46208

NELSON, KENNETH LOWELL, acct.; b. Fargo, N.D., Nov. 12, 1949; s. E. O. and Jewell A. N.; B.A. in Acctg., Moorhead State Coll., 1971. Cost acct. Northwest Airlines, Inc., St. Paul, 1973-78; v.p. customer service SES, Inc., St. Paul, 1978-80; dir. fin. Escanaba & Lake Superior R.R. Co., Wells, Mich., 1980—, Rail Investments, Wells, 1980—; pres. K.L. Nelson and Assos., Inc., Wells. Served with U.S. Army, 1971-73. C.P.A. Home: 903 Saint Clair Saint Paul MN 55105 Office: Wells MI 49894

NELSON, LEROY ELBURN, veterinarian; b. Arlington, Wash., June 5, 1926; s. Carl S. and Francis Viola (Eidem) N.; D.V.M., Iowa State U. 1949; student U. Minn., 1944-45; m. Julia Jeanne McAllister, Jan. 1, 1950; children—Julia, Paul, Nancy. Practice veterinary medicine, Bricelyn, Minn., 1949-71; veterinary med. officer U.S. Dept. Agr., Albert Lea, Minn., 1971—. Mem. Sch. Bd., Bricelyn, 1965-72, Volunteer Fire Dept. 1951-77; treas. Volunteer Relief Assn., 1967-69; pres. Band Parents Assn., 1972. Mem. AVMA, Minn., South Central (pres. 1957), So. Minn. (pres. 1970) veterinary med. assns., Am. Assn. Food Hygiene Veterinarians, No. Iowa Veterinary Med. Assn., Nat. Assn. Fed. Veterinarians (Minn. rep. 1973-77). Trustee Bricelyn Luth. Ch., 1974-77. Home: Box 365 Bricelyn MN 56014 Office: Bricelyn MN 56014

NELSON, MERLIN DEAN WILLIAM, accountant; b. Norfolk, Nebr., Nov. 22, 1943; s. Oscar Reuben and Esther L. (Schmidt) N.; ed. public schs.; m. Sandra Lee Davalos, Feb. 27, 1965; children—Renee Marie, Ramon Reuben. Sales clk. Katz Drug Co., Topeka, 1964-65; with Frito Lay Inc., Topeka, 1965-66, Pacific Gamble Robinson, Topeka, 1966-68; cost accountant Ohse Meat Products, Inc., Topeka, 1968—, office mgr., acctg. supr., 1980—. Served with U.S. Army, 1961-64. Roman Catholic. Home: 427 Emmett St Topeka KS 66616 Office: PO Box 1658 3215 E 6th St Topeka KS 66601

NELSON, PATRICIA REVER, educator; b. Rockford, Ill., Nov. 7, 1932; d. George F. and Ruth E. (Whitlock) Rever; B.S. in Edn., Edgewood Coll., 1966; m. Harry W. Nelson. Bookkeeper, Amerock Hardware Co., Rockford, 1952, Lillian's, Inc., Rockford, 1967-68; elem. tchr. in Milw., Chgo., Northfield, Ill., Mpls., 1953-67; reading specialist Fairview Sch. Dist. 300, Carpentersville, Ill., 1968—. Mem. Assn. Children with Learning Disabilities, Fox Valley Assn. Children with Learning Disabilities, Internat. Reading Assn., Assn. for Supervision and Curriculum Devel. Certified in learning disabilities, Ill.; specialist in elementary reading. Home: 415 S 2d St West Dundee IL 60118 Office: Fairway and Wren Rds Carpentersville IL 60110

NELSON, PAUL AUGUSTINE, educator; b. Milw., Aug. 31, 1945; s. Alfred C. and Mary (Reinhardt) N.; B.S., U. Wis., Milw., 1966; M.S., U. Wis., Madison, 1967, 72, Ph.D., 1974. Instr., Mich. Technol. U., Houghton, 1972-74, asst. prof. mgmt. sci., 1974-78, asso. prof., 1978—, dir. M.S. in Bus. Adminstrn. program, 1975—, pres. faculty senate, 1976-79; cons. Dept. Energy. Bd. dirs. Copper County United Way, Houghton, 1975—, drive chmn., 1980. Served to lt. U.S. Army, 1967-69. Mem. Am. Econ. Assn., Ops. Research Soc. Am., Sigma Xi, Phi Kappa Phi. Author: Geothermal Energy in the Western United States: Innovation Versus Monopoly, 1978; contbr. articles in field to tech. publs. Home: 1617 Anthony St Hancock MI 49930 Office: School of Business Michigan Technological University Houghton MI 49931

NELSON, ROBERT EDDINGER, mgmt. and devel. cons. co. exec.; b. Mentone, Ind., Mar. 2, 1928; s. Arthur Irven and Tural Cecile (Eddinger) N.; B.A., Northwestern U., 1949; L.H.D., Iowa Wesleyan Coll., 1969; m. Carol J., Nov. 24, 1951; children—Janet K. Nelson Callighan, Eric P. Asst. dir. alumni relations Northwestern U., Evanston, Ill., 1950-51, 54-55; v.p. and dir. pub. relations Iowa Wesleyan Coll., Mt. Pleasant, 1955-58; vice chancellor for devel. U. of Kansas City, 1959-61; v.p. instl. devel. Ill. Inst. of Tech., Chgo., 1961-68; pres. Robert Johnston Corp., Oak Brook, Ill., 1968-69, Robert E. Nelson Assos., Inc., Elmhurst, Ill., 1969—; dir. Chautauqua Workshop in Fund Raising and Instl. Relations, 1970-74, Snelling & Snelling, Inc., 1974-79; nat. conf. chmn. and program dir. Am. Coll. Pub. Relations Assn., 1961; trustee, Iowa Wesleyan Coll., 1962-68; faculty mem. Ind. U. Workshops on Coll. and Univ. Devel., 1963-65, Lorretto Heights Summer Inst. for Fund Raising and Pub. Relations, 1964-68; mem. Pub. Review Panel for Grants Programs, Lilly Endowment, Inc., 1975. Served with U.S. Army, 1951-54. Mem. Council on Fin. Aid to Edn. (bd. dirs. 1957-63), Public Relations Soc. Am., Nat. Soc. Fund Raisers, Nat. Small Bus. Assn., Chgo. Soc. Fund Raising Execs., Blue Key, Delta Tau Delta. Methodist. Clubs: Execs., Econ., Union League (Chgo.); Monroe; Masons. Author chpt. in Handbook of Coll. and Univ. Adminstrn., 1970. Home: 5 Oak Brook Club Dr N101 Oak Brook IL 60521 Office: 180 W Park Suite 10 Elmhurst IL 60126

NELSON, ROBERT HENSHAW, mfg. co. exec.; b. Detroit, Jan. 16, 1934; s. Harry Monroe and Elizabeth James (Jones) N.; B.S., Mich. State U., 1957; M.S., Kans. State U., 1960; m. Catherine Casteel Saunders, Jan. 24, 1959; 1 son, Robert Henshaw. Adminstrv. asst. to pres. Shatterproof Glass Corp., Detroit, 1960-62; sr. mktg. analyst Internat. Mineral & Chem. Corp., Skokie, Ill., 1962-64; mktg. research mgr. Cryovac div. W.R. Grace, Duncan, S.C., 1964-66; pres. Estan Mfg. Co., Troy, Mich., 1966-71; pres., owner R.A. Young Ind., Inc., Fraser, Mich., 1973—, Master Industries, Sterling Heights, Mich., 1975—; tchr. bus. orgn. Furman U., 1963-64; head bus. seminar Lawrence Inst. Tech., 1968. Served in U.S. Army, 1957-59. Mem. Engring. Soc. Detroit, Birmingham Power Squadron. Republican. Clubs: Birmingham Athletic, Birmingham Village Players; Grosse Pointe Yacht. Home: 1438 Kensington Rd Bloomfield Hills MI 48013 Office: 34190 Doreka St Fraser MI 48026

NELSON, ROJEAN EVELYN, civic worker; b. Wilcox, Nebr., Oct. 20, 1927; d. August and Anna Angelina (Adam) Jesse; student Kearney (Nebr.) State Tchrs. Coll., 1946; m. Ward Stanley Nelson, Aug. 13, 1950; children—Kevin Ward, Kirk August. Public sch. tchr., 1946-54; substitute tchr., 1960-76; sec.-bookkeeper Wilcox Corp., 1972-76; sec. Jim Reiss Ins. Agy., Wilcox, 1977—. Sec. Holdrege (Nebr.) Women's Bowling Assn., 1966—; bd. dirs. Nebr. Women's Bowling Assn., 1970-77, sgt.-at-arms, 1977—; pres. Phelps County Democratic Women, 1975-79; sec. Phelps County Dem. Central Com., 1972-76; mem. Nebr. Dem. Central Com., 1978—; Sunday sch. tchr. Fridhem Lutheran Ch., Funk, Nebr., 1962—, sec. ch. council, 1976-79; post pres. Am. Legion Aux., 1979—. Home: Route 1 Box 149 Wilcox NE 69882 Office: Jim Reiss Agy Wilcox NE 68982

NELSON, SANDRA JEAN, educator; b. Hillsboro, N.D., Apr. 18, 1950; d. Clifford A. and Inez M. (Wolff) Christenson; B.S. magna cum laude, Mayville State Coll., 1971; m. Lynn Cameron Nelson, Nov. 26, 1971; children—Nicole Heather, Eric Ryan. Substitute tchr./driver edn. instr. Hope (N.D.) Public Sch., 1972-73; sec. Mayville (N.D.) State Coll., 1973-74; tchr. Jamestown (N.D.) Public Schs., 1974—. Mem. Nat. Bus. Edn. Assn., Am. Vocat. Assn., N.D. Vocat. Assn., N.D. Office Edn. Assn., Profl. Edn. Assn., Delta Kappa Gamma, Delta Pi Epsilon. Roman Catholic. Home: 1108 10th Ave SE Jamestown ND 58401 Office: Jamestown Sr High Sch 3d Ave SE Jamestown ND 58401

NELSON, THOMAS ROY, writer; b. Deadwood, S.D., July 30, 1957; s. John Edward and Olga Marie (Girardi) N.; B.S. in Journalism, S.D. State U., 1979; m. Melodee Sharlet Stell, Aug. 18, 1978. Asst. football coach Yankton (S.D.) Coll., 1980, dir. public affairs, 1979-81; producer Miss Yankton Pageant, 1979—; producer, dir., publicity dir. local pageants of Miss America Pageant Orgn., 1977—; copy writer Dakota Advt., Inc., Yankton, 1980—. Cert. football and basketball ofcl., S.D. Mem. Council for Advancement and Support Edn., Coll. Sports Info. Dirs. Am., Nat. Assn. Intercollegiate Athletics, Alpha Psi Omega. Democrat. Roman Catholic. Clubs: Yankton Morning Optimists, Yankton Coll. Booster, Yankton Elks. Home: 1800 John St Yankton SD 57078 Office: Gurney Seed and Nursery 2d and Capitol Yankton SD 57079

NELSON, TOM, state senator; B.S., Mankato State Coll.; m. Margaret Nelson; children—Jeff, Connie, Beth. Tchr. social studies, Austin, Minn.; mem. Minn. Senate, 1976—. Former city councilman, Austin; mem. Minn. State Health Coordinating Council. Mem. Democratic-Farmer-Labor party. Office: 23K State Capitol St Paul MN 55155*

NELSON, WARREN BRYANT, commodity brokerage co. exec.; b. Manhattan, Kans., Sept. 29, 1922; s. Oscar William and Eda Caroline (Hokanson) N.; B.S. cum laude in Agrl. Econs., Kans. State U., 1942, postgrad., 1950; postgrad. Am. U., 1947; m. Betty Lou Wiley, Dec. 24, 1944; children—Barbara Ann, David William, Marcia Lynn, Robert Warren. Statistician agrl. div. Bur. Census, U.S. Dept. Commerce, Washington, 1945-48, Statis. Reporting Service, U.S. Dept. Agr., Topeka, 1948-50; price analyst Longstreet Abbott & Co., St. Louis, 1951-59, partner, 1959-69; sec. Clayton Brokerage Co., St. Louis, 1959-69, exec. v.p., 1969-72, pres., 1972-77, vice chmn. bd., 1977—. Served to lt. USAAF, 1942-45. Decorated D.F.C. with 2 oak leaf clusters, Air medal with 3 oak leaf clusters. Mem. Chgo. Bd. Trade, Chgo. Merc. Exchange, Internat. Monetary Market, N.Y. Cotton Exchange, Winnipeg Grain Exchange. Republican. Lutheran. Clubs: Union League (Chgo.); St. Louis. Home: 839 Elm Tree Ln Kirkwood MO 63122 Office: 7701 Forsyth Blvd Suite 300 Clayton MO 63105

NELSON, WILLIAM ANDREW, farmer; b. Williams, Iowa, Jan. 1, 1914; s. William Henry and Olive Rebecca (Blair) N.; student public schs., Dodge Center, Minn.; m. Ona Ruth Kellar, Sept. 28, 1936; children—William D., Donna M., Daryl G. Route salesman Kraft Foods Co., 1936-46, br. mgr., 1946-51, product mgr., 1951-61, mktg. mgr., 1961-67, v.p. sales and ops., 1967-73; pres. Huntsinger Farms, Inc., Eau Claire, Wis., 1973—, aldo dir.; pres. Silver Spring Gardens, Eau Claire, 1974—; dir. Am. Nat. Bank. Mem. Chippewa Valley council Boy Scouts Am. Mem. Nat. Food Distbrs. Assn. (mfrs. council). Republican. Methodist. Clubs: Masons, Shriners, Elks. Office: Huntsinger Farms Inc PO Box 360 Eau Claire WI 54701

NEMEC, JANET LEE, educator; b. St. Louis, July 5, 1948; d. Leo Charles and Norma Lee (Gehrs) Warren; A.B., Harris Tchrs. Coll., 1970; M.A., U. Mo., St. Louis, 1974; Ph.D., St. Louis U., 1978; m. Donald John Nemec, Mar. 6, 1971; children—Donald Lee, John Charles. Tchr., St. Louis Public Sch. Dist., 197—73; tchr. Valley Park (Mo.) Sch. Dist., 1973-78; asso. prof. Maryville Coll., 1979-80; asst. prof., tchr. corps sch. based tchr. educator St. Louis U., 1978—; cons. classroom discipline, individualized instrn. Mem. Assn. for Supervision and Curriculum Devel., Council for Exceptional Children, Nat. Soc. Study Edn., Phi Delta Kappa (v.p. 1981-82). Roman Catholic. Home: 1936 Lanchester Ct Chesterfield MO 63017 Office: Saint Louis U 221 S Grand St Saint Louis MO 63103

NEMEC, STANLEY S., physician; b. Yugoslavia, June 16, 1911; s. Adolf and Josefina (Koblizek) N.; M.D., St. Louis U., 1936; m. Katherine M. Vidakovich Barr, June 15, 1940; children—Edward S., Mary K., Charles S., Robert S., Louise K., Dorothy K., Barbara K. Gen. med. practice, 1936-43; radiologist, St. Louis City Hosp., 1943-46; practice medicine specializing in radiology, 1946—; cons. radiologist Wabash R.R. Woodland Hosp., Moberly, Mo.; radiologist St. Charles Clinic, Marian Hosp.; asst. in radiology St. Louis U. Sch. Medicine. Diplomate Am. Bd. Radiology, Nat. Bd. Med. Examiners, Fellow Am. Coll. Radiology; mem. Radiology Soc. N.A., A.M.A., So. Med. Assn., St. Louis Med. Soc., St. Louis Soc. Neurology and Psychiatry. Author: History of the Croatian Settlement in St. Louis, 1931; Yugoslav Sokol Almanac, 1933. Editor: Sokol Magazine, 1931-34, The Koch Messenger, 1939. Contbr. articles to profl. jours. Home: 2870 S Lindbergh Blvd Huntleigh Village St Louis County MO 63131 Office: Suite 1 6500 Chippewa St St Louis MO 63109

NEPOTE, HAZEL ELLEN, bank exec.; b. Robinson, Ill., Oct. 5, 1921; d. Henry Elmer and Effie Mae (Matheny) York; B.A. in Edn., U. Ill., 1942; m. Peter A. Nepote, Dec. 26, 1942; children—Peter Anthony, John Lynn. Sec., Keokuk C. of C. (Iowa), 1958-61; real estate officer Keokuk Savs. Bank & Trust Co., 1964—, personnel mgr., 1973—, trust officer, 1974—. Mem. Keokuk Personnel Forum, 1975—; bd. dirs. Lee County (Iowa) Mental Health Assn. Named Woman of Yr., Keokuk, 1967. Mem. Nat. Assn. Bank Women (treas. 1977, sec. 1978), Iowa Realtors Assn., Beta Sigma Phi. Republican. Roman Catholic. Club: Soroptomists. Home: 2819 Middle Rd Keokuk IA 52632 Office: 501 Main St Keokuk IA 52632

NESBIT, ROBERT CARRINGTON, historian; b. Ellensburg, Wash., July 16, 1917; s. Sidney Shaw and Verna Mildred (Carrington) N.; B.A., Central Wash. Coll., 1939; M.A., U. Wash., 1947, Ph.D., 1957; m. Marie Richert, Nov. 24, 1942. Tchr., Cashmere (Wash.) Pub. Schs., 1939-41; state archivist Wash., 1951-57; adminstrv. asst. Wash. Dept. Gen. Adminstrn., 1958-59, supr. purchasing, asst. dir., 1959-62; asso. prof., chmn. dept. history Extension div. U. Wis., Madison, 1962-68, prof., asso. chmn. dept. history, 1967—. Served with USAAF, 1941-46. Wis. History Found. grantee, 1971-72; Nat. Endowment for Humanities grantee, 1980-82. Mem. Orgn. Am. Historians. Author: He Built Seattle: A Biography of Judge Thomas Burke, 1961; Wisconsin, A History (award of merit Am. Assn. State and Local History 1975), 1973. Home: 5613 Varsity Hill Dr Madison WI 53705 Office: 3211 Humanities Bldg U Wis Madison WI 53706

NESHEIM, ROBERT OLAF, mfg. co. exec.; b. Monroe Center, Ill., Sept. 13, 1921; s. Olaf M. and Sena M. (Willms) N.; B.S. in Agr. with highest honors, U. Ill., 1943, M.S., 1950, Ph.D., 1951; postgrad. Harvard U., 1971; m. Doris Howes Calloway, 1981; children—Barbara Mowry, Sandra Rankin, Susan Yost. With Haldermann Farm Mgmt. Service, Wabash, Ind., 1946-48; swine research specialist Gen. Mills, Detroit, 1951-52; mgr. swine feed research, livestock feed research Quaker Oats Co., Barrington, Ill., 1952-64, dir. research/devel., 1967-69, v.p., 1969-77, v.p. sci. and tech., Chgo., 1977—; prof. head dept. animal sci. U. Ill., Urbana, 1964-67; mem. food and nutrition bd. Nat. Acad. Sci., 1972-78; mem. Food Safety Council, 1976—; mem. Nutrition Found., 1970—, trustee, 1978-80; mem. food update bd. Food and Drug Law Inst., 1980—, vice chmn., 1981; mem. food adv. com. Office Tech. Assessment, U.S. Congress, 1974-80; trustee bioscis. info. service Biol. Abstracts, 1978—, chmn., 1982; dir. First Nat. Bank & Trust Co. of Barrington. Bd. dirs. Buehler YMCA, Palatine, 1969—, chmn., 1974-76; mem. Barrington Fire and Police Commn., 1974-79, sec., 1976-79; exec. bd. N.W. Suburban Council Boy Scouts Am., 1973—. Served to capt. U.S. Army, 1943-46. Mem. AMA, Grocery Mfrs. of Am., Fedn. Am. Socs. Exptl. Biology (treas. 1974-76, 77-78), Nat. Nutrition Consortium, Am. Inst. Nutrition, AAAS, Nutrition Today Soc., Soc. Nutrition Edn., Inst. Food Technologists, Am. Soc. Animal Sci., Am. Public Health Assn. Clubs: Barrington Hills Country, Mchts. and Mfrs. Home: 201 E Chestnut St Apt 7D Chicago IL 60611 Office: Quaker Oats Co Merchandise Mart Plaza Chicago IL 60654

NESMITH, LESLIE WALLACE, ophthalmologist, retinal surgeon; b. Lawrence, Kans., Sept. 7, 1940; s. Dean D. and Norma Roy (Wallace) N.; B.S., U. Kans., 1962; M.D., Kans. U., 1966; m. Elizabeth Ann Duley, Nov. 23, 1968; children—Trent L. W., Brooke L.W., Seth L.W., Britt L.W., Cade L.W. Intern Kans. U. Med. Center, Kansas City, 1966-67, resident, 1969-72; retinal fellowship Mass. Eye and Ear Infirmary, Harvard U., and Retina Found., Boston, 1972-73; practice medicine specializing in ophthalmology and retinal surgery, Wichita, Kans., 1974—; asst. clin. prof. surgery U. Kans., Wichita. Served with USAF, 1967-69. Diplomate Am. Bd. Ophthalmology. Fellow ACS, Internat. Coll. Surgeons; mem. Am., Kans., Sedgwick County med. assns., Am. Acad. Ophthalmology and Otolaryngology. Contbr. articles to med. jours. Home: Rural Route 3 Box 161-C Augusta KS 67010 Office: 3333 E Central Suite 504 Wichita KS 67208

NESS, LARRY DEAN, mfg. co. exec.; b. Austin, Minn., July 27, 1947; s. LeRoy Herman and Mabel Doris (Redwing) N.; A.A., Austin State Jr. Coll., 1967; B.S. in Agr. Engring. (Univ. scholar, Beta Sigma Phi scholar), N.D. State U., 1969, M.S., 1973; m. Nancy Jean Timm, Nov. 28, 1969; children—Christopher Alan, Sara Jean. Civil, agrl. engr. U.S. Forest Service, Billings, Mont., 1969; design engr. George A. Hormel & Co., Austin, 1973-75; waste applications mgr., applications mgr. Lindsay Mfg. Co. (Nebr.), 1975-81; tech. mgr. Lindsay Internat. Sales Corp., 1981—. Mem. ch. council Trinity Luth.

Ch. Served with U.S. Army, 1969-71. NSF trainee, 1971-72. Mem. Am. Soc. Agrl. Engrs., Irrigation Assn. (past vice chmn. waste water resources com.), Water Pollution Control Assn., Phi Kappa Phi. Home: 1668 28th Ave Columbus NE 68601 Office: PO Box 605 Columbus NE 68601

NESS, ORDEAN GERHARD, educator; b. Buxton, N.D., Oct. 4, 1921; s. Ole Thomas and Gerda (Johnson) N.; B.A. with highest honors, U. N.D., 1942; M.A., U. Wis., 1947, Ph.D. (fellow), 1953. Instr., Syracuse U., 1947-49; cons., personnel policies officer Office of Sec. of Army, 1950-52; asst. prof. Pa. State U., 1953-55; asst. prof. U. Wis., Madison, 1955-59, asso. prof., 1959-61, prof. communication arts, 1961—, asso. chmn. dept. speech, 1961-70, asso. dir. articulated instrnl. media program, 1964-66, prof. theatre and drama, 1973-80, chmn. dept., 1973-75, chmn. dept. communication arts, 1975-80, prof. dept. comparative lit., 1978-80, chmn. faculty div. humanities, 1976-77, exec. com., 1974-77, 80—; mem. U. Wis. System Adv. Task Force on Telecommunications; free-lance stage, TV and radio actor-dir.; patron Madison Civic Repertory Theatre, Madison Community Access Center; acad. program cons. Served to 1st lt. U.S. Army, 1942-46, capt., 1950-52. Mem. Speech Communication Assn., Nat. Collegiate Players, Nat. Assn. Ednl. Broadcasters, Broadcasting Edn. Assn., AAUP, Am. Council for Arts, Internat. Communication Assn., Am. Film Inst., Central States Speech Assn., Wis. Hist. Soc., Wis. Acad. Scis., Letters and Arts, Am., Wis. theatre assns., Wis. Communication Assn. (named outstanding communications instr. 1981), Consortium for Arts, Wis. Council for Arts, U. Wis., U. N.D. alumni assns., Bascom Hill Soc., Nature Conservancy, Center for Study of Dem. Instns., Friends of Channel 21, Wis. Public Radio Assn., Wis. Assn. Alcohol and Drug Abuse, Phi Beta Kappa, Delta Sigma Rho, Blue Key, Phi Eta Sigma, Phi Beta (hon. patron). Author: (with A.T. Weaver) The Fundamentals and Forms of Speech, 1957, 63; An Introduction to Public Speaking, 1961. Deptl. editor Speech Tchr., 1955-63. Contbr. articles to profl. jours. Home: PO Box 5452 Madison WI 53705. *Communication is a human being's rarest gift—but a gift with strings attached. Central to all human endeavors, communication is every person's responsibility. One of my first mentors in "speech" believed that "it is no wonder that communication fails; the wonder is that we communicate at all." Out of respect for the complexities of the process, I have devoted my career to its study and practice.*

NESSE, ANTON STEPHAN, radiologist; b. Bergen, Norway, Apr. 25, 1938; s. Harold and Esther (Stephansen) N.; came to U.S., 1957, naturalized, 1962; B.S. (Med. Research fellow), U. Minn., 1961, M.D., 1963; m. Kaye R. Kellgreen, July 13, 1978; children—Brian Scott, Dawn Michelle. Intern, Hennepin County Gen. Hosp., Mpls., 1963-64; resident radiology U. Minn., Mpls., 1966-70; clin. instr. radiology U. Minn.-Mpls. VA Hosp., 1970—; radiologist Suburban Radiologic Cons. Ltd., Mpls., 1970—; staff Unity, Mercy hosps., Mpls., 1970—. Served as flight surgeon USAF, 1964-66. Mem. AMA, Alpha Omega Alpha, Phi Rho Sigma, Theta Chi. Home: 7541 Van Buren St NE Fridley MN 55432 Office: 6600 France Ave S Minneapolis MN 55435

NESTERENKO, DIMITRI A., structural engr.; b. Kiev, Ukraine, USSR, May 23, 1909; s. Atanazy and Maria (Mikulinski) N.; C.E., Tech. State U., Warsaw, Poland, 1935; m. Herta Reichardt, Oct. 22, 1939;children—Elizabeth, Alexander. Came to U.S., 1948, naturalized, 1954. Field engr. City of Sochaczew, Poland, 1935-36; city engr., Otwock, Poland, 1936-44; structural design specialist Stanley Cons., Inc. (formerly Stanley Engring. Co.), Muscatine, Iowa, 1948-55, prin., chief structural engr., 1955—, v.p., 1972—, also dir. tech. staff, 1978—; structural cons. engr., 1977—. Registered profl. engr., Iowa, Mo., Ky., Wis., Alaska, Ohio; structural engr., Ill. Mem. Nat. Soc. Profl. Engrs., Am. Concrete Inst., Iowa Engring. Soc. Mem. Greek Orthodox Ch. Author math. work pub. by Stanley Engring. Co., also numerous tech. articles. Home: 3306 Spinning Wheel Ct Muscatine IA 52761 Office: Stanley Bldg Muscatine IA 52761

NESWALD, BARBARA ANNE, mktg. co. exec.; b. N.Y.C., Jan. 14, 1935; d. Edward and Veronica (Presby) Lutz; Regents scholar, Hunter Coll., N.Y.C.; divorced; children—Kurt Thomas, Linda Neswald Hunt, Elizabeth Neswald Williams. Media dir. R.M. Klosterman Inc., Los Angeles, 1960-64; copy writer, Los Angeles, 1964-73; copy chief Broadway Dept. Stores, Los Angeles, 1973-76; creative dir. Lucky Stores, Inc., Buena Park, Calif., 1976-79; v.p. advt. and communications Top Value Enterprises Co., Dayton, Ohio, 1979—; adv. bd. Los Angeles Trade Tech. Coll., 1976-77. Recipient various advt. awards. Mem. Women in Communications, Am. Women in Radio and TV, Nat. Acad. TV Arts and Scis., Dayton Advt. Club. Office: 3085 Woodman Ave Kettering OH 45429

NETSCH, DAWN CLARK, state senator; b. Cin., Sept. 16, 1926; B.A. with distinction, Northwestern U., 1948, J.D. magna cum laude, 1952; m. Walter A. Netsch. Admitted to Ill. bar; individual practice law, Washington, Chgo.; law clk. U.S. Dist. Ct. Chgo.; adminstrv. and legal aide Ill. Gov. Otto Kerner, 1961-65; prof. law Northwestern U., 1965—; mem. Ill. Senate. Del. Ill. Constl. Conv.; adv. bd. Nat. Program Ednl Leadership, LWV, Mus. Contemporary Art, Ill. Welfare Assn. Democrat. Author: (with Daniel Mandelker) State and Local Government in a Federal System; contbr. articles to legal jours. Office: State Capitol Springfield IL 62707*

NEU, ARTHUR ALAN, lawyer; b. Carroll, Iowa, Feb. 9, 1933; s. Arthur Nicholas and Martha Margaret (Frandsen) N.; B.S. in Bus. Adminstrn., Northwestern U., 1955, J.D., 1958; LL.M., Georgetown U., 1961; m. Mary Naomi Bedwell, Apr. 4, 1964; children—Eric, Mara, Towle. Admitted to Iowa bar; practiced in Carroll, 1962—; senator State of Iowa, 1967-72, lt. gov., 1972-78; city atty. Carroll, 1978—. Mem. Iowa Bd. Regents, 1979—. Served with U.S. Army, 1958-62. Mem. Iowa Bar Assn., Am. Bar Assn. Republican. Presbyterian. Clubs: Rotary, Elks. Home: Route 2 Carroll IA 51401 Office: 721 N Main St Carroll IA 51401

NEUBAUER, CHARLES FREDERICK, journalist; b. Elmhurst, Ill., Feb. 13, 1950; s. Fred Charles and Dolores Jeanne (Pries) N.; B.S. in Journalism, Northwestern U., 1972, M.S., 1973; m. Sandra Carol Bergo, Oct. 4, 1975. Investigator, Better Govt. Assn., Chgo., 1971-73; investigative reporter Chgo. Today, 1973-74, Chgo. Tribune, 1974—. Co-recipient Pulitzer prize for local investigative reporting, 1976; recipient Edward Scott Beck award for domestic reporting Chgo. Tribune, 1980. Home: 1015 Dobson St Evanston IL 60202 Office: Chgo Tribune 435 N Michigan Ave Chicago IL 60611

NEUBERG, FRANK JOSEPH, interior designer; b. Cicero, Ill., Sept. 8, 1914; s. Frank and Anna (Prucha) N.; A.Sc., Morton Coll., 1935; student Art Inst. Chgo., 1948; m. Marilyn J. Lawrence, Sept. 12, 1975; children—Laurel, Paul. Staff, Derk Smit & Co., Chgo., 1935-39; owner, operator Interior Designers Workshop, Chog., 1939-43; staff Reinkin & Sons, Chgo., 1946-50; owner, operator F. Neuberg Interiors, Indian Head Park, Ill., 1950—; prof. interior design Coll. of DuPage, 1977—; color cons.; appraiser. Served with arty., U.S. Army, 1943-46; ETO. Decorated Bronze Star. Methodist. Home and Office: 208 Cascade Dr Indian Head Park IL 60525

NEUCE, EDWIN OLANDO, editor; b. Morgantown, W.Va., Sept. 3, 1922; s. Thornton Olando and Elizabeth (Gutherie) N.; student pub. schs., Morgantown; b. Nina Lynne Foltz, Mar. 24, 1943; 1 dau., Carol Lynne Neuce Davidson. Police officer, Front Royal, Va., 1950-58; office mgr. No. Va. Daily, Front Royal, 1958-59; feature editor Dominion-News, Morgantown, 1959-60; news editor Coin World, Sidney, Ohio, 1961-72; editor Linn's Stamp News, Sidney, 1972—; mem. mgmt. planning group Amos Press Inc., Sidney. Mem. Sidney City Council, 1973-74. Served with U.S. Army, 1940-45. Recipient Outstanding Citizen award Sidney Jaycees, 1966. Mem. Am. Philatelic Soc., Soc. Philatelic Americans, Am. Numismatic Assn. Presbyterian. Clubs: Kiwanis, Moose. Author: Basic Knowledge for the Coin Collector, 1962; Price Guide for the Collector of U.S. Paper Money Errors, 1968; editor: Linn's World Stamp Almanac, 1976. Home: 1013 Juniper Way Sidney OH 45365 Office: 911 Vandemark Rd Sidney OH 45365

NEUENSCHWANDER, FREDERICK PHILLIP, bus. exec.; b. Akron, Ohio, Mar. 19, 1924; s. Willis Lee and Esther (Mayer) N.; student Franklin and Marshall Coll., 1942-43, U. Akron, 1946-48; m. Mary Jane Porter, Mar. 19, 1948; children—Carol, Frederick Philip, Lynn, Dean, Richard. Chief insp. Retail Credit Co., Akron, 1948-55; exec. v.p. Wadsworth (Ohio) C. of C., 1955-62, Wadsworth Devel. Corp., 1955-62, Wooster (Ohio) C. of C., 1962-63, Wooster Expansion, Inc., 1962-63; dir. devel. dept. State of Ohio, Columbus, 1963-71; exec. v.p. James A. Rhodes & Assos., Columbus, 1971-74; prin. F.P. Neuenschwander & Assos., Columbus, 1975—. Mem. adv. council Small Bus. Adminstrn. Exec. dir. Wadsworth United Fund, Inc., 1956-62; pres. Templed Hills, Inc.; pres. Central Ohio exec. bd. Boy Scouts Am.; vice-chmn. Ohio Water Commn., Ohio Expns. Commn.; chmn. Ohio Water and Sewer Rotary Fund Commn.; mem., past chmn. Midwest Gov.'s Adv. Council; sec. Ohio Devel. Council, Ohio Devel. Finance Commn. Adv. council Rio Grande Coll.; 1st chmn. bd. trustees Ohio Transp. Research Center; bd. dirs. League Against Child Abuse, United Ch. Bd. for World Ministries. Served with AUS, 1943-46. Named Outstanding Young Man of Year, Wadsworth Jr. C. of C., 1958; recipient SIR award for directing outstanding state indsl. devel. program N. Am., 1966, 68, Ohio Gov.'s award 1967. Mem. Am., Gt. Lakes indsl. devel. councils, C. of C. Execs. of Ohio, Huguenot Soc. Am., Am. Legion, Ohio Soc. N.Y. (res. v.p.). Mem. United Ch. of Christ (property mgmt. com. Ohio Conf.). Club: Worthington Hills Country. Home: 1155 Clubview S Worthington OH 43085 Office: 2066 Henderson Rd Worthington OH 43085

NEUHARD, JAMES RICHARD, lawyer; b. Milton, Pa., May 21, 1944; s. Robert F. and Margret (LeDuc) N.; B.S., U. Notre Dame, 1966; J.D., U. Mich., 1969. Admitted to Mich. bar, 1969; law clk. Mich. Supreme Ct., 1969-71; staff atty. State Appellate Defender's Office, Detroit, 1971-72, dir., 1972—; mem. adv. com. ct. reporters Mich. Supreme Ct., 1975—, jud. planning com., 1977—; cons. Nat. Center Def. Mgmt.; mem. adjudication com. Office of Criminal Justice Programs, 1975-79; mem. Nat. Study Commn. on Def. Services Task Force, 1976-77; lectr. Mem. Mich. Bar Assn., Detroit Bar Assn., Nat. Lawyers Guild, Mich. State Bar (dir. criminal law sect. 1974-75, chmn. defender systems and services com. 1975-77), Criminal Def. Attys. Mich. (founding; treas. 1977-78, 80—, pres. 1978-80, edn. com. 1977—), Nat. Legal Aid and Defender Assn. (dir. 1975-79; chmn. appellate council 1975-76; chmn. defender com. 1977—), Nat. Defender Inst. (dir. 1978—), Editor: Michigan Speakers Manual Against the Death Penalty; contbr. articles to legal jours. Home: 25660 Southfield Rd #203 Southfield MI 48075 Office: 1200 6th Ave 3N Detroit MI 48226

NEUMAN, STEPHANIE SELLORS, clin. psychologist; b. Pueblo, Colo., Dec. 14, 1945; d. John and Catherine (Swing) Sellors; B.A., Miami U., 1967; M.A., Case Western Res. U., 1974, Ph.D., 1976. Social worker, spl. edn. tchr., 1967-72; clin. psychologist, research dir. Mental Devel. Center, Cleve., 1973-77; psychology cons. Cuyahoga County Bd. Mental Retardation, Cleve., 1974-77; research coordinator State of Ohio Dept. Mental Health and Mental Retardation, Cleve., 1977—; staff psychologist Cleve. Met. Gen. Hosp., 1978—; asst. prof. dept. psychiatry Sch. Medicine Case Western Res. U., Cleve., 1978—; cons. psychologist United Meth. Children's Home, Berea, Ohio, 1977-81; pvt. practice clin. psychology, 1980—; cons. Hanna Perkins Sch., Lake Ridge Acad., Council Econ. Opportunities, Cleve., 1974-77. Mem. Am. Psychol. Assn., Am. Orthopsychiat. Assn., Ohio Psychol. Assn., Cleve. Psychol. Assn. (exec. v.p.). Home: 15515 Van Aken Blvd Shaker Heights OH 44120 Office: 26900 Cedar Rd Beachwood OH 44122

NEUMANN, FREDERICK LLOYD, plant breeder; b. Waterloo, Iowa, Apr. 9, 1949; s. Lloyd Frederick and Leita Evangeline (Otto) N.; B.S., Iowa State U., 1972, M.S., 1974; m. Diane Marie Brown, Aug. 18, 1973; children—Bradley, Brian. Research dir., plant breeder Ames Seed Farms Inc. (Iowa), producers hybrid popcorn seed, 1973—; mem. research com. Popcorn Inst., Chgo., 1976—. Treas., Laurel Tree Nursery Sch., Inc., 1981—. Mem. Am. Soc. Agronomy, Phi Kappa Phi, Gamma Sigma Delta. Republican. Episcopalian. Home: 2884 Monroe Dr Ames IA 50010 Office: Rural Route 3 Ames IA 50010

NEUNER, ANDREW MICHAEL, assn. exec.; b. Belleville, Ill., Dec. 10, 1941; s. Andrew Joseph and Melva Opal (Amlung) N.; B.A., Blackburn Coll., 1964; M.A., U. Kans., 1966; m. Donna Jean Keppler, Apr. 4, 1964. Youth dir. Springfield (Ill.) YMCA, 1964-69; asst. dir. Assn. Systematics Collections, Lawrence, Kans., 1978—. Mem. Soc. Vertebrate Paleontology, AAAS, Sigma Xi. Office: Mus Natural History U Kans Lawrence KS 66045

NEVILLE, MICHAEL KEVIN, paper distbn. co. exec.; b. Bklyn., Aug. 19, 1941; s. Michael Edward and Eleanor Rose (Murphy) N.; B.S. in Econs., Villanova U., 1963; m. Diana J. Campbell, Aug. 17, 1968; children—Michael Edward, Jennifer Anne. Sales rep. Springs Mills, Inc., N.Y.C., 1964-67, Continental Can Co., N. Eng., Phila., Detroit, 1968-73; mktg. mgr. Gt. Plains Bag Corp., subs. Continental Can, 1973-74; pres., owner Taylor Martin Papers, Inc., Ft. Wayne, Ind., 1974—; adv. bd. Druth Packaging Corp. Cons. Jr. Achievement. Served with Army N.G., 1963-69. Mem. Nat. Paper Trade Assn., Ft. Wayne Club of Printing House Craftsman, Ft. Wayne In-Plant Printing Mgrs. Orgn. Roman Catholic. Clubs: Summit, Orchard Ridge Country. Home: 1248 W Sherwood Terr Fort Wayne IN 46807 Office: 4621 Executive Blvd Fort Wayne IN 46808

NEVIN, JOHN J., tire and rubber co. exec.; b. Jersey City, Feb. 13, 1927; s. Edward Vincent and Anna (Burns) N.; B.S., U. Calif., 1950; M.B.A., Harvard U., 1952; m. Anne Filice, June 16, 1951; children—Stanley James, John Joseph, Richard Charles, Paul Edward, Gerald Patrick, Mary Anne. With Ford Motor Co., Dearborn, Mich., 1954-71, v.p. mktg., 1969-71; with Zenith Radio Corp., Chgo., 1971-79, pres., 1979, chmn., chief exec. officer, 1977-79; with Firestone Tire and Rubber Co., Akron, Ohio, 1979—, chmn. bd., chief exec., 1980—; dir. First Chgo. Corp., First Nat. Bank Chgo., FMC Corp. Gen. chmn. Detroit United Found., 1970. Served with USNR, 1945-46. Office: 1000 Milwaukee Ave Glenview IL 60025

NEVINNY-STICKEL, HANS BORIS, physician, tumor inst. adminstr.; b. Innsbruck, Austria, Jan. 12, 1927; came to U.S., 1954, naturalized, 1963; s. Hans and Zweta (Kotzewa) N.-S.; M.D., Leopold Franzens Universität Medizin. Fakultät, Innsbruck, Austria, 1951; M.S. in Hygiene, Sch. Public Health Harvard U., 1961; m. Dagmar Tirala, July 31, 1951; children—Victoria, Corinne, Philip. Asst. in pathol. anatomy U. Innsbruck, Austria, 1951-52; med. asst. U. Bern, Switzerland, 1953; surg. asst. U. Florence, Italy, 1953; intern and resident, Burlington, Vt., R.I., Boston, 1954-58; research fellow and asso. Harvard Med. Sch., Boston, 1958-70; dir. Alfred & Hilda Strauss Tumor Inst., L.A. Weiss Hosp., Chgo., 1970—; research asso. Children's Cancer Research Found. and Peter Bent Brigham Hosp., Boston, 1962-70; clin. asso. prof. medicine Coll. Medicine, U. Ill.; cons. Westside VA Hosp., Chgo. Bd. dirs. Am. Cancer Soc. Recipient Andreas Vesalius medal, 1966. Mem. Am. Assn. Cancer Research, Am. Soc. Clin. Oncology, Am. Assn. for Cancer Edn., Eastern Coop. Oncology Group, N.Y. Acad. Scis. Researcher cancer chemotherapy. Home: 251 King Muir Rd Lake Forest IL 60045 Office: 4646 N Marine Dr Chicago IL 60640

NEVLING, LORIN IVES, JR., mus. adminstr.; b. St. Louis, Sept. 23, 1930; s. Lorin I. and Rose Elizabeth (Meyer) N.; B.S., St. Mary's Coll., 1952; postgrad. U. Notre Dame, 1952-53; A.M., Washington U., St. Louis, 1957, Ph.D. (Van Blarcom scholar), 1959; m. Janet Frances Sullivan, June 1, 1957; children—Lorin, Laura, Mark, James, John. Teaching asst. U. Notre Dame, 1953; teaching asst. Washington U., 1955-58, lectr. botany, summer 1958; research asst. flora of Panama, Mo. Bot. Garden, St. Louis, 1957-58, 59; asst. curator Arnold Arboretum, Harvard U., Boston, 1959-61, asso. curator, 1961-69, asso. curator Gray Herbarium, 1963-72, curator, 1969-73, mem. faculty arts and scis., 1966-73, lectr. biology, 1969-73, coordinator bot. systematic collections, 1972-73; curator Field Mus. Natural History, Chgo., 1973—, chmn. dept. botany, 1973-77, asst. dir. sci. and edn., 1978-80, dir., 1980—; lectr. biol. scis. Northwestern U., Evanston, Ill., 1974—; adj. prof. biol. scis. No. Ill. U., De Kalb, 1974—; cons. biol. research resources program NSF, 1975, 76; cons. to Charles T. Branford Co., pubs., 1970-73; mem. adv. bd. Sta. WBEZ, 1981—; mem. adv. council Projecto Flora Amazonica, 1977-80. Area rep. Youth for Understanding, 1976-79; asst. cubmaster Jamaica Plains council Boy Scouts Am., 1969-72, committeeman Downers Grove (Ill.) council, 1973-74, 76; mem. Open Spaces Task Force, Boston, 1971; mem. exec. bd. Jamaica Hills Assn., 1972-73; bd. dirs. Ill. Inst. Natural Resources, 1979—. Served with U.S. Army, 1953-55. Recipient Outstanding Vol. award United Way Met. Chgo., 1978; NSF grantee, 1970-73, 78-78. Fellow AAAS; mem. Am. Inst. Biol. Scis. (governing bd. 1974-77), Am. Assn. Museums, Bot. Soc. Am., Assn. for Tropical Biology (travel grantee 1966), Internat. Assn. Plant Taxonomy, Am. Soc. Plant Taxonomists (pres. 1977, council 1974-78, George R. Cooley award 1970), Linnean Soc. London, Internat. Assn. Botanic Gardens, Sociedad Botanica de Mex., Sigma Xi. Asso. editor Rhodora, 1964-70; mem. editorial bd. Anales del Instituto de Biologia, Mex., 1970-74; contbr. numerous articles on botany and flora distbn. to sci. jours. Office: Field Museum of Natural History Chicago IL 60605

NEWBERG, FAYE ROSALIND, acctg. and data processing exec.; b. Cleve., Nov. 4, 1923; d. Barney W. and Ethel (Siegel) Desberg; student pub. schs., Cleveland Heights, Ohio; children—Dennis Scott, Judith Ann Briskey. Bookkeeper, The Higbee Co., Cleve., 1941-42; asst. personnel dept. William Taylor & Sons, Cleve., 1942-43; sr. personnel cons. acctg. and data processing specialist The Career Professionals, Inc., Cleve., from 1975, now dir. acctg. and data processing. Leader, Girl Scouts U.S.A., 1954-59; den mother Cub Scouts, Boy Scouts Am., 1953-56; active ARC Bloodmobile, 1953-55. Cert. personnel cons. Mem. Am. Mgmt. Assn., Cert. Personnel Cons. Soc., Council Jewish Women, Smithsonian Instn. Club: B'nai B'rith Women (profl. and bus. v.p.), Park Synagogue Sisterhood, Socialite Single, Pythian Sister's, Sunshine Girls (pres.). Office: 666 Euclid Ave Cleveland OH 44114

NEWBERGER, SHEL, packaging exec.; b. Chgo., Nov. 30, 1925; s. Oscar and Daisy N.; B.A., U. Chgo., 1944; m. Natalie Bernard, Oct. 22, 1946; children—Steven, Richard, David, Jill. Packaging salesman Cleary Box Co., Chgo., 1946-48, Chippewa Paper Products, Chgo., 1948-63, Lanzit Corrugated Box Co., Chgo., 1950-63, Consol. Packaging Corp., Chgo., 1960-63; pres., Apollo Containers, Inc., Evanston, Ill., 1963—, prin., pres., Boyer Corp., Evanston, 1976—. Alderman, Evanston, 1967-71; officer Evanston Recreation Bd., 1971—. Served with U.S. Army, 1944-46. Mem. Chgo. Assn. Commerce and Industry, Evanston C. of C. Home: 100 Dempster St Evanston IL 60202 Office: 2902 Central St Evanston IL 60201

NEWBERN, MARY RUTH, steel co. sales person; b. Cleve., Nov. 27, 1951; d. Philip and Mary W. Newbern; student Alliance Francaise, Paris, 1972; B.A., Baldwin-Wallace Coll., 1973; postgrad. Princeton U., 1973-74, Austin-Peay State U., 1978; m. Robert S. Williams, Feb. 4, 1974; children—Joy C Williams, Robert S. Williams III, Philip Newbern Williams. Adminstrv. asst. Drug Abuse Centers, Inc., Cleve., 1972-73; tchr. Newburgh (N.Y.) City Schs., 1974-75; employee relations coordinator Kaiser Found., Cleve., 1976-77; exec. asst. to pastor Phillips Temple Ch., Toledo, 1977-79; sales asst. U.S. Steel Corp., Cleve., 1979—; reporter Christian Index, 1970-73; free-lance reporter, 1972. Recipient sales award U.S. Steel Corp., 1979. Mem. Am. Psychol. Assn., Twenty-First Congl. Dist. Caucus, Smithsonian Assos., YWCA. Mem. Christian Meth. Episcopal Ch. Home: 2918 Minnie Ave Cleveland OH 44104

NEWBERRY, GEORGE WILLIAM, educator; b. Denver, Feb. 12, 1927; s. Everitt Franklin and Frances Ethel (Suggs) N.; B.A. in Psychology, U. Denver, 1956, M.A. in Speech Pathology, 1959; Ph.D. in Spl. Edn., Communications Disorders, St. Louis U., 1972; married; children—Karen, Deborah, Melissa, Melinda, George William II. Exec. asst. speech clinic U. Denver, 1956-62; asso. prof., chmn. dept. communication disorders St. Louis U., 1962—. Commr. police, Crestwood, Mo., 1971-72; mem. intrastate planning council, Title VI adv. Mo. State Dept. Edn., 1974—, mem. adv. council Inservice Tng. and Personnel Preparation, 1977—; public works commr. City of Crestwood, 1976-78; mem. extension council Mo. U., 1976-79. Mem. Am. Speech, Lang. Hearing Assn., Mo. Speech, Lang. Hearing Assn., Speech and Hearing Assn. Greater St. Louis, Phi Delta Kappa, Sigma Alpha Eta. Recipient certificates of recognition Wash. U. Orthodontic Study Group, Scott AFB Med.-Dental Group. Cert. in speech pathology Am. Speech and Hearing Assn. Home: 8758 Sturdy Dr Crestwood MO 63126 Office: 3733 W Pine Saint Louis MO 63108

NEWBERRY, ROBERT LUCIAN, clergyman, assn. exec.; b. Manitowoc, Wis., June 16, 1943; s. Lucian Leray and Olive Marian (Benedict) N.; B.A., Ottawa (Kans.) U., 1966; M.Div., Central Baptist Theol. Sem., Kansas City, Kans., 1969; m. Sherill Anne James, June 23, 1968; children—Robert, Melissa. Ordained to ministry Baptist Ch., 1969; pastor 1st Baptist Ch., Merrill, Wis., 1969-71, Stafford, Kans., 1971-73; minister of edn. 1st Baptist Ch., Hutchinson, Kans., 1973-76; pastor 1st Baptist Ch., Belleville, Kans., 1976-79, 1st Bapt. Ch., Indianola, Iowa, 1979—; exec. dir. Republic County Econ. Devel. Dept., Belleville, 1976-79; chmn. Four Rivers Tourism Task Force, 1978-79; sec.-treas. N.E. Kans. Regional Tourism Bd., 1979; mem. religious com. Assn. Retarded Persons, Merrill, Wis., 1970-71; mem.

Indianola (Iowa) Drug Abuse and Alcoholism Commn., 1981—; sec.-treas. Indianola Ministerial Assn., 1980-81. Recipient Master Sec. award Optimists, 1973. Mem. Mid-Am. Bapt. Ministers Council. Republican. Club: Lions. Home: 807 N Howard St Indianola IA 50125 Office: PO Box 204 Indianola IA 50125

NEWBOLD, DONALD REX, supermarket chain exec.; b. Aurora, Mo., Aug. 4, 1946; s. Ward Eugene and Retha (Bell) N.; B.S. in Acctg., S.W. Mo. State U., 1968. Auditor, U.S. Army Audit Agy., St. Louis, 1968-70; acctg. James E. Newbold, C.P.A.'s, Aurora, 1971-72; controller, asst. sec.-treas. Roswil, Inc., Ramey Supermarkets, Springfield, Mo., 1973—. Served with AUS, 1969-70. Mem. Ozark Empire Grocers Assn. Home: 1629 W Katella St Springfield MO 65807 Office: 3259 E Sunshine St Springfield MO 65804

NEWBY, RICHARD PROUTY, clergyman; b. Des Moines, Apr. 13, 1923; s. James Moore and Bertha (Prouty) N.; B.A., William Penn Coll., 1945; m. Doris Prignitz, June 1, 1945; children—Darlene Ann, James Richard, John Charles. Pastor Soc. of Friends Ch.; pastor, Pleasant Plain, Iowa, 1945-47, Mpls., 1947-58, Muncie (Ind.) Friends Ch., 1958-67, University Friends Ch., Wichita, Kans., 1967-73, College Ave. Friends Ch., Oskaloosa, Iowa, 1973-74, Friends Meml. Ch., Muncie, 1974—. Presiding clk. Iowa Yearly Meeting of Friends, 1955-58; asst. presiding clk. Ind. Yearly Meeting of Friends, 1978—; chmn. bd. on Christian edn. Friends United Meeting, 1955-66; pres. Delaware County Council Chs., 1965-66, Wichita Council Chs., 1970-71. Chmn. Muncie Mayor's Com. on Human Relations, 1962-63, Muncie Human Rights Commn., 1981—. Bd. dirs. Am. Friends Service Com., 1960-64; trustee William Penn Coll., 1955-58, Earlham Coll., 1962-67, 77—, Friends U., Wichita, 1970-74; bd. advisers Earlham Sch. Religion, 1976—. Recipient award of merit William Penn Coll., 1957. Mem. Delaware County Ministerial Assn. (pres. 1961-62). Home: 605 S Rambler Rd Muncie IN 47304 Office: Friends Memorial Ch Adams and Cherry Sts Muncie IN 47305

NEWELL, DAVID R., state legislator; b. Oakland, Calif., Oct. 14, 1946; A.A., Norfolk Jr. Coll., 1967; B.S., U. Nebr.-Omaha, 1971, postgrad.; m. Arlene Paider, Mar. 30, 1974; children—John, Sarah. Mem. Nebr. Legislature, 1976—. Former state pres., now Nat. Committeeman Young Democrats; adminstrv. asst. to dir. adminstrv. services state exec. and central coms. Democratic Party. Served with U.S. Army, 1967-69; Vietnam. Mem. Am. Legion, Phi Alpha Theta. Address: Room 1406 State Capitol Lincoln NE 68509

NEWELL, VIRGINIA SHAW, ret. educator; b. Eau Claire, Wis., Jan. 15, 1901; d. La Forrest and Caroline (Wingen) Newell; student Eau Claire Normal Sch., 1919-21; B.A., U. Wis., Madison, 1924, postgrad., 1964-68; postgrad. Northwestern U., 1941; M.A., Catholic U. Am., 1951. Tchr., Eau Claire Sr. High Sch., 1924-43; tchr., drama dir. Adams-Friendship High Sch., Adams, Wis., 1951-54; tchr. English and speech, drama dir. Westfield (Wis.) High Sch., 1954-55; tchr. English, drama dir. Medford (Wis.) High Sch., 1955-57; tchr. English and speech, drama dir. Marinette, Wis., 1957-63; tchr., dir. forensics, dir. contest plays Adams-Friendship High Sch., 1963-66; tchr. Title I remedial and devel. reading, 1966-70; free-lance writer. Vol. Adams County unit Am. Cancer Soc., 1972-75, crusade chmn., 1975, bd. dirs., 1975-77, recipient Cert. of Merit, 1977; pres. Adams County Assn. Republican Women, 1969-73; publicity chmn. Adams County Rep. Party, 1973-76; vice chairperson, 1976; coordinator congressman's re-election campaign, 1972; sponsor Nat. Rep. Congressional Com., 1976; mem. Winnebago County Rep. Women, Nat. Fedn. Rep. Women, Rep. Nat. Com. Served to lt. Women's Res., USCG, 1943-46. Ann. fellow Intercontinental Biog. Assn.; mem. Res. Officers Assn. U.S. (life), AAUW, Winnebago County Ret. Tchrs. Assn. (life), Wis. Ret. Tchrs. Assn. (life), Winnebago County Ret. Tchrs. Assn., Smithsonian Assos., Nat. Ret. Tchrs. Assn., Cath. U. Am. Alumni Assn., Nat. Travel Club, Delta Kappa Gamma Soc. Internat., Half Century Club of U. Wis. Roman Catholic. Author: (radio play) Charity, Inc., 1941; asst. editor: Stories and Poems from the First Grade through the Eighth, 1924; contbr. articles to profl. jours. Home: 200 Merritt Ave Apt 202 Oshkosh WI 54901

NEWEY, PAUL DAVIS, lawyer, investigator; b. Mpls., July 4, 1914; s. Paul S. and Mary (Yonan) N.; A.A., Central YMCA, 1935; J.D., John Marshall Law Sch., 1940; A.B., Detroit Inst. Tech., 1947; diploma U.S. Treasury Dept. Law Enforcement Sch., 1943; spl. courses U.S. Govt. and Mil. Intelligence Schs., 1951-53; m. Viola W. Raymond, Dec. 16, 1943; children—Paul Sarkhoshe II, Davis Raymond, Dean Alan, Arthur Tyler. Admitted to Ill. bar, 1946; squad leader Bur. Census, Dept. Commerce, 1940; officer Uniformed Force U.S. Secret Service, 1940-42; agt. Bur. Narcotics Treasury Dept., 1942-47; pvt. practice law, real estate, ins. broker, Chgo., 1948-51; spl. rep. CIA, 1951-57; asst. state's atty.-investigator, County of Cook, Ill., 1957-58, asst. state's atty.-chief investigator, chief of state's atty.'s police, 1958-60; pvt. practice law, Chgo., 1961-65; spl. investigator, Chgo., 1961—; partner law firm Adamowski, Newey & Adamowski, Chgo., 1965—. Sec., dir. Master Fishing Gear, Inc., 1956-57. Served as pvt. AUS, 1941; 1st lt., CIC, 1949-54. Recipient Medal of Merit and elected to Hall of Fame, Nat. Police Officers Assn. Am., 1960; Distinguished Citizen award Assyrian-Am. Welfare Council, 1970; citation merit John Marshall Law Sch., 1970. Mem. Am., Ill., Chgo. bar assns., Internat. Assn. Investigators and Spl. Police (chmn. bd. dirs. 1963—), N. Am. Inst. Police Sci. (dir. 1961—), N. Am. Detective Agy. (dir. 1961—), Spl. Agts. Assn. (3d v.p. Chgo. chpt. 1978-80), U.S. Treasury Agts. Assn. (pres. 1970-71), John Marshall Law Sch. Alumni Assn. (dir. 1968—, treas. 1973-75), Fed. Criminal Investigation Assn., Internat. Assn. Chief Police, Am. Judicature Soc., Chgo. Assn. Commerce and Industry, Ill. Assn. Chiefs Police. Mem. Apostolic Cath. Assyrian Ch. of East. Mason (32 deg., Shriner). Clubs: Chicago Congregational (pres. 1963-64, dir. and trustee 1962-65); Starcraft. Home: 1034 W Altgeld St Chicago IL 60614 Office: 11 S LaSalle St Chicago IL 60603

NEWGENT, FRANK WILLIAM, JR., social service adminstr.; b. East St. Louis, Ill., Nov. 14, 1926; s. Frank William and Mildred (Auten) N.; A.B., Central Coll. Mo., 1947; M.A., U. Chgo., 1951; m. Mary Maurine Mobberly, Dec. 21, 1946; children—Kevin Newgent Dartt, Eric William. Child welfare worker Ill. Dept. Pub. Welfare, 1949-50; child welfare worker Ill. Soldiers and Sailors Children's Sch., 1951-53, child welfare supr., 1954-57; child guidance counselor Ill. Inst. for Juvenile Research, 1953-54; adminstrv. rev. cons. Wis. Div. for Children and Youth, 1957-59, chief community services, 1959-60, asst. dir., 1960-61, dir., 1961-68; adminstr. Div. Family Services, Dept. Health and Social Services, 1968-77; dep. asst. sec. Human Devel. Services, U.S. Dept. HEW, 1977; dir. Wyalusing Acad., Prairie du Chien, Wis., 1978—. Del., White House Conf. on Children and Youth, 1960; leader Workshop on Child Welfare Adminstrn., Columbia Sch. Social Work, 1964; mem. adv. council in pub. welfare HEW, 1964-66, mem. state and local adminstrv. adv. com. on family assistance, 1970-72; chmn. Midwest Regional Conf., Child Welfare League Am., Milw., 1965; del., forum leader White House Conf. on Children, 1970. Bd. dirs. Madison Community Welfare Council, 1961-66, Wis. Council on Human Concerns, 1978—; mem. adv. council execs. Child Welfare League Am., 1973-75. Mem. Nat. Assn. Social Workers (treas. S. Central Wis. chpt. 1959-61), Acad. Certified Social Workers, Am. Public Welfare Assn. (dir. 1966-67, 73-76, v.p. 1977), Wis. Public Welfare Assn., Wis. Welfare Council. Contbr. articles to profl. jours. Home: 1010 S 15th St Prairie du Chien WI 53821 Office: 601 S Beaumont Rd Prairie du Chien WI 53821

NEWHOUSE, RICHARD H., JR., state senator; b. Louisville, Jan. 24, 1924; s. Richard H. and Annie Louise (Singleton) N.; B.S., Boston U., 1950, M.S., 1952; J.D., U. Chgo., 1960; m. Katherine Vetterlein; children—Suzanne, Richard, Holly. Admitted to Ill. bar; individual practice law, Chgo.; mem. Ill. Senate, 1966—. Del. Democratic Nat. Conv., 1980. Served with USAAF, 1943-45. Named Best Legislator Ind. Voters Ill.; recipient Best Legislator award Am. Legion; Outstanding Public Servant Cook County Bar Assn.; Senator of Yr. Bapt. Ministers Conf. Chgo. Mem. Chgo. Bar Assn., Black Legislators Assn. (founder, pres., dir.), Adlai Stevenson Inst., Ill. State Hist. Soc., Nat. Urban Coalition. Address: 5533 S Cornell Chicago IL 60634*

NEWKIRK, DONALD RICHARD, trade assn. exec.; b. Hamilton, Ohio, Jan. 5, 1927; s. Stanton Mathew and Mary Elizabeth (Gallaher) N.; B.S. in Bus. Adminstrn., Miami U., Oxford, Ohio, 1949; m. Peggy Wills, Dec. 9, 1976; children—Melinda, Debra, Jeff, Dan, Stephany. Mgr. in planning, advt., purchasing Champion Paper Co., Hamilton, 1949-52; adminstrv. asst. Mercy Hosp., Hamilton, 1952-53; asst. adminstr. Children's Hosp., Cin., 1953-56, Meml. Hosp., Fremont, Ohio, 1956-59; pres. Ohio Hosp. Assn., Columbus, 1959—; mem. clin. faculty Ohio State U. Sch. Allied Med. Professions and Coll. Medicine; mem. adv. bd. dirs. Direct Relief Found., Santa Barbara, Calif.; mem. Ohio Dept. Health Hosp. Adv. Council; dean's asso. Miami U. Coll. Bus. Adminstrn. Vice chmn. bd. trustees First Community Ch., Columbus, 1974; chmn. bd. First Community Village, Columbus, 1977-78. Served with USN, 1945-46. Decorated Order of Merit (Ecuador). Fellow Am. Coll. Hosp. Adminstrs. (chmn. 1980-81); mem. Am. Hosp. Assn., Am. Soc. Assn. Execs. (cert. assn. exec.), Public Relations Soc. Am. (cert.), Internat. Hosp. Fedn., Ohio Trade Assn. Execs., Partners of Ams. (steering com. of Ohio/Parana, Brazil com.). Clubs: University, Athletic, Kiwanis (Columbus). Contbr. articles to profl. jours. Office: 21 W Broad St Columbus OH 43215

NEWLAND, JAMES I., stockgrower; b. Belle Fourche, S.D., Feb. 12, 1911; s. Wilbur F. and Lucille C. (King) N.; m. Velma L. Bourne, Sept. 5, 1943; children—Robert J., Wilbur H. Stockgrower, Belle Fourche, S.D. and Colony, Wyo., 1920—; coop. weather observer, 1954—; pres., dir. Fed. Land Bank Assn., Belle Fourche, 1970-76. Mem. Am. Scotch Highland Breeders Assn. (past pres.), Am. Nat. Cattlemen's Assn. (past dir.), S.D. Sheepgrowers Assn., S.D. Stockgrowers Assn. (dir.), Wyo. Stockgrowers Assn., Mont. Stockgrowers Assn., Nat. Woolgrowers Assn., Wyo. Woolgrowers Assn., Mont. Woolgrowers Assn. Democrat. Methodist. Clubs: K.P., Moose. Home: Via Belle Fourche SD 57717

NEWMAN, BARBARA MILLER, devel. psychologist; b. Chgo., Sept. 6, 1944; d. Irving George and Florence (Levy) Miller; student Bryn Mawr Coll., 1962-64; A.B. with Honors, U. Mich., 1966, Ph.D., 1971; m. Philip R. Newman, June 12, 1966; children—Samuel Asher, Abraham Levy, Rachel Florence. Lectr. psychology U. Mich., Ann Arbor, 1971-72, research asso. Inst. Social Research, 1971-72; Asst. prof. psychology Russell Sage Coll., Troy, N.Y., 1972-77, asso prof., 1977-78; asso. prof., chmn. dept. family relations and human devel. Ohio State U., Columbus, 1978—. Mich. Scholars fellow, 1966; recipient Horace H. Rackham research prize, 1970-71. Mem. Eastern, Am. psychol. assns., Soc. for Research in Child Devel., AAAS, N.Y. Acad. Scis. Jewish. Author: The College Classroom: Conflict, Change and Learning, 1971; Development Through Life: A Psychosocial Approach, 1975, 2d edit., 1979; Development Through Life: A Case Study Approach, 1976; Infancy and Childhood: Development and Its Contexts, 1978; An Introduction to the Psychology of Adolescence, 1979; Personality Development through the Life Span, 1980; Living: The Process of Adjustment, 1981. Contbr. articles interpersonal processes, adolescence to profl. publs. Home: 1969 Chatfield Rd Columbus OH 43221 Office: Dept Family Relations and Human Devel Ohio State U Columbus OH 43221

NEWMAN, CAROLE HERMINE SPITZER, educator; b. N.Y.C., July 12, 1944; d. Edward Ralph and Kay (Katz) Spitzer; B.Ed., U. Miami, 1965; M.A., U. Akron, 1975, postgrad. 1977—; m. Isadore Newman, July 2, 1966; children—David and Matthew (twins). Tchr. public schs., Fla., N.Y., Ill., Ohio, 1965-73; instr. U. Akron (Ohio), 1979—; guest lectr. in field. Mem. adv. bd. Practical Edn. for Parents, Summit County, 1981; mem. Summit County Juvenile Ct. Women's Bd., 1981—; Sisterhood bd. dirs. Temple Israel, Akron, 1980-82; v.p. edn. Woman's Am. Orgn. for Rehab. through Tng., 1972-74, donor chmn., 1975, community and Am. affairs chmn., 1981-82. Mem. Phi Lambda Theta. Clubs: Hadassah, Faculty Women's, PTA. Author: (with Newman, Frye and Bluemfeld) An Introduction to the Basic Concepts and Techniques of Measurement and Evaluation, 1974; (with Isadore Newman) Conceptual Statistics for Beginners, 1977; contbr. articles to profl. jours. Address: 2995 Stanley Rd Akron OH 44313

NEWMAN, FRED COLBY, ins. co. exec.; b. Pulaski, Va., Sept. 22, 1931; s. Elmer Dexter and Mary Lydia (Gross) N.; B.S. in Bus. Adminstrn., Va. Poly. Inst., 1958; cert. Vale Tech. Inst., 1959, Am. Ednl. Inst., 1971, Coll. Ins., 1978; m. Mary Lou Meade, Aug. 6, 1955; children—Michael, Matthew, Charles. Claim trainee Glens Falls Ins. Co., 1959, claim rep., supr., br. claim mgr., exec. asst., 1959-70; staff asst. Gt. Am. Ins. Cos., Cin., 1970, exec. asst., 1971-74, dir. field claims, 1974-78, asst. v.p. claims, 1978-79, v.p. claims, 1979—; v.p. Agrl. Excess & Surplus Lines Ins. Co., Agrl. Ins. Co., Am. Nat. Fire Ins. Co. Served with USAF, 1951-55. Republican. Baptist. Club: Cin. Home: 810 Kipp Dr Cincinnati OH 45230 Office: 580 Walnut St Cincinnati OH 45202

NEWMAN, M. W., editor; b. N.Y.C., 1917; B.A. in Journalism, U. Wis., 1938; m. Nancy Newman. Formerly with Indpls. Times, Greensboro (N.C.) Daily News, Hoboken (N.J.) Observer; joined Chgo. Daily News as copyreader, 1945, successively, rewrite man, gen. assignment reporter, book editor, 1971-78, editor arts and amusements dept. and Panorama mag., 1973-78; writer Chgo. Sun-Times, 1978—; editor Inland Architect mag., 1969-80. Address: c/o Sun-Times 401 N Wabash Chicago IL 60611

NEWMAN, MERLE EDWARD, business exec.; b. Guthrie County, Iowa, Sept. 24, 1934; s. Clarence Elmer and Martha Josephina Carolina (Guttenfelder) N.; student sales and mgmt. Drake U., 1961-64; m. Gwendolyn May Dutler, Sept. 13, 1957; children—Ronald Wayne, Roger Merle, Richard Lane. Vice pres. Casey's Gen. Stores, Inc., Des Moines, 1970—; pres. Consol. Bldg. Systems, Inc., Des Moines, 1971—. Patentee heat pump and heat recovery system. Home: 6897 2d Ave Des Moines IA 50313 Office: 1277 E Broadway Des Moines IA 50313

NEWMAN, MURIEL KALLIS STEINBERG, art collector; b. Chgo., Feb. 25, 1914; d. Maurice and Ida (Nudelman) Kallis; Art Inst. Chgo., 1932-36, Ill. Inst. Tech., 1940's, U. Chgo., 1950's; m. Jay Steinberg, Apr. 1938; 1 son, Glenn D.; m. 2d, Albert H. Newman, May 14, 1955. Painter, 1930's and 1940's; dir. 20th Century Painting and Sculpture Com. of Art Inst. Chgo., 1955-78, also mem. com. for purchasing, 1955-78; governing mem. of Art Inst. Chgo., 1955—, benefactor, 1976—; pioneer collector of Am. abstract expressionist art, 1949—. Mem. bd. govs. Landmarks Preservation Council, Chgo., 1966-78; mem. U. Chgo. Woman's Bd., 1960-78, Art Inst. Chgo. Woman's Bd., 1953—, also maj. benefactor; trustee Chgo. Sch. of Architecture Found., Archives of Am. Art, Mus. of Contemporary Art, Chgo.; hon. life trustee Met. Mus. Art of N.Y. Recipient Scroll Recognition of Pub. Service, U.S. Dept. of State, 1958. Mem. Chgo. Hist. Soc. (mem. Guild), Antiquarian Soc. of Art Inst. Chgo. Clubs: Arts, Casino (Chgo.). Address: 179 E Lake Shore Dr Chicago IL 60611

NEWMAN, NANCY BLITZSTEN, pub. relations exec.; b. Chgo.; d. Harry and Alice Eleanor (Karno) Blitzsten; student Cape Cod Theatre Sch.; B.A., B.S., U. Chgo. Coll.; m. M.W. Newman. Former editor nat. directory safety films Nat. Safety Council, Chgo.; later staff writer Chgo. Sun-Times and Chgo. Daily News; then pub. relations staff writer U. Chgo. Hosps. and Clinics; former asst. dir. pub. relations Michael Reese Hosp. and Med. Center, Chgo.; later pub. relations dir. Ravenswood Hosp. Med. Center, Chgo.; account supr. Manning, Selvage & Lee Mid-Am., 1973—. Bd. dirs. Urban Gateways, 1975-77. Mem. Publicity Club Chgo., Public Relations Soc. Am., Arts Club Chgo. Cookbook and food columnist Chgo. Sun-Times. Home: 433 W Briar Pl Chicago IL 60657 Office: 233 N Michigan Ave Chicago IL 60601

NEWMAN, PHILIP ROBERT, psychologist; b. Utica, N.Y., Dec. 17, 1942; s. Samuel M. and Sara Rose (Dumain) N.; A.B. with high distinction, U. Mich., 1964, Ph.D. (Woodrow Wilson fellow 1964, Univ. fellow 1964-66, Horace H. Rackham Research scholar 1969-71), 1971; m. Barbara Miller, June 12, 1966; children—Samuel Asher, Abraham Levy, Rachel Florence. Asst. prof. psychology U. Mich., Ann Arbor, 1971-72; asst. prof. psychology Union Coll., Schenectady, 1972-76; dir. human behavior curriculum project Am. Psychol. Assn., Washington, 1977-81; pvt. practice psychology, Columbus, Ohio, 1978—; cons. Agy. Instructional TV, 1979. Mem. Am. Psychol. Assn., Internat. Assn. Applied Psychology, Internat. Sociol. Assn., Soc. Psychol. Study Social Issues, Am. Sociol. Assn., Nat. Council Family Relations, Groves Conf. Marriage and Family, Eastern Psychol. Assn., Midwestern Psychol. Assn., Western Psychol. Assn., N.Y. Acad. Sci., Phi Beta Kappa, Sigma Xi, Phi Kappa Phi. Author: (with B. Newman) Development through Life: A Psychosocial Approach, 1975, 2d edit., 1979; Infancy and Childhood Development and Its Contexts, 1978; An Introduction to the Psychology of Adolescence, 1979; Personality Development through the Life Span, 1980; Living: The Process of Adjustment, 1981; editor: (with B. Newman) Development Through Life: A Case Study Approach, 1976. Home and Office: 1969 Chatfield Rd Columbus OH 43221

NEWMAN, RALPH GEOFFREY, bookseller, author, cons.; b. Chgo., Nov. 3, 1911; s. Henry and Dora (Glickman) N.; Litt.D., James Milliken U. (Lincoln Coll.), 1950, Knox Coll.; LL.D., Iowa Wesleyan Coll.; Litt.D., Rockford Coll.; m. Estelle Hoffman (div.); children—Maxine Newman Brandenburg, Carol Jacqueline Parry; m. 2d, Patricia L. Simon, 1972. Founder, pres. Abraham Lincoln Book Shop, Inc., Chgo., 1933—; owner Americana House, pubs., 1947—; pres. Lincoln's New Salem Enterprises, Inc., 1952—, Ralph Geoffrey Newman, Inc., Chgo., 1967—; appraiser, cons. rare manuscripts and archives: archivist City of Chgo., 1979—. Pres. bd. dirs. Chgo. Pub. Library, 1965-79; pres. Urban Libraries Council, 1967-78; mem. library council U. Notre Dame; former pres. Adult Edn. Council Greater Chgo.; trustee Lincoln Coll. Served with USNR, 1944-45. Recipient diploma of honor Lincoln Meml. U., 1952; Am. of Year award Independence Hall Assn., 1958; Nevins-Freeman award for Civil War history, 1975. Fellow Royal Soc. Arts London; mem. Civil War Round Table Chgo. (founder 1940), Abraham Lincoln Assn. (dir.), Ulysses S. Grant Assn. (pres.), Stephen A. Douglas Assn. (pres.), Am., Ill., Iowa, Kans., Chgo. hist. socs., Am. Legion, Am. Booksellers Assn., Bibliog. Soc. Am., Lincoln Fellowship of So. Calif., Pa., Wis., Phi Alpha Theta. Clubs: Caxton, Press, Arts; Sangamo (Springfield, Ill.). Author: (with Otto Eisenschiml) The American Iliad, 1947. Editor: The Diary of a Public Man, 1945; The Railsplitter, 1950; (with Otto Eisenschiml and E.B. Long) The Civil War, 1956; The Abraham Lincoln Story (radio series), 1958-59; Lincoln for the Ages, 1960; (with Otto Eisenschiml) Eyewitness, 1960; (with E.B. Long) The Civil War Digest, 1960; Pictorial Autobiography of Abraham Lincoln, 1962; Abraham Lincoln, An Autobiographical Narrative, 1970; Abraham Lincoln: His Story in His Own Words, 1975; Abraham Lincoln's Last Full Measure of Devotion, 1981. Home: 175 E Delaware Pl Chicago IL 60611 Office: 18 E Chestnut St Chicago IL 60611

NEWNUM, RAYMOND LAVERN, internist; b. Kingman, Ind., June 18, 1925; s. Robert P. and Sylvia Grace (Alward) N.; student Purdue U., 1943-44; B.S. in Anatomy and Physiology, Ind. U., Bloomington, 1948, M.D., 1951; M.Sc., U. Minn., 1958; m. Betty Lou Coffing, Dec. 20, 1944; children—Kathleen Sue Newnum Roetzer, Janice Marie Newnum Sbrocchi, Betsy Rae, Paul Douglas, Lisa Dawn. Rotating intern Ind. U., 1951-52; gen. practice medicine, Hagerstown, Ind., 1952-55; resident in internal medicine Mayo Found., Rochester, Minn., 1955-58; cons. in internal medicine Carle Clinic, Urbana, Ill., 1958-61; practice medicine specializing in internal medicine, Evansville, Ind., 1961-75; founder, pres. Tri-State Internal Medicine, Inc., Evansville, 1975—; pres. staff St. Mary's Hosp., 1970-71, chief of medicine, 1965-67, clin. instr. medicine, 1973-77, cons. internal medicine, 1961-77; asst. prof. medicine Ind. U. Served with USNR, 1943-47. Diplomate Am. Bd. Internal Medicine. Fellow A.C.P. (life); mem. AMA, Ind., Vanderburgh County med. socs., Evansville, Ind. Soc. Internal Medicine (bd. dirs.), Am. Soc. Internal Medicine. Mem. Ch. Christian Fellowship. Home: 6710 Washington Ave Evansville IN 47715 Office: 801 Saint Marys Dr Evansville IN 47715

NEWPHER, JAMES ALFRED, JR., mgmt. cons.; b. New Brighton, Pa., Nov. 14, 1930; s. James Alfred and Olive Myrtle (Houlette) N.; B.S., U. Pa., 1952; M.B.A., Wharton Sch. U. Pa., 1957; m. Mildred Taylor, Aug. 23, 1953. Indsl. engr., Corning Glass Works (N.Y.), 1957-58, plant supr., 1958-60, prodn. supt., 1960-61, plant mgr., 1961-63, dept. mgr. advance products, 1963-64; asso. Booz, Allen & Hamilton, Inc., Chgo., 1964-69; v.p., mng. officer Lamalie Assos., Chgo., 1969-73; pres., chief exec. officer Newpher & Co., Inc., Chgo., 1973—; dir. D.B. Corkey Co., The Selden Co., Design Tech., Inc. Served with USN, 1951-56. Decorated Purple Heart. Mem. Naval Res. Assn., Inst. Mgmt. Cons., Res. Officers Assn. Presbyn. Club: Metropolitan Chgo. Home: 1655 We-Go Trail Deerfield IL 60015 Office: 2215 York Rd Suite 202 Oakbrook IL 60521

NEWSOM, GENE ALAN, agr. cooperative exec.; b. Pennsville, Ohio, Dec. 8, 1936; s. Clarence Thomas and Jennie Lucille (Smith) N.; B.S., Ohio State U., 1960; m. Lorinda Rose Larimer, June 1, 1958; children—Deborah Jo, Darla Jean, Thomas Alan. With Amstutz Hatchery, Orrville, Ohio, 1961; partner Tastee Egg Co., Marietta, Ohio, 1961-63; mgr. Northwest Ohio Poultry Assn., Napoleon, Ohio, 1963-67; mem. staff food div. Landmark, Inc., Columbus, Ohio, 1967-70, ops. coordinator food div., 1970-75, mgr. egg mktg. and food distbn., 1975-80, mgr. food div., 1981—; mem. adv. bd. Ohio State U. Poultry Dept. and Coll. Agr.; sec., dir. N. Am. Poultry Coop., N.Y.C.,

1978—; dir. Ag Foods, Burlington, N.J.; chmn. bd. dirs. Egg Clearinghouse, Durham, N.H., 1979—; dir. United Egg Producers, Atlanta; dir., past pres. Midwest Egg Producers, Davenport, Iowa; mem. Nat. Egg Price Study Com., Atlanta; mem. Am. Egg Bd. Task Force. Past chmn. pastor-parish com. William St. United Methodist Ch., now mem. adminstrv. bd. Recipient Golden Egg award Ohio Poultry Industry, 1979. Mem. Columbus Sales Exec. Club, Delaware County (Ohio) State U. Alumni Assn. (dir., past pres.). Club: Masons, Shriners, Kiwanis. Home: 144 Devon Rd Delaware OH 43015 Office: 35 E Chestnut St Columbus OH 43216

NEWSOM, JOHN WALTON, motion picture co. exec.; b. Durham, N.C., July 24, 1919; s. Marion Eugene and Annie Laurie (Long) N.; B.S., U.S. Naval Acad., 1941; postgrad. U. Md., 1954; m. Faye Nelson, Dec. 17, 1945; children—Jennifer Marie, John Walton, Elizabeth Nelson. Commd. ensign U.S. Navy, 1941, advanced through grades to capt., 1958; served in Jamaica, Panama, China, S. Am., South Pacific; ret., 1964; v.p. Centron Films Co., Lawrence, Kans., 1964—; prof. naval sci. U. Kans., 1958-61. Active local Boy Scouts Am., United Way, Big Bros./Big Sisters; chmn. Lawrence Meml. Hosp. Endowment Assn., 1971; mem. Douglas County-Lawrence Planning Commn., 1968-72. Decorated unit citation Letter of Commendation (3), USN. Mem. Public Relations Soc. Am., Internat. Assn. Bus. Communicators, Mktg. Communications Execs. Internat., U.S. Naval Acad. Alumni Assn. Republican. Methodist. Clubs: Army-Navy (Washington); Lawrence Country, Lawrence Rotary (pres. 1967-68; chmn. dist. govs. conf. 1966). Home: 3008 Nathan Dr Lawrence KS 66044 Office: 1621 W 9th St Lawrence KS 66044

NEWTON, GEORGE, musician; b. Kankakee, Ill., Jan. 18, 1908; s. George Andrew and Helen Hall (Coy) N.; A.B., Princeton U., 1929; postgrad. (sch. fellow) Juilliard Sch. Music, 1929-33; m. Melba Florence Nesbit, Dec. 26, 1944; 1 dau., Lucy Park. Solo singer in recital and oratorio, 1930—; instr. voice Ball State U., 1936-74; pvt. tchr. singing, Indpls., 1933—; lectr., lecture-recitalist at convs., workshops, 1950—. Fellow Am. Inst. Vocal Pedagogy; mem. Nat. Assn. Tchrs. Singing (regional gov., nat. dir., founder Indpls. chpt.), Music Tchrs. Nat. Assn., Am. Musicol. Soc. Republican. Presbyterian. Clubs: Indpls. Athletic, Portfolio, Parrhesian. Contbr. numerous articles on singing and composers, translations to profl. jours. Home: 747 N Graham Ave Indianapolis IN 46219

NEWTON, JOHN MILTON, univ. adminstr., psychologist; b. Schenectady, Feb. 25, 1929; s. Harry Hazleton and Bertha A. (Lehmann) N.; B.S., Union Coll., 1951; M.A., Ohio State U., 1952, Ph.D., 1955; m. Elizabeth Ann Slattery, Sept. 11, 1954; children—Patricia, Peter, Christopher. Research psychologist electric boat div. Gen. Dynamics Corp., Groton, Conn., 1957-60; asst. prof. psychology U. Nebr., Omaha, 1960-63, asso. prof., 1963-66, prof., 1966—, chmn. dept., 1967-74, dean Coll. Arts and Scis., 1974—; cons. in field, 1960-72. Served to 1st lt. Med. Service Corps, U.S. Army, 1955-57. Lic. psychologist, Nebr. Mem. Midwestern Psychol. Assn., Am. Psychol. Assn., Psychonomic Soc., Am. Assn. Higher Edn. Club: Rotary (Omaha). Research and publs. in field. Home: 5611 Jones St Omaha NE 68106 Office: Coll Arts and Scis U Nebr Omaha NE 68182

NEWTON, LINDA HUFFT, educator, communications cons.; b. Junction City, Kans., Aug. 5, 1940; d. Robert and Gail (Carter) Hufft; B.A., William Jewell Coll., 1962; M.A., U. Mo., Columbia, 1963; postgrad. Kans. U. Med. Center, 1966; m. Grundy Earl Newton, Aug. 9, 1963; children—Lance Madison, Clinton Graham. Speech therapist public schs., Independence, Mo., 1963-66; mem. faculty William Jewell Coll., Liberty, Mo., 1966—, asst. prof. communications, 1969—; cons. bus. and govt., 1972—; vis. prof. Harlaxton Coll., Grantham, Eng., 1980. Vol., Met. Orgn. to Combat Sexual Assaults, 1977—; loaned exec. Nat. Alliance Businessmen, 1973-76. Kansas City Council Higher Edn. grantee; Office. Vocat. Rehab. grantee. Mem. Internat. Transactional Analysis Assn., Speech Assn. Am., Central State Speech Assn., Mo. Speech Assn., Alpha Delta Pi. Presbyterian. Author: Therapy Made Fun, 1975. Office: William Jewell Coll Liberty MO 64068

NEWTON, NILES, psychologist, educator; b. N.Y.C., Jan. 19, 1923; d. Edward and Fanny (Scott) Rumely; B.A., Bryn Mawr Coll., 1945; Ph.D., Columbia U., 1952; m. Michael Newton, Mar. 27, 1943; children—Elizabeth W. Newton Reed, Frances L. Newton Stuntz, Edward Robson, Warren Polk. Research asso. obstetrics Sch. Medicine, U. Pa., Phila., 1952-55; mem. faculty (part-time) Sch. Medicine U. Miss., Jackson, 1955-66; asst. prof. div. psychology, dept. neurology and psychiatry Northwestern U. Med. Sch., Chgo., 1966-68, asso. prof., 1968-73, prof. dept. psychiatry, 1973-80, prof. behavioral sci. dept. psychiatry and behavioral scis., 1980—; mem. bd. consultants Am. Found. for Maternal and Child Health, N.Y.C., 1978—, v.p., 1981—; mem. internat. sci. com. 3d Internat. Congress of Psychosomatic Medicine in Ob-Gyn., London, 1971, mem. internat. organizing com. 4th Internat. Congress Psychosomatic Medicine in Ob-Gyn., Israel, 1974; mem. profl. adv. bd. La Leche League Internat., 1972—. Work group recorder White House Conf. on Childhood and Youth, 1960; bd. dirs. Family Focus, Chgo., 1977—. Recipient Spl. award Miss. Psychol. Assn., 1966; NIMH research fellow, 1949-51. Fellow Am. Psychol. Assn.; mem. Midwestern Psychol. Assn., Internat. Childbirth Edn. Assn. (dir. 1960-66, newsletter editor 1960-64), Internat. Soc. Psychosomatic Ob-Gyn. (exec. sec. 1974-80, founder 1971, v.p. 1980—), Soc. for Research in Child Devel., Am. Psychosomatic Soc., Internat. Acad. Sex Research, Soc. for Med. Anthropology, Am. Anthrop. Assn., Children's Home and Aid Soc. of Ill. (trustee 1979—), Sigma Xi. Author: Family Book of Child Care, 1957; contbr. chpts. in field to books on obstetrics; contbr. numerous articles on psychosomatic obstetrics to profl. jours.; columnist Chgo. Tribune, 1973-74; asso. editor Birth and Family Jour., 1975—; editorial bd. Psychology of Women Quar., 1978-80, Child and Family, 1962-67. Home: 2440 N Lakeview Chicago IL 60614 Office: Northwestern U Med Sch 303 E Chicago Ave Chicago IL 60611

NEWTON, RICK MARCUS, educator; b. St. Louis, May 8, 1949; s. Morris Eldon and Dolores (Bradford) N.; B.A. summa cum laude, Washington U., St. Louis, 1971; Raphael Demos scholar, Coll. Year in Athens, 1969-70; M.A. (grad. fellow), U. Mich., 1972, Ph.D., 1975; postgrad. Am. Acad. in Rome, 1973; m. Evangeline Stamatia Vlanton, Aug. 20, 1972; children—Joanna Alexandra, Olympia Stephanie. Asso. prof. classical studies Kent (Ohio) State U., 1975-80, asso. prof., 1980—. Bd. dirs. Hellenic Cultural Center, Pitts., Greek Sch. of Annunciation Greek Orthodox Ch., Akron, Ohio. Recipient Disting. Tchr. award Kent State U., 1979, research grantee, 1977, 79; research fellow Am. Sch. Classical Studies, Athens, 1977. Mem. Am. Philol. Assn., Am. Vergilian Soc., Classical Assn. Middle West and South, Ohio Classical Conf., Modern Greek Studies Assn., Phi Beta Kappa. Greek Orthodox. Contbr. articles to profl. jours. Home: 520 Rellim Dr Kent OH 44240 Office: Dept of Classical Studies Kent State University Kent OH 44242

NEWTON, ROGER GERHARD, physicist; b. Landsberg, Germany, Nov. 30, 1924; came to U.S., 1946, naturalized, 1949; s. Arthur and Margaret (Blume) N.; A.B. summa cum laude, Harvard U., 1949, M.A., 1950, Ph.D., 1953; m. Ruth Gordon, June 18, 1953; children—Julie, Rachel, Paul. Teaching fellow Harvard U., 1951-52; mem. Inst. Advanced Study, Princeton, N.J., 1953-55, 79; asst. prof. physics Ind. U., Bloomington, 1955-58, asso. prof., 1958-60, prof., 1960-78, Disting. prof., 1978—, chmn. math. physics program, 1964—, chmn. dept. physics, 1973-80; sr. NSF fellow U. Rome, 1962-63; CNRS fellow U. Montpellier, France, 1971-72, U. Geneva, 1972; cons. Gulf Research Corp. Pres., Bloomington Civil Liberties Union, 1968. Served with U.S. Army, 1946-47. Recipient Bowdoin prize Harvard U., 1948. Fellow Am. Phys. Soc.; mem. N.Y. Acad. Sci., Fedn. Am. Scientists, AAUP, AAAS, Phi Beta Kappa, Sigma Xi. Author: Scattering Theory of Waves and Particles, 1966; The Complex J Plane, 1964. Asso. editor Jour. Math. Physics, 1967-70, 73-76. Contbr. articles to profl. jours. Home: 1023 S Ballantine Bloomington IN 47401 Office: Physics Dept Indiana Univ Bloomington IN 47405

NG, SAMUEL YUWAI, research and devel. engr.; b. Hong Kong, Oct. 21, 1940; s. Fook-Man and Kwok-Ching (Chui) N.; came to U.S., 1963, naturalized, 1977; B.S., Hong Kong Bapt. Coll., 1962; M.S., U. Miss., 1965; Ph.D., Okla. State U., 1970; m. Virginia Thuc-Hoa, Dec. 26, 1970; children—Randy, Debbie. Teaching asst. Hong Kong Bapt. Coll., 1961-62, instr., 1962-63; research asst. U. Miss., 1963-65, research engr., 1965; research asst. dept. civil engring. Okla. State U., 1965-70; geotech. engr., sr. project engr. Soil Exploration Co., St. Paul, 1970-79, prin. engr., dir. research and devel., 1979-80; adv. soil mechanics div. dept. civil and mineral engring. U. Minn., 1979—. Social activities chmn. Elim Youth Group T.S.T. Bapt. Ch., Hong Kong, 1960-61; deacon Chinese Christian Fellowship, St. Paul, 1971-77, 79-80, chmn. bd. deacons, 1981—, chmn. evangelism and missions com., 1977-80, adult Sunday Sch. tchr., 1978—. Christian Student scholar and distinction scholar Hong Kong Bapt. Coll., 1961, David J. Carver Jr. Meml. Fund scholar U. Richmond, 1964, U. Miss. fgn. student scholar, 1964; registered profl. engr., Minn., Iowa, Wis., Wyo., N.D., S.D. Mem. ASCE, Transp. Research Bd.-NRC, Internat. Soc. Soil Mechanics and Found. Engring., Engring. Inst. Can., Minn. Geotech. Soc., Sigma Xi, Phi Kappa Phi. Baptist.

NGUYEN, HIEP, chemist; b. Hanoi, Vietnam, Aug. 6, 1929; came to U.S., 1975, naturalized, 1981; s. Ung Van and Hien Thi (Pham) N.; pharmacist, Coll. Pharmacy, Saigon, Vietnam, 1956; B.Sc., U. Paris, 1965, Ph.D. in Pharmacy, 1966; m. Lien Phuong Thi Ngo, Mar. 3, 1970; children—Thanh Huong Thi, George Binh Hiep. Tech. dir. Unitex Labs., Vietnam, 1967-70; owner, dir. Biothera Labs., Vietnam, 1970-75; prof. pharmaceutics Coll. Pharmacy, U. Saigon (Vietnam), 1967-75; dir. quality control Upsher-Smith Labs., Mpls., 1975—. Bd. dirs. Vietnamese Alliance Minn.; active Amber Woods Homeowners Assn. Mem. Minn. Chromatography Forum. Buddhist. Contbr. chpt. in book. Home: 18605 33d Ave N Plymouth MN 55447 Office: 14905 23d Ave N Minneapolis MN 55441

NIBLETTE, ROBERT KENNETH, clin. psychologist; b. Hackensack, N.J., Aug. 4, 1943; s. Howard Taylor and Eleanor Pearl (McEachern) N.; B.A. (Coll. scholar, Am. Legion scholar), Hamilton Coll., 1966; postgrad. Western Mich. U., 1966-67; M.A., Wayne State U., Detroit, 1974, Ph.D., 1976; m. Judith Mae Hacking, Jan. 31, 1964; children—Robert Kenneth II, James William. Psychologist, Wayne County Child Study Clinic, Detroit, 1968-69; clin. psychology intern Mental Hygiene Clinic, Allen Park (Mich.) VA Hosp., 1969-71; psychologist Plymouth Center Human Devel., Northville, Mich., 1971-73, Northville Residential Tng. Center, 1973-76, Coldwater (Mich.) Regional Center for Devel. Disabilities, 1976—; pvt. practice clin. psychology, Coldwater, 1979—. Former pres. Westminster Pl. Coop., Taylor, Mich.; chmn. Parents Ad Hoc Com. for Busing in Coldwater. VA internship grantee, 1969-71; USPHS grantee, 1967-68. Mem. Am. Assn. Mental Deficiency, Am. Psychol. Assn., Psi Chi. Research on auditory and tactile sensory interaction, biofeedback, relaxation, and retarded adults. Home and Office: 834 Buccaneer Ln Coldwater MI 49036

NICHIPORUK, WALTER, chemist; b. Poland, Sept. 5, 1919; came to U.S., 1946, naturalized, 1952; s. Alex Andrew and Anna Josephine (Radchuk) N.; student U. Warsaw, 1938-39; U. Munich, 1946; M.S., U. Chgo., 1950; m. Elizabeth Kellner, Aug. 14, 1958; 1 son, Brian. Technologist, Enrico Fermi Inst., U. Chgo., 1950-52; chemist Calif. Inst. Tech., Pasadena, 1952-68; research asso. Ariz. State U., Tempe, 1968-74; cons. chemist, Tempe, 1974-77; chemist U.S. Dept. Energy, Argonne, Ill., 1977—; mem. translation panel Plenum Publ. Corp., N.Y.C., 1967-77. Served with UNRRA, Germany, 1945-46. Fellow Meteoritical Soc.; mem. Am. Chem. Soc., Internat. Assn. Geochemistry and Cosmochemistry, Geochem. Soc., Sigma Xi. Asso. editor Bibliography of Meteorites, 1953; translator, reviser (V.V. Cherdyntsev) Raprostranennost' Khimicheskikh Elementov, 1961; contbr. articles to profl. jours. Home: 107 W 65th Lake Dr Westmont IL 60559 Office: US Dept Energy/New Brunswick Lab Argonne IL 60439

NICHOL, JOHN BRUCE, hosp. adminstr.; b. Chgo., Feb. 21, 1941; s. David McGreggor and Eloise (Kincaid) N.; student W.Va. Inst. Tech., 1959-61, Northwestern U., 1961-62; B.S. in Psychology, U. Mich., 1969. Tng. cons. Precision Mgmt. Co., Kansas City, Mo., 1969-72; dir. edn. Internat. Assn. Assessing Officers, Chgo., 1973-76; dir. sales tng. Commerce Clearing House, Chgo., 1977; instructional developer King Faisal Specialist Hosp. and Research Centre, Riyadh, Saudi Arabia, 1977-80; cultural cons., Kalamazoo, 1980-81; orientation supr. King Abdul Aziz Airbase Hosp., Dhahran, Saudi Arabia, 1981—. Mem. Am. Soc. Health Manpower Edn. and Tng., Am. Soc. Tng. and Devel., Internat. Cons. Found., Soc. Intercultural Edn., Tng. and Research. Editor: Property Assessment Valuation, 1977; photographer: The American in Saudi Arabia, 1980; contbr. articles to profl. jours. Home: 1075 Wall Lake Dr Delton MI 49046 Office: Personnel Services King Abdul Aziz Airbase Hosp Dhahran Internat Airport PO Box 570 Dhahran Saudi Arabia

NICHOL, ROBERT JAMES, lumber co. exec.; b. Sandusky, Mich., Nov. 29, 1949; s. James Leroy and Mary Catherine (Moore) N.; student Central Mich. U., 1971-72, St. Clair County Community Coll., 1972-77; m. Cheryl Lynn Trowhill, June 20, 1970; children—Tracie Renae, Marcus Robert. Partner, Nichol Lumber Co., Deckerville, Mich., 1972-75, v.p., 1975-80, pres., 1980—. Served with U.S. Army, 1968-71. Mem. Jaycees. Republican. Methodist. Clubs: Lions (v.p. 1981—), Huron Shores Golf (treas. 1981—). Home: 3646 Pine St Deckerville MI 48427 Office: Nichol Lumber Co 3742 N Main St Deckerville MI 48427

NICHOL, WILLIAM E., state legislator; b. Windsor, Colo., Mar. 12, 1918; grad. Nebr. Wesleyan U.; m. Ruth Ellis, Nov. 29, 1941; children—James C., Linda Harsch. Mem. Nebr. Legislature, 1974—. Commr., Scotts Bluff County, Nebr.; former mayor, councilman, Scottsbluff. Office: U Nebr Panhandle Sta Scottsbluff NE 69361*

NICHOLAS, CHARLES THOMAS, steel and aluminum roofing and siding mfg. exec.; b. Indpls., Mar. 31, 1949; s. Charles and Marcella (Hadjieff) N.; B.S., Ind. U., 1971; m. Marsha Lynne, June 23, 1973; children—Tara Lynne, Todd Stephen. Real estate broker F.C. Tucker Co., Indpls., 1971-72; state trooper State of Ind., Charlestown, 1972-76; sales rep. Gifford-Hill & Co., Inc., Louisville, 1976-78, gen. mgr., Jefferson, Ohio, 1978—. Mem. Ind. U. Alumni Assn., Aircraft Owners and Pilots Assn., Kappa Sigma. Republican. Methodist. Home: 366 Kathleen Dr Jefferson OH 44047 Office: Gifford-Hill & Co Inc 352 E Erie St Jefferson OH 44047

NICHOLAS, HAROLD JOSEPH, biochemist; b. St. Louis, Mar. 1, 1919; s. Joseph Lucas and Alma (Beger) N.; B.S. in Chem. Engring., Mo. Sch. Mines and Metallurgy, 1941; Ph.D. in Biochemistry, St. Louis U., 1950; m. Dorothy Jean Reinhold, May 24, 1952; children—Mark, Christopher. Asst. prof. biochemistry dept. U. Kans., Lawrence, 1950-53; asst. prof. Ob-Gyn dept. U. Kans., Kansas City, 1953-60, asso. prof., 1960-63; asst. prof. dept. biochemistry St. Louis U., 1963-72, prof., 1972—, dir. exptl. medicine Inst. Med. Edn. and Research, 1962—. Mem. Am. Acad. Neurology (asso.), Endocrine Soc., Am. Soc. Biol. Chemists, Am. Soc. Plant Physiology, Am. Soc. for Neurochemistry (charter), Am. Chem. Soc., Am. Inst. Chemists, Pan Am. Med. Soc. (asso.), Sigma Xi (pres. St. Louis U. chpt. 1975), Tau Beta Pi. Contbrs. articles in field of terpene biochemistry, brain biochemistry and liquid crystals to profl. jours.; patentee in field of liquid crystals. Home: 12456 Merrick Dr Creve Coeur MO 63141 Office: Inst Med Edn and Research 1605 S 14th St Saint Louis MO 63104

NICHOLS, ROBERT CHARLES, clin. psychologist; b. Morristown, N.J., Apr. 20, 1941; s. Charles Taylor and Mae Miller N.; B.A., Lafayette Coll., 1963; Ph.D., U. Tenn., 1973; m. Barbara Van Til, Aug. 12, 1967; children—Linda Alison, Laura Beth. Clin. psychologist Bay Area Guidance Center, Bay City, Mich., 1971-74, clin. supr., 1974—, asst. dir., 1980—; pvt. practice clin. psychology, Bay City, 1975—. Mem. Am. Psychol. Assn. Home: 625 Green Ave Bay City MI 48706 Office: 201 Mulholland Bay City MI 48706

NICHOLS, ROBERT LEE, food mfg. co. exec.; b. Clarksburg, W.Va., Nov. 4, 1924; s. Clarence Garfield and Reatha Maude (Berry) N.; student W.Va. Bus. Coll., 1944, U. Detroit, 1959; m. Vianne Hope Demaray; children—Donna Beth, Michael Alan, Jeffrey Mark. Sales rep. Kellogg Sales Co., Battle Creek, Mich., 1944-50, dist. mgr., 1950-61, asst. div. mgr., 1961-64, sales promotion dir., 1964-69, exec. v.p., gen. sales mgr., 1969-71, pres., 1976-78; group exec. v.p., dir. Kellogg Co., Battle Creek, 1978—; pres. Mrs. Smith's Frozen Foods Co., 1979—, also dir.; pres. Fearn Internat. Inc., 1971-76, dir., 1971—; dir. Cereal Inst., 1976-79, Am. Frozen Food Inst., 1979—; bd. govs. Acad. Food Mktg., St. Joseph U., 1976. Exec. v.p., bd. dirs. Jr. Achievement of Battle Creek, 1970-71. Mem. Battle Creek Area C. of C. Clubs: Battle Creek Country, Masons, Scottish Rite. Office: 235 Porter St Battle Creek MI 49016

NICHOLS, THEODORE GEORGE, hosp. engr.; b. Chgo., July 27, 1927; s. Michael Feodor and Sophia (Lewandowski) N.; Student Wright Jr. Coll., 1950-53, Ill. Inst. Tech., 1956-61; m. Barbara McKillip, Mar. 14, 1975; children by previous marriage—Michael J., Julie Ann, Theodore George. Supt., Paschen Contractors, Ill. and Ind., 1947-56; dir. phys. plant Ill. Inst. Tech. Research Inst., Chgo., 1956-69; dir. engring. Rush Presbyn. St. Luke's Med. Center, Chgo., 1969—. Deacon, sec. council St. Andrews Ch., 1966-68; com. chmn., instl. rep. Chgo. Area Council Boy Scouts Am., 1967-68. Mem. Am. Hosp. Assn., Inst. Plant Maintenance, Western Soc. Engrs., Chgo. Supts. Assn. Supervised constrn. 1st indsl. nuclear reactor, 1955. Home: 111 Fernwood Dr Glenview IL 60025 Office: 1753 W Congress Pkwy Chicago IL 60612

NICHOLS, THOMAS HOGAN, steel fabricating co. exec.; b. Kansas City, Mo., Feb. 14, 1926; s. Harold F. and Bess V. (Hogan) N.; B.S., Ind. U., 1950; B.S. in Metallurgy, Purdue U., 1959; bus. certificate U. Chgo., 1962; m. Patricia A. Young, June 7, 1952; children—Patricia J., Susan T. Salesman, U.S. Steel Corp., Chgo., 1950-53; quality control supr. Taylor Forge & Pipe Co., Gary, Ind., 1953-55; asst. supt. prodn. control Youngstown Steel Co., East Chicago, Ind., 1955-70; exec. v.p. Sherman-Reynolds Co., Chgo., 1972—; dir. 240 Venture Land Devel. Co. Adviser Jr. Achievement, Chgo.; cons. Dawson Skill Center, Chgo.; bd. dirs. Chgo. State U.; mem. Joint Hosp. Fund Com. Lake County (Ind.), 1972-74. Served with U.S. Army, 1944-46. Recipient Boss of Yr. award Hammond (Ind.) Jr. C. of C., 1964; certificate of merit Jr. Achievement, Chgo., 1960. Mem. Am. Iron and Steel Inst., Ind. U. Alumni Club, Midwest Alumni Club U. So. Calif., Parents Club U. So. Calif. Republican. Presbyterian. Clubs: Masons, Shriner. Home: 697 Old Barn Rd Barrington IL 60010

NICHOLS, VIRGINIA LLOYD, personnel exec.; b. Inverness, Fla., Feb. 6, 1921; d. Strauss L. and Ida Mae (Baker) Lloyd; B.S., Fla. State Coll. for Women, 1942; m. Ralph Charles Nichols, Dec. 31, 1947; 1 dau., Cheryl Nichols Campbell. Home economist Fla. Power Corp., St. Petersburg, 1942-47; state home economist Graybar Electric Co., Jacksonville, Fla., 1950-55; home economist Ind. and Mich. Electric Co., South Bend, Ind., 1956-58; with Snelling & Snelling, South Bend, 1970-78, asst. mgr., 1973-74, gen. mgr., 1974-75, v.p. ops., 1975-78; pres., gen. mgr. Nichols & Assos., Inc., d/b/a Snelling & Snelling, Merrillville, Ind., 1978—, Highland, Ind., 1981—, mem. nat. exec. council Snelling & Snelling, 1981-82. Bd. dirs. Family and Childrens Center, South Bend, 1962-70, Better Bus. Bur. N.W. Ind., 1981—; chmn. Joan E. Snelling Meml. Com.; mem. adv. bd. Projects with Industry, Goodwill Industries Michiana, South Bend, 1975-78; mem. Republican Precinct Com., 1958-70; deacon Sunnyside Presbyterian Ch., 1962-66. Recipient nat. citation Goodwill Industries, 1976, numerous award Snelling and Snelling. Mem. N.W. Ind. Personnel Assn. (v.p. 1980-82), Nat. Assn. Personnel Cons., Am. Soc. Personnel Adminstrn., Smithsonian Instn. Soc., Nat. Audubon Soc., Bus. and Profl. Womens Club. Clubs: Conservation of Kosciuosko County, Conservation of Ind. Author: Eating Right Can Be Fun, 1955. Office: 1000 E 80th Place Twin Towers # 302S Merrillville IN 46410

NICHOLS, WILLIAM CURTIS, JR., clin. psychologist, family therapist; b. Fayette, Ala., Apr. 16, 1929; s. William Curtis and Eva (Hargett) N.; A.B., U. Ala., 1953; Ed.D., Columbia U., 1960; postgrad. U. Colo., 1963; m. Alice Mancill, May 29, 1954; children—A. Camille, William Mancill, David Paul. Asst. prof. U. Ala., 1960-63; prof. Samford U., 1963-65; postdoctoral fellow in psychotherapy Merrill-Palmer Inst., 1963-64, mem. psychotherapy faculty, 1965-69; pvt. practice psychology, Grosse Pointe, Mich., 1969-73; prof. home and family life, dir. marriage and family counseling Fla. State U., 1973-76; pvt. practice clin. psychology and family therapy, Birmingham, Mich., 1976—. Mem. Detroit Mayor's Commn. on Children and Youth, 1966-69; v.p. Family and Children Services Oakland (Mich.), 1981—. Served with C.E., U.S. Army, 1948-49. Recipient Service award Ala. Assn. Mental Health, 1963; Spl. award for outstanding contbns. Fla. Assn. Marriage and Family Counselors, 1976; Disting. Service award Mich. Assn. Marriage

Counselors, 1979. Fellow Am. Assn. Marriage and Family Therapists (Spl. award for outstanding contbns., 1976, 78, pres. 1981-82), Am. Orthopsychiat. Assn.; mem. Am. Psychol. Assn., Nat. Council Family Relations (dir. 1969-77, 79-80, pres. 1976-77). Democrat. Presbyterian. Founding editor Jour. Marital and Family Therapy, 1974-76; editor Family Relations (formerly Family Coordinator), 1970-76. Home: 31829 Sheridan Dr Birmingham MI 48009 Office: 30200 Telegraph Rd Suite 455 Birmingham MI 48010

NICHOLS-JOHNSON, VICTORIA RAYE, physician; b. Springfield, Ill., Nov. 21, 1944; d. George Ray and Vesta Victoria (Meek) Nichols; B.S., U. Ill., 1966; M.D., U. Mich., 1970; m. Louis Chism Johnson, Dec. 14, 1974; children—Marguerita V., Victoria Susan. Intern, Mayo Clinic, Rochester, Minn., 1970-71, resident, 1971-75; staff physician Planned Parenthood of Rochester (Minn.), 1972-75; clin. asst. prof. obstetrics and gynecology So. Ill. U. Sch. Medicine, Carbondale, 1976, asst. prof. obstetrics and gynecology, Springfield, 1977—; med. dir. Planned Parenthood, Springfield, 1979-80. NIMH research fellow, 1967-68; Sloan Found. Nat. Med. fellow, 1967-70; diplomate Am. Bd. Obstetrics and Gynecology. Fellow Am. Coll. Obstetricians and Gynecologists; mem. Am. Fertility Soc., Ill. Med. Assn., Am. Med. Women's Assn., AAUW, Delta Sigma Theta. African Methodist Episcopal Ch. Club: Springfield Right-to-Life. Contbr. articles in field to profl. jours.; composer: From Now On We are As One, 1974 (musical composition). Home: 240 Deerhead Ln Springfield IL 62704 Office: So Ill Univ Sch Medicine 800 N Rutledge PO Box 3926 Springfield IL 62708

NICHOLSON, MARION CRAWFORD, mfrs. rep., former mayor; b. College Park, Ga., Jan. 31, 1917; s. William Malcolm and Marion Melissa (Neely) N.; certificate aero. engring. Ga. Inst. Tech., 1940; m. Catherine Vaughn Wise, Apr. 5, 1947; children—Catherine Marion, Barbara Ann. With Atlanta Constn. Pub. Co., 1937-40; sta. mgr. Eastern Air Lines, St. Louis, Memphis and Lake Charles, La., 1940-53; owner, operator M.C. Nicholson & Assos., mfrs. sales rep., St. John, 1953—, Aetna Metal Products Co., St. John, 1973—; councilman, St. John, 1974, mayor, 1974-77. Pres. PTA concil Normandy Sch. System, 1966-67. Mem. Nat. Assn. Mfrs. Agts., St. Louis Bd. Elec. Trade. Democrat. Presbyterian. Address: 3901 Engler Ave St Louis MO 63114

NICHOLSON, NANCY VIOLA SNIDER, educator; b. Lachine, Mich., May 28, 1923; d. John William and Edna (Mills) Snider; B.A., U. Mich., 1946, M.A., 1947, Ph.D., 1962; m. Fred Nicholson, May 24, 1967 (div. Oct. 1968). English instr. Iowa State Tchrs. Coll., Cedar Falls, 1947-48; instr. Alpena (Mich.) Community Coll., 1953-54; asst. prof. U. N.Y. State Tchrs. Coll., Cortland, N.Y., 1955-56; instr. supr. Columbia Thcrs. Coll., Afghanistan, 1956-57; instr. Tufts U., Medford, Mass., 1957-60; asso. prof. Clarion State Coll., Clarion, Pa., 1963-66; asso. prof. Wis. State U., LaCrosse, 1966-67; lectr. Eastern Mich. U., Ypsilanti, 1967-69; prof. English, So. U., Baton Rouge, 1969-71; research on folklore, Lachine, Mich., 1971-74; lectr. U. Isfahan (Iran), 1974-76; vis. prof. grad. studies U. Paraiba (Brazil), 1976-77; asso. prof. U. Tabriz (Iran), 1977-78, Women's Coll., U. Riyadh (Saudi Arabia), 1979-80; lectr. Jinan (China) U., 1981—; seminar dir. Ford Found., U. Pitts. summer 1964. Founded library in South India, 1954, social work in India, 1954. Mem. Hindustani Assn., U. Mich. (pres. 1954), Modern Lang. Assn., Coll. English Assn., AAUW, AAUP, League of Women Voters. Contbr. articles in field to profl. jours. Home: Lachine MI 49753

NICHOLSON, THEODORE H., ednl. adminstr.; b. Chgo., July 27, 1929; B.S., Loyola U., Chgo., 1951; M.S. (State of Ill. Vets scholar), No. Ill. U., 1955; postgrad., Rockford Coll., 1955; Ph.D. (NDEA fellow, 1966-67), U. Wis., Madison, 1968; children—Craig, Kimberlee, Christine, Rhonda. Tchr., Morris Kennedy Sch., Winnebago County, Ill., 1951-53, Rockford (Ill.) Public Schs., 1953-55, evening sch., 1956-60; prin. Marsh Schs., Dist. 58, Winnebago County, 1955-59, supt., 1959-66; supt. Dearborn Twp. Sch. Dist. 8, Dearborn Heights, Mich., 1968-69, Wilmington (Ohio) City Sch., 1969-72; supr. schs., Wausau, Wis., 1972—; vis. prof. Central State U., Wilberforce, Ohio, 1969-70; teaching asst., research asst., lectr. U. Wis., summer 1976; lectr., cons. Univ. Council Ednl. Adminstrn.; v.p. N.C. Data Processing Center, 1974—. Active Central Wausau Progress, 1973—. Served with USN, 1943-46. Recipient Citizenship award City of Rockford, 1960, 64; Community Leader award Sta. WXCO, Wausau, 1974. Mem. Am. Assn. Sch. Adminstrs., Wis. Ednl. Research Assn., Wis. Assn. Sch. Dist. Adminstrs., Am. Assn. Supervision and Curriculum Devel., C. of C. (edn. com.), Phi Delta Kappa. Clubs: Elks, Optimists. Contbr. articles in field to profl. publs. Office: 407 Grant St Wausau WI 54401

NICHOLSON, WILLIAM NOEL, clin. neuropsychologist; b. Detroit, Dec. 24, 1936; s. James Eardly and Hazel A. (Wagner) N.; A.B., Wittenberg U., 1959; M.Div., Luth. Theol. Sem., Phila., 1962; Ph.D. (HEW fellow), Mich. State U., 1972; m. Nancy Ann Marshall, June 15, 1957; children—Ann Marie, Kristin, Scott. Ordained to ministry Lutheran Ch., 1962; parish pastor Our Savior Luth. Ch., Saginaw, Mich., 1962-69; psychologist Ingham-Eaton-Clinton Mental Health Bd., 1971-72; psychologist Bay-Arenac Mental Health Bd., 1972-74; dir., psychologist Riverside Center, Bay City, Mich., 1974-75; pres. Bay Psychol. Assos., P.C., Bay City, 1975—; cons. Gov.'s Office of Drug Abuse, 1972-74. Cert., Nat. Register Health Care Providers in Psychology. Mem. Am. Psychol. Assn., Midwest Psychol. Assn., Mich. Psychol. Assn., Soc. Behavioral Medicine, Mental Health Assn. (pres. Bay-Arenac Chpt. 1981). Lutheran. Clubs: Bay City Yacht, Rotary. Author: A Guttman Facet Analysis of Attitude-Behaviors Toward Drug Users by Heroin Addicts and Mental Health Therapists, 1972; contbr. articles to profl. jours. Office: Allen Medical Bldg 200 S Wenona St Bay City MI 48706

NICHTER, JAMES WALTER, educator; b. Logansport, Ind., July 16, 1935; s. Walter Martin and Lillian H. (Grosh) N.; B.S., Ohio State U., 1964; M.B.A., Oklahoma City U., 1967; m. Margery Ann Siferd, Jan. 8, 1955; children—Charles W., Michael B., Katrina L. Enlisted USAF, 1954, advanced through grades to capt., 1968; base procurement officer Wakkanai Air Sta., Hokkaido, Japan, 1967-70; transp. officer Chauute AFB (Ill.), 1971-74; ret., 1974; instr. acctg. Canby (Minn.) Area Vocat.-Tech. Inst., 1975—; pres. Marnick, Inc., Mpls., 1970-71. Pres., Canby Community Players Inc. Recipient citation Gov. Tokyo, 1960-62. Mem. Am. Vocat. Assn., Minn. Edn. Assn. (mem. state negotiations council), Canby Edn. Assn. (chief negotiator), Canby C. of C. Clubs: Golf (treas.), Masons (sr. steward), Eagles (treas.) (Canby). Home: 306 Orlano Ave Canby MN 56220 Office: Hwy 68 W Canby MN 56220

NICKELL, LOUIS G., chem. co. exec.; b. Little Rock, July 10, 1921; s. Louis G. and Caroline Idene (Brasher) N.; B.S., Yale U., 1943, M.S. (Eaton fellow), 1947, Ph.D. (Sterling fellow, Sheffield fellow), 1949; m. Natalie Wills, Sept. 30, 1942; children—Natalie Wills, Louis Edward, Mary Barbara. Research asso. Bklyn. Bot. Garden, 1949-51; head phytochemistry lab. Pfizer, Inc., Bklyn., 1951-61; dir. research Hawaiian Sugar Planters Assn., Honolulu, 1961-75; v.p. research div. W.R. Grace Co., Columbia, Md., 1975-78; v.p. research and devel. Velsicol Chem. Corp., Chgo., 1978—. Served with USMC, 1942-45. Mem. Am. Soc. Plant Physiologists (treas. 1976—), Am. Chem. Soc., Plant Growth Regulator Working Group (chmn. 1980-81), Soc. Economy Botany, Chi Phi. Mem. editorial bd. Antimicrobial Agents and Chemotherapy, 1972-77. Home: 3730 N Lake Shore Dr Chicago IL 60613 Office: Velsicol Chem Corp 341 E Ohio St Chicago IL 60611

NICKELS, ROBERT EDWARD, outdoor products mfg. co. exec.; b. Detroit, Jan. 23, 1943; s. William Edward and Winifred Jane (Hocking) N.; B.S., Mich. State U., 1965, M.B.A., 1966; postgrad. Standford Exec. Program, 1978; m. Carol Lee Johnson, Jan. 26, 1963; children—Tracy Lee, Robbie Lynn. Dept. mgr. mfg. Procter & Gamble, Chgo., 1967-69; with Roper Lawn Products, 1969-78, v.p. mfg., 1977-78; exec. v.p. Roper Outdoor Products, Bradley, Ill., 1978-81, pres., 1981—, also pres. Roper Corp., 1981—; dir. Wilkens Parts & Equipment. Bd. dirs. Roper Found. Republican. Presbyterian. Clubs: Elks, Bon Vivant Country. Home: 9 Bristol Green Bourbonnais IL 60914 Office: Roper Outdoor Products Broadway and Schuyler Bradley IL 60915

NICKEY, KARYL KRISTINE, acct.; b. Elmhurst, Ill., Oct. 1, 1950; d. Edward Albert and Verna Eulalia (Bergdahl) N.; student Western Ill. U., 1968-69; B.A. in Acctg. (Farmers Ins. Group scholar), B.A. in Psychology, North Central Coll., 1977. Billing and accounts payable clk. NBC, 1972-75; acct. Oak Brook Devel. Co., 1976-77; acctg. mgmt. trainee A.C. Nielsen Co., Northbrook Ill., 1977-78, supr. payroll and payroll taxation, 1978-80; corp. payroll mgr. Brunswick Corp., Skokie, Ill., 1980—. Tchr. swimming to handicapped ARC; founder, coach Villa Park Swim Team, 1967-69; vol. Good Shepherd Hosp., Barrington, Ill., unit co-chmn. vols. for ob-gyn, 1980-82; mem. Horsemasters Drill Team; appeared in film Your Emotions. Mem. Nat. Assn. Accts. (asso. dir. meetings Chgo. chpt. 1979-80, dir. meetings 1980-81, program dir. 1981-82). Club: Riding (Barrington Hills, Ill.). Office: 1 Brunswick Plaza Skokie IL 60077

NICOLAON, GILBERT ANDRE, scientist; b. Paris, May 1, 1940; came to U.S., 1969; s. Auguste Leon and Germaine (LeGoff) N.; student Ecole Superieure de Chimie Industrielle de Lyon, 1960-63; Ingenieur E.S.C.I.L., Faculte des Sciences de Lyon, 1963, Ph.D. in Chemistry, 1968. Asst. prof. U. Lyon (France), 1968-69; research asso. Clarkson Coll. Tech., Potsdam, N.Y., 1969-72; research scientist Alsthom-Exxon, Massy, France, 1972-75; cultural and sci. attache French Embassy, Houston, 1976-79, sci. attache, Chgo., 1979—. Decorated chevalier des Palmes Academiques. Mem. Am. Chem. Soc., AAAS, Soc. Automotive Engrs., Sigma Xi. Contbr. articles to internat. jours. Patentee in field. Home: 1030 N State St Chicago IL 60610 Office: 401 N Michigan Ave Chicago IL 60611

NICOLAZZI, ROBERT JOSEPH, tractor co. exec.; b. Kenosha, Wis., Dec. 19, 1938; s. John Seccondo and Mary Anne (Gianeselli) N.; B.B.A. in Fin., U. Notre Dame, 1960; M.B.A., Mich. State U., 1979; m. Judith Marie Thomey, Nov. 10, 1962; children—Steven J., Deborah A., Richard J. With tractor ops. Ford Motor Co., 1960—, procurement planning mgr., Antwerp, Belgium, 1965-68, product program timing mgr., Troy, Mich., 1968-71, dist. sales mgr., Memphis, Richmond and Albany, 1971-76, gen. mktg. mgr. world-wide ops., Troy, 1976-80, gen. ops. mgr. tractor ops.-Europe, Brussels, Belgium, 1980; gen. sales mgr. tractor internat. ops., Troy, Mich., 1981—. Home: 3664 Ridgeland Rd West Bloomfield MI 48033 Office: 2500 E Maple Rd Troy MI 48084

NICOLET, PAULA ANN, clin. social worker; b. Alton, Ill., Sept. 17, 1940; d. Paul Alcide and Opal Marie (Hamilton) N.; B.A. in Psychology and Sociology, So. Ill. U., Edwardsville, 1962; M.S.W. with final honors, Washington U., 1969. Caseworker, Cook County Dept. Public Aid, Chgo., 1962-65; casework rep., coordinator spl. projects Oak Forest (Ill.) Hosp., 1965; regional caseworker, service staff Dept. Public Aid State of Ill., Belleville, 1965-67; caseworker II group work coordinator Madison County (Ill.) Dept. Public Aid, Edwardsville, 1969-71; dir. social services St. Joseph's Hosp., Highland, Ill., 1971—; adj. faculty St. Louis U., Washington U., St. Louis, Eastern Ill. U., Charleston; vis. lectr. social work and sociology So. Ill. U., Edwardsville; cons. in field. Bd. dirs. Madison County Mental Health Center, Alton, Ill., 1972-79, pres., 1974-79; bd. dirs. Hospice Madison County, Inc., Eastern Madison County Nutritional Services; mem. Health Systems Agy. St. Louis. Cert. social worker, Ill. Mem. Acad. Cert. Social Workers, Nat. Assn. Social Workers, Am. Hosp. Assn., Ill. Soc. Hosp. Social Work Dirs. (chmn. profl. papaers com. 1981), Soc. Hosp. Social Service Dirs., Am. Public Health Assn., AAUW (dir. 1973-77, v.p. 1974-76). Home: 809 Sycamore Highland IL 62249 Office: 1515 Main St Highland IL 62249

NICOLL, DAVID, magazine pub.; b. St. Louis, Jan. 3, 1929; s. Thadius Warsaw and Virginia (Feilbach) Taylor; student Kenyon Coll., 1946-47, U. Toledo, 1948-51; m. Dorothy Novielli, Dec. 16, 1967; children by previous marriage—David, Andrew Taylor, Jeffery Scott, Rebecca Lynn. Test pilot, sales mgr. Navion div. Tusco Corp., Galveston, Tex., 1957-59; sales mgr. Bellanca Aircraft Co., Alexandria, Minn., 1959-63; pub. Airport Services Mgmt. mag., Mpls., 1963—; comml. pilot. Served with USAF, 1955-56. Mem. Nat. Air Transp. Assn., Am. Assn. Airport Execs., Aircraft Owners and Pilots Assn. Republican. Home: 8549 Irwin Rd Minneapolis MN 55437 Office: 731 Hennepin Ave Minneapolis MN 55403

NICOLOSI, STEPHEN LOUIS, chemist; b. N.Y.C., Feb. 13, 1950; s. Louis Joseph and Angelina N.; student Suffolk County Community Coll., 1968-69; B.S., SUNY, Stony Brook, 1973, M.S., 1979. Chemistry asso. dept. nuclear energy Brookhaven Nat. Lab., Upton, N.Y., 1973-80; research scientist nuclear and flow systems sect. Battelle Columbus Labs. (Ohio), 1980—; participant Japan-U.S. Seminar on High Temperature Gas Cooled Reactor Safety Tech., 1977. Mem. AAAS, Am. Phys. Soc., Math. Assn. Am., Am. Nuclear Soc. Office: Battelle Columbus Lab 505 King Ave Columbus OH 43221

NIDAY, JAMES LOREN, ednl. supr./cons.; b. Gallipolis, Ohio, Jan. 26, 1932; s. Carlos Graham and Margena R. (Stillings) N.; B.A./B.S., Bowling Green State U., 1958, M.Ed., 1970, Ph.D. (NDEA fellow), 1978, Fullbright scholarship, Hebrew U., Jerusalem, Israel, 1981; m. Ruth Anne Casteel, Aug. 26, 1956; children—Lorinda Sue Niday Keefer, Cindra Ann Niday Stratton, Elizabeth Jean Niday Hubbell, James Loren. Tchr. English, dramatics and history Eastwood High Sch., Pemberville, Ohio, 1958-61; tchr. English and dramatics Johnson Park Jr. High Sch., Columbus, 1961-63; sch.-ct. liaison officer, dept. pupil personnel Columbus City Schs., 1963-68; supt. Hancock County Home, Findlay, Ohio, 1968-70; prin. Louis C. DeBrosse Elem. Sch. O.Y.C., Liberty Center, Ohio, 1970-71; doctoral fellow, instr. Bowling Green (Ohio) State U., 1971-73, mem. adv. and policy council for dean Coll. Edn., 1972-73, Williams County rep. adv. com., dept. ednl. adminstrn. and supervision, 1976—; prin. Hilltop Middle and High Schs., Millcreek-West Unity Schs., West Unity, Ohio, 1973-76; secondary supr., cons., grad. faculty, B.G.S.U. Williams County Schs., Bryan, Ohio, 1976—; chmn. Juvenile Conf. of Franklin County, 1966-67; mem. curriculum and transcript com. Ohio Youth Commn., 1970-71; mem. expansion and rev. com. Williams County 4-H Program, Bryan, 1976-78; mem. adult basic edn. adv. com. Four County Joint Vocat. Sch., Archbold, Ohio, 1976-82. Deacon, United Methodist Ch., 1973—; mayor Village of Custar, Ohio, 1971-73. Served with USN, 1950-54. Mem. Ohio Sch. Bds. Assn., Ohio Assn. Supervision and Curriculum Devel. (treas.), Northwestern Ohio Assn. Supervision and Curriculum Devel., Ohio Sch. Suprs. Assn., Internat. Brotherhood Magicians, Met. Owners N.Am., Phi Delta Kappa (NW Ohio chpt. pres. 1980-81), Kappa Delta Pi. Clubs: Masons (pres.), Lions, Crosley Automobile. Home: 126 S Defiance St West Unity OH 43570 Office: Williams County Schs Court House Bryan OH 43506

NIDEA, HIGINIO MORCOSO, physician; b. Philippines, Jan. 11, 1933; came to U.S., 1969, naturalized, 1975; s. Luciano B. and Marciana N. (Morcoso) N.; A.A., U. St. Tomas, 1953, M.D., 1958; M.P.A., U. Philippines, 1966; M.P.H., Johns Hopkins U., 1971; m. Zenaida T. Alvarez, Jan. 31, 1958; children—Luis Virgilio, Anthony Andrew, Joseph Albert, Robert Francis. Intern, U.S. Air Force Hosp., Clark AFB, Philippines, 1957-58; fellow in epidemiology N.Y. Med. Coll., 1969-71; chief enteroviruses sect. Dept. Health, Philippines, 1959-69; instr. dept. sanitary engring. Nat. U. Philippines, 1967-69; chief Hosp. Infection Surveillance and Control Sect., hosp. epidemiologist, vice chmn. hosp. infection com. VA Hosp., Hines, Ill., 1971-75; pvt. practice gen. and indsl. medicine, Cicero, Ill. WHO fellow in virology, 1960. Fellow Am. Soc. Contemporary Medicine and Surgery, Am. Public Health Assn.; mem. AMA, Ill. Med. Soc., Chgo. Med. Soc., Ill. Public Health Assn., Am. Soc. Microbiology, Soc. for Epidemiologic Research. Republican. Assemblies of God. Contbr. articles to profl. jours. Home: 163 Maple Ave Hillside IL 60162

NIDETZ, MYRON PHILIP, med. adminstr., health delivery systems cons.; b. Chgo., Dec. 29, 1935; s. David J. and Rose Y. (Yudell) N.; B.S., U. Ill., 1958; M.B.C., Hamilton Inst., Phila., 1972; M.P.A., Roosevelt U., 1981; m. Linda Freeman, Dec. 18, 1960; children—Julia, Allison. Dir., Union Coop. Eye Care Center, Chgo., 1961-65; dir. med. adminstrv. services Michael Reese Hosp. and Med. Center, Chgo., 1966-75; asso. dir. program to improve med. care and health services in correctional instns. AMA, 1975-79; exec. dir. N. Central Dialysis Centers, Chgo., 1979—. Active Suburbar Health Systems Agy., Oak Park, Ill. Served with U.S. Army, 1959-60. Fellow Am. Acad. Med. Adminstrs., Am. Public Health Assn.; mem. Assn. Hosp. Med. Edn., Am. Acad. Polit. and Social Sci., Am. Geriatrics Soc., Am. Hosp. Assn., AMA, Inst. of Soc., Ethics and Life Scis., Gernotol. Soc., Royal Soc. Health. Home: 14800 S Minerva Ave Dolton IL 60419 Office: 55 E Washington St Chicago IL 60602

NIEBLER, CHESTER JOHN, lawyer; b. Milw., Jan. 5, 1915; s. John J. and Margaret (Burkard) N.; Ph.B. summa cum laude, Marquette U., 1937; J.D. magna cum laude, 1939; m. Lorraine M. Millmann, Mar. 30, 1940; children—John H., Anne N. (Mrs. James McNamara), Joseph C., Paul F. Admitted to Wis. bar, 1939; practiced in Milw., 1945-69, Menomonee Falls, 1969—; ct. commr., 1961—; dir. numerous corps.; lectr. legal aspects profl. archtl. and engring. liability. Bd. govs. St. Thomas More Soc. Mem. Wis., Milw., Waukesha, bar assns., Am. Trial Lawyers Assn., Am. Judicature Soc., Woolsack Soc. (sec. 1966, dir. 1966-67), Marquette Law Alumni Assn. (dir. 1963-70), Alpha Sigma Nu, Delta Sigma Rho, Sigma Nu Phi. Club: Kiwanis (dir. 1956-58). Co-editor Marquette Law Rev., 1938-39. Home: N 84 W 16300 Menomonee Ave Menomonee Falls WI 53051 Office: PO Box 444 Menomonee Falls WI 53051

NIEBYLSKI, LEONARD MARTIN, physicist; b. Detroit, Nov. 11, 1925; s. Joseph M. and Sophia (Kalenchuk) N.; B.S., Wayne State U., 1949, M.S., 1952; postgrad. U. Mich., 1953-54, U. Calif. at Los Angeles, 1961, Harvard, 1972; m. Jeannette S. Horozaniecki, July 31, 1950; children—David, Richard, Margaret, Bruce, Mary, Roger, Charles, Mark, Amy. Research physicist Pioneering Research div., Ethyl Corp., Ferndale, Mich.; 1950-67, asso., 1967-71, sr. research asso., 1971—. Served with USAAF, 1944-46. Mem. Am. Soc. Testing and Materials, Electron Microscopy Soc. Patentee in field. Contbr. articles to profl. jours. Home: 32365 Robinhood St Birmingham MI 48010 Office: 1600 W 8 Mile Rd Ferndale MI 48220

NIED, WALTER H., JR., motel exec.; b. Dearborn, Mich., Apr. 25, 1951; s. Walter Henry and Ann Nied; student Northwestern Mich. Coll., 1969-71; B.S., Ferris State Coll., 1974; postgrad. Central Mich. U., 1976-78; m. Kathleen J. Armstrong, Nov. 17, 1973; 1 son, Jason Andrew. Comml. pilot, 1971-74; v.p., treas., gen. mgr. Indian Trail Lodge, Inc., Traverse City, Mich., 1974—. Vol., Probate Ct., Traverse City, 1975—; mem. Grand Traverse Republican Fin. Com., 1978—. Mem. Traverse City Area C. of C., West Mich. Tourist Assn., Mich. Lodging Assn., Am. Hotel Motel Assn., Internat. Orgn. Hotel Motel Mgrs., Traverse City Jaycees (dir. 1975-76). Clubs: Traverse City Flying, Kiwanis (dir. 1978—), Northwestern Mich. Coll. Wigwam (dir. 1977, pres. 1979-80), Elks. Home: 818 Ave D Traverse City MI 49684 Office: 877 Munson St Traverse City MI 49684

NIEDLING, HOPE HOTCHKISS, dietitian; b. Meriden, Ill., Feb. 14, 1922; d. Bert and Myrle Glenn (Vaughn) Hotchkiss; student North Central Coll., 1939-40; B.S., U. Ill., 1943; M.S. in Food Sci. and Nutrition, U. Wis. 1974; m. Ivan Martin Niedling, June 26, 1948. Teaching dietitian U. Hosp., Balt., 1944; dietitian public sch. cafeterias, Balt., 1944-48; dir. admisions Thomas Sch. Retailing, Phila., 1954-55; instr. foods U. Wis., Stevens Point, 1967-68; food service supr. instr. Mid-State, N.Central and Fox Valley Tech. Insts., Wis., 1973-75; cons. dietitian nursing homes in Wis., 1973—. Chmn., Village of Plover Cancer Fund Drive, 1977-78; pres. Portage County Republican Women, 1969-74; bd. dirs. Stout Found., U. Wis., 1977—, mem. exec. com., 1978—. Recipient Loyalty award U. Ill., 1978, award of merit U. Ill. Home Econs. Assn., 1979. Mem. Am. Dietetic Assn., Wis. Dietetic Assn., No. Wis. Dietetic Assn. (pres. 1971-73), Soc. for Nutrition Edn., Nutrition Today Soc., Nutritionists in Bus., DAR (sec. 1977-80, 1st vice regent 1980—, nat. state vice regents club 1980—), May-osh-ing chpt. DAR (organizing regent 1972-73, chpt. regent 1973-77, chpt. registrar 1977—), Colonia Dames XVII Century (2d v.p. 1979-81, 1st v.p. 1981—), Daus. Am. Colonists, Nat. Assn. Registered Parliamentarians, Wis. Public Health Assn. (mem. aging com. 1974-78), Portage County Humane Soc. (sec. 1973—), Wis. Fedn. Women's Clubs (pres. 1980—), Gen. Fedn. Women's Clubs (bd. dirs. 1980—), U. Ill. Alumni Assn. (dir. 1973-79), NCCJ (disting. merit citation 1976, vice chmn. Wis.), AAUW (pres. Stevens Point br. 1968-72, scholarship award 1970, state corr. sec. 1971-73), Gamma Sigma Delta, Epsilon Sigma Omicron. Methodist. Clubs: Order Eastern Star, Order of Amaranth, Order White Shrine of

Jerusalem, Stevens Point Area Woman's (pres. 1970-74, 76-78). Address: 1008 3rd St Stevens Point WI 54481

NIEHAUS, WILLIAM ROGER, newspaper exec.; b. Cin., June 10, 1932; s. George Anthony and Lorine Rosemary (Bennett) N.; B.S. in Physics Xavier U., 1954; M.S. in Physics (Univ. fellow), St. Louis U., 1956; m. Marian Camille Martinson, Oct. 21, 1961; children—Theodore, David, Jennifer, Thomas, Juliet, Natalie. Engring. cons. Allstates Design & Devel. Co., Cin., 1959-61; engring. physicist Thompson-Ramo-Wooldridge Co., Cleve., 1961; head of aerothermodynamics systems analysis Aeronca Mfg. Corp., Middletown, Ohio, 1961-65; engring. cons. Belcan Corp., Montgomery, Ohio, 1965-70; research dir. E.W. Scripps Co., Cin., 1970—. Bd. dirs. Montgomery Baseball Assn., 1972—; mem. Montgomery Recreation Commn., 1978—. Served as 1st lt. ordnance U.S. Army, 1956-58. Mem. Am. Inst. Aeros. and Astronautics, Am. Inst. Indsl. Engrs., Internat. Newspaper Promotion Assn., Am. Newspaper Pubs. Assn., Nat. Rifle Assn. (life), Sigma Xi. Republican. Roman Catholic. Patentee. Home: 10240 Pendery Dr Cincinnati OH 45242 Office: 1100 Central Trust Tower Cincinnati OH 45202

NIEHOFF, KARL RICHARD BESUDEN, stock exchange exec.; b. Cin., May 11, 1943; B.A., U. Cin., 1967. Vice pres., sec. Weil Roth & Irving, Inc., Cin., from 1976; chmn. Cin. Stock Exchange, from 1978, pres., 1979—, also mem. exec., ops. coms.; v.p., trustee Cin. Stock and Bond Club. Trustee, sec. Contemporary Arts Center Cin.; past trustee Tangeman Fine Arts Gallery, U. Cin. Clubs: Cin. Country, University, Miami, Keenland Assn. Address: Cin Stock Exchange 205 Dixie Terminal Bldg Cincinnati OH 45202

NIEHOFF, MARILEE SCHULTZ, bus. and edn. cons.; b. Horicon, Wis.; d. Carl J. and Myra (Mellenthien) Schultz; B.S. with honors, Ill. State U., 1972, M.S., 1973, Ph.D., 1976; m. Carl Niehoff; children—Nan Niehoff Miller, Kay C. Niehoff Eynatten, Janet A., Sally M., Carl III. Tchr., Metcalf Lab. Sch., Normal, Ill., 1973-75; asst. prof. elem. edn. Ill. State U., Normal, 1976-77; vis. asst. prof. psychology Kent (Ohio) State U., 1977-78; tng. coordinator Firestone Tire & Rubber Co., Akron, Ohio, 1978-80; bus. and edn. cons. M.S. Niehoff and Assos., Kent, Ohio, 1980—. Mem. Am. Soc for Tng. and Devel., Am. Assn. for Higher Edn., Am. Psychol. Assn., Assn. Specialists in Group Work, Assn. for Humanistic Psychology, Am. Personnel and Guidance Assn. Unitarian. Contbr. articles in field to profl. jours. Home: 7702 Diagonal Rd Kent OH 44240

NIELD, JOHN B., counselor educator; b. Montpelier, Idaho, Feb. 23, 1941; s. LaVar B. and Rhena Emily (Wilkes) N.; B.A., Idaho State U., 1967, M.A., 1969, Ed.D., 1976; m. Karla Anne Nelson, July 5, 1963; children—Kip J., Tani Kim, Suzette. Counselor Snake River Jr. High Sch., Blackfoot, Idaho, 1968-69; sch. psychologist White Pine County Schs., East Ely, Nev., 1969-70; dir. child devel.-family counseling, also instr. psychology No. Nev. Community Coll., Elko, 1970-74; asst. prof. psychology, counseling edn. Pittsburg (Kans.) State U. 1976—; cons. in field Bd. dirs. Head Start, Elko, 1973-74. Mem. Am., Kans. personnel and guidance assns., Assn. Counselor Edn. and Supervision, Kans. Assn. Counselor Edn. and Supervision, Am. Assn. Marriage and Family Therapists (clin. mem.), N.Am. Soc. Adlerian Psychology (del. assembly 1980—). Mem. Ch. Jesus Christ of Latter-Day Saints. Home: 401 W Quincy St Pittsburg KS 66762 Office: Room 115 Hughs Hall Pittsburg State U Pittsburg KS 66762

NIELSEN, CARL EBY, physicist; b. Los Angeles County, Calif., Jan. 22, 1915; s. Charles Harry and Josie Elizabeth (Musselman) N.; A.B., U. Calif., Berkeley, 1934, Ph.D., 1941; m. Imogene Herron, June 26, 1938; children—Paul, Sylvia, Robert. Instr. physics U. Calif., Berkeley, 1941-45, lectr., 1945-46; asst. prof. U. Denver, 1946-47; asst. prof. Ohio State U., Columbus, 1947-53, asso. prof., 1953-64, prof., 1964—; scientist Midwestern U. Research Assn., Madison, Wis.,1960-61; vis. scientist Culham Lab., U.K. Atomic Energy Authority, 1966; vis. scientist Max Planck Inst. Plasma Physics, Munich, 1969, 70, 72, 73, 74 summers; cons. Oak Ridge Nat. Lab., Lawrence Livermore Lab., Los Alamos Sci. Lab., Argonne (Ill.) Nat. Lab., Jet Propulsion Lab., Calif. Inst. Tech. Ford fellow, CERN, Geneva, 1958-59. Mem. Internat. Solar Energy Soc., Am. Phys. Soc., Phi Beta Kappa. Unitarian. Co discoverer negative mass instability in ion beams, 1959; research in salt gradient solar ponds, 1973—; contbr. articles to profl. jours. Home: 8030 Sawmill Rd Dublin OH 43017 Office: Dept Physics Ohio State U Columbus OH 43210

NIELSEN, FORREST HAROLD, research nutritionist; b. Junction City, Wis., Oct. 26, 1941; s. George Adolph and Sylvia Viola (Blood) N.; B.S., U. Wis., 1963, M.S., 1966, Ph.D., 1967; m. Emily Joanne Currie, June 13, 1964; children—Forrest Erik, Kistin Emily. NIH grad. fellow dept. biochemistry U. Wis., Madison, 1963-67; research chemist Human Nutrition Research Inst., Agrl. Research Service, U.S. Dept. Agr., Beltsville, Md., 1969-70, research chemist Grand Forks (N.D.) Human Nutrition Research Center, Sci. and Edn. Adminstrn., 1970—; research asso. U. N.D., Grand Forks, 1971—. Served with U.S. Army, 1967-69. Mem. Am. Inst. Nutrition, Internat. Assn. Bioinorganic Scientists, Soc. Environ. Geochemistry and Health, Soc. Exptl. Biology and Medicine, N.D. Acad. Sci., Sigma Xi. Lutheran. Author works in field; mem. editorial bd. Biol. Trace Element Research, 1979—. Office: Box 7166 University Station Grand Forks ND 58201

NIELSEN, LLOYD CHARLES, supt. schs.; b. Racine, Wis., Jan. 7, 1926; s. Johannes and Dagmar Rasmunsen N.; B.S., Lawrence Coll., 1950; M.Ed., Harvard U., 1955, Ed.D., 1963; m. Clare Ann Frank, June 16, 1951; children—Peter, Mary, Laura. Tchr., Merrill (Wis.) Sr. High Sch., 1950-53, prin., 1955-57; tchr. Washington Park High Sch., Racine, 1953-55; prin. Monroe (Wis.) Sr. High Sch., 1957-60; asst. supt. schs. Minnetonka (Minn.) Pub. Schs., 1962-66; supt. schs. Monongalia County Schs., Morgantown, W.Va., 1966-67, Roseville (Minn.) Area Schs., 1967—; vis. lectr. Winona State U., U. Minn., St. Cloud State U., Mankato State U. Mem. Met. Council Land Use Planning Adv. Com., 1976-80, Gov.'s Ednl. Policy Task Force, 1979-81. Served with USAAF, 1944-46; PTO. Recipient service awards YMCA. Mem. Am. Assn. Sch. Adminstrs. (pres.-elect, v.p.), Nat. Soc. for Study of Edn., Assn. for Supervision and Curriculum Devel., Minn. Assn. Sch. Adminstrs. (pres.), Suburban Sch. Supts. (pres.). Clubs: Rotary, Nat. Appaloosa Horse. Home: 3674 Big Fox Rd Saint Paul MN 55110 Office: Roseville Area Schs 1251 W County Rd B-2 Roseville MN 55113

NIELSEN, ROGER PAUL, computer co. exec.; b. Racine, Wis., Oct. 16, 1942; s. Paul J. and Carol Louise (Mannering) N.; B.S. in Elec. Engring., U. Wis., 1967; M.S., U. So. Calif., 1970; M.B.A., UCLA, 1975; m. Sandra Lee Bupp, Jan. 20, 1968; 1 son, Erik Paul. Project mgr. Hughes Aircraft Co., Culver City, Calif., 1971-73; mgr. fed. mktg. Data Gen. Corp., Washington, 1973-80; dir. original equipment mfr. mktg. div. NCR Corp., Dayton, Ohio, 1980—. Served with USAF, 1963-71. USAF scholar, 1965-67. Mem. Am. Mktg. Assn., Am. Mgmt. Assn., IEEE, Eta Kappa Nu. Episcopalian. Club: Rotary. Home: 46 Park Rd Dayton OH 45419 Office: NCR Corp 1700 S Patterson Blvd Dayton OH 45479

NIEMAN, TIMOTHY ALAN, analytical chemist; b. Cin., Dec. 31, 1948; s. Everett Orville and Emma (Hoffmeier) Nieman; m. Sandra Toth, Aug. 29, 1970. B.S., Purdue U., 1971; Ph.D., Mich. State U., 1975. Grad. asst. in chemistry Mich. State U., 1971-75; asso. prof. chemistry U. Ill. at Urbana-Champaign, 1975—. Mem. Am. Chem. Soc., Soc. Applied Spectroscopy, Alpha Chi Sigma, Phi Beta Kappa, Phi Lambda Upsilon. Mich. State U. Chemistry Dept. fellow, 1971-74; Eastman Kodak fellow, 1973-74; Am. Chem. Soc. Analytical Div. fellow, 1974-75. Contbr. articles to Analytical Chemistry jour. Home: 204 E McHenry St Urbana IL 61801 Office: Sch Chem Scis U Ill Urbana IL 61801

NIEMANN, CHARLES MICHAEL, computer service co. exec.; b. Belleville, Ill., Oct. 20, 1938; s. Eugene H. and Marie Emily (Stewart) N.; A.A. Belleville Area Coll., 1965; B.S. Washington U., 1966, B.A., 1966; M.S.C., St. Louis U., 1970; children—Karen Lynn, Steven Michael. Fin. Analyst Chrysler Corp., Detroit, 1966-67; budget dir. Cerro Corp., Sauget, Ill., 1968-70; corp. budget dir. Intertherm Inc., St. Louis, 1970-; gen. mgr. McDonnel Automation Co., Belleville, 1970—; mem. faculty (part-time) Belleville Area Coll., 1970—; dir. Belleville Indsl. Devel. Corp., 1976-77, Belleville New Industries, 1976—. Mem. adv. bd. Sch. Dist. 201 Co-op Edn., 1970—; mem. Sunset Legis. Adv. Commn., St. Clair County, 1976—; mem. bd. Mayor's Prayer Breakfast Com., Belleville, 1976—; adv. City and County Affairs Com., Belleville, 1972-73; chmn. adv. bd. Sch. Dist. 201 Coop. Edn., 1980-81. Served with U.S. Army, 1957-60. Mem. Belleville Area C. of C. (1st v.p. 1975-76, pres. 1976-77, treas. 1974-75), Metro East C. of C. Assn. (pres. 1976-77), Ill. Police Assn. Clubs: Elks, Optimist (bd. govs. 1975-76). Home: 520 A Morgan St Apt 2 Belleville IL 62221 Office: 1704 N Belt W Belleville IL 62223

NIEMEYER, GLENN ALAN, coll. adminstr.; b. Muskegon, Mich., 1934; s. John and Johanna (Walhout) N.; B.A., Calvin Coll., 1955; M.A., Mich. State U., 1959, Ph.D., 1962; m. Betty Sikkenga, July 8, 1955; children—Kristin, Alexis, Sander. Social sci. tchr. Grand Haven (Mich.) Christian Sch., 1955-58; asst. prof. history Grand Valley State Colls., Allendale, Mich., 1963-66, asso. prof., 1966-70, prof., 1970—, dean Coll. Arts and Scis., 1970-73, v.p. colls., 1973-76, v.p. acad. affairs, 1976—, provost, 1980—; commr. North Central Assn., 1979—, evaluator, 1974—; mem. Mich. Council State Coll. Pres.'s, 1973—. Trustee, Calvin Coll., 1974-80; trustee Unity Christian High Sch., 1978—, pres., 1979-80. Mem. Am. Assn. Higher Edn., Am. Council Edn., Am. Hist. Assn., Orgn. Am. Historians. Mem. Christian Ref. Ch. Author: The Automotive Career of Ransom E. Olds, 1963; also articles. Office: Grand Valley State Colleges Allendale MI 49401

NIEMEYER, MAXINE BREWER, ins. exec.; b. Detroit, Jan. 14, 1920; d. Daniel Frederick and Ella (Case) Niemeyer; student Detroit Coll. Bus., 1938-39, Exec. Sec. Asso. (hon.), 1960; grad. Dale Carnegie course, 1946; student Wayne U., 1958, Wayne State and U. Mich. Extension Schs., 1961-64, 65—. Gen. office clk. Hart Sewing Machine Supplies Co., Detroit, 1938-39; cashier, sec. N.Am. Life Assurance Co., Detroit, 1939-41, office mgr., 1942-43; office mgr. L.A. Walden & Co., Detroit, 1943-46; asst. office mgr. Dr. Ralph H. Pino, Ophthalmologist, Detroit, 1946-48; registrar Leadership Tng., Inc., Detroit, 1948-50; sec. to mgr. market analysis and dealer orgn dept. Sales div. Chevrolet Motor Co., Detroit, 1950-56; office mgr., sec. to Walter R. Cavanaugh, C.L.U., 1956—, corp. sec. 1958—, mgr. policyholders service and sales promotion, 1966; owner and pres. M.B. Niemeyer CLU & Assos., 1966—; advanced underwriting cons., agt., surplus lines agy. mgr. Phoenix Mut. Life; registered rep. Phoenix Equity Planning Corp. Trustee, Am. Coll. Named Detroit Sec. of Yr. Detroit chpt. Nat. Secs. Assn. Internat., 1960, One of Top Ten Working Women Central Bus. Dist. Assn., Detroit, 1965; C.L.U.; lic. life ins. counselor. Mem. Profl. Secs. Internat. (pres. Detroit chpt. 1962-64), Detroit Assn. Life Underwriters (pres. 1974-75), Am. Soc. C.L.U.'s (regional dir.; pres. Detroit chpt. 1973-74), Fin. and Estate Planning Council Detroit, Life Ins. Leaders Mich., Mich. Assn. Life Ins. Counselors, Internat. Assn. Fin. Planners, Alpha Iota Internat. (chpt. pres. 1944). Presbyterian. Club: Soroptimist (pres. 1972—) (Grosse Pointe, Mich.). Home: 1792 Vernier Rd Grosse Pointe Woods MI 48236 Office: 3000 Town Center Suite 202 Southfield MI 48075

NIESSE, JOHN EDGAR, materials engr.; b. Indpls., Nov. 30, 1927; s. John Leo and Jessie Louise (Pohlig) N.; B.S., U.S. Naval Acad., 1950; M.S., Mass. Inst. Tech., 1956, Sc.D., 1958; m. Elaine Corinne Morin, Dec. 27, 1958; children—John A., Ann L. With textile dept. Carborundum Co., Niagara Falls, N.Y., 1966-67, mgr., 1961-66; sect. mgr. metals and ceramics AVCO Corp., Lowell, Mass., 1967-72; sr. research group leader Monsanto Co., Durham, N.C., 1972-75, engring. supt., St. Louis, 1975—. Served with U.S. Navy, 1950-55; capt. Res. Registered profl. engr., Mo. Mem. Am. Ceramic Soc., Nat. Assn. Corrosion Engrs., Am. Soc. Metals. Author tech. papers. Home: 424 Glan Tai Dr Manchester MO 63011 Office: Monsanto Co 800 N Lindbergh Blvd Saint Louis MO 63166

NIESZ, GEORGE MELVIN, tool and die co. exec.; b. Norwood, Ohio, Aug. 6, 1926; s. George John and Anita Agnes Lucille (Chialastri) N.; student pub. schs., Norwood and Deer Park; m. Evelyn Catherine Rayburn, Oct. 18, 1946; children—Nancy L., George J., Jr. Profl. baseball player St. Louis Cardinals Orgn., 1944-45; tool and die maker Steelcraft Mfg. Co., Cin., 1946-51; supt., mgr. Abco Tool & Die Co., 1951-70; founder, pres. Niesz Tool & Die Co., Cin., 1970—. State dir., v.p. Sycamore-Deer Park Jr. C. of C., 1956-59. Ky. Col. Mem. Am. Soc. Metals, Soc. Mfg. Engring., Cin. C. of C., Anderson Twp. C. of C. Republican. Clubs: Masons (32 deg); Shriners. Patentee portable tool attachment; chess champion. Home: 4171 Winesap Ct Cincinnati OH 45236 Office: PO Box 44147 Cincinnati OH 45236

NIEUBUURT, JOHN EDWARD, realtor; b. Chgo., Mar. 27, 1931; s. Edward John and Minnie (Riemersma) N.; student U. Wyo., 1953; grad. Realtors Inst., 1970; m. Beatrice T. Tallackson, Feb. 2, 1957; children—Pamela, John Edward. Asso. Edward J. Nieubuurt Realtor, Chgo., 1949-52; partner Nieubuurt Realtors, Evergreen Park and Tinley Park, Ill., 1956-74; asst. v.p. Nat. Assn. Realtors, Chgo., 1974—. Pres. bd. dirs. Holland Home for Aged, Chgo., 1966-68. Chmn. real estate examining com. Ill. Dept. Registration and Edn., 1971-73. Served with USAF, 1952-56. Mem. Nat., Ill. (dist. v.p. 1968) assns. real estate bds., Nat. Assn. Ind. Fee Appraisers (chpt. treas. 1970), Chgo.'s South Side Real Estate Bd. (pres. 1968), Southwestern Suburban Bd. Realtors (pres. 1966-67), Home: Route 3 Box 56C Country Club Estates Fontana WI 53125 Office: 430 N Michigan Ave Chicago IL 60611

NIEUWSMA, MILTON JOHN, public relations exec.; b. Sioux Falls, S.D., Sept. 5, 1941; s. John and Jean (Potter) N.; B.A., Hope Coll., Holland, Mich., 1963; postgrad. Wayne State U., 1963-65; M.A., Sangamon State U., 1978; m. Marilee Gordon, Feb. 1, 1964; children—Jonathan, Gregory, Elizabeth. Public info. officer Wayne State U., Detroit, 1963-69; public relations dir. Sinai Hosp., Detroit, 1969-72; dir. div. officer services Am. Hosp. Assn., Chgo., 1972-73; asst. prof. journalism Wayne State U., Detroit, 1974; dir. public relations and devel. Meml. Med. Center, Springfield, Ill., 1975-79; v.p. for public affairs Grant Hosp., Chgo., 1979—; governing mem. Chgo. Zool. Soc., 1981—. Bd. dirs. Springfield (Ill.) Boys Clubs, 1979-80, Sangamon County Heart Assn., 1978-80; public relations chmn. Sangamon County Heart Fund Campaign, 1978; pres. Ford Com., 1975-76; bd. dirs. United Meth. Housing Corp., Detroit, 1968-70. Recipient Malcolm T. MacEachern citation Acad. Hosp. Public Relations, 1971, 72, Malcolm T. MacEachern award of merit 1972; Merit award Springfield Public Relations and Advt. Fed., 1976. Mem. Public Relations Soc. Am., Nat. Assn., Hosp. Devel., Acad. Hosp. Public Relations, Am. Soc. Hosp. Public Relations, Am. Hosp. Assn., Ill. Hosp. Public Relations Soc., Springfield Public Relations/Advt. Fedn. Republican. Presbyterian. Contbr. articles in field to profl. jours. Home: 322 Scottswood Rd Riverside IL 60546 Office: 550 W Webster Ave Chicago IL 60614

NIEVES, RAFAEL, state ofcl.; b. Camuy, P.R., Apr. 15, 1932; s. Jose and Maria (Rosa) N.; came to U.S., 1950; B.A., DePaul U., Chgo., 1956; M.A., Governors State U., 1979; postgrad. Union Grad. Sch.; m. Betty Carrillo, Apr. 18, 1964; 1 son, Jose Rafael. Caseworker, Cook County Dept. Public Aid, Chgo., 1955-62; mem. Peace Corps, Venezuela, 1962-64; exec. dir. dept. human resources, Westtown, Chgo., 1964-69; coordinator uptown Chgo. Model Cities Program, 1969-70; coordinator Title III-B program OEO, dir. 16th point program region V, HEW, Chgo., 1970-73; mem. Ill. Pardon and Parole Bd., 1973-78; mem. Ill. Prisoner Rev. Bd., 1978—. Lang. prof. Fed. Regional Coll., Malcolm X Coll., 1973; dir., social sci. workshop, inter societal studies Northwestern U. for Stateville Prison inmates, 1972-73; mem. Nat. Council on Crime and Delinquency. Founder YMCA, Petare, Venezuela, 1963; Midwest Conf. Spanish Speaking People Am., 1968. Recipient Guaicaipuro de Oro for best TV program, Caracas, 1963. Mem. U.S. Assn. Paroling Authorities, Am. Correctional Assn. Contbr. articles to profl. jours. Home: 848 S Laflin St Chicago IL 60607 Office: Room 420 160 N LaSalle St Chicago IL 60601

NIGHTINGALE, EDMUND ANTHONY, educator, cons. transp. economist; b. St. Paul, July 17, 1903; s. Edmund Alexander and Katherine Ellen (Eagan) N.; B.B.A., U. Minn., 1933, M.A., 1936, Ph.D., 1944; m. Lauretta A. Horejs, June 5, 1937; children—Edmund Joseph, Paul Lawrence. With operating dept. various railroads, 1920-33; teaching asst. econs. U. Minn., 1933-36, instr. in econs., transp., 1936-44, asst. prof., 1944-47, asso. prof., 1947-52, prof., 1952-72, prof. emeritus, 1972—, dir. insts. in rail transp., 1948-49. Cons. to Mpls. Mayor's Citizen Adv. Com. on streetcar and bus matters, 1952-54; cons. transp. economist. Editorial statistician Minn. State Planning Bd., 1936; prin. indsl. specialist, prin. transp. economist WPB, Washington, 1942-43; cons. transp. economist to Minn. Resources Commn., Minn. Iron Range Resources and Rehab. Commn., 1941-48; cons. to dir. mil. traffic service Office Sec. Def., Washington, 1950-53; cons. Minn. Legis. Interim Com. to Study R.R. and Warehouse Commn., 1956-57; mem. Transp. Research Adv. Com., U.S. Dept. Agr., 1960-63, mem. adv. com. mktg. research and service programs, 1963-66; mem. Gov.'s Transit Authority Study Com., 1964-69; research cons. Mid-Am. Gov.'s Transp. Council, 1965-72; cons. Minn. Pub. Service Commn., 1965-72, U.S. Dept. Transp., 1969-70. Mem. Gov's Transp. Adv. Com., 1968-72. Chmn. Highlands dist. Indianhead council Boy Scouts Am., 1955-58, mem.-at-large, exec. bd., 1958-74. Recipient diploma of honor internat. prize jury VIII Pan-Am. Congress, Washington, 1953; St. George award, Cath. Com. Scouting Archdioces St. Paul, 1960. Registered practitioner ICC. Mem. Am. Soc. Traffic and Transp., Transp. Club Mpls. and St. Paul, AAUP, Am. Econ. Assn., Am. Agr. Econ. Assn., Assn. ICC Practitioners (pres. chpt. 1957-58; regional v.p. 1961-63, chmn. com. edn. for practice 1971-73), Internat. Assn. Assessing Officers, Nat. Tax Assn. (com. on taxation pub. utility and transp. 1971—), Midwest Econs. Assn., Royal Econ. Soc., Nat. (legis. com. 1969—), N.W. (mem. legislative com. 1952-69, chmn. 1960-67) assns. shippers adv. bds., Asso. Traffic Clubs Am. (v.p. edn. and research 1958-62, v.p. W. N. Central States 1962-63; Distinguished Transp. Educator, 1966), Transp. Research Forum, Beta Gamma Sigma, Beta Alpha Psi, Alpha Kappa Psi. Clubs: Transp., Campus (Mpls.). Co-author: Aviation in Minnesota, 1952; Foreign Trade via the St. Lawrence Seaway, 1965; Transportation Problems and Policies in the Trans-Missouri West, 1967. Contbr. to Freight Traffic Management at Installations of the Military Depts., Dept. of Defense, rev. edit., 1952. Contbr. articles econs., taxation, transp. jours. Home: 2120 Niles Ave St Paul MN 55116 Office: Grad Sch Bus Adminstrn University of Minn Minneapolis MN 55455

NIGHTINGALE, EDMUND JOSEPH, clin. psychologist; b. St. Paul, Jan. 10, 1941; s. Edmund Anthony and Lauretta Alexandria (Horejs) N.; student Nazareth Hall Prep. Sem., 1959-61; A.B., St. Paul Sem., 1963; A.B. magna cum laude, Cath. U. of Louvain (Belgium), 1965, M.A., 1967, S.T.B. cum laude, 1967; postgrad. U. Minn., 1971; M.A., Loyola U., Chgo., 1973, Ph.D. in Clin. Psychology, 1975; m. Marie Arcara, Apr. 9, 1978; 1 son, Edmund Bernard. With Cath. Archdiocese of St. Paul and Mpls., 1967-73; intern in clin. psychology Michael Reese Hosp. and Med. Center, Chgo., 1973-74, W. Side VA Hosp., Chgo., 1974-75; staff psychologist, student counseling center, Loyola U., Chgo., 1975; staff psychologist and clin. coordinator of inpatient unit, drug dependency treatment center Hines (Ill.) VA Hosp., 1975-79, acting chief drug dependency treatment center, 1979-80; chief psychology VA Med. Center, Danville, Ill., 1980—; mem. personnel bd. Archdiocese of St. Paul and Mpls., 1968-70; lectr. psychology, Loyola U., Chgo., 1975; asst. professorial lectr. psychology, St. Xavier Coll., Chgo., 1975-78; adj. asst. prof. psychology in psychiatry, Abraham Lincoln Sch. Medicine, Med. Center U. Ill., Chgo., 1977—; adj. prof. psychology Purdue U., 1981—. Bd. dirs. Inst. Postgrad. Studies, Ill. Psychol. Assn., 1978-80, chmn. acad. sect., 1981—. Registered psychologist, Ill.; certified Nat. Registry of Health Service Providers in Psychology. Mem. Am. (clin. psychology, public service, psychoanalysis and psychotherapy divs.), Ill. (clin. psychology and acad. sects.) psychol. assns., Assn. for Advancement of Psychology, Internat. Soc. Hypnosis, Am. Group Psychotherapy Assn., Am. Acad. Psychotherapists, Am. Soc. Clin. Hypnosis. Founding editor: Louvain Studies, 1966. Home: 92 Country Club Dr Danville IL 61832 Office: VA Med Center Danville IL 61832

NIKISHIN, IGOR FEDOR, surgeon; b. Kharkov, Russia, Dec. 25, 1917; s. Fedor F. and Maria A. (Dikarev) N.; came to U.S., 1949, naturalized, 1954; A.B., French Lyceum Prague, Czechoslovakia, 1936; M.D., Charles U., Prague, 1941; children—Nina, Alexander, Michael, Igor. Intern, George August U. Med. Sch., Goettingen, Germany, 1941-42, resident, 1942-46; chief surgeon 326th Res. Detachment Mil. Govt. Hosp., Brit. Army of the Rhine, 1945-47, sr. med. officer hdqrs. 509, 1947-48; sr. med. officer 609 Hdqrs. Control Commn. Germany, 1948-49; chmn. dept. surgery, sr. attending surgeon Aultman Hosp., Canton, Ohio, 1970—; asst. prof. surgery George August U., Goettingen, Germany, 1943-47; sr. attending surgeon Timken Mercy Hosp., Canton, 1959—; asso. prof. dept. human anatomy NE Univs. Coll. Medicine. Pres., Canton Symphony Assn., 1964-68, East Central Heart Assn., 1965-67; bd. dirs. Am. Cancer Soc., 1976; bd. dirs. AmDoc., Santa Barbara, Calif., 1965-69. Diplomate Am. Bd. Surgeons, Am. Bd. Abdominal Surgeons. Mem. AMA, Am. Soc. Abdominal Surgeons, ACS, Am. Coll. Angiology, Am. Geriatrics Soc., Ohio State Med. Assn., Ohio State Surg. Assn., N.Y., Ohio acads. scis., Med. Educators Assn. N.E. Ohio, Stark County Med. Soc. Club: Canton. Contbr. articles to profl. jours.

Home: 5646 Channel Dr NW Canton OH 44718 Office: 214 Dartmouth Ave SW Canton OH 44710

NIKKEL, VERNON LLOYD, protective structures and instl. turf products mfg. co. exec.; b. Goessel, Kans., May 26, 1928; s. Henry P. and Martha (Dirksen) N.; B. Music Edn., Bethany Coll., 1950; M.S., Kans. State Tchrs. Coll., 1961; m. Lennea Oetinger, June 11, 1950; children—Greta Ann, Sanford Louis. Mgr., Emma Creek Stock and Grain Farm, McPherson Kans., 1942—; tchr. music Weskan (Kans.) public schs., 1950-53, Roxbury (Kans.) public schs., 1953-57; dir. music Hesston (Kans.) unified public schs., 1957-64; v.p. indsl. relations Excel Inc., Hesston, 1964—, dir., 1965—; pres. Hesston Devel., Inc., 1972-76. Mem. Tri County Community Health Bd. of Harvey County, Kans., 1965-71; councilman of Hesston, Kans., 1961-63, mayor, 1967-69; mem. Substance Abuse Bd. of Harvey County, 1976—; sec. Harvey County Orch. Assn., 1973-79; Sunday sch. tchr. United Methodist Ch., Hesston, 1962—, treas. bldg. com., 1969-70; camp dir. Family Week Camp at Rocky Mountain Mennonite Camp, 1966-70; dir. music Kans. West United Meth. Conf., 1975-77; mem. Wichita Ann. Conf. Council of Ministries, United Meth. Conf., 1976—; mem. Kans. Balance of State Pvt. Industry Council, 1979—, now chmn.; mem. CETA/Balance of State Manpower Planning Council, 1979—. Recipient citation Kans. Dept. Employment Security, 1976; Harvey County Community Mental Health award, 1971, Alumni award of merit Bethany Coll., 1980. Mem. Am. Soc. Personnel Adminstrs. (dist. dir. 1970-77, regional v.p. Kans. Assn. of Commerce and Industry (chmn. unemployment compensation sub-com. 1975), Fine Arts council of Harvey County, Newton (Kans.) C. of C. (chmn. local industry com. 1976—). Republican. Clubs: Lions, Elks. Home: 230 S Weaver St Hesston KS 67062 Office: 200 S Ridge Rd Hesston KS 67062

NIMEE, LYNN ELIZABETH, educator; b. Chgo., Aug. 17, 1932; d. Evan B. and Gladys (Davis) Baily; B.S. in Edn., Western Ill. U., Macomb, 1954; m. Joseph Nimee; children—Jolynn, Jennifer, Joseph. Tchr., Hall High Sch., Spring Valley, Ill., 1954-57, librarian, 1959-66; tchr. Putnam County High Sch., Granville, Ill., 1957-59; unit media dir. Spring Valley (Ill.) Elementary Sch. Dist. #99, 1968—, dir. adult basic edn., 1977-80. Chmn. Bureau County Heart Assn., 1972-74. Mem. Am., Ill. library assns., Am., Ill. (v.p. 1976, dir. 1974, 75) assns. sch. librarians, AAUW, Nat. Ill. edn. assns. Certified media specialist, high sch. English tchr., Ill. Home: Rural Route #1 Spring Valley IL 61362 Office: 800 N Richard Spring Valley IL 61362

NIMR, ABDULLATIF MOHAMED, physician; b. Bait ala, Palestine, Nov. 6, 1943; came to U.S., 1970, naturalized, 1978; s. Mohamed Amer and Fatima Mohamed (Abdel Rahman) N.; M.B., B.Ch., Alexandria (Egypt) Med. Sch., 1969; m. Soad M. El-Taki, Dec. 26, 1969; children—Heba, Haney. Intern, St. Vincent Hosp., Toledo, 1970-71; resident Med. Coll. Ohio, 1971-75, Ferguson Clinic, Grand Rapids, Mich., 1975-76; practice medicine specializing in surgery, Toledo, 1976—; mem. staff Toledo Hosp., St. Luke's Hosp., Maumee, Ohio; mem. staff St. Vincent Hosp., Toledo, also chief sect. colon and rectal surgery; clin. asso. prof. Med. Coll. Ohio, Toledo, 1977—; v.p. Drs. Blank and Nimr, Inc., Toledo, 1978—. Fellow A.C.S., Am. Soc. Colon and Rectal Surgeons; mem. Acad. of Medicine of Lucas County, AMA, Ohio State Med. Soc., Toledo Surg. Soc., Islamic Center. Club: Toledo. Office: 3100 W Central St Toledo OH 43606

NIMROD, JOHN J., state senator; b. Chgo.; student U. Ill., Ill. Inst. Tech.; B.S., Northwestern U., 1950; m. D. Ingeborg; 4 children. Cons. engr. design and prodn.; pres. plastics firm, Barrington, Ill.; now mem. Ill. Senate. Asst. to chmn. Ill. Indsl. Commn.; asst. dir. Ill. Dept. Revenue; asst. to pres. Cook County (Ill.) Bd. Commrs.; former auditor Niles Twp.; Republican commiteeman Niles Twp. Served with U.S. Army, World War II, Korea. Mem. Twp. Ofcls. Cook County (past pres.), Am. Legion, Amvets, Skokie Civil Def. (past dir.). Presbyterian. Clubs: Chgo. Athletic Assn., Masons, Shriners. Office: State Capitol Springfield IL 62706*

NIMS, CHARLES FRANCIS, clergyman, egyptologist; b. Norwalk, Ohio, Oct. 19, 1906; s. Joel Benjamin and Grace (Wildman) N.; student U. Toledo, 1924-25; A.B., Alma Coll., 1928; B.D., McCormick Theol. Sem., 1931; Ph.D., U. Chgo., 1937; m. Myrtle Eileen Keillor, Apr. 18, 1931. Ordained to ministry Presbyn. Ch., 1931; pastor, First Ch., Eldorado, Ill., 1940-43; research asst. Oriental Inst., 1934-40; staff Sakkarah Expdn., Egypt, 1934-36; staff Epigraphic Survey, 1937-39; egyptologist Epigraphic Survey, 1946-63, field dir., 1964-72; research asso. dept. Oriental lang. U. Chgo., 1948-67, faculty mem., 1960-61, asso. prof., 1967-70, prof., 1970-72, emeritus, 1972—; staff mem. Chgo. Archeol. Expdn., Tolmeita, Libya, 1954, 56, 57, 58; lectr. adult edn. Field Mus. Natural History, 1976. Mem. Found. Egyptologique Reine Elizabeth, Egypt Exploration Soc., Soc. Bibl. Lit., Am. Oriental Soc., Am. Photog. Soc. Am Schs. Oriental Research, Mil. Chaplains Assn. U.S., AAUP, Am. Research Center in Egypt, L'Association Internationale pour l'Étude du Droit Pharaonique (hon. pres.); ordinary mem. Deutsches Archaologisches Instut; asso. mem. L'Institut d' Egypte. Served as chaplain (capt.) U.S. Army, 1943-46. Author: (with H.H. Nelson et al) Medinet Habu IV, 1940; (with Prentice Duell) Mastaba of Mereruka, 1938; (with G.R. Hughes) Reliefs and Inscriptions in Karnak, III, 1954; Medinet Habu V-VIII (with G.R. Hughes), 1957-70; Thebes of the Pharoahs, 1965; (with E.F. Wente) The Tomb of Kheruef, 1980, The Temple of Khonsu, I, 1979; (with William Murnane) The Temple of Khonsu, II, 1981. Contbr. articles to profl. jours. Home: 5540 Blackstone Ave Chicago IL 60637 Office: Oriental Inst U Chgo Chicago IL 60637

NIMS, JAMES CARVER, orgn. exec.; b. Brattleboro, Vt., Nov. 18, 1943; s. Fred Loran and Shirley Carver N.; student Burdett Coll., 1969-71; m. Helen Louise Renaud, Jan. 22, 1972; children—Jennifer, Carrie, Shirley. Purchasing agt. Brattleboro (Vt.) Meml. Hosp., 1969-72; dir. purchasing Alliance (Ohio) City Hosp., 1972-75; sales mgr. D.T. Air Filter Products Co., Alliance, 1975-77; exec. dir. Alliance Area United Way, 1977—. Mem. adv. bd. Stark County CETA; mem. membership com. Alliance YMCA; pres. Carnation City Festival Bd., gen. chmn. festival, 1981; mem. Stark County Community Edn. Bd. Served with USN, 1962-66. Recipient Community citation City of Sebring (Ohio), 1980. Cert. purchasing mgr. Am. Purchasing Soc. Mem. Vt. Purchasing Soc. (founding pres.), Internat. Mgmt. Council (Man of Yr. award 1975, 78, past pres. Alliance chpt.), Alliance Social Service Assn. (past pres.). Democrat. Roman Catholic. Clubs: Rotary (bd. dirs.), Elks, Taylorcraft Flying. Home: 2525 Edgewood Ave Alliance OH 44601 Office: Alliance Area United Way 210 E Main St Alliance OH 44601

NINKE, ARTHUR ALBERT, cons. accountant; b. Coloma, Mich., Aug. 20, 1909; s. Paul F. and Theresa Grace (Warskow) N.; student accounting Internat. Bus. Coll., 1928; diploma commerce Northwestern U., 1932; m. Claudia Wagner, Sept. 13, 1930; children—Doris (Mrs. Leroy Hart), Donald, Marion, George, Arthur Albert, Thomas, Mark, Albert. Auditor, Arthur Andersen & Co., C.P.A.'s, Chgo., 1929-36, St. Louis, 1950-55, Midwest Stock Exchange, 1936-41, SEC, 1942-45; expense controller Butler Bros., Chgo., 1946-49; office mgr. Hargis Electronics, 1956-59; auditor HUD, Detroit, 1960-64; owner Urban Tech. Staff Assos., cons. urban renewal projects and housing devel., Detroit, 1965—; pres. Simplified Systems & Service, 1978—, Complete Bus. Service, Dallas, 1979—, Loving Shepherd Nursing Home, Warren, Mich., 1981—; sec. Gideons Detroit North Woodward, 1981—. Controller, Lake Superior Research and Devel. Inst., Munising, Mich., 1973-76; pres. Luth. Friendship Homes, Inc., 1975—; mng. dir. Family Evangelism Found., 1977—; controller S.E. Mich. Billy Graham Crusade, 1976-77. Mem. Nat. Soc. Pub. Accountants, Nat. Assn. Housing and Redevel. Ofcls. (treas. Mich. 1973-75), Luth. Center Assn. (treas. 1975-81, dir. 1975-81), Internat. Luth. Laymen's League (treas. S.E. Mich. 1971-75, dir. 1976—), Am. Mgmt. Assn. Author: Family Bible Studies. Developer simulated machine bookkeeping system; trade mark holder Record-Checks-Systems, 1981—. Home: 12937 Santa Clara St Detroit MI 48235 Office: 18415 James Couzens Blvd Detroit MI 48235

NISBET, THOMAS ALBERTIS, JR., mfg. co. exec.; b. Raeford, N.C., May 27, 1924; s. Thomas Albertis and Bonnie Dixie (McBryde) N.; student U. N.C., Chapel Hill, 1942-43, 46-47; m. Emilia Colamarino, Jan. 5, 1979; 1 son, James C.; children from previous marriage—Christy Nisbet Foster, Cindy Nisbet Holton, Dixie Nisbet Fleck, Thomas A. III. With Internat. Harvester Co., Memphis, 1947-49; with Gen. Motors Corp., various locations, 1949-79, regional dir., Chgo., 1969-71, mgr. field ops., Detroit, 1971, mgr. heavy duty truck sales Chevrolet Motor div., Detroit, 1971-79; v.p., gen. mgr. Ottawa (Kans.) Truck div. Gulf & Western Mfg. Co., 1979—. Elder, dean, supt. Sunday sch., chmn. Christian edn. Forest Hills Presbyterian Ch., Charlotte, N.C. Served with USN, 1943-46; CBI, PTO. Mem. Am. Trucking Assn. Found., Calif. Trucking Assn., Soc. Auto Engring., Am. Truck Hist. Soc. Democrat. Office: 415 E Dundee St Ottawa KS 66044

NISBETH, G. RICHARD, banker; b. Potsdam, N.Y., Nov. 28, 1947; s. George R. and Adriana (Bettini) N.; B.S. in Fin., Fla. Atlantic U., 1970; m. Ardith Austin, July 2, 1977; 1 son, Eric. With St. Joseph Valley Bank, Elkhart, Ind., 1973—, v.p., dir. corp. planning, 1976-78, sr. v.p., 1978—. Bd. dirs. Elkhart Water Works, Elkhart Concert Club, Big Bros./Big Sisters, Elkhart. Mem. Planning Execs. Inst., Midwest Planning Assn., Nat. Assn. Accountants, Am. Mktg. Assn., Alpha Tau Omega. Episcopalian. Home: 1507 Ash Dr W Elkhart IN 46514 Office: 121 W Franklin St Elkhart IN 46514

NITSCHKE, CHARLES ALBERT, architect; b. Columbus, Ohio, July 15, 1928; s. Andrew Gunning and Carrie (Fiedler) N.; B.Arch., Ohio State U., 1951; m. Sally Moore, Nov. 29, 1953; children—Christopher Moore, Caren, David Rathburn. Designer Tully & Hobbs, Columbus, 1953-55; partner Downie W. Moore-Charles A. Nitschke, architects, Columbus, 1955-60; prin. C. Nitschke & Assos., Columbus, 1960-72; partner Nitschke Godwin Bohm, architects, Columbus, 1972-76; prin. Nitschke Assos. Inc., Columbus, 1976—. Instr. architecture Ohio State U., Columbus, 1955-60; v.p., dir. Columbus Properties, Inc., 1970—; v.p. Nitschke Bros., Inc., Columbus, 1972—; occasional lectr. architecture, city planning and redevel. econs. Ohio State U., U. Wis., others. Founding bd. dirs. Columbus Landmarks Found., 1977—. Served with USNR, 1951-53. Recipient Plan awards, Jr. League of Columbus, 1966, 68. Mem. Columbus C. of C. (mem. downtown action com. 1972-79), Volunteers Am. (v.p., dir. 1972—), AIA (bd. dirs. 1967-74, pres. 1973), Urban Land Inst., Nat. Trust Historic Preservation, Am. Inst. Planners (asso.), Alpha Tau Omega. Episcopalian (lay reader). Clubs: Ohio State U. Faculty, Rotary (dir. 1981—), University (Columbus). Home: 6570 Plesenton Dr Worthington OH 43085 Office: 31 E Gay St Columbus OH 43215

NITTI, JOHN ANTHONY, photoengraving co. exec.; b. Chgo., July 26, 1953; B.S. in Mktg. and Fin., So. Ill. U., 1975; postgrad. in law No. Ill. U., 1975-76; also profl. seminars; m. Joy L. Brown, Sept. 2, 1978. Internal auditor Beatrice Foods Corp., Chgo., 1976-79; photo engraver, mgr. Collins Miller & Hutchings, Chgo., 1979—; speaker orientation program Graphic Arts Tech. Found.; tchr. statis. sampling. Recipient 4 top sales awards Kinney's Show Corp 500 Club, 1970-71; Outstanding Sr. award So. Ill. U., 1975, Outstanding Mktg. Student award, 1975; Wall St. Jour. award, 1975; So. Ill. U. Pres.'s scholar, 1971-75; Ill. State scholar, 1971-75; Eastman Kodak Acad. Excellence scholar, 1974-75; Justinian Soc. Lawyers scholar, 1975-76; C.P.A., Ill. Mem. Am. Mktg. Assn., ARC Life Savers, Beta Gamma Sigma (v.p. chpt. 1973-75), Phi Kappa Phi. Roman Catholic. Office: 333 W Lake St Chicago IL 60606

NITZ, ALBERT JOSEPH, educator; b. Atchison, Kans., Apr. 13, 1952; s. Robert LaVern and Rosemary Felicitas (Soerries) N.; A.A., Highland Jr. Coll., 1972; B.S., U. Kans. 1974, postgrad., 1980—. Substitute tchr. Unified Sch. Dist. 409, Atchison, 1975; tchr. Halstead (Kans.) Grade Sch., 1975-77; intermediate math tchr. Valley Heights Grade Sch., Blue Rapids, Kans., 1977-80; substitute tchr. Unified Sch. Dist. 497, Lawrence, Kans., 1980—. Mem. NEA, Kans. Edn. Assn., U. Kans. Alumni Assn. and Edn. Soc., Valley Heights Edn. Assn. (sec. 1978-79). Roman Catholic. Home: 1435 Santa Fe Atchison KS 66002 Office: 931 W 28th St Lawrence KS 66044

NITZ, TERRY EDWIN, housing mfg. co. exec.; b. St. Joseph, Mich., May 1, 1944; s. Leonard Harry and Gloria Ann (Swope) N.; B.S. in Mktg., Ferris State Coll., Big Rapids, Mich., 1980; m. Patricia Lynn Chipman, June 7, 1971; children—Justin Mathew, Kimberly Lynn. Dock ops. supr. Squire Dingee Co., Baroda, Mich., 1962—; supr. stock dept. Heathkit Co., Benton Harbor, Mich., 1964; mgr. men's suit dept. Libin's Varsity Shop, Kalamazoo, 1971-72; mgr. men's clothing and furnishings Montgomery Ward & Co., Kalamazoo, 1972-78; sales mgr. South Park Homes, Inc., Reed City, Mich., 1978-80; mgr. Doyle's Mobile Home Center, Inc., Columbus, Ohio, 1980—. Served with USAF, 1966-70. Mem. Am. Mktg. Club, Profl. Bus. Orgn. Lutheran. Clubs: Lions, Photography, USO (v.p.). Home: 493 Knob Hill W Columbus OH 43228 Office: 6200 S High St Columbus OH 43137

NOBLE, CLARA DOWLING, cons. in social welfare adminstrn.; b. Jackson, Mich., Mar. 22, 1924; d. Martin Cedric and Marjorie Hills D.; student Conn. Coll., 1941-42; B.S. in Chemistry, Mich. State U., 1945; M.S.W., U. Mich., 1971; m. Russell Edwin Noble, June 28, 1945; children—Richard Cedric, Martha Louise, Sally Ann, Mary Catherine. Research biochemist U. Mich. Hosp., Ann Arbor, 1947-50; flavor chemist, Jackson, Mich., 1950-53; exec. dir. Jackson YWCA, 1964-65; exec. coordinator Mich. Community Coordinated Child Care Council, Lansing, 1971-73; dir. human services asso. program Jackson Community Coll., 1975-77, cons. family and child programs, 1980—; social worker Head Start, Jackson, 1966-68, family devel. program devel., planning, 1977-80, dir., 1980—; adj. prof. Spring Arbor (Mich.) Coll., 1980—. Mem. bd. dirs. Mich. Mid-South Health Systems Agy., 1979—, Mich. 4-C Council, 1976-80; bd. dirs., chmn. planning div. United Way, Jackson, 1974-80; bd. dirs. Spaulding for Children, 1971—, pres., 1975-78; bd. dirs. Jackson Women's Symphony, 1974; trustee, pres. Jackson Literary & Art Assn., 1976—. Cert. social worker. Mem. Nat. Assn. Social Workers, Nat. Assn. for Edn. Young Children, Nat. Head Start Assn., Nat. Council Prevention Child Abuse/Neglect, Phi Kappa Phi, Tau Sigma, Sigma Chi Gamma. Club: Kappa Kappa Gamma Alumni. Home: 1728 Maybrook Rd Jackson MI 49203

NOBLE, ELLSWORTH GLENN, writer; b. Sioux City, Iowa, Sept. 2, 1902; s. Lincoln and Zada Belle (Gardner) N.; B.A., Coe Coll., 1927; postgrad. U. Iowa, 1927, U. Nebr., 1932-33; m. Lillian Peterka, June 8, 1933. Reporter, Morning Republican, Findlay, Ohio, 1922-23, 25, Mankato (Minn.) Free Press, 1924; partner drug store, Table Rock, Nebr., 1928-29; area circulation mgr. Omaha Bee-News, 1929-30; interviewer, then field rep. Nat. Reemployment Service, 1934-37; area mgr. Nebr. Employment Service, Nebraska City, 1937-67; dir. Wildwood Center, cultural center, mus., arts-crafts facility, Nebraska City, 1967-76, mem. bd., 1967-79. Mem. Nebr. Writers Guild (v.p. 1956), Brownville Hist. Soc. (charter, dir. 1956-62, pres. 1962, editor quar. 1956-60), Nebr. Hist. Soc. Author: Colorful Old Brownville, 4th edit., 1978; John Brown and the Jim Lane Trail, 1977; Historically Eventful Nebraska City, 1981. Home: 502 N 17th St Nebraska City NE 68410

NOBLE, HOWARD BATES, orthopaedic surgeon; b. Pocatello, Idaho, Aug. 3, 1939; s. Wallace Bert and Melrhea (Parker) N.; B.A., U. Wash., 1961; M.D., Bowman Gray Med. Sch., 1965. Intern, Passavant Meml. Hosp., Chgo., 1965-66; resident Northwestern U., 1968-72; practice medicine specializing in orthopaedic surgery, Chgo., 1972; attending physician Northwestern Meml., Children's Meml., Grant hosps.; team physician Chgo. Bulls; instr., mem. exec. com., dir. Center Sports Medicine, Northwestern U. Med. Sch.; cons. Peoples Gas Co. Mem. adv. com. Ill. Gov.'s Council on Health and Fitness. Served with USNR, 1966-68. Travelling fellow James IV Soc. Surgeons, 1975. Diplomate Am. Bd. Orthopaedic Surgery. Fellow A.C.S., Am. Acad. Orthopaedic Surgeons; mem. AMA, Am. Assn. Ry. Surgeons, Ill. State Med. Soc. (chmn. sports medicine com.), Chgo. Med. Soc. Contbr. articles to profl. jours. Address: 233 E Erie St Chicago IL 60611

NOBLITT, HARDING COOLIDGE, polit. scientist; b. Marion, N.C., Oct. 31, 1920; s. Walter Tate and Nellie Mae (Horton) N.; B.A., Berea Coll., 1942; M.A., U. Chgo., 1947, Ph.D., 1955; m. Louise Hope Lester, July 3, 1943; 1 son, Walter Thomas. Mem. faculty Concordia Coll., Moorhead, Minn., 1950—, prof. polit. sci., 1956—, Wije Disting. prof., 1979—, chmn. dept., 1964-72. Democratic candidate for Congress, 1962; del. Dem. Nat. Conv., 1964; chmn. Profs. for Johnson-Humphrey, Minn., 1964; chmn. platform com. Dem. State Conv., 1968; mem. Gov's Citizens Council on Aging, 1963-68; mem. Minn. Higher Edn. Coordinating Bd., 1971-81, sec., 1974-75, pres., 1979-80. Served with AUS, 1943-46; ETO. Recipient 1st ann. Great Tchr. award Concordia Coll., 1960. Mem. Am. Polit. Sci. Assn., Acad. Polit. Sci., Am. Acad. Polit. and Social Sci., Am. Legion, VFW, Phi Kappa Phi, Pi Gamma Mu, Tau Kappa Alpha, Pi Kappa Delta. Democrat. Presbyterian (elder). Edit. bd. Discourse: A Review of the Liberal Arts, 1957-67, acting editor, 1959-60. Home: 2014 S 4th St Moorhead MN 56560 Office: Dept Polit Sci Concordia Coll Moorhead MN 56560

NOE, FRANCES ELSIE (MRS. ROBERT DAVIES), physician; b. Beacon Falls, Conn., May 23, 1923; d. Alfred and Edith (Carlson) Noe; B.A., Middlebury Coll., 1944; M.N., Yale, 1947; M.D., U. Vt., 1954; m. Robert Davies, June 16, 1956; children—Kenneth Roger, Ralph Eric. Intern, Mary Hitchcock Meml. Hosp., Hanover, N.H., 1954-55; fellow cardiovascular research Mich. Heart Assn., 1955-56; resident pulmonary div. Henry Ford Hosp., Detroit, 1956-57; fellow cardiopulmonary research Wayne State U. Coll. Medicine, 1957-58, instr. anesthesia dept., 1958-61, asst. clin. prof. anesthesia dept., 1961-65, 76—; asso. staff, div. research Sinai Hosp. of Detroit, 1965-70, chief pulmonary physiology sect., div. research, 1970—. Mem. Am. Soc. Anesthesiologists, Sigma Xi. Contbr. articles in field to profl. jours. Home: 1601 Kirkway Bloomfield Hills MI 48013 Office: Sinai Hosp Detroit MI 48235

NOETZELMANN, DAVID CHARLES, plastics engr.; b. Lewellen Nebr., Aug. 31, 1943; s. Henry C. and Ethel M. (Hutchison) N.; student Am. Sch., Chgo., 1961-62; m. Gladys E. Smith, Apr. 6, 1962; children—Sandra, David Charles, Paul. Jr. engr. Midwec, Oshkosh, Nebr., 1963-65, quality assurance engr., 1966-69, quality control mgr., 1970-78, sr. mfg. engr., Sidney, Nebr., 1978-79, product engr. mgr., Scottsbluff, Nebr., 1979-81, dir. quality assurance, 1981—; quality control mgr. CEBU, Philippines Complex, 1980-81; mem. Modern Plastics adv. panel, 1974-80. Mem. Grace Lutheran Ch. Mem. Soc. Plastics Engrs., Garden County Jaycees. Club: Elks. Home: Lake Minatare Minatare NE 69356 Office: 10 S Skyport Dr Scottsbluff NE 69361

NOFFSINGER, DONALD ALLEN, pub. co. exec.; b. Defiance, Ohio, Apr. 18, 1929; s. Obert M. and Mazie V. (Etter) N.; B.S. in Commerce, Internat. Coll., 1949; postgrad. U. Calif. at San Diego, 1959-61, Anderson Coll., 1964; B.S., Ball State U., 1974, M.B.A., 1980; LL.D. (hon.), Anderson Coll., 1980; m. Birdie F. George Smith, May 21, 1955; 1 son, Mark A.; stepchildren—Gregory L. Smith, Ronald D. Smith, Randall G. Smith. With dist. accounting office Burroughs Corp., Chgo., 1949-50; accounting supr. Gen. Motors Corp., Defiance, 1950-59; in charge financial forecasting Convair astronautics div. Gen. Dynamics Corp., San Diego, 1959-61; sec.-treas., sr. v.p. Warner Press, Inc., Anderson, Ind., 1961-74, exec. v.p., 1974, pres., 1975—, also dir.; partner Orange Blossom Gardens Devel. Co., Anderson, 1964—; dir., mem. exec. com. Laymen Life Ins. Co., Anderson; dir. Comml. Service Co., Asso. Cos., Inc., Anderson. Mem. City Council, Defiance, 1958-59, pres. pro tem, 1958-59; mem. Redevel. Commn., Anderson, 1968-70, v.p., 1968-69, pres., 1969-70; dir. Wilson Boys Clubs, Inc.; mem. exec. council Ch. of God. Bd. dirs. Nat. Bd. Ch. Extension and Home Missions, Ch. of God, Anderson, Ind., Community Hosp. Anderson and Madison County, Jr. Achievement of Madison County, Inc., Anderson YMCA, Anderson Symphony Orch., Mid-Am. council Boy Scouts Am. Served with AUS, 1948-55. Mem. Am. Mgmt. Assn., Nat. Assn. Accountants, Am. Accounting Assn., Presidents Assn., Protestant Ch. Owned Publishers Assn. (pres. 1979-80, dir.), Coop. Publ. Assn. (v.p. 1980—), Anderson C. of C., Urban League. Clubs: Anderson Country, Optimist (v.p. 1965-66, pres. 1971-72, lt. gov. 1972-73) (Anderson), Masons. Home: 310 Ravenview Ct Anderson IN 46011 Office: PO Box 2499 Anderson IN 46011

NOGAJ, RICHARD JOSEPH, cons. environ. engr.; b. Chgo., Feb. 17, 1938; s. Joseph John and Loretta Elizabeth (Kowalczyk) N.; B.S. in Civil Engring., Ill. Inst. Tech., 1960, M.S. in San. Engring., 1963; m. Barbara Ann Fitzmaurice, Aug. 22, 1959; children—Debra, Thomas, John. Civil engr. Met. San. Dist. Greater Chgo., 1960-61; mgr. engring. Clow Corp., Melrose Park, Ill., 1961-70; dir. engring. Keene Corp., Aurora, Ill., 1970-73; head dept. san. engring. Harza Engring. Co., Chgo., 1973-75; pres. RJN Environ. Assos., Wheaton, Ill., 1975—. Bd. dirs. Marion Park, Inc., 1977—, Du Page County (Ill.) Health Systems Agy., 1977—. Registered profl. engr., Ill. Mem. Water Pollution Control Fedn., ASCE, Nat., Ill. socs. profl. engrs. Roman Catholic. Club: Wyncliff Swim. Contbr. articles on wastewater treatment to tech. publs. Patentee wastewater treatment process equipment. Home: 27W147 Fleming Dr Winfield IL 60190 Office: 213 S Wheaton Ave Wheaton IL 60187

NOGG, ROBERT STERLING, accountant, mfg. co. exec., real estate developer; b. Omaha, July 20, 1942; s. Ezra Leo and Sarah Irene (Sterling) N.; B.B.A., U. Okla., 1964; student U. Nebr., 1977,

Wharton Sch. U. Pa., 1978; children—Dana, Jennifer. Staff acct. Peat, Marwick, Mitchell & Co., C.P.A.'s, 1964-65; sr. acct. Elmer Fox, Westheimer & Co., C.P.A.'s, Omaha, 1965-67; partner, co-founder Frankel Nogg & Co., Omaha, 1968—; pres. Indsl. Label Corp., Omaha, 1974-77, Bocage Real Estate Inc., 1972—; v.p. Nogg Fruit Co., 1975-77, Ski Racquet Inc., 1976-78; partner GNF Co. Real Estate, 1973-77, Pacific Properties Co., 1974-78, Firehouse Dinner Theatre, 1973-78; guest lectr. Creighton U., U. Nebr.; adv. Open Elem. Sch., 1977; counselor SBA, 1974-76. Chmn. bd. dirs. Phillip Sher Home for Aged, 1974; mem. nat. leadership cabinet UJA, 1976; treas., bd. dirs. Omaha Civic Opera, 1976-78; co-chmn. leadership cabinet Omaha Jewish Philanthropies, 1976; bd. dirs. Temple Israel, 1975-77, Jewish Fedn.; adv. Jr. Achievement; com. mem. Loveland Sch. PTA, 1977-78. Mem. Am. Inst. C.P.A.'s, Nebr. Soc. C.P.A.'s (chmn. rev. com. 1975, ethics com. 1974), Joslyn Art Soc., Nat. Assn. Ski Dealers. Clubs: Temple Mens, Highland Country, Omaha Racquet, Tennis, B'nai B'rith, Ak-Sar-Ben. Exhbn. photography Jewish Community Center, 1978. Home: 728 Sunset Trail Omaha NE 68132

NOGGLE, LAWRENCE WESLEY, mech. engr.; b. Dayton, Ohio, Oct. 9, 1935; s. William Henry and Lula Evelyn (O'Dell) N.; B.M.E., Gen. Motors Inst., 1959; B.A., Simpson Coll., 1965; M.Sc., Ohio State U., 1972, Ph.D., 1973; postgrad. Indsl. Coll. of Armed Forces, 1980-81; m. Alwilda June Yount, Nov. 20, 1952; children—Lawrence Wesley, Yvonne, Grant, Matthew, Dorinda. Coop. student, jr. project engr. Gen. Motors Corp., Indpls. and Oak Ridge, 1954-61; aerospace engr. USAF, Wright-Patterson AFB, Ohio, 1961-62; computer room supr. Wells Fargo Bank, San Franciso, 1962-65; research engr. Boeing Co., Seattle, 1965-66; aerospace engr., sr. aerospace engr., study mgr. aero. systems div. Wright Patterson AFB, 1966-76, program mgr., mission area planner, 1976—; tchr. Simpson Coll., 1962-63. Active PTA, Little League, Brookville Band Boosters. Gen. Motors Corp. fellow, 1954-58, USAF fellow, 1970-71; recipient Outstanding Performance award USAF, 1968, 69, 73, 74, 80. Mem. AIAA (tech. com. air transp. systems 1978—), Air Force Assn., Ohio State U. Alumni Assn., Gen. Motors Inst. Alumni Assn., Sigma Xi, Tau Beta Pi, Chi Alpha Omega. Mem. Christian and Missionary Alliance Ch. Contbr. articles to profl. jours. Home: 12257 Air Hill Rd Brookville OH 45309 Office: Aeronautical Systems Div Wright Patterson AFB OH 45433

NOHA, EDWARD J., ins. co. exec.; b. 1926; B.B.A., Pace Coll.; married. With Dept. Justice, 1944-52, Met. Life Ins. Co., 1952-55; exec. v.p. Allstate Ins. Co., 1955-74; chmn. bd., pres., chief exec. officer Continental Casualty Co.; chmn. bd., pres., chief exec. officer Continental Assurance Co., Chgo.; chmn. bd. Nat. Fire Ins. Co. of Hartford, Inc., Transcontinental Ins. Co. Office: Continental Casualty Co CNA Plaza Chicago IL 60685*

NOLAN, CAROLE RITA, broadcasting co. exec.; b. Chgo., Jan. 28, 1932; d. Martin Francis and Caroline Rita (Alton) N.; B.A., DePaul U., 1954, M.A., 1961. Tchr. Chgo. public schs., 1954-61, sci. cons., 1961-66, dir. instructional TV, 1966-71; dir. bur. telecommunications and broadcasting, mgr. Sta. WBEZ-FM, Chgo., 1971—; mem. faculty Northeastern U., 1964-65, De Paul U., 1975—; cons. Comptons Ency., 1964-65, Chgo. Area Sch. TV, 1964-72, Ill. TV Adv. Council, 1969. Bd. dirs. Am. Chamber Symphony, Ella Flagg Young Women Adminstrs., Chicagoland Radio Info. Services. Mem. Nat. Assn. Ednl. Broadcasters, Ill. Assn. Supervision and Curriculum, Chgo. Network, Nat. Pub. Radio, Japan Am. Soc., DePaul Univ. Alumni Assn., Delta Kappa Gamma. Office: 228 N LaSalle Chicago IL 60601

NOLAN, DAVID P., civil engr.; b. Euclid, Ohio, Mar. 26, 1953; s. Michael J. and LaVerne A. (Pepper) N.; B.S. in Civil Engring., Ohio No. U., 1975. Civil engr. Osborn Engring. Co., Cleve., 1975-77, Medusa Corp., Cleve., 1977—. Registered profl. engr., Ohio, Mich., Pa., Wis., Ga. Mem. ASCE, Nat. Soc. Profl. Engrs., Charlevoix Jaycees, Tau Beta Pi, Omicron Delta Kappa, Alpha Phi Gamma. Clubs: Mayfield Village Racquet, Charlevoix Yacht. Home: 535 Petoskey Ave Charlevoix MI 49720 Office: Bells Bay Rd Charlevoix MI 49720

NOLAN, JOSEPH THOMAS, chem. co. exec.; b. Waterbury, Conn., Apr. 11, 1920; s. Thomas Francis and Mary Margaret (Gaffney) N.; A.B., Holy Cross Coll., 1942; M.A. in English, Boston U., 1945; Ph.D. in Econs., N.Y. U., 1972; m. Virginia Theodate Tappin, May 6, 1943; children—Carol (Mrs. Francois Rigolot), David J. Washington corr. UPI, 1943-49; writer, editor N.Y. Times, N.Y.C., 1949-55; mgr. editorial and press services RCA Corp., N.Y.C., N.Y., 1955-62; sr. v.p. corp. communications Chase Manhattan Bank, N.Y.C., 1962-74; prof. journalism and public affairs, U. S.C., Columbia, 1974-76; v.p. public affairs Monsanto Co., St. Louis, 1976—. Bd. dirs. United Way Greater St. Louis. Mem. Public Relations Soc. Am., Regional Commerce and Growth Assn. (bd. dirs.). Contbr. numerous articles to various mags. Home: 2316 Putter Lane St Louis MO 63131 Office: Monsanto Co 800 N Lindbergh Blvd St Louis MO 63166

NOLAN, SANDRA JEAN, mgmt. cons.; b. Milw., May 26, 1947; d. Harry Ernest and Mary Patricia Polley; B.S., U. Wis., Milw., 1974; m. Timothy M. Nolan, July 29, 1967; children—Tracy, Stephanie, Alissa. Pres. Early Learners Child Devel. Centers, Inc., Milw., 1971—; v.p. Nolan Assos., Inc., Milw., 1973-78, Innovative Tng. and Devel. Assos., Inc., Milw., 1973—. Mem. Am. Mgmt. Assn., Am. Soc. Tng. and Devel. Office: 759 N Milwaukee St Milwaukee WI 53202

NOLAND, GARY LLOYD, job placement co. exec.; b. Lindsborg, Kans., July 29, 1942; s. Willard Lloyd and Florence Lizzie (Waggoner) N.; B.S., Central Mo. State U., 1971, M.S., 1974; postgrad. U. Mo., 1976-79. Vice pres. sales First Nat. Land Co., Scottsdale, Ariz., 1961-66; mid-mgmt. instr. State Fair Community Coll., Sedalia, Mo., 1972-74, dir. job placement, 1974-79; dir. Statewide Job Placement Service, Sedalia, 1979—. Served with U.S. Army, 1966-68. Decorated Commendation medal, Air medal. Mem. Nat. Assn. Industry-Edn. Coop., Am. Vocat. Assn., Mo. Assn. Community and Jr. Colls., Mo. Tchrs. Assn., Mo. Guidance Assn., Mo. Vocat. Assn., Mo. Coll. Personnel Assn., Midwest Coll. Placement Assn., Coll. Placement Council. Clubs: Lions, Moose, Masons, Elks. Author: Help Yourself to Successful Employment, 1975. Home: Route 1 Mora MO 65345 Office: Statewide Job Placement Service 1900 Clarendon Rd Sedalia MO 65301

NOLAND, GEORGE BRYAN, univ. adminstr.; b. Ft. Ogden, Fla., Mar. 7, 1926; s. George Bryan and Alice Lucille (Lepage) N.; B.S., U. Detroit, 1950, M.S., 1952; Ph.D., Mich. State U., 1955; m. Mildred Theresa Filipp, Sept. 6, 1952; children—Michael Thomas, Elizabeth Ann, Susan Marie, Linda Ann, Carol Marie. Instr. biology U. Dayton (Ohio), 1955-57, asst. prof., 1957-60, asso. prof., 1960-65, prof., 1965—, chmn. biology dept., 1963-76, dean grad. studies and research, 1976-79, asso. provost, 1979—; instl. rep. Council Grad. Schs., Ohio Bd. Regents Adv. Com. on Grad. Studies. Served with USN, 1943-46. Named Prof. of Year, U. Dayton, 1968. NSF grantee, 1965-66, Kresge Found. grantee, 1965-66, Research Corp. grantee, 1966-67, HEW grantee, 1968-72. Mem. AAAS, Nat. Council Univ. Research Adminstrs., Am. Assn. Higher Edn., Am. Inst. Biol. Sci., Sigma Xi. Author: General Biology, 1979; (with others) General Biology, 3d edit., 1975. Office: U Dayton 300 College Park Dayton OH 45469

NOLAND, MARION SEYMOUR, nutritionist; b. Claresholm, Alta., Can., Feb. 2, 1930; d. Ferdinand Brown and Lucy Mary (Hart) Seymour; came to U.S., 1956, naturalized, 1964; B.S. in Home Econs., U. Man., 1952; M.S. in Dietetics, Ohio State U., 1954; M.A. in Counseling, U. Mo., Kansas City, 1969; m. Norman Asbury Noland, Feb. 2, 1964. Instr. Sch. Home Econs. U. B.C., Vancouver, Can., 1953-55; asst. prof. Sch. Nursing U. Tex. Med. Branch, Galveston, 1956-60; asso. prof. dept. dietetics and nutrition U. Kans. Med. Center, Kansas City, 1960-66; counselor Franklin Smith Elementary Sch., Blue Springs, Mo., 1969-71, 1974-76; pvt. practice cons. nutritionist and counselor, Blue Springs, 1976—. Recipient U. Man. Home Econs. award, 1952; Singer Co. award, 1952; certified profl. counselor Profl. Counselors Assn., 1968. Mem. Am. Dietetic Assn. (registered dietitian), Am. Personnel and Guidance Assn., Mo. State Tchrs. Assn., Am. Mental Health Counselors Assn., Cons. Nutritionists Groups, AAUW (v.p. 1974-76), Blue Springs Community Educators Assn., Tex. League for Nursing, League of Women Voters, Beta Sigma Phi (chpt. pres.), Sigma Delta Epsilon. Mem. Unity Sch. of Christianity Ch. Clubs: Lake Tapawingo Women's (v.p. 1971-73). Author, pub. Nutrition and Special Diet Helpletter, 1977—. Contbr. articles to Jour. Home Econs., Am. Jour. Clin. Nutrition, Jour. Am. Dietetic Assn., 1955-65. Home and Office: 1700 Dana Dr Blue Springs MO 64015

NOLAND, WAYNE BARNETT, mfg. co. exec.; b. Spirit Lake, Iowa, Nov. 13, 1918; s. Fred Alvard and Nora Lucinda (Cook) N.; student public schs., Earlham, Iowa; m. Ruth Ellen Smith, June 2, 1941; children—Barbara Jo, Alice Marie, Gary Chester, Larry Fred. Engr., mgr. mfg. Woodford Mfg. Co., Des Moines, 1943-70; pres. Noland Mfg. Co., Inc., Carlisle, Iowa, 1970—. Quaker. Patentee in field. Home: 340 Crescent Dr Carlisle IA 50047 Office: 100 E School St Carlisle IA 50047

NOLES, MAX HAROLD, ins. co. exec.; b. Rotan, Tex., July 19, 1933; s. George Allen and Gladys Irene (Strickland) N.; B.A.S., U. Houston, 1955; m. Nancy Ray Edwards, Apr. 21, 1956; children—Mark Randall, Michelle Rae. Mgr. engring. publns. The Travelers Ins. Co., Hartford, Conn., 1966-72; mgr. products devel. Internat. Safety Acad., Macon, Ga., 1972-73; dir. comml. loss control Nationwide Ins., Columbus, Ohio, 1973—. Served with U.S. Army, 1956-58. Cert. safety profl. Mem. Am. Soc. Safety Engrs. (profl.), Am. Bus. Communication Assn. Office: 1 Nationwide Plaza Columbus OH 43216

NOLL, CHARLES GORDON, physicist; b. Sunbury, Pa., Dec. 2, 1948; s. J. Herman and Helen Elisabeth (Gelnett) N.; B.A., Bloomsburg (Pa.) State Coll., 1970; M.S., Ohio State U., Columbus, 1974, Ph.D., 1975; m. Alice Marie Walters, Dec. 20, 1971; children—Carlton Leigh, Benjamin Douglass. Lectr. physics Ohio State U., 1975-76; researcher research and devel. United McGill Corp., Columbus, 1976-78, corp. physicist, Groveport, Ohio, 1978—; cons. environ. problems. Mem. Am. Phys. Soc., IEEE, Electrostatics Soc. Am., Sigma Xi, Sigma Pi Sigma. Author: Ensemble Theory for Electrostatic Precipitation, 1980; Computer Aided Research Tools for Pilot Testing of Pollution Control Equipment, 1981. Home: 121 Academy Ct Gahanna OH 43230 Office: One Mission Park Groveport OH 43125

NOLLAN, RICHARD CHARLES, religious printing and pub. co. exec.; b. Neenah, Wis., Oct. 29, 1935; s. Walter Theodore and Emily Anne (Vondrachek) N.; student Northwestern U., eves. 1958-62. Mgr. data processing Wine & Spirits Liquor Co., Chgo., 1957-67, Gold Seal Liquors Co., Chgo., 1967-72; dir. mgmt. info. services J.S. Paluch Co., Chgo., 1972—. Served with USMC, 1953-57; Korea. Mem. Assn. Computing Machinery, Data Processing Mgmt. Assn., Computer Soc. Roman Catholic. Club: N. Am. Hunting. Home: 3946 W Estes St Lincolnwood IL 60645 Office: 1800 W Winnemac Ave Chicago IL 60640

NOLOT, MERVIN JOSEPH, planning agy. adminstr.; b. DePauw, Ind., July 18, 1946; s. Cecil Joseph and Lula Mae (Smith) N.; B.S. in Polit. Sci., Ind. State U., 1971, M.A. in Public Adminstrn. (grad. asst.), 1973; m. Barbara Anne, July 19, 1980; 1 dau., Jacqueline Marie. Regional planner West Central Ind. Econ. Devel. Dist., Terre Haute, 1973-76, transp. planner, 1976-77, exec. dir., 1977—. Served with U.S. Army, NG, 1966-72. Mem. Am. Soc. Public Adminstrn., Ind. Planning Assn. Roman Catholic. Office: 121 S 3d St Terre Haute IN 47808*

NOLT, LOUISE, educator; b. New Philadelphia, Ohio, July 9, 1922; d. Enos Dale and Edna Lucille (Thompson) N.; A.B. in History, Biology and Edn., Manchester Coll., 1944; M.A. in History, Case Western Res. U., 1962. Tchr. Coesse (Ind.) High Sch., 1944-45, Sidwell Friends Sch., Washington, 1945-46; membership clk., med. records librarian Group Health Assn., Washington, 1946-47; tchr. history, govt., geography Springfield High Sch., Akron, Ohio, 1948—; tchr. English to Hmong refugees Internat. Inst., Akron, summer 1981; bd. dirs. Summit Fed. Credit Union, Akron, 1951—. Teller, Ch. of the Brethren Ann. Confs., 1977-81, women's work cabinet No. Ohio, 1980-81. Martha Holden Jennings Found. of Cleve. Jennings scholar, 1978. Mem. Am. Hist. Assn., NEA, Ohio Edn. Assn., Northeastern Ohio Edn. Assn., Kappa, Kappa Iota. Home: 1211 Girard St Akron OH 44301 Office: 2966 Sanatorium Rd Akron OH 44312

NOOT, ARTHUR EDWARD, state ofcl.; b. Mpls., Feb. 4, 1933; B.A., U. Minn., 1958; M.A., U. Pa., 1968; m. Linnaia D. Koch; 3 children. Caseworker I, Mower County (Minn.) Welfare Dept., 1959-61; caseworker I and II, Hennepin County (Minn.) Welfare Dept., 1961-64; dir. I, Chisago County (Minn.) Welfare Bd., 1964-66; with Minn. Dept. Public Welfare, 1968-72, state welfare commr., 1979—; from dir. fin. assistance to dep. dir. Ramsey County (Minn.) Welfare Dept., 1972-79; past part-time instr. Lakewood Jr. Coll., White Bear Lake, Minn. Served with USN, 1951-55; Korea. Author articles in field.

NOPPER, RALPH JACOB, civil engr.; b. Toledo, July 5, 1916; s. Charles Joseph and Martha Elizabeth (Rippel) N.; B.Engring., U. Toledo, 1939; m. Roberta R. Newcomb, July 31, 1943; children—Linda E. (Mrs. Kenneth J. Keiser). Structural engr. A. Bentley & Sons Co., Toledo, 1937-38; constrn. engr. E.B. Badger & Sons Co., Boston, 1938-39; engr., H.C. Baker Co., Toledo, 1939-40; chief maintenance engr. Libbey-Owens-Ford Co., Toledo, 1940-81; self-employed as cons. engr., Toledo, 1940—. Registered profl. engr., Ohio. Mem. ASCE (pres. Toledo sect. 1954), Nat., Ohio, Toledo (pres. 1953) socs. profl. engrs., Toledo Tech. Council (pres. 1952-53). Home: 3710 Harley Rd Toledo OH 43613

NORAGON, JACK LEROY, state ofcl.; b. Lincoln, Nebr., Apr. 5, 1937; s. Claude LeRoy and Frances Bernice (Laun) N.; student (Washington Semester scholar), Am. U., 1958; B.A., Doane Coll., 1959; postgrad. U. Nebr., 1960; Ph.D., Ohio State U., 1968; m. Patricia Ann Handwerk, June 21, 1969; children—Michele Lea, Melinda Rae. Tchr., South Sioux City (Nebr.) public schs., 1959-61; instr. Denison U., Granville, Ohio, 1966-68; asst. prof. Oberlin (Ohio) Coll., 1968-69; asst. prof. Cleve. State U., 1969-76; research asso. Ohio Legis. Service Commn., Columbus, 1976-78, sr. research asso., 1978—; lectr. Ohio State U., Marion, 1980-81; polit. cons. Chmn. AAUP state and fed. govt. com. Cleve. State U., 1972-73, 75-76. Ford Found Legis. intern, 1964-65. Mem. AAUP, Am. Polit. Sci. Assn., Midwest Polit. Sci. Assn., Ohio Assn. Economists and Polit. Scientists, ACLU, Pi Sigma Alpha, Phi Alpha Theta. Congregationalist. Contbr. articles to profl. jours. Home: 1015 Beechview Dr S Worthington OH 43085 Office: Ohio Legis Service Commn State House Columbus OH 43215

NORD, EVANS ALLEN, broadcasting co. exec.; b. Carver, Minn., Apr. 15, 1917; s. Frank W. and Elin A. (Johnson) N.; B.A., Augustana Coll., 1939; m. Jean White, June 9, 1956; children—Stephen C., Nancy, Allen, Cynthia, Thomas. Program dir. Sioux Falls (S.D.) Broadcast Assn., 1939-42; sta. mgr. KELO, 1946-49; gen. mgr. Midcontinent Broadcasting Co., Sioux Falls, 1949-60, gen. mgr., 1960-75, pres., gen. mgr. Stas. KELO-LAND div., 1975—; v.p., dir. Wayne-Evans & Assos. (Mpls.); mem. Legis. Com. S.D. Broadcasters, chmn., 1968—; sales adv. com. TV Bur. Advt.; mem. S.D. State Bd. Engring. and Archtl. Examiners, 1970-78. Bd. dirs. YMCA, 1958—, Sioux Valley Hosp., 1967-77; gen. chmn. United Fund, 1967; state chmn. Mental Health, 1964; state chmn. Radio Free Europe, 1962-63; mem's com. Japan Internat. Christian U., 1965-78; state chmn. S.D. vol. com. U.S. Bonds, 1977—; steering com. Salvation Army, 1970-71; former pres. and fund drive chmn. Augustana Alumni Assn.; fellow Augustana Coll.; parents adv. com. U. S.D., 1965-73; citizens adv. com. Urban Renewal Program, 1967-73; chmn. S.D. Battleship Commn., 1962—; chmn. Nat. Security Seminar, 1963; co-chmn. Citizens Com. Med. Edn., 1972-75; health sci. adv. council U. S.D., 1975—; bd. dirs. S.D. Easter Seals, 1976—; cancer crusade chmn. S.D., 1977-78; chmn. bd. S.D. chpt. Am. Cancer Soc., 1978-80; bd. dirs. S.D. Council Econ. Edn., 1978-81. Served to capt. USNR, 1942-46. Named Boss of Yr., Jr. C. of C., 1964, Advt. Man of Yr., 1972; recipient Citizen of Week award, 1967, Disting. Service award United Community Services, 1967, Friend of Youth award Optimists Club of Sioux Falls, 1971, Cosmopolitan Disting. Service award, 1975, Disting. Service award S.D. Med. Assn., 1978. Mem. Sioux Falls Area C. of C. (dir. 1961-65, pres. 1961), Navy League U.S. (pres. Sioux Falls council), Greater S.D. C. of C., S.D. Broadcasters Assn. (dir. 1967-73, state pres. 1954-55), S.D. Res. Officers Assn. (past pres., Reservist of Yr. 1962), Sioux Falls Area C. of C., Internat. Radio and TV Soc., Am. Legion, VFW, Naval Res. Assn., Ret. Officers Assn., Nat. Hon. Broadcasting Soc. Republican. Baptist. Clubs: Masons, Shriners, Elks, Sertoma. Home: 1000 S Garfield Ave Sioux Falls SD 57105 Office: 501 S Phillips Ave Sioux Falls SD 57102

NORDAAS, HAAKON NJAAL, home bldg. co. exec.; b. Stavanger, Norway, Oct. 20, 1919; came to U.S., 1938, naturalized, 1945; s. Halvar and Anna (Stangeland) N.; grad. high sch.; m. Mavis Thompson, Oct. 28, 1966; children—Linda, Robert, Perry, Dawn. Owner, pres., treas. Nordaas Am. Homes, Minnesota Lake, Minn., 1949—; pres. Am. Distbg. Co., Am. Advt. Co.; dir. Farmers Nat. Bank. Served with U.S. Army, 1945. Mem. Nat. Assn. Home Builders, Nat. Office Products Assn., Nat. Restaurant Assn. (Contractor of Yr. award 1974, 75), Am. Legion, U.S. C. of C. Republican. Lutheran. Club: Sons of Norway. Office: Nordaas Am Homes Hwy 22 Box 116 Minnesota Lake MN 56068

NORDBY, EUGENE JORGEN, orthopaedic surgeon; b. Abbotsford, Wis., Apr. 30, 1918; s. Herman Preus and Lucille Violet (Korsrud) N.; B.A., Luther Coll., Decorah, Iowa, 1939; M.D., U. Wis., 1943; m. Olive Marie Jensen, June 21, 1941; 1 son, Jon Jorgen. Intern, Madison (Wis.) Gen. Hosp., 1943-44, asst. in orthopedic surgery, 1944-48; practice medicine specializing in orthopaedic surgery, Madison, Wis., 1948—; pres. Bone and Joint Surgery Assos., S.C., 1969—; chief staff Madison Gen. Hosp., 1957-63, bd. dirs., 1957-76; asso. clin. prof. U. Wis. Med. Sch.; chmn. Wis. Physicians Service, 1979; dir. Wis. Regional Med. Program; bd. govs. Wis. Health Care Liability Ins. Plan; dir. Chgo. Madison and No. Railroad; chmn. trustees S.M.S. Realty Corp. Pres. Norwegian Am. Museum, Decorah, Iowa. Served to capt. M.C., AUS, 1944-46. Recipient Distinguished Service award Luther Coll., 1964. Decorated Knight 1st class Royal Norwegian Order St. Olav, 1979. Mem. Am. Acad. Orthopaedic Surgeons (dir. 1972-73), Clin. Orthopaedic Soc., Assn. Bone and Joint Surgery (pres. 1972), Internat. Soc. Study Lumbar Spine, State Med. Soc. Wis. (chmn. 1968-76, treas. 1976—; Council award 1976), Wis. Orthopaedic Soc., Dane County Med. Soc., Phi Chi. Lutheran. Club: Nat. Exchange. Asso. editor Clin. Orthopaedics and Related Research, 1964—. Home: 6234 S Highlands Madison WI 53705 Office: 2704 Marshall Ct Madison WI 53705

NORDEEN, DALE ARRON, financial assn. exec.; b. Madison, Wis., Dec. 23, 1927; s. Frank Edward and Pearl (Day) N.; B.A. in Accounting with honors, U. Wis., 1950; m. Nora Ellen Haley, Aug. 26, 1950; children—Kathy, Chris, Andy. Bus. trainee Gen. Electric, Madison, 1950-52; auditor Ernst & Ernst, C.P.A.'s, Madison, 1952-55; mgr. Hill Farms Devel. U. Wis., 1956-58; clk. First Fed. Savs. & Loan, 1948-49, auditor, 1955, asst. treas., 1956-60, v.p., treas., 1960-61, dir., 1961, pres., 1962—, chmn. bd., 1977—; vice-chmn., dir. Fed. Home Loan Bank of Chgo., 1974. Chmn. Wis. Housing Finance Authority, 1974-75, 77-79; pres. Central Madison Council, 1980; bd. dirs. Jr. Achievement, 1970-79; bd. dirs., chmn. Methodist Hosp., 1981—; sec. Madison Devel. Corp., 1980. Served with USNR, 1945-46. Lic. real estate broker, ins. agt.; C.P.A. Mem. U.S. Savs. and Loan League, Wis. Savs. and Loan League (pres. 1971, Outstanding Service award 1974). Home: 4206 Yuma Dr Madison WI 53711 Office: 202 State St Madison WI 53703

NORDEEN, PEGGY ANN, advt. exec.; b. Muscatine, Iowa, July 27, 1946; d. Gene E. and Marylou Nordeen; B.A. in Journalism and English, U. Iowa, 1968. Gen. assignment news reporter Davenport (Iowa) Times-Democrat, 1966-69; with Sperry-Boom Inc., Chgo., 1970-78, v.p., dir. 1976-78; pres. Starmark, Inc., Chgo., 1978—. Mem. Viking Ship Restoration Com., Chgo., 1979; Iowa Realtors Assn.

scholar, 1964. Mem. Am. Mktg. Assn. (v.p. communications Chgo. chpt. 1974), Publicity Club Chgo. (sec., dir. 1973-74), Gamma Phi Beta. Mem. Christian Ch. (Disciples of Christ). Office: Starmark Bldg 706 N Dearborn St Chicago IL 60610

NORDLAND, GERALD J(OHN), mus. adminstr.; b. Los Angeles, July 10, 1927; s. Arthur Andre and Doris Monica (Johnston) N.; A.B., U. So. Calif., 1948, J.D., 1950; m. Mary Lou Lindstrom, Aug. 29, 1948 (div. 1972); children—Brady Lynn, Todd Jefferson. Art critic various mags. and newspapers, 1955-64; dean Chouinard Art Inst., Los Angeles, 1960-64; dir. Washington Gallery Modern Art, Washington, 1964-66, San Francisco Mus. Art, 1966-72, Frederick S. Wight Art Gallery, UCLA, 1973-77, Milw. Art Mus., 1977—. Commr. Calif. State Fair, 1974-76. Served with U.S. Army, 1953-55. Gaston Lachaise Found. grantee, 1973-74. Mem. Assn. Art Museum Dirs. Clubs: University, Arts (Chgo.). Author: Paul Jenkins, 1972; Gaston Lachaise—The Man and His Work, 1974. Office: Milwaukee Art Mus 750 N Lincoln Memorial Dr Milwaukee WI 53202

NORDLIE, ROBERT CONRAD, biochemist, educator; b. Willmar, Minn., June 11, 1930; s. Peter Conrad and Myrtle (Spindler) N.; student Gustavus Adolphus Coll., 1948-49; B.S. in Edn., St. Cloud (Minn.) State Coll., 1952; M.S., U. N.D., 1957, Ph.D. (NIH fellow), 1960; m. Sally Ann Christianson, Aug. 23, 1959; children—Margaret, Melissa, John. Teaching and research asst. biochemistry U. N.D. Med. Sch., Grand Forks, 1955-60, Hill research prof. biochemistry, 1962-74, Chester Fritz distinguished prof. biochemistry, 1974—; NIH fellow Inst. Enzyme Research, U. Wis., 1960-61; mem. biochemistry study sect. NIH. Cons. enzymology Oak Ridge, 1961—. Served with AUS, 1953-55. Mem. Am. Soc. Biol. Chemists, Am. Chem. Soc., AAAS, Internat. Union Biochemists, Am. Soc. for Microbiology, Soc. for Exptl. Biology and Medicine, Nat. Inst. Nutrition, Brit. Biochem. Soc., Sigma Xi, Alpha Omega Alpha. Club: Elks. Editorial bd. Biochimica et Biophysica Acta. Research, publs. on enzymology relating to metabolism of various carbohydrates in mammaliam livers. Home: 162 Columbia Ct Grand Forks ND 58201

NORDLING, BERNARD ERICK, lawyer; b. Nekoma, Kans., June 14, 1921; s. C.R. Ebben and Edith (Freeburg) N.; A.B., McPherson Coll., 1947; student George Washington U., 1941-43; LL.B., J.D., Kans. U., 1949; m. Barbara Ann Burkholder, Mar. 26, 1949; children—Karen, Kristine, Leslie, Erick, Julie. Clerical employee FBI, 1941-44; admitted to Kans. bar, 1949; practiced in Hugoton, Kans., 1949—; mem. firms Kramer & Nordling, 1950-65, Kramer, Nordling & Nordling, 1966—; city atty., Hugoton, 1951—; county atty. Stevens County (Kans.), 1957-63. Sec., Raycolor, Inc., Hugoton, 1968-81; exec. sec. S.W. Kans. Royalty Owners Assn., 1968—; Kans. mem. legal com. Interstate Oil Compact Commn., 1969—, mem. supply tech. adv. com. Nat. Gas Survey, FPC, 1975-77; mem. Kans. Energy Adv. Council, 1975-78, exec. com., 1976-78. Mem. Hugoton Sch. Bds., 1954-68, pres. grade sch. bd., 1961-66; pres. Stevens County Library Bd., 1957-63. Trustee McPherson Coll., 1971-81, mem. exec. com., 1975-81. Served with AUS, 1944-46. Mem. Nat. Honor Soc., Nat. Assn. Royalty Owners (bd. govs. 1980—), Order of Coif. Home: 218 N Jackson St Hugoton KS 67951 Office: 209 E 6th St Hugoton KS 67951

NORDLUND, DONALD E., agribus. exec., lawyer; b. Stromsburg, Nebr., Mar. 1, 1922; s. Elmer C. and Edith O. (Peterson) N.; B.A., Midland Coll., 1943, LL.D. (hon.), 1975; J.D., U. Mich., 1948; m. Jane Houston, June 5, 1948; children—Craig, William, Sally, Peter. Admitted to Ill. bar, 1949; asso. firm Stevenson, Conaghan, Velde & Hackbert, Chgo., 1948-56; counsel A.E. Staley Mfg. Co., ecatur, Ill., 1956-58, v.p. law and adminstrn., 1958-65, pres., 1965-80, chief exec. officer, 1973—, chmn., 1975—, also dir.; dir. Amsted Industries, Citizens Nat. Bank Decatur, Ill. Bell Telephone Co., Sentry Ins. Co., Sundstand Corp.; mem. Chgo. Bd. Trade. Trustee, Millikin U., 1960—, chmn. bd. trustees, 1979; bd. dirs. Decatur Meml. Hosp., 1966-75. Served with U.S. Army, 1943-46, 50-52; Korea. Mem. Am. Bar Assn., Chgo. Bar Assn. Clubs: Decatur, Country of Decatur, Tavern of Chgo. Office: 2200 Eldorado St Decatur IL 62525

NORDSTRAND, RAYMOND WILLIAM, broadcasting co. exec., publisher; b. Evanston, Ill., Sept. 13, 1932; s. Nels Eric and Frida Elise (Kuehl) N.; B.A., Northwestern U., 1953, M.S., 1956; m. Susan Diana Ports, June 15, 1963; 1 dau., Susan Erika. Instr. econs. Northwestern U., 1953-55; announcer Sta. WFMT-FM, Chgo., 1953-57, asst. mgr., 1957-63, comml. mgr., 1963-68, sta. mgr., 1968-70, gen. mgr., 1970—; pres. WFMT, Inc., 1970—; pub. Chgo. Mag., 1970—. Co-producer nationally syndicated radio program Midnight Spl.; syndicator radio series Chgo. Symphony, Chgo. Lyric Opera. Treas., trustee Broadcasting Found. Am.; trustee Chgo. Symphony Orch.; chmn., trustee Cinema Chgo.; v.p., trustee Old Town Sch. Folk Music. Recipient Maj. Armstrong award for Midnight Spl. program, 1971; named Outstanding Citizen by resolution of mayor and City Council Chgo., 1973, 78. Mem. Concert Music Broadcasters Assn. (exec. com., chmn. 1975-76), Nat. Radio Broadcasters Assn., City and Regional Mag. Assn. (dir. 1979—, research dir. 1981—), Phi Beta Kappa. Contbr. articles in field to profl. jours. Office: 303 E Wacker Dr Chicago IL 60601

NORDSTROM, HARRISON BERNARD, railroad supply co. exec.; b. St. Paul, Feb. 22, 1932; s. Harry Bernard and Dorothy Kathrine (Driscoll) N.; B.S., Purdue U., 1958; m. Judith Ann O'Brien, May 20, 1961; children—Anne Driscoll, Cecily Mills, Harrison Bernard III. Sales engr. Magnus Metal Corp., 1958-63; pres. Roaring Fork Realty Corp., Aspen, Colo. 1963-68; v.p. Intext-ICS World Ltd., Scranton, Pa., 1968-71; v.p. sales Holland Co., Lombard, Ill., 1971-80; pres. Railroad Mech. Devices Inc., 1980—, Nordek Corp., 1981—. Served with USN, 1952-56. Mem. ASME, Newcomen Soc. N.Am. Club: Chicago Athletic Assn. Office: 528 S Batavia Ave Batavia IL 60510

NORLING, RAYBURN EDWIN, agribus. co. exec.; b. Willmar, Minn., Nov. 25, 1934; s. Albin Joseph and Huldah Sophia (Skoglund) N.; B.S. in Bus. Adminstrn., Gustavus Adolphus Coll., 1956; m. Harriet Joanne Peterson, Aug. 25, 1956; children—Gaye, Jodi, Torry. Accountant, Burroughs Corp., St. Louis, 1956-57; office mgr. Willmar Poultry Co., Inc. (Minn.), 1958-65, plant mgr., 1965-70, hatchery div. mgr., 1970-81, exec. v.p., 1975—, also dir.; dir. Farm Service Elevator Co., Willmar, Norling Bros. Silo Co., Inc., Svea, Minn.; dir. West Central Industries, 1970-79, pres., 1973-75. Bd. regents Golden Valley (Minn.) Luth. Coll., 1980-81. Served with U.S. Army, 1957. Mem. Willmar C. of C. (dir.), Minn. Turkey Research and Market Devel. Council (dir., pres. 1975-81), Minn. Turkey Growers Assn. (dir. 1975-81, pres. 1980-81). Republican. Lutheran. Willmar Golf; Sons of Norway. Home: 7131 Long Lake Rd Willmar MN 56201 Office: Box 753 Willmar MN 56201

NORMAN, CHARLES HENRY, radio sta. exec.; b. St. Louis, June 13, 1920; s. Charles Henry and Grace Vincent (Francis) N.; B.S., U. So. Calif., 1942; Salesman, announcer Sta. WTMV, East St. Louis, Ill., 1948-51; disk jockey Sta. WIL, St. Louis, 1951-56; owner, mgr. Sta. WGNU, St. Louis, 1961—. Served with U.S. Navy, 1943-46. Mem. Nat. Assn. Broadcasters, Greater St. Louis Radio Assn., St. Louis Ambassadors. Office: PO Box 178 Saint Louis MO 63166

NORMAN, FORREST ALONZO, lawyer; b. Renton, Pa., Nov. 21, 1929; s. Forrest Alonzo and Nellie Elizabeth (Corley) N.; B.B.A., Case Western Res. U., 1952, J.D., 1954; m. Christine Dende, July 5, 1954; children—Sally, Forrest Alonzo III, William. Admitted to Ohio bar, 1954; Mem. firm Gallagher, Sharp, Fulton, Norman & Mollison and predecessor firms, Cleve., 1956—. Served with AUS, 1955-56. Mem. Internat. Soc. Barristers, Def. Research Inst. Inc. (v.p. 1973-75, dir. 1975-79, v.p. public relations 1978-79), Fedn. Ins. Counsel (v.p. 1974-75, dir. 1975-79, sec.-treas. 1979-80, exec. v.p. and pres.-elect 1980-81, pres. 1981), Internat. Soc. Barristers, Am. Bd. Trial Attys., Nat. Assn. R.R. Trial Counsel, Internat. Assn. Ins. Counsel, Order of Coif, Delta Theta Phi. Clubs: Shaker Heights Country, Union, Masons. Home: 2977 Courtland Blvd Shaker Heights OH 44122 Office: 6th Floor Bulkley Bldg Cleveland OH 44115

NORMAN, JOHN WILLIAM, oil co. exec.; b. Harrisburg, Ill., Sept. 4, 1910; s. Walter Jacob and Clarissa May (Bush) N.; student pub. schs., Saline County, Ill.; m. Marcella Mary Souheaver, July 2, 1937. Dist. mgr. Martin Oil Co., 1936-54; with Am-Bulk Oil Co. (name changed to Norman Oil Co., 1960), Lisle, Ill., 1949—, pres., 1960—; dir. 1st Ogden Corp., Bank Hinsdale, Bank Lockport; chmn. bd. Bank of Lisle. Served with USNR, 1943-44. Mem. VFW, Am. Legion. Home: 4333 Main St Lisle IL 60532 Office: 1018 Ogden Ave Lisle IL 60532

NORMAN, RONALD VICTOR, library exec.; b. Venice, Calif., July 10, 1929; s. Victor Stephen and Violet B. (Aughton) N.; B.A., U. N.Mex., 1952; M.Div., Lutheran Sch. Theology, Chgo., 1960; M.A. in L.S., U. Denver, 1970; m. Anita Louise Redstrom, June 5, 1953; children—Ronald Stephen, Jennifer Lynn, Mark Andrew. Ordained to ministry Lutheran Ch., 1960; pastor Trinity Luth. Ch., Dalton, Nebr., 1960-64, St. Paul Luth. Ch., Auburn, Nebr., 1964-69; telecommunications network coordinator Tex. State Library, Austin, 1970-71; library dir. Kearney (Nebr.) Pub. Library, 1971—. Served with USN, 1953-56. Mem. ALA, Nebr. Library Assn., Am. Soc. Info. Sci., Mountain-Plains Library Assn. Democrat. Home: 3607 6th Ave Kearney NE 68847 Office: 2020 1st Ave Kearney NE 68847

NORMOYLE, JOHN LOUIS, writer, editor, public relations exec.; b. Chgo., Mar. 27, 1922; s. John Joseph and Catherine Henrietta (Shrodi) N.; grad. Morton Jr. Coll., 1947; B.S., Northwestern U., 1952; m. June Rose Bastlin, Sept. 8, 1947 (div. Sept. 1969); children—Janice, Judy, Joyce, Jennifer. Asso. editor Brick and Clay Record mag., Chgo., 1950-53; publicity supr. Allstate Ins. Co., Skokie, Ill., 1953-60; account exec. Philip Lesly Co., Chgo., 1960-62; pub. relations dir. Alberto Culver Co., Chgo., 1963; exec. v.p. Compass 4 Pub. Relations, Chgo., 1964-67; dir. press info. Bonsib Advt., Fort Wayne, Ind., 1968-69; mng. editor Lab. Medicine mag., Chgo., 1969-77; dir. public info. Am. Soc. Clin. Pathologists, Chgo., 1977-80; prin. Normoyle Writing/Editorial Services, Chgo., 1981—. Guest lectr. pub. relations and journalism Mich. State U., East Lansing, 1965-66, Columbia Coll., Chgo., 1961, YMCA Central Coll., Chgo., 1970-71, U. Ill., 1973, Chgo. Med. Coll., 1974-75, Northwestern U., 1976, Sangamon Coll., Springfield, Ill., 1977. Served with AUS, 1942-45. Decorated Bronze Star medal, Purple Heart with oak leaf cluster. Recipient Honor award for best feature writing, Publicity Club of Chgo., 1962, award for best continuing pub. relations campaign, 1964. Mem. Chgo. Press Club, Mensa. Author: The News Release Format, 1956. Contbr. articles to profl. jours. Home and Office: 1630 W Farwell Ave Chicago IL 60626

NORRIS, ALAN EUGENE, judge; b. Columbus, Ohio, Aug. 15, 1935; s. James Russell and Dorothy A. (Schrader) N.; certificate Sorbonne, 1956; B.A., Otterbein Coll., 1957; LL.B., N.Y. U., 1960; m. Nancy Jeanne Myers, Apr. 15, 1962; children—Tom Edward Jackson, Tracy Elaine. Admitted to Ohio bar, 1960; law clk. Chief Justice Kingsley A. Taft, 1960-61; partner firm Metz, Bailey, Norris & Spicer, Westerville, 1963-80; mem. Ohio Ho. of Reps. from 27th Dist., 1967-80; judge 10th Dist. Ct. Appeals, 1981—. City prosecutor, Westerville, 1962-66; mem. Zoning Bd. of Appeals, 1962-66, chmn., 1966; mem. Ohio Constl. Revision Commn., 1971-77. Chmn. Ohio Am. Revolution Bicentennial Commn., 1972-80. Mem. Franklin County Republican Central Com., 1962-80; mem. com. on suggested state legislation Council State Govts., 1967-76; mem. reapportionment com. Nat. Legis. Conf., 1973-75, chmn., 1974-75, mem. ethics, elections and reapportionment com., 1975-80. Trustee, United Methodist Children's Home. Recipient Jaycee Disting. Service award, 1967, Spl. Achievement award Otterbein Coll., 1973; named Legislator of Year, Ohio Acad. Trial Lawyers, 1972. Mem. Am., Ohio, Columbus bar assns., Ohio Hist. Soc., Otterbein Coll. Alumni Assn. (pres. 1971-72). Clubs: Masons, Kiwanis. Contbr. articles to profl. jours. Home: 58 W College Ave Westerville OH 43081 Office: 369 S High St Columbus OH 43215-4578

NORRIS, AUDREY BLESSING, supt. schs.; b. Washington, Dec. 6, 1924; d. John Frederick and Ethel Mae (Robinson) Blessing; B.A., Am. U., 1947; M.A., George Washington U., 1952; Ed.D., Case Western Res. U., 1969; m. Aug. 22, 1947. Tchr., Rockbridge County (Va.) schs., 1947-49, Arlington County (Va.) schs., 1949-53, Anderson Jr. High Sch., Cin., 1953-54; curriculum coordinator and supr. Hamilton County (Ohio) Schs., 1954-60; dir. curriculum, secondary supr. Willoughby Eastlake (Ohio) City Schs., 1960-64, dir. curriculum and research, 1964-75; asso. prof. U. Cin., 1964-73; dep. supt. curriculum and planning Jackson (Mich.) Pub. Schs., 1973-74; supt. schs. Maple Heights (Ohio) City Schs., 1974—; adj. asso. prof. Cleve. State U. Recipient Outstanding Service award Hamilton County Tchrs. Assn., 1960. Mem. Am. Assn. Sch. Adminstrs., Assn. for Supervision and Curriculum Devel., Am. Ednl. Research Assn., NEA, Ohio Edn. Assn., Buckeye Assn. Sch. Adminstrs., Ohio Assn. for Supervision and Curriculum Devel. (pres.), Phi Delta Kappa, Delta Kappa Gamma, Phi Delta Epsilon, Cairn Terrier Club Am. Presbyterian. Clubs: Cin. Kennel, Cleve. Women's City, Cin. Women's City. Office: 5305 Northfield Rd Apt 319 Bedford Heights OH 44146 also 5500 Clement Dr Maple Heights OH 44137

NORRIS, BRUCE ARTHUR, grain mcht., profl. hockey team exec.; b. Chgo., Feb. 19, 1924; s. James and Marguerite (Loris) N.; A.B., Yale U., 1945. With Norris Grain Co., N. Miami, Fla., 1947—, pres., 1952—, chmn. bd., 1956—; chmn. bd. Norin Corp., N. Miami; pres., chmn. Detroit Red Wings; pres. Norris Cattle Co., Ocala, Fla.; dir. C., R.I.&P. Ry., West Indies Sugar Co., Maple Leaf Mills., Ltd. Clubs: Chgo. Athletic, Chgo., Tavern, Lake Shore (Chgo.); Onwentsia (Lake Forest, Ill.); Everglades (Palm Beach, Fla.). Office: Detroit Red Wings 600 Civic Center Dr Detroit MI 48226*

NORRIS, FREDERICK THOMAS LEE, city ofcl., fin. services exec.; b. Wilmington, N.C., Nov. 6, 1936; s. Russel C. and Grace L. (Rivenbark) N.; student Beloit Coll., 1954-57, Worsham Coll. Mortuary Sci., 1957-58, De Paul U., 1965-66; m. Virginia Annett Eckhoff, June 29, 1957; children—Lynda Lee, Fred Thomas, Jr., Brenda Lee. Funeral dir. Norris Funeral Home, St. Charles, Ill., 1957—; credit mgr. Gen. Motors Acceptance Corp., Evanston, Ill., 1959-65; sr. credit analyst Brunswick Corp., Chgo., 1965-70; with SCM Corp., 1970—, fin. services mgr., Oakbrook, Ill., 1970—; dir. Dunham Bank, St. Charles, Ill., 1976—; instr. Chgo. Inst. Credit, 1975-78; alderman, City of St. Charles, 1968-77, mayor, 1977—. Chmn. DuKane Valley Council Mayors, 1980-81; commr. Cultural Art Center, 1978—; pres. St. Charles Park Found., Inc., 1975—; bd. dirs. Baker Community House and Recreation Center, 1975—, Tri-City Family Project, 1971—. Recipient Disting. Service award St. Charles Jaycees, 1972, also named Jaycee Man of Year, 1968. Mem. Am. Mgmt. Assn., Chgo. Midwest Credit Mgrs. Assn. Clubs: Lion; Rotary; Mason (Shriner); Moose. Home: 44 Stirrup Cup Ct St Charles IL 60174 Office: 2 E Main St Saint Charles IL 60174 also 3121 Butterfield Rd Oak Brook IL 60521

NORRIS, G. KENNON, realty co. exec.; b. Kearney, Nebr., Apr. 16, 1929; s. George E. and Mable S. (Nieman) N.; B.A., Kearney State Coll., 1950; m. Margaret M. Schlagel, May 20, 1951; children—Deborah, Sandra, Jennifer, Kyle. Sch. tchr., coach, Woodston, Kans., 1950-51; divisional sales mgr. Hybrid Seed Corn Co., Spencer, Iowa, 1953-63; with Spencer Realty, 1963—, pres., 1974—. Pres. YMCA, Spencer, 1977—. Mem. Nat. Assn. Realtors, Iowa Assn. Realtors (asso. v.p. 1970), Spencer C. of C., Iowa Great Lakes Bd. Realtors (pres. 1970-71). Served with AUS, 1951-53. Home: 2101 W 11th St Spencer IA 51301 Office: 1823 Hwy Blvd Spencer IA 51301

NORRIS, JULIUS MAURICE, social service agy. exec.; b. Chgo., Apr. 11, 1944; s. James Harry and Zelma (Brown) N.; student West Point Mil. Acad.; B.A. in Music, Gov.'s State U., 1975; cert. John Marshall Law Sch., 1976. Dir. job bank devel. Youthpower, Inc., Chgo., 1966-69; asst. dist. exec. Boy Scouts Am., Chgo., 1969; adminstr. Marion Bus. Coll., Gary, Ind., 1975—; pres., founder Peoples Coalition and the Centralized Job Bank, Chgo., 1975—. Mem. Chgo. Bicentennial Com., 1976; research chmn. Gary Minority Bus. Com., 1972-74; mem. 7th Dist. Police Steering Com., 1975—. Served with N.G., 1962-66. Decorated Gold medallion N.G., 1965. Mem. Nat. Assn. Community Developers, Englewood Interagy. Council, Phi Beta Sigma. Baptist. Office: Peoples Coalition 5829 S Calumet Ave Chicago IL 60637

NORRIS, ROBERT MIRANDA, physician; b. Oviedo, Spain, Sept. 3, 1923; s. Theodore F. and Lillian (Norris) Miranda; B.A., U. Oviedo, 1942; M.D., U. Madrid (Spain), 1949, U. Havana (Cuba), 1951; m. Maruja Gonzalez, Nov. 18, 1951; children—Robert, Josephine. Came to U.S., 1957, naturalized, 1962. Gen. practice medicine, Havana, 1951-57; intern Passavant Memi. Hosp., Chgo., 1957-58; basic ophthalmology U. Ill. Med. Sch., 1958-59; resident ophthalmology City Hosp. Center, N.Y.C., 1959-61; practice medicine specializing in ophthalmology, Rockford, Ill., 1961—; with Canfield Clinic, Rockford, 1961-79, asso. med. dir., chief ophthalmology, 1973-79; asso. prof. ophthalmology Rockford Sch. Medicine. Diplomate Am. Bd. Ophthalmology. Fellow Am. Acad. Ophthalmology, A.C.S., Royal Soc. Health, Soc. Eye Surgeons; mem. A.M.A. Club: Rockford Country. Home: 3510 Val Mark Terrace Rockford IL 61107 Office: 414 Executive Pkwy Rockford IL 61107

NORRIS, SARAH ANN, sch. adminstr.; b. Cramerton, N.C., July 13, 1936; d. Leo Alphus and Mary Lee (Phillips) N.; A.B. in Edn., Marion (Ind.) Coll., 1957; M.A. in Edn., Ball State U., Muncie, Ind., 1961, lic. in Secondary Sch. Adminstrn., 1979; postgrad. Vanderbilt U., summer 1970. Tchr. math. Oak Hill Sch. Corp., Mier, Ind., 1957-61; tchr., counselor Marion (Ind.) Community Schs., 1961-62, dean of girls, counselor, 1962-64, dean of girls, 1964-74, adminstrv. asst., 1974—, dir. Title III program 1970. Mem. exec. bd. Grant County March of Dimes, 1971-79, chmn., 1974-79, campaign chmn., 1972-74; asst. Sunday sch. supt. Wesleyan Ch., Marion, 1977-80; bd. dirs. Grant-Blackford Mental Health Clinic, 1978—, treas., 1980-81, v.p., 1981-82. Mem. Assn. for Supervision and Curriculum Devel., Sch. Employees Fed. Credit Union (clk. supervisory com.), Marion Community Schs. Adminstrs. Assn. (pres., 1981—), Am. Bus. Women's Assn. (pres. 1974-75, corr. sec. 1981-82), Delta Kappa Gamma (treas. 1980-82). Republican. Home: 3818 S Edgewater Ct Marion IN 46952 Office: Marion Community Sch 720 N Miller Ave Marion IN 46952

NORRIS, WILLIAM C., corp. exec.; b. Inavale, Nebr., July 14, 1911; s. William H. and Mildred A. (McCall) N.; B.S., U. Nebr., 1932; m. Jane Malley, Sept. 15, 1943; children—W. Charles, George, Daniel, Brian, Constance, Roger, Mary N., David. Sales engr. Westinghouse Electric Mfg. Co., Chgo., 1935-41; v.p., gen. mgr. Engrng. Research Assos., 1946-55; v.p., gen. mgr. Univac div. Sperry Rand Corp., 1955-57; pres. Control Data Corp., 1957—, now chmn. bd., chief exec. officer, chmn. policy com.; bd. dirs. N.W. Bank Corp., N.W. Growth Fund, Tronchemics, Inc. Trustee Hill Reference Library; adv. com. White House Conf. on Balanced Nat. Growth and Econ. Devel., 1978—. Served to comdr. USNR, 1941-46. Office: Control Data Corp 8100 34th Ave S Minneapolis MN 55440*

NORTH, JEFFREY WILLIAM, reprographic engr.; b. Chgo., Jan. 12, 1948; s. Edward Martin and Valerie Anne N.; student De-Vry Inst. Tech., 1970-72; 1 dau., Stephanie Anne North. With quality control dept. Robertson Photo Mechanix, Des Plaines, Ill., 1970-72; salesman, cons. Cushing & Co., Chgo., 1972-76; prodn. and product mgr. Century Blue, Chgo., 1976-77; repor-graphics mgr. Procon, Inc., Des Plaines, 1977—. Vice pres. St. Ita's Fathers' Club, 1977, 78. Served with U.S. Army, 1966-69; Vietnam. Mem. Ill. Printers Assn., Mini Max Assn., Blue Printer Assn., Combines Gt. Lakes Navy Assn., U.S. Navy League, Vets Assn., Am. Legion. Author: Modern Drafting Techniques for Quality Reproductions, 1977; inventor in field. Home: 325 Oak Meadow Ct Schaumburg IL 60193 Office: Procon Inc 30 UOP Plaza Des Plaines IL 60016

NORTH, ROGER STEPHEN, jewelry co. exec.; b. Phila., Jan. 26, 1948; s. Roger Parker and Judith Ann (Girard) N.; diploma Radio/TV Broadcasting, Elkins Inst., Dallas, 1973; B.A. in Communications Arts and Scis. magna cum laude, Western Mich. U., 1975; m. Betty Kay Louwenaar, May 6, 1978; 1 dau., Lindsey Julia. Founder Silverbird Jewelry Supply Co., Kalamazoo, 1976, chief exec. officer, 1976—. Chmn. bd. dirs. Vine Neighborhood Assn., 1980—; bd. dirs. Kalamazoo Small Bus. Devel. Corp.; mem. Central Bus. Dist. Task Force. Home: 616 Village St Kalamazoo MI 49008 Office: 723 S Westnedge Ave Kalamazoo MI 49007 also 821 S Westnedge Kalamazoo MI 49007

NORTH, WILLIAM STANLEY, mfg. co. exec.; b. Chgo., May 1, 1911; s. Francis Stanley and Julia (Morgan) N.; B.S.M.E., Harvard U., 1934, postgrad., 1935; m. Sarah Jackson, 1934; children—Sarah Randolph, Elizabeth Holmes; m. 2d, Patricia Cathcart Armstrong, Mar. 20, 1958 (dec. Nov. 1978); 1 stepson, James Cathcart Armstrong; m. 3d, Margo Reid Donald, Dec. 11, 1979; stepchildren—Alasson Donald, Mrs. Sangwoo Ann, Mrs. James Leonard, Mrs. Gordon Wilson. With Union Spl. Corp., Chgo., 1935—, engr. and salesman, personnel dir., 1941-44, v.p., 1944-47, asst. gen. mgr., 1947-52, pres., gen. mgr., 1952-74, chmn., chief exec. officer, 1974-76, chmn., 1976—; dir. Portec Inc. Past chmn. Lawson YMCA, Chgo.; bd. dirs., v.p., past pres. Lyric Opera Chgo.; trustee, past pres. Allendale Sch. Boys; bd. dirs., v.p., past treas. Lake Forest Open Lands Assn.; governing mem. Chgo. Symphony Orch. Mem. Ill. Mfg. Assn. (past pres.), Midwest Indsl. Mgmt. Assn. (past pres.). Republican. Episcopalian (past sr. Warden). Clubs: Univ., Harvard, Campfire, Casino (past gov.), Commonwealth (past pres.), Comml. (Chgo.); Onwentsia (past gov.), Old Elm (past gov.), Winter (past pres.)(Lake Forest, Ill.); Tin Whistles (Pinehurst, N.C.); Pine Valley (N.J.) Golf; U.S. Srs. Golf Assn.; Gulf Stream Bath and Tennis (bd. govs.) Gulf Stream Golf (v.p., bd. govs.); Royal and Ancient Golf of St. Andrews (Fife, Scotland). Home: 1490 N Green Bay Rd Lake Forest IL 60045 also 3224 N Ocean Blvd Delray Beach FL 33444 Office: 400 N Franklin St Chicago IL 60610

NORTHCOTT, JOHN EDWARD, clergyman; b. Toledo, Aug. 15, 1939; s. John William and Adele Kathrine (Kieper) N.; B.A., Gustavus Adolphus Coll., 1962; M.Div., Luther Northwestern Sems., 1965; D.Min., Consortium for Higher Edn. Religious Studies/United Theol. Sem., Dayton, 1981; m. Mary Anne Kern, June 22, 1962; children—John Christian, Lisa Marie. Ordained to ministry Lutheran Ch. Am., 1965; asst. chaplain Bethesda Luth. Hosp., St. Paul, 1964-65; pastor Arborg (Man., Can.) Luth. Parish, 1964-68, St. Pauls Luth. Ch., Grandville, Mich., 1968-72, Gethsemane Luth. Ch., Berkley, Mich., 1972-80; sr. pastor Cana Evang. Luth. Ch., Berkley, 1980—. Counselor, Berkley-Huntington Woods Youth Assistance. Mem. Acad. Paris Clergy. Home: 1978 Earlmont Rd Berkley MI 48072 Office: 2119 Catalpa Dr Berkley MI 48072

NORTHOUSE, RICHARD A., computer co. exec.; b. Lanesboro, Minn., Apr. 2, 1938; s. LaVerne J. and Selma L. (Breno) N.; B.S. in Elec. Engring., U. Wis., Madison, 1966, M.S., 1968; M.S. in Computer Sci., Purdue U., 1970, Ph.D. (NASA-Am. Soc. Engring. Edn. fellow 1970-71), 1971; m. Marcia M. Ninneman, Aug. 13, 1961; children—Rodger Allen, Nicole Marie. Expeditor, Am. Motors Co., 1958-61; news photographer Milw. Sentinal, 1961-64; vis. scientist NASA, 1970-71; mem. faculty U. Wis., 1971-75; pres. Compco, Milw., 1975—. Active local YMCA, PTA, Boy Scouts Am., Youth Softball League. Summer fellow NSF, 1967, 68. Mem. Assn. Computing Machines, IEEE (chmn. Milw. sect. Computer Soc. 1972-73). Author numerous papers in field. Office: 7110 W Fond du Lac Ave Milwaukee WI 53218

NORTHRUP, ARTHUR HARRY, lawyer, economist; b. Indpls., June 3, 1920; s. Leonard Evart and Margaret (Couden) N.; B.A. in Econs. with honors, Harvard U., 1942, M.B.A., 1946; J.D., U. Mich., 1949; m. Anne Mary Holmes, July 31, 1948; children—Arthur Harry, Nancy Anne Northrup Eastman, m. 2d, Deborah Lee Norris, Sept. 19, 1969; children—Heather Lynn, Christopher A., Holly Margaret. Quality control engr. Wright Aero. Corp., 1943-44; admitted to Ind. bar, 1949; since practiced in Indpls.; mem. firm Gregg, Fillion, Hughes & Northrup, 1951-70, firm Martz, Beattey, Hinds & Wallace, 1970-78; individual practice law, 1978—; lectr. econs. Earlham Coll., 1949, Butler U., 1950-57, 59-76; asst. city atty., Indpls., 1951-54, 68-76; mem. Ind. Ho. of Reps., 1969-70; gen. counsel Ind. Consumer Finance Assn., 1954-74, Ind. Restaurant Assn., 1951-56. Sec. Ind. Corps. Survey Commn., 1958-77, mem., 1978—. Pres. Washington Twp. Republican Club, 1966-68; sec. bd. dirs. Summer Mission for Sick Children. Served with USNR, 1944-46. Mem. Am., Seventh Circuit, Ind. (chmn. probate trust and real estate sect.), Indpls. bar assns., Am. Legion (past post comdr.), S.A.R. (pres. Ind. 1956). Republican. Episcopalian. Clubs: Century (pres. 1960), Ind. Harvard (pres. 1954), Harvard Bus. Sch. (pres. 1955), U. Mich. (pres. Indpls. alumni 1975-77) (Indpls.), Meridian Hills Country, Contemporary, Players. Editor: Forms for Indiana Corporations, 1966, 77. Contbr. articles on trusts, income tax and other tax laws to profl. jours. Home: 7770 N Pennsylvania Indianapolis IN 46240 Office: 130 E Washington St Indianapolis IN 46204

NORTHUP, WILLIAM CARLTON, acct.; b. Columbia, Mo., Dec. 1, 1930; s. Lansford Lionel and Elsie Rebecca (Eaton) N.; B.S. in Statistics, U. Mo., 1953, M.B.A., 1974; m. Sharon Joan Carlson, June 27, 1970; children—Richard Carlton, Karen Frances. Research asso. Mo. Crippled Children's Service, Columbia, 1968-69, asst. supt. research and records, 1969-70, supt., 1970-76; broker London Commodity House, Inc., Chgo., 1976-77; chief accountant Nat. Congress PTA, Chgo., 1977-78; mgmt. analyst fin. systems for health and hosps. Cook County Governing Commn., Chgo., 1978-79; acct. V Cook County Hosp., 1979—; controller, dir. pub. health statistics, coordinator automatic data processing, supt. ins. Mo. Crippled Children's Service; asst. prodn. mgr., chief estimator, account exec. Am. Press; spl. advisor to Gov. Mo. on printing and pub., 1965. Mem. Columbia Fin. Study Commn., 1974, steering com. Columbia Town Meeting, 1976; bd. dirs. Camp Wannanoya, 1976; mem. steering com. Teen Auto Club, 1972; vol. probation officer Boone County Juvenile Office, 1971-72. Mem. Am. Mgmt. Assn., Am. Statis. Assn., Mo. Pub. Health Assn., Assn. M.B.A. Execs., Hosp. Fin. Mgmt. Assn., Mensa, Delta Sigma Pi. Republican. Baptist. Club: Optimists. Home: 24 Williamsburg Terr Evanston IL 60203 Office: 1825 W Harrison St Chicago IL 60612

NORTON, LOUISE CHARNETTE, dietitian; b. Plattsburg, Mo., Nov. 17, 1941; d. Robert Rea and Helen Louise (Ditmars) N.; student Central Mo. State Coll., 1958-61; B.S., U. Mo., 1963; postgrad. Chabot Coll., 1968; M.S. (Allied Health grantee), U. Mo., 1976; postgrad. U. Wis., 1976, U. Mo., 1978. Dir. food mgmt. Stouffer Food Corp., Cleve., 1963-67; dir. dietary services Motion Picture Country Home and Hosp., Woodland Hills, Calif., 1967-68, Laurel Grove Hosp., Castro Valley, Calif., 1968; area dietitian Homan Food Services, Los Angeles, 1968-69; dir. dietary services Lutheran Hosp. Soc., Santa Monica, Calif., 1969-73; info. specialist Coll. Home Econs., U. Mo., Columbia, 1973-74; product mgr. dietary products div. Am. Hosp. Supply, Chgo., 1974-76; dir. dietetics Bethany Med. Center, Kansas City, Kans., 1976—. Mem. Federated Republican Women of Clay County, Am. Dietetic Assn., Mo. Dietetic Assn., Kansas City Dist. Dietetic Assn., Am. Home Econs. Assn., Mo. Home Econs. Assn., Greater Kansas City Home Econs. Assn., Am. Soc. Hosp. Food Service Adminstrs., Gamma Sigma Delta, Omicron Nu, Phi Upsilon Omicron. Mem. Ch. of Brethren. Clubs: Prairie Cottage Extension, P.E.O. Home: 9953 N Cherry St Kansas City MO 64155 Office: Bethany Med Center 51 N 12th St Kansas City KS 66102

NOTEIS, VICTORIA LYNN, architect; b. Kansas City, Mo., Aug. 2, 1953; d. Earl Tennyson and Betty Jo (Odam) N.; B.Arch., Kans. State U., 1976; m. Mark Randall Davis, June 7, 1975. Field surveyor Topeka-Shawnee County Met. Planning Commn., 1974; teaching asst., asst. instr. architecture graphics Kans. State U., 1975-76, research asso., 1976; architect, office mgr. Charles F. McAfee Architects and Planners, Kansas City, Mo., 1977-79; architect Patty, Berkebile, Nelson Assos., Kansas City, Mo., 1979-80; corp. dir. Simmons/Schafer/Noteis Inc., cons., Kansas City, Mo., 1980—. Vice pres. for Mo. polit. affairs Greater Kansas City Women's Polit. Caucus, 1979, pres., 1980—; del. Mo. Women's Polit. Caucus, 1979; sec. Democratic Task Force, Nat. Women's Polit. Caucus. Mem. AIA (asso.), Nat. Trust for Historic Preservation, Tau Sigma Delta. Democrat. Methodist. Office: 815 City Center Square 1100 Main St Kansas City MO 64105

NOTHHELFER, GEORGE ANTHONY, safety council adminstr.; b. Mpls., Sept. 12, 1915; s. George Anthony and Marie Elizabeth (Poelzer) N.; student Duluth Jr. Coll., 1935-38; B.A. cum laude, U. Minn., 1958; m. Charlotte Ruth Hicken, June 21, 1941; children—George Park, Catherine Marie. Asst. to safety dir. Oliver Iron Mining Co., Duluth, Minn., 1943; safety dir. Duluth C. of C. Safety Bur., 1944-59; mgr. Omaha Safety Council, 1959—. Mem. Omaha Mayor's Traffic Safety Adv. Com., 1965—; mem. State of Nebr. Dept. Motor Vehicles Health Adv. Bd., 1980—; mgr. Metro Area Tng. Consortium, 1980—. Cert. adult edn. instr. in safety and related subjects. Mem. Am. Soc. Safety Engrs., Am. Soc. Tng. and Devel. Episcopalian. Clubs: Masons (32 deg., Shriner), Rotary. Home: 10223 Wright St Omaha NE 68124 Office: 2707 Gomez Ave Omaha NE 68107

NOTO, JOHN EDWARD, JR., psychologist; b. Chgo., Dec. 4, 1947; s. John Edward and Josephine (Muchia) N.; B.S., U. Wis., 1970; M.S., Ill. State U., 1974; Ph.D., Fielding Inst., 1982; m. Lynda Miles, Nov. 30, 1974; children—Steven, Daniel. Staff psychologist LaSalle County Comprehensive Community Mental Health Center, Ottawa, Ill., 1974-76; staff therapist child and family dept. Tri-City Comprehensive Community Mental Health Center, Highland, Ind., 1976-78; outpatient coordinator mental health unit Alexian Bros. Med. Center, Elk Grove, Ill., 1978—. Mem. Am. Psychol. Assn., Midwest Psychol. Assn., Soc. for Psychol. Study Social Issues, Assn. for Birth Psychology. Contbr. articles to profl. jours. Home: 1081 Cypress Ln Elk Grove Village IL 60007 Office: 800 W Biesterfield Rd Elk Grove Village IL 60007

NOTOWIDIGDO, MUSINGGIH HARTOKO, mfg. co. exec.; b. Indonesia, Dec. 9, 1938; s. Moekarto and Martaniah (Brodjonegoro) N.; B.M.E., George Washington U., 1961; M.Sc., N.Y. U., 1966, postgrad., 1970; m. Sihar P. Tambunan, Oct. 1, 1966 (dec. Nov. 1976); m. 2d, Joanne S. Gutter, June 3, 1979; 1 son, Matthew Joseph. Cons., Dollar Blitz & Assos., Washington, 1962-64; ops. research analyst Am. Can Co., N.Y.C., 1966-69; prin. analyst Borden Inc., Columbus, Ohio, 1969-70, mgr. ops. research, 1970-71, mgr. ops. analysis and research, 1972-74, asst. gen. controller, officer, 1974-77, corp. dir. info. systems/econ. analysis, officer, 1977—; adj. lectr. Grad. Sch. Adminstrn. Capital U. Mem. Fin Execs. Inst. (chmn. profl. devel., mem. bd. Columbus), Ops. Research Soc., Inst. Mgmt. Sci., Am. Mgmt. Assn., Nat. Assn. Bus. Economists, Long Range Planning Soc., Am. Statis. Assn., Soc. Mgmt. Info. Systems. Republican. Club: Racquet. Home: 4532 Carriage Hill Ln Upper Arlington OH 43220 Office: 180 E Broad St Columbus OH 43215

NOVACK, RICHARD M., constrn. co. exec.; b. Boston, July 14, 1932; s. Lawrence and Pearl (Meirick) N.; student civil engring. U. Mass.; m. Claire Rosenfeld, Oct. 30, 1955; children—Karyn Lee, Lawrence James. Supt., engr., estimator Gil Wyner Co., Inc., Malden, Mass., 1951-52, 55-56, 58; project mgr., estimator A.R.T. Constrn. Co., Newport, R.I., 1956-57; v.p., dir. Edward R. Marden Corp., Allston, Mass., 1958-70; v.p. Hannan Co., Cleve., 1970—. Served with C.E., U.S. Army, 1953-54. Home: 24775 Hilltop Dr Beachwood OH 44122 Office: 23200 Chagrin Blvd Cleveland OH 44122

NOVAK, JAMES F., elec. engr.; b. Oak Park, Ill., Sept. 5, 1926; s. James and Mary (Bartunek) N.; B.E.E., Ill. Inst. Tech., 1952; m. Lorraine Waisnor, Aug. 16, 1952; children—Ann Marie, James Edward. With Jensen Mfg. Co., Schiller Park, Ill., 1952—, chief engr. Jensen Sound Labs. div. Pemcor, Inc., 1969-74, v.p. engring., 1974—. Served with USNR, 1944-47. Audio Engring. Soc. fellow. Mem. IEEE (sr.), Acoustical Soc. Am. Club: Moose. Research loudspeaker enclosure design. Patentee in field. Contbr. articles to profl. jours. Office: 4136 N United Pkwy Schiller Park IL 60176

NOVAK, JAMES LOUIS, mfg. plant mgr.; b. Crosby, Minn., Dec. 7, 1939; s. Louis R. and Annie (Plovich) N.; student St. Cloud Tech. Sch., 1957-58; m. Kathleen L. Cartie, June 29, 1963; children—Jodi Kay, Jaimi Louise. With Woodland Container Co., Crosby, Minn., 1959—, plant mgr., 1979—. Mem. Am. Forestry Assn. Home: N Lake Shore Crosby MN 56441 Office: 312 1st Ave NW Crosby MN 56441

NOVAK, MELVIN ANDREW, mech. engr.; b. Campbell, Ohio, Dec. 20, 1935; s. Andrew John and Katherine Agnes (Skorich) N.; B. Engring., Youngstown U., 1967; m. Josephine F. Caggiano, Oct. 1, 1955; children—Debra Josephine, Russell Andrew, Dina Marie. With Jones and Laughlin Steel Corp. (formerly Youngstown Sheet & Tube Co.), East Chicago, Ind., 1955—, shops planning engr., 1968-69, chief stationary engr. 1969-79, supt. shops dept., 1979—. Served with USNR, 1952-60. Recipient Supervisory Improvment Program award Youngstown Sheet & Tube Co., 1972, 73, 76; cert. mgr. Inst. Cert. Profl. Mgrs. Mem. Mahoning Valley Mgmt. Assn., Nat. Mgmt. Assn., Assn. Iron and Steel Engrs., East Chicago C. of C. Home: 8602 Baring Ave Munster IN 46321 Office: 3001 Dickey Rd East Chicago IN 46312

NOVAK, RICHARD FRANCIS, pathologist, educator; b. Chgo., May 4, 1932; s. Frank S. and Marie L. (Kawula) N.; B.S., Loyola U., Chgo., 1953, M.D., 1957; m. Rose J. Ippolito, June 23, 1956; children—Catherine Ann, Richard Francis, James I. Intern, Madison (Wis.) Gen. Hosp., 1958, resident, 1959; resident Cook County Hosp., Chgo., 1959-62; asst. pathologist Swedish-Am. Hosp., Rockford, Ill., 1962-63; clin. instr. pathology Coll. Medicine, U. Ill., 1962-63; asso. dir. labs. St. Anthony Hosp., Rockford, 1963-69; asst. dir. No. Ill. Blood Bank, Rockford, 1963-69; dir. clin. lab., dir. program for med. tech. Loyola U. Hosp., Chgo., 1969-72; asst. prof. pathology Stritch Sch. Medicine, Loyola U., Chgo., 1969-72; prof. pathology, chmn. dept. Rockford Sch. Medicine, U. Ill., 1972—; pathologist Rockford Meml. Hosp., 1972-77, chmn. dept. pathology, v.p. med. affairs, 1977-79; cons. blood bank program Ill. Dept. Health, 1972-78. Diplomate Am. Bd. Pathology. Fellow Coll. Am. Pathologists, Am. Soc. Clin. Pathologists; mem. AMA, Am., Ill. (sec.-treas. 1970-74) assns. blood banks, Ill. Soc. Pathologists (pres. 1976-77), Ill. Pathology Soc., Ill. Med. Soc., Winnebago County Med. Soc. Roman Catholic. Contbr. artilces in field to profl. jours. Home: 3292 Andover Dr Rockford IL 61111 Office: 2400 N Rockton Ave Rockford IL 61103

NOVICK, MARVIN, accountant; b. N.Y.C., July 16, 1931; s. Joseph and Anna (Leichter) N.; B.B.A., CCNY, 1952; M.B.A., N.Y. U., 1955, postgrad., 1958—; m. Margaret Ann Blau, Apr. 10, 1960; children—Jeffrey, Stuart, Barry. Staff accountant various acctg. firms, N.Y.C., 1954-58; sr. analyst Ford Motor Co., Detroit, 1958-61; v.p. ops. and fin. Mich. Blue Cross Blue Shield, Detroit, 1961-70; controller Handleman Co., Detroit, 1971; v.p. fin. Meadowbrook, Inc., Southfield, Mich., 1971-73; partner J.K. Lasser & Co., Southfield, 1973-77; partner Touche Ross & Co., internat. acctg., Detroit, 1977—. Pres., trustee Oak Park (Mich.) Bd. Edn., 1966-72; pres., v.p., treas., trustee Temple Beth El, Birmingham, Mich., 1967—; pres., trustee Mich. Assn. Emotionally Disturbed Children, 1968—; chairperson Democratic 18th Congl. Dist., Mich., 1972-74; pres., trustee Providence Hosp., Southfield, 1973—. Served with U.S. Army, 1954-55. Mem. N.Y. State Soc. C.P.A.'s, Am. Inst. C.P.A.'s, Mich. Assn. C.P.A.'s, Data Processing Mgmt. Assn. Jewish. Office: 200 Renaissance Ct Detroit MI 48243

NOVOTNY, DONALD STEVE, rubber co. exec.; b. Columbus, Nebr., Apr. 11, 1942; s. Stephen Alois and Mildred June (Houfek) N.; B.S.E., Wayne State Coll., 1964; Ph.D., U. Nebr., 1970; m. Marianne Kay Hookstra; children—Jill Ann, Brent Lee, Curt Jason. Tchr. Allen (Nebr.) Public Schs., 1964-65, Winside (Nebr.) Public Schs., 1965-66; chemist Goodyear Tire & Rubber Co., Lincoln, Nebr., 1970-74, project chemist, 1974-75, tech. supr., Windsor, Vt., 1975-77, devel. mgr., St. Marys, Ohio, 1977-79, v.p. devel., Wabash, Ind., 1979—. Area fin. chmn. Boy Scouts Am., 1978-79; active Jr. Achievement, 1973-74. NDEA fellow, U. Nebr., 1966-69. Mem. Am. Chem. Soc., Sigma Xi, Kappa Mu Epsilon, Lambda Delta Lambda (nat. pres. 1963). Patentee in field. Home: 208 Sunset Dr North Manchester IN 46962 Office: PO Box 507 Wabash IN 46992

NOVOTNY, VLADIMIR, civil engr., educator; b. Olomouc, Czechoslovakia, Aug. 30, 1938; s. Vladimir and Frantiska (Havrankova) N.; came to U.S., 1969; diploma in Engring., Tech. U. Brno (Czechoslovakia), 1963, Candidate of Sci., 1968; Ph.D. in Environ. Engring., Vanderbilt U., 1971; m. Lynn E. Braasch, June 14, 1975; children—Paul, Eric. Research engr., Hydraulic Research Inst., Brno, Czechoslovakia, 1962-69, acting head Inst., 1966-67; research engr. Vanderbilt U., Nashville, 1969-71; sr. cons. engr. Asso. Water & Air Resources Engrs., Nashville, 1971-73; asso. prof. dept. civil engring. Marquette U., Milw., 1973—; cons. in water pollution control and mgmt. to various govtl. agys. and industries, 1972—. Internat. Joint Commn. for Great Lakes grantee, 1975-77; registered profl. engr., Wis. Mem. Water Pollution Control Assn., Internat. Assn. on Water Pollution Research, Internat. Water Research Assn., Assn. Environ. Engring. Profs., Am. Water Resources Assn. (v.p. Wis. sect. 1978), Am. Automobile Assn. Club: Sokol (Milw.). Contbr. numerous articles on water quality mgmt. to profl. jours.; also books. Home: W 132 N11589 Forest Dr Germantown WI 53022 Office: 1515 W Wisconsin Ave Milwaukee WI 53233

NOWACKI, JOHN JOSEPH, architect; b. Detroit, Nov. 14, 1951; s. Leonard Raymond and Jeanne Frances (Parker) N.; B.Arch. cum laude, U. Detroit, 1973, M.Arch., 1975. Archtl. designer Max Sabaroff & Co., Detroit, 1976-77; sr. facilities architect Detroit Edison Co., 1977—; archtl. cons. Pres. parish council St. Frances Cabrini, Allen Park, Mich. Registered architect, Mich. Mem. Engring. Soc. Detroit. Club: K.C. (Allen Park). Home: 15402 White Ave Allen Park MI 48101 Office: Detroit Edison Co 2000 2d Ave Detroit MI 48226

NOWAK, CHESTER JOSEPH, optometrist; b. Chgo., Jan. 30, 1923; s. Peter Joseph and Josephine (Starsiak) N.; O.D., Ill. Coll. Optometry, 1945; m. Florence J. Wardach, Feb. 14, 1943; children—Sandra Jane, Susan Micheline, Sharlene Joyce, Pamela Jo, Robert Chester, Jerome Cyril. Pvt. practice optometry, Chgo., 1946-56, Niles, Ill., 1956—; sch. lectr. children's visual problems. Recipient Optometric Recognition award Nat. Eye Research Found., 1981. Mem. Nat. Eye Research Found., Better Vision Inst. Roman Catholic. Club: K.C. Author: What Parents Should Know About Their Children's Eye Vision, 1972; The Brain's Vision, 1981. Patentee devices for diagnosing and correcting eye abstract fusion. Office: 8150 N Milwaukee Ave Niles IL 60648

NOWICKI, SUSAN ANN, assn. exec.; b. Detroit, Sept. 30, 1945; s. Carl Louis and Mary Louise (Waitz) N.; B.S., Mich. State U., 1974; postgrad. Roosevelt U., Chgo. Writer communications div. United Dairy Industry Assn., Chgo., 1975-78; asst. dir. communications, editor bull. Am. Acad. Orthopaedic Surgeons, Chgo., 1978—. Mem. Women in Communications (chmn. career conf. Chgo. chpt. 1981, treas. 1981-82), Am. Mktg. Assn., Public Relations Soc. Am., Internat. Assn. Bus. Communicators. Democrat. Presbyterian. Home: 1318 E Algonquin St Schaumburg IL 60195 Office: 444 N Michigan Ave Suite 1500 Chicago IL 60611

NOWOSIELSKI, LAWRENCE ALEXANDER, clin. psychologist; b. Detroit, Nov. 22, 1944; s. Alexander Stanley and Charlotte Beatrice (Mikulski) Nowosielski; B.A., U. Mich., 1967; M.A., U. Detroit, 1972. Instr., Detroit Bd. Edn., 1967-68; social worker Mich. Wayne County Dept. Social Services, Detroit, 1968-71; sch. psychologist Lakeview Pub. Schs., St. Clair Shores, Mich., 1971-79; clin. psychologist Eastwood Community Clinic, Detroit. 1974—. Cert. psychol. examiner, cert. social worker, sch. psychologist, Mich. Mem. Am. Psychol. Assn., Mich. Psychol. Assn., Macomb County Psychol. Assn., Mich. Assn. Sch. Psychologists, Nat. Assn. Sch. Psychologists, Am. Orthopsychiatric Assn., Nat., State edn. assns., Psy Chi. Roman Catholic.

NUCCITELLI, SAUL ARNOLD, civil engr.; b. Yonkers, N.Y., Apr. 25, 1928; s. Agostino and Antoinette (D'Amicis) N.; B.S., N.Y.U., 1949; M.C.E., 1954; D.C.E., M.I.T., 1960; m. Concetta Orlandi, Dec. 23, 1969; 1 son, Saul A. Asst. civil engr. Westchester County Engrs., N.Y.C., 1949-51, 53-54; project engr. H.B. Bolas Enterprises, Denver, 1954-55; asst. prof., research engr., U. Denver, 1955-58; mem. staff M.I.T., 1958-60; asst. prof. engring. Cooper Union Coll., N.Y.C., 1960-62; pvt. practice cons. engring., Springfield, Mo., 1962—; dir. Bell Savs. & Loan Assn., Springfield; organizer Met. Nat. Bank, Springfield. Pres. Downtown Springfield Assn.; adv. council Mo. Public Drinking Water, Park Central Hosp. Served with C.E., U.S. Army, 1951-53. Recipient Cert. of Appreciation, Mo. Mcpl. League, 1981. Registered profl. engr., N.Y., Mo., Colo., Conn., Mass.; lic. land surveyor, Mo., Colo., Conn., Mass. Mem. Nat., Mo. socs. profl. engrs., ASCE, Boston Soc. Civil Engrs., Am. Concrete Inst., Am. Inst. Steel Constrn., Am. Welding Soc., ASTM, Am. Soc. Mil. Engrs., Springfield C. of C. Named Mo. Cons. Engr. of Yr. 1973. Contbr. articles to profl. jours. Home: 2919 Brentmoor Ave Springfield MO 65804 Office: 122 Park Central Sq Springfield MO 65806

NUFRIO, RONALD MICHAEL, educator; b. Richmond, Ind., Apr. 10, 1947; s. Rocco Michael and Marie Johannah (Stracke) N.; B.S. in Edn., Ball State U., 1969; M.S. in Edn., 1977; U. Dayton, 1977; m. Janet Borchers, June 27, 1973; children—Elizabeth, David. Tchr. English, Anna (Ohio) High Sch., 1969—. Named Tchr. of Yr., U. Dayton/Western Ohio Edn. Assn., 1980, Anna Schs., 1980; Martha Holden Jennings scholar, 1981. Mem. Western Ohio Edn. Assn. (mem. exec. com. 1975-78), Anna Local Edn. Assn. (pres. 1972-73), Ohio Edn. Assn., NEA, Shelby County English Tchrs. Assn. (pres. 1981-82), Ohio Modern Lang. Tchrs. Assn., Nat. Council Tchrs. English. Clubs: Anna Community (pres. 1970-72), Kiwanis (pres. 1977). Contbr. articles in field to profl. jours. Home: 206 Hall Ave Sidney OH 45365 Office: Anna High Sch 2d St Anna OH 45302

NUGENT, JOHNNY WESLEY, state senator; b. Cleves, Ohio, July 18, 1939; s. Carl H. and Velma (Holland) N.; grad. high sch.; m. Nancy C. Whiteford, 1960; 1 dau., Suzette. Owner, mgr. Nugent Tractor Sales, 1968—; mem. Ind. State Senate, 1979—. Bldg. commr., Dearborn County, Ind., 1967-74. Named Ky. Col. Baptist. Clubs: Masons, Shriners. Office: Ind State Capitol Indianapolis IN 46204*

NUHFER, EDWARD BERNARD, petrologist; b. Parkersburg, W.Va., Sept. 5, 1943; s. Edward Phillip and Mary Agnes (McNerney) N.; A.A., Potomac State Jr. Coll., 1963; B.S., W.Va. U., 1966, M.S., 1967; Ph.D., U. N.Mex., 1979. Petroleum geologist Chevron Oil Co., New Orleans, 1967-69; instr. Marietta (Ohio) Coll., 1970-75; econ. geologist W.Va. Geol. Survey, 1975-77, research petrologist, electron microscopist, 1977-79; asst. prof. geology U. Wis., Platteville, 1979—, also faculty research asso. U.S. Geol. Survey, 1980—; adj. prof. W.Va. U., 1978-79; instr. YMCA; instr. W.Va. Martial Arts Assn., 1978-79. Shell Merit fellow, 1970; NSF grantee. Mem. Am. Inst. Profl. Geologists, AIME (v.p. Upper Miss. Valley sect.), Geol. Soc. Am., Nat. Assn. Geology Tchrs., Soc. Profl. Well Log Analysts, Microbeam

Analysis Soc., Sigma Xi. Democrat. Contbr. articles to profl. jours. Office: Geoscis Dept U Wis Platteville WI 53818

NUN, EDWARD WALTER, ins. and financial exec.; b. Ohiowa, Nebr., Sept. 23, 1911; s. Anton and Anna (Sieber) N.; diploma Lincoln (Nebr.) Sch. Commerce, 1930; m. Lucile M. Bartels, Jan. 30, 1940; children—Catherine, Richard, Jane. Bookkeeper, Nat. Bank Commerce, Lincoln, 1930-31; postal clk., Ohiowa, 1932-36; bookkeeper Lytton (Iowa) Savs. Bank, 1936-37; with Pioneer Credit Corp., Fairmont, Minn., 1937-40; cashier, exec. officer 1st Nat. Bank, Wilmont, Minn., 1940-43; rent div. inspector Office of Price Adminstrn., 1943; with Ute (Iowa) State Bank, 1946—, cashier, exec. officer, 1946-68, pres., 1969—. Mem. Iowa State Banking Bd., 1957-61. Mem. Monona County (Iowa) Planning and Zoning Commn., 1971—; city clk., Ute, 1947-63; Democratic committeeman, St. Claire Twp., 1957-80. Served with AUS, 1943-46; PTO. Mem. Am. Legion, V.F.W., Ute Comml. Club. Democrat. Lutheran. Address: Ute IA 51060

NUNEMAKER, WESLEY, grain and livestock rancher, utility assn. exec.; b. Langdon, Kan., July 9, 1919; s. Joseph J. and Gladys Mary (Kabler) N.; student Southwestern Coll., Winfield, Kans., 1937-38, Kan. State U., 1938-39; m. Twila Virl Reece, Aug. 22, 1937; children—Marcia (Mrs. Jack Castleberry), Wayne Wesley. Farm, ranch mgr., operator, Langdon, Kans., 1940—. Dir. Ark. Valley Electric Co-op. Assn., Inc., 1955-61, 73—, chmn., 1959-61. Dist. bd. chmn. Lerado Cemetery, 1952-58; mem. Reno County Extension Council, 1949-53, chmn., 1951-53; active United Fund and Christian Rural Overseas Program drives Bell Twp., 1959-62; twp. committeeman Agrl. Stablzn. and Conservation Service, 1960-66; mem. Reno County Spl. Edn. Bd. of Control, 1973. Bd. dirs. Local High Schs., 1952-73; trustee Hutchinson Community Jr. Coll., 1959—, chmn., 1959-60, 67-68, 73-74, 78-79; bd. dirs. Central Kans. Area Vocat. Tech. Sch., 1975—, pres. 1978-79; trustee Kans. Electric Power Coop., 1976—. Recipient Kans. Master Farmer award, 1973. Mem. Kans. Farm Bur., Kans. Wheat Growers Assn., Kans. Farm. Mgmt. Assn., Top Farmers Am. Assn., Reno County Bankers Soil Conservation (mem. awards selection com. 1953), Kans. Master Farmer Assn. (pres. 1976—). Mem. Christian Ch. (elder 1971—, Sunday sch. supt. 1941-46). Home: Langdon KS 67549

NUNLEY, CHARLES EUGENE, sch. supt.; b. Ross County, Ohio, Nov. 1, 1928; s. Charles D. and Myrtle M. Nunley; B.S., Ohio U., 1956, Ed.M., 1958; Ed.S., Bowling Green State U., 1964; Ed.D., U. Akron, 1970; m. Ann Lynn Darby, Aug. 26, 1956; children—Terri, David. Tchr., Pike County (Ohio) schs., 1953-54, prin., 1954-58, supt., 1958-60; supt. Gibsonburg (Ohio) schs., 1960-62; supt. Marysville (Ohio) schs., 1962-67, Ashland (Ohio) schs., 1967-72, Pemberton Twp., N.J., 1972-75, Lorain (Ohio) schs., 1975—. Mem. adv. bd. Salvation Army, Lorain, 1976—; trustee Lorain Found., 1977—; bd. dirs. Fireland council Boy Scouts Am., 1978—. Served with inf., U.S. Army, 1951-53. Mem. Am. Assn. Sch. Adminstrs., Ohio Assn. Sch. Adminstrs., Mid-Am. Assn. Sch. Adminstrs., Lorain Urban League (v.p. 1978—), Phi Delta Kappa (pres. 1979-80). Clubs: Rotary (v.p. 1979-80, pres. 1980-81, team leader group study exchange to Chile, 1981), Masons. Home: 2744 Skyline Dr Lorain OH 44053 Office: 1020 7th St Lorain OH 44052

NUNN, ARTHUR SHERMAN, JR., physiologist, educator; b. Independence, Mo., Nov. 9, 1922; s. Arthur Sherman and Marian Louella (Greene) N.; B.S., Kans. State U., 1955; M.S., State U. Iowa, 1959, Ph.D., 1960; m. Dorothy Wilhelmina Miller, July 24, 1950; children—Pamela and Patricia (twins), Dorothy Kay, William Arthur, Frances Marie. USPHS fellow U. Ill., Urbana, 1955-56, State U. Iowa, Iowa City, 1958-60; instr. physiology St. Louis U. Sch. Medicine, 1960-62; asst. prof. physiology U. Miami (Fla.) Sch. Medicine, 1962-63, asso. prof., 1963-67; prof. physiology Ind. U. Sch. Medicine, Indpls., 1967—; cons. USPHS, 1974-78. Served with USN, 1940-47. Mem. Am. Physiol. Soc., Midwest Membrane Transport Group, Phi Kappa Phi, Omicron Kappa Upsilon. Home: 9308 Jutland Ct Apt A Indianapolis IN 46250 Office: Dept Physiology Sch Medicine 1100 W Michigan Ave Indianapolis IN 46202

NUNN, PHILIP CLARK, III, mgmt. scientist; b. Cin., Apr. 4, 1933; s. Philip Clark and Frances Kay (Patton) N.; student Kenyon Coll., 1951-53; B.A., Aquinas Coll., 1969; postgrad. Western Mich. U., 1970-78; m. Hildegarde Loretta Bauer, Jan. 17, 1953; children—Annette, Catherine, Margaret, Christopher. With Lear Siegler, Inc., Grand Rapids, Mich., 1957-70, devel. project coordinator, 1962-70; mgr. environ. systems devel. Nat. Sanitation Found., Ann Arbor, Mich., 1970-74; dir. urban and environ. studies inst. Grant Valley State Colls., Allendale, Mich., 1974-80; internat. coordinator research and devel. Amway Corp., Ada, Mich., 1980—; adj. prof. F. E. Seidman Grad. Coll. of Bus. and Adminstrn., 1976—. Health dir. Cin. area Boy Scout Camp, 1952; regular panel mem. Soundings weekly radio program WOOD-AM and FM, Grand Rapids, Mich., 1973—; vice chmn. community health planning sect. W. Mich. Health Systems Agy., 1976—; mem. central planning com. W. Mich. Comprehensive Health Planning Unit, 1973-76; chmn. environ. simulation sect. Summer Computer Simulation Conf., 1972; bd. dirs. Kent County Conservation League, 1964-65. Served with USAF, 1953-57. Kenyon Coll. scholar, 1951. Mem. AAAS, Soc. Gen. Systems Research (chmn. orgn. and mgmt. studies 1970-74), Soc. for Computer Simulation, Alpha Delta Phi. Episcopalian. Contbr. articles in field to profl. jours. Home: 201 Netherfield St Comstock Park MI 49321 Office: Research and Devel Project Control Amway Corp Ada MI 49355

NUNNELEE, THOMAS FREDERICK, funeral dir., mortician; b. Cairo, Ill., Aug. 25, 1944; s. Edward Eugene and Marie Lucille (Ohmes) N.; grad. Ky. Sch. Mortuary Sci., 1968; student S.E. Mo. State U., 1963, Memphis State U., 1965-67; m. Mary Alice Waltemath, Apr. 20, 1968; children—Christina Marie, Thomas F. With Nunnelee Funeral Chapel, Inc., Sikeston, Mo., 1968—, v.p., 1976—; Scott County coroner, 1980—. Bd. dirs. Kenny Rogers United Cerebral Palsy Center; pres. Scott County Young Democrats, 1976-77. Recipient Disting. Service award Sikeston Jaycees, 1979. Mem. Nat. Funeral Dirs. Assn., Mo. State Funeral Dirs. Assn., S.E. Mo. Funeral Dirs. Assn., Country Music Assn., Mo. Sheriff's Assn. (hon.). Democrat. Roman Catholic. Clubs: Jaycees, Eagles, K.C., Elks. Office: 205 N Stoddard St Sikeston MO 63801

NUSBAUM, WILLIAM CARD, elec. products co. exec.; b. Columbus, Ohio, Feb. 20, 1923; s. Christian and Marion (Trout) N.; B.S., Case Inst. Tech., 1944; M.B.A., Harvard U., 1955; m. M. Joyce McGilliard, Apr. 3, 1954; children—Cynthia Hess, William Card, Bradford Noel. Sales engr. Leed and Northrup Co., 1946-48; regional sales mgr. Tracerlab Inc., 1949-51; sales account exec., jet div. TRW, 1952-54; exec. asst. to chief exec. officer Emerson Electric Co., St. Louis, 1955-62, v.p. adminstrn. DayBrit div., 1962-63, v.p. sales White Rodgers div., 1963-66, exec. v.p. Ridge Tool Co. div., 1966-70, corporate v.p. corporate devel., 1971—. Founder, St. Louis Corporate Growth Assn.; trustee St. Louis Council Boy Scouts Am., 1973-76, Miss. Valley Jr. Achievement, 1975—; bd. dirs. Whitfield Sch., 1974—. Served to lt. (j.g.) USNR, 1944-46. Republican. Office: Emerson Electric Co 8100 W Florissant St Saint Louis MO 63136

NUTT, PAUL CHARLES, systems engr., educator; b. Dowgiac, Mich., Sept. 14, 1939; s. Charles E. and Isabell E. (Brigham) N.; B.S. in Indsl. Engring., U. Mich., 1962, M.S., 1963; Ph.D., U. Wis., 1974; m. Nancy Davis, Sept. 9, 1963; children—Suzanne, Lynn, Charles. Indsl. engr. TRW, Inc., Corp. Cons. Group, Cleve., 1963-64, Eastman Kodak Co., Rochester, N.Y., 1964-67; dir. planning Wis. Regional Med. Program, Inc., Madison, 1967-72; cons. health groups and health planning agys., 1972—; asst. prof. grad. program hosp. and health services adminstrn., faculty mgmt. sci. dept. indsl. and systems engring. Ohio State U., Columbus, 1974-78, asso. prof., 1978—; mem. project monitoring teams Health Resources Adminstrn., HEW, 1973—, Nat. Center for Health Services Research, 1973—; project team mem. Urban Inst., 1980—. Ohio Dept. of Health grantee, 1978—, HEW grantee, 1973-76. Registered profl. engr., Wis., Mich. Mem. Acad. of Mgmt., Profl. Engring. Soc., Am. Inst. Decision Scis., Inst. Mgmt. Sci., Sigma Xi. Author: Evaluation Concepts and Methods: Shaping Policy for the Health Adminstrator, 1981; asso. editor Mgmt. Sci., Acad. of Mgmt. Rev.; contbr. 70 articles to profl. jours. Home: 1637 Scottsdale Ave Columbus OH 43220 Office: 1583 Perry St Columbus OH 43210

NUTTER, DANIEL LYON, librarian, coll. adminstr.; b. Alcester, S.D., Jan. 16, 1932; s. Fayette Alonzo and Enolia Lottie (Lyon) N.; B.A., Southeastern Okla. State U., 1956; M.L.S., North Tex. State U., 1967, postgrad., 1980—; m. Elizabeth Jane Mohnkern, Dec. 21, 1963; children—Margaret Enolia, Charles Arthur. Librarian, Buna (Tex.) Ind. Sch. Dist., 1956-61, Clarendon (Tex.) Coll., 1961-66, Hamshire-Fannett (Tex.) Ind. Sch. Dist., 1966-67, East Tex. Bapt. Coll., 1967-68; dir. library Southwestern Coll., Winfield, Kans., 1968—; past trustee Winfield Public Libarary. Recipient Outstanding Service award East Tex. Bapt. Coll., 1968. Mem. ALA, Coll. and Research Library Assn., Kans. Library Assn., Mountain Plains Library Assn., Pvt. Acad. Libraries, Clarendon Jaycees (Outstanding Jaycee 1965), Blue Key, Sigma Tau Gamma, Alpha Sigma Lambda. Democrat. Methodist. Club: Lions (Key Lion 1976). Office: 100 College St Winfield KS 67156

NUZMAN, CARL EDWARD, hydrologist; b. Topeka, Aug. 5, 1930; s. Loren Manuel and Lorraine Lillian (Bowler) N.; B.S. in Agrl. Engring., Kans. State U., 1953; M.S. in Water Resources Engring., U. Kans., 1966; m. Janet Ruth Steck, Aug. 23, 1952. Engr. div. water resources Kans. Bd. Agr., Topeka, 1957-65; hydrologist Kans. Water Resources Bd., Topeka, 1965-66; hydrology supr., sales engr. Layne-Western Co., Inc., Shawnee Mission, Kans., 1967—. Treas. local sch. bd., 1958-59. Served to 1st lt. USAF, 1953-56. Registered profl. engr., Kans., Mo. Mem. Am. Soc. Agrl. Engrs., ASCE, Am. Geophys. Union, Kans. Engring. Soc. (sec.-treas. 1965-68, Outstanding Young Engr. award Topeka chpt. 1965), Nat. Soc. Profl. Engrs., Alpha Kappa Lambda, Sigma Tau, Steel Ring. Elk. Contbr. articles to profl. jours.; author, inventor. Home: Route 1 Silver Lake KS 66539 Office: PO Box 1322 Mission KS 66222

NWANGWU, PETER UCHENNA, pharmacologist; b. Umuahia, Nigeria, June 13, 1949; came to U.S., 1972; s. Sidney Nwokeke and Phoebe (Akueke) N.; B.A., U. Nebr., Lincoln, 1974, M.S., 1976, Pharm.D., Ph.D., 1979; m. Patience Okaro, June 3, 1978. Instr. chemistry SUNY, Syracuse, 1975; chmn. bd. PUN Labs., Inc., Omaha, 1979—; asst. prof. pharmacology and toxicology, dir. clin. research Fla. A&M U., Tallahassee, 1979—; cons. clin. toxicology. Bd. dirs. Calvary Baptist Ch., Omaha, 1978-80. Recipient Research Excellence award U. Nebr. Med. Center, 1979. Mem. AAAS, Am. Fedn. Clin. Research, Acad. Pharm. Research, Am. Pharm. Assn., Nat. Pharm. Alliance (tech. and regulatory com.), Am. Assn. Colls. Pharmacy, Nebr. Soc. Clin. Pharmacists, Internat. Platform Assn., Sigma Xi, Phi Eta Sigma, Rho Chi. Contbr. articles to profl. jours. Home: 4314 Franklin Omaha NE 68111 Office: Sch Pharmacy Fla A&M Univ Tallahassee FL 32307

NYE, MIRIAM MAURINE BAKER, writer; b. Castana, Iowa, June 14, 1918; d. Horace Boies and Hazel Dean (Waples) Hawthorn; B.A., Morningside Coll., 1939, postgrad., 1957-58; postgrad. U. Ariz., 1973, U. S.D., 1975-77, New Coll., U. Edinburgh (Scotland), 1974; m. Carl E. Baker, June 21, 1941 (dec. 1970); children—Kent Alfred, Dale Hawthorn; m. 2d, John Arthur Nye, Dec. 25, 1973. Tchr. jr. high sch., Rock Falls, Ill., 1939-41, Moville (Iowa) Community Sch., 1957-62, Woodbury Central Community Sch., Climbing Hill, Iowa, 1962-64; homemaking columnist Sioux City (Iowa) Jour.'s Farm Weekly, 1953-81; author: Recipes and Ideas From the Kitchen Window, 1973; But I Never Thought He'd Die: Practical Help for Widows, 1978; speaker, Iowa, Nebr., Minn., S.D. Counselor, Iowa State U., 1972—; county adv. Iowa Children's and Family Services, 1980—; mem. public relations com. Farm Bur., Woodbury County, 1980—. Recipient Alumni award Morningside Coll., 1969; Service award Woodbury County Fair, 1969; Friend of Extension award Iowa State U. Extension Assn., 1981. Mem. AAUW, Iowa Fedn. Women's Clubs (dist. creative writing chmn. 1978-80), Common Cause, Alpha Kappa Delta, Sigma Tau Delta. Methodist. Home and Office: Box 193 Route 2 Moville IA 51039

NYHUS, ORRIN ROY, ammunition mfg. co. exec.; b. Cumberland, Wis., July 26, 1947; s. Orrin Edgar and Lorraine Evelyn N.; student Brown Inst., 1966; m. Linda Kay Rust, Oct. 12, 1968; children—Aaron Jon, Dawn Rae. Industry control specialist, inventory control and sales Goodyear, St. Paul, 1966-67; indsl. salesman Newark Co., Mpls., 1968-69; supt. plant security and protection, contract adminstr. Fed. Cartridge Corp., New Brighton, Minn., 1969—. Recipient various certs. in mgmt. and related fields. Mem. Am. Law Enforcement Assn., Am. Def. Preparedness Assn. Republican. Office: Twin Cities Army Ammunition Plant New Brighton MN 55112

NYKIEL, FRANK PETER, diversified co. exec.; b. Chgo., Dec. 30, 1917; s. Joseph and Ann (Jerz) N.; B.S. in Acctg., U. Ill., 1941; m. Marie Papa, Mar. 1, 1942; children—Carol Ann (Mrs. Thomas J. Barta), Frank Peter II. With Arthur Andersen & Co., C.P.A., Chgo., 1947-52, sr. acct., 1951-52; with Consumers Co., Chgo., 1952-60, exec. v.p., 1959-60; v.p., treas. Miss. Valley Barge Line Co., St. Louis, 1960-62, exec. v.p., dir., 1962—, (merger Miss. Valley Barge Line Co. and Chromalloy Am. Corp. to Valley Line Co., 1968), v.p. marine-fin., dir. Chromalloy Am. Corp., 1968-70, vice chmn. bd. fin., dir., 1970, now pres., chief exec. officer; chmn. bd., chief exec. officer, dir. Water Treatment Corp., 1968-71. Served with USAAF, World War II. C.P.A. Clubs: Mo. Athletic; Sunset Country. Office: Chromalloy Am Corp 120 S Central Ave Saint Louis MO 63105

NYLANDER, VIRGIL CHARLES, psychologist, educator; b. Denver, Feb. 27, 1943; s. Virgil Herman and Marie Dorthy (Molander) N.; B.S., Colo. State U., 1967, M.S., 1969; Ph.D., Iowa State U., 1977; m. Gayle Diane Soderberg, Sept. 11, 1964; 1 child, Lisen Harris. With Boeing Aircraft Corp., 1969; mem. faculty U. Wis., River Falls, 1969—, chmn. dept. psychology, 1979—. Mem. Am. Psychol. Assn., Midwest Psychol. Assn., AAAS, Nat. Conf. on Use of Computers in Psychology, Soc. for Neurosci. Methodist. Clubs: Masons, Scottish Rite (Eau Clair, Wis.); Shriners (Madison). Home: 622 Sunset Ln River Falls WI 54022 Office: 153 CSH Univ Wisconsin River Falls WI 54022

NYMAN, RUTH ANN, pub. co. exec.; b. Ames, Iowa, May 28, 1945; d. Walter Talbot and Mildred Harriet (Deal) Farley; B.S., Westmar Coll., 1967; postgrad. Iowa State U., 1967-68; m. Garrett Merle Nyman, Aug. 10, 1968; children—Nicholas Guy, Nathan Garrett. Copywriter, Better Homes and Gardens, Meredith Corp., Des Moines, 1968-75, merchandising and mktg. promotion mgr., 1975-78, mail order books promotion mgr., 1978-80, mail order books mgr., 1980-81, mktg. mgr. crafts catalog and home products, 1981—. Active United Way, Des Moines. Mem. Des Moines Profl. Advt. Assn., Des Moines C. of C. Republican. Lutheran. Office: 1716 Locust St Des Moines IA 50336

NYQUIST, IRENE MAE, chem. co. patent exec.; b. Washington, Feb. 18, 1931; d. Leo W. and Susan (Cox) Cote; B.S., St. John's U., Bklyn., 1952; postgrad. (Fulbright scholar) U. Reading (Eng.), 1953-54; M.S., U. Minn., 1955; M.A., Central Mich. U., 1974; m. Richard Allan Nyquist, Jan. 28, 1956; children—Richard H., Jean, Kathryn, Robert. Chemist, Dow Chem. Co., Midland, Mich., 1955-56, office supr. legal dept., 1975-80, patent info. specialist patent dept., 1980—. Mem. Midland Public Schs. Curriculum Council, 1973-77, sec., 1974-75; mem. Midland Community Relations Commn., 1978—. Mem. Saginaw Valley Patent Law Assn., Sigma Xi. Democrat. Lutheran. Home: 3707 Westbrier Terr Midland MI 48640 Office: Dow Chem Co Patent Dept 1776 Bldg Midland MI 48640

NYSTROM, JOHN NORMAN, state senator; b. June 16, 1933; s. Clifford and Agnes N.; student Iowa State U.; m. Joanne Barnes; children—Eric, Ellen, Monica. Mem. Iowa Ho. of Reps, 1971-72; Iowa Senate, 1973—. Mem. Iowa State Republican Central Com., 1969-70. Served with U.S. Army; Korea. Mem. Am. Legion, C. of C. Baptist. Clubs: Elks, Shriners, Masons. Office: State Capitol Des Moines IA 50319*

NYSTROM, PAUL CLIFDON, educator; b. St. Paul, June 23, 1940; s. Donald T. and Thelma Irene (Searle) N.; B.S. in Econs., U. Minn., 1962, M.A. in Public Adminstrn., 1966, Ph.D. in Indsl. Relations, 1970; m. Carol Jean Lewis, Jan. 20, 1962; children—Leigh Erik, Joy Beth. Asst. prof. mgmt. Sch. Bus. Adminstrn., U. Wis., Milw., 1969-74, asso. prof., 1974-78, prof., 1978—, asst. dean, 1970-72. Mem. Acad. Mgmt., Am. Inst. Decision Scis., Am. Psychol. Assn., Am. Sociol. Assn., Indsl. Relations Research Assn., Inst. Mgmt. Scis. Contbr. numerous articles to profl. jours.; co-editor: Prescriptive Models of Organizations, 1977; Handbook of Organizational Design, vols. 1 and 2, 1981; asso. editor Mgmt. Sci., 1975—. Home: 4764 N Larkin St Whitefish Bay WI 53211 Office: Sch Bus Adminstrn U Wis Milwaukee WI 53201

OAK, VISHNU VITTHAL, educator; b. Bombay, India, Nov. 30, 1895; s. Vitthal Anant and Sitabal V. (Marathe) O.; came to U.S., 1922, naturalized, 1948; A.B. in English and History, U. Bombay, 1920; M.A. in Econs., U. Calif., Berkeley, 1923; B.S. in Journalism, U. Oreg., 1924; M.S. in Bus., U. Iowa, 1932; Ph.D. in Econs. and Sociology, Clark U., 1937; m. Evangeline Mary Pullen, Sept. 13, 1945; children—Sarojini Evangeline, Vishnu Narahar. Instr. Howard U., spring 1926; prof. econs. Wiley Coll., 1926-27; prof. econs. Wilberforce (Ohio) U., 1927-30, prof. bus., 1939-41, prof. sociology, 1941-49, editor quar., dir. pub. relations, 1941-49; prof. econs. and sociology Lincoln U. of Mo., 1930-32; prof., chmn. social sci. div. Langston U., 1932-33; prof. bus. Samuel Houston Coll., 1935-36, N.C. Coll., Durham, 1937-39; prof. social scis. Harris Tchrs. Coll., St. Louis, 1949-65; prof. bus. Lane Coll., 1966-67; prof., chmn. social sci. div. Rust Coll., 1967-69, Edward Waters Coll., 1969-71; prof. div. bus. Voorhees Coll., Denmark, S.C., 1971-72, chmn. div. bus., 1972-76; prof., dir. bus. adminstrn. Morris Coll., Sumter, S.C., 1976-78; dean acad. affairs Daniel Payne Coll., 1978. Mem. AAUP, ACLU, Am. Friends Soc., Common Cause, NAACP, Public Citizen. Independent Democrat. Unitarian. Author: England's Educational Policy in India, 1925; The Negro Newspaper, 1948, reprinted, 1971; The Negro's Adventure in General Business, 1949, 2d edit., 1971. Home: 324 W Perrin Ave Springfield OH 45506

OAKAR, MARY ROSE, congresswoman; b. Cleve.; B.A., Ursuline Coll., Cleve., 1962; M.A., John Carroll U., Cleve., 1966; postgrad. Columbia U., 1967—. Clk., Higbee Co., 1956-58; long distance operator Ohio Bell Telephone Co., 1957-62; instr. English and drama Lourdes Acad., Cleve., 1963-70; asst. prof. English, speech and drama Cuyahoga Community Coll., 1968-75; mem. 95th-96th Congresses from 20th Ohio Dist. Ward leader Cuyahoga County Democratic Com., 1972-76; mem. Cleve. City Council, 1973-76; state central committeewoman 20th Congl. Dist., 1974; trustee Fedn. for Community Planning, Health and Planning Commn., Community Info. Service, Soc. for Crippled Children, Nationalities Services Center, YWCA. Recipient Outstanding Service award OEO, 1973-75, Community Service awards Am. Indian Center, 1973, Nationalities Service Center, 1974, Club San Lorenzo, 1976. Home: 1892 W 30th St Cleveland OH 44113 Office: 427 Cannon House Office Bldg Washington DC 20515

OAKES, RAVENNA LOU, bank exec.; b. Ottawa, Kans., Jan. 29, 1938; d. Otho Richard and Lily Elizabeth (Solon) Bateman; B.A. cum laude in Psychology and Human Relations, U. Kans., 1967; m. Joe Duane Oakes, June 10, 1955 (div. 1969), children—Brian David, Bradley Duane, Melanie Lyn. Programmer, Hallmark Cards, 1969-71; clin. psychologist, programmer, analyst Johnson County (Kans.) Mental Health Center, 1971-74; data processing supr. Cogna Systems, Inc., Chgo., 1974-77; data processing dir., officer Globe Life Ins. Co., Chgo., 1977-78; data processing cons. Tri-State Data Services, Oak Brook, Ill., 1978-79; computer services product mgr. First Nat. Bank of Chgo., 1979—. NDEA fellow, 1967-69. Mem. Am. Mensa Ltd. (nat. sec. governing bd. 1981—). Home: Skokie IL

OAKLEY, PATRICIA ANN KING, mathematician, educator; b. Winchester, Ky., Apr. 8, 1932; d. Richard Simpson and Mary Leona (Kirk) King; student Miami U., Oxford, Ohio, 1950-51; B.A. in Edn., Northeastern Ill. U., 1971; M.S., No. Ill. U., 1976, adminstrv. cert., 1978; m. Robert Lewis Oakley, Mar. 17, 1951; children—Robert Jeffrey, Cheryl Sue, Mark Stephen. In personnel relations Armco Steel Corp., Middletown, Ohio, 1951-53; tchr. math. High Sch. Dist. 211, Palatine, Ill., 1971—. Pres., N.W. Suburban Council PTA's, 1963-65, also pres. Pleasant Hill PTA; mem. Bd. Edn., Sch. Dist. 15, Palatine, 1965-71. Recipient awards Northeastern Ill. U., 1971. Mem. Nat. Council Tchrs. Math., Assn. for Supervision and Curriculum Devel., Ill. Council Tchrs. Math., Am. Fedn. Tchrs., Ill. Congress PTA's (life), Northeastern Ill. U. Alumni Assn., No. Ill. U. Alumni Assn., Kappa Delta Pi. Republican. Episcopalian. Club: Pres.'s (No. Ill. U.). Home: 4440 Dawngate Ln Rolling Meadows IL 60008 Office: William Fremd High Sch 1000 S Quentin Rd Palatine IL 60067

OAKS, GILBERT EARL, JR., internat. fin. cons.; b. Monterey, Calif., July 16, 1944; s. Gilbert E. and Wanda F. (Stevenson) O.; B.S. in Elec. Engring., Findlay Engring. Coll., 1966, B.S. in Mech. Engring.; M.B.A., Frostburg State Coll., 1974; Ph.D. in Internat. Fin., Am. Western U., Okla., 1981; m. Carolyn Shonka, Nov. 26, 1966; 1 son. Engr., Panhandle Eastern Co., Kansas City, Mo., 1962-66, AEC, Kansas City, 1966-69, chief engr., 1969-70, fin. analyst, 1970-71, spl. asst. tech. affairs, Washington, 1971-74; pres. Oaks Mgmt. Associates Internat., Elm Grove, Wis., 1974—, cons. to various banks and fin.

firms, 1974—; profit cons. J.C. Penney Co., Milw., Wis., 1974-76, regional mgr., Milw., 1976—. Dist. commr. Potawatomi council Boy Scouts Am., 1977—. Mem. Internat. Assn. Fin. Planners, Internat. Soc. Financiers, Mortgage Bankers Assn. Am., Assn. M.B.A. Execs., Internat. Solar Energy Soc., Ind. Bus. Assn. Wis., Internat. Assn. Bus. and Fin. Cons., Am. Inst. Indsl. Engrs., Nat. Assn. Fin. Cons. Republican. Mem. Christian Ch. Pub. Internat. Financialist, 1980—. Home: 3030 Nassau Dr Brookfield WI 53005 Office: PO Box 234 Elm Grove WI 53122

OANCEA, ROD JOHN, corp. exec.; b. Bucharest, Romania, Nov. 15, 1937; s. John and Elena (Bratianu) O. (Am. citizen); B.S. in Elec. Engring., U. Pitts., 1961, postgrad. 1965; M.B.A., Purdue U., 1972. Designer, Houser and Carafas Engring. Co., Pitts., 1958-63; engr. Swindell Dressler, Pitts., 1963; design engr., constrn. engr., project mgr. U.S. Steel Corp., Pitts., 1964-75; cons. engr. Altos Hornos del Mediteraneo-Madrid (Spain), 1975; pres. Enterprise T. & E.S. Co., Pitts. and Chgo., 1975—. Active Chgo. Council on Fgn. Relations, Internat. Visitors Center-Chgo., Art Inst. Chgo., Nat. Soc. Hist. Preservation. Served with USAF, 1961. Mem. Nat. Soc. Profl. Engrs., Internat. Trade Club, IEEE, Iron and Steel Assn., Chgo. Hist. Soc. Internat. Entrepreneurs Assn., Secretariat OAS, Am. Security Council, Chgo. Hist. Soc., Smithsonian Inst., Chgo. Lyric Opera Council, Am. Def. Preparedness Assn. Republican. Clubs: Good Fellowship, Toastmasters Internat., University. Office: PO Box 8259 Chicago IL 60680 also PO Box 9679 Pittsburgh PA 15256

OATMAN, PATRICIA MURPHY, corp. services co. ofcl.; b. St. Paul, Apr. 22, 1955; d. Richard Joseph and Genevieve Lorraine (Brokaw) Murphy; B.A. in English, Coll. of St. Catherine, 1977; m. Michael James Oatman, Sept. 16, 1977. Public relations intern The St. Paul Cos., Inc., 1976-77; communications asst. Gelco Corp., Eden Prairie, Minn., 1977-79, communications specialist, 1979-81, mgr. communications projects, 1981, mgr. internal communications, 1981—. Mem. Public Relations Soc. Am., Internat. Assn. Bus. Communicators, Women in Communications. Office: One Gelco Dr Eden Prairie MN 55344

O'BANNON, FRANK LEWIS, lawyer, state senator; b. Louisville, Jan. 30, 1930; s. Robert Pressley and Rosella Faith (Dropsey) O'B.; A.B., Ind. U., 1952, J.D., 1957; m. Judith Mae Asmus, Aug. 18, 1957; children—Polly, Jennifer, Jonathan. Admitted to Ind. bar, 1957, since practiced in Corydon; partner firm Hays, O'Bannon & Funk, 1966-80, O'Bannon, Funk & Simpson, 1980—; mem. Ind. State Senate, 1970—, minority floor leader, 1979—, asst. minority floor leader, 1972-76; pres., dir. O'Bannon Pub. Co., Inc. Served with USAF, 1952-54. Mem. Ind. Dem. Editorial Assn. (pres. 1961), Am. Judicature Soc., Am. Bar Assn., Ind. Bar Assn. Democrat. Methodist. Office: 303 N Capitol St Corydon IN 47112

OBENOUR, RALPH EUGENE, loss control ofcl.; b. Marion, Ohio, Feb. 4, 1925; s. Ivan M. and Fairydale G. (Jones) O.; B.S. in Edn., Ohio No. U., 1949; postgrad. Bowling Green State U., 1951-54; m. Julia M. Clary, Nov. 18, 1945; children—Grayden L., Janice E., Daryl E. Ada (Ohio) high sch. tchr., 1949-55; loss control engr. Gates, McDonald & Co., Columbus, Ohio, 1955-69, dir. loss control tng., 1970-75, western regional mgr. Oakland, Calif., 1975-78, dir. loss control services, Columbus, 1978—; tng. dir. Brown Paper Co., Kalamazoo, 1969-70; cons., instr. various corps. Served with USAF, 1943-45. Decorated D.F.C., Air medal with clusters. Cert. safety profl. Mem. Am. Soc. Safety Engrs., Vets. of Safety. Republican. Mem. Christian Ch. (Disciples of Christ). Participant various loss control and tng. programs. Office: Box 1944 Columbus OH 43216

OBER, DAVID LAWRENCE, engring. co. exec.; b. Kansas City, Mo., Oct. 2, 1936; s. David Wendell and Maude Pearl (Ferguson) O.; A.Sci., Kansas City Jr. Coll., 1957; B.S.C.E., Finlay Engring. Coll., 1963; m. Carol Enola Gohres, Apr. 4, 1958; children—Daniel Gregory, Cynthia Lynn, Steven Christopher. Design engr. Lloyd T. Thorp, Cons. Engr., Prairie Village, Kans., 1962-65; design engr. Black & Veatch, Cons. Engrs., Kansas City, Mo., 1965-66, asso. planner, 1966-68, project planner, 1968-71, design engr., 1971-77, project coordinator, 1977-79, sr. planner, 1979-81, asso. project mgr., 1981—. Volunteer worker Heart of Am. United Way campaign, Kansas City, 1972-74; dir. Post Oak Farm Homeowners Assn., Lenexa, Kans., 1974—; flotilla staff officer USCG Aux., 1981—; asst. scoutmaster Boy Scouts Am., Lenexa, Kans., 1971—, troop chaplain, 1972-73, named to Order of Arrow Honor Camping Soc., 1974. Recipient Honor award, Frontiersmen Drum and Bugle Corps, 1973; Certificate of Merit, YMCA, 1967. Christian Ch. (elder 1974-77, chmn. deacons 1970). Home: 7900 Noland Rd Lenexa KS 66215 Office: 1500 Meadowlake Pkwy Kansas City MO 64114

OBERG, GARY RICHARD, physician; b. Chgo., Aug. 18, 1946; s. Richard Arthur and Jean Elizabeth (Griffiths) O.; B.A., DePauw U., 1968; M.D., Loyola U., Chgo., 1972. Intern, Children's Meml. Hosp., Chgo., 1972-73, adj. attending physician, 1976—; resident in pediatrics Rush-Presby.-St. Luke's Med. Center, Chgo., 1973-75; individual practice medicine specializing in gen. pediatrics, pediatric and adult allergy-clin. ecology, Crystal Lake, Ill., 1975—; attending physician McHenry Hosp.; adj. attending physician, vis. faculty dept. pediatrics Rush Med. Coll.; med. cons. Spl. Edn. Dist. McHenry County, 1975-78; mem. neonatal and maternal task force and wellness task force Health Systems Agy. Kane-Lake-McHenry County, 1977; chmn. consumer evaluation Rockford (Ill.) Perinatal Center, 1978; mem. governing bd. McHenry County Nutrition Edn. Network; med. cons. Nutra Lunch Program, Dist. 47, Crystal Lake, Ill., 1978—. Diplomate Am. Bd. Pediatrics, Nat. Bd. Med. Examiners. Fellow Am. Acad. Pediatrics, Soc. Clin. Ecology; asso. fellow Am. Acad. Allergy; mem. AMA, Ill. Med. Soc., McHenry County Med. Soc., Pan Am. Allergy Soc. Contbr. articles to med. jours. Home: 4702 Shady Oaks Ln Crystal Lake IL 60014 Office: College Hill Profl Bldg Suite F 4911 Route 31 Crystal Lake IL 60014

OBERHAMER, DOUGLAS ROY, trade assn. exec.; b. St. Paul, Apr. 22, 1949; s. Roy Raymond and Hulda Wilhemina (Gens) O.; grad. high sch.; m. Deborah Lynn Hallett, May 28, 1977; children—Jason Douglas, Kimberly Joy. Sales mgr. Hilton Hotels Corp., St. Paul, 1969-71; adminstrv. asst. to exec. v.p. Water Conditioning Assn. Internat., Wheaton, Ill., 1971-74; exec. dir. Water Quality Assn., Lombard, Ill., 1974—; dir. Water Quality Research Council, Ground Water Council, 1976-77, Water Quality Improvement Standards and Certification Council. Served with USAF, 1969-71. Recipient award for youth Optimists, 1967; Distinguished Service award ARC, 1967; certified assn. exec. Mem. Am., Chgo. socs. assn. execs., European Water Conditioning Assn. (dir.). Republican. Home: 2348 Appleby Dr Wheaton IL 60187 Office: 477 E Butterfield Rd Lombard IL 60148

OBERHAUSER, JOSEPH FRANCIS, data processor; b. Toledo, May 26, 1947; s. Francis Joseph and Marie Hilda (Bauer) O.; B.S. in Bus. Adminstrn. cum laude, Bowling Green State U., 1968-74; M.B.A. in Mgmt. Info. Systems, U. Minn., 1976. Programmer, analyst Lathrop Co., gen. contractors, Toledo, 1968-70; data systems mgr. Systemedia div. N.C.R. Corp., Wahington Court House, O., 1970-71, ind. systems and programming cons. Toledo sales office, 1971-72; sr. systems cons. Arthur Young & Co., C.P.A., Toledo, 1972-74; applications analyst, software engr., applications product mgr. Datapoint Corp., San Antonio, 1976—. Certificate in data processing Inst. for Certification of Computer Profls. Served in U.S. Army, 1965-68; Vietnam. Mem. Soc. Certified Data Processors, Assn. for Computing Machinery, Bowling Green State U. Alumni Assn., Delta Sigma Pi (founding mem., v.p. Bowling Green State U. chpt.), Phi Kappa Phi. Roman Catholic. Home: 1520 Lawnview Ave Toledo OH 43607 Office: 9725 Datapoint Dr M67 San Antonio TX 78284

OBERHOLTZER, JOHN CLAYTON, lawyer; b. Cleve., Sept. 11, 1942; s. Clayton J. and Winefred E. (Graham) O.; grad. Coll. of Wooster, 1964; LL.B., Western Res. U., 1967; m. Janet L. Bartter, June 20, 1965; children—Julie, John Jacob, Joy. Admitted to Ohio bar, 1967, Fla. bar, 1979, U.S. Supreme Ct. bar, 1981; partner Oberholtzer, Filous & Chase, Medina, 1967—; pres., Minn. Title Agy. of Medina, Inc.; dir. Mack Industries, Inc., WDBN Radio. County commr. Medina County, 1971-78, pres. bd. commrs., 1975-77; chmn. housing com. NE Ohio Area Co-ordinating Agy., 1972-73; former mem. Five County Mass Transp. Study Adv. Com., Tri County Manpower Consortium; past bd. dirs. Medina County United Appeal; trustee United Fund, United Torch Drive; bd. dirs. Flat Rock Children's Home; amateur soccer referee. Mem. Am., Ohio, Medina County bar assns., Comml. Law League of Am. Methodist. K.P., Kiwanian (pres. Medina 1974-75). Home: 875 Damon Dr Medina OH 44256 Office: 230 S Court St Medina OH 44256

OBERLE, KEVIN RAY, mktg. communications specialist; b. Columbus, Ohio, Nov. 24, 1948; s. Raymond Zeigler and Kathern Viola (Hickerson) O.; B.S. in Communication (Zousmer Meml. award), Ohio U., 1971. Broadcast technician Sta. WLWC-TV, Columbus, 1971; prodn. asst. Sta. WSTV-TV, Steubenville, Ohio, 1972; dir. Sta. WTVN-TV, Columbus, 1972-74; broadcast technician Sta. WLWC-TV, Columbus, 1974; community relations dir. Goodwill Industries of Central Ohio, Inc., Columbus, 1974-77, pub. relations cons. Goodwill Industries Am., Inc., Washington, 1976-77; regional field rep. St. Jude Childrens Research Hosp., Memphis, 1977-78; mktg. communications specialist splty. materials dept. Gen. Electric Co., Worthington, Ohio, 1978—. Mem. spl. events com. United Way Franklin County. Served with Signal Corps, U.S. Army, 1971-72. Mem. Pub. Relations Soc. Am., Nat. Acad. TV Arts and Scis., Internat. TV Assn., Columbus Advt. Fedn. Club: Kiwanis. Home: 1150-A Fountain Ln Columbus OH 43213 Office: 6325 Huntley Rd Worthington OH 43085

OBERLIN, DONALD JERRY, gen. contractor; b. Bryan, Ohio, June 8, 1947; s. Charles Franklin and Donna Vee (Shough) O.; B.S. in Edn., Bowling Green State U., 1969; m. Marsha Mae Gerencser, June 15, 1968; children—Gabriel, Benjamin, Matthew. Indsl. arts tchr. Perrysburgy (Ohio) High Sch., 1969-70, Hicksville, Ohio, 1970-73; gen. contractor Black Swamp Builders, Inc., Antwerp, Ohio, 1973—; gen. contractor/partner Tri-State Solarcrete Bldg. Systems, Antwerp, 1979—; solar energy instr. N.W. Tech. Coll., Archbold, Ohio, 1980—. Bd. dirs. Antwerp Community Improvement Corp., 1975—. Licensed constrn. supt., Allen County, Ind., Ft. Wayne, Ind. Mem. N.E. Ind. Solar Collective, Antwerp Jaycees (pres. 1977). Home: PO Box 43B Route 1 Antwerp OH 45813 Office: 319 S Main St Antwerp OH 45813

OBERLIN, FLORENCE GRACE, educator; b. Wheatland, Mich., Aug. 14, 1912; d. Clarence Dale and Grace Emma (Chamberlin) O.; B.A. with honors in Math., Oberlin Coll., 1933; M.A., Mich. State U., 1944; postgrad. U. Mich., 1950, 56, U. Buffalo, 1959, U. Wash., 1954, Wayne State U., 1949, 60, 73, Mich. State U., 1951. Tchr. upper elem. grades public schs., Bancroft, Mich., 1935-37 Pontiac, Mich., 1939-41; tchr. Ionia (Mich.) Jr. High Sch., 1937-39; tchr. math Wayne (Mich.) Meml. High Sch., 1941-78, chmn. math. dept., 1954-60, 68-73, counselor, 1949-78, chmn. counseling, 1960-66, 73-78; acad. adv. nursing program. U. Toledo (Ohio), 1978-79; lectr. math. U. Mich., Dearborn, 1979—; guest faculty mem. Mich. State U., summer 1945. Mem. Am. Personnel and Guidance Assn., NEA, Am. Fedn. Tchrs., Nat. Council of Math. Tchrs., Sch. Sci. and Math. Assn., Nat. Vocat. Guidance Assn. Congregationalist. Club: Wayne Ladies Literary. Contbr. articles on counseling to profl. publs.; Florence Oberlin scholarship named in her honor. Home: 35800 Michigan Ave Wayne MI 48184 Office: Room 1184 Univ Mall U Mich 4901 Evergreen Rd Dearborn MI 48128

OBERMAN, MOISHE DAVID, mag. pub.; b. Springfield, Ill., Mar. 3, 1914; s. Harry and Ida (Guralnik) O.; student St. Louis Coll. Pharmacy, 1931-33; m. Bobbye Friedman, Oct. 8, 1939; children—Michael Alan, Martin Jay, M.H. William, Marjorie Ann. Scrap metals broker, Springfield, 1937-41; founder Scrap Age Mag., 1944, Mill Trade Jour., 1963, Waste Age Mag., 1969, Encyclopedia of Scrap Recycling, 1976; pres., editor, pub. 3 Sons Pub. Co., Niles, Ill., 1944; pres. Emde Realty Devel. Corp., Springfield, 1957-63; exec. sec. Midwest Scrap Dealers Assn., Springfield, 1941; treas. North Shore Investments, Highland Park, Ill., 1968; exec. dir. Springfield Area Devel. and Tourist Commn., 1963-68; mem. Ill. Inst. Environ. Quality Solid Waste Task Force Com., 1971. Pres. Ill. Assn. Jewish Centers, 1934-40; editor congregation publs., treas. North Suburban Synagogue Beth El. Mem. War Production Bd., 1942-44. Recipient Meritorious Service award for outstanding contbns. to iron and steel industry St. Louis Steel Assn., 1961. Mem. Nat. Solid Waste Mgmt. Assn., Am. Pub. Works Assn. (solid waste mgmt. task force), Execs. Inc. (pres. 1963-67), Am. Soc. Assn. Execs., Internat. Platform Assn., Nat. Press Club, Springfield Jr. C. of C. (pres. 1946-47), Springfield Assn. Execs., Springfield Assn. Commerce and Industry. Jewish. Club: B'nai B'rith (sec. 1935-39, pres. 1942-45). Home: 857 Stonegate Dr Highland Park IL 60035 Office: 6311 Gross Point Rd Niles IL 60648

OBERMILLER, STANLEY MATHEW, retail trade co. exec.; b. Norman County, Minn., Dec. 1, 1914; s. Frank and Josephine (Rubash) O.; student Marquette U., 1936-37, N.D. State U., 1940-41; m. Elaine Bursch, Jan. 26, 1946; children—Michael, Karen. Dep. county auditor Mahnomen County, Minn., 1937-40; sales exec. Ford Motor Co., Fargo, N.D., 1945-49; propr., mgr. Elaine's Store, Thief River Falls, Minn., 1949-52; pres. Palette Shop, Inc., Milw., 1953—; dir. Nat. Art Industries, Inc., 1971—. Bd. dirs. Milw. Sch. of the Arts. Served with USAAF, 1942-45. Recipient Hall of Fame award Nat. Art Materials Trade Assn., 1977. Mem. Wis. Rural Artists Assn., Milw. Assn. of Commerce, Illustrators and Designers of Milw., Nat. Art Materials Trade Assn. (dir. 1958-67, pres. 1963-65), Wis. Painters and Sculptors. Roman Catholic. Club: K.C. (past grand knight) Columnist. Art Material Trade News, 1971—. Home: 4332 W Grace Ave Mequon WI 53092 Office: 409 E Michigan St Milwaukee WI 53202

OBERROTMAN, ALAIN MAURICE, mgmt. cons.; b. Paris, France, Mar. 17, 1951; s. Joseph and Janine (Binder) O.; came to U.S., 1955, naturalized, 1961; B.S. in Accounting cum laude, U. Ill., 1972; M.B.A. cum laude, U. Chgo., 1974. Mgmt. cons. to MARCOR, Chgo., 1972-74, to Touche Ross & Co., Chgo., 1974-78; asst. to pres. Mark Controls Corp., Skokie, Ill., 1978-79; asst. controller MCC Powers, Skokie, 1979-81; pres. Oberrotman & Assos., mgmt. cons., 1981—; research cons. to N.Y. U. dept. acctg., N.Y.C., 1974—; guest lectr. U. Chgo., 1975-76, Northwestern U., Loyola U., Milliken U., 1976. Supernumerary, Lyric Opera Chgo., 1979-80. Recipient Bronze medal for sabre fencing Israel World Games, 1973. C.P.A., Ill. Mem. Nat., Am. acctg. assns., Am. Inst. C.P.A.'s, Ill. Soc. C.P.A.'s, Planning Execs. Inst., Fin. Execs. Inst., Am. Fin. Assn., Midwest Planning Assn. Author: SEC Replacement Cost Accounting: A Guide to Implementation; also articles. Home: 1952 N Cleveland Chicago IL 60614 Office: 3400 Oakton St Skokie IL 60076

OBERST, BYRON BAY, physician; b. Omaha, Mar. 15, 1923; s. Byron Bay and Claire Matilda (Healy) O.; B.A., U. Omaha, 1943; M.D., U. Nebr., 1946; m. Mary Catherine Nadolny, Dec. 27, 1945; children—Byron Joseph, Terrence Martin, Matthew Robert. Intern, U. Nebr. Hosp., Omaha, 1946-47, resident in pediatrics, 1947-48; resident Henry Ford Hosp., Detroit, 1950-51; practice medicine specializing in pediatrics, Omaha, 1951—; instr. pediatrics Wayne U. Sch. Medicine, Henry Ford Hosp. Sch. Nursing, Detroit, 1950-51, Creighton Coll. Medicine, 1951-54, St. Catherine's Sch. Nursing, Omaha, 1952-55; faculty U. Nebr. Coll. Medicine, 1951—, asso., 1954—, asso. prof., 1969—, dir. adolescent clinic, 1960-63, clin. prof. pediatrics, 1977—; adj. prof. psychology Bellevue (Nebr.) Coll., 1966-68; staff mem. Children's Meml. Hosp., 1951—, treas. staff, 1958, dir. adolescent clinic, 1967-70, pres. staff., 1968-70; clinician in charge nursery, mem. infection control com. Nebr. Meth. Hosp., 1957-60; asst. clinician for heart diseases Nebr. Services for Crippled Children, 1953-60; pediatrician in charge pediatrics, newborns Bishop Clarkson Meml. Hosp., 1963-76; pediatrician in chief Archbishop Bergan Mercy Hosp., 1965-66; guest lectr. civic orgns., ch. young people's groups, schs., tchr. groups. Bd. dirs. Operation Bridge, Suburban Youth Guidance Counselling Service, 1968-73; active Boy Scouts Am., 1951-67, troop scoutmaster, 1960-67; founder, bd. dirs. Omaha STAAR Program for Sch. Learning Disabilities, 1968—; mem. com. on health planning Health Planning Council of Midlands, 1976-79; hon. life mem. PTA. Served to capt. M.C., AUS, 1948-50. Sch. Health Physicians fellow, 1970-73. Fellow Am. Acad. Pediatrics (chmn. Nebr. chpt. 1976-79, chpt. chmn. com. on med. practice 1971-76, numerous other coms.); mem. AMA, (Recognition award 1969, 73, 76), Nebr. (com. on mental health 1971), Omaha-Douglas County (com. on edn. 1971), Pan Am. med. socs., NW, Nebr. (pres. 1958) pediatric socs., Midwest Clin. Soc. (chmn. sect. pediatrics 1957), Soc. for Adolescent Medicine (charter, mem. com. on med. practice 1971-79), Soc. for Computer Medicine (chmn. com. on standards 1974-77, 81—), Gt. Plains Orgn. for Perinatal Health Care, Nat. Assn. Children's Learning Disabilities (hon. life). Republican. Roman Catholic. Author: Practical Guidance for Pediatric and Adolescent Office Practice, 1973; contbr. articles to profl. jours. Home: 307 S 93d St Omaha NE 68114 Office: 12808 Augusta Ave Omaha NE 68144

OBERSTAR, JAMES L., congressman; b. Chisholm, Minn., Sept. 10, 1934; s. Louis and Mary (Grillo) C.; B.A. summa cum laude, St. Thomas Coll.; postgrad. in French, Laval U., Que., Can.; M.A. in Govt. (scholar), Coll. Europe, Bruges, Belgium; postgrad. in govt. Georgetown U.; m. Marilynn Jo Garlick, Oct. 12, 1963; children—Thomas Edward, Katherine Noelle, Ann-Therese, Monica Rose. Adminstrv. asst. to Congressman John A. Blatnik, 1963-74; adminstr. Pub. Works Com., U.S. Ho. of Reps., 1971-74; mem. 94th-97th Congresses from 8th Minn. Dist. Mem. Am. Polit. Sci. Assn. Home: 317 NW 9th St Chisholm MN 55719 Office: 2351 Rayburn House Office Bldg Washington DC 20515*

OBEY, DAVID ROSS, congressman; b. Okmulgee, Okla., Oct. 3, 1938; s. Orville John and Mary Jane (Chellis) O.; B.S. in Polit. Sci., U. Wis., 1960, M.A., 1962; m. Joan Therese Lepinski, June 9, 1962; children—Craig David, Douglas David. Mem. Wis. Assembly from Marathon County, 1963-69, asst. minority leader, 1967-69; mem. 91st-97th Congresses from 7th Dist. Wis., mem. Democratic steering com., vice chmn. house Dem. study group, mem. appropriations com., house budget com., subcoms. on labor, HEW and fgn. ops., chmn. commn. adminstrv. rev. Mem. adminstrv. com. Wis. Democratic Party, 1960-62. Named Edn. Legislator of Year rural div. NEA, 1968; recipient Legis. Leadership award Eagelton Inst. Politics, 1964. Home: 831 Dunbar St Wausau WI 54401 Office: 2230 Rayburn House Office Bldg Washington DC 20515*

OBLINGER, JOSEPHINE KNEIDL HARRINGTON (MRS. WALTER L. OBLINGER), state legislator; b. Chgo., Feb. 14, 1913; d. Thomas William and Margaret (Kneidl) Harrington; B.S., U. Ill., 1933; J.D., U. Detroit, 1968; L.H.D., Sioux Empire Coll., 1966; m. Walter L. Oblinger, Apr. 27, 1940; 1 son, Carl D. Tchr. Lanphier High Sch., Springfield, Ill., 1951-62; clk. Sangamon County, assessor Capital Twp., Springfield, 1962-69; asst. dir. Ill. Dept. Registration and Edn., Springfield, 1970—; exec. dir. Gov.'s Com. on Voluntary Action, 1970-73; asst. to pres. Lincoln Land Community Coll., 1973-77; dir. Ill. Dept. on Aging, 1977-78; mem. Ill. Ho. Reps., 1978—. Sec. Springfield and Sangamon County Community Action, 1965-70 pres., 1970-74; mem. finance com. Child and Family Service, Springfield, 1965-70; mem. Nat. Com. for Day Care of Children, 1960—; pres. Springfield Fedn. Tchrs. AFL-CIO, 1957-59, Ill. Fedn. Tchrs. AFL-CIO, 1959-63; mem. adv. com. to Gov.'s ACTION Office; mem. Planning Consortium for Services to Children in Ill., pres., 1978-79; chmn. mothers' march Sangamon County March of Dimes, 1980. Officer, Repulican Women's Luncheon Club, 1959—, pres., 1963-67; chmn. Sangamon County Rep. com., 1965—; pres. Ill. Fedn. Rep. Women. Del. to White House Conf., 1960. Bd. dirs., pres. Sangamon-Menard County Council on Alcoholism and Drugs, Nat. Center Vol. Action; mem. bd. Sangamon County Salvation Army, Ret. Sr. Vol. Program. Mem. Ill. Assn. County Clks. and Recorders (pres.), Am. Bus. Women's Assn., Am., Ill., Sangamon County bar assns., Am. Assn. Vol. Services Coordinators (dir., chmn. pub. policy com.), N.A.A.C.P. (exec. bd.), Urban League, Am. Arbitration Assn., U. Ill. Alumni Assn., Nat. Assn. Counties, Nat. Assn. Recorders and Clks., Sangamon County Hist. Soc., Ill. Council Continuing Edn. (exec. com.), P.E.O., Kappa Delta Pi, Sigma Delta Pi, Delta Delta Delta. Clubs: Springfield Women's; Altrusa (pres. 1968-70, dir.) (Springfield). Home: Rural Route 1 Sherman IL 62684 Office: Room 1129 Stratton Office Bldg Springfield IL 62706

O'BRIEN, CHARLES RICHARD, JR., educator; b. Boston, Nov. 10, 1934; s. Charles R. and Dorothy Margaret (DeBesse) O'B.; B.A., St. John's U., Boston, 1956; M.S., N.D. State U., 1968; Ed.D., U. Wyo., 1972. Dir. religious edn., Framingham, Mass., 1963-66; dir. of guidance Cardinal Muench Sem., Fargo, N.D., 1966-69; asst. prof. edn. N.D. State U., Fargo, 1969-73; asso. prof. counselor edn. Western Ill. U., Macomb, 1974—, dir. Univ. Counseling Center, 1978—; pastoral adviser Norfolk County (Mass.) Hosp., 1960-63, Waltham (Mass.) Hosp., 1973-74; guidance cons. Diocese of Fargo, 1966-73, Newman Found., Ill., 1974; vis. lectr. Fitchburg State Coll., Fitchburg, Mass., 1973-74; research cons. Office of Employment Security, N.D., 1972-72; cons. Ill. Office Edn., 1976, 77; lectr. profl. and community orgns. Recipient cert. of recognition Ill. Guidance and Personnel Assn., 1977, Presdl. Merit award Western Ill. U., 1978. Mem. Am., Midwestern psychol. assns., Am. Coll. Personnel Assn., Am. Personnel and Guidance Assn. (cons. European br. 1977), Phi Delta Kappa, Phi Kappa Phi, Kappa Delta Pi. Roman Catholic. Contbr. numerous articles on counseling to profl. Jours.; editorial bd. Counseling and Values. Home: 1334 Parkview Dr Macomb IL 61455 Office: 127 Sherman Hall Western Illinois Univ Macomb IL 61455

O'BRIEN, DENNIS ERROL, pharmacist; b. Blue Island, Ill., May 25, 1948; s. Earl E. and Dorthy H. (Rusnak) O'B.; B.S. in Pharmacy, U. Toledo, 1974; student Kent State U., 1966-69; m. Barbara Ann McCormick, July 1, 1972; children—Michael Dennis, Lisa Marie. Pharmacist, Gray Drug Co., Toledo (Ohio) area, 1974, DePaul Pharmacy, Strongsville, Ohio, 1974-75, mgr., 1974-75; pharmacist-mgr. Shaker Square Pharmacy, Shaker Heights, Ohio, 1975-76, Mannino Leader Pharmacy, Mentor, Ohio, 1976-81, Speice Drug, Chagrin Falls, Ohio, 1981—; dir. Ohio Pharmacy Polit. Action Com. Cert. surg. appliance fitter. Mem. Nat. Assn. Retail Druggists (consumer relation com.), Ohio State Pharm. Assn. (dir. 1979-81), Northeastern Ohio Acad. Pharmacy (pres. 1978-79), Am. Pharm. Assn., U.S. Jaycees, Ohio Jaycees, Phi Kappa Tau (pres. 1968-69). Republican. Lutheran. Columnist Ask Your Pharmacist, News Herald, 1971—. Office: 31 N Main St Chagrin Falls OH 44022

O'BRIEN, ELMER JOHN, educator, librarian; b. Kemmerer, Wyo., Apr. 8, 1932; s. Ernest and Emily Catherine (Reinhart) O'B.; A.B., Birmingham So. Coll., 1954; Th.M., Iliff Sch. Theology, 1957; M.A., U. Denver, 1961; m. Betty Alice Peterson, July 2, 1966. Ordained to ministry Methodist Ch., 1957; pastor Meth. Ch., Pagosa Springs, Colo., 1957-60; circulation-reference librarian Boston U. Sch. Theology, Boston, 1961-65; asst. librarian Garrett-Evang. Theol. Sem., Evanston, Ill., 1965-69; librarian, prof. United Theol. Sem., Dayton, Ohio, 1969—. Abstractor, Am. Bibliog. Center, 1969-73. Mem. Am. Theol. Library Assn. (head bur. personnel and placement 1969-73, dir. 1973-76, v.p. 1977-78, pres. 1978-79), AAUP, Delta Sigma Phi, Omicron Delta Kappa, Eta Sigma Phi, Kappa Phi Kappa. Club: Torch International. Author: Bibliography of Festschriften in Religion Published Since 1960, 1972. Home: 7818 Lockport Blvd Centerville OH 45459

O'BRIEN, GEORGE MILLER, congressman; b. Chgo., June 17, 1917; s. Matthew J. and Isabel (Hyde) O'B.; A.B., Northwestern U., 1939; J.D., Yale U., 1947; m. Mary Lou Peyla, Sept. 6, 1947; children—Caryl Isabel O'Brien Bloch, Mary Deborah O'Brien Treadwell. Admitted to Ill. bar, 1947; sr. partner O'Brien & Garrison, Joliet, 1966—; mem. 93d-97th Congresses from 17th Dist. Ill., mem. appropriations com. Chmn., Will County chpt. ARC, 1957-58; pres. Joliet-Will County Community Chest Program; mem. Will County Bd. Suprs., 1956-64; mem. Legis. Adv. Com. to Northeastern Ill. Planning Commn., 1971-72; mem. Ill. Ho. of Reps., 1970-72, mem. exec. and judiciary II coms. Served to lt. col. USAAF, 1941-45. Recipient Distinguished Service award Joliet Boys' Club. Mem. Am., Ill., Chgo., Will County bar assns., Trial Lawyers Assn. Ill., Am. Legion, VFW, Phi Beta Kappa. Roman Catholic. Clubs: Elks, Rotary, Union League (Chgo.). Office: 2439 Rayburn House Office Bldg Washington DC 20515

O'BRIEN, JEAN VIVIAN, sch. adminstr.; b. Chgo., Oct. 5, 1920; d. John and Emanuella (DeStefano) Pellettieri; B.E., Chgo. Tchrs. Coll., 1942; M.A., Northwestern U., 1947; M.S., Chgo. State U., 1971; m. John Joseph O'Brien; Nov. 21, 1944; children—Jill Louise, Judith Ann, John David. With Chgo. Bd. Edn., 1952-80, coordinator instructional services Dist. 5 Office, 1976-80; prin. St. James Elem. Sch. Catholic Archdiocese of Chgo., 1980—; lectr. Chgo. State U., 1971-76; writer, cons. in field. NSF grantee, 1947-48; recipient Juliette Low award Girl Scouts U.S.A., 1958; Com. Dedicated Tchr. award, 1971; Educator of Yr. award Phi Delta Kappa, 1980. Mem. Chgo. Reading Assn. (pres. 1965-67), Adjustments Tchrs. Council (pres. 1970), PTA, Assn. Supervision and Curriculum Devel., Nat. Assn. Elem. Sch. Prins., Archdiocesan Prins. Assn., Nat. Sci. Tchrs. Assn., Delta Kappa Gamma. Office: 140 North Ave Highwood IL 60040

O'BRIEN, MICHAEL VINCENT, environ. engr.; b. Chgo., Aug. 22, 1946; s. Vincent F. and Bernice Ann (Coffey) O'B.; B.A., U. Puget Sound, 1970; M.P.H., U. Minn., 1975, M.A., Hubert H. Humphrey Inst. Public Affairs, U. Minn., 1977; m. Marsha L. Mills, Sept. 14, 1974; children—Erin Moire, Michael Vincent. Pollution control insp. City of Mpls., 1971-73; teaching asst. extension div. U. Minn., Mpls., 1976; research asst. Environ. Quality Council, State of Minn., Mpls., 1976; environ. specialist environ. and safety dept. United Power Assn., Elk River, Minn., 1977, environ. engr., 1978, supr. permits and monitoring, lands div., 1978—; chmn. transmission task force Minn./Wis. Power Suppliers Group, 1980—. Pres. recreation bd. City of Elk River, 1980—. EPA fellow, 1973-75. Mem. Air Pollution Control Assn. (v.p. Upper Midwest sect. 1981). Contbr. articles on environ. pollution control to tech. publs. Home: 821 Gates St Elk River MN 55330 Office: United Power Assn Elk River MN 55330

O'BRIEN, PATRICK MICHAEL, library adminstr.; b. Newport, R.I., Mar. 17, 1943; s. Joseph Xavier and Loretta C. (DeCotis) O'B.; B.A. in English Literature, Merrimack Coll., North Andover, Mass., 1964; M.L.S., U. R.I., 1965; m. Roberta Jean Luther, Nov. 27, 1977; children—Megan MacRae, Brendan Watters. Chief of reference Newsweek Mag. Editorial Library, 1965-72; asst. dir. research FIND/SVP-The Info. Clearing House, N.Y.C., 1973-74; chief bus. and industry div. Chgo. Public Library, 1975, asst. commr. central library and cultural center, 1975-79; dir. Cuyahoga County (Ohio) Public Library, Cleve., 1979—; mem. hist. archives com. of clk. Circuit Ct. of Cook County, Ill., 1977-78; chmn. cooperative collection devel. com. Ill. State Library, 1976-78; bd. examiners City Service Commn. of Milw., Milw. Public Library; mem. Depository Library Council to Public Printer, 1977-79; pres. bd. dirs. Cleve. Area Met. Library System, 1980-82. Participant, Leadership Cleve. Program, 1981. Mem. ALA (dir. reference and adult services div. 1978—, pres. public libraries systems sect. 1981), Am. Soc. Info. Sci., Ohio Library Assn., Spl. Libraries Assn., Am. Mgmt. Assn. Club: Chgo. Athletic Assn. Contbr. articles in field. Office: 4510 Memphis Ave Cleveland OH 44144

O'BRIEN, VIRGINIA LEE HUNT, occupational therapist; b. Fort Worth, Jan. 27, 1954; d. Foster Samuel and Beverly Ann (Thornhill) Hunt; B.S. in Occupational Therapy with Distinction, U. Wis., 1976; m. William Dennis O'Brien, June 17, 1978; 1 dau., Katherine Maureen. Head occupational therapy dept. North Tex. Easter Seal Rehab. Center, Wichita Falls, Tex., 1977-78; program coordinator phys. disabilities occupational therapy dept. Madison (Wis.) Gen. Hosp., 1978-79; head dept. occupational therapy dept. Southview Acres Health Care Center, St. Paul, Minn., 1979-81; student coordinator St. Croix Therapy, Inc., Edina, Minn., 1981—. Asso. student leader Campus Life, East Madison, Wis., 1971-72; student campus dir. Bapt. Student Union, Univ. Wis., Madison, 1973-76. Recipient Scholarship, Madison Tchrs. Assn., 1972. Mem. Am. Occupational Therapy Assn., Minn. Occupational Therapy Assn. Democrat. Baptist. Home: 1949 Wilson Ave #105 Saint Paul MN 55119 Office: 7400 Metro Blvd Edina MN 55435

OBRZUT, FLORENCE THERESE, nurse; b. Chgo., Feb. 23, 1921; d. Charles and Sophie (Pierzchalski) Kuzminski; student Loyola U., Chgo., 1943-45, 48-49, 59-60, U. Ill., 1973, Chgo. City Coll., 1957-58; R.N., South Chicago Hosp., 1947; B.S., St. Mary-of-the-Woods Coll., 1977; m. Adam Joseph Obrzut, Oct. 4, 1958; children—Maribeth, Susan. Machine operator Cuneo Press, 1941, Stone Container, 1941-42; clk. U.S. Steel Co., 1943-44; head nurse emergency dept. South Chicago Community Hosp., Chgo., 1947—. Registered nurse, Ill., Ind. Mem. ARC Nurses Alumnae, Emergency Dept. Nurses Assn., VFW Ladies Aux. Republican. Roman Catholic. Home: 9530 Marigold Ln Munster IN 46321 Office: 2320 E 93d St Chicago IL 60617

OBST, GEORGE JAY, med./dental employment and office services exec.; b. Bklyn., Mar. 21, 1939; s. Joseph Jay and Pearl Louise (Newmark) O.; B.A., Alfred U., 1960; M.S., L.I. U., 1963; m. Carol Adler, June 24, 1961; children—Amy, Pamela, Matthew. Social investigator N.Y.C. Dept. Welfare, 1960-62; asst. v.p. Chem. Bank, N.Y.C., 1962-70; v.p. ops. Heritage Dental Labs. div. Sybron Corp., Romulus, Mich., 1970-79; pres. Dental Lab. div., Codesco Inc., Phila., 1979-80, Met. Med. Placement, Mpls., 1980—. Served with U.S. Army, 1961-62. Home: 6936 Moccasin Valley Rd Edina MN 55435 Office: 7250 France Ave S Edina MN 55435

OCASEK, OLIVER ROBERT, state legislator; b. Bedford, Ohio, Nov. 2, 1925; s. Jack Barney and Olive (Drabek) O.; B.S., Kent State U., 1946, M.A., 1951, LL.D., 1975; LL.D., Ohio Coll. Podiatric Medicine, 1977; Litt. D. (hon.), U. Akron, 1978; D.Public Service (hon.), Rio Grande Coll., 1979; m. Virginia Mae Hejduk, June 18, 1955. Tchr. public schs., Summit County, Ohio, 1946-51, prin., 1951-60; prof. edn. U. Akron, 1960-79, prof. emeritus, 1979—; mem. Ohio Senate, 1958—, pres. pro tem., 1975-78, pres., 1979-81; nat. vice chmn. Council State Govts., 1979-80. Pres. bd. trustees Akron YMCA, 1974-75; chmn. Ohio YMCA Youth in Govt.; mem. exec. com. Goodwill Industries Summit County; elder Northfield (Ohio) Presbyterian Ch., 1958-79; trustee Sagamore Hills Twp. (Ohio), 1949-60. Recipient Disting. Service awards Assembly Govt. Employees, 1976, NEA, 1975, Ohio Edn. Assn., 1971, Ohio Assn. Public Sch. Employees, 1974, others. Mem. Council State Govts., Nat. Conf. State Legislators. Democrat. Club: Masons. Office: Ohio Senate Statehouse Columbus OH 43215

OCEPEK, ANTHONY STEVEN, broadcasting exec.; b. Barberton, O., Aug. 3, 1938; s. Anthony and Josephine Helen (Jastraub) O.; B.S., Kent State U., 1960; m. Margaret Benes; children—Beth, Mark, Paul. With Westinghouse Broadcasting Co. KYW-TV, Cleve. and Phila., NBC-WKYC-TV, Cleve.; pres. WPVL, Painesville, O., 1970—; pres. Capital Communications, Inc.; v.p. WHOK, Inc.; dir. Lake County Nat. Bank. Bd. dirs. Lake County Hist. Soc., Holden Arboretum, Lake County Devel. Council. Mem. Nat., Ohio assns. broadcasters, Painesville Area C. of C. (dir.). Rotarian. Home: 9045 Baldwin Rd Kirtland Hills OH 44060 Office: 1 Radio Pl Painesville OH 44077

OCHBERG, FRANK MARTIN, clinician-exec., psychiatrist; b. N.Y.C., Feb. 7, 1940; s. Gerald and Belle (Solomon) O.; A.B., Harvard U., 1961; M.D., Johns Hopkins U., 1965; postgrad. Stanford U., 1966-69; m. Lynn J. Wescott, July 1, 1962; children—Billie Jennifer, Jesse Frank, Abigail Kathryn. Intern, USPHS Hosp., San Francisco, 1965-66; resident in psychiatry Stanford U. Med. Center, 1966-69; Asst. to dir. NIMH, Bethesda, Md., 1969-71; asso. regional health dir. HEW, San Francisco, 1971-73; dir. mental health services div. NIMH, 1973-76, asso. dir. NIMH, 1977-79; cons. New Scotland Yard, London, 1976-77; dir. Mich. Dept. Mental Health, Lansing, 1979-81; med. dir. St. Lawrence Mental Health, 1981—; practice medicine specializing in psychiatry, Lansing, 1981—; clin. prof. Mich. State U.; cons. FBI; adv. U.S. Secret Service; pres. Victimization and Tng. Inst. Served with USPHS, 1966-81. Recipient commendation FBI, Scotland Yard, Am. Psychiat. Assn. Fellow Am. Psychiat. Assn. (chmn. council nat. affairs 1978, mem. com. on women); mem. Assn. Research in Nervous and Mental Disease (v.p. 1972), Nat. Com. Patients Rights (founding). Co-editor: Violence and the Struggle for Existence, 1970; Victims of Terrorism, 1982. Office: 1201 W Oakland Lansing MI 48915

O'CONNELL, LAURENCE JOSEPH, theologian, educator; b. Chgo., May 12, 1945; s. Joseph John and Eleanor Margaret (Coleman) O'C.; B.A., St. Mary's Coll., 1963; M.A., U. Louvain, 1970, S.T.B., 1970, S.T.L., 1972, Ph.D. in Religious Studies, 1976, S.T.D. in Theology, 1976; m. Angela Marion Schneider, Sept. 5, 1970; 1 son, Coleman Brian. Asst. to dir. systematic theology U. Louvain, 1974-76; asst. prof. theol. studies St. Louis U., 1976-79, dir. corp. ministry program, 1976-79, asso. prof. theol. studies, 1979—, acting chmn. dept., 1977-79, chmn. dept., 1979—. Mem. Assn. Clin. Pastoral Edn. (bd. dirs.), Assn. Supervision and Curriculum Devel., Soc. Advancement in Edn. for Ministry, Assn. Theol. Field Educators, Am. Acad. Religion, Coll. Theology Soc., Cath. Theol. Soc. Am., Nat. Assn. Cath. Chaplains. Roman Catholic. Office: 3634 Lindell Blvd Saint Louis MO 63108

O'CONNELL, WILLIAM JAMES, mil. officer; b. Chico, Calif., Aug. 15, 1950; s. Glen Wayne and Helen Viola (York) McCord; A.A., Butte Jr. Coll., Durham, Calif., 1968-70; B.A., Calif. State U., 1974; postgrad. U. Nebr.; m. Cheryl Lin Morrow, Mar. 10, 1979. Commd. 2d. lt. U.S. Marine Corps, 1974, advanced through grades to capt., 1979; student Naval Flight Officer Sch., Pensacola, Fla., 1975, Air Def. Sch., 29 Palms, Calif., 1977; sr. air dir. Marine Air Control SQ-7, Camp Pendleton, Calif., 1978-79; student Weapons & Tactics Sch., Marine Corps Air Sta., Yuma, Ariz., 1979; tactical air ops. officer Marine Air Control SQ-4, Futenma Okinawa, Japan, 1979-80, marine officer instr. NROTC Unit, U. Nebr., Lincoln, 1980—. Decorated Nat. Def. medal, Sea Service ribbon. Mem. Am. Legion, Ind. Order of Foresters. Republican. Home: 3305 N 63rd St Lincoln NE 68507 Office: NROTC Unit U Nebr Lincoln NE 68588

O'CONNOR, JAMES JOHN, utility exec.; b. Chgo., Mar. 15, 1937; s. Fred James and Helen Elizabeth (Reilly) O'C.; B.S., Holy Cross Coll., 1958; M.B.A, Harvard U., 1960; J.D., Georgetown U., 1963; m. Ellen Louise Lawlor, Nov. 24, 1960; children—Fred, John, James, Helen Elizabeth. Admitted to Ill. bar, 1963; with Commonwealth Edison Co., Chgo., 1963—, asst. to chmn. exec. com., 1964-65, comml. mgr., 1966, asst. v.p., 1967-70, v.p., 1970-73, exec. v.p., 1973-77, pres., 1977—, chmn., 1980—; dir. Borg-Warner Corp., Esmark, Talman Home Fed. Savs. & Loan Assn., Bell & Howell Co. Civilian aide to sec. Army for Ill., 1978-80; bd. dirs. Chgo. unit Am. Cancer Soc., chmn. bd., 1971-73; bd. dirs. Chgo. Boys' Clubs, v.p., 1970—; bd. dirs. Leadership Council for Met. Open Communities, v.p., 1976—; bd. dirs. Lyric Opera Chgo., Spl. Children's Charities, Arthritis Found., Cath. Charities Chgo., Reading is Fundamental; trustee Adler Planetarium, Children's Home and Aid Soc. of Ill., Michael Reese Med. Center, Field Mus., Northwestern U., Mus. Sci. and Industry, St. Xavier Coll.; past chmn. bd. Chgo. Conv. and Tourism Bur.; bd. dirs., chmn. Chgo. Urban League; trustee Coll. Holy Cross; mem. exec. bd. Boy Scouts Am.; v.p. adv. bd. Mercy Hosp.; chmn. bd. Citizenship Council Met. Chgo.; mem. citizens bd. U. Chgo.; exec. v.p. Hundred Club Chgo.; bd. govs. Chgo. Heart Assn. Served with USAF, 1960-63. Named One of Chgo.'s 10 Outstanding Young Men, Chgo. Jr. Assn. Commerce and Industry, 1970. Mem. Am., Ill., Chgo. bar assns., Chgo. Assn. Commerce and Industry (dir.), Assos. Harvard U. Grad. Sch. Bus. Adminstrn. Roman Catholic. Clubs: Comml., Econ., Chgo., Chgo. Commonwealth, Met. (Chgo.). Home: 9549 Monticello Ave Evanston IL 60203 Office: PO Box 767 One First Nat Plaza Chicago IL 60690

O'CONNOR, JOHN JOSEPH, automotive mfg. co. exec.; b. Springfield, Mass., June 21, 1937; s. Patrick Joseph and Marguerite Lillian (Costello) O'C.; B.S. in Bus. Adminstrn., Kent (Ohio) State U., 1960; postgrad. U. Akron (Ohio), 1963; m. Carol Jean Cressman, June 13, 1959; children—Colleen Theresa, Shaun Michael. Prodn. supr. Goodyear Tire & Rubber Co., Akron, 1958-60; with indsl. relations dept. Ford Motor Co., Canton, Ohio, 1960-67, mgr. indsl. relations, Canton, 1969-71, Indpls., 1971—, mem. community relations com., 1969—; indsl. relations research analyst, labor relations staff Ford World Hdqrs., 1967-69; dir., mem. exec. com. Mut. Med. Ins., Inc. (Blue Shield of Ind.), 1973—; Mem. personnel adv. com. City of Carmel, Ind., 1977—; active 500 Festival Assos. Designated Sagamore of Wabash, Gov. Ind., 1976. Mem. Am. Soc. for Personnel Adminstrn. (accredited), Ind. Mfrs. Assn., Ind. C. of C. (personnel and labor relations com., workmans compensation com.), Ind. Soc. of Chgo., Indpls. Personnel Assn., Ind. Personnel Assn. Republican. Roman Catholic. Clubs: Highland Golf and Country (Indpls.); Carmel Racquet. Home: 13 Rolling Springs Ct Carmel IN 46032 Office: 6900 Enblish Ave Indianapolis IN 46206

O'CONNOR, LAWRENCE MICHAEL, health care fin. exec.; b. Indpls., Jan. 8, 1942; s. Thomas F. and Joan Mary (Szawatkowski) O'C.; student U. Md., 1960, Long Beach City Coll., 1962; A.S., U. Cin., 1972; m. Nancy Lee Jeffryes, Jan. 16, 1965; children—Kelley Michelle, Sean Michael. Mgr. customer service P.R. Mallory, Indpls., 1963; mgr. consumer loan Midland Co., Indpls., 1964; mgr. consumer loan Welfare Finance, Cin., 1965-69; mgr. credit card dept. Fifth/Third Bank, Cin., 1969-71; mgr. patient accounts Providence Hosp., Cin., 1971-73; reimbursement specialist Gen. Hosp., Cin., 1973-75; mgr. patient accounts St. Francis-St. George Hosp., Inc., Cin., 1975—; fin. cons., broker, 1978—. Served with USMC, 1959-63. Mem. S.W. Ohio Hosp. Fin. Mgmt. Assn. (dir.). Republican. Roman Catholic. Home: 435 Hillbrook Dr Cincinnati OH 45238 Office: 1860 Queen City Ave Cincinnati OH 45214

O'CONNOR, MARGARET ANNE, oil co. advt. ofcl.; b. Springfield, Mass., Jan. 27, 1953; d. John Francis and Francine Marie (Provost) O'C.; B.A., Webster Coll., 1976; postgrad. U. Mo., 1981—. Advt. coordinator Guth Lighting, St. Louis, 1978-79; asst. mgr. mailroom, print shop and publs. depts. Clayton Brokerage, St. Louis, 1979-80; advt. coordinator Site Oil Co., Clayton, Mo., 1980—; sec. St. Louis Psychotherapy Inst. tng. seminars, 1979-80. Office: 50 S Bemiston St Clayton MO 63105

O'CONNOR, MICHAEL JOSEPH, state senator; b. Sioux Falls, S.D., Dec. 15, 1928; s. Michael Joseph and Hazel Theresa (Lundquist) O'C.; student U. S.D., 1948-49; B.A., Augustana Coll., 1951; m. Barbara May Brown, 1950; children—Deborah Ann, Michael Joseph II, Theresa Louise, Mary Catherince. Dir. Sioux Empire State Fair, 1964—; pres. O'Connor Prodns, Inc.; mem. S.D. Ho. of Reps., 1971-72, S.D. Senate, 1973-78, 81—. Precinct chmn. Democratic party, 1969-70; pres. Dem. Forum, 1969-70; state chmn. adv. bd. SBA. Served with USMC, 1946-48, USMCR, 1948-51. Recipient Disting. Service award Jaycees, 1960; Outstanding Layman's award S.D. Chiropractors Assn., 1974. Mem. S.D. Comml. Printers Assn., S.D. C. of C. Baptist. Club: Tastmasters. Office: State Legislator State Capitol Pierre SD 57501*

O'CONNOR, NANCY JEANNE, nurse; b. Omaha, Aug. 19, 1951; d. Steve and Regina May (Van Buren) Hoody; B.S. in Nursing, Creighton U., Omaha, 1973; postgrad. U. Minn., 1977-78; m. Timothy Edward O'Connor, Dec. 22, 1973. Orthopedic staff nurse A. Bergan Mercy Hosp., Omaha, 1973-74; instr. med-surg. nursing Creighton U. Nursing Coll., 1974-75; ICU-CCU nurse Fairview Hosp., Mpls., 1975-76; dir. nurses Shriners Hosp., Mpls., 1976—; speaker in field. Devel. fund coordinator Creighton U., 1973. Mem. Am. Nurses Assn., Minn. Nurses Assn. (dist. legis. liason 1975-76, 79-80), Nebr. Nurses Assn. Roman Catholic. Office: 2025 E River Rd Minneapolis MN 55414

O'CONNOR, SARA ANDREWS, theater exec.; b. Syracuse, N.Y., Apr. 5, 1932; d. Harlan Francis and Ethel (Hoyt) Andrews; m. Boardman O'Connor, Aug. 26, 1955 (div. 1969); children—Ian, Douglas; B.A. with high honors, Swarthmore Coll., 1954; M.A. in Drama, Tufts U., 1955. Asso. producer Co. of the Four, 1959-65; asso. producer Theatre Co. of Boston, 1965-68, producer, 1969-71; pub. relations dir. Repertory Theatre, New Orleans, 1968-69; gen. mgr. Cherry County Playhouse, summer, 1970; mng. dir. Cin. Playhouse, 1971-74, Milw. Repertory Theater, 1974—; v.p. League Resident Theatres; pres., bd. dirs. Theatre Communications Group; bd. dirs. Theatre X, Internat. Theatre Inst.; cons. Found. for Extension and Devel. Am. Profl. Theatre; mem. theater policy panel Nat. Endowment for Arts. Mem. Actors Equity Assn., Wis. Theatre Assn. Office: 929 N Water St Milwaukee WI 53202

O'DELL, FREDERICK CHARLES, JR., surgeon; b. Bad Axe, Mich., Sept. 23, 1924; s. Frederick Charles and Charlotte (Herrington) O.; A.B., U. Mich., 1946, M.D., 1949; m. Deborah Lincoln, Oct. 29, 1955; children—Winnifred Charlotte, Catherine Hobbs, Mary Lincoln. Intern U. Mich. Hosp., 1949-50, resident 1949-55; registrar in surgery St. Bartholomews Hosp., London, 1955-56; practice medicine specializing in surgery, Alpena, Mich., 1956—; mem. staff Alpena Gen. Hosp. Pres. Alpena Community Concert Assn., 1976—; trustee Alpena Community Found., 1974—. Served with USN, 1951-53. Mem. AMA, Midwest Surg. Assn., ACS, Frederick A. Coller Sur. Soc. Episcopalian. Home: 445 Island View Dr Alpena MI 49707 Office: 615 W Chisholm St Alpena MI 49707

O'DELL, LYNN MARIE LUEGGE (MRS. NORMAN D. O'DELL), librarian; b. Berwyn, Ill., Feb. 24, 1938; d. George Emil and Helen Marie (Pesek) Luegge; student Lyons Twp. Jr. Coll., La Grange, Ill., 1957; student No. Ill. U., Elgin Community Coll., U. Ill., Coll. of DuPage; m. Norman D. O'Dell, Dec. 14, 1957; children—Jeffrey, Jerry. Sec., Martin Co., Chgo., 1957-59; librarian Carol Stream (Ill.) Pub. Library, 1964—; exec. com. Du Page County Library System, 1967, 68, 71—. Active Carol Stream unit Central DuPage Hosp. Aux. Named Woman of Year, Wheaton Bus. and Profl. Woman's Club, 1968. Mem. ALA, Carol Stream Hist. Soc. (v.p.), Library Adminstrs.' Conf. No. Ill. Club: Carol Stream Woman's (sec. 1968, 1st v.p. 1969). Lutheran (organist). Home: 182 Yuma Ln Carol Stream IL 60187 Office: 616 Hiawatha Dr Carol Stream IL 60187

O'DELL, RICHARD FREDERICK, historian; b. Lansing, Mich., Oct. 16, 1914; s. George Maywood and Edna Blanche (Spindler) O'D.; B.A., Mich. State U., 1935; M.A., U. Mich., 1939, Ph.D. in History, 1948; m. Louise Sprau, Jan. 26, 1940; children—Dorothy Louise O'Dell Clore, Richard Frederick. Tchr., Mt. Morris (Mich.) Jr. High Sch., 1939-40, prin. Sr. High Sch., 1940-41; instr. Navy V-12 Program, U. Mich., 1943-46; asso. prof. history Evansville (Ind.) U., 1947-48; asso. prof. history No. Mich. U., Marquette, 1949-52, prof., 1952-74, head dept. history, 1957-63, prof. emeritus, 1975—; pres. Upper Peninsula Child Guidance Clinic, Marquette, 1962-65. Chmn., Upper Peninsula Mental Health Planning Com., 1964-65. Alfred H. Lloyd fellow U. Mich., 1948-49. Mem. Am. Hist. Assn., Hist. Soc. Mich. (trustee 1949-52, v.p. 1951-52), AAUP, Marquette County Hist. Soc. (trustee 1950-78, pres. 1956-59), Phi Kappa Phi, Alpha Phi

Omega. Home: 321 E Hewitt Ave Marquette MI 49855 Office: Dept of History Northern Mich Univ Marquette MI 49855

ODEN, RUMOR LAMAR, ins. co. exec.; b. Sylacauga, Ala., May 29, 1910; s. Lawler and Sally (Horten) O.; A.B., Miles M Coll., 1933; B.A., Wayne State U., 1950; postgrad. U. Mich., 1959-60, Dale Carnegie Human Relations, 1966, Wake Forest U., 1970; m. Mary Lou Jefferson, July 31, 1948; children—William S., LaMaretta. Tchr. public schs., Birmingham, Ala., 1934-35; agt., asst. mgr. Atlanta Life Ins. Co., 1936-42; asst. dir. Gt. Lakes Mut. Life Ins. Co., Detroit, 1942-64; agy. dir., dir. Winston Mut. Life Ins. Co., Winston-Salem, N.C., 1964-73; tng. dir. Chgo. Met. Mut. Assurance Co., 1973—; asst. dean Cosmopolitan C. of C. Free Sch. Bus. Mgmt., Chgo., 1975-78. Bd. dirs. Bethlehem Child Care Center, Winston-Salem, 1965, 73. Mem. Russell Woods Assn. (v.p. 1962-64), Detroit Council Ins. (pres. 1961-63), Nat. Ins. Assn. (v.p. 1972-73, Spl. Agy. Officers award 1978, Spl. Agy. award 1978), Chgo. Ins. Assn. (pres. 1975-78), Detroit Mgmt. Underwriters Assn. Episcopalian. Home: 4850 Lake Park Chicago IL 60615 Office: 5316 W Harrison Chicago IL 60644

O'DILLON, RICHARD HILL, physician; b. Watkinsville, Ga., Dec. 11, 1934; s. Herman Thomas and Elizabeth (Hill) O'D.; B.S., U. Ga., 1956; M.D., Med. Coll. Ga., 1960. Intern, Athens (Ga.) Gen. Hosp., 1960-61; resident Grady Meml. Hosp., Atlanta, 1963; practice medicine, specializing in clin. investigation, Rochester, N.Y., 1964—; asst. med. dir. Strasenburgh Labs., 1964-65, asso. med. dir., 1966; group dir. product devel., dir. clin. research Merrell-Nat. Labs., Cin., 1966-75, group dir. gastrointestinal clin. research, 1975-78; dir. clin. research Duphar Labs., Inc., 1979—. Served as capt. USAF, 1961-62. Mem. AMA, So. Med. Assn., N.Y. Acad. Scis., Am. Acad. Dermatology, Ohio Med. Assn., Acad. Medicine Columbus and Franklin County, Am. Geriatrics Assn., AAAS, Gamma Sigma Epsilon, Phi Eta Sigma, Alpha Epsilon Delta, Delta Phi Alpha. Home: 728 Bluffview Dr Worthington OH 43085 Office: 1080 Kingsmill Pkwy Columbus OH 43229

ODOM, JOANNA BETH, accountant; b. Indpls., May 7, 1949; d. Ralph Harold and Betty Ruth (Marcum) Slaughter; B.S., Ind. U., 1971; M.B.A., Butler U., 1980; m. John Odom, Feb. 23, 1968; children—Cara Rene, Lora Beth. Office mgr. First Holding Corp., Indpls., 1968-74; statistician Firstmark Fin., Indpls., 1974-76; controller Mallory Overseas, Indpls., 1976-79; acct. P.R. Mallory & Co., Mallory Timers Co., Indpls., 1979—; tax adviser, 1973—. Coach girls' softball teams, 1977-78; active ARC, 1965—. Mem. Am. Mgmt. Assn., Nat. Assn. Female Execs., Am. Soc. Profl. and Exec. Women, Nat. Jogging Assn., Mensa. Home: 236 E North St Westfield IN 46074 Office: Mallory Timers Co 3029 E Washington St Indianapolis IN 46206

ODON, ROBERT ARTHUR, automotive co. analyst; b. Cross Plains, Tenn., Aug. 4, 1943; s. Robert Lee and Annie Mai Craft (Walker) O.; A.A., Sinclair Community Coll., 1975; m. May 28, 1968 (div.); children—Robert A., Roxanne A. Stock chaser NCR, 1967; assembly worker Delco Moraine div. Gen. Motors Corp., 1967-70, supr., 1971, tool inspection clk., 1972-78, shipping specialist, 1978, transp. analyst, 1978—. Served with USAF, 1962-67; active Res. Mem. Air Force Sgts. Assn., Am. Legion, Delta Nu Alpha. Democrat. Roman Catholic. Club: Miami Valley Traffic. Office: 1420 Wisconsin Blvd Dayton OH 45401

O'DONNELL, CLETUS FRANCIS, bishop; b. Waukun, Iowa, Aug. 22, 1917; s. Patrick E. and Isabelle A. (Duffy) O'D.; M.A., St. Mary of Lake Sem. (Ill.), 1941; J.C.D., Cath. U. Am., 1945. Ordained priest Roman Cath. Ch., 1941; asst. pastor Our Lady of Lourdes Ch., Chgo., 1941-42; vice chancellor Archdiocese of Chgo., 1947-60, vicar, gen. counsel, 1961; apptd. titular bishop Abrittum, aux. bishop Chgo., 1960; consecrated bishop, 1960; pastor Holy Name Cathedral, Chgo., 1966; bishop Diocese of Madison (Wis.), 1967—. Chmn. Am. Bd. Cath. Missions, 1966—, Nat. Cath. Edn. Assn., 1975—. Recipient C. Albert Koob award Nat. Cath. Edn. Assn., 1978. Address: 15 E Wilson St Madison WI 53711*

O'DONNELL, DAVID RICHARDSON, civil engr.; b. Bishop, Calif., June 2, 1937; s. Herbert Preston and Minerva Elizabeth (Richardson) O.; A.A., Am. River Community Coll., 1959; B.S., U. Idaho, 1961; children—Derek T., Irene Denise. Jr. civil engr. Calif. Dept. Water Resources, Sacramento, 1962-67; hydraulic engr. Pioneer Service & Engring. Co., Chgo., 1969-72; hydraulic structures engr. Harza Engring. Co., Chgo., 1973-75; chief engring. dept. Urban Planning Consultants, Inc., Chgo., 1975-77, Milw. Pollution Abatement Program; now asso. engr. City of Detroit. Served with U.S. Army, 1961-62. Registered profl. engr., Del., Pa., N.J., Ill., Ind., Iowa, Mich. Mem. ASCE, Am. Water Works Assn., Water Pollution Control. Fedn., Nat. Soc. Profl. Engrs. Republican. Home: 111 Cadillac Sq Apt 12 I Detroit MI 48226 Office: 735 Randolph St Detroit MI 48226

O'DONNELL, MARTIN THOMAS, food co. exec.; b. Chgo., Feb. 20, 1937; s. Martin and Barbara (Flaherty) O'D.; B.S., Loyola U., Chgo., 1960; M.B.A., U. Chgo., 1964. Math. tchr. Chgo. pub. schs., 1961-62; bus. analyst Exxon Corp., Baton Rouge, 1964-65; staff analyst sales and fin. depts. Inland Steel Corp., Chgo., 1966-70; diversification analyst G.D. Searle & Co., Skokie, Ill., 1970-74; corp. devel. specialist Libby, McNeill & Libby, Inc., Chgo., 1974, mgr. real estate, 1974-76, asst. to treas., 1976-78, asst. treas., 1978—. Served to lt. U.S. Army, 1960-61. Mem. Chgo. Council Fgn. Relations, Cash Mgmt. Practitioners Assn., Assn. Corp. Growth, Midwest Planning Assn., Planning Execs. Inst., N.Am. Soc. Corp. Planning, Nat. Assn. Corporate Real Estate Execs., Indsl. Devel. Research Council. Roman Catholic. Club: Execs. (Chgo.). Home: 2820 W Chase St Chicago IL 60645 Office: 200 S Michigan Ave Chicago IL 60604

O'DONNELL, THOMAS JAMES, educator; b. Ottawa, Ill., Nov. 7, 1938; s. Thomas Edmund and Margaret (Guilfoyle) O'D.; B.A., U. Notre Dame, 1960; M.A., U. Ill., 1966, Ph.D., 1970; m. Linda Kuhfuss, Jan. 29, 1966; 1 dau., Erin Elizabeth. Teaching asst. U. Ill., 1965-67; asst. prof. English, U. Kans., 1970-76, asso. prof., 1977—. Hurley scholar, 1958-60; NEA grantee, 1977-78. Mem. MLA, AAUP. Democrat. Author: The Confessions of T. E. Lawrence, 1979. Home: Box 126A Rural Route 2 Lawrence KS 66044 Office: U Kans Dept English Wescoe Hall Lawrence KS 66045

O'DOWD, MARY MEL, educator, author; b. Monticello, Wis., June 26, 1917; d. Andrew Martin and Roseanne (Brogan) Dowd; B.A., St. Xavier Coll., 1952; M.A., Cardinal Stritch Coll., Milw., 1961; Ph.D., U. Md., 1973. Tchr., Chgo. and Burlington (Iowa) Parochial Schs., 1938-54; elem. sch. prin., Burlington, 1954-59; tchr. multiply handicapped, Potomac, Md., 1959-62; curriculum specialist Archdiocese of Chgo., 1962-68, edn. dir. Head Start, 1965-68; edn. dir. Capital Head Start, Washington, 1968-71; instr. sci. of human ecology U. Md., 1971-73; asst. prof. Sch. Edn., U. Wis., Milw., 1974-80; contbr. articles to profl. jours.; author: Methodology in Early Childhood Education. Bd. dirs. Marion Nursing Home, Milw. Mem. Soc. Research in Child Devel., Nat. Assn. Childhood Edn., Internat. Assn. Edn. Young Children, Wis. Assn. Infant and Toddler Devel., Mercy Higher Edn. Confs. Roman Catholic. Address: 2924 E Hartford Ave Milwaukee WI 53211

ODVARKA, ROBERT CHARLES, dentist; b. Omaha, Jan. 5, 1926; s. V.L. and Helen (Stenicka) O.; B.S., U. Nebr., 1951, D.D.S., 1953; m. Arlene Mae Fayman, Aug. 16, 1947; children—Sandra Odvarka Weeder, Robert Scott, Scott Brian. Gen. practice dentistry, Clarkson, Nebr., 1953—. Vice pres. Clarkson Bd. Edn., 1961-64. Served with AUS, World War II. Mem. ADA, Acad. Gen. Dentistry, Am. Legion, VFW, Internat. Platform Assn. Republican. Presbyterian. Home: Drawer F 523 Pine St Clarkson NE 68629 Office: Drawer F 244 Pine St Clarkson NE 68629

O'DWYER, JOANNE INEZ, data processing exec.; b. Chgo., Oct. 13, 1936; d. John Adolph and Emmy (Schneckenberger) Bruland; B.A., U. Colo., 1958. Account rep. Royal Globe Ins. Cos., Chgo., 1961-64; with Milw. Gear Co., 1965-72, data processing mgr., 1970-72; partner AIS Computer Services, Milw., 1972-73, Ozauk Computer Services, Grafton, Wis., 1973-75; pres. Moraine Data Services, Inc., Hartford, Wis., 1975—. Mem. Pvt. Industry Council, Washington County, Wis., 1979—; chmn. Washington County Library Planning Com., 1974-78; mem. twp. ad hoc park com. Richfield Twp., 1973-74, mem. crime prevention com., 1975-77; mem. adv. council Trees for Tomorrow Environ. Center, Wis., 1975—, chmn. transp. com., 1979—; charter mem. treas. Friends for Battered Women of Washington County, 1978-79, treas., 1979-80; mem. Boulder (County) Republican Bd., 1957-58; sec. Colo. State Rep. Orgn., 1958; pres. Niles Twp. (Ill.) Young Rep. Orgn., 1960-62; del. Washington County (Wis.) Rep. Orgn., 1980—. Mem. PACE (treas. 1980-81), IBM Small Systems Users Group (charter pres. 1970-72), Honeywell Users Group (pres. 1978-79, dir. 1977—), Data Processing Mgmt. Assn. (chpt. sec. 1977-79, dir. 1977—), Alpha Omicron Pi. Lutheran. Club: Gen. Fedn. of Women's (charter club pres. 1970-71, club pres. 1978-79, dist. conservation div. chmn. 1976—, state corr. sec. 1978-80, state 1st v.p. 1980-81, state pres. 1982—). Home: 3428 Lovers Ln Slinger WI 53086 Office: 51 E Sumner St Hartford WI 53027

OEHMKE, THOMAS HAROLD, publisher, author, lawyer; b. Detroit, Nov. 13, 1947; s. Harold W. and Elizabeth A. (Ryerse) O.; Ph.B., Wayne State U., 1969, J.D., 1973; children—Theodore, Jason. Admitted to Mich. bar, 1973, U.S. Supreme Ct. bar, 1977; tchr. St. Edward Sch., Detroit, 1967-69, Stephenson (Mich.) High Sch., 1969-70; labor relations analyst and tng. dir. Employers Assn. Detroit, 1970-73; lobbyist, urban economist New Detroit, Inc., 1973-79; individual practice law, Detroit, 1973—; dir., pub. Am. Law Research Inst., 1978—. Resource person Gov.'s Commn. on Worker's Disability Compensation, 1974-75; mem. com. Gov.'s Mich. Econ. Action Council, 1975-76; mem. Wayne County Bus. and Comml. Devel. Council, 1975-77, Mayor's Econ. Devel. Planning Adv. Council, 1975-77, Gov.'s State Fair Planning Com., 1977, Mayor's Overall Econ. Devel. Planning Com., 1978—; chmn. Mich. chpt. Ams. Democratic Action, 1979-80. Mem. Assn. Trial Lawyers Am., Nat. Def. Exec. Res., State Bar Mich., Am., Detroit bar assns., Commercial Panel Arbitrators, Am. Arbitration Assn., Detroit Research Assos., Assn. Am. Pubs. Author: Sex Discrimination in Employment; Michigan Incorporation Manual; Michigan Corporation Law, 1982 Supplements; The Civil Litigation Manual; (with others) Mich. Appeals Manual, 2d edit.; editor Mich. Divorce Manual, 3d edit; The Commercial Arbitration Manual. Home: 13548 Tacoma Ave Detroit MI 48205 Office: 517 E Larned Detroit MI 48226

OENES, ERWIN JULIAN, accountant; b. Chgo., Feb. 16, 1929; s. Bert M. and Elsa Helen (Zastrow) O.; B.B.A., U. Wis., 1953; m. Sondra Mae Bird, May 1, 1954; children—Wayne Bruce, Any Sue. Accountant, Ernst & Ernst, Chgo., 1953-56; tax mgr. Trane Co., LaCrosse, Wis., 1956-67; controller Combined Paper Mills, Inc., Combined Locks, Wis., 1967-70; pres., treas. Oenes & Paul, S.C., Appleton, Wis., 1970—; dir., officer M M & T, Inc., others. Served with USAF, 1946-49. C.P.A. Mem. Nat. Assn. Accountants (pres. No. Wis. chpt.), Wis. Inst. C.P.A.'s. Lutheran. Club: Elks. Home: 1305 S Lehmann Ln Appleton WI 54911 Office: 2999 W Spencer St Appleton WI 54911

OESTREICH, KARL LYNN, cons.; b. Two Rivers, Wis., Oct. 7, 1942; s. Karl E. and Sally (Beitzel) O.; B.S., U. Wis., 1965; m. Jeanenne LaMarsh; children—Karl Lynn, Nicole Marie. Systems analyst Firestone Tire & Rubber Co., Akron, 1965-68; prodn. control supr. Baxter Labs., Morton Grove, Ill., 1968-71; gen. prodn. mgr. Intercraft Industries, Chgo., 1971-73; corp. materials mgr. Rust-Oleum Corp., Evanston, Ill., 1973-80; asso. cons. Austin Co., Evanston, Ill., 1980—. Mem. exec. bd. North East Ill. council Boy Scouts Am., 1975—; trustee Village of Morton Grove, 1975-77; Republican precinct capt.; chmn. Morton Grove Police and Fire Com., Morton Grove Traffic and Safety and Civil Def. Com. Cert. practitioner inventory mgmt. Mem. Assn. Protection Adopted Triangle (dir., treas.), Am. Prodn. Inventory Control Soc., Am. Mgmt. Assn., No. Ill. Indsl. Assn. Republican. Home: 7409 Davis St Morton Grove IL 60013 Office: 820 Davis St Evanston IL 60204

OESTREICH, RICHARD PETER, rehab. adminstr.; b. Watertown, Wis., Dec. 12, 1938; s. Ruben John and Frances Mary (Weyland) O.; M.A., Cath. U. Am., 1965; M.A. in Behavioral Disabilities, U. Wis., 1970; m. Mary Anne Roth, Apr. 13, 1968; children—Joseph Richard, Jill April. Rehab. dir. Goodwill Industries of Central Ohio, 1971-74; adminstr. Ohio Rehab. Services Commn., 1974-77; exec. dir. Nat. Rehab. Assn., Washington, 1977-79; rehab. services coordinator Vision Center of Central Ohio, Columbus, 1979—; dir. adv. council Research and Tng. Center, Stout U.; dir. Nat. Industries for the Severely Handicapped. Mem. Nat. Rehab. Assn., Am. Personnel and Guidance Assn., Nat. Rehab. Counseling Assn. Office: 1393 N High St Columbus OH 43201

OFFENBECKER, SUSAN KAYE, nurse; b. Grand Rapids, Mich., Sept. 8, 1948; d. Charles and Lois L. (Steele) Sikkema; L.P.N., Grand Rapids Jr. Coll., 1968; A.D.N. with high distinction, Ferris State Coll., Big Rapids, Mich., 1973; student Nazareth Coll., Kalamazoo, 1978—; m. Adam Lee Offenbecker, Sept. 23, 1975. Practical nurse Grand Rapids Osteo. Hosp., 1967-74, surgery scrub nurse, 1972-73, charge nurse, inservice coordinator, team leader emergency resuscitation team, 1973-74; charge nurse Blodgett Meml. Med. Center, Grand Rapids, 1974-78, head nurse, 1978; dir. emergency care center St. Mary's Hosp., Grand Rapids, 1978—; cons. Emergency Nursing Task Force on Continuing Edn.; cons. Nursing 79, 1979—; nurse rep. West Mich. Critical Care Policy and Rev. Bd.; mem. task force 2 Health and Facilities Commn., Mich. Dept. Public instr. ARC. Cert. emergency nurse. Mem. West Central Mich. Emergency Dept. Nurses Assn. (pres. 1977-82), Mich. Emergency Services Health Council (bd. dirs.), Nat. Assn. Female Execs., Am. Bus. Women's Assn., Kent County Emergency Med. Council (charter, sec. 1981). Methodist. Home: 21 Union St NE Grand Rapids MI 49503 Office: 200 Jefferson St Grand Rapids MI 49503

OFFENHISER, ANDREW BREWSTER, business exec.; b. Palo Alto, Calif., May 28, 1926; s. Paul Lloyd and Edith (Wise) O.; student U. Ill., 1943-44, 1946-47; A.B., Colby Coll., 1949; M.B.A., Stanford U., 1955; m. Helen Louise Forker, Nov. 1, 1952; 1 dau., Nancy Louise. Passenger dept. Burlington R.R., 1950, Pa. R.R., 1951, supr. service Pa. R.R., 1951-53; div. head traffic dept. J.C. Penney Co., N.Y.C., 1956-60; asst. traffic mgr., 1960, civic affairs co-ordinator, pub. relations dept., 1961-64, regional pub. relations co-ordinator, 1964-73, regional pub. relations mgr., 1973-76; with Gen. Growth Mgmt. Corp., Des Moines, 1976-81; exec. cons. Am. City Bur./Beaver Assos., Rosemont Ill., 1981—. Mem. solicitations panel, adv. com. on solicitations Nat. Better Bus. Bur., mem. adv. com. contbns. execs. United Community Funds and Councils Am.; bd. dirs. Des Moines Symphony Assn. Served with USNR, 1944-46. Mem. Am. Retail Fedn. (state orgn. com.), SAR, United Way Am. Corporate Assos., Soc. Mayflower Descs., Sigma Alpha Epsilon. Republican. Episcopalian. Home: 42 N Wise Ave Freeport IL 61032 Office: 9501 W Devon Rosemont IL 60018

OFFERMAN, JAMES MICHAEL, writer, producer; b. Mpls., July 21, 1949; s. Douglas Bernard and Lillian Violet (Johnson) O.; B.A. in Journalism and Mass Communication, U. Minn., 1971, M.A. in Advt. Research, 1973. Video gernalist Hennepin County Gen. Hosp., 1973-74; reporter, editor Twin Cities Courier, 1974-75; mktg. and promotional dir. Centerpiece Records, 1975-77, Variety Artists Internat., 1977; creative dir. BBD & Offerman Advt., Mpls., 1977-78; creative dir. Pickwick Internat., Inc., 1978-81; sr. writer, producer Hoffman-York Advt., Inc., Mpls., 1981—. Winner 3 awards for advt. excellence Nat. Assn. Record Merchandisers; CLIO award finalist. Mem. Advt. Fedn. Minn., Art. Dirs./Copywriters Club Minn. Research on effects of claim substantiation on persuasiveness in advt. Home: 2757 Ewing Ave S Minneapolis MN 55416 Office: Suite 1300 7900 Xerxes Ave S Minneapolis MN 55431

OFFERMANN, GLENN WALTER, librarian; b. Waterloo, Ill., May 20, 1936; s. Armin W. and Luella C. (Dann) O.; B.S., Concordia Tchrs. Coll., 1958; M.A.L.S., U. Chgo., 1965; Ph.D., So. Ill. U., 1977; m. Marilyn C. Wirth, July 19, 1958; children—Brian, Brenda. Prin., tchr. St. Stephen's Lutheran Sch., Atkins, Iowa, 1958-60; librarian Luther High Sch. South, Chgo., 1960-67; head librarian Concordia Coll., St. Paul, 1967—; bd. dirs. Cooperating Libraries in Consortium, St. Paul, 1969—; mem. Council Minn. Acad. Library Dirs., 1975—; trustee J.J. Hill Reference Library, St. Paul, 1976—. Archivist, Minn. South dist. Lutheran Ch.—Mo. Synod, 1975—. Mem. Luth. Edn. Assn., ALA, Minn. Library Assn., Concordia Hist. Inst. Lutheran. Office: Concordia Coll Saint Paul MN 55104

OFFINGER, WALTER EUGENE, JR., assn., exposition and trade show mgmt. co. exec.; b. Zanesville, Ohio, Oct. 6, 1942; s. Walter E. and Margaret O. (Owens) O.; student Muskingum Coll., 1963; B.A. in Business, Denison U., 1964; m. Sarel Duberstein, May 5, 1973; Personnel planning and service mgr. F & R Lazarus Co., Columbus, Ohio, 1964-68; pres., owner Offinger Mgmt. Co., Zanesville, 1968—. Asso. bd. dirs. Bethesda Hosp.; bd. dirs. Zanesville Art Center. Served with USAF, 1964-70. Recipient Nat. Assn. Exposition Mgrs. Certificate of Outstanding Scholastic Achievement in Expn. Professionalism, 1975. Mem. Am. Soc. Assn. Exec., Nat. Assn. Expn. Mgrs., Midwest Toy and Hobby Assn., Ind. Soc. Assn. Execs., Trade Show Bar., Mid-Am. Craft Hobby Assn., Southwestern Craft-Hobby Assn., Columbus Conv. Bur., Ohio Trade Assn., Hobby Industry Am., Nat. Rifle Assn. (life), Am. Forestry Assn. (life), Nat. Audubon Soc. (life), Bass Anglers Sportsmen's Soc. (life), Ducks Unlimited, Nat. Geog. Soc. (life). Republican. Lutheran. Clubs: Masons, Shrine, Rotary, Zanesfield Rod and Gun, Zanesville Country. Home: 475 W Highland Dr Zanesville OH 43701 Office: 1100 Brandywine Blvd PO Box 2188 Zanesville OH 43701

OFFNER, PAUL, state legislator; b. Bennington, Vt., Aug. 7, 1942; s. Richard and Philippa (Gerry) O.; B.A., Amherst Coll., 1964; Ph.D., Princeton U., 1970. Legis. asst. U.S. Senate, 1971-72; mem. Wis. Assembly, Madison, 1974-76, Wis. Senate, 1976—. Democrat. Office: Room 4 S State Capitol Madison WI 53702

OFFUTT, BERCH RANDALL, psychologist; b. Kansas City, Mo., May 20, 1938; s. Frederick Berch and Mae Louise (Hord) O.; B.A., Hamline U., 1961; M.A., U.S. Internat. U., 1972, Ph.D., 1975; m. Rae Lynn Johnson, June 7, 1961; children—Jonathan Berch, Jeffrey Littleton, Elisabeth Jane. Asst. regional dir. N.D. State Hosp., Jamestown, 1973-75; research asso., treas. Dakota Research Assos., Jamestown, 1974-75; counselor Family Counseling Center, Jamestown, 1975; clin. psychologist S.E. Mental Health Center, Fargo, N.D., 1975-76; co-dir. Profl. Assos. for Continuing Edn., Fargo, 1976—; dir. Personal Resource Center, Fargo, 1976—; pvt. practice psychology, Fargo, 1976—; cons. South Valley Spl. Edn. Program, 1976—; adj. prof. N.D. State U., 1977—. Served with USNR, 1962-66. Mem. Am. Psychol. Assn., Assn. for Humanistic Psychology, Assn. for Advancement of Psychology, N.D. Psychol. Assn., Minn. Psychol. Assn. Democrat. United Methodist. Club: Masons. Home: 1026 N 7th St Fargo ND 58102 Office: 205 Professional Bldg 100 S 4th St Fargo ND 58103

OGANOVIC, NICHOLAS JOSEPH, mgmt. and personnel cons., former govt. ofcl.; b. Chisholm, Minn., Dec. 22, 1912; s. Dan and Angeline (Danculovic) O.; B.E., State Tchrs. Coll., St. Cloud, Minn., 1934; M.A., U. Minn., 1940; m. Helen Sperl, Oct. 14, 1948; 1 son, Robert Nicholas. Coordinator-tchr., also asst. prin.-tchr. pub. sch. systems, Brainerd and Lakefield, Minn., 1934-40; personnel officer, regional adminstr. Nat. Youth Adminstrn., St. Paul, 1940-43; with U.S. Civil Service Commn., 1943-71, dir. bur. deptl. operations, 1958-60, dep. exec. dir. commn., 1960-65, exec. dir., 1966-71; prof. adminstrn. Minn. Met. State U., St. Paul, 1971-80; mgmt. and personnel cons., 1981—. Recipient Pub. Personnel award President's Com. Employment Handicapped, 1962, Gold medal commr.'s award Civil Service Commn., 1962, Career Service award Nat. Civil Service League, 1963. Mem. Am. Soc. Pub. Adminstrn., Pub. Personnel Assn., Govt. Coll. Council, Am. Psychol. Assn., Soc. for Advancement Mgmt. Home: 2215 Mitchell Ave St Paul MN 55119

OGDEN, ALVIN CHARLES, ednl. adminstr.; b. Orion, Kans., Feb. 1, 1930; s. Benjamin Harrison and Ethel Naomi O.; B.S., Kans. State U., 1954; M.Ed., U. Kans., 1963; postgrad. U. Ill., 1970-73; m. Ann Porter, May 29, 1954; 1 dau., Karen. Coach, tchr. Lyons (Kans.) Jr. High Sch., 1954-56, Vance Sch., Kansas City, Kans., 1956-58; profl. sales rep. Wm. H. Rorer Pharms., greater Kansas City and Eastern Kans., 1958-60; ter. mgr. Univis, Inc., Kans., Mo., Colo., Nebr.,

1960-62; counselor Leavenworth (Kans.) High Sch., 1962-64; dir. pupil personnel services Bonner Springs (Kans.) High Sch., 1964-67; counselor Lawrence (Kans.) High Sch., 1967-68; dean of students Oak Park-River Forest High Sch., Oak Park, Ill., 1968—. Served with U.S. Army, 1947-49. Mem. Am. Personnel and Guidance Assn., Am. Sch. Counselors Assn., Oak Park-River Forest High Sch. Tchrs. Assn. Episcopalian. Home: 221 N Kenilworth Ave Oak Park IL 60302 Office: 201 N Scoville Oak Park IL 60302

OGDEN, RUSSELL LEE, educator; b. Isabel, Ill., Nov. 10, 1923; s. Clarence Haney O.; B.S., Eastern Ill. U., 1947; M.A., U. No. Colo., 1952, Ed.D., 1964; m. Marianne Johnson, Feb. 9, 1951; children—Sally Jo Ogden Rudolph, James Russell, Suzanne Marie. Tchr., Kansas (Ill.) Community Unit Sch. Dist. No. 3, Kansas High Sch., 1947-55; supr. student tchrs. Eastern Ill. U., Kansas (Ill.) High Sch., 1953-55; asst. prof. dept. bus. Eastern Mich. U., Ypsilanti, 1956-63, asso. prof. Coll. Bus., 1964-67, prof., 1967—, undergrad. academic adviser, 1966-69, freshman and transfer admissions, 1967-69, faculty senator-at-large, 1971-74, del.-at-large faculty council, 1975-77, chmn. com. acting dean coll., Coll. of Bus. rep. to creative teaching com. 1980-81, chmn. accrediting com. dept. home econs., coordinator commencement exercises, fall 1981. Pres. Parent Tchrs. Orgn. Roosevelt Campus Sch., Eastern Mich. U., 1964-65; trustee Ypsilanti Bd. Edn., 1976—, also v.p.; mem. West Jr. High Parent Adv. Group, Ypsilanti, 1965-66; cons. low income counselors dept. housing and urban devel. State of Mich., 1973; cons. Consumer Edn. Council, Ypsilanti, 1973-76, Sci. Research Assos., State of Mich., 1975; exec. advisor com. Ypsilanti High Sch. Choral Program, 1979-80. Served with AUS, 1943-47. Recipient Outstanding Service citation Eastern Mich. U. chpt. Phi Sigma Epsilon, 1974, Outstanding Tchr. Coll. Bus., Eastern Mich. U., 1978. Mem. Nat., Mich. (asst. editor Bull. 1957-58) bus. edn. assns., AAUP (treas. chpt. 1975-77), Phi Delta Kappa, Delta Pi Epsilon, Alpha Kappa Psi (Outstanding Educator in Coll. Bus. 1969-70, 75, Outstanding Educator of Yr. 1978, 25 Year Service citation 1974), Pi Omega Pi, Psi Kappa Alpha. Club: Mich. Schoolmasters (chmn. bus. edn. div. 1958-59) (Ann Arbor). Editorial cons. Introduction to Modern Business (Musselman, Hughes), 1958, Personal Finance Textbook, 1977, 79, Personal Finance Today, 1979, Modern Personal Finance, 1979, Personal Finance, 1981; ednl. cons. Personal Finance, 1979, Personal Finance Today, 1979, Modern Personal Finance, 1979. Home: 1206 Grant St Ypsilanti MI 48197

OGDEN, SYLVESTER ORVILLE, mining co. exec.; b. Paris, Mo., Oct. 29, 1935; s. Lester Hugh and Anastasia (Koziczkowski) O.; A.A., Hannibal LaGrange Coll., 1959; B.S. in Engring., U. Mo., 1961, M.S., 1964; M.B.A., Central Mich. U., 1971; m. Martha Jane Peterman, Feb. 15, 1964; children—Stasia Lynette, John Michael. Mgr. hydrocarbons and energy Dow Chem. Co., Midland, Mich., 1961-72; v.p. Youghiogheny & Ohio Coal Co., Cleve., 1972-76, pres., St. Clairsville, 1978—; v.p. Westmoreland, Coal Co., Colorado Springs, 1976-78; pres. Colo. Westmoreland, Inc., Colorado Springs, 1976-78; dir. Aurora Industries, Inc., Ravencliffs Devel. Co. Colo. del. to White House Conf. on Balanced Nat. Growth and Econ. Devel., 1978. Bd. dirs. Ohio Valley Med. Center. Served with U.S. Army, 1955-57. Recipient Denver Fed. Exec. Bd. award for Achievement in Environ. Protection. Mem. Rocky Mountain Coal Mining Inst., Am. Inst. Chem. Engrs., Nat. Coal Assn., Bituminous Coal Operators Assn., Ohio Mining and Reclamation Assn., Sigma Iota Epsilon. Club: Belmont Hills Country. Home: Route 1 Spaceview Ridge Saint Clairsville OH 43950 Office: PO Box 1000 Saint Clairsville OH 43950

O'GEARY, DENNIS TRAYLOR, contracting and engring. co. exec.; b. Waverly, Va., Feb. 20, 1925; s. King William and Mary Virginia (Traylor) O'G.; surveying degree Tri-State U., 1943; B.S. in Civil Engring., Ill. Inst. of Tech., 1947; m. Alice Stuart Baum, Aug. 3, 1947; children—Dennis Patrick, Mary Alice O'Geary Burton, Elizabeth Christina. Resident engring. trainee Va. Hwy. Dept., Richmond, 1947-50; civil engring. supt. Wiley Jackson Co., Roanoke, Va., 1950-57; engr., asst. estimator, project mgr., v.p. and asst. to area mgr. S.J. Groves & Sons Co., Mpls. and Springfield, Ill., 1957-77, v.p., area mgr., 1978—. Served with USNR, 1943-46. Mem. ASCE, Am. Concrete Inst., Soc. Am. Mil. Engrs., Internat. Oceanographic Found., Cousteau Soc. Methodist. Home: Rural Route 2 Rochester IL 62563 Office: 1104 W Reynolds St Springfield IL 62705

OGILVIE, RICHARD BUELL, lawyer, former gov. Ill.; b. Kansas City, Mo., Feb. 22, 1923; s. Kenneth S. and Edna Mae (Buell) O.; B.A., Yale U., 1947; J.D., LL.D. (hon.), Chgo.-Kent Coll. Law, 1949; LL.D. (hon.), Lincoln Coll., Millikin U., Ill. Wesleyan U., Lake Forest Coll., MacMurray Coll., Greenville Coll.; m. Dorothy Louise Shriver, Feb. 11, 1950; 1 dau., Elizabeth. Admitted to Ill. bar, 1950; practiced in Chgo., 1950-54, 55-58, 61-62, 73—; asst. U.S. atty., Chgo., 1954-55; spl. asst. to U.S. atty. gen., Chgo., 1958-61; sheriff Cook County (Ill.), 1962-66; pres. Bd. Commrs. Cook County, 1966-68; gov. of Ill., 1968-73; partner firm Isham, Lincoln & Beale, 1973—; trustee Milw. R.R., 1979—; dir. CNA Fin. Corp., Jewel Cos., Fansteel Corp., Chgo. Bd. Options Exchange, LaSalle St. Fund, Chgo. Mercantile Exchange. Chmn., Young Republican Orgn. Cook County, 1953-54. Served with AUS, 1942-45. Mem. Am., Ill., Chgo., Fed. bar assns., Phi Alpha Delta, Beta Theta Pi. Presbyterian. Clubs: Masons; Chgo., Glen View, Tavern, Old Elm, Casino, Sangamo. Office: 1 First Nat Plaza Chicago IL 60670

O'HALLORAN, CHARLES, librarian; b. Denver, Dec. 7, 1926; s. Charles and Jane (Parry) O'H.; B.A., U. Colo., 1950; student Western State Coll. Colo., 1953; M.A., U. Denver, 1954; m. Genevieve Miller, July 14, 1952; children—Paul M., Joan C., Hugh J. Tchr., Ft. Morgan, Colo., 1950-52, Denver, 1952-53; asst. reference librarian Kansas City (Mo.) Pub. Library, 1954-56, readers adviser, 1956-59; dir. Rosenberg Pub. Library, Galveston, Tex., 1959-64; state librarian Mo. State Library, Jefferson City, 1964—; interim commr. higher edn. State of Mo., 1976-77. Served with AUS, 1946-47. Mem. Am., Mo. library assns., Rocky Mountain Ry. Club. Contbr. profl. jours. Home: 119 Douglas Dr Jefferson City MO 65101 Office: 308 E High St Jefferson City MO 65101

O'HALLORAN, MICHAEL JAMES, pediatrician; b. Mpls., Jan. 20, 1941; s. Raymond J. and Patricia M. (Friede) O'H.; B.S., John Carroll U., 1963; M.D., Creighton U., 1967; m. Martha Helen Bergan, Aug. 14, 1965; children—Teresa Erin, Patrick Joseph, Peggy Sue. Intern, Good Samaritan Hosp. and Med. Center, Portland, Oreg., 1967-68; resident in pediatrics Good Samaritan Hosp., Phoenix, 1970-72; practice medicine specializing in pediatrics, Eau Claire, Wis., 1972—; mem. staff Midelfort Clinic, 1972—, corp. dir., 1978—; mem. staff Sacred Heart Hosp., Luther Hosp., Eau Claire; med. dir. West Central Wis. Cerebral Palsy Evaluation Clinic. Served as capt. U.S. Army, 1968-70. Diplomate Am. Bd. Pediatrics. Fellow Am. Acad. Pediatrics; mem. Northwestern Pediatric Soc., Irish and Am. Paediatric Soc., AMA (Physicians' Recognition award 1976, 80), State Med. Soc. Wis., Eau Claire-Dunn-Pepin Tri-County Med. Soc. Home: 1312 Cummings Ave Eau Claire WI 54701 Office: 733 W Clairemont Ave Eau Claire WI 54701

O'HALLORAN, RICHARD EUGENE, hosp. exec.; b. Chgo., May 17, 1932; B.A., St. Martin's Coll., Wash., 1954; postgrad. Loyola U., Chgo., 1959; m. Josephine Komenski, Apr. 9, 1955; children—Barbara, Rick, Daniel, Nancy. Plant divisional, corporate personnel dir. Amphenol-Borg, Bunker Ramo Corp., Los Angeles, Wis., Chgo., 1957-69; asst. adminstr. St. Francis Hosp., Evanston, Ill., 1969-75, asso. adminstr., 1975-76, v.p. ops., 1976—; dir. St. Anne and St. Elizabeth hosps., Chgo., 1978—; corporate dir. personnel Sisters of St. Francis Health Services, 1970—; dir. Investment Advisory Com., Sisters of Providence St. Mary of the Woods Coll., Terra Haute, Ind. Active YMCA, Downers Grove, Ill., 1969—. Served with AUS, 1955-56. Mem. Am. Soc. for Personnel Adminstrn., Am. Coll. Hosp. Adminstrs., Am. Hosp. Assn., Chgo. Hosp. Council, N. Suburban Assn. for Health Resources, Am. Mgmt. Assn., Hosp. Mgmt. Systems Soc., Chgo. Hosp. Personnel Mgmt. Assn., Nat. Alliance Businessman, Evanston C. of C., Am. Legion. Roman Catholic. Club: Moose. Office: St Francis Hosp 355 Ridge Ave Evanston IL 60202

OHANNES, DONALD SAMUEL, ins. co. exec.; b. Chgo., Mar. 14, 1937; s. Samuel O. and Nellie (Shimon) O.; B.S., San Jose State U., 1961; A.M., Roosevelt U., 1968; m. Barbara June Fagan, June 21, 1969; children—Carrie Ann, Lawrence Kennedy. Staff, IRS, Chgo., 1965-67; analyst mcpl. bonds John Nuveen & Co., Inc., Chgo., 1967-69; stockbroker Ill. Co., Chgo., 1969-72; sr. investment mgr. Allstate Ins. Co., Northbrook, Ill., 1972—. Capt. 3d. precinct, 42d ward Chgo. Republican party, 1970-72; adv. com. Ill. State Scholarship Commn., 1978—. Mem. Chgo. Mcpl. Analysts Soc. (pres. 1979-80). Presbyterian. Clubs: Glenbrook Racquet (Northbrook, Ill.); Whitehall (Chgo.). Office: Investments Allstate Ins Co Allstate Plaza Northbrook IL 60062

O'HARA, ARTHUR NORWOOD, tool mfg. co. exec., museum exec.; b. Elyria, Ohio, Feb. 2, 1910; s. Edward S. and Gertrude (Keller) O'H.; m. Muriel E. Steane, Dec. 2, 1931. Engaged in heavy constrn. equipment mfg., 1927-72; cons. to tool industry, 1959-72; officer, dir. Lorain Tool Enterprises (Ohio), 1958—; bus. mgr. Gt. Lakes Hist. Soc. Museum, Vermilion, Ohio, 1971—; mem. N.E. Ohio Inter-Mus. Council, 1973—. Sec. Lake Erie Firelands Tourist Council, 1976—. Mem. Inter-Lake Yachting Assn. (rec. sec. 1977—, pres. trustees 1975, commodore 1971), Ohio Travel Assn., Lorain County Arts Council, Vermilion C. of C., U.S. Yacht Racing Union. Republican. Congregationalist. Clubs: U.S. Power Squadron, Gt. Lakes Cruising (port capt. 1980—), Vermilion Boat (commodore 1965), Internat. Order Blue Gavel (Eastern v.p.), Shriners. Author articles on Gt. Lakes history and yachting, also weekly newspaper column Tell Tale, 1968—. Address: 480 Main St Vermilion OH 44089

OHL, FRANCES BODFISH, interior designer; b. Coleman, Mich.; d. John Henry and Metta Cleveland (Whitehead) Bodfish; B.A., Ohio State U., 1933; cert. N.Y. Sch. Interior Design, 1937; m. William John Ohl, Sept. 27, 1940; 1 son, Charles John. Owner, mgr. Frances Ohl for Interiors, Hinsdale, 1972—. Officer, dir. LWV, 1959-62; trustee Village of Hinsdale, 1975-79; bd. dirs. Hinsdale-Oak Brook Area Community Chest, 1970-73; officer PTA, 1950-59. Mem. Mich. Congress Parents and Tchrs. (life), Hinsdale C. of C. (pres., dir. 1972-77), Nat. Home Fashions League, AAUW, Chi Omega. Club: Hinsdale Womens'. Home: 109 S Quincy St Hinsdale IL 60521 Office: 110 S Washington St Hinsdale IL 60521

OHLE, JOHN ROBERT, univ. adminstr.; b. Steubenville, Ohio, May 25, 1947; s. Robert E. and Eleanor Jane (Bolander) O.; B.A., Ohio No. U., 1969; postgrad. Hamma Sch. Theology, 1969-71; M.A., Bowling Green State U., 1974; m. Kirsten R. Lindquist, Sept. 5, 1970; children—Robert Paul, Andrew Martin (dec.), John Michael, Thomas Martin. Asst. to dean students Wittenberg U., Springfield, Ohio, 1970-71; tchr., coach River View Sch. Dist., Warsaw, Ohio, 1971-73; asso. dean students Muskingum Coll., New Concord, Ohio, 1973-74; dir. alumni and spl. programs, dir. devel. Ohio No. U., Ada, 1974-78; v.p. instnl. advancement Nebr. Wesleyan U., Lincoln, 1978—. Mem. Council for Advancement and Support Edn., Nebr. Ind. Coll. Found. Republican. Lutheran. Home: 7630 Willard Ave Lincoln NE 68507 Office: 50th and St Paul Sts Lincoln NE 68504

OHLSSON, JOHN ALLAN, dentist; b. Stambaugh, Mich., Dec. 26, 1935; s. John Erich and Hildur Elin (Soderquist) O.; B.S., Mich. State U., 1958, M.S. in Microbiology, 1960; D.D.S., U. Mich., 1966; m. Lois Gail Whitfield, Oct. 18, 1958; 1 son, Donald Paul. Staff researcher Wyandotte Chems. Corp., 1960-62; research technician dental materials dept. U. Mich. Dental Sch., 1963-65; dentist Oakland (Mich.) County Health Dept., 1966-71; staff dentist Oakland County Community Coll., 1967-72; pvt. practice dentistry, Rochester, Mich., 1966—. Fellow Acad. Gen. Dentistry; mem. ADA, Internat. Clin. Prosthetic Assn., Am. Profl. Practice Adminstrn., Am. Soc. Dentistry Children, Am. Public Health Assn., Fedn. Dentaire Internat., Mich. Dental Assn. (alt. rep. 1979), Oakland County Dental Soc., Detroit Dist. Dental Soc., Mich. Assn. of Professions, Creation Research Soc., U. Mich. Alumni Soc., Mich. State U. Alumni Soc., Rochester Jaycees (v.p. 1968-71), Greater Rochester C. of C., Alpha Chi Sigma, Tri Beta. Lutheran. Home: 300 Camelot Way Rochester MI 48063 Office: 811 Oakwood Dr Rochester MI 48063

OHM, MERVIN ROBERT, mfg. exec.; b. Olney, Ill., Nov. 30, 1939; s. John Francis and Anna Margaret (Harper) O.; student Chosun U., Kyung Hee U.; B.S. in Bus. Adminstrn., Franklin U., 1963; postgrad. Feng Chia U. Mil. adviser to Republic of China, 1964-66; ops. engr. Am. Bridge div. U.S. Steel Co., Gary, Ind., 1966-67; sr. supr. prodn. Uniroyal, Joliet (Ill.) Army Ammunition Plant, 1967-70; co-owner Tip Top Motel, Olney, 1970-75; asst. advt. dir. Olney Daily Mail, 1975-78; contract procurement and prodn. specialist Opportunity Center, Inc., 1978-80; prodn. planning and control exec. Union Fronderburg Corp., 1980—; v.p. Oleon Coins, Inc., Joliet, 1967-70. Dist. chmn. Am. Ind. Party, 1972-76. Served with AUS, 1957-66. Mem. Am. Legion, Olney C. of C. (legis. com. 1971-76), Franklin U. Alumni Assn., Epsilon Delta Chi. Club: Eagles. Home: 1501 E York St Olney IL 62450 Office: 1 Union Dr Olney IL 62450

OHNO, MITSUGI, glassblower; b. Tochigi, Japan, June 28, 1926; s. Shigeo and Tsuya (Ohgane) O.; came to U.S., 1961, naturalized, 1970; m. Kimiyo Nagayama, Oct. 13, 1953; children—Tsutomu, Hiroko, Julie. Glassbower, U. Tokyo, 1947-61, Kans. State U., Manhattan, 1961—; works include: USS Constitution (at Eisenhower Museum), 1971, Independence Hall (at White House), 1972, U.S. Capitol (at Smithsonian), 1975, Ohno Klein bottle, 1975, Anderson Hall, Kans. State U., 1976, and others. Recipient Yoshikawa-Eiji prize for cultural merit, Tokyo, 1979, Walter Harrison award Kans. State U. Home: 2808 Nevada St Manhattan KS 66502 Office: Dept Chemistry Cardwell Hall Kansas State Univ Manhattan KS 66506

OHREN, JOSEPH ALBERT, mfg. co. exec.; b. Litchfield, Ill., June 22, 1931; s. Joseph Peter and Marie Theresa (Leitschuh) O.; B.S., U. Ill., 1959, M.S., 1963, Ph.D., 1965; m. Beverly Ann Koehler, Sept. 7, 1957; children—Joseph Michael, Mary Jane. Pilot plant technician Pet Inc., Greenville, Ill., 1959-60; group leader Central Soya Co., Chgo., 1965-66; product mgr. Ross Labs., Columbus, Ohio, 1966-69; devel. mgr. Fairmont Food Co., Omaha, 1969-73; tech. sales mgr. Grain Processing Corp., Muscatine, Iowa, 1973—. Republican precinct committeeman Bloomington Twp. (Iowa), 1980—; co-chmn. fin. com. St. Mary's Roman Cath. Co., Muscatine, 1975-77. Served with AUS, 1951-53; Korea. Decorated Combat Inf. Badge; fellow NIH, 1964. Mem. Am. Assn. Cereal Chemists (chmn. new products sessions 1979), Inst. Food Technologists (publicity chmn. Iowa sect. 1976). Republican. Club: Elks. Developer new food products. Home: Rural Route 1 Box IA147 Muscatine IA 52761 Office: 1600 Oregon St Muscatine IA 52761

OILAR, JOHN RAY, artist, writer, historian; b. Lafayette, Ind., Jan. 22, 1949; s. Kenneth Raymond and Anna Belle (Kessinger) O.; B.A., Western N.Mex. U., 1971. Public sch. tchr., 1972-78; computer operator Purdue U., 1978-79, staff writer religion and history Spirit newspaper, 1979-81; writer Sport Scene newspaper, 1981—; author 200 papers and articles on religion, history and sociology; art work included in Artists/U.S.A. Mem. Alpha Phi Omega, Kappa Delta Pi, Blue Key, Sigma Tau Delta, Pi Gamma Mu. Republican. Lutheran. Home: 813 S 10th St Lafayette IN 47905

O'KEEFE, BETH EGAN, psychologist; b. Springfield, Ill., Aug. 27, 1945; d. James Michael and Margaret M.L. (Kuhn) Egan; A.B., Mt. St. Scholastica Coll., Atchison, Kans., 1967; M.S., St. Louis U., 1970, Ph.D., 1971; m. Rip L. O'Keefe, June 27, 1969; children—Kelly Egan, Casey Egan, Quinn Egan. Psychology intern Alton (Ill.) State Hosp., 1968; trainee VA Hosp., Jefferson Barracks, Mo., 1968-70, John Cochran VA Hosp., St. Louis, 1970-71; staff psychologist Comprehensive Community Mental Health Center, Rock Island, Ill., 1971-72, coordinator psychol. services, 1972—; adj. asst. prof. St. Ambrose Coll., Davenport, Iowa, 1976-77. Bd. dirs. Neighborhood Health Center, Rock Island, Ill., 1973-77; mem. budget com. United Way of Rock Island and Scott Counties, 1977; mem. mental health subcom. Illowa Health Systems Agy., Davenport, 1976-77. Mem. Am., Ill., Rock Island County (v.p. 1978—) psychol. assns. Office: 2701 17th St Rock Island IL 61201

O'KEEFE, GERALD FRANCIS, bishop; b. St. Paul, Mar. 30, 1918; s. Francis Patrick and Lucille Mary (McDonald) O'K.; B.A., St. Thomas Coll., 1944; LL.D., St. Ambrose Coll., 1967; L.H.D., Marycrest Coll., 1967; LL.D., Loras Coll., 1967. Ordained priest, Roman Cath. Ch., 1944; instr. St. Thomas Mil. Acad., 1944-45; chancellor Archdiocese of St. Paul, 1945-61; consecrated bishop, 1961; aux. bishop St. Paul, 1961-67; pastor St. Paul Cathedral, 1961-67; bishop Diocese of Davenport (Iowa), 1967—. Home: 1430 Clay St Davenport IA 52804 Office: 2706 Gaines St Davenport IA 52804

O'KEEFE, ROBERT GEORGE, podiatrist; b. Chgo., Nov. 2, 1950; s. John Robert and Mildred (Brown) O'K.; B.S., Loyola U., Chgo., 1973; D. Podiatric Medicine, Ill. Coll. Podiatric Medicine, 1977; m. Anne Elizabeth O'Donnell, Aug. 17, 1974; 1 dau., Kathleen Meghan. Resident in reconstructive foot surgery Northlake (Ill.) Hosp., 1977-78; asso. prof. dept. surgery Ill. Coll. Podiatric Medicine, Chgo., 1981—; practice podiatry, Chgo., 1978—; mem. teaching staff Northlake Community Hosp., 1978—. Mem. Am. Podiatry Assn., Ill. Podiatry Soc. Home: 1137 N Potter Rd Park Ridge IL 60068 Office: 5420 N Harlem St Chicago IL 60656

O'KEEFE, THOMAS JOSEPH, metall. engr.; b. St. Louis, Oct. 2, 1935; s. Thomas and Hazel (Howard) O.; B.S., Mo. Sch. Mines, 1958; Ph.D., U. Mo., Rolla, 1965. m. Jane Gilmartin, Aug. 31, 1957; children—Thomas, Kathleen, Matthew, Daniel, Margaret Mary, Robert. Process control engr. Dow Metal Products, Madison, Ill., 1959-61; asst. prof. metall. engring. U. Mo., Rolla, 1965-68, asso. prof., 1968-72, prof., 1972—; research technologist NASA, Houston, Tex., summer 1965; research metall. engr. Ames Lab. (Iowa), 1966-67; research metall. engr., cons. Cominco Ltd., Trail, B.C., Can., 1970-71. Mem. Am. Inst. Mining and Metall. Engrs. (dir. 1976-77, 79—), Can. Inst. Metallurgy, Alpha Sigma Mu, Sigma Xi, Tau Beta Pi, Phi Kappa Theta (dir. 1965-77). Recipient certificate of commendation Phi Kappa Theta, 1970; named one of Outstanding Young Men of Am., U. Mo., Rolla, 1970, recipient Alumni Merit award, 1971, Outstanding Teaching award, 1979. Home: 5 Crestview Dr Rolla MO 65401 Office: Material Research Center Univ Mo Rolla MO 65401

OLDERMAN, GERALD MYRON, health care exec.; b. N.Y.C., July 16, 1933; s. Cass and Hilda (Klein) O.; B.S. in Chemistry, Rensselaer Poly. Inst., 1958; M.S., Seton Hall U., 1971, Ph.D., 1972; m. Myrna Ruth Schwartz, Aug. 3, 1958; children—Sharon, Neil, Lisa. Research chemist Nat. Cash Register Co., Dayton, Ohio, 1958-61; with Johnson & Johnson, New Brunswick, N.J., 1961-78, v.p. research and devel., 1975-78, dir. Surgikos div. 1972-78; v.p. research and devel. Am. Convertors div. Am. Hosp. Supply Corp., Evanston, Ill., 1978—, dir., 1978—. Served with USMC, 1954-56. Recipient Robert Wood Johnson medal, 1969. Mem. Assn. Advancement of Med. Instrumentation, Am. Soc. Artificial Internal Organs, Am. Soc. Extracorporeal Technicians, Am. Chem. Soc., Fiber Soc., INDA, the Assn. of Nonwovens Industry (corp. rep.), Nat. Fire Protection Assn., Health Industry Mfrs. Assn. (industry rep. to Nat. Fire Protection Assn.). Home: 3487 Summit Ave Highland Park IL 60035 Office: 1740 Ridge Ave Evanston IL 60201

OLDFATHER, CHARLES EUGENE, lawyer; b. Brady, Nebr., Oct. 7, 1927; s. Harold and Marcia (Hazlett) O.; student U. Colo., 1945, Kearney (Nebr.) State Tchrs. Coll., 1946-48, U. Cal. at Berkeley, 1949; A.B., U. Nebr., 1950; J.D. with distinction, U. Mich., 1953; m. Diane C. Harris, June 15, 1957; children—David H., Jane S. Admitted to Nebr. bar, 1953, since practiced in Lincoln; asso. Cline, Williams, Wright & Johnson, 1953-58; partner Cline, Williams, Wright, Johnson & Oldfather, 1958—. Trustee U. Nebr. Found.; past pres. Family Service Assn. Lincoln; past v.p., bd. dirs. Nebr. Soc. for Prevention Blindness. Served with Adj. Gen. Div., AUS, 1946-48. Mem. Am., Nebr., Lincoln bar assns., Lincoln C. of C. (past dir.), Phi Kappa Psi, Phi Delta Phi. Republican. Presbyn. Club: Lincoln Country. Bd. editors U. Mich Law Rev. 1952-53. Home: 6719 Old Cheney Rd Lincoln NE 68516 Office: 1900 First Nat Bank Bldg Lincoln NE 68508

OLDHAM, HOWELL G., supt. schs.; b. Atoka, Okla., Jan. 31, 1925; s. Jack V. and Mildred D. (Surrell) O.; Asso. Sci., Cameron State Coll., Okla., 1948; B.A., Hastings Coll., 1950; Mus.M. (Ak-Sarben scholar), U. Nebr., 1958, Ed.D., 1966; m. Mary Ann Hitchler, Aug. 11, 1945; children—Jack E., Suzanne Oldham Gallagher, Jeffrey Lynn, Gregg A. Tchr., music dir. Gibbon (Nebr.) Pub. Schs., 1950-54; music specialist Grand Island (Nebr.) Pub. Schs., 1954-60, coordinator instrumental music, 1960-69; supt. Gothenburg (Nebr.) Pub. Schs., 1969—; dir., mgr. Grand Island Municipal Band, 1961-69; mem. music com. Nebr. Centennial, 1964-65; music cons. Nebr. State Arts Council, 1966-70; guest dir., contest judge various Nebr. dists., 1967-77; grad. asst. U. Nebr., Lincoln, summers 1959-60, vis. prof. ednl. adminstrn., summer 1976. Mem. Gov.'s Council on Nebr. Cultural Resources, 1965. Served with USAAF, 1943-44. Inst. Devel. Ednl. Activities fellow, 1970, 72, 74, 75, 77; Danforth/NASE fellow, 1976; recipient Rotary award for Outstanding Teaching Grand Island Rotary Club, 1956; Partner in Progress award Grand Island C. of C., 1969. Mem. Am. Assn. Sch. Adminstrs., Nebr. Council Sch. Adminstrs. (legis. com. 1970-74), Am. Legion, Gothenburg C. of C., Phi Theta Kappa, Phi Delta Kappa, Pi Kappa Lambda, Central Nebr. Musicians Assn. (sec. 1961-69). Clubs: Elks, Kiwanis, Gothenburg Service. Home: 803 13th St Gothenburg NE 69138 Office: 1415 Ave G Gothenburg NE 69138

OLDHAM, LOWELL TINCHER, ret. dentist; b. Moberly, Mo., Sept. 29, 1910; s. Rufus Kent and Lula (Tincher) O.; D.D.S., U. Ia., 1933, Cert. Orthodontics, 1934, M.S., 1934; m. Wyntrice Earwood, Apr. 15, 1934; 1 son, Thomas E. Research asst. U. Ia., 1933-34, research asst. Child Welfare Sta. U. Ia., 1933-34; pvt. practice dentistry, specializing in orthodontics, Mason City, Iowa, 1934-75, ret., 1975. Served with AUS, 1943-45. Life mem. Am. Assn. Orthodontists, Iowa State Dental Assn. (past pres. North Central dist.), Iowa State Orthodontic Soc. (past pres.), Am. Dental Assn., Midwestern Soc. Orthodontists, Am. Bd. Orthodontics (charter mem. Coll. of Diplomates), Omicron Kappa Upsilon. Clubs: Elks, Euchre & Cycle, Masons, Shriners, Jesters. Home: B-101 Ambassador East II 502 S Ohio Mason City IA 50401

OLDHAM, PHYLLIS VIRGINIA KIDD, librarian; b. Lafayette, Ind., Mar. 19, 1926; d. Hulbert Haven and Grace Ellene (Doup) Kidd; B.S., Purdue U., 1948, M.S., Butler U., 1966; children—Stephen Kidd. Tchr. English, Jefferson High Sch., Lafayette, 1950; tchr., librarian Tudor Hall Sch., Indpls., 1954-70; librarian Park Tudor Sch., 1970—. Dist. dir. People-to-People Student Ambassador Program, 1970—; chmn. bd. Central Christian Ch., Indpls., 1979-81; mem. adv. bd. Indpls. Zool. Soc. Mem. ALA, Marion County Librarians Assn. (pres. 1969-72), Ind. Media Educators, Kappa Delta Pi, Delta Kappa Gamma (treas. Alpha Eta chpt. 1974-80), Pi Beta Phi. Home: 7015 Warwick Rd Indianapolis IN 46220 Office: 7200 N College St Indianapolis IN 46240

OLDS, DAVID ALLEN, social worker; b. Cleve., Sept. 7, 1951; s. Bruce A. Edwards and Nola Lydia (Wrentmore-Edwards) Olds; B.S. in Social Work, Ohio State U., 1973, M.S. in Social Work, 1976; m. Patricia Lynne Wagner, Sept. 7, 1974; 1 dau., Megan Anne. Child care worker, Bellefaire-University Heights, Ohio, 1974-75; instr. Urbana (Ohio) Coll., 1977-78, Clark Tech. Coll., Springfield, Ohio, therapist Oesterlen Services Youth, Springfield, 1976-79; 1978-79;/program dir., therapist Children's Home Wheeling (W.Va.), 1979—; pvt. practice psychotherapy, 1977—. Bd. dirs. No. Panhandle Head Start, 1981—. Mem. Nat. Assn. Social Workers. Office: 14 Orchard Rd Wheeling WV 26003

O'LEARY, FRANCIS BERNARD, librarian; b. N.Y.C., Oct. 6, 1926; s. Bernard and Bridget (O'Sullivan) O'L.; B.S., Manhattan Coll., N.Y.C., 1949; M.S. L.S., Columbia U., 1952; m. Antoinette M. Walbroel, Sept. 26, 1964; 1 son, Paul. Zoology-botany librarian Columbia U., 1949-53, asst. librarian for natural scis., 1953-57; librarian Inst. Tech., U. Minn., 1957-60; librarian Med. Center, St. Louis U., 1960—; project dir. Med. Library Network Bistate Regional Med. Program, 1970-73. Mem. Grand Jury, Bronx County, N.Y., 1956-57; rep. Assn. Coll. and Reference Libraries to 4th Nat. Conf. on Health in Colls., N.Y.C., 1953. Mem. Spl. Libraries Assn. (pres. Greater St. Louis chpt. 1963-64), AAUP, Med. Library Assn. (chmn. med. schs. sect. 1968-69), AAAS. Club: Naval Records. Author articles in field. Editor: Science Reference Notes (Columbia), 1954-57. Home: 5865 Delor St Saint Louis MO 63109 Office: 1402 S Grand Blvd Saint Louis MO 63104

O'LEARY, JOHN RICHARD, civil engr., educator; b. Chgo., June 23, 1948; s. John Francis and Mary Margret (Kelly) O.L.; B.S. (scholar), Ill. Inst. Tech., 1974, M.S.C.E., 1974; Ph.D. (Engring. Research fellow), U. Tex., Austin, 1980; m. Debra J. O'Leary, June 21, 1974; children—John Edward, Kelly Ann. Engring. analyst Sargent & Lundy Engrs., Chgo., 1971-74, staff cons., 1980—; engr. scientist Tracor Aerospace Co., Austin, 1977-80; asst. prof. structural mechanics Ill. Inst. Tech., Chgo., 1980—; cons. to industry. Mem. ASME, Am. Acad. Mechanics, ASCE (asso.), Sigma Xi (asso.), Tau Beta Pi. Roman Catholic. Contbr. articles to profl. jours. Office: Civil Engring Dept Ill Inst Tech Chicago IL 60616

O'LEARY, ROBERT WHITE, lawyer, assn. exec.; b. New Bedford, Mass., Dec. 3, 1943; s. Francis White and Eileen May (Boyle) O'L.; B.S., U. Mass., 1965; M.P.A., SUNY, Albany, 1968; J.D., Suffolk U., Boston, 1973. Adminstrv. asst. N.Y. State Health Dept., Albany, 1965-66; asst. dir. Hosp. Assn. N.Y. State, Albany, 1966-68; exec. v.p. Mass. Hosp. Assn., Burlington, 1968-74; admitted to Ill. bar, 1978; pres. Ill. Hosp. Assn., Oak Brook, 1974—; bd. dirs. Tri-State Hosp. Assembly; bd. dirs., exec. com., chmn. public affairs com. Ill. Cancer Soc.; pres. Ill. Hosp. Joint Ventures, Inc., Ill. Hosp. Research and Ednl. Found., Ill. Provider Trust, Ill. Compensation Trust, Ill. Risk Mgmt. Services, Assn. Mgmt. Resources. Mem. Gov. Mass. Task Force for Reorgn. State Govt., 1972, Gov. Ill. Transition Task Force, 1976-77. Mem. Am. Soc. Hosp. Execs., State Hosp. Assn. Execs. Forum, Am. Bar Assn., Ill. Bar Assn., Chgo. Bar Assn. Roman Catholic. Office: 1200 Jorie Blvd Oak Brook IL 60521

O'LEARY, THOMAS HOWARD, corp. exec.; b. N.Y.C., Mar. 19, 1934; s. Arthur J. and Eleanor (Howard) O'L.; A.B., Holy Cross Coll., 1954; postgrad. U. Pa. Wharton Sch., 1959-61; m. Barbara A. McDonough, Aug. 13, 1977; children—Mark, Timothy, Thomas Howard, Denis, Daniel, Mary Frances. Asst. cashier First Nat. City Bank, N.Y.C., 1961-65; asst. to chmn. fin. com. Mo. Pacific R.R. Co., St. Louis, 1966-70, v.p. fin., 1971-76, chmn. fin. com. 1976—, also dir.; treas. Mo. Pacific Corp., St. Louis, 1968-71, v.p. fin., 1971-72, exec. v.p., 1972-74; dir., chmn. bd. Mississippi River Transmission Corp., 1974—; dir. Mo. Pacific Corp., 1972—, pres., 1974—; dir. Merc. Bancorp., Merc. Trust Co., N.A., Interco Inc., Kroger Co. Trustee, St. Louis U.; commr. St. Louis Area council Boy Scouts Am. Served to capt. USMC, 1954-58. Clubs: Blind Brook, Wall St., Chgo. Office: 9900 Clayton Rd Saint Louis MO 63124

OLEGARIO, GIL FORTUNATO SEVILLA, pathologist, nuclear physician; b. Lingayen, Pangasinan, Philippines, Oct. 18, 1933; s. Fortunato Garcia and Agripina Marino (Sevilla) O.; came to U.S., 1958, naturalized, 1968; A.A. in Pre-medicine, U. Santo Tomas, Manila, Philippines, 1952, M.D., 1957; m. Rosario Velasco Gatchalian, Apr. 18, 1958; children—Gilda Ruby, Gil Francis. Extern, adjunct gen. practice resident, Pangasinan Provincial Hosp., Dagupan City, Philippines, 1957-58; rotating intern, Bklyn. Hosp., N.Y., 1958-59, 1959-60, resident in pathology, 1960-61; practice medicine specializing in gen. practice, Mangatarem, Pangasinan, Philippines, 1961-62; resident in pathology, Bklyn-Cumberland Hosp. Med. Center, Bklyn., 1963-65, Beth Israel Med. Center, N.Y.C., 1965-66; asst. pathologist, Maimonides Med. Center, Bklyn., 1966-67, 1969-70, asst. dir. labs., 1970-72, asso. pathologist, 1971-72; asso. pathologist, Manhasset (N.Y.) Med. Center, 1967-69; asso. pathologist, Beyer Meml. Hosp., Ypsilanti, Mich., 1973-75, Annapolis Hosp., Wayne, Mich., 1975—; clin. instr. pathology, U. Santo Tomas, Manila, 1962-63, State U. N.Y., Downstate Med. Center, Bklyn., 1969-72. Served from lt. to capt. M.C. Res., Armed Forces of Philippines, 1962-63. Diplomate Am. Bd. Pathology, Am. Bd. Nuclear Medicine. Fellow Am. Soc. Clin. Pathologists, Coll. Am. Pathologists; mem. AMA, N.Y., Kings County med. socs., N.Y. Pathol. Soc., Pathologists Club, Am. Soc. Cytology, Washtenaw County, Mich. State med. socs. Roman Catholic. Home: 3031 Warwick Rd Ann Arbor MI 48104 Office: Annapolis Hosp 33155 Annapolis Ave Wayne MI 48184

OLEJNICZAK, DOMINIC, Realtor, football exec.; b. Green Bay, Wis., Aug. 18, 1908; s. John A.B. and Victoria (Marshall) O.; ed. U. Wis., U. Chgo.; m. Regina Bettine, Nov. 24, 1938; children—Thomas, Mark. Owner realty firm, Green Bay, 1955—; pres. Green Bay Packer Football Corp., 1958—. Mem. Gov.'s Commn. on Mass Urban Transp., 1953-54; mem. City Council, Green Bay, 1936-44, mayor, 1945-55. Mem. Land Bank Assn. (past sec.), Wis. League Municipalities (past pres.). Roman Catholic (treas. congregation 1944—). Club: Elks. Office: care Green Bay Packers 1265 Lombardi Ave Green Bay WI 54303*

OLENDORF, WILLIAM CARR, SR., artist; b. Deerfield, Ill., Apr. 18, 1924; s. Harry A. and Beatrice (Carr) O.; B.A., Washington and Lee U., 1946; postgrad. Harvard U., 1946; m. Marry Gillies, Mar. 10, 1943; children—William Carr, Donald. Advt. mgr. Sci. and Mechanics mag., 1946-50; regional sales mgr. Better Homes & Gardens, 1950-55; account supr. Kling Studios, 1955-57; account exec. Leo Burnett, 1957-60; exec. v.p. Tobias & Olendorf, 1960-65; account supr. Foote, Cone & Belding, 1965-70; pres. Olendorf Promotions, Inc., Chgo., Chgo. 200 Galerie, Inc., 1970—; exhibited in one-man shows at Galerie Marcel Bernheim Paris, 1963; group exhbns. include Chgo. Artists Show, Art Inst. Chgo., 1965, Riccardo's Restaurant & Gallery, Chgo., 1967—, Galerie Marcel, Bernheim, Paris, 1971, Galerie Herder, Stockholm, 1973, Colby's Chgo., 1976, Am. Artist Show, Marshall Field Galleries, Chgo., 1978, Cogswell Gallery, San Francisco, Dayton Art Inst., Galerie Benita, Mykonos, Greece, Air Force Mus., Dayton, Scott Gallery, N.Y.C., Vincent Price Gallery, Los Angeles, Merrill Chase Galleries, Chgo.; works represented pvt. and public collections including Abbott Labs., Chgo., Am. Airlines, N.Y.C., Borg Warner, Chgo., Chgo. Bd. of Trade, Chgo. and Washington, First Nat. Bank of Chgo., Foote, Cone & Belding, Chgo. and N.Y.C., Gould Inc., Chgo., J. Walter Thompson, Chgo., Ky. Horsepark, Lexington, Nat. Tourist Burs. Stockholm, Copenhagen, Helsinki, Pullman Corp., Chgo., Readers' Digest, Chgo. and N.Y.C., Ringling Bros. Barnum & Bailey Circus, Washington, Russian Trade Commn., Moscow, SAS Scandinavian Airlines, N.Y.C. and Stockholm, Standard Oil Co., Chgo., U. Ill., Chgo., Wrigley Co., Chgo. Served with USNR, 1942-46. Rockefeller Found. grantee, 1957; awards Chgo. Vicinity Show, Art Inst. Chgo., 1967, Art in Am., N.Y.C., 1964. Mem. Artists Guild Chgo., USAF Art Program, Sigma Alpha Epsilon. Republican. Episcopalian. Clubs: Cliff Dwellers (Chgo.), Racquet (Miami); Wellington, Palm Beach Polo and Country (Fla.). Office: 9 E Ontario St Chicago IL 60611

OLINGER, JOHN CHARLES, seismograph co. exec.; b. Lamar, Colo., Dec. 2, 1950; s. Charles Forrest and Edna Dorothy (Palmer) O.; student Garden City Jr. Coll., 1969-71; A.S., Harvard, 1971; B.S., Ft. Hays Kan. State Coll., 1973, M.A., 1976. Permit agt. Petty-Ray Geophys. Co., Houston, 1976—. Mem. Am. Hist. Assn., Am. Assn. for Advancement of Slavic Studies, Nat. Assn. of Outlaw and Lawman History, Kans. Corral of the Westerners. Republican. Mem. Ch. of God. Contbr. articles to profl. jours. Address: 711 Jefferson St Hugoton KS 67951

OLIVAREZ, JUAN ROJELIO, ednl. adminstr.; b. Alice, Tex., Nov. 5, 1949; s. Alfinio and Anne (Nava) O.; B.A., Aquinas Coll., 1971; M.A., Wayne State U., 1975; postgrad. Mich. State U., 1979—; m. Mary Tychyj, May 22, 1971; children—Elias, Samuel. Tchr., Grand Rapids (Mich.) Public Schs., 1971-73, sch. psychologist, 1975-80, supr. spl. edn., 1980—; sch. psychologist intern Detroit Public Schs., 1974-75; research asst. Mich. State U., 1978-80; bd. dirs. Grand Rapids Child Guidance Clinic, 1975—. Bd. dirs. W. Mich. Public TV, 1981—; bd. dirs. Hispanic Scholarship Fund, Inc., Grand Rapids, 1980—; pres., 1981-82. Mem. Council Exceptional Children, Mich. Assn. Sch. Psychologists, Mich. Assn. Children with Learning Disabilities, Assn. Supervision and Curriculum Devel. Home: 1144 E Chippewa St SE Grand Rapids MI 49506 Office: 143 Bostwick St NE Grand Rapids MI 49503

OLIVER, CHERYL DARLENE, career planning/edn. specialist; b. Ridgway, Pa., Apr. 30, 1948; d. Ernest Laverne and Rose Lee (Wilkerson) O.; B.A. in Psychology, U. Mo., 1976, M.A. in Counseling, 1977, Ed.S. in Adminstrn., 1979; div.; children—Michelle Renee Biggs, Melissa Dawn Biggs. Counselor/trainer Women Employable, Independence, Mo., 1977-79; test adminstr. U. Mo., Kansas City, 1977-80; career planning specialist Kansas City Power & Light Co. (Mo.), 1979—; owner, cons. Career Synergistics, Kansas City, Mo., 1980—; mem. planning bd. Career Crossroads; state coordinator Mo. Career Planning and Adult Devel. Network; mem. Chancellor's Com. on Implementation Title IX, U. Mo., 1976; mem. parent adv. bd. Early Childhood Edn. Program, 1976, editor Bd. News, 1975; mem. edn. task force Regional Commn. on Status Women, 1980. Mem. Assn. Women in Psychology, Am. Soc. Profl. and Exec. Women, Nat. Assn. Female Execs., Am. Personnel and Guidance Assn., Am. Soc. Tng. and Devel., Nat. Women's Polit. Caucus, NOW, Quill and Scroll (life). Writer, Univ. News, U. Mo., 1978; editor Mo. Career Planning and Adult Devel. Newsletter, 1981; mem. publ. rev. bd. U. Mo., 1977. Home: 5623 Charlotte Kansas City MO 64110

OLIVER, JOHN WATKINS, judge; b. Cape Girardeau, Mo., Dec. 17, 1914; s. Robert Burett and Jessie (McCreery) O.; A.B., U. Mo., 1934, LL.B., 1936; m. Gertrude Field, Jan. 24, 1940; children—John Watkins II, Gertrude, Jane, David. Admitted to Mo. bar, 1936; practiced in Kansas City, 1936-62; U.S. judge, Western Dist. Mo., 1962—, formerly chief judge; mem. Jud. Conf. U.S. Standing Com. on Adminstrn. Probation, 1963—. Chmn. bd. of election commrs., Kansas City, 1950-54; mem. Mo. Bd. Law Examiners, 1952-62. Bd. dirs. Mo. Law Sch. Found., Am. Law Inst. Mem. Am., Kansas City bar assns., Mo. State Bar (gov. 1945-46), Lawyers Assn. Kansas City (dir. 1942), Am. Judicature Soc., Mo. Hist. Soc. Mem. Soc. of Friends. Office: Room 404 US Court House 811 Grand Ave Kansas City MO 64106*

OLIVER, RUSSELL LEE, coll. dean; b. Eau Claire, Wis., Sept. 13, 1930; s. Myrl L. and Mahala M. (Sorlie) O.; B.S., U. Wis., Eau Claire, 1956; M.A., U. Minn., 1956; Ed.D., U. No. Colo., 1964; m. Jean E. Anderson, July 26, 1958; children—Cynthia, Daniel, Karen, Rebecca. Tchr., prin., counselor Wis. high schs., 1956-63; supr. student tchrs. U. Wis., Stevens Point, 1964-67, dean Univ. Center, 1968-73, prof. edn., 1973-78, dean Sch. Edn., 1979—. Served with USNR, 1950-54. Mem. Assn. Supervision and Curriculum Devel., Am. Assn. Colls. Tchr. Edn., Central Wis. Edn. Assn. Lutheran. Office: COPS U Wis 440 Stevens Point WI 54481

OLIVER, SYLVIA ELLEN BASSETT (MRS. WILLARD CHELSEA OLIVER), librarian; b. South Bend, Ind., Mar. 24, 1921; d. Clark and Lillian (Geer) Bassett; B.S., S.W. Tex. U., 1942; M.L.S., U. Mo., 1969; m. Willard Chelsea Oliver, Jan. 10, 1942; children—Jeffrey David, Jill Jeanette (Mrs. James Pilkington). Tchr., Moberly (Mo.) Jr. High Sch., 1954-55, Westran High Sch., Huntsville, Mo., 1955-58, Springfield Twp. Jr. High Sch., Michigan City, Ind., 1958-59; dir. Little Dixie Regional Library, Moberly, 1962-73; librarian Moberly Area Jr. Coll., 1973—. Founder, mem. exec. com. Randolph County Council Social Agys., Moberly, 1973-79. Bd. dirs. Randolph County United Fund. Mem. ALA (councilor 1974-78), Mo. Library Assn. (exec. bd. pub. relations com. 1970-73, exec. bd. outreach round table 1971-73), Mo. Assn. Social Welfare (bd. dirs. E. Central div. 1973—). Baptist. Clubs: Lioness (pres. Huntsville, Mo. 1973-74); Altrusa (pres. Moberly, Mo. 1974-75). Home: Route 2 Huntsville MO 65259

OLIVIA, LAWRENCE ANTHONY, assn. exec.; b. 1933; m.; four children; B.S., Pa. State U., 1959, M.S., 1970. With Sterling Hotel Corp., Wilkes-Barre, Pa., summers 1957-58; steward, banquet mgr. Wilson Lodge, Wheeling, W.Va., 1958-59; asst. food and beverage mgr. Nittany Lion Inn, State College, Pa., 1959-64; supr. coll. food service ops. Instl. Food Research and Services, Pa. Dept. Pub. Instrn. and Pa. State U., 1964-67, instr. food service and housing adminstrn., 1967-70; adminstr. dept. habitational resources U. Wis., Stout, 1970-75; dir. program devel. Ednl. Inst., Am. Hotel and Motel Assn., East Lansing, Mich., 1975—; owner/operator Vee Gee's Lighthouse Restaurant, Lansing, 1980—; pres. Fox Hills Enterprises, Inc., 1980—; project dir. Food and Nutrition Services, Dept. Agr.; adviser Cahners Books, Inc.; lectr. numerous profl. orgns. Recipient H.B. Meek Hospitality Educator of Year award, 1976. Mem. Am., Mich., Lansing (chmn. Nutrition Week 1976) dietetic assns., Am., Mich. home econs. assns., Am. Assn. Housing Educators, Am. Assn. Ret. Persons, Travel Research Assn., Travel Industry for Environment, Am. Vocat. Assn. (asso.), Nat. Assn. Profl. Industry Trainers, Council on Hotel, Restaurant and Instl. Edn. (past dir.), Pa. State Hotel and Restaurant Soc. (pres.), Pa. State Alumni Assn., Coll. Human Devel. Alumni Assn. (past dir.). Contbr. articles to profl. jours. Address: 1039 Fox Hills Dr East Lansing MI 48823

OLLHOFF, BARBARA JEAN, educator; b. Wausau, Wis., July 12, 1947; d. Franklin H. and Myrtle (Giese) Ollhoff; B.Edn., U. Wis., Whitewater, 1969, M.S., 1974; grad. Fashion Inst. of Tech., 1969. With Manchester's Dept. Store, Madison, Wis., 1968, Liberty House Dept. Store, Honolulu, 1973; instr. Waukesha County Tech. Inst., Pewaukee, Wis., 1969—; cons. in field. Student advisor Distributive Edn. Clubs Am., 1969-80. Mem. Am. Vocat. Assn., Wis. Assn. Vocat. and Adult Edn., NEA, Wis. Edn. Assn., Wis. Assn. Distributive Edn. (Instr. of Yr. 1978-79), Distributive Edn. Club of Am. Lutheran. Contbr. articles to profl. jours. Office: 800 Main St Pewaukee WI 53072

OLLIS, HESTER GREY, ins. agency exec.; b. Eldorado, Okla., Mar. 19, 1914; d. Embry G. and Gladys Gertrude (Wood) West; m. Lawrence Woodbridge Ollis, Oct. 21, 1934; children—Ronald Arkwright, Hester Elizabeth Ollis Massey. Partner, sec. Ollis and Co., Springfield, Mo., 1955-60, v.p., 1960-70, pres., 1970-72, v.p., dir., 1972—. Treas. steering com. Goals for Springfield, 1972-73; membership chmn. Community Concert Assn., 1970-71; pres. St. Anne's Guild, St. John's Episcopal Ch. Recipient 25 Yr. Citation for service Greene County Crippled Children and Adults. Mem. Springfield Assn. Ind. Ins. Agts (sec. treas), Drury Coll. Women's Aux. (pres.). Republican. Clubs: Soroptimists Internat., P.E.O. (corr. sec., v.p., treas. chpt. FN), Harriet E. Shepard Saturday (pres.). Home: 3745 E Monroe Springfield MO 65804 Office: 2274 E Sunshine Springfield MO 65804

OLOFSON, TOM WILLIAM, business exec.; b. Oak Park, Ill., Oct. 10, 1941; s. Ragnar V. and Ingrid E. O.; B.B.A., U. Pitts., 1963; m. Jeanne Hamilton, Aug. 20, 1960; children—Christopher, Scott. Various mgmt. positions Bell Telephone Co. of Pa., Pitts., 1963-67; sales mgr. Xerox Corp., Detroit, 1967-68, nat. account mgr., Rochester, N.Y., 1968, mgr. govt. planning, Rochester, 1969, mgr. Kansas City (Mo.) br., 1969-74; corp. v.p. health products group Marion Labs., Inc., Kansas City, Mo., 1974-78, sr. v.p., 1978-80; exec. v.p., dir. Electronic Realty Assn., Inc., 1980—; dir. Optico Industries, Kalo Labs., Am. Stair-Glide, Marion Health and Safety, Marion Sci., Marion Internat., Kansas City Bank & Trust Co., ASG Corp., ICP, Inc. Mem. Menninger Found.; trustee Barstow Sch., Village United Presbyn. Ch. Mem. Omicron Delta Kappa, Sigma Chi. Republican. Presbyterian. Club: Kansas City. Home: 4808 W 87th St Prairie Village KS 66207 Office: 4900 College Blvd Overland Park KS 66201

O'LOUGHLIN, JOHN KIRBY, ins. co. exec.; b. Bklyn., Mar. 31, 1929; s. John Francis and Anne (Kirby) O'L.; B.A. in Econs., St. Lawrence U., Canton, N.Y., 1951; m. Janet R. Tag, July 5, 1952; children—Robert K., Steven M., Patricia A., John A. State agt. Royal Globe Ins. Group, 1953-58; with Allstate Ins. Co., 1958—, mktg. v.p., group v.p., then exec. v.p., 1972—, pres. Allstate Life Ins. Co., 1977—; chmn. bd. Allstate Ins. Co. and Life Co. Can., 1976—; dir. Allstate Ins. Co., Allstate Life Ins. Co., Allstate Ins. Co. Can., Northbrook P&C Co., Northbrook E&S Co., Northbrook Life Ins. Co., Allstate ENTR, Inc. Trustee St. Lawrence U.; elder First United Presbyn. Ch., Lake Forest, Ill. Served to capt. USMCR, 1951-53. Mem. Sales and Mktg. Execs. Internat. (dir.), Alpha Tau Omega. Clubs: Met. (Chgo.); Knollwood (Lake Forest, Ill.); Lahinch Golf (County Clare, Ireland). Home: 752 N Waukegan Rd Lake Forest IL 60045 Office: Allstate Plaza Bldg F-8 Northbrook IL 60062

OLSEN, CLARENCE RANDALL, educator; b. Benton, Ky., Aug. 16, 1932; s. Clarence and Alma Idell (East) O.; B.S., Murray State Coll., 1959, M.A., 1960; Ph.D., Mich. State U., 1969; m. Shirley A. Ferguson, Sept. 14, 1958; children—Nina Ann, Dawn Lee, Cara Lynn. Tchr., dean students Barstow (Calif.) High Sch., 1960-66; instr. Mich. State U., East Lansing, 1967-69; asst. prof. edn. U. Conn., Storrs, 1969-72; mem. faculty Chgo. State U., 1972—, prof., 1975—, chairperson dept. curriculum and instrn., 1972—. Served with U.S. Navy, 1951-55. Mott Found. intern, 1966-67. Mem. Am. Assn. Sch. Adminstrs., Assn. Supervision and Curriculum Devel., Nat. Community Edn. Assn., Phi Delta Kappa. Democrat. Co-author: The Role of the School in Community Education, 1969; contbr. articles to profl. jours. Office: Chicago State Univ 95th St and King Dr Chicago IL 60628

OLSEN, DOUGLAS ALFRED, engring. co. exec., scientist; b. Mpls., Oct. 10, 1930; s. Alfred Julius and Lydia Victoria (Strand) O.; B.A., Gustavus Adolphus Coll., 1953; M.S., U. Iowa, 1955, Ph.D., 1960; m. Jeanne Marie Lindberg, Aug. 16, 1958; children—Victoria, Elliot, Valerie. Devel. chemist Bemis, Inc., Mpls., 1955-57; sr. research scientist Honeywell, Inc., Hopkins and Mpls., 1959-63; project leader Archer Daniels Midland Co., Mpls., 1963-67; dept. head Litton Systems, Inc., Mpls., 1967-70; v.p., treas. Bio-Medicus, Inc., Minnetonka, Minn., 1970-75, dir., 1970-76; pres. PMD, Inc., Eden Prairie, Minn., 1975—, also dir. Research asso. biochemistry U. Minn., 1973-76; vis. prof. Tech. U. Denmark, 1974. Mem. Citizens League, 1973—. Served with Chem. Corps, AUS, 1956. Registered profl. engr., Minn. Mem. Am. Chem. Soc., AAAS, Am. Soc. Artificial Internal Organs, AAUP, Sigma Xi, Alpha Chi Sigma, Phi Lambda Upsilon. Episcopalian. Adv. editor Progress in Surface and Membrane Sci., 1969-77; editorial cons. Polymer Digests, 1969-70. Contbr. articles to profl. jours. Patentee in field. Home: 4106 Linden Hills Blvd Minneapolis MN 55410 Office: 12985 Pioneer Trail Eden Prairie MN 55344

OLSEN, HAROLD LOUIS, mech. engr.; b. Chgo., Dec. 31, 1925; s. Arthur L. and Louise E. Olsen; B.S., Cornell U., 1948; M.S., Purdue U., 1951; m. Marlene C. Lukitsch, July 2, 1951; children—Paul D., David A., Philip S., Janet G. Designer of aircraft heating and air conditioning Pacific Airline Equipment Co., Chgo., 1946-48;

application engr. Allis Chalmers, Milw., 1948-51; designer heating, air conditioning and refrigeration systems Harry F. Wilson & Assos., Milw., 1951-52; designer of railway and bus air conditioning Waukesha (Wis.) Motor Co., 1952-53; designer Wis. State Bur. Engring., Madison, 1953-55; pres., chief mech. engr. Olsen & Evans, Madison, 1954-78; chief mech. engr. Donohue & Assos., Madison, 1978—. Served with USN, 1943-46. Registered profl. engr., Wis., Iowa, Mich., Minn., Ill. Fellow Constrn. Specifications Inst.; mem. ASHRAE. Lutheran. Club: Kiwanis. Home: 5713 Dorsett Dr Madison WI 53711 Office: Donohue & Assos 6325 Odana Rd Madison WI 53719

OLSEN, JANUS FREDERICK, III, library adminstr.; b. Portland, Oreg., Jan. 4, 1942; s. Janus Frederick and Edna Mae (Petersen) O.; B.F.A. in Art Edn., U. S.D., 1964; postgrad. Luther Theol. Sem., St. Paul, 1964-65; M.L.S., U. Western Ont. (Can.), 1971; m. Doris Marie Scheetz, Apr. 19, 1974. Successively reference librarian, head cataloging and tech. processing, field coordinator in-service tng. public and instl. librarians, cons. to tribal, public, organizational, sch. and govt. libraries, acting asst. dir., acting dir. S.D. State Library Commn., Pierre, 1971-73; dir. Mitchell (S.D.) Public Library, 1973-80; dir. Alexander Mitchell Public Library, Aberdeen, S.D., 1980—. S.D. Interium Documents Study Commn., 1972, Mitchell Prehistoric Indian Village Commn., 1974-75; chmn. Davison County Centennial Commn., 1975; edn. chmn. Mitchell Bicentennial Commn., 1975-77; pres. Mitchell Area Arts Council, 1976. Served with arty. U.S. Army, 1965-67. Mem. Am. Library Assn., S.D. Library Assn. (pres. 1977, chmn. centennial com. 1981—, chmn. ad hoc com. on state union catalog of audio-visual materials), Mountain Plains Library Assn. (exec. bd. 1977), Can. Library Assn., Corn Palace Reading Council (pres. 1975), Mitchell Right-to-Read Com., Aberdeen Assn. Adminstrs. (sec.), Oscar Howe Cultural Center, Mitchell C. of C., Internat. Soc. Artists. Lutheran. Club: Am. Legion. Contbr. articles in field to profl. jours. Home: 1619 12th Ave SE Aberdeen SD 57401 Office: 519 S Kline St Aberdeen SD 57401

OLSEN, ORVILLE VERNON, city ofcl.; b. Temple, N.D., Mar. 2, 1917; s. Hans Christen and Elsie Anna (Rynning) O.; certs. U. Wis., 1974; m. Arlene E. Egge, Nov. 1, 1946; children—Steven Blaine, Cheryl Rennae, David Bryan, Maureen Lynne. Farmer, Temple, 1932-38; constrn. worker Noel Constrn. Co., Jamestown, N.D., 1938-42, constrn. foreman, 1945-47; owner, operator Olsen Constrn. Co., Williston, N.D., 1947-71; bldg. insp. City of Williston, 1971—; pres. Apollo Splty. Inc., Williston, 1974—. Served with inf., U.S. Army, 1942-45. Decorated Croix de Guerre, Vermillion Star, campaign medals. Mem. Bldg. Ofcls. and Code Adminstrns. Internat. Lutheran. Clubs: Am. Legion, Moose. Patentee scaffold plank connectors. Home: 2713 7th Ave W Williston ND 58801 Office: Apollo Specialty Inc Box 1585 Williston ND 58801

OLSEN, SAMUEL RICHARD, JR., printing co. exec.; b. Hamilton, Ohio, May 1, 1938; s. Samuel Richard and Hazel Mildred (Berg) O.; Asso. Applied Sci., Rochester Inst. Tech., 1961; children—Kristin, Erika, Samuel Richard III; m. 2d, Roberta Apa, June 1, 1974; children—Lonnie, Erik. Vice-pres. mfg. Datagraphic N.Y., Inc., Rochester, N.Y., 1965-68; pres., chief exec. officer Form Service, Inc., Schiller Park, Ill., 1968—; pres., chief exec. officer Dealers Press, Inc., Rosemont, Ill., 1973—, also dir; v.p., dir. Form Service West, Inc., Camarillo, Calif.; founder, chief exec. officer Bus. Form Service East, Inc., Balt., 1980. Served with USMC, 1960-63. Recipient Voight award Graphic Arts Tech. Found., 1981. Mem. Nat. Bus. Forms Assn. (officer, dir.), Forms Mfg. Credit Interchange (chmn. 1973-74), Printing Industries Am., Nat. Assn. Printers and Lithographers. Home: 772 Halbert Ln Barrington IL 60010 Office: 9555 Ainslie St Schiller Park IL 60176

OLSHER, HARVEY JAY, drug co. exec.; b. Chgo., Dec. 31, 1939; s. Jacob and Anne (Leader) O.; B.S., Northwestern U., 1961; M.B.A., U. Chgo., 1981; m. Nancy Doyle Palmer, Aug. 26, 1979; children by previous marriage—Cindy, Scott, Steven. Exec. v.p. Foremost Sales Promotions, Inc., Chgo., 1961-77; dir. franchising Bresler's 33 Flavors, Chgo., 1977; dir. mktg. programs and advt., Louis Zahn Drug Co., Melrose Park, Ill., 1977—. Mem. Beta Gamma Sigma. Home: 321 N Pinecrest St Bolingbrook IL 60439 Office: 1930 George St Melrose Park IL 60439

OLSON, ALLEN INGVAR, gov. N.D.; b. Rolla, N.D., Nov. 5, 1938; s. Elmer Martin and Olga (Sundin) O.; m. Barbara Benner, Aug. 29, 1964; children—Kristin, Robin, Craig; B.S. in Bus. Adminstrn., U. N.D., 1960, J.D., 1963. Admitted to N.D. bar, U.S. Supreme Ct. bar; asst. dir. N.D. Legis. Council, 1967-69; partner firm Conmy, Rosenberg, Lucas & Olson, 1969-72; atty. gen. N.D., 1972-80; gov. N.D., 1981—; chmn. N.D. Law Enforcement Council; bd. dirs. Bank of N.D. and State Mill and Elevator, N.D. Indsl. Commn. Vice pres. Dakota Zool. Soc. Mem. N.D. Bar Assn., Masons, Elks, Exchange Club. Named Man of Year, Am. Religious Town Hall Found., 1977. Office: Office of Governor State Capitol Bismarck ND 58501

OLSON, ARNE PETER, nuclear engring. cons.; b. Kimberley, B.C., Can., Aug. 9, 1939; s. Peter and Maud Peggy (Jensen) O.; B.A.Sc., U. B.C., 1964; Sc.D., M.I.T., 1967; m. Carol Marion Slater, July 4, 1964; children—Jennifer Jane, Stephanie Lara, Arne Peter. Asso. nuclear engr. Argonne (Ill.) Nat. Lab., 1967-73; mgr. Nuclear Services Corp., Campbell, Calif., 1974-78; dir. Sci. Applications, Inc., Oak Brook, Ill., 1978-80; pres. Arne P. Olson Corp., Western Springs, Ill., 1980—; cons., Argonne Nat. Lab., Commonwealth Edison Co. M.I.T. Inst. fellow, 1964-65. Mem. Am. Nuclear Soc., AAAS. Club: M.I.T. of Chgo. Contbr. articles to profl. jours. Address: 4029 Grand Ave Western Springs IL 60558

OLSON, BYRON LOUIS, chemist; b. Akron, Ohio, Aug. 14, 1942; s. Louis Nels and Mary Virginia (Rous) O.; B.S., U. Akron, 1964; Ph.D., Case Western Res. U., 1970; m. Patricia Ann Thomas, June 28, 1969; children—Ann-Marie, Michael. Postdoctoral fellow Ind. U., 1970-72; asso. prof. preventive dentistry and biochemistry Ind. U. Schs. Dentistry and Medicine, Indpls., 1972—. Served with AUS, 1964-66. NIH grantee. Mem. Am. Chem. Soc., Internat. Assn. Dental Research, Chem. Soc. London, N.Y. Acad. Scis., Am. Assn. Dental Schs., Am. Heart Assn. Sigma Xi. Roman Catholic. Author: (with others) Chemistry and Nutrition for the Dental Hygienist, 1980. contbr. articles to profl. jours. Home: 146 Sherman Dr Carmel IN 46032 Office: 410 Beauty Ave Indianapolis IN 46202

OLSON, DANIEL ROBERT, chemist; b. Gary, Ind., July 7, 1949; s. Robert Francis and Winifred Adrienne (Dempelein) O.; B.A., Ind. U., 1971; m. Heather Lynne Lasenby, Mar. 25, 1972; children—Erik Daniel, Kirstin Mae Marie. Chemist, East Chicago (Ind.) San. Dist., 1970-72, chief chemist, 1975—; tchr. metal analysis Ivy Tech. Sch., Gary, Ind., 1977. Served with U.S. Army, 1972-75. Registered profl. sanitarian, Ind. Mem. Am. Chem. Soc. Methodist. Office: 5200 Indianapolis Blvd East Chicago IN 46312

OLSON, DOLORES MARGARET, nurse; b. Kenosha, Wis., Mar. 14, 1926; d. Joseph and Margaret Mary (Langer) Lourigan; R.N., St. Luke's Hosp., Racine, Wis., 1947; student U. Wis. Extension, 1960-62, Carthage Coll., Kenosha, 1969-71, Marquette U., Milw., 1975, U. Wis. Parkside, Kenosha, 1976; B.S., Coll. St. Francis, Joliet, Ill., 1979; postgrad. U. Ill., 1979—; m. Donald Olson, May 11, 1957 (dec.); children—Christine Mays, Dale, Thomas. Staff nurse St. Luke's Hosp., 1947-52; indsl. nurse Johnson Motors, Waukegan, Ill., 1953-54; staff nurse Kenosha Meml. Hosp., 1954-60, P.M. supr., 1960-64, central supply supr., 1964-65, clin. supr. gen. surg. service and ICU, 1965-69, clin. supr. maj. surgery and ICU, 1969-73, divisional supr. surg. services, 1973-78, asst. dir. nursing, 1978-79, v.p. nursing, 1979—. Liaison com. U. Wis., Milw. and U. Wis. Parkside. Mem. Am. Hosp. Assn., Am. Soc. Nursing Service Adminstrs., Am. Nurses Assn., Wis. Nurses Assn., Kenosha Dist. Nurses Assn., Assn. Hosp. Nursing Adminstrs. Greater Milw. Area, Greater Milw. Area Nursing Service and Nursing Edn. Adminstrs., Am. Heart Assn., Wis. Lung Assn., Kenosha-Racine Ostomy Club, Kenosha Meml. Hosp. Aux., Smithsonian Assos. Roman Catholic. Clubs: Bus. and Profl. Women's, Kenosha Meml. Hosp. Employees. Home: 7852 10th Ave Kenosha WI 53140 Office: Kenosha Memorial Hospital 6308 8th Ave Kenosha WI 53140

OLSON, DONALD GEORGE, univ. computer services adminstr.; b. Minot, N.D., May 16, 1941; s. George James and Ellen (Ranta) O.; B.M.E., U. N.D., 1963; M.M.E., N.D. State U., 1968; 1 son, Todd B. Analyst, programmer Bur. Reclamation, Denver, 1963-66; asst. dir. computer center N.D. State U., Fargo, 1966-69; data processing mgr. U. Calif. Sci. Lab., Los Alamos, 1969-74; dir. data processing nat. assessment ednl. progress Edn. Commn. States, Denver, 1974-77; staff mgr. Mountain Bell, Denver, 1977-80; dir. computer services Mankato (Minn.) State U., 1980—; cons. in field. Registered profl. engr., certified data processor. Mem. AAAS, Assn. Computing Machinery, YMCA, Phi Delta Theta. Republican. Presbyterian. Home: 1336 N 4th St Mankato MN 56001 Office: Computer Services Box 45 Mankato State U Mankato MN 56001

OLSON, JAMES CLIFTON, educator, univ. pres.; b. Bradgate, Iowa, Jan. 23, 1917; s. Arthur Edwin and Abbie (Anderson) O.; A.B., Morningside Coll., 1938, LL.D., 1968; M.A., U. Nebr., 1939, Ph.D., 1942, Litt.D., 1980; m. Vera Blanche Farrington, June 6, 1941; children—Elizabeth, Sarah Margaret. Instr., N.W. Mo. State U., 1940-42; dir. Nebr. State Hist. Soc., 1946-56; lectr. U. Omaha, 1947-50; OAS prof. Am. history El Colegio de Mexico, 1962; lectr. history U. Nebr., Lincoln, 1946-54, asso. prof., 1954-56, prof., 1956-68, chmn. dept. history, 1956-65, asso. dean Grad. Sch., 1965-66, dean, 1966-68, dir. grad. devel. program, 1965-66, vice chancellor for grad. studies, 1968; chancellor U. Mo., Kansas City, 1968-76, interim pres., 1976, pres. U. Mo., 1977—; vis. prof. U. Colo., Boulder, summer 1965; expert cons. Dept. Air Force, 1946-52; group sec. Gt. Plains Conf. on Higher Edn., U. Okla., 1956; dir. United Telecommunications, Inc., Standard Milling Co.; chmn. adv. com. to coordinating bd. for higher edn. State of Mo., 1978-79, 81-82. Bd. dirs. Harry S. Truman Library Inst., 1968—, v.p., 1977-81, pres., 1981—; v.p. Kansas City Public TV, Inc., 1972-77; bd. dirs. St. Louis Symphony Soc., 1977—, Kansas City Philharmonic, 1974—; bd. dirs. Mid-Am. Arts Alliance, 1974—, chmn., 1977-81; trustee Midwest Research Inst., 1976—; chmn. hist. adv. com. Dept. Army, 1980—. Served with USAAF, 1942-46. Recipient Mont. Heritage award State Hist. Soc. Mont., 1958; Woods faculty fellow U. Nebr., 1959-60. Mem. Orgn. Am. Historians (exec. com. 1963-66), Am. Hist. Assn. (com. on coms. 1965-68), Am. Assn. for State and Local History (regional v.p. 1956-62, pres. 1962-64, editorial com. 1958-62), Western History Assn., Nebr. History Soc. (pres. 1962-68), Nebr. Writers Guild (pres. 1951-53), Mississippi Valley Hist. Assn. (sec.-treas. 1953-56), Nebr. History and Social Studies Tchrs. Assn. (pres. 1957-58), Am. Council on Edn., Assn. Am. Univs. (chmn. com. grad. edn. 1979-80), Mo. Council on Public Higher Edn. (pres. 1977-78), AAUP (v.p. U. Nebr. chpt. 1958-59), Mid-Am. State Univs. Assn. (chmn. 1979-80), Assn. Urban Univs. (pres. 1973-75), Univ. of Mid-Am. (chmn. bd. 1979-80), Nat. Assn. State Univs. and Land-Grant Colls. (com. on fine arts 1978— com. on internat. affairs 1981—), Inter-Am Orgn. Higher Edn. (exec. com. N.Am. 1980—, v.p. 1981—), Phi Beta Kappa, Phi Kappa Phi, Pi Gamma Mu, Omicron Delta Kappa. Clubs: Cosmos (Washington); Rotary (Columbia); Mission Hills Country (Kansas City, Mo.); Country of Mo. Office: 321 University Hall Columbia MO 65211

OLSON, KENNETH LOWELL, explosives co. exec.; b. Wentworth, S.D., Sept. 9, 1931; s. Martin Lowell and Luella O.; student schs. Decorah, Iowa; m. Helen Elaine Jacobson, July 8, 1955; children—Mark, Karla, Judy. Sales mgr. beer distbn. co., 1954-67; with Olson Explosives Inc., Decorah, Iowa, 1967—, v.p., gen. mgr., 1971—, also dir. Served with U.S. Army, 1951-53. Republican. Lutheran. Clubs: Elks, Sons of Norway. Home: 1304 Blue Grass Dr Decorah IA 52101 Office: Rural Route 1 Box 384 Decorah IA 52101

OLSON, MARY MARGARET SHAMSHOIAN, high sch. prin.; b. Racine, Wis., May 14, 1951; d. Edward and Rose (Kashian) Shamshoian; B.S. in Math., U. Wis., Parkside, 1973; M.S. in Curriculum and Instrn., U. Wis., Milw., 1978; postgrad. (Roman Catholic Archiodiocese Milw. scholar) Marquette U., Milw., 1981; m. Mark Edward Olson, June 12, 1976. Mem. faculty St. Catherine High Sch., Racine, 1973—, chmn. dept. math., then curriculum dir., 1971-80, asst. prin. academics, 1980—; bd. dirs. Marzbed Armeian Sch.; rep. Racine Area Inservice Planning Com. Recipient Outstanding Tchrs. award Archdiocese Milw., 1978, 79. Mem. Assn. Supervision and Curriculum devel., Wis. Assn. Supervision and Curriculum Devel., Phi Delta Kappa. Mem. Armenian Apostolic Ch. Home: 2032 Orange Ave Racine WI 53403 Office: 1200 Park Ave Racine WI 53403

OLSON, MILDRED MARIE, advt. agy. ofcl.; b. Denver, Jan. 13, 1946; d. Waldo and Miriam (Young) O.; B.A., Colo. Coll., 1968. Editorial asst. Seventeen Mag., N.Y.C., 1969-70; copywriter N.W. Ayer, Chgo., 1970-73; v.p., asso. creative dir. Needham, Harper & Steers, Chgo., 1973-77; v.p., creative dir. J. Walter Thompson Co., Chgo., 1977—. Home: 2100 Lincoln Park W Chicago IL 60614 Office: J Walter Thompson Co 875 N Michigan Ave Chicago IL 60611

OLSON, NANCY SUZANNE, fashion co. exec.; b. Crookston, Minn., Feb. 22, 1938; d. Solon Hubert and Orpha Florence (Love) Gullickson; B.A., Concordia Coll., Moorhead, Minn., 1960; M.S., U. Minn., 1968; m. Arvid L. Olson, Nov. 26, 1960; children—Daniel, David. Tchr. home econs. dept. Circle Pines Jr. High Sch., 1960-61; home econs. tchr. Minnetonka East Jr. High Sch., 1966-68; chmn./coordinator apparel specialist program Anoka (Minn.) Vocat. Tech. Inst., 1968-72; pres. Fashion Services, Inc., Mpls., 1972—; cons. sewing notions div. 3M Co., 1972-73; instr. creative learning center Control Data Corp., 1972-73. Bd. dirs., officer Minn. Montessori Found., 1968-74. Mem. Am. Home Sewing Assn., Am. Home Econs. Assn., The Fashion Group, Am. Fedn. Radio and TV Artists. Lutheran. Author: Patterngrams, 2d edit., 1980; patentee in field. Home: 412 Arthur St Edina MN 55343 Office: 600 1st Ave N Minneapolis MN 55403

OLSON, NORMA JEAN, educator; b. Des Moines, Dec. 3, 1930; s. Floyd Robert and Faye (Spears) Brown; B.S., U. Iowa, 1952; M.A., U. Minn., 1966, Ph.D., 1978; m. Alfred Barber Olson, July 21, 1950; children—Cheri Lynne, Alan Kent. Mem. faculty North Hennepin Community Coll., Mpls., 1966-67, 70—, prof. bus., 1970—; mem. faculty Arapahoe Community Coll., 1967-69, Normandale Community Coll., 1969-70; cons. St. Benedictine Coll., Gen. Mills, U. Iowa, State of Minn. Mem. NEA, Minn. Edn. Assn., Minn. Bus. Edn., North Central Bus. Educators, AAUW, Am. Soc. Tng. Dirs., Am. Bus. Women's Assn., Delta Pi Epsilon. Democrat. Methodist. Home: 4510 W 65th St Shawnee Mission KS 66208 Office: 7411 85th Ave N Minneapolis MN 55445

OLSON, O(SCAR) WILLIAM, lawyer, transp. co. exec.; b. Oak Park, Ill., Feb. 1, 1927; s. Oscar William and Eudora (Landstrom) O.; A.B., DePauw U., 1949; J.D., John Marshall Law Sch., 1953; m. Margaret Greiner; children—Peter W., Stephen W., Martha L. Admitted to Ill. bar, 1953, U.S. Supreme Ct. bar; pres., chmn. bd. Safeway Precision Products, Pompano Beach, Fla., 1968—, Intercontinental Steel Corp., Chgo., 1965—; chmn. bd., pres., chief exec. officer South Suburban Safeway Lines, Inc., Harvey, Ill., 1970—; pres., chmn. bd. Safeway Enterprises, Inc., Chgo., Barr Industries, Inc., Intercontinental Sales, Ltd., Intercontinental Services, Ltd., Illectric Industries, Inc., Dahltron Corp. (all Chgo.). Served with USAAF, 1944-46: ETO. Mem. Am., Ill., Chgo. bar assns. Clubs: Monroe, Union League, Chgo. Athletic Assn., Execs.; Edgewood Valley Country (LaGrange, Ill.). Home: 15W121 81st St Hinsdale IL 60521 Office: 20 N Clark St Suite 2200 Chicago IL 60602

OLSON, RICHARD E., mayor; b. Aurora, Ill., Aug. 3, 1929; student U. Ill., 1948; grad. Drake U., 1951; m. Cleojean Meredith, Mar. 28, 1951; children—Meredith, Dave, Dana, Brad. Former salesman Minn. Mining Corp.; with Bankers Life Co., 1954-68, salesman, then asst. supr. home office, asst. mgr., Des Moines, agy. mgr., 1960-68; councilman, Des Moines, 1968-71, mayor, 1972—. Mem. Alpha Tau Omega. Office: City Hall E 1st Locust St Des Moines IA 50307 also 610 Liberty Bldg Des Moines IA 50309

OLSON, RICHARD WENDELL PALMER, artist; b. Rockford, Ill., Aug. 14, 1938; s. Palmer B. and Corrine (Anderson) O.; B.S., U. Wis., 1960, M.S., 1961, M.F.A., 1962; m. Kathleen Wolke, Oct. 22, 1966; 1 son, Kevin. Chmn. art dept. Milton (Wis.) Coll., 1961-62; asst. prof. art Clarion (Pa.) Coll., 1962-63; mem. faculty Beloit (Wis.) Coll., 1963—, prof. art, 1976—, chmn. dept., 1969-77, 81-82; juror, cons., guest curator, gallery mgr. Wright Art Center, Beloit, Wis.; designer logo and name City Beloit Transit System, cover designs Beloit Poetry Jour.; rep. permanent collections rare book dept. Wallace Library, Rochester (N.Y.) Inst. Tech., Sohm Archiv, Markingronin, W.Ger., Stempelplaats Archive, Amsterdam, Mus. Contemporary Art, Chgo., Mus. Modern Art, N.Y.C., Library Sch. of Art Inst. Chgo., Lund (Sweden) U. Archive of Exptl. Art. Recipient Gimbels award painting, 1961, Gimbel-Schuster award sculpture, 1969, Mayer award painting, 1960, Cullister grant offset printing, 1978; Cullister grantee, Europe, 1977. Included in Artifacts at the End of a Decade, 1981. Office: Art Dept Beloit Coll Beloit WI 53511

OLSON, RUSSELL A., lt. gov. Wis.; b. Chgo., Feb. 19, 1924; student U. Ill. Farmer; mem. Wis. Ho. of Reps., 1960, 62, 66, 68, 72, 74, 76; lt. gov. State of Wis., Madison, 1978—. Served with USMCR, 1942-46. Mem. Farm Bur., Am. Legion, VFW, Wis. Cattlemen's Assn. Republican. Club: Eagles. Office: Office of Lt Gov 22 East State Capitol Madison WI 53702

OLSON, SCOTT E., architect; b. Chariton, Iowa, Dec. 28, 1945; s. J. Donald and Mary Helen O.; B.Arch., Iowa State U., 1969; m. Carol Marie Gergen, Apr. 4, 1974. With Leo Peiffer & Assos., Architects, Cedar Rapids, Iowa, 1969-79, partner, 1976-79; prin. Olson Popa Novak, Architects, P.C., Marion, Iowa, 1979—; vice-chmn. Cedar Rapids Bldg. Bd. Appeals. Bd. dirs. Linn County unit Am. Cancer Soc., Jr. Achievement, Cedar Rapids, Cedar Rapids Conv. Bur., Cedar Rapids-Marion Fine Arts Council, Cedar Rapids Art Center (treas.), Boys Acres, Discovery Village; mem. Five Seasons Center Commn., Linn County Bd. Rev. Served with AUS, 1970-71. Registered architect, Iowa. Mem. AIA, Nat. Council Archtl. Registration Bds., Nat. Trust for Historic Preservation, Czech Heritage Found., Inc., NAACP, Indian Creek Nature Center, Iowa State Alumni Assn., Cedar Rapids C. of C. (dir.), Marion C. of C. (pres.-elect), Greater Downtown Cedar Rapids Assn., Inc. Republican. Presbyn. Clubs: Elmcrest Country, Elks, Cedar Rapids Jaycees, Cedar Rapids Rotary, Linn County Cyclone. Home: 4070 Hickory Hill Ln SE Cedar Rapids IA 52403 Office: 790 11 St Marion IA 52302

OLSON-HELLERUD, LINDA KATHRYN, sch. guidance dir.; b. Wisconsin Rapids, Wis., Aug. 26, 1947; d. Samuel Ellsworth and Lillian (Dvorak) Olson; B.S., U. Wis. at Stevens Point, 1969, teaching cert., 1970, M.S.T., 1972; postgrad. U. Wis. at Madison, 1969-70; M.S., U. Wis. at Whitewater, 1975; Ed.S., U. Wis.-Stout, 1978. Clk., Univ. Counseling Center, U. Wis., Stevens Point, 1965-69; elementary sch. tchr., Wisconsin Rapids, 1970-76, sch. counselor, 1976-79, dist. elem. guidance dir., 1979—. Active Wisconsin Rapids Hosp. Aux. Mem. NEA, Wisconsin Rapids Edn. Assn., Am. Personnel and Guidance Assn., Am. Sch. Counselor Assn., Wis. Sch. Counselor Assn., Assn. for Measurement and Evaluation in Guidance, AAUW, Community Career Edn. Assn. Mem. Moravian Ch. Club: Hosp. Aux. Women's. Home: 120 11th St N Wisconsin Rapids WI 54494 Office: Bd Edn 510 Peach St Wisconsin Rapids WI 54494

OLSTON, MARY KAY, sch. psychologist; b. Milw., Oct. 27, 1949; d. Gordon Rhodes and Mary Anne (Popp) Olston; B.A., Carroll Coll., 1970; M.S., U. Wis. at Milw., 1971. Asso. sch. psychologist Milw. Pub. Schs., 1971-74, sch. psychologist, 1974—; research asst. U. Wis., Madison, 1973-76. Lic. sch. psychologist. Mem. Am. Psychol. Assn., Wis. Sch. Psychol. Assn., Nat. Assn. Sch. Psychologists, Milw. Area Assn. Psychologists in Schs., Milw. County Psychol. Assn., Alliance Française (librarian 1980-82). Home: 10541 W Woodward Ave Wauwatosa WI 53222 Office: 3620 N 18th St Milwaukee WI 53206

OLSZEWSKI, CHARLES CHESTER, educator; b. Detroit, Mar. 8, 1952; s. Chester John and Marcella Regina (Wojsznayowicz) O.; B.S. in Gen. Engring., Mich. State U., 1979. Elec. and mech. technician Lansing Elec. Motors (Mich.), 1973-77; mem. adj. faculty engring. tech. Lansing Community Coll., 1977-80, instr. engring. tech., 1980—; adj. faculty Agrl. Inst., Mich. State U., 1980. Apptd. to Office for Young Children Planning Bd., 1979. Mem. Assn. Supervision and Curriculum Devel., Mich. Educators Energy Forum (asso.). Home: 409 Leslie St Lansing MI 48912 Office: Lansing Community Coll Engring Tech Dept 419 N Capital St Lansing MI 48912

OLWAN, SALLI RINKER, oil and gas devel. co. exec.; b. Warren, Ohio, Aug. 8, 1943; d. Edward Earl and Helen Louise (Miller) Smither; student in ct. reporting Stautzenberger Bus. Coll., 1961, in amateur ham radio Macomber Vocation Coll., 1964, in basic real estate Howell Town & Country, Inc., 1969, in data processing Cleary Coll., 1979—; m. Jack Rhodes Rinker, Dec. 14, 1963; m. 2d Casim Emmett Olwan, Oct. 22, 1976. Asst. dir. Toledo Bldg. Congress, 1966-69; owner, operator SJR Acctg. Services, Toledo, 1968-77, C & S Tobacco Bar, Toledo, 1971-76; sec.-treas. RSA Corp., Ann Arbor, Mich., 1968—; dir. RSA Corp., Thor Petroleum Corp., Acry-Dent Supply Co., Capital Income & Realty Corp. Mem. Republican Nat. Congl. Com. Mem. Am. Mgmt. Assn., Nat. SBA, Toledo Symphony Orch. Assn., Smithsonian Assos., Worldwide Sportsmen Club. Episcopalian. Clubs: Toledo Ski, Nomads. Home: 3075 Plumbrook Rd

Maumee OH 43537 Office: 213 E Washington St Ann Arbor MI 48108

O'MAHONEY, MICHAEL TERRENCE, psychologist; b. Chgo., May 7, 1943; s. James Fanahan and Mary Terese (Roche) O'M.; B.S., Ill. Inst. Tech., 1969, M.S., 1970, Ph.D., 1972; m. Linda Ann Bliznik, May 30, 1967; children—Jean Marie, Michael T., Maura Elizabeth. Research scientist Inst. for Juvenile Research, Chgo., 1968-72; instr. psychology Ill. Inst. Tech., Chgo., 1972-75; dir. research and evaluation Mental Health Center of LaSalle County, Ottawa, Ill., 1974-75; vis. prof. St. Xaviers Coll., Chgo., 1975; asst. prof. psychiatry U. Ill. Med. Sch., 1973-75; asst. dir. psychol. services Cook County Sch. Nursing, Chgo., 1972-75; asst., prof. psychiatry Northwestern U. Med. Sch., Chgo., 1975—; coordinator clin. services, out-patient dept. Inst. of Psychiatry, Northwestern Meml. Hosp., Chgo., 1975—. Served with U.S. Army, 1964-67. Mem. Am., Ill. psychol. assns. Home: 296 Hagans St Elmhurst IL 60126 Office: 259 E Erie St Chicago IL 60611

O'MALLEY, JOAN ELIZABETH, sch. adminstr.; b. Chgo., Mar. 11; d. Arthur Stephen and Anna Catherine (Manning) O.M.; B.Ed., Chgo. Tchrs. Coll., 1940; M.B.A., Northwestern U., 1960; postgrad. Stanford U., 1963; D.ED., Nova U., 1974. Acct., United Air Lines, Chgo., 1941-56; tchr., counselor Chgo. Public Schs., 1956-69, operations analysis coordinator, 1969-75, prin. high sch., 1975—; rep. to Nat. Assn. Secondary Sch. Prins./HEW Conf. on Ednl. Planning, 1976. Bd. dirs. South Loop Planning Bd., Chgo., 1980-82. Mem. Chgo. Prins. Assn., Zonta Internat., Am. Assn. Supervision and Curriculum Devel., Big Sisters, Ill. Sch. Prins. Assn., Am. Personnel and Guidance Assn., Ill. Vocat. Assn., Northwestern U. Profl. Women's Assn., Delta Kappa Gamma, Phi Chi Theta. Home: 1115 S Plymouth Ct Chicago IL 60605 Office: 606 S State St Chicago IL 60605

O'MALLEY, PAUL EDWARD, popcorn co. exec.; b. Shirley, Ind., Dec. 5, 1941; s. James and Mary Elizabeth (Spencer) O'M.; B.S., Purdue U., 1965; postgrad. Bowling Green State U., 1974-76; m. Carol Elizabeth Leavitt, Sept. 18, 1965; children—Heather Spring, Lesha Chloe. Prodn. supr. Carnation Co., Oconomowoc, Wis., 1970-72; prodn. mgr. Hunt-Wesson Foods, Inc., Perrysburg, Ohio, 1972-77; plant mgr. Robert A. Johnston Co., Milw., 1977-80; gen. mgr. Orville Redenbacher Popcorn div. Hunt-Wesson Foods, Inc., Valparaiso, Ind., 1980—. Bd. dirs. Sylvan Manor Homeowner's Assn., 1981-84, treas., 1981-82. Served with USAF, 1965-70. Decorated Air medal with three oak leaf clusters, Vietnam Service medal, Armed Forces Expeditionary medal, Presdl. Citation. Mem. Nat. Mgmt. Assn., Popcorn Inst., Valparaiso C. of C. Republican. Club: Rotary (Valparaiso, Ind.). Home: 127 Southport Ct Valparaiso IN 46383 Office: PO Box 468 Valparaiso IN 46383

O'MARA, THOMAS PATRICK, info. systems co. exec.; b. St. Catharine's, Ont., Can., Jan. 17, 1937; s. Joseph Thomas and Rosanna Patricia (Riordan) O'M.; B.S., Allegheny Coll., 1958; M.S., Carnegie Inst. Tech., 1960; m. Nancy Irene Rosevear, Aug. 10, 1968; children—Patricia Catharine, Tracy Irene, Sara Megan. Mktg. analyst U.S. Steel, Pitts., 1960-65; dir. information systems Screw & Bolt Corp., Pitts., 1965-68; v.p., gen. mgr. toy div. Samosonite Corp., Denver, 1968-73; regional mgr. Hertz Corp., Denver, 1973-75; asst. to chmn. Allen Group, Melville, N.Y., 1975-76; group exec., v.p. fin. and adminstrn. Bell & Howell Co., Chgo., 1976-77, corp. controller, 1977-78; corp. v.p., pres. audio-visual/optics group, 1978—. Served with U.S. Army, 1961-66. Mem. Fin. Execs. Inst., Sigma Alpha Epsilon. Clubs: Knollwood, Economic (Chgo.). Home: 1262 W Deerpath Rd Lake Forest IL 60045 Office: Bell Howell 7100 McCormick Rd Chicago IL 60645

O'MEARA, EDWARD THOMAS, bishop; b. St. Louis, Aug. 3, 1921; s. John and Mary (Fogarty) O'M.; student Kenrick Sem., 1943-46; S.T.D., Angelicum U., Rome, 1953. Ordained priest Roman Cath. Ch., then became monseignor, ordained bishop, 1972; asst. pastor St. Louis Cathedral, 1952-55; asst. nat. dir. Soc. for Propagation of the Faith, 1956-60, dir. St. Louis area, 1960-67, nat. dir., N.Y.C., 1967-79; archbishop of Indpls., 1979—. Editor Mission mag., World mission mag. Home: Chancery Office 1350 N Pennsylvania St Indianapolis IN 46202*

O'MELIA, DONALD C., lawyer; b. Rhinelander, Wis., May 24, 1917; s. Albert James and Eva (Hildebrand) O'M.; U. Notre Dame, 1939; LL.B., Marquette U., 1941; m. Margaret L. McDonald, June 7, 1937 (dec.); children—Nora Ann (Mrs. Donald Bluhm), Michael John, Mary (Mrs. David Peterson), Patricia (Mrs. Louis E. Widule), Susan (Mrs. James Jankowski), Christine (Mrs. James Kasson), Donald C., Margaret (Mrs. David Gillis), Brian, David, Dennis; m. 2d, Doris H. Danner, July 3, 1981. Admitted to Wis. bar; pvt. practice, 1941-43; dist. atty. Oneida County, 1943-49; now sr. mem. firm O'Melia Law Offices, S.C., Rhinelander, Dir., Martin Ins. Co., Heart of Lakes Savs. & Loan, Rhinelander Telephone Co. Mem. Gov.'s 1st Conf. Home and Family, Milw., 1966, Gov.'s Council Phys. Activity and Sports, 1965—; mem. Rhinelander High Sch. Bd. Edn., 1955-78, Oneida County Safety Com., Wis. Gov.'s Council on Phys. Fitness, 1968—; dist. chmn. Boy Scouts Am. Del. Republican Nat. Conv., 1960, Wis. Rep. Conv., 1944-73; chmn. Oneida Rep. Com.; state chmn. Lawyers for Nixon-Agnew, 1968; bd. dirs. St. Mary's Hosp., Wis. Judicare, Inc. Served with USMCR, 1937-41, AUS, 1944-45. Mem. Am. Judicature Soc., Wis. Bar Found., State Bar Wis. (gov. 1960-64, exec. com. 1964-65, 66-67, pres. 1965-66; Spl. Merit award), Milw., Oneida County (past pres.) bar assns., Wis. Dist. Attys. Assn. (pres. 1946-47, sec.-treas. 1944-45), Wis. Acad. Trial Lawyers, Bar Assn. of 7th Fed. Circuit, Rhinelander C. of C. (dir.), Wis. Cancer Soc. (chmn. state legacy com. 1965-71), Am. Legion, Delta Theta Pi. K.C. (advocate), Eagle (trustee 1944-45), Lion. Clubs: Rhinelander Country (dir. 1956-57), Dilemma. Home: 203 Pleasant St Rhinelander WI 54501 Office: 4 S Stevens St Rhinelander WI 54501

OMMEN, DUANE FRANCIS, psychologist; b. Fulda, Minn., Feb. 12, 1934; s. Henry P. and Ella Marie Ommen; B.S., S.D. State U., 1959, M.S., 1960; postgrad. U. Minn., 1961-62; m. Illa Mae Felton, May 9, 1959; children—Cindy, Paul, Jackie. Employee counselor Mpls. Gas Co., 1960-61, personnel dir., 1961-62, supr. employee counseling, 1962-63, mgr. manpower devel and orgn. planning, 1963-67, mgr. mktg., 1967-72, dir. planning and control, 1972—. Served with U.S. Army, 1953-56. Mem. Am. Psychol. Assn., Minn. Psychol. Assn. Republican. Methodist. Clubs: Mason, Mpls. Athletic. Home: 3232 Xenia Ave N Minneapolis MN 55422 Office: Minn Gas Co 700 Linden Ave W Minneapolis MN 55403

ONDREJKA, JOSEPH EDWARD, mfg. co. exec.; b. Whiting, Ind., June 5, 1923; s. Joseph Victor and Pauline (Nedrost) O.; B.S., Ind. U., 1948; m. Theresa M. Lesniak, Aug. 31, 1946; 1 dau., Denise E. Office mgr. Lummus Co., East Chicago, Ind., 1946-56, Morrison Constrn. Co., Hammond, Ind., 1956-63; adminstrv. mgr. Guy F. Atkinson Co., San Francisco, 1963-77; v.p. fin. Centro-Metalcut, Inc., Rockford, Ill., 1977—, Morgardshammar, Inc., 1980—; treas. Rapid Granulator, Inc., 1978—. Served to 1st lt. USAF, 1943-45. Decorated Purple Heart, D.F.C., Air medal. Mem. Am. Assn. Cost Engrs., Am. Legion. Roman Catholic. Club: Forest Hill Country. Office: 2730 Eastrock Dr Rockford IL 61125

ONDREY, JOSEPH THOMAS, printing co. exec.; b. Cleve., May 15, 1923; s. Joseph Jacob and Elizabeth Gertrude (Feld) O.; B.S., Miami U., Oxford, Ohio, 1946; M.B.A., Case Western Res. U., 1972; m. Teri Tatary, Jan. 10, 1948; children—Carol, David, Thomas, James. Vice-pres. sales promotion William Feather/Printers, Cleve., 1948-61; pres. Mueller Printing Co., Cleve., 1961-71; pres. J.T. Ondrey Assos., Inc., Chagrin Falls, Ohio, 1971-75; sr. v.p. Davies/Wing, Inc., 1980—; editor/pub. Gt. Lakes Jour., Cleve., 1962—; pub. Children's Playmate mag., Cleve., 1961—. Councilman, City of Orange (Ohio), 1955-64, pres., 1967-68. Served to capt., USAAF, 1943-45. Decorated Air Medal with 2 clusters. Mem. Am. Angus Assn., League Am. Wheelmen, Mensa, Sigma Chi. Golden Keys awardee Club Printing House Craftsmen N.Y., 1967. Home: 17444 Ravenna Rd Chanticleer Farm Burton OH 44021 Office: 1278 W 9th St Cleveland OH 44113

O'NEAL, DAVID CORTLAND, lt. gov. Ill.; b. Belleville, Ill., Jan. 24, 1937; s. Floyd Cortland and Edna Ruth (Barrow) O'N.; student McKendree Coll., 1955-56; B.S., St. Louis Coll. Pharmacy, 1962; m. Sandra Finley, Dec. 26, 1958; children—Allison, Kelly. Pres., Westown Pharmacy, Inc., Belleville, 1962-70; sheriff St. Clair County, 1970-76; lt. gov. Ill., 1977—. Mem. adminstrn. justice task force East West Gateway Council, 1971—; mem. Ill. Law Enforcement Commn., 1971-73; chmn. Tech. Advisory Com. on Aging, abandoned mines land reclamation council; chmn. Gov.'s Spl. Commn. on State Mandated Programs; chmn. Ill. Senior Citizens Legis. Forum. Trustee, McKendree Coll., St. Louis Coll. of Pharmacy. Mem. Young Republicans, Mens Rep. Club. Bd. dirs. Okaw Valley council Boy Scouts Am., St. Clair County Health and Welfare Council, Metro-East Health Council. Served with USMC, 1956-59. Recipient Distinguished Service award Belleville Jaycees, 1971; named Outstanding Young Reps., 1971, Humanitarian of the Year, 1973, Outstanding Young Rep. of Nation, 1975. Mem. Belleville C. of C., Madison-St. Clair Profl. Pharmacy Assn. Office: Office of Lt Gov State House Springfield IL 62706

O'NEAL, WILLIAM EDDIE, ednl. adminstr.; b. Ruleyville, Miss., Apr. 5, 1939; s. William and Lueida (Dollison) O'N.; B.S., Ball State U., 1961, M.A., 1965, Ed.D., 1976; m. Carolyn Green, June 13, 1959; 1 son, Keith. Tchr., Muncie (Ind.) Community Schs., 1961-67, counselor, supr. Muncie Southside High Sch., 1968-72, asst. prin., 1972-74; fellow Ind. Public Sch. Council Study, 1975-76; asst. supt. Anderson (Ind.) Community Schs., 1976—; cons. Ind. Dept. Public Instrn. Dir., United Way; bd. dirs. YMCA; vice chmn. St. John's Hosp. Bd. Health Com.; v.p. Community Action. Mem. Assn. Children with Learning Disabilities, Assn. Sch. Curriculum Devel., Ind. Assn. Public Sch. Supts., NAACP, Urban League. Clubs: Paramount (past pres.), Rotary. Home: 36 Cambridge Ct Anderson IN 46012 Office: 30 W 11th St Anderson IN 46016

O'NEIL, EDWARD JOSEPH, newspaper exec.; b. Dayton, Feb. 10, 1930; s. Edward J. and Rita K. (McKenny) O'N.; student U. Dayton, 1947-48; m. Virginia R. Butz, Apr. 26, 1952; children—Michael J., David E., Stephen C., Daniel J., Susan E., Joanne C. Sports writer, editor Dayton Daily News, Miami (Fla.) Daily News, Sporting News, St. Louis, Champaign-Urbana (Ill.) Gazette, 1948-66; with Dayton Newspapers, Inc., 1966—, advt. dir., 1974—. Served with USAF, 1950-53. Mem. Dayton Advt. Club (past pres.), Ohio Newspaper Advt. Execs. (pres.), Internat. Newspaper Advt. and Mktg. Execs. (mem. exec. com., dir.). Clubs: Sycamore Creek Country, Dayton Racquet. Home: 4817 James Hill Rd Kettering OH 45429 Office: Dayton Newspapers Inc 4th and Ludlow Sts Dayton OH 45401

O'NEIL, KEITH (KEITH SMITH), entertainment prodn. co. exec.; b. Van Nuys, Calif., Dec. 13, 1946; s. Ottis and Jimmie Smith; student Don Martin Sch. Radio and TV Arts and Scis., 1962-66; m. Donna Jean Krupp, July 14, 1967; children—Brian Lee, Julie Ann. Musician, 1958-65; announcer, chief engr. Sta. KSFV, San Fernando, Calif., 1965; announcer, program dir. Sta. KTOT, Big Bear Lake, Calif., 1966; announcer, music dir. Sta. KHOF-FM, Glendale, Calif., 1966-67; ops. mgr. Stuart Broadcasting Co., Sta. KRGI-AM, Grand Island, Nebr., 1967-74, Sta. KWTO, Springfield, Mo., 1974-79; pres. Ramblin' Prodns. (prodns./syndication co.), Springfield, 1979—. Chmn. adv. bd. S.W. Mo. dist. Easter Seals, 1975, pres. state adv. bd. Mo. Easter Seals Soc., 1976. Mem. Country Music Assn. Mem. Assembly of God Ch. Office: Ramblin' Prodns 430 S Glenstone St Suite C Springfield MO 65802

O'NEIL, MICHAEL GERALD, bus. exec.; b. Akron, Ohio, Jan. 29, 1922; s. William Francis and Grace (Savage) O'N.; A.B., Coll. of Holy Cross, 1943; postgrad. Sch. Bus., Harvard, 1948; LL.D., U. Akron, 1962, Ashland, Coll., 1967; m. Juliet P. Rudolph, Jan. 7, 1950 (div.); children—Michael, Gregory, Jeffrey, Shawn, Julie, Nancy, Susan; m. 2d, Jean Bowman, Oct. 2, 1981. With Gen. Tire Co., 1947—, staff inter-plant ops., Venezuela, 1947-48, dir., 1950—, exec. asst. to pres., 1951-60, pres., 1960—, chmn. bd., 1981—, mem. exec., finance coms.; dir., chmn. bd. Aerojet-Gen. Corp.; dir. 1st Nat. Bank of Akron. Served as lt. USAAF, 1944-45. Clubs: Portage Country, Akron City; Detroit Athletic, Sharon Golf. Office: One General St Akron OH 44329

O'NEIL, PENNY FELTON, univ. adminstr.; b. Baton Rouge, June 20, 1947; d. Joseph P. Felton and Reva B. Bota; B.S. in Bus. Adminstrn., Ohio State U., 1971; M.B.A., Xavier U., 1978; m. William J. O'Neil, Sept. 7, 1968; 1 son, Michael Sean. Salary analyst, personnel services Ohio State U., Columbus, 1972-73, job analyst, personnel services, 1973-76, asst. dir., registration services systems, office of registration services, 1976-77, dir. adminstrv. services, office of registration services, 1977-79, asst. univ. treas., 1979—. Office: Treasurer's Office Ohio State U 240 Lincoln Tower Columbus OH 43210

O'NEIL, THOMAS FRANCIS, broadcasting and rubber co. exec.; b. Kansas City, Mo., Apr. 18, 1915; s. William and Grace Agnes (Savage) O'N.; A.B., Holy Cross Coll., 1937; m. Claire Miller McCahey, June 15, 1946; children—Shane, Eileen, Mark, Conn, Claire, Liam, Grace, Carol, Owen. With Gen. Tire & Rubber Co., Akron, Ohio, 1937-41, 46—, dir., 1948—, v.p., 1950-60, vice chmn. bd., 1960, chmn., 1961-81; v.p., dir. The Yankee Network, Boston, 1948-51; pres., dir. RKO Gen., Inc., N.Y.C., 1955-66, chmn. bd., 1966-76, now chmn. exec. com.; dir. Frontier Airlines, Inc., Flintkote Co. Served to lt. USCG, World War II. Office: Gen Tire & Rubber Co One General St Akron OH 44329

O'NEILL, ARDEN GLENN LANE, appraiser; b. Flint, Mich., June 5, 1929; s. George Richard and Mildred Odena (Baker) O'N.; student U. Md.; grad. Nat. Coll. Chiropractic, 1952; m. Jeanne Parrotte, Dec. 20, 1956; children—Laurie Jean, Lane Arden. Adjuster, appraiser Western Adjustment & Inspection Co. (merged with Gen. Adjustment Bur.), Flint, 1956-73; pres., sr. residential appraiser Associated Appraisal Service, Inc., Burton, Mich., 1973—; pres. Teon, Inc., Burton, 1974-81. Served with USAF, 1952-56. Mem. Soc. Real Estate Appraisers (past chpt. pres.), Nat. Acad. Conciliators (conciliator), Flint Bd. Realtors, Genesee County Assessors Assn., Am. Arbitration Assn. (arbitrator), Home Builders Assn. Flint. Methodist. Clubs: Bristol-Hill Kiwanis; Flint Elks. Home: 2432 Valley Lane Dr Grand Blanc MI 48439 Office: 1423 E Bristol Burton MI 48529

O'NEILL, ARTHUR J., bishop; b. East Dubuque, Ill., Dec. 14, 1917; student Loras Coll., Dubuque, Iowa, St. Mary's Sem., Balt. Ordained priest Roman Cath. Ch., 1943; bishop of Rockford (Ill.), 1968—. Office: 1245 N Court St Rockford IL 61101*

O'NEILL, BETTY, oil co. exec.; b. Canton, Ohio, May 19, 1938; d. Elmer George and Mary Josephine (Monter) O'N.; degree in fashion merchandising Stevens Career Coll., 1961; student Malone Coll.; m. Morgan W. Roderick, Jr., Nov. 6, 1979; 1 son, David William. Fashion coordinator Stern & Mann's, Canton, 1962-68; fashion and sales coordinator Kenneth Beauty Salons and Products, Inc., N.Y.C., 1968-72; dir. fashion merchandising McKinley Tech. Inst., Canton, 1971-72; fashion and sales coordinator Fashion 220 Cosmetics, Aurora, Ohio, 1972-75; v.p. Amtex Oil and Gas Inc., Canton, 1975—; fashion cons. Gay Gibson Dress Co. Docent Canton Art Inst.; active Canton Civic Ballet; chmn. Ruff Community Forum. Recipient Career award Fashion Grop of Cleve., 1970. Mem. Ohio Oil and Gas Assn., Smithsonian Assos., Network, Inc. Republican. Roman Catholic. Clubs: Juli-Fe View Country, Four Seasons Swim, Petroleum, Skyland Pines. Home: 2010 Woodlawn St NW Canton OH 44708 Office: 573 Citizens Savs Bldg Canton OH 44702

O'NEILL, CLAIRE BERNADETTE, security services corp. ofcl.; b. Chgo., Sept. 29, 1943; d. Harold William and Clara Jeannette (Pape) Glavin; student Immaculata Sch., Chgo.; m. Patrick F. O'Neill, Sept. 30, 1961; children—Kathleen Claire, Patrick Sean. Asst. service mgr. Jewel Food Stores, Chgo., 1961-65; civil service examiner Chgo. Park Dist., 1969-79; dist. mgr. Burns Internat. Security Services, Inc., Hinsdale, Ill., 1979-80, asst. mgr. nuclear unit, Bensenville, Ill., 1980-81, nuclear personnel specialist, 1981—. Active Chgo. Park Dist. Air and Water Show, 1971—, awards, 1977, 78; active 47th Ward Regular Dem. Orgn.; mem. Ravenswood Conservation Com., 1975-78. Mem. Am. Soc. Indsl. Security, Chgo. Park Dist. Employees Assn. (dir., chmn. publicity com. 1976-79), Nat. Assn. Female Execs., Am. Soc. Profl. and Exec. Women, Chgo. Police Wives Assn. (sec. 1969-70). Roman Catholic. Creator, writer column Park Pal, Parkways, 1977-79. Office: 252 James St Bensenville IL 60106

O'NEILL, JOHN, lawyer; b. Logansport, Ind., July 24, 1939; s. Donald D. and Virginia B. O'N.; student Wabash Coll., 1958-61; B.S., Ind. U.-Purdue U. at Indpls., 1968, J.D., 1971; children—Shawn, Johnna, Taylor. Admitted to Ind. bar, 1971; partner firm Hirschauer & O'Neill, Logansport, 1971—; dir., atty. Community State Bank (Royal Center, Ind.); county atty. Cass County, Ind., 1972—; atty. Pioneer Community Sch. Corp., Cass County Plan Commn., 1972—, Cass County Drainage Bd., 1972-78. Pres. Cass County United Way, 1977, Cass County A.R.C., 1978; trustee Meml. Hosp. Served with U.S. Army, 1965-67. Mem. Am. Bar Assn., Ind. Bar Assn., Cass County Bar Assn. Republican. Clubs: Masons, Elks. Home: 2412 North St Logansport IN 46947 Office: 220 4th St Logansport IN 46947

O'NEILL, JOHN JOSEPH, audiologist, educator; b. DePere, Wis., Dec. 6, 1920; s. John Joseph and Elizabeth (Murray) O'N.; B.S., Ohio State U., 1947, Ph.D., 1951; m. Dorothy J. Arnold, Dec. 28, 1943; children—Katherine, Thomas, John, Philip. Instr., Ohio State U., Columbus, 1949-51, asst. prof., 1951-57, asso. prof., 1957-59; faculty U. Ill., Champaign, 1959—, prof. speech and hearing sci. Coll. Medicine, 1965—. Served with Inf., U.S. Army, 1942-46. Decorated Purple Heart, Bronze Star with oak leaf cluster; recipient Disting. Alumnus award Ohio State U., 1969. Fellow Am. Speech, Lang. and Hearing Assn. (honors 1979); mem. Am. Psychol. Assn., Acoustical Soc. Am., Acad. Rehabilitative Audiology. Democrat. Roman Catholic. Author: (with H.J. Oyer) Visual Communication, 1961; Hard of Hearing, 1964; Applied Audiometry, 1966. Home: 1113 W Church St Champaign IL 61820 Office: University of Illinois 901 S 6th St Champaign IL 61820

O'NEILL, MICHAEL STEVEN, clin. psychologist; b. Oakland, Calif., Dec. 10, 1944; s. Francis Carroll and Ellen Geraldine (Harper) O'N.; B.S., Brigham Young U., 1965; M.A., U. Utah, 1968, Ph.D., 1974; m. Claudia Moss, Jan. 11, 1964; children—Timalyn, Malachi Merritt, Morggan Patrick. Asso. psychologist, Childrens Center, Salt Lake City, 1969-71; dir. children services Med Nebr. Community Mental Health Center, Grand Island, 1971-74, clin. dir., 1974-75; pvt. clin. practice specializing in children and adolescents, Grand Island, 1975—; advisor cons. mental health, tng. office Nebr. Head Start, 1973—; dir. Family/Child Center, 1980—; pres. Grasslands Press. Bd. dirs. Childrens Village Grand Island, 1973-75, YMCA, Grand Island, 1975—; mem. bd. edn. Grand Island Public Schs. USPHS fellow, 1965. Mem. Mem. Am., Midwestern, Rocky Mountain, Nebr. psychol. assns., Nebr. Soc. Profl. Psychologists, Am. Soc. Psychologists in Pvt. Practice, Assn. Children with Learning Disabilities, Nat. Soc. Autistic Children, Sigma Xi. Home: 1603 Gretchen Ave Grand Island NE 68801 Office: 321 W 2d St Grand Island NE 68801

O'NEILL, TIMOTHY JAMES, retail co. exec.; b. Cadillac, Mich., Dec. 14, 1949; s. Jack Whyte and Dorothy Ann (Kroth) O'N.; student Regis Coll., 1967-69; B.A. in Bus. Adminstrn., Aquinas Coll., Grand Rapids, Mich.; m. Mary Diane Stilwell, June 27, 1970; children—Molly Ann, Brian James. With Ace Hardware, Cadillac, 1963-68, Nat. Biscuit Co., Cadillac, 1968, Maurer Office Supply, 1970; owner O'Neill Office Supply Co., Cadillac, 1971-76; pres. O'Neill Office Center, Inc., 1976—, O'Neill Co., 1976—. Pres., Wexford County Easter Seal Soc., 1976-77; bd. dirs. United Way of Wexford County, 1973-75, sec., 1974; bd. dirs. City of Cadillac Police and Firemen's Pension Trust, 1977-81, pres., 1979—; mem. adv. bd. Wexford-Missaukee Vocat. Center, 1972-79. Recipient Geyer's Dealer Topics Nat. Dealer award, 1979. Mem. Cadillac Area C. of C., Cadillac Area Retailers Assn., Nat. Office Products Assn., Nat. Office Machines Dealers Assn., Mich. Retail Hardware Assn., Nat. Retail Hardware Assn., Nat. Fedn. Ind. Bus. Republican. Roman Catholic. Club: Cadillac Rotary (pres. 1976-77). Home: 515 Oak St Cadillac MI 49602 Office: 116 W Harris St Cadillac MI 49601

O'NEILL, WILLIAM JAMES, JR., transp. co. exec.; b. Cleve., Aug. 28, 1933; s. William James and Dorothy (Kundtz) O'N.; B.S. cum laude, Georgetown U., 1955; J.D., Harvard U., 1958; m. Deborah J. Baker, Oct. 22, 1966; children—Alec M., Sara L., Jessie A., Laura E. Admitted to Ohio bar, 1958; gen. counsel Leaseway Transp. Corp. and subs.'s, 1961-67, East coast group head, Phila., 1967-68; v.p. East coast group, 1968-69, sr. v.p., Cleve., 1969-74, pres., chief operating officer, 1974-80, exec. v.p. planning and devel., 1980—. Trustee, Dyke Coll. Corp., O'Neill Bros. Found., Gilmour Acad., Bluecoats, Inc. (all Cleve.). Served to capt. USAF, 1958-61. Recipient Air Force Commendation medal with oak leaf cluster; named Man of Year, Gilmour Acad., 1974. Mem. Pvt. Truck Council, Am. Trucking Assn. (pvt. carrier conf.), Truck Renting and Leasing Assn. (pres. 1980-81, dir.). Roman Catholic. Clubs: Chagrin Valley Hunt, Country, Cleve. Polo. Home: Hunting Valley OH Office: 3700 Park East Dr Cleveland OH 44122

ONG, JOHN DOYLE, rubber products co. exec.; b. Uhrichsville, Ohio, Sept. 29, 1933; s. Louis Brosee and Mary Ellen (Liggett) O.; B.A., Ohio State U., 1954, M.A., 1954; LL.B., Harvard U., 1957; m. Mary Lee Schupp, July 20, 1957; children—John Francis Harlan,

Richard Penn Blackburn, Mary Katherine Caine. Admitted to Ohio bar, 1958; asst. counsel B.F. Goodrich Co., Akron, Ohio, 1961-66, group v.p., 1972-73, dir., 1973—, exec. v.p., 1973-74, vice chmn. bd., 1974-75, pres., 1975-77, pres. and chief operating officer, 1978-79, pres., chmn. bd., chief exec. officer, 1979—; asst. to pres. Internat. B.F. Goodrich Co., Akron, 1966-69, v.p., 1969-70, pres., 1970-72; dir. Cooper Industries, Kroger Co., Ohio Bell Telephone Co. Vice pres. exploring Gt. Trail council Boy Scouts Am., 1974-77; bus. adv. com. Transp. Center, Northwestern U., 1975-78. Trustee St. John's Home for Girls, Painesville, 1969-71, Kent State U. Found., 1974-76, Bexley Hall Sem., Rochester, N.Y., 1974—; trustee Western Res. Acad., Hudson, Ohio, 1975—, pres. bd. trustees, 1977—; trustee Case Western Res. U., 1980—; nat. trustee Nat. Symphony Orch., 1975—; pres. bd. trustees Akron Community Trusts; adv. bd. Blossom Music Center; bus. adv. council Carnegie Mellon U., 1978—. Served with Judge Adv. Gen.'s Corps, AUS, 1957-61. Mem. Ohio Bar Assn. (corp. counsel sect. bd. govs. 1962-73, chmn. 1970), Rubber Mfrs. Assn. (dir.), Chem. Mfrs. Assn. (dir.), Hudson Library and Hist. Soc. (pres. 1971-72, trustee), Conf. Bd., Phi Beta Kappa, Phi Alpha Theta. Episcopalian. Clubs: Akron City, Portage Country (Akron); Links, Union League (N.Y.C.); Union (Cleve.); Rolling Rock (Ligonier, Pa.); Country of Hudson (Ohio); Met. (Washington); Castalia (Ohio) Trout. Home: 230 Aurora St Hudson OH 44236 Office: 500 S Main St Akron OH 44318

ONG, WALTER JACKSON, clergyman, educator, author; b. Kansas City, Mo., Nov. 30, 1912; s. Walter Jackson and Blanche Eugenia (Mense) O.; A.B., Rockhurst Coll., 1933; Ph.L., St. Louis U., 1940, A.M., 1941, S.T.L., 1948; Ph.D., Harvard U., 1955; various hon. degrees. Newspaper, comml. positions until 1935; entered Soc. of Jesus, 1935, ordained priest, Roman Catholic Ch., 1946; instr. English and French, Regis Coll., Denver, 1941-43; asst. in English, St. Louis U., 1944-47, instr., 1953-54, asst. prof., 1954-57, asso. prof., 1957-59, prof., 1959—, prof. humanities in psychiatry Sch. Medicine, 1970—, Univ. prof. humanities, 1981—. Mem. Fulbright nat. selection com., France, 1957-58, chmn., 1958; regional asso. Am. Council Learned Socs. 1957-66; mem. White House Task Force on Edn., 1966-67; mem. Nat. Council on Humanities, 1968-74, vice chmn., 1971-74; co-chmn. adv. com. on sci., tech. and human values Nat. Endowment for Humanities, 1974-78; mem. Rockefeller Found. Commn. on Humanities, 1978-80. Guggenheim fellow, 1949-50, 51-52; fellow Center Advanced Studies, Wesleyan U., Middletown, Conn., 1961-62, Sch. Letters, Ind. U., 1965—; fellow Center for Advanced Study in Behavioral Scis., Stanford, 1973-74; vis. prof. U. Calif., 1960; Terry lectr. Yale, 1963-64; vis. lectr. U. Poitiers, 1962; Berg prof. English, N.Y. U., 1966-67; McDonald lectr. McGill U., 1967-68; Willett vis. prof. humanities U. Chgo., 1968-69; nat. Phi Beta Kappa vis. scholar, 1969-70; Lincoln lectr. Central and West Africa, 1973-74; Messenger lectr. Cornell U., 1979-80. Adv. bd. John Simon Guggenheim Meml. Found.; trustee Nat. Humanities Faculty, 1968-76, chmn., 1974-76. Decorated chevalier l'Ordre des Palmes Académiques (France). Fellow Am. Acad. Arts and Scis.; mem. AAUP, Renaissance Soc. Am. (adv. council 1957-59), MLA (pres. 1978), Modern Humanities Research Assn., Nat. Council Tchrs. English, Cambridge Bibliog. Soc. (Eng.), Catholic Commn. Intellectual and Cultural Affairs (exec. com. 1962-63), Milton Soc. of Am. (pres. 1967), Phi Beta Kappa, Alpha Sigma Nu. Author: Frontiers in American Catholicism, 1957; Ramus, Method, and the Decay of Dialogue, 1958; Ramus and Talon Inventory, 1958; Am. Cath. Crossroads, 1959; The Barbarian Within, 1962; In the Human Grain, 1967; The Presence of the Word, 1967; Rhetoric, Romance and Technology, 1971; Why Talk?, 1973; Interfaces of the Word, 1977; Fighting for Life: Contest, Sexuality, and Consciousness, 1981; co-author, editor: Darwin's Vision and Christian Perspectives, 1960; Knowledge and the Future of Man, 1968. Editor: Petrus Ramus and Audomarus Talaeus, Collectaneae praefationes epistolae, orationes, 1969; Petrus Ramus, Scholae in liberales artes, 1970. Editorial bd. Studies in English Literature, 1962—; editorial adv. bd. Philosophy and Rhetoric, 1967—, The English Literary Renaissance, 1969—, Manuscripta, 1957—, others. Contbr. articles, chpts. learned and popular publs. Address: St Louis University Saint Louis MO 63103

ONODA, BRIGHT YASUNORI, physician; b. Cosmopolis, Wash., July 25, 1921; s. Sanjuru and Yaeko (Shingai) O.; B.S., Hillsdale (Mich.) Coll., 1948; M.D., U. Mich., 1952; m. Teresa Peters, Aug. 13, 1976; children—Carol, Paul. Intern, Harper Hosp., Detroit, 1952-53; resident U. Chgo. Clinics, 1956-57, St. Luke's Hosp., Chgo., 1957-58; dir. dept. anesthesiology Augustana Hosp., Chgo., 1973—, med. dir. respiratory care dept., 1968—, also mem. exec. com., treas. med. staff. Bd. dirs. Augustana Hosp., 1978—. Served in U.S. Army, 1945-48. Diplomate Am. Bd. Anesthesiology. Fellow Am. Coll. Anesthesiologists; mem. AMA, Chgo. Med. Soc., Am. Soc. Anesthesiologists, Ill. Soc. Anesthesiologists, Am. Legion. Home: 9023 Tamaroa Skokie IL 60067 Office: 411 W Dickens Chicago IL 60614

ONOFRIO, ANGELO MICHAEL, counseling psychologist; b. Chgo., June 26, 1947; s. Angelo M. and Lucille Marie (Bagnolia) O.; B.A. with distinction, U. Ill., 1969; M.A. in Counseling Psychology, Roosevelt U., 1974. Tchr. of reading and English, Hyde Park High Sch., Chgo., 1970-71; tchr. St. Joseph High Sch., Westchester, Ill., 1971-72; grad. asst. Coll. of Edn., Roosevelt U., Chgo., 1972-74; reading therapist and counselor Student Counseling Service, U. Ill., Chgo., 1974; English tutor Alexander-Smith Acad., Chgo., 1974-75; counselor Morton Coll., Cicero, Ill., 1975—, also instr. English, 1975—. Mem. Am., Ill. personnel and guidance assns., Nat. Council Tchrs. of English, Nat. Vocat. Guidance Assn., U. Ill., Roosevelt U. alumni assns. Democrat. Roman Catholic. Home: 1005 Des Plaines Ave Forest Park IL 60130 Office: 3801 S Central Ave Cicero IL 60650

ONOFRIO, CATHERINE FRANCES, educator; b. Chgo., Mar. 8, 1953; d. Louis and Margaret Sophie (Nicholson) O.; B.S.E.E., DePaul U., 1974, M.A. with distinction, 1979; postgrad. U. Chgo., 1980—. Tchr., Bernard Moos Sch., Chgo. Bd. Edn., 1974-76, Duke Ellington Br. Sch., 1976-78, basic skills resource tchr. Burbank Sch., 1978-79, basic skills tchr., 1979—, also volleyball coach, girl's basketball coach, tchr. sign lang.; instr. Inst. Fin. Edn. Cert. K-9 tchr., supr., adminstr., Ill; cert. K-3 tchr., Chgo. Mem. Assn. for Supervision and Curriculum Devel., Council for Basic Edn., Assn. Tchrs. Educators, Gregorians (sec.), Phi Delta Kappa, Kappa Delta Phi. Clubs: Cath. Alumni, De Paul Booster. Office: 2035 N Mobile St Chicago IL 60639

OPDAHL, KEITH MICHAEL, educator; b. Cook County, Ill., Nov. 4, 1934; s. Olaf Solomon and Florence Hilda (Holmquist) O.; B.A., Denison U., 1956; M.A., U. Ill., 1957, Ph.D., 1961; m. Martha Donovan, June 5, 1965; children—Michael, Cristina. Teaching asst. U. Ill., 1957-61; instr. U. Wis., 1961-64, asst. prof., 1964-67; asst. prof. English, DePauw U., Greencastle, Ind., 1967-69, asso. prof., 1969-77, prof., 1977—. DePauw-Ford Found. fellow, 1967, 68, 69, 71, 72, 74; Fulbright fellow, 1971-72. Mem. MLA. Author: The Novels of Saul Bellow, 1967. Office: DePauw U 304 Asbury St Greencastle IN 46135

OPFERMAN, CHARLES ROBERT, architect; b. Waukegan, Ill., Dec. 8, 1951; s. Charles Robert and Constance (Tribou) O.; student Case Western Res. U., 1970-72; B.S. with honors in Archtl. Studies, U. Wis. Milw., 1974, M.Arch., 1981. Supt., C.M. Assos. of Milw., Inc., 1976-77, estimator, 1977-78, v.p. ops., 1978—. Mem. AIA, Soc. Am. Value Engrs. Home: 1029 E Kewaunee St Milwaukee WI 53202 Office: 6323 W Douglas Ave Milwaukee WI 53218

OPHEIM, VERNON HOLMEN, musician; b. Alta., Can., Dec. 29, 1931; s. Ingvald Pederson and Mattie Opheim; came to U.S., 1953, naturalized, 1963; student Augsburg Coll., Mpls., 1950-51; B.A. in Music Edn., Concordia Coll., 1954; M.M., Mac Phail Sch. Music, 1966; D.M.A., U. Ill., 1971; m. Avis Leone Walwick, Apr. 5, 1955; children—Kathryn, Mayme, Kara. Tchr., Moorhead (Minn.) public schs., 1955-66; mem. faculty U. Ill., Urbana, 1966-69, U. Maine, Orono, 1969-72; asso. prof. music U. Minn., Duluth, 1972—; choral clinician, adjudicator, 1959—. Maurice and Lillian Knutson conducting scholar, 1954. Mem. Am. Choral Dirs. Assn. (dir. Minn. chpt.), Coll. Music Soc., Am. Musical Soc., Music Educators Nat. Conf., NEA. Lutheran. Home: 1826 Vermilion Rd Duluth MN 55803 Office: Music Dept Univ Minn Duluth MN 55812

OPITZ, DAVID WILMER, businessman, state senator; b. Port Washington, Wis., Dec. 15, 1945; s. Wilmer Charles and Ella B. (Lonesdale) O.; B.S. Carroll Coll., 1968; m. Nancy Opitz, Dec. 29, 1979. Biologist, Aqua-Tech, Inc., Port Washington, 1968-73, sales and tech. rep., 1973-76, pres., 1976—; mem. Wis. Assembly, 1972-79, Wis. Senate, 1979—. Republican. Club: Elks.

OPSAL, JANICE MARJORIE, nurse; b. Hector, Minn., Apr. 20, 1932; d. David LeRoy and Luverne Dora Carlson; student St. Paul Bible Coll., 1953, Bethel Coll., 1954; R.N., Swedish Hosp., 1953; B.S. in Public Health Nursing, U. Minn., 1962; m. Donald A. Opsal, Aug. 28, 1953; children—Lori, Michael. Staff nurse Swedish Hosp., Mpls., 1953-56; office nurse, mgr. doctor's office, Mpls., 1956-58; staff nurse Douglas County Hosp., Alexandria, Minn., 1958-59; county public health nurse Douglas County, Alexandria, 1959-61; nurse dir. program practical nursing Alexandria Area Tech. Inst., 1962—; chair adv. com. nursing edn. to Higher Edn. Coordinating Bd., 1978-79. Pres. Alexandria Baptist Women's Soc., 1975-76. Mem. Am. Nurses Assn., Minn. Nurses Assn., Am. Vocat. Assn., Minn. Vocat. Assn., Nat. League Nursing, Minn. League Nursing, NEA, Minn. Edn. Assn. Club: Alexandria Euterpean (pres. 1965-66). Home: Route 1 Box 860 Lake Darling Alexandria MN 56308 Office: 1601 Jefferson St Alexandria MN 56308

O'QUINN, MILTON LAFAYETTE, bus. machines co. exec.; b. Chgo., Apr. 19, 1944; s. John William and Cleodia L. (Dawkins) O'Q.; B.A., Houston-Tillotson Coll., 1967; postgrad. U. Chgo. Grad. Sch. Bus., 1968-71; children—Lynn, Milton Lafayette, John, Lisa. Sales rep. Lever Bros., 1967; account rep. Procter & Gamble, 1968-71; account rep. Xerox Corp., Chgo., 1971-73, systems specialist, Mpls., 1974-76, sales mgr., 1976-78, br. mgr. sales, 1978-80, region sales ops. mgr. Midwest Region, Des Plaines, Ill., 1980—; br. dir. Chgo. Youth Centers, Altgeld-Roseland, 1975-77. Bd. dirs. South Shore Community Center, Chgo., Marcy-Newberry Assn.; v.p. West Side Assn. for Community Action, 1974-75; co-founder O'Quinn Royal Gladiators Drum and Bugle Corp. Mem. Bloomington C. of C., Am. Legion, Kappa Alpha Psi. Home: 2240 Hassell Rd Hoffman Estates IL 60195 Office: 3000 Des Plaines Des Plaines IL 60018

ORAZEM, FRANK, economist; b. Slovenia, Yugoslavia, Jan. 19, 1925; came to U.S., 1949, naturalized, 1954; s. Marko and Marija (Merhar) O.; Dr.rer.pol., Karl Franzens U., Graz (Austria), 1949; M.S., Kans. State U., 1953; Ph.D., Iowa State U., 1956; m. Slava Furlan, June 30, 1953; children—Mark, Peter, Mary Anne, Thomas, Helena. With Dept. Agr., 1954-56; mem. faculty Kans. State U., 1956—, prof. econs., 1966—; Fulbright lectr., vis. prof. U. Naples (Italy), 1964-65; cons. FAO, India, 1978. Served with AUS, 1950-52. Recipient Gamma Sigma Delta award, 1973; social scis. grad. faculty award Kans. State U., 1973, sr. faculty award, 1980. Mem. Am. Agrl. Econs. Assn., Am. Assn. Advancement Slavic Studies, Assn. Social Econs. Author: Production Economics: Theory with Applications (with J. Doll), 1978. Address: 609 Bertrand St Manhattan KS 66502

ORCHARD, ELWOOD FRANK, mfg. co. exec.; b. Sanilac County, Mich., Oct. 20, 1936; s. Frank Herbert and Alma Dale O.; B.A., Mich. State U., 1959; M.B.A., Wayne State U., 1973; m. Leota Mae Munger, Sept. 7, 1957; children—Lori Michelle, Wendy Lea, Marti June. Acct., Price Waterhouse & Co., Detroit, 1964-68; with Ford Motor Co., Dearborn, Mich., 1968-75; dir. audit services, Internat. Multifoods, Mpls., 1975—. Served to 1st lt., USAF, 1959-64. C.P.A., Minn. Mem. Am. Inst. C.P.A.'s, Minn. Soc. C.P.A.'s, Inst. Internal Auditors. Club: Mpls. Athletic. Home: 6613 Dakota Trail Edina MN 55435 Office: 1200 Multifoods Bldg 8th St and Marquette St Minneapolis MN 55402

ORDINACHEV, MILES DONALD, educator; b. St. Louis, Oct. 23, 1926; s. Delmar Marko and Ann Louise (Allen) O.; B.S., Washington U., St. Louis, 1968, postgrad. computer sci., 1975, grad. media specialist, 1980; M.A. in Edn., 1980; m. Joan Slinkard Harter, Mar. 11, 1978; children from previous marriage—Linda, Jean. With Midwest Pipe & Supply Co., St. Louis, 1944-47, Bailey Tech. Sch., St. Louis, 1950-53; dir. instr. Mo. Tech. Sch., St. Louis, 1953-63; instruction programmer Perceptual Devel. Labs., St. Louis, 1963-66; tchr., chmn. indsl. electronics dept. South County Tech. High Sch., Sunset Hills, Mo., 1966—. Mem. Am., Mo. vocat. assns., Spl. Sch. Dist. Community Tchrs. Assn. (pres. 1969-70), Mo., Greater St. Louis tchrs. assns., Midwest Soc. Individual Psychology, Assn. Supervision and Curriculum Devel. Clubs: Masons, Shriners, Computer. Home: 9541 Avila Dr Affton MO 63123 Office: 12721 W Watson Rd Sunset Hills MO 63127

OREFFICE, PAUL FAUSTO, chem. co. exec.; b. Venice, Italy, Nov. 29, 1927; s. Max and Elena (Friedenberg) O.; came to U.S., 1945, naturalized, 1951; B.S. in Chem. Engring., Purdue U., 1949; m. Franca Giuseppina Ruffini, May 26, 1956; children—Laura Emma, Andrew T. With Dow Chem. Co., various internat. locations, 1955—, pres. Dow Chem. Inter-Am., Ltd., Sao Paulo, Brazil and Bilbao, Spain, 1967-69, v.p., dir. fin. services Dow Chem. Internat., Inc., Coral Gables, Fla., 1969-70, v.p. finance Dow Chem. Co., Midland, Mich., 1970-74, v.p., treas., 1974-75, pres., 1978—, pres. Dow Chem. U.S.A., 1975-78, also dir.; dir. 1st Midland Bank & Trust Co., Midland, Conn. Gen. Ins. Co., Dow Corning. Nat. bd. dirs. Jr. Achievement; trustee Am. Enterprise Inst., Midland Community Center; mem. policy com. Bus. Roundtable; bd. govs. Purdue U. Found. Served with AUS, 1951-53. Decorated Encomienda del Merito Civil (Spain), 1966. Mem. Chem. Mfrs. Assn. (chmn.). Office: Dow Center Midland MI 48640

ORENDORFF, WILLIAM RADCLIFFE, banker; b. Kirksville, Mo., Dec. 21, 1949; s. Joseph Richard and Evelyn Gertrude (Radcliffe) O.; B.S. in Bus. Adminstrn., U. Mo., Columbia, 1971; m. Judith Ann McCune, July 19, 1969; 1 son, Edward Charles. Visual mdse. mgr. Sears, Roebuck & Co., Lawton, Okla. and Columbia, Mo., 1971-73; communications cons. Gen. Telephone Co. of Midwest, Columbia, Mo., 1973-74; sales rep. Equitable Life Assurance Soc. of U.S., 1974-75; asst. trust officer First Nat. Bank, Kirksville, 1977—; mem. student loan com. Mo. Dept. Higher Edn. Bd. dirs., pres.-elect Spring Lake Inc.; bd. dirs. Kirksville Community Center, Kirksville Cardio-Pulmonary Resuscitation Tng. Center; chmn. Adair County Heart Assn.; capt. retail div. Adair County United Fund Campaign; bd. dirs., treas., chmn. finance com. Kirksville Family YMCA. Served with U.S. Army, 1975-77. Mem. Mo. Bankers Assn. (compliance com.), Kirksville C. of C., Kirksville Jr. C. of C. (dir.). Methodist. Home: Spring Lake PO Box 306 Kirksville MO 63501 Office: First Nat Bank PO Box 289 Kirksville MO 63501

ORFANOS, MINNIE, librarian; b. Hinsdale, Ill., Dec. 10, 1921; d. Antonious George and Catherine (Lekatsos) Orfanos; Ph.B., Northwestern U., 1954; M.A. in L.S., U. Mich., 1958. Library clk. Chgo. Pub. Library, 1940-43; library asst. Dental Sch. Library, Northwestern U., Chgo., 1943-45, asst. librarian, 1945-50, acting librarian, 1950-52, librarian, 1952—. Sec. governing bd. Midwest Regional Med. Library, 1971-72, vice chmn., 1973, pres., 1974; cons., surveyor for Assn. Canadian Faculty of Dentistry, 1970-72; mem. grant rev. com. NIH, 1974; mem. Northwestern U. Library Council, 1975—; cons. dental libraries. Recipient Merit award for distinguished service to dentistry Am. Coll. Dentists, 1967. Mem. Med. Library Assn. (dental group chmn. 1952, sec. Midwest regional group 1957, pres. 1968; exchange com. 1964, chmn. exchange com. 1965—, exec. com. Midwest group 1965—, cons. to coms., fin. trustee 1976-77), Am. Assn. Dental Schs., Sigma Phi Alpha. Roman Catholic. Contbr. articles to profl. publs. Compiler list of textbooks for dental curriculum Acad. Ednl. Devel., 1977. Home: 45 Wilmette Ave Glenview IL 60025 Office: 311 E Chicago Ave Chicago IL 60611

ORFIELD, GARY ALLAN, polit. scientist; b. Mpls., Sept. 5, 1941; s. Myron Willard and Melba Berniece (Lindseth) O.; B.A. summa cum laude, U. Minn., 1963; M.A., U. Chgo., 1965, Ph.D., 1968; m. Antonia Marie Stoll, May 24, 1963; children—Amy, Sonia, Rosanna. Asst. prof. U. Va., 1967-69; asst. prof. politics and public affairs Princeton U., 1969-73; scholar-in-residence U.S. Civil Rights Com., Washington, 1972-73; research asso. Brookings Inst., Washington, 1973-77; asso. prof. U. Ill., Urbana, 1977-80, prof. dept. polit. sci. and Inst. Govt., 1980-81; prof. dept. polit. sci. U. Chgo., 1981—; chmn. Nat. Inst. Edn. Study Group on Desegregation Research, 1979-81; cons. Ford Found., HUD, Rand Corp., Ill. Office Edn., sch. bds.; chmn. tech. assistance com. Chgo. Desegregation Plan, Ill. State Bd. Edn.; bd. dirs. Fund for an Open Soc., Policy Studies Orgn., 1980. Woodrow Wilson fellow, 1963-64; Danforth fellow, 1963-67; Falk fellow, 1963-65; Brookings fellow, 1966-67; Carnegie research grantee; Twentieth Century Fund research grantee, 1981-82. Democrat. Roman Catholic. Author: The Reconstruction of Southern Education: The Schools and the 1964 Civil Rights Act, 1969; Congressional Power: Congress and Social Change, 1975; Must We Bus? Segregated Schools and National Policy, 1978; Toward a Strategy for Urban Integration, 1981. Office: Dept Polit Sci Pick Hall U Chgo Chicago IL 60637

ORKIN, LOUIS H., lawyer; b. Cleve., Dec. 30, 1930; s. William H. and Dorothy K. (Kaspy) O.; J.D., Boston U., 1954; m. Charlotte Simon, July 10, 1959; children—Linda, Laura, Steven. Admitted to Ohio bar, 1954; asst. atty. gen. State of Ohio, 1957-59; individual practice law, 1959-60; asst. law dir. and pros. atty. Cleveland Heights (Ohio), 1961-64; partner firm Weiner, Orkin, Abbate & Suit, and predecessor firms, Beachwood, Ohio, 1964—; law dir., prosecutor City of Bedford (Ohio), 1964-73; pros. atty. Shaker Heights (Ohio), 1964—; law dir., prosecutor City of Beachwood, 1973—; acting judge Cleveland Heights Municipal Ct., 1969-72; prosecutor Hunting Valley (Ohio), 1977—; Village Solicitor Orange Village (Ohio), 1977—, Woodmere Village (Ohio), 1979—; Spl. Counsel to state atty gen.; asst. to pres., gen. counsel Peoples Bldg. & Loan Co.; adj. prof. mcpl. law Cleve. State Law Sch., 1974—. Mem. Am. Bar Assn., Ohio Bar Assn., Cleve. Bar Assn., Cuyahoga County Bar Assn., Nat. Assn. Mcpl. Law Officers, Ohio Assn. Attys. Gen., Am. Soc. Hosp. Attys. (charter mem.), Am. Trial Lawyers Assn., Ohio Acad. Trial Lawyers, Cuyahoga County Law Dirs. Assn., Suburban East Bar Assn. (v.p.). Home: 23400 Ranch Rd Beachwood OH 44122 Office: 24200 Chagrin Blvd Beachwood OH 44122

ORLOCK, ROBERT EUGENE, computer services co. exec.; b. Chgo., June 9, 1925; s. Arthur J. and Verona J. (Murphy) O.; B.A., UCLA, 1952; m. Dorothy Drummond, Sept. 13, 1961. With Bank of Am., 1948-58, Fireman's Fund Inc., 1958-61, Continental Assurance, 1961-64, Stanley Publ. Co., 1964-74; pres., owner Orlock Co., Inc., Chgo., 1974—. Served with USN, 1942-46. Clubs: Glen Oak Country, Plaza. Home: 3 Wheaton Center Wheaton IL 60187 Office: 230 N Michigan Ave Chicago IL 60601

ORLOPP, MARILYNN JEANETTE, ednl. adminstr.; b. Milw., Sept. 30, 1948; d. Walter E. and Annette C. (Lawonn) Schueler; B.S., U. Wis., 1971, postgrad. 1973—; m. Richard Orlopp, Jan. 15, 1972; 1 son, Daniel Richard. Distributive edn. tchr. Germantown (Wis.) Public Schs., 1972-77, Milw. Pub. Schs., 1977-79; adminstr. Germantown Public Schs., 1979—; coordinator lodging/tourism specialty program Wis. Distributive Edn. Clubs Am. Conf. Staff, 1974-79. Recipient Mktg. Student of the Yr. award Waukesha County Tech. Inst., 1969. Mem. Wis. Assn. Secondary Distributive Edn. Tchrs. (pres. 1976-77), Wis. Assn. Vocat. Educators, Am. Vocat. Educators, Wis. Assn. Secondary Vocational Adminstrs., Distributive Edn. Clubs Am. (nat. award 1969, service award Wis. chpt. 1981). Office: W180 N11501 River Ln Germantown WI 53022

ORMOND, BETTY LOU (HAYDEN), employment agency exec.; b. LaPlata, Mo., Dec. 31, 1931; d. Laurice P. and Cecil J. (Whitfield) Hayden; ed. high sch.; m. Walter James Ormond, Apr. 12, 1952; children—Becky Sue, John Joseph. Various secretarial, clerical positions, Ill., 1949-59; specialist consumer relations Audio Products div. Gen. Electric Co., Decatur, Ill., 1959-69; mgr. Kelly Services, Decatur, 1969—; owner, mgr. Ormond Personnel Center, Decatur, 1972—; lectr. in field. Chairperson membership Decatur Convs. and Tourism Bur., 1975-76; bd. dirs. Jr. Achievement Decatur, 1977-81; bd. dirs. Pvt. Industry Council (CETA), 1979—, chmn., 1980-81; mem. Macon County Zoning Bd. Appeals, Decatur, 1977-81; mem. Richland Community Coll. Sex Equity Project Bd., 1978-80; adv. bd. Project Expand, Interagy. Sch. Dist. 61 and U. Ill., 1981—. Recipient Small Bus. award, 1981. Mem. Met. Decatur C. of C. (dir. 1976-78), Nat., Ill. (dir. 1976-78, pres. downstate chpt. 1976-77) employment assns., Nat. Personnel Assos. Presbyterian. Clubs: Altrusa of Decatur. Home: 4654 Hale Dr Decatur IL 62526 Office: 2645 N Oakland St Suite A Decatur IL 62526

ORNBERG, MARY KATHERINE, transp. exec.; b. Chgo., Aug. 3, 1947; d. Raymond P. and Pauline (Hanes) Czarnecki; div.; children—Richard, Catherine. With Fed. Express, 1977—, city mgr., Peoria, Ill., 1980—. Mem. Peoria C. of C., Peoria Airport Authority, Women in Mgmt. Club: Newcomers. Office: 1900 Maxwell Rd Peoria IL 61607

ORNDORFF, JAMES ALLEN, JR., civil engr.; b. Hanover, Pa., Oct. 31, 1949; s. James Allen and Dolores Elaine (Adams) O.; B.S. in Civil Engring., Pa. State U., 1971, M.S. in Civil Engring., 1974; m. Diane Lynn Kohler, Sept. 22, 1973. Faculty research asst. Pa. State U., 1972-74; design engr. Chgo. Bridge & Iron Co., Oak Brook, Ill., 1975—. Served with U.S. Army, 1974. Registered profl. engr., Ill. Republican. Patentee in field. Home: 541 Kenilworth Ave Glen Ellyn IL 60137 Office: 800 Jorie Blvd Oak Brook IL 60521

O'ROURKE, EDWARD WILLIAM, bishop; b. Downs, Ill., Oct. 31, 1917; s. Martin and Mary (Hickey) O'R.; student St. Henry's Coll., Belleville, Ill., 1935-38; B.A., St. Mary of the Lake Sem., Mundelein, Ill., 1940, M.A., 1942, S.T.L., 1944; Licentiate of Philosophy, Aquinas Inst., River Forest, Ill., 1960. Ordained priest Roman Cath. Ch., 1944, bishop, 1971; asst. chaplain Newman Found., U. Ill., 1944-59; exec. dir. Nat. Cath. Rural Life Conf., Des Moines, 1960-71; bishop of Peoria, Ill., 1971—. Dir. refugee resettlement Diocese of Peoria, 1948-59; chmn. arbitration com. Nat. Conf. Cath. Bishops, 1973-76; chmn. priorities com. Peoria United Fund, 1972-73; bd. dirs. Internat. Vol. Services, 1960-71; trustee Cath. Relief Services, 1978-80; chmn. bd. Am. Coll. Louvain, 1977-80. Recipient John Henry Newman award, 1959, Nat. Cath. Rural Life Conf. Disting. Service award, 1973. Club: KC Author: Marriage and Family Life, 1955; Fundamentals of Philosophy, 1956; Gift of Gifts, 1977; Self Help Works, 1978; Living Like a King, 1979; Roots of Human Rights, 1981. Editor Cath. Rural Life mag., 1960-71. Address: 607 NE Madison Ave PO Box 1406 Peoria IL 61655

O'ROURKE, EDWARD WILLIAM, bishop; b. Downs, Ill., Oct. 31, 1917; s. Martin and Mary (Hickey) O'R.; student St. Henry's Coll., Belleville, Ill., 1935-38; B.A., St. Mary of the Lake Sem., Mundelein, Ill., 1940, M.A., 1942, S.T.L., 1944; Licentiate of Philosophy, Aquinas Inst., River Forest, Ill., 1960. Ordained priest Roman Cath. Ch., 1944, bishop, 1971; asst. chaplain Newman Found., U. Ill., 1944-59; exec. dir. Nat. Cath. Rural Life Conf., Des Moines, 1960-71; bishop of Peoria, Ill., 1971—. Dir. refugee resettlement Diocese of Peoria, 1948-59; chmn. arbitration com. Nat. Conf. Cath. Bishops, 1973-76. Chmn. priorities com. Peoria United Fund, 1972-73. Bd. dirs. Internat. Vol. Services, 1960-71; trustee Cath. Relief Services; chmn. bd. Am. Coll. Louvain. Recipient John Henry Newman award, 1959, Nat. Cath. Rural Life Conf. Disting. Service award, 1973. K.C. (4 deg.). Author: Marriage and Family Life, 1955; Fundamentals of Philosophy, 1956; Gift of Gifts, 1977; Self Help Works, 1978; Living Like a King, 1979. Editor: Cath. Rural Life Mag., 1960-71. Address: 607 NE Madison Ave Peoria IL 61603

O'ROURKE, J. TRACY, mfg. co. exec.; b. Columbia, S.C., Mar. 14, 1935; s. James Tracy and Georgia Adella (Bridges) O'R.; B.S.M.E., Auburn U., 1956; m. Lou Ann Turner, Mar. 19, 1954; 1 son, James Tracy. Teflon specialist duPont Co., Wilmington, Del., 1957-61; pres., chief exec. officer LNP Corp., Malvern, Pa., 1961-71; v.p. Carborundum, Niagara Falls, N.Y., 1971-75; exec. v.p. Chemetron, Chgo., 1975-78; sr. v.p. Allen Bradley Co., Milw., 1978—. Served to 1st lt. USAF, 1957-59. Office: 1201 S 2d St Milwaukee WI 53201

O'ROURKE, JAMES TIERNAN, art museum dir.; b. Langdon, N.D., July 20, 1933; s. Joseph M. and Mildred G. (Gustafson) O'R.; B.A., Concordia Coll., Moorhead, Minn., 1956. Founder, 1960, since dir. Rourke Gallery, Moorhead; instr. painting and design Moorhead State U., 1965-66; instr. art history N.D. State U., 1969; exec. dir., bd. dirs. Plains Art Mus., Moorhead, 1975—; v.p. Wahpeton (N.D.) Art Gallery, 1972-76; adv. panel Minn. Arts Bd., 1977—; mem. Moorhead Mayor's Art Adv. Panel, 1974-79; one-man shows include Fergus Falls (Minn.) Gallery, 1979, Dacotah Prairie Mus., Aberdeen, S.D., 1980, 2d Crossing Gallery, Valley City, N.D., 1980. Served with AUS, 1957-60. Recipient Bismarck (N.D.) art citation award, 1969, N.D. State Arts Council Achievement award 1980. Mem. Am. Assn. Museums, Plains Archtl. Heritage Found. (v.p., dir.). Home: 316 S 5th St Moorhead MN 56560 Office: 521 Main Ave Moorhead MN 56560

O'ROURKE, TERENCE JAMES, newspaper editor; b. Mpls., Oct. 29, 1926; s. James Thomas and Irene Catherine (Feeney) O'R.; student Gustavus Adolphus Coll., 1944; B.S., U. Minn., 1946, B.A. in Journalism, 1949; m. Shirley Ann Larson, Aug. 23, 1952; children—Karen, Kathryn, Mary Ellen, Kevin. With Rapid City (S.D.) Daily Jour., 1949-53; successively copy editor, news editor, city editor, mng. editor Gary (Ind.) Post-Tribune, 1953—; instr. Valparaiso U. Former pres. N.W. Ind. Boys Club; active Lake County Area United Way. Served as ensign, USNR, 1943-47. Mem. Ind. AP Mng. Editors Assn. (past pres.), Hoosier Press Assn., AP Mng. Editors, Am. Soc. Newspaper Editors, Merrillville C. of C. (dir.). Roman Catholic. Club: Lions (past pres.). Office: 1065 Broadway Gary IN 46410

ORR, BRUCE ALAN, real estate co. exec.; b. Des Moines, Jan. 3, 1948; s. Delbert Vernon and Betty Jean (Brown) O.; B.B.A., U. Iowa, 1970, postgrad., 1975-76. Mgmt. intern civil service Washington, 1970; nat. dir. youth affairs VA, Washington, 1971-72; coordinator ambulatory clinics Iowa City VA Hosp., 1972-73, asst. chief staff, 1973-76; gen. partner Medivestments Co., Iowa City, 1976—; pres. Orr Corp., Iowa City, 1976-80; pres. Melrose Corp., Iowa City, 1977—; cons., lectr. in field; dir. Regency Gardens Devel. Corp.; pres., chief exec. officer Urban Housing Mgmt., Ltd., 1980—. Mem. Nat. Small Bus. Assn. Home: 300 Samoa Ct Iowa City IA 52240 Office: 1200 Park Ave Muscatine IA 52761

ORR, CARL CLIFTON, ins. agy. exec.; b. Jonesboro, Ill., Apr. 1, 1915; s. John and Jessie Marie O.; ed. high sch.; m. Elizabeth N. Graham, Jan. 25, 1936; children—Kathryn Ann Orr Harvey, Carla J. Orr Brooks. Ins. salesman Country Cos., Union County, Ill., 1937-39, agy. mgr., Williamson County, Ill., 1939-40, Union County, 1940-44, 46-61, Williamson, Union, and Johnson Counties, Jonesboro, Ill., 1961—. Served with U.S. Army, 1944-46; ETO, MTO. C.L.U. Mem. So. Ill. Assn. Life Underwriters, Am. Soc. C.L.U.'s, Agy. Mgrs. Conf., Nat. Assn. Life Underwriters. Home: 112 Apple Ln Anna IL 62906

ORR, DARRELL CLARK, mfg. co. fin. exec.; b. Grand Forks, N.D., Sept. 29, 1938; s. Raymond Clark and Bernice (Anderson) O.; B.S. in Indsl. Mgmt., U. N.D., 1960; M.B.A. in Fin. Mgmt., Loyola U., Chgo., 1972; m. Maureen Scully, Jan. 30, 1960; children—Julie, Suzanne, Jeffrey. Asst. plant controller Nat. Can Corp., 1963-66, plant controller, 1966-67, group controller, 1967-68, mfg. methods specialist, 1968-70, adminstrv. asst., 1970-71, asst. plant mgr., 1971-72; corp. mgr. ops. analysis ATO Inc., 1972-73, div. controller George J. Meyer div., 1973-76, v.p., controller George J. Meyer Mfg. div., 1976-77, v.p. fin. and Latin Am. ops., 1977-79, v.p. fin. and internat. ops., 1979-81; v.p. fin. Heil Co., Milw., 1981—; dir. acctg. and adminstrn. Heil Co., Milw., 1979—. Bd. dirs. Trinity Meml. Hosp. Found., Cudahy, Wis., 1975. Served to 1st lt. U.S. Army, 1960-63. Mem. Nat. Assn. Accountants, Fin. Execs. Inst. Home: 12003 W Burdick Ave West Allis WI 53227 Office: 777 E Wisconsin Ave Suite 2800 Milwaukee WI 53202

ORR, EARL LAWTON, obstetrician-gynecologist; b. Savannah, Ga., July 12, 1934; s. Alfonso and Geneva Zenobia (Marks) O.; B.S., N.C. U., 1955; M.D., Meharry Med. Coll., 1960; m. Suzanne M. Harwood, Aug. 21, 1969 (dec. Aug. 1974); children—Alfonso, Rhonda, Vanessa, Andrea. Intern, Wilford Hall Hosp., San Antonio, 1960-61; resident Huron Rd. Hosp., Cleve., 1962-65, St. Vincent Hosp., Toledo, 1965-66; practice medicine specializing in obstetrics and gynecology, Chgo., 1967—; chief cons. gynecologist Louise Burg Hosp., 1969—; cons. Chgo. Bd. Health, 1969—; dir. obstetrics-gynecology Martin L. King Health Center, Chgo., 1968-74, Tabernacle Hosp., Chgo., 1974—; sr. attending St. Francis Cabrini Hosp., Chgo., 1976—; clin. asso. Chgo. Med. Sch., 1967-74. Fellow A.C.S., Internat. Coll. Surgeons, Am. Coll. Obstetrics and Gynecology, Am. Fertility Soc.; mem. AMA, Ill. Med. Assn., Chgo. Med. Soc. (profl. orientation com. 1972-74), Am. Assn. Gynecologic Laparoscopists. Roman Catholic. Home: 2825 S Michigan Ave Chicago IL 60616 Office: 3233 Martin L King Dr Chicago IL 60616

ORR, KENNETH FRANCIS, JR., drug mfg. co. ofcl.; b. Chgo., Oct. 18, 1946; s. Kenneth Francis and Agnes (Dhuysser) O.; B.S., So. Ill. U., 1970; m. Jane Czuj, Aug. 1, 1970; children—Kimberly, Thomas. Sr. copywriter CNA Fin., Chgo., 1970-73; dir. advt. N.Am. Co., Chgo., 1973-75; mktg. communications mgr. Travenol Labs., Deerfield, Ill., 1975—; cons. mfg. cos. Recipient 9 awards for graphic presentation, 2 for direct mail campaigns. Mem. Midwest Pharm. Advertisers Club, Med. Mktg. Assn. Roman Catholic. Mng. editor Infection Control and Urol. Care, 1975—. Home: 526 Bryant Ave Glen Ellyn IL 60137 Office: 1 Baxter Pkwy Deerfield IL 60015

ORR, KENNETH THOMAS, computer systems scientist; b. Pittsburg, Kans., May 10, 1939; s. Thomas Everett and Nell Thelma (Davis) O.; B.A., Wichita State U., 1960; m. Marlene B. Samra, Dec. 28, 1963; children—Nancy Marie, Judith Ann, Kathryn Elisabeth, Paige Marlene. Programmer, Boeing Airplane Co., Wichita, Kans., 1960; programmer U. Chgo., 1961-63; programmer/analyst Lutter & Maremont, Chgo., 1963-64; systems analyst Service Bur. Corp., Chgo., 1964-67; v.p. info. systems Daniel D. Howard & Assos., Chgo., 1967-70; dir. info. and communication systems State of Kans., Topeka, 1970-73; v.p. advanced systems Langston, Kitch & Assos., Topeka, 1973-80; pres. Ken Orr & Assos., Topeka, 1980—. Mem. Nat. Assn. State Info. Systems (regional dir. 1970-73), Chgo. Assn. for Computing Machinery (chpt. chmn. 1969-70), IEEE. Author: Structured Systems Development, 1977; Structured Requirements Definition, 1981; contbg. editor Infosystems Mag., 1977-81. Home: 104 Woodlawn St Topeka KS 66606 Office: 715 E 8th St Topeka KS 66607

ORR, ROBERT DUNKERSON, gov. Ind.; b. Ann Arbor, Mich., Nov. 17, 1917; s. Samuel Lowry and Louise (Dunkerson) O.; B.A., Yale U., 1940; postgrad. Harvard Bus. Sch., 1940-42; hon. degrees Ind. State U., 1973, Hanover Coll., 1974, Butler U., 1977; m. Joanne Wallace, Dec. 16, 1944; children—Robert Dunkerson, Susan Orr Dunn, Marjorie R. Orr Hail. Officer, dir. Orr Iron Co., 1946-50, Sign Crafters, Inc., 1957-74, Hahn, Inc., 1957-69, Indian Industries, Inc., 1962-73; mem. Ind. Senate, 1968-72; lt. gov. Ind., 1973-81, gov., 1981—; dir. Dixson, Inc., Grand Junction, Colo. Leader, Fgn. Ops. Adminstrn. evaluation team to Vietnam, 1954; pres. Buffalo Trace council Boy Scouts Am., 1957-58; v.p. Evansville's Future, Inc., 1958-62; chmn. Vanderburgh County Republican Com., 1965-71; alt. del. Rep. Nat. Conv., 1956, 76; trustee Hanover Coll., Willard Library, Evansville YMCA, 1950-70. Served to maj. AUS, 1942-46. Decorated Legion of Merit. Mem. Scroll and Key Soc., Delta Kappa Epsilon. Presbyterian (elder, trustee, deacon). Clubs: Oak Meadow Golf, Meridian Hills, Columbia; Rotary. Office: 206 State House Indianapolis IN 46204

ORR, ROY JOSEPH, hosp. exec.; b. Bethany, Mo., Sept. 15, 1952; s. Jay Cedric and Carolyn Mae (Ellis) O.; A.A., Platte Coll., 1972; B.S., U. Mo., Columbia, 1974; M.Rehab. Adminstrn., U. San Francisco, 1981; m. Patrice Marie Kuta, Aug. 11, 1973; 1 dau., Sarah DuLaine. Occupational therapist Midwestern Rehab. Center, Omaha, 1974-76, chief occupational therapist, 1977-80, dept. dir., 1979-80; dir. phys. medicine Archbishop Bergan Mercy Hosp., Omaha, 1980—. Bd. dirs. Nebr. chpt. Arthritis Found., 1977—, 2d v.p., 1977-78, pres., 1980—. Mem. Assn. Med. Rehab. Dirs. and Coordinators Am. Occupational Therapy Assn., Nebr. Occupational Therapy Assn. (1980 del. People-to-People tour Europe, USSR). Roman Catholic. Home: 12911 Corby St Omaha NE 68164 Office: Archbishop Bergan Mercy Hosp 7500 Mercy Rd Omaha NE 68124

ORR, VICTOR DARRYL, engr.; b. Poplar Bluff, Mo., Aug. 17, 1944; s. Charles Victor and Jewell Elizabeth (Evenson) O.; m. Linda Jarell, Sept. 6, 1969; 1 son, David. B.S., U. Mo., Rolla, 1970, M.S., 1971. Registered profl. engr., Mo. Co-owner, engr. Trotter Assos., Dexter, Mo., 1971—; city rep. Bootheel Regional Planning Commn., 1973—; mem. Dexter Planning and Zoning Commn., 1973—. Mem. Nat., Mo. (Outstanding Young Engr. of Yr. 1977), socs. profl. engrs., Profl. Engrs. in Pvt. Practice, Am. Water Works Assn., Dexter C. of C., Water and Sewerage Conf., Phi Kappa Phi, Chi Epsilon. Recipient Outstanding Young Engr. of Yr., SE Mo. chpt. Mo. Soc. Profl. Engrs., 1977; contbr. articles to profl. jour. Home: Route 3 Orchard Lake Subdivision Dexter MO 63841 Office: 100 Ridgetop Dr Dexter MO 63841

ORSELLO, ALBERT LOUIS, human service agy. exec.; b. St. Paul, Mar. 12, 1947; s. Louis Patrick and Teresa Bridget (Pariana) O.; B.A., St. Mary's Coll., 1969; M.S., Winona State U., 1972; postgrad St. Thomas Coll., 1971-72, Loyola U. Chgo., 1974-75, U. Minn., 1971-72; 1 dau., Delia Sunshine. Tchr., Grace High Sch., Mpls., 1969-70, chmn. dept. counseling, 1970-71; chmn. dept. counseling Acad. Holy Angels, Mpls., 1972-74; mgr. Del Fiacco's Italian Eatery, St. Paul, 1974-76; founder, exec. dir. Person Edn.-Developmental Edn., Mpls., 1972—; cons. U.S. Office Edn. Bd. dirs. Grantsmanship Center Los Angeles. Mem. Am. Personnel and Guidance Assn., Minn. Personnel and Guidance Assn., Minn. Chem. Dependency Assn., Nat. Assn. Prevention Profls., Sales and Mktg. Execs. Roman Catholic. Club: K. C. Home: 701 Bedford St Saint Paul MN 55101 Office: 4225 3d Ave South Minneapolis MN 55409

ORSZULAK, RICHARD STEWART, acct.; b. Girard, Kans., Oct. 4, 1957; s. John Andrew and Cleo Nadine (Shaffer) O.; B.S. in Bus. Adminstrn., Pittsburg (Kans.) State U., 1979. Acct., Biron, Inc., Chanute, Kans., 1981—. Mem. Am. Econ. Assn., Nat. Assn. Accts. Republican. Baptist. Home: Rural Route 2 Box 58-1 Chanute KS 66720 Office: 910 W Elm St Chanute KS 66720

ORTEGA, CARLOTA AYALA, sch. counselor; b. Piedras Negras, Mex. (parents Am. Citizens); d. Jose Angel and Antonia (de Hoyos) Ayala; B.A. summa cum laude, Saginaw Valley State Coll., 1974; M.A., Central Mich. U., 1975, Guidance and Counseling Edn. Endorsement, 1977; Ed.D., Wayne State U., 1981; m. Guadalupe F. Ortega, Apr. 11, 1942; children—Yvonne Ortega Tutunjian, David R., Joseph G. Ct. interpreter U.S. Narcotics and Immigration Authorities, 1944-47; sec. Saginaw (Mich.) Planned Parenthood, 1967-70; employment interviewer Mich. Employment Security Commn., Saginaw, 1970-74; secondary sch. tchr., Saginaw, 1974; Sch. Counselor Saginaw Pub. Schs., 1974—; supr. Mid-Mich. Bilingual Bicultural Program at Saginaw Valley State Coll. for Bay City Sch. Dist., 1978—; field reader HEW Office Edn.; cons. tchrs. inservice tng. Bd. dirs. United Migrant Opportunities, 1960-61; commr. Saginaw Human Relations Commn., 1970-74; mem. La Raza Citizens Adv. Com. to State Bd. of Edn., 1974-75. Doctoral fellow U.S. Dept. Edn., 1978. Mem. Mich. Personnel and Guidance Assn., Am. Personnel and Guidance Assn., Mich. Elementary and Middle Sch. Prins. Assn., Mich. Assn. for Specialist in Group Work, North Central Guidance Assn. of Mich., Nat. Assn. Bilingual Edn. Am. Legion, Am. Legion Aux., League Women Voters, Alpha Mu Gamma. Home: 1842 Coolidge St Saginaw MI 48603

ORTHWEIN, WILLIAM COE, mech. engr.; b. Toledo, Jan. 27, 1924; s. William Edward and Millie Minerva (Coe) O.; B.S., Mass. Inst. Tech., 1946; M.S., U. Mich., 1957, Ph.D., 1959; m. Helen Virginia Poindexter, Feb. 1; children—Karla Frances, Adele Diana, Maria Theresa. Aerophysicist, Gen. Dynamics Co., Ft. Worth, 1951-52; research asso. U. Mich., 1952-59; adv. engr. IBM Corp., Owego, N.Y., 1959-61; dir. Computer Centers, U. Okla., Norman, 1961-63; research scientist Ames Lab., NASA, Moffett Field, Calif., 1963-65; mem. faculty So. Ill. U., Carbondale, 1965—, prof. engring., 1967—; cons. in field. Pres. Jackson County (Ill.) Taxpayers Assn., 1976. Served with AUS, 1943-46. Registered profl. engr., Ill., Ind., Ky. Mem. ASME (Outstanding Service award 1972), Ill. Soc. Profl. Engrs. (chmn. salary and employment com. 1974, chmn. ad hoc com. continuing edn. 1975), Soc. Exptl. Stress Analysis. Tensor Soc., Soc. Mining Engrs., Am. Gear Mfrs. Assn., Am. Acad. Mechanics, Nat. Rifle Assn., Aircraft Owners and Pilot Assn., Sigma Xi. Mormon. Author papers, revs. Home: PO Box 3332 Carbondale IL 62901 Office: So Ill Univ Carbondale IL 62901

ORTIZ, EDUARDO, physician; b. Bucararmanga, Colombia, Aug. 21, 1937; came to U.S., 1965, naturalized, 1979; s. Pedro A. and Sofia (Mendez) O.; M.D., Javeriana U., 1962; m. Martha L. Garavito, Dec. 2, 1961; children—Eduardo, Xavier, Oscar. Intern, St. Joseph Hosp., Providence, 1965-66; resident in Ob-Gyn, Henry Ford Hosp., Detroit, 1967-70; practice medicine specializing in obstetrics and gynecology, Adrian, Mich., 1971—; mem. staff Emma L. Bixby Hosp. Mem. AMA, A.C.S., Am. Assn. Gynecol. Laparoscopists, Mich. Med. Soc., Lenawee County Med. Soc., Am. Coll. Obstetricians and Gynecologists. Roman Catholic. Club: Rotary. Office: 227 Riverside St Adrian MI 49221

ORTLEB, EDWARD PAUL, sch. adminstr.; b. St. Louis, June 2, 1932; s. Paul K. and Anita Ortleb; B.A., Harris Tchrs. Coll., 1955; M.A., Washington U., St. Louis, 1959, Advance Grad. Cert., 1963; m. Bernadette C. Burke, Mar. 19, 1955; children—Diane, Kathy. Tchr., St. Louis public schs., 1955-61, coordinator sci., gifted classes, 1963-66, supr. elem. sci., 1966-69, sci. supr., 1969-79, facilitator of instrn., 1979—; lectr. Harris Tchrs. Coll., 1959-61; student tchr. supr. Washington U., 1962-63, mem. adj. faculty dept. biology, 1969—. Bd. dirs. St. Louis Cancer Soc., 1969-75; mem. commn. McDonnell Planetarium, 1970—. Served with U.S. Army, 1955-57. Recipient Mo. Sci. Educator award, 1972; NSF fellow, 1961-62. Mem. Sci. Tchrs. Mo. (pres. 1974-75), Nat. Sci. Tchrs. Assn. (dist. dir. 1974-76, pres. 1978-79), Nat. Sci. Supr. Assn., Mo. Acad. Sci., Herpetologist League, Nat. Audubon Soc., St. Louis Naturalist Club, Assn. Supervision and Curriculum Devel., St. Louis Audubon Soc. (dir. 1969-75), Phi Delta Kappa. Roman Catholic. Contbr. articles to profl. jours. Home: 5663 Pernod Ave Saint Louis MO 63139 Office: 721 Pendleton Ave Saint Louis MO 63108

ORTMAN, WILLIAM ANDREW, SR., lawyer; b. Detroit, Mich., Mar. 22, 1934; s. Frank J. and Marcella Pauline (Gfell) O.; B.A., Wayne State U., 1958; grad. Bus. Sch. U. Mich., 1960; J.D. (regional outstanding student 1962, scholarship certificate and key, jurisprudence awards), U. Detroit, 1963; m. Lavina Mae Ladson, June 29, 1957; children—William A., Nancy Lee, Merrie Jo, Kristy Ann, Keira Therese. Radio sta. mgr., 1953-56; para-legal Ortman Co., 1956-60, real estate broker, co-partner, 1956—; indsl. relations analyst FoMoCo, 1960-62; pub. info. specialist Dept. Def., Detroit, 1962-63; admitted to Mich. bar, 1963, Ohio Fed. bar, 1963; sr. atty. firm Ortman & Ortman, Detroit, 1964—; polit. campaign specialist, 1968—; real-estate, mortgage broker, 1956—; cons. pub. relations and advt., 1962—; lectr. St. Joseph Comml. Coll., 1961-62. Bd. govs., past dean Detroit Metro. Alumni Senate; councilman, Farmington Hills area, 1968-75; nominee Mich. Supreme Ct., 1972. Served with U.S. Army, 1953-56. Mem. Am., Mich., Oakland bar assns., Delta Theta Phi, Alpha Kappa Delta. Clubs: Detroit Athletic, German-Am. Cultural Center, Elks. Contbr., author and editor of nat., State and local legal jours. Home: 28010 S Harwich Dr Farmington Hills MI 48018 Office: 2238 Commonwealth Bldg Detroit MI 48226

ORVIS, ALAN LEROY, med. physicist; b. Cleve., May 2, 1921; s. Harvey Willard and Helen Louise (Gerlach) O.; B.S., Westminster (Pa.) Coll., 1944; certificate meteorology U. Calif. at Los Angeles, 1943; M.S., Case Inst. Tech., 1949; Ph.D., U. Tex., 1952; m. Jennie Morgan, Aug. 30, 1947; children—James Alan, Joan Morgan. Grad. asst. physics Case Inst. Tech., 1946-48, instr., 1948-49; teaching fellow physics U. Tex., Austin, 1949-50, instr., 1950-52; instr. biophysics Mayo Grad. Sch. Medicine, U. Minn., Rochester, 1956-59, asst. prof., 1959-67, asso. prof., 1967—; cons. in biophysics Mayo Clinic, Rochester, 1952—, radiol. safety officer, 1954—; mem. Adv. Com. Radiation Safety, Minn. State Bd. Health, 1960—, chmn., 1964-69; mem. Biomed. Users Group, Los Alamos, Meson Prodn. Facility, 1969—. Served to capt. USAAF, 1943-46. Mem. Am. Assn. Physicists in Medicine, Am. Geophys. Union, Soc. Nuclear Medicine, Health Physics Soc. (dir. chpt. 1968-71, pres. 1971-72), AAAS, Am. Assn. Physics Tchrs., Minn. Soc. Radiologic Technologists (hon.), Minn. Radiol. Soc., Minn. Acad. Sci., Sigma Xi, Sigma Pi Sigma. Author sci. publs. in field; contbr. chpts. to several books. Home: 2512 Crest Ln SW Rochester MN 55901 Office: Curie Pavilion Mayo Clinic Rochester MN 55901

ORWOLL, GREGG S. K., lawyer; b. Austin, Minn., Mar. 23, 1926; s. Gilbert M. and Kleonora (Kleven) O.; B.S., Northwestern U., 1950; J.D., U. Minn., 1953; m. Laverne M. Flentie, Sept. 15, 1951; children—Kimball G., Kent A., Vikki A., Tristen A., Erik G. Admitted to Minn. bar, 1953, U.S. Supreme Ct. bar, 1973; asso. firm Dorsey, Owen, Marquart, Windhorst and West, Mpls., 1953-59, partner, 1959-60; asso. counsel Mayo Clinic, Rochester, Minn., 1960-63, gen. counsel, 1963—; gen. counsel, dir. Rochester Airport Co., 1962—, sec., 1962-81, v.p., 1981—; gen. counsel Mayo Med. Services, Ltd., 1972—; asst. sec. Mayo Found., Rochester, 1972-76, sec., 1976—; adj. prof. William Mitchell Coll. Law, St. Paul, 1978—. Trustee Minn. Council on Founds., 1977—; pres. Rochester Council of Chs., 1968-69; mem. bd. advisors YWCA, Rochester, 1966-72; bd. dirs. Rochester Med. Center Ministry, Inc., 1975-81, Zumbro Luth. Ch., 1962-64, 77-79, pres., 1964-65; bd. dirs. Rochester YMCA, 1966-70; trustee Courage Found., 1974-80, YMCA-YWCA Bldg. Corp., 1966-73. Served with USAAF, 1944-45. Mem. Am. Soc. Hosp. Attys., Minn. Soc. Hosp. Attys. (dir. 1981—), Minn. State Bar Assn. (chmn. legal med. com. 1977—), Am. Bar Assn., Olmsted County Bar Assn. (v.p. 1977-78 pres. 1978-79), Rochester C. of C., Phi Delta Theta, Phi Delta Phi. Republican. Lutheran. Contbr. articles to legal and medico-legal publs.; editorial bd. Minn. Law Rev., 1952-53. Office: Mayo Clinic 200 1st St SW Rochester MN 55901

ORYSHKEVICH, ROMAN SVIATOSLAV, physician, physiatrist, dentist, educator; b. Olesko, Ukraine, Aug. 5, 1928; s. Simeon and Caroline (Deneszczuk) O.; came to U.S., 1955, naturalized, 1960; D.D.S., Ruperto-Carola U., Heidelberg, Germany, 1952, M.D., 1953; Ph.D. cum laude, Rupert-Charles U., Heidelberg, 1955; m. Oksana Lishchynsky, June 16, 1962; children—Marta, Mark, Alexandra. Research fellow in cancer Exptl. Cancer Inst., Rupert-Charles U., 1953-55; rotating intern Coney Island Hosp., Bklyn., 1955-56; resident in diagnostic radiology N.Y. U. Bellevue Med. Center and Univ. Hosp., 1956-57; resident, fellow in phys. medicine and rehab. Western Res. U. Highland View Hosp., Cleve., 1958-60, also orthopedic surgery Met. Gen. Hosp., Cleve., 1959; asst. chief rehab. medicine service VA West Side Med. Center, Chgo., 1961-74, acting chief, 1974-75, chief, 1975—; dir. edn. integrated residency tng. program U. Ill. Affliated Hosp., 1974—; clin. instr. U. Ill., 1962-65, asst. clin. prof., 1965-70, asst. prof., 1970-75, asso. clin. prof., 1975—. Founder, pres. Ukrainian World Med. Mus., Chgo., 1977; founder, 1st pres. Am. Mus. Phys. Medicine and Rehab., 1980—. Diplomate Am. Bd. Phys. Medicine and Rehab.; cert. electromyography and electrodiagnosis. Fellow Am. Acad. Phys. Medicine and Rehab., Am. Congress Rehab. Medicine, mem. Assn. Acad. Physiatrists, AAUP, Am. Assn. Electromyography and Electrodiagnosis, Ill. Soc. Phys. Medicine and Rehab. (pres., bd. dirs. 1979-80), Ukrainian Med. Assn. N.Am. (bd. dirs., pres. Ill. chpt. 1977-79, fin. mgr. 17th med. conv. and congress, Chgo. 1977, adminstr. and conv. chmn. 1979), World Fedn. Ukrainian Med. Assns. (co-founder 1977, 1st exec. sec. for research and sci. 1977-79), Internat. Rehab. Medicine Assn., Rehab. Internat. U.S.A., Nat. Assn. VA Physicians, AAAS, Assn. Med. Rehab. Dirs. and Coordinators, Nat. Rehab. Assn., Nat. Assn. Disability Examiners, Nat. Rehab. Counseling Assn., Nat. Congress on Rehab. Homebound and Institutionalized Persons, Am. Acad. Manipulative Medicine, Assn. Am. Med. Colls. (individual mem.), Am. Med. Writers Assn., Pan Am. Med. Assn., Biofeedback Research Soc. Am., Chgo. Soc. Phys. Medicine and Rehab. (pres., founder 1978-79), Ill. Rehab. Assn., Ukrainian Acad. Med. Scis. (founder, pres. 1979-80), Gerontol. Soc., Internat. Soc. Electrophysiol. Kinesiology, Internat. Assn. Univ. Profs. and Lectrs., Internat. Soc. Prosthetics and Orthotics, Fedn. Am. Scientists, Internat. Platform Assn. Ukrainian Catholic. Author and editor: Who and What, 1978. Contbr. articles profl. jours.; splty. cons. in phys. medicine and rehab. to editorial bd. Chgo. Med. Jour., 1978—. Home: 1819 N 78th Ct Elmwood Park IL 60635 Office: 820 S Damen Ave Chicago IL 60612

OSBORN, DONALD DEAN, elec. engr.; b. Villisca, Iowa, Apr. 5, 1922; s. Ned Cecil and Blanche (Winter) O.; student State U. Iowa, 1943-44, U. Mo. 1946-47; B.S. in Elec. Engring., Iowa State U., 1949; m. Emogene Faye Strausbaugh, Nov. 26, 1949; children—Larry Jay, David Lee, Melvin Randall, Patricia Ann Osborn Phelps. With Stanley Cons., Inc., Muscatine, Iowa, 1949—, head elec. design dept., 1962-70, head elec. systems group, 1970-77, v.p., 1972—, head transmission and distbn. group, 1977-80, chief elec. engr. specializing in design of electric power transmission and distbn. lines; mem. Am. Nat. Standards Com. on Wood Poles; mem. Nat. Elec. Safety Code Subcom.; mem. ICA engring. team studying feasibility of electric power system for Republic of Liberia, W. Africa, 1958. Served as pfc. 83d Inf. Div., U.S. Army, 1943-46; ETO. Registered profl. engr., Iowa, Ill., Ky., Colo., Ariz., S.D., Alaska, Ala., Ohio, Wis. Mem. IEEE (sr.), Power Engring. Soc. (towers, poles and conductors subcom., past chmn., mem. working group on wood structures, working group standard dictionary), Indsl. Applications Soc. (rural elec. power com.), Iowa Engring. Soc., Nat. Soc. Profl. Engrs., Iowa Geneal. Soc. Republican. Presbyn. Designer 1st maj. transmission line in permafrost region of Alaska, 1965. Home: Rural Route 4 Box 134 Muscatine IA 52761 Office: Stanley Cons Inc Stanley Bldg Muscatine IA 52761

OSBORN, KENNETH LOUIS, financial exec.; b. Belleville, Ill., Jan. 9, 1946; s. William Arthur and Louise Mary (Brueggemann) O.; B.B.A., U. N.Mex., 1968; m. Roberta Marie Vodicka, Oct. 23, 1971; 1 son, David Anthony. Auditor, Ernst & Ernst, Albuquerque, 1968; budge mgr. Rockwell Internat., Chgo., 1970-74; mgr. internat. acctg. Allied Van Lines, Chgo., 1974-76; fin. mgr. Sealy, Inc., Chgo., 1976-79; sr. fin. analyst Newark Electronics, Chgo., 1979-80, internat. dir. credit, 1980—; fin. cons. Sealy, Inc. Served with AUS, 1968-70. Decorated Air medal. Roman Catholic. Club: Moose. Office: 500 N Pulaski St Chicago IL 60624

OSBORNE, ARTHUR ELLSWORTH, JR., dept. store exec.; b. Chgo., May 21, 1920; s. Arthur Ellsworth and Esther Irene (Harrison) O.; student, Grinnell (Iowa), 1942; m. Barbara Jane Rupp, May 21, 1943; children—Arthur Ellsworth III, Richard Harrison, David Charles. Asst. to dir. personnel Marshall Field & Co., 1945-46, group mgr. fine jewelry, 1947-65, v.p. women's apparel, 1966-71, v.p., gen. mgr., 1972-75, sr. v.p., 1975—, dir., 1976—, pres. Chgo. div., 1977-79, corp. exec. v.p., 1979—. Chmn. Chgo. crusade Am. Cancer Soc., 1975, vice chmn. Chgo. chpt., 1976-79, chmn., 1979-81; chmn. State St. Council 1972-77; bd. dirs. Evanston Hosp., 1974—, Chgo. Hist. Soc., 1976—, Chgo. Boys Clubs, 1978—, Chgo. Crime Commn., 1979—. Served to capt. USAAF, 1942-45. Decorated D.F.C., Purple Heart, Air medal, Presdl. Citation. Mem. Nat. Retail Merchants Assn. (exec. com. 1973), Chgo. Assn. Commerce and Industry (dir. 1979—). Episcopalian (vestry). Clubs: Chicago, Glen View, Mid-America, Carlton. Home: 1531 Palmgren Dr Glenview IL 60025 Office: 25 E Washington St Chicago IL 60690

OSBORNE, BYRON LINDLEY, clergyman, educator; b. Greensboro, N.C., Mar. 27, 1894; s. Lindley Ellard and Ada Sylvania (Hendricks) O.; student Cleve. Bible Coll., 1913-16; Th.B., Marion Coll., 1927; M.A., Winona Sch. Theology, 1930; D.D., Taylor U., 1950; m. Ruth Frances Malone, Sept. 6, 1917; children—Ruth Elisabeth, Emma Geraldine, Byron Lindley, Hendricks Malone. Ordained to ministry Friends Ch., 1917; pastor Friends Ch., Franklin, Va., 1917-20; prof. Greek and English bible Malone Coll., Canton, Ohio, 1920-51, pres., 1951-60; dist. supt. Friends Ch., Cleve. Dist., 1935-47; editor Evang. Friend organ of Friends Ch., 1935-47; co-founder Accrediting Assn. of Bible Colls., 1949; frequent lectr. in Bible confs.; ret., 1960; chmn. Christ for Cleve. Evangelistic Com., 1949-50; chmn. Evang. Friends Conf., 1947-50; ednl. dir. Nat. Holiness Assn., 1946-47. Republican. Author: The Man and His Messages, 1935; The Malone Story, 1970; The Investment of a Life, 1976. Address: 808 McDowell Rd NE North Canton OH 44721

OSELAND, NANCY L., twp. ofcl.; b. Joliet, Ill., Sept. 3, 1940; d. James Donaldson and Charlotte H. (McPhee) O.; student Joliet Jr. Coll., 1957-59. Tax rep. Chgo. Title & Trust Co., 1960-64; clk. Will County Treasurer's Office, Joliet, 1964-66, clk. Will County Bd. Review, 1966-67; dep. Joliet Twp. Assessor's Office, 1968-75, chief dep. supr. assessments, 1975-78, supr. assessments, 1978—. Mem. Nat. Assn. Ind. Fee Appraisers, Internat. Assn. Assessing Officers, Ill. Assessing Officers. Office: Will County 20 W Washington St Joliet IL 60431

O'SHAUGHNESSY, MARIE MARGUERITTE, educator; b. Pontiac, Mich., Mar. 21, 1924; d. Charles Stuart and Marie Pearl (Collingwood) Morton; B.A. with honors, Olivet Coll., 1946; postgrad. Wayne State U., 1957-58; M.A. in Guidance, Oakland U., 1975; Mary Grove Coll., 1978; m. George B.E. June, Mar. 21, 1946 (div.); children—Doris Sharon, Laura Kathryn, Alice Dawn, George W.M., Stephen Charles, Jennifer Ellen; m. 2d, Alvin C. O'Shaughnessy, Apr. 14, 1967; stepchildren—Laurel, Kathleen, Roxanne, Sheila. Tchr. 2d grade McConnell Sch., Pontiac, 1948; substitute tchr. West. Bloomfield and Dublin (Mich.) schs., 1956-58; social worker Mich. Social Service, Pontiac, 1966-68; tchr. 2d and 3d grades Four Towns Sch., Waterford, Mich., 1970—; counselor for substance abuse. Cert. tchr. Mem. NEA, Mich., Waterford edn. assns., Am. Personnel and Guidance Assn., Am. Sch. Counselors Assn., Mich. Elementary Sch. Guidance Assn., AAUW, NOW. Quaker. Home: 4695 Forest Dr Pontiac MI 48054 Office: 6370 Cooley Lake Rd Pontiac MI 48045

O'SHEA, LYNNE EDEEN, farm equipment mfg. co. exec.; b. Chgo., Oct. 18, 1945; d. Edward Fisk and Mildred (Lessner) O'Shea; B.J., U. Mo., 1968, B.A., 1968, M.A., 1971; Ph.D. in Internat. Communications, Northwestern U., 1977; m. James David Thybony, Dec. 22, 1973. Writer, The Columbia Missourian, 1965-68; writer/editor Mo. Regional Med. Program, Columbia, 1967-68; pres. O'Shea Advt. Agy., Dallas, 1968-69; exec. asst. U.S. Hos. of Reps., Washington, 1969-70; brand mgr. Procter & Gamble, Cin., 1971-73; account exec. Foote, Cone & Belding, 1973-76; account supr. The First Nat. Bank of Chgo., 1976-78; v.p. Foote, Cone & Belding, Chgo., 1978-79; account supr. Kraft, Inc., 1979; corp. v.p. Internat. Harvester, Chgo., 1979—; vis. faculty Mich. State U., E. Lansing, 1978, Northwestern U., Evanston, Ill., 1978, Wayne State U., Detroit, 1979; lectr. in mktg. Grad. Sch. Bus., U. Chgo., 1979-80. Cons., Voluntary Action Center, United Way of Chgo., 1973-75; founder, chmn. Ill. Women's Olympic Com., 1976—; Ill. del. U.S. Olympic Com., N.Y.C., 1978—; cons. YWCA, Chgo., 1978—; advt./campaign mgr. various Rep. Congressional campaigns, 1968-72; bd. dirs. Off-the Street Club, Chgo., 1978—; mem. adv. bd. Grad. Sch. Bus., U. Ill., 1980—. Recipient numerous Eagle Fin. Advt. awards, Chgo., 1978; Am. Assn. Advt. Agencies research grantee U. Mo., 1970-71. Mem. World Am. Assn. Public Opinion Research, Midwest Assn. Public Opinion Research, World Future Soc., Council on Fgn. Relations, Public Relations Soc. Am., The Network. Republican. Episcopalian. Author: A Q-Methodological Approach to the Use of Advertising in Politics, 1971; Adam's Apple: A Q-Study of the Value Congruences that are Shaping Mankind's Future, 1977. Home: 3720 N Lake Shore Dr Chicago IL 60613 Office: 401 N Michigan Ave Chicago IL 60611

O'SHEE, VINCENT RICHARD, obstetrician, gynecologist; b. Clonmel, County Tipperary, Ireland, Apr. 4, 1927; came to U.S., 1957, naturalized, 1962; s. James John and Annie Mary (Naughton) O'S.; S.J., Belvedere Coll., Dublin, Ireland, 1944; M.B., B.Ch., B.A.O., Nat. U. Ireland, 1956; m. Irene Finnegan, Aug. 16, 1956; children—Marianne, Louise, Jean, Laura, Eileen, James. Intern, Detroit Meml. Hosp., 1957-58, resident, 1958-62; mem. staffs Detroit-Macomb Hosps. Assn., 1962—, Holy Cross Hosp., Detroit, 1962—; practice medicine, specializing in ob-gyn, Sterling Heights, Mich., 1962—. Mem. Mich. Med. Soc., Macomb Med. Soc. Roman Catholic. Clubs: Ancient Order of Hibernians, Friendly Sons of St. Patrick. Home: 1047 Whittier Grosse Pointe Park MI 48230 Office: 40580 Van Dyke Sterling Heights MI 48078

OSHINSKI, WILLIAM JOSEPH, business exec.; b. Chgo., June 18, 1933; s. Edward Joseph and Mae O.; B.S., U. Ill., 1955; m. Barbara Ann Anderson, Oct. 1, 1955; children—Allen, Paul. Indsl. engring. mgr. Playskool Inc., Chgo., 1966-70; mgr. mfg. Bauer Electric Co., Chgo., 1970-71; exec. v.p. Patton Consultants, Des Plaines, Ill., 1971-79; v.p. mgmt. cons. div. Austin Co., Evanston, Ill., 1979—; cons. in field, 1971—. Served with USNR, 1955-57. Mem. Am. Inst. Indsl. Engrs. (sr.), Indsl. Mgmt. Soc. (sr.). Republican. Contbr. sect. to ency., articles to profl. jours. Home: 636 S Arlington Heights Rd Arlington Heights IL 60005 Office: Austin Co 820 Davis St Evanston IL 60201

OSKEY, D. BETH, banker; b. Red Wing, Minn., Dec. 23, 1921; d. Alvin E. and Effie D. (Thompson) Feldman; student U. Wis., River Falls, 1939-41; B.A., Met. State U., Minn., 1975; grad. degree in banking, U. Wis., 1973, postgrad. in banking, 1977; student in interior decorating LaSalle Extension U., Chgo., 1970; m. Warren B. Oskey, Sept. 27, 1941; children—Jo Cheryl, Warren A., Peter (dec.), Jeffrey L. Officer, Hiawatha Nat. Bank, Hager City, Wis., 1959—, cashier, 1978-79, pres., 1979, exec. v.p., dir., sec. bd. dirs., 1959—, sec., mem. discount com.; with First Nat. Bank of Glenwood, Glenwood City, Wis., 1965— pres., exec. v.p., 1979—, dir., sec. bd., 1965—, sec., mem. discount com.; speaker on women in banking. Banking com. Vo-Tech Sch., Red Wing, Minn.; former officer civic orgns. Mem. Ind. Bankers Am., Wis. Bankers Assn., Am. Bankers Assn. Republican. Lutheran. Club: Minn. Fedn. Women's Clubs (treas., pres. dist. III, 1978—). Home: 1022 Hallstrom Dr Red Wing MN 55066 Office: Hiawatha National Bank Hager City WI 54014

OSMANSKI, JOHN EDWARD, mgmt. cons.; b. Nanticoke, Pa., Apr. 16, 1915; s. Frank Edward and Ann (Czechowicz) O.; student Haverford Coll., 1933-35; B.Ed., U. Hawaii, 1937, M.Ed., 1939; M.B.A., Stanford U., 1945; m. Margaret Mason Logan, Oct. 18, 1947; children—Edna-Ann, Margaret, Susan. Dir. indsl. relations Island Creek Coal Co., Huntington, W.Va., 1950-63, Am. Laundry Machinery Co., Cin., 1963-68, gen. mgr. ops., 1968-73; v.p. devel., 1973-74; pres. New Era, Inc., Cin., 1974—; prof., dir. placement No. Ky. U., Highland Heights, 1975—. Chmn. stewardship Cin. Presbytery, 1968-74. Served with USAAF, 1941-45. Mem. Cin. Personnel Assn., Am. Soc. Profl. Consultants, NAM (mem. labor council 1978), Indsl. Inst. (past dir.), Cin. C. of C. (chmn. edn. com. 1976-80). Libertarian. Presbyterian. Club: Glendale Lyceum. Home: 360 Albion Cincinnati OH 45246 Office: 330 University Center Highland Heights KY 41076

OSMOND, JOHN DEXTER, JR., radiologist; b. Cleve., Nov. 14, 1913; s. John Dexter and Nellie A. (Pratt) O.; A.B., Denison U., 1935; M.D., Western Res. U., 1939; m. Jean M. Lindstrom, June 15, 1937; children—John Dexter III, Jean Osmond Schneider, Charles D., Mark W. Intern, asst. resident in obstetrics and gynecology and radiology Cleve. City Hosp. and Univ. Hosp., 1939-41, Cleve. Clinic Found., 1945-47; asso. radiologist Univ. Hosps., Cleve., 1947, Drs. Hill and Thomas Radiology Group, 1948—; dir. radiology Euclid Gen. Hosp. (Ohio), 1947-71; asso. clin. prof. radiology Case Western Res. U. Bd. trustees Cleve. Health Edn. Mus., 1961—, pres., 1965-74, chmn. bd., 1974-78, hon. chmn., 1978—. Served from 1st lt. to maj. M.C., AUS, 1941-45. Decorated 2 Bronze Stars; recipient Alumni citation Denison U., 1966; Distinguished Alumnus award Case Western Res. U. Sch. Medicine, 1972; Order of Merit, Boy Scouts Am., 1965, Silver Beaver award, 1966. Diplomate Am. Bd. Radiology. Fellow Am. Coll. Radiology; mem. Acad. Medicine Cleve. (pres. 1961-62), Cleve. Med. Library Assn. (trustee 1965-68), Ohio Med. Assn., AMA, Cleve., Ohio radiol. socs., Radiol. Soc. N.Am., Am. Roentgen Ray Soc., Eastern Radiol. Soc. (pres. 1977-78), Phi Beta Kappa, Omicron Delta Kappa, Phi Gamma Delta, Nu Sigma Nu. Republican. Presbyterian. Clubs: Cleve. Country, Cleve. Skating; Royal Poinciana Golf (Naples, Fla.). Contbr. articles to profl. jours. Home: 32899 S Woodland Rd Cleveland OH 44124 Office: 1611 S Green St Euclid OH 44121

OSSOFF, ROBERT HENRY, head and neck surgeon; b. Beverly, Mass., Mar. 25, 1947; s. Michael Max and Eve Joan (Kladky) O.; B.A., Bowdoin Coll., 1969; D.M.D., Tufts Dental Sch., 1973; M.D., Tufts Med. Sch., 1975; 1 son, Jacob. Intern, Northwestern Meml. Hosp., Chgo., 1975-76; resident in otolaryngology Northwestern Med. Sch., Chgo., 1976-80, NIH Research fellow dept. otolaryngology, 1977-78, Am. Cancer Soc. clin. fellow, 1980-81; practice medicine specializing in head and neck surgery, Chgo., 1975—; mem. staff Children's Meml. Hosp., Chgo., 1980-81; asst. prof. Northwestern Dental and Med. Schs., 1980—. Trustee, Ill. Biolaser Inst., Chgo., 1981—. Recipient Lederer-Pierce award, Chgo. Laryngol. Soc., 1978. Mem. AMA, A.C.S., Am. Acad. Oral Medicine, Am. Council Otolaryngology, Am. Acad. Oral Pathology, Soc. Ear, Nose and Throat Advances in Children. Jewish. Contbr. articles to profl. jours. Home: 2741 Harrison St Evanston IL 60201 Office: 303 E Chicago Ave Chicago IL 60611

OSTBY, DONALD HAROLD, environ. engr.; b. Muskegon, Mich., Feb. 17, 1927; s. Ernest Harold and Evelyn (Roberts) O.; B.S., M.E., U. Wash., Seattle, 1951; m. Mary E. Shaw, Feb. 14, 1951; children—Michael Lee. Vice pres. engring. Lakey Foundry Corp., Muskegon, 1951-70; engring. cons. Nat. Chinese Govt., 1970-71; chief engr. East Muskegon Roofing & Sheet Metal Co., Muskegon, 1972-73; environ. engr Sealed Power Corp., Muskegon, 1973-79; dir. research and devel. Mich. Boiler & Engring., 1979—, Mike Volk Co., Mansfield, Ohio, 1980—. Served with USN, 1944-48. Decorated Purple Heart. Mem. Am. Foundry Soc., Plant Engrs. Soc. Patentee air pollution control equipment. Home: 838 Forest Ave E Muskegon MI 49442

OSTEN, DONALD WALTER, marketing co. exec.; b. Bklyn., Mar. 20, 1923; s. Walter Charles and Paula (Osten) Gigerich; A.B., Clark U., 1947, M.A., 1948; postgrad. Am. U., 1950-52; m. Eleanor Louise Beckley, Aug. 31, 1946; children—Richard Donald, David Walter. Media and research dir. Larrabee Asso., advt., Washington, 1953-56; asst. marketing dir., asso. media dir. Gardner Advt. Co., St. Louis, 1956-63; media dir. plans review com. BBD&O, Chgo., 1963-65; founder, pres. Media/Marketing Service Center, Western Springs, Ill., 1965—, chmn. bd. 1968—. Lectr. marketing and advt. Roosevelt U., Chgo., 1968—. Mem. steering com. Western Springs (Ill.) Bicentennial Commn., 1974-76; dep. coordinator emergency services, Western Springs, 1976—; scoutmaster Boy Scouts Am., Western Springs, Ill., 1972-80, mem. exec. bd. West Suburban Council, 1981—. Served with USMCR, 1942-43, USNR, 1943-46. Recipient Vigil Honor, Order of the Arrow, Boy Scouts Am. Mem. Am. Mgmt. Assn., NAMA. Republican. Presbyn. Club: Broadcast Advt. Home: 4106 Clausen Ave Western Springs IL 60558 Office: 4365 Lawn Ave Western Springs IL 60558

OSTER, MERRILL JAMES, publisher, farmer, author, lectr.; b. Cedar Falls, Iowa, May 30, 1940; s. Harland James and Pearl Rosetta (Smith) O.; B.S. in Agrl. Journalism (Sears and Roebuck scholar, Spokesman scholar), Iowa State U., 1961; M.S. in Agrl. Journalism, U. Wis., 1962; m. Carol Jane Dempster, June 1, 1962; children—David, Leah Jane. Grad. asst. U. Wis., 1961; asst. radio-TV farm dir. Sta. WKOW, Madison, 1961-62; asst. editor Crops and Soils mag., Madison, 1962, Ford Farming and Ford Almanac mags., 1964-67; editor Top Farmer Intelligence, Woodstock, Ill., 1967-69; pres. Communication Consultants, Cedar Falls, 1969—, Oster Farms and Pork Pro, Inc., Cedar Falls, 1971—, Hometowner, Inc., Cedar Falls, 1976—, Cedar Terrace Developers, Inc., Cedar Falls, 1977—; pres., pub. Commodities Mag., Inc., Cedar Falls, 1975—; chmn. Commodity Communications Corp., Lombard, Ill., 1981—; pres. Oster Communications, Inc., 1981—; lectr. Land and commodity futures Profl. Farmers Inst., 1973—; instr. Grad. Sch. Banking, U. Wis., 1976—. Bd. dirs. Emmaus Bible Sch., Oak Park, Ill., treas., 1978, vice chmn., 1979; pres. bd. dirs. Christian Heritage Sch., 1977-79, 81—; chmn. bd. trustees Downing Avenue Gospel Chapel, 1978-79; mem. alumni achievement fund com. Iowa State U., 1980—. Named Outstanding Young Alumnus, Iowa State U., 1975. Mem. Am. Assn. Agrl. Editors, Nat. Assn. Agrl. Marketers, Am. Soc. Farm Mgrs. and Rural Appraisers (instr.), Profl. Farmers Am. (founder, pres. 1973—), Cedar Falls C. of C. (dir. 1975-78), Alpha Zeta, Sigma Delta Chi. Republican. Clubs: Rotary; Sunnyside Country (Waterloo, Iowa); Beaver Hills Country (Cedar Falls). Author: Commodity Futures for Profit, 1978; Multiply Your Money Through Commodity Trading, 1979; Multiply Your Money Trading Soybeans, 1981; contbr. numerous articles, bulls. and spl. reports on food, agr., commodity futures to profl. publs. Home: Rural Route 4 Cedar Falls IA 50613 Office: 219 Parkade Cedar Falls IA 50613

OSTERKAMP, WAITE ROBERT, hydrologist; b. Clayton, Mo., Nov. 7, 1939; s. Clifton Grover and Constance Elizabeth (Waite) O.; B.A.Geology, U. Colo., 1961, B.A. in Chemistry, 1963; M.S. (B.S. Butler scholar), U. Ariz., 1970, Ph.D., 1976; m. Marilynn Spear Bowie, June 15, 1963; children—Jeffrey Mark, Lauryl Alyce. Chemist, U.S. Geol. Survey, Denver, 1965, Helena, Mont., 1966-68, hydrologist, Tucson, 1971-73, Lawrence, Kans., 1974—; research asst. U. Ariz., Tucson, 1969, teaching asso., 1970. Mem. AAAS, Am. Geol. Soc., Nat. Water Well Assn., Sierra Club, Sigma Gamma Epsilon. Contbr. articles to profl. jours. Home: 2628 Bardith Ct Lawrence KS 66044 Office: 1950 Ave A Capus West U Kans Lawrence KS 66044

OSTERMEYER, ELMER HENRY, transp. co. exec.; b. Indpls., June 27, 1922; s. Elmer H. and Jessie F. (Bowlus) O.; B.S., Notre Dame U., 1948; m. Joan M. Melody, Apr. 17, 1948; children—John, Kathy, David, Lisa. Sec., treas. Dad's Root Beer Bottling Co., Madison, Wis., 1948-51; with Am. Red Ball Transit Co., Indpls., 1951—, pres., 1979—. Bd. dirs. 500 Festival Assn., 1972-73. Served with U.S. Army, 1943-46. Mem. Am. Movers Assn., Ind. Motor Truck Assn., Nat. Def. Transp. Assn., Better Bus. Bur. (dir.). Republican. Roman Catholic. Clubs: Hillcrest Country, Notre Dame (Indpls.). Established Eddie Sachs Scholarship Award. Office: American Red Ball Transportation Co PO Box 1127 Indianapolis IN 46206

OSTERMUELLER, RALPH EDWARD, mgmt. cons., bus. broker; b. St. Louis, Nov. 5, 1940; s. Joseph Albert and Martha (Jaworek) O.; B.S. in Commerce, St. Louis U., 1962; m. Dorothy J. Hannis, June 29, 1963; children—Joseph Stephen, Kristin Rose, Erik Thomas, Katherine Martha. Accountant, sr. auditor S.D. Leidesdorf & Co., St. Louis, 1962-66; auditor, treas., Webster Groves Bank & Trust Co. (Mo.), 1966-67; mgmt. cons. Peat Marwick Mitchell, St. Louis, 1967-71; v.p., controller Stockyards Bank, Oklahoma City, 1971-72; nat. rep. HBE Corp., St. Louis, 1972-75; dept. head, mgmt. cons., dir. govt. services Alexander Grant & Co., St. Louis, 1976-81; midwest mgr. for merger and acquisitions services VR Bus. Brokers, St. Louis, 1981—; pres. Ostermueller & Assos., Inc., 1981—. Chmn. audit and fin. com. City of Des Peres (Mo.), 1979-81; precinct capt. Gravois Twp. Republican Club, 1966-68. Served with U.S. Army, 1962-63. Recipient Outstanding Sr. award St. Louis U., 1962; C.P.A., Mo. Mem. Am. Inst. C.P.A.'s, Mo. Soc. C.P.A.'s, Webster Grove C. of C. (bd. dirs. 1966-68), Orgn. Devel. Consultants (internat. dir. 1979—). Club: Town and Country Racquet. Office: One Corporate Hill 1655 Des Peres Rd Saint Louis County MO 63131

OSTFELD, ALEXANDER MARION, advt. agy. exec.; b. St. Louis, Feb. 13, 1932; s. Simon and Margaret (Fishmann) O.; B.S., Washington U., St. Louis, 1953; postgrad. St. Louis U., 1953-56. Mktg. mgr. lighting div. Emerson Electric Co., St. Louis, 1955-59; dir. research and media Frank Block Assos., St. Louis, 1959-61; research and media supr. Compton Advt., Chgo., 1961-65; media and mktg. supr. Leo Burnett Advt., Chgo., 1965-68; dir. mktg. and account planning, v.p. McCann-Erickson, Chgo., 1968-72, Kenyon & Eckhardt, Chgo., 1972; now dir. Canadian and internat. ops. A. Eicoff & Co., Chgo. Cons. Am. Assn. Advt. Agys. Mem. Am. Mktg. Assn. (sec. St. Louis 1956-57), Internat. Platform Assn., Broadcast Advt.

Club, Am. Research Found. Clubs: Chgo. Exec.; Hadlock Hunt (Cary, Ill.). Home: 391 Poplar Ave Elmhurst IL 60126 Office: 520 N Michigan Ave Chicago IL 60611

OSTIEN, J. KEITH, clin. psychologist; b. Kano, Nigeria, Aug. 21, 1947 (parents Am. citizens); s. J. Bruce and Jean Elizabeth (Trout) O.; B.A., Houghton Coll., 1969; M.A., Mich. State U., 1970, Ph.D., 1979; m. Helen Marjorie Parker, June 26, 1976; children—Jennifer Karen, Kathryn Helen. Staff psychologist Genesee County Community Mental Health, Flint, Mich., 1973-74, clin. supr., adminstr. acute care in-patient unit, 1974; research asst. Mich. State U., 1974-75; clin. psychologist Psychol. Evaluation and Treatment Center, East Lansing, Mich., also clin. psychologist Ingham County Probate Ct., 1975—; cons. Nat. Dist. Attys. Assn. Conv., 1975, Victim-Witness Program on Domestic Violence, 1978, local agencies; guest TV shows to discuss domestic violence and divorce-related problems. Served with AUS, 1970-72. Decorated Joint Services Commendation medal, Meritorious Service medal; lic. psychologist, Mich. Mem. Mich. Psychol. Assn., Am. Psychol. Assn. Home: 427 LaSalle Blvd Lansing MI 48912 Office: 4990 Northwind Dr Suite 235 East Lansing MI 48823

OSTRAND, JANET LOUISE, psychologist; b. Highland Park, Ill., May 25, 1945; d. Walter August and Lucille Louise (Gerken) O.; B.S., U. Ill., 1968, M.A., 1970, Ph.D., 1973; m. Thomas Hubert Plaisance, Apr. 24, 1976; 1 son, Paul Thomas Plaisance. Intern, Chgo. Read Mental Health Center, 1971; asst. supr. to counseling practicum U. Ill., Urbana, 1972; psychotherapist Rehab. Center, U. Ill., Urbana, 1973; psychologist counseling service U. Ill., Chgo. Circle, 1973—; pvt. practice, Chgo., 1976—; dir. Chgo. Psychol. Guidance Center, 1981—; mem. psychol. services Highland Park (Ill.) Hosp., 1979—; mem. council Nat. Register Health Service Providers in Psychology. Mem. Am. Psychol. Assn., Kappa Delta Pi. Contbr. articles to profl. jours. Office: University Hall Univ Ill Chicago IL 60680

OSTREM, JOHN STANLEY, regional govt. ofcl.; b. LaCrosse, Wis., Apr. 28, 1943; s. Jerome Sherman and Ann Josephine (Paulson) O.; student Hamline U., 1961-62; B.A. in Arch., U. Minn., 1965; M.A. in Urban Studies, Mankato State Coll., 1972; m. Eloise Jane Kinneberg, June 27, 1965; children—Jill, Joy, Janel. Asso. planner Olmsted County Dept. Devel., Rochester, Minn., 1968-71; regional planner Rochester-Olmsted Council Govts., 1972-73; planning dir. Headwaters Regional Devel. Commn., Bemidji, Minn., 1973-76, exec. dir., 1976—. Served with AUS, 1966-68. Decorated Bronze Star. Mem. Minn. Assn. Regional Commns. (exec. vice chmn. 1977-78), Am. Planning Assn., Minn. Planning Assn. Lutheran. Clubs: Rotary, Elks. Home: 2807 Birchmont Dr Bemidji MN 56601 Office: PO Box 586 722 15th St Bemidji MN 56601

OSTROM, GARY WILLIAM, newspaper exec.; b. Chgo., May 4, 1943; s. Bengt William and May Evelyn (Bertelsen) O.; B.A., Stetson U., 1965; M.A., U. Fla., 1967; m. H. Kay Peete, Feb. 14, 1969; children—Carol Allison, Clay William. Reporter intern Miami (Fla.) News, 1963; public service coordinator Miami Herald, 1969-73; circulation mktg. mgr. Phila. Inquirer and Daily News, 1973-76; mktg. mgr. Muskegon (Mich.) Chronicle, 1976—. Sec., Goodfellows, Inc., 1977—; elder 1st Presbyterian Ch., Muskegon; active United Way of Muskegon, 1977—. Served with U.S. Army, 1967-68. Decorated Bronze Star. Mem. Internat. Circulation Mgrs. Assn., Internat. Newspaper Promotion Assn., Internat. Newspaper Advt. and Mktg. Execs. Assn., Muskegon Area C. of C. Home: 3465 Rood Rd Muskegon MI 49441 Office: 981 3d St Muskegon MI 49443

OSTROV, JON WILLIAM, mktg. exec.; b. N.Y.C., Sept. 15, 1950; s. Albert M. and Doris (Julian) O.; B.S., Ithaca Coll., 1972; student London Poly. Inst., 1971. Asst. dir. advt. Louis Ostrov Shoe Co., Barberton, Ohio, 1972-73; account exec. Lang, Fisher and Stashower Advt., Inc., Cleve., 1973-75; dir. advt. Brown Derby, Inc., Walton Hills, Ohio, 1975-78, dir. mktg., 1978-80; field mktg. mgr. Continental Restaurant Systems div. Foodmaker, Inc., 1980—; dir. Louis Ostrov Shoe Co., 1976—. Mem. Alpha Epsilon Rho. Office: 26777 Lorain Rd Suite 714 North Olmsted OH 44070

OSWALD, JAMES OLIVER, univ. adminstr.; b. Millersburg, Ohio, June 1, 1944; s. John A. and Ida (Lenhart) O.; B.A., Cedarville Coll., 1967; B.S., Central State U., 1967; M.A., U. Akron, 1980; m. Ruth Ann Mast, Nov. 23, 1962; children—Todd Anthony, Lori Anne. Tchr. coll. English and journalism, coach West Holmes High Sch., Millersburg, 1967-68; editor employee communications Rubbermaid, Inc., Wooster, Ohio, 1968-79; mgr. internat. communications United Telephone Co. Ohio, Mansfield, 1969-71; dir. dept. univ. publs. U. Akron, Ohio, 1971—. Mem. NEA, Internat. Assn. Bus. Communicators, AAUP, Am. Assn. Higher Edn., Ohio Edn. Assn., Univ. and Coll. Designers Assn., Council Advancement and Support of Public Relations Soc. Am. Republican. Mennonite. Clubs: Akron Press. Home: 306 Washington Blvd Orrville OH 44667 Office: University of Akron 225 S Forge St Akron OH 44325

OTIS, JAMES CORNISH, judge; b. St. Paul, Mar. 23, 1912; s. James Cornish and Winifred (Brill) O.; B.A., Yale U., 1934; LL.B., U. Minn., 1937; m. Constance S. Dillingham, Apr. 6, 1974; children by previous marriage—Emily T., James D., Todd H. Admitted to Minn. bar, 1937; partner firm Otis, Faricy & Burger, St. Paul, 1937-48; municipal judge City St. Paul, 1948-54; judge 2d Dist. Ct. Minn., St. Paul, 1954-61; asso. justice Supreme Ct. Minn., 1961—. Trustee Hamline U., Amherst Wilder Found., Minn. Nature Conservancy, Minn. Bar Found. Mem. Inst. Jud. Adminstrn., Am., Minn. bar assns., Am. Judicature Soc., Nat. Council Crime and Delinquency, Phi Delta Phi. Unitarian. Home: 7 Crocus Hill Saint Paul MN 55102 Office: 230 State Capitol Saint Paul MN 55155

O'TOOLE, JEANNE MARIE, hosp. educator; b. Chgo., Sept. 18, 1924; d. Dennis Joseph and Eleanor Marie (Fleming) O'Toole; B.A., Mt. Mary Coll., 1946; M.A., St. Xavier U., 1966; Ph.D., Loyola U., Chgo., 1972. Supr., Hartford Accident and Indemnity Co., Chgo., 1946-53; supr. personnel Carson Pirie Scott & Co., Chgo., 1953-57; tchr. Evergreen Park Sch. Dist., 1957-69; dir. edn. Meml. Hosp., Elmhurst, Ill., 1975—; lectr., Loyola U., Chgo., 1969—. Chmn. ednl. planning Beverly Area Planning Assn., 1973-75; mem. finance com. Christ the King Sch. Bd., 1973-75, pres. bd., 1974-76; mem. exec. adv. bd. Loyola U., Chgo., 1972—, chmn. grad. sch. fund raising drive, 1973, pres. Chgo. Alumnae Assn., 1975. Recipient Fellowship, Loyola U., 1970. Mem. PTA (life), AAUP, Am. Hosp. Assn., Council Basic Edn., History Edn. Soc., Delta Kappa Gamma, Phi Delta Kappa. Republican. Roman Catholic. Club: Big Sand Lake (Phelps, Wis.). Home: 10401 S Menard Ave #109 Oak Lawn IL 60453

OTRICH, GEORGE HAMILTON, ret. supt. schs.; b. Jonesboro, Ill., Aug. 26, 1918; s. Charles O. and Mabel (Hileman) O.; student Wofford Coll., 1944; B.S., So. Ill. U., 1947, M.S., 1950, Ed.S., 1956, postgrad., 1956-60; postgrad. Washington U., 1959; Ph.D., So. Ill. U., 1965; m. Mildred Adams, July 26, 1939; 1 dau., Janet Marie. Tchr., Jerseyville (Ill.). Elem. Sch., 1941-47; tchr. social studies, coach, athletic dir., asst. prin. Anna (Ill.) Jr. High Sch., 1947-59; supt. schs. Union County, Ill., 1959-79. Chmn. edn. com. for Union County, White House Conf. Children and Youth, 1960. Bd. dirs. Stinson Meml. Library, 1959-78. Served from pvt. to 2d lt. U.S. Army, 1942-45. Mem. NEA, Ill. Assn. County Supts. Schs. (pres. 1973), Sch. Masters Club, Am., Ill. assns. sch. adminstrs., Rural Edn. Assn., Am. Legion, Phi Delta Kappa. Democrat. Baptist. Contbr. chpts. in books; also articles to profl. jours. Home: 206 Walnut St Jonesboro IL 62952

OTT, ROGER ARTHUR, surgeon; b. Dubuque, Iowa, Aug. 12, 1930; s. Arthur William and Gertrude (Manders) O.; B.S. magna cum laude, Loras Coll., 1951; M.D., Loyola U., Chgo., 1955; m. Luanus McDermott, June 11, 1955; children—Roger Arthur, Lezlie Erin, Judson William, Kristin Feeley, Jennifer Alane, Stefanie Ann, Sarah Lynn, Alison Suzanne. Intern, Cook County Hosp., Chgo., 1955-56, resident surgery, 1959-63; clin. instr. surgery U. Ill., 1960-62; surgeon Med. Assos., Dubuque, 1963—; mem. staff Mercy Hosp., 1963—, chief of staff, 1967; mem. staff Finley, Xavier Hosps. Served to capt. M.C., AUS, 1956-58. Recipient Bruno Epstein Achievement award Cook County Hosp., 1956. Diplomate Am. Bd. Surgery. Fellow A.C.S.; mem. A.M.A., Iowa, Dubuque County med. socs., Midwest, Western surg. assns., Karl Meyer Surg. Soc., Iowa Acad. Surgeons, Am. Med. Soc. Vienna, Phi Chi. Home: 300 Fremont St Dubuque IA 52001 Office: 1000 Langworthy St Dubuque IA 52001

OTTE, DORIS MINNIE, graphic arts co. rep.; b. Iowa, May 22, 1928; d. LeRoy and Minnie Elizabeth (Swanson) Johnson; student public schs.; m. Darrel Paul Otte, Sept. 7, 1947; children—Curtis Darrel, Marianne Doris. With Cramer's Jewelry, Clarinda, Iowa, 1940-56; dir. vols. Iowa Mental Health, 1956-61; with Clarinda Co., graphic arts, 1961-67; with Black Dot, graphic arts, Crystal Lake, Ill., 1967—, customer service rep., 1971—; editorial cons., tchr. typesetting markup. Mem. Page County (Iowa) 4-H, 9 yrs., state 4-H queen, 1947; 4-H leader Buchanan Twp., 1947-52; chmn. Jr. Miss scholarship program, McHenry County, 1979—. Mem. Bus. and Profl. Women (chpt. pres. 1960), Am. Bus. Women's Assn. (organizer chpt. 1978, pres. 1978-79; Woman of Yr. award 1979). Lutheran. Club: China Painters. Editor: Coal Mining of Yesterday, 1979. Home: 431 Linn Ave Crystal Lake IL 60014 Office: Crystal Lake IL 60014

OTTE, KARL HENRY, research engr., educator; b. Chgo., Feb. 20, 1904; s. Paul C. and Mileta (Olbert) O.; B.S., Armour Inst. Tech., 1926, M.E., 1933; S.M., Mass. Inst. Tech., 1928; m. Maxine Muriel Roehl, June 10, 1950. Mech. engr. F.J. Littell Machine Co., 1926-27; mech. engr. on foundry devel. Hawthorne Plant, Western Electric Co., 1928-32; sr. indsl. engr. supr. devel. improved methods E.J. Brach & Sons, 1933-41; mech. engr. on research in printing equipment R. R. Donnelley & Sons, Inc. (all Chgo.), 1942; bldg. process engr. supervising process engring. dept. Milw. (Wis.) Ordnance Plant U.S. Rubber Co., 1942-43; mech. engr. supervising engring. research and devel. equipment Purity Bakeries Service Corp., Chgo., and its successor Am. Bakeries Co., 1943-63; asst. prof. mech. engring. U. Ill., Chgo.; lectr. in machine design Lewis Inst. Bd. dirs. St. Paul's House (home for aged). Registered profl. engr., Ill. Fellow Am. Soc. M.E.; mem. Nat. Soc. Profl. Engrs., Am. Mgmt. Assn., Western Soc. Engrs., Am. Foundrymen's Soc., Am. Soc. Engring. Edn. Clubs: University, Massachusetts Institute Technology (Chgo.). Patentee. Home: 1005 S Knight Ave Park Ridge IL 60068 Office: University of Ill Chgo Circle Chicago IL 60680

OTTE, RAY MARION, JR., banker; b. Scottsbluff, Nebr., Mar. 19, 1946; s. Ray Marion and Elaine Mary Ann (Stevens) O.; B.S., U. Nebr., Lincoln, 1969; student Schs. of Banking, Omaha, 1976-78; m. Linda Lee Talley, Aug. 1, 1970; children—Jordan Stevens, Nathan Hedges, Adrian Springman. With Edwardsville Nat. Bank and Trust Co. (Ill.), 1965-66, Gateway Bank, Lincoln, Nebr., 1966-68, Scottsbluff Nat. Bank and Trust Co., 1968; asst. v.p. Minatare State Bank (Nebr.), 1970-74; v.p., cashier Bank of Gering (Nebr.), 1974—, also dir. City of Gering Planning Commr., 1978—, vice chmn., 1981—; active Artist-in-Schs. Com., Gering Public Schs., 1977-81, chmn., 1978-81; rep. Nebr. Rep. State Central Com., 1976—; exec. com. Scotts Bluff County Rep. Com., 1972—. Mem. Bank Adminstrn. Inst., Am. Bankers Assn., Nebr. Bankers Assn., Scottsbluff-Gering C. of C. (mem. Outriders, 1978—), Jaycees (treas. Nebr. Jaycees, 1979, dist. dir. 1977, Keyman award Nebr. Jaycees, 1979, outstanding Jaycee, Gering, 1977). Presbyterian. Club: Elks. Home: 1920 21st St Gering NE 69341 Office: 1540 10th St Gering NE 69341

OTTEN, RALPH FRIEDRICH, osteopathic physician; b. Phila., Apr. 28, 1933; s. John Friedrich and Eva Marie (Muz) O.; B.S., Temple U., Phila., 1955; D.O., Phila. Coll. Osteopathy, 1959; m. Ethel May Wilson, Apr. 12, 1958; children—Carol, Kristin, Richard, Susan. Intern, Grand Rapids (Mich.) Osteo. Hosp., 1959-60; resident in internal medicine Green Cross Gen. Hosp., Cuyahoga Falls, Ohio, 1969-70, Chgo. Osteo. Hosp., 1970-72; chief nuclear medicine Jackson (Mich.) Osteo. Hosp., 1973—; mem. faculty Mich. State U., E. Lansing, 1973—, prof. osteo. medicine, 1978—. Mem. Am. Osteo. Assn., Am. Coll. Osteo. Internists, Am. Osteo. Coll. Nuclear Medicine, Soc. Nuclear Medicine, S. Central Osteo. Assn., Mich. Assn. Osteo. Phys. and Surg. Republican. Lutheran. Home: 1001 Brighton Rd Jackson MI 49203 Office: 309 W Fee Hall Mich State Univ East Lansing MI 48824

OTTENFELD, MARSHALL, mktg. research co. exec.; b. Chgo., Jan. 15, 1937; s. Leo and Sadie (Patt) O.; B.A., U. Chgo., 1959; M.A., Roosevelt U., 1968; m. Gloria Jean Zilke, Dec. 28, 1960; children—David Joel, Jonathan Lawrence, Jennifer Lynn, Heather Anne. Study dir. Chgo. Tribune, 1962-64; project dir. Gardner Advt. Co., N.Y.C., 1964-65; research asso. Advt. Research Found., N.Y.C., 1965-66; research asso. pharm. products div. Abbott Labs., North Chicago, Ill., 1966-70; sr. v.p., dir. mktg. research D'Arcy-MacManus & Masius, Inc., Chgo., 1970—, also chmn. U.S. research operating com.; pres. Mid-Am. Research, Chgo., 1970—; lectr. mktg. Roosevelt U. Asst. scout master Boy Scouts Am., Deerfield, Ill., 1978—. Served with AUS, 1961-62. Mem. Am. Mktg. Assn., Advt. Research Found., Research Practices Council, Qualitative Research Council, Am. Assn. Public Opinion Research, Midwest Assn. Public Opinion Research, Am. Acad. Polit. and Social Sci., Zeta Beta Tau. Jewish. Club: Internat. Home: 1050 Summit Dr Deerfield IL 60015 Office: 200 E Randolph Dr Chicago IL 60015

OTTENWELLER, ALBERT HENRY, bishop; b. Stanford, Mont., Apr. 5, 1916; s. Charles and Mary (Hake) O.; student St. Joseph's Coll., 1934-36; A.B., Cath. U. Am., 1943. Ordained priest Roman Catholic Ch., 1943; asso. pastor St. John's Ch., Delphos, Ohio, 1943-49, St. Richard's Ch., Swanton, Ohio, 1959-61; pastor St. Joseph's Ch., Blakeslee, Ohio, 1961-62, O.L. of Mt. Carmel, Bono, Ohio, 1962-68, St. John's Delphos, Ohio, 1968-76, St. Michael Ch., Findlay, Ohio, 1976-77; bishop Diocese of Steubenville (Ohio), 1977—; consecrated aux. bishop of Toledo, 1974; chmn. Bishops Laity Com., 1978-81. Home: 609 N 7th St Steubenville OH 43952 Office: 422 Washington St Steubenville OH 43952

OTTERSBERG, WALTER HUGO, health care products mfg. co. exec.; b. Flushing, N.Y., Oct. 15, 1937; s. Fred and Lena (Haas) O.; B.A. in Physics, Queens Coll., 1967; m. Frances Vera Goepper, Aug. 3, 1963; 1 son, Karl Henry. Tech. writer Kollsman Instrument Corp., N.Y.C., 1958-59, staff engr., 1959-67, corporate radiation safety officer, 1962-67; staff physicist Leesona-Moos Labs., Great Neck, N.Y., 1967-68; project engr. Emerson Electric Co., St. Louis, 1968-70; sr. project engr. product engring. dept. Zimmer-U.S.A., Inc., Warsaw, Ind., 1970-71, devel. engr., 1971-72, research engr., 1972-74, sr. devel. engr., 1974-77, group devel. mgr. Hosp. Equipment Products, 1977—, sec. new product and patent com., 1978. Pres. Madison Sch. Communications Council, Warsaw, 1974-75. Registered profl. engr., Ind. Mem. Nat. Soc. Profl. Engrs., Ind. Soc. Profl. Engrs., Med. Electronics and Data Soc., Soc. Photo-Optical and Instrumentation Engrs. Lutheran. Club: Lions. Patentee in field. Home: 1823 Crescent Dr Warsaw IN 46580

OTTESON, SCHUYLER FRANKLIN, univ. dean; b. Mondovi, Wis., July 17, 1917; s. Hans and Elizabeth (Meyer) O.; student Eau Claire State Tchrs. Coll., 1935-37; Ph.B., U. Wis., 1939; M.B.A., Northwestern U., 1940; Ph.D., Ohio State U., 1948; m. Marie Lila Rothering, 1940; children—Judith Marie, Martha Jean, Karn Wilma, John Christian. Research asst. exec. com. Fair Store, Chgo., 1940-42; asst. buyer Montgomery Ward & Co., 1942-43; instr. econs. and bus. adminstrn. Ohio Wesleyan U., 1943-44, asst. prof., 1944-46; asst. prof. marketing Ind. U., 1946-48, asso. prof., 1948-52, prof., 1952—, asso. dir. Bur. Bus. Research, 1947-49, dir., 1954-60, chmn. of marketing dept., 1960-65, chmn. Dr. Bus. Adminstrn. Program, 1965-71, dean Sch. Bus., 1971—, also dir. Internat. Bus. Research Inst.; bd. dirs. Am. Assembly of Collegiate Schs. of Bus., 1978-82, pres., 1981; pres. Center for Leadership Devel., 1976—. Mem. ednl. adv. com. Chgo. Bd. Trade, 1952-55, chmn. com., 1954-55. Mem. Am., Midwest econs. assns., Ind. Acad. Social Scis. (pres. 1969-70), Am. Marketing Assn. (pres. 1965-66), Am. Statis. Assn., Alpha Delta Sigma, Beta Gamma Sigma (gov. 1978-82). Author: (with T.N. Beckman) Cases in Credits and Collections, 1949; (with William G. Panschar and James M. Patterson) Marketing: The Firm's Viewpoint, 1964. Editor: Marketing—Current Problems and Theories, 1952; Business Horizons, 1957-66. Contbr. articles profl. publs. Home: 512 S Jordan Ave Bloomington IN 47401

OTTO, DAVID GORDON, plastics mfg. co. exec.; b. Massillon, Ohio, Feb. 28, 1947; s. Dick Gordon and Doris Mae (Longworth) O.; B.S., U. Akron, 1969; m. Ann K. Darnell, Mar. 22, 1969; children—Heather Ann, Michael David. With O'Neils, Akron, Ohio, 1969-74; personnel mgr. Lee Turzillo Contracting Co., Richfield, Ohio, 1974-76, Smithers-Oasis, Kent, Ohio, 1976—. Mem. Am. Soc. Personnel Adminstrn., Am. Compensation Assn., Am. Soc. for Tng. and Devel. Republican. Episcopalian. Office: Smithers-Oasis 919 Marvin Ave Kent OH 44240

OTTO, HARLEY JOHN, assn. exec.; b. Richfield, Kans., May 5, 1928; s. John and Hazel (Petersen) O.; B.S., Colo. State U., 1952; Ph.D., Cornell U., 1956; student U. Hawaii, 1950-51; m. Sara Elizabeth Kenyon, Sept. 12, 1953; children—Judith Ann Otto Petsch, Sandra Sue. Asst. prof. dept. plant breeding Cornell U., Ithaca, N.Y., 1956-57; asst. prof. dept. agronomy, 1957-58; from asst. prof. to prof. agronomy U. Minn., St. Paul, 1958-75; exec. v.p. Minn. Crop Improvement Assn., St. Paul, 1975—, dir. and sec., 1959-75; dir. Assn. Ofcl. Seed Certifying Agys., 1963—, Minn. Agrl. Chems. Assn., 1961-64, hon. pres., 1964. Named Hon. Premier Seed Grower, Minn. Crop Improvement Assn., 1964. Mem. Am. Soc. Agronomy, Am. Soybean Assn., Minn. Soc. Assn. Execs., Assn. Ofcl. Seed Certifying Agys. Club: Rotary. Office: 1900 Hendon Ave Saint Paul MN 55108

OTTO, KLAUS, physicist, phys. chemist; b. Friedrichroda, Germany, Sept. 18, 1929; came to U.S., 1960, naturalized, 1967; s. Theodor M.W.A. and Gertrud (Gohla) O.; Vordiplom, U. Hamburg (W. Ger.), 1954, Diplom, 1957, Dr. rer. nat., 1960; m. Christa Thomsen, Nov. 16, 1962; children—Ina N., Peter N. Research asst. U. Hamburg, 1959-60; postdoctoral fellow Argonne (Ill.) Nat. Lab., 1960-62; sr. research scientist Ford Motor Co., Dearborn, Mich., 1962-73, prin. research scientist asso., 1973-81, staff scientist, 1981—. Mem. Am. Chem. Soc., AAAS, Mich. Catalysis Soc. (pres. 1980-81), Deutsche Bunsengesellschaft, N.Y. Acad. Scis., Sigma Xi (treas. Ford chpt. 1969-80). Contbr. numerous articles, revs. to profl. publs. Home: 35173 W Six Mile Rd Livonia MI 48152 Office: Sci Research Staff Ford Motor Co Dearborn MI 48121

OTTO, LUTHER BENEDICT, research sociologist, clergyman, educator; b. Galva, Iowa, Apr. 17, 1937; B.A., Corcordia Sr. Coll., 1959; M.Div., Concordia Theol. Sem., 1962; M.S., U. Wis., 1963, Ph.D. (J.H. Kolb scholar) in Social Psychology, 1973; m. Nancy Arlene Hannaman, June 2, 1961; children—Nathan Scott, Timothy Mark, Stephen Andrew. Ordained to ministry Luth. Ch. Mo. Synod, 1962; sr. pastor Immanuel Luth. Ch., Madison, Wis., 1962-65; sr. pastor, dir. Calvary Luth. Chapel and Student Center, U. Wis., Madison, 1965-67; dir. devel. Adult Christian Edn. Found., Madison, 1967-69; research asst. dept. sociology U. Wis., Madison, 1969-72, project dir., 1972-73; asst. prof. dept. sociology Wash. State U., Pullman, 1973-76, mem. grad. faculty, 1975-76, acting dir. Social Research Center, 1975-76, asso. prof., 1976; fellow Center for Study of Youth Devel., Boys Town, Nebr., 1976—, dir. research div., 1977—; mem. basic sociocultural research rev. com. Dept. Health and Human Services, 1981—; cons. to various ednl. orgns., state and fed. agys., 1971—; editorial cons. to various pubs., 1973—; reviewer HEW, 1975—, NSF, 1977—, NIMH, 1976—. Mem. steering com. Ednl. Needs Assessment of State of Wash., 1974-75; bd. dirs. Luth. Med. Center, Omaha, 1979—. Mem. Am. Sociol. Assn., Internat. Sociol. Assn., Am. Ednl. Research Assn., Soc. Research Adminstrs., Nat. Council on Family Relations, Nat. Council U. Research Adminstrs., AAAS. Contbr. articles to jours. in sociology and edn., religious publs.; asso. editor Sociology of Edn., 1977—. Home: 518 S 127th St Omaha NE 68154 Office: Center for Study of Youth Development Boys Town NE 68010

OTZMAN, ROSEMARY KATHERINE, editor; b. Detroit, Feb. 15, 1937; d. Stephen John and Marian Ann (Silvenis) Kuchta; B.A., Albion Coll., 1958; postgrad. Mich. State U., U. Mich., Wayne State U., U. No. Colo.; m. Gerald Otzman, June 9, 1958 (div.); children—Gerald (dec.), William Robert, James Harold; m. 2d, Joseph Zurakowski, Jan. 19, 1975. Freelance writer, 1965-74; spl.

writer Detroit News, 1971-74; editor The Review, Richmond, Mich., 1974—; newscaster WSMA Radio, Marine City, Mich., 1971—; mng. editor Sommerville Communications, Inc., Richmond, 1976—. Mem. exec. bd. Otsikita council Girl Scouts Am., 1971, Humanity House Alcoholic Treatment Center, 1972-73; mem. North Macomb Crime Prevention Exec. Bd., 1977-78. Recipient Communicators award 4-H Clubs, 1977; Communicator of Yr. award Farm Bur. Macomb County, 1978. Home: 11974 Sharon Lee St Romeo MI 48065 Office: 68830 Main St Richmond MI 48062

OUGHTON, JAMES HENRY, JR., bus. exec., farmer; b. Chgo., May 14, 1913; s. James H. and Barbara (Corbett) O.; student Dartmouth Coll., 1931-35; m. Jane Boyce, Jan. 23, 1940; children—Diana (dec.), Carol Oughton Biondi, Jr., Pamela Oughton Powell, Deborah. Pres., dir. L.E. Keeley Co., Dwight, Ill., 1936—, Nev. Corp.; past adminstr. The Keeley Inst., Dwight, 1938—; v.p., dir 1st Nat. Bank of Dwight, 1946—, Ill. Valley Investment Co.; farmer, farm mgr., livestock feeder, Ill.; sec., dir. Dwight Indsl. Assn.; past mem. Ill. Ho. of Reps. Co-chmn. 1st Indsl. Conf. on Alcoholism, 1948; chmn. Midwest Seminar on Alcoholism for Pastors, 1957, 58, 59, 60; chmn. adv. bd. Ill. Dept. Corrections; chmn. Gov.'s Task Force on Mental Health Adminstrn., 1971-72; chmn. adv. bd. Ill. Dept. Mental Health; dir., mem. exec. bd., Corn Belt council Boy Scouts Am. Served as lt. (j.g.) USNR, 1944-46; PTO. Republican. Episcopalian. Clubs: Univ., Union League (Chgo.). Address: 103 W South St Dwight IL 60420

OUTCALT, MERLIN BREWER, social worker; b. Reedsburg, Wis., Aug. 26, 1928; s. Raymond and Ruby (Brewer) C.; B.S., Ind. U., 1955, M.A. in Social Service, 1957; m. Ruth Ann Auble, Sept. 22, 1950; children—Roger Lee, Dennis Alan, Steven Len. Probation officer Marion County Juvenile Ct., Indpls., 1957-59; supr., exec. dir. Travelers Aide Soc., Cin., 1959-65; exec. dir. Methodist Youth Service, Chgo., 1965-68; child care cons. United Meth. Health and Welfare Ministries, Chgo., 1968-74; exec. dir. group child care cons. services U. N.C., Chapel Hill, 1974-77; exec. dir. Webster-Cantrell Hall, Decatur, Ill., 1977—. Bd. dirs. Meth. Children's Home, Raleigh, N.C., 1976-77, Decatur Area Council of Community Services, 1980—; chmn. Decatur Area Agy. Execs. Forum, 1980-81; mem. Grace United Meth. Ch., Decatur, 1977—; lay leader Decatur Dist. United Meth. Ch., 1979—; mem. United Meth. Central Ill. Conf. Bd. of Ch. and Soc., 1980—. Served with AUS, 1950-52. Mem. Acad. Cert. Social Workers, Nat. Assn. Social Workers, Nat. Assn. Health and Welfare Ministries, Child Care Assn. of Ill. (dir. 1980—). United Methodist. Club: Decatur Rotary (sgt.-at-arms 1979-80). Author papers, reports in field. Home: 1811 Burning Tree Dr Decatur IL 62521 Office: 1942 E Cantrell St Decatur IL 62521

OUTCALT, ROGER LEE, social worker; b. Indpls., Aug. 14, 1951; s. Merlin Brewer and Ruth Ann (Auble) O.; B.A. in Sociology and Psychology, Ind. Central U., 1973; M.S.W. (stipendee Salvation Army Family Services 1976), Ind. U., 1977; m. Roberta Sue Coombs, Aug. 27, 1972; children—Jared Michael, Cherrylynn Marie. Caseworker, then casework supr. Salvation Army Family Services, Indpls., 1974-79, asst. dir., 1979—; adj. lectr. Ind. U. Sch. Social Work, 1978—; counselor sr. high youth Southport (Ind.) United Methodist Ch., 1975-80, coordinator athletic activities, 1974—. Bd. dirs. Gleaners Food Bank of Indpls., Inc. Mem. Nat. Assn. Social Workers, Acad. Cert. Social Workers, Nat. Assn. Christians in Social Work. Club: Kiwanis. Home: 5338 Birch Ln Greenwood IN 46142 Office: 234 E Michigan St Indianapolis IN 46204

OVERBERG, PAUL JOSEPH, actuary; b. Toledo, Feb. 25, 1926; s. Frank and Frieda (Bohnett) O.; B.B.A., U. Toledo, 1948; M.A., U. Mich., 1950; m. Lottie Marie Modlinski, Apr. 3, 1948; children—Cynthia Ann, Debra Denise, David Paul. Asst. actuary, actuarial student Pan Am. Life, New Orleans, 1950-54; asst. actuary Am. United, Indpls., 1954-57; group actuary Security Mut., Binghamton, N.Y., 1959-61, asso. actuary, 1957-59; actuary Allstate Life Ins. Co., Northbrook, Ill., 1961-63, chief actuary, 1963—, v.p., 1964-74, sr. v.p., 1974—, also dir.; v.p. Cross-Country Life Ins. Co. (merged into Northbrook Life Ins. Co. 1980); actuary Allstate Life Ins. Co. Can., 1964—, valuation actuary, 1977—; asst. sec. Allstate Ins. Co., 1963-77 sr. v.p., chief actuary, dir. Northbrook Life Ins. Co., 1978—. Served as aviation cadet USAAF, 1944-45. Fellow Soc. Actuaries; mem. Ill. C. of C., Am. Acad. Actuaries, Nat. Assn. Securities Dealers (former gov.), Canadian Inst. Actuaries, Chgo. Actuarial Club. Republican. Roman Catholic. Clubs: Lake Forest; Execs. Chgo. Home: 1223 W Inverlieth Ra Lake Forest IL 60045 Office: Allstate Plaza Northbrook IL 60062

OVERBY, MONESSA MARY, counselor, nun; b. Staples, Minn., Sept. 7, 1932; d. Joseph Melvin and Marie Frances (Fellman) O.; B.S., Coll. of St. Teresa, 1964; tng. Gestalt Center, Mpls., 1974-76; M.S., Winona State U., 1978. Joined Order Sisters of St. Francis; tchr. pub. schs., Clarissa, Minn., 1952; tchr. pvt. schs., Austin, Minn., 1955, Tracy, Minn., 1956-60, Owatonna, Minn., 1960-64; elem. sch. adminstr., tchr., Lake City, Minn., 1964-70; pastoral asso. St. Edward's Parish, Austin, 1970-76; campus minister Winona (Minn.) State U., 1976-81; counselor in pvt. practice, Winona, 1978—; group psychotherapist Family Services Assn., La Crosse, Wis., 1981-82. Chmn., Mental Health Adv. Com. Austin, 1974-75; del. Democratic county convs., 1968, 73, 74, 75, 76, 78, election judge, 1978, 79, 80. Winona State U. grad. asst., 1976-78, 77. Mem. Am. Personnel and Guidance Assn., Assn. of Humanistic Psychology, Assn. Specialists in Group Work, Cath. Campus Ministry Assn., Minn. Specialists in Group Work, (founding pres. 1981), AAUW. Roman Catholic. Home: 357 W Howard St Winona MN 55987 Office: 475 Huff St Winona MN 55987 also 2350 South Ave La Crosse WI 54601

OVERBY, OSMUND RUDOLF, art historian; b. Mpls., Nov. 8, 1931; s. Oscar R. and Gertrude C. (Boe) O.; B.A., St. Olaf Coll., 1953; B.Arch., U. Wash., 1958; M.A., Yale U., 1960, Ph.D., 1963; m. Barbara Ruth Spande, Mar. 20, 1954; children—Paul, Katherine, Charlotte. Architect, U.S. Nat Park Service, summers 1959, 62, 63, 65, 68, 69, 70, 73, Hist. Am. Bldgs. Survey, 1960-61; lectr. dept. fine arts U. Toronto, Can., 1963-64; mem. faculty dept. art history and archaeology U. Mo., Columbia, 1964—, prof. art history, 1979—, chmn. dept. art history, 1967-70, 75-77, dir. Mus. Art and Archaeology, 1977—; cons. and panelist Nat. Endowment for Humanities, 1974—; counselor St. Louis Landmarks Assn., 1977—; adv. to Heritage/St. Louis Survey, 1974—; chmn. Task Force on Hist. Preservation, City of Columbia, 1977-78. Served with U.S. Army, 1953-55. Kress Found. grantee, 1971; Rehmann scholar, 1964. Mem. Soc. Archtl. Historians (editor Jour. 1968-73, dir. 1968-73, 77—, editor proc. seminar on architecture 1975), Coll. Art Assn., Midwest Art History Soc. (dir. 1975-78), Nat. Trust Hist. Preservation (bd. advisers 1974—, exec. com. 1978—), Mo. Heritage Trust (pres. 1976-79), Mo. Adv. Council Hist. Preservation. Lutheran. Author: (with Carolyn Toft) Laclede's Landing, a History and Architectural Guide, 1977, The Old St. Louis Post Office, 1979; contbr. articles on hist. Am. bldgs. to scholarly publs.; contbr. book revs. in field. Home: 1118 W Rollins Rd Columbia MO 65201 Office: Mus Art and Archaeology U Mo Columbia MO 65211

OVERFIELD, LESTER DELMER, realtor; b. North Lewisburg, Ohio, May 21, 1920; s. Lester Delmer and Bertha Meyer (Noyes) O.; m. Eva Rose Donahoe, May 24, 1941; children—William Robert, Edward Lester, Thomas Paul. Model making apprenticeship NCR Corp., Dayton, 1945-48, draftsman, mechanisms designer, 1948-52, design engr., 1952-72, design engr. financial terminal systems, Waterloo, Canada, 1972-75, quality engr., Dayton, Ohio, 1975-80; realtor, referral and relocation dir. Century 21 Vintage Realty, Inc., Vandalia, Ohio, 1980—. Dist. commnr. Miami Valley council Boy Scouts Am., 1968-69. Served with AUS, 1940-45. Decorated Bronze Star medal. Mem. Butler C. of C. (dir. 1952-54), Vandalia Charter Commn. (vice-chmn. 1958), Am. Soc. Mech. Engrs. Club: Lions (pres. 1967-68), Vandalia. Patentee document sorting control mechanism. Home: 750 Kenbrook Dr Vandalia OH 45377 Office: Century 21 Vintage Realty 147 W National Rd Vandalia OH 45377

OVERGAARD, BJORN, surgeon; b. Goteborg, Sweden, May 16, 1927; s. Thomas Elsasser and Ammy Elin Sofia (Holmgren) O.; M.D., Kungl. Karolinska Medico-Kirurgiska Inst., Stockholm, Sweden, 1957; m. 2d, Margareta Karin Setterberg, Feb. 11, 1971; children—Hans, Malin, Niklas, Carl. Resident in surgery Univ. Hosp., Goteborg, Central Hosp., Karlstad, Sweden, 1957-66; clin. fellow in surgery Royal Victoria Hosp., Montreal, Que., Can., 1960-61; asst. chief surg. service County Hosp., Kungalv, Sweden, 1966-71; intern Iowa Lutheran Hosp., Des Moines, 1971-72; staff physician VA Hosp., Des Moines, 1973—, asso. chief of staff, 1981—; clin. asso. in surgery U. Iowa Coll. Medicine, 1979—. Served as lt. (s.g.) M.C., Royal Swedish Navy, 1966. Merck, Sharp & Dohme research fellow, McGill U., 1960-61. Recipient AMA physicians recognition awards 1974, 77, 80. Fellow A.C.S.; mem. Assn. VA Surgeons, Nordic, Swedish surg. socs., Polk County Med. Soc., Swedish Med. Assn., Nat. Assn. VA Physicians. Republican. Lutheran. Club: Rotary. Contbr. articles to profl. jours. Home: 3328 Douglas Ave Des Moines IA 50310 Office: VA Med Center 30th & Euclid Sts Des Moines IA 50310

OVERGAARD, HOLGER CHRISTIAN, printing co. exec.; b. Cedar Falls, Iowa, July 14, 1916; s. Neils and Mettie Christine (Christiansen) O.; B.A., U. No. Iowa, 1941; postgrad. Columbia U., 1942, Ind. U., South Bend, 1965, Goshen Coll., 1965; m. Edith May Scott, Dec. 20, 1945; children—David Christian, Richard Nelson, Robert Joseph, Thomas Scott. Bookkeeper, Bank of Am., Santa Barbara, Calif., 1935-37; tchr. high schs., Ind., Iowa, 1941-42; owner, mgr. Overgaard's Dairy, Sioux City, Iowa, 1946-51; with Woodmen Accident and Life, Lincoln, Nebr. and South Bend, Ind., 1954-62; v.p. health Ind. Liberty Life, Grand Rapids, Mich., 1974-75; pres. Artcraft Printers, Inc., South Bend, Ind., 1975—. Republican nominee for mayor of South Bend, 1979; regional technician Census Program, 1970; field supr., adminstr. PEP Program, Ind., 1973-74; bd. dirs. No. Ind. council Boy Scouts Am., 1960—, chmn. bd. dirs. Salvation Army; pres. John Marshall Sch. PTA, 1963-64; mem. St. Joseph County Council. Served with USNR, 1942-46, 51-54, capt. Res. ret. Recipient Silver Beaver award, Boy Scouts Am. Mem. Health Underwriters Assn. (internat. pres. 1967-68), Ind. Res. Officers Assn. (pres. 1969-70), Internat. Health Underwriters Assn. (regional dir., v.p.), St. Joseph County Meml. Day Soc. (pres.). Republican. Lutheran. Mason (Shriner), Kiwanian (lt. gov. 1980-81). Home: 1958 Briar Way South Bend IN 46614 Office: 834 Portage Ave South Bend IN 46616

OVERHOLSER, RONALD LEE, actor, scriptural character impressionist; b. Washington, Ind., June 25, 1942; s. James Ora and Jewel Emily (Wise) O.; pvt. voice lessons Mrs. John Sellman and Roger Nye of Bowdoin Coll. (Maine); student Johnson Bible Coll., Knoxville, 1964, Cin. Bible Coll., 1968-70. Various clerical and manual positions, 1963-66; narrator The Good Life, N.Am. Christian Conv., Cin. Riverfront Stadium, 1972; has portrayed numerous Bibl. characters for schs., chs. and colls. including: Messiah, Paul of Tarsus, 12 disciples; designer 14 costumes for portrayals; interpreter Miami Purchase Assn. Mem. ARC, Friends of Cin. Parks. Served with USN, 1960-63. Winner, Internat. Platform Conv. Talent Previews, Washington, 1974. Fellow Intercontinental Biog. Assn.; mem. Internat. Platform Assn., Am. Soc. Distinguished Citizens, Smithsonian Inst. (nat. asso.). Mem. Christian Ch. Home: 5104 Hawaiian Terr Cincinnati OH 45223

OVERHOLT, STEVEN LOWELL, otolaryngologist, army officer; b. Decorah, Iowa, July 26, 1946; s. Edwin Lowell and Thelma Orletta (Amundsen) O.; B.A. magna cum laude, Luther Coll., 1968; M.D., U. Chgo., 1972; m. Connie Marlow, June 20, 1971; children—Lesley Erin, Russell Colin. Intern, Gundersen Clinic, LaCrosse (Wis.) Luth. Hosp., 1972-73; resident in gen. surgery St. Lukes Hosp., St. Louis, 1973-74, resident in otolaryngology Barnes Hosp., St. Louis, 1974-78; commd. capt. M.C., U.S. Army, 1978, advanced through grades to maj., 1978; chief otolaryn. service, Ft. Leonard Wood, Mo., 1978-79; asst. chief otolaryn. service Fitzsimons Army Med. Center, Aurora, Colo., 1979-80; staff Gundersen Clinic, LaCrosse, Wis., 1980—; clin. instr. U. Colo. Med. Sch. Diplomate Am. Bd. Otolaryngology, Nat. Bd. Med. Examiners. Fellow Am. Acad. Otolaryngology, Am. Council Otolaryngology. Lutheran. Home: 1008 Park LaCrosse WI 54601 Office: Gundersen Clinic LTD 1836 South Ave LaCrosse WI 54601

OVERHOLT, WILLIAM ALVIN, univ. adminstr.; b. Elkins, W.Va., May 23, 1917; s. Gilbert Henry and Ethel Mae (Beall) O.; B.A., Davis and Elkins Coll., 1937; M.A., Boston U., 1941, Ph.D., 1951; m. Dorothea Carolyn Donenwirth, May 12, 1944; children—William H., Carolyn Overholt Talbot. With YMCA, Canton, Ohio, 1937-40, state extension sec., Charleston, W.Va., 1947-49, nat. student staff, Mpls., 1949-54; protestant chaplain, asst. prof. religion in higher edn. Boston U., 1954-70, asso. dean student affairs, 1970-73; dean student affairs U. Ill. Med. Center, Chgo., 1973—; leader, U.S.-USSR student exchanges, 1961, 66, 77, U.S. China Study tour, 1978; sabbatical prof. Central Philippine U., 1963-64. Served with USAAF, 1943-46. Mem. Nat. Assn. Student Personnel Adminstrs., AAUP, Am. Coll. Personnel Assn., Inst. of Soc., Ethics and the Life Scis., Soc. for Health and Human Values, Am. Assn. for UN, Phi Delta Kappa. Methodist. Contbr. articles in field to profl. jours.; editor: Exploring Humanistic Health Science Education, 1977; Fostering Ethical Values in the Education of Health Professionals, 1976. Home: 5149 Riverview Dr Lisle IL 60532 Office: 1737 W Polk St Chicago IL 60612

OVERMIER, JAMES BRUCE, psychologist, educator; b. Queens, N.Y., Aug. 2, 1938; s. James J. and Emma Annette (Carlton) Wheelwright; A.B., Kenyon Coll., 1960; M.A., Bowling Green State U., 1962; M.A. (NIH fellow), U. Pa., 1964, Ph.D., 1965; m. Judith Ann Smith, Aug. 19, 1962; 1 dau., Larisa Nicole. Mem. faculty U. Minn., Mpls., 1965—, prof. psychology, 1971—, researcher, exec. officer Center for Research in Human Learning, 1973-78, 80—. NSF fellow, 1971-72; Nat. Acad. Sci. exchange fellow, 1972; Fulbright Hays lectr., 1980. Fellow Am. Psychol. Assn.; mem. Psychonomics Soc. (sec. treas. 1981—), AAUP (pres. 1981-82), Animal Behavior Soc., Delta Kappa Epsilon. Editorial bd. Behavioral Brain Research, 1979—, Physiological Research, 1982—, Jour. Exptl. Psychology, 1971-74; editor: Learning and Motivation, 1973-76; contbr. numerous articles to profl. jours. Office: 75 E River Rd Minneapolis MN 55455

OVERTON, GEORGE WASHINGTON, lawyer; b. Hinsdale, Ill., Jan. 25, 1918; s. George Washington and Florence Mary (Darlington) O.; A.B., Harvard U., 1940; J.D., U. Chgo., 1946; m. Jane Vincent Harper, Sept. 1, 1941; children—Samuel Harper, Peter Darlington, Ann Vincent. Admitted to Ill. bar, 1947; counsel Wildman, Harrold, Allen & Dixon, Chgo. Bd. dirs. Open Lands Project, pres., 1978-81; bd. dirs. Chgo. Bar Found., Ill. Inst. Continuing Legal Edn. (chmn.). Mem. Am., Ill., Chgo. (bd. mgrs. 1981—) bar assns., Assn. Bar City N.Y. Home: 5648 S Dorchester Ave Chicago IL 60637 Office: One IBM Plaza Chicago IL 60611

OWEN, BRUCE WILMOT, fin. and engring. cons.; b. Perry County, Pa., Nov. 26, 1922; s. Wilmot Ayres and Margaret Katheryn (Wilson) O.; B.S. in Mech. Engring., Lehigh U., 1948; M.B.A., Case Western Res. U., 1956; m. Lois Jean Tedrow, Oct. 18, 1968; children—Kimberley, Gail, Cynthia, Connie. Engr. NACA, Cleve., 1948-50; Bryant Heater Co., Cleve., 1950-52; estimator Wean Equipment Co., Euclid, Ohio, 1952-54; engr. Addressograph-Multigraph Corp., Euclid, 1954-64; prin. cons. engr. Latech Cons., Willowick, Ohio, 1965—; pres. Latech Developers, Willoughby, Ohio, 1975—; v.p., Problem Solvers, Inc., Beechwood, Ohio, 1972—; asso. Herman Realty, Beechwood, 1977—; Sec. Ocen Assos., Inc., Willoughby, 1974—. Served with USAAF, 1942-45. Decorated Air Medal, D.F.C. Mem. Nat. Soc. Profl. Engrs., Ohio Soc. Profl. Engrs., Cleve. East Soc. Profl. Engrs. Presbyterian. Home and Office: 30410 Thomas St Willowick OH 44094

OWEN, GEORGE EDWIN, JR., sound and communications mfg. co. exec.; b. Chgo., Mar. 26, 1926; s. George Edwin and Elizabeth Owen; B.E.E., Kans. State U., 1950; M.E.E., Northwestern U., 1962; M.B.A., U. Chgo., 1971; m. Josephine Frances DeRose, June 6, 1953; children—Mary Lynn, Frank Joseph, Edward George, Elizabeth Josephine, Anne Therese. Devel. engr. Motorola Inc., Chgo., 1950-57, project engr., 1957-66, chief engr., 1966-68, dir. audio product engring., 1968-74; product mgr. Quasar Electronics Corp., Franklin Park, Ill., 1974-76; group product mgr. Motorola Auto div., Shaumburg, Ill., 1976-79; v.p. engring. Rauland-Borg Corp., Chgo., 1979—. Served with USNR, 1944-46. Mem. Sigma Xi, Sigma Tau, Eta Kappa Nu. Patentee audio and radio tech. Home: 1316 N 12th Ave Melrose Park IL Office: Rauland Borg Corp 3535 W Addison St Chicago IL 60618

OWEN, MICKEY, real estate, constrn. and devel. co. exec.; b. Evansville, Ind., Mar. 10, 1939; s. Lloyd Nelson and Margaret Marie (Gonterman) O.; B.S.M.E., Evansville Coll., 1957-63; student Ind. U. Sch. of Law, 1963; m. Ruth Ann Stephan, Feb. 21, 1959; children—Marc Allen, Christina Marie, Bryan Keith. Designer heating and air conditioning George Koch Sons, Inc., Evansville, Ind., 1959-63; project engr. U.S. Naval Avionics Facility, Indpls., 1963-67; design group supr. Emerson Electric, St. Louis, 1967-70; group engr. McDonnell Douglas, St. Louis, 1970-72; owner, pres. Owen Real Estate, Constrn., Investment and Devel. Co., St. Charles, Mo., 1972—; owner, pres. Eastern Mo. Properties, Inc.; owner Owen Farms, Williamburg, Mo. Bd. dirs. Mo. Indsl. Devel. Council, St. Charles City/County Library Dist., St. Charles County YMCA, St. Peter's Civic Progress. Lic. real estate broker, Mo., Iowa, Ark., Kans. Mem. Nat. Assn. Realtors, St. Charles County Bd. Realtors (dir., sec. 1974), St. Charles Home Builders (pres., 1977, dir.), St. Louis Home Builders Assn., Nat. Inst. Farm and Land Brokers, Am. Polled Hereford Assn., St. Louis Real Estate Exchange Group. Patentee in field. Home: 3344 Ridgeway Dr Saint Charles MO 63301 Office: 1411 AB Hwy 94S Saint Charles MO 63301

OWEN, ROBERT FREDERICK, physician; b. Poplar Bluff, Mo., Oct. 19, 1927; s. John Clarence and Lydia Anna (Laverty) O.; A.B. summa cum laude in Biology, Princeton U., 1948; M.D., Yale U., 1952; m. Edith Suzanna Trugly, June 11, 1960; 1 dau., Suzanne Marie. Intern, Barnes Hosp., St. Louis, 1952-53; resident in internal medicine Washington U., St. Louis, 1953-54, 56-58, also St. Louis City Hosp.; instr. clin. medicine Washington U. Sch. Medicine, 1958—, cons. Arthritis and Connective Tissue Diseases Clinic, 1958-78; practice medicine specializing in internal medicine and rheumatology, St. Louis, 1958—; mem. staff Mo. Bapt. Hosp., St. Luke's Hosp., Christian Hosp. N.E.-N.W., Deaconess Hosp. Served as capt. M.C., U.S. Army, 1954-56. Diplomate Am. Bd. Internal Medicine. Mem. A.C.P., AMA, Mo. State Med. Assn., St. Louis Met. Med. Soc., Phi Beta Kappa., Sigma Xi, St. Louis Rheumatism Soc. Home: 12 Hacienda Dr Saint Louis MO 63124 Office: 525 Saint François St Florissant MO 63031

OWEN, RUSSELL M., coll. pres.; b. Crosby, Minn., Nov. 27, 1922; s. Russell McKinley and Evelyn Doris (Perry) O.; B.S., U.S. Naval Acad., 1945; M.S., U. Wis., 1951, Ph.D., 1955; m. Patricia Frances Riley, Sept. 5, 1953; children—Jay R., Kay Linda. Tchr., coach St. Croix Falls (Wis.) High Sch., 1948-49, Waukesha (Wis.) High Sch., 1949-50, Shawano (Wis.) High Sch., 1950-53; research, teaching asst. U. Wis., 1953-55; head football coach Winona State Coll., 1955-58; dean adminstrn. Wayne (Nebr.) State Coll., 1958-66; chief of party No. Nigeria Tchr. Edn. Project, 1966-68; dep. dir. Center for the Study of Sch. Fin., U. Wis., 1968-69; prof. higher edn. Ball State U., Muncie, Ind., 1969-71; pres. Southwestern Mich. Coll., Dowagiac, 1971—. Trustee, Mid-Continent Regional Edn. Lab.; chmn. Central States Colls. and Univ. Research Orgn.; chairperson Mich. Community Colls. Mission and Roles Subcom. Served with USNV, 1942-48. Mem. Nebr. Coll. Conf. (pres.), Nat. Assn. Intercoll. Athletics Faculty Reps. (nat. v.p.), U.S. Naval Acad. Alumni Assn., U.S. Naval Acad. Athletic Assn., U. Wis. Alumni Assn., Phi Delta Kappa. Clubs: Pickwick, (Niles, Mich.); Point O'Woods Country (Benton Harbor, Mich.). Contbr. articles to profl. jours. Office: Southwestern Mich Coll Dowagiac MI 49047

OWENS, B(OBBIE) D(EANE), univ. pres.; b. Grant City, Mo., Jan. 17, 1935; s. Arthur Leslie and Leota Crystal (Wilson) O.; B.S. in Bus. Adminstrn., N.W. Mo. State U., 1956-69; Ph.D. in Applied Econs., U. Pa., 1962; m. Eleanor Sue Wright, Aug. 17, 1957; children—Brent Arthur, Kevin Wright. Mem. grading and standardization panel Am. Coll. Life Underwriters Center Ins. Edn., Bryn Mawr, Pa., 1961-63; asst. prof. bus. adminstrn. Bowling Green (Ohio) State U., 1962-65, asst. to pres., asso. prof., 1967-68, v.p. research and fin. affairs, prof. fin. and ins., 1968-71; pres. U. Tampa (Fla.), 1971-77, N.W. Mo. State U., Maryville, 1977—; chmn. bd. Centurian Fin., Inc., 1973-76; cons. ins., fin. instns.; pres., dir. BEKO, Inc. Mem. exec. bd. Tampa United Fund, 1972-77; mem. Fla. Council of 100, 1974-76; trustee Bowling Green State U. Found., 1968-71; bd. dirs. Tampa ARC, 1972-77, Fla. Gulf Coast Symphony, 1972-77; mem. Edgar Snow Sci. and Cultural Del. to People's Republic of China, 1980. Served with USAF. Recipient Theta Chi Outstanding Faculty award, 1969; N.W. Mo. State U. Disting. Alumni award, 1972; Educator of Yr. award Kappa Delta Pi, 1973; Exec. of Yr. award NW Area Chpt. Nat. Secs. Assn., 1980. S.S. Huebner Found. fellow, 1959-62; Am. Council Edn. fellow. Mem. Young Pres. Orgn., Am. Econ. Assn., Acad. Mgmt., Am. Soc. C.L.U.s, Charter Property Liability Underwriters, Tau Kappa Epsilon (dir. 1978—). Clubs: Rotary, Masons, Moila Country (St. Joseph); Maryville Golf and Country. Author: Teach-In Viability of Change, 1971. Contbr. articles to profl. jours. Office: Northwest Mo State Univ Maryville MO 64468

OWENS, CRAIG RANDALL, businessman; b. Columbus, Ind., Jan. 18, 1953; s. Russell Eugene and Alice Jean (Essex) O.; student Hotel & Restaurant Mgmt., Northwood Inst., West Baden, Ind., 1974; student Vincennes U., 1979—; m. Martha J. Owens; 1 son, Daren Russell. Food and beverage controller French Lick (Ind.) Sheraton, 1975-76, purchasing/inventory control, 1976-79; asst. food and beverage mgr. Marriott Hotel, Clarksville, Ill., 1979-80; asst. mgr. Electrolux, Inc., New Albany, Ind., 1980—. Republican. Home: 1813 Greentree Blvd Apt 172 Clarksville IN 47130 Office: 2574 Charlestown Rd New Albany IN 47150

OWENS, DWIGHT RAY, microbiologist; b. Hickory Creek, Tex., Nov. 15, 1942; s. Sim Francis and Kathleen (Butler) O.; B.S., East Tex. State U., 1964, M.S., 1965; m. Linda Kay Vandiver, June 3, 1969; 1 dau., Shari. Microbiologist, Ark. Livestock and Poultry Commn., Little Rock, 1966-68; microbiologist U. Mo., Coll. of Vet. Medicine, Columbia, 1968-78; microbiologist, lab. mgr. Harlan Industries, Inc., Cumberland, Ind., 1978—. Mem. Am. Soc. Microbiology, Am. Acad. Microbiology, Soc. for Applied Microbiology, Am. Assn. Lab. Animal Sci., S. Central Assn. Clin. Microbiology, Internat. Orgn. Mycoplasmology, Sigma Xi. Democrat. Clubs: Masons, Shriners. Contbr. numerous articles in field to sci. jours. Home: 1131 Golfview Dr Apt C Carmel IN 46032 Office: Harlan Industries Inc PO Box 29176 298 E County Line Rd Cumberland IN 46229

OWENS, JAMES HAMILTON, JR., structural engring. cons.; b. N.Y.C., Dec. 17, 1913; s. James H. and Olga (Von Hartz) O.; student Mass. Inst. Tech., 1935-37; B.S., Johns Hopkins U., 1953, M.S., 1958; m. Helen Purdy Nixdorff, May 3, 1938: children—Helen Pierpont, James Hamilton, Alan Schuyler, Alexander Hamilton. Engr. and draftsman Faisant & Kooken Consulting Engrs., Balt., 1945-49; asso. engr. City of Balt. Dept. Pub. Works, 1949-50; sr. stress analyst, group engr. Martin Co., Balt., 1950-59; sr. stress analyst Fairchild Stratos Corp., Hagerstown, Md., 1959-62; staff engr. Bendix Corp., Ann Arbor, Mich., 1962-72; structural designer, analyst AM Gen. Corp., Detroit, 1972-74; sr. engr. Aeronca Corp., Middletown, Ohio, 1976-77; cons. structural design and analysis to various machine mfg. cos., 1972—; lectr. flight structures aerospace engring. dept. U. Mich., Ann Arbor, 1963-65. Mem. Am. Inst. Aeros. and Astronautics. Democrat. Club: Kiwanis. Author: (with D.C. Chang) Belleville Springs Simplified, 1970. Home and Office: 1859 Country Club Rd Ann Arbor MI 48105

OWENS, LLOYD, stockbroker; b. Balt., Feb. 10, 1930; s. Hamilton and Olga (von Hartz) O.; A.B., Johns Hopkins U., 1952; M.B.A., Case Western Res. U., 1962; m. Luvean Moore, Jan. 1, 1955; children—Luvie Moore, Elizabeth Von Hartz, Edward Lloyd Hamilton. Research asso. Horizons, Inc., Cleve., 1952-59; product mgr. Brush Instruments, Cleve., 1960-66; dist. mgr. Cahners Pub. Co., Denver, 1966-71; regional mgr. CNA Fin. Corp., 1972-75; account exec. Blunt Ellis & Loewi, Inc., Skokie, Ill., 1975-79, Kidder Peabody & Co., Chgo., 1979—; part-time instr. investments. Treas., Lake Shore Unitarian-Universalist Soc., 1978—. Served as 1st lt. USAR, 1952-60. Mem. Johns Hopkins U. Alumni Assn. Ill. (pres. 1977-80). Clubs: Univ. (Chgo.); Rowfant (Cleve). Patentee in field (2). Contbr. articles to tech. jours. Home: 922 Elm St Winnetka IL 60093 Office: 125 S Wacker Dr Chicago IL 60606

OWENS, RICHARD GEORGE, mental health adminstr.; b. Clinton, Iowa, June 1, 1946; s. Murray Riley and Margaret McBain (Owens) O.; B.A., Hope Coll., 1968, tchr. cert., 1970; M.A., Mich. State U., 1979, postgrad., 1979; m. Susan Elizabeth Sentman, June 15, 1968; 1 son, Joshua Morgan. Designer, draftsman Stone Container Corp., Chgo., 1968-69; chmn. art dept. Covert (Mich.) public schs., 1970-73; staff writer, art cons. United Educators, Inc., Lake Bluff, Ill., 1972-74; client supr. work activity center Allegan County Com. Mental Health Services, Allegan, Mich., 1974-75, supr. sheltered workshop, 1975-76; prodn. supr. Celebration Candle, Hart, Mich., 1976-77; direct care worker Alternative Services, Inc., Royal Oak, Mich., 1978-79, home mgr., 1979-80, Lansing area adminstr., 1980—, chmn. ad hoc com. on staff tng. and devel., 1981—; instr. adult edn. Pres., Saugatuck Renaissance Guild, 1974-75. Mem. Assn. Supervision and Curriculum Devel., State Wide Care Assn., East Lansing Arts Workshop. Presbyterian. Author: Ceramics As A Career, 1973; Kohoutek and the Queen, 1974. Home: 1301 I University Village East Lansing MI 48823 Office: 1606 Greencrest St East Lansing MI 48823

OWNBY, PAUL DARRELL, educator; b. Salt Lake City, Nov. 9, 1935; s. Paul William and Isabel Hope (Pearson) O.; B.S., U. Utah, 1961; M.S. (Kaiser Aluminum & Chem. Co. fellow), Mo. Sch. Mines and Metallurgy. 1962; Ph.D. (Kennecott Copper fellow), Ohio State U., 1967; m. Nina Rose Mugleston, Aug. 31, 1961; children—Melissa, Heather, Kirsten, Shannon, Paul William, Evan Darrell, Martha. Research ceramist Battelle Meml. Inst., Columbus, Ohio, 1963-68; asst. prof. U. Mo., Rolla, 1968, asso. prof., 1969-74, prof. ceramic engring., 1974—; vis. scientist Max Planck Institut fur Werkstoff Wissenschaften, Stuttgart, Germany, 1974-75; dir. Rinco, Inc., Rolla, Mo., 1972-77; cons. Battelle Meml. Inst., Columbus, 1968-70, Dynasil Corp. Am., 1969-74, 79—, Eagle Picher Industries, Inc., 1970—, McDonnell Douglas Astronautics Co., 1974-76, Monsanto Co., 1979—, A.P. Green Refractories Co., 1979-80, Mead Office Systems, 1980—. Neighborhood commr. Central Ohio dist. Boy Scouts Am., 1966-67, instl. rep.. 1970, 73-74, troop com., 1961-62, 70-74, chmn., 1973, instl. head, 1979—. Battelle Meml. Inst. fellow, 1973. Mem. Am. Ceramic Soc., Am. Vacuum Soc., Ceramic Edn. Council, Keramos, Sigma Xi. Republican. Mem. Ch. Jesus Christ of Latter-day Saints. Inventor in field. Home: 8 Burgher Dr Rolla MO 65401 Office: U Mo Rolla MO 65401

OYLER, LARRY WATTS, city ofcl.; b. Peru, Ind., Feb. 20, 1949; s. Harry Kenneth, Jr., and Hazel Del (Watts) O.; B.S., Purdue U., 1977. City councilman, City of Peru, 1975-78, mayor, 1978, 80—. Dem. precinct committeeman; mem. Peru Planning Commn. Served with U.S. Army, 1969-71; Vietnam. Decorated Bronze Star. Mem. Ch. of Christ. Office: 19 E 3d St Peru IN 46970

OYLER, ROBERT LEON, personnel services co. exec.; b. Jackson, Miss., Feb. 17, 1944; s. John G. and Sara Catherine (Beckley) O.; B.A., Butler U., 1966; M.S., U. Wis., 1968; m. JoAnn C. Darden, Mar. 9, 1979. Exec. dir. Wis. Council on Developmental Disabilities, 1969-73; pres., gen. mgr. Life Style Services, Inc., Madison, Wis., 1973—, chmn. bd. Mem. Adminstrv. Mgmt. Soc. (bd. dirs.), Am. Soc. Personnel Adminstrs., Nat. Assn. Personnel Cons., Wis. Assn. Personnel Cons., Inter-City Personnel Cons., Madison C. of C., Phi Eta Sigma, Sigma Chi. Club: Madison. Contbr. article to Am. Jour. Health. Home: 2700 Waunona Way Madison WI 53713 Office: 415 W Main Madison WI 53713

OZAROWSKI, ETHEL, acctg. technician; b. Waupaca, Wis., Apr. 12, 1911; d. Charles Rueben and Goldie (Hirshorne) Bierman; Ph.B., U. Chgo., 1932; B. Dramatic Arts, Art Inst. Chgo., 1937; m. Stanley Ozarowski, May 17, 1969. Acctg. technician Office of Chief of Fin. U.S. Army, Chgo., 1943-45, Fin. Center, St. Louis, 1945-50, hdqrs. 5th Army, Chgo., 1950-56, Adminstrn. Center, Chgo., 1956-61, chief analysis and reconciliation sect., fin. and acctg. div., Area Support Command, Chgo., 1961-72, acctg. technician, comptroller directorate, Hdqrs. Ft. Sheridan, Ill., 1972—, recipient cert. of service Dept. of Army, 1978, also ofcl. commendation for outstanding performance, 1980, cert. of appreciation, 1981. Mem. U.S. Army Fin. Assn. (charter), U. Chgo. Alumni Assn., U. Chgo. Service League. Contbr. poems to profl. publs. Represented in anthology A Book of Chicago Poets, 1964. Home: 2730 Lawndale Ave Evanston IL 60201 Office: US Army Hdqrs Ft Sheridan IL 60037

OZIER, CECIL RUSSELL, constrn. exec.; b. Cumberland County, Ill., July 1, 1900; s. Richard Simms and Lena Lottie (Webber) O.; student pub. schs. Cumberland County and Greenlaws Bus. Coll., Flora, Ill.; m. Gleena Morefield, Apr. 16, 1921 (dec. 1957); children—Darrell Simms, Mervyn Watts; m. 2d, Dorothy A. Seeber, Nov. 19, 1958. In bldg. industry, 1925—, as individual propr., 1925-47, bldg. homes in Champaign-Urbana, Ill.; pres., dir. Ozier-Weller, Inc., developers Garden Park, other sub-divs., in Ill., 1947—. Community Homes, Inc., Bel Air Builders, Inc., Danville Community Builders, Inc., 1950—; pres. Ozier Homes, Inc., Fairlawn Village, Inc.; sole owner Ozier-Weller Homes, Inc. Fl., 1950—; developer land in P.R.; chem. experimentation, mining, refining rare earths for use in def., Cin., Colorado Springs, Laramie, Wyo.; active in oil and gas prodn., Ill.; lectr. U. Ill., mortgage bankers groups, builders. Mem. Operations Trade Group, on tour Europe, 1956. Active YMCA. Methodist (ofcl. bd., past lay leader). Home: 608 W John St Champaign IL 61820 Office: 2000 N Mattis Ave PO Box 581 Champaign IL 61820

OZINGA, FRANK M., state senator, banker; b. Chgo., Aug. 30, 1914; s. Martin and Wilma (Hoving) O.; A.A., Central YMCA Coll., Chgo., 1934; J.D., Chgo.-Kent Coll. Law, 1938; m. Grace Stob, 1938; children—Wilma Ozinga Molenhouse, Martin F., Ronald, Janice Ozinga Hoffman, Marcia. Admitted to Ill. bar; chmn. bd., gen. counsel First Nat. Bank Evergreen Park (Ill.); mem. Ill. State Senate, 1956, 73—, chmn. exec. com. Justice of peace, Worth Twp., Ill., 1937-41; del. Republican Nat. Conv., 1980. Served to lt. (j.g.) USN, 1944-46; PTO. Mem. Am. Bar Assn., Am. Judicature Soc., Nat. Soc. State Legislators, Am. Legion. Club: Lions. Office: 307 State Capitol Springfield IL 62706*

PACE, STANLEY CARTER, mfg. co. exec.; b. Waterview, Ky., Sept. 14, 1921; s. Stanley Dan and Pearl (Carter) P.; B.S., U. Ky., 1940; postgrad. U.S. Military Acad., 1943; M.S. Calif. Inst. Tech., 1949; m. Elaine Cutchall, Aug. 21, 1945; children—Stanley, Lawrence, Richard. With TRW, Inc., 1954—, v.p., gen. mgr. Tapco group (now Equipment Group, 1958-71, exec. v.p., 1965-77, head Automotive Worldwide, 1971-77, asst. to pres., 1976-77, pres., chief operating officer, 1977—, also dir.; dir. Lamson & Sessions, Nat. City Bank, Republic Steel. Mem. exec. bd. Greater Cleve. council Boy Scouts Am.; bd. dirs. Greater Cleve. Growth Assn., United Way Sers.; trustee Mus. Arts Assn., Cleve. Served with AC U.S. Army, 1943-47, USAF, 1947-54. Decorated Air medal with 2 Bronze Oak Leaf clusters, Purple Heart. Recipient Silver Antelope award, Boy Scout Am., 1976. Mem. N.A.M. (dir., dist. vice chmn. Midwest div.). Clubs: Pepper Pike, Union (Cleve.). Office: 23555 Euclid Ave Cleveland OH 44117

PACELLI, ANTHONY DANIEL, ins. co. exec.; b. Chgo., Apr. 17, 1944; s. Rocco Salvatore and Grace Ruth P.; B.A., St. Mary's Coll., 1967; postgrad. DePaul U., 1967-69; M.B.A., Roosevelt U., 1972. Gen. acct. Food Marketers, Westchester, Ill., 1971-73; staff acct. Bankers Life & Casualty Co., Chgo., 1973-74; cost acct. Guarantee Trust Life Ins. Co., Chgo., 1974-78, acctg. supr., 1978—, ABC project leader, 1980—. Served with U.S. Army, 1969-71. Decorated Bronze Star, Purple Heart with oak leaf cluster. Recipient Fellow Life Mgmt. Inst.; mem. Ins. Acctg. Statis. Assn., Life Office Mgmt. Assn., Am. Mgmt. Assn., Am. Legion. Republican. Roman Catholic. Clubs: Societa Aleanza Ricigilianese. Home: 291 Yorkfield Elmhurst IL 60126 Office: 2537 W Montrose Ave Chicago IL 60638

PACHUT, JOSEPH F., JR., educator; b. Little Falls, N.Y., Mar. 6, 1950; s. Joseph F. and Marion E. (Steinberg) P.; B.A. in Geology (N.Y. State Regents scholar), SUNY, Oneonta, 1972; Ph.D. in Geology, Mich. State U., 1977; m. Elizabeth A. Battisti, June 3, 1972; children—Jennifer E., Melissa N. Grad. teaching asst. geology dept. Mich. State U., East Lansing, 1972-77; instr. Delta Coll., University Center, Mich., 1975, Albion (Mich.) Coll., 1975; asst. prof. geology Ind. U.-Purdue U., Indpls., 1977—. NDEA fellow, 1975; Ind. U.-Purdue U., Indpls. summer faculty fellow. Mem. AAAS, Paleontol. Soc., Soc. Econ. Paleontologists and Mineralogists, Sigma Xi. Contbr. articles in field to profl. publs., paper to profl. confs. Office: 925 W Michigan St Indianapolis IN 46202

PADBERG, MILDRED TRUE, occupational therapist; b. Melrose, Mass., June 16, 1932; d. Donald Wilbur and Natalie Emma (Smith) True; B.S., Tufts U., 1955; grad. Boston Sch. Occupational Therapy, 1955; M.Ed., U. Ill., 1980; m. Daniel Ivan Padberg, Aug. 5, 1956; children—Susan, Jean, Carol. Sr. occupational therapist Spl. Children's Center, Ithaca, N.Y., 1966-72; resource tchr., occupational therapist DeWitt Jr. High Sch., Ithaca, 1973-75; occupational therapist Ford-Iroquois County Spl. Edn. Assn., Elliott, Ill., 1980—. Served to lt. (j.g.), USNR, 1955-57. Mem. Am. Occupational Therapy Assn., Ill. Occupational Therapy Assn., Champaign County Hist. Soc., Phi Delta Kappa, Kappa Delta Pi. Republican. Club: U. Ill. Women's. Home: 1505 Alma Dr Champaign IL 61820 Office: PO Box 216 Elliott IL 60933

PADDA, KULWANT SINGH, ednl. adminstr.; b. India, Jan. 5, 1938; s. Bela Singh and Parsin Kaur (Uppal) P.; M.S. in Physics, U. Tex., 1969; M.S. in Statistics, So. Ill. U., 1979; m. Gurdeep Kaur, June 27, 1963; children—Gurpreet, Harjot. Math. statistician Dept. Energy, Argonne, Ill., 1979-80; adminstrv. asst. II, Desegregation and Monitoring Office, St. Louis Public Schs., 1980—. Trustee, Sikh Study Circle, St. Louis, 1980—. Mem. Am. Statis. Assn., Ops. Research Soc. Am. Home: 12543 Sunview Dr St Louis MO 63141 Office: St Louis Public Schools 911 Locust St Saint Louis MO 63101

PADEN, ROBERT CHARLES, mental hosp. adminstr.; b. Colby, Kans., May 4, 1942; s. Homer Ernest and Harriet Eloise (McCafferty) P.; B.A., Wichita State U., 1967, M.A., 1973; postgrad. U. Ill., 1975—; m. Carolyn Lee Erwin, July 29, 1972; children—Matthew Lee, Lezlie Diane. Staff psychologist Jacksonville (Ill.) State Hosp., 1969-71; sr. staff mem. Psychosocial Rehab. Research project Adolf Meyer Mental Health Center, Decatur, Ill., 1971-73, mental health program adminstr., 1974-79, asst. supt. clin./profl. support services, 1979—; program evaluator Macon County (Ill.) Day Probation/Edn. Program, Decatur, 1973-74. Mem. Ill. Rehab. Counseling Assn. (dir. 1978-80), Am. Psychol. Assn., Nat. Rehab. Assn. Home: 1614 W Harrison St Decatur IL 62526 Office: 2310 E Mound Rd Decatur IL 62526

PADIA, ARVIND DHARAMSHI, chemist; b. Jetpur, Gujarat, India, May 7, 1948; s. Dharamshi Jivabhai and Amritben (Dharamshibhai) P.; B.S. in Chemistry, Kotak Inst. Sci., Rajkot, India, 1968; B.S. in Chem. Engring., Ind. Inst. Tech., 1972; m. Chandramani Gordhandas Kiri, Nov. 15, 1976. Research and devel. chemist, Leepoxy Plastics, Fort Wayne, Ind., 1973-76; devel. chemist Hardman, Inc., Bellville, N.J., 1976-77; sr. chemist product devel. Edmont div. Becton, Dickinson and Co., Coshocton, Ohio, 1978—. Mem. Am. Chem. Soc. Club: Jaycees. Home: 58040 Rose Ln West Lafayette OH 43845 Office: 1300 Walnut St Coshocton OH 43812

PADILLA, DONALD G., pub. relations agy. exec.; b. Carroll, Iowa, Apr. 1, 1921; s. J. Torres and Mabel (Smith) P.; B.A., U. Iowa, 1947; m. Dagny May Stenehjem, Jan. 31, 1942; children—Doreen, Douglas, Jeri. Reporter, photographer, picture editor Cedar Rapids (Iowa) Gazette, 1947-50; picture editor Des Moines Register and Tribune, 1950-52; asso. news dir., chief photography Sta. WTCN and WCTN-TV, Mpls., 1952-54; asso. news dir. Sta. WCCO-TV, Mpls., 1954-55; specialist in film documentaries Continental Films, 1955-56; publicity and promotion dir. Minn. Statehood Centennial Commn., 1956-58; co-founder, pres. Padilla and Sarjeant, Inc., Mpls., 1958-61; pres. Padilla, Sarjeant, Sullivan and Speer, Inc., Mpls., 1961-71; pres., chmn., chief exec. officer Padilla and Speer, Inc., Mpls., 1971—; co-owner Crow River Farms, Minnetonka, Minn. Bd. regents Augsburg Coll., Mpls.; bd. dirs. Courage Found., Minn. Newspaper Found., Mpls., Westwood Found, Ebenezer Found., Multi Resources Center, Mpls.; mem. exec. council Minn. Hist. Soc., St. Paul. Served with USAAF, 1942-46. Recipient St. Olaf medal King Olav V of Norway; King's medal King Carl XVI Gustav of Sweden, 1976, Vesterheim medal, 1978; Outstanding Service award Minn. Press Club, 1973; Outstanding Achievement award Nat. Press Photographers Assn., 1954; others. Mem. Pub. Relations Soc. Am. (Meritorious Service citation 1971, 73), Nat. Investor Relations Inst. (charter), U. Iowa Alumni Assn., Republican. Lutheran. Clubs: Mpls. Athletic, Golden Valley Country, Minn. Press, Shriners (Mpls.). Home: 2253 Wildwood Circle Minnetonka MN 55343 Office: 224 Franklin Ave W Minneapolis MN 55404

PADMORE, JOEL MACKIE, chemist; b. Macy, Nebr., Dec. 8, 1938; s. William Geer and Mildred Elanor P.; B.A., U. Nebr., Omaha, 1960; Ph.D., Mont. State U., 1964; m. Carol Ann Coffey, Aug. 19, 1960; children—Susan, Robert, John. Prof. chemistry U. S.D., Vermillion, 1964-79; state chemist, dir. S.D. State Chem. Lab., Vermillion, 1979—. Mem. Assn. Ofcl. Analytical Chemists, Am. Chem. Soc., Assn. Am. Feed Control Ofcls., Assn. Am. Plant Food Control Ofcls., Assn. Am. Pesticide Control Ofcls., Assn. Food and Drug Ofcls. Lutheran. Club: Lions (pres. 1978-80) (Vermillion). Home: 1200 Crestview Dr Vermillion SD 57069 Office: State Chem Lab Vermillion SD 57069

PADY, DONALD STUART, librarian; b. Kansas City, Mo., Aug. 17, 1937; s. Stuart McGregor and Rose Annie (Maw) P.; B.A., U. Kans., 1959; M.S., Emporia State U., 1962; M.A., Iowa State U., 1977; m. Carol Lee Tulloss, June 1, 1958; children—Patricia Ann, Peter John, Laura Jean, David Sean. Librarian Ariz. State U. Library, 1962-66, Kans. State U. Library, 1966-68; reference librarian Iowa State U. Library, 1968—, asso. prof., 1978—, bibliographer, 1968—; cons. for computer applications in libraries and museums, 1972—. Served with U.S. Army, 1957-58. Carnegie Research grantee, 1958-59. Mem. Soc. for Study of Midwestern Lit., Spl. Libraries Assn., Iowa Local History and Mus. Assn. Democrat. Presbyterian. Club: Masons. Author: Scientific, Agricultural and Technological Artifacts Among Iowa's Libraries, Museums and Private Collections, 1978; editor: Annual Bibliography of Midwestern Literature in Mid-America, 1973—.

PAES, MAURO MARIA, cardiologist; b. Assolna Goa, India, Aug. 22, 1945; came to U.S., 1970, naturalized, 1973; d. Bonifacio Marciano and Malaquina (Silva-Lobo) P.; I.Sc., St. Xavier Coll., 1962; M.B., B.S., U. Bombay, 1968; m. Sol Esperanza Bermudez, Dec. 6, 1973; children—Michelle Lisa, Mellisa Ann, Sarah Lynn. Intern, Phila. Gen. Hosp., 1970-71; resident Michael Reese Hosp. and Med. Center, 1972-73, Mercy Hosp. and Med. Center, 1974-75; practice medicine specializing in cardiology, Chgo., 1975—; mem. staff Mercy Hosp. and Med. Center, 1975—, asso. dir. cardiac surveillance unit, 1977—; partner Henry Schmitz Med. Group, 1975—; clin. asst. prof. medicine Abraham Lincoln Sch. of Medicine, U. Ill., Chgo. Fellow Am. Coll. Chest Physicians, Am. Coll. Cardiology, Inst. Medicine Chgo., Am. Heart Assn., A.C.P.; mem. AMA, Am. Soc. Echocardiography, Ill. Med. Soc., Chgo. Med. Soc. Home: 424 Ridgeview St Downers Grove IL 60515 Office: 55 E Washington St Chicago IL 60602

PAGANI, ALBERT LOUIS, air force officer; b. Jersey City, Feb. 19, 1936; s. Alexander and Ann P.; B.S., U.S. Naval Acad., 1957; M.B.A., So. Ill. U., 1971; postgrad. Indsl. Coll. Armed Forces, 1974, Air War Coll., 1977; m. Beverly Cameron Good, Feb. 23, 1971; children—Penelope, Deborah, Michael. Commd. lt. USAF, 1957, advanced through grades to Col., 1978; chief spl. requirements Hdqrs. Mil. Air Lift Command, Scott AFB, Ill., 1972-74, chief airlift mgmt., 1978-81, dir. tech. and spl. ops. plans and concepts, 1981, dir. command and control, 1982—; comdr. 627 Mil. Airlift Support Squadron, Mildenhall, Eng., 1974-75, 435 Tactical Airlift Group, Mildenhall, 1975-76, dep. comdr. Rhein Main Air Base, Frankfurt, Germany, 1976-78. Decorated Bronze Star, Air medal, Meritorious Service medal with 3 oak leaf clusters, Air Force Commendation medal with 2 oak leaf clusters, Vietnam Cross of Gallantry. Mem. Nat. Def. Transp. Assn., Airlift Assn., Soc. Logistics Engrs., Air Force Assn., Mensa. Club: Daedalions. Home: 1307 Pinehurst Dr OFallon IL 62269 Office: Hdqrs MAC/DOC Scott AFB IL 62225

PAGANO, RONALD JOSEPH, sch. adminstr.; b. Arnold, Pa., Aug. 15, 1950; s. Joseph and Janine (Yanuzzo) P.; B.A., Susquehanna U., 1972; M.Ed., Westminster Coll., 1977; postgrad. Akron U., 1979—; m. Karla Elaine Pahl, June 9, 1973; children—Carrin, Nicholas. High sch. social studies tchr. Leetonia (Ohio) Schs., 1973-75; high sch. social studies tchr., elem. sch. tchr. Struthers (Ohio) Schs., 1975-79; elem./secondary sch. prin. Lowellville (Ohio) Schs., 1979—. Active Lowellville Businessmen's Assn., 1981—. Named Outstanding Young Man in Am., 1979. Mem. Assn. for Supervision and Curriculum Devel., Ohio Assn. Secondary Sch. Adminstrs. Phi Delta Kappa. Club: Struthers Lions. Home: 120 Como St Struthers OH 44471 Office: Lowellville High Sch 2 E Grant St Lowellville OH 44436

PAGE, CLARENCE EUGENE, TV broadcaster; b. Dayton, Ohio, June 2, 1947; s. Clarence Hannibal and Maggie Lee (Williams) P.; B.S. in Journalism, Ohio U., 1969; m. Leanita McClain, May 28, 1974. Reporter, asst. city editor Chgo. Tribune, 1969-80; dir. community affairs WBBM-TV, Chgo., 1980—; instr. journalism Northwestern U. Served with AUS, 1969-71. Recipient award for best community service UPI, 1980, Edward Scott Beck award, 1976. Mem. Chgo. Area Broadcast Public Affairs Assn. (rec. sec. 1981-82), Chgo. Acad. TV Arts and Sci. (dir.), Chgo. Assn. Black Journalists, AFTRA. Unitarian. Contbr. freelance articles to Wash. Monthly, Playboy, Chgo. Reader. Office: 630 N McClurg Ct Chicago IL 60611

PAGE, DAVID ALAN, engring. co. exec.; b. St. Louis, June 11, 1951; s. David Richard and Grace Marie (Craven) P.; B.S., U. Mo., 1973, M.B.A., 1978; m. Karen S. Koebbe, May 20, 1972; children—Carrie Ann, David Joseph, Joseph Richard. Indsl. engring. trainee Nat. Steel Corp., Granite City (Ill.) Steel Div., 1973-74, indsl. engr., 1974-75, supr. capital and profit planning, 1975-76, supr. budgetary planning, 1976-78, gen. supr. fin. planning, 1978, asst. gen. foreman galvanized products, 1978-79; dir. ops. Fox & Cole, civil engring. and surveying, 1979—, pres., 1980—; faculty Webster Coll., 1977—. Mem. Am. Inst. Indsl. Engrs. (v.p. 1972-73), Am. Iron and Steel Inst. (steel fellows program 1976-79), Am. Mgmt. Assn., Assn. Iron and Steel Engrs. Roman Catholic. Home: 5816 Bristlecone St Saint Louis MO 63129

PAGE, DOZZIE LYONS, educator; b. Tiptonville, Tenn., Apr. 13, 1921; d. Lessie LeRoy and Carrie (Oldham) Lyons; B.S.Ed., Chgo. Tchrs. Coll., 1968; M.S.Ed., Chgo. State U., 1976; M.A. in Bus. Edn., Govs. State U., 1979; m. Eugene Page, Dec. 22, 1973; children—Rita, Gerald. Cashier receptionist Unity Mut. Life Ins. Co., Chgo., 1939-47; sec. United Transport Service Employees Union, Chgo., 1947-51; sec. to dir. YMCA West Side, Chgo., 1951-53; sec., office mgr. Joint Council Dining Car Employees AFL CIO, Chgo., 1957-59; sr. stenographer Chgo. Police Dept., 1962-65; tchr. office practice Manpower Devel. Tng. Act, Chgo. Bd. Edn., 1965-67; tchr., coordinator distributive edn. Dunbar Vocational High Sch., Chgo., 1968—. Mem. Office Occupations Club, Distbr. Edn. Club, Chgo. Urban League, Chgo. Bus. Tchrs. Assn., Ill., Am. personnel and guidance assns., Am. Vocat. Assn., Nat., Ill. bus. edn. assns., Chgo. State U. Alumni Assn., Phi Delta Kappa. Home: 6127 Justine St S Chicago IL 60636 Office: 3000 ML King Dr Chicago IL 60616

PAGE, RUTH, dancer; b. Indpls.; d. Lafayette and Marian (Heinly) Page; student Tudor Hall, Indpls., N.Y.C.; D.H.L. (hon.), DePaul U., 1980, Ind. U., 1982; m. Thomas Hart Fisher, Feb. 8, 1925 (dec.). Dancer with Pavlowa at age of 15; performed in leading role of J. Alden Carpenter's The Birthday of the Infanta, produced by Chgo. Opera Co., 1919, later in N.Y.C.; toured U.S. as prin. dancer with Adolph Bolm's Ballet, later appeared in London with Mr. Bolm; premiere danseuse 2d Music Box Revue, N.Y.C., 1921-23, Chgo. Allied Arts performances, 1924, 25, 26; studied under Enrico Cecchetti at Monte Carlo, 1925; premiere danseuse Mcpl. Opera Co., Buenos Aires, Ravinia Opera Co., 1926-31; guest soloist with Met. Opera Co., 1926-28; guest artist at enthronement ceremonies for Emperor Hirohito, Japan, 1928; performed series of Am. dances before Sophil Soc., Moscow, 1930; ballet dir. Chgo. Opera, 1934-37, 42-43, 45; dir. Fed. Theatre Dance Project, Chgo., 1938-39; S. Am. tour with first dance group as co-dir. Page-Stone Ballet, 1940; guest choreographer with Bentley Stone, dancer Frankie and Johnny for Ballet Russe de Monte Carlo, 1945; guest choreographer, dancer The Bells for Ballet Russe de Monte Carlo, 1946, Billy Sunday, 1948; Impromptu au Bois, and Revanche, Les Ballets des Champs-Elysees, 1951, Royal Festival Ballet, Vilia, 1953; co-dir. Les Ballets Americains, Theatre des Champs Elysees, Paris, 1950; ballet mistress Chgo. Lyric Opera, 1954-69; choreographer, dir. Ruth Page's Chgo. Opera Ballet, 1956-66, Ruth Page's Internat. Ballet, 1966-70; choreographer Merry Widow Ballet, 1956, Susanna and the Barber, 1957, Salome, 1957, Triumph of Chastity, 1958, El Amor Brujo, 1958, Camille, 1958, Carmen, 1959, Fledermaus, 1960, Concertino, 1961, Mefistofela, 1962, Bullets or Bon-Bons, 1965, Nutcracker, 1965—, Carmina Burana, 1966, Bolero, 1967, Dancer's Ritual, 1968, Alice in the Garden, 1970, also Alice in Wonderland and Alice Through the Looking Glass at Pitts. Ballet Theatre, 1971, Catulli Carmina, 1973, Chain of Fools, 1973, Alice in Wonderland ballet, 1978, Frankie and Johnny, produced by Dance Theater of Harlem, Covent Garden, London, 1981, N.Y.C., 1982; lectr. tour Ruth Page's Invitation to the Dance, 1971-72. Recipient award Adult Council Greater Chgo., 1963; citation outstanding service Ballet Guild Chgo. Mem. Chgo. Nat. Assn. Dance Masters (hon.). Clubs: Arts, Friday, Racquet (Chgo.). Contbr. to mags. Address: Ruth Page Found Sch Dance 1016 N Dearborn St Chicago IL 60610

PAGE, SALLY JACQUELYN, univ. adminstr.; b. Saginaw, Mich., July 8, 1943; d. William Henry and Doris Effie (Knippel) P.; B.A., U. Iowa, 1965; M.B.A., So. Ill. U., 1973. Copy editor, C.V. Mosby Co., St. Louis, 1965-69; edit. cons. Edit. Assos., Edwardsville, Ill., 1969-70; research adminstr. So. Ill. U., 1970-74, asst. to pres., affirmative action officer, 1974-77; civil rights officer U. N.D., Grand Forks, 1977—, lectr. mgmt., 1978—; polit. comentator Sta. KFJM, Nat. Public Radio affiliate, 1981. Pres., Pine to Prairie council Girl Scouts U.S.A., 1980—; mem. employment com. Ill. Commn. on Status of Women, 1976-77; mem. Bicentennial Com. Edwardsville, 1976, Bikeway Task Force Edwardsville, 1975-77. Mem. AAUW (dir. Ill. 1975-77), Am. Assn. Affirmative Action, Soc. Research Adminstrs., M.B.A. Assn. Republican. Presbyterian. Home: 3121 Cherry St Grand Forks ND 58201 Office: Univ ND Grand Forks ND 58202

PAGE, WALTER SHARP, JR., assn. exec.; b. Columbus, Ohio, July 16, 1917; s. Walter Sharp and Esther (Johnson) P.; student Denison U., 1934-35; B.A., M.A., Ohio State U., 1939; m. Eva Johnson, Mar. 1, 1941; children—Frances Johnson, Walter Sharp. Community sec. Winston-Salem (N.C.) YMCA, 1939-40; field rep., state campaign dir. N.C. Tb Assn., 1940-42; exec. sec. Passaic County (N.J.) Tb and Health Assn., 1947-49; program cons. Am. Heart Assn., 1949-50; exec. v.p. Ohio affiliate Am. Heart Assn., Columbus, 1952—. Mem. Gov.'s Task Force on Environ. Protection, 1971. Served to maj. AUS, 1942-46, 50-52. Decorated Bronze Star with 2 oak leaf clusters. Mem. Staff Soc. Heart Assns. (pres. 1958-59), Ohio Pub. Health Assn. (chmn. vol. health agy. sec. 1966-68, pres. 1971-72), Phi Delta Theta. Methodist. Clubs: Rotary, Univ. (Columbus). Home: 1544 Guilford Rd Columbus OH 43221 Office: 6161 Busch Blvd Columbus OH 43229

PAGEL, RICHARD FREDERICK, metallurgist; b. Beckingen, Germany, May 28, 1920; s. Richard and Paula A. (Roth) P.; m. Frieda H. Stallinger, Sept. 28, 1952; children—Carmen L., Ricarda L.; B.S. in Metall. Engring., U. Idaho, 1949. Research metallurgist Cerro de Pasco Corp., LaOroya, Peru, 1949-52; plant metallurgist Am. Zinc Co., Dumas, Tex., 1952-55, research engr., Sauget, Ill., 1955-71, chief metallurgist, 1973—. Mem. Moose. Patentee electrolytic zinc refining, wastewater treatment; contbr. articles to profl. jours. Home: Belleville IL 62221 Office: AMAX Zinc Co PO Box 2347 East St Louis IL 62202

PAGET, JOHN GEORGE, JR., fin. and mktg. exec.; b. Detroit, Apr. 7, 1942; s. John George and Shirley (Nicholas) P.; B.S. in Mktg., Calif. Western U., 1980, M.B.A. in Fin., 1981; m. Celia A. Iacampo, May 8, 1971; children—Cleve Geoffrey, Nicholas John, Annmarie. Mktg. rep. Univac div. Sperry Rand Corp., Cleve., 1967-70; sales mgr. Midwestern div. Ampex Computer Products Corp., 1971-72; sales mgr. Ohio area Mohawk Data Scis. Corp., 1972-74; regional sales mgr. Midwestern div. Data Transmission Corp., 1974-75; v.p., gen. mgr. Traveletter Corp., Bellevue, Wash., from 1975; now nat. accounts mgr. Docutel Corp., Dallas. Served with U.S. Army, Mem. Am. Mgmt. Assn., Wash. Council on Fgn. Trade, U.S. Parachute Assn. (cert. instr., class D license). Club: Sons of Italy (trustee) (Bellevue). Home: 12803 Lynn Dr Chesterfield OH 44026

PAGET, SAM S., chem. mfg. co. exec.; b. Bridgeport, Conn., Jan. 9, 1947; s. Louis S. and Edith S. P.; B.S. in Bus. Adminstrn., Lehigh U., 1968; m. Cathy Shogan; children—Jonathan, Wendy. Auditor, Brout Isaacs & Co., C.P.A.'s, Bridgeport, Conn., 1969-71; v.p. Qonaar Corp., Elk Grove Village, Ill., 1971-79; v.p. Bell Chem. Co., Chgo., 1979-81, chief operating officer, 1981—. Served with U.S. Army. Office: 411 N Wolcott Ave Chicago IL 60622

PAHREN, HERBERT ROGER, govt. ofcl.; b. St. Bernard, Ohio, Oct. 20, 1929; s. Aloysius John and Bernadine Marie (Telintelo) P.; Chem. E., U. Cin., 1952; M.S., Purdue U., 1958; m. Mary Katherine Bachmann, Oct. 22, 1955; children—Roger, Kathleen, Barbara, Patrice. Chem. engr., AEC, 1952-55; san. engr. USPHS, Cin., Boston, Denver, 1955-66; dep. regional dir. Fed. Water Pollution Control Adminstrn., Boston, 1966-72; indsl. adviser EPA, Cin., 1972-75, research mgr., 1975—, employee of yr., 1978. profl. engr., Ohio. Mem. Am. Water Works Assn., Water Pollution Control Assn., Sigma Xi, Alpha Chi Sigma. Roman Catholic. Contbr. articles water pollution control to profl. publs. Home: 9413 Shadyoak Ct Cincinnati OH 45231 Office: EPA 26 W St Clair St Cincinnati OH 45268

PAINE, CARLTON BENTLEY, clin. psychologist; b. Lincoln, Nebr., Nov. 4, 1939; s. Charles Bentley and Hazel Marie (Beechner) P.; B.A., Nebr. Wesleyan U., 1962; M.A., U. Mo., Columbia, 1964, Ph.D., 1971; m. Judith Anne Umberger, June 21, 1963; children—Liza Anne, Heather Lynn, Jennifer Leigh. Intern, Greater Kansas City (Mo.) Mental Health Found. and U. Mo. Med. Sch., 1966-67, instr. U. Mo. Sch. Medicine, Kansas City, 1967-71; cons. Otoe County Mental Health Clinic, Nebraska City, Nebr., 1971-73; asso. in clin. psychology U. Nebr., Lincoln, 1971-80; program dir. Community Mental Health Center of Lancaster County, Lincoln, 1971-80; clin. psychologist Health Central, Lincoln, 1980-81; sch. clin. psychologist Nebr. Wesleyan U., Lincoln, 1973—; pvt. practice clin. psychology; profl. adv. Lancaster County Mental Health Assn., 1974-76. Pres. Eastridge Recreation Assn., 1981; past mem. Emergency Med. Services Council. USPHS trainee, 1964-65. Mem. Am. Psychol. Assn., Nebr. Psychol. Assn., Nebr. Soc. Profl. Psychologists, Zeta Psi, Psi Chi. Democrat. Unitarian. Contbr. book review and article to profl. publs. Home: 201 Carolyn Ct Lincoln NE 68510 Office: Suite 201F 3701 O St Lincoln NE 68510

PAINTER, MILTON MCFARLAND, mfg. co. exec.; b. Friars Point, Miss., Dec. 6, 1920; s. Milton McFarland and Ernestine (Cobb) P.; B.A., La. State U., 1942; m. Frances Elwanda Groves, Apr. 4, 1955; children—Michael Cobb, Cynthia Lee, Judy Frances. Creative dir., merchandising dept. Walgreen Drug Stores, Chgo., 1946-50; account exec. Chek-Chart Corp., 1950-53; asst. dir. advt. and sales promotion Ency. Brit., Inc., 1953-56; advt. supr., canned meat div. and frozen food div. Libby, McNeil & Libby, 1956-66; account exec. Young & Rubicam, Inc., 1966-68; advt. and sales promotion mgr. Westclox div. Gen. Time Corp., LaSalle, Ill., 1968-72; advt. and sales promotion mgr. Republic Molding Corp., Chgo., 1972—. Served to tech. sgt. USAAF, 1942-45; to lt. col. USAFR, 1946-80. Mem. Smithsonian Assos., Res. Officers Assn., Ill. Sheriffs Assn., SAR, Sons of Confederate Vets., Mil. Order Stars and Bars, Daggers, Sigma Alpha Epsilon. Home: 881 Darlington Ln Crystal Lake IL 60014

PAINTER, NANCY FARRAR, counselor; b. St. Louis, Sept. 6, 1926; d. Benedict and Ruth (Gregg) Farrar; A.B., Wells Coll., 1948; m. Paul Painter, Sept. 2, 1949; children—Jeffrey, Gregg, Lucy, Anne, Benedict, Thomas. Coll. counselor Family Guidance, Inc., St. Louis, 1973—; area rep. Am. Field Service, St. Louis, 1974—, trustee, 1981—. Founding bd. dirs. Jr. Kindergarten, St. Louis, 1961-70; mem. St. Louis Council Expt. in Internat. Living, 1968-74; bd. dirs. Planned Parenthood, St. Louis, 1970-76, Washington U. Child Guidance Clinic, 1970-76, Internat. Inst., 1981—; mem. allocation panel United Fund, 1973-76. Kettering Internat. fellow, 1980. Episcopalian. Clubs: Jr. League, Pioneers. Author: Guidebook to College Admissions, 1978; contbr. chpt. to book NACAC Guide to Admission Counseling. Home: 6 Glenview Rd Saint Louis MO 63124 Office: 450 N Lindbergh Saint Louis MO 63141

PAISLEY, DENNIS LEE, physicist, cons.; b. Macomb, Ill., May 16, 1942; s. Lyle H. and Clarice C. (Ward) P.; B.S. in Physics, Western Ill. U., 1965; M.S. in Physics, Xavier U., 1973; m. Daisy I. Fernetti; 1 son, Dennis Lyle. Physics instr. Scioto (Ill.) High Sch., 1964-65; engr. div. hwys. State of Ill., Peoria, 1965-67; sr. research physicist Mound Lab. Monsanto Research Corp., Miamisburg, Ohio., 1967-80; prin. physicist Calspan Corp., Buffalo, 1980-81; research physicist U. Dayton (Ohio) Research Inst., 1981—; cons. in ultra-high speed photography, laser photography, streak photography, hydro diagnostics, explosives, shock and detonation phenomena. Mem. Soc. Photoinstrumentation Engrs. Club: Lions. Author publs. in field. Home: 708 St Dunstan Ct Dayton OH 45449

PAKER, PHILLIP ERROL, retail co. info. mgr.; b. Chgo., July 8, 1945; s. Abraham Daniel and RoseJoy (Noren) P.; B.A. in Bus. Adminstrn., Bellevue (Nebr.) Coll., 1967; postgrad. DePaul U., 1978; m. Diane Marie Breon, July 12, 1966; children—Edward Phillip, Mathew Shane, Deborah Ann, Aaron David, Joshua Nathaniel. Systems rep., sr. programmer analyst Honeywell, 1969; cons. PEPI Consulting, Chgo., 1969—; data base analyst Continental Nat. Assurance, 1976-78; mgr. data base systems and adminstrn. consulting COMSI, Oak Brook, Ill., 1978-79; mgr. data base adminstrn. Target Stores, Fridley, Minn., 1979—. Served with USAF, 1965-69. Mem. M.B.A. Assn., Nat. Rifle Assn. Home: 22603 Cedar Dr Bethel MN 55005 Office: 1080 73d Ave NE Fridley MN 55432

PAKIS, VAL, engring. mgr.; b. Cleve., Sept. 22, 1924; s. Val and Mary (Hribar) P.; B.S. in Elec. Engring., Mont. State Coll., 1950; m. Therese Molinski, Jan. 31, 1948; children—Val, Fred, Laura. With Illuminating Co., Cleve., 1948-51, Reliance Electric Co., Cleve., 1951, Austin Co., 1951-55; with W.W. Clark Corp., Cleve., 1955—, engring. mgr., 1973—. Mem. City Planning Commn., Willowick, Ohio, 1974-76. Served with Paratroops, U.S. Army, 1943-46. Decorated Bronze Star, Purple Heart. Mem. Cleve. Engring. Soc., IEEE, Internat. Assn. Elec. Insps. Republican. Home: 377 Clarmont Rd Willowick OH 44094 Office: 1251 E 286 St Euclid OH 44132

PALACIO, JUNE ROSE, dietitian; b. Hove, Sussex, Eng., June 14, 1940; d. Alfred and Doris Winifred (Blanch) Payne; B.S., U. Calif., Berkeley, 1963; dietetic intern Mills Coll., Oakland, Calif., 1963-64; m. Moki Moses Palacio, Nov. 30, 1968. Asst. dir. dept. food service and residence halls Mills Coll., 1964-66; staff dietitian Servomation-Bay Cities, Oakland, 1966-67; commissary mgr. Host Internat., Inc., Honolulu, 1967-74; dir. dietary services Straub Clinic and Hosp., Honolulu, 1974—; instr. Kapiolani Community Coll., Honolulu, U. Hawaii Sch. Public Health. Named Boss of Year, Honolulu Bus. and Profl. Women's Assn., 1975. Mem. Am., Hawaii dietetic assns., Soc. Nutrition Edn., U. Calif. Berkeley Alumni Assn. Republican. Episcopalian. Home: 100 Wilson Ct Manhattan KS 66506

PALBYKIN, DONALD JOHN, aviation exec.; b. Oak Park, Ill., Oct. 11, 1929; s. Albert Alfred and Cecilia Mary (Keiper) P.; student pub. and parochial schs.; m. Elizabeth Mae Perry, May 29, 1948; children—Stephen, Alan, Martin, Julie, Debra, Susan, Ann Marie. Laborer, Studebaker Corp., 1948-56; chief pilot Stockert Flying Service, 1956-59; asst. pres. Wheel Horse, 1959-66; pres. Skystream, Inc., Plymouth, Ind., 1966-76; owner bus. and apt. bldgs.; pres. Palbykin Enterprises; pres. Paladay Industries, Inc., mfr. modular homes, 1980—. Club: Plymouth Country. Home: 310 N Michigan St Penthouse 500 Plymouth IN 46563 Office: Plymouth Bldg Plymouth IN 46563

PALENCHAR, ROBERT EDWARD, diversified industry exec.; b. Detroit, Apr. 8, 1922; s. John Peter and Irene Ann (Repicky) P.; A.B. in Econs. and Personnel Adminstrn., U. Notre Dame, 1942; postgrad. U. Mich., 1943; m. Ethel Lindsay, Sept. 10, 1942; children—Patricia Ann (Mrs. Richard K. Atchinson), James Lindsay. With Ex-Cell-O Corp., Detroit, 1949-62, dir. indsl. relations, 1962; v.p. employee relations automotive div. Budd Co., Detroit, 1962-66; v.p., dir. employee relations Sunbeam Corp., Chgo., 1966-69; v.p. personnel and pub. relations Esmark, Inc., 1969-77, v.p. corp. affairs and personnel, 1977—, dir. subholding cos. Pres., Esmark, Inc. Found., 1971—. Served with U.S. Army, 1943. Mem. Chgo. Bd. Commerce, Bus. Roundtable (labor-mgmt. com.), Ill. C. of C., Notre Dame Alumni Assn., Am. Mgmt. Assn., Conf. Bd. Club: Mid-America (Chgo.). Home: 64 Joyce Ct Glen Ellyn IL 60137 Office: 55 E Monroe St Chicago IL 60603

PALERMO, ANTHONY, JR., elec. engr.; b. Cleve., Sept. 22, 1926; s. Anthony and Sblendora (Palange) P.; m. Margaret Theresa Packer, July 28, 1951; children—Thomas, David, Patricia, Steven, Nancy, James, Jeanne; student U. Dayton, 1944, U. Ind., 1945; B.S.E.E., Case Inst. Tech., 1949. Engr., Picker Corp., Cleve., 1949-58, sr. engr., 1959-62, chief engr. indsl. products group, 1962-64, engring. mgr. indsl. products group, 1964-72, cons. engr., 1972-75, engring. mgr. x-ray generators spl. systems group, 1975—; profl. musician, 1949—. Active Boy Scouts Am., 1961-62; publicity chmn., mem. speakers bur. S. Euclid Hist. Soc., 1972—, pres., 1977—. Mem. Am. Nat. Standards Inst., Am. Soc. for Metals, Little Red Schoolhouse Hist. Soc., Cleve. Musicians Union, Theta Chi. Clubs: Lander Haven Country, Pioneer Investment. Contbr. articles, chpts. to profl. jours., texts; author: Our Own Little Red Schoolhouse, 1976; holder numerous patents. Home: 1715 Biltamy Blvd South Euclid OH 44121 Office: 600 Beta Dr Mayfield OH 44143

PALETTA, FRANCIS XAVIER, plastic surgeon; b. New Kensington, Pa., Nov. 4, 1915; s. Frank and Mary (Fillipelli) P.; ed. Duquesne U., 1932-34; M.D., Marquette U., Milw., 1938; m. Janet Hausman, Oct. 6, 1973; children—Deane, Mary, Francis Xavier, Christian, David, Richard, Kathy, Stephen. Intern, St. Francis Hosp., Pitts., 1939; Cancer fellow Barnard Skin and Cancer Hosp., St. Louis, 1939-41; surg. resident U. Va. Hosp., 1941-43; resident in plastic surgery Columbia Presbyn. Hosp., N.Y.C., 1946-48; practice medicine specializing in plastic surgery, St. Louis, 1948—; chief plastic surgery St. Louis U. Med. Center, 1948—, prof. clin. surgery, 1950—, dir. cleft palate and craniofacial clinic, 1948, dir. tng. program plastic surgery, 1957; chief plastic surgery Cardinal Glennon Hosp. Children, 1957; mem. staff Cochran's VA Hosp., St. Louis City Hosp., St. Mary's Health Center, St. Johns Hosp. Served to maj. M.C., AUS, 1943-46. Recipient 1st Marquette U. Med. Alumni award cancer research, 1942. Diplomate Am. Bd. Surgery, Am. Bd. Plastic Surgery. Mem. Am. Soc. Plastic and Reconstructive Surgery (past pres.), A.C.S., Plastic Research Council, Am. Soc. Surgery Hands, Am. Burn Assn., Soc. Head and Neck Surgeons, Am. Assn. Plastic Surgeons, Central Surg. Assn., Am. Cleft Palate Assn., St. Louis Surg. Soc. (past pres.). Roman Catholic. Clubs: Serra, University, Algonquin Golf. Author: Pediatric Plastic Surgery, 1967; History of American Society Plastic and Reconstructive Surgery, 1968; contbr. chpts. to book, also articles to profl. jours. Office: 1035 Bellevue St Saint Louis MO 63117

PALIA, CHARLES CANTARDO, ednl. adminstr.; b. Spring Valley, Ill., Sept. 5, 1923; s. Cantardo and Mary Lou (Barto) P.; B.S. in Zoology, So. Ill., 1950; M.S., No. Ill.U., 1960; m. Enise M. Nanni, Aug. 2, 1947; children—Charles, David Damian. Tchr. math. and sci. Spring Valley Elementary Schs., 1950-60; prin. Lincoln Sch., Spring Valley, 1960-64; supt. schs., Spring Valley, 1964—. Post adviser Explorer Scouts; active civil def., Salvation Army, A.R.C., Tri-County Humane Soc. Bd. dirs. Spring Valley Assn. City Library, 1965-71; pres. adult bd. Spring Valley Youth Center. Served with USNR, 1942-45. Recipient Silver Beaver award Boy Scouts Am., 1971. Mem. Ill. Assn. Mental Health, Ill. Assn. Sch. Adminstrs., Bur. County Adminstrs., Ill. Sch. Bd. Assn., Am. Legion, Bqr.-Marshal-Putnam Tri-County Spl. Ednl. Coop. (chmn. 1971—), Am. Sch. Food Service Assn. Clubs: K.C., Rotary (pres. Spring Valley 1974-75). Home: 325 W Minnesota St Spring Valley IL 61362 Office: 800 N Richard Ave Spring Valley IL 61362

PALLASCH, MAGDALENA HELENA (MRS. BERNHARD MICHAEL PALLASCH), artist; b. Chgo., Sept. 6, 1908; d. Frank and Anna (Meier) Fixari; student Chgo. Acad. Fine Arts, 1922-26, Am. Acad. Fine Arts, 1926-30, U. Chgo., 1960, Art Inst. Chgo.; pvt. study with Joseph Allworthy, 1935-38; m. Bernhard Pallasch, Nov. 26, 1931; children—Bernhard Michael, Diana Pallasch Miller. Contbr. two murals and ten life size figures for Century of Progress Exhbn., Chgo., 1933-34; free-lance portrait artist, subjects include Cardinal Cody, Chgo., 1958—; represented in permanent collections Loyola U., Chgo., Barat Coll., Lake Forest, Ill., Internat. Coll. Surgeons, Chgo. Mem. Presentation Ball Aux.; mem. President's Club, Loyola U., also mem. women's bd. Recipient first award for still life Arts Club, N.Y.C., 1960; First award Nat. League Am. Pen Women, 1972; 1st place and best of show State Exhibit, Springfield, Ill., 1973; 1st award Chgo. Woman's Club, 1978. Mem. Nat. League Am. Pen Women (v.p. Chgo. br. 1966-68, art chmn. 1978-80, Margaret Dingle Meml. award 1979), Friends of Austria, Friends of D'Arcy Gallery of Medieval and Renaissance Art. Clubs: Ill. Cath. Women (gov. 1979—), Cuneo Meml. Hosp. Aux. (dir.), Fidelitas (dir.). Home and studio: 723 Junior Terr Chicago IL 60613

PALLMANN, MARGOT SIMONS, mathematician, educator; b. Stolberg, W. Germany, Dec. 13, 1927; d. Hubert J. and Bernadette (Waleffe) Simons; came to U.S., 1963, naturalized, 1978; B.A., U. Cologne, 1953, M.A., 1955; M.A., Washington U., 1971, Ph.D. (NDEA grad. fellow), 1975; m. Albert J. Pallmann, June 26, 1958; 1 son, Thomas R. Instr., City-Gymnasium, Cologne, W. Germany, 1955-57; instr., head physics div. Private Coll. Prep. Sch., Cologne, 1957-59; prof., chmn. dept. physics U El Salvador, C. Am., 1961-63; instr. U. Mo., St. Louis, 1965-68; instr. math. Washington U., St. Louis, 1973-77, lectr. math., 1977-78, adj. faculty summer sch., 1977-81; asst. prof. math. Harris-Stowe State Coll., St. Louis, 1977—. Mem. Am. Math. Soc., Math. Assn. Am., Assn. Women in Math., Nat. Council Tchrs. of Math. Home: 9 Middlesex Dr Saint Louis MO 63144 Office: 3026 Laclede Ave Saint Louis MO 63103

PALLO, MICHAEL STEPHEN, fisheries biologist; b. Independence, Mo., June 2, 1951; s. Mike J. and Evelyn N. Pallo; B.S. in Zoology, N.W. Mo. State U., Maryville, 1973, M.S. in Biology with spl. honors, 1974; m. Christi Jaye Hass, July 21, 1979. Fisheries research asst. N.W. Mo. State U., 1973-74; environ. health sanitarian City of Independence, 1975-76; asso. fisheries scientist NALCO Environ. Scis., Northbrook, Ill., 1976-79; environ. specialist Ill. Power Co., Decatur, 1979—. Cert. fisheries scientist. Mem. Am. Fisheries Soc., Nat. Wildlife Fedn., Muskies, Inc. (chpt. dir.). Author papers in field. Home: 3555 Dove Dr Decatur IL 62526 Office: 500 S 27th St A17 Decatur IL 62525

PALM, ERNEST THEODORE, surgeon; b. Missoula, Mont., Apr. 2, 1922; s. Ernest A. and Edith Anna (Cling) P.; B.A., Gustavus Adolphus Coll., 1942; B.S., U. Minn., 1944, M.B., 1945, M.D., 1946; m. Muriel Charlotte Larson, June 5, 1947; children—Augusta Jane, David, Barbara, William. Intern, Hahnemann Med. Sch. and Hosp., Phila., 1945-46; resident in surgery Swedish-St. Barnabas Hosp., Mpls., 1963-67; mem. staff Met. Med. Center, Fairview-Southdale

Hosp., Meth. Hosp., Mpls. Diplomate Am. Bd. Surgery. Recipient Ross award for sci. lit., 1964. Fellow A.C.S.; mem. AMA, Minn. State, Hennepin County med. socs., Minn., Mpls. surg. socs., Am. Physicians Art Assn. Lutheran. Contbr. articles in field to med., surg. jours., yearbooks. Home: 144 W Minnehaha Pkwy Minneapolis MN 55419 Office: 1202 Metropolitan Med Bldg Minneapolis MN 55404

PALMATIER, MARION BABILLA, dispatcher; b. Gary, Ind., Nov. 18, 1925; d. Sam L. and Theresa Marie Babilla; student Ind. U., 1944-46, Western Ky. State Tchrs. Coll., 1946, Western Mich. Coll., 1946-47; m. Robert A. Palmatier, Dec. 21, 1946; children—David Eugene, Denise Marie. Receptionist, switchboard operator Progressive Welder, Vicksburg, Mich., 1950-53; transp. clk. Western Mich. Univ., Kalamazoo, 1961-68, work order clk., radio dispatcher, 1968-73, cost and billing clk. phys. plant, 1973-75, sec., billing clk. communication and transp., 1975-77, dispatcher, 1977—. Mem. Adminstrv. Profl. Assn., Woman's Commn. Western Mich. U. Presbyterian. Home: 1326 Hardwick Kalamazoo MI 49002 Office: Physical Plant Oakland Dr Kalamazoo MI 49008

PALMER, KATHRYN MAIRE, nurse educator; b. Carbondale, Ill., Feb. 1, 1939; d. Frank Allen and Molene Maire (Jenkins) Baker; R.N., Maumee Valley Hosp., 1960; student So. Ill. U., 1961; B.S., U.S. Nursing Trainingship grantee, 1969-71), Med. Center U. Ill., 1971, M.S. (Ill. State Public Health grantee, 1971-73), 1973; postgrad. U. Ill., Champaign, 1976—; m. Leroy Palmer, Nov. 8, 1961; children—Kimberly Ann, John Christopher, Dana Elaine. Multiple clin. nursing appointments, Ohio, Ill., 1960-69; instr. Chgo. City Colls., 1973-74; asst. prof. Chgo. State U., 1974-76; instr. Parkland Community Coll., Champaign, Ill., 1976-77; clin. instr. Carle Found. Hosp., Urbana, Ill., 1977—; asso. dir. nursing, dir. edn. Bethany Hosp., Chgo.; cons. ednl. staff. Edn. Profl. Devel. Act fellow, 1977-78. Mem. Am. Public Health Assn., Am. Vocat. Assn., Nat. Assn. for Advancement of Black Americans in Vocat. Edn., AAUP, Phi Delta Kappa, Kappa Delta Pi. Baptist. Clubs: Cook County Bar Aux., Nat. Barristers Wives.

PALMER, KAYTON ROY, clergyman; b. McHenry County, N.D., Aug. 3, 1925; s. Nick William Guvakosky and Agnes (Nechiporenko) Guvakosky Palmer; A.A., U. N.D., 1948; A.B., U. Calif., Berkeley, 1949; B.D., Princeton U., 1957; m. Marilyn Elizabeth Schuler, June 8, 1962; children—David Christian, Katherine Elizabeth. Ordained to ministry Presbyn. Ch., 1957; pastor Valley Parish of Angus-Tabor, Euclid, Minn., 1957-61, Keystone Presbyn. Ch., Keywest, Minn., 1957-61; asst. pastor House of Hope Presbyn. Ch., St. Paul, 1961-65; sr. pastor 1st Presbyn. Ch., Aberdeen, S.D., 1965-70; real estate salesman Spring Co., Roseville, Minn., 1971-73; pastor Czech Brethren Presbyn. Ch., Silver Lake, Minn., 1973—; mem. Presbytery Council Minn. Valleys, 1977—; chmn. Minn. Valleys Risk Evangelism Com., 1977-80; mem. program cabinet Minn. Council Chs., 1975—, chmn. region 6 E, 1975-79, bd. dirs., 1980—; chmn. Minn. Valleys Ecumenical Com., 1980—; mem. ecumenical com. Synod of Lakes and Prairies, 1980—. Bd. dirs. Midway br. YMCA, St. Paul; bd. dirs. Dist. 425 Sch. Bd. Minn., 1975-81, chmn., 1980-81; emergency med. technician Vol. Ambulance Service Silver Lake, 1975—, sec., 1976-78; mem. Crow River Pupil Studies Services Coop. Joint Powers Dist. 937, Hutchinson, Minn., 1976—, chmn., 1980-81. Served with USNR, 1943-46. Mem. U. Calif. Alumni Assn. Home and Office: 100 W Main St Silver Lake MN 55381

PALMER, MARGARET LOUISE, speech and lang. pathologist; b. Flint, Mich., Sept. 18, 1935; d. Frederick William and Sylvia Elvira (Mattsen) P.; B.A., Mich. State U., 1959, M.A., 1967. Speech and lang. pathologist Ingham Intermediate Sch. Dist., Mason, Mich., 1959—; cons. Ednl. Consultation Center. Lic. pvt. pilot. Mem. Am. Speech and Hearing Assn. (certificate of clin. competence), Council of Exceptional Children, Mich. Speech and Hearing Assn., Aircraft Owners and Pilots Assn., Phi Kappa Phi. Home: 408 Durand St East Lansing MI 48823 Office: 2630 W Howell Rd Mason MI 48854

PALMER, MARK THOMAS, systems analyst; b. Detroit, Aug. 24, 1948; s. Thomas Albert and Elaine Elizabeth (Trafeli) P.; B.A., Mich. State U., 1970; cert. of programming, honors grad. Control Data Inst., 1974; m. Norma Jean Henning, Mar. 24, 1973; children—Audrey Jean, Ryan Thomas. Computer operator Automated Service Bur., Detroit, 1974; systems engring. coordinator, retail systems NCR Corp., Detroit, 1974-80; systems analyst, major retail products Winkelman's, Inc., Detroit, 1980—; pres. Palmer Enterprises, mgmt. cons. Group leader Gt. Books Found. Am. Cancer Soc. Scholar, 1963. Mem. Nat. Space Inst. and Planetary Soc. Roman Catholic. Office: Winkelman's Inc 25 Parsons St Detroit MI 48201

PALMER, ROBERT R., performing arts adminstr.; b. Chicago, Sept. 8, 1950; B.A. cum laude, Augustana Coll., Rock Island, Ill., 1973; M.A. in Arts Adminstrn., U. Wis.-Madison, 1975. Mgr., U. Wis.-Madison Symphony Orchs., 1974-75, Madison Civic Music Assn., 1975—; tchr. music appreciation U. Wis. Extension, Madison Area Tech. Coll. Treas., mem. exec. com. of bd. dirs. Dane County Arts Council, 1979-80. Mem. Beta Gamma Sigma, Omicron Delta Kappa, Phi Mu Alpha, Alpha Phi Omega. Office: 211 N Carroll St Madison WI 53703

PALMER, ROBERT TOWNE, lawyer; b. Chgo., May 25, 1947; s. Adrian Bernhardt and Gladys (Towne) P.; B.A., Colgate U., 1969; J.D., U. Notre Dame, 1974; m. Ann Therese Darin, Nov. 9, 1974; 1 son, Justin Darin. Admitted to Ill. bar, 1974, D.C. bar, 1978, U.S. Supreme Ct. bar, 1978; law clk. Hon. Walter V. Schaefer, Ill. Supreme Ct., 1974-75; asso. firm McDermott, Will & Emery, Chgo., 1975-81, partner, 1982—; mem. adj. faculty Chgo-Kent Law Sch., 1975-77, Loyola U., 1976-78. Bd. dirs. Orch. of Ill. Assn., 1981—. Mem. Am. Bar Assn., Ill. State Bar Assn., Chgo. Bar Assn., D.C. Bar Assn., Bar Assn. 7th Federal Circuit, Orch. of Ill. Assn. (dir., mem. exec. com. 1980—), Mensa. Republican. Episcopalian. Clubs: Chgo., Univ. Chgo., Saddle & Cycle. Home: 5555 N Sheridan Rd Chicago IL 60640 Office: 111 W Monroe St Chicago IL 60603

PALMER, WILLIAM DARRELL, state senator; b. Iowa City, Jan. 13, 1935; s. George Darrell and Florence Iona (Middour) P.; student pub. schs., Iowa; m. Evelyn Lucille Johnson, June 1953; children—William Nick, Tony Robert, Amanda Kaye. Mem. Iowa Ho. of Reps., 1965-69; mem. Iowa Senate from 32d Dist., 1969—, chmn. appropriations com., 1975-78, also ranking mem.; mem. budget and fin. com. Nat. Conf. State Legislators. Bd. dirs. Highland Meml. Gardens. Democrat. Methodist. Club: Masons. Home: 2948 Easton Blvd Des Moines IA 50317 Office: 1340 E 33d St Des Moines IA 50317

PALMERSHEIM, THERESA ANN, free-lance writer; b. Rockford, Ill., Aug. 29, 1950; d. John P. and Ellen L. (McNeil) McHugh; B.A., St. Catherine's Coll., St. Paul, 1972; M.S., Am. U., Washington, 1980; m. Lawrence A. Palmersheim, June 17, 1972. Reporter, Catholic Bull. Newspaper, St. Paul, 1971-72; editor Allstate Ins. Co., Northbrook, Ill., 1972-75; mgr. employee publs. McCormick & Co., Inc., Hunt Valley, Md., 1975-80; free-lance writer, 1980—. Mem. Public Relations Soc. Am., Sigma Delta Chi (awards 1972). Home: 4580 Horizon Circle Eagam MN 55123

PALMISANO, MICHAEL ROBERT, athletic adminstr., educator; b. Cleve., Oct. 9, 1942; s. Michael P. and Agatha Barbara (Caputo) P.; B.S. in Edn., U. Mich., 1964; Ed.M., Miami U., Ohio, 1966; m. Linda Diane Martin, Aug. 26, 1967; children—Ryan, Jason, Nicole. Instr. of health, phys. edn. and recreation Ohio No. U., Ada, 1966-71, head varsity wrestling coach, asst. football coach, 1966-71, supr. student tchrs., 1968-71, pres. faculty senate, 1968-69; asst. prof. health, phys. edn. and recreation U. Nebr., Omaha, 1971-79, head varsity wrestling coach, 1971-79; adminstrv. asso. dept. intercollegiate athletics U. Mich., Ann Arbor, 1979—, dir. of promotions, mktg. and spl. events, 1979—; instr. wrestling Jewish Community Center, Omaha, 1976-77; dir. Omaha Soccer Sch., 1977-79; dir. Mike Palmisano's Mid-Am. Summer Wrestling Camp, Omaha, 1972-79; coordinator Explorer Olympics, 1976-78; participant Seasonal Weekly TV Show, channel 26, Omaha, 1975-79; 1st alt. coach and mgr. U.S. Wrestling Freestyle, World Games, Moscow, 1972; instr. golf YMCA, 1973-74; guest speaker numerous service clubs, 1966-81. Fund raiser Am. Cancer Soc., 1976-78; mem. Douglas County (Nebr.) Election Bd. Commn., 1977-78. Recipient Achievement award Cleve. Exchange Club, 1960. Mem. AAHPER, Am. Assn. Colls. Tchr. Edn., U.S. Wrestling Fedn., Nat. Collegiate Athletic Coaches Assn., AAUP, Nat. Collegiate Athletic Assn., Phi Kappa Alpha. Roman Catholic. Contbr. articles on phys. edn. and athletics to profl. publs.; producer TV film Championship Wrestling, 1976; Ohio AAU wrestling champion, 1958-63; Mich. AAU wrestling champion, 1961, 63, 64. Office: 1000 S State St Ann Arbor MI 48109

PALMITER, HARRY ALVA, editor; b. Edgerton, Wis., Dec. 14, 1922; s. Louis Orsamus and Carrie Eliza (Thompson) P.; B.S., U. Wis., 1950; m. Marjory E. Roeber, Dec. 16, 1950; children—Lynn E., Steven Jay. Mem. editorial staff Olsen Publ. Co., Inc., Milw., 1950; asst. editor, 1951, mgr. spl. services div., 1953-58; promotions chief, markets div. Wis. Dept. Agr., Madison, 1958-62; with Cheese Reporter, Madison, 1962—, editor, pub., 1962—. Active Boy Scouts Am., Madison, 1971—. Served with AUS, 1943-46. Mem. Internat. Milk and Food Sanitarians, Wis. Dairy Tech. Soc., Wis. Cheese Makers Assn. (hon. life), Northeastern Wis. Cheese and Buttermakers Assn. (hon. life), Alpha Gamma Rho. Presbyterian (elder 1966—). Home: 917 Lorraine Dr Madison WI 53705 Office: 6401 Odana Rd Madison WI 53719

PALMORE, JULIAN IVANHOE, III, mathematician, educator; b. Balt., Sept. 26, 1938; s. Julian I. and Josephine Keith (Shellman) P.; B. in Engring. Physics, Cornell U., 1961; M.A. in Math., U. Ala., 1964; M.S.E. in Aerospace Sci., Princeton U., 1965; M.S. in Astronomy, Yale, 1966, Ph.D., 1967; Ph.D. in Math., U. Calif., Berkeley, 1973; m. Barbara Bland Hawkins, May 27, 1967; children—Andrew Hanson, Rebecca Keith. Research engr. NASA, Huntsville, Ala., 1961-64; asso. staff mem. Boeing Co., Seattle, 1966; research asso. U. Minn., Mpls., 1967-68; vis. fellow Princeton (N.J.) U., 1968; instr. math. M.I.T., Cambridge, 1973-75; vis. asst. prof. dept. math. U. Mich., Ann Arbor, 1975—77; asst. prof. math. U. Ill., Urbana, 1977-80, asso. prof., 1980—, fellow Center Advanced Study, 1979; lectr. various univs. including Purdue U., 1976, U. Chgo., 1976, Brown U., 1973, U. Houston, 1978, Oberwolfach, Ger., 1978, 81, U. Md., 1974, 80, Los Alamos Sci. Lab., 1980-81, Northwestern U., 1980, U. Cin., 1981; participant NSF regional conf., U. N.C., Chapel Hill, 1976; NSF lecture Tufts U., 1979; mem. panel of judges Faculty Open Fellowships, Lilly Endowment, Inc., 1979, 80, 81, 82. Served with USN, 1961—64. Lilly Teaching fellow, 1974—75; NSF grantee, 1974—. Fellow Royal Astron. Soc.; mem. Am. Math. Soc., Planetary Soc., Sigma XI. Contbr. articles on research in math. and celestial mechanics to sci. jours. Office: Math Dept Univ Ill 1409 W Green St Urbana IL 61801

PALUZZI, JEANNE GERRITSEN, public relations counselor; b. Zeeland, Mich., Sept. 18, 1934; d. Gerrit John and Mary (Staal) Gerritsen; student Calvin Coll., Grand Rapids, Mich., 1952-53, Wayne State U., 1970-76; m. Rocco Paluzzi, Apr. 7, 1956 (div. Apr. 1971); children—Jeanna Marie, Nicholas, Paul, Karen Adele. Asst. to dir. public affairs Smith Hinchman & Grylls, Inc., Detroit, 1972-73; co-mgr. public relations Albert Kahn Asso., Detroit, 1973-74; owner Jeanne Paluzzi & Co., Detroit, 1974-76; public relations exec. Young & Rubicam, Inc., Detroit, 1976-79; owner, pres. JGP Public Relations, Inc., 1979—. Mem. cable TV adv. com., Livonia; mem. Wayne 2d dist. Republican com.; mem. Rep. Women's Task Force; bd. dirs. Hemophilia Found. of Mich., Met. Detroit YWCA. Recipient Demmy award, 1976; United Found. award, 1977. Mem. Public Relations Soc. Am. (accredited), Women in Communications Inc. (program chmn. nat. conv. 1978, chmn. fin. com. Detroit chpt. 1977-78, v.p. 1978-79, v.p. public relations 1979-81), Nat. Assn. Women Bus. Owners (v.p. public relations Mich. chpt. 1979-81), Adcraft of Detroit, Bus./Profl. Advt. Assn., Livonia C. of C. (dir.), Nat. Women's Polit. Caucus. Clubs: Detroit Press, Renaissance, Detroit Econ., Women's Econ. Home and Office: 17315 Rougeway St Livonia MI 48152

PAMER, FRANK PAUL, lawyer; b. Akron, Ohio, Jan. 4, 1914; s. Frank and Amelia (Vasarhely) P.; B.S., Kent State U., 1938, M.A., 1941; B.Law, Akron Law Sch., 1953, J.D., 1968; m. Ruth Eileen Pansler, Jan. 23, 1943; children—Fred Kelly, Dorothy Kay. Real estate broker, ins. broker, Akron, Ohio, 1948-53; admitted to Ohio bar, 1953, U.S. Dist. Ct. bar, 1957; practice law, Akron, 1953—; pres. Rubber Industry Credit Exchange, 1953-68; gen. counsel Toy Balloon Mfrs. U.S., 1953-68; pres. Kenmore Bd. Trade, 1970-71, bd. dirs., 1958-78. Served as lt. USNR, 1943-47. Mem. Ohio Bar Assn., Akron Bar Assn., Phi Alpha Theta, Tau Phi Alpha. Republican. Lutheran. Clubs: Kiwanis (past pres.), Masons (32 deg.), Shriners, Jesters. Home: 2066 Brookshire Rd Akron OH 44313 Office: 992 Kenmore Blvd Akron OH 44314

PAN, PETER NAW YANK, mfg. co. exec.; b. N.Y.C., Feb. 1, 1942; s. Wen Yuan and Julia W.T. Pan; B.E.E., Rensselaer Poly. Inst., 1963, M.E.E., 1965; Ph.D. in Physics, Tex. Christian U., 1970; postgrad. Harvard U. Bus. Sch., 1975; m. Carolyn L. Benjamin, July 23, 1963; children—Victoria, Michael, William. Sr. research scientist Continental Group Inc., Chgo., 1970-72, mgr. research and devel., 1972-77; v.p. Paxall Inc., Chgo., 1977—; exec. v.p., gen. mgr. Thiele Engring. Co., Mpls., 1979-80, pres., 1980—; exec. dir. PHP Inc., Mpls., 1980. Bd. dirs. Country Club Hills (Ill.) Library Bd., 1970-72; mem., pres. Sch. Dist. 160 Bd., 1971-77. Recipient Humanitarian of Yr. award Jaycees, 1970. Mem. IEEE, Tex. Acad. Sci., Soc. Mfg. Engrs., Am. Inst. Physics, Sigma Xi. Contbr. articles to profl. jours.; patentee in field. Home: 18408 Timber Ridge Dr Minnetonka MN 55343 Office: 7225 Bush Lake Rd Minneapolis MN 55435

PANAR, LEONARD BARTOK, ednl. adminstr.; b. N.Y.C., Feb. 19, 1949; s. Leonard Alfred and Marion (Barbero) P.; B.A. cum laude, Bklyn. Coll., 1972; M.A., Columbia U., 1974, M.Ed., 1975; m. Marie Antoinette Lovallo, Aug. 27, 1978; 1 son, Gregory Matthew. Tchr. art Lincoln High Sch., N.Y.C., 1972-73; co-dir. Ziegfield Gallery, N.Y.C., 1974-75; coordinator Cooper Hewitt Mus., N.Y.C., 1975-76; media cons. N.Y. Soc. for Ethical Culture, N.Y.C., 1976-78; admissions officer Columbia U., 1972-79; dir. admissions Kansas City (Mo.) Art Inst., 1979—, fgn. student advisor; chmn. dirs. of admission Union Ind. Colls. Art, also mem. editorial bd. Mem. Nat. Assn. Schs. Art, Coll. Art Assn., Am. Assn. Coll. Registrars and Admissions Officers, Nat. Art Edn. Assn. Author: The Artist/Teacher and Professional Art Schools, 1979; Art Education 1860-1900, 1978. Office: 4415 Warwick Blvd Kansas City MO 64111

PANCERO, JACK BLOCHER, restaurant exec.; b. Cin., Dec. 27, 1923; s. Howard and Hazel Mae (Blocher) P.; student, Ohio State U., 1941-44; m. Loraine Fielman, Aug. 4, 1944; children—Gregg Edward, Vicki Lee. Partner, Howard Pancero & Co., Cin., 1948-66; stockbroker Gradison & Co., Cin., 1966-70; real estate asso. Parchman & Oyler, Cin., 1970-72; v.p. Gregg Pancero, Inc., Kings Mills, Ohio, 1972—. Methodist. Clubs: Western Hills Country, Cincinnati, Engrs. Table, Masons, Shrine; Wilderness Country (Naples, Fla.). Home: 5730 Pinehill Ln Cincinnati OH 45238 Office: Kings Island Columbia Rd Kings Mills OH 45034

PANDE, SHARAD CHANDRA, radiologist; b. Ujjain, M.P., India, Dec. 5, 1937; s. Badriprasad and Dwarkabai (Joshi) P.; M.B., B.S., M.D., Gajra-raja Med. Coll., Gwalior M.P., India, 1958. Intern, Resurrection Hosp., Chgo., 1964-65; resident Mt. Sinai Hosp., Chgo., 1964; instr. Northwestern U., Chgo., 1965-66; radiologist Selkirk Mental Hosp., Selkirk, Man., Can., 1969—. Fellow Royal Coll. Physicians and Surgeons (Can.); affiliate mem. Royal Soc. Medicine (Eng.). Home: Selkirk Mental Hosp Selkirk MB R1A 2B5 Canada

PANDYA, NAVIN CHANDRA NARMADA SHANKER, engr.; b. Mangrol, India, Jan. 30, 1928; came to U.S., 1957, naturalized, 1970; s. Narmada Shanker and Rambhaben N. Joshi P.; B.Civil Engring., Gujarat U., 1954; M.S. in Civil Engring., Wayne State U., 1959; doctoral candidate U. Mich.; m. Snehlata P. Joshi, Apr. 29, 1954; children—Sonal, Pranav, Prashant. Chief civil engr. Atul Products, India, 1954-57; instr. Wayne State U., Detroit, 1959-62; designer, project engr. Giffels Assos., Inc., Southfield, Mich., 1962-73, dir. computer applications, 1973-78, dir. advance techs., 1978; mng. partner Real Investment Co., Universal Investment Devel. Co.; cons. in field; mem. various nat. coms. Pres. Cultural Soc. of India, 1975—; v.p. Bharatiya Temple, 1976. Registered profl. engr., Mich. Mem. ASCE (pres. SE Br. Mich. Sect., 1975-76). Am. Concrete Inst., Soc. Computer Applications in Engring., Planning, Arch., Chi Epsilon. Club: Toastmasters Internat. (pres. 1978). Contbr. papers to confs., articles to profl. jour. Home: 27460 Everett St Southfield MI 48076 Office: 25200 Telegraph Rd Southfield MI 48037

PANEC, WILLIAM JOSEPH, lawyer; b. Pawnee City, Nebr., June 22, 1937; s. Albert and Thelma I. (Sebring) P.; B.S., U. Nebr., 1962, J.D., 1965; m. Carolyn R. McVitty, Aug. 17, 1963. Admitted to Nebr. bar, 1965, since practiced in Fairbury; county judge Jefferson County (Nebr.), 1965-70, county atty., 1973-75; mem. Nebr. Jud. Qualifications Commn., 1968-70; organizer Nebr. Jud. Reform; chmn. Region XIV Crime Commn., 1969-71, cons. on law enforcement and criminal justice, 1971-79; cons. Regions VIII, IX and XIV Regional Jail Study, 1972; profl. instr. Nebr. Law Enforcement Adv. Council, 1972—; village atty. Diller (Nebr.), 1975—; bd. dirs. Housing Authority, City of Fairbury, 1979—; chmn. law day Jefferson County, 1972, 73. Served with AUS, 1955-56. Recipient Nebr. State Farmer degree, 1955. Mem. Am., Nebr., Jefferson County bar assns., Nebr. County Judges Assn. (v.p., pres.), Am. Judicature Soc., Nebr. Assn. Trial Attys., Assn. Trial Attys. Am., Internat. Footprint Assn., U. Nebr. Alumni Assn., Delta Theta Phi. Methodist (trustee). Clubs: Masons, Elks. Author: Probate Procedures and the Uniform Probate Code. Home: 1529 G St Fairbury NE 68352 Office: 610 D St Fairbury NE 68352

PANETHIERE, HENRY ANDREA, state senator; b. Kansas City, Mo., May 3, 1914; s. Frank and Mary (Cosentino) P.; A.B., U. Mo., 1949, J.D., 1952; children—Vicki Panethiere Kontras, Henry Andrea, Darrell, Gary L. Asso. firm Panetheier & Helfland, 1952—; mem. Mo. Senate, 1976—. Bd. govs. UNICO; pres. Arthritis Found. Served with U.S. Army, 1941-48. Mem. Kansas City Bar Assn. Club: KC Office: 1301 Traders Bank Bldg 1125 Grand Ave Kansas City MO 64106*

PANG, JOSHUA KEUN-UK, trade co. exec.; b. Chinnampo, Korea, Sept. 17, 1924; s. Ne-Too and Soon-Hei (Kim) P.; came to U.S., 1951, naturalized, 1968; B.S., Roosevelt U., 1959; m. He-Young Yoon, May 30, 1963; children—Ruth, Pauline, Grace. Chemist, Realemon Co. Am., Chgo., 1957-61; chief-chemist chem. div. Bell & Gossett Co., Chgo., 1961-63, Fatty Acid Inc., div. Ziegler Chem. & Mineral Corp., Chgo., 1963-64; sr. chemist-supr. Gen. Mills Chems. Inc., Kankakee, Ill., 1964-70; pres., owner UJU Industries Inc., Broadview, Ill., 1971—, also dir. Bd. dirs. Dist. 92, Lindop Sch., Broadview, 1976—; chmn. Proviso Area Sch. Bd. Assn., Proviso Twp., Cook County, Ill., 1976-77; bd. dirs. Korean Am. Community Services, Chgo., 1979-80. Mem. Am. Chem. Soc., Am. Inst. Parliamentarians (region 2 treas. 1979-81, region 2 gov. 1981-82), Internat. Platform Assn., Ill. Sch. Bd. Assn., Chgo. Area Parliamentarians, Parliamentary Leaders in Action (pres. 1980-81), Nat. Speakers Assn. (dir. Ill. chpt. 1981-82). Club: Toastmasters (dist. gov. 1970). Home: 2532 S 9th Ave Broadview IL 60153 Office: PO Box 351 Broadview IL 60153

PANGBORN, DOMINIC JOSEPH, designer, illustrator; b. Seoul, Korea, July 29, 1952; s. Spencer James and Mary Helen (Hoffman) P.; came to U.S., 1962, naturalized, 1966; A.A., Chgo. Acad. Art, 1975; m. Delia C. Lipa, Oct. 25, 1975; 1 son, Oliver Dominic. Designer, Ed Jaster Studio, Chgo., 1971-76; multi-media designer Wilding Div., Southfield, Mich., 1976-77; designer, illustrator Al Hutt Assos., Detroit, 1977-79; partner, designer Herman/Pangborn, Detroit, 1979—; exhibited group show Master Eagle Gallery, N.Y.C., 1978; works published in Playboy mag., 1978, Communication Arts mag., 1979. Recipient Communication Arts Award of Excellence, 1979; 1st pl. award Detroit Scarab Show, 1980. Home: 771 Fisher St Grosse Pointe MI 48230 Office: 450 W Fort St Detroit MI 48226

PANNWITT, ELIZABETH JUNE, mgmt. tng. and devel. cons.; b. Evanston, Ill., Nov. 16, 1947; d. Fred J. and Barbara (Semple) Pannwitt; B.A., Grinnell Coll., 1969; postgrad. U. S. Fla., 1970-71. Editor, 1st Nat. Bank Tampa, 1969-71; dir. The Innovators, 1st Nat. Bank Tampa, 1971-73; acct. exec. Daniel J. Edelman Public Relations, Chgo., 1973-75; dir. Great Ideas Touring Corp. Art Collection, Container Corp. Am., Chgo., 1975-76, mgr. employee communications, 1976-78, mgr. employee tng. and devel., 1978-81; pvt. practice mgmt. tng. and devel. cons., 1981—. Mem. Women in Communications (v.p. 1976-78), Am. Soc. Tgn. and Devel. Home: 360 W Wellington St #2-C Chicago IL 60657

PANSINO, SALVATORE ROCCO, electronics engr., scientist, human relations cons.; b. Monongahela, Pa., Apr. 15, 1935; s. Rocco Fred and Theresa Vee (Malena) P.; B.S. in Engring., Carnegie Inst. Tech., 1957; M.S., Franklin and Marshall Coll., 1961; postgrad. U. Pitts., 1961-63; Ph.D., Carnegie-Mellon U., 1968; LL.B., LaSalle U., 1976; m. Vivian Sue Nahar, Apr. 26, 1958; children—Cynthia Claire, Vivian Diana, Sondra Sue, Nancy Elaine. Microwave engr. Bendix Corp., York, Pa., 1957-61; research asst. U. Pitts., 1961-63; project engr. Carnegie-Mellon U., Pitts., 1963-68; electronics instr. Forbes Trail Tech. Sch., Monroeville, Pa., 1963; project mgr., electronics group leader, mem. planning staff Babcock & Wilcox Research Center, Alliance, Ohio, 1967—; instr. Mt. Union Coll., 1980, Youngstown State U., 1980-81. Chmn. Jaycees, 1979, editor, 1971, recipient awards. NSF grantee, 1963-67; recipient human relations award Dale

Carnegie; Explorer Scouts award, 1969; Disting. service award Jaycees. Mem. IEEE, U.S. Tennis Assn., Sigma Pi Sigma. Clubs: Alliance Racquet, Toastmasters (pres., v.p. publicity, chmn. bd., area gov., Toastmaster of Yr., Disting. Toastmaster), Babcock & Wilcox Employees (pres., chmn. bd., trustee). Home: 2480 Crestview Ave Alliance OH 44601

PANTZER, KURT FRIEDRICH, JR., lawyer; b. Indpls., May 24, 1928; s. Kurt Friedrich and Katharine Hunter (Ferriday) P.; B.A., Yale U., 1950; J.D., Harvard U., 1955; m. Elizabeth Elliott Kennedy, Aug. 25, 1951; children—Elizabeth E., Katharine H. Pantzer Lange, Kurt Friedrich III, Julia F. Admitted to Ind. bar, 1955; practiced in Indpls., 1955—; partner Royse, Travis, Hendrickson & Pantzer, 1966—; dir., sec. Aircraft and Electronic Specialties, Inc., Avon, Ind., 1961—; pres. Ind. Neuromuscular Research Lab., Inc., 1970—. Pres. Estate Planning Council Indpls., 1977-78. Treas., 11th Congressional Dist. Republican Central Com., 1964-66; pres. Marion County Election Bd., 1981—. Bd. dirs. Marion County Muscular Dystrophy Found., 1958-78, pres., 1960-62; bd. dirs. Greater Indpls. chpt. The Myasthenia Gravis Found., 1970-77, chmn., 1970-72; bd. dirs. Booth Tarkington Civic Theatre, Indpls., pres., 1977-80. Served to 1st lt. U.S. Army, 1951-53. Decorated Bronze Star. Fellow Am. Coll. Probate Counsel; mem. Am., Ind., Indpls. bar assns., Internat. Acad. Estate and Trust Law (academician). Presbyterian (deacon). Clubs: Columbia, Manor House, Dramatic (pres. 1980-81), Players, Lambs (dir. 1962—). Author: Documentary Evidence, 1961; Unauthorized Practice of Law, 1962; Pre-Nuptial Agreements, 1973; Probate Fees, 1976; Orphans' Deduction, 1977. Co-editor: Trusts, Wills, Estate Adminstration and Taxes, Parts 1 and 2, 1963. Home: 9401 Spring Mill Rd Indianapolis IN 46260 Office: 111 Monument Circle Suite 500 Indianapolis IN 46204

PANZARELLA, PHILIP PATRICK, govt. engring. ofcl.; b. N.Y.C., Mar. 17, 1939; s. John J. and Josephine C. (Cassella) P.; B.S., St. Louis U., 1960; M.S., Air Force Inst. Tech., 1965; M.S. in Mgmt., M.I.T., 1979; m. Susan K. Barga, Sept. 3, 1966; children—Michael A., Gregory S., David J. Project engr. USAF, Eglin AFB, Fla. 1960-63; test dir. Directorate of Flight Test Aero. Systems Div., Wright Patterson AFB, Ohio, 1965-76, chief modification engr., Airborne Laser Lab., 1976-78, tech. dir. 4950th Test Wing, 1980—. Mem. Xenia (Ohio) Bd. Edn. adv. group, 1980-81. Served with USAF, 1960-69. Decorated Air Force Commendation medal with 2 oak leaf clusters; Sloan fellow, M.I.T., 1979-80; registered profl. engr., Calif. Mem. System Safety Soc., Soc. Flight Test Engrs., Am. Meteorol. Soc. Roman Catholic. Club: Engrs. Contbr. articles to profl. jours. Office: 4950 AM Wright Patterson AFB OH 45433

PANZER, HAROLD JAY, physician; b. N.Y.C., June 7, 1909; s. Hermann and Martha Panzer; A.B., Nebr. Wesleyan U., 1933, M.A., 1937; M.D., U. Nebr., 1937; m. Mary Luella Keller, Mar. 31, 1956; children—James Frederick, John, Barbara Jean, Robert. Intern, Nebr. Methodist Hosp., Omaha, 1937; gen. practice medicine, Bassett Nebr., 1939-71, Ainsworth, Nebr., 1971—; mem. staff Rock County Hosp., Bassett, Brown County Hosp., Ainsworth, Nebr. Served with U.S. Army, 1937-39. Fellow Am. Soc. Abdominal Surgeons; mem. Am. Thoracic Soc., AMA, Nebr. Med. Assn., Holt and Northwest County Med. Soc. (past pres.). Republican. Methodist. Clubs: Elks, Commercial, Odd Fellows, Masons. Address: N Harrington St Ainsworth NE 69210

PAPADAKIS, CONSTANTINE NICHOLAS, civil engr.; b. Athens, Greece, Feb. 2, 1946; s. Nicholas and Rita (Mashiotti) P.; came to U.S., 1969, naturalized, 1978. diploma Nat. Poly. U. Athens, 1969; M.S., U. Cin., 1970; Ph.D., U. Mich., 1973; m. Eliana Apostolides, Aug. 28, 1971. Hydraulic engring. cons. Commonwealth Assos., Jackson, Mich., James F. MacLaren Ltd., Willowdale, Ont., 1973-74; postdoctoral scholar dept. civil engring. U. Mich., Ann Arbor, 1973-74; adj. asst. prof. George Washington U., Washington, 1975-76; vis. asso. prof. Mich. State U., 1978; engring. specialist, then asst. chief engr. Bechtel, Inc., Gaithersburg, Md. and Ann Arbor, Mich., 1974-81; v.p., mgr. hydraulics-hydrology div. STS Cons.'s, Ltd., Ann Arbor, 1981—; adj. asso. prof. U. Mich., 1976—; co-founder, pres. PD&M Inc., Ann Arbor, 1976—; teaching fellow U. Mich., 1971-73, U. Cin., 1969-71. Horace W. King grantee civil engring. dept. U. Mich., 1971-73; recipient merit awards Bechtel Inc., 1974-79; registered profl. engr., Mich., Va., Greece. Mem. ASCE (br. pres. 1980-81, treas. Mich. sect. 1981-82), ASME (chmn. fluid transients com. 1978-80), Internat. Assn. Hydraulic Research, Am. Mgmt. Assn., Tech. Chamber Greece, Am. Water Resources Assn., Am. Geophys. Union, Sigma Xi, Tau Beta Pi, Chi Epsilon. Greek Orthodox. Author: Problems on Strength of Materials, 1968, Sewer Systems Design, 2d edit., 1969; Solutions to Problems in Fluid Mechanics, 1975; editor Fluid Transients and Acoustics in the Power Industry, 1978; Pump-Turbine Schemes, 1979; Small Hydro-Power Fluid Machinery, 1980; contbr. 20 tech. articles to profl. jours. Home: 1420 Bardstown Trail Ann Arbor MI 48105 Office: 3001 S State St Suite 1014 Ann Arbor MI 48104

PAPADAKIS, EAMMANUEL PHILIPPOS, automotive co. exec.; b. N.Y.C., Dec. 25, 1934; s. Philippos Emmanuel and Helen (Eastman) P.; B.S. in Physics, M.I.T., 1956, Ph.D., 1962; M.Mgmt., U. Mich., 1979; m. Stella Christopher, Sept. 4, 1960; children—Susan H., Philip E., Christopher E., Nicholas E. Mem. tech. staff Bell Telephone Labs., Allentown, Pa., 1962-69; dept. head Panametrics, Inc., Waltham, Mass., 1969-73; prin. staff engr. Ford Motor Co., Detroit, 1973-75, supr., 1975—; partner E & S Antiques, Redford, Mich., 1978—. Fellow Acoustical Soc. Am. (Biennial award 1968); mem. Am. Phys. Soc., Am. Soc. Quality Control, ASTM, IEEE, Am. Soc. for Nondestructive Testing (Mehl Honor Lecture 1979), Sigma Xi. Democrat. Greek Orthodox. Contbr. articles to profl. jours.; asso. editor IEEE Trans. Sonics & Ultrasonics, 1972—; asso. tech. editor Materials Evaluation, 1975—; patentee in field. Office: 24500 Glendale Ave Detroit MI 48239

PAPAY, ANDREW GEORGE, chem. engr.; b. K. Achaia, Greece, Oct. 10, 1924; s. George P. and Martha (Paparodis) P.; B.S., Athens U., 1951; M.S. (grad. fellow 1957-58), Colo. Sch. Mines, 1959; D.Eng., Athens Tech. U., 1974; came to U.S., 1957, naturalized, 1966; m. Vasso Skiadas, Dec. 12, 1960; children—Martha, Tinna. Sr. research engr. Mobil Oil Research & Devel. Co., Paulsboro, N.J., 1959-69; supr. Stauffer Chem. Co., Dobbs Ferry, N.Y., 1969-71; asso. dir. technology Edwin Cooper Inc., St. Louis, 1971—. Mem. Soc. Automotive Engrs., Coordinating Research Council, Am. Soc. Lubrication Engrs. (chmn. St. Louis), ASTM. Greek Orthodox. Patentee in field. Contbr. articles to profl. jours. Asso. editor Lubrication Engring., 1977—. Home: 897 Rusticmanor Circle Manchester MO 63011 Office: 125 Lafayette Ave Saint Louis MO 63104

PAPEZ, DONALD WESLEY, marketing exec.; b. Albion, Nebr., June 21, 1923; s. John S. and Olive (Maricle) P.; student Doane Coll., 1941-42, Colo. Coll., 1943-44; B.S., U. Nebr., 1947; grad. Inst. Internat. Studies, Geneva, 1949; m. Simone Girod de Boeck, Dec. 6, 1947; children—Ronald, Chantal. Staff mem. UN Secretariat Econ. Commn. for Europe, Geneva, 1949-53; sr. econ. and marketing research analyst Matson Nav. Co., San Francisco, 1954-64; v.p. Ceco Mktg. Research Inc., San Francisco, 1964-68, Transam. Research Corp., San Francisco, 1968-70; dir. eastern Can., Wm. Wrigley Jr. Co., Ltd., Toronto, Ont., 1971-74, dir. mktg. research, Chgo., 1975—. Served to lt. (j.g.) USNR, 1943-46. Mem. Am. Mktg. Assn. (bd. govs., nat. dir. 1967-69), Econ. Round Table San Francisco (pres. 1960). Episcopalian. Club: Univ. (Chgo.). Home: 1120 N Lake Shore Dr Chicago IL 60611 Office: 410 N Michigan Ave Chicago IL

PAPLAUSKAS, LEONARD PAUL, research adminstr.; b. Wiesbaden, Germany, June 22, 1949; s. Leonardas P. and Emilija A. Paplauskas; B.S., Loyola U., 1970; Ph.D., So. Ill. U., 1974; m. Lynn Verhoeven, Nov. 25, 1972; 1 son, Grant Peter. Asst. sec. U.S. Adopted Names Council, AMA, Chgo., 1974; research adminstr. Health and Hosps. Governing Commn. of Cook County, Chgo., 1975-76; asst. dir. Office Research and Sponsored Programs, Northwestern U., Evanston, Ill., 1976—; cons. in field. Mem. Nat. Council Univ. Research Adminstrs., Soc. Research Adminstrs., Am. Soc. Microbiology, AAAS. Roman Catholic. Home: 14036 Concord Dr Orland Park IL 60462 Office: 633 Clark St Evanston IL 60201 also 303 E Chicago Ave Chicago IL 60611

PAPLAUSKAS, LYNN ELLEN, cons.; b. Montreal, Que., Can., Dec. 22, 1944; d. Clarence Peter and Frances Ellen (Dixon) Verhoeven; B.A., St. Xavier Coll., 1965; m. Leonard Paul Paplauskas, Nov. 25, 1972; 1 son, Grant Peter. Research technician Stritch Sch. Medicine, Maywood, Ill., 1965-66; electron microscopy technologist U. Ill., Chgo., 1966-68; scientist Alpha Research and Devel. Co., Blue Island, Ill., 1968-71; electron microscopist Nalco Chem. Co., Chgo., 1972; researcher So. Ill. U., Carbondale, 1972-74; chief electron microscopy Cook County Hosp., Chgo., 1974-80; v.p. Infi-Tek Assos., Chgo., 1976—. Mem. Am. Soc. Electron Microscopy, Ill. Micros. Soc., Midwest Soc. Electron Microscopists, Defenders of Wildlife, Audubon Soc., Nat. Wildlife Fedn. Baptist. Contbr. articles to profl. jours. Home and Office: 14036 Concord Dr Orland Park IL 60462

PAPLINSKI, WILLIAM ELLIOTT, librarian; b. New Kensington, Pa., Aug. 29, 1944; s. Chester John and Alta Ann (Elliott) P.; B.A., Kent State U., 1970; M.L.S., U. R.I., 1974; m. Cheryl Joan Alexander, Nov. 6, 1971; 1 son, Aaron Elliott. With U. R.I. Library, Kingston, 1972-74, Willard (Ohio) Meml. Library, 1974-77; dir. Troy-Miami County Pub. Library, Troy, Ohio, 1977—. Vice pres. Troy Council Chs., 1981. Served with USN, 1965-67. Recipient Award of Outstanding Service, Literacy Council, Troy. Mem. ALA, Ohio Library Assn., Am. Soc. Public Adminstrn. Presbyterian (deacon 1977—). Club: Masons. Home: 65 Cricket Lane Troy OH 45373 Office: 419 W Main St Troy OH 45373

PAPONE, ALDO, bus. exec.; b. Genoa, Italy, Aug. 16, 1932; came to U.S., 1956, naturalized, 1956; s. Alexander and Ines (Mantegazza) P.; B.B.A., U. Genoa, 1955; m. Sandra Cataleta, July 2, 1955; 1 dau., Renata. With R.H. Macy Co., N.Y.C., 1956-74, v.p., asst. gen. mdse. mgr., 1971, sr. v.p. 1972, dir. exec. com., chmn. mdse com., 1972-74, sr. v.p., gen. mgr. travel div., 1974; dir., sr. v.p. Am. Express Internat., Inc., N.Y.C., 1974-80, pres., 1975, sr. v.p., 1974-80, pres. card div., 1979-80; dir., pres. Am. Express Co. of Egypt Ltd. and Spain, 1974-80; dir., chmn. Am. Express Co. of Greece, 1974-80; pres. Am. Express SAI, Italy, 1974-80; exec. v.p. Dayton Hudson Corp., Mpls., 1980, vice chmn., 1981—; dir. Club Med, Inc., N.Y.C., 1976-80, Warner Amex Cable Communications Corp., 1979-80. Mem. United Cerebral Palsy Assn. campaign com., 1976-79; vice chmn. travel and tourism industry adv. council Commerce Com., U.S. Senate, 1979—; chmn. adv. bd. Congressional Travel and Tourism Caucus, 1980—; trustee Minn. Opera, 1980—; bd. dirs. St. Paul Chamber Orch., 1980—. Roman Catholic. Contbr. articles to profl. jours. Home: 1355 Shoreline Dr Wayzata MN 55391 Office: 777 Nicollet Mall Minneapolis MN 55402

PAPP, JOHN PAUL, physician; b. Cleve., Aug. 28, 1938; B.A., Coll. Wooster, 1960; M.D., Ohio State U., 1964; m. Mary Ann Peters; children—Mary Lynn, John, James. Intern, Cleve. Clinic, 1964-65; resident in medicine U. Mich. Med. Center, Ann Arbor, 1967-69, fellow in gastroenterology, 1969-71, NIH trainee, 1970-71, teaching asso. dept. internal medicine, 1969-70; practice medicine specializing in internal medicine, subsplty. gastroenterology, Grand Rapids, Mich., 1971—; asst. clin. prof. dept. medicine Coll. Human Medicine, Mich. State U., 1973-76, asso. clin. prof., 1976—; mem. staff Blodgett Meml. Med. Center. Bd. dirs. Kent County unit Am. Cancer Soc., 1972-74. Served to lt., M.C., U.S. Navy, 1965-67. Diplomate Am. Bd. Internal Medicine. Fellow ACP, Am. Coll. Gastroenterology (trustee 1980—, chmn. nat. affairs com. 1981—); mem. Am. Gastroent. Assn., Am. Soc. Gastrointestinal Endoscopy (chmn. audit com. 1972-74, councilor 1978-82), Mich. Soc. Gastrointestinal Endoscopy (v.p. 1975-77, pres. 1977-78), Mich. Soc. Internal Medicine (sec.-treas. 1979-81, pres. elect 1981—), AMA, Mich. State Med. Soc. (vice chmn. spltys. caucus 1981—), Kent County Med. Soc., Detroit Gastroent. Soc., Am. Assn. Study Liver Diseases. Contbr. articles to med. jours. Office: 1900 Wealthy SE Grand Rapids MI 49506

PAPPAJOHN, JOHN GEORGE, financial cons.; b. St. Luke's, Greece, July 31, 1928 (parents Am. citizens); s. George and Maria (Zanios) P.; B.Sc., U. Iowa, 1952; m. Mary Limberis, Sept. 10, 1961; 1 dau., Ann. Agent, Aetna Life Ins. Co., Mason City, Iowa, 1953-58; gen. agt. Occidental Life Ins. Co., Mason City, 1958-63; co-founder, exec. v.p. Guardsman Life Ins. Co., Des Moines, 1963-69; pres. Ins. Investors, Inc., Des Moines, 1963-69, Guardsman Ins. Investors, Inc., Des Moines, 1965-69, Jo-Tel-So, Inc., Mason City, 1966—, Equity Dynamics Inc., John Pappajohn & Assos. Inc., Equimatics, Inc., Evia Ltd., Fedinco, Inc., Jay Barmish Loan Co., Agrl. Bus. Credit Corp. (all Des Moines); pres., dir. Ashworth Plaza Corp., Des Moines; mng. partner Ashworth Plaza Ltd.; v.p. State St. Investments Corp., Mason City; dir. Key Labs., San Diego, Tech-S Corp., Detroit, Curries Mfg., Mason City, Am. Trencher Inc., Delhi, Iowa, Iowa Gateway Inc., Keokuk, Shirlamar Inc., Des Moines, ISCO, Inc., Cin., Tech-S, Inc., Detroit, TESI, San Diego, GNAT Computers, San Diego, Data Law, Denver, Vitalmetrics, San Diego, Coratomic, Inc., Indiana, Pa., Valpar, Tucson, Home Health Care of Am., Santa Ana, Calif., Bio Corp., Denver, Staodynamics, Inc., Longmont, Colo.; gen. partner Growth Equities Ltd. Trustee Des Moines Art Center; bd. dirs., sec. Big Bros. Am.; chmn. Iowa Citizens for Arts. Mem. Internat., Nat. assns. merger and acquisition consultants, Nat. Assn. Life Underwriters, Soc. Fin. Analysts, Soc. Advancement Mgmt., Nat. Assn. Life Cos., Investment Bankers Assn., Internat. Assn. Fin. Planners, Assn. Corp. Growth, Inst. Bus. Appraisers, Consultants Com. of 100, U. Iowa Alumni Assn., Order of Ahepa, Phi Gamma Delta. Republican. Orthodox. Clubs: Masons, Shriners, Des Moines, Univ., Embassy, Country (Des Moines). Home: 7301 Benton Dr Des Moines IA 50322 Office: 2116 Financial Center Des Moines IA 50309

PAPPAS, ANTHONY VINCENT, JR., ednl. testing co. exec.; b. Phila., Oct. 1, 1942; s. Anthony Vincent and Emily Veronica (DeLaurentis) P.; B.A., LaSalle Coll., 1964; M.A., U. Miss., 1973, Ph.D., 1975; children—Anthony Vincent III, Kristina, Michael. Consumer fin. mgr. Sylvan Pools, Doylestown, Pa., 1968-71; asst. vice chancellor, asst. prof. psychology U. S.C., 1975-80; asst. dir. career planning services Am. Coll. Testing, Iowa City, 1980—. Mem. S.C. Adv. Com. on Gerontology, 1978-80; mem. S.C. Appalachian Edn. TV Satellite Adv. Com., 1976-80; chmn. membership Community Concerts, Spartansburg, S.C., 1979. Dept. Labor Manpower fellow, 1972-73; grantee Office Edn., 1978-79, CETA, 1979-80, others. Mem. Am. Personnel and Guidance Assn., Nat. Vocat. Guidance Assn., Am. Psychol. Assn., Nat. Assn. Student Personnel Adminstrs., Adult Edn. Assn. Contbr. numerous articles to profl. jours. Home: 404 6th St Apt D5 Coralville IA 52241 Office: PO Box 168 Iowa City IA 52243

PAQUETTE, ELMER GORDON, research physicist; b. Janesville, Wis., June 26, 1922; s. Nathan Winfield and Elsie (Orlena) P.; B.S., Milton (Wis.) Coll., 1949; children—Kerry Alan, Nichelle, Wendy Denise. Apprentice machinist, journeyman Parker Pen, Janesville, 1940-42; tchr. Antigo (Wis.) Jr. High Sch., 1949-51; research physicist Bjorksten Research Labs., Madison, Wis., 1951-68, dir. of physics, 1968—. Mem. Sch. Bd., Cambridge, Wis., 1962-63. Served with USAF, 1942-46. Recipient cert. of recognition NASA, 1981. Registered profl. engr., Wis.; registered profl. designer. Contbr. articles to profl. jours. Home: 326 Phlox Dr Madison WI 53713 Office: PO Box 9444 Madison WI 53715

PARADIES, BRIAN JOHN, publishing co. exec.; b. Chgo., July 18, 1941; s. LeRoy John and Evelyn Alice (Gollnick) P.; student DePaul U., 1959-61; B.S. in Fin., No. Ill. U., 1964; M.B.A., Loyola U., Chgo., 1972; m. Nancy Mary Gonciarz, Apr. 8, 1967; children—Michelle, Kevin. Mktg. analyst Bankers Life & Casualty Co., Chgo., 1965-72; direct mail mgr. Bell & Howell Schs., Chgo., 1972-74; gen. mgr. Sakanovsky & Co., Evanston, Ill., 1974-75; asst. dir. direct mktg. Playboy Enterprises, Inc., Chgo., 1975—. Served with U.S. Army, 1965. Mem. Chgo. Assn. Direct Mktg. (dir. 1980-81, sec.-treas. 1981-82), Direct Mail Mktg. Assn. Roman Catholic. Office: 919 N Michigan Ave Chicago IL 60611

PARAMORE, DOROTHY JEAN (DOTTIE PAIGE), advt. exec.; b. Topeka, Kans., July 10, 1929; d. Warren Gilbert and Vivian Alice (Neiswender) P.; B.S. in Radio and Speech, Kans. State U., 1951. Women's dir. Sta. WREN, Topeka, 1951-54; women's dir. Sta. WIBW, Topeka, 1955-59, promotion dir., 1957-59; copy and media dir. Patterson Advt. Agency, Inc., Topeka, 1959—, also dir.; guest lectr. Washburn U., 1963. Bd. dirs. Topeka Arts Council, 1977. Recipient Silver Medal award in Advt., Profl. Advt. Club Topeka, 1968. Mem. Am. Women in Radio and TV (v.p. Heart of Am. chpt. 1959), Kans. (treas. 1973-74), Topeka (pres. 1964) press women, Women in Communications (v.p. Topeka br. 1967), Nat. League Am. Pen Women (pres. Topeka br. 1972-74), Topeka C. of C. (chmn. women's div. 1966), Delta Delta Delta. Methodist. Club: Order Eastern Star. Home: 1731 Randolph St Topeka KS 66604 Office: 2900 Plass Ct Topeka KS 66611

PARASCANDOLA, JOHN LOUIS, sci. historian; b. N.Y.C., July 14, 1941; s. Louis Salvatore and Ann (Guido) P.; B.S., Bklyn. Coll., 1963; M.S., U. Wis., Madison, 1968, Ph.D., 1968; m. Elisa Castellon, June 1, 1963; children—Mark, Linda. Macy postdoctoral research fellow in history of medicine and biol. sci. Harvard U., 1968-69; asst. prof. history of pharmacy and history of sci. U. Wis., Madison, 1969-73, asso. prof., 1973-80, prof., 1980—. Recipient Edward Kremers award, 1980. NSF grantee, 1971-76; Am. Acad. Arts and Scis. grantee, 1977-81; NIH grantee, 1979-83. Mem. Internat. Acad. History of Pharmacy, Am. Inst. History of Pharmacy (dir. 1973-81, gen. editor publs. 1973-81), Am. Assn. History Medicine, History of Sci. Soc., Internat. Soc. History of Pharmacy, Am. Assn. Colls. Pharmacy. Contbr. numerous articles on history of biomed. sci. to profl. jours. Office: 4308 Chamberlin Hall U Wis Madison WI 53706

PARDO-KEGER, LYNN MICHELE, artist, educator; b. Lakewood, Ohio, Sept. 16, 1950; A.S., Cuyahoga Community Coll., 1972; B.A., Cleve. State U., 1977; m. Lawrence Keger, Feb. 8, 1980. Art instr. Lakewood (Ohio) Bd. Edn. and Recreation Dept., 1968, 70, 79; art instr., artist Dept. Recreation Cleve.; pvt. art cons. Mem. New Orgn. for Visual Arts. Lutheran. Address: 17819 Webb Cliff Dr Lakewood OH 44107

PAREDES, AUGUST VICTOR, cardiologist; b. Arequipa, Peru, Apr. 16, 1929; s. Carlos Augusto and Rosa Amelia (Alvarez) P.; came to U.S., 1955, naturalized, 1960; M.D., U San Marcos, Lima, Peru, 1955; m. Margaret Connor, Jan. 19, 1956; children—Mark, Nancy, Christopher, Anne Marie, Patrick, Jacquelyn, Michael, Peggy. Intern, Michael Reese Hosp., Chgo., 1955-56, resident, 1956-58, fellow in cardiology, 1958-60; practice medicine specializing in cardiology, 1961—; mem. staff Ingalls Meml. Hosp., Harvey, Ill., 1961—, dir. cardiology, 1968; mem. staff Michael Reese Hosp., Chgo.; dir. Mobile Intensive Care Network S. Cook County, 1975; pres. S. Suburban Cardiology, Ltd., 1971—; chmn. Mobile Intensive Cardiac Care Com., Chgo. Heart Assn., 1975—. Served with Peruvian Navy, 1953-54. Recipient Meritorious Service award Chgo. Heart Assn., 1975, Outstanding Citizen award S. Suburban C. of C., Chgo. 1977. Fellow Am. Coll. Cardiology, Inst. Medicine Chgo.; mem. Peruvian Soc. Cardiology, Am. Soc. Internal Medicine, Michael Reese Alumni Assn., AMA, Ill. State, Chgo. med. socs., Am. Heart Assn. Home: 783 Brookwood Olympia Fields IL 60461 Office: 71 W 156th St Harvey IL 60426

PARENT, JOSEPH DOMINIC, cons.; b. Boston, Aug. 4, 1910; s. Joseph Emile and Mary Brigid (Smyth) P.; B.S. in Chem. Engring., Cath. U. Am., 1929; M.S., Rensselaer Poly. Inst., 1931; postgrad. U. Md., 1931-32; Ph.D. in Chem. Engring., Ohio State U., 1933; m. Margaret Mary Madden, Feb. 15, 1941; children—J. Dennis, Mary M. (Mrs. Joseph Warnemuende), Margaret (Mrs. Anthony Knapp), Gerard T., Ellen (Mrs. Gregory Caputo), Mary T. (Mrs. Robert Essig), Christine (Mrs. Francis Zeman), Joan (Mrs. John Houser). Asst. prof. chemistry Loyola U., Chgo., 1935-42; asso. prof. chem. engring., Kans. State U., Manhattan, 1942-43; dean students Inst. Gas Tech., Chgo., 1943-53, cons., 1972—; cons. The Peoples Gas Light & Coke Co., Chgo., 1953-72. Mem. Am. Chem. Soc., Am. Inst. Chem. Engrs., Am. Gas Assn., Sigma Xi, Alpha Delta Gamma, Phi Lambda Upsilon, Alpha Chi Sigma. Elk. Home: 614 Linden Ave Wilmette IL 60091 Office: 3424 S State St Chicago IL 60616

PARFET, RAY T., JR., pharm. co. exec. Dir., Upjohn Co., 1958—, v.p., 1958-59, exec. v.p. charge research, legal, financial and personnel activities, 1960-62, pres., gen. mgr., 1962-69, chmn. bd., chief exec. officer, 1969—; dir. 1st Nat. Bank & Trust Co. Mich., Kalamazoo, The Aro Corp., Bryan, Ohio, Gilmore Bros. Dept. Store, Kalamazoo, Union Pump Co., Battle Creek, Mich. Bell, Detroit, 1st Am. Bank Corp., Kalamazoo. Trustee, Bronson Meth. Hosp., Kalamazoo, Nat. 4-H Council, Washington, Mem. Pharm. Mfrs. Assn. (past chmn., past dir.), Internat. Fedn. Pharm. Mfrs. Assns. (past dir.). Office: 7000 Portage Rd Kalamazoo MI 49001

PARIS, BILLY GENE, ins. co. exec.; b. Harrisburg, Ill., Jan. 9, 1938; s. Arvle Ernest and Bonnie Louise (Dalton) P.; B.S. in Bus. Adminstrn., U. Md., 1960; student Ins. Inst. Am., 1971; C.L.U., Am. Coll., 1976; R.H.U., Nat. Assn. Health Underwriters, 1979; m. Dorothy Margaret DeMartinis, June 14, 1958; children—Michael A., Denise M., Christopher R. Policeman, Montgomery County, Md., 1959-64; claims adjuster Nationwide Ins. Co., 1964-67, agt., 1967-68, dist. sales mgr., 1968-73, regional sales tng. mgr., 1973-75, regional sales mgr., Indpls., 1975—. Active, Mountaintop Taxpayers Assn., 1978-80. Served with USMCR, 1956-62. Named Regional Sales Mgr.

of Yr., Nationwide Ins. Co., 1975-79, recipient Pres.'s award, 1977, 80; named Ky. Col., 1980. Mem. Nat. Assn. Health Underwriters, Am. Soc. C.L.U.'s, Nat. Assn. Life Underwriters. Roman Catholic. Home: 5202 Sherwood Ct Carmel IN 46032 Office: 941 E 86th St Suite 207 Indianapolis IN 46024

PARISH, PRESTON SEITER, pharm. co. exec.; b. Chgo., Nov. 10, 1919; s. Preston and Louise (Vesley) P.; A.B., Williams Coll., 1941; m. Suzanne U. DeLano, Apr. 17, 1948; children—Barbara Parish Gibbs, Katharine Parish Miller, P. William, Preston L., David C. Salesman, Am. Flange and Mfg. Co., N.Y., Chgo., Los Angeles, 1946-47, resident mgr. Can. subs., 1947-49; prodn. engr. Upjohn Co., Kalamazoo, Mich., 1949-55, dir., 1955-58, v.p., dir., 1958-60, exec. v.p., dir., 1960-69, vice chmn. bd., chmn. exec. com., 1969—; dir. Am. Nat. Bank and Trust Co., Kalamazoo, Am. Nat. Holding Co., Kalamazoo; chmn. Kal-Aero, Inc., Kalamazoo; trustee W.E. Upjohn Unemployment Trustee Corp., Kalamazoo, 1963—, chmn., 1976—. Trustee Bronson Methodist Hosp., 1959—, Williams Coll., Williamstown, Mass., 1965—, Holderness Sch., Plymouth, N.H., 1968-76; past trustee Eaglebrook Sch., Deerfield, Mass.; chmn. Kalamazoo Aviation History Mus., 1978—; mem. nat. bd. Jr. Achievement, 1979—, vice chmn., 1981; adv. bd. Found. Student Communication, Inc., Princeton, N.J., 1973—. Served to maj. USMC, 1941-46, col. Res. ret. Decorated Bronze Star. Mem. Nat. Alliance of Businessmen (past chmn.), Food and Drug Law Inst. (dir., chmn.), Conf. Bd., Warbirds of Am. (hon. dir., past pres.), Nat. Bus. Aviation Assn. (dir.). Office: 7000 Portage Rd Kalamazoo MI 49001

PARISH, SHEILA DIANE, educator; b. Rockford, Ill., Feb. 1, 1947; d. Donald Allen and Mabel Amanda (Johnson) P.; A.B., U. Ill., 1969, M.A.T.S.S., 1972. Tchr. social studies Dist. 118, Danville, Ill., 1969-78, 79-81, chmn. dept. social studies, 1981—; student tchr. supr. U. Ill., 1978-79. Mem. Ill. Council Social Studies, Nat. Council Social Studies, Assn. Supervision and Curriculum Devel., Soc. History Edn., Phi Delta Kappa, Kappa Delta Pi. Office: Danville High Sch Fairchild and Jackson Sts Danville IL 61832

PARK, CHAN HYUNG, physician, educator; b. Seoul, Korea, Aug. 16, 1936; s. Chung Suh and Yoon Sook (Yuh) P.; came to U.S., 1964, naturalized, 1976; M.D., Seoul Nat. U., 1962, M.S., 1964; Ph.D., U. Toronto, 1972; m. Mary Hyungrok Kim, Apr. 16, 1966. House staff Seoul Nat. U. Hosp., 1962-64; intern St. Francis Gen. Hosp., Pitts., 1964-65; resident in medicine U. Miami and Jackson Meml. Hosp., Miami, Fla., 1966-68; fellow in oncology-hematology Brown U. and Roger Williams Gen. Hosp., Providence, 1972-74; practice medicine specializing in internal medicine and med. oncology, Kansas City, Kans., 1974—; asst. prof. medicine Kans. U. Med. Center, Kansas City, 1974-80, asso. prof., 1980—. Recipient Research Career Devel. award USPHS, 1979. Mem. Am. Fedn. Clin. Research, Internat. Soc. Exptl. Hematology, Cell Kinetics Soc., Am. Assn. Cancer Research, Am. Soc. Clin. Oncology, Am. Soc. Hematology. Home: 9137 Grandview Dr Overland Park KS 66212 Office: 39th and Rainbow Sts Kansas City KS 66103

PARK, HONG YOUL, economist; b. Choong-Nam, Korea, Mar. 1, 1938; s. Bong Rae and Sung Yeu (Yoon) P.; B.A., Kyung Hee U., Seoul, Korea, 1962; M.A. in Econs., Seoul Nat. U., 1966; M.B.A., Fairleigh Dickinson U., 1970; Ph.D. in Econs., Utah State U., 1975; m. Chung Soo, Feb. 19, 1966; children—Jenny, Helene, Anne, Sonia. Teaching asst. Kyung Hee U., Seoul, 1966-68; payroll bookkeeper Fairleigh Dickinson U., Rutherford, N.J., 1968-70; research asst. Utah State U., 1971-75; asst. prof. econs. Saginaw Valley State Coll., University Center, Mich., 1975-78, asso. prof., 1978—, dir. Center for Econ. and Bus. Research, 1979—. Mem. Am. Econ. Assn., Econometric Soc., Regional Sci. Assn., Western Econ. Assn., Mid-Continent Regional Sci. Assn., World U., Mid-Mich. Korean Soc. (pres.). Contbr. articles to profl. jours. Office: 2250 Pierce Rd University Center MI 48710

PARK, JOSEPH DALE, educator; b. Hartford, Ky., Dec. 11, 1947; s. William Carson and Helen Mae (Hardesty) P.; B.S., Purdue U., 1969, M.S., 1978; m. Elizabeth Louise Meunier, June 14, 1969; children—Travis, Aaron, Jeremy. Tchr., Henryville (Ind.) High Sch., 1969-70; tchr. vocat. agr. Indian Creek High Sch., Trafalgar, Ind., 1970—. Mem. Nat. Vocat. Agr. Tchrs. Assn., Am. Vocat. Assn., Ind. Vocat. Assn., Ind. Vocat. Agr. Tchrs. Assn., Ind. Young Farmers Assn., Trafalgar Young Farmers Assn. Republican. Roman Catholic. Home: Route 3 Box 112 Franklin IN 46131 Office: Indian Creek High School Route 2 Box 3E Trafalgar IN 46181

PARK, TERRY PAUL, psychologist; b. Sioux Falls, S.D., July 22, 1951; s. Ronald Paul and Patricia Sue Park; B.S., U. S.D., 1973, M.A., 1975, Ph.D., 1978; m. Kathleen Hayes Oksol, Jan. 2, 1981. Clin. psychologist Dakota Mental Health Center, Mitchell, S.D., 1978—, chief psychologist, 1980—. Mem. Am. Psychol. Assn., S.D. Psychol. Assn., Phi Beta Kappa. Home: 700 1/2 E Havens St Mitchell SD 57301 Office: 910 W Havens Mitchell SD 57301

PARK, THOMAS CHOONBAI, educator; b. Bookchong, Korea, May 21, 1919; came to U.S., 1956, naturalized, 1972; s. Heeun and Jongsoon (Kim) P.; diploma with honors, Tchrs. Coll., Seoul Nat. U., 1941; B.A. with honors, U. Fla., 1958, M.A., 1959, Ed.D., 1961; m. Whasoon Hong, Feb. 7, 1942; children—James Jingoo, Susan S. Kim, John Jinoh, Doris S., Betty S. Master tchr. Hongwon (Korea) Public Sch., 1941-43, Hinode Public Sch., Wonsun, Korea, 1943-45; instr. music Hamhung (Korea) Normal Sch., 1945-46; instr. Coll. Edn., Seoul Nat. U., 1946-56; prof., registrar Fla. Meml. Coll., St. Augustine, 1961-65; asst. prof. edn. St. Cloud (Minn.) State U., 1965-66, asso. prof., 1966-69, prof., 1969—. Mem. Am. Assn. Higher Edn., Assn. Supervision and Curriculum Devel., NEA, AAUP (sec. local chpt. 1968-69), Minn. Edn. Assn., Phi Kappa Phi (sec.-treas. local chpt. 1974-79), Kappa Delta Pi. Republican. Methodist. Author: Norai Kongboo, 6 vols., 1950; (with Elisabeth H. Dietz) Folksongs of China, Japan, Korea, 1964; Curriculum for Schools in a Democratic Society, 1979. Home: 1133 Kilian Blvd SE Saint Cloud MN 56301 Office: Coll Edn St Cloud State U Saint Cloud MN 56301

PARKE, HARRY MORRIS, indsl. distributor; b. Toledo, Oct. 23, 1920; s. Harry Wiswall Parke and Marie Louise (Hahn) P.; B.B.A., U. Toledo, 1942; m. Margaret Jean Beat, July 25, 1942; children—Richard Blake, Catherine Jean Parke Hollingsworth. Pres., M.I. Wilcox Co., Toledo, 1958-60; v.p. indsl. sales Bostwick-Braun Co., Toledo, J.T. Wing Co., Detroit, 1964-73; pres. Bingham, Inc., Cleve., 1973-76; v.p. market devel. The W.M. Pattison Supply Co., Cleve., 1976-78; pres. Cleve. Tool & Supply Co., 1978-80, N. Central Indsl. Supply Co., Mansfield, Ohio, 1978-80; owner, pres. Parke Supply Co., Avon Lake, Ohio, 1980—; breeder thoroughbred horses. Served to lt. col. USMCR. Mem. Nat. Indsl. Distbrs. Assn., Cleve. Indsl. Distbrs. Assn., U. Toledo Alumni Assn., Phi Kappa Psi. Republican. Episcopalian. Club: Rotary. Home: 32821 Tanglewood Ct Avon Lake OH 44012 Office: PO Box 5 Avon Lake OH 44012

PARKER, ADAJUNE, consumer specialist; b. Oak Hill, Ill., Mar. 15, 1938; d. Delbert Vernon and Nellie Adelaide (Hayes) Helle; B.S. in Home Econs., Bradley U., 1961; postgrad. No. Ill. U., 1973, 74; m. William Robert Parker, June 18, 1961; children—Rebecca June, Phyllis Ann. Asst. dept. mgr. Marshall Field and Co., Oak Park, Ill., 1961; home econs. tchr. Forest Park (Ill.) Jr. High Sch., 1962-64, Glenbard East High Sch., Lombard, Ill., 1964-65; Vocat. foodservice and home econs. tchr. Lisle (Ill.) Community High Sch., 1969-74; extension advisor Licking County Coop. Extension Service, Newark, Ohio, 1975-76; consumer specialist, dir. home environ. lab. program Underwriters Labs., Inc., Northbrook, Ill., 1976-80, sec. consumer advisory council, sponsor rep. to Chgo. Area consumer sounding-board; lectr., speaker consumer product safety and foodservice sanitation; freelance consumer specialist and cons., Newark, Ohio, 1980—; instr. Chgo. City-Coll., 1976-79; foodservice cons. Dupage Area Vocat. Edn. Authority, 1974. Health dept. steering com. Orchard-brook Homeowners Assn., 1976; Bicentennial Commn. Licking County, 1975-76; 4-H Program Review Com., 1975-76, county fair advisor/judge, 1975; active Walkathon Communications, March of Dimes, 1973, 74; reporter foodservice div. advisory council Dupage Area Vocat. Edn. Authority, 1969-74; vol. hot lunch coordinator Bethany Luth. Sch., Naperville, Ill., 1966-68; Brownie leader, Woodridge, Ill., 1969-71. Recipient disting. service award Nat. Inst. for Foodservice Industry, 1977. Mem. Elec. Womens Roundtable (sec. Chgo. chpt., 1978-79, treas., 1979-80, nat. conf. program co-chmn., 1979), Am. Home Econs. Assn., Home Economists in Bus., Internat. Microwave Power Inst.-Cooking Appliance Sect., Ill. Home Econs. Assn., Soc. Consumer Affairs Profls., Kappa Omicron Phi. Methodist. Clubs: Newcomers Bridge, Orchardbrook Assn. Editor consumer advisory council bulletin, 1977-80; contbr. consumer articles, Newark Advocate, 1974-76; editor monthly newsletter for coop. extension service, 1975-76; editor UL Trends, 1980; radio program Homemakers Cues and Clues sta. WCLT, Newark, 1974-76; contbr. research papers, news releases, articles to publs. in field. Home: 52 Victoria Dr Newark OH 43055 Office: PO Box 2173 Newark OH 43055

PARKER, CHARLES WALTER, JR., equipment co. exec.; b. nr. Ahoskie, N.C., Nov. 22, 1922; s. Charles Walter and Minnie Louise (Williamson) P.; B.S. in Elec. Engring., Va. Mil. Inst., 1947; Dr. Engring. (hon.), Milw. Sch. Engring., 1980; m. Sophie Nash Riddick, Nov. 26, 1949; children—Mary Parker Hutto, Caroline Davis, Charles Walter III, Thomas Williamson. With Allis-Chalmers Corp., 1947—, dist. mgr., Richmond, Va., 1955-57, Phila., 1957-58, dir. sales promotion industries group, Milw., 1958-61, gen. mktg. mgr. new products, 1961-62, mgr. mktg. services, 1962-66, v.p. mktg. public relations and mktg., 1966-70, v.p., dep. group. exec., 1970-72, v.p. staff group exec. communications and public affairs, 1972—; dir. Heritage Wis. Corp., Internat. Gen. Ins. Corp. Mem. Greater Milw. Com.; vice chmn. United Way of Milw.; gen. chmn. Met. Milw. United Fund, 1975; trustee Milw. Boy Scouts Trust Fund; bd. dirs., Jr. Achievement, Better Bus. Bur., 1976—; trustee Univ. Sch. Milw., 1978-80, Carroll Coll.; bd. regents Milw. Sch. Engring. Served to capt. AUS, 1943-46; ETO. Decorated Bronze Star. Mem. Am. Mktg. Assn. (dir. 1976-78), Wis. C. of C. (pres. 1974-76), IEEE (asso.), Sales and Mktg. Execs. Internat. (pres., chief exec. officer 1974-75), Pi Sigma Epsilon, Kappa Alpha. Home: 2907 E Linnwood Ave Milwaukee WI 53211 Office: PO Box 512 Milwaukee WI 53201

PARKER, CLYDE ALVIN, psychologist; b. Odgen, Utah, Mar. 17, 1927; s. Thomas and Reka Jacoba (Van Braak) P.; B.S., Brigham Young U., 1952, M.S., 1952; Ph.D., U. Minn., 1957; m. Ilene Kendell, Dec. 27, 1950; children—Thomas, Gregory, Camille, Lisa. Asso. prof. edn., chmn. counseling center Brigham Young U., Provo, Utah, 1957-64; faculty U. Minn., Mpls., 1964—, prof., chmn. dept. ednl. foundations, 1974—; psychologist Center Counseling and Therapeutic Services, McKay Dee Hosp., Ogden, Utah. Served with USNR, 1945-46. Mem. Am. Psychol. Assn., Am. Personnel and Guidance Assn., Phi Kappa Phi, Mormon. Author: Counseling Theory and Counselor Education, 1968; Psychological Consultation in the Schools, 1975. Office: McKay Dee Hosp Center Counseling and Therapeutic Services 3939 Harrison Blvd Ogden UT 84409

PARKER, DOROTHY MAY, educator; b. Painesville, Ohio, June 25, 1947; d. William Harry and Eileen Alberta (Snow) B.; student Kent State U., 1965-66; B.A., Miami U., Ohio, 1969; M.Ed., Bowling Green State U., 1976; m. David Brent Parker, Aug. 24, 1968. Tchr., Lakota High Sch., Liberty Center, Ohio, 1969-72, Robinson Jr. High Sch., Toledo, 1972-73, Sylvania High Sch., Toledo, 1973-76, Sylvania Southview High Sch., 1976—. John R. Williams Meml. scholar, 1965. Mem. Internat. Reading Assn., Assn. Supervision and Curriculum Devel., NEA, Ohio Edn. Assn., Sylvania Edn. Assn. (pres.), Delta Kappa Gamma, Am. Field Service (pres. Sylvania chpt., area rep. 1982). Home: 4950 W Central St Toledo OH 43615 Office: 7225 Sylvania Ave Sylvania OH 43615

PARKER, EDWARD ALAN, textbook editor; b. Cin., Aug. 17, 1946; s. William Arthur and Lucille Grant (Lake) P.; B.B.A., U. Cin., 1969, M.B.A. (Southwestern Pub. Co. fellow), 1970. Asst. prof. Xavier U., Cin., 1970-76; asst. prof., chmn. dept. bus. Spalding Coll., Louisville, 1976-78; editor bus. and econs. textbooks South-Western Pub. Co., Cin., 1978—; mktg. cons., Cin. and Louisville, 1972-78. Trustee, Ky. Assn. Specific Perceptual Motor Disability, 1978-80; active United Metro Way Campaign, 1976-77; chmn. bd. deacons Kenwood Bapt. Ch., 1973-75, chmn. Bd. Christian Edn., 1982. Mem. Advt. Club Louisville (dir. 1978), Am. Mktg. Assn., Delta Sigma Pi. Republican. Home: 5291 Belleview Rd Cincinnati OH 45242 Office: 5101 Madison Rd Cincinnati OH 45227

PARKER, FRANCES THERESA, Realtor; b. Windber, Pa., July 12, 1935; d. Gazel Frank and Agnes Stella (Zadio) Roza; cert. Thornton Community Coll., 1977; student Real Estate Inst., 1978; children—Terrance Lee Poddam, Robert S. Hall, Gregory Lee Parker. Sales rep. Top Value Realty, Chgo., 1966-73, Bovenkerk Realty, South Holland, Ill., 1973-76, Thomas D. Murphy, Inc., Red Oaks, Iowa, 1976, Regent Realtors, Calumet City, Ill., 1978—, Swepco (Southwestern Petroleum Co.), Ft. Worth, 1978—; also distbr. Amway Products. Mem. Am. Mgmt. Assn., Calumet City C. of C., St. Vick's Women's Club. Democrat. Roman Catholic. Office: Amway Corp Ada MI

PARKER, FRED, wholesale co. exec.; b. Cleve., Feb. 25, 1946; s. William Henry and Lura Ella (McGhee) P.; B.B.A., Cleve. State U., 1977, M.B.A., 1980; Cert. in Real Estate, Cuyahoga Community Coll., 1970. Advisor, Aircraft & Missile Overseas div. Lear Siegler, Inc., Oklahoma City, 1968-74; field advt. dir. Time, Inc., N.Y.C., 1974-77; area mgr. Quaker Oats Co., Columbus, Ohio, 1977-79; U.S. zone mgr. B. Allright Cos., Inc., Cleve., 1979—; advt./research cons. Asst. dir. Regional Growth Council of Advisors, Cleve., 1980—. Served with USAF, 1963-67. Recipient Community Civic award African-Am. Culture Club, 1977. Mem. Internat. Specialty Merchandisers Assn. (dir. 1979—), Nat. Wholesale Marketers Assn. of Execs. Republican. Club: Mansfield Country and Golf. Home: 12004 Woodland Ave Cleveland OH 44120 Office: 11814 Buckeye Rd E Cleveland OH 44120

PARKER, JAMES JOHN, elec. engr.; b. Oak Park, Ill., June 16, 1947; s. John J. and Marjorie (Grohmann) P.; B.S. in E.E., Marquette U., 1971; B.S. in Bus. Adminstrn., Elmhurst Coll., 1981; m. Mary P. Nash, Oct. 21, 1972; children—Elizabeth Ann, John James, Patricia Mary. Student engr. Motorola Consumer Products, Franklin Park, Ill., 1968-70, engring. asso., 1972-74; co-op engr. Warwick Electronics, Niles, Ill., 1971-72; engr. Quasar Electronics, Inc., Franklin Park, 1974-76; sr. project engr. Motorola Data Products, Carol Stream, Ill., 1976-79; sr. project engr. Zenith Radio Corp., Glenview, Ill., 1979—; faculty Wright Jr. Coll., Chgo., part-time 1975-80. Advisor, Jr. Achievement, Chgo., 1972-78. Mem. IEEE, Midcon (vice chmn. public relations 1979, chmn. spl. exhibits 1981), Delta Mu Delta. Editorial adv. bd. Electronic Products Mag., 1976-77. Home: 421 Berkley Ave Elmhurst IL 60126 Office: 1000 Milwaukee Ave Glenview IL 60025

PARKER, JAMES MITCHELL, mktg. co. exec.; b. Chgo., Sept. 3, 1931; s. Robert Barnett and Bonnie (Mitchell) Chidester; student Wilson Jr. coll., 1949-51; B.S., U. Ill., 1955; M.B.A., U. Chgo., 1969; 1 dau., Ginger. Asso. producer Lee Parker Productions, Chgo., 1955-59; sales exec. Borg-Warner Corp., Chgo., 1959-65; account supr. Perrin & Assos., Chgo., 1966-69; pres. Parkton Corp., Ellsworth, Kans., 1969-72; v.p. Dynamark Corp., Chgo., 1972-77; pres. United Mktg. Corp., Chgo., 1977—. Served to lt. U.S. Army, 1951-53. Mem. Exec. Club, Exec. Program Club. Clubs: Chgo. Athletic; Flossmoor Country. Patentee improved lawn mower. Home: 1117 Leavitt Ave Flossmoor IL 60422 Office: 35 E Wacker Dr Chicago IL 60601

PARKER, JAMES ROBERT, educator, athletic dir.; b. Midland, Mich., Aug. 6, 1952; s. Robert Leroy and Jeannette Evelyn (Graczyk) P.; B.S., Alma Coll., 1974; M.A., Central Mich. U., 1976; m. Dawn Suzanne Savich, Sept. 20, 1975. Asst. basketball and baseball coach Alma Coll., 1974-75; mem. faculty Blackburn Coll., Carlinville, Ill., 1975—, also basketball coach, dir. men's and women's athletics. Mem. AAHPER, Nat. Assn. Collegiate Dirs. Athletics. Republican. Presbyterian. Office: Dawes Gym Blackburn Coll Carlinville IL 62626

PARKER, MARYLAND (MIKE), broadcasting exec.; b. Oklahoma City, Feb. 5, 1926; d. Clarence N. and Minzola (Perkins) Davis; student U. Ark., Pine Bluff, 1970-71; student Marymount Coll., 1974-77; m. John Harriss Parker, Nov. 25, 1944 (dec.); children—Norma Jean Parker Brown, Janice Kay Parker Shelby, Joyce Lynn, John H. (dec.), Cherie D. Parker Hite, Patrick Scott, Charles Roger. Beautician, Maryland's Ho. of Beauty, Salina, Kans., 1964-69; youth adv. NAACP, Salina, 1970-72; newspaper reporter BACOS Newsletter, Salina, 1971-77; radio announcer Kina's BACOS Report, Salina, 1973—. Mem. Salina County Democratic Women, 1960—; part-time vol. Salvation Army, Salina, 1979—; bd. dirs. Salina Child Care Assn. Mem. NAACP (life), Nat. Fedn. Press Women, Kans. Press Women, Internat. Platform Assn., VFW Aux., Am. Legion Aux. Mormon. Home: 920 Birch Dr PO Box 705 Salina KS 67401 Office: PO Box 778 Salina KS 67401

PARKER, PAUL LANGE, food co. exec.; b. Des Moines, Apr. 27, 1921; s. Addison Melvin and Ida Louise (Lange) P.; B.A., Dartmouth Coll., 1943; J.D., U. Iowa, 1948; m. Allegra Willis, Sept. 6, 1947; children—Hugh C., Melissa W., Paul W. Admitted to Iowa bar, 1948; pvt. practice law, Des Moines, 1948-56; asst. county atty. Polk County, Iowa, 1950-52; mem. Iowa Ho. of Reps., 1953-55; exec. asst. Gov. of Iowa, 1955-56; gen. mgr. Canadian ops. Gen. Mills, Inc., Toronto, Ont., 1960-62; gen. internat. div. mgr. Gen. Mills, Inc., Mpls., 1962-64, v.p., dir. public relations, 1965-69, sr. v.p. employee and public relations, 1969-76, exec. v.p., chief adminstrv. officer, 1976—; trustee Farmers & Mechanics Savings Bank, Mpls., 1970—; dir. Equitable of Iowa, Des Moines, 1975—, Burlington No., St. Paul, 1976—. Trustee Simpson Coll., Indianola, Iowa, 1967—. Served with USN, 1943-46. Home: 785 N Ferndale Rd Wayzata MN 55391 Office: 9200 Wayzata Blvd Minneapolis MN 55440

PARKER, PAUL LEROY, ednl. adminstr.; b. New Richmond, Ind., July 21, 1919; s. James and Evadne (Young) P.; B.S. in Bus. and Phys. Edn., Central Normal U., Danville, Ind., 1940; M.S. in Adminstrn., Purdue U., Lafayette, Ind., 1952; children—Lanny, Mike, Susan. Prin. Bainbridge (Ind.) Schs., 1959-63; supt. Redkey (Ind.) Pub. Schs., 1963-64, Harrison-Washington Community Sch. Corp., Gaston, Ind., 1964—. Pres., E. Central Study Council, 1974-81; bd. dirs. Delaware County Mental Health Assn. Mem. Ind. Assn. Pub. Sch. Supts., Am. Assn. Sch. Adminstrs. Club: Optimists (past pres.). Home: Rural Route 14 Box 419 Muncie IN 47302 Office: Rural Route #1 Gaston IN 47342

PARKER, RAYMOND LEROY, med. data systems co. ofcl.; b. Detroit, Oct. 8, 1924; s. Peter and Kornelia (Gosky) P.; B.S. in Elec. Engring. (Bomber scholar), U. Mich., 1950; m. Dorothy Cieslak, Aug. 2, 1947; children—Constance, Margaret, Barbara. Design engr. Burroughs Corp., Detroit, 1951, asst. supt., 1955-57, supt., 1957-66, supt. assembly ops. Downington (Pa.) plant, 1966-68, quality control mgr., 1968-71, cons. Croydan (Eng.) plant, 1972, product assurance mgr. Plymouth (Mich.) plant, 1974-80; quality assurance mgr. Medtronic Med. Data Systems Div., Ann Arbor, Mich., 1980—. Bd. dirs. Nat. Home Respiratory Care Center S.E. Mich., 1977—. Served with USNR, 1943-46. Mem. Am. Soc. for Quality Control, IEEE. Roman Catholic. Home: 36817 Rayburn St Livonia MI 48154 Office: 2311 Green Rd Ann Arbor MI 48105

PARKER, ROBERT AMOS, fin. planning co. exec.; b. Bragg City, Mo., June 3, 1935; s. Ira Clofic and Lizzie Bell (Holmes) P.; B.S., Ark. State U., 1958; M.P.H., U. N.C., 1962; m. Mon; 1 dau., Natasha. Adminstrv. asst. dist. 4, Mo. Div. Health, Poplar Bluff, 1958-61; asst. health officer East Orange (N.J.) Health Dept., 1962-66; asst. regional dir. regional office VII, Office Comprehensive Health Planning, HEW, Kansas City, Mo., 1966-69; vis. faculty dept. health care adminstrn. Washington U., St. Louis, 1969-74; exec. dir. Alliance for Regional Community Health, Inc., St. Louis, 1969-76; v.p. fin. mgmt. concepts Gerald Siegel & Assos., St. Louis, 1976-81; gen. agt. Continental Assurance Co., St. Louis, 1981—. Bd. dirs. Family Planning Council, 1977-79, mem. exec. com., 1978-79. Served to 2d lt. U.S. Army, 1958-60, capt. Res., 1966-69. Mem. Am. Public Health Assn., Mo. Public Health Assn., Am. Comprehensive Health Planning Assn., St. Louis Soc. Assn. Execs. Home: 1971 Beacon Grove Saint Louis MO 63141 Office: Robert A Parker & Assos 1971 Beacon Grove Dr Saint Louis MO 63141

PARKER, ROBERT RUDOLPH, podiatrist; b. Carthage, Ill., Nov. 10, 1927; s. Elmer B. and Lena Parker; D.P.M., Ill. Coll. Podiatric Medicine, 1952; m. Beverly E. Phillipi, June 11, 1951; children—Mary Elizabeth, Robert Mitchell. Practice podiatry, Springfield, Ill., 1952—. Served with USN, 1945-46. Diplomate Am. Bd. Podiatric Medicine. Mem. Sangamon County Podiatry Soc. (pres.), Ill. Podiatry Soc. (pres. Zone III), Am. Podiatry Assn. Roman Catholic. Clubs: Am. Bus., Elks, Sangamo, Island Bay Yacht. Home: 18 W Hazel Dell Springfield IL 62707 Office: 1209 S 4th St Springfield IL 62703

PARKER, RUTH JUNE, travel co. exec.; b. Chgo., June 8, 1923; d. Thomas Donald and Clara Elizabeth (Moody) Gately; student Bryant Stratton Bus. Sch., 1942, also LaSalle Extension U., N.Y. U., U. Wis., Harvard Sch. Bus.; children—Cheryl Ann, Helen Joyce. Owner, Gifts by R. J. Fortune, Chgo., 1954-57; sales mgr. Osborne Kemper Thomas, Chgo., 1957-60; v.p. sales Salesbuilders, Inc., Chgo., 1960-63; territorial mgr. Sears Roebuck, Chgo., 1963-66; pres. Jet-a-Way, Inc., Wis., 1968-71; pres. Parker Universal Travel, Racine, Wis., 1973-76; dir. group sales Presley Tours, Inc., Belleville, Ill.,

1976—; pres. Parkinton Assos., Belleville, 1976—; coordinator real estate investment seminars; v.p. Real Estate Investors Credit Union (v.p.); lectr. to various orgns. to numerous states. Organizer pilot program Widowed Persons Service, 1977, pres., 1977-78; organizer Tours for Deaf; bd. dirs. Mo. Property and Apt. Owners, 1978-80; mem. bus. adv. council Nat. Republican Com., Washington, 1980; bd. advs. Edn. Advancement Inst. Mem. Nat. Assn. Female Execs., Bus. Advt. Council, Am. Assn. Ret. Persons, Bus. and Profl. Women, Mo. Apt. Assn., St. Louis Apt. Assn. (dir.), Internat. Platform Assn., Friends of China (coordinator tours of China). Club: Belleville Travel. Home and Office: 7 Windmill Ct Belleville IL 62221

PARKER, W. GARY, banker; b. Hattiesburg, Miss., June 26, 1944; s. Charles P. and Nell M. P.; B.S. in Bus. Adminstrn., U. Ariz., 1966; postgrad. Armstrong Coll., 1975; M.B.A. in Banking, Golden Gate U., 1978; m. Judith K. Merkle, Dec. 6, 1973; stepchildren—James, John. Area mgr. Reading Dynamics, 1966-70; sales mgr. Burroughs Corp., Oakland, Calif., 1970-74; with Bank of Am., Corp. Electronic Banking, Chgo., 1974—, sales mgr., 1980. Mem. exec. bd. Boy Scouts Am., 1978; bd. dirs. Anchorage Handicapped Workshop; fund raiser United Way; vol. worker Home for Handicapped Children. Mem. Bank Mktg. Assn., Jaycees, C. of C. Republican. Club: Toastmasters.

PARKER, WAYNE FREDERICK, heat processing equipment exec.; b. Sylvania, Ohio, Nov. 10, 1927; s. Harry Costello and Edna Johanna (Kubitz) P.; student U. Toledo, 1946-53; m. Martha M. McQuade, Sept. 21, 1973; 1 dau. by previous marriage, Sharon L.; stepchildren—Deborah L. Kelley Weisbrod, David M. Kelly, Vicki L. Kelley, Kathye A. Kelley, Bryan J. Kelley. With surface div. Midland-Ross Corp., Toledo, 1944—, beginning as draftsman, insp., successively elec. designer, elec. engr. and safety coordinator, estimator, product engr., project elec. engr., tech. service specialist, systems supr., mgr. quality assurance, 1944-77, mgr. product assurance, 1977—; lectr.; cons. product liability laws, codes, standards and interpretations. Former pres. Redeemer Lutheran Ch. Served with AUS, 1946-48. Recipient youth leadership outstanding award Jr. Achievement, 1971. Mem. Indsl. Heating Equipment Assn., Nat. Fire Protection Assn., Am. Nat. Standards Inst., Am. Gas Assn. (Hall of Flame 1975), Am. Soc. Quality Control. Clubs: Anthony Wayne Toastmasters (pres. 1965), Heather Downs Country (Toledo), Elks, Masons. Contbr. articles to trade jours. Home: 2156 Chadbury Ln Toledo OH 43614 Office: 2375 Dorr St Toledo OH 43691

PARKER, WILLIAM HOOPER, III, environ. engr.; b. Westbrook, Maine, May 4, 1937; s. William Hooper and Anne (Delaney) P.; B.S., U. Maine, 1960; M.S., Northeastern U., 1966; M.E.M., U. Detroit, 1981; m. Joan Currier, June 17, 1959; children—Laurie Jean, Michael Currier, Suzan Elizabeth, Julie Ann. Project engr. Camp Dresser & McKee, Cons. Engrs., Boston, 1962-72; v.p. Camp Dresser & McKee & CDM Internat., Boston, 1972-79; sr. v.p., regional mgr. Camp Dresser & McKee, Inc., Detroit, 1979-81, regional mgr. East Central Region, Detroit, 1981—; partner CDM/Mich. Commr., Reading Municipal Light Dept., 1973-75. Served to 1st lt. C.E., U.S. Army, 1960-62. Registered profl. engr., Mich., Ohio, Ill., Ky., Named Young Engr. of Year Mass. Soc. Prof. Engrs., 1971. Mem. ASCE, Am. Water Works Assn., Am. Public Works Assn., Nat. Soc. Profl. Engrs., Engring. Soc. Detroit, Inst. Engrs. Singapore. Republican. Roman Catholic. Club: Economic of Detroit. Home: 235 Touraine St Grosse Pointe Farms MI 48236 Office: 615 Griswold St Detroit MI 48226

PARKEVICH, TAMAR GILSON, nursing adminstr.; b. Toledo, Nov. 5, 1942; d. Richard Leland and Margaret White (Welsh) Gilson; B.S.N., Ohio State U., 1964, M.S., 1970; m. James Parkevich, Apr. 23, 1972; 1 son, James Ryan. Staff nurse Children's Hosp., Columbus, Ohio, 1964-65, clin. instr., 1965-66, evening supr., 1966, asst. dir. evenings, 1966-68, interim dir. nursing services, 1970, in-patient nursing dir., 1970-72, acting dir. nursing, 1972-73, asso. exec. dir., dir. nursing, 1973—; clin. instr. Ohio State U., Sch. of Nursing, Columbus, 1970—; adv. council Grant Hosp., Otterbein Coll. Sch. Nursing, 1979—. Volunteer, various health-related orgns. fund campaigns; adv. council Columbus Practical Sch. of Nursing, Columbus Public Schs., 1973, 74, 78, 79; adv. council Ohio Action for Newborns, 1976. Nat. Health Tng. grantee, 1968-70. Mem. Am. Soc. for Nursing Service Adminstrs. (del., health care info. exchange program to several countries 1980), Ohio Soc. for Hosp. Nursing Service Adminstrs. (sec. 1974-75), Ohio Hosp. Assn., Nat. League for Nursing, Ohio League for Nursing, Central Ohio League for Nursing (steering com., vice chmn. 1979-80), Am. Nurses Assn., Assn. for Child Care in Hosps., Ohio Action for Newborns, Columbus Hosp. Nursing Service Dirs. Assembly, Sigma Theta Tau. Contbr. articles in field to profl. jours.; co-editor, contbg. author patient edn. textbook. Home: 4390 Dublin Rd Columbus OH 43220 Office: 700 Childrens Dr Columbus OH 43205

PARKIN, EVELYN HOPE, ret. med. social worker; b. Owatonna, Minn., d. Wilbur L. and Verta (Cowles) P.; B.A., Carleton Coll., 1931; postgrad. U. Minn., 1939-41. Pediatric social worker, instr. field work U. Minn. Hosps., 1941-45; pediatric med. social worker, supr. Med. Social Service Dept., Mayo Clinic, Rochester, Minn., 1946-53, dir. Med. Social Service Dept., 1953-75, voting mem., 1972-75, emeritus staff, 1975—. Bd. dirs. Minn. Heart Assn., 1959-64; mem. nat. com. Am. Heart Assn., 1958-62; treas. Young Republican League Rochester, 1962; sec. Olmsted County Rep. Com., 1953-55; bd. dirs. YWCA, Rochester, 1953-54; sec. bd. dirs. Mayo Clinic Credit Union, 1958-65, 65-68. Mem. Nat. Assn. Social Workers (exec. com. Minn. sect. 1964-65), Minn. Welfare Conf. (sec. 1954), AAUW (asst. treas. 1953-54), Am. Hosp. Assn., D.A.R. Presbyterian. Clubs: Mayo Clinic Women's (pres. 1950-52), Carleton Coll. Alumni. Home: 502 15th Ave SW Rochester MN 55901 Office: Mayo Clinic Rochester MN 55901

PARKINSON, GEORGE AMBROSE, ednl. adminstr.; b. Columbus, Ohio, Jan. 22, 1899; s. Daniel Homer and Cynthia Catherine (English) P.; B.S., Ohio State U., 1922, M.A., 1923; postgrad. U. Chgo., 1930; Ph.D., U. Wis., 1929; m. Mildred Jane Smith, June 17, 1920 (dec.); children—Virginia Jane, George (dec.), Daniel Smith; m. 2d, Myrtle Volger, June 20, 1975. Prin., Parkinson High Sch., Zanesville, Ohio, 1916-17, Ripley High Sch., Greenwich, Ohio, 1917-18; instr. math. Worthington (Ohio) High Sch., 1921-23; instr. engring. math. U. Wis., 1923-27; asst. prof., chmn. dept. math. Milw. extension div. U. Wis., 1927-29, asso. prof., 1929-40, asst. dir. in charge evening classes, 1934-40, dir., prof., 1945-56; vice provost, dir. bus. affairs, prof. U. Wis., Milw., 1956-58; dir. Milw. Area Tech. Coll., 1958-68, dir. emeritus, cons. to bd., 1968—; cons. on evaluation manpower programs GAO, 1969—, Am. Assn. Jr. Colls.; chmn. Albert S. Puelicher Meml. Scholarship Com., 1969—. Trustee, Midwestern Ednl. TV, Inc., 1961—, v.p., 1964—; mem. policy bd. Great Plains Nat. Instructional TV Library, 1962—. Served with USN, 1918-19, 40-45. Recipient Meritorious Service award Students Milw. Tech. Coll., 1968, award of honor Wisdom Soc., 1970. Mem. SAR (bd. govs. Wis. soc. 1953—, Gold medal 1959, Patriot's medal 1972), Am. Tech. Edn. Assn. (nat. trustee 1962—), Navy League (dir. Milw. council 1947—), Am. Math. Soc., Math. Assn. Am. (chmn. Wis. sect. 1935-36), Adult Edn. Assn. U.S.A., Am. Vocat. Assn., Am. Soc. Engring. Edn., Am. Vocat. Edn. Research Assn., Assn. Pub. Sch. Adult Educators U.S., Wis. Assn. Vocat. and Adult Edn. (citation 1968), Sigma Xi, Phi Eta Sigma, Phi Delta Kappa, Pi Mu Epsilon, Gamma Alpha, Alpha Kappa Psi, Phi Theta Kappa. Presbyterian. Clubs: Univ., Press (life, Headliner award 1968), Statesmen's (Milw.); Univ. (life) (Madison, Wis.); Masons (supreme council), Shriners. Author: Vocational and Technical Education in a Decade of Change, 1974; A Brief Introduction to Analytic Geometry, 1944; (with D.S. Parkinson) Education, Man and Society, 1952; contbr. articles to profl. jours. Home: Rural Route 2 Box 662 Oostburg WI 53070 Office: 1015 N 6th St Milwaukee WI 53203

PARKS, MURRILL DOUGLAS, veterinarian; b. Chickasha, Okla., Mar. 28, 1931; s. Murrill Douglas and Dora Mae (Baker) P.; student Okla. U., 1948-49, Oklahoma City U., 1950, Oklahoma State U., 1950-51; B.S., Colo. State U., 1956, D.V.M., 1961; m. Shirley Ann Singleton, July 4, 1960; children—Douglas Craig, Bellamy Ann, James Gregory. Research and mgmt. biologist Alaska Fish and Wildlife Service, 1955-59; gen. practice veterinary medicine, Ogallala, Nebr., 1959—. Mem. Ogallala Planning Commn., 1970-71. Served with U.S. Army, 1951-54. Decorated Korea medal with 4 Bronze Stars. Mem. Am., Nebr. vet. med. assns., Beta Beta Beta, Am. 1st Day Cover Soc. Democrat. Methodist. Clubs: Rotary, Elks. Home and Office: 303 E 9th St Ogallala NE 69153

PARKS, OATTIS ELWYN, geologist; b. Atlanta; s. James E. and Jennie O. Parks; B.A. in Geology, Emory U., 1947; M.A., Tex. Christian U., 1954; m. Loretta I. Latulippe, Jan. 5, 1959; children—Oattis Elwyn, Henry B., Camilla F., Michelle M., Richard Dumais. Mem. faculty Fla. State U., 1965-67; guest lectr. U. Mass., Fla. A&M U., 1964-67; v.p. exploration and devel. AMAX Coal Co., Indpls., 1967-72; v.p. AMAX Internat., Indpls., London, 1972-74; founder, pres. NEWCO Engring. & Coal Devel. Co., Inc., Indpls., 1975—; pres. NEWSEL, Inc., Indpls., 1977—. Served to col. USAF, 1940-64; ETO. Decorated Presdl. citation, Army Commendation medal, USAF Commendation medal with 2 oak leaf clusters, D.F.C., Silver Star, Air medal with 4 oak leaf clusters. Mem. Assn. Profl. Geol. Scientists, Geol. Soc. Am., Soc. Econ. Geologists, Ind. Acad. Sci. Presbyterian. Clubs: Indpls. Athletic, Masons. Author tech. papers in field. Office: 8060 Knue Rd Suite 132 Indianapolis IN 46250

PARKS, ROBERT HILL, educator; b. Newberry, S.C., Oct. 8, 1921; s. Robert Gilbert and Lucy Suber (Hill) P.; B.S., Clemson U., 1943; M.Ed., U. Mo., Columbia, 1971, cert. specialization adult edn., 1973; children from 1st marriage—Diane R., Martin H.; children from 2d marriage—Lillian A., William A. Enlisted as pvt. U.S. Army, 1943, commd. cpl., 1943, advanced through grades to maj.; brigade exec. officer, 7th Inf. Div., Korea, 1965-66; chief, supply support services U.S. Army Electronics Support Command, Fort Monmouth, N.J., 1966-67; security, plans and ops. officer Tuy Hoa Subarea Command, Vietnam, 1967-68; exec. officer, 4th Bn., U.S. Army Sigma Corps Sch., Fort Monmouth, N.J., 1968-69; ret., 1969; tchr. Central (Mo.) Sch. Dist. R-6, 1970-71; tchr. Mo. Div. Corrections, 1973-74, vocat. edn. supr., 1974—. Decorated Bronze Star, Purple Heart, Army Commendation medal. Mem. Am. Vocat. Assn., Nat. Employment and Tng. Assn., NRA, (life), Ret. Officers Assn., Mo. Correction Assn. Baptist. Club: United Sportsmens. Home: Route 7 Chateau Villa 30 Jefferson City MO 65101 Office: 911 Missouri Blvd Jefferson City MO 65101

PARKS, THOMAS AQUINAS, mfg. co. exec.; b. Cleve., Nov. 4, 1929; s. Jonathan B. and Marian Mae (Campbell) P.; B.A., State U. Iowa, 1954; postgrad. U. Ill., 1965; m. Judith Fausch; children—David Jonathan, Sandra Anne. Dept. head internat. sales div. Collins Radio Co., Cedar Rapids, Iowa, 1954-58; asst. export sales mgr. Amana Refrigeration, Inc. (Iowa), 1958-62; export sales mgr. Cedar Rapids Engring. Co., 1962-64, gen. sales mgr., 1964-65, v.p. sales, dir., 1966-68, pres., 1968—; pres. Kwik-Way Industries, 1969—; pres. Kwik-Way Ltd. (Can.), 1969—; chmn., dir. Line-O-Tronics Inc., 1972—; chmn. bd. Material Products Co., Rock Island, Ill., 1972—; dir. A/L Sports, Inc., Chgo. Fgn. affairs speaker Speakers Bur., Cedar Rapids C. of C., 1958—, chmn. Fgn. Trade Bur., 1956-62, bd. dirs., 1974-77; council v.p. Boy Scouts Am., 1976—; trustee Cedar Rapids Children's Home, 1974—, Coe Coll., 1977—; bd. dirs. Cedar Rapids Symphony Assn., 1975-77. Served with USAF, 1951-53. Republican. Club: Cedar Rapids Country. Home: Timberlake Estates Swisher IA 52338 Office: 701 American Bldg Cedar Rapids IA 52401

PARKS, WILLIAM ROBERT, univ. adminstr.; b. Lincoln County, Tenn., Oct. 13, 1915; s. Benjamin N. and Minnie A. (Taylor) P.; B.A., Berea Coll., 1937, LL.D. (hon.), 1966; M.A., U. Ky., 1938, D.Sc. (hon.), 1973; Ph.D., U. Wis., 1948; LL.D., Drake U., 1968; L.H.D., Westmar Coll., 1968; m. Ellen R. Sorge, July 1, 1940; children—Andrea, Cynthia. Economist bur. agrl. econs. Dept. Agr., 1940-48; prof. govt. Iowa State Coll., 1948-56; prof. agrl. econs. U. Wis., 1956-58; dean of instrn. Iowa State U., 1958-61; v.p. academic affairs, 1961-65, pres., 1965—. Cons. TVA, part-time 1956-57, also Dept. Interior; dir. Northwestern Bell Telephone Co., Central Life Assurance Co. Trustee Coll. Retirement Equity Fund, U. of Mid-Am. Served to lt. (j.g.) USNR, 1943-46. Mem. Assn. Am. Univs. (pres. 1977, chmn. 1978), Mid-Am. State Univs. Assn. (pres. 1965), Nat. Assn. State Univs. and Land Grant Colls. (pres. 1973). Contbr. articles to profl. jours. Home: The Knoll Iowa State U Ames IA 50010

PARMATER, JOHN ROGER, marine contractor; b. Lansing, Mich., Jan. 9, 1941; s. John Lioneland Beatrice (Algate) P.; B.S. in Civil Engring., U. Colo., 1965; m. Mary Catherine Holmes, July 11, 1959; children—Tama, Troy. Engr., Caterpillar Tractor Co., Peoria, Ill., 1965-67; gen. mgr. United Glazed Products Co., Lansing, Mich., 1967-71; with Bultema Dock & Dredge Co., Muskegon, Mich., 1971—, exec. v.p., 1979-80, pres., dir., 1980—; pres., dir. La Crosse Dredging Co., Muskegon, 1980—; v.p., dir. Bultema Marine Transp. Co., Canonie-Bultema Pacific Corp.; dir. Canonie Constrn. Co. Mem. ASCE, Soc. Naval Architects and Marine Engrs., Marine Tech. Soc., Nat. Assn. Dredging Contractors, Young Pres.'s Orgn. Clubs: Muskegon Country, West Shore Tennis, Century. Home: 438 Melody Ln North Muskegon MI 49445 Office: 559 E Western Ave Muskegon MI 49443

PARMER, DAN GERALD, veterinarian; b. Wetumpka, Ala., July 3, 1926; s. James Lonnie and Virginia Gertrude (Guy) P.; student Los Angeles City Coll., 1945-46; D.V.M., Auburn U., 1950; m. Donna Louise Kesler, June 7, 1980; 1 son, Dan Gerald; 1 dau. by previous marriage—Linda Leigh. Gen. practice vet. medicine, Galveston, Tex., 1950-54, Chgo., 59—; staff veterinarian Chgo. Commn. Animal Care and Control, 1974—; tchr. Highlands U., 1959. Served with USNR, 1943-45; PTO; served as staff veterinarian and 2d and 5th Air Force veterinarian chief USAF, 1954-59. Recipient Veterinary Appreciation award U. Ill., 1971. Mem. Ill. (chmn. civil def. and package disaster hosps. 1968-71), Nat., Chgo. (bd. govs. 1969-72, 74—, now pres.-elect), South Chgo. (pres. 1965-66) veterinary med. assns., Am. Animal Hosp. Assn. (dir.), Ill. Acad. Vet. Practice, Nat. Assn. of Professions, Am. Assn. Zoo Veterinarians, Am. Assn. Zool. Parks and Aquariums, VFW. Democrat. Clubs: Masons, Shriners, Kiwanis, Midlothian Country, Valley Internat. Country. Discoverer Bartonellosis in cattle in N.Am. and Western Hemisphere, 1951; co-developer bite-size high altitude in-flight feeding program USAF, 1954-56. Address: 7953 S Cicero Ave Chicago IL 60652

PARR, THOMAS CHARLES, retail exec.; b. Mansfield, Ohio, May 29, 1942; s. Robert Fredrick and Dorothy Pauline (Hassinger) P.; student public schs. Columbus, Ohio; m. Jane Elaine Kropp, Feb. 17, 1963; children—Connie Sue, Thomas Andrew. Dept. mgr. IGA, Columbus, Ohio, 1958-66; firefighter Upper Arlington Fire Div., Columbus, Ohio, 1966—, paramedic coordinator, 1979—; pres. Parr Emergency Product Sales, Inc., Galloway, Ohio, 1974—. Recipient World Champion 1st Aid Competition team award, 1973; named Franklin County Fireman of Yr., 1974, Central Ohio Heart Assn. Vol. of Yr., 1974. Mem. Ohio Assn. Emergency Med. Services (pres. 1975-79), Nat. Assn. Emergency Med. Technicians. Lutheran. Home and Office: 6106 Bausch Rd Galloway OH 43119

PARRISH, BARRY JAY, advt. agy. exec.; b. Chgo., Sept. 3, 1946; s. Hy J. and Shirley F. (Fimoff) Perelgut; B.A., Columbia Coll., 1968; M.B.A., U. Chgo., 1971; 1 son, Jeffrey Scott. Asst. advt. mgr. Libby McNeill & Libby, Chgo., 1965-67; creative dir./account exec. Bozell & Jacobs, Chgo., 1969-72; account supr. Dailey & Assos., San Francisco, 1972-75; v.p./account supr. internat. Arthur E. Wilk Advt., Chgo., 1975-76; exec. v.p. Shaffer/MacGill & Assos., Chgo., 1976—; TV commls. judge CLIO awards, 1978, 79, U.S. Film Festival, 1980. Served with USMC, to 1972. Recipient awards Houston Internat. Film Festival, Nat. Employment Assn., others. Mem. Am. Mgmt. Assn., Chgo. Council on Fgn. Relations, Art Inst. Chgo., Lincoln Park Zool. Soc. Club: Chgo. Advertising. Contbr. articles to profl. jours., newspapers, mags. Home: 210 E Pearson St Chicago IL 60611 Office: Shaffer/MacGill & Assos 410 N Michigan Ave Chicago IL 60611

PARRISH, JAMES HILLIARD, librarian; b. Nashville, May 23, 1926; s. Joseph Warren and Katherine (Cooper) P.; B.S., Middle Tenn. State U., 1953; M.L.S., George Peabody U., 1955. Spl. student asst. Vanderbilt U. Med. Library, Nashville, 1953-55; circulation, reference librarian U. Tenn., Martin br., 1955-57; reference librarian Air U., Maxwell AFB, Ala., 1957-60, Sch. Aerospace Medicine, San Antonio, 1960-63; head library services NASA Tech. Library, Houston, 1963-64; asst. med. librarian U. Ky., Lexington, 1964-66; acting dir. Falk Library, U. Pitts., 1967-68, asst. librarian, 1966-67; librarian Hawaii Med. Library, Honolulu, 1969-71; prof., coordinator for extramural programs U. Ill. Med. Center, Library of Health Scis., Chgo., 1971—; invited speaker 4th Internat. Congress on Med. Librarianship, Belgrade, Yugoslavia, 1980. Served with USNR, 1944-46, 50-52. Mem. Spl. Libraries Assn., Med. Library Assn., AAUP. Home: 4235 N Keeler St Apt 1C Chicago IL 60641 Office: 1750 W Polk St Chicago IL 60612

PARRISH, JIM W., lawyer; b. Great Bend, Kans., Aug. 25, 1946; s. Clement Crane and Ruth Elizabeth (Cox) P.; A.A., Pratt (Kans.) Community Jr. Coll., 1967; B.S., Kans. State U., 1970; J.D. cum laude, Washburn U., 1973; m. Nancy Elaine Buchele, Jan. 31, 1970; children—Leslie, Tyler. Admitted to Kans. bar, 1973; mem. Kans. Ho. of Reps., 1973-74; mem. Kans. Senate, 1975-80, asst. minority leader, 1977-80; exec. v.p., dir. devel., sec., gen. counsel Show Biz Pizza Place, Inc., 1980—; corp. sr. v.p. Brock Hotel Corp., 1981—; partner firm Colmery, McClure, Funk, Letourneau & Entz, Topeka, 1978—. Served with USAR, 1970-79. Mem. Kans. Bar Assn., Topeka Bar Assn., Sigma Delta Chi. Democrat. Office: 2209 W 29th St Topeka KS 66611

PARRISH, MATTHEW DENWOOD, mental health adminstr.; b. Washington, Apr. 1, 1918; s. Forrest Denwood and Alice Lorena (Flynn) P.; B.A., U. Va., 1939; M.D., George Washington U., 1950; m. Marilyn Kay Parrish; children—Denwood, John, Stephen, Megan. Intern, Letterman Gen. Hosp., San Francisco, 1951; psychiat. resident Walter Reed Gen. Hosp., Washington, 1954; commd. officer U.S. Army, advanced through grades to col., 1967; div. psychiatrist, Korea, 1954-55, U.S. Army Dispensary, Yokohama, 1955-56; chief psychiatrist, Ft. Belvoir, Va., 1956-60; asst. chief psychiatrist Office Army Surgeon Gen., 1960-62; chief psychiat. service U.S. Army Hosp., Frankfurt am Main, 1962-65; chief psychiatry dept. Walter Reed Army Inst. Research, Washington, 1965-67; chief psychiatrist for combat theatre, Viet Nam, 1967-68; chief psychiatrist Office Army Surgeon Gen., Washington, 1968-70; psychiat. cons. Blackman's Devel. Center, Washington, 1969-72; cons. Md. Drug Abuse Program, Va. Dept. Vocat. Rehab., Fairfax, 1969-72; tng. program exec. Ill. Dept. Mental Health and Developmental Disabilities, Chgo., 1972—; supt. Singer Zone Center, Rockford, Ill., 1974—; clin. prof. psychiatry Abraham Lincoln Sch. Medicine, U. Ill., Chgo., 1973-77, Rockford Sch. Medicine, 1978—. cons. Ch. of Jesus Christ of Latter-day Saints, Potomac Stake, Washington, 1969-75. Mem. governing bd. Family Services, Alexandria, Va., 1959-62. Served with U.S. Army, 1941-45. Decorated Air medal with oak leaf, Legion of Merit with oak leaf. Fellow Am. Psychiat. Assn.; mem. Am. Soc. Group Psychotherapy and Psychodrama, Soc. Med. Cons. to Armed Forces, Assn. Mil. Surgeons. Editor-in-chief U.S. Army Vietnam Med. Jour., 1967-68. Home: 1854 Telemark Dr Rockford IL 61108 Office: 4402 N Main St Rockford IL 61103

PARRISH, NANCY ELAINE BUCHELE, educator, state senator; b. Cedar Vale, Kans., Nov. 9, 1948; d. Julian Milton and Vergie May (Bryant) Buchele; B.S. in Edn., Kans. State U., 1970; M.S. in Spl. Edn., U. Kans., 1974; m. James Wesley Parrish, Jan. 31, 1970; children—Leslie Elgin, Tyler Jonathan. Tchr., Topeka Public Schs., 1970-75; spl. edn. tchr. Topeka State Hosp., 1975-81; mem. Kans. Senate, 1980—; mem. edn. task force Council of State Govts., 1981—. Bd. dirs. Mental Health Assn., Topeka, Boys Club, Topeka; mem. East Topeka Council on Aging; bd. advisors Sch. of Future. Mem. Order Women Legislators, NEA, Council for Exceptional Children, LWV. Democrat. Office: Room 403 State Capitol Bldg Topeka KS 66612

PARROTT, LAVERNE WILLIAM, air and hydraulic cylinders mfg. co. ofcl.; b. Jackson, Mich., May 31, 1928; s. Albert Asahel and Pearl Agnes (Marshall) P.; student Jackson Community Coll., 1976-77; m. Lorraine Emma Hall, Oct. 18, 1947; children—James William, Diana Lynn Parrott Midgley, Brad Charles, With Union Steel Co., Albion, Mich., 1946-54, Decker Nut Mfg. Co., Albion, 1954-59; with Tomkins-Johnson Co., Jackson, 1959—, asst. foreman, 1971—, quality control supr., 1975—. Pres. North Parma (Mich.) Cemetery Assn., 1977—; active North Parma Meth. Ch., 1981—. Mem. Am. Soc. Quality Control, Am. Soc. Non-Destructive Testing. Clubs: Oddfellows, Moose, Rebekahs. Home: 10750 Maines Rd Parma MI 49269 Office: 2425 W Michigan St Jackson MI 49202

PARSON, ROBERT EUGENE, JR., statistician, research systems analyst; b. East Chicago, Ind., May 30, 1950; s. Robert Eugene and Mary (Pazdur) P.; B.S. in Chemistry and Biochemistry, Purdue U., 1972; M.S. in Stats. and Applied Math., Rochester Inst. Tech., 1978; m. Maureen B. Gelfand, Apr. 11, 1977; 1 son, Sean Michael. Research scientist Pharm. div. Pennwalt Corp., Rochester, N.Y., 1972-78; research systems analyst Genesee Computer Co., Rochester, 1978-79; mgr. analytic systems group Office Public Policy Analysis, Am. Hosp. Assn., Chgo., 1979-81; staff analyst resource utilization unit, bus. systems ops. Allstate Ins. Co., Northbrook, Ill., 1981—. Mem. Inst. Math. Stats., Am. Statis. Assn., Am. Soc. Quality Control, Soc. Indsl. and Applied Math., Am. Chem. Soc., Biometry Soc. Home: 6915 Hawthorne Ln Hanover Park IL 60103 Office: Allstate Ins Co Allstate Plaza CO6 Northbrook IL 60062

PARSONS, DANA LEE, lawyer; b. Sedalia, Mo., Feb. 4, 1941; d. Gilbert Leroy and Erna Verna (Steiner) Parsons; B.A., U. Mo., Kansas City, 1963, M.A., 1965, J.D., 1976; 1 son, Charles Dana. Admitted to Mo. bar, 1977; faculty Kans. State U., Pittsburg, 1965-66, Kennedy Coll., Wahoo, Nebr., 1967-68, U. Nebr., Omaha, 1968-71; tchr. Kansas City (Mo.) Sch. Dist., 1977-78; atty. Blue Cross-Blue Shield, 1978—; individual practice law, Kansas City, 1977—. Mem. Fed., Mo., Kansas City bar assns., AAUW, NOW, Kansas City Assn. Women Lawyers, LWV. Club: Altrusa. Home and Office: 409 W 90th St Kansas City MO 64114

PARSONS, FREDERICK AMBROSE, educator; b. Mpls. Feb. 21, 1916; s. Olof and Volborg (Anderson) P.; B.E., St. Cloud State Coll., 1939; postgrad. Colo. U., 1941; M.A., U. Minn., 1947, Ed.S., 1970; m. Margaret C. Anderson, June 20, 1943; children—Gretchen, Mark, Christine. Tchr., Delano (Minn.) High Sch., 1940-43, prin., 1943-47; supt. schs. Delano, 1947—. Mem. Am., Minn., assns. sch. adminstrs., Met. Supts. Assn., U. Minn. Alumni Assn., Tau Kappa Alpha, Kappa Delta Pi, Phi Delta Kappa. Mason. Address: Delano MN 55328

PARSONS, FREDERICK MILLER, real estate exec.; b. Pen Argyle, Pa., Feb. 21, 1918; s. Lyonal George and Winifred (Miller) P.; student Wharton Sch., U. Pa., 1935-36, Churchman Bus. Coll., 1936-39; m. Marjorie Edith Strout, Feb. 22, 1941; children—Lyona Kay, Adrienne Lee. Sec., Parsons Bros. Slate Co., 1946-51; judge Minor Jud. Ct., Northampton County, Pa., 1951-57; propr. tax rep., chief appraiser Bethlehem Steel Corp., 1957-67; mgr. property taxes U.S. Gypsum Co., 1967-73; mgr. internat. real estate and property taxes Morton-Norwich Products, Inc., Chgo., 1973—; lectr. in field. Served with U.S. Army, 1943-45; PTO. Mem. Internat. Assn. Assessing Officers, Nat. Assn. Property Tax Reps. (cert.), Indsl. Devel. Research Council. Methodist. Club: River Forest Golf. Home: 155 N Harbor Dr Chicago IL 60601 Office: 110 N Wacker Dr Chicago IL 60606

PARSONS, JAMES BENTON, fed. judge; b. Kansas City, Mo., Aug. 13, 1911; s. James Benton and Maggie (Virgia) P.; A.B., James Millikin U., 1934; M.A., U. Chgo., 1946, LL.D., 1949; also hon. degrees; m. Amy Maxwell, Dec. 24, 1952 (dec.); 1 son, Dieter K. Faculty, Lincoln U. Mo., 1934-40, asst. to dean of men, instr. polit. sci., acting head music dept., 1938-40; supr. pub. schs., Greensboro, N.C., 1940-42; faculty John Marshall Law Sch., Chgo.; asst. corp. counsel City of Chgo., 1949-51; asst. U.S. atty., Chgo.; judge Superior Ct. of Cook County, Ill., 1960-61; judge U.S. Dist. Ct., No. Dist. of Ill., Chgo., 1961—, chief judge, 1977—. Active Boy Scouts Am., mem. nat. exec. bd., mem. adv. bd. Reading Research Found.; mem. citizens com. U. Ill., Champaign; mem. pres.'s council St. Ignatius Coll. Prep. Sch., Chgo.; mem. centennial anniversary com. Loyola U., Chgo.; hon. chmn. Chgo. Conf. on Religion and Race and Tri-Faith Employment Ser.; exec. bd. Chgo. Community Music Found.; adv. bd. Ill. Masonic Hosp., Chgo. Trustee Millikin U., Decatur, Ill., Ada S. McKinley Community Sers.; bd. dirs. Harvard-St. George Sch., Chgo., Leukemia Research Found., Chgo., Mercy Halfway House Corp., Chgo.; nat. bd. trustees NCCJ. Home: 2801 King Dr Chicago IL 60616 Office: US Dist Ct US Courthouse 219 S Dearborn St Chicago IL 60604*

PARSONS, JAMES FREDERICK, mfg. co. exec.; b. N.Y.C., Feb. 8, 1920; s. James Franklin and Anne Marie (McGill) P.; M.E., Stevens Inst. Tech., 1942; m. Adrienne M. Morris, Dec. 16, 1944; children—Edwina Mary, Meredith Ann, Adrienne Mary. Gen. sales mgr. Econ. Machinery Co., Worcester, Mass., 1952-62; v.p. mktg. George J. Meyer Mfg. Co., Milw., 1962-68; pres. SS Systems div. ATO, Inc., Milw., 1968-75; v.p., gen. mgr. Simplicity Engring. Co., Durand, Mich., 1975-79; group v.p. Gen. Steel Industries, Inc., St. Louis, 1980—; cons. Counselor, Jr. Achievement, 1969-70; chmn. fin. lay com. Milw. Roman Catholic Archdiocese, 1970-71. Served with USN, 1942-45; PTO. Registered profl. engr., Mass. Mem. Packaging Inst., Am. Foundrymen's Assn., Conveyor Equipment Mfrs. Assn., Inst. Scrap Iron and Steel. Clubs: Univ. (Milw.): Oakland Hills Country. Home: 2627 Covington Pl Birmingham MI 48010 Office: PO Box 566 Birmingham MI 48012

PARSONS, JOANNE HUNTER, home economist, educator; b. Greene County, Iowa, June 20, 1952; d. Floyd Clare and Wilma Irene (Clipperton) Hunter; B.S. in Home Econs. Edn. with high distinction, Iowa State U., 1974; postgrad. in counseling and religion N.Am. Bapt. Sem., 1976, United Theol. Sem., New Brighton, Minn., 1977; M.A. in Home Econs. Edn., U. Minn., 1980, postgrad., 1980—; m. Mark Hunter Parsons, Aug. 16, 1975. Cons., instr. nutrition edn. workshops various schs. and agys., Iowa, Kans., Utah, Israel, Minn., 1972—; tchr. home econs. Mpls. Public Sch., 1974-76, curriculum developer and evaluator, 1979-80; project coor., Vocat. Parent and Family Edn. Network, Minn. Tech. Inst., 1981-82; Family Educator, Family Sev. of Greater St. Paul, 1982—; edn. dir. and youth coordinator United Meth. Ch., Fairfax, Minn. and Presbyn. Ch., Worthington, Minn., 1976-78; grad. asst. U. Minn., 1978-81; lectr. home econs. edn. U. Wis.-Stout, Menomonie, fall 1979; intern Minn. Senate, 1978; intern, cons. Pillsbury Co., Mpls., 1981; teaching asso. in home econs. edn. U. Minn., St. Paul, 1980—. Del. to Democratic-Farm-Labor Party dist. conv., 1980; 4-H leader, 1974-76; adult and family ministries coordinator Lino Lakes Meth. Ch., 1981-82. Recipient Outstanding All-U. Sr. award Iowa State U. Alumni, 1974; Minn. Home Econs. Assn. scholar, 1978-79; U.S. Office Edn. fellow, 1978-81. Mem. Am. Home Econs. Assn., Minn. Home Econs. Assn. (chmn. public affairs com.), Am. Vocat. Assn., Soc. Nutrition Edn., Council on Anthropology and Edn., Mortar Bd., Phi Delta Kappa, Phi Upsilon Omicron, Pi Lambda Theta, Alpha Lambda Delta, Kappa Delta Pi, Omicron Nu, Phi Kappa Phi, Gamma Sigma Delta. Democrat. Methodist. Home: 7500 Lake Dr Lino Lakes MN 55014

PARSONS, KEITH I., lawyer; b. Davenport, Iowa, Apr. 28, 1912; s. Alfred and Cora Pearl (McDowell) P.; Ph.B., U. Chgo., 1933, J.D., 1937; m. Lorraine Watson, June 28, 1939; children—Robert, Susan, James. Asst. to sec. U. Chgo., 1934-37; admitted to Ill. bar, 1938, since practiced in Chgo. asst. chief, later chief legal div. Chgo. Ordnance Dist., 1942-46; partner firm Milliken, Vollers & Parsons, 1946-64; partner firm Ross, Hardies, O'Keefe, Babcock & Parsons, 1965—. Mem. Hinsdale (Ill.) Bd. Edn., 1957-63, pres., 1959-63; mem. Chgo. Crime Commn., 1960—; mem. citizens bd. U. Chgo., 1964—. Mem. bd. govs. Ill. State Colls. and Univs., 1970-73. Served to lt. col. AUS, 1942-46. Mem. Am., Ill., Chgo. (past chmn. corp. law com.; mem. bd. mgrs. 1967-69) bar assns., Econ. Club Chgo., Law Club, Legal Club (past pres.), Phi Beta Kappa, Psi Upsilon. Clubs: Chicago, University, Commonwealth (Chgo.); Hinsdale Golf; Chikaming Country (Lakeside, Mich.). Office: One IBM Plaza Chicago IL 60611

PARSONS, PETER PEABODY, automobile co. exec.; b. Lock Haven, Pa., Aug. 3, 1930; s. Frederick Henry and Elizabeth Tracy (Peabody) P.; B.M.E., Lehigh U., 1953; postgrad. (Sloan program fellow) Stanford U., 1968: m. Antoinette Frances Schultes, June 5, 1971; 1 son, Jeffrey Michael; children by previous marriage—Janet Elizabeth, Sally Mary, Diane Jean. With Fisher Body div. Gen. Motors Corp., Warren, Mich., 1953—, sr. engr. in charge, 1977—. Mem. Soc. Automotive Engrs., Am. Soc. Body Engrs. Republican. Home: 2459 Chelsea Ln Troy MI 48084 Office: 30001 Van Dyke St Warren MI 48090

PARSONS, SAMUEL DALE, agrl. engr.; b. Brazil, Ind., Sept. 4, 1939; s. Ray Edison and Vera Pauline (Ames) P.; B.S., Purdue U., 1961; M.S., Cornell U., 1964; Ph.D., Mich State U., 1975; m. Jane Ann Evans, June 11, 1961; children—Samuel Dale, William E. Design engr. Cummins Engine Co., Columbus, Ind., 1961-63; extension agr. engr. Purdue U. and Coop. Extension Service, Lafayette, Ind., 1964—, asso. prof. dept. agrl. engring., 1975—; cons. various agrl. equipment firms. Mem. Am. Soc. Agrl. Engrs., Am. Forage and Grassland Council, Sigma Xi, Tau Beta Pi, Gamma Sigma Delta, Epsilon Sigma Phi. Office: Agrl Engring Dept Purdue U Lafayette IN 47905

PARTAIN, CARL STANLEY, optometrist; b. Harrisburg, Ill., May 16, 1942; s. Carl and Mary Agnes (Stanley) P.; student U. Ill., 1960-62; O.D., Ill. Coll. Optometry, 1965; m. Judith Ann Lawson, Oct. 29, 1967; children—Joe, Jonathan, Jill. Practice optometry, Flora, Ill., 1965-66, Hoopeston, Ill., 1970—. Served with AUS, 1967-68. Mem. Am., Ill., Eastern Ill. (pres. 1973) optometric assns., Hoopeston C. of C., Hoopeston Jr. C. of C. (dir. 1971). Home: 827 E Maple St Hoopeston IL 60942 Office: Rural Route 3 851 E Orange St Hoopeston IL 60942

PARTENHEIMER, ALBERT PHILLIP, camera repair shop propr., acct.; b. Huntingburg, Ind., Oct. 29, 1928; s. William G. and Helen L. (Gumz) P.; B.S. in Mktg., U. Evansville, 1950; grad. with honors Nat. Camera Repair, Englewood, Colo., 1962; m. Lillian Walter Keach, June 7, 1950; children—Lillian Kay Partenheimer Freschly, Emma Lou Partenheimer Bednarik. Pres., founder Camera Engrs. Corp. Inc., 1962-71; owner, operator Al Partenheimer Camera Repair, Evansville, Ind., 1971—, also engring. plant acct. So. Ind. Gas & Elec. Co., Evansville, 1972—. Served with Army N.G., 1948-50. Mem. Soc. Photo Technicians. Mem. United Ch. of Christ. Home and Office: 1850 Lodge Ave Evansville IN 47714

PARTYKA, LEONARD ROLFE, wire and cable co. exec.; b. Chgo., Sept. 30, 1945; s. Leonard F. and Beverly (Rolfe) P.; B.S., So. Ill. U., 1968, M.B.A., 1970; m. Barbara K. Berube, May 14, 1966; children—Holly Rae, Cortney Quinn. Research asst. Bur. Bus. Research, So. Ill. U., 1968-70; Mktg. mgr. corporate services Continental Ill. Nat. Bank & Trust Co., Chgo., 1970-72; dist. sales mgr. Dearborn Wire & Cable Co., Rosemont, Ill., 1972-76, nat. sales mgr., 1976-78, v.p. sales and mktg., 1978. Mem. Pi Sigma Epsilon. Office: Dearborn Wire & Cable Co 9299 Evenhouse Ave Rosemont IL 60018

PARZEN, PHILIP, educator; b. Tussyn, Poland, June 28, 1916; s. Samuel and Sarah (Getzel) P.; B.S. in Physics, Coll. City N.Y., 1939; M.S. in Physics, N.Y. U., 1946, Ph.D. in Applied Math, 1953; m. Trude Rosenthal, Aug. 7, 1949; children—Stanley, Julia. Dir. research Parzen Assos., Mineola, N.Y., 1957-60; chief space physics Republic Aviation, Farmingdale, N.Y., 1960-62; staff engr. Astro Electronics div. RCA, Princeton, N.J., 1962-68; pvt. cons., Princeton, 1968-69; prof. info. engring. U. Ill. Chgo. Circle, 1969—. Asst. scoutmaster George Washington council Boy Scouts Am., Princeton, 1962-64. Mem. IEEE (sr.), Pi Mu Epsilon. Contbr. articles to profl. jours. Patentee in field.

PASCAL, HAROLD SAUNDERS, health care exec.; b. Coffeyville, Kans., Mar. 16, 1934; s. Michael William and Jacqueline V. P.; B.S., So. Meth. U., 1956; M.B.A., Ga. So. U., 1973; m. Dinah L. Filkins, Aug. 13, 1955; children—Lee Ann, Tracey Michele. Commd. 2d. lt. U.S. Army, 1957, advanced through grades to maj., 1967; served med. service dept.; asso. exec. dir. Gen. Hosp., Humana Inc., Ft. Walton Beach, Fla., 1974-75, adminstr. Sarasota (Fla.) Palms Hosp., 1975-76, exec. dir. Llano (N.Mex.) Estacado Med. Center, 1976-77; pres. Americana Hosp. Co. (Cenco Inc.), Monticello, Ill., 1977-80, Continental Health Care Ltd., 1980—. Pres. PTA, San Antonio, 1969-70; bd. dirs. NE Sch. Dist., San Antonio, 1968-69; dir. community blood drive, San Francisco, 1964-65. Decorated Bronze Star, Air Medal, Purple Heart, Cross of Gallantry, Combat Med. Badge. Mem. Am. Coll. Hosp. Adminstrs., Am. Acad. Med. Adminstrs., Am. Hosp. Assn., Am. Soc. Hosp. Engrs., Ill. Hosp. Assn., Fla. Hosp. Assn., Fedn. Am. Hosps. (dir.), Psi Chi. Presbyterian. Clubs: Hunter Riding (pres., 1972-73), Rotary, Toastmasters. Author: Plight of the Migrant Worker, 1974; Installation Supply Procedures, 1968; programmed text on Supply Procedures, 1969; Dictionary of Supply Terms, 1969. Home: 10 S 321 Jaime Ln Hinsdale IL 60521 Office: 101 N Scoville Oak Park IL 60302

PASCHAL, WILLIAM BARRON, mech. engr.; b. Chgo., Feb. 26, 1948; s. William Kiernan and Sophie Marie (Kaczmar) P.; B.S. in Mech. Engring., U. Ill., Chgo., 1971; m. Rosanne A. Pancerz, May 27, 1972. Project engr. Sherwin Stenn Engrs. Inc., Chgo., 1969-76; project supr. heating, ventilating and air conditioning Sargent and Lundy Engrs., Chgo., 1976—; cons. on bldg. design and constrn. to architects and owners. Registered profl. engr., Ill. Mem. ASME, Am. Soc. Heating, Refrigerating, Air Conditioning Engrs., Am. Nuclear Soc., Ill. Soc. Radiologic Technologists. Roman Catholic. Home: 1725 Taylor St Downers Grove IL 60516 Office: 55 E Monroe St Chicago IL 60603

PASCHKE, ED F., artist, educator; b. Chgo., June 22, 1939; s. Edward and Waldrine (Mackiewicz) P.; B.F.A., Sch. Art Inst. Chgo., 1961, M.F.A., 1970; m. Nancy E. Cohn, Nov. 22, 1968; children—Marc, Sharon. Chmn. art dept. Northwestern U., Evanston, Ill.; exhibited in major mus., U.S., Europe. Served in U.S. Army, 1962-64. Office: Dept Art Northwestern U Evanston IL 60201

PASCOE, BRIAN JOSEPH, design spray finishing systems co. exec.; b. Tacoma, Aug. 1, 1947; s. Raymond F. and Margaret M. Pascoe; student U. Wis. Whitewater, 1965-72; brokers lic. Wis. Sch. Real Estate, 1972; m. Mary A.J. Jackson, Aug. 26, 1967; 1 son, Joseph. Research asst. RBP Chem., Milw., 1968-77; partner Acme Finishing Equipment, Inc., Milw., 1977—; owner Broker's Assos. Realty, Delafield, Wis., 1973—; pres. AFE Chemicals, Inc., Milw. Alderman for 1st Ward, Delafield, 1977—. Mem. Delafield C. of C. (pres. 1978, Man of Yr. 1979). Roman Catholic. Club: Delafield-Summit Lions (v.p. 1977-79, pres. 1980). Home: W 36 Main St Delafield WI 53018 Office: 4940 N 32d St Milwaukee WI 53018

PASCOE, PERCY WILLARD, JR., editor; b. Little Rock, Jan. 31, 1930; s. Percy Willard and Oma Mae (Grizzle) P.; student pub. schs., Little Rock, St. Louis; m. Delma Lucille Huff, Sept. 27, 1967. Founder editor Cuba (Mo.) Free Press, 1960—. Served with USAF, 1951-55. Recipient Tilghman Cloud Meml. Editorial award Mo. Press Assn., 1975, Best Editorial Page award, 1975; Best Advt. Idea award Met. Newspaper Services, 1975; Best Investigative Story, 1979; Best Front Page, 1980; 1st Place award for gen. excellence. Mem. Mo. Press Assn. (Blue Ribbon Newspaper award 1968, 72), Mo. Ad Mgrs. (pres. 1976-77), Nat. Newspaper Assn. (Blue Ribbon awards 1975-82), Soc. Profl. Journalists, Sigma Delta Chi. Democrat. Mem. Ch. of Christ. Home: Route 2 Cuba MO 65453 Office: 110 S Buchanon St Cuba MO 65453

PASEK, MICHAEL ANTHONY, computer technologist; b. Duluth, Minn., Sept. 5, 1951; s. Antone William and Helene (Tunsky) P.; ed. pub. schs., tech. schs. and colls. Operator, Bd. Pensions, Lutheran Ch. in Am., 1973-75; corp. mgr. Microtex Corp., Cloquet, Minn., 1975-79; v.p. internat. ops. Microtex Corp., Mpls., 1979-81, pres., 1981—; systems programmer NCR Comten, Inc., 1977-80, supr./sr. systems programmer, network software devel., 1980—; mem. Data Communications Adv. Panel. Home: 9741 Foley Blvd NW Coon Rapids MN 55433 Office: 2700 N Snelling Roseville MN 55113

PASKY, ROBERT, III, educator; b. Detroit, Sept. 14, 1950; s. Robert and Ruth Virginia (Moirn) P.; B.A., Wayne State U., 1972, M.Ed., 1977; postgrad. U. Conn., 1978-80; m. Karen P. Nowakowski, Jan. 21, 1977; children—Catherine Leigh and Jennifer Leigh (twins). Tchr., Detroit pub. schs., 1973-76; acad. service officer, curriculum designer Dept. Family Medicine, Wayne State U., Detroit, 1977-78; dir. curriculum and evaluation Dept. Family Medicine U. Conn., Storrs, 1978-80; asst. to dir. family practice and dir. behavioral sci. Dept. Family Medicine, Rockford (Ill.) Sch. Medicine, U. Ill., 1980—; ednl. cons.; pvt. practice family therapy, Rockford, 1978—; adj. faculty Detroit Coll. of Bus. 1977-78, St. Joseph Coll., Conn., 1978-79, Post Coll., Conn., 1979-80, Central Conn. State Coll., 1979-80, Kiswaukee Coll., Ill., 1980—. Wayne State U. grad. profl. scholar, 1975-77. Mem. Am. Assn. Higher Edn., Assn. for Supervision and Curriculum Devel., Am. Edn. Research Assn., Soc. Tchrs. Family Medicine, Phi Delta Kappa. Republican. Presbyterian. Contbr. articles to profl. jours. Home: 1012 Nassau Pkwy Rockford IL 61107 Office: 1601 Parkview Ave Rockford IL 61101

PASSALACQUA, SALVATORE ANTHONY, mfg. co. exec.; b. Wyandotte, Mich., Apr. 26, 1949; s. Joseph and Nancy Mary (Randazzo) P.; B.B.A., Eastern Mich. U., 1971; m. Susan M. Vettraino, Oct. 26, 1973; children—Marc, Jason, Nicholas. Supr., Touche Ross, Detroit, 1971-77; controller, v.p. fin., treas., Jack Haines, Detroit, from 1977, now v.p., gen. mgr. C.P.A., Mich. Mem. Am. Inst. C.P.A.'s, Mich. Soc. C.P.A.'s, Detroit Tooling Assn. Republican. Roman Catholic. Clubs: Recess; Detroit Athletic. Office: 2761 Stair St Detroit MI 48209

PASSMAN, RICHARD HARRIS, educator; b. Providence, Sept. 22, 1945; s. Carl and Ruth Ilse (Oberlander) P.; B.A., Brown U., 1967; M.A., Temple U., 1970; Ph.D., U. Ala., 1972; m. Jane Aline Horvitz, June 22, 1969; children—Elana, Joshua. Intern in clin. psychology U. Minn., 1972; instr. psychology U. Ala., Tuscaloosa, 1971; asst. prof. psychology U. Wis.-Milw., 1972-78, asso. prof. 1978—; dir. psychol. services Head Start, Pawtucket, R.I., 1968; psychol. cons., staff child psychology instr. Head Start, Providence, 1969; dir. psychol. services Head Start, East Providence-Bristol County, R.I., 1969; staff psychologist U. Ala. Psychology Clinic, 1971. Bd. dirs. Milw. Mental Health Assn. USPHS fellow U. Ala., 1969-71, NIMH fellow U. Minn., 1971-72. Mem. Am., Midwestern psychol. assns., Soc. Research in Child Devel. Contbr. articles to profl. jours. Home: 310 E Calumet Rd Fox Point WI 53217 Office: Psychology Dept U Wis Milwaukee WI 53201

PASZYNA, SISTER MARY ANNELLE, nun, occupational therapist; b. Chgo., Jan. 24, 1947; d. Walter Frank and Bernice Mary (Pozniak) P.; A.A., Felician Coll., 1968; B.S., Mt. Mary Coll., 1972. Joined Felician Sisters, Roman Cath. Ch., 1965; tchr. elementary sch., 1968-69; nursing asst. Our Lady of Good Counsel Infirmary, Chgo., 1969-70, activity dir., 1972-74; occupational therapist St. Mary's Home for the Aged, Manitowoc, Wis., 1974—; mem. adv. com. Lakeshore Tech. Inst., 1976-78. Registered occupational therapist. Mem. Am. Occupational Therapy Assn., Wis. Occupational Therapy Assn. Address: 2005 Division St Manitowoc WI 54220

PATACH, DOROTHY MARIE, nurse, educator; b. Omaha, Dec. 4, 1923; d. John Charles and Marie (Satorie) P.; diploma in nursing U. Nebr., 1944, B.S. in Home Econs., 1968; B.S. in Nursing, U. Omaha, 1956, M.S. in Nursing Edn., 1961. Asst. supr., clin. instr. operating rooms U. Nebr. Sch. Nursing and Hosp., 1945-48; instr., operating room supr. Bishop Clarkson Meml. Hosp. and Sch. Nursing, Omaha, 1949-55; instr. Jennie Edmundson Meml. Hosp. Sch. Nursing, Council Bluffs, Iowa, 1956-59; head dept. nursing and med. tech. U. Omaha, 1959-70; asst. prof., asst. to dean Coll. Arts and Scis. for coordination nursing and allied health edn. U. Nebr., Omaha, 1970—. Recipient recognition for vol. continued edn. Nebr. Nurses Assn., 1974-76, 76-78. Mem. Am. Nurses Assn., Nat. League Nursing, AAUP, AAUW, AAAS, U. Nebr. Coll. Nursing Alumni Assn., Tri Beta, Kappa Delta Pi. Republican. Club: U. Nebr. Faculty Women. Contbr. articles to profl. newsletters and jours. Home: 1822 N St Omaha NE 68107 Office: U Nebr at Omaha Allwine Hall 212 60th and Dodge Omaha NE 68182

PATALANO, FRANK ANTHONY, ins. co. exec.; b. Bellows Falls, Vt., Dec. 6, 1941; s. Giro Raphael and Giavanna (Muscemici) P.; student U. Md., 1962-64; B.S., U. Vt., 1967; M.B.A., U. Chgo., 1976; m. Gladys Rushing, July 21, 1962; children—Rhonda, Stephanie. Jr. mfg. engr. IBM, Essex Junction, Vt., 1967; asst. dir. planning-budgeting systems State of Vt., Montpelier, 1967-68; exec. dir. Ark. Planning Commn., State of Ark., Little Rock, 1968-71; dir. Office of Planning and Analysis, State of Ill., Springfield, 1971-73; exec. asst. to chmn. CNA Financial Corp., Chgo., 1973-75; exec. asst. to chmn. CNA Ins. Cos., 1975-76, v.p. group ops., 1976-78, v.p. services, 1978-80, v.p. profl. liability div., 1980—. Mem. Chgo. Crime Commn., 1974—; trustee Ill. 2000 Found., 1979-80. Served with USAF, 1959-64. Mem. Ill. Coll. Podiatric Medicine (trustee). Republican. Roman Catholic. Home: 3818 Russett Ln Northbrook IL 60062 Office: CNA Plaza Chicago IL 60685

PATCHAK, RUSSELL GEORGE, accountant; b. Chgo., Oct. 10, 1924; s. Joseph E. and Wilhelmina (Washack) P.; B.S. in Bus. Adminstrn., Northwestern U., 1949; C.P.A., U. Ill., 1951; m. Mary Ann Koler, Apr. 26, 1947; children—Randall Richard, Debra Sue. With George W. Peterson & Co., C.P.A.'s, Chgo., 1949-51, Peter Shannon & Co., C.P.A.'s, Chgo., 1951-55; pvt. practice as accountant, Chgo. and Homewood, Ill., 1955—; partner Milano-Patchak & Co., C.P.A.'s, Chgo., 1963-65, Ash Investments, Homewood, 1963—; pres. R. Patchak & Co., Ltd., Homewood, 1977— dir. various corps. Served with AUS, 1943-46. Mem. Am. Inst. C.P.A.'s, Ill. Soc. C.P.A.'s, C.P.A.'s of So. Cook County (pres. 1963-64), Computer Accountants Assn. Home: 15305 Aubrieta Ln Orland Park IL 60462 Office: Profl Arts Bldg 18227 Harwood Ave Homewood IL 60430

PATEL, DAKSHA ASHOK, neonatologist; b. Baroda, India, Mar. 28, 1941; d. Madhukant Natwarlal and Manjulaben Madhukant Mehta; B.S., M.B., Bombay U., 1965; m. Ashok R. Patel, Nov. 7, 1965; children—Ashlesha, Urjeet. Intern, Mercy Hosp., Buffalo, 1965-66; resident in pediatrics E.J. Meyer Meml. Hosp., Buffalo, 1967; resident in pediatrics and neonatology Cook County Hosp., Chgo., 1968-70; clin. asso. prof. Loyola U., Chgo., 1981—; neonatologist Columbus Hosp., Chgo., 1972—, co-dir. nursery, 1979—; mem. staff Children's Meml. Hosp., Chgo., 1981—. Fellow Am. Acad. Pediatrics. Home: 1900 N Hudson St Chicago IL 60614 Office: 2520 N Lakeview St Chicago IL 60614

PATEL, DILIPKUMAR GORDHANBHAI, physician; b. Nairobi, Kenya, Feb. 13, 1948; s. Gordhanbhai L. and Kamlaben G.; came to U.S., 1971, naturalized, 1977; M.D., Baroda Med. Coll., 1971; m. Surjeet Risam, Sept. 22, 1972; children—Roopal, Hiten. Intern,

Mercy Hosp. and Med. Center, Chgo., 1972, resident in internal medicine, 1973-75, chief resident, 1974-75; practice medicine, specializing in internal medicine, Elmhurst and Oak Park, Ill., 1975—; attending staff dept. medicine W. Suburban Hosp., Oak Park, 1975—, also Meml. Hosp. DuPage County, Elmhurst. Diplomate Am. Bd. Internal Medicine. Mem. AMA, Ill. Med. Soc., Chgo. Med. Soc., ACP, Am. Soc. Internal Medicine. Office: 135 S Kenilworth Elmhurst IL 60126 also 126 E Vallette St Elmhurst IL 60126

PATEL, JAYANT AMBALAL, pharmacist; b. Indore, India, May 23, 1935; s. Ambalal Jeshingbhai and Hiraben Ambalal P.; came to U.S., 1959, naturalized, 1973; B.S. in Chemistry, U. Saugor, 1957, in Pharmacy, 1958; M.S., U. Mich., 1961, Pharm.D., 1966; m. Kala Jashbhai, May 28, 1954; children—Visha, Neeta, Rita, Manish. Pharmacist, Ernest Labs., India, 1958-59, U. Mich., Ann Arbor, 1961; pharmacist, dir. drug analysis lab. Univ. Hosp., Ann Arbor, 1964—. Recipient grant Roche Co., 1969, Achievement award Am. Soc. Hosp. Pharmacists Research Edn. Found., 1976; registered pharmacist, Mich. Mem. Am. Soc. Hosp. Pharmacists (contbg. editor jour.), AAAS, Rho Chi. Hindu. Home: 474 Larkspur St Ann Arbor MI 48105 Office: 1601 Ann St Ann Arbor MI 48109

PATEL, LOKANATH, metall. and materials engr.; b. Kuntara, India, June 1, 1943; s. Kamal Lochan and Khatkuri (Nayak) P.; came to U.S., 1969, naturalized, 1977; B.S., Utkal U., 1965; B.S., Indian Inst. Tech., 1968; M.S., U. Tenn., Knoxville, 1981; M.S., Va. Poly. Inst., 1973; m. Basanti Patel, Jan. 9, 1969; children—Veena, Suman Kumar. Materials and processes engr., nuclear power generation div. Babcock & Wilcox Co., Lynchburg, Va., 1973-75; materials and metal. engr. John Deere & Co., Moline, Ill., 1977—. ASG Glass Industries fellow, 1971-73; Nat. Merit scholar, 1961-68. Mem. Am. Soc. Metals, Am. Inst. Mining Metall. Engrs., Am. Welding Soc., Am. Ceramic Soc. Contbr. articles to profl. jours. Home: 611 E 5th St Coal Valley IL 61240 Office: Deere & Co Plow & Planter Works 501 3d Ave Moline IL 61265

PATEL, MEHROO MINOO, physician; b. Bombay, India, May 5, 1930; d. Kavasji Shapurji and Dina Kavasji (Nania) Kanga; M.B.B.S., U. Bombay, 1955; M.S., 1961; m. Minu Kaikhashru Patel, Mar. 6, 1967; children—Cyrus, Deena. Research asso. in surg. research Hektoen Inst., Chgo., 1967-69; research and edn. asso. West Side VA Hosp., Chgo., 1970-71; asso. prof. Malcolm X Coll., Chgo., 1971-72; staff physician Portes Center Prevention Center, Chgo., 1972—; research asst. prof. surgery Med. Sch. U. Ill., Chgo., 1969—, asst. prof. dept. public health Coll. Nursing, 1977—. Diplomate Am. Bd. Family Practice. Fellow Royal Coll. Surgeons Edinburgh, Am. Acad. Family Physicians; mem. AMA, Ill. Med. Soc., Chgo. Med. Soc., Am. Acad. Family Physicians. Mem. Zoroastrian Assn. Chgo. Office: 33 W Huron St Chicago IL 60610

PATEL, PRAVINCHANDRA VALLABHBHAI, microbiologist; b. Ahmedabad, India, Sept. 1, 1935; d. Vallabhbhai Lallubhai and Sakerben Vallabhbhai P.; came to U.S., 1970; B.S. in Microbiology, Gujarat U., India, 1957, M.S. in Indsl. Microbiology, 1959; Ph.D. in Applied Microbiology, U. Strathclyde, Glasgow, Scotland, 1968; m. Joti Patel, Feb. 2, 1964; children—Hitashvi, Preya. Microbiologist, Alembic Chem. Works Co., Baroda, India, 1959-65; research fellow McMaster U., Hamilton, Ont., Can., 1969-71; bacteriologist No. Ohio Med. Lab., Cleve., 1972-74; clin. microbiologist Woman's Gen. Hosp., Cleve., 1974—. Can. NRC research fellow, 1969-71. Mem. AAAS, Am. Soc. Microbiology, Am. Acad. Microbiology, Soc. Indsl. Microbiology. Home: 1632 Joann Dr Parma OH 44134

PATEL, VIRENDRA CHATURBHAI, engineer; b. Mombasa, Kenya, Nov. 9, 1938; s. Chaturbhai S. and Kantaben N. (Rai) P.; came to U.S., 1969, naturalized 1975; B.Sc., with honors, Imperial Coll., London, 1962; Ph.D., Cambridge (Eng.) U., 1965; m. Manjula Patel, May 29, 1966; children—Sanjay, Bindiya. Sr. asst. in research Cambridge U., 1965-69; vis. prof. Indian Inst. Tech., Kharagpur, India, 1966; cons. Lockheed Ga. Co., Marietta, 1969-70; asst. prof. energy engring. U. Iowa, Iowa City, 1971-72, asso. prof., 1972-75, prof., 1975—, chmn. div. energy engring., 1976—, chmn. mech. engring. program, 1979—, research engr. Iowa Inst. Hydraulic Research, 1971—; vis. prof. U. Karlsruhe (Ger.), 1980-81; cons. in field; mem. Iowa Gov.'s Science Adv. Council, 1977—. Recipient Sr. U.S. Scientist award Alexander von Humboldt Found., 1980-81. Mem. AIAA, Internat. Towing Tank Conf. (resistance com. 1978—), ASME, Sigma Chi, Pi Tau Sigma. Author: Three Dimensional Turbulent Boundary Layers, 1972; contbr. articles to profl. jours. Home: 1212 Teg Dr Iowa City IA 52240 Office: Div Energy Engring Univ Iowa Iowa City IA 52242

PATERSON, PHILIP Y., physician; b. Mpls., Feb. 6, 1925; s. Donald Gildersleeve and Margaret (Young) P.; B.S., U. Minn., 1946, M.B., 1947, M.D., 1948; m. Virginia Lee Bray, Mar. 22, 1947; children—Anne, Peter, Benjamin. Intern, Mpls. Gen. Hosp., 1948-49; research fellow div. infectious diseases Tulane U. Sch. Medicine, 1949-50, instr. medicine, Am. Heart Assn. research fellow, 1950-51; Am. Heart Assn. research fellow dept. microbiology U. Va. Sch. Medicine, 1953, asst. resident and co-resident in medicine univ. hosp., 1953-55, asst. prof. microbiology, instr. medicine, established investigator Am. Heart Assn., 1955-57; med. officer Lab. Immunology, Nat. Inst. Allergy and Infectious Diseases, NIH, Bethesda, Md., 1957-60; vis. asst. prof. microbiology N.Y. U., 1957-60, asso. prof. medicine, 1960-65; asso. prof. medicine, dir. Samuel J. Sackett Research Labs. and chief sect. infectious diseases, dept. medicine Northwestern U., 1965-66, Samuel J. Sackett prof. medicine and chief infectious diseases, hypersensitivity sect., dept. medicine Northwestern U.-McGaw Med. Center, 1966-72, Samuel J. Sackett prof. medicine and microbiology, chief infectious diseases, hypersensitivity sect., 1972-75, prof. microbiology-immunology, chmn. dept. microbiology-immunology Northwestern U. Med. and Dental Schs., 1975—; Christine Larsen lectr. Sch. Medicine, Albuquerque, 1973; Disting. lectr. Ann. Meeting, Assn. Am. Physicians and Western sect. Am. Fedn. Clin. Research, Carmel, Calif., 1974; Grace Faillace Meml. lectr. Leo Goodwin Inst. Cancer Research, Nova U., 1978; Ernest Witebsky Meml. lectr. 6th Internat. Convocation on Immunology, Niagara Falls, N.Y., 1978; Joseph E. Smadel Meml. lectr. Ann. meeting, Infectious Diseases Soc. Am., Atlanta, 1978; mem. drug evaluation com. Nat. Multiple Sclerosis Soc., 1973—; mem. immunol.-microbiol. research study com. Am. Heart Assn., 1978-81; mem. internat. med. adv. bd. Internat. Fedn. Multiple Sclerosis Socs., 1973—; mem. adv. panel Am. Bd. Med. Lab. Immunology, 1978—; cons. Gt. Lakes Naval Base, Ill., 1967-74. Served to capt. M.C., USAR, 1951-53. Mem. Am. Fedn. Clin. Research, AAAS, Am. Soc. Microbiology. Am. Assn. Immunologists, Harvey Soc., Am. Soc. Clin. Investigation, Infectious Diseases Soc. Am. (Gold medal 1978), Central Soc. Clin. Research, Am. Rheumatism Assn., Assn. Am. Physicians, Am. Clin. and Climatol. Assn., Sigma Xi, Alpha Omega Alpha. Editor and contbg. author: (with others) The Biological and Clinical Basis of Infectious Diseases, 1975, 2d edit., 1980; contbr. numerous articles, chpts. and revs. on neuroimmunology, host-parasite interactions and infectious diseases to profl. jours.; mem. editorial bd. Procs. Soc. Exptl. Biology and Medicine, 1968-73, 1977—, Cellular Immunology, 1969—, Infection and Immunity, 1970—, Clin. and Exptl. Immunology, 1970—, Clin. Immunology and Immuno-pathology, 1978—, Jour. Clin. and Lab. Immunology, 1979—, Jour. Immunology, 1981—; asso. editor Jour. Infectious Diseases, 1979—. Office: 303 E Chicago Ave Chicago IL 60611

PATHAK, DEV S., mktg. analyst, educator; b. Ahmedabad, India, Nov. 18, 1942; s. Shankerlal C. and Champa S. (Raval) P.; came to U.S., 1965, naturalized, 1975; LL.B., Gujarat U., India, 1965; M.S. in Econs., So. Ill. U., 1966; M.B.A. in Mktg., Mich. State U., 1969, D.B.A., 1972; m. Diane L. Dallas, Nov. 21, 1970; 1 son, Jay Ryan. Instr. Saginaw Valley Coll., University Center, Mich., 1970-71, asst. prof., 1971-73; asst. prof. Phila. Coll. Textiles and Sci., also dir. Inst. Research in Textile Mktg., 1973-74; asso. prof. Appalachian State U., Boone, N.C., 1974-76, asso. dir. Bur. Econ. and Bus. Research, 1975-76; asso. prof. pharmacy adminstrn. dept. Ohio State U., Columbus, 1976-78; prof. pharmacy adminstrn. U. Ill. Med. Center, Chgo., 1978-80; prof. and chmn. pharmacy adminstrn., prof. mktg. Ohio State U., Columbus, 1980—; mktg. cons. Fla. Internat., Whirlpool, Inc., Second Nat. Bank of Saginaw, Walgreen Drug Stores, Health Info. Design, Inc. Mem. Acad. Mgmt., Assn. Consumer Research, Am. Pharm. Assn., Am. Mktg. Assn., Am. Assn. Colls. Pharmacy, Am. Inst. Decision Scis. (acad. affairs com. 1975-77), Am. Soc. Hosp. Pharmacists. Author: Marketing Professional Pharmacy Services; Student Involvement Guide to Accompany Marketing Principles: The Management Process, 1977; contbr. articles to profl. publs. Home: 7739 Strathmore Rd Dublin OH 43017 Office: Coll Pharmacy Ohio State U 500 W 12th Ave Columbus OH 43210

PATNAUDE, RAYMOND FRANCIS, JR., mfg. co. exec.; b. South Ind., Mar. 6, 1947; s. Raymond Francis and Beulah Irene (Biddle) P.; A.B., U. Notre Dame, 1969; M.A., 1971; M.S. in Bus. Adminstrn., Ind. U., 1978; m. Dianne Peczkowski, Aug. 24, 1968; children—Raymond III, Courtney. Tchr., St. Mary's Assumption Sch., South Bend, 1969-70, St. Monica's Sch., Mishawaka, Ind., 1970-71, Stanley Clark Sch., South Bend, 1971-73; asst. dir. safety Tucker Freight Lines Inc., South Bend, 1974-75, dir. personnel, 1975-79; mgr. indsl. relations Garden City Fan, Niles, Mich., 1979—. Mem. Am. Soc. Personnel Adminstrs. Home: 21326 Teton Ct South Bend IN 46628 Office: 1701 Terminal Rd Niles MI 49120

PATRICH, BERMA RUTH, counselor; b. Granite City, Ill., Nov. 23, 1937; d. Hayden Brildon and Pearl Eva (Tate) Atchley; B.A., So. Ill. U., Edwardsville, 1975, M.S. (grad. asst. 1976), 1977, Ed.S., 1979; m. John Mitchell Patrich, Feb. 6, 1954; children—Joy Darlene, Fay Marlene, Paul Mitchell. Various sales and office positions, 1955-59; research staff asst. Ednl. Opportunity Center, St. Louis, 1976-77, counselor, 1977-81; coordinator transfer services St. Louis U., 1981—. Pres. King s Daus. Women's Missionary Council, First Assembly of God Ch., Granite City, 1955. Mem. Am. Personnel and Guidance Assn., Nat. Employment Counselor Assn., Consortium Vocat. Edn. and Employers. Democrat. Home: 2109 Dawn Pl Granite City IL 62040 Office: St Louis Univ Saint Louis MO 63103

PATRICK, ELIZABETH MILLER, ednl. adminstr.; b. Lorain, Ohio, Jan. 6, 1925; d. John Stewart and Rubie Ann (Moore) Miller; student Ohio Wesleyan U., 1941-42; B.S., N.Y. Coll. Tchrs., Buffalo, 1945; M.A., No. Mich. U., 1970; postgrad. Wayne State U., 1971, So. Ill. U., 1970, 73; m. Bruce W. Patrick, Feb. 28, 1948; children—Ralph Stewart, Margaret Ann. Tchr. home econs. Kenmore (N.Y.) Jr. High Sch., 1945-48; co-owner, co-operator Patricks Landing Resort and Boat Shop, Cedarville, Mich., 1948—; tchr. secondary and elem. classes Les Cheneaux Schs., Cedarville, 1962-70; curriculum resource cons. Eastern Upper Peninsula Intermediate Sch. Dist., Sault Ste. Marie, Mich., 1970-72; dir. Regional Ednl. Media Center 22, Sault Ste. Marie, 1972—; sec. Regional Ednl. Media Center Adv. Council, 1972—; sec. Profl. Devel. Adv. Council, 1980; coordinator Profl. Devel. for Eastern Upper Peninsula Tchrs. Mem. Les Cheneaux Community Schs. Bd. Edn., 1958-62, pres., 1959-62. Mem. Nat. Assn. Regional Media Centers, Mich. Intermediate Media Assn. (sec. 1979-80), Mich. Assn. Media in Edn., Assn. Supervision and Curriculum Devel., Assn. Ednl. Communication and Tech., Les Cheneaux Hist. Soc., Alpha Delta Kappa. Mem. Cedarville Union Ch. Club: Les Cheneaux Yacht. Home: 1 Park Ave Cedarville MI 49719 Office: Eastern Upper Peninsula Intermediate Sch Dist PO Box 883 Armory Pl Sault Sainte Marie MI 49783

PATRICK, JOHN JOSEPH, educator; b. East Chicago, Ind., Apr. 14, 1935; s. John W. and Elizabeth (Lazar) P.; A.B., Dartmouth Coll., 1957; Ed.D., Ind. U., 1969; m. Patricia Grant, Aug. 17, 1963; children—Rebecca, Barbara. Social studies tchr. Roosevelt High Sch., East Chicago, 1957-62, Lab. High Sch., U. Chgo., 1962-65 research asso. Sch. Edn., Ind. U., Bloomington, 1965-69, asst. prof., 1969-74, asso. prof., 1974-77, prof. edn., 1977—; bd. dirs. Biol. Scis. Curriculum Study, 1980—; ednl. cons. Mem. Nat. Council Social Studies, Assn. Supervision and Curriculum Devel., Social Sci. Edn. Consortium, Council for Basic Edn., Soc. History Edn., Phi Delta Kappa. Author: Progress of the Afro-American, 1968; The Young Voter, 1974; (with L. Ehman, Howard Mehlinger) Toward Effective Instruction in Secondary Social Studies, 1974; (with R. Remy) Civics for Americans, 1980; (with Mehlinger) American Political Behavior, 1972. Home: 3512 Westminster Way Bloomington IN 47401 Office: 513 N Park St Bloomington IN 47401

PATRICOLO, JOHN ANDREW, recruiting and mgmt. cons. co. exec.; b. Detroit, Mar. 2, 1948; s. Andrea and Carole Emily (Sinelli) P.; B.A., Wayne State U., 1970. Chief counselor Bendix Field Engring., Detroit, 1970-72; personnel analyst, supr. records mgmt. Blue Cross of Mich., Detroit, 1973-76, asst. mgr. claims pricing, 1976-77; recruitment mgr. Campbell-Ewald Advt. Co., Detroit, 1977-81; personnel dir. Sandy Corp., Southfield, Mich., 1977—; pres. RMC Assos., Inc., recruiting and mgmt. cons. co., Southfield, 1981—. Chmn. citizens adv. bd. Oakland County Community Coll., 1974-78. Mem. Am. Records Mgmt. Assn. (program chmn. 1974-75, v.p. 1975-76, pres. 1977-78). Home: 2296 Rose St Howell MI 48843 Office: Suite 132 Harvard Plaza 29350 Southfield Rd Southfield MI 48076

PATRICOSKI, THOMAS STANLEY, physician; b. Mt. Carmel, Pa., May 8, 1932; s. Peter Paul and Ellen (De Manincor) P.; B.S., St. Vincent Coll., 1959; M.D., Jefferson Med. Coll., 1963; m. Marie L. Andruscauage, Oct. 24, 1953; children—Paul, Michael, Ann, Christopher, Matthew, Amy, Joseph, Eve, Joy. Intern, Little Co. of Mary Hosp., Evergreen Park, Ill., 1963-64; practice medicine specializing in family medicine, Chgo., 1974—; sr. attending physician Little Co. Mary Hosp., 1964—, chmn. dept. family practice, 1972-77, pres. staff, 1980—, sr. attending mem. dept. family practice St. George Hosp., Chgo., 1969-72; sr. attending dept. family practice Palos Community Hosp., Palos Heights, Ill., 1972—, chmn. dept., 1979—. Served to 1st lt. Med. Service Corps, U.S. Army, 1952-57. Diplomate Am. Bd. Family Practice, Am. Bd. Med. Examiners. Fellow Am. Acad. Family Physicians; mem. AMA, Ill., Chgo. (pres. Calumet br. 1971) med. socs., Cath. Physicians Guild, Ill. Acad. Family Physicians (pres. Beverly chpt. 1974—), N.W.T. Med. Assn., A. Louis Rosi Med. Soc. (Guadalajara, Mex.). Club: Salon Unltd. Home: 12210 S 86th Ave Palos Park IL 60464 Office: 3754 W 95th St Evergreen Park IL 60642

PATTERSON, AMOS CLEVELAND, educator; b. Sallisaw, Okla., Nov. 2, 1942; s. Grover Cleveland and Ruby Louise (Cameron) P.; B.S., Ind. U., 1969, M.S., 1971, Ed.D., 1980; m. Elaine Stein, June 22, 1974; 1 dau., Amy Yvonne. Quality control technician Gen. Motors Co., Indpls., 1962-64, Chrysler Corp., Kokomo, Ind., 1964-67; dir. instructional services and devel., Ind. State Univ., Bloomington, 1969-74; mem. faculty U. Toledo, Ohio, 1974—, prof. ednl. tech., 1974—, chmn. dept., 1974—; internat. cons. tng. and human resources devel., 1969-81; speaker field ednl. tech., 1972—. Active 4-H Youth programs, Fulton County, Ohio. Recipient Merit award in profl. devel. Assn. Ednl. Communications and Tech., 1979; Outstanding Tchr. award U. Toledo, 1980. Mem. Ohio Ednl. Library Media Assn. (dir., pres.), Assn. Ednl. Communications and Tech. (mem. com.), Nat. Soc. Performance and Instrn., Am. Soc. Tng. and Devel., Assn. Supervision and Curriculum Devel., Nat. Marine Edn. Assn., Phi Delta Kappa, Am. Contract Bridge League. Democrat. Contbr. numerous articles to various publs. Home: Route 1 Box 185 Metamora OH 43540

PATTERSON, C. RICHARD, jeweler, gemologist; b. Garden City, Kans., May 18, 1939; s. Orville Merritt and Bessie Pauline (Chuesberg) P.; student U. Kans., 1957-59; B.S. in Bus. Adminstrn., Kans. State U., 1961; grad. Gemological Inst. Am., 1966; m. Marcia Jo Allen, Apr. 5, 1975; 1 dau., Somer Lee. Sec., treas. William V. Thompson Co., Kansas City, 1961-62; sec., treas. Patterson Jewelry, Inc., Garden City, 1962-76, chief exec. officer, 1976—; pres. Patterson Mfg. Co., Garden City, 1973—, Carriage Diamond Services, Inc., Garden City, 1980—. Bd. dirs. Miss Kans. Scholarship Pageant, 1964-71; bd. dirs. YMCA, Garden City, 1974-75. Mem. Am. Gem Soc. (cert., recipient Golden Loupe award 1970), Am. Jewelry Designers Guild, Gemmological Assn. Great Britain, Retail Jewelers Am., Kans. Retail Jewelers, Jewelers Vigilance Com., Jewelry Industry Council. Republican. Clubs: Elks, Masons. Research on colored stones, cubic zirconia as a diamond imitation. Office: 318 N Main St Garden City KS 67846

PATTERSON, GLORIA JEAN, counselor; b. Toledo, Nov. 18, 1941; d. Joseph Bankert and Wilhelmina (Pistole) Sprinkle; B.A., Olivet Nazarene Coll., 1965; M.Ed. in Counseling, U. Toledo, 1975; m. Charles Leon Patterson, Oct. 1, 1966. Tchr., Toledo Pub. Schs., 1963-64, substitute tchr., 1970-75; tchr. Mason (Mich.) Consol. Schs., 1964-66; job developer Concentrated Employment Program, Toledo, 1968-70; counselor St. Joseph Central Catholic High Sch., Fremont, Ohio, 1976-78, Fassett Jr. High Sch., Oregon, Ohio, 1978-79; edn. coordinator Grace Community Center, Toledo, 1979—. Adv. sr. scouts Maumee Valley council Girl Scouts U.S.A. Mem. Am., Ohio personnel and guidance assns., Am. Sch. Counselor Assn., NAACP. Methodist. Home: 3134 Kimball Ave Toledo OH 43610

PATTERSON, HARLAN RAY, educator; b. Camden, Ohio, June 27, 1931; s. Ernest Newton and Beulah Irene (Hedrick) P.; B.S., Miami U., 1953, M.B.A., 1959; Ph.D., Mich. State U., 1963; m. Carol Lee Reighard, July 31, 1970; children—Kristan Lee, Elizabeth Jane (previous marriage), Leslie, Nolan Gene. Asst. prof. finance U. Ill. at Urbana, 1962-66; asso. prof. finance Ohio U., Athens, 1966-77, prof., 1977—; fin. cons. Research projects for Bank of Am., Morgan Guaranty Trust, Am. Investment Corp., City Pub. Service Bd. of San Antonio. Chmn. Athens Adv. Bd., Ohio State scholarship com. of Rainbow for Girls. Served as officer USN, 1953-56. Stonier fellow, 1961; Found. Econ. Edn. fellow, 1965, 67, 69, 71; vis. prof., fellow Chgo. Merc. Exchange, 1971. Mem. Phi Beta Kappa, Beta Gamma Sigma, Phi Eta Sigma, Omicron Delta Epsilon, Pi Kappa Alpha, Alpha Kappa Psi. Republican. Mason (32 deg., Shriner). Contbr. articles in field to profl. and acad. jours.

PATTERSON, HARRY OSCAR, educator; b. Omaha, Feb. 1, 1919; s. Harry Oscar and Viva (Mills) P.; A.B., U. Omaha, 1940; M.A., U. Nebr., 1951; Ed.D., Wayne State U., 1964; m. Annette Montgomery, June 30, 1946; children—Nancy Gail, Jody Lynn. Asst. prof. Baldwin-Wallace Coll., 1949-52; research asst. Standard Oil of Ohio, 1952-53; prof. psychology Gen. Motors Inst., Flint, Mich., 1953—. Served with U.S. Navy, 1942-46. Lic. psychologist, Mich. Mem. Am. Psychol. Assn., N. Central Reading Assn. (chmn. bd. dirs.), Biofeedback Soc. Mich., Am. Soc. Clin. Hypnosis. Home: 5069 Shady Oak Trail Flint MI 48504 Office: 1700 W 3d Ave Flint MI 48502

PATTERSON, JAMES D'WOLF, advt. co. exec.; b. Evanston, Ill., July 23, 1944; s. John Graham and Elizabeth D'Wolf (Archer) P.; B.A., Brown U., 1966; m. Pamela Lynn Resnik, Aug. 11, 1973. Account exec. Tatham, Laird & Kudner, Chgo., 1967-72, Grey-North, Chgo., 1972-74, Earle Ludgin, Chgo., 1974-76; account supr. Bozell & Jacobs, Chgo., 1976-77; account exec. Leo Burnett Co., Inc., 1977—. Bd. dirs. St. Leonards House, 1975—. Home: 3228 N Volz Dr W Arlington Heights IL 60004 Office: Leo Burnett Co Inc 1 Prudential Plaza Chicago IL 60601

PATTERSON, LARRY GEORGE, hosp. adminstr.; b. Iola, Kans., June 1, 1934; s. Dwight Burdett and Lois Valentine (Steele) P.; B.S., Iowa U., 1956; M.S., Northwestern U., 1963; m. Nola Maye Smith, Aug. 19, 1955; children—Sharon Lynn, Karen JoAnn. Commd. 2d lt. U.S. Army, 1956, advanced through grades to lt. col., 1980, ret., 1981; hosp. adminstr. Graham County Hosp., Hill City, Kans., 1980—. Active City Council, sch. bd.; bd. dirs. Health Systems Agy. III. Decorated Navy Cross. Recipient Marine and Sailors medal. Fellow Am. Coll. Hosp. Adminstrs.; mem. Am. Hosp. Assn., Kans. Hosp. Assn. Clubs: Elks, Lions, Res. Officers Assn., VFW (service officer, chmn. emergency med. service Region 5), Am. Legion. Home: 1015 W McFarland Dr Hill City KS 67642 Office: 304 Prout Hill City KS 67642

PATTERSON, LLOYD WILLIAM, air force officer; b. Britton, S.D., July 4, 1946; s. Chester Addison and Viola Marie (Hatch) P.; student Falcon Air-to-Air Missile Sch., Lowry AFB, Colo., 1964-65, extension U. Alaska, 1966; B.S., U.S. Air Force Acad., 1970; student Basic Flying Tng., Vance AFB, Okla., 1970-71, Upgrade Flying Tng., Eglin AFB, Fla., 1971, Castle AFB, Calif., 1972-73, Squadron Officer Sch., Maxwell AFB, Ala., 1976; M.A. in Communication Studies with distinction, Calif. State U., Sacramento, 1979; grad. Def. Info. Sch., Ft. Benjamin Harrison, Ind., 1979, Air Command and Staff Coll., Wright-Patterson AFB, Ohio, 1980; m. Sharon Ann Decker, June 4, 1970; children—Christine Joy, Shelly Ann, Brian Scott. Served as enlisted man U.S. Air Force, 1964-66, commd. 2d lt., 1970, advanced through grades to maj., 1981; served as reconnaissance pilot Nakhon Phanom Royal Thai AFB, Thailand, 1971-72; assigned to Beale AFB, Calif., 1972-78, wing duty controller, 1976-78; public affairs officer Hdqrs. Air Force Logistics Command, chief div. community relations, Wright-Patterson AFB, 1979-80, public affairs office Hdqrs. Air Force Logistics Command, chief spl. projects div., 1980-81; chief public affairs Air Force Acquisition Logistics div., Wright-Patterson AFB, 1981—. Scoutmaster Troop 2 Buttes Area council Boy Scouts Am., 1974-76; media center chmn., mem. Dayton (Ohio) Air Fair Com., 1980-81; Lead singer Kingdom Quartet gospel quartet, Enon, Ohio, 1980-81; mem. Nat. Collegiate Championship Skeet Team in Am. Style Skeet, 1969; mem. 2d Pl. Internat. Style Skeet Team, 1969; mem. Nat. Collegiate Championship Skeet Team in Internat. Style Skeet, 1970; mem. 1st Pl. Postal Div. Skeet Team for Assn. Coll. Unions Intercollegiate Tournaments, 1970. Decorated D.F.C., Air medal with 2 oak leaf clusters, Air Force Commendation medal (U.S.); Cross of Gallantry with palm, (Republic of Vietnam). Mem. Air Force Assn. (life; jr. officer adv. council exec. com.), Assn. Grads. USAF Acad., Am. Def. Preparedness Assn., Nat. Assn. Underwater Instrs., Profl. Assn. Diving Instrs., Calif. Assn. Four Wheel Drive Clubs Inc., Sacramento Valley Varmints Four Wheel Drive Club (sgt. at arms 1977, pres. 1978, safety officer 1979). Club: Wright-Patterson AFB Aero (dir.). Mem. Ch. of Christ. Home: 2635 Fowler Rd Springfield OH 45502 Office: AFALD/PA Wright-Patterson AFB OH 45433

PATTERSON, LUCILLE JOAN, author, lyricist, educator; b. Chgo.; d. William Leon and Hortense Adele (Brooks) Washington; B.A., DePaul U., 1962; M.A., Northeastern Ill. U., 1973; m. Owen J. Patterson II, June 17, 1956 (div.); children—Karin Janine, Owen Jeremiah III. Tchr. English, speech, Spanish, journalism and Afro-Am. lit. Chgo. Pub. Schs., 1962-66, 68—, Cook County Dept. Pub. Aid, 1966-68; Upward Bound tchr. Barat Coll., Lake Forest, Ill., 1976, Loyola U., Chgo., 1977; chmn. dept. English, Carver Area High Sch., 1977-78; instr. Chgo. Sun-Times Tchr. Inst., 1974-76; pres. WAPA Press; writer criterion reference testing program Chgo. Bd. Edn., 1980; editor Stinkin' Onion Publs.; dir., founder Young Peoples Writers Workshop; participant poetry series DuSable Mus. of Afro-Am. History, 1981. Recipient award for contbns. to arts and letters Nat. News Media Women, 1974, award for contbns. to journalism Loyola U. Upward Bound Program, 1977, U. Chgo.-Blum-Kovler Ednl. award, 1978. Mem. Nat. Council Tchrs. English, Ill. Assn. Tchrs. English (minority task force 1981), Ill. Speech and Theatre Assn., Assn. Study Afro-Am. Life and History. Episcopalian. Club: English of Greater Chgo. Author: Sapphire (poetry), 1972; Moon in Black (poetry and short stories), 1974. Songwriter for jazz ensemble. Daughter of the Hawk, 1975; (poetry) Windy City Rhythms, 1975, Raindrops and Mud Puddles, 1977; producer, writer, choreographer Touch the Sisters, 1978. Home: 8555 S Prairie Ave Chicago IL 60619 Office: 13100 S Doty Ave Chicago IL 60627

PATTERSON, RICHARD GEORGE, engring. co. exec.; b. Cascade, Iowa, May 26, 1928; s. George Samuel and Mary Anna (Heffernen) P.; B.S. in Elec. Engring., Purdue U., 1949, M.S. in Elec. Engring., 1950; m. Jeanne Lundberg, Oct. 10, 1953; children—Christa, Courtney. Project engr. Honeywell Inc., Mpls., 1956-66, sec. head, 1966-68, engring. mgr., 1968-72, sec. head, 1972-74, engring. mgr. 1974-81, chief engr., 1981—. Mem. AIAA, Tau Beta Pi, Eta Kappa Nu. Roman Catholic. Patentee autothrottle, servo loop synchronizer. Home: 4336 Avondale Rd Minneapolis MN 55416 Office: 2600 Ridgway Pkwy Minneapolis MN 55413

PATTERSON, RICHARD HENRY, psychiatrist; b. Milw., June 15, 1931; s. Richard John and Gertrude (Biegel) P.; B.S., Marquette U., 1953, M.D., 1956. Intern, St. Joseph's Hosp., Milw., 1956-57; psychiat. resident Colo. Psychopathic Hosp., Denver, 1957-58, The Asso. Psychiat. Tng. Program Milw., 1960-62; staff psychiatrist Milw. Sanitarium Found.; practice medicine specializing in psychiatry, Milw., 1962—; sec., treas. Philstan Psychiat. Clinic, S.C.; cons. Social Security Adminstrn., Bur. Hearings and Appeals, 1966—; psychiat. cons. Blue Cross/Blue Shield of Wis., Curative Rehab. Center; chmn. operating com., mem. peer rev. com. Milw. Health Protection Plan. Served to capt. M.C., USAF, 1958-60. Diplomate Am. Bd. Psychiatry and Neurology. Mem. AMA, Am., Wis. (chmn. 3d party payments com., pres.-elect) psychiat. assns., Med. Soc. Milw. County (surg. care operating com. Blue Shield Plan). Home: 4110 W Martin Dr Milwaukee WI 53208 Office: 3070 N 51st St Milwaukee WI 53210

PATTERSON, RUSSELL JAMES, veterinarian; b. San Francisco, June 13, 1932; s. Russell James and Dorothy Luella P.; A.A., Monterey Peninsula Coll., 1963; B.S., D.V.M., U. Calif., Davis, 1967; m. Carmen Joy Kleinkopf, Feb. 14, 1953; children—Michael Kent, Sheri Lin. Precision sheet metal specialist Ampex Corp., Redwood City, Calif., 1956-57; mgr. consumer loan dept. Crocker Nat. Bank, San Francisco, 1957-61; veterinarian Petaluma (Calif.) Veterinary Hosp., 1967-68, partner, 1968-69, propr., 1969-70; pres., chmn. bd. Animal Health Associates, 1970-77; mgr. small animal veterinary services Ralston Purina Co., St. Louis, 1977—. Bd. dirs. Sonoma Mountain County (Calif.) Water Dist., 1968-72. Served to sgt. USAF, 1952-56; Korea. Mem. AVMA, Mo. Vet. Med. Assn., St. Louis Vet. Med. Assn., Am. Animal Hosp. Assn., Am. Assn. Indsl. Veterinarians, Nat. Wildlife Fedn., Audubon Soc., Aircraft Owners and Pilots Assn., Smithsonian Assos., Am. Radio Relay League, Cal Aggie Alumni Assn., Exptl. Aircraft Assn. Contbr. articles in field to profl. jours. Home: 4 Bitterfield Ct Ballwin MO 63011 Office: Checkerboard Square Saint Louis MO 63188

PATTERSON, SAMUEL CHARLES, educator; b. Omaha, Nov. 29, 1931; s. Robert Foster and Garnet Marie (Jorgensen) P.; B.A., U. S.D., 1953; M.S., U. Wis., 1956, Ph.D., 1959; m. Suzanne Louise Dean, June 21, 1956; children—Polly Ann, Dean Foster, Grier Edmund. Asst. prof. polit. sci. Okla. State U., Stillwater, 1959-61; asst. prof. U. Iowa, Iowa City, 1961-64, asso. prof., 1964-67, prof., 1967—; vis. prof. U. Wis., 1962, U. Okla., 1968-78, U. Essex, Colchester, Eng., 1969-70. Served with U.S. Army, 1953-55. Social Sci. Research Council fellow, 1961, 67. Mem. Internat. Polit. Sci. Assn., Am. Polit. Sci. Assn., Midwest Polit. Sci. Assn. (pres. 1980-81), Phi Beta Kappa, Phi Kappa Phi, Pi Sigma Alpha. Author: (with R.D. Hedlund and G.R. Boynton) Representatives and Represented, 1975; (with M.E. Jewell) The Legislative Process in the United States, 3d edition, 1977; (with G. Loewenberg) Comparing Legislatures, 1979; (with R.B. Ripley and R.H. Davidson) A More Prefect Union, 1979; editor: American Legislative Behavior, 1968; (with J.C. Wahlke) Comparative Legislative Behavior: Frontiers of Research, 1972; editor: Am. Jour. of Polit. Sci., 1970-73. Home: 431 S Summit St Iowa City IA 52240 Office: Department of Political Science 310A Schaeffer Hall University of Iowa Iowa City IA 52242

PATTERSON, WILLIS CHARLES, bass; b. Ann Arbor, Mich., Nov. 27, 1930; s. James (stepfather) and Kathleen (Gulley) P.; m. Frankie Audreymae Bouyer, June 21, 1958; children—Sharon Lynelle, Kevin Charles, Shelia Kathleen; B.Mus., U. Mich., 1958, M.Mus., 1959. Instr. music So. U., Baton Rouge, 1959-61; asst. prof. music Va. State Coll., Petersburg, 1962-68; prof. music U. Mich., Ann Arbor, 1968-71, prof. music, dir. Men's Glee Club, 1970-75, prof. music, chmn. voice dept., 1976—, asso. dean for acad. affairs Sch. Music, 1979—; profl. bass soloist with orchs. throughout U.S.; song recitalist. Mem. Ann Arbor Citizens Recreation Adv. Com., 1970-76; music adv. com. State Council of Arts, 1974—. Mem. Nat. Assn. Tchrs. Singing, Nat. Assn. Negro Musicians, NAACP, Alpha Phi Alpha. Club: Rotary. Recipient Marian Anderson award for singers, 1959; Fulbright grantee, 1965-66. Author: Anthology of Art Songs of Black American Composers, 1977. Home: 2906 Brandywine Blvd Ann Arbor MI 48104

PATTISON, MARK ANDREW, newspaper exec.; b. Detroit, July 6, 1956; s. Robert James and Jeannine (Gilberte) P.; student Oakland U., 1974-75; B.A. in Journalism, Wayne State U., 1978, postgrad., 1978-81. Mem. sports dept. Detroit Free Press, 1978-80; writer popular music column Detroit Monitor, Fraser, Mich., 1979—; with Northeast Detroiter-Harper Woods, Herald, Detroit, 1978—, mng. editor, 1978—. Mem. parish council St. David Ch., Mich., 1978-80, chmn. Christian service commn., 1979-80, sec. edn. commn., 1975-77; choir dir., folk choir dir. St. Ignatius Ch., Detroit, 1977—. Roman Catholic. Office: 15522 E Eight Mile Detroit MI 48205

PATTON, BARBARA ELAINE, educator; b. Cin., Sept. 21, 1934; d. Oscar Charles and Mildred Bethel (Hagan) P.; R.N., Jewish Hosp. Cin. Sch. Nursing, 1955; B.S.N., U. Cin., 1970, M.Ed., 1974, postgrad., 1976, 77, 80, 82. Staff nurse Cin. Gen. Hosp., 1955-56; occupational health nurse Western-So. Life Ins. Co., Cin., 1956-63; with Jewish Hosp. Cin. Sch. Nursing, 1963-79, chmn. prins. nursing, 1970-75, instr. med.-psychiat. nursing, 1975-79; instr. diversified health occupations Scarlet Oaks Career Devel. Campus-Great Oaks Joint Vocat. Sch. Dist., Cin., 1979-81; Health and Safety Coor., 1981—. Fund raiser Am. Heart Assn., 1970-81, Nat. Kidney Found., 1975-81, Am. Cancer Soc., 1970-81; deaconess Bond Hill United Presbyn. Ch., 1968-70; mem. Elk Lake Shores Property Owners Assn., 1974—. Mem. Am. Nurses Assn., Nat. League for Nursing, Am. Vocat. Assn., Ohio Nurses Assn., Ohio Vocat. Assn., Jewish Hosp. Cin. Sch. Nursing Alumni Assn., Kappa Delta Pi. Home: 1403 Beaverton Ave Cincinnati OH 45237

PATTON, DONNA SUE, publishing co. ofcl.; b. Eldorado, Ill., May 19, 1949; d. John Charles and Alta Lee (Cox) P.; B.S., So. Ill. U., 1971. Home econs. tchr. Flora Twp. Sch., Flora, Ill., 1971-75, High Sch. Dist. 214, Arlington Heights, Ill., 1975-78; advt. rep. Co-Ed/Forecast Mags., Chgo., 1978-80, Chgo. mgr., 1980-81; advt. rep. Chgo. office Reader's Digest, 1981—. Mem. home econs. adv. council Eastern Ill. U. Mem. Kraft Consumer's Right to Know bd., Ill. Home Econs. Curriculum Council, 1980—. Mem. Am. Home Econs. Assn., Ill. Home Econs. Assn., Ill. Vocat. Home Econs. Tchrs. Assn., Am. Vocat. Assn., Home Economists in Bus. Clubs: Agate, Women's Advt. of Chgo. (dir. 1980-82). Home: 2828 N Burling St Chicago IL 60657 Office: 111 E Wacker Dr Chicago IL 60601

PATTON, EARL DEAN, ednl. adminstr.; b. Eldorado, Ill., Oct. 3, 1922; s. Ernest H. and Lola A. (Overton) P.; certificate So. Ill. Normal U., 1940; B.S. in Edn., So. Ill. U., 1947, M.S. in Edn., 1952; Ed.D., U. Ill., 1962; m. Catherine Gaynelle Dent, Dec. 25, 1948; children—James Kevin, John Brian. Tchr., elementary prin. Gallatin and Saline County Schs., Ill., 1940-43; grad. asst., instr. history So. Ill. U. at Carbondale, 1947-48; supt. schs. City of Shawneetown, Ill., 1948-50; supr. elementary schs., Virginia, Ill., 1950-51; prin. elementary and jr. high sch., Salem, Ill., 1951-53; dir. instrn., asst. supt. and acting supt. schs., Kankakee, Ill., 1953-57; research asso. U. Council Tchr. Edn., U. Ill. at Urbana, asso. dir. Ill. Curriculum Program, Office of Ill. Supt. Pub. Instrn., Springfield, 1957-59; gen. asst. supt. schs., Champaign, Ill., vis. lectr. U. Ill. at Urbana, 1959-63; supt. schs. Culver City (Cal.), Unified Sch. Dist., 1963-69; supt. schs. Dist. 186, Springfield, Ill., 1969-73; adj. prof. ednl. adminstrn. Western Ill. U., Macomb, 1972—; asst. state supt. edn. Ill. Office of Edn., Springfield, 1973-78; head Office of Ombudsman, Ill. Office Edn., Springfield, 1975-78; cons. Southwestern Ednl. Lab., Long Beach, Calif., 1978—; vis. prof. adminstrn. Sangamon State U., Springfield, 1973—. Mem. instrn. resources council, equal ednl. opportunity com. Ill. State Supt. of Pub. Instrn., 1962-70, mem. gen. adv. coms., 1962-70; research cons. U. Wis. at Milw., 1963, North Central Assn. Colls. and Secondary Schs., 1964. Sacramento County (Calif.) Schs., 1964, Nuclear Sci. Curriculum Project, Calif., 1967, Project Capital, Springfield, 1970-72. Bd. dirs. United Fund, Boy Scouts Am., YMCA, Urban League, Mental Health Assn. Served to capt. AUS, 1943-46. Decorated Bronze Star; named Distinguished Citizen Kankakee C. of C., 1955; recipient Pub. Relation award Sch. Mgmt., Rutgers U., 1961; Distinguished Ednl. Service awards Copley Press, City of Culver City, Los Angeles County Bd. Suprs., 1969; Citizen of Year award Frontiers Internat., 1972-73, Distinguished Service award Ill. Curriculum Council, 1975; Mentor Graham award Ill. Ednl. Consortium, 1977; spl. commendation Ill. Office Edn., 1978; Career Recognition resolution Ill. Ho. of Reps., 1978. Mem. NEA, Am. Assn. Sch. Adminstrs., Ill. Sch. Adminstrs. Assn. (pres. 1973, Citation 1974), Nat. Soc. Study of Edn., U. Ill., So. Ill. U. alumni assns., Phi Delta Kappa, Kappa Delta Pi. Mason (32 deg.). Rotarian, Elk. Home: 49 Inverness Rd Springfield IL 62704

PATTON, JAN CHEVALIER, ednl. cons.; b. Mountain Grove, Mo., Oct. 7, 1940; d. James Robert and Beulah E. (Wheatcraft) Chevalier; B.S. in Edn., U. Mo., Columbia, 1963; M.Ed., Bowling Green State U., 1977, Ph.D., 1981; m. Robert Allen Patton, Mar. 28, 1964; 1 son, James Robert. Tchr. French, English, Columbia City Schs., 1963-67; tchr. French, Bowling Green (Ohio) City Schs., 1968-70, English tchr. and dept. chairperson, 1974-79; secondary cons. Findlay (Ohio) City Schs., 1980—; mem. subcom. on secondary English, Ohio Gov.'s Commn. on Articulation, 1981. Vol., United Way, Heart Fund, March of Dimes; trustee First United Methodist Ch., Bowling Green. Mem. Nat. Council Tchrs. English, Assn. Supervision and Curriculum Devel., Delta Gamma Alumnae. Club: P.E.O. Sisterhood. Home: 946 Fairview Ave Bowling Green OH 43402 Office: 227 S West St Findlay OH 45840

PATTON, NOEL THOMAS, mfg. co. exec.; b. Fort Wayne, Ind., Dec. 16, 1945; s. Bennie Noel and Marcella (Branstrator) P.; B.Philosophy with honors, Ind. U., 1969; postgrad. Harvard Bus. Sch., 1977. Salesman Patton Electric Co., Inc., Fort Wayne, 1967-69, sales mgr., 1969-70, exec. v.p., 1970-73, pres., chmn., 1973—. Chmn. Ind. Students for Robert Kennedy, 1968; campaign dir. Students and Faculties for Birch Bayh, 1968. Rhodes scholar candidate, 1967. Mem. Doubles, Le Club (N.Y.C.); Eagle (Gstaad, Switzerland). Patentee electric fans. Home: 8227 Westridge Rd Fort Wayne IN 46825 Office: PO Box 128 New Haven IN 46774

PATTON, RAY BAKER, urban planner, investment broker, economist; b. Enid, Okla., Jan. 24, 1932; s. Dwight Lyman Moody and Opal (Hembre) P.; B.A., U. Okla., 1955, M.R.C.P., 1960, M.A.P.A., 1969; m. Gloria Ruth Chambers, June 6, 1954; children—David Baker, Dayna Erin. Asst. dir. planning San Joaquin, Calif., 1959-61; dir. planning City of Norman (Okla.) and planning cons. U. Okla., Norman, 1961-65; dir. planning Oklahoma City, 1965-67; dir. planning St. Louis County, Mo., 1967-71; pres. Creative Environments, Inc., Clayton, Mo., 1972-74; chmn. Creative Consultants, Inc., Clayton, 1972-75; pres., chmn. bd. dirs. Patton Real Estate, Inc., Success Power, Inc., St. Louis, 1976-81; prin. Raymond B. Patton & Assos., Ballwin, Mo., 1975-81; dir. pub. works and planning, health commr., zoning enforcement officer City of Des Peres, Mo., 1977-79; zone mgr. Investors Diversified Services, Chesterfield, Mo., 1980-81; investment broker, fin. planner A.G. Edwards & Sons, Inc., Clayton, 1981—. Mem. faculty Nat. Inst. Farm and Land Brokers, 1971-76. Scoutmaster, St. Louis Area council Boy Scouts Am., 1976-80, vice chmn. adult tng., 1977—. Served with USMC, 1955-58. Named Outstanding Mcpl. Employee, State of Okla., 1963. Mem. Am. Inst. Cert. Planners, Nat. Assn. Home Bldrs., Urban Land Inst., Lambda Chi Alpha (pres. 1953-54). United Methodist (minister of music, Ballwin 1979—). Club: Kiwanis (Moberly, Mo.). Contbr. articles to profl. jours. Home: 610 Morewood Ct Saint Louis MO 63011 Office: Suite 295 Pierre Laclede Center 7733 Forsyth Blvd Clayton MO 63105

PATZER, ROLAND DIETZ, ednl. cons.; b. East Cleve., Apr. 27, 1927; s. Juluis and Marie Patzer; B.S., Kent (Ohio) State U., 1951, B.S. in Edn., 1954, M.A., 1957; m. Joan Fiocca, Dec. 28, 1950; children—Roland Dietz, Nancy Carolyn. Interpreter, Twin Coach Co., Kent, 1951-52; adminstrv. asst. Kent State U., 1952-53, asst. dir. Kent State Union, 1953-55, asst. dean of men, 1955-58, asst. dean of men and dir. student activities, 1958-61; dean of men U. Vt., Burlington, 1961-66, chief student personnel officer, 1964-66, dean of student personnel, 1966-67, dean of students, 1967-73; edn. program specialist U.S. office of Edn., Washington, 1972-73; pres. Urbana (Ohio) Coll., 1973-79; internat. program cons. Ohio Coll. Assn., Columbus, 1979—; guest lectr. various workshops and insts., 1967-71; cons. U. Center, Boston, 1968, Dept. Justice, 1969, U. Hartford, 1970; host and co-producer monthly TV series, 1970-72; profl. tenor oratorio soloist various mus. orgns. in U.S., 1948-61; choir dir. chs. in Cleve., 1948-73, Akron, Ohio, Washington, 1972-73. Chmn. profl. div. Burlington (Ohio) Community Chest, 1963-64; mem. Burlington Public Sch. System Bldg. Adv. Com., 1971-73; mem. vestry Episcopal Ch. of the Epiphany, 1977—; bd. dirs. Shelburne Arts Festival, 1966-68, Burlington Boys Club, sec.; bd. dirs. Citizens Scholarship Found. of Burlington, 1968-72, United Fund, 1968-72, So. Ohio Coll., 1980—. Served with M.C., U.S. Army, 1945-47. Mem. Ohio Coll. Assn. (dir. 1973-79), Assn. of Ind. Colls. of Ohio (mem. legis. relations com. 1973-79), Nat. Assn. of Student Personnel Adminstrs., Am. Coll. Personnel Assn., Council for Advancement of Small Colls. Club: Rotary. Contbr. articles on coll. edn. and adminstrn. to profl. publs. Home: 60 Rue St Clair Urbana OH 43078 Office: Ohio Coll Assn 45 W 11th Ave Columbus OH 43210

PAUDEL, PADAM PRASAD, radiation oncologist; b. Mitkyina, Burma, Jan. 2, 1937; s. Rudra Prasadand Indra Devi Paudel; came to U.S., 1971, naturalized, 1977; M.B., B.S., Inst. Medicine, Rangoon, Burma, 1965; m. Dalbir Amar Kumari, Nov. 18, 1967; 2 children—Sanjay, Vijay, Ravi. Intern, Ravenswood Med. Center, Chgo., 1971; resident in radiology Michael Reese Hosp., Chgo., 1972-74, Meml. Sloan Kettering Hosp., N.Y.C., 1973; staff physician U. Mich. Hosp., Ann Arbor, 1974-76; dir. radiation oncology dept. Meml. Hosp., Elmhurst, Ill., 1977—; asst. prof. Loyola U. Med. Sch., Maywood, Ill.; cons. physician Hinsdale (Ill.) Sanitroium, Central DuPage Hosp. Diplomate Am. Bd. Radiology. Fellow Am. Coll. Internat. Physicians; mem. AMA (Physicians Recognition award 1980), Am. Coll. Radiology, Am. Soc. Therapeutic Radiologists. Hindu. Home: 398 Shady Ln Elmhurst IL 60126 Office: Dept Radiation Oncology Memorial Hosp Elmhurst IL 60126

PAUL, DAVID LEWIS, real estate developer; b. N.Y.C., May 1, 1939; s. Isadore and Ruth (Goldstein) P.; B.S. in Econs., U. Pa., Isadore and Ruth (Goldstein) P.; B.S. in Econs., Wharton Sch., U. Pa., 1951; M.B.A., Columbia U., 1965, J.D., 1967; Ph.D. in Planning, Harvard U., 1968; children—David J., Michael M. Developer Hawthorne Towers, Montclair, N.J., 1967, Colony House, Lakewood, N.J., 1968, Pequannock (N.J.) Shopping Plaza, 1969, Townhouse of Amherst (Mass.), 1971, Brandywine Village, Amherst, 1972, Shrewsbury Mass., 1973, Regency Hyatt House, Sarasota, Fla., 1974, Tall Oaks Village, Weymouth, Mass., 1975, Somerset Village, Ft. Lauderdale, Fla., 1977, Green Knolls, Brockton, Mass., 1977, Am. Furniture Mart, Chgo., 1979, others; chmn. bd., chief exec. officer Westport Co. Trustee, Mt. Sinai Med. Center, N.Y.C., U. City N.Y., Mt. Sinai Hosp., N.Y.C., Mt. Sinai Sch. Nursing and Neustadter Convalescent Center, N.Y.C.; bd. dirs., governing mem. Lincoln Center Repertory Theatre, N.Y.C. Clubs: Standard, Mid-Am. (Chgo.). Author: The Effect of the AFL-CIO Merger on Centralization, 1961; Progressive Architecture, 1967. Office: 666 N Lake Shore Dr Chicago IL 60611

PAUL, EILEEN SUSAN, brewing co. exec.; b. El Paso, Tex., Nov. 30, 1943; d. Ralph Dewey and Bettie Jane (Payne) P.; B.A., Coll. of Mt. St. Vincent, 1967; M.B.A., U. Wis., 1978. Nat. tng. mgr. Manpower, Inc., Chgo., 1969-71, dir. ops., 1971-73; sales promotion coordinator Miller Brewing Co., Milw., 1973-75, asst. brand mgr., 1975-77, brand devel. mgr. new products, 1978-79, brand mgr. Miller High Life, 1979-80, mgr. mktg. services, 1980—; bus. adv. com. U. Wis.-Milw., 1978-79. Mem. United Fund Speakers' Bur., 1974-76. Mem. Am. Mktg. Assn. (pres. 1975-76, census adv. com. 1977-79, mktg. mgmt. council 1980-82), Am. Mgmt. Assn., Tempo (dir. 1981—). Clubs: Milw. Advt., Toastmasters, Miller Brewing Co. Mgmt. (dir. 1977-81). Home: 425 W Willow Ct Fox Point WI 53217 Office: 3939 W Highland Blvd Milwaukee WI 53201

PAUL, GABRIEL (GABE), baseball exec.; b. Rochester, N.Y., Jan. 4, 1910; s. Morris and Celia (Snyder) P.; ed. pub. schs., Rochester; m. Mary Frances Copps, Apr. 17, 1939; children—Gabriel, Warren, Michael, Jennie Lou, Henry. Reporter, Rochester Democrat and Chronicle, 1926-28; publicity mgr., ticket mgr. Rochester Baseball Club, 1928-34, traveling sec., dir., 1934-36; publicity dir. Cin. Baseball Club, 1937, traveling sec., 1938-48, asst. to pres., 1948-49, v.p., 1949-60, gen. mgr., 1951-60; v.p., gen. mgr. Houston Baseball Club, 1960-61; gen. mgr. Cleve. Baseball Club, 1961-63; pres., treas., gen. mgr. Cleve. Indians, Inc., 1963-72; pres., treas. Cleve. Soccer, Inc., 1967-68; pres., partner N.Y. Yankees, 1973-77; pres. Cleve. Indians, 1978—. Trustee various bus., civic and charitable instns. Served with inf. U.S. Army, 1943-45. Named Major League Exec. of Year, Sporting News, 1956, 74, United Press Exec. of Yr., 1976, Sports Exec. of Year, Gen. Sports Time, 1956, Baseball Exec. of Yr. Boston Baseball Writers Assn., 1974, 76; recipient J. Lewis Comiskey Meml. award Chgo. chpt. Baseball Writers Assn. Am., 1961, Bill Slocum award N.Y. chpt., 1976, Emil Fuchs award Boston Baseball Writers Assn., 1968, 76 Sports Touch of Learning award, 1976; inducted into Ohio Baseball Hall of Fame, 1980. Clubs: Shaker Heights (Ohio) Country; Cleve. Athletic; Palma Ceia Country (Tampa, Fla.); Skyline Country (Tucson).

PAUL, JAMES CHARLES, aeronautical engr.; b. Manistee, Mich., June 8, 1948; s. Virgil James and Dorothy Margaret (Hardy) P.; B.S.E., U. Mich., 1970, M.S.E., 1972. Dir. systems devel. Internat. Husky, Inc., Bloomfield, Hills, Mich., 1973-76; v.p. Airflow Sci. Corp., Plymouth, Mich., 1975—; v.p. Attached Flow Corp., Ann Arbor, Mich., 1980—. U. Mich. teaching fellow, 1971-73; registered profl. engr., Mich. Mem. Nat. Soc. Profl. Engrs., Mich. Soc. Profl. Engrs. Home: 706 Dewey Ave Ann Arbor MI 48104 Office: 352 N Main St Plymouth MI 48170

PAUL, PROSPER FREDERICK, hotel-motel exec.; b. Mansfield, Mass., July 31, 1932; s. Alexander J. and Blanche (Dion) P.; B.S., U. Mont., 1954; m. Mary Ellen F. Truckner, Nov. 7, 1964; children—Kevin, Jeffrey Mark. Asst. mgr. Hotel Florence, Missoula, Mont., 1957-59, gen. mgr., 1959-63; gen. mgr. Abbey Resort, Lake Geneva, Wis., 1963-64; innkeeper Holiday Inn, Jackson, Mich., 1964—. Served to 1st lt. AUS, 1955-57. Mem. Am. Hotel and Motel Assn. (dir. 1961-63), Mich. Hotel and Motor Hotel Assn. (treas. 1972-73, pres. 1974-75). Rotarian. Home: 1951 Elmhurst Ln Jackson MI 49201 Office: 2000 Holiday Inn Dr Jackson MI 49201

PAUL, RICHARD HENRY, chem. engr.; b. Kentland, Ind., Feb. 24, 1919; s. Otto Adolph and Marie Maud (Ford) P.; B.S. in Chem. Engring., Purdue U., 1941, A.A.S. in computer tech., 1967; m. Billie Louise Speitel, June 30, 1944; children—Richard Frederick, Jefferson

Ford, John William, David Henry. With Uniroyal Inc., Indpls., 1941-80, mgr. devel. engring. 1972-76, mgr. quality control, tech. mgr., 1976-78, quality assurance specialist, 1978-80; v.p. tech. services Indpls. Rubber Co., 1980—; U.S. del. Internat. Standards Orgn. Mem. Tire and Rim Assn. (chmn. tube and valve standards subcom. 1975), Soc. Automotive Engrs. (tire valve com.), Rubber Mfrs. Assn., Purdue U. Alumni Assn. Presbyterian. Patentee conically molded and slot-formed inner tubes, also amphibious tires. Home: 7848 W 88th St Indianapolis IN 46278 Office: 549 E Georgia St Indianapolis IN 46202

PAULISSEN, JAMES PETER, physician, public health adminstr.; b. Chgo., Aug. 14, 1928; s. Joseph Edward and Louise Catherine (Muno) P.; student Loyola U., Chgo., 1946-49, M.D. cum laude, Stritch Sch. Medicine, 1953; M.P.H., Johns Hopkins U., 1966; m. Lorraine A. Polly, Sept. 11, 1954; children—Linda, Steven, Mark, Daniel. Intern, Milw. County Hosp., 1953-54; resident in pediatrics Milw. Children's Hosp., 1957-59; practice medicine specializing in pediatrics Wauwatosa (Wis.) Children's Clinic, 1959-65; chief Bur. of Maternal and Child Health, Ill. Dept. Public Health, Springfield, 1966-70, chief div. family health, 1970-76; exec. dir. DuPage County Health Dept., Wheaton, Ill., 1976—; dir. Suburban Cook-DuPage Health Systems Agy. Del., White House Conf. Children, 1970; mem. Gov.'s Adv. Council on Developmental Disabilities, 1973-76; mem. Ill. Commn. on Children, 1976—; mem. Ill. TB Adv. Bd., 1980—; Served with USAF, 1954-56. Diplomate Am. Bd. Pediatrics. Fellow Am. Acad. Pediatrics, Am. Public Health Assn.; mem. AMA, Ill. State Med. Soc., Ill. Public Health Assn. (past pres.), Ill. Assn. Maternal and Child Health (past pres.), DuPage County Med. Soc., Ill. Assn. Public Health Adminstrs., Comprehensive Health Council Met. Chgo. (past pres., dir.). Roman Catholic. Office: 111 N County Farm Rd Wheaton IL 60187

PAULSEN, RICHARD WALLACE, data processing mgr.; b. Blue Island, Ill., Aug. 9, 1945; s. Richard Wallace and Betty Lucille (Frobish) P.; student Carson Coll., 1966-67; B.S. in Bus. Adminstrn., U. Nev., 1972, M.B.A., 1980; student law DePaul U., 1975-76; m. Mildred Stephenson Baker, July 16, 1964 (dec. Jan. 1977); children—David Charles, John Stanley, Claire Jane, Kristen Irene; m. 2d, Elizabeth Susan Riley, Nov. 24, 1978; 1 son, Richard James. Materials and testing engr. State of Nev. Dept. Hwys., 1964-69, computer programmer, analyst, 1969-72; computer systems analyst Nev. Dept. Employment Security, 1972-74; 2d v.p. corp. lending systems Continental Bank, Chgo., 1974—, mgr. multiple systems divs. including Europe and Chgo.; initiated EDP rehab. program Nev. State Prison-Nev. Employment Security Dept., 1972-74. Trustee, Avery Loonley Sch. Recipient Outstanding Grad. award State of Nev., 1969; certified data processor. Mem. Soc. Mgmt. Info. Systems, Am. Inst. Banking, Omicron Delta Epsilon, Beta Gamma Sigma. Unitarian. Home: 736 Ridgeview Downers Grove IL 60516 Office: 231 S LaSalle St Chicago IL 60693

PAULSEN, ROBERT THOMAS, elec. supply co. exec.; b. Chicago Heights, Ill., Mar. 10, 1924; s. Paul Frederick and Vera Gladys P.; B.S., Ill. Inst. Tech., 1947; postgrad. Northwestern U. Sch. Bus., 1949-50, Harvard U. Sch. Bus., 1956, Stanford U., 1960; m. Patricia Salisbury Elsam, Nov. 10, 1945; children—Jeffrey Thomas, Dale Melissa. Sales mgr. Electric Supply, Hammond, Ind., 1954-56, v.p., br. mgr., 1956-74, exec. v.p. Electric Supply subs. IV Internat., 1975-78, chmn., 1978-79; pres. Electric Supply Co. subs. Crescent Electric, Melrose Park, Ill., 1980—; dir. Calumet Nat. Bank, Hammond, Inc. Served with U.S. Navy, 1943-46. Mem. Assn. Iron and Steel Engrs., Electric Assn. Chgo. (past pres.), Western Soc. Engrs. Clubs: Met. (Chgo.); Flossmoor Country, Lake Michigan. Office: 1950 N Mannheim Melrose Park IL 60160

PAULSON, LYNDA R., tng. specialist; b. Indpls., Oct. 18, 1939; d. Alfred E. and Mary Louise (Gladden) Fitch; B.A., Ind. U., 1961; m. Bernard N. Mariano, Dec. 10, 1975; children by previous marriage—Phillip Todd Paulson, Paige Anne Paulson. Mgr., Margies Bridal Salon, Melrose Park, Ill., 1967-68; account exec. Sheraton Hotel, Oak Brook, Ill., 1968-70; regional sales mgr. Dale Carnegie Inst., Westchester, Ill., 1970-79; pres., founder Success Strategies, Inc., Clarendon Hills, Ill., 1979—; individual speech coach; instr. Am. Mgmt. Assn., Dale Carnegie courses. Recipient awards for prodn. and instrn. Dale Carnegie Inst.; named to Who to Look for in '81, Entree Mag. Mem. Nat. Assn. Women Bus. Owners, Women in Mgmt. (Charlotte Danstrom entrepreneur award 1981), Am. Mgmt. Assn. Republican. Clubs: Willowbrook Racquet, Oak Brook Racquet. Developer retail sales seminar for bus. owners and key personnel. Home and Office: 23 Kane Ct Clarendon Hills IL 60514

PAULSON, WILLIAM LEE, state supreme ct. justice; b. Valley City, N.D., Sept. 3, 1913; s. A.P. and Inga G. Paulson; B.A., Valley City State Tchrs. Coll., 1935; J.D. U. N.D., 1937; m. Jane E. Graves, Sept. 8, 1938; children—John T., Mary (Mrs. Mikal Simonson). Admitted to N.D. bar, 1937; practiced in Valley City, 1937-66; state's atty. Barnes County, 1941-50, 59-66; asso. justice N.D. Supreme Ct., 1967—. Mem. N.D. Combined Law Enforcement Council, 1969; mem. nat. awards jury Freedoms Found., Valley Forge, Pa., 1969, 71, 77. Mem. alumni adv. bd. U. N.D., 1971—. Recipient Disting. Alumni award Valley City State Coll. Alumni Assn., 1981. Mem. Am., N.D. (ex officio mem. com. unified court system) bar assns., N.D. States Attys. Assn. (pres. 1964), Nat. Dist. Attys. Assn. (state dir. 1963-65), Valley City Jr. C. of C. (pres. 1943, Outstanding Jaycee award 1945, dist. v.p. 1945-46), Valley City C. of C. (dir. 1960, 61). Episcopalian (chancellor N.D. 1965—). Clubs: Masons, Shriners, Elks, Eagles, K.P. Home: 1009 E Highland Acres Rd Bismarck ND 58501 Office: Supreme Ct State Capitol Bismarck ND 58505

PAVA, BARRY MICHAEL, chem. co. ofcl.; b. Chgo., Dec. 15, 1943; s. Joseph Leonard and Rose Indarosa (Stein) P.; student U. Ill., 1961-63; B.S. in Chemistry, Elmhurst Coll., 1967; postgrad. in bus. adminstrn. Columbia U., 1968-69; m. Kathe Jane Wardecker, Mar. 1, 1969; children—Jorie Marlene, Joelle Meagan. Cosmetic applications mgr. Felton Internat., Bklyn., 1969-70; midwest sales mgr. flavor/essence, Monsanto Chem. Co., N.Y.C., 1970-73; nat. sales mgr. fragrance, Stepan Chem. Co., Northbrook, Ill., 1973-79; v.p. sales Belmay Co., Inc., Long Island City, N.Y., 1979—. Commr. Bartlett Park Dist., 1976—, pres., 1978-81; mem. Bartlett Ambutol Commn., 1977-78; vol. fireman Bartlett and Countyside Fire Protection Dist. Recipient certificates of appreciation Kiwanis, Jaycees, Lions. Mem. Soc. Cosmetic Chemists, Inst. Food Technologists, Am. Chem. Soc. Democrat. Jewish. Contbr. article in field to publ. Home: 110 Jervey Ln Bartlett IL 60103

PAVEL, GARY JOE, state govt. ofcl.; b. Seward, Nebr., Apr. 28, 1946; s. Joseph Robert and Lillian Marie (Soukup) P.; B.S. in Bus. Adminstrn., U. Nebr., 1969; m. Patricia F. Andersen, May 27, 1972; children—Stephanie, Melissa, Brent. Chief internal auditor Lincoln Telephone & Telegraph Co. (Nebr.), 1970-74; audit supr. Office of Nebr. State Auditor, Lincoln, 1974-76, chief acct. Bd. Ednl. Lands and Funds, State of Nebr., 1976-77, county audit mgr. Office of Nebr. State Auditor, 1977—. Served with U.S. Army, 1969-70; Vietnam. Decorated Army Commendation medal (2); C.P.A., Nebr. Mem. Am. Inst. C.P.A.'s, Nebr. Soc. C.P.A.'s, Assn. Govt. Accts. (v.p. 1981-82), Am. Legion, VFW. Republican. Roman Catholic. Home: 4801 Grassridge Rd Lincoln NE 68512 Office: State Capitol Room 2303 Lincoln NE 68509

PAVELKA, ELAINE BLANCHE, mathematician, educator; b. Chgo., Feb. 4; d. Frank Joseph and Mildred Bohumila (Seidl) P.; B.A., M.S., Northwestern U.; Ph.D., U. Ill. Mathematician, Northwestern U. Aerial Measurements Lab., Evanston, Ill.; instr. Leyden Community High Sch., Franklin Park, Ill.; prof. math. Morton Coll., Cicero, Ill. Mem. Am. Ednl. Research Assn., Am. Math. Assn. of Two-Year Colls., Am. Math. Soc., Mensa, Assn. Women in Math., Canadian Soc. History and Philosophy of Math., Ill. Council Tchrs. of Math., Ill. Math. Assn. for Community Colls., Intertel, Math. Assn. Am., Math. Action Group, Ga. Center for Study of Learning Teaching Mathematics, Nat. Council Tchrs. of Math., Sch. Sci. and Math. Assn., Spl. Interest Group Research in Math. Edn., Soc. Indsl. and Applied Math., Northwestern U., U. Ill. alumni assns., Pi Mu Epsilon, Sigma Delta Epsilon. Home: 1900 Euclid Ave Berwyn IL 60402 Office: Morton Coll 3801 S Central Ave Cicero IL 60650

PAVLENKO, VICTOR VICTOROVICH, community and organizational devel. cons. co. exec.; b. Chgo., July 9, 1944; s. Victor Z. and Lucy Pavlenko; B.S., Valparaiso U., 1967; M.Div., Wartburg Theol. Sem., 1971; m. Nancy Arndt, Dec. 23, 1966; children—Laura Anna, Catherine Kay. Mktg. cons. Morse Press, Medford, Oreg., 1967; program dir. River Valley Community Action Agy., Dubuque, Iowa, 1967-70; ordained to ministry Lutheran Ch., 1971; student pastor St. John and St. Paul Luth. chs., Dubuque, Iowa, 1968-70; asst. pastor Canton (S.D.) Lutheran Ch., 1970-73; exec. dir. CENCOAD, Inc., Sioux Falls, S.D., 1973—; exec. dir. Sioux Falls Area Edn. Work Council, 1977—; cons. Northwestern Bell Telephone Co.; mem. continuing edn. faculty Mich. State U., 1978—. Bd. dirs. Canton Inwood Hosp., 1975—, Upper Midwest Environ. Mediation Center, Mpls.; vice chmn. All Saints Sch. Bd., Sioux Falls. Named Citizen of Yr., Canton C. of C., 1977; Outstanding Young Men of Am., U.S. Jaycees, 1977. Home: 616 E 2d St Canton SD 57013 Office: 2118 S Summit St Sioux Falls SD 57105

PAWL, RONALD PHILLIP, physician; b. Chgo., July 26, 1935; s. Phillip Joseph and Ruby Helen (Graham) P.; B.S., Loyola U., Chgo., 1957, M.D., 1961; m. Mary Margaret Rohner, July 11, 1959; children—Mary, Linda, Diane, Julie, Matthew, Michael. Intern, Resurrection Hosp., Chgo., 1961-62; resident in surgery VA Hosp., Hines, Ill., 1962-63; resident in neurosurgery U. Ill., 1962-66, asst. prof. neurosurgery, 1969-73, asso. prof., 1973—; practice medicine specializing in neurosurgery, Chgo., 1968—, Lake Forest, Ill., 1974—; mem. staff Ill. Masonic Med. Center, pres. staff, 1974-75; mem. staff Lake Forest Hosp. Hon. trustee Ill. Masonic Med. Center, 1975-79, trustee, 1979—. Served with AUS, 1966-67. Diplomate Am. Bd. Surgery. Fellow A.C.S.; mem. Central Neurosurg. Soc. (past pres.), Ill. Neurosurg. Soc. (sec.-treas. 1975-77, v.p. 1978-81), AMA, Am. Assn. Neurol. Surgeons, Congress Neurol. Surgeons, Chgo. Neurol. Soc. (sec.-treas. 1979-80, v.p. 1980-81, pres. 1981-82). Roman Catholic. Club: Masons. Home: 1221 Loch Ln Lake Forest IL 60045 Office: 912 Wood St S Chicago IL 60612

PAWLEWSKI, NORMAN LEONARD, state public health ofcl.; b. Buffalo, May 28, 1934; s. William and Estelle P.; B.S. in Acctg. with honors, U. Buffalo, 1960; postgrad. Nat. Center for Disease Control Tng. Program, intermittently 1962-70; postgrad. in public adminstrn. Drake U., 1973-74; m. Rose Marie Fiscarelli, June 19, 1965; children—David Brian, Dawn Marie. Partner cocktail lounge and restaurant, Lancaster, N.Y., 1960-62; with USPHS, 1962-70, adminstrv. asst. Iowa Dept. Health, Des Moines, 1967-69, dep. chief preventive med. service, 1969-70; asst. to commr. public health Iowa Dept. Public Health, Des Moines, 1970-73, acting commr. public health, 1973, commr. public health, 1973—. Served with U.S. Army, 1953-55. Republican. Evangelical Christian. Home: 3707 SW 28th St Des Moines IA 50321 Office: Lucas Office Bldg Des Moines IA 50319

PAWLIK, JOHN MICHAEL, II, investment banker; b. Buffalo, Dec. 6, 1954; s. John Joseph and Marie Rita (Luthi) P.; B.S., SUNY, Buffalo, 1975; M.B.A., U. Pa., 1980; J.D., Buffalo Law Sch., 1980. Investigative asso. N.Y. State Commn. on Jud. Conduct, Buffalo, Albany, N.Y.C., 1976-77; research fellow Higher Edn. Fin. Research Inst., U. Pa., Phila., 1979-80; admitted to Pa. bar, 1980; asso. John Nuveen & Co., Inc., Chgo., 1980—; adj. asst. prof. Glassboro (N.J.) State Coll., 1978-79; lectr. Medaille Coll., 1976-77. Mem. Mayor's Adv. Bd. of Buffalo Environ. Mgmt. Commn., 1975; mem. govt. structures task force Greater Buffalo Devel. Found., 1976-77. Mem. Wharton Grad. Alumni Assn., Beta Gamma Sigma, Omicron Delta Epsilon. Republican. Roman Catholic. Club: Wharton (Phila.). Opinion editor Wharton Jour., 1979-80. Office: 209 S LaSalle St Chicago IL 60604

PAWLITSCHEK, DONALD PAUL, bus. cons.; b. Heron Lake, Minn., Aug. 5, 1941; s. Paul P. and Marion (Erickson) P.; student Southwest Tech. Inst., 1960, Mankato State Coll., 1965-66; m. Korrine Kunerth, Oct. 9, 1965; children—Andrew, Jennifer, Heidi, Sarah, Benjamin. Farmer, Heron Lake, 1967-73; pres. Dundee Steel Inc., 1973-75, Alpha Prime Inc., Heron Lake, 1975-80, Prime Ventures, Inc., 1980—; dir. Am. Search and Referral Co. Served with AUS, 1960. Mem. Nat. Assn. Fin. Cons., Am. Entrepreneurs Assn., Am. Legion. Conservative. Roman Catholic. Club: Elks. Patentee livestock flooring. Address: Rt 2 Heron Lake MN 56137

PAWLOW, MARY LOUISE, educator; b. Franklin, Tenn., Oct. 30, 1944; d. Roy Dixon and Mattie Lou (McMahon) Stephens; B.A., Vanderbilt U., 1966; postgrad Middle Tenn. State U., 1972-77; m. Stephen A. Pawlow, June 2, 1979; 1 dau., Lara Elizabeth. Tchr. math Hillwood High Sch., Nashville, 1966-68, David Lipscomb High Sch., 1968-72, Spencer Youth Center, 1972-78; tchr. math Fort Zumwalt High Sch., O'Fallon, Mo., 1978—, St. Mary's Coll., O'Fallon, 1980—. Collector Cancer Crusade; vol. Heart Fund. Delta Kappa Gamma scholar, 1976-77. Mem. Nat. Council Tchrs. Math, Assn. Supervision and Curriculum Devel., NEA, Mo. Edn. Assn., Mo. Math Tchrs., Delta Kappa Gamma, Pi Mu Epsilon. Republican. Home: 313 Morningside Dr Saint Peters MO 63376 Office: Dept Math St Marys Coll O'Fallon MO 63366

PAWLOWSKI, THOMAS JOSEPH, JR., wholesale gemstone co. exec., former naval officer; b. Chgo., Oct. 14, 1923; s. Thomas Joseph and Marie Bonaventure (Gasiarowski) P.; student Ill. Inst. Tech., 1941-42; B.S., U.S. Naval Acad., 1947; student Naval Supply Corps Sch., 1947-48; diploma Air U. Grad. Sch., 1961; m. Evelyn Bernadette Sternowski, June 21, 1947; children—Carol Ann, Thomas Joseph III, Barbara Eve, Diane-Marie, Janet Marie. Commd. ensign U.S. Navy, 1947, advanced through grades to capt., 1968; supply officer on USS Mason, USS Orion, 1948-60; logistic coordinator Bur. Supplies and Accounts and Def. Logistics Agy., Washington, 1961-68; dir. weapons systems coordination div., ships parts control center, Mechanicsburg, Pa., 1968-71; dir. office planning and mgmt., dep. comdr. def. logistics services center, Battle Creek, Mich., 1971-74; dir. logistics Naval Ships Weapons Systems Engring. Sta., Port Hueneme, Calif., 1974-77; ret., 1977; owner, pres. T.J.P. Enterprises, gemstones, Libertyville, Ill., 1978—. Bd. dirs. Community Services Battle Creek, Mich., 1973-74; lay eucharistic minister U.S. Naval Chapel, Port Hueneme, 1975-77. Decorated Meritorious Service medal, Joint Services Commendation medal. Mem. Nat. Assn. Catholic Laity, U.S. Naval Supply Corps Alumni Assn. (life), U.S. Naval Acad. Alumni Assn. (life), Ret. Officers Assn. (life), Soc. Logistics Engrs. Home: 921 Jeremy Ln Libertyville IL 60048 Office: PO Box 385 Libertyville IL 60048

PAWULA, JOHN STEPHEN, automated material handling co. exec.; b. Chgo., June 12, 1938; s. Stephen and Frances Mary (Jusczyk) P.; student U. Kans., 1957-58, bus. sch., service schs.; m. Kathleen Sophie Flasza, Aug. 12, 1961; children—Michael Brent, Lisa Frances. Radio and TV inspector Zenith Radio Corp., 1960; field engr. Barrett Elec. Corp., Northbrook, Ill., 1960-66, chief field engr., 1966-71, mgr. systems engring., 1971-72, asst. gen. mgr., 1972—, v.p. sales, 1977—. Served with USAF, 1956-60. Roman Catholic. Home: 1113 S Walnut St Arlington Heights IL 60005 Office: 630 Dundee Rd Northbrook IL 60062

PAXTON, ALBERT ELWYN, chrome plating co. exec.; b. Chgo., May 19, 1902; s. Frederick H. and Harriet I. (Griffiths) P.; B.S., U. Ill., 1925; m. Edna Marjorie Rehm, July 11, 1930; children—Marilyn V., Nancy L. Editor, Mill Supplies, McGraw-Hill Publs., Chgo., 1926-34, mgr., N.Y.C., 1934-37; mgr. engring. New Record-Constrn. Methods, N.Y.C., 1938-45, publisher, 1945-48; v.p. western region McGraw Hill Pub. Co., Chgo., 1945-67; pres. Nova Chrome, Inc., Franklin Park, Ill., 1967—. Clubs: Chgo., Univ., Westmoreland Country. Office: Nova Chrome Inc 3200 Wolf Rd Franklin Park IL 60131

PAYAN, HUSHANG MOFAKHAM, pathologist; b. Iran, Jan. 1, 1925; s. Ali M. and Bel M. P.; came to U.S., 1952, naturalized, 1960; M.D., U. Teheran, 1951; m. Irene Ruszkowski; children—Leila, John. Intern, Jewish Meml. Hosp., N.Y.C., 1953; resident Queens Gen. Hosp., N.Y.C., 1954-58; practice medicine specializing in pathology, 1960—; asst. pathologist Booth Meml. Hosp., N.Y.C., 1958-60; dir. labs. VA Hosp., Clarksburg, W.Va., 1965-68, Bell Meml. Hosp., Ishpeming, Mich., 1968—; asst. prof. pathology N.Y. Med. Coll., N.Y.C., 1960-65; asso. prof. pathology U. W.Va., 1965-68; clin. asst. prof. pathology U. Wis., Madison, 1968—. Diplomate Am. Bd. Pathology. Mem. AMA, Mich. State, Marquette County med. socs., Am. Coll. Pathologists, Soc. Clin. Pathologists, Internat. Acad. Pathologists, Am. Soc. Exptl. Pathologists, N.Y. Acad. Scis. Contbr. articles to med. jours. Home: 681 Mather Ave Ishpeming MI 49849 Office: Bell Meml Hosp Ishpeming MI 49849

PAYNE, GARY L., supt. schs.; b. Gallipolis, Ohio, Sept. 9, 1935; s. Raymond A. and Frances Payne; B.S., Ohio State U., 1957; M.E., Kent State U., 1965; Ed.D., Rutgers U., 1976; m. Mary Jane Keifer, Jan. 31, 1958; children—Allison, Andrea, Gary, Jr., Angela. Dir. music Barberton (Ohio) public schs., 1957-60; dir. instrn. in music Canton (Ohio) public schs., 1960-65; guidance counselor Canton (Ohio) public schs., 1965-66; prin. Churchill Jr. High Sch., East Brunswick, N.J., 1969-72; guidance counselor Westfield (N.J.) public schs., 1966-67, asst. prin., 1966-69, dir. secondary edn., 1972-74, dir. instrn. K-12, 1974-76, asst. supt. instrn. K-12, 1976-77; supt. schs. Wyoming (Ohio) City Schs., 1977—; mem. governing bd. Spl. Edn. Regional Resource Center, Cin., 1980-81. Chmn. for edn. United Appeal, 1979-80. Mem. Am. Assn. Sch. Adminstrs., Assn. Supervision and Curriculum Devel., Phi Delta Kappa. Club: Kiwanis. Contbr. articles to various publs. Home: 394 Circlewood Lane Wyoming OH 45215 Office: 500 Grove Ave Wyoming OH 45215

PAYNE, MARGARET RALSTON, educator; b. Louisville, Jan. 31, 1946; d. Henry Morris and Rena Belle (Owens) Ralston; B.A., Kalamazoo Coll., 1968; M.A., Kent State U., 1971; student U. Sierra Leone, 1966-67; m. James Edward Payne, Dec. 11, 1976; 1 dau., Maya Renee. Asst. prof. psychology Kent (Ohio) State U., 1972-78, asst. dean devel. services, 1974—; cons. to Kent State U., Gen. Assistance Center Ohio, 1974, 77, Portage County (Ohio) Headstart, 1974-79, Kent State U. Regional Police Acad., 1975, Midwest Assn. Community Health Centers, Inc., 1977, Detroit Pub. Schs., 1978. Bd. dirs. Portage County Community Action Council, 1979—. Ohio Rehab. Services Commn. grantee, 1974, 75; HEW grantee, 1974, 78-81. Mem. Am. Psychol. Assn., Midwestern Psychol. Assn., Nat. Assn. Black Psychologists, Am. Assn. Higher Edn., Nat. Assn. Women Deans, Adminstrs. and Counselors, Ohio Assn. Women Deans, Adminstrs. and Counselors, Mid-Am. Assn. Equal Opportunity Program Personnel, Ohio Assn. Equal Opportunity Program Personnel, Delta Sigma Theta, Omicron Delta Kappa. Club: Links. Home: 237 Rellim Dr Kent OH 44240 Office: 106 Kent Hall Kent State U Kent OH 44242

PAYNE, NELLIE MARIA DE COTTRELL, zoologist, entomologist; b. Cheyenne Wells, Colo., Dec. 11, 1900; d. James Edward and Mary Emmeline (de Cottrell) P.; B.S., Kans. State Coll., 1920, M.S., 1921; Ph.D., U. Minn., 1925; student U. Vienna, 1930-31. Asst. entomologist Kans. State Coll., 1918-21; asst. instr. entomology U. Minn., 1923-25; instr. math. and chemistry Lindenwood Coll., St. Charles, Mo., 1921-22; fellow NRC, 1925-27; mem. biol. abstracts sci. staff, Phila., 1927-33; lectr., fellow U. Minn., 1933-37; asst. research entomologist Am. Cyanamid Co., Stamford, Conn., 1937-44, biologist, 1944-57; lit. chemist Velsicol Chem. Corp., Chgo., 1957-70; cons. entomology and agrl. chem. lit., 1970—; with Marine Biol. Lab., Woods Hole, Mass., summers, Marine Biol. Lab., Plymouth, Eng., 1930; guest investigator Biologisches Versuchanstalt, Berlin-Delhem, Germany, 1931. Co-founder, Stamford (Conn.) Cath. Library, endowment trustee, 1974—. Fellow AAAS, Entmol. Soc. Am.; mem. N.Y. Acad. Sci., Am. Soc. Zoologists, N.Y. Entomol. Soc., Am. Chem. Soc. (counselor 1972—), Sigma Xi, Phi Kappa Phi, Iota Sigma Pi (nat. v.p. 1966-72), Sigma Delta Epsilon. Republican. Roman Catholic. Contbr. tech. jours. Home: 2908 W Fletcher St Chicago IL 60618

PAYNE, W(ILLIAM) SPENCER, surgeon; b. St. Louis, Mar. 22, 1926; s. Richard Johnson and Mary Matthews P.; student DePauw U., 1944-45, Haverford Coll., 1945-46; M.D., Washington U., St. Louis, 1950; M.S., U. Minn., 1960; m. Maureen J.S. Divertie, Oct. 3, 1959; children—Susan Mary, William Spencer, Sarah Elspeth. Intern, St. Louis City Hosp., 1950-51, resident in internal medicine, 1951-52, resident in gen. surgery, 1954-55; resident in gen. surgery Mayo Grad. Sch., Rochester, Minn., 1955-58, resident in thoracic surgery, 1958-61; practice medicine specializing in surgery, Rochester, 1962—; cons. thoracic and cardiovascular surgery, dept. surgery Mayo Clinic and Mayo Found., Rochester, 1962—; prof. surgery Mayo Med. Sch., 1974—; mem. staff Rochester Methodist Hosp., St. Mary's Hosp., Rochester State Hosp. Served as lt. M.C., USNR, 1952-54. Recipient Howard K. Gray award Mayo Assn., 1959. Mem. Am. Surg. Assn., Am. Assn. for Thoracic Surgery, Soc. Thoracic Surgeons, A.C.S., Am. Coll. Chest Physicians, Central Surg. Assn., Minn. Surg. Soc., Internat. Assn. for Study of Lung Cancer, Mayo Alumni Soc. for Thoracic Surgery, Priestley Soc., Internat. Soc. for Diseases of the Esophagus. Presbyterian. Clubs: Univ. (Rochester). Author: The Esophagus, 1974; contbr. numerous articles to med. jours. Office: Mayo Clinic Rochester MN 55901

PAYNE, WILLIAM JOSEPH, ednl. adminstr.; b. Chgo., Oct. 27, 1945; s. William Thomas and Ardele J. (Beberger) P.; B.B.A., St. Norbert Coll., 1967; C.L.U., Am. Coll. Life Underwriters, 1974. Sales mgr. Prudential Ins. Co., Chgo., 1970-74; account mgr. Wilson Learning, Eden Prairie, Minn., 1974-76; pres. Payne & Assos., Addison, Ill., 1976-77; dir. instruction Wilson Learning Corp., Eden Prairie, 1977—. Bd. dirs. Ridgewood Condominiums, 1980-82. Served to capt. Mil. Police Corps, U.S. Army, 1968-70. Decorated Army Commendation medal. Mem. Am. Soc. C.L.U.'s, Assn. of Humanistic Psychology, Am. Soc. Tng. and Devel., Nat. Soc. Performance and Instrn. Home: 8952 D Neill Lake Eden Prairie MN 55344 Office: 6950 Washington St Eden Prairie MN 55344

PAZIK, GEORGE JAMES, editor, pub.; b. Milw., Apr. 7, 1921; s. Richard Francis and Josephine (Bartos-Bucek) P.; B.S., U. Wis., 1944; m. Bernice Emily Thiele, June 19, 1943; children—Marjorie Anne, Carol Sue. Mgr., Pazik's Delicatessen, Milw., 1946-54; owner. Kitchens by Pazik, Milw., 1952-59; exec. dir. Upper 3d St Comml. Assn., Milw., 1959-64; exec. v.p., founder Northtown Planning and Devel. Council, Milw., 1964-74; editor, pub. Fishing Facts mag., Menomonee Falls, Wis., 1970—. Chmn. Milwaukee County Expressway and Transp. Commn., 1971-74; chmn. Wis. state com. of U.S. Commn. on Civil Rights, 1970-72. Served with U.S. Army, 1944-46. Recipient Human Relations award Milw. Council B'nai B'rith, 1968. Mem. Outdoor Writers Assn. Am., AAAS, Sierra Club, Wilderness Soc. Lutheran. Home: 8549 N Service Dr Unit 204 Milwaukee WI 53223 Office: N84 W13660 Leon Rd Menomonee Falls WI 53051

PEAK, LARRY MARTIN, counseling psychologist, social worker; b. Wichita, Kans., Nov. 6, 1945; s. Boyd Dewey and Betty Maxine (Taylor) P.; B.A., Wichita State U., 1967; M.S., U. Mo., 1969; Ph.D., Kans. State U., 1975; m. Carol Ann Albright, June 3, 1966; children—Brian, Christopher, Nathan, Nicholas. Social worker Lutheran Social Service, Wichita, 1969; instr. Kans. State U., 1973-75; asst. prof. social work, 1979-81; outpatient services mgr. Pawnee Mental Health Center, Manhattan, Kans., 1974-81; pvt. practitioner Assos. in Psychol. and Family Services, 1981—. Bd. dirs., treas. Manhattan (Kans.) Youth Care Inc., 1974-79; v.p. PTA, Marlatt Sch., Manhattan, 1977-78, pres., 1978-79. Served as capt. Med. Service Corps., U.S. Army, 1969-73. NIMH trainee, 1967-69. Mem. Am. Psychol. Assn., Nat. Assn. Social Workers. Home: 1608 Baltimore Terr Manhattan KS 66502 Office: 142 N Emporia St Manhattan KS 67202

PEAK, WILBUR JAMES, cons. pub. relations; b. Quincy, Ill., Mar. 6, 1907; s. Roy Thomas and Violetta (Lay) P.; B.S., Knox Coll., 1928; m. Ruth Visny, Aug. 28, 1937; children—Kathy Ann Peak Miller, Thomas J. Accountant, Ill. Bell Telephone Co., 1928, supr., 1936, supr. tng., 1938, employee info. supr., 1942, pub. relations and demonstrations supr., 1945, gen. info. mgr., 1949, asst. v.p., 1955-71; cons. pub. relations, 1971—; dir. State Bank of Geneva (Ill.). Recipient Achievement award Knox Coll., 1968. Mem. Telephone Pioneers Am., Chgo. Jr. C. of C. (life mem., pres. 1942-43), Chgo. Assn. Commerce and Industry, Pub. Relations Clinic, Pub. Relations Soc. Am. (pres. 1963). Methodist. Clubs: Masons, Press, Lake Shore (pres. 1963-64), Publicity (pres. 1955-56), Tavern, Headline, Econ., Knox Alumni (pres. 1950) (Chgo.), Lions. Home: 301 Charles St Geneva IL 60134

PEAPPLES, GRACE AGNES, ednl. adminstr.; b. Muskegon, Mich., Feb. 16, 1936; d. John and Rebecca Lillian (Harrison) Middlecamp; student Muskegon Community Coll., 1954-57; B.Ed., Wayne State U., 1960; M.A., Eastern Mich. U., 1968, specialist in Ednl. Leadership, 1975; m. Robert W. Peapples, Jan. 25, 1956 (div.); children—Carrie Lynn, Ronald John. Tchr., remedial reading instr. Thorne Elem. Sch., Dearborn Heights, Mich., 1960-70, asst. elem. prin., 1970-76, prin., 1976—; vis. lectr. Eastern Mich. U., 1976-78; Dale Carnegie instr., 1980—. Mem. adv. council Inkster (Mich.) YWCA, 1978-79. Mem. Mich. Elem. and Middle Sch. Prins., Nat. Assn. Elem. Sch. Prins., League Cooperating Prins., Mich. Assn. for Individually Guided Edn., Mich. Reading Assn., Mich. Assn. Children with Learning Disabilities, Westwood Adminstrs. Assn. (pres. 1974-75, 76-77, 78-79), Mich. Assn. for Supervision and Curriculum Devel., Pi Lambda Theta. Presbyterian. Home: 9314 Rosedale Blvd Allen Park MI 48101 Office: 25251 Annapolis St Dearborn Heights MI 48125

PEARL, IRWIN ALBERT, chemist; b. Seattle, Dec. 25, 1913; s. Louis and Lena (Stusser) P.; B.S., U. Wash., 1934; M.S., 1935, Ph.D., 1937; m. Lillian Aronin, Dec. 24, 1938; children—Cheryl Pearl Rubin, Hugh Stuart. Supr. labs. Wash. Dept. Conservation and Devel., 1938-40; research asso. U. Wash., 1940-41; sr. research asso. Inst. Paper Chemistry, Appleton, Wis., 1941-76; cons. in chemistry, Appleton, 1977—. Bd. dirs. Moses Montefiore Congregation, Appleton, 1950-69, chmn., 1955; chmn. United Jewish Charities, 1951-55. Fellow N.Y. Acad. Scis.; mem. TAPPI (chmn. wood chemistry div. 1971), Forest Products Research Soc. (chmn. wood conversion div. 1960), Am. Chem. Soc. (exec. com. cellulose and wood chemistry div. 1964), Phytochem. Soc. N.Am., Outagami Philatelic Soc. (past pres.), Wis. Fedn. Stamp Clubs (past pres.), Am. Philatelic Soc., Brit. Assn. Palestine and Israel Philatelists, Soc. Israel Philatelists. Club: B'nai Brith. Author: Chemistry of Lignin, 1967. Contbr. articles on wood chemistry and related subjects to profl. jours. Home: 2115 N Linwood Ave Appleton WI 54911

PEARSALL, THOMAS EDWARD, educator; b. N.Y.C., Oct. 28, 1925; s. Lewis and Anna V. (Farrell) P.; A.B. magna cum laude, Colgate U., 1949; M.A., U. Tex., 1956; Ph.D., U. Denver, 1960; m. Anne K. Chimato, Sept. 1, 1946; children—Mark, Susan, Morgan, David. Asso. prof. English, USAF Acad., Colo., 1959-69; prof. tech. communication U. Minn., St. Paul, 1969—, head dept. rhetoric, 1979—; dir. Communication Sci., Inc.; cons. to Medtronic, Inc., St. Paul Cos. Served in USAF, 1949-69. Named Twin Cities Tech. Communicator of the Yr., 1975; recipient Distinguished Tech. Communication award Soc. for Tech. Communication, 1974. Asso. fellow Soc. for Tech. Communication (program chmn. internat. tech. communication conference 1978). mem. MLA, Nat. Council Tchrs. English, Council Programs in Tech. and Sci. Communication (pres. 1974-78). Co-author: Reporting Tech. Info., 1968, 4th edit., 1980; Better Spelling, 1971; How to Write for the World of Work, 1977, 2d edit., 1982; author: Teaching Tech. Writing, 1975, Audience Analysis for Tech. Writing, 1969. Home: 2098 Folwell St Saint Paul MN 55108 Office: Dept of Rhetoric University of Minnesota Saint Paul MN 55108

PEARSE, PAUL THEODORE, broadcast advt. exec.; b. Montclair, N.J., Jan. 5, 1943; s. Bernard Paul and Isabel (Hussa) P.; B.A., Mich. State U., 1965; postgrad. Wayne State U. 1967-68; m. Gail Ann Schollenberger, Oct. 9, 1965; children—Jennifer Ann, Jessica Alexandra. Broadcast media buyer/planner Campbell-Ewald Advt., Detroit, 1965-67; account exec. Blair TV, Detroit, 1968-77, v.p. sales, 1977-79, v.p., gen. mgr., 1980—; radio/tv cons. Mich. State U., 1980—; cons. in field. Served as lt., USN, 1970-76. Mem. Sta. Reps. Assn. (pres. 1970-72), Mich. Assn. Broadcasters, Detroit Advt. Assn., Detroit Advt. Athletic League (pres. 1969—). Repbulican. Roman Catholic. Clubs: Players, Detroit Golf. Office: 1811 Fisher Bldg Detroit MI 48202

PEARSON, GERALD WILLIAM, chem. co. exec.; b. Detroit, Mar. 4, 1933; s. Mark L. and Daisy Bernice (Dibble) P.; B.S. in Chem. Engring., Mich. State U., 1955; grad. Advanced Mgmt. Program, U. Tex., 1970; m. Mary Frances Speck, Oct. 15, 1954; children—Dennis Mark, Kim Michelle. With Dow Chem. Co., 1955—, pres. Industrias Dow, Argentina, 1970-71, mng. dir. Dow Quimica do Brazil, 1972-74, corp. dir. product research, Midland, Mich., 1975-77, v.p., gen. mgr. Dow Chem. Investment Fin. Corp. and gen. mgr. organic chems. dept., 1978-80; comml. v.p. Dow Chem. Can., Ltd., Sarnia, Ont., 1980—, also dir.; dir. Piramides Brasilia, Banco Cidade, Spuma Pac. Served to capt U.S. Army, 1957-58. Mem. Am. C. of C. in Argentina, Synthetic Organic Chem. Mfrs. Assn. (dir., sr. v.p. 1980), Soc. Plastics Industries (Can. bd. 1981, exec. com.), Can. Chem. Producers Assn. (bus. econs. com. 1981), Tau Beta Pi. Republican. Episcopalian. Home: Rural Route 2 Camlachie ON N0N 1E0 Canada Office: PO Box 1012 Modeland Rd Sarnia ON N7T 7K7 Canada

PEARSON, JOHN EDGAR, ins. co. exec.; b. Mpls., Jan. 17, 1927; s. Edgar Clarence and Viola Esther (Quist) P.; student Gustavus Adolphus Coll., 1944-45, Northwestern U., 1945-46; B.B.A., U. Minn., 1948; m. Sharon M. Nessler, Nov. 4, 1950; children—Cynthia Lynn, Thomas Calvin. Sales trainee Minn. Mining & Mfg. Co., St. Paul, 1948-49; group rep. Northwestern Nat. Life Ins. Co., Seattle, 1949-51; salesman Marsh & McLennan Inc., Seattle, 1951-53; with Northwestern Nat. Life Ins. Co., Mpls., 1953—, pres., chief exec. officer, dir., 1975—, chmn., 1981—; chmn. bd. North Atlantic Life Ins. Co., 1980—, No. Life Ins. Co.; dir. Northwestern Nat. Bank. Active United Way; Republican precinct committeeman, 1970-71; bd. dirs. Found. Health Care Evaluation, 1971-75, Meth. Hosp., 1979—, Mpls. Soc. Fine Arts, 1980—, Greater Mpls. Met. Housing Corp.; chmn. Mpls. Urban Coalition, 1978-80. Served with USNR, 1944-46. Mem. Ins. Fedn. Minn. (chmn. 1981—), Am. Council Life Ins. (dir. 1979—), Health Ins. Assn. Am. (dir. 1979—), Mpls. C. of C. (dir.). Clubs: Masons, Mpls., Minikahda Country (Mpls.). Edina Country, Rotary. Home: 5027 Wooddale Ln Edina MN 55424 Office: 20 Washington Ave S Minneapolis MN 55440

PEARSON, LOUISE MARY (MRS. NELS K. PEARSON), mfg. co. exec.; b. Inverness, Scotland, Dec. 14, 1919 (parents Am. citizens); d. Louis Houston and Jessie M. (McKenzie) Lenox; grad. high sch.; m. Nels Kenneth Pearson, June 28, 1941; children—Lorine (Mrs. Ronald Walters), Karla (Mrs. John Rapp). Dir. Wauconda Tool & Engring. Co., Inc., Algonquin, Ill., 1950-80; reporter Oak Leaflet, Crystal Lake, Ill., 1944-47, Sidelights, Wilmette, Ill., 1969-72, 79-82. Active Girl Scouts U.S.A., 1955-65. Recipient award for appreciation work with Girl Scouts, 1965. Clubs: Antique Automobile of Am. (Hershey, Pa.); Veteran Motor Car (Boston); Classic Car of Am. (Madison, N.J.). Home: 125 Dole Ave Crystal Lake IL 60014

PEARSON, MILO LORENTZ (LON), educator; b. Murray, Utah, Feb. 13, 1939; s. Milo Willard and Gulli Victoria (Peterson) P.; B.A. magna cum laude, U. Utah, 1965, M.A., 1968; Ph.D. (NDEA Title IV fellow 1966-69), UCLA, 1973; postdoctoral fellow Johns Hopkins U., 1975-76; m. Janet Stepan, Oct. 7, 1961; children—Russell, Stephanie, Robert, Richard, Sharon. Asst. instr. U. Utah, Salt Lake City, 1965-66; asso. instr. UCLA, 1969-70; instr. Spanish, U. Mo., Rolla, 1970-73, asst. prof., 1973-77, asso. prof., 1977—, head lang. div., 1977-80, varsity coach men's soccer, 1979-80, asst. varsity coach, 1980—, head coach women's varsity soccer, 1982—. Served with Army N.G., 1961-62. NSF fellow, 1971, 73; Nat. Endowment Humanities fellow, 1981; recipient Award of Merit, Big Piney dist. Boy Scouts Am., 1981. Mem. Internat. Inst. Iberoamerican Literature, Am. Assn. Tchrs. Spanish and Portuguese, MLA (Del. Assembly for Midwest and Rock Mountain States), Midwest MLA, Linguistic Soc. Am., Mo. Philol. Assn., Ark. Philol. Assn., Fgn. Lang. Assn. Mo. (mem. exec. bd. 1973—, cited for disting. service), Phi Kappa Phi. Mormon (2d counselor Bishopric of Rolla ward). Club: Optimists Internat. Author: Nicomedes Guzman: Proletarian Author in Chile's Literary Generation of 1938, 1976. Contbr. articles in field to profl. jours. Home: 933 E 7th St Rolla MO 65401 Office: Dept Humanities University Missouri Rolla MO 65401

PEARSON, NELS KENNETH, mfg. co. exec.; b. Algonquin, Ill., May 2, 1918; s. Nels Pehr and Anna (Fyre) P.; student pub. schs.; m. Louise Mary Houston Lenox, June 28, 1941; children—Lorine Marie Pearson Walters, Karla Jean Pearson Rapp. Assembler, Oak Mfg. Co., Crystal Lake, Ill., 1936-38, machine operator, assembly line foreman, 1938-43, apprentice tool and die maker, 1946-50; co-founder, pres. Wauconda Tool & Engring. Co., Inc., Algonquin, 1950—; co-founder, treas. Kenmode Tool & Engring. Co., Inc., Algonquin, 1960-72. Mem. McHenry County Edn. and Tng. Com., 1961—, treas., 1961—. Served with AUS, 1943-46. Mem. Am. Soc. Tool and Mfg. Engrs. Clubs: Moose, Antique Auto, Classic Car, Vet. Motor Car, Horseless Carriage. Home: 125 Dole Ave Crystal Lake IL 60014 Office: Huntley Rd Algonquin IL 60102

PEARSON, NORMAN, town planning cons., author; b. Stanley, County Durham, Eng., Oct. 24, 1928; s. Joseph and Mary (Pearson) P.; came to Can., 1954; B.A. with honors in Town and Country Planning, U. Durham (Eng.), 1951; Ph.D. in Land Economy, Internat. Inst. Advanced Studies, 1979; M.B.A., Pacific Western U., 1980; m. Gerda Maria Josefine Riedl, July 25, 1972. Cons. to Stanley Urban Dist. Council, U.K., 1946-47; planning asst. Accrington Town Plan and Bedford County Planning Survey, U. Durham Planning Team, 1947-49; planning asst. to Allen and Mattocks, cons. planners and landscape designers, Newcastle upon Tyne, U.K., 1949-51; adminstrv. asst. Scottish Div., Nat. Coal Bd., Scotland, 1951-52; planning asst. London County Council, U.K., 1953-54; planner Central Mortgage and Housing Corp., Ottawa, Ont., Can., 1954-55; planning analyst City of Toronto Planning Bd., 1955-56; dir. of planning Hamilton Wentworth Planning Area Bd., Hamilton, Ont., Can., 1956-59; dir. planning for Burlington (Ont.) and Suburban Area Planning Bd., 1959-62, also commr. planning, 1959-62; pres. Tanfield Enterprises Ltd., London, Ont., Can., 1976—, Norman Pearson Planning Assos. Ltd., Can., 1981; cons. in planning, 1962—; life mem. U.S. Com. for Monetary Research and Edn., 1976—; spl. lectr. in planning McMaster U., Hamilton, 1956-64, Waterloo (Ont.) Luth. U., 1961-63; asst. prof. geography and planning U. Waterloo (Ont.), 1963-67; asso. prof. geography U. Guelph (Ont.), 1967-72; prof. polit. sci. U. Western Ont., London, 1972-77; mem. Social Scis., Econ. and Legal Aspects Com. of Research Adv. Bd. Internat. Joint Commn., 1972-76; cons. to City of Waterloo, 1973-76, Province of Ont., 1969-70; adviser to Georgian Bay Regional Devel. Council, 1968-72; real estate appraiser, province of Ont., 1976—. Pres. Unitarian Ch. of Hamilton, 1960-61. Served with RAF, 1951-53. Decorated knight Sovereign Order St. John of Jerusalem. Fellow Royal Town Planning Inst. (Bronze medal award 1957), Royal Econ. Soc.; mem. Internat. Soc. of City and Regional Planners, Am., Canadian insts. planners, Canadian Polit. Sci. Assn. Clubs: Masons, Empire; Ontario; University (London). Author: (with others) An Inventory of Joint Programmes and Agreements Affecting Canada's Renewable Resources, 1964. Editor, co-author (with others) Regional and Resource Planning in Canada, 1963, rev. edit., 1970; editor (with others) The Pollution Reader, 1968. Contbr. numerous articles on town planning to profl. jours. and chpts. in field to books. Home: 223 Commissioners Rd East London ON N6C 2S9 Canada Office: PO Box 5362 Station A London ON N6A 4L6 Canada

PEARSON, ROBERT EDWIN, psychiatrist; b. Toledo, Apr. 29, 1923; s. Albin Lawrence and Elizabeth Genevieve (Christ) P.; B.S., Wayne State U., 1949, M.D., 1952; children—Robert, Michael, Barbara, Eric, Brian, Katherine. Intern, Highland Park (Mich.) Gen. Hosp., 1952-53; gen. practice medicine, Boyne City, Mich., 1953-66; resident in psychiatry Traverse City (Mich.) Regional Psychiat. Hosp., 1966-69, chief receiving service, 1969-71, asst. dir. psychiat. edn., 1971-78, dir. div. adult psychiatry, 1978—; asst. clin. prof. psychiatry Mich. State U., 1971—. Served with U.S. Army, 1941-45. Decorated D.F.C., Air medals (13). Fellow Am. Soc. Clin. Hypnosis (ann. award 1972, past pres.), Soc. Clin. and Exptl. Hypnosis; mem. Am. Soc. Clin. Hypnosis Ednl. and Research Found. (chmn. 1976-77, ann. award 1976), AMA, Am. Psychiat. Assn., Am. Psychol. Assn., Mich. State Med. Soc. Contbr. articles to profl. jours. Home and Office: 1001 W 11th St Traverse City MI 49684

PEARSON, ROBERT LEONARD, educator; b. Allamakee County, Iowa, July 25, 1927; s. Leonard Victor and Mabel Julia (Swenson) P.; B.B.A., State U. Iowa, 1959, M.A., 1961; m. Donna M. Moellering, July 17, 1955; children—Tracy, Eric. Barber, Monona, Iowa, 1949-51, 55-57; tchr. bus. edn. public schs., Humboldt, Iowa, 1960-66; tchr., head dept. vocat. office occupations Iowa Central Community Coll., Ft. Dodge, 1966—. Bd. dirs., v.p. Shelter Care of N. Central Iowa, 1980—; bd. dirs. Fellowship of Christian Athletes, 1977—. Served with USN, 1945-46, USAF, 1951-55. Mem. NEA, Iowa Bus. Edn. Assn., Iowa Office Edn. Coordinator's Assn. (pres. 1971), Iowa Vocat. Assn., Am. Vocat. Assn. Democrat. Methodist. Club: Elks. Home: 2336 7th Ave N Fort Dodge IA 50501 Office: 330 Ave M Fort Dodge IA 50501

PEARSON, RODGER HUGH, state ofcl.; b. Albany, Calif., July 21, 1943; s. Bernard Victor and Marjorie (Henriks) P.; B.S. in Animal Sci., Wash. State U., Pullman, 1966; married; children—Deborah, Kesiah, Bruce. Regulatory services dir. S.D. Dept. Agr., Pierre, 1969-80, sec. agr., 1980—. Served in U.S. Army, 1966-68. Mem. Pierre Jaycees (dir. 1972-77), Nat. Assn. State Depts. Agr., Izaak Walton League. Republican. Club: Elks. Home: 1020 N Central St Pierre SD 57901 Office: Anderson Bldg Pierre SD 57501

PEARSON, ROY HAROLD, savs. and loan exec.; b. Galesburg, Ill., June 10, 1920; s. Roy and Jennie (Palmquist) P.; grad. Browns Bus. Coll., Galesburg, 1939; cert. Grad. Sch. Savs. and Loan Assns., Ind. U., 1963; m. Rosa J. Johnson, June 9, 1946; 1 dau., Mary Jo Pearson Eklund. With Fidelity Fed. Savs. & Loan Assn., Galesburg, 1939—, sec.-treas., 1954-57, v.p., 1957-66, exec. v.p., 1966-71, pres., 1971—, dir., 1968—; vice-chmn. bd. Fed. Home Loan Bank Chgo., 1972. Pres., treas. Galesburg Civic Music Assn., 1966; pres. St. Mary's Hosp. Found., Galesburg, 1979-82; vice-chmn. Christian radio fellowship com. Sta. WDLM-FM, 1978-82. Served with U.S. Army, 1942-45. Mem. Ill. Savs. and Loan League (chmn. fed. com. 1974-75), Fed. Savs. and Loan Council Ill. (dir., pres. 1973), Galesburg C. of C. (pres. 1972-73), Inst. Fin. Edn., Galesburg Real Estate Bd. Baptist. Club: Galesburg Exchange (pres., dist. gov. 1960).

PEASE, DONALD JAMES, congressman; b. Toledo, Sept. 26, 1931; s. Russell Everett and Helen Mary (Mullen) P.; B.S. in Journalism, Ohio U., Athens, 1953, M.A. in Govt., 1955; Fulbright scholar Kings Coll., U. Durham, (Eng.), 1954-55; m. Jeanne Camille Wendt, Aug. 29, 1953; 1 dau., Jennifer. Mem. Ohio Senate, 1965-66; mem. Ohio Ho. of Reps., 1969-74; mem. Ohio Senate, 1975-76; mem. 95th-96th Congresses from Ohio. Chmn., Oberlin Pub. Utilities Commn., 1960-61; mem. Oberlin City Council, 1961-63. Served with U.S. Army, 1955-57. Home: 140 Elm St Oberlin OH 44074

PEASE, EDWARD ALLAN, lawyer, state senator; b. Terre Haute, Ind., May 22, 1951; s. Robert Richard and Joanna Rose (Pilant) P.; A.B. with distinction (Wendell Willkie scholar), Ind. U., Bloomington, 1973, J.D. cum laude, Indpls., 1977; postgrad. Memphis State U., 1975-76, Ind. State U., 1978-79. Gen. law clk. appellate and contracts div. Office Ind. Atty. Gen., Indpls., 1974-75; nat. dir. alumni affairs Pi Kappa Alpha Frat., Memphis, 1975-76; admitted to Ind. bar, 1977; partner firm Thomas, Thomas & Pease, Brazil, Ind., 1977—; mem. Ind. Senate, 1980—; dir. 1st Bank & Trust Co. Clay County. Bd. dirs. Brazil-Clay County YMCA, Ind. Asbury Towers, Greencastle; lay leader 1st United Meth. Ch., Brazil; mem. exec. bd. Wabash Valley council Boy Scouts Am., 1972—, v.p., 1977—. Recipient Silver Beaver award Boy Scouts Am., 1975. Mem. Ind. Bar Assn., Phi Beta Kappa. Republican. Clubs: Columbia (Indpls.); Rotary. Office: PO Box 194 Brazil IN 47834

PEAVEY, RUSSELL GUY, JR., pharmacist; b. Flint, Mich., Oct. 15, 1929; s. Russell Guy and Marion Francis P.; B.S. in Pharmacy, Ferris Inst., Big Rapids, Mich., 1951; m. Dolores R. Brown, Sept. 1, 1950; children—Paula Jean, Johnny Guy, Jeffrey Alan. Pharmacist, Mut. Drugs, Niles, Mich., 1951-52, Gutes Drugs, Owosso, Mich., 1952-54; pharmacist, mgr. Gould Drug Co., Mt. Pleasant, Mich., 1954-67; chief pharmacist Mt. Pleasant Regional Center for Devel. Disabilities, 1967—. Methodist. Club: Masons. Office: Mount Pleasant Regional Center PO Box 448 Mount Pleasant MI 48858

PECARO, DANIEL THOMAS, radio and TV sta. exec.; b. Chgo., Jan. 24, 1926; s. William and Rose Catherine Kopke P.; B.S., DePaul U., 1950; m. Nancy Jean Mihills, Apr. 15, 1950; children—Timothy Scott, Daniel Drew. Tchr., sports coach Chgo. Pub. Schs., 1950-55; radio producer, dir., writer WGN radio, Chgo., 1955-57, prodn. supr., 1957-58, asst. program mgr., 1958-60, program mgr., 1960-62, program mgr. WGN-TV, 1962-65, group P program mgr. WGN-TV, KDAL-TV, KWGN-TV, 1965-66, v.p., group program chmn., 1966-67, v.p., gen. mgr. WGN-TV, 1967-72, exec. v.p., gen. mgr., 1972-74, exec. v.p., gen. mgr., dir. WGN Continental Broadcasting Co., 1974-75, pres., chief exec. officer, 1975—; pres. WGN Colo. Inc., also dir.; dir. KDAL Inc., WGN Continental Sales Co. Mem. program policy adv. com. Catholic TV Network, Archdiocese Chgo., 1975—; bd. dirs. Chgo. Boys Clubs, 1976—. Served with Amphibious Corps USNR. Mem. Nat. Assn. Broadcasters (TV bd. dirs.). Clubs: Oak Park Country, Execs., Economic. Home: 2955 N Oak Park Ave Chicago IL 60634 Office: 2501 W Bradley Pl Chicago IL 60618

PECK, MELISSA JANE, marketing research co. ofcl.; b. Milw., Aug. 27, 1955; d. Emmett James and Judith B. (Birenholtz) P.; B.S. in Marketing Mgmt., Syracuse U., 1977. Project supr. Conway/Milliken Corp., Chgo., 1977-79; account supr. Tele-Research/TRIM, Inc., Chgo., 1979-81, v.p., 1982—. Mem. Am. Mktg. Assn. (registrar Chgo. Midwest Research Conf. 1980-81, vice chmn. 1982). Home: 3450 Elaine Pl Chicago IL 60657 Office: One E Wacker Dr Chicago IL 60601

PECK, ROBIN LEE, ednl. adminstr.; b. Painesville, Ohio, May 1, 1942; s. Neil McKinley and Shirley Waltina (Palmer) P.; B.S., Kent State U., 1964, M.Ed., 1968; m. Gale Lucile Ells, June 26, 1965; children—Heather Lyn, Shane Edward. Tchr. indsl. arts Kenston Middle Sch., Chagrin Falls, Ohio, 1964-70, guidance counselor, 1970-71, asst. prin., 1972-77; prin. Ledgemont High Sch., Thompson, Ohio, 1977-78; dir. secondary edn. Geauga County Dept. Edn., Chardon, Ohio, 1978—. Lt., v.p. Hambden Vol. Fire Dept.; mem. Hambden Twp. Bd. Trustees, 1980—. Cert. EMT. Mem. Assn. Supervision and Curriculum Devel., Sigma Phi Epsilon. Republican. Home: 13645 Radcliffe St Chardon OH 44024 Office: 401 South St Chardon OH 44024

PECK, SUZANNE WEXLER, mgmt. cons.; b. Chgo., Oct. 12, 1945; d. Louis A. and Ruth Marie (Lewis) W.; B.Sc., Northwestern U., 1967; m. Abe Peck, Mar. 19, 1977. Tng. specialist Interaction Assos., San Francisco, 1971-73; exec. dir. Internat. Bus. Communications Inst., San Francisco, 1973-76; mgr. Erhard Seminars Tng., San Francisco, 1974-76; v.p. Leopold & Assos., Chgo., 1977—, also dir.; instr. Dominican Coll. San Rafael, Calif., 1973-74. Mem. Northwestern Club Chgo., Oak Brook Assn. Commerce and Industry, Am. Soc. Tng. and Devel., Assn. Humanistic Psychology, Internat. Giraffe Appreciation Soc. Office: 2650 N Lakeview St Chicago IL 60614

PECKENPAUGH, DONALD HUGH, psychologist, ednl. cons.; b. East Chicago, Ind., Aug. 11, 1928; s. George Martin and Thelma Mintia (Anderson) P.; Ph.B., U. Chgo., 1948, A.M., 1954, Ph.D. (NIMH fellow), 1968; m. Mary Frances Dreesen, Sept. 2, 1950; children—Ann Dreesen, Eve Louise. Psychologist, sch. adminstr., Gary, Ind., 1950-58, Munster, Ind., 1958-65; cons., Pitts., 1967-68; supt. schs., West Bend, Wis., 1967-69, Duluth, Minn., 1969-72, Birmingham, Mich., 1972-78, Palos Hills, Ill., 1978-79; psychologist, cons. N.W. Ind. Spl. Edn. Coop., Crown Point, Ind., 1979—; pvt. practice cons. Served with U.S. Army, 1952-54. Mem. Am. Assn. Sch. Adminstrs., Sch. Mgmt. Study Group, Assn. Supervision and Curriculum Devel., Nat. Soc. for Study Edn., Phi Delta Kappa. Author books, including: Closing a School, 1977; The Public School as Moral Authority, 1977. Home: 3 Brook Ln Palos Park IL 60464 Office: 2150 W 97th Ave Crown Point IN 46307

PECKHAM, BILLIE JEAN, sch. adminstr.; b. Bonnersdale, Ark., Nov. 20, 1930; d. Thomas Verner and Esther Lillian (Wallis) Lambert; B.A. in Elementary and Secondary Edn., Union Coll., Lincoln, Nebr., 1956; M.A. in Ednl. Adminstrn., U. Kans., 1977; reading specialist, Washburn U., Topeka, 1980; m. Daniel Hammond Peckham, June 8, 1952; children—Kim Wendall, John Mark. Elem. sch. tchr., 1950-52, 54-56; overseas worker, 1961-65; edn. supr. Seventh-Day schs. schs., Kans. and Nebr., 1977-80, asso. supt., 1981—. Mem. Assn. Supervision and Curriculum Devel., Internat. Reading Assn., Delta Kappa Gamma. Home: 6816 Fountaindale St Topeka KS 66614 Office: 3440 Urish Rd Topeka KS 66614

PECKINPAUGH, PHILIP EARL, water conditioning co. exec.; b. Muncie, Ind., June 5, 1946; s. Robert Ephraim and Audrey Vivian (Rawlings) P.; A.B., U. Cin., 1968; M.B.A., Ind. U., 1972; m. Janet Lee Bartchy, Jan. 25, 1969. Dir. spl. edn. Perry Sch. Dist., Massillon, Ohio, 1968-70; mgr. internat. personnel dept. Borg-Warner Corp., Chgo., 1972-73; v.p. Peck Water Systems Inc., Canton, Ohio, 1973-77, pres., 1977—. Bd. dirs. Canton Urban League, 1977, Jr. Achievement of Stark County, 1978—, Better Bus. Bur. N.E. Ohio, 1978—. Cert. water conditioning specialist. Mem. Canton Jaycees (dir. 1974), Ohio (pres. 1977), U.S. water quality assns., Canton C. of C. Presbyterian. Club: Canton Rotary (dir. 1978—). Home: 8640 Foxglove Ave NW Clinton OH 44216 Office: 1434 Cleveland Ave NW PO Box 9006 Canton OH 44711

PECSOK, MARILYN WIEGAND, civic worker; b. Indpls., Nov. 19, 1929; d. Homer Louis and Florence (Randel) Wiegand; A.B. in Romance Langs., De Pauw U., 1951; M.S. in Edn., Butler U., 1955; m. John Gilbert Pecsok, July 14, 1962. Tchr. elem. grades, supr. student tchrs. Indpls. Pub. Schs., 1951-62. Advt. coordinator 500 Festival Program, 1978; vice precinct committeewoman Noblesville Republican Com., 1963-66; chmn. adv. council Vol. Bur., 1969-72; v.p. Hoosier Capital council Girl Scouts U.S.A., 1969-72; v.p. community projects Jr. League, Indpls., 1968-69; sch. vol. council Indpls. Public Schs., 1972-74; sec., v.p. Ind. chpt. Cystic Fibrosis Research Found., 1972, 75, bd. dirs., 1976-77, 80—; pres. United Way League, 1978-79; chmn. residential div. United Way, 1979, mem. admissions com., 1978-81; chmn. local arrangements Ind. Gov.'s Conf. on Libraries and Info. Services, 1979; bd. dirs. Indpls. chpt. ARC, 1974-80, Community Service Council, 1978, Children's Bur. Indpls., 1981—; treas. Children's Bur. Aux., 1979-81, v.p., 1981—; mem. Indpls. Day Nursery Aux. Bd., 1975—; mem. Child Abuse and Neglect Council, 1980—; pres. Breath of Life Guild, 1973-74, 81—; alumni bd. Butler U., 1979-80, sec., 1981—. Recipient hon. award Gov. of Ind., 1976, Those Spl. People award Women in Communications, 1969. Mem. AAUW (pres. Indpls. br. 1962-64, state bd., library chmn. 1964-68), DAR (regent Jonathon Jennings chpt. 1968-70), Women's Archtl. League (pres. 1965-66), Classic Car Club (sec.-treas. Ind. region 1976-78), Milestone Car Soc. (exec. sec. 1977-79), Mortar Bd. (pres. alumnae 1965), Phi Beta Kappa (pres. Ind. Alpha chpt. 1970-72), Theta Sigma Phi, Delta Kappa Gamma (pres. chpt. 1966-68, pres. Indpls. council 1970-72), Kappa Kappa Kappa (pres. 1971-72, state chmn. 1977—), Pi Beta Phi (pres. house corp. 1955-62, pres. Indpls. alumnae 1966-68, chmn. alumnae adv. council 1978-79). Presbyterian. Home: 4716 E 75th St Indianapolis IN 46250

PEDERSON, DAVID DAVIS, psychologist, hypnotherapist, psychic; b. Duluth, Minn., Oct. 30, 1933; s. Charles and Leila M. (Davis) P.; B.A., U. No. Iowa, 1976, M.A., 1977; M.A., U. Sussex (Eng.), 1976; m. Lorena Collmann, Jan. 14, 1953; children—David C., Derek C. Television news dir. KIFI-TV, Idaho Falls, Idaho; news anchorman KGLO-TV, Mason City, Iowa; pvt. practice psychol. counseling, hypnotherapy, Mason City, 1971—; profl. psychic; lectr. in field; dir. Midwestern Inst. Parapsychology, 1967-73. Counselor in adult edn. program North Iowa Area Community Coll., 1976—. Served with U.S. Army, 1949-56. Decorated Purple Heart, Silver Star; recipient Pub. Service award USAF, 1974. Mem. Am. Personnel and Guidance Assn., Ia. Assn. Life Long Learning, SEARCH of Minn., VFW, Am. Legion, Assn. for Ethical Hypnosis. Republican. Author: The Heroic Thieves, 1955; Sunday Is a Day of . . ., 1956. Home: 1200 Meadowbrook Dr Mason City IA 50401 Office: PO Box 262 Mason City IA 50401

PEDERSON, ROBERT MURWIN, communication exec.; b. Jamestown, N.D., June 23, 1951; s. Murwin James and Jane Margaret (Schwartz) P.; B.A., No. Ill. U., 1973, M.A. in Speech Communications, 1975; m. Phyllis Lynn Paxton, Aug. 26, 1972; children—Jennifer Diane, Nicholas R. Sales mgr. Media Masters Inc., DeKalb, Ill., 1972-73; TV prodn. mgr. No. Ill. U., DeKalb, 1973-76; dir., writer Sta. WREX-TV, Rockford, Ill., 1976; writer, producer State Farm Ins. Cos., Bloomington, Ill., 1976—; photographer E. & L Trucking, Palos Heights, Ill., 1975—. Vol. worker United Way, DeKalb, 1975. Mem. Nat. Assn. Ednl. Broadcasters (mem. producer's council 1975-77, mgr.'s council 1975-77). Methodist. Author: Life Claim Investigations Workbook, 1977; (videotapes) Wichita Falls, Texas, April 10, 1979; telephone Techniques, 1980; Estate Analysis, 1981; Agency Manager/Health Marketing, 1981; (audio tapes) IRA-KEOGH-TSA, 1979/81; Business Life Insurance, 1981; Corporate Retirement Plans, 1981; Property and Casualty Claim Investigation, 1981. Home: 2204 Clearwater Bloomington IL 61701 Office: One State Farm Plaza Bloomington IL 61701

PEDERSON, VERNON R., judge; b. Surrey, N.D., Sept. 11, 1919; s. John and Tilda (Torgerson) P.; B.S.C., U. N.D., 1947, Ll.B., 1949, J.D., 1969; m. Evelyn I. Kraby, Oct. 11, 1952; children—Kathy, Mary. Admitted to N.D. bar, 1949; asso. firm Benjamin A. Bradford, Minot, N.D., 1949-51; spl. agt., atty. Office Price Stblzn., Fargo, N.D., 1951-53; spl. asst. atty. gen., gen. counsel N.D. State Hwy. Dept., Bismarck, 1953-74; justice N.D. Supreme Ct., Bismarck, 1975—. Served with U.S. Army, 1941-45. Mem. Am. Bar Assn., N.D. Bar Assn., Am. Judicature Soc., Inst. Jud. Adminstrn. Lutheran. Office: State Capitol Bismarck ND 58505

PEDICINI, LOUIS JAMES, truck trailer co. exec.; b. Detroit, June 29, 1926; s. Louis I. and Myra Ann (Bergan) P.; B.S.E.E., Wayne U., 1955; m. Ellen Sylvia Mulden, June 5, 1948; 1 son, Eric Louis. Dept. head Gen. Motors Corp., 1948-58; exec. v.p. Lester B. Knight & Assos., Inc., Chgo., 1959-76; exec. v.p. ops. Pullman Trailmobile, Chgo., 1976-81; mng. dir. Ingersoll Engrs., Inc., Rockford, Ill., 1981—. Served with U.S. Army, 1944-46. Fellow Inst. Brit. Foundrymen; mem. Am. Foundrymen's Soc. (past dir.). Republican. Clubs: Skokie Country (Glencoe, Ill.); Plaza (Chgo.). Home: 405 Sheridan Rd Kenilworth IL 60043 Office: 707 Fulton St Rockford IL 61101

PEDIGO, HOWARD KENNETH, steel fabricating co. exec.; b. Charleston, Ill., Aug. 5, 1931; s. Clarence and Cecil (Elliot) P.; B.S. in Civil Engring., Rose Poly. Inst., 1953; M.B.A., Ohio State U., 1963; m. Doris Dean Mullins, Mar. 21, 1954; children—Susan Kay, John Jay. Stress analyst Bendix Corp., South Bend, Ind., 1955-61; project engr. Wright Field, Dayton, Ohio, 1961-63; project mgr. TRW Corp., Cleve., 1963-64; exec. v.p. Universal Tank & Iron Co., Indpls., 1964—. Chmn., United Way Hendricks County (Ind.), 1973; bd. dirs. United Way Greater Indpls., 1975-77; bd. indsl. adviser Rose-Hulman Inst. Served to 1st lt. U.S. Army, 1953-55. Registered profl. engr., Ala., Ill., Ind., N.J., Ohio, Tenn., Wis. Mem. ASCE, Am. Water Works Assn. (steel tank com.), Steel Plate Fabricators Assn., Rose Tech. Alumni (class agt. 1971-73), Lambda Chi Alpha. Methodist. Club: Elks. Home: 633 Elm Dr Plainfield IN 46168 Office: 11221 Rockville Rd Indianapolis IN 46231

PEDOTO, GERALD JOSEPH, steel mfg. co. supr.; b. Jersey City, Jan. 5, 1948; s. Salvatore Joseph and Rosalie (Benigno) P.; B.S., Bowling Green State U., 1970; M.B.A., U. Akron, 1976; m. Karen Sue Knutty, June 28, 1975; children—Deborah Louise, Donald Lee, Timothy Scott. Trainee indsl. engring. Timken Co., Canton, Ohio, 1970, asso. indsl. engr., 1972-73, supervisory candidate, 1973-74, foreman product inspection, 1974-75, supr. indirect labor, 1975-80, supr. heat treatment, 1980—. Active United Way, YMCA fund drs. Served with U.S. Army, 1970-72; Korea. Decorated Army Commendation Medal; cert. mgr. Inst. Cert. Profl. Mgrs. Mem. Internat. Mgmt. Council, Nat. Mgmt. Assn., Assn. M.B.A. Execs., Alpha Tau Omega, Beta Gamma Sigma, Omicron Delta Kappa. Republican. Mem. United Ch. of Christ. Home: 3419 Cain St NW North Canton OH 44720 Office: Gambrinus Bearing Plant Timken Co 1835 Dueber Ave SW Canton OH 44706

PEDRAJA, RAFAEL RODOBALDO, food scientist; b. Sagua la Grande, Cuba, Oct. 21, 1929; s. Jesus M. and Ursula H. (Dulzaides) P.; came to U.S., 1953, naturalized, 1962; B.S., Superior Sch. Arts and Trades (Havana), 1947; M.S., U. Havana, 1950, Ph.D., 1952; m. Gladys Hortensia Ochoa, Jan. 23, 1954; children—Ralph Kelvin, Amy Ann. Auditor chemist Chas. Martin Co., Havana, Cuba, 1953; chemist, bacteriologist Specialty Products div. Borden Co., Elgin, Ill., 1953-56; research chemist Griffith Labs., Inc., Chgo., 1956-62; tech. dir. Am. Dry Milk Inst., Chgo., 1962-65; tech. dir. Food Products div. Superior Tea & Coffee Co., Chgo., 1965-67; v.p. research devel. and quality assurance Booth Fisheries div. Consol. Foods Corp., Chgo., 1967—; lectr. sci. and tech. topics related to food industry; mem. U.S. del. to Codex Alimentarius Commn., sponsored by FAO and WHO of UN, 1972—; spl. hon. tech. councilor to Chamber of Fisheries of Nicaragua, 1972—; mem. food sci. and tech. indsl. adv. bd. U. So. Miss., 1974; judge Putnam Food awards Food Processing mag., 1971—. Mem. Am. Chem. Soc., AAAS, Am. Dairy Sci. Assn., Am. Assn. Cereal Chemists, Inst. Food Tech., Am. Soc. Microbiology, Nat. Fisheries Inst. (mem. tech. com. 1970—), Nat. Shrimp Breaders and Processors Assn. (mem. tech. com. 1968—), Am. Soc. Heating, Refrigeration and Air Conditioning Engrs. (mem. tech. com. 1972—). Contbr. articles to sci. jours. Mem. editorial adv. bd. Food Processing mag., 1971—. Home: 2804 White Pine Dr Northbrook IL 60062 Office: 2 N Riverside Plaza Chicago IL 60606

PEDRAM, MANOUCHEHR (MANNY), educator; b. Tehran, Iran, Mar. 26, 1926; came to U.S., 1955, naturalized, 1966; s. Abootaleb and Sharie-Badre-Sadat (Khoii) P.; student Tehran U. Faculty of Law, 1950-53; B.A., Washburn U., 1957; M.S., U. Kans., 1959, Ph.D., 1963; m. Marilyn B. Crist, Jan. 27, 1961; children—Jaleh Denise, Cyrus Andre. Secondary social sci. tchr. Kans. Boys Indsl. Sch., Topeka, 1962-65; social studies tchr. Denver Public Sch. System, 1965-68; secondary edn. specialist, program monitor Mid-Continent Regional Ednl. Lab., Kansas City, Mo., 1968-74; asso. prof. edn. Graceland Coll., Lamoni, Iowa, 1974-79; dir. Internat. Student Counseling Center and coop. urban tchr. edn. program Kansas City, Mo., 1979—. Pres., UN Assn. Greater Kansas City, 1978—; mem. Kansas City Mayor's UN Ann. Program Com., 1978—; bd. dirs. Center for World Community, 1978—; mem. Mayor's Corps of Progress, 1980. Mem. Philosophy of Edn. Soc., Am. Ednl. Studies Assn., Phi Delta Kappa. Democrat. Moslem. Contbr. articles, monographs, book revs. to profl. jours. Home: 8903 Holly St Kansas City MO 64114 Office: 617 W 33 St Kansas City MO 64111

PEDROTTY, JOHN RICHARD, metal cleaning co. exec.; b. Mishawaka, Ind., June 14, 1924; s. Francis Walter and Elizabeth (Cutson) P.; B.N.S., U. Notre Dame 1944; B.S. in Bus. Adminstrn., U. Notre Dame, 1947; m. Gladys May Mercer, May 17, 1947; children—John Richard, Joseph A., James C., Jeffrey F. Field engr. Wheelabrator Frye Corp., Mishawaka, 1947-51; gen. mgr. Indsl. Metal Cleaning Corp., St. Louis, 1951-60, pres., 1960—. Alderman, City of Woodson Terrace (Mo.), 1956-57. Served with USN, 1944-46. Mem. Am. Soc. for Metals, (chpt. chmn. 1979-80), Met. St. Louis Engring. Guidance Council. Roman Catholic. Office: 801 Cass Ave Saint Louis MO 63106

PEEBLER, CHARLES DAVID, JR., advt. and public relations co. exec.; b. Waterloo, Iowa, June 8, 1936; s. Charles D. and Mary E. (Barnett) P.; student Drake U., 1954-56; m. Tonita Worley, Nov. 12, 1979; children—David, Mark, Todd. With Bozell & Jacobs, Internat., Inc., Omaha, 1958—, v.p., mem. plans bd., 1960, pres., 1965, chief exec. officer, 1967, chmn. bd., 1975, pres., chief exec. officer, 1979—; dir. U.S. Nat. Bank of Omaha. Exec. com. United Way of Am., 1960—, nat. exec. com., 1973-76; gen. campaign chmn. United Community Services, 1966; cons. com. SAC, 1973—. Named Religious Heritage of Am. Man of Yr., 1971, Omaha Citizen of the Yr., 1975; recipient Silver medal Omaha Fedn. Advt., 1978. Mem. Am. Assn. Advt. Agencies (dir. 1975—), Young Pres.'s Orgn. (Western area v.p. 1965—, dir., exec. com.), Nat. Outdoor Advt. Inst. (dir. 1968—). Republican. Clubs: Marco Polo (N.Y.C.); Bermuda Dunes (Calif.); Omaha Press, Omaha Plaza, Highland Country (Omaha); Ak-Sar-Ben (councillor 1967, gov. 1976). Contbr. numerous articles to advt. publs. Home: 10530 Pacific St Omaha NE 68114 Office: 10250 Regency Circle Omaha NE 68114

PEEBLES, WILLIAM, real estate developer; b. Oconomowoc, Wis., Apr. 21, 1936; s. Robert William and Frances Alma (Lathrop) P.; B.S., U. Wis., 1958; grad. Wis. Realtors Inst., 1970, Dale Carnegie Inst., 1972; m. Allene Kay Sedlmayr, July 9, 1960; children—Ross William, Robb Allan, Raymond John, Renda Kay. Partner, Peebles Dairy Farm, Oconomowoc, 1958-73; real estate broker specializing in farms and land sales, 1964-70; founder Luxury Homes, Inc., Watertown, Wis., 1970—, pres., 1971—; founder The Plus Devel. Corp., Watertown, 1978—; exec. mng. dir. Hidden Meadows Assn., Watertown, 1979—. Active Boy Scouts Am., Ashippun, Wis., 1975—, troop chmn., 1979—; mem. Recreation Bd. City of Oconomowoc, 1966-69; treas. Waukesha County Conservation Alliance, 1968, sec., 1969, v.p., 1970; youth chmn. Trees for Tomorrow Camp and Projects, Oconomowoc, 1966-69; manufactured housing industry rep. and speaker to Wis. gov. hearings on laws, adminstrv. rules and taxation and consumer needs, 1970-79. Recipient Ser. Plaque, Wis. Mfrd. Housing bd. dirs., 1978. Mem. Wis. Manufactured Housing Assn. (bd. dirs. 1972-79, treas. 1974-79), Waukesha County Bd. Realtors, Wis. Realtors Assn., Nat. Realtors Assn. Methodist. Club: Toastmasters (pres. 1974, 76). Home: 37788 Mapleton Rd Oconomowoc WI 53066 Office: Luxury Homes Inc Hidden Meadows Pkwy Watertown WI 53094*

PEELLE, EVAN, mgmt. cons. behavioral scientist; b. N.Y.C., Oct. 10, 1944; d. William and Vivian (Segal) Sallee; B.S. in Edn., Wayne State U., Detroit, 1966; M.A. in Edn., U. Mich., Ann Arbor, 1973, M.A. in Psychology, 1975, Ph.D. in Behavioral Scis., 1980; 1 dau., Rebecca Ann. Tchr., counselor, adminstr, 1966-72; cons., trainer, mgr. U. Mich., 1972-77; sales mgr. Printing and Pub. Co., Brighton, Mich. 1977-78; dir. research and devel., Plymouth, Mich., 1978-81; pres. Evan Peelle & Asso. Inc. Ann Arbor, Mich., Internat. Survival Inst., Coral Gables, Fla., asso., Bus. Edn. Div. of Dun & Bradstreet, N.Y.C., 1981—. Fellow Explorers Club; mem. Nat. Geog. Soc. Office: PO Box 2748 Ann Arbor MI 48106

PEENEY, GEORGIANA HARRIET, engr.; b. Evanston, Ill., Oct. 9, 1906; d. Edward Anderson and Clara Matilda (Schnell) P.; B.S. in Civil Engring., M. Indsl. Engring., Northwestern U., 1929. Engr., Curtis Lighting, Inc., Chgo., 1929-32, Victor Pearlman Co., Chgo., 1932-33; free lance drafting and engring., 1933-36; engr. Dept. Pub. Works, Evanston, Ill., 1936-42, 46-47, Office Chief Ordnance, U.S. Army, 1942-46, Lansing B. Warner, Inc., Chgo., 1947-74; pvt. practice, 1974—; mem. Ill. Profl. Engring. Exam. Com., 1976-77. Recipient silver medal, award of merit Soc. Am. Mil. Engrs., 1945; Alumni Merit award Northwestern U., 1949. Registered profl. engr., Ill. Mem. Ill. Soc. Profl. Engrs., Nat. Soc. Profl. Engrs., Western Soc. Engrs. (life mem.; chmn. profl. women's div., vice chmn. publs. com.), Soc. Am. Mil. Engrs., Am. Ordnance Assn., Soc. Women Engrs. (nat. public relations chmn.), AAUW, Bus. and Profl. Women's Club of Evanston (chmn. radio and TV com., news service com.), Northwestern U. Alumni Assn. (dir. 1959-62), Evanston Hist. Soc., Sigma Sigma Delta. Republican. Presbyterian. Home: 2226 Colfax St Evanston IL 60201

PEERCY, ROGER RAY, soc. ofcl.; b. Dayton, Ohio, Jan. 5, 1951; s. Albert and Maxine (Layne) P.; B.S., Cumberland Coll., 1975; M.B.A., U. Dayton, 1979; m. Sally Eiler, June 7, 1975; 1 dau., Meghan. Proposal, grant adminstr. Clinton County Community Action, 1975-76; with Chem. Abstracts Service div. Am. Chem. Soc., Columbus, Ohio, 1976—, contracts coordinator, 1980—. Served with U.S. Army, 1971-72. Decorated Bronze Star. Mem. Direct Mail-Mktg. Assn., Am. Mgmt. Assn., Am. Chem. Soc. Home: 8505 Ohio Wesleyan Ct Lancaster OH 43130 Office: PO Box 3012 Columbus OH 43210

PEET, HOWARD DAVID, educator, author; b. Fargo, N.D., Oct. 7, 1930; s. Howard M. and Beatrice K. (Gunness) P.; B.A., Macalester Coll., 1956; B.S. in English, Moorhead State U., 1962, M.S., 1965; postgrad. U. Minn., 1966-67; m. Jacquelyn M. Hegge, June 20, 1953; children—Terry H., Pamela D. Trainer, Retail Credit Co., 1956-57; trumpet The Palmer Orch., Kliff Riggs Orch.; faculty dept. English, N.D. State U., Fargo, 1965—, asso. prof. English, 1972—; cons. to Prentice-Hall, Inc., 1978—. Served with USN, 1949-50, 52-53; Korea. Recipient Distinguished Educator award N.D. State U., 1977. Mem. Nat. Council for Tchrs. English, Nat. Reading Assn., N.D. Council for Tchrs. English, N.D. Edn. Assn., AAUP, Am. Legion. Club: Masons. Author: (with J.E. Coomber) WordSkill, 11 vols., 1979; (with Allan Glatthorn) The English Book, 6 vols., 1980; editor: Beyond the Furrow (Hiram M. Drache), 1976, Tomorrow's Harvest, 1978; contbr. numerous articles on vocabulary devel. to profl. jours. Home: 2450 15 St S Fargo ND 58103 Office: SE 212-A North Dakota State Univ Fargo ND 58105

PEHLER, JAMES CLETUS, educator, state senator; b. Grand Rapids, Minn., Feb. 23, 1942; s. James V. and Adelaide (Abts) P.; B.S., St. Cloud State U., 1965, M.A., 1967; m. Beverly Rueckert, June 11, 1966; children—James, Karl. Instr., St. Cloud (Minn.) State U., 1967—; mem. Minn. Ho. of Reps., 1972-80, Minn. Senate, 1980—. Mem. state bd. dirs., mem. exec. com. Minn. Heart Assn.; chmn. Minn. Heart Fund, 1980; mem. Miss. River Pkwys. Commn., Legis. Commn. Waste Mgmt.; former mem. community edn. adv. bd. Big Bros. and Big Sisters Adv. Bd.; chmn. area com. Employment of Handicapped; active YMCA Youth in Govt. Mem. Nat. Conf. State Legislatures. Mem. Democratic-Farmer-Labor Party. Roman Catholic. Office: Room 306 State Capitol Saint Paul MN 55155

PEKAREK, ROBERT CHARLES, psychologist; b. Cleve., Sept. 9, 1938; s. Thomas and Johanna (Miller) P.; B.S., Purdue U., 1963, M.S., 1967, Ph.D. (fellow), 1969; m. Mary Ann Hulburt, Nov. 29, 1969; children—Kristina Lynn, Brian, Robert. Dir. activities and orgns., asst. dean men Fla. State U., Tallahassee, 1967-69; pvt. practice marriage and family counseling, 1969-73; dir. White House Conf. on

Children and Youth, Fla. Bur. of Planning, Tallahassee, 1970-71; nat. follow-up dir. White House Confs. on Children and Youth, Washington, 1971-72; psychologist Medina & Thompson Inc., Chgo., 1973-78; pres. Indsl. Psychology Ltd., Chgo., 1978—; dir. N.Am. Biologicals, Miami, Fla., 1976-80. Served as 1st. lt. USAF, 1963-65. Mem. Am. Psychol. Assn., Alpha Tau Omega, Kappa Delta Pi, Phi Delta Kappa. Presbyterian. Author: Florida's Children and Youth, 1971. Home: 1220 Wild Rose Ln Lake Forest IL 60045 Office: 444 N Michigan Ave Chicago IL 60611

PELANDA, KATHERINE BRAZAR, speech pathologist; b. Canton, Ohio, Aug. 29, 1931; d. Paul and Anna (Matasich) Brazar; B.S. in Edn., Kent State U., 1953, M.Ed. (Elks grantee), 1964; m. Raymond V. Pelanda, Apr. 25, 1953; children—Raymond P., Kevin L., Melanie A., Kenneth B. Adminstrv. dir. Community Rehab. Clinic, Canton, 1952-56; speech therapist Massillon (Ohio) Pub. Schs., 1956-57, Jackson Local Schs., Massillon, 1961-63, Alliance (Ohio) Pub. Schs., 1964-66; grad. asst. Kent State Child Study Center, 1962-63; mem. faculty, drama and speech dept. Mt. Union Coll., Alliance, 1963-64, 67-68; dir. developmental programs Kent State U., Salem (Ohio) campus, 1964-80; supr. Stark Speech and Hearing Clinic, Canton; registered rep. Investor's Diversified Services, 1978—; dir. edn. and research Massillon (Ohio) State Hosp., 1980-81, asst. supt., 1981—. Bd. dirs. Stark County Mental Health Assn., 1960-75, chmn. speakers bur., 1962-70, program chmn., 1970-72; sec. Stark County Ecumenical Assn., 1971-72; chmn. lease and contracts com. Stark County Bd. Mental Health and Retardation, 1975—, sec., 1977-79, pres., 1979, 80; mem. Stark County Developmental Disabilities Treatment Task Force, 1977—; chmn. sesquicentennial year St. John The Baptist Roman Catholic Ch., 1974. Mem. Am. Speech and Hearing Assn. (cert. clin. competence), Kappa Delta Pi, Gamma Phi Beta. Author: (with K. Ward) Speak Your Piece, 1976. Home: 915 24th St NE Canton OH 44714 Office: Massillon State Hosp Massillon OH

PELKEY, DONNA LEE, personnel adminstr.; b. Detroit, July 13, 1951; d. Wilfred Leo and Leona Christine (Kernkamp) Boening; student (Bd. Govs. scholar), Wayne State U., 1969-70; R.N. (Bd. Trustees scholar), Grace Hosp. Sch. Nursing, 1973; student U. Detroit, 1977—; m. Glenn T. Pelkey, Nov. 10, 1973; 1 dau., Melissa Christine. With Litton Industries, Southfield, Mich., 1969-70; staff nurse St. Joseph Hosp., Mt. Clemens, Mich., 1973-76, head nurse, 1976-78, nurse recruiter, 1978, mgr. employment, 1978—, in-house lectr. techniques, legal aspects interviewing, 1976—. Bd. dirs. Macomb Area Work Edn. Council, 1979-81. Mem. Nat. Assn. Nurse Recruiters, Mich. Assn. Nurse Recruiters, Am. Soc. Profl. and Exec. Women, Am. Mgmt. Assn., Am. Soc. for Hosp. Personnel, Am. Hosp. Assn., Greater Detroit Area Assn. Hosp. Personnel Adminstrs., Alpha Sigma Lambda (chancellor Alpha Beta chpt.). Club: Order Eastern Star. Office: St Joseph Hosp 215 North Ave Mount Clemens MI 48043

PELLETIER, ALCID MILTON, psychologist; b. Bridgeport, Conn., Aug. 27, 1926; s. Alcid L. and Mary Jane (Auger) P.; A.A., Graceland Coll., 1951; B.A. in Psychology, U. Mo., Kansas City, 1971; M.A. in Psychology, Western Mich. U., 1972, Ed.D., 1975; children—Paulette, Alcid Milton, Lionel, Debra, Jon, Jacques, Teresa, Melanie, William, Scott, Angelique. Ordained to ministry, Reorganized Church of Jesus Christ of Latter Day Saints, 1951, assigned to transfers, Ont., Can., Ill., Pa., Mo., Mich., 1951-72; chief forensic psychology, Kent County Jail, Grand Rapids, Mich., 1972-74; asst. to med. dir., clin. coordinator, chief psychologist, chief admissions officer, Kent Oaks Hosp., Grand Rapids, 1974-78; adminstr. Mich. Med. Weight Control Clinics, Grand Rapids, Lansing, Kalamazoo, 1978; owner, pres. Center for Human Potential, P.C., Grand Rapids, 1978—; pvt. practice psychology, Grand Rapids; cons. Family Services Assn., Grand Rapids, 1972-74; instr. Calhoun County Juvenile Ct., 1974-77, Grand Valley State Colls., 1975, Western Mich. U., 1974; instr. nursing Butterworth Gen. Hosp., 1974; instr. New Clinic for Women, 1974, 77, 78; condr. workshops for Mich. Supreme Ct., annually 1973-78, probate cts., Mich. Dept. Social Services, 1977, 78. Mem. sheriff's adv. com., 1976-78; mem. Human Devel. Assn., Mt. Vernon, Ill., 1959, Kent County Mental Health Assn., Mich. Soc. for Mental Health. Served with U.S. Army, 1945-46. Recipient certificate of appreciation for profl. services Western Mich. U., 1974; lic. psychologist, Mich., also certified rehab. counselor. Mem. Am., Mich. psychol. assns., Am., Mich. personnel and guidance assns., Assn. Counselor Edn. and Supervision, Am. Rehab. Counselors Assn., Mich., Am. socs. clin. hypnosis, Am. Coll. Hosp. Adminstrs., Internat. Assn. Clin. and Exptl. Hypnosis, Insts. Religion and Health. Republican. Contbr. articles to profl. jours., speeches to confs. in fields of use of hypnosis as treatment. Home: 2951 Vineland NE Grand Rapids MI 49508 Office: 2953 Vineland NE Grand Rapids MI 49508

PELLETT, KENT LOUIS, editor; b. Salem, Mo., Feb. 12, 1904; s. Frank Chapman and Ada Eugenie (Neff) P.; B.S., Iowa State Coll., 1928; m. Marie Summerbell, June 23, 1929; children—Franklin, David, Susan Pellett Penn. Partner, Pellett & Porter, Printers, Hamilton, Ill., 1921-24; co-owner, co-editor Lehigh (Iowa) Valley Argus, Ft. Dodge (Iowa) Independent, 1929-35; freelance writer Ft. Dodge, 1935-42; mng. editor Soybean Digest, Hudson, Iowa, 1942-67, editor, 1967-73; editor Co-Op-Co News, Hudson, 1943-67; editor Soybean Blue Book, 1947-73; editor Late News, Newsletter, 1953-72. Mem. Hudson Comml. Club (sec. 1943), Iowa State Ames Commons Club (pres. 1926). Mem. Community Ch. (dir., chmn. 1959-60). Club: Lions (pres. 1964-65). Author: Pioneers in Iowa Horticulture, 1941; Livestock Feeding, 1952. Home: PO Box 126 Hudson IA 50643

PELOSO, THOMAS JOSEPH, JR., state ofcl.; b. Port Huron, Mich., Jan. 29, 1923; s. Thomas Joseph and Mary Sophia (Marigold) P.; B.S., U. Notre Dame, 1948, postgrad., 1948; postgrad. U. Mich., 1963. Probation and parole agt. Mich. Dept. Corrections, Detroit, 1948-56; field rep., chief claims Fair Employment Practices Commn. Mich., Detroit, 1956-63; dir. enforcement Mich. Dept. Civil Rights, Detroit, 1964-70, dep. exec. dir., 1970-76, chief dep. dir., 1976—. Bd. dirs. Cath. Youth Orgn., Detroit Urban League; pres. Historic Boston-Edison Assn. Served with AUS 1943-45. Decorated Air medal. Mem. Nat. Assn. Human Rights Workers, Am. Soc. Indsl. Security, Locksmith Security Assn., Associated Locksmiths Am., NAACP, Internat. Assn. Human Rights Agencies, Clubs: Rotary, Detroit Boat, Renaissance. Home: 2027 W Boston Blvd Detroit MI 48206 Office: 1200 6th Ave Detroit MI 48226

PELOZA, STANLEY JOSEPH, hosp. ofcl.; b. Vele Mune, Istria, Yugoslavia, May 16, 1919; s. John and Anna (Zadkovic) P.; came to U.S., 1928, naturalized, 1928; student St. Louis U., 1946-48, Duquesne U., Pitts., 1957-58, Ind. U., 1963-64; m. La Rita Inez Russell, Feb. 28, 1941; 1 dau., Stana Jo Peloza Bowman. Enlisted in USMC, 1937, advanced through ranks to sgt. maj., 1961; service in China, Hawaii and U.S., Philippines, Okinawa, South Vietnam; bn. sgt. maj., acting div. sgt. maj. 3d Marine Div., Fleet Marine Force Far East, 1964-65; 2d Force Service Regt., Camp Lejeune, N.C., 1966-67; ret., 1967; mem. mgmt. staff Wishard Meml. Hosp., Indpls., 1968—, supt. bldgs., 1968-78, mem. staff security dept., 1978—, asst. dir. hosp. security, mem. infection control and safety coms., 1969-77; bd. dirs. United Hosps. Service, Inc., Indpls., 1975-77, chmn. stadardization com., 1975-76. Mem. Naval Fleet Res. Assn., Marine Corps Assn., Croatian Fraternal Union, Ind. Sheriffs Assn. (asso.), Devon Civic League. Roman Catholic. Clubs: Elks, K.C. (4 deg.). Home: 4340 Ashbourne Ln Indianapolis IN 46226 Office: Wishard Meml Hosp 1001 W 10th St Indianapolis IN 46202

PELTON, CHARLES LEONARD, physician; b. Mitchell, S.D., Nov. 22, 1940; s. Paul F. and Irene (Briggs) Anderson; B.S. in Medicine, U. S.D., 1968; M.D., U. Kans., 1970; m. Lois Myers-Pelton; children—Cynthia, Charles, Christine. Salesman, S.E. Massengill Co., 1962-64; intern Sioux Valley Hosp., Sioux Falls, S.D., 1970-71; practice medicine specializing in family practice, Hoven, Gettysburg, S.D., 1971-77, Aberdeen, S.D., 1977—; mem. clin. faculty U. S.D. Med. Sch. Chmn. Aberdeen Area Child Protection Team, 1977—. Fellow Am. Acad. Family Practice; mem. Am. Assn. Sex Educators, Counselors and Therapists, AMA, S.D. State Med. Assn., Am. Soc. Clin. Hypnosis, Flying Physician's Assn., Am. Assn. Marriage and Family Therapy (clin.), Soc. for Sci. Study of Sex, Inc., Internat. Human Learning Resources Network. Republican. Club: Elks. Author: Doctor, My Bill Is Too High, 1978; The Sex Book for Those Who Think They Know it All. Mem. physician adv. panel Med. World News. Home: 1811 N Jay Aberdeen SD 57401 Office: 201 S Lloyd Suite 230 Aberdeen SD 57401

PEMBAUR, BERTOLD JOSEPH, physician; b. Salzburg, Austria, Aug. 24, 1919; s. Friedrich Paul and Berta (Radauer) P.; M.D., U. Innsbruck (Austria), 1945; came to U.S., 1951, naturalized, 1961; m. Joan Elizabeth Bruder, Oct. 2, 1954; children—Odilie, Berthold, Robert, Derrick, Lisa. Intern, Univ. Hosp., Innsbruck, 1948-51; resident in medicine Deaconess Hosp., Cin., 1951-52, mem. attending staff, 1967—; resident in medicine/surgery St. Francis Hosp., Cin., 1953-54; practice medicine, Cin., 1954—; attending staff Good Samaritan Hosp.; courtesy staff Providence Hosp., Cin.; med. dir. Rockdale Med. Center; clin. instr. dept. family medicine Coll. Medicine U. Cin. Mem. task force Avondale Task Force Planning Team, 1976-77. Recipient Hon. award Am. Acad. Gen. Practice-Cancer Control br. USPHS, 1968. Diplomate Am. Bd. Family Practice. Fellow Am. Acad. Family Physicians (charter); mem. AMA, Austrian Acad. Medicine, Am., Ohio acads. family physicians, Ohio Med. Assn., Southwestern Ohio Soc. Family Physicians, Cin. Acad. Medicine. Republican. Roman Catholic. Club: Bankers. Office: 430 Rockdale Ave Cincinnati OH 45229

PEMBERTON, ERNEST HUGH, glass container co. mgr.; b. Marion, Ind., Nov. 28, 1943; s. Ernest Harm and Beatrice Ann (Wilson) P.; student U. Cin., 1961-62; B.S.M.E., Purdue U., 1966; postgrad. U. Toledo, 1970-71; m. Judith Kay Cox, Aug. 31, 1963; children—Tony, Shawn. With Gen. Tire & Rubber Co., Marion, 1962-63; with Owens-Ill., Inc., Toledo, 1966—, beginning as engring. mgmt. trainee, successively project engr., Central Region automatic inspection engr., 1971-73, mfg. engr., auto inspection mgr., automatic inspection sect. head, 1974-75, finished products mgr. Glass Container div., 1975—; leader seminars on automatic inspection in bottle bus. Vice pres. Glendale Grade Sch. PTA; cubmaster Cub Scouts Am.; communication chmn. Boy Scouts Am. Mem. ASME, Am. Soc. Quality Control, Am. Mgmt. Assn., Purdue Alumni Assn, Onized Club. Republican. Methodist. Club: Masons. Patentee in field. Home: 2427 Orchard St Toledo OH 43606 Office: PO Box 1035 Toledo OH 43666

PENBERTHY, STANLEY JOSIAH, JR., publisher; b. Des Moines, Sept. 3, 1921; s. Stanley Josiah and Beatrice Ann (Voith) P.; student Drake U., Des Moines, 1940-43; m. Dorothea Oehmke, July 7, 1945; 1 son, Robert Bruce. Engaged in broadcasting, 1941-56; freelance radio, TV, motion picture actor, narrator, 1956—; v.p. Fed. I-D Equipment Corp., Dearborn, Mich., 1956-62; pres. Publishers, Inc., Detroit, 1976—. Bd. dirs. Sleeping Bear Dunes Citizens Council, Traverse City, Mich., 1970-75. Mem. Adcraft Club Detroit, Detroit Execs. Assn. (dir.), Screen Actors Guild, AFTRA (past dir.), Alpha Tau Omega (past alumni pres.). Congregationalist. Club: Masons (33 deg.). Author, producer, narrator nat. radio series These Were Our Presidents, 1975. Home: 35560 Heritage Ln Farmington MI 48024 Office: 500 Temple Ave Detroit MI 48201

PENCE, JEAN VIRGINIA COTTRELL (MRS. ROBERT PENCE), Realtor; b. Chgo., July 12, 1925; d. William Roscoe and Sophie (Kumlacky) Cottrell; grad. Gregg Bus. Coll., 1943; m. Robert Pence, June 14, 1947; children—Marjorie (Mrs. Raymond Tuinstra), Robert. Sales asso. William W. Knight Co., LaGrange, Ill., 1962-70, v.p., sales mgr., 1970-76; pres. Pence & Co., 1977—. Mem. S.W. Suburban Council on Aging, 1971-72; chmn. LaGrange March of Dimes, 1972; mem. go-getters com. WTTW-TV, 1967-72, chmn. LaGrange com., 1973-74. Mem. Nat. Inst. Real Estate Brokers (mem. Ill. asso. com. 1971), Nat., Ill. (edn. com. 1972—, legis. com. 1975—) assns. real estate bds., Women's Council Realtors (pres. chpt. 1979-81), LaGrange Bd. Realtors (sec.-treas. 1973-75, chmn. edn. com. 1972-74), Speakers Bur. Ill. Assn., Hinsdale Bus. and Profl. Women's Club (press chmn. 1971-72), DAR. Conglist. (treas. women's assn. 1971-72). Club: Woman's (sec. 1967-68) (LaGrange Park, Ill.). Office: 42 S LaGrange Rd LaGrange IL 60525

PENCE, LELAND HADLEY, research chemist; b. Kearney, Mo., Oct. 1, 1911; s. Samuel Anderson and Rose Louise (Reid) P.; student Stanford U., 1928; B.S., U. Fla., 1932; M.S., U. Mich., 1933, Ph.D., 1937; m. Mary Ellen Elliott, Aug. 6, 1938; children—Jean, Daniel, Elizabeth. Research chemist Biochem. Research Found. of Franklin Inst., Phila., 1937-39; instr. chemistry Reed Coll., 1939-42, asst. prof., 1942-45; sr. scientist Difco Labs., Inc., Detroit, 1945—; research chemist Mayo Found., Rochester, Minn., summer 1940; research fellow Calif. Inst. Tech., spring 1943. Fellow AAAS; mem. Am. Chem. Soc., Tissue Culture Assn., Am. Soc. Microbiology, Sigma Xi. Republican. Presbyterian (trustee 1969-75, 78—). Club: Circumnavigators. Research on carcinogens, estrogens, bile acids, steroids, cardiolipin, lecithins, serological reagents, fluorescent antibodies, phytohemagglutinin, mitogens, chromosome reagents, lectins, immunochemistry, monoclonal antibodies. Home: 972 Alberta Ave Ferndale MI 48220 Office: 920 Henry St Detroit MI 48201

PENCEK, TERRENCE LYLE, med. educator; b. Berwyn, Ill., Aug. 24, 1947; s. Robert Joseph and Lillian (Stefula) P.; B.S., Valparaiso U., 1969; Ph.D. (NSF trainee), Ill. Inst. Tech., 1975; M.D. (DuPage Med. Soc. scholar, Sandoz award), Rush Med. Coll., 1981; m. Pamela Fay Turner, Aug. 11, 1973. Asst. prof. dept. physiology and neurology Rush Med. Coll., Chgo., 1977-81, instr. dept. neurology, 1976; mem. Multiple Sclerosis Center, Rush-Presbyn.-St. Luke's Med. Center, Chgo., 1980—. Nat. Multiple Sclerosis Soc. grantee, 1976-78; NIH grantee, 1977. Mem. Am. Physiol. Soc., Biophys. Soc., AMA, N.Y. Acad. Sci., Soc. for Neurosci., Chgo. Med. Soc., Sigma Xi. Lutheran. Contbr. articles to profl. jours. Home: 919 Brookwood St Bensenville IL 60106 Office: 1725 W Harrison St Chicago IL 60612

PENDERGRASS, PRESLEY WADE, coll. ofcl., clergyman; b. Scottsboro, Ala., Dec. 28, 1934; s. Theodore R. and Elsie B. (Barclay) P.; B.A., Samford U., 1957; M.Div., So. Bapt. Theol. Sem., 1962, Th.M., 1964; Ed.M., U. Fla., 1970, Ed.D., 1971; m. Paula Belcher, July 5, 1957; children—Kimberley Anne, Shannon Dawn. Tchr., Kate Duncan Smith Sch., Grant, Ala., 1957-58; ordained to ministry Bapt. Ch., 1957; minister First Bapt. Ch., Grant, Ala., 1957-58; asst. br. librarian Louisville Free Public Library, 1958-61; minister Central Bapt. Ch., Hawesville, Ky., 1959-62; tchr. Louisville elem. and secondary public schs., 1962-63; minister First Bapt. Ch., Hawthorne, Fla., 1964-66; vol. various community orgns., Gainesville, Fla., 1966-68; asso. minister and adminstr. First Bapt. Ch., Gainesville, 1966-68; minister First Bapt. Ch., MacIntosh, Fla., 1968-71; asso. prof. edn. and psychology Pikeville (Ky.) Coll., 1971-73, prof. 1973-78, chmn. div. of human devel., 1976-78; dir. Mid-Appalachian Tchr. Edn. Program, Pikeville Coll. and Pike County Sch. System, 1973-77; adj. grad. instr. Morehead (Ky.) State U., 1973-78; dean acad. affairs Oakland (Ind.) City Coll., 1978—; cons. div. edn. Furman U., Greenville, S.C., 1975. Bd. dirs. Mid-South Tchr. Corps Network, Nashville, 1976-77, Southeastern Tchr. Corps Network, 1974-76. Mem. Am. Ednl. Studies Assn., Assn. Supervision and Curriculum Devel., Assn. Tchr. Educators, AAUP, Am. Assn. Univ. Adminstrs., Phi Delta Kappa. Republican. Club: Kiwanis. Home: 731 N Polk Dr Oakland City IN 47660 Office: Oakland City Coll Lucretia St Oakland City IN 47660

PENDERGRASS, R. A., educator; b. Bakersfield, Mo., Feb. 21, 1944; s. Roy Lester and Hester (Hasseltine) P.; B.S. in Edn. (Regent's scholar, 1962), SW Mo. State U., 1965; M.Ed., U. Mo., 1968; Ed.D., Wash. State U., 1973; m. Paula B. Wealand, June 3, 1966; 1 dau., Amber Rene. Tchr. Dora (Mo.) Public Schs., 1965-66, Seymour (Mo.) Schs., 1966-67, Stafford (Mo.) Schs., 1967-68; instr., dir. social studies Lincoln U. Lab. Sch., Jefferson City, Mo., 1968-70; asst. prof. U. Houston, 1973-76; sr. cons. Region X Edn. Service Center, Richardson, Tex., 1976-78; asso. prof. edn. Wright State U., Dayton, Ohio; cons. Houston Ind. Sch. Dist., Tchr. Corps Projects State of Wash. Active NOW, ACLU, Common Cause; caucus del. Pullman Democratic Com., 1977. Recipient certificate of appreciation Tex. State Tchrs. Assn., 1975. Mem. Assn. for Supervision and Curriculum Devel., Assn. Tchr. Educators, Phi Delta Kappa (research grantee, 1973). Democrat. Mem. Church of Christ. Co-author: Teaching Strategies: A Guide to Better Instruction, 1980; contbr. articles to jours. Home: 6230 Troy Frederick Tipp City OH 45371 Office: Wright State Univ Dayton OH 45435

PENDLETON, THELMA BROWN, phys. therapist, health service adminstr.; b. Rome, Ga., Jan. 30, 1911; d. John O. and Alma (Ingram) Brown; diploma Provident Hosp. Sch. Nursing, 1931; certificate Loyola U., 1942, Northwestern U., 1946; m. George W. Pendleton, Mar. 2, 1946; 1 son, George William. Pediatric nurse Rosenwald Found., Chgo., 1931-32; staff nurse Vis. Nurse Assn., Chgo., 1932-45; chief phys. therapy Provident Hosp., Chgo., 1946-55; phys. therapy cons. Parents Assn., Inc., Chgo., 1956-60; cons. United Cerebral Palsy of Greater Chgo.'s Pipers Portal Schs., 1961-63, dir., 1963-64; dir. phys. therapy services LaRabida Children's Hosp. and Research Center, Chgo., 1964-75; mem. nat. com. Joint Orthopedic Nursing Adv. Services, 1947-55; clin. supr., instr. programs in phys. therapy Northwestern U. Med. Sch., Chgo., 1947-55, 64-75; cons. United Cerebral Palsy, 1970-75; lectr. Japanese service com. on Cerebral Palsy, 1970; mem. Ill. Phys. Therapy Exam. Com., 1952-62. Recipient certificate of Commendation CSC Cook County (Ill.), 1961, Citation of Merit, Wands Cerebral Palsy Unit, 1961. Mem. Am., Ill. phys. therapy assns., Ill. League Nursing, Provident Hosp. Nurses Alumni Assn. Democrat. Clubs: Washington Park Swimming, Tu-Fours Bolivia. Author: Low Budget Gournet, 1977; contbr. articles on phys. therapy to profl. jours. Address: 2631 S Indiana Ave Chicago IL 60616

PENFIELD, BEVERLY HOFFMAN, diagnostic clinic adminstr.; b. Cleve., Jan. 13, 1943; d. William P. and Margaret H. Hoffman; B.S., Kent State U., 1965, M.Ed., 1970; children—Janine, Jennifer. Elem. tchr. public schs., Ohio, 1965-67, 68-69; learning disabilities specialist Fairview Park, Ohio, 1970-71, 72-77; learning disabilities supr. Cuyahoga County (Ohio) Bd. Edn., 1977-80; instr., student teaching supr. Cleve. State U., 1977-78; instr. Kent State U., 1977-81; ednl. cons. Cuyahoga Spl. Edn. Service Center, 1975-81; clin. dir. Notre Dame Coll. Diagnostic Clinic, South Euclid, Ohio, 1981—. Active Fairview Park Jr. Women's Club, 1969-81, Girl Scouts of Am., 1977-81; bd. dirs. chpt. 947 Council for Exceptional Children, 1979-81. Recipient Cert. Appreciation gifted com. Fairview Park Bd. Edn., 1979-80, Cert. Appreciation Ohio Conf. of Council Exceptional Children, 1980. Mem. Council for Exceptional Children, Cleve. Assn. Children and Adults with Learning Disabilities, Ohio Assn. Gifted and Talented Children. Co-editor, developer Student Learning Profile, 1980, Competency-Based Tutor Training Program for Cuyahoga County, 1981; contbr. articles to profl. publs. Home: 18849 W Valley Dr Fairview Park OH 44126 Office: Notre Dame Coll Diagnostic Clinic 4545 College Dr South Euclid OH 44121

PENG, YENG-KAUNG, research scientist; b. Shanghai, China, Dec. 14, 1948; came to U.S., 1977; s. Shaw-Chang and Wei-Lam P.; M.S., U. Nebr., 1978, Ph.D., 1980. Marine engr. Engring. Research Center, U. Nebr., Lincoln, 1973-76, research asst., 1977-78, research asso., 1978-80, research scientist, 1981—. Mem. ASME, Am. Nuclear Soc., AM. Soc. Engring. Edn., Sigma Xi. Condr. research delayed-neutron yields of thermal fission of uranium-235, optical properties of zircaloy and its oxide by ellipsometry. Office: 204 NEC U Nebr Lincoln NE 68588

PENICK, ELIZABETH CARNEL, psychologist; b. New Orleans, July 17, 1934; d. Rawley M. and Marie (Sells) P.; B.A., Sophie Newcomb Coll., 1957; student U. London, 1958; M.Sc., Tulane U., 1960; Ph.D., Washington U., St. Louis, 1975. Intern clin. psychology Washington U., St. Louis, 1962-63; dir. psychology lab. St. Louis Children's Hosp., 1964-68; instr. dept. psychiatry Washington U., 1966-74; cons. psychology to local schs., St. Louis, 1968-69; dir. community psychol. services Malcolm Bliss Mental Health Center, St. Louis, 1969-74; research project dir. dept. psychiatry U. Ky., Lexington, 1974-77, asst. prof. dept. psychiatry U. Ky. Med. Center, 1976-77; asso. prof. dept. psychiatry Kans. U. Med. Center, Kansas City, 1977—, dir. div. psychology, dept. psychiatry, 1980—; coordinator alcohol dependency treatment unit VA Hosp., Kansas City, Mo., 1978-80, research project dir., 1977-78; mem. profl. adv. bd. Judevine Found. for Autistic Children, St. Louis, 1970-74. Mem. Lt. Gov.'s Task Force on Mental Health Problems in Times of Disaster, 1973-74. Mem. Am. Psychol. Assn., Evaluation Research Soc., Sigma Xi. Contbr. articles to profl. jours. Home: 4725 Black Swan Dr Shawnee KS 66216 Office: Kans U Med Center 39th and Rainbow Kansas City KS 66103

PENICK, MICHAEL ROBIN, mfg. co. exec.; b. Hannibal, Mo., June 5, 1947; s. Harry Jewel and Lauretta (Roush) P.; B.S.B.A., U. Mo., Columbia, 1971; M.A., Webster Coll., 1980; m. Diana Lewis, Dec. 14, 1973; children—Brooke Lauren, Darcy Erin. Field underwriter N.Y. Life Ins. Co., Boonville, Mo., 1975-76; supr. workmen's compensation Office of Adminstrn., State of Mo., Jefferson City, 1976-77; asst. personnel mgr. foundry products div. Gould, Inc., St. Louis, 1977-78; personnel mgr. Jackes-Evans Mfg. Co., St. Louis, 1978—. Mem. adv. bd. Jefferson County Jr. Coll. Mem. Am. Assn. Indsl. Mgmt., Assn. Industries of Mo., Am. Soc. Personnel Adminstrn., Personnel Roundtable. Home: 515 Ranch Manchester MO 63011 Office: 4427 Geraldine St Louis MO 63115

PENILLA, ANTONIO RESUMA, physician; b. Quezon, Philippines, Nov. 18, 1943; came to U.S., 1967, naturalized, 1976; A.A., U. Santo Tomas, 1963, M.D., 1967; s. Fortunato Libranda and Crisanta (Resuma) P.; m. Rose Ann Walther, Nov. 14, 1970; children—Mary Lisa, James Michael, John Michael. Intern, St. Louis County Hosp., St. Louis, 1968; resident in internal medicine St. Mary's Health Center, St. Louis, 1970-72; asso. Knight-McCarthy Internists, Inc., St. Louis, 1972-74; practice medicine specializing in internal medicine, St. Louis, 1974-79; fellow in cardiology St. Louis U. Sch. of Medicine, 1979-81, clin. asst. prof. medicine, 1981—. Mem. Am. Coll. Cardiology, Am. Coll. Chest Physicians, Am. Soc. Internal Medicine, AMA, Mo. Med. Assn., St. Louis Met. Med. Soc. Roman Catholic. Home: 17 Deer Creek Woods Saint Louis MO 63124 Office: 12255 DePaul Dr Bridgeton MO 63044

PENKAVA, ROBERT RAY, radiologist; b. Virginia, Nebr., Jan. 30, 1942; s. Joseph Everet and Velta Mae (Oviatt) P.; A.B., B.S., Peru State Coll., 1963; M.D., U. Nebr., 1967; m. Mary Kathryn Secrest, Apr. 6, 1973; 1 dau., Ashley Secrest. Intern, Lincoln (Nebr.) Gen. Hosp., 1967—68; resident Menorah Med. Center, Kansas City, Mo., 1968-71, chief resident, 1970-71; asso. radiologist Deaconess Hosp., Evansville, Ind., 1973—, chmn. continuing med. edn. com.; med. dir. Sch. Radiol. Tech., Ind. State U., Evansville. Chmn. profl. div. United Way of So. Ind.; bd. dirs. S.W. Ind. Pub. Broadcasting, Inc.; chmn. So. Ind. Health Systems Agy.; bd. dirs. Southwestern Ind. PSRO. Served to maj. U.S. Army, 1971—73. Recipient Sci. Tchr. of Year award Lewis and Clark Jr. High Sch., 1963. Mem. AMA. Am. Coll. Radiology, Am. Roentgen Ray Soc., N.Am., Bluegrass, Tri-State (past pres.) radiol. socs., Evansville Med. Radiol. Assn. (v.p.), Ind. State, Vanderburgh County (treas., dir., chmn. fin. com.) med. socs. Contbr. articles to profl. jours. Office: 611 Harriett St Evansville IN 47710

PENMAN, ALLEN STUART, cons. psychologist; b. Williston, N.D., June 16, 1920; s. Roy R. and Daisy M. (Huntington) P.; B.S., U. Ill., 1947, M.S., 1948, Ph.D., 1951; m. Jean M. Kron, Dec. 28, 1946; children—Geoffrey, Steven, Patricia. Chief psychologist VA Hosp., St. Cloud, Minn., 1951-57; cons. psychologist Rohrer, Hibler & Replogle, Detroit, 1957-58, mng. partner, Toronto, Ont., Can., 1958-66, gen. partner, Chgo., 1966-68, sr. partner, 1968-73, chmn., chief exec. officer, 1973—, also dir.; dir. Rohrer, Hibler & Replogle Internat. (Europe), 1st Fed. Savs. & Loan Assn. Chgo. Bd. dirs. Hinsdale (Ill.) Community House, 1971, Robert Crown Center for Health Edn., Suburban Hosp., Chgo. Theol. Sem.; bd. mgrs. Chgo. Met. YMCA; trustee Found. U. Ill. Served with USAAF, 1942-45. Mem. Am., Ill. psychol. assns., Chgo. Sunday Evening Club (trustee), Newcomen Soc., Execs. Club Chgo. Republican. Lutheran (chmn. ch.). Clubs: Met., Monroe (Chgo.); Ruth Lake Golf and Country. Editor, contbg. author Managing Through Insight, 1968. Home: 530 Princeton Rd Hinsdale IL 60521 Office: 55 E Monroe St Chicago IL 60603

PENN, RICHARD KNIGHT, radio sta. exec.; b. Columbus, Ohio, May 24, 1941; s. Morgan Covan and Ruth (Willoughby) P.; B.B.A., Ohio U., 1965; 1 son, John Andrew. Account exec. Kayser Roth Industries, Columbus, Ohio, 1965-67; account exec. Nationwide Communications, WRFD-WNCI Radio, Columbus, 1967-70, sales mgr., 1970-71; account exec. Rounsville Radio, WFUN Radio, Miami, Ohio, 1971-76; gen. sales mgr. KKDJ, Combined Communications, Los Angeles, 1976-77, gen. mgr. KTAR-KBBC, Phoenix, 1977-78, pres., gen. mgr. WWWE-WDOK, Cleve., 1972-79; v.p., gen. mgr. NBC owned-operated WKOX-FM, Chgo., 1979—. Bd. dirs. Steppenwolf Theatre, 1981. Mem. Nat. Assn. Broadcasters, Ill. Broadcasters Assn., Radio Broadcasters Chgo., Broadcast Advt. Club Chgo. (bd. dirs.). Office: NBC Merchandise Mart Chicago IL 60654

PENNELL, JOHN SPEAR, lawyer; b. Jackson, Mich., Jan. 7, 1916; s. Henry R. and Stella (Spear) P.; A.B., U. Mich., 1938, J.D., 1940; m. Era Northcutt, Nov. 30, 1946; children—William, Jeffrey, Patricia. Admitted to Mich. bar, 1940, Ill. bar, 1941; asso. in law U. Mich. Law Sch., 1940-41; asso. McDermott, Will & Emery, Chgo., 1941-51, partner, 1951—; cons. fed. income tax project Am. Law Inst.; lectr. various tax insts. Tulane U. Tax Inst., N.Y.U. Tax Inst., U. Miami Tax Conf. (adv. com. 1964—), U. Chgo. Fed. Tax Conf., Mid-Am. Tax Conf., Ark. Fed. Tax Inst., Ky. Inst. Fed. Taxation, Ala. Ann. Fed. Tax Clinic, So. Fed. Tax Inst., Inst. Fed. Taxation U. So. Calif., Hawaii Tax Inst. Served to capt. AUS, 1942-46. Decorated Order Cross of Italy. Mem. Am. (chmn. com. on partnerships tax sect. 1965-68, council sect. taxation 1970-73, vice chmn. sect. 1971-73, chmn. elect sect. 1976—), Ill. (chmn. sect. on fed. taxation 1958-59, vice chmn. adv. council Inst. on Continuing Edn. 1962-69, chmn. 1969-71), Chgo. (chmn. com. on fed. taxation 1974-75) bar assns., State Bar Mich. Clubs: Union League (pres. 1976-77), Metropolitan, Executive (Chgo.); Midday; Westmoreland Country. Co-editor partnership dept. Jour. Taxation. Home: 1030 Romona Rd Wilmette IL 60091 Office: 111 W Monroe St Chicago IL 60603

PENNER, AUDREY LESLIE, educator; b. Galena, Kans., Apr. 25, 1942; d. Hal Chesler and Leslie (Bliss) Leonard; B.S., Kans. State U., Emporia, 1960; M.A., U. No. Colo., 1964; Ed.S., Pittsburg State U., 1972; m. Delmar Gene Penner, Feb. 3, 1967; 1 son, John David. Tchr., elem. schs. Santa Anna, Calif., 1964-66, Jefferson County, Colo., 1966-67, Los Angeles, 1968-71, Galena, Kans., 1971-74; prin. elem. sch., Galena, 1974-77; dir. elem. edn. Public Schs. Carl Junction, Mo., 1977—. Dir. blood program ARC, recipient spl. service award, 1976; bd. dirs. Jasper County Child Advocacy Council. Mem. Assn. Curriculum Devel., Nat. Assn. Elem. Prins. Presbyterian. Club: Briarbrook Golf and Country. Home: 1 Par Ln Carl Junction MO 64834 Office: PO Box 4 Carl Junction MO 64834

PENNING, TIMOTHY GERARD, radiologic technologist; b. Hermann, Mo., Feb. 26, 1954; s. John L. and Gloria (Neumann) P.; B.S. in Radiologic Tech., U. Mo., Columbia, 1976, M.Ed. 1977; m. Joann Marie Korman, Aug. 16, 1975. Staff radiologic technologist U. Mo. Med. Center, Columbia, 1977; ednl. coordinator radiologic tech. Franciscan Hosp., Rock Island, Ill., 1977—. Coach Daniel Boone league Little League Baseball, Columbia, 1976. Mem. Am. Soc. Radiologic Technologists (edn. com. 1980-81), Ill. Soc. Radiologic Technologists (state v.p. 1980-81), Rock Island Jaycees (dir. 1978—, outstanding 1st yr. mem. 1979), Kappa Delta Pi, Phi Kappa Phi. Roman Catholic. Contbr. articles to profl. jours. Home: 2315 20th Ave Rock Island IL 61201 Office: Franciscan Hosp 2701 17th St Rock Island IL 61201

PENNINGTON, LEA GIBLYN, psychologist; b. Freeport, N.Y., June 9, 1935; d. Leo Frederick and Edna (Decker) Giblyn; B.A. in Sociology, Hofstra U., 1957; M.S. in Sch. Psychology, U. Wis., 1960; m. Leonard W. Pennington, Jr., Dec. 26, 1969; children—Christopher Leonard, Meredith Lea. Playground asst. Freeport Pub. Schs., 1951-52, playground instr., 1953-57, tchr., 1957-59, psychologist, 1960-61; tchr. Madison (Wis.) Pub. Schs., 1961-63, psychologist, 1963—, psychologist spl. lang. clinic, summers 1967-72. Mem. Nat., Wis. edn. assns., Nat., Wis. assns. sch. psychologists, Madison Tchrs. Assn., Madison Met. Sch. Dist. Reading Council, Alpha Delta Kappa, Pi Delta Epsilon, Phi Epsilon. Editorial bd. Issues Jour., Madison Met. Sch. Dist. Home: 6309 Landfall Dr Madison WI 53705 Office: 545 W Dayton St Madison WI 53703

PENNINGTON, LEONARD WILLIAM, JR., psychologist; b. Washington, Apr. 14, 1930; s. Leonard William and Selma Nina (Lackey) P.; B.S., Richmond Profl. Inst., Coll. William and Mary, 1952, M.S., 1954; postgrad. U. Wis., 1958—; m. Lea Giblyn Kroll, Dec. 26, 1969; children—Christopher Leonard, Meredith Lea; children by previous marriage—Scott William, Pamela Ann. Psychologist, Wis. Dept. Health Social Services, Madison, 1956-63; sch. psychologist Madison Pub. Schs., 1963-68; supr. sch. psychol. services Wis. Dept. Pub. Instruction, Madison, 1968—; instr. emotional health and curriculum U. Wis.; staff psychologist Wis. Diagnostic Center; cons. Minn. Dept. Pub. Instrn.; pvt. practice psychology; mem. coordinating bd. Nat. Council Accreditation of Tchr. Edn.; mem. Gov's. Commn. Status Women, Wis. Bd. dirs. Family Services Soc., Madison. Served with M.I., AUS, 1954-56. Mem. Nat. Assn. Sch. Psychologists (regional dir., co-chmn. accreditation, credentialing and tng. com.), Am., Wis., Dane County (Wis.) psychol. assns., Wis. Sch. Psychologists Assn. Episcopalian. Contbr. articles in field to profl. jours. Home: 6309 Landfall Dr Madison WI 53705 Office: 125 S Webster St Madison WI 53702

PENNINGTON, TERRANCE CARLYLE, forest products mfg. co. exec.; b. Englewood, N.J., Mar. 30, 1948; s. Vincent Carlyle and Valeria Elaine (Epps) P.; student Montclair State Coll., 1960-68; B.A. in Bus. Adminstrn. and Psychology, Capital U., 1981; m. Deborah Cross, Dec. 20, 1969; children—Chevion, Terrence, La-Toya, Letitia, Tiffany. Employment rep., mgr. employment Container div. Seatrain Lines, Inc., Weehawken, N.J., 1973-76; personnel adminstr. Church & Dwight Co., Inc., Piscataway, N.J., 1976-79; human resources specialist Mead Advanced Systems Group, Mead Corp., Dayton, Ohio, 1979-80; mgr. human resources Mead Digital Systems, Dayton, 1980—. Mem. Am. Mgmt. Assn., Nat. Urban Affairs Council. Office: 3800 Space Dr PO Box 3230 Dayton OH 45431

PENNY, TIMOTHY JOE, state senator; b. Mansfield Twp., Freeborn County, Minn., Nov. 19, 1951; s. Jay C. and Donna J. (Haukoos) P.; B.A. in Polit. Sci., Winona State U., 1974; m. Barbara Christiansen, Oct. 18, 1975; children—Jamison, Joseph, Molly. Mem. Minn. State Univ. Bd., 1974-77; mem. Minn. Senate, 1976—. Mem. New Richland Jaycees. Mem. Democratic Farm Labor Party. Lutheran. Club: Waseca Pals. Office: Room 121 State Capitol Saint Paul MN 55155

PENRY, RICHARD EARL, surgeon; b. Belgrade, Nebr., June 10, 1912; s. John William and Minnie Frances (Peters) P.; B.S., U. Nebr., 1941, M.D., 1941; m. Martha Ann Pfingsten, Mar. 31, 1941; children—Kandis Lynn Penry Haggstrom, Deborah Ann Penry Lewis, John Jay (dec.). Intern, Immanuel Deaconess Inst., Omaha, 1941-42; resident in gen. surgery Ft. Campbell, Ky., 1942-43, 136th Evacuation Hosp. U.S. Army, 1943-45, Ft. Jackson, S.C., 1945-46; individual practice medicine, specializing in gen. surgery, Hebron, Nebr., 1945—; chief of staff Thayer County Meml. Hosp., Hebron, 1975—. Mem. bd. Hebron Municipal Airport, 1950-60; bd. edn. Hebron Pub. Schs., 1960-67. Served as surgeon, U.S. Army, 1941-46. Mem. Nebr., S. Central med. socs., Am. Acad. Family Practice, Am. Soc. Abdominal Surgeons, Internat. Bd. Proctology, Nat. Assn. Legions Honor. Republican. Lutheran. Clubs: Masons, K.T., Shriners, Rotary (pres. Hebron 1955-56). Home: 534 N 4th St Hebron NE 68370 Office: Bryan Bldg Hebron NE 68370

PENTECOSTE, JOSEPH CLARENCE, educator; b. Selma, Ala., July 30, 1918; s. Joseph C. and Georgia A. (Watson) P.; A.A., Wilson Jr. Coll., 1950; B.A., Roosevelt U., 1954; M.A., Northeastern Ill. State Coll., 1968; postgrad. Chgo. State U., 1977; Ph.D., Purdue U., 1972; children—Joseph, Maria Faith. Dir. publicity and edn. United Farm and Metal Workers Union, 1941-52; chmn. fair employment practices commn. Farm-Equipment Elec. Workers, 1952-54; publicity dir. Nat. Negro Labor Council, 1946-50; dir. counseling Warehouse Workers Union Local 500, 1954-59; asso. Hall & Brock Research Assos. and Accountants, 1959-63; counselor, youth worker Victor Oleander Boys Club, Chgo., 1966-67; asst. psychologist to psychologist in pvt. practice, Chgo., 1967-68; research dir. Better Boys Found., Chgo., 1968-70; asst. prof. inner city studies Northeastern Ill. State Coll., 1969-72, asso. prof., 1972—; chmn. dept. Afro-Am. studies Ind. U. N.W., Gary, 1972—; cons. in field. Mem. Am., Midwest psychol. assns., Soc. Psychol. Study of Social Issues, Assn. Black Psychologists, Am. Edn. Research Assn., AAUP, Assn. Study of Afro-Am. Life and History, Assn. Social and Behavioral Scientists, Council Advancement of Psychol. Professions and Scis., Psi Chi, Phi Delta Kappa, Kappa Alpha Psi. Author: The Systems of Poverty, 1977; contbr. articles to profl. jours. Office: 3400 Broadway Gary IN 46408

PENTICO, ROBERT LEE, data processing exec.; b. Des Moines, Nov. 9, 1942; s. Lee Lincoln and Anna Mary (Hybl) P.; B.A., Central Coll., 1964; m. Nancy Elizabeth Oliver, June 15, 1963; children—Robb, Shanna, Jodi. Methods analyst Employers Mutual Cos., Des Moines, 1964-66, systems analyst, 1966-68, sr. systems analyst, 1968-73, mgr. computer services, 1973-75; systems and data processing mgr. Gen. Growth Properties, Des Moines, 1975-77; pres. Kirke-Van Orsdel Computer Services, Des Moines, 1977-79; gen. mgr. TLS Data Processing Services, Des Moines, 1979—. Area dir. United Campaign, 1974; mgr. Boy Scouts Am., 1965-66. Mem. Assn. Systems Mgmt. (past pres.), Nat. Accountants Assn. Republican. Methodist. Club: Young Men's Breakfast. Home: 720 39th St West Des Moines IA 50265 Office: 202 E Des Moines St Des Moines IA 50316

PEPER, CHRISTIAN BAIRD, lawyer; b. St. Louis, Dec. 5, 1910; s. Clarence F. and Christine (Baird) P.; A.B. cum laude, Harvard, 1932; LL.B., Washington U., 1935; LL.M. (Sterling fellow), Yale, 1937; m. Ethel C. Kingsland, June 5, 1935; children—Catherine K. (Mrs. Kenneth B. Larson), Anne C. (Mrs. John M. Perkins), Christian B. Admitted to Mo. bar, 1934, since practiced in St. Louis; partner Peper, Martin, Jensen, Maichel & Hetlage. Lectr. various subjects Washington U. Law Sch., St. Louis, 1943-61; partner A.G. Edwards & Sons, 1945-67; pres. St. Charles Gas Corp., 1953-72; chmn. St. Louis Steel Casting Inc., Hydraulic Press Brick Co. Mem. vis. com. Harvard Div. Sch., 1964-70. Trustee St. Louis Art Mus. Mem. Am., Mo., St. Louis bar assns., Order of Coif, Phi Delta Phi. Roman Catholic. Clubs: Noonday, University, Harvard (St. Louis); East India, Devonshire (London). Contbr. articles to profl. jours. Home: 1454 Mason Rd Saint Louis MO 63131 Office: 720 Olive St Saint Louis MO 63101

PEPPER, JOHN ENNIS, JR., soap and detergent mfg. co. exec.; b. Pottsville, Pa., Aug. 2, 1938; s. John Ennis and Irma (O'Conor) P.; B.A. magna cum laude, Yale U., 1960; m. Frances Graham Garber, Sept. 9, 1967; children—John, David, Douglas, Susan. With Procter & Gamble Co., 1963—, div. mgr. internat., So. Europe, 1977-78, v.p., div. mgr. package soaps and detergents, Cin., 1978-80, group v.p. package soap and detergent div., bar soap and household cleaning products div., 1980—. Trustee Cin. Med. Center Fund; bd. dirs. Cin. Symphony Orch. Served with USN, 1960-63. Mem. Nat. Alliance Businessmen (chmn. communications com. 1979—). Clubs: Yale, Queen City. Office: Procter & Gamble Co 6th and Sycamore Sts Cincinnati OH 45202

PEPPING, RAYMOND AUSTIN, aerospace co. exec.; b. St. Louis, Nov. 8, 1918; s. Fred W. and Beatrice M. (Murray) P.; B.S. in Mech. Engring., Washington U., St. Louis, 1941, M.S., 1942; m. Sue S. Sheffield, Jan. 21, 1950; children—Janet Ellen, Eric Philip. With McDonnell Douglas Corp., St. Louis, 1946—, now v.p. space programs; mem. NACA Flutter Subcom., 1951-55, NASA research adv. com. on missile and space vehicle aerodynamics, 1961-65. Served to capt. USAAF, 1942-46. Mem. Aircraft Industries Assn. (aircraft research and testing com., flutter subcom. 1947-55, ad hoc space group com. 1979—). Office: PO Box 516 Saint Louis MO 63166

PERARO, JAMES SALVATORE, physicist; b. Enfield, Conn., June 19, 1935; s. James Salvatore and Moresta Mary (Santanella) P.; B.A., Am. Internat. Coll., 1957; M.S., Franklin and Marshall Coll., 1968. Physicist, Pratt & Whitney Aircraft, Middletown, Conn., 1959-61; research physicist Armstrong Cork Co., Lancaster, Pa., 1961-76; sr. scientist Owens Corning Fiberglas, Granville, Ohio, 1976—. Mem. ASTM (chmn. tech. com. on dynamic mech. properties), N. Am. Thermal Analysis Soc., Soc. Rheology, Am. Phys. Soc. Democrat. Roman Catholic. Club: Am. Contract Bridge League (dir.). Patentee in field. Home: 63 Salem Ct Reynoldsburg OH 43068 Office: PO Box 415 Route 16 Granville OH 43023

PERCY, CHARLES HARTING, U.S. senator; b. Pensacola, Fla., Sept. 27, 1919; s. Edward H. and Elisabeth (Harting) P.; A.B., U. Chgo., 1941; LL.D., Ill. Coll., 1961, Roosevelt U., 1961; H.H.D., Wilmette U., 1962, LL.D., Lake Forest Coll., 1962, Bradley U., 1963, Defiance Coll., 1965; L.H.D., Nat. Coll. Edn., 1964, Northwestern U., 1966; m. Jeanne Valerie Dickerson, June 12, 1943 (dec.); children—Valerie Jeanne (dec.) and Sharon Lee (Mrs. John D. Rockefeller IV) (twins), Roger; m. 2d, Loraine Diane Guyer, Aug. 27, 1950; children—Gail, Mark. Sales trainee, apprentice Bell & Howell, 1938, mgr. war coordinating dept., 1941-43, asst. sec., 1943-46, corp. sec., 1946-49, pres., 1949-61, chief exec. officer, 1951-63, chmn. bd., 1961-66; sales promotion Crowell-Collier Pub. Co., 1939; U.S. senator from Ill., 1967—. Dir., Nat. Recreation and Park Assn.; co-chmn. NCCJ, Chgo., 1951, 54; mem. Bus. Adv. Council; spl. ambassador and personal rep. Pres. U.S. to presdl. inauguration ceremonies in Peru and Bolivia, 1956. Past chmn. Fund for Adult Edn., Ford Found.; trustee U. Chgo.; mem. citizens bd., bd. dirs. alumni found., Cal. Inst. Tech., until 1967. Chmn. Republican Com. on Program and Progress, 1959, Rep. Platform Com. Nat. Conv., 1960. Served as lt. USNR, 1943-45. Named one of 10 outstanding young men of 1949, U.S. Jr. C. of C., Business Man of Year, Saturday Review, 1962, Alumnus of Year, U. Chgo. Alumni Assn., 1962, Father of Year, Nat. Father's Day Com., 1973; recipient World Trade award, World Trade Award Com., 1955; Nat. Sales Execs. Mgmt. award, 1955; French Legion of Honor, 1961, Statesmanship award Harvard Sch. Assn., Chgo., 1962, Abraham Lincoln Centre award for humanitarian service, 1962. Mem. Phi Delta Phi, Alpha Delta Phi. Clubs: Chicago, Economic (past dir.), Executives (past dir.), Commercial (Chgo.). Author: Growing Old in the Country of the Young, 1974; I Want to Know about the United States Senate, 1976. Office: Senate Office Bldg Washington DC 20510

PEREZ, CARLOS A., radiologist, educator; b. Colombia, Nov. 10, 1934; came to U.S., 1960, naturalized, 1970; B.S., Universidad de Antiquia, Medellin, Colombia, 1952, M.D., 1960; m. Blanca; children—Carlos S., Bernardo, Edward P. Rotating intern Hosp. Universitario Saint Vincente de Paul, Medellin and Caldas, Colombia, 1958-59; resident in radiology Hosp. Universitario del Valle, Cali, Colombia, 1959-60; resident in radiology Mallinckrodt Inst. Radiology, Washington U. Sch. Medicine, 1960-63, instr. in radiology, 1964-66, asst. prof. radiology, 1966-67, asso. prof., 1967-72, prof., 1972—, dir. div. radiation oncology, 1976—; fellow in radiotherapy M.D. Anderson Hosp. and Tumor Inst., U. Tex., Houston, 1963-64; chmn. hyperthermia subcom., chmn. membership com., mem. exec. com. Radiation Therapy Oncology Group; chmn. com. on radiation therapy, mem. exec. com. Southeastern Cancer Study Group; mem. written exam. com. Am. Bd. Radiology. Mem. Internat. Assn. Study Lung Cancer, Am. Soc. Clin. Onco- logy, Am. Radium Soc., Am. Assn. Cancer Research, Am. Assn. Cancer Edn., Am. Coll. Radiology, Radiol. Soc. N.Am., Brit. Inst. Radiology, Assn. Univ. Radiologists, AAAS, AMA, Mo. Radiol. Soc., Mo. Acad. Sci., Mo., St. Louis med. socs., Greater St. Louis Soc. Radiologists, Radiation Research Soc., Soc. Surg. Oncologists, Am. Soc. Therapeutic Radiologists. Contbr. articles to profl. publs.; editorial bd. Yearbook of Cancer, 1973—; asso. editor, mem. editorial bd. Internat. Jour. Radiation Oncology, Biology and Physics, 1975—. Home: 9243 Clayton Rd Saint Louis MO 63124 Office: Div Radiation Oncology 4511 Forest Park Blvd Saint Louis MO 63108

PEREZ, HECTOR ROB, advt. and prodn. co. exec.; b. Chgo., Sept. 14, 1948; s. Angel and Rose (Garza) P.; A.A., Morton Coll., 1969; B.A., Columbia Coll., 1975; postgrad. Govs. State U.; m. Betty S. Slezak, May 6, 1971; children—Luke, Ronica, Milisa. Producer, Sta. WMAQ-TV, Chgo., 1975-76; pres. Luron Prodns., Inc., Chgo., 1976—; producer TV documentaries on Chgo. Hispanic Community. Served with USMC, 1969-71. Recipient EMMY award, Chgo., 1978; certs. of commendation, comdg. gen. Marine Force Pacific, 1970, 71. Mem. Chgo. Assn. Commerce and Industry. Roman Catholic. Club: Hispano Am. Jaycees (pres. 1978). Home: 16132 Long St Oak Forest IL 60452 Office: 233 N Michigan Ave Suite 2022 Chicago IL 60601

PEREZ, PAMELA EDYTHE, ednl. adminstr.; b. Cleve., Dec. 23, 1948; d. Joseph David and Cornelia Frances (Shy) Smith; B.S., Ohio State U., 1971; M.Ed., Cleve. State U., 1981; m. Francis Perez, Jan. 2, 1981. Tchr. English, Proviso E. High Sch., Maywood, Ill., 1973-78; tchr. English, Kirk Middle Sch., East Cleveland, 1978-80, curriculum specialist, 1980—. Ratner Miller Shafron Found. grantee, 1967-71. Mem. Assn. Supervision and Curriculum Devel., Nat. Council Tchrs. English, Greater Cleve. Council English Tchrs., Delta Sigma Theta. Office: 14410 Terrace Rd East Cleveland OH 44112

PEREZ-FERREIRO, ERNESTO SERGIO, surgeon, physician; b. Havana, Cuba; came to U.S., 1960, naturalized, 1969; s. Ernesto L. Perez-Ferrer and Josefina Ferreiro-De Leon; B.S., Champagnat Sch., Cuba; M.D. in Medicine and Surgery, U. Madrid (Spain), 1960; D.Med. and Surg., U. Havana, 1960; m. Ingrid E. Carlson, Apr. 22, 1979. Intern, Augustana Hosp., Chgo., 1961; resident in internal medicine Michael Reese Hosp., Chgo., 1962, Mercy Hosp., Chgo., 1963; practice medicine specializing family practice, Chgo., 1964—; cons. physician Portes Cancer Prevention Center, Northwestern U., 1977—; staff physician Chgo. Dept. of Health, 1977—. Mem. Oak Brook Civic Assn. Diplomate Am. Bd. Family Practice. Fellow Am. Acad. Family Physicians, Interam. Coll. Physicians and Surgeons; mem. Cuban Med. Assn. in Exile, Royal Soc. of Medicine of Gt. Brit., Ill. State Med. Soc., Chgo. Med. Soc., Ill. Acad. Family Physicians, AMA (Physicians Recognition award 1977, 78, 80). Roman Catholic. Office: 33 W Huron St Chicago IL 60610

PERINCHIEF, ROBERT Y., educator; b. Spring Lake, N.J., Jan. 31, 1931; B.S. in Music Edn., Trenton (N.J.) State U., 1957; M.A. in Music Edn., Columbia Tchr. Coll., N.Y.C., 1958, Ed.D. in Music Edn., 1964; married; 3 children. Instr. music No. Valley Regional High Sch., Demarest, N.J., 1956-57; instr. music Essex Fells (N.J.) Sch., 1957-58; instr. music Mahwah (N.J.) Pub. Schs., 1959-66; prof. music U. Wis., Whitewater, 1966—, coordinator Arts Outreach,

1977—, coordinator univ. conferencing and media-based edn., 1980—. Mem. NEA (life), Music Educators Nat. Conf. (life), Am. (life), Wis. choral dirs. assns., Coll. Music Soc. (life), Wis. Music Educators Conf., Midwest Kodaly Music Educators Am., Orgn. Am. Kodaly Educators (exec. sec.), Phi Mu Alpha Sinfonia (life). Authored Kodaly music edn. teaching materials. Recipient U. Wis. Excellence in Teaching award, 1973; Phi Mu Alpha Sinfonia Fraternity Orpheus award, 1973; cert. music tchr., N.J., Wis. Home: 1148 W Highland St Whitewater WI 53190 Office: Continuing Edn U Wis Whitewater WI 53190

PERINE, DAVID ANDREW, social worker; b. St. Louis, Sept. 28, 1946; s. O.D. and Beulah (Sykes) P.; B.A., Lincoln U., Jefferson City, Mo., 1971; M.S.W., Washington U., St. Louis, 1973; m. Martha Ann Levingston, June 14, 1969; children—David Andrew, Alissa Lynette and Alison Lynette (twins). Recreational supr. Mo. Div. Welfare, 1966; instr., coll. placement counselor Sophia Study Center, St. Louis, 1969-72; caseworker II, Family and Children's Service Greater St. Louis, 1973-76; planning asso. Greater St. Louis Health Systems Agy., 1976-78; social work coordinator Center Family Mental Health, St. Louis, 1978—; dir. child care services St. Louis Housing Authority, 1980—; part-time instr. Forest Park Community Coll., St. Louis; part-time lectr. George W. Brown Sch. Social Work, Washington U.; practicum instr. George Warren Brown Sch. Social Work, Washington U.; mem. black adoption task force Family and Children's Services Greater St. Louis; cons. in field. Mem. parent adv. council University City (Mo.) Title I Program; treas. Holy Met. Missionary Baptist Ch., St. Louis. Recipient various awards; Eleanor Roosevelt scholar, 1966. Mem. Nat. Assn. Social Workers, Acad. Cert. Social Workers, Nat. Assn. Black Social Workers, Nat. Urban League, NAACP, Alpha Phi Alpha, Iota Phi Lambda. Home: 7624 Cornell Ave Saint Louis MO 63130 Office: 3827 Enright Ave Saint Louis MO 63108

PERINO, ANTHONY RALPH, psychologist; b. Peoria, Ill., Apr. 24, 1942; s. Sam Ralph and Helen C. (Wagner) P.; B.S., Bradley U., 1965, M.A., 1966; Ph.D., So. Ill. U., 1971; m. Patricia E. Polansky, Oct. 8, 1966; children—Gina M., Gregory S. Dir. adolescent services Zeller Mental Health Center, Peoria, Ill., 1971-76; clin. asst. prof. psychiatry Peoria Sch. Medicine, U. Ill., 1973—; psychologist St. Francis Hosp., 1976-78, 81—; Mem. adv. council Phoenix Products, 1979—. Served with U.S. Army, 1966-69. Decorated Commendation medal. Mem. Am. Psychol. Assn., Council for Nat. Register of Health Services Providers in Psychology, Phi Kappa Phi. Roman Catholic. Home: 6408 N Camelot Peoria IL 61615 Office: 515 NE Glen Oak Peoria IL 61603

PERK, WAYNE LEE, printing press mfg. co. ofcl.; b. Chgo., June 25, 1943; s. Joseph F. and Elsie W. P.; B.S. in Bus. Adminstrn., Kans. State U., 1966, B.A. in Advt., 1966; m. Dorothy Delasso, Feb. 3, 1979. Dir. publs. J.T. Ryerson & Son, Chgo., 1967-68; dir. communications Zurich-Am. Ins. Cos., Schaumburg, Ill., 1968-80; dir. sales promotion and advt., graphic systems div. Rockwell Internat., Chgo., 1981—; bd. dirs. Ins. Advt. Conf. Mem. Ill. State C. of C. (rep.), Northwest Assn. Commerce and Industry, Chgo. Assn. Commerce and Industry (rep.), Sigma Delta Chi. Office: 3100 S Central Ave Chicago IL 60650

PERKETT, WILLIAM OLIVER, univ. dean; b. Traverse City, Mich., Aug. 24, 1922; s. Oliver B. and Margaret E. (Fick) P.; B.B.A., U. Oreg., 1952; M.B.A., U. Wash., Seattle, 1955, Ph.D., 1963; m. Jane B. Courtade, May 4, 1946; children—Lynnae, Mozelle, Venetia, Jeffrey, Megan. Asso. prof., then prof. bus. adminstrn. Gonzaga U., Spokane, Wash., 1964-66, v.p. fin. and planning, 1966-70; dean Sch. Bus., Haille Selassie U., Addis Ababa, Ethiopia, 1970-75; dean Sch. Bus. Adminstrn., U. Wis., La Crosse, 1976—; dir. Midnite Money Corp.; cons. to industry. Served with AUS, 1942-46. Decorated Purple Heart; Ford fellow, 1965; research grantee various fed. agys. Mem. Am. Mgmt. Assn., Am. Mktg. Assn., S.W. Fedn. Associated Scis. Author articles, reports in field. Office: 224 North Hall U Wis La Crosse WI 54601

PERKINS, DONALD SHELDON, diversified retailing co. exec.; b. St. Louis, Mar. 22, 1927; s. Arthur and Edna Ann (Meinert) P.; B.A., Yale, 1949; M.B.A., Harvard, 1951; m. Phyllis Elizabeth Babb, June 9, 1951; children—Elizabeth Perkins Hill, Jervis, Susan Perkins Getzendanner. With Jewel Cos., Inc., 1953—, v.p., gen. mgr. routes dept., 1961-63, dir., 1962—, exec. v.p. 1963-65, pres. 1965-70, chmn., 1970—, chmn. exec. com., 1980—, dir. Aurrera, S.A., Mexico City, Time, Inc., LaSalle St. Fund, AT&T, Inland Steel Co., Cummins Engine Co., Corning Glass Works, G.D. Searle & Co., Freeport-Memoran, Inc., Thyssen-Bornemisza (Monaco); internat. council Morgan Guaranty Trust Co. Bd. dirs. Assos. Harvard Bus. Sch.; trustee Ford Found., Brookings Instn., Johnson Found., Northwestern U., chmn. United Way/Crusade of Mercy, Chgo. Mem. Bus. Council. Clubs: Chgo., Econ., Commonwealth, Comml. (pres.) (Chgo.); Univ. (N.Y.C.); Glen View (Golf, Ill.); Old Elm (Sheridan, Ill.). Office: Jewel Cos Inc One First Nat Plaza Chicago IL 60603

PERKINS, D'WAYNE JOSEPH, automobile dealer sales mgr.; b. Kansas City, Mo., Apr. 28, 1948; s. Harold Joseph and Charlene Armenta (Lasley) P.; student (scholar) U. Mo., Kansas City, 1966-68; degree in data processing, Worth Bus. Coll., 1969; children—D'Michael Anthony, Marchita LaSean. Fin. mgr. Sherrill Minter Ford, Kansas City, Kans., 1970-75; sales mgr. Broadway Ford, Inc., Kansas City, Mo., 1975—. Served with M.P., AUS, 1968-70. Decorated Army Commendation Medal. Mem. Big Wheel Sales Mgrs. Club, Alpha Phi Alpha. Democrat. Baptist. Office: 3401 Broadway Kansas City MO 64111

PERKINS, JAMES PATRICK, advt. agy. exec.; b. Chgo., Dec. 6, 1939; s. John Alfred and Mary Grace (Quinlan) P.; student U. Ill., 1959-60, Western Ill. U., 1961; m. Sarah Reed Simkins, Sept. 13, 1975; children—Brian Patrick, Kevin Matthew. Sales and mktg. exec. Glidden-Durkee, 1964-65; advt. mgr. Amvar Chem. Co., 1965-69; indsl. coatings rep. Benjamin Moore Co., 1969-71; account exec. JTC Advt., 1971-74; creative dir., pres. Laven, Fuller & Perkins Advt.-Mktg., Chgo., 1974—. Dir., Mem. adv. bd. Booth Meml. Hosp., Salvation Army, Chgo., 1978-81. Served with U.S. Army, 1961-62 Mem. Bank Mktg. Assn. Roman Catholic. Home: 1314 Scott Winnetka IL 60093 Office: 233 E Ontario Chicago IL 60611

PERKINS, JOHN HAROLD, banker; b. Chgo., Aug. 28, 1921; s. Harold Reed and Roschen (Baker) P.; B.S., Northwestern U., 1943; m. Len Welborn, June 24, 1944; children—John H., Robert G., Reed F. With Continental Ill. Nat. Bank & Trust Co., Chgo., 1946—, asst. cashier, 1949-52, 2d v.p., 1952-56, v.p., 1956-65, sr. v.p., 1965-68, exec. v.p., dir., 1968-71, vice chmn., 1971-73, pres., 1973—; pres. Continental Ill. Corp., 1973—; prin. Chgo. United; dir. PEFCO (Pvt. Export Funding Corp.), Pillsbury Co.; pres. Am. Bankers Assn., 1978-79, now dir.; bd. govs. Midwest Stock Exchange. Bd. dirs. Nat. Minority Purchasing Council; trustee Northwestern U., Com. for Econ. Devel., Chgo. Symphony Orch., Episcopal Diocesan Found., Underwriters Labs., Michael Reese Hosp. and Med. Center. Served with USNR, 1943-46. Mem. Assn. Res. City Bankers, Phi Beta Kappa, Delta Tau Delta. Clubs: Wall St. (N.Y.C.); Indian Hill (Winnetka, Ill.); Met. (Chgo. and Washington); Bankers, Little La Salle St., Econ., Chgo., Univ., Carlton, Comml., Bond (Chgo.); Old Elm (Ft. Sheridan, Ill.). Office: care Regina Wells Continental Bank 231 S LaSalle St Chicago IL 60693

PERKINS, JOHN ROBERT, advt. exec., musician; b. Schenectady, Mar. 7, 1938; s. John R. and Catherine (Brown) P.; B.S., U. Ky., 1960; M. Sacred Music, So. Bapt. Coll., 1964; m. Sharon Lynn Cook, Aug. 24, 1958; children—Karon E., Laura L., Melissa A. Asst. research met. Bethlehem Steel Co., Lackawanna, N.Y., 1960; dir. research, account exec. Jayme Orgn., Cleve., 1960-65; asso. media dir.-indsl. products Meldrum & Fewsmith, Cleve., 1965-67; supr. marketing services Taylor-Winfield Corp., Warren, Ohio, 1967-68, mgr. promotion and mktg., 1968-69; account exec. Campbell-Ewald Co., 1969-74, account supr., 1974-76; copy chief Delco Remy div. Gen. Motors Corp., Anderson, Ind., 1976—. Fellow AAAS; mem. Am. Inst. Mining and Metall. Engrs., Assn. Indsl. Advertisers, Ky. Soc. Profl. Engrs. Clubs: Masons, K.T., Shriners, Edgewood Country, Detroit Adcraft. Contbr. articles to profl. jours. Composer, arranger, condr. sacred music, French hornist various local orchs., 1960—. Home: 3422 Berkeley Rd Anderson IN 46011 Office: 2401 Columbus Ave Anderson IN 46011

PERKINS, JOHN ROBERT, ambulance service exec.; b. Milw., Dec. 3, 1940; s. John Edward and Gertrude Mae (Clarke) P.; student U. Minn., 1959-61; m. Patricia K. Lemke, May 6, 1967; children—Lara M., Ryan. Owner, mgr. Gold Cross Ambulance Service, Inc., Rochester, Minn., 1962—. Named Outstanding Young Man, City of Rochester, 1975. Mem. Nat. Assn. Emergency Med. Technicians (charter), Nat. Registry Emergency Med. Technicians, Minn. Emergency Care Assn. Clubs: Masons, Shriners. Home: 1006 14th Ave SW Rochester MN 55901 Office: Gold Cross Ambulance Service 1005 6th St NW Rochester MN 55901

PERKINS, LINN BRUCE, hosp. adminstr.; b. Binghamton, N.Y., July 16, 1925; s. Carl Herbert and Lillian (Bruce) P.; B.A., Amherst Coll., 1949; M.H.A., Washington U., St. Louis, 1951; m. Nancy Marks, Aug. 18, 1951; children—Scott, Anne, Priscilla, John. Asst. adminstr., asst. dir., asso. dir., asso. exec. dir. Christ Hosp., Cin., 1951-70; exec. dir. St. Louis Childrens Hosp., 1970—. Chmn. bd. Episcopal-Presbyn. Found. for Aging, Inc.; trustee Diocesan Investment Trust, Inc. Served with inf., AUS, 1943-46; ETO. Mem. Soc. Adminstrv. Assos., Nat. Assn. Childrens Hosps. and Related Instns. (chmn. bd.), Am. Hosp. Assn., Mo. Hosp. Assn., St. Louis Met. Hosp. Assn. (chmn. bd.), Council Teaching Hosps. Home: 16 Rio Vista St Ladue MO 63124 Office: 500 S Kingshighway Saint Louis MO 63110

PERKINS, M(INER) THOMAS, clergyman, pastoral care adminstr.; b. Omaha, Apr. 5, 1934; s. Kenneth K. and Margaret Cecilia (Hope) P.; B.A., Nebr. Wesleyan U., 1956; B.D., So. Meth. U., 1960, M.S.T., 1966; M.S.W., U. Nebr., 1974; m. Cara Ruth Hutchinson, Sept. 8, 1957; children—M(iner) Thomas II, Lance N. Ordained to ministry United Meth. Ch., 1960; minister Chester-Hubbell United Meth. Ch., Chester, Nebr., 1961-64, Fontana (Kans.) United Meth. Ch., 1964-66; chaplain Nebr. Meth. Hosp., Omaha, 1966-69; dir. Uta Halee Home for Girls, Omaha, 1969-73, Equilibria Med. Center, Omaha, 1973-75; minister Maplewood United Meth. Ch., Omaha, 1975-78; dir. pastoral care W. Nebr. Gen. Hosp., Scottsbluff, 1978—; cons. to Cath. Diocese of Omaha, 1978, United Meth. Met. Ministries, 1966-78; therapist Panhandle Mental Health Center, 1979; guest Bellevue Coll., 1969; lectr. Creighton U. Coll. Medicine, 1972, Concordia Coll., 1977, U. Nebr., 1977-78. Vol. dir. Personal Crisis Service, 1968-70; co-chmn. Com. on Youth of Douglas County, Nebr., 1972-73; mem. com. Omaha Mayor's Commn. on Status of Women, 1972-74; mem. Omaha Public Schs. Spl. Edn. Adv. Com., 1969-73, Omaha-Douglas County Health Dept. on Edn., 1974; candidate State Legis., Nebr., 1974; mem. profl. edn. com. Nebr. div. Am. Cancer Soc.; bd. dirs. Scotts Bluff County Am. Cancer Soc., Scotts Bluff County YMCA, 1979, Cluster Six Council PTA, 1976-78; pres. Nebr. Hospice Assn. Recipient Human Relations award Omaha Public Sch. System, 1978; cert. pastoral care. Mem. Nat. Assn. Social Workers (v.p. Nebr. chpt. 1975-77, Social Worker of Year award 1977); Acad. of Cert. Social Workers, Perkins Sch. Theology Alumni Council. Democrat. Club: Kiwanis.

PERKINS, MARVIN DEUANE, real estate broker; b. Hoyt, Kans., Nov. 5, 1934; s. David Elmer and Gladys Lucille (Vaught) P.; B.A.I.S., Columbia Coll., 1975; m. Virginia Lee Hoyt, Sept. 9, 1956; children—Bradley Allen, Trudy Lynn, Tracy Scott. Sales mgr. George B. Emery Jr., real estate and ins., Topeka, 1963-64, Gerlach Marcy Co., realtors, Topeka, 1965-67; owner M.D. Perkins Agy., real estate, Topeka, 1967-68, 70-74; partner Coin-op. Laundry P & W Enterprises, Topeka, 1963-76; v.p. Thomas E. Crosley & Assos., realtors, Topeka, 1975-76; appraiser-broker Griffith & Blair, Inc., Topeka, 1976-78; v.p. Quail Creek Real Estate Co., Inc., Topeka, 1978-80; pres. Quail Creek Edn. Co., Inc., Topeka, 1978-80; owner M.D. Perkins Agy., Realtor, Topeka, 1980—, Profl. Ednl. Resources of Kans. Inst., Topeka, 1981—; lectr. in field; treas. Topeka Bd. Realtors, 1972. Pres., Tecumseh Sch. Parent-Tchr. Orgn., 1973-74; trustee Topeka Twp., 1977—; clk., 1965-68, justice of peace, 1973-74; chmn. Topeka Bd. Equal Opportunity in Housing Com., 1975; bd. govs. Kans. Grad. Realtors Inst., 1975—, dean, 1977. Served to maj. AUS, 1968-69; Vietnam; to lt. col. Res., 1969—. Decorated Bronze Star; named Realtor of Yr., Topeka, 1977; Ky. col., 1978; hon. dep. marshal Dodge City, 1979; cert. rev. appraiser, real estate counselor, residential specialist. Mem. Eastboro Mchts. Assn. (dir. 1974-75), Shawnee Heights Boosters Club (dir. 1975-77), Assn. U.S. Army (dir. 1970-72), Topeka Housebuilders Assn. (v.p. 1963), Topeka Real Estate Bd., Kans. Assn. Realtors (v.p. zone 1, 1978, 79), Nat. Assn. Realtors, Realtors Nat. Mktg. Inst., Nat. Guard Assn. Kans. and U.S., Ind. Fee Appraisers (pres. chpt. 1979-81), VFW, Am. Legion. Methodist (adminstrv. bd.). Clubs: Optimists (v.p. Shawnee Heights 1974), Toastmasters (edn. v.p. Topeka chpt. 1963), Masons, Shriners, Lake Shore Country (pres. 1973). Research new methods appraisal. Home: 2426 SE 37th St Topeka KS 66605 Office: MD Perkins Agy Realtor 3300 SW 29th St Topeka KS 66614

PERKINS, WILLIAM H., JR., financial co. exec.; b. Rushville, Ill., Aug. 4, 1921; s. William H. and Sarah Elizabeth (Logsdon) P.; ed. Ill. Coll.; m. Eileen Margaret Nelson, Jan. 14, 1949; 1 son, Gary Douglas. Legis. rep. CNA Fin. Corp., Chgo., 1949-79; pres. Howlett & Perkins Assos., Ltd., Chgo., 1979—. Mem. Nat. Armed Forces Mus. Adv. Bd. of Smithsonian Instn., 1964—; mem. Ill. AEC, 1963—, sec., 1970—; mem. Ill. Traffic Safety Adv. Council; sgt.-at-arms Dem. Nat. Conv., 1952, 56, del.-at-large, 1964, 68, 72; spl. asst. to chmn. Dem. Nat. Com., 1960; mem. Presdl. Inaugural Com., 1961, 65, 69, 73. Served with AUS, 1944-46; aide to prime minister and Brit. ambassador at founding of UN, 1945. Mem. Ill. C. of C. (chmn. legis. com. 1971), Ins. Fedn. Ill. (pres. 1965—, also dir.), Chgo. Assn. Commerce and Industry (legis com.), Health Ins. Assn. Am. Methodist. Clubs: Masons, Shriners; Ill. Athletic (Chgo.); Sangamo (Springfield, Ill.); Riverside (Ill.); Fed. City (Washington). Home: 52 N Cowley Rd Riverside IL 60546 Office: 188 W Randolph St Suite 2900 Chicago IL 60601

PERLMAN, LAWRENCE, lawyer, bus. exec.; b. St. Paul, Apr. 8, 1938; s. Irving and Ruth (Mirsky) P.; B.A., Carleton Coll., 1960; J.D., Harvard U., 1963; m. Medora Scoll, June 18, 1961; children—David, Sara. Admitted to Minn. bar, 1963; law clk., fed. judge, 1963-64; asso. partner, firm Fredrikson, Byron, Colborn, Bisbee Hansen & Perlman, and predecessor firms, Mpls., 1964-75; v.p., sec., gen. counsel Medtronic Inc., Mpls., 1975, exec. v.p., 1975-78; sr. partner firm Oppenheimer, Wolff, Foster, Shepand and Donnelly, Mpls., St. Paul, and Brussels, Belgium, 1978-80; v.p., gen. counsel sec. law and govt. relations Control Data Corp., 1980—; dir. CPT Corp., Am. Med. Systems, Inc., Magnetic Peripherals, Inc.; adj. prof. law U. Minn., 1974-76, 79-80; lectr. Minn. Continuing Legal Edn. Chmn., Minn. Fgn. Policy Assn., 1972; mem. Mpls. Bd. Estimate and Taxation, 1973-75; chmn. Mpls. Municipal Fin. Commn., 1978-79; bd. dirs. Walker Art Center, 1975—, Hennepin Center for Arts, 1977—, Mpls. Urban League, 1972-74, Hennepin County chpt. ARC, 1976-79. Mem. Am., Minn. (chmn. banking, corp. and bus. law sect.), recipient Outstanding Author award, 1975), Hennepin County bar assns., Am. Law Inst., Phi Beta Kappa. Club: Minneapolis. Home: 2366 W Lake of Isles Pkwy Minneapolis MN 55405 Office: Control Data Corp Box O Minneapolis MN 55440

PERLMUTTER, JERRY, psychologist, educator; b. Atlantic City, July 6, 1932; s. Irving and Yetta Rachel P.; B.S., CCNY, 1954; postgrad. Merrill-Palmer Inst., 1954-55; M.A., U. Chgo., 1964, Ph.D., 1966; children—David, Rachel. Staff psychologist Ill. State Psychiat. Inst., Chgo., 1960-66, asst. chief psychologist, 1966-67; dir. tng. Chgo. Metrozone N., Ill. Dept. Mental Health, 1967-69; asso. prof. behavioral sci. Grad. Sch., George Williams Coll., Downers Grove, Ill., 1969—; pres. Cons. for Personal and Organizational Enrichment, Chgo., 1968—. Served with U.S. Army, 1955-57. Mem. Am. Psychol. Assn., Nat. Tng. Labs. Inst. Applied Behavioral Sci., Am. Group Psychotherapy Assn., Am. Soc. Clin. Hypnosis, Psi Chi. Jewish. Office: George Williams Coll 555 31st St Downers Grove IL 60515

PERRAULT, GARY EUGENE, engr.; b. Ogdensburg, N.Y., Mar. 29, 1950; s. Clarence Eugene and Edna Loraine (Hughes) P.; B.S. in Ceramic Engring., Alfred U., 1974; m. Ivy Christine Dillemuth, Aug. 31, 1974; children-Mark Ian, Matthew Dion. Tech. service engr. Union Carbide Corp., Cleve., 1974-75, product engr., 1975-76; sales engring. trainee Mobil Oil Corp., Cleve., 1976, sales engr., Rockford, Ill., 1977-78, lubrication engr., Schaumburg, Ill., 1978—. Mem. Canton (N.Y.) Narcotic and Drug Commn., 1969-70; instr. Cleve. Jr. Achievement. Mem. Am. Soc. Lubrication Engrs., Soc. Mfg. Engrs., Am. Inst. Plant Engrs. Democrat. Lutheran. Clubs: Triumph Sportscar, Masons. Home: 2808 Edelweiss Rd Rockford IL 61109 Office: Mobile Oil Corp 600 Woodfield Dr Schaumburg IL 60195

PERRET, MAURICE EDMOND, educator; b. La Chaux-de-Fonds, Switzerland, May 19, 1911; s. Jules Henri and Henriette Marie (Leuba) P.; Bac. es Lettres, U. Zurich (Switzerland), 1930; Licence es Lettres, U. Neuchatel (Switzerland), 1940; M.A. (Internat. House fellow 1940-42), U. Calif. at Berkeley, 1942; Doctorat es Lettres, U. Lausanne (Switzerland), 1950. Tchr., Petropolis and Lycee Francais, Rio de Janeiro, Brazil, 1935-37; asst. consulate Switzerland, San Francisco, 1942-43; del. internat. com. Red Cross, Washington, 1943-45; del. Aid to Arab Refugees, Palestine, 1949-51; asst. Internat. Telecommunication Union, Geneva, Switzerland, 1951-52; librarian La Chaux-de-Fonds, Switzerland, 1953-54; asst. Oltremare, Rome, Italy, 1955-56; prof. Avenches, Switzerland, 1957-63; prof. geography, map librarian U. Wis., Stevens Point, 1963—. Curator Roman Mus., Avenches, Switzerland, 1960-63. Mem. city council Avenches, Switzerland, 1961-63. Served with Swiss Army, 1939-40. Mem. Assn. Am. Geographers, Nat. Council Geog. Edn., Am. Geog. Soc., Wis. Acad. Scis., Arts and Letters, Societe vaudoise de geographie (v.p. 1960-63), Fedn. Swiss Geog. Socs. (v.p. 1961-63). Club: Travelers Century. Editorial com. Atlas Switzerland, 1960-63. Contbr. articles to profl. jours. Office: Geography Dept U Wis Stevens Point WI 54481

PERRY, ANN J., biochemist; b. Newark, Feb. 17, 1922; d. Stanley R. and Lillian E. (Cronley) Jelliffe; student (prize scholar), U. Rochester, 1939-41; B.A. in Chemistry, U. Calif., Berkeley, 1944; M.S. in Organic Chemistry, La. State U., Baton Rouge, 1954; Ph.D. in Phys. Biochemistry (Eye Research fellow, 1956-58), Northwestern U. Med. Sch., 1960; 1 dau., Joan E. Research asso. Chgo. Med. Sch. Research Inst., 1961-63; research asso. Northwestern U. Med. Sch., Chgo., 1963-65, Am. Dental Assn., Chgo., 1965-76; asso. faculty Ind. U. Northwest, Gary, 1974—; research biochemist VA Med. Center, North Chicago, Ill., 1978—; speaker sci. confs. Vol. Dem. presdl. campaign, 1976. Prin. investigator USPHS research grants dental biochemistry, 1971-74; certified clin. lab. dir., HEW. Mem. N.Y. Acad. Scis., Soc. for Complex Carbohydrates, Sigma Xi, Sigma Pi Sigma, Sigma Delta Epsilon. Reviewer, contbr. articles to profl. jours. in field. Home: 18448 Roy St Lansing IL 60438 Office: VA Medical Center North Chicago IL 60064

PERRY, ANTHONY JOHN, hosp. adminstr.; b. Dighton, Mass., Oct. 19, 1919; s. Antone and Jessie P.; B.S. in Edn., State Coll. Mass. at Bridgewater, 1942; M.S. in Hosp. Adminstrn., Northwestern U., 1952; m. Harriet M. McGirr, Nov. 26, 1949; children—Joan Perry Markward, Martha. Flight supt. Trans World Airlines, Lisbon, Portugal, 1946-47; sta. mgr. Peruvian Internat. Airlines, N.Y.C., 1947-49; with adminstrn. Decatur and Macon County Hosp. (now Decatur Meml. Hosp.), Decatur, Ill., 1952—, adminstr., 1961—, exec. v.p., 1969-74, pres., 1974—; v.p., treas. Hosp. Shared Services Inc., 1979—; v.p. Multihosp. Mut. Ins. Ltd.; corp. mem. Health Care Service Corp. (Blue Cross/Blue Shield Plan). Bd. dirs. South Central Ill. Health Planning Council, 1969—, Vol. Hosps. Am., 1977—; mem. adv. bd. Grad. Studies Center, Millikin U., Decatur. Served with USAAF, 1942-46. Fellow Am. Coll. Hosp. Adminstrs.; mem. Am. Hosp. Assn. (chmn. council on fin. 1977-79, trustee, mem. regional adv. bd. 5, mem. com. on equity in payment for not for profit hosps. 1981—), Ill. Hosp. Assn. (pres. 1972, chmn. rate rev. steering com. 1979—), Northwestern U. Alumni Assn. (exec. council). Clubs: Decatur Country, Decatur. Home: 421 Hackberry Dr Decatur IL 62521 Office: 2300 N Edward St Decatur IL 62526

PERRY, DONALD EDWARD, vol. and tng. coordinator; b. Mondovi, Wis., Aug. 27, 1942; s. Dean Goss and Amy May (Olson) P.; B.A., Augsburg Coll., 1971; Cert. Mgmt. in Human Services, U. Minn., Mpls., 1979; m. Kathleen Jo Thorp., Jan. 22, 1966; 1 son, Bryce Colin. Probation and parole officer Minn. Dept. Corrections, St. Paul, 1971-72; probation and parole officer Anoka (Minn.) County Corrections, 1972-74; adminstrv. dir. Minn. Sheriff's Boys Ranch, Isanti, Minn., 1974-75; vol. and tng. coordinator Anoka County (Minn.) Corrections, 1977—; cons. adult edn., mgmt.-supervisory skills vocat. schs., White Bear, Minn. Served with USN, 1965-71. Recipient Outstanding Vol. Program citation Nat. Council Juvenile and Family Ct. Judges, 1980. Mem. Minn. Assn. County Probation Officers (pres. 1979), Minn. Corrections Assn. (newsletter editor 1979-80), Am. Soc. Tng. and Devel., Minn. Assn. Vol. Dirs., Assn. Vol. Adminstrs. Lutheran. Home: 24381 Riverbank Ln Rural Route 1 Box 152 Isanti MN 55040 Office: Corrections Dept Courthouse Anoka MN 55303

PERRY, ESTON LEE, banker; b. Wartsburg, Tenn., June 16, 1936; s. Eston Lee and Willimae (Heidle) P.; B.S., Ind. State U., 1961; m. Alice Anne Schmidt, Oct. 21, 1961; children—Julie Anne, Jeffrey John. With Oakley Corp., 1961-81, owner, operator Oakley

Pharmacies, Terre Haute, Ind., 1961-70, corp. treas., dir., 1965-79; officer Ind. State Bank, Terre Haute, 1975-80, corp. v.p., 1981—; dir. Oakley Found. Bd. dirs., adv. bd. Terre Haute Salvation Army, 1978-79; mem. Vigo County (Ind.) Welfare Bd.; pres. Terre Haute Bd. Aviation Commrs., 1968-70; chmn. Wabash Valley March of Dimes Airlife, 1965-70; bd. dirs. Jr. Achievement of Wabash Valley, 1981. Served with U.S. Army, 1955-57. Mem. Am. Bankers Assn., Ind. Bankers Assn., Ind. Aviation Trades Assn., Ind. Airport Ofcls. Assn., Wabash Valley Pilots Assn. (past pres.), Presidents Assos. of Ind. State U. Clubs: Ind. State U. Varsity; Lions, Elks (Terre Haute). Home: 124 Madison Blvd Terre Haute IN 47803 Office: 18 S 16th St Terre Haute IN 47807

PERRY, GEORGE WILLIAM, communications co. exec.; b. Central City, Ill., Sept. 23, 1925; s. George and Florence May (Gott) P.; B.S.C., Northwestern U., 1955; m. Elaine Lois Berezin, Jan. 13, 1951; children—Robin A., Eric T. Freelance actor, announcer, radio, TV, recordings, film, vaudeville, theatre, Chgo., 1938-53; orders and service mgr. RCA Rec. Studios, Chgo., 1951-53; asst. dir. radio and TV, Nat. Safety Council, Chgo., 1953-61, mem. pub. info. conf., 1961-76; exec. sec. Chicago Unlimited Inc., 1961—; charter mem., treas. Joseph Jefferson Awards Com., 1969-73; bd. advisers Vets. Bedside Network, 1972—; mem. steering com. Midwest Seminar Videotape and Film, Chgo., 1974-75; mem. adv. com. Chgo. arts, entertainment and media industry Labor Inst. Human Enrichment, Inc., 1980—. Publicity dir. Oakton Cub Scouts, Evanston, 1968. Served with USAAF, 1943-45. Mem. Nat. Acad. TV Arts and Scis. (exec. dir. Chgo. chpt. 1961-73), Goodman Sch. Drama Alumni Assn. (exec. sec. 1977-79). Editor: CU Directory, CU Digest, Weekly, 1961—. Office: 203 N Wabash Ave Suite 1020 Chicago IL 60601

PERRY, HAROLD, radiation therapist; b. Hamtramck, Mich., June 26, 1924; s. James Arthur and Ida B. (Hill) P.; student Wayne State U., 1941-43, Cornell U., 1944; M.D., Howard U., 1948; m. Agnes Marie Barnes, June 12, 1948; children—Harold Arthur, Karen Fanchon, Michael Elliott. Intern, Freedmen's Hosp., Washington, 1948-49, resident in radiology, 1949-52; resident in radiation therapy Meml. Hosp. for Cancer and Allied Diseases, N.Y.C., 1952, 55, Olin-Squibb Sr. fellow, 1964; Kress fellow in radiation therapy Meml. Hosp., dept. biophysics Sloan-Kettering Inst., N.Y.C., 1956-57; asst. prof. radiology U. Cin., 1957-63, asso. prof., 1963-66; clin. asso. prof. radiology Wayne State U., 1966-68, adj. asso. prof., 1969-73, clin. asso. prof., 1973—; pvt. practice medicine specializing in radiation therapy, Detroit, 1966—; asso. mem. staff S.W. Oncology Group, Detroit, 1976—; mem. staffs Sinai, Detroit VA hosps., S. Macomb Hosp., Warren, Mich.; dir. radiation therapy Abraham and Anna Srere Radiation Therapy Center, Sinai Hosp., Detroit, 1966—, chmn. dept. radiation therapy, 1981—; bd. dirs. Mich. Cancer Found., Detroit, 1968—; mem. hosp. adv. council S.E. Mich. Regional Med. Program, 1969—, mem. radiation therapy adv. council, 1969—, chmn., 1978—; mem. exec. com. Mich. Cancer Found., 1970—, co-dir. radiation therapy network Met. Detroit Cancer Control Program, 1974—, chmn. radiation therapy adv. panel, 1976—, vice chmn. bd., 1976—; lectr. Internat. Symposium Fundamentals in Tech. Progress, Liège, Belgium, 1979; Wm. E. Allen, Jr. lectr. Nat. Med. Assn., 1979; spl. lectr. 7th Internat. Use of Computers in Radiation Therapy, Japan, 1980. Served with AUS, 1942-46, as capt. M.C., USAF, 1953-55. Diplomate Am. Bd. Radiology. Fellow Am. Coll. Radiology; mem. AAAS, N.Y. Acad. Scis., Am. Radium Soc., Radiol. Soc. N.Am., Am. Soc. Therapeutic Radiologists (chmn. com. on edn. 1968-69), AMA, Wayne County (Mich.) Med. Soc., Mich. Radiol. Soc. (pres. 1977-78), Mich. Soc. Therapeutic Radiologists (pres. elect 1981), Detroit Cancer Club, Nat. Med. Assn., Am. Soc. Clin. Oncology, Am. Assn. Physicists in Medicine (asso.), Kappa Pi. Contbr. articles to profl. jours. Home: 287 Orange Lake Dr Bloomfield Hills MI 48013 Office: 6767 W Outer Dr Detroit MI 48235

PERRY, IRVING CHESTER, III, petroleum trader; b. Phila., Jan. 18, 1943; s. Irving Chester and Erma (McNeil) P.; B.A., Lake Forest Coll., 1965; m. Dayanne Schurecht, Aug. 27, 1966; 1 son, London Schade. Sr. mgmt. trainee Brit. Overseas Airways Corp., London, 1968-69; founder, owner ITEC Internat. Ltd., Palatine, Ill., 1969—, pres. 1970—, chmn. bd. dirs., 1970—; founder, co-owner, pres., chmn. bd. dirs. ITEC Oil Co. Ltd., Palatine, 1976—; pres. ITEC Trading Co., Ltd., Palatine; tchr. local courses in fin. and real estate; mem. O'Hare Group for Industry and Bus., 1972—. Served with AUS, 1965-68; Vietnam. Decorated Bronze Star, Air medal, Purple Heart, Army Commdation medal. Mem. Barrington Bd. Realtors (dir. 1974—), Barrington C. of C., Chgo. Real Estate Bd., Internat. Real Estate Fedn., Nat. Inst. Farm and Land Brokers, Nat. Inst. Real Estate Brokers, Am. Petroleum Inst., Kappa Sigma. Mem. Religious Soc. Friends. Clubs: Barrington Bath and Tennis, Chgo. Oil Men's. Home: 200 Coolidge St Barrington IL 60010 Office: 119 E Palatine Rd Suite 205 Palatine IL 60067

PERRY, NANCY ESTELLE, psychologist; b. Pitts., Oct. 30, 1934; d. Simon Warren and Estelle Cecelia (Zaluski) Reichard; B.S., Ohio State U., 1956, M.A. in Psychology, 1969, Ph.D. in Psychology (Ednl. Profl. Devel. Act fellow), 1973; m. John Cleveland; children—Scott, Karen, Elaine. Nurse, various locations, 1956-63; sch. psychologist public schs., Columbus, Ohio, 1970-72; human devel. specialist Madison County (Ohio) Schs., 1972-75; pvt. practice clin. psychology, cons., Worthington, Ohio, 1975-80; tchr. U. Wis., Milw., 1980—; pvt. practice Milw. Devel. Center, 1980—. Ohio Dept. Edn. grantee, 1973-76. Mem. Am. Psychol. Assn., Ohio Psychol. Assn., Orgnl. Devel. Network, Internat. Assn. Applied Social Scientists, Nat. Assn. Sch. Psychologists, Am. Assn. Marriage and Family Counselors. Home: 2210 W Cleveland Ave Mequon WI 53092 Office: 1500 E Capital Dr Shorewood WI 53211

PERRY, OSCAR L., SR., clergyman; b. Blytheville, Ark., Apr. 9, 1935; s. Will and Lettie (Lewis) P.; D.D. (hon.) in Religious Sci. and Art, 1975; m. Darlene Burgess, Feb. 14, 1954; children—Oscar L., Brenda K. Ordained to ministry Pentecostal Ch., 1954; asst. pastor Power House Ch. God in Christ, 1955-69; pastor Mt. Sinai Ch., Indpls., 1969—; plant mgr. Carter Indsl. Service, Anderson, Ind., 1976—; v.p. Inst. of Religious Sci., Inc., Gary, Ind., 1975-77; state evangelist Ind. North. Mem. Am. Hort. Soc. Home: 516 Central Way Edgewood IN 46011 Office: PO Box 2739 Anderson IN 46011

PERRY, PAUL, flavor chemist; b. N.Y.C., May 12, 1926; s. Samuel J. and Gertrude (Fishoff) P.; B.S. in Chemistry, L.I. U., 1949; M.S. in Chemistry, Poly. Inst. Bklyn., 1953, B.S. in Chem. Engring., 1953, Ph.D. in Chemistry, 1957; postdoctoral student Pa. State U., 1958; m. Leatrice Oster, Sept. 12, 1948; children—Gail Madelaine, Lisa Randie. Chemist, L. Baron Co., Yonkers, N.Y., 1949-51; chief flavor chemist Globe Extract Co., Bklyn., 1951-58; v.p. flavors V&E Kohnstamm Co., Bklyn., 1958-65; dir. research and devel. Fries & Fries Co., Cin., 1965-70; dir. flavor dept. Warner-Jenskinson Inc., St. Louis, 1970—; sr. scientist 7-Up; vis. prof. U. Mo.; cons. Orthodox Union. Served with AUS, 1943-46. Decorated Purple Heart, D.S.C. Mem. Chem. Sources Assn. (pres. 1978), Am. Assn. Cereal Chemists (pres. 1976-77), Inst. Food Technologists (chmn. 1958-59), Flavor Chemists Soc., Am. Chem. Soc., Candy Technologists Assn., Am. Soc. Enologists, Soft Drink Technologists Assn., Flavor and Extract Mfrs. Assn., Essential Oil Assn., Am. Jewish Congress, Jewish Fedn., Christian and Jewish Assn., Anti-Defamation League, NAACP. Club: B'nai B'rith. Author numerous articles, patentee in field. Home: 731 Wayfield Dr Olivette MO 63132 Office: 121 S Meramec St Clayton MO 63105

PERRY, ROBERT JOSEPH, lawyer; b. Glenford, Ohio, Nov. 19, 1932; s. Elmer L. and Claudia (Vinson) P.; B.A., Ohio State U., 1955, J.D., 1961; postgrad. U.S. Fgn. Service Inst., 1957; m. Jane E. Brazik, 1979; children—Scott Warren, Elaine Marie Schwendeman, Karen Elizabeth; 1 stepson, Richard J. Brazik. Vice consul, 3d sec. Am. embassy, Mexico, 1957-59; admitted to Ohio bar, 1962; practiced in Columbus, 1962—; asso. DeVennish & Hague, 1962; asst. atty. gen. State of Ohio, 1963-65; asso. Fontana, Ward & Kaps, 1965-70; partner Fontana, Ward, Kaps & Perry, 1970-77, Perry & Boyuk, 1978—. Asst. scoutmaster Boy Scouts Am., 1968-73; pres. Ohio State U. Law Sch. Republican Club, 1961; trustee Columbus Legal Aid Soc., 1979-81, Columbus Law Library Assn., 1980-82, Pastoral Counseling Services, Inc., 1981—; mem. task force on student legal services Ohio State U., 1980-81. Served with USAF, 1951-53. Mem. Am., Ohio (chmn. prepaid legal services com. 1975-76), Columbus (bd. govs. 1975-79, sec.-treas. 1979-80, pres. 1981—) bar assns., Columbus Bar Found., Ohio Assn. Attys. Gen. (treas. 1978, sec. 1979), Order Demolay (Legion of Honor), Delta Sigma Phi, Phi Delta Phi. Republican. Lutheran. Clubs: University, Masons. Home: 6201 Alrojo St Worthington OH 43085 Office: 150 E Broad St Columbus OH 43215

PERRY, WENDY RUTH, occupational therapist; b. Medicine Hat, Alta., Can., Dec. 15, 1951; came to U.S., 1965, naturalized, 1980; d. John Alexander and Ruth (Gandier) Perry; B.S., Ohio State U., 1974. Chief occupational therapist Elkes Aidmore Hosp., Atlanta, 1975-76; staff occupational therapist Ga. Bapt. Hosp., Atlanta, 1976-77; staff/team leader occupational therapist II and III, Talmadge Meml. Hosp., Augusta, Ga., 1977-80; dir. occupational therapy Redwood Sch. & Rehab. Center, Ft. Mitchell, Ky., 1980-81; staff occupational therapist Soc. for Crippled Children, Lakewood, Ohio, 1981—; guest instr. occupational therapy Med. Coll. Ga., Augusta, 1977-80; cons. in field. Mem. Am. Occupational Therapy Assn., Ohio Occupational Therapy Assn. Ga. Occupational Therapy Assn., Center for Study of Sensory Integrative Dysfunction. Club: Sierra. Home: 2684 Mayfield Rd Apt 101 Cleveland Heights OH 44106 Office: 14587 Madison Ave Lakewood OH 44107

PERSHING, ROBERT GEORGE, telecommunications co. exec.; b. Battle Creek, Mich., Aug. 10, 1941; s. James Arthur and Beulah Francis P.; B.S.E.E., Tri-State Coll., Angola, Inc., 1961; m. Diana Kay Prill, Sept. 16, 1961; children—Carolyn, Robert. Communications engr. Am. Elec. Power, Ind., N.Y. and Ohio, 1961-69; design supr. Wescom, Inc., Ill., 1969-74; dir. engring. Tellabs, Inc., Lisle, Ill., 1974-78; pres. Teltrend, Inc., West Chicago, Ill., 1979—, also dir.; engring. cons. Mem. IEEE. Office: 1020 Carolina Dr West Chicago IL 60185

PERSKY, SEYMOUR HOWARD, lawyer; b. Chgo., May 22, 1922; s. Joseph E. and Bertha (Solomon) P.; A.A. magna cum laude, City Coll., Chgo., 1949; B.A., Roosevelt U., 1952; J.D., DePaul U., 1952; postgrad. Northwestern U., 1961-62; m. Beverly M. Lipsky, July 8, 1962; children—Jonathan E., Abbe Joan. Admitted to Ill. bar, 1952, U.S. Supreme Ct. bar, 1965; resident counsel Mid-West Loan Co., Chgo., 1953-58; sr. partner firm Persky, Phillips & Berzock, Chgo., 1961-63; practiced in Chgo., 1963—; pub. defender Narcotics Ct., Municipal Ct. of Chgo., 1964—; lectr. Truman Jr. Coll.; mem. Mid Am. Commodity Exchange, Internat. Monetary Market (Chgo. Merc. Exchange). Vice pres. Peoples Rehab. Found., Yiddish Theater Assn.; bd. govs. Israel Bonds of Greater Chgo., chmn. young peoples div., 1970-72, chmn. lawyers div., 1973-74, pres. Prime Minister's Club; bd. govs. Ida Crown Jewish Acad.; bd. dirs. Hillel Torah North Suburban Day Sch., Skokie, Ill. 1973, Arie Crown Day Sch., 1977—, Skokie Valley Synagogue, 1977—; partner DePaul U. Coll. Law; mem. endowment bd. DePaul U. Served with USAAF, 1941-44. Mem. Am., Ill. (chmn. subcom. unauthorized practice law com. 1962), Chgo. (criminal law com., def. prisoners com.) bar assns., Ill. Acad. Criminology, Decalogue Soc., Def. Lawyers Assn., Am. Trial Lawyers Assn., Nat. Trust for Historic Preservation, Lex Legio DePaul U., Soc. Fellows DePaul U., DePaul U. Alumni Assn (chmn. alumni class 1952), Chgo. Assn. Commerce and Industry, Landmarks Preservation Council, Greater N.Mich. Ave. Assn., Mensa, Nu Beta Epsilon. Clubs: City, Covenant of Ill. (vice chmn. library com.), Execs., Lincoln Park Builders (Chgo.). Home: 65 Prospect Ave Highland Park IL 60035 Office: 105 W Madison St Chicago IL 60602

PERSON, MARJORIE PERRY, educator; b. Mound City, Mo., Sept. 14, 1917; d. David Clinton and Nelle Katherine (Yous) Perry; B.S. in Edn., NW Mo. State U., 1940; M.B.A., Ind. U., Bloomington, 1956, D.B.A., 1965; m. Paul Manning Person, May 23, 1940 (dec. 1943); 1 son, William Paul. Tchr. Mound City Pub. Schs., 1946-54; instr. bus. NW Mo. State U., 1954-55; asst. prof. bus., 1956-62; asso. prof. bus. adminstrn. Idaho State U., Pocatello, 1963-65; asst. prof. bus. adminstrn., Ind. U. at Fort Wayne, 1965-69, asso. prof., 1969—; vis. prof. mktg. U. Nev., Las Vegas, 1972-73; cons., bd. dirs. Arnolt Corp., Warsaw, Ind., 1968-72; exec. v.p., dir. JMB Enterprises, Inc., Fort Wayne, 1968-72. Nonservice fellow Ind. U., Bloomington, 1961-62; Summer Faculty fellow, Ind. U. Fort Wayne, 1972; named Outstanding Educator, Alpha Delta Kappa, Fort Wayne, 1972; recipient Distinguished Teaching award Ind. U., Fort Wayne, 1970. Mem. Am. Mktg. Assn., Pi Omega Pi, Delta Pi Epsilon, Beta Gamma Sigma, Alpha Sigma Alpha. Republican. Club: Eastern Star. Co-editor: The Challenge of Change, Marketing Readings, 1974; contbr. articles in field to profl. jours. Home: 1206 3 Rivers Apts N Fort Wayne IN 46802 Office: Ind Univ-Purdue Univ Fort Wayne IN 46805

PERYER, FREDERICK WILLIAM, musician, ednl. adminstr.; b. Flint, Mich., Aug. 22, 1932; s. Samuel Richardson and Eva Alice P.; Mus.B., Western Mich. U., 1956; postgrad. U. Mich., Flint, 1957-59; m. Marjorie Ann Carey, June 11, 1956; children—Marianne, Marcia, Marilyn, Michelle. Music tchr. Flint Public Schs., 1956-69, Carman Sch. Dist., Flint, 1969-73; personnel mgr. Flint Symphony Orch., 1970-73, mng. dir., 1973—; asst. to mng. dir. Flint Inst. Music, 1972-73, mng. dir., 1973-81, exec. dir., 1981—; profl. tuba player, 1956—; tuba tchr. Charles Stewart Mott Community Coll. and U. Mich., Flint; producer musical enrichment programs Charles Stewart Mott Found., 1956—; orchestral condr., 1956-64. Festival and public relations coms. Flint Bicentennial Commn., 1975-76; mem. Greater Flint Arts Council, Flint Area Conv. and Tourist Council; bd. dirs. Flint Hist. Theater. Mem. Am. Symphony Orch. League (mgmt. mem.), Mich. Orch. Assn. (dir.), Assn. Coll., Univ. and Community Arts Adminstrs., Met. Orch. Mgrs. Assn. (chmn. Mid-West region), Am. Fedn. Musicians, Flint Area C. of C. Club: Kiwanis. Musical arranger for Gen. Motors Corp. and TV productions. Office: 1025 E Kearsley St Flint MI 48503

PESCH, LEROY ALLEN, physician, educator, health and hosp. cons., corp. exec.; b. Mt. Pleasant, Iowa, June 22, 1931; s. Herbert Lindsey and Mary Clarissa (Tyner) P.; student State U. Iowa, 1948-49, Iowa State U., 1950-52; M.D. cum laude, Washington U., St. Louis, 1956; m. Donna J. Stone, Dec. 28, 1975; children from previous marriage—Christopher Allen, Brian Lindsey, Daniel Ethan; stepchildren—Christopher Scott Kneifel, Linda Suzanne Kneifel. Intern, Barnes Hosp., St. Louis, 1956-57; research asso. NIH, Bethesda, Md., 1957-59; asst. resident medicine Grace-New Haven Hosp., New Haven, 1959-60; clin. fellow Yale Med. Sch., New Haven, 1960-61, instr. medicine, 1961-62, asst. prof. medicine, 1962-63, asst. dir. liver study unit, 1961-63; asso. physician Grace-New Haven Hosp., 1961-62; asso. prof. medicine Rutgers U., New Brunswick, N.J., 1963-64, prof., 1964-66, chmn. dept. medicine, 1965-66; asso. dean, prof. medicine Stanford Sch. Medicine, 1966-68; mem. gen. medicine study sect. NIH, 1965-70, chmn., 1969-70; dean, dir. univ. hosps. SUNY, Buffalo, 1968-71; spl. cons. to sec. for health HEW, 1970—; prof. div. biol. scis. and medicine U. Chgo., 1972-77; prof. pathology Northwestern U., 1977-79; health and hosp. cons.; pres. Concept Group, Inc., Chgo., 1976-77; pres. L.A. Pesch Assos., Inc., Chgo., 1977—; chmn. bd., chief exec. officer Health Resources Corp. Am., 1981—; dir. Lakeside Bank. Bd. dirs. Buffalo Med. Found., 1969-72, Health Orgn., Western N.Y., 1968-71; trustee Michael Reese Hosp. and Med. Center, Chgo., 1971-76, pres., chief exec. officer, 1971-77; mem. exec. bd. Auditorium Theatre Council, Chgo.; trustee W. Clement and Jessie V. Stone Found., Joffrey Ballet; adv. council Congl. Award. Served with USPHS, 1957-59. Mem. Am. Assn. Study of Liver Diseases, Am. Fedn. Clin. Research, Am. Soc. Biol. Chemists, AAAS, Sigma Xi, Alpha Omega Alpha. Clubs: Buffalo, Standard, Internat. Quadrangle, Mid-Am., Capitol Hill, Acapulco Yacht, Chicago Yacht. Contbr. articles on internal medicine to profl. jours. Home: 333 N Mayflower Rd Lake Forest IL 60045 Office: 303 E Ohio St Chicago IL 60611

PESEK, WILLIAM BENEDICT, landscape architect; b. Marshall, Minn., June 28, 1945; s. Frank James and Rita Mary (Jelen) P.; student S.D. State U., 1963-65, U. Minn., 1965-68; m. Carole Otte, Sept. 25, 1971; 1 dau., Cristina Otte. Peace Corps vol., Arecibo, P.R., 1968-69; vol. VISTA, Muskegon, Mich. and Mpls., 1969-71; asst. landscape supr. Coll. of St. Catherine, St. Paul, 1971-72; landscape architect Dept. Community Services, City of St. Paul, 1972—; pres. Burton Eateries, Inc., Marshall, Minn.; v.p. Gzorkios, Inc., Canby, Minn., also Otte & Pesek Assos. Mem. Am. Soc. Landscape Architects. Home: 1420 Portland Ave Saint Paul MN 55104 Office: City Hall Annex 3d Floor Saint Paul MN 55102

PESHKIN, SAMUEL DAVID, lawyer; b. Des Moines, Oct. 6, 1925; s. Louis and Mary (Grund) P.; B.A., U. Iowa, 1948, J.D., 1951; m. Shirley Isenberg, Aug. 17, 1947; children—Lawrence Allen, Linda Ann. Admitted to Iowa bar, 1951, since practiced in Des Moines; partner Bridges & Peshkin, 1953-66, Peshkin and Robinson, 1966—; chmn. Iowa Bd. Law Examiners, 1970-76. Bd. dirs. Sch. Religion, U. Iowa, U. Iowa Old Gold Devel. Fund, 1955—, Iowa Meml. Union, 1957—, State U. Iowa Found., 1957—. Served with USNR, 1943-45. Fellow Am. Bar Found., Internat. Soc. Barristers; mem. Internat., Inter-Am., Am. (bd. govs. 1973—, ho. of dels. 1968—, chmn. standing com. on membership 1959—), Iowa State (pres. jr. bar sect. 1958-59, bd. govs. 1958-59, chmn. com. on ann. meeting 1953—, award of merit 1974), Polk County bar assns., Am. Law Inst., Am. Judicature Soc., State U. Iowa Alumni Assn. (pres. 1957—, dir., 1951—). Home: 3000 Grand Ave Apt 613 Des Moines IA 50312 Office: 1010 Fleming Bldg Des Moines IA 50309

PESKE, PATRIC O., psychologist; b. Akron, Ohio, Sept. 21, 1942; s. Robert Wilhelm and Eileen Michele (Doherty) P.; B.A., Akron U., 1968, M.A., 1972; postgrad. Case Western Res. U., 1969, Temple U., 1971-72, U. Chgo., 1975; m. Nancy Lee Pokorosky, Nov. 20, 1967; 1 son, Arthur Z. Aleksandor. Sr. asst. to dir. personality research Hay Exec. Mgmt., Phila., 1970-72; intern child study psychologist Wadsworth-Rittman (Ohio) Edn. Systems, 1972-73; pvt. practice psychiatric cons., Phila., 1970-72, Akron, 1972-73; child study psychologist Genesee Intermediate Edn. System, Flint, Mich., 1973—; dir. Pro Media Consultants; lectr. psychology Gen. Motors Inst., Flint, 1973-77; instr. psychology and modern Life, continuing edn. dept. Mott Community Coll., Flint, 1977—; internat. lectr. psychol. and Rorschach techniques; exec. dir. Rorschach Seminars, Workshops for Advanced Profl. Edn., Workshops for Tchrs. Mem. Internat. Congress for Sci. Study Rorschach and other Projective Methods, Internat. Congress Study Art and Psychopathology, Am. Assn. Learning Disabilities, Nat., Internat. assns. sch. psychologists, Am. Psychol. Assn. (ethics com., child advocacy com.), Internat. Rorschach Soc. (chmn., U.S. del.), Nat. Rorschach Soc. (exec. dir., pres.), Soc. Personality Assessment, Internat. Platform Assn., ACLU (sec., dir.), Brit. Projective Methods Soc., Psi Chi. Author charter of childrens rights proposals and books and articles in field. Home: PO Box 7149 Flint MI 48507

PETACQUE, ARTHUR MARTIN, journalist; b. Chgo., July 20, 1924; s. Ralph David and Fay Nora (Brauner) P.; student U. Ill., 1941-42; m. Regina June Battinus, Dec. 10, 1944; children—Susan Wendy Petacque Leshin, William Scott. Investigative reporter, columnist Chgo. Sun-Times, 1943—. Cons. World Book Ency. Recipient Pulitzer prize for local investigative reporting, 1974; Jacob M. Scher award Northwestern U., 1964; Marshall Field award, 1968; Nat. Big Story awards NBC; 5 A.P., 7 UPI awards, including best spot news coverage award UPI, 1980; Dante award Joint Civic Com. Italian Ams., 1980; Giant award for journalism Ed Kelly Sports Program, 1982; named outstanding journalist Villa Scalabrini, Little Flower; Prime Minister of Israel medal, 1976. Mem. Sigma Delta Xi, Sigma Alpha Mu. Jewish. Office: 401 N Wabash St Chicago IL 60611

PETCHENIK, EDWARD M., surgeon; b. Clinton, N.Y., Dec. 25, 1919; s. Patrick and Bridget (McCabe) P.; grad. sch., Plattsburgh, N.Y.; student Plattsburgh Normal Sch.; M.D., Albany Med. Coll., 1944; post-grad. work, Postgrad. Med. Sch. and Hosp., and N.Y. Polyclinic; m. Nora Loomis, Oct. 15, 1950. Practice medicine, Kingston, N.Y., 1950; chief of staff, Augustana Hosp.; chmn. clinics County Com. for Prevention Tb; chmn. County Pub. Health Co. Bd. mgrs. Training Sch. for Boys, Hudson; now v.p., bd. mgrs. Tb Hosp. Democrat. Clubs: K.C., Elks. Home: 872 Pines Winnetka IL 60093

PETERHANS, LOUIS RAYMOND, JR., aluminum products mfg. co. exec.; b. Evanston, Ill., Oct. 14, 1949; s. Louis R. and Rosemary (Rudersdorf) P.; B.A., St. Thomas Coll., 1971; M.B.A., Loyola U., Chgo., 1972; m. Mary Carol Toebber, June 1, 1974. Fin. planning mgr. Nichols-Homeshield, Aurora, Ill., 1977—; instr. quantitative methods St. Thomas Coll., St. Paul, 1969-71. Chmn., bd. dirs. Holy Cross Parish Credit Union, 1979. Served with USAF, 1973-77. Mem. Assn. M.B.A. Execs. Home: 214 N Lincoln St Batavia IL 60510 Office: 1470 Farnsworth Ave Aurora IL 60507

PETERING, HAROLD GEORGE, educator; b. LaPorte, Ind., Oct. 8, 1910; s. George Herman and Magdalena S. (Droege) P.; B.S., U. Chgo., 1935; Ph.D., U. Wis., 1938; m. Eva C. Petersen, Mar. 4, 1939; children—Christine L, David H., Marion L. Asst. prof. Mich. State U., East Lansing, 1938-41; sr. scientist E.I. duPont Co., New Brunswick, N.J., 1941-45; sr. research scientist Upjohn Co., Kalamazoo, Mich., 1945-66; asso. prof. U. Cin., 1966-69, prof. dept. environ. health, 1969-78, prof. emeritus, 1978—. Mem. Am. Chem. Soc., AAAS, Am. Soc. Biol. Chemists, Am. Assn. Cancer Research, Am. Inst. Nutrition, Sigma Xi, Phi Beta Kappa. Lutheran. Club: Torch. Home: 6662 Plantation Way Cincinnati OH 45224

PETERS, ALVERA KAE, savs. and loan exec.; b. Washington, Mo., Aug. 24, 1951; d. Allen Robert and Vera Schulte (Kriete) P.; B.S. cum laude, SW Mo. State U., 1973. Savs. counselor, loan clk. Prudential Savs. & Loan Assn., Union, Mo., 1973-74, area coordinator community relations, 1974-78, regional dir. mktg., 1978-80, asst. v.p. mktg., 1980—. Publicity chmn. City of Union Bicentennial Celebration, 1976; mem. fine arts com. E. Central Coll., Union; bd. dirs. E. Central Coll. Found. Mem. AAUW (treas. Franklin County br. 1975-76), Am. Legion Aux., Franklin County Hist. Soc. Republican. Mem. United Ch. Christ. Home: PO Box 135 Union MO 63084 Office: 8020 Forsyth Blvd Clayton MO 63105

PETERS, BRENDA BROWN, banker; b. Pineville, La., Oct. 22, 1949; d. Murry and Lucille Marie (Blackman) B.; B.S. in Bus. Adminstrn., So. U., 1967-71; m. Jerome Edward Peters, Oct. 14, 1978. Compensation analyst Harris Bank, Chgo., 1971-76; compensation analyst First Nat. Bank of Chgo., 1976-78, personnel adminstr., 1978-80, personnel officer, 1980—. Mem. Nat. Assn. Female Execs., Am. Mgmt. Assn., Am. Compensation Assn., Am. Soc. Personnel Adminstrs., Am. Bankers Assn., Chgo. Compensation Assn., Delta Sigma Theta. Office: First National Bank of Chicago One First National Plaza Chicago IL 60670

PETERS, ELOISE KEPPEL, elec. corp. mgr.; b. Pittston, Pa., Apr. 22, 1942; d. Henry Robert and Edna Louise (Keppel) Carichner; B.A., U. R.I., 1964; M.A., U. Chgo., 1978; children—Lisa, Bradley. With Personnel Devel., Inc., Palatine, Ill., 1972-77, Spiegel, Inc., Oak Brook, Ill., 1978-79; mgr. tng. and devel. Sun Elec. Corp., Crystal Lake, Ill., 1979—; tchr. women's program Harper Coll., Palatine; founder, pres. Nat. Network of Women in Sales. Adv. bd. McHenry County Coll. Mem. Am. Soc. Tng. and Devel., Ill. Soc. Tng. and Devel. Home: 338 N Benton St Palatine IL 60067 Office: One Sun Pkwy Crystal Lake IL 60014

PETERS, GERALD LEROY, educator; b. Dayton, Ohio, Apr. 4, 1939; s. Roy E. and Mildred E. (Hull) P.; B.S., Manchester Coll., 1961; electronic technician cert. United Electronic Inst., 1968; M.S., U. Dayton, 1978; postgrad. Wright State U., 1977—; m. Lynn L. Harry, Aug. 6, 1960; children—Roy H., Gerald D., Susan R., Betsy L. Tchr. public schs., New Lebanon, Ohio, 1961-66, Clayton, Ohio, 1966-78, head dept. math. instrn. Northmont High Sch., 1972-78; curriculum specialist Montgomery County (Ohio) Office Edn., 1978—; owner, operator Electronic Remote Control Systems, 1963—; pres. Northmont Tchrs. Assn., 1976-77. Clk.-treas. Perry Twp. (Ohio) Trustees), 1968—; active Eversole Ch. of the Brethren, New Lebanon, trustee, 1979—, fin. chmn., 1977-80, deacon, 1975—, chmn. ch. bd., 1978. Mem. Assn. Supervision and Curriculum Devel., Ohio Assn. Supervision and Curriculum Devel., S.W. Ohio Assn. Supervision and Curriculum Devel., Ohio Sch. Suprs. Assn., Ohio Council Math. Tchrs., Ohio Assn. Trustees and Clks., Montgomery County Assn. Trustees and Clks., Am. Radio Relay League, Dayton Amateur Radio Assn., Acad. Model Aeros. Republican. Club: Flying Aero Sport Teams. Home: 12450 Amity Rd Brookville OH 45309 Office: 451 W 3d St Dayton OH 45422

PETERS, J(OHN) DOUGLAS, lawyer, educator; b. Dover, N.H., Jan. 23, 1948; s. John Phillip and Helen Irene (Hurst) P.; B.A. cum laude, U. N.H., 1971; J.D., U. Toledo, 1975; m. Christine K. Consales, June 13, 1973. Program dir. H.H. Lung Assn., 1971-72; exec. dir. 4th Ohio Area Profl. Standards Rev. Council, Toledo, 1974-75; admitted to Mich. bar, 1975; asso. firm Charfoos and Charfoos, p.c., Detroit, 1975—; adj. asst. prof. law and medicine U. Toledo, Coll. Law, 1977—, Wayne State U. Sch. Medicine, 1980—; legal dir. Mich. Med. Schs. Council of Deans Med.-Legal Project, 1978—. Mem. smoking and health com. Occupational Health Com., Am. Lung Assn., Detroit, 1977—. HEW grantee, 1978-80. Mem. Am. Bar Assn., Mich. Bar Assn., Detroit Bar Assn., State Bar Mich. (chairperson com. medicolegal problems), Assn. Trial Lawyers Am., Am. Soc. Hosp. Attys., Nat. Health Lawyers Assn., Mich. Trial Lawyers Assn., Am. Soc. Law and Medicine, Psi Chi. Author: The Law of Medical in Michigan, 1981; contbr. articles to legal and med. jours.; asso. editor U. Toledo Law Rev.; editor-in-chief Discovery, 1972-74. Office: 4000 City National Bank Bldg Detroit MI 48226

PETERS, JAMES WILLIAM, human resource mgmt. cons.; b. Park Falls, Wis., Feb. 16, 1950; s. William Ralph and Agnes Grace P.; B.A., U. Wis., Milw., 1972, M.A., 1981; m. Janet Meade Mahoney, Aug. 26, 1973; children—Jahna Meade, Christopher Ryan. Tech. recruiter Mgmt. Recruiters, 1972-75; asso. cons. human resources Wargo & Co., Inc., Milw., 1975-77, sr. prin., 1977-79, v.p. human resource cons., 1979—; pres. Midwest Human Resource Planners Group, Chgo., 1981-82. Mem. Am. Soc. Personnel Adminstrs., Human Resource Planning Soc. Republican. Roman Catholic. Club: Athletic (Milw.). Office: 260 Regency Ct Milwaukee WI 53286

PETERS, JEANNE ELIZABETH FISHER, educator, artist; b. Chgo., Dec. 23, 1923; d. Frank T. and Helen Mary (Shepperd) Fisher; student North Park Coll., 1943; A.B., Coll. of Wooster, 1948; postgrad. Northeastern Ill. U., 1964; m. Herbert M. Peters, Sept. 27, 1952; children—Margaret Lynn, Linda Anne. Sec., lab. worker Battel Meml. Inst., Columbus, Ohio, 1948-52; sec. Rauland Corp., Chgo., 1960-64; tchr. public schs., Chgo., 1964-79, 81—, tchr. Bethlehem Luth. Sch., Evanston, Ill., 1979-80. Recipient PTA award, 1973. Mem. Smithsonian Inst. Lutheran. Pioneered Open Court reading method Reilly Sch., Chgo. Home: 4729 N Leamington Ave Chicago IL 60630

PETERS, JEROME FRANK, credit union exec.; b. Milw., June 14, 1917; s. Jerome Michael and Meta A. (Pinz) P.; student pub. schs., Chgo.; m. Armella L. Dapper, Jan. 13, 1940 (div. Apr. 1981); children—Jerome Frank, Susan T.; m. 2d. Quan I. Elisevson, Oct. 17, 1981. Treas., gen. mgr., dir. Am. United Cab Assn. Credit Union, Chgo., 1953-56; field rep. Ill. Credit Union League, Chgo., 1956-57; treas., gen. mgr., dir. East Moline (Ill.) Works Credit Union, 1957-65, State Capitol Credit Union, St. Paul, 1965—; pres., dir. Minn. On-Line, Inc. Mem. Credit Union Execs. Soc., Minn. League Credit Unions (dir. 1968-69, 79—, sec. 1981—, Disting. Leadership award), Credit Union Nat. Assn. (dir. 1979—), North Star Chpt. Credit Unions (pres. 1969-71). Recipient citation for meritorious service rendered on behalf of entire Credit Union Movement, 1971, Fin. Stblzn. award, 1975. Home: 200 S Winthrop St Saint Paul MN 55119 Office: 95 Sherburne Ave Saint Paul MN 55103

PETERS, JOANN CAROL, data mgmt. officer; b. Joliet, Ill., June 17, 1932; d. Paul Raymond and Martha Leonelda (Gallo) Senter; grad. U.S. Army Mgmt. Engring. Tng. Activity, 1978, Biomed. Program, UCLA, 1978, Wright Patterson Air Force Tng. Center, 1979; m. John Calvin Peters, May 20, 1951; 1 son, Calvin John. Clk. typist U.S. Army Procurement and Supply Agy., Joliet, Ill., 1959; indsl. specialist U.S. Army Munitions Command, Joliet, Ill., 1960—; mgmt. analyst U.S. Armament Command, Rock Island, Ill., 1963; program analyst U.S. Armament Readiness Command, Rock Island, Ill., 1971, contract data mgmt. officer, 1976—, devel. counselor, 1980—. Chmn. Heart Assn., 1977—; pres. Little League, 1964. Mem. Am. Def. Preparedness Assn., Am. Ordnance Assn. Roman Catholic. Clubs: Rock Island Arsenal Women's Fifteen Year; Toastmistresses; Moose. Contbr. to support of 15 children, U.S. and abroad. Home: 16 Watch Hill Rd Rock Island IL 61201 Office: Rock Island Arsenal Rock Island IL 61299

PETERS, JOSEPH HARLAN, savs. and loan exec.; b. Coffeyville, Kans., Feb. 21, 1920; s. Phillip John and Florence (Harris) P.; A.A., Coffeyville Jr. Coll., 1940; A.B., Baker U., 1942; m. Geraldine Carr, Feb. 8, 1947; children—Susan Jo, Julie Lynn. With Blue Valley Fed. Savs. & Loan Co., Kansas City, Mo., 1946—, successively clk., asst. sec., 1946-52, v.p., 1952-61, dir., 1955—, pres. mng. officer, 1961—; dir. United Mo. Bank of Blue Valley, Kansas City, Mo. Mem. Independence Bd. Edn., 1966-72; trustee Jackson County 4-H Found.; trustee Baker U., Baldwin City, Kans., 1972-80, Mt. Washington Cemetery. Served with USNR, 1943-46. Recipient Distinguished Service award Independence Jr. C. of C., 1954; hon. fellow Harry S. Truman Library Inst. (life). Mem. Mil. Order World Wars (life), Am. Savs. and Loan Inst. (chpt. pres. 1948), Mo. (pres.), Kansas City (chpt. pres. 1965-66), savs. and loan leagues, Kansas City Real Estate Bd., Kansas City, Independence chambers commerce, Blue Valley Mfrs. and Bus. Mens Assn. (pres. 1966-67), Am. Royal Assn. (gov. 1974—), Am. Legion, Delta Tau Delta (Nat. Achievement award 1976). Democrat. Presbyterian (elder). Club: Masons. Home: 2510 Grand Ave Kansas City MO 64108 Office: 6515 Independence Ave Kansas City MO 64125

PETERS, LARRY DEAN, gallery adminstr., curator; b. Manhattan, Kans., July 15, 1938; s. Ralph Eugene and Vera Adalaid (Watkins) P.; B.F.A., Washburn U., 1962; M.F.A., So. Ill. U., 1965; m. Joyce L. Laton, Sept. 14, 1974. With Topeka (Kans.) Public Library, 1965—, gallery dir., 1973—. Bd. dirs. Topeka Arts Council, 1981—; mem. visual arts adv. panel Kans. Arts Commn., 1975-81. Mem. Am. Assn. Mus., Mountain Plains Mus. Assn., Kans. Mus. Assn. (dir. 1980—), Kans. Artists Craftsman Assn. Democrat. Office: 1515 W 10th Topeka KS 66604

PETERS, NATHANIEL ASHBY, III, educator, psychologist; b. Kansas City, Mo., Mar. 29, 1941; s. William Ashby and Nina Muriel (Ottman) P.; B.A., U. Kans., 1963; M.A., Columbia U., 1966; Ph.D., U. Wis., 1971; postgrad. in family therapy dept. psychiatry Georgetown U., 1976—; m. Juanita Inez del Regato, June 17, 1967; children—Christopher William Ashby, Charles Andrew Ottman. Tchr., N.Y. Philanthropic League, N.Y.C., 1964-66, Kansas City, Mo., 1966-68; research asso. Wis. Research and Devel. Center for Cognitive Learning, Madison, 1968-70; asst. dir. reading and lang. center Oakland Schs., Pontiac, Mich., after 1970, now dir. Learning Assessment Clinic, Communication Enhancement Center; cons. Oakland County Community Mental Health Bd., 1973—; adj. prof. Marygrove Coll., Detroit, 1971—. NDEA fellow, 1963; Elk's Club Found. grantee, 1964-65. Mem. Am., Mich. psychol. assns., Assn. for Children with Learning Disabilities, Internat. Reading Assn., Nat., Mich. assns. sch. psychologists, Mich. Reading Assn., Nat. Reading Conf., Orton Soc., Internat. Neuropsychology Soc., Phi Delta Kappa. Author: (with others) Reading Problems: A Multidisciplinary Perspective, 1977. Contbr. articles to profl. jours. Home: 2498 Pineview Dr West Bloomfield MI 48033 Office: 2100 Pontiac Lake Rd Pontiac MI 48054

PETERS, ROBERT PAUL, sch. prin.; b. Elyria, Ohio, Dec. 28, 1925; s. Robert Frank and Mary Martha (Lange) P.; B.A. in Math., Valparaiso U., 1949; M.Ed. in Guidance, Kent State U., 1955; M.Ed. in Ednl. Adminstrn., 1957; m. Dorothea L. Husemann, June 9, 1951; children—Robert William, Paul Edgar. Tchr., coach Chatham (Ohio) Local Sch., 1949-50, LaGrange (Ohio) High Sch., 1951-53; tchr., prin. Keystone High Sch., LaGrange, 1953-55; tchr., counselor Avone Lake (Ohio) High Sch., 1955-58, asst. prin. Learwood Jr. High Sch., 1958-69, prin., 1969—; mem. Ohio com. N. Central Assn. Colls. and Secondary Schs. Choir dir. Faith Lutheran Ch., Avon, 1971—; bd. dirs. Mighty Goliath Prodn. theater group, 1975. Served with AUS, 1944-46; ETO. NSF fellow, 1957; Nat. Inst. Life Ins. fellow, 1967 (both Miami U., Oxford, Ohio). Mem. Nat. Assn. Secondary Sch. Prins., Ohio Assn. Secondary Sch. Adminstrs. Republican. Office: 340 Lear Rd Avon Lake OH 44012

PETERSEN, DIETRICH LINDE, mfg. co. exec.; b. Pana, Ill., Sept. 3, 1933; s. Alfred C. and Gladyce E. (Anderson) P.; B.S., Millikin U., 1955; M.Litt., U. Pitts., 1959, Ph.D., 1968; m. Marjorie J. Beatty, Aug. 27, 1955; children—Erich K., Kurt F., Krista M., Heidi A. Sr. staff engr. and supr. Westinghouse Air Brake Co., Pitts., 1955-65; mgr. advt. materials Allis-Chalmers, West Allis, Wis., 1965-67; asst. prof. Sch. Bus. Adminstrn. Marquette U., Milw., 1967-69; research staff mem. Inst. for Def. Analysis, Washington, 1969-70; gen. mgr. services Fiat-Allis Co., Chgo., 1970-75; v.p., dir. mfg. Perkins Diesel Corp., Canton, Ohio, 1975-78; pres. Perkins Diesel Corp., 1978-79, v.p., gen. mgr. Clark Egt. Crane div., 1979-81; v.p., group exec. Union Metal Mfg. Co., 1981—; lectr. Sangamon State U., Springfield, Ill., 1972-74, Stark Tech. Coll., 1977. Mem. adv. bd. Malone Coll., Canton, 1977—. Mem. Canton C. of C. (edn. subcom. 1977-78). Methodist. Contbr. articles on econs. to profl. jours. Home: 2273 Radford NW North Canton OH 44720

PETERSEN, DONALD EUGENE, automobile co. exec.; b. Pipestone, Minn., Sept. 4, 1926; s. William L. and Mae (Pederson) P.; B.M.E., U. Wash., 1946; M.B.A., Stanford U., 1949; m. Jo Anne Leonard, Sept. 12, 1948; children—Leslie Carolyn, Donald Leonard. With Ford Motor Co., Dearborn, 1949—, asst. to v.p. N.Am. ops., 1965-66, car product planning mgr., 1966-69, exec. dir. adminstr. engring. and indsl. design, 1969, v.p. car planning and research, 1969-71, v.p. truck and recreation products ops., 1971-75, exec. v.p. diversified products ops., 1977, exec. v.p. internat. automotive ops., 1977-80, pres., chief operating officer, 1980—, dir., 1977—. Bd. trustees Cranbrook Ednl. Community, Bloomfield, Mich., 1973—. Served with USMCR, 1946-47, 51-52. Mem. Soc. Automotive Engrs., Engring. Soc. Detroit, Phi Beta Kappa, Sigma Xi, Tau Beta Pi. Episcopalian. Clubs: Renaissance, Bloomfield Hills Country. Office: Ford Motor Co Am Rd Dearborn MI 48121

PETERSEN, DONNA LEE, hosp. printing and postal services mgr.; b. Omaha, Oct. 23, 1948; d. S. Edwin and A. June (Blackman) Jones; student public schs., Omaha; m. James H. Petersen, Dec. 16, 1972; 1 son, James H. With, Bishop Clarkson Meml. Hosp., Omaha, 1968—, mgr. printing and postal services, 1969—. Mem. In-Plant Printing Mgmt Assn. (v.p. 1980—), Omaha Mail Mgrs. Assn. Republican. Office: Clarkson Meml Hosp 44th & Dewey Ave Omaha NE 68105

PETERSEN, EDWARD SCHMIDT, assn. exec., physician; b. Chgo., Nov. 19, 1921; s. William F. and Alma C. (Schmidt) P.; student Harvard U., 1943, M.D., 1945; m. Zoe A. Bakeeff, June 11, 1944; children—Catherine P. Mack, Edward B. Rotating intern St. Luke's Hosp., Chgo., 1945-46; residency medicine U. Chgo., 1948-51; pvt. practice, Chgo., 1951-53; mem. staff Northwestern Med. Sch., Chgo., 1953-72; asst. dir. dept. undergrad. med. edn. AMA, Chgo., 1972-76, dir., 1976—, co-sec. liaison com. med. edn., 1976—; asso. prof. medicine Northwestern U., Chgo., 1964-72, asso. dean, 1960-72, lectr., 1972—; chmn. Com. Hosps. and Clinics, Ill. Dept. Pub. Aid, 1961-70; v.p. Inst. Medicine, Chgo., 1971-74, pres., 1975-76. Bd. dirs. Hull House, 1962-70; exec. com. health div. Welfare Council Chgo., 1956-62. Served with M.C., AUS, 1946-48. Diplomate Am. Bd. Internal Medicine. Recipient Danielson award hist. writing, 1972. Fellow A.C.P.; mem. Assn. Am. Med. Colls. (chmn. Midwest Group on student affairs 1967-69), Lake Assn. Lake Geneva (Wis.) (v.p. 1972-76), Chgo. Soc. History Medicine, (dir. 1974-77), Westerners Chgo. (dir. 1972-80). Clubs: Lake Geneva Yacht, Lake Geneva Country; Racquet (Chgo.). Contbr. articles diabetes, med. edn., med. history to profl. publs. Home: 1350 Astor St Chicago IL 60610 Office: 535 N Dearborn St Chicago IL 60610

PETERSEN, JERRY D., sch. prin.; b. Modesto, Calif., Jan. 4, 1947; s. Loren Harvey and Ruth Ann (Dodge) P.; B.S., Mankato State U., 1969; M.S.Ed., Western Ill. U., 1973, Ed.S., 1974; postgrad Iowa U., 1979—; m. Linda Kay, Sept. 15, 1967; children—April, James. Tchr., dean students, asst. prin. Newman Central Catholic High Sch., Sterling, Ill., 1969-73; asst. prin. Olympia High Sch., Stanford, Ill., 1974-76; asso. prin. Clinton (Iowa) High Sch., 1976-80; prin. Bettendorf (Iowa) High Sch., 1980—; cons. teaching/learning style, stress mgmt. Usher, Asbury United Meth. Ch. Named Educator of Yr., Clinton Jr. C. of C., 1980. Mem. Iowa Assn. Secondary Sch. Prins., Nat. Assn. Secondary Sch. Prins., Iowa Assn. Supervision and Curriculum Devel., Assn. Supervision and Curriculum Devel., Phi Delta Kappa. Club: Rotary. Office: 3333 18th St Bettendorf IA 52722

PETERSEN, JOHN LAURENS, mktg. co. exec.; b. Omaha, July 11, 1943; s. J. Allan and Evelyn R. Petersen; B.S. in Elec. Engring., John Brown U., 1965; m. Janet Diane Carter, July 22, 1967; 1 son, John Carter-Laurens. Advt. mgr. Russ Reid Co., Park Ridge, Ill., 1970; asst. to pres. Embosograph Display Mfg. Co., Chgo., 1971-72; v.p. Family Concern Inc., Wheaton, Ill., 1974-79; pres. John L. Petersen & Assos., Chgo., 1979—, Lakeshore Communications Corp., Chgo., 1979—. Pres., Near North Housing Corp., 1971-78, Cabrini-Green Legal Aid Clinic, 1974-78; sec. Chgo.-Orleans Housing Corp., 1971-79, pres., 1979—; bd. dirs. Near North Community Orgn., 1979—. Served to lt. USN, 1966-69, to comdr. Res. Decorated Air medal (3), Navy Commendation medal; cert. transp. aircraft navigator. Mem. Naval Res. Assn. Exec. editor Family Concern Series, 1979; author in field. Office: 704 N Wells St Chicago IL 60610

PETERSEN, LYNDELL, state senator; b. July 4, 1931; B.S. in Animal Sci.; married; 1973; 2 children. County extension agt.; mem. S.D. Senate, 1976—. Bd. dirs. Central States Fair, Clarkson-Mt. View Nursing Bd., First Step Pre-sch. Republican. Clubs: Masons, Cosmopolitan. Office: State Capitol Pierre SD 57501*

PETERSEN, ROLAND FREDERICK, editor, pub.; b. Chgo., Aug. 3, 1930; s. Frederick Christian and Elizabeth (Kutzik) P.; student Sioux Falls (S.D.) Coll., 1948-50; B.A. in Sociology, Roosevelt U., Chgo., 1955; M.S. in Indsl. and Labor Relations, Loyola U., Chgo., 1960; m. Esther Sypek, Nov. 11, 1954 (dec. July 1970); children—Grant Charles, Mark Vaughn; m. 2d, Madeline Porter Coyne, Mar. 1, 1975. Indsl. engr. Western Elec. Co., Chgo., 1956-64, labor relations investigator, 1964-66; personnel mgr. St. Regis Paper Co., Chgo., 1966-67; employment mgr. John Plain & Co., Chgo., 1967-68; sales rep. Digest Publs., Inc., Chgo., 1968-74, pres., treas., dir., 1974—, pub. Police Digest. Served with USMC, 1952-53. Mem. Chgo. Police Lts. Assn. (hon.). Republican. Baptist. Home: 3400 N Lakeshore Dr Chicago IL 60657 Office: 2234 W Irving Park Rd Chicago IL 60618

PETERSEN, SUSAN ROSE, counselor; b. Ontario, Calif., Jan. 19, 1946; d. Donal Christian and Elaine (Browne) Petersen; B.A. in Psychology, St. Louis U., 1968; M.A., U. Mo., St. Louis, 1976. Supr., Project, Inc., St. Louis, 1968-70, evaluator, 1970-72, chief counselor, 1972-77, coordinator rehab., services, 1977—; guest lectr. U. Mo., St. Louis, 1970—. Mem. Am. Personnel and Guidance Assn., Nat. Rehab. Assn., Mo. Rehab. Assn., Vocat. Evaluation and Work Adjustment Assn. (pres. elect 1977-78). Roman Catholic. Home: 481 Brightspur Ln Ballwin MO 63011 Office: 6301 Manchester Saint Louis MO 63139

PETERSEN, MRS. WILLIAM J. (BESSIE RASMUS PETERSEN), orgn. exec., club woman; b. Cherokee, Iowa, June 30, 1902; d. Andrew John and Singni (Nystedt) Rasmus; B.A., State U. Iowa, 1926, M.A., 1930; m. William John Petersen, Sept. 25, 1937. Speech pathologist Rockefeller Found. Mental Hygiene Clinic for Iowa, Iowa City, 1926-28; instr. speech, phonetics U. Iowa, 1928-37; organizer, dir. U. Iowa, Articulatory Speech Clinic, 1928-37; lectr., speech pathology U. Nebr., summers 1931, 37, 38, 39, 40, 41; lectr. Butler U., summer 1937; cons. spl. edn. Iowa Dept. Pub. Edn., 1948-50; asst. dir. Iowa State Hist. Soc. Tours, 1948—. Mem. com. White House Conf. on Spl. Edn., 1929. Mem. Girl Scout Council, 1938-41. Mem. Needlework Guild of Am. (pres. 1939), AAUW (pres. 1940), Iowa Speech and Hearing Assn., Iowa Bus. and Profl. Women's Club, Iowa State Hist. Soc., League Women Voters Iowa Fedn. Women's Clubs, Sigma Xi, Chi Omega. Mem. Order Eastern Star. Club: University. Home: 329 Ellis Ave Iowa City IA 52240

PETERSEN, WILLIAM JOHN, writer, educator; b. Dubuque, Iowa, Jan. 30, 1901; s. Charles Lewis and Bertha Louise (Helm) P.; B.A., U. Dubuque, 1926; M.A., U. Iowa, 1927, Ph.D., 1930; LL.D. (hon.), Iowa Wesleyan Coll., 1958; m. Bessie Josephine Rasmus, Sept. 25, 1937. Grad asst., fellow U. Iowa, 1926-30, instr. history, 1930-36, lectr. history, 1936—, asso. prof., 1948-69; research asso. State Hist. Soc. Iowa, 1930-47, supt., 1947-72; hist. lectr. Am. Sch. Wild Life, summers 1932, 36-40, Drake U. Tours, summers 1933, 34; prof. history Washington U., St. Louis, summers 1940, 41, 65, Iowa Wesleyan Coll., summers 1962, 63. Bd. dirs. Alvord Meml. Commn., 1940; mem. Iowa Centennial Com., 1946; chmn. Johnson County Red Cross War Fund, 1945. Recipient Iowa Library Assn. award for best contbn. to Am. lit. by an Iowan, 1937. Mem. Am., So., Miss. Valley (editorial bd. 1953-56) hist. assns., Soc. Am. Archivists, Am. Acad. Polit. and Social Sci., Minn., Kans. hist. socs., State Hist. Soc. Iowa, Phi Kappa Delta, Pi Gamma Mu, Zeta Sigma Pi, Delta Upsilon. Republican. Presbyterian. Clubs: Iowa Author (pres. 1940-42); Propeller (Quad City); Westerners, Cliff Dwellers, Caxton (Chgo.); Research (sec.-treas. 1944-46) Triangle, S.P.C.S. Rotary, C. of C. (Iowa City), Masons (32 deg.). Author: True Tales of Iowa (with Edith Rule), 1932; Two Hundred Topics in Iowa History, 1932; Steamboating on the Upper Mississippi, 1937, rev. edit., 1968; Iowa: The Rivers of Her Valleys, 1941; A Reference Guide to Iowa History, 1942; Iowa History Reference Guide, 1952; The Story of Iowa, 2 vols., 1952; Mississippi River Panorama: Henry Lewis Great National Work, 1979; Towboating on the Mississippi, 1979. Editor: (John Plumbe, Jr.) Sketches of Iowa and Wisconsin, 1948; (Isaac Galland) Galland's Iowa Emigrant, 1950; (John B. Newhall) A Glimpse of Iowa in 1846, 1957; author-editor: The Pageant of the Press, 1962; The Annals of Iowa-1863; Illustrated Historical Atlas of the State of Iowa in 1875 (A.T. Andreas), 1970; contbr. to profl. mags. Home: 329 Ellis Ave Iowa City IA 52240

PETERSON, ARLENE JULIETTE, constrn. co. exec.; b. Winner, S.D., Apr. 27, 1936; d. Elwood Lloyd and Geneva Carolyn (Mayes) Miller; B.S., Black Hills State Coll., 1968; children—Richard Allen, Dean Allen. Tchr. pub. schs., Meade County, S.D., 1959-60; spl. edn. tchr. Title I Program, New Underwood, S.D., 1960-72; office mgr. Overhead Drive Co., Rapid City, S.D., 1972-75; office mgr. Dean Kurtz Constrn. Co., Rapid City, 1975—, sec.-treas., 1976—, dir., 1979—. Mem. Asso. Gen. Contractors Am., Women in Constrn.

Republican. Lutheran. Home: 2110 6th Ave Rapid City SD 57701 Office: PO Box 1917 Rand Rd Rapid City SD 57709

PETERSON, ARTHUR GENE, automobile mfg. corp. exec.; b. Northwood, Iowa, Feb. 17, 1931; s. Henry Otto and Pearl Cornelia (Orpen) P.; B.B.A., U. Minn., 1960; M.B.A., Wayne State U., 1971; children—Patricia, Debra, Heidi, Greta. Rate clk. Interstate System, St. Paul, 1954-60; trainee M&St.L Rwy., Mpls., 1960-61; distbn. supr. Green Giant Co., LeSueur, Minn., 1961-63; transp. analyst Ford Motor Co., Dearborn, Mich., 1963—. Fin. sec. Scandinavian Festival Com., 1978-80, v.p., 1980-81. Served with USAF, 1948-52. Mem. ICC Practitioners Assn. (dir. Gt. Lakes chpt.), Sons of Norway (v.p. lodge 1979, pres. 1980, 81). Lutheran. Home: 4410 Jonathon Ln Dearborn MI 48126 Office: Ford Motor Co Rotunda at Southfield Dearborn MI 48121

PETERSON, ARTHUR PAUL, JR., steel co. exec.; b. Chgo., June 20, 1923; s. Arthur Paul and Lillian Susanne (Hummel); B.A., DePauw U., 1946; postgrad Purdue U., 1946-48; m. Idella Felice Fields, July 2, 1944; children—Sheryl Lynn, Arthur Paul, Patricia Sue. Asst. prof. math. Purdue U., 1946-48, asst. prof. naval engring., 1948-50; sales mgr. Alprodco, Inc., Kempton, Ind., 1950-51; with Ingersoll Johnson Steel, New Castle, Ind., 1951-81, v.p. sales, 1971-81; mgr. midwest region Voest-Alpine Internat. Corp. N.Y., New Castle, 1981—; dir. Pan Am. Bridge Co., New Castle, 1960-61. Committeeman Republican 7th Precinct, New Castle, 1951-53; mem. budget com. United Fund., New Castle, 1974-76; bd. advisors Goodwill Industries, Indpls.; chmn. adminstrv. bd., trustee, vice chmn. fin. commn. First United Methodist Church, New Castle. Served with U.S. Navy, 1943-46; capt. Res. ret. Deocrated Bronze Star with Combat V; recipient Boy Scout Leadership award, 1961. Mem. Naval Res. Assn., Res. Officers Assn., Navy League U.S., U.S. Naval Inst., Am. Mgmt. Assn., Sigma Chi. Clubs: Kiwanis, Westwood Country, Mason, Elks. Home: 1150 Woodlawn Dr New Castle IN 47362 Office: PO Box 1011 New Castle IN 47362

PETERSON, C(ARL) DONALD, justice state supreme ct.; b. Mpls., Feb. 2, 1918; s. Karl Emil and Emma Marie (Sellin) P.; B.A. cum laude, U. Minn., 1939; J.D. with honors, U. Ill., 1941; m. Gretchen Elaine Palen, Dec. 6, 1952; children—Barbara Elaine, Craig Donald, Mark Bradley, Polly Suzanne, Todd Douglas, Scott Jeffrey. Admitted to Minn. bar, 1941, to practice before U.S. Supreme Ct., 1950; partner firm Howard, Peterson, LeFevere, Lefler, Hamilton & Pearson, 1941-66; asso. justice Minn. Supreme Ct., St. Paul, 1967—; chmn. Minn. News Council, 1971-80; co-chmn. Nat. Task Force of 20th Century Fund. Mem. Minn. Ho. of Reps., 1959-63; Republican candidate for lt. gov. State of Minn., 1962; elder, congregation pres. Christ Presbyterian Ch., Edina, Minn. Served with USAAF, 1942-45, with USAF, 1951-52. Decorated Bronze Star; named Outstanding Legislator; recipient Disting. Service to Journalism award Minn. Newspaper Assn., 1977, award of merit Sigma Delta Chi, 1979. Mem. Am., Minn. bar assns, Hennepin County Bar Assn., Inst. Jud. Adminstrn., Am. Law Inst., Am. Judicature Soc. Clubs: Minn., Torske Klubben. Office: 230 State Capitol Bldg Saint Paul MN 55155

PETERSON, CLIFFORD "SKIF", artist; b. Longmont, Colo., May 22, 1947; s. Sigurd Gustav and Isabelle Claire (McCauley) P.; A.B. cum laude, Harvard U., 1972; M.S. in Environ. Design, Notre Dame U., 1977. Dir., Aqualibria Textiles, Los Angeles, 1969; artist-in-residence Gary (Ind.) Public Schs., 1975; dir. Farmhouse Studio, Inc., La Porte, Ind., 1974—, pres., 1981—; one-man shows include: M.I.T., 1971, Indpls. Mus. Art, 1975, Mus. Decorative Art, Copenhagen, 1977; work represented in permanent collections. Bd. advisors Environic Found. Internat.; Marshall fellow, 1975-76. Mem. Screen Printing Assn. Internat., Assn. Harvard Alumni. Address: 2215 E 350 N La Porte IN 46350 also Jack Denst Designs Mdse Mart 6-117 Chicago IL

PETERSON, COLLIN C., state senator; b. Fargo, N.D., June 29, 1944; s. Lauren Peterson and Della (Askegaard) P.; B.A., Moorhead State U., 1966; Pres., Peterson & Aukerfelt, Ltd., 1966—; mem. Minn. Senate, 1977—. Served with U.S. Army, 1963-69. Recipient Disting. Service award Detroit Lakes Jaycees, 1975. Mem. Am. Inst. C.P.A.s Becker County Council Alcoholism, Am. Fedn. Musicians, Jaycees. Lutheran. Office: State Capitol St Paul MN 55155*

PETERSON, DARREL LEE, state senator; b. Fairmont, Minn., Mar. 8, 1939; student Mankato State U., 1957-59; B.S., U. Minn., 1961; m. Candace Prouix, 1960; children—Anne Kristen, Mary Kathryn, Elizabeth Catherine. Farmer, 1961—; mem. Minn. Ho. of Reps., 1974-78, minority leader, 1976-78; mem. Minn. Senate, 1980—. Mem. task force food supply Nat. Conf. State Legislators; mem. adv. com. small bus. State of Minn.; chmn. Martin County Spl. Edn. Coop.; mem. East Chain Bd. Edn., Fairmont Bd. Edn. Mem. Alpha Zeta. Republican. Club: East Chain Sportsman's. Office: 138 State Office Bldg St Paul MN 55155*

PETERSON, DAVID ALLEN, virologist; b. Hayward, Wis., Nov. 29, 1938; s. Allen H. and Faith I. (Olsen) P.; B.S., Wis. State U., Stevens Point, 1966; M.S., Ind. U., 1970, Ph.D., 1971; m. Bonnie J. Sablovitch, May 29, 1964; children—Frank A., Ruth A. Postdoctoral research fellow dept. microbiology Rush-Presbyn.-St. Luke's Med. Center, Chgo., 1970-71; asst. prof. dept. microbiology Rush U. Coll. Health Scis., Chgo., 1975-81, asst. prof. dept. microbiology Rush Med. Coll., 1971-81, safety and environ. control officer dept. microbiology, 1971-81; asst. scientist med. staff Rush-Presbyn.-St. Luke's Med. Center, 1971-81, chief diagnostic virology lab. dept. microbiology, 1971-81; lectr. Cook County Grad. Sch. Medicine, 1975-81; clin. project mgr. Abbott Labs., North Chicago, 1981—. Served with USAF, 1957-61. Mem. Am. Soc. Microbiology, AAAS, Soc. Exptl. Biology and Medicine, Tissue Culture Assn., Ill. Soc. Microbiology. Congregationalist. Contbr. articles to profl. jours. Home: 461 Edens Ln Northfield IL 60093

PETERSON, DONALD, state senator; b. Mar. 30, 1930; grad. high sch.; married; 2 children. Pres., Yaggie Mills-Grain Processing and Feed Mfg., Yankton, S.D., Feed Processing Wholesaling, Bridgewater, S.D.; mem. S.D. Ho. of Reps., 1976-78, S.D. Senate, 1978—. Former mem. Vermillion City Commn., Bridgewater City Commn.; exec. bd., trustee Yankton Coll. Mem. Yankton C. of C., S.D. Rail Users Assn. (pres.). Lutheran. Republican. Office: State Capitol Pierre SD 57501*

PETERSON, DONALD ROBERT, chem. engr.; b. Ogallala, Nebr., Nov. 28, 1929; s. John Edward and Bessie Iona (Miller) P.; m. Mary Louise Forney, Dec. 28, 1958; children—Kirstin, Eric. B.Sc., U. Nebr., 1961, B.Ch.E., 1961. Staff chemist Dale Electronics, Inc., Columbus, Nebr., 1961-63, sr. materials engr., 1963—, mgr. chemistry lab., 1965—. Chmn., Columbus City Republican Party, 1968; chmn. Platte County Republican Party, 1972-73; mem. Columbus (Nebr.) City Council, 1974—; police commr. City of Columbus, 1974—. Mem. Am. Electroplaters Soc. (sec., treas., v.p. Nebr. Iowa br. 1972-77), Platte County Hist. Soc., C. of C., Masons (Shriner), Rotary Club, Pawnee Shrine Club, Delta Sigma Phi, Elks Club, Pawnee Motor Patrol. Home: 1870 25th Ave Columbus NE 68601 Office: Dale Electronics Inc PO Box 609 Columbus NE 68601

PETERSON, DOUGLAS ARTHUR, physician; b. Princeton, N.J., Sept. 13, 1945; s. Arthur Roy William and Marie Hilma (Anderson) P.; B.A., St. Olaf Coll., 1966; Ph.D. in Organic Chemistry, U. Minn., 1971, M.D., 1975; m. Virginia Kay Eng, June 24, 1967; children—Rachel, Daniel, Rebecca. Lab. asst. St. Olaf Coll., 1965-66; teaching asso. U. Minn., 1966-68, research asst., 1968-71, now clin. asst. prof. medicine; postdoctoral fellow U. Pitts., 1971-72; resident in medicine Hennepin County Med. Center, Mpls., 1975-78; practice medicine, specializing in internal medicine, Bloomington-Lake Clinic, Mpls., 1978—; dir. cardiac rehab. program Lutheran Deaconess Hosp., Mpls., 1979—, dir. med. edn., 1979—. Bd. dirs. Rolling Acres Home for Mentally Retarded Children, Mpls. Alworth scholar, 1966-69; St. Olaf scholar, 1963-65; Dupont Summer fellow, 1967, 69; Mobil Summer fellow, 1968. Diplomate Am. Bd. Internal Medicine. Mem. AAAS, AMA, Minn. Med. Assn., Am. Bd. Internal Medicine, Phi Beta Kappa, Alpha Omega Alpha. Lutheran. Office: 3017 Bloomington Ave S Minneapolis MN 55417

PETERSON, ELIZABETH ANN, educator; b. Jackson, Mich., Dec. 20, 1936; d. Allan Guy and Cecilia Ann (Beiswanger) Weatherwax; B.S., Lindenwood Coll., 1959; M.A., Eastern Mich. U., 1965; m. Jay Alvin Peterson, Aug. 15, 1959; children—Scott Allan, Jacqueline Cecile. Tchr., Spl. Sch. Dist. of St. Louis County, St. Louis, 1959-61, 65-67; tchr. educable mentally retarded E. Jackson (Mich.) Public Schs., 1964-65, 67-69; dir. White Wing Sch., Nashua, N.H., 1970-72; cons. Cape Elizabeth (Maine) Public Schs., 1973-74; ednl. resource tchr. Ft. Zumwalt Pub. Schs., O'Fallon, Mo., 1975-79; itinerant learning disability tchr., ednl. examiner St. Charles (Mo.) Public Schs. 1979-80, ednl. resource tchr., supr. evaluation, 1980—; mem. com. to write guidelines for ednl. resource program Mo. Dept. Edn.-Inservice State Prison, 1976. Active in voter registration, co-chmn. county fund raising, Republican Party, 1963—. Recipient Award for service to a tchr./cadet program Ft. Zumwalt Tchr. Cadet program, 1979. Mem. Am. Assn. on Mental Deficiency, Council of Exceptional Children, Mo. Tchrs. Assn., Phi Delta Kappa. Club: Lindenwood Alumni, Order of Eastern Star. Home: 251 Mill Run Ln Saint Charles MO 63301 Office: 1916 W Elm St Saint Charles MO 63301

PETERSON, ETHEL MARIE, sch. counselor; b. Dodge City, Kans., Oct. 31, 1933; d. Henry Lindberg and Myrtle May (Smith) P.; A.A., Dodge City Community Coll., 1955; B.S. in Elem. Edn., Ft. Hays State Coll., 1960, M.S. in Elem. Edn., 1967, cert. in counseling, 1977; postgrad. Colo. State U., 1971, Pittsburg (Kans.) State Coll., 1964. Elem. tchr. Kismet (Kans.) Public Sch., 1955-58, Sunnyside Sch., Dodge City, 1958-76; elem. counselor Unified Sch. Dist. 443, Dodge City, 1976—. Co-chair Dodge City chpt. Nat. Com. Prevention of Child Abuse, 1976—; bd. dirs. PALS, Inc., 1978-79; adv. bd. emergency foster care Kans. Children's Service League; precinct committeewoman Ford County Democratic Party, 1978—; pres. Dodge City Area Council Retarded Children, 1967; bd. dirs., rec. sec. Kans. Tchrs. Hall of Fame, 1981—; bd. dirs. Dodge City chpt. Am. Diabetes Assn., 1981—. Named Dodge City's Master Tchr., 1975; recipient citation for profl. service to tchrs. of Kans., 1969. Mem. NEA (nat. bd. dirs. 1975-81, bd. dirs. Kans., exec. com. Dodge City; chmn. women's concerns com. 1980—), Kans. Edn. Assn., Dodge City Edn. Assn., Am. Personnel and Guidance Assn., Kans. Personnel and Guidance Assn., S.W. Kans. Personnel and Guidance Assn., Am. Sch. Counselors Assn., Ft. Hays Alumni Assn. (life), Kans. Congress Parents and Tchrs. (life), Phi Delta Kappa. Unitarian. Home: 2315 Melencamp Dodge City KS 67801 Office: 1000 2d Ave Dodge City KS 67801

PETERSON, GALE EUGENE, mus. dir.; b. Sioux Rapids, Iowa, May 23, 1944; B.S. in History, Iowa State U., 1965; M.A., U. Md., 1968, Ph.D., 1973. Teaching asst. U. Md., 1965-66, 67-68, instr. history, 1971-72; instr. Cath. U. Am., 1972-73; prin. investigator Gregory Directory project Orgn. Am. Historians, 1973-75; asst. prof. Purdue U., 1975-76; dir. U.S. Newspaper project Orgn. Am. Historians, 1976-79; dir. Cin. Hist. Soc., 1978—; research asst. Living History Farms project Smithsonian Instn., 1966-67, 70. Mem. Orgn. Am. Historians, Am. Hist. Assn., ALA, Am. Assn. State and Local History. Author handbooks, articles in field. Address: Cin Hist Soc Eden Park Cincinnati OH 45202*

PETERSON, HOWARD LOUIS, state senator; b. Stanton, Iowa, Mar. 22, 1914; s. William August and Anna (Ossian) P.; student Luther Coll., 1933-34; B.S., U. Nebr., 1937, postgrad., 1939; m. Jeanne Phyllis Backlund, June 22, 1939; children—Richard, Roger, Ronald, Robert. With Agrl. Extension Service, 1937-44; exec. dir. Nebr. Farm Bur. Fedn., 1944-47; with Lincoln Service & Supply Co., 1947-62; dir. estate planning Midland Lutheran Coll., 1965-69; v.p., trust officer comml. Nat. Bank & Trust Co., 1969-76; with Peterson Bros. Distbg. Co., 1977-78; dir. devel. Stuhr Mus. Found., also mem. Nebr. Senate, 1980—. Pres., Messiah Luth. Ch. Council, 1958-60, Grand Island Gideon Camp, 1973-74; chmn. Great Plains Power Agy., 1976-77; bd. dirs. Luth. Hosp. and Homes Soc., 1954-66; mayor City of Grand Island, 1964-68; co-chmn. Nat. Corn Picking Contest, 1962; pres. Grand Island Community Chest, 1960, Overland Trails Council Boy Scouts Am., 1972, Silver Beaver award, 1973; adv. bd. Luth. Meml. Hosp., 1954-68; chmn. Agrl. Ward Bd., World War II; bd. dirs. Midland Luth. Coll. Recipient service award Grand Island Community Chest, 1960, alumni award Midland Luth. Coll., 1974. Mem. Grand Island Area C. of C. (pres. 1979). Republican. Lutheran. Club: Grand Island Kiwanis (past pres., lt. gov. div. 1976). Office: Dist 35 State Capitol Lincoln NE 68509

PETERSON, JAMES MATTHEW, anthropologist/archaeologist; b. Rockford, Ill., May 12, 1946; s. Kenneth Jerome and Constance Hildegard (Sapiega) P.; B.A., Lewis U., 1969; M.A., Sangamon State U., 1980. With U.S. Peace Corps, Dominican Republic, Philippines, 1973-78; field/lab. supr. for Prehist. archaeol. sites Ill. State Mus., Springfield, 1980—. Served with U.S. Army, 1969-71. Decorated Army Commendation medal. Mem. Am. Anthropol. Assn., Am. Ethnol. Soc., Soc. for Humanistic Anthropology, Soc. for Applied Anthropology, Midwest Ad Hoc Com. on Philippine Studies. Contbr. articles to profl. jours. Home: 2609 Hooker Ave Rockford IL 61108 Office: Ill State Mus Archaeol Research Spring at Edwards Springfield IL 62706

PETERSON, JAN MARIE, advt. co. ofcl.; b. Mpls., Feb. 14, 1954; d. Leo John and Jeanne A. Feider; A. Chem. Engring. Tech. (tech. scholar), S.W. State U., 1974; B.S. with distinction in Tech. Communications, U. Minn., 1976; m. Brad A. Peterson, May 20, 1978. Tech. writer, coordinator advt. and product publicity Minco Products, 1976-79; coordinator, mgr. advt. and publicity Despatch Industries, Mpls., 1979-81; account mgr. Martin Communications, Mpls., 1981—; freelance writer. Mem. Bus. and Profl. Advt. Assn., Soc. Tech. Communications. Office: 312 Central Ave Minneapolis MN 55414

PETERSON, JERROLD M(ELVIN), economist; b. Mpls., Jan. 5, 1940; s. Melvin Leslie and Ruth E. P.; B.A., Knox Coll., 1962; M.A., U. Ill., 1967, Ph.D., 1970; m. Jory Henry, Sept. 8, 1962; children—Gregory, James, Matthew. Teaching asst. U. Ill., 1967-69; asst. prof. econs. U. Minn., Duluth, 1969-74, asso. prof., 1974-80, prof., 1980—, dir. Bur. Bus. and Research, 1979—. Served with U.S. Army, 1962-64. Recipient Outstanding Faculty award U. Minn. at Duluth Student Assn., 1974. Mem. Am. Econ. Assn., Western Econ. Assn., Assn. Bus. and Econ. Research, Midcontinent Regional Service. Republican. Presbyterian. Editor, co-author Duluth Bus. Indicators, 1979—. Home: 354 Kenilworth Duluth MN 55803 Office: Dept Econs U Minn Duluth MN 55812

PETERSON, JOHN BURL, artificial breeding co. exec.; b. Stark City, Mo., May 26, 1919; s. John Bunyan and Fern Lulu (Borden) P.; B.S. in Agr., U. Mo., 1947; M.S., U. Mo., 1948; m. Velma LaVada Holmes, June 9, 1949; children—Karl, Kurt. Asst. county agrl. agt. Mt. Vernon, Mo., 1948; asst. prof. animal husbandry Cornell U., Ithaca, N.Y., 1948-50; dist. extension dairyman U. Tenn., Knoxville, 1950-53; research asso. Am. Breeders Service, Madison, Wis., 1953-58, frozen semen field supr., 1958-64, mgr. frozen semen storage and distbn.,; cons. on cryogenic storage equipment design. Served to capt., USAAF, 1942-45. Mem. Am. Dairy Sci. Assn. Republican. Lutheran. Club: Dairy Shrine. Patentee in field. Home: 1954 Melrose St Madison WI 53704 Office: PO Box 7070 Madison WI 53707

PETERSON, KENNETH ALLEN, SR., sch. adminstr.; b. Hammond, Ind., Jan. 20, 1939; s. Chester E. and Bertha (Hornby) P.; B.Ed. cum laude, Chgo. State U., 1963; M.S., Purdue U., 1970; NSF grantee U. Iowa, 1964-65; postgrad. U. Ill., 1977-81; m. Marilyn M. Musson, Jan. 3, 1961; children—Kimberly, Kari, Kenneth Allen. Tchr., Markham (Ill.) Sch. Dist. 144, 1961-67; prin. Brookwood Sch., Glenwood (Ill.) Sch. Dist. 1967, 1967-77, prin. Hickory Bend Sch., 1977-78, dir. spl. edn., 1978-80, asst. supt. schs., 1981—; mem. No. Ill. Planning Commn. for Gifted Edn. Chmn. Steger (Ill.) Bicentennial Commn., 1976; vice chmn. Ashkum dist. Boy Scouts Am., recipient Order of Arrow; program com. South Cook County council Girl Scouts U.S.A.; mem. Steger Community Devel. Commn. Mem. Council Exceptional Children, Assn. Supervision and Curriculum Devel., Nat. Assn. Elem. Sch. Prins., P.T.A. (life), Kappa Delta Pi. Republican. Lutheran. Home: 3208 Phillips Ave Steger IL 60475 Office: 201 Glenwood Dyer Rd Glenwood IL 60425

PETERSON, MARTHA ELIZABETH, coll. pres.; b. Jamestown, Kans., June 22, 1916; d. Anton R. and Gail (French) Peterson; A.B., U. Kans., 1937, M.A., 1943, Ph.D., 1959; postgrad. Northwestern U., Columbia U.; L.H.D., Chatham Coll., 1968, Med. Coll. Pa., 1970, Molloy Coll., 1971, Mundelein Coll., 1972, Pace Coll., 1974, U. Wis., 1975, Temple U., 1975; D. Letters and Laws, Columbia, 1968. Douglas Coll., 1968; LL.D., Hofstra U., 1969, Austin Coll., 1972, Hamilton Coll., 1974, Drury Coll., 1975, W.Va. Wesleyan Coll., 1976, Beaver Coll., 1977; Dr. Pedagogy, R.I. Coll., 1975. Instr., U. Kans., 1942-46, asst. dean women, 1946-52, dean women, 1952-56; dean women U. Wis., 1956-63, asst. to pres., 1963, univ. dean students, 1963-67; pres. Barnard Coll., also dean in Columbia U., 1967-75; pres. Beloit Coll., 1975—. Dir. Met. Life Ins. Co., Exxon Corp., First Wis. Corp., United Banks Ill., Rock Savs. Assn., R.H. Macy & Co. Mem. exec. com. commn. ind. colls. and univs.; mem. Pres.'s Commn. White House Fellowships, Rhodes Scholarship Com. Wis.; trustee U. Notre Dame, Chatham Coll., Pitts., 1965—, Com. Econ. Devel.; bd. dirs. Council Fin. Aid to Edn.; vice chmn. Wis. Gov.'s Tax Reform Commn.; mem. vis. com. Am. Council Learned Socs. Recipient Charles Evans Hughes award, 1975; Spirit of Achievement award Albert Einstein Coll. Medicine, 1975; named to U. Kans. Women's Hall Fame, 1972. Mem. Am. Council Edn. (student personnel commn. 1956-59, commn. acad. affairs 1970—, chmn. exec. com. 1971—), Nat. Assn. Women Deans and Counselors (exec. bd. 1959-61, pres. 1965-67), Nat. Assn. Ind. Colls. and Univs. (dir. 1976-77), Intercollegiate Assn. Women Students (nat. adviser 1953-55, 59-61), Am. Arbitration Assn. (dir.), Mortar Board, Phi Beta Kappa, Sigma Xi, Pi Lambda Theta, Phi Kappa Phi. Office: Beloit Coll Beloit WI 53511

PETERSON, MILDRED OTHMER (MRS. HOWARD R. PETERSON), lectr., writer, librarian, civic leader, world traveler; b. Omaha, Oct. 19, 1902; d. Frederick George and Freda Darling (Snyder) Othmer; student U. Iowa, 1919, U. Nebr., 1921-23, Northwestern U., 1935, U. Chgo., 1943, m. Howard R. Peterson, Aug. 25, 1923 (dec. Feb. 1970). Asst. Central High Sch. Library, Omaha, 1915-19; asst. Tech. High Sch. Library, 1919-20; asst. purchasing agt. Met. Utilities Dist., 1920-21; asst. U. Nebr. Library, 1921-23; tchr. piano, dir. choir, Harlan, Iowa, 1924-26; dir. pub. relations and gen. asst. Des Moines Pub. Library, 1928-35; broadcaster weekly book programs WHO and other Iowa radio stas.; columnist, writer Mid-West News Syndicate, Des Moines Register and Tribune, editor Book Marks, 1929-35; writer for Drug Topics, Drug Trade News, others, No. Ill., 1935; writer, spl. asst. ALA, Chgo. 1935-59, Chgo. Tribune, 1941-59; travel writer Hyde Park Herald, 1974—; lectr. on travel, fgn. jewelry and internat. relations, 1940—; lectr. SS. Rotterdam of Holland Am. Line, 1971; lectr. tours U.S., Can., Mexico, 1970—; Del. 1st Assembly Librarians Ams., Washington, 1947. Chgo. Chmn. India Famine Relief, 1943; a founder, pres. Pan Am. Bd. Edn., 1955-58; a founder, pres. Internat. Visitors Center, 1952-56; rep. Chgo. at State Dept. Conf. on Community Services to Fgn. Visitors, also a founder COSERV (Nat. Council for Community Services to Internat. Visitors), Washington, 1957; mem. exec. bd., awards com. Mayor's Com. on Chgo. Beautiful; mem. Ill. Gov.'s Com. on Sao Paulo (Brazil), Partners of Am., chancellor's com. U. Nebr. Former bd. dirs. council, troop leader Girl Scouts U.S.A.; mem. centennial com. Hyde Park Union Ch., also 75th anniversary com.; bd. dirs. YWCA, recipient Outstanding Service award; women's bd. Camp Brueckner-Farr, Grad. Bapt. Student Center. Decorated Uruguayan medal, 1952; Internat. Eloy Alfaro medal, 1952, Order of Carlos Manuel de Cespedes (Cuba); Order of Vasco Nunez de Balboa (Panama); cited by Chgo. Sun, Ill. Adult Edn. Council, 1953; recipient scholarship in Latin-Am. field U. Chgo. and Coordinator Inter-Am. Affairs, U.S. Govt., 1943; world understanding merit award Chgo. Council on Fgn. Relations, 1955; Distinguished Service award Hospitality Center, 1958; Distinguished Service medal U. Nebr., also U. Nebr. Alumni Assn., 1963, Distinguished Achievement award, 1975; Ambassador of Friendship award Am. Friendship Club, 1963; merit award YWCA, 1964, Distinguished Service award, 1975; Civic salute WMAQ radio, Chgo., 1965; Distinguished Service award Pan-Am. Bd. Edn., 1966, also founders award, 1968; Laura Hughes Lunde Meml. award Citizens Greater Chgo., 1968; Friendship award Philippine Girl Scouts, 1971; Distinguished Service award OAS, 1971; named Woman of Year, Friends of Chgo. Sch. and Workshop for Retarded, 1975; Distinguished Service trophy Fedn. Latin Am. Orgns., 1976. Fellow Am. Internat. Acad. (life mem.); mem. Nat. Council Women U.S., English Speaking Union, Japan-Am. Com., U.S.-China Friendship Assn., Internat. House Assn. (v.p.), Pan-Am. Bd. Edn., Chgo. Better Films and TV Council, U.S.-China Friendship Assn., U.S. Capitol, Ill., Nebr., Chgo., Hyde Park (charter mem. award 1978) hist. socs., Field Mus. Natural History, Lincoln Park Zool. Soc., Citizenship Council Met. Chgo., Oriental Inst., Am. Heritage Council, Am., Ill. (local arrangements conf. com. 1976, 78) library assns., Soc. Woman Geographers (pres. Chgo. chpt., v.p. internat. 1978—), Council Fgn. Relations (speakers bur.), Nat. Assn. Travel Ofcls. (Chgo. Tribune rep.), Pan. Am. Council (a founder), Library Internat. Relations, U. Nebr. Alumni Assn. (past pres. local chpts.), U. Nebr. Found., U. Chgo. Internat. House Assn. (v.p. 1976—), Art Inst. Chgo., U. Chgo. Service League (past bd. mem.), Am. Legion Aux. (mem. state bds. Iowa and Ill.), AAUW, League Women Voters, Children's Benefit League, United Negro Coll. Fund Bd., Renaissance Soc.,

Peruvian Arts Soc., Hispanic Soc. Chgo., Chgo. Acad. Scis. (woman's bd.), Chgo. Chamber Orch. Assn., John G. Shedd Soc., Japan Am. Soc., Friends Chgo. Pub. Library, Chgo. Symphony Soc., Citizens Greater Chgo., Found. for Ill. Archaeology, Cook County Hosp. Aux., Dyslexia Guild, Lyric Opera Guild, Crossroads Student Center, Internat. Platform Assn., Alpha Delta Pi (past pres. local alumnae chpts., editor Adephean 1938-39, woman of year award U.S. and Can. 1955), Xi Delta. Mem. Order Eastern Star. Clubs: South Shore Country, College, Quadrangle, Ill. Athletic, University of Chicago Dames, Iowa Authors, Lakeside Lawn Bowling, Hyde Park Neighborhood, Travellers Century. Contbr. articles to newspapers, periodicals, encys. and yearbooks; lectr.; visited and photographed with husband and alone 216 fgn. countries and large islands, including China. Address: 5834 Stony Island Ave Chicago IL 60637

PETERSON, NORMAN LEWIS, elec. control systems engr.; b. Milw., Feb. 23, 1919; s. Roy Norman and Olive (Sprecher) P.; B.E.E., Marquette U., 1944; m. Ann Marie Czerwinski, Mar. 6, 1943; children—Jean Ann, Norman Roy, Christine, Leif. Test engr. test dept. Cutler Hammer Co., Milw., 1941-44, elec. engr., 1944-59; chief engr. Allen Electric Co., Milw., 1959-62; sr. devel. engr. Rexnord Co., Milw., 1962-65; chief engr. Repete Corp., Milw., 1965-68, pres., 1968—. Patentee in field. Home: 4629 N 100 St Wauwatosa WI 53225 Office: 7933 N 73d St Milwaukee WI 53223

PETERSON, PAUL O., educator, athletic dir.; b. Falmouth, Maine, Sept. 4, 1916; s. Hans and Ella Christine (Hansen) P.; B.A., Dana Coll., 1941; M.A., U. Nebr., 1951; m. Ruth Irene Hansen, Oct. 3, 1942; children—Brian, Brent, Beth. Tchr., Craig High Sch., 1941-42; mem. faculty dept. phys. edn. Dana Coll., Blair, Nebr., 1942—, athletic dir., 1942, chmn. phys. edn., 1946—. Chmn. chpt. ARC, 1952—. Mem. AAHPER, Nebr. Alliance for Phys. Edn. Republican. Lutheran. Office: Dana Coll Blair NE 68008

PETERSON, RALPH HENRY, lawyer; b. Hunter, N.D., Aug. 26, 1922; s. Henry R. and Ella C. (Peterson) P.; B.S., U. Minn., 1945, J.D., 1947; m. Marjorie C. Youngquist, Sept. 25, 1948; children—Charlotte, Patricia, Carol, Anita. Admitted to Minn. bar, 1947, since practiced in Albert Lea; mem. firm Peterson, Chesterman, Erickson, Anderson & Hareid, P.A., and predecessor firms, 1947—; sec., gen. counsel Bridon Cordage, Inc., Albert Lea, 1975—; dir. Jobs, Inc., 1st Northwest Nat. Bank of Albert Lea, Edwards Mfg. Co., Olson Mfg. Co., Upin Enterprises, Inc., Upin Co., Inc., Upin Investment Co., 1st State Bank of Emmons (Minn.), St. Paul Clothiers of Hibbing, Inc., St. Paul Clothiers of LaCrosse, Inc., Lake Chapeau Farms, Inc., Albert Lea Indsl. Devel. Corp. Mem. Minn. Bd. Edn., 1967-75, pres., 1971-72; supr., Town of Albert Lea, 1954-58; chmn. Freeborn County Republican Com., 1956-57; chmn. bd. trustees Lea Coll. Mem. Am., Minn., 10th Jud. Freeborn County bar assns., Albert Lea C. of C. (past com. chmn.), Gamma Eta Gamma. Lutheran. Rotarian. Asso. editor: Minn. Law Rev., 1946. Home: 929 Lakeview Blvd Albert Lea MN 56007 Office: 402 S Washington Ave Albert Lea MN 56007

PETERSON, RANDOLPH W., state senator; J.D., U. Minn., 1979; m. Jennifer Bloom. Mem. Minn. Senate, 1980—. Mem. Democratic-Farmer-Labor party. Office: 27 State Capitol St Paul MN 55155*

PETERSON, RAYMOND WILLIAM, JR., mass transit exec.; b. Emporia, Kans., Sept. 8, 1943; s. Raymond William and Evelyn Lucille (Hayworth) P.; B.S., Pan Am. U., 1973; M.Urban Planning, Tex. A&M U., 1974; m. Modesta Munoz, Aug. 16, 1969; children—Cassandra, Robert James. Transp. planner City of Springfield (Mo.), 1975-77; city planning dir. City of Pharr (Tex.), 1977-78; transit analyst City Utilities, Springfield, 1978-79; supr. transit, 1979—; night instr. environ. planning S.W. Mo. State U., Springfield, 1976-77. Served with U.S. Navy, 1963-68; Vietnam. Mem. Am. Planning Assn., World Future Soc., Am. Public Transit Assn. Home: 1668 E Belmont St Springfield MO 65802 Office: 301 E Central St PO Box 551 Springfield MO 65801

PETERSON, RICHARD, state legislator; b. Meadow Grove, Nebr., Dec. 3, 1928; grad. high sch.; m. Kathryn Kuhl, May 7, 1950; children—Michael, Sandra, Karen Julie, Richard, James. Farmer, beekeeper, Norfolk, Nebr.; mem. Nebr. Legislature, 1980—. Former vice chmn. Madison County (Nebr.) Republican Party; former mem. Nebr. Rep. Central Com.; former pres. rural and parochial sch. bds.; del. Rep. Nat. Conv., 1980. Mem. C. of C., Farm Bur., Nebr. Honey Producers, Nebr. Agr. Council. Lutheran. Address: Route 2 Box 346 Norfolk NE 68701*

PETERSON, RICHARD ELSWORTH, physician; b. Seattle, Aug. 27, 1921; s. Arthur Oscar and Agnes Victoria (Ericson) P.; B.S., U. Wash., 1942; B.M.S., M.D., Northwestern U., 1946; m. Lois Fay Scott, Aug. 5, 1955; children—Margaret Ann, Christina Marie, Andrew Scott, Sarah Rebecca, Karen Linnea. Intern, Emergency Hosp., Washington Med. Center, 1946-47; resident in internal medicine VA Med. Center, Van Nuys and Long Beach, Calif., 1947-51; faculty U. Iowa Coll. Medicine, Iowa City, 1952—, asst. prof. medicine, 1960-63, asso. prof. medicine and radiology, 1963-66, prof. medicine and radiology, 1966—, mem. nuclear medicine staff Univ. Hosps., 1963-78; chief nuclear medicine service VA Med. Center, Iowa City, 1953—. Chmn. nuclear medicine residency rev. com. Accreditation Com. on Grad. Med. Edn., 1979—. Served to capt. M.C., AUS, 1946-48. Diplomate Am. Bd. Internal Medicine, Am. Bd. Nuclear Medicine. Mem. AMA (sect. council on nuclear medicine 1978-80), Federated Council Nuclear Medicine Orgns. (vice chmn. 1978-81), N.Y. Acad. Sci., A.C.P., Am. Soc. Internal Medicine, Central Soc. Clin. Research., Soc. Nuclear Medicine (sec. 1965-68, treas. 1968-69), Am. Bd. Nuclear Medicine (founding mem. 1972), Am. Coll. Nuclear Physicians (Iowa del. 1977, sec. 1981—). Presbyterian. Contbr. chpts. to books, papers to profl. lit. Office: Nuclear Medicine Service VA Med Center Iowa City IA 52240

PETERSON, ROBERT AUSTIN, mower mfg. co. exec.; b. Sioux City, Iowa, July 5, 1925; s. Austen W. and Marie (Mueller) P.; B.S., U. Minn., 1946, B.A., 1947; m. Carol May Hudy, May 17, 1952; children—Roberta, Richard, Thomas, Bruce. Credit mgr. New Holland Machine div. Sperry Rand Corp., Mpls., 1952-61; credit mgr. Toro Co., Mpls., 1961-68, treas., 1968-70, v.p. finance, after 1970, now v.p., treas., internat. finance officer and pres. Toro Credit Co.; dir. State Bond & Mortgage, State Bond Ins. Co., Turf Care Products, Toronto, Ont., Can., Norton Corp., Phoenix, Turf Products Corp., Boston, Agri-Tech, Montreal, Que., Can., L.L. Johnson Distbg., Denver. Chmn., Prior Lake Spring Lake Watershed Dist., 1970—; chmn. mem. bd. dirs. Prior Lake Bd. Edn., 1965-71; chmn. Scott County Republican Party, 1969-70. Bd. dirs. Scott Carver Mental Health Center, 1969-73. Served to ensign USNR, 1943-46. Mem. Financial Execs. Inst. Clubs: Prior Lake Yacht (dir.); Decathlon Athletic (Mpls.), Mpls. Home: 14956 Pixie Point Circle SE Prior Lake MN 55372 Office: 8009 34th Ave Minneapolis MN 55420

PETERSON, ROBERT EUGENE, lawyer; b. Fulton County, Ind., Mar. 8, 1930; s. Clarence Cleveland and Beulah Marie (Russell) P.; B.S., Purdue U., 1952; J.D., Ind. U., 1964; m. Martha Ann Coplen, Sept. 12, 1965; children—Matthew Alan, Elaine Elizabeth. Admitted to Ind. bar, 1964, U.S. Dist. Ct. So. Ind., 1964; farmer, Rochester, Ind., 1954-56; auditor County of Fulton, Ind., 1957-60; mem. Ind. State Senate, 1961-68, 77-80; individual practice law, Rochester, Ind., 1965—. Democratic nominee for lt. gov. Ind., 1980. Served with U.S. Army, 1952-54. Decorated Bronze Star. Mem. Ind. U. Law Alumni Assn. (pres. 1978), Am. Bar Assn., Ind. State Bar Assn., Fulton County Bar Assn. Democrat. Clubs: Kiwanis (lt. gov. Ind. 1972), Masons, Scottish Rite. Office: 100 W 9th St Rochester IN 46975

PETERSON, ROBERT LLOYD, mfg. co. exec.; b. Nebr., July 14, 1932; grad. U. Nebr., 1951; m. Oct. 4, 1952; children—Mark R., Susan P. Student cattle buyer Wilson & Co., 1951-52; cattle buyer Jim Boyle Order Buying, 1954-56, R & C Packing Co., 1956-61; cattle buyer plant mgr., v.p. carcass prodn. IBP, 1961-69; v.p. ops. Spencer Foods, 1969-71; pres. Madison Foods, Inc., 1971-76; pres. Iowa Beef Processors, Inc., Dakota City, Nebr., 1976—, also chief exec. officer, dir. Served with U.S. Army, 1952-54. Club: Sioux City Country. Office: Iowa Beef Processors Inc Dakota City NE 68731

PETERSON, ROY RICHARD, ins. co. ofcl.; b. McKeesport, Pa., Oct. 5, 1924; s. Roy John and Sarah Elizabeth P.; B.S., Indiana State U. of Pa., 1953; m. Mary Lou Neal, June 22, 1966; children—Kimberly Joy, Mark Richard. With Ins. Co. N. Am., Cin., 1953—, now mgr. loss control dept. Served with U.S. Army, 1943-45. Decorated Bronze Star with five oak leaf clusters. Profl. safety engr., Calif.; cert. product safety mgr. Internat. Product Safety Mgmt. Cert. Bd. Mem. Am. Soc. Safety Engrs. (cert.), Motor Vehicle Fleet (safety dir., nat. com. motor fleet suprs. tng.). Club: Couples First Presbyn. Ch. Mt. Washington (past pres.). Home: 1225 Fagin Run Rd New Richmond OH 45157 Office: 1800 DuBois Tower Cincinnati OH 45202

PETERSON, VERNON JEROME, radiologist; b. Elkhorn, Iowa, Feb. 20, 1942; s. Alva Raymond and Gladys Tena May (Johnson) P.; student Union Coll., 1960-62; B.S. in Chemistry, Denver U., 1964; M.D. with honors, Loma Linda U., 1968; m. Beverly Jo Owen, July 29, 1962; children—Tamara Lynn, Scott Allen. Intern, Riverside County and Univ. Teaching Hosp., 1968-69; resident in radiology U. Mo., Columbia, 1969-73; diagnostic radiologist Radiology and Nuclear Medicine Profl. Assn., Topeka, 1974—; instr. radiology U. Mo., 1973-74; active staff Stormont-Vail, St. Francis, Meml. hosps. Served to capt. M.C., AUS, 1970-72. Named Outstanding Intern Riverside Hosp., 1968-69. Diplomate Am. Bd. Radiology. Mem. Am. Coll. Radiology, Radiol. Soc. N.Am., Kans., Shawnee County med. socs., AMA, Alpha Omega Alpha. Republican. Seventh-day Adventist. Home: 4730 Brentwood St Topeka KS 66606 Office: 310 Medical Arts Bldg 10th and Horne Sts Topeka KS 66604

PETERSON, VICTOR LEIGHTON, coll. adminstr.; b. Seattle, July 10, 1926; s. Marcus Daniel and Velma Ruby (Shaw) P.; A.B. in Sociology, Augustana Coll., 1949; postgrad. Garrett Theol. Sem., 1950-52, George Williams Coll., 1953-56; m. Doris Boruff, Aug. 26, 1951. Boys work sec. YMCA of Met. Chgo., 1953-58, br. exec., 1958-63; exec. YMCA of Hammond (Ind.) Area, 1963-71; fund raising cons., 1971-72; dir. devel. Planned Parenthood Assn. Chgo., 1972-73; dir. fund devel. Rockford (Ill.) Coll., 1974-77, v.p. devel., 1977-80; v.p., inst. adv. Central YMCA Community Coll., Chgo., 1980—. Republican. Methodist. Home: 1912 Prairie Square Schaumburg IL 60195 Office: 211 W Wacker Dr Chicago IL 60606

PETERSON, WAYNE WILLIAM, advt. art studio exec.; b. Milw., July 19, 1950; s. Wayne Eugene and Diane Josephine (Lasnicka) P.; A. in Comml. Art, Milw. Area Tech. Sch., 1970; B.F.A., U. Wis., Milw., 1973; m. Joanne Marie Foti, Oct. 27, 1973; children—Christine Marie, Amy Katherine. Prodn. artist Hubbard Asso., Milw., 1970-72; packaging designer Milprint Inc., Milw., 1972-73; asst. art dir. Country Beautiful Corp., Waukesha, Wis., 1973-74; acct. exec. Frank Bercker Studios, Milw., 1974; art dir. R.L. Meyer Advt., Milw., 1975; mgr. art direction and prodn. James Jeffords & Assos., Milw., 1976; art dir. The Brady Co., Milw., 1977; owner, pres. Wayne Wm. Peterson Design & Illustration Ltd., Muskego, Wis., 1978—. Served with NG U.S. Army, 1970-76. Recipient Cert. of Excellence Milw. Soc. Communicating Arts, Ltd., 1978. Mem. The Free Lance Artists Guild (founder, pres.). Republican. Roman Catholic. Clubs: Four Winds Tae Kwon Do, Croation Fraternal Lodge. Co-author cartoon strip The Sea Turkeys, 1979. Home and Office: S68 W 16962 Martin Dr Muskego WI 53150

PETERSON, WILLIAM MC CLURE, cons. engr.; b. Detroit, Feb. 14, 1930; s. Signor and Frances Elizabeth (McClure) P.; student Lawrence Inst. Tech.; m. Carol Lynn Straub, June 20, 1975; children—Shelly Frances, Carl Eric, Paul David, Mark Edward, Stephen Alan. Prodn. mgr. Cargill Detroit Corp., 1951-59; v.p. Olsen Mfg. Co., Inc., Royal Oak, Mich., 1959-68, dir., 1960-68; v.p., dir. Hydramet Amm., Inc., Royal Oak, 1968-78; pres. Peterson Engring., Inc., Alpena, Mich., 1978-81; engring. mgr. Mohr Machinery Co., Detroit, 1981—; mem. task com. guarding power presses Cemented Carbide Producers Assn. Served with USMCR, 1948-50; comdr. USCG Aux., 1980. Mem. Soc. Mfg. Engrs. (sr.), Am. Ceramic Soc., Am. Nuclear Soc., Soc. Carbide and Tool Engrs., Am. Def. Preparedness Assn., Nat. Wildlife Fedn., U.S. Power Squadron, Boat Owners Assn. U.S. Republican. Club: Elks. Patentee lubricating devices, method for compacting powders. Home: 4060 Nordstrom Birmingham MI 48010 Office: PO Box 1148 Dearborn MI 48121

PETRELLA, RUSSELL CONRAD, clin. and forensic psychologist; b. Buffalo, Aug. 21, 1951; s. Albert John and Connie M. (Nelson) P.; B.A., Syracuse U., 1973; Ph.D. (NIMH fellow, 1973-75), Washington U., St. Louis, 1978; m. Nancy Sue Swartz, Aug. 8, 1975. Clin. psychology intern, Spring Grove Hosp. Center, Balt., 1975-76; clin. asst. behavior therapy clinic Washington U., St. Louis, 1977-78; asso. dir. evaluation unit Center for Forensic Psychiatry, Ann Arbor, Mich., 1978-81, chmn. dept. psychology, 1981—; part time faculty Wayne State U.; cons. Fed. Correctional Inst., Milan, Mich. Mem. Am. Psychol. Assn., Am. Psychology-Law Soc. Roman Catholic. Speaker at profl. convs. Office: PO Box 2060 Ann Arbor MI 48106

PETRI, HENRY LAW, ret. mfg. co. exec.; b. Brookline, Mass., Nov. 9, 1914; s. Gunther Hector Petri and Gertrude Dennison (Bement) Petri Dennison; grad. Gov. Dummer Acad., 1935; m. Avalo Brown, Mar. 23, 1943; children—Pamela Dennison Humphrey, Stephanie Petri Lord. With Filene's, Boston, 1936-40; with United Carr Fastener (later merged with TRW), Cambridge, Mass., 1940-45, sales engr., Detroit, 1945-57, dist. sales mgr. Ucinite div., 1957-72, mgr. customer relations and sales rep. Carr div. TRW, Southfield, Mich., 1972-81, ret., 1981. Mem. Am. Soc. Body Engrs., Soc. Automotive Engrs. Episcopalian. Club: Country of Detroit. Home: 97 Handy Rd Grosse Pointe Farms MI 48236 Office: 21311 Civic Center Dr Southfield MI 48075

PETRI, THOMAS EVERT, U.S. congressman; b. Marinette, Wis., May 28, 1940; s. Robert George and Marian Ingrid (Humleker) P.; B.A., Harvard U., 1962, LL.B., 1965. Admitted to Wis. bar, 1965; with Peace Corps, Somalia, 1966-67; mem. Wis. Senate, 1973-79; mem. 96th and 97th Congresses from 6th Dist. Wis. Candidate for U.S. Senate from Wis., 1974; Office: Room 1024 Longworth House Office Bldg Washington DC 20515

PETRICK, RONALD DALE, mfg. co. exec.; b. Sandusky, Ohio, Mar. 12, 1942; s. Joseph and Marian Lucille (Jones) P.; B.B.A., Ohio Dominican Coll., 1974; M.B.A., Xavier U., 1976; student Capital U., 1960-62; m. Joanne Luckino Petrick, May 20, 1978. Mgr. tech. service Glidden Durkee div. SCM Corp., Cleve., 1963-68; mgr. market devel. Chem. div. Borden Inc., Columbus, 1968-77; mktg. mgr. Liqui-Box Corp., Worthington, Ohio, 1977-78; product mktg. mgr. epoxy glass laminates Gen. Electric Co., Coshocton, Ohio, 1978—; mem. adj. faculty Otterbein Coll., Ohio Dominican Coll. Mem. alumni bd. Ohio Dominican Coll., pres., 1977-78, mem. presdl. search com. Recipient Theodore Hoffman award Borden Inc., 1974, 75, 76; Mktg. Innovation award Gen. Electric Co., 1980. Mem. Am. Mktg. Assn. Republican. Lutheran. Home: 154 Aldrich Rd Columbus OH 43214 Office: 1350 S 2d St Coshocton OH 43812

PETRIE, BRUCE INGLIS, lawyer; b. Washington, Nov. 8, 1926; s. Robert Inglis and Marion McClurg (Douglas) P.; B.B.A., U. Cin., 1948, J.D., 1950; m. Beverly Ann Stevens, Nov. 3, 1950; children—Laurie Ann, Bruce Inglis, Karen Elizabeth. Admitted to Ohio bar, 1950; asso. firm Kunkel & Kunkel, Cin., 1950-51; asso. firm Graydon, Head & Ritchey, Cin., 1951-56, partner, 1957—. Mem. Ohio Ethics Commn., 1974-75; mem. bd. Charter Com. Greater Cin., 1952-76; mem. Green Areas adv. com. Village of Indian Hill, Ohio, 1969-80, chmn., 1976-80; mem. Bd. Edn. Indian Hill Exempted Village Sch. Dist., 1964-67, pres., 1967; mem. adv. bd. William A. Mitchell Center, mental health center, 1969—; mem. sta. WGUC-FM Community Bd., 1974—, chmn., 1974-76; bd. dirs. Murray Seasongood Good Govt. Fund. Served with USMCR, 1944-46. Recipient Young Man of Year Distinguished Service award Jr. C. of C., 1959; Pres.'s award for Excellence, U. Cin., 1976. Fellow Ohio State Bar Assn. Found., Am. Bar Found.; mem. Am., Ohio State (modern cts. com. 1965—, chmn. 1977-80, council dels. 1976, dir. OBAR Automated Research Corp. 1974-77), Cin. (exec. com., pres. 1980-81), bar assns., Cin. Lawyers Club, Am. Judicature Soc. (dir., Herbert Lincoln Harley award 1973), Cincinnatus Assn. (exec. com. 1972-75; Spl. award 1980), U. Cin. Law Sch. Alumni (chmn. 1974-75), Order of Coif, Lit. Club Cin., Sigma Chi. Presbyterian (elder, trustee, deacon). Clubs: University (gov. 1972-75), Cincinnati Country (Cin.). Home: 5940 Crabtree Ln Cincinnati OH 45243 Office: 5th 3d Center 511 Walnut St Cincinnati OH 45202

PETRIE, RICHARD EDWIN, indsl./interior designer; b. Chgo., Mar. 11, 1931; s. Edwin R. and Mildred A. (Jindra) P.; diploma Art Inst. Chgo., 1958; student U. Ill., 1964-65; m. Sept. 16, 1961. Indsl. designer Palma-Knapp Assos., River Forest, Ill., 1958-60; indsl./interior designer Whirlpool Corp., Benton Harbor, Mich., 1960-74; owner Richard Petrie Interiors, Kalamazoo, 1974—. Served with USAF, 1950-54. Mem. Indsl. Designers Soc. Am., AIA. Clubs: Mchts. and Mfrs., Park. Contbr. articles to profl. jours. Home: 421 Sunview St Kalamazoo MI 49002

PETROFSKY, JERROLD SCOTT, physiologist; b. St. Louis, May 5, 1948; s. Phillip and Jeanette (Zebrack) P.; A.B., Washington U., 1970; Ph.D., St. Louis U., 1974; m. Cheryl L. Petrofsky, June 22, 1974; 1 dau., Melissa. Postdoctoral fellow St. Louis U., 1974-76, asst. prof. physiology, 1976-79; dir. bioinstrumentation lab., asso. prof. biomed. engring. Wright State U., Dayton, 1979—; cons. USAF, 1977—, Eastman Kodak, 1979. NIH grantee, 1979—. Mem. Am. Physiol. Soc., Am. Coll. Sports Medicine, IEEE, Bioengring. Soc., Sigma Xi. Jewish. Contbr. articles to profl. jours. Home: 1591 Hillside Dr Dayton OH 45432 Office: Dept Engring Wright State U Dayton OH 45435

PETROS, SOPHIE KARIPIDES (MRS. THOMAS S. PETROS), home economist, dir. pub. relations; b. Canton, Ohio, Nov. 4, 1932; d. Constantine N. and Martha (Sideropoulos) Karipides; student Ohio State U., 1950-52; B.S. in Journalism, Northwestern U., 1954; m. Thomas S. Petros, Jan. 10, 1960; 1 son, Dean. Tchr. home econs. St. Charles Borromeo Environment House, Chgo., 1958; publicity-promotion asst. Toni Co., Chgo., 1954-55; TV account exec. Yardis Advt. Co., Phila., 1955-56; TV writer, demonstrator Crestline Co., Chgo., 1957; home service rep. Peoples Gas Light & Coke Co., Chgo., 1957-62; dir. pub. relations and advt., sec. Dial On Corp., Milw., 1962—; condr. gourmet cooking show WISN-TV, Milw., 1971—; free-lance food demonstrator, TV commls., 1956—; owner, operator Sophie Kay's Fine Dining. Chmn., Hope for Hope Fund, Canton, 1954. Recipient debate award Nat. Forensic League, 1950. Mem. Am. Fedn. Television and Radio Artists, Am. Home Econs. Assn., Home Econs. in Bus., Northwestern U. Alumni Assn., Theta Sigma Phi, Alpha Xi Delta. Mem. Greek Orthodox Ch. Author: Sophie Kay's Step-by-Step Cook Book, 1972; Sophie Kay's Family Cookbook, 1974; International Menu Cookbook, 1976; Junior Chef Cookbook, 1977; Sophie Kay's Yogurt Cookery, 1978; Sophie Kay's Pasta Cookery, 1979; The Chicken Cookbook, 1981. Home: 15325 Westover Rd Elm Grove WI 53122 Office: 5171 S 108 St Hales Corners WI 53130

PETROSS, PRECIOUS DORIS, personnel adminstr.; b. Chgo., d. Joseph and Olive (Williams) Johnson; B.A., U. Mich., Flint, 1967; M.A., Eastern Mich. U., 1974; J.D., Detroit Coll. Law, 1982; m. Robert G. Petross (div.); children—Charles Howard, Janice Elaine Petross Habashe, Michael Alan. Personnel technician City of Flint (Mich.), 1967-69, sr. personnel technician, 1969-72; asst. personnel dir. Hurley Med. Center, Flint, 1972-74, personnel dir., 1974-80, asst. med. center dir. for human resources, 1980—; personnel cons.; participant oral appraisal bds. State of Mich. and City of Flint. Adv. bd. Mott Community Coll. Social Work Tech. Program, 1976—; bd. dirs. Fairwinds council Girl Scouts U.S.A., 1977—; active LWV, Urban League of Flint. Recipient Human and Race Relations award St. James Meth. Episcopal Ch., 1977; Black Women's Polit. Leadership Caucus award, 1976; named Woman of Year, 1978; Nat. Civil Service League fellow, 1971. Mem. Internat. Personnel Mgmt. Assn., Am. Hosp. Assn., Mich. Hosp. Personnel Dirs. Assn., Am. Soc. Hosp. Personnel Adminstrn., Flint Personnel Assn., AAUW, Nat. Assn. Negro Bus. and Profl. Women's Clubs, U. Mich. Alumnae Assn., Zeta Phi Beta. Baptist. Clubs: Snow Birds Ski, Genesee Temple Elks. Office: Hurley Med Center 1 Hurley Plaza Flint MI 48502

PETROVS, VALDIS IVARS, rubber mfg. co. exec.; b. Lubeck, Germany, Feb. 22, 1947; came to U.S., 1950, naturalized, 1963; s. Pierre Jacques and Livia Petrovs Fridenbergs; B.S. in Mgmt. Sci., Case Inst. Tech., 1968; M.B.A., Case Western Res. U., 1971; m. Georgia Jean Apple, June 8, 1969. Bus. intern TRW Inc., Cleve., 1968-70, adminstrv. asst., 1970-71, prodn. scheduler, 1971-73, prodn. control supr., 1973-74; prodn. control mgr. Imperial Clevite, Inc., Milan, Ohio, 1974-77, injection molding mgr., 1977-78; plant mgr. elastomer products div., 1978—; instr. Firelands Coll. of Bowling Green State U., Huron, Ohio. Mem. Am. Prodn. and Inventory Control Soc. (founder, past pres. Sandusky chpt.). Home: 1222 Marina Dr Huron OH 44839 Office: Imperial Clevite Inc Lockwood Rd Milan OH 44846

PETRUNGARO, CHARLES EUGENE (GINO), architect, developer; b. Chgo., Aug. 2, 1937; s. Joseph P. and Rose A. (La Valle) P.; B.A., Notre Dame U., 1960; m. Janet Ann Boswell, Nov. 24, 1962; children—Eugene, Joseph, Lisa, Laura. Project architect Joseph Bagnola & Assos., Architects, and Engrs., 1960-61; sole owner

Petrungaro & Assos., Architects and Engrs., Melrose Park, Ill., 1961—; architect, engr. Leyden Twp., 1963—. Mem. Elmwood Park (Ill.) Planning Commn., 1967-75. Recipient Emerson Meml. prize, 1958; Rambusch award, 1959; three monogram awards U. Notre Dame; winner internat. competition Design Derby, 1958; Lord Warner fellow, 1959-60; Mem. Soc. Am. Registered Architects, Nat. Council Archtl. Registration Bds. Republican. Roman Catholic. Clubs: Nat. Monogram, U. Notre Dame, Chgo. Club of U. Notre Dame. Contbr. articles to Notre Dame Tech. Rev. Office: 2227 N Mannheim Rd Melrose Park IL 60164

PETTAPIECE, MERVYN ARTHUR (BOB), educator; b. Detroit, May 27, 1941; s. Alvy Merrill and Thelma Margaret (Mattson) P.; B.A., Mich. State U., 1963, 67; M.Ed., Wayne State U., 1971, ednl. specialist cert., 1973, Ed.D. (Univ. grad. profl. scholar), 1980; m. Sandra Marie Howe Alber, Aug. 26, 1977; 1 dau., Lori; stepchildren—Michelle Howe, Erin Howe. Tchr. math. Hutchins Jr. High Sch., Detroit, 1968-71; tchr. math. No. High Sch. Detroit, 1971-72, tchr. social studies, 1972—; tchr. Community High Sch., Detroit, 1977—; part-time instr. Coll. Edn., Wayne State U. Mem. adv. bd. Met. Detroit Youth Found., 1977-80. Mem. Nat. Assn. Core Curriculum, Mich. Council for Social Studies, Mich. Assn. Core Curriculum (sec.-treas.), Phi Delta Kappa. Home: 14341 Artesian Detroit MI 48223 Office: 9026 Woodward Detroit MI 48202

PETTINELLI, VINCENT DODDIS, human services co. exec.; b. Houston, Jan. 29, 1944; s. Vincent and Nicolina A. (Doddis) P.; B.A., U. St. Thomas, 1967; M.SW., Tulane U., 1970; m. Judith Bowles, Sept. 28, 1974; 1 son, Matthew Joseph. Supr. counselors Jewish Community Center, New Orleans, 1968-70; dir. edn. Mental Health Assn. for Houston/Harris County, Houston, 1970-71; dir. regional services Midlands Center, Dept. Mental Retardation State of S.C., Columbia, 1971-74; dep. commr. mental retardation dept. public welfare State of Pa., Harrisburg, 1974-76, acting dep. sec. Office Mental Retardation, 1976-77; dir. Joint Mental Health and Mental Retardation Adv. and Review Commn., Columbus, Ohio, 1977; dir. bd. Community Residential Center's, Inc., Cin., 1978; pres. Prescriptive Mgmt. Services, Inc., Columbus, 1977-78; pres. VOCA Corp., Columbus, 1978—, also dir.; asst. prof. social work U. S.C., 1971-74; asst. prof. Temple U., 1974-77; adj. prof. Ohio State U., 1978—; cons. in field. Mem. profl. adv. com. on mental health and mental retardation technology Columbus Tech. Inst. Qualified mental retardation profl., Ohio. Mem. Acad. Cert. Social Workers, Nat. Assn. Social Workers, Am. Assn. Mental Deficiency, Am. Mgmt. Assn. Presbyterian. Home: 4754 Smoketalk Ln Westerville OH 43081 Office: 1350 W 5th Ave Suite 217 Columbus OH 43212

PETTINER, ROSEMARY HENDERSON, interior designer; b. Mitchell, Ind., July 20, 1944; d. Willard H. and Edith C. (Fry) Terrell; B.A., Ind. U., 1968; m. Robert L. Pettiner, Apr. 1, 1979; children—(by previous marriage) Joel M. Henderson, Jessica Rose Henderson; pvt. practice interior design, 1969—; owner Etcetera Assoc., Indpls., 1979—; participant St. Margaret's Guild Decorator Showhouse, 1978-79. Exec. dir. United Way, Bedford, Ind., 1974; mem. adv. council Region V, SBA, Indpls.; nat. project chmn. communications liaison Northwood Inst. Nat. Women's Bd., also communications liaison chmn. Indpls. chpt., admissions/campus liaison chmn. Indpls. chpt., chmn. auction com.; v.p. Nat. Sports Resources Corp.; constrn. mgr. for restoration of 2 major Victorian era hotels in So. Ind. Mem. Contract Furnishings Council of Am., Kappa Kappa Kappa, Delta Delta Delta. Mem. adv. bd. Interior Design mag., 1977; contbr. articles to profl. jours. Home: 3684 Walden Pl Carmel IN 46032 Office: Pettiner Agy 101 E Carmel Dr #200 Carmel IN 46032

PETTIT, KELLY BROOKS, metals recycling furnace mfg. co. exec.; b. Wichita, Kans., Jan. 7, 1953; s. Donald Leroy and Bette Jean P.; student U. Kans., 1971-75. Aircraft salesman also commuter pilot Clopine Aircraft Co., Topeka and Lawrence Aviation (Kans.), 1970-75, part-time salesman, pilot United Corp., Topeka, 1970-75, sales mgr., 1975-78, pres., 1978—; chmn. bd., pres., chief exec. officer United Corp. Cert. airline transp. pilot. Mem. Topeka C. of C., Inst. Scrap Iron and Steel, Nat. Assn. Recycling Industries, Delta Upsilon. Republican. Episcopalian. Clubs: Topeka Country, Masons (32 deg.), Shriner. Home: 7630 Robin Ct Topeka KS 66604 Office: 1947 N Topeka Ave Topeka KS 66608

PETTIT, MARLIN HAZEN, design and furnishings co. exec.; b. Oskaloosa, Iowa, Sept. 14, 1942; s. Hazen C. and Rhea Ferne (Shultz) P.; S.B., Mass. Inst. Tech., 1964; student in Law, U. Va., 1965-66; M.B.A. (Stein, Roe fellow), Harvard U., 1968; m. Maureen T. Kelly, Aug. 8, 1970; children—R. Mark, K. Nicole. Internat. fin. specialist, corp. treas.'s office Chrysler Corp., Detroit, 1968-70; pres. Cimarron Corp., Detroit, 1970-71; sr. fin. analyst J.L. Hudson Co., Detroit, 1971, gen. mgr. contract div., 1972-75; pres., treas., chief exec. officer Contract Interiors, Inc., Detroit, 1975—; exec. v.p. Contract Craftsmen, Inc., Fraser, Mich., 1978—. Active Citizens Research Council of Detroit, Big Bros. Recipient Beaver Key, Mass. Inst. Tech., 1964. Mem. Nat. Office Products Assn. Roman Catholic. Clubs: Econ. of Detroit, Detroit Athletic, Renaissance. Office: 511 Woodward Ave Detroit MI 48226

PETTY, ELIJAH EDWARD, chem. processing co. exec.; b. Terre Haute, Ind., June 12, 1920; s. Curtis and Bonnie Belle (Reed) P.; M.E., U. Ariz., 1943; B.S. in Chem. Engring., U. Okla., 1947; m. Nelda Morris, Nov. 8, 1942; children—Montie Curtis, Vicki Ann. Mgr., Anderson Clayton Edible Oil Plant, Sao Paulo, Brazil, 1959-62, Armour Edible Oil Plant, Kankakee, Ill., 1963-66; supt. refineries Archer Daniels Midland Co., Decatur, Ill., 1966-68; v.p. M. Neumonz & Son, N.Y.C., 1968-73; pres. Petco Internat., Mt. Zion, Ill., 1973—; pres. I. & I. Co., Ltd.; chmn. bd. I. & I. Co., Ltd. (Ireland); tech. dir. AGRIMA (Rio de Janeiro); chief exec. officer DIKTIC Inc.; v.p. M&E Engring.; pres. Chem. Agrl. Processes, Inc.; cons. oil seed processing FAO, UN Indsl. Devel. Orgn., Am. Soybean Assn., Fgn. Agr. Service, U.S. Dept. Agr., numerous fgn. cos. and govts. Adv. com. Jacksonville (Ill.) Sch. Bd. Adv. Com.; chmn. Jacksonville Community Chest. Served with AUS, 1943-46. Registered profl. engr., Tex. Mem. Am. Oil Chemists Soc. Patentee continuous hydrogenation. Home: Rosewood Acres Mount Zion IL 62549 Office: PO Box 309 Mount Zion IL 62549

PETTY, ERIC D., state senator; B.A. with honors, Occidental Coll., 1975; M.B.A., Wharton Sch. U. Pa., 1977; m. Pamela Berendt. Mgr. corp. communications Donaldson Co., Inc.; mem. Minn. Senate, 1980—. Mem. Democratic-Farmer-Labor party. Office: 24E State Capitol St Paul MN 55155*

PETTY, JUDITH NELL, govt. ofcl.; b. Columbia, Pa., Sept. 25, 1947; d. Sylvester L. and Dorothy P. (Lieberknecht) Nell; B.A., Ohio State U., 1968; postgrad. Ind. U., 1969-70; m. Robert R. Petty, Aug. 10, 1974; children—Matthew Robert, Travis Joseph. Mgmt. trainee U.S. Dept. Commerce, Bur. Census, Jeffersonville, Ind., 1969-72, sr. procedures writer, 1972-75, supervisory mgmt. analyst, dep. EEO officer, 1975-77, asst. br. chief geography br., 1977-79, asst. program mgr. for adminstrn., data preparation div. 1980 census, 1979-81, processing office mgr. Decennial ops., 1981—. Adv., Meth. Youth Fellowship, 1972-73; Leader Girl Scouts U.S.A., 1973-74; mem. Barbour Manor Sixth-Class City Steering Com., 1975; coach Say Soccer, 1981. Recipient letter of commendation 1970 Decennial Census, U.S. Census Bur. Mem. Am. Statis. Assn., Assn. Female Execs., LWV (chmn. voter services 1974). Derby City Federally Employed Women (pres. 1975). Presbyterian. Club: Louisville Ski. Office: 1201 E 10th St Jeffersonville IN 47132

PETTY, RICHARD EDWARD, psychologist, educator; b. Garden City, N.Y., May 22, 1951; s. Edmund and Josephine (Serzo) P.; B.A. with high honors, U. Va., 1973; M.A., Ohio State U., 1975, Ph.D., 1977; m. Virginia Lynn Oliver, Aug. 5, 1978. Asst. prof. psychology U. Mo., Columbia, 1977-81, asso. prof., 1981—. NIMH grantee, 1978; NSF grantee, 1980. Mem. Am. Psychol. Assn., Midwestern Psychol. Assn., AAAS, Soc. Psychophysiol. Research, Soc. Exptl. Social Psychologists, Assn. Consumer Research. Author: (with others) Cognitive Responses in Persuasion, 1981; (with J. Cacioppo) Attitudes and Persuasion, 1981, Social Psychophysiology, 1982. Office: McAlester Hall U Mo Columbia MO 65211

PETWAY, JESSE LEE, public schs. adminstr.; b. Rocky Mount, N.C., Sept. 24, 1944; s. Jesse J. and Ada E. (Randolph) P.; B.A. in Math., N.C. A&T State U., 1965; M.A. in Math., U. Detroit, 1972; postgrad. Western Mich. U.; m. Diane Elma Savage, July 27, 1979; 1 son, Jesse Jerhome. Computer programmer Bur. Census, Suitland, Md., 1967; tchr. math. Pontiac (Mich.) Public Schs., 1965-68, secondary math. cons., 1968-71, supr. evaluation, 1971-73, supr. curriculum devel., 1973-79, dir. curriculum and staff devel., 1979—; cons. in proposal writing and leadership devel.; adj. prof. Oakland U., Rochester, Mich., 1971-72. Team leader Pontiac Human Relations Com., 1968-72. Recipient Meritorious Achievement award Pontiac Operation Propel, 1979. Mem. Assn. for Supervision and Curriculum Devel., Am. Assn. Sch. Adminstrs., Am. Ednl. Research Assn., Mich. Ednl. Research Assn., Nat. and Mich. Alliance of Black Educators, Mich. Assn. for Supervision and Curriculum Devel., Pontiac Urban League, NAACP, Kappa Alpha Psi. Baptist. Contbr. articles on teaching methods to profl. publs. Home: PO Box 4353 Auburn Heights MI 48057 Office: 25 S Sanford St Pontiac MI 48057

PETZING, CHARLES EDWARD, state ofcl.; b. Vandalia, Ill., May 23, 1951; s. Raymond H. and Rose Marie (Dust) P.; A.S., Lake Land Coll., 1971; student Eastern Ill. U., 1971-72; B.A., Sangamon State U., 1981, postgrad. 1981—. Legis. asst. to Rep. Roscoe D. Cunningham, Ill. Ho. of Reps., 1973-77; data technicion Ill. Dept. Trans., Springfield, 1977-81, environmentalist, 1981—. Alt. del. Republican Nat. Conv., 1976; mem. Ill. Rep. Com. Task Force, 1975, precinct committeeman; bd. dirs. Ill. Young Rep. Orgn. Mem. Ill. Assn. Hwy. Engrs. Republican. Roman Catholic. Clubs: Elks, K.C. Office: 126 E Ash St Springfield MO 62706

PETZOLD, FRITZ HERBERT, transit adminstr.; b. Freital, Germany, Feb. 21, 1937; s. Walter Bruno and Charlotte C. P.; came to U.S., 1953, naturalized, 1958; student Wright Jr. Coll., 1961-65; B.S., U. Ill., 1970; m. Karen J. Schmutte, June 23, 1973; children—Brian, Patrick, Erika, Markus. Operator printing press Chippewa Paper Products Co., Chgo., 1953-59; bus operator Chgo. Transit Authority, 1959-65, project mgr. engring. dept.-capital improvements transp., 1974—; mech. engr., project engr. dept. aviation Chgo. Pub. Works, 1970-74. Registered profl. engr., Ill. Mem. ASME, Nat. Soc. Profl. Engrs. Office: Chgo Transit Authority Room 7-155 Mdse Mart PO Box 3555 Chicago IL 60654

PEVERLY, DAVID EMERY, real estate mgr.; b. Decatur, Ill., Nov. 29, 1940; s. Joseph Emery and Doris Isabel (Ferrill) P.; student Decatur public schs.; m. Patricia Ann Shea, Apr. 24, 1965; children—Christine, Heather, Janet. Enlisted U.S. Coast Guard, 1960, advanced through grades to chief warrant officer, 1976; ret., 1981; real estate mgmt. engr. Turley-Martin Co., St. Louis, 1981—. Mem. USCG Chief Warrant and Warrant Officers Assn. (past pres.), Refrigeration Engrs. Soc. Republican. Lutheran.

PEW, STEPHEN DWIGHT, mental health adminstr.; b. McCook, Nebr., Apr. 5, 1947; s. Harlow Clinton and Veda Elizabeth (McKeown) P.; B.A., U. Nebr., 1970, M.A., 1971, Ph.D., 1978; m. Caren Handleman, Nov. 1, 1975; 1 son, Ethan Handleman. Dir. behavior shaping unit Eastern Nebr. Community Office of Retardation, Omaha, 1971-73, dir. program devel. and tng., 1973-74, behavioral systems analyst, 1975-76, acting dir., 1977; dir. Eastern Nebr. Community Office of Mental Health, Omaha, 1979—; vis. asst. prof. U. Nebr., Lincoln, 1977-79. Vol. probation counselor Lincoln Probation System, 1970. Mem. Am. Psychol. Assn., Soc. Pediatric Psychology, Am. Mental Health Counselors Assn. Republican. Presbyterian. Office: 885 S 72nd St Omaha NE 68114

PFANNENSTIEL, DONALD JOSEPH, florist; b. Hays, Kans., Oct. 11, 1945; s. Victor and Cecelia (Younger) P.; B.S., Fort Hays State U., 1968; m. Ann E. Beeler, Aug. 12, 1967; children—Stacy Leann, Stephanie Lynn, Shelly Renee. Art supr. United Sch. Dist. 237, Smith Center, Kans., 1968-70; tchr. art and photography United Sch. Dist. 427, Belleville, Kans., 1970-74; owner, mgr. Holiday Floral, Belleville, 1970-72; owner, operator, mgr. Belleville Greenhouses & Floral, 1974-79; mgr. Hutchinson Floral Inc. (Kans.), 1979—; owner Beloit (Kans.) Floral, 1976-78, Mankato (Kans.) Floral, 1977-78. Mem. bd. edn. United Sch. Dist. 427, 1977—; instl. rep. Boy Scouts Am., 1978-79. Recipient numerous awards for floral designs. Mem. Soc. Am. Florists, Kans. Florists Assn., Florists Transworld Delivery (state pres. 1978-79), Telefloral, Belleville C. of C., Republic County Recreation Assn., Am. Inst. Floral Designers, Kans. Assn. Floral Artists. Clubs: Lions, Eagles, Elks. Home: 612 Newport St Hutchinson KS 67501 Office: 521 E 11th St Hutchinson KS 67501

PFEIFER, JAMES HENRY, agronomist; b. Emmetsburg, Iowa, Jan. 2, 1948; s. Celestine John and Lucille Elizabeth (Drees) P.; B.S., S.D. State U., 1969, M.S., 1971; m. Mary Joan Penney, June 7, 1969; 1 son, Jason Stuart. Lab instr. S.D. State U., Brookings, 1968-69, research asst., 1969-71; fertilizer and agrl. chem. specialist Farmland Industries, Aberdeen, S.D., 1971-75; fertilizer and ag chem. div. mgr. S.D. Wheat Growers, Aberdeen, 1975—. Served with U.S. Army, 1971, Army N.G., 1972-74. Mem. S.D. Fertilizer and Agrl. Chem. Assn. (bd. dirs. 1976—, pres. 1978), Jr. C. of C., Soil Sci. Soc. Am., Am. Soc. Agronomy. Republican. Roman Catholic. Club: Elks. Home: 1524 N Jackson St Aberdeen SD 57401 Office: PO Box 1460 Aberdeen SD 57401

PFEIFER, PAUL E., lawyer, state senator; b. Bucyrus, Ohio, Oct. 15, 1942; B.A., Ohio State U., 1963, J.D., 1966; m. Julia; children—Lisa, Beth Ann, Kurt. Admitted to Ohio bar, partner firm Cory, Brown & Pfeifer, Bucyrus; asst. atty. gen. State of Ohio, 1967-70; rep. Ohio Legislature, 1971-72, mem. Ohio State Senate, 1976—; asst. pros. atty. Crawford County, 1973-76. Mem. Crawford County Ohio State U. Alumni Assn. (pres.). Republican. Methodist. Home: 3234 Keiss Rd Bucyrus OH 44820 Office: 221 S Poplar St Bucyrus OH 44820

PFISTER, LINDA ARLENE, ednl. cons. and researcher; b. Lima, Ohio, July 11, 1947; d. Clare Russell and Beulah Pauline (Zeisloft) Pfister; B.S., Bowling Green State U., 1969, M.A., 1971; m. Joseph E. Keilholtz, July 20, 1968. Curriculum specialist, bus. and office edn. tchr. Toledo (Ohio) pub. schs., 1969-71; project asso., comprehensive career edn. model Center for Vocat. and Tech. Edn., Ohio State U., 1971-72; supr. career devel., div. vocat. edn. Ohio Dept. Edn., Columbus, 1972-75; program service officer Coll. Entrance Exam. Bd., N.Y.C., 1974-79; research specialist Nat. Center for Research in Vocat. Edn., Ohio State U., Columbus, 1979-81, asso. dir., 1981—. Mem. Am. Vocat. Assn., Nat. Vocat. Guidance Assn., Am. Personnel and Guidance Assn. Home: 2604 N 4th St Columbus OH 43202 Office: Nat Center for Research in Vocat Edn Ohio State U Columbus OH

PFISTER, SANDRA LYNN, robot co. adminstr.; b. Detroit, Nov. 16, 1947; d. Robert E. and Dorothy V. (Heighes) P.; robot tng. course, 1977 A.B.A., Schoolcraft Coll., 1980; student Eastern Mich. U., 1980—, Macomb Community Coll., 1981. Dist. claims asst. Ins. Co. Dist. Office, Olympic Ins./Transam. Corp., Southfield, Mich., 1968-69; personnel asst., sec. Nat. Can Corp., Livonia, Mich., 1969-70; adminstrv. asst. Crown Alum Co., Inc., Livonia, 1970-72; ops. and adminstrv. asst. Complete Auto Transit Inc., Southfield, 1972-73; fin., adminstrv. mgr. Unimation, Inc., Farmington, Mich., 1975—, office adminstr. Prab Robots, Inc., Detroit, 1981—. Cert. profl. sec. Mem. Robot Inst. Am., Assn. Finishing Processes, Soc. Mfg. Engrs., Robotics Internat. of SME (founding mem., co-chmn. Human Factors Div. 1980, chpt. 2nd vice chmn. 1981-82 Steering/exec. com., edn. task force, robots adv. com., Cert. of Appreciation 1980), Adminstrv. Mgmt. Soc., Profl. Secs. Assn., Nat. Assn. Female Execs. Office: 5944 E Kilgore Rd Kalamazoo MI 49003

PFLAGER, RUTH WOOD, radio and TV consumer advocate; b. Springfield Mass., Mar. 3, 1917; d. Walter Guy and Mabel (Munson) Wood; B.S., U. Mass., 1938; postgrad. Northwestern U., 1939-40; m. Miller S. Pflager, Aug. 31, 1940; children—Sandra P. Wischmeyer, Charlene P. Balistrere, William Wood, Jessie Ruth. Program chmn., v.p. Radio and TV Council Greater Cleve., Inc., 1973-75, pres., 1975-77, exec. dir., 1977-79. Mem. Communications Commn., Greater Cleve. Interchurch Council, 1972—, vice chmn., 1981-82; communications coordinator Ch. Women United in Cleve., 1974-80, bull. editor, 1974-78, honor award, 1980; chmn. media concerns Ch. Women United in Ohio, 1979—; chmn. Mental Health Inst., 1981, 82. Recipient Outstanding Service award Radio-TV Council, 1977. Mem. AAUW (br. pres. 1977-79, com. on women Ohio div. 1979-80, Ohio div. chmn. task force on media concerns 1981-82), Am. Council Better Broadcasts (life mem., sec. 1979—, v.p. 1981—), Nat. Assn. Better Broadcasting, Nat. Citizens Com. for Broadcasting, Orange Hist. Soc. Methodist. Club: Women's City (mem. mental health com. 1974—) (Cleve.). Home: 4349 S Hilltop Dr Chagrin Falls OH 44022 Office: Room 1219 University Tower Cleveland OH 44115

PFLEAGER, REBECCA MORSE, educator; b. New Britain, Conn., Sept. 8, 1943; d. Royal Harrison and Marjorie (Goodrich) Morse; B.S., Ohio State U., 1965, M.A., 1977; m. Robert Wayne Pfleager, Dec. 21, 1968. Tchr., Gahanna (Ohio) Lincoln High Sch., 1965-66; tchr. Stygler Rd. Jr. High Sch., Gahanna, 1966-75; tchr. Gahanna Middle Sch. W., 1975—, mem. math. resource room com., 1979—; exec. liason officer Franklin County (Ohio) Sch. Employees Fed. Credit Union, 1970-81, dir., 1981—; mem. Franklin County Met. Educator's Polit. Action Com., 1968-79. Martha Holden Jennings Found. scholar, 1977-78. Mem. Assn. Supervision and Curriculum Devel., Nat. Council Tchrs. Math., NEA, Ohio Edn. Assn., Ohio Middle Sch. Assn. (rep. to state exec. bd. central region 1980-82), Jefferson Local Edn. Assn. (dir.), Gahanna-Jefferson Edn. Assn., Delta Kappa Gamma. Office: 350 Stygler Rd Gahanna OH 43230

PFLUG, IRVING JOHN, biol. engr.; b. Ind., Sept. 17, 1923; s. Fred Lewis and Josephine Susan (Meyer) P.; B.S., Purdue U., 1946, B.S. in Agrl. Engring., 1948; M.S., U. Mass., 1950, Ph.D. in Food Sci., 1953; m. E. Charlotte Hoglund, 1973: children—Nancy, Mark, Ann, Jane. Asst. instr. agrl. engring. Purdue U., 1946-48; asst. prof., then asso. prof. engring. U. Mass., 1948-54; prof. agrl. engring., food sci. Mich. State U., 1954-67; prof. food sci., nutrition and public health U. Minn., Mpls., 1967—; food and pharm. industry cons. Served with U.S. Army, 1943-46. Mem. Am. Soc. Microbiology, Inst. Food Technologists, ASHRAE, Internat. Inst. Refrigeration, Brit. Microbiology Soc., Internat. Assn. Milk, Food and Environ. Sanitarians, Sigma Xi, Phi Tau Sigma, Alpha Zeta. Lutheran. Club: Masons. Contbr. articles to profl. jours. Home: 10 E Oaks Rd St Paul MN 55110 Office: Environ Sterilization Lab U Minn 100 Union St SE Minneapolis MN 55455

PHAIR, GRETCHEN MUELLER, speech pathologist; b. Marinette, Wis., Jan. 19, 1913; d. George Anton and Margarethe Louisa (Uecke) Mueller; B.S., U. Wis., Madison, 1944, M.S., 1946; m. George Milton Phair, Sept. 7, 1946. Tchr., Marinette County, Wis., 1930-39; speech therapist Madison (Wis.) Pub. Schs., 1944-46; supr. speech therapy Bur. for Handicapped Children, Dept. Pub. Instrn., State of Wis., Madison, 1946-74; pvt. practice speech therapy; cons. Cleft Palate program U. Wis. Med. Sch.; instr. U. Utah summer sessions, 1954, 56. Chmn. bd. dirs. Friend of the Waisman Center, 1975-77; tutor, Lauback Literacy program. Fellow Am. Speech and Hearing Assn.; mem. Council for Exceptional Children, Wis. Speech and Hearing Assn. (honors 1955, 74), Am. Cleft Palate Assn., Friends of Channel 21, Zeta Phi Eta (Distinguished Service award, 1971), Sigma Alpha Eta. Clubs: West Side Garden, Friends of Arboretum, Friends of Waisman Center. Coordinator movies Wis. Cleft Palate Story (Golden Reel award), 1955; M.R. Mental Retardation, 1967; author chpt. in Voice and Speech Disorders, 1962; contbr. articles in field to profl. jours. Home: 306 Westmorland Blvd Madison WI 53705

PHAN, HUU THANH, physician; b. Saigon, Vietnam, Jan. 24, 1941; s. Phan Van Huych and Ho Thi Gianh; M.D., U. Saigon, 1968; m. Nguyen Ai Trinh, Dec. 19, 1966; children—Phuong, Diep, Suong. Intern, Wayne State U. Hosp., Detroit, 1972-73, resident in gen. surgery, 1973-77; asso., fellow in cardiovascular surgery William Beaumont Hosp., Royal Oak, Mich., 1977-78; mem. active staff Pontiac (Mich.) Gen. Hosp., 1978—, Crittenton Hosp., Rochester, Mich., 1981—. Served to capt. M.C., Army of Vietnam, 1968-72. Mem. Mich. State Med. Soc., Oakland County Med. Soc. Budhist. Office: Pontiac Gen Hosp 1701 Baldwin Ave Pontiac MI 48055

PHANEENDRANATH, BANGALORE RAGHAVENDRACHAR, crop scientist; b. Nelamangala, India, Apr. 11, 1943; s. G. B. Raghavendrachar and Sundaramma Raghavendrachar; B.Sc., U. Agrl. Sci., Bangalore, 1966; M.S., Miss. State U., 1971; Ph.D., Rutgers U., 1977. Asst. agrl. officer Karnataka State Dept. Agr., Madhugiri, India, 1966-67; hort. asst. Karnataka State Hort. Dept., Madhugiri, 1967-68; research asst. Miss. State U., State College, 1969-71; research intern Rutgers U., New Brunswick, N.J., 1972-77; research asst. Ohio State U., Columbus, 1977-78; seed technologist Growers' Seed Assn., Lubbock, Tex., 1979-81; dir. research, prodn. and quality control Ag-One Seeds Inc., Washington Court House, Ohio, 1981—. Mem. Am. Soc. Agronomy, Crop Sci. Soc. Am., Soc. Comml. Seed Tech., Am. Oil Chemists Soc., Nat. Cottonseed Products Assn., Sigma Xi. Club: Pinchoppers Bowling (pres. 1980-81). Office: 648 Miami Trace Rd SW Washington Court House OH 43160

PHANSALKAR, ARVIND GANGADHAR, psychiatrist; b. Poona, India, Jan. 19, 1944; s. Gangadhar Vasudeo and Umabai (Gangadhar) P.; came to U.S., 1971; M.B.B.S., Poona U., 1968, M.D., 1971; m. Jyotsna K-Tambe, Nov. 17, 1972. Intern, Thana, Bombay, India,

1967; lectr. pharmacology U. Poona, 1968-71; resident in psychiatry St. Louis U. Med. Center, Mo. Inst. Psychiatry, 1972-75; clin. instr. psychiatry U. Ill., 1975-79; mem. faculty U. Wis., Milw., 1979—; staff psychiatrist Singer Mental Health Center, 1975-79; pvt. practice psychiatry, Milw., 1979—; attending psychiatrist Luth. Hosp., Sacred Heart Hosp., Kettle Moraine Hosp., Milw. Psychiat. Inst., 1979—; cons. Cath. Social Services, Ill. Div. Vocat. Rehab. Diplomate Am. Bd. Psychiatry and Neurology. Mem. Ill. Psychiat. Soc., Wis. Psychiat. Assn., Am. Psychiat. Assn., India Cultural Assn., Maharashtra Mandal. Contbr. articles to profl. jours. Home: 5780 Timberlane Rd New Berlin WI 53151 Office: 2130 N Mayfair Milwaukee WI 53226

PHELAN, JOHN DENSMORE, ret. ins. co. exec., bus. cons.; b. Kalamazoo, Aug. 31, 1914; s. John and Ida (Densmore) P.; B.A. magna cum laude, Carleton Coll., 1935; m. Isabel McLaughlin, July 31, 1937; children—John Walter, William Paul, Daniel Joseph. With Hardware Muts., Stevens Point, Wis., 1936-45; with Am. States Ins. Co., Indpls., 1945-79, chmn., to 1979, now dir. subs.'s Am. States Life Ins. Co., Am. Economy Ins. Co., Am. States Ins. Co. Tex., Am. Union Ins. Co. of N.Y., Am. Preferred Ins. Co.; dir., mem. exec. com. Indpls. Power & Light; mem. advisory council Timberland Corp., Newmarket, N.H.; chmn. Percifield-Phelan Ins. Agy., Columbus, Ind. Past pres. Marion County Assn. for Mental Health; trustee, chmn. C.P.C.U.-Loman Found. Mem. C.P.C.U. Soc. (nat. past pres.), C.L.U. Soc., Phi Beta Kappa. Presbyterian. Clubs: Indpls. Athletic; Woodland Country; 100 of Indpls.; El Conquistador Country (Bradenton, Fla.). Author: Business Interruption Primer, 1st edit., 1949; contbr. articles profl. trade publs. Home: 307 Woodland Ln Carmel IN 46032 Office: 500 N Meridian St Indianapolis IN 46207

PHELAN, MARGARET MARIE, bus. research cons. co. exec.; b. Kansas City, Mo., July 8, 1924; d. William Michael and Grace (Magaw) P.; B.S. in Bus., Kans. State U., 1945; M.A. in Library Sci., Rosary Coll., 1969. Various secretaial positions, Kansas City, Mo. and Ankara, Turkey, 1945-58; export mgr. Coleman Instruments, Maywood, Ill., 1958-60; mgr. info. services Heidrick and Struggles, Inc., Chgo., 1960-76; owner Phelan Bus. Research, Shawnee Mission, Kans., 1976—. Mem. Reagan/Bush Planning Task Force, 1980—; mem. Presdl. Personnel Office Transition Team, 1980. Home and Office: 9603 Nieman Pl Shawnee Mission KS 66214

PHELAN, WILLIAM HENRY, internist; b. Albany, N.Y., Sept. 15, 1926; s. Thomas William and Helen (Rausch) P.; B.S. magna cum laude, Coll. of Holy Cross, 1949; M.D., Albany Med. Coll., 1953; m. Evlyn Doreen May, Jan. 18, 1958; children—John M., William H., Jr., Thomas W., Julie Anne, Elizabeth M. Rotating intern Albany Hosp., 1953—54; resident in internal medicine Presbyterian Hosp., Chgo., 1954-56, chief resident, 1957, attending staff, 1957—, adv. com. dept. medicine, 1975-78; instr. in medicine U. Ill., 1956—64, clin. asst. prof., 1964—69, clin. assn. prof., 1969—71; assn. prof. medicine Rush Med. Coll., 1971—, mem. faculty council, 1973—76; practice medicine specializing in internal medicine, cardiology, Chgo., 1957—. Bd. dirs. Chgo. Heart Assn., 1969—75. Served with USN, 1945—46. Diplomate Am. Bd. Internal Medicine, Nat. Bd. Med. Examiners. Fellow A.C.P., Am. Coll. Chest Physicians; mem. Am. Heart Assn., N.Y. Acad. Sci., Am., Chgo. socs. internal medicine, AMA, Ill., Chgo. med. socs., Alpha Omega Alpha. Club: Northbrook Racquet. Contbr. articles in field. Home: 702 Waukegan Rd Glenview Il 60025 Office: 122 S Mich Ave Chicago IL 60603

PHELPS, NAN DEE HINKLE (MRS. ROBERT PHELPS), artist; b. London, Ky.; d. John W. and Lula May (Weaver) Hinkle; ed. Cin. Art Acad. m. Robert Phelps, Apr. 9, 1927; children—Alma Phelps Lamb, Wilmarie, Donna Phelps Beer, Paul R., Robbie, John Robert. One-woman shows: Galerie Etienne, N.Y.C., Cin. Mus.; exhibited in group shows: Paula Insen, N.Y.C., Cin. Art Mus., Copley Soc., Bos., Pallette Club, Lynn Katler Gallery, N.Y.C.; mural Trinidad Island, Lima, Peru, numerous others Ohio area; executed 17 murals in chs., homes, instn.; represented in permanent collections at Ford Motor Co., Pulaski (Va.) C. of C., Lincoln Sch., other schs., numerous pvt. collections; executed murals in churches and residences. Mem. Copley Soc. Club: The Brush Easel (Hamilton, Ohio). Address: 1721 Green Wood Ave Hamilton OH 45011

PHELPS, RICHARD ALLEN, advt. agy. exec.; b. South Bend, Ind., Jan. 4, 1947; s. Devon Garber and Dorothy Elizabeth (Stevens) P.; B.A. in Journalism, Purdue U., 1969; M.S., Northwestern U., 1978; postgrad. Alaska Meth. U., 1970-71. In advt. sales Chgo. Tribune, 1972-74, Gen. Telephone Directory Co., Chgo., 1974-75; salesman Gallery of Homes, Hoffman Estates, Ill., 1975-76; sales mgr. Val-Pak, Arlington Heights, Ill., 1976-77; advt. sales mgr. Family Ad Weekly, Des Plaines, Ill., 1977; editor Gourmet Merchandizing, Evanston, Ill., 1978-79; owner, pres. Phelps Advt. & Mktg. Inc., Palatine, Ill., 1978—. Served with U.S. Army, 1969-71. Mem. Sigma Delta Chi, Kappa Tau Alpha. Presbyterian. Home: 712 Mariner Point Schaumburg IL 60194 Office: 330 W Colfax St Palatine IL 60067

PHELPS, RICHARD FREDERICK, basketball coach; b. Beacon, N.Y., July 4, 1941; s. Richard Bruce and Margaret Adele (Sullivan) P.; B.S. in Commerce, Rider Coll., 1963; M.A. in Bus. Edn., 1964; m. Teresa K. Godwin, June 25, 1965; children—Karen, Richy, Jennifer. Head basketball coach St. Gabriel's High Sch., Hazleton, Pa., 1965-66; asst. basketball coach U. Pa., 1966-70; head basketball coach Fordham U., N.Y.C., 1970-71, U. Notre Dame, 1971—. Named Coach of Yr., N.Y. Basketball Writers Assn., 1971, Phila. Coll. Basketball Writers Assn., 1971. Office: U Notre Dame Notre Dame IN 46556*

PHETTEPLACE, BETTY HELENA (MRS. JOSEPH ARTHUR PHETTEPLACE), curator; b. Sterling, Ill., Dec. 24, 1916; d. Thomas and Oral (Leland) Shelkey; grad. high sch.; m. Joseph Arthur Phetteplace, June 25, 1936; 1 adopted son, Larry Charles. Curator, Phetteplace Mus., Wauzeka, Wis., 1956—. Lapidary tchr. State Youth Camp, Lomira, Wis., 1949-54. Mem. Midwest Fedn. Mineralogical and Geol. Socs. Methodist. Home: Wauzeka WI 53826 Office: Phetteplace Museum 115 Inlay Ave Wauzeka WI 53826

PHIBBS, CLIFFORD MATTHEW, surgeon; b. Bemidji, Minn., Feb. 20, 1930; s. Clifford Matthew and Dorothy Jean (Wright) P.; B.S., Wash. State U., 1952; M.D., U. Wash., 1955; M.S., U. Minn., 1960; m. Patricia Jean Palmer, June 27, 1953; children—Wayne Robert, Marc Stuart, Nancy Louise. Intern, Ancker Hosp., St. Paul, 1955-56; resident in surgery U. Minn. Hosps., 1956-60; practice medicine specializing in surgery, Oxboro Clinic, Mpls., 1962—; mem. staff St. Barnabas Hosp.; mem. staff Fairview-Southdale Hosp., 1965—, chief of surgery, 1970-71, sec.-treas., 1971-72, chmn. intensive care unit, 1973-76; clin. asst. prof. U. Minn., Mpls., 1975—. Bd. dirs. Bloomington (Minn.) Bd. Edn., 1974—, treas., 1976—; mem. adv. com. for jr. coll. study City of Bloomington, 1964-66, mem. community facilities com., 1966-67, adv. youth study commn., 1966-68; vice chmn. bd. Hillcrest Meth. Ch., 1970-71; mem. Bloomington Adv. and Research Council, 1969-71; bd. dirs. Bloomington Symphony Orch., 1976—; dir. bd. mgmt. Minnesota Valley YMCA, 1970-75; bd. govs. Mpls. Met. YMCA, 1970—. Served to capt. M.C., U.S. Army, 1960-62. Diplomate Am. Bd. Surgery. Mem. AMA (Physician's Recognition awards 1969, 73-76, 76—), Minn. Med. Assn., Minn. Acad. Medicine, Minn., Mpls. surg. socs., Hennepin County Med. Soc., Pan-Pacific Surg. Assn., A.C.S. Club: Jaycees. Contbr. articles to med jours. Home: 9613 Upton Rd S Minneapolis MN 55431 Office: 9820 Lyndale Ave S Minneapolis MN 55420

PHILIP, FRANK STUART, educator; b. Chgo., Dec. 14, 1943; s. Robert Stuart and Pearl Dodds (Foster) P.; B.A., Mich. State U., 1966, M.A. (Tng. Tchrs. of Tchrs. fellow), 1972, postgrad., 1977—; m. Gloria G. Goncoe, Nov. 5, 1967; children—Brandy, Bradley. Tchr. art Waverly Schs., Lansing, Mich., 1972-76, dir. A.R.T.S. project, 1977—; dir. Mich. Arts Advocacy Program, 1981-82. Tenor Opera Guild Greater Lansing, 1972—. Served with USN, 1967-71. Recipient grants Title IVc, 1976, Mich. Council Arts, 1979, 81-82. Mem. Mich. Art Edn. Assn., NEA, Mich. Sch. Public Relations Assn., Assn. Supervision and Curriculum Devel., Mich. Ednl. Research Assn., Mich. Edn. Assn., NEA, Mich. Alliance for Arts Edn., Phi Delta Kappa. Presbyterian. Home: 2056 LacDuMont St Haslett MI 48840 Office: 5601 W Michigan Ave Lansing MI 48917

PHILIP, JAMES PEYTON, JR., state senator, food products co. mgr.; b. Elmhurst, Ill., May 26, 1930; s. James Peyton and Elsa (Gerhardt) P.; student Kansas City Jr. Coll., 1949-50, Kans. State Coll., 1952-53; m. Nancy Britz Ramey; children—Cynthia Kay, Jase, Randall, Kevin. Asst. mgr. Edison Bros. Stores, Inc., 1949-53; sales rep. Pepperidge Farm, Inc., 1953-54, sales promotion supr., 1960, sales promotion mgr., 1960-62, dist. sales mgr., 1962—; mem. Ill. Ho. of Reps., 1966-72, 72-74, Ill. State Senate, 1975—. Del. Republican Nat. Conv., 1980; treas. Elmhurst Young Rep. Club, 1960; chmn. DuPage County (Ill.) Young Rep. Orgn., 1961-63; adminstrv. asst. to chmn. bd. Ill. Young Reps., 1963, jr. nat. committeeman, 1963-65, pres., 1965-74; auditor York Twp., 1965—; chmn. DuPage County Republican Central Com., 1969—. Served with USMC, 1950-52. Mem. Suburban Bus. Mgmt. Council, Grocery Mgmt. and Sales Exec. Club Chgo., Am. Legion. Episcopalian. Clubs: Elks, Shriners. Office: DuPage County Hdqrs 224 S Washington St Wheaton IL 60187*

PHILIP, ROLAND STEPHEN, surgeon; b. N.Y.C., Dec. 16, 1938; s. Marcin and Antoinette (Schwartz) P.; A.B., Cornell U., 1960; M.D., U. Louvain (Belgium), 1966; m. Claire E. Elkon, Apr. 23, 1967; children—Joseph Bernard, Sarah Elizabeth. Intern, St. Luke's Hosp., Newburg, N.Y., 1965-66; intern, then resident in surgery Kings County Hosp., Bklyn., 1966-68; surg. fellow Cleve. Clinic, 1970-73; mem. surg. staff, partner Ohio Permanente Med. Group, Cleve., 1973—; area chief surgery Kaiser Found. Hosp.; sr. clin. instr. Case Western Res. U. Med. Sch. Chmn. eastside undergrad. secondary sch. com. Cornell U. Served as officer M.C., USAF, 1968-70. Fellow A.C.S.; mem. Soc. Critical Care Medicine (founding mem., sec. Ohio chpt.), Rupert Turnbull Surg. Soc. (pres.), Acad. Medicine Cleve. Jewish. Clubs: Cornell (Cleve.), Cleve. Skating. Contbr. articles med. jours. Home: 2325 Delamere Dr Cleveland Heights OH 44106 Office: 2475 East Blvd Cleveland OH 44120

PHILIPON, RUTH WEDGWOOD, artist; b. Toronto, Ont., Can., Oct. 21, 1933; d. Reginald Abraham and Kathleen Wedgwood (Duncan) Dennison; student Chgo. Acad. Fine Arts, 1952-54, Chgo. Art Inst., 1952-54, 67-70, Polytechnic Sch. London, 1956, Academie de la Grande Chaumiere, Paris, 1956; m. Phillip James Philipon, Feb. 15, 1958; 1 son, Dion Demetri Wedgwood. Fashion illustrator, designer Charles A. Stevens Co., Chgo., 1954-55, 59-62; illustrator Carson, Pirie, Scott, Chgo., 1958; freelance illustrator Marshall Fields, RX Cosmetics, Dr. Scholl's, Chgo., 1965-66; one-woman shows Anderson-Marsh Gallery, St. Petersburg, Fla., 1977, 78, 79, 80, Bergstrom Mus., Neenah, Wis., 1975, Brown County Library, Green Bay, Wis., 1977, Arts Center, St. Petersburg, 1978, Stables Gallery, Hastings, Eng., 1981, Elliot Gallery, Eckerd Coll., St. Petersburg, 1981; exhibited in group shows Circle Gallery, Chgo., 1971, Women in the Arts, Oshkosh, 1975, Milw., 1976, Festival of States, St. Petersburg, 1976, 77, 78, 80-81, Neville Mus., Green Bay, 1976, 77, Marine Bank, Milw., 1979; represented in permanent collections Milw. Art Center, Rahr-West Mus., Manitowoc, Wis.; owner, mgr. Tria Gallery of Contemporary Art, Ellison Bay, Wis., 1970—; exhbn. designer Maritime Mus., Gills Rock, Wis., 1977. Mem. Top of the Thumb Assn. (art dir.), Gills Rock Assn., Wis. Women in Arts, Peninsula Arts Assn., Chgo. Council on Fgn. Relations, Smithsonian Assos., Door County Environ. Assn. Author, illustrator: Mykonos, 1977; initiated Guild of Door County Artists scholarship, 1975. Address: Route 1 Box 221 Ellison Bay WI 54210

PHILIPPS, LOUIS EDWARD, hosp. data system mfg. co. exec.; b. Duluth, Minn., Feb. 7, 1906; s. Carl Frederick Ferdinand and Sarah Marguerithe (Mortenson) P.; student Duluth pub. schs.; m. Gladys Victoria Monsen, Nov. 13, 1930. Engr., Cleve. Radioelec. Co., 1946-48; v.p., gen. mgr. Radio Systems, Inc., Cleve., 1948-50, Royal Communications, Inc., Cleve., 1950-56; dir. engrng. Auth Elec. Co., N.Y.C., 1956-59; chief engr. Hosp. Products div. Motorola-Dahlberg Co., Mpls., 1959-63; founder, pres., chmn. bd. Medelco, Inc., Schiller Park, Ill., 1964-74; founder, chmn. bd. DATX Corp., Chgo., 1975—. Named Father of the Hosp. Systems Industry, Am. Hosp. Assn., 1974. Mem. IEEE (sr.). Republican. Presbyterian. Clubs: Anvil (East Dundee, Ill.), Eastern Star, Masons, Shriners. Patentee in field. Office: 303 E Ohio St Chicago IL 60611

PHILIPSON, WILLARD DALE, educator, univ. adminstr.; b. Sleepy Eye, Minn., Mar. 18, 1930; s. Walter and Alice Anna (Rasmussen) P.; B.S., U. Minn., 1953, M.A., 1959, Ph.D., 1967; m. Sylvia Eileen Olson, Sept. 26, 1953; children—Andrew Will, Jennifer Dale, Pamela Elizabeth. Instr. agrl. engrng. U. Minn. at Morris, 1959; audio visual materials advisor Audio Visual Edn. Service, Mpls., 1960-63; asst. prof., head ednl. film library No. Ill. U., DeKalb, 1963-66; asso. prof., dir. audio visual library services U. Minn., Mpls., 1966-78, prof. curriculum and instrn. systems, 1978—. Active mem. Commn. on Minn. Civil Service Exec. Mgmt. Tng., St. Paul, 1969-71, Troop 401, Boy Scouts Am., St. Paul, 1972-75, chmn. fund dr., 1974-75; mem. Citizens for Libraries, Legis. Com., St. Paul, 1976—. Served with USN, 1953-58. Decorated Nat. Service medal, Naval Res. medal, Armed Force Campaign ribbon; recipient Adult Educator of Yr. award 1973; Sears, Roebuck & Co. scholar, 1952; service award Gov. LeVander, Minn. 1969; Silver Reel award Consortium of Univ. Film Centers, 1979. Mem. Naval Res. Assn., Assn. Ednl. Communicatons and Tech., Adult Edn. Assn., Assn. Supervision and Curriculum Devel., Minn. Ednl. Media Orgn., Alpha Tau Alpha. Editor Audio-Visual Jour., 1966-78. Home: 3020 N Chatsworth St Saint Paul MN 55113 Office: Peik Hall 159 Pillsbury Dr Minneapolis MN 55455

PHILLIPS, BERT EUGENE, mfg. co. exec.; b. Quincy, Ill., May 8, 1919; s. John Herbert and Zella Mae (Long) P.; student U. Ill., 1938-39; student Quincy (Ill.) Coll., 1940-41, D.Indsl. Mgmt. (hon.), 1977; LL.D. (hon.) Tri-State U., 1974; m. Helen J. Grummon, Jan. 23, 1943; children—Eric W., Julia Phillips Gleason. With Clark Equipment Co., 1948—, gen. mgr. constrn. machinery div., 1966-67, exec. v.p., 1967-70, pres., 1970—, chmn. bd., 1979—; dir. Amsted Industries, Exxon Corp., Mass. Mut. Life Ins. Co., Whirlpool Corp. Trustee Tri-State U. Mem. Machinery and Allied Products Inst. (exec. com.). Office: Circle Dr Buchanan MI 49107*

PHILLIPS, BETTY GOLISH, educator; b. Sullivan County, Ind., Mar. 20, 1936; d. John and Tressie Eunice (Bunch) Golish; B.S. cum laude in Vocat. Home Econs., Ind. State U., 1963, M.S. in Home Econs., 1964, Edn. Specialist, 1973; m. Dale Smith Phillips. Home econs. tchr., Carlisle, Ind., 1964-65; home econs. tchr. Sullivan (Ind.) High Sch., 1966—, dept. chmn. home econs. dept., 1968—; dist. coordinator Future Homemakers Am., 1972-79, mem. state adv. bd., 1972-81; cons. Consumer Edn. Program, 1970-71. Sec., County Comprehensive Health Council, 1975-76; bd. dirs. Sullivan County Assn. Retarded Citizens, 1974-77; sec. County March of Dimes, 1976-79, vice-chmn., 1980-81; mem. Local Drug Council, 1975-78; community worker Head Start, 1970-77. Recipient Young Educator award Jr. C. of C., 1970, Woman of Yr. award Bus. and Profl. Women's Club, 1978; named Tchr. of Year, Family Circle and Am. Home Econs. Assn., 1974. Mem. Internat. Fedn. Home Econs., Am. Tchr. Educators, Women's Elks Found., NEA, Am. Home Econs. Assn., People-to-People Internat., Ind. Vocat. Home Econs. Assn. (merit award 1980), Ind. State Tchrs. Assn., Ind. Home Econs. Assn., Nat. Assn. Vocat. Home Econs. Tchrs., Delta Kappa Gamma (scholarship 1971, grant 1977). Methodist. Home: 202 Cross St Sullivan IN 47882 Office: 220 W Wolfe St Sullivan IN 47882

PHILLIPS, CAROLE ANN, educator; b. Princeton, Ill., Nov. 1, 1936; d. Ward Elwood and Anna Victoria (West) Birkey; B.S., Ill. State U., 1961; M.Ed., Macalester Coll., 1970; M.S. of Ed., No. Ill. U., 1975; postgrad. Salzburg (Austria) Coll., 1978; m. Bobby Elwood Phillips, Aug. 15, 1963; children—Keith Robert. Tchr., Walnut (Ill.) Pub. Schs., 1956-57, Wyanet (Ill.) Pub. Schs., 1958-60, Princeton (Ill.) Elementary Schs., 1960-63, Batavia (Ill.) Pub. Schs., 1963-71; with Hinsdale (Ill.) Health Mus. (now Robert Crown Center for Health Edn.), 1972-74; guidance counselor Aurora (Ill.) Central Cath. High Sch., 1974-81; tchr. math., physics and chemistry Valley Lutheran High Sch., St. Charles, Ill., 1981—; cons. to Region V HEW, Chgo., 1972-74; lectr. in field. Named Outstanding Phys. Sci. Tchr. of Chgo. Met. Region, Bell Labs., 1980. NSF grantee, 1969-70. Mem. NEA, Am. Guidance and Personnel Assn., Nat. Vocational Guidance Assn. Mem. United Ch. of Christ. Contbr. articles in field to profl. jours. Home: 1212 N Brandywine Circle Batavia IL 60510 Office: Valley Luth High Sch 701 Geneva Rd Saint Charles IL 60174

PHILLIPS, DAVID RALPH, restaurant exec.; b. Detroit, Dec. 31, 1941; s. Ralph Ernest and Dorthy Mable (Linke) P.; student Henry Ford Coll., 1960-61, Culinary Inst. Am., New Haven, 1962-63; m. Gale Sandra Phillips, Jan. 4, 1964; children—Brian David, Amy Gale. Asst. mgr. Schensul's Cafeteria, Grand Rapids, Mich., 1964; dining room mgr. J.L. Hudson, Detroit, 1965-69; mgr. food service Oakland U., 1970-71; owner, mgr. Gray Gables Inn, Charlevoix, Mich., 1971—. Weblos leader Scenic Trails council Boy Scouts Am. Served with U.S. Army, 1965. Recipient Gov.'s award State of Mich., 1976. Mem. C. of C. (dir. 1972-76). Methodist. Clubs: Lions, Masons. Listed in Guiness Book of World Records for creation of world's largest cherry pie. Home and Office: 308 Belevedere St Charlevoix MI 49720

PHILLIPS, GLENN ALLEN, educator, retail co. asso.; b. Des Moines, Aug. 3, 1948; s. Walter Russell and Loretha Joyce (Larson) P.; B.A., U. No. Iowa, 1971, postgrad., summers 1971, 72. Instr. bus. East Buchanan (Iowa) High Sch., 1971-73; substitute instr. Cedar Rapids Schs., 1973; with Iowa Electric Light and Power Co., Cedar Rapids, 1973-80, procurement quality technician, 1973-75, supr. elec. generating plant, nuclear, 1975-80; office asso. Gordon Jewelers, Cedar Rapids, 1981—; instr. adult night class Kirkwood Community Coll., Cedar Rapids, 1973—, mem. adv. com. office edn., 1978—; instr. Hamilton Bus. Coll., Cedar Rapids, 1981—. Bd. dirs. Iowa Electric Light & Power Co. Employees Credit Union, 1976—. Mem. Am. Mgmt. Assn., Phi Beta Lambda. Home: 244 Drinkward NW Cedar Rapids IA 52405

PHILLIPS, HOLLAND WOODFORD, internat. trade cons.; b. Grand Rapids, Minn., Apr. 30, 1932; s. Holland W. and Irene R. (Johnson) P.; B.B.A., U. Minn., 1955; m. Betty M. O'Neill, Mar. 26, 1955; children—Michael Stephen, Lynn Holly, Ronn Patrick. Partner, pres. Capital Electronics, Inc., St. Paul, 1960-68; v.p. Overseas Mktg. Group, Inc., Balt., 1968-73; dir. internat. div. Leslie Internat., Chgo., 1973-75; founder, pres. Holland W. Phillips & Assos., Ltd., internat. trade cons., Romeoville, Ill., 1975—; lectr. Elmhurst Coll. Vice commodore, bd. dirs. Mpls. Aquatennial, 1966-67. Mem. Chgo. Council Fgn. Relations, Internat. Trade Club Chgo., West Suburban Internat. Trade Club (pres. 1978—). Author: Complete Export Checklist, 1977; contbr. articles on internat. trade and export devel. to profl. jours. Home: 411 Wildwood Ct Romeoville IL 60441

PHILLIPS, INEZ EVALYN, commodity broker; b. Lakin, Kans., Oct. 9, 1919; d. Charles Winfield and Hannah Alida (Johnson) Rosebrook; student Salt City Bus. Coll., 1936-38; m. Frank Phillips, 1936 (dec. 1966); children—Kelley, Terry, Kerry, Vicki, Kirby. Exec. dir. Western Kans. counties Nat. Multiple Sclerosis Assn., Garden City, 1967-69; commodity broker, stock broker Goffe-Carkener Blackford, Garden City, 1969-72; account exec., br. mgr. Heinold Commodities and Heinold Securities, Garden City, 1972—; dir. Western State Bank, Garden City; tchr. Garden City Community Coll. County chmn., vice chmn., precinct committeewoman Democratic Party. Mem. Nat. Bus. Women, Garden City C. of C. (dir.), Am. Legion Aux. Presbyterian. Home: 1602 Belmont Pl Garden City KS 67846 Office: 403 Campus Dr Garden City KS 67846

PHILLIPS, J. STEPHEN, univ. dean; b. Dover, Ohio, Jan. 3, 1939; s. Delbert C. and Margaret Jane P.; B.S., Bowling Green State U., 1961; M.A., Tenn. Tech. U., 1965; now postgrad. U. Cin.; m. Carla W. Garrett, Aug. 14, 1965; children—Stephanie Leigh, Matthew Stephen. Tchr., Dover Bd. Edn., 1964-65; grad. asst. Tenn. Tech. U., 1965-66; dir. student services Ohio U., Chillicothe, 1966-73, asst. dean, coordinator continuing edn., 1973—; instr. Nat. Assn. Ct. Adminstrn.; tchr. ednl. psychology and stats. Bd. dirs. Roweton's Boys Ranch, 1970—; mem. Mid-Ohio Health Planning Bd., 1975—; exec. bd. S. Central Ohio Consortium Bus., 1980—. Served as 1st lt. U.S. Army, 1961-64. Human Services Tech. Program grantee, 1974-81; Ohio Assn. Mcpl. Ct. Clks. grantee, 1975-81. Mem. Am. Soc. Tng. and Devel., Am. Assn. Higher Edn., Am. Assn. Jr. Colls., Nat. Assn. Ct. Adminstrs. Republican. Presbyterian. Clubs: YMCA, Symposiarchs. Home: 1299 Betty Ln Chillicothe OH 45601 Office: Ohio U PO Box 629 Chillicothe OH 45601

PHILLIPS, JOAN KARIN, humanist counselor, hosp. adminstr.; b. Chgo., May 27, 1932; d. Ben and Vivien Dorothy (Federman) Rosenfield; B.A. in Communication Arts, Columbia Coll., 1970; M.A. in Cultural Studies, Governors State U., 1973, M.A. in Human Learning and Devel. (fellow in humanistic psychology 1973-74), 1974; Ph.D. in Psychology, Northwestern U., 1978. Tchr., performing artist, piano, voice, folk guitar, Chgo., 1962—; exec. mgr. Chgo. offices Boys Town of the Desert, 1966-69; asst. registrar Columbia Coll., Chgo., 1969-70, dir. admissions, fgn. student adviser, records evaluator, 1970-76; coordinator Learning Exchange, Evanston, 1973; founder, dir. Humanist Center, New Directions, Chgo., 1973—; human relations cons., group workshop facilitator Communications Labs., Tinley Park, Ill., 1974—; edn. and pub. relations coordinator, instr. Samuel and Melvin A. Kopp Center for Continuing Edn., Honey

Creek, Wis., and Evanston, Ill., 1975—; Tai Chi instr., Chgo., 1975—; convenor, activities coordinator TORI Assos., Midwest, Chgo., 1975—; free-lance tech. and pub. relations writer, Chgo., 1975—; adminstr. Rush-Presbyn. St. Luke's Med. Center, 1976—; cons., writer Kornhaber, Manka & Assos., Community Therapists, Crestwood, Ill., 1979—; facilitator SAR workshops Northwestern U. Foster children's advocate, crisis intervention hot-line Vol. Dept. Children and Family Services, 1977; active Rainbow Soc. for Deaf; mem. choir Ch. of Atonement. Mem. Nat. Assn. Women Deans, Adminstrs. and Counselors, Ill. Assn. Coll. Admissions Counselors, Assn. for Humanistic Psychology, Am. Humanist Assn., Ethical Humanist Soc., Nat. Assn. Fgn. Student Affairs, Am., Ill. assns. collegiate registrars and admissions officers, Oasis, Midwest Center for Human Potential, NOW, Profl. Women's Network (chief coordinator 1979-80), Chgo. Mus. Contemporary Art, Field Mus. Natural History, Lincoln Park Zool. Soc., Costeau Soc.; S.W. Suburban Women's Liberation Coalition, TORI Assos. Internat., Chgo. Chamber Choir, Grant Park Symphony Chorus. Episcopalian. Author, editorial cons. self-awareness and personal growth textbooks for S.W. suburban Chgo. jr. coll. system.

PHILLIPS, JOHN MILTON, lawyer; b. Kansas City, Mo., Dec. 16, 1915; s. John and Atha (Dennis) P.; A.B., U. Kans., 1937; J.D., Harvard, 1940; m. Mary Hamilton Bracken, Aug. 29, 1942; children—Mary Bracken, Patricia Ann, Jean Hamilton, John Milton, Daniel Dennis. Admitted to Mo. bar, 1940; asso. firm Stinson, Mag & Fizzell, 1940-46, partner, 1946—. Trustee Philharm. Assn. of Kansas City, pres., 1965-67; former v.p. dir. Am. Symphony Orch. League 1965-67; past bd. dirs. Kansas City chpt. ARC. Served from pvt. to capt. AUS, 1942-46. Mem. Citizens Assn. Kansas City (past pres.), Kansas City Council on Edn. (past pres.), Am. Bar Assn., Mo. Bar Assn., Acad. Social and Polit. Sci., SR, Mil. Order of World Wars, Phi Gamma Delta, Delta Sigma Rho. Republican. Episcopalian. Clubs: Kansas City, Harvard. Home: 311 W 99th St Kansas City MO 64114 Office: 2100 Ten Main Center Kansas City MO 64105

PHILLIPS, JOSHUA, mgmt. cons.; b. N.Y.C., Dec. 15, 1936; s. Eli and Hilda (Peters) P.; B.A. in Chemistry, Williams Coll., 1957; M.B.A., U. Pa., 1959; m. Rheva Betensky, Dec. 24, 1961; 1 son, Jason. Comml. devel. rep. The Nat. Cash Register Co., Dayton, Ohio, 1959-60; corp. bus. devel. specialist Nalco Chem. Co., Chgo., 1960-67; mgmt. cons. A.T. Kearney & Co., Inc., Chgo., 1967-71; exec. v.p., dir. Environ. Recreation Systems, N.Y.C. and San Juan, P.R., 1971-72; asst. to pres. Pioneer & Conco Mortgage Co., Chgo., 1973-74; pres. J. Phillips & Assos., Highland Park, Ill., 1974—; lectr. Am. Mgmt. Assn., Chgo., 1968—. Active Cub Scouts Am., 1973-75. Served with U.S. Army, 1957-58, 61-62. Mem. Am. Chem. Soc., Comml. Devel. Assn., Chem. Mktg. Research Assn., Midwest Chem. Mktg. Assn., Williams, Wharton Grad. Sch. alumni assns., Phi Sigma Kappa. Club: Deer Creek Racquet (Highland Park). Address: 1725 Northland Ave Highland Park IL 60035

PHILLIPS, LEO DONOVAN, real estate developer; b. Phila., May 7, 1936; s. Leo E. and Helen E. (Egan) P.; student Georgetown U., 1954-57; B.S. in Econs. and Polit. Sci., Xavier U., 1959; married, Feb. 27, 1965; children—Michael, Cara. Methods engr. Gen. Motors Corp., Detroit, 1959-63; pres. Fin. Planning Services, Birmingham, Mich., 1963-73; mng. partner Kern Property Assos. Bloomfield Hills, Mich., 1973-76; developer and gen. partner Lone Pine Office Bldg. and Lone Pine/Bloomfield Office Center, Bloomfield Hills, 1976—; propr., pres. Leo D. Phillips & Co., Bloomfield Hills, 1975—. Mem. Urban Land Inst., Builder Owners Mgrs. Assn. of Detroit, Fraternal Order of Police. Republican. Roman Catholic. Club: Optimist. Home: 1004 Wimbleton St Birmingham MI 48008 Office: 525 N Woodward Bloomfield Hills MI 48013

PHILLIPS, MARGARET JOSEPHINE, educator, lectr., calligrapher; b. Sandusky, Ohio, Mar. 19, 1943; d. Armenio and Lidia (Arduini) Phillips; B.S., Bowling Green State U., 1965; M.A., George Washington U., 1969; postgrad. Firelands Coll., part-time. Tchr. 6th grade Randolph Village Elementary Sch., Landover, Md., 1965-68, tchr. learning disabilities, 1968-69; tchr. 6th grade Bataan Elementary Sch., Port Clinton, Ohio, 1969-70; tchr. learning disabilities Portage Elementary Sch., Gypsum, Ohio, 1970-77; tchr. English, Port Clinton High Sch., 1977—. Mem. governing bd. Tri-County Vol. Counselors, Inc.; trustee Vol. Probation Officers, Inc.; v.p. Immaculate Conception Catholic Sch. Bd., 1978-81. Mem. Nat. Council Tchrs. English, N.W. Ohio, Ohio edn. assns., AAUW (2d v.p. 1976-78), George Washington U. Gen. Alumni Assn., Am. Fedn. Tchrs., Bowling Green State U. Found., Port Clinton C. of C., Delta Kappa Gamma. Democrat. Roman Catholic. Home: 311 11th St Port Clinton OH 43452 Office: Port Clinton High Sch 821 Jefferson St Port Clinton OH 43452

PHILLIPS, MICHAEL DEON, state ofcl.; b. Fairfield, Ill., June 13, 1951; s. Martin T. and Cora J. Phillips; B.S., M.S., Central Mo. State U., 1978. Indsl. safety cons. State of Ill., Chgo., 1979—. Mem. Am. Soc. Safety Engrs. Republican. Baptist. Office: Dept Indsl Safety State of Ill 160 N LaSalle St Chicago IL 60601

PHILLIPS, NORA COLLINS, educator; b. Nashville, Oct. 14, 1934; d. Nathan Sherlockree and Katherine Anne (Toy) Collins; B.S., Akron U., 1955, postgrad., 1975; M.S. in Supervision, Kent State U., 1978; m. Leonard E. Phillips, July 7, 1955; children—Katherine, Kimberly. Tchr., parochial schs., Akron, Ohio, 1956-66; substitute tchr., public and parochial schs., 1966-68; Akron, 1970-74; head start tchr. Akron, 1974; adminstr. Edgewood Day Care Center for emotionally disturbed children, tchr. sci. and English to learning ltd. Public Schs., Canton, Ohio, 1975—; worker Census Bur., 1979-80. Mem. NAACP, Canton Profl. Educators Assn., Exceptional Children Scholarship Com., Delta Sigma Theta, Iota Phi Lambda. Home: 872 Packard Dr Akron OH 44320 Office: 521 W Tuscarawas St Canton OH 44702

PHILLIPS, PHILIP KAY, iron and steel products mfg. co. exec.; b. Kansas City, Mo., Jan. 3, 1933; s. Ernest Lloyd and Mildred Blanche (Moser) P.; B.A., Bob Jones U., Greenville, S.C., 1958; postgrad. Central Mo. State U., 1977-78; m. Constance Diana Lucas, June 12, 1955; children—John Allen, David Lee, Stephen Philip, Daniel Paul, Joy Christine. Ordained minister Baptist Ch., 1959; pastor Mt. Moriah Baptist Ch., Clarksburg, Mo. 1958-59; security officer Mo. Dept. Corrections, Jefferson City, Mo., 1959-64; field mgr. office Darby Corp. and Piping Contractors Inc., Kansas City, Kans., 1965-72, safety and security dir. Darby Corp. and Leavenworth Steel Inc., Kansas City, 1972—. Mem. planning com. Kans. Gov.'s Indsl. Safety and Health Conf., 1977-78, chmn. mfg. sect., 1978. Mem. Nat. Safety Council, Nat. Safety Mgmt. Soc., Am. Soc. Safety Engrs. (chpt. exec. com. 1980-81, treas. chpt. 1981—), Kans. Safety Assn. (v.p., mem. exec. com. 1979-80). Home: 3205 NE 66th St Gladstone MO 64119 Office: Darby Corp and Leavenworth Steel Inc 1st and Walker Sts Kansas City KS 66110

PHILLIPS, RICHARD MILES, machine tools co. exec.; b. Akron, Ohio, May 11, 1935; s. Wilmer Miles and Thelma Evelyn (Cooper) P.; student U. Akron, 1957-58, Pierce Coll., 1964-65; m. Merida M. Vough, July 4, 1953; children—Steven Miles, Michael Richard. Pres., chmn. bd. Phillips Precision Drilling Systems Inc., Tallmadge, Ohio, 1971-78, Three/Phase Electronics Corp., Kent, Ohio, 1975-78, Phillips Indsl. Properties Inc., Kent, 1974—, Software & Computer Service Inc., Ravenna, 1975-78, MSM Leasing & Sales, Stow, Ohio, 1975—, Phillips Precision Drilling Systems, Tallmadge, Ohio, 1979—. Chmn., Republican Party City of Stow, Ohio, 1972-73. Served with AUS, 1952-56. Mem. Stow Jaycees (pres. 1957-58), Am. Soc. Metals, Am. Soc. Tool Mfg. Engrs. Home: 3247 Patty Ann St Stow OH 44224 Office: PO Box 234 239 West Ave Tallmadge OH 44278

PHILLIPS, TERRY LEMOINE, elec. engr.; b. Washington, July 27, 1938; s. Clifford LeMoin and Dorothy Louise (Schuman) P.; B.S., Purdue U., 1964, M.S., 1966; m. Lynne Ann Bruce, Aug. 12, 1962; children—Susan Rae, Stephen Kirk. Asso. program leader, data processing Purdue U. Lab. Applications of Remote Sensing, West Lafayette, 1966-71, program leader, 1971-74, dep. dir., 1974—; cons. AID, Computer Scis. Corp. Scoutmaster, explorer adviser Boy Scouts Am.; sports coordinator, youth sports, Battleground, Ind.; elder, deacon Presbyterian Ch. Served with USN, 1956-59. Mem. IEEE (sr.), Assn. Computing Machinery, Data Processing Mgmt. Assn. (co-founder, v.p., pres. Sagamore chpt.), Tau Beta Pi, Eta Kappa Nu. Club: Rotary (dir., treas.). Home: 1522 E 600 N West Lafayette IN 47906 Office: 1220 Potter Dr West Lafayette IN 47906

PHILLIPS, VEL, state ofcl.; b. Milw, Feb. 18, 1924; d. Russell Lowell and Thelma (Payne) Rodgers; B.S., Howard U., 1946; LL.B., U. Wis., 1951; m. W. Dale Phillips, Nov. 7, 1947; children—Dale Franklin, Michael Damon. Admitted to Wis. bar, practiced in Milw.; legislator Milw. Common Council; judge br. 13 Milw. County Children's Ct.; lectr. dept. Afro-Am. studies U. Wis.-Milw.; vis. prof. U. Wis. Law Sch., Carroll Coll., Waukesha, Wis.; now sec. of state State of Wis., Madison. Recipient Jr. Achievement award, 1957, Milw. Star award, 1967, Woman of Yr. award Milw. Sentinel, 1967, Alumni Achievement award Howard U., 1960, numerous others. Mem. Wis. Bar Assn., Milw. Bar Assn., Nat. Council Juvenile Ct. Judges, Milw. Council on Alcoholism (dir.), Day Care and Child Devel. Council Am., NAACP (dir.), AAUW. Democrat. Office: 244 W Washington Ave Madison WI 53702*

PHILLIPS, WALLY, radio announcer; ed. Schuster-Martin Sch. Drama; children—Holly, Todd, Jennifer. TV and radio personality stas. WJEF, Grand Rapids, Mich., 1947, WSAI, Cin., 1948-50, WCPO, Cin., 1950-52, WLW, Cin., 1952-56, WGN, Chgo., 1956—. Served with USAAF, World War II. Office: 2501 Bradley Pl Chicago IL 60618

PHILLIPS, WAYNE WOODROW, II, lawyer; b. Norwalk, Ohio, Sept. 14, 1945; s. Wayne Woodrow and Iverna Martha (Sherman) P.; B.A., Ohio No. U., 1967, J.D., 1972; m. Patricia Smith, Jan. 10, 1981. Admitted to Ohio bar, 1972, Ind. bar, 1973; acct. Edward R. Moyer, C.P.A., Bellevue, Ohio, 1967-70; tax acct. Kern, Linnemeier & Co., C.P.A.'s, Ft. Wayne, Ind., 1972-74; partner firm Stubbins, Phillips & Co., Zanesville, Ohio, 1974—; dir. Killbuck Inc., Buckeye Water Service, Buckeye Well Surveys, Inc. Chmn. bd. dirs. Zanesville Goodwill Industries, 1976—; treas. Friends of the Library, Zanesville, 1976-77. Named Zanesville Citizen of the Month, May, 1977. Mem. Am. Bar Assn., Ohio State Bar Assn., Ind. State Bar Assn., Muskingum County Bar Assn., Ohio Soc. C.P.A.'s, Am. Inst. C.P.A.'s, Am. Assn. Atty-C.P.A.'s, Ohio Oil and Gas Assn, Zanesville Jaycees (treas. 1975-76, pres. 1976-77), Ohio Jaycees (asst. treas. 1977-78, treas. 1978-79; senator). Republican. Episcopalian. Clubs: Zanesville Quarterback (treas. 1978-81), Mason. Home: 260 Skyline Dr Zanesville OH 43701 Office: 925 Military Rd Zanesville OH 43701

PHILLIPS, WILLIAM GEORGE, business exec.; b. Cleve., Mar. 3, 1920; s. Edward George and Ina Marie (Cottle) P.; A.B., Antioch Coll., 1942; m. Laverne Anne Evenden, Aug. 7, 1943; children—Karen Anne (Mrs. David F. Berry), Connie Allynette (Mrs. Richard Tressel), Scott William. Pub. accountant Price Waterhouse & Co., Cleve., 1945-48; tax accountant Glidden Co., Cleve., 1948-52, asst. treas., 1952, treas., dir., 1953-67, adminstrv. v.p., 1963-64, pres., 1964-67, chief exec. officer, 1967, pres. Glidden-Durkee div. SCM Corp., 1967-68; pres., chief exec. officer Internat. Multifoods Corp. (formerly Internat. Milling), Mpls., 1968-70, chmn. bd., 1970—; dep. chmn. Mpls. Fed. Res. Bank, 1979-82, chmn., 1982—, also dir.; dir. Soo Line R.R. Co., N. Am. Life and Casualty Co., Firestone Tire & Rubber Co., No. States Power Co. Bd. overseers U. Minn. Coll. Bus. Adminstrn.; nat. corp. adv. bd. United Negro Coll. Fund; exec. com. U.S.-Iran Joint Bus. Council; adv. bd. Nat. Alliance Businessmen; bd. dirs. Mpls. Downtown Devel. Corp., Minn. State Council on Econ. Edn.; mem. pres.'s adv. bd. Am. Diabetes Assn.; adv. bd. Inst. Internat. Edn.; trustee Hamline U., 1979—; bd. dirs. Mpls. Found.; trustee Mpls. Soc. Fine Arts, Nat. Jewish Hosp. at Denver, Ednl. Research Council Am. Served to lt., inf. AUS, 1942-45. Mem. Conf. Bd., U.S. C. of C. (dir., mem. U.S.-Can. com., exec. com., regional v.p. Northwestern region), Ohio Soc. C.P.A.s, Grocery Mfrs. Am. (dir.), Conf. Bd. Mem. Community Ch. Clubs: Lafayette, Minneapolis (bd. govs.), Woodhill Country. Home: 2610 W Lafayette Rd Excelsior MN 55331 Office: 1200 Multifoods Bldg Minneapolis MN 55402

PHILPOTT, LARRY LA FAYETTE, horn player; b. Alma, Ark., Apr. 5, 1937; s. Lester and Rena (Owens) P.; B.S., Ga. So. Coll., 1962; Mus.M., Butler U., 1972; m. Elise Robichaud, Nov. 24, 1962; Daniel. Mem. N.C. Symphony, 1960, Savannah (Ga.) Symphony, L'Orchestre Symphonique de Quebec (Que., Can.), 1962-64; prin. horn player Indpls. Symphony Orch., 1964—, Flagstaff Summer Festival, 1968—; instr. in horn Butler U., De Pauw U.; artist in-residence Ind.-Purdue Indpls.; appeared with Am. Shakespeare Theatre, summer 1965, Charlottetown Festival, summers 1967-68. Served with USN, 1956-60. Mem. Internat. Horn Soc., Coll. Music Soc., Am. Fedn. Musicians, Internat. Conf. Symphony and Opera Musicians, Phi Mu Alpha Sinfonia. Home: 740 Spring Mill Ln Indianapolis IN 46240 Office: Indpls Symphony 4600 Sunset Ave Indianapolis IN 46208

PHIPPS, RENEE ELIZABETH, mfg. co. ofcl.; b. Oceanside, Calif., Sept. 2, 1951; d. Norman H. and Frances M. P.; B.S., Auburn U., 1973. Jr. analyst Allis-Chalmers Corp., Wichita Falls, Tex., 1973, scheduling supr., 1973-74, programmer analyst, Jackson, Miss., 1974-75, sr. programmer analyst, 1975-76, supr. coll. relations and career devel., Milw., 1976—. Mem. Nat. Soc. Women Engrs. (pres. Milw. sect. 1979-80), So. Coll. Placement Assn., Rocky Mt. Coll. Placement Assn., Midwest Coll. Placement Assn., Wis. Career Planning and Placement Assn., Auburn Alumni Assn. Roman Catholic. Office: 1205 S 70th St West Allis WI 53214

PHOENIX, NANCY MAE, human services adminstr.; b. Appleton, Wis., Nov. 25, 1951; d. Edward Peter and Eunice Margaret (Schmeichel) Jochman; grad. public adminstrn. U. Wis., Green Bay, 1979. Staff asst., public relations coordinator Youth Resources Council, Green Bay, Wis., 1977-78; project asst., fiscal adminstr., youth advocate Youth Devel. Tng. Project, Youth Resources Council and Wis. Assn. for Youth, 1978; dir. Youth Resources Council of Brown County, Inc., Green Bay, 1978-80, Vol. Action Center, 1980—; cons. Assos. Community Tng., Inc., 1979—. Pres., N.E. Neighborhood Assn., 1976-78, treas., 1979; v.p. Wis. Assn. Vols. in Adult and Juvenile Justice, 1978; bd. dirs. Wis. Assn. for Youth, 1978, Early Childhood Project of Brown County, 1978-80, Juvenile Justice Personnel Devel. Center, 1978; chmn. Neighborhood Preservation Commn., 1976-78; sec. Teen Involvement and Leadership Tng., Inc., 1978-80; v.p. Council United Way Agys., 1981, pres., 1982; sec. N.E. Wis. Assn. Vol. Coordinators, 1981. Recipient Environ. award of Year, U. Wis., Green Bay, 1971. Mem. Am. Soc. Public Adminstrn., LWV. Home: 1360 E Mason St Green Bay WI 54301

PIATT, WILLIAM MAC-A-CHEEK, curator; b. West Liberty, Ohio, Sept. 12, 1914; s. John MacA Cheek and Kathryn (Sullivan) P.; student U. Dayton, 1947-48; m. Frances Monahan, Apr. 6, 1942; children—William Mac-a-Cheek II, Margaret (Mrs. P.J. Eckert). With State Capitol Ins. N.C., 1946-47, Gen. Foods Corp., Dayton, Ohio, 1947-48; curator, co-owner Piatt Castle, West Liberty, 1948—. Co-chmn. Ohio Sesquicentennial for West Liberty, 1953, Sesquicentennian, 1967. Served with M.C., AUS, 1938-46. Decorated Bronze Star, Purple Heart. Mem. DAV, Am. Legion (post service officer), VFW, Ohio Travel Council (charter mem., dir., recipient Paul Sherlock award 1977), Tecumseh Tourist Council (founding pres. 1971), Logan County Tourist Assn. (founder 1971), West Liberty Bus. Assn., Bellefonatine C. of C. (dir. tourist div. 1965-71), Discover Am. Travel Orgn., 40 and 8. Roman Catholic. Clubs: K.C. (4 deg.), Lions. Address: RD 2 West Liberty OH 43357

PICCIONE, JAMES JOSEPH, food co. exec.; b. Columbus, Ohio, Oct. 16, 1938; s. James R. and Rose Marie (Gerardi) P.; student public schs., Columbus; m. Barbara E. Thompson, Mar. 18, 1957; children—Toni Maria, Vicki Lynn, Joseph James, Juli Anne. With Schiffs Shoe Co., Columbus, 1953-57; sales mgr. O.G. Sandbo Co., Columbus, 1957-67; pres., dir. Gage Foods, Melrose Park, Ill., 1967—, Dale Foods, Melrose Park, 1972—; pres. Cap Chem. Co., Melrose Park, 1979—; dir. Capitol Food Industries, Chgo. Residence asst. Devonshire Civic Assn., 1961-62. Served with USN, 1956. Mem. Am. Camping Assn., Am. Sch. Food Service Assn., Chgo. C. of C., Round Table Club, 100,000 Club. Republican. Roman Catholic. Office: 1501 N 31st Ave Melrose Park IL 60160

PICKENS, ROBERT BRUCE, bus. exec.; b. Uniontown, Pa., May 20, 1926; s. Joseph Abraham and Margaret Gertrude (Brown) P.; B.S. in Bus. Adminstrn., Waynesburg Coll., 1950; m. Mary Ellen Evans, Sept. 9, 1950; children—Laura Gail Pickens Martin, Rachel Diane, David Bruce. Vice pres., dir. Home Bottle Gas Corp., Uniontown, Pa., 1950-51; jr. accountant Tenney & Co., Uniontown, 1951-52, sr. accountant, 1952-56; mgr. of reports budgets and procedures Hosp. Service Assn. Western Pa., Pitts., 1956-57; auditor and analysis officer U. Pitts., 1957-58; sr. accountant Eugene A. Conniff Co., Pitts., 1958-59; mgr. Sheppard & Co., Pitts., 1959-63; supr. Alexander Grant & Co., Chgo., 1963-65; asst. to the treas. CTS Corp., Elkhart, Ind., 1965, gen. auditor, 1965-66, controller, 1966-81, cons., 1981—. Served with AC U.S. Army, 1944-45. C.P.A., Pa., Ill., Ind. Mem. Accounting Research Assn., Am., Pa. insts. C.P.A.'s, Ill. Soc. C.P.A.'s Ind. Assn. C.P.A.'s. Republican. Presbyterian. Home: 3322 Calumet Ave Elkhart IN 46514 Office: 905 N West Blvd Elkhart IN 46514

PICKERING, ALAN JAY, assn. exec.; b. Joplin, Mo., Mar. 21, 1928; s. Walter Roscoe and Evelyn Faye (Ebenstein) P.; student U. Colo., 1946, Joplin Jr. Coll., 1947; B.S., U. Kan., 1949; M.Div., McCormick Sem., U. Chgo., 1952; Ph.D., Hebrew Union Coll., 1956; m. M. Kay McCollough, July 2, 1980; children by previous marriage—Nancy, Keith, Scott; stepchildren—Cari, Christi. Ordained to ministry, Presbyn. Ch., 1952; minister Ladoga (Ind.) Presbyn. Ch., 1952, Venice Presbyn. Ch., Ross, Ohio, 1952-56; asso. dir. United Ministries in Higher Edn., Lawrence, Kans., 1957-59, dir., U. Nebr., Lincoln, 1960-70; pres. Echo Air Taxi Corp., Lawrence, Kans., 1957-62; prof. comparative religion U. Kans., 1957-60, U. Nebr. Sch. Religion, 1960-70; career devel. cons., nat. bd. YMCA, Mpls., 1970-75; region asso. for career devel., fiscal and personnel mgmt. Mid-Am. Region of YMCA's, Mpls., 1975-80, dep. region exec., 1974-80; nat. tng. mgr. YMCA in U.S.A., Rosemont, Ill., 1980—; community faculty Met. State U., Mpls., 1976-80; cons. Citizens Long-Range Planning Com., Bloomington Public Schs., 1978-79. Pres., Center for Performing Social Scis., Mpls., 1975-80. Served with USN, 1945-46. Louis M. Rabinowitz Interfaith fellow, 1952-56; recipient Wis. YMCA Outstanding Service award, 1980, many others. Mem. Assn. Profl. Dirs. YMCA's, Acad. Cert. Profl. Dirs. of YMCA's in U.S.A., Am. Soc. Tng. and Devel., Am. Mgmt. Assn., Am. Radio Relay League. Clubs: Metro Area Repeater Assn., Twin City FM. Book rev. editor Perspective Mag., 1978—; contbr. articles to profl. jours. Office: 6400 Shafer Ct Suite 175 Rosemont IL 60018

PICKERING, JOSEPH RANDALL, life ins. co. exec.; b. Topeka, June 21, 1924; s. Joseph Walter and Nina (Kelley) P.; B.S. in Bus. Adminstrn., U. Calif., Berkeley, 1950; postgrad. U. Man. (Can.), 1950-51; m. Marie Fox, Apr. 22, 1950; children—Jeanne, Randall, Nina, Roger. Actuarial asst. Prudential Ins. Co., 1951-53; asst. dir. Mut. of N.Y., 1953-61; with IDS Life Ins. Co., Mpls., 1961—, exec. v.p., 1970-79, chief actuary, 1975, pres., 1979—. Served with USMCR, 1942-45. Fellow Soc. Actuaries; mem. Am. Acad. Actuaries (charter mem.), Am. Council Life Ins. (dir. 1981—). Club: Twin Cities Actuarial. Office: IDS Life Ins Co IDS Tower Minneapolis MN 55402

PICKETT, FLOYD CARL, ins. co. exec., cons.; b. Des Moines, Sept. 21, 1905; s. William Carl and Barbara (Kronmueller) P.; student public schs., Des Moines; m. Luella C. Peterson, Aug. 1, 1928; children—Barbara Lue, David Floyd. Clerical and claims examiner So. Surety Co., Des Moines, 1922-28, St. Louis, 1928-30, bond claims examiner, N.Y.C., 1930-32; claims examiner liquidation bur. N.Y. State Ins. Dept., N.Y.C., 1932-37; dept. mgr. Home Ins. Co., N.Y.C., 1937-65; v.p. Excel Mortgage Ins. Corp., Bettendorf, Iowa, 1965-74; cons. ins. regulations, Davenport, Iowa, 1974—; 2d v.p. Sovereign Life Ins. Co., Santa Barbara, Calif., 1979—. Mem. Ins. Soc. N.Y., Soc. Fin. Examiners. Presbyterian. Clubs: Hon. Order Blue Goose, Hon. Order Ky. Cols. Contbr. articles to profl. jours. Home and Office: 2501 Jersey Ridge Rd Davenport IA 52803

PICKLE, ROBERT DOUGLAS, lawyer, diversified industry exec.; b. Knoxville, Tenn., May 22, 1937; s. Robert Lee and Beatrice Jewel (Douglas) P.; A.A., Schreiner Mil. Inst., Kerrville, Tex., 1957; B.S. in Bus. Adminstrn., U. Tenn., Knoxville, 1959, J.D., 1961; honor grad. seminar Nat. Def. U., 1979; m. Rosemary Elaine Noser, May 9, 1964. Admitted to Tenn. bar, 1961, Mo. bar, 1964, U.S. Ct. Mil. Appeals bar, 1962, U.S. Supreme Ct., 1970; atty. Brown Shoe Co., Inc., St. Louis, 1963-69, asst. sec., atty., 1969-74; sec., gen. counsel Brown Group, Inc., St. Louis, 1974—; Miltary Acad. Liaison Officer, U.S. Miltary Acad. West Point, N.Y., 1979—; Provisional judge Municipal Ct., Clayton, Mo., summer 1972; chmn. Clayton Region attys. sect., profl. div. United Fund Greater St. Louis Campaign, 1972-73, team capt., 1974—. Served to col. JAG Corps, U.S. Army, 1961-63. Mem. Am., Tenn., Mo., St. Louis County bar assns., Bar Assn. Met. St. Louis, St. Louis Bar Found. (dir. 1979—), Am. Soc. Corp. Secs. (treas. St. Louis regional group 1976-77, sec. 1977-78, v.p. 1978-79, pres. 1979-80), U. Tenn. Gen. Alumni Assn. (pres., dir. St. Louis chpt. 1974-76, 80-82), U.S. Trademark Assn. (dir. 1978—), Tenn. Soc. St. Louis, Scabbard and Blade, Kappa Sigma, Phi Delta Phi, Phi Theta Kappa, Beta Gamma Sigma, Phi Kappa Phi. Republican. Presbyn. Club: University (dir. 1976—, v.p. 1976-77, sec. 1977—) (St. Louis). Home: 214 Topton Way Saint Louis MO 63105 Office: 8400 Maryland Ave Saint Louis MO 63105

PICKMAN, MICHELE DENISE, med./surg. mktg. research co. exec.; b. Columbus, Ohio, Feb. 25, 1947; d. Robert Alan and Louise Theodora (Kahn) Lazar; student Northwestern U., 1969-70; B.A., U. Wis., 1968; m. Steven Pickman, Mar. 18, 1972. Research/teaching asst. dept. psychiatry Northwestern U. Med. Sch., Chgo., 1968-70; sr. project dir. Dietz-Leonhard Corp., Chgo., 1970-75; pres. Pickman & Assos. Med. Mktg., Chgo., 1975—; prin. The Pickman-Klein Group, Chgo.; cons. in field. B'nai B'rith merit scholar, 1964. Mem. Am. Mktg. Assn., Pharm. Mktg. Research Group, Med. Surg. Mktg. Research Group. Home: 1561 Asbury Ave Winnetka IL 60093 Office: 400 N Michigan Ave Chicago IL 60611

PICKUP, LILLIAN ERICKSON, social service adminstr., nurse; b. Joliet, Ill., Aug. 13, 1947; d. Edward Axel and Magda (Anderson) Erickson; R.N., Presbyterian St. Luke's Hosp. Sch. Nursing, Chgo., 1967; certificate Summer Sch. Sch. Alcohol Studies Rutgers U., 1977; children—Kimberlie Ann, Khristie Marie. Staff nurse Lutheran Gen. Hosp., Park Ridge, Ill., 1967-68; acting asst. dir. nursing Fairview Hosp., Chgo., 1968-71, Chgo. Lakeshore Hosp., 1971-73; supr. psychiat. nursing N.E. Community Hosp. on Lake, Chgo., 1973-76; dir. emergency services alcoholism and drug dependance program Luth. Welfare Services Ill., Chgo., 1976—; cons., lectr., condr. seminars on alcoholism; vol. Niles (Ill.) Lions Club Glaucoma Screening, 1970, 71, 75, Niles blood drives, 1973-74. Recipient certificate of appreciation Niles Lions Club, 1970, 71, 75; cert. alcoholism counselor. Mem. Am. Nurses Assn., Ill. Alcoholism, Drug Dependance Assn., Ill. Group Psychotherapy Assn., Ill. Alcoholism Counselors Alliance, Nat. Nurses Assn. on Alcoholism. Presbyterian. Office: 5517 N Kenmore St Chicago IL 60640

PIEART, MARC ALLEN, drug chain co. ofcl.; b. Des Moines, June 17, 1951; s. Donald Allen and Norma Mae (Kenyon) P.; B.B.A., U. Wis., Whitewater, 1973; m. Terry Lynne Lindeman, June 2, 1973; 1 dau., Tracy. Service mgr. Turnstyle div. Osco Drug, Inc., Chgo., 1974-76, liquor mgr., domestics mgr., 1976-77, ops. asst., 1977; electronic point of sale coordinator Osco Drug, Inc., Oak Brook, Ill., 1977-78, mgr. payroll and benefits, 1978—. Tutor disadvantaged children. Lutheran. Home: 1068 Almond Dr Aurora IL 60506 Office: Osco Drug Inc 1818 Swift Dr Oak Brook IL 60521

PIECEWICZ, WALTER MICHAEL, lawyer; b. Concord, Mass., Jan. 27, 1948; s. Benjamin Michael and Cecelia (Makuc) P.; A.B. magna cum laude, Colgate U., 1970; J.D., Columbia U., 1973; m. Anne T. Mikolajczyk, Oct. 28, 1978; 1 dau., Tiffany Anne. Admitted to Ill. bar, 1973; mem. firm Levenfeld, Kanter, Baskes & Lippitz, Chgo., 1973-78, Boodell, Sears, Sugrue, Giambalvo & Crowley, Chgo., 1978—; dir. No. Data Systems, Inc. Mem. Am. Bar Assn., Ill. Bar Assn., Chgo. Bar Assn., Chgo. Estate Planning Council, Internat. Bus. Council, Phi Beta Kappa. Democrat. Roman Catholic. Home: 1103 N Lombard Ave Oak Park IL 60302 Office: Boodell Sears Sugrue Giambalvo & Crowley 69 W Washington St Chicago IL 60602

PIERCE, DANIEL MARSHALL, lawyer, state legislator; b. Chgo., Mar. 31, 1928; s. Hyman A. and Thelma (Udwin) P.; A.B., Harvard U., 1949, LL.B., 1952; m. Rhoda Ann Pierce; children—Andrew, Anthony, Theodore. Admitted to Ill. bar, 1952; asso. Ross, McGowan, Babcock & O'Keefe, Chgo., 1954-59; partner Stebbins & Pierce, Chgo., 1959-66; partner Altheimer & Gray, Chgo., 1966—; mem. Ill. Ho. of Reps., 1964—, now chmn. Ill. Econ. and Fiscal Com., vice chmn. Energy Resources Com. Mem. Ill. Reapportionment Commn., 1963; chmn. renewable energy subcom. Nat. Conf. State Legislatures, 1978—. Democratic state central committeeman, 1962-66, 70—. Bd. dirs. Cove Sch., Evanston, Ill. Served to 1st lt. USAF, 1952-54. Mem. Am., Ill., Chgo. bar assns. Club: Harvard of Chgo. Home: 2756 Oak St Highland Park IL 60035 Office: 1 IBM Plaza Chicago IL 60611

PIERCE, DANNIE EUGENE, ins. co. exec.; b. Mobile, Ala., Dec. 7, 1949; s. Clifton Lee and Margie Lou P.; A.B., Columbus Tech. Inst., 1974; B.S., Franklin U., 1977; m. Beverly Renee Beynon, Aug. 30, 1969. With Jeffrey Mining Co., Columbus, Ohio, 1969-77, systems analyst, 1975-77; sr. systems analyst Acceleration Life Co., Columbus, 1977-79, mgr. systems and programming, 1979-81, spl. projects coordinator, 1981—. Served with U.S. Army; 1970-72; Vietnam. Mem. Assn. Systems Mgmr. (chmn. nominations, awards), Data Processing Mgmt. Assn. (treas.), Digital Equipment Corp. Users Soc. (asso.). Baptist. Home: 5065 Grandon Dr Hilliard OH 43026 Office: 155 E Broad St Columbus OH 43215

PIERCE, DAVID PAUL (DEE), agri-service co. exec.; b. Marion, Ohio, Dec. 22, 1934; s. Donald Paul and Myrtle Ellen (Bonsel) P.; student pub. schs., Marion; m. Janis E. Worthington, June 19, 1955; children—Donald Paul, Deanna Lynn. With E.E. Drumm Nash Sales, 1954-58; self-employed, 1958-60; sales rep. Nickles Bakery, Marion, 1960-63; with Blank's Agri-Service, Marion, 1963—, now v.p., sales mgr. Served with USNR, 1952-54. Mem. Nat. Fertilizer Solutions Assn. Republican. Baptist. Home: 1916 Somerlot Hoffman Rd W Marion OH 43302 Office: Blank's Agri-Service 560 Barks Rd W Marion OH 43302

PIERCE, DONALD FRED, law pub. exec.; b. Granite City, Ill., Feb. 28, 1932; s. Fred Arthur and Agnes Ester (Shier) P.; student U. Ill., 1950-51; B.A. in Bus., Washington U., St. Louis, 1954; children—Donald Fred, Robert Craig. Mgr., Shier & Pierce Builders, Cahokia, Ill., 1954-58; salesman Oliver Parks Realty Co., Caholia, 1958-60; pvt. practice real estate broker, Cahokia, 1960-61; pres. Graham-Pierce Legal Printers, Inc., Fairview Heights, Ill., 1961—. Served with U.S. Army, 1954. Republican. Presbyterian. Club: Exchange (Fairview Heights). Home: 214 Laurel Dr Fairview Heights IL 62208 Office: 2007 Highway 50 W Fairview Heights IL 62208

PIERCE, EDWARD CHARLES, physician, state senator; b. Three Rivers, Mich., Jan. 3, 1930; s. Melvin Charles and Lucille Emily (Bobb) P.; B.A., U. Mich., 1955, M.D., 1959; m. Mary Lee Baisch, Aug. 28, 1954; children—Lynne, Janet, Paul, Amy. Intern, St. Joseph Mercy Hosp., Ann Arbor, Mich., 1959-60; gen. practice medicine, Ann Arbor, 1960-78; mem. Mich. Senate, 1979—. Mem. Ann Arbor City Council, 1964-66. Democrat. Office: Senate Office Bldg Lansing MI 48909*

PIERCE, JEAN WILLIAMS, educator; b. Evergreen Park, Ill., Feb. 4, 1947; d. Raymond Theodore and Elizabeth Dorothy Williams; B.A., Purdue U., 1969; M.A., Northwestern U., 1972, Ph.D., 1976; m. Louis Dean Pierce, Apr. 3, 1971. Tchr., Glen Oak Sch., Glen Ellyn, Ill., 1969-71; asst. prof. Northern Ill. Univ., DeKalb, 1974-80, asso. prof. ednl. psychology, 1980—. No. Ill. U. grantee, 1980-81. Mem. Am. Ednl. Research Assn., Soc. Research Child Devel., Mid-Western Ednl. Research Assn. (sec. 1978-80, publ. editor 1980—). Contbr. articles to profl. jours. Office: Dept of Learning and Devel Northern Ill Univ DeKalb IL 60115

PIERCE, JERRY EARL, pub. co. exec.; b. Hinsdale, Ill., Aug. 3, 1941; s. Earl and Adeline A. (Zaranski) P.; B.S., U. Ill., 1964; m. Carol Louise Martin, Aug. 15, 1964; children—Patricia, Barbara, Linda, Bradley. With R.R. Donnelley & Sons, Chgo., 1964-70; with Western Pub. Co., Racine, Wis., 1970—, nat. pubs. sales mgr., 1975—; pres. Pierce Sale Co., Inc.; v.p., sec. Savers Clubs Am., Inc. Served to 1st lt. U.S. Army, 1968-70. Mem. Printing Industry Am., Sales and Mktg. Execs. Republican. Episcopalian. Clubs: Canterbury Country, Cleve. Advt. Home: 19551 North Park Blvd Shaker Heights OH 44122 Office: 24200 Chagrin Blvd Cleveland OH 44122

PIERCE, RALPH, cons. engr.; b. Chgo., Apr. 14, 1926; s. Charles and Fay (Reznik) P.; B.E.E., Northwestern U., 1946; m. Adrian H. Rosengard, Sept. 3, 1978; children—Marc Fredrick, Deborah Ann, Elizabeth Allison. Test engr. Am. Elec. Heater Co., Detroit, 1946-47; sr. asso. engr. Detroit Edison Co., 1947-52; sec., chief utility engr. George Wagschal Assos., Detroit, 1952-58; sr. partner Pierce, Yee & Assos., Engrs., Detroit, 1958-73; mng. partner Harley Ellington Pierce Yee Assos., 1973—; mem. Dept. Commerce Mission to Yugoslavia. Served to ensign USNR, 1944-46; comdr. Res. ret. Registered profl. engr., Mich., Ind., Ill., Ohio, Ky., N.Y., Washington, Fla., Can. Mem. Nat. Council Engring. Examiners, Nat. Soc. Profl. Engrs., Engring. Soc. Detroit, IEEE, Soc. Coll. and Univ. Planners, Illuminating Engring. Soc., Mich. Soc. Architects (asso.). Home: 5531 Pebbleshire Rd Birmingham MI 48010 Office: 26111 Evergreen Rd Southfield MI 48076

PIERCE, ROBERT HARVEY, state agy. exec.; b. Chgo., Dec. 12, 1927; s. Joseph Claire and Alice (Helfer) P.; B.Arch., Ill. Inst. Tech., 1958; m. Rita Ann Mierle, May 26, 1962 (div. Jan., 1976); children—Jan Scott, Eric Thomas, Todd Christopher. Chief architect Okinawa, Lyon Assos., 1964-69, chief architect Asia, chief engr. Bangkok, 1969-72; project adminstr. Bertrand Goldberg Assos., Chgo., 1972-75; sr. project mgr. Capital Devel. Bd., 1975-76, supr. higher edn., 1976-79, mgr. No. Region ops., 1979—. State of Ill. rep. on Chgo. Constrn. Coordinating Com., 1979—. Bd. dirs. Ada S. McKinley Settlement House, 1957-58. Served with USN, 1946-53. Mem. Am. Inst. Architects, Soc. Am. Mil. Engrs., VFW, Alpha Sigma Phi. Patentee bearing mark timer for use on submarines. Home: 541 W Oakdale Apt 518 Chicago IL 60657 Office: 180 N LaSalle St Suite 320 Chicago IL 60601

PIERCE, SHELBY CRAWFORD, oil co. exec.; b. Port Arthur, Tex., May 26, 1932; s. William Shelby and Iris Mae (Smith) P.; B.S.E.E., Lamar State Coll. Tech., Beaumont, Tex., 1956; student M.I.T. Program for Sr. Execs., 1980; m. Marguerite Ann Grado, Apr. 2, 1954; children—Cynthia Dawn, Melissa Carol. With Amoco Oil Co., 1956—, zone supr., gen. foreman, maintenance, 1961-67, operating supt., 1967-69, coordinator results mgmt., Texas City (Tex.) refinery, 1969-72, dir. results mgmt., corp. hdqrs., Chgo., 1972-75, ops. mgr. refinery, Whiting, Ind., 1975-77, asst. refinery mgr., 1977-79, dir. crude replacement program, Chgo., 1979-81, mgr. refining and transp. engring., 1981—. Fin. chmn. Bay Area council Boy Scouts Am., 1974; chmn. bd., chmn. fin. com. Methodist Ch., 1967-72. Mem. Sigma Tau. Republican. Home: 18840 Loomis Ave Homewood IL 60430 Office: 200 E Randolph Dr Chicago IL 60601

PIERCE-BABA, JAE ANN, occupational therapist; b. Herington, Kans., July 11, 1953; d. Glenn Edward and Shirley May (Locke) Pierce; student Kans. State U., 1971-73; B.S. in Occupational Therapy, U. Kans., 1976. Occupational therapist Univ. Hosps., Madison, Wis., 1975, Crippled Children's Nursery Sch., Kansas City, Mo., 1976, N.Y. U. Med. Center, Goldwater Meml. Hosps., N.Y.C., 1976; head occupational therapist Geriatric/Diversified United, St. Joseph (Mo.) State Hosp., 1976-78; staff occupational therapist Children's Rehab. Unit, Family Guidance Center, St. Joseph, 1978-80; now pvt. practice occupational therapy, Kansas City, Mo.; cons. in field; lectr. in field. Bd. dirs. Mental Health Assn., St. Joseph, Mo., 1977-80. Mem. Assn. for Severely Multihandicapped, Am. Occupational Therapy Assn., Kans. Occupational Therapy Assn., Parents and Children Together, Assn. for Children with Learning Disabilities. Episcopalian. Contbr. articles to profl. jours. Address: 2616 Manhattan St Wichita KS 67204

PIERSON, DAVID LOWELL, orch. mgr.; b. Hamilton, Ohio, Jan. 21, 1949; s. Raymond Charles and Irma Lucille (Vizedom) P.; B.Mus. Edn., Ind. U., 1972, M.A. in Arts Adminstrn., 1976; m. Deboral Pfleeger, June 11, 1977. Music tchr. Lurnen High Sch., Liverpool, N.S.W., Australia, 1972-73; asst. mgr. Dayton Philharm. Orch. Assn., Inc., 1976-77, gen. mgr., 1977—; cons. Ohio Arts Council. Adv. com. music program Career Acad, Dayton Public Schs., 1979-81; bd. deacons Covenant Presbyn. Ch., 1981—. Ind. U. Arts Adminstrn. Program fellow, 1974-76. Mem. Orgn. Ohio Orchs. (dir. 1980), Am. Symphony Orch. League, Ohio Citizens Com. for Arts, Pi Kappa Lambda. Club: Rotary. Home: 515 Southwood St Springfield OH 45504 Office: 125 E First St Dayton OH 45402

PIETREK, ANNE MARY, ednl. coordinator; b. La Crosse, Wis., Aug. 15, 1939; d. Arthur Raymond and Helen Margaret (McGrath) Brisson; grad. St. Francis Sch. Nursing, 1960; m. Francis John Pietrek, Apr. 8, 1961; children—Michael Raymond, Mary Frances. Office nurse Dr. C.F. Meyer and Clinic, Independence, Wis., 1964-70; staff nurse Trempealeau County Health Center, Whitehall, Wis., 1971-72, dir. alcoholism program, 1972-73, inservice and staff devel. coordinator, 1973—; CPR program coordinator Western Wis. Tech. Inst., 1975—. Pres., Independence Parochial Sch. Bd., 1977—. Mem. Am. Soc. Health Edn. and Manpower Tng., Wis. Soc. Health Edn. and Manpower Tng., Am. Nurses Assn., Western Wis. Inservice Educators Assn., LaCrosse Dist. Nurses Assn. (v.p. 1978—). Roman Catholic. Home: 606 Ash St Independence WI 54747 Office: Route 2 Whitehall WI 54773

PIETROFESA, JOHN JOSEPH, educator; b. N.Y.C., Sept. 12, 1940; s. Louis John and Margaret (Proietti) P.; B.E. cum laude, U. Miami, 1961, M.Ed., 1963, Ed.D., 1967; m. Diana Pinto, June 8, 1963; children—John, Paul. Counselor, Dade County (Fla.) pub. schs., 1965-67; faculty Wayne State U., Detroit, 1967—, prof. edn., 1974-77, div. head theoretical and behavioral founds., 1977—; cons. to various schs., hosps. and univs. Served to 1st lt. Mil. Police Corps, AUS, 1963-65. Mem. Am. Psychol. Assn., Am., Mich. personnel and guidance assns., Assn. Counselor Edn. and Supervision, Phi Delta Kappa. Author: The Authentic Counselor, 1971; School Counselor as Professional, 1971; Counseling and Guidance in the Twentieth Century, 1971; Elementary School Guidance and Counseling, 1973; Career Development, 1975; Career Education, 1976; College Student Development, 1977; Counseling: Theory Research and Practice, 1978; editorial bd. Counseling and Values, 1972-75. Home: 2437 Clawson Royal Oak MI 48073 Office: 319 Education Wayne State U Detroit MI 48202

PIETZ, RUDY J., food co. exec.; b. Carmine, Tex., Sept. 4, 1931; s. Rudolph G. and Hertha (Jacob) P.; student Blinn Coll., 1948-49; m. Consuelo Dominguez, Apr. 21, 1971; children—Julia, Laura, Rosemary, Arleen. With Austex div. Frito-Lay, Inc., 1950-65, plant mgr., Conyers, Ga., 1965, with Belle Products div., Houston, 1966-69; plant mgr. Chun King Frozen Food Plant, RJR Foods, Inc., Jackson, Ohio, 1969—. Republican. Episcopalian. Elk, Rotarian. Home: 22 Payne St Jackson OH 45640 Office: 100 E Broadway Jackson OH 45640

PIFER, LEWIS ARTHUR, broadcast engr.; b. Newark, July 15, 1945; s. Lewis Arthur and Mary Ellen (Albee) P.; grad. San Bernardino Valley Coll., 1970; m. Sherry Robbins, Oct. 18, 1969; children—Evertt James, Cynthia Lynn. Master control technician KVCR-TV, San Bernardino, Calif., 1969-70; asst. chief engr. KXFM/KDUO, San Bernardino, 1970; chief engr. KCKC Radio Sta., San Bernardino, 1970-71; chief engr. WMIX AM & FM, Mt. Vernon, Ill., 1971-74; field service engr. Harris Broadcast Products, Quincy, Ill., 1974—. Mem. Soc. Broadcast Engrs., Quincy Jr. C. of C. (service award 1976, dir. 1978-79), Western Ill. Amateur Radio Club, Am. Radio Relay League (life). Home: 1001 N 11th St Quincy IL 62301 Office: PO Box 4290 Quincy IL 62305

PIHERA, LAWRENCE JAMES, advt. agy. exec.; b. Cleve., Jan. 9, 1933; s. Charles and Dorothy P.; student U. Hawaii, Cooper Sch. Art, Cleve. Inst. Art; m. Patricia Dunn, Aug. 22, 1955; children—Lauren, Scott. Advt. mgr. Johnson Rubber Co. and subs., 1957-58; creative dir. Mansfield Advt. (Ohio), 1958-60, G. W. Young Public Relations, Dayton, 1960-70; pres. Phiera Advt. Assos., Inc., Centerville, Ohio, 1970—. Bd. dirs. Centerville Fine Arts Commn. Served with USN. Recipient 1st Place Advt. Writing, 1970, 71, 74, 76, 77, 78. Mem. Soc. Bus. Cons., Art Center Dayton, Dayton Advt. Club, Centerville C. of C. (bd. dirs.). Author: Making of a Winner, 1972; editor McCall Spirit, 1970; architecture critic Instl. Mgmt. mag.; contbr. articles to profl. jours.

PIKAART, LEN, mathematician, educator; b. Nutley, N.J., Jan. 4, 1933; s. Leonard Gascoigne and Janette Theodora (Hendricks) P.; student U.S. Naval Acad., 1952-55; B.A. with distinction, U. Va., 1959, M.Ed., 1960, Ed.D., 1963; m. Constance Natalie Headapohl, Nov. 6, 1954; children—Leonard Frederick, William Edward, Lori Janette, Lucinda Corinne. Tchr. math. jr. and sr. high schs., Arundel County (Md.), 1955-56; sr. research asst. and instr. div. ednl. research U. Va., Charlottesville, 1960-62, instr. div. math. Sch. Engring., 1962-63; asst. prof. math. edn. U. Ga., Athens, 1963-67, head dept. math. edn., 1966-69, asso. prof. math. edn., 1967-71, prof. math. edn., 1971-74, dir. Ednl. Profl. Devel. Act Program for math. suprs., 1968-70, program for doctoral study in math. edn., 1964-74; Robert L. Morton prof. math. edn. Ohio U., Athens, 1974—; cons. to Center for Internat. Math. Edn. Info., U. Chgo., 1968, E.L. Kizziah Co., Rome, Ga., 1965-74, U.S. Office of Edn., 1969-74; participant Internat. Congress in math. edn., Lyon, France, 1969, Berkeley, Calif., 1980. Served to sgt. with arty. U.S. Army, 1956-58. Postdoctoral fellow N.Y. U., 1970-71. Mem. Math. Assn. Am. (cons. com. undergrad. program in math. 1968), Am., Nat., Ohio (pres.-elect 1981—), Ga. (pres. 1972-73) councils tchrs. math., AAUP, Am. Ednl. Research Assn. (steering com. spl. interest group for research in math. edn. 1968-69), Phi Delta Kappa (pres. U. Ga. chpt. 1967-68, del. biennial council 1967, 69). Clubs: Kiwanis, Athens Aero (pres. 1980-82). Author: (with K. J. Travers) Mathematics Teaching, 1977; asst. editor The Arithmetic Tchr., 1967-70; contbr. articles on edn. in math. to profl. pubs. Home: 27 Utah Pl Athens OH 45701 Office: McCracken Hall Ohio U Athens OH 45701

PIKARSKY, MILTON, transp. ofcl.; b. N.Y.C., Mar. 28, 1924; s. Abraham J. and Celia (Kaufman) P.; B.C.E., CCNY, 1944; postgrad. Ill. Inst. Tech., 1947-56, M.S. in Civil Engring., 1969; postgrad. DePaul U., 1959-60; children—Joel Jay, Amy Jo. Asst. engr. N.Y.C. R.R., Chgo., 1944-57; cons. civil engr., Chgo., Gary, Ind., Dearborn, Mich., 1955-60; engr. Dept. Pub. Works, Chgo., 1960-64, commr., 1964-73; chmn. Chgo. Transit Authority, 1973-75; chmn. Regional Transit Authority (RTA), Chgo., 1975—; dir. transp. research Research Inst., Ill. Inst. Tech., 1979—, research prof., 1979—; adj. prof. U. Ill.; mem. steering com. Nat. League of Cities' Com. on Transp. and Communication, 1968; mem. steering com. Urban Mass Transp. Adv. Council, U.S. Dept. Transp.; mem. Engrs. Joint Council Panel on Tech. Assessment, 1973; mem. transp. adv. com. Fed. Energy Adminstrn., 1976; nat. adv. com. Inst. Aviation, U. Ill., 1976; mem. adv. com. basic transp. research studies Mass. Inst. Tech. Center Transp. Studies; mem. adv. council to dept. civil and urban engring. U. Pa.; mem. steering com. Nat. Energy Users Conf. for Transp.; mem. com. for transit and hwy. funding Chgo. Assn. Commerce and Industry; sec.-treas. Council Univ. Transp. Centers; cons. to Govt. Argentina for Buenos Aires Met. Rys.; rep. edn. div. Public Transit Adv. Council; mem. group council Transp. Research Bd. Trustee Children's World Montessori Sch. Park Ridge; mem. indsl. adv. com. Coll. Engring., U. Ill. Named Chicagoan of Year in Architecture and Engring., Chgo. Jr. Assn. Commerce and Industry, 1967; Outstanding Engring. award for Chgo. Central Filtration Plant, Nat. Soc. Profl. Engrs.; named One of Top 10 Pub. Works Men-of-Year, 1969; Townsend Harris medal City Coll. N.Y., 1969; Chgo.'s Outstanding Leader in Transp. award Soc. of Little Flower, 1969. Fellow ASCE (Civil Govt. award 1973), Am. Assn. Advancement of Sci.; mem. Nat., Ill. socs. profl. engrs., Am. Ry. Engring. Assn., Am. Road Builders Assn. (chmn. council urban mass transp.), Inst. for Rapid Transit (com. on govt. affairs), Western Soc. Engrs. (past pres.), Transp. Research Bd. (exec. com., chmn.), Nat. Acad. Engring. (BART impact com., com. pub. engring. policy, civil engring. peer com.), Am. Public Transit Assn., Chi Epsilon, Lambda Alpha. Clubs: Econ., Chgo. Engrs., Ground Hog (pres.). Office: 10 W 35th St Chicago IL 60616

PIKE, LENNOX ALEXANDER, physician; b. Belize City, Belize, July 19, 1936; came to U.S., 1977; s. Lennox Alexander and Rosenell Adella (Arnold) Pike; M.B.B.S., U. London, 1961; D.P.H., U. Toronto (Ont., Can.), 1972; m. Margaret Euphemia Ewing, Dec. 12, 1964; children—Karen Michelle, Sherilyn Ann, Lisa Alexandra. Intern, Univ. Coll. W.I., Kingston, Jamaica, 1961; chief anesthesiology, Belize City Hosp., 1964-72, chief of staff, 1970-72; chief med. office Govt. of Belize, 1972-77; chief resident physician Kirwood Gen. Hosp., Detroit, 1978-79; med. dir. Wilshire Clinic, Detroit, 1979—; prof. tropical medicine Mich. State U. in Belize, 1973-74. Chmn. med. com. Mich./Belize Partners of the Ams., 1978—. Pan Am. Health Orgn./WHO fellow, 1971-72; Commonwealth fellow, 1968-69. Fellow Royal Coll. Surgeons (Eng.); mem. Brit. Med. Assn., Am. Public Health Assn., AMA, Am. Acad. Family Physicians. Club: Birmingham Racquet. Composer: Coronation March, 1973; Almighty Father With Thy Hand, 1960. Home: 27166 Selkirk St Southfield MI 48076 Office: 746 Collingwood St Detroit MI 48202

PIKE, ROBERT WILLIAM, communication cons. co. exec.; b. Chgo., Apr. 22, 1947; s. Louis Gustav and Patricia May (Svenson) P.; B.A. in Pastoral Tng., Moody Bible Inst., Chgo., 1970. Licensed to preach, 1970; asst. pastor Indian Hill Chapel, Ingleside, Ill., 1967-70; sr. v.p. Master Edn. Industries, Denver, 1970-73; v.p. Personal Dynamics, Inc., Mpls., 1974-79; adminstr. U. LaVerne (Calif.), 1975-79; pres. Profl. Edn. Inst., Mpls., 1979—; condr. leadership devel. programs for businesses, instns., colls. and univs., 1974—; prin. Communication Cons., 1979—; dir. profl. edn. programs Coll. St. Scholastica, Duluth, Minn., 1979-80. Mem. adv. bd. Christian Berets, 1977—; trustee Chapel Hill (Minn.) Acad., 1977-80. Served with USNR, 1965-72. Recipient numerous service awards. Mem. Am. Soc. Tng. and Devel. (chmn. tng. with religious assn. spl. interest group 1977, 79, nat. dir. 1980-81), Salesman With A Purpose (1st v.p. S.E. Denver chpt. 1974), Am. Personnel and Guidance Assn., Nat. Assn. Evangelicals. Club: Calhoun Beach. Author: The Psychology of Selling; The Psychology of Management; author seminar texts on leadership, attitudes, motivation, others; contbr. articles to profl. publs. Home: 939 11th Ave S Hopkins MN 55343 Office: 5620 Lincoln Dr Edina MN 55436

PILAS (PILAS-WOOD), PEGGY, advt. agy. exec.; b. Chgo., July 2, 1950; d. James Paul and Carol Pilas; B.S., U. Tex., 1972; M.S.J., Northwestern U., 1974; m. Arthur M. Wood, Mar. 15, 1980. Account exec. Young & Rubicam Inc., N.Y.C., 1974-75; TV cons. White House, Washington, 1975-76; account exec. J. Walter Thompson, Chgo., 1977-78, account supr., 1978—; mktg. cons. to polit. campaigns. Mem. exec. bd. 43d Ward Republican Orgn., Chgo., 1979, Flexible Careers, Chgo., 1980; bd. dirs. Landmark Preservation Council Ill., 1982. Recipient cert. leadership YWCA Met. Chgo., 1980, named Outstanding Young Woman of Yr., 1978. Mem. Young Execs. Club, Women's Advt. Club Chgo., Republican Assos. Office: J Walter Thompson 875 N Michigan Ave Chicago IL 60611

PILENZO, RONALD COSMO, assn. exec.; b. Detroit, Oct. 7, 1928; s. Angelo and Mary Pilenzo; B.B.A. cum laude, U. Detroit, 1961, M.B.A., 1964; m. Lorna Gloria Polimadei, Oct. 29, 1955; children—Paula Leslie, Christopher Ronald. Various exec. positions Ford Motor Co., 1956-67; prin. mgmt. cons. R.E. Danto Assos., Inc., Detroit, 1967-68; corp. personnel dir. Allied Supermarkets, Inc., Detroit, 1968-71; dir. manpower and orgn. devel. Evans Products Co., Boston, Mass., 1971-75; corp. dir. compensation and mgmt. devel. Internat. Multifoods Corp., Mpls., 1975-80; pres., chief exec. officer Am. Soc. Personnel Adminstrn., Berea, Ohio, 1980—. guest lectr. profl. socs. and bus. groups. Served with USAF, 1950-54. Mem. Am. Soc. Personnel Adminstrn. (v.p. profl. services 1979-80; Outstanding Nat. Com. Chmn. 1977, 78, 79, dir. 1977-80), Am. Soc. Assn. Execs., World Fedn. Personnel Mgmt. Assns., Am. Compensation Assn., Am. Soc. Tng. and Devel. Club: Capitol Hill (Washington). Contbr. articles on personnel adminstrn. to profl. publs.; reviewer career lit. Home: 333 Tanglewood Ln Bay Village OH 44140 Office: 30 Park Dr Berea OH 44017

PILLA, ANTHONY MICHAEL, bishop; b. Cleve., Nov. 12, 1932; s. George and Libera (Nista) P.; student St. Gregory Coll. Sem., 1952-53, Borromeo Coll. Sem., 1955, St. Mary Sem., 1954, 56-59; B.A. in Philosophy, John Carroll U., Cleve., 1961, M.A. in History, 1967. Ordained priest Roman Catholic Ch., 1959; asso. St. Bartholomew Parish, Middleburg Heights, Ohio, 1959-60; prof. Borromeo Sem., Wickliffe, Ohio, 1960-72, rector-pres., 1972-75; mem. Diocese Cleve. Liturgical Commn., 1964-69, asst. dir., 1969-72; sec. for services to clergy and religious personnel Diocese Cleve., 1975-79; titular bishop of Scardona, aux. bishop of Cleve. and vicar Eastern region Diocese of Cleve., 1979, apostolic adminstr. Diocese, 1980, bishop of Cleve., 1981—; trustee Borromeo Sem., 1975-79; trustee, mem. bd. overseers St. Mary Sem., 1975-79; adv. bd. permanent diaconate program Diocese of Cleve., 1975-79, mem. hospitalization and ins. bd., 1979. Trustee, Cath. U., 1981—; bd. dirs. Cath. Communications Found., 1981—. Mem. Nat. Cath. Edn. Assn. (dir. 1972-75), U.S. Cath. Conf., Nat. Conf. Cath. Bishops, Cath. Conf. Ohio. Address: 1027 Superior Ave Cleveland OH 44114

PILLIOD, CHARLES JULE, JR., rubber co. exec.; b. Cuyahoga Falls, Ohio, Oct. 20, 1918; s. Charles Jule and Julia (Sullivan) P.; student Muskigum Coll., 1937-38, Kent State U., 1938-40; m. Marie Elizabeth Jacobs, June 15, 1946; children—Christine Marie Pilliod Earhart, Charles Jule, Mark Alan, Stephen Matthew, Renee Elizabeth. With prodn. squadron Goodyear Tire & Rubber Co. 1941; salesman Goodyear Internat. Corp., 1945-47, mgr., dir. Panama, field rep. Costa Rica, 1947-51, field rep., Chile, Bolivia, Peru, 1951-53, asst. sales mgr., Peru, 1953, sales mgr., Colombia, 1954-56, comml. mgr., Brazil, 1956-59, mng. dir., Brazil, 1959-63, sales dir., Eng., 1963-64, mng. dir., Eng., 1964-66, dir. ops., Akron, Ohio, 1966-67, v.p., 1967-71, pres., 1971-72; v.p. Goodyear Tire & Rubber Co., 1971, exec. v.p., dir., 1971-72, pres., 1972-74, chmn. bd., 1974— chief exec. officer, 1973—; dir. CPC Internat., Inc., Mfrs. Hanover Corp., Mfrs. Hanover Trust Co., Communications Satellite Corp., Continental Group, Inc. Trustee U. Akron, Mt. Union Coll., Alliance, Ohio. Served to capt. USAAF, 1942-45. Mem. U.S.-Mex. C. of C., Rubber Mfrs. Assn., Bus. Council, Bus. Roundtable. Office: 1144 E Market St Akron OH 44316

PILLON, NANCY HARGIS BACH, educator; b. Jackson, Ky., July 28, 1917; d. Grannis and Evelyn (Crawford) Bach; student Lees Jr. Coll., 1934-36; B.A., Western Ky. State U., 1939; M.S. in Library Sci., U. Ky., 1957, Ed.D., 1967; m. Richard Walsh Pillon, Oct. 6, 1950 (div.); 1 son, Richard Crawford. Librarian Breathitt County High Sch., Jackson, Ky., 1939-42, tchr., librarian, 1952-60; instr. library sci. No. Ill. U., Dekalb, 1960-65; asst. prof. library sci. U. Ky., Lexington, 1965-69; prof. library sci. Ind. State U., Terre Haute, 1969—, acting chmn. dept. library sci., 1971, 77. Chmn. conf. Indian Sch. Library Suprs., 1969-73; former mem. Ind. State Com. Certification Sch. Librarians, 1971—; dir. inst. tng. sch. librarians Higher Edn. Act, 1969. Served with USNR, 1942-46, USN, 1946-50. Mem. ALA, Am. Assn. Library Schs., D.A.R. (chpt. regent 1958-60). Democrat. Presbyterian. Home: 2375 Ohio St Terre Haute IN 47803

PILLSBURY, GEORGE STURGIS, state senator; b. Crystal Bay, Minn., July 17, 1921; s. John S. and Eleanor (Lawler) P.; A.B., Yale U., 1943; m. Sally Whitney, Jan. 4, 1947; children—Charles Alfred, George Sturgis, Sarah Kimball, Katharine Whitney. Pres., Sargent Mgmt. Co.; mem. Minn. Senate; dir. Whitney Land Co., Pillsbury Co. Mem. Smithsonian Assos. (nat. dir.). Clubs: Woodhill, Minnetonka Yacht, Mpls. Athletic, Mpls.; Minnesota (St. Paul); River (N.Y.C.); Seminole Golf (Palm Beach, Fla.). Home: 1320 Bracketts Point Rd Wayzata MN 55391 Office: 930 Dain Tower Minneapolis MN 55402

PILLSBURY, JOHN SARGENT, JR., ins. co. exec.; b. Mpls., Oct. 28, 1912; s. John Sargent and Eleanor (Lawler) P.; B.A., Yale U., 1935; LL.B., U. Minn., 1940; m. Katharine Harrison Clark, June 11, 1936; children—John Sargent, Donaldson Clark, Lynde Harrison, Katharine Pillsbury Jose. Various positions Pillsbury Mills, Inc., 1936-37; admitted to Minn. bar, 1940; asso. Faegre & Benson, Mpls., 1940-45, partner, 1946-56; pres. Northwestern Nat. Life Ins. Co., 1956-69, chmn., 1969-77, chief exec. officer, 1969-77, chmn. bd., 1978-81, also dir.; dir. NW Bell Telephone Co., Boise Cascade Corp.; trustee Wells Fargo Mortgage and Equity Trust. Life dir. Minn. Orchestral Assn.; trustee Dunwoody Indsl. Inst.; founding trustee Twin Cities Pub. TV. Served from lt. (j.g.) to lt. comdr., air combat intelligence, USNR, 1942-45. Mem. Am., Minn., Hennepin County bar assns., Phi Delta Phi, Order of Coif. Republican. Congregationalist. Clubs: Minneapolis, Minnetonka Yacht, Woodhill Country (Mpls.); Yale (N.Y.C.). Address: 930 Dain Tower Minneapolis MN 55402

PIMMEL, MICHAEL JOSEPH, mfg. co. ofcl.; b. St. Louis, Dec. 12, 1944; s. Vernon Leo and Dorothy Gertrude (Dunsworth) P.; A.A., St. Louis Community Coll., 1968; B.S., Washington U., 1974; m. Valerie Jeane Reinert, June 21, 1969; 1 dau., Michelle Renee. Indsl. engr. Ford Motor Co., Mahwah, N.J., 1968-69; personnel officer Washington U., St. Louis, 1969-74; dir. indsl. relations Contico Internat., Inc., St. Louis, 1974-79; div. mgr. indsl. relations and personnel Gulf & Western Industries, Inc., Danville, Ill., 1979—. Bd. advisors Hazelwood (Mo.) Sch. Dist., 1977-79; mem. steering com. Greater St. Louis United Way, 1977-79; pres. Danville Soccer Assn., 1979—. Mem. Am. Soc. Personnel Adminstrn., St. Louis Indsl. Relations Assn., Greater St. Louis Indsl. Relations Research Assn., Am. Assn. Indsl. Mgmt., Nat. Safety Council. Roman Catholic. Office: 1625 E Voorhees St Danville IL 61832

PINDERA, JERZY TADEUSZ, mechanics scientist, educator; b. Czchow, Poland, Dec. 4, 1914; s. Jan Stanislaw and Natalia Lucia (Knapik) P.; came to Can., 1965, naturalized, 1975; B.S. in Mech. Engring., Tech. U., Warsaw, 1936; M.S. in Aero. Engring., Tech. Univs. Warsaw and Lodz, 1947; D. Tech. Scis., Polish Acad. Scis., 1959; D. Habil. in Applied Mechanics, Tech. U. Cracow, 1962; m. Aleksandra-Anna Szal, Oct. 29, 1949; children—Marek Jerzy, Maciej Zenon. Asst. Lot Polish Airlines, Warsaw, 1947; lab. head Aero. Inst., Warsaw, 1947-52, Inst. Metallography, Warsaw, 1952-54; dep. prof., head lab. Polish Acad. Scis., Warsaw, 1954-59; head lab. Bldg. Research Inst., Warsaw, 1959-62; vis. prof. mechanics Mich. State U., East Lansing, 1963-65; prof. mechanics U. Waterloo (Ont., Can.), 1965—; cons. in field; vis. prof., France, Ger. Served with Polish Army, 1939. Registered profl. engr., Ont. Mem. Can. Soc. Mech. Engring., Gesellschaft fuer angewandte Mathematik und Mechanik, Soc. Exptl. Stress Analysis, ASME, Société Française des Mécaniciens, Soc. Engring. Sci., N.Y. Acad. Scis., Assn. Profl. Engrs. Province Ont. Chmn. Internat. Symposium Exptl. Mechanics U. Waterloo, 1972. Editorial adv. bd. Mechanics Research Communications, 1974—. Contbr. to books, articles to profl. publs. in exptl. mechanics. Home: 310 Grant Crescent Waterloo ON N2K 2A2 Canada Office: Dept Civil Engring U Waterloo Waterloo ON N2L 3GI Canada

PINEDA, MAURICIO HERNÁN, reproductive physiologist; b. Santiago, Chile, Oct. 17, 1930; came to U.S., 1970; s. Teófilo Pineda García and Bértila Pinto Bouvret; D.V.M., U. Chile, 1955; M.S., Colo. State U., 1965, Ph.D., 1968; m. Rosa A. Gómez, July 26, 1956; children—Ana María, Jorge H., Monserrat. Reproductive physiology-endocrinology trainee U. Wis., Madison, 1970-72; fellow in reproductive physiology Colo. State U., Fort Collins, 1972-74, research asso., 1972-78; asso. prof. physiology Iowa State U., Ames, 1979—. Mem. Soc. Study Reproduction, Soc. Study Fertility, Am. Soc. Vet. Physiol. Pharmacology, Sigma Xi, Phi Kappa Phi, Beta Beta Beta. Contbr. articles to profl. jours. Office: Iowa State U Dept Physiology and Pharmacology Vet Medicine Ames IA 50011

PINET, FRANK SAMUEL, univ. dean; b. Topeka, Nov. 8, 1920; s. Frank Leo and Hattie Blanche (McClure) P.; B.S., U. Kans., 1942, M.B.A., 1947, Ph.D., 1955; postgrad. Harvard U. Sch. Bus. Adminstrn., 1943-44; m. Winifred Sarann Meyer, Jan. 27, 1956; children—Christopher Paul, Nancy Ann, Rosemary, Winifred Suzanne, Caroline Michele. Faculty, U. Kans., Lawrence, 1946—, asso. dean, prof. Sch. Bus., 1969—; vis. prof. OEC, Italy, 1959-60; dir. Dold Foods, Inc.; cons. Peoples Gas Systems, Chgo., Dillon Cos., Inc., Panhandle Eastern Pipeline Co., Gen. Telephone & Electronics Corp., others. Served to lt. comdr. USN, 1942-46, 50-52. Recipient Outstanding Teaching award Standard Oil Co. (Ind.), 1973, Henry A. Bubb Outstanding Teaching award, 1972, Outstanding Educator in Am. awards, 1973, 74, 75; Mortar Bd. Outstanding Educator, 1980; Ford Found. fellow, 1961-62. Mem. Am. Econ. Assn., Indsl. Relations Research Assn. Author: Probated Estates in Kansas, 1940 and 1950, 1956. Home: 704 W 12th St Lawrence KS 66044 Office: U Kans 202 Summerfield Hall Lawrence KS 66045

PING, CHARLES JACKSON, univ. pres.; b. Phila., June 15, 1930; s. Cloudy J. and Mary M. (Marion) P.; B.A., Southwestern at Memphis, 1951; B.D., Louisville Presbyn. Theol. Sem., 1954; Ph.D., Duke, 1961; m. Claire Oates, June 5, 1951; children—Andrew, Ann Shelton. Asso. prof. philosophy Alma Coll., 1962-66; prof. philosophy Tusculum Coll., 1966-69, v.p., dean faculty, 1967-68, acting pres., 1968-69; provost Central Mich. U., Mt. Pleasant, 1969-75; pres. Ohio U., Athens, 1975—. Dir. Nationwide Corp. Advisory Bd., Inst. for Ednl. Mgmt., Harvard U. Adv. bd. Ind. Coll. Program Northwest Area Found. Mem. Am. Philos. Assn., Am. Council Acad. Deans, Am. Assn. Higher Edn. Author: Meaningful Nonsense, 1966, also articles. Office: Ohio U Office of Pres Athens OH 45701

PINGEL, JOHN HENRY, health physicist, environmentalist; b. Bowler, Wis., Feb. 28, 1914; s. Ernest William and Emma Whilmina (Gluesing) P.; student U. Wyo., 1933-34, U. Wis. Central State, 1936-38; tchrs. cert. U. Mich. and U. Wis., 1942, B.S. in Engring. and Physics, 1948; M.P.H. (fellow), U. Mich., 1960; m. Helen Olga Habeck, Feb. 7, 1942; 1 son, John Edward. Tchr., 1937-42; jr. scientist, asso. scientist, asso. supr. health physics sect. Argonne (Ill.) Nat. Lab., 1948-67; head environ. protection sect. safety div. Chgo. operations office AEC-ERDA, 1967-76; cons., Downers Grove, Ill., 1976—; expert IAEA, 1978-79. Served with Signal Corps, AUS, 1942-46. Cert. health physicist Am. Bd. Health Physics; cert. radiol. def. tchr., Ill. Mem. Health Physics Soc. (nat. sec., pres. Midwest chpt.), Am. Indsl. Hygiene Assn., Am. Conf. Govtl. Indsl. Hygienists, Am. Future Soc., Am. Nuclear Soc., AAAS., Theosophical Soc., Self-Realization Fellowship, Sigma Xi. Author: Radiation Accidents and Emergencies in Medicine, Research and Industry, 1965; contbr. articles sci. jours. Home and Office: 6730 Fairview Ave Downers Grove IL 60516

PINKELMAN, FRANKLIN CHARLES, state govt. ofcl.; b. Toledo, May 2, 1932; s. Theodore B. and Henrietta M. (King) P.; B.S. in Acctg., U. Detroit, 1957, M.B.A., 1963; m. Elizabeth Jean Kirwan, Apr. 30, 1960; children—Franklin, James, Nancy, Michael, Brian, Katherine. Auditor, Marvin J. Polewach, C.P.A., Birmingham, Mich., 1957-59, Miller, Bailey & Co., C.P.A.'s, Detroit, 1959-64, Nat. Bank Wyandotte-Taylor (Mich.), 1961-64; asst. prof. U. Detroit, 1964-66; dep. auditor-gen. State of Mich., 1966—; mem. exec. com. Midwestern Intergovtl. Audit Forum; adj. prof. Western Mich. U., Aquinas Coll.; adv. council to dean Bus. Sch., Central Mich. U. Bd. dirs. Wyandotte Assn. Service Clubs, 1963, Northville Little League Baseball, 1977-78. Served with AUS, 1953-55. C.P.A., Mich.; cert. internal auditor. Mem. Am. Inst. C.P.A.'s, Council State Govts. (chmn. fin. reporting task force), Nat. Council Govtl. Acctg., Mich. Assn. C.P.A.'s, Nat. Legis. Conf. (exec. com. 1969-70, chmn. post audit planning com. 1969-70), Inst. Internal Auditors (past pres. Detroit chpt.). Author papers in field. Home: 44942 Byrne Dr Northville MI 48167 Office: 333 S Capitol Ave Suite A Lansing MI 48913

PINKELTON, NORMA BERTHA HARRIS, nurse, educator; b. Phila., Oct. 15, 1927; d. Robert Reynolds and Olivia (Gilbert) Harris; grad. Lincoln Sch. for Nurses, N.Y.C., 1950; B.S.N., U. Cin., 1963, M.S.N., 1965, Ed.D. (NDEA fellow), 1976. Nurse phychiat. med. and surg. unit Bellevue Hosp., N.Y.C., 1950-53; staff nurse surgery, Mt. Sinai Hosp., N.Y.C., 1953-56; pvt. and semi-pvt. nurse Luth. Hosp., N.Y.C., 1955-56; pub. health nurse Pub. Health Dept., Phila., 1956-57; labor and delivery nurse, Chestnut Hill Hosp., Phila., 1957-58; supr., staff nurse Cin. Gen. Hosp., 1958-61; counselor research project, Cin., 1965-67; asso. prof. Coll. Nursing and Health, U. Cin., 1967-79, dir. minority nurse recruitment and retention project, 1978-80; adj. prof. Afro-Am. studies U. Cin.; asst. health commr. profl. services Cin. Health Dept., 1980—; pvt. practice family marriage and individual counseling, Cin.; bd. trustees Children's Hosp. Med. Center, Cin. Bd. dirs. Mental Health, Mental Retardation-Children's Services, Winton Hills Med. and Health Centers, Inc. Mem. Am. Nurses Assn., Nat. League Nurses, Am. Public Health Assn., Nat. Network Women Mgrs. in Health, Child Health Assn., Mental Health Assn., AAUP, Black Faculty Assn., Black Nurses Assn., Sigma Theta Tau. Episcopalian. Home: 3808 Dunloe Ave Cincinnati OH 45213 Office: Cin Health Dept 3101 Burnet Ave Cincinnati OH 45229

PINKERTON, DOREEN ANN, legal adminstr.; b. East Chicago, Ind., July 7, 1946; d. Alfred Paul and Elizabeth Bianucci; grad. Hammond (Ind.) Bus. Coll., 1967; m. Kirk A. Pinkerton, Apr. 1, 1977; children by previous marriage—Lori Ann Dixon, Grayden Charles Dixon. Ct. reporter Lake County Criminal Ct., 1965-68; legal sec. Given Dawson & Cappas, 1972-74; office mgr., legal adminstr. Goldsmith, Goodman, Ball & Van Bokkelen, Highland, Ind., 1975—; participant 9th Ann. Inst. Law Office Mgmt., Toronto, 10th Ann. Inst., Denver. Mem. Nat. Assn. Legal Secs. (pres. Lake County chpt.), Assn. Legal Adminstrs. Home: 41 Glendale Park Hammond IN 46320 Office: 3737 45th St Highland IN 46322

PINKERTON, JAMES RONALD, sociologist; b. Milw., Dec. 1, 1932; s. Adam Brownlie and Florence Louise (Korn) P.; B.A., Carroll Coll., Waukesha, Wis., 1954; M.B.A., U. Wis., Madison, 1958, M.S., 1962, Ph.D. (teaching asst.), 1965; m. Marjorie Jean Glass, June 29, 1957; children—Steven James, Kathryn Lynn. Ins. and real estate salesman A. B. Pinkerton Agy., Green Bay, Wis., 1958-59; asst. prof. sociology Eastern Mich. U., Ypsilanti, 1964-65; asst. prof. rural sociology U. Mo., Columbia, 1965-69, asso. prof., 1969—. Served with U.S. Army, 1954-56. Wis. Assn. Ins. Agts. scholar U. Wis., 1957, NIH tng. fellow, 1964; Manpower Adminstrn., U.S. Dept. Labor research grantee, 1973, Summer Manpower Research Inst. faculty fellow, 1968, 69. Mem. Am. Sociol. Assn., Population Assn. Am., Rural Sociol. Soc., AAUP, Midwest Sociol. Soc. Presbyterian. Clubs: Art League, Track (Columbia, Mo.). Author: Outdoor Recreation and Leisure: A Reference Guide and Selected Bibliography, 1969; Socioeconomic Determinants of Urban Poverty Area Workers' Labor Force Participation and Income, 1978; Social Assessment for Mark Twain National Forest, 1981. Home: 1014 Westport Dr Columbia MO 65201 Office: Dept Rural Sociology U Mo Columbia MO 65211

PINKERTON, RICHARD LADOYT, univ. dean; b. Huron, S.D., Mar. 5, 1933; s. Abner Pyle and Orral Claudine (Arneson) P.; B.A. (La Verne Noyes scholar), U. Mich., 1955; M.B.A., Case Western Res. U., 1962; Ph.D. (Nat. Assn. Purchasing Mgmt. fellow), U. Wis., 1969; m. Sandra Louise Lee, Aug. 28, 1965; children—Elizabeth, Patricia. Sr. market research analyst Harris-Intertype Corp., Cleve., 1957-61; mgr. sales devel. Triax Co., Cleve., 1962-64; coordinator mktg. programs Mgmt. Inst., U. Wis., 1964-67, dir. exec. programs Grad. Sch. Bus., asst. prof. mktg., 1969-74; prof. mgmt., dean Grad. Sch. Adminstrn., Capital U., Columbus, Ohio, 1974—; cons. dep. asst. sec. USAF, Washington, 1972-76; cons. House of Vision, Chgo., Control Products div. Amerace Corp., Union, N.J., United Shoe Machinery, Boston, Union Carbide Corp., N.Y.C., Westinghouse, Pitts., Ansul Co., Marinette, Wis., Esna, Ltd., Toronto, Ont., Can.; mem. Wis. Gov.'s Exec. Conf. on Mktg. and Research and Devel., 1969-70. Bd. govs. Hannah Neil Home for Children, Columbus, 1975-78; trustee Ohio Council Economic Edn., 1976—. Served as 1st lt. USAF, 1955-57; ret. lt. col. Res. Mem. Am. Mktg. Assn. (chpt. pres. 1972-73; bd. publs. 1973-74), Nat. Assn. Purchasing Mgmt. (nat. chmn. acad. planning), Sales Mktg. Execs. Internat., Air Force Assn., Res. Officers Assn. U.S., Bus. and Econ. Forum Wis. (program dir. 1972-73), Beta Gamma Sigma, Alpha Kappa Psi, Phi Gamma Delta. Club: Downtown Kiwanis (Columbus). Author: (with K. Lawyer) Small Business Success: Operating and Executive Characteristics, 1963; Curriculum for Purchasing, 1969; also articles. Home: 200 S Chesterfield Rd Columbus OH 43209

PINKERTON, ROBERT BRUCE, mfg. co. exec.; b. Detroit, Feb. 10, 1941; s. George Fulwell and Janet Lois (Hedke) P.; student M.I.T., 1959-61; B.S. in Mech. Engring., Detroit Inst. Tech., 1965; M.A.E., Chrysler Inst. Engring., 1967; J.D., Wayne State U., 1976; m. Barbara Ann Bandfield, Aug. 13, 1966; 1 son, Robert Brent. Various engring. positions Chrysler Engring. Office, Chrysler Corp., Highland Park, Mich., 1967-73, supr. body engring., 1973-76, sr. body engr., 1976-78, emissions and fuel economy planning specialist, 1978-80; dir. engring. Replacement div. TRW, Inc., Cleve., 1980—; mem. Mich. Adv. Com. on Vehicle Inspection and Maintenance, 1979-80. Mem. Soc. Automotive Engrs., Cleve. Engring. Soc. Episcopalian. Clubs: Darrow Racquet, Redwood. Home: 7337 Valerie Ln Hudson OH 44236 Office: 8001 E Pleasant Valley Rd Cleveland OH 44131

PINKHAM, ELEANOR HUMPHREY, librarian; b. Chgo., May 7, 1926; d. Edward Lemuel and Grace Eleanor (Cushing) Humphrey; A.B., Kalamazoo Coll., 1948; M.S. in L.S. (Alice Louise LeFevre scholar), Western Mich. U., 1967; m. James Hansen Pinkham, July 10, 1948; children—Laurie Sue, Carol Lynn. Pub. services librarian Kalamazoo Coll., 1967-68, asst. librarian, 1968-70, library dir., 1971—; vis. lectr. Western Mich. U. Sch. Librarianship, 1970—, mem. adv. bd., 1977—, also adv. bd. Inst. Cistercian Studies library, 1975—. Mem. ALA, Mich. Library Assn. (chairperson acad. div. 1977-78), Mich. Library Consortium (exec. council 1974-80, chairperson 1977-78), AAUP, Beta Phi Mu. Presbyterian (elder 1969—). Home: 2519 Glenwood Dr Kalamazoo MI 49008 Office: 1200 Academy St Kalamazoo MI 49007

PINKSON, EUGENE S(TINIER), govt. safety specialist; b. Pine Level, Ala., Oct. 12, 1919; s. Stinier and Pascena (Wright) P.; student Tuskegee Inst., 1949-52, U. Cin., 1960-61, Miami U., 1961-62; 2 children. Med. technologist VA Med. Center, Tuskegee, Ala., 1949-52; chem. technician Robert A. Taft Center, Bur. Radiol. Health, Cin., 1959-69, phys. sci. research asst., Falls Church, Va., 1949-52; radiation technologist FDA, Rockville, Md., 1971-74; safety specialist Region VI, compliance safety health officer Occupational Safety and Health Adminstrn., Dallas, 1974-78, Region V, Chgo., 1980—, Milw., 1979-81. Served with U.S. Army, World War II; ETO. Mem. Am. Soc. Safety Engrs. Democrat. Baptist. Office: Clark Bldg Room 400 633 W Wisconsin Ave Milwaukee WI 53203

PINKUS, CRAIG ELDON, lawyer; b. Indpls., Feb. 8, 1943; s. Seymour and Virginia M. (Schwartz) P.; A.B. magna cum laude, Butler U., 1965; J.D., Harvard U., 1968; m. Mary M. Mosby, Sept. 29, 1979; 1 son, Aaron. Admitted to Ind. bar, 1968, U.S. Supreme Ct. bar, 1971; asso. firm Barnes, Hickam, Pantzer & Boyd, 1968-69; exec. dir. Ind. Civil Liberties Union, Indpls., 1969-71; chief counsel Legal Services Orgn., Indpls. Inc., 1971-72; partner firm King, Pinkus & Beeler, Indpls., 1972-78, Mitchell, Yosha & Hurst, 1980—; individual practice law, Indpls., 1978-80; host, writer program Family and Consumer Law, Ind. Higher Edn. TV Service, 1974; chief counsel Marion County (Ind.) Prosecutor, 1976-78; dir. Indy Runners, Inc., Village Records, Inc. Mem. Am. (Silver Gavel award 1975, Inst. on Computer in Litigation 1979, 80), Ind., Indpls. bar assns., Bar Assn. 7th Circuit. Democrat. Jewish. Contbr. article to profl. jour. Home: 7828 W 88th St Indianapolis IN 46278 Office: 2220 N Meridian St Indianapolis IN 46208

PINNELL, ROY JOHN, banker; b. Taylorville, Ill., Mar. 27, 1946; s. Charles Royce and Mary Corono (Corso) P.; certificate banking courses Springfield Coll., 1970, 72, 75, 75, So. Ill. U., 1973; m. Sue Ann Grant, June 20, 1965; children—Trene Suzanne, Trent Anthony.

Assembler, Caterpillar Tractor Co., Decatur, Ill., 1965; collector Heights Finance Co., Taylorville, Ill., 1965-66, asst. mgr., 1966, mgr., 1966-69; salesman Hopper-Grant Ford, Inc., Taylorville, 1969; collection mgr. First Trust Bank, Taylorville, 1969-71, loan officer, 1971-73, asst. v.p., 1973-75, v.p., 1975-77; pres., chmn. bd. State Bank of Keyesport (Ill.), 1977—, dir., 1978—. Coach Biddy Basketball; chmn. fireworks City of Taylorville. Recipient Pres.'s award Optimist Club. Mem. Am. Bankers Assn., Ill. Bankers Assn., Tri-County Bankers Assn., Jr. C. of C. (Outstanding Young Man Am. award 1976). Home: Rural Route 1 Keyesport IL 62253 Office: State Bank of Keyesport PO Box 9 Keyesport IL 62253

PINNELL, WILLIAM GEORGE, univ. ofcl.; b. Clarksburg, W.Va., Sept. 6, 1922; s. George Mason and Anna (Wagner) P.; A.B., W.Va. U., 1950, M.A., 1952; Dr. Bus. Adminstrn., Ind. U., 1954; m. Dortha Elizabeth Graham, June 25, 1946; 1 dau., Georgia Pinnell Stowe. Asst. dean Ind. U. Sch. Bus., 1954-56, became asso. dean, 1956, acting dean, 1959, dean Sch. Bus., 1963-71, v.p., treas., 1971-74, exec. v.p., 1974—; dir. Central Soya Co., Inc., Kroger Co.; trustee Am. Fletcher Mortgage Investors. Served to lt. (j.g.) USNR, 1942-47. Mem. Am., Midwest econ. assns., Am. Finance Assn., Ind. Acad. Social Scis., Internat. Bus. Edn. Assn., Midwest Bus. Adminstrn. Assn., Regional Sci. Assn., Beta Gamma Sigma, Beta Alpha Psi, Sigma Iota Epsilon, Alpha Kappa Psi. Methodist. Club: Bloomington Country (dir.). Author: An Analysis of the Economics Base of Evansville; co-author Case Study of a Depressed Area. Mem. editorial bd. Business Horizons, 1959—. Contbr. articles to profl. jours. Home: 2700 Pine Lane-Bittner Woods Bloomington IN 47401

PINSKI, JAMES BERNARD, dermatologist; b. New Orleans, Oct. 31, 1934; s. Max James and Vera Bernice (Holberg) P.; B.A., U. Ill., 1955, B.S., 1956, M.D., 1959; m. Dee Cass, Aug. 26, 1957; children—Kevin Scott, David Alan, Michael James. Served to maj. M.C., AUS, 1959-66; intern Brooke Gen. Hosp., San Antonio, 1959-60; resident in dermatology Letterman Gen. Hosp., San Francisco, 1960-63; chief dermatology service U.S. Army Hosp., Heidelberg, W. Ger., 1963-66; practice medicine specializing in dermatology, Chgo., 1966—; mem. staff Riverside Hosp., St. James Hosp.; asst. clin. prof. dermatology Northwestern U. Med. Sch. Mem. Internat. Soc. Dermatol. Surgery, Internat. Soc. Tropical Dermatology, A.C.P., AMA, Assn. Mil. Dermatologists, Am. Soc. Dermatol. Surgery, Noah Worcester Dermatol. Soc., Chgo. Med. Soc., Chgo. Dermatol. Soc., Ill. Med. Soc., Internat. Soc. Wines and Foods, Phi Beta Kappa, Alpha Omega Alpha. Clubs: B'nai B'rith, Safari. Contbr. articles to med. jours. Home: 175 E Delaware St Chicago IL 60611 Office: 55 E Washington St Chicago IL 60602

PINSKY, STEVEN MICHAEL, radiologist, educator; b. Milw., Feb. 2, 1942; s. Leo Donald and Louise Miriam (Faldberg) P.; B.S., U. Wis., 1964; M.D., Loyola U., Chgo., 1967; m. Sue Brona Rosenzweig, June 12, 1966; children—Mark Burton, Lisa Rachel. Resident in radiology and nuclear medicine U. Chgo., 1968-70, chief resident in diagnostic radiology, 1970-71, asso. prof. radiology and medicine, 1973—; dir. nuclear medicine Michael Reese Med. Center, Chgo., 1973—; dir. nuclear medicine tech. program Triton Coll., River Grove, Ill., 1974—. Served to maj., M.C., U.S. Army, 1971-73. Am. Cancer Soc. research fellow, 1969-70. Mem. Am. Coll. Nuclear Physicians (Ill. del.), Soc. Nuclear Medicine (trustee 1979—), Soc. Medicine (pres. central chpt. 1980-81). Contbr. chpts. to books, articles to med. jours. Office: Michael Reese Med Center 2929 S Ellis Ave Chicago IL 60616

PINT, MICHAEL JOSEPH, state govt. ofcl.; b. Decorah, Iowa, Oct. 3, 1943; s. Joseph John and Marcella Gladys (Bersie) P.; B.A. in Bus. Adminstrn., State Coll. Iowa, Cedar Falls, 1965; grad. Rutgers U. Stonier Grad. Sch. Banking, 1974; m. Joyce Holthaus, Sept. 5, 1964; children—Kimberly Anne, Stephen. With Fed. Res. Bank Mpls., 1967-79, officer supervision and regulations dept., 1967-75; commr. banks, chmn. commerce commn. State of Minn., 1979—; mem. regulations adv. com. Fed. Res. Bank Mpls., 1980—. Club: Elks. Office: 500 Metro Sq Bldg 7th and Robert Sts St Paul MN 55101

PINTAR, MILAN MIK, physicist, educator; b. Celje, Yugoslavia, Jan. 17, 1934; s. Richard and Milena (Kovac) P.; B.Sc., U. Ljubljana, 1958, M.Sc., 1964, Ph.D., 1966; m. Sandra Dawn Burt, Nov. 7, 1974; children—Richard, Katarina, Andrej. Research fellow Inst. J. Stefan, Ljubljana, 1957-66; postdoctoral fellow McMaster U., Hamilton, Ont., Can., 1966-67; asst. prof. physics U. Waterloo (Ont., Can.), 1967-69, asso. prof., 1969-75, prof., 1975—; chmn. Internat. Summer Sch. Nuclear Magnetic Resonance, 1969—; cons. Ont. Cancer Found. Recipient Nat. award Sci., B. Kidric, Ljubljana, 1965, Student Research award Presern, Ljubljana, 1956; NRC grantee, 1967—; NIH grantee, 1973-76; Med. Research Council grantee, 1973-74. Mem. Internat. Soc. Magnetic Resonance (sec.-gen.), Can. Assn. Physicists, Am. Phys. Soc., Ampere Soc. Editor: NMR Introductory Essays, 1976; mem. editorial bd. Bull. Magnetic Resonance, 1980—. Home: 134 Dunbar S Waterloo ON N2L 2E9 Canada Office: Dept Physics U Waterloo ON N2L 3G1 Canada

PINTO, PATRICK RICHARD, indsl. psychologist; b. Buffalo, June 21, 1945; s. Patrick R. and Rita (DeMeo) P.; B.S., Fordham U., 1966; M.S. in Indsl. Psychology, Purdue U., 1968; Ph.D., U. Ga., 1970; m. Eileen Ann Smyntek, Sept. 3, 1966; children—John P., David P., Susan K. Personnel research cons. Xerox Corp., Rochester, N.Y., 1966-69; asso. prof. indsl. relations and psychology U. Minn., Mpls., 1970—; pres. Performance Improvement Assos., St. Paul, Minn., 1973—; vis. prof. U. B.C., 1980-81. Lic. cons. psychologist; mem. Arbitration Panel, Minn. Bur. Mediation Services. Mem. Am. Psychol. Assn., Human Resource Planning Soc., Acad. Mgmt., Nat. Soc. Performance and Instrn., Phi Beta Kappa. Contbr. articles to profl. jours. Home: 2243 W Hoyt Ave Saint Paul MN 55108 Office: Univ Minn 271 19th Ave S Minneapolis MN 55455

PINTO, RICHARD ANTHONY, metal working mfg. co. exec.; b. N.Y.C., Nov. 23, 1927; s. Anthony and Nancy (O'Malley) P.; B.Engring., Yale U., 1948; m. Constance M. Langmann, Apr. 7, 1956; children—James Richard, Cecilia Anne, Mary Constance. With Abex Corp. and predecessor Am. Brake Shoe Co., Chicago Heights, Ill., 1949—, exec. v.p. castings group, 1979—, pres. cast products group 1980—, also dir.; dir. Amsco, Mexicana, Lloyds Burton. Mem. Am. Soc. for Metals, Machinery and Allied Products Inst., Mktg. Council. Roman Catholic. Club: Hinsdale Golf. Home: 1339 Laurie Lane Hinsdale IL 60521 Office: Abex Corp 389 E 14th St Chicago Heights IL 60411

PIOTROWSKI, ROMAN EUGENE, advt. exec.; b. Utica, N.Y., Nov. 18, 1931; s. Roman and Ella Gladys (Rosinski) P.; A.Arts and Sci., SUNY, 1951; m. Mary Teresa Kelly, May 22, 1964; children—Marc Roman, Luke Edward, Dorothy Anne. Asst. mgr. Neisner Bros., Evanston, Ill., 1951-52, 56; research market analyst Pabst Brewing Co., Chgo., 1956-58; market analyst J.R. Brady Co., Chgo., 1958; classified auto advt. mgr. Chgo. Daily News, 1958-60; classified auto advt. mgr. Chgo. Sun Times/Chgo. Daily News, 1960, retail advt. sales, 1960-64, nat. advt. sales, 1964-74, co-op mgr., 1974-78; advt. sales mgr. Suburban Sun Times, Elk Grove Village, Ill., 1978—; dir. Newspaper Advt. Co-op Network, 1978-81. Bd. dirs. City of Hope, Chgo., 1976-78; mem. Republican. Nat. Com., 1980-81. Served with USN, 1952-56. Recipient Marshall Field award, 1977; decorated Joint Service Commendation medal. Mem. Navy Supply Corps Assn. (dir. 1980—), Navy Res. Assn., Navy League, Naval Order of U.S., Res. Officers Assn., Assn. of Naval Aviation, Blue Jackets Assn., Ill. Sheriffs Assn., River Park Athletic Assn. for Blind, Sovereign Hospitaller Order of St. John. Republican. Roman Catholic. Clubs: Food Products of Chgo. (pres. 1976-80, chmn. bd. 1980), Off the St., Grocery Mfg. Sales Execs., Jowl, Pickwick Country. Home: 2432 Fontana Dr Glenview IL 60025 Office: 411 Busse Rd Elk Grove Village IL 60007

PIPITONE, PHYLLIS LUIS (MRS. THOMAS A. COX), psychologist, educator, lectr.; b. Chgo.; d. Max and Julia Antionette (Walkey) Luis; student Chgo. Conservatory Music, Chgo. Tchrs. Coll., Peabody Conservatory Music, So. Meth. U., McGill U., Montreal; B.A., U. Akron, M.A.; Ph.D. (NIMH grantee), Kent State U.; children—Guy, Daniel, Paul. Pvt. practice psychologist, Akron, Ohio, 1967-79; psychologist, instr. Kent (Ohio) State U.; instr. piano and theory Music Acad., Chgo. Mem. Council for Exceptional Children, Am. Psychol. Assn., Nat. Assn. Sch. Psychologists, Am. Soc. Psychical Research, Kent PSI Research Group, Mensa, Tuesday Mus. Club, Weathervane Theatre Women's Bd. Home: 224 Pheasant Run Wadsworth OH 44281

PIRSCH, CAROL MCBRIDE, telephone co. ofcl., state senator; b. Omaha, Dec. 27, 1936; d. Lyle Erwin and Hilfrie Louise (Lebeck) McBride; student U. Miami, Oxford, Ohio, U. Nebr., Omaha; m. Allen I. Pirsch, Mar. 28, 1954; children—Pennie Elizabeth, Pamela Elaine, Patricia Eileen, Phyllis Erika, Peter Allen, Perry Andrew. Mem. data processing staff Omaha Public Schs.; with Western Electric Co., Omaha; legal sec., Omaha; office mgr. Pirsch Food Brokerage Co., Inc., Omaha; supr. community relations Northwestern Bell Telephone Co., Omaha; mem. Nebr. State Senate. Bd. dirs. Adams Sch. PTA and N.W. High Sch. PTSA, U. Nebr., Omaha Parents Assn.; Brownie leader Girl Scouts U.S.A.; mem. Mayor's Commn. Status of Women; del. White House Conf. of Families; mem. Republican County Central Com.; del. state and county Rep. convs.; deacon Benson Presbyterian Ch. Recipient Golden Elephant award; Outstanding Legis. Leadership award Nat. Orgn. Victim Assistance; justice of peace. Mem. Orgn. Women Legislators, Tangier Women's Aux. Clubs: Pilot, Omaha Women's. Office: Dist 10 Room 1126 State Capitol Lincoln NE 68509*

PISCOPO, JOSEPH ANTHONY, sci. co. exec.; b. Marysville, Calif., Sept. 1, 1944; s. John Michael and Marjorie Maxine (Sadler) P.; B.S., U. Ill., 1965; m. Mary Lou Vecchiollo, Nov. 29, 1969; children—Philip Joseph, Thomas Alan. Programmer U.S. Army Ammunition Plant, Joliet, Ill., 1965-66; lead programming mgr. Montgomery Ward & Co., Chgo., 1966-68; v.p. tech. research and devel. Consumer Systems Corp., Oak Brook, Ill., 1968-69; pres. Pansophic Systems Inc., Oak Brook, Ill., 1969-80, chmn., 1980—, also dir. Certificate in data processing. Mem. Software Industry Assn. (dir. 1971-73), Am. Mgmt. Assn. Research software, computer sci. Office: 709 Enterprise Dr Oak Brook IL 60521

PISTILLI, MICHAEL FRANCIS, chemist; b. Chgo., Dec. 21, 1942; s. Michael Francis and Mary Ann (Armato) P.; B.A., Lewis U., 1965; m. Tina Mary Lisner, Nov. 16, 1968; children—Andrea, Michael Francis Jr. Chemist, Marquette Cement Research Lab., Chgo., 1965-67; chemist Material Service Corp., Chgo., 1967-75; research chemist Portland Cement Assn., Skokie, Ill., 1975-77; lab. mgr. Am. Admixtures & Chem. Corp., Chgo., 1977-81, tech. mgr., 1981—. Served with USMCR, 1966-72. Mem. Am. Ceramic Soc., Am. Concrete Inst., ASTM, Transp. Research Bd. Roman Catholic. Office: 5909 N Rogers St Chicago IL 60646

PISTNER, STEPHEN LAWRENCE, retail co. exec.; b. St. Paul, Mar. 14, 1932; s. Leopold and Prudence Charolette (Selcer) P.; student U. Wash.; B.A., U. Minn., B.S., 1953; m. Jane Evelyn Golden, Sept. 30, 1971; children—Paul David, John Alan, Betsy Ann. Pres., chief exec. officer Target Stores, Inc., Mpls., 1973-76, chmn., chief exec. officer, 1976; exec. v.p. Dayton Hudson Corp., Mpls., 1976-77, pres., chief operating officer, 1977-81, also dir.; pres., chief exec. officer Montgomery Ward, 1981—. Bd. dirs. Chgo. Symphony Orch.

PITBLADO, JOHN MACDONALD, mfg. co. exec.; b. Mpls., Jan. 25, 1918; s. James MacDonald and Jennie Serena (Bark) P.; B.S. in Chem. Engring., U. Minn., 1940; m. Jeanne Oistad, Jan. 21, 1942; children—James MacDonald, Judy Pitblado Skoglund. Chem. engr. U.S. Steel Corp. South Works, Chgo., 1940-41, Mobil Oil Co., Milw., 1941-43; with 3M Co., 1946—, v.p. abrasives, adhesives, bldg. service and chems. group, 1975-79, corp. dir., 1978—, pres. U.S. ops., 1979—; dir. Josten's, Inc. Bd. dirs. United Way Mpls., 1980—, Minn. Public Radio, 1980; trustee Sci. Mus. Minn., Mpls., 1980—. Served with USNR, 1943-46. Mem. St. Paul C. of C. (dir. 1979—). Address: 3M 3M Center Bldg 220-14 St Paul MN 55144

PITT, GEORGE, lawyer; b. Chgo., July 21, 1938; s. Cornelius George and Anastasia (Geocaris) P.; B.A., Northwestern U., 1960, J.D., 1963; m. Barbara Lynn Goodrich, Dec. 21, 1963; children—Elizabeth Nanette, Margaret Leigh. Admitted to Ill. bar, 1963; asso. firm Chapman and Cutler, Chgo., 1963-67; partner firm Borge and Pitt, and predecessor, 1968—. Served to 1st lt. AUS, 1964. Mem. Am., Ill., Chgo. bar assns., Phi Delta Phi, Phi Gamma Delta. Home: 872 Burr Ave Winnetka IL 60093 Office: 120 S LaSalle St Chicago IL 60603 also 20 Exchange Pl New York NY 10005

PITT, HY, mgmt. cons.; b. Boston, Nov. 28, 1920; s. Morris and Rebecca (Silberstein) P.; B.S. in Math., U. Wis., Madison, 1948, M.S., 1949; m. Jeanne D. Goldstein, Apr. 11, 1943; children—Barbara, Daniel, Ronald, Rebecca. Statis. analyst Oscar Mayer & Co., Madison, 1956-62; mgr. statis. services and quality control United Fruit Co., Boston, 1962-67; dir. Edn. and Tng. Inst., Am. Soc. Quality Control, Milw., 1967-70; dir. Mgmt. Acad., Bayer and McElrath, Inc., Milw., 1970-73; pres. Pitt Tng. Assos., Milw., 1973—; instr. math. U. Wis., Madison, 1950-56. Pres. Glendale (Wis.) Concerned Citizens, 1972—, Madison Sch. PTA, 1958. Served with USAAF, 1942-46. Fellow Am. Soc. Quality Control (testimonial awards 1973, 78); mem. Am. Statis. Assn., Math. Assn. Am., European Orgn. Quality Control, Inst. Food technologists, Nat. Space Inst. Contbr. articles in field to profl. jours. Address: 6810 N Neil Pl Milwaukee WI 53209

PITTELKO, ROGER DEAN, clergyman; b. Elk Reno, Okla., Aug. 18, 1932; s. Elmer Henry and Lydia Caroline (Nieman) P.; A.A., Concordia Coll., 1952; B.A., Concordia Sem., St. Louis, 1954, M.Div., 1957, S.T.M., 1958; postgrad. Chgo. Luth. Theol. Sem., 1959-61; Th.D., Am. Div. Sch., Pineland, Fla., 1968, D.Div., 1977; m. Beverly A. Moellendorf, July 6, 1957; children—Dean, Susan. Ordained to ministry, Lutheran Ch.-Mo. Synod, 1958; vicar St. John Luth. Ch., S.I., N.Y., 1955-56; asst. pastor St. John Luth. Ch., New Orleans, 1958-59; pastor Concordia Luth. Ch., Berwyn, Ill., 1959-63; pastor Luth. Ch. of the Holy Spirit, Elk Grove Village, Ill., 1963—; mem. Commn. on Worship, Luth. Ch.-Mo. Synod. Mem. Luth. Acad. for Scholarship, Concordia Hist. Inst. Republican. Clubs: Maywood (Ill.) Sportsman; Itasca (Ill.) Country. Author: Guide to Introducing Lutheran Worship. Contbr. articles to jours. Home: 64 Grange Rd Elk Grove Village IL 60007 Office: 666 Elk Grove Blvd Elk Grove Village IL 60007

PITTS, ROBERT DUANE, ednl. adminstr.; b. Rockford, Mich., Feb. 16, 1932; s. Ralph Hays and Mildred (Jewell) P.; student Moody Bible Inst., 1950-52; A.B., Greenville Coll., 1955; M.Div., No. Bapt. Theol. Sem., 1958; M.A. (NDEA fellow), U. Mich., 1964; Ed.D. (NDEA fellow), Ind. U., 1969; m. Marsha E Weir, Aug. 15, 1952; children—Debra, Gregory, Sheila. Credit interviewer Marshall Field & Co., Chgo., 1955-59; ordained to ministry Bapt. Ch., 1958; asst. pastor Temple Bapt. Ch., St. Paul, 1959-61; asst. supt. Lydia Children's Home, Chgo., 1961-62; tchr. English, Greenville (Mich.) High Sch., 1962-63; dir. public relations and devel. Oakland City (Ind.) Coll., 1964-67; asst. dean, asso. prof. Geneva Coll., Beaver Falls, Pa., 1969-73; dean, Taylor U., Upland, Ind., 1973-79, v.p. acad. affairs, 1979—, prof., 1973—; mem. acad. commn. Council for Advancement of Small Colls., 1974-77; bd. dirs. AuSable Inst. for Environ. Studies, 1973—, exec. com., 1975-78, chmn. bd., 1978—; mem. Deans Council Christian Coll. Consortium, 1973—, chmn., 1978-81; interim pastor First Bapt. Ch., Ellettsville, Ind., 1968, Beaver Falls, 1972-73. Deacon First Bapt. Ch., Beaver Falls, 1970-73, moderator, 1972-73; head usher Evang. Mennonite Ch., Upland, 1979-80. Mem. Am. Assn. Higher Edn., AAUP, Am. Assn. Univ. Adminstrs., Profl. Organizational Devel. Network, Evang. Theol. Soc., Am. Conf. Acad. Deans, Ind. Conf. Acad. Deans (chmn. 1977-78), Am. Assn. Coll. Registrars and Admissions Officers, Coll. and Univ. Personnel Assn., Phi Delta Kappa, Alpha Kappa Sigma, Alpha Phi Gamma, Chi Alpha Omega. Republican. Office: Reade Ave & 3d St Upland IN 46989

PITZER, DONALD ELDEN, historian, educator; b. Springfield, Ohio, May 6, 1936; s. Elden C. and Gladys Marie (Weller) P.; student Messiah Coll., 1955-57; A.B., Wittenburg U., 1958; M.A., Ohio State U., 1962, Ph.D., 1966; m. Mariann Hershey, Aug. 20, 1960; children—Tonja Sue, Donald Elden. Instr., Messiah Coll., Grantham, Pa., 1959-61; teaching asso. Ohio State U., Columbus, 1963-66; manuscript librarian Ohio Hist. Soc., Columbus, summer, 1966; asst. prof. history Taylor U., Upland, Ind., 1966-67; prof. history Ind. State U., Evansville, 1967—, dir. Center for Communal Studies, 1976—; dir. Historic Communal Socs. Confs., 1974—; historian New Harmony Commn. of Ind., 1973—. Recipient Outstanding Prof. award Ind. State U., 1979. Mem. Am. Hist. Assn., Ind. Hist. Soc., Orgn. Am. Historians, Nat. Hist. Communal Socs. Assn. (exec. dir. 1975—). Author: New Harmony's First Utopians, 1979; contbr. articles in field to scholarly jours., chpts. to books; editor: Robert Owen's American Legacy, 1972. Home: 614 Agathon Dr Evansville IN 47712 Office: 8600 University Blvd Evansville IN 47712

PIZER, IRWIN HOWARD, librarian, educator; b. Wellington, N.Z., Oct. 16, 1934 (parents Am. citizens); s. Harry and Cecelia (Cohen) P.; B.S., Antioch Coll., 1957; M.S., Columbia U., 1960. Librarian, asso. prof. med. history Upstate Med. Center, SUNY, Syracuse, 1964-69, dir. biomed. communication network, 1966-70; asso. dir. libraries SUNY, Buffalo, 1969-71; univ. librarian, prof. library adminstrn. U. Ill. Med. Center, Chgo., 1971—; dir. Regional Med. Library, Region VII, Nat. Library of Medicine, 1980—. Bd. dirs. Ranch Triangle Conservation Assn., Chgo., 1971-74, pres., 1973; bd. dirs. Lincoln Park Conservation Assn., 1972-73. Mem. Med. Library Assn. (Murray Gottlieb prize 1964, continuing edn. com. 1963-66, sr. adviser 1967-68, mem. goals and structure com. 1969-73, dir. 1975-78), Internat. Fedn. Library Assns. and Instns. (chmn. sect. biol. and med. scis. libraries 1977—, sec. div. spl. libraries 1979-81, chmn. div. 1981—, mem. profl. bd. 1981—, chmn. working group 5th Internat. Congress Med. Librarianship), Spl. Libraries Assn., Upstate N.Y.-Ont. Med. Library Assn. (hon.), Sigma Xi. Contbg. author World Ency. of Library and Info. Sci., 1980; Handbook of Medical Library Practice, 4th edit., 1981. Mem. editorial bd. Internat. Jour. Spl. Libraries, 1981—. Contbr. articles to profl. jours. Home: 1875 N Fremont St Chicago IL 60614 Office: 1750 W Polk St Chicago IL 60612

PIZZI, ANTHONY CHARLES, accountant; b. Hancock, Mich., June 25, 1953; s. Antonio and Catherine P.; B.A., Alma Coll., 1975; student Mich. Tech. U., 1971-72. Staff acct. Cybulski & Turnquist, P.C., Houghton, Mich., 1975-77; officer Turnquist & Pizzi, P.C., 1978—. Bd. dirs. Portage Lake Multi-Ednl. Services, Inc., 1977—, treas., 1977-79; bd. dirs. Calumet Area Community Band, Inc., 1977—, pres., 1977-79; treas. Houghton County Republican Com., 1977-78, vice chmn., 1976, chmn., 1979—; mem. 11th Congl. Dist. (Mich.) Rep. Exec. Com., 1976—; mem. Mich. Rep. State Com., 1981-83; del. Mich. Rep. Conv., 1974—; Rep. candidate for county treas., 1976. C.P.A., Mich.; treas. Houghton chpt. ARC, 1980—. Mem. Mich. Assn. C.P.A.'s, Am. Inst. C.P.A.'s. Clubs: Lions (treas. Hancock 1976-78, v.p. 1979-81, pres. 1981-82), Mich. Tech. Huskies, Mich. Tech. President's, Elks, Alma Coll. Pres.'s. Office: 417 Shelden Ave Houghton MI 49931

PLANJE, THEODORE JOHN, univ. dean; b. St. Louis, Mar. 17, 1919; s. George and Edna (Johnston) P.; B.S. in Ceramic Engring., Mo. Sch. Mines and Metallurgy, 1940; postgrad. Mass. Inst. Tech., 1940-41; Ph.D. in Ceramic Engring., U. Mo., 1950; m. Miriam Louise Kelting, Aug. 8, 1942; children—Theodore John, Curtis E. Instr. ceramic engring. U. Mo. at Rolla (formerly Mo. Sch. Mines and Metallurgy), 1946-50, asst. prof., 1950-52, asso. prof., 1952-55, prof., chmn. dept. ceramic engring., 1955-64, dir. Sch. Mines and Metallurgy, 1964-65, dean, 1965—, also dir. of Space Sci. Research Center. Served to capt. USAAF, 1941-46. Registered profl. engr., Mo. Fellow Am. Ceramic Soc. (past pres.); mem. Am.Inst. Mining, Metall. and Petroleum Engrs., Nat. Inst. Ceramic Engrs., Am. Soc. for Engring. Edn., Rolla C. of C., Keramos, Sigma Xi, Tau Beta Pi, Sigma Gamma Epsilon. Contbr. articles tech. publs. Patentee in field. Home: 2 McFarland Dr Rolla MO 65401*

PLANT, MARCUS LEO, educator; b. New London, Wis., Nov. 10, 1911; s. George Henry and Margaret (McGinty) P.; B.A., Lawrence Coll., 1932, M.A., 1934; J.D., U. Mich., 1938; m. Geraldine Hefter, Dec. 27, 1944; children—Margaret Ann, Elizabeth, Mark, Nancy. Admitted to Wis. bar, 1939, N.Y. bar, 1946, Mich. bar, 1949; pvt. practice Miller, Mack & Fairchild, Milw., 1938-44, Cahill, Gordon, Zachry & Reindel, N.Y.C., 1944-46; prof. law U. Mich., 1946—. Rep. of U. Mich. in Intercollegiate Conf. of Faculty Reps., 1955-79, sec., 1956-79; mem. U.S. Olympic Com., 1969-72; trustee Lawrence U., 1972-79. Mem. Nat. Collegiate Athletic Assn. (pres. 1967-69), Delta Tau Delta, Order of Coif, Tau Kappa Alpha. Author: Cases on the Law of Torts, 1953; (with Burke Shartel) The Law of Medical Practice, 1959; (with Wex S. Malone) Cases and Materials on Workmen's Compensation, 1963; (with W.S. Malone, Joseph W. Little) Cases and Materials on the Employment Relation, 1974; (with Malone and Little) Cases and Materials on Workers' Compensation and Employment Rights, 1980. Home: 2311 Woodside Rd Ann Arbor MI 48104

PLANTE, JULIAN GERARD, educator; b. St. Paul; s. Roland Joseph and Marion Magdalen (Herold) P.; M.A., Fordham U., 1963, Ph.D., 1972. Asst. to pres. Elmer R. Davis & Assos., mgmt. cons., N.Y.C., 1964-66; asst. prof. classics City Coll., City U. N.Y., 1964-66; research prof. classics, dir. Hill Monastic Manuscript Library, St. John's U., Collegeville, Minn., 1966—; guest prof. Manchester Coll. (Ind.), 1972; cons. reorgn. library Augustinian Hist. Inst., N.Y.C., 1967-68; mem. adv. bd. Bakken Mus. of Electricity in Life, Mpls.,

1977—. Decorated Lalibela cross Patriarch Ethiopian Orthodox Ch., 1973. Mem. Minn. (exec. bd. 1971-74), St. Cloud Area geneal socs., Minn. Hist. Soc., Stearns County Hist. Soc., AAUP, Am. Philol. Assn., Medieval Acad. Am., Medieval Assn. Midwest (v.p. 1981-82, pres. 1982—), Vergilian Soc., Am. Papyrological Soc., Conseil Internat des Archives, Soc. Internat. des Papyrologistes. Clubs: Moose; Univ. of St. Paul. Contbr. articles to profl. jours. Home: 111 Park Ave S Saint Cloud MN 56301 Office: Hill Monastic Manuscript Library Saint Johns U Collegeville MN 56321

PLASKET, RICHARD LAWRENCE, mgmt. cons.; b. Moorestown, N.J., May 27, 1936; s. George Kellum, Sr., and Martha Longstreth (Rouse) P.; A.B., Western Md. Coll., 1958; M.B.A., George Washington U., 1963; m. Elizabeth Carolyn Flohr, Apr. 25, 1959; children—Richard Lawrence, Caryl L. Commd. 2d lt. U.S. Army, 1958, advanced through grades to lt. col., 1973; served project mgr. Army Personnel Systems, U.S. Army Personnel Command, 1970-75, dir. mgmt. info. systems U.S. Army Recruiting Command, 1975-78, ret., 1978; dir. internal mgmt. services Health Care Service Corp., Chgo., 1978-81; mgmt. cons., 1981—; lectr. mgmt. seminars Harvard U. Decorated Legion of Merit, Bronze Star. Mem. Assn. for Systems Mgmt. (chpt. pres., mem. of year 1978-79), Project Mgmt. Inst., Am. Mgmt. Assn. Clubs: Lake Zurich Lions, Chgo./Suburban Cairn Terrier, Cairn Terrier Club Am.; Masons (Moorestown, N.J.); Chesapeak Scottish Rite (Balt.). Home and office: 21815 N Old Rand Rd Lake Zurich IL 60047

PLATT, GEORGE MILO, univ. adminstr.; b. Rapid City, S.D., Jan. 1, 1931; s. George Lee and Josephine M. (Paulson) P.; B.S., S.D. State U., 1953; M.A., Syracuse U., 1955, Ph.D., 1962. Asst. prof. U. S.D., 1962-65, U. Iowa, 1965-69; dir. planning and instl. research Wichita (Kans.) State U., 1969-79, asso. v.p., 1979—; Ford Found. adv. to secs. of local govt., East and West Pakistan, 1963, 65-66, 68. Served with AUS, 1955-57. Mem. Am. Soc. for Public Adminstrn., Am. Polit. Sci. Assn., Midwest Polit. Sci. Assn., Western History Assn., Soc. for Coll. and Univ. Planning. Author: (with Richard O. Niehoff) Local Government in East Pakistan, 1964; (with Alan L. Clem) A Bibliography of South Dakota Government and Politics, 1965, (with others) Administrative Problems in Pakistan, 1966. Home: 3527 E 15th St Wichita KS 67208 Office: Wichita State U Wichita KS 67208

PLATTS, JOHN, appliance co. exec.; b. Detroit, Nov. 19, 1917; s. Ralph E. and Mary E. (Snyder) P.; student U. Toledo, 1938-39; m. Dorothea M. Sleeper, Nov. 24, 1940; children—Pamela, Polly, Melissa. With Whirlpool Corp., 1941—, dir. purchases laundry plants, St. Joseph, Mich., 1954-55, works mgr. laundry plants, 1955-56, gen. sales mgr., 1956-57, gen. mgr. refrigeration plant, v.p. refrigeration product group, Evansville, Ind., 1957-62, corp. pres., Benton Harbor, Mich., 1962-77 chmn. bd., chief exec. officer, 1971—; dir. Shell Oil Co., Sears Bank & Trust Co., Clark Equipment Co. Mem. adv. council Coll. Engring., U. Notre Dame; mem. nat. execs. com. Nat. Council Crime and Delinquency; sr. mem. Conf. Bd.; trustee Citizens Research Council Mich. Mem. ASHRAE. Clubs: Chgo., Union League, Met. (Chgo.); Point O' Woods Country, Berrien Hills (Benton Harbor, Mich.). Office: Whirlpool Corp Adminstrv Center US 31 N Benton Harbor MI 49022

PLAUT, ERIC ALFRED, psychiatrist; b. N.Y.C., Nov. 16, 1927; s. Alfred and Margaret (Blumenfeld) P.; B.S., Columbia U., 1949, M.D., 1953; m. Eloine Raab, Sept. 5, 1976. Intern, Montefiore Hosp., Bronx, 1953-54; psychiat. resident Worcester (Mass.) State Hosp., 1954-55, Mass. Meml. Hosp., Boston, 1956-57; cons. psychiatrist Mass. Dept. Corrections, 1957; fellow in student health psychiatry U. Calif., Berkeley, 1957-58; practice medicine, specializing in psychiatry, Berkeley, 1958-74; staff psychiatrist Kaiser Hosp., Oakland, Calif., 1958-62, Cowell Meml. Hosp., Berkeley, 1958-62; cons. psychiatrist Bur. Indian Affairs, Dept. Interior, 1967-68; program chief Berkeley Mental Health Services, 1968-71; dep. commr. Ind. Dept. Mental Health, Indpls., 1974-76; commr. Conn. Dept. Mental Health, Hartford, 1976-81; asso. dir. Inst. Psychiatry, Northwestern Meml. Hosp., also vice chmn. dept. psychiatry Northwestern U. Med. Sch., Chgo., 1981—; asst. clin. prof. psychiatry U. Calif. Med. Sch., San Francisco, 1958-74; asso. clin. prof. psychiatry U. Ind. Med. Sch., Indpls., 1975-76; clin. prof. psychiatry U. Conn. Med. Sch., Farmington, 1978-81, Yale U. Med. Sch., New Haven, 1979-81; cons. Assembly Sci. Adv. Council, Calif. Legislature, 1970; chmn. Bay Area Region, Calif. Conf. Local Mental Health Dirs., 1970-71; mem. task force on access and barriers, Pres.'s Commn. on Mental Health, 1977—; gen. partner Vanguard Investments, Berkeley, 1971-78. Bd. dirs. ACLU, Berkeley, 1960-65; mem. psychiatry panel Grad. Med. Edn. Nat. Adv. Com., 1979-81. Served with USN, 1944-46. Diplomate Am. Bd. Psychiatry and Neurology. Fellow Am. Psychiat. Assn. (cons. task force on govt. relations 1973-76, chmn. com. on public info. 1975-76, mem. com. on certification in adminstrv. psychiatry 1979—); mem. No. Calif. Psychiatric Soc. (chmn. com. on law and legis. 1968-72, legis. rep. 1972-74, councillor 1972-73, pres.-elect 1973-74), Calif. Med. Assn. (alt. del. 1968-71), Alameda-Contra Costa Med. Assn. (chmn. mental health com. 1972), Conn. Med. Soc., Nat. Assn. State Mental Health Program Dirs. (dir.). Mem. editorial bd. Yale Psychiat. Quar., 1976-81; contbr. articles to profl. jours. Home: 1418 Judson Ave Evanston IL 60201 Office: Inst Psychiatry Northwestern Meml Hosp 320 E Huron St Chicago IL 60611

PLAWECKI, DAVID ANTHONY, state senator; b. Detroit, Nov. 8, 1947; s. Edward and Lakodya C. (Popek) P; B.S.M.E., Gen. Motors Inst. Tech., Flint, Mich., 1970; M.B.A., U. Mich., 1977; m. Linda Rose Chantres, Apr. 11, 1970; 1 son, Brent David. Jr. engr. hydramatic div. Gen. Motors Corp., Ypsilanti, Mich., 1970; mem. Mich. Senate, 1971—, majority floor leader, chmn. labor and retirement com. Mem. Kingswood-Crestwood Civic Assn., 1973—. Chmn., Young Dems. Club, 1968-69; mem. exec. bd. Dearborn Heights (Mich.) Dem. club, 1969-73, vice chmn., 1970-71; treas. 15th congl. dist. Dem. orgn., 1970, mem. exec. bd., 1970—; mem. exec. bd. 16th congl. dist. Dem. orgn., 1971—, 19th dist., 1971-72. Bd. dirs. Center Internat. Transp. Exchange, Mich. Quality of Work Life Council, Inc. Mem. Jaycees, Goodfellows, Polish League Am. Vets., Polish Am. Congress, U. Mich. Alumni Assn., Gen. Motors Inst. Alumni Assn. Club: K.C. Youngest state senator in Mich. history. Home: 1157 N John Daly St Dearborn Heights MI 48127 Office: Mich State Senate Lansing MI 48909

PLESKAC, JOHN JOSEPH, JR., indsl. engr.; b. David City, Nebr., Feb. 16, 1942; s. John J. and Marie R. (Sypal) P.; B.S. in Indsl. Engring., U. Nebr., Omaha, 1967; M.S. I.M.S.E., U. Nebr., Lincoln, 1975; m. Marilyn Kay Juranek, June 6, 1964; children—Lisa K., Shari L., John R. Supr. wired equipment mfg. Western Elec. Co., Omaha, 1966-68, supr. prodn. control, 1968-71, supr. tng., 1971-74, indsl. engr., 1974-75, planning engr., 1975-79, sr. planning engr., 1979—. Co-founder, pres. Holling Heights Parent-Tchrs. Orgn., 1970-72; mem. planning com. Millard Sch. Dist., 1974-75, Douglas County 4-H Ice Skating Com., 1975—; active in student career guidance U. Nebr., Omaha, 1975—. Named Outstanding Undergrad. student U. Nebr., Omaha, 1967; registered profl. engr., Nebr. Mem. Am. Inst. Indsl. Engrs. (sr., pres., 1972-73), Nat. Soc. Profl. Engrs., U. Nebr. at Omaha Alumni Assn. (dir. 1981—), Alpha Pi Mu, Gamma Pi Sigma. Office: Western Elec Co PO Box 14000 W Omaha Sta Omaha NE 68114

PLETCHER, RICHARD HAROLD, educator; b. Elkhart, Ind., May 21, 1935; s. Raymond Harold and Annabelle Mary (Aurand) P.; B.S. in M.E., Purdue U., 1957; M.S., Cornell U., 1962, Ph.D., 1966; m. Carol Jean Robbins, June 9, 1957; children—Douglas Alan, Laura Jean, Cynthia Robbins. Instr. mech. engring. Cornell U., Ithaca, N.Y., 1961-64; sr. research engr. United Aircraft Research Labs., East Hartford, Conn., 1965-66; mem. faculty Iowa State U., Ames, 1967—, prof. mech. engring., 1976—; cons. Caterpillar Tractor Co., Peoria, Ill., ARO, Inc., Arnold Air Force Station, Tenn., Gen. Electric Co., Phila. Served with U.S. Navy, 1957-60. Registered profl. engr., Iowa. Mem. ASME, AIAA, Am. Soc. Engring. Edn., AAUP, Sigma Xi, Sigma Delta Chi, Pi Tau Sigma, Tau Beta Pi, Phi Kappa Phi. Presbyterian. Mem. editorial adv. bd. Numerical Heat Transfer, 1980—; contbr. articles to various publs. Home: 411 Oliver Ave Ames IA 50010 Office: Dept Mech Engring Iowa State U Ames IA 50011

PLEZBERT, MICHAEL JOSEPH, marriage and family counselor; b. Chgo., July 1, 1934, s. Michael and Regina (De Cristopher) P.; B.S., Evangel Coll., 1969; M.S. in Guidance and Counseling, Southwestern Mo. State U., 1972; postgrad. U. Calif., Santa Cruz, 1973-75, Heed U., Hollywood, Fla.; m. Janice Sherrill Pietrini, Feb. 13, 1965; 1 son, Michael Paul. Tchr. spl. edn. Spokane (Mo.) Sch. Dist., 1969-70; psychologist, counselor Family Service Assn., Watsonville, Calif., 1970-72; adult instr. hosp. adminstrn. and psychology Santa Cruz Dept. Edn., 1972-75; pres. Inst. Personal and Family Communications, Springfield, Mo., 1975—; marriage, family and child guidance counselor and cons.; public speaker. Mem. Mo. Gov.'s Com. on Employment of Handicapped. Served with AUS, 1956-64. Mem. Greene County Mental Health Assn., Nat. Autistic Soc., Nat. Council Family Relations, Nat. Assn. Social Workers, Am. Personnel and Guidance Assn. Mem. Assemblies of God Ch. Club: Lions. Office: Institute for Personal and Family Communications Springfield MO 65803

PLIER, ROBERT EDWIN, fin. co. exec.; b. Port Washington, Wis., Apr. 8, 1947; s. Emil T. and Edna Plier; B.B.A., U. Wis., Whitewater, 1969; postgrad. Bradley U., 1977, 78. Sr. staff accountant Clifton, Gunderson & Co., C.P.A.'s, Peoria, Ill., 1969-74; treas. Peoria Disposal Co., 1974—. Bd. dirs. Boys Club Peoria, 1977-78. Mem. Am. Mgmt. Assn., U.S. Jaycees (treas. 1978-79), Ill. Jaycees (state chaplain 1975-76, dir. children's camp, 1977-79, ambassador, 1976—), Am. Inst. C.P.A.'s, Nat. Assn. Accountants, Ill. Soc. C.P.A.'s. Club: Kennel Lake Sportsmen's. Home: 1049 E Jefferson St Morton IL 61550

PLOCHER, DAVID WAYNE, physician; b. Shakopee, Minn., July 9, 1949; s. Edward Benjamin and Paula Martha (Hill) P.; student U.S. Naval Acad., 1967-68, Mankato State U., 1968-69; B.A. magna cum laude in Biology, U. Minn., 1971, M.D., 1975; m. Michelle Ann Monti, May 5, 1979. Resident in medicine U. Minn. Hosp., Mpls., VA Hosp., Mpls., St. Paul Ramsey Med. Center, United Hosps., St. Paul, 1975-78; practice medicine specializing in internal medicine, St. Paul, 1978—; cons. United Hosps., St. Joseph's Hosp., St. Paul. Diplomate Am. Bd. Internal Medicine. Mem. St. Paul Soc. Internatl. Medicine, Ramsey County Med. Soc., Minn. Med. Assn., Alpha Omega Alpha. Lutheran. Office: 1215 Lowry Medical Arts Bldg Saint Paul MN 55102

PLOESER, WALTER CHRISTIAN, ins. cons., diplomat; b. St. Louis, Jan. 7, 1907; s. Christian D. and Maud Elizabeth (Parr) P.; student City Coll. of Law and Fin., St. Louis; LL.D., Norwich U., 1948; Dr. hon. causa, Nat. U. Asuncion, Paraguay; m. Dorothy Annette Mohrig, Aug. 17, 1928; children—Ann Ploeser Bergan, Sally Ploeser Chapel III. In ins. bus., St. Louis, 1922—; founder firm Ploeser, Watts & Co., 1933, organized subs. Marine Underwriters Corp., 1935, former pres.; now cons.; founder Ins. Inst. Mo., 1938, pres., 1938-40; past pres. Grant, Ploeser & Assos., Inc., nat. and internat. pub. relations, offices in Mexico City, Washington, St. Louis, South Bend, Ind.; pres. Walter C. Ploeser Co.; dir. Webster Groves Trust Co.; U.S. ambassador to Republic of Paraguay, 1957-59, to Costa Rica, 1970-72. Mem. Mo. Legislature, 1931-32; chmn. 5th dist. com. fin. and budget Rep. Nat. program Com., 1937-39; mem. 77th, 78th, 79th and 80th Congresses from 12th Mo. dist.; mem. appropriations com., Rep. steering com., chmn. select com. on small bus. chmn. subcom. on govt. corps.; mem. econ. adv. com. U.S. Senate com. on banking and currency, 1953-54; Rep. nat. committeeman for Mo., 1964-66; chmn. bd. Salvation Army, 1967-70; former trustee Shriners Hosp. for Crippled Children, St. Louis, Scottish Rite Found.; Mo. DeMolay Ednl. Fund; chmn. Scottish Towers Residence Found. Recipient Nat. Religious award Ams. United, 1976; Freedoms Found. award, 1949; decorated Grand Cross Republic of Paraguay, 1959. Mem. Miss. Valley Assn. (pres. 1955, chmn. bd. 1956) DeMolay Legion of Honor, Ins. Bd. St. Louis, St. Louis C. of C. (chmn. nat. affairs com. 1964-66), C. of C. Met. St. Louis (dir.). Republican. Clubs: Masons (33 deg.), Shriners; Order of DeMolay (supreme council, grand master internat. 1952; Sovereign grand insp. gen. Scottish Rite in Mo.); Mo. Athletic, St. Louis Triple A Golf. Home: 275 Union Blvd Saint Louis MO 63108 Office: 3633 Lindell Blvd Saint Louis MO 63108

PLOGHOFT, MILTON ERNEST, educator; b. Atlantic, Iowa, May 15, 1923; s. Grover Cleveland and Jennie Ora (Freeman) P.; B.S.Ed., N.W. Mo. State U., 1949; M.S., Drake U., 1951; postgrad. U. Mo., 1953-54, U. Minn., 1955; Ed.D., U. Nebr., 1957; m. Zella I. Mitchell, May 22, 1923; children—Milton Eugene, Philip, Shelley, Tara. Tchr. public jr. high sch., Quitman, Mo., 1943-44, Coin, Iowa, 1944-45; elem. prin, public schs., Audubon, Iowa, 1946-50; elem. supr., public schs., Kearney, Nebr., 1950-52, McCook, Nebr., 1952-56; prin. Univ. Sch., Ohio U., Athens, 1957-58; asso. prof. elem. edn. U. Nebr., Lincoln, 1958-62; dir. AID Project, Kano, Nigeria, 1963-65; prof. curriculum Ohio U., 1965—, dir. Social Sci. Center, 1966—; vis. lectr. Faculty Pedagogy, U. Saigon, 1971; cons. Internat. Sch., Santiago, Chile, 1971; program devel. dir. AID Ohio U. Team to Govt. Botswana, 1980; George Gund Found. grantee, dir. 1st nat. conf. on Children and TV, 1979; mem. Nebr. State Merit System, 1959-61, chmn., 1960-61. Served with U.S. Army, 1942-43. George Gund Found. grantee, 1981. Mem. NEA, Assn. Supervision and Curriculum Devel., Nat. Assn. Elem. Sch. Prins., Nat. Council for Social Studies. Democrat. Unitarian. Club: Kiwanis. Author: The Emerging Elementary School Curriculum, 1963; (with A. Shuster) Social Science Education in the Elementary School, 1971; Education for the Television Age, 1981. Home: 133 Longview Heights Athens OH 45701 Office: 206 McCracken Hall Ohio U Athens OH 45701

PLUCKER, ORVIN LOWELL, supt. schs.; b. Emery, S.D., July 18, 1922; s. John E. and Johannah (Olthoff) P.; student Sioux Falls Coll., 1940-41; B.A. cum laude, Augustana Coll., 1943; M.Ed., U. S.D., 1948; Ed.D., U. Colo., 1951; m. Mavis Appleton, Mar. 3, 1945; 1 dau., Mary Kathryn. Tchr. public schs., Alexandria, S.D., 1943-44, Canton, S.D., 1944-48; dir. curriculum public schs., Yankton, S.D., 1948-49; instr. U. Colo., Boulder, 1949-51; dir. instrn. Independence (Mo.), 1951-54, supt. schs., 1954-62; pres. Kansas City (Kans.) Jr. Coll., 1962-66; supt. schs. Kansas City (Kans.), 1962—; educator in residence U. Kans., 1973; dir. Anchor Savs. & Loan Co., Kansas City, Kans. Bd. dirs. Mid-continent Ednl. Lab., Kansas City, Mo., 1965—, v.p., 1967, pres., 1968—; mem. Kans. Gov.'s Commn. Sch. Finance, 1968; bd. dirs., exec. com. West Central Area YMCA, Kansas City, Kans., pres., 1964, sec., 1966-69; bd. dirs., v.p. YMCA of Rockies, Estes Park, Colo.; bd. dirs. Mid-Am. region YMCA, Urban League, Kansas City, Mo., Sci. Pioneers, Kansas City, Mo., Heart Assn., Kansas City, Kans., United Fund, Kansas City, Kans., Central Bapt. Sem., Kansas City, Kans.; chmn. Kansas City (Kans.) Commn. Formation of City Govt., 1981; bd. dirs. Kansas Valley March of Dimes, pres., 1979. Recipient Disting. Service award Jaycees, Independence, 1958; YMCA Disting. Service award, 1964, Man of Yr. award, 1972. Mem. Kansas City (Kans.) C. of C. (dir. 1976-79, vice-chmn. 1981), Am. Assn. Sch. Adminstrs., Kans. Assn. Sch. Adminstrs. (dir.), Wyandotte County Council Govts. (founder, pres. 1967—), Met. Sch. Supts. Assn. Kansas City (charter dir.), United Sch. Adminstrs. Kans. (dir. 1970—, pres. 1973-74), Horace Mann League (pres.-elect 1981), Kans. Sch. Masters (pres. 1973-74), Conf. Sch. Supts. in Cities with Populations over 100,000 (chmn. exec. com. 1976—), Phi Delta Kappa. Baptist (deacon). Clubs: Masons (32 deg.), Shriners, Rotary (pres. Kansas City 1968-69, dir. 1968—; chmn. internat. group study exchange com. 1967-69). Home: 2235 Washington Blvd Kansas City KS 66102 Office: 625 Minnesota St Kansas City KS 66101

PLUMMER, CARY D., foundry exec.; b. Marion, Ind., May 2, 1948; s. Ralph Y. and Vera P.; B.S. in Mgmt. Sci., Ball State U., 1980; m. Sandra K. Branagin, May 25, 1968; children—Mark B., Kelly D. Personnel mgr. Frank Foundries Corp., Muncie, Ind., 1970—. Mem. East Central Ind. Personnel and Indsl. Relations Assn., Ind. Personnel Assn., Golden Key. Baptist. Home: Rural Route 1 Springport IN 47386 Office: 1324 S Brotherton St Muncie IN 47302

PLUMMER, KENNETH ALEXANDER, health services exec.; b. Chgo., Mar. 28, 1924; s. Alexander Oliver and Estella Marie (Koziol) P.; student N. Central Coll., 1940-41, the Citadel, 1941-42, Far Eastern U. (Philippines), 1946-48; m. Marie M. Ricci, Oct. 10, 1943; children—Pamela, Diane, Kenneth, Stacy. Commd. 2d lt. U.S. Army, 1943, advanced through grades to col., 1966, ret., 1970; dir. Ancilla Domini Health Services, Inc., Des Plaines, Ill., 1970—; cons. Cambodian Refugee Program for Cath. Relief Services; moderator, instr. Air War Coll. Non-Resident Program; installed med. relief teams in Cambodian refugee camps. Mem. govt. affairs com. Chgo. Assn. Commerce and Industry, 1976-79. Decorated numerous mil. awards; recipient Assn. of U.S. Army citation, 1961; Res. Officers Assn. award, 1964; Cath. Relief Service award, 1980; Ancilla Domini Sisters award, 1980. Mem. Mil. Order World Wars (comdr. 1962-63), Hosp. Pub. Relations Soc., Chgo. Council on Fgn. Relations, Assn. U.S. Army, Ret. Officers Assn., Am. Hosp. Assn., Cath. Hosp. Assn. Roman Catholic. Club: Oak Park. Contbg. author Command Gen. Staff Review, 1961-64; editor Health Services Quarterly, 1974-79; contbr. Mgmt. Rev. Home: 415 N Elmwood St Oak Park IL 60302 Office: 2300 E Devon Ave Des Plaines IL 60018

PLUMMER, PAUL JAMES, telephone co. mgr.; b. Scottsbluff, Nebr., Aug. 3, 1946; s. Virgil Frank and Helen Louise (Hultberg) P.; B.A., U. Nebr., 1968; postgrad. Platte Coll., 1974-75; M.B.A., U. Iowa, 1982; m. Pamela Lee Purdom, June 26, 1976. With Gen. Telephone Co. of the Midwest, 1968—, div. traffic supr., Columbus, Nebr., 1969-75, div. traffic mgr., Columbia, Mo., 1975-78, labor relations adminstr., Grinnell, Iowa, 1978-79, labor relations mgr., 1979-82, compensation and services mgr., 1982—. Active, services Boy Scouts Am. Mem. Am. Assn. Personnel Adminstrn., Personnel Mgmt. Assn. Columbia (exec. bd. dirs., 1st v.p. 1975-78). Episcopalian. Clubs: Optimist (past pres. Columbus, Nebr., lt. gov. Nebr. 1973-74), Elks. Home: 106 14th Ave Grinnell IA 50112 Office: 11 11th Ave Grinnell IA 50112

PLUNKETT, CHARLES WALTER, ry. exec.; b. Franks, Mo., May 2, 1926; s. Charley Amos and Ethel M. (Rockey) P.; grad. high sch. With Rock Island R.R., Chgo., 1943-58, supr. constrn. signal dept., 1959-62; ops. mgr., sales engr. Matisa Equipment Corp., Chicago Heights, Ill., 1962-67; asst. chief engr. Mo. Pacific R.R., St. Louis, 1967-68; gen. mgr. sales Jackson Vibrators, Inc., Chgo., 1969-70, v.p. r.r. sales, 1970, exec. v.p. r.r. products, 1973; pres. Comml. Quality Feed Center, Inc., Lebanon, Mo., 1973—, Material Cons., Inc., Lebanon, 1975—; pres., bus. mgr., dir. Served with USAAF, 1944-46. Decorated Purple Heart, D.F.C., Air Medal. Mem. Ry. Engring-Maintenance and Supplies Assn. (dir. 1968-71), Ry. Engring. Assn., Roadmasters and Maintenance of Way Assn., Lebanon C. of C. (dir.). Clubs: Union League (Chgo.); Optimists. Home: Washington Apts Lebanon MO 65536 Office: 274 W Pierce St Lebanon MO 65536

PLUNKETT, MELBA KATHLEEN, mfg. co. exec.; b. Marietta, Ill., Mar. 20, 1929; d. Lester George and Florence Marie (Hutchins) Bonnett; student public schs.; m. James P. Plunkett, Aug. 18, 1951; children—Julie Marie Plunkett Hayden, Gregory James. Co-founder, 1961, since sec.-treas., dir. Coils, Inc., Huntley, Ill. Mem. U.S. C. of C., Ill. Mfg. Assn., Ill. C. of C., Ill. Notary Assn. Roman Catholic. Home: Route 1 Sleepy Hollow Rd West Dundee IL 60118 Office: 11716 Algonquin Rd Huntley IL 60142

POAGE, GEORGE RICHARD, historian; b. Gallatin, Mo., July 25, 1914; s. George Naylor and Linda Lane (Doolin) P.; student Harvard U., 1932-33; B.A. summa cum laude, U. No. Iowa, 1951; M.A., U. Iowa, 1952, Ph.D., 1954; m. Patricia Ann Lowe, May 20, 1946; 1 dau., Susan Kathleen. Cryptanalist, War Dept., Washington, 1941-42; instr. history, U. Iowa, 1952-53, univ. fellow, 1953-54, vis. prof. German history, 1966-67; asst. prof. history U. No. Iowa, 1954-59, asso. prof., 1959-65, prof., 1965—, chmn. exec. council Coll. Behavioral Scis., 1967-72, chmn. univ. faculty, 1972-74; dir. Iowa High Sch. Model UN, 1965—; bd. dirs. Iowa div. UN Assn., 1965—, Council on Internat. Relations and UN Affairs, 1967-73, UN Assn. of U.S.A., 1973-80, nat. council, 1980—; chmn. Gov. Iowa's Com. on UN, 1976-79. Served with Signal Corps, U.S. Army, 1942-45; MTO. Decorated Silver Battle Star; recipient citation for outstanding service Gov. Iowa, 1975; Roswell Garst Meml. award UN Assn., 1979. Mem. Am. Hist. Assn., Conf. Group for Central European History, AAUP (pres. U. No. Iowa chpt. 1957). Democrat. Presbyterian. Club: Masons. Home: 1421 W 18th St Cedar Falls IA 50613 Office: 309 Sabin Hall U of No Iowa Cedar Falls IA 50613

POCHOPIEN, DONALD JOHN, biochemist; b. Harvey, Ill., Nov. 28, 1946; s. John Joseph and Wanda Lottie (Litko) P.; B.S., Loyola U., Chgo., 1968; Ph.D., Ill. Inst. Tech., Chgo., 1972. Dir. biochemistry Central Community Hosp., Chgo., 1973—; cons. biochemistry St. Anthony's Hosp., Chgo., 1977—, Franklin Blvd. Community Hosp., Chgo., 1980—. Mem. Am. Assn. Clin. Chemistry (chmn. Chgo. sect. 1979). Club: Pine Point Ski. Contbr. articles in field to profl. jours. Home: 5415 N Sheridan Rd Chicago IL 60640 Office: 5701 S Wood St Chicago IL 60636

PODLESAK, GEORGE EDWARD, contract specialist; b. Chgo., Jan. 3, 1916; s. John and Anna (Hoch) P.; A.A., Morton Jr. Coll., 1937; A.A., Northwestern U., 1942, B.S. in Bus. Adminstrn., 1949, M.B.A., 1952; m. Flora Rita Coglianese, Sept. 25, 1954; children—Janice, Dennis, Georgiana. Asst. to mgr. Edgewood Valley Country Club, Willow Springs, Ill., 1938-42; cost analyst Electromotive div. Gen. Motors Corp., McCook, Ill., 1939-52; staff cost-price analyst Mid Central Air Procurement Dist., Chgo., 1952-53; chief contract div. contracting officer AFPRO Ford Aircraft Engine div., Ford Motor Co., Chgo., 1952-59; chief contract div. contracting officer WCMR Detachment 1, Vandenberg AFB, Calif., 1959-61; contract cons. Central Contract Mgmt. Region,

Wright-Patterson AFB, Ohio, 1961-63; adminstrv. contracting officer Chgo. Contract Mgmt. Dist., Chgo., 1963-65; procurement analyst, compensation S.P., chief termination settlement div. contracting officer DLA DCASR, Chgo., 1965—. Served with USAAF, 1942-46; col. Res. (ret.). Warranted contracting officer; lic. real estate broker; cert. profl. contract mgr. Mem. Nat. Contract Mgmt. Assn., Reserve Officers Assn., Am. Legion, Northwestern U. Mgmt. Alumni Assn., Delta Sigma Pi, Delta Mu Delta. Roman Catholic. Office: DLA DCASR Chgo O'Hare Internat Nat Airport PO Box 66475 Chicago IL 60666

PODOLIN, LEE JACOB, health planning exec.; b. Buffalo, Oct. 23, 1930; s. David J. and Helen J. (Feldman) P.; B.A., U. Rochester, 1952; M.P.A., Syracuse U., 1953; M.P.H., Yale U., 1959, m. Catherine McIntosh, Nov. 22, 1956; 1 son, George Philip. Statis. analyst Eastman Kodak Co., Rochester, N.Y., 1956-57; asst. dir. Montefiore Hosp., N.Y.C., 1958-63; dir. facility planning Health & Hosp. Planning Corp., N.Y.C., 1963-68; exec. dir. Met. Health Planning Corp., Cleve., 1968-76; exec. dir. Milw. Regional Med. Center, 1976—; asst. clin. prof. Med. Coll. Wis., Milw., 1976—; adj. asst. prof. Case Western Reserve U., Cleve., 1970-76; adj. instr. Ohio State U., Columbus, 1974-76; mem. med. assistance adv. council Dept. HEW, 1970-72. Trustee Village of Fox Point, 1980—, Fox Point-Bayside Joint Library, 1980—; bd. dirs. Fox Point Found., 1980-81. Served with U.S. Army, 1953-56. Fellow Am. Pub. Health Assn.; mem. Am. Assn. for Comprehensive Health Planning (trustee 1973-76), Am. Hosp. Assn., Am. Coll. Hosp. Adminstrs. Club: Univ. (Mil.). Home: 7415 N Lombardy Rd Fox Point WI 53217 Office: 9001 Watertown Plank Rd Milwaukee WI 53226

POE, JOAN BARBARA, wholesale co. exec.; b. Cedar Falls, Iowa, June 9, 1932; d. Stanley Walter and Norma Louise (Blecke) Seroke; student Iowa State Tchrs. Coll., 1950-52; m. Ellsworth Poe, Sept. 15, 1951 (dec. 1971); children—Stanley, David, Thomas, Melinda, Susan, Michael. Pres. Buchanan Wholesale Co., Waterloo, Iowa, 1979—, Crystal Ice & Cold Storage Co., Waterloo, 1980—, Standard Distbg. Co., beer distbrs., Waterloo, 1971—. Bd. dirs. Waterloo Jr. Achievement, 1975—; mem. Iowa Commn. Status Women, 1974—; mem. athletic policy div. council U. No. Iowa, Cedar Falls, 1978—. Mem. Waterloo C. of C. (dir. 1976-78), Cedar Falls C. of C. (dir. 1978-80), Nat. Beer Wholesalers Assn. (nat. com.), Iowa Wholesale Beer Distbr. Assn. (sec. 1977—, v.p. 1979—). Republican. Lutheran. Home: 1310 Lilac Ln Cedar Falls IA 50613 Office: 403 Chestnut St Waterloo IA 50703

POEL, RUSSELL JOHN, educator; b. Muskegon, Mich., July 24, 1934; s. Abel John and Fanny (Vander Wall); A.B., Calvin Coll., 1956; Ph.D. in Chemistry, Mich. State U., 1965; m. Mary Joan Dirkse, 1956; children—Barbara Jo, Richard James, Patricia Jean. Instr. dept. chemistry North Central Coll., Naperville, Ill., 1962-65, asst. prof., 1965-69, asso. prof., 1969-77, prof., 1977—. Elder, Wheaton Christian Ref. Ch., 1977-80; bd. dirs. Roseland Christian Ministries Center, 1975—, mem. fin. com., 1975—; bd. dirs. Stategic Christian Ministry Found., 1969—, pres., 74-76, treas., 1981—; bd. dirs. Naperville Little League, 1975—, pres., 1977-81. Recipient Rueben Blessing Athletic Service award, 1974, 77. Mem. Am. Chem. Soc., Midwest Assn. of Chemistry, Tchrs. in Liberal Arts Colls., AAUP, Sigma Xi. Club: Kiwanis (editor newsletter 1978, dir. 1978—). Office: Dept Chemistry North Central College Naperville IL 60566

POELVOORDE, ANDREW AUGUST, gen. contractor; b. Moline, Ill., June 7, 1928; s. August Alois and Leontine (Vindevogel) P.; m. Rose Marie Schatteman, Aug. 27, 1951; children—Theresa, Susan, Michael, Kaye. Pres., Andrew A. Poelvoorde Constrn. Co., Silvis, Ill., 195—. Served with USN, 1946-48. Roman Catholic. Home: 701 Ivy Ln Silvis IL 61282 Office: 541 1st Ave N Silvis IL 61282

POETKER, FRANCES LOUISE, florist; b. Cin., Apr. 16, 1912; d. Charles Benjamin and Louise (Johnston) Jones; B.A., Vassar Coll., 1933; M.A., U. Cin., 1934; m. Joseph G. Poetker, Aug. 10, 1937. Buyer, Mabley & Carew Dept. Store, Cin., 1933-35; owner Jones the Florist, Cin., 1942—; dir. Cin. Bell Telephone Co.; co-chmn. flower decorations Winter Olympics, 1980; dir. profl. flower shows, N.Y. and France, commentator wedding shows. Mem. honors com. U. Cin.; pres.'s com. Xavier U., Cin.; exec. com. Cin. Opera; v.p. Air Pollution Control League Cin.; bd. dirs. Bethesda Hosp., Cin.; mem. Cin. Beautiful Com. Recipient award of appreciation Dept. Agr., 1962, Sylvia award floral excellence, 1976; Belle Skinner Clark fellow, 1930; named Woman of Year, Cin. Enquirer, 1978; named to Floricultural Hall of Fame. Mem. Am. Hort. Soc. (dir.), Soc. Am. Florists, Florists Transworld Delivery Assn. (commentator), Am. Acad. Florists (dir. emeritus), Allied Florists Assn. Cin., Profl. Florist Commentators Internat., MacDowall Soc., McMicken Soc. Lutheran. Clubs: Travel (pres., dir.), Women's, Symphony, Banker's (Cin.); Garden of Am. (mem.-at-large), Town. Co-author: Wild Wealth, 1971; (newspaper column Fun With Flowers, 1949; contbr. articles to mags. Actress, designer 3 syndicated movie shorts for profession. Office: 1037 E McMillan St Cincinnati OH 45206

POETKER, JOEL SMITH, educator; b. Jackson, Ohio, Oct. 1, 1934; s. Norman Oakly and Lola Wanda (Smith) P.; student Ohio Wesleyan U., 1952-54; A.B., Muskingum Coll., 1958; M.A., Miami U., Oxford, Ohio, 1961; Ph.D., Ohio State U., 1971; m. Mabel Marie Riegel, Sept. 12, 1954; children—Susan Johnson, Ann, Samuel. Tchr., Middletown (Ohio) Sr. High Sch., 1958-61, Bexley (Ohio) High Sch., 1961-65; teaching asso. edn. Ohio State U., Columbus, 1968-70; asso. v.p. academic affairs, prof. history and social studies edn. State U. N.Y. Coll. at Buffalo, 1970—, chmn. dept., 1972-76. Recreation dir. City of Bexley, 1965-67. Served with U.S. Army, 1954-56. John Hay humanities fellow Williams Coll., 1963; Gen. Electric econs. fellow Purdue U., 1964. Mem. Am. Hist. Assn., Nat. Council Social Studies, N.Y. State Council Social Studies, Can. Assn. Social Studies, Phi Delta Kappa, Phi Alpha Theta, Phi Gamma Delta. Presbyterian. Author: The Fourteen Points, 1969; The Monore Doctrine, 1968. Contbr. articles to profl. publs. Home: 98 N High St Jackson OH 45640 Office: 519 Grover Cleveland Hall State U NY Coll Elmwood Ave Buffalo NY 14222

POFFENBERGER, THOMAS, educator; b. Pitts., Aug. 9, 1921; s. Millard C. and Rebecca R. (Siviter) P.; B.A., Mich. State U., 1948, M.A., 1949, Ed.D., 1954; m. Shirley Briggs, Aug. 30, 1947; children—Pamela, Mark. Advanced fellow Merrill Palmer Inst., Detroit, 1949-50; asso. prof. and specialist family relations agrl. extension service Oreg. State U., Corvallis, 1951-53; asso. prof. family sociology U. Calif., Davis, 1953-61; asso. prof. child devel. Iowa State U., Ames, 1961-65; vis. prof. child devel. U. Baroda, India, 1961-65; cons. family planning Ford Found., New Delhi, India, 1965-68; sr. specialist East-West Center, Honolulu, 1968-69; prof. edn. and population planning U. Mich. Sch. Public Health, Ann Arbor, 1969—, dir. program in population planning, 1977-79; pvt. practice (part-time) clin. psychology, Oreg., 1951-53, Calif., 1961-65. Served with USN, 1942-46. Cert. psychologist, Calif. Fellow Am. Psychol. Assn., Soc. for Applied Anthropology. Contbr. articles on psychology and population to profl. jours. Home: 1050 Wall St Apt 5-C Ann Arbor MI 48105 Office: School Public Health Univ Michigan Ann Arbor MI 48109

POGGE, FRANKLYN WILLIAM, chem. engr.; b. Council Bluffs, Iowa, Jan. 24, 1942; s. Francis William and Leah Letti Pogge; B.S. in Chemistry, Creighton U., Omaha, 1964, postgrad., 1964-66; m. Donna Jean Grayson, Feb. 17, 1968; 1 dau., Stephanie Janine. Lab. analyst, then chemist Council Bluffs City Water Works, 1962-66; with Kansas City (Mo.) Water Dept., 1966—, chief water supply div., 1978—; chmn. Mo. Operation Cert. Bd., 1978-79. Mem. fin. com. local Girl Scouts, 1977—, mem. bd. Winding River Council, 1979—; div. chmn. Friends of Girl Scouting, 1978-79. Recipient Dr. Warren A. Kramer Tech. Achievement award Mo. sect. Am. Water Works Assn., 1973; registered profl. engr., Mo. Mem. Nat. Soc. Profl. Engrs., Am. Chem. Soc. (chmn. Kansas City sect. 1976), Soc. Applied Spectroscopy (past chmn. Kansas City sect.), Am. Water Works Assn. (lectr., chmn. standards com. carbon dioxide 1979-80). Roman Catholic. Author papers in field. Home: 6719 N Hickory St Kansas City MO 64118 Office: 1 NW Briarcliff Rd Kansas City MO 64116

POGWIZD, TAD ANTHONY, training systems engr.; b. Chgo., Apr. 21, 1943; s. Thaddeus Michael and Amelia Marie (Kurzawa) P.; B.B.A., Loyola U., Chgo., 1966; student U. Chgo., 1975-76; m. Grace Mary Mikaitis, Apr. 28, 1972; children—Jason, Aaron. Orgn. analyst Health Care Service Corp., Chgo., 1971-73, adminstr. Assessment Center, 1973-76, mgr. tng. and devel., 1979—; dir. assessment services Blue Cross-Blue Shield Assn., Chgo., 1976-79; cons. Center for Performance Improvement. Guest lectr. Lake Forest Coll., Triton Coll. Served with AUS, 1966-68. Mem. Assn. for Performance Improvement, Am. Soc. Tng. and Devel., Ill. Tng. Dirs. Assn. Home: 4205 Applewood Ln Matteson IL 60443 Office: 233 N Michigan Ave Chicago IL 60601

POHL, KENNETH ROY, electronics co. exec.; b. Beloit, Wis., Nov. 11, 1941; s. Walter John and Ruth Margret (Wieck) P.; student Wis. State Coll., Whitewater, 1959-60, Milton Coll., 1963-66; A.A. in Liberal Arts; m. Deloris Jean Harris, Sept. 22, 1970. With Beloit Corp., 1960-63; mgr. trainee Faimly Fin. Corp., 1966; with Chrysler Corp., 1966-67; owner, operator bowling alley and lounge, 1967-68; with Automatic Electric Co., Genoa, Ill., 1968-69; buyer Fox Corp., Janesville, Wis., 1969-70; materials mgr. Clinton Electronic Corp., Loves Park, Ill., 1970-72, import-export mgr., supr. sales adminstrn., 1972-80, import-export mgr., corp. gen. traffic mgr., 1980—, distbn. mgr., 1981—; dir. Air-Pack Enterprises Inc., Schaumburg, Ill. cons. internat. transp.; mem. Midwest Shippers Adv. Fed. Maritime Commn. Founder, exec. dir. Tri-State All Star Bowling Assn.; adv. Ladies Profl. Tournament Bowlers. Mem. Am. Prodn. and Inventory Control Soc., Ill. State C. of C. (internat. com. for trade and investments). Lutheran. Clubs: Lions, Rock River Valley Traffic; World Trade (charter mem.) (Northern, Ill.). Home: 134 Carry Dr PO Box L Clinton WI Office: 6701 Clinton Rd Box 2277 Loves Park IL 61131

POHORSKY, WILLIAM B., assn. exec.; b. Cedar Rapids, Iowa, Mar. 4, 1928; s. Ben Franklin and Besse (Easker) P.; B.A., Coe Coll., 1955; postgrad. State U. Iowa, 1955-56, Mich. State U., 1958-64; m. Betty Lou Nejdl, Oct. 30, 1949; children—Jane, Jean, John, Joan, James. Exec. asst. Cedar Rapids C. of C., 1957-60; exec. dir. Greater Downtown Cedar Rapids Assn., Inc., 1960—. Cubmaster Boy Scouts Am., Cedar Rapids, 1968-69; mem. adv. com. Mt. Mercy Coll., 1977—, Kirkwood Community Coll., 1976—; mem. Linn County 6th Jud. Dist. Adv. Com. and Jail Renovation Com., 1975—; bd. dirs. Salvation Army, Cedar Rapids, 1977—; active various charitable orgns.; bd. dirs. Linn County Sr. Center, 1977—; mem. Cedar Rapids-Marion Area Council of Chs., 1963-66; mem. adv. manpower council CETA, 1975—; elder Presbyn. Ch., Cedar Rapids, 1963—, mem. bd. trustees, 1960-63, chmn., 1964; mem. Mayor's Jobs for Vets. Com., 1971; mem. Internat. Yr. of Disabled Persons Com. Served with USN, 1946-48, USAFR, 1952-72. Recipient Gov. award for service to handicapped, 1976; certificate of award Kirkwood Community Coll., 1976; Exemplary Service award Cedar Rapids Police Dept., 1973; U.S. Nat. Security Seminar award, 1966; Council of Chs. award, 1965. Mem. Linn County Czech Heritage Found., C. of C., Reserve Officers Assn. of Linn County (pres. 1967), Coe Coll. Alumni Assn., U.S. Power Squadron, Internat. Oceanographic Found., Urban Land Inst., Nat. Parking Assn., Internat. Downtown Exec. Assn., Am. C. Of C. Execs., Iowa C. of C. Execs. Presbyterian. Clubs: Kiwanis, Elks, Cedar Rapids Exec., Cedar Rapids Travel Men, Iowa State Travel Men. Contbr. articles in field to profl. jours. Home: 1016 29th St NE Cedar Rapids IA 52402 Office: 904 American Bldg Cedar Rapids IA 52401

POINSETT, SALLYANN BOUGHEY, educator; b. Trenton, N.J., Jan. 1, 1938; d. Elmer Elsworth and Frances Ellen (McCann) Boughey; B.S., Trenton State Coll., 1959; M.A., U. Mich., 1973, Ph.D., 1976; m. Frederick George Poinsett, Aug. 8, 1959; children—Scott Christopher, Craig Jeffrey, Paige Beth. Asst. prof. Oakland U., Rochester, Mich., 1974-76; dir. counseling, dir. Project WILL (Women in Leadership Learning Project), Barat Coll., Lake Forest, Ill., 1976-80; cons. Ednl. Leadership IMPACT Program, Wayne County Intermediate Sch. Dist., Wayne, Mich., 1980—; cons., trainer in edn., govt. and bus. Danforth Asso., 1978—. Mem. Am. Coll. Personnel Assn., Am. Personnel and Guidance Assn., Am. Soc. Tng. and Devel., Am. Assn. Sex Educators, Counselors and Therapists, Phi Delta Kappa. Author: A Woman's Introduction to Leadership Learning; WILL Resource Guide: Developing Leadership Programs; exec. producer film and videotape Soar at WILL. Home: 30650 Bruce Ln Franklin MI 48025 Office: 33500 Oak Barn Rd Wayne MI 48184

POINSETTE, DONALD EUGENE, bus. exec., value mgmt. cons.; b. Fort Wayne, Ind., Aug. 17, 1914; s. Eugene Joseph and Julia Anna (Wyss) P.; student Purdue U., 1934, Ind. U., 1935-37, 64; m. Anne Katherine Farrell, Apr. 15, 1939; children—Donald J., Eugene J., Leo J., Sharon Poinsette Smith, Irene Poinsette Snyder, Cynthia Poinsette West, Maryanne Poinsette Stohler, Philip J. With various cos., 1937-39; metall. research and field sales cons. P.R. Mallory Corp., 1939-49; dist. sales mgr. Derringer Metall. Corp., Chgo., 1949-50; plant engr. Cornell-Dubilier Electric Corp., Indpls., 1950-53; with Jenn-Air Corp., Indpls., 1953-74, purchasing dir., 1953-71, mgr. value engring. and quality control, 1969-74; bus. mgmt. cons. Mays and Assos., Indpls., 1974-76; Named to U.S. Finder's List, Nat. Engrs. Register, 1956. Pres., Marian Coll. Parents Club, Indpls., 1969-70; com. mem. Boy Scouts Am. Nat trustee Xavier U., 1972-73, Dad's Club, Cin. Mem. Nat. Assn. Purchasing Mgmt., Indpls. Purchasing Mgmt. Assn., Soc. Am. Value Engrs. (certified value specialist; sec.-treas. Central Ind. chpt. 1972-73), Soc. Ret. Execs. Indpls. C. of C., Ind. U., Purdue U. alumni assns., Columbian (pres. 1972-73), Triad choral groups, Internat. Platform Assn., Tau Kappa Epsilon. Club: K.C. (4 deg.). Home: 5760 Susan Dr E Indianapolis IN 46250

POIRIER, BROOKE ELIZABETH, public relations counselor; b. San Luis Obispo, Calif., Aug. 12, 1942; d. Vincent Brian and Jane Elizabeth (Strosnyder) Curran; B.A., Washburn U., 1966; M.B.A., U. Mo., Kansas City, 1976; m. Constant John Poirier, III, Apr. 19, 1969; 1 son, Desmond Constant. Reporter, Topeka Capital-Jour., 1965-67; fin. reporter, asst. to bus. editor Kansas City Star, 1968-69; public affairs officer Model Cities Dept., City of Kansas City, Mo., 1969-72; coordinator media relations Am. Nurses Assn., Kansas City, 1972-75; pres. MarCom, Inc., Kansas City, 1976-78; dir. public relations dept. Bernstein, Rein & Boasberg, Inc., Kansas City, 1978-81; v.p. The Boasberg Co., Kansas City, 1981—. Mem. Public Relations Soc. Am. (accredited), Beta Gamma Sigma. Episcopalian. Office: 800 W 47th St Kansas City MO 64112

POLAKOFF, DONALD MILES, assn. exec.; b. Shelbyville, Ind., Dec. 7, 1933; s. Maurice Howard and Helen Elizabeth (Behrendt) P.; B.S., Ind. U., 1956; m. Jackie Lou Hawkins, Mar. 8, 1958; children—Susan, Jennifer. Indsl. relations dir. Shelby Mfg. Co., Shelbyville, 1958-61, plant mgr., 1962-68; v.p. Ind. Mfrs. Assn., Indpls., 1968—; instr. suprs. inst. Ind. Central Coll., Indpls., 1968-75; mem. adv. council Vocat. Tech. Services Center, Ind. State U., Terre Haute, 1975-77; mem. research adv. com. Ind. Bd. Vocat. Tech. Edn., 1975-77; mem. Ind. Manpower Planning Council, 1973, Ind. Manpower Devel. Council, 1974-76, Ind. Adv. Com. on Day Care Services, 1969, Ind. Manpower Devel. Council, 1974-76; chmn. Hoosier State Apprenticeship Conf., 1973, 75, 77, 79, 81; mem. curriculum adv. com. Vincennes U., 1975—; field coordinator Youth for Understanding, Exchange Student Program. 1972—; mem. Pvt. Industry Council, Ind. Balance of State, 1980—. Served with CIC, AUS, 1956-58. Mem. Ind. Personnel Assn. (dir.), Personnel Assn. Indpls. (dir.), Ind. Manpower Research Assn. Republican. Jewish. Clubs: Elks, Eagles, Moose. Home: PO Box 178 Shelbyville IN 46176 Office: 115 N Pennsylvania St Indianapolis IN 46204

POLASCIK, MARY ANN, ophthalmologist; b. Elkhorn, W.Va., Dec. 28, 1940; d. Michael and Elizabeth (Halko) Polascik; B.A., Rutgers U., 1967; M.D., Pritzker Sch. Medicine, 1971; m. Joseph Elie, Oct. 2, 1973; 1 dau., Laura Elizabeth Polascik. Jr. pharmacolgist Ciba Pharm. Co., Summit, N.J., 1961-67; intern Billings Hosp., Chgo., 1971-72; resident in ophthalmology U. Chgo. Hosp., 1972-75; practice medicine specializing in ophthalmology, Dixon, Ill., 1975—; pres. McNichols Clinic, Ltd.; cons. ophthalmology, Dixon Devel. Center; mem. staff Katherine Shaw Bethea Hosp., Dixon, Dixon Devel. Center Hosp. Bd. dirs. Sinissippi Mental Health Center. Mem. AMA, Ill. State Med. Soc., Ill., Am. assns. ophthalmology, Am. Assn. Physicians and Surgeons, AAUW, Alpha Sigma Lambda. Roman Catholic. Clubs: Dixon Country, Galena Territory. Office: 120 S Hennepin Ave Dixon IL 61021

POLCAR, GERTRUDE ELIZABETH, judge; b. Cleve., Oct. 10, 1916; d. Martin and Gertrude M. (Jirele) Polcar; student Leland Stanford Jr. U., 1935-36; A.B. in Law, U. Chgo., 1938, J.D., 1940. Admitted to Ohio bar, 1941, U.S. Supreme Ct. bar, 1981; individual practice law, Parma, 1942-44, 50-56, 60-71; asst. atty. gen. of Ohio, 1945-49, 57-59; councilman City of Parma, 1960-68; mem. Ohio Ho. of Reps. from Dist. 51, 1969-71; judge Parma Municipal Ct., 1972—, presiding and adminstrv. judge, 1976-77, 82—; v.p.-at-large Greater Cleve. Safety Council. Mem. Republican State Central Com. from 20th Dist., 1954-64; mem. Citizens League, South Ridge Civic Assn. Recipient superior jud. service awards Supreme Ct. Ohio, 1975, 76, June, 77, 78, 79, 80, 81. Mem. Ohio, Cuyahoga County, Parma bar assns., Bar Assn. Greater Cleve., Cleve. Women Lawyers' Assn., Ohio Municipal Judges Assn. (exec. com.), Greater Cleve. Municipal Judges Assn. (pres.), Ohio Jud. Conf., Am. Judges Assn. Clubs: Order Eastern Star, Ladies' Oriental Shrine N.Am. Home: 7060 Ridge Rd Parma OH 44129 Office: 5750 W 54th St Parma OH 44129

POLCZYNSKI, JAMES JOHN, educator; b. Milw., Dec. 18, 1949; s. Stanley Anthony and Ruth Ann (Rehorst) P.; B.B.A., U. Wis., Milw., 1972; M.B.A., U. Wis., Madison, 1973; Ph.D., Marquette U., 1978; m. Joan Carol Beere, July 9, 1977. Lectr. bus. mgmt. U. Wis., Parkside, 1973-77, asst. prof. bus. mgmt., 1977-80, asso. prof. mgmt., 1981—; cons. mgmt., civic orgns., Wis. Recipient U. Wis. Disting Teaching award, 1974. Mem. Nat. Assn. Mktg. Mgmt. Educators (mem. instnl. membership com.), Nat. Acad. Mgmt., Midwest Acad. Mgmt., Midwest Bus. Adminstrn. Assn. Author: Concepts and Practices of Management and Organization, 1979; Concepts and Practices of Management: A Book of Readings, 1981. Home: 2125 E Oak St Oak Creek WI 53154 Office: Div Bus U Wis Parkside Kenosha WI 53141

POLIAN, HAROLD, investment banker; b. Omaha, Oct. 14, 1893; s. John Albert and Ida Louise (Brandt) P.; LL.B., Creighton U., 1921; m. Gladys L. Fessenden, 1921; children—Virginia Avalon, Maxine Lenore. With Peters Trust Co., Omaha, 1921-26; investment banker Smith Polian & Co., Omaha, 1927—; chmn. bd. So. Calif. Water Co., Los Angeles, Edison Sault Electric Co., Sault Ste. Marie, Mich.; pres. Smith Polian Co. Mem. Nebr. Investment Bankers Assn. (past pres.), Omaha C. of C., Am. Legion. Clubs: Union League (Chgo.); Omaha, Happy Hollow. Home: 2527 Country Club Ave Omaha NE 68104 Office: 1623 Farnam St Suite 700 Omaha NE 68102

POLICASTRO, ANTHONY JOSEPH, mech. engr.; b. Elizabeth, N.J., Mar. 5, 1946; s. Anthony George and Etta (Gigante) P.; B.S., Columbia U., 1966, M.S., 1967, Eng. Sc.D. (NASA fellow), 1970; m. Laurie Marie Zeman, June 13, 1976. San. engr. N.Y.C. Health Dept., summer 1966; engr. Argonne (Ill.) Nat. Lab., 1970—; cons. Swedish Meteorol. and Hydrol. Inst., 1976, Rudjer Boskovic Inst. and Boris Kidric Inst., Yugoslavia, 1976; adj. asso. prof. So. Ill. U. at Cardondale, 1976—; cons. IAEA, 1978, 79. Grantee Nuclear Regulatory Commn., 1976, Electric Power Research Inst., 1977, 80, Dept. Energy, 1980. Mem. Internat. Center Heat and Mass Transfer, AIAA, ASME, Internat. Assn. Great Lakes Research. Roman Catholic. Contbr. articles to profl. jours. Home: 1260 Andrus Ave Downers Grove IL 60516 Office: 9700 Cass Ave S Argonne IL 60439

POLICH, JOHN EDMUND, environ. cons. co. exec.; b. Sturgeon Bay, Wis., Oct. 12, 1945; s. John J. and Frieda A. (Krueger) P.; B.S., U. Wis., 1968; m. Mary A. Gibson, Aug. 26, 1972; children—Joshua, Sarah. Project engr. Cities Service Co., East Chicago, Ind., 1968-70, Borg Warner Co., Parkersburg, W. Va., 1970-71; pollution control engr., asst. to head enforcement Met. San. Dist. Chgo., 1971-72; mgr. environ. services div. Erickson Chem. Co., Chgo., 1972-73; asso., pres. Gabriel & Assos., Chgo., 1973—, also founder. Mem. Chgo. Indsl. Water, Waste and Sewage Group (sec. 1974-75, pres. 1978-79). Address: 1439 W George St Chicago IL 60657

POLING, ALAN DALE, psychopharmacologist; b. Grafton, W.Va., Oct. 24, 1950; s. Howard Taft and Ruth Jean P.; B.A., Alderson-Broaddus Coll., 1972; M.A., W.Va. U., 1974; Ph.D., U. Minn., 1977. Cons., Minn. Public Sch. Dist. 287, Mpls., 1977; research asso. U. S.C., Columbia, 1977-78; asst. prof. dept. psychology Western Mich. U., Kalamazoo, 1979—; acting prin. investigator USPHS grants, 1977-78. Mem. Behavioral Pharmacology Soc., Am. Psychol. Assn., Assn. Behavior Analysis. Contbr. numerous articles to profl. jours. Home: 2722 Mt Olivet St Kalamazoo MI 49004 Office: Dept Psychology Western Mich U Kalamazoo MI 49008

POLITE, MICHAEL FRANCIS, sch. adminstr.; b. Galesburg, Ill., Aug. 24, 1950; s. Douglas W. and Mary V. Polite; B.A., Knox Coll., 1972; M.S., U. Chgo., 1976; m. Danica Hurley, May 11, 1974; 1 son, Adam. Tchr., Sch. Dist. 75, Mundelein, Ill., 1974-77, dir. inservice project, 1977-81, dir. spl. services and inservice project, 1979-80, prin., inservice dir., 1980—; condr. profl. workshops on behavior devel. of children. Served with USAR, 1972-78. Mem. Ill. Prins. Assn., Assn. Supervision and Curriculum Devel. Office: 1200 N Midlothian St Mundelein IL 60060

POLK, BEN, state legislator; b. Hamburg, Iowa, Jan. 24, 1930; student, U. Nebr., 1952, St. Louis U., 1954. Mem. Ill. Ho. of Reps. from 36th Dist., 1972—, minority whip 81st Gen. Assembly, 1978-79; adminstrv. asst. to U.S. Rep. Tom Railsback, 1965-72. Vice chmn. Rock Island County Republican Central Com., 1966-70; mem. Council on Alcoholism; bd. dirs. Rock Island County chpt. ARC; bd. dirs. Lutheran Welfare. Served with USMC, 1948-52. Recipient Friends to Edn. award Ill. Office Edn., 1975, 76, 77, Legislator of Year award Ill. Edn. Assn., 1976. Republican. Lutheran. Clubs: Jaycees (past state v.p. Nebr., past pres. Quint City Council). Office: House of Representatives Springfield IL 62706

POLK, EDWARD JOHN, indsl. engr., educator; b. Scottdale, Pa., Aug. 17, 1922; s. John and Ann P.; B.Indsl.Engring., Gen. Motors Inst., 1949; M.S., Mich. State U., 1958; m. Geraldine Juliette, Nov. 21, 1959; children—Sandra Ann, Jeanne Marie. Work standards engr., foreman Fisher Body Co., Cleve., 1946-50; supr. indsl. engring. Ford Motor Co., Highland Park, Ill., 1950-51; asso. prof. indsl. engring. Gen. Motors Inst., Flint, Mich., 1951—. Served with USN, 1944-46. Mem. Am. Inst. Indsl. Engrs., Saginaw Valley Engring. Council, Alpha Pi Mu. Author: (with others) Advanced Methods and Work Standards, 1977; (with others) Methods Analysis and Basic Time Study, 1978. Home: 1532 Flushing Rd Flushing MI 48433 Office: 1700 W 3d Ave Flint MI 48502

POLK, GLORIA HARRIS, speech pathologist; b. Norfolk, Va., Aug. 27, 1944; d. Ellis James and Annie Gertrude (Smith) Harris; B.A., Hampton (Va.) Inst., 1966; M.A., Western Mich U., 1967; m. Silas William Polk, III, Mar. 26, 1971; children—John Elder, Audra Alise. Speech and lang. pathologist Elkhart (Ind.) County Assn. for Retarded, Elkhart, 1968-69; mgr. speech, lang. and audiology dept. Wyandotte (Mich.) Gen. Hosp., 1969-77; v.p. Speech, Lang. and Audiology Programs, Inc., Cons., Detroit, 1976—; clin. supr., lectr. Wayne State U., Detroit, 1979—; part-time instr. Wayne County Community Coll., 1979—. Chmn. improvement com. Hartwell-Grove Block Club, Detroit, 1976-77. Mem. Am. (com. on pvt. practice), Mich. (v.p. community and hosp. services 1975-77) speech and hearing assns., Mich. Speech Pathologists in Clin. Practice. Mem. United Ch. Christ. Club: Sunday Bridge. Contbr. articles to profl. confs. Home: 18105 Fairfield St Detroit MI 48221 Office: 571 Manoogian Hall Wayne State U Detroit MI 48202

POLK, SOL HALFRED, retail co. exec.; b. Chgo., May 14, 1917; s. Henry H. and Yetta (Ryan) P.; student public schs., Chgo. Pres., Polk Bros., Inc., Melrose Park, Ill., 1935—. Bd. dirs. Chgo. Better Bus. Bur., Coyne Electronics Inst., Chgo. Heart Assn., Clarence Darrow Community Center, Am. Heritage Found.; dir. bd. econ. devel. Ill. Div. Tourism. Served in U.S. Army, 1943-46. Named Brand Name Retailer of Yr., Brand Name Found., 1961, 67. Mem. Nat. Appliance and TV-Radio Dealers Assn. (dir.), Sales and Mktg. Execs. Club, Young Pres. Orgn., Chgo. Assn. Commerce, Action Com. Internat. Devel., Com. Econ. and Cultural Devel. Chgo., Chgo. Execs. Club, Ill. C. of C. Office: 8311 W North Ave Melrose Park IL 60160*

POLLEY, HOWARD FREEMAN, physician; b. Columbus, Ohio, Nov. 12, 1913; B.A., Ohio Wesleyan U., Delaware, 1934, D.Sc. (hon.), 1965; M.D., Ohio State U., 1938; M.S., U. Minn., 1945; m. Georgiana Redrup, June 5, 1938; children—Alice, Mary Ann, William. Intern, St. Luke's Hosp., Chgo., 1938-39, resident, 1939-40; fellow Mayo Grad. Sch., U. Minn., 1940-43; first asst. in rheumatology Mayo Clinic, Rochester, Minn., 1942-43, cons. in medicine and rheumatic diseases, 1943-46, 48—, cons. in phys. medicine, 1946-48, head sect. of medicine, 1962-66, chmn. div. rheumatology, dept. medicine, 1966-76, sr. cons. rheumatology, 1976—; mem. adv. council Nat. Inst. Arthritis, Metabolism and Digestive Diseases, NIH, Bethesda, Md., 1972-76; mem. nat. arthritis adv. bd. NIH, 1981—; mem. Nat. Arthritis Commn., 1975; instr. phys. medicine Mayo Grad. Sch., U. Minn., 1947-48, instr. medicine, 1948-50, asst. prof., 1950-54, asso. prof., 1954-60, prof., 1960-72, prof. medicine Mayo Med. Sch., 1972—. Vice pres. Arthritis Found., 1966-68, mem. exec. bd., bd. dirs., 1964-68; trustee Ohio Wesleyan U., 1967-78, 79—, mem. exec. com., 1970-72, chmn. student affairs com. of bd., 1970-72. Recipient Alumni Achievement award Ohio State U., 1958. Diplomate Am. Bd. Phys. Medicine. Fellow A.C.P.; mem. Central Soc. for Clin. Research, AMA, Zumbro Valley Med. Soc., Am. Rheumatic Assn. (Spl. citation 1951, pres. 1964-65), Indian (hon.), Japan (hon.), USSR (hon.) rheumatism assns., Nat. Soc. Clin. Rheumatologists (founder, 1st pres.), Sociedad Uruguaya de Rheumatologia (hon.), Societe Francaise de Rheumatologie (hon.), Sigma Xi, Alpha Omega Alpha. Author: (with others) Physical Examination of the Joints, 1965; sr. author: Rheumatologic Interviewing and Physical Examination of the Joints, 2d edit., 1978; asso. editor Arthritis and Rheumatism, 1960-64. Office: Dept Internal Medicine Div Rheumatology Mayo Clinic Rochester MN 55901

POLLITT, GERTRUDE STEIN, clin. social worker, psychotherapist; b. Vienna, Austria, Sept. 12, 1919; d. Julius and Sidoni (Brauch) Stein; came to U.S., 1949, naturalized, 1951; B.A., Roosevelt U., 1954; M.A., U. Chgo., 1956; certificate Chgo. Inst. Psychoanalysis, 1963; m. Erwin P. Pollitt, Jan. 13, 1951. Resident social worker Anna Freud, Essex, Eng., 1944-45; dep. dir. UN, U.S. Zone, Germany, 1945-48; psychiat. social worker Jewish Children's Bur., Chgo., 1955-63; pvt. practice as psychiat. and clin. social worker, Glencoe, Ill., 1961—; condr. seminars; cons. Winnetka Community Nursery Sch., 1962-63, North Shore Congregation Israel Nursery Sch., 1966-69, Oakwood Home for Aged, 1980. Fellow Am. Orthopsychiat. Assn., Ill. Soc. Clin. Social Workers; mem. Nat. Registry Health Care Providers in Clin. Social Work, Acad. Certified Social Workers, Nat. Assn. Social Workers (chmn. pvt. practice com. 1967-70), Lic. Clin. Social Workers Calif., Menninger Found., Child Care Assn. Ill. Author articles in field. Home: 481 Oakdale Ave Glencoe IL 60022

POLLNOW, GILBERT FREDERICK, chemist, computer programmer; b. Oshkosh, Wis., Jan. 17, 1925; s. Arthur Ewald and Alma Clara (Sonnenberg) P.; B.S., U. Wis., Oshkosh, 1950; M.S., U. Iowa, 1951, Ph.D. (Office Naval Research fellow), 1954; m. Katherine L. Kaye, Apr. 7, 1973; children by previous marriage—Nicole Denise, Steven John. Research scientist Dow-Corning Corp., Midland, Mich., 1954-58; research scientist Allis-Chalmers Mfg. Co., Milw., 1958-61; prof. chemistry, computing specialist U. Wis., Oshkosh, 1961—; cons. chem. accidents; worldwide cons. sci. computer programming. Served with USN, 1942-46. NSF lectr., summer 1968, 70-71; NSF/CAUSE grantee, 1976-78. Mem. Am. Chem. Soc. (nat. tour speaker 1971, 74, chmn. N.E. Wis. sect. 1968), AAAS, Sigma Xi. Club: Elks. Patentee in field. Home: 103 W South Park Ave Oshkosh WI 54901 Office: Dept Chemistry U Wis Oshkosh WI 54901

POLLOCK, DAVIS ALLEN, ins. co. exec.; b. Douds, Iowa, Aug. 31, 1942; s. Davis Edwin and Bertha Dorothy (Barker) P.; B.S., Drake U., 1964; m. Marcia Tedrow, Jan. 1, 1965; children—Eric, Kirsten. With Central Life Ins., Des Moines, 1964—, v.p. corp. planning, 1979—. Fellow Soc. Actuaries; mem. Am. Acad. Actuaries, Des Moines Actuaries Club, Kappa Mu Epsilon, Omicron Delta Kappa. Republican. Methodist. Club: Mason. Home: 4229 Foster Dr Des Moines IA 50312 Office: 611 5th Ave Des Moines IA 50309

POLLS, IRWIN, aquatic biologist; b. Thunder Bay, Ont., Can., Oct. 30, 1944; came to U.S., 1954, naturalized, 1963; s. Joseph and Fanny (Segal) P.; B.S., U. Ill., 1967; M.S. Oreg. State U., 1970. Aquatic biologist research and devel. dept. Met. San. Dist. of Greater Chgo., 1971—. Served with U.S. Army, 1970-71. Decorated Bronze Star, Air medal. Mem. Internat. Assn. Water Pollution Research, Societas Internationalis Limnologiae. Jewish. Office: Rural Route 2 Box 226 Roselle IL 60172

POLUGA, CHARLES, educator; b. Wheeling, W.Va., Apr. 14, 1944; s. Chester and Stella (Stus) P.; B.A., Coll. Steubenville, 1966; M.A., U. Akron, 1969; m. Judith Takacs, Dec. 16, 1972; children—Adam, Danielle (dec.), Nathan. Asst. prof. math. Kent State U., Ashtabula, Ohio, 1968—. Mem. NEA, AAUP, Ohio Edn. Assn. Roman Catholic. Author: (with Daniel L. Auvil) Elementary Algebra, 1978. Home: 1470 Cherry Ln Ashtabula OH 44004 Office: Kent State University 3325 W 13th St Ashtabula OH 44004

POLYDORIS, STEVEN NICHOLAS, mfg. co. exec.; b. Evanston, Ill., Sept. 12, 1954; s. Nicholas George and Gloria Anne (Lucas) P.; student Drake U., 1972-73, Northwestern U., 1973-77. With Wilder Engring. Co., 1978; pres. ENM Co., Chgo., 1979—. Home: 128 16th St Wilmette IL 60091 Office: 5150 Northwest Hwy Chicago IL 60630

POMA, PEDRO ALFONSO, obstetrician, gynecologist; b. Peru, Mar. 11, 1938; came to U.S., 1966; s. Cesar and Rosa (Herrera) P.; B.Medicine, San Marcos U., 1964, Physician-Surgeon, 1965; m. Lydia Maria Marca, Mar. 27, 1965; children—Ana Elizabeth, Alfonso Martin. Intern, Central Hosp., Lima, 1964; resident in obstetrics and gynecology San Marcus U. Grad. Sch., 1965-66; resident Cook County Hosp., Chgo., 1966-71; resident obstetrics and gynecology, pathology Northwestern U., Chgo., 1969; asst. prof. obstetrics and gynecology Loyola U., Chgo., 1973—; vice chmn. dept. obstetrics and gynecology Mt. Sinai Hosp., Chgo., 1975-80; lectr. Cook County Grad. Sch. Medicine, 1977—; chmn. dept. obstetrics and gynecology Gottlieb Meml. Hosp., Melrose Park, Ill., 1981—. Fellow A.C.S., Am. Coll. Obstetricians and Gynecologists, Chgo. Gynecol. Soc.; mem. Chgo. Med. Soc. (sec. br., treas. 1977-78, pres. 1978—), Central Assn. Obstetricians and Gynecologists, AMA, Am. Fertility Soc. Roman Catholic. Contbr. articles to profl. publs.; also bi-monthly sci. newspaper column. Contbg. editor in ob-gyn Ill. Med. Jour. Office: 1200 Superior St Suite 402 Melrose Park IL 60160

POMERANTZ, SHERWIN BERNARD, data processing exec.; b. N.Y.C., Nov. 18, 1939; s. Sidney and Anna (Simons) P.; B.S. in Indsl. Engring., N.Y. U., 1960; M.S. in Mech. Engring. (teaching fellow), U. Ill., 1962; m. Barbara Sue Rashbaum, Jan. 27, 1962; children—Shari, Deborah. Instr. mech. engring. U. Ill., Champaign, 1960-62; instr. engring. drawing Cuyahoga Community Coll., Cleve., 1962-64; controller Masten Corp., Chgo., 1964-1966; pres. founder Controls for Industry Inc., Chgo., 1966—. Pres., Allied Jewish Sch. Bd. Met. Chgo., 1975-78; pres. Maine Twp. Jewish Congregation, Des Plaines, Ill., 1976-78; pres. bd. Jewish Edn. Met. Chgo., 1981—; pres. Midwest region United Synagogue Am., 1978-81, also chmn. council regional presidents; bd. dirs. World Council of Synagogues, 1979—. Served to capt. Signal Corps U.S. Army, 1962-64. Named Man of Yr., Israel Bond Orgn., 1973. Mem. ASME, Chgo. Assn. Commerce and Industry, Mensa, Alpha Epsilon Pi (nat. v.p.). Weekly columnist Chgo. Jewish Post and Opinion, 1975-78; contbr. articles to profl. jours. Home: 8812 Church St Des Plaines IL 60016 Office: 2635 Peterson Ave Chicago IL 60659

POMERANZ, JEROME RAPHAEL, dermatologist; b. Newark, Dec. 29, 1930; s. Raphael and Zina (Rubinow) P.; B.A., George Washington U., 1952; M.D., Boston U., 1956; m. Barbara Barna, May 1978; children—Russell Carl, William Eric, Emily Suzanne. Rotating intern Kings County Hosp., 1956-57; intern in pathology Johns Hopkins Hosp., Balt., 1957-58, asst. physician out patient dept. allergy clinic, 1963-65; fellow in medicine (dermatology) Johns Hopkins U. Sch. Medicine, 1960-63, fellow in medicine (allergy and infectious disease), 1963-65; dir. dermatology Cleve. Met. Gen. Hosp., 1965—, pathologist in charge skin pathology, 1967—; asso. prof. dermatology Case Western Res. U. Sch. Medicine, 1971—, asst. prof. pathology, 1967—; mem. com. to rev. use of ionizing radiation for treatment of benign diseases Nat. Acad. Scis., 1975—. Served with M.C., U.S. Army, 1958-60. Diplomate Am. Bd. Dermatology. Fellow A.C.P., Am. Acad. Dermatology; mem. Am. Dermatol. Assn., Am. Soc. Dermatopathology, Soc. Investigative Dermatology, Assn. Profs. Dermatology, Am. Fedn. Clin. Research, AAAS, Cleve. Dermatol. Soc. (pres. 1973-75), N.Y. Acad. Scis., Cleve. Soc. Pathologists (asso.), Cleve. Acad. Medicine. Club: Ripon. Home: 490 Merrimak Dr Berea OH 44017 Office: 3395 Scranton Rd Cleveland OH 44109

POMEROY, ELWAINE F(RANKLIN), lawyer; b. Topeka, June 4, 1933; s. Charles Franklin and Ada Frances (Owen) P.; A.B., Washburn U., 1955, J.D., 1957; m. Joanne Carolyn Bunge, Sept. 30, 1950; children—Janella Ruth, Duane Franklin, Carl Fredrick. Admitted to Kans. bar, 1957, since practiced in Topeka; sr. partner Pomeroy and Pomeroy, 1964—; pres. Topeka Escrow Service, Inc. Mem. Kans. State Senate, 1969—; Republican precinct committeeman, 1961-80; mem. Kans. Jud. Council, 1977—; commr. Nat. Conf. Commrs. on Uniform State Laws, 1979—. Mem. Am., Kans., Topeka bar assns. Mason, Eagle. Author: (with others) Principles of Accounting, 1957. Home: 1619 Jewell St Topeka KS 66604 Office: 1415 Topeka Ave Topeka KS 66612

POMINVILLE, HENRY ARTHUR, lawyer; b. Grosse Pointe Farms, Mich., Mar. 11, 1933; s. Arthur Henry and Esther Elizabeth (Stephens) P.; B.J., U. Mo., 1957; LL.B., Wayne State U., 1964; m. Mary Valerie Stackpoole, June 6, 1959; children—Stephen Eric, Lauretta Ann, Garrett Arthur, Kyle Edwin, Kathleen Ann. Newsman, UP Internat., 1957-58; with IRS, 1959-64; admitted to Mich. bar, 1964; staff atty. The Dow Chem. Co., Midland, Mich., 1964-65; asst. U.S. atty. U.S. Dept. Justice, Bay City, Mich., 1965-66; asst. pros. atty. Bay County (Mich.), 1966; practice law, Bay City, 1966—; dir. Internat. Terminals, Inc., Bay City. Mayor, City of Bay City, 1969-72; mem. Bay County Democratic Exec. Com., 1969-71. Served with AUS, 1953-55. Mem. Am., Bay County (treas. 1966-68), Lawyer-Pilots bar assns., State Bar Mich., Am., Mich. trial lawyers assns., Maritime Law Assn. U.S., U.S. Navy League (chpt. v.p. 1970), Kappa Tau Alpha, Delta Theta Phi. Clubs: K.C., Elks, Bay City Country. Office: 314 Davidson Bldg 916 Washington Ave Bay City MI 48706

POMMREHN, RICHARD JUNIOR, publishing co. exec.; b. Iowa City, Apr. 17, 1924; s. Arthur R. and Leone K. (Dick) P.; student U. Louisville, 1944, Westminster Coll., 1944-45; B.B.A., Tulane U., 1947; M.A., Drake U., 1953; m. Patricia A. Bahr, June 6, 1952; 1 son, Mark R. Accountant, Standard Oil Co., Des Moines, 1947-51; dir. research Wallaces Farmer, mag., Des Moines, 1951, Wis. Agriculturist Mag., Racine, 1951—; dir. research Prairie Farmer mag., Chgo., 1957—; asst. gen. mgr. Wallace Homestead Co., Des Moines, 1973, gen. mgr., 1974—, v.p., 1977—; v.p., mgr. Agrl. Insight, 1967—; dir. research Midwest Unit Farm Publs., 1969—; mem. census adv. com. on agrl. statistics, 1962—, chmn., 1981—; pres. Farm Publ. Reports, 1981—. Served with USNR, 1944-47. Methodist (state bd. mission 1969-73). Home: 1225 18th St West Des Moines IA 50265 Office: 1912 Grand Ave Des Moines IA 50305

PONGUDOM, WILAIVAN, nurse; b. Thailand, May 5, 1943; came to U.S., 1971, naturalized, 1981; d. Peg-Tang and Boonrkong (Pongudom) Sae-Tia; B.S. in Nursing, cert. in midwifery, Siriraj Sch. Nursing, Bangkok, 1966; M.Ed., Loyola U., Chgo., 1976. Teaching asso. Ramathibodi Sch. Nursing, Mahidol U., Bangkok, 1966-71; staff nurse operating room Sheridan Rd. Pavilion, Rush-Presbyn-St. Luke's Hosp., Chgo., 1972-77; night nursing supr. Thorek Hosp. and Med. Center, Chgo., 1977—. Mem. Am. Soc. Eve. and Night Nursing Suprs., Nay. Intravenous Therapy Assn. Buddhist. Office: 850 W Irving Park Rd Chicago IL 60613

PONKA, LAWRENCE JOHN, indsl. engr.; b. Detroit, Sept. 1, 1949; s. Maximilian John and Leona May (Knobloch) P.; A.A., Macomb County Community Coll., 1974; B.S. in Indsl. Mgmt., Lawrence Inst. Tech., 1978; postgrad. Central Mich. U., 1980—; m. Jane Marie Hamilton, Oct. 25, 1975. Engr.'s asst. Army Tank Automotive Command, 1967-68; with Sperry & Hutchinson Co., Southfield, Mich., 1973, Chrysler Corp., Detroit, 1973; with Gen. Motors Corp., Warren, Mich., 1973—, engring. systems coordinator engring. staff, 1976—, now current product engring. Served with USAF, 1968-72; Vietnam, Japan, Okinawa. Decorated Air Force Commendation medal. Mem. Soc. Automotive Engrs., Engring. Soc. Detroit, Nat. Corvette Owners Assn., DAV. Roman Catholic. Home: 403 Castell Rochester MI 48063 Office: Gen Motors Corp 12 Mile and Mound Rds Warren MI 48090

PONSOLDT, WILLIAM RAYMOND, diversified mfg. co. exec.; b. Cleve., July 30, 1941; s. Raymond Samuel and Margaret (Farmer) P.; B.S. with honors, Fairleigh Dickinson U., 1963; m. Mariane Ponsoldt, Oct. 5, 1963; children—William Raymond, Tracy, Christopher. Chmn., Am. Realty Corp., Milw., 1963—, chmn. Munchen-Nassau Trading Co. Ltd., Bahamas, 1968—; chmn. bd., chief exec. officer Erie Controls, Milw., 1977—. Republican. Clubs: Cat Cay (Bahamas), Western Racquet, Exchecquer. Office: Erie Controls 4000 S 13th St Milwaukee WI 53221

PONT, JOHN, ins. agt.; b. Canton, Ohio, Nov. 13, 1927; s. Bautista and Susie (Sikurinec) P.; B.S., Miami U., Oxford, Ohio, 1952, M.S., 1956; m. H. Sandra Stoutt, June 23, 1956; children—John W., Jennifer Ann, Jeffrey David. Profl. football player, Can., 1952-53; instr., freshman football-basketball coach Miami U., 1953-55, head football coach, asst. prof., 1955-62; head football coach Yale, 1963-65; head football coach, prof. Ind. U., Bloomington, 1965-73; prof., head football coach Northwestern U., Evanston, Ill., 1973-77, athletic dir., 1975-80; agt. Equitable Assurance, Cin., 1981—. Athletic dir. Jewish Community Center, Canton, 1953; mem. Pres.'s Council on Phys. Fitness; mem. legis. spl. com. on recruiting Nat. Collegiate Athletic Assn.; v.p. NCAA Council, 1979-80. Chmn. Ind. Easter Seal, 1968-69; chmn. Ind. div. Cancer Crusade, 1969. Bd. dirs. Multiple Sclerosis, Chgo. council Boy Scouts Am. Served with USNR, 1945-47. Named Football Coach of Year, Coaches Assn., 1967, Football Writers' Coach of Year, 1967; named to Miami U. Hall of Fame, 1968; recipient Significant Sig award, 1968. Mem. Am. Football Coaches Assn. (chmn. ethics com.), Blue Key, Sigma Chi (sec. 1951), Phi Epsilon Kappa (pres. 1951), Omicron Delta Kappa. Republican. Address: 3900 Carew Tower Cincinnati OH 45202

POOLE, CHARLES DAVID, constrn. co. exec.; b. Cleve., Sept. 5, 1941; s. Claton Dever and Frances Elizabeth (Brown) P.; B.S., Andrews U., 1963; B.S.E., U. Mich., 1964; m. Rose Marie Kuerbiss, Aug. 25, 1963; children—Charles, Laurence, Kathleen. Vice pres. Poole Constrn. Co., Inc., Berrien Springs, Mich., 1964-76, pres., 1977—. Mem. Nat. Soc. Profl. Engrs. Adventist. Home: 400 Poole Berrien Springs MI 49103 Office: 500 Poole Dr Berrien Springs MI 49103

POOLE, DAVID HENRY, elec. engr.; b. Kansas City, Mo., Sept. 14, 1935; s. Paul Morris and Sarah Elizabeth (Hanna) P.; B.S. in Elec. Engring., Ill. Inst. Tech., 1973; m. Louise Mary Naus, Oct. 15, 1977; children by previous marriage—Christyne Marie, David Henry. Draftsman, Arthur Anderson Co., Chgo., 1959-60; draftsman, elec. designer Scam Instrument Co., Chgo., 1960-64; applications engr. electric furnace dept. Whiting Corp., Harvey, Ill., 1966-81; project engr. Republic Steel Corp., Chgo., 1981—; dir. Allsup Carbon Refractor Products Co. Mem. Reavis High Sch. Dist. 220 Sch. Bd., 1974-77, sec. bd., 1976-77. Served with USAF, 1955-58. Roman Catholic. Home: 14541 University St Dolton IL 60419 Office: 11600 S Burley Ave Chicago IL 60617

POOL-LEFFLER, NANCY, radio sta. exec.; b. St. Louis County, Mo., Dec. 4, 1920; d. Oscar S. and Ruth Aline (Hutchinson) Moessmer; student William Woods Coll., 1938-39; B.A., Washington U., St. Louis, 1941; m. Victor W. Leffler, June 9, 1979. Announcer, Sta. WTMV, St. Louis, 1937-41; account exec., media buyer, copywriter D'Arcy Advt., St. Louis, 1940-43; owner asst. mgr. Channel 2 TV, St. Louis, 1962-64; Diversified Media Unltd., St. Louis, 1966-70; with v.p., gen. mgr. Sta. KSHE, St. Louis, 1970—; owner Moessmer Corp., St. Louis, 1977—. Mem. Mo. Broadcasters. Republican. Home: 1299 S McKnight Rd Saint Louis MO 63117 Office: 9434 Watson Rd Saint Louis MO 63126

POOTS, CLIFFORD ALLAN, real estate broker, developer, contractor, appraiser, certified property mgr.; b. Newton, Iowa, Jan. 29, 1934; s. Clifford Lyman and Helen May (Cool) P.; student Simpson Coll., 1953, Iowa State U., 1953, U. Iowa, 1956-59; m. Kathleen M. LaBudde, Aug. 17, 1957; children—Michael Allan, Patricia Ann. Real estate broker, developer, Coralville, Iowa, 1960—; officer, dir. various corps., 1963—; asst. instr. mech. engring. State U. Iowa, 1957-59. Hon. trustee Cedars Home Children, 1972. Served with AUS, 1954-55. Recipient archtl. design awards Iowa State U., Iowa Homebuilders Assn., 1965-67. Home: 10 Olde Hickory Ridge Lakewood Hills Coralville Iowa City IA 52241 Office: PO Box 5095 Coralville Br Iowa City IA 52241

POPARAD, PAUL CARL, nurse; b. Gary, Ind., July 29, 1946; s. Nick Paul and Ruth Marie (Schultz) P.; A.D. in Nursing, Ind. Central Coll., Indpls., 1967; B.S. in Life Sci., Ind. State U., Terre Haute, 1969; diploma hosp. exec. devel., St. Louis U., 1978; health facilities adminstrn. lic., Ohio State U., 1978; m. Mary Ann Konopasek, Nov. 25, 1972; children—Amanda, David, Nathaniel. Mem. nursing staff St. Anthony Hosp., Terre Haute, 1969-75; adminstr. George Ade Meml. Hosp., Brook, Ind., 1975-79; dir. nursing service St. Anthony Med. Center, Crown Point, Ind., 1979—; bd. dirs. No. Ind. Health Systems Agy., 1978—, chmn. nominating com., 1975-80, exec. com., 1980-82; active local ARC, Assn. Retarded Citizens. Mem. Ind. Hosp. Assn. (pres. Midwest dist. 1978-79), Ind. Soc. Nursing Service Adminstrn.

POPE, JAMES RICHARD, architect; b. Mason City, Iowa, Oct. 26, 1932; s. Ivan O. and Elizabeth E. (Sears) P.; B.S. in Archtl. Engring., Iowa State U., 1959. Chief draftsman Krusmark & Krusmark Architects, Casper, Wyo., 1962; prin. Scott Engring., Watertown, S.D., 1963-65; partner Robel & Pope Architects, Watertown, 1966-71; pres. Pope Architects Inc., Watertown, 1972—. Served with USN, 1956-59; Korea. Mem. AIA. Home: 486 N Lake St Watertown SD 57201 Office: 26 N Broadway Watertown SD 57201

POPE, JEAN GROVE, psychologist, educator; b. Cin., June 12, 1927; d. Fred E. and Gertrude (Welch) Grove; B.S., Purdue U., 1966; M.Ed., U. Cin., 1969, Ed.D., 1977; m. Jack H. Pope, Aug. 24, 1946; children—Michael, Nancy, Holly. Tchr., Eastern Hills Elementary Sch., Cin., 1966-67; sch. psychologist Clermont County (Ohio) Pub. Schs., Batavia, 1969-74, Hamilton County (Ohio) Pub. Schs., Cin., 1974-75, instr. Clermont Coll., Batavia, 1975—; dir. Counseling

Center, Edgecliff Coll., Cin., 1978-79; psychologist, care center Christ Hosp., 1979—. Mem. Nat., Ohio assns. sch. psychologists, Am., Cin. psychol. assns., Ohio Orgn. Human Service/Mental Health Educators, Kappa Delta Pi. Home: 6944 Miami Bluff Dr Cincinnati OH 45227 Office: Kenwood Psychological Services Cincinnati OH 45236

POPE, JOHN DAWSON, III, lawyer; b. Butte, Mont., May 29, 1913; s. John Dawson and Abbie Esther (Shaw) P.; student Mont. State Sch. Mines, 1929-30; B.S., Mont. State U., 1933; J.D., Harvard U., 1936; postgrad. M.I.T., 1936; m. Eileen Dodds, June 27, 1981; children—John Daniel (dec.), Judith Anne, Elizabeth Pope Hoummers. Admitted to Mo. bar, 1937; since practiced in St. Louis; asst. patent atty. Monsanto Chem. Co., St. Louis, 1936-39; asso. firm Haynes & Koenig, St. Louis, 1939-50; partner firm Koenig & Pope and successor, St. Louis, 1950-63; mem. firm John D. Pope III, 1964-76; partner firm Pope & Fishel, 1977-79, pres., 1978-79; pres. John D. Pope P.C., 1979—; lectr. Washington U., St. Louis, 1964; mem. bd. admissions U.S. Dist. Ct., Eastern Dist. Mo., 1964-70, chmn., 1969-70. Mem. Am. Chem. Soc., AAAS, U.S. Trademark Assn. (lawyers adv. com. 1952-54, 57-59, 63-66, 74-77), Am. Patent Law Assn., Am., Fed. bar assns., Mo. Bar, Bar Assn. Met. St. Louis (chmn. patent sect. 1958-59), Phi Kappa Phi. Clubs: Mo. Athletic, Media (St. Louis). Editor Am. Philatelic Congress Book, 1954. Home: 926 Lanyard Ln Kirkwood MO 63122 Office: 818 Olive St Saint Louis MO 63101

POPE, JOHN WARING, investment accounts adminstr.; b. Chgo., Jan. 9, 1913; s. Henry and Adele Freida Pope; Ph.B., U. Wis., 1935; cert. of completion Grad. Sch. Bus. Adminstrn., Harvard U., 1939; m. Elizabeth Louise Davis, Aug. 25, 1938; children—John W., Henry Dewitt, E. Jane, Sabina West, Roger Conant. Asst. to pres. and chmn. Bear Brand Hosiery Co., Chgo. and Kankakee, Ill., 1935-42, dir., 1945-55; asst. to pres. and chmn. Paramount Textile Machinery Co., Chgo. and Kankakee, 1935-42, v.p., 1945-65, also dir.; asst. chief insp., asst. to personnel dir. Quaker Oats Ordnance Corps, Grand Island, Nebr., 1942-44; prodn. planner, personnel asst. Douglas Aircraft Corp., Park Ridge, Ill., 1944-45; pres., dir. Pope Brace Co., Chgo. and Kankakee, 1955-65, pvt. practice investment accounts mgmt., Chgo. and Winnetka, Ill., 1948—; dir., v.p., sec. Pope Found., Inc., 1937—; owner, operator farm, Ill., 1951-60. Mem. Investment Analysts Soc. Chgo., Fin. Analysts Fedn., Inst. Chartered Fin. Analysts, Sigma Phi. Republican. Mem. Winnetka Congregation Ch. Clubs: Chgo. Farmer's, Indian Hill. Home and Office: 649 Locust St Winnetka IL 60093

POPE, RONALD RUSSELL, educator; b. Chico, Calif., Aug. 22, 1942; s. Russell B. and F. Helen (Moore) P.; student Monterey Inst. Fgn. Studies, summer, 1963; B.A. in Econs., U. Calif., Riverside, 1964; M.A. in Russian Area Studies, UCLA, 1966; postgrad. Sch. Theology, Claremont, Calif., 1964-65; Ph.D. in Internat. Relations, U. Pa., 1975; m. Susan Ann Scoville, Aug. 14, 1965; children—Carrie, Amy, Bryan. Spl. lectr. Boise (Idaho) State Coll., 1968-70; research analyst Fgn. Policy Research Inst., Phila., 1971-72; lectr. Community Coll. of Phila., 1975-76, Montgomery County Community Coll., Pa., 1976, Beaver Coll., Glenside, Pa., 1975-76; vis. asst. prof. polit. sci. Temple U., Phila., 1976; asst. prof. dept. polit. sci. Ill. State U., Normal, 1976—; regional rep. and cons. Field Inst., Citizen Exchange Council, 1979—. Trustee Wesley Found., Ill. State U., 1981—. Served to capt. USAF, 1967-71. Fellow H.B. Earhart 1971-73, Henry Salvatori, 1972-73. Mem. Am. Assn. for Advancement of Slavic Studies. Democrat. Methodist. Mem. adv. com. Soviet Law and Govt.; jour. transls., 1972—; contbr. articles on internat. relations and Soviet fgn. policy to profl. jours.; contbr. book revs. in field. Office: Dept Political Science Illinois State Univ Normal IL 61761

POPE, SARAH GEORGINA, physician; b. N.S., Can., Oct. 29, 1940; d. George Donovan and Hughena (Mac Innis) Donovan; came to U.S., 1969; B.Sc. in Chemistry, Mt. St. Vincent Coll., 1960; M.D., Ottawa U., 1964; m. Dec. 14, 1968; children—Sarah, Patrick. Intern, Ottawa (Can.) Gen. Hosp., 1964-65; resident Royal Victoria Hosp., 1966-68; resident Henry Ford Hosp., Detroit, 1969, asso. radiologist, 1970-73; asso. radiologist Sinai Hosp. of Detroit, 1973—, dir. residency tng. program, 1973—. Mem. AMA, Wayne County Med. Soc., Am. Coll. Radiology, Mich. Radiol. Soc., Am. Soc. Nuclear Medicine. Home: 1884 Balmoral Dr Detroit MI 48203 Office: 6767 W Outer Dr Detroit MI 48235

POPE, SHARON KAY, ednl. adminstr.; b. Kansas City, Mo., Dec. 27, 1944; d. Allen David and Mildred Maybel (Wilcox) P.; B.S. cum laude, U. Mo., 1966, M.Ed., 1967, Ph.D., 1971; m. Bob Callis, Sept. 4, 1971. Adminstrv. asst. U. Mo., Columbia, 1967-68, asst. dir. women student affairs, 1968-69, grad. asst. Inst. Personnel Work, 1969-70, asst. dir. Center for Student Life, 1974—; instr. edn. U. Mo., Kansas City, 1970-71, asst. prof. edn., counseling psychologist, 1971-72, asst. dir. testing and counseling center, asst. prof. edn., 1972-73; mem. adv. bd. Women's Resource Service, U. Mo., Kansas City, 1970-72. Recipient award of merit Mo. Personnel Assn., 1979. Lic. psychologist, Mo. Mem. Am. (pres. 1977), Mo. (planning com. 1973) coll. personnel assns., Am., Mo. (chmn. research on changing women's roles 1973) personnel and guidance assns., Nat. Vocat. Guidance Assn., Assn. Counselor Educators and Suprs., Mo. Psychol. Assn., Mo. Guidance Assn., U. Mo. Columbia Edn. Alumni Assn. (dir. 1969-72), Pi Lambda Theta, Phi Delta Kappa, Delta Gamma. Club: Columbia Dance. Home: Route 4 Box 205 Columbia MO 65201 Office: 106 Read Hall U Mo Columbia MO 65201

POPLAR, GEORGIA ANNE, nursing home adminstr.; b. Toledo, Nov. 13, 1924; d. Norman George and Thelma LaVere (DeMoss) Scott; grad. St. Vincent's Hosp. Sch. Nursing, 1946; B.S.N., Mary Manse Coll., 1970; M. Ed., U. Toledo, 1974; m. Frank A. Poplar, Oct. 26, 1946 (dec.); children—Janice Ann, Kenneth F. Mem. nursing staff Riverside Hosp., Toledo, 1952-65, dir. nursing service, 1965-70; dir., coordinator nursing service Flower Hosp., Crestview Center, Sylvania, Ohio, 1970; adminstrv. dir. Lake Park Hosp., Sylvania, 1972—. Fellow Am. Coll. Nursing Home Adminstrs.; mem. Am. Coll. Hosp. Adminstrs., Nat. League Nursing. Roman Catholic. Home: 3628 Sylvanwood Dr Sylvania OH 43560 Office: 5100 Harroun Rd Sylvania OH 43560

POPLAWSKI, JOSEPH WALTER, closure mfg. co. exec.; b. Chgo., July 8, 1932; s. Joseph and Catherine P.; m. Geraldine Snell, May 24, 1952; children—Joseph, Thomas, Jerald, Julianne, Scott. With Phoenix Closures Co., Chgo., 1953—, v.p. mfg., 1978—. Chmn. Mohawk council Boy Scouts Am., Chgo., 1963-65. Served with U.S. Army, 1949-52. Office: 2444 W 16th St Chicago IL 60608

POPOVICH, PETER STEPHEN, lawyer; b. Crosby, Minn., Nov. 27, 1920; s. Peter and Rose Mary (Mihelich) P.; A.A., Hibbing Jr. Coll., 1940; B.A., U. Minn., 1942; J.D. (Minn. Bar Assn. scholar 1946), St. Paul Coll. Law, 1946; children—Victoria Ann, Dorothy Rose, Stephen Peter, Susan Jane. Admitted to Minn. bar, 1947, Fed. bar, 1947, U.S. Supreme Ct. bar, 1956; practiced in St. Paul, 1947—; mem. firm Peterson, Popovich, Knutson & Flynn, St. Paul, 1947—. Counsel, Minn. Sch. Bds. Assn., 1961—, Minn. Broadcasters Assn., 1970—, various sch. dists., 1947—; chmn. planning com., St. Mary's Point, 1970-77; mem. Minn. Bd. Continuing Legal Edn., 1975—, Minn. Lawyers Public Offices Commn., 1979—. Mem. State Coll. Bd., 1965-69; mem. Higher Edn. Coordination Com., 1968-69. Mem. Minn. Ho. of Reps., 1953-63. Mem. Am., Minn., Ramsey County, Washington County bar assns., Minn. Hist. Soc. (exec. council 1958—), Nat. Orgn. Legal Problems in Edn. (dir. 1976-79), Gamma Eta Gamma. Home: 1400 River Rd St Marys Point Route 1 Lakeland MN 55043 Office: 314 Minnesota Bldg St Paul MN 55101

POPPA, RICHARD ALLEN, trade assn. exec.; b. Indpls., Nov. 5, 1951; s. Richard Francis and Marjorie June (Miller) P.; B.S. in Polit. Sci., Ball State U., 1974; m. Kimberly A. Parks, June 1, 1974. Spl. agt. Coll. Life Ins. Co., Muncie, Ind., 1974; mgr. Ponderosa Steak House, Anderson, Ind., 1974-75, MCL Cafeteria, Anderson, 1975-76; program coordinator, adminstrv. asst., staff writer Ind. Dept. Commerce, Indpls., 1976-79; solar cons. State of Ind.; exec. asst. Ins. Inst. Ind., Indpls., 1979—. Mem. Perry Twp. Sch. Bd., 1978-81. Recipient Ind. Gov.'s Public Service Fellowship award, 1976. Mem. Ind. Soc. Assn. Execs. (dir.), Southport Jaycees, Ball State U. Alumni Assn. (past pres., bd. govs. Indpls. area, also council). Home: 2403 Appleton Dr Indianapolis IN 46227 Office: One N Capitol Suite 330 Indianapolis IN 46204

POPPE, WASSILY, chemist; b. Riga, Latvia, Nov. 10, 1918; s. Wilhelm and Barbara (Gogotoff) P.; student Kaiser Friedrich Wilhelm U., Berlin, 1936-39; cand. chem., U. Tubingen (Germany), 1947; dipl. chem. Inst. Tech. Stuttgart (Germany), 1949; Ph.D., U. Pitts., 1966; m. Larissa Heffner, Oct. 16, 1942; 1 dau., Katherine Poppe Zawadzkas. Came to U.S., 1959, naturalized, 1965. Chemist, Dr. Hans Kittel Chem. Lab., Germany, 1949-50; devel. chemist Karl Worwag Lack & Farbenfabrik, Germany, 1950-51, prodn. mgr. paint Pinturas Iris, Venezuela, 1951-53; lab. supr. Pinturas Tucan, Venezuela, 1953-54, tech. dir., 1954-57, plant mgr. paint prodn. 1957-59; chemist PPG Industries Springfield, Pa., 1959-64; research asst. phys. chemistry U. Pitts., 1964-66; group leader surface chemistry Avisun Corp., Marcus-Hook, Pa., 1966-68; research asso. Amoco Chems., Naperville, Ill., 1968—. Fellow Am. Inst. Chemists; mem. Am. Chem. Soc., Sigma Xi. Home: 105 Main St Lombard IL 60148 Office: PO Box 400 Naperville IL 60540

POPPELBAUM, WOLFGANG JOHANN, physicist; b. Frankfurt, Germany, Aug. 28, 1924; s. Hermann and Edith (Baumann) P.; M.S., Lausanne U., 1948, Ph.D., 1953. Came to U.S., 1957. Prin. investigator charge circuit research group Digital Computer Lab. U. Ill., 1954—, dir. Info. Engring. Lab., 1973—. Fellow IEEE; mem. Swiss, Am. phys. socs., Sigma Xi. Author: Computer Hardware Theory; also articles to profl. jours. Home: 2007 S Anderson Urbana IL 61801 Office: Digital Computer Lab U Ill Urbana IL 61801

POPPEN, HENRY ALVIN, state senator; b. DeSmet, S.D., Feb. 12, 1922; s. Otto H. and Sena (Fransen) P.; B.A., Huron Coll., 1949; m. Lorna Mildred Meyer, 1952; children—Elizabeth Ann, Nanette Mildred. Partner, Poppen Bros., DeSmet, 1954-69; mem. S.D. Senate, 1966—. Crew leader Agrl. Census, Kingsbury-Miner County, S.D., 1959, 60; chmn. Kingsbury County Republican party, 1960-65; chmn., supr. Spirit Lake Twp. Bd., 1964—. Mem. S.D. Stockgrowers, Kingsbury County Farm Bur., Kingsbury County Hist. Soc. (pres.). Presbyterian. Club: Masons. Office: State Capitol Pierre SD 57501*

POPPLETON, GERTRUDE ELIZABETH SHOGREN, social service adminstr.; b. Pitts., Apr. 16, 1931; d. Paul William and Gertrude Elizabeth (Curry) Shogren; B.A., Grove City Coll., 1953; M.A., U. Pitts., 1955; student U. Wis., 1975-79, Pa. State U., summer, 1952; m. Robert Glenn Poppleton, June 24, 1955; children—Eric David, Lisa Roberta. Grad. asst. Western Psychiat. Inst., U. Pitts. Med. Sch., 1953-55; tchr. kindergarten Wilkinsburg Public Sch., Pitts., 1955-58; dir. Louis Child Care Center, Pitts., 1958-59; orientation leader classes for new mothers to work as asst. tchrs., Indpls., 1965-70; pres. Glendale Co-op Nursery Sch., 1963-65; ednl. cons. Ind. Assn. for Edn. of Young Children, 1967-70; vol. coordinator Pleasant Run Children's Home, Indpls., 1970-71, adminstr., 1971—; advisor Indpls. Council Parent Coops., 1966—. Sunday sch. tchr. Boys Reformatory, Grove City, Pa., 1951-53, Swissvale Presbyn. Ch., Pitts., 1951-60, Presbyn. Ch., New Orleans, 1960-63, Meth. Ch., Indpls., 1963-67, Orchard Park Presbyn. Ch., Carmel, Ind., 1967—. Mem. Nat. Assn. Edn. Young Children, Ind. Assn. Edn. Young Children, Coop. Tchrs. Orgn., Indpls. Council Parent Coops., Parent Co-op Preschs. Internat. (Outstanding Service award 1971, Dist. award 1969), Ind. Press Women, AAUW, Ind. Assn. Residential Child Care Agys. (pres.), Community Service Council, Mortar Board, Alpha Theta Mu. Author: New Voices in American Poetry, 1975, 76; Are You Going to Teach Today, Mommy?. Home: 8 Forest Bay Ln Rural Route 1 Cicero IN 46034 Office: 1404 S State St Indianapolis IN 46203

POPRICK, MARY ANN, psychologist; b. Chgo., June 25, 1939; d. Michael and Mary (Mihalcik) P.; B.A., De Paul U., 1960, M.A., 1964; Ph.D., Loyola U., Chgo., 1968. Intern psychology Elgin (Ill.) State Hosp., 1961-62; staff psychologist, 1962; staff psychologist Ill. State Tng. Sch. for Girls, Geneva, 1962-63, Mt. Sinai Hosp., Chgo., 1963-64; lectr. psychology Loyola U. at Chgo,, 1964-67; asst. prof. Lewis U., Lockport, Ill., 1967-70, asso. prof., 1970-75, chmn. dept. psychology, 1968-72; adj. asso. prof. South Chgo. Community Hosp. Sch. Nursing, Lewis U., 1975; postdoctoral intern clin. psychology Ill. State Psychiat. Inst., Chgo., 1972-73; pvt. clin. practice, asso. with David Psychiat. Clinic Ltd., S. Holland, Ill., 1973—; mem. asso. sci. staff Riveredge Hosp., Forest Park, Ill., 1975, 76. Co-chmn. commn. on personal growth and devel. Congregation 3d Order St. Francis of Mary Immaculate, Joliet, Ill., 1970-71. Mem. Am., Midwestern, Calif., Ill. (sec.-treas. acad. sect. 1975-77, chairperson acad. sect. 1978-79, chmn. program com. 1981-82, sec. 1979-81), pres.-elect 1981-82) psychol. assns., Assn. Advancement of Psychology, AAUP, AAAS, Kappa Gamma Pi, Psi Chi (sec. 1964-65, pres. 1965-66). Home: 547 Marquette Ave Calumet City IL 60409 Office: 645 E 170th St South Holland IL 60473

PORAT, AVNER M., mgmt. cons. co. exec.; b. Tel Aviv, Israel, June 20, 1939; s. Eldad and Meriam P.; B.A., Hebrew U., 1962; M.B.A., U. Pitts., 1965, Ph.D., 1968; m. Joan Gelfund, Aug. 28, 1965; children—Ilana, Gil. Research asso. U. Pitts., 1965-68; asst. prof. Sch. Bus., U. Rochester, N.Y., 1968-70; partner Hay Assos., Chgo., 1970—; dir. Pollak Internat. Ford Found. fellow, 1967-68; Fulbright scholar, 1964-67. Mem. Am. Psychol. Assn., Beta Gamma Sigma. Contbr. articles to profl. jours. Office: Hay Assos 1 E Wacker Dr Chicago IL 60601

PORCO, CARMEN, real estate mgmt. exec.; b. Steubenville, Ohio, Apr. 29, 1947; s. Carmine and Theresa (Rotell) P.; B.A., Alderson-Broaddus Coll., 1969; M.Div., Andover Newton Theol. Sch., 1972; m. Marilyn Ruth Cheyne, June 5, 1971; children—John, Dorothy. Urban minister Nat. Ministries, Boston, 1969-71; mgr. Columbia (Md.) Interfaith Housing, 1972-73; cluster mgr. Desert Cluster, Riverside, Colton and Coachella, Calif., 1973-74; asst. v.p. Nat. Housing Ministries, Milw., 1974—; pres. Consulting, Planning Devel. Services, Milw., 1979—; instr. U. Wis. Extension; mem. City of Madison Housing Task Force; bd. dirs. La Casa Evanjelica. Treas. Dem. Party of Wis., 1978-81, chmn. Century Club, 1980; bd. dirs. Milw. Christian Center, 1977—; mem. bd. of outreach First Bapt. Ch., Madison, 1980-81. Mem. Inst. Real Estate Mgmt. (instr., cert. property mgr., legis. affairs com., HUD liaison com.), Madison Assn. Realtors, Wis. Assn. Homes for the Aged, Nat. Leased Housing Assn., Madison Bd. Realtors. Home: 2810 Willard Ave Madison WI 53704 Office: 3730 W Greentree Rd Milwaukee WI 53209

POROD, ROBERT FRANCIS, devel. engr.; b. Chgo., Oct. 10, 1946; s. Rudolph F. and Lorraine J. (Budzynski) P.; A.A., Morton Jr. Coll., 1966; B.S. in Mech. Analysis and Design Engring., U. Ill., Chgo., 1968; m. Janet M. Przybyl, Aug. 24, 1968; children—Robert Francis, Karyn M., Eric J. Sr. devel. and product engr. Hawthorne sta. Western Electric Co., Chgo., 1968—. Pres., Med. Engring. Devel. Group, 1977—; publicity chmn. Lincoln PTA, 1976-77; bd. dirs. South Cicero Baseball Assn., 1978-81; campaign chmn. Cicero Community Chest, 1979-80; mem. bd. Our Lady of Charity Grade Sch., 1980-81, pres., 1981. Mem. ASME (asso.), Western Soc. Engrs. (asso.; Charles Ellet award 1976), U. Ill. Alumni Assn. (life, alumni recognition award 1980), Polish Nat. Alliance. Roman Catholic. Club: Hunting and Fishing. Home: 3235 S 60th Ct Cicero IL 60650 Office: Hawthorne Sta Dept 8365 Chicago IL 60623

PORRETTA, LOUIS PAUL, educator; b. Malvern, Ohio, Sept. 24, 1926; s. Peter A. and Rosa (Tersigne) P.; B.A., Eastern Mich. U., 1950; Ed.M., Wayne State U., 1959, Ed.D., 1967; m. Elizabeth M. Murphy, Oct. 13, 1951; children—Leslie Elizabeth, Paul Louis, Jeffrey Mark. Tchr. elem. sch. Mason Consol. Sch., Erie, Mich., 1952-53, tchr., prin., 1953-54; prin. Mason Jr. High Sch., Erie, Mich., 1954-59; asst. prof. edn. Eastern Mich. U., Ypsilanti, 1959-62, asso. prof., 1962-66, prof. edn., 1967-71, prof. dept. curriculum and instruction, 1974—, dir. Office Internat. Projects, 1979—; chief-of-party Nat. Tchr. Edn. Center, Somalia, 1967-70; mem. edn. survey team AID, Botswana, Lesotho and Swaziland, 1970, sr. adv. U. Botswana, Lesotho and Swaziland, 1972-74; campus coordinator Swaziland Primary Curriculum Devel. Project, AID, 1978; chief-of-party projects AID, Swaziland, 1975-78, Yemen, 1981—. Chmn. March of Dimes, Westenaw County, Mich., 1956. Mem. Assn. Tchr. Educators, Inst. Internat. Edn., AAUP, Assn. for Supervision and Curriculum Devel., Phi Delta Kappa, Pi Gamma Mu. Club: Ypsilanti Rotary. Home: 719 Cornell St Ypsilanti MI 48197 Office: Eastern Mich Univ Ypsilanti MI 48197

PORT, FRIEDRICH KONRAD, nephrologist; b. Heidelberg, Germany, Mar. 17, 1938; came to U.S., 1965; s. Johannes M. and Lucie G. (Roewer) P.; M.D., U. Erlangen/Nürnberg (West Germany), 1964; M.S., U. Minn., 1975; m. Evelyn Ann Kastner; children—Angela, Joseph, James. Intern, City Hosp., Forchheim, W. Ger., 1965, Fitkin Meml. Hosp., Neptune, N.J., 1965-66; resident U. Würzburg (W. Ger.), 1967, Mayo Grad. Sch. Medicine, Rochester, Minn., 1968-72; asso. cons. Mayo Clinic, Rochester, 1972-73; dir. hemodialysis unit U. Mainz (W. Ger.), 1973-74; asst. prof. U. Mich., Ann Arbor, 1974-78, acting chmn. nephrology div., 1977-78, asso. prof. internal medicine, 1978—; chief hemodialysis unit VA Med. Center, Ann Arbor, 1974—; mem. sci. adv. bd. Kidney Found. Mich., 1978—; mem. exec. com. Mich. Ed-Stage Renal Disease Network Coordinating Council, 1980—. Fellow ACP; mem. Am. Soc. Nephrology, Am. Fedn. Clin. Research, Am. Soc. Artificial Internal Organs, Internat. Soc. Nephrology, Internat. Soc. Artificial Organs, European Dialysis and Transplant Assn., Sigma Xi. Contbr. articles to profl. jours. Office: B2954 CFO Bldg U Hosp Ann Arbor MI 48109

PORTA, JOHN CHARLES, constrn. engr.; b. St. Louis, May 18, 1953; s. Charles A. and Savina A. P.; Engring. degree Drury Coll., 1972; m. Nancy Siteman, Sept. 20, 1978 (div. Jan. 1980). With Charles Porta Co. Inc., St. Louis, 1970—, v.p. estimating, 1973-75, exec. v.p., 1975—, also dir.; pres. Design for Living; pres. Cap Devel., Inteno Concepts by Porta, Inc., Porta Properties. Co-chmn. Businessmen's Com. for Vincent Schoemell for Mayor of St. Louis, 1981—; chmn. St. Louis Young Ambassadors, bd. dirs. St. Louis Ambassadors, 1981—. Mem. Profl. Businessman's Club (rec. sec.), Am. Soc. Profl. Estimators (cert. appreciation 1977, pres. chpt. 19 1976-77), Concrete Council St. Louis, St. Louis Jaycees, Constrn. Specifications Inst. (cert. appreciation 1977), Sons of Bosses Clubs. Roman Catholic. Clubs: Media, Lions, Mo. Athletic. Democrat. Contbr. articles on constrn. estimating to profl. jours. Home: 19 Williamsbury Est Saint Louis MO 63131 Office: 2200 S 59th St Saint Louis MO 63110

PORTE, ALVIN ROBERT, writer, producer; b. N.Y.C., Jan. 23, 1930; s. Jack and Frances Catherine (Derison) P.; B.A., Met. State U., 1977; M.A., U. Minn., 1981; m. Bonnie Berger Barnum, Feb. 15, 1975; children—Steven Brett, Ariel Suzanne, Trina Jan. Writer, Grey Advt. Agy., N.Y.C., 1955-57, Norman, Craig & Kummel, N.Y.C., 1958-60; mgr. advt. Revlon Corp., N.Y.C., 1960-62; v.p. Ted Bates & Co., N.Y.C., 1962-69, Clyne Maxon, N.Y.C., 1969-70; exec. v.p. ZEA Mktg., N.Y.C., 1970-72; dir. mktg. Carmichael-Lynch, Mpls., 1972-75; free-lance writer, Mpls., 1976-78; writer, producer program devel. KTCA-TV, Twin Cities Public TV, St. Paul, 1979—. Mem. Mpls. Citizen's Cable Telecommunication adv. com., 1978-79; exec. com. bd. dirs. U. Minn. Community Video Center, 1973-78; mem. FM radio acquisition task force U. Minn., 1977-78; mem. Twin Cities Press Rev. Bd., 1979-80. Served with USN, 1949-50. Mem. Am. Film Inst., Nat. Assn. Ednl. Broadcasters. Methodist. Author: Broadcasting Handbook, 1981; contbr. articles to profl. jours. Home: 2221 Minneapolis Ave Minneapolis MN 55406 Office: 1640 Como Ave Saint Paul MN 55108

PORTE, BLOSSOM TOVROV, publishing co. exec.; b. Chgo., Nov. 16, 1915; d. Joseph and Sadie (Glassman) Tovrov; B.A., U. Chgo., 1937; postgrad. Northwestern U. Sch. Journalism, 1941-44; m. Ned H. Porte, Sept. 3, 1938; children—Andrew J., Phillip L. Writer, Chgo. Sun, 1941-45; dir. pub. relations Childrens Meml. Hosp., Chgo., 1965-71; cons. Health Communications, 1971-77; pres. Health Edn. Publs., Chgo., 1977—; pub. For Your Good Health, The Healthy Child, The Present Pace, Stay Safe; pres. HEP, Inc. Recipient 13 MacEachern awards, 1965-71. Nat. Cancer Inst. grantee, 1975. Mem. Am. Soc. Hosp. Pub. Relations (dir. 1968-71, nat. pres. 1972-74), Am. Acad. Hosp. Pub. Relations (dir. 1968-74), Chgo. Hosp. Pub. Relations Soc. (past pres.). Contbr. articles to profl. publs. Office: 221 N LaSalle St Chicago IL 60601

PORTER, BARRY LAVON, state librarian; b. Cedar City, Utah, Oct. 3, 1942; s. LaVon and Alta (Haycock) P.; B.S., So. Utah State Coll., 1967; M.L.S., Brigham Young U., 1970; m. Gayle Willis, Sept. 3, 1965; children—Donald, Michelle, Jeffrey, Steven, Jared. Bookmobile librarian Utah State Library Commn., 1967-68, reference librarian, 1968-73; dir. Iowa State Library Commn., 1973—; exec. sec. Utah Library Assn., 1972; trustee Bibliog. Center for Research, Rocky Mountain region, 1973—, pres. bd., 1978, 79. Mem. Chief Officers of State Library Agys. (chmn. continuing edn. com. 1978, 79, 81), Western Council State Librarians (v.p. 1981). Mormon. Home: 521 31st St West Des Moines IA 50265 Office: Historial Bldg Des Moines IA 50319

PORTER, CLOYD ALLEN, state legislator; b. Huntley, Ill., May 22, 1935; s. Cecil and Myrtle (Fisher) P.; grad. high sch.; m. Joan Ellen Hawkins, July 25, 1959; children—Ellen Joan, Lee Ann, Jay Allen, Joli Sue. Partner, Cecil W. Porter & Son Trucking, 1955-70; treas.

Burlington Sand and Gravel, 1964-70; owner Cloyd A. Porter Trucking, 1970-72; sales rep. John Lynch Chevrolet, 1971-74; mem. Wis. State Assembly from 43d Dist., 1972—, mem. com. fin. instns., com. energy, com. environ. resources, spl. com. energy conservation; mem. Fox River Watershed com. So. Wis. Regional Planning Council, 1975-77, chmn. subcom., 1975-77; mem. Intergovtl. Council Racine County (Wis.), 1971-74; v.p. bd. dirs. Racine County Planning Council Health and Social Services, 1971-72, exec. com., 1969-72; chmn. Town of Burlington (Wis.), 1971-74; Presdl. elector, 1980. Vice-chmn., Burlington br. Goodwill Industries, 1971; chmn. state and met. affairs Wis. Jaycees, 1963, state v.p., 1969, adminstrv. asst., 1970, exec. v.p., 1971; pres. Burlington Jaycees, 1968, 1st v.p., 1967, dir., 1965; mem. bd. restoration fund dr. St. Mary's Catholic Ch., 1977-79, mem. athletic bd., 1972-81; mem. Burlington Soap Box Derby Com., 1963-72, co-dir., 1971; coach Burlington Minor League, 1972-74; mem. promotion com. Burlington Air Show, 1971-73; bd. dirs. Burlington Coop. Playsch., 1976-81. Recipient numerous awards, including: Burlington Jaycee of Yr. award, 1966; Disting. Service award City of Burlington, 1969; Outstanding Citizen award Burlington VFW, 1972; cert. of appreciation Kiwanis Club Lake Geneva, 1975; hon. mem. Racine County Fire Chiefs Assn., 1976; cert. of merit Village of East Troy, 1979; award Wis. Vet. Edn. Com., 1980; recognition of support Lake Geneva Fire Dept., 1980. Republican. Roman Catholic. Clubs: Toastmasters; Burlington Flying, K.C. (council; 4th deg.), Rotary (Burlington). Home: 28322 Durand Ave Burlington WI 53105 Office: Room 320 N Capitol Bldg Madison WI 53702

PORTER, DAVID JAMES, sch. prin.; b. Marion, Ala., Sept. 26, 1942; s. Wilmer James and Ellen Clementine (Perry) P.; B.A., Central State U., Wilberforce, Ohio, 1964; M.A., U. Mich., 1971; Ed.D., Wayne State U., 1981; m. Marjorie Curtis Porter, Aug. 12, 1978; children—Kyra Noelle, Ellen Jamae. Tchr. public schs., Milw., 1964, Detroit public schs., 1964-74; staff coordinator Cerveny Elem. Sch., Detroit, 1974-75, asst. prin. Houghton Elem. Sch., 1975-80, Cerveny Middle Sch., 1980-81, prin. Bagley Elem. Sch., 1981—; cons. Nat. Inst. Edn., Washington; Mem. NAACP, Assn. Supervision and Curriculum Devel., Nat. Alliance Black Sch. Adminstrs., Met. Alliance Black Sch. Educators, Orgn. Sch. Adminstrs. and Suprs., Am. Fedn. Sch. Adminstrs., Kappa Alpha Psi (life), Pi Lambda Theta, Phi Delta Kappa. Methodist. Office: 8100 Cutis St Detroit MI 48221

PORTER, DAVID STEWART, judge; b. Cin., Sept. 23, 1909; s. Charles Hamilton and Caroline (Pemberton) P.; A.B., U. Cin., 1932, J.D., 1934; m. Marjorie Ellis Porter, July 28, 1956; children by previous marriage—Mary Porter Greaves, Margaret Porter Alexander, Elizabeth Porter Blistein. Admitted to Ohio bar, 1934, Tenn. bar, 1935; individual practice law, Troy, Ohio, 1936-49; judge Common Pleas Ct., Miami County, Ohio, 1949-66; judge U.S. Dist. Ct. So. Dist. Ohio, Cin., 1966-77, chief judge, 1977-79, sr. judge, 1979—; faculty adv. Nat. Coll. State Trial Judges, 1964-65. Bd. dirs. Ohio Blue Cross, Dettmer Hosp., Troy. Recipient Disting. Alumni award U. Cin. Coll. Law, 1980. Mem. Ohio Common Pleas Judges Assn. (past pres.), Am. Bar Assn., Ohio Bar Assn., Cin. Bar Assn., Miami County Bar Assn., Am. Judicature Soc.

PORTER, DEAN ALLEN, museum adminstr., artist; b. Gouverneur, N.Y.; B.A. Harpur Coll., Binghamton, N.Y., 1961; M.A. in Art History, SUNY, Binghamton, 1966, Ph.D. in Art History, 1974; m. Carol Ann DuBrava; children—Kellie Ann, Tracie Ann. Admissions counselor Harpur Coll., 1961-64; curator art Gallery U. Notre Dame, 1966-74, asso. prof. art history, 1966—, dir. Snite Museum Art, 1974—; numerous one-man shows, 1968—. Bd. dirs. Michiana Arts and Scis. Council. Samuel H. Kress fellow, 1972—. Mem. Coll. Art Assn. Am., Am. Assn. Mus., Mid-Am. Coll. Art Assn., Ind. Art Commn. (mem. adv. panel). Contbr. articles in field to profl. jours. Office: Art Gallery University of Notre Dame Notre Dame IN 46556

PORTER, DONALD GAMALIEL, floor covering co. exec.; b. Marion, Ohio, Nov. 10, 1920; s. Talmage Newton and Mabel (Wottring) P.; B.Arch., Ohio State U., 1943; m. Jean Alice McCoskey, Nov. 27, 1943; children—Talmage Newton, Stephen Donald. Purchasing agt. Wallace F. Ackley Co., Columbus, Ohio, 1946-48; salesman Wilson Floors Co., Columbus, 1948-70, v.p. sales and mktg., 1970-77; pres. Porter Interior Surfaces Inc., Columbus, 1977—; instr. Builders Exchange Sch., Columbus, 1972—. Mem. Brookside Civic Assn., Worthington, Ohio, 1956—. Served with AUS, 1943-46. Mem. Constrn. Specifications Inst. (tech. com. awards 1968—), Builders Exchange Columbus (dir. 1970), Alpha Rho Chi. Methodist (trustee 1952-58). Clubs: Masons, Shriners, Univ. (Columbus); Ohio State U. Faculty. Home: 6541 Winston Ct Worthington OH 43085 Office: 6145 Dolan Pl Dublin OH 43017

PORTER, GEORGE DARWIN, computer mfg. co. exec.; b. Dayton, Pa., July 25, 1937; s. Melvin Clair and Mary Gladys (Thomas) P.; diploma Robert Morris Sch., Pitts., 1957; m. Charlotte Louise Ferkan, June 8, 1963; children—George Darwin, II, Faye Ellen, Joseph Clair, David Eugene. Mgr. data processing Magnetics, Inc., Butler, Pa., 1961-62, 63-67; computer operator Mellon Bank, Pitts., 1962-63; systems and procedures mgr. Dresser Industries Co., Bradford, Pa., 1967-68; info. systems mgr. Standard Transformer Co., Warren, Ohio, 1968-69; v.p. sales Pryor Corp., Chgo., 1969—; instr. data processing Pa. State U. Extension, Butler, 1966. Pres. North Rd. Elementary Sch. PTA, Warren, Ohio, 1974-75; lay pres. congregation St. Paul's Luth. Ch., Warren, 1974. Served with U.S. Army, 1958-61; ETO. Recipient numerous sales awards Pryor Corp., 1971-80. Mem. Data Processing Mgmt. Assn., Assn. Systems Mgmt. Republican. Clubs: Avalon Swim and Tennis, Masons. Home: 4272 Aleesa Dr SE Warren OH 44484 Office: PO Box 830 280 N Park Ave Warren OH 44482

PORTER, HELEN VINEY (MRS. LEWIS M. PORTER, JR.), assn. exec., lawyer; b. Logansport, Ind., Sept. 7, 1935; s. Charles Lowry and Florence Helen (Kunkel) V.; A.B., Ind. U., 1957; J.D., U. Louisville, 1961; m. Lewis Morgan Porter, Jr., Dec. 26, 1966; children—Alicia Michelle, Andrew Morgan. Admitted to Ind. and Ill. bars, 1961, U.S. Supreme Ct. bar, 1971; atty. office chief counsel Midwest regional office IRS, Chgo., 1961-73; asso. regional atty. litigation center Equal Employment Opportunity Commn., Chgo., 1973-74; practice in Northbrook, Ill., 1974—; partner firm Porter & Andersen, Chgo., 1979-80; lectr. Law in Am. Found., Chgo., summer, 1973, 74; asso. prof. No. Ill. U. (formerly Lewis U. Coll. Law), Glen Ellyn, Ill., 1975-79; lectr. women's rights and fed. taxation to bar assns. Fellow Am. Bar Found.; mem. Women's Bar Assn. Ill. (pres. 1972-73), Fed. (pres. Chgo. chpt. 1974-75), Ill. (del. 1972-78) bar assns., Nat. Assn. Women Lawyers (pres. 1973-74) Home: 225 Maple Row Northbrook IL 60062 Office: 225 Maple Row Northbrook IL 60062

PORTER, JOHN EDWARD, congressman, lawyer; b. Evanston, Ill., June 1, 1935; s. Harry H. and Florence B. (Vahle) P.; student M.I.T., 1953-54; B.S. in Bus. Adminstrn., Northwestern U., 1957; J.D. with distinction, U. Mich., 1961; m. Kathryn Cameron Porter; children—John Clark, David Britton, Ann Lindsay. Admitted to Ill. bar, 1961, U.S. Supreme Ct. bar; atty. civil div., appellate sect. Dept. Justice, Washington, 1961-63; practice law, Evanston, 1963-80; mem. Ill. Ho. of Reps. from 1st Dist., 1973-79; mem. 96th-97th Congresses from Ill., mem. com. on appropriations, subcoms. on fgn. ops., labor, health and human services, edn. and D.C. Chmn. lawyers sect. United Community Services of Evanston, 1965, 67; bus. and industry chmn. Evanston March of Dimes, 1968-69; mem. East Evanston Community Conf., 1969-75. Co-counsel Evanston Republican Club, 1967-70; precinct capt., mem. exec. bd., area chmn. Evanston Regular Rep. Orgn., 1968—; pres. Evanston Young Rep. Club, 1968-69; gen. counsel Cook County Young Rep. Orgn., 1965; v.p. polit. affairs Niles Twp. Young Rep. Orgn., 1966; hdqrs. chmn. Evanston Citizens for Ogilvie, 1966; charter mem. Evanston Rep. Workshops, 1967; bd. dirs. Legal Assistance Found. Cook County, 1967-72, North Cook County Legal Adv. Bd., 1967-72; bd. dirs. YMCA, 1970-75, adv. bd., 1975—; treas. S.E. Evanston Assn., 1967-68, bd. dirs., 1967-69; trustee Evanston Hist. Soc., 1970-73, Cove Sch. for Perceptually Handicapped Children, 1974-76. Served with U.S. Army Res., 1958-64. Named Outstanding Legislator, Independent Voters Ill., 1974, League Conservation Voters, 1974, Chgo. Crime Commn., 1976. Mem. Am., Ill., Chgo., N.W. Suburban bar assns., Evanston C. of C. (past com. chmn.). Presbyn. Club: Univ. (past v.p., dir.) (Evanston). Asst. editor: Mich. Law Rev., 1960-61. Home: 1124 Sheridan Rd Evanston IL 60202 Office: 2100 Ridge Ave Evanston IL 60204

PORTER, JOHN WILSON, univ. pres.; b. Fort Wayne, Ind., Aug. 13, 1931; s. James Richard and Ola (Phillips) P.; A.A. (hon.), Schoolcraft Coll., 1979; B.A., Albion Coll., 1953; M.A., Mich. State U., 1957, Ph.D., 1962; L.H.D., Adrian Coll., 1970, U. Detroit, 1979; Ed.D. (hon.), Detroit Inst. Tech., 1978; LL.D., Western Mich. U., 1971, Eastern Mich. U., 1975, Mich. State U., 1977; Dr. Pub. Adminstrn., Albion Coll., 1973; H.H.D., Kalamazoo Coll., 1973, Detroit Coll. Bus., 1975, Madonna Coll., Livonia, Mich., 1977, U. Detroit, 1979; m. Lois Helen French, May 27, 1961; children—Stephen James, Donna Agnes. Counselor, Lansing Pub. Schs., 1953-58; cons. Mich. Dept. Pub. Instrn., 1958-61; dir. Mich. Higher Edn. Assistance Authority, 1961-66; asso. supt. for higher edn. Mich. Dept. Edn., 1966-69, state supt. schs., 1969-79; pres. Eastern Mich. U., Ypsilanti, 1979—; pres. Council Chief State Sch. Officers, 1977; mem. Nat. Commn. Reform of Secondary Edn., 1972-75, Nat. Adv. Council Career Edn., 1974—, Coll. Entrance Exam. Bd., 1979—, Nat. Commn. Financing Post-Secondary Edn., 1972-75, Nat. Commn. Performance-Based Edn., 1974, Nat. Commn. on Manpower Policy, 1974-79; dir. Mich. Bell Telephone Co. Mem. Local Draft Bd. 264, 1967—; mem. Pres.'s Commn. Mental Health Task Panel Mental Health and Family, 1977-80; bd. dirs. Council Chief State Sch. Officers, 1974-79, Nat. Sch. Vol. Program, 1978-79; adv. bd. Women's Ednl. Equity Communications Network, 1977; bd. dirs. Mich. Internat. Council; mem. Nat. Adv. Council Social Security, 1977-79; trustee Mich. Joint Council Econ. Edn., 1977-79, Coll. Bd., 1980—, Nat. Urban League, Charles S. Mott Found., 1980—, Thomas Alva Edison Found., 1980—. Nat. Urban League. Recipient Phi Beta Sigma Delta Kappa cert., 1970; recognition Mich. Legislature, 1970; Disting. Service award Ind. Colls. and U. Mich., 1974, Mich. Assn. Secondary Sch. Prins., 1974; Distinguished Alumni award Albion Coll., 1970, Mich. State U., 1979; Pres.'s award Nat. Alliance Black Sch. Educators, 1977; Freedom Bell award, 1977; Anthony Wayne award Wayne State U. Coll. Edn., 1979; citation Detroit Bd. Edn., 1979; others. Club: Econ. (dir.) (Detroit). Appeared on CBS Bicentennial Minute, 1976. Home: 600 W Forest St Ypsilanti MI 48197 Office: Eastern Mich U Ypsilanti MI

PORTER, LANA GARNER, communications co. exec.; b. Salem, Ill., Dec. 31, 1943; d. Marion E. and Belva M. (Hayden) Garner; B.A., Murray State U., 1965, M.A., 1972; M.B.A., Ohio State U., 1980; m. Michael E. Porter, June 7, 1964; 1 dau., Catherine Diane. Tchr. jr. high sch. French, Hopkinsville, Ky., 1964-66; tchr. high sch. English, French and speech, Benton, Ky., 1966-69; instr. Murray (Ky.) State U., 1969-70; ednl. researcher Battelle Meml. Inst., Columbus, Ohio, 1970-73; coordinator of info., research, and devel. Planned Parenthood of Columbus, 1973-76; account exec. Ohio Bell Telephone Co., Columbus, 1976-78, adminstrv. mgr., Cleve., 1978-79, industry mgr., 1979—. Trustee, sec. Cerebral Palsy of Columbus, 1977-78; trustee United Cerebral Palsy of Cuyahoga County, 1979—. Mem. Am. Mgmt. Assn., Am. Soc. Profl. and Exec. Women, Jr. League, Alpha Omicron Pi Alumna. Republican. Presbyterian. Home: 163 Elm Ct Chagrin Falls OH 44022 Office: Ohio Bell Telephone Co 1020 Bolivar St 4th Floor Cleveland OH 44115

PORTER, LAURELLEN, educator; b. Louisville, Ill., Oct. 5, 1933; d. Andrew and Golda (Hume) Porter; A.B., U. Ill., 1954, M.A., 1958, Ph.D., 1968. Tchr., Potomac (Ill.) Grade Sch., 1954-55; tchr. English, Bellflower (Ill.) High Sch., 1955-57; grad. asst. U. Ill., Urbana, 1957-58; tchr. English, social sci. Warren High Sch., Monmouth, Ill., 1958-61; residence hall dir. U. Ill., Urbana, 1961-64, grad. student and fellow, 1964-66; asst. prof. history and govt. William Woods Coll., Fulton, Mo., 1966-67; asst. prof. polit. sci. Ind. State U., Terre Haute, 1967-73, asso. prof. polit. sci., 1973—; participant Nat. Symposium on Agrl. Policy, 1977. Dir., Eugene V. Debs Found., Terre Haute, 1977—; mem. state policy bd. Ind. Women Polit. Caucus, 1977-78; v.p. W. Central Ind. Women's Polit. Caucus, 1978-79; pres. Ind. State U. local Am. Fedn. Tchrs., 1980—. U. Ill. Charles E. Merriam fellow, 1965-66; Ind. Com. for Humanities grantee, 1976. Mem. Am. Polit. Sci. Assn., Midwest Polit. Sci. Assn., AAUP, AAAS, Am. Assn. Advancement of Humanities, Ind. Acad. Social Scis., Phi Beta Kappa. Democrat. Contbr. articles in field to profl. jours. Home: 1833 S Brown Ave Terre Haute IN 47803 Office: Holmstedt Hall Ind State Univ Terre Haute IN 47809

PORTER, LEE, ednl. adminstr.; b. Syracuse, N.Y., Sept. 26, 1937; s. Kenneth Donald and Madeline (Beeman) P.; B.S., SUNY, Oswego, 1958, Ed.D., 1969; M.A., Syracuse U., 1960; m. Betty Ann Tarkowski, July 17, 1970. Program adminstr. Syracuse U., 1967-71, exec. dir. Evening Coll., 1971-76; asso. dean continuing edn. U. Ariz., 1976-77; dean Coll. Continuing Edn. and Met. Services, Roosevelt U., 1977—; cons. in field; mem. various visitation coms. for coll. accreditation, 1977—; bd. dirs. Ednl. Network for Older Adults, 1977-80, pres., 1979; host, producer Event, weekly TV show, 1966-76. Bd. dirs. Ariz. Consortium for Edn. of Social Services, 1976-77, v.p., 1978; bd. dirs. Internat. Center, Syracuse, 1975-76. Served with Air N.G., 1955-61. Grantee, S and H Found., 1968, Fund for Improvement of Postsecondary Edn., 1977-79, Sloane Found., 1978, others. Mem. Adult Edn. Assn., Assn. Continuing Higher Edn., Nat. Univ. Continuing Edn. Assn., Chgo. Met. Higher Edn. Council, Ill. Council Continuing Higher Edn. Author: Degrees For Sale, 1972; contbr. articles, chpts. to profl. publs.; editorial adv. bd. Franklin Watts Pubs., 1978—. Home: 6372 Hampshire Ct Lisle IL 60532 Office: 430 S Michigan Ave Chicago IL 60605

PORTER, LEWIS PAUL, educator; b. Canton, Ohio, Feb. 28, 1947; s. Chape Stewart and Helen Lavada (Bigley) P.; B.A., Malone Coll., 1970; M.A., Kent State U., 1974; postgrad. Sorbonne, U. Paris, summer 1975, Ohio State U., 1978—. Tchr. English and French, Lake Local Schs., Hartville, Ohio, 1971-72, Youngstown (Ohio) City Schs., 1975-78, Columbus (Ohio) City Schs., 1978—; organist Bethel Lutheran Ch., 1969-72; organist-choir dir. Grace Luth. Ch., 1972-78; organist Faith Luth. Ch., 1979—. Mem. Am. Guild Organists, Am. Assn. Tchrs. French Council for Basic Edn., Assn. for Supervision and Curriculum Devel. Home: 1437-F Highland St Columbus OH 43201 Office: 5151 Karl Rd Columbus OH 43229

PORTER, MARC DAVID, research chemist; b. Columbus, Ohio, June 7, 1955; s. Merle Dempesy and Mary Lee (Wiley) P.; B.S. cum laude, Wright State U., 1977, M.S., 1979; postgrad. (Univ. Chemistry Dept. fellow) Ohio State U.; m. Shelley Jean Coldiron, Feb. 14, 1981. Grad. research asso. Wright State U., Dayton, Ohio, 1978-79, grad. research asso. Brehm Lab., 1980—; grad. teaching asso. Ohio State U., Columbus, 1980; cons. Wright-Patterson AFB, 1980. NSF grantee, 1977. Mem. Am. Chem. Soc., Am. Soc. for Mass Spectrometry, AAAS, Ohio Acad. Sci. Contbr. chpt. to book, articles to profl. jours. Home: 720 N King St Xenia OH 45385 Office: Brehm Lab Wright State U Dayton OH 45435

PORTER, STUART WILLIAMS, investment co. exec.; b. Detroit, Jan. 11, 1937; s. Stuart Perlee and Alma Bernice (Williams) P.; B.S., U. Mich., 1960; M.B.A., U. Chgo. (Am. Accounting Assn. fellow), 1967, postgrad., 1967-68; m. Myrna Marlene Denham, June 27, 1964; children—Stuart, Randall. Investment mgr., partner Weiss Peck & Greer Investments, Chgo., 1978—. Chmn., Crusade of Mercy, 1973; chmn. investment com., v.p. bus. affairs com. Presbytery of Chgo. Served with USAF, 1961-62. Recipient award for excellence in bus. and accounting Fin. Exec. Inst., 1966. Mem. Midwest Pension Conf., Investment Analysts Soc. Chgo., Fin. Analysts Fedn., Investment Tech. Symposium N.Y., Beta Gamma Sigma. Presbyterian. Clubs: Renaissance (Detroit); Forest Grove Tennis (Palatine, Ill.); Turnberry Country (Crystal Lake, Ill.); Economic, Chgo. Athletic. Home: 130 Wyngate Dr Barrington IL 60010 Office: 30 N LaSalle St Chicago IL 60602

PORTER, TERENCE CLIFTON, lawyer; b. St. Joseph, Mo., Dec. 13, 1934; s. Ernest Clifton and Helen Francis (Denny) P.; B.S. in Agr., J.D., U. Mo., 1958; m. Joyce Newman, June 2, 1956; children—Katherine, Michael, David, Susan. Admitted to Mo. bar, 1958; with firm Clark & Becker, Columbia, Mo., 1958-60, Becker & Porter, 1960-61, Welliver, Porter & Cleveland, 1962-70, Porter, Sprick & Powell, 1970-78, Terence C. Porter, 1979—; partner Porter & Porter Investment & Rental Co., 1963—; sec., dir. Boone County Devel. Co., Hilton Inn of Columbia. Served to lt. U.S. Army, 1958. Mem. Am., Mo. bar assns., Def. Research Inst. Democrat. Presbyterian. Club: Kansas City. Home: 1129 Danforth Circle Columbia MO 65201 Office: 10 N Garth Columbia MO 65201

PORTERFIELD, H. WILLIAM, plastic surgeon; b. Hagerstown, Md., Sept. 24, 1929; s. Hubert L. and Florence C. P.; B.A., U. Va., 1950; M.D., Jefferson Med. Coll., 1955; m. Linda A. Obenauf, Nov. 19, 1977; children—Scott, Jeff, Wendy, Todd, Marli. Intern, Akron (Ohio) City Hosp., 1955-56, resident, 1956-58; resident in plastic surgery Ind. U. Med. Center, 1958-60; practice medicine specializing in plastic and reconstructive surgery, Columbus, Ohio, 1960—; asso. clin. prof. surgery Ohio State U. Chmn. bd. dirs. Ohio Med. Polit. Action Com., 1974—. Mem. Am. Soc. Plastic and Reconstructive Surgeons (pres. 1981-82), AMA (del. from Ohio 1975—), Acad. Medicine Columbus and Franklin County (pres. 1968), Physicians Health Plan of Central Ohio (pres. 1979—), Ohio State Med. Assn., ACS, Am. Cleft Palate Assn., Am. Assn. Plastic Surgeons, Am. Soc. Aesthetic Plastic Surgery. Republican. Office: 1100 Morse Rd Columbus OH 43229

PORTH, CAROL MART, mfg. corp. exec.; b. Cleve., June 15, 1950; d. Maurice and Lena Claire (Friedman) Mart; B.A., Ohio State U., 1971; m. Robert Porth, Aug. 26, 1979. Formerly dir. advt. Front Row Theatre, Cleve., account exec. Martin J. Simmons Advt., Chgo., Sta. WLUP, Chgo.; advt., sales promotion mgr. Bally Mfg. Corp., Chgo., 1978—; mem. Advt. Age Sounding Bd., Chgo., 1980-81. Recipient Mark of Excellance award Midtec Paper Corp., 1980. Mem. Am. Soc. Profl. and Exec. Women, Nat. Female Execs. of Am., Bus./Profl. Advt. Assn. Office: Bally Mfg Corp 2640 W Belmont Ave Chicago IL 60618

PORTTEUS, ELNORA MARIE MANTHEI, librarian; b. Rosendale, Wis.; d. H. R. and Anna M. (Kentop) Manthei; student Oshkosh State Coll., 1937-39; B.S., U. Wis., 1941; M.A., Kent State U., 1954; m. Paul Portteus, Oct. 19, 1942; children—Carrie Jo (Mrs. J.P. Thomas), Lane Paul, Andre Eugene. Librarian, tchr. Racine-Kenosha Normal Sch., 1942; library asst. Fed. Res. Bank of Cleve., 1943; asst. librarian Indsl. Relations Counselors N.Y., 1947-48; librarian Findlay (Ohio) City Schs., 1948-58; asst. prof. Sch. Library Sci., Kent (Ohio) State U., 1958-65, now adj. asso. prof.; dir. ednl. media services Cleve. Bd. Edn., 1965—; cons. Coop. Ednl. Services, Columbus, 1956-65; adv. bd. H.W. Wilson Standard Catalogue Series; dir. NDEA Inst., 1965; mem. adv. bd. library tech. program Cuyahoga Community Coll. Chmn., Findlay Council Youth Serving Agys., 1954-56. Recipient 1st place Ency. Brit. Sch. Library, 1967; Disting. Alumna award, Kent State U., 1967. Mem. AAUW, Am. (chmn. adv. com. Midwest Program on Airborn TV Instrn. 1964-68, recipient John Cotton Dana publicity award, 1967, 70, 1st v.p., pres. 1972-74), Ohio (pres. 1957-58) assns. sch. librarians, Ohio Library Assn. (chmn. book exam. center com. 1964-65, chmn. scholarship com. 1965-67, named Ohio Librarian of Yr. 1972), ALA, Beta Phi Mu, Delta Kappa Gamma. Club: Order Eastern Star. Contbr. articles to profl. jours.; reviewer Library Jour. Home: 7357 West Lake Blvd Kent OH 44240 Office: 10600 Quincy Ave Cleveland OH 44106

POSAVAC, EMIL JAMES, psychologist, educator; b. Pitts., July 29, 1939; s. Emil Edward and Catherine Elizabeth (Anstine) P.; B.S., Carnegie-Mellon U., 1961; M.A., U. Ill., Urbana, 1968, Ph.D., 1969; m. Wendy Cook, Aug. 10, 1963; 1 son, Steven Scott. Asst. prof. psychology Loyola U., Chgo., 1969-73, asso. prof., 1973-79, prof., 1979—; cons. health care research. Naurice Nesset research fellow Luth. Gen. Hosp., Park Ridge, Ill., 1973-75. Mem. AAAS, Am. Psychol. Assn., Evaluation Network, Midwestern Psychol. Assn. Author: Program Evaluation: Methods and Case Studies, 1980; editor: Impacts of Program Evaluation on Mental Health Care, 1979; contbr. articles to profl. jours. Home: 8153 Kolmar St Skokie IL 60076 Office: 6525 N Sheridan Rd Chicago IL 60626

POSCH, JOSEPH LOUIS, surgeon; b. St. Paul, Dec. 26, 1915; s. Louis Gustav and Frances Martha (Kurz) P.; B.S cum laude, St. Thomas Coll., 1938; M.D., U. Minn., 1942; m. Martha Jane Stark, May 2, 1942; children—Mary Katherine Posch Gebeck, Joseph Louis. Intern, City of Detroit Receiving Hosp., 1942-43, fellow in surgery, 1943-44, resident in surgery, 1946-49, chief of staff, 1965; practice medicine specializing in surgery, Detroit; dir. hand surgery Hand Center, Harper-Grace Hosp., Detroit Med. Center, Wayne State U.; mem. staff Hutzel Hosp., Detroit Gen. Hosp., St. Joseph Mercy Hosp., Mt. Carmel Mercy Hosp., Children's Hosp. of Mich., St. John's Hosp., Sinai Hosp., Bon Secours Hosp., VA Hosp., USPHS Hosp.; clin. prof. surgery Coll. Medicine, Wayne State U., 1973, Rehab. Services Adminstrn.; HEW trainee in rehab. medicine (hand surgery), micro-surgery research lab. Wayne State U. Served with M.C., U.S. Army, 1944-46; ETO. Diplomate Am. Bd. Surgery. Mem. Am. Soc. for Surgery of the Hand, Am. Assn. for Surgery of Trauma, AMA, A.C.S., Indsl. Med. Assn., Detroit, Central, Western, Midwest surg. assns., Acad. Surgery of Detroit, Detroit Surg. Soc., Mich., Wayne County med. socs., Am. Soc. for Plastic and Reconstructive Surgery (asso.), Mich., Detroit, hist. socs., Detroit Inst. Arts Founders Soc., Anthony Wayne Soc., Grosse Pointe Power Squadron, Phi Chi. Roman Catholic. Clubs: Detroit Athletic, Grosse Pointe Yacht, K.C.

Contbr. articles to profl. jours. Home: 73 Webber Pl Grosse Pointe Shores MI 48236 Office: 1408 Kales Bldg 76 W Adams St Detroit MI 48226

POSEY, DAISY LYNETTE, ednl. adminstr.; b. Shelby, Miss., June 8, 1945; d. Eddie and Sarah (Gibson) Anderson; B.Sci. Edn., Central State U., 1968; M.A. in Edn., Case-Western Res. U., 1973; postgrad. Cleve. State U., 1979—; m. James LeRoy Posey, Dec. 20, 1969; children—Vida Jamille, Danny Darius James. Stenographer, Fed. Res. Bank, Cleve., summers 1965-67; tchr. East Cleveland (Ohio) City Schs., 1968-79, curriculum specialist, 1979—. Mem. Assn. Supervision and Curriculum Devel., Nat. Assn. Elem. Sch. Prins. Club: Internat. Toastmistress. Author: A Handbook: Exceptional Children, Teaching Strategies, 1979. Office: 13916 Mayfair Ave East Cleveland OH 44112

POSKO, THOMAS CHARLES, mech. engr.; b. Chgo., May 13, 1947; s. James L. and Marie F. (Mangan) P.; ward of Robert J. and Frances Murphy; A.S. in Archtl. Engring., Milw. Sch. Engring., 1968, B.S. in Archtl. Engring., 1973; student Loras Coll., 1965-67; m. Mary D. Marangelli, Sept. 4, 1971; 1 son, Michael Edward. Coop. engr., jr. engr. Joseph P. Jansen Co., Milw., 1968-70; project engr., v.p. R.J. Miller Assos., Milw., 1973-80; pres. Posko Associates, Inc., Pewaukee, Wis., 1980—; lectr. Milw. Sch. Engring., 1978-80. Active Chgo. council Boy Scouts Am., 1960-64; bd. dirs. Milw. Sch. Engring. Alumni Assn., 1978—. Served with USNR, 1969-72. Recipient Achievement award Milw. Sch. Engring., 1968; registered profl. engr., Wis., Mich., Ill. Mem. Constrn. Specifications Inst. (dir. 1977-79), ASHRAE, ASME, Scientists and Engrs. of Milw., Am. Inst. Plant Engrs. Republican. Roman Catholic. Club: Wisconsin. Home: Delafield WI 53018 Office: 1390 Capitol Dr Pewaukee WI 53072

POSNER, JUDITH LOIS, fine arts corp. dir.; b. Milw., Sept. 22, 1941; d. Sol. J. and Miriam F. (Posner) Kahn; B.S. in Fine Art, U. Wis., 1963; m. Jeffry A. Posner, Aug. 17, 1963; children—Wendy Lee, David Adam. Asst. dir. Gallery 12, Daytons, Mpls., 1963-64; partner, dir. fine arts Jeffry A. Posner Corp., Judith L. Posner & Assos., Inc., Milw., 1973—. Mem. corporate bd. Mt. Sinai Med. Center, recipient Hands That Serve award, 1976, chairwoman art purchases com., mem. aux.; mem. women's welfare bd. Mental Health Assn. Mem. Milw. Art Center, Milw. Symphony League and Ballet League. Home: 7945 N Fairchild Rd Milwaukee WI 53217 Office: 7641 N Port Washington Rd Milwaukee WI 53217

POSPISHIL, LLOYD LABAR, lawyer; b. West Point, Nebr., May 19, 1911; s. Paul and Matilda Alice (Yunek) P.; B.A., U. Nebr., 1932, LL.B., 1933, J.D., 1968; m. Margaret E. Reuter, July 14, 1937. Admitted to Nebr. bar, 1933; practiced in Schuyler, 1933—; county atty. Colfax County, 1935-39, 43-51, now dep. county atty.; city atty. Schuyler, 1942-43, 58-60, 62-64; staff legal officer Naval Air Intermediate Tng. Command, 1943-45; judge Ct. Indsl. Relations, 1961-67; dir. First Nat. Bank, Schuyler, FNS, Inc., Schuyler, Clarkson Bank (Nebr.); counsel U.P. R.R.; mem. Nebr. Supreme Ct. Nominating Commn. U. Nebr. rep. Internat. Intercollegiate Debate with U. Oxford, Eng., 1930; mayor Schuyler, 1940-42; bd. dirs. Meml. Hosp., Schuyler, 1953-57, 71-77; mem. governance commn. U. Nebr. Served to lt. comdr. USNR, 1943-46. Fellow Am. Coll. Probate Counsel; mem. Schuyler C. of C. (pres.), Nat. Forensic Soc., Nebr. Assn. Trial Lawyers (pres.), Am. (mem. coms.), Nebr. (adv. com. 1951-75), 6th Jud. Dist., Colfax County (pres.) bar assns., Nebr. Bar Found. (dir. 1977—), Am. Legion (Distinguished Citizen award 1957, 74, dist. comdr., Nebr. vice comdr., nat. vice chmn. Americanism commn., dept. judge adv.), Cheminot Nat., 40 and 8, Delta Sigma Rho. Club: Rotary (pres.; Paul Harris Found. fellow 1978). Contbr. articles to profl. jours. Home: 425 B St Schuyler NE 68661 Office: 324 E 11th St Schuyler NE 68661

POSTHUMA, ALBERT ELWOOD, surgeon; b. Grand Rapids, Mich., Apr. 25, 1919; s. Gerrit Pylman and Alice (Mandemaker) P.; A.B., Calvin Coll., 1940; M.D., U. Mich., 1943, M.S. 1949; m. Jean L. Swann, Aug. 17, 1974; children by previous marriage—Beth Alicia Posthuma Jenkins, Ann Maureen Posthuma Lustig, Jane Marie, Sue Swann Frankforter. Intern, St. Mary's Hosp., Grand Rapids, 1943-44, resident, 1944-46, 48-50; practice medicine specializing in surgery, 1950—; cons. surgeon St. Mary's Hosp., 1972—, chief of staff, 1972-78; cons. surgeon Ferguson-Drost-Ferguson hosps. Pres., Kent County Med. Found., 1979. Served from 1st lt. to capt. AUS, 1946-48. Recipient citation U. Mich., 1949. Diplomate Am. Bd. Surgery. Fellow A.C.S.; mem. Pan-Pacific Surg. Assn., Kent County Med. Soc. (pres. 1978-79). Club: Blythefield Country. Home: 2117 Osceola Dr Grand Rapids MI 49507 Office: 153 Lafayette SE Grand Rapids MI 49502

POSTICH, GEORGE, univ. adminstr.; b. North Chicago, Ill., Mar. 24, 1930; s. Rade and Minnie (Svilar) P.; B.S. in Polit. Sci., U. Wis., 1952; M.B.A., Harvard U., 1964; postgrad. Bowling Green State U.; m. Margaret Anne Jordan, June 14, 1952; children—Steven, Kevin, Kathryn, Mary, Anne, Shawn, Shane. Commd. ensign U.S. Navy, 1952, advanced through grades to capt., 1972; served in various mgmt. positions, fin. mgmt. systems positions and inventory mgmt. positions, including planning officer, 1969-72, exec. officer Electronic Supply Office, Gt. Lakes, Ill., 1972-74, exec. officer Navy Fin. Center, Cleve., 1974-75; ret., 1975; v.p. ops. Bowling Green State U., 1975—; asst. prof. U. N.Mex., 1954-56; Dept. Def. coordinator for Cleve. Nat. Air Show and Air Races, 1971; operating chmn. fund-raising dr. Orange and Los Angeles County Navy Relief Fund, 1965; mem. Wood County Airport Authority. Decorated Meritorious Service medal, Navy Commendation medal with gold star; recipient award for mil. merit Chgo. Tribune, 1952. Mem. Bowling Green C. of C. (trustee), Ret. Officers Assn., Inter Univ. Council Fiscal Officers, Nat. Assn. Coll. and Univ. Bus. Officers, U. Wis. Alumni Assn., Phi Beta Kappa, Phi Eta Sigma, Phi Kappa Phi. Clubs: Harvard Bus. Sch. (Cleve.); Falcon, also Presidents (Bowling Green State U.). Office: 911 Adminstrn Bldg Thurstin St Bowling Green OH 43403

POTENTE, EUGENE, JR., interior designer; b. Kenosha. Wis., July 24, 1921; s. Eugene and Suzanne Marie (Schmit) P.; Ph.B., Marquette U., 1943; postgrad. Stanford U., 1943, N.Y. Sch. Interior Design, 1947; m. Joan Cioffe Potente, Jan. 29, 1946; children—Eugene J., Peter Michael, John Francis, Suzanne Marie. Founder, pres. Studios of Potente, Inc., Kenosha, Wis., 1949—; pres., founder Archtl. Services Assos., Kenosha, 1978—, Bus. Leasing Services of Wis. Inc., 1978—; nat. v.p. Inter-Faith Forum on Religion, Art and Architecture; mem. State Capitol and Exec. Residence Bd., 1981—. Sec., Kenosha Symphony Assn. Served with AUS, 1943-46. Mem. Am. Soc. Interior Designers, Inst. Bus. Designers (mem. Wis. bd.), Sigma Delta Chi. Roman Catholic. Clubs: Rotary, Kenosha Country, Elks. Home: 6634 3d Ave Kenosha WI 53140 Office: 914 60th St Kenoshaw WI 53140

POTHAST, HENRY LYNN, sch. social worker; b. Marshalltown, Iowa, Apr. 2, 1952; s. Lester Raymond and Annie (Dunham) P.; student Marshalltown Community Coll., 1970-71; B.A., U. Iowa, 1974, M.S.W., 1981; postgrad. U. No. Iowa, 1977-78; m. June Dubberke, Feb. 14, 1976; 1 dau., Emily Ann. Youth services worker Iowa Tng. Sch. for Boys, Eldora, 1974-75, youth counselor I, 1975-78, youth counselor II, 1978-79, instr. high sch. equivalency, 1975-77; social worker Area Edn. Agy. 6, Eldora, 1981—. Mem. Nat. Assn. Social Workers, Phi Beta Kappa. Club: DeMolay (orator 1969-70). Home: Rt 1 Box 158 Hubbard IA 50122 Office: Area Edn Agy 6 Eldora IA 50627

POTTEN, DENNIS FRANK, travel agy. exec.; b. Rockville Center, L.I., Sept. 30, 1950; s. Eugene Albert and Katherine Louise (Koenderman) P.; student Millikin U., 1968-69; B.A., U. Maine, 1972; m. Christine Marie McCollough, Aug. 30, 1970; 1 son, Timothy McCollough. Travel agt. Franklin Travel Agy., Decatur, Ill., 1968-69; internal auditor Executive Airlines, Boston, 1969-71; travel agt. Tradewinds Travel, Portland, Saco, Maine, 1971-73, Baker Travel Service, Champaign, Ill., 1973-74; pres. Franklin Travel, Champaign, 1974—, World Wide Travel, Rantoul, Ill., 1981—; exec. vice-pres. Travel Development, Inc., Champaign, Ill., 1978—. Trustee, Ill. Assn. for Retarded Citizens. Mem. Am. Soc. Profl. Cons., Champaign C. of C., Urbana C. of C. Presbyn. Home: 1619 Bassett Ln Champaign IL 61820 Office: 1509 S Neil St Champaign IL 61820

POTTER, ARNEL DEWAINE, chemist; b. Fairview, Idaho, Nov. 1, 1931; s. Ellis Duane and Mary Arzella (Jamison) P.; B.S., Brigham Young U., Provo, Utah, 1953; Ph.D., U. Utah, 1959; m. Dona Louise Nielsen, Apr. 22, 1955; children—Elizabeth Dianne, Rosemary Ann, William, Vernon, Cynthia. Chemist, Union Carbide Co., 1958-61; chemist-adv. scientist Continental Can Co., 1961-69; sr. scientist, group leader Uniroyal Inc., 1969-71; sr. scientist W.H. Brady Co., 1971-76; asst. research dir. Reilly Graphics Co., 1976-77; research dir. Zipatone Inc., Hillside, Ill., 1977—. Hal Youngman scholar, 1949; fellow Am. Cancer Soc., 1955-59. Mem. Am. Chem. Soc., Soc. Plastics Engrs. Republican. Home: 490 S Waukegan Rd Lake Forest IL 60045 Office: 150 Fencl Ln Hillside IL 60162

POTTER, DIANE SUE, social worker; b. Pontiac, Ill., Feb. 17, 1944; d. Claire Snyder and Gladys Frances (Ahrends) P.; B.A., Eureka (Ill.) Coll., 1966; M.S.W., W.Va. U., 1971. Tchr. English, Fairbury (Ill.)-Cropsey High Sch., 1966-67; social worker Lincoln (Ill.) State Sch., 1968-69; adoption social worker The Baby Fold, Normal, Ill., 1971-73; social worker Norwalk (Conn.) Hosp., 1973-77; pediatric social work specialist U. Iowa Hosps. and Clinics, Iowa City, 1977—. Mem. Assn. Care of Children in Hosps. Mem. Disciples of Christ Ch. Office: Dept Social Service U of Iowa Hosps and Clinics Iowa City IA 52240

POTTER, GEORGE HARRIS, banker; b. Pitts., Dec. 15, 1936; s. William Sommerville and Katharine Thayer (Rockwell) P.; B.A., Colgate U., 1959; postgrad. U. Pitts., 1963, Rutgers U., 1966; m. Nicole Sue Enfield, May 1, 1977; children—Clara Potter Mokher, George Harris, Faris F., Jonathan R., Kristin B. Weir, David B. Weir, Jr., Jennifer B. Weir. Life underwriter Equitable Life Assurance Soc. U.S., Pitts., 1958; asst. cashier Pitts. Nat. Bank, 1959-64; v.p. SE First Nat. Bank of Miami, Fla., 1964-79; v.p. regional banking div. Central Nat. Bank of Cleve., 1979—; dir. Motive Parts Co., Pitts., 1963-64, Pitts. Testing Lab., 1973—. Adv. dir. Vanguard Sch., Coconut Grove, Fla., 1968-79; dir. fund raising New Cleve. Campaign, 1979—. Mem. Greater Cleve. Growth Assn. Republican. Congregationalist. Clubs: University (Pitts.); River Oaks Racquet (Rocky River, Ohio); Colgate (pres. 1981), Hermit (Cleve.); Clifton Beach (Lakewood, Ohio). Office: 800 Superior Ave Cleveland OH 44114

POTTER, GEORGE WILLIAM, mining exec.; b. St. Louis, Aug. 5, 1930; s. George William and Fay Marguerite (Finch) P.; B.A., U. Mo., Kansas City, 1952; m. Emily Louise Withers, Feb. 11, 1956; 1 dau., Anne Finch. Pres., Ortiz Mines, Inc., Joplin, Mo., 1962-64, chmn. bd., 1964—; one man shows Barn Gallery, Kansas City, Mo., 1974, Fountain Valley Sch., Colorado Springs, Colo., 1975, U. Leyden (Netherlands), 1977; books (under pseudonym E.L. Withers) include: The House on the Beach, 1957; The Salazar Grant, 1959; Diminishing Returns, 1960; Heir Apparent, 1961; The Birthday, 1962; Royal Blood, 1964. Mem. Republican Senatorial Com., 1978—; bd. dirs. Winfred L. and Elizabeth C. Post Meml. Art Reference Library, 1977—, Kansas City Ballet, 1976-79. Recipient Mo. Writers award, 1967. Mem. Authors Guild, Friends of Art, Hist. Found. Kansas City, Nat. Trust for Hist. Preservation, Soc. Fellows Nelson Gallery Found. Home: 1239 W 61st Terr Kansas City MO 64113 Office: PO Box 211 Joplin MO 64802

POTTER, NORMAN RODNEY, psychologist; b. New London, Conn., Oct. 27, 1927; s. Kirby Safford and Lucy Ann (Carter) P.; B.A., U. Conn., 1952; M.S., Trinity U., 1959; Ph.D., Okla. State U., 1966; m. Mary Elizabeth Wallace, Nov. 23, 1950; children—Steven Douglas, Janice Linn, Jeffrey Curtis. Research psychologist various Air Force Labs., 1953-60; engring. psychologist Human Engring. Lab., Griffiss AFB, N.Y., 1960-63; chief Personnel Subsystems Br., Wright-Patterson AFB, Ohio, 1966-69; chief Systems Support Office, Human Resources Lab., Brooks AFB, Tex., 1969-70; asst. prof. biometry La. State U. Med. Center, New Orleans, 1970-73; sr. scientist Systems Research Labs., Dayton, Ohio, 1973-77, chief scientist human factors engring. div., 1977, mgr. div., 1977—; human factors cons. Army-Navy-Air Force Aircrew Standardization Panel, 1966-69, Joint Services Task Force Two, 1966-67; mem. Human Factors Group Joint Services Task Force Eight, 1968. Mem. adv. group for internal reorgan. La. Heart Assn., 1972. Served with USAF, 1952-70. Decorated Air Force Commendation medal with two oak leaf clusters; licensed psychologist, Ohio, Tex. Mem. Am., Southeastern psychol. assns., Soc. Engring. Psychologists, Human Factors Soc., Sigma Xi, Psi Chi. Contbr. articles in field to profl. jours. Home: 2988 Southfield Dr Xenia OH 45385 Office: 2800 Indian Ripple Rd Dayton OH 45440

POTTER, ROBERT LAWRENCE, communications researcher; b. Buffalo, July 27, 1943; s. William Ervin and Mildred Katharine (Poppenberg) P.; B.S. summa cum laude in Elec. Engring. (N.Y. State scholar), SUNY, Buffalo, 1964; S.M. in Elec. Engring., M.I.T., 1965; m. Louise Marie Hayek, Feb. 3, 1968; children—Amy Katherine, Eric Rudolph. In electronic switching devel. Bell Telephone Labs., Naperville, Ill. and Holmdel, N.J., 1964-69, operator systems design, 1969-77; asst. mgr. exchange systems design AT&T, Parsippany, N.J., 1977-79, supr. product devel., public services mktg., 1979-80, operator systems planning Bell Telephone Labs., Naperville, Ill., 1980—. Named Student Engr. of Yr., Erie County chpt. N.Y. State Soc. Profl. Engrs. Mem. IEEE, AAAS, Assn. Computing Machinery, U.S. Power Squadrons (sr.), Sigma Xi, Tau Beta Pi, Phi Eta Sigma. Republican. Baptist. Patentee telephone circuitry. Home: 843 E Gartner Rd Naperville IL 60540 Office: Bell Telephone Labs Naperville and Warrenville Rds Naperville IL 60566

POTTER, THOMAS DARK, service cos. exec.; b. Huntsville, Ala., May 1, 1933; s. Leroy Van and Annie Mae (Cagle) P.; A.A., Macomb Community Coll., Warren, Mich., 1958; postgrad. U. Mich., 1968-73, Washington U., St. Louis, 1967; m. Martha Ann, June 19, 1958; children—Robert, Julia, Katherine. Tech. rep. Philco Co., Phila., 1956-57; radio interference analyst Burroughs Co., Detroit, 1957-58; instrumentation technician Bendix Co., Detroit, 1958-59; sales engr. Comtel Corp., Detroit, 1960-68; chmn. Liuper Inc., Warren, Mich., 1968—, Dearper Inc., Warren, 1968—, also dir.; owner Potters Programs, St. Clair Shores, Mich., 1976—; dir. Pletzer, Inc. Served with USCG, 1952-56. Mem. South Eastern Mich. Computer Orgn., Nat. Fedn. Ind. Bus., Soc. Asso. Franchise Owners, C. of C. Democrat. Home: 22444 Lakeland St St Clair Shores MI 48081 Office: Suite 601 30500 Van Dyke St Warren MI 48093

POTTS, GLENN THOMAS, economist; b. Danville, Ill., Jan. 11, 1950; s. Edgar W. and Maxine (Menagh) P.; B.A. in Econs. with honors, MacMurray Coll., 1972; M.S., Iowa State U., 1974, Ph.D., 1976; m. Jeanette Ramsey, Jan. 16, 1971; 1 son, Edward. Asst. prof. econs. U. Wis., River Falls, 1976—. Mem. Midwest Econs. Assn. Office: Dept Econs U Wis River Falls WI 54022

POULIN, MAUREEN JOAN, educator; b. Haverhill, Mass., Nov. 14, 1949; d. Alfred Dominic and Rosemarie Augustine (Dolfe) Poulin; B.S., U. Kans., 1972; M.A., U. Mo., Kansas City, 1975; 1 son, Michael Jeremy. Primary tchr. Our Lady of Lourdes Sch., Raytown, Mo., 1972-74; psychometrist North Kansas City Pub. Schs., Kansas City, Mo., 1975-76, learning specialist, 1976-77, cons. gifted and talented program, 1976-77, psychometrist, 1977-80, learning specialist, 1980—. Mem. Am. Personnel and Guidance Assn., Council Exceptional Children, Kappa Delta Pi. Roman Catholic. Home: 1536 A Mews Dr Kansas City MO 64131 Office: 2000 NE 46th St Kansas City MO 64116

POULOSE, KUTTIKATT PAUL, physician; b. Cochin, India, Sept. 2, 1935; came to U.S., 1972; s. Paul K. and Mariamkutty P. (Maliakal) P.; M.B., B.S., Med. Coll., Trivandrum, India, 1958, M.D. in Internal Medicine, 1964; m. Queeny Mayne, June 11, 1962; children—Anil, Abraham, Benjamin. Intern, Med. Coll. Hosps., Trivandrum, 1959-60, resident, 1960-64; resident VA Hosp.-Kings County Hosp., Bklyn., 1972-76; asst. prof. internal medicine Med. Coll., Calicut, India, 1968-72; chief dept. medicine VA Med. Center, Leavenworth, Kans., 1975—, dir. continuing med. edn., 1977—, acting chief of staff, 1976-77, chief of staff, 1980—; asst. clin. prof. neurology Kans. U., 1976-81, asso. clin. prof. neurology, 1981—. Cert. in internal medicine, India; diplomate Am. Bd. Psychiatry and Neurology. Fellow A.C.P., Royal Coll. Physicians of Can.; mem. Am. Acad. Neurology. Roman Catholic. Contbr. articles to profl. jours. Home: 1111 Santa Fe St Leavenworth KS 66048 Office: VA Medical Center Dept Medicine Leavenworth KS 66048

POUND, JAMES BUCHANAN, chem. mfg. co. exec.; b. St. Louis, Aug. 22, 1940; s. Orville R. and Callie Doris P.; student U. Mo., 1959-60; B.S. in Bus. Adminstrn., Gen. Sci. and Zoology, N.E. Mo. State U., 1960-64; m. Charlotte Pound, Aug. 25, 1962; children—Michael Jeffrey, Mark Alan. Material control supr. Electronics and Space div. Emerson Electric Co., St. Louis, 1965-66, mgr. prodn. control, 1966-68, sr. buyer, 1968-69, purchasing mgr. Indsl. Controls div., 1969-70, program mgr. corp. procurement and corp. scrap mgr., 1970-79, corp. energy coordinator, 1973-75, mgr. Facilities Services Property Mgmt. div., 1979-80, dir. purchasing Alco Controls div., 1980-81; dir. materials mgmt. Calgon Corp. Subs. Merck & Co. Inc., 1981—. Active Boy Scouts Am., Jr. Achievement; chmn. ad hoc citizens com. St. Charles City Sch. Dist. (Mo.). Clubs: Bogey Hills Country, Ambassadors, Masons, Shriners. Office: Calgon Corp 7501 Page Ave Saint Louis MO 63166

POURIAN, HEYDAR, economist, educator; b. Tehran, Apr. 23, 1948; came to U.S., 1972, naturalized, 1978; s. Pasha and Moneer (Hamidi-Khaleghi) P.; student Nat. U. Iran, 1966-70, B.A., 1972; English lang. cert. U. Mich., 1972; M.A. (Internat. Scholar), U. Wis., Oshkosh, 1974; Ph.D., U. Wis., Milw., 1980; public econs. cert. M.I.T., summer, 1979. Research asst. dept. econs. and C. of C., U. Wis., Oshkosh, 1974; teaching asst. dept. econs. U. Wis., Milw., 1975-78, lectr. econs., dept. econs. and Sch. Bus. Adminstrn., 1978-79; asst. prof. econs. U. Mo., St. Louis, 1979—. Recipient Grad. Sch. award U. Wis., Milw., 1975. Mem. Am. Econ. Assn., Econometrics Soc., Western Econ. Assn., History of Econs. Soc., AAUP, ACLU, UN Assn. of U.S.A., Omicron Delta Epsilon, Phi Kappa Phi (charter mem. U. Mo. at St. Louis chpt.). Contbr. papers to profl. confs.; participant interviews Public Broadcasting Service, Sta. KWMU, St. Louis Globe-Democrat, 1980. Home: 4426 D Normandy Trace Ct Normandy MO 63121 Office: Dept of Economics Univ Missouri Saint Louis MO 63121

POVISH, KENNETH JOSEPH, bishop; b. Alpena, Mich., Apr. 19, 1924; s. Joseph Francis and Elizabeth (Jachcik) P.; A.B., Sacred Heart Sem., Detroit, 1946; M.A., Cath. U. Am., 1950; grad. student No. Mich. U., 1961, 63. Ordained priest Roman Cath. Ch., 1950; asst. pastorships, 1950-56; pastor in Port Sanilac, Mich., 1956-57, Munger, Mich., 1957-60, Bay City, Mich., 1966-70; dean St. Paul Sem., Saginaw, Mich., 1960-66, vice-rector, 1962-66; bishop of Crookston, Minn., 1970-75, Lansing, Mich., 1975—; bd. consulators Diocese of Saginaw, 1966-70; instr. Latin and U.S. history St. Paul Sem., 1960-66. Bd. dirs. Cath. Charities Diocese Saginaw, 1969-70. Mem. Mich., Bay County hist. socs. Kiwanian. Weekly columnist Saginaw and Lansing diocesan newspapers. Home: 1348 Cambridge Lansing MI 48910 Office: 300 W Ottawa St Lansing MI 48933

POWDRILL, GARY LEO, plant engring. mgr.; b. Butte, Mont., Nov. 26, 1945; s. Harold Holmes and Genevieve Marie (Tansey) P.; B.S., Gonzaga U., 1969; M.B.A., U. Detroit, 1973; m. Marsha A. McKeon, Oct. 6, 1979. Plant design engr. Ford Motor Co., Sterling Heights, Mich., 1969-73, div. plant engr. Chassis div., 1973-74, supr. plant engring. sect., Indpls. plant, 1974-78, mgr. plant engring., 1978-80, mgr. engring. and facilities, 1980—. Mem. Indpls. Mayor's Tech. Adv. Com., 1975—. Licensed profl. engr., Ind. Mem. Ind. Soc. Profl. Engrs. Roman Catholic. Elk. Home: Rural Route 1 Box SC8 New Palestine IN 46163 Office: 6900 English Ave Indianapolis IN 46206

POWELL, BARRY BRUCE, classicist; b. Sacramento, Apr. 30, 1942; s. Barrett Robert and Anita Louise (Burns) P.; B.A. with highest distinction U. Calif., Berkeley, 1963, Ph.D., 1970; M.A., Harvard U., 1965; m. Patricia Ann Cox, Sept. 9, 1967; children—Elena Melissa, Adam Vincent. Asso. in classics U. Calif., Berkeley, 1968; asst. prof. English and comparative lit. No. Ariz. U., 1969-73; asst. prof. classics U. Wis., Madison, 1973-76, asso. prof., 1976—, chmn. dept. classics, 1977—; public broadcasting adv. in Egyptian topics. AMVETS nat. scholar, 1959-60, Gen. Motors nat. scholar 1960-63; Woodrow Wilson fellow, 1965-66; Wis. Alumni Research Found. grantee, 1973, 76, 78, 79. Fellow Am. Soc. Papyrologists; mem. Am. Philol. Assn., Archaeol. Inst. Am., Phi Beta Kappa. Author: Composition by Theme in the Odyssey, 1977; contbr. articles to profl. jours., 1970—, poetry and short fiction to lit. jours., 1976-78. Home: 2521 Kendall Ave Madison WI 53705 Office: Box 921 Van Hise Hall 1220 Linden Dr U Wis Madison WI 53706

POWELL, DON RICHARD, psychologist; b. Bklyn., Aug. 14, 1950; s. Robert B. and Yvette (Steinmetz) P.; B.A., U. Mich., 1971; Ph.D. cum laude, U. Mich., 1978; m. Nancy Talberg, July 18, 1976. Instr. psychology dept. U. Mich., Ann Arbor, 1971-76; sr. staff psychologist Inst. for Behavior Change, Ann Arbor, Mich., 1977-78; v.p. Smoke Stoppers, Inc., Ann Arbor, 1978-79; regional dir. div. health promotion services Am. Health Found., Southfield, Mich., 1979—; TV and radio talk show guest; cons. to pvt. industries and U.S. govt. Mem. Am. Psychol. Assn., Am. Public Health Assn., Midwest Psychol. Assn. Home: 34106 Northwick Rd Farmington Hills MI 48018 Office: 3000 Town Center Suite 2900 Southfield MI 48075

POWELL, DWIGHT EDWARD, social worker; b. Pine Bluff, Ark., Feb. 16, 1948; s. James Curtis and Lyvonne Dozie (Jones) P.; B.A., Roosevelt U., Chgo., 1971; M.S.W. (fellow), U. Ill., 1975; m. Marsandra Mayberry, Aug. 19, 1973; 1 son, Ryan Thomas. Specialist in aging Mayor's Office of Sr. Citizens, Chgo., 1970-72; adult probation officer adult probation dept. Cook County, Chgo., 1973-76; social worker United Charities of Chgo., 1976—; supr./team leader outpatient/adult-elderly-family services Englewood Community Health Center, Chgo.; cons. Morningside Apts., Wentworth Nursing Center; instr. dept. sociology Chgo. State U. Mem. adv. bd. Substance Abuse Program, Chgo.; vice chmn. Children's Network, Chgo. Cert. social worker, Ill. Mem. Ill. Probation, Parole and Correctional Assn., Nat. Assn. Social Workers, Children's Network, Am. Assn. Ret. Persons, Nat. Registry Health Care Providers for Psychiat. Social Workers. Contbr. articles to profl. jours. Home: 8231 S Jeffery Blvd Chicago IL 60617 Office: 800 N Clark St Chicago IL 60610

POWELL, GEORGE EVERETT, JR., motor freight co. exec.; b. Kansas City, Mo., June 12, 1926; s. George Everett and Hilda (Brown) P.; student Northwestern U.; m. Mary Catherine Kuehn, Aug. 26, 1947; children—George Everett III, Nicholas K., Richardson K., Peter E. With Riss & Co., Inc., Kansas City, Mo., 1947-52, treas., 1950-52; with Yellow Freight System, Inc., Kansas City, Mo., 1952—, pres., 1957-68, chmn. bd., 1968—; dir. 1st Nat. Charter Corp., Butler Mfg. Co. Trustee, mem. exec. com. Mid-West Research Inst., Kansas City, Mo., 1961—, chmn. bd. trustees, 1968—; bd. govs. Kansas City Art Inst., 1964—, chmn. bd. trustees, 1973-75. Served with USNR, 1944-46. Mem. Kansas City C. of C. (bd. dirs. 1965-68). Home: 1040 W 57th St Kansas City MO 64113 Office: Yellow Freight System Inc 10990 Roe Overland Park KS 66207

POWELL, IRA CHESLEY, choral music conductor; b. Luling, Tex., Apr. 20, 1930; s. Ira Milton and Margaret Elizabeth (Anderson) P.; student Baylor U., 1946-47; B.S., Wayland Coll., 1950; M. Sacred Music, Southwestern Baptist Theol. Sem., 1956; D. Music Edn., U. Okla., 1969; m. Elinor Cora Van Dyke, Dec. 31, 1974. Minister of music First Baptist Ch., Norman, Okla., 1961-67; mem. music faculty U. Mo., Columbia, 1967—; choral and vocal clinician and adjudicator; bass oratorio soloist; cons. ch. music; musical dir. Community United Methodist Ch., Columbia, Mo.; co-founder, pres. Galaxy Games, Inc. Named Hon. Citizen of Norman (Okla.), 1967. Mem. Nat. Assn. Tchrs. of Singing (Mo. gov. 1973-77), Am., Mo. choral dirs. assns., Pi Kappa Lambda, Phi Mu Alpha Sinfonia. Republican. Methodist. Home: 1200 S Glenwood St Columbia MO 65201 Office: Music Dept Univ Missouri Columbia MO 65201

POWELL, JAMES MICHAEL, environ. engr.; b. Chgo., Aug. 2, 1952; s. Robert Morris and Joan (Glasser) P.; B.S. in Biochemistry - B.S. in Geography, U. Iowa, 1974; M.S. in Environ. Engring., U. Fla., 1975; m. Cheri Lynn Axel, Aug. 12, 1978; children—Emily A., Joseph B., Carrie E. Staff environ. engr. Stanley Cons., Muscatine, Iowa, 1975-77, air quality planning tech. mgr., 1977-81, sr. environ. engr., 1979-81, project mgr., 1981—. Coach, Muscatine YMCA Swim Club, 1975—. U.S. EPA Air Pollution Training grantee, 1974-75. Mem. Air Pollution Control Assn. (dir. upper Midwest sect. 1979—), Iowa Engring. Soc. (chpt. pres. 1980-81), Am. Meteorol. Soc., Nat. Weather Assn., Nat. Soc. Profl. Engrs., Am. Public Works Assn. Jewish. Clubs: Muscatine Y's Men's, Elks. Author: Hurricane Adaptations in Florida, 1974; (with others) Integration of Monitoring, Modeling and Laboratory Analysis, 1979. Office: Stanley Bldg Muscatine IA 52761

POWELL, JEROME EVAN, ins. agency exec.; b. Dallas, Mar. 30, 1935; s. Harry E. and Myrtle H. (McAlear) P.; B.S., U. Dayton, 1957; m. Constance J. Griffiths, May 10, 1958; children—Lisa M., Judith L., Amy E. Retail store mgr. Gen. Tire Co., Pitts., 1957-60; brokerage cons., asst. mgr. Conn. Gen. Life Ins. Co., Chgo., 1960-65; v.p., sec.-treas. Assurance Agy., Arlington Heights, Ill., 1965—; dir. Community Bank of Hanover Park. Bd. dirs., pres. Inverness Village Assn.; bd. dirs. Barrington Area Council of Govts. Mem. Nat. Assn. Life Underwriters, Million Dollar Round Table. Republican. Roman Catholic. Club: Inverness Golf. Home: 1600 Pheasant Trail Inverness Palatine IL 60067 Office: 1114 N Arlington Heights Rd Arlington Heights IL 60004

POWELL, JOHN HAYES, univ. adminstr.; b. Hissop, Ala., July 8, 1941; s. John S. and Willie Mae (McKinney) P.; B.S., Tuskegee (Ala.) Inst., 1964; M.Urban Planning, U. Mich., Ann Arbor, 1977; m. Shirley Joan Hochstedler, Oct. 31, 1964; children—Angela, Edward, Christopher. Field sec. SNCC (Student Non-violent Coordinating Com.), Miss. and Ala., 1959-63; tchr. Detroit public schs., 1964-67; social worker Wayne Dept. Social Services, Detroit, 1967-68; compliance officer Trade Union Leadership Council, Detroit, 1968; ordained to ministry Mennonite Ch., 1971; pastor Mennonite Ch., Wichita, Kans., 1968-69; exec. dir. Minority Ministries Council, Elkhart, Ind., 1969-74, African/Afro-Am. Inter-Mennonite Unity Conf., Ann Arbor, 1972—; Mich. dir. Am. Friends Service Com., Ann Arbor, 1974-77; asst. dir. community servs. U. Mich., 1977—; sec. Nexus Corp.; cons. in field. Chmn. Arbor Heights Center, 1974—, Washtenaw County Coalition Against Aparthied, 1977-78; mem. affirmative action com. Am. Friends Service Com., 1978—; mem. citizens advisory com. racial balance and ednl. opportunity Ann Arbor pub. schs., 1978—; commr. Ann Arbor Human Rights Commn., 1978—; trustee Ann Arbor Bd. Edn., 1979—. Mem. Nat. Assn. Sch. Personnel Adminstrs., NOW. Author: A History of Kenyan/Afro-American Relationships, 1972, Toward a Unified Black Theology, 1972, Squatter Settlements in Developing Countries: Possible Solutions, 1978; also articles. Office: 2204 Michigan Union Ann Arbor MI 48109

POWELL, MARVIN, psychologist, educator; b. Syracuse, N.Y., May 5, 1924; s. William and Gussie (Chainov) P.; A.B., Syracuse U., 1947, M.S. in Edn., 1949, Ph.D., 1952; m. Rita T. Cohen, June 16, 1951; children—Jeffrey A., Linda B., Laura W. Asst. prof. Western Reserve U., Cleve., 1952-61; dir. psychol. services, guidance and research Willoughby-Eastlake Schs. (Ohio), 1956-61; prof. dept. learning and devel. No. Ill. U., DeKalb, 1961—; cons. Found. Individualized Evaluation and Research, Inc., DeKalb, 1970—, pres., 1975. Served with USAAF, 1943-46. Fellow Am. Psychol. Assn., AAAS; mem. Soc. Research in Child Devel., Sigma Xi, Phi Delta Kappa. Jewish. Author: The Psychology of Adolescence, 1963, 2d edit., 1971; Psychosomatic Ailments in Childhood and Adolescence, 1967; Readings in Adolescent Psychology, 1971; Individual Progression, 1970; Introduction to Educational Psychology, 1971; Youth Critical Issues, 1972; contbr. articles in field to psychol. and ednl. jours. Office: Dept Learning and Devel No Ill U DeKalb IL 60115 also 248 1/2 E Lincoln St DeKalb IL 60115

POWELL, MAXINE BELL, orgnl. cons.; b. Kosciusko, Miss., Feb. 10, 1935; d. Albert W. and Susan (Stuckey) Bell; B.S., Jackson State U., 1956; postgrad (NSF fellow) N.Mex. State U., 1959, (Case Western Res., U., 1962, U. Cin., 1966-67; postgrad. Nat. Tng. Labs. courses, 1974-76; m. Lavatus V. Powell, Jr., Nov. 23, 1956 (div. Jan. 1978); children—Robin LaJoyce, Judith LaVonne, Lavatus V. III. Tchr., Lanier High Sch., Jackson, Miss., 1956-59, Walnut Hills High Sch., Cin., 1959-60, 62-64, 65-67; research library mgr. U.S. Indsl. chems. div. Nat. Distillers Corp., Cin., 1961; with Procter & Gamble Co., Cin., from 1970, mgr. tech. info., 1972-75, sect. head research and devel., tech. transfer, from 1976, sect. head soap and toilet goods services; now mgmt. and orgnl. cons. Chmn. unit United Appeal, 1974; trustee Resident Arts and Humanities Consortium, 1974-76. Mem. AAAS, Am. Soc. Info. Sci., Delta Sigma Theta, NAACP, Orgnl. Devel. Network, Nat. Tng. Labs, Alpha Kappa Mu. Home: 2 Revel Ln Cincinnati OH 45217

POWELL, WILLIAM ALFRED, physician; b. Washington, Feb. 16, 1931; s. Alfred Gottwals and Margaret Prudence (Appel) P.; A.A., George Washington U., 1951, M.D., 1959; A.B., Ohio Wesleyan U., 1953; M.A., Williams Coll., 1955; m. Miriam Louise Stauffer, July 7, 1956; children—William Neven, Robert Alfred, Perri Linn, Laura Ann. Intern, resident in gen. practice USPHS Hosp. Div., 1959-62; practice medicine specializing in family practice, Millersburg, Ohio, 1962—; chmn. utilization rev. com. spl. care unit and phys. therapy dept., trustee, treas. Pomerene Hosp.; preceptor in family medicine Ohio State U, Northeastern Ohio Coll. Medicine. Chmn. Millersburg Village Planning Commn., 1973-81. Diplomate Am. Bd. Family Practice. Mem. Ohio Med. Assn., Holmes County Med. Soc., Am. Acad. Family Physicians, Ohio Acad. Family Physicians. Republican. Methodist. Clubs: Millersburg Rotary (v.p. 1979). Family Motor Coach Assn., Masons (master 1971). Home: 115 S Alexander St Millersburg OH 44654 Office: 9 W Adams St Millersburg OH 44654

POWELL-BROWN, ANN, educator; b. Boonville, Mo., Mar. 19, 1947; d. Edward Marsh and Ethel M. (Benton) Powell; B.S., Central Mo. State U., 1969, M.S.E., 1975; postgrad. U. Mo., Kansas City; m. Richard Lee Brown, Dec. 29, 1978. Tchr., Gulfport and Biloxi (Miss.) Schs., 1969-70; mem. adj. staff Providence Coll., Taichung, Taiwan, 1971-72; mem. reading and learning disabilities staff, Kansas City (Mo.) Bd. Edn., 1973-78, mem. learning disabilities identification team, 1978-79, mem. spl. edn. placement com., 1979—; v.p., bd. dirs. Nat. Tutoring Inst., 1976; adj. faculty Ottawa Coll., 1980, instr. English as 2d lang., 1976-77; adj. faculty U. Mo., Kansas City, 1981; speaker various orgns. Mem. public affairs com. Jewish Community Center, 1978; v.p. Com. for Indochinese Devel., 1977; mem. edn. council Episcopal Diocese Western Mo., 1977; founder, bd. dirs. Friends of St. Mary's. Mem. Am. Anthrop. Assn., Am. Ethnological Soc., Council Edn. and Anthropology, Council Exceptional Children, Assn. Children with Learning Disabilities, Internat. Reading Assn., Doctoral Student Spl. Interest Group, Internat. Relations Council, Friends of Art Soc., AAUW, Gray Panthers, Pi Lambda Theta. Democrat. Episcopalian. Club: Grace Challinor Guild. Home: 501 Knickerbocker Pl Kansas City MO 64111 Office: Kansas City Bd Edn 1211 McGee St Kansas City MO 64106

POWER, JOYCE HAWKINS, cons. co. exec.; b. Detroit, Apr. 30, 1946; d. Frederick Bowen and Julia Jane (Oliphant) Hawkins; B.A., No. Ill. U., DeKalb, 1968; M.Ed. (grantee), U. Cin., 1971, Ed.D. (grantee), 1975; 1 dau., Julia Lynne. Ednl. cons., Cin., 1975—; ednl. dir. Adolescent Family Center, Cin., 1978-80; pres. Adscience; dir. Power Learning Systems, also Project Read Summer Program, Cin., 1977—; cons. to bus. in package design and instructional design. Mem. Cin. Commn. Human Services, 1980—. Mem. Orton Soc. (dir.), Alpha Lambda Delta, Pi Beta Phi. Home: 7134 Goldengate St Cincinnati OH 45244 Office: PO Box 30139 Cincinnati OH 45230

POWERS, ANTHONY WILLIAM, JR., banker; b. Indpls., Sept. 18, 1946; s. Anthony William and Rosalie P.; B.S.I.M., Purdue U., 1968; postgrad. U. Chgo., 1968-69; m. Teresa Ann Kolkana, Dec. 28, 1969; children—Timothy, Katharine. Applications analyst Control Data Corp., 1968-69; cons. staff, mgr. Arthur Andersen & Co., 1969-76; v.p. No. Trust Co., 1976-79; sr. v.p. Nat. Sharedata, Schaumburg, Ill., 1979-81. Active Indian Guides and Indian Princess programs YMCA, Cub Scouts. Republican. Roman Catholic. Office: Suite 151 1365 Wiley Rd Schaumburg IL 60195

POWERS, EARL HERSHEL, entrepreneur; b. Tell City, Ind., May 5, 1934; s. Archie E. and Mabel (Hobbs) P.; B.S., Western Ky. U., 1961; m. Sharon A. Grimes, Jan. 15, 1972; children from previous marriage—Allen, Patricia, Kimberly, Lisa Fentress, Jeff Fentress. Account exec. Wolverine World Wide, Rockford, Mich., 1961-67; owner The Ky.-Ind. Corp., coal, First Nat. Mortgage Co., Inc., Evansville, Ind.; dir. The Ind.-Ky. Minerals, Ltd., Powers Bros. Realty and Ins., Koal Industries Corp., Inc. Pres. ch. council Zion United Ch. Christ, Newburgh, Ind.; bd. dirs. Good Samaritan Home. Served with USNR, 1954-58. Recipient Silver Key award for condominium design U.S. Steel, 1973; named hon. Ky. col., Boss of Yr., Ind. Diamond chpt. Am. Bus. Women's Assn., 1981. Mem. C. of C., Nat. Home Builders Assn. (nat. outstanding achievement award 1974), Nat. Inst. Real Estate Brokers, Evansville Bd. Realtors, Multiple Listing Service, LaSalle Law Alumni Club, Indiana Soc. of Ohio, Indiana Soc. of Chgo., UN Assn., Phi Delta Kappa. Mason (Shriner), Elk. Clubs: Tri State Racquet. Office: 5200 Washington Ave Evansville IN 47715

POWERS, JAMES BRUCE, educator; b. Cin., Oct. 29, 1940; s. John Rankin and Elizabeth Almyra (White) P.; B.S., U.S. Naval Acad., 1962; M.A., U. Cin., 1964; m. Catherine Edith Tarbell, June 27, 1964; children—Anne Elizabeth, David Evan, Robert Bruce. Tchr. social studies Indian Hill High Sch., Cin., 1964—, chmn. dept., 1976—. Vol., Alcoholic Drop-In Center, 1973-75; bd. dirs. Housing Opportunities Made Equal, 1977-79, 2d v.p., 1979. Served with USN, 1958-62. William R. Coe fellow, Stanford U., 1970; USA/USSR exchange tchr., 1972. Mem. Am. Hist. Assn., Nat. Council Social Studies, Nat. Edn. Assn., Indian Hill Classroom Tchrs. Assn., Cin. Hist. Soc., Ohio Edn. Assn., Ohio Council Social Studies, Phi Alpha Theta. Roman Catholic. Author: Justice and Power: A Primer in Political Philosophy, 1977. Home: 6110 Cherokee Dr Cincinnati OH 45243 Office: 6845 Drake Rd Indian Hill OH 45243

POWERS, KATHRYN DOLORES, social adminstr.; b. Chgo., Dec. 17, 1929; B.A., Colgate-Rochester U., 1951; M.S.W., Smith Coll., 1964. Child welfare worker, supr. Cook County Dept. Public Aid Children's Div., Chgo., 1953-68; dir. program Central Bapt. Children's Home/Family Services, Lake Villa, Ill., 1968—; pres. bd. dirs. Community Residential Network, Inc., 1978-79; instr. field work U. Wis., 1975-76; mem. habilitation/rehab. task force Health Systems Agency, Kane, Lake and McHenry counties, Ill., 1979. Recipient Spl. Merit citation Am. Bapt. Homes and Hosps. Assn., 1979. Mem. Nat. Assn. Social Workers, Acad. Cert. Social Workers. Home: 309 Milwaukee St Lake Villa IL 60046 Office: Box 218 Lake Villa IL 60046

POWERS, ODELL EUGENE, business exec.; b. Peoria, Ill., May 2, 1928; s. Clarence O. and Beulah P. (Fernandez) P.; B.A., Bradley U., 1952; m. Elizabeth Marie Johnson, Mar. 12, 1950; children—Mark Daniel, Kristin Lynne, Julianne Lynne, Elizabeth M. Mng. dir. Caterpillar Mitsubishi, Inc., Tokyo, 1963-67; dir. internat. fin. and adminstrn. Honeywell, Inc., Mpls., 1967-69, v.p., Brussels, 1969-71, v.p. parent co., also exec. v.p. Honeywell-Europe, 1971-73; pres., chief exec. officer Turbodyne Corp., Mpls., 1973-76, chmn., chief exec. officer, 1976-78; chmn., chief exec. officer Worthington Compressors Co., Holyoke, Mass., 1976-78; pres., chief operating officer, dir. McGraw-Edison Co., Rolling Meadows, Ill., 1979-80; pres., chief operating officer S.J. Groves & Sons Co., Mpls., 1980—; dir. Internat. Multifoods, Mpls. Trustee, Bradley U., Peoria. Served with AUS, 1946-47. Mem. U.S. C. of C. (internat. trade subcom.). Republican. Presbyterian. Clubs: Minneapolis, Minikahda Country (Mpls); Chicago; Deepdale Golf (N.Y.); Tucson Nat. Golf; Metropolitan (N.Y.C.). Office: PO Box 1267 Minneapolis MN 55440

POWERS, ROBERT M., mfg. co. exec.; b. 1931; B.S., Emory U., 1952, M.S., 1953, Ph.D., 1958; married. With A.E. Staley Mfg. Co., agrl. and indsl. products, 1958—, v.p. agrl. products group; then exec. v.p., 1975-80, pres., chief operating officer, 1980—. Served with AUS, 1954-55. Address: 2200 Eldorado St Decatur IL 62525

POYNTON, JOSEPH PATRICK, aerospace engr.; b. Chgo., Aug. 28, 1934; s. Joseph P. and Marvel E. (Gaffney) P.; B.S. Aero. Engring., U. Notre Dame, 1956, M.S. Aero. Engring., 1958; m. Betty Jeanne Gorman, Oct. 1, 1971; 1 dau., Jeanne Louise. Teaching fellow U. Notre Dame, 1956, research asst., 1957; aerodynamics engr. Douglas Missiles Co., Santa Monica, Calif., 1958-59; sr. aerodynamic engr. Honeywell Inc., Mpls., 1959-64; sr. design engr. Fgn. Technology div., Dayton, Ohio, 1964; sr. aerospace engr. Lockheed Space & Missiles Co., Sunnyvale, Calif., 1965-66; supervisory aerospace engr. U.S. Army-Dept. Def. Army Aviation Research and Devel. Command, St. Louis, 1966—, program decision rev. chmn. for aircraft survivability equipment, also supr. chem. and biol. protection. Mem. Am. Inst. Aeros. and Astronautics, Am. Helicopter Soc., Sigma Xi. Roman Catholic. Author tech. papers. Home: 9624 Yorkshire Estates Crestwood MO 63126 Office: PO Box 209 Saint Louis MO 63166

POZULP, NAPOLEON CHARLES, II, psychologist; b. Chgo., Nov. 1, 1947; s. Harry Lawrence and Bernice Pozulp; student U.S. Mcht. Marine Acad., 1965-68; B.A., Ind. U., 1970; M.A., No. Ill. U., 1973, Ph.D., 1976. Clin. therapist Rush-Presbyn.-St. Lukes Med. Center, Chgo., 1976-77; sr. therapist Tri-City Mental Health Center, East Chicago, Ind., 1977-79; dir. Asso. Cert. Psychologists, Chgo., 1979—; cons. in field. Mem. Am. Psychol. Assn., Ill. Psychol. Assn. Contbr. articles to profl. jours.; editor Psychology News, 1980—. Home: 12500 S 91st Ave Palos Park IL 60464 Office: 625 N Michigan Ave Suite 500 Chicago IL 60611

POZZI, FRANCIS THOMAS, sch. prin.; b. Jersey City, Mar. 23, 1939; s. Frank Anthony and Helen Frances (Wandell) P.; B.S., Seton Hall U., 1963, M.A., 1967; Ph.D., Miami U., Oxford, Ohio, 1979; m. Carol Elaine Armstrong, Dec. 23, 1967; children—Michele Elaine, Maribeth Frances. Tchr., St. Joseph's Elem. Sch., 1959-63, Union City, N.J., Hillsborough Sch., Belle Mead, N.J., 1963-64, Clarkstown Central Sch. Dist., New City, N.Y., 1967-69, Franklin Elem. Sch., North Bergen, N.J., 1964-68; tchr., Dayton Public Schs., from 1969, now prin. Jefferson Primary Sch. Mem. Ohio Assn. Elem. Sch. Prins., Nat. Assn. Elem. Sch. Prins., Assn. Supervision and Curriculum Devel., Dayton Adminstrs. Assn., Phi Delta Kappa. Roman Catholic. Home: 188 E Floyd Ave Dayton OH 45415 Office: 1223 N Euclid Ave Dayton OH 45407

PRAEGER, HERMAN ALBERT, JR., research agronomist; b. Claflin, Kans., Jan. 2, 1920; s. Herman Albert and Gertrude Edna (Grizzell) P.; B.S., Kans. State U., 1941, M.S., 1947, Ph.D., 1977; 1 dau., Gwenneth Irene. Commd. lt., U.S. Army, 1941, advanced through grades to lt. col., 1973; mem. faculty Command and Gen. Staff Coll., 1963-67; comdg. officer U.S. Army Support Group, Joint Security Area, Korea, ret., 1973; research agronomist Kans. State U., Manhattan, 1978—; adminstr. improvement of pearl millet program AID, 1978—. Decorated Legion of Merit, Bronze Star with 3 oak leaf clusters, Medal for Merit, Joint Services Commendation medal, Army Commendation medal with oak leaf cluster, Purple Heart. Mem. Assn. U.S. Army, Am. Soc. Agronomy, AAAS, Crop Sci. Soc. Am., V.F.W. Republican. Episcopalian. Club: Elks. Home: 3008 Gary Ave Manhattan KS 66502 Office: Throckmorton Hall Kans State U Manhattan KS 66506

PRAEGER, SUSAN GRAY, nurse, educator; b. Princeton, N.J., Aug. 18, 1948; d. Richard Quinn and Margaret (Reilly) P.; B.A., Colo. State U., 1970; M.S., N.Y. Med. Coll., 1973; Ed.D., U. No. Colo., 1980; m. Gregory R. Bernhardt, Aug. 10, 1974; 1 dau., Sarah Praeger Bernhardt. Labor and delivery perinatal nurse specialist U. Kans. Med. Center, 1974-75; instr. nursing U. Utah, 1975-76; staff nurse, clin. coordinator Weld County Gen. Hosp., Greeley, Colo., 1976-78; instr. nursing U. Wyo., 1977-79; asst. prof. nursing Wright State U., Dayton, Ohio, 1980—. Mem. Assn. Humanistic Edn., Nat. League Nursing, Assn. Supervision and Curriculum Devel., Kappa Delta Pi. Home: 690 Omar Circle Yellow Springs OH 45387 Office: Sch Nursing Wright State U Dayton OH 45435

PRAGER, DAVID, justice Kans. Supreme Ct.; b. Fort Scott, Kans., Oct. 30, 1918; s. Walter and Helen (Kishler) P.; A.B., U. Kans., 1939, LL.B., 1942; m. Dorothy Schroeter, Sept. 8, 1945; children—Diane, David III. Admitted to Kans. bar, 1942; practiced in Topeka, 1946-59; dist. judge, Topeka, 1959-71; asso. justice Supreme Ct. Kans., 1971—; lectr. law Washburn Law Sch., 1948-68. Served to lt. USNR, 1943-46. Mem. Am., Kans., Topeka bar assns., Order of Coif, Phi Beta Kappa, Phi Delta Theta, Phi Delta Phi. Home: 5130 SW 53d St Topeka KS 66610 Office: Kans Jud Center Topeka KS 66612

PRAGER, JAMES SCOTT, social worker; b. N.Y.C., Apr. 18, 1948; s. Alfred and Cecile P.; B.A., U. Hartford, 1971; M.S.W., Wash. U., 1973. With Wiltwyck Sch., Yorktown Heights, N.Y., 1973-74, St. Cabrini Home, West Park, N.Y., 1974-75; social worker Watkins Glen (N.Y.) Day Hosp., 1976-79, Battle Creek (Mich.) Child Guidance and Adult Clinic, 1979—. Bd. dirs. Temple B'nai Israel, Kalamazoo, Mich., 1980-81. Cert. social worker, N.Y., Mich. Mem. Nat. Assn. Social Workers, Nat. Conf. on Social Welfare, Internat. Conf. Social Welfare. Jewish. Home: 90 Greentree Ln Apt 28B Battle Creek MI 49015 Office: 155 Garfield St Battle Creek MI 49017

PRALL, ELMER CLARENCE, dentist; b. Lamoni, Iowa, Mar. 9, 1902; s. Oscar Edward and Eleanor Margaret (Gibbons) P.; A.A., Graceland Coll., 1923, U. Iowa, summers, 1920-22, 24, 26; D.D.S., U. Iowa, 1930; m. Irma Caroline Reihman, June 25, 1927; 1 dau., Paula (Mrs. White). Tchr., athletic coach Iowa High Schs., 1920-22, 23-24, 26-27; gen. practice dentistry, Mount Vernon, Iowa, 1930—. Pres., Mount Vernon chpt. ARC, 1947, v.p., water safety chmn., 1948-76. Mem. Mount Vernon City Council, 1934-76; mem. tax com. Iowa League Municipalities, 1936. Fellow Am. Coll. Dentists (pres. Iowa sect. 1980); mem. Am. Soc. Dentistry for Children (unit pres. 1955), Am. (life), Iowa (supt. clinics. 1950, chmn. ins. council 1956-64) dental assns., University Dist. (pres. 1950, sec. 1945-50, 68—), Cedar Rapids (pres. 1944-45) dental socs., Pierre Fauchard Acad., Alumni Assn. Dental Coll. U. Iowa (pres. 1957, treas. 1958-65), Mount Vernon C. of C. (pres. 1933). Methodist (trustee 1971-74). Lion (pres. 1937). Home: 419 S 2d St Mount Vernon IA 52314 Office: 125 1st St W Mount Vernon IA 52314

PRANGE, JAMES ROBERT, Realtor; b. Hammond, Ind., Apr. 27, 1936; s. William Edward and Mildred Lorraine (Hutchinson) P.; grad. high sch., Grad. Realtors Inst., 1974; m. Marilyn Joyce Lavery, June 29, 1970; children—James Allen, Thomas Michael, Cynthia Sue. Electrician, No. Ind. Pub. Service Co., Crown Point, Ind., 1957-61; salesman Burkhardt Schmal Realty Inc., Crown Point, 1961-63; broker, owner Lake County Realty, Inc., and Prange Devel. Co.,

1963—. Owner Jamar Properties mgmt., 1970—; pres. Triangle Constrn. Co., 1976—, Burgundy Builders, 1977—, Wide World of Travel, 1977—. Served with AUS, 1955-57. Mem. Home Builders Assn. (dir., 1973-74), South Lake County Bd. Realtors, Merrillville C. of C., Nat. Assn. Realtors, Nat. Inst. Real Estate Brokers, Ind. Realtors Inst., Nat. Assn. Ind. Fee Appraisers (v.p., 1969-71), Crown Point C. of C. Methodist. Home: 349 Devon Rd Valparaiso IN 46383 Office: 8695 Broadway St Merrillville IN 46410

PRASAD, ANANDA SHIVA, med. educator; b. Buxar, Bihar, India, Jan. 1, 1928; s. Radha Krishna and Mahesha (Kaur) Lall; B.Sc. with honors, Patna (India) Sci. Coll., 1946, M.B.B.S., 1951; Ph.D., U. Minn., 1957; m. Aryabala Ray, Jan. 6, 1952; children—Rita, Sheila, Ashok, Audrey. Came to U.S., 1952, naturalized, 1968. Intern, Patna Med. Coll. Hosp., 1951-52; resident St. Paul's Hosp., Dallas, 1952-53, U. Minn., 1953-56, VA Hosp., Mpls., 1956; instr. dept. medicine Univ. Hosp., U. Minn., Mpls., 1957-58; vis. asso. prof. medicine Shiraz (Iran) Med. Faculty, Nemazee Hosp., 1960; asst. prof. medicine and nutrition Vanderbilt U., 1961-63; mem. faculty, dir. div. hematology dept. medicine Wayne State U., Detroit, 1963—, asso. prof., 1964-68, prof., 1968—; mem. staff Detroit Gen. Hosp., VA Hosp., Allen Park, Mich.; mem. trace elements subcom. Food and Nutrition Bd., NRC-Nat. Acad. Scis., 1965-68; chmn. com. 5 Trace Elements in Human Nutrition Commn. IV Internat. Union Nutritional Scis., 1980—. Trustee Detroit Internat. Inst., Detroit Gen. Hosp. Research Corp., 1969-72, Pfizer scholar, 1955-56; recipient research recognition award Wayne State U., 1964, Am. Coll. Nutrition award, 1976. Diplomate Am. Bd. Nutrition. Fellow A.C.P., Internat. Soc. Hematology; mem. Am. Soc. Clin. Nutrition (awards com. 1969-70), Am. Fedn. Clin. Research (pres. Mich. 1969-70), Am. Inst. Nutrition (trace elements panel), Am. Physiol. Soc., Am. Soc. Clin. Investigation, Am. Soc. Hematology, Assn. Am. Physicians, Central Soc. Clin. Research, Soc. Exptl. Biology and Medicine (councillor Mich. 1967-71), Wayne County Med. Soc., AMA (Goldberger award 1975), Internat. Soc. Internal Medicine, Sigma Xi. Club: Cosmos (Washington). Author: Zinc Metabolism, 1966; Trace Elements in Human Health and Disease, 1976; co-editor: Zinc Metabolism: Current Aspects in Health and Disease, 1977; Trace Elements and Iron in Human Metabolism, 1978; editor Am. Jour. Hematology; contbr. articles to profl. jours. Office: 540 E Canfield Ave Detroit MI 48201

PRASUHN, LLOYD WAYNE, veterinarian; b. Beamsville, Ohio, June 28, 1930; s. Carl Henry and Ellen Victoria (Neal) P.; D.V.M., Ohio State U., 1954; m. Mary Zinn Squibb, Nov. 7, 1963. Practice of vet. medicine, New Palestine, Ind., 1956-57; veterinarian Lake Shore Animal Hosp., Chgo., 1957—, pres., dir., 1963—; cons. Wilson Labs., Beatrice Foods, Kimberly-Clark Corp., Parke-Davis, Ralston Purina, Affiliated Labs.; editor D.V.M. News mag., 1969-72; editor-in-chief Veterinary Digest, 1976-80. Mem. adv. bd. manpower devel. and tng. act Ill. Dept. Labor, 1971—. Pres. Lake Shore Found. for Animals, 1966—. Served as capt. USAF, 1954-56. Mem. AMVA, Ohio, Ill. State, Chgo. vet. med. assns., Am. Animal Hosp. Assn., Am. Vet. Radiology Soc., Am. Acad. Vet. Cardiology, Am. Vet. Neurology Assn., Nat. Wildlife Fedn., Lincoln Park Zool. Soc., Humane Soc. U.S., Am. Humane Assn., Internat. Veterinary Acupuncture Soc. (treas. 1976-81). Phi Eta Sigma, Phi Zeta. Lutheran. Clubs: International, Whitehall. Contbr. articles to publs. Home: 225 W Division St Chicago IL 60610

PRATT, DAN EDWIN, chemist, educator; b. High Point, N.C., Feb. 7, 1924; s. C. Daniel and Carol Druscilla (Wyatt) P.; student U. Tampa, 1946-47; B.S., U. Ga., 1950, M.S., 1952; postgrad. Va. Poly. Inst., 1954, Emory U. Law Sch., 1955-56; U. Mass., 1954-55; Ph.D. (fellow) Fla. State U., 1962; m. Mana Clariece Peacock, Aug. 29, 1959; 1 dau., Mana Lisa. Asst. prof. food chemistry U. Ga., Athens, 1955-60; asso. prof., research scientist dept. food sci. and nutrition U. Wis., Madison, 1964-69; prof., food scientist, Purdue U., West Lafayette, Ind., 1969—; del. Internat. Congress Food Scientists, Tokyo, 1978; vis. scientist Republic of China, 1978, Natick Army Research and Devel. Labs., 1980. Served with USMCR, 1942-45. Fellow Am. Inst. Chemists; mem. Nat. Inst. Food Scientists (sec. Inst.), Inst. Food Technologists, Ga. Acad. Sci., N.Y. Acad. Sci., Sigma Xi, Phi Kappa Phi, Pi Mu Epsilon, Phi Tau Sigma (exec. sec. 1969). Clubs: Optinestment; Lafayette Toastmasters (pres.). Contbr. numerous sci. articles to profl. jours. Home: 1600 Northwestern Ave West Lafayette IN 47906 Office: Dept Foods and Nutrition Purdue Univ West Lafayette IN 47906

PRATT, PHILIP, fed. judge; b. Pontiac, Mich., July 14, 1924; s. Peter and Helen (Stathis) P.; student U. Chgo., 1943-44; LL.B., U. Mich., 1950; m. Mary Charlotte Hill, July 26, 1952; children—Peter, Laura, Kathleen. Admitted to Mich. bar, 1951; asst. pros. atty., Oakland County, Mich., 1952; practice law in Pontiac, 1953-63; circuit judge 6th Jud. Circuit Mich., 1963-70; judge U.S. Dist. Ct., Eastern Dist. Mich., Detroit, 1970—. Served with OSS, AUS, 1943-46. Decorated Bronze Star medal. Mem. Am., Mich., Oakland County (pres. 1959-60) bar assns., Am. Judicature Soc. Office: US Courthouse Detroit MI 48226

PRATT, WILLIAM CROUCH, JR., educator; b. Shawnee, Okla., Oct. 5, 1927; s. William Crouch and Irene (Johnston) P.; B.A., U. Okla., 1949; M.A., Vanderbilt U., 1951, Ph.D., 1957; m. Anne Cullen Rich, Oct. 2, 1954; children—Catherine Cullen, William Stuart, Randall Johnston. Rotary Internat. fellow U. Glasgow (Scotland), 1951-52; instr. English, Vanderbilt U., 1955-57; instr. Miami U., Oxford, Ohio, 1957-59, asst. prof. English, 1959-64, asso. prof., dir. freshman English, 1964-68, prof., 1968—; adviser Ohio Poetry Circuit, 1964—; Fulbright-Hays lectr. in Am. lit., prof. Am. lit. Univ. Coll., Dublin, Ireland, 1975-76; resident scholar Miami U. European Center, Luxembourg, fall 1976; lectr. Yeats Internat. Summer Sch., Eire, 1979, 81, 82. Served to lt. USNR, 1953-55. Mem. Modern Lang. Assn., Nat. Council Tchrs. English (Ohio awards chmn. 1967-69), Coll. Conf. on Composition, Communication, Internat. Contemporary Lit. and Theatre Soc., Soc. Study So. Lit., Phi Beta Kappa, Sigma Alpha Epsilon. Republican. Episcopalian. Club: Butler County (Ohio) Torch. Author: The Imagist Poem, 1963; The Fugitive Poets, 1965; The College Writer, 1969; contbr. essays, translations, poems, revs. to lit. jours., books. Home: 212 Oakhill Dr Oxford OH 45056 Office: Dept of English Miami U Oxford OH 45056

PRAY, BRUCE S., clergyman, psychologist; b. Haverhill, Mass., June 5, 1926; s. Roland Call and Elsie (Stevens) P.; B.S., Houghton Coll., 1962; M.Div. Colgate-Rochester Div. Sch., 1966; M.S., Alfred U., 1968; m. Rose Mary Barios, Oct. 30, 1948; children—Steven, Ronald, Karen, Bruce, Douglas, Shirley, Elsie, John, Gerry. Clin. tng. Willard State Hosp., 1962, Gowanda State Hosp., 1963; intern VA Hosp., Sioux Falls, S.D., 1971. Ordained to ministery, Presbyn. Ch., 1956; patrolman Gen. Electric Co., Schenectady, 1948-53; pastor Howard Union Ch., Howard, N.Y., 1960-66; chaplain Bath (N.Y.) VA Hosp., 1966-68; guidance counselor, Kimball, S.D., 1968-69; sch. psychologist Flandreau (S.D.) Ind. Sch., 1969-76; pvt. practice sch. psychology, Pipestone, Minn., 1976-77; dir. spl. edn. Aberdeen area Bur. Indian Affairs, 1977—, also cons. bur., Washington; stated supply pastor Minn. Valley Presbytery, 1970—, serving Turner County Presbyn. Ch., 1970-74, Rushmore Presbyn. Ch., 1975-77, Emmanuel Presbyn. Ch., 1977-78, Beaver Creek Presbyn. Ch., 1978-80, State Line Presbyn. Ch., 1980—; del. to profl. meetings. Contbr. articles to profl. jours. Home: 114 W 1st Ave Flandreau SD 57028

PRAY, RALPH RUSTIN, physician; b. Fargo, N.D., Feb. 2, 1943; s. Laurence Gesner and Helen Louella (Van Atta) P.; B.A., Grinnell Coll., 1965; M.D., U. Iowa, 1969; m. D. Jean Reay, Apr. 5, 1969; children—Sarah Elaine, Gregory David. Intern, Harborview Med. Center, Seattle, 1969-70; resident in internal medicine U. Iowa Hosps. and Clinics, Iowa City, 1970-73; practice specializing in internal medicine, Des Moines, 1973—; mem. staff Iowa Methodist Med. Center, Broadlawns Polk County Hosp.; instr. internal medicine Iowa Meth. Med. Center. Diplomate Am. Bd. Internal Medicine. Fellow A.C.P., mem. AMA, Iowa, Polk County med. socs., Am. Soc. Internal Medicine, Med. Library Club, Alpha Omega Alpha. Presbyterian. Clubs: Masons, Des Moines Golf and Country, West Des Moines Breakfast. Home: 4616 Western Hills Dr West Des Moines IA 50265 Office: 1221 Center St Suite 15 Des Moines IA 50309

PREBE, WILLIAM FRANCIS, automotive and truck parts co. exec.; b. Toledo, O., Aug. 27, 1922; s. Kaiser and Gertrude Mary (Hurley) P.; B.B.A., U. Toledo, 1949; m. Jeanette Marie Burtscher, July 2, 1949; children—Ronald William, Susan Lynette. With Dana Corp., automotive and truck parts mfr., Toledo, 1952—, market research mgr., 1966-68, corp. economist, 1969—, v.p., economist, 1976—; adj. prof. U. Toledo; lectr. Cleve. State U., 1976—. Area bd. Salvation Army, Mental Health, Adult Rehab. Center. Served to lt. (j.g.) USNR, 1942-46, 50-52. Mem. Am. Statis. Assn., Nat. Assn. Bus. Economists, Automotive Market Research Council (pres. 1980-81), Fourth Dist. Economists Round Table, U. Toledo Bus. Alumni Assn. (sec. 1972-73). Club: K.C. Contbr. articles to profl. publs. Home: 3620 Orchard Trail Toledo OH 43606 Office: PO Box 1000 Toledo OH 43697

PREBLE, ROBERT CURTIS, JR., life ins. exec.; b. Oak Park, Ill., Dec. 19, 1922; s. Robert Curtis and Dorothy (Seidel) P.; B.A. (Meml. fellow), Amherst Coll., 1947; M.B.A., Harvard U., 1949, grad. 61st Advanced Mgmt. Program; m. Lidia Blazik, May 29, 1963. Asst. to gen. supt., asst. buyer Carson Pirie Scott & Co., Chgo., 1949-52; sales dept. Northwestern Mut. Life Ins. Co., Chgo., 1952-53, Nat. Life Ins. Co., Chgo., 1953-59; prin. Preble Assos., Chgo., 1959—; pres.-treas. Variable Annuity Life Ins. Agys., Inc.; pres., treas. Savs. Plans Inc., cons. Iowa Savs. & Loan League; dir. Scandia Savs. & Loan Assn. (Iowa); dir. World Book Life Ins. Co.; consul of Bolivia, 1968-71; hon. consul of Colombia; mem. adv. bd. Ill. Dept. Ins., 1965-70. Dep. regional chmn. Democratic Nat. Fin. Com., 1952; bd. dirs. McCormick Theol. Sem. Served to 1st lt. AUS, 1943-46; PTO. Recipient service award Chgo. council Boy Scouts Am., 1962, C.L.U. Mem. Newcomen Soc., Soc. Colonial Wars, Assn. for Advanced Life Underwriting (founding pres. 1957-58), Am. Soc. C.L.U.'s (pres. Chgo. chpt. 1963-64), Nat. Assn. Life Underwriters (life mem. Million Dollar Round Table 1956—), Mil. Order World Wars, Chgo. Council Fgn. Relations (dir. 1971-77), Associated Harvard Alumni (dir.), Harvard Bus. Sch. Assn. (exec. council), Inst. Internat. Edn. (Midwest advisory bd.), Chi Psi (trustee ednl. trust). Democrat. Presbyterian. Clubs: University, Chicago, Economic, Harvard Bus. Sch. (past pres.), Amherst (past pres.), Harvard (Chgo.). Home: 300 N State St Chicago IL 60610 Office: 401 N Wabash St Suite 519 Chicago IL 60611

PRELAS, MARK ANTONIO, nuclear engr.; b. Pueblo, Colo., July 2, 1953; s. George B. and Katheryn (Beck) P.; B.S. in Engring. Sci., Colo. State U., 1975; M.S. in Nuclear Engring., U. Ill., Champaign-Urbana, 1976, Ph.D. (ERDA trainee, univ. fellow), 1979; m. Rosemary Roberts, May 21, 1979. Research scientist, research reactor U. Mo., Columbia, 1980—, asst. prof. nuclear engring., 1979—. Mem. AAAS, Am. Nuclear Soc., Am. Phys. Soc., Am. Soc. Engring. Edn., IEEE, Mo. Acad. Sci., Sigma Xi. Author papers in fusion and energy conversion. Home: 1904 LoveJoy Ln Columbia MO 65201 Office: 0039 Nuclear Engring U Mo Columbia MO 65211

PRENDERGAST, MARY KATHRYN, mathematician; b. Evergreen Park, Ill., Nov, 16, 1942; d. Francis Justine and Ann (Lanigan) Foley; B.S., Mundelein Coll., 1963; M.A., Loyola U., 1965; m. William Patrick Prendergast, Nov. 21, 1964; children—William Francis, Patrick Joseph. Asso. prof. mathematics Richard J. Daley Coll., Chgo., 1966—, sec. mathematics dept., 1968—, faculty advisor, 1974—. Mem. Math. Assn. Am., Am. Math. Assn. of Two-Yr. Colls. Home: 10109 S Parke Ave Oak Lawn IL 60453 Office: 7500 S Pulaski Rd Chicago IL 60652

PRENTICE, DIXON WRIGHT, asso. justice Ind. Supreme Ct.; b. Sellersburg, Ind., June 3, 1919; s. Walter E. and Maude (Wilson) P.; LL.B., Ind. U., 1942; m. Phyllis Catherine Ropa, Dec. 20, 1941; children—Penelope Prentice Rauzi, Peter K., William W. Admitted to Ind. bar; partner firm Prentice & Prentice, Lawyers, Jeffersonville, Ind., 1946-71; partner Green Tree Assos., Jeffersonville, 1968-73; asso. justice Ind. Supreme Ct., Indpls., 1971—; mem. Nat. Commn. Uniform State Laws, 1979—. Served with U.S. Navy, 1942-46; lt. comdr. USNR Ret. Mem. Am. Bar Assn., Ind. Bar Assn. (ho. of dels. 1954-56, bd. mgrs. 1964-66), Clark County Bar Assn. (pres. 1953), Indpls. Bar Assn., Am. Judicature Soc., Ind. Judges Assn. Clubs: Meridian Hills Country, Elks. Office: 306 State House Indianapolis IN 46204

PRENTICE, STEWART WEBSTER, r.r. exec.; b. Cin., May 4, 1919; s. Robert James and Grace Webster (Lombard) P.; student U. Oreg., 1946; student hotel-motel mgmt. La Salle U., 1968; m. Cindy Kovic Two; foster children—Carol, Robert, Debra; children—Kari, John. Mgr., Hotpoint Country Club, Mukwonago, Wis., 1937-40; mgr. advt. dept. Chgo. Daily News, 1940-43; chief clk. Alton R.R., Chgo., 1943-44, asst. supr. Chgo. Union Sta., 1943-44; dispatcher Western Ind. R.R., Chgo., 1944-47, traffic dir., Chgo., 1947—. Served with AUS, 1940-46. Mem. Asso. Traffic Clubs Am., Exptl. Aviation Assn. Am., Delta Nu Alpha. Methodist. Home: 800 Circle Ave Forest Park IL 60130

PRENZLOW, ELMER JOHN CHARLES, JR., clergyman, educator; b. Norfolk, Neb., Apr. 4, 1929; s. Elmer Edward and Alvina Carolina (Henning) P.; B.A., Northwestern Coll., 1950; B.D., Evang. Luth. Theol. Sem., 1953; postgrad. U. Minn., 1957-61; M.S. in Ednl. Psychology, U. Wis., 1969; m. Karen McHarg DeMoss, July 4, 1980; 1 son, Elmer Carl III. Ordained to Luth. Ch., Mo. Synod, 1953; parish pastor St. Paul Luth. Ch., Bloomer, Wis., 1953-62; chaplain Univ. Luth. Chapel, U. Wis., Milw., 1962-78; prof. Spencerian Bus. Coll., Milw., 1963-78, chmn. humanities dept., 1969-72; dir. devel. and public relations S. Wis. dist. Luth. Ch.-Mo. Synod, 1979—. Mem. Wis. State Legis. com. for Kerner Report, Madison, 1968-70, U.S. Justice Dept. Commn. Law Enforcement Goals and Standards, 1970-73; mem. ad hoc adv. panel Nat. Inst. Corrections, U.S. Dept. Justice and U.S. Bur. Prisons, 1972—; mem. 9th Congl. dist. U.S. Ser. Acad. Selection Rev. Bd., 1979—. Bd. dirs. Patricia Stevens Career Coll., Milw., Wis. Inst. Social Research and Devel. Mem. Am., Wis. psychol. assns. Republican. Optimist. Contbr. articles to denominational jours. Home: 4073 W Rivers Edge Circle #1 Brown Deer WI 53209 Office: 8100 W Capitol Dr Milwaukee WI 53222

PREROST, FRANK JOSEPH, psychologist, educator; b. Chgo., Jan. 20, 1948; s. Joseph John and Emily Lisa (Dubina) P.; B.S., U. Ill., 1970; M.A., DePaul U., 1973, Ph.D., 1975. Intern psychologist Children's Meml. Hosp, Chgo., 1972-73; asst. professorial lectr. St. Xavier Coll., 1974-75; asst. prof., coordinator community psychology Lewis U., Lockport, Ill., 1975-78; asst. prof., dir. field experiences Western Ill. U., Macomb, 1978-80, asso. prof., dir. field experiences, 1980—; pvt. practice psychotherapy, 1975—. Mem. Am., Ill., Midwestern psychol. assns., Soc. Pediatric Psychology, AAAS, U. Ill. Alumni Assn. Roman Catholic. Contbr. articles to profl. jours. Home: 8245 S California Ave Chicago IL 60652 Office: Dept Psychology Western Ill U Macomb IL 61455

PRESKA, MARGARET LOUISE ROBINSON, univ. pres.; b. Parma, N.Y., Jan. 23, 1938; d. Ralph Craven and Ellen Elvira (Niemi) Robinson; B.S. summa cum laude, SUNY, Brockport, 1957; M.A., Pa. State U., 1961; Ph.D., Claremont (Calif.) Grad. Sch., 1969; postgrad. Manchester Coll., Oxford (Eng.) U., summer 1973; m. Daniel C. Preska, Jan. 24, 1959; children—Robert, William, Ellen. From instr. to asso. prof. history and govt. U. LaVerne (Calif.), 1968-75, acad. dean, 1972-75; instr. Starr King Sch. Ministry, Berkeley, Calif., summer 1975; v.p. acad. affair, EEO officer Mankato (Minn.) State U., 1975-79, pres., 1979—; trustee Fielding Inst.; bd. dirs. Minn. Council Econ. Edn.; mem. commn. on govtl. relations, pres.'s Com. on collegiate athletics Am. Council Edn.; dir. No. State Power Co., Inc. Sec., Pomona Sign Study Commn., 1965-66; pres. Pomona Valley (Calif.) chpt. UN Assn., 1968-69, Unitarian Soc. Pomona Valley, 1968-69, Pomona (Calif.) chpt. LWV, 1972-74, Lincoln Elem. Sch. PTA, Pomona, 1973-74; mem. Pomona City Charter Revision Commn., 1972; exec. bd. Twin Valley council Boy Scouts Am., 1978; bd. dirs. Mankato Salvation Army, 1979—. Named Outstanding Alumna, Claremont Grad. Sch., 1979, Disting. Educator, 1980; grantee Carnegie Found., 1974. Mem. Am. Assn. Univ. Adminstrs. (dir. found.), Am. Assn. State Colls. and Univs., AAUW, Women's Equity Action League, Mankato C. of C. (dir.), P.E.O., Phi Kappa Phi, Pi Lambda Theta, Delta Kappa Gamma, Kappa Delta Pi. Mem. Democratic-Farmer-Labor Party. Club: Benedicts Dance. Office: Box 24 Mankato State U Mankato MN 56001

PRESS, ALLAN N., psychologist, educator; b. Hartford, Conn., Apr. 22, 1942; s. Lowis and Betty (Tobin) P.; S.B. in Math., M.I.T., 1964; M.A. in Psychology, Clark U., 1967, Ph.D., 1972; m. Marilynn B. Osterkamp, Oct. 20, 1978. Chief programmer Clark U. Computer Center, Worcester, Mass., 1966-67, research asst. dept. psychology, 1967-69, programmer and statistician dept. psychology, 1969-70; asst. prof. dept. psychology Kans. State U., Manhattan, 1970-74; research asso. Sch. Social Welfare, U. Kans., Lawrence, 1974-75, asso. prof., 1975—; cons. human relations, program evaluation, 1978—. NIMH grantee, 1972-77. Mem. Am. Psychol. Assn., Nat. Assn. Social Workers. Contbr. articles to jours. in psychology. Home: 1115 W Campus Rd Lawrence KS 66044 Office: Twente Hall Univ of Kansas Lawrence KS 66045

PRESSLER, LARRY, U.S. Senator; b. Humboldt, S.D., Mar. 29, 1942; s. Antone Lewis and Lorretta (Claussen) P.; B.A., U. S.D., 1964; diploma in Econs. (Rhodes scholar), Oxford (Eng.) U., 1966; M.A., Harvard U., 1971, J.D., 1971. Mem. 94th-95th Congresses from 1st Dist. S.D.; mem. U.S. Senate from S.D., 1979—; mem. commerce, fgn. relations, sci. and transp. coms., Spl. com. on aging, Republic senatorial campaign com., also subcoms.; sec. U.S. del. Inter-Parliamentary Union for 97th Congress. All-Am. del. 4-H Agrl. Fair, Cairo, 1961. Served to 1st lt. AUS, 1966-68; Vietnam. Recipient Nat. 4-H Citizenship award, 1962, Report to Pres. 4-H award, 1962. Mem. Am. Assn. Rhodes Scholars, VFW, DAV, Am., D.C. bar assns., Am. Legion, Phi Beta Kappa. Club: Lions. Home: 700 New Hampshire Ave NW Washington DC 20037 Office: 411 Russell Senate Office Bldg Washington DC 20510

PRESTLEY, KENNETH LEE, graphic designer; b. Morrison, Ill., Oct. 7, 1946; s. Leroy Charles and Marjorie June (Rhymer) P.; A.A., So. Ill. U., 1966; m. Thelma Irene Hartsfield, July 30, 1964; 1 son, Clinton Lee. With Desaulnier & Co., Moline, Ill., 1966-68; art dir. D.R. Light Co., Moline, 1970-72; creative dir. Wilson and Lund Co., Moline, 1972-73; creative dir. Fanning Advt. Co., Bettendorf, Iowa, 1973-74; with Hired Hand Visual Communications, Inc., Davenport, Iowa, 1974—; owner, v.p. Prestley & Prestley Advt. & Public Relations, Inc., Davenport 1979—; mem. Quad City Devel. Group. Bd. dirs. Humane Soc. Scott County, 1976—. Recipient 1st place award Iowa Trout Stamp competition, 1976. Mem. Davenport C. of C., Nat. Audubon Soc., Humane Soc. U.S.A., Graphic Artists Guild N.Y., Quad Cities Advt. Assn., Iowa Art Dirs. Assn., Advt. Fedn. Dubuque, Am. Advt. Fedn. Republican. Baptist. Clubs: Davenport, Rock Island Arsenal Golf. Artist, Iowa Trout stamp, 1976. Home: 14 Van Villa Ct Bettendorf IA 52722 Office: 1218 E 37th St Davenport IA 52807

PRESTON, ELIZA HOYT, editor; b. Columbia, Mo., Dec. 12, 1936; d. Charles Edwin and Frances Gertrude (Reynolds) Barkshire; A.B., U. Mo., 1955, B.J., 1956, M.A.; m. J. E. Sutherland, May 23, 1981. Reporter, feature writer Daily Republican Times, Ottawa, Ill., 1956-61; asso. editor Irving Cloud Pub. Co., Lincolnwood, Ill., 1961-63; asst. editor Sci. Research Assos., Chgo., 1963-64; instr., pub. editor, extension div. Coll. Agr., U. Mo., Columbia, 1965-73; editor consumer info. services Sears, Roebuck & Co., Chgo., 1973-80, asst. dir. corp. contbns. and memberships, 1980—. Chmn. pub. relations com. Boone County (Mo.) Assn. Mental Health, 1970-73. Mem. Am. Assn. Agrl. Coll. Editors, AAUW, Newberry Library Assos., Chgo. Council Fgn. Relations, Kappa Epsilon Alpha, Sigma Delta Chi, Theta Sigma Phi, Delta Delta Delta, P.E.O. Contbg. editor Mo. Today. Home: 187 Asbury Ave Evanston IL 60202

PRESTON, NAOMI ELIZABETH, mfg. co. exec.; b. Cleve., Mar. 30, 1955; d. Nicholas N. and Mary Preston; B.S., Denison U., 1977; postgrad. Western Mich. U., 1979—. Mktg. research analyst Yee Minard & Assos., Lathrup Village, Mich., 1977-78; mktg. research analyst new products Kellogg Co., Battle Creek, Mich., 1978-80, asst. product mgr., 1980—. Chmn. spl. gifts com. United Way, Battle Creek. Mem. Am. Mktg. Assn., Phi Beta Kappa, Sigma Xi. Home: 5185 East R Ave Kalamazoo MI 49002 Office: 235 Porter St Battle Creek MI 49016

PRESTON, WILBUR DEAN, credit reporting and collection exec.; b. Mealy, Ky., Oct. 14, 1943; s. Homer W. and Marie (Ward) P.; B.S., Pikeville Coll., 1965; m. Wanda Lou Franklin, May 29, 1965; children—Gregory, Jeffrey. Tchr. public schs., Clark County, Ohio, 1965-70; reporting mgr. Credit Bur., Dayton, Ohio, 1970-74, sec., treas., gen. mgr., 1975-78; v.p., gen. mgr. Trans Union Credit Info. Co., Dayton, 1978—. Mem. Associated Credit Bureaus Ohio (dir. 1979—), Associated Credit Bur. Inc. (Bronze Leadership award 1977, mem. nat. credit reporting div. com.), Dayton Credit Execs. Assn. (sec. 1975—). Home: 3429 Loggerhead Ct Dayton OH 45414 Office: Trans Union Credit Info Co 115 E 3rd St Dayton OH 45402

PREUSS, ROGER E(MIL), artist; b. Waterville, Minn., Jan. 29, 1922; s. Emil W. and Edna (Rosenau) P.; student Mankato Comml. Coll., Mpls. Sch. Art; m. MarDee Ann Germundson, Dec. 31, 1954 (dec. Mar. 1981). Painter of nature art; one man shows St. Paul Fine

Art Galleries, 1959, Albert Lea Art Center, 1963, Hist. Soc. Mont., Helena, 1964, LeSueur County Hist. Soc. Mus., 1976; exhibitions include Midwest Wildlife Conf. Exhbn., Kerr's, Beverly Hills, Calif., 1947, Joslyn Meml. Mus., Omaha, 1948, Minn. Centennial, 1949, Federated Chaparral Authors, 1951, Nat. Wildlife Art, 1951, 52, N.Am. Wildlife Art, 1952, Ducks Unltd. Waterfowl exhibit, 1953, 54, St. Paul Winter Carnival, 1954, St. Paul Gallery Art Mart, 1954, Salmagundi Club, 1968, Grand Central Art Galleries, N.Y.C., 1971, Stanley Gallery, Nairobi, Kenya, 1973; Galleria Colosseo, Rome, 1974, Holy Land Conservation Fund Exhbn., Tel Aviv, La Galerie Mouffe, Paris, Merrill's Gallery Fine Art, Taos, N.Mex.; represented in permanent collections Demarest Meml. Mus., Hackensack, N.J., Smithsonian Hall of Philately, N.Y. Jour. Commerce, Mont. Hist. Soc., Voyageurs Nat. Park Interpretative Center, Inland Bird Banding Assn., Minn. Capitol Bldg., Mont. State U., Wildlife Am. Collection, LeSueur Hist. Soc., Lucky'leven, VFW, Mpls., Nat. Wildlife Fedn. Collection, Stark Mus., Orange, Tex., Minn. Ceremonial House, Harris Fine Arts Center of Brigham Young U., U.S. Wildlife Service Fed. Bldg., Ft. Snelling, Minn., VA Hosp., Mpls., Luxton Collection, Banff, Alta., Can., Inst. Contemporary Arts, London, Mont. Capitol Bldg., Goldblatt Collection, Lyons, Ill., Minn. Dept. Econ. Devel., St. Paul, numerous galleries and pvt. collections; designer Fed. Duck Stamp, U.S. Dept. Interior, 1949, Commemorative Centennial Pheasant Stamp, 1981. Former judge ann. Goodyear Nat. Conservation Awards Program. Del. Nat. Wildlife Conf.; bd. dirs. Voyageurs Nat. Park Assn., Deep-Portage Conservation Found., N. Am. Conservation Hall and Mus., Wetlands for Wildlife U.S.A.; pres. Wildlife Am.; dir. Minn. Conservation Fedn., 1952-54; panelist Sportsman's Roundtable, WTCN-TV, Mpls., 1953—; seminar instr. Minn. Coll. Art and Design. Served in USNR, World War II. Recipient Silver medal for wildfowl sculpture Nat. Sportsmans Show, 1951; Minn. Outdoor award, 1956; Patron of Conservation award, 1956; Minn. Sports Champion award, 1958; 1st award Am. Indsl. Devel. Council; citation of merit V.F.W.; award of merit Mil. Order Cootie, 1963; Nat. Art Print of Year award, 1973; merit award Minn. Waterfowl Assn., 1976; Mark Twain knighthood Mark Twain Soc., 1978; Silver medal Nat. Soc. SAR, 1978; honor degree U.S. Vets. Venison Program, 1980; named Wildlife Conservationist of Year, Sears Found.-Nat. Wildlife Fedn. Program, 1966, Am. Bicentennial Wildlife Artist, 1976; named to Water, Woods and Wildlife Hall of Fame, 1977; hon. Ky. Col.; hon. mem. Ont. Chippewa Nation of Can., 1957. Fellow Internat. Inst. Arts (life), Soc. Animal Artists N. Am. Mycol. Assn.; mem. Nat. Audubon Soc., Internat. Sci. Info. Service, Nat. Wildlife Fedn. (nat. wildlife week chmn. Minn.), Minn. Ducks Unltd. (dir.), Minn. Artists Assn. (past v.p., dir.), Soc. Artists and Art Dirs., Outdoor Writers Am., Am. Artists Profl. League, Mpls. Soc. Fine Arts, Wildlife Soc., Zool. Soc., Minn. Mycol. Soc. (pres. emeritus, hon. life), Minn. Conservation Fedn. (hon. life), Deep Portage Conservation Found. (dir.), Le Sueur Hist. Soc. (hon.), Fairbault Art Center (hon. life), Pheasants Inc. (hon.), Waseca Arts Council (hon. life). Clubs: Beaverbrook (hon. life), Minn. Press; Explorers (N.Y.C.). Contbr. to Christmas Echos, 1955, Wing Shooting, Trap & Skeet, 1955; Along the Trout Stream, 1979; also illustrations and articles in periodicals. Asso. editor: Sports and Recreation mag., Out-of-Doors mag. Compiler and artist; Outdoor Horizons, 1957; Twilight over the Wilderness, 1972; featured artist Art West, 1980; ltd. edit. prints of wildfowl, 1981; appeared in film Your BFA - Care & Maintenance; contbr. Educators Guide to Science Materials; paintings and text Minnesota Today. Creator Preuss Wildlife Calendar; inventor Wildlife Am. Calendar. Studio: 2224 Grand Ave Minneapolis MN 55405

PREUSS, RONALD STEPHEN, lawyer, educator; b. Flint, Mich., Dec. 1, 1935; s. Edward Joseph and Harriette (Beckwith) P.; B.A., U. Mo., 1957, M.A., 1963; J.D., St. Louis U., 1973; student U. Calif., Berkeley, 1979, Worcester Coll., Oxford U., 1979; 1 son, William Stephen. Mem. faculty St. Louis Jr. Coll. Dist., 1965—, asst. prof. English, 1972—; admitted to Mo. bar, 1973; partner Anderson, Preuss & Zwibelman, St. Louis, 1974—. Served with U.S. Army, 1958. Mem. Mo. Bar Assn., St. Louis Bar Assn., Am. Bar Assn., AAUP, Tabard Inn. Author: Laudamus Te and Other Poems, 1962; The St. Louis Gourmet, 1979. Co-editor: Criterion, 1961-62; columnist Capital Courier, 1962-64. Home: 32 Conway Cove Chesterfield MO 63017 Office: 222 S Meramec St Suite 300 Clayton MO 63105

PREVOST, ARLENE TRAVIS, educator; b. Huntington, W.Va., July 4, 1939; d. James Wesley Travis and Marjorie (Walker) Travis Coleman; B.S.Ed., Wilverforce U., 1961; M.Ed., Clev. State U., 1972; m. Herman B. Prevost, Dec. 22, 1970. Tchr., Attica (N.Y.) Central High Sch., 1961-64; tchr. Cleve. Public Schs., 1964—, chmn. dept. bus. edn. Lincoln West High Sch., 1976—. Mem. exec. bd. Mt. Pleasant Community Council, 1971-75. Recipient citation N.Y. chpt. Future Farmers Am., 1962. Mem. Cleve. Area Bus. Tchrs. Assn. (dir., pres. 1976-77), Am. Vocat. Assn., Nat. Bus. Edn. Assn., N. Central Bus. Edn. Assn., Ohio Bus. Tchrs. Assn., Ohio Vocat. Edn. Assn., AAUW (rec. sec. 1978-80), Delta Sigma Theta (pres. 1981—). Contbg. writer: Reading in the Content Area, 1979.

PREYSZ, LOUIS ROBERT FONSS, JR., business cons.; b. Elkins, W. Va., July 15, 1916; s. Louis Robert Fonss and Lucile (Falardeau) P.; student U. Ky., 1946-47; m. Lucille Parks, Oct. 17, 1941 (dec. May 1981); children—Louis Robert Fonss III, Carole Preysz Carmichael, Marsha, James Jay, Lorentz Dreyer. Asst. to pres. North Star Corp., Indian Head Mining Co., Hazard, Ky., 1948-51; controller Meadow River Lumber Co., Rainelle, W.Va., 1951-55; agt. insp. Internal Revenue Service, Cin., 1955; controller Creamery Package Mfg. Co. (merged into St. Regis Paper Co.), Chgo., 1956-64, sec., Toronto, Ont., Can., 1956-64; v.p., treas. Gisholt Machine Co. (merged into Giddings & Lewis Inc.), Madison, Wis., 1964-66, dir. Gisholt Gt. Britain, London, Gisholt-Italia, Milan, 1964-70, exec. v.p., 1966-70, v.p. Giddings & Lewis, Inc. (parent co.), Fond du Lac, Wis., 1967-70; corp. cons., 1970—; chmn. exec. com., dir. T and T Tech., Inc., Madison, 1972, chmn. bd., chief exec. officer, 1972-73; fin. cons. to bd. dirs. Meadow River Lumber Co., Rainelle (co. merged into Ga. Pacific Corp.), 1970-72; cons. to bd. dirs. Norland Corp., Ft. Atkinson, Wis., 1971—; dir. Preysz Precision Instruments, Inc., Madison; cons. Cordis Corp., Miami, Fla., 1972—. Bd. dirs. Madison YMCA, 1967-70. Served to capt. USMC, 1936-46. C.P.A., Ill., W.Va. Mem. Am. Inst. C.P.A.'s, W.Va. Soc. C.P.A.'s, Athletic Congress of U.S.A., Berea Coll. Alumni Assn., Ret. Marine Officers Assn. Episcopalian. Clubs: Milw. Athletic; Chgo. Athletic Assn. Address: Route 1 Drake Rd Poynette WI 53955

PRICE, ANNE ELIZABETH, ednl. adminstr.; b. St. Louis, Apr. 25, 1925; d. Calvin Marion, Sr., and Sallie Elizabeth (Edwards) P.; B.A. in Edn., Stowe Tchrs. Coll., 1946; M.A. Ed., U. Chgo., 1948; Ph.D. in Edn., St. Louis U., 1981. Tchr. elem. sch. St. Louis Public Schs., 1946-50, reading clinician, 1950-52, lang. arts cons., 1952-60, prin. elem. sch., 1960-70, curriculum specialist, 1970-72, exec. dir. curriculum services div., 1972-79, area supt. magnet and spl. schs., 1979—; instr. literacy program Sta. KMOX-TV, 1960-73; co-author, dir. Home-Sch. Partnership Model, HEW, U.S. Office of Edn., Washington, 1969-76. Life mem. NEA, Mo. State Tchrs. Assn., Nat. Assn. Elem. Sch. Prins., U. Chgo. Alumni Assn., Pi Lambda Theta, Phi Delta Kappa; mem. Internat. Reading Assn., Assn. Supervision & Curriculum Devel. (dir. 1978-81). Office: Saint Louis Public Schs 721 Pendleton at Enright Saint Louis MO 63108

PRICE, BARBARA JEAN, govt. ofcl.; b. Coatopa, Ala., Mar. 12, 1944; d. Ollis and Daisy (Saunders) Atkins; B.A., U. Mich., 1965; postgrad. in bus. adminstrn., U. Toledo, 1969-71; m. Foster Price, Mar. 5, 1972. Tchr., Toledo public schs., 1965-68; with Toledo Civil Service Commn., 1969—, chief examiner, 1975-78, recruitment and exam. adminstr., 1978-79, commr., 1979—; pres. Q&A Consultants, 1980—. Chmn., Gt. Lakes Assessment Council, 1979. Urban League fellow, 1963-65; Lavina Laible fellow, 1964-65. Mem. Internat. Assn. Personnel Women (pres.-elect 1979-80), Toledo Mgmt. Assn., Internat. Personnel Mgmt. Assn. (assessment council), Bus. Owners Assn., Toledo Inter-Organizational Task Force. Office: 1100 Jackson St Toledo OH 43624

PRICE, BUDDY ALAN, podiatrist; b. Miami, Fla., Feb. 1, 1953; s. Grover Eugene and Beatrice (Shapiro) P.; student Rollins Coll., 1970-73; B.S. in Podiatric Medicine, Ill. Coll. Podiatric Medicine, 1979, D.P.M. cum laude, 1979. Sr. extern Chgo. and Ottawa (Ill.) hosps., 1978; resident in podiatric medicine Northlake (Ill.) Community Hosp., 1979-80; resident in podiatry Children's Meml. Hosp. and Schriner's Children's Meml. Hosp., both Chgo., 1979-80; surg. dissection instr. Ill. Coll. Podiatric Medicine, Chgo., 1980—; practice gen. podiatry Munster (Ind.) Foot Clinic, 1980—, Lake Shore Foot Clinic, Chgo., 1980—; surg. faculty Northlake Community Hosp.; asso. surg. staff Gary (Ind.) Meth. Hosp., Broadway Community Hosp., Merrillville, Ind., 1980—; surg. staff Surgicare Center, Chicago Heights, Ill., 1980—. Active, Big Bros. Am., Orlando, Fla., 1972-73. Cert. to CPR, Am. Heart Assn.; registered podiatrist, Ind., Ill., Fla., Calif. Mem. Ill. Podiatry Soc., Lake County Podiatry Assn., Am. Soc. Podiatric Dermatology, Am. Podiatry Assn., Am. Coll. Foot Surgeons, Kappa Tau Epsilon. Democrat. Jewish. Contbr. articles to profl. jours. Office: 668 W Diversey Pkwy Chicago IL 60614

PRICE, CARL E(DWIN), clergyman; b. Parkersburg, W.Va., Nov. 9, 1931; s. Carl W. and Wanda Evelyn (Johnson) P.; A.B., Marietta Coll., 1956; M.S.T., Wesley Theol. Sem., 1959; D.D. (hon.), Adrian Coll., 1977; m. Patricia A. Smyth, June 13, 1959; children—Mark, Samuel, David. Ordained to ministry United Methodist Ch., 1959; pastor 8 rural chs. Palestine Circuit, W.Va. Conf., 1953-56, First Meth. Ch., Lonaconing, Md., 1956-59, Broad St. Meth. Ch., Trenton, 1959-60, Allentown (N.J.), Meth. Ch., 1960-62, St. Marks Meth. Ch., Detroit, 1965-68; asso. pastor First Meth. Ch., Birmingham, Mich., 1962-65; sr. minister Central United Meth. Ch., Pontiac, Mich., 1968-73, First United Meth. Ch., Midland, Mich., 1973—; Gen. and Jurisdictional Conf. del., 1976, 80; mem. North Central Jurisdictional Com. on Ministry of United Meth. Ch., 1976-80; chmn. Bd. Ordained Ministry, Detroit Conf., 1976-80. Mem. exec. bd. Lake Huron Area council Boy Scouts Am. Served with USMC, 1951-52. Paul Harris fellow. Mem. Midland Clery Assn., Soc. John Wesley. Club: Rotary (Midland). Author: Trails and Turnpikes, 1968; Worship without Walls, 1980; contbr. articles to ch. jours. Office: 315 W Larkin St Midland MI 48640

PRICE, CHARLES MELVIN, Congressman; b. East St. Louis, Ill., Jan. 1, 1905; student St. Louis U.; m. Geraldine M. Freelin, July 7, 1952; 1 son, William Melvin. Newspaper corr. East St. Louis Jour., St. Louis Globe-Democrat; sports editor East St. Louis News-Rev.; sec. to Congressman Edwin M. Schaefer, 1933-43; mem. 79th-97th congresses from 23d Ill. Dist. Mem. St. Clair County Bd. Suprs., 1929-31. Mem. Am. Legion, AMVETS, Nat. Press Club. Clubs: Moose, Eagles, Elks, K.C., Order of Hibernians. Office: Room 2110 Rayburn House Office Bldg Washington DC 20515

PRICE, CHARLES MORGAN, lawyer; b. Chgo., July 17, 1898; s. L. Morgan and Eva (Lapham) P.; A.B., Northwestern, 1920, J.D., 1923; m. Elinor Rew, Oct. 8, 1932; children—Henry Morgan, Rew (Mrs. Donald F. Carne), Charles Morgan. Admitted to Ill. bar, 1923, partner firm Price, Cushman, Keck, Mahin & Cate, and predecessor firms, Chgo., 1923—. Mem. Am., Ill., Chgo. bar assns., Delta Upsilon, Phi Delta Phi. Republican. Episcopalian. Clubs: Chgo.; Glen View. Home: 1500 Lake Shore Dr Chicago IL 60610 Office: 8300 Sears Tower 233 S Wacker Dr Chicago IL 60606

PRICE, FAYE HUGHES, mental health adminstr.; b. Indpls.; d. Twidell W. and Lillian Gladys (Hazlewood) Hughes; A.B. with honors (scholar 1939-43), W.Va. State Coll., 1943; postgrad. social work (scholar) Ind. U., 1943-44; M.S.W., Jane Addams Sch., U. Ill., 1951; student summer insts. U. Chgo., 1960-65; m. Frank Price, Jr., June 16, 1945; 1 dau., Faye Michele. Supr. youth activities Flanner House, Indpls., 1945-47; program dir. Parkway Community House, Chgo., 1947-56, dir., 1957-58; dir. social services Chgo. Dept. Health, 1958-61, dir. community services, 1961-65, asso. dir. planning and devel., 1965-69, regional program dir., 1969-75, asst. dir. mental health, 1975, acting dir., 1976, acting adminstrv. dir., 1976—; cons. various health, welfare and youth agencies; instr. U. Ill., U. Chgo., Atlanta U., George Williams U.; lectr. Chgo. State U., U. Ill., other profl. workshops, seminars and confs. Active mem. Art Inst. Chgo., Bravo chpt. Chgo. Lyric Opera, Chgo. Urban League, Southside Community Art Center, Chgo., Chgo. YWCA, 9897 Parnell Ave. Block Club, Chgo., DuSable Mus., Chgo. Recipient scholarship Mt. Zion Baptist Ch., 1938-39, Fisk U., 1943; Mother-of-Year award Chgo. State Women's Club, 1975. Mem. Nat. Assn. Social Work, Acad. cert. Social Workers, Ill. Welfare Assn., Ill. Group Psychotherapy Soc., Nat. Conf. on Social Welfare, Council on Social Work Edn., Center for Continuing Edn. of Ill. Mental Health Insts., Am. Group Psychotherapy Assn., Am. Public Health Assn., Ill. Public Health Assn., Zonta Internat. (Chi South Side chpt.), Alpha Gamma Phi, Alpha Kappa Alpha, NAACP, U. Ill. Alumni Assn., Nat. Council Negro Women, Municipal Employees Soc. Chgo. Episcopalian. Clubs: Jack and Jill of Am. (asso.), Links Inc. (Chgo. chpt., nat. exec. council), Chums Inc. (Chi chpt.), Les Cameos Social. Office: Richard J Daley Center Chgo Dept Health Bur Mental Health Room 2853 Chicago IL

PRICE, GENEVA ELLEN, educator; b. Creston, Iowa, Oct. 13, 1934; d. Roy David and Jessica Beatrice (Lyon) Bell; A.A., Centerville (Iowa) Community Coll., 1962; B.S. in Edn., Social Studies and English, N.E. Mo. State Tchrs. Coll., Kirksville, 1965, M.Ed. in Spl. Edn., 1968; div.; children—Lynita Clarice Price Brown, Denise Michelle Price Lewis. English tchr., Hedrick High Sch., Hedrick, Iowa, 1965-66; spl. edn. tchr., Davis County Community Sch., Bloomfield, Iowa, 1967—. Sec. Davis County Hist. Soc. 1975-76; pres. Davis County Assn. Retarded Citizens, 1973—; area bd. dirs. Assn. Retarded Citizens, 1980—; county adv. for mentally handicapped and devel. disabled; mem. Dist. Specialized Child Health Bd., Devel. Disabilities Council, Dist. Planning Core Group for Mentally Retarded and Devel. Disabled; bd. dirs., com. on Critical Issues Iowa State Assn. Retarded Citizens; adv. hearings on rights for develop mentally dsabled; active Girl Scouts U.S.A. Mem. NEA, Iowa Edn. Assn., Davis County Community Local Edn. Assn. Clubs: Bloomfield Bus. and Profl. Women's (pres. 1977-79, dist. com. chmn. public relations 1979-80, dist. membership chmn. 1980-81, found. chmn. 1981-82), Meth. Women's Circle (chairperson 1976-77). Certified, Iowa; specialist in workshops pertaining to sexuality and the handicapped. Home: 508 W Poplar Bloomfield IA 52537 Office: 200 W Locust St Bloomfield IA 52537

PRICE, GEORGE EDWARD, computer phototypesetting co. exec.; b. Chgo., June 20, 1940; s. Edward August and Maxine Leland (Crow) P.; A.A. with honors, Lincoln Coll., 1961; B.S. with honors, Bradley U., 1963. Pres., Graphic Sales, Inc., Chgo., 1968—. Mem. St. Cornelius Sch. Bd., Chgo., 1980—. Served to capt. USAF, 1964-68. Mem. Printing Industry Ill., Chgo. Assn. Commerce and Industry, Printing Industry Am., Ill. Typographical Assn. Republican. Roman Catholic. Home: 5444 N Lotus Ave Chicago IL 60630 Office: 550 W Jackson Blvd Suite 419 Chicago IL 60606

PRICE, JOHN MICHAEL, photographer; b. Indpls., Oct. 10, 1936; s. Chester Morris and Sarah Elizabeth (Ferguson) P.; grad. high sch.; m. Madalene Wing, May 8, 1956; children—Teresa Kay, Michael Chester. Farmer; owner, photographer Price Portrait Studio, Lizton, Ind., 1967—; owner Agri-Photo Belt Buckles. Cons., judge photography 4-H workshops, state and county fairs (Ind.), high schs., 1967—. Supt. agrl. displays 4-H fairs, Ind., 1966—; mem. youth adv. council Hendricks County (Ind.), 1970-71; pres. band boosters New Salem (Ind.) High Sch., 1970; instr. leather craft local orgns. Recipient honors 4-H Club Continued Service, 1971, 73. Mem. profl. photographers Am., Ind. Address: Box 159 Rd 900 N Lizton IN 46149

PRICE, LUCILE BRICKNER BROWN, ret. personnel adminstr.; b. Decorah, Iowa, May 31, 1902; d. Sidney Eugene and Cora (Drake) Brickner; B.S., Iowa State U., 1925; M.A., Northwestern U., 1940; m. Maynard Wilson Brown, July 2, 1928 (dec. 1937); m. 2d, Charles Edward Price, Jan. 14, 1961. Asst. dean of women Kans. State U., Manhattan, 1925-28; mem. bd. student personnel adminstrn. Northwestern U., Evanston, Ill., 1937-41; with personnel research dept. Sears, Roebuck & Co., Chgo., 1941-42; overseas club dir. ARC, Eng., 1942-43, Africa, 1943, Italy, 1944-45; dir. Child Edn. Found., N.Y.C., 1946-56; del. Mid-Century White House Conf. Children and Youth, 1950; mem. Iowa State Extension Adv. Com., 1973-75, Winneshiek County (Iowa) CSC, 1978-80, 82—; mem. Decorah (Iowa) Tree Com., 1978-82. Bd. dirs. NE Iowa Mental Health Center, pres., 1960-61; trustee Porter House Mus. Recipient Alumni Merit award Iowa State U., 1975. Mem. Am. Coll. Personnel Assn. (life), AAUW (Gift award 1977; dir. Decorah br. 1965-75; life), Norwegian-Am. Museum (life, Vesterheim fellow), Winneshiek County Hist. Soc. (life), Internat. Platform Assn., DAR, Common Cause, Am. Overseas Assn. (life; nat. bd. 1960-79), Pi Lambda Theta, Chi Omega. Instrumental in building of house designed specifically for retirement living; active on Historic Preservation com. of AAUW which secured grants from Nat. Endowment for Humanities, Nat. Endowment for Arts, also listing on Nat. Register Historic Places. Address: 508 W Broadway Decorah IA 52101

PRICE, MARGARET ANN, civic worker; b. Westfield, Ill., Feb. 16, 1921; d. Harry Albert and Margaret Remington (Madison) Day; student Lincoln Trail Coll., 1972-76; m. William Keith Price, Nov. 11, 1941; children—Richard Keith, Robert Kent. Pres., Jr. Woman's Club, Ill. Fedn. Women's Clubs, 1956-57, pres. Minerva Club, 1962-64, pres. 23d Dist., 1976-78; regent James Halstead, Sr. chpt. DAR, 1976-78, pressbook chmn. for Ill., 1979-80; leader Cub Scouts, Wabash Valley council Boy Scouts Am., 1954-60, v.p. cub scouting, 1980—; pres. local United Meth. Women, 1963-67, 70-71, 79—, pres. Olney Dist., 1970-74; dean So. Ill. Conf. Sch. Christian Mission, United Meth. Women, 1978-79; mem. state nominating com. Church Women United, 1981-83; pres. Crawford County Fedn. Rep. Women, 1981-83. Recipient SilVer Fawn award Boy Scouts Am., 1972; Outstanding Community Service award Robinson C. of C., 1981. Republican. Methodist. Mem. Crawford Meml. Hosp. Aux. Editor: Chimes, quar. publ. United Meth. Women. Home: 307 St Petersburg Robinson IL 62454

PRICE, MARGARET STAFFORD, business exec.; b. Belleville, Ill., Feb. 12, 1944; d. John and Helen Klich; student Belleville Jr. Coll., 1961; m. Herschel Price, Mar. 27, 1966; children—Denni, Melissa, Teresa. With Playboy Clubs, 1963—, owner, mgr. St. Louis Playboy Club, 1976—. Pres., Suburban League chpt. AMC Cancer Research Center and Hosp., Denver, 1974-76, hosp. bd. dirs., 1977-79, pres. St. Louis Council of Auxiliaries, 1981—. Mem. NOW, Variety Club, Jewish Hosp. Aux. Home: 18 Sackson Woods Creve Coeur MO 63141 Office: 6926 S Lindbergh Saint Louis MO 63125

PRICE, MARJORIE ANN, educator; b. N. Vernon, Ind., Feb. 21, 1919; d. Oscar G. and Kathryne K. (Weller) P.; B.S., Ariz. State U., Tempe, 1947; M.Ed., U. Nev., Reno, 1957; Ed.D., U. Mo., Columbia, 1968. Instr. phys. edn. U. Nev., Reno, 1947-50, instr., 1957-59; phys. edn. tchr. Carson City (Nev.) Pub. Schs., 1951-55; staff U. Ariz., 1959-64; asst. prof. U. Mo., Columbia, 1964-67; instr. Miami U., Oxford, Ohio, 1967, prof., 1971—, chmn. dept. phys. edn., 1967-77. Mem. AAHPER, Midwest Assn. Health, Phys. Edn. and Recreation, Ohio Assn. Health, Phys. Edn. and Recreation, Midwest Assn. Phys. Edn. and Coll. Women (pres. 1978-79). Home: 3571 Kehrwood Oxford OH 45056 Office: Dept Phys Edn Miami U Oxford OH 45056

PRICE, NORMAN EDWARD, mfg. co. exec.; b. Cleve., Sept. 15, 1953; s. Edward and Carolyn Christine P.; B.Comml. Sci., Tiffin U., 1975. Asso. buyer Bendix Autolite, Fostoria, Ohio, 1974-77, buyer Bendix Brake and Steering, South Bend, Ind., 1977-79, group sr. buyer Bendix Heavy Vehicles Systems Group, Elyria, Ohio, 1979—. Mem. Nat. Assn. Purchasing Mgmt., Cleve. Regional Minority Bus. Council. Home: 2280 W River Rd #A15 Elyria OH 44035 Office: 901 Cleveland St Elyria OH 44035

PRICE, ROBERT EUGENE, banker; b. Fayette County, Ind., Oct. 21, 1929; s. James Thomas and Geneva (McClain) P.; grad. Stonier Grad. Sch. Banking, Rutgers U., 1970; m. Nancy Kay Riggs, Mar. 2, 1957; children—Deron James, David Lewis. With Central State Bank, Connersville, Ind., 1947—, asst. cashier, mktg. officer, 1951-58, v.p., 1959-69, exec. v.p., 1969-71, pres., chmn., 1971—; pres., chmn. Central Ins. Agency, Connersville, 1971—, Central State Realty Corp., Connersville, 1971—, Central State Travel Agency, Connersville, 1974—; nat. dir. from Ind., Ind. Bankers Assn. Am., 1980—. Pres., Jr. Achievement Connersville, 1972. Served with U.S. Army, 1951-53. Recipient Connersville Distinguished Citizen's award, 1976; Jaycee Distinguished Service award, 1955, 62, Award of Merit, 1974. Mem. Independent Bankers Assn. Ind. (pres. 1976-77), C. of C. (pres. 1962), Downtown Connersville (pres.). Democrat. Episcopalian. Clubs: Country, Elks, Masons (33 deg.), K.T. (grand comdr. Ind. 1978-79). Home: PO Box 102 Connersville IN 47331 Office: 531 Central Ave Connersville IN 47331

PRICE, RONN LEE, security systems co. exec.; b. Middletown, Ohio, July 22, 1952; s. Charles Burton and Ruth Mildred (Gillum) P.; B.S., Ariz. State U., 1975; m. Paula Ann Muraski, Aug. 5, 1977. Pres., founder Futuristic Security Systems, Inc., Cin., 1975—; founder, pres. U.S. Computer Systems, Inc., Cin.; v.p. Cal Crim Futuristic Alarm, Inc. Mem. Nat. Burglar and Fire Alarm Assn. (v.p. Cin. chpt.), Cin. Homebuilders Assn., Dayton Homebuilders Assn., Middletown C. of C. Home: 8297 Saint Andrews Dr West Chester OH 45069 Office: 3625 Hauck Rd Cincinnati OH 45241

PRICE, THOMAS EMILE, export sales, investment, fin. co. exec., sports assn. ofcl.; b. Cin., Nov. 4, 1921; s. Edwin Charles and Lillian Elizabeth (Werk) P.; B.B.A., U. Tex., 1943; postgrad. Harvard U., 1944; m. Lois Margaret Gahr Matthews, Dec. 21, 1970; 1 dau. by previous marriage, Dorothy Elizabeth Wood Price; stepchildren—Bruce Albert, Mark Frederic, Scott Herbert, Eric William Matthews. Co-founder Indsl. Waxes, Inc., 1946, sec., 1946-75, treas., 1946-76, pres., 1975-76; co-founder Climax Products Corp., Cin., 1953, sec., 1957-59, treas., 1956-57, v.p., 1953-57; co-founder Price Y Cia, Inc., Cin., 1946—, sec., 1946-75, treas., 1946—, pres., 1975—, also dir.; co-founder Premium Finishes Sales, Inc., Cin., 1963—, pres., 1975—, also dir.; co-founder Price Paper Products Corp., Cin., 1956, treas., 1956—, pres., 1975—, sec., 1956-75, also dir.; mem. Cin. Regional Export Expanison Com., 1961-63; dir. Central Acceptance Corp., 1954-55; founding mem. and dir. Cin. Royals Basketball Club Co., 1959-73. Referee Tri-State Tennis Championships, 1963-68, Western Tennis Championships, 1969-70, Nat. Father-Son Clay Court Championships, 1974—, Tennis Grand Masters Championships, 1975-77, 80; vol. coach Walnut Hills High Sch. Boys Team, Cin., 1970—; chmn. and coach Greater Cin. Jr. Davis Cup, 1968-78; co-founder Tennis Patrons of Cin., Inc., 1951, trustee, 1951—, pres., 1958-63, 68; co-founder Greater Cin. Tennis Assn., 1979. Participant in fund raising drives Cin. Boys Amateur Baseball Fund; chmn. Greater Cin. YMCA World Service Fund Drive, 1962-64; trustee Cin. World Affairs Inst., 1957-60, gen. chmn., 1959. Served to 1st lt. USAAF, 1943-46; ETO. Elected to Western Hills High Sch. Sport Hall of Honor; named hon. Almaden Grand Master, 1980. Mem. Cin. Fgn. Credit Club, Cin. World Trade Club (pres. 1959), U.S. Trotting Assn., Cin. Hist. Soc., U.S. Lawn Tennis Assn. (trustee 1959-60, 62-64, chmn. Jr. Davis Cup com. 1960-62, mem. jrs. and boys championships com. 1960—, founder of Col. James H. Bishop award 1962), Ohio Valley (trustee 1948—, Gillespie award 1957, Dredge award 1973, pres. 1952-53), Western (trustee 1951—, mem. championships adv. com. 1969-78, pres. 1959-60, Melvin R. Bergman Disting. Service award 1979) tennis assns., Cin., Eastern Hills indoor tennis clubs, Assn. Tennis Profls. (nat. adv. com. 1979—), Phi Gamma Delta. Republican. Presbyterian. Clubs: Cin. Country, Univ., Cin. Tennis (pres. 1957-58, advisory com. 1959—). Nationally ranked boys 15, 1936, jr. tennis player, 1939. History columnist Tennis Talk Greater Cin., 1978-80. Home: 504 Williamsburg Rd Cincinnati OH 45215 Office: 924-929 Dixie Terminal Bldg Cincinnati OH 45202

PRICE, VICTOR DOUGLAS, author; b. Lansing, Mich., Sept. 16, 1949; s. Victor David and Inez Mildred (Denstaedt) P.; student Lansing Community Coll., 1974-78, Mich. State U., 1972-76; 1 son, Richard Douglas. With Woolco Dept. Stores, Okemos, Mich., 1973-74; area store mgr. Summit Corp., New Britain, Conn., 1974-76; mgmt. cons., Lansing, 1979—; cons. Allson Originals, Lansing, 1974-79, B & S Enterprises, Lansing, 1975-79, Denstaedt's, Lansing, 1975-79. Author: Who Do You Seek, 1975; And the Game Begins, 1977; To Mother, 1977; Rememberings, the Soul of a Man, 1979; The Gambler, 1979. Address: 311 E Rouse St Lansing MI 48910

PRICHARD, ROBERT DONALD, safety engr.; b. Sac City, Iowa, July 5, 1944; s. Donald Robert and Mary Rose (Bye) P.; B.S., Iowa State U., 1971, M.S. in Indsl. Safety, 1976; Ed.S., Central Mo. State U., 1980; m. Lynda Lou Ray, Mar. 1, 1969; children—Eric Todd, Kelly Michelle. Synchrotron operator Iowa State U., 1967-72; safety engr. Royal Ins. Co., Des Moines, 1976—. Lt. Comdr. U.S. Navy Res., 1962-66, 72-75. Cert. safety profl. Mem. Am. Soc. Safety Engrs., Naval Res. Assn., Epsilon Pi Tau, Phi Kappa Phi. Home: 107 3d Ave Slater IA 50244 Office: 1025 Ashworth West Des Moines IA 50265

PRIEBE, BERL EASTMAN, state senator, farmer; b. Lone Rock, Iowa, May 31, 1918; s. Clarence and Amy (Bond) P.; grad. high sch.: m. Madelyn Paetz, 1938; children—Constance, Paula, Gary. Farmer, Algona, Iowa; now mem. Iowa State Senate. Pres. Kossuth County Fair Bd.; dir. North Iowa Fair; 4-H leader. Mem. Izaak Walton League, Kossuth County Beef and Pork Producers Assn., Iowa State Beef and Pork Producers Assn., Farm Bur., Coop. Elevators, Rural Electric Coop. Lutheran. Clubs: Gun, Saddle, Algona Country. Office: State Senate State Capitol Des Moines IA 50319*

PRIEDE, JANIS, research analyst; b. Hausach, W. Ger., Sept. 21, 1948; came to U.S., 1951, naturalized, 1958; s. Karlis Olgerts and Bertha (Pilins) P.; B.S., U. Ill., 1971; M.A., No. Ill. U., 1975. Mgmt. analyst programmer dept. computing services No. Ill. U., 1971-75, research asso. Office Budget and Planning, 1976—. Alderman, City of DeKalb (Ill.), 1975-79; vice chmn. DeKalb County Democratic Central Com., 1978-80; sec. DeKalb County Health Planning Com., 1979, chmn., 1980; v.p. regional bd. Comprehensive Health Planning of N.W. Ill.; mem. Statewide Health Coordinating Council, 1981—. Recipient Commemorative award for service DeKalb City Council, 1979; Ill. State scholar, 1966. Mem. U.S. Jaycees (treas. DeKalb chpt. 1976-77), Am. Contract Bridge League, Omicron Delta Kappa. Lutheran. Home: 1307 W Lincoln Hwy Apt 6112 DeKalb IL 60115 Office: Office Budget and Planning No Ill U DeKalb IL 60115

PRIEDEMAN, WILLIAM ROBBINS, mktg. services co. exec.; b. St. Paul, Dec. 2, 1925; s. George Walter and Cecil (Robbins) P.; B.S., Yale U., 1949; M.B.A., Harvard U., 1951; m. Nancy Katharin Gaver, Apr. 25, 1953; children—Katharin Robbins, William Robbins. Pres. Mpls. Ornamental Iron Co., 1957-63; pres. Consol. Engring. Inc., Mpls., 1963-65; corporate services Piper Jaffray & Hepwood, Mpls., 1965-67; v.p. Waters Instruments, Rochester, Minn., 1967-71, cons., 1971-73; pres. Sci. Med. Inc., Mpls., 1973-75; pres. W.R. Priedeman Asso., Wayzata, Minn., 1975—; community faculty Metro State U.; dir. MGK Inc. Served with AC U.S. Army, 1943-46. Clubs: Lafayette, 555. Home: 19400 Cedarhurst St Wayzata MN 55391 Office: 1421 E Wayzata Blvd 251D Wayzata MN 55391

PRIEHS, GEORGE WILLIAM, corp. exec.; b. Mt. Clemens, Mich., May 24, 1907; s. Edward Carl and Mathilda Amelia (Burdenam) P.; B.A., U. Mich., 1930; postgrad. U. Wis., U. London; m. Hermine Soukup, Oct. 25, 1933; children—Marolyn Louise, Sandra Suzanne. Nat. publicity dir. Nat. Thrift Com., N.Y.C., 1931-32; with toy dept. R.H. Macy Co., N.Y.C., 1931-32; pres. Priehs Dept. Store, Priehs Realty Co. and J. Priehs Merc. Co., Inc., Mt. Clemens, 1933—; sr. partner Medea Corp., Mt. Clemens, 1956-72, Clemens Center Co., 1966-70; drama critic Mich. Daily, Wis. Cardinal; writer Fairchild Publs. Mem. Mt. Clemens City Planning Commn., 1956-71, War Prodn. Retail Trade Adv. Com., Washington, World War II; mem. Presdl. Steering Com., Washington, 1981—. Recipient Wisdom Award of Honor, 1970, Brookfield Clothing Acad. award, 1961; hon. gen. 1st Fighter Wing USAF. Mem. Nat. Retail Mchts. Assn. (pres. smaller stores div.), Mich. Retailers Assn., AIM, Am. Ordnance Assn., Am. Judicature Soc., AF Assn., U.S., Mich. hist. socs., Alpha Tau Omega. Clubs: Selfridge Air Force Officers (hon.), U. Mich. Alumni (emeritus club), Elks, Macomb County Old Crowd, St. Joseph Hosp. Century, Detroit Econ. Home: 24805 Crocker Blvd Mount Clemens MI 48043 Office: 60 66 Macomb St Mount Clemens MI 48043

PRIEST, CHARLES JOSEPH, mfg. co. exec.; b. River Rouge, Mich., May 18, 1924; s. William K. and Ada Regina (Plunkett) P.; B.A. in Chemistry, Trinity U., 1954; m. Annie Louise Tullos, Jan. 5, 1945; children—Sydney Lee, Jo Ann, Mary Katheryn. Coating supr. E. Tex. Pulp & Paper Co., Evadale, Tex., 1954-58; tech. supt. C.A. Venezolana de Pulpa Y Papel Co., Venezuela, 1958-60; supr. tech. services Continental Can Co., Augusta, Ga., 1960-67; br. mgr. Cesco Inc., Charleston, S.C., 1967-70; tech. Augusta Pub. Schs., 1970-74; process chemist Inland Container Corp., Newport, Ind., 1974—, tech. supt., 1975—; cons. of wastewater treating, 1975—. Served with USNR, 1943-46. Mem. Vermillion County Improvement Assn., TAPPI, Nat. Council of Paper Industry for Air and Stream Improvement. Mem. Rock Ch. Author articles. Home: 1704 Vermilion Danville IL 61832 Office: PO Box 428 Newport IN 47966

PRIESTER, SHARON PATRICIA, mathematician; b. Endicott, N.Y., Jan. 3, 1942; d. Joseph Edward and Suzanne (Yusko) Prebish; B.S., SUNY, Oneonta, 1962; M.A., Western Mich. U., 1967; m. David C. Priester, Aug. 12, 1967; children—David C., Patrick, Ann, Kristin, Jennifer. Tchr., Jennie F. Snapp Jr. High Sch., Endicott, N.Y., 1963-66, W.K. Kellogg Jr. High Sch., Battle Creek, Mich., 1967-68; instr. math Ill. State U., Bloomington, 1969-71, 74—; cons. St. Clare-Holy Trinity Schs., Bloomington. Dir. pre-sch. religion Holy Trinty Ch., 1974-76; dir. publicity PTO, Centennial Sch., 1975-77; tres. Holy Trinity Bd. Edn., 1978—; pres. swim team YMCA, Bloomington-Normal, 1979-81. Mem. Nat. Council Tchrs. Math, Ill. Council Tchrs. Math, Assn. Supervision and Curriculum Devel. Roman Catholic. Home: 206 Radliff Rd Bloomington IL 61701 Office: Dept Math Ill State U Normal IL 61761

PRIMICH, THEODORE, sheet metal and machinery mfg. co. exec.; b. Manassas, Va., May 28, 1915; s. John and Mary (Zudock) P.; student Gary (Ind.) pub. schs.; m. Katherine Pollak, Jan. 30, 1938; children—Geraldine Mary, Katherine Jean. Vice pres. G.W. Berkheimer Co., Gary, 1936-46; pres. Gary Steel Products Corp., Gary, 1945—; v.p. Primich Warehouse Co., Gary, 1955-77; pres. Primich Engineered Products. Mem. Air Distribution Inst., Ind. Mfrs. Assn., Ind. State, Gary C. of C.'s, Nat. Assn. Mfrs., Nat. C. of C., Midwest Indsl. Mgmt. Assn., N.Am. Heating and Air Conditioning Assn. Club: Lions, Gary Country. Patentee numerous items. Home: 1937 W 61st Pl Merrillville IN 46410 Office: 4400 W 9th Ave Gary IN 46406

PRIMO, MARIE NASH, mgr. shopping centers; b. Clarksburg, W.Va., Dec. 10, 1928; Frank and Josephine (DiMaria) Nash; student public schs., Clarksburg; m. Joseph C. Primo, Sept. 27, 1953; 1 dau., Joan E. Sec., Nat. Bank Detroit, 1945-46; exec. sec. Cutting Tool Mfrs. Assn., Detroit, 1946-50; adminstrv. asst. Irwin I. Cohn, atty., Detroit, 1950—; mgr. Bloomfield Shopping Plaza, Birmingham, Mich., 1959—, North Hill Center, Avon Twp., Mich., 1957—, Drayton Plains Shopping Center (Mich.), 1958—, South Allen Shopping Center, Allen Park, Mich., 1953-77, Huron-Tel Corner, Pontiac, Mich., 1977—; officer, dir., numerous privately held corps. Mem. steering com., treas. Univ. Liggett Antiques Show, 1971-76, mem. adv. com., 1977-80; mem. parents com. Wellesley (Mass.) Coll., 1979—. Mem. Met. Mus. Art, Founders Soc. Detroit Inst. Arts, Mich. Humane Soc., Detroit Sci. Center, Detroit Hist. Soc., Detroit Zool. Soc., Smithsonian Assos., Hist. Soc. Mich., Grosse Pointe War Meml. Assn., Grosse Pointe Public Library Assn., Detroit Grand Opera Assn., Internat. Biog. Assn. Roman Catholic. Club: Women's Econ. Home: 1341 N Renaud Rd Grosse Pointe Woods MI 48236 Office: 2290 1st National Bldg Detroit MI 48226

PRIMUS, MARY JANE DAVIS, social worker; b. Marion, Iowa, May 31, 1924; d. Lawrence Henry and Verna Leona (Suman) Davis; B.S., Iowa State U., 1950; m. Paul C. Primus, Aug. 23, 1955; children—Kenneth Roy, Donald Karl. Asst. cashier First State Bank, Greene, Iowa, 1942-46; tchr. Oskaloosa (Iowa) pub. schs., 1950-52; extension home economist Iowa State U., Oskaloosa-Eldora, 1952-57; homemaker, dist. supr. Iowa Dept. Social Service, Webster City, 1970-77. Substitute tchr. Eldora Pub. Schs., 1966-68; homemaker health aide supr. Mid-Iowa Community Action OEO, Iowa Dept. Social Service, 1968-69. Den mother Boy Scouts Am., Steamboat Rock, Iowa, 1966-71; leader Girl Scouts Am., Steamboat Rock, 1969-72; mem. Iowa State U. Extension Family Living Council, Hardin County, 1961-65; outreach chmn. Iowa Family and Children Services, 1966-72; field days women's program chmn. Iowa Soil Conservation, 1968. Mem. Am. Home Econs. Assn., Nat. Council Homemaker-Home Health Aide Services, Nat. League Am. Pen Women, Nat. Soc. Lit. and the Arts, Soil Conservation Soc. Am., Am. Legion, Internat. Platform Assn., P.E.O. Mem. Ch. of Christ (pres. 1963-65). Mem. Order Eastern Star. Club: Federated Women's (Steamboat Rock). Author: Through the Window, 1973; Through the Window Twice, 1974; Tracery Windows, 1975; Shuttered Windows, 1977; Wings, 1979; Wings II, 1980; area news corr., 4 newspapers; columnist Iowa Wildlife Fedn.; contbr. poems to various publs. Office: Steamboat Rock IA 50672

PRINCE, RICHARD, univ. dean; b. Chgo., Sept. 18, 1922; s. William and Kate Prince; B.S. in Chemistry, U. Chgo., 1947, M.S. in Edn., 1948, Ph.D. in Ednl. Adminstrn., 1957; m. Catherine Yff, Mar. 7, 1944; children—Richard John, David William. Tchr. high sch. sci., 1947-51; prin. Chgo. Christian High Sch., 1951-58; registrar Trinity Christian Coll., Palos Heights, Ill., 1958-61; mem. faculty Chgo. State U., 1961-73, dean grad. div. and extension services, 1973—. Mem. Trinity Christian Coll. and Elim Christian Sch. Bd., 1972-78; group leader Lynwood Christian Reformed Ch., Lynwood, Ill., 1968-78. Served with AUS, 1943-46. Mem. AAUP, Phi Delta Kappa. Office: Chgo State Univ 95th St and King Dr Chicago IL 60628

PRINCE, THOMAS RICHARD, educator; b. New Albany, Miss., Dec. 7, 1934; s. James Thompson and C. Florence (Howell) P.; B.S., Miss. State U., 1956, M.S., 1957; Ph.D. in Accountancy, U. Ill., 1962; m. Eleanor Carol Polkoff, July 14, 1962; children—Thomas Andrew, John Michael, Adrienne Carol. Instr., U. Ill., 1960-62; mem. faculty Northwestern U., 1962—, prof. acctg. and info. systems, 1969—, chmn. dept. accounting and info. systems Grad. Sch. Mgmt., 1968-75; cons. in field; dir. Applied Research Systems, Inc. Served to 1st lt. AUS, 1957-60. C.P.A., Ill. Mem. Am. Accounting Assn., Am. Inst. C.P.A.'s, Am. Econ. Assn., Inst. Mgmt. Scis., Fin. Execs. Inst., AAAS, Ill. Soc. C.P.A.'s, Nat. Assn. Accts., Alpha Tau Omega, Phi Kappa Phi, Omicron Delta Kappa, Delta Sigma Pi, Beta Alpha Psi. Congregationalist. Author: Extension of the Boundaries of Accounting Theory, 1962; Information Systems for Management Planning and Control, 3d edit., 1975. Home: 303 Richmond Rd Kenilworth IL 60043 Office: Leverone Hall Northwestern U Evanston IL 60201

PRINCE, VIRGINIA FAYE DIXON, educator; b. Big Springs, Mo., July 23, 1919; d. William Marcellus and Cassie Mae (Walker) Dixon; A.A., Hannibal-LaGrange Coll., 1946; B.A., N.E. La. State Coll., 1956; M.Ed., Southwestern La. U., 1959; postgrad. U. Mo., 1948, U. Hawaii, 1952, 53, So. Ill. U., 1960-64, degree certificate of specialist So. Ill. U., 1969; m. A. E. Prince, Aug. 7, 1949 (dec. Sept. 30, 1980). Sec. to pres. Hannibal-LaGrange Coll., 1946-48; tchr. pub. schs., Center, Mo., 1947-48, Honolulu, 1952-54, Monroe, La., 1954-56, Jennings Mo. 1958—; dietitian Hannibal-LaGrange Coll., 1948-50; sec. to pastor Auckland (New Zealand) Bapt. Tabernacle, 1951-52. Mem. Internat. Reading Assn., Assn. Childhood Edn., NEA, Mo., St. Louis tchrs. assns., Am. Bell Assn., Alpha Delta Kappa, Kappa Delta Pi. Republican. Baptist. Mem. Order Eastern Star. Home: 8932 Berkay St Louis MO 63136

PRINDAVILLE, LAWRENCE ALLEN, psychologist; b. Dixon, Ill., Dec. 28, 1947; s. Raphael Edward and Florence Margarite (Reis) P.; B.S., Loyola U., Chgo., 1970; M.S., Western Ill. U., 1974; m. Gloria M.; children—Sara Meghan, Laura Beth. Psychologist, Sinnissippi Mental Health Center, Dixon, Ill., 1972—, coordinator sustaining care program, 1976-80, dir. clin. services, 1980—. Fellow Am. Orthopsychiat. Assn.; mem. Am. (asso.), Ill. psychol. assns., Ill. Assn. Master Psychologists, Am. Mental Health Counselors Assn. Home: 1315 Prescott St Dixon IL 61021 Office: Sinnissippi Mental Health Center Dixon Sterling Freeway Dixon IL 61021

PRINGLE, MARY BETH, educator; b. Lansing, Mich., July 20, 1943; d. Gordon H. and Lucile R. (Drake) P.; B.A., U. Denver, 1964, M.A., 1967; Ph.D. (fellow), U. Minn., 1977; m. Harvey A. Siegal, Mar. 18, 1978; 1 son. Teaching asst. English dept. U. Denver, 1966-67; instr. Southwest Mo. State U., Springfield, 1967-69, Iowa State U., Ames, 1969-72; teaching asso. dept. English, U. Minn., Mpls., 1973-75; instr. dept. English, Wright State U., Dayton, Ohio, 1975-76, asst. prof., 1976-80, asso. prof., 1980—; founder, partner Writing Assos., Inc., Dayton, 1977—. Recipient Outstanding Teaching award Wright State U., 1980. Mem. MLA, Midwest Modern Lang. Assn., Assn. for Lit. and Linguistic Computing, Popular Culture Assn., Virginia Woolf Soc., Am. Bus. Communication Assn., Women's Caucus for Modern Langs., Women's Studies Assn., Phi Kappa Phi, AAUP. Author: (with Anne Stericker) Sex Roles in Literature, 1980; (with Marshall Rosenswet) A Guide to Labor Relations, 1981; (with Pierre Horn) The Prostitute in Modern Literature; contbr. articles on lit. criticism to profl. publs.; contbr. book revs. to lit. jours. Home: North Lake Ln 8497 St Route 48 Waynesville OH 45068 Office: English Dept Wright State Univ Dayton OH 45435

PRINS, CONRAD, ins. and real estate exec.; b. Sioux County, Iowa, July 3, 1920; s. John and Henrietta Louise P.; student Sanborn (Iowa) public schs.; m. Gladys J. Post, July 24, 1943; children—Dennis Lee, Bruce Wayne, Cheryl Rae, Bryan Conrad. Pres., Prins Ins., Inc., Sanborn, Iowa, 1946—, Prins Real Estate, Sanborn, 1946—; exec. v.p. Iowa Premium Service Co., 1973—; adv. council Lemars Mut. Ins. Co., State Automobile and Casualty Underwriters. Mem. Sanborn City Council, Sanborn Sch. Bd.; pres. Sanborn Improvement Corp. Served with USNR, 1942-45; PTO. Mem. Pres.'s Club Continental Western Ins. Mem. Iowa Profl. Ins. Agts. (pres. 1979-80), Nat. Profl. Ins. Agts., Iowa Ind. Ins. Agts., Nat. Ind. Ins. Agts., Sanborn C. of C. (past pres.). Home: 308 W 7th St Sanborn IA 51248 Office: 301 Main St Sanborn IA 51248

PRINZ, LEON MARVIN, urologist; b. Chgo., Nov. 14, 1930; s. George and Helen P.; B.S. in Medicine, U. Ill., 1952, M.D., 1954; m. Dora Pinsky, July 3, 1955; children—Michael, Steven, Paul, Carolyn, Linda. Practice medicine specializing in urology, Chgo., 1961—; clin. asso. prof. surgery U. Chgo. Med. Sch.; attending physician Michael Reese Hosp. Fellow A.C.S., Internat. Coll. Surgeons; mem. Michael Reese Alumni Assn. (pres.). Office: 104 S Michigan Ave Chicago IL 60603

PRITCHARD, CLAUDIUS HORNBY, JR., coll. pres.; b. Charleston, W.Va., June 28, 1927; s. Claudius Hornby and Katherine Ellison P.; B.A., Hampden Sydney Coll., 1950; M.A., Longwood Coll., 1965; Ph.D., Fla. State U., 1971; m. Marjorie Pullen, Aug. 9, 1952; children—Virginia Aiken, Katherine Winston, Olivia Reynolds, Claudius V. Loan teller, Am. Nat. Bank, Danville, Va., 1950-53; asst. cashier Planters Bank & Trust Co., Farmville, Va., 1953-55; asst. to pres. Hampden Sydney (Va.) Coll., 1955-57, bus. mgr., treas., 1957-67, v.p. devel., 1967-71; sr. budget analyst for edn. State of Fla., Tallahassee, 1971-72; pres. Sullins Coll., Bristol, Va., 1972-76; v.p. adminstrn. Maryville Coll., St. Louis, 1976-77, pres., 1977—. Bd. dirs. Episcopal Day Sch., Bristol, Va.; trustee, Logan Coll., St. Louis. Served with USNR, 1945-46. Fla. State U. fellow, 1969-70; Arthur Vining Davis fellow, ACE Inst. Coll. Pres., 1974. Mem. Am. Assn. Higher Edn., AAUP, So. Hist. Assn., Phi Kappa Phi, Omicron Delta Kappa. Republican. Presbyterian. Club: University (St. Louis). Author: Colonel D. Wyatt Aiken (1828-1887): South Carolina's Militant Agrarian, 1970. Home: 15514 Easy Ridge Ct Chesterfield MO 63017 Office: 13350 Conway Rd Saint Louis MO 63141

PRITZKER, JAY ARTHUR, lawyer; b. Chgo., Aug. 26, 1922; s. Abraham Nicholas and Fanny (Doppelt) P.; B.Sc., Northwestern U., 1941, J.D., 1947; m. Marian Friend, Aug. 31, 1947; children—Nancy (dec.), Thomas, John, Daniel, Jean. Asst. custodian Alien Property Adminstrn., 1947; admitted to Ill. bar, 1947, since practiced in Chgo.; partner firm Pritzker & Pritzker, 1948—; chmn. bd. Hyatt Corp., Hyatt Internat., Marmon Group, Inc.; dir. Continental Air Lines, Elsinore Corp.; partner Chgo. Mill & Lumber Co., Mich.-Calif. Lumber Co. Trustee, U. Chgo. Served as aviator USNR, World War II. Mem. Am., Chgo. bar assns. Clubs: Standard, Comml., Lake Shore, Mid-Day, Arts, Vince (Chgo.). Office: 2 First Nat Plaza Chicago IL 60603

PRITZKER, ROBERT ALAN, mfg. co. exec.; b. Chgo., June 30, 1926; s. Abram Nicholas and Fanny (Doppelt) P.; B.S. in Indsl. Engring., Ill. Inst. Tech., 1946; grad. student bus. adminstrn., U. Ill.; m. Irene Dryburgh, Feb. 15, 1980; children by previous marriage—James Nicholas, Linda, Karen. Engaged in mfg., 1946—; pres., dir. GL Corp., The Marmon Group Inc., Chgo., Mormon Industries, Inc., Trans Union Corp., The Colson Co.; dir. Hyatt Corp., Peoples Energy Corp., Hyatt Internat. Corp., Chgo., Salem Corp., Pitts., Rego Group, Inc. Vice pres., bd. dirs. Pritzker Found., Chgo.; trustee vice chmn., Ill. Inst. Tech. Office: 39 S LaSalle St Chicago IL 60603

PROBST, WILDENA GEORGIA, speech pathologist; b. Kremlin, Okla., July 13, 1939; d. George Coverdale and Wilma Elizabeth (French) Probst; B.A., U. Okla., 1962. Speech pathologist Wichita (Kans.) Pub. Schs., 1962-63, Larned (Kans.) City Schs., 1964-66, Coldwater (Kans.) Unified Dist. #300, 1967; pvt. practice speech pathology, Protection, Kans., 1965—. Mem. Am. Speech and Hearing Assn. Democrat. Address: Lexington Route Ashland KS 67831

PROCHNOW, HERBERT VICTOR, banker; b. Wilton, Wis., May 19, 1897; s. Adolph and Alvina (Liefke) P.; B.A., U. Wis., Madison, 1921, M.A., 1922, LL.D. (hon.), 1956; Ph.D., Northwestern U., 1947; Litt.D. (hon.), Millikin U., 1952; LL.D. (hon.), Ripon Coll., 1950, Northwestern U., 1963, Lake Forest Coll., 1964; D.H.L. (hon.), Thiel Coll., 1965, Monmouth Coll., 1965, U. N.D., 1966; m. Laura Virginia Stinson, June 12, 1928 (dec. Aug. 1977); 1 son, Herbert Victor. Prin., Kendall (Wis.) High Sch.; asst. prof. bus. adminstrn. Ind. U.; advt. mgr. Union Trust Co., Chgo.; with First Nat. Bank of Chgo., 1933-73, pres., dir., 1962-68, hon. dir., 1968-73; dir. Banco di Roma, Chgo.; sec. Fed. Res. Adv. Council, 1945—; spl. cons. sec. state, 1955, 57; dep. under sec. state econ. affairs, 1955-56; alt. gov. Internat. Bank and IMF, 1955-56. Chmn., U.S. del. GATT, Geneva, 1956; mem. U.S. del. Colombo Conf., Singapore, 1955, OECD, Paris, 1956; pres. Internat. Monetary Conf., 1968, now cons., hon. mem.; lectr. Loyola U., Northwestern U., dir. summer Grad. Sch. Banking, U. Wis., 1945—; fin. columnist Chgo. Tribune, 1968-70. Treas., Nat. 4-H Clubs,

1962-69; former trustee McCormick Theol. Sem., Evanston Hosp. Served with AEF. Decorated comdr. Order of Vasa (Sweden); comdr.'s cross Order of Merit (W.Ger.); recipient award Harvard Bus. Sch. Assn., 1965, Ayres Leadership award Stonier Grad. Sch. Banking, Rutgers U., 1966, Silver Plaque award NCCJ, 1967. Mem. Am. Econ. Assn., Chgo. Assn. Commerce and Industry (pres. 1964-65), Chgo. Council Fgn. Relations (pres. 1966-67), Nat. Assn. Bus. Economists, Fgn. Policy Officers Assn., Am. Finance Assn., Beta Gamma Sigma (nat. honoree). Clubs: Chicago Sunday Evening (trustee), Univ., Chgo., Comml., Mid-Day, Rotary, Union League (Chgo.); Bankers, Executives, Glen View. Author: Great Stories from Great Lives (an anthology), 1944; Meditations on the Ten Commandments, 1946; The Toastmaster's Handbook, 1949; Term Loans and Theories of Bank Liquidity, 1949; Successful Speakers Handbook, 1951; 1001 Ways to Improve Your Conversations and Speeches, 1952; Meditations on the Beatitudes, 1952; The Speaker's Treasury of Stories for All Occasions, 1953; The Toastmaster's and Speaker's Handbook, 1955; The Speaker's Handbook of Epigrams and Witticisms, 1955; Speaker's Treasury for Sunday School Teachers, 1955; The New Guide for Toastmasters, 1956; A Treasury of Stories, Illustrations, Epigrams and Quotations for Ministers and Teachers, 1957; The New Speaker's Treasury of Wit and Wisdom, 1958; A Family Treasury of Inspiration and Faith, 1958; Meditations on the Lord's Prayer, 1957; The Complete Toastmaster, 1960; Speaker's Book of Illustrations, 1960; Effective Public Speaking, 1960; 1000 Tips and Quips for Speakers and Toastmasters, 1962; 1400 Ideas for Speakers and Toastmasters, 1964; Tree of Life, 1972; Speaker's Source Book, 1969; A Speaker's Treasury for Educators, Convocation Speakers, 1973; The Speaker's and Toastmaster's Handbook, 1973; co-author: The Next Century is America's, 1938; Practical Bank Credit, 1939, rev. edit., 1963; The Public Speaker's Treasure Chest, 1942, rev. edit., 1964, 77; A Dictionary of Wit, Wisdom and Satire, 1962; The Successful Toastmaster, 1966; A Treasury of Humorous Quotations, 1969; Quotation Finder, 1971; The Changing World of Banking, 1974; The Toastmaster's Treasure Chest, 1979; editor: American Financial Institutions, 1951; Determining the Business Outlook, 1954; Federal Reserve System, 1960; World Economic Policies and Problems, 1965; The Five-Year Outlook for Interest Rates, 1968; The One-Bank Holding Company, 1969; The Eurodollar, 1970; The Five-Year Outlook for Interest Rates in the United States and Abroad, 1972; Dilemmas Facing the Nation, 1979; Bank Credit, 1981. Home: 2950 Harrison St Evanston IL 60201 Office: 1 First Nat Plaza Chicago IL 60670

PROCHNOW, HERBERT VICTOR, JR., banker, lawyer; b. Evanston, Ill., May 26, 1931; s. Herbert V. and Laura (Stinson) P.; A.B., Harvard U., 1953, J.D., 1956; A.M., U. Chgo., 1958; m. Lucia Boyden, Aug. 6, 1966; children—Thomas Herbert, Laura. Admitted to Ill. bar, 1957; with 1st Nat. Bank Chgo., 1958—, atty., 1961-70, sr. atty., 1971-73, counsel, 1973—, adminstrv. asst. to chmn. bd., 1978-81. Mem. Am., Ill., Chgo. (chmn. com. internat. law 1970-71) bar assns., Am. Soc. Internat. Law, Phi Beta Kappa. Clubs: Chicago; Harvard (N.Y.C.); Legal, Law, Onwentsia, Economic, Executives, University (Chgo.). Author: (with Herbert V. Prochnow) The Public Speaker's Treasure Chest, 1977; The Toastmaster's Treasure Chest, 1979; The Changing World of Banking, 1973; also articles in legal publs. Home: 226 Ravine Forest Dr Lake Bluff IL 60044 Office: 1 First Nat Plaza Chicago IL 60670

PROKOP, GAIL JEAN, occupational therapist; b. Chgo., Apr. 7, 1955; d. Robert John and Jean Marie (Padour) Prokop; B.S. in Occupational Therapy, U. Ill., 1979. Staff occupational therapist Home Health Care Service, Hillside, Ill., 1979. Central Du Page Hosp., Winfield, Ill., part-time, 1979; dir. occupational therapy In Home Health Care Service, Hillside, 1979—; occupational therapy cons. for blind/deaf children, Du Page/West Cook Regional Spl. Edn. Assn., Oak Sch., Dist. 181, Hinsdale, Ill., 1980—; supr. students U. Ill. Chgo. Med. Center, 1979—. Mem. Am. Occupational Therapy Assn., Ill. Occupational Therapy Assn. Club: NoMads Ski. Mng. editor Communique, 1980-82. Office: In Home Health Care Service of Suburban Chicago West Inc 4415 W Harrison St Hillside IL 60162

PROMENSCHENKEL, JAMES JOSEPH, data processing exec.; b. Gibsonburg, O., Dec. 30, 1944; s. Joseph Francis and Mildred Lucille (Kirsch) P.; B.S.B.A., Bowling Green State U., 1972; student Weber State Coll., 1967-68, U. Alaska, 1968-70; M.B.A., Central Mich. U., 1980; m. Sally Joyce Schmidt, Aug. 24, 1968; children—Joyce Anne, Kimberly Sue. Systems analyst Blue Cross Central Ohio, Columbus, 1973-74; programmer/analyst Ohio Nat. Bank, Columbus, 1974-75, State of Ohio, Columbus, 1975-78; data base adminstr. Pub. Employees Retirement System, Columbus, 1978-80; data processing quality assurance analyst Gold Circle Stores, Columbus, 1980-81; mgmt. cons. for data processing Peat, Marwick, Mitchell & Co., Columbus, 1981—. Served with USAF, 1966-70. Mem. Nat. Mgmt. Assn., Assn. Computer Machinery, Assn. Systems Mgrs., Data Processing Mgmt. Assn., Ohio Jaycees (outstanding chpt. mgmt. v.p. 1978-79), Columbus Jaycees (life, Jaycee of Year 1978, exec. v.p. 1978-79), Columbus C. of C. (mem. data processing task force). Club: Toastmasters. Home: 3135 Aleshire Dr Dublin OH 43017 Office: 277 E Town St Columbus OH 43215

PRONKO, NICHOLAS HENRY, psychologist, educator; b. McKees Rocks, Pa., Feb. 28, 1908; s. Michael John and Dorothy P.; B.A., George Washington U., 1941; M.A., Ind. U., 1941, Ph.D., 1944; m. Geraldine Allbritten, Dec. 16, 1953. Lectr., Shriverham and Biarritz Am. univs., 1946; asst. prof. CCNY, 1946-47; prof. psychology Wichita (Kans.) State U., 1947-78, prof. emeritus, 1978—. Fulbright lectr. Istanbul U., 1952-53; Ford Found. vis. prof. Cracow U. (Poland), 1959; Rothschild fellow Technion, Haifa, Israel, 1963. Fellow Am. Psychol. Assn., Kans. Psychol. Assn., Am. Soc. for Clin. Hypnosis, Kans. Soc. for Clin. Hypnosis, AAAS, Phi Beta Kappa, Sigma Xi. Author: (with Bowles) Empirical Foundations of Psychology, 1951; Textbook of Abnormal Psychology, 1963; Panorama of Psychology, 1969; Psychology From the Standpoint of an Interbehaviorist, 1980. Home: 525 Longford Ln Wichita KS 67206

PROPST, JANETT FAY, nursing adminstr.; b. Sedalia, Mo., July 2, 1933; d. Harry Walter and Georgia A. (Vestal) Pasley; diploma Burge Sch. of Nursing, 1954; m. Kenneth Lee Propst, Aug. 21, 1955; children—Kerry Leigh, Jeffrey Clark. Staff nurse operating room Wadsworth VA Hosp., Leavenworth, Kans., 1954-55; staff nurse med. surg. dept. Kansas City (Mo.) VA Hosp., 1955-57; staff nurse operating room Independence (Mo.) Sanitarium and Hosp., 1958-65, head nurse operating room, 1965-69; asso. dir. nurses, dir. operating rooms Menorah Med. Center, Kansas City, Mo., 1969-71; patient care coordinator operating rooms, recovery room, labor and delivery Kansas City (Mo.) Coll. Osteo. Medicine Center for Health Scis., 1971-73; asso. dir. nurses, dir. operating rooms and recovery room Trinity Luth. Hosp., Kansas City, Mo., 1973—. Mem. Am. Nurses Assn., Assn. of Operating Room Nurses (dir. Greater Kansas City chpt. 1970-73, pres. 1977-78, chmn. nat. editorial com. 1977, chmn. nat. com. nominations 1979-80, nat. sec. 1980), Mo. Nurses Assn. (dir. 1975—, mem. bylaws com. 1975—), 2d Dist. Mo. Nurses Assn. (dir. 1975-77, chmn. bylaws com. 1975-76). Mem. Christian Ch. Office: Trinity Lutheran Hosp 31st and Wyandotte Streets Kansas City MO 64108

PROST, JOHN CHARLES, ins. co. exec.; b. Detroit, Oct. 16, 1936; s. John L. and Kathryn E. Prost; B.A., Mich. State U., 1959; m. Lucinda Hendricks, July 25, 1959; children—Kathryn E., Elizabeth J. Asst. purchasing agt. Hupp Corp., 1958-59; spl. agt. Northwestern Mut. Life Ins. Co., 1959-61; brokerage mgr. Occidental Life Ins. Co., Detroit, 1961-63, Colonial Life Ins. Co., Detroit, 1963-65; br. mgr. Dominion Life Ins. Co., Detroit, 1965—. Mem. campaign staff Cavanagh for Mayor Detroit, 1962, 65, Romney for Gov. Mich., 1964; mem. Citizens Com. for Better Transp., Detroit, 1964; mem. exec. com. Republican Citizens Mich. 14th Congressional Dist., 1966; chmn. Grosse Pointe Park Rep. Club, 1971, 72; pres. Grosse Pointe PTA/Parent Tchr. Orgn. Council, 1975-76; mem. Grosse Pointe Park City Council, 1979. Recipient Presdl. award of honor Detroit Jaycees, 1964-67; Distinguished Service award Grosse Pointe Jaycees, 1968; citation for civic accomplishments Mich. Senate, 1977. Mem. Mich. State (pres. 1976-77), Detroit (pres. 1970-71) assns. life underwriters, Detroit Gen. Agts. and Mgrs. Assn. (pres. 1977), Fin. and Estate Planning Council Detroit, Greater Detroit C. of C., Am. Coll. Life Underwriters (Gold Key Soc.), Grosse Pointe Park Civic Assn. (pres. 1977), Grosse Pointe Jaycees (founder), Kappa Alpha Mu, Sigma Alpha Epsilon. Roman Catholic. Clubs: Detroit Athletic, Econ. of Detroit; Grosse Pointe Power Squadron. Home: 652 Pemberton Rd Grosse Pointe Park MI 48230 Office: 4000 Town Center Suite 303 Southfield MI 48075

PROTEAU, ROSEANNE VITULLO, pediatrician; b. Chgo., Sept. 26, 1936; d. Ralph N. and Elvira (Liambo) Vitullo; B.A., Clarke Coll., 1958; M.D., Loyola U., Chgo., 1962; m. Paul Joseph Proteau, Sept. 2, 1967; children—Paul Michael, Susan Marie. Intern, Resurrection Hosp., Chgo., 1962-63; resident in pediatrics Presbyn.-St. Luke's Hosp., Chgo., 1963-65, chief resident, 1965-66, dir. Birth Defects Spl. Treatment Center, 1972—; attending pediatrician Mile Sq. Health Center, Chgo., 1966-73; med. dir. Misericordia Homes for Retarded Children, Chgo., 1972—; asst. prof. pediatrics Rush Med. Sch., 1972—; cons. Madden Zone Center; mem. Ill. Gov.'s Adv. Council on Developmental Disabilities, 1973—. Mem. St. Mary's Sch. Bd., Riverside, Ill., 1974-77, sec., 1974-75, vice chmn., 1976-77; bd. dirs. Riverside Community Fund, 1978-81. NIH fellow, 1974. Diplomate Am. Bd. Pediatrics. Fellow Am. Acad. Pediatrics; mem. Chgo. Pediatric Soc., Ill., Chgo. med. socs., AMA. Roman Catholic. Home: 278 Longcommon Rd Riverside IL 60546 Office: 2916 W 47th St Chicago IL 60632 also 1753 W Congress Pkwy Chicago IL 60612

PROTHE, ELDON D., finance co. exec.; b. Beatrice, Nebr., Apr. 21, 1940; s. Walter H. and Clara E. P.; B.A., Valparaiso U., 1962; m. H. Jeanne Yuill, June 27, 1970; children—James, Gregory. Asst. acct. Peat, Marwick, Mitchell & Co., Chgo., 1962-64, audit sr., 1964-69, audit supr., 1969-71; asst. controller, 1971-74, tax mgr. USLIFE Credit Corp., Schaumburg, Ill., 1974-79, v.p., controller, 1979—. C.P.A., Ill. Mem. Am. Inst. C.P.A.'s, Ill. Soc. C.P.A.'s. Lutheran. Office: 1027 E State Pkwy Schaumburg IL 60195

PROTHRO, WINSTON BOONE, ret. public health adminstr.; b. Ferndale, Ark., Dec. 19, 1911; s. George and Ida Emily (Jones) P.; B.A., Baylor U., 1934; B.S., U. Ark., 1937, M.D., 1939; M.P.H., U. Mich., 1948; m. Jewell Maxine Nash, Nov. 12, 1942; children—Nelda Mae, Mary Estella, Winston Boone; m. 2d, Esther Kangas Jamieson, Oct. 13, 1978. Intern, Charity Hosp., New Orleans, 1939-40; dir. health dist. #3, Ark. State Health Dept., Arkadelphia, 1940-41; dir. El Paso (Tex.) City-County Health Dept., 1941-45, Kalamazoo City-County Health Dept., 1945-52, Grand Rapids (Mich.)-Kent County Health Dept., 1952-76; asso. dir. Mich. Dept. Public Health, Lansing, 1976-79, ret., 1979; chief med. examiner Kent County (Mich.); non-resident lectr. Sch. Public Health U. Mich.; chief sect. contagious disease control El Paso County Hosp., 1941-45; med. staff Blodgett Meml. Med. Center and Butterworth Hosp.; exec. dir. Community Health Service, 1964-76; med. dir. Kent County Civil Defense, 1954-76; founder, bd. dirs. Kent County Health Council, 1958-63; mem. Comprehensive State Health Planning Council, 1968-75; mem. Central Planning Unit W. Mich. Health Systems Agency Bd., chmn. public health tech. advisory com., chmn. ad hoc com. health services for Lake County; apptd. State Advisory Council on Alcoholism; health officer liaison rep. to State Health Advisory Council, 1974-76. Charter mem. bd. dirs. United Community Services, mem. planning div., 1959-63; founder, bd. dirs. Kent County Coordinating Council for the Aging, 1957-63, Kent County Mental Health Center, 1956-63; mem. regional interagency com. on mental retardation West Central Dist. council Mich. Assn. Regional Med. Program for Heart, Cancer and Stroke; bd. dirs., exec. and planning coms. Kent County Community Action Program; charter bd. dirs., exec. com. Neighborhood Health Services (award of merit 1974); bd. dirs. local chpt. Planned Parenthood Assn., Nat. Found. (March of Dimes), Am. Cancer Soc. (disting. service award Kent County unit 1965), Mich. Soc. Crippled Children and Disabled Adults, Sr. Neighbors; environ. health advisory com. to Ferris State Coll.; mem. Mich. Soc. for Mental Health, Mich. Lung Assn., Urban League, Project Rehab., Intergovtl. Employees Assn.; consistory, council on care, usher Central Reformed Ch. of Grand Rapids. Served to 1st lt. USAAF, 1941. Recipient public service award Mich. Dental Soc., 1977, distinguished service awards, Kent County Bd. Commrs., 1977, V.K. Volk award Mich. Soc. Gerontology, 1981. Diplomate Am. Bd. Preventive Medicine and Public Health. Fellow Am. Coll. Preventive Medicine (charter mem.), Am. Public Health Assn. (named to honor roll public health dirs. by assn. and U.S. C. of C., 1954-56); mem. Am. Assn. Public Health Physicians (charter), Mich. Health Officers Assn. (pres. 1957, various terms bd. dirs.; Disting. Service award 1964, 76), Mich. Sch. Health Assn. (pres. 1956-57), Mich. Med. Soc. (ho. of dels. 1971-75, coms. public and environ. health, rheumatic fever and CD, emergency med. services), Kent County Med. Soc. (disting. service award 1977), Mich. Public Health Assn. (dir. 1965-69, ho. of dels. 1971-75, coms.), Phi Chi. Clubs: Rotary, Elks, Woodmen of the World. Contbr. articles to profl. med. jours. Home: 2081 Lac DuMont Haslett MI 48840

PROTTER, HAROLD EDWIN, broadcasting co. exec.; b. N.Y.C., Dec. 21, 1941; s. Joseph Protter; B.S., U. Conn., 1962, postgrad., 1963; m. Gail Louis Brekke. Nat. sales mgr. Sta. WDCA-TV, Washington; sales mgr. Telerep, Detroit and St. Louis; v.p., gen. mgr. Sta. WXIX-TV, Cin.; exec. v.p., chief operating officer Sta. KPLR-TV, St. Louis, 1974—. Mem. Ind. TV Sta. Assn. (exec. com. dir.), Nat. Acad. TV Arts and Scis. (pres. St. Louis chpt.), Concerned Broadcasters Using Intercity Video Transmissions Facilities (chmn.). Office: 4935 Lindell Blvd Saint Louis MO 63108

PROUTY, GARRY FRANKLYN, psychologist; b. Syracuse, N.Y., Aug. 21, 1936; s. Cyrus and Rita (McFall) P.; student Buffalo State Tchrs. Coll., 1954-57; B.A., U. Buffalo, 1959; postgrad. (LaVerne Noyes scholar) U. Chgo., 1966; 1 dau., Gwen Allison. Teaching fellow dept. sociology U. Buffalo, 1961-62; chief psychologist Kennedy Job Tng. Center, Palos Park, Ill., 1966-70; dir. mental health program Prairie State Coll., Chicago Heights, Ill., 1970-74; pvt. practice as psychologist, Park Forest, Ill., 1968-72; psychologist Southwell Inst., Olympia Fields, Ill., 1972—; adj. prof. Union Grad. Sch., Yellow Springs, Ohio, 1972-74; mem. adv. bd. S. Suburban Council on Alcoholism, 1978; psychol. cons. Found. I Drug Abuse. Fellow Chgo. Psychotherapy Center, 1975-77. Fellow Am. Orthopsychiat. Assn.; mem. Am. Psychol. Assn. (asso.), Am. Sociol. Assn., Internat. Soc. for Study of Symbols. Editorial bd. Psychotherapy Theory, Research and Practice, 1970—, Jour. Mental Imagery, 1977—. Home: 1232 Birch Rd Homewood IL 60430 Office: Southwell Institute 2601 Lincoln Olympia Fields IL 60461

PROXMIRE, WILLIAM, U.S. senator; b. Lake Forest, Ill., Nov. 11, 1915; s. Theodore Stanley and Adele (Flanigan) P.; A.B., Yale U., 1938; M.B.A., Harvard U., 1940, M.A. in Pub. Adminstrn., 1948; m. Ellen Hodges; children—Theodore Stanley, Elsie Stillman, Douglas Clark. Pres. Artcraft Press, Waterloo, Wis., 1953-57; U.S. senator from Wis., 1957—. Nominee for gov. Wis., 1952, 54, 56; assemblyman Wis. legislature, 1951. Democrat. Home: 4613 E Buckeye Rd Madison WI 53716 Office: 5241 Dirksen Office Bldg Washington DC 20510*

PRUCKA, JOSEPH ALLEN, mfg. co. exec.; b. Omaha, May 17, 1933; s. Frank Hiram and Margret (Dawson) P.; transp. cert. U. Kans., 1954; B.A., B.S. U. Tenn., 1957; cert. distbn. and warehouse Drake U., 1978; m. Ardith Gibby, Apr. 3, 1957; children—Marjorie Ann, Leslie Jo. With Prucka Transp., Inc., Chgo., 1957-59, terminal mgr., 1959; pres. and gen. mgr. Himarco Inc., Omaha, 1965-75; with Interstate Motor Freight System, Des Moines, Chgo., 1959-65, ops. mgr., 1964-65; v.p., dir. Nebr. Transport Terminals, Inc., Omaha, 1962-77, Delaware Transport Terminals, Inc., Chgo. and Omaha, 1962-77; nat. mgr. distbn. and traffic Cook Paint and Varnish Co., Kansas City, Mo., 1977—; dir. Cornhusker Farms, Inc., Nebr. Transport Terminals Inc., Omaha Terminal Warehouse, Inc., Himarco Inc., Prucka Transp. Services. Served with USMC, 1951-53; Korea. Mem. Am. Mgmt. Assn., Pvt. Truck Council Am., Pvt. Carrier Council, Delta Tau Delta Alumni Assn., Delta Nu Alpha. Republican. Presbyterian. Clubs: Traffic and Transp. of Kansas City, Sertoma. Home: 1610 NE Redbud Ln North Kansas City MO 64116 Office: 919 E 14th Ave North Kansas City MO 64116

PRUIS, JOHN J, bus. exec.; b. Borculo, Mich., Dec. 13, 1923; s. Ties J. and Trientje (Koop) P.; B.S., Western Mich. U., 1947; M.A., Northwestern U., 1949, Ph.D., 1951; Litt.D., Yeungnam U., Taegu, Korea, Ind. State U.; m. Angeline Rosemary Zull, Sept. 14, 1944; children—David Lofton, Daniel J., Dirk Thomas. Tchr. pub. schs., Mich., 1942-43; supervising tchr. Campus Sch., Western Mich. U., 1947-48; instr. speech U. No. Iowa, 1951-52; from asst. prof. to asso. prof. speech So. Ill. U., 1952-55; mem. faculty Western Mich. U., 1955-68, sec. bd. trustees, 1964-68, v.p., 1966-68; pres. Ball State U., Muncie, Ind., 1968-78; v.p. corp. relations Ball Corp., 1978—. Cons., evaluator, exec. bd. N. Central Assn., 1959—, bd. dirs., 1972—, v.p., 1976-77, pres., 1977-78. County drive chmn. Kalamazoo Community Chest, 1964. Bd. dirs. Kalamazoo chpt. Am. Cancer Soc., 1963-68, Ball Meml. Hosp., United Fund Delaware County, Muncie Symphony Orch., Muncie Big Bros./Big Sisters. Served with USNR, 1943-46; capt. Res. Mem. Am. Assn. Higher Edn., Muncie C. of C., Speech Communication Assn. Presbyterian. Club: Rotary. Home: 305 N Brentwood Ln Muncie IN 47304

PRUNCKLE, TAIT CHARLES, real estate and constrn. exec.; b. Chgo., Sept. 22, 1949; s. John Peter and Ann T. (Leaskis) P.; B.S., Roosevelt U., 1975; m. Elizabeth Markey, Oct. 11, 1975; 1 son, Christopher. Jr. acct. Lemont (Ill.) Mfg. Co., 1972-74; asst. controller Berger Group, Chgo., 1975-78; controller Olympia Fields (Ill.) Country Club, 1978-81, controller Podcor Constrn. Co. and Podolsky & Assos. Ltd., Rosemont, Ill., 1981—. Mem. Nat. Assn. Accts., Chgo. Assn. Hospitality Accts., Club Accts. Assn. Democrat. Roman Catholic. Home: 10400 S Bell St Chicago IL 60643 Office: Podolsky & Assos Ltd 9655 Bryn Mawr Ave Rosemont IL 60018

PRY, ROBERT HENRY, electronic co. exec.; b. Dormont, Pa., Dec. 28, 1923; s. William Henry and Marie Eda (Freeman) P.; student Tex. A. & M. U., 1941-42, Okla. State U., 1943, U. Manchester (Eng.), 1945; B.S. in Physics, Tex. A. & I. U., 1947; M.A. in Physics, Rice U., 1949, Ph.D., 1951; m. Claude Marcelle Freyss, Dec. 20, 1947; children—Phillip Paul, Terry Allen, Pamela Lee, Patricia Ann, David Robert. Research asso. research labs. Gen. Electric Co., Schenectady, N.Y., 1951-60, mgr. alloys studies, 1960-62, mgr. properties studies, 1962-65, mgr. liaison and transition, 1965-67, mgr. metallurgy and ceramics lab., 1968-73, research and devel. mgr. elec. sci., and engring., 1973-76; v.p. research and devel. Combustion Engring. Co., Stamford, Conn., 1976-77; exec. v.p. research and devel. Gould Inc., Rolling Meadows, Ill., 1977—. Mem. indsl. adv. council U. Ill.; mem. vis. com. U. Pa. Served with Signal Corps, U.S. Army, 1943-46. Fellow AAAS, Am. Soc. Metals; mem. Research Dirs. Assn. of Chgo., Am. Phys. Soc., Am. Inst. Physics, Am. Inst. Mining Metallurgy and Petroleum Engrs., IEEE, Am. Mgmt. Assn., Indsl. Research Inst., Nat. Lab. Task Force, Metal Properties Council (dir.). Holder 5 patents in field; contbr. book chpt. and over 20 articles in field to profl. jours. Home: 21038 Andover Rd Kildeer IL 60047 Office: Gould Inc 10 Gould Center Rolling Meadows IL 60008

PRYOR, BARBARA WRIGHT, educator, concert artist; b. Stamps, Ark., May 30, 1934; d. Joseph Dudley and Bernyce Eleanor (Hayes) Wright; B.E., Chgo. State U., 1961; M.A., Roosevelt U., 1978; M.Ed., Chgo. Conservatory Music, 1967; m. Harry Leonard Pryor, Jr., June 26, 1954; 1 son, Harry Leonard III. Tchr. Am. history and govt. Wendell Phillips Upper Grade Center, Chgo., 1961-63; 8th grade tchr. George T. Donoghue Sch., Chgo., 1963-78; contralto soloist, dir. music St. James United Meth. Ch., Chgo., 1966-74; chorale dir. Duke Ellington, 1968; soloist Quinn Chapel A.M.E. Ch., Chgo., 1978—; guidance counselor George T. Donoghue Sch., Chgo. Public Sch. System, 1979—. Bd. dirs. Soc. Black Cultural Arts, Inc., 1978—, chmn. artist selection com., 1978—; active Chgo. Lyric Opera Guild. Recipient Outstanding Tchr. of Year award Chgo. Public Schs., 1977. Mem. Am. Personnel and Guidance Assn., Am. Sch. Counselor Assn., AAUW, Nat. Assn. Negro Musicians, Ill. Assn. Supervision and Curriculum Devel., Chgo. Music Assn., Roosevelt U. Alumni Assn., Phi Delta Kappa. United Methodist. Composer: Hear Us, We Beseech Thee, 1968. Home: 8258 Morgan St Chicago IL 60620 Office: 707 E 37th St Chicago IL 60653

PRYOR, DAVID BRUCE, psychoanalyst; b. Detroit, Dec. 30, 1934; s. Thomas Marion and Alice (Wurfel) P.; B.A., U. Mich., 1957, M.S., 1958; Ph.D., Mich. State U., 1962; m. Carolyn Gale Barnard, Dec. 24, 1966; children—Benjamin Carl, Aurora Dawn, Amanda Zoe. Postdoctoral fellow Menninger Found., Topeka, 1963-65; asst. prof. psychology and psychiatry U. Mich., Ann Arbor, 1965-76; faculty Mich. Psychoanalytic Inst., 1978—; pvt. practice psychotherapy and psychoanalysis, 1967—. Mem. Am. Psychoanalytic Assn., Am. Psychol. Assn., Mich. Psychoanalytic Assn., Soc. Projective Techniques. Clubs: Huron Portage Yacht, Pinckney Running. Editor Mich. Psychoanalytic Soc. newsletter, 1978—. Home: 1482 Nita St Pinckney MI 48169 Office: 2200 Fuller Rd Ann Arbor MI 48105

PRYOR, WILLIAM LEE, III, computer co. exec.; b. New London, Conn., Sept. 24, 1929; s. William Lee and Mary Day (Rouse) P.; student Johns Hopkins U., 1948-50, U.S. Naval Acad., 1951-52; B.A., Northwestern U., 1954; m. Lorie Schultz, Sept. 23, 1974; children—Bill, John, Kiley, Alex, Liz, Jennifer, Tory, Sue. Data processing salesman IBM, Evanston, Ill., 1956-58; advt. salesman Times-Life, Chgo., 1958-59; founder, pres. Pryor Corp., Chgo., 1959—. Bd. dirs. Chgo Council Fgn. Relations, 1962-65, Big Bros.,

Chgo., 1974-79; mem. Chgo. Crime Commn. Served with U.S. Army, 1955-57. Mem. Data Processing Mgmt. Assn., Assn. Data Processing Service Orgn., Young Pres.'s Orgn. Republican. Episcopalian. Clubs: Chgo. Yacht, Racquet of Chgo., Saddle & Cycle Country, Army and Navy. Office: 400 N Michigan Ave Chicago IL 60611

PRYSAK, MICHAEL F., obstetrician, gynecologist; b. Detroit, Jan. 31, 1945; s. Stanley and Frances (Wojewnik) P.; B.S., U. Detroit, 1966; Ph.D. (NDEA fellow 1966-68, NSF fellow 1968-69), Vanderbilt U., 1969; M.D., U. Mich., 1973; m. Charlene Jean Prieur, June 1, 1973; children—Kristen Ann, Geoffrey Michael, Kelly Grae. Intern, resident in Ob-Gyn Med. Coll. Va., 1973-77; practice medicine specializing in Ob-Gyn, Richmond, Va., 1977-79, Detroit, 1979—; program dir. Ob-Gyn St. John Hosp., Detroit, 1979—; clin. asst. prof. Wayne State U. Med. Sch., Detroit, 1979—. Fellow Am. Coll. Ob-Gyn; mem. Am. Chem. Soc., AMA, Hudnall Ware Soc., Sigma Xi. Home: 579 N Brys Grosse Pointe Woods MI 48236 Office: 22101 Moross Rd Detroit MI 48236

PSAROUTHAKIS, JOHN, mfg. co. exec.; b. Canea, Crete, Greece, June 29, 1932; s. Michael and Stamatia (Tsikouldani) P.; B.S., Mass. Inst. Tech., 1957, M.S., 1962; Ph.D., U. Md., 1965; Program for Execs., Carnegie-Mellon U., 1968; m. Inga Lundgren, Aug. 1, 1959; children—Michael, Peter. Dept. mgr. Thermo Electron Corp., Waltham, Mass., 1958-62; research dept. mgr., nuclear div. Martin Marietta Corp., Balt., 1962-66; dir. tech. and new product planning Allis Chalmers Corp., Milw., 1966-70; group v.p. internat. operations and internat. corporate devel. Masco Corp., Taylor, Mich., 1973-77, corp. v.p. planning and engring., 1970-73; pres. J.P. Industries, Inc., Ann Arbor, Mich., 1977—; former chmn. Masinco A.G., Switzerland; pres. Mariani SpA, Italy; dir. Century S.p.A., Corp., Italy, Holzer Co. GmbH, Germany, EMCO Ltd., Can. Recipient Disting. Young Scientist award Md. Acad. Sci., 1965. Mem. Am. Mgmt. Assn., Am. Metals Soc., Bus. Internat., Conf. Bd., Mich. C. of C. Club: Liberty Lawn Tennis (Ann Arbor). Contbr. articles to profl. jours. Patentee in field. Home: 2119 Melrose St Ann Arbor MI 48104 Office: 825 Victors Way Ann Arbor MI 48104

PTAK, LOUIS RICHARD, chem. engr.; b. Chgo., May 13, 1916; s. Joseph and Antoinette (Stopka) P.; B.S., U. Lwow (Poland), 1938; m. Helen R. Komperda, July 1, 1944; children—Patricia, Richard, Louis Richard, John, Joseph. With Tech. Center, Continental Can Co., Chgo., 1943—, mgr. product and engring. standards, 1977—. Served as 2d lt. U.S. Army, 1938-41. Decorated Purple Heart; Croix de Guerre (France). Mem. Am. Chem. Soc., Packaging Inst., Inst. Food Technologists. Home: 5317 Johnson Ave Western Springs IL 60558

PU, PIN HSIU, pathologist, lab. dir.; b. Shanghai, China, Feb. 11, 1924; s. Yien Bei and Hsiu Ching (Chang) P.; came to U.S., 1949, naturalized, 1962; B.S., St. Johns U., Shanghai, China, 1944, M.D., 1947; m. Elise Yao, May 25, 1948; children—Lillian, Steve, Sheila, Debbie. Pathologist, St. Anthony Hosp., Terre Haute, Ind., 1960-67, Mary Sherman Hosp., Sullivan, Ind., 1963-67, Valley Med. Lab., Terre Haute, Ind., 1963-67; pathologist, dir. labs. Dunklin County Meml. Hosp., Kennett, Mo., 1968—; cons. pathologist Dexter Meml. Hosp. (Mo.), 1970—, Pemiscot County Meml. Hosp., Hayti, Mo., 1971—, Presnell Hosp., Kennett, Mo., 1968—; dir. SE Mo. Found. Med. Care; dir. SE Mo. Profl. Standard Rev. Orgn.; chmn. rev. com. Bootheel Comprehensive Health Planning Council, 1972-76. Diplomate Am. Bd. Pathology. Methodist. Office: 611 Teaco Rd Kennett MO 63857

PUCCINELLI, ALVIN EMIL, advt. agy. exec.; b. Santa Cruz, Calif., May 9, 1938; s. Emilio Joseph and Clara (Kronberger) P.; B.S. in Bus. Adminstrn., Northwestern U., 1961; m. Beatrice Khano, May 31, 1969; 1 dau., Leslie Claire. Trainee, acct. exec. Campbell-Mithun Inc., Chgo., 1962-64, media supr., 1965-67, acct. supr., 1968-72, v.p. acct. supr., 1976-79, v.p., mgmt. supr., 1979—; dir. advt. Orient region N.W. Airlines, Tokyo, 1973-75. Republican. Club: Mensa. Home: 3620 Bernay Dr Northbrook IL 60062 Office: 111 E Wacker Dr Chicago IL 60601

PUCEL, JOHN CHARLES, clin. psychologist; b. Mpls., Feb. 16, 1945; s. William F. and Olive (Soderberg) P.; A.A., Ely Jr. Coll., 1965; B.A. summa cum laude, U. Minn., Duluth, 1967; M.A. (NDEA grad. scholar), U. Mo., Ph.D., 1972; m. JoAnna Petritz, Sept. 9, 1967; 1 dau., Janet. Mgr. Boundary Waters Canoe Outfitters, Ely, Minn., 1964-71; coordinator mental health asso. tng. program VA Hosp., St. Cloud, Minn., 1972-76, staff psychologist alcohol treatment program, 1976-77, coordinator Chem. Dependency Center, 1977—; pvt. practice clin. psychology, St. Cloud; asst. prof. St. Cloud State U., 1972-78, Coll. of St. Benedict, 1972-77; pres. Human Service Forum, 1976; mem. Central Minn. Drug Adv. Bd., 1976-79, Central Minn. Health Systems Agy. Task Force on Mental Health/Chem. Dependency. Mem. choir Newman Center Ch. Named Outstanding Young Citizen in St. Cloud, Jaycees, 1980; recipient VA commendation for upward mobility tng., 1976. Mem. Central Minn. Chem. Dependency Profls., Am. Psychol. Assn. Roman Catholic. Club: Rotary (dir. St. Cloud 1976-79, v.p. 1982). Contbr. articles to profl. pubis. Home: Rural Route 5 Wayside Addition Saint Cloud MN 56301 Office: CDC 116C VA Medical Center Saint Cloud MN 56301

PUCKETT, HELEN LOUISE, tax cons. co. exec.; b. Ripley, Ohio, Oct. 29, 1934; d. Joseph and Gladys Muriel (Madden) Haney; student Columbus Bus. U., 1971; m. Marvin R. Puckett, May 29, 1953 (dec.); children—Steven W., Thomas J. Office mgr. Al-Win Tng., Inc., West Jefferson, Ohio, 1971—, sec.-treas., 1971—, agt., 1977-79; notary public, 1975—. Sunday Sch. tchr. London (Ohio) Ch. of Christ, 1975—, pres. Women's Fellowship, 1979-81. Home: 130 Columbia Ave London OH 43140 Office: 485 Glade Run Rd West Jefferson OH 43162

PUCKORIUS, PAUL RONALD, water treatment, cooling water and pollution control cons.; b. Chgo., Apr. 7, 1930; s. Paul Joseph and Lucy (Adulis) P.; B.A., North Central Coll., Naperville, Ill., 1953; postgrad Northwestern U., 1953-54; m. Joyce Elaine Heinzman, Feb. 14, 1953; children—Susan, David, Cynthia. With Nalco Chem. Co., Chgo., 1948-69, product mgr. cooling water, 1963-65, mgr. cooling water chems. dept., 1965-69; v.p., exec. v.p. Zimmite Corp., Cleve., 1969-76; owner, pres. P.R. Puckorius & Assos. Inc., Cleve., 1976—; mem. adv. bd. Internat. Water Conf. Leader, Explorer Scouts, 1964, active Boy Scouts Am., 1964-72; hon. bd. dirs. Clague Playhouse Theatre; mem. vestry Episcopal Ch., 1964-69, 70-72. Served with Ill. N.G., 1949-58. Mem. Nat. Assn. Corrosion Engrs. (chmn. coms.), Korean Inst. Chem. Engrs. (hon.), Engrs. Soc. Western Pa., Am. Chem. Soc., Am. Water Works Assn., Am. Petroleum Inst., Am. Inst. Chem. Engrs., ASTM, Am. Electroplaters Soc., Cooling Tower Inst. (pres. 1979-80). Author: (with others) Cooling Water Primer, 1971; also articles in profl. jours., papers presented at profl. confs. Patentee in water treatment chemicals. Home: 20800 Valley Forge Dr Cleveland OH 44126 Office: Box 4846 Cleveland OH 44126

PUDLO, EDMUND MARION, chemist; b. Chgo., June 20, 1927; s. Louis John and Apolonia Mary (Krol) P.; B.S., De Paul U., 1950; m. Regina Suzanne Samborski, Apr., 1953; children—Robert, Richard, Raymond. Chemist indsl. coatings Armstrong Paints Co., Chgo., 1950-57; mgr. chem. coatings lab. Mobil Chem. Co., Kankakee, Ill., 1957—. Served with USAAF, 1945-46. Mem. Fedn. Socs. Coatings Tech. Clubs: Elks, Moose. Home: 27 Guildford Dr Bourbonnais IL 60914 Office: 901 N Greenwood St Kankakee IL 60901

PUEPPKE, GLENN HOWARD, furniture co. exec., farmer; b. Amenia, N.D., Apr. 12, 1927; s. Howard Monroe and Malinda Wilhelmina (Judisch) P.; student Concordia Coll., 1945-46; m. Letha Pauline Mitchell, Sept. 4, 1948 (dec.); children—Steven, David, Eric, Howard, Clinton; m. 2d, Ruth Bernice Kleinsasser, Sept. 19, 1965. With Macklanborg Supply Co., Oklahoma City, 1947, Collins, Dietz, Morris Co., Oklahoma City, 1948-50; farmer nr. Erie, N.D., 1950—; pres. G & G Transport Co., Erie, 1960-66; co-founder Arkota Industries, furniture mfg. co., Valley City, N.D., 1971—, vice chmn., 1970—; pres. Pan African Traders Ltd., 1980—; mem. N.D. Trade Mission to Middle East, 1976; N.D. del. People's Republic of China, 1978; mem. adv. com. CCREC Power Coop. Pres., Erie (N.D.) Sch. Bd., 1965-67, Dakota Sch. Bd., 1970-81; chmn. Cass County 4C's, 1966. Bd. dirs. St. Lukes Hosp., 1958-60. Mem. Nat. Sunflower Growers Assn., Red River Valley Bean Growers Assn., N.D. Farm Bur., Profl. Farmers Am., Internat. Platform Assn., Eagles, Alpha Epsilon Sigma. Mem. Ch. of God (vice chmn. N.D. mission 1971-73). Republican. Home: Erie ND 58029

PUETZ, WAYNE EDWARD, polit. scientist, educator; b. Joliet, Ill., Feb. 20, 1946; s. Arthur A. and Anne C. (Scheri) P.; B.A. with high honors, Lewis U., 1968; M.A., Georgetown U., 1970; m. Dale Duda, July 9, 1977. Asst. dept. mgr. Hardlines Corp., retail outlets, Joliet, Ill., 1963-68; vis. prof. polit. sci. dept. Hanover (Ind.) Coll., 1975; prof. law and govt. Coll. St. Francis and Joliet Jr. Coll., Joliet, 1975—; faculty Bolingbrook High Sch., Bolingbrook, Ill., 1975-76; dir. gifted program Jane Addams Sch., Bolingbrook, Ill., 1977-79; prof. ednl. adminstrn. Nat. Coll. Edn., Evanston, Ill., 1979—; dir. gifted program Bolingbrook High Sch., 1979—, Valley View Sch. Dist., 1980—; researcher role technosci. progress and internat. law. Mem. Friends and Parents of Gifted Children. Named Outstanding Young Educator, Bolingbrook (Ill.) Jaycees, 1978. Mem. Am. Polit. Sci. Assn., Am. Soc. Internat. Law, Center for Study of Presidency, Delta Epsilon Sigma, Pi Sigma Alpha. Home: 1321 N William St Joliet IL 60435

PUGHE, JOHN EDWARD, purchasing exec.; b. Barmouth, North Wales, U.K., Oct. 18, 1932; came to U.S., 1949, naturalized, 1954; s. Thomas Norman and Mary Caroline (Williams) P.; B.A., Mich. State U., 1955; M.B.A., Rollins Coll., 1965; m. Frances Mary Udvarnoky, Aug. 27, 1955; children—Charles Edward, Thomas John, Roberta Mary. Sr. buyer Aeroquip Corp., Jackson, Mich., 1956-58; purchasing mgr. Martin Co., Orlando, Fla., 1958-67; dir. procurement Bendix Corp., Avionics Div., Ft. Lauderdale, Fla., 1967-76, corp. purchasing officer, Southfield, Mich., 1976—. Pres., Men of Presbyn. Ch. of Am., Ft. Lauderdale, 1975-76; bd. dirs. Inner-City Bus. Improvement Forum, Detroit, 1979—. Cert. purchasing mgr. Mem. Nat. Assn. Purchasing Mgmt. (v.p. 1975-76, dir. 1975-76), Cambrian Welsh Soc. of S. Fla. (pres. 1974-76), Nat. Minority Purchasing Council, Machinery and Allied Products Inst., Purchasing Mgmt. Assn. Detroit, Theta Xi. Club: Lions. Contbr. articles to profl. jours.; editor: Aljian's Purchasing Handbook, Sect. 25, 4th edit. 1981. Home: 1255 Rugby Circle Bloomfield Hills MI 48013 Office: Bendix Exec Offices Southfield MI 48037

PUGLIESE, JOSEPH MARGIOTTI, geophysicist; b. Pitts., Aug. 19, 1936; s. Sebastian Charles and Grace (Margiotti) P.; B.S. in Geophysics and Geochemistry, Pa. State U., 1958; m. Ann Marie Johnson, Apr. 12, 1969; 1 dau., Marie Christina. Geophysicist, Bur. Mines U.S. Dept. Interior, College Park, Md., 1958-65, geophysicist project engr., Mpls., 1965-68, head thermal and elec. fragmentation lab., Mpls., 1968-70, geophysicist, environ. specialist, mining engr., sr. research investigator, adviser, team leader, Mpls., 1970—. Adviser, tchr. seminars in field including Canadian Mines dept., Ottawa, U.S. C.E., others; tech. adviser met. clean air com. Mpls., 1974—. Vol. Little Bros. Poor, Mpls., St. Paul, 1972—. Served with USNR, 1959. Mem. Twin Cities Geologists, Internat. Soc. Rock Mechanics, Sigma Gamma Epsilon. Roman Catholic. Author tech. papers research rock disintegration, pre-mine planning. Home: 5016 18th Ave S Minneapolis MN 55417 Office: 5629 Minnehaha Ave S Minneapolis MN 55417

PULFER, LESLIE LOUIS, state ofcl.; b. Elgin, Iowa, Jan. 22, 1932; s. John and Ida (Fischer) P.; A.A., Iowa State U., 1966; B.B.A., Ill. State U., 1971; m. Wilma Wettstein, July 18, 1954; children—Jeffrey, Kathleen, Eldon, Doris. With Rath Packing, Waterloo, Iowa, 1951-52, Borden Milk Co., Pekin, Ill., 1956-59, Standard Brands, Inc., Pekin, 1959-71; ops. mgr. Soldwedel All Star Dairy, Canton, Ill., 1972; asst. adminstr. Bur. Animal Health Ill. Dept. Agr., Springfield, 1972—; pres. New World Sweeteners, Eureka, Ill., 1979—; cons. Standards Brands, 1959-71, Malt Products Co., 1972-78. Advisor, Jr. Achievement, Pekin Ill., 1959-64; pres. Boys Club of Pekin, 1969-71; v.p. bd. dirs. Jr. Achievement, 1963-71; pres. Shade Youth Camp, 1975-79, Pekin Leaders of Youth, 1963-65. Served with USMC, 1951-52. Recipient Herbert Hoover award, 1974; Bronze Keystone award, Boys' Clubs Am., 1978; named Man of Distinction, Am. Legion, 1965, others. Mem. Inst. Food Tech., Iowa Dairy Industry Club, Tazewell County Farm Bur., Am. Mgmt. Assn., Inst. Internal Auditors, Am. Legion (comdr. 1964). Republican. Apostolic Christian Ch. Clubs: Pekin Celestial Investment (pres. 1981—), Iowa State Alumni, Ill. State Alumni, Boys, Keystone, Giraffe (charter). Patentee in field. Home: 1504 S 7th St Pekin IL 61554 Office: State Fairgrounds Springfield IL 62706

PULFORD, ROBERT JESSE (BOB), profl. hockey team exec.; b. Newton Robinson, Ont., Can., Mar. 31, 1936. Formerly center Toronto Maple Leafs; past center, capt. Los Angeles Kings, also formerly coach; was coach, now gen. mgr. Chgo. Black Hawks. Office: care Chgo Black Hawks 1800 W Madison St Chicago IL 60612*

PULLEN, JAMES RALPH, educator; b. Oklahoma City, Feb. 16, 1936; s. Ralph and Anna Margaret (Kiely) P.; m. Janice Louise Robinson, Dec. 9, 1965; 1 son, James Arthur; B.S., U. Mo., 1958, M.Ed., 1963; Ed.D., U. S.D., 1971. With Dept. Def., Germany and P.R., 1963-65; high sch. counselor, Casper, Wyo., 1965-67; counselor, dir. adult edn., Keokuk, Iowa, 1967-69; asso. prof. Central Mo. State U., Warrensburg, 1971—; cons. human relations USAF. Vice pres. Johnson County Mental Health Assn., 1974; bd. dirs. Warrensburg Planned Parenthood Assn., W.Central Mo. Mental Health Center, 1979-81. Served with USNR, 1958-60. HEW grantee, 1973-75. Mem. Am. Personnel and Guidance Assn., Mo. Personnel and Guidance Assn. (treas.), Am. Psychol. Assn., NEA, AAUP, Phi Delta Kappa. Clubs: Masons, Rotary. Contbr. articles to profl. jours. Home: Route 2 Northfield Warrensburg MO 64093

PULLIAM, EUGENE SMITH, publisher; b. Kans., 1914; s. Eugene C. and Myrta (Smith) P.; A.B., DePauw U., 1935, LL.D., 1973; m. Jane Bleecker, 1943; children—Myrta, Russell, Deborah. Reporter United Press, Chgo., Detroit and Buffalo burs., 1935-36; news editor radio sta. WIRE, Indpls., 1936-41; city editor Indpls. Star, 1947-48; mng. editor Indpls. News, 1948-62; now pub. Indpls. Star and Indpls. News; exec. v.p. Central Newspapers, Inc.; pres. Phoenix Newspapers Inc. Past vice pres. U.S. Golf Assn. Co-founder St. Richard's Sch. Served as lt. USNR, 1942-46. Mem. Am. Soc. Newspaper Editors, Am. Press Inst. (dir.), Am. Newspaper Pubs. Assn. (past pres. found.), Hoosier State Press Assn. (treas.), Ind. Acad., Delta Kappa Epsilon, Sigma Delta Chi. Episcopalian. Rotarian. Clubs: University (Indpls.); Crooked Stick (Carmel, Ind.); Woodstock; Links (N.Y.C.); Pine Valley Golf; Royal and Ancient Golf. Co-author textbook. Home: 8830 Pickwick Dr Indianapolis IN 46260 Office: Indianapolis News Indianapolis IN 46206

PULLIAM, FREDERICK CAMERON, supt. schs.; b. Mesa, Ariz., Jan. 3, 1936; s. Frederick Posy and Nathana Laura (Cameron) P.; AA., Hannibal LaGrange Coll., 1955; A.B., Grand Canyon Coll., 1958; M.Ed., U. Mo., Columbia, 1966, Ed.S., 1976, Ed.D., 1981; m. Deborah Jean Botts, June 1, 1979; children by previous marriage—Cameron Dale, Joy Renee. Tchr., Centerview (Mo.) Public Schs., 1958-59; ordained to ministry So. Baptist Conv., 1955; minister Bethel Bapt. Ch., Kansas City, Mo., 1959-61; adminstr. Fiti'uta, Manu'a sch., Am. Samoa, 1966-69; cons. in fin. Mo. State Tchrs. Assn., Columbia, 1969-79; supt. schs. Midway Heights C-VII, Columbia, 1979—; cons. sch. fin., curriculum improvement. Mem. Columbia Am. Revolution Bicentennial Commn. Inst. Devel. Ednl. Activity fellow, 1969, 80, 81. Mem. Mo. Assn. Sch. Adminstrs., Mo. Assn. Supervision and Curriculum Devel., Nat. Assn. Supervision and Curriculum Devel., Mo. Assn. Elem. Sch. Prins., Nat. Assn. Elem., Kindergarten and Nursery Educators, Phi Delta Kappa. Republican. Clubs: Kiwanis, Masons, Shriners. Contbr. articles to profl. jours. Home: 35 Sandalwood Ct Route 5 Columbia MO 65201 Office: Midway Heights Sch Dist Route 5 Columbia MO 65201

PUMPER, ROBERT WILLIAM, microbiologist; b. Clinton, Iowa, Sept. 12, 1921; s. William R. and Kathrine M. (Anderson) P.; B.A., U. Iowa, 1951, M.Sc., 1953, Ph.D., 1955; m. Ruth J. Larkin, June 24, 1951; 1 son, Mark. Asst. prof. Hahnemann Med. Coll., Phila., 1955-57; prof. microbiology U. Ill. Coll. Medicine, Chgo., 1957—; cons. pathology St. James Hosp., Chicago Heights, Ill.; Raymond B. Allen Med. lectr., 1970, 74, 76. Served with USAAF, 1942-46. Diplomate Am. Soc. Microbiology. Mem. Tissue Culture Assn., Sigma Xi, Phi Rho Sigma. Lutheran. Co-author: Essentials of Medical Virology, 1975; contbr. articles profl. jours. Home: 18417 Argyle Ave Homewood IL 60430 Office: Dept Microbiology 808 S Wood St Chicago IL 60680

PUNDT, RICHARD ARTHUR, lawyer, inventor; b. Iowa City, Iowa, Apr. 18, 1944; s. Arthur Herman and Johanna Celeste (Pasterik) P.; B.A., State U. Iowa, 1966; J.D., Drake U., 1969; m. Joyce Kay Schoenfelder, Dec. 1, 1968; children—Vincent Arthur, Jennifer Johanna, Heather Ann. Temporary claims dep. Iowa Employment Security Commn., 1968-69; admitted to Iowa bar, 1969; staff atty. Polk County Legal Aid, Office Econ. Opportunity, 1969; spl. agt. FBI, 1969-71; law asso. Keys & Crawford, Cedar Rapids, 1971-72, Faches, Klinger & Gloe, Cedar Rapids, 1972-75, Silliman, Gray & Stapleton, Cedar Rapids, 1975—; dir. Cedar Rapids Profl. Football Corp., 1972-73, pres., 1972-73. Exec. dir. Iowans for Rockerfeller, 1968; exec. dir. Polk County Republican Com. 1968-69; mem. Linn County Rep. Central Com., 1972—; chmn. Linn County Rep. party, 1977-78; asst. atty. Linn County, 1972-76. Mem. Am., Iowa, Linn County bar assns., Metro Athletic Assn. (dir. 1976—). Roman Catholic. Club: Sertoma. Home: 4118 Hickory Hill Ln SE Cedar Rapids IA 52403 Office: 807 American Bldg Cedar Rapids IA 52401

PUNTNEY, DOYLE EUGENE, coal co. exec.; b. Mt. Vernon, Ill., Mar. 9, 1945; s. Denzil D. and Leona Mae (Veatch) P.; B.A. in Bus. Adminstrn., Central Meth. Coll., Fayette, Mo., 1968; m. Gayle Elizabeth Cobb, June 15, 1968; children—Kevin Mathew, Kristin Lynn. Jr. accountant Main Lafrentz, St. Louis, 1968-70; mgr. corporate accounting Arch Mineral Corp., St. Louis, 1970-73, mgr. sales accounts and distbn., 1973-74; account mgr. Amax Coal Co., Indpls., 1975-77; v.p. sales Circle City Coal Corp., Indpls., 1977-80; regional sales mgr. MAPCO Coals, Inc., 1980—; student tchr. accounting Central Meth. Coll. Methodist. Home: 844 Plymouth Rock Dr Des Peres MO 63131

PURCELL, EDWARD KENNETH, clergyman; b. Broadhead, Ky., Sept. 18, 1923; s. Edward Jefferson and Minnie (Owens) P.; Th.B., Frankfort Pilgrim Coll., 1949; B.A., Taylor U., 1950; Th.M., Am. Theol. Inst., 1952, Th.D., 1955; m. Louella Marie Hahn, Oct. 25, 1941; children—Edward Daniel, Barbara Lou, Minnie Rose, Timotheus Samuel. Ordained to ministry Wesleyan Ch., 1949; staff mem. Taylor U. and pastor ch., Gas City, Ind., 1951; missionary, dist. supt. S. Am., 1952, supt., Curacao, Netherlands Antilles, 1953-58, promoter missions, 1958-59; pastor, Detroit, 1959-62, Denver, 1962-65, Fredonia, Kans., 1965-67, Clay Center, Kans., 1967-70, Alva, Okla., 1970-74, Oklahoma City, 1974-79, Scott City (Mo.) Wesleyan Ch., 1979—; asst. supt. Colo. Dist., 1965-66. Served with USN, 1943-46. Mem. Internat. Platform Assn., Ministerial Alliance (past pres., sec., treas.). Contbr. articles to religious jours. Home: 503 Crites St Scott City MO 63780

PURCELL, MARY ELAINE (BURKEY), mgmt. cons.; b. Columbus, Ohio, Aug. 10, 1944; d. Wayne W. and Betty Jane (Warren) Burkey; B.A. in Edn., Capital U., 1966. Tchr., Columbus public schs., 1966-68, Reynoldsburg (Ohio) public schs., 1968-71; women's affairs coordinator Ohio Dept. Personnel, Columbus, 1972-73; chief tng. Ohio Dept. Adminstrv. Services, Columbus, 1973-75; mgmt. cons. Colburn & Assos., Columbus, 1975-78; pres. Mary Purcell & Assos., Cin., 1978—; mem. faculty Columbus Tech. Inst., Hocking Tech. Coll., Clark Tech. Coll.; Ohio's rep. to Midwest Intergovtl. Tng. Com.; mem. Ohio Gov.'s Speakers' Bur. Mem. campaign staff Celeste for Gov. Ohio, 1978. Recipient cert. recognition SBA, 1978. Mem. Columbus Met. Club, Am. Soc. Tng. and Devel., Am. Soc. Public Adminstrn., Met. Exchange Cin, Internat. Public Mgmt. Assn. Office: 10921 Reed Hartman Cincinnati OH 45242

PURCELL, ROBERT HARRY, fin. service co. exec.; b. Beatrice, Nebr., July 21, 1943; s. Harry C. and Anita (Finley) P.; B.S., U. Nebr., 1965, J.D., 1968; m. Linda Jo Cook, Sept. 6, 1964; children—Gregory, Jennifer, Christopher. Tax specialist Arthur Andersen & Co., Omaha and Cin., 1968-73; dir. taxes Ward Foods, Inc., Chgo., 1973-77; tax counsel Walter E. Heller Internat. Corp., Chgo., 1977-80, v.p. corp. planning, 1980—. Mem. Internat. Fiscal Assn., Am. Bar Assn., Am. Inst. C.P.A.'s, Planning Execs. Inst., Ill. Soc. C.P.A.'s, Nebr. Soc. C.P.A.'s, Nebr. Bar Assn., Execs. Club Chgo. Home: 1020 Mallard Dr Palatine IL 60067 Office: 105 W Adams St Chicago IL 60603

PURCELL, TERRY ALLAN, retail exec.; b. Paducah, Ky., Sept. 20, 1948; s. Allan Edward and Ruth Lorene P.; B.S., Murray State U., 1972; m. Marilyn Jean Robbearts, Dec. 1, 1973; children—Danielle, Gavin. With CMC Corp., various locations, 1976—, v.p., regional sales mgr., Atlanta, 1979, St. Louis, 1979-80, v.p. sales, St. Louis, 1980—. Served with USAR, 1968-76. Named Store Mgr. of Yr., Montgomery Ward Co., 1973. Mem. Am. Mgmt. Assn. Republican. Lutheran. Club: Masons. Home: 549 Timberridge St Saint Charles MO 63301 Office: 12115 Lackland Rd Suite 150 Saint Louis MO 63141

PURDY, DONALD KEITH, mortician; b. Greenfield, Iowa, June 15, 1925; s. Clifford Floyd and Juanita Marie (Cox) P.; diploma Kans. Coll. Mortuary Sci., Kansas City, 1948; m. Marianne Seegers, Oct. 3, 1948; 1 son, Mark Donald. Engaged in mortuary bus., 1946—. Served with AUS, 1943-45. Decorated Bronze Star. Mem. Am. Funeral Homes Assn. (past dir.), Nat. Funeral Firs. Assn., Asso. Funeral Dirs. Service, Iowa Funeral Dirs. Assn., Am. Legion, VFW, Council Bluffs Fish and Game Protective Assn. Republican. Lutheran. Clubs: Elks, Optimist (pres. Council Bluffs 1963-64, internat. v.p. 1980-81; various awards). Address: 140 Norton Ave Council Bluffs IA 51501

PURFEERST, CLARENCE MARK, grain and hog farmer, state senator; b. Faribault, Minn., June 30, 1928; s. Mark P. and Amelia E. (Charpentier) P.; student Faribault public schs.; m. Rosie Paquette, Jan. 26, 1949; children—Judy, Jane, Jim, Joe, Mary, Amy. County ofcl. Dept. Agr.; grain and hog farmer, Faribault; mem. Minn. State Senate, 1970—. Mem. Faribault Sch. Bd.; former nat. and state officer Jaycees. Mem. Rice County Farmers Union (pres.). Clubs: Elks (pres.), Eagles. *

PURIFOY, CECIL ERNEST, JR., educator; b. Houston, Sept. 22, 1927; s. Cecil E. and Ruth Agnes (Dupre) P.; B.S., U. Tex., 1949; M.A., Mich. State U., 1952, Ph.D., 1970. Tchr. public schs., Prince George's County, Md., 1954-55, Houston, 1955-64; mem. faculty Mich. State U., 1964-66, U. Tenn., 1966-71; mem. faculty Ball State U., Muncie, Ind., 1971—, asso. prof. English, 1979—; continuing edn. cons. public schs. Mich. State U. fellow, 1950-54, 64-66. Mem. ALA, Nat. Council Tchrs. English, Children's Lit. Assn., Midwest Modern Lang. Assn., Phi Delta Kappa. Contbr. articles to profl. publs. Home: 4501 Wheeling St Muncie IN 47304 Office: 207 D English Bldg Ball State U Muncie IN 47306

PURNELL, JOHN HENRY OSCAR, mfg. co. exec.; b. Newark, Md., Feb. 28, 1946; s. Herbert and Alice (Richards) P.; M.S., U. Tenn., 1972; m. Sheila Long, May 24, 1968; children—Eric, Greg. Tng. coordinator Union Carbide, Oak Ridge, 1972-76, system and procedures specialist, 1976-78; corp. tng. and devel. mgr. Camcar-Textron, Rockford, Ill., 1978-79, corp. tng. and spl. program mgr., 1979—; cons. U. Tenn. Ednl. Opportunities Center. Mem. Am. Soc. Tng. and Devel. (Minority Network Trainer of Yr. award 1980, regional v.p. 1981-82), Winneabago County Opportunities Industrialization Center, Ill. Mfg. Assn., Pvt. Industry Council, Rockford C. of C. Methodist. Home: 6241 Legend Ln Rockford IL 61109 Office: 424 Eighteenth Ave Rockford IL 61101

PURSELL, CARL DUANE, Congressman; b. Plymouth, Mich., Dec. 19, 1932; B.A., Eastern Mich. U., 1957, M.A., 1962; LL.D. (hon.), Madonna Coll.; m. Peggy Jean Brown, 1956; children—Philip, Mark, Kathleen. Educator, small bus. owner; mem. Mich. Senate, 1971-76, mem. appropriations com.; mem. 95th and 97th Congresses from 2d Mich. Dist., mem. Edn. and Labor Com., Sci. and Tech. Com.; past mem. Mich. Crime Commn. Mem. Wayne County Bd. Commrs., 1960-70. Named Outstanding Young Man of Year Jr. C. of C., 1965; recipient Outstanding Environ. Legislator in Mich. award Fed. Environ. Protection Agy., 1976. Served as officer, inf., U.S. Army, 1957-59. Republican. Office: 1414 Longworth House Office Bldg Washington DC 20515*

PURVIS, DOROTHY LA RUE, telephone co. service adminstr.; b. Indpls., Sept. 20, 1934; d. Frank Edward and Alberta Kellem (Jessup) Simko; student Coll. St. Thomas, 1979; children—Dawn P. Jensen, Patricia La Rue Dumond, Wesley J. La Rue, Mark H. La Rue, Diane E. La Rue. Long distance telephone operator, 1951-63; sr. clk. network mgmt. Ind. Bell Telephone, Indpls., 1963-65, traffic engr., 1965-70; separations mgr. Continental Telephone, St. Paul, 1970-73, div. traffic engring. mgr., 1973-77, network services adminstr., 1977-78, network mgmt. center task force, 1979-80, div. network service adminstr., 1980—; active seminars in field. Women in Mgmt. cert. Coll. St. Catherine, 1978. Mem. Nat. Assn. Female Execs. Republican. Roman Catholic. Home: 10650 Brunswick Rd Bloomington MN 55438 Office: 6053 Hudson Rd Saint Paul MN 55119

PUTBRESE, CHARLES EDWARD, broadcast exec.; b. Auburn, Iowa, Aug. 24, 1931; s. Edward O. and Marjorie I. Putbrese; B.A., Drake U., 1953; M.A., Ball State U., 1973; m. Kay Kinley, Nov. 22, 1953; children—Steven, Kevin, Mark, Daniel, John, Heather, Keith. Commd. U.S. Air Force, 1954; chief Tech. Services div. Dist. 70 Hdqrs., Wiesbaden, Germany, 1970-74, asst. comdr., 1972-74; comdr. Dist. 33 Def. Investigative Service, Kansas City, Mo., 1974-75, ret., 1975; dir. operational surveys and analysis dept. Operational Systems, Inc., 1975-76; now pres. Norseman Broadcasting Corp. and gen. mgr. Sta. KWKY-AM, Des Moines. Mem. Crime Prevention and Law Enforcement Com., City of Des Moines. Decorated Meritorious Service medal, Air Force Commendation medal (3). Office: PO Box 662 Des Moines IA 50303

PUTH, JOHN WELLS, mfg. co. exec.; b. Orange, N.J., Mar. 14, 1929; s. Lenard G. and Elizabeth (Wells) P.; B.S. cum laude, Lehigh U., 1952; m. Betsey Leeds Tait, Mar. 1, 1952; children—David Wells, Jonathan Craig, Alison Leeds. With Purolator Products, Rahway, N.J., 1955-62; pres., dir. Bridgeport Hardware Mfg. Corp. (Conn.), 1962-65; v.p., div. gen. mgr. H.K. Porter Co., Inc., Pitts., 1965-72; pres., chief exec. officer Disston Inc., Pitts., 1972-75; pres., chief exec. officer, dir. Vapor Corp., Chgo., 1975—; dir. Clevite Imperial Co., Chgo., L.B. Foster Co., Pitts., Nihon Regulator, Japan, Central Nat. Bank, Chgo. Home: 180 De Windt Rd Winnetka IL 60093 Office: 5420 W Howard St Niles IL

PUTNAM, CLYDE CHARLES, JR., lawyer; b. Iowa City, June 30, 1911; s. Clyde C. and Clara F. (Rittenmeyer) P.; student U. Iowa, 1931; LL.B., Drake U., 1934; m. Dorothy Rolofson, May 5, 1946; children—Tom, Kim. Admitted to Iowa bar, 1934; partner Putnam, Putnam & Putnam, Des Moines, 1934—. Mem. Mayor's Com. Civil Def., Des Moines, 1958. Served with AUS, 1942-46. Mem. Internat. Assn. Ins. Counsel, Iowa Acad. Trial Lawyers, Iowa Def. Lawyers Assn., Iowa (bd. govs. 1972—, jud. nominating commn. 1968—), Polk County (pres. 1970-71) bar assns., Iowa Res. Officers Assn. (pres. 1949). Mason (Shriner). Home: 1919 56th St Des Moines IA 50310 Office: 940 Des Moines Bldg Des Moines IA 50309

PUTNAM, DAVID ARMS, computer co. exec.; b. Mpls., Mar. 31, 1937; s. Norcross and Ruth Ann (Vigoren) P.; B.S., Beloit Coll., 1959; M.S., U. Iowa, 1962; m. Karen Maria Nielsen, June 18, 1960; children—Steven, Jeffrey, Kenneth. Tchr. schs., Chgo. and Iowa City, Iowa, 1959-64; systems analyst Univac, 1964-65; mgr. design data processing Lear Siegler, Inc., Grand Rapids, Mich., 1965-68; v.p. L. and H. Computer Co., Chgo., 1968-70; dir. computer info. services U.S. League of Savs. Assns., Chgo., 1970-76; dir. data shops Systems Mgmt. Inc. (SMI), Chgo., 1976-78, v.p. mktg., 1978-80, chief exec. officer Roads, Inc., 1980—; tchr. computer sci. Roosevelt U., 1973; mem. nat. review bd. Nat. Home Study Council, 1973-74. Mem. Data Processing Mgmt. Assn., Soc. Certified Data Processers, Chgo. Assn. Commerce and Industry, Am. Soc. Assn. Execs. (affiliate), SAR. Author home study course Computer Programming Concepts, 1968. Creator BIO-CURVE R method of computerized biorhythmic analysis, 1971. Home: 6525 Taylor Dr Woodridge IL 60515 Office: 20301 Ventura Blvd Woodland Hills CA 91364

PUTZIER, JOHN LEONARD NEWELL, chem. mfg. co. ofcl.; b. Canton, Ohio, May 21, 1951; s. Jack Henry and Gwendolyn Iverne (Hicks) P.; B.S.I.M., U. Akron, 1973; m. Kathryn Marie Ann Munka, Nov. 12, 1976. Sr. asst. mgr. Household Fin. Corp., Ravenna, Ohio, 1973-75; fin. analyst examiner I div. banks U.S. Dept. Commerce, Columbus, Ohio, 1975; clk.-treas. Woodridge Bd. Edn., Cuyahoga Falls, Ohio, 1975-76; communications, community relations PPG Industries Inc., Barberton, Ohio, 1976-77, coordinator labor relations, 1977-78, mgr. employment, 1978-80, mgr. employee benefits adminstrn., 1980-81, mgr. benefits and salary adminstrn., gen. office, Pitts., 1981—. Account rep. Nat. Alliance of Businessmen, 1976-77; adviser Jr. Achievement Greater Akron, 1977-79, Mem. Am. Soc. Personnel Adminstrn. (dir.-at-large 1978-80, sec., 1981, v.p., 1982; adv. U. Akron student chpt. 1978-79), Beta Gamma Sigma; Internat. Wildlife Fedn., Medina County Humane Soc. Club: City (Pitts.). Home: 232 Baldwin St Wadsworth OH 44281 Office: PPG Industries Inc One Gateway Center Pittsburgh PA 15222

PUYEAR, ROBERT BREWER, chem. co. exec.; b. Cape Girardeau, Mo., Aug. 21, 1932; s. Hugh Gates and Isabel (Brewer) P.; B.S.Ch.E., Mo. Sch. Mines, 1954; M.S. in Indsl. Adminstrn., Purdue U., 1967; m. Donna G. Timmons, Feb. 14, 1960; children—Jill B., Timothy H., Sue Ellen. Engr., Union Carbide Corp., Kokomo, Ind., 1954-55, 57-61, group leader, 1961-67, product mgr., coatings service dept., Bethel, Conn., 1967-68, Indpls., 1969; materials specialist Monsanto Co., St. Louis, 1970-71, supt. materials engring., 1971-74, mgr. materials technology sect., 1974—. Served with C.E., AUS, 1955-57. Registered profl. engr., Mo., Calif. Mem. Materials Technology Inst. (co-founder, 1st chmn., dir.), Nat. Assn. Corrosion Engrs., Am. Inst. Chem. Engrs., Am. Soc. Metals, Am. Mgmt. Assn. Methodist. Patentee oxidation-resistant coatings. Home: 226 River Valley Dr Chesterfield MO 63017 Office: 800 N Lindbergh Blvd St Louis MO 63166

PYEATT, JOHN SAMUEL, owner lumber co.; b. Denver, Apr. 1, 1931; s. John Samuel and Myra Syrena (Loy) P.; B.S. in Engring., Princeton U., 1952; M.S. in Engring., Lehigh U., 1953; m. Nancy K. Davis, Apr. 27, 1957; children—John, Katherine. Plant supt. Monsanto Chem. Co., Long Beach, Calif., 1957-60, process engr., Springfield, Mass., 1960-61; owner, operator Coerper Lumber Co., Milw., 1961—, Brookfield Lumber Co. (Wis.), 1974—. Served with C.E., USNR, 1953-57. Mem. Wis. Retail Lumbermen's Assn. Republican. Episcopalian. Clubs: Wis.; Hoo Hoo (pres. 1968) (Milw.). Home: N 93 W 15048 Hillside Ln Menomonee Falls WI 53051 Office: Coerper Lumber Co 2161 N 30th St Milwaukee WI 53208

PYLE, BEATRICE ALZIRA, educator; b. West Chester, Pa., May 21, 1922; d. Norman James and Audrey (Dilks) Pyle; B.S., Gettysburg Coll., 1944; M.S. in Hygiene and Phys. Edn., Wellesley Coll., 1946; certificate U. Oslo, 1960. Instr. Gettysburg Coll., 1938-40, Vassar Coll., 1946-52; tchr. pub. schs., Winnetka, Ill., 1952-57; asso. prof. phys. and health edn. Miami U., Oxford, Ohio, 1957—. Mem. Am. Pub. Health Assn., Royal Soc. Health Can. and Eng., Nat., Ohio edn. assns., AAHPER (coordinator aquatic insts. for aquatic council), Ohio Coll. Assn., Am. Camping Assn., AAUW, Ohio, Midwest assns. health, phys. edn. and recreation. Author: Small Craft: An Instructional Textbook for Teachers; Anatomy Handbook; Kinesiology Laboratory Manual. Home: 119 N Campus Ave Oxford OH 45056

PYLE, GEORGE WALTER, city mgr.; b. Morrill, Kans., Mar. 20, 1927; s. George Vernon and Nellie Ellen (Bundy) P.; B.A., U. Kans., 1948; m. Donna May Bower, Sept. 6, 1953; children—George B., Eric A., Christopher E., Mary Lynn. Adminstrv. asst. City of Kansas City, Mo., 1952-57; city mgr., McCook, Nebr., 1957-67; city mgr., Hutchinson, Kans., 1967—. Mem. Internat. City Mgmt. Assn., League Kans. Municipalities (dir. 1974-75), League Kansas Municipalities (v.p. 1979-80, pres. 1981—), Kans. Assn. City Mgrs. (pres., dir. 1973-74). Home: 112 W 19th St Hutchinson KS 67501 Office: 125 East Ave B Hutchinson KS 67501

PYUN, SEONG KYUN, obstetrician, gynecologist; b. Seoul, Korea, Sept. 23, 1938; s. Woo Chang and Chung (Sook) P.; came to U.S., 1964, naturalized, 1976; M.D., Yonsei U. Coll. Medicine, 1964; m. Boo Whan Oh, Oct. 30, 1964; 2 daus., Jean, Sandra. Intern, Euclid (Ohio) Gen. Hosp., 1965; resident in obstetrics and gynecology Wayne State U., Detroit, 1966-70; fellow dept. pathology Hutzel Hosp., Detroit, 1971; program dir. St. Joseph Mercy Hosp., Detroit, 1971-73; practice medicine specializing in obstetrics and gynecology, St. Clair, Mich., 1973—; pres. profl. corp. Diplomate Am. Bd. Obstetricians and Gynecologists. Fellow Am. Coll. Obstetricians and Gynecologists; mem. AMA, St. Clair County, Mich. State med. socs., Mich. Soc. Obstetricians and Gynecologists. Club: Rotary (St. Clair). Home: 200 Hawthorne St Saint Clair MI 48079 Office: 132 Trumbull Saint Clair MI 48079

QUAAL, WARD LOUIS, broadcasting exec.; b. Ishpeming, Mich., Apr. 7, 1919; s. Sigfred Emil and Alma Charlotte (Larson) Q.; A.B., U. Mich., 1941; LL.D., Mundelein Coll., 1962, No. Mich. U., 1967, DePaul U., 1974; D. Pub. Service (hon.), Elmhurst Coll., 1967; L.H.D., Lincoln Coll., 1968; m. Dorothy Graham, Mar. 9, 1944; children—Graham Ward, Jennifer Anne. Announcer, writer radio station WDMJ, Marquette, Mich., 1936-37; announcer, writer, producer WJR, Detroit, 1937-41; spl. events announcer-producer WGN, Chgo., 1941-42, asst. to gen. mgr., 1945-49; exec. dir. Clear Channel Broadcasting Service, Washington, 1949-52; asst. gen. mgr. Crosley Broadcasting Corp., Cin., 1952, v.p., asst. gen. mgr., 1953-56; v.p., gen. mgr. WGN, Inc., Chgo., 1956-61, exec. v.p., pres., 1961-74; chmn. bd. United Telecom Corp., 1974—; pres. Ward L. Quaal Co., 1974—; dir. Christine Valmy, Inc., Universal Resources Corp.; dir. WLW Radio, Inc., also chmn. exec. com.; pres., chief exec. officer Clear Channel Broadcasting Service, 1964-74; bd. dirs. Assn. Maximum Service Telecasters, Inc., 1954-73. Chmn. exec. com. Council for TV Devel., 1969-73; bd. dirs. Broadcasters Found.; bd. dirs. Chgo. Better Bus. Bur., chmn., 1964-67; pres., dir. Broadcast Pioneers, 1962-63; bd. dirs. Farm Found., 1960-72; chmn. exec. com., dir., vice chmn. Research and Edn. Found., also nat. gov., immediate past chmn. Assn. Better Bus. Burs. Internat.; bd. dirs. Sears, Roebuck Found., 1970-74, Internat. Radio and TV Found.; mem. ethics com. Am. Advt. Fedn.; mem. bd. control collegiate athletics U. Mich.; trustee Mundelein Coll., 1964-72, Hillsdale (Mich.) Coll., 1968-72. Served as lt. USNR, 1942-45. Recipient Distinguished Alumnus award U. Mich., 1967; Washington honor medal Freedoms Found. Valley Forge, 1969, 71, 72; named Broadcast Man of Year, 1968; Chgo. Advt. Club Man of Year, 1969; Ill. Broadcaster of Year, Ill. Broadcasters Assn., 1973; recipient Distinguished Service award Nat. Assn. Broadcasters, 1973; Outstanding Achievement in Field of Communications award Brandeis U., 1973; Advt. Man of Year Golden medallion Chgo. Advt. Club, 1969; named Communicator of Year, Jewish United Fund; recipient Key to Loyola, Loyola U., Chgo., 1971; named to Better Bus. Bur. Hall of Fame, 1975. Mem. Delta Tau Delta. Clubs: Mid-Am. (Chgo.); Lakeside Country (Hollywood, Calif.); Bankers (San Francisco); El Niguel Country (South Laguna, Calif.); Kenwood Golf and Country, Internat. (Washington); Exmoor Country; Marco Polo (N.Y.C.). Author: (with Leo A. Martin) Broadcast Management, 1968, (with James A. Brown) 2d edit., 1976. Home: 1706 Northfield Sq Northfield IL 60093 Office: Suite 370 O'Hare Plaza 5725 E River Rd Chicago IL 60631

QUADER, ATHER A., research engr.; b. Hyderabad, India, Oct. 10, 1941; s. A. Taher M. A. and Saeed Linissa (Begun) Kader; B.E. in Mech. Engring., Osmania (India) U., 1962; Ph.D. in Mech. Engring., U. Wis., 1969; m. M. J. Parveen, Mar. 26, 1968; children—Sameena, Salmaan. Research asst. U. Wis., 1963—; asso. sr. research engr. Gen. Motors Research Labs., Warren, Mich., 1968-74, sr. research engr., 1974—, now staff research engr. Recipient Horning Meml. award Soc. Automotive Engrs., 1974, Arch T. Colwell award, 1976, award for excellence in oral presentation, 1976, 78. Mem. Soc. Automotive Engrs. (readers com., Horning Meml. Award bd.), AAAS, Combustion Inst. Office: Gen Motors Research Labs Warren MI 48090*

QUALLY, ROBERT LEE, communications co. exec., graphic designer, filmmaker; b. Denver, Aug. 24, 1947; s. Ebner Milton and Alberta (Jackson) Q.; A.A., Northeastern Jr. Coll., 1970; B.F.A., Colo. State U., 1972. Partner, Quill Images, Fort Collins, Colo., 1970-72; sr. designer Salesvertising, Inc., Denver, 1972-74; design dir. Stephens, Biondi, DeCicco, Chgo., 1974; v.p., creative dir., producer Lee King & Partners, Inc., Chgo., N.Y.C., Los Angeles, 1974-79; pres., creative dir. Qually & Co., Inc., Evanston, Ill., Chgo., 1979—. Served with USNG, 1968-74. Recipient Clio awards in design, art direction, producing and writing; Gold medal Art Dirs. Club. Mem. Am. Inst. Graphic Arts (medal), Soc. Typographic Art, Indsl. Graphics Internat., Chgo. Advt. Club, Chgo. Soc. Communication Arts, Colo. State U. Alumni Assn. (life). Republican. Club: Chgo. Athletic Assn. Author: 8 1/2" x 11", The Story of a Graphic Designer, 1980; patentee in field. Office: 2238 Central St Evanston IL 60201

QUANDT, DANIEL JON, assn. exec.; b. Fargo, N.D., Oct. 13, 1952; s. Werner F. and Grace H. (Hjelmstad) Q.; B.A. in Broadcast Journalism, U. N.D., 1976; m. Kyle R. Knutson, June 21, 1975; 1 dau., Erin Ruth. Asst. prodn. mgr., camera operator Sta. KTHI-TV, Grand Forks, 1972-74, news dir., 1977-81; dir. Grand Forks Conv. and Visitors Bur., 1981—; anchorman U. N.D. TV news, 1974, producer, dir., news dir., 1974-75, student news asst. Office of Univ. Relations 1975-76, staff announcer Sta KFJM, 1976; cons. in field. Lic. 3d class radiotelephone operator, FCC. Mem. Nat. Press Photographers Assn., U.S. Jaycees, Sigma Delta Chi. Lutheran. Clubs: Eagles, Elks. Home: 1418 13th Ave S Apt 1 Grand Forks ND 58201 Office: PO Box 1177 Grand Forks ND 58201

QUANDT, DAVID MYLO, mech. engr.; b. Mpls., Aug. 9, 1946; s. Werner Frank and Grace H. (Hjelmstad) Q.; grad. St. Luke's Sch. Radiol. Tech., Fargo, N.D., 1968; B.S. in M.E., N.D. State U., 1971; m. Kristine Knutson, June 30, 1973; children—Brett David, Erik Todd. Sales engr. Schilling Trane, Indpls., 1972-73; project engr. Meridian Trane, Indpls., 1973-74, Paul R. Hosler, Inc., Indpls., 1974-75; project mgr. Stanley Cons., Inc., Indpls., 1976-81; dir. mktg. P.R. Duke Constrn. Co., Inc., Indpls., 1981—. Councilman, Messiah Lutheran Ch., 1976—. Served with USAR, 1970-76. Registered profl. engr., Ind., Ky., Ohio; registered technician Am. Registry Radiol. Technologists. Mem. ASME, Nat., Ind. socs. profl. engrs., Profl. Engrs. in Constrn. (chmn.). Home: 517 Marstella Dr Brownsburg IN 46112 Office: 5455 W 86 St Indianapolis IN 46268

QUANSTROM, ROY FRED, coll. adminstr., clergyman; b. Gary, Ind., Mar. 4, 1934; s. Roy Fred and Isabella Mary (Ulrich) Q.; A.B. in Math., Eastern Nazarene Coll., 1956; M.A. in Religion, Olivet Nazarene Coll., 1969; m. Shirley Ann Martin, June 11, 1954; children—Mark Roy, Joan Ardath, Stephen Roy, Lynne Renee. Computer programmer Chrysler Missile Corp., Detroit, 1956-58; systems programmer Ford Motor Co., Dearborn, Mich., 1958-60; systems engr. IBM, Cleve., 1960-64; ordained to ministry Ch. of the Nazarene, 1967; pastor chs., Avon Lake, Ohio, 1960-64, Brookfield, Ill., 1964-70, Pontiac, Mich., 1970-73, Port Huron, Mich., 1973-77; dir. devel. and admissions Olivet Nazarene Coll., 1977—. Mem. Nazarene Devel. Officers Assn. (chmn. 1980), Am. Assn. Collegiate Registrars and Admissions Officers. Contbr. articles to religious jours. Home: 649 Olde Oak Bourbonnais IL 60914 Office: Olivet Nazarene Coll Kankakee IL 60901

QUAYLE, DAN, senator; b. Indpls., Feb. 4, 1947; s. James C. and Corinne (Pulliam) Q.; B.A. in Polit. Sci., DePauw U., Greencastle, Ind., 1969; postgrad. Ind. U. Law Sch., 1970-74. m. Marilyn Tucker, Nov. 18, 1972; children—Tucker Danforth, Benjamin Eugene, Mary Corinne. Admitted to Ind. bar, 1974. Ct. reporter, pressman Huntington (Ind.) Herald-Press, 1965-69, asso. pub., gen. mgr., 1974-76; mem. Consumer Protection div. Atty. Gen.'s Office, 1970-71; adminstrv. asst. to Gov. Edgar Whitcomb, 1971-73; dir. Ind. Inheritance Tax Div., 1973-74; mem. 95th-97th Congresses from 4th Ind. Dist.; tchr. bus. law Huntington Coll., 1975. Mem. Assn. Retarded Citizens. Mem. Ind., Huntington bar assns., Ft. Wayne Press Club, Hoosier State Press Assn., Huntington C. of C. Club: Rotary. Home: 7 N Jefferson St Huntington IN 46750 Office: 254 Russell Senate Office Bldg Washington DC 20510

QUAYLE, VIRGINIA WINGET, educator; b. Monroe, Utah, Jan. 11, 1927; d. Elmer and Florence S. (Wilson) Winget; B.S., Utah State U., 1949; M.A., U. Wis., 1972; m. Calvin King Quayle, Aug. 5, 1949; children—Susanne, Pamela, Gordon Calvin. Clk., typist, registrar's office Utah State U., Logan, 1949-50; receptionist Latter-day Saints Hosp. and Residence Halls, Madison, Wis., 1950-51; instr. English, librarian Fall Creek (Wis.) High Sch., 1966; instr., head, communication dept. Dist. One Tech. Inst., Eau Claire, Wis. 1966—. Mem. Am. Vocat. Assn., Internat. Listening Assn., Wis. Communication Assn. Mormon. Author: Individualized Composition, 1976; (with Judy Rice) Effective Listening, 1981. Home: 3756 Halsey St Eau Claire WI 54701 Office: District One Technical Institute Clairemont Ave Eau Claire WI 54701

QUEEN, DANIEL, cons. elec. engr.; b. Boston, Feb. 15, 1934; s. Simon and Ida (Droker) Q.; student U. Chgo., 1951-54; m. Helen Pantazopoulos, Mar. 23, 1957; 1 son, Aaron Jacob. Quality control mgr. Magnacord, Inc., Chgo., 1955-57; project engr. Revere Camera Co., Chgo., 1957-62; dir. engring. for Amplivox products Perma Power Co., Chgo., 1962-70; prin. engr. Daniel Queen Assos., Chgo., 1970—, pres. Daniel Queen Labs., Inc., 1980—; chmn. Am. Nat. Standards Subcom. PH 7-6, mem. com. PH-7; mem. standards com. P8-5 Electronic Industries Assn. Bus. mgr. 5300-5500 Gladys Block Club, Chgo., 1970—. Fellow Audio Engring. Soc.; mem. IEEE (sr.), Am. Nat. Standards Inst. (sec. S-4 com., mem. PH-7 com.), Audio Engring. Soc. (chmn. papers, U.S. convs. 1980), Acoustical Soc. Am. (chmn. Chgo. regional chpt. 1976-78, mem. engring. acoustics com.) Midwest Acoustics Conf. (pres. 1971-72), Chgo. Acoustical and Audio Group (pres. 1969-70), Assn. Ednl. Communications and Tech., Soc. Motion Picture and TV Engrs. (mem. audio rec. and reprodn. com.), ASTM, AAAS, Catgut Acoustic Soc. Contbr. papers to profl. jours., also articles to trade and popular mags.; editorial bd. Jour. Audio Engring. Soc., 1978—. Address: 5524 W Gladys Ave Chicago IL 60644

QUEZADA-DIAMONDSTEIN, MARIA DEL SOCORRO, polit. scientist; b. Loma Linda, Calif., Sept. 16, 1949; d. Jose Ramiro Quezada M. and Margarita Medrano de Quezada; teaching degree Instituto Pedagogico de Chihuahua (Mex.), 1967; B.A., U. Tex., Austin, 1970; postgrad. Sorbonne, Paris, 1971, Sophia U., Tokyo, 1973; M.A. in Polit. Sci., U. Tex., El Paso, 1977; postgrad. U. Chgo., 1979—; m. Bert M. Diamondstein, Aug. 11, 1978; 1 dau., Socorro Mayuko. Coordinator, lectr. workshops in social scis. and humanities Centro de Estudios Generales, Chihuahua, 1971-72; import-export supr. Admiral Corp. Am., Ciudad Juarez, Mex., 1974-75; instr. polit. sci. U. Tex., El Paso, 1975-78, El Paso Community Coll., 1978; asst. survey dir. III, Nat. Opinion Research Center, U. Chgo., 1979—; also condr. workshops; asst. to pres. U. Autonoma de Chihuahua, 1971-72; prodn.-mktg. researcher Duraplay de Parral, 1973-74; mem. nat. Chicano research network Inst. for Social Research, U. Mich., 1980—. Recipient prize for oil painting Banco Comercial Mexicano Ann. Art Exhbn., 1968; U. Calif., San Diego grantee, 1978. Mem. Latin Am. Studies Assn., Pi Sigma Alpha. Roman Catholic. Office: 6030 S Ellis Ave Chicago IL 60637

QUICK, GUY HAYDEN, ins. co. exec.; b. Crawfordsville, Ind., May 4, 1920; s. Guy Hayden and Helen Naomi (Eltzroth) Q.; student Ill. State U., 1938-41; m. Martha Malinda March, Nov. 6, 1942; children—Guy Hayden, III, Jeffry March, Jean Marie. Joined Chem. Corps, U.S. Army, 1942, commd. 2d lt., Ordnance Corps, 1943, advanced through grades to lt. col., 1962; faculty Army Bomb Disposal Sch., 1943-46; bomb disposal officer JTF-1, Bikini atomic bomb tests, 1946; asso. prof. mil. sci. Hofstra Coll., Hempstead, N.Y., 1951-55; sr. ammunition advisor Republic of Korea Army, 1955-57; ops. officer, insp. gen.'s office Def. Atomic Support Agy., Sandia Base, N.Mex., 1957-59; chief tech. inspection div., insp. gen.'s office Hdqrs. U.S. Army Pacific, Ft. Shafter, Hawaii, 1959-63, ret., 1963; with Fireman's Fund Ins. Cos., St. Louis, 1964-70, Davenport, Iowa, 1970-73, Detroit, 1973—, mgr. loss control depts., 1970—; mem. Mayor's Explosive Safety Commn., Florissant, Mo., 1968-70; pres. Scott County (Iowa) Safety Council, 1972-73; bd. dirs., recruiting chmn. Mich. Safety Conf. Cert. safety profl.; registered profl. engr., Calif. Mem. Am. Soc. Safety Engrs. (profl. mem.; pres. chpt. 1978-79), Vets. of Safety, Nat. Safety Mgmt. Soc., Nat. Fire Protection Assn., Nat. Safety Council, Ret. Officers Assn., Am. Def. Preparedness Assn., Am. Assn. Ret. Persons, System Safety Soc., Mil. Order World Wars, Nat. Assn. Watch and Clock Collectors. Home: 31207 Kendall St Livonia MI 48154 Office: 23777 Greenfield Rd Southfield MI 48075

QUICK, WILLIAM KELLON, clergyman; b. Marlborough County, S.C., May 20, 1933; s. Douglas and Virginia S. (Stubbs) Q.; A.A., Pfeiffer Coll., 1952; B.A., Randolph-Macon Coll. for Men, 1954; M.Div., Duke U., 1958; D.D., Pfeiffer Coll., 1972; m. Barbara Elizabeth Campbell, Jan. 8, 1955; children—Stephen Kellon, Kathryn Elizabeth, David Christopher, Paul Sanders. Ordained to ministry Methodist Ch., 1956; asso. pastor Broad St. Meth. Ch., Richmond, Va., 1952-54, Camp Glenn, Morehead City, N.C., 1954-55; pastor Bahama Circuit, 1955-59, First Meth. Ch., Zebulon, N.C., 1959-63, St. James Meth. Ch., Greenville, N.C., 1963-69, Trinity Meth. Ch., Durham, N.C., 1969-74; sr. minister Met. United Meth. Ch., Detroit, 1974—. Trustee, Louisburg Coll., 1962-70, Meth. Coll., 1970-76, Scarritt Coll., Nashville, 1978-80, Adrian Coll., 1980—; mem. Gov's Good Neighbor Council, N.C., 1965-69, chmn. Pitt County, N.C., 1967-69; mem. Durham County Reorganizational Com., 1971-73; mem. Internat. Freedom Festival Com., 1978-81; bd. dirs. New Center Area Council, Detroit, 1979—; host Open Doors, Sta. WDIV-TV, 1978—. Named Outstanding Young Man of Yr., Zebulon Record, 1959; recipient Disting. Alumnus award Pfeiffer Coll., 1968, Disting. Service award Center City Ch. Council, 1974. Mem. Nat. Meth. TV Presence and Ministry, 1980-84; mem. exec. com., program com. World Meth. Council, 1976-86; mem. exec. com. Nat. Meth. Bicentennial Com., 1981-84; v.p. Gen. Commn. on Communications, 1980-84; mem. exec. com. Contact Teleministries Am., Inc., 1980—; mem. exec. com. Christian Communication Council Met. Detroit, 1976-82. Democrat. Methodist. Clubs: Downtown Rotary, Economic, Athletic (Detroit). Contbr. articles in field to profl. jours. Home: 18450 Scarsdale Rd Detroit MI 48223 Office: 8000 Woodward Ave Detroit MI 48202

QUIE, ALBERT HAROLD, gov. Minn.; b. nr. Dennison, Minn., Sept. 18, 1923; s. Albert K. and Nettie (Jacobson) Q.; B.A. in Polit. Sci., St. Olaf Coll., 1950; hon. degrees St. Olaf Coll., Gordon Coll., Greenville Coll., Gettysburg Coll., Buena Vista Coll., Capital U., Gallaudet Coll.; m. Gretchen Hansen, June 5, 1948; children—Fredric, Jennifer, Daniel, Joel, Benjamin. Dairy Farmer; mem. Minn. Senate, 1955, 57; mem. 85th-95th Congresses from 1st Minn. dist.; mem. com. edn. and labor, standards of ofcl. conduct com.; gov. Minn., 1979—. Past soil conservation dist. dir. Named Young Man of Year, Minn. Jr. C. of C., 1957; recipient Disting. Alumni award St. Olaf Coll.; Legis. Statesmanship award Council Exceptional Children; Ann. award Nat. Council Local Adminstrs.; citation Am. Vocat. Assn.; Distinguished Govt. award Minn. Speech and Hearing Assn., others; named Distinguished Citizen of Agr., Nat. Milk Producers Fedn., 1974. Republican. Home: Dennison MN 55018 Office: Gov's Office 130 State Capitol Saint Paul MN 55155

QUIGG, DONALD DAVID, sales exec.; b. Quincy, Ill., Mar. 11, 1947; s. Charles Leroy and Laura Kay (Bower) Q.; student Culver-Stockton Coll., 1965-66; B.S., Quincy Coll., 1969. Salesman, Selby Implement Co., Inc., Quincy, 1972-73; expediter Broadcast Products div. Harris Corp., Quincy, 1974-76; comml. applicator field crops pest control, dist. mgr. Nachurs Plant Food Co., Mendon, Ill., 1976—; distbr. Conklin Co., Inc., Mendon, 1979—. Assessor, Mendon Twp. (Ill.), 1978—. Served with Army N.G., 1970. Mem. Smithsonian Assos., Nat. Rifle Assn., Twp. Ofcls. of Ill., Unity Jaycees (pres.). Democrat. Lutheran. Clubs: Meyer Gun and Boat, Mendon Lions. Home and office: Rural Route 2 Mendon IL 62351

QUIGGLE, LYNN KAY WUTSCHKE, psychotherapist; b. Northfield, Minn., Dec. 18, 1951; d. Kenneth Earl and Patricia Ruth (Bailey) Wutschke; B.A. magna cum laude, U. Minn., 1973, M.S.W., 1977; m. Scott S. Quiggle, July 28, 1973. Psychiat. social worker No. Community Mental Health Center, Ashland, Wis., 1977-79; psychotherapist Human Devel. Center, Duluth, Minn., 1980—; lectr. on family and individual dynamics, condr. workshops and seminars on personal growth, stress mgmt. Mem. Women's Network, Northwoods Women (co-founder), NOW. Home: 2332 Jefferson St Duluth MN 55812 Office: 1401 E 1st St Duluth MN 55805

QUINN, CHARLES LEWIS, judge; b. Garrett, Ind., Dec. 23, 1941; s. Franklin Charles and Goldie Ellen (Lewis) Q.; A.B., Manchester Coll., 1964; J.D., Ind. U., 1967. Admitted to Ind. bar, 1967, U.S. Supreme Ct. bar, 1973; mem. legal dept. Midwestern United Life Ins. Co., Fort Wayne, 1967-69; law clk. Allen Superior Ct., Fort Wayne, 1969; mem. firm Smith & Quinn, Auburn, Ind., 1969-75; judge Garrett (Ind.) City Ct., 1974-75, DeKalb County Ct., Auburn, Ind., 1976-77, DeKalb Superior Ct., Auburn, 1977—; DeKalb County examiner for com. on character and fitness Ind. Bd. Law Examiners. State chmn. Ind. Young Republicans, 1973-75; chmn. adminstrv. bd. Garrett United Meth. Ch., 1977-79; trustee Garrett Library, 1974-79, Auburn Community Theatre; mem. exec. com. No. Ind. Health Systems Agy., Inc., 1974-78. Recipient Bronze and Silver medallions N.E. Ind. Heart Fund Drive; bd. dirs. Big Bros. and Sisters N.E. Ind., 1974-75. Mem. Ind. Judges Assn. DeKalb County (past pres.), Am. Bar Assn., Nat. Trust Historic Preservation, Auburn C. of C. (pres. 1973-74), Manchester Coll. and Ind. U. Alumni assns. Republican. Methodist. Clubs: Masons, Scottish Rite. Home: 718 N Main St Auburn IN 46706 Office: Court House Auburn IN 46706

QUINN, CHRISTINE AGNES, radiologist; b. Cleve., Sept. 23, 1946; d. Paul Leo and Estelle Christine Quinn; B.A., Marquette U., 1967; M.D., Med. Coll. Pa., 1971; m. Paul C. Janicki, July 11, 1970; 1 dau., Sarah Christine. Intern, St. Luke's Hosp., Cleve., 1971-72; resident in diagnostic radiology Cleve. Clinic Found., 1972-75, radiologist, 1975—. Diplomate Am. Bd. Radiology. Mem. Radiol. Soc. N.Am., Am. Coll. Radiology, Soc. Nuclear Medicine, Ohio, Cuyahoga County med. socs., AMA. Contbr. to CRC Handbook Series, Vol. II, 1977; contbr. articles to profl. jours. Home: 2436 Loyola Rd University Heights OH 44118 Office: Cleveland Clinic Foundation 9500 Euclid Ave Cleveland OH 44106

QUINN, ROBERT WESLEY, JR., investment co. exec.; b. Newark, Feb. 22, 1948; s. Robert Wesley and Elizabeth Francis (Campbell) Q.; B.A., Baldwin Wallace Coll., 1970; m. Cynthia Gail MacLeod, Sept. 6, 1969; children—Scott MacLeod, Brian Campbell, Elizabeth Allen. Investment officer Banker Trust Co., N.Y.C., 1971-73; mcpl. specialist Smith Barney & Co., N.Y.C., 1974; investment officer Central Nat. Bank, Cleve., 1974-75; pres., chief ops. officer Gelfand, Quinn & Assos., Inc., Cleve., 1975—. Active Bus. in Action; mem. fundraising com. Cleve. Orch. Served with USN, 1968-71. Mem. Cleve. Soc. Security Analysts, N.E. Ohio Fin. Mgrs. Soc. Republican. Presbyterian. Club: Shaker Heights Country. Home: 17712 Berwyn Rd Shaker Heights OH 44120 Office: Leader Bldg Cleveland OH

QUINN, WILLIAM JOHN, lawyer, coll. adminstr.; b. St. Paul, May 8, 1911; s. William J. and Celina (LaRocque) Q.; B.A., St. Thomas Coll., 1933, LL.D. (hon.), 1959; LL.B., U. Minn., 1935; m. Floy Isabelle Heinen, July 2, 1942; children—William J., George, Patrick, Richard, Floy, Maureen, Michaele, Shannon. Admitted to Minn. bar, 1935; individual practice law, St. Paul, 1935-37; asst. U.S. atty. Dist. Minn., 1937-40; atty. Soo Line R.R., Mpls., 1940-42, asst. commerce counsel, 1945, commerce counsel, 1945-52, asst. gen. counsel, 1952, gen. counsel, 1952-54, v.p., 1953-54; spl. agt. FBI, 1942-45; gen. solicitor Chgo., Milw., St. Paul & Pacific R.R. Co., 1954-55, v.p., gen. counsel, 1955-58, pres., 1958-66; pres., chief exec. officer Chgo., Burlington & Quincy R.R., Chgo., 1966-70; chmn, chief exec. officer Chgo. Milw., St. Paul & Pacific R.R. Co., 1970-78; vice chmn. Burlington No., Inc., 1970; pres., chmn. Chgo. Milw. Corp., 1972-78; dir. Clow Corp., Nat. R.R. Pass Corp. Chmn. bd. trustees Loyola U. Chgo., 1978—; bd. dirs. St. Francis Hosp., Evanston, Ill.; mem. adv. council Coll. Bus. Adminstrn., U. Notre Dame; bd. dirs. Catholic Charities, Chgo.; mem. exec. bd. Chgo. council Boy Scouts Am.; trustee Coll. St. Thomas; trustee emeritus Nat. Jewish Hosp. Mem. Am. Bar Assn., Minn. Bar Assn., Hennepin County Bar Assn., Ill. Bar Assn., Chgo. Bar Assn., Chgo. Assn. Commerce and Industry. Clubs: Econ., Execs., Comml., Chgo., Mid-Day, Mid-Am., Skokie Country. Office: 111 Washington St Chicago IL 60602

QUINT, JUNE KISER, public schs. bus. mgr.; b. Hancock County, Ill., July 29, 1922; d. Claude E. and Hazel S. (Schaad) Kiser; student Gem City Coll., 1940-41, Parkland Coll., 1971-72, Ill. State U., 1973-74. Civil Service clk. Chanute AFB, Ill., 1942-47; sec., office mgr. Rantoul (Ill.) City Schs., 1947-65, bus. mgr., legis. coordinator, 1965—. Exec. trustee Ill. Mcpl. Retirement Fund, 1970-76, v.p., 1975-76; nat. sec. Impact Area Schs., 1972; mem. data processing adv. com. Office of Supt. Public Instrn., Ill., 1973-76; governing bd. Regional Ednl. Data Info. Coop., 1974-78. Named Business Woman, Mo. Bus. and Profl. Women, 1973; Ill. Ednl. Adminstr. of Yr., 1980. Mem. Nat. Secs. Assn. (state pres. 1961-62), Ill. Assn. Ednl. Secs., Ill. Assn. Sch. Bus. Ofcls. (legis. com. 1973-75, Assn. Sch. Bus. Ofcls. of U.S., Nat. Assn. Sch. Affiliates (dir. 1971-74), Nat. Assn. Fed. Impacted Schs. (pres. 1980-81), Epsilon Sigma Alpha. Republican. Home: 624 E Sangamon Ave Rantoul IL 61866 Office: 400 E Wabash Ave Rantoul IL 61866

QUINTANILLA, ANTONIO PAULET, physician, educator; b. Peru, Feb. 8, 1927; s. Leandro Marino and Edel Paulet Q.; came to U.S., 1963, naturalized, 1974; Ph.D., San Marcos U., 1948, M.D., 1957; m. Mary Parker Rodriguez, May 2, 1958; children—Antonio Paulet, Angela, Francis, Cecilia, John. Asso. prof. physiology U. Arequipa, Peru, 1960-63; asso. in physiology Cornell U., N.Y., 1963-64; prof. physiology U. Arequipa, 1964-68; asso. prof. medicine Northwestern U., 1969-80, prof., 1980—; chief renal sect. VA Lakeside Hosp., 1976—; mem. adv. bd. Kidney Found. Ill., Am. Fedn. Clin. Research. Fellow A.C.P.; mem. Chgo. Heart Assn. (hypertension council), Central Soc. Clin. Research, Am. Soc. Clin. Pharmacology and Therapeutics, Am., Internat. socs. nephrology, Chgo. Soc. Internal Medicine. Contbr. articles on renal disease to med. jours.; also chpts. in books. Home: 500 Ridge Ave Evanston IL 60202 Office: 333 E Huron St Chicago IL 60611

QUITMEIER, NANCY EILEEN, occupational therapist; b. Des Moines, Nov. 10, 1951; d. Daniel Raymond and Jane Thompson (Pettengill) Wessling; B.S. with highest distinction in Occupational Therapy, U. Kans., 1975; m. William Michael Quitmeier, Dec. 29, 1973; 1 dau., Lesley Michelle. Occupational therapy aide Menorah Med. Center, Kansas City, Mo., 1974-75; in-patient occupational therapist Tri-County Community Mental Health Center, North Kansas City, Mo., 1975-80, community placement program occupational therapist, 1980—; cons. in field. Mem. Am. Occupational Therapy Assn., Mo. Occupational Therapy Assn., Kans. Occupational Therapy Assn. Office: 2900 Hospital Dr North Kansas City MO 64116

QUO, PHILLIP C., engring. co. exec., educator; b. Fukien, China, Oct. 4, 1930; came to U.S., 1955, naturalized, 1974; m. Consuelo Yao, Aug. 5, 1932; children—Marcia Ann, Stacey Dagmar, Geoffrey Quintin, Brian Christopher; LL.B., J.D., Nat. Amoy (China) U., 1949; B.S. in Mech. Engring., U. Kans., 1960, M.S. in Mech. Engring., 1965. Mech. designer, power plant div. Black and Veatch Cons. Engrs., Kansas City, Mo., 1960-64, project engr., 1964-66; lectr. Finley Engring. Coll., Kansas City, Mo., 1964-66; with A.M. Kinney, Inc., Cin., 1966—, dir. computing engring., 1966-75, acting dir. power and nuclear engring., 1968-70, v.p., 1975—; adj. lectr. U. Cin., 1968-71, adj. asso. prof., 1971-74, adj. prof. civil engring., 1974—. Mem. AAUP, Am. Nuclear Soc. (papers review and publs. com., power div. 1974—), Engring. Soc. Cin. (chmn. energy com. 1974-76, chmn. environ. profl. interest com. 1976-77, dir. bd. 1977-79, v.p. 1979-80, pres. 1980-81), ASME (dir. Cin. sect. 1969-71, vice chmn. 1972-73, chmn. 1973-74, v.p. Ohio council 1974-77, chmn. honors and awards com. Gt. Lake Region V, sec. Region V 1978-80, sr. del. nat. agenda conf. 1973-75, nat. policy bd. gen. engring. dept. 1974—, policy bd. edn. dept. 1975-76, nat. metric study com. 1975—, editor Metric News 1975—, mem. nat. nominating com. 1977-78, chmn. com. 1978-79, nat. gen. awards com. 1979-82, vice chmn. 1981-82, cert. of awards Nat. Council 1974, 76, 78, 80), Pi Tau Sigma, Sigma Tau, Alpha Sigma Lambda (hon.). Recipient citation Kansas City Internat. Club, 1959; citation Kansas City Jr. Achievement Assn., 1966; Profl. Accomplishment in Industry of Year award Tech. and Sci. Socs. Council of Cin., 1976, Community Service in Industry of Year award, 1980. Author: Introduction to Fortran Programming for Engineers, 1967; CPM and Network Diagramming, 1970; chpt. in Process Plant Design Handbook, 1982; contbr. papers to profl. publs. Home: 12067 Deerhorn Dr Cincinnati OH 45240 Office: 2900 Vernon Pl Cincinnati OH 45219 also Univ Cincinnati Cincinnati OH 45221

QURAESHI, ZAHIR AHMED, educator; b. Poona, India, Jan. 31, 1946; came to U.S., 1967; s. Raschid and Akila (Khan) Q.; B.Sc. with honors, U. Karachi (Pakistan), 1966; B.S. in Chem. Engring. cum laude, Ind. Inst. Tech., 1970; M.B.A., Mich. State U., 1972, Ph.D., 1978. Indsl. analyst Indsl. Engring. Cons., Karachi, 1965; managerial cons. PakCon, Karachi, 1965-67; mktg. analyst Eastern Tex., Karachi, 1972-73; research asst. Bur. Bus. and Econ. Research, Mich. State U., 1973-78; asst. prof. mktg. Western Mich. U., 1978—; cons. bus. and mktg. Named Student of Yr., Pakistan Youth Students Orgn., 1965. Mem. Am. Mktg. Assn., Acad. Mktg. Sci., Acad. Internat. Bus., World Future Soc., Beta Gamma Sigma, Iota Tau Kappa. Contbr. articles to profl. jours.; co-editor: International Business-1977: A Selection of Current Readings, 1977; International Business—1979: A Selection of Current Readings, 1979. Home: 215 N Sage 3A Kalamazoo MI 49007 Office: Coll Bus Western Mich U Kalamazoo MI 49008

RAABE, HAZEL UDSETH, educator; b. Summit, S.D., Apr. 26, 1917; B.S., Ellendale (N.D.) State Coll.; M.S., No. State Coll., Aberdeen, S.D.; m. Stanley Raabe; children—William John II, Suzanne. Tchr. 2d grade Frederick (S.D.) county schs.; tchr. reading and English, Wilmot (S.D.) schs.; librarian, tchr. English, elementary prin. Java (S.D.) schs.; reading specialist Mobridge (S.D.) Ind. Schs., 1974—. Past stewardship sec. St. Paul's Lutheran Ch., Java; precinct chairperson Dem. party. Mem. NEA, S.D., Mobridge, Java (past pres.) edn. assns., AAUW, Bridge City Concert Assn., Sons of Norway, Am. Assn. Ret. Persons, Sons of Sherman's March, Delta Kappa Gamma. Clubs: Marathon Bridge, Women's Bridge, Country, Women's Golf League, Christian Women's, Women of Moose, Naomi Circle, Westerners' Trail Boss, Life Health Spa. Home: 702 2d Ave W Mobridge SD 57601 Office: 601 E 4th St Mobridge SD 57601

RAACK, BARBARA JEAN, advt. exec.; b. Berwyn, Ill., Aug. 13, 1943; d. Albert Henry and Loretta Mae (Bartelt) R.; B.A., U. Ill., 1965. Freelance writer, Champaign, Ill., summer 1965; creative dir. Kane Advt., Bloomington, Ill., 1965-67; dir. advt. services Profl. div. Helene Curtis, Chgo., 1967-77; dir. advt. services White Hen Pantry div. Jewel Cos., Elmhurst, Ill., 1977—. Recipient cert. of appreciation USMC, 1978, 79. Home: 1S188 Eliot Ln Villa Park IL 60181 Office: 666 Industrial Dr Elmhurst IL 60126

RABAN, MORTON, educator; b. St. Louis, Oct. 18, 1940; s. Samuel and Viola (Bierman) R.; B.A., Harvard U., 1962; Ph.D., Princeton U., 1967; m. Mary Sheldon, Apr. 29, 1980; 1 son, David. Chemist, Research Inst. for Medicine and Chemistry, Cambridge, Mass., 1962-63; instr. Princeton (N.J.) U., 1966-67; asst. prof. chemistry Wayne State U., Detroit, 1967-70, asso. prof., 1970-74, prof., 1974—. Am. Chem. Soc. grantee, 1967-72; NIH grantee, 1968—; NSF grantee, 1969-81; A.P. Sloan fellow, 1970-74. Mem. Am. Chem. Soc., Royal Soc. Chemistry (London), Sigma Xi. Contbr. articles to profl. jours. Home: 6888 W Dartmoor St West Bloomfield MI 48033 Office: Wayne State Univ 335 Chemistry Detroit MI 48202

RABB, GEORGE B., zoologist; b. Charleston, S.C., Jan. 2, 1930; s. Joseph A. and Teresa C. (Redmond) R.; B.S., Coll. Charleston, 1951; M.A., U. Mich., 1952, Ph.D., 1957; m. Mary Sughrue, June 10, 1953. Teaching fellow zoology U. Mich., 1954-56; curator, coordinator research Chgo. Zool. Park, Brookfield, Ill., 1956-64, asso. dir. research and edn., 1964-75, dep. dir., 1969-75, dir., 1976—; pres. Chgo. Zool. Soc., 1976—; research asso. dept. psychology U. Chgo., 1960—; research asso. Field Mus. Natural History, 1965—; lectr. dept. zoology U. Chgo., 1965—, mem. Com. on Evolution Biology, 1969—. Fellow A.A.A.S.; mem. Am. Soc. Ichthyologists and Herpetologists (pres. 1978), Herpetologists League, Soc. Systematic Zoology, Soc. Mammalogists. Soc. Study Evolution, Ecol. Soc. Am., Am. Soc. Zoologists, Soc. Study Animal Behavior, Am. Assn. Museums, Am. Soc. Naturalists, Am. Assn. Zool. Parks and Aquariums (dir. 1979-80), Internat. Union Dirs. Zool. Gardens, Sigma Xi. Office: Chgo Zool Park Brookfield IL 60513

RABBERS, NORMAN LLOYD, structural engr.; b. Kalamazoo, Dec. 31, 1925; s. Oscar Archibald and Nellie Hertha (Jones) R.; student Oberlin Coll., 1943-44; B.S.E. in Civil Engring., U. Mich., 1946; postgrad. Western Mich. U., 1946, Northwestern U., 1972; m. Jean Von Holten; children by previous marriage, David, Kenneth, Thomas, Vicki; stepchildren—Larry and Terri Von Holten. Hwy. engr. Mich. Hwy. Dept., 1946-47; engring. draftsman L. C. Kingscott Co., Kalamazoo, 1947-48; structural designer Sargent & Lundy, Chgo., 1948-50, structural design engr. and structural project engr., 1953-63, structural project engr., systems and standards adminstr., 1974-79; structural design engr. Floyd G. Brown, Marion, Ohio, 1952-53; partner Upper Peninsula Engring. Assos., Chgo., 1963-64; structural project engr. Pioneer Service & Engring. Co., 1964-67; dir. bus. devel., De Leuw, Cather & Co., Chgo., 1967-70; practice civil and structural engring., 1970-71; project mgr. Mark Lovejoy & Assos., Inc., Burr Ridge, Ill., 1971-72; mgr. civil div. The Engr. Collaborative, Chgo., 1972-73; v.p. ops. Ervin Engring. Ill., Oak Brook, 1973-74; power group project engr. Darin & Armstrong, Inc., Southfield, Mich., 1979-80; mgr. power engring. Detroit Black & Veatch, Detroit, 1980-81. Mem. nat. exec. com. Y-Indian Guides, YMCA, 1960-69; bd. dirs. B.R. Ryall YMCA, Wheaton, Ill., 1961-70, chmn., 1968-69; vice chmn. DuPage (county, Ill.) Planning Council, 1967-69; mem. Darien (Ill.) Econ. Devel. Commn., 1973-74; mem. planning com. Chgo. Met. Housing and Planning Council, 1977-79. Served to capt. USMCR, 1943-46, 50-52. Registered profl. engr., Ill., Mich., Ohio; registered structural engr., Ill. Fellow ASCE (chmn. urban planning and devel. Ill. sect. 1968-69). Republican. Lutheran. Home: 720 Coachman Dr Apt 4 Troy MI 48084

RABE, CHARLES CASTENS, coll. pres.; b. Steeleville, Ill., July 14, 1916; s. Charles H. and Emma (Castens) R.; student Valparaiso U., 1935-37; B.S. in Pharmacy, St. Louis Coll. Pharmacy, 1939; M.S., Mass. Coll. Pharmacy, 1950, D.Sc. (hon.), 1966; m. Martha Zority, June 12, 1948; children—Constance Anne, Pamela Martha. Sales rep. Merck, Sharp & Dohme, St. Louis, 1939-41, Warner-Lambert Co., Mo., Ill., Iowa, 1941-42; instr., asst. prof. St. Louis Coll. Pharmacy, 1942-48, asso. prof., 1950-54, pres., 1961—; teaching fellow Mass. Coll. Pharmacy, 1948-50; asst. to sec. Am. Pharm. Assn., Washington, 1954-57; mgr. profl. relations Roerig div. Pfizer, Inc., N.Y.C., 1957-61. Trustee O.J. Cloughly Ednl. Found., Pharmacists Ins. Trust. Recipient Distinguished Alumnus award Alumni Assn. St. Louis Coll. Pharmacy, 1963. Mem. Am. Pharm. Assn. (v.p. 1978-79), Nat. Assn. Retail Druggists, Am. Coll. Apothecaries, Mo. Pharm. Assn., Kappa Psi, Rho Chi. Republican. Presbyn. Clubs: Univ., Greenbriar Hills Country. Home: 530 Flanders Dr Warson Woods MO 63122 Office: 4588 Parkview Pl Saint Louis MO 63110

RABIN, BARRY EDWARD, psychiatrist; b. Chgo., Oct. 1, 1942; s. Henry and Rebecca (Itzkowitz) R.; M.D., U. Ill., 1967; m. Nancy Joan McGonagill, Apr. 7, 1973; children—Jason, Jennifer, Jessica. Chief resident in psychiatry Loyola U. Hosp., Chgo., 1973, dir. psychiatry resident edn., dir. inpatient psychiatry unit, 1973-75; med. dir. Cicero (Ill.) Mental Health Center, 1973-74; dir. alcohol treatment unit Alexian Bros. Med. Center, Chgo., 1975; clin. dir. psychiatry service St. Joseph Hosp., Elgin, Ill., 1975—; practice medicine specializing in psychiatry, Elgin, 1975—; cons. Ill. Dept. Mental Health, Elgin Mental Health Center; asst. clin. prof. Loyola U. Med. Sch.; bd. dirs. Elgin Community Concern Alcoholism and Drug Abuse; adv. bd. Elgin Community Coll. Served with USAR, 1968-70; Vietnam. Diplomate Am. Bd. Psychiatry and Neurology (examiner). Mem. Am. Assn. Dirs. Psychiat. Residency Programs, Ill. Assn. Gen. Hosp. Psychiatrists. Office: 860 Summit St Elgin IL 60120

RABIN, JOSEPH HARRY, mktg. research co. exec.; b. Chgo., Dec. 12, 1927; s. Morris and Libby (Broder) Rabinovitz; B.Sc., Roosevelt U., 1950; M.B.A., DePaul U., 1951; m. Barbara E. Leader, Oct. 31, 1954; children—Marc Jay, Michelle Ann, Deborah Susan. Account exec. Gould, Gleiss & Benn, 1951-56; asst. dir. mktg. research Paper Mate Co., Chgo., 1956-63; pres. Rabin Research Co., Chgo., 1963—. Pres. Mather High Sch. Council, 1972-74; bd. dirs. Market Research Inst., 1973, 74, Ner Tamid Synagogue, 1976—, Jewish Vocat. Service, 1977-80; mem. adv. council U. Toledo Coll. Bus. Adminstrn., 1976-77. Served with AUS, 1946-47. Mem. Am. Mktg. Assn. (chpt. pres. 1961-62, nat. dir. 1973-75, nat. v.p. mktg. research 1978-79, census adv. com. 1978-81, nat. pres. 1981-82), Assn. Consumer Research, Am. Statis. Assn. (chpt. pres. 1962-63), Am. Assn. Pub. Opinion Research. Home: Apt 308 7061 N Kedzie Chicago IL 60645 Office: 520 N Michigan Ave Chicago IL 60611

RABINOVITZ, ADOLPH J., physician, pathologist; b. Chgo., July 3, 1927; s. Samuel and Esther Hannah (Callner) R.; A.A., Herzl Jr. Coll., 1946; B.S. in Chemistry, Roosevelt U., 1948; M.D., U. Ill., 1952; m. Miriam Pogrund, June 19, 1951; children—Esther Ann, Isaac Aaron, Rena Ruth, Don Joseph. Intern, Cook County Hosp., Chgo., 1952-53; resident in pathology U. Ill. Research and Edn. Hosp., Chgo., 1953-54, 56-57, Augustana Hosp., Chgo., 1957-59; pathologist Lutheran Gen. Hosp., Park Ridge, Ill., 1959-60; research asso. dept. pathology Michael Reese Hosp., Chgo., 1961-63; asso. pathologist St. Anne's Hosp., Chgo., 1960-72, dir. labs., 1972-75; dir. labs. St. Elizabeth Hosp., Chgo., 1972-75; dir. clin. labs., dir. dept. nuclear medicine Augustana Hosp., Chgo., 1975—; clin. asst. prof. pathology U. Ill. Coll. Medicine, Chgo., 1964—; mem. dept. med. biophysics and nuclear medicine Hadassah Hosp.-Hebrew U. Jerusalem, 1981-82. Served with AUS, 1946-47, USAF, 1954-56. Diplomate Am. Bd. Pathology, Am. Bd. Nuclear Medicine. Mem. AMA, Ill. State, Chgo. med. socs., Am. Soc. Clin. Pathologists, Coll. Am. Pathologists, Chgo. Path. Soc. Jewish. Book rev. staff Jour. AMA, 1977-79. Office: Augustana Hosp 411 W Dickens St Chicago IL 60614

RABON, WILLIAM JAMES, JR., architect; b. Marion, S.C., Feb. 7, 1931; s. William James and Beatrice (Baker) R.; B.S. in Arch., Clemson (S.C.) Coll., 1951; B.Arch., N.C. State Coll., 1955; M.Arch., Mass. Inst. Tech., 1956. Designer archtl. firms in N.Y.C. and Birmingham, Mich., 1958-61; designer, asso. John Carl Warnecke and Assos., San Francisco, 1961-63, 63-66, Keyes, Lethbridge and Condon, Washington, 1966-68; prin. archtl. partner A.M. Kinney and William J. Rabon Assos., Cin., 1968—; v.p., dir. archtl. design A.M. Kinney, Inc., Cin., 1977—; lectr. U. Calif., Berkeley, 1963-65; asst. prof. archtl. design Catholic U. Am., 1967-68; prin. works include Kaiser Tech. Center, Pleasanton, Calif. (Indsl. Lab. of Year award), 1970; Clermont Nat. Bank, Milford, Ohio, 1971; Pavilion bldg. Children's Hosp. Med. Center, Cin. (AIA Design award), 1973; EG&G, Hydrospace, Inc., Rockville, Md. (AIA Design award), 1970; Mead Johnson Park, Evansville, Ind. (Indsl. Research Lab. of Year hon. mention), 1973; Hamilton County Vocat. Sch., Cin., 1972; hdqrs. lab. EPA, Cin., 1975; Arapahoe Chem. Co. Research Center, Boulder, Colo. (Indsl. Research Lab. of Year award 1976; Concrete Reinforced Steel Inst. Nat. Design award), 1976; NALCO Chem. Co. Research Center, Naperville, Ill., 1980; Proctor & Gamble-Winton Hill Tunnel, Cin. (AIA Design award), 1978; Toyota Regional Center, Cin., 1980. Served to 1st lt. AUS, 1951-53; Korea. Decorated Silver Star, Bronze Star with V device, Purple Heart; M.I.T. Grad. Sch. scholar, 1955-56; Fulbright scholar, Italy, 1957-58. Mem. AIA (Design award 1980). Office: 2900 Vernon Pl Cincinnati OH 45219

RACH, ROY DEAN, engr.; b. Edwardsburg, Mich., Apr. 24, 1930; s. Edward Carl and Edna Elberta (Dargin) R.; B.S. in Physics, Ind. U., 1971; M.S. in Mfg. Adminstrn., Western Mich. U., 1980; m. Delores Ann Irvin, Nov. 24, 1951; children—Kathryn Ann, Thomas Dean, Karen Lynn. Product service mgr. Lab. Equipment Corp., St. Joseph, Mich., 1965-72; instrumentation engr. J.A. Jones Constrn. Co., Donald C. Cook Nuclear Plant, Bridgman, Mich., 1972-73; plant engr. Modern Plastics Corp., Benton Harbor, Mich., 1973-75; engring. and maintenance mgr. Dynac Corp., St. Joseph, 1975-78; plant maintenance engr. Watervliet Paper Co. (Mich.), 1978-80; maintenance and performance engr. Ind. & Mich. Electric Co., Bridgman, Mich., 1980—; instr. Lake Mich. Coll., Benton Harbor; cons. Wightman Assos., St. Joseph. Served with USN, 1951-55. Registered profl. engr., Mich.; certified flight instr. Mem. Nat., Blossomland profl. engr. socs., Instrument Soc. Am., Am. Phys. Soc., Nat. Flight Instr. Assn. Baptist. Home: Route 1 Box 34 Old Pipestone Rd Eau Claire MI 49111

RACHESKY, STANLEY ROBERT, entomologist; b. Red Bank, N.J., Feb. 28, 1939; s. Alex and Rose (Albert) R.; B.S. in Zoology, Kans. State U., 1963, M.S. in Entomology, 1966; m. Carole Prochazka, June 5, 1965; children—Peter, Stacey. Urban entomologist U. Ill. Co-op. Extension Service, Chgo., 1966-80, pesticide adviser, 1966-80, mass media coordinator, 1973-80; pres. S. Rachesky & Assos., integrated pest mgmt. cons., Glen Ellyn, Ill., 1971—; instr. Coll. DuPage, Glen Ellyn, Ill., 1971, William Rainey Harper Jr. Coll., Palatine, Ill., 1972, Triton Jr. Coll., River Grove, Ill., 1973; lectr. entomology to various colls., clubs, 1966—; TV appearances Chgo. stas. WBBM, WGN, WLS and WMAQ, 1966—; mem. Ill. Turfgrass Found., 1966—. Mem. Sch. Bd. Dist. 13, Bloomingdale, 1973—. Served with M.C., AUS, 1958-60. Mem. Entomol. Soc. Am., Nat. Environ. Health Assn., Environ. Mgmt. Assn., Garden Writers Assn. Am., Ill. (cons. 1974—), Nat. pest control assns., Am. Forestry Assn., Ill. Mosquito Control Assn., Nat. Assn. County Agts. Am. (Feature Story award 1975), Ill. Landscape Contractors Assn. (exec. sec. 19—), Kans. Entomol. Soc., Pi Chi, Gamma Sigma Delta. Contbr. articles on research in pesticides to profl. jours.; columnist Chgo. Tribune, 1967—. Author: Getting Pests to Bug Off, 1978. Home: 665 Forest Ave Glen Ellyn IL 60137 Office: 526 Crescent Blvd Glen Ellyn IL 60137

RACHIE, GEORGE LOUIS, dentist; b. Mpls., Apr. 20, 1919; s. Elias and Amanda Marie (Lein) R.; B.A., U. Minn., 1945, D.D.S., 1945; m. Lucille Margaret Schumann, July 19, 1946; children—Susan (Mrs. William Hibbard), Jeanne (Mrs. Todd Andrew Teske), Thomas George. Practice dentistry, Mpls., 1946-65, Edina, Minn., 1965—. Chmn. troop Boy Scouts Am., 1971-73; pres. Minn. Pioneer Park, Annandale. Served to 1st lt. Dental Corps USNR, 1945-47. Mem. Am. Acad. Prosthetics, Am., Minn. prosthetic socs., Children Dental Soc., Acad. Gen. Practice, Am., Mpls. dental assns., International Dentaire, Sons of Norway, Silver Spur, Grey Friars, Psi Omega. Lutheran. Optimist. Club: Ys Mens (Mpls.). Home: 5603 Interlachen Circle Edina MN 55436 Office: 535 Southdale Med Bldg Edina MN 55435

RACKOFF, JOHN M(ICHAEL), metal working mfg. exec.; b. Pitts., Sept. 26, 1950; s. Raymond and Barbara (Weinberg) R.; B.A. in Polit. Sci., U. Denver, 1972; M.B.A., George Washington U., 1976; m. Melinda Taylor Gowell, June 24, 1973. Exhibits specialist Nat. Archives, Washington, 1972-73; adminstrv. aide HUD, Washington, 1973-75; sales mgr. ASKO Inc., Amsterdam, Holland, 1976-78, v.p., Chgo., 1978—. Mem. Am. Iron and Steel Engrs., Am. Soc. for Metals, Am. Mktg. Assn., Am. Technion Soc., Art Inst. Chgo. Clubs: Ravisloe Country, Whitehall. Office: 15600 Vincennes Rd South Holland IL 60473

RADAMUS, VAIKE LAINE, interior designer; b. Tallinn, Estonia, July 3, 1920; came to U.S., 1964, naturalized, 1973; d. Eduard and Agathe Henriette (Boeckler) Mandel; B.S. in Interior Design summa cum laude, U. Minn., 1968; m. Dec. 28, 1949 (dec. 1975); 1 son, Aldo. Statistician, Hector's Dept. Store, Copenhagen, Denmark, 1945-48; sec., interior designer Argentine Lutheran Ch., Buenos Aires, 1950-64; interior designer, dir. design Gen. Office Products Co., Mpls., 1968—, exec. design cons., 1979—. Recipient 1st prize Halo/ASID Nat. Lighting Competition, 1981. Mem. Am. Soc. Interior Designers, AIA (design asso.). Lutheran. Clubs: Mpls. Woman's, Estonian Soc. Minn., NW Raquet. Office: 4521 Hwy 7 Minneapolis MN 55416

RADCLIFF, WILLIAM FRANKLIN, lawyer; b. Fredericksburg, Ind., May 21, 1922; s. Samuel Pearl and Hester Susan (Sherwood) R.; B.A., Yale U., 1948; J.D., Ind. U., 1951; m. Margery Anne Glass, Aug. 18, 1962 (dec. May 1980); children—Forrest Lee, Stephanie Anne; foster children—Cheryl Lynn, Sandra Lee, Richard Alan, Lezlie Laverne. Admitted to Ind. bar, 1951; with firm DeFur, Voran, Hanley, Radcliff & Reed, and predecessors, Muncie, Ind., 1951—, partner, 1954—; dir., mem. exec. com. Am. Nat. Bank and Trust Co. of Muncie; dir. Ben Zeigler Co., Inc., Muncie; dir., sec. Muncie Tennis and Country Club. Pres., Delaware County Mental Health Assos., 1962-63; a founder Ind. Mental Health Meml. Found., 1962, sec., 1962—; bd. dirs. Delaware County Cancer Soc., Goodwill Industries Delaware County. Served with AUS, 1940-46; PTO; lt. col. Res., ret. Mem. Am., Ind., Muncie bar assns., Muncie-Delaware County C. of C. (pres. 1972-73). Clubs: Masons, Exchange (pres. 1962); Delaware Country (pres. 1974), Muncie (Muncie). Home: 1809 N Winthrop Rd Muncie IN 47304 Office: 320 S High St Muncie IN 47305

RADDEN, JAMES DAVID, county coroner; b. Kankakee, Ill., Feb. 24, 1945; s. Maurice F. and Marianna J. (Graner) R.; student Burlington Coll., 1963-64, Wis. Inst. Mortuary Sci., 1965, St. Louis U., 1978; m. Barbara E. Christenson, Aug. 6, 1966; children—Cynthia Lynn, James M. Dir., Baldus-Radden Funeral Home, Belleville, Ill., 1966-74; chief dep. ct. clks. St. Clair Circuit Clks. Office, 1974, chief dep. small claims div., 1976; coroner St. Clair County, Belleville, Ill., 1976—; dir. Baldus-Radden Funeral Home; tchr. medicolegal deaths. Chmn. Belleville Empty Stocking Fund, 1967-68; former pres. and v.p. United Methodist Men; bd. dirs. Belleville Jaycees, 1965. Cert. in sudden infant death syndrome, identification and care mgmt. U.S. Consumer Product Safety Commn. Mem. St. Clair County Funeral Dirs. Assn. (pres. 1967), Ill. Coroners Assn. (v.p. 1979), Internat. Med. Examiners and Coroners Assn., Ill. Funeral Dirs. Assn., Nat. Funeral Dirs. Assn., Federated Funeral Dirs. Assn., Belleville Area C. of C. Republican. Clubs: Belleville Lions (pres. 1967), Belleville High Twelve (pres. 1977), Shriners, Masons, Moose, Eagles. Research on violent deaths in St. Clair County. Home: 21 S 35th St Belleville IL 62223 Office: Coroners Office 5th and F Sts Belleville IL 62220

RADELET, LOUIS AUGUST, educator; b. Green Bay, Wis., Dec. 10, 1917; s. John B. and Alice C. (Bodart) R.; B.A. cum laude, Notre Dame U., 1939, M.A. magna cum laude in Polit. Sci., 1947, postgrad., 1948; m. Elizabeth Grace Delaney, June 20, 1942; children—John, Joseph, Ann, Michael, Timothy, David, Steven, Kevin. Instr., Notre Dame U., South Bend, Ind., 1948-51; part-time dir. Ind. regional office NCCJ, South Bend, 1948-51, ednl. dir. five-state E. Central div., Detroit, 1951-52, dir. Commn. on Community Orgns., N.Y.C., 1952-54, dir. nat. program ops., 1954-59, dir. nat. program devel., 1959-63; prof. Sch. Police Adminstrn. and Public Safety, Mich. State U., East Lansing, 1963—, dir. numerous workshops in human relations U. Mich., Notre Dame U., U. Montreal, Adelphi U.; founder, asso. dir. Nat. Inst. on Police and Community Relations, Mich. State U., 1955-63, dir., 1963-70, coordinator Nat. Center on Police and Community Relations, 1965-73, dir. Mich. Inst. on Community Relations and Adminstrn. of Justice, 1970—; mem. Mich. Commn. on Crime, Delinquency and Criminal Adminstrn., 1966-68; cons. Pres.'s Commn. on Law Enforcement and Adminstrn. of Justice, 1966-67, Nat. Adv. Commn. on Civil Disorders, 1967-68; chmn. Mich. State U. Com. on Public Safety, 1972-73; mem. Acad. Council, Acad. Policies Com. of Coll. Social Sci. Served to 2d lt. U.S. Army, 1941-46. Fellow Soc. for Values in Higher Edn.; mem. Adult Edn. Assn. of U.S., AAUP, Acad. of Criminal Justice Scis., Midwest Assn. Criminal Justice Educators, Mich. Assn. Criminal Justice Educators, Internat. Assn. of Chiefs of Police, Nat. Assn. Intergroup Relations Ofcls. (past v.p.), Council Nat. Orgns. for Children and Youth (past mem. exec. com.), Phi Kappa Phi. Author: Police and Community, 1973, 77, 80; contbr. numerous articles in field to profl. jours.; co-editor: (with A. F. Brandstatter) Police and Community Relations, 1968. Home: 223 Lexington Ave East Lansing MI 48823 Office: 560 Baker Hall Mich State U East Lansing MI 48824

RADEN, LOUIS, tape and label corp. exec.; b. Detroit, June 17, 1929; s. Harry M. and Joan (Morris) R.; B.A., Trinity Coll., 1951; postgrad. N.Y. U., 1952; m. Mary K. Knowlton, June 18, 1949; children—Louis III, Pamela, Jacqueline. With Time, Inc., 1951-52; with Quaker Chem. Corp., 1952-63, sales mgr., 1957-63; exec. v.p. Gen. Tape & Supply, Inc., Detroit, 1963-68, pres., chmn. bd., 1969—; pres. Mich. Gun Clubs, 1973-77. Fifth reunion chmn. Trinity Coll., 1956, pres. Mich. alumni, 1960-75, sec. Class of 1951, 1981—; trustee, Mich. Diocese Episcopal Ch. Recipient Key Man award Greater Hartford Jaycees, 1957. Mem. Nat. Rifle Assn. (life), Nat. Skeet Shooting Assn. (life, nat. dir. 1977-79), Greater Detroit Bd. Commerce, Mich. C. of C., C. of C. U.S., Theta Xi (life; Disting. Service award 1957, alumni pres. 1952-57). Republican. Clubs: University; Detroit Golf, Detroit Gun. Home: 1133 Ivy Glen Circle Bloomfield Hills MI 48013 Office: 7451 W Eight Mile Rd Detroit MI 48221

RADER, DAVID L., ins. co. exec.; b. Columbus, Ohio, Nov. 2, 1946; s. Earl R. and Ruth R.; student Wittenberg U., 1964-66; B.A., Ohio State U., 1968; m. Martha Cardwell, Sept. 9, 1967. Research asso. Ohio Legislature, 1968-70; asso. exec. dir. Ohio Med. Assn., Columbus, 1971-76; v.p., sec. Physicians Ins. Co. Ohio, Columbus, 1976-80; sec. Pico Life Ins. Co., Columbus, 1978-80, pres., 1981—; dir. Ky. Med. Ins. Co., Ind. Physicians Ins. Co. Past mem. Planning Commn. Upper Arlington, Ohio. Clubs: University (Columbus); Moundbuilders Country. Home: 2740 Crafton Park Columbus OH 43221 Office: Box 281 Pickerington OH 43147

RADKE, HERBERT KARL, ind. oil producer, petroleum marketer; b. Chelsea, Okla., Jan. 25, 1934; s. William Carl and Laura J. (Doening) R.; student Okla. Sch. Accountancy and Law, Tulsa, 1960-61; m. Linda Clair Hester, Dec. 20, 1962; children—Meredith Lynn, Herbert Karl. Route salesman Anderson Music Co., Chelsea, 1955-62; pres., gen. mgr. Radke Oil Co. Inc., McPherson, Kans., 1962—. Served with AUS, 1953-55. Recipient award Texaco, Inc., 1962. Mem. Kans. Oil Marketers Assn., McPherson C. of C., McPherson Advt. Council. Republican. Lutheran. Clubs: Kiwanis, Elks. Guitarist Merry Valley Boys, Pryor, Okla., 1949-51. Home: 1489 N Walnut St McPherson KS 67460 Office: 1060 W Kansas St McPherson KS 67460

RADKE, LESSIE EMBRY, nurse; b. Louisville, Mar. 5, 1940; d. Donald W. and Donna Ann Embry; student U. Louisville, 1958-59; R.N., St. Joseph's Sch. of Nursing, 1962; m. John David Radke, June 16, 1962 (div.); children—John David II, Sarah Ann. Nurse, Mayo Clinic, Rochester, Minn., 1963-66, Case Western Res. U. Hosps., Cleve., 1966-68, St. Marys Health Center, St. Louis, 1968-75, St. Anthonys Med. Center, St. Louis, 1975-77; operating room supr. Incarnate Word Hosp., St. Louis, 1977—. Registered nurse, Minn., Ohio, Mo. Mem. Am. Nurses Assn., Assn. Operating Room Nurses (dir. 1976-78, v.p. 1978—). Lutheran. Home: 141 Horseshoe St Kirkwood MO 63122 Office: Incarnate Word Hosp 3545 Lafayette St Saint Louis MO 63104

RADMACHER, CAMILLE J., librarian; b. Monmouth, Ill., Apr. 14, 1917; d. Harry M. and Esther (Greenleaf) R.; student Monmouth Coll., 1935-37. With adult dept. Warren County Library, Monmouth, 1937-48, head county librarian, 1948—, exec. dir. Western Ill. Library System, 1965—; exec. dir. Nat. Library Week in State of Ill., 1959. Mem. Monmouth Coll. Community Concert Lecture Bd., 1967-72; mem. adv. com. Ill. State Library, 1962-72. Mem. Ill. Library Assn. (Ill. Librarian Citation award 1967), Women's Nat. Book Assn., DAR. Methodist. Clubs: Order Eastern Star, Altrusa (treas. 1968-69). Home: 500 N 1st St Monmouth IL 61462 Office: 60-62 Public Sq Monmouth IL 61462

RADMER, MICHAEL JOHN, lawyer; b. Wisconsin Rapids, Wis., Apr. 28, 1945; s. Donald Richard and Thelma Loretta (Donahue) R.; B.S., Northwestern U., 1967; J.D., Harvard U., 1970; m. Debra B. Petrik, Sept. 14, 1974; children—Christina Nicole, Ryan Michael. Admitted to Minn. bar, 1970; asso. firm Dorsey, Windhorst, Hannaford, Whitney & Halladay, Mpls., 1970-76, partner, 1976—; sec. or gen. counsel rep. for 13 investment cos., including St. Paul Securities, Inc.; instr. Hamline U. Sch. Law. Mem. Am. Bar Assn., Minn. Bar Assn., Hennepin County Bar Assn. Club: Mpls. Athletic. Contbr. articles to profl. jours. Home: 4329 E Lake Harriet Pkwy Minneapolis MN 55409 Office: Dorsey Windhorst Hannaford Whitney & Halladay 2200 1st Bank Pl E Minneapolis MN 55402

RADOCHONSKI, STEPHEN PETER, dentist; b. Chgo., Apr. 22, 1919; s. Peter Simon and Stephanie Charolette (Noga) R.; student DePaul U., 1937-40; D.D.S., Loyola U., Chgo., 1944; m. Jeanette Marie Kolodziejczyk, Sept. 9, 1944; children—Bernard S., Paul B., Donna M. Practice dentistry, Chgo., 1945—. Mem. elem. sch. bd. dist. 124, Evergreen Park, Ill., 1970-76; sec. Fire and Police Commn. Evergreen Park, 1971—, pres., 1978—. Served as lt. USNR, 1942-45. Named hon. alumnus St. Cyril and Methodius Sem., Orchard Lake, Mich., 1960. Mem. Acad. Gen. Dentistry, Dental Arts Soc. Chgo. (pres. 1950-51), Internat. Prosthodontic Conf. Soc., ADA, Ill., Chgo. (chmn. table clinics) dental socs., Am. Legion, 40 and 8, Holy Name Soc. (pres. St. Camilius 1949), Delta Sigma Delta. Clubs: Polish Nat. Alliance Lodge; Elks; Beverly Country, Holy Cross Hosp. Physicians and Dentists, New City Lions (pres. 1952-53) (Chgo.). Home: 9641 S Ridgeway Ave Evergreen Park IL 60642 Office: 6302 W Archer Ave Chicago IL 60638

RADOVANOV, RADMILA, physician; b. Belgrad, Yugoslavia, Nov. 17, 1934; d. Cvetko and Jelena (Kandic) Lazarevic; M.D., Med. U. Belgrad, 1960; m. Milan Radovanov, Nov. 8, 1959; children—Jelena, Nicol; came to U.S., 1967, naturalized, 1972. Intern, St. Francis Hosp., Wichita, Kans., 1968-69, resident, 1969-72; practice medicine specializing in radiology Newton (Kans.) Radiologists Assn., 1972—; mem. staff Bethel Deaconess Hosp., Newton. Diplomate Am. Bd. Radiology. Mem. AMA, Kans. Med. Soc., Am. Coll. Radiology, Women Med. Assn. Club: Racquet. Home: 8705 Stoneridge Wichita KS 67206 Office: 500 Main St Newton KS 67114

RADWAN, ALEX ANDREW, publisher; b. Gary, Ind., Jan. 28, 1953; s. H. Steve and Anne Aurielia R.; A.A., Thornton Jr. Coll., 1972; B.S. in Mktg. Adminstrn. summa cum laude, Calumet Coll., 1975; m. Cecilia M. Posko, June 5, 1976; 1 son, Christopher Eric. Br. mgt. trainee Calumet Nat. Bank, Hammond, Ind., 1969-72; acct. Sherwin Williams Co., Chgo., 1973-75; sales rep. McGraw-Hill Dodge Constrn. News, Chgo., 1975-79, pub., 1979—. Mem. Constrn. Specifications Inst. Roman Catholic. Office: 230 W Monroe St Chicago IL 60606

RADY, JOHN MORTIMER, pipeline co. exec.; b. Chgo., Feb 16, 1921; s. Mortimer D. and Clara J. (Wiegers) R.; Ph.B., U. Detroit, 1947, LL.B., 1949; m. Shirley M. Moore, Nov. 4, 1950; children—John Mortimer, Paul Moore, Jane Kathryn, Thomas More. Admitted to Mich. bar, 1949; war materiel expediter Rolls-Royce, Inc., Detroit, 1941-42; asso. counsel legal dept. Mich. Wis. Pipe Line Co., 1949-67; sec. Great Lakes Gas Transmission Co., Detroit, 1967-80, gen. atty., 1969-73, v.p., 1972-78, sr. v.p., 1978-80, gen. counsel, 1973-80; v.p. Am. Natural Service Co. and v.p., sec. Am. Natural Resources Co. (both Detroit), 1981—. Active United Fund. Served with USNR, 1942-45. Mem. Am. Gas Assn., Am., Fed. Energy, Detroit bar assns., State Bar Mich., Greater Detroit C. of C., Interstate Natural Gas Assn. Am., Midwest Gas Assn., Econ. Club Detroit, Gamma Eta Gamma. Republican. Roman Catholic. Clubs: Detroit Athletic; Birmingham (Mich.) Athletic. Home: 367 Suffield St Birmingham MI 48009 Office: One Woodward Ave Detroit MI 48226

RAFFERTY, GENEVIEVE KENNEDY, social service agy. adminstr.; b. Davenport, Iowa, Jan. 21, 1922; d. Thomas Cyril and Mabel Veronica (Finefield) Kennedy; B.A., St. Ambrose Coll., 1942; postgrad. U. Iowa, 1972; m. Daniel J. Rafferty, Aug. 22, 1942; children—Daniel D., Michele M., Genevieve, Thomas K., Eileen M., Margaret M., Sheila M. Real estate saleswoman Manhard Realty, Moline, Ill., 1950-59; substitute tchr., Rock Island, Ill., 1963-67; head start tchr., Rock Island-Scott County Dept. Social Services, 1966; public welfare worker Scott County Dept. Social Services, Davenport, Iowa, 1967-72; exec. dir. Info., Referral and Assistance Service, Rock Island, 1972—; commr. Rock Island Housing Authority; mem. Quad-City Council on Crime and Delinquency, 1977-80; mem. Rock Island County Council on Alcoholism, 1976—; dir. Quint-City Drug Abuse. Mem. Nat. Assn. Social Workers (Social Worker of Yr., Quad City chpt. 1973), Iowa Council Info. and Referral Providers, Nat. Conf. Social Welfare, Ill. Welfare Assn., NOW, Alliance of Info. and Referral Services. Republican. Roman Catholic. Office: 2002 3d Ave Rock Island IL 61201

RAFFERTY, SANDRA LEA, occupational therapist; b. St. Louis, May 7, 1944; d. George W. and Frances E. (Lantow) R.; student Ind. U., 1962-63; B.S. in Occupational Therapy, Washington U., 1966; postgrad. U. Calif., Berkeley, 1971; M.A., San Francisco State U., 1975; cert. riding instr. Acorn Hill Equestrian Center, 1974; m. Ronald C. Walchshavser, Jan. 17, 1981. Occupational therapist David P. Wohl Meml. Mental Health Inst., St. Louis, 1966-67, Sonoma State Hosp. for the Mentally Retarded and Physically Handicapped, Eldridge, Calif., 1967-70; cons. occupational therapist Sonoma (Calif.) Convalescent Hosp., 1968-69; tchr.'s aide Polly Priest Bus. Sch., Vallejo, Calif., 1970; occupational therapist Solano County Dept. Public Health, Vallejo, 1971-72; tchr. orthopedically handicapped Spl. Sch. Dist., St. Louis County, 1974-79; founder, exec. dir., riding instr. Therapeutic Horsemanship, St. Louis, 1974—; instr. (part-time) program in occupational therapy Washington U., St. Louis, 1979—; cons. occupational therapist Jefferson County (Mo.) Commn. for Handicapped, 1979—; tchr. workshops on therapeutic horsemanship, 1975—. Nat. Health Found. scholar, 1962-66. Mem. Am. Occupational Therapy Assn., N.Am. Riding for the Handicapped Assn. (dir. 1978—), U.S. Combined Tng. Assn., Am. Horse Protection Assn., U.S. Dressage Fedn. Presbyterian. Address: Route 1 PO Box 369 Troy MO 63379

RAFTERY, SUSAN ROSE, sociologist; b. Norwalk, Ohio, Oct. 9, 1952; d. William J. and Corris (Myers) R.; B.A., Ohio State U., 1974, M.S., 1980. Asso. rural life dir. Cath. Diocese Toledo, 1981—; instr. sociology Bowling Green (Ohio) State U., 1981—; cons. Charles F. Kettering Found. Mem. Rural Sociol. Soc., Am. Studies Assn., Phi Kappa Phi. Democrat. Roman Catholic. Home: 20805 Mermill Rd Rudolph OH 43462 Office: Dept Sociology Bowling Green State U Bowling Green OH 43403

RAGHEB, MAGDI M. H., nuclear engr., educator; b. Alexandria, Egypt, Nov. 25, 1946; s. Mohammed and Nehmat (El Sfrafi) R.; M.Sc., U. Wis., Madison, Ph.D.; m. Barbara Rose Wesolek, Feb. 16, 1980. Research scientist Brookhaven Nat. Lab., Upton, N.Y., summers 1975, 81; research asso. Oak Ridge Nat. Lab., summer 1979; asst. prof. nuclear engring. U. Ill., Urbana, 1979—; cons. Brookhaven Nat. Lab. Mem. Am. Nuclear Soc., AAAS, Sigma Xi. Home: 401 Edgebrook Dr Champaign IL 61820 Office: 223 Nuclear Engring Lab U Ill Urbana IL 61801

RAGLAND, SAM BENTON, JR., cons.; b. Fort Benton, Mont., Oct. 8, 1936; s. Sam Benton and Madeline Elizabeth (Fultz) R.; B.B.A., U. Mont., 1959; m. Sandra J. Taylor, Dec. 25, 1963; children—Laura Joan, Deborah Sue, Daniel Coy. Asst. v.p. sales planning and promotion Union Bank, Los Angeles, 1963-70; asst. v.p., dir. bus. devel. First City Nat. Bank, Houston, 1970-73; v.p., dir. mktg. Ohio Nat. Bank, Columbus, 1973-77; exec. v.p. Fin. Tng. Resources, Columbus, 1978—. Served with U.S. Army, 1960-63. Mem. Am. Mgmt. Assn., Am. Mktg. Assn., Bank Mktg. Assn., Sales and Mktg. Execs. Assn. Republican. Mem. Christian Ch. Club: Sawmill Athletic (Columbus). Home and office: 1838 Victorian Ct Columbus OH 43220

RAGSDALE, ROY LEE, supt. schs.; b. Cullman, Ala., Oct. 31, 1941; s. Marvin J. and Bessie Ragsdale; student Middle Tenn. State U., 1963-64; A.B., Trevecca Nazarene Coll., 1966; M.S. in Edn. with distinction, Ark. State U., 1969; postgrad. U. Mo., 1967-68, State Coll. Ark., 1967, U. Utah, 1967, U. Miss., 1969-72, Washington U., 1970-71; Ed.D., Ph.D. with high honors, St. Louis U., 1976; m. Cheryl E. Lloyd, June 1974. Tchr., Senath-Hornersville Sch. Dist., Mo., 1966; tchr. music and supr. Southland Sch. Dist., Mo., 1966-68; grad. asst. sch. adminstrn. Ark. State U., summers, 1967, 68; dir. elem. edn. South Pemiscot Consol. Sch. Dist., Steele and Holland, Mo., 1968-69; jr.-sr. high sch. prin. Valley Park Sch. Dist., St. Louis County, Mo., 1969-70; asst. high sch. prin. Bayless Sch. Dist., St. Louis County, 1970-71; asst. high sch. prin. Belvidere (Ill.) Community Sch. Dist., 1971-72, also tchr. adult evening classes, 1971-72; high sch. prin. Dupo (Ill.) Community Unit Sch. Dist., 1972-77; supt. schs. Nashville (Ill.) Community Consol. Sch. Dist. 49, 1977-79, Central Community Unit Sch. Dist. 301, Burlington, Ill., 1979—; chmn. high sch. athletic conf., 1975-76; participant numerous profl. workshops and confs., 1968—. Dir. Dupo Community Choir, 1976, Central Community Choir, 1980—; minister music and edn. Fox Valley First Ch. of the Nazarene, St. Charles, Ill., 1979—. Mem. Am. Assn. Sch. Adminstrs., Ill. Assn. Sch. Adminstrs., Assn. for Supervision and Curriculum Devel., Assn. Sch. Bus. Ofcls. U.S. and Can., Ill. Assn. Sch. Bus. Ofcls., Ill. Assn. Sch. Personnel Adminstrs., Ill. Assn. Sch. Bds., Phi Delta Kappa, Kappa Delta Pi. Republican. Author: Ten Commandments for Success, 1977; contbr. articles to profl. publs. Home: 43W845 Empire Rd Saint Charles IL 60174 Office: PO Box 396 Burlington IL 60109

RAHMAN, SYED (MUKHLESUR), radiologist; b. Dacca, Bangladesh, Dec. 19, 1939; came to U.S., 1974, naturalized, 1981; s. Syed Lutfor and Amena (Bano) R.; M.B.B.S., Chittagong Med. Coll., Dacca U., 1964; D.M.R.T., London U., 1971, A.B.R., 1976; m. Saleha Rahman, Aug. 17, 1965; children—Sabina, Adnan, Sarmina. Intern, Med. Coll. Hosp., Dacca; fellow in nuclear medicine Toronto (Ont., Can.) Gen. Hosp., 1968-69; resident in radiology Glasgow (Scotland) U. Hosp., 1971-74, sr. registrar in radiology, 1973-74; chief resident in radiology lMethodist Hosp., Bklyn., 1974-75; fellow in radiology Meml. Sloan Kettering Cancer Center, N.Y.C., 1975; asst. prof. radiol. oncology U. Va., 1975-77; dir. radiol. therapy dept. Riverside Hosp., Columbus, Ohio, 1977-79; chief sect. therapeutic radiology Grant Hosp., Columbus, 1979—. Mem. Radiol. Soc. N.Am., Am. Soc. Therapeutic Radiology, Am. Coll. Radiology, AMA, Franklin County Med. Assn. Home: 4278 Edgehill Dr Columbus OH 43220 Office: 309 E State St Columbus OH 43215

RAHMANN, JOHN CHARLES, television sta. exec.; b. Tarentum, Pa., Aug. 11, 1927; s. Carl Antone and Dorothy Lucille (Klein) R.; B.S., U. Md., 1960; M.B.A., Syracuse U., 1962; grad. Army Lang. Sch., Command and Gen. Staff Coll., 1961; postgrad. George Washington U., 1968—; m. Margaret Lane Shattuck, July 27, 1954; children—John Charles, Pamela Lane, Susan Marion. Commd. 2d lt. U.S. Army, 1947, advanced through grades to lt. col., 1964; ret., 1967; teaching fellow George Washington U., 1968; dir. adminstrn., dep. gen. mgr. WETA-TV, Washington, 1969-71; sr. v.p. WTTW-TV, Chgo., 1972—. Decorated Joint Services Commendation medal, Army Commendation medal, Bronze Star, Purple Heart, Combat Inf. badge; recipient Nat. Pub. TV Devel. award, 1973. Mem. Ret. Officers Assn., Chgo. Assn. Commerce and Industry. Home: 199 Hazel St Glencoe IL 60022 Office: 5400 N St Louis St Chicago IL 60625

RAHN, ROBERT LEE, ins. co. exec.; b. Freedom, Wis., Feb. 13, 1918; s. Robert Julius and Lulu (Wait) R.; student public schs., Appleton, Wis.; m. Wilma Denzer, June 15, 1946; 1 son, Bruce Alan. With, Inst. of Paper Chemistry, Appleton, Wis., 1936-37; with Aid Assn. for Lutherans, 1937—, 2d v.p. property mgmt. 1976—. Mem. bd. appeals Little Chute, Wis., 1971—; mem. housing tech. adv. com. East Central Wis. Regional Planning Commn., 1979—. Mem. Bldg. Owners and Mgrs. Assn. (bd. govs. 1980—). Lutheran. Club: Rotary (dir. 1967-69, pres. 1970-71). Home: 1511 E Main St Little Chute WI 54140 Office: Aid Assn for Lutherans 4321 N Ballard Rd Appleton WI 54919

RAILSBACK, THOMAS F., congressman; b. Moline, Ill., Jan. 22, 1932; s. Fred Harold and Elizabeth (Johnston) R.; B.A., Grinnell Coll., 1954, LL.D.; J.D., Northwestern U., 1957; LL.D., Monmouth Coll.; m. Patricia Sloan, Aug. 27, 1955; children—Kathryn, Julie, Margaret, Lisa. Admitted to Ill. bar, 1957; practice law, Moline; became mem. Ill. Ho. Reps., 1963; mem. 90th-97th Congresses from 19th Ill. Dist., mem. judiciary com., select com. narcotics abuse and control; rep. U.S.-France Parliamentary Exchange Program, U.S.-Japan Parliamentary Exchange Program, Rep. Task Force Internat. Econ. Devel.; chmn. Ill. Republican del. to Congress. Former pres. alumni bd. dirs. Grinnell Coll. Served with AUS, 1957-59. Recipient Alumni award Grinnell Coll., 1973, Flandrau award Nat. Council on Crime and Delinquency, 1974, others. Mem. Am., Ill. (former pres. Younger Mems. Conf.), Rock Island County bar assns., Phi Gamma Delta, Blue Key. Conglist. Home: 2800 12th St Moline IL 61265 Office: 2104 House Office Bldg Washington DC 20515 also Fed Bldg Rock Island IL 61201

RAIM, ROLAND LEO, musician, band dir.; b. Cedar Rapids, Iowa, Mar. 12, 1936; s. Leo Anton and Libbie Marie (Vesely) R.; Mus.B., U. Iowa, 1958, M.A., 1965; m. Nancy Ann Springer, Aug. 7, 1966; children—Jay Roland, Janelle Joy. Band dir., Milledgeville, Ill., 1958-59, Lone Tree, Iowa, 1959-63; dir. instrumental music Cedar Rapids (Iowa) Community Schs., 1965—; musician, guest condr., soloist Cedar Rapids Municipal Band. Sec. Cedar Rapids Community Concerts Assn., 1968-77; dir. programs Cedar-Rapids-Marion Fine Arts Council, 1970-75; pres. Czech Heritage Found., 1977, 79, Czech Fine Arts Found., 1976. Mem. NEA, Music Educators Nat. Conf., Iowa Band Masters Assn., Assn. Coll. Univ. and Community Arts Adminstrs. Home: 1455 Parkview Dr Marion IA 52302

RAINBOW-EARHART, KATHRYN ADELINE, physician; b. Wheeling, W.Va., Mar. 21, 1921; d. John Henry and Addaline (Holly) Rainbow; B.S., Fort Valley State Coll., 1942; M.D., Meharry Med. Coll., 1948; m. William Earhart, July 29, 1966; children by previous marriage—Frederic B., Holly R. Bryant. Intern, Harlem Hosp., N.Y.C., 1948-49; pediatric resident Mercy-Douglas, Children's hosps., Phila., 1949-50, Freedman's Hosp., Washington, Nat. Found. for Infantile Paralysis fellow, 1950-52; NIMH psychiat. residency fellow Menninger Sch. Psychiatry, Topeka, 1962-65, grad., 1965; pvt. pediatric practice, Rocky Mount, N.C., 1952-54; staff physician Lakin State Hosp., W.Va., 1954-60, supt., 1960-62; staff psychiatrist Topeka State Hosp., 1965-79, Shawnee Community Mental Health Center, Inc., 1979-81, Kans. Reception and Diagnostic Center, 1981—; adviser to Psychiat. Aide Orgn., 1969-71, 77-79. Bd. dirs. The Villages, Topeka, Mobile Meals, Hospice of Topeka, Topeka Assn. Retarded Children, 1972-78. Recipient 5-years Service to Humanity pin Lakin State Hosp., 1961, 25 years service to humanity plaque Meharry Med. Coll., 1973. Mem. Am., Nat., Kans. med. assns., W.Va. (pres. 1961-62), Shawnee County med. socs., Am. Med. Women's Assn., Am. Psychiat. Assn., Black Psychiatrists Am., Menninger Sch. Psychiatry Alumni Assn., Mental Health Assn. Shawnee County, NAACP, Quota Internat. (pres. chpt. 1976-77), Links (pres. chpt. 1976-78), Alpha Kappa Alpha. Mem. St. John A.M.E. Ch. Home: 2916 Kentucky Ave Topeka KS 66605 Office: 3817 E Sixth St Topeka KS 66607

RAINE, DIANNA LEE, ednl. media adminstr.; b. Cleve., Jan. 31, 1944; d. Charles P. and Alberta (Garraway) Rose; B.A., Adrian Coll., 1966; M.S., Eastern Mich. U., 1972; Ed.S. in Instructional Tech., U. Toledo, 1981; m. Albert Raine, Aug. 8, 1970; 1 son, Chad Albert. Recreation dir. Adrian (Mich.) Tng. Sch., 1965-72; media dir. Regional Center, Lenawae Intermediate Sch. Dist., Adrian, 1972—. Mem. Blissfield (Mich.) Com. for Cable TV Franchising, 1981. Cert. tchr., Mich. Mem. Nat. Assn. Regional Media Centers, Mich. Intermediate Media Assn., Mich. Assn. Media in Edn. (bd. dirs.), Nat. Campers and Hikers Assn. (chpt. sec.). Methodist. Home: 11757 Berkey Blissfield MI 49228 Office: 4107 N Adrian Adrian MI 49221

RAINER, DONALD LEEVAN, banker; b. Albia, Iowa, Mar. 19, 1926; s. Herman Lester and Vesta Ida (Meek) R.; B.S., N.E. Mo. State U., 1952; M.B.A., Iowa State U., 1977; m. Josephine Iris McCarty, June 2, 1948; children—Deborah Ann, Randall Lee. Tchr. public schs., Edison, Nebr., Winthrop and Newhall, Iowa, 1952-58; sales mgr. North Iowa Hatcheries, Osage, 1958-59; fieldman Farm Bur., Fayette, Iowa, 1959-63; asst. cashier Bank of Fayette, 1963-66, Security State Bank, Pine Island, 1966-68; v.p., loan Adminstr. Decatur County State Bank, Leon, Iowa, 1968-73; with Bankers Trust Co., Des Moines, 1973—, v.p., agr. specialist, 1978—. Mem. Iowa Vocat. Edn. Council; chmn. bd. dirs. Decator County Hosp., 1972-73; chmn. bd. trustees United Meth. Ch., 1971; active Boy Scouts Am. Served with AF, USN, 1944-46. Mem. Iowa Bankers Assn., Farmers Grain and Livestock Assn., Am. Inst. Banking, Assn. M.B.A. Execs. Republican. Home: 702 S 5th St Grimes IA 50111 Office: 110 S Main Grimes IA 50111

RAINES, GLENN ALLEN, agronomist; b. Paola, Kans., Feb. 25, 1944; s. Lester Clifford and Lillie May (Wilson) R.; B.S., Kans. State U., 1967, M.S., 1977. Research technician U.S. Dept. Agr., Sci. and Edn. Adminstrn., Newell, S.D., 1972-73; soils farm supt. Mich. State U., East Lansing, 1973-75; area agronomist U. Ill., Champaign, 1977—, supt. Orr Research Center, 1978—. Served with USAF, 1967-71. Cert. profl. agronomist, profl. soil scientist, profl. crop scientist Am. Registry Cert. Profls. in Agronomy, Crops and Soils. Mem. Am. Soc. Agronomy, Crop Sci. Soc. Am., Soil Sci. Soc. Am., Ill. Forage and Grassland Council. Mem. Christian Ch. Club: Mount Sterling Optimists (bd. dirs. 1980-81, v.p. 1981-82). Home: 307 W North St Mount Sterling IL 62353 Office: PO Box 212 Perry IL 62362

RAINEY, BAZELLA GIOTTO, III, hosp. adminstr.; b. Clarksdale, Miss., Mar. 5, 1943; s. Bazella Giotto and Vera Lee (Sledge) R.; student Delta State U., 1968-69, Tougaloo Coll., 1959-61; certificate N.Y. Inst. Photography, 1964; A.B. cum laude, U. Detroit, 1976; m. Janet Gail Osborn, Aug. 6, 1978; children—Valentia Therese, Chandra Lynette, Bazella Giotto, IV; stepchildren—Seth Thomas, Amy Loren. Photographer, salesman H.O. Pippen Photographers, Jackson, Miss., 1965-66; tchr. basic adult edn. Coahoma Opportunities, Inc., Clarksdale, Miss., 1966-67; counselor, coordinator Bolivar County Community Action Program, Cleveland, Miss., 1966-67; news dir. WGPR, Inc., Detroit, 1969-71; staff announcer WJBK-TV, Southfield, Mich., 1971-74; sales service rep. Sci. Med. Labs. of Detroit, 1976-77; dir. communications St. Joseph Mercy Hosp., Pontiac, Mich., 1977—; hypnosis instr. Community Services div. Wayne County Community Coll., Detroit; mem. Oakland County Emergency Med. Services Council, mem. com. on communications, 1977-79. Pres. Pitcher-McKinney Community Council, Greydale 197 Block Club; past pres. North Suburban Postal Customers' Council; mem. Mayor's Community Leadership Council N.W. Detroit, 1976-77; bd. dirs. Mich. Emergency Patrol, 1973-74; instr. judo YMCA, 1972-73; del. state conv. Miss. Young Democrats, 1966. Served with USAF, 1961-65. Mem. Am. Soc. Hosp. Engring., Telecommunications Assn. Health Care in S.E. Mich. (pres.), Am. Mgmt. Assn., Soc. Profl. Journalists, Nat. Assn. to Advance Ethical Hypnosis (former mem. nat. exec. bd., past pres. Mich. chpt. 1), Alpha Epsilon Rho. Roman Catholic. Club: Kiwanis Internat. Home: 652 Pearson St Ferndale MI 48220 Office: St Joseph Mercy Hosp 900 Woodward St Pontiac MI 48053

RAINVILLE, ROGER HAROLD, pub. affairs and pub. relations cons.; b. Chgo., Nov. 18, 1940; s. Harold and Mariann (Pack) R.; A.B., Dartmouth Coll., 1962; M.A., U. Pa., 1966; m. Jane Young, 1967; children—Lynn, Keith. Founder, owner Roger Rainville & Assos., Ltd., Chgo., 1966—; White House advanceman, 1972-76; cons. to real estate and urban planning firms, 1968—. Campaign mgr. Sen. Dirksen for Re-election, 1968; dir. E.M. Dirksen Congressional Leadership Research Center, 1969-72; lectr. Urban interstate hwy. projects 1969—; bd. dirs. Family Guidance Center, Inc., 1970-79, treas., 1974-76; campaign mgr. city, county, state and fed. elections, 1966—; pres. North Shore Health Found., 1979—. Served to 1st lt. USAF, 1962-65. Mem. Chgo. Council Fgn. Relations, Internat. Wildlife Fedn., Internat. Visitors Center. Clubs: Dartmouth, Press (Chgo.); Elephant (exec. dir. 1976-80) (Evanston, Ill.). Home: 1626 Lincoln St Evanston IL 60201 Office: 612 N Michigan Ave Suite 616 Chicago IL 60611

RAITT, JOHN WELLESLEY, musician; b. Chgo., Oct. 17, 1923; s. Charles Henry and Vie Clinton (Hanna) R.; student Chgo. Mus. Coll., 1946-48; m. Marjorie Ann McLain, May 13, 1950; children—Michael John, Leslie, Barbara, Robin. With Chgo. Civic Orch., 1942, 46, Ark. State Symphony, Little Rock, 1947-48; asst. prin. bassoonist Chgo. Symphony Orch., 1949—; faculty Sherwood Mus. Coll., Chgo., 1951-61, Roosevelt U., Chgo., 1951-57; prin. bassoon Ravinia Festival, Highland Park, Ill., 1962. Served with USAAF, 1943-46. Home: 1510 E Fremont St Arlington Heights IL 60004 Office: 220 S Michigan Ave Chicago IL 60604

RAJCHEL, JAMES MICHAEL, ednl. adminstr.; b. East Chicago, Ind., June 7, 1946; s. Joseph Aloysius and Lottie Harriet (Wajda) R.; B.Music Edn., VanderCook Coll. Music, Chgo., 1968; M.Ed., Loyola U., Chgo., 1973; Ed.S., Purdue U., 1982; m. Kathleen Marie Kogut, Aug. 3, 1968; 1 dau., Bonnie Marie. Dir. bands Sch. Dist. #155, Calumet City, Ill., 1968-78; prin. Woodrow Wilson Elem. Sch. and dist. spl. edn. coordinator, 1978—. Supt., Sch. of Christian Living, St. Michael The Archangel Polish Nat. Cath. Ch., East Chicago, 1969-78, chmn. parish com., 1981—. Mem. Ill. Prins. Assn., Ill. Assn. Supervision and Curriculum Devel., Assn. Supervision and Curriculum Devel., Am. Fedn. Musicians, VanderCook Coll. Music Alumni Assn. (pres. elect 1980-82), Phi Delta Kappa. Home: 4814 Baring Ave East Chicago IN 46312 Office: Woodrow Wilson Sch Wentworth Ave and Memorial Dr Calumet City IN 60409

RAJENDRA, KUNWAR, engr.; b. Lahore, India (now Pakistan), Sept. 10, 1938; s. Ram Murti and Raj Rani Pawsey; came to U.S., 1970; B.S. in Civil Engring., Roorkee U., India, 1960; Ph.D., Mich. State U., 1980; m. Shanno Tandon, Dec. 6, 1963; children—Archana, Rachana, Anuja. Engr., State of India, 1961-70; project engr., coordinator high energy physics, Mich. State U., East Lansing, 1971-74; transp. coordinator City of Lansing (Mich.), 1974—; vis. faculty Mich. State U.; speaker profl. confs.; cons. Lectr. stress mgmt. and yoga Mich. State U., 1971—. Registered profl. engr., Mich. Mem. Inst. Transp. Engrs. (chmn. subcom. research needs in transp. in developing countries), Transp. Research Bd., ASCE (urban transp. econs. com.), Indian Roads Congress. Contbr. articles to profl. jours. Home: 5244 Bluehaven Dr East Lansing MI 48823 Office: 2d Floor Washington Sq Annex City Hall Lansing MI 48933

RAJPUT, AQIL KHAN, data processing exec.; b. Mundawar, India, July 1, 1944; s. Rafi Khan and Mijazan A. (Rao) R.; came to U.S., 1975, naturalized, 1975; M.S., U. Sind, 1967; m. Jane Mary Thompson, Oct. 29, 1974; children—Sabina Saerah, Amira Mijazan. Research asst. Harrods Ltd., London, 1971-74; officer Brit. Railways, London, 1974-75; sr. programmer Harley-Davidson Motor Co., Milw., 1975; project statistician City of Milw., 1975-79; systems devel., data processing Mortgage Guaranty Ins. Corp., Milw., 1979; exec. dir. RAFI, Inc., Milw., 1979—. Fellow Royal Statis. Soc.; mem. Data Processing Mgmt. Assn., Am. (sec.-treas. Milw. chpt. 1977-79, chpt. pres. 1979—), Sind U. statis. assns., Ops. Research Soc. Am. (1st vice chmn. Milw. chpt. 1977-78), Inst. Mgmt. Scis., Canadian Ops. Research Soc., Internat. Assn. Survey Statisticians, Assn. Computing Machinery, Inst. Mgmt. Scis. (chmn. Milw. chpt. 1978—), Am. Soc. Quality Control (chmn. 24th indsl. seminar Milw. chpt. 1978), Statis. Sci. Assn. Can. Asso. editor: Al-Manar. Home: 8869 W Appleton Ave Milwaukee WI 53225 Office: PO Box 2151 Milwaukee WI 53201

RAJU, PUTHANKURISSI SANKARANARAYAN, educator; b. Kerala State, India, Sept. 14, 1950; came to U.S., 1971, naturalized, 19—; s. Puthankurissi Appuier and Rajam Sankaranarayan; B.Tech., Indian Inst. Tech., 1971; M.S. (univ. fellow), U. Ill., Champaign-Urbana, 1976, Ph.D., 1977; m. Revathy Athmaraman, July 9, 1978. Mem. faculty Pa. State U., 1975-80, asst. prof. mktg., 1976-80; asst. prof. mktg. U. Ill., Chgo., 1980—. Ford Found. fellow, 1977. Mem. Am. Mktg. Assn., Assn. Consumer Research, Am. Inst. Decision Scis. Address: Dept Mktg Box 4348 U Ill Chicago IL 60680

RAJU, SATYANARAYANA GOTTUMUKKALA VENKATA, elec. engr.; b. Undi, India, Jan. 8, 1934; came to U.S., 1961, naturalized, 1975; s. Subba G. and Subbamma R.; B.S., Andhra U., 1955; M.Tech., Indian Inst. Tech., 1959; Ph.D., Poly. Inst. Bklyn., 1965; m. June 12, 1955; children—Jaya, Uma. Sr. research asst. Phys. Research Labs., Ahmedabad, 1959-61; asst. prof. Clarkson Coll. Tech., 1965-67; asst. prof. Ohio U., Athens, 1967-68, asso. prof., 1968-72, prof. elec. engring., 1972—, chmn. dept., 1973—. Grantee NSF, NASA, Dept. Energy. Mem. IEEE (sr.), Am. Soc. Engring. Edn., Internat. Fedn. Automatic Control, Eta Kappa Nu, Sigma Xi. Club: Rotary. Contbr. articles to profl. jours. Home: 11 Lamar Dr Athens OH 45701 Office: Dept Elec Engring Ohio U Athens OH 45701

RAKOCZY, JOSEPH RONALD, civil and environ. engr.; b. Chgo., Apr. 24, 1949; s. Joseph C. and Henrietta (Mach) R.; B.S. in Chem. Engring., Ill. Inst. Tech., 1971, postgrad. in environ. engring., 1974-77. Asst. civil engr. Met. San. Dist. Greater Chgo., 1971-74, asso. civil engr., 1974-77, sr. civil engr., 1977—, project engr. Chgo. Tunnel and Reservoir Plan; instr., speaker, cons. urban hydrology and flood control reservoir design; seminar instr. stormwater detention design and urban hydrology Chgo. chpts. Am. Soc. Plumbing Engrs., Ill. Soc. Profl. Engrs. Recipient plaque of appreciation Chgo. chpt. Nat. Soc. Profl. Engrs.; registered profl. engr., Ill. Mem. ASCE, Water Pollution Control Fedn., Central States Water Pollution Control Assn., Am. Inst. Chem. Engrs. (asso.), Nat. Audubon Soc., Cousteau Soc., Nature Conservancy, Sierra Club, Wilderness Soc., Natural Resources Def. Council. Home: 121 W Glenlake Ave Park Ridge IL 60068 Office: 666 N Lake Shore Dr Chicago IL 60611

RALL, KENNETH LOEM, radiologist; b. Independence, Mo., Feb. 11, 1935; s. Albert A. and Roberta F. R.; B.S., Central Mo. State U., 1956; M.D., U. Mo., 1960; m. Sara B. Thoma, May 27, 1956; children—Kenneth, Susan, Kurt. Intern, Pontiac (Mich.) Gen. Hosp., 1960-61; resident U. Mo., Columbia, 1961-64; practice medicine specializing in radiology, 1966—; mem. staffs Boone County Hosp., Cooper County Hosp., Woodland Hosp.; clin. asso. prof. radiology U. Mo., 1966—; mem. staff Radiology, Inc., Columbia, 1966—. Active Boy Scouts Am., 1967—. Served with U.S. Army, 1964-66. NIH fellow, 1965-66; Am. Cancer Soc. fellow, 1963-64. Diplomate Am. Coll. Radiology. Mem. AMA, Mo. State, So. med. assns., Radiol. Soc. N.Am. Presbyterian. Clubs: Cosmopolitan Internat., Masons,

Shriners. Home: 1121 Danforth St Columbia MO 65201 Office: 1502 E Broadway Columbia MO 65201

RALSTON, MARY AGNES, lectr., writer; b. Caledonia, Ill., d. William D. and Agnes (Kelly) Ralston; student Rockford Coll., U. Wis. Extension; B.S., Northwestern U. Lectr., free lance writer. Mem. Nat. Assn. Bank Women, Council for Wis. Writers, AAUW, Indsl. and Ednl. Counselors Assn., Asso. Bus. Writers Am., Wis. Regional Writers Assn., Wis. Press Women, Nat. Fedn. Press Women, Women in Communications, Authors Guild, Authors League Am., Am. Profl. Inst., Milw. Press Club, Kappa Alpha Theta. Club: Tempo. Author: How to Return to Work in an Office, 1973. Contbr. numerous articles to profl., trade jours. Home: 1006 E State St Milwaukee WI 53202

RAMADANOFF, DIMITER, engring. and research cons.; b. Kustendil, Bulgaria, Oct. 8, 1900; s. Christo Ivan and Elena (Stoyanova) R.; came to U.S., 1920, naturalized, 1938; B.S. in Elec. Engring., U. Ill., 1924; Ph.D. in Physics, Cornell U., 1932; m. Thelma A. Briggs, Sept. 12, 1926; 1 son, David Dimitri; McMullen research scholar, instr. elec. engring. Cornell U., 1926-37; research elec. engr., physicist Nat. Carbon Co. div. Union Carbide Corp., Cleve., 1937-58, gen. cons. Carbon Products div., 1958-65; engring. and research cons., Berea, Ohio, 1965—. Fellow IEEE; mem. Inst. Aeros. and Astronautics, Soc. Lubrication Engrs., Soc. Automotive Engrs., Sigma Xi, Phi Kappa Phi. Patentee aircraft and automotive elec. equipment. Address: 661 Grayton Rd Berea OH 44017

RAMAEKERS, PATRICK JOSEPH, life ins. salesman; b. Humphrey, Nebr., Nov. 25, 1945; s. Edward Henry and Cecilia Barbara Ramaekers; student Omaha U., 1966-67; C.L.U., 1979; m. Shirley A. Mohr, Nov. 16, 1966; 1 son, Nichlas Joseph. Engaged in life ins. bus., 1967—; gen. mgr. Am. Nat. Life Ins. Co., Omaha, 1971—. Active local Am. Heart Assn., Am. Cancer Soc., Boys Club, A.R.C. Served with USNR, 1965. Recipient numerous ins. salesmanship awards. Mem. Nat. Life Underwriters Assn., Gen. Agts. Mgmt. Com., Million Dollar Round Table (state membership chmn. 1969—), Life Underwriters Polit. Action Com., Omaha Assn. Life Underwriters (pres. 1979—), Nebr. Assn. Life Underwriters, Omaha Assn. Fin. Planners. Roman Catholic. Author articles in field. Home: 321 N 130th St Omaha NE 68154 Office: 6818 Grover St Suite 201 Omaha NE 68106

RAMAKRISHNAN, VENKATASWAMY, educator; b. Coimbatore, India, Feb. 27, 1929; s. Venkataswamy and Kondammal (Krishnaswamy) R.; came to U.S., 1969; B.E., U. Madras (India), 1952, D.S.S., 1953; D.I.C. in Hydropower and Concrete Tech., Imperial Coll. (Eng.), 1957; Ph.D., Univ. Coll., U. London (Eng.), 1960; m. Vijayalakshmi Unnava, Nov. 7, 1962; children—Aravind, Anand. Lectr., P.S.G. Coll. Tech., U. Madras (India), 1952-55, asst. prof., 1960-61, prof., head dept. civil engring., 1961-69; vis. prof. S.D. Sch. Mines and Tech., Rapid City, 1969-70, prof. civil engring., 1970—, dir. concrete tech. research, 1970-71, head grad. div. structural mechs. and concrete tech., dept. civil engring., 1971—; cons. architecture and structural engring., India. Founding mem. PSGR Children's Sch., 1961—; founding dir., now v.p. World Open U. Columbo Plan fellow, 1955-60; named Outstanding Educator Am., 1975; recipient Pres.'s award S.D. Sch. Mines and Tech., 1980. Mem. Internat. Assn. Bridge and Structural Engring., ASCE (vice chmn. constrn. div. publs. com.), Am. Concrete Inst. (chmn. subcom. gen. considerations for founds., pres. Dakota chpt.), Instn. Hwy. Engrs. (London), Transp. Research Bd. (mech. properties of concrete com., performance of concrete phys. aspects com., curing of concrete com.), Am. Soc. Engring. Edn., Internat. Council Gap-Graded Concrete Research and Application (sec.), Nat. Soc. Profl. Engrs., Am. Soc. Engring. Edn., Sigma Xi (chpt. treas., mem. numerous coms.). Author: Ultimate Strength Design for Structural Concrete, 1969; contbr. articles to profl. jours. and procs. Home: 1809 Sheridan Lake Rd Rapid City SD 57701

RAMBERT, GORDON ARTHUR, corp. exec.; b. Rochester, N.Y., Mar. 6, 1922; s. Arthur Frederick and Mildred (Baker) R.; B.S., Lehigh U., 1949; m. Jeanne Audrey Bucher, Dec. 27, 1947; children—Paul A., Cynthia L., Gregory N., Michele M. Personnel mgr. Jamestown Malleable Iron Corp. (N.Y.), 1955-58; mgr. compensation Todd div. Burroughs Corp., Rochester, 1958-64; asst. sec., dir. personnel Consol-Vacuum Corp., Rochester, 1964-66; v.p. indsl. relations Joslyn Mfg. & Supply Co., Chgo., 1966-70; pres. Rambert and Co., Inc., mgmt. cons., Lake Bluff, Ill., 1970—; adv. cons. on exec. compensation Midwest Indsl. Mgmt. Assn. Served with Signal Corps AUS, 1942-46. Mem. Am. Soc. Personnel Adminstrn. (dir. 1968—, treas. 1970, 71), Indsl. Relations Assn., Indsl. Relations Research Assn., N.A.M. (indsl. relations com.), Lambs (dir.). Home: 641 Williams Ct Gurnee IL 60031 Office: 11 N Skokie Hwy Lake Bluff IL 60044

RAMER, JAMES LEROY, profl. engr.; b. Marshalltown, Iowa, Dec. 7, 1935; s. LeRoy Frederick and Irene (Wengert) R.; student U. Iowa, 1953-57; M.S. in Civil Engring., Washington U., St. Louis, 1976, M.A. in Polit. Sci., 1978; m. Jacqueline L. Orr, Dec. 15, 1957; children—Sarah T., Robert H., Eric A., Susan L. Civil engr. U.S. State Dept., Del Rio, Tex., 1964; project engr. H. B. Zachry Co., San Antonio, 1965-66; civil and constrn. engr. U.S. Army C.E., St. Louis, 1967-76, tech. advisor for planning and nat. hydropower coordinator, 1976-78, project mgr. for EPA constrn. grants, Milw., 1978-80; chief architecture and engring. HUD, Indpls., 1980-81; pvt. practice civil engring., 1981—; adj. faculty civil engring. Washington U., 1968-78, U. Wis., Milw., 1978-80. Mem. ASCE, Nat. Soc. Profl. Engrs., Soc. Am. Mil. Engrs., AAUP. Lutheran. Club: Optimists Internat. Home: Route 1 Box 51 Fortuna MO 65034 Office: 405 E Morgan St Tipton MO 65081

RAMEY, RALPH EMERSON, JR., univ. adminstr.; b. Columbus, Ohio, Dec. 4, 1928; s. Ralph Emerson and Margaret Jessie (Tanner) R.; B.S., Ohio State U., 1950, M.S. in Natural Resources, 1976; m. Jean Alice Waldschmidt, May 26, 1951; children—John Louis, Carolyn Louise, James Andrew. Sales rep. Pfizer Labs., 1953-65, Highlights for Children, 1965-66; recreation supr. Ohio Div. of Parks and Recreation, 1966-69; supr. Public info. Columbus and Franklin County Met. Park Dist., 1969-73; lectr. Ohio State U. Sch. Natural Resources, 1970-73; now dir. Glen Helen, nature preserve Antioch Coll., Yellow Springs, Ohio. Chmn., Ohio Natural Areas Council; trustee Little Miami, Inc.; mem. Ohio Recreation and Resources Com. Served with U.S. Army, 1951-52. Recipient Green leaf award PP364 Nature Conservancy, 1973. Mem. Nature Conservancy (past chmn., dir. Ohio chpt.), Ohio Conservation and Outdoor Edn. Assn. (past pres.), Ohio Biol. Survey (trustee), Ohio Wildlife Mgmt. Assn., Outdoor Writers Ohio (past sec.-treas.), Assn. Interpretive Naturalists, Ohio Hist. Soc., Wilderness Soc., Nat. Parks and Conservation Assn., Ohio Environ. Council (trustee). Contbr. articles to profl. jours. Office: 405 Corry St Yellow Springs OH 45387

RAMIG, DAVID LAWRENCE, podiatrist; b. Mitchell, S.D., July 3, 1951; s. Clifford Lawrence and Vergie Lee (Cahoy) R.; B.S. in Biology, U. Cin., 1973; D.P.M., Ohio Coll. Podiatric Medicine, 1977; m. Leigh Ann Ellis, Dec. 21, 1972; children—David, Jenny, Christy, Kevin. Resident in podiatric surgery Cleve. Foot Clinic, 1977-78; practice podiatric medicine and surgery, Red Oak, Iowa, 1978—; adj. clin. instr. Ohio Coll. Podiatric Medicine. Mem. Red Oak Park Bd., 1981—. Recipient Clin. Proficiency award Ohio Coll. Podiatric Medicine, 1977. Mem. Am. Podiatry Assn., Iowa Podiatry Soc., Am. Coll. Sports Medicine, Am. Coll. Foot Surgeons (asso.), Am. Public Health Assn. Club: Elks. Home: 1903 Sunnyslope Red Oak IA 51566 Office: 502 Reed Red Oak IA 51566

RAMLER, WARREN JOSEPH, radiation equipment co. exec.; b. Joliet, Ill., Jan. 1, 1921; s. John George and Anna Louise (Kohlmeyer) R.; B.S. in Elec. Engring., Ill. Inst. Tech., 1943, M.S. in Elec. Engring., 1953; postgrad. Carnegie-Mellon U., 1943-46, U. Pitts., 1943-46; m. Ruth E. Wilder, Sept. 4, 1943; children—John W., Richard W., Barbara Anne. Instr. elec. engring. and physics Carnegie Inst. Tech., 1943, 44, 46; elec. engr. Tenn. Eastman Corp., Oak Ridge, 1944-46; sr. scientist, project dir. low energy accelerators Argonne (Ill.) Nat. Lab., 1946-73, cons., 1973—; gen. mgr. Radiation Polymer Co. div. PPG Industries, Plainfield, Ill., 1973-80; sr. v.p. RPC Industries, Plainfield and Hayward, Calif., 1980—; cons. to univs. and industry. Asso. chmn. Boy Scouts Am., Elmhurst, Ill., 1956-60; mem. sci. adv. com. York High Sch., 1962. Mem. IEEE, Am. Phys. Soc., Am. Mgmt. Assn., AAAS, N.Y. Acad. Scis., U.S. Power Squadron, Eta Kappa Nu, Tau Beta Pi, Rho Epsilon. Home: 15 Buckingham Dr Prestbury Aurora IL 60504

RAMNATH, RAMCHANDRA, plastic surgeon; b. Bombay, India, Aug. 8, 1929; s. K.S. Ramchandra and Chelli (Ammal) Iyer; came to U.S., 1962, naturalized, 1976; B.S., M.B., U. Bombay, 1954; m. Irmgard Pfitzer, June 20, 1963; children—Urmila, Albert, Erik, Michelle. Intern, Elizabeth (N.J.) Gen. Hosp., 1962-63; resident in surgery Provident and St. Agnes Hosps., Balt., 1962-66; resident in plastic surgery Christ Hosp., Cin., 1966-69; practice medicine specializing in plastic surgery, Dayton, Ohio, 1970—; mem. staff St. Elizabeth Med. Center, Miami Valley Hosp., Good Samaritan Hosp., Kettering Med. Center, Children's Med. Center; asst. clin. prof. surgery Wright State U. Sch. Medicine; cons. in plastic surgery Dayton VA Center. Diplomate Am. Bd. Plastic Surgery. Fellow Internat. Coll. Surgeons, mem. AMA, Ohio State, Pan Am. med. assns., Montgomery County Med. Soc., Dayton Surg. Soc., Internat. Cosmetic Surgery Assn., Assn. Surgeons India, Am. Soc. Plastic and Reconstructive Surgery, Ohio Valley Plastic and Reconstructive Soc., Sashruta Soc. Clubs: East Dayton Optimist, Lions; Ghatkoper (India). Home: 430 E Schantz Ave Dayton OH 45409 Office: 3080 Ackerman Blvd Dayton OH 45429

RAMON, PACIFICO CRUZ, JR., pathologist; b. Manila, Philippines, Feb. 25, 1936; s. Pacifico N. and Adriana G. (Cruz) R.; A.A., Letran Coll., Manila, 1953; M.D., U. St. Thomas, Manila, 1958; m. Maria Luisa Buenafe; children—Dulcie Marie, Darryl Anthony. Intern, Jamaica (N.Y.) Hosp., 1959-60, resident in pathology, 1960-64, asso. pathologist, 1964-74; asso. pathologist St. John's Hosp., Queens, N.Y.C., 1966-68; pathologist and dir. labs. Cass County Meml. Hosp., Atlantic, Iowa, 1974—; cons. pathologist Audubon (Iowa) County Meml. Hosp., Manning (Iowa) Gen. Hosp., 1974—; asst. clin. prof. pathology Sch. Medicine, Creighton U., Omaha. Diplomate Am. Bd. Pathology. Fellow Coll. Am. Pathologists, Am. Soc. Clin. Pathologists, Internat. Acad. Pathology, Am. Soc. Cytology, Assn. Clin. Scientists; mem. AMA, Iowa Med. Assn., Iowa Assn. Pathologists, Cass County Med. Soc., Atlantic C. of C. Roman Catholic. Club: Rotary. Home: 101 E 21st St Atlantic IA 50022 Office: 1501 E 10th St Atlantic IA 50022

RAMP, ALVON DENEAL, mgmt. cons.; b. Dixon, Ill. Sept. 10, 1947; s. Jacob Levi and Bertha Mae (Rucker) R.; B.S. in Math., No. Ill. U., 1969; M.B.A., Loyola U., Chgo., 1977; m. Jeryl Ann McGreevy, Aug. 25, 1968; children—Alette Christine, Patrick Christian, Megan Ann. Systems programmer No. Ill. U., DeKalb, 1968-70; adminstrv. systems analyst Coll. of DuPage, Glen Ellyn, Ill., 1970-72, asso. dir. data processing and programming, 1972-74, dir. data processing, 1974-78; mgmt. cons. Cara Corp., Oak Brook, Ill., 1978-81, mgr. field services, Lombard, Ill., 1981—; instructional specialist for data processing Boulder (Colo.) Valley Schs., 1972; instr. Coll. of DuPage, 1971-72, Waubonsee Community Coll., Sugar Grove, Ill., 1970-72; EDP cons., 1971—. Pack master Cub Scouts, Wheaton, Ill. Mem. Data Processing Mgmt. Assn., Ill. Assn. Ednl. Data Systems (dir.), Lincoln Sch. PTA, Loyola U. of Chgo. Grad. Sch. Bus., No. Ill. U. alumni assns., S.E. Wheaton Homeowners Assn. Roman Catholic. Home: 1522 Gainesboro Dr Wheaton IL 60187 Office: 1010 Jorie Blvd Suite 124 Oak Brook IL 60521

RAMSEY, CHARLES HENRY, mental health cons.; b. Bay City, Mich., July 18, 1915; s. David Alger and Harriet Janet (Kellogg) R.; B.A. summa cum laude, Central Mich. U., 1948; M.A., U. Mich., 1953; m. Mertie Alice Stanley, May 16, 1942; children—Alice Denise, Lisa Ann. Social worker Saginaw (Mich.) County Schs., 1948-53; dir. juvenile ct. services Saginaw County juvenile div. Probate Ct., 1953-57; chmn. social work dept. Saginaw Public Schs., 1958-65; dep. supt., dir. spl. edn. Tuscola County Intermediate Sch. Dist., Caro, Mich., 1965-69; Dept. Mental Health rep. to Mental Retardation Cadre and cons. on spl. edn., Lansing, Mich., 1969, regional adminstr. Region II, dir. children and youth services, Lansing, 1978-81, ret., 1981; now cons. various children's agys. Chmn., Mich. Juvenile Services Tng. Council, 1973-77, Referent Group for Minimal Objectives for Mental Health Edn., Lansing, 1975-76; mem. Mich. Mental Health Reps. for Children and Youth, 1975; mem. state task force Family Life Edn. and Family Planning for Handicapped, 1975-76; bd. dirs. Big Bros., Saginaw, 1953-60, Alcohol Info. Center, Saginaw, 1955-65, Adult Mental Health Clinic, Saginaw, 1960-62. Served with USCG, 1941-45. Mem. Am. Assn. Psychiat. Services to Children, Am. Assn. Mental Deficiency, Council for Exceptional Children, Nat. Rehab. Assn., Mich. Soc. for Study of Adolescence. Methodist. Contbr. articles in field to profl. jours. Home: 3031 Thorncrest Dr SE Grand Rapids MI 49506

RAMSEY, DAVID SELMER, hosp. adminstr.; b. Mpls., Feb. 19, 1931; s. Selmer A. and Esther D. R.; B.S., U. Mich., 1953, M.S., 1954, M.H.A., 1962; m. Elinor Corfield, Aug. 15, 1953; children—Scott, Stewart, Thomas. Cancer research asso. Detroit Inst. Cancer Research, 1954-61; asso. adminstr. Harper Hosp., Detroit, 1962-72; adminstr. Iowa Meth. Med. Center, Des Moines, 1972—; dir. Iowa Savings & Loan Assn., Des Moines. Mem. Am. Coll. Hosp. Adminstrs. (regent), Am. Mgmt. Assn., Assn. Rehab. Dirs., Am. Hosp. Assn., Soc. Advancements Mgmt., Iowa Hosp. Assn. (chmn. 1979-80), Execs. Assn. Des Moines (pres. 1976-77), Alumni Assn. U. Mich. (pres.). Club: Wakonda. Contbr. articles on cancer research to profl. jours. Home: 2825 Caulder St Des Moines IA 50321 Office: 1200 Pleasant St Des Moines IA 50308

RAMSEY, RICHARD RALPH, lawyer, state legislator; b. Osceola, Iowa, Nov. 23, 1940; s. Jospeh D. and Ardis R. (Bowlsby) R.; B.A. in History, U. No. Iowa, 1963; J.D., U. Iowa, 1966; m. Natalie J. Green, Sept. 27, 1968; children—Adam Todd, Angela Ruth, Aaron Nathaniel, Aimee Rebecca. Admitted to Iowa bar, 1966, since practiced in Osceola; county atty. Clarke County (Iowa), 1968-72; mem. Iowa Senate, 1973—, asst. minority leader, chmn. com. energy and ethics, pres. pro tem, 1981—. Served with U.S. Army, 1966-68; Vietnam. Office: 231 S Main St Osceola IA 50213

RAMSEY, WILLIAM LEE, ednl. adminstr.; b. Loveland, Ohio, Jan. 1, 1927; married, 3 children. B.A., B.S. in Edn., 1948; M.A. in Edn. Adminstrn., Xavier U., 1956; Ph.D. in Adminstrn., U. No. Colo. at Greeley, 1960. Supt. Rossford (Ohio) City Schs., 1961-65; supt., pres. Penta-County Vocat. Sch., Owens Tech. Coll., Toledo, 1965-68; prof. high edn., Colo., Ohio, 1957-68; dist. dir. Milw. Area Tech. Coll., 1968—; cons. in field; lectr. in field. Bd. dirs. Aerospace Found. 1970— (pres. 1975—), Milw. council Adult Learning, 1969—, Greater Milw. Survey Social Welfare, Health Services Inc., 1971—, Midwestern Ednl. T.V. Inc., 1971—, Student Leadership Services, Wis., 1973—. Mem. councils Nat. Aerospace Edn., 1966—, Nat. Sch. house Constrn., 1966—, Opportunities Industrialization Center, Citizens, 1969—, mem. coms. Ohio Sch. Dist. Orgn. Survey, 1966, Wis. Acad. Programs, 1972—; Milw. Mayor's Model Cities Project, 1968—, Sch. Masters Club Inc., 1968—, area Milw. Employment Handicapped, 1969—, We-Milwaukeeans Sub-Com., 1970—. Mem. NEA, Ohio Edn. Assn., Am. Assn. Sch. Adminstrs., Am. Vocat. Assn., Am. Assn. Higher Edn., Am. Assn. Community Jr. Colls., North Central Assn. Colls., Wis. Assn. Vocat. Adult Edn., Wis. Assn. Vocat., Tech. Adult Edn. Adminstrs., Kellett Task Force on Edn., Milw. Mental Health Assn., Phi Delta Kappa. Contbr. numerous articles to profl. jours. Home: 21810 Locksley Ln Brookfield WI 53005 Office: 1015 N 6th St Milwaukee WI 53203

RAMSEYER, JAMES ALBERT, silicon chemistry mfg. co. exec.; b. Bay County, Mich., Apr. 19, 1940; s. Herbert Samuel and Naomi Ida (Gudeman) R.; B.S., Saginaw Valley State Coll., 1970; M.B.A., Central Mich. U., 1972; m. Marlene M. Reeves, Mar. 30, 1961; children—Bethany, Debra, Wendy, Natalie. Sr. technician Dow Corning Corp., Midland, Mich., 1968-70, tech. service and devel., 1971-73, corp. profl. personnel, 1973, supr. plant personnel, safety, security and tng., 1973-76, corp. edn. and personnel devel., 1976-81, mgr. edn. and tng., 1981, mgr. Midland plant personnel, 1981—; lectr. in field. Tchr. Sunday Sch., Apostolic Christian Ch., Bay City, Mich., 1963-67, supt. Sunday Sch., 1967-68, minister, 1968—; ordained minister Apostolic Christian Ch., 1968. Served with U.S. Army, 1959-61, 61-62. Mem. Am. Soc. Personnel adminstrn. (pres. chpt. 1975-76, dist. dir. region X 1974-75, regional v.p. 1976-77, nat. treas. 1978-79, Outstanding Regional Vice Pres. award 1976, 77), Am. Soc. Tng. and Devel., Soc. Assessment Systems Practitioners (founder, 1st pres. 1980). Republican. Patentee abalative material for heat shields in spacecraft, 1971. Home: 312 Sylvan Ln Midland MI 48640 Office: Dow Corning Corp 3901 S Saginaw Rd Midland MI 48640

RAMSLAND, MAXWELL O., real estate appraiser and cons.; b. Duluth, Minn., Aug. 13, 1939; s. Maxwell O. and Virginia (Mendenhall) R.; B.A., U. Minn., 1963; m. Betty S. Golden, Sept. 23, 1967; children—Austin W., Kathryn S. Staff appraiser Equitable Life Assurance Soc. U.S., Washington, 1964-68; asso. Wilbur S. Ratcliffe & Assos., Washington, 1968-70, C. Robert Boucher & Assos., Washington, 1970-71; cons. and appraiser real estate, Duluth, 1971-77; pres. Ramsland & Vigen Inc., Duluth, 1977—. Bd. dirs. Minn. Higher Edn. Facilities Authority, St. Luke's Hosp., Duluth, Duluth Grad. Med. Edn. Council. Mem. Am. Soc. Appraisers (dir. ednl. found. 1972—), Am. Inst. Real Estate Appraisers (dir. Minn. chpt. 1978—), Soc. Real Estate Appraisers, Am. Arbitration Assn. Club: Kitchi Gammi. Contbr. articles to profl. publs. Home: 2401 E 1st St Duluth MN 55812 Office: Torrey Bldg Duluth MN 55802

RAMSTAD, JAMES M., state senator, lawyer; b. Jamestown, N.D., May 6, 1946; s. Marvin Joseph and Della Mae (Fode) R.; B.A., U. Minn., 1968; J.D. with honors, George Washington U., 1973. Adminstrv. asst. to speaker Minn. Ho. Reps., 1969; spl. asst. to Congressman Tom Kleppe, 1970; admitted to N.D. bar, D.C. bar, 1973, U.S. Supreme Ct. bar, 1976, Minn. bar, 1979; practiced in Jamestown, 1973, Washington, 1974-1978, Mpls., 1979—; mem. Minn. Senate from Dist. 43, 1980—; instr. Am. govt. Montgomery (Md.) Coll., 1974; adj. prof. Am. U., Washington, 1975-78. Bd. dirs. Children's Heart Fund, Northwest YMCA, Lake County Food Bank, Normandale Coll. Found., Minn. Alpha Found. Served as 1st lt. U.S. Army Res., 1968-73. Mem. Am., Fed., Minn., Hennepin County, D.C., N.D. bar assns., Nat. Assn. Criminal Def. Lawyers, Nat. Legal Aid and Defender Assn., Trial Lawyers Assn. Minn., George Washington Law Assn., Assn. Trial Lawyers Am., U. Minn. Alumni Assn. (nat. dir.), Am. Legion, Northwest Met. C. of C., Plymouth Civic League, Phi Beta Kappa, Phi Delta Theta. Republican. Clubs: Mpls. Athletic, Nat. Press, Lafayette, U. Minn. Alumni (past pres. Washington), Lions. Home: 1869 Zanzibar Ln Plymouth MN 55447 Office: 136 State Office Bldg Saint Paul MN 55155

RANADE, VINAYAK VASUDEO, chemist; b. Wani, India, Feb. 5, 1938; came to U.S., 1964, naturalized, 1967; s. Vasudeo Narsinh and Sharayu Vasudeo R.; Ph.D. in Organic Chemistry, U. Bombay, 1964; m. Meghana, Aug. 27, 1964; 1 dau., Tanuja. Research asso. U. Mich., Ann Arbor, 1965-75; radiochemist Abbott Labs., North Chicago, Ill., 1975—. Recipient G. Czerniak prize for Nuclear Medicine and Radiopharmacology, 1974. Council Sci. and Indsl. Research fellow, 1962-64. Fellow Am. Inst. Chemists; mem. Am. Chem. Soc., Acad. Pharm. Scis., Sigma Xi. Referee Jour. Medicinal Chemistry. Contbr. articles in field to profl. jours. Home: 1219 Deertrail Ln Libertyville IL 60048 Office: D-463 AP-9 Abbott Labs North Chicago IL 60064

RANCOUR, JOANN SUE, registered nurse; b. Elyria, Ohio, Nov. 10, 1939; d. Joseph and Ann (Donich) Sokol; diploma M.B. Johnson Sch. Nursing, 1960; B.S. in Profl. Arts, St. Josephs Coll., N. Windham, Maine, 1981; student in psychology Alfred Adler Inst., Chgo., 1976—, Lorain County Community Coll., 1973-75, Ursuline Coll., Cleve., 1976; m. Richard Lee Rancour, July 29, 1961; children—Kathleen Ann, Donna Marie. Staff nurse Elyria Meml. Hosp., 1960-62, 72-75, head nurse psychiat. unit, 1975-79; sec-treas. Alfred Adler Inst. Cleve., 1978-79; detention home nurse Domestic Relations Ct. Lorain County, Elyria, Ohio, 1980; staff nurse VA Med. Center, Breckville, Ohio, 1981—. Active PTA, yearbook com.,

1969-70, co-chmn. ways and means, 1971; Dem. poll worker, 1971-72; sec. St. Mary's Confrat. Christian Doctrine Program, 1970-71. Mem. Am. Nurses Assn. (cert. generalist practitioner psychiat. and mental health nursing practice), Ohio Nurses Assn., N.Am. Soc. Adlerian Psychology, Nat. League for Nursing, Internat. Platform Assn. Roman Catholic. Home: 205 Denison Ave Elyria OH 44035

RANDA, GEORGE BRANT, auditor; b. Mineola, N.Y., Jan. 25, 1943; s. George John and Elin Margareta (Brant) R.; B.A., Baldwin-Wallace Coll., 1970. Trust dept. adminstrv. asst. Nat. City Bank, Cleve., 1966-70; ops. supr. Merrill, Lynch, Inc., Cleve., 1970-72; sr. internal auditor Union Commerce Bank, Cleve., 1972—. Bd. dirs. Center Repertory Theatre, 1977-79; ex-officio bd. mem. Greater Cleve. Growth Assn., 1977-78; pres. Cleve. Jaycee Found.; active Citizens League Cleve. Named Outstanding Cleve. Jaycee, 1975, 79. Mem. Jr. Chamber Internat. (life, senator), Ohio Jr. C. of C. (metro chmn. 1977-78), Cleve. Jr. C. of C. (pres. 1976-77, chmn. bd. 1977-78). Editor CJC Forum, 1973-74. Home: 6521 State Rd Parma OH 44134

RANDALL, BOOKER TALIAFERRO, paper mfg. co. exec.; b. Pascagoula, Miss., Apr. 16, 1948; s. Booker T. and Florine D. Randall; B.S., Tenn. State U., 1970, M.S., 1971; m. Judy E. Barnes, Aug. 26, 1972; children—Julian B., Jason A. Adminstrv. asst., employee relations Internat. Paper Co., Moss Point, Miss., 1972-75, asst. mgr. employee relations, Panama City, Fla., 1975-76, supr. employee relations, Peoria, Ill., 1976-79, divisional employee relations mgr., Kansas City, Kans., 1979—. Mem. Am. Soc. Personnel Adminstrn. Baptist. Home: 9541 Outlook Dr Overland Park KS 66201 Office: International Paper Co 7930 State Line Rd Prairie Village KS 66207

RANDALL, DICK, advt. and public relations co. exec.; b. Port Chester, N.Y., Nov. 12, 1945; s. Gene and Frances (Grandazzo) Cicatelli; B.A., Marquette U., 1967; m. Maureen Russell, Aug. 17, 1966; children—Gregory, Katharine. Writer, news reporter Sta. WISN-TV, Milw., 1966-67; news reporter, anchorman Sta. WEMP, Milw., 1967-70; consumer reporter, anchorman Sta. WISN-TV, Milw., 1970-71; pres. Aquarius Prodns., Inc., Waukesha, Wis., 1977—; adj. instr. Marquette U. Parish asst. St. Anthony on the Lake, Pewaukee, Wis. Served with USNR, 1968—. Mem. Am. Fedn. TV and Radio Artists, Milw. Advt. Club, Better Bus. Bur. Milw., Sigma Delta Chi, Roman Catholic. Home: W278 N2968 Rocky Point Rd Pewaukee WI 53072 Office: 280 Regency Ct Suite 200 Waukesha WI 53186

RANDALL, JAMES R., food products co. exec.; b. 1924; B.S. in Chem. Engring., U. Wis., 1948; married. Tech. dir. Cargill Inc., 1948-68; v.p. prodn. and engring. Archer-Daniels-Midland Co., Decatur, Ill., 1968-69, exec. v.p., 1969-75, pres., dir., 1975—. Served in U.S. Army, 1943-46. Office: Archer-Daniels-Midland Co 4666 Faries Pkwy Box 1470 Decatur IL 62525*

RANDALL, JOHN DANIEL, JR., lawyer; b. Cedar Rapids, Iowa, July 30, 1935; s. John Daniel and Margaret (Graham) R.; B.A., State U. Iowa, 1958, LL.B., 1959; m. Melissa Lyon, Nov. 10, 1962; 1 son, John Daniel III. Admitted to Iowa bar, 1959; asso. John D. Randall Law Office, Cedar Rapids, 1959—. Vice pres. exec. com. Old Shad's Assn., Shattuck Sch., Minn., 1972-76. Mem. Am. (gen. practice sect. council 1967-73, vice chmn. com. on coms. 1967-68, membership com. 1967-74, lay assts. to lawyers com. 1969-70, utilization lay assts. to lawyers com. 1970-72, budget and fin. com. 1972-76, sub-com. legal assts. 1972-75), Iowa, Linn County bar assns., Cedar Rapids C. of C., Sigma Nu, Phi Alpha Delta. Clubs: Univ. Athletic, Masons, Shriners. Home: PO Box 2131 330 1st St SE Cedar Rapids IA 52406 Office: 330 1st St SE Cedar Rapids IA 52407

RANDALL, PATRICIA LORENE, clin. social worker; b. Springfield, Mo., Nov. 14, 1942; d. James Joseph and Bertha (Sperandio) R.; B.A. in Sociology, Mt. St. Scholastica Coll., 1964; M.S.W., St. Louis U., 1966. Staff mem., clin. social worker Family and Children's Service of Greater St. Louis, 1966-80, dir. Clayton (Mo.) dist. office, 1981—. Del. gov.'s adv. bd. Mo. White House Conf. on Families, 1979-80; chmn. St. Louis County Schs. Agys. Com. on Youth, 1969-71; mem. Block Partnership, 1971-72. Cert. Acad. Cert. Social Workers. Mem. Nat. Assn. Social Workers (del. state bd. 1977-79), Am. Assn. Marriage and Family Therapy, Am. Group Psychotherapy Assn., Mo. Assn. Social Welfare. Roman Catholic. Clubs: St. Francis Xavier Parish Singles Group, Christian Life Community. Home: 728 Lilac Ave Webster Groves MO 63119 Office: 107 S Meramec St Clayton MO 63105

RANDALL, PRISCILLA RICHMOND (MRS. RAYMOND V. RANDALL), public relations exec.; b. Arlington, Mass., Mar. 19, 1926; d. Harold B. and Florence (Hoefler) Richmond; student Wellesley Coll., 1943-44, Garland Sch., 1944-46, Winona State U. extension, 1967—; m. Raymond V. Randall, Mar. 2, 1946; children—Raymond R., Priscilla, Susan. Publicity and publs. coordinator Rochester (Minn.) Meth. Hosp., 1960-66, pub. relations cons., 1966-69; pub. relations dir. Sheraton-Rochester Hotel, Rochester, 1969-71; owner, sr. cons. Ideas Unltd., Rochester, 1971—; sr. cons. Med. Travel; pres. Randall Travel, Inc., Rochester, 1977—, SABU, Inc., 1972-74; travel writer, 1976—; producer TV show Priscilla's World, 1972-75. Mem. Am. Soc. Hosp. Public Relations Dirs., Internat. Platform Assn., Acad. Hosp. Public Relations, Public Relations Soc. Am. (accredited), Coordinated Health Communications Soc. (sec.-treas. 1970), Rochester Meth. Hosp. Aux. (pres. 1955-57), Inst. Cert. Travel Agts. (life), Women Ind. Bus. Owners. Club: Zonta. Editor: Inside Story, Rochester Meth. Hosp. News, 1960-69. Address: 611 Memorial Pkwy Rochester MN 55901

RANDALL, THEODORE JOSEPH, SR., systems program exec.; b. Springfield, Ill., Jan. 4, 1936; s. James Otis and Eura Marie (Burgess) R.; B.A. in Urban Studies, Wright State U., 1975; M.P.A., U. Dayton, 1978; m. Alice Marie Hitt, Jan. 24, 1956; children—Alice Eura Marie, Theodore Joseph, Roy Vincent, Mark Otis, Eric Jerome. Budget analyst City of Dayton (Ohio), 1975-76, mgmt. analyst, 1976, asst. to dir. human resources, 1976-77, intergovtl. affairs analyst, 1977—; adj. prof. Sinclair Coll., Wilmington (Ohio) Coll.; dir. resources project U.S. CSC; coordinator Data Collection Project, student internship allication and implementation; mem. Montgomery County Planning Subcom. 5-year plan, phys. resources com. Miami Valley Regional Planning Commn. Precinct leader Democratic Party, 1968-70; area dir. levy renewal Mental Health and Mental Retardation, 1977; chmn. fin. com., vice chmn. Children's Services Bd., 1977—; trustee Chaminade/Julienne High Sch.; EEO Affirmative Action rep., also Leadership Dayton rep. Aero. System div. Wright-Patterson AFB; mem. fin. devel. com. Arthritis Found. Served with USAF, 1955-59. Named Employee of Year, City of Dayton, 1978; recipient grant City of Dayton, 1971. Mem. Am. Soc. Public Adminstrn. (pres.), Social Workers Guild, Affiliated Socs., Greater Cin. Intergovtl. Tng. Council, Pi Sigma Alpha. Roman Catholic. Club: K.C. Home: 1335 Amherst Pl Dayton OH 45406 Office: Wright-Patterson AFB OH 45433

RANDALL, WILLIAM CLYDE, utilities exec.; b. Lake City, Minn., Oct. 29, 1949; s. Howard C. and Ardis E. (Fick) R.; A.A., Rochester State Jr. Coll., 1969; B.A. in Biology/Chemistry, Mankato State U., 1971. Asst. chemist EPA Research Project, S.B. Foot Tanning Co., Red Wing, Minn., 1972-74, chief chemist, 1974-75; dir. pub. utilities City of Red Wing, 1976—. Recipient cert. U. Wis. Mgmt. Inst., 1976; cert. as class A wastewater treatment plant operator Minn. Pollution Control Agy., 1976. Mem. Am. Water Works Assn., Water Pollution Control Fedn., Central States Water Pollution Control Assn., Minn. Wastewater Operators Assn. Methodist. Clubs: Lake City Country, Red Wing Rifle and Pistol. Home: 617 Grace St Red Wing MN 55066 Office: 229 Tyler Rd N Red Wing MN 55066

RANDLE, LEONARD SHENOFF, profl. baseball player, found. exec.; b. Long Beach, Calif., Feb. 12, 1949; s. Issac and Ethel (Smith) R.; B.S., Ariz. State U., 1970; m. Jacqueline Corr, Dec. 25, 1975. Third base player Chgo. Cubs, 1980—; pres. Lenny Randle Underprivileged Found., N.Y.C., 1977—.

RANDOLPH, DONALD APPLEBY, building materials mfg. co. exec.; b. Biscoe, Ark., May 3, 1939; s. Almarine Leon and Bennie Lee (Appleby) R.; B.S. in Chemistry, Ark. A.M.&N. Coll., Pine Bluff, 1960; M.A. in Chemistry, Fisk U., 1962; postgrad. U. Chgo., 1971-73; m. Edna Ruth Watkins, Sept. 30, 1962; children—Donald Appleby, Daron Anthony. Analytical chemist Am. Can Co., Maywood, Ill., 1962-66; advanced analytical chemist U.S. Gypsum Co., Des Plaines, Ill., 1966-68, group leader, 1968-71, analytical testing mgr., 1971-74, research mgr., 1974—; cons. in field. Coach Briarcliffe Community Youth Baseball & Basketball, Wheaton, Ill., 1977—; treas. Pack 382, Dupage Area council Boy Scouts Am., Wheaton, 1977—. Recipient Cert. of Appreciation, U.S. Gypsum Co., 1976. Mem. Am. Chem. Soc., Soc. Applied Spectroscopy, Chgo. Gas Chromatography Discussion Group, Am. Inst. Chem. Engrs., Am. Mgmt. Assn., Kappa Alpha Psi (dir. Youth Guidance Found., Maywood-Wheaton chpt.). Methodist. Author chpt. Ency. of Indsl. Chem. Analysis, 1971; founder, editor U.S. Gypsum Co. Research Center news mag., 1968-70. Home: 1605 S Prospect St Wheaton IL 60187 Office: 1000 E Northwest Hwy Des Plaines IL 60016

RANDOLPH, KENNETH HENRY, veterinarian; b. McCausland, Iowa, June 23, 1923; s. Clarence Raymond and Lillian Henrietta (Litscher) R.; B.S., Iowa State U., 1943, M.S., D.V.M., 1950; m. Carmaleta Frances Stephens, Dec. 21, 1946; children—Joylene Ann, Kerry Alden, Jody Lee. Grad. asst. dept. anatomy Iowa State U., 1947-50; pvt. veterinary practice, Lost Nation, Iowa, 1950—. Mem. Lost Nation City Council, 1957-62. Served with AUS, 1944-46. Mem. AVMA, Eastern Iowa, Iowa veterinary med. assns., Soc. Gentle Doctor, Lost Nation Businessmen's Assn. (pres. 1979), Phi Kappa Phi, Alpha Zeta. Republican. Presbyterian (elder 1962-75). Clubs: Masons, Shriners, Order Eastern Star, Lost Nation Booster, Cyclone Century. Home: 304 Esther St Lost Nation IA 52254 Office: 311 Main St Lost Nation IA 52254

RANDOLPH, LILLIAN LARSON, ins. co. exec.; b. Spokane, Wash., May 3, 1932; d. Charles P. Larson; B.A., U. Wash., 1953, M.A., 1956; Ph.D., U. Calif., Berkeley, 1966; postgrad. N.Mex. State U., Las Cruces, 1975-78; m. Philip Randolph, Nov. 12, 1952; children—Marcus P., Andrew L. Asst. prof. Calif. State U., Hayward, 1965-68; lectr. U. Tex., El Paso, 1968-69, Loyola U., Chgo., 1977-79; instr. N.Mex. State U., 1973-74, DePaul U., Chgo., 1977-79; programmer-systems analyst CNA Ins. Co., Chgo., 1980—. Mem. W. Tex. Council Govts., 1976-77. Recipient profl. awards. Mem. Am. Inst. Planners (pres. W. Tex. 1975-76), AAUP. Club: Toastmistress (pres. region V, 1976). Author: The Fundamental Laws of Government Organizations, 1971; Third-Party Settlement of Disputes in Theory and Practice, 1973. Home: 408 Wilshire Dr W Wilmette IL 60091 Office: CNA Ins Co CNA Plaza Chicago IL 60685

RANGSITHIENCHAI, PISIT, physician; b. Bangkok, Thailand, May 8, 1947; came to U.S., 1971; s. Kee Han and Pek Eng (Hau) Lau; M.D., Chulalongkorn U., Thailand, 1970; m. Thusnee Lowsitisukdi, Jan. 14, 1973; children—Allan, Alice. Intern, Chulalongkorn U. Hosp., Bangkok, Thailand, 1970-71; resident pediatrics Michael Reese Hosp., Chgo., 1971-74; fellow in allergy La Rabida U. Chgo. Inst., 1974-76, asst. prof., 1978—; practice medicine specializing in allergy, Oak Forest, Ill. and Chgo., 1976—; adj. prof. Chgo. Coll. Osteo. Medicine, 1978—. Diplomate Am. Bd. Pediatrics, Am. Bd. Allergy and Immunology. Mem. AMA, Am. Acad. Allergy, Ill. Med. Soc., Chgo. Med. Soc., Ill. Soc. Allergy and Clin. Immunology, Thai Med. Council. Buddhism. Office: 5601 Victoria Dr Oak Forest IL 60452 also 10401 S Kedzie Ave Chicago IL 60429

RANK, HUGH (DUKE), educator; b. Chgo., Nov. 3, 1932; s. Hugh Anthony and Margaret Francis (McGreevy) R.; B.A., U. Notre Dame, 1954, M.A., 1955, Ph.D., 1969; m. Lee Mary Novak, Aug. 30, 1958; children—Elizabeth, Christopher, James-Jonathan, David. Mem. faculty U. Notre Dame (Ind.), 1959-60, Ariz. State U., Tempe, 1960-62, St. Joseph's Coll., Rensselaer, Ind., 1962-67; Fulbright prof. Copenhagen, 1967-68; mem. faculty Sacred Heart U., Bridgeport, Conn., 1968-72; prof. English, Governors State U., Park Forest South, Ill., 1972—. Served to 1st lt. U.S. Army, 1955-58. Notre Dame scholar, 1954-55, fellow, 1960-61. Mem. Nat. Council Tchrs. English (George Orwell award 1976), Conf. on Coll. Composition and Communication, Rhetoric Soc., Ill. Consumer Educators. Author: The American Scene, 1969; The U.S.A. Today: A Commentary, 1972; Edwin O'Connor, 1974; Language and Public Policy, 1974; Intensify-Downplay, 1976; The Counter-Propaganda File, 1977; Persuasion, 1980; contbr. articles and poetry to profl. jours. Home: 834 Pin Oak Ln Park Forest South IL 60466 Office: Dept English Governors State Univ Park Forest South IL 60466

RANKIN, MICHAEL RAE, mortgage banker; b. Coffeyville, Kans., July 16, 1945; s. Sam Harrison and Irene (Kochwelp) R.; B.S., Central Mo. State U., 1967; M.B.A., S.W. Mo. State U., 1976; m. Deborah K. Harmon, Aug. 31, 1968; children—Heather Rae, Ashley Mae, Summer Kae. With Central Mortgage Bancshares, Inc., Springfield, Mo., 1970—, sr. v.p., dir., chief exec. officer mortgage banking div., 1972—. Chmn., Springfield Airport Commn.; bd. dirs. Ozarks council Boy Scouts Am. Served as 1st lt. U.S. Army, 1967-70; Vietnam. Decorated Bronze Star with oak leaf cluster; cert. mortgage banker. Mem. Am., Mo. (dir., treas.) mortgage bankers assns., S.W. Mo. Better Bus. Bur. (dir.). Lutheran. Clubs: Rotary (dir.), Twin Oaks Country. Home: 1934 E Lark St Springfield MO 65804 Office: MPO Box 631 Springfield MO 65801

RANNEY, BROOKS, gynecologist; b. Daytona Beach, Fla., Jan. 31, 1915; s. Milo Miles and Ruth Farrell (Schertz) R.; B.A., Oberlin Coll., 1936; M.D., Northwestern U., 1940, M.S. in Physiology, 1948; m. Ruth Vail Snow, Oct. 14, 1939 (dec. 1979); children—Robert Lawrence, David Francis, Carol Elizabeth; m. 2d, Viona Inez Voy, Aug. 29, 1981. Intern Wesley Meml. Hosp., Chgo., 1940, resident, 1945-48; practice medicine specializing in ob-gyn, Yankton, S.D., 1948—; prof., chmn. dept. ob-gyn U. S.D., 1952-76; chmn. dept. ob-gyn Yankton Clinic, 1948—, Sacred Heart Hosp., 1948—, Yankton State Hosp., 1948—. Mem. Yankton City Commn., 1960-66, mayor, 1965. Served to maj. M.C. AUS, 1941-45; ETO. Fellow A.C.S.; mem. Central Assn. Obstetricians and Gynecologists (pres. 1975), Am. Coll. Obstetricians and Gynecologists (pres. 1982),; Am. Fertility Soc., Am. Cytol. Soc. Mem. United Ch. of Christ. Contbr. chpts. to books, articles to profl. jours. Home: 705 W 10th St Yankton SC 57078 Office: 1104 W 8th St Yankton SD 57078

RANNEY, MICHAEL OMAR, fund raising cons.; b. Cleve., Oct. 14, 1945; s. Omar Steele and Dorothy Mae (Phillips) R.; B.A., Allegheny Coll., 1967; M.P.A., U. Pitts., 1969. Dir., Ohio Gov.'s Youth Action Program, Columbus, Ohio, 1972-74; chief bur. delinquency prevention Ohio Youth Commn., Columbus, 1974-75; exec. dir. Crawford County Drug/Alcohol Planning Commn., Meadville, Pa., 1975-77; scheduler Citizens with Celeste, Columbus, 1977-78; asst. exec. dir. Alvis House, Columbus, 1978-81; v.p. Bill Heim Co., Alexandria, Ohio, 1981—. Trustee Youth Adv. Services. Mem. Nat. Soc. Fund Raising Execs. (sec. Central Ohio chpt. 1981—), Public Relations Soc. Am. Club: Downtown Kiwanis (Columbus). Home: 143 Midcliff Dr Columbus OH 43213 Office: Box 32 Alexandria OH 43001

RANOUS, CHARLES ALBERT, educator; b. Ann Arbor, Mich., July 18, 1912; s. Adelbert and Cora (Sink) R.; A.B., U. Mich., 1936, M.A., 1938; postgrad. Columbia U., 1949-53; m. Dorothy Diefendorf, June 7, 1940; 1 son, Karl E. Instr. English and speech U. Tenn., 1938-42, Drake U., 1944-47; instr. Air Force and Army programs Memphis State Coll. and U. Oreg., 1942-44 asst. prof., head freshman English, Fairleigh Dickinson U., 1949-53; tech. writer IT&T Labs., Nutley, N.J., 1953-57; tech. editor, engr. mgmt. staff Burroughs MECD, Detroit, 1957-60; asso. prof. tech. writing U. Wis., Madison, 1960-77, prof., 1977—; editorial cons. Mem. IEEE (sr.), Profl. Group on Edn., Am. Bus. Communication Assn. Republican. Club: Madison Technical. Author: (with Dunn and Allen) Learning Our Language, 1950; Communication for Engineers, 1964; (with D. Ranous) The Inner Zone, 1968; The Engineer's Interfaces, 1974; contbr. articles to profl. jours. in English, edn., engring. Home: 1321 Rosedale Madison WI 53714

RANSHAW, WILLIAM ALBERT, mfg. co. exec.; b. Oxford, Iowa, Jan. 14, 1928; s. George Albert and Bessie Marie (Hebl) R.; B.S.C., U. Iowa, 1951; m. Joanna Marie Files, Feb. 4, 1950; children—Barbara Kathleen, William Craig, Steven James. Cost acctg. mgr. Square D Co., Cedar Rapids, Iowa, 1957-65, plant acct., Los Angeles, 1965-67; corp. acctg. mgr. Penick and Ford Ltd., Cedar Rapids, 1967-77; controller Hwy. Equipment Co., Cedar Rapids, 1977—. Treas., Hawkeye Area council Boy Scouts Am., Cedar Rapids, 1975-81. Served with U.S. Army, 1945-47. Mem. Cedar Rapids C. of C., Nat. Assn. Accts. Methodist. Home: 431 Red Fox Rd SE Cedar Rapids IA 52403 Office: 616 D Ave NW Cedar Rapids IA 52405

RANSOM, EVELYN NAILL, linguist, educator; b. Memphis, Apr. 20, 1938; d. Charles Rhea and Evelyn (Naill) R.; A.A., Mt. Vernon Jr. Coll., 1958; B.A., Tulane U., 1960; M.A., N.Mex. Highlands U., 1965; Ph.D. (NDFL fellow), U. Ill., 1974. Teaching asst. N.Mex. Highlands U., 1963-64; instr. U. Wyo., 1965-66; teaching asst. U. Ill., 1966-70; asso. prof. linguistics Eastern Ill. U., Charleston, 1970—; speaker at confs. Faculty Research Grant, EIU, 1982. Mem. Linguistic Soc. Am. (workshop leader Summer Inst. 1980). Contbr. articles to profl. jours. Home: 4 Wildwood R1-35 Mahomet IL 61853 Office: Dept of English Eastern Illinois University Charleston IL 61920

RANSOM, HENRY KING, surgeon, educator; b. Jan. 21, 1898; s. Fred C. and Gayle (King) R.; A.B., U. Mich., 1920, M.D., 1923, M.S. in Anatomy, 1934. Intern U. Mich. Hosp., 1923-24, asst. resident, 1924-25, instr. in surgery, 1925-26, sr. instr. in surgery, 1926-29, asst. prof., 1929-33, asso. prof., 1933-50, prof., 1950-68, acting chmn. dept. surgery, 1957-59, prof. emeritus, 1968—; surgeon Univ. Hosp., 1930-67; surgeon emeritus St. Joseph Mercy Hosp., 1942-60; cons. Ann Arbor VA Hosp., 1950-70. Diplomate Am. Bd. Surgery. Mem. Washtenaw County, Mich. State med. socs., AMA (vice chmn. sect. surgery and gen. abdominal 1956-57), A.C.S., Am., Western, Central (founder, pres. 1952-53), Frederick A. Coller (pres. 1952-55), St. Paul (Minn.), Internat. surg. socs., Soc. Surgery Alimentary Tract, Am. Gastroenterological Assn., Surgeons Club, Acad. Surgery Detroit, Flint Acad. Surgery, Galens Hon. Med. Soc., Alpha Omega Alpha (pres. 1922-23), Phi Kappa Phi, Phi Sigma, Phi Chi. Mem. editorial bd. Archives Surgery, 1956-63. Contbr. numerous articles to med. jours. Office: U Mich Med Sch Ann Arbor MI 48109

RANZ, FRANK STEPHEN, elec. engr.; b. Blue Ash, Ohio, Oct. 31, 1918; s. William R. and Alvina (Snook) R.; B.S. in Elec. Engring., U. Cin., 1940; m. Joan M. Ranz. Engr. R.K. LeBlond Machine Tool Co., Cin., 1940-41, Nat. Automatic Tool Co., Richmond, Ind., 1941-42, Yarnall Waring Co., Phila., 1946-47, W.K. Millholland Machinery Co., Indpls., 1947-51; owner, pres. Frank S. Ranz Co., machine tool distbrs., Cin., 1951—. Served as lt. AUS, 1942-46. Republican. Clubs: Kenwood Country, Masons (32 deg.), Shriners. Patentee in field. Home: 4668 E Galbraith Cincinnati OH 45236 Office: 4668 E Galbraith Cincinnati OH 45236

RAO, PURUSHOTHAMA, metallurgist/electrochemist; b. Mulbagal, India, Oct. 3, 1940; came to U.S., 1964, naturalized, 1974; s. Sripada and Kaveri-Bai Rao; B.E., Indian Inst. Sci., 1962; M.S., U. Minn., 1966; m. Rama P., Nov. 11, 1964; children—Veena, Sridhar. Teaching asst. dept. metallurgy Indian Inst. Sci., Bangalore, 1962-64; research metallurgist Gould Nat. Batteries, St. Paul, 1966-71; process engr. Gould, Inc., Automotive Battery Div., St. Paul., 1971-77, mgr. advanced engring., 1977—. Recipient Gould Sci. Achievement award, 1974, 79. Mem. AIME, Electrochem. Soc. Hindu Soc. of Minn. Contbr. articles to profl. jours.; editor Newsletter of Hindu Soc. Minn., 1979-80; patentee in field. Home: 1210 Carlson Lake Ln Eagan MN 55123 Office: PO Box 43140 Saint Paul MN 55164

RAO, TADIKONDA LAKSHMI KANTHA, anesthesiologist; b. Rajampet, India, Nov. 23, 1946; s. Atchuta T. and Lakshmi Rao; B.Sc., Govt. Arts Coll., 1963; M.D., Pondicherry Med. Coll., 1971; m. Vyjayanthi Rao, Oct. 9, 1971; children—Usha, Vijay, Madhavi. came to U.S., 1972, naturalized, 1976. Registrar, dept. anesthesiology Pondicherry Med. Coll., India, 1970-72; intern, resident Cook County Hosp., Chgo., 1972-74, asso. chmn. clin. anesthesia, 1975-77; practice medicine specializing anesthesiology, Chgo., 1976-81; asso. prof. Loyola U. Med. Center, Maywood, Ill., 1978, also med. dir. ambulatory surg. center. Mem. AMA, Internat. Anesthesia Research Soc., Ill. Med. Assn., Chgo. Med. Soc., Am. Soc. Anesthesiologists, Am. Soc. Regional Anesthesia, Chgo. Soc. Anesthesiologists, Soc. Cardiovascular Anesthesiologists, Ill. Soc. Anesthesiologists. Contbr. articles to profl. jours. Home: 135E 20th St Lombard IL 60148 Office: 2160 S 1st Ave Maywood IL 60153

RAPHAEL, RICK, writer; b. N.Y.C., Feb. 20, 1919; s. Louis Nevin and Viola (Felix) R.; B.A., U. N.Mex., 1952; postgrad. U. Philippines, 1938, Boise State Coll., 1961; m. Donna Edith Swenson, May 19, 1972; children—Christopher, Patricia, Melanie Raphael Swensen, Karen Raphael Pleak, Teresa, Stephanie Raphael Martinez. Editor, reporter Albuquerque Jour., 1946-50, Denver Post, 1950-51, Ariz. Republic, Phoenix, 1951-53, San Bernardino (Calif.) Sun, 1953-56, Middleton (N.Y.) Record, 1956-58, Idaho Daily Statesman, Boise,

1958-59; news dir., polit. editor Sta. KBOI-TV, Boise, 1959-63; press sec., exec. asst. U.S. Senator Frank Church, Washington, 1963-69; legis. rep. J.C. Penny Co., Mpls., 1969-74, sr. govt. relations rep., 1974-79; ret., 1979; lectr. polit. sci. Coll. Idaho, 1960-61, George Washington U., Am. U., Washington, 1964-66. Bd. dirs. State Govtl. Affairs Council. Served to capt. AUS, 1936-45. Decorated Bronze Star with oak leaf and valor clusters, Purple Heart with oak leaf cluster; named Outstanding Nat. Producer-Dir. TV Documentary News, Nat. Radio and TV News Dirs. Assn., 1962. Mem. Nuclear Energy Writers Assn., Sci. Fiction Writers Assn., Guthrie Found., U.S. Ski Assn., Nat. Geog. Soc., Minn. Press Club, Jefferson Forum, Sigma Delta Chi. Episcopalian. Club: Tower. Author: The Thirst Quenchers, 1965; Code Three, 1966; The Defector, 1980; The President Must Die, 1981; contbr. articles, short stories, novellas to mags. Home: 3320 Niagara Ln Minneapolis MN 55441

RAPKIN, JEROME, def. industry exec.; b. Wilmington, Del., Aug. 1, 1929; s. Harry and Ida (Hermann) R.; B.S. in Marine Engring., U.S. Naval Acad., 1952; M.S. in E.E., U.S. Naval Postgrad. Sch., 1959; postgrad. Armed Forces Staff Coll., 1965, Catholic U. Am., 1978; m. Janet Vansant, Nov. 4, 1954; children—Keith, Leigh, Paige. Commd. ensign U.S. Navy, 1952, advanced through grades to capt., 1979; dir. Surface Warfare Systems Naval Sea Systems Command, Washington, 1974-75; comdr. Destroyer Squadron 26 Surface Force Atlantic, Norfolk, Va., 1975-78; head surface to surface warfare, chief naval ops., Washington, 1978; dir. programs and budget Chief Naval Material, Washington, 1979; v.p. engring. devel. Ocean Systems div. Gould, Inc., Cleve., 1979-. Decorated Navy Meritorious Service medal, Navy Commendation medal with gold star. Mem. Am. Def. Preparedness Assn., U.S. Naval Inst., Aerospace Industries Assn. Am., Navy League U.S. (v.p. Cleve. council 1979—). Home: 12345 Valley Vista Rd Chesterland OH 44026 Office: 18901 Euclid Ave Cleveland OH 44117

RAPOZA, RITA SANDRA, counseling psychologist; b. Captain Cook, Kona, Hawaii, Nov. 26, 1943; d. Herbert and Virginia (Bernabe-Tellas) R.; B.A. in History cum laude, Chaminade Coll., Honolulu, 1966; M.L.S., U. Hawaii, 1968; Ph.D. in Counseling, U. Minn., 1974. Tchr., James Campbell High Sch., Oahu, Hawaii, 1966-67; reference librarian Mankato (Minn.) State U., 1968-70; counseling psychologist trainee VA, Mpls., 1970-72; teaching asst. U. Minn., Mpls., 1970-71; counselor Mounds View Sch. Dist. 621, St. Paul, 1972-75; asst. prof. Coll. Edn., counseling psychologist U. Western Ont., London, Ont., Can., 1975-77; human devel. systems cons., 1977; dir. mktg. for customer contact products Wilson Learning Corp., Eden Prairie, Minn., 1977—. Mem. Am. Psychol. Assn., Am. Personnel and Guidance Assn. Roman Catholic. Co-editor: Career Development and Counseling of Women, 1978; contbr. articles profl. jours. Home: 7511 Bittersweet Dr Eden Prairie MN 55344 Office: 6950 Washington Ave S Eden Prairie MN 55344

RAPP, GEORGE ROBERT, univ. adminstr.; b. Toledo, Ohio, Sept. 19, 1930; s. George Robert and Gladys Mae (Warner) R.; B.A. in Geology and Mineralogy, U. Minn., 1952; Ph.D. in Geochemistry, Pa. State U., 1960; m. Jeanette Messner, June 15, 1956; children—Kathryn, Karen. Asst. prof. S.D. Sch. Mines and Tech., Rapid City, 1957-65; asso. prof., 1960-65; asso. prof. geology and geophysics Univ. Minn., Mpls., 1965-75; prof. geology and archeology, dean Coll. Letters and Sci., U. Minn., Duluth, 1975—; chmn. Consortium for Interdisciplinary Archael. Sci., 1980—. NSF postdoctoral fellow, 1963-64; Fulbright-Hays Sr. Research fellow, Greece, 1972-73. Fellow Geol. Soc. Am.; mem. Nat. Assn. Geology Tchrs. (pres.), Assn. Field Archaeology (pres.), AAAS (life), Mineral. Soc. Am., Archaeol. Inst. Am., Soc. Archeol. Sci., Mineral. Soc., Mineral. Assn. Can., Soc. Environ. Geochemistry and Health, Soc. Mining Engrs., Soc. Am. Archaeology, Soc. Profl. Archaeologists, Sigma Xi. Author books including: Messenia Expedition, 1972; Encyclopedia of Minerals, 1974; Nichoria Excavation, 1978; Archaeological Geology of Troy, 1981; Contbr. articles to profl. jours. Home: 1410 Brainerd Ave Duluth MN 55811 Office: U Minnesota Duluth MN 55812

RARDIN, JOHN ARTHUR, pub. co. exec.; b. Charleston, Ill., Apr. 29, 1930; s. John Briggs and Margaret Fayette (Hopper) R.; B.S., Eastern Ill. U., 1954; M.S., U. Ill., 1961; m. Rosemary Boyd, Jan. 17, 1952; children—Byron, Erin, Jerrine, John A. Newspaper editor Eastern Ill. U., Charleston, 1951; editor, Charleston Daily News, 1952, 1955-57; financial editor Champaign-Urbana (Ill.) Courier, 1959-62; research asst. Ill. Bus. Review, Champaign-Urbana, 1956-59; tchr., Rockford and Des Plaines, Ill., 1963-66; owner Rardin Graphics, Charleston, 1966—; pres., Graphic Creations, Inc., Charleston, 1970—; v.p. G.I.R.E. Internat. Inc., Charleston, 1980—. Served with AUS, 1952-54. Mem. Nat. Pilots Assn., Aircraft Owners and Pilots Assn., Ill. Press Assn., Ill. Pilots Assn., Charleston C. of C., Am. Inst. Parliamentarians, Pi Delta Kappa. Clubs: Rotary, Toastmasters (area gov. 1981). Home: 1003 Monroe St Charleston IL 61920 Office: 617 18th St Charleston IL 61920

RASCHKE, ALFRED CHARLES, pump mfg. co. exec.; b. Chgo., Aug. 4, 1924; s. Alfred Henry and Gladys Merle (Emery) R.; grad. Exec. Devel. Program, U. Mich., 1966, Advanced Mgmt. Program, Harvard U., 1973; m. Loraine Maude Twigg, Aug. 31, 1946; children—Loral Jean, Charles Allen. With Minn. Mining & Mfrs. Co., Chgo., 1942-50, br. office mgr., 1950; pres. Bennett Pump Co., Muskegon, Mich., 1950—; dir. Hackley Bank & Trust, N.A., Muskegon, Enterprise Brass Works. Sect. chmn. United Way of Muskegon County; mem. city council City of Whitehall, 1952-58, mayor, 1958. Served with U.S. Army, 1943-46. Mem. Am. Petroleum Inst., Gasoline Pump Mfrs. Assn. (chmn.), Muskegon Mfrs. Assn. (dir.), Harvard Bus. Club Western Mich. Episcopalian. Clubs: Century (bd. govs.) (Muskegon). Office: Bennett Pump Co PO Box 597 Muskegon MI 49443

RASHEED, SHAMS, pediatrician, neonatologist; b. Gurdaspur, India, Feb. 17, 1936; came to U.S., 1972; s. Abdur and Kaniz Fatima (Chaudhry) Rashid; diploma Faculty Sci., Govt. Coll., Lahore, Pakistan, 1954; diploma child health Royal Coll. Phys. and Surg., Glasgow, Scotland, 1971; M.B., B.S., Nishter Med. Coll., Multan, Pakistan, 1962; m. Amtul Wadud Khan, Oct. 29, 1969; children—Sairah, Saba, Bilal. House physician N. Lonsdale Hosp., Barrow-in-Furness, Eng., 1963-64; sr. house physician in geriatrics Monkmoor Hosp., Shrewsbury, Eng., 1964-65; sr. house physician in pediatrics Gen. Hosp., Boston, Eng., 1965-66, Children's Hosp., Sunderland, Eng., 1966-67; sr. house physician in internal medicine Royal Infirmary, Sunderland, 1967-68; registrar in pediatrics/neonatology Royal Aberdeen (Scotland) Childrens Hosp., 1968-72; resident in pediatrics Mt. Sinai Hosp., Chgo., 1972-73; chief resident in pediatrics Newark Beth Israel Hosp., 1973-74; fellow in neonatology U. Conn. Health Center, Farmington, 1974-76; asst. prof. dept. pediatrics U. N.D. Sch. Medicine, Minot, 1976—; dir. neonatology ICU, Trinity Hosp., Minot; mem. N.D. Task Force on Perinatal Care. Diplomate Am. Bd. Pediatrics. Asso. fellow Am. Acad. Pediatrics; mem. Gt. Plains Orgn. Perinatal Care. Islam. Home: 3 Glacial Point Minot ND 58701 Office: 20 Burdick Expressway N Minot ND 58701

RASMUS, ROBERT NELSON, bldg. materials mfg. co. exec.; b. Chgo., Sept. 17, 1925; s. Walter E. and Edith C. (Nelson) R.; B.S. in Gen. Engring., U. Ill., 1948; M.M.E., Cornell U., 1949; m. Annette E. Avery, Dec. 28, 1951; children—John, Richard. Vice pres. mfg. Masonite Corp., Chgo., 1965-70, v.p., gen. mgr. Bldg. Products div., 1970-71, group v.p. board products group, 1971-74, exec. v.p., 1975-76, pres., 1976—, chief exec. officer, 1977—, also dir.; dir. Employers Ins. of Wausau. Served with AUS, 1943-46. Decorated Bronze Star with oak leaf cluster. Conglist. Clubs: Econ., Met., Tower (Chgo.). Home: 59 Lakewood Dr Glencoe IL 60022 Office: 29 N Wacker Dr Chicago IL 60606

RASMUSSEN, GARY HOWARD, ednl. adminstr.; b. Sterling, Ill., July 17, 1943; s. Howard Carl and Laurel Olmstead (Mathews) R.; B.A., Ariz. State U., 1969, M.A., 1969; Ed.D., Vanderbilt U., 1980; children—David, Anne. Tchr. educable mentally retarded Milw. public schs., 1969-72, acting prin./tech. trainable mentally retarded, 1972-75, diagnostic instructional specialist, 1975; shift supr., control dept./computer center First Wis. Nat. Bank, Milw., 1969-74; supr. Milwaukee County Handicap Recreation Program, Milw., 1974-75; coordinator exceptional edn. Sch. Dist. of Kettle Moraine, Wale, Wis., 1975-78, dir. supportive services, 1978-80, bus. mgr., 1981—; participant Joint Wis./Minn. Spl. Edn. Leadership Workshop, 1977; lectr. in field. Mem. adv. com. Job Service Project, Waukesha County, 1975-76; vol. worker Milw. Fine Arts, United Performing Arts Fund; mem. parent adv. com. Shorewood public schs., 1979-80; active campaign worker various village ofcls. Recipient Am. Legion award, 1957. Mem. Council Exceptional Children (pres. 1979-80), Wis. Council Adminstrs. of Spl. Edn. (regional asst. 1980-81), Wis. Council Adminstrs. of Pupil Services, United Assn. for Retarded Citizens, Wis. Assn. Sch. Bus. Ofcls., Phi Delta Kappa, Sigma Phi Epsilon. Republican. Episcopalian. Club: Robert Allen Nothing Down Investment. Contbr. articles to profl. jours. Office: PO Box 39 Wales WI 53183

RASMUSSEN, GLEN RUSSELL, coll. pres.; b. Chgo., Apr. 23, 1921; s. Halfdan and Ruth (Seversen) R.; B.S., Wayne State U., Detroit, 1947, M.A., 1949; Ph.D., U. Mich., 1953; LL.D. (hon.), Chung-ang U., Seoul, Korea, 1975; m. Joyce Elaine Marion, Mar. 27, 1944; children—Carol, Paul, Neil, David, Steven. Asso. prof. U. Mich., 1952-62; v.p., acad. dean Carthage Coll., Kenosha, Wis., 1963-68; v.p. acad. affairs Morningside Coll., Sioux City, Iowa, 1968-72; pres. Findlay (Ohio) Coll., 1972—. Bd. dirs. Findlay United Way, 1976-79. Served with AUS, 1942-46. Mem. Ohio Coll. Assn. (dir.), Assn. Ind. Colls. and Univs. Ohio (dir.), Ohio Found. Ind. Colls. (trustee), Findlay Area C. of C. (dir. 1975-79). Lutheran. Clubs: Findlay Rotary, Findlay Country, Findlay Symposium. Contbr. articles to profl. jours. Office: 1000 N Main St Findlay OH 45840

RASMUSSEN, ROSS H., farmer; b. Lincoln, Nebr., Jan. 24, 1917; s. Louis J. and Grace A. (Kennedy) R.; B.S. in Agr., U. Nebr., 1942; m. Alice Willa Hoegemeyer, Oct. 16, 1943; children—Ruth Ann McMaster, Janice Kay Belohlavy, Nina Beth Kavich. Farmer, pres. Rossway Hybrids, Nu-Dwarf Farms, Inc., Hooper, Nebr. Mem. Nebr. State Senate, 1960-68; mem. Dodge County Bd. Suprs., 1958-60; chmn. Dodge County Democrats, 1959-60; dir. Nebr. Hall of Fame. Served with AUS, 1943-45. Decorated Bronze Star; recipient Disting. award Nebr. Schoolmasters, 1964; Disting. Service award Dept. Rural Edn., 1965. Mem. Nebr. Council Tchr. Edn., Agrl. Research Council, Nebr. Council Econ. Edn., Nat. Orgn. Legal Problems Edn., Turf Grass Council, Nebr. Assn. Former State Legislators (pres. emeritus, founder), Am. Legion, 40 and 8, V.F.W., Gamma Sigma Delta. Lutheran. Club: Westerners. Patentee (6). Home: Hooper NE 68031

RASMUSSEN, RUTH, state agy. ofcl.; b. Stanton, Mich., Apr. 4, 1919; d. William E. and Ella Luce (Palmer) Rasmussen; B.A., Mich. State U., 1951, M.A., 1953; J.D., Cooley Law Sch., 1977. Research dir. Mich. Fair Employment Practices Commn., 1963-64; with Mich. Dept. Civil Rights, 1964—, dep. dir. programs, 1972-75, dir. dept., 1975—; asst. prof. econs. Ferris State Coll., Big Rapids, Mich., 1959-62. Asst. dir. United Community Chest, Lansing, Mich. Mem. Internat. Assn. Ofcl. Human Rights Agencies (pres.), Nat. Assn. Human Rights Workers, NAACP (life), Pi Kappa Phi. Roman Catholic. Office: 125 W Allegan St Lansing MI 48913*

RASTAS, VYTAS PRANAS, veterinarian; b. Lithuania, May 10, 1922; s. Pranas and Josephine R.; came to U.S., 1951, naturalized, 1957; student Baltic U., 1946-48, Hannover (Ger.) Vet. Coll., 1948-51; V.M.D., U. Pa., 1954; m. A. Jane Rosell, June 2, 1956; children—Carolyn, John, Paul, Christine. Fed. meat insp., South St. Paul, 1954-55; pvt. vet. practice, Morris, Minn., 1955-58; with Wis. Dept. Agr., Madison, 1958—, vet. diagnostician animal health lab., 1962—. Mem. Wis., Lithuanian vet. med. assns. Roman Catholic. Home: 2406 Jonquil Rd Madison WI 53711 Office: 6101 Mineral Point Rd Madison WI 53705

RASTOGI, ANIL KUMAR, research scientist; b. India, July 13, 1942; came to U.S., 1969, naturalized, 1978; s. R.S. and K.V. Rastogi; B.Sc. with honours, Lucknow U., 1963, M.S., 1964; Ph.D. in Polymer Sci., McGill U., Montreal, 1969; m. Anjali Capur, Mar. 18, 1970; children—Priya, Sonya. Mem. staff Owens-Corning Tech. Center, Granville, Ohio, 1969—, lab. supr., 1975-76, lab. mgr. materials tech. labs., 1976-79, lab. mgr. product devel. labs., 1979-80, research dir., 1980—; adv. bd. Central Ohio Tech. Coll.; lectr., cons. in field. Bd. dirs. Licking County Family Services Assn.; sect. chmn. local United Way. Fellow Nat. Research Council Can., 1966-69. Mem. Am. Mgmt. Assn., Am. Chem. Soc., Soc. Plastics Engrs., Sigma Xi. Club: Toastmasters (past pres.). Author, patentee in field. Home: 538 Knoll Dr Granville OH 43023 Office: Owens-Corning Fiberglas Tech Center Granville OH 43023

RATANATHARATHORN, VORAVIT, med. oncologist; b. Thonburi, Thailand, Dec. 25, 1946; s. Siau Noong and Shuling Tsia (Koh) Koh; B.M.S., Mahidol U., 1969, M.D., 1971. Intern, Grace Hosp., Detroit, 1972-73; resident Thomas Jefferson U., Phila., 1973-75; med. oncology fellowship Wayne State U., 1975-77, asst. prof. oncology, 1977—, head protected environment unit and hematologic oncology, 1977—. Diplomate Am. Bd. Internal Medicine, Am. Bd. Med. Oncology. Mem. Am. Coll. Physicians, AAAS, Wayne County Med. Soc., Mich. State Med. Soc., N.Y. Acad. Scis. Seventh-day Adventist. Contbr. articles to profl. jours. Home: 2049 Beverly St Berkley MI 48072 Office: 3990 John R St Detroit MI 48201

RATCHESON, RICHARD J., brewing co. exec.; b. Chgo., Apr. 21, 1945; s. Maurice and Kate (Davidow) R.; B.A. in Journalism, U. Okla., 1968; m. JoAnn Snyder, May 3, 1970; 1 son, Zachary. Exec. tng. program Kenyon & Eckhardt Advt., Chgo., 1968; asst. advt. mgr. Pabst Brewing Co., Milw., 1968-72, advt. mgr., 1972-78, asst. to exec. v.p., 1978-79, v.p. sales, 1979-80, v.p., sr. brand mgr., 1980—; dir. Ardvark Corp., Milw., Internat. Inst., Milw. Mem. exec. com. Holiday Folk Fair, 1972-77, chmn. nominating com., 1980—; mem. Vol. Advt. Council Milw., 1971-72. Clubs: Milw. Ad (dir., sec. 1976-77, chmn. edn. com. 1977-78); Milw. Athletic. Home: 4470 N Ardmore St Shorewood WI 53211 Office: 917 W Juneau St Milwaukee WI 53201

RATCLIFFE, MYRON FENWICK, investment mgmt. exec., banker; b. Evanston, Ill.; s. James Lewis and Jean (Gardner) R.; B.S., U. Ill., 1925; m. Margaret Archibald; 1 dau., Elizabeth Ratcliffe Heinze. With Goldman, Sachs & Co., N.Y.C., 1925-33; adminstr. fin. codes NRA, 1934-35; syndicate mgr. Lehman Bros., N.Y.C., 1936-49; partner Bache & Co., Chgo., 1949-56; pres. Miami Corp., Chgo., 1956-77, Cutler Oil & Gas Corp., 1956-77; chmn. bd., dir. Nat. Blvd. Bank of Chgo., 1956-80, hon. life dir., 1981—; dir. Miami Corp., Chgo., Cutler Oil & Gas Corp., Nat.-Standard Co., Niles, Mich. Bd. govs. Midwest Stock Exchange, 1949-56; trustee Children's Home and Aid Soc. Ill. Served as lt. col. AUS, 1942-46. Decorated Legion of Merit. Clubs: Masons, Bond, Chicago, Casino, Mid-Am. (Chgo.); Indian Hill Country (Winnetka); Old Elm (Ft. Sheridan, Ill.); Birnam Wood Golf (Santa Barbara, Calif.). Home: 82 Indian Hill Rd Winnetka IL 60093 Office: 410 N Michigan Ave Chicago IL 60611

RATH, GARY D., educator; b. Fargo, N.D., Dec. 25, 1948; s. Albert H. and Mary (Lang) R.; B.S., Valley City State Coll., 1970; M.S., U. N.D., 1974, postgrad. 1974-78; postgrad N.D. State U., 1970-71, Mont. State U., 1976. Staff writer Valley City (N.D.) Times-Record, 1967-70; bus. and history tchr. McKenzie County Sch. Dist., Watford City, N.D., 1970-72; vocat. bus. and office edn. tchr. Langdon (N.D.) High Sch., 1972—; part-time instr. adult courses Lake Region Jr. Coll., Devils Lake, N.D., 1979—. Pres., Langdon Ambulance Service, 1978-80. Registered emergency med. technician, emergency care technician, N.D.; Am. Heart Assn. Basic Life Support Instr. Mem. NEA, N.D. Edn. Assn., Langdon Edn. Assn. (past pres.), N.D. Bus. Edn. Assn. (past pres.), Am. Vocat. Edn. Assn., N.D. Vocat. Edn. Assn., Nat. Bus. Edn. Assn., N.D. Assn. EMT's-ECT's, Delta Pi Epsilon, Pi Omega Pi. Democrat. Lutheran. Clubs: N.D. Right to Life Assn., Cavalier County Right to Life Assn. Home: Rural Route 2 Box 27 Langdon ND 58249 Office: Langdon High Sch Langdon ND 58249

RATH, PATRICIA MINK, educator, author; b. Chgo.; d. Dwight L. and Margaret (Strom) Mink; A.B., Oberlin Coll.; M.S. in Merchandising, Simmons Coll.; postgrad. U. Ill., Northwestern U.; 1 son, Eric Clemence. Bd. dirs. Ill. Found. for Distbv. Edn., Inc. Mem. Am. Mktg. Assn., LWV, Am. Vocat. Assn., Chgo. Council Fgn. Relations. Author: (with Ralph E. Mason) Marketing and Distribution, 1968, 74, Marketing Practices and Principles, 3d edit., 1980; (with Ralph E. Mason and Lloyd J. Phipps) Succeeding on the Job, 1970, Supervising on the Job, 1971; Career Education Kit, 1977. Address: 1037 Cherry St Winnetka IL 60093

RATHGEB, HAROLD DEAN, JR., materials exec.; b. Alton, Ill., July 3, 1942; s. Harold Dean and Dorothy Mae (Brady) R.; student Monmouth Coll., 1960-64; B.S. in Edn., So. Ill. U., Edwardsville, 1966; M.A. in Mgmt. and Bus. Adminstrn., Webster Coll., 1977, M.A. in Procurement Mgmt., 1981; cert. in data processing St. Louis U., 1980. Tech. writer Laclede Steel Co., St. Louis, 1966-69, sr. tech. writer, 1969-74, systems engr., 1974-77, systems and procedures analyst, 1977-81; materials mgr. Micro-Term, Inc., St. Louis, 1982—. Hon. fellow Harry S. Truman Library Inst.; mem. Nat. Assn. Purchasing Mgmt., Am. Prodn. and Inventory Control Soc. (certified), Tau Kappa Epsilon, Phi Theta Kappa. Clubs: St. Louis Tip Toppers. Home: 300 Mansion House Center Apt 315 Saint Louis MO 63102 Office: Laclede Steel Co 10 S Broadway Saint Louis MO 63102

RATHI, MANOHAR, physician; b. Beawar, India, Dec. 25, 1933; s. Bagtawarmal and Sitadevi (Laddha-Palod) R.; M.B., B.S., Rajasthan (India) U., 1961; D.C.H., Royal Coll. Surgeons and Physicians, London, 1964; came to U.S., 1969; m. Kamla Jajoo, Feb. 21, 1960; children—Sanjeev, Rajeev. Resident house physician in pediatrics and internal medicine hosps. in India and Eng., 1961, 63-64; casualty med. officer Bombay Hosp., 1961-62; resident sr. house physician pediatrics Gen. Hosp., Oldham, Eng., 1964-65; registrar physician in pediatrics hosp. in Newcastle-on-Tyne and Ashington, Eng., 1965-68; fellow neonatology Methodist Hosp., Bklyn., 1969-70, chief resident, 1969-70, chief div. neonatology, asst. attending pediatrics, 1971-73; clin. instr. pediatrics Downstate Med. Center, Bklyn., 1971-72; dir. newborn medicine, coordinator pediatric edn., asst. dir., sr. attending div. pediatrics Little Company of Mary Hosp., Evergreen Park, Ill., 1972-74, cons. neonatologist, 1974—; dir. perinatal medicine Christ Hosp., Oak Lawn, Ill., 1974—, chmn. dept. pediatrics, 1980—; asst. prof. pediatrics Rush Med. Coll., Chgo., 1974-79, asso. prof., 1979—. Grantee Hummel Found., 1976-77. Diplomate Am. Bd. Pediatrics with subsplty. neonatal perinatal medicine. Recipient Outstanding New Ill. Citizen award, 1978. Fellow Am. Acad. Pediatrics; mem. AMA (Physicians Recognition award 1971, 74), N.Y. State, Kings County, N.Y., Ill., Chgo. med. socs., Chgo. Pediatric Soc. Contbr. numerous articles to med. jours. Home: 9221 S Tripp Ave Oak Lawn IL 60453 Office: 4440 W 95th St Oak Lawn IL 60453

RATHKAMP, WALTER ROBERT, endocrinologist; b. Williamsburg, Va., Sept. 5, 1942; s. Walter Frank and Helen Martha (Seostrom) R.; B.S., Cornell U., 1964; M.A., Ind. U., 1968, Ph.D., 1972; m. Anita Louise Roschelle, July 7, 1968; children—Walter Thad, Samuel Martin, Joshua Raymond. Postdoctoral fellow Ind. U., 1972-73; tchr. Peace Corps, Ethiopia, 1964-66; asst. prof. Ind. U.-Purdue U., 1973; mem. faculty Saginaw Valley State Coll., University Center, Mich., 1973—, asso. prof. biology, chmn. dept., 1977—. Active local Big Bros., Little League; elder Countryside Presbyn. Ch., Saginaw, Mich., 1978—. Recipient Franc A. Landee award for teaching excellence Saginaw Valley State Coll., 1980. Mem. AAAS, Ind. Acad. Sci., Mich. Acad., N.Y. Acad. Sci., Sigma Xi. Author papers in field. Office: SUSC 2250 Pierce Rd University Center MI 48710

RATHKE, ROGER HARRY, advt. agy. exec.; b. Rockford, Ill., Oct. 30, 1934; s. Herbert W. and Dorothy A. (Perlee) R.; B.S. with honors (Raymond Bill Meml. fellow), U. Wis., 1959, M.A., 1960; m. Nancy K. Horn, June 21, 1958; children—Elizabeth, Kathryn, Susan. Account exec. Stephan & Brady Inc., Madison, Wis., 1959-61; exec. v.p. Steiger-Rathke Devel. Co., Phoenix, 1961-65; account exec. Howard H. Monk & Assos., Rockford, 1966-74; exec. v.p. Benson/Rathke & Assos., Rockford, 1974-79; pres. Rathke Blair Kerns & Frost, Inc., Rockford, 1979—. Republican precinct committeeman, 1970-72, campaign mgr. Congressman John B. Anderson, 1970, area campaign coordinator Gov. Richard Ogilvie, 1972; trustee Keith Country Day Sch., 1968-74; v.p. Y Men's Club, 1974; vice chmn. United Way Fund Dr., 1977; bd. dirs. Public TV of Rockford, 1981—, Rockford Art Assn., 1980—; mem. steering com. Rockford Regional/Urban Design Assistance Team Study, 1980-81. Served with AUS, 1954-56. Mem. No. Ill. Advt. Club, Rockford Council of 100. Home: 5630 Inverness Dr Rockford IL 61107 Office: Rathke Blair Kerns & Frost Inc 1639 N Alpine Rd Rockford IL 61107

RATHMANN, DONALD JULIUS, owner food service co.; b. Milw., May 10, 1923; s. Otto C. and Hulda (Olson) R.; B.A., U. Wis., 1948; m. Virginia Lillian Delano, Sept. 6, 1947; children—Ronald, Sharon, Karen, Stuart. Editor, advt. mgr. Cour Rev., Barrington, Ill., 1949; pub. Delaware County Herald, Earlville, Iowa, 1950; dairy distbr., 1951; owner, operator Rathmann Food Service, Green Bay, Wis., 1952—. Pres. Green Bay Diabetes Assn., 1979-80. Served with U.S. Army, 1943-45. Mem. Am. Meat Processors Assn. Republican. Unitarian. Club: Lions (pres. 1970-71, sec. 1978-79) (Green Bay).

Home: 3533 Briar Ct Green Bay WI 54301 Office: Rathmann Food Service 1711 Industrial Dr Green Bay WI 54302

RATIGAN, WILLIAM, author, historian; b. Detroit; s. Bernard Joseph and Bertie (Laing) R.; student U. Detroit, 1931; A.B., U. Tenn. at Chattanooga, 1935; M.A., Mich. State U., 1961, Ph.D., 1963; m. Eleanor Dee Eldridge, Sept. 12, 1935; children—Patsy Ratigan Ranger, Anne Ratigan Pelton, Bobbie Laing (dec.), Shannon Leitrim. Continuity dir., producer NBC, Denver, 1937-40, supervisor NBC Far Eastern Listening Post, 1940-42, mng. news editor Western Div., supr. commentators and war corrs. PTO, 1942-45, news editor, scriptwriter UN Conf., 1945; short story and serial writer Curtis Pub. Co. and other mag. chains, 1946—; founder Dockside Press, Charlevoix, Mich., 1954—; founder counseling center Public Schs. Charlevoix, 1959—; sr. extension lectr. Mich. State U., 1962—; staff mem. NDEA Counseling Inst., 1962; vis. lectr. Fla. State U., 1965, U. Wis. at Milw., 1966, 68, U. Miami, 1967; Duneland Dimension series lectr. Ind. Dunes Nat. Lakeshore, 1981; mem. at large U.S. Adv. Council Naval Affairs, 1957—; cons. Smithsonian Instn. on tech. devel. of Great Lakes craft, 1959—; writer in residence Kingswood Sch., 1981. Adopted chief Ottawa Indian Tribe, 1957; named Knight of Mark Twain, 1970; William Ratigan Collection at Bentley Hist. Library, U. Mich. Mem. Am. Psychol. Assn., Am. Personnel and Guidance Assn., Mich. Acad. Profl. Educators (charter), Blue Key, Phi Kappa Phi. Author: Soo Canal! (foreword by Gen. Douglas McArthur), 1954, 2d edit., 1968; Young Mr. Big, 1955; Hiawatha and America's Mightiest Mile, 1955; The Adventures of Captain McCargo, 1956; Straits of Mackinac, 1957; The Blue Snow, 1958; Tiny Tim Pine, 1958; Adventures of Paul Bunyan and Babe, 1958; The Long Crossing, 1959; Highways Over Broad Waters, 1959; Great Lakes Shipwrecks and Survivals, 1960, 69, 77; Conflicts Within Counseling, 1964; Great Lakes Shipwrecks and Survivals, 1980; (with others) Theories of Counseling, 1965, 2d edit., 1972, A View from Within, 1967. Editor centennial facsimile edit. The Song of Hiawatha, 1955. Contbr. to The Great Lakes Reader, 1966, Ency. Americana, 1968—; research on Great Lakes. Home: (summer) 223 Park Ave Charlevoix MI 49720 also (winter) PO Box 543 Dunedin FL 33528 Office: The Dockside Press 1 Shipyard Row Box 1 Charlevoix MI 49720

RATKOVICH, JOHN MARK, lawyer, inventor; b. Chgo., Sept. 28, 1936; s. John Mark and Marie (Schackle) R.; B.B.A. (Evans scholar), Wis. U., 1958; J.D., Loyola U., 1966; m. Evely Joan Architect, Oct. 24, 1959; children—Diana, John Mark, David, Kristina, Marlaina, Aaron. Admitted to Ill. bar, 1965; individual practice law, Elmhurst, Ill., 1974—; with Tower Oil and Tech. Co., Chgo., 1974—. Mem. Chgo. Bar Assn., Inventors Soc. Am. (pres.). Inventor hunting arrow with electronic transmitter, elbow-rest for use in holding binoculars. Office: 529 S Hough Barrington IL 60010

RATLEDGE, EARL THORNTON, JR., indsl. engr., educator; b. Chgo., Jan. 8, 1928; s. Earl T. and Emily (Goebel) R.; student Aurora Coll., 1947-48, U. Ill., 1949-50; B.S., Ill. State U., 1951; M.S., U. Wis., 1961; m. Jane Bloodgood, Mar. 24, 1953; children—Lynn Kay, Earl Thornton III, Jill Anne, Beth Lea. With engring. dept. McKee Door Co., Aurora, Ill., 1946-48; tchr. Benton Harbor (Mich.) public schs., 1953-54; design engr. Security Indsl. Services, Port Washington, Wis., 1955-56; asso. prof. indsl. engring. U. Wis., Milw., 1954—; mem. drafting adv. com. Cedarburg (Wis.) schs., 1968-70, chmn. vocat. adv. com., 1966-68; cons. engring. design and graphics, 1970—. Scoutmaster, Bay Lakes council Boy Scouts Am., 1970-76, dist. scouting chmn., 1976-80; mem. campsite selection com. YMCA, Milw., 1970; judge Marquette Sci. Fair, Wis., 1965. Served to 1st lt. USAF, 1951-53. Recipient Silver Beaver award Boy Scouts Am., 1979. Mem. Am. Soc. Engring. Edn. (asso. editor mag. 1971-75, reviewer Annals edit. 1977-78, nat. coordinator Effective Teaching Inst. 1974-76, dir. sect. 1971, 72), Wis. Indsl. Edn. Assn., Wis. Acad. Scis., Arts and Letters, Sigma Xi, Iota Lambda Sigma, Phi Delta Kappa (chpt. pres. 1959-60). Methodist. Author: (with W.M. Christman) Basic Graphics for Engineers, 1968, 2d edit. with workbook, 1970, Basic Multi-View Projection, 1972; Graphics for Communication Workbook, 1972; contbr. articles to profl. jours.; producer tape slides for engring. graphics instrn. Office: Dept Indsl and Systems Engring Coll Engring U Wisconsin Milwaukee WI 53201

RATNER, MARK ALAN, educator; b. Cleve., Dec. 8, 1942; s. Max and Betty (Wohlvert) R.; B.A., Harvard U., 1964; Ph.D., Northwestern U., 1969; m. Nancy Ball, June 16, 1969; children—Stacy, Daniel. Amanuensis, Aarhus U., Denmark, 1969-70; asst. prof. chemistry N.Y. U., 1970-74, asso. prof., 1974-75; asso. prof. Northwestern U., Evanston, Ill., 1975-79, prof., 1980—, asso. dean Coll. Arts and Scis., 1980—. Sloan fellow, 1974-76. Fellow Am. Phys. Soc.; mem. AAAS, Am. Chem. Soc., Chem. Soc., Sigma Xi. Jewish. Contbr. articles to profl. jours. Home: 25 Locust Rd Winnetka IL 60093 Office: Dept Chemistry Northwestern Univ Evanston IL 60201

RAU, JEROLD MATTHEW, dermatologist; b. Wichita, Kans., July 3, 1939; s. Peter Joseph and Clara Theresa (Scheer) R.; B.A., U. Wichita, 1961; M.D., U. Kans., 1965; m. Jacqueline Anne Nickerson, Aug. 8, 1970. Intern, Fitzsimons Army Gen. Hosp., Denver, 1965-66; resident Walter Reed Army Hosp., Washington, 1966-69; commd. capt., M.C., U.S. Army, 1964, advanced through grades to lt. col., 1969-73; asst. chief dermatology Walter Reed Hosp., 1969-70; mem. faculty George Washington U., Georgetown U. Med. Schs., Washington, 1969-70; chief dermatology 225th Sta. Hosp., Munich, W.Ger., 1970-71; chief 130th Sta. Hosp., Heidelberg, W.Ger., 1971-73; chief cons. U.S. Army, Europe, 1971-73; chief dermatology Kansas City (Kans.) VA Hosp., 1973—; asst. prof. medicine U. Kans., 1973-77, asso. prof., 1977—; asso. clin. prof. U. Mo., Kansas City, 1977—; spl. cons. U.S. Army, 1974—. Pres., Kansas City (Mo.) Community Neighborhood Assn., 1976—. Diplomate Am. Bd. Dermatology, Am. Bd. Pathology. Mem. AMA, Mo., Jackson County med. socs., Kansas City (pres. 1980—), Mo. (dir. 1979—) dermatol. socs., Am. Acad. Dermatology, Soc. Internat. Dermatology and Tropical Medicine. Contbr. articles to profl. jours. Home: 6024 Morningside Dr Kansas City MO 64113 Office: 315 Nichols Rd Suite 235 Kansas City MO 64112

RAU, JOHN EDWARD, banker; b. Milw., June 19, 1948; s. Edward J. and Grace Barbara (Kutschenreuter) R.; B.A., B.S., Boston Coll., 1970; M.B.A., Harvard, 1972. Dir. corporate devel. 1st Chgo. Corp., Chgo., 1973-74, corporate officer finance and treasury, 1975; mgr. planning and adminstrn. 1st Nat. Bank Chgo., 1976-77, mgr. Central Operations Group, 1977-78, gen. mgr. internat. trade fin., 1979-80; exec. v.p. Exchange Nat. Bank Chgo., 1980—; asst. prof. finance Master Program, Chgo. Inst. Postgrad. Edn. in Bus. Election judge Project LEAP, 1976; bd. contbrs. Henrotin Hosp., 1975. Asso. dir. Chgo. Child Care Soc., 1978—. Served with U.S. Army, 1970-71. Harvard-Goldman, Sachs Sr. Finance fellow, 1971-72; Finnegan Outstanding Grad. grantee, 1969-70. Mem. Assn. Masters in Bus. Adminstrn., Art Inst. Chgo., Am. Mgmt. Assn. (instr.). Clubs: Harvard Bus. Sch., Harvard, Athletic Assn. (Chgo.); Mid-Town. Author: (with D.J. Vitale) Dividend Policy, The Corporate Treasurers Handbook, 1976. Home: 1310 Ritchie Ct Chicago IL 60610 Office: 130 S LaSalle St Chicago IL 60603

RAU, MARY THERESE, health care center adminstr.; b. Lewistown, Mont., Sept. 24, 1927; d. Frank J. and Rose Etheldreda (Costelloe) R.; B.A., St. Mary Coll., Leavenworth, Kans., 1949; M.S., U. Notre Dame, 1958; M.A., U. Kans., 1976. Tchr. secondary schs., Kansas City, 1958-65, Billings, Mont., 1965-67; prin. secondary sch., Billings. 1967-75; dir. admissions St. Mary Coll., Leavenworth, 1976-80; dir. edn. Marian Health Center, Sioux City, Iowa, 1980—; communications cons. E.S.U., Inc., Lawrence, Kans., No. Border Pipeline Co.; cons. Council for Advancement Small Colls. Mem. Juvenile Ct. Adv. Bd., 1968-72; mem. Siouxland Med. Edn. and Coordinating Com., 1981—; mem. Human Relations Council, 1972-75. Mem. Am. Soc. Tng. and Devel., Am. Soc. Health Manpower Edn. and Tng. Democrat. Roman Catholic. Office: Box 3168 Sioux City IA 51102

RAUCH, IRMENGARD, linguist, educator; b. Dayton, Ohio, Apr. 17, 1933; d. Konrad and Elsa (Knott) Rauch; student Nat. U. Mexico, summer 1954; B.S. with honors, U. Dayton, 1955; M.A., Ohio State U., 1957; postgrad. (Fulbright fellow) U. Munich (W.Ger.), 1957-58; Ph.D. (dissertation grantee summer 1962), U. Mich., 1962; m. Gerald F. Carr, June 12, 1965; children—Christopher, Gregory. Instr. German and linguistics U. Wis., Madison, 1962-63, asst. prof., 1963-66; asso. prof. German, U. Pitts., 1966-68; asso. prof. German and linguistics U. Ill., 1968-72, prof., 1972—; prof. U. Calif., Berkeley, 1979-80. Named Outstanding Woman on Campus, U. Ill. Radio Sta. WILL, 1975; research grantee U. Wis., summer 1966, U. Ill., 1975, 76, 77, 78, 79, U. Calif., Berkeley, 1979, 80; NSF and Linguistics Soc. Am. travel grantee, 1972; Nat. Endowment for Humanities grantee, 1978. Mem. Linguistics Soc. Am., Modern Lang. Assn., Am. Assn. Tchrs. German, Societas Linguistica Europaea, Internat. Linguistic Assn., AAAS, AAUP, Phonetics Assn., Semiotic Soc. Am., Alpha Sigma Tau, Delta Phi Alpha. Author: The Old High German Diphthongization: A Description of a Phonemic Change, 1967; co-editor: Approaches in Linguistic Methodology, 1967, Spanish edit., 1974; Der Heliand, 1974; Linguistic Method: Essays in Honor of Herbert Penzl, 1979; The Signifying Animal: The Grammar of Language and Experience, 1980; contbr. articles to profl. jours. Home: 200 Cherry Ln Villa Grove IL 61956 Office: Dept Germanic Languages and Literatures U Illinois Urbana IL 61801

RAUFEISEN, RAYMOND ROBERT, advt. exec.; b. Rochester, N.Y., Nov. 21, 1930; s. Raymond W. and Eleanor R. (Froelicher) R.; B.A., U. Ill., 1955; postgrad. Northwestern U., 1957-58; m. Phyllis Arlene Luebbers, Feb. 5, 1955; children—David Craig, Julie Christine, Lisa Marie. Vice pres. Edelstein-Nelson Advt. Agy., Chgo., 1957-61; advt. mgr. Illinois Tool Works Inc., Elgin, 1961-62, Sloan Valve Co., Franklin Park, Ill., 1962—. Served with U.S. Army, 1955-57. Mem. Bus./Profl. Advt. Assn. (dir. 1978-79, treas. 1981-82). Republican. Episcopalian. Club: Tropicana Swim and Tennis (trustee 1974—). Home: 1540 Fairfield Ln Hoffman Estates IL 60195 Office: 10500 Seymour Ave Franklin Park IL 60131

RAUSCH, GEORGE JAY, JR., bookseller; b. Aurora, Ill., Apr. 9, 1930; s. George Jay and Esther M. (Boudreau) R.; B.A., N. Central Coll., Naperville, Ill., 1955; M.A., U. Ill., 1958, Ph.D., 1960, M.L.S., 1961; m. Diane Lynn Kolb, June 12, 1973. Chief social sci. div., library lectr. in history Wash. State U., 1962-68; dir. libraries Drake U., Des Moines, 1968-73; dean libraries Kans. State U., Manhattan, 1973-81; cons. in field. Served with AUS, 1951-54. Mem. ALA, Kans. Library Assn. Author: The Detective Short Story: A Bibliography and Index, 1974.

RAUSCHEL, ARNETTE MARIE MURRAY, ednl. cons.; b. Chgo., Dec. 17, 1934; d. Arnett Bedford Francis and Hazel Marie (Lumpkins) Murray; B.S., U. Ill., 1957; M.S., Coll. Racine, 1974; Ph.D., So. Ill. U., 1981; div.; children—Victor, Vincent, Victoria. Tchr., Holy Child High Sch., Waukegan, Ill., 1957-60; tchr. Zion (Ill.) Elem. Dist. No. 6, 1969-70, Title I dir., 1970-76; ednl. cons. reading, tchrs. centers, gifted edn. Ill. State Bd. Edn., Springfield, Ill., 1976—; cons. U.S. Dept. Edn., NEA. Vol. workshop leader Springfield Housing Authority, 1980; Right-to-Read dir. Zion-Benton Twp., 1974-76; mem. Zion Environ. Commn., 1974. Mem. Am. Assn. Sch. Adminstrs., Assn. Tchr. Educators, Ill. Assn. Supervision and Curriculum Devel., Am. Assn. Supervision and Curriculum Devel. Home: 2908 Woodward Ave Springfield IL 62703 Office: 100 N 1st St Springfield IL 62777

RAVEN, PETER HAMILTON, botanist, garden adminstr.; b. Shanghai, China, June 13, 1936; s. Walter Francis and Isabelle Marion (Breen) R.; A.B., U. Calif., Berkeley, 1957; Ph.D., UCLA, 1960; m. Tamra Gail Engelhorn, Nov. 29, 1968; children—Alice Catherine, Elizabeth Marie, Francis Clark. NSF postdoctoral fellow Brit. Mus., London, 1960-61; taxonomist Rancho Santa Ana Botanic Garden, Claremont, Calif., 1961-62; asst., asso. prof. biol. scis. Stanford U., 1962-71; dir. Mo. Bot. Garden, Engelmann prof. botany Washington U., St. Louis, 1971—. Commr., Tower Grove Park, St. Louis, 1971—. NSF grantee. Fellow AAAS, Calif. Acad. Scis., Am. Acad. Arts and Scis.; mem. Nat. Acad. Scis., Royal Danish Acad. Arts and Scis. (fgn. mem.), others. Clubs: Univ., Noonday. Author books; contbr. numerous articles to profl. jours. Office: Mo Bot Garden PO Box 299 Saint Louis MO 63166

RAVES, PETER HARLEY, product engr.; b. London, Eng., Mar. 12, 1930; s. Henry Alfred and Josephine Esther (Smart) R.; came to U.S., 1969; higher nat. cert. in mech. engring. S.E. Essex Tech. Coll. (Eng.), 1963; m. Ena Joyce Williamson, Aug. 17, 1957; children—Amanda Jane, Mark Andrew, Melanie Ann. Phys. test lab. supr. Ford Motor Co., Eng., 1956-64, sr. devel. engr., 1964-67, sr. test engr., 1967-70; sr. product engr. Kelsey Hayes Co., Romulus, Mich., 1970—. Served with Brit. Army, 1951-53. Mem. Soc. Automotive Engrs. Home: 18303 Ridge Rd Northville MI 48167 Office: 38481 Huron River Dr Romulus MI 48174

RAVITCH, MICHAEL MARK, ednl. psychologist, educator; b. Balt., Jan. 23, 1943; s. Mark M. and Irene R. Ravitch; A.B., Franklin and Marshall Coll., 1966; M.A., Tchrs. Coll. Columbia U., 1968; Ph.D., Stanford U., 1977; m. Myrnice McCormick, Dec. 22, 1968; 1 dau., Lara Michelle. Elem. tchr. N.Y.C., 1968-69; program evaluator various ednl. contracts Stanford (Calif.) U., test officer, mem. faculty Calif. State U., Hayward, 1969-73; asst. prof. edn., asso. med. edn. U. Rochester, 1973-77; asst. prof. med. edn. Office Med. Edn. Research and Devel., Coll. Human Medicine, Mich. State U., East Lansing, 1977—; U.S. Office Edn.-HEW research trainee, 1970-72. Recipient Morrisania Community Project award, 1969. Mem. Am. Ednl. Research Assn., AAAS, Am. Psychol. Assn., Internat. Assn. Applied Psychology, Nat. Council on Measurement in Edn., Soc. for Med. Decision Making, Am. Assn. for Cancer Edn. Adv. editor Jour. Ednl. Measurement; contbr. articles to profl. jours.; research on physicians' clin. decision making. Office: Office of Medical Education Research and Development A 202 E Fee Hall Michigan State Univ East Lansing MI 48824

RAWITCH, ALLEN BARRY, biochemist; b. Chgo., Dec. 29, 1940; s. Samuel and Jean (Riefman) R.; student Pierce Coll., 1958-60; A.A., U. Calif. at Los Angeles, 1961, B.S., 1963, Ph.D., 1967; m. Patricia Nan Karlan, July 21, 1962; children—Bruce Howard, David Andrew. Research fellow U. Ill., 1967-69; asst. prof. chemistry Kent State U., 1969-73, asso. prof., 1973-75; asso. prof. dept. biochemistry U. Kans. Med. Center, Kansas City, 1975—; cons. chiefs of police pub. service communications, Portage County, Ohio, 1974-75; research scientist Mid Am. Cancer Center Program. Res. police officer City of Overland Park (Kans.), 1978—. Recipient NIH Research Career Devel. award, 1973; NIH grantee, 1971—; NSF grantee, 1970-72; Nat. Heart Assn. grantee, 1976-77. Mem. Am. Chem. Soc., Am. Soc. Biol. Chemists, AAAS, Sigma Xi. Home: 10112 Oakridge Dr Overland Park KS 66212 Office: Dept Biochemistry U Kans Med Center Kansas City KS 66103

RAWLINGS, CHARLES ADRIAN, biomed. engr., educator; b. Paducah, Ky., Nov. 11, 1936; s. James A. and Frances J. (Oldani) R.; student Paducah Jr. Coll., 1954-55; B.S. in Elec. Engring., U. Ill., 1959; M.S. in Engring., So. Ill. U., 1965, Ph.D. in Physiology and Engring., 1974; postgrad. U. Utah, 1960, El Camino Coll., 1961. Engr., Sperry Rand, Salt Lake City, 1959-61; field engring. tng. rep. Autonetics div. of N.Am. Aviation, Anaheim, Calif., 1961-64, sr. logistics field engr. Space and Info. Systems div., Downey, Calif., 1965-66; lectr. So. Ill. U., Carbondale, 1965-74, instr., 1964-65, asst. prof. dept. elec. scis. and systems engring., 1974-78, asso. prof., 1978—, dir. biomed. engring., 1980—, dir. Seminar in Biomed. Instrumentation, 1972—, cons., 1969—; mem. tech. staff Autonetics div. N.Am. Rockwell, Anaheim, Calif., 1966-69; chmn. Bd. Examiners for Biomed. Equipment Technicians, 1975-79, chmn. cert. commn., 1979-81. Mem. IEEE, Instrument Soc. Am. (sr. mem., bd. dirs. 1979—, pres.-elect 1981-82), Assn. for Advancement of Med. Instrumentation, Am. Soc. Hosp. Engring., Mensa, Soc. Biomed. Equipment Technicians (lifetime hon.). Contbr. articles on med. instrumentation and biomed. engring. to profl. jours. Home: 1430 E Walnut St Carbondale IL 62901 Office: Coll Engring and Tech So Ill U Carbondale IL 62901

RAWLINGS, EDWIN WILLIAM, cons., former food co. exec., ret. air force officer; b. Milroy, Minn., Spet. 11, 1904; s. Frank Henry and Ella Mae (Frazier) R.; B.A., Hamline U., 1927, D.B.A. (hon.), 1945; M.B.A., Harvard U., 1939; H.H.D. (hon.), U. Dayton, 1954; L.L.D. (hon.), Ohio Wesleyan U., 1957, Hendrix Coll., 1957, Miami U., Oxford, Ohio, 1957; Dr.Bus.Adm. (hon.), Tufts U., 1959; m. Muriel Peterson, July 17, 1930; children—Peter E., Charles F., Richard W., John F. Reporter, St. Paul Pioneer Press and Dispatch, 1925; asst. dept. mgr. Dayton Co., Mpls., 1927-29; commd. 2d lt. AC, U.S. Army, 1930, advanced through grades to gen., 1954; comdg. gen. Air Materiel Command, Wright-Patterson AFB, Ohio, 1951-59; ret., 1959; fin. v.p. Gen. Mills, Inc., Mpls., 1959, exec. v.p., 1960-61, pres., 1961-67, chmn. bd., 1967-68, dir., 1959-76, ret., 1968; cons. Gen Mills, Inc.; dir. Magnetic Controls Co., Mpls. Bd. dirs. Air Force Acad. Found., Inc., Colorado Springs, Colo. Decorated D.S.M. with oak leaf cluster, D.F.C.; comdr. Order Brit. Empire (Eng.); recipient Gen. William E. Mitchell award Am. Legion Aviators Post, 743, 1957. Republican. Methodist. Club: Mpls. Home: 2765 Shadywood Rd Excelsior MN 55331 Office: 1914 First Bank Pl W Minneapolis MN 55402

RAWLINGS, GARY DON, environ. engr.; b. Houston, Tex., Feb. 6, 1948; s. William Lee and Sarah Jeanette (Lanham) R.; B.S., SW Tex. State U., 1970, M.S., 1971; Ph.D. (Tex. Expt. Sta. grantee), Tex. A&M U., 1974. Program mgr. environ. engring. research and devel. sect. Monsanto Research Corp., Dayton, Ohio 1974—, formerly project. mgr. EPA Project, Dayton, now mgr. internat. mktg. for nuclear sources. Mem. Air Pollution Control Assn., Am. Soc. Chem. Engrs., Sigma Xi, Alpha Chi. Author: (with B. W. Cornaby) Management of Toxic Substances in Our Ecosystem, 1981; contbr. 56 articles to EPA publs. and symposiums. Home: 2932 Asbury Ct Miamisburg OH 45342 Office: 1515 Nicholas Rd Dayton OH 45418

RAWN, EDWIN LEROY, educator; b. Alma, Mich., July 6, 1938; s. William E. and Dortha (Wright) R.; B.M.E., Alma (Mich.) Coll., 1961; M.A. in Secondary Sch. Adminstrn., Central Mich. U., Mt. Pleasant, 1968; Edn. Specialist in Sch. Adminstrn., Central Mo. State U., Warrensburg, 1974; Ed.D. in Ednl. Adminstrn., U. Mo.-Columbia, 1979. Team leader edn. treatment St. Joseph (Mo.) State Hosp., 1969-71; asst. prin. N. Harrison R-III Sch. Dist., Eagleville, Mo., 1971-73; supt. Sheridan (Mo.) R-II Schs., 1974-76, North Andrew R-VI, 1976-77; asst. state chmn. Mo.-N.Central Assn., 1977-79; research asso. dept. ednl. adminstrn. U. Mo., 1980—. Mem. commr.'s staff Pony Express council Boy Scouts Am., 1969—, Great River Council, 1979; first aid instr. ARC, Sheridan, Mo., 1970—. Mem. Mo. State Tchrs. Assn., Phi Kappa Phi, Phi Delta Kappa. Certified in adminstrn., Mo., Mich. Home: 2300 West Blvd S Columbia MO 65201 Office: 7 Hill Hall U Mo Columbia MO 65211

RAWSKI, THOMAS MARK, supermarket exec.; b. Toledo, Dec. 28, 1947; s. Walter John and Genevieve Ursula (Jenczewski) R.; student Bowling Green State U., 1965-67; B.B.A., U. Toledo, 1970, postgrad., 1973-74. Employment interviewer Toledo Edison Co., 1970-73, employment mgr., 1973-75; Affirmative Action coordinator Seway Food Town, Inc., Maumee, Ohio, 1975-76, tng. coordinator, 1976—. Advisor, Jr. Achievement, 1974-78; firm chmn. United Way, 1975-81; mem. career devel. adv. com. Toledo public schs., 1977-81; mem. tribute to women in industry com., adult programming com. YWCA, Toledo, 1979-81. Served with U.S. Army Res., 1970-76. Mem. Am. Soc. Personnel Adminstrn. (dist. dir. Region VIII 1980), Am. Soc. Tng. and Devel., Toledo Personnel Mgmt. Assn. (pres. 1978-79), Toledo Indsl. Recreation and Employee Services Council. Clubs: Toledo Ski, K.C. Home: 1238 Hidden Ridge Dr Toledo OH 43615 Office: 1020 Ford St Maumee OH 43537

RAY, CHARLES DEAN, neurosurgeon; b. Americus, Ga., Aug. 1, 1927; s. Oliver Tinsley and Katherine (Broadfield) R.; A.B., Emory U., 1950; M.S., U. Miami (Fla.), 1952; M.D., Med. Coll. Ga., 1956; m. Roberta L. Mann, Dec. 17, 1978; children—Bruce, Kathy, C. Marlene, Thomas, John, Blythe. Intern, Baptist Meml. Hosp., Memphis, 1956-57; resident, research asso. in neurosurgery U. Tenn. Hosp., Memphis, 1957-62; fellow, research asst. Mayo Clinic and Found., Rochester, Minn., 1962-64; asst. prof. neurosurgery, lectr. bioengring. Johns Hopkins Med. Sch., 1964-68; chief dept. med. engring. F. Hoffmann-LaRoche, Basel, Switzerland, also lectr. U. Basel, 1968-73; practice medicine specializing in neurosurgery, Mpls., 1973—; pres. Charles D. Ray, Ltd.; mem. staff Sister Kenney Inst., Children's, Abbott-Northwestern hosps.; clin. asso. prof. U. Minn. Med. Sch.; sr. cons. Medtronic, Inc.; adviser med. devices FDA; chmn. com. materials and devices World Fedn. Neurosurg. Socs.; dir. Herman Miller, Inc., Zeeland, Mich., Newart Sci., Wayzata, Minn. Mem. vestry St. Martin's Episcopal Ch., Wayzata. Served with USNR, 1945-49. Diplomate Am. Bd. Neurol. Surgery. Cert. clin. engr. Fellow ACS, Royal Soc. Health; mem. Am., Pan-Am. med. assns., Am. Assn. Neurol. Surgeons, Congress Neurol. Surgeons, W. Ger. Armed Forces Med. Soc., IEEE, Internat. Fedn. Med. Biol. Engring., Internat. Soc. Stereotaxic and Functional Neurosurgery, ASTM, Internat. Orgn. Standardization, Assn. Advancement Med. Instrumentation, AAAS, Bioengring. Soc., Minn., Hennepin County med. socs., Minn. Neurosurg. Soc., Sigma Xi, Alpha Omega Alpha, Psi Chi. Clubs: Cosmos, Lafayette, Mpls. Author: Principles of

Engineering Applied to Medicine, 1964; Medical Engineering, 1974; also monographs, numerous articles. Home: 19550 Cedarhurst Wayzata MN 55391 Office: Inst for Low Back Care 2737 Chicago Ave Suite 1750 Minneapolis MN 55407

RAY, DARRELL DEAN, dentist; b. Fairfax, Mo., Dec. 5, 1927; s. Nicholas Jerome and Edna R.; B.A., Tarkio Coll., 1952; D.D.S., U. Mo., 1956; m. J. Natalie Hart, Aug. 30, 1952; children—David, Cynthia, Michelle. Practice dentistry, Shenandoah, Iowa, 1957; intern VA, Wadsworth, Kans., 1956-57. Bd. dirs. ARC, 1964, Porters Lake Lutheran Center, Am. Legion War Meml. Trust. Served with USN, 1946-48. Mem. Am. Legion (post comdr. 1962), Shenandoah C. of C. (dir. 1977—), Tarkio Coll. Alumni Assn. (pres. 1969), ADA, Iowa Dental Assn. (pres. 1976-77, treas. 1981—), S.W. Iowa Dental Assn., Internat. Coll. Dentists, Am. Coll. Dentists, Acad. Gen. Dentistry, Pierre Fauchard Acad., Am. Prosthodontic Soc., Chgo. Dental Soc. (asso.), U. Iowa Dental Alumni Assn. (dir. 1981—). Republican. Lutheran. Club: Rotary (pres. 1968). Home: 2 Country Club Ln Shenandoah IA 51601 Office: 118 N Blossom St Shenandoah IA 51601

RAY, FRANK DAVID, govt. agy. ofcl.; b. Mt. Vernon, Ohio, Dec. 1, 1940; s. John Paul and Lola Mae (Miller) R.; B.S. in Edn., Ohio State U., 1964, J.D., 1967; m. Julia Anne Sachs, June 11, 1976. Admitted to Ohio bar, 1967, U.S. Supreme Ct., 1971; legal aide to atty. gen. Ohio, 1965-66; bailiff probate ct., Franklin County, Ohio, 1966-67, gen. referee, 1967-68; with firm Stouffer, Wait and Ashbrook, Columbus, Ohio, 1967-71; jour. clk. Ohio Ho. of Repts., 1969-71; dist. dir. SBA, 1971—. Mem. Upper Arlington (Ohio) Bd. Health, 1970-75; pres. Buckeye Republican Club, 1970, Franklin County Forum, 1970; chmn. Central Ohio chpt. Nat. Found.-March of Dimes, 1974-77; trustee Columbus Acad. Contemporary Art, 1976. Recipient Service award Nat. Found.-March of Dimes, 1974, 75, 76, 77; named Ohio Commodore, 1973. Clubs: Ohio State U. Pres., Shrine. Home: 4200 Dublin Rd Columbus OH 43220

RAY, JAMES ALLEN, mfg. co. exec.; b. Lexington, Ky., Feb. 21, 1931; s. Allen Brice and Elizabeth Logan (Simpson) R.; B.S. in Geology, U. N.C., 1958; M.S., N.C. State Coll., 1961; m. Mary Ruth Johnston, June 8, 1958; children—James Edward, Allen Bruce, John David. Chief petrographic research Master Builders div. Martin Marietta Corp., Mantua, Ohio, 1959-73, asst. dir. research, 1973-77, dir. research, 1977-78, v.p. research, 1979-80, v.p. creative research, 1980—. Served with USAF, 1951-55. Recipient Jefferson Cup, Martin Marietta Corp., 1977. Mem. Mineral. Soc. Am., Mineral. Soc. Can., Am. Ceramic Soc., Am. Concrete Inst., ASTM, Res. Officers Assn. (life), Air Force Assn., Nat. Rifle Assn. (life), Washington Legal Found. (life), Am. Security Council. Republican. Patentee in field. Home: 9891 Stamm Rd Mantua OH 44255 Office: 23700 Chagrin Blvd Cleveland OH 44112

RAY, JOHN WALKER, physician; b. Columbus, Ohio, Jan. 12, 1936; s. Kenneth Clark and Hope (Walker) Ray; A.B. magna cum laude, Marietta Coll., 1956; M.D. cum laude, Ohio State U., 1960; postgrad. Temple U., 1964, Mt. Sinai Hosp. and Columbia U., 1964, 66, Northwestern U., 1967, 71, U. Ill., 1968, U. Ind., 1969, Tulane U., 1969; m. Susanne Gettings, July 15, 1961; children—Nancy Ann, Susan Christy. Intern, Ohio State U. Hosps., Columbus, 1960-61, clin. research trainee NIH, 1963-65, resident dept. otolaryngology, 1963-65, 1966-67, resident dept. surgery 1965-66, instr. dept. otolaryngology, 1966-67, 70-75, clin. asst. prof., 1975—; active staffs Bethesda, Good Samaritan hosps., Zanesville, Ohio, 1967—; courtesy staff Ohio State U. Hosps., Columbus, 1970—. Past pres. Muskingum chpt. Am. Cancer Soc. Served to capt. USAF, 1961-63. Recipient Barraquer Meml. award, 1965; named Ky. col., 1966. Diplomate Am. Bd. Otolaryngology. Fellow A.C.S., Am. Soc. Otolaryn. Allergy, Am. Acad. Otolaryngology, Am. Acad. Facial Plastic and Reconstructive Surgery; mem. Muskingum County Acad. Medicine, Am., Ohio (del.) med. assns., Columbus Ophthalmol. and Otolaryngol. Soc. (pres.), Ohio Soc. Otolaryngology (past pres.), Pan-Am. Assn. Otolaryngology and Bronchoesophagology, Pan-Am. Allergy Soc., Am. Council Otolaryngology, Am. Soc. Contemporary Medicine and Surgery, Phi Beta Kappa, Alpha Tau Omega, Alpha Kappa Kappa, Alpha Omega Alpha, Beta Beta Beta. Republican. Presbyterian. Contbr. articles to sci., med. jours. Collaborator, surg. motion picture Laryngectomy and Neck Dissection, 1964. Office: 2927 Bell St Zanesville OH 43701

RAY, MRS. ROBERT D., wife of Iowa gov.; b. Colombus Junction, Iowa, May 16, 1928; d. Herbert F. and Eva (Hickman) Hornberger; B.S. in Edn. cum laude, Drake U., 1950; m. Robert D. Ray, Dec. 22, 1951; children—Randi Sue, Lu Ann, Vicki Jo. Tchr. elementary sch., 1950-55. Active United Campaign, Heart Fund, March of Dimes, Easter Seals, Mental Health drives, Polk County (Iowa) Cancer Soc., Campfire Girls, ARC, Fedn. Republican Women; mem. Foster Grandparents Adv. Com.; trustee Mamie Eisenhower Birthplace Found.; hon. state chairperson Internat. Year of the Child; state chmn. Iowa Friendship Force; hon. adviser Women in Bus. Midwest Regional Conf.; hon. chmn. Internat. Yr. Disabled Persons, 1981-82. Recipient Nat. Alumni Assn. Centennial award Drake U., 1981. Mem. Polk County Attys. Wives, Drake Nat. Alumni Assn. (dir. 1970—), Mid-Am. Arts Alliance, Zonta (hon.), P.E.O., Beta Sigma Phi, Kappa Delta Phi, Kappa Beta Kappa, Alpha Delta Kappa, Omicron Delta Kappa, Delta Kappa Gamma, Chi Omega. Address: 2300 Grand St Des Moines IA 50312

RAY, RICHARD SCHELL, veterinarian, educator; b. Awtwerd, Ohio, May 21, 1928; s. Alton D. and Dorothy (Schell) R.; B.A., Ohio State U., 1950, D.V.M., 1955, M.Sc., 1958, Ph.D., 1963; m. Diane Maxine Foster, June 12, 1954; children—Kathleen F., David A., Elizabeth A. Practice vet. medicine, Toledo, 1955; instr. Ohio State U., Columbus, 1955-63, asst. prof., 1963-67, asso. prof., 1967-73, prof. vet. clin. sci., 1973—; cons. forensic pharmacology and metabolic diseases. Recipient Lab. of Yr. award U.S. Harness Writers Assn., 1970; recipient various grants. Fellow Am. Coll. Vet. Pharmacology and Therapeutics; mem. Am. Chem. Soc., Am. Assn. Vet. Clinicians, Am. Assn. Equine Practitioners, Am. Soc. Vet. Physiologists and Pharmacologists, Assn. Drug Detection Labs., Assn. Ofcl. Racing Chemists, World Assn. Vet. Physiologists, Pharmacologists and Biochemists, Phi Zeta, Omega Tau Sigma, Alpha Sigma Phi. Republican. Methodist. Clubs: Masons, Eastern Star. Contbr. articles to profl. jours. Home: 2752 Folkstone Rd Columbus OH 43220 Office: 1935 Coffey Rd Columbus OH 43221

RAY, ROBERT D., gov. Iowa; b. Des Moines, Sept. 26, 1928; s. Clark A. and Mildred (Dolph) R.; B.A. in Bus. Adminstrn., Drake U., 1952, J.D., 1954; hon. degrees Central Coll., Iowa Wesleyan Coll., Grinnell Coll., Still Osteo. Coll., Cornell Coll., St. Ambrose Coll., Upper Iowa Coll., Westmar Coll., Luther Coll.; m. Billie Lee Hornberger, Dec. 21, 1951; children—Randi Sue, Lu Ann, Vicki Jo. Admitted to Iowa bar, 1954; mem. firm Lawyer, Lawyer & Ray, Des Moines, 1954-69; owner Emmet Broadcasting Co.; gov. State of Iowa, 1969—; mem. exec. com. Nat. Gov.'s Conf., 1970—, also com. on rural and urban devel., com. on natural resources and environ. mgmt., 1974-75; mem. exec. com. Republican Govs. Assn., 1970—, chmn. policy council, 1975-76; chmn. Midwest Gov.'s Conf., 1972, Nat. Gov.'s Conf., 1975-76, Iowa Exec. Council; v.p. exec. com. Council State Govts.; mem. Adv. Commn. Intergovtl. Relations; chmn. del. govs. to Japan, People's Republic of China, 1972-74, USSR, 1975; spl. adviser to Adv. Com. Intergovtl. Affairs vice chmn. Rep. Gov.'s Assn., 1976-77; mem. subcoms. clean air mgmt., fgn. trade, tourism task force Nat. Gov.'s Assn.; hon. vice chmn. nat. distinguished guests com. Am. Legion, 1977-78. State chmn. March of Dimes, 1960-62; hon. adviser nat. council Boy Scouts Am.; chmn. Iowa Republican party, 1963-68, Midwest Assn. Rep. State Chmn., 1965-68; chmn. Nat. Rep. State Chmns. Assn., 1967-68; chmn. platform com. Rep. Nat. Conv., 1976; bd. dirs. Family Service Des Moines; hon. chmn. Everett McKinley Dirksen Library; hon. trustee Am. Acad. Achievement; chmn. Geol. Bd. Iowa; hon. bd. dirs. Make Today Count, Burlington, Iowa, Practicing Law Inst. Served with AUS, 1946-48. Recipient Nat. Distinguished Service award Future Farmers Am., 1970; Distinguished Alumni award Drake U.; named One of Am.'s 200 Rising Young Leaders, Time Mag., 1974. Chmn. Edn. Commn. of the States (past v. chmn.). Mem. Iowa Acad. Trial Lawyers, Am. Trial Lawyers Assn., Iowa State, Polk County, Am. bar assns., Nat. Reading Council, Order of Coif, Alpha Zeta, Delta Theta Phi, Alpha Kappa Psi, Omicron Delta Kappa, Sigma Alpha Epsilon. Mem. Disciples of Christ Ch. Home: 2300 Grand Ave Des Moines IA 50312 Office: State Capitol House Des Moines IA 50319

RAY, ROBERT DURANT, physician, educator; b. Cleve., Sept. 21, 1914; s. Clifford A. and Edna B. (Durant) R.; student U. Calif., Berkeley, 1932-37, M.A., 1938, Ph.D., 1948; M.D., Harvard U., 1943; Med.Dr.Sci. honoris causa, U. Umea, Sweden, 1972; m. Genevieve Triau, Dec. 19, 1953; children—Francis, Robert, Esten, Gisele, Charles. Surg. intern Peter Bent Brigham Hosp., Boston, 1943; resident Children's Hosp., Boston, 1944-45, U. Calif., San Francisco, 1949; asst. prof. U. Wash. Sch. Medicine, Seattle, 1948-51; asso. prof., head orthopedic surgery U. Wash., Seattle, 1951-56; prof., head dept. orthopedics Presbyn. St. Luke's Med. Center, 1956-71, U. Ill. Research Edn. Hosp., Chgo., 1956—. Served to capt. U.S. Army, 1945-47. Recipient Kappa Delta award for outstanding research in orthopaedics, 1954, 70. Mem. AAAS, Am. Assn. Orthopedic Surgeons, Am. Assn. Anatomists, ACS, AMA, Am. Orthopedic Assn., Assn. of Bone and Joint Surgery, Chgo. Orthopedic Soc., Internat. Coll. Surgeons, Internat. Soc. Orthopedic Surgery and Traumatology. Home: 227 Dempster St Evanston IL 60201 Office: 840 S Wood St Chicago IL 60612

RAY, ROY L., mayor of Akron (Ohio); b. Akron, July 16, 1939; s. Charles H. and Geneva L. (Edwards) R.; B.S. in Bus. Adminstrn., U. Akron, 1962, postgrad. in bus. adminstrn., 1972—; m. Frances M. Jordan, Aug. 24, 1968; children—Christopher Lee, Brian Edward. Sales rep. Goodyear Internat. Co., Akron, 1962-67; stockbroker Francis I. DuPont Investment Firm, Akron, 1967-69; research analyst City of Akron, 1969-72, dep. service dir., 1972-73, mem. Public Utilities Commn., 1973-74, budget dir., 1974-77, fin. dir., 1977-80, mayor, 1980—; guest lectr. U. Akron, Kent State U. Precinct committeeman Summit County Republican Com.; mem. Goals for Greater Akron Area, Downtown Redevel. Com.; trustee Ohio Mcpl. League. Mem. Internat. City Mgrs. Assn., Mcpl. Fin. Officers Assn., U.S. Conf. Mayors, Nat. League Cities, Omicron Delta Kappa, Phi Kappa Tau. Club: Kiwanis. Office: City Hall 166 S High St Akron OH 44308

RAY, WILLIAM THEODORE, state ofcl.; b. New Haven, Mar. 20, 1916; s. William Howard and Malinda Catherine (Miller) R.; student Oberlin (Ohio) Coll., 1934-36, Cleve. Coll., part-time 1938-40; LL.D. (hon.), Oakland City (Ind.) Coll., 1976; m. Alice Brokenburr, Sept. 12, 1942; children—Linda A., William V., Alan B., Paul S. Engaged in real estate and ins., Indpls., 1946—; exec. asst. to gov. Ind., 1973-80; dir. Ind. Dept. Fin. Instns., 1980—; organizer, dir. Midwest Nat. Bank, Indpls. Mem. Met. Sch. Dist. Washington Twp., 1968-72, pres., 1970; bd. dirs. Indpls. Found., United Way Indpls., Indpls. chpt. NAACP, Commn. Downtown Indpls., Ind. council Boy Scouts Am. Served with AUS, 1941-46. Decorated Bronze Star. Mem. Conf. State Bank Suprs., NAACP (life), Nat. Bd. Realtors, Ind. Bd. Realtors. Republican. Presbyterian. Clubs: Guaranter, Clowes Hall. Office: 1024 State Office Bldg Indianapolis IN 46204

RAYBELL, GLENNA JEAN, social worker; b. Poulsbo, Wash., June 29, 1932; d. Glen E. and Ruby (Nupp) R.; B.S., Mary Coll., 1961; M.S.W., U. Ill., Chgo., 1971. Coordinator youth services, psychologist, social worker Chgo. Mental Health Div., 1968-72; chmn. dept. history St. Mary's Central High Sch., Bismarck, N.D., 1965-68; mem. N.D. Gov.'s Commn. on Status of Women, 1972-73; mem. N.D. Parole Bd., 1973-74; social worker VA, Sioux Falls, S.D., 1974-77; asst. prof. U. S.D., 1977-78; dir. social work program Mt. Marty Coll., Yankton, S.D., 1978-79; clin. dir. Luther Youngdahl Human Relations Center, Owatonna, Minn., 1979-81; mem. Southeastern Minn. Health Systems Agy. Mental Health Task Force, 1981; bd. dirs. Minn. Sudden Infant Death Center, 1981; pvt. practice psychotherapy and hypnotherapy; mem. Annunciation Priory, Bismarck. Pres., N.D. Women's Coalition, 1973-74; mem. county exec. bd. Democratic Non-Partisan League Party, 1973-74, state platform com., state del., 1974; del. Nat. Dem. Mid-Term Conv., 1974; a founding mem. N.D. Coordinating Council for ERA, 1974-76. Mem. Acad. Cert. Social Workers, N.D. Council Social Studies (pres. 1967-68), Nat. Assn. Social Workers, N.D. Assn. Social Workers, Pilgrim Soc., Womens Ordination Conf. (dir. 1976). Roman Catholic. Home: Annunciation Priory Apple Creek Rd Bismarck ND 58501 Office: St Alexius Hosp 9th and Thayer Ave Bismarck ND 58501

RAYBORN, RANDALL LEE, educator; b. Rushville, Ill., May 14, 1934; s. Orville Lee and Dorothy Fern (Beatty) R.; student U. Ill., 1952-54; B.S., Western Ill. U., 1957; M.Ed., Loyola U., Chgo., 1964; m. Nancy Ellen Sehnert, Nov. 24, 1956; children—Michael, James, LeeAnn, Mark, Robin. Tchr., Chgo. Public Schs., 1957-58, Rhodes Sch., River Grove, Ill., 1958-61, Kenton Sch., Skokie, Ill., 1961-63; guidance dir. Marian High Sch., Chicago Heights, Ill., 1963-64, St. George High Sch., Evanston, Ill., 1964-67; counselor Maine West High Sch., Des Plaines, Ill., 1967—. Founder, Oakton Community Coll., 1969. Served with Ill. Army N.G., 1957-62. Mem. NEA, Ill. Edn. Assn., Am. Personnel and Guidance Assn., Am. Sch. Counselor Assn. (licensure cons. region 5), Ill. Guidance Personnel Assn. (senator, state licensure com. 1973-79), Ill. Sch. Counselor Assn. (mem. governing bd., secondary v.p., certificates of recognition 1975-79), Delta Sigma Phi. Roman Catholic. Home: 1480 Perry St Des Plaines IL 60016 Office: 1755 S Wolf Rd Des Plaines IL 60018

RAYMOND, MARGARET (BETH) PEAKE, planning & research social services co. exec.; b. Tahlequah, Okla., June 22, 1941; d. Jesse J. and Mary Louise (Breuninger) P.; B.S. in Edn., Northeastern Okla. State U., 1963; M.S.W. (Cherokee Nation of Okla. grantee 1972-74, David Logan fellow 1973-74), U. Okla., Norman, 1974; m. Elgie Victor Raymond, Dec. 30, 1977; children—Reid Scott, Gary Drew, Lisa LaDawn, Victor Jason. Tchr. elem. public schs., Gallup, N.Mex., O'Falon, Mo., Bristow, Okla., 1960-69; dir. talent search Oklahomans for Indian Opportunity, Norman, 1974-75; spl. asst. to dir. Minn. Alcohol and Drug Authority, St. Paul, 1975-78; tribal planner Cherokee Nation of Okla., Tahlequah, 1978; dir. planning and program devel. 1st Phoenix Am. Corp., Mpls., 1978—, v.p., 1981—; mem. Nat. Indian Bd. on Alcohol and Drug Abuse, 1975-81; mem. community services rev. com. Nat. Inst. on Alcohol Abuse and Alcoholism, 1979-81; mem. Nat. Adv. Council on Drug Abuse, 1981-83. Mem. United Indian Planners Assn., Nat. Congress Am. Indians. Research in field. Home: 2649 Longfellow Ave Minneapolis MN 55407 Office: 2025 Nicollet Ave Suite 204 Minneapolis MN 55404

RAYNOR, JOHN PATRICK, univ. pres.; b. Omaha, Oct. 1, 1923; s. Walter V. and Mary Clare (May) R.; A.B., St. Louis U., 1947, M.A., 1948 L.Ph., 1949, S.T.L., 1956; Ph.D., U. Chgo., 1959. Joined S.J., 1941, ordained priest Roman Cath. Ch., 1954; tchr. St. Louis U. High Sch., 1948-51, asst. prin., 1951; instr. dept. edn., asst. to dean Coll. Liberal Arts, Marquette U., Milw., 1960, asst. to v.p. academic affairs, 1960-62, v.p. academic affairs, 1962-65, pres. Marquette U., 1965—; dir. Kimberly-Clark Corp.; mem. N. Central Assn. Colls. and Secondary Schs., also cons., examiner; sponsor United Negro Coll. Fund; mem. Wis. Higher Ednl. Aids Bd. Corp. mem. United Community Services of Greater Milw.; mem. energy mgmt. policy com. City of Milw.; mem. Goals for Greater Milw. 2000 Project; hon. bd. dirs. Goethe House, Milw. Recipient Distinguished Service award Edn. Commn. of the States, 1977. Mem. Met. Milw. Assn. Commerce, Citizens Govtl. Research Bur., Greater Milw. Com., Internat. Fedn. Cath. Colls. and Univs., Nat. Cath. Edn. Assn., Am. Council Edn., Wis. Assn. Ind. Colls. and Univs. (past pres.), Assn. Jesuit Colls. and Univs. dir., exec. com.), NCCJ (past pres.), Phi Beta Kappa, Phi Delta Kappa, Alpha Sigma Nu. Home: 615 N 11th St Milwaukee WI 52233

READ, ROBERT BENJAMIN, city ofcl.; b. Detroit, Apr. 30, 1918; s. Benjamin K. and Adah M. (Lloyd) R.; B.S., U. Wis., 1943; m. Lydia Emma Porte, July 11, 1953. Field engr. Consoer, Townsend & Assos., Chgo., 1946; constrn. engr. Dept. Pub. Works Madison (Wis.), 1947-69, pub. works planning engr., 1969—. Mem. adv. bd. Madison Area Tech. Coll., 1971-79. Served with USNR, 1943-46. Registered profl. engr., Wis. Mem. Wis. (dir. 1963-65, v.p. 1967-71, Profl. Engr. in Govt., 1975, Engr. of Year in Govt. award 1974, Pres.'s Achievement award 1974, Resolution of Distinguished Service 1974, Engr. of Year 1978), Nat. (dir. 1971-74) socs. profl. engrs., ASCE, Am. Pub. Works Assn. Presbyterian (deacon 1973-76). Clubs: Masons, Shriners, DeMolay Legion of Honor. Home: 645 Charles Ln Madison WI 53711 Office: 210 Monona Ave Madison WI 53709

READINGER, DAVID M., state senator; b. Des Moines, Dec. 23, 1935; s. Max O. and A. Evelyn R.; B.S., Drake U., 1962. Former mem. Iowa Ho. of Reps., now mem. Iowa Senate. Mem. Urbandale Jaycees, LWV Lutheran. Clubs: Lions, Urbandale Boosters, Drake Nat. "D". Office: State Senate State Capitol Des Moines IA 50319*

REAGAN, MARGARET A., ednl. adminstr.; b. Beaver Falls, Pa., Dec. 1, 1949; d. William J. and Helen G. Reagan; B.S.Ed., Ill. State U., 1972, M.S.Ed., 1977. Tchr., Hancock County Schs., Chester, W.Va., 1972-75; instr. Ill. State U., Normal, 1979; field rep. U.S. Commerce Dept., Govt. div., Chgo., 1979-80; tchr. Ottawa (Ill.) Elem. Sch. Dist., 1980-81; prin. Effingham (Ill.) Unit Sch. Dist., 1981—. Mem. Assn. Supervision and Curriculum Devel., Ill. Prins. Assn. Home: 501 S 5th St Apt 2 Effingham IL 62401 Office: West Side School Effingham IL

REAGEN, MICHAEL VINCENT, state ofcl.; b. Jersey City, N.J., July 27, 1942; s. Vincent T. and Jeanette M. (Jameson) R.; B.S., Fordham U., 1964; M.S. (James Webb scholar), U. Ill., 1965; Ph.D., Syracuse U., 1972; postgrad. Wayne State U., 1969; m. Susan Carol Koplinka, Sept. 10, 1966; children—Jane, Erin, Jennifer. Asst. to pres. Maria Regina Coll., Syracuse, N.Y., 1966-69; directing research fellow Syracuse U. Research Corp., 1972-74; program adminstr. Continuing Edn. Center for Public Service, Syracuse U., 1969-72, adj. faculty, 1971-79; pres. Asso. Orgnl. Cons., Inc., Syracuse, 1974; county adminstr. Onondaga County (N.Y.), 1975-79; cons. in field; commr. Iowa State Dept. Social Services, Des Moines, 1979—; vis. lectr. Drake U., Inst. Pub. Affairs and Adminstrn., 1980-81; adj. faculty U. Iowa Sch. Social Work, 1981—; sr. instr. Inst. for Local Public Service, Syracuse, 1974-77; vis. lectr. Central N.Y. Police Acad., 1971-75, Criminal Justice Inst., Onondaga Community Coll., 1975; dir. Inst. for Devel. Exec. Ability, 1973, Inst. for Drug Edn., Syracuse, 1971-72, Agway, Inc., 1973; vis. lectr. U.S. Army Chaplain's Sch., 1971-72; co-dir. Maxwell Internat. Devel. Agy., 1969-71; cons. in field. Mem. State Criminal Justice Adv. Bd. to Gov. Iowa, 1980—, mgmt. tng. adv. bd., 1980—; mem. Drake U. Adv. Com. for Inst. Pub. Affairs and Adminstrn., 1980—; mem. Rep. Forum, 1978; corporate mem. United Way of Syracuse, 1978; bd. dirs. Urban League, Syracuse, 1978; vice chmn. Boy Power Dinner, Boy Scouts Am., Syracuse, 1978; mem. met. com. Greater Syracuse YMCA, 1976-77; bd. dirs. Urban League, Syracuse, 1976-77, Onondaga Rep. Citizens Com., 1976-77; usher Holy Cross Roman Cath. Ch., Dewitt, N.Y., 1976-77; gen. chmn. visit of U.S. Pres. Gerald Ford to Syracuse, 1976; mem. citizens adv. bd. Onondaga County Correctional Facility, 1973-75. Recipient Young Man of the Yr. award, Greater Syracuse Jr. C. of C., 1978; citation for quality leadership in probation, Ad Hoc Com. of Onondaga County Probation Officers Assn., 1978; James Webb Young scholar, U. Ill., 1965. Mem. Am. Soc. Public Adminstrn., (pres. Iowa chpt. 1981—), Am. Public Welfare Assn., N.Y. Criminal Justice Educators Assn., N.Y. State Assn. of Counties Human Services, Alpha Delta Sigma, Alpha Kappa Psi. Contbr. articles to profl. jours. Office: Hoover State Office Bldg Des Moines IA 50319

REAMS, BERNARD DINSMORE, JR., lawyer, educator; b. Lynchburg, Va., Aug. 17, 1943; s. Bernard Dinsmore and Martha Eloise (Hickman) R.; B.A., Lynchburg Coll., 1965; M.S., Drexel U., 1966; J.D., U. Kans., 1972; m. Rosemarie Bridget Boyle, Oct. 26, 1968; children—Andrew Dennet, Adriane Bevin. Instr., asst. librarian Rutgers U., Camden, N.J., 1966-69; admitted to Kans. bar, 1973; asst. prof. law and librarian U. Kans., Lawrence, 1969-74; asst. prof. law and librarian Washington U., St. Louis, 1974-76, asso. prof., 1976, prof., 1976—. Mem. Am., Spl. library assns., Am. Assn. Law Libraries, Am. Bar Assn., Beta Phi Mu, Phi Delta Phi, Order of Coif. Author: Law for the Businessman, 1974; (with Wilson) Segregation and the Fourteenth Amendment in the States, 1975; (with Kettler) Historic Preservation Law: An Annotated Bibliography, 1976; Reader in Law Librarianship, 1976; (with Haworth) Congress and the Courts: A Legislative History 1787-1977, 1978; (with Ferguson) Federal Consumer Protection: Laws, Rules and Regulations, 1979; The Internal Revenue Acts of the United States 1909-1950, 1979; Federal Price and Wage Control Programs 1917-1979: Legislative Histories, 1980. Adv. editor Historical Writings in Law and Jurisprudence, 1980. Office: Washington U Sch Law Box 1120 Saint Louis MO 63130

REANEY, JAMES CRERAR, educator, poet, playwright; b. Ont., Can., Sept. 1, 1926; s. James Nesbitt and Elizabeth Henrietta (Crerar) R.; B.A., U. Toronto, 1948, M.A., 1949, Ph.D., 1957; D.Litt., Carleton U., 1975; D.Letters, McMaster U., 1979; m. Colleen Thibaudeau, Dec., 1951; children—James Stewart, Susan Alice. Lectr., asst. prof. English U. Man., 1949-60; prof. English U. Western Ont., London, Can., 1960—. Recipient Massey award, 1960; Chalmers award, 1974, 75, 76. Fellow Royal Soc. Can.; mem. Assn. Can. Univ. Tchrs. (pres. 1959-60), League Can. Poets, Can. Theatre Co-op. Mem. United Ch. Author: Colours in the Dark, 1969; Masks of Childhood, 1972; Poems, 1972; Listen to the Wind, 1972; Apple Butter and Other Plays for Children, 1973; 14 Barrels from Sea to Sea, 1977; The Dismissal, 1978. Plays include: Sticks and Stones: The Donnellys Part I, 1975; Handcuffs: The Donnellys Part III, 1977. Office: Dept English Univ Western Ont London ON N6A 3K7 Canada

REARDON, JOHN EDWARD, mayor; b. Kansas City, Kans., Aug. 23, 1943; s. Joseph E. and Helen (Cahill) R.; B.S. in History and Govt., Rockhurst Coll., Kansas City, Mo., 1965; m. Helen Kasick, June 18, 1966; children—Joseph, Kathleen. Tchr., head social studies dept. Arrowhead Jr. High Sch., Kansas City, Kans., 1966-72; register of deeds Wyandotte County/Kansas City, Kans., 1972-75; mayor of Kansas City (Kans.), 1975—; mem. Kansas City Devel. Corp. Bd. dirs. Kansas City United Way. Recipient Loyalty Day award VFW; named Outstanding Young Kansan, Jaycees, 1978, also numerous certs. of appreciation. Mem. U.S. Conf. Mayors, Kans. League Municipalities (v.p.), Kansas City C. of C. Democrat. Roman Catholic. Club: Central Ave. Optimists. Home: 1513 Tauromee St Kansas City KS 66102 Office: 701 N 7th St Kansas City KS 66101

REARDON, JOHN THOMAS, ret. state judge Ill.; b. Quincy, Ill., Mar. 3, 1910; s. Patrick J. and Katherine (Daniels) R.; J.D., St. Louis U., 1932; LL.D., Quincy (Ill.) Coll., 1979; m. Mildred Moller, Sept. 1, 1934; children—Constance Reardon Kaltenbach, Sharon Reardon Gibbons, Judith Reardon Rossmiller. Admitted to Ill. bar, 1933; corp. counsel City of Quincy, 1936-41; master in chancery Circuit Ct., Adams County (Ill.), Quincy, 1941-44; state's atty. Adams County, 1944-52; judge, Circuit Ct. Ill., 8th Circuit, Quincy, 1957-78, chief judge, 1963-75, appellate judge, 1976-78, ret., 1978; pres. justice 4th Dist. Appellate Ct., 1978—; chmn. Ill. Supreme Ct. Downstate Ct. Reorgn. Com., 1963; mem. exec. com. Ill. Jud. Conf., 1963-69; chmn. Ill. Chief Judges Conf., 1965-69; chmn. Nat. Conf. State Trial Judges, 1969. Active Community Chest, Quincy, co-chmn. ann. dr., 1939, chmn., 1940; co-chmn. St. Mary Hosp. dr., Quincy, 1961, mem. adv. bd., 1959-67; chmn. Quincy Coll. dr., 1947-49, mem. adv. bd., 1960-66; co-chmn. Christian Bros. High Sch. dr., Quincy, 1957, mem. adv. bd., 1962-66; chmn. Easter Seal dr., Quincy, 1967; active drs. for Blessing Hosp. and other community campaigns. Recipient Alumni Merit award St. Louis U., 1966. Fellow Am. Bar Found.; mem. Am. (chmn. div. jud. adminstrn. 1974-75), Ill., Adams County bar assns., Am. Judicature Soc., Nat. Conf. State Trial Judges (exec. exec. com. 1963-70), Ill. State's Attys. Assn. (pres. 1950), Ill. Circuit and Appellate Judges Assn. (pres. 1964-64). Clubs: Lions, K.C. (4 deg.). Home: 4143 Coachlight Ct Quincy IL 62301

REASONER, GREGORY ALAN, robotics co. personnel mgr.; b. Marion, Ohio, July, 18, 1953; s. Irl and Nancy Jane Reasoner; B.A., Miami U., Oxford, Ohio, 1976, M.S., 1977; Dir. counseling services Chatfield Coll., 1977-78; dir. personnel Smith Clinic, Marion, 1978-80; corp. mgr. manpower and staffing Borden, Inc., Columbus, Ohio, 1980-81; mgr. personnel Advanced Robotics Corp., Hebron, Ohio, 1981—; instr. Marion Tech. Coll., 1979-80; chmn. personnel council Marion Area C. of C., 1980-81. Mem. Am. Soc. Personnel Adminstrn., Marion Econ. Council, Med. Group Mgmt. Assn., Marion Assn. Tng. and Devel. Home: 5037 Marion-Bucyrus Rd Marion OH 43302 Office: Advanced Robotics Corp Newark Industrial Park Bldg 8 Route 79 Hebron OH 43025

REAVES, CHARLES EDWIN, physician; b. Gulfport, Miss., July 16, 1942; s. Thomas B. and Jessie A. (Roberts) R.; B.S., U. Miss., 1964, M.D., 1967; postgrad. Armed Forces Inst. Pathology, 1973; m. Sandra Joyce Carter, July 5, 1964; children—Valerie Clarisse, Charles Edwin. Intern, USAF Med. Center, Keesler AFB, Miss., 1967-68; resident USAF Med. Center, San Antonio, 1971-74; practice medicine specializing in dermatology, Pine Bluff, Ark., 1976-78, Galesburg, Ill., 1978—; clin. asst. prof. dermatology U. Ark. Sch. Medicine, 1976—; cons. dermatology Area Health Edn. Center program, Pine Bluff, 1976-78; mem. staff Galesburg Clinic Assn., St. Marys Hosp., Galesburg Cottage Hosp.; cons. Galesburg Mental Health Center; asst. clin. prof. dermatology Peoria (Ill.) Sch. Medicine, 1979—. Mem. Republican Com., Jefferson County, Ark., 1976-78; bd. dirs. Knox County Symphony Orch., Galesburg, Ill., 1979—, Knox County chpt. Am. Cancer Soc. Served to lt. col., M.C., USAF, 1967-76. Diplomate Am. Bd. Dermatology. Fellow Am. Acad. Dermatology, Am. Soc. Dermatopathology; mem. A.C.P., Am. Venereal Disease Assn., AMA, Am. Soc. for Dermatologic Surgery. Presbyterian. Contbr. articles on dermatology to med. jours. Home: 220 Illini Dr Galesburg IL 61401 Office: 3315 N Seminary St Galesburg IL 61401

REBBECK, LESTER JAMES, JR., artist; b. Chgo., June 25, 1929; s. Lester J. and Marie L. (Runkle) R.; B.A.E., Art Inst. Chgo., 1953, M.A.E., Art Inst. Chgo. and U. Chgo., 1959; m. Paula B. Phillips, July 7, 1951; 1 son, Lester J. Asst. prof. art William Rainey Harper Coll., Pallatine, Ill., 1967-72; dir. Countryside Art Gallery (Ill.), 1967-73; gallery dir. Chgo. Soc. Artists, 1967-68; now artist, tchr.; one man exhbns. include: Harper Jr. Coll.; group exhbns. include: Univ. Club, Chgo., 1980, Art Inst., Chgo., 1953. Served with U.S. Army, 1951-52. Mem. NEA, Ill. Edn. Assn., Ill. Art Educators Assn., Chgo. Soc. Artists, Coll. Art Assn., Art Inst. Chgo. Alumni Assn. Republican. Presbyterian. Home: 2041 Vermont St Rolling Meadows IL 60008

REBEIZ, CONSTANTIN ANIS, educator; b. Beirut, July 11, 1936; s. Anis C. and Valentine A. (Choueyri) R.; came to U.S., 1969, naturalized, 1975; B.S., Am. U. Beirut, 1959; M.S., U. Calif. at Davis, 1960, Ph.D., 1965; m. Carole Louise Conness, Aug. 18, 1962; children—Paul A., Natalie, Mark J. Dir. dept. biol. scis. Agrl. Research Inst., Beirut, 1965-69; research asso. U. Calif. at Davis, 1969-71; asso. prof. plant physiology U. Ill., Urbana-Champaign, 1972-76, prof., 1976—. Mem. Am. Soc. Plant Physiologists, Comité Internat. de Photobiologie, Am. Soc. Photobiology, AAAS, Lebanese Assn. Advancement Scis. (exec. com. 1967-69), Sigma Xi. Mem. Greek Orthodox Ch. Club: Explorers (fellow). Research and publs. in plant physiology and biochemistry. Home: 301 W Pennsylvania Ave Urbana IL 61801 Office: Vegetable Crops Bldg U Ill Urbana-Champaign IL 61801

REBER, DONALD DAVID, ret. supt. schs.; b. Allentown, Pa., Sept. 16, 1915; s. Charles A. and Hattie (Smith) R.; B.S., Franklin-Marshall Coll., 1937; M.A., Lehigh U., 1948; post-grad. Harvard U., 1942, Stanford U., 1948-52; Ed.D., U. So. Calif., 1958; m. Alma A. Yons, Aug. 23, 1941; children—Donna G. Reber Ebell, Jane M. Reber Grady, Becke A. Reber McKnight. Sch. tchr., prin., Coopersburg, Pa., 1937-42; prin., Allentown, Pa., 1945-48, Punahou Sch., Honolulu, 1948-50; prin., supt. schs., Lynwood, Calif., 1950-59; supt. schs., Claremont, Calif., 1959-63, Lyons Twp. High Sch. and Jr. Coll., LaGrange, Ill., 1963-80, ret., 1980; asso. prof. Claremont Grad. Sch., 1959-62, U. So. Calif., 1959-63. Bd. govs. LaGrange Community Meml. Hosp.; bd. dirs. United Fund, W. Suburban YMCA, W. Suburban Heart Assn. Served with USNR, 1941-45. Named Lynwood Man of Year, 1959; recipient Honor medal Freedoms Found., 1959; named Ednl. Adminstr. of Year, IAES, 1976; Eisenhower exchange fellow, Europe, 1958-59. Mem. Am., Ill. assns. sch. adminstrn., N. Central Assn. (dist. dir. Ill.), No. Ill. Supts. Round Table, Ill., Nat. (hon. life), Calif. (hon. life) parent-tchs. assns., Phi Delta Kappa. Congregationalist. Club: Kiwanis. Contbr. articles to ednl. jours. Home: 421 Blackstone St LaGrange IL 60525

REBER, WILLIAM ELWOOD, mental health adminstr.; b. Dayton, Ohio, Nov. 17, 1937; s. Eldred Thurmon and Ailene (Penick) R.; B.A., Ohio U., Athens, 1960; M.S. in Social Adminstrn., Case Western Res. U., 1962; m. Maryann Shollenbarger, Sept. 9, 1961; children—Eric William, Elizabeth Anne. Clin. social worker Lucas County Children's Services Bd., Toledo, 1962-64; clin. supr., sr. clin. therapist Lutheran Social Services, Toledo, 1964-68; successively supr. spl. projects, dir. profl. services, asso. dir. Family Services Greater Toledo, 1968-75; exec. dir. East Center Community Mental Health, Toledo, 1975—; mem. adj. faculty Mary Manse Coll., Toledo, 1968-72, U. Toledo Community Coll., 1972-74, Ashland (Ohio) Coll., 1979-81; trustee Community Mental Health Center West, 1969-74; mem. nat. steering com. dirs. profl. services Family Service Assn., Am., 1972-75; mem. Gov. Ohio Task Force Adoption, 1971-72; cons. in field, 1968—. Mem. Nat. Assn. Social Workers (cert. recognition N.W. Ohio chpt. 1975), Am. Assn. Marriage and Family Therapists, Acad. Cert. Social Workers, Nat. Council Community Mental Health Adminstrs., Alpha Kappa Delta. Address: 4222 Elmway Dr Toledo OH 43614

REBONE, WILLIAM FREDERICK, mfg. corp. exec.; b. Detroit, Nov. 15, 1913; s. Jacob R. and Elizabeth (Weithoff) R.; student St. Joseph's Comml. Coll., 1930; B.S. in Mech. Engring., U. Mich., 1944; m. Idamae Bacon, Dec. 31, 1966; children—William Frederick, Richard J., Margaret E., Kelly G., Bradley M. With Packard Car Co., Detroit, 1939-45, NuEra Gears, New Bedford, Mass., 1945-64, Napco Industries, Hopkins, Minn., 1964-74; v.p. mfg. Hanauer Machines, Inc., Avon, Minn., 1974-80; regional mgr., Columbia Gear, Avon, Minn., 1981—; cons. St. Cloud (Minn.) Area Vocat. and Tech. Inst. Mem. Soc. Mfg. Engrs. Republican. Roman Catholic. Home: 1816 13th Ave SE Saint Cloud MN 56301 Office: Columbia Gear Avon MN 56310

RECK, W(ALDO) EMERSON, ednl. pub. relations specialist, ret. writer; b. Gettysburg, Ohio, Dec. 28, 1903; s. Samuel Harvey and Effie D. (Arnett) R.; A.B., Wittenberg U., 1926; A.M., U. Iowa, 1946; LL.D., Midland Coll., 1949; m. Hazel Winifred January, Sept. 7, 1926; children—Phyllis Jean Reck Welch, Elizabeth Ann Reck Lada. Reporter, Springfield (Ohio) News, 1922-26; publicity dir. Midland Coll., Fremont, Nebr., 1926-28, dir. pub. relations, prof. journalism, 1928-40; dir. pub. relations Colgate U., 1940-48; v.p. Wittenberg U., Springfield, Ohio, 1948-70, v.p. emeritus, 1970—; pub. relations specialist Cumerford Corp., Ft. Lauderdale, Fla., 1970-78; hist. columnist Springfield (Ohio) Sun, 1973-79; spl. corr. AP, 1928-38; mng. editor Fremont Morning Guide, 1939; vis. lectr. pub. relations State U. Iowa, summers 1941, 42, U. Wyo., summer 1948; co-dir. Seminar on Pub. Relations for High Edn., Syracuse U., summers 1944, 45, 46. Recipient award Am. Coll. Pub. Relations Assn. for Distinguished Service, 1942, for Outstanding Achievement in Interpretation of Higher Edn., 1944, 47; award Council for Advancement and Support of Edn., 1977; medal of honor Wittenberg U., 1982. Mem. Am. Coll. Pub. Relations Assn. (v.p. in charge research 1936-38, editor assn. mag. 1938-40, pres. 1940-41, chmn. plans and policies com. 1944-50, dir. 1956, historian 1967-76), Luth. Coll. Pub. Relations Assn. (pres. 1951-53), Pub. Relations Soc. Am. (nat. jud. council 1952), Assn. Am. Colls. (com. on pub. relations 1945-48), AAUP, Springfield C. of C. (dir. 1958-60), Council for Advancement and Support Edn., Nat. Luth. Ednl. Conf. (chmn. com. pub. relations 1949-50), Ohio Coll. Pub. Relations Officers (pres. 1954-55), Archives Assos., Nat. Hist. Soc., Abraham Lincoln Assn., Ohio Hist. Soc., Smithsonian Assos., Nat. Trust Historic Preservation, Omicron Delta Kappa, Sigma Delta Chi, Pi Delta Epsilon, Delta Sigma Phi, Blue Key, Elbeetian Legion. Author: Public Relations: a Program for Colleges and Universities, 1946; (with others) The American Colleges, 1949, Public Relations Handbook, 1950, 60, 67; The Changing World of College Relations, 1976; Abraham Lincoln's Last 24 Hours, 1982; editor: Publicity Problems, 1939; College Publicity Manual, 1948; contbr. to ednl., profl. and hist. publs. Mem. commn. on ch. papers, 1951-62, cons. com. dept. of press, radio and TV United Luth. Ch., 1955-60; mem. commn. on ch. papers Luth. Ch. in Am., 1962-64, 70-72, mem. exec. com., also chmn. com. periodicals of bd. publ., 1962-72, mem. mgmt. com. Office of Communications, 1972-76; chmn. pub. relations com. Council Protestant Colls. and Univs., 1961-65. Home: 61 Hedgely Rd Springfield OH 45506

RECTENWALD, GARY MICHAEL, systems engr.; b. Toledo, Dec. 31, 1949; s. Edgar E. and Dorothy C. (Antieau) R.; B.S. (cum laude), Ohio State U., 1971, M.S. in Computer Sci., 1972, M.B.A., 1978. Programmer trainee Ohio State U., 1970-71, grad. research asso., 1971-72; application systems programmer, 1972-77, mgr. application systems programming, 1977-78; mem. Instrn. and Research Computer Center; systems engr. IBM, Columbus, 1978—. Mem. Ohio State U. Marching Band, 1967-75 (most inspirational bandsman 1973), Phi Beta Kappa, Beta Gamma Sigma, Kappa Gamma Sigma, Pi Mu Epsilon, Kappa Kappa Psi. Roman Catholic. Home: 1572 Ramblewood Ave Columbus OH 43220 Office: IBM 140 E Town St Columbus OH 43215

REDBURN, DENNIS BURTON, educator; b. Mangum, Okla., Feb. 26, 1936; s. Wilbur B. and Mary Elizabeth (Koehle) R.; B.S., Austin Coll., 1958; Ed.M., E. Tex. State Coll., 1964, Ph.D., 1966; m. Doris Jean Tolbert, Aug. 17, 1956; children—Rebecca Denise Redburn Warner, Arra Elizabeth. High sch. tchr. Commerce (Tex.) Public Schs., 1958-64, athletic dir., 1961-64; teaching fellow E. Tex. State U., Commerce, 1964-66; prof. edn. Ball State U., Muncie, Ind., 1966—, coordinator student teaching programs, 1970—. United Fund Drive team leader Munice YMCA, 1975-76, membership team leader, 1976-77. Mem. Am. Fedn. Tchrs., Nat. Assn. of Tchr. Educators, Ind. Assn. of Tchr. Educators (pres. 1974-75, Recognition award 1974, 75, 76, 77, Outstanding Service award 1978-79), Kappa Delta Phi, Phi Delta Kappa. Democrat. Methodist. Author: (with Joe Hollis, etal) Guidelines for Implementing Doctoral Degree Programs in Teachers College, 1969; editor: Handbook for Supervising Student Teachers, 1970-79; editor, cons. Putting It All Together With Insight Unlimited, 1979. Home: 3205 W Noel Dr Muncie IN 47305 Office: TC 815 Ball State Univ Muncie IN 47306

REDDY, NELLURI LAKSHMINARAYANA, tech. cons.; b. Sanugaringapuram, India, Aug. 17, 1936; came to U.S., 1967; s. Ramakrishna and Andal R.; M.A., U. Madras, 1956, M.Sc., 1957, Ph.D., 1963; married; 1 dau., Nasera. Mgr. communication system U. Minn., 1974-77; mgr. tech. services Minn. Edn. Computing Consortium, 1977-80; sr. tech. cons. Control Data Corp., Arden Hills, Minn., 1980—; tchr. spl. classes U. Minn. Mem. Assn. Computing Machinery, IEEE. Hindu. Home: 3043 N Wilder St Roseville MN 55113 Office: 4201 N Lexington Ave Arden Hills MN 55112

REDENBAUGH, ROBERT EARL, sales exec.; b. Toledo, June 26, 1924; s. Clifford E. and Sylvia (Reynolds) R.; student Yale U., 1943-44; B.S. in Mech. Engring., Washington U., St. Louis, 1949; m. Jacqueline M. McDonald, June 12, 1948; 1 dau., Patricia Ann. With Lincoln-St. Louis div. McNeil Corp., 1942—, product engr., 1946-53, sales mgr. original equipment mfrs. div., St. Louis, 1953—. Served with AUS, 1944-46. Decorated Purple Heart. Mem. Am. Soc. Agrl. Engrs., Am. Def. Preparedness Assn. (life). Home: 1570 St Denis St Florissant MO 63033 Office: 4010 Goodfellow Blvd Saint Louis MO 63120

REDER, ROBERT PAUL, shoe co. exec.; b. Cin., Sept. 26, 1927; s. Joseph Bernard and Emma (Tellmann) R.; B.S. cum laude, Xavier U., 1948; m. Patricia Ann Christian, Nov. 27, 1948; children—Thomas J., Karen Ann, Mary Sharen, Robert Paul. Plant controller Electric Auto-Life Co., Cin., 1949-58; controller, asst. gen. mgr. OKT Inc., Cin., 1958-63; controller Trailmobile div. Pullman, Inc., Cin., 1963-65; v.p., group controller U.S. Shoe Corp., Cin., 1965—; dir. Western Star Loan & Bldg. Assn., Cin. Served to lt. AUS, 1948-49. Mem. Financial Execs. Inst., Nat. Assn. Accountants, Pi Alpha Phi. Roman Catholic (lay deacon 1970—). Home: 7236 Green Farms Dr Cincinnati OH 45224 Office: 1658 Herald Ave Cincinnati OH 45212

REDGRAVE, JOHN ROBERT, heavy machinery mfg. co. exec.; b. Phila., Nov. 9, 1925; s. DeWitt Clinton and Hope (Pillsbury) R.; M.E., Rittenhouse Coll., 1948; m. Nancy Jean Rosendale, Aug. 17, 1951; children—Martyn Robert, Timothy Douglas, John Robert, Barbara Jean. Regional sales mgr. Beloit Corp., Portland, Oreg., 1963-67, gen. mgr. control systems div., Beloit, Wis., 1967-70, v.p. sales, 1974-77; pres. Beloit Sorel Walmsley, Ltd., Sorel, Que., Can., 1970-74, also dir.; chmn., pres. Dolphin Machining Inc., South Beloit, Ill., 1977—; dir. Beloit Savs. Bank. Vice chmn. Citizen's Adv. Com., Beloit, 1968-70; sec. bd. dirs. Meml. Hosp.; del. White House Conf. Small Bus.; mem. Small Bus. Action Council of Ill.; mem. steering com. Gov.'s Conf. Small Bus.; chmn. Conf. on Small Bus. for Green Rock and Walwatto County (Wis.). Served with USNR, 1943-46. Mem. Nat. Assn. Parliamentarians, Robert's Rules Assn. (chmn. 1965), Am. Mgmt. Assn., Ind. Businessmen's Assn. Wis., Nat. Fed. Ind. Businessmen's C. of C. (action council), Am. Inst. Parliamentarians, Ill. Mfg. Assn., TAPPI. Clubs: Rotary, Beloit Country (dir.). Home: 3709 Oak Lane Dr Beloit WI 53511 Office: 540 Eastern Ave Beloit IL 61080

REDLIN, ROLLAND, state senator, farmer; b. Lambert, Mont., Feb. 29, 1920; ed. U. Wash., N.D. State Coll.; m. Christine Nesje; children—Ilene, Jeannette, Lisa, Daniel, Steven. Vice-pres. bank, agrl. agt. and farmer; mem. N.D. State Senate, 1958-64, 73—; mem. Congress from N.D., 1964-66. Pres., Christ Luth Ch., 1973—. Office: ND State Senate State Capitol Bismarck ND 58505*

REDONDO, DIEGO, pediatrician; b. Barranquilla, Colombia, Apr. 22, 1936; s. Diego and Regina (Villarreal) R.; came to U.S., 1953, naturalized, 1973; A.A., Christian Bros. Coll., 1955; M.D., Tulane U., 1961; m. Susan Biebel, Feb. 16, 1963; children—Diego, Dorothy, Peter, Ramon. Intern, Charity Hosp., New Orleans, 1961-62; resident in pediatrics Children's Meml. Hosp., Chgo., 1962-64, chief resident in pediatrics, 1964-65, fellow in hematology, 1965-66; practice medicine specializing in pediatrics, Deerfield, Ill., 1966—; asst. prof. clin. pediatrics Northwestern U. Med. Sch.; bd. dirs. Children's Meml. Hosp., 1976—. Mem. Gov's. Transition Task Force, Ill., 1972-73; mem. Ill. Bd. Higher Edn., 1974—, vice chmn., 1979—; chmn. Ill. Ednl. TV Commn., 1976—. Fellow Am. Acad. Pediatrics; mem. Ill. State, Lake County med. socs., AMA. Roman Catholic. Author: (with Edith Freund) Growing Up Healthy, 1976. Home: 1345 Montgomery Dr Deerfield IL 60015 Office: 956 Deerfield Rd Deerfield IL 60015

REDSHAW, WARD FULLER, audio-visual co. exec.; b. Great Falls, Mont., Mar. 31, 1923; s. Thomas Alfred and Elvina Anne (Fuller) R.; student U. Md., 1958-59, Army Command and Gen. Staff Coll., 1960; m. Margaret MacPherson, Feb. 9, 1946; children—Neil, Barbara, Janet Redshaw Prochnow, Mark. Commd. 2d lt., U.S. Army, 1950, advanced through grades to maj., 1962, ret. as chief pictorial officer, 1963; with Keuffel & Esser Co., engring. and audio-visual, Dallas, 1963-65, Chgo., 1965-66; mfrs. rep. Vern Schultz & Assos., Crystal Lake, Ill., 1966-69; propr. Redshaw Audio-Visual Co., mfrs. rep., also bus. cons., Libertyville, Ill., 1969—; instr., also bd. dirs. Nat. Audio-Visual Assn., 1972-75, exec. council and ind. rep. council 1972—. Decorated Combat Infantryman's badge, Army Commendation medal with 2 oak leaf clusters; cert. media specialist Nat. Audio-Visual Assn. Mem. Chicagoland Electronic Reps. Assn. (v.p. 1979-82), Profl. Photographers Am. (photog. craftsman degree). Presbyterian. Club: Masons. Home: 15087 W Redwood Ln Libertyville IL 60048 Office: 1641 N Milwaukee Ave Libertyville IL 60048

REEBIE, SKIP, Realtor; b. Chgo., Mar. 18, 1940; s. Owen J. and Jane P. R.; B.B.A., U. Tex., El Paso, 1963; grad. Realtors Inst., 1979; m. Patricia A. Porth, Nov. 16, 1963; children—Scott, Jenny, Kate. Salesman, Am. Hosp. Supply Co., Cleve., Mpls., 1968-77; real estate salesman, land developer, Prior Lake, Minn., 1977—. Active various civic orgns., Prior Lake; mem. Prior Lake Fire Dept. and Rescue Squad. Served to lt. USN, 1963-68. Emergency med. technician. Mem. Nat. Bd. Realtors, Minn. Assn. Realtors, Mpls. Bd. Realtors, Prior Lake C. of C. (pres.), Lake Assn., VFW. Lutheran. Clubs: Optimists (dir.), Yacht, Rotary (Prior Lake). Home: 3592 Willow Beach Trail Prior Lake MN 55372 Office: Prior Lake Bank Bldg Prior Lake MN 55372

REECE, DAVID ANDREW, hosp. adminstr.; b. Midland, Mich., Apr. 18, 1948; s. William Andrew and Mary Barbara (Murphy) R.; B.S. in Bus. Adminstrn., Central Mich. U., 1970; M.S. in Hosp. and Health Services Adminstrn., Ohio State U., 1973; m. Frances Marie Burns, Aug. 1, 1970; children—Scott Kenneth, Matthew David. Adminstrv. resident Kettering (Ohio) Med. Center, 1972; asst. v.p. Midland Hosp. Center, 1973-76, v.p., 1976-77, v.p., sec., 1977-79, v.p. for ops., sec., 1979—; bd. dirs. East Mich. Emergency Med. Services; tchr. health care mgmt. Northwood Inst., Midland, 1975-76; lectr. Eastern Mich. U., 1976; mem. Midland County Ambulance Bd., 1976—; mem. emergency med. services com. East Central Mich. Health Systems Agy. Recipient Traineeship award USPHS, 1972. Mem. Am. Coll. Hosp. Adminstrs., Mich. Hosp. Assn., Am. Hosp. Assn., Am. Mgmt. Assn. Republican. Episcopalian. Club: Midland Country. Contbr. articles to profl. jours. Home: 805 Heathermoor St Midland MI 48640 Office: 4005 Orchard Dr Midland MI 48640

REECE, WILBUR TAYLOR, dentist; b. Normal, Ill., Aug. 23, 1910; s. John Stewart and Estella Jennie (Schaeffer) R.; B.E., Ill. State U., 1932; M.A., U. Chgo., 1937; D.D.S., Northwestern U., 1949; m. Lois

Conover, Mar. 15, 1935 (dec. Oct. 1968); children—John C., Sharon Reece Clark; m. 2d, Mildred Welch, Nov. 28, 1969. Sci. tchr., prin. high sch., Petersburg, Ill., 1932-36; sci. tchr. Elmhurst (Ill.) Jr. High Sch., 1936-40; research asst. Ill. Edn. Assn., Springfield, 1941-43, 1946; gen. practice dentistry, Springfield, Ill., 1949—. Trustee, Ill. Dental Service, non profit dental service corp., 1969—, chmn. bd., 1981—. Served with USNR, 1943-46; lt. Res. ret. Fellow Am. Acad. Gen. Dentistry; Am. Coll. Dentists; mem. Ill. Dental Soc. (chmn. com. legis. 1960-68), G.V. Black Dist. Dental Soc. (pres. 1962-63), Kappa Delta Pi, Phi Delta Kappa, Delta Sigma Delta., Am. Legion, ADA, Ill. Acad. Gen. Dentistry (pres. 1981—), Fedn. Dentaire Internat., Chgo. Dental Soc., Forty and Eight. Congregationalist (moderator 1970-71). Contbr. to profl. publs. in field. Home: 58 Andover Dr Springfield IL 62704 Office: 425 W Ash St Springfield IL 52704

REED, DONALD IRVING, assn. exec.; b. Oak Park, Ill., June 25, 1929; s. Samuel Irving and Pearl Hart (Kniffen) R.; B.A., Ripon Coll., 1951; m. Beverly Burner Cram, July 17, 1954; children—Diana, David. Design engr. Internat. Harvester Co., Melrose Park, Ill., 1956-59; with Nat. Marine Mfrs. Assn., Chgo., 1959—, dir. engring., 1971—, also exec. sec. Trailer Mfrs. Assn. (an affiliate). Served with U.S. Army, 1951-56; comdr. Ill. wing CAP. Mem. Soc. Automotive Engrs. (chmn. specialized vehicle and equipment council), Am. Boat and Yacht Council (div. dir. standards div.), Soc. Naval Architects and Marine Engrs., Am. Def. Preparedness Assn., Aircraft Owners and Pilots Assn., Nat. Rifle Assn., Internat. Orgn. for Standardization (U.S. del. leader to internat. meetings), ASTM (panel chmn.). Home: 1216 3d Ave Des Plaines IL 60018 Office: 401 N Michigan Ave Chicago IL 60611

REED, E. SMITH, JR., mech. engr.; b. Washington, Dec. 8, 1945; s. E. Smith and Josephine (Lewis) R.; B.S. in Mech. Engring., U. Ark., 1968; m. Virginia Ann Burch, June 13, 1970; children—Robyn Cathleen, Karen Lindsay, S. Alexander. Production engr. ordnance div. Honeywell Inc., Mpls., 1968-70; chief product engr. Toro Co., Mpls., 1970-79; engring. mgr. Sweepers, Tennant Co., Mpls., 1979—. Elder, Faith Presbyn. Ch., 1974—. Recipient James F. Lincoln Found. award, 1976; registered profl. engr., Minn. Mem. Minn. Soc. Profl. Engrs., Soc. Automotive Engrs., Phi Delta Theta. Inventor of golf course greens spikers and greens clippings discharge device. Home: 20225 Cottagewood Ave Deephaven MN 55331 Office: 701 N Lilac Dr Minneapolis MN 55440

REED, EDSEL SHERWOOD, radiologist; b. Bowen, Ky., Aug. 19, 1923; s. George W. and Mattie Elizabeth (Palmer) R.; B.S., Morehead State U., 1943; M.D., U. Louisville, 1946; m. Allie Carey, Dec. 23, 1947; children—Patricia Jayne Reed Tate, Cynthia Lynn, Edsel Sherwood. Intern, Good Samaritan Hosp., Lexington, Ky., 1947, U. Pa., 1950-51; resident in radiology U. Louisville, 1948-51, asst. in radiology 1948-50, instr., 1951, 58-68, asst. clin. prof., 1969—; staff med. isotopes U. Tex., Houston, 1957; pvt. practice radiology, St. Joseph, Mo., 1953-56; asso. radiologist, asst. dir. dept. radiology Miners Meml. Hosp. Assn., Harlan, Ky., 1956-58; dir. radiology Clark County Meml. Hosp., Jeffersonville, Ind., 1958—; chief med. staff, 1973; pres. Radiology Assos. Inc., 1969-71. Deacon, 1st Bapt. Ch., Jeffersonville, 1969—, vice chmn., 1980. Served with AUS, 1943-46, to capt. USAR, 1951-53. Diplomate Am. Bd. Radiology. Mem. Clark County Med. Soc. (pres. 1962), Greater Louisville Radiology Soc. (pres. 1970), Ind. Med. Assn., AMA, Ind. Roentgen Soc., Am. Coll. Radiology, Radiol. Soc. N.Am., Ky., Ind. hist. socs. Clubs: Masons, Elks, Shriners. Contbr. articles to profl. jours. Home: 111 Pawnee Dr Jeffersonville IN 47130 Office: 1220 Missouri Ave Jeffersonville IN 47130

REED, GARETH LAVERNE, elec. co. exec.; b. Cedar Rapids, Iowa, Dec. 22, 1932; s. John Ivan and Florence Lorene (Larson) R.; B.S., Iowa State U., 1954; M.S., U. N.Mex., 1958; Ph.D., U. Md., 1966; M.B.A., U. Mich., 1974; m. LaVonne Doris Bartels, June 13, 1954; children—Richard K., Robin R., Kathryn S. Sr. engr. N.Am. Aviation, Canoga Park, Calif., 1958-62; project engr. Martin-Marietta, Balt., 1962-67; dir. product devel. Allis Chalmers, Milw., 1967-70; dir. corporate planning Masco Corp., Detroit, 1970-72, div. gen. mgr., 1972-80; v.p., officer JP Industries, Ann Arbor, Mich., 1980—. Served to capt. USAF, 1955-58. Mem. Am. Inst. Chem. Engrs., Soc. Mfg. Engrs., Am. Mgmt. Assn., Tau Beta Pi, Pi Tau Sigma, Sigma Xi. Lutheran. Contbr. articles to profl. jours. Inventor in field. Home: 3670 Chatham Way Ann Arbor MI 48105 Office: 825 Victors Way Ann Arbor MI 48104

REED, GEORGE RENNISON, educator; b. Detroit, Feb. 8, 1922; s. George Rennison and A. Beatrice (Weaver) R.; A.B., Albion Coll., 1953; M.A., Western Mich. U., 1956; Ed.D., Mich. State U., 1970; m. Virginia May O'Dell, June 29, 1946; children—Karen Virginia, Ann Marie, Susan Kay. Tchr., Albion (Mich.) public schs., 1953-54; tchr., prin. Kellogg Consol. Schs., Hickory Corners, Mich., 1954-61; asst. supt. Galesburg-Augusta Community Schs., Galesburg, Mich., 1961-63; asst. prof. edn. Albion (Mich.) Coll., 1963-69, asso. prof., 1969-77, prof., 1977—, acting chmn. dept. edn., 1967-68. Trustee Augusta (Mich.) Village Council, 1959-61. Served with AUS, 1942-45. Mem. AAUP, NEA, Mich. Edn. Assn., Mich. Acad. Sci., Arts and Letters, Phi Beta Kappa, Omicron Delta Kappa. Methodist (trustee 1967—). Clubs: Duck Lake Country, Athelstan, Rotary. Methodist (trustee 1967-75). Home: 1582 E Michigan Ave Albion MI 49224

REED, JOHN ELWYN, nurse anesthesist; b. La Harpe, Ill., Aug. 31, 1930; s. William Sherman and Mary Jane (Jameson) R.; R.N., Broadlawns Polk County Hosp. Sch. Nursing, 1955; diploma anesthesia Lancaster Gen. Hosp., 1956; m. Lorraine Irene Ciha, June 18, 1955; children—Connie Sue, Douglas John, Deanna Lynn, Roger Neal, Darin Lee, Tammi Joleen. Staff anesthetist Lancaster (Pa.) Gen. Hosp., 1956-57, Murphy Meml. Hosp., Red Oak, Iowa, 1957-58; chief anesthetist Broadlawns Polk County Hosp., Des Moines, 1958—. Pres., Saylor Twp. (Iowa) Fire Dept., 1970-74; pres. Polk County Fire Fighters, 1974-75; bd. dirs. Emergency Med. Communication Center Des Moines, 1972-75, Central Iowa Emergency Med. Services Council, 1977—. Recipient Ike of Yr. award, 1972. Mem. Iowa Assn. Nurse Anesthetists (pres. 1967-69), Am. Assn. Nurse Anesthetists, Iowa Firemen's Assn., Polk County Firemen's Assn., Central Iowa Emergency Med. Services Assn., Izaac Walton League Am. (pres. trail 1975-76). Home: 5305 NE 5th St Des Moines IA 50313 Office: Broadlawns Med Center 18th and Hickman Sts Des Moines IA 50314

REED, JOHN SHEDD, railway exec.; b. Chgo., June 9, 1917; s. Kersey Coates and Helen (Shedd) R.; grad. Hotchkiss Sch., 1935; B.S., Yale, 1939; m. Marjorie Lindsay, May 4, 1946; children—Ginevra Coates, Lindsay Keith, Helen Shedd, Peter Shedd, John Shedd. With A., T. & S.F. Ry., 1939—, beginning as test dept. asst., Topeka, successively spl. rep. to gen. supt. transp., Chgo., transp. insp., Amarillo, Tex., trainmaster, Slaton, Tex., Pueblo, Colo., 1952, supt. Mo. div., Marceline, Mo., asst. to v.p., Chgo., 1954, exec. asst. to pres., 1957, v.p., finance, 1959-64, v.p. exec. dept., 1964-67, pres., 1967-78, chmn., chief exec. officer, 1968—; pres. Santa Fe Industries, 1968-78, chmn., chief exec. officer, 1973—; dir. No. Trust Co., Dart Kraft, Inc. Served from ensign to lt. comdr. USNR, 1940-46. Clubs: Chicago; Old Elm, Shoreacres, Onwentsia. Home: 301 W Laurel Ave Lake Forest IL 60045 Office: 224 S Michigan Ave Chicago IL 60604

REED, JOHN WALTER, elec. co. exec.; b. Wichita, Kans., Nov. 29, 1935; s. Jerry Harrison and Zelda Mae (Wilson) R.; student Utah State U., 1953-57, U. Wichita, 1959-61; m. Betty LaRee Larsen, Sept. 11, 1961; children—Shauna, Robert, Linda, Paul, Cecelia. With Boeing Co., Wichita, 1958-62; data process systems programmer U. Utah, Salt Lake City, 1968-73; data processing mgr., sr. analyst Asso. Food Stores, Salt Lake City, 1973-76; pres. Reed & Fugate, Inc. Wichita, 1976—; instr. data processing Stevens Henegar Coll., Salt Lake City, 1969-74. Scoutmaster, chmn. unit commn. Great Salt Lake and Quivera councils Boy Scouts Am., Eagle Scout, recipient Order of Arrow; elders quorum pres. Ch. Jesus Christ Latter-day Saints, high counciler, bishop's counselor, bishop. Mem. Nat. Fedn. Ind. Bus. Research and Edn., Nat. Small Bus. Assn., Auto Service Council. Home: 15320 E 47th St S Derby KS 67037 Office: 350 Indiana St Wichita KS 67214

REED, JOSEPH HARRY, office systems exec.; b. Columbia, Mo., Aug. 16, 1943; s. Roy Lawrence and Albina Mary (Zuzack) R.; student U. Mo., 1961-64; B.S. in B.A., Central Mo. State U., 1969; m. Katherine Marie Hogan, Sept. 1, 1979; children—Maureen, Joseph. Computer programmer Butler Mfg., Kansas City, Mo., 1965-68, programmer-analyst, 1968-72; sr. programmer-analyst Blue Cross of Kansas City, 1972-74; contract services mgr. Informatics, Inc., Chgo., 1974-76, br. service mgr., 1976-77; sr. cons. Alexander Grant & Co., Chgo., 1977-78, sr. computer audit specialist, 1979-81, office systems mgr., 1981—; tchr. theory and practice of computer systems controls. Mem. Am. Mgmt. Assn. Home: 806 S Myrtle St Kankakee IL 60901 Office: 600 Prudential Plaza Chicago IL 60601

REED, MARILYN DAVIS, educator; b. Cin., June 2, 1928; d. Charles Bradley and Lenore (Musser) D.; B.F.A., Ohio State U., 1950, M.A., 1970, Ph.D., 1980; m. Eldis O. Reed, Sept. 4, 1948; children—Peggy, Nancy Jeanne. Tchr. Fishinger Sch., Upper Arlington, Ohio, 1959-72; coordinator informal alternative classrooms Upper Arlington, Ohio, 1972—; pres. Ed Lums The Ohio State Univ., Columbus, 1978-79. Mem. Nat. Council Tchrs. English, Nat. Council Tchrs. Math., Internat. Reading Assn., Assn. Supervision and Curriculum Devel., Phi Delta Kappa. Home: 735 Highland Dr Columbus OH 43214 Office: 1780 Barrington Rd Columbus OH 43221

REED, MARY JO, librarian; b. Oklahoma City, Sept. 29, 1935; s. Clifton Gore and Muriel Audrey Webb; B.S., Okla. State U., 1957; M.S., Pittsburg State U., 1970, Ed.S., 1980; m. Paul Hudson Reed, July 28, 1975; children—Jeffrey Lee, Jonathan Lynn, Joel Lonnie Clark. Librarian, tchr. lit. Holy Name Jr. High Sch., Coffeyville, Kans., 1964-68; library supr. Unified Sch. Dist. No. 445, Coffeyville, 1968—. Mem. United Sch. Adminstrs., ALA, Am. Assn. Sch. Librarians, Kans. Library Assn., Kans. Assn. Sch. Librarians, Internat. Assn. Sch. Librarianship, Kans. Assn. Edn. and Communication Tech., Bus. and Profl. Women, AAUW, Phi Delta Kappa, Alpha Delta Kappa. Club: Kans. Dinner. Home: 701 Willow St Coffeyville KS 67337 Office: 615 Ellis St Coffeyville KS 67337

REED, PETER JOHN EDWARD, accountant; b. London, Feb. 24, 1940; s. John Edward and Daisy Irene Reed; came to U.S., 1970; student West London Coll. Commerce, 1953-57; M.S. in Mgmt., Aquanis Coll., Grand Rapids, Mich., 1981; m. Kathleen Elizabeth Johnson, Apr. 4, 1964; children—Julian Peter, Grant Thomas. Sr. accountant Spain Bros., Chartered Accountants, London, 1957-64; controller R.J. Fulwood & Bland, Shropshire, Eng., 1964-66; systems analyst City of Birmingham (Eng.), 1966-68; group chief acct. Lilleshall Co., Shropshire, 1968-70; nat. dir. EDP auditing Seidman & Seidman, Grand Rapids, Mich., 1973—. Fellow Inst. Chartered Accountants; asso. Inst. Cost and Mgmt. Accountants, Inst. Chartered Secs.; mem. Brit. Computer Soc., Assn. Systems, Brit. Inst. Mgmt., Data Processing Assn., Inst. Internal Auditors, EDP Auditors Assn., Am. Inst. C.P.A.'s, Mich. Assn. C.P.A.'s. Republican. Roman Catholic. Office: 700 Union Bank Plaza Grand Rapids MI 49502

REED, PHILIP G., book illustrator, designer; b. Park Ridge, Ill., Jan. 17, 1908; s. John Wesley and Grace C. (Hibbard) R.; grad. Art Inst. Chgo., 1930; m. Nancy L. Price, April 30, 1954 (div. Sept. 1980); children—Keith O., Scott H., Ian Campbell. Founded Broadside Press, Barrington, Ill., 1930-33, Katonah, N.Y., 1933-36, Park Ridge, Ill., 1936-39; founder Philip Reed, Printer, Ltd., 1977; dir. The Monastery Hill Press, Chgo., 1939-43; founded Printing Office of Philip Reed, 1946, pres., 1948—; asso. A. & R. Roe Printers, St. Joseph, Mich., 1956-73; work exhibited in Moscow Am. Nat. Exhbn. Served with C.E., AUS, 1943-45. Recipient awards for printing design Chgo. Soc. Typographic, Arts, 1937, 40, 47, 51-53, book design, 1951; nominee Caldecott medal, 1963. Mem. Am. Inst. Graphic Arts (50 books of year 1939, 40, 47, 51-53, 63, printing for commerce 1937, 49, 50-56). Republican. Episcopalian. Club: Cliff Dwellers. Specialist in book design and illustration. Home and Office: 2901 Cleveland Ave Saint Joseph MI 49085

REED, ROBERT GEORGE, III, petroleum co. exec.; b. Cambridge, Mass., Aug. 9, 1927; s. Robert George and Marjorie (Furber) R.; B.A., Dartmouth Coll., 1949; grad. Advanced Mgmt. Program, Harvard Bus. Sch., 1970; m. Maggie L. Fisher, Mar. 22, 1974; children—Sandra R. McNickle, Valerie, Jonathan J., John-Paul. Prin., Robert G. Reed Co., Boston, 1949-57; trainee Tidewater Oil Co., Phila., 1957, asst. mgr., N.Y.C., 1958, mktg. mgr. Eastern div., 1958-61, home office mktg. mgr., Los Angeles, 1961-64, asst. gen. mgr. Western div., 1964; retail mktg. mgr. Cities Service Oil Co., Tulsa, 1964-66, v.p. mktg., dir., 1966-72; group v.p. refining, mktg. and transp. Tesoro Petroleum Corp., San Antonio, 1972-76, exec. v.p., 1976-79; chmn. bd., chief exec. officer Clark Oil & Refining Corp., Milw., 1979-81; pres., chief exec. officer Clark Oil & Refining Corp. div. Apex Oil, St. Louis, 1981—; dir. Marine Corp., Marine Nat. Exchange Bank, First Houston Energy. Served with USNR, 1945-46. Mem. Nat. Petroleum Refiners Assn. (dir. 1973—), Am. Petroleum Inst. (gen. com. mktg. 1963-64, 69-76, budget and planning com. 1969-77). Clubs: Milw. Country, Milw. Athletic, Univ. Home: 200 S Brentwood Blvd #19D Saint Louis MO 63105 Office: 212 S Central Ave Saint Louis MO 63105

REEDER, EILEEN BERENDT, bus. cons.; d. Edward and Hilda Christina (Buchholz) Berendt; M.Ed., U. Mo. at Kansas City; M.B.A., So. Ill. U., Edwardsville, 1973; m. John Charles Reeder; children—John Robert, Valerie Ann, Deborah Eileen. Bus. cons. extension bus. and industry program U. Mo., St. Louis, 1974—. Mem. Am. Mktg. Assn., Am. Statis. Assn., AAUW. Methodist. Office: 522 Olive St 2d Floor Saint Louis MO 63101

REEDS, JAMES ALEXANDER, II, humanist, educator; b. Kansas City, Mo., Nov. 16, 1921; s. Ralph Edgar and Wanda Alice (Nelson) R.; B.A., U. Iowa, 1948, M.A., 1949; M.A., U. Mich., 1959, Ph.D., 1966; m. Hedy Newman, Sept. 20, 1946; children—James Alexander III, Susan Esther. Teaching fellow German, U. Iowa, Iowa City, 1948-50; tchr. German, English, Fargo (N.D.) High Sch., 1950-52; instr. German, speech, Pa. State U., Altoona, 1952-58; Fulbright instr. English, Leopoldinum II, Detmold, W. Ger., 1956-57; instr. English, U. Detroit, 1962-65; asst. prof. English, U. Wis.-Milw., 1966-69, asso. prof. linguistics, English, U. Mo., Kansas City, also dir. English as fgn. lang., 1969—; v.p. Gen. Linguistics Corp., Kansas City, 1975—. Served with U.S. Army, 1942-46. IBM grantee, 1965. Mem. MLA, Am. Translators Assn., Am. Lit. Translators Assn., AAUP, Linguistic Soc. Am., Nat. Council Tchrs. English, Am. Assn. Tchrs. German, Delta Phi Alpha, other orgns. Author: (with Harris Winitz) Comprehension and Problem Solving as Language Acquisition Strategies, 1973; Phonetics, a Manual for Listening, 1979. Home: 200 E 56th St Kansas City MO 64113 Office: Speech Sci Lab 5216 Rockhill Rd U Mo Kansas City MO 64110

REEGER, HAROLD LAWRENCE, moving/storage exec.; b. Chgo., Feb. 11, 1936; s. Harold John Reeger and Catherine Rita (Browne) Berg; B.S., U.S. Naval Acad., 1958; m. Janice Kathryn Speck, June 14, 1958; children—Stacy, Christopher, Susan, Sharon, Matthew. Owner, operator bookkeeping, ins. service, Albuquerque, 1970-71; retail sales Sears, Roebuck & Co., Chgo., 1972-75; freelance sales ins., Chgo., 1975-76; gen. mgr. corp. Atlas Galleries, Inc., Chgo., 1976-80; bus. mgr. Adams Werner Kennelly Co., Inc., Chgo., 1980—. Chmn. fund raising to build shrine to St. Jude, Marina, Calif., 1963-64; v.p. sports com. Our Lady of Grace Sch., Chgo., 1975, pres., 1975-76. Served with USN 1958-70, comdr. Res. ret. Decorated Vietnamese Cross of Gallantry. Mem. Naval Res. Assn., Aircraft Owners and Pilots Assn., Res. Officers Assn., U.S. Naval Inst. Roman Catholic. Home: 2554 N Bernard St Chicago IL 60647 Office: Adams Werner Kennelly Co Inc 55 E Pershing Rd Chicago IL 60653

REEGO, WILLIAM ANDREW, mfg. co. exec.; b. Chgo., Oct. 2, 1929; s. Andrew and Emily R.; B.S.A. with honors, U. Ill., 1955; M.B.A. with distinction, Northwestern U., 1970; m. Violet M. Belcaster, June 4, 1955; children—John Joseph, James Andrew, Jennifer. Salesman, IBM, 1955-56; mgr. adminstrv. services Arthur Andersen & Co., Chgo., 1956-65; dir. mgmt. info. systems, corporate controller Joslyn Mfg.-Supply Co., Chgo., 1965-74; v.p. fin. Clow Corp., Oak Brook, Ill., 1974—. Served with USAF, 1951-52. C.P.A., Ill. Mem. Fin. Execs. Inst. (dir. 1979—). Home: 3856 Brittany St North Brook IL 60062 Office: 1211 W 22d St Oak Brook IL 60521

REENTS, AUGUST CURTIS, chem. engr.; b. Oak Hill, Ill., Sept. 15, 1921; s. August and Kathryn E. (Plack) R.; B.S., Bradley U., Peoria, Ill., 1943; M.S., Iowa State U., 1947; m. June Ruppert, Jan. 8, 1944; children—David G., Doris J., Donald C. With Ill. Water Treatment Co., 1946-72; founder, 1972, since partner, v.p. Techni-Chem., Inc., Belvidere, Ill. Served as lt. (j.g.) USN, 1943-46. Mem. Am. Chem. Soc. (past officer water and waste div.), Am. Inst. Chem. Engrs. Club: University. Patentee in field. Address: 4411 Dunbar Pl Rockford IL 61111

REES, JANE L., home economist; b. Carbondale, Pa.; B.S., Syracuse U., 1945; M.S., Columbia U., 1947; Ph.D., Pa. State U., 1959. Asst. prof. Rutgers U., New Brunswick, N.J., 1953-56; exec. dir. Am. Home Econs. Assn., Washington, 1966-67; prof., chmn. dept. home econs. and consumer scis. Miami U., Oxford, Ohio, 1958—; dir. Cin. Gas & Electric Co. Fulbright awardee, 1964; recipient fellowships. Mem. AAUW, P.E.O., Delta Gamma. Clubs: Miami U. Faculty (pres. 1968-69); Hamilton City. Home: 940 Silvoor Ln Oxford OH 45056 Office: 260 McGuffey Miami U Oxford OH 45056

REES, THOMAS KREIDLER, mfg. co. exec.; b. LaPorte, Ind., Feb. 24, 1924; s. Benjamin C. and Helen F. (Kreidler) R.; B.S., Ind. U., 1947; m. Margaret E. Huyler, July 2, 1949; children—Thomas K., Michael H., William R., John B. Salesman, Swift & Co., Davenport, Iowa, 1947-48; mgr. tobacco dept. Sears, Roebuck & Co., Memphis, 1948-50; sales rep. Gen. Outdoor Advt. Co., Peoria and Chgo., 1950-59; Chgo. sales rep. Kubin-Nicholson Corp., 1959-72, v.p., partner, 1972-80, pres., 1980—. Area chmn. Wilmette (Ill.) United Fund, 1968-69; area chmn. Republican Party, 1964, precinct capt., 1960, 63. Served with USAAF, 1942-45. Named Salesman of Yr., Gen. Outdoor Advt., 1955. Mem. Printing Inst. Am., Outdoor Advt. Assn. Republican. Roman Catholic. Club: Mich. Shores. Office: 333 N Michigan Ave Chicago IL 60601

REES, WARREN JAMES, judge; b. Anamosa, Iowa, Aug. 2, 1908; s. Barlow G. and Anna (Lowe) R.; student Grinnell Coll., 1926-27; m. Alma Davis, Aug. 20, 1938; children—Mary Ann (Mrs. R. Ashley Lyman), William (dec.). Clk. Dist. Ct., Jones County, Iowa, 1929-32; admitted to Iowa bar, 1934; pvt. practice law, Anamosa, 1934-63; county atty., Jones County, 1939-45; judge 18th and 8th Jud. Dists. Iowa, 1963-69; justice Iowa Supreme Ct., 1969-80; sr. judge Jud. Dept., State of Iowa, 1980—. Chmn., Jones County Republican Central Com., 1938-50; mem. Rep. State Central Com., 1950-54; trustee Cornell Coll., Mt. Vernon, Iowa, Herbert Hoover Birthplace Found. Mem. Am., Iowa, Jones County bar assns., Am. Judicature Soc., Order of Coif. Methodist. Mason (Shriner), Lion. Home: 608 W Crane St Anamosa IA 52205 Office: Jones County Courthouse Anamosa IA 52205

REESE, ALAN FLOYD, human resource cons.; b. Barberton, Ohio, Oct. 17, 1940; s. Nelson F. and Yvonne Reese; B.S., Purdue U., 1964; M.B.A., St. Francis U., 1970; m. Carol Ann Cohoon, Sept. 26, 1964; children—Daisy Lynn, Marshal Alan. Sales mktg. staff George A. Hormel Co., Ind., 1964-70, mem. coll. recruiting staff, Austin, Minn., 1970-75; mgr. selection and placement Allied/Mills/Continental Grain Co., Chgo., 1975-79; personnel mgr. McGraw Edison Co., Chgo., 1979-81; human resource cons. Costello, Erdlen & Co., Chgo., 1981—; instr. Dale Carnegie, 1973—. Bd. dirs. YMCA, 1978-80. Mem. Indsl. Relations Assn. Chgo., Northwest Indsl. Council, Midwest Coll. Placement Assn., Am. Soc. Personnel Adminstrn., Internat. Jaycees. Clubs: Toastmasters, YMCA Men's. Home: 1128 George Ln Naperville IL 60540

REESE, JOHN GILBERT, lawyer; b. Newark, Ohio, July 7, 1925; s. Everett David and Martha Grace (Miller) R.; student Phillips Acad. Andover, 1941-43; B.A., Ohio State U., 1949, J.D., 1952; m. Louella Catherine Hodges, Sept. 9, 1951; children—Martha Grace, Sarah Sherwood, Gilbert Hodges, Lucius Everett, Megan. Admitted to Ohio bar, 1952, since practiced in Newark; partner Reese, McNenny, Pyle & Drake, 1966—. Dir. Park Nat. Bank of Newark; State Savs. Co., Columbus, Southgate S.C. Corp., B & L Motor Freight, Inc., Capitol Corp.; chmn. bd. First Fed. Savs. & Loan Assn. of Newark. Safety dir. City of Newark, 1955; mem. Newark City Council, 1956-57; city atty., 1958-62. Chmn. nat. council Ohio State U. Coll. Law; pres. Thomas J. Evans Found.; trustee Central Ohio Tech. Coll.; chmn. governing com. Licking County Found.; trustee Dawes Arboretum, Columbus Mus. Art; trustee, pres. YMCA. Served with M.C., AUS, 1943-46. Named Outstanding Man of Year Jr. C. of C., 1955. Mem. Am., Ohio, Licking County (pres.) bar assns., Newark Area C. of C. (pres.), Newark Fedn. Musicians. Presbyterian. Clubs: Columbus, Presidents of Ohio State U. (Columbus, Ohio); Moundbuilders Country (Newark); Granville (Ohio) Tennis, Elks, Rotary. Home: 693 Tall Oaks Ct Newark OH 43055 Office: 36 N 2d St Newark OH 43055

REESE, WILLIAM, JR., ednl. adminstr.; b. Gary, Ind., Aug. 17, 1950; s. William and Reesie A. (Parker) R.; B.S., Ball State U., 1972, M.A.E., 1974, adminstrv. certificate, 1975. Social studies tchr.

Tolleston Jr. High Sch., Gary (Ind.) Community Sch. Corp., 1972-75, adminstrv. intern Froebel Middle Sch., 1975-76, adminstrv. asst. Pulaski Sch., 1976-80, dean students Wirt High Sch., 1980-81; asst. prin. Edison Middle Sch., 1981—; bd. dirs. Lake County Fed. Employees Credit Union, 1979-81. Mem. NAACP, Assn. Supervision and Curriculum Devel., Lake County Secondary Prins. Assn., Gary Secondary Prins. Assn., Gary Hist. Soc., Omega Psi Phi. Mem. Ch. of Christ Holiness. Home: 1433 W 15th Ave Gary IN 46407 Office: 5th Ave and Burr St Gary IN 46404

REEVES, JAMES EARL, podiatrist; b. Atwood, Kans., Aug. 21, 1953; s. Kay Loren and Constance Kay Reeves; A.A., Hutchinson Community Jr. Coll., 1973; B.S., Emporia State U., 1975; D.P.M., Calif. Coll. Podiatric Medicine, 1978; m. Lyn Higley, Aug. 22, 1973; children—Sierra Leigh, Brianna Dee. Resident in surgery Lindell Hosp., St. Louis, 1978-79; practice podiatric medicine, Lawrence, Kans., 1979—. Mem. Kans. Podiatry Assn., Am. Podiatry Assn., Lawrence C. of C. Mem. Disciples of Christ Ch. Club: Masons. Home: 2429 Missouri St Lawrence KS 66044 Office: 1203 Iowa St Lawrence KS 66044

REEVES, PATRICK ALOYSIUS, advt. agy. owner; b. Cin., Apr. 21, 1939; s. Morris Leslie and Bernice Gertrude (Farfsing) R.; B.B.A., U. Cin., 1963; children—Patricia Pierson, Jennifer Elizabeth. Writer, Cin. Gas & Electric Co., 1960-64; sr. copywriter Northlich Stolley, Inc., 1964-66; creative dir. Clinton E. Frank, Inc., Cin., 1966-68, Ralph Jones Co. (name now Fahlgren & Ferriss), Cin., 1968-70; pres., creative dir. Reeves Advt., Inc., Cin., 1970—. Mem. steering com. Young Republican Club, 1962-66; bd. dirs. Com. 100, U. Cin., 1964-67; pres. Music for Kids, Inc., 1966-75; mem. Ohio steering com. Reagan for Pres., 1979, 80; public relations mgr. Businessmen for Reagan, Cin., 1979, 80. Served with U.S. Army, 1956-57. Mem. N.Y. Art Dirs. Club, Queen City Council Performing Arts (v.p., dir.). Republican. Methodist. Home: 3421 Pape Ave Cincinnati OH 45208 Office: 714 Victory Tower 2330 Victory Pkwy Cincinnati OH 45206

REEVES, RONALD GLENN, coll. adminstr.; b. Terre Haute, Ind., Aug. 6, 1935; s. Roy Theodore and Mary Edith (Bogard) R.; B.S. in Elec. Engring., Rose Hulman Inst. Tech., 1958. Supt. engring. div. Union Carbide/Ethyl Corp., Terre Haute, 1959-67; faculty Rose-Hulman Inst. Tech., Terre Haute, 1967—, v.p. for devel. 1971—. Treas., Banks of the Wabash Festival, 1979—; bd. dirs. Wabash Valley council Boy Scouts Am., 1980—, Family Service Assn. of Terre Haute, 1981—. Served to 2d lt. C.E., U.S. Army, 1958-59. Registered profl. engr., Ind. Mem. Nat. Soc. Profl. Engrs., Am. Soc. Engring. Edn., Council Advancement and Support Edn., Alpha Tau Omega. Lutheran. Clubs: Kiwanis, Elks, Aero. Home: 634 S 32nd St Terre Haute IN 47803 Office: Rose-Hulman Inst Tech 5500 Wabash Ave Terre Haute IN 47803

REGAGNON, PAUL, bioanalyst; b. Mexico, D.F., Mex., Nov. 5, 1916; s. Antoine and Ana M. (Rangel) R.; came to U.S., 1944, naturalized, 1945; B.B.Sc., Colegio Frances De La Salle, 1935; postgrad. U. National de Mexico, 1936, 38-43; m. Opal Faye McHenry, July 28, 1949; children—Donnie May, Tom H., Peggy D., Paulette, Diana, Daniel P. With Sid Richardson Refining Co., 1948-49, Eddy Clinic, Hays, Kans., 1953-70; with Laughlin Hosp. & Clinic, Inc., Kirksville, Mo., 1970-78, dir. of labs., 1953-78; with Logan County Hosp., Oakley, Kans., 1978—. Chmn. blood com. Adair County chpt. ARC, 1970-78. Served with U.S. Army, 1944-47, 49-53. Diplomate Am. Bd. Bioanalysis. Mem. AAAS, Am. Assn. Bioanalysts, Med. Electronics and Data Assn., Am. Chem. Soc., Heart of Am. Assn. Blood Banks, Am. Legion. Mormon. Home: Rural Route 1 Grinnell KS 67738 Office: 211 Cherry St Oakley KS 67748

REGENSTEIN, JOSEPH, JR., mfg. co. exec.; b. Chgo., 1923; grad. Brown U., 1945. Chmn. bd., pres., chief exec. officer, dir. Arvey Corp., Chgo. Office: Arvey Corp 3450 N Kimball Chicago IL 60618*

REGGIO, VITO ANTHONY, mgmt. cons.; b. Rochester, N.Y., Dec. 17, 1929; s. Salvatore and Carrie Angelina (LoRe) R.; student Middlebury Coll. Grad. Sch. Modern Langs., 1948; B.S., Purdue U., 1952; postgrad. (Inter-Univ. Exchange fellow) grad. schs. univs. Ala., Tenn., Ky., 1952-53; m. Mary Ann Dolores Pippie, Sept. 28, 1957; children—Salvatore, Angela. Position classifier Navy Dept. Office Indsl. Relations, Indpls., 1955-56; asso. prin. Bus. Research Corp., mgmt. cons., Chgo., 1956-60; dir. personnel mgmt. cons. services Ebasco Services, Inc., Chgo., 1960-77; pres. Reggio and Assos., Inc., Human Resources Consultants, Chgo., 1977—. Served with Adj. Gen. Corps, AUS, 1953-55. Mem. Am. Mgmt. Assn., Am. Compensation Assn., Am. Soc. Personnel Adminstrn., Indsl. Relations Assn. Chgo., Western Soc. Engrs. Home: 441 S 6th Ave La Grange IL 60525 Office: 547 W Jackson Blvd Chicago IL 60606

REGITZ, SUSAN YOUNG, interior designer; b. Elkhorn, Wis., Sept. 4, 1941; d. Gerald Ordway and Margeret Webster (Vietch) Young; B.F.A. in Interior Design, U. Denver, 1963; m. Norman William Regitz, Dec. 21, 1963; children—Norman William, Drew Young. Contract designer Marshall Field & Co., Chgo., 1963-64; with Desks, Inc., Chgo., 1964, Marshall Field & Co., Oakbrook, Ill., 1971; owner, operator Regitz Interiors, West Chicago, Ill., 1972—; antique dealer, 1972—; lectr. Am. Indian art of S.W. Republican. Mem. United Ch. of Christ. Home and Office: 425 W Washington St West Chicago IL 60185

REGNER, DAVID JOSEPH, fin. cons., state senator; b. Chgo., Mar. 9, 1931; s. Joseph H. and Catherine Ann R.; B.S., DePaul U., 1958; m. Aug. 10, 1957; 1 son, David M. Sr. programmer Universal Oil Prodn., 1960-62; sr. research analyst Allstate Ins., 1962-66; ins. agt., fin. cons., Mt. Prospect, Ill., 1966—; pres. Regner Enterprise, airplane rental, D. J. Regner & Assos., public and govtl. relations; mem. Ill. Ho. of Reps., 1967-73, Ill. Senate, 1973—; twp. auditor, 1964-66. Served with U.S. Army. Republican. Club: Jaycees (pres. local chpt. 1964, state v.p. 1965, internat. dir. 1966).

REGULA, RALPH, lawyer, congressman; b. Beach City, Ohio, Dec. 3, 1924; s. O.F. and Orpha (Walter) R.; B.A., Mt. Union Coll., 1948; LL.B., William McKinley Sch. Law, 1952; m. Mary Rogusky, Aug. 5, 1950; children—Martha, David, Richard. Sch. adminstr. Stark County Bd. Edn., 1948-55; admitted to Ohio bar, 1952; practiced law, Navarre; mem. Ohio Ho. of Reps., 1965-66, Ohio Senate, 1967-72; mem. 93d-97th congresses from 16th Dist. Ohio; partner Regula Bros. Mem. Pres.'s Commn. Fin. Structures and Regulation, 1970-71; mem. Ohio Bd. Edn., 1960-65; mem. adv. bd. Walsh Coll., Canton, Ohio. Trustee Mt. Union Coll., Alliance, Ohio, Stark County Hist. Soc., Stark County Wilderness Soc. Served with USNR, 1944-46. Recipient Community Service award Navarre Kiwanis Club, 1963; Meritorious Service in Conservation award Canton Audubon Soc., 1965; Ohio Conservation award Gov. James Rhodes, 1969; named Outstanding Young Man of Year, Canton Jaycees, 1957; Legislative Conservationist of Year, Ohio League Sportsman, 1969. Mem. Am., Ohio, Stark County bar assns. Republican. Episcopalian. Home: 8787 Erie Ave SW Navarra OH 44662 Office: 2209 Rayburn House Office Bldg Washington DC 20515

REHE, ROLF FRIEDRICH, typographer; b. Zwickau, Germany, May 28, 1935; s. Fritz and Melanie (Mueller) R.; came to U.S., 1960, naturalized, 1966; B.A., Ind. U., 1970, M.A., 1972. Apprentice, E. Schwendt, Schw. Hall (Germany), 1949-52, journeyman typesetter, 1952-60; dir. typographic design Roger Typesetting Co., Indpls., 1963-67; instr. Herron Sch. Art, Ind./Purdue U., Indpls., 1972-75, asst. prof., 1975-78, asso. prof., 1978—; dir. Design Research Internat., Carmel, Ind. Mem. pub. relations bd. Indpls. chpt. ARC, 1974—; adv. bd. Advt. Prodn. Art Inst., Ltd., St. Louis, 1976—. Recipient Best of Show award Ind. Art Dirs. Club Ann. Contest, 1974, Outstanding Vol. award Indpls. chpt. ARC, 1977. Mem. Assn. Typographique Internationale, Soc. for Typographic Arts, AAUP, Sigma Delta Chi. Roman Catholic. Clubs: Carmel Toastmasters (pres. 1976-77); Athenaeum Turners (Indpls.). Author: Typography: How to Make It Most Legible, 1972, rev. edit., 1976. Contbr. articles to trade publs. Home: 520 Lark Dr Carmel IN 46032 Office: 1701 N Pennsylvania St Indianapolis IN 46202

REHFELD, LARRY E., govt. service agy. exec.; b. Aberdeen, S.D., Nov. 26, 1948; s. Walter W. and Gertrude B. R.; B.S. cum laude, No. State Coll., 1973; m. Jamie A. Gardner, Aug. 30, 1969; children—Lara M., Christopher G. Ct. officer 11th Dist. County Ct., Aberdeen, 1970-73; program coordinator Dist. IV Planning and Devel. Commn., Aberdeen, 1973-76; exec. dir. N.E. Council Govts., Aberdeen, 1976—. Recipient Disting. Service award Foster Grandparents Program. Mem. Am. Soc. Public Adminstrn., Nat. Assn. Devel. Orgns., Nat. Assn. County Ofcls., Plains Assn. Regional Councils (chmn.), Aberdeen C. of C., Nat. Assn. County Execs. (state coordinator). Republican. Lutheran. Club: Archery. Office: 615 S Main St Aberdeen SD 57401*

REHKOPF, CHARLES FREDERICK, ch. exec.; b. Topeka, Dec. 24, 1908; s. Frederick A. and Mary G. (Jennings) R.; B.S., Washburn Coll., 1932; certificate Episcopal Theol. Sch., 1935; m. Dorothy A. Getchell, July 30, 1936; children—Frederick, Jeanne, Susan. Civil engr. Kans. Engring. Co., Topeka, 1927-30; rector Trinity Episc. Ch., El Dorado, Kans., 1935-44, St. John's Eipsc. Ch., St. Louis, 1944-52; archdeacon and exec. sec. Diocese Mo., Protestant Episc. Ch., St. Louis, 1953-76; chmn. dept. research and planning Met. Ch. Fedn. Greater St. Louis, 1954-64; chmn. div. adminstrn. Mo. Council Chs., 1965-68, chmn. div. communications, 1970-72, chmn. div. Christian unity, 1972-73; registrar Diocese of Mo., 1949—; staff Episc. Ch., Webster Groves, Mo., 1976—. Trustee Episcopal Presbyn. Found. for Aging, Inc., mem. Religious Pub. Relations Council. Mem. Soc. Am. Archivists, Hist. Soc. Protestant Episc. Ch. (dir.). Editor The Historiographer's News Letter; author articles pub. profl. jours. Home: 642 Clark Ave Webster Groves MO 63119 Office: 1210 Locust St Saint Louis MO 63103

REHNER, HERBERT ADRIAN, writer, educator; b. Vincennes, Ind., Dec. 14, 1926; s. Herbert O. and Anna-Blanche (Chapman) R.; A.B., Ind. State U., M.A., 1948; LUD, Royal Acad. Dramatic Art, U. London, 1949, student Acad. Arts and Design in Mex., Litt.D., 1960; Litt.D., Brantridge Forest Sch., Eng., 1967. Tchr., Ind. State U., 1947-48; lectr. Royal Acad. Dramatic Art, 1949-50; head theatre dept. Wilson Br., Chgo. City Coll., 1950-68, head speech dept., 1959-68, chmn. and prof. speech and drama, 1968—; producer, dir. Shawnee Summer Theatre, Greene County, 1960; pres. Ind. Acad. Dramatic Art, 1953-56; producer, dir. profl. tour of You Can't Take It with You for Def. Dept., Europe, 1959; programs over radio sta. WBOW and WIHI, 1946-48; summer producer White Barn Profl. Theater, Terre Haute, Ind.; cultural rep. Internat. Theater Inst., Chgo., 1955; dir. All City Chicago Drama Festival, 1957; dir. Shakespeare on TV, 1961, 69; producer Guys and Dolls, Chgo., 1960, Westward the River hist. drama, 1967; mgr. theatre tour to S. Pacific, Dept. Def., 1971; dir. TV variety hour, Seoul, Korea, 1971; prod. Profl. Performing Equity Co., Drama Guild, Chgo., 1972-75; mng. producer Sta. WKKC, Chgo., 1978; producer Swapface, Profl. Performing Co., 1978, Sinbad and the Magic Mystery, 1979; producer, dir. 227 (2d pl. Nat. Lorraine Hansberry award), 1978, 80; Balluster Ballads, 1980. Contracted to develop 5 curricula, also design performing arts center for new university, Iran, 1973; designer profl. theatre Bloomfield, Ind., 1979; host Community Coll. Conv., Ill. Theatre Assn., 1981. Fulbright grant to study in Eng. and Europe; James Yard award for human relation NCCJ, 1960; named Chgo. Tchr. of Year, 1965; recipient Kate Moremont travel grant, 1965. Mem. Speech Assn. Am., Sadlers Wells-Old Vic Assn., Soc. Midland Authors, ANTA (Chgo. bd. 1960-61), Theta Chi, Theta Alpha Phi (nat. v.p. 1968, 72-74, nat. pres. 1974-76, nat. council 1977—), Blue Key. Club: Players (N.Y.C., hon.). Author: Sons of the Prairie, 1950; Pastime of Eternity, 1948; The Dramatic use of Oral Interpretation and Choral Speaking, 1951; The Constant Heritage, 1952; Out of this Land, 1954; Practical Public Speaking, 1957; Communication Through Speaking, 1959, rev., 61, 62, 65, 68, 77, 78; Speaking in Public, 1961; Activities In Living and Speaking, 1965, rev., 1967, 73; nat. editor Cue mag., 1962-64. Home: Valhalla Star Route 1 Owensburg IN 47453 Office: 6904 S Harvard Ave Chicago IL 60621

REICH, JACK EGAN, ins. exec.; b. Chgo., June 17, 1910; s. Henry Carl and Rose (Egan) B.; student Purdue U., 1928-31; LL.D. (hon.), Butler U., 1973; m. Jean Grady, Apr. 30, 1935; children—Rosemary (Mrs. Jerry Semler), Judith (Mrs. Dan Hoyt). With Inland Steel Co., East Chicago, Ind., 1925-31; field dir. gross income tax and employment security divs. State of Ind., 1933-40; field dir. Ind. C. of C., 1940-52, exec. v.p., 1952-62; chmn., pres. Indpls Water Co., 1962-67, now mem. exec. com., dir.; chmn. bd., chief exec. officer Am. United Life Ins. Co.; dir., past pres. Assn. Ind. Life Ins. Cos.; dir. Ins. Systems Am.; dir., exec. com. Am. Fletcher Corp., Am. Fletcher Nat. Bank & Trust Co.; dir. First Nat. Bank East Chicago. Bd. dirs., past pres. Greater Indpls. Progress Com.; bd. govs., past chmn. Asso. Colls. Ind.; bd. govs., past chmn. bd., pres. United Way Greater Indpls.; past mem. bd. lay trustees St. Mary-of-the-Woods Coll.; bd. dirs. Indpls. Neighborhood Housing, Inc., Commn. for Downtown, Corp. Community Council; mem. adv. bd. Jr. League Indpls., St. Vincent Hosp.; pres., bd. dirs. Ind. Legal Found.; Ind. chmn. 1981 campaign United Negro Coll. Fund. Mem. Ind. (dir., past chmn.), Indpls. (dir.) chambers commerce, Pi Kappa Alpha. Clubs: Columbia, Econ. (past pres.), Indpls. Athletic, Indpls. Press, Meridian Hills Country, 100 Club (Indpls.). Home: 7404 N Pennsylvania St Indianapolis IN 46240 Office: One W 26th St Indianapolis IN 46206

REICH, LARRY LYNN, mfg. co. exec.; b. Decatur, Ill., July 27, 1943; s. Frederick W. and Mildred (Ballinger) R.; student Milliken U., 1961-63; A.A.S. in Electronics, Devry Inst. Tech., 1965; B.B.A. cum laude, Loyola U., 1977. Asst. dir. Bell & Howell Schs., Chgo., 1965-77; mgr. manpower planning and devel. Sweetheart Cup Corp., Chgo., 1977—. Leader, Tri-Ridge council Boy Scouts Am., Chgo. Mem. Am. Soc. Tng. and Devel., Adult Edn. Assn., Ill. Tng. and Devel. Assn., Alpha Sigma Nu. Lutheran. Office: 7575 S Kostner St Chicago IL 60652

REICHENBACH, NANCY LYNN, pharm. co. mgr.; b. Evanston, Ill., Sept. 4, 1952; d. Gilbert Carl and Beatrice Pearlene (Shemwell) R.; B.Bus. with honors, Western Ill. U., 1974. Employment interviewer Diversey Chems., Des Plaines, Ill., 1974-75, supr. recruitment and compensation, 1975-76; employment supr. field ops. div. Addressograph Multigraph, Schaumburg, Ill., 1976-77; sr. employment counselor pharm. div. G.D. Searle & Co., Skokie, Ill., 1977-78, mgr. employment, 1978-79, sr. compensation analyst, 1979-80, mgr. compensation, 1980-81, mgr. compensation and orgn. planning Searle Pharms., Inc., Skokie, 1981—. Recipient cert. of Leadership, YWCA Met. Chgo., 1980. Mem. Am. Mgmt. Assn., Am. Soc. Personnel Adminstrn., Soc. Personnel Adminstrs. Greater Chgo., Am. Compensation Assn., Internat. Assn. Personnel Women, Employment Mgmt. Assn. Home: 710 F Cobblestone Circle Glenview IL 60025 Office: 4901 Searle Pkwy Skokie IL 60077

REICHERT, JACK FRANK, mfg. co. exec.; b. West Allis, Wis., Sept. 27, 1930; s. Arthur Andrew and Emily Bertha (Wallinger) R.; cert. in mktg. U. Wis., Milw., 1957; grad. Advanced Mgmt. Program, Harvard U., 1970; m. Corrine Violet Helf, Apr. 5, 1952; children—Susan Marie, John Arthur. With Gen. Electric Co., 1948-57; with Brunswick Corp., 1957—, v.p. mktg., 1967-71, v.p. mktg. Mercury Marine div., 1971-72, pres., 1972, corporate v.p., 1974, group v.p. marine power group, 1974-77, pres., chief operating officer, 1977—, also dir.; dir. Sanshin Industries Co., Ltd., Japan; hon. dir. Nat. Exchange Bank, Fond du Lac, Wis. Bd. dirs. McCormick Theol. Sem., Chgo.; indsl. chmn. United Fund, Fond du Lac, 1977; trustee Carroll Coll., Waukesha, Wis. Served with U.S. Army, 1951-53. Recipient Distinguished Alumnus of Yr. award, U. Wis., Milw., 1979. Mem. Am. Mgmt. Assn., Beta Gamma Sigma. Presbyterian. Clubs: Knollwood (Lake Forest, Ill.); Pres. Club, Loyola U. Chgo.; Harvard Bus. Sch. of Chgo. Office: 1 Brunswick Plaza Skokie IL 60077

REICHERT, NORMAN VERNON, transp. co. exec.; b. Berwyn, Ill., Apr. 17, 1921; s. John G. and Valeria (Hoffman) R.; B.S. in Bus. Adminstrn., Northwestern U., 1943; postgrad. Harvard U., 1943-44; m. Wilma Eleanor Catey, Feb. 5, 1944; children—Susan, Norman V. Accountant, Arthur Young & Co., Chgo., 1946-50; central fin. staff, controller styling div. Ford Motor Co., Dearborn, Mich., 1950-61; asst. treas. Philco Ford Corp., Phila., 1961-69; asst. treas. United Air Lines, Inc., 1969-72; v.p. fin., treas. Trailer Train Co., Chgo., 1972—, Railbox Co., Chgo., 1974—; v.p. fin., treas., dir. Railgon Co., Chgo., 1979—; dir. Hamburg Industries, Inc., Augusta, Ga., Calpro, Inc., Riverside, Calif., Delpro, Inc., Wilmington, Del., Acorn Industries, Jacksonville, Fla. Served to lt. USNR, 1943-46. C.P.A., Ill. Mem. Am. Inst. C.P.A.'s, Fin. Execs. Inst., Newcomen Soc., Beta Alpha Psi, Sigma Alpha Epsilon. Clubs: Union League, Knollwood, Execs. Home: 921 Grandview Ln Lake Forest IL 60045 Office: 101 N Wacker Dr Chicago IL 60606

REICHLE, GREGORY CHARLES, burial vault mfg. co. exec.; b. Chgo., Nov. 6, 1943; s. Richard George and Catherine Ann (Schulte) R.; B.S., Xavier U., 1965; M.A., Loyola U., Chgo., 1968; m. Shelley Thomson, Apr. 2, 1978; children by a previous marriage—Suzanne, Michael, David and James (twins). Tchr., Marian Central High Sch., Woodstock, Ill., 1966-69; with Saginaw Wilbert Vault Corp., Saginaw, Mich., 1969-72; pres. Am. Wilbert Vault Corp., Chgo., 1972—, also dir.; cons. to various vault cos.; dir. Wilbert, Inc., Nat. Polymer Concrete, Inc., Coburn Wilbert Vault Corp., New Baden Wilbert Vault Corp., Reichle & Assos., Inc., St. Louis Wilbert Vault Co., Wilbert Enterprises, Inc. Mem. Nat. Concrete Burial Vault Assn., Funeral Dirs. Services Assn., Ill. Funeral Dirs. Assn., Wilbert Mfrs. Assn. Republican. Roman Catholic. Club: Lions (pres. 1981—). Home: 1020 Troost St Forest Park IL 60130 Office: American Wilbert Vault Corp 1015 Troost Forest Park IL 60130

REICHMAN, GEORGE ALBERT, agronomist; b. Belgrade, Mont., Sept. 24, 1925; s. Lawrence Everett and Alice Lorania (Holdiman) R.; B.S., Mont. State Coll., Bozeman, 1950, M.S., 1954; m. Virginia Mae Baum, Oct. 26, 1952; children—Lawrence William, Alice Marie. Soils technician U.S. Bur. Reclamation, Miles City, Mont., 1949; asst. in soils Mont. State Coll., Bozeman, 1950-54; soil scientist U.S. Dept. Agr., Mandan, Mont., 1954—; adj. prof. N.D. State U., Fargo, N.D., 1979—. Served with USNR, 1943-46. Mem. Am. Soc. Agronomy, Soil Sci. Soc. Am., Western Soc. Soil Sci., Soil Conservation Soc. Am., N.D. Acad. Sci., Orgn. Profl. Employees in Dept. Agr. Presbyterian. Club: Rotary. Contbr. articles to profl. publs. Home: 306 Sixth Ave NW Mandan ND 58554 Office: PO Box 459 No Great Plains Research Center South on Hwy 6 Mandan ND 58554

REICHNER, ROBERT JAMES, accounting co. exec.; b. Warren, Ohio, Nov. 21, 1944; s. Stephen and Lillian (Simon) R.; B.S., Duquesne U., 1966; M.B.A., Northwestern U., 1967; m. Lucille Patrick Hoyle, Jan. 20, 1973; children—Robert James II, Danielle Marie. Sr. accountant Arthur Andersen & Co., Chgo., 1967, 69-71; pres. Robert J. Reichner & Assos. Inc., Wilmette, Ill., 1971—; partner Reichner & Nykiel, Wilmette, 1974-75; lectr. in field. Founding com. Chgo. Community Ventures Inc., 1971—. Served with U.S. Army, 1967-69. Decorated Bronze Star. Home and office: 807 Chestnut St Wilmette IL 60091

REID, CLYDE MYER, microbiologist, educator; b. Birmingham, Ala., Jan. 15, 1930; s. Fred Reid and Alma Arlene Reid McDonald; B.A., Rust Coll., 1954; Med. Technologist, Homer G. Phillips Sch. Med. Tech., 1955; postgrad. St. Louis U., 1957-58, 66-68; m. Elsa Maxine Sydner, July 30, 1955; children—Sandra, Kim, Clyde, Jannette. Lab. supr. De Paul Hosp. Lab., St. Louis, 1955—; instr. microbiology St. Louis U. Sch. Medicine, 1958—; lab. dir., pres. Reid Lab. Inc., St. Louis, 1960—. Active Boy Scouts Am.; exec. bd. McKnight Sch. Parent Tchr. Orgn., 1972-73, treas., 1974-75. Served with AUS, 1950-52. Diplomate Am. Soc. Clin. Pathologists. Mem. Am. Soc. Microbiology, Am. Soc. Clin. Pathology Tech., Mo., Am., St. Louis socs. med. tech. Home: 847 Saxony Ct University City MO 63130 Office: 1402 S Grand St Saint Louis MO 63104

REID, JAMES MARSHALL, physicist, educator; b. Wayne, Mich., July 12, 1933; s. Bert C. and Inez H. Reid; B.S., Eastern Mich. U., 1958; M.A.T.S., Mich. State U., 1970; m. Sue Ann Wright, June 16, 1962; 1 dau., Robyn Meredith. Tchr., Honors Sci. Inst., East Lansing, Mich., 1958; tchr. Lansing (Mich.) Public Schs., 1958—, tchr. physics Sexton High Sch., 1958—; asso. prof. U. Wis.-Superior, summers 1969-74; cons. Harvard Project Physics, 1966-68. Mem. Am. Assn. Physics Tchrs. (Innovative Tchr. award 1973), NEA (life), Mich. Sci. Tchrs. Assn., Mich. Edn. Assn. (life). Lutheran. Home: 1300 Pettis St Lansing MI 48910 Office: 102 McPherson St Lansing MI 48915

REID, JOHN EDWARD, lawyer, forensic cons.; b. Chgo., Aug. 16, 1910; s. Thomas and Margaret (Hanley) R.; student Loyola U., Chgo., 1930-31; J.D., DePaul U., 1936; m. Margaret McCarthy, July 26, 1941. Began testing subjects with polygraph Chgo. Police Sci. Crime Detection Lab., 1940, inventor polygraph for detection false rises in blood pressure, 1944; revised questioning technique in lie detector tests, 1947; established John E. Reid & Assos. Lab for Lie Detection, Chgo., 1947; founder Reid Coll. for Detection of Deception; devised Reid Report and Reid Survey psychol. questionnaires to determine job applicant and employee honesty. Mem. Chgo. Crime Commn. Fellow Am. Acad. Forensic Scis.; mem. Am. Polygraph Assn. (dir.), Ill. Polygraph Soc., Am. Acad. Polygraph Examiners (past pres.), Internat. Assn. Arson Investigators, Spl. Agts. Assn. (past pres.). Author: (with Fred. E. Inbau) Lie Detection and Criminal Interrogation; Criminal Interrogation and Confessions; Truth and Deception, The Polygraph (Lie Detector) Technique; also articles on lie detection, criminal interrogation. Home: 44 Park Ln Park Ridge IL 60068 Office: 215 N Dearborn St Chicago IL 60601

REID, MARGARET GILPIN, economist; b. Man., Can., Jan. 27, 1896; came to U.S., 1927, naturalized, 1938; d. John Clements and Martha (Sparling) R.; B.S. in Home Econs., U. Man., Winnipeg, 1921, LL.D. (hon.), 1960; Ph.D., U. Chgo., 1931. Lectr., Ont. (Can.) Agrl. Coll., Guelph, 1921-27; asst. prof. econs. Conn. Coll., 1929-30; asst. prof. econs. Iowa State Coll., 1930-36, asso. prof., 1936-39, prof., 1940-45; economist Exec. Office of Pres., Washington, 1943-44; head family econs. div. Dept. Agr., Washington, 1945-48; prof. econs. U. Ill., Champaign, 1948-51; prof. home econs. and econs. U. Chgo., 1951-54, prof. econs., 1954-61, prof. econs. emeritus, 1961—. Social Sci. Research Council grantee, 1961-62; Social Security Adminstr. grantee, 1963-68. Fellow Am. Econs. Assn. (disting.); mem. Am. Statis. Assn. Author books including: Food for People, 1943, 2d edit., 1976; Housing and Income, 1962, 2d edit., 1974; contbr. articles to profl. publs. Home: 1155 E 56th St Chicago IL 60637 Office: Foster Hall U Chgo 1130 E 59th St Chicago IL 60637

REID, WILLIAM HOWARD, psychiatrist; b. Dallas, Apr. 10, 1945; s. Howard Clinton and Lucile (Brock) R.; B.A., U. Minn., 1966, M.D., 1970; M.P.H., U. Calif., Berkeley, 1975. Intern, U. Calif., Davis, 1970-71, resident in psychiatry, 1973-75; clin., research and forensic psychiatrist, asso. prof., vice chief of staff Nebr. Psychiat. Inst., Omaha, 1977—; lectr. in psychiatry Northwestern U., vis. asso. prof. and forensic cons. Rush Med. Coll., 1978-81; chair research sect. Cross Keys Internat. Conf. Psychiat. Aspects of Terrorism; v.p. Nat. Assn. State Mental Health Research Insts. Served with M.C., AUS, 1971-73. Diplomate Am. Bd. Psychiatry and Neurology. Mem. Am. Psychiat. Assn., Nebr. Psychiat. Soc. (exec. council), AMA, Assn. Advancement of Psychotherapy, AAAS, Am. Acad. Psychiatry and the Law, Internat. Platform Assn. Author: The Psychopath: A Comprehensive Study of Antisocial Disorders and Behaviors, 1978; Psychiatry for the House Officer, 1979; Basic Intensive Psychotherapy, 1980; The Treatment of Antisocial Syndromes, 1981; contbr. articles to sci. jours. Composer 15 mus. compositions. Office: Nebraska Psychiatric Institute 602 S 45th St Omaha NE 68106

REIDDA, PHIL, psychologist; b. Hackensack, N.J.; s. Benedict and Vera (Sandino) R.; B.A., U. Hartford, 1961; M.S., Coll. City N.Y., 1963; Ph.D., Ill. Inst. Tech., 1971; m. Ellen Kapsis, Dec. 27, 1958; children—Barry, Sloane. Psychometrist, N.Y. U. Testing Center, N.Y.C., 1963; psychology intern Chgo. State Hosp., 1963-64, psychologist, 1964-65; psychologist Lakeview-Uptown Community Mental Health Center, Chgo., 1966-67, Harbor Light Out-Patient Clinic, 1965-66; dir. Garfield Park Community Mental Health Center, Chgo., 1966-70; coordinator of research and evaluation Chgo. Bd. Health, 1970-71; clin. cons. psychologist Affiliated Psychologists, Ltd., Chgo., 1971—; instr. psychology Elmhurst (Ill.) Coll., 1967-81; instr. Chgo. Med. Sch., 1982—. Served with USNR, 1948-50. Mem. Am., Ill. (standards and tng. com.) psychol. assns., Ill. Group Psychotherapy Soc. Contbr. articles to profl. jours. Home: 1440 Glencoe Highland Park IL 60035 Office: 2544 W Montrose Chicago IL 60618

REIDER, JAMES WILLIAM, hosp. security ofcl.; b. Mpls., June 25, 1952; s. William H. and Marilyn M. (Fish) R.; student Defiance Coll., 1970-72, U. Denver, 1972-74, U. Minn., 1974—; m. Mary K. Johnson, July 10, 1976; children—Christina Marie, Jessica Anne. Safety and security mgr. K-Mart Corp., Mpls., 1974-76; ops. and safety mgr. Park Detective Agy., Inc., Mpls., 1976-77; ops. mgr. Twin City Security, 1977; security and safety officer Hennepin County Med. Center, Mpls., 1977-78, safety officer, 1978-81; corp. dir. security Abbott-Northwestern Hosp., Mpls., 1981—; cons. safety and security. Active CAP, 1962-80, capt., 1978-80; mem. com. to draft city fire regulations ordinances for health care facilities Mpls. Fire Dept., 1980-81. Cert. health care safety profl., exec. level. Mem. Am. Soc. Safety Engrs., Nat. Safety Mgmt. Soc., Am. Soc. Indsl. Security, Am. Soc. for Hosp. Risk Mgmt., Sigma Phi Epsilon. Office: 2727 Chicago Ave S Minneapolis MN 55407

REIFF, GUY GENE, educator; b. Los Angeles, May 8, 1926; s. Emil and Marcelle (Erhart) R.; B.S., U. So. Calif., 1952; M.A., Colo. State Coll., 1955; Ph.D., U. Mich., 1964; m. Geraldine Bruce, June 12, 1955; children—Sheri, Teri, Craig. Athletic coach Calif. Mil. Acad., Los Angeles, 1948-50, St. John's Acad., Los Angeles, 1950-52; grad. fellow recreation Colo. State Coll., Greeley, 1952-53; athletic coach, dir. phys. edn. program Coll. High Sch., Greeley, 1953-55; asst. prof. phys. edn. Colo. State Coll., Greeley, 1955-60; instr. phys. edn. U. Mich., Ann Arbor, 1960-64, asst. prof., 1964-67, asso. prof., 1967-71, prof. phys. edn., 1971—; cons. HEW, Ednl. Testing Service, U.S. Golf Found., Pres.'s Council on Phys. Fitness and Sports. Served with USN, 1943-46. Fellow AAHPER, Am. Coll. Sports Medicine; mem. AAUP. Contbr. articles to profl. jours.; asso. editor Research Quarterly, 1970—. Home: PO Box 417 Lakeland MI 48143

REIGEL, DON, former corp. exec.; b. Deer River, Minn., Sept. 4, 1914; s. Jake and Marion (Shabel) R.; B.A., cum laude, Carleton Coll., 1936; postgrad. Minn. Sch. Bus., 1942; grad. Command and General Staff Coll., Fort Leavenworth, Kans., 1963; postgrad. in polit. sci. Mankato (Minn.) State Coll.; m. Mary Jane Scott, Oct. 24, 1942; children—Marc, Kent. Auditor, Stearns Lumber Co., Hutchinson, Minn., 1936-42; advt. mgr. U.S. Check Book Co., Omaha, 1946-50, Journ.-Chronicle Co., Owatonna, Minn., 1950-56; pub., owner Photo News, Owatonna, 1956-73; pres. Reigel Corp., 1973-79; info. officer vocat. rehab./econ. devel. State of Minn., 1974—. Tchr. U. Omaha and Van Sant Sch. of Bus., Omaha, 1946-50, Mankato State Coll., 1972-73, Rasmussen Sch. Bus., 1978-79, Globe Bus. Coll., 1981—. Pres. Owatonna Community Chest, 1954; dist. chmn. Wasioja dist. Boy Scouts of Am., 1955-56; chmn. long range planning and research com. Minn. United Meth. Conf. Mem. Minn. Ho. of Reps. from Steele County, 1968-70. Bd. dirs. Paul Watkins Home, Winona, 1966-72. Served to capt. AUS, 1942-46; to lt. col. Res. Mem. Minn. Newspaper Assn. (chmn. advt. com. 1962-63), Nat. Editorial Assn. Clubs: Sr. Active, Rotary (sec. 1955-76), Masons, Minneapolis Athletic, Am. Legion. Home: 558 E South St Owatonna MN 55060

REIGLE, LYNN LEROY, accountant; b. Flint, Mich., June 26, 1944; s. Lewis William and Edith Lucielle (Chrombie) R.; A.A., Delta Coll., 1964; B.B.A., Saginaw Valley State Coll., 1974; m. Gay Adolphine Zacharias, June 26, 1965; 1 son, Gerald Lewis. Dept. mgr. Arlans Dept. Store, Saginaw, Mich., 1964-66; social worker Mich. Dept. Social Services, Saginaw, 1966-72; controller State Asphalt Corp., Saginaw, 1974-76; controller, treas. Mahon Indsl. Corp., Saginaw, 1976-80; controller Equipment Distbg. Co., 1980—. Mem. Nat. Assn. Accts., Am. Acctg. Assn., Ind. Accts. Assn. Mich., Am. Legion. Roman Catholic. Home: 3177 Sapphire Way Apt 802 Saginaw MI 48603 Office: Equipment Distbg Co 1455 Agricola Dr Saginaw MI 48604

REILE, ELLSWORTH SAMUEL, clergyman; b. Hebron, N.D., Mar. 21, 1928; s. Samuel Andrew and Lydia (Lang) R.; B.A. in Religion, Union Coll., 1949; m. Norma Jean Johnson, Feb. 2, 1947; 1 dau., Cindy Reile Tarr. Ordained to ministry Seventh-day Adventist Ch., 1953; dist. pastor Colo. Conf., 1949-54; departmental dir. Kans. Conf., Topeka, 1954-57; youth dir. Ga.-Cumberland Conf., Atlanta, 1957-59, So. Calif. Conf., Glendale, 1959-64, So. Union Conf., Atlanta, 1964-68; pres. Carolina Conf., Charlotte, N.C., 1968-77, Mid-Am. Union Conf., Lincoln, Nebr., 1978—. Home: 6112 S 25th St Lincoln NE 68512 Office: PO Box 6127 Lincoln NE 68506

REILLY, EDWARD FRANCIS, JR., state senator; b. Leavenworth, Kans., Mar. 24, 1937; s. Edward F. and Marian C. (Sullivan) R.; B.A., U. Kans., 1961. Vice pres. Ed Reilly & Sons, Inc., Leavenworth, 1967—; pres. Westside Village, Inc., Leavenworth, 1968-79, Yllier Lake Estates, Inc., Easton, Kans., 1965-79; v.p. First State Bank of Lansing, 1979—; mem. Kans. Ho. of Reps., 1963-64; mem. Kans. State Senate, 1964—, asst. majority leader, 1977—, vice-chmn. govtl. orgn., chmn. ins. subcom., chmn. fed. and state affairs com. Cultural chmn. Christian Youth Orgn.; del. to Republican Nat. Conv., Miami Beach, Fla., 1968; chmn. Leavenworth County Radio Free Europe Fund, 1972; bd. dirs. Kaw Valley Heart Assn., 1971-77, St. John's Hosp., Leavenworth, 1970-79, sec.; bd. dirs. Leavenworth Assn. for Handicapped, 1968-69, ARC, Leavenworth chpt., Kans. Blue Cross/Blue Shield, 1969-72. Mem. Leavenworth C. of C. (hon. dir. 1970-73), Assn. U.S. Army (Henry Leavenworth award 1960), Kansas City (Kans.) C. of C., Leavenworth Hist. Soc. (dir. 1968-73), Ancient Order of Hibernians. Republican. Roman Catholic. Clubs: Kiwanis (dir. 1969-70), K.C., Elks. Home: 430 Delaware Leavenworth KS 66048

REILLY, FRANK KELLY, educator; b. Chgo., Dec. 30, 1935; s. Clarence Raymond and Mary Josephine (Ruckrigel) R.; B.B.A., U. Notre Dame, 1957; M.B.A., Northwestern U., 1961; M.B.A., U. Chgo., 1964, Ph.D., 1968; m. Therese Adele Bourke, Aug. 2, 1958; children—Frank Kelly, Clarence Raymond, Therese B., Edgar B. Trader, Goldman Sachs & Co. stocks, Chgo., 1958-59; security analyst Technology Fund, Chgo., 1959-62; asst. prof. U. Kans., Lawrence, 1965-68, asso. prof., 1968-72; prof. bus., asso. dir. div. bus. and econ. research U. Wyo., Laramie, 1972-75; prof. fin. U. Ill., Urbana, 1975-81; Bernard J. Hank prof. bus. adminstrn., dean Coll. Bus. Adminstrn., U. Notre Dame, 1981—. Arthur J. Schmidt Found. fellow, 1962-65; U. Chgo. fellow, 1963-65; chartered fin. analyst. Mem. Midwest Bus. Adminstrn. Assn. (pres. 1974-75), Southwestern, Eastern (dir. 1979—, pres.-elect 1981), Western (exec. com. 1973-75), Am. fin. assns., Fin. Analysts Fedn., Fin. Mgmt. Assn. (v.p. 1977—), Nat. Bur. Econ. Research, Beta Gamma Sigma. Roman Catholic. Author: Investment Analysis and Portfolio Management, 1979; Investments, 1982; editor: Readings and Issues in Investments, 1975; asso. editor Fin. Rev., 1979, Fin. Mgmt., 1977—, Quar. Rev. Econs. and Bus., 1979. Home: 17385 Turnberry Ct Granger IN 46530 Office: Coll Bus Adminstrn U Notre Dame Notre Dame IN 46556

REILLY, JEANETTE P., psychologist; b. Denver, Oct. 19, 1908; d. George Lindsey and Marie (Bloedorn) Parker; A.B., U. Colo., 1929; M.A., Columbia U., 1951, Ed.D., 1959; m. Peter C. Reilly, Sept. 15, 1932; children—Marie Reilly Heed, Sara Jean Reilly Wilhelm, Patricia Ann Reilly Davis. Lectr. psychology Butler U., Indpls., 1957-58, 60-65; chief psychologist Cerebral Palsy Clinic, Ind. U. Med. Center, Indpls., 1961-62, VA Outpatient Clinic, Indpls., 1965-66; pvt. practice clin. psychologist, Indpls., 1967—; asso. mem. staff St. Vincent's Hosp. Mem. women's council U. Notre Dame, 1953—; trustee Hanover (Ind.) Coll., 1975—; mem. Community Hosp. Found., Indpls., 1978—; mem. Nat. Register of Health Service Providers in Psychology, 1975—. Mem. Am. Psychol. Assn., Am. Personnel and Guidance Assn., Am. Vocat. Guidance Assn., Midwestern Psychol. Assn., Ind. Psychol. Assn., Central Ind. Psychol. Assn., Mortar Bd., Pi Lambda Theta, Kappa Delta Pi. Home and office: 1015 Stratford Hall Indianapolis IN 46260

REIMER, JUDY ELLEN, nursing adminstr.; b. Filer, Idaho, Apr. 24, 1938; d. Daniel Melvern and Florence Pauline (Slatter) Shank; grad. Bethel Deaconess Sch. Nursing, 1960; student Kearney State Coll., 1972—; m. Richard L. Reimer, Sept. 8, 1960; children—R. Anthony, Matt W., Curtis D. Staff nurse Lima (Ohio) Meml. Hosp., 1960-63; pediatric staff nurse Weld County Hosp., Greeley, Colo., 1962, 63; staff nurse Mary Lanning Hosp., Hastings, Nebr., 1966-68, supr., 1968-74, dir. staff devel., 1974—; chmn. Project Shared Hosp. Assn. for Resources and Edn., 1974-75; mem. state program com. Nebr. Organ Retrieval System, Inc., 1979—. Mem. profl. edn. com. Am. Cancer Soc. Mem. Am. Nurses Assn., Nebr. Nurses Assn. (pres. Dist I), Dist. Nurses Assn. (Disting. Service award 1978). Republican. Methodist. Club: Faculty Wives. Home: 811 N Lincoln Ave Hastings NE 68901 Office: 715 N St Joseph Ave Hastings NE 68901

REIN, FAITH KATHLEEN, YWCA exec.; b. Schenectady, N.Y., Nov. 6, 1934; s. Herbert Dyer and Kathleen Virginia (Drumm) Johnson; student Ohio U., 1953-54; A.A.B.A., U. Toledo, 1975; B.S. in Gerontology (fellow), Bowling Green (Ohio) State U., 1978; m. Don Carris Rein, Dec. 27, 1972; children—Linda Faith (Mrs. Loren Marcee), David Mackey, Frederick Mackey, Paul Mackey, Diane Mackey. Asst. community club awards dir. WOHO Radio, 1970; program dir. YWCA, Toledo, 1971-76, exec. dir., 1977—. Mem. recreation adv. com. Owens Tech. Coll.; treas., bd. dirs. R.S.V.P. Cert. food service mgr., Ohio. Mem. Exec. Forum, Council Jr. Cotery Federated Clubs of Toledo (pres. 1968), Maumee Fedn. Garden Clubs (pres. 1967). Republican. Methodist. Club: Zonta (exec. com.). Home: 3060 Villa Dr Toledo OH 43614 Office: 1018 Jefferson Ave Toledo OH 43624

REINER, MARY, ins. co. exec.; b. Wooster, Ohio, Aug. 15, 1942; d. Glenn Ward and Blanche Anna (Rehm) Wirth; B.S., Wheaton (Ill.) Coll., 1964; M.B.A., Loyola U., Chgo., 1972; m. David Reiner, May 31, 1969 (div. Dec. 1975). Various positions Montgomery Ward Co., Chgo., 1966-73, mgmt. selection systems mgr., 1973-75, retirement plan mgr., 1975-76; salaried benefits mgr. Interlake Inc., Chgo., 1977-79; orgn. devel. mgr. Zurich Ins. Co., Schaumburg, Ill., 1979—. Bd. dirs. Lincoln Park Conservation Assn., 1975; sec. Lincoln Central Assn., 1974, pres., 1975. Mem. Am. Compensation Assn., Employee Relocation Council, Am. Mgmt. Assn., N.W. Indsl. Council, Am. Soc. for Personnel Adminstrn., N.W. Suburban Assn. Commerce and Industry (transp. com. 1980-81). Republican. Presbyterian. Club: Chgo. Health. Office: Zurich Ins Co 213 Martingale Rd Schaumburg IL 60196

REINERTSON, JAMES WAYNE, pediatrician; b. Des Moines, Jan. 25, 1927; s. Adolph Jennings and Bonnie Viola (Wald) R.; B.A., Luther Coll., 1948; M.S.P.H., U. N.C., 1949; postgrad. Wayne U., 1952-54; M.D., U. Iowa, 1959; m. Beverly Elaine Sampson, June 6, 1948; children—Mark Wayne, Marilee. Asso. research parasitologist Parke, Davis & Co., 1949-54; intern Mercy Hosp., Cedar Rapids, Iowa, 1959-60; resident in pediatrics, Wyeth pediatric fellow Blank Meml. Hosp., Des Moines, 1960-62; practice medicine specializing in pediatrics, Cedar Rapids, 1962—; mem. staff St. Lukes Meth. Hosp., 1962—, pres., 1979—; staff Mercy Hosp.; instr. Cedar Rapids Med. Edn. Program. Mem. ch. council First Lutheran Ch., 1965-71; bd. dirs. Linn County Assn. Retarded Citizens, 1972—. Diplomate Am. Bd. Pediatrics. Fellow Am. Acad. Pediatrics; mem. AMA, Iowa, Linn County med. assns. Lutheran. Developer exptl. drug amebiasis. Home: 1130 27th St Cedar Rapids IA 52402 Office: 411 10th St SE Cedar Rapids IA 52403

REINHARD, KEITH LEON, advt. agy. exec.; b. Berne, Ind., Jan. 20, 1935; s. Herman L. and Agnes Verena (Liechty) R.; student pvt. schs., Berne; children by previous marriage—Christopher, Timothy, Matthew, Geoffrey, Jacqueline; m. 2d, Rose-Lee Simons, Nov. 7, 1976; 1 dau., Rachel. Comml. artist Kling Studios, Chgo., 1953-55; mgr. tech. communications dept. Magnavox Co., Ft. Wayne, Ind., 1955-61; creative/account exec. Biddle Co., Bloomington, Ill., 1961-64; pres. Needham, Harper & Steers, Chgo., 1980—, also dir. Protestant Episcopalian. Office: 303 E Wacker Dr Chicago IL 60601

REINHARD, SHEILA MARY, educator; b. Phila., Feb. 1, 1952; d. Harold Joseph and Eileen Patricia (Murray) R.; B.S., U. Dayton, 1973; M.Ed., Kent State U., 1978, Ed.S., 1980. Tchr. mentally retarded Madison Plains Local Sch. Dist., London, Ohio, 1973-76; behavior disorder tchr. Parmadale Sch., Parma, Ohio, 1976-78; learning disabilities tchr. Buckeye Local Sch. Dist., Medina, Ohio, 1978-80; spl. needs coordinator Medina County Vocat. Center, 1980—. Mem. Council Exceptional Children, Ohio Vocat. Assn., Am. Vocat. Assn., Ohio Vocat. Assn. Spl. Needs Personnel, Ohio Tchrs. Exceptional Children, Medina County Vocat. Edn. Assn., Ohio Edn. Assn., NEA, Mensa. Democrat. Roman Catholic. Home: 454 Georgia Ave Elyria OH 44035 Office: Medina Vocational Center 1101 W Liberty St Medina OH 44256

REINHART, EDWARD JOHN, JR., educator; b. Chgo., Mar. 26, 1943; s. Edward John and Dorothy Phillis (Grabert) R.; B.S., Ill. State U., 1965; M.S., Chgo. State U., 1969; postgrad. No. Ill. U., 1972; Ph.D., Purdue U., 1974; m. Bonnie Lee Zabelka, Dec. 17, 1966; children—Edward John III, Eric Victor. Tchr. indsl. arts Normal (Ill.) Community High Sch., 1965-66; tchr. indsl. arts Evergreen Park (Ill.) High Sch., 1966-70, audio visual dir., 1968-70; prof., chairperson occupational edn. dept. Chgo. State U., 1970—. Cubmaster, Pack 349, Boy Scouts Am., Lemont, Ill., 1976-78, awards chmn. Boy Scout Troop 49, 1979—; v.p. Brodperek PTA, Lemont, 1975-76, treas., 1976-77; instr. scuba diving Profl. Assn. Diving Instrs., 1978—. Davte grantee research for solar energy, 1978-79. Mem. Am. Indsl. Arts Assn., Am. Vocational Assn., Nat. Council Energy and Power, Ill. Indsl. Edn. Assn., Ill. Vocational Assn., Ill. Assn. Electricity and Electronic Educators. Roman Catholic. Contbr. articles to profl. jours. Office: Chgo State U 95th and King Dr Chicago IL 60628

REINHEIMER, JANE KORTE, editor, pub.; b. Stamps, Ark., June 26, 1943; d. Allison Oscar and Anna Mae (Stubbe) Haltom; student Trinity Christian Coll., 1978; m. Quintin K. Reinheimer, Sept. 20, 1978. Personnel mgr. Nat. Outdoor Advt. Bur., 1963-68; exec. sec. Worth Twp. Youth Commn., Worth, Ill., 1970-77; press sec. to twp. supr., Town of Worth, 1977-78; exec. sec. to gen. counsel, corp. sec. Inolex Corp., Chgo., 1978-79; editor, pub., pres. Patriot Press, Inc., Palos Hills, Ill., 1979—. Bd. dirs. United Way of Oak Lawn, 1979—; v.p. Girls Scouts of South Cook County Council, 1972-74; pres. Am. Luth. Ch. Women, Trinity Luth. Ch., 1974. Mem. Palos Hills C. of C. (dir. 1979). Author: (poetry) Hot and Cold Running Happy!, 1979. Address: 8249 Holly Ct Palos Hills IL 60465

REINHOLD, EDNA FRANCES, librarian; b. Clinton, Ill., June 15, 1935; d. Pavey Evert and Leila Fern (Bennett) Jones; B.S., MacMurray Coll. for Women, 1958; M.S. in Library Sci., U. Ill., 1965; postgrad. in mgmt. Washington U., St. Louis, 1970, 71; postgrad. in edn. U. Mo., St. Louis, 1975; m. James Frank Reinhold, May 11, 1968. Asst. circulation dept. Decatur (Ill.) Public Library, 1958-61, asst. reference dept., 1961-65, chief central public services, 1965-66, acting city librarian, 1966, supr. adult services, 1966-68; prin. librarian circulation dept. St. Louis Public Library, 1968-70, chief librarian readers' sers., 1970-73, chief librarian humanities and social scis., 1973—. Mem. Am. Library Assn., Spl. Libraries Assn., Mo. Library Assn., Greater St. Louis Library Club, Alpha Lambda Delta, Beta Phi Mu. Democrat. Unitarian. Home: 10 Plaza Sq Apt 402 Saint Louis MO 63103 Office: St Louis Public Library 1301 Olive Saint Louis MO 63103

REINSCH, ALBERT LEE, ednl. adminstr.; b. St. Louis, Aug. 31, 1932; s. Albert John and Ethel Dolly (Wilson) R.; A.A., St. Johns Coll., 1953; A.B., Washington U., St. Louis, 1959; M.A.Ed., 1962, Ph.D., 1977; M.S., Mich. State U., 1964; m. Apryl Ann Saulich, Apr. 2, 1966; children—Albert Lee, Kristine Anne, Heather Lynne. Tchr., Hope Luth. Sch., 1956-57; tchr. high sch., Central, Beaumont and Northwest schs., St. Louis, 1959-69; asst. prin. Northwest High Sch., 1969-73, prin. Cleveland High Sch., 1973-80; asst. dep. supt. St. Louis Public Schs., 1980—; dist. mgr. I.C.S., 1968-69. State dir. Smoke Watchers Internat., 1971-73. Served with U.S. Army, 1954-56. NSF fellow, 1964-65; Parsons Blewett Found. fellow, 1964-65; Danforth Found. fellow, 1974-75. Mem. Mo. Fedn. Tchrs. (pres. 1967-69), St. Louis Tchrs. Union (treas. 1966-68), Nat. Assn. Secondary Sch. Prins., Assn. for Supervision and Curriculum Devel., St. Louis Adminstrs. Assn., Nat. Assn. Sch. Adminstrs. Home: 4941 Deepwood Ct Saint Louis MO 63128 Office: 911 Locust St Saint Louis MO 63101

REINSDORF, JERRY MICHAEL, bus. exec., lawyer; b. Bklyn., Feb. 25, 1936; s. Max and Marion (Smith) R.; B.A., The George Washington U., 1957; J.D., Northwestern U., 1960; m. Martyl F. Rifkin, Dec. 29, 1956; children—David Jason, Susan Janeen, Michael Andrew, Jonathan Milton. Admitted to D.C., Ill. bars, 1960; atty. staff regional counsel IRS, Chgo., 1960-64; asso. law firm Chapman & Cutler, 1964-68; partner law firm Altman, Kurlander & Weiss, 1968-74; of counsel firm Katten, Muchin, Gitles, Zavis, Pearl & Galler, 1974-80; gen. partner Carlyle Real Estate Ltd. Partnerships, 1971-72; chmn. bd. The Balcor Co., Skokie, Ill., 1974—; mng. partner TBC Films, 1975—; chmn. bd. Chgo. White Sox, 1981—; dir. Ednl. Tape Rec. for Blind; lectr. John Marshall Law Sch., 1966-68; dir. Real Estate Securities and Syndication Inst., 1972-76. Bd. dirs. Chgo. Gastro-Intestinal Research Found. Co-chmn., Ill. Profls. for Sen. Ralph Smith, 1970. C.P.A., Ill.; cert. specialist in real estate securities. Mem. Am., Ill., Chgo., Fed. bar assns., Order of Coif, Omega Tau Rho. Author: (with L. Herbert Schneider) Uses of Life Insurance in Qualified Employee Benefit Plans, 1970. Office: 10024 Skokie Blvd Skokie IL 60077

REIS, HEIDI MARY, mgmt. cons.; b. Sturgeon Bay, Wis., Sept. 12, 1953; d. John Peter and Gloria Kathryn (Weber) R.; B.A., St. Norbert Coll., 1975; student U. Salzburg (Austria), 1973-74; Asso., A.T. Kearney, Inc., Chgo., 1975-80, mgr., 1981—. Mem. Internat. Word Processing Assn., Am. Mgmt. Assn. Co-author: Handbook of Business Problem Solving, 1980; also articles. Office: 222 S Riverside Plaza Chicago IL 60606

REISMAN, ARNOLD, educator; b. Lodz, Poland, Aug. 2, 1934; s. Isadore and Rose (Joskowitz) R.; came to U.S., 1946, naturalized, 1955; B.S., UCLA, 1955, M.S., 1957, Ph.D., 1963; m. Ellen Gay Kronheim, Aug. 3, 1980; children by previous marriage—Miriam Jennie, Ada Jo, Deborah Fawn, Nina Michelle. Design engr. Los Angeles Dept. Water and Power, 1955-57; asso. prof. Calif. State U., Los Angeles, 1957-66; prof. U. Wis., Milw., 1966-68; prof. ops. research Case Western Res. U., Cleve., 1968—; vis. prof. Hebrew U., Jerusalem, 1975, Japan-Am. Inst. Mgmt. Sci., Honolulu, 1975, Bus. Econ. and Quantitative Methods, U. Hawaii, Honolulu, 1971; asso. research engr. Western Mgmt. Sci. Inst., U. Calif. at Los Angeles,

1964-65; coordinator programs between Inst. Mgmt. Scis. and AAAS, 1971-74; examiner North Central Assn. Colls., Univs. and Secondary Schs., 1971; v.p. Univ. Assos., Inc., Cleve., 1968—; expert witness Solicitor Gen., Dept. Labor, 1969-70, U.S. Equal Opportunities Commn., 1976-79; atty. gen. State of Ohio, 1981; cons. to asst. sec. HEW, 1971-72, Office Program Planning and Evaluation, U.S. Office Edn., Pan Am. Health Orgn., 1972—; cons. in gen. field systems analysis numerous corps. and instns. U.S. del. to Internat. Fedn. Ops. Research Socs., Conv., Dublin, Ireland, 1972. Review bd. mem. Lake Erie Regional Transp. Authority, 1974-75; mem. del. assembly Jewish Community Fedn. Cleve., 1974—; mem. Shaker Heights (Ohio) Citizens Adv. Com., 1972—; founder, bd. dirs. Greater Cleve. Coalition on Cost Effectiveness of Health Care Services; trustee Hillel Found. Named Cleve. Engr. of the Year, 1973. Registered profl. engr., Calif., Wis., Ohio. NSF fellow, 1963. Fellow AAAS (council); mem. Ops. Research Soc. Am., Inst. Mgmt. Scis., ASME, Am. Soc. Engring. Edn., AAUP, Am. Inst. Indsl. Engrs., N.Y. Acad. Sci., Phi Delta Kappa, Sigma Xi. Contbr. over 100 articles to profl. jours.; contbr. chpts. to books; author: Managerial and Engineering Economics, 1971; Systems Approach and the City, 1972; Industrial Inventory Control, 1972; Health Care Delivery Planning, 1973; System Analysis for Health Care Services, 1979; Computer System Selection, 1980; Materials Management for the Health Services, 1981, others; series editor: Operations Management, 1975-78; asso. editor: Socio Economic Planning Sciences. Home: 18428 Parkland Dr Shaker Heights OH 44122 Office: Case Western Reserve U Dept Operations Research Cleveland OH 44106

REISMAN, BETTY LOU, educator; b. Youngstown, Ohio, Nov. 9, 1941; d. Bernard and Florence Esther (Liebermann) Reisman; B.A., Case Western Res. U., 1963; M.A., Kent State U., 1965, Ph.D., 1977. Asst. dean students State U. Coll. at Buffalo, 1965-68; asst. dean student affairs Clarion (Pa.) State Coll., 1968-69; asst. dir. housing, adj. instr. sch. psychology and counseling State U. N.Y. Coll. at Oswego, 1969-75; organizational specialist Kent State U., 1976-77, mem. grad. faculty, 1977; counselor U. Md., Balt. County, 1977-78; dir. student/staff devel. Ohio State U., 1978-79; asso. prof. counselor edn. Wayne State U., Detroit, 1979—, coordinator student personnel specialist program, 1979—; adviser Hillel Group, 1973. Mem. Am. Coll. Personnel Assn., Am. Coll. and U. Housing Officers, Nat. Assn. Women Deans, Adminstrs. and Counselors (exec. bd. 1977-78), N.Y. Assn. Women Deans, Adminstrs. and Counselors (mem. adv. bd. 1973-75), Mich. Assn. Women Deans, Adminstrs. and Counselors, Am. Personnel and Guidance Assn., Nat. Vocat. Guidance Assn., Mich. Coll. Personnel Assn. (exec. bd. 1981-82), Sigma Psi. Author monographs; asst. editor Urban Educator, 1979—; contbr. articles to profl. jours. Home: 3475 5th Ave Youngstown OH 44505

REISS, IRA LEONARD, sociologist, educator; b. N.Y.C., Dec. 8, 1925; s. Philip and Dorothy (Jacobs) R.; B.S., Syracuse U., 1949; M.A., Pa. State U., 1951, Ph.D., 1953; m. Harriet Marilyn Eisman, Sept. 4, 1955; children—David, Pamela, Joel. Mem. faculty Bowdoin Coll., Brunswick, Maine, 1953-55, Coll. William and Mary, Williamsburg, Va., 1955-59, Bard Coll., Annandale, N.Y., 1959-61, U. Iowa, Iowa City, 1961-69; prof. dept. sociology U. Minn., Mpls., 1969—, dir. U. Minn. Family Study Center, 1969-74; cons. in field. Served with U.S. Army, 1944-46. NIMH grantee, 1960-64; recipient award Ednl. Found. for Human Sexuality, 1970; award for best theory and research article of year Nat. Council Family Relations, 1980. Mem. Midwest Sociol. Soc. (pres. 1971-72), Nat. Council Family Relations (pres. 1979-80), Soc. for Sci. Study Sex (pres. 1980-81), Am. Sociol. Assn. (pres. family sect. 1975-76), AAUP, Internat. Acad. Sex Researchers. Democrat. Jewish. Author books in field including: Premarital Sexual Standards in America, 1960; Social Context of Premarital Sexual Permissiveness, 1967; Contemporary Theories About the Family, 1979; Family Systems in America, 3d edit., 1980. Office: Dept Sociology U of Minn Minneapolis MN 55455

REISS, MARY LORANGER, state ednl. adminstr.; b. Superior, Wis., Feb. 19, 1934; d. Egbert Fletcher and Mary J. Loranger; B.S., Wayne State U., 1955; M.A., U. Mich., 1965, Ph.D., 1971; children—Eric, Merritt. Health and sci. cons. Oak Park (Mich.) schs., 1961-63, sch.-community coordinator, 1963-65; edn. cons. Wayne County (Mich.) Intermediate Schs., 1965-70; cons. Mich. Dept. Edn., 1970-73, dir. adult extended learning service area, Lansing, 1978—; dir. allied health occupations Washtenaw Community Coll., 1973-74; dir. div. continuing edn. N.Y. State Edn. Dept. Albany, 1974-78; asso. prof. sociology Oakland Community Coll., 1967-69; guest lectr. various univs., colls., including Tchrs. Coll., Columbia U., CCNY; N.Y. State Dept. Edn. rep. Public Exec. Project, 1978; mem. Mich. Gov.'s Cons. Task Force on Volunteerism, 1979—; mem. Mich. Dept. Labor Task Force on Policy Analysis, 1979—; mem. Task Force on Implementation of State of Mich. Full Employment Act, 1979—. Recipient State award Mich. Welfare League, 1965. Mem. Nat. Assn. Public Continuing Adult Edn., Mich. Assn. Public Adult Community Edn., Mich. Community Edn. Assn., Nat. Council State Dirs. Adult Edn. Research in field. Office: Leonard Plaza 309 N Washington Lansing MI 48909

REISTER, RAYMOND ALEX, lawyer; b. Sioux City, Iowa, Dec. 22, 1929; s. Harold William and Anna (Eberhardt) R.; A.B., Harvard, 1952, LL.B., 1955; m. Ruth Elizabeth Alkema, Oct. 7, 1967. Admitted to N.Y. bar, 1956, Minn. bar, 1960; asso. firm Paul, Weiss, Rifkind, Wharton & Garrison, N.Y.C., 1955-56; asso. firm Dorsey, Windhorst, Hannaford, Whitney & Halladay, Mpls., 1959-63, partner, 1964—; instr. law U. Minn. Extension Div., 1964-66. Served to 1st lt. AUS, 1956-59. Mem. Am. Coll. Probate Counsel, Am., Minn., Hennepin County bar assns., Internat. Acad. Estate and Trust Law, Mpls. Soc. Fine Arts (trustee), Minn. Hist. Soc. (dir.). Clubs: Minneapolis, Harvard of Minn. (pres. 1969-70). Editor (with Larry W. Johnson) Minnesota Probate Administration, 1968. Home: 93 Groveland Terr Minneapolis MN 55403 Office: 2300 1st Nat Bank Bldg Minneapolis MN 55402

REITAN, DANIEL KINSETH, educator; b. Duluth, Minn., Aug. 13, 1921; s. Conrad Ulfred and Joy Elizabeth R.; B.S.E.E., N.D. State U., 1946; M.S.E.E., U. Wis., 1949, Ph.D., 1952; m. Marian Anne Stemme, July 16, 1946; children—Debra Leah, Danielle Karen. Control engr. Gen. Electric Co., Schenectady, N.Y., 1946-48; transmission line engr. Gen. Telephone Co., Madison, Wis., 1949-50; mem. faculty Coll. Engring. U. Wis., Madison, 1952—, prof. elec. and computer engring., 1962—, dir. power systems simulation lab., 1968—; cons. in field. Served with U.S. Army, World War II. Recipient Outstanding Tchr. award Polygon Engring. Council. Registered profl. engr., Wis. Mem. IEEE, IEEE Power Engring. Soc., Conf. Internat. des Grands Reseaux Electriques a Haute Tension, Am. Soc. Engring. Edn., Wis. Acad. Scis., Am. Wind Energy Assn., Sigma Xi, Tau Beta Pi, Eta Kappa Nu, Kappa Eta Kappa. Lutheran. Contbr. articles to profl. jours. Patentee in field. Office: Elec and Computer Engring Dept 1425 Johnson Dr Madison WI 53706. *I believe that one's career professionalism and perseverance are key factors in success. In one's personal life, the family should be the center, but not the circumference, about which all activities revolve.*

REITMEISTER, NOEL WILLIAM, fin. planner, investment, ins. and commodity broker; b. Bklyn., Aug. 12, 1938; s. Morris G. and Anna (Miller) R.; B.A. in Economics, Queens Coll., 1960; M.B.A. in Indsl. Psychology and Bus., CUNY, 1969; diploma N.Y. Inst. Fin., 1969; grad. Coll. Fin. Planning, 1974; Ph.D. in Econs. and Fin. Counseling, Am. Western U., 1981; m. Elaine Schendelman, Sept. 16, 1961; children—Gregg Allen, Stephen Michael. Account exec. duPont Walston, Chgo., Gary and Merrillville, Ind., 1969-74; sr. investment broker A.G. Edwards & Sons, Merrillville, 1974-79, v.p.-investments, 1979—; partner Nat. Property Investors, Ind. Investments; ltd. partner Petro Lewis, Oil Income Funds, Nora Assos.; vice chmn. bd. Menorah Credit Union, 1979-81, chmn., 1981—; dir. Arctic Exploration, Inc.; co-founder Leader Publs.; guest speaker, lectr. univs.; cons. and lectr. Calumet Coll. (Ind.); lectr. Purdue U., Hammond, Ind. Bd. dirs. South Suburban HELP, 1968-69; trustee Temple Anshe Sholom, 1975—; local troop coordinator Boy Scouts Am., 1977-78; mem. Anti-Defamation League Cabinet, 1978-80; v.p. Chgo. B'nai B'rith Council, charter mem. The Havorah. Served with USAR, 1960-66. Cert. fin. planner; cert. fin. examiner Coll. Fin. Planning; registered rep. N.Y. Stock Exchange, Am. Stock Exchange, Midwest Stock Exchange, Pacific Stock Exchange, Boston Stock Exchange, PBW Exchange, Chgo. Bd. Trade, Chgo. Mercantile Exchange, Comex, NASD, Chgo. Options Exchange; lic. broker, N.Y., N.J., Conn., Mass., Ohio, Fla., Ariz., Okla., Ill., Ind. Mem. Michiana Fin. Planning, Inst. Certified Fin. Planners, Chgo. Assn. Fin. Planners, Internat. Assn. Fin. Planners (charter), Internat. Soc. Registered Reps., Spl. Edn. Service Support Assn. (co-founder, treas.). Clubs: Masons, Shriners, B'nai B'rith (pres. lodge). Home: 2246 Flossmoor Rd Flossmoor IL 60422 Office: 8300 Mississippi Merrillville IN 46410

REIZEN, MAURICE S., state ofcl.; b. Detroit, Feb. 24, 1919; s. Max and Minna (Chad) R.; B.A., U. Mich., 1940, M.S. in Public Health, 1946; tchrs. cert. Wayne State U., 1946; M.D., U. Rochester (N.Y.), 1950; m. Leanor Grossman, July 18, 1943; children—Mark E., Nancy E. Reizen Serlin, Bruce J. Intern, Grace Hosp., Detroit, 1950-51; pvt. group practice, Warren, Mich., 1951-66; dir. Ingham County (Mich.) Health Dept., 1966-70; dir. Mich. Dept. Public Health, Lansing, 1970-80, chief bur. personal health services, 1981—; asso. prof. medicine Coll. Human Medicine, Mich. State U., East Lansing, 1966—; non-resident lectr. U. Mich., Ann Arbor, 1974—. Served with USAAF, 1941-45. Fellow Am. Acad. Family Physicians; mem. AMA (Physicians Recognition award 1969), Mich. Med. Soc. (citation 1978, 81), Assn. State and Territorial Health Officers (pres. 1974). Home: 1915 Tomahawk Rd Okemos MI 48864 Office: 3500 N Logan St Lansing MI 48909

RELFORD, ARTHUR DOUGLAS, psychiat. social worker; b. E. St. Louis, Ill., July 14, 1925; s. Floyd A. and Frances (Price) R.; B.S. in Edn., So. Ill. U., Carbondale, 1950; M.S.W., Washington U., St. Louis, 1972; children—Linda, Regina, Patricia, Angela, Arthur Douglas II, Robin, Anthony, Juanita, Teresa, Christopher, Darlene. Profl. pianist, trombonist, arranger and composer, St. Louis, 1942—; dir. Sch. Music, Mound Bayou (Miss.) High Sch., 1952-53; band dirs. Lyons (Ga.) Indsl. High Sch., 1955-57; caseworker Ill. Dept. Public Aid, East St. Louis, 1960-72; chief narcotic addiction rehab. act counselor Narcotics Service Council, St. Louis, 1972-74; psychiat. social worker II, St. Louis State Hosp. and Community CLinic, St. Louis, 1974—; grad. sch. practicum instr. St. Louis U., Washington U., U. Mo., St. Louis. Served with USAAF, 1944-46. Cert. social worker, Ill. Mem. Acad. Cert. Social Workers, Nat. Assn. Social Workers, Nat. Assn. Black Social Workers, Am. Correctional Assn., Acad. Criminal Justice Scis., Ill. Welfare Assn., Mo. Assn. Social Welfare, Alpha Phi Alpha. Home: PO Box 14155 St Louis MO 63178 Office: 3927 Olive St St Louis MO 63108

RELFORD, REGINA FRANCES, rehab. counselor; b. St. Louis, Mar. 16, 1952; d. Arthur D. and Clote V. Relford; B.S. in Adminstrn. of Justice, So. Ill. U., Carbondale, 1973; M.Ed., Loyola U., Chgo., 1977. Intern, St. Clair County (Ill.) Criminal Justice System, 1973; rehab. counselor Ill. Div. Vocat. Rehab., Chgo., 1974-79, mem. dir.'s counselors' adv. com., 1975-79; adminstrv. asst. to dep. dir. Ill. Bur. Vocat. Rehab. Services, Springfield, 1979—. Mem. Nat. Rehab. Assn., Am. Personnel and Guidance Assn. Roman Catholic. Home: PO Box 3531 Merchandise Mart Bldg Chicago IL 60654 Office: 200 E Randolph Dr Chicago IL 60601

RELLE, FERENC MATYAS, chemist; b. Gyor, Hungary, June 13, 1922; came to U.S., 1951, natrualized, 1956; s. Ferenc and Elizabeth (Netratics) R.; B.S. in Chem. Engring., Jozsef Nador Poly. U., Budapest, 1944, M.S., 1944; m. Gertrud B. Tubach, Oct. 9, 1946; children—Ferenc, Ava, Attila. Lab. mgr. Karl Kohn Ltd. Co., Landshut, W. Ger., 1947-48; resettlement officer IRO, Munich, 1948-51; chemist Farm Bur. Coop. Assn., Columbus, Ohio, 1951-56; indsl. engr. N. Am. Aviation, Inc., Columbus, 1956-57; research chemist Keever Starch Co., Columbus, 1957-65; research chemist Ross Labs., div. Abbott Labs., Columbus, 1965-70, research scientist, 1970—; cons. in field. Chmn. Columbus and Central Ohio UN Week, 1963; pres. Berwick Manor Civic Assn., 1968; trustee Stelios Stelson Found., 1968-69. Mem. Am. Chem. Soc. (alt. councilor 1973, chmn. long range planning com. Columbus sect. 1972-76, 78-80), Am. Assn. Cereal Chemists (chmn. Cin. sect. 1974-75), Internat. Tech. Inst. (adv. dir. 1977—), Nat. Intercollegiate Soccer Ofcls. Assn., Am. Hungarian Assn., Hungarian Cultural Assn. (pres. 1978-81), Ohio Soccer Ofcls. Assn., Ohio High Sch. Athletic Assn., Germania Singing and Sport Soc. Presbyterian. Club: Civitan (gov. Ohio dist. 1970-71, pres. Eastern Columbus 1962-64, 72-73; internat. gov. of yr. 1971, various awards). Home: 3487 Roswell Dr Columbus OH 43227 Office: 625 Cleveland Ave Columbus OH 43216

REMER, RICHARD CHARLES, banker; b. Des Moines, July 6, 1944; s. Vernon Ralph and Jane Viola (Bush) R.; B.A. in Econs., U. Iowa, 1966, M.A., 1970; m. Deanne Marie Anderson, Oct. 27, 1973; 1 son, Michael Edward. With N.W. Brenton Nat. Bank, Des Moines, 1970—, sr. v.p., 1979—, dir., 1981—. Mem. Johnston Bd. Adjustment, 1977—, sec., 1977, 78, 79; treas. Johnston Bus. Assn., 1978, pres., 1979. Served with U.S. Army, 1967-69. Mem. Am. Bankers Assn., Am. Inst. Banking. Republican. Congregationalist. Clubs: Johnston Lions, N.W. Des Moines Rotary. Home: 5204 N W 64th Pl Des Moines IA 50323 Office: 2805 Beaver Ave Des Moines IA 50310

REMICH, ANTONE FORD, holding co. exec.; b. Chgo., June 15, 1939; s. Antone Charles and Florence (Ford) R.; B.S. in Metall. Engring. and Indsl. Mgmt., Purdue U., 1961; M.B.A. in Fin. and Ops. Mgmt. (Dean's scholar 1968-70), Northwestern U., 1970. Mgmt. cons. Haskins & Sells, Chgo., 1970-72; bus. analyst Trans Union Corp., 1972-75, mgr. program and bus. devel., Lincolnshire, Ill., 1975—. Bd. dirs., v.p. scouting, dir. high adventure program N.E. Ill. council Boy Scouts Am., 1976-79. Served to col. USAR, 1961—. Decorated Silver Star, Bronze Star, Air medal, Army Commendation medal, Combat Inf. Badge. Co-author: Bank Costs for Planning and Control, 1972. Home: 711 Shepard Ct Gurnee IL 60031 Office: 90 Half Day Rd Lincolnshire IL 60015

REMICK, ROBERT JEROME, electrochemist; b. Williamsport, Pa., Dec. 16, 1945; s. Robert Jervine and Katherine Jane (Reiff) R.; B.S., Lock Haven (Pa.) State Coll., 1968; M.Ed., Millersville (Pa.) State U., 1972; Ph.D., Pa. State U., 1978; m. Joyce Marie Villello, Aug. 24, 1968. Tchr. chemistry Middletown (Pa.) public schs., 1968-75; research asst. Pa. State U., 1975-78; research supr. Inst. Gas Tech., Chgo., 1978—. Pres. Royalton (Pa.) Borough Council, 1972-75. Mem. Am. Chem. Soc., AAAS, Electrochem. Soc., Sigma Xi (chpt. research award 1977). Republican. Lutheran. Author, patentee in field. Office: 3424 S State St Chicago IL 60616

REMINGER, RICHARD THOMAS, lawyer; b. Cleve., Apr. 3, 1931; s. Edwin Carl and Theresa Henrietta (Bookmyer) R.; A.B., Case-Western Res. U., 1953; J.D., Cleve.-Marshall Law Sch., 1957; m. Billie Carmen Greer, June 26, 1954; children—Susan Greer, Patricia Allison, Richard Thomas. Admitted to Ohio bar, 1957, Pa. bar, 1978, U.S. Supreme Ct. bar, 1961; personnel and safety dir. Moton Express, Inc., Cleve., 1954-58; mng. partner firm Reminger & Reminger Co., L.P.A., Cleve., 1958—; dir. U.S. Truck Lines, Inc. Del., Cardinal Casualty Co.; mem. nat. claims council adv. bd. Comml. Union Assurance Co., 1980—; lectr. transp. law Fenn Coll., 1960-62, bus. law Case-Western Res. U., 1962-64. Mem. joint com. Cleve. Acad. Medicine and Greater Cleve. Bar Assn. Trustee Cleve. Zool. Soc., Andrew Sch., Huron Road Hosp., Cleve. Served with AC, USNR, 1950-58. Mem. Fedn. Ins. Counsel, Trial Attys. Am. (mem. sect. litigation, also tort and ins. practice), Fed., Am. (com. on law and medicine, profl. responsibility com. 1977—), Internat., Ohio, Cleve. (chmn. med. legal com. 1978-79, profl. liability com. 1977—) bar assns., Motor Carrier Lawyers Assn., Cleve. Def. Attys. Assn., Am. Soc. Hosp. Attys., Soc. Ohio Hosp. Attys., Ohio Assn. Civil Trial Attys., Am. Judicature Soc., Def. Research Inst. (law inst. com. 1977—), Maritime Law Assn. U.S., Am. Coll. Law and Medicine. Clubs: Mayfield Country (dir. 1977—, pres. 1980—), Union, Cleve. Playhouse, Hermit (pres. 1973-75) (Cleve.); Lost Tree (Fla.). Home: 34000 Hackney Rd Hunting Valley OH 44022 Office: Leader Bldg Cleveland OH 44114

REMMERT, BERNARD WAYNE, funeral dir.; b. El Paso, Ill., June 18, 1929; s. Otto A. and Sophie S. (Menssen) R.; Mortuary Sci. degree Butler U., 1954; grad. Ill. Coll. Mortuary Sci., 1955; m. Phyllis Ann Vincent, June 29, 1952; children—Debra Remmert Beschorner, Linda A., Gary L. Mgr., Vincent Meml. Home, Roanoke, Ill., 1955-65; owner, mgr. Remmert Nursing Home, Roanoke, 1957-62; owner, dir. Remmert Funeral Home, Roanoke, 1965—; owner Remmert Ambulance Service, 1965—; owner, dealer Remmert Memls., 1967—; owner, mgr. Lorene's Dress Shop, 1969-79; v.p. Roanoke Enterprises, Inc., 1971-77; partner Remmert Bros. Farm, Eureka, Ill. Mem. Roanoke Benson Unit 60 Bd. Edn., 1966-72, pres., 1971-72; 1st scoutmaster troop 461 Boy Scouts Am., Roanoke, 1956; pres. congregation Lutheran Ch., 1959-60, elder, 1974-78. Served with U.S. Army, 1951-53. Mem. Roanoke Jaycees (charter pres. 1962), Nat. Funeral Dirs. Assn., Ill. Funeral Dirs. Assn., Dist. 8 Ill. Funeral Dirs. Assn. (pres. 1966). Republican. Lutheran. Club: Rotary. Home: 711 Randolph St Roanoke IL 61561 Office: 123 E Broad St Roanoke IL 61561

REMPERT, LAWRENCE ARNOLD, engr.; b. Oak Park, Ill., Oct. 14, 1942; s. Arnold William and Eleanor Emma (Melchin) R.; B.S. in E.E., Purdue U., 1964, M.S. in E.E., 1966; m. Susan Hopkins Wrenn, June 24, 1967; children—Laura Louise, Carl Halder. Mem. tech. staff RCA Labs., Princeton, N.J., 1966-70; tech. advisor to patent dept., corp. staff RCA, Princeton, 1970-72; sr. project engr. Esterline Angus Instrument Co., Indpls., 1972-77, chief digital engr., 1977-79, engring. mgr. digital products, 1979—. Recipient outstanding achievement award RCA Labs., 1969. Mem. Instrument Soc. Am., Tau Beta Pi, Eta Kappa Nu. Episcopalian. Club: Danville (Ind.) Optimist. Patentee in field. Home: 540 N Washington St Danville IN 46122 Office: 1200 Main St Speedway IN 46224

RENCHER, MARK JULIUS, machining co. exec.; b. Huntington, N.Y., Apr. 19, 1947; s. Julius Kilian and Wanda Anne (Kurpita) R.; B.Mech. Engring., U. Detroit, 1969, M.Engring. in Mfg., 1977; M.A., Ball State U., 1974; m. Charlene Starman, May 20, 1972. Jr. engr. LTV Aerospace Corp., Warren, Mich., 1966-68; asso. engr. Burroughs Corp., Plymouth, Mich., 1973-76; tech. asst. to pres. Cleary Devel. Inc., Madison Heights, Mich., 1976—. Served with USAF, 1969-73; mem. Ohio Air NG. Certified mfg. technologist. Mem. ASME, Soc. Die Casting Engrs., Soc. Mfg. Engrs., Mfg. Engring. Inst. U. Detroit, Soc. Plastic Engrs., Am. Powdered Metallurgy Inst. Roman Catholic. Home: 6722 Langle St Clarkston MI 48016 Office: 32033 Edward St Madison Heights MI 48071

RENDLEMAN, GEORGE FRANKLIN, JR., physician; b. St. Louis, Aug. 31, 1929; s. George Franklin and Lorraine (Meyer) R.; B.S., Northwestern U., 1951; M.D., U. Mo., 1958; postgrad. St. Louis U. Law Sch., 1952-54; m. Nancy Lou Smith, Aug. 2, 1963; children—George Franklin III, Carl Christian. Intern, resident St. Louis City Hosp., Ohio State U. Group, 1958-63; practice medicine specializing in surgery, St. Louis, 1963—; pres. Med-Surg., Inc.; mem. staff Deaconess, Mo. Bapt., St. Anthony's, Incarnate Word, Lutheran hosps. Diplomate Am. Bd. Surgery. Fellow A.C.S.; mem. AMA, Mo. State, St. Louis med. assns., Sigma Nu, Phi Beta Pi. Presbyterian. Mason (32 deg., Shriner). Home: 2 Vista Brook Ln Saint Louis MO 63124 Office: 818 Olive St Saint Louis MO 63101

RENDLEN, ALBERT LEWIS, state supreme ct. justice; b. Hannibal, Mo., Apr. 7, 1922; s. Charles E. and Norma (Lewis) R.; B.A., U. Ill., 1943; J.D., U. Mich., 1948; m. Dona Meeker; children—Albert Lewis, Susan Virginia. Admitted to Mo. bar, 1948; practice in Hannibal 1948-74; U.S. commnr. Eastern Dist. Mo., 1953-55; judge St. Louis dist. Mo. Ct. Appeals, 1974-77; justice div. 1, Mo. Supreme Ct., 1977—. Chmn. Mo. Republican Com., 1973-74; bd. regents N.E. Mo. State Coll., 1973-75; mem. nat., dist. adv. council SBA, 1970 bd. dirs. United Fund, 1970; mem. Marion County Family Planning Council, 1965, Marion County Welfare Commn., 1964; pres., 1948, Dist. council Boy Scouts Am., 1949. Served with AUS, 1943-46; to comdr. USCGR, 1951-70. Mem. Am. Bar Assn., Mo. Bar Assn., Hannibal C. of C., VFW, Am. Legion, Navy League, Res. Officers Assn. (past chpt. pres.). Address: Supreme Ct Bldg Jefferson City MO 65101

RENIER, JAMES J. B., bus. systems mfg. co. exec., scientist; B.S. in Chemistry, Coll. St. Thomas; Ph.D. in Phys. Chemistry, Iowa State U. With AEC and Esso Corp., to 1956; with Honeywell, Inc., Mpls., 1956—, corp. v.p. and gen. mgr. data systems ops., 1970-74, v.p. aerospace and def. group, 1974-76, group v.p., 1976-78, corp. exec. v.p., 1978-79, pres. control systems, 1979—, also dir. Office: Honeywell Inc Honeywell Plaza Minneapolis MN 55408*

RENN, LOUIS MATTHEW, heavy equipment mfg. co. exec.; b. Louisville, Dec. 18, 1935; s. Louis M. and Cecilia M. (Schnurr) R.; B.S., Purdue U., 1960; m. Mary Sue Bachman, Aug. 19, 1967; children—Christopher, Mary Beth, Anne. Indsl. engr. Corning Glass Works (N.Y.), 1960-63; supt. inspection, quality assurance supt. Internat. Harvester Co., Louisville, 1963—, mgr. product quality, 1979—. Mem. So. Ind. Dist. Bd. Edn., 1978—, pres., 1979-81. Served with USAF, 1960. Cert. quality engr., Ky. Mem. Am. Soc. for Quality Control (chief proctor cert. com. 1980-81, chmn. Louisville sect. 1978-79), Am. Foundrymen's Soc. (vice chmn. Kentuckiana chpt. 1981), Productivity Internat., Kappa Sigma. Republican. Roman Catholic. Clubs: Toastmasters (sec. 1979), K.C. Author: The 5/1 Quality Manual, 1980. Home: 1344 Miller Ln New Albany IN 47150

Office: Internat Harvester Co 5005 Crittenden Dr Louisville KY 40221

RENNEKE, EARL WALLACE, state senator; b. St. Peter, Minn., Mar. 10, 1928; s. John Gottfried and Olga (Strand) R.; student U. Minn.; m. Marjorie Elizabeth Eckberg, 1951; children—Rochelle, Lynnette, Kristin. Farmer, LeSueur, Minn.; mem. Minn. Senate, 1969—. Vice chmn. Sibley County Republican party, 1966-67, chmn., 1968-69. Mem. Minn. Farm Bur. Fedn. Lutheran. Office: 121A State Office Bldg St Paul MN 55155*

RENNINGER, LA DONNA JEAN TROUTMAN, social worker, child therapist; b. Walla Walla, Wash., July 5, 1949; d. Elder Marvin W. and Lillian P. (Trautman) Troutman; B.A. in Psychology and Sociology, Columbia Union Coll., 1971; M.S.W. (Univ. scholar), Wayne State U., 1978; m. George C. Renninger, Apr. 18, 1971. Takoma Park (Md.) exchange student, Jequie, Brazil, 1969; unit mgr. Washington San. and Hosp., Takoma Park, Md., 1969-71; tchr. Bermuda Inst., St. George's Secondary, 1971-74; office mgr. Chubb & Son/Colonial Life/Satullo Co., Detroit, 1974-76; social worker St. Ambrose Project, Detroit, 1977-79; sch. social worker, child therapist Roseville (Mich.) Community Schs., 1978—; cons. in field. Active state lobbying for edn. legis., children's rights, abuse and neglect prevention legis. Cert. clin. social worker. Mem. Am. Assn. Psychiat. Services for Children, Nat. Assn. Social Workers, Nat. Assn. Sch. Social Workers, Acad. Cert. Social Workers, Mich. Inter-Profl. Assn., Mich. Assn. Emotionally Disturbed Children, Am. Fedn. Tchrs. (rep. 1978-80). Clubs: Stamp Collectors; Campers of Mich. (Guthrie Lakes). Home: 1520 Linwood Ave Royal Oak MI 48067 Office: 18975 Church St Roseville MII 48066

RENNINGER, MARILYN H., nun; b. Hoagland, Ind., Jan. 5, 1935; d. Henry S. and Cecilia (Hoffman) R.; B.A., Coll. St. Francis, 1968; M.A., DePaul U., 1975. Joined Franciscan Sisters of the Sacred Heart, Roman Catholic Ch., 1953; tchr., St. Joseph Sch., Dyer, Ind., 1956-60; tchr., St. Charles Sch., Ft. Wayne, Ind., 1960-64, teaching asst. prin., 1964-67; teaching prin. St. Mary Sch., Park Forest, Ill., 1967-70, prin., 1970-74; mem. Gen. Council, Franciscan Sisters of the Sacred Heart, Mokena, Ill., 1974-79, superior gen., 1979—. Cert. tchr., adminstr., Ill. Mem. Nat. Cath. Ednl. Assn., Nat. Assn. Elem. Sch. Prins., Fedn. Franciscan Sisters U.S., Cath. Hosp. Assn., Internat. Union Superiors Gen., Consortium Perfectae Caritatis, Soc. Religious Vocations, Inst. Religious Life. Developed, implemented curriculum for multi-aged classes. Home and Office: Rural Route 1 Saint Francis Woods Mokena IL 60448

RENO, OTTIE WAYNE, former judge; b. Pike County, Ohio, Apr. 7, 1929; s. Eli Enos and Arbannah Belle (Jones) R.; Asso. in Bus. Adminstrn., Franklin U., 1949; LL.B., Franklin Law Sch., 1953; J.D., Capital U., 1966; grad. Coll. Juvenile Justice, U. Nev., 1973; m. Janet Gay McCann, May 22, 1947; children—Ottie Wayne II, Jennifer Lynn, Lorna Victoria. Admitted to Ohio bar, 1953; practiced in Pike County; recorder Pike County, 1957-73; common pleas judge Probate and Juvenile divs. Pike County, 1973-79. Mem. adv. bd. Ohio Youth Services, 1972-74. Mem. Democratic Central Com. Camp Creek precinct, 1956-72; sec. Pike County Central Com., 1960-70; chmn. Pike County Democratic Exec. Com., 1971-72; del. Dem. Nat. Conv., 1972; mem. Ohio Dem. Central Com., 1969-70; Dem. candidate 6th Ohio dist. U.S. Ho. of Reps., 1966; pres. Scioto Valley Local Sch. Dist., 1962-66. Recipient Distinguished Service award Ohio Youth Commn., 1974; 6 Outstanding Jud. Service awards Ohio Supreme Ct.; 15 times Ala. horsehoes pitching champion; named to Nat. Horseshoe Pitchers Hall of Fame; mem. internat. sports exchange, U.S. and Republic South Africa, 1972. Mem. Ohio, Pike County (pres. 1964) bar assns., Nat. Council Juvenile Ct. Judges, Am. Legion. Mem. Ch. of Christ. Author: Story of Horseshoes, 1963; Pitching Championship Horseshoes, 1971, 2d rev. edit., 1975. Home: 148 Reno Rd Lucasville OH 45648

RENSEL, LLOYD ALOYSIUS, univ. adminstr; b. Cleve., May 25, 1921; s. Lloyd R. and Florence Marie (Mahoney) R.; A.B. in Psychology, U. Dayton, 1943; m. Bette J. Hempelman, Aug. 21, 1943; 1 son, John Edward. Employee counselor White Motor Co., Cleve., 1945—46; dir. testing services, coordinator student employment U. Dayton (Ohio), 1946—; cons. McGraw-Hill Calif. Test Bur., 1970—76. Chmn., St. Brendan Fund Raising Program, 1961—64. Served with U.S. Army, 1942—45. Recipient Chpt. award Montgomery County U. Dayton Alumni Assn., 1953; Parish award, 1965; Sponsor's award U. Dayton Arena, 1967; cert. of appreciation U. Dayton, 1971. Mem. Nat. Vocat. Guidance Assn., Am., Ohio, Miami Valley personnel and guidance assns., Nat. Catholic Counselors Assn., Nat. Travel Club, U. Dayton Alumni Assn., Univ. Colleagues Assn. Clubs: Optimists, K.C. Democrat. Roman Catholic. Home: 5177 Scarsdale Dr Dayton OH 45440 Office: Univ Dayton Dayton OH 45469

RENTER, LOIS IRENE HUTSON, librarian; b. Lowden, Iowa, Oct. 23, 1929; d. Thomas E. and Lulu Mae (Barlean) Hutson; B.A. cum laude, Cornell Coll., Iowa, 1965; M.A., U. Iowa, 1968; m. Karl A. Renter, Jan. 3, 1948; children—Susan Elizabeth, Rebecca Jean, Karl Geoffrey. Tchr. Spanish, Mt. Vernon (Iowa) High Sch., 1965-67; head librarian Am. Coll. Testing Program, Iowa City, Iowa, 1968—; vis. instr. U. Iowa Sch. Library Sci., 1972—. Mem. Am. Soc. Info. Sci., ALA, Spl. Libraries Assn., Phi Beta Kappa. Methodist. Home: 1125 29th St Marion IA 52302 Office: Box 168 Iowa City IA 52243

RENTSCHLER, ALVIN EUGENE, mech. engr.; b. Havre, Mont., Oct. 24, 1940; s. Alvin Joseph and Pauline Elizabeth (Browning) R.; B.S., Mont. State U., 1964; m. Marilyn Joan Bostrom, Dec. 7, 1974; children—Elizabeth Louise, Richard Eugene, Alison Lynn. Dist. mgr. Woodmen Accident and Life Co., Helena, Mont., 1966-69; profl. med. rep. Abbott Labs., Great Falls, Mont., 1969-72; design engr. Anaconda Co. (Mont.), 1974-77; ops. and maintenance engr. Rochester (Minn.) Meth. Hosp., 1977—; mem. engring. coordinating com. Franklin Heating Sta., 1977—. Bd. dirs. Mont. affiliate Am. Diabetes Assn., 1975-78, pres. Butte-Anaconda chpt., 1974-77; mem. citizens adv. com. Rochester Area Vocat.-Tech. Inst., 1978—. Recipient Greatest Achievement award Combined Tng., Inc., 1977. Mem. ASME, Am. Soc. Hosp. Engrs., Am. Hosp. Assn. Mem. Covenant Ch. Office: 201 W Center St Rochester MN 55901

RENTSCHLER, WILLIAM HENRY, bus. cons.; b. Hamilton, Ohio, May 11, 1925; s. Peter Earl and Barbara (Schlosser) R.; grad. Berkshire Sch., Sheffield, Mass.; A.B., Princeton, 1949; m. Sylvia Gale Angevin, Dec. 20, 1948; children—Sarah Yorke Rentschler Mittendorf, Peter Ferris, Mary Angevin, Phoebe Mason; m. 2d, Martha Snowdon, Jan. 20, 1967; 1 dau., Hope Snowdon. Reporter, Cin. Times-Star, 1946; successively reporter, exec. trainee, asst. to exec. editor Mpls. Star & Tribune, 1949-53; mgr. pub. relations The Northern Trust Co., Chgo., 1953, mgr. pub. relations and advt., 1953-54, 2d v.p., 1954-56; pres. Martha Washington Kitchens, Inc., 1957-68, Stevens Candy Kitchens, Inc., 1957-66; investor closely-held cos., 1970—; bus. and mktg. cons., 1973—; chmn. Cherokee Assos., 1978—, HR Assos., 1979—, Medart, Inc., 1981, Lochinvar Corp., 1981—; dir. Am. Internat. Investments, Inc.; commentator radio sta. WBEZ/FM; freelance writer. Spl. adviser Pres.'s Nat. Program for Vol. Action, 1969; bd. dirs. Better Boys Found., John Howard Assn., Fellowship of Christian Athletes; Republican candidate U.S. Senate, 1960, 70; chmn. Ill. Citizens for Nixon, 1968; pres. Young Reps. Ill., 1957-59; exec. com. United Rep. Fund Ill., 1963-69; former trustee Rockford Coll., Goodwill Industries. Recipient 1st ann. Buddy Hackett award for service to young men, 1968. Clubs: Onwentsia (Lake Forest, Ill.); Execs., Economic, City, Tavern (Chgo.); Princeton (N.Y.C.). Home: 301 Oakdale Ave Lake Forest IL 60045

REPP, DUANE LESLIE, engine and generator distbn. exec.; b. South Bend, Ind., Apr. 26, 1931; s. Earl C. and Marie A. (Zepka) R.; B.S. in Mech. Engring., Purdue U., 1953; m. Shirline L. Bierbaum, Apr. 14, 1956; children—Duane M., Mark A., Thomas S. Sales engr. Cummins Engine Co., Columbus, Ind., 1953, 55-57, indsl. sales supr., 1957-58, regional rep., Chgo., 1958-60, regional mgr., N.Y.C., 1960-62, constrn. and indsl. div. mgr., 1962-66, div. mgr., 1966-70, gen. mgr. N.Am. sales and service, Columbus, 1970-72, chmn. indsl. distbr. council, 1978, pres. Cummins Wis., Inc., Milw., 1972—; pres. DMT Corp., Milw., 1973—; dir. First Nat. Bank Wauwautosa; mem. Perkins Distbr. Council, 1981—. Chmn., Met. Hwy Users Comf., Milw., 1973-81; vice-chmn. Wis. Hwy. Users Conf., 1981—; trustee Univ. Lake Sch., Hartland, Wis., 1975—, v,p., 1981—; chmn. fund dr. St. Clare Ch., North Lake, Wis., 1975-76; mem. Chenequa Village Planning Commn., 1978—; commr. Lake Area Communication System, 1979-80. Served with USAF, 1953-55. Recipient President's E award, 1979. Mem. U.S., Milw. chambers commerce, Wis. Mfrs. Assn., Milw. World Trade Assn., Wis. Motor Carriers, Wis. Equipment Distbrs. Assn. (v.p. 1979-80, pres. 1980-82), Am. Automobile Assn. (dir. Wis. div. 1976—), Hwy. Users Fedn. (dir. 1977-80). Republican. Roman Catholic. Clubs: Kiwanis, Wisconsin, Chenequa Country (dir. 1978—, sec. 1978-79, v.p. 1979-80, pres. 1981-82). Office: 1921 S 108th St Milwaukee WI 53227

REPPERGER, DANIEL WILLIAM, elec. engr.; b. Charleston, S.C., Nov. 24, 1942; s. Daniel William and Mary (Schurer) R.; B.S.E.E., Rensselaer Poly. Inst., 1967, M.S.E.E., 1968; Ph.D. in Elec. Engring., Purdue U., 1973; m. Ruth S. Hammond, Nov. 26, 1968; children—Lisa Ann, Daniel William. Teaching asst., David Ross research fellow Purdue U., 1968-73; NRC postdoctoral fellow, 1973-74; systems analyst Systems Research Lab., Dayton, Ohio, 1974-75; systems analyst Aerospace Med. Research Lab., Wright Patterson AFB, Dayton, 1975—; lectr. math. dept. Air Force Inst. Tech., 1977-78. NATO grantee, 1978. Mem. IEEE (Schuck award 1979), AAAS, Internat. Assn. Math. Modeling, Ohio Soc. Profl. Engrs., N.Y. Acad. Scis., Sigma Xi, Sigma Phi Epsilon, Tau Beta Pi, Eta Kappa Nu, Dayton Natural History Soc., Amateur Athletic Union, U.S. Judo Assn. Roman Catholic. Contbr. articles to profl. jours. Home: 711 Kirkwood Dr Vandalia OH 45377 Office: Bldg 33 Air Force Aerospace Med Research Lab Wright Patterson AFB Dayton OH 45433

RESLER, PAUL EDWARD, optometrist; b. Pittsburg, Kans., Aug. 21, 1922; s. L.M. and Margaret (Kelly) R.; A.B., Kans. U., 1948; B.S., Ill. Coll. Optometry, 1952, O.D., 1953; m. Marion M. Twardokus, Oct. 8, 1953; children—John L., Tammy J. Pvt. practice optometry, Kans., 1953-58; mem. edn. dept. Plastic Contact Lens Co., Chgo., 1959-60; dir. St. Louis Wesley-Jessen, 1960-64, regional mgr. Midwest, St. Louis, 1965-67; pvt. practice, Florissant, Mo., 1967—, Chesterfield, Mo., 1975—; pres. Resler Optometry Inc., 1974—; co-chmn. membership com. Nat. Eye Research Found. Served with USN, 1942-46. Fellow Nat. Eye Research Found. (Distinguished Service award 1974), Internat. Orthokeratology Soc.; mem. Am., Mo., St. Louis optometric assns., Am. (life), Mo. (life) optometric founds., Am. Pub. Health Assn., Florissant Fine Arts Council (charter), St. Louis Art Mus. (life), St. Louis Symphony Soc. (sustaining), Heart of Am. Contact Lens Soc., Better Vision Inst., Friends of St. Louis Zool. Soc. (life). Clubs: Elks, Rotary. Internat. lectr. contact lenses. Home: 1660 Featherstone Dr Saint Louis MO 63131 Office: 14386 Woodlake Dr Woodsmill Profl Campus Chesterfield MO 63017

RESNIK, MARVIN, optometrist; b. Kiev, Russia, Jan. 24, 1921; s. Jacob and Anna (Cohen) R.; came to U.S., 1929, naturalized, 1943; student Case Inst. Tech., 1937-38; B.Sc., Ohio State U., 1939, O.D., 1946; student U. Wyo., 1943, State U. Iowa, 1943; m. Elizabeth Stalnaker, Nov. 28, 1942; children—Judy, Charles. Practice optometry, East Akron, Ohio, 1946—. Trustee Ohio Lions Eye Research Found. (charter). Served with AUS, 1942-46. Decorated Bronze Star. Mem. Am., Ohio optometric assns. Jewish (soloist congregation choir 1947-73). Mason (Shriner), Lion (pres. 1965-66); mem. B'nai B'rith. Home: 202 Durward Rd Akron OH 44313 Office: 863 E Market St Akron OH 44305

RESTIVO, RAYMOND M., health assn. exec., pub. health cons.; b. Chgo., Aug. 19, 1934; s. Frank M. and Angeline (Franzone) R.; B.S.A., Loyola U., Chgo., 1956; certificate pub. health adminstrn. U. Ill., 1968; C.A.E., 1978; m. Sharon Restivo; children—Laura, Maria, Mark, Susan, Steven, John, Tony. Adminstrv. asst. to pres. of S.K. Culver Co., Chgo., 1954-59; projects coordinator Chgo. Heart Assn., 1959-66, exec. dir., 1973—; pub. health adminstr. Chgo. Bd. Health, 1966-73, mem. advisory com., 1967-73, mem. editorial rev. com. for newsletter, 1968-73; cons. community health to various pub., vol. and ofcl. health agys., 1962—; del. to Pub. Service Inst. of City of Chgo., 1973; notary pub., Cook County (Ill.), 1971—; mem. oral bd. examiners for cardiovascular technologist, City of Chgo. Civil Service Commn., 1971-73. Sec., Morris Fishbein, Jr. Meml. Fund, 1973—; mem. Zoning Bd. Appeals, Forest Park, Ill., 1964-68; mem. Health Services Task Force, Oak Park, Ill., 1974-75; bd. dirs. Chgo. Health Research Found., 1976—; mem. Planning Com. 4th Nat. Congress Quality of Life AMA, 1977-78. Recipient Meritorious Service award Village of Oak Park, 1975. Mem. Ill. Pub. Health Assn. (mem. policy com. 1971-73, mem. health issues com. 1972-73), Am. Pub. Health Assn., Am. Heart Assn. Profl. Staff Soc., Am. Soc. Assn. Execs., Chgo. Soc. Assn. Execs., Am. Mgmt. Assn., Nat. Assn. of Emergency Care Technicians, Epidemiology Club of Chgo., City of Chgo. Exec. Devel., Loyola U. alumni assns. Clubs: Tower, University. Contbr. articles on heart disease to profl. publs. Office: 20 N Wacker Dr Chicago IL 60606

RESZKA, ALFONS, computer systems architect; b. Imielin, Poland, Dec. 17, 1924; s. Alfons and Maria (Galazka) R.; B.Sc., U. London, 1954; M.S. in E.E., Northwestern U., 1960; Ph.D., Northwestern U., 1976; m. Betty Reszka; children—Ann, Elizabeth, Alfred, Cathrine. Engr., British Jeffrey Diamond, Wakefield, Eng., 1954-55; lectr. Bradford (Eng.) Tech. Coll., 1955-56; engr. A.C. Nielson, Chgo., 1956-59; with Teletype Corp., Skokie, Ill., 1959-80, project dir., 1969-75, sr. staff engr., 1975-80; cons. data base mgmt. systems Bell Labs., Naperville, Ill., 1980—; prof. info. sci. Northeastern Ill. U., Chgo., 1980—. Mem. IEEE, Computer Soc., Tech. Com. of Computer Architecture. Patentee in electronics. Home: PO Box 373 Northbrook IL 60062 Office: Bell Labs 1100 Naperville Rd Naperville IL 60566

RETZER, MARY ELIZABETH HELM (MRS. WILLIAM RAYMOND RETZER), librarian; b. Balt.; d. Francis Leslie C. and Edna (Smith) Helm; B.A., Western Md. Coll., 1940; M.A., Columbia U., 1946; postgrad. George Washington U., Ind. U., U. Ill., Ill. State U., Bradley U.; Ph.D., Western Colo. U., 1972; m. William Raymond Retzer, June 28, 1945; children—Lesley Elizabeth, April Christine. Mem. faculty Rockville (Md.) Bd. Edn., 1940-47, elementary supr., 1945-47; cons. librarian Bergan High Sch., 1964-67; condr. library sci. course in reference Bradley U., 1966—; librarian Hines Elementary Sch., 1963-66, Roosevelt Jr. High Sch., 1966-69; head librarian Manual High Sch., Peoria, Ill., 1969—. Instr. water safety courses ARC, summers 1940—; pres. women's bd. Salvation Army, 1952-54; mem. Crippled Children's Adv. Com., Peoria, 1957-60; mem. women's adv. bd. Peoria Journal Star, 1970-73; active various community drives. Mem. ALA, Ill., Ill. Valley (pres. 1971-72) library assns., NEA, Ill. (audio visual com. 1972-74), Peoria edn. assns., AAUW, Internat. Platform Assn., Ill. Assn. Sch. Librarians (certification com. 1973-75). Republican. Presbyn. Mem. Order Eastern Star. Clubs: Ill. State University Administrators, Willowknolls Country. Home: 1317 W Moss Ave Peoria IL 61606

RETZER, WILLIAM RAYMOND, ret. indsl. hygiene engr.; b. Bklyn.; s. William Michael and Mildred Adalaide (Engles) R.; B.S. in Chem. Engring., Lehigh U., 1934; s. Elizabeth Helm, June 28, 1945; children—Lesley Elizabeth, April Christine Meacham. Control chemist Dupont Co., Nat. Lead Co., 1934-36; indsl. hygiene and safety engr. Pulmosan Co., 1936-34, Ky. Health Dept., 1940-42, Md. Health Dept., 1946-47; indsl. hygiene and safety engr. East Peoria plant Catepillar Tractor Co., 1947-68, worldwide plants, 1968-77. Mem. Peoria mayor's coms. noise and smoke abatement; mem. Ill. Com. Indsl. Hygiene. Served to maj. USAAF, 1942-46. Diplomate Am. Bd. Indsl. Hygiene. Mem. Am. Indsl. Hygiene Assn., Am. Acad. Indsl. Hygiene, Am. Pub. Health Assn. Club: Shriners, Masons (Scottish Rite). Home: 1317 W Moss Ave Peoria IL 61606

RETZLAFF, WAYNE ALFRED, utility co. exec.; b. Cooperstown, N.D., July 17, 1942; s. Carrol Bernard and Shirley Lucille (Watne) R.; student U. N.D., 1961; A. in Bus. Adminstrn., Dakota Bus. Coll., Fargo, N.D., 1964; m. Elaine Marie Erickson, June 26, 1965; children—Sara, Dirk, Angela, Marja, Cody. With No. States Power Co., Fargo, 1964-70; radio communication sales rep. Motorola, Inc., Schaumburg, Ill., 1970-73, zone sales mgr., 1973-75, utility account exec. in N.D. and S.D., 1975-77; gen. mgr. McKenzie Electric Coop., Inc., Watford City, N.D., 1977—. Vice chmn. Watford City Planning Commn., 1978-81; bd. dirs. Upper Mo. Luth. Bible Camp, Epping, N.D., 1979-81. Mem. Watford City Assn. Commerce (dir. 1979—), N.D. Rural Electric Coop. Mgrs. Assn., N.D. Power Use Council (dir. 1979—, pres. 1981), N.D. Jaycees (Outstanding Chpt. Pres. award 1981), Bismarck Jaycees (pres. 1971), Am. Legion. Clubs: Rotary, Elks, Eagles. Home: 703 Park Ave E Watford City ND 58854 Office: East of City Watford City ND 58854

RETZLOFF, DAVID GEORGE, educator; b. Pitts., Feb. 19, 1939; s. John Joseph and Georgia Ruth (Hook) R.; B.S., U. Pitts., 1963, M.S., 1965, Ph.D., 1967; postgrad. Kans. State U., 1970-73, U. Houston, 1974-75; m. Debra Rae Renz, July 31, 1971. Wetenschaplijk medewerker U. Delft (The Netherlands), 1967-68; research asso. U. Colo., Boulder, 1968-69; asst. prof. Kans. State U., Manhattan, 1969-73; research engr. Exxon Research and Engring. Co., Baytown, Tex., 1973-75; asst. prof. chem. engring. U. Mo., Columbia, 1975—. Served with USAF, 1956-60. Mem. AAAS, Am. Inst. Physics, Am. Chem. Soc., Am. Inst. Chem. Engring., Am. Math. Soc., Sigma Xi. Republican. Roman Catholic. Home: 1461 S Mesa Dr Columbia MO 65201 Office: U Mo Dept Chem Engring Columbia MO 65201

REUBEN, DON H., lawyer; b. Chgo., Sept. 1, 1928; s. Michael B. and Sally (Chapman) R.; B.S., Northwestern U., 1949, J.D., 1952; m. Evelyn Long, Aug. 27, 1948 (div.); children—Michael Barrett, Timothy Don, Jeffrey Long, Howard Ellis; m. 2d, Jeannette Hurley Haywood, Dec. 13, 1971; stepchildren—Harris Hurley, Jeannette Hope, Edward Gregory. Admitted to Ill. bar, 1952; practiced with firm Kirkland & Ellis, Chgo., 1952-78; now sr. partner Reuben & Proctor; gen. counsel for Tribune Co. and subsidiaries, Chgo. Bears Football Club, Inc., Catholic Archdiocese of Chgo.; spl. asst. atty. gen. State of Ill., 1963-64, 69—; counsel spl. session Ill. Ho. of Reps., 1964, for Ill. treas. for congl., state legis. and jud. reapportionment, 1963—; spl. fed. ct. master, 1968-70. Dir. Lake Shore Nat. Bank. Mem. citizens adv. bd. to Sheriff Cook County, 1962-66; mem. jury instrns. com., 1963-68, com. rules Ill. Supreme Ct., 1963-73; mem. pub. relations com. Nat. Conf. State Trial Judges; mem. Chgo. Better Schs. Com., 1968—, Chgo. Crime Commn., 1970—; mem. supervisory panel Fed. Defender Program. Mem. nat. legacy com. Multiple Sclerosis Soc., also vice chmn. Central region; bd. dirs. Lincoln Park Zool. Soc., United Cerebral Palsy Assn. Chgo.; mem. citizens bd. Loyola U. of Chgo.; trustee Northwestern U., Pitzer Coll.; exec. com. U. Chgo. Citizen's Com., vis. com. Law Sch., 1975-78. Mem. Ill., Chgo. (chmn. subcom. on propriety and regulation of contingent fees com. devel. law 1966-69) Am. (standing com. on fed. judiciary 1973-79) bar assns., Am. Law Inst., Am. Judicature Soc., Fellows Am. Bar Found., Bar Assn. 7th Fed. Circuit, Am. Coll. Trial Lawyers (com. on complex litigation, former mem. rule 23 com.), Internat. Acad. Trial Lawyers, Ill. Trial Lawyers Assn., Assn. Trial Lawyers Am., Am. Arbitration Assn. (nat. panel arbitrators) Phi Eta Sigma, Beta Alpha Psi, Beta Gamma Sigma, Order of Coif. Clubs: University, Chicago, Tavern, Mid-Am., Chgo. Yacht, Mid-Day (Chgo.); Comml.; Dunham Woods Riding. Lectr. on libel, slander, privacy and freedom of press, corporate takeovers and trial tactics. Home: 2430 Lake View Ave Chicago IL 60614 Office: 19 S LaSalle St Chicago IL 60603

REUSS, CARL FREDERICK, sociologist, ch. orgn. exec.; b. Phila., June 7, 1915; s. Charles F. and Marie (Kick) R.; B.S., U. Va., 1934, M.S., 1935, Ph.D., 1937; m. Thelma Lucille Steinmann, June 24, 1938; children—Paula Lucille (Mrs. Robert Schanz), Ellen Marie (Mrs. Thomas Jeppesen), Betty Jeanne (Mrs. Wayne Shovelin). Asst. rural sociologist State Coll. Wash., 1937-44; social sci. analyst U.S. Dept. Agr., Berkeley, Calif., 1944; prof. sociology Capital U., 1944-48; dean of faculty Wartburg Coll., 1948-51; exec. sec. Bd. for Christian Social Action, Am. Luth. Ch., Columbus, Ohio, 1951-60; dir. research and analysis Am. Luth. Ch., Mpls., 1960-81, exec. asst. to pres. bishop, 1981—. Sec. Commn on Inner Missions, Luth. World Fedn., 1952-63; mem. com. on church and soc. World Council Chs., 1954-61; del. 1968 assembly World Council Chs.; del. assemblies Luth. World Fedn., 1957, 63, 70; mem. various coms. Lutheran Council U.S.A. Bd. dirs., v.p. conf. religious leaders Nat. Safety Council, 1973-78. Mem. Am. Sociol. Assn., Rural Sociol. Soc., Nat. Council Family Relations, Phi Kappa Phi, Alpha Kappa Delta. Editor: The Christian in His Social Living, 1960, Conscience and Action, 1971. Home: 5311 Vincent Ave S Minneapolis MN 55410 Office: 422 S 5th St Minneapolis MN 55415

REUSS, HENRY S(CHOELLKOPF), congressman; b. Milw., Feb. 22, 1912; s. Gustav A. and Paula (Schoellkopf) R.; A.B., Cornell U., 1933; LL.B., Harvard, 1936; m. Margaret Magrath, Oct. 24, 1942; children—Christopher, Michael, Jacqueline, Anne. Admitted to Wis. bar, 1936, practiced in Milw., 1936-55; lectr. Wis. State Coll., Milw., 1950-51; asst. corp. counsel Milwaukee County, 1939-40; asst. gen. counsel OPA, Washington, 1941-42; dep. gen. counsel Marshall Plan, Paris, France, 1949; spl. prosecutor Milw. County Grand Jury, 1950; personal counsel to Sec. State in reapportionment case Wis. Supreme Ct., 1953; mem. 84th-97th congresses from 5th Dist. Wis. Mem. legal adv. com. Nat. Resources Bd., Washington, 1948-52; chmn. Joint Economic Com. Mem. Milw. Sch. Bd., 1953-54; chmn. clubs and orgns. com. Milw. March of Dimes, 1953; nat. adv. bd. Am. Youth

Hostels. Bd. visitors Cornell U. Coll. Arts and Scis. Served from 2d lt. to capt. 63d, 75th Inf. Divs., AUS, 1943-45; chief price control br. Office Mil. Govt. Germany, 1945. Decorated Bronze Star. Mem. Children's Service Soc. (dir.), Jr. Bar Assn. of Milw. (vice chmn.), Milwaukee County (chmn. constn. and citizenship com.), Milw. bar assns., Chi Psi Alumni Assn. (v.p.). Club: Milw. City. Alumni trustee Harvard Law Rev., 1956-60. Author: The Critical Decade, 1964; Revenue Sharing, Crutch or Catalyst, 1970; On the Trail of the Ice Age, 1976; To Save Our Cities, 1977. Home: 517 E Wisconsin Milwaukee WI 53202 Office: 2413 Rayburn House Office Bldg Washington DC 20515 also 517 E Wisconsin Ave Milwaukee WI 53202

REUTER, HELEN HYDE, psychologist; b. McGehee, Ark., July 26, 1917; d. John Lloyd and Sallie Elizabeth (Holcomb) Hyde; B.A., Westmar Coll., 1965; A.M., U. S.D., 1969; L.H.D., Sioux Empire Coll., 1970; Ph.D., Northgate Grad. Sch., 1979; m. George S. Reuter, Jr., Aug. 18, 1956; children—Don N., M. Allan, K.L. Postmaster, College Heights, Ark., 1952-65; counselor various pub. schs., 1965-70; sch. psychologist New Madrid County (Mo.) Pub. Schs., 1970-75, Oak Park and River Forest (Ill.) high schs., 1975—; cons. in field. Named Mother of Yr., Monticello, Ark., 1960. Mem. Ill. Psychol. Assn., Nat. Assn. Sch. Psychologists, AAUW, P.E.O., Council Exceptional Children, Assn. Learning Disabilities, Profl. Counselors Assn., Psi Chi, Alpha Chi, Phi Delta Kappa, Delta Kappa Gamma. Democrat. Baptist. Author: (with G.S. Reuter, Jr., A.M. Mintz) One Blood, 1964; (with G.S. Reuter) Democracy and Quality Education, 1965; contbr. articles to profl. jours. Home: 430 Geneva Ave Bellwood IL 60104 Office: 201 N Scoville Ave Oak Park IL 60302

REVERE, AMIE LEE, educator; b. East St. Louis, Ill., Aug. 30, 1935; d. Howard and Viola Brooks; B.S., Central State U., Ohio, 1957; M.Ed., Miami U., Ohio, 1970; children—Bridget Renee, Shelly Alane, Lorna Irene. Tchr., Public Schs. Cleve., 1957-58, Dayton (Ohio), 1959-69; dir. community sch. Dayton Bd. Edn., 1969-71, asst. prin., 1971-75; dir. curriculum and instrn. Jefferson Twp. Bd. Edn., Dayton, 1975-79, asst. supt., 1978-81; adj. prof. U. Dayton, 1975-81, asst. prof., 1981—. Vice pres. Montgomery County Parks and Recreation Bd., 1980, 81. Kettering Found. fellow, 1976; named Outstanding Woman of Yr., Iota Phi Lambda, 1981. Mem. S.W. Assn. Supervision and Curriculum Devel., Ohio Assn. Supervision and Curriculum Devel., Assn. Supervision and Curriculum Devel., Phi Delta Kappa, Delta Kappa Gamma, Alpha Kappa Alpha. Baptist. Home: 6169 Dayton Farmersville Rd Dayton OH 45418 Office: 300 College Park U Dayton Dayton OH 45469

REX, LINDA KAY, retail exec.; b. Ft. Madison, Iowa, Jan. 24, 1949; d. Richard Thomas and Dorothy May Hall; student Indian Hills Community Coll., Ottumwa, Iowa; m. James Wesley Rex, Apr. 2, 1966; 1 dau., Lissa Dawn. With Rider Nursery & Floral Co., Farmington, Iowa, 1971-77, Harmeier Tax Service, 1977-78; clk. Van Buren County Ct. House, Keosauqua, Iowa, 1977-78; pres. R-2 Inc., agrl. and recreation supplies, Bonaparte, Iowa, 1974—; owner R-2 Supply, retail store and tax service, Bonaparte, 1975—; sales agt. Van Buren Realty, 1981; horse trainer and owner, 1965—. Founder, 1975, since leader Trot Right In 4-H Club; bd. dirs. Van Buren Riding Club, 1977, sec-treas., 1978-79; chmn. Bonaparte Pony Express Riders for Easter Seals, 1977-78; treas., tourist promotion dir., mem. budget and legis. coms. Van Buren Devel. Assn., 1980, adminstrv. asst., 1980-81; bd. dirs. Van Buren County Fair, 1981; project dir. Van Buren Fine Arts Council, 1981. Mem. Nat. Family Opinion. Author articles in field. Address: Rural Route 2 Bonaparte IA 52620

REY, LUCY DAVIS, sociologist, educator; b. Oklahoma City, Sept. 26, 1938; d. Howard and Dorothy (Kennedy) Davis; B.A., Wellesley Coll., 1960; M.A., U. Chgo., 1964; Ph.D. (fellow), U. Notre Dame, 1976; m. Charles Albert Rey, Aug. 20, 1960; children—Kristin, David. Tchr. social studies Thornton Twp High Sch., Harvey, Ill., 1962-64; instr. (part-time) Western Mich. U., Kalamazoo, 1974-75; asst. prof. Kalamazoo Coll., 1975-76; asst. prof. sociology and anthropology North Central Coll., Naperville, Ill., 1976—. Mem. Citizens Adv. Bd., Naperville public schs., 1977; mem. Naperville Task Force, YWCA, 1978; mem. ministry and council com. Unitarian-Universalist Ch. of DuPage county, Ill., 1977—; mem. area advisory council Cook County-DuPage County Health Systems Agency, 1979—. Mem. Am. Sociol. Assn., Midwestern Sociol. Assn., Ill. Sociol. Assn., Nat. Council on Family Relations, Sociologists for Women in Soc., Soc. for Values in Higher Edn., Phi Beta Kappa. Contbr. articles to profl. jours. Office: North Central College Naperville IL 60540

REYELTS, ALAN DUANE, data processing exec.; b. Breckenridge, Minn., Dec. 9, 1947; s. Marcus Conrad and Clara Kathern (Ludwig) R.; A.S. in Computer Sci., State Sch. Sci., N.D., 1967; m. Judith H. Goodejohn, Oct. 22, 1965; children—Stacy, Stephanie. Owner, operator A.D.R. Cons. Services, Thompson, N.D., 1970—; with Minnkota Power Corp., Grand Forks, N.D., 1968-75, programming mgr., 1972-75; dir. mgmt. info. systems Lystads, Inc., Grand Forks, N.D., 1975-80, adminstrv. asst. to pres., 1980—; mem. faculty U. N.D., Grand Forks, 1979—; lectr. in field; counsellor on careers, 1975—. Mem. parish bd. Luth. Ch., Thompson, 1978—, pres., 1978—. Club: Athletic Boosters. Contbr. articles to profl. jours. Home: 533 Crescent Dr Thompson ND 58278 Office: PO Box 1718 Grand Forks ND 58201

REYER, STEVEN ELLIOTT, educator; b. Los Angeles, May 31, 1950; s. Elliott E. and Jean P. R.; B.S., U. Wis., Milw., 1972, M.S., 1973; postgrad. U. Ill., 1973-75; Ph.D., Marquette U., 1978; m. Barbara Joan Merker, Mar. 17, 1979; stepchildren—Brian, Sara. Engr. Wis. Telephone Co., Milw., 1969-71; cons. Astronautics Corp. Am., Milw., 1973, Harris Inc., Quincy, Ill., 1976; lectr., research asso. U. Wis., Milw., 1975-77, asst. prof. elec. engring., 1978—. Mem. Amateur Radio Emergency Service, Milw., 1968—. Frank Rogers Bacon Found. fellow, 1972, 77. Mem. IEEE, Am. Radio Relay League, Sigma Xi, Tau Beta Pi, Phi Kappa Phi, Phi Eta Sigma. Author: (with Robert J. Colbert) Top Ten Data Book, 1971. Contbr. articles in field to profl. jours. Home: 8664 N Pelham Pkwy Bayside WI 53217 Office: PO Box 784 Milwaukee WI 53201

REYMOND, RALPH DANIEL, radiologist; b. Geneva, Mar. 31, 1937; s. Ernest and Dolores (Francini) R.; came to U.S., 1950, naturalized, 1955; A.B. in Physics and Egyptology, Johns Hopkins U., 1959, M.A. in Physics, 1963; M.D., 1967; m. Patricia Ann Bulger, Feb. 4, 1961; 1 son, Eric Daniel. Intern Md. Gen. Hosp., Balt., 1967-68; resident in radiology Johns Hopkins Hosp., Balt., 1968-72; radiologist in radiology and nuclear medicine, Topeka, 1972—; clin. asst. prof. therapeutic radiology U. Kans. Med. Sch., 1975—; physicist Harry Diamond Labs., Dept. Army, Washington, summers 1957-66; jr. instr. physics Johns Hopkins U., 1960-62. Bd. dirs. Topeka Zoo, 1972-75. Diplomate Am. Bd. Radiology, Nat. Bd. Med. Examiners. Mem. Am., So., Kans. med. assns., Am. Radium Soc., Royal Soc. Medicine (London), Radiol. Soc. N. Am., Am. Coll. Radiology, Am. Med. Soc. Vienna, Am. Phys. Soc., Am. Assn. Physicists in Medicine, Am. Coll. Nuclear Physicians, Kans. Radiol. Soc., AAAS, Med. and Chirurg. Faculty Md., Nat. Assn. Residents and Interns, Am. Coll. Nuclear Medicine, Am. Research Center Egypt. Republican. Clubs: Rolls-Royce Owners, Saturday Night Literary. Patentee in field. Home: 2816 MacVicar Ave Topeka KS 66611 Office: 310 Med Arts Bldg 10th and Horner Sts Topeka KS 66604

REYNAERT, EDWARD ANDREW, chem. co. exec.; b. Detroit, Aug. 24, 1938; s. Andrew J. and Helen M. (Zvara) R.; B.S.E.E., Detroit Inst. Tech., 1962. Engr., Ford Motor Co., Detroit, 1962-64; with Gen. Electric, Syracuse, N.Y., 1964-66; mgr. Electric dept. Dow Chem. Co., Midland, Mich., 1966-79; tech. specialist Dow Corning, Midland, 1979—; elec. cons. Mem. exec. com. Republican Party, 1976-79. Mem. IEEE (sec. working group on insulator contamination 1980, bd. dirs. Arnold Center 1979—), Nat. Mgmt. Assn. (bd. dirs. 1972-73). Republican. Roman Catholic. Club: 4-H. Office: 10330 Hercules Dr Freeland MI 49623

REYNES, WENDY WARNER, pub.'s rep.; b. Boston, Sept. 29, 1944; d. Philip Russell and Elizabeth (Patton) Warner; A.A., Conn. Coll., 1966; m. Jose (Tony) Antonio Reynes, III, Apr. 26, 1969; children—Jose (Tad) Antonio, Gabrielle Elizabeth. With Foote, Cone & Belding, N.Y.C., 1966-68; advt. sales rep. Cosmopolitan Mag., N.Y.C., 1968-69, Co-Ed Mag., N.Y.C., 1969-70; asst. product mgr. Avon Products, N.Y.C., 1970; advt. sales rep., Magazine Networks, N.Y.C. and Chgo., 1970-72; midwest mgr. advt. sales, Girl Talk Mag., Chgo., 1972-75; div. mgr. advt. sales, Pattis Group, Chgo., 1975-79; pres. Reynes & Assos., Chgo., 1979—. Bd. dirs. Multiple Sclerosis, 1974—, St. Joseph's Sch. PTA, 1979-80, Marriage Encounter, 1976—; active Jr. League Greenwich, Conn., 1965-67, Jr. League N.Y.C., 1967-75. Mem. City Regional Mag. Assn., Advt. Assn. Clubs: Agate (v.p., dir.), Women's Advt. Club Chgo. (chmn. Ad Women of Yr. 1970—), Touhy, Michigan Ave., North Shore Country, Wilmette Tennis, Court House, East Bank. Home: 1701 Forest Ave Wilmette IL 60091 Office: Reynes & Assos Inc 2 N Riverside Plaza Chicago IL 60606

REYNOLDS, ARTHUR RICHARD, social worker; b. Columbus, Ohio, Sept. 26, 1946; s. Arthur Charles and Jane Frances (Davis) R.; B.S. in Social Work, Ohio State U., Columbus, 1968, M.S.W., 1970; m. Georgia Lyn Browning, June 1, 1968; children—Mark Browning, Jill Margaret. Mem. staff N. Central Mental Health Center, Columbus, 1974—, coordinator adult intermediate care program, chmn. med. records rev. com. and developmental disabilities task force, 1979—; individual practice, Columbus; mem. adj. faculty Coll. Social Work, Ohio State U. Bd. trustees, chmn. agy. com., host family Columbus Area Internat. Program, 1978—. Served with U.S. Army, 1970-74. Decorated Army Commendation medal with oak leaf cluster; cert. alcoholism counselor. Mem. Acad. Cert. Social Workers, Nat. Assn. Social Workers (mem. Registry Clin. Social Workers), Nat. Registry Health Care Providers in Clin. Social Work (charter). Home: 5157 Northtowne Blvd Columbus OH 43229 Office: 978 S Front St Columbus OH 43206

REYNOLDS, BARBARA GERTRUDE, hosp. personnel dir.; b. London, Ont., Can., Dec. 14, 1936; d. Albert Andrew and Gertrude Isabelle (Wilson) Wood; student Kingsway Coll., 1953, Columbia Union Coll., 1954-55; B.S. in Bus. Adminstrn., Franklin U., 1980; m. James Carl Reynolds, Aug. 28, 1955; children—James Marcus, Julie Dianne. Tchr. typing Kingsway Coll., Ont., 1965-66; real estate sales rep. George Sullivan Real Estate, Whitby, Ont., 1966-68; exec., legal and med. sec. various firms and instns., 1955-56, 62-65, 68-73; adminstrv. asst. McKay-Dee Hosp., Ogden, Utah, 1973-76; personnel dir. Harding Hosp., Worthington, Ohio, 1976—. Recipient Outstanding Achievement award Harding Hosp., 1978; accredited personnel mgr. Mem. Hosp. Personnel Mgmt. Assn. (sec.-treas.), Am. Soc. Hosp. Personnel Adminstrn., Am. Hosp. Assn., Ohio Hosp. Assn., Am. Mgmt. Assn. Seventh-day Adventist. Home: 826 Griswold St Worthington OH 43085 Office: 445 E Granville Rd Worthington OH 43085

REYNOLDS, FRANK ELON, twp. ofcl.; b. Detroit, Oct. 3, 1931; s. Elon Hudson and Marion Selma (Morgan) R.; student Gen. Motors Inst., 1949-51; B.S. in Archtl. Engring., Lawrence Inst. Tech., 1962; M. Urban Planning, Wayne State U., 1971; postgrad. U. Mich., 1978—; m. Ilene Joan Rowland, May 28, 1955; children—Rick Evan, Robin Ilene, Randi Elaine, Reed Rowland. Engring. asst. Berry Door Corp., Birmingham, Mich., 1957; archtl. designer Gen. Motors Tech. Center, Warren, Mich., 1958-68; chief product engr. Fruehauf Bldgs. div. Fruehauf Co., Ypsilanti, Mich., 1969-70; city planner City of Phoenix, 1971; prin. planner City of Pontiac (Mich.), 1971-73; planning dir. Twp. of West Bloomfield, West Bloomfield, Mich., 1973—; pres. Air Plan Aerial Photography. Tchr. aviation ground sch., adult edn. programs West Bloomfield, Walled Lake and Clarkston, Mich. Served with USN, 1951-53; USMC, 1953-56, 66-68. Registered community planner, Mich.; cert. flight instr. FAA. Mem. Am. Planning Assn., Mich. Soc. Planning Ofcls. (Honor award 1980), Am. Inst. Cert. Planners. Republican. Presbyterian. Author: Oblique Aerial Photography for Urban Planning, 1981. Home: 6455 Waterford Hill Terr Waterford MI 48095 Office: Twp of West Bloomfield 4460 Orchard Lake Rd West Bloomfield MI 48033

REYNOLDS, HARRY AARON, JR., veterinarian, educator; b. Lumberton, N.J., Feb. 6, 1928; s. Harry Aaron and Bertha Rose (Smith) R.; A.B., Gettysburg Coll., 1952; V.M.D., U. Pa., 1956; M.S., U. Ill., 1963, Ph.D., 1966; m. Ann Jane Rowell, Nov. 28, 1959; children—Jennifer Smith, John Wilson. Mem. faculty Sch. Vet. Medicine, U. Pa., 1956-59; USPHS fellow in pathology U. Ill., 1960-63; mem. faculty U. Ill., Coll. Vet. Medicine, Urbana, 1963—, asso. prof. pathology, 1968—, chmn. div. pathology, 1969—; cons. U. Chgo. Sch. Medicine; mem. faculty Grad. Coll., U. Ill. Practice vet. medicine, Delanco, N.J., 1956-59. Served with USMC, 1946-49. Recipient Disting. Tchr. award Norden Labs., 1970. Mem. Internat. Acad. Pathology, AAAS, AAUP, N.Y. Acad. Sci., Am. Vet. Med. Assn., Midwest Assn. Vet. Pathologists, Eastern Ill. Vet. Med. Assn., Nat. German Shorthaired Pointer Assn. (trustee, 1st v.p.), Wilderness Soc., Wildlife Fedn., Scabbard and Blade, Sigma Xi, Phi Zeta, Beta Beta Beta, Chi Gamma Iota, Phi Sigma, Gamma Sigma Delta, Sigma Chi, Alpha Psi, Omega Tau Sigma. Home: 12 Briar Cliff Mahomet IL 61853 Office: Coll Vet Medicine U Ill Urbana IL 61820

REYNOLDS, JOHN FRANCIS, ins. co. exec.; b. Escanaba, Mich., Mar. 29, 1921; s. Edward Peter and Lillian Margaret (Harris) R.; B.S., Mich. State U., 1942; m. Dorothy Gustafson, May 1, 1946; children—Lois Reynolds Janson, Peggy Reynolds Ventura, Michael. Asst. v.p., bond mgr. Wolverine Ins. Co., Battle Creek, Mich., 1955-64, v.p. underwriting, 1964-69; Midwestern zone underwriting mgr. Transamerica Ins. Co., Battle Creek, 1969-73, v.p., Midwestern zone mgr., 1975—; pres., gen. mgr. Candian Surety Co. subs. Transamerica Ins. Co., Toronto, Ont., Can., 1974-75. City commr., Battle Creek, 1967-69. Mem. Mich. Assn. Ins. Cos. (past chmn.). Office: Transamerica Ins Co PO Box 667 Battle Creek MI 49016

REYNOLDS, JOHN W., dist. judge; Green Bay, Wis., Apr. 4, 1921; s. John W. and Madge (Flatley) R.; Ph.B., U. Wis., 1946, LL.B., 1949; m. Patricia Ann Brody, May 26, 1947 (dec. Dec. 1967); children—Kate M. Reynolds Lindquist, Molly A. Reynolds Jassoy, James B.; m. 2d, Jane Conway, July 31, 1971; children—Jacob F., Thomas J., Frances P., John W. III. Admitted to Wis. bar, 1949, since practiced in Green Bay; dist. dir. price stblzn., 1951-53, U.S. commr., 1953-58; atty. gen. State of Wis., 1958-62; gov. State of Wis., 1963-65; U.S. dist. judge Eastern Dist. Wis., 1965-71, chief judge, 1971—. Mem. Am., Wis. State, Brown County bar assns., Am. Law Inst. Democrat. Office: Room 471 US Courthouse 517 E Wisconsin Ave Milwaukee WI 53202

REYNOLDS, JOSEPH DANIEL, investment adviser; b. Syracuse, N.Y., Apr. 2, 1938; s. Howard John and Anne Marie (Hurley) R.; B.S., Rochester Inst. Tech., 1959; M.S., Elmira Coll., 1963; postgrad Syracuse U., 1962-64; m. Margaret McCarthy, Aug. 22, 1959; children—Mary Anne, Suzanne, Patrick, Daniel, Kathryn, Sean, Michael, Margaret. Coach, bus. tchr., high sch., Sherrill, N.Y., 1959-66; stockbroker Hayden Stone Co., Syracuse, N.Y., 1966-70, Hardy Co., Syracuse, 1970-71; sr. v.p., dir. Gradison & Co., Inc., Cin., 1971-78; owner, pres. J.D. Reynolds Co., Cin., 1978—. NSF grantee, 1964. Mem. Market Technicians Assn. Republican. Roman Catholic. Clubs: Terrace Park Country, Terrace Park Swim and Tennis. Home: 620 Floral Ave Terrace Park OH 45174 Office: 706 Indian Hill Rd Terrace Park OH 45174

REYNOLDS, KATHLEEN MARIE, occupational therapist, educator; b. Decatur, Ill., Jan. 15, 1952; d. Maurice D. and Vera L. (Headrick) R.; B.S., Western Mich. U., 1974; M.S., Wayne State U., 1979. Occupational therapist D.& D Health Assos., Oak Park, Mich., 1975-76, Rehab. Inst., Detroit, 1976-78; research project dir. Jewish Vocat. Service, Detroit, 1978-80; mem. staff occupational therapy Riley Hosp. for Children, Indpls., 1981—; mem. faculty div. allied health scis. Ind. U. Sch. Medicine, Indpls., 1980-81; mem. faculty psychology dept. Purdue U., Indpls., 1980-81. Mem. Am. Occupational Therapy Assn., Mich. Occupational Therapy Assn., Ind. Occupational Therapy Assn., World Fedn. Occupational Therapists, Am. Assn. Mental Deficiency, Am. Acad. Cerebral Palsy and Devel. Medicine, Delta Zeta Alumnae Assn. Contbr. articles on vocat. rehab. and occupational therapy to profl. jours.; author book revs. Home: 5615 Fjord Dr Suite C Indianapolis IN 46250 Office: CH 311 1100 W Michigan St Indianapolis IN 46223

REYNOLDS, L. MICHAEL, cable tv co. exec.; b. Beloit, Wis., Apr. 30, 1948; s. Maurice Herbert and Marie Dorothy R.; B.S., U. Wis., 1970; m. Patricia Ann R., Aug. 15, 1970; children—Dana Marie, Kari Elizabeth, Anne Catherine. Program mgr. Teleprompter Cable TV, Dubuque, Iowa, 1970-71, Johnstown, Pa., 1972-74; gen. mgr. Teleprompter, Sault Ste. Marie, Mich., 1974-75, Winona, Minn., 1975-76; gen. mgr. Teleprompter Cable TV, Rochester, Minn., 1976-79, Grosse Pointe, Mich., 1980—. Mem. Minn. Cable Communications Assn. (sec. 1976-79), N. Central Cable TV Assn. (pres. 1980). Lutheran. Home: 740 University Grosse Pointe MI 48230 Office: Teleprompter Cable TV 19245 Mack Ave Grosse Pointe Woods MI 48236

REYNOLDS, LARRY ROYCE, social worker; b. Imperial, Nebr., Jan. 7, 1944; s. John R. and Thelma Lucille (Walters) R.; B.A., U. Nebr., 1971; M.S.W., Washington U., St. Louis, 1973; postgrad. U. Wis., 1977—; m. Shelly Dea Shelmadine, Apr. 5, 1969 (div. Nov. 1979); 1 son, Scott Thaddeus. Instr., Moraine Park Tech. Inst., Fond du Lac, Wis., 1975-76; psychiat. social worker Fond du Lac County Mental Health Center, 1973—; behaviorial psychotherapist Inst. Human Services, Inc., Fond du Lac, 1979-81; cons. psychotherapist Meta Resource Center, St. Agnes Hosp., Fond du Lac, 1981—; clin. cons. Linden Center, Fond du Lac. Served with U.S. Army, 1965-67. Cert. completion hypnotherapy Soc. Clin. Exptl. Hypnosis, 1975. Mem. Nat. Assn. Social Workers, Acad. Cert. Social Workers. Democrat. Methodist. Office: Saint Agnes Hosp Fond du Lac WI 54935

REYNOLDS, ROBERT FRANKLIN, bldg. contractor; b. Vanatta, Ohio, July 18, 1923; s. James Calvin and Edith May (Hughes) R.; student pub. schs., Vanatta and Newark, Ohio; m. Mary Martha Gleckler, Mar. 9, 1945; 1 dau., Sandra Lynna Miller. Dairy and hog farmer, St. Louisville, Ohio, 1947-56; carpenter Rockwell Mfg. Co., Newark, Ohio, 1955-56; owner, operator R.F. Reynolds Co., Newark, 1957—. Served with U.S. Army, 1943-46; PTO. Mem. Nat., Ohio, Licking County homebuilders assns. Republican. Lutheran. Club: Licking Springs Trout and Golf. Address: 746 Robin Hood Dr Newark OH 43055

REYNOLDS, ROY ROBERT, civil engr.; b. Shreveport, La., Nov. 30, 1946; s. Orland Anderson and Della Mae (Faught) R.; B.S., La. Tech. U., 1969; m. Beverly Gayle Johnson, May 22, 1971; children—Byron Earle, John Anderson. With Servitron, Inc., 1969-74, transitman, Shreveport, 1969-70, project engr., Shreveport, 1970-71, project engr., estimator, Baton Rouge, 1971-72, contracting engr., estimator, Kansas City, Mo., 1972-74; civil engr. Sverdrup & Parcel & Assos., Inc., St. Louis, 1974-79; r.r. sect. leader Huckleberry R.R., Genesee County Parks and Recreation Commn., Flint, Mich., 1979—. Deacon, So. Baptist Ch., 1978—; operator exhibits Agrl. Hall of Fame and Nat. Center, Bonner Springs, Kans., summers 1966-67. Registered profl. engr., La. Mem. Am. Ry. Engring. Assn., Nat. Model R.R. Assn. (life), Tau Beta Pi. Republican. Home: 6005 E Dodge Rd Mt Morris MI 48458 Office: G-5055 Branch Rd Flint MI 48506

REYNOLDS, RUBY JEAN, nurse; b. Bowling Green, Mo., Jan. 1, 1932; d. William and Leola (Hampton) Robinson; diploma Kansas City Gen. Hosp. and Med. Center, 1964; B.A., Stephens Coll., Columbia, Mo., 1975; postgrad. U. Mo., Kansas City, 1975-76; m. Clarence C. Reynolds; children—Maurice L. Davis, Bernice E. Franklin. Head nurse Kansas City (Mo.) Gen. Hosp., 1964-65; with St. Joseph Hosp., Kansas City, Mo., 1965—, adminstrv. asst. patient services, 1978—; CPR instr. trainer Am. Heart Assn., 1976—, CPR faculty affiliate Kansas City chpt., 1976—. Chmn. dept. Christian Edn., United Meth. Ch., Kansas City, 1979. U. Colo. grantee, 1969-70. Mem. Am. Nurses Assn., Mo. Nurses Assn., Dist. Nurses Assn., Assn. Nursing Adminstrs. Methodist. Home: 3842 E 63d St Kansas City MO 64130

REYNOLDS, WILLIAM PRESTON, railroad exec.; b. Janesville, Wis., Aug. 24, 1940; s. James William and Helen Sophia (Pitzen) R.; student U. Wis., 1959-60; B.A., Milton Coll., 1964. Claims examiner U.S. R.R. Retirement Bd., Chgo., 1965-68; sta. clk., receiver, transit technician Chgo. Transit Authority, 1969—; secondary sch. tchr. Stephenson Town (Wis.) High Sch., 1964-65; owner-mgr. Jackson Harbor Inn, Washington Island, Wis. Mem. Lake View Citizens Council, Landmarks Preservation Council; mem. Chgo. Sch. Architecture Found. Named Chgo. Transit Authority Employee of Year, 1970. Mem. Omnibus Soc. Am. (dir. 1974-76), Central Electric Rail Fans Assn. (activities dir. 1969-70), R.R. Club Chgo., Ill. Psychic Research Soc., Wis. Electric Ry. Hist. Soc., Spiritual Frontiers Fellowship. Republican. Roman Catholic. K.C. (4 deg.). Home: 1119 Hannah Ave Forest Park IL 60130 Office: Room 7-133 Merchandise Mart 222 N Bank Dr Chicago IL 60654

REYNOLDSON, WALTER WARD, chief justice Iowa Supreme Ct.; b. St. Edward, Nebr., May 17, 1920; s. Walter Scorer and Mabel Matilda (Sallach) R.; B.A., State Tchrs. Coll., 1942; J.D., U. Iowa, 1948; m. Janet Aline Mills, Dec. 24, 1942; children—Vicki (Mrs. Gary Kimes), Robert. Admitted to Iowa bar, 1948; practice in Osceola, 1948-71; justice Iowa Supreme Ct., 1971-78, chief justice, 1978—; lectr. seminar Sch. Law, Drake U., 1968; county atty. Clarke

County (Iowa), 1953-57. Trustee, Clarke County Community Hosp., Osceola; pres. bd. dirs. Osceola Ind. Sch. Dist. Served with USNR, 1942-46. Recipient Osceola Community Service award, 1968. Mem. Iowa (chmn. com. on legal edn. and admission to bar 1964-71), Am. bar assns., Iowa Acad. Trial Lawyers, Am. Coll. Trial Lawyers. Contbg. author: Trial Handbook, 1969. Home: Rural Route 2 Osceola IA 50213 Office: State Capitol Bldg Des Moines IA 50319

REZMERSKI, WILLIAM EDWARD, cons. co. exec.; b. Ridgway, Pa., July 2, 1945; s. John James and Augusta Ruth (Dickinson) R.; B.A. in Psychology, Calif. State Coll., 1972; M.Ed. in Ednl. Psychology, Edinboro State Coll., 1973; postgrad. U. S.D., 1977-78; m. Cathy Ann Smalley, Sept. 4, 1971; children—Hayley Ann, Hilary Ruth. Sch. psychologist Northwest Tri-County Intermediate Unit, Edinboro, Pa., 1974-77; v.p. tng. Personal Dynamics, Mpls., 1978-80; v.p. mktg. Performax Systems Internat., Inc., Mpls., 1980—; mng. partner Progressive Learning Assos., Mpls., 1981—. Served with U.S. Army, 1966-70. Decorated Bronze Star, Army Commendation medal. Recipient St. Joseph Soc. scholar, 1963; named Ednl. Coordinator of Yr., Personal Dynamics, 1977. Mem. Am. Soc. Tng. and Devel. Home: 13060 Ferris Ct Apple Valley MN 55124 Office: 12805 State Hwy 55 Minneapolis MN 55441

RHEA, ULYSSES SIMPSON, chemist; b. Smith's Grove, Ky., Oct. 22, 1934; s. James Oscar and Maggie (Stark) R.; B.S., Knoxville Coll., 1957; postgrad. Xavier U., 1959, 64, 68; m. Bennie Louise Singleton, June 15, 1957; 1 dau., Stephanie. Research lab. technician Children's Hosp. Research Found., Cin., 1957; phys. sci. technician USPHS, 1959-68, research chemist, Cin., 1968—; lectr. in field. Vice pres. Ken-Sil-Ridge, 1973-75. Cert. equal employment opportunity counselor, 1980. Mem. AAAS, Sigma Xi. Baptist. Club: Laymen's Movement. Contbr. articles to profl. jours. Office: 1090 Tusculum Ave Cincinnati OH 45226

RHEE, KENNY KWANGHYO, radiation oncologist; b. Sunchun, Korea, Nov. 6, 1943; came to U.S., 1972, naturalized, 1980; s. Kwan Young and Ok Hwa R.; M.D., Cath. Med. Coll., Seoul, 1968; m. Joanne Junghae Cha, Mar. 29, 1972; 1 dau., Monica C. Intern, Hutzul Hosp., Detroit, 1972-73; resident in radiation therapy Harper Hosp., Detroit, 1973-76; fellow radiation therapy Rush-Presbyn. St. Luke's Med. Center, Chgo., 1976-77; staff dept. therapeutic radiology Mercy Hosp., Urbana, Ill., 1977—, med. dir. radiation therapy, 1977—; clin. instr. clin. medicine U. Ill., Urbana, 1979—. Served with Korean Army, 1968-71. Mem. Am. Coll. Radiology, Am. Soc. Therapeutic Radiologists, Brit. Inst. Radiology, Radiol. Soc. N.Am., AMA, Ill. Med. Soc., Champaign County Med. Soc., Ill. Radiol. Soc. Office: 1400 W Park Ave Urbana IL 61801

RHIEW, HYOMYEONG BENJAMIN, psychiatrist; b. Seoul, Korea, May 14, 1939; s. Choon-San and Sun-Ae (Chang) R.; M.D., Seoul Nat. U., Korea, 1964; came to U.S., 1967; m. Dongsun Shin, June 7, 1967; children—Albert, Catherine, Margaret, Patricia. Intern, Detroit-Macomb Hosps. Assn., Detroit, 1967-68; resident Phila. Gen. Hosp., 1968-70, Detroit Psychiat. Inst., 1970-71; staff psychiatrist, sect. dir. Northville (Mich.) State Hosp., 1971-75; pvt. practice psychiatry, Detroit and Livonia, Mich., 1972—; staff psychiatrist Adult Psychiat. Clinic, Detroit, part time 1971-72; attending psychiatrist Detroit Meml. Hosp., 1977—, Ardmore Acres Hosp.; cons. psychiatrist Samaritan Health Center, Alexander Blain Hosp., S.W. Detroit Hosp., Dearborn Med. Center; clin. ward dir. Detroit Psychiat. Inst., 1975—; clin. asst. prof. Wayne State U., 1976—. Served with Korean Army, 1964-67. Diplomate Am. Bd. Psychiatry and Neurology. Mem. AMA, Mich. Psychiat. Soc., Am. Psychiat. Assn., Mich. State, Wayne County med. socs. Home: 25451 Liberty Ln Farmington Hills MI 48018 Office: 615 David Whitney Bldg Detroit MI 48226

RHOADES, THOMAS PERRY, III, automotive co. exec.; b. Indpls., Jan. 16, 1941; s. Thomas Perry and Frances Elizabeth (Kirkpatrick) R.; student U. Va., 1959-62; B.A., Northland Coll., Ashland, Wis., 1964; m. Myra Gertrude Aichholz, Jan. 24, 1970; children—Melinda Ann, Thomas Perry IV. Reporter, Daily Item, Port Chester, N.Y., 1964-65; reporter Kansas City Star, 1965-66, copy editor, 1967-69; pub. relations specialist Ford Motor Co., N.Y.C., 1969-70, Ford div., Dearborn, Mich., 1970-74, Lincoln-Mercury div., Dearborn, 1974-76, asst. pub. relations mgr. Ford Parts and Service div., Livonia, Mich., 1976-78, editorial planning asso., corp. info. and service office, public relations staff, Dearborn, 1978-80, public relations mgr. spl. vehicle ops., 1981—. Served with U.S. Army, 1965-67. Mem. Pub. Relations Soc. Am., Internat. Motor Press Assn., Northland Coll. Alumni Assn. (past bd. dirs.). Episcopalian. Clubs: Detroit Press, Players. Home: 588 Lincoln Rd Grosse Pointe MI 48230 Office: Am Rd Dearborn MI 48121

RHOADES, WALTER FLOYD, chem. engr., paint mfg. co. exec.; b. King City, Calif., Sept. 3, 1916; s. Walter F. and Mabel E. (Long) R.; B.S., U. Calif., Berkeley, 1940; M.S., Calif. Inst. Tech., 1942; m. Lorene Dry, Feb. 22, 1958; children—Suzanne L., Barbara L. Mgr. resin dept. Calif. Ink Co., Berkeley, 1940-49; tech. dir. Pacific div. DeSoto, Inc., Berkeley, 1949-54, gen. mgr. Southwestern plant, Garland, Tex., 1955-57, v.p., dir. merchandising, Chgo., 1958-62; pres., dir. Standard T Chem. Co., Inc. subs. Montgomery Ward, Chgo., 1962-81, chmn. bd., dir., 1981—. Trustee Bapt. Theol. Union, Chgo. Served to capt. AUS, 1942-46. Mem. Nat. Paint and Coatings Assn. (dir.). Republican. Baptist. Clubs: Union League, Michigan Shores; Chandlers Landing Yacht (Rockwall, Tex.). Home: 2432 Meadow Dr N Wilmette IL 60091 Office: Standard T Chem Co Inc 140 S State St Chicago IL 60603

RHOADS, MARK QUENTIN, state senator, indsl. real estate broker; b. Hinsdale, Ill., Dec. 3, 1946; s Herbert Graves and Mary Margaret (Gurrie) R.; student George Washington U., 1966-68; B.A. in Polit. Sci., Loyola U., Chgo., 1971; postgrad. Am. U., 1973. Office aide to U.S. Senator Everett M. Dirksen, Washington, 1967; legis. research aide to Congressman Edward J. Derwinski, Washington, 1973; broker, comml. investment div. Rich Port Realtors, Oak Brook, Ill., 1977—; mem. Ill. State Senate, 1976—; co-founder Am. Legis. Exchange Council, 1973. Bd. dirs. Ill. Conservative Union, 1974—; mem. Ill. Econ. and Fiscal Commn., 1977-80, Ill. Election Laws Commn., 1977-80. Named Outstanding Area Citizen, La Grange Area Jaycees, 1976. Mem. DuPage County Bd. Realtors, La Grange Bd. Realtors, Phila. Soc., Jaycees. Republican. Roman Catholic. Clubs: Kiwanis, K.C. Office: 600 Hillgrove Ave Western Springs IL 60558

RHOADS, WILLIAM SCHLOMER, chem. co. exec.; b. Harrisburg, Pa., Apr. 2, 1922; s. Kenneth Myer and Mary Morrow (Schlomer) R.; B.A. in Chemistry, Gettysburg Coll., 1943; m. Marion Susanne Boyer, Apr. 9, 1949; children—Carol, Richard, Susanne, Kimberly. With Atlas Powder Co., Wilmington, Del., 1947-52; salesman Kenneth M. Rhoads & Sons, Harrisburg, 1952-54, Cowles Chem. Co., Cleve., 1954-56; with Stepan Chem. Co., Northfield, Ill., 1956—, v.p., gen. mgr. surfactants, 1974-79, v.p. internat., 1979—. Served to 1st lt. USMC, 1943-46. Mem. Am. Chem. Soc., Cosmetic Chemists Soc. Republican. Episcopalian. Club: Knollwood. Home: 694 S Ridge Rd Lake Forest IL 60045 Office: Stepan Chem Co Edens and Winnetka Rd Northfield IL 60093

RHODES, ARTHUR EDWARD, utility exec.; b. Seymour, Mo., Sept. 19, 1925; s. Washington Hope and Lillie Mae (Cawthra) R.; student pub. schs.; m. Nadine Ruth Fauscett, Dec. 23, 1966. Pressman, Mountain Grove (Mo.) Jour., 1946-50; shop foreman Mansfield (Mo.) Mirror newspaper, 1950-56; editor Sho-Me Live Wire, Marshfield, Mo., 1956-60; with G & T Sho-Me Power Corp., Marshfield, 1960—, dir. pub. relations, 1966-73, dir. personnel and pub. relations, 1974-75, mgr. dept. personnel and pub. relations, 1975-79, mgr. adminstrv. and community affairs dept., 1979—. Chmn., Mo. Ozarks Mem. Services Group, 1974—. Pres., Webster County Fair Bd., 1968-69; chmn. publicity Webster County Red Cross, 1963-65; v.p. Ozark Area Community Action Corp., 1968-72. Chmn. Webster County Republican Com., 1972-73. Chmn. bd. dirs. Webster County OEO, 1966-72. Served with C.E., AUS, 1943-46; ETO. Recipient 1st place award photography Nat. Rural Electrification Coop. Assn., 1964. Mem. Springfield Personnel Assn., Am. Legion. Mem. Christian Ch. (elder). Rotarian. Club: Marshfield. Home: 706 NW Hubble Dr Marshfield MO 65706 Office: 301 W Jackson St Marshfield MO 65706

RHODES, DONALD ELLSWORTH, lawyer, ins. co. exec.; b. New Castle, Pa., Oct. 21, 1915; s. Oscar E. and Alice R. (Heasley) R.; A.B., Grove City Coll., 1937; LL.B., U. Mich., 1948; postgrad. in ins. mgmt. U. Wis.-Madison, 1965-66; m. Emily Swanson, June 15, 1940; children—Susan Rhodes Stefanski, Jeffrey E. Draftsman, Bell Telephone Co. of Pa., New Castle, 1937-38; draftsman Pa. Dept. Hwys., New Castle, 1938-39; mgr. Retail Credit Co., Johnstown and Beaver, Pa., 1939-41; supr. drafting Curtiss-Wright Corp., Beaver, also Caldwell, N.J., 1941-46; admitted to Mich. bar, 1948; dir. Citizens Mut. Ins. Co. (name later changed to Citizens Ins. Co. of Am.), Howell, Mich., 1948—; dir. Beacon Ins. Co. Am., Columbus, Ohio, Am. Select Ins. Co., Columbus, Econ. Devel. Corp. Howell. Chmn., Mich. Auto No-Fault Legal Com., 1972-73, Howell Citizens Adv. Com. on Schs., 1956-58; co-chmn. Howell Area United Fund, 1969. Bd. dirs. Lansing (Mich.) Mental Health Clinic, 1956-61, pres., 1959-60; trustee Child and Family Services of Mich. Inc. Mem. State Bar of Mich. (chmn. com. ins. law 1958-59), Am. Bar Assn., Fedn. Ins. Counsel (v.p. 1961), Ins. Fedn. Ohio (mem. legis. com., exec. com.), Mich. Ins. Lawyers Council (pres. 1960), Mich. Ins. Info. Service (gov. 1967-71), Mich. Assn. Mut. Ins. Cos. (pres. 1969-70), Mich. Assn. Ins. Cos. (chmn. legis. com., 1971—), Mich. Ins. Edn. Assn., Howell Area C. of C. (pres. 1964), Highlander Athletic Boosters (pres. 1969-70), Pi Gamma Mu, Nu Lambda Phi. Presbyterian (elder 1969). Mason (Shriner, K.T.), Elk; mem. Order of Eastern Star. Home: 1444 Crest Rd Howell MI 48843 Office: 645 W Grand River Ave Howell MI 48843

RHODES, JAMES ALLEN, gov. Ohio; b. Jackson County, Ohio, Sept. 13, 1909; s. James Allen and Susan (Howe) R.; student Ohio State U.; m. Helen Rawlins, Dec. 18, 1941; children—Suzanne, Saundra, Sharon. Columbus city auditor 1941-44, mayor 1944-53; auditor Ohio, 1953-62; gov. of Ohio, 1963-70, 75—. Past nat. pres. AAU; del. Pan-Am. Sports Congress, Internat. Sports Fedn.; mem. adv. com. Profl. Golfer's Assn.; mem. U.S. Olympic Com.; mem. Columbus Bd. Edn., 1937-40; founder Nat. Caddie Assn., Inc., All-Am. Newspaper Boys Scholarships, Columbus Boys Club. Presbyterian. Mason (32 deg.). Kiwanian. Author: Johhny Shiloh, 1958; The Trial of Mary Todd Lincoln, 1959; The Court Martial of Commodore Perry, 1960. Office: Office of Governor State House Columbus OH 43215*

RHODES, JOHN AMMON, educator; b. Chgo., June 7, 1947; s. Glenn D. and Elizabeth Irene (Gloss) R.; B.S., No. Ill., 1969, M.S. in Edn., 1970, C.A.S. in Edn., 1975, Ed.D., 1979; m. Rosemary Ann Franklin, June 14, 1969; children—Jodi Ann, Scott Ammon, Amy Ann. Tchr. biology Aurora (Ill.) West High Sch., 1968, Lincoln Sch., Dist. 44, Lombard, Ill., 1969-71; tchr., asst. to prin. Highland Hills Sch., Dist. 44, Lombard, 1971-73; curriculum cons., research asst. Inst. for Ednl. Research, Downers Grove, Ill., 1973-75; tchr., head math. dept., head sci. and computer sci. depts., curriculum dir. Avery Coonley Sch. for Bright and Gifted Children, Downers Grove, Ill., 1973—; instr. gifted edn. No. Ill. U., 1976; instr. computer sci. Governor's State U., 1980. Mem. Ill. Math. League, Assn. Supervision and Curriculum Devel., Ill. Assn. Supervision and Curriculum Devel., Ill. Jr. Acad. Sci., Ill. Sci. Tchrs. Assn., Mu Alpha Theta, Phi Sigma. Office: 1400 W Maple St Downers Grove IL 60515

RHOTEN, JULIANA THERESA, sch. prin.; b. N.Y.C., June 28; d. Julius Joseph and Gladys Maude (Grant) Bastian; B.A., Hunter Coll., 1954; M.S., 1956; Ed.S., U. Wis., Milw., 1977; m. Marion Rhoten, Aug. 7, 1956; 1 son, Don Carlos. Tchr. elem. schs., Milw., 1957-65, reading specialist, 1965-71, adminstr., 1971-80; prin. Ninth St. Sch., Milw., 1980—. Mem. Assn. Supervision and Curriculum Devel., Internat. Reading Assn., Nat. Council Tchrs. English, Adminstrs. and Suprs. Council, Phi Delta Kappa, Alpha Kappa Alpha. Home: 7222 N 99th St Milwaukee WI 53224 Office: 1723 N 9th St Milwaukee WI 53205

RIBORDY, DENIS EUGENE, drug co. exec.; b. East Chicago, Ind., July 20, 1929; s. Myrel I. and Lela (Hunsley) R.; B.S. in Pharmacy, Butler U., 1952; m. Carolyn Ann McClurg, June 20, 1954; children—Cheryl, Scott, Nancy, Mark. Partner Hill Drug Co., Augusta, Ga., 1954; pres. Ribordy's Pharmacy, Gary, Ind., 1955; founder, pres. Ribordy Drugs Inc., retail chain, Highland, Ind., 1955—; dir. Gary Nat. Bank, No. Ind. Public Service Co.; chmn. bd. Affiliated Drug Stores, Inc., N.Y.C., 1978-79, now dir.; mem. editorial adv. bd. Post Tribune. Pres. Gary Downtown Council, 1962, Ogden Dunes (Ind.) Home Owners Assn., 1972; pres. Town Bd. Trustees Ogden Dunes, 1974—; bd. dirs. N.W. Ind. Better Bus. Bur., 1959—, v.p., 1969—; adv. bd. Butler U. Coll. Pharmacy, 1964—, trustee Methodist Hosp., Gary, 1970—, pres. bd. trustees, 1974-78; trustee City Meth. Ch., 1968-74; bd. dirs. Chgo. Motor Club, 1980—; chmn. Gary ARC, 1975-76; mem. adv. bd. Ind. U. Northwest. Served with AUS, 1952-54. Recipient Boss of Yr. award Am. Bus. Women's Assn., 1966; Man of Yr. award Navy League, 1979; A. H. Robins Bowl of Hygeia award, 1967. Mem. Lake County (pres. 1957-58), Ind., Am. pharm. assns., Nat. Assn. Retail Druggists (chmn. merchandising com. 1974), Nat. Assn. Chain Drug Stores (adv. com. 1980—), N.W. Ind. Assn. Commerce and Industry (dir. 1978—, v.p. 1981), Gary U. Club (pres. 1972), Ind. Soc. Chgo. Clubs: Gary Univ., Masons, Jesters, Shriners, Gary Country. Home: 530 40 Diana Rd Ogden Dunes IN 46368 Office: Ribordy Drugs Inc 9626 Cline Ave Highland IN 46322

RICE, ARTHUR RAYMOND, computer service & machine tool exec.; b. Lexington, Va., Oct. 27, 1940; s. Raymond Guy and Frances Allene (Spangler) R.; student Ind. U. NW; m. Diana Charmaine Sage, June 5, 1971; children—Alicia Rene, Anthony Rea, Dianna Michele; adopted stepchildren—Lisa Marie, Mark Timothy. With industry control dept. Gen. Electric Co., Salem, Va., 1964-66, with process computer dept. Phoenix, Ariz., 1966-68, with installation and service engring., div. Chgo., 1968—, service supr. digital processors, 1975-77, mgr. machine tool/computers Kansas City unit, 1978—. Served with USAF, 1959-64. Republican. Baptist. Home: 11200 Grandview Overland Park KS 66210 Office: 10550 Barkley Overland Park KS 66210

RICE, CARL VENTON, lawyer, bus. exec.; b. Lovilla, Iowa, Mar. 27, 1898; s. Walter Scott and Ida Isabelle (Chamberlain) R.; LL.B., U. Kans., 1918; m. Ruth Burton, Nov. 13, 1919 (dec. 1968); children—Ruth Isabelle Rice Mitchell, Carlene V. Rice Lind, Mary E. Rice Wells, Grace L. Rice Muder; m. 2d, Virginia Docking, 1978. Admitted to Kans. bar, 1918, U.S. Supreme Ct. bar, 1933; practiced in Kansas City, Kans., 1919-81; chmn. bd., pres. Pierce Industries, Inc., Andersen, Ind., 1954-64; now v.p. Rodar Leasing Corp., Kansas City, Kans. and Tampa, Fla., Fairfax Spltys., Kansas City, Kans., Graham Products Co., Kansas City, Kans., 3654 Cypress Corp., Tampa, Mission Groves, Inc., Ft. Pierce, Fla.; Hwy. commr. State of Kans., 1931-33; regional counsel RFC, 1933-38, CCC, 1934-50, Def. Plant Corp., 1941-50; counsel Kans. Banking Dept., 1937-39. Mem. exec. com. Democratic Nat. Com., 1948-52. Served with F.A., U.S. Army, World War I. Track Nat. Champion All-Am., 1917-18. Mem. Am. Bar Assn., Kans. State Bar Assn., Delta Theta Phi. Clubs: Kansas City, Indian Hills Country (Kansas City, Kans.); Pelican Yacht (Ft. Pierce). Home: 2108 Washington Blvd Kansas City KS 66102 Office: 600 Security Nat Bank Bldg Kansas City KS 66101

RICE, DAVID MYERS, interior designer; b. Balt., June 24, 1931; s. Franklin Chester and Dorothy Bell (Myers) R.; student U. Nebr., Omaha; m. Sara Elizabeth White, Dec. 27, 1947 (dec.). Staff designer J.L. Brandeis & Sons, Omaha, 1955-66, Orchard & Wilhelm Co., Omaha, 1966-67; owner, designer David M. Rice, Inc., Omaha, 1968—; owner D.M. Rice, Key West Inc. (Fla.), 1977; adv. interior design dept. U. Nebr., Omaha, Lincoln, 1970—, Met. Tech. Community Coll., 1974—. Bd. dirs., past mem. exec. com. Opera/Omaha; mem. nat. council Met. Opera, 1981—; founding mem. Inter-Racial Fellowship of Balt. Served with U.S. Army. Mem. Am. Soc. Interior Designers (mem. exec. council 1978, chmn. profl. practice com. 1978, mem. exec. com. 1977, past pres. Nebr.-Iowa chpt.), Internat. Fedn. Interior Designers (del.), Nat. Trust for Hist. Preservation. Home and Office: 524 N 65th St Omaha NE 68132 also 1025 Fleming St Key West FL 33040

RICE, EDWARD AUGUSTUS, SR., educator; b. Richmond, Va., Apr. 8, 1929; s. James E. and Annie Y. R.; B.S., Va. Union U., 1949; M.A., Columbia U., 1952; M.B.A., U. Conn., 1963; m. Josie Alberta Wigfall, Aug. 18, 1952; children—Patricia G., Edward Augustus, Audrey L. Commd. 2d lt. U.S. Air Force, 1950, advanced through grades to maj., 1971; mem. research faculty Sch. Aerospace Medicine, San Antonio, 1962-66; asst. dir. USAF Nuclear Energy Center, Wright-Patterson AFB, Ohio, 1966-71, ret., 1971; asst. prof. bus. adminstrn. Central State U., Wilberforce, Ohio, 1971—, chmn. dept., acting dean bus. adminstrn., 1974—; dir. Capsulated Systems, Inc.; pres. bd. dirs. Central State U. Credit Union, Inc. Mem. Yellow Springs (Ohio) Sch. Bd., 1971-75; pres. Green County Joint Vocat. Sch. Bd., 1974-75. Decorated Air Force Commendation medal. Mem. Am. Nuclear Soc., Midwest Bus. Adminstrn. Assn., Miami Valley Consortium, Ohio Bus. Tchrs. Assn., AAUP, Alpha Phi Alpha. Contbr. articles to profl. jours. Home: 678 Omar Circle Yellow Springs OH 45387 Office: Central State U Wilberforce OH 45384

RICE, JOHN EDWARD, indsl. parts brokerage co. exec.; b. Washington, Oct. 13, 1952; s. Jack Earl and Yvonne (Hoffman) R.; B.A., U. Iowa, 1974; m. Kirsten Hartwig, Aug. 26, 1978; 1 dau., Kira Leigh. Circulation mgr. Interstate Shopper, Iowa City, Iowa, 1973-74; sales engr. Wahl & Wahl Co., Des Moines, 1973-74, Am. Koyo Corp., Westlake, Ohio, 1975-78; pres. Transcom, Inc., Mpls., 1978—. Recipient People are Great award Pepsi Cola and WFIL TV, 1969. Mem. Iowa City Jaycees (Spark Plug award 1973), Burnsville Jaycees (v.p. chpt. mgmt., Jaycee of Yr. award 1980). Republican. Christian Scientist. Club: Calhoun Beach (Mpls.). Office: PO Box 1064 Burnsville MN 55337

RICE, MARILYN JUNE, state govt. ofcl.; b. St. Louis, Oct. 19, 1947; d. Edward and Juanita A. Pressgrove; A.A., Rend Lake Jr. Coll., 1968; B.S., Murray State U., 1971; M.A., Sangamon State U., 1980; postgrad. So. Ill. U., 1981—. With State of Ill., Springfield, 1971—, statistician for controllers, 1971-75, legis. liaison Ill. Capital Devel. Bd., 1975-77, adminstrv. asst. to dir. Ill. Dept. Law Enforcement, 1977-81; exec. asst. to supt. Ill. Dept. Correction Tng. Acad., Springfield, 1981—; tchr., evaluation specialist corrections law. Legisl. rep. Ill. Fedn. Bus. and Profl. Women's Orgn.; aide to Ill. rep., Ill. Gen. Assembly, 1976-77. Mem. Am. Soc. Tng. and Devel., Am. Corrections Assn., AAUW, Ill. Fedn. Bus. and Profl. Women, Am. Legion Aux. (past local officer). Baptist. Contbr. articles to Bus. and Profl. Women publs. Research publs. on effects of delayed justice. Home: 319 Durkin Dr Springfield IL 62704 Office: 1301 Concordia Ct Springfield IL 62702

RICE, PAUL FREDERICK, structural engr.; b. Mandan, N.D., Dec. 8, 1921; s. Paul Frederick and Claire Olive (Des Jardins) R.; B.S., N.D. State Coll., 1941; postgrad. Ill. Inst. Tech., 1942; M.S., Mass. Inst. Tech., 1947; postgrad. U. Mich., 1953-57; m. Joan Carol Cannon, June 22, 1946; children—Paul Frederick, Clair Patrick, John Cassius, Richard Clay. Structural design engr. Cunningham-Limp Co., Detroit, 1947-49; structural field engr. Mich., Portland Cement Assn., Chgo., 1949-54; tech. dir. Am. Concrete Inst., Detroit, 1954-58; v.p. engring. Concrete Reinforcing Steel Inst., Chgo., 1958—; chmn. Concrete Improvement Bd. Detroit, 1955-56; vice chmn. Reinforced Concrete Research Council, ASCE, 1974-76. Served with C.E., AUS, 1942-46; ETO. Registered profl. engr., Mich.; registered structural engr., Ill. Fellow ASCE, Am. Concrete Inst.; mem. Am. Welding Soc., ASTM, Structural Engs. Assn. Ill., Reinforced Concrete Research Council. Editor, author: Concrete Reinforcing Steel Institute (CRSI) Handbook, 1968, 71, 75, 78; co-author: Structural Design Guide to ACI Building Code, Structural Design Guide to AISI Specifications. Home: 2033 Sherman Ave Evanston IL 60201 Office: 933 N Plum Grove Rd Schaumburg IL 60195

RICE, STANLEY MILTON, pharm. co. exec.; b. Bloomington, Ind., Aug. 17, 1951; s. F. Milton and LaRitta Pauline R.; B.S., Ind. State U., 1973; postgrad. Ind. U., 1974; m. Deborah Ann Zimmerman, Nov. 25, 1975; children—Stephanie Ann, Christina Elaine. Dist. rep. Am. Cancer Soc., Indpls., 1974-76; asst. microbiologist Central Pharms., Inc., Seymour, Ind., 1976—, asst. prodn. mgr., 1979—. Pres., v.p. Am. Cancer Soc.; deacon First Assembly of God Ch. Mem. Am. Soc. Microbiology (asso.), Drug Chem. and Allied Trader Assn. Home: Route 2 Box 52A North Vernon IN 47265 Office: 116 128 E 3d St Seymour IN 47274

RICH, JEFFREY ALAN, lawyer; b. Cleve., July 10, 1945; s. Henry and Ida (Mart) R.; B.A. with distinction in Polit. Sci., Ohio State U., 1967; J.D., Cleve. State U., 1970; m. Leslie Stratton, Aug. 2, 1969; children—Jordan Joy, Courtney Stratton. Spl. asst. to pres. Cleve. State U., 1970; law clk. Ohio Supreme Ct. Justice, 1970-71; asst. legislative counsel to gov. Ohio, 1971-72; admitted to Ohio bar, 1970, U.S. Supreme Ct. bar, U.S. Tax Ct., Fed. Dist. Cts. in Ohio; mem. firm Teaford, Rich & Dorsey, Columbus, Ohio, 1972—; tchr. Capital U., Columbus, 1974. Alt.-at-large del. Democratic Nat. Conv., 1976;

chmn. Bd. Zoning Appeals, Village of Dublin; chmn. liaison com. Muirfield Assn.; pres. Indian Hills Residents Assn. Mem. Am. Bar Assn., Am. Arbitration Assn., Am. Assn. Trial Lawyers, Ohio Bar Assn., Franklin County Assn. Trial Lawyers, Columbus Bar Assn., Dublin C. of C., Cleve. State U. Center Alumni Assn. Clubs: Athletic (Columbus); Country (Muirfield Village, Ohio). Home: 8803 Narin Ct Dublin OH 43017 Office: 100 E Broad St Columbus OH 43215

RICH, RUTH ANNE, concert pianist, music educator; b. Salisbury, N.C., Dec. 20, 1941; d. Arthur L. and Helen (Wall) R.; Mus.B., Fla. State U., 1963; Mus.M., Peabody Conservatory, 1964; lic. (Fulbright grantee) Ecole Normale de Musique de Paris, 1965; diplome de virtuosite (Fondation des Etats-Unis grantee) Schola Cantorum de Paris, 1966; lic. Royal Acad. Music, London, 1966; D.M.A., Eastman Sch. Music, 1974. Artist-in-residence Mercer U., Macon, Ga., 1966-67; asst. prof. Lawrence U., Appleton, Wis., 1967-68, Valdosta (Ga.) State Coll., 1971-74; asso. prof. music Kansas City Conservatory, U. Mo., 1974—; soloist with maj. orchs., Paris, Lisbon, Portugal, Europe, the Orient, U.S. Recipient 1st prize Marie Morrisey Keith Nat. Piano Contest, 1961; 1st prize biennial piano contest Nat. Fedn. Music Clubs, 1963. Mem. Music Tchrs. Nat. Assn., Mo. Music Tchrs. Assn., Phi Kappa Phi, Sigma Alpha Iota, Pi Kappa Lambda. Contbr. articles in field to prof. publs. Home: 203 Huntington Rd Kansas City MO 64113 Office: Conservatory of Music 4949 Cherry St Kansas City MO 64110

RICHARD, JACK, artist; b. Akron, Mar. 7, 1922; s. John Peter and Maude Anna (Williams) R.; student Chgo. Profl. Sch. Art, 1940-42, Kent State U., 1953-54, Akron U., 1947-48, U. Ohio, 1958-58. One-man shows: Canton (Ohio) Art Inst., Ambassador Coll. Gallery, Pasadena, Calif., 1969, Cuyahoga Valley Art Sch., French Colony Gallery, Gallopolis, Ohio, 1975; exhibited in group shows; represented in permanent collection: Canton Art Inst., Taylor Meml., Albany, Ohio; executed portraits Pres. and Mamie Eisenhower, also murals; dir. Cuyahoga Valley Art Center, 1952-62, Almond Tea Galleries, Cuyahoga Falls, 1962—; conservator, lectr. Served with AUS, 1942-45. Huntington Hartford Internat. fellow. Mem. Fifty Am. Artists, Internat. Platform Assn. Home and studio: 2250 Front St Cuyahoga Falls OH 44221

RICHARD, LOUIS PAUL, food co. exec.; b. Oak Park, Ill., Mar. 25, 1933; s. Paul Anthony and Verna Lucretia (Elwood) R.; B.A., Monmouth Coll., 1956; B.S. in Mech. Engring., Case Inst. Tech., 1956; M.S., Purdue U., 1959; m. Diane M. Dietrich, May 27, 1961; children—Steven W., Paul A. Research engr. Martin Marietta Co., 1960-61; v.p. Richards Food Corp., Melrose Park, Ill., 1962-72, pres., 1972—. Mem. Nat. Nutrition Foods Assn. (dir.), Inst. Food Technologists, Am. Assn. Cereal Chemists, Nat. Assn. Splty. Foods Trade, Nat. Food Distbrs. Assn., Tau Beta Pi, Pi Tau Sigma, Sigma Omicron Mu. Office: 4520 James Pl Melrose Park IL 60160

RICHARDS, EARL FREDERICK, elec. engr.; b. Detroit, Mar. 11, 1923; s. Earl F. and Esther Stancer (Branning) R.; B.S. in E.E., Wayne U., 1951; M.S. in E.E., Mo. Sch. Mines and Metallurgy, 1961; Ph.D. in E.E., U. Mo., 1971; m. Marjorie P. Holt. Jan. 12, 1946; children—Dennis Lee, Laura Lee. Project engr. Pa. Salt Mfg. Co., Wyandotte, Mich., 1952-53; elec. engr. Revere Copper & Brass, Inc., Detroit, 1954-58; plant engr., elec. engring. U. Mo., Rolla, 1958—; tchr. U. Detroit, 1956-58; research asso. Argonne (Ill.) Nat. Lab., 1963; cons. Firestone Rubber Corp., 1954-56, Electronic Control Corp., Detroit, 1950-51. Served with OSS, 1942-46. Registered profl. engr. Mo., Mich. Mem. Sigma Xi, Tau Beta Pi, Eta Kappa Nu, Theta Xi. Roman Catholic. Club: Lions. Home: 8 Hyer Ct Rolla MO 65401 Office: Dept Elec Engring U Mo Rolla MO 65401

RICHARDS, FRANCIS LEE, physician; b. Ashland, Nebr., Feb. 19, 1908; s. Earl Webster and Ida Belle (Wortman) R.; A.B., Doane Coll., 1932; M.D., U. Nebr., 1938; m. Dorothy Waters Hamilton, Jan. 29, 1938; 1 son, Donald Lee. Intern, University Hosp., Omaha, 1938-39; practice medicine specializing in eye, ear, nose and throat, Kearney, Nebr., 1946—; mem. staff Good Samaritan Hosp., Kearney, chief of staff, 1953-54; pres. Valley Plaze Corp., 1967—; charter mem., chmn., dir. Kearney State Bank. Mem. Kearney City Council, 1961-63; mayor, Kearney, 1963-78; mem. So. Route Commn., 1976—; hon. mem. Kearney Vol. Fire Dept. Served with AUS, 1941-46. Recipient distinguished service award Cosmopolitan Internat., 1967. Mem. AMA, Nebr. Acad. Ear, Nose Throat, Kearney C. of C. (dir. 1956-57). Republican. Presbyterian (deacon 1953-54, trustee 1949-50, elder 1980—). Mason, Elk. Club: Cosmopolitan (pres. 1955). Home: 3206 1st Av Kearney NE 68847 Office: 214 W 25th St Kearney NE 68847

RICHARDS, GILBERT FRANCIS, mfg. exec.; b. Prairieburg, Iowa, Nov. 2, 1915; s. Raymond D. and Theresa (O'Connor) R.; student Tilton Acad.; LL.D. (hon.), Ursinus Coll., 1973; m. Mary Elizabeth Hanchett, May 13, 1959; children—Patricia Richards Roorda, Michael, Sheri Stanton McManus, Jan Stanton Johnson, Lauri Stanton Taylor, James Stanton, Mary Elizabeth. Dist. mgr. Permanente Cement Co., 1944-45; dist. sales mgr. Kaiser Gypsum Co., 1945-48, gen. sales mgr., 1948-52; gen. sales mgr. Kaiser Metal Products, 1952-56; v.p. sales Sharples Corp., 1956-58; sales mgr. Airframe, The Budd Co., 1958-59, v.p. sales, 1959-65, v.p., gen. mgr. automotive div., 1965-68, pres., gen. mgr. automotive div., 1968-71; pres., chief exec. officer Budd Co., 1971-74, chmn. bd., chief exec. officer, 1974-80, chmn. bd., 1980—; dir. Fed. Mogul Corp.; supervisory bd. Thyssen Industrie AG. Bd. dirs. Detroit Renaissance. Mem. Soc. Automotive Engrs. Clubs: Economic (dir.) (Detroit); Bloomfield Hills (Mich.) Country; Eldorado Country (Calif.); Marrakesh Country (Calif.); Capitol Hill; Yondotega. Home: 1009 Stratford Ln Bloomfield Hills MI 48013 Office: 3155 W Big Beaver Rd Troy MI 48084

RICHARDS, KURT FRED, chem. engr.; b. Cleve., July 8, 1923; s. Ernst Fred and Ernestine Anna (Racek) R.; B.Chem. Engring., Cornell U., 1948; diplome de Langue, Alliance Francaise, Paris, 1975; m. Winifred Ann Parker, June 25, 1949; children—Paul, Carl, Eric. Technologist, Amoco Chemicals Corp., Chgo., 1950-57; sr. tech. rep. Exxon Chem. Co., N.Y.C., Akron, 1957-69; sr. engr., mktg. specialist H.K. Ferguson Co., Cleve., Paris, Riyadh, Saudi Arabia, 1973-77; mgr. bus. devel. Procon Internat. Inc., Des Plaines, Ill., 1977-79; dir. engring. devel. Cunningham-Limp Internat., Birmingham, Mich., 1979-81. Mem. Lake County (Ind.) Planning Commn., 1955, North Olmsted (Ohio) Planning Commn., 1967-74, chmn., 1974. Served with Inf., AUS, 1943-46. Decorated Combat Infantryman Badge, Bronze Star; Ohio Dept. Edn. fellow, 1940; John McMullen Indsl. scholar, 1942-48. Mem. Am. Chem. Soc., Am. Inst. Chem. Engrs., Nat. Water Supply Improvement Assn., French-Am. C. of C. Lutheran. Patentee in teflon plastics and oil additives; editor The Indicator, 1957-59. Home: 5176 W Park Dr North Olmsted OH 44070 Office: Davy McKee Corp 6200 Oak Tree Blvd Cleveland OH 44131

RICHARDS, LACLAIRE LISSETTA JONES (MRS. GEORGE A. RICHARDS), social worker; b. Pine Bluff, Ark.; d. Artie William and Geraldine (Adams) Jones; B.A., Nat. Coll. Christian Workers, 1953; M.S.W., U. Kans., 1956; postgrad. Columbia U., 1960; m. George Alvarez Richards, July 26, 1958; children—Leslie Rosario, Lia Mercedes, Jorge Ferguson. Psychiat. supervisory, teaching, community orgn., adminstrv. and consultative duties Hastings Regional Center, Ingleside, Nebr., 1956-60; supervisory, consultative and adminstrv. responsibilities for psychiat. and geriatric patients VA Hosp., Knoxville, Iowa, 1960-70, 71-74, Fed. women's program coordinator, 1972-74, equal employment counselor, 1969-74; chief social worker, adult female service Mental Health Inst., Cherokee, Iowa, 1974-77; outpatient social worker VA Center, Sioux Falls, S.D., 1978—, also EEO counselor; field instr. for grad. students from U. Mo., 1966-67, also equal employment opportunity counselor, 1969-70, 71-74, com. chmn., 1969-70; field instr. Drake U., 1969-70, 73, also U. Iowa, U. No. Iowa, Morningside Coll., Buena Vista Coll., Westmar Coll., Hastings Coll., Wm. Penn Coll., Central Coll.; mem. adj. asst. prof. dept. social behavior U. S.D.; instr. minority studies Augustana Coll.; mem. civil rights com. Mental Health Inst. Mem. Knoxville Juvenile Adv. Com., 1963-65, 68-70, sec., 1965-66, chmn., 1966-68; sec. Urban Renewal Citizens' Adv. Com., Knoxville, 1966-68; canvasser community fund drives, Knoxville; bd. dirs., sec., exec. com., personnel com. Vis. Nurse Assn., 1979—; mem. edn. com. 1st United Meth. Ch., Sioux Falls. Mem. Nat. Assn. Social Workers (co-chmn. Nebr. chpt. profl. standards com. 1958-59, chmn. minority affairs com. 1979-80, pres. S.D. chpt. 1980—), Acad. Cert. Social Workers, AAUW (sec. Hastings chpt. 1958-60), S.D. AMA Aux., 7th Dist. Med. Aux. United Methodist (past Sunday sch. tchr. adult div.; mem. commn. on edn. and missions 1968-74, chmn. health and welfare commn. 1973-74, mem. edn. com. 1979—, mem. task force experimental styles ministry and leadership). Home: 1701 Ponderosa Dr Sioux Falls SD 57103

RICHARDS, PHILIP HARVEY, coll. adminstr., mgmt. cons. firm exec.; b. Hart, Mich., Sept. 7, 1924; s. Eugene Carson and Ruby Mae (Bettin) R.; B.S., U. Omaha, 1952, M.S., 1955; Ed.D., U. Nebr., 1964; postgrad. Denver U., 1965-66; m. Gloria Jean Heller, Dec. 30, 1946; children—Gloria, Rodger, Phyllis, Susan, Russell, Rodney. Sch. adminstr. Westside Community Sch., Omaha, 1955-63; asst. prof. Drake U., Des Moines, 1963-64, Denver, U., 1964-66; asso. prof., chmn. edn. dept. Trinity U., San Antonio, 1966-68; prof. edn., dean extended programs div. Coll. St. Scholastica, Duluth, Minn., 1968—; v.p. Zelrich Co., Duluth, 1979—; pres. Richards Enterprises, Duluth, 1978—. Trustee Operation Aware, 1974-81; mem. Duluth Visitor and Conv. Bur., 1973-81. Served with AUS, 1943-44. Named Ednl. coordinator of Yr., Personal Dynamics Inst., 1980. Mem. N.Am. Assn. Summer Session (regional v.p. 1978-80), Am. Soc. Tng. and Devel., Am. Mgmt. Assn., Council for Experiential Learning, Am. Assn. for Colls. Tchr. Edn. Republican. Lutheran. Club: Rotary. Author: Family Designed Learning, 1976, also children's stories, film strips. Home: 2118 Abbotsford St Duluth MN 55803 Office: Coll Saint Scholastica 1200 Kenwood Ave Duluth MN 55811

RICHARDS, THOMAS JEFFREY, physicist; b. Berwyn, Ill., Feb. 28, 1944; s. James Henry and Caroline Emily (Patha) R.; B.A., Lake Forest Coll., 1966; M.A., Wake Forest U., 1968; Ph.D., St. Louis U., 1972. Sr. research engr. Caterpillar Tractor Co., Peoria, Ill., 1973-76, project engr., 1976-81, staff engr., 1981—. Mem. Am. Phys. Soc., AAAS. Patentee in field. Office: Research Dept TC-E Caterpillar Tractor Co Peoria Il 61629

RICHARDS, WILLIAM ARNOLD, banker; b. Aurora, Ill., Oct. 30, 1922; s. William Wilson and Ethel (Reynolds) R.; student Northwestern U., 1939-40, U. Hawaii, 1945; grad. Grad. Sch. Banking, U. Wis., 1951; m. Bernice Whitney, Apr. 22, 1945 (dec.); children—Patricia, Barbara. Cashier, Farmers State Bank, Lostant, Ill., 1945-55, pres., dir., 1981—; with First Trust & Savs. Bank, Kankakee, Ill., 1955—, pres., dir., 1981—; pres., dir. Micro Data Corp., Kankakee, 1969—; chmn., dir. Electronic Funds Ill., Chgo., 1978-81. Past pres. United Way, Community Service Council, Salvation Army. Served with USMC, 1940-45. Mem. C. of C. Republican. Methodist. Club: Lions. Home: Rural Route 2 Woodlea Rd Kankakee IL 60901 Office: 1 Dearborn Square Kankakee IL 60901

RICHARDSON, DEAN EUGENE, banker; b. West Branch, Mich., Dec. 27, 1927; s. Robert F. and Helen (Husted) R.; A.B., Mich. State U., 1950; LL.B., U. Mich., 1953; postgrad. Stonier Grad. Sch. Banking, 1965; m. Barbara Trytten, June 14, 1952; children—Ann Elizabeth, John Matthew. With Indsl. Nat. Bank, Detroit, 1953-55; with Mfrs. Nat. Bank, Detroit, 1955—, v.p. adminstrn., 1964-66, sr. v.p., 1966-67, exec. v.p., 1967-69, pres., chief exec. from 1969, now chmn., dir.; chmn. bd. dirs. Mrs.-Detroit Internat. Corp., 1973—; gov. Adela Corp. of Luxembourg, Atlantic Internat. Bank of London; dir. Detroit Edison Co., R.P. Scherer Corp., Tecumseh Products Co. Served with USNR, 1945-46. Mem. Mich., Detroit bar assns., Assn. Res. City Bankers, Am. Inst. Banking, Mens Forum, Robert Morris Assos., Econ. Club Detroit (dir.), Newcomen Soc. N.Am. Episcopalian. Clubs: Detroit Athletic, Detroit, Country of Detroit, Masons. Office: Mfrs Nat Corp 100 Renaissance Center Detroit MI 48243

RICHARDSON, EMANUEL ROSS, govt. ofcl.; b. Richmond, Va., Dec. 23, 1924; s. George C. and Lelia Ann (Gibbs) R.; B.S., Hampton Inst., 1950; M.A., Central Mich. U., 1973; Cornell U. Law Sch., 1950-53; m. Irene Hortense Burnette, Dec. 1, 1963; children—Angela Dawn, Eric Bernard. Substitute tchr. secondary schs., Richmond, 1953-54; recreation dir. City of Richmond, 1953-54; group leader and supply commodity mgr. officer U.S. Naval Aviation Supply Office; exec. agt. for retail agreements U.S. Air Force Logistics Command, Wright-Patterson AFB, Ohio, 1963-70, systems analyst, 1970-77, fgn. mil. sales program mgr. Aero. Systems div., 1977—; propr. A to Z Rental Center, Xenia, Ohio, 1969-71. Pres. Wilberforce Community Property Owners and Voters Assn., 1966-68; chmn. Xenia Area Human Relations Council, 1969-72; sec. treas. Greene County chpt. Greene-Montgomery Health and Welfare Planning Council, 1972-76; mem. affirmative action com. Xenia Pub. Schs., 1977; treas. Greene County Farm City Tour Com., 1976-77; mem. pres.'s club Nat. Democratic Party Com., Washington, 1977-78; trustee Dayton Opera Assn. Served with U.S. Army, 1943-46, 55-58. Decorated Bronze Star (3). Mem. Air Force Assn., Am. Def. Preparedness Assn., Assn. for the Study of Afro-Am. Life and History (state sec.), Xenia C. of C., NAACP (negotiating com. 1976—), Am. Legion, Greene County Hist. Soc. Democrat. Episcopalian. Clubs: Kiwanis, Optimist; Town and Country (pres.). Home: PO Box 512 Wilberforce OH 45384 Office: US Air Force Aeronautical Systems Div Wright Patterson AFB OH 45433

RICHARDSON, GAYLE ELWIN, ins. agy. exec.; b. East Orange, N.J., Apr. 10, 1911; s. Glenn Ellison and Gabriella (Clyne) R.; B.A., U. Mich., 1932; postgrad. John Marshall Law Sch., 1933-34, Grad. Sch. Social Work, Northwestern U., 1934-36, Sch. Bus., U. Minn., 1940-41; m. Bernice M. Richardson, June 5, 1937; 1 son, William B. Asst. v.p., asst. to exec. v.p. Am. States Ins. Co., Indpls., 1944-47; state mgr. Ind., Gen. Ins. Cos. of Am. and SAFECO, Indpls., 1947-57; owner, operator G.E. Richardson Agy., Indpls., 1958—; lectr. ins. Ind. U., 1951-70; panel moderator, ins. program Sta. WLWI-TV, Indpls., 1964-65. Past pres. Marion County Cancer Soc.-Little Red Door; mem. fin. com. United Fund of Indpls.; mem. fin. com., bd. dirs. North Meth. Ch., Indpls. Recipient spl. citation for service to ins. industry Nat. Soc. C.P.C.U.-Continental Assurance Co., 1962; C.P.C.U., 1952, C.L.U., 1965. Mem. Nat. Soc. Chartered Property and Casualty Underwriters (past pres. Indpls. chpt.), Nat. Soc. Chartered Life Underwriters, Nat. Assn. Life Underwriters, Nat. Assn. Health Underwriters, U. Mich. Alumni Assn. Republican. Clubs: Contemporary, Masons (Indpls.). Author: Behind the Fine Print, 1961; Who Pays?, 1967; Am I Covered?, 1973. Home: 5367 Graceland St Indianapolis IN 46208 Office: 804 Investor's Trust Bldg Indianapolis IN 46204

RICHARDSON, GEORGE BOWN, sales exec.; b. Akron, Ohio, Nov. 3, 1926; s. William Samuel and Margaret (Bown) R.; B.S. in Commerce, U. Va., 1950; m. Helen Miller, Dec. 1, 1956; 1 dau., Denise. Nat. mgr. indsl. maintenance and transp. sales Glidden Co., 1950-59; pres., chmn. bd. R/C Assos., Inc., R/C-NSO, Inc., Beachwood, Ohio, 1949—. Served with USMCR, 1944-46; PTO. Mem. Elec. League Cleve., Nat. Elec. Mfrs. Reps. Assn. (bd. govs.). Republican. Episcopalian. Club: Country of Cleve. Home: 2840 Lander Rd Pepper Pike OH 44124 Office: 24100 Chagrin Blvd Beachwood OH 44122

RICHARDSON, JOHN ADKINS, art scholar, educator; b. Gillette, Wyo., Oct. 24, 1929; s. John Wesley and Joyce L. (Adkins) R.; B.A., Eastern Wash. State U., 1951; M.A., Columbia U., 1952, Ed.D., 1958; children—Christopher, Robin; m. 3d, Glenda Marie Lawhorn. Prof. art and design State U. N.Y., Geneseo, 1957-58, Fresno (Calif.) State Coll., 1958-59, So. Ill. U., Edwardsville, 1959—. Author: Modern Art and Scientific Thought, 1971; Art: The Way It Is, 1974; The Complete Book of Cartooning, 1976. Home: 802 W High St Edwardsville IL 62025 Office: Box 64 Southern Illinois Univ Edwardsville IL 62025

RICHARDSON, JOHN BIXLER, savs. and loan exec.; b. St. Louis, Dec. 15, 1951; s. Preston Allan and Pearl Lurlene R.; A.A. in Bus., Drury Coll. With Charles E. Scheidt, real estate appraisals, 1973-74; v.p. ins. div. Mut. Fed. Savs. & Loan Assn., 1974; br. mgr. Farm & Home Savs. Assn., St. Louis, 1974-76, asst. sec., 1976—; founder, pres. Richardson Corp., 1981—; cons. fins. Bd. dirs. University City Loop Spl. Bus. Dist. Commn., 1981—. Mem. University City C. of C. (pres. 1977-78). Home: 13 Overbrook Dr Ladue MO 63124 Office: 6680 Delmar Blvd Saint Louis MO 63130

RICHARDSON, JOSEPH HILL, physician; b. Rensselaer, Ind., June 16, 1928; s. William Clark and Vera (Hill) R.; M.S. in Medicine, Northwestern U., 1950, M.D., 1953; m. Joan Grace Meininger, July 8, 1950; children—Lois N., Ellen M., James K. Intern, U.S. Naval Hosp., Great Lakes, Ill., 1953-54; fellow in medicine Cleve. Clinic, 1956-59; individual practice medicine specializing in internal medicine and hematology, Marion, Ind., 1959-67, Ft. Wayne, Ind., 1967—. Served to lt. MC USNR, 1954-56. Diplomate Am. Bd. Internal Medicine. Fellow ACP, AAAS; mem. Am. Fedn. for Clin. Research, Am. Med. Writers Assn., AMA. Mason. Contbr. articles to med. jours. Home: 8726 Fortuna Way Fort Wayne IN 46815 Office: 3010 E State Blvd Fort Wayne IN 46805

RICHARDSON, JOSEPH LEONARD, mfg. co. exec.; b. Kansas City, Mo., Apr. 23, 1940; s. Joseph and Genevieve A. R.; B.A. in Sociology, Lincoln U., 1964; m. Jacqueline O. Webb, July 24, 1976; 1 dau., Jolawn. Employment rep. Butler Mfg. Co., Kansas City, 1968-69, div. employee relations mgr., Mpls., 1970-72; cons. John Tschohl & Assos., Mpls., 1972-73; acct. rep. Mgmt. Recruiters, Mpls., 1973-76; tng. mgr. The Toro Co., Bloomington, Minn., 1976-79; owner, pres. J.R. & Assos., Inc., Mpls., 1979—. Pres. Pan Hellenic Council, 1977—, Great Circle Factory; bd. dirs. Greater Kansas City Jr. Achievement, 1964, Phyllis Wheatley House, Mpls., 1971-72. Served with M.P., AUS, 1964-68; Vietnam. Decorated Army Commendation medal with oak leaf cluster; named Rookie of Year, Minn. Employment Assn., 1974. Mem. Am. Soc. Tng. and Devel., Twin City Personnel Assn., Am. Soc. Personnel Adminstrs., Alpha Phi Alpha. Club: Investment (pres. 1971-73). Methodist. Home: 11505 22d Ave S Burnsville MN 55337 Office: 101 W Burnsville Pkwy Burnsville MN 55337

RICHARDSON, JUDITH MONK, ednl. adminstr.; b. Des Moines, Nov. 19, 1942; d. James Harrison and Margaret Harriet (Winder) Monk; B.A., Drake U., 1965, M.S., 1972, Ed.D., 1979; m. Dennis G. Norris, Feb. 18, 1965 (dec.); children—Lisa Dawn; m. Darrel L. Richardson, Mar. 18, 1970; 1 son, Sean Robert. Tchr. English, Weeks Jr. High Sch., Des Moines, 1966-71, project coordinator, 1972-75; vice prin. Brody Jr. High Sch., Des Moines, 1976-79; vice prin. curriculum Des Moines Tech. High Sch., 1980—; cons. curriculum planning, grant devel., talented and gifted to various schs., 1976—. Mem. Am. Fedn. Tchrs. (sec. 1967-69), NEA, Council Exceptional Children, Assn. Supervision and Curriculum Devel., Am. Vocat. Assn., Vice Prins. Assn. Republican. Methodist. Home: 740 42d St West Des Moines IA 50265 Office: Des Moines Tech High Sch 1800 Grand St Des Moines IA 50309

RICHARDSON, MILDRED TOURTILLOTT, sch. and clin. psychologist; b. North Hampton, N.H., May 8, 1907; d. Herbert Shaw and Sarah Louise (Fife) Tourtillott; B.A., Bates Coll., 1930; M.A., U. Mich., 1948; Ed.S., Butler U., 1961; Ph.D., Ind. U., 1965; m. Harold Wellington Richardson, June 25, 1932; children—Elizabeth R. Ruben, Constance R. Van Valer, Carol-Louise Eads. Tchr. math. Norwich (Conn.) Free Acad., 1930-32; war emergency tchr. sci., Port Huron, Mich., 1943-45; dir. psychol. services and guidance Franklin (Ind.) Community Sch. Corp., 1956-64; intern Sch. Psychology, Devereux Found., 1964-65; sr. sch. psychologist Devereux Found., Devon, Pa., 1965-75, cons. clin. tng., 1975-78; tchr. psychology of spl. edn. Pa. State U., 1966-68; clin. asso. prof. Hahnemann Med. Coll., Phila., 1975-78; pvt. practice psychology, 1970—; psychologist spl. services Johnson County (Ind.) public schs., 1978—; asso. prof. edn. Ind. U., Bloomington, 1980—; cons. to public schs. on ednl. psychology, sch. psychology, pre-sch. edn.; participant Internat. Sch. Psychology Colloqium, 1975, Resource for Emotionally Handicapped Children and Adolescents, 1979—. Lic. psychologist, Pa., Ind.; diplomate Am. Bd. Profl. Psychology (exam. com. Midwest region 1981—. Fellow Am. Psychol. Assn.; mem. Internat. Council Psychologists, Phi Kappa Phi. Baptist. Contbr. articles on sch. edn. to profl. jours. Home: 477 S Oakwood Dr Greenwood IN 46142 Office: 500 Earlywoods Dr Franklin IN 46131

RICHARDSON, MYRTLE, abstracter, judge; b. Jefferson County, Ohio, July 2, 1907; d. Thomas and Blanche (Whitecotton) Heinselman; student Kansas State Tchrs. Coll., 1926; A.A., Dodge County Community Coll., 1978; m. Harold Richardson, Mar. 4, 1929 (div.); 1 dau., Nancy Lee (Mrs. Donald W. Ridgway). Tchr. pub. schs. Edwards County, Kans., 1924-28; reporter, advertiser Kinsley Graphic, Kinsely, Kans., 1928-35; editor, advt. mgr. S. Standard, McMinnville, Tenn., 1935-36; mgr. Kinsley Graphic, 1937-41; abstracter H.F. Thompson, Kinsley, 1943-54; editor Kinsley Mercury, 1954-57; abstracter, Kinsley, 1957—; owner, mgr. Richardson Abstract Co.; probate judge, Kinsley, 1958-68; police judge, City of Kinsley, 1958-68. Bd. dirs. United Drive, 1947-57; mem. bd. Edwards County chpt. ARC, 1940-50; community and project leader 4-H Club, 1943-52; community and project leader Edwards County 4-H Who's Who Club, 1943-52; pres. PTA, 1940-44; vice chmn. Edwards County Dem. Central Com., 1956-81, chmn., 1981—; charter mem. Edwards County Dem. Women's Federated Club, pres., 1970—, dist. dir., 1981—. Mem. C. of C. (Sec.-mgr. 1947-54), Edwards County Hist. Soc. (historian 1950). Nat. Council Juvenile Ct. Judges, Internat. Platform Assn., S. Central Kan. Probate Judges Assn. (pres. 1966). Author: Oft' Told Tales, a history of Edwards County, Kansas, to 1900, 1976. Home: 120 N 2d St Kinsley KS 67547 Office: 218 W 8th St Kinsley KS 67547

RICHARDSON, ROBERT LOWELL, mfg. exec.; b. Detroit, Oct. 8, 1938; s. Melvin James and Caroline Kathern (Herbert) R.; B.A., Olivet (Mich.) Coll., 1961; m. Janet Lois Thoresen, Feb. 12, 1966; children—Robert Gary, Thomas James, Joseph Lowell. Writer, exec. Jam Handy Orgn., Detroit, 1961-68; tng. dir., mktg. mgr., v.p. Jervis B. Webb Co., Farmington Hills, Mich., 1968—, also mgr., dir. Campbell, Henry & Calvin, Inc., Farmington Hills, 1974—. Active, Boys Clubs Detroit, Boy Scouts Am., Leadership Detroit, Detroit YMCA, Farmington Community Center. Served with AUS, 1961. Mem. Am. Def. Preparedness Assn., Am. Foundrymen's Soc., Assn. Iron and Steel Engrs., Engring. Soc. Detroit, Material Handling Inst., NAM, Nat. Def. Exec. Res., Soc. Mfg. Engrs., Adcraft Club Detroit, Econ. Club Detroit. Clubs: Detroit Athletic, Hundred (Detroit). Contbr. articles to periodicals. Home: 953 Dursley Bloomfield Hills MI 48013 Office: Jervis B Webb Co Webb Dr Farmington Hills MI 48018

RICHARDSON, ROY, mfg. co. exec.; b. Chgo., Mar. 22, 1931; s. John George and Margaret Beattie (Henderson) R.; B.A. in Psychology, Macalester Coll., 1952; M.A. in Labor and Indsl. Relations, U. Ill., 1953; Ph.D. in Indsl. Relations, U. Minn., 1969; m. Mary C. Westphal, May 16, 1970; children—Beth Allison, Jessica, Adam, Roman, Alexis. With Honeywell, Inc., Mpls., 1956-70, corp. manpower mgr., 1967-70; mgr. Manpower Devel. and Tng. Internat. Harvester, Chgo., 1970-73; dir. personnel U. Minn., 1973-75; v.p. human resources Onan Corp., Mpls., 1975—; pres. Personnel Surveys, Inc., Mpls., 1978-80. Vice pres. Mpls. Urban League, 1962-64. Recipient Disting. Citizens award City of Mpls., 1964. Mem. Am. Soc. Personnel Adminstrs., Am. Compensation Assn., U. Minn. Indsl. Relations Alumni Soc. (dir. 1979—, pres. 1981). Republican. Episcopalian. Club: Edina Country. Author: Fair Pay and Work, 1971. Home: 5509 Goya Ln Edina MN 55436 Office: 1400 73d Ave NE Minneapolis MN 55432

RICHARDSON, VICTOR ARNOLD, educator; b. Spring Valley, Minn., Mar. 10, 1944; s. Douglas Donald and Anne Christine (Lemke) R.; A.A., Austin State Jr. Coll., 1964; B.S., U. Minn., 1966, M.A., 1979; m. Clarice Gertrude Lindeman, May 31, 1969; children—Melanie, Craig, Janelle. Instr. vocat. agr. Jeffers (Minn.) High Sch., 1966-69; instr. high sch. and adult vocat. agr. Storden-Jeffers Sch., 1969-73; vets. agr. instr. Owatonna (Minn.) High Sch., 1973-77, adult agr. instr., 1979—; edn. cons. Minn. Farmers Union. Pres. St. John Lutheran Ch., 1981. Mem. Owatonna Edn. Assn., Minn. Edn. Assn., NEA, Minn. Vocat. Assn., Am. Vocat. Assn., Minn. Vocat. Agr. Instrs. Assn. (membership sec. 1980-81, v.p. 1981-82), Nat. Vocat. Agr. Tchrs. Assn. Lutheran. Club: Owatonna Exchange. Author: Rewarding Returns from an Ingenious Investment, 1980. Home: 351 13th St SW Owatonna MN 55060 Office: 333 E School St Owatonna MN 55060

RICHERT, DAVID DEAN, bank exec.; b. Milw., Nov. 10, 1945; s. Howard E. and Dorothy A. R.; student La. State U., 1963-64, U. Wis., 1969-73; m. Sharon Trotts, Dec. 11, 1965; children—Michele, Christopher. Programmer various state, fed. agys., S.D., 1967-68; project leader ins. programs Northwester Nat. Ins., 1968-70; sr. analyst/ops. research Schlitz Brewery, Milw., 1970-73; analyst data bank, mgr. systems programs Milw. Ins. Co., 1973-76; supr. tech. support and edn. Cutler Hammer Inc., Milw., 1976-79; capacity planning mgr. First Wis. Nat. Bank, Milw., 1979-80, data processing officer, info. center mgr., 1980—; lectr. and instr. in field. Served with U.S. Army, 1965-67. Mem. Assn. Computing Machinery, Assn. System Mgmt., Data Processing Mgmt. Assn., Inst. Software Engring., various EDP user groups. Home: 2602 N 116th St Wauwatosa WI 53226 Office: First Wis Nat Bank 777 E Wisconsin Ave Milwaukee WI 53202

RICHEY, CLARENCE BENTLEY, agrl. engr., educator; b. Winnipeg, Man., Can., Dec. 28, 1910 (parents Am. citizens); s. Raus Spears and Emily Cornelia (Bentley) R.; B.S. in Agrl. Engring., Iowa State U., 1933; B.S. in Mech. Engring., Purdue U., 1939; m. Marguerite Anne Jannusch, Dec. 27, 1936; children—David Volkman, Stephen Bentley. Time study engr. David Bradley Mfg. Works (Ill.), 1933-36; instr. Purdue U., 1936-41; asst. prof. Ohio State U., 1941-43; head devel. engr. Electric Wheel Co., Quincy, Ill., 1943-46; project engr. Harry Ferguson, Inc., Detroit, 1946-47; sr. project engr. Dearborn Motors Corp., Detroit, 1947-54; supr., chief research engr. Ford Tractor Div., Birmingham, Mich., 1954-62; chief engr. Fowler (Calif.) div. Massey-Ferguson, Inc., 1964-69; product mgmt. engr. Massey-Ferguson, Ltd., Toronto, Ont., Can., 1969-70; asso. prof. agrl. engring. Purdue U., West Lafayette, Ind., 1970-76, prof. emeritus, 1976—. Farm equipment cons. Ford Found., Allahabad, India, 1963. Fellow Am. Soc. Agrl. Engrs. (recipient Cyrus Hall McCormick medal 1977). Editor in chief: Agricultural Engineers' Handbook, 1961. Contbr. bulls., articles to profl. publs. Patentee farm equipment. Home: 2217 Delaware Dr West Lafayette IN 47906 Office: Agricultural Engineering Bldg Purdue U West Lafayette IN 47907

RICHEY, ROBERT WAYNE, ednl. adminstr.; b. Bradley, Ill., July 6, 1928; s. Robert Walter and Ina Lee (Thompson) R.; B.A. with honors, So. Ill. U., 1954, M.A., 1958; m. Anita Joann Sweeney, Jan. 7, 1950; children—Robert Bruce, Rebecca Lynn, Pamela Ann, Mary Beth (dec.). Budget officer State of Kans., Topeka, 1956-66; exec. sec. Iowa Bd. Regents, Des Moines, 1966—. Mem. Iowa Coordinating Council for Post High Sch. Edn., 1969—; mem. Iowa Planning Council on Developmental Disabilities, 1974—; mem. nat. adv. council Nat. Center for Higher Edn., 1974—; mem. Iowa Higher Edn. Facilities Commn., 1967-71; mem. adv. com. to Nat. Commn. on Correctional Edn., 1974-76, Iowa Coll. Aid Commn., 1981 and various others. Served with U.S. Army, 1946-47. Mem. State Higher Edn. Exec. Officers, commn., 1981 and various others. Home: 1441 7th Des Moines IA 50314 Office: Grimes State Office Bldg Des Moines IA 50319

RICHIE, ERNEST CARL, mfg. co. exec.; b. Mannheim, Germany, Aug. 25, 1912; s. Carl and Maria (Aberle) R.; came to U.S., 1954, naturalized, 1959; M.S. in Electronics, Tech. U. Berlin, 1936; m. Gertrude E. Heyartz, Apr. 22, 1948; children—Peter Carl, Patricia Monica, Raymond Ronald. Mgr. electronics factory Gen. Electric Co., Buenos Aires, 1938-54, dir., 1952-54; works mgr. tuner div. Sarkes Tarzian, Inc., Bloomington, Ind., 1954-77; pres. Tuner Service Corp., Bloomington, 1965—; gen. mgr. Sarkes Tarzian Mexicana, 1967-77; exec. v.p. Eastern Electronic Co., Taipei, 1970-77; pres. Cableconverter Service Corp., Bloomington, 1977-78; cons. Tonfunk, Karisruhe, Germany, 1961, Dean Bros., Indpls., 1961-65. Author: Appliances, 1945; Radio Equipment for FM, 1945; contbr. articles to profl. jours. Home: 316 Lakewood Dr Bloomington IN 47401 Office: Tuner Service Corp 537 S Walnut St Bloomington IN 47401

RICHMAN, ERIC THOMAS, podiatrist; b. N.Y.C., Jan. 9, 1950; s. Ernest and Dorothy (Miller) R.; B.S., Ohio State U., 1972; D.P.M., Pa. Coll. Podiatric Medicine, 1977; m. Vivian Freezman, July 1, 1973; children—Jessica, Amy. Pvt. practice podiatry Wooster, Ohio, 1978—; mem. staff Wayne Gen. Hosp., 1980—, Wooster Community Hosp., 1980—. Bd. dirs. Wayne-Holmes County Diabetes Assn., 1980—, Wayne County Crippled Children and Adults Assn., 1981—. Mem. Mideastern Acad. Ohio Podiatry Assn. (chmn. continuing edn. 1979—, treas. 1981), Am. Podiatry Assn., Ohio Podiatry Assn., Am. Assn. Hosp. Podiatrists, Ohio State U. Alumni Assn. Wayne County (sec.-treas. 1981—), Wooster Jaycees. Club: Rotary. Home: 1560 Willoughby Dr Wooster OH 44691 Office: 118 E North St Wooster OH 44691

RICHMAN, JOHN MARSHALL, food co. exec.; b. N.Y.C., Nov. 9, 1927; s. Arthur and Madeleine (Marshall) R.; B.A., Yale U., 1949; LL.B., Harvard U., 1952; m. Priscilla Frary, Sept. 3, 1951; children—Catherine Richman Roddy, Diana H. Admitted to N.Y. State bar, 1953, Ill. bar, 1973; asso. firm Leve, Hecht, Hadfield & McAlpin, N.Y.C., 1952-54; mem. law dept. Kraft, Inc., 1954-63, gen. counsel Sealtest Foods div., 1963-67, asst. gen. counsel, 1967-70, v.p., gen. counsel, 1970-73, sr. v.p., gen. counsel, 1973-75, sr. v.p. adminstrn., gen. counsel, 1975-79, dep. chmn., 1979, chmn. bd., chief exec. officer Kraft, Inc., 1979; chmn. bd., chief exec. officer Dart & Kraft, Inc., Northbrook, Ill., 1980—. Congregationalist. Clubs: Executives, Econ., Mid-Am. (Chgo.); Union League (N.Y.C.); Westmoreland Country (Wilmette, Ill.). Office: Dart & Kraft Inc 2211 Sanders Rd Northbrook IL 60062

RICHMOND, HAROLD WAYNE, physician; b. Oakdale, La., July 11, 1925; s. Harold Easborn and Essie (Seals) R.; B.S., U. Southwestern La., 1946; M.D., La. State U., 1948; m. Frances Alexa Womack, Sept. 30, 1950; children—Mark Kimbrough. Intern, Confederate Meml. Med. Center, Shreveport, La., 1948-49, resident surgery and orthopedics, 1949-50; pvt. practice gen. medicine and surgery, Oakdale, 1953-60; med. dir. Cummins Engine Co., Inc., Columbus, Ind., 1960-74, corporate med. dir., 1974—. Co-founder, med. dir. Columbus Occupational Health Center, 1970—. Served to lt. (j.g.), M.C., USNR, 1951-53. Recipient Ind. Good Samaritan award, 1979; diplomate Am. Bd. Preventive Medicine, Am. Bd. Family Practice (also recert.). Fellow Am. Coll. Preventive Medicine, Am. Acad. Family Practice, Am. Acad. Occupational Medicine, Royal Soc. Medicine (affiliate). Clubs: Harrison Lake Country; Columbia (Indpls.). Home: 3960 Waycross Dr Columbus IN 47201 Office: 605 Cottage Av Columbus IN 47201

RICHMOND, JOHN A., mech. engr.; b. Boston; B.S., Yale U., 1954. Process engr., supr. quality control and process engring. Remington Arms Co., Inc., Bridgeport, Conn. and Park Forest, Ill., 1954-59; asst. to product mgr. Gen. Am. Transp. Corp., Chgo., 1959-60, dist. mgr., 1960-63, sales rep., N.Y.C., 1963-68, gen. mgr. Cleve. transp. div., 1968-69; asso. Heidrick and Struggles, Inc., Cleve., 1969-73, mgr., Cleve., 1973-74, v.p., mgr., 1974-81, sr. v.p., dir., Midwest regional mgr., 1981—. Office: Heidrick and Struggles Inc 1100 Superior Ave Suite 930 Cleveland OH 44114

RICHMOND, QUINTON BLAINE, accountant; b. New, W.Va., Mar. 7, 1924; s. Calvin H. and Nora Ellen (Garten) R.; student Southeastern Bible Coll., 1950-51; B.A., Southwestern Bible Inst., 1952, Th.B., 1952; m. Patricia Lee Haley, Oct. 4, 1944; children—Carolyn Sue Richmond Terry, Larry Dean, Ronald David. Ordained to ministry Gen. Council of Assemblies of God, 1955; pastor chs., Kaufman, Tex., 1952-54, Dallas, 1954-56, New Carlisle, Ohio, 1963-66; accountant, auditor States Seed Co., Inc., Garland, Tex., 1952-53; with Indsl. Towel Co., Dallas, 1953-54; contract statistician Chance Voight Aircraft Corp., Dallas, 1954-55; auditor Tex. Automatic Sprinkler Corp., Dallas, 1955; accountant Wright-Patterson Air Force Base, Ohio, 1955-56; supr. cost accountant Dayton Air Force Depot, Dayton, Ohio, 1956-60; supervisory accounting tech. Detroit Air Force Contract Mgmt. Dist., 1960-61, contract specialist, 1961-63; contract price analyst/negotiator Wright Patterson AFB, Ohio, 1963-74; accountant, corporate officer, pres., chmn. bd. dirs. South Ohio Profl. Service & Sales Co., Inc., Dayton, 1973—; owner Beauty World Salon, Dayton, 1975—. Served with USNR, 1942-44. Recipient cert. of merit Nat. Small Bus. Assn., 1977. C.P.A., Ohio. Mem. Nat. Soc. Pub. Accountants. Composer songs. Home: 2860 Nacoma Pl Kettering OH 45420 Office: 3108 Wilmington Pike Dayton OH 45429

RICHMOND, RICHARD (DICK) THOMAS, journalist; b. Parma, Ohio, May 16, 1933; s. Arthur James and Frances Marie (Visosky) R.; A.B., Washington, U., St. Louis, 1961; m. Charlotte Jean Schwoebel, Dec. 18, 1954; children—Kris Elaine, Leigh Alison, Paul Evan. Bur. mgr. UPI Newspictures, St. Louis, 1961-62; asst. picture editor St. Louis Post-Dispatch, 1962-64, editor of color sect., 1964-80, columnist, 1971—; v.p. Golden Royal Enterprises, St. Louis, 1976-78; pres. OroQuest Press, Inc., St. Louis, 1977; dir. U.S. Mortgage & Investment Corp., 1977—; pres. Magalar Mining, 1979—. Served with USAF, 1953-57. Author: (with Roy Volker) Treasure Under Your Feet, 1974; In the Wake of the Golden Galleons, 1976. Home: 307 Lebanon Ave Belleville IL 62221 Office: Post-Dispatch 900 N Tucker Blvd Saint Louis MO 63101

RICHMOND, WILLIAM FREDERICK, life ins. agt.; b. Jackson, Mich., July 18, 1938; m. Fred L., Jr. and Mary Eileen (Reilly) R.; B.B.A., U. Mich., 1960; C.L.U., 1968; m. Marilyn Jean Wheeler, June 18, 1960; children—William Frederick, John M., David S. Engaged in ins. sales, 1960—; br. mgr. Northwestern Nat. Life Ins. Co., Jackson, 1972—. Served with Mich. N.G., 1962. Mem. Nat. Assn. Life Underwriters, Gen. Agts. and Mgrs. Assn., Mich. Assn. Life Underwriters, Jackson Assn. Life Underwriters (past pres.), Sales and Mktg. Execs. Club (dir.). Republican. Roman Catholic. Clubs: Jackson Country, Town, Elks. Home: 4725 Brich Haven Jackson MI 49201 Office: Box 50 1 Jackson Sq Jackson MI 49204

RICHTER, FRANZ ALLBERT, artist, graphic designer, sculptor; b. Seattle, Oct. 16, 1942; s. Fritz and Tredella Leona (Myhre) R.; student Hamline U., St. Paul, 1960-61, U. Minn., Mpls., 1961, 63-65, St. Cloud (Minn.) State U., 1963, Art Center Sch., Los Angeles, 1962. Woodworker, craftsman William J. Ketelle & Co., Los Angeles, 1961-62; graphic design cons. Grebner/Schoen & Assos., St. Paul, 1964-72, Minn. Writers' Pub. House, 1973; sculptor Tokheim Stoneware, Dawson, Minn., 1973—; owner, prin. designer Richter Graphics, Clarkfield, Minn., 1977—; one-man shows: Coffman Meml. Union, U. Minn., 1964, Chippewa County Library, Montevideo, Minn., 1974; miniature folk sculpture pieces distributed by Nord Hus Scandinavian Shop, St. Paul; record jacket design for John Koerner, Folk Singer, 1974; book designs include: Fifty-Five Leap Frogs (Gregory W. Bitz, artist and poet), 1969, Parrot in the Wheat, 1971, Watch the Turtle, 1972; illustrator Old Man Rubbing His Eyes, 1975; cover illustrator 20 Poems of Tomas Tranströmer (Swedish), 1970, Raingather, 1973, The Well Digger's Wife, 1974, Open to the Wind, 1978. Mem. Mpls. Soc. Fine Arts, Southwestern Minn. Arts and Humanities Council, Minn. Crafts Council, Yellow Medicine County Hist. Soc. Mem. Sons of Norway Democratic-Farm-Labor Party. Lutheran. Asso. editor Nickel and Dime Quar., 1969-70. Home: Rural Route 2 Clarkfield MN 56223

RICHTER, ROBERT CHARLES, business exec.; b. Heidelberg, Germany, Oct. 14, 1951; s. Arley Charles and Portia Dorcus (Tatum) R.; B.S., Miami U., Oxford, Ohio, 1973; M.B.A., Bowling Green State U., 1979; m. Lee Ann Esterly, June 23, 1973; children—Erin Marie, Brody Charles. Analyst, Ohio Casualy Ins. Group, Hamilton, Ohio, 1973-74; asst. to pres. Gen. Ohio Savs. & Loan Corp., Findlay, Ohio, 1974-76, asst. sec., asst. treas., 1976-78, corp. sec., 1978-80; controller Venture group Dana Corp., Toledo, 1981—; v.p., treas. Diamond Fin. Holdings, Toledo, 1981—, Potomac Leasing Co., Toledo, 1981—; chmn. adv. bd. thrift services Automatic Data Processing, Cin., 1979—. Mem. Fin. Com. Humane Soc. Hancock County. Mem. Fin. Mgrs. Soc. Savs. Assns., Beta Gamma Sigma. Democrat. Episcopalian. Clubs: Exchange, ELks. Home: 5562 State Route 12 W Findlay OH 45840 Office: 1609 Henthorne Dr Maumee OH 43537

RICHTER, ROBERTA BRANDENBURG (MRS. J. PAUL RICHTER), educator; b. Osborn, Ohio, Dec. 29; d. Warren F. and Mary M. (Davis) Brandenburg; student Miami-Jacobs Coll., 1930, Wittenberg U., 1930-31, Coll. Music, U. Cin., U. Dayton, 1954, 64; B.S., Miami U., Oxford, Ohio, 1958, M.Ed., 1959; postgrad. Wright State U., 1966-70, Ohio State U., 1969—; m. Jean Paul Richter, Oct. 6, 1934; 1 son, James Paul. Bus. mgr. T.D. Peffley, Inc., 1929-32; sec., prodn. mgr. Delco Products div. Gen. Motors, 1932-34; exec. sec. LWV, 1935-38, Elder & Johnston Dept. Store, 1938-40; cts. and conv. reporter Montgomery County, 1940-46; adminstrv. asst. Ch. Fedn. Greater Dayton (Ohio), 1946-50; audio-visual cons. schs., chs. Twyman Films, 1950-53; legal asst. Nadlin Law Offices, 1953-58; instr. stenotype, office practice Miami-Jacobs Coll., Dayton, 1952-59; tchr. stenotype and bus. edn., guidance counselor Stebbins High Sch., Dayton, 1958-81; vocat. guidance coordinator Mad River Planning Dist., Montgomery County, Ohio, 1968-74; test coordinator Miami U. dist. Ohio Achievement Tests, State Bd. Edn.; adviser Nat. Honor Soc.; lectr. in field; profl. cellist; instr. workshops in stenotype and ct. reporting, prof. Wright State U., Dayton, 1970—; owner Dayton Stenographic Studio. Supt., tchr., adviser youth div. Grace United Meth. Ch., Dayton, 1942-72, sec. adminstrv. bd., 1940—, past pres. Ex-cel Club, mem. council on ministries, 1970-73, work area, Christian social concerns, Christian missions Women's Soc. Christian Service; counselor Camp Miniwanca, Am. Youth Found., 1953-68; circle leader United Meth. Women, 1976—. Mem. Am., Ohio, Miami Valley personnel and guidance assns., Nat. Bus. Tchrs. Assn., Ohio Bus. Tchrs. Assn., Am., Ohio sch. counselor assns., Nat. Shorthand Reporters Assn., Nat., Ohio edn. assns., Nat. Vocat. Guidance Assn., Ohio Assn. Counselors, Deans and Adminstrs., Dayton Bus. Soc. (v.p. 1969-79), Internat. Platform Assn., AAUW, Pub. Speaker Bur., Council World Affairs, Delphian (past pres.), League Women Voters (past pres., dir., treas.), World Trade Club, Greater Dayton C. of C., Bus. and Profl. Women, Pi Omega Pi. Clubs: Order Eastern Star, Progressive Mothers (chmn. program Dayton 1969-70), World Traveler. Author numerous ednl. handbooks, pamphlets. Contbr. articles to profl. jours. Home: 3865 Seiber Ave Dayton OH 45405

RICKBEIL, CLARA EVELYN SHELLMAN (MRS. RAYMOND E. RICKBEIL), club woman; b. Gibson City, Ill.; d. Kilian and Anna Marie (Johnson) Shellman; grad. Brown's Bus. Coll., Champaign, Ill., 1922; student U. Ill., 1927-28; m. Raymond Earl Rickbeil, May 8, 1930. Office sec. Ford County Farm Bur., Gibson City, Ill., 1922-26; secretarial position Raymond E. Rickbeil, C.P.A., Springfield, Ill., 1928-61, Ernst & Ernst, Springfield, 1961-65. Program chmn. 21st dist. Ill. Fedn. Women's Clubs, 1968-69, corr. sec., 1969-71, dir., 1971-73; mem. nat. adv. bd. Am. Security Council; mem. Republican Women's Club Sangamon County, Nat. Fedn. Rep. Women Mem. Sangamon County Farm Bur., Child and Family Service Sangamon County; mem. Abraham Lincoln Meml. Garden Fund, Inc.; bd. dirs. Carrie Post King's Daus. Home for Women, 1967-69, also mem. Willing Circle. Recipient award for work pub. accounting legislation Ill. Soc. C.P.A.'s, 1956. Mem. U. Ill. Alumni Assn., Am. Legion Aux., YWCA, Sangamon County Hist. Soc., Meml. Hosp. Aux., Abraham Lincoln Assn., Am. Assn. Ret. Persons. Republican. Presbyterian. Mem. Order Eastern Star. Clubs: Springfield Woman's (reception com. 1962-63, social com. 1963-64, corr. sec. 1972-74), Mariama (chpt. chmn., mem. bd. 1969-71), Amateur Musical, Zonta (treas. 1954-57, finance chmn. 1957, 63, 66, service chmn. and mem. service com. 1953-62, mem. fin. com. 1967-79), Sangamo, U. Ill. Presidents; Three Hills Extension Homemakers (reporter 1982) (Kerrville, Tex.). Home: 937 Feldkamp Ave Springfield IL 62704

RICKERT, RICHARD MICHAEL, engr. b. Bklyn., Aug. 17, 1936; s. Richard and Louisa (Hofbauer) R.; A.B., Columbia U., 1958, B.S. in Elec. Engring., 1959, M.S. in Elec. Engring., 1960; m. Carla Schmidt, Jan. 16, 1961; children—Richard, Louisa, Adam. Mem. tech. staff Bell Telephone Labs., Indpls., supr. advanced home communication systems, 1964—. Mem. IEEE (editor newsletter Central Ind. sect. 1969-71), Phi Beta Kappa, Eta Kappa Nu, Tau Beta Pi, Indpls. Art Mus., Children's Mus., Smithsonian Assos. Club: K.C. Contbr. articles to profl. jours. Patentee in field. Office: 2525 Shadeland Ave Indianapolis IN 46206

RICKETTS, WILLIAM DALE, engring. and constrn. co. exec.; b. Greensburg, Kans., Feb. 14, 1929; s. Howard Hutchison and Isalone Mamie (Harrison) R.; m. Phyllis Jane Aguilera, June 17, 1948; children—Vernon Dale, Cheryl Kay, Howard Duane. Field constrn. mgr. Procon, Inc., Des Plaines, Ill., 1951-64; pres., dir. field ops. Litwin Constrn., Wichita, Kans., 1964-69; pres., chief exec. officer World-Wide Constrn. Services, Inc., Wichita, Kans., 1969—; now also v.p., dir. Ricketts Constrn. & Investments, Wichita; pres. U.S. Gasohol Corp., Wichita, also Lockeford, Calif. Mem. Nat. Soc. Profl. Engrs., ASME, Am. Inst. Chem. Engrs., ASTM, Am. Welding Soc., The Presidents Assn. Mason, Elk. Home: 7546 Plaza Ln Wichita KS 67206 Office: PO Box 8126 Wichita KS 67208

RICKGARN, RALPH LEE VURNE, univ. ofcl.; b. Slayton, Minn., June 1, 1934; s. Henry William and Alma Lenora Theodora (Swan) R.; B.A. cum laude, U. Minn., 1960, M.A., 1964, M.A., 1981; m. Glenys Agatha Neville, June 18, 1966; 1 dau., MerLynne Ann. Asst. to v.p. for devel. U. Minn., Mpls., 1964-65, sr. residence hall dir. Territorial Hall, 1971-72, prin. residence hall dir. Centennial Hall, from 1972, now sr. housing adminstr.; analyst Dept. Def., Washington, 1965-68; dean of students Ricker Coll., Houlton, Maine, 1968-71; cons. Served with U.S. Army, 1954-57. Recipient Public Service award U. Minn. Police Dept., 1974; Regents scholar, 1974-82.

Mem. Am. Personnel and Guidance Assn., Am. Coll. Personnel Assn. (Commn. III award 1980-81), Assn. Coll. and Univ. Housing Officers, Minn. Personnel and Guidance Assn., Minn. Coll. Personnel Assn., Minn. Decoy Collectors Assn., Pi Lambda Phi. Episcopalian. Home: 3536 Colfax Ave S Minneapolis MN 55408 Office: Centennial Hall U Minn 614 Delaware St SE Minneapolis MN 55455

RICKMAN, DARRELL GLENN, bank exec.; b. Kennett, Mo., Mar. 7, 1949; s. Russell and Earline R.; student Albion Coll., 1967-68, Ark. State U., 1970-71, U. Mich., 1971-73, Lansing Community Coll., 1978-79; m. Mary Lynn, Aug. 13, 1977; children—Shari, Staci. With Household Fin. Corp., Flint, Mich., 1970-74; with Mich. Nat. Bank, Flint and Lansing, 1974—, asst. v.p., credit officer bankard div., Lansing, 1975—; instr. Lansing Community Coll. Active, Big Bros. of Greater Flint, 1975-76, Jr. Achievement, Flint, 1976-77; coach boys baseball and women's softball. Served with USAF, 1968-70. Winner citizenship award VFW, 1967, I Dare You award, 1967. Mem. Am. Inst. Banking (pres., 1979, mem. dist. council, 1980, state com., 1980-81, bd. govs., 1977-81, bankard instr., 1978-81). Baptist. Club: Downtown Coaches. Office: PO Box 30993 Lansing MI 48909

RICKS, BERNARD E., auto mfg. co. exec.; b. Boscobel, Wis., Jan. 25, 1914; s. Clarence G. and Idllie Bell (Hubanks) R.; B.S.M.E., Detroit Inst. Tech., 1943; m. Ruth M. Guenther, Sept. 29, 1946; children—William (adopted), Jeff, Jon, Michal. With TRW, various locations, 1940—, dir. quality control and reliability, Warren, Mich, 1962—71, dir., coordinator quality control and relations, automotive world wide, Warren, 1971—. Mem. Soc. Auto. Engrs., Am. Soc. Quality Control, Am. Mgmt. Assn. Presbyterian. Clubs: Birmingham Country, Spring Lake Country, Recess, Masons. Patentee in field. Home: 17630 Oakwood Spring Lake MI 49456 Office: 34201 Van Dyke St Warren MI 48092

RIDDLE, MAXWELL, newspaper columnist; b. Ravenna, Ohio, July 29, 1907; s. Henry Warner and Mary E. (Fitz-Gerald) R.; B.A., U. Ariz., 1929; m. Martha A. Hurd, Mar. 31, 1933; children—Betsy (Mrs. Richard H. Whitmore), Henry W. III. Turf editor, columnist NEA Service, 1930, 39; kennel editor, columnist, pets columnist Cleve. Press, 1938-69; columnist Columbia Features, Inc., 1959-66; columnist Ledger Syndicate, 1966-73, Scott Editor Service, 1973—, Allied Feature Syndicate, 1975—; all breed dog judge, fgn. countries, 1955. U.S., 1960—. Recipient Cruikshank medal, 1941; Dog Writer of Year, 1949, 61; Dogdom's Man of the Year, 1968, Dog. Journalist of Year, 1970, 72. Mem. Ohio Dog Owners Assn., Dog Writers Assn. (past pres.), Sigma Delta Chi, Delta Upsilon. Clubs: Western Reserve Kennel, Ravenna Kennel. Author: The Springer Spaniel, 1939; The Lovable Mongrel, 1954; This Is The Chihuahua, 1959; The Complete Book of Puppy Training and Care, 1962; Dog People are Crazy, 1966; Your Show Dog, 1968; A Quick Guide to the Standards of Show Dogs, 1972; (with Mrs. M.B. Seeley) The Complete Alaskan Malamute, 1976. The Complete Brittany Spaniel, 1974; The New Shetland Sheepdog, 1974; The Wild Dogs in Life and Legend, 1979; Your Family Dog, 1981, also articles in field. Contbr. New Dog Ency., 1967, Internat. Dog Ency., 1972, World Book Ency. Asso. editor Dog World Mag., 1961—. Home: PO Box 286 Ravenna OH 44266

RIDDLE, THOMAS WAYNE, educator; b. Delano, Calif., Feb. 3, 1943; s. LeRoy James and Elna Marie (Anderson) R.; B.A., Whitworth Coll., 1964; M.A., Wash. State U., 1971, Ph.D., 1976; student Occidental Coll., 1960-61; m. Linda L. Lee, Dec. 27, 1966; children—Camille Kathleen, Joel Thomas. Social studies tchr., South Kitsap, Wash., 1966-68, Seattle, 1968-69; teaching asst. Wash. State U., Pullman, 1970-75; instr. S.W. Tex. State U., San Marcos, 1975-77; instr. Hasting (Nebr.) Coll., 1977-79, asst. prof. history, 1979—. Regional humanist Nebr. Com. for Humanities, 1977—; dist. dir. Hastings History Day, 1980—. Mem. AAUP, Am. Assn. for Advancement of Humanities, Am. Hist. Assn., Orgn. Am. Historians. Presbyterian. Home: 302 W 7th St Hastings NE 68901 Office: Dept History Hastings Coll Hastings NE 68901

RIDEN, MICHAEL DAVID, nuclear engr.; b. Maryville, Tenn., July 2, 1947; s. William Walter and Grace Ella (Elrod) R.; B.S. in Nuclear Engring., U. Tenn.-Knoxville, 1974; m. Perry Dene Thyberg, Mar. 28, 1970; children—Chad Michael, Kirk David, Eric Wesley. Area mgr. Field Enterprises Ednl. Corp., Maryville, 1973-74; asst. engr. Duke Power Co., Oconee Nuclear Sta., Seneca, S.C., 1974-78; reactor insp. Region III, U.S. Nuclear Regulatory Commn., Glen Ellyn, Ill., 1978-79; gen. mgr. Chgo. Barra Corp. Am., Wheaton, Ill., 1979—; ordained deacon Presbyn. Ch. U.S., 1976; deacon Presbyn. Ch., Seneca, 1976-77. Served with USAF, 1967-71. Decorated Air Force Commendation medal; recipient Air Force Meritorious award, 1971. Mem. Am. Nuclear Soc. Home: 22W302 Hackberry Dr Glen Ellyn IL 60137 Office: 929 W Liberty Dr Wheaton IL 60187

RIDENOUR, C. THOMAS, univ. adminstr.; b. St. Paris, Ohio, July 24, 1926; s. Carl Thomas and Carrie (Mackan) R.; student St. Lawrence U., 1944-45, Coll. of Holy Cross, 1945-46; B.S., Ohio State U., 1951; m. Frances Rozum, Sept. 13, 1947; children—Michael, Andrea, Carla, Paul. Internal auditor Procter & Gamble, Cin., 1951; staff acct. Keller, Kirschner, Martin & Clinger, C.P.A.'s, Columbus, Ohio, 1952-57; controller Ohio State U., Columbus, 1957—. Served with USNR, 1944-46. Mem. Ohio Soc. C.P.A.'s, Am. Inst. C.P.A.'s, Nat. Assn. Coll. and Univ. Bus. Officers. Roman Catholic. Home: 4512 Zeller Rd Columbus OH 43214 Office: 1800 Cannon Dr Columbus OH 43210

RIDGWAY, GEORGE MARTIN, computer cons. co. exec.; b. Rockford, Ill., Aug. 15, 1936; s. William Franklin and Marjorie Ann (Bolin) R.; Ph.B., Northwestern U., 1966; postgrad. U. Colo., 1966-67; m. Nanette Marie Populorum, Dec. 23, 1961; children—Philip Esta, Paul Franklin, Elizabeth Ann. Program analyst Abbott Labs., Chgo., 1960-66; systems mgr. Colo. Interstate Computer Services, Colorado Springs, 1966-67; mgr. computer services Greyhound, Chgo., 1967-68, asst. to pres., 1968-69; founder Systems Mgmt., Des Plaines, Ill., 1969—, also pres.; partner H&R Leasing; pres. R-Lease; cons. Joint Commn. on Accreditation Hosps., 1974-75, HEW, 1974-75. Treas., Republican County Com., 1967-73, precinct committeeman, 1965-67. Served with AUS, 1957-59. Mem. Presidents Assn., Assn. Computing Machinery, Assn. for Data Processing Service Orgns., Data Processing Mgmt. Assn., Am. Contract Bridge League. Presbyterian (deacon). Home: 681 Monticello Circle Lake Forest IL 60045 Office: 10400 W Higgins Rd Rosemont IL 60018

RIDINGS, JAMES SIDNEY, engring. co. exec.; b. Escanaba, Mich., Nov. 14, 1946; s. Sidney Charles and Mavis Ethel (LaFaver) R.; B.S. in Edn., No. Mich. U., 1972; m. Marsha Lynne Hess, Oct. 25, 1975; children—Lyndsay Dyan, Joshua Hazer. Personnel rep. Fluor Utah, San Mateo, Calif., 1973-76; personnel rep. Ralph M. Parsons, Pasadena, Calif., 1976-77, mgr. project personnel adminstrn., 1977-78; dir. employee relations Procon Inc., Des Plaines, Ill., 1978—. Served with U.S. Army, 1966-68. Decorated Bronze Star medal, Purple Hearts (2). Mem. Am. Mgmt. Assn., Am. Soc. Personnel Adminstrs., Am. Soc. Tng. and Devel. Methodist. Club: Elks. Home: 2015 Sprucewood St Lindenhurst IL 60046 Office: 30 UOP Plaza Des Plaines IL 60016

RIDLEN, JULIAN LEON, state govt. ofcl.; b. Macon County, Ill., Feb. 4, 1940; s. Charles F. and Doris O. (Franklin) R.; B.A., Anderson (Ind.) Coll., 1963; J.D., George Washington U., 1967; m. Susanne Lee Smith, June 1, 1963. Tchr., Emerson Inst., also Washington Hall Jr. Coll., Washington, 1966-68; legal researcher, writer NEA, Washington, 1967-68; admitted to Ind. bar, 1967; mem. firm Smith & Ridlen, Logansport, 1968—; judge Logansport City Ct., 1969-78; treas. State of Ind., 1979—. Chmn. Cass County (Ind.) Bicentennial Com., 1974-76; pres. Cass County Youth Services Bur., 1971, Cass County chpt. ARC, 1971-73; v.p., bd. dirs. Logansport United Fund, 1972; v.p. Cass County Mental Health Assn., 1971-74; mem. Cass County Bd. Election Commrs., 1970; mem. staff Republican. Nat. Com., 1963-64; elder Calvary Presbyn. Ch., Logansport, 1971—. Recipient Disting. Service award Logansport Jaycees, 1971, Boss of Year award Logansport chpt. Nat. Secretaries Assn., 1976, Golden Deeds award Logansport Exchange Club, 1976, 78. Mem. Nat. Assn. State Treasurers, Nat. Assn. State Auditors, Comptrollers and Treasurers, Am. Bar Assn., Ind. Bar Assn., Cass County Bar Assn., Cass County Hist. Soc. (pres. 1974-78), Phi Alpha Delta. Clubs: Kiwanis, Elks, Eagles, Moose. Office: 242 State Office Bldg Indianapolis IN 46204

RIDZON, JAMES RONALD, orthodontist; b. Canton, Ohio, Mar. 25, 1941; s. Joseph John and Marcella Norma (McMahan) R.; student John Carroll U., 1959-61; B.S., Western Res. U., 1963, D.D.S., 1965, M.S., 1971; m. Marilyn Lee McQuern, July 3, 1965; children—Richard, Susan. Asso. in practice gen. dentistry, Canton, 1968-70; asso. in practice orthodontics, Wooster, Ohio, 1970-72; pvt. practice orthodontics, Massillon, Ohio, 1972—. Served as lt. U.S. Navy, 1965-68. Recipient award of achievement Am. Coll. Dentists. Mem. Royal Soc. Health, ADA, Ohio Dental Assn., Omicron Kappa Upsilon. Roman Catholic. Home: 5772 West Blvd NW Canton OH 44718 Office: 3140 Lincoln Way E Massillon OH 44646

RIECKER, JOHN E(RNEST), lawyer, bank exec.; b. Ann Arbor, Mich., Nov. 25, 1930; s. Herman H. and Elizabeth (Wertz) R.; A.B. with distinction, U. Mich., 1952, J.D. with distinction, 1954; m. Margaret Ann Towsley, July 30, 1955; children—John Towsley, Margaret Elizabeth. Admitted to Mich. bar, 1954, Calif. bar, 1955, bar U.S. Tax Ct., U.S. Supreme Ct. Bar, U.S. Treasury Bar; asso. law firm Bonisteel & Bonisteel, Ann Arbor, 1954-55; partner firm Francis, Wetmore & Riecker. Midland, Mich., 1958-65; partner firm Gillespie Riecker & George, Midland, 1966-78, Riecker, George, Hartley & Van Dam, P.C., 1978—; chmn. bd. First Midland Bank & Trust Co., 1970-78; sec., dir. numerous Mich. corps. Mem. NAM trade mission to EEC, 1964. Trustee, treas. Delta Coll., 1965-68; mem. bd. mgrs. United Fund Midland 1960-64; sec. Midland City Charter Rev. Com., 1964, mem. Spl. Charter Commn., 1972; mem. Midland Found., 1974; mem. Bd. Ethics State of Mich., 1976—; asst. sec. Mich. Molecular Inst., Dow Found., Towsley Found. Ann Arbor; mem. exec. com. Mich. United Fund, 1970-72; bd. govs. Northwood Inst., 1969-71; benefactor U. Mich.; bd. dirs. U. Mich. Devel. Council, 1974—, Central Mich. U. Devel. Council, 1978—; bd. govs. Cranbrook Acad. Art, 1980—; chmn. Matrix: Midland, 1981-82. Served as 1st lt., Judge Adv. Gens. Corps, AUS, 1955-58; now capt. Res. Mem. Midland County (pres. 1962-63), Am., Calif., Mich. (tax council) bar assns., Midland C. of C. (pres. 1971), Phi Beta Kappa, Phi Kappa Phi, Phi Eta Sigma, Sigma Iota Epsilon, Alpha Delta Phi, Phi Delta Phi. Republican. Episcopalian. Clubs: Benmark, Midland Country, Saginaw, Saginaw Valley Torch; Detroit Athletic, Renaissance; Travis Pointe Country (Ann Arbor); Rotary; President's (U. Mich). Mem. bd. editors Mich. Law Rev., 1953-54. Contbr. articles to profl. jours. Home: 3211 Valley Dr Midland MI 48640 Office: 414 Townsend St Midland MI 48640

RIECKER, MARGARET ANN TOWSLEY (MRS. JOHN E. RIECKER), polit. worker, found. exec.; b. Ann Arbor, Mich., Nov. 9, 1933; d. Harry A. and Margaret (Dow) Towsley; B.A., Carleton Coll., 1954; postgrad. Mt. Holyoke Coll., 1955; m. John E. Riecker, July 30, 1955; children—John Towsley, Margaret Elizabeth. Vice chmn. Midland County Republican Com., Midland, Mich., 1962—; vice-chmn. 10th Congl. Dist. (Mich.) Com., 1964—; spl. asst. for women's affairs Rep. state chmn. Mich., 1966—; 1st vice chmn. Mich. Rep. party, 1968—; mem. Rep. Nat. Com. from Mich., 1970—, mem. exec. com., 1973—. Trustee Herbert H. & Grace A. Dow Found., 1962—, Harry A. and Margaret D. Towsley Found., 1961—; trustee Central Mich. U., 1974—, chmn. bd., 1976—; chmn. Mich. Council of Founds., 1981—; mem. women's bd. trustees Northwood Inst., Midland, 1965—; bd. dirs. Detroit Inst. Tech., 1979—; mem. Midland Center for Arts, Midland Community Concerts; benefactor U. Mich., 1978—. Mem. Midland Symphony Guild, Carleton Coll. Alumni Assn., Midland Art Assn. Clubs: Women's Study, Midland Country, Zonta, Northwood Town and Campus (sec. 1967—), University of Michigan President's. Address: 3211 Valley Dr Midland MI 48640

RIEDEL, RICHARD DOUGLAS, ophthalmologist; b. Ludlow, Ky., Jan. 29, 1943; s. Eugene Douglas and Josephine Ann (Kelly) R.; B.A., Thomas More Coll., 1964; M.D., U. Louisville, 1968; m. Nancy Ann Katzen, June 11, 1965; children—Andrew, Christopher, Kimberly. Intern, Presbyn.-St. Luke's Hosp., Chgo., 1968-69; resident in ophthalmology U. Cin., 1972-75; practice medicine specializing in ophthalmology, Cin., 1975—; pres. Hyde Park Eye Physicians and Surgeons, Inc.; mem. staff Deaconess, Children's, Bethesda, Christ hosps. (all Cin.); clin. instr. U. Cin. Med. Sch. Served to lt. comdr. M.C., USN, 1970-72. Diplomate Am. Bd. Ophthalmology. Fellow Am. Acad. Ophthalmology; mem. Am. Assn. Ophthalmologists, Internat. Glaucoma Congress, Am. Intraocular Implant Soc., Am. Soc. Contemporary Ophthalmology, Cin. Ophthalmol. Soc., Ohio State Med. Soc., Cin. Acad. Medicine, Alpha Omega Alpha. Office: 3666 Paxton Ave Cincinnati OH 45208

RIEDL, FRANK WILLIAM, physician; b. Chatham, Ont., Can., Apr. 22, 1940; s. Frank and Helen (Bernath) R.; M.D., U. Western Ont., 1965; m. Mary Lynne Lampitt, Apr. 27, 1968; children—Becky Elizabeth, Craig Allan Lampitt, Jennifer Lynne, Frank Douglas. Intern, St. Joseph's Hosp., London, Ont., 1965-66; resident U. Alta. Hosp., Edmonton, 1966-67; family practice medicine, Petrolia, Ont., 1967—; home physician Lambton Twight Haven, Petrolia, 1970-71; chief staff Charlotte Elleanor Englehart Hosp., Petrolia, 1970-71, trustee, 1970-71, 77-78. Mem. adv. bd. Ont. Addiction Research Found., Lambton, 1971-74. Served with RCAF, 1961-64. Fellow Ont. Geriatrics Research Soc.; mem. Canadian, Ont. med. assns., Canadian, Ont. colls. family physicians, Coll. Physicians and Surgeons Ont., Southwestern Ont. Anaesthetists Soc., Lambton County Med. Soc. (pres. 1977-78). Roman Catholic. Club: Rotary (pres. 1979-80). Home: 513 Queen St Petrolia ON N0N 1R0 Canada Office: 4141 Lorne Ave Petrolia ON N0N 1R0 Canada

RIEDMANN, WILLIAM JOSEPH, lawyer; b. Omaha, Dec. 19, 1941; s. William J. and Elizabeth (Welch) R.; J.D., Creighton U., 1965; m. Agnes A. Czerwinski, Aug. 17, 1963; children—Elizabeth, William. Admitted to Nebr. bar, 1965; asso. firm Kennedy, Holland, DeLacy & Svoboda, Omaha, 1965-68, partner, 1968-72; sr. partner firm Riedmann & Kruger, Omaha, 1972-81, Matthews, Cannon & Riedmann, Omaha, 1981—; dir. Sawyer's Safety Service Inc.; lectr. nursing and law Creighton Meml. Hosp., St. Joseph Hosp., St. Mary's Coll. Mem. Omaha Symphony Council, 1971—; mem. Omaha Citizens Crime Commn., 1967; spl. asst. to Mayor for Implementation of Crime Commn. Recommendations, 1968; chmn. Lawyers Com. Heart Fund Drive, 1969; mem. Mayor's Crime Study Com., 1969; mem. com. Omaha Hearing Sch. Fund Drive, 1968, United Community Services Fund Drive, 1969; chmn. probation com. United Community Services Cts. Correction and Legal Services Task Force, 1970; bd. dirs. Crime Crisis Council. Mem. Omaha, Nebr., Am. bar assns., Nebr. Assn. Trial Attys. (pres. 1978—), Omaha Barristers Club (pres. 1967), Def. Counsel Assn. Nebr. (pres. 1972), Phi Alpha Delta. Republican. Roman Catholic. Club: Omaha Ski (dir. 1970-72). Home: 2322 S 91st St Omaha NE 68124 Office: 318 S 19 St Omaha NE 68102

RIEDY, JOHN K., business exec.; b. Chgo., June 29, 1916; s. Elmer B. and Evelyn (Marcoe) R.; m. Mary Eileen Grogan, Feb. 8, 1941; children—Robert D., John M., Michael J. Vice pres. Florsheim Shoe Co., Chgo., 1957-66, pres., 1967-70, chmn. bd., 1970—; pres., chief operating officer Interco, Inc., St. Louis, 1970-81, vice chmn. bd., 1981, chmn. bd., chief exec. officer, 1981—. dir. First Nat. Bank St. Louis, Pet Inc., Union Electric Co. Home: 200 S Brentwood Blvd Clayton MO 63105 Office: 10 Broadway Saint Louis MO 63102

RIEGEL, FARALD LLOYD, accountant; b. Dayton, Ohio, Sept. 26, 1940; s. James Lloyd and Olive Anne (Heiden) R.; student Ohio State U., 1960-62; B.S., Wright State U., 1969, M.B.A., 1972; m. Mary Carolyn Paige, Sept. 25, 1969; children—James Lloyd, Paige Renee Anne. Supr., Bertram Plotnick Co., C.P.A.'s, Dayton, 1972-73; pvt. practice acctg., Dayton, 1973—. Served with U.S. Army, 1958-60. Mem. Am. Inst. C.P.A.'s, Ohio Soc. C.P.A.'s, Nat. Soc. Pub. Accountants, Pub. Accountants Soc. Ohio, Nat. Assn. Accountants, Dayton Tax Club. Club: Trailsend. Home: 3204 Allendale Dr Kettering OH 45409 Office: 4140 Linden Ave Dayton OH 45432

RIEGER, HELEN BREEDEN HEDRICK (MRS. WRAY MONTGOMERY RIEGER), emeritus mus. curator; b. Columbia, Mo., Oct. 13, 1903; d. Earle Raymond and Helen Breeden (Seidensticker) Hedrick; B.S., U. Mo., 1925; postgrad. Pomona Coll., 1926-27; m. Wray Montgomery Rieger, Sept. 15, 1927; children—Helen B. (Mrs. John Robert Anderson), Wray Montgomery. Substitute tchr., Chgo., 1927-28, Kirksville, Mo., 1941-57; curator E. M. Violette Mus., Kirksville, 1958-79, curator emeritus, 1979—; archivist N.E. Mo. State U., Kirksville, 1966-79. Bd. dirs. Sojourners Public Library, 1946-70, 81-82. Mem. Alpha Gamma Delta. Baptist. Clubs: Sojourners, University Dames (pres. 1937) (Kirksville). Home: 516 Halliburton Ave Kirksville MO 63501

RIEGER, MITCHELL SHERIDAN, lawyer; b. Chgo., Sept. 5, 1922; s. Louis and Evelyn (Sampson) R.; A.B., Northwestern U., 1944; J.D., Harvard, 1949; 1 dau., Karen Rieger Gross Cooper; step-children by previous marriage—Jill Felsenthal Levi, Susan Felsenthal, Linda Felsenthal Hanan, James Geoffrey Felsenthal; m. Pearl Handelsman, June 10, 1973; stepchildren—Steven B. Newman, Mary Ann Malarkey, Nancy L. Newman. Admitted to Ill. bar, 1950; asso. firm Rieger & Rieger, Chgo., 1950-54; asst. U.S. atty. No. Dist. of Ill., 1954-60, chief tax div., 1954-55, chief criminal div., 1955-58, first asst. 1958-60; asso. gen. counsel SEC, Washington, 1960-61; partner firm Schiff Hardin & Waite and predecessor, Chgo., 1961—; instr. law John Marshall Law Sch., Chgo., 1952-54. Past pres., dir. Park View Home. Mem. Chgo. Crime Commn. Served to comdr. USNR, 1943-46, ret. 1967. Fellow Am. Coll. Trial Lawyers; mem. Am., 7th Circuit, Ill., Chgo., Fed. (pres. Chgo. chpt. 1959-60, nat. v.p. 7th dist. 1960-61) bar assns., Am. Judicature Soc., Phi Beta Kappa. Clubs: Metropolitan, Law, The Standard (Chgo.), Lake Shore Country (Glencoe). Contbr. articles to profl. jours. Home: 4950 Chicago Beach Dr Chicago IL 60615 Office: 7200 Sears Tower 233 S Wacker Dr Chicago IL 60606

RIEGER, PEARL HANDELSMAN, ednl. psychologist; b. Chgo., Feb. 8, 1928; d. Meyer and Anne (Goldkin) Handelsman; B.A., U. Mich., 1948; M.A., U. Chgo., 1974; m. Mitchell Sheridan Rieger, June 10, 1973; children from previous marriage—Steven B. Newman, Mary Ann Malarkey, Nancy L. Newman. Speech therapist Michael Reese Hosp. and Med. Center, Chgo., 1948-51; ednl. diagnostician Ancona Montessori Sch., Chgo., 1974-77; cons. ednl. diagnostician U. Chgo. Lab. Schs., Harris Sch., Ancona Montessori Sch., 1974-80; pvt. practice psychoednl. diagnostics, Chgo., 1974—; mem. Wolf, Liese, Rieger & Schwartz Psychol. Assos.; part-time faculty Roosevelt U.; trustee Chgo. Inst. Psychoanalysis; chmn. bd. com. Barr Harris Center Study of Separation and Loss During Childhood, 1976—; psychoednl. diagnostician One-to-One Learning Center, Wilmette, Ill.; v.p. bd. govs. U. Chgo. Lab. Schs., 1966-69, 74-75. Mem. women's bd. Jewish Fedn. Met. Chgo., 1952-60, Michael Reese Hosp., 1955-69, Jewish Community Centers, 1956-61. Mem. Am. Psychol. Assn. (asso.), Council Exceptional Children, Assn. Children with Learning Disabilities, Am. Speech and Hearing Assn., Zeta Phi Eta, Pi Lambda Theta. Jewish. Club: Quandrangle. Home and Office: 4950 Chicago Beach Dr Chicago IL 60615

RIEGLE, DONALD WAYNE, JR., Senator; b. Flint, Mich., Feb. 4, 1938; s. Donald Wayne and Dorothy (Fitchett) R.; B.A. in Bus. Adminstrn. and Econs., U. Mich.; M.B.A., Mich. State U., 1961; postgrad. Harvard Bus. Sch., 1964-66; m. Lori Hansen; children—Catherine Anne, Laurie Elizabeth, Donald Wayne III. Faculty Mich. State U., 1960-61; sr. pricing analyst IBM, 1961-64; cons. Harvard-Mass. Inst. Tech. Joint Center on Urban Studies; mem. 90th-94th Congresses Mich. 7th Dist.; mem. U.S. Senate from Mich., 1976—, mem. budget com., com. on banking, housing and urban affairs, com. on labor and human resources, com. on commerce, sci. and transp.; fellow-in-residence John Kennedy Inst. for Politics, Harvard, 1971. Recipient Distinguished Alumni award U. Mich. Bus. Adminstrn. Soc., 1967; named one of 10 Outstanding Young Men in Am., U.S. Jaycees, 1967; one of 200 Nat. Leaders Under Age 45, Time mag., 1974. Mem. Beta Gamma Sigma. Democrat. Author: O Congress, 1972. Office: Dirksen Senate Office Bldg Washington DC 20510

RIEGLE, EARL WILFORD, warehouse mgr.; b. Pawnee Rock, Kans., Mar. 26, 1920; s. Logan John and Laura Rose (Brown) R.; student public schs.; m. Ruth Lois Vogler, Sept. 8, 1943; children—Phillip Earl, John Frederick. With Boeing Co., Wichita, Kans., 1942-45; asst. mgr. Wilson & Co., Wichita, 1945-52; from foreman to mgr. Wichita Ice & Cold Storage Co., 1952-74; mgr. Comml. Distbn. Center, Independence, Mo., 1974—. Mem. Internat. Assn. Refrigerated Warehouses (sec.-treas. Mo. Valley chpt. 1977), Kansas City Warehousemen's Assn. (sec. 1979). Republican. Home: 16912 E 3d Terr S Independence MO 64056 Office: 16500 E Truman Rd Independence MO 64050

RIEGLE, ROBERT ROY, meat packing co. exec.; b. Greenville, Ohio, July 30, 1927; s. Alvin N. and Nola M. (Dickey) R.; student Internat. Coll., 1952-53; m. Donna L. Rogers, Nov. 21, 1954; children—Kirk, Karen Riegle Weingart. Accountant, Coopers & Lybrand, Fort Wayne, 1953-67; mgr. corp. accounting Peter Eckrich & Sons, Inc., Fort Wayne, 1967-69; v.p., sec., controller E.W. Kneip, Inc., Forest Park, Ill., 1969—, also dir. Mem. Am. Inst. C.P.A.'s, Ind. Assn. C.P.A.'s, Nat. Inst. Controllers, Nat. Assn. Accountants, Adminstrv. Mgmt. Soc. Club: Lions (pres. 1975). Home: 3903

Saratoga Ave Downers Grove IL 60515 Office: 7501 Brown Ave Forest Park IL 60130

RIEHL, EMIL JOSEPH, state legislator; b. Raleigh, N.D., Jan. 1, 1925; s. Melchor Karl and Emma (Wagner) R.; m. Irene Gustin, June 24, 1946; children—David, Judy, Thomas, Andrew, Colette, Margaret, Emilie, James, William, Richard. Pres., Mor-Gran-San Electric Coop., Inc., 1971-80, dir., 1963-81; mem. N.D. Ho. of Reps., 1976—. Mem. Raleigh Sch. Bd., 1953-56. Democrat. Roman Catholic. Clubs: Lions, K.C. Address: Box 50 Rural Route 1 Raleigh ND 58564

RIELLY, JOHN EDWARD, assn. exec.; b. Rapid City, S.D., Dec. 28, 1932; s. Thomas J. and Mary R.; B.A., St. Johns U., Minn., 1954; Ph.D., Harvard U., 1961; Fulbright scholar London Sch. Econs. and Polit. Sci., 1955-56; m. Elizabeth Downs, Dec. 28, 1957 (annulled 1976); children—Mary Ellen, Catherine Ann, Thomas Patrick, John Downs. With Alliance for Progress program Dept. State, 1961-62; fgn. policy asst. to Senator and Vice Pres. Hubert H. Humphrey, 1963-69; cons. Office European and Internat. Affairs, Ford Found., N.Y.C., 1969-70; sr. fellow Overseas Devel. Council, Washington, 1970-71; exec. dir. Chgo. Council on Fgn. Relations, 1971-74; pres., 1974—; cons. NSC, White House, 1978-80. Mem. Grad. Sch. Arts and Scis. adv. bd. Harvard U.; trustee St. Johns U., Minn. Mem. N.Y. Council on Fgn. Relations, Am. Council on Germany, China Council of Asia Soc., Trilaterial Commn., Commn. U.S. Brazilian Relations, Am. Polit. Sci. Assn. Clubs: Harvard (N.Y.C.); Mid Am., Michigan Shores, Chgo.; Met. (Washington). Edit. bd. Fgn. Policy, 1974—. Contbr. articles to profl. jours. Home: 2021 Kenilworth Ave Wilmette IL 60091 Office: 116 S Michigan Ave Chicago IL 60603

RIELY, PHYLLIS ELEANOR, microbiologist; b. Welshfield, Ohio, Jan. 25, 1918; d. Clifford James and Ethel Belle (Corliss) Brunton; student Capital U., Columbus, Ohio, 1936-39; student med. tech. Huron Rd. Hosp., Cleve., 1940-41; m. Charles Riely, Nov. 28, 1941; children—Terrence, Patricia, Maura, Shawn. Systems microbiologist Fairchild Hiller, Farmingdale, N.Y., 1960-66; mgr. med. product devel. Internat. Paper, Tuxedo, N.Y., 1969-71; dir. med. products E/W Med. Products, Syosset, N.Y., 1971-73; mgr. biomed. regulatory affairs Pall Corp., Glen Cove, 1973-74; mgr. microbiol. devel. Marion Labs., Kansas City, Mo., 1974—. Fellow Royal Acad. Health; mem. Am. Soc. Microbiology, Pharm. Mfrs. Assn. (com. environ. microbiology). Republican. Methodist. Contbr. articles to sci. publs.; patentee in field. Home: 111 W 99th Terr Kansas City MO 64114 Office: 10236 Bunker Ridge Rd Kansas City MO 64137

RIEMAN, DWIGHT WALKER, educator; b. Berlin, Pa., Mar. 30, 1918; s. George S. and Emma (Walker) R.; A.B., Juniata Coll., 1940; M.S., Case Western Res. U., 1949; m. Emily Hutton Griest, Jan. 11, 1947; children—Eliot, Janice, Michael, Elizabeth. Psychiat. social worker Fed. Employee Mental Health Clinic, USPHS, Washington, 1946-50; cons. psychiat. social worker Tex. Dept. Health, 1950-60, chief psychiat. social worker, 1960-65; adminstrv. cons. community services Tex. Dept. Mental Health, Austin, 1965-68; asso. prof. Social Work Extension Program, U. Mo., Coll. Public and and Community Services, Columbia, 1968—; program dir. NIMH continuing edn. projects, 1970-73, 75-78; cons. on prodn. film "Community Mental Health", Mental Health Film Bd., N.Y.C., Hollywood, Calif., 1959; cons. Mid-Continent Inst., Nat. Assn. Social Workers, 1965, Confs. Chief Psychiat. Social Workers in State Mental Health Programs, USPHS, Region IV, 1965, Ga. Dept. Pub. Health, Community Mental Health Services, 1966, Greater Kansas City Mental Health Found., Inst. for Pupil Study, 1967. Served with M.C., AUS, 1944-45. Mem. Nat. Assn. Social Workers (del. Mo. council, Region VI cons. continuing edn. 1972-73), Nat. Conf. on Social Welfare, Acad. Certified Social Workers, Council on Social Work Edn., Mo., Tex. (past v.p., treas.) social welfare assns. Contbr. to Consultation in Social Work Practice, 1963; Mental Health and the Community-Problems, Programs and Strategies, 1969; Consultation in Community Mental Health Services, 1973; Staff Board Collaboration in Community Mental Health Programs, 1979; More Than Shelter—Social Services in Public Housing, 1979. Home: 405 S Garth St Columbia MO 65201 Office: 628 Clark Hall U Mo Columbia MO 65211

RIEMER, KENNETH KARL, health care co. exec.; b. Chgo., Oct. 21, 1940; s. Gottlieb and Emily Riemer; B.S. in Bus. Adminstrn., Elmhurst Coll., 1962; m. Karen Dorn, June 29, 1963; children—Jill, Julie, Jodi. Mgmt. trainee, asst. order mgr. Ralston Purina, 1962-66; corp. coll. relations mgr. Emerson Electric, St. Louis, 1966-70; personnel supr. Boatmen's Bank, St. Louis, 1970-72; dir. personnel Vis. Nurse Assn., St. Louis, 1972-77; v.p. human resources Spectrum Emergency Care, Creve Coeur, Mo., 1977—. Bd. dirs. Murphy Blair Housing Devel., St. Louis, 1970-72; pres. bd. dirs. Planned Parenthood, St. Louis, 1979—. Home: 414 Cannonbury St Webster Groves MO 63119 Office: 970 Executive Pkwy Creve Coeur MO 63141

RIESS, JOHN DAVID, psychologist; b. Evanston, Ill., Oct. 5, 1939; s. John Howard and Ethel Jane (Richardson) R.; B.A., Hanover Coll., 1962; M.S., So. Ill. U., 1966, postgrad., 1966-67; m. Phyllis Ann Evans, Nov. 26, 1964; children—John Howard, Jana Kathryn. Intern, Anna (Ill.) State Hosp., 1964-65; psychologist Ill. Security Hosp., 1965-66, Galesburg (Ill.) State Research Hosp., 1967—; part-time instr. Carl Sandburg Jr. Coll., 1967-81. Author: Analytic American: Contract Bridge Quantification and Natural Bidding in their Irreducible Basics; contbr. articles to profl. jours. Home: 984 Willard St Galesburg IL 61401 Office: Galesburg Mental Health Center N Seminary St Galesburg IL 61401

RIETBERG, WAYNE A., educator; b. E. Grand Rapids, Mich., May 8, 1939; s. Albert A. and Margaret (Joling) R.; married, 4 children. B.A. in Edn., Calvin Coll., Grand Rapids, 1961; M.A. in Edn., Mich. State U., E. Lansing, 1970; m. Marilyn Buteyn. Tchr. Byron Center (Mich.) Pub. Schs., 1961-65, reading cons., 1965-66, coordinator fed. projects, 1966-71, prin., 1969—. Chief Indian Guides Kentwood YMCA, 1975-76; bd. dirs. South YMCA, 1976—. Mem. Nat., Mich. assns. elementary sch. prins., Internat., Mich. reading assns., Assn. Supervision Curriculum Devel., Kent County Curriculum Council, Kent County Elementary Sch. Prins. Assn., Assn. Evaluation Elementary Schs., Phi Delta Kappa. Home: 1730 Mapleview St SE Kentwood MI 49508 Office: 8064 Byron Center Ave Byron Center MI 49315

RIETZ, EDWARD GUSTAVE, educator; b. Chgo., Feb. 24, 1911; s. Edward Jacob and Emily Olive (Olsen) R.; B.S., U. Chgo., 1933, M.S., 1935, Ph.D., 1938. Chemist, U.S. FDA, Chgo., 1939-42; research chemist U.S. Dept. Agr., Albany, Calif., 1942-46; asso. prof. U. Fla., Gainesville, 1946-52; prof., chmn. dept. Chgo. City Colls., 1952—; vis. prof. U. Ill., Chgo., 1956—; vis. asso. prof. chemistry St. Louis U., 1955; ednl. coordinator Rush Med. Coll., Chgo. Active Rec. for the Blind; bd. dirs. Family Counseling Service Evanston and Skokie Valley, 1975—; chmn. bd. trustees Nat. Chem. Exposition. Served with USNR, 1943-46; PTO; capt. USNR ret. Recipient award of merit Chgo. Assn. Technol. Socs., 1981. Mem. Am. Chem. Soc. (councilor 1973—, chmn. Chgo. sect. 1973; trustee Chgo. sect.; Disting. Service award 1981), Ret. Officers Assn., Episcopalian. Club: Cliff Dwellers (Chgo.). Author: (with others) Chemical and Biological Warfare Defense, 1952; (with Pollard) Problems in Organic Chemistry, 1952. Contbr. articles to profl. jours. Home: 2948 N Laramie Ave Chicago IL 60641

RIETZ, ROBERT ROY, neurophysiologist; b. Mitchell, S.D., Apr. 3, 1946; s. Roy K. and Yvonne Virginia (Young) R.; B.A., U. S.D., 1968; Ph.D., U. Tenn., 1973; M.D., Creighton U., 1979; m. Elaine Dianna Dewey, June 5, 1966; children—Roy K., Tricia M., Rebecca A., Robin L. Postdoctoral fellow Emory U. Sch. Medicine, Atlanta, 1973-75; asst. prof. physiology Creighton U. Sch. Medicine, Omaha, 1975—. USPHS fellow, 1969-71. Mem. Am. Physiol. Soc., Soc. Neurosci., AAAS, Sigma Xi, Tau Kappa Epsilon. Lutheran. Research in skeletal muscle control by central nervous system. Office: Creighton Univ Omaha NE 68178

RIFAI, GHASSAM MOUTEIH, urologist; b. Syria, Sept. 15, 1936; came to U.S., 1966, naturalized, 1976; s. Mohamed Mouteih and Zuhnieh (Khateeb) R.; M.D. with honors, Damascus U., 1962; m. Rania A. Azim, Sept. 21, 1978; children—Tom, Ronnie. Surg. resident N.Y. PolyClinic, 1966-67; rotating intern Highland Park (Ill.) Gen. Hosp., 1967-68; resident in urology William Beaumont Hosp., Royal Oak, Mich., 1968-71; chief resident in urology Hammot Med. Center, Erie, Pa., 1973-74; practice medicine specializing in urology, Allen Park, Mich., 1974—; pres. G.M. Rifai, M.D., P.C., 1978—; mem. staff Seaway Hosp., Trenton, Mich., 1974—, chief of surgery, 1980-81; mem. staff Heritage Hosp., Taylor, Mich., 1972—, mem. patient care evaluation com., 1978—; med. officer UN Relief Agy., Damascus, 1965-66. Served with Syrian Army, 1962-65. Diplomate Am. Bd. Urology. Mem. Am. Coll. Emergency Physicians, Wayne County Med. Soc., Arab Med. Assn. (pres.-elect Mich. chpt.). Office: 6540 Park St Allen Park MI 48101

RIFFE, VERNAL G., JR., state legislator; b. New Boston, Ohio, June 26, 1925; s. Vernal G. and Jewell (Adkins) R.; student Ohio U., Ins. Agy. Mgmt. Sch. Miami U., Oxford, Ohio; m. Thelma Cooper, 1948; children—Cathy Riffe Skiver, Verna Kay, Mary Beth, Vernal G. III. Pres., Sherman, Riffe & Bennett Ins. Agy., Inc.; v.p., dir. Mchts. and Mfrs. Mut. Ins. Co.; dir. Mark Man Investment Co.; mem. Ohio Ho. of Reps., 1959—, now speaker. Mem. at large Ohio State Democratic Com. Served with USAAF, 1943-45; ETO. Mem. Am. Legion, Bus. and Profl. Men's Assn. Club: Masons. Office: Ohio Ho of Reps Columbus OH 43215*

RIGDON, RONALD MILTON, mgmt. cons.; b. Balt., Jan. 15, 1937; s. Leland Sanford and Betty Berniece (Roe) R.; student Kansas City (Mo.) Art Inst., 1958-60, William Jewell Coll., Liberty, Mo., 1955-58, 62-63; m. Arlene June Eddington, May 26, 1962; children—Ryan Todd, Rebecca Erin. Field adjuster CNA Ins. Corp., Kansas City, Mo., 1962-63; asst. mgr. Anchor Fin. Corp. Ins. Agy., Overland Park, Kans., 1963-64; mgr. First Mortgage Investment Co. Ins. Agy., Kansas City, Mo., 1964-67; pres. Programming Inst., Mission, Kans., 1967-70, RMR & Assos., Inc., Overland Park, 1970—; dir. Assn. Cons., Inc., Scheduling Systems, Inc. First v.p. Johnson County Mental Health Assn., 1968-70, Kans. Mental Health Assn., 1969-70. Mem. Mgmt. Cons. Inst., Profl. Ins. Mass-Mktg. Assn., Am. Mgmt. Assn., Assn. Chief Exec. Officers, Am. Profl. Assn. Group Ins. Adminstrs., U.S. Dressage Fedn., Kansas City Dressage Soc. Republican. Baptist. Author: Work Flow-Cost Reduction a Management Control System, 1978. Home: 12200 Big Bone Trail Olathe KS 66061 Office: 8300 W 110th St Suite 200 Overland Park KS 66210

RIGG, ROBINSON PETER, ins. co. exec.; b. Blackpool, Eng., Jan. 13, 1918; s. Robinson Patrick and Lilian Mary (Clough) R.; came to U.S., 1969; A.B., U. Liverpool (Eng.), 1939; m. Jane Lane Chadwick, Apr. 3, 1952. Vice chmn. Fgn. Office Whitley Council, German sect., 1947-52; pub. editor Indsl. Screen, London, 1957-62; indsl. firm corr. Financial Times, London, 1958-63; communications cons., 1963-69; chmn. indsl. film corrs. group, 1966-69; public relations asso. Combined Ins. Co. Am., Chgo., 1969-72, dir. public relations advt., 1972, v.p., 1972-81, v.p. public service, 1981—; mng. dir. Robin Publs. Ltd., London, 1957—; dir. Adeline Pl. Mansions Mgmt. Ltd., London. Dir. public relations Congressional Award, 1981—, Internat. Fedn. Keystone Youth Orgns., 1980—; trustee Ill. Council Econ. Edn., 1977—. Served with Brit. Army, 1939-46. Fellow Royal Photog. Soc.; mem. Public Relations Soc. Am., Inst. Public Relations (Eng.), Internat. Public Relations Assn., Inst. Journalists (Eng.), Soc. Authors, Health Ins. Assn. Am. (chmn. consumer relations com.), Inst. Dirs. Clubs: Sportsman's, Royal Automobile (London); Press (Chgo.); Michigan Shores (Wilmette, Ill.). Author Audiovisual Aids & Techniques, 1969; contbr. to Indsl. Advt. Mgrs. Handbook, 1968, Dirs. Handbook, 1970, The Times, Financial Times, The Dir., Investors Chronicle. Home: 2769 Asbury Ave Evanston IL 60201 Office: 500 Skokie Blvd Northbrook IL

RIGGS, BYRON LAWRENCE, JR., physician; b. Hot Springs, Ark., Mar. 24, 1931; s. Byron Lawrence and Elizabeth Ann (Patching) R.; student U. Ark., 1948-51, B.S., 1953, B.S. in Medicine, 1955, M.D., 1955; M.S. in Medicine, U. Minn., 1962; m. Janet Templeton Brewer, June 24, 1955; children—Byron Kent, Ann Templeton. Intern, Lettermen Army Hosp., San Francisco, 1958-59; resident internal medicine Mayo Grad. Sch. Medicine, 1958-61; asst. to staff Mayo Clinic, Rochester, Minn., 1961, mem. staff internal medicine and metabolism Mayo Clinic and Found., 1962—; instr. medicine U. Minn., 1962—, asst. prof., 1967-70, asso. prof., 1970—; prof. medicine Mayo Med. Sch., 1974—; chmn. div. endocrinology and metabolism Mayo Clinic and Med. Sch., 1974—; mem. gen. medicine B study sect. NIH. Served with M.C., AUS, 1956-58. Recipient Mayo Found. Postgrad. Travel award, 1961; Kappa Delta award Am. Acad. Orthopedic Surgery, 1972. Royal Soc. Medicine Found. traveling fellow, 1973. Diplomate Am. Bd. Internal Medicine. Fellow A.C.P.; mem. Am. Diabetes Assn., AMA, Minn., Zumbro County med. socs., Am. Soc. Clin. Investigation, Endocrine Soc., Am. Fedn. Clin. Research (councillor Midwest sect.), Am. Soc. Bone and Mineral Research, Central Soc. Clin. Research (councillor), Central Clin. Research Club, AAAS, N.Y. Acad. Scis. Contbr. articles to profl. jours. Research in metabolism. Home: 432 SW 10th Ave Rochester MN 55901 Office: 200 SW 1st St Rochester MN 55902

RIGGS, JEANETTE TEMPLETON, civic worker; b. Little Rock, Mar. 13, 1933; d. Donald M. and Fay (Templeton) Brewer; student Little Rock U., 1950-51, Tex. Coll. for Women, 1951-52; B.S., U. Ark., 1955; m. Byron Lawrence Riggs, June 1955; children—Byron Kent, Ann Templeton. Founder, Rochester (Minn.) Ballet Guild, 1970, pres., 1974; mem. establishing bd., exec. bd. Rochester Arts Council, 1972, producer, dir. T.S. Elliot's The Rock, 1970; founder, performer So. Minn. Ballet Co., 1974; sponsor Nat. Ballet Cos., Rochester, 1970-75; exec. bd. for restoration 1875 Pattern Book House, Rochester Heritage Assn., 1975-77; exec. bd. Savino Ballet Nat., 1975-78; founder, exec. bd. Citizens Action Com., 1977-79; asso., commentator Women, Cable TV Program for Women, Rochester, 1979; mem. Mayor's Com. on Drug Abuse, 1979-80; mem. Olmsted County Steering Com. for George Bush, 1979-80, a founder, mem. exec. bd. Olmsted County Republican Women's Orgn., 1979—, mem. Olmsted County Rep. Central Com., 1979—, exec. bd. issues com., 1979-80. Home: 432 SW 10th Ave Rochester MN 55901

RIGHTER, WALTER CAMERON, clergyman; b. Phila., Oct. 23, 1923; s. Richard and Dorothy Mae (Bottomley) R.; B.A., U. Pitts., 1948; M.Div., Berkeley Div. Sch., 1951, D.D., 1972; m. Marguerite Jeanne Burroughs, Jan. 26, 1946; children—Richard Stanton, Rebecca Jean. Ordained to ministry Episcopal Ch., 1951; vicar All Saints Ch., Aliquippa, Pa., 1951-54; rector Ch. of Good Shepherd, Nashua, N.H., 1954-71; consecrated bishop, 1972; bishop diocese of Iowa, Des Moines, 1972—; mem. exec. com. Protestant Episcopal Ch., U.S.A., 1979—, mem. Domestic and Fgn. Missionary Soc., 1979—. Bd. dirs. Orchard Place Home for Children, Des Iowa, 1975—, Door of Faith Mission, Des Moines; past bd. dirs. Protestant Home for Children, Nashua, 1954-70; trustee Nashua Public Library, 1968-71. Served with AUS, 1943-45; ETO. Fellow Coll. Preachers Washington Cathedral; mem. Newcomen Soc. Clubs: Masons, Rotary (dir.). Contbr. articles to religious publs. Address: 225 37th St Des Moines IA 50312

RIGSBY, DONALD MARK, data processing co. exec.; b. Wichita Falls, Tex., Sept. 22, 1951; s. William Edwin and Mary (Jeter) R.; B.A. in Bus., Northwestern Okla. State U., 1974; m. Paula Gay Kindred, Apr. 5, 1975; children—Erin Michelle, Penni Lynn. Mktg. rep. Burroughs Corp., Wichita, Kans., 1974-78, dist. sales mgr., St. Louis, 1978-80, br. mgr., 1980—. Deacon Harvester Baptist Ch. Republican. Home: 4 Millspring Ct Saint Charles MO 63301 Office: Burroughs Corp 11975 Westline Industrial Dr Saint Louis MO 63141

RIKER, CHARLES MARR, III, banker; b. Chgo., Apr. 27, 1938; s. Charles Marr II and Mary Jeanne (Handy) R.; student Ill. State Normal U., 1964; grad. So. Ill. U. Sch. Banking, 1971; M.B.A., Pacific Western U., 1981; m. Barbara Jean Schierer, Sept. 5, 1964; children—Kimberly Marie, Deborah Sue, Charles Marr IV. Asst. mgr., sec. Pontiac Savs. & Loan Assn. (Ill.), 1964-69; v.p., cashier Manteno State Bank (Ill.), 1969-74; pres., chief exec. officer State Bank of Herscher (Ill.), 1974—, also dir. Alderman, Pontiac, 1966-69, named outstanding alderman City of Pontiac, 1968; pres. Livingston County Young Republican Club, 1965-66. Served with USN, 1956-60. Mem. Am., Ill. bankers assns., Herscher C. of C. (pres. 1981). Roman Catholic. Clubs: Lions, Moose, Kiwanis (treas. 1967). Home: 524 4th St Herscher IL 60941 Office: 10 Tobey Dr Herscher IL 60941

RIKIMARU, YUKI, archtl. designer, planner; b. Sacramento, Oct. 7, 1927; s. Joseph Iwasuke and Kiyono (Aramaki) R.; A.B. in Architecture, San Mateo City Coll., 1949; B.A. in Architecture Washington U., St. Louis, 1953; m. Kaoru Goto, Nov. 8, 1958; children—Raymond Kenji, Loryn Tamiko. Archtl. draftsman William B. Ittner, St. Louis, 1953-55; archtl. designer Russell, Mulgardt Schwarz, Van Hoeflin, St. Louis, 1956—; archtl. partner W.B. Kromm Asso., St. Louis, 1957—; prin. Kromm Rikimaru & Johansen Inc., architects, St. Louis, 1960—; v.p. Kromm, Rikimaru, Johansen & Aach Inc., architects, engrs. and planners, St. Louis, 1972, Archtl. Mgmt. Group Inc. Served with AUS, 1946-47. Mem. AIA, Nat. Council Archtl. Registration Bds., Mo. Council Architects. Prin. archtl. works include: Maplewood Municipal Bldg., St. Louis, 1961; Mineral Area Coll., Flat River, Mo., 1966; Fulton (Mo.) Juvenile Center, 1967; Delmar Gardens Nursing Home, St. Louis, 1968; Columbia (Mo.) Regional Hosp., 1972. Office: 112 S Hanley Rd St Louis MO 63105

RIKKER, LESLIE DENES, engring. co. exec.; b. Hungary, Mar. 12, 1937; s. Josef and Ilona (Egri) R.; came to U.S., 1957, naturalized, 1962; diploma in power engring., Budapest (Hungary) Inst. Tech., 1950-55; m. Cecilia Eva Mucska, Feb. 15, 1957; children—George Leslie, Eva Katerina. Plant engr. Budapest Motor Casting, 1955-56; engr. Combustion Engring. East Chgo. Div., 1957-60, Raymond Div., Chgo., 1960-64, asst. squad leader, 1962-64; designer Nat. Engring. Co., Chgo., 1964, sr. mech. engr., 1965-67, asst. chief mech. engr., 1969-71, v.p. 1973-76, exec. v.p., 1976—, also dir. Recipient cert. of appreciation Dept. Commerce, 1971, 72. Mem. Am. Foundrymen Soc. Roman Catholic. Club: Union League (Chgo.). Patentee in field. Home: 15441 Betty Ann Ln Oak Forest IL 60452 Office: 20 N Wacker Dr Chicago IL 60606

RILEY, DONALD ALAN, mfg. co. info. systems exec.; b. Youngstown, Ohio, July 11, 1937; s. Perry W. and Dorothy E. (Battin) R.; B.S. in Bus. Adminstrn., Youngstown U., 1960; diploma U.S. Army Command Gen. Staff Coll., 1974, Indsl. Coll. Armed Forces, 1976; postgrad. bus. adminstrn. Ohio State U., 1964-65; children—Robert Alan, Kathleen Joyce. Commd. 2nd lt. U.S. Army, 1960, advanced through grades to maj., 1967; asst. prof. mil. sci. Ohio State U., 1964-65; comdg. officer signal co., 1st air cavalry div., Vietnam, 1966-67; chief EDP facility, Ft. Leavenworth, Kans., 1967-70; mgr. data processing Kansas City (Mo.) div. Bendix Corp., 1970—. Active Boy Scouts Am., YMCA, PTA. Served as col. USAR, 1970—. Decorated Bronze Star medal, Army Commendation medal, Air medal. Mem. Bendix Mgmt. Club, U.S. Army Res. Assn., Theta Chi. Home: 11128 E 85th St Raytown MO 64138 Office: PO Box 1159 Kansas City MO 64141

RILEY, JAMES JOSEPH, union exec.; b. Cleve., Nov. 12, 1919; s. Frank James and Mary Jane (Connor) R.; B.S., Western Res. U., 1940; m. Ruth Marie Pearce, Apr. 10, 1939; children—Janet M., Nancy C., Catherine A., James F., Thomas M., Dennis J., Ruth E., Mary H., John R. Mem. Cleve. Motion Picture Operators Union, Local 160, 1941—; partner Electric Speed Indicator Co., weather instrument maker, Cleve., 1965-67; bus. agt. Internat. Alliance of Theatrical Stage Employees and Moving Picture Operators of U.S. and Can., Cleve., 1967-78, internat. gen.-sec. treas., N.Y.C., 1978—, internat. trustee, 1969-78; v.p. Union Label dept. AFL-CIO, 1980—. Served to lt. USNR, 1943-46; PTO. Roman Catholic. Editor Bull., Internat. Alliance Quar., 1978—. Home: 15801 Edgecliff Rd Cleveland OH 44111 Office: Suite 601 1515 Broadway New York NY 10036

RILEY, LYMAN GUYTON, cons. evangelism; b. Little Sioux, Iowa, May 13, 1918; s. Elias Lyman and Anna Marie (Johnson) R.; A.S., Graceland Coll., 1937; B.A., Trinity Coll., Sioux City, 1938; m. Velma Ruth Benson, Feb. 23, 1939; children—Patricia (Mrs. Robert L. Wallis), Linda Maureen (Mrs. Dennis Steele). Prin., St. Joseph High Sch., Salix, Iowa, 1937-38; dist. mgr. Econs. Lab., St. Paul, 1939-43; mgr. Meramec Caverns, Stanton, Mo., 1946-49; owner, mgr. Onondaga Cave, Leasburg, Mo., 1950-67; dir. Woodland Hills Camp Found., 1971—. Vice pres. Meramec Basin Corp., Kirkwood, Mo., 1962-67. Chmn. Mo. Travel Commn., 1958-63. Mem. Republican County Com., 1968-77. Bd. dirs. Nat. Youth Found., St. Louis, 1973-75. Mem. Am. Cave Men (pres. 1946-50, Cave Man of year 1962, 63, 64), US 66 Assn. (dir. 1947-66), Meramec Basin Assn. (pres. 1964-67), Nat. Assn. Travel Ofcls. Mem. Reorganized Ch. Jesus Christ Latter-day Saints (elder). Clubs: Masons, Shrine, Lion, Rotary. Home: Route 1 Leasburg MO 65535

RILEY, VERNETTE E., hosp. adminstr.; b. Kewaskum, Wis., Dec. 8, 1932; B.S.N., U. Iowa, 1975, M.A. in Nursing Adminstrn., 1978; children—Richard R., Nancy E. Head nurse Mercy Hosp., Des Moines, 1954-56, asst. dir. nursing, 1961-71, asso. dir. nursing, 1971-78, v.p., 1978—. Mem. Am. Soc. Nursing Adminstrs., Iowa Soc. Nursing Adminstrs., Nat. League Nursing, Am. Nurses Assn. Lutheran. Club: Des Moines Women's. Home: 2620 Sherwood Dr

Des Moines IA 50310 Office: Mercy Hospital 6th and University Ave Des Moines IA 50314

RIMPILA, JULIAN JOHN, gastroenterologist; b. Chgo., Apr. 19, 1940; s. Charles Einar and Verna Catherine (Swanson) R.; B.A., Knox Coll., 1962; M.S., U. Chgo., 1966, M.D., 1966; m. Beverly Rose Dahlen, Apr. 30, 1966; children—John-Eric, Carl, Kari, Siiri, Heidi. Intern in medicine Northwestern U.-Evanston Hosp., 1966-67, resident in internal medicine, 1967-70; fellow in gastroenterology U. Chgo., 1973-76; practice medicine specializing in gastroenterology, Chgo., 1976—; mem. med. staff Grant Hosp., Henrotin Hosp., Gottlieb Hosp.; mem. cons. staff Christ Hosp. Asst. scoutmaster Boy Scouts Am., Westchester, Ill., 1980—; councillor U. Chgo. Alumni Council, 1976-80. Served with M.C., U.S. Army, 1970-73. Recipient Leadership and Service award Boy Scouts Am., 1978, 79, 80. Mem. ACP, AMA, Am. Soc. Gastrointestinal Endoscopy, Chgo. Med. Soc., Assn. U.S. Army, Res. Officers Assn. U.S., Am. Scandinavian Found., Sigma Xi. Republican. Lutheran. Mem. editorial bd. Medicine on the Midway, 1980—. Home: 11049 Windsor Dr Westchester IL 60153 Office: Suite 406 505 N Lake Shore Dr Chicago IL 60611

RINDOKS, ROLAND RAYNARD, steel co. exec.; b. East Chicago, Ind., June 16. 1925; s. Peter Stanley and Anna (Simon) R.; student Fenn Coll., 1944, Purdue U. Extension, 1946-47; m. Lillian Stone, Aug. 19, 1950; children—Roland Raynard, Bruce, Kurt, Brian. With M.W. Kellogg Constrn. Co., East Chicago, 1947-48; mech. designer Design Service, Inc., Chgo., 1948-49, Sumner S. Sollitt Constrn. Co., 1949-50; owner, mgr. Boulevard Pharmacy, East Chicago, 1950-53; mech. designer Petroleum Piping Contractors, Hammond, Ind., 1953-54; asst. plant engr. Gen. Am. Transp. Corp., East Chicago, 1954-62; project engr. Jones & Laughlin Steel Co. and precessor co., East Chicago, 1962—. Served with USAAC, 1943-46. Roman Catholic. Home: 7013 Ridgeland Ave Hammond IN 46324 Office: 3001 Dickey Rd East Chicago IN 46312

RINEHART, RAY DEE, county ofcl.; b. Liberal, Kans., Mar. 23, 1947; s. Oliver Joe and Margaret Marie (Wilburn) R.; student Southwestern Coll., Winfield, Kans., 1965-66; m. Karen Ann Johnston, Jan. 25, 1974. Farmer, Liberal, 1966-70; dispatcher City of Liberal, 1970-73, patrolman, 1973, dir. emergency preparedness, 1973, vol. fire fighter, 1973-76, fulltime fireman, 1976-78; fire chief County of Seward, Liberal, 1977—, dir. emergency preparedness, 1979—; sec. Region II, S.W. Kans. Emergency Med. Services, 1981—. Pres., Seward County Safety Council, 1975—; bd. dirs. United Way Seward County, 1975—, Cimarron chpt. ARC, 1979—. Democrat. Club: Elks. Home: 515 Starlight Dr Liberal KS 67901 Office: Box 1194 Liberal KS 67901

RINEHART, RAYMOND GEORGE, indsl. exec.; b. Waukegan, Ill., Mar. 31, 1922; s. Horace and Irene R.; student Northwestern U., St. Vincent's Coll., 1941-46; m. Winifred, May 24, 1947; children—R. Michael, John, Judy, Susan, Patricia, Robert. With Clow Corp., Chgo., 1947—, pres., dir., 1967-80, chief exec. officer, 1968-76, chmn. bd., pres., chief exec. officer, 1976-80, chmn. exec. com., 1980—; dir. VSI Corp., Pasadena, Calif., First Fed. Savs. & Loan Assn. of Chgo., Kewaunee Sci. Equipment Corp. (N.C.). Active Rehab. Inst. Chgo., United Settlement Appeal; bd. dirs. ARC, 1969-80, also past chmn.; trustee Community Fund Corp.; past chmn. adv. bd., mem. exec. com. Coll. Bus. Adminstrn., U. Notre Dame. Served with USAAF, 1941-46. Mem. Ductile Iron Pipe Research Assn. (past chmn., mem. exec. com.), Nat. Clay Pipe Inst. (dir.), Chgo. Assn. Commerce and Industry (past dir.), Econ. Club Chgo., Newcomen Soc. Clubs: Butler Nat. Golf; Hinsdale Golf; Chicago, Room 503, Commercial (Chgo.); Metropolitan. Address: Clow Corp 1211 W 22d St Oak Brook IL 60521

RING, GERALD JOHN, real estate developer; b. Madison, Wis., Oct. 6, 1928; s. John George and Mabel Sarah (Rau) R.; student pub. schs., Madison; m. Armella Marie Dohm, Aug. 20, 1949; children—Michael J., James J., Joseph W. With Sub-Zero Freezer Co., Madison, 1948-70, mfr.'s rep., 1954-70; founder, sec.-treas. Parkwood Hills Corp., Madison, 1965—; founder, sec.-treas. Park Towne Devel. Corp., Madison, 1969—; past chmn., exec. com. CUMIS Ins. Soc.; past chmn., chmn. exec. com. CUNA Mut. Ins. Soc., CUNA Mut. Ins. Group, Cudis Ins. Soc.; chmn. CMCI Corp.; treas. CUNADATA Corp., 1974-81. Pres., Wis. Credit Union League, 1965-67, bd. dirs., 1958-79; mem. Wis. Credit Union Rev. Bd., 1967—, chmn., 1973-76. Served with USMC, 1951-53. Mem. Aircraft Owners and Pilots Assn., CUNA Credit Union Nat. Assn. (dir. 1964-81), Greater Madison C. of C. (dir. 1976—, chmn. 1980). Roman Catholic. Club: Rotary. Home: 721 Anthony Ln Madison WI 53711 Office: 6622 Mineral Point Rd Madison WI 53705

RING, LEONARD M., lawyer; b. Tauragena, Lithuania, May 11, 1923; s. Abe and Rose (Kahn) R.; brought to U.S., 1930, naturalized, 1930; student N.Mex. Sch. Mines, 1943-44; LL.B., DePaul U., 1949, J.D., 1971; m. Donna R. Cecrle, June 29, 1959; children—Robert Steven, Susan Ruth. Admitted to Ill. bar, 1949; since practiced in Chgo.; spl. asst. atty. gen. State Ill., 1967-72; spl. atty. Ill. Dept. Ins., 1967-73; spl. trial atty. Met. San. Dist. Greater Chgo., 1967-77; lectr. civil trial, appellate practice, tort law Nat. Coll. Advocacy, San Francisco, 1971, 72; guest lectr. civil trial practice U. Chgo. Law Sch., 1973; mem. com. jury instrns. Ill. Supreme Ct., 1967-71, 73—; nat. chmn. Attys. Congl. Campaign Trust, Washington, 1975-79. Trustee Roscoe Pound-Am. Trial Lawyers Found., Washington, 1974-80; chmn. bd. trustees Avery Coonley Sch., Downers Grove, Ill., 1974-75. Served with USA, 1943-46. Decorated Purple Heart. Fellow Am. Coll. Trial Lawyers, Internat. Acad. Trial Lawyers, Internat. Soc. Barristers; mem. Soc. Trial Lawyers, Appellate Lawyers Assn. (pres. 1974-75), Assn. Trial Lawyers Am. (nat. pres. 1973-74), Ill. Trial Lawyers Assn. (pres. 1966-68), Chgo. Bar Assn. (bd. mgrs. 1971-73), Am., Ill. bar assns., Lex Legio (pres. 1976-78). Club: Oak Brook Polo (Ill.); Metropolitan, Monroe (Chgo.). Author: (with Harold A. Baker) Jury Instructions and Forms of Verdict, 1972; contbr. chpts. to books, articles to profl. jours. Home: 6 Royal Vale Dr Oakbrook IL 60521 Office: 111 W Washington St Chicago IL 60602

RINGER, ALFRED VICTOR, lawyer; b. Williamsport, Ind., Nov. 10, 1903; s. Victor Howard and Alice (Thomas) R.; A.B. with distinction, Ind. U., 1926, J.D., 1928; m. Dorothy Evelyn Slabaugh, Apr. 19, 1929; children—Thomas L. William A., Joan L. (Mrs. John Larson). Admitted to Ind. bar, 1927, U.S. Dist. Ct., 1928; practiced in Williamsport, 1928—; pros. atty. Warren Circuit Ct., Ind., 1935-40; atty. Town of Williamsport, 1940-72; atty. Warren County, Williamsport, 1953-70. Mem. Am., Ind. (pres. 6th dist. 1952; bd. mgrs. 1964-66), 7th Circuit bar assns., Ind. Bar Found. (dir., pres. 1972-73), Am. Judicature Soc., Ind. Soc. Chgo., Shrine, Phi Beta Kappa, Phi Delta Phi, Sigma Nu. Republican. Presbyn. Mason (Scottish Rite); Elk, Rotarian (dist. gov. 1951-52). Club: Columbia (Indpls.). Home: 311 Lincoln St Williamsport IN 47993 Office: 110 N Monroe St Williamsport IN 47993

RINGHOFER, JOSEPH FRANK, bus. services co. exec.; b. Chgo., May 15, 1936; s. Joseph Frank and Eleanor (McGee) R.; B.S.I.E., Indsl. Engring. Coll., Chgo., 1964; M.S.I.R., Loyola U., Chgo., 1978; m. Mariann Hall, Apr. 4, 1959; children—Joseph Frank III, Daniel, Jonathan. Indsl. engr. Tuthill Pump Co., Chgo., 1959-65; indsl. engr. Interlake Steel div. Howell Co., St. Charles, Ill., 1965-68, plant engr., 1968-70, supt., 1970-73, mgr. indsl. relations, 1973-76; mgr. employee and community relations Allis Chalmers Corp., Batavia, Ill., 1976—. Exec. bd. Two Rivers council Boy Scouts Am., 1973-81; sec. St. Charles (Ill.) Fire Dept., 1968-81, pres., 1981—. Served with USN, 1956-58. Mem. Valley Indsl. Assn. (pres. 1981), Kane DuPage Personnel Assn., Am. Mgmt. Assn., Am. Soc. Personnel Adminstrn., Indsl. Relations Research Assn., Nat. Safety Council, Jaycees (pres. St. Charles 1968), St. Charles C. of C. (v.p. 1974), Batavia C. of C. (v.p. 1979). Assn. for Ind. Devel. (v.p.). Clubs: Kiwanis (pres. St. Charles 1971-72), Rotary (pres. Batavia 1979-80), Moose, St. Charles Hockey. Home: 4N 150 Thornetree Rd Saint Charles IL 60174 Office: 1500 N Raddant Rd Batavia IL 60510

RINGO, BOYD COLBURN, civil engr.; b. Tulsa, May 16, 1927; s. Boyd Riley and Helen (Colburn) R.; B.S. in Archtl. Engring., Washington U., 1950, M.S. in Civil Engring., 1954; Ph.D. in Civil Engring., U. Mich., 1964; postgrad. Mich. State U., 1956-58; m. Marie Helen Smolicek, Sept. 13, 1948; children—Kim Ellen, Lynn Ann, William Colburn. Archtl. draftsman Gallmaier Engring. Co., Oklahoma City, 1950-51; asst. project engr. Granco Steel Products Co., Granite City, Ill., 1951-52; structural designer Sverdrup & Parcel Consulting Engrs., St. Louis, 1952-54; instr. dept. civil engring. Mich. State U., East Lansing, 1954-57, asst. prof., 1957-61; asst. prof. dept. of civil engring. U. Cin., 1961-64, asso. prof., 1964-67, prof., 1967—; cons. to various indsl. and mfg. firms, 1955—; reviewer for McGraw Hill Book Co., 1966; judge for Lincoln Arc Welding Found. Competition, 1964, 69; lectr. on tornadoes and structural damage to CD and the community, 1974—. Committeeman, Dan Beard council Cub Scouts Am., 1968-72, asst. scoutmaster, 1972—; Sunday sch. tchr. Faith Luth. Ch., Cin., 1972-74; committeeman Roselawn Luth. Ch., Cin., 1978—. Served with USN, 1945-46. Recipient Entry of Merit award Lincoln Arch Welding Found., 1975; registered profl. engr., Mich., Mo., Ohio. Mem. ASCE (faculty adviser 1962-64, reviewer Jour. for structural div. 1968-72), Am. Concrete Inst. (ednl. activities com. 1972-78), Am. Inst. Steel Constrn. (Spl. Citation award 1972), Am. Soc. Engring. Edn. (Western Electric Fund award for Teaching Excellence 1976), Tau Beta Pi, Chi Epsilon, Pi Mu Epsilon. Author: (with J.F. McDonough and C.J. Keaney) Use of Computer by the Practicing Civil Engineer, 1967; contbr. articles on structural design and engring. edn. to profl. jours.; developed the structural curriculum for undergrad. and grad. courses at U. Cin. Home: 9098 Arrowhead Ct Cincinnati OH 45231 Office: Mail Loc 71 Univ of Cincinnati Cincinnati OH 45221

RINGO, MIRIAM K., cons.; b. N.Y.C.; B.A., Hunter Coll.; M.A., U. Chgo.; 3 children. Former economist War Manpower Commn.; research asst. Inland Steel Co.; staff dir. Gov.'s Com. on Unemployment; asst. to Gov. Otto Kerner, Springfield, Ill.; dir. Ill. State Dept. Personnel; staff dir., mem. adv. com. on research U.S. Employment Service; staff dir. Ill. Commn. on Labor Law; former dir. personnel Office Ill. Sec. State, Springfield; former dir. ops. Ill. Ho. of Reps., Springfield; now cons., writer. Mem. Jane Austen Soc. Author: Nobody Said It Better, 1980. Home: 16 W 220 97th St Hinsdale IL 60521

RINKENBERGER, DONALD S., social worker; b. Gridley, Ill., Jan. 6, 1932; s. Burl E. and Olive (Krug) R.; student St. Francis Coll., Milw., 1949-51; B.A., St. Mary of Lake U., 1954; M.S.W., Loyola U., Chgo., 1962; m. Dorothy Ann Grande, June 13, 1964; children—Ann Marie, Mary Therese, James Andrew. State sales rep. N. Central Ins. Co., St. Paul, 1956-58; social worker Big Bros. Inc., Mpls., 1958-60, 62-64, supr., 1962-64, camp dir., 1963-66; social worker Mpls. Public Schs., 1964-67; coordinator secondary and social work aides, 1967-74, inservice coordinator, adminstr. East Area Tchr. Center, 1974-76, social worker, 1976—. Instr. Met. Community Coll., Mpls., part time, 1970-76. Vol., Big Bros., 1955-78; mem. bldg. and edn. com. St. Joseph the Worker Ch., 1976—; chmn. steering organizational com. Northwest Community Coop., 1979, pres. bd. dirs., 1980-81; bd. dirs. First Call for Help, United Way, Hennepin County, 1981. Served with AUS, 1954-56. Recipient grant Mpls. Found., 1955. Mem. Nat. Assn. Social Workers (cons. editor jour. 1981), Acad. Cert. Social Workers, Mpls. Sch. Social Workers Forum, Minn. Sch. Social Workers Assn. (exec. sec. 1970-81), Mpls. Fedn. Tchrs. Roman Catholic. Office: 3611 20th Ave S Minneapolis MN 55407

RINKENBERGER, KENNETH WAYNE, seed co. ofcl.; b. Watseka, Ill., Nov. 20, 1952; s. William Robert and Marjorie Louise R.; B.S. in Agrl. Communications, U. Ill., 1973; M.B.A., Ill. State U., 1979; m. Devon Lee Nussbaum, Dec. 29, 1974; children—Brandon, Jarod, Candice, Kristen. With Funk Seeds Internat., Bloomington, Ill., 1974—, copywriter, 1974, market research analyst, 1974-77, public relations mgr., 1977-80, mgr. advt. and public relations, 1980—; mktg. cons. Chmn. Ill. Ag Day, 1979; chmn. Ill. Checkoff Publicity Com., 1980. Mem. Nat. Agri-Marketers Assn., Am. Agrl. Editors Assn. Home: 18 Devon Bloomington IL 61701 Office: PO Box 2911 Bloomington IL 61701

RINSLEY, DONALD BRENDAN, psychiatrist; b. N.Y.C., Jan. 31, 1928; s. Louis and Annamay (Hindle) R.; A.B. with honors, Harvard, 1949, postgrad., 1949-50; M.D., Washington U., St. Louis, 1954; diploma in child psychiatry honoris causa Menninger Found., 1975; m. Jacqueline Ann Louk, May 28, 1955. Intern pediatrics St. Louis Children's Hosp., 1954-55; fellow in psychiatry Menninger Found., Topeka, 1955-56, 58-60; staff psychiatrist Dept. Justice, U.S. Med. Center for Fed. Prisoners, Springfield, Mo., 1956-58; resident psychiatrist Topeka State Hosp., 1955-56, 58-60, asst. chief adolescent unit, children's sect., 1960-68, chief, 1968-70, dir. sect., 1970-75; asso. chief psychiatry edn. Topeka VA Hosp., 1975—; cons. psychiatrist C.F. Menninger Meml. Hosp., 1976—; asst. in pediatrics Washington U. Sch. Medicine, St. Louis, 1954-55; faculty gen. psychiatry, Menninger Sch. Psychiatry, Topeka, 1960—, faculty child psychiatry, 1968—, exec. and tng. faculty in child psychiatry, 1969-75, 77-79; asso. clin. prof. psychiatry U. Kans. Sch. Medicine, 1970-77, clin. prof., 1977—. Sr. asst. surgeon to surgeon USPHS, 1956-80. Recipient Edward A. Strecker Meml. award Inst. Pa. Hosp., 1968. Spencer Found. fellow in advanced studies Menninger Found., 1976-79, fellow in interdisciplinary studies, 1979—. Diplomate in psychiatry Am. Bd. Psychiatry and Neurology. Fellow Am. Psychiat. Assn. (br. chmn. com. research 1964-65), Am. Coll. Psychoanalysts, Royal Soc. Health, AAAS, N.Y. Acad. Scis., Am. Orthopsychiat. Assn., Am. Assn. Children's Residential Centers; mem. Assn. for Research Nervous and Mental Disease, Am. Soc. Adolescent Psychiatry, Am. Acad. Psychoanalysis, Am. Acad. Child Psychiatry, Canadian Psychiat. Assn. (corr.), Am. Assn. Psychiat. Services for Children, Argentine Assn. Child and Adolescent Psychiatry and Psychology (hon.), Sigma Xi (zone cons. to chpt.-at-large 1969-71, mem. com. on membership-at-large 1972-75). Club: Harvard-Radcliffe of Kansas City. Editorial bd. Psychiat. Quar. Adolescent Psychiatry, Bull. of Menninger Clinic; hon. cons. editor Argentine Jour. Child and Adolescent Psychiatry and Psychology. Contbr. articles to profl. publs. Home: 4521 W 33d Street Terr Topeka KS 66614 Office: 2200 SW Gage Blvd Topeka KS 66622

RINSLEY, JACQUELINE ANN LOUK, hosp. adminstr.; b. Chgo., Apr. 5, 1933; d. John Lancelot and Margaret Elizabeth (Zeilinger) Louk; student Washington U., St. Louis, 1951-52; diploma in nursing St. Luke's Hosp. Sch. Nursing, 1955; m. Donald Brendan Rinsley, May 28, 1955 (div. Jan. 1982). Psychiat. nurse Topeka State Hosp., 1955-56, sect. head nurse, 1955-56; gen. and pediatric nurse St. John's Hosp., Springfield, Mo., 1956-57, Burge Hosp., 1957-58; head pediatric nurse Stormont-Vail Hosp., Topeka, 1958-60; psychiat. nurse. Kans. Neurol. Inst., Topeka, 1960-70, adminstr. Honey Bee Lodge, 1970-80, dir. nursing edn., coordinator continuing edn., 1980-81. Mem. Am. Nurses Assn., Kans. State Nurses Assn., Am. Assn. for Mental Deficiency, Nat. Rehab. Assn., Nat. Audubon Soc., Am. Mus. Nat. History, Smithsonian Assos., Zeta Tau Alpha. Republican. Lutheran. Home: 3301 W 30th Street Terr Topeka KS 66614 Office: Kansas Neurological Institute 3107 W 21st St Topeka KS 66604

RIORDAN, DONALD ROBERT, SR., health ins. co. exec.; b. Bklyn., May 2, 1931; s. Dennis Aloysius and Helen Octavia (Mansell) R.; B.S., Marquette U., Milw., 1954; m. Mary Carol Perry, Nov. 28, 1953; children—Donald, Dennis, Robert, Timothy, Phillip, Kathleen, John. Sr. auditor Arthur Young & Co., C.P.A.s, Milw., 1954-59; mgr. audit and tax Schwerman Trucking Co., Milw., 1959-64; sr. auditor A.O. Smith Corp., Milw., 1964-66; controller Associated Hosp. Service, Milw., 1966-72, asst. v.p., 1972-73; v.p. fin., then sr. v.p. internat. adminstrn. Blue Cross N.E. Ohio, Cleve., 1972-76, pres., chief exec. officer, 1976—; bd. dirs. Blue Cross Assn., Health Services, Inc.; bd. dirs., com. mem. Met. Health Planning Corp. Cleve.; mem. Greater Cleve. Coalition Health Care. Mem. coms. Cleve. State U. C.P.A., Ohio. Mem. Am. Health Planning Assn. (dir.), Ohio Soc. C.P.A.s, Treas. Club Cleve., Cleve. Bus. Economists Club, Fedn. Community Planning, Greater Cleve. Growth Assn., Roman Catholic. Club: Cleve. Athletic. Office: 2066 E 9th St Cleveland OH 44115

RIORDAN, JOHN JOSEPH, accountant, minerals mining and processing co. ofcl.; b. Chgo., Dec. 22, 1946; s. John Stephen and Joan Matilda (Matuszyk) R.; B.S. in Acctg., Loyola U., Chgo., 1972; M.B.A. in Fin., U. Chgo., 1979; m. Sandra Grace Formusa, Nov. 23, 1974; 1 dau., Christina Marie. Staff auditor S.D. Leidesdorf, C.P.A.'s, 1972-75; internal auditor Internat. Minerals Chem. Corp., 1975-76, mgmt. advisor fin., 1976-79, mgr. fin. Imcore div. Olivine Products, 1979, mgr. fin. planning and analysis Industry Group, Imcore div., Des Plaines, Ill., 1979—; lectr. acctg. Northwestern U., 1979—. Corp. chmn. alumni fund raising U. Chgo., 1980, chmn., Mt. Prospect, Ill., 1980. Named No. 1 Acctg. Instr. Evanston Campus of Northwestern U., 1979-80. Designer copyrighted flow diagram of acctg. cycle. Home: 2011 Wintergreen St Mount Prospect IL 60056

RIORDAN, RAY JOSEPH, trade assn. exec.; b. Green Bay, Wis., Jan. 27, 1916; s. Daniel E. and Florence E. (Brooks) R.; student St. Norbert Coll., 1933-35; B.S., Marquette U., 1937; m. Eileen Kelly, June 25, 1941; children—Mary Eileen (Mrs. Richard Harper), Ray Joseph, Patrick D., Robert H. Editor, pub. Tri County News, Pulaski, Wis., 1938-41; salesman Yellow Pages, Mich., Wis. and Ind., 1941-42; telephone engr. Hercules Powder Co., Wilmington, Del., 1942-43; comml. mgr. Gen. Telephone Co., Wausau and Madison, Wis., 1943-46; comml. mgr. 6 state area Central Telephone Co., LaCrosse, Wis., 1946-52; exec. v.p. Wis. State Telephone Assn., Madison, 1952—; pres. Shamrock Affiliates, Madison, 1959—; sec.-treas. Wis. State Telephone Found., Madison, 1965—, N.E. Telephone Co., Pulaski, 1950—; mem. Wis. Emergency Number Systems Bd., 1981—. Mem. Council Telephone Execs. (pres. 1962, 70), Ind. Telephone Pioneers (pres. Badger chpt. 1954-55). Clubs: Elks, Madison, Black Hawk Country. Home: 6711 N Dunlap Hollow Rd Mazomanie WI 53560 Office: 617 N Segoe Rd Suite 202 Madison WI 53705

RIORDAN, ROBERT FREDERICK, energy research co. exec.; b. Los Angeles, May 24, 1942; s. Francis Xavier and Edna Elizabeth (Parris) R.; B.S. in Engring., U.S. Naval Acad., 1964; M.S. in Meteorology, Naval Postgrad. Sch., 1971; m. Pamela Elizabeth Sutton, June 4, 1964; children—Robert Patrick, Elizabeth Parris, Anastasia Marie. In bus. devel. Wilson & Co., Salina, Kans., 1975-76; pres. Riordan Enterprises Ltd., Salina, 1977-78; energy research coordinator State Kans. Energy Office, Topeka, 1978-79; dir. applied energy research and public service program U. Kans. Center Research, Inc., Lawrence, 1979—; mem. rev. panel for solar thermal program Dept. Energy, 1980-81; cons. Jet Propulsion Lab., 1980—; mem. Kans. Solar Energy Adv. Com., 1976-78; chmn. Tri-Govt. Energy Usage Commn., 1977-78. Pres., St. Mary's Parish Council, 1977-78. Served to lt. comdr. USN, 1964-75. Mem. AAAS, U.S. Naval Acad. Alumni Assn. (Outstanding Naval Acad. Info. Officer Kans. 1978), Lawrence C. of C., Kans. Solar Energy Soc. (dir. 1976-78), Sigma Xi. Roman Catholic. Clubs: Elks, Rotary (dir. 1977-78). Office: 2291 Irving Hill Dr Lawrence KS 66045

RIPP, WILLIAM ROBERT, state senator, dairy farmer; b. Dimock, S.D., Dec. 30, 1924; s. Henry Peter and Bertha Helen (Kabeiseman) R.; ed. public and parochial schs. Breeder purebred cattle, Dimock; mem. S.D. State Extension Adv. Bd., 1966-68; pres. Hutchinson County Extension Bd., 1960-68; mem. S.D. Senate, 1970—. Mem. Sch. Bd., 1965-70; clk. Twp. Bd., 1960-70. Mem. Nat. Holstein Cattle Assn. Republican. Roman Catholic. Club: K.C. (state dep. 1962-63). Home and Office: Dimock SD 57331

RIPPY, FRANCES MARGUERITE MAYHEW, educator, editor; b. Ft. Worth, Sept. 16, 1929; d. Henry Grady and Marguerite Christine (O'Neill) Mayhew; B.A., Tex. Christian U., 1949; M.A., Vanderbilt U., 1951, Ph.D. (fellow), 1957; postgrad. Birkbeck Coll. U. London (Eng.), 1952-53; m. N. Merrill Rippy, Aug. 29, 1955 (dec. Sept. 1980); children—Felix O'Neill, Conrad Mayhew, Marguerite Hailey. Teaching fellow Vanderbilt U., Nashville, 1951-52; instr. Tex. Christian U., 1953-55; instr. to asst. prof. Lamar State U., 1955-59; successively asst., asso., prof. dept. English, Ball State U., Muncie, Ind., 1959—; asso. prof., 1964-68, prof., 1968—; dir. English doctoral studies, 1966—, vis. prof. U. Puerto Rico, summers 1959, 60, 61, Sam Houston State U., summer, 1957; cons., evaluator North Central Assn. Colls. and Schs., 1973—. Treas., Friends of Muncie Pub. Library, 1976-78. Named Danforth Asso., 1965—; Danforth summer grantee, 1962; MacClintock research scholar, 1965. Mem. Modern Lang. Assn., Am. Soc. 18th Studies (charter), Johnson Soc. Central Region (sec. 1961-62), Coll. English Assn., Nat. Council Tchr. English, AAUP, Ind. Coll. English Assn., Ind. Council Tchrs. English. Editor Ball State U. Forum. Author articles in profl. jours. Home: 4709 W Jackson St Muncie IN 47304

RIPPY, WILLIAM FRANCIS, property and assets mgmt. co. exec.; b. Salem, Ill., Mar. 22, 1944; s. William Byron and Mary Martha (Stevenson) R.; B.S. in Bus. Adminstrn., Greenville Coll., 1965; m. Barbara Gail Olsen, Sept. 25, 1965; children—Steven Todd, Beth Anne, Megan Lynn, Lee Ann. Sales rep. IBM, 1965-67; data processing officer Bank of Ill., 1967-69; owner Bill Rippy Real Estate, Mt. Vernon, Ill., 1969-72; v.p. mktg. Fin. Computing Corp., St. Louis, 1972-74; v.p. Unicon, designers, builders, Highland, Ill., 1974-76; regional mgr. Linclay Corp., Kansas City, Mo., 1976-79; pres. Cohen Asset Mgmt., Inc., Kansas City, Mo., 1979—. Drive chmn. Jefferson County United Fund, 1970-71; state chmn. polit. action com. Farmers Union, 1971. Mem. Mo. Builders Assn. (chmn. legis. com. 1976). Democrat. Methodist. Home: 2109 Sunvale Dr Olathe KS 66061 Office: 1100 Main St Kansas City MO 64105

RIPS, LANCE JEFFREY, psychologist, educator; b. Omaha, Dec. 19, 1947; s. Norman Julian and Barbara Joy (Taxman) R.; B.A., Swarthmore Coll., 1970; Ph.D., Stanford U., 1974. Asst. prof. behavioral scis. U. Chgo., 1974-81, asso. prof., 1981—. Recipient Research Scientist Devel. award NIMH, 1979—; NSF fellow, 1970-74. Mem. Psychonomics Soc., Am. Psychol. Assn., Linguistic Soc. Am., Cognitive Sci. Soc., Phi Beta Kappa. Cons. editor Memory and Cognition, 1975-81, Cognitive Psychology, 1981—; research on natural concepts and deductive reasoning. Office: 5848 S University Ave Chicago IL 60637

RISELEY, MARTHA SUZANNAH HEATER (MRS. CHARLES RISELEY), psychologist, educator; b. Middletown, Ohio, Apr. 25, 1916; d. Elsor and Mary (Henderson) Heater; B.Ed., U. Toledo, 1943, M.A., 1958; Ph.D., Toledo Bible Coll., 1977; student Columbia U., summers 1943, 57; m. Lester Seiple, Aug. 27, 1944 (div. Feb. 1953); 1 son, L. Rolland, III; m. 2d, Charles Riseley, July 30, 1960. Tchr. kindergarten Maumee Valley Country Day Sch., Maumee, Ohio, 1942-44; dir. recreation Toledo Soc. for Crippled Children, 1950-51; tchr. trainable children Lott Day Sch., Toledo, 1951-57; psychologist, asst. dir. Sheltered Workshop Found., Lucas County, Ohio, 1957-62; psychologist Lucas County Child Welfare Bd., Toledo, 1956-62; tchr. educable retarded, head dept. spl. edn. Maumee City Schs., 1962-69; pvt. practice clin. psychology, 1956—; instr. spl. edn. Bowling Green State U., 1962—; instr. Owens Tech. Coll., 1973; interim dir. rehab. services Toledo Goodwill Industries, summer 1967, clin. psychologist Rehab. Center, 1967—; mem. staff Toledo Mental Health Center, 1979—. Dir. camping activities for retarded girls and women Camp Libbey, Defiance, Ohio, summers 1951-62; group worker for retarded women Toledo YWCA, 1957-62; guest lectr. Ohio State U., 1957. Mem. Ohio Assn. Tchrs. Trainable Youth (pres. 1956-57), NW Ohio Rehab. Assn. (pres. 1961-62), Toledo Council for Exceptional Children (pres. 1965), Greater Toledo Assn. Mental Health, Nat. Assn. for Retarded Children, Ohio Assn. Tchrs. Slow Learners, Am. Assn. Mental Deficiency, Am. Soc. Psychologists in Marital and Family Counseling, Psychology and Law Soc., Am. (asso.), Ohio, NW Ohio (sec.-treas. 1974-77, pres. 1978-79) psychol. assns., Ohio Psychol. Assn. (continuing edn. com. 1978—), NEA, AAUW, Am. Soc. Psychologists in Pvt. Practice (nat. dir. 1976—), State Assn. Psychologists and Psychol. Assts., Bus. and Profl. Women's Club, (pres. 1970-72), Ohio Fedn. Bus. and Profl. Women's Clubs (dist. sec. 1970-71, dist. legis. chmn. 1972-74), Toledo Art Mus., Women's Aux. Toledo Bar Assn., Zonta Internat. (local pres. 1973-74, 78-79, area dir. 1976-78), Maumee Valley Hist. Soc., MBLS PEO (chpt. pres. 1950-51), Toledo Council on World Affairs, Internat. Platform Assn. Baptist. Home: 322 River Rd Maumee OH 43537 Office: 706 Madison Ave Toledo OH 43624

RISH, SEYMOUR ABRAHAM, acct., assn. exec.; b. Chgo., May 23, 1921; s. David and Nettie (Rothenberg) R.; grad. Chgo. Jr. Coll., 1941; m. Jean Jacobson, Sept. 3, 1944; 1 son, L. David. Owner, mgr. S.A. Rish, tax acct., auditor, Chgo., 1947-59; founder, exec. sec. Nat. Assn. Enrolled Fed. Tax Accts., Chgo., 1960—, pres. 1960-62, sec., 1964-65, sec.-treas., 1961-62, exec. sec., 1963-72, also editor assn. publ., exec. dir. Ill. assn., 1972—, dir. nat. affairs, 1972—. Treas., Am. Blood Research Soc., Chgo., 1956-69, pres., 1969—; dist. v.p. Pterson Park (Ill.) Improvement Assn., 1962-65.

RISLEY, TODD ROBERT, educator, scientist; b. Palmer, Alaska, Sept. 8, 1937; s. Robert and Eva Lou R.; A.B. with distinction in Psychology, San Diego State Coll., 1960; M.S., U. Wash., 1963, Ph.D., 1966; m. Marguerite Risley; 1 son, Todd Michael. Asst. prof. psychology Fla. State U., Tallahassee, 1964-65; research asso. Bur. Child Research, U. Kans., Lawrence, 1965-77, sr. scientist, 1977—, asst. prof. dept. human devel., 1967-69, asso. prof., 1969-73, prof., 1973—; pres. Center for Applied Behavior Analysis, 1970—; dir. Lawrence Day Care Program, 1970—, Johnny Cake Child Study Center, Mansfield, Ark., 1973-74; vis. prof. U. Auckland (N. Z.), 1978; acting dir. Western Carolina Center, Morganton, N.C., 1981; cons. Alaska Dept. Health and Social Service, 1979, Logos Research Inst., Van Nuys, Calif., 1979, Pa. State U. Coll. Human Devel., 1979, Eastern Oreg. Hosp. and Tng., Center, 1977—, Nashville Police Dept., 1975—, Luton Mental Health Center, Nashville, 1975—, Nat. Inst. Drug Abuse, 1975, Western Carolina Retardation Center, 1975—, Mont. State Survey on Mental Health and Aging, 1975, N.C. Div. Mental Health, 1975, R.I. Div. Mental Health, 1975, numerous others; cons. Children's Asthma Research Inst. and Hosp., Denver, 1970—, Nat. U. Mex., Mexico City, 1970, Gen. Motors Inst., Kansas City, Kans., 1970, Regional Intervention Project, George Peabody Coll., Nashville, 1969—, Kans. State Dept. Social Welfare, 1968, Cerebral Palsy Center, Kansas City, Mo., 1966, Rehab. Inst., So. Ill. U., 1966, Inst. Behavior Modification, HEW, Washington, 1966, OEO, Washington, 1966, numerous others; co-chmn. Fla. task force on use of behavioral procedures in state programs for retarded, 1974—; mem. resident abuse investigating com., div. retardation Fla. Dept. Health and Rehab. Services, 1972—; mem. counci sci. advs. Nat. Asthma Center, 1974-78; mem. adv. com. Nat. Inst. Edn., 1974; mem. rev. panel Ill. Dept. Mental Health, 1974-75; mem. spl. study sect. Nat. Inst. Aging, 1976; mem. adv. com. Social Research Inst., U. Utah, 1977—; mem. nat. planning com. Nova Behavioral Conf. on Aging, 1976-79; lectr. Co-pres., Pinckney Neighborhood Assn., 1976-77, Cordley Sch. PTA, 176-77; mem. com. on day care Lawrence Schs., 1977-78; co-pres. Pinckney Sch. PTA, 1979-80. NIMH grantee, 1971-72, 72-73; Nat. Center Health Services Research grantee, 1976-79; Nat. Inst. Edn. grantee, 1973; numerous others. Fellow Am. Psychol. Assn. (dir. div. 25, 1974-77, div. com. guidelines for human experimentation); mem. AAAS, Am. Assn. Mental Deficiency, Assn. Advancement of Behavior Therapy (dir. 1975-80, pres. 1976-77, com. regulation of behavioral practice 1975-77, publs. bd. 1975-80, legis. com. 1976, chmn. profl. rev. com. 1977—; series editor Readings in Behavior Therapy 1977—), Soc. Behavioral Medicine, Assn. Behavior Analysis, Sigma Xi. Editor Jour. Applied Behavior Analysis, 1971-74, mem. editorial bd., 1967-70, 76-79; mem. editorial bd. Jour. Exptl. Child Psychology, 1969-71; Behaviorism: A Forum for Critical Discussion, 1971—, Jour. Personalized Instruction, 1975—, Jour. Organizational Behavior Mgmt., 1977—, Jour. Applied Research in Mental Retardation, 1979—, Edn. and Treatment of Children, 1979—, Behavior Modification, 1980—, Analysis and Intervention in Developmental Disabilities, 1980—; contbr. revs. and numerous articles to profl. jours.; adv. editor Advances in Child Clin. Psychology, 1976—; mng. editor Behavior Therapy, The Behavior Therapist, Behavioral Assessment, 1977-80. Co-author: The Infant Center, 1977; Shopping with Children: Advice for Parents, 1978; The Toddler Center, 1979; contbr. chpts. to books in field. Office: U Kans Lawrence KS 66045

RISS, ROBERT BAILEY, fin. co. exec.; b. Salida, Colo., May 27, 1927; s. Richard R. and Louise (Roberts) R.; B.S. in Bus. Adminstrn., U. Kans., 1949; children—Edward Stayton, G. Leslie, Laura Bailey, Juliana Warren. Pres., Riss Internat. Corp., Kansas City, Mo., 1950-80, chmn. bd., 1964—; founder, pres., chmn. bd. Republic Industries, Inc., Kansas City, 1969—; pres. Grandview Bank & Trust Co., 1969-80, chmn. bd., 1969—; chmn. bd., treas. Columbia Properties, Inc., Kansas City, 1969—; chmn. bd. Johnson Motor Lines, Inc., Charlotte, N.C., 1979-81; mem. exec. com. ERC Corp., Kansas City, 1979-80, mem. fin. com., 1977-80, dir., 1976-80; adv. dir. United Mo. Bank of Kansas City, 1978-80; pres., chmn. bd. Dominion

Banqueshares, Kansas City, 1980—. Pres. Boys Club of Kansas City, Mo., 1956; officer United Fund Campaign, 1952-54; chmn. Muscular Dystrophy Assn. Fund Drive of Greater Kansas City Area, 1955; mem. Kansas City Crime Commn., 1955-56; mem. adv. com. Am. Field Service, 1968-72; bd. dirs. Kansas City Area council Boy Scouts Am., 1971—, Mission Hills Homes Assn., 1973, Downtown, Inc., Kansas City, Mo., 1970—; bd. govs. Agrl. Hall of Fame, 1975—; bd. dirs. American Royal Assn., 1979—, v.p., 1980—; bd. govs. Safety Council, 1952-56; trustee U. Kans. Endowment Assn., 1970—, mem. exec. com., 1974—, vice-chmn., 1980—. Named Most Outstanding Young Man in State of Mo., U.S. Jr. C. of C., 1956; recipient Silver Beaver award Boy Scouts Am., 1972; Fred Ellsworth medallion U. Kans., 1979, Disting. Service citation, 1976. Mem. Kansas U. Alumni Assn. (pres. 1969-70, dir. 1968-74). Clubs: Kansas City (chmn. exec. com., 1st v.p. 1973); Univ.; Olympic; Ponte Vedra; Farmington Country; N.Y. Athletic; Garden of Gods; Mission Hills Country. Home: 9202 W 71st St Merriam KS 66204 Office: Riss Internat Corp 215 W Pershing Ave Kansas City MO 64108

RISSER, FRED A., state senator; b. Madison, Wis., May 5, 1927; student Carleton Coll., U. Wis., Madison; B.A., U. Oreg., 1950; LL.B., 1952; 3 children. Admitted to Wis. bar; mem. Wis. Assembly, 1956-60, Wis. Senate, 1962—, pres. senate, pres. pro tem, 1975, 77, minority leader, 1967-73. Del. Dem. Nat. Conv., 1960, 64; chmn. Wis. Electoral Coll., 1964. Served with USN, World War II. Address: Room 235 South State Capitol Madison WI 53702*

RISTAU, DANIEL DEAN, hosp. adminstr.; b. Fremont, Nebr., Jan. 29, 1952; s. Donald H. and Phyllis E. (Pischke) R.; B.S. in Bus. Adminstrn., U. Nebr., 1975; M.H.A., Duke U., 1978. Fin. analyst Nebr. State Dept. Health, Lincoln, 1975-76; mgr. housekeeping Duke U. Med. Center, Durham, N.C., 1977-78; asst. adminstr. Johnson County Meml. Hosp., Buffalo, Wyo., 1978, Ami Holt Meml. Nursing Home, 1978; adminstr. Gregory (S.D.) Community Hosp., 1978-81, Rosebud Nursing Home, 1978-81; adminstr. Luth. Hosps. and Homes Soc. Am., 1981—; emergency med. technician. Leader, Catholic youth group. Mem. Am. Coll. Hosp. Adminstrs., Am. Hosp. Assn., S.D. Hosp. Assn. (v.p. Dist. IV 1981-82), S.D. Health Care Assn. Clubs: K.C., Rotary (bd. dirs. 1979). Office: 1202 Westrac PO Box 2087 Fargo ND 58107

RISTOLA, EUGENE GUSTAF, electronics engr.; b. Withee, Wis., Mar. 18, 1920; s. Nestor and Gunilla (Alline) R.; B.S., U. Wis., 1947; m. Mary Jane Hubbard, July 28, 1950; 1 son, Stephen Eugene. Electronic design engr. Collins Radio Co., Cedar Rapids, Iowa 1947-60, adminstrv. mgr. research div., 1960-64, mem. tech. staff electronics research dept., 1964-69, mem. inertial navigation systems dept., 1969-71; engring. mgr. Norand Corp., Cedar Rapids, 1971-75; mem. avionics div. Collins Radio Group Rockwell Internat., 1976—, Active Boy Scouts Am. Served with AUS, 1943-46. Mem. IEEE, Internat. Platform Assn., Eta Kappa Nu. Lutheran (mem. finance com.). Club: Toastmasters Internat. Home: 4208 Northwood Dr NE Cedar Rapids IA 52402

RITCHERSON, RODERICK ANTHONY, savs. & loan exec.; b. Houston, June 29, 1950; s. Lewis Henry and Velma Joyce R.; B.S. in Phys. Edn., U. Wis., 1972. Copywriter, Stephan & Brady Advt., Madison, Wis., 1972-75; advt., public relations dir. Home Savs. & Loan, Madison, 1975-77, v.p. mktg., 1977—. Active United Way, Madison. Mem. Madison Advt. Fedn. (dir. 1976-78). Sales and Mktg. Execs. Madison, Savs. Instns. Mktg. Soc. Am. Home: 1210 Pontiac Trail Madison WI 53711 Office: Home Savings & Loan 2 S Carroll St Madison WI 53703

RITTENHOUSE, DAVID RAYMOND, investment co. exec.; b. Griswold, Ill.; s. Edward F. and Mary E. (Griswold) R.; B.A. cum laude, U. Mich., 1933; m. Cornelia Arnos, June 14, 1933; children—Barbara, Linda, Susan, Sally. Vice pres. Securities Inc., Toledo, 1937-46; pres. Rittenhouse Motors, Inc., Toledo, 1946-71, Toledo Discount Co., 1950—. Served with USNR, 1944-46. Mem. Toledo Bd. Edn., also past pres.; mem. Ohio Bd. Edn.; trustee Toledo Mus. Art, 1969—. Mem. Toledo C. of C. (v.p.), Toledo Automobile Club (dir.), Phi Beta Kappa, Phi Kappa Phi, Beta Theta Pi. Mem. First Congl. Ch. Clubs: Rotary (pres. Toledo), Hermits, Belmont Country, Toledo. Home: 10641 Cardiff Rd Perrysburg OH 43551 Office: 309 N Reynolds Rd Toledo OH 43615

RITTER, GREGORY HUGH, ednl. adminstr.; b. St. Paul, Feb. 16, 1946; s. Winfield Arthur and Mary Jean (Thompson) R.; B.S., U. Minn., 1968; M.Div., United Theol. Sem., New Brighton, Minn., 1974; m. Barbara Anne Berzak, Mar. 14, 1970; children—Anne-Jean, William, Catherine. Tchr. English, Mpls. South High Sch., 1968-70; ordained to ministry United Presbyn. Ch., 1974; asso. pastor Congl. Ch., Rochester, Minn., 1972-73, Oak Grove Presbyn. Ch., Bloomington, Minn., 1974-78; dir. ch. relations United Theol. Sem., New Brighton, 1978-79, v.p. devel., 1979—; bd. dirs., sec. Alfred Adler Inst. Minn., 1980—; mem. Bloomington Youth Commn., 1976-78; mem. Big Bros., 1976-78. Mem. Council Advancement and Support Edn., North Suburban C. of C. Home: 602 Driftwood Rd New Brighton MN 55112 Office: 3000 5th St NW New Brighton MN 55112

RITTER, HUBERT AUGUST, obstetrician, gynecologist; b. St. Louis, Aug. 30, 1924; s. Hubert C. and Louise (Laipple) R.; A.B., Westminster Coll., 1945; M.D., St. Louis U., 1948; m. Harriette Hudson, Feb. 27, 1949; 1 dau., Lisa. Intern, St. Louis U. Hosp., 1948-49, resident, 1950-53; practice medicine specializing in ob-gyn, St. Louis, 1955—; founder Ritter Ob-Gyn Assos., Inc., St. Louis, 1969—; acting chmn. ob-gyn St. Louis U., 1976, also clin. prof. Served with USN, 1949-55. Recipient Key to City St. Louis from Mayor J. Poelker for community serivce, 1975. Fellow Am. Coll. Obstetricians and Gynecologists, A.C.S.; mem. AMA (trustee 1976—, pres. Edn. and Research Found. 1977—), Mo., So. med. assns., St. Louis Med. Soc. (hon.), St. Louis Gynecol. Soc. (pres. 1978-79), Internat., Am. fertility socs. Presbyterian. Clubs: St. Louis, Old Warson Country, St. Louis, St. Louis Skeet and Trap, Masons (32 deg.), Shriners. Contbr. articles to med. jours. Office: 1035 Bellevue Ave Suite 208 Saint Louis MO 63117

RITZ, BERYL GENEVA, dietitian; b. Beresford, S.D., May 5, 1920; d. Albert and Bertyne O. (Tollefson) Birkland; student U. S.D., 1938-39; B.S. in Foods and Nutrition, Iowa State U., 1942, postgrad., 1958; postgrad. S.D. State U., 1971; m. John Richard Meyer, Sept. 17, 1944 (dec. 1955); children—Judith F. Meyer Ripke, John A., Sally B.; m. 2d, Lawrence Henry Ritz, July 15, 1967. Dietetic intern Miami Valley Hosp., Dayton, Ohio, 1942, Army Sta. Hosp., Ft. Leonard Wood, Mo., 1943; dietitian U.S. Army Hosp., Santa Maria, Calif., 1943-45; head dietitian Sioux Valley Hosp., Sioux Falls, S.D., 1947-48; asst. chief dietitian VA Med. Center, Sioux Falls, 1949-51; asst. chief dietetic service VA Med. Center, Hot Springs, S.D., 1961-64; chief dietetic service VA Med. Center, Sioux Falls, 1964—; resource person for nutrition S.D. Nursing Home Assn., 1970-74; mem. S.D. White House Conf. on Aging, 1972; nutrition cons. Sr. Citizens Center, Sioux Falls, United Cerebral Palsy Community Living Center and Sch. Troop leader Girl Scouts U.S.A., 1961-64; active United Fund, 1977, recipient Key Campaigner award; coordinator Fed. Women's Program. Served with M.C., AUS,

1943-45. Recipient award for contbn. to edn. programs in food sci. S.D. State U., 1977; Cost Reduction Contbr. award Adminstr. Vets. Affairs, 1975. Mem. Am. Dietetic Assn., S.D. Dietetic Assn. (charter mem., exec. bd., past pres., del., chmn. public relations, chmn. registration), Nutrition Today Soc. (charter mem.), AAUW, Nutrition Council S.D. (exec. bd.), Iowa State U. Alumni Assn. Lutheran. Clubs: Sons of Norway, Sioux Falls Republican Women's (pres. 1980—). Home: 1601 S Hawthorne St Sioux Falls SD 57105 Office: 2501 W 22d St Sioux Falls SD 57105

RIVERS, EDWARD ALEXANDER, educator, counselor; b. White Cloud, Mich., Apr. 29, 1914; s. Alexander Baxter and Sarah Winifred Rivers; student Kent State U., 1950-51; B.A., Case Western Res. U., 1955, M.A., 1960; postgrad. Mich. State U., 1963, Marquette U., 1965, U. Mich., 1966-67, Ball State U., 1968, U. Wis., Milw., 1970; m. Joan Marie Franz, June 29, 1963; children—Michael, Melanie. Tchr. English, social studies and reading, Cleve., 1955-61; tchr. English and reading, Grand Rapids, Mich., 1961-63, Milw., 1963-65; faculty Continuation Sch. Milw. Inst. Tech., 1965-68; counselor gen. edn. Milw. Area Tech. Coll., 1968—. Sec. Cleve. Baha'i Community Local Spiritual Assembly, 1959-61. Served with U.S. Army, 1941-47. Mem. Am. Fedn. Tchrs., Wis. Fedn. Tchrs., Council for Occupational Edn., Wis. Adult Vocat. Edn. Assn. Home: RFD 1 Sumac Rd Plymouth WI 53073 Office: 1015 N 6th St Milwaukee WI 53203

RIVERS, GEORGE RONALD, market analyst; b. Charleston, S.C., Nov. 8, 1941; s. Peter and Mary Rivers; B.A., U. Wis.; children—Laura, Naomi, Ronny. Dir. public relations, dir. publicity Broom St. Theater, Madison, Wis., 1969-71; multi-media specialist, adminstrv. asst. Dept. Public Instrn., Madison, 1971-73; counselor Tellurian, Madison, 1976-77; analyst CUNA Mut. Ins. Group, Madison, 1977—. Bd. dirs. Middleton (Wis.) Welfare Dept., 1974-77; mem. Middleton Com. for Redevel., 1974-76; v.p. Soul-Ful Shack, Halfway Ho., Madison, 1970-72, pres., 1972-75. Served with USAF, 1961-65. Mem. Am. Mgmt. Assn. Western Buddhist. Author: Original Poetry, 1974; Equal Love, 1976. Office: 5910 Mineral Point Rd Box 391 Madison WI 53701

RIVES, JAMES HENRY, JR., structural engr.; b. Bessemer, Ala., Mar. 9, 1931; s. James Henry and Bessie Lillian (Hardy) R.; B.S. in Civil Engring., U. Ala., 1954; m. Mary Jo Wiggins, Jan. 14, 1954; children—James Gordon, Thomas Scott. Structural engr. So. Services, Inc., Birmingham, Ala., 1955-62; prin. engr. Barnard & Burk, Inc. cons. engrs., Baton Rouge, 1962-72; mgr. engring. Gibbs & Hill, Inc., Omaha, 1972—. Coach, Baton Rouge Little League, 1965-69, Am. Legion Baseball, 1970; mem. indsl. cons. group Southeast Community Coll., Milford, Nebr., 1975—. Served with AUS, 1953-55. Recipient Am. Def. award U.S. Govt., 1955. Mem. Nat. Soc. Profl. Engrs., Profl. Engrs. Nebr., La. Engring. Soc. (sec., vice chmn. 1971-72), Am. Concrete Inst., Am. Welding Soc., Theta Tau, Theta Chi. Episcopalian (mem. vestry Birmingham, Ala. 1962, Baton Rouge, La. 1968-70, mem. sch. bd. Baton Rouge 1969-70). Clubs: Piedmont (sec. bd. govs. 1969-70), Skyhawk Flying (v.p. 1978-80), Acadian (dir. 1971-72). Home: 2206 S 138th St Omaha NE 68144 Office: 8420 W Dodge Rd Omaha NE 68114

RIVES, STANLEY GENE, educator; b. Decatur, Ill., Sept. 27, 1930; s. James A. and Frances (Bunker) R.; B.S., Ill. State U., 1952, M.S., 1955; Ph.D., Northwestern U., 1963; m. Sandra Lou Belt, Dec. 28, 1957; children—Jacqueline Ann, Joseph Alan. Instr. W.Va. U., 1955-56, Northwestern U., 1956-58; asst. prof. Ill. State U., Normal, 1958-63, asso. prof., 1963-67, prof., 1967-80, asst. dean Coll. Arts and Scis., 1968-70, dir. W.K. Kellogg Faculty and Instructional Devel. Program, 1977-80, chmn. gen. speech area dept. speech, 1968-70, asso. dean faculties, 1970-72, dean undergrad. instrn., 1972-80, asso. provost, 1976-80, acting provost, 1979-80; v.p. acad. affairs, prof. Eastern Ill. U., Charleston, 1981—; vis. prof. U. Hawaii, 1963-64. Trustee, Nat. Debate Tournament, 1967-75. Served with AUS, 1952-54. Mem. Central States, Ill. speech assns., Speech Communication Assn., Am. Midwest (pres. 1961-63) forensic assns., AAUP, Am. Assn. Higher Edn., Theta Alpha Phi, Pi Kappa Delta, Pi Gamma Mu. Author: (with Donald Klopf) Individual Speaking Contests: Preparation for Participation, 1967; (with Gene Budig) Academic Quicksand: Trends and Issues in Higher Education, 1973; (with others) Academic Innovation: Faculty and Instructional Development at Illinois State University, 1979; The Fundamentals of Oral Interpretation, 1981; contbr. articles to profl. jours. Home: 2308 Andover Pl Charleston IL 61920 Office: Office of Vice Pres Academic Affairs Eastern Ill U Charleston IL 61920

RIVLIN, GERALD BENJAMIN, stock broker; b. Columbus, Ohio, Mar. 4, 1929; s. Solomon and Rose L. Rivlin; B.S. in Acctg. and Mgmt., U. Ill., 1950; m. Helene Mabel Rivlin, Dec. 16, 1950; children—Deborah, Sandra, Jeffrey, Annette. Asst. corp. v.p. Goldblatt Bros. Dept. Stores, Chgo., 1950-56; account exec. Walston & Co., Chgo., 1956-61; account exec. Rodman & Renshaw, Chgo., 1961-64, partner, 1964—, sr. v.p., 1977—; pres., dir. Windy City Acceptance Corp. Pres. Beth Hillel Congregation, Wilmette, Ill., 1966-69; bd. govs. Israel Bonds, Chgo., 1967—; bd. dirs. Midwest region United Synagogue, 1966-72. Served with AUS, 1951-53. Recipient Disting. Service award State of Israel, 1973; named Man of Year, State of Israel Bonds, 1970, Beth Hillel Men's Club, 1966. Mem. N.Y. Stock Exchange, Chgo. Analysts Soc. Republican. Jewish. Club: B'nai B'rith (Wilmette). Home: 822 Westwood Ln Wilmette IL 60091 Office: 209 S LaSalle St Chicago IL 60604

RIZZA, PETER JOSEPH, JR., edn. cons.; b. Brookline, Mass., Jan. 21, 1947; s. Peter J. and Madge M. (Horton) R.; B.S. in Edn., Boston U., 1968, Ed.M., 1972; Ph.D., Pa. State U., 1974; m. Elizabeth Virginia Solis-Cohen, July 5, 1970; children—Daniel Hays, Emily Katherine. Tchr. math. Wayland (Mass.) High Sch., 1968-72; grad. asst. acad. curriculum div. Pa. State U., 1972-74; ednl. cons. Control Data Corp., Bloomington, Minn., 1974—, computer-based edn. specialist, 1974-76, mgr. acad. products, 1976-78, mgr. product specification and design, 1978-80; cons. Edn. Tech. Center, 1981—; tech. cons. AID, Brasilia, Brazil, 1975-76; instr. and field coordinator NSF, 1972-73. Recipient Tarpon award Control Data Corp., 1977, also Outstanding Achievement award, 1981, Outstanding Young Men of Am. Award, 1975. Mem. Soc. for Applied Learning Tech., Am. Ednl. Research Assn., Assn. of Computing Machines, Assn. of Edn. Data Systems, Council for Basic Edn., Assn. for Devel. of Computer Based Instructional Systems, Phi Delta Kappa. Contbr. articles on computer based edn. to profl. publs.; also papers presented to nat. and internat. confs.

RIZZI, JOSEPH VITO, retail exec.; b. Berwyn, Ill., Dec. 5, 1949; s. Joseph and Mary Catherine (Mancini) R.; B.S. in Commerce summa cum laude, DePaul U., 1971, M.B.A., U. Chgo., 1973; J.D. magna cum laude, U. Notre Dame, 1976; m. Candace Kunz, June 24, 1972; 1 dau., Jennifer. Admitted to Ill. bar, 1976; law clk. to judge U.S. Dist. Ct. No. Dist. Ill., 1976-77; exec. v.p. T.B.R. Enterprises, Inc., Downers Grove, Ill., 1977—. Mem. Nat. Retail Merchants Assn., Am. Bar Assn., Ill. Bar Assn., Delta Epsilon Sigma. Roman Catholic. Asso. editor Notre Dame Lawyer, 1975-76; contbr. articles to profl. publs. Home: 6824 Meadowcrest Dr Downers Grove IL 60515 Office: 7323 Lemont Rd Downers Grove IL 60515

RIZZO, ANGELYN RENA, newspaper exec.; b. Chgo., June 30, 1937; d. Reno Giacomo and Anne Rose (Loro) R.; student Marquette U., 1954-57; B.S. in Journalism, Purdue U., 1959. Advt. copywriter, sales mag. editor Continental Casualty Co., Chgo., 1959-60; editor internal employee mag., dir. employee relations Johnson and Johnson, Chgo., 1960-62; with Lafayette (Ind.) Jour. and Courier, 1963—, mng. editor, 1979—. Mem. Am. Soc. Newspaper Editors, AP Mng. Editors Assn. Roman Catholic. Office: 217 N 6th St Lafayette IN 47901

ROACH, DOROTHY ANNETTE, legal sec.; b. Jasper, Ind., Oct. 18, 1953; d. William George and Eileen Zelma (Seitz) Schaber; A.S., Vincennes U., 1974; m. Jerald Allen Roach, June 17, 1972. Sec. credit dept. Gimbel-Bond Dept. Store, Vincennes, Ind., 1972-75; legal sec./asst. Shake, Lewis, Kixmiller, Sturm & Smith, Vincennes, 1975—; instr. Vincennes U., 1980—. Mem. Knox County Assn. Legal Secs., Ind. Assn. Legal Secs., Nat. Assn. Legal Secs. (gov. 1979—), Vincennes Fedn. Bus. and Profl. Women, Ind. Fedn. Bus. and Profl. Women, Nat Fedn. Bus. and Profl. Women (dist. dir. 1979-80, state new club expansion chmn. 1980-81, state rec. sec. 1981-82). Republican. Lutheran. Club: Bus. and Profl. Women's (editor monthly pub. The Tattler 1976—). Home: Route 6 Box 14 Vincennes IN 47591 Office: PO Box 393 Vincennes IN 47591

ROACH, JOHN ROBERT, archbishop; b. Prior Lake, Minn., July 31, 1921; s. Simon J. and Mary V. Roach; B.A., St. Paul Sem.; M.A., U. Minn. Ordained priest Roman Catholic Ch., 1946; named domestic prelate, 1966; instr. St. Thomas Acad., 1946-50, headmaster, 1951-68; rector St. John Vianney Sem., 1968-71; aux. bishop St. Paul and Mpls., 1971; pastor St. Charles Borromeo Ch., Mpls., 1971, St. Cecilia Ch., St. Paul, 1973-75; archbishop of St. Paul and 1975—. Apptd. vicar for parishes, 1971-75; vicar for clergy, 1972-75; mem. Priests Senate, 1968-72; pres. Priests Senate and Presbytery, 1970; Episcopal moderator Nat. Apostolate for Mentally Retarded, 1974-77. Chmn., Com. on Accreditation Pvt. Schs. in Minn., 1952-57; mem. adv. com. Coll. Entrance Exam. Bd., 1964. Trustee, St. Paul Sem., Coll. of St. Thomas, St. Thomas Acad., Coll. of St. Catherine, Visitation Convent and Sch., Cath. U. Am. Mem. Minn. Cath. Edn. Assn. (pres. 1959-61), Assn. Mil. Colls. and Schs. U.S. (pres. 1961-62), N.Central Assn. Colls. and Secondary Schs. (adv. com. 1963-66), Am. Council Edn. (del. 1963-65), Am. Assn. Theol. Schs. (dir.), Nat. Conf. Cath. Bishops (v.p. 1977, pres. 1980-83). Office: 226 Summit Ave St Paul MN 55102

ROACH, RONALD THOMAS, ins. broker; b. Martinton, Ill., Feb. 6, 1926; s. John and Aldea (Benoit) R.; grad. high sch.; m. Esther Duclos Wehling, June 18, 1966; step-children—David A., Sandra (Mrs. David Webster). Salesman Leatherman Ins. Agy., Woodland, 1960-61; owner Ronald T. Roach Ins. Agy., Martinton 1960—; salesman Eaken Realty, Watseka, 1966-69; real estate broker Ronald T. Roach Ins. & Real Estate, Martinton, 1969—; pres. Miller-Roach Ins. Agy., Donovan, Ill., 1973—. Village trustee, Martinton, 1955, village clk., 1960—; clk. Martinton Twp., 1967—. Served with M.C., AUS, 1951-53. Mem. Iroquois-Ford Counties Bd. Realtors, Twp. Ofcls. Ill. Assn. Am. Legion, V.F.W. Roman Catholic. Home: 201 S 2d St Martinton IL 60951 Office: PO Box 11 Martinton IL 60951

ROACH, SALLY ANN, advt. agy. exec.; b. Decatur, Ill., June 27, 1947; d. Neal Francis and Beverly Ann (Thompson) R.; B.A. in Fine Arts, Eastern Ill. U., 1969. Tchr., Wauconda (Ill.) Sch. System, 1969-70; acct. mgr. Reuben H. Donnelley Corp., Chgo., 1970-76; founder, pres. Communications Planning Corp. Am., Chgo., 1976—. Mem. Chgo. Council on Fgn. Relations, Chgo. Assn. Commerce and Industry. Office: 303 E Ohio St Suite 2704 Chicago IL 60611

ROACHE, ESTHER WILSON (MRS. FRED W. ROACHE), civic worker; b. Osgood, Ind.; d. Clarence B. and Alice (Garrigues) Wilson; student Franklin Coll., 1915-16, Ind. U., 1919; m. Fred W. Roache, June 12, 1942 (dec. 1960). Asst. cashier Aurora (Ind.) State Bank, 1936-50, cashier, 1950-56; v.p. 1st Nat. Bank, Aurora, Ind., 1956-65, dir., 1956-76, dir. emeritus, 1976—. Sec.-treas. Dearborn County Council Social Action 1962-74; mem. Gov. Commn. of the Arts, 1964-66; exec. sec. Hillforest Hist. Found., 1956—; sec.-treas. Southeastern Ind. Recreational Council, 1963-74, dir., 1964; sec. Southeastern Ibdiaba Econ. Occupational Council, 1978; bd. dirs. Tri State Air Com., 1970-72, Historic Hoosier Hills Inc. Named 1 of 10 Greater Cin. Women of Year, Cin. Enquirer, 1971; recipient citation for service to historic preservation Ind. U. Preservation Conf., 1980. Mem. Nat. Assn. Bank Women, D.A.R. (regent Col. Archibald Lochry chpt. 1969-71), Aurora C. of C. (dir.), Tri Kappa, Delta Delta Delta, Aurora Research Club. Home: 415 Manchester St Aurora IN 47001

ROAN, FRANK JOSEPH, lawyer; b. Pitts., May 2, 1925; s. Frank Joseph and Margaret Loretta (Gordon) R.; student Amherst Coll., 1942-43; J.D., St. Louis U., 1948; m. Elfieda L. Gillespie, Dec. 23, 1945; children—Catherine (Mrs. Robin A. deTurk), Beverly (Mrs. Wilson J. Seldon, Jr.). Admitted to Ill. bar, 1949, Fla. bar, 1976; practiced in Marion, to 1955; asso. firm Rathje, Kulp, Sabel & Sullivan, Chgo., 1955-63; partner Shorey, Floberg & Roan, Chgo., 1963-65, Ross, Hardies, O'Keefe, Babcock, McDugald & Parsons, Chgo., 1965-70; sr. partner Roan & Grossman, Chgo., 1970—. Mem. adv. council Ill. Inst. Continuing Legal Edn., 1961-73, exec. com., 1972-73; counsel Ill. Election Laws Commn., 1962—, co-drafter Election Code 1972. Asst. atty. gen. of Ill., 1949-53. Served with USNR, 1943-46. Fellow Am. Coll. Probate Counsel (Ill. chmn. 1977-79); mem. Am., Ill. (chmn. jr. bar 1952-54, vice chmn. probate and trust law 1960-61), Chgo., Fla. bar assns., Law Club Chgo., Legal Club Chgo. Clubs: Monroe, Univ. (Chgo.); Glen Oak Country (Glen Ellyn, Ill.); Sara Bay Country (Sarasota, Fla.). Author: (with others) Administering Illinois Estates, 1969; (with others) Creditors Rights in Illinois, 1968. Home: 1409 Burr Oak Rd 201A Hinsdale IL 60521 also 5855 Midnight Pass Rd Sarasota FL 33581 Office: 55 W Monroe St Chicago IL 60603 also 1803 Glengary St Sarasota FL 33581

ROAN, RICHARD LEE, med. diagnostic imaging co. exec.; b. Massillon, Ohio, Aug. 6, 1938; s. Calvin G. and Irene M. (Richards) R.; B.S. in Secondary Edn., Wittenberg U., 1960; m. Patricia Jeanne Roan, Aug. 25, 1971; children—Kelly Ann, David Stewart, Joseph Wilson. Dist. sales mgmt. and tng. mgmt. Allstate/Nationwide Ins. Co., 1965-73; platform speaker, motivator Am. Salesmasters Inc. Denver, 1973-75; pvt. practice cons., Massillon, 1975-79; dir. sales tng. program Picker Internat. Med. Corp., Cleve., 1979—. Mem. membership council St. Paul's Luth. Ch., Massillon, 1979—, Sunday sch. tchr., 1979—. Mem. Nat. Assn. Tng. Dirs., Nat. Speakers Assn., Ohio Speakers Forum, Picker Mgmt. Assn. Club: Sideliners. Office: 595 Miner Rd Cleveland OH 44143

ROARK, LAVERNE WALDO, computer cons.; b. Canute, Okla., Jan. 23, 1922; s. Waldo Walton and Luella Gertrude (Cox) R.; student Kans. State Tchrs. Coll., 1941-43; m. Donnetta Molz, Feb. 15, 1947; children—Sandra K. Broadstreet, LaNita Rae (Mrs. Thomas M. Dick). Owner, mgr. W-R Grocery Store, Johnson, Kans., 1945-48; tool attendant Boeing Airplane, Wichita, 1948-52, sr. systems analyst, 1958-70; owner farm, Animas, N.Mex., 1952-55; cons., program mgr. Boeing Computer Service, Inc., Wichita, Kans., 1970-80; engring. computer cons. Boeing Mil. Aircraft Co., Wichita, 1980—. Served with USAF, 1943-45. Mason. Home: 11204 Valley Hi Ct Wichita KS 67209 Office: 3801 S Oliver St Wichita KS 67210

ROBA, WILLIAM HENRY, educator; b. Moline, Ill., Mar. 8, 1946; s. Roy Clarence and Elsie Preciosa (Knaack) R.; A.B., Augustana Coll., Rock Island, Ill., 1968; M.A., Cornell U., 1971; Ph.D., U. Iowa, 1979; m. Sylvia Linea Lee, June 10, 1967; children—Jennifer Sarah, Allison Courtney. Chmn. social sci. dept. Palmer Jr. Coll., Davenport, Iowa, 1971-74; asso. planner criminal justice Bi-State Met. Planning Commn., Rock Island, 1974-76; instr. interdisciplinary studies Black Hawk Coll., Moline, 1976-77; asst. prof. St. Ambrose Coll., 1978-79, Scott Community Coll., Davenport, 1979—; cons. in field. Trustee Davenport Pub. Library, 1972—; del. Iowa Democratic Nominating Com., 1972. NDEA grantee, 1968-70. Mem. Am., Iowa library assns., Am. Studies Assn., Soc. Study Midwest Lit., Phi Alpha Theta, Pi Kappa Delta. Unitarian. Contbr. articles to profl. jours. Home: 1137 Kirkwood Blvd Davenport IA 52803 Office: Belmont Rd Bettendorf IA 52722

ROBBENNOLT, GENE, state legislator S.D.; b. Gettysburg, S.D., Mar. 8, 1936; s. Max and Mary (McDonnell) R.; grad. high sch.; m. Donna Bown, May 21, 1955; children—Mark, Michelle, Stephan. Farmer, rancher, Gettysburg, 1956—; mem. S.D. Ho. of Reps., 1972—. Dir., Potter County Grain Coop. Mem. Sch. Bd., Gettysburg, 1965-72; County Democratic chmn., 1963-72. Served with AUS, 1954-56. Mem. Farmers Union, Nat. Farmers Orgn. Roman Catholic. Club: Gettysburg Country. Address: Route 2 Box 10 Gettysburg SD 57442

ROBBERT, LOUISE BUENGER, historian, educator; b. St. Paul; d. Albert and Myrtle (Rubbert) Buenger; B.A., Carleton Coll., 1947; M.A., U. Cin., 1948, B.Ed., 1949; Ph.D., U. Wis., 1955; m. George S. Robbert, Sept. 17, 1960; 1 son, George Harold. Instr., Smith Coll., 1954-55; instr. Hunter Coll., 1957-60, St. Louis Coll. Pharmacy, 1960-62; asst. prof. Tex. Tech U., 1962-63, 64-74, asso. prof., 1974-75; adj. asso. prof. history U. Mo.-St. Louis, 1978—. Fulbright scholar, Italy, 1955-57; Am. Council Learned Socs. grantee, 1960. Mem. Mediaeval Acad. Am., Am. Hist. Assn., Econ. History Assn. Lutheran. Club: Wednesday (St. Louis). Contbr. articles to profl. jours. Home: 15 S Seminary Terr Saint Louis MO 63105 Office: Dept History U Mo-St Louis 8001 Natural Bridge Rd Saint Louis MO 63121

ROBBINS, BOB, electrical service co. exec.; b. Ottawa, Ill., May 8, 1934; s. Chester M. and Helen Robbins; B.S. in B.A., U. Denver, 1959; A.B.A., Pueblo Jr. Coll., 1961; A.S. in Elec. Engring., Richland Community Coll., 1977; m. Melba James, Feb. 1, 1974; children—James, Malinda, Robert, Terry, Felicia, Halena, Gregory. Vice pres. Space Com Inc., Colorado Springs, Colo., 1961-70; chief engr. Robbins Electric Service Co., Mulberry Grove, Ill., 1970—; instr. basic electricity and safety, civic and med. groups. Served with AUS, 1951-54: Korea. Mem. IEEE, Am. Mfrs. Assn. Office: PO Box 11303 Saint Louis MO 63105

ROBBINS, DONALD JEROME, educator; b. Parsons, Kans., July 11, 1940; s. Robert Franklin and Evelyn Lavonne (Singleton) R.; A.A., Parsons Jr. Coll., 1960; B.S., Pittsburg State U., 1965, M.S., 1966; Ph.D., Kans. State U., 1973; m. Sandra Sue Bretches, June 5, 1960. Instr. biology/chemistry St. Joseph (Mo.) Jr. Coll., 1965-67; prof. biology Mo. Western State Coll., St. Joseph, 1967—. Served with USNR, 1960-62. NDEA grantee, 1965. Mem. Mo. State Tchrs. Assn., Mo. Acad. Sci., Sigma Xi. Methodist. Clubs: Masons, K.T. Author: (with others) Laboratory Inquiries into Principles of Biology, 4th edit., 1980. Office: 4525 Downs Dr Saint Joseph MO 64507

ROBBINS, EDWARD LOUIS, educator; b. Eaton, Ind., Feb. 11, 1933; s. Ora Clayton and Marcella Pearl (Smoot) R.; B.S., Ball State U., 1958, M.A., 1959; postgrad. (grad. fellow) Wayne State U., 1960, (NDEA fellow) No. Colo. U., 1965; Ed.D., Ind. U., 1971; m. Beverly Ann Williams, Jan. 31, 1954; children—Ann, Kay. Elementary sch. tchr. Fort Wayne (Ind.) community schs., 1958-66; dir. Title I ESEA, Ind. Dept. Pub. Instrn., Indpls., 1966-69; vis. lectr. Ind. U., Bloomington, 1969-71; asst. prof. edn. Ind. U.-Purdue U., Indpls., 1971-74, asso. prof., 1974—; dir. Ind. Head Start Supplementary Tng., 1969-76, Comprehensive Tng. Program for Tchrs. of Reading, 1972-73; community resource Model Cities Schs. Town Meeting, Indpls., 1972. Served with AUS, 1953-55. Mem. Nat. Soc. Study Edn., Am. Ednl. Research Assn., Internat. Reading Assn., Assn. Supervision and Curriculum Devel., Kappa Delta Pi, Phi Delta Kappa. Methodist. Author: Handbook for Volunteer Tutors, 1971; (with Blanton, Laffey, Smith) POWER Reading Program, 1972; (with Carl Smith) Robbins and Smith Reading Tests, 1972; Testing Program, Macmillan Series R Basal Reading Program, 1975. Editor: Ind. Reading Quar., 1970-71, 78-81. Home: 7346 Shamrock Dr Indianapolis IN 46217 Office: 902 N Meridian St Indianapolis IN 46204

ROBBINS, FREDERICK CHAPMAN, physician; b. Auburn, Ala., Aug. 25, 1916; s. William J. and Christine (Chapman) R.; A.B., U. Mo., 1936, B.S., 1938; M.D., Harvard, 1940; D.Sc. (hon.), John Carroll U., 1955, U. Mo., 1958; LL.D., U. N.Mex., 1968; m. Alice Havemeyer Northrop, June 19, 1948; children—Alice, Louise. Sr. fellow virus disease NRC, 1948-50; staff research div. infectious diseases Children's Hosp., Boston, 1948-50, asso. physician, asso. dir. isolation service, asso. research div. infectious diseases, 1950-52; instr., asso. in pediatrics Harvard Med. Sch., 1950-52; dir. dept. pediatrics and contagious diseases Cleve. Met. Gen. Hosp., 1952-66; asso. pediatrician U. Hosps., Cleve., 1952—; prof. pediatrics Case-Western Res. U., 1952—, dean Sch. Medicine, 1966—; vis. scientist Donner Lab., U. Calif., 1963-64. Served as maj. AUS, 1942-46; chief virus and rickettsial disease sect. 15th Med. Gen. Lab.; investigations infectious hepatitis, typhus fever and Q fever. Decorated Bronze Star, 1945; received 1st Mead Johnson prize application tissue culture methods to study of viral infections, 1953; co-recipient Nobel prize in physiology and medicine, 1954; Med. Mut. Honor Award for 1969. Diplomate Am. Bd. Pediatrics. Mem. Am. Epidemiol. Soc., Am. Acad. Arts and Scis., Am. Soc. Clin. Investigation (emeritus mem.), Am. Acad. Pediatrics, Soc. Pediatric Research (pres. 1961-62, emeritus mem.), Am. Assn. Immunologists, Soc. Exptl. Biol. and Medicine, Am. Pediatric Soc., Nat. Acad. Scis., Nat. Inst. Medicine, Am. Philos. Soc., Phi Beta Kappa, Sigma Xi, Phi Gamma Delta. Home: 2467 Guilford Rd Cleveland Heights OH 44118 Office: 2119 Abington St Cleveland OH 44106*

ROBBINS, NORMAN NELSON, lawyer; b. Detroit, Sept. 27, 1919; s. Charles and Eva (Gold) R.; J.D., Wayne State U., 1943; m. Elaine Helen Israel, June 22, 1946; children—Aimee Carol (Mrs. Stephen B. Malkin), Susan Lynn (Mrs. Ira Stuart Jacobs). Admitted to Mich. bar, 1943, practice specializing in family law, Detroit, 1946—; lectr. Inst. Continuing Legal Edn. under auspices of U. Mich., Ann Arbor, and Wayne State U., Detroit, 1971-75; instr. Eastern Mich. U., Ypsilanti, 1973. Pres. Wayne County (Mich.) unit Am. Cancer Soc., 1969-74, recipient achievement award, 1974. Bd. dirs. Mich. State Bd. Marriage Counselors, 1968-78, chmn. bd., 1971-77; bd. dirs. Mich. State Bd. Vets. Trust Fund, 1964-78, chmn. bd., 1974; hon. life mem. Wayne County unit Am. Cancer Soc. Served to capt. USMCR, 1943-46. Named Mich. State Judge Adv., Am. Legion, 1966-67; named Boss of the Year, Southfield Bus. and Profl. Women, 1972; recipient Pub. Service commendation Sta. WOMC, 1974; Mich. Minuteman Gov.'s award, Mich. Minuteman citation of honor Jewish War Vets. Fellow Am. Acad. Matrimonial Lawyers; mem. Mich. Interprofl. Assn. Marriage, Divorce and the Family (pres. 1967-70, 78-80, trustee); mem. Am., Detroit (chmn. family law com. 1967-74), Oakland bar assns., State Bar of Mich. (chmn. family law com. 1969-71, chmn. family law sect. 1974-75), Am. Judicature Soc., Am. Arbitration Assn., Am. Legion (vice-comdr. Mich. dept. 1964-65, comdr. Detroit dist. 1963-64), Am. Assn. Marriage and Family Law Counselors (disting. affiliate). Mason. Author: Domestic Relations Form Book, 1972. Editor: State Bar Mich. Family Law Jour. Contbr. numerous articles on family law to The Family Coordinator and other profl. jours. Home: 23071 Riverside Dr Southfield MI 48075 Office: 30400 Telegraph Rd Suite 452 Birmingham MI 48010

ROBBINS, OREM OLFORD, ins. co. exec.; b. Mpls., Feb. 5, 1915; s. Douglas Ford and Grace (Rorem) R.; B.B.A. with distinction, U. Minn., 1936; B.S.L., William Mitchell Coll. Law, 1946, J.D. cum laude, 1948; m. Margaret Linderberg Thomson, July 4, 1968; children—Ford, Ross, Gail, Cynthia (Mrs. David Rothbard). Admitted to Minn. bar, 1948; with Northwest Bell Tel. Co., Mpls., 1936-47; dep. dir. Savs. Bond div. U.S. Treasury Dept., 1947-49; agt. Conn. Gen. Life Ins. Co., Mpls., 1949-59; founder-chmn. Security Life Ins. Co. of Am., Mpls., 1956—; chmn. bd., pres. Security Am. Fin. Enterprises, Inc.; chmn. bd. Congress Life Ins. Co., Santa Ana, Calif.; mem. faculty bus. ins. and estate planning U. Minn. Ext. Div. Chmn. bd. dirs. Meth. Hosp.; bd. dirs. Family and Children's Service, Goodwill Industries; trustee, treas. Hamline U.; mem. bd. pensions Minn. conf. United Meth. Ch. Served as Col. U.S. Army ret. Decorated Legion of Merit. Fellow Life Office Mgmt. Assn.; mem. Am. Soc. CLUs, Minn. State Bar Assn., Nat. Eagle Scout Assn., Res. Officers Assn., Assn. U.S. Army, Am. Legion (past comdr.), Delta Sigma Pi, Beta Gamma Sigma. Clubs: Skylight, Mpls., Minikahda, Masons. Home: 77 Woodland Circle Edina MN 55424 Office: 1200 2d Ave S Minneapolis MN 55403

ROBEDEAU, WILLIAM FRANK, refrigeration co. exec.; b. Toledo, June 21, 1939; s. Frank Clarence and Lolita Mae R.; B.S. in Mech. Engring., U. Toledo, 1964, M.S. in Indsl. Engring., 1976; m. Georgia Ann Dominique, July 1, 1961; children—Debra Jean, Mark Charles. Asst. chief engr. Ransom & Randolph Co., Toledo, 1966-68; asst. plant mgr. Doehler Jarvis div. NL Industries, Toledo, 1970-74; project engr. Samborn, Steketee, Oatis & Evans, Toledo, 1974-75; chief engr. Floating Floors, Inc., Toledo, 1975-76; mgr. engr. data systems Hussmann Refrigerator Co., Bridgeton, Mo., 1976—. Adviser, Jr. Achievement, 1977-79; mem. troop adv. council Boy Scouts Am., 1977-79. Served to 1st lt. AUS, 1964-66. Registered profl. engr., Ohio, Mo. Mem. ASHRAE, Nat. Soc. Profl. Engrs., Mo. Soc. Profl. Engrs. Roman Catholic. Home: 714 Guenevere Dr Ballwin MO 63011 Office: Hussmann Refrigerator Co 12999 St Charles Rock Rd Bridgeton MO 63044

ROBERSON, LAWRENCE R., automotive co. exec.; b. Birmingham, Ala., Aug. 26, 1946; s. Mack E. and Aressa R.; student Harvard U., 1966; B.S. in Math., Ala. A. & M. U., 1967; M.B.A., Ind. U., 1970. Systems engr. IBM, Huntsville, Ala., 1967-68, fin. analyst, Harrison, N.Y., 1969; supr. fin. analysis Ford Motor Co., Dearborn, Mich., 1970—. Recipient Outstanding Young Men in Am. award, 1972. Mem. Am. Mgmt. Assn., Nat. Black M.B.A. Assn. (past pres. Detroit chpt.), Alpha Phi Alpha. Baptist. Home: 15745 Greenfield St Detroit MI 48227 Office: Ford Motor Company Dearborn MI 48121

ROBERTO, MARCUS AURELIUS, state senator; b. New Milford, Ohio, Nov. 26, 1930; s. Americo Dominic and Anna (Laurito) R.; B.S., Kent State U., 1957, M.A., 1960; J.D., Akron Sch. Law, 1972; m. Marjorie Jean Hope; children—Cathleen Roberto Rufener, John, Elizabeth, Marcuss. Practice law, Ravenna, Ohio, 1957—; mem. Ohio Ho. of Reps., 1971-76, Ohio Senate, 1977—. Served with USAF, 1950-54. Recipient Martha Holden Jennings award, 1967-68. Mem. Am. Legion, Grange. Club: Rotary. Office: State Senate Columbus OH 43216*

ROBERTS, C. PAT, congressman; b. Topeka, Apr. 20, 1936; s. Wes and Ruth R.; B.A. in Journalism, Kans. State U., Manhattan; m. Franki Fann, Nov. 10, 1969; children—David, Ashleigh, Anne, Wesley. Newspaper editor, pub., Litchfield Park, Ariz., 1962-67; adminstrv. asst. to Sen. Frank Carlson of Kans., 1969-80, to Congressman Keith Sebelius, 1980; mem. 97th Congress from Kans. 1st Dist., 1980—. Served to 1st lt. USMC, 1962; capt. USMCR. Republican. Methodist. Club: Toastmasters. Office: 1428 Longworth Office Bldg Washington DC 20515*

ROBERTS, CHARLES CHESTER, JR., mech. engr.; b. New Bedford, Mass., May 6, 1944; s. Charles Chester and Janina (Patykula) R.; B.S. in M.E., Worcester Tech. Inst., 1966, M.S. in M.E., 1967; Ph.D., U. N.Mex., 1972; m. Lydia Justine Laquer, June 15, 1972. Devel. engr. Jamesbury Corp., Worcester, Mass., 1967-68; mech. engr. Yuma (Ariz.) Proving Ground, 1968-70; mem. tech. staff Bell Labs., Naperville, Ill., 1972-76; sr. profl. engr. Packer Engring. Assos., Naperville, 1976-79; pres. C. Roberts, cons. engrs., Warrenville, Ill., 1979—; cons. heat transfer, probabilistic design, computer design techniques, structural analysis, explosion analysis, accident reconstrn., skiing biomechanis. Served with AUS, 1968-70. Registered profl. engr., Ill.; cert. profl. ski instr. Mem. ASME, AIAA, ASHRAE, ASTM, Assn. Energy Engrs. Inst. Environ. Scis., Sigma Tau. Roman Catholic. Clubs: North Shore Yacht, Toastmasters. Contbr. articles on heat pipe design, probabilistic design and temperature measurements to tech. jours. Patentee in field. Office: 27W776 Greenview St Warrenville IL 60555

ROBERTS, CLARENCE NELSON, historian, educator; b. Sturgeon, Mo., Dec. 11, 1912; s. W. Everett and Burbie (Schultz) R.; B.S., U. Mo., 1935, M.A., 1936, Ph.D., 1950; m. Ruth Elizabeth Gee, July 1, 1944. Instr. history Hannibal-LaGrange Coll., Hannibal, Mo., 1936-39, U. Mo., Columbia, 1939-41; mem. faculty Kemper Mil. Sch., Boonville, Mo., 1941-42; mem. faculty dept. history U. Mo. Sch. of Mines and Metallurgy, Rolla, 1942-50; prof. history North Central Coll., Naperville, Ill., 1950—, chmn. dept. history, 1950—. Sunday sch. tchr. Evang. United Brethren Ch., 1952-62, ch. historian, 1950-75. Mem. Orgn. Am. Historians, Ill. State Hist. Soc., Mo. Hist. Soc., Miss. Valley Hist. Assn., Historians of Met. Chgo., DuPage Hist. Soc. Republican. Author: History of Missouri School of Mines, 1946; A History of Brick and Tile Industry, 1950; A History of Refractories Industry, 1951; North Central College-A Century of Liberal Education, 1960; contbr. articles on Am. history to scholarly jours. Office: Dept History North Central College Naperville IL 60540

ROBERTS, CLINT R., congressman; b. Presho, S.D., Jan. 30, 1935; student Black Hills State Coll.; m. Beverly Anne Dittman; children—Dera, Schelle, Clayton, Kristie. Farmer-rancher, Presho; mem. S.D. Senate, 1972-78, pres. pro tem.; sec. agr. State S.D., 1979-80; mem. 97th Congress from S.D. 2d Dist. Past v.p. S.D. Jaycees; bd. dirs. S.D. Cowboy and Western Heritage Hall of Fame. Mem. Wheatgrowers Assn., Stockgrowers Assn., C. of C., Farm Bur., Screen Actors Guild. Republican. Methodist. Clubs: Shriners, Lions,

Elks. Address: 1009 Longworth House Office Bldg Washington DC 20515*

ROBERTS, DONALD GAYLORD, mental health adminstr.; b. Youngstown, Ohio, Aug. 29, 1926; s. Thompson Charles and Mary A. (McRoberts) R.; B.S., Youngstown U., 1961; M.S.W., U. Pitts., 1965; m. Barbara E. Lewis; children—Keith H., Bruce A., Charlene A. With scheduling and billing dept. Youngstown Sheet & Tube Co., 1947-53; investigator Security Service, Inc., Youngstown, 1953-55; probation officer, traffic referee Mahoning County Juvenile Ct., Youngstown, 1955-63, founder juvenile jury, 1958; exec. dir. Columbiana County Mental Health Center, Lisbon, Ohio, 1965—, Columbiana County Mental Health Bd., 1969—; instr. criminal justice Youngstown State U., 1969—; sec., treas. Steel Valley Aviation, Inc., 1970—; v.p. Am. Boarding Homes, Inc., 1981—. Mem. Children Service Bd. of Mahoning County, Youngstown, 1979—; scout master; explorer adv. Boy Scouts Am. Served with U.S. Army, 1945-46. Mem. Nat. Assn. Social Workers, Am. Assn. Marriage and Family Therapy, Assn. Mental Health Adminstrs., Aircraft Owners and Pilots Assn. Club: Kiwanis. Home: 19 Overlook Blvd Struthers OH 44471 Office: 40722 State Route 154 Lisbon OH 44432

ROBERTS, ELIZABETH ANN, educator; b. Denver, July 1, 1944; d. Harold M. and Dorothy M. (Black) R.; B.A. in History (Colo. Joint Honor Scholar), Adams State Coll., 1967, M.A. in Speech/Theatre, 1968; postgrad. Purdue U., 1971-72, Ohio U., 1980—. Instr. speech and oral interpretation, asst. dir. theatre Coll. of Wooster (Ohio), 1968-70; grad. asst., dept. communications Purdue U., West Lafayette, Ind., 1971-72; instr. speech/theatre, dir. individual events and readers theatre Ohio No. U., Ada, 1973-77, dir. communication skills program, asst. prof. speech/theatre, 1977—, parliamentarian Coll. Arts and Scis., 1973-80; teaching asso. Sch. Interpersonal Communication, Ohio U., Athens, 1980—; oral communications cons. to area high schs. Mem. Soc. for Tech. Communications, Speech Communication Assn., Internat. Communication Assn., Central States Speech Assn., Speech Communications Assn. Ohio, AAUW, Mortar Bd., Pi Kappa Delta (sec.-treas. Province-of-the-Lakes 1976-79), Theta Alpha Phi, Alpha Psi Omega, Alpha Omicron Pi (chpt. adviser 1979-80). Republican. Home: 34-409 N McKinley Athens OH 45701 Office: Sch of Interpersonal Communication Ohio U Athens OH 45701

ROBERTS, GEORGE CHANDLER, educator; b. Lafayette, Ind., Nov. 25, 1931; s. Charles Raymond and Lucile Emily (Chandler) R.; B.S. with distinction, Purdue U., 1953; A.M., Ind. U., 1954, Ph.D., 1962; m. Elizabeth Ann Domagalski, June 21, 1967; 1 dau., Emily Elizabeth. Mem. faculty Ind. U., Jeffersonville, 1958-59, U. Ark., Fayetteville, 1959-66; mem. faculty Ind. U. N.W., Gary, 1966—, asso. prof. polit. sci. 1971—. Del. Ind. Democratic Conv., 1954, 58; candidate for Ind. State Senate, 1958. Served with U.S. Army, 1954-56. Mem. Ind. Acad. Social Scis. (pres. 1980—), Center for the Study of Presidency, Pi Sigma Alpha. Contbg. author: The 1964 Election in the Southwest, 1966; author (with E.B. McPheron) Apportionment in Indiana, 1957. Office: Indiana University Northwest Gary IN 46408

ROBERTS, JAMES CARROLL, lab. dir.; b. Greencastle, Ind., Sept. 19, 1939; s. James Russall and Carol (Goodenough) R.; student Carroll Coll., 1980—; m. Ruthann Conners, June 25, 1970; children—Sherry, Heather, Holly. Instr., Alverno Coll. and U. Wis., LaCrosse, dir. Nuclear Lab. and Ultrasound Program, St. Mary's Hosp., Milw., 1964—, dir. Nuclear Med. Sch., Milw., 1967—. Mem. Whitefish Bay Police, 1971—. Served with USN, 1959-64; USCGR, 1965—. Mem. Am. Soc. Radiol. Technologists, Registry of Nuclear Medicine Cert. Bd., Registry Med. Technologists, Soc. Nuclear Medicine, Soc. Nuclear Medicine Technologists, Am. Soc. Clin. Pathologists, Am. Registry Radiol. Technologists, Am. Nuclear Soc., Wis. Soc. Nuclear Med. Technologists (past pres.), Am. Mgmt. Assn. Clubs: Masons, Shriners. Office: PO Box 503 Milwaukee WI 53201

ROBERTS, JAMES LESTER, journalist; b. Quincy, Ill., Apr. 27, 1954; s. Donald J. and D. Hilda R.; B.A. in Polit. Sci., B.S. in Bus. Adminstrn., Ill. Wesleyan U., 1977. Reporter, Radio Sta. KRIX-RRXL-FM, Kirksville, Mo., 1977-78; reporter Kansas City (Mo.) Dispatch, 1978-79; asso. editor Liberty (Mo.) Tribune, 1979-82; editor Trenton (Mo.) Republican-Times, 1982—. Office: PO Box 548 Trenton MO 64683

ROBERTS, JO ANN WOODEN, ednl. adminstr.; b. Chgo., June 24, 1948; d. William Dean and Annie Mae (Wardlaw) Dean Wooden; B.S., Wayne State U., 1970, M.Ed., 1971; Ph.D., Northwestern U., 1977; children—Edward Allen, Hillary Ann. Speech pathologist Holy Cross Hosp., Chgo., 1971; speech pathologist Chgo. Bd. Edn., 1971—, now coordinator program for speech and lang.; instr. Mayfair City Community Coll., Chgo., 1975-76; project dir. Ednl. Testing Service, Evanston, Ill., 1976; cons. Frank Cassell and Assos., Evanston, Nat. PUSH Program, Chgo.; author edn. programs, cons. and lectr. in field. Mich. ednl. grantee, 1969-70, ednl. fellow, 1970-71. Founder, pres. Alliance Concerned Black Educators, 1979; bd. dirs. Thresholds, Beatrice Caffrey Youth Service, Inc. Mem. Chgo. Assn. Sch. Speech Therapists, Am. Speech and Hearing Assn., Ill. Speech and Hearing Assn., Black Speech, Lang. and Hearing Assn., Christian Bus. and Profl. Women's Club Phi Delta Kappa. Roman Catholic. Author: Learning to Talk, 1975. Home: 5000 S Cornell Ave Apt 5B Chicago IL 60615 Office: 228 N LaSalle St Chicago IL 60601

ROBERTS, JOAN MARIE, educator; b. Wall, Pa., Sept. 28, 1932; d. Thomas Robert and Helen Lydwein (Ryan) McGranahan; B.S., Wayne State U., 1954, M.A., 1957, Ph.D., 1962; m. Robert L. Roberts, July 1, 1966. Research asst. Lafayette Clinic, Detroit, 1956-62, research asso., 1962-63; instr. Wayne State U. Sch. Medicine, Detroit, 1963-66; asst. prof. U. Detroit Sch. Dentistry, 1966-71, asso. prof., 1971—; cons. Detroit Meml. Hosp., 1963-66. USPHS research grantee, 1964-71; Seed grantee, 1973-76. Mem. Radiation Research Soc., AAAS, Am. Psychol. Assn., Am. Assn. Dental Schs., AAUP, Sigma Xi. Roman Catholic. Contbr. articles to profl. jours. Home: 136 E Sunnybrook Rd Royal Oak MI 48073 Office: 2985 E Jefferson St Detroit MI 48207

ROBERTS, JOHN GERALD, marketing exec.; b. Salem, Ohio, Aug. 15, 1936; s. John Morgan and Shirley Virginia (Ward) R.; B.M.E., Youngstown State U., 1963; m. Rose Mary Tomsello, Apr. 19, 1963; children—Kenneth, Steven, Gayle, Kathy, Scott, Donna. Various mktg. mgmt. positions B.F. Goodrich, Troy, Ohio, 1963-74; dir. product mktg. B.F. Goodrich Engring. Systems, Akron, Ohio, 1974-78; dir. mktg. I.T.T. Harper, Morton Grove, Ill., 1978—. Served with U.S. Army, 1954-57. Home: 677 Monterey Dr Crystal Lake IL 60014 Office: 8200 Lehigh St Morton Grove IL 60053

ROBERTS, JOSEPH FRANCIS, JR., pub. co. exec.; b. Chgo., Nov. 24, 1941; s. Joseph F. and Anne C. (Mitchell) R.; student U. Ill., Chgo., 1961, DePaul U., 1965; m. Rita L. Mele, Mar. 2, 1968; children—Joseph F. III, Cynthia Marie. Circulation mgr., asst. treas. Bettendorf Pub. Ltd., Chgo., 1963-68; pub., gen. mgr. Collateral Media div. Standard Rate & Data Service, Inc., Skokie, Ill., 1968-73; sr. v.p., gen. mgr. Nat. Register Pub. Co., Skokie, 1973-76; gen. mgr. info. products group Automated Mktg. Systems, Inc., Chgo., 1976—; chmn. Chgo. Midwest Direct Mktg. Day, 1972, 76. Commr., Schaumburg (Ill.) Park Dist., 1973-81, pres., 1976-77, v.p., 1974-75, sec.-treas., 1978-79, treas., 1980; cubmaster Boy Scouts Am., 1976-80, scoutmaster, 1980—, named Cubmaster of Year, 1980. Mem. Am. Mktg. Assn., Nat. Press Club, Chgo. Assn. Direct Mktg. (v.p. 1977). Republican. Clubs: Meadow, Masons. Home: 885 Asbury Ln Schaumburg IL 60193 Office: 310 S Michigan Ave Chicago IL 60604

ROBERTS, JUDITH S., entertainment co. public relations exec.; b. Jacksonville, Fla.; d. Robert R. and Betty S. (Sagvold) R.; B.S. in Journalism and Internat. Polit. Sci., Northwestern U., 1966. Reporter, Chgo. Tribune, 1968-72, Milw. Jour., 1973; news assignment editor Sta. WBBM-TV, CBS, Chgo., 1974-76; mgr. press relations Northwestern U., 1976-77; nat. news media rep. Am. Hosp. Assn., Chgo., 1977-79; mgr. public relations Playboy Enterprises, Inc., Chgo., 1979—; lectr. journalism Northwestern U.; lectr various univs. Mem. jr. governing bd. Chgo. Symphony Orch.; bd. dirs. John Howard Assn. Recipient Pulitzer prize for gen. local reporting Chgo. Tribune, 1973. Mem. Chgo. Women in Broadcasting, Publicity Club N.Y., Chgo. Council Fgn. Relations, Internat. Visitors Center. Clubs: Chgo. Press, Young Execs. Chgo. Home: 1360 N Lake Shore Dr Chicago IL 60610 Office: 919 N Michigan Ave Chicago IL 60611

ROBERTS, LEIGH MILTON, educator; b. Jacksonville, Ill., June 9, 1925; s. Victor Harold and Ruby Harriet (Kelsey) R.; B.S., U. Ill., 1945, M.D., 1947; m. Marilyn Edith Kadow, Sept. 6, 1946; children—David, Carol (Mrs. Thomas Mayer), Paul, Nancy. Intern, St. Francis Hosp., Peoria, Ill., 1947-48; resident U. Wis. Hosps., Madison, 1953-56; gen. practice medicine, Macomb, Ill., 1948-50; staff psychiatrist Mendota (Wis.) State Hosp., 1956-58; prof. psychiatry U. Wis. Med. Sch., Madison, 1959—, acting chmn. dept. psychiatry, 1972-75. Mem. spl. rev. bd. Wis. Parole Bd. for Sex Crimes Law, 1962—; cons. Wis. Div. Mental Hygiene, 1965-78, VA, Milw., 1962-75, VA, Madison, 1977—. Mem. Dane County Devel. Disabilities Bd., 1972-77; mem. Wis. State Planning Coms., Mental Health, 1963-65, Health, 1969-71, Vocat. Rehab., 1966-68, Mental Health Centers, 1967-71, Mental Health Adv., 1973-78; pres. Wis. Council Chs., 1976-78. Bd. dirs. Meth. Hosp., Madison, Madison Campus Ministry, Dane County Rehab. House, Dane County Assn. Mental Health, St. Benedict Center; trustee North Central Coll. Served with USNR, 1943-45, 50-53. Decorated Bronze Star medals, Purple Heart. Diplomate Am. Bd. Neurology and Psychiatry. Fellow Am. Psychiat. Assn. (area rep. 1976-80); mem. Wis. Psychiat. Assn. (pres. 1967). Methodist (gen. council ministries 1973-80). Editor: Community Psychiatry, 1966; Comprehensive Mental Health, 1968. Contbr. articles to profl. jours. Home: 7924 Deer Run Rd Cross Plains WI 53528 Office: 600 Highland Ave Madison WI 53792

ROBERTS, LOREN BRITTON, ednl. adminstr.; b. Mpls., Nov. 17, 1929; s. Loren Britton and Elizabeth Agnes (Hicks) R.; student Ohio Wesleyan U., 1948-50, Cleve. Coll., 1950-51; B.S., Ohio State U., 1957, M.Ed., 1961; postgrad. U. Cin., 1967, 72, Wright State U., 1975-76; m. Juanita Ellen Dundon, Dec. 27, 1961; children—Jonathan Britton, Stephen Charles. Asst. circulation mgr. Sun-Press, Cleve., 1950; salesman Confedn. Life Assn., Cleve., 1952-53; tchr. Olentangy High Sch., Delaware County, Ohio, 1957-59; tchr., adminstr. Marengo High Sch., Morrow County, Ohio, 1959-60; adminstr., guidance counselor Indian Lake High Sch., Logan County, Ohio, 1960-63; guidance counselor Stivers High and Wilbur Wright High Sch., Dayton, Ohio, 1963-65; vis. tchr. and supr. adminstrn. bldg. Bd. Edn., Dayton, 1965-70, 71-73, dir. student action services and security, 1974—, designee to hear recommendations for expulsions and appeal of suspensions, 1976—. Ruling elder, chmn. stewardship and fin. College Hill Presbyn. Ch., 1967-69; mem. at large adminstrv. bd. Concord United Meth. Ch., 1972—, mem. fin. com., 1974—, mem. choir, 1975—, also chmn. bldg. com. outdoor activity center, chmn. adminstrv. bd., 1980—; scoutmaster Troop 55, Boy Scouts Am., 1973-80, chmn. Gt. N.W. Dist., 1980—. Recipient Disting. merit award and Wood Badge, Boy Scouts Am., 1979, Silver Beaver award, 1981. Mem. Ohio Ednl. Assn., Dayton Classroom Tchrs. Assn., Western Ohio Vis. Tchrs. Assn., Ohio Vis. Tchrs. Assn., Ohio Sch. Suprs. Assn. Republican. Home: 6000 Romaine Dr Dayton OH 45415 Office: 348 W 1st St Dayton OH 45402

ROBERTS, MERLE E., mgmt. co. exec.; b. New Kensington, Pa., June 8, 1928; s. Merle B. and Marie E. Roberts; B.S., U. Pitts., 1949; M.B.A., Case-Western Res. U., 1952; m. Dorothy Bougher, July 1, 1950; children—Cynthia Grace, Lisa Bogumill, Keith, Courtney. Pres., owner Roberts Assos., Inc., Columbus, Ohio, 1964—; pres. The Food Group, Inc., Columbus, 1975-81; dir. Internat. Seaway, Colamco Inc.; Splty. Cars Co.; pres. Chrysalis Corp., Family Security Agy.; mem. faculty Case-Western Res. U., 1953-55, Cleveland State Coll., 1954-56, Capital U., 1962-64, Ohio State U., 1964-68. Mem. U.S. Senatorial Adv. Bd., 1980-81. Republican. Presbyn. (elder, dir.). Address: 2646 Alliston Ct Columbus OH 43220

ROBERTS, ROY, marketing exec.; b. Chgo., June 18, 1927; s. Irwin Leon and Berenice Muriel (Lindenthal) R.; B.A., Stanford U., 1950; m. Marian Cecily Fried, Dec. 14, 1952; children—Julia Ann, Charles Harry. Asst. account exec. Ruthrauff & Ryan, Chgo., 1951-52; account exec. Bozell & Jacobs, Chgo., 1952-56; advt. mgr. Duraclean Internat., Deerfield, Ill., 1956-57; v.p. Home Arts Guild Corp., Chgo., 1957-69, pres., 1969—, owner, 1969—. Served with AUS 1945-47. Mem. Am. Marketing Assn., Marketing Research Assn., Alpha Delta Sigma. Office: 35 E Wacker Dr Chicago IL 60601

ROBERTS, VIRGIL DEAN, state legislator; b. Mindoro, Wis., Apr. 13, 1922; s. Earl Edwin and Eva Grace (Radcliffe) R.; student Winona State Coll., 1958-61; m. Alice Marie Evenson, Jan. 20, 1945; children—Ann, Joan, Gordon, Janet. Train dispatcher Milw. Rd., 1943—; mem. Wis. Gen. Assembly, 1970—; dir. Bank of Holmen (Wis.). Mem. sch. bd. Mindoro (Wis.) area schs., 1952-58. Mem. Am. Train Dispatchers Assn., LaCrosse Area Fedn. Luth. Men (pres. 1968-70). Democrat. Lutheran. Club: Lions (treas. 1966-68). Home: 308 Park Ln Holmen WI 54636 Office: State Capitol Madison WI 53702

ROBERTS, WILLIAM KEITH, indsl. psychologist; b. Arcola, Ill., Dec. 19, 1922; s. Dewey N. and Anna E. (Franklin) Roberts; m. Patricia R. Park, June 12, 1948; children—Christopher, Scott, Andrew, Theodore, Rebecca; B.S., Purdue U., 1950, M.S., 1951. Instr. psychology Gen. Motors Inst., Flint, Mich., 1951, personnel evaluation specialist, 1953-54, supr. edn. and tng. Gen. Motors Corp., Linden, N.J., 1954-56; adminstr. tng. and devel. Am. Standard Corp., N.Y., 1956-59; mgr. mgmt. devel. Raytheon Co., Lexington, Mass., 1959-64; personnel and organizational cons. Abbott Labs., North Chgo., Ill., 1964-66; mgr. tng. and devel. services Allis-Chalmers Corp., Milw., 1966-79; pres. W.K. Roberts & Assos., Mgmt. Cons., 1979—; v.p. group studies R.I. Thompson & Assos., 1980—; instr. U. Wis. extension div., 1971—. Pilot USAAF, 1943-45; pilot psychology br. Aeromed. Lab., USAF, 1951-53. Registered psychologist, Ill. Mem. Am. Soc. Tng. and Devel., Am. Psychol. Assn. Contbr. articles to profl. jours. Home: 2390 Hannemann Rd Grafton WI 53024 Office: 17700 W Capitol Dr Brookfield WI 53005

ROBERTSON, A. JOHN, JR., acctg. cons. and tax co. exec.; b. Mpls., Dec. 25, 1937; s. Alvin J. and Ruth (Whalen) R.; B.S. cum laude, Coll. Holy Cross, Worcester, Mass., 1958; m. Joan Davies Morahan, June 22, 1962; 1 dau., Ellen Meredith. With Peat, Marwick, Mitchell & Co., 1960-65, 68—, partner, 1968—, mng. partner, Rome, 1968-72, partner-in-charge of European tng., Paris, 1972-73, sr. regional partner France, Spain and N. Africa, Paris La Defense, France, 1973-79, mng. partner, St. Louis, 1979—; asst. corp. controller Otis Elevator Co., 1965-68. Bd. dirs. Arts and Edn. Council, 1980—; v.p. Green Room Assn. of St. Louis Symphony Orch., 1981—. Mem. Fin. Execs. Inst., Am. Inst. C.P.A.'s, N.Y. Soc. C.P.A.'s, Mo. Soc. C.P.A.'s, Ill. Soc. C.P.A.'s, Nat. Assn. Accts. Clubs: Am. (pres. 1978-79), Polo de Paris, Maxim's Bus. (Paris); Dance St. Louis (pres. 1980—), Old Warson Country, St. Louis, Racquet, Noonday (St. Louis). Home: 4 Upper Ladue Rd Saint Louis MO 63124 Office: 720 Olive St Saint Louis MO 63101

ROBERTSON, ABEL ALFRED LAZZARINI, JR., pathologist; b. St. Andrews, Argentina, July 21, 1926; s. Abel Alfred Lazzarini and Margaret Therese (Anderson) R.; came to U.S., 1952, naturalized, 1957; B.S., Coll. D.F. Sarmiento, Buenos Aires, Argentina, 1946; M.D. cum laude, U. Buenos Aires, 1951; Ph.D., Cornell U., 1959; m. Irene Kirmayr Mauch, Dec. 26, 1958; children—Margaret Ann, Abel Martin, Andrew Duncan, Malcolm Alexander. Fellow tissue culture div. Inst. Histology and Embryology, U. Buenos Aires Sch. Medicine, 1947-49; surg. intern Hosp. Ramos Majia, Buenos Aires, 1948-50; fellow in tissue culture research Ministry of Health, Buenos Aires, 1950-51; resident Hosp. Nacional de Clinicas, Buenos Aires, 1950-51; head blood vessel bank and organ transplants Research Center, Ministry of Health, Buenos Aires, 1951-53; fellow dept. surgery and pathology Cornell U. Sch. Medicine, N.Y.C., 1953-55; asst. vis. surgery U. Hosp. N.Y., N.Y.C., 1955-60; asst. prof. research surgery N.Y. U. Postgrad. Med. Sch., N.Y.C., 1955-56; asst. vis. surgeon Bellevue Hosp., N.Y.C., 1955-60; asso. prof. research surgery N.Y. U. Postgrad. Med. Sch., 1956-60, asso. prof. pathology Sch. Medicine and Postgrad. Med. Sch., 1960-63; staff mem. Cleve. Clinic Found. Div. Research, 1963-73, prof. research, 1972-73; asso. clin. prof. pathology Case Western Res. U. Sch. Medicine, Cleve., 1968-72, prof. pathology, 1973—, dir. interdisciplinary cardiovascular research, 1975—. Research fellow N.Y. Soc. Cardiovascular Surgery, 1957-58; mem. research study subcom. of heart com. N.E. Ohio Regional Med. Program, 1969—. Recipient Research Devel. award NIH, 1961-63. Fellow Am. Coll. Cardiology, Am. Coll. Clin. Pharmacology, Am. Heart Assn. (nominating com. council on arteriosclerosis 1972), Royal Microscopical Soc. (Gt. Britain), Royal Soc. Promotion Health (Gt. Britain), Am. Geriatrics Soc., N.Y. Acad. Scis., Cleve. Med. Library Assn.; mem. AAAS, Am. Assn. Pathologists and Bacteriologists, AAUP, Am. Inst. Biol. Scis., Am. Judicature Soc., Am. Soc. Cell Biology, Am. Soc. Exptl. Pathology, Am. Soc. Nephrology, Assn. Am. Physicians and Surgeons, Assn. Computing Machinery, Electron Microscopy Soc. Am., Internat. Acad. Pathology, Internat. Cardiovascular Soc., Internat. Soc. Cardiology (sci. council on arteriosclerosis and ischemic heart disease 1960-64), Internat. Soc. Nephrology, Internat. Soc. Stereology, Pan Am. Med. Assn. (life, councillor in angiology 1966-72), Reticuloendothelial Soc., Soc. Cryobiology, Tissue Culture Assn., Ohio Soc. Pathologists, Electron Microscopy Soc. Northeastern Ohio (pres., trustee 1966-68), Heart Assn. Northeastern Ohio, N.Y. Soc. Cardiovascular Surgery, N.Y. Soc. Electron Microscopists, Cuyahoga County Med. Soc., Cleve. Soc. Pathologists, Sigma Xi. Mem. internat. editorial bd. Atherosclerosis, Jour. Exptl. and Molecular Pathology, 1964—. Contbr. articles to profl. jours. Home: 3596 Beverly Hills Dr Rocky River OH 44116 Office: 2085 Adelbert Rd Cleveland OH 44106

ROBERTSON, BILLY O'NEAL, sch. adminstr.; b. Columbia, S.C., Mar. 27, 1930; s. William Anglo and Ollie Vandora (Freeman) R.; student Furman U., 1955-58; B.A., U. Louisville, 1959; M.A., Ind. U., 1962; postgrad. Mich. State U., 1971-74; m. Helen Noreen Oglesby, May 21; children—Larry, Ronald, Marcia. Tchr.-librarian North Central Sch., Ramsey, Ind., 1959-61; tchr.-librarian Dennis Jr. High Sch., Richmond, Ind., 1961-63; sch. library supr. Greeley (Colo.) Pub. Schs., 1963-65; dir. media Pub. Schs. Lincoln (Nebr.), 1965-70; coordinator instructional media Pub. Schs. Midland (Mich.), 1970—; asso. prof. library and audio visual U. Nebr. Served with USAF, 1948-50, 50-51. Recipient Media Educator award Nebr. Ednl. Media Assn., 1970. Mem. Mich. Library Assn. (chmn. sch. sect.), Nat. Council Accreditation of Tchr. Edn., ALA, Assn. Ednl. Communications and Tech., Mich. Assn. Media in Edn., Assn. Supervision and Curriculum Devel., Am. Ednl. Research Assn. Democrat. Baptist. Clubs: Lions, Gideons. Home: 4411 Swede Rd Midland MI 48640 Office: 600 Carpenter St E Midland MI 48640

ROBERTSON, GARY JEROME, ednl. pub. co. exec., psychologist; b. Mattoon, Ill., Apr. 4, 1938; s. James Monroe and Eleanor Nadine (Brick) R.; B.S., Eastern Ill. U., 1961; M.A., Columbia U., 1962, Ph.D., 1967; M.B.A., 1976; m. Librada Carino, July 6, 1974. Tchr., Oak Park (Ill.) public schs., 1961; editor test dept. Harcourt Brace Jovanovich, N.Y.C., 1964-66, mng. editor test dept., 1966-70, asst. dir. ednl. measurement div. The Psychol. Corp., Harcourt Brace Jovanovich, 1970-76; dir. test publs. div. Am. Guidance Service, Circle Pines, Minn., 1976—; pres. Ednl. Test Bur., Circle Pines, 1980—; cons. U.S. Office of Edn., Bur. Edn. for Handicapped, Nat. Inst. Edn., Am. Council Edn. NDEA fellow, 1961-64. Mem. Am. Psychol. Assn., Am. Ednl. Research Assn., Nat. Council Measurement in Edn., Internat. Reading Assn., Planetary Soc., Kappa Delta Pi, Sigma Tau Delta. Presbyterian. Contbr. chpts. to books, articles to ednl. jours. Home: 36 W Golden Lake Rd Circle Pines MN 55014 Office: Publishers Bldg Circle Pines MN 55014

ROBERTSON, JAMES EDWARD, tire and motor supply co., investment co. exec.; b. St. Joseph, Mo., Nov. 27, 1931; s. James Leo and Laura E. (Rupp) R.; grad. St. Joseph Jr. Coll., 1951; m. Jolene Ann O'Connor, Sept. 3, 1956; children—Mike, Jina, John, Jan. With Leo Robertson Tire & Motor Supply, Inc., St. Joseph, 1952—, pres., dir., 1959—; partner Robertson Bros., St. Joseph, 1964—; chmn., dir. Citizens State Bank, Seneca, Kans., 1971-76; pres. Seneca Bancshares, 1972-78, dir., 1972—; sec.-treas., 1st Mo. Bancshare; sec.-treas., dir. Kans. BanCorp., Kansas City, 1970-78, Central Bank Shares, Hutchinson, Kans., 1970-73; dir. Belt Nat. Bank, St. Joseph, Ameribanc of St. Joseph, 1974-79; adv. dir. Home State Bank, Kansas City, Kans., 1970-77. Chmn., Mayor's Drug Abuse Commn., 1970-78; pres., bd. dirs. J. Leo Robertson Found., 1965—; bd. dirs. St. Joseph Public Sch. System, 1968-76, v.p., 1973-75, pres., 1975-76, chmn. fin. com., 1975-76; pres., bd. dirs. New Life Inner City, 1969-74; trustee George Bode Trust, St. Joseph, 1976—; bd. dirs. St. Joseph Hosp., 1973—; bd. dirs. Mo. State Sch. Bd., 1978—, pres., 1981—. Served with USAF, 1951-52. Mem. Nat. Tire Dealers and Retreaders Assn., Am. Mgmt. Assn., Soc. Advancement of Mgmt., C. of C. Roman Catholic. Home: 35 Stonecrest St Saint Joseph MO 64506 Office: 1801 Frederick St Saint Joseph MO 64501

ROBERTSON, JOHN MARVIN, agrl. computer co. exec.; b. Kincaid, Kans., Feb. 10, 1932; s. John M. and Laura C. (Guffey) R.; B.S. in Agr., Oreg. State U., 1955, Ed.M., 1961; Ph.D. in Agrl. Edn., Mich. State U., 1970; m. Sara Helen Ethredge, Apr. 28, 1972; children—Susan, Cheryl, John Marion, Doris, John Thomas. Dir. adult edn. and tchr. Moro (Oreg.) Schs., 1957-68; mayor City of

Moro, 1963-67; cons. and intern Mich. State Govt., 1968-70; asst. prof. vocat. edn. dept. U. Ga., Athens, 1970-73; vis. prof. Ohio State U., Columbus, summer, 1972, research specialist, 1973-75; exec. dir. Pardner Systems, Columbus, 1973-76; dist. mgr. employee/mgmt. devel. ICS, Norman, Okla., 1976-77; agrl. bus. coordinator Southwest State U., Marshall; Minn., 1977-79; partner Rural America Enterprises, Marshall, Minn., 1979—. Mem. Am. Soc. of Farm Mgrs. and Rural Appraisers, Minn. Farm Mgrs. and Appraisers, Marshall Area C. of C. (mem. agr. com. 1977-81), Nat. Vocat. Agrl. Tchr. Educators, Am. Vocat. Assn., Oreg. Vocat.-Agrl. Tchrs. Assn. (pres.). Episcopalian. Club: Toastmasters. Contbr. articles on vocat. edn. to profl. publs. Office: Rural America Enterprises 707 N 7 Box 14 Marshall MN

ROBERTSON, JOSEPH EDMOND, indsl. grain processing co. exec.; b. Brownstown, Ind., Feb. 16, 1918; s. Roscoe Melvin and Edith Penina (Shields) R.; B.S., Kans. State U., 1940, postgrad., 1940; m. Virginia Faye Baxter, Nov. 23, 1941; 1 son, Joseph Edmond. Cereal chemist Ewing Mill Co., 1940-43, flour milling engr., 1946-50, feed nutritionist, 1951-59; v.p., sec. Robertson Corp., Brownstown, Ind., 1960-80, pres., 1980—. Pres. Jackson County (Ind.) Welfare Bd., 1948-52. Served with USAAF, 1943-45. Mem. Hardwood Plywood Mfrs. Assn. (v.p. affiliate div. 1971-73), Am. Assn. Cereal Chemists, Assn. Operative Millers, Am. Legion, Brownstown C. of C. (dir. All Am. city program 1955), Kans. State U. Alumni Assn. (life), Blue Key, Phi Delta Theta, Phi Kappa Phi, Alpha Mu. Presbyn. (elder 1954-69). Elk. Clubs: Country (Seymour, Ind.); Hickory Hills Country (Brownstown, Ind.). Home: Route 2 Lake and Forest Club Brownstown IN 47220 Office: 200 Front St Brownstown IN 47220

ROBERTSON, JUDITH IRENE, city ofcl.; b. East Chicago, Ind., Aug. 14, 1943; d. John Wesley and Irene (Kandalec) R.; B.A., U. Md., 1974; programming tech. cert. Control Data Inst., 1972. Jr. acct. George Mazur Enterprises, Washington, 1967-72; bookkeeper United Consol. Industries, Balt., 1975; fin. dir. City of Hammond (Ind.) Dept. Planning and Devel., 1976—, mem. Mayor's Budget Adv. Com., 1981—. Mem. Mcpl. Fin. Officers Assn. Democrat. Roman Catholic. Home: 433 Locust St Hammond IN 46324 Office: Hammond Dept Planning and Devel 7324 Indianapolis Blvd Hammond IN 46324

ROBERTSON, NANCY LEE, occupational therapist; b. Hibbing, Minn., June 1, 1951; d. James H. and Gertrude (Hansen) R.; B.S. in Occupational Therapy, U. Minn., 1973. Staff occupational therapist Crippled Children's Hosp. and Sch., Sioux Falls, S.D., 1973-77, Rapid City (S.D.) Rehab. Hosp., 1977-79, dir. occupational therapy, 1979—, mem. faculty Center for Study of Sensory Integrative Dysfunction, instr. various workshops; cons. occupational therapist Custer (S.D.) State Sch., 1978. Mem. Am. Occupational Therapy Assn., S.D. Occupational Therapy Assn. (pres., 1977-79, del. nat. congress, mem., chmn. various coms.). Republican. Lutheran. Club: Rapid City Kennel. Trainer, handler show dogs. Home: Box-92 Black Hawk SD 57718 Office: 2809 5th St Rapid City SD 57701

ROBERTSON, ROBERT SCOTT, profl. basketball coach; b. Ft. Smith, Ark., Feb. 1, 1930; student U. Tex., Ark., La. Tech. U., Ruston. Coach, La. Tech. U., 1964-74, New Orleans Jazz, Nat. Basketball Assn., 1974-75, Chgo. Bulls, 1978-79, Detroit Pistons, 1980—. Address: Detroit Piston Pontiac Silverdome 1200 Featherstone St Pontiac MI 48057*

ROBERTSON, VIRGINIA FAYE, chemist, dietitian; b. Manhattan, Kans., Oct. 7, 1918; d. Arthur A. and Laura Belle (Falkenrich) Baxter; B.S., Kans. State U., 1939, postgrad. 1941; m. Joe E. Robertson, Nov. 23, 1941; 1 son, Joseph E. Clinician-technician Mayo Clinic, Rochester, Minn., 1939-40; research asst. metabolism studies Kans. State U., Manhattan, 1940-41; dir. cereal research, testing Ewing Mill Co., Brownstown, Ind., 1942-44; mem. staff food dehydration studies Pub. Service Co. Ind., Brownstown, 1944; with Robertson Corp., Brownstown, 1946—, dietary cons., 1949—. Fgn. mission sec. New Albany Presbyterial Assn., So. Ind. Dist., 1950; pres. Presbyn. Women's Fellowship, Brownstown, 1971-77. Mem. AAUW, Pi Beta Phi, Psi Iota (pres. Brownstown chpt. 1948). Clubs: Seymour (Ind.) Country; Hickory Hills Country, Lake and Forest (Brownstown). Home: Box A Lake and Forest Club Brownstown IN 47220 Office: 100 Front St Brownstown IN 47220

ROBESON, MARK D., motor carrier co. exec.; b. Columbus, Kans., Sept. 6, 1911; s. Daniel Webster and Minnie (Colvin) R.; B.A., U. Kans., 1935; m. Katherine M. Willard, Jan. 23, 1937; children—Mark D., Daniel F. Trust cons. City Nat. Bank & Trust Co., Kansas City, Mo., 1936-47; 1st v.p. Riss & Co., Kansas City, Mo., 1947-53; chmn. fin. com. Yellow Freight System, Inc., Shawnee Mission, Kans., 1953—, also dir. Chmn. Western Hwy. Inst., San Francisco, 1969; bd. dirs., chmn. Nat. Safety Council, Chmn., 1979-81; trustee Am. Trucking Assn. Found.; pres. Am. Trucking Assns., Inc., 1969; regional dir. Office Emergency Transp., 1967—; mem. Urban Transp. Adv. Council, 1968-74; mem. Pres.'s Transp. Task Force, 1969—; mem. exec. com. transp. research Nat. Acad. Scis., 1979. Chmn. Kans. Econ. Devel. Commn., 1963-65. Bd. dirs. ENO Found., Westport, Conn., 1974—; bd. dirs. Kans. Council Econ. Edn., 1970-72, pres., 1972-74; hon. chmn. YWCA, Kansas City, 1973—. Served to lt. USNR, 1942-45. Mem. Transp. Assn. Am. (dir. 1968—, Seley award 1979), Nat. Def. Transp. Assn. (v.p., dir. 1974-79). Home: 6420 Sagamore Rd Mission Hills KS 66208 Office: Yellow Freight System Inc 10990 Roe Blvd Shawnee Mission KS 66207

ROBIE, FRED SMITH, coll. pres.; b. Aspinwall, Pa., Mar. 7, 1920; s. George Randolph and Blanche (Hilliard) R.; B.A., U. Pitts., 1941; M.A., U. Mich., 1949; Ph.D., U. Pitts., 1970; m. Mary Louise Kent, May 9, 1943; children—William Randolph, Nancy Ann, Fred Kent. Instr. speech W.Va. U., 1946-47; asst. prof. U. Pitts., 1947-51, alumni dir., 1960-67, asst. dir., dir. admissions, 1967-70; spl. agt. FBI, 1951-60; pres. Jefferson Tech. Coll., Steubenville, Ohio, 1970—; cons./evaluator N. Central Assn. Commn. on Instns. of Higher Edn., 1974—, commr., 1981. Pres., Steubenville Area United Way, 1977-78; campaign chmn. Jefferson County Heart Assn., 1974-78, pres., 1980-81; bd. dirs. Fort Steuben council Boy Scouts Am. Served to capt. U.S. Army, 1942-46; PTO. Ford. Found. grantee, 1968-69. Mem. Ohio Assn. Tech. Colls. (pres. 1974), Steubenville Area C. of C. (v.p. 1977-79). Presbyn. Clubs: Rotary, Williams Country, Mason. Home: 1718 Williams Pl Steubenville OH 43952 Office: 4000 Sunset Blvd Steubenville OH 43952

ROBINDER, CATHERINE MAE FITZPATRICK, mathematician; b. East Moline, Ill., July 24, 1922; d. Walter H. and Belva M. (Westerfield) Fitzpatrick; A.B. cum laude, Augustana Coll., 1956; M.S., U. Iowa, 1961; m. Wallace R. Robinder, Nov. 5, 1966. Draftsman, Rock Island (Ill.) Arsenal, 1942-45, Swanson & Maiwald, Architects, Moline, Ill., 1946-47; mathematician-engr. Rock Island Arsenal, 1948-77; cons. field stress analysis, 1970—. Recipient Rock Island Arsenal spl. award for published article, 1966, for outstanding analysis work, 1960, 69, 75. Mem. Am. Math. Soc., AAUW (br. treas. 1962-65), Illowa Gem and Mineral Soc., Rock Island County Hist. Soc., Embroiders Guild Am., Am. Needlework Guild, Potnam Mus., Sigma Xi. Baptist (chmn. music com. 1963-80, fin. sec. 1956-63, youth work com. 1954—). Club: Blackhawk Gem and Mineral (v.p., program chmn. 1967, pres. 1973). Home: 2115 25th Ave Rock Island IL 61201

ROBINER, DONALD MAXWELL, lawyer; b. Detroit, Feb. 4, 1935; s. Max and Lucia (Chassman) R.; A.B., U. Mich., 1957; J.D., Case Western Res. U., 1961; m. Linda Goodman, June 29, 1958; children—Steven Ralph, Lawrence Alan. Admitted to Ohio bar, 1961; with firm Gaines, Stern, Schwarzwald & Robiner, Co., L.P.A. and predecessor firms, Cleve., 1961-81, partner, 1967-71, prin., dir., officer, 1971-81; prin., dir., officer firm Schwarzwald, Robiner Wolf & Rock, L.P.A., Cleve., 1981—; mem. Ohio Bd. Bar Examiners, 1974-79; dir., officer Richard L. Bowen & Assos. Inc., Fenwick Corp. Game Trek of N. Madison, Inc.; asst. dir. law City Mayfield Heights, 1961-66. Mem. Cuyahoga County Republican Exec. Com., 1978. Mem. Greater Cleve. Bar Assn., Cuyahoga County Bar Assn., Ohio State Bar Assn., Am. Bar Assn., Ohio Acad. Trial Lawyers, Assn. Trial Lawyers Am., Cuyahoga County Law Dirs. Assn., Ohio Council Sch. Bd. Attys., Nat. Council Sch. Bd. Attys., Jewish Community Fedn. Cleve. Club: Commerce. Home: 23512 E Silsby Rd Beachwood OH 44122 Office: 1300 E 9th St 616 Bond Ct Cleveland OH 44114

ROBINS, ELI, psychiatrist, neurochemist; b. Houston, Feb. 22, 1921; s. Abe and Ida (Schaffer) R.; B.A., Rice U., 1940; M.D., Harvard, 1943; m. Lee Nelken, Feb. 22, 1946; children—Paul, James, Thomas, Nicholas. Asst. in psychiatry Harvard, 1944-45; Boston U., 1948; intern Mt. Sinai Hosp., N.Y.C., 1944; resident Mass. Gen. Hosp., Boston, 1944-45, McLean Hosp., Waverly, Mass., 1945-46, Pratt Diagnostic Hosp., Boston, 1948-49; instr. neuropsychiatry Washington U., St. Louis, 1951-52, asst. prof. psychiatry, 1953-56, asso. prof., 1956-58, prof., 1958-66, head dept. psychiatry, 1963-75, Wallace Renard prof., 1966—. Served to capt. U.S. Army, 1946-48. Recipient career research award USPHS, 1961-63; gold medal Soc. Biol. Psychiatry, 1974; Paul H. Hoch award Am. Psychopath. Assn., 1977; Award of Merit, St. Louis Med. Soc., 1978; Salmon Medalist, New York Academy of Med., 1981. Diplomate Am. Bd. Am. Bd. Psychiatry and Neurology. Fellow Am. Psychiat. Assn., Royal Coll. Psychiatrists, Am. Coll. Neuropsychopharmacology (hon.); mem. Am. Soc. Clin. Investigation, Am. Soc. Biol. Chemists, Soc. Biol. Psychiatry, Psychiatric Research Soc., Am. Psychopath. Assn. Internat. Soc. Neurochemistry, Assn. for Research in Nervous and Mental Disease (v.p. 1960), Soc. Neurosci. Contbr. articles to med. jours. Office: 4940 Audubon Saint Louis MO 63110

ROBINS, GARY BRUCE, beverage co. exec.; b. Columbus, Ohio, June 6, 1946; s. Louis and Sara (Kahn) R.; student Ohio State U., 1964-66; m. Constance Kiefer, Aug. 11, 1967; children—Dean, Chad, Bret, Zach. Salesman, Excello Wine Co., Columbus, 1967-70, v.p., 1971—; pres. Hi-State Beverage Co., Columbus, 1977—, also dir.; v.p. The Robins Beverage Group, 1980—. Active United Jewish Fund, 1970—; bd. dirs. Jewish Family Service, 1975; mem. Columbus Conv. and Visitors Bur.; mem. Columbus Quincentennial Exposition 1992; bd. dirs. Am. ORT Fedn., 1981—, Columbus Jewish Fedn., 1981—. Mem. Wholesale Beer Assn. Ohio, Nat., Beer Wholesalers Assn., Wine and Spirits Wholesalers Am., Ohio Wholesale Wine Dealers Assn., Columbus Mfrs. Reps. Assn., Columbus C. of C., Ohio C. of C. Clubs: B'nai B'rith, Winding Hollow Country, Columbus Men's ORT. Home: 389 S Merkle Rd Columbus OH 43209 Office: 949 King Ave Columbus OH 43212

ROBINS, MARJORIE MCCARTHY (MRS. GEORGE KENNETH ROBINS), civic worker; b. St. Louis, Oct. 4, 1914; d. Eugene Ross and Louise (Roblee) McCarthy; A.B., Vassar Coll., 1936; diploma St. Louis Sch. Occupational Therapy, 1940; m. George Kenneth Robins, Nov. 9, 1940; children—Carol Robins Von Ariz, G. Stephen, Barbara A. Robins Foorman. Mem. Mo. Library Commn., 1937-38; mem. bd. St. Louis Jr. League, 1945, 46; mem. bd. Occupational Therapy Workshop of St. Louis, 1941-46, pres., 1945, 46; mem. bd. Ladue Chapel Nursery Sch., 1957-60, 61-64, pres. bd., 1963, 64; past regional chmn. United Fund; past mem. St. Louis Met. Youth Commn., St. Louis Health and Welfare Council; bd. dirs. Internat. Inst. of St. Louis, 1966-72, 76-82, sec., 1968, 2d v.p., 1969, 70, v.p., 1981; bd. dirs. Mental Health Assn. St. Louis, 1963-70, Washington U. Child Guidance and Evaluation Clinic, 1968-78; bd. dirs. Central Inst. for Deaf, 1970—, v.p., 1975-76, pres., 1976-78; bd. dirs. Met. St. Louis YWCA, 1954-63, 64-70, pres. bd., 1960-63, trustee, 1977—; mem. nat. bd. YWCA, 1967-79, nat. v.p., 1973-76; vol. tchr. remedial reading clinic St. Louis City Schs., 1968-71; trustee John Burroughs Sch., 1960-63, John Burroughs Found., 1965—, Roblee Found., 1972—, Nat. YWCA Retirement Fund, 1979—; bd. dirs. Gambrill Gardens United Meth. Retirement Home, 1979—, Thompson Retreat Center, 1981—; v.p. bd. dirs. Springboard to Learning Inc., 1980, 81. Clubs: Vassar (sec. and pres. 1939-40), Wednesday (dir. 1968-70, 77-79, 80—) (St. Louis). Home: 45 Loren Woods Saint Louis MO 63124

ROBINS, NORMAN ALAN, steel co. exec.; b. Chgo., Nov. 19, 1934; s. Irving and Sylvia (Robbin) R.; S.B. in Chem. Engring., M.I.T., 1955, S.M. in Chem. Engring., 1956; Ph.D. in Math., Ill. Inst. Tech., 1972; m. Sandra Ross, June 10, 1956; children—Lawrence Richard, Sherry Lynn. With Inland Steel Co., East Chicago, Ind., 1956—, beginning as metallurgist, successively research metallurgist, asst. mgr. processing systems and controls div., asso. mgr. processing systems and controls div., dir. process research, 1957-77, v.p. research, 1977—. Mem. Homewood-Flossmoor High Sch. Sch. Bd., 1974-77. Mem. AIME (Nat. Open Hearth Conf. award 1972), Am. Inst. Chem. Engrs., Am. Iron and Steel Inst. (Regional Tech. Meeting award 1967, 72), Indsl. Research Inst., Math. Assn. Am. Patentee in field. Office: 3001 E Columbus Dr East Chicago IN 46312

ROBINSON, BARBARA EMMA VIOLA, ednl. counselor; b. Bermuda, Mar. 30, 1938; came to U.S., 1957, naturalized, 1978; d. Julien Cornelius and Ellen Clare (Andrews) Jones; B.A. in English, Atlantic Union Coll., Mass., 1960; M.A.T., Andrews U., 1975, M.A. in Edn., 1977, postgrad. in Ednl. and Counseling Psychology, 1978—; children—Miranda, Carmen, Neil. Tchr. secondary English, Berkeley Inst., Bermuda, 1960-61; free lance writer Fame mag.; reporter, personality columnist Royal Gazette and Bermuda Sun, 1961-72; tchr. English secondary sch. Inst. of Seventh-day Adventists, Bermuda, 1973-74; head tchr., personal adjustment coordinator Gateway Rehab. Center, Berrien Springs (Mich.) Sch. Community Edn., 1976-78; counselor Niles (Mich.) Sr. High Sch., 1978-80; Head Start coordinator Niles Community Schs., 1980—; psychologist Family & Children's Center, Mishawaka, Ind. State of Mich. tuition grantee, 1979—. Mem. Am. Personnel and Guidance Assn., Am. Sch. Counselor Assn., Assn. Measurement and Evaluation in Guidance, Assn. of Non-White Concerns in Personnel and Guidance, Berrien-Cass County Counselors Assn., Mich. Edn. Assn. Seventh-day Adventist. Contbr. article Jour. Adventist Edn. Home: Berrien Springs MI 49103 Office: Niles Community Schs Fairland Center Niles MI 49120

ROBINSON, BRUCE DOUGLAS, architect; b. Toronto, Ont., Can., May 4, 1949; came to U.S., 1960, naturalized, 1967; s. Howard Willan and Phyllis Lillian (Brannigan) R.; B.S. in Architecture, U. Cin., 1973; M.Arch. (Regent's fellow), UCLA, 1976; m. Janice Franks, June 30, 1973; 1 son, Jonathan Ross. Project designer Wood Kock & Grier Architects, Cin., 1973-74; teaching asso. UCLA, 1975-76; researcher, designer Solar Resources, Inc., Los Angeles, 1975-76; dir. project design Taft Broadcasting/Kings Prodns., Cin., 1976—; guest lectr. U. Cin. Registered architect, Ohio; cert. Nat. Council Archtl. Registration Bds. Mem. A.I.A., Nat. Trust Hist. Preservation, Scarab, Delta Phi Delta. Methodist. Designer Nat. Football Found. Coll. Football Hall of Fame, 1978; project architect Canada's Wonderland, theme park for Toronto, 1979. Office: Kings Productions 1932 Highland Ave Cincinnati OH 45219

ROBINSON, BRUCE FAIRBAIRN, telephone co. exec.; b. Joliet, Ill., Aug. 28, 1921; s. Edwin and Salome (Fairbairn) R.; B.S. in Elec. Engring., Tex. A&M U., 1944; B.S. in Elec. Engring., U. Ill., 1946; m. Elizabeth Jane VanSant, June 29, 1946; children—Lesley Ann, Doug Bruce. With Fed. Telephone & Radio Corp., 1946-50, tech. adviser, 1949-50; state equipment maintenance supr. Mich. Asso., 1950-51, equipment engr., 1951-53; gen. bldg. and equipment engr. Gen. Telephone Co. of Mich., Muskegon, 1953-58, chief engr., engring. and constrn. dir., 1958-77, v.p. network engring. and constrn., 1977—. Bd. dirs. Econ. Devel. Com. Norton Shores, 1975—. Served with Signal Corps, U.S. Army, 1942-45. Mem. IEEE (sr.). Republican. Methodist. Clubs: Exchange Elks. Office: Gen Telephone Co of Mich 455 Ellis St Muskegon MI 49443

ROBINSON, CHARLES DOUGLAS, cons. engr.; b. Springfield, Ohio, Aug. 17, 1945; s. Charles Robert and Geraldine Dawn (Saddoris) R.; student U. Cin., 1963-67; B.S.C.E., U. Toledo, 1968, M.S.Ch.E., 1971; m. Susan Elnora Marzetta, Aug. 27, 1966; 1 dau., Jennifer Ann. Engr., project engr. Jones & Henry Engrs., Ltd., Toledo, Ohio, 1967-72; project engr., asso. Post, Buckley, Schuh & Jernigan, Inc., Miami, Fla., 1972-75; project mgr. Warren & Van Praag, Inc., St. Louis, 1975-77, asso., dir. san. engring., office co. mgr., Decatur, Ill., 1977-78; v.p., dir. san. engring. and Midwest ops. Airan Consultants, Inc., Coral Gables, Fla., 1978-80; owner C.D. Robinson Cons. Engrs., Decatur, 1980—; lectr. in field. Trustee San. Dist. of Decatur, 1978; mem. St. Louis East-West Gateway Coordinating Council Task Force, 1976-77; mem. Macon County (Ill.) Govtl. Task Force, 1980-81. Registered profl. engr., Ohio, Fla., Ill., Mo., Iowa. Mem. Nat. Soc. Profl. Engrs., ASCE (sec. environtl. exec. com. S. Fla. sect. 1974), Water Pollution Control Fedn. Central States Water Pollution Control Assn., Am. Cons. Engrs. Council (mem. nat. adv. com. 1977-78, 79—), Ill. Soc. Profl. Engrs. (pres. Central Ill. sect. 1981-82), Am. Waterworks Assn., Decatur C. of C. (chmn. environ. issues com. 1981—). Democrat. Home: 2263 Straza Ct Decatur IL 62526

ROBINSON, DAVID ANDREW, retail office furniture and systems co. exec.; b. Cape Girardeau, Mo., Jan. 29, 1950; s. Bill C. and Mary S. Robinson; B.S., Purdue U., 1972; M.B.A., Butler U., 1978; m. Cheryl L. Lotspeich, Oct. 4, 1980. Asst. mgr. Justrite Systems, Inc., Crawfordsville, Ind., 1972-73; asst. mgr. Red Lobster Inns of Am., Indpls., 1973; sales rep. Shaw-Walker Co., Indpls., 1973-79, br. mgr., St. Louis, 1979—. Commr., asst. dist. commr., Cub commr. Crossroads of Am. council Boy Scouts Am., 1975—. Mem. Adminstrv. Mgmt. Soc., Kappa Kappa Psi. Mem. Christian Ch. Club: Lions. Office: Shaw Walker Co 1 Mercantile Center Suite 2801 St Louis MO 63101

ROBINSON, DELIA MAE, mental health adminstr.; b. Omaha, Nov. 16, 1934; d. Robert and Sarah Ethel (Speese) Gardner; B.B.A., Lincoln U., Mo., 1955; M.S.W., U. Nebr., Omaha, 1974; children—Walter George, Waddell Craig. Caseworker, St. Louis County Dept. Public Welfare, Maplewood, Mo., 1957, St. Louis City Dept. Welfare, 1958-59, Douglas County (Nebr.) Dept. Welfare, Omaha, 1959-65; counselor Women's Job Corps Center, Omaha, 1966; child protective service worker Douglas County Social Service, Omaha, 1967-68, casework supr., 1968-73; psychiat. social worker Douglas County Hosp. Community Mental Health Center, Omaha, 1974-75; dir. social service dpt. Douglas County Hosp./Annex, 1975-80; cons. Native Am. Alcoholism Program, Omaha, NAACP, Omaha. Mem. adv. bd. Woodson Center, 1968-70, ENCOMH South Clinic, 1977-78. Mem. Nebr. Welfare Assn., Nat. Assn. Social Workers (sec. Nebr. chpt.), Nat. Assn. Black Social Workers, Nat. Soc. Hosp. Social Work Dirs., Nebr. Soc. Hosp. Social Work Dirs., Alpha Kappa Alpha. Democrat. Baptist. Home: 5822 Taylor St Omaha NE 68104 Office: 4102 Woolworth Ave Omaha NE 68105

ROBINSON, ELIOT FINLEY, architect; b. Detroit, July 19, 1918; s. Mitchell Barther and Alma (Finley) R.; B.A. in Econs., U. Mich., 1939; M.Arch., Harvard U., 1942; m. Sarah Winston, June 28, 1949; children—Peter, Lydia, Suzanne, Sarah. Project dir. Albert Kahn, Inc., 1946-49; liaison architect Eero Saarinen & Assos., Bloomfield Hills, Mich., 1949-53; pvt. practice architecture, Birmingham, Mich., 1953-58; asso. Frederick Stickel Assos., Birmingham, 1961—; pres. Beacon Bldg. Products Co., Detroit, 1958-61; asst. prof. Lawrence Inst. Tech., 1956. Chmn., mem. Birmingham Planning Bd., 1957—; pres., trustee Bloomfield Art Assn. Mem. adv. bd. dirs. City and Country Sch. Bloomfield Hills. Served to lt. comdr. USNR, 1942-45. Decorated Bronze Star medal. Registered architect, Mich. Mem. AIA. Club: Harvard. Patentee support bracket. Home: 572 Linden Rd Birmingham MI 48009 summer Old Bennington VT 05201 Office: 2900 W Maple Troy MI 48084

ROBINSON, ERNEST LEON, aquatic biologist; b. Hopewell, Va., July 12, 1926; s. Benjamin and Irene (Spencer) R.; B.S., Youngstown Coll., 1954; B.S., U. Cin., 1955-56, postgrad., 1959-60; m. Daphne Marie Williams, Mar. 29, 1959; children—Leon Spencer, Todd Claiborne, Kent Williams. Research aquatic biologist EPA, Cin., 1954—. Pres. bd. dirs. Wesley Child Care Center, 1978-79, v.p., 1981—; pres. bd. dirs. Coalition of Neighborhoods, 1979—; bd. dirs. Nat. Neighbors, 1980—. Served with U.S. Army, 1945-47, 48-49. Mem. Sigma Xi, Alpha Phi Alpha. Republican. Methodist. Home: 708 E Mitchell Ave Cincinnati OH 45229 Office: EPA 3411 Church St Cincinnati OH 45244

ROBINSON, GEORGE ALBERT, accountant; b. Elgin, Ill., Dec. 2, 1941; s. Joseph and Myrtle Louise (Beyer) R.; student Elgin Community Coll., 1964-65; m. Christine Ann Schneider, Sept. 2, 1961; children—Brian, Karen, Jaclyn. Accountant, Grant Motor Sales, Lake Zurich, Ill., 1959-60, W. Ray Davis & Asso., pub. accountant, Elgin, 1960-69; owner George A. Robinson Tax and Acctg. Service, Elgin, 1969—. Mem. Nat. Soc. Pub. Accountants, Independent Accountants Assn. Ill. (chpt. pres. 1971-72), Assn. Enrolled Agts. Home: 240 S Edison Ave Elgin IL 60120 Office: 20 Woodland Ave PO Box 633 Elgin IL 60120

ROBINSON, GLADYS MABEL CHAMBERS (MRS. CARL TAPLEY ROBINSON), educator; b. New Orleans, Dec. 5, 1909; d. Oscar Louis and Susie Elizabeth (Lang) Chambers; A.B., Northwestern State Coll., 1929; M.S., U. Chgo., 1931, postgrad., 1947, 68; postgrad. Tulane U., 1932, Marine Biol. Lab., Woods Hole, Mass., 1938, U. Ill., 1955-57, Ill. Inst. Tech., 1964-65; m. Carl Tapley Robinson, Dec. 24, 1932. Asst. prof. biology Tougaloo (Miss.) Coll., 1931-41, U. Akron (Ohio), 1942-48; instr. George William Coll., Downers Grove, Ill., 1949-50, prof. biology, 1959-75, prof. emeritus, 1975—, dir. div. natural scis., 1965-73; instr. Cook County Sch. Nursing, Chgo., 1950-59. Recipient Golden Apple award for excellence in teaching, student body George Williams Coll., 1972, Gladys C. Robinson Marsh named in honor, 1975. Ford Found.

scholar, 1953, NSF scholar, 1964-65, 65, 68. Mem. Bot Soc. Am., Am. Inst. Biol. Sci., Assn. Midwest Coll. Biology Tchrs., Ill. Acad. Sci., Phi Sigma, Sigma Delta Epsilon. Democrat. Baptist. Home: 7920 S Lafayette St Chicago IL 60620 Office: 555 31st St Downers Grove IL 60515

ROBINSON, GLENN HUGH, soils agronomist; b. Rosedale, Ind., May 20, 1912; s. William Albert and Margaret Lorene (Brown) R.; student Ind. State Tchrs. Coll., 1932-35; B.S., Purdue U., 1938, M.S. (Eli Lilly fellow), 1940; Ph.D., U. Wis., Madison, 1950; m. Tiur Augustina Hutabarat, Mar. 10, 1976; children by previous marriage—Glenn Philip, Joan E., Albert L. Asst. prof. agronomy Purdue U., Lafayette, Ind., 1940-42; asso. soil surveyor U.S. Dept. Agr., Salinas, Calif., 1942-44, Raleigh, N.C., 1944-46, Madison, 1946-51, soil correlator Bur. Plant Industry, Knoxville, Tenn., 1951-53, sr. soil correlator Soil Conservation Service, Blacksburg, Va., 1953-61; sr. soil scientist FAO, Guiana, 1961-64, Tanganyika, 1964, sr. soil scientist, project mgr., Sudan, 1964-69, Thailand, 1969-73, Indonesia, 1973-75; sr. soil specialist U.S./Saudi Arabia Joint Econ. Commn., Riyadh, 1976-80; free-lance cons. in soil survey and land classification for agrl. devel., Carbon, Ind., 1980—. Pres., Oregon (Wis.) Sch. Bd., 1948-50, Oregon PTA, 1948-50. Recipient cert. of merit U.S. Dept. Agr., 1977. Mem. Am. Soc. Agronomy, Soil Sci. Soc. Am., Internat. Soil Sci. Soc., Sigma Xi. Methodist. Clubs: Masons, Rotary. Home and office: Box 210A Rural Route 1 Carbon IN 47837

ROBINSON, HAROLD DOUGLAS, mech. engr., mfg. co. exec.; b. Dayton, Ohio, Nov. 8, 1945; s. Walter Merle and Hazel Edna (Lyons) R.; B.S.M.E., Gen. Motors Inst., 1968; 1 dau., Patricia Ann. Service engr. Delco Products div. Gen. Motors Corp., Dayton, 1969-71, sr. sales engr., Detroit, 1972-77, engring. design supr., Dayton, 1978-80, mfg. mgr., 1980—. Delco Products chmn. Community Blood Center blood drive, 1980. Mem. Soc. Automotive Engrs. Republican. Methodist. Design supr. McPherson type strut damper. Office: 2000 Forrer Blvd Kettering OH 45429

ROBINSON, JACK F(AY), clergyman; b. Wilmington, Mass., Mar. 7, 1914; s. Thomas P. and Ethel Lincoln (Fay) R.; A.B., Mont. State U., 1936; D.B., Crozer Theol. Sem., 1939; A.M., U. Chgo., 1949, postgrad., 1950-52; m. Eleanor Jean Smith, Sept. 1, 1937 (dec. 1966); 1 dau., Alice Virginia Dungey; m. 2d, Lois Henze, July 16, 1968. Ordained to ministry Baptist Church, 1939; minister Bethany Ch., American Falls, Idaho, 1939-41, 1st Ch., Council Grove, Kans., 1944-49; ordained (transfer) to ministry Congl. Ch., 1945; minister United Ch., Chebanse, Ill., 1949-52, 1st Ch., Argo, Ill., 1954-58, Congl. Ch., St. Charles, Ill., 1958-64; asso. minister Plymouth Congregational Ch., Lansing, Mich., 1964-66; tchr. Chgo. Pub. Schs., 1966-68; minister Waveland Ave. Congl. Ch., Chgo., 1967-79, First Congregational Ch., Des Plaines, Ill., 1979—. Asso. Hyde Park dept. Chgo. YMCA, 1942-44. U. Chgo. Library 1952-54; chmn. com. evangelism Kans. Congl. Christian Conf., 1947-48; city chmn. Layman's Missionary Movement, 1946-51; trustee Congl. and Christian Conf. Ill., v.p., 1963-64; mem. exec. council Chgo. Met. Assn. United Ch. of Christ.; mem. gen. bd. Ch. Fedn. Greater Chgo. Library board Council Grove, 1945-49; city chmn. NCCJ, 1945-49; dean Northside Mission Council United Ch. of Christ, 1975-77. Mem. Am. Soc. Ch. History, Am. Acad. Polit. Sci., Am. Hist. Assn., C. of C. (past dir.), Internat. Platform Assn. Author: The Growth of the Bible, 1969; From A Mission to a Church, 1976. Home: 2614 Lincolnwood Dr Evanston IL 60201 Office: PO Box 4578 Chicago IL 60680

ROBINSON, JAMES DAVID, musician, educator; b. Yoakum, Tex., Oct. 23, 1951; s. Raymond Lee and Violet Juanita (McDowell) R.; B.Music Edn., W. Tex. State U., Canyon, 1974, M.Mus., 1976; m. Susan Annette Willis, Mar. 12, 1977. Grad. asst. W. Tex. State U., 1974-76; mem. faculty William Jewell Coll., Liberty, Mo., 1976—, asst. prof. voice, 1979—, dir. Opera Workshop, 1976-80; baritone Kansas City Lyric Opera Co., 1978-80; minister of music Rockwood Bapt. Ch., Independence, Mo., 1978-80, Liberty Manor Bapt. Ch., Liberty, Mo., 1980—. Summer grantee William Jewell Coll., 1978. Mem. Nat. Assn. Tchrs. Singing, Am. Guild Mus. Artists, Mo. Music Men, Phi Mu Alpha Sinfonia, Kappa Kappa Psi, Alpha Chi, Alpha Psi Omega. Baptist. Home: 584 E Mill Liberty MO 64068 Office: William Jewell Coll Liberty MO 64068

ROBINSON, JAMES RICHARD, mech. and nuclear engr.; b. Michigan City, Ind., June 20, 1942; s. Gordon William and Irene Francis (Murray) R.; engring. technician cert. Inst. Cert. Engring. Technicians, 1969; diploma archtl. drawing and designing Internat. Corr. Schs., 1970; diploma bus. mgmt. LaSalle Extension U., 1972; m. Linda K. Robinson, July 29, 1966; children—Scott Anthony, Marcy Lynn. Draftsman, Hay's Corp., Michigan City, 1960-61; head plant/project draftsman Weil McLain Mfg. Co., Michigan City, 1962-63; sr. draftsman F.W. Dwyer Mfg. Co., Michigan City, 1963-66; sr. designer Union Tank Car Co., East Chicago, Ind., 1966-67; sr. designer Superior Engring. Corp., Hammond, Ind., 1967-69; sr. nuclear project engr. Morrison Constrn. Co., Hammond, 1969-79; asst. to gen. mgr. ops. Kemlite Corp., Joliet, Ill., 1979-80; asso. Splty. Engring. and Equipment Co. Inc., Mokena, Ill., 1980-81; pres. Solar-Shield Control Co., New Lenox, Ill., 1981—. Served with USAF, 1963. Mem. ASME, Am. Soc. Cert. Engring. Technicians, Inst. Cert. Engring. Technicians. Republican. Home: 420 Livingston Dr New Lenox IL 60451

ROBINSON, MAX, television news broadcaster; b. Richmond, Va., May 1, 1939; s. Maxie Cleveland and Doris (Jones) R.; student Oberlin Coll., 1957-58, Ind. U., 1959-60; LL.D. (hon.), N.C. A&T State U., 1979; L.H.D. (hon.), Va. Union U., 1981; D.Public Service (hon.), Voorhees Coll., 1981; D.Lit. (hon.), Va. State U., 1981; m. Beverly Hamilton, Apr. 1, 1973; children—Mark, Maureen, Michael, Malik. Corr., cameraman Sta. WTOP-TV, Washington, 1965, anchorman, 1969-78; corr. Sta. WRC-TV, Washington, 1965-69; anchorman ABC Network News, N.Y.C., 1978—; asso. prof. communicative arts Fed. City Coll., 1968-72; journalist in residence Coll. William and Mary. Served with USAF, 1959-60. Recipient Journalist of Year award Capital Press Club, 1967; NEA award, 1966; Nat. Emmy award, 1967, Regional Emmy award (2), 1967; award Ohio State U., 1967; Outstanding News Reporting award D.C. C. of C., 1978; Communication and Leadership award Toastmasters Internat., 1978, Chgo. State U., 1979, Congress Nat. Black Chs., 1979; Heritage award Coll. William and Mary, 1981; Martin Luther King, Jr. Meml. Drum Maj. for Justice award, 1981, Disting. Recognition award Detroit City Council, 1981; named Hon. Citizen Indpls., 1978, Houston, 1978, Cin., 1979, Atlanta, 1979; Max Robinson Day decreed in D.C., 1978, Richmond, 1978, Norfolk, Va., 1981, Atlanta, 1981, Highland Park, Mich., 1981, Fulton County, Ga., 1981; Nat. Media award Capital Press Club, 1979; decorated knight comdr. Order African Redemption (Liberia), 1972. Mem. Sigma Delta Chi. Office: 190 N State Chicago IL 60601

ROBINSON, PAULETTE HILTON, vocat. educator; b. Taylorsville, Miss., July 8, 1948; d. William and Claudia Mae (Shelby) R.; B.B.A., U. Oreg., 1973; M.Ed., Oreg. State U., 1977; doctoral candidate (Rubel scholar), Ohio State U., 1980; m. Warren Laroy Robinson, Jr., Oct. 4, 1970; children—Micah Andre, Gabriella Dominique. Office asst. Nero Industries, Portland, Oreg., 1973-74; supr., instr. Portland Opportunities Industrialization Center, Inc., 1974-76; adminstrv. intern Oreg. Dept. Edn., 1976-77; coordinator David Douglas Sr. High Sch., Portland, 1977-78; state supr. Ohio Dept. Edn., 1978-80; grad. research asso. Nat. Center Research in Vocat. Edn., Columbus, 1980-81; vocat. devel. specialist U.S. Dept. Labor, Job Corps, Seattle, 1981—; cons. Office of Edn., Portland Urban League, Portland State U. Pres., Sherwood PTA, Columbus. Recipient cert. for outstanding service Supt. Edn. State of Oreg., 1978; named Corpswoman of Month, Tong Point Job Corps, Astoria, Oreg., 1968. Mem. Ohio Vocat. Assn., Nat. Assn. Advancement Black Ams. in Vocat. Edn. (sec.), Nat. Assn. State Suprs. Bus. and Office Edn., Am. Vocat. Assn., Nat. Assn. Vocat. Edn. Spl. Needs Personnel. Editor Newsnotes of Nat. Assn. Vocat. Edn. Spl. Needs Personnel, 1979-80. Home: 4502 Drifton Dr Columbus OH 43227 Office: 909 First Ave Room 1145 Seattle WA 98144

ROBINSON, PEARL MARIE, ednl. adminstr., dietitian; b. Marshfield, Mo., Oct. 8, 1915; d. Louis Sylvester and Mattie Azalie (White) Petty; student schs. Marshfield, Mo.; m. Joel F. Robinson, Dec. 13, 1933; children—Jack, Joe Bill, Janice. Gen. supr. food buying and menu planning, dietitian Marshfield (Mo.) Schs., 1958—; mem. lunch workshop com., Springfield, Mo., 1977—. Sunday Sch. tchr. First Bapt. Ch., 1950-75. Clubs: Bus. and Profl. (pres. 1967), Rebecca Lodge (chaplain 1973-79, vice grand 1979—, noble grand 1980, 81). Home: 227 E Bedford St Marshfield MO 65706 Office: Junior High Bldg Commercial St Marshfield MO 65706

ROBINSON, PHYLLIS ELEANOR TAYLOR, ednl. cons.; b. Inkster, Mich., Sept. 20, 1946; d. Hervey Alene and Janie Louise (Crittendon) Taylor; B.S., Wayne State U., 1968, M.A., 1972; Ph.D., U. Mich., 1978; m. Phil Clayton Robinson, Dec. 17, 1976; children—Marcia Lynn, Robert Edward. Tchr., Peck Elem. Sch., Detroit, 1968-70; coordinator outreach tutorial program St. Martin de Porres High Sch., Detroit, 1968-70; adminstrv. asst. devel. career guidance project Detroit public schs., 1970-73; career edn. cons. for 36 local sch. dists, Wayne County, Mich., 1973—; adj. prof. U. Mich., Ann Arbor, 1978—, Wayne State U., Detroit, 1979—; cons. social work program VA Hosp., Allen Park, Mich., 1979, instl. workshop teams Eastern Mich. U., 1975-78, Mich. State U., 1976-79; mem. adv. bd. Ednl. Resources Info. Center, Ann Arbor, Mich., 1978—. Chairperson, Friends of Lula Belle Stewart Center, 1979-80; bd. dirs. Met. Detroit council Girl Scouts U.S., 1977-80, chairperson career guidance and spl. projects, 1976—; mem. planning com. United Community Services of Met. Detroit, 1978-80; mem. bd. Christian edn. Plymouth United Ch. of Christ, 1979—. Recipient Disting. Service citation U.S. Office Edn., 1976, citation Girl Scouts U.S., 1977, Nat. Assn. Industry-Edn. Cooperation, 1978, Mich. Dept. Edn., 1977, 78. Mem. Assn. for Supervision and Curriculum Devel., Am. Personnel and Guidance Assn., Mich. Sch. Counselors Assn., Nat. Assn. for Industry Edn. Cooperation, Nat. Council for Negro Women, NAACP, Nat. Assn. for Career Edn., Mich. Assn. Career Edn., Mich. Council for Women in Ednl. Adminstrn., Alpha Kappa Alpha. Democrat. Contbr. articles on career edn. to profl. publs. Home: 1367 Joliet St Detroit MI 48207 Office: Wayne City Intermediate Sch Dist 33500 Van Born Rd Wayne MI 48184

ROBINSON, RENAULT ALVIN, police assn. exec.; b. Chgo., Sept. 8, 1942; s. Robert S. and Mabel (Stevenson) R.; B.A., Roosevelt U., 1970; M.A., 1971; postgrad. (urban fellow) Northwestern U., 1972-73; m. Annette Richardson, Feb. 23, 1963; children—Renault Alvin, Brian, Kivu, Kobie. With Chgo. Post Office, 1960-62; printer, Union Tank Car Co., Chgo., 1963-64; patrolman, Chgo. Police Dept., 1964—; pres. Afro-Am. Patrolmen's League, Chgo., 1968-70, exec. dir., 1970—. Mem. Com. on Fgn. and Domestic Affairs, Chgo. Forum, 1971—. Bd. dirs. League to Improve the Community, Chgo. Recipient Citizens award Malcolm X Coll., 1972; Cabrini Green Alternative High Sch., 1972; Outstanding Service award NIU Black Arts Festival, 1971; Appreciation award Youth for Christ Choir, 1973; Outstanding Young Man award Chgo. South End Jr. C. of C., 1970; Community Service awards Black Olympics Com., 1973, Nat. Assn. Black Social Workers, 1974; Dr. Martin Luther King Jr. award SCLC, 1975; Image award League Black Women, 1975; I am my Brother's Keeper award Policemen for a Better Gary, 1975; AABS award excellence, 1976; Service to Community award Newspaper Guild, 1976; Humanitarian Service award Centers New Horizons, 1976; Gratitude award Kiwanis Club of Roseland, 1976; Affirmative Action award Breadbasket Comml. Assn., 1976; Affirmative Action, Pub. Service award Cook County Bar Assn., 1976; named Man of Year, Guardians Police Orgn., 1975. Mem. Nat. Black Police Assn. (nat. info. officer). Office: PO Box 49122 Chicago IL 60649

ROBINSON, RICHARD HARDING, JR., mech. engr.; b. Denver, Apr. 7, 1956; s. Richard Harding and Janet Lee (Hamilton) R.; B.S.M.E. with distinction (Gates Found. scholar, Owens-Corning scholar, Consolidation Coal Co. scholar, Davidson scholar), Purdue U., 1978; m. Jill Elizabeth Fortner, July 14, 1979. Design engr. Clark Equipment Co., Battle Creek, Mich., 1978-79, sr. design engr. new products, 1979-81. Registered engr.-in-tng., Ind. Mem. ASME (asso.), Purdue U. Alumni Assn., Phi Kappa Phi, Pi Tau Sigma. Inventor uprights for lift truck. Home: 6750 Marlow St Portage MI 49002 Office: 525 N 24th St Battle Creek MI 49016

ROBINSON, ROBERT JOHN, physician; b. Georgetown, Ky., Mar. 19, 1945; s. Frank Edmund and Ina Mae (Wicker) R.; B.S., Bob Jones U., 1967; M.D., Ind. U., 1971; m. Gail Diane Shoemaker, Aug. 19, 1967; children—Rod, Sheila, Wendy, Heidi. Intern, U. Colo., 1971-72, Denver Health and Hosp. Corp., 1972; gen. staff Marion County Health and Hosp. Corp., Indpls., 1972-73; practice family medicine, Indpls., 1973—; sec. ob-gyn. dept. St. Francis Hosp., Indpls., 1977-80; preceptor Ind. U. Sch. Medicine, 1977-80; founder New Life Adoption Agy., Inc. PTA pres. South Side Christian Sch.; bd. dirs. Ind. Bapt. Coll., Life Action Ranch; mem. adv. bd. Ind. Com. for Preservation Life; coach Franklin Twp. Little League Basketball; Sunday Sch. tchr. Emmanuel Bapt. Ch. Diplomate Am. Bd. Family Practice. Mem. AMA, Ind. Med. Assn., Marion County Med. Soc., Exptl. Aircraft Assn., Antique Airplane Assn., Internat. Aerobatics Club. Baptist. Home: Route 1 Box 38A Greenwood IN 46142 Office: 6745 S Gray Rd Indianapolis IN 46227

ROBINSON, SALLY WINSTON, artist; b. Detroit, Nov. 2, 1924; d. Harry Lewis and Lydia (Kahn) Winston; B.A., Bennington Coll., 1947; student Cranbrook Acad. Art, 1949; grad. Sch. Social Work, Wayne U., 1948, M.A., 1972; M.F.A., Wayne State U., 1973; m. Eliot F. Robinson, June 28, 1949; children—Peter Eliot, Lydia Winston, Suzanne Finley, Sarah Mitchell. Psychol. tester Detroit Bd. Edn., 1944; pyschol. counselor and tester YMCA, N.Y.C., 1946; social caseworker Family Service, Pontiac, Mich., 1947; instr. printmaking Wayne State U., Detroit, 1973—. One person shows U. Mich., 1973, Wayne State U., 1974, Klein-Vogol Gallery, 1974, Rina Gallery, 1976, Park McCullough House, Vt., 1976, Williams Coll., 1976, Arnold Klein Gallery, 1977; exhibited group shows Bennington Coll., Cranbrook Mus., Detroit Inst. Art, Detroit Artists Market, Soc. Women Painters, Soc. Arts and Crafts, Bloomfield Art Assn., Flint Left Bank Gallery, Balough Gallery, Detroit Soc. Women Painters, U. Mich., U. Ind., U. Wis., U. Pittsburg, Toledo Mus., Krannert Mus.; represented collections, Detroit, N.Y.C., Birmingham, Bloomfield Hills; tchr. children's art Detroit Inst. Art, 1949-50, now artistic advisor, bd. dirs. drawing and print orgn. Bd. dirs. Planned Parenthood, 1951—, mem. exec. bd., 1963—; bd. dirs. P.T.A., 1956-60, Roeper City and Country Sch., U. Mich. Mus. Art, 1978; trustee Putnam Hosp. Med. Research Inst., 1978; mem. Gov.'s Commn. Art in State Bldgs., 1978-79. Mem. Detroit Artists Market (dir. 1956—), Bennington Coll. Alumnae Assn. (regional co-chmn. 1954), Detroit Soc Women Painters, Birmingham Soc. Women Painters (pres. 1974-76), Bloomfield Art Assn. (program co-chmn. 1956), Founders Soc. Detroit Inst. Art. Unitarian (mem. Council 1963—). Clubs: Village Women's (Birmingham, Mich.); Women's City (co-ordinator art shows 1950) (Detroit). Home: 572 Linden Rd Birmingham MI 48009 also 7 Monument Circle Old Bennington VT 05201

ROBINSON, WALTER STITT, JR., historian; b. Matthews, N.C., Aug. 28, 1917; s. Walter Stitt and Mary Irene (Jamison) R.; B.A. summa cum laude, Davidson Coll., 1939; M.A., U. Va., 1941, Ph.D., 1950; m. Constance Lee Mock, Mar. 18, 1944; children—Ethel Barry, Walter Lee. Asst. prof. history Florence (Ala.) State Coll., 1946-47, asso. prof., 1947-48; asst. prof. U. Kans., Lawrence, 1950-54, asso. prof., 1954-59, prof., 1959—, chmn. dept., 1968-73; mem. Nat. Civil War Centennial Commn., 1961-65; mem. Kans. Com. for Humanities, 1971-78, chmn., 1976, 77. Adminstrv. bd. 1st United Methodist Ch., Lawrence; mem. exec. com. bd. dirs. Kans. Sch. Religion. Served to capt. U.S. Army, 1941-45. Decorated Bronze Star; Social Sci. Research Council grantee, 1959-60; Am. Philos. Soc. grantee, 1967; recipient Distinguished Scholarship award U. Kans., 1976. Mem. Am., So. hist. assns., Orgn. Am. Historians (chmn. program com. 1959), Kans. State (dir.), Douglas County (dir., mem. exec. com., pres. 1979-81) hist. socs., Raven Soc., Phi Beta Kappa, Phi Alpha Theta (internat. council 1977-79, internat. adv. bd. 1980—). Author: Land Grants in Virginia, 1607-1699, 1957; The Southern Colonial Frontier, 1607-1763, 1979; mem. editorial bd. 18th century bibliography in Philol. Quar., 1975-78; contbr. articles in field to Jour. So. History, Miss. Valley Hist. Rev., others. Home: 801 Broadview Dr Lawrence KS 66044 Office: Dept History Univ Kansas Lawrence KS 66045

ROBINSON, WILLIAM LESLIE, coll. adminstr.; b. Cleve., June 1, 1933; s. James and Agnes (Mawhinney) R.; student Coll. Wooster, 1957-59; B.S., Ohio No. U., 1960-61; postgrad. Bowling Green U., 1961-64; m. Gretchen E. Yant, July 29, 1961; children—Todd William, Staci Elizabeth. With Cleve. Indians Baseball Co., 1950-53; dean of men Ohio No. U., Ada, 1961-70, dean of admissions, 1970-79, dir. student activities, 1979—, asso. prof., 1970—. Mem. Ada Sch. Bd., 1975—, pres., 1979—. Served with AUS, 1953-55. Recipient Outstanding Alumni award Ohio No. U., 1970. Mem. Ohio Assn. Coll. Admissions Counselors (life), Assn. Coll. Admissions Counselors, Am. Coll. Personnel Assn., Omicron Delta Kappa (gen. council). Lutheran. Club: Meadowink Country (dir.). Home: 608 Conley Ada OH 45810 Office: Ohio No U Ada OH 45810

ROBINSON, WILLIAM NATHANIEL, educator; b. St. Joseph, Mo., May 7, 1919; s. William Eugene and Maude (Cummings) R.; B.S., U. Ariz., 1947; B.S., U. Kans., 1950, M.E., 1953; Ed.D., U. Neb., 1965; m. Analee June McClung, Aug. 25, 1946; children—June Ann Sutley, William Steuart. Dep. county sch. supt., Pima County, Ariz., 1947-49; tchr., prin. Sabetha (Kans.) High Sch., 1950-54; prin. Holyrood (Kans.) High Sch., 1954-58; asst. prof. edn. Tarkio Coll., 1958-64; prof. edn. Fort Hays (Kans.) State U., 1964—; cons. North Central Kans. Regional Resource Center; mem. Kans. Title IV Adv. Council. Chmn., March of Dimes, Holyrood, 1956. Bd. dirs. Cedar Bluff North Shore Lake Assn. Served with USAAF, 1940-43. Mem. Nat. Assn. Secondary Sch. Prins., NEA, Kans. Edn. Assn., Kans. Classroom Tchr. Commn., Soc. Profs. Edn., Ellsworth County Tchrs. Assn. (pres. 1956), Phi Delta Kappa. Presbyn. (deacon 1967-70, trustee 1970-73). Lion. Author: American Education: Its Organization and Control, 1968. Contbr. articles to various jours. Home: 2906 Hillcrest St Hays KS 67601 Office: Edn Dept Fort Hays State U Hays KS 67601

ROBLES, RICARDO JULIO, agribus. co. exec.; b. Panama City, Panama, Mar. 21, 1926; s. Rogelio and Sibila (Ramirez) R.; B.S. (Kellogg Found. scholar), Carleton Coll., 1947; m. Johanna Sienko, May 26, 1951; children—Richard, John, Jeffrey, Jane. With Cargill, Inc., various locations, 1947—, v.p., Mpls., 1981—, pres. Cargill Americas Inc., Mpls., 1971—, mgr. Pan Am dept., Mpls., 1981—; chmn. bd. Latin Am. Agribus. Devel. Corp., 1978—; dir. Flagship Banks Inc., Miami, Fla. Republican. Roman Catholic. Office: Cargill Inc Pan Am Dept PO Box 9300 Minneapolis MN

ROBLING, JOHN STEVENS, publishing co. exec.; b. Clinton, Iowa, May 16, 1922; s. Christopher M. and Mary (Stevens) R.; student Dowling Coll., 1939-41; B.J., U. Mo., 1943; m. Charlotte L. Fitz Henry, July 6, 1946; children—Mary Charlotte, Stevens, Christopher, Julia. Editor, A.P., Chgo., 1943-45; pub. relations mgr. Meredith Pub. Co., Des Moines, 1945-51; dir. advt. and pub. relations McCall Corp., N.Y.C., 1951-57; dir. Nat. Library Week, Nat. Book Com., N.Y.C., 1957-61; v.p. advt. and pub. relations Ency. Brit., Inc., Chgo., 1961—, v.p. public affairs, 1981—; cons. This Week Mag., 1958-59; mem. steering com. Nat. Library Week, N.Y., 1964-67; chmn. Ill. State Com. for Library Week, 1966; mem. Citizens Com. for Chgo. Pub. Library, 1969; dir. Nat. Citizens Com. to Save Edn. and Library Funds, 1969; alt. del. White House Conf. on Libraries; mem. adv. com. Center for the Book, Library of Congress. Chmn. pub. relations planning com. Am. Ednl. Publs. Inst., 1968-69; treas. Des Moines Child Guidance Center, 1950; pres. Polk County Young Democrats, 1949; trustee Winnetka Pub. Library Bd., 1968-74, Ill. Library Bd., 1972-78; bd. dirs. Chgo. Pub. Library Friends, Civitas Found. Served with AUS, 1942-43. Recipient Spl. Honor citation Am. Assn. Sch. Librarians, 1967, Campbell Meml. award Ill. Library Assn.; Faculty/Alumni award U. Mo., 1980. Mem. Pub. Relations Soc. Am. (Silver Anvil award for Better Homes and Gardens, 1948, Ency. Brit. 1967). Clubs: Grolier (N.Y.C.); Nat. Book League (London); Chgo. Arts, Chgo. Press, Chgo. Racquet, Caxton. Contbr. articles to profl. jours. Home: 50 W Schiller St Chicago IL 60610 Office: 425 N Michigan Ave Chicago IL 60611

ROCCAFORTE, PETER, hosp. sci. officer; b. Sicily, Italy, Mar. 19, 1940; came to U.S., 1950; s. Joseph and Santa Francesca (Messina) R.; B.S., Northeastern Ill. U., 1970; M.S., Chgo. State U., 1973; Ph.D., Ill. Inst. Tech., 1976; children—Gina, Marcus. Biomed. electronic technician Michael Reese Hosp., Chgo., 1961-64; biomed. engr. Hektoen Inst., Chgo., 1965-75; sci. officer Cook County Hosp., Chgo., 1975—; research asst. prof. U. Ill. Med. Sch., 1979—. Registered psychologist, Ill. Mem. Am. Psychol. Assn., AAUP. Contbr. in field. Home: 1711 W Thorndale St Chicago IL 60660 Office: 627 S Wood St Chicago IL 60612

ROCCO, JAMES ROBERT, civil engr.; b. Orange, N.J., Jan. 18, 1953; s. Jerry Arnold and Anna R.; B.S. in Civil Engring., N.J. Inst. Tech., 1974; m. Lori Ellen Jacops, Jan. 29, 1977; children—Jerrold Edward, Jennifer Lynn. Jr. engr., mktg. div. Standard Oil Co. (Ohio), Columbus, 1974-75, constrn. and maintenance engr., mktg. div., 1975-76, region engr., mktg. div., 1976-77, constrn. and maintenance supr., mktg. div., 1977-79, constrn. and maintenance mgr., mktg. div., 1979—. Public affairs trustee Village of Reminderville (Ohio). Mem. ASCE (asso.). Roman Catholic. Home: 10326 Smugglers Cove

Aurora OH 44202 Office: Standard Oil Co (Ohio) 4850 E 49 St Cleveland OH 44115

ROCH, LEWIS MARSHALL, II, ophthalmic surgeon; b. Mineola, Tex., Aug. 13, 1934; s. Lewis Marshall and Gladys Irene (Hoover) R.; B.A., U. Tex., 1954, M.D., 1959; m. Lois Afton Price; children—Lewis Marshall III, Katrina Ann. Intern USPHS Hosp., Boston, 1959-60; resident ophthalmology USPHS Hosp., New Orleans, 1960-63, dep. chief ophthalmology, 1963-64; chief ophthalmology USPHS Hosp., Seattle, 1964-67; practice medicine specializing in ophthalmology, Muncie, Ind., 1967—; attending ophthalmic surgeon Ball Meml. Hosp., Muncie, chmn. dept. surgery, 1973, 81, chmn. clin. staff, 1975. Served with USPHS, 1959-67. Diplomate Am. Bd. Ophthalmology. Fellow Am. Acad. Ophthalmology and Otolaryngology, A.C.S.; mem. AMA, So. Med. Assn., Soc. Eye Surgeons Internat. Eye Found., Contact Lens Assn. Ophthalmologists, Am. Assn. Opthalmology, Ind. Acad. Ophthalmology and Otolaryngology, Muncie Acad. Medicine (past pres.), Am. Intra-Ocular Implant Soc. Home: 2006 Robinwood Dr Muncie IN 47304 Office: 708 W White River Blvd Muncie IN 47303

ROCHE, WILLIAM MICHAEL, ins. co. exec.; b. Evanston, Ill., Feb. 26, 1929; s. Gerald Carte and Gladys LeMae (Elmore) R.; B.S., U. N.Mex., 1951; m. Marilyn L. D'Amour, Dec. 1, 1951; children—Peter J., Michael F., Karen D., Jeffrey A., Steven P., Jeri A. Pres., W. M. Roche & Assos., Park Ridge, Ill., 1952—; football coach St. George High Sch., Evanston, 1953-57; cons. Christian Bros. Ins. Program, 1956—. Founder, chmn. bd. Chgo. Minor Hawks Hockey Found., 1967—; chmn. Heart Fund, 1970—. Served with U.S. Army, 1950-52. Mem. Leading Producers Roundtable, Chgo. Bd. Underwriters, Nat. Assn. Health Underwriters, Nat. Collegiate Athletic Assn., U. N.Mex. Alumni Assn. (dir. 1978—), Am. Coll. Hockey Coaches Assn., VFW. Republican. Roman Catholic. Office: 18 S Northwest Hwy Park Ridge IL 60608

ROCHETTO, EVELYN MARIE, educator; b. Chgo.; d. Lucius J. and Clara M. (Jung) Young; Ph.B., Northwestern U., 1952; m. Paul A. Rochetto, June 9, 1937. Profl. musician, 1930-50; membership sec. Internat. Soc. for Gen. Semantics, 1950-55, exec. sec., 1955-68, dir., 1952-68; tchr. Aurora Coll., 1968—; counselor State of Ill., 1970—. Pres., Chgo. Story League. Dir. Pan Am. Bd. Edn. Mem. AAUW (pres. Chgo. br. 1956—, mem. bd. 1953—), Am. Legion Auxiliary (mem. bd.), Alpha Sigma Lambda (dir.). Club: Woman's University (pres. 1966—). Home: 5240 Sheridan Rd Chicago IL 60640

ROCHFORD, E(DWARD) MICHAEL, priest; b. Chgo., May 20, 1937; s. Edward Michael and Julia Agnes (Merrick) R.; B.A., St. Mary of Lake Sem., Mundelein, Ill., 1958, S.T.B., 1960, M.A., 1961; M.S.W., U. Ill., 1968. Ordained priest Roman Catholic Ch., 1962; asso. pastor Resurrection Ch., Chgo., 1962-71; pastor St. Thomas of Canterbury Parish, Chgo., 1971—; co-founder, pres. Austin Clergy Council, 1965-69; co-founder, mem. bd. Cath. Com. Urban Ministry, 1979-81, Amos Temporary Help Services, 1976-79. Co-founder, v.p. Orgn. Better Austin, 1965-70; co-founder, chmn. bd. Prologue Alternative High Sch., 1974—, Uptown Peoples Action Program, 1971—. Recipient Golden Key award City of Chgo., 1970, Outstanding Clergyman award North Side Internat. Festival, 1978. Mem. Assn. Chgo. Priests, Nat. Assn. Social Workers. Roman Catholic. Clubs: K.C., Shamrock-American. Author articles, poems. Address: 4827 N Kenmore Ave Chicago IL 60640

ROCHFORD, JAMES M., mfg. co. exec.; b. Chgo., Oct. 1, 1921; s. James and Ellen (Kane) R.; student FBI Nat. Exec. Inst.; Northwestern U., Traffic Inst.; DePaul U.; m. Lois J. Fallon, May 9, 1946; children—Jeanne, Joan, Elizabeth. With Chgo. Police Dept., 1947-57, first dept. supt., 1968, supt., 1974-77; with Bally Mfg. Corp., Chgo., 1977—, v.p. corporate security, v.p. corporate affairs govt. relations, dir.; dir. Continental Air Transp. Served with U.S. Army, 1942-46. Decorated Bronze Star medal with oak leaf cluster. Recipient Supts. Award of Valor, Chgo. Police Dept.; Pub. Service award, others. Mem. Internat. Assn. Chiefs of Police, Ill. Assn. Chiefs of Police, Am. Legion, Amvets, V.F.W. Roman Catholic. Club: Ridgmoor Country. Home: 6881 N Tonty St Chicago IL 60646 Office: 2640 W Belmont St Chicago IL 60618*

ROCK, PHILIP JOSEPH, state senator, lawyer; b. Chgo., May 4, 1937; s. Joseph and Kathryn (Crimmins) R.; J.D., Loyola U., 1964; m. Sheila Graber, 1964; children—Kathleen, Meghan, Colleen, John Joseph. Admitted to Ill. bar, 1964; partner firm Rock Fusco, Reynolds & Hineghan, Chicago, 1973—; mem. Ill. State Senate, 1971—, asst. minority leader, 1973, asst. majority leader, 1975, 77, pres., 1979. Mem. Ill. Dem. central com., 1970—; committeeman Oak Park Dem. Twp., 1978; del. Dem. Nat. Conv., 1980; mem. Dem. Nat. Com., 1980—. Mem. Am. Bar Assn., Ill. Bar Assn., Chgo Bar Assn. Roman Catholic. Office: State Capitol Springfield IL 62706

ROCKS, JAMES ENGEL, educator; b. Cleve., May 26, 1939; s. Francis Joseph and Earla Elizabeth (Engel) R.; A.B., Western Res. U., 1961; M.A., Duke U., 1962, Ph.D., 1966; m. Judith Tredway, June 30, 1973. Asst. prof. English, Tulane U., New Orleans, 1965-72; asst. prof. English, Loyola U. of Chgo., 1972-77, asso. prof., 1977—, asst. chmn. dept., 1979-80, dir. grad. programs, 1980—. James B. Duke fellow, 1962-64. Mem. Modern Lang. Assn. Episcopalian. Contbr. articles to profl. jours. Office: 6525 N Sheridan Rd Chicago IL 60626

RODABAUGH, MARY JANE, educator; b. Napoleon, Ohio, Aug. 2, 1917; d. Daniel and Sophia Wilhemina (Ruetz) Gorman; B.A., B.S. in Edn., Capital U., Columbus, Ohio, 1939; M.A., Ohio State U., 1945; m. James H. Rodabaugh, Nov. 9, 1946. Tchr. social studies and English, Mt. Zion (Ohio) High Sch., 1939-43; tchr., chmn. history dept. Columbus Sch. for Girls, 1955-63; instr. Kent (Ohio) State U., 1963-65, asst. prof., 1965-67; instr. Miami U., Oxford, Ohio, 1967-69, asst. prof. dept. tchr. edn., 1969—. John Hay fellow Williams Coll., 1965. Mem. NEA, Higher Edn. Assn., Ohio Edn. Assn., Nat., Ohio councils social studies, LWV, (dir. Oxford), Phi Delta Kappa. Author: (with James H. Rodabaugh) Nursing in Ohio: A History, 1951; (with Parker LaBach) Common Learnings: Core and Interdisciplinary Team Approaches, 1969. Home: 105 Olde Farm Rd Oxford OH 45056 Office: 307 A McGuffey Miami U Oxford OH 45056

RODDIS, WILLIAM HENRY, banker; b. Marshfield, Wis., Nov. 6, 1917; s. Hamilton and Catherine Sara (Prindle) R.; student Mass. Inst. Tech., 1937-40; m. Setsuko Manabe, 1967; children—Grace, Thomas. Plant mgr. Roddis Plywood Corp., Marshfield, Wis., 1946-56, corporate sec., 1946-60, dir., 1951-60; profl. specialist Weyerhaeuser Co., Longview, Wash., 1961-62; v.p. Swords Veneer Ill., 1962-64; dir. Citizen's Nat. Bank & Trust Co., Marshfield, 1972—. Mem. Wood County Bd. Suprs., 1943-44. Served with USNR, 1944-46. Mem. Aircraft Owners and Pilots Assn., Forest Products Research Soc., Mayflower Soc., Soc. Colonial Wars (dep. gov. gen. 1978—), SAR (nat. trustee Wis. soc. 1978—), Huguenot Soc. Wis. (pres. 1979-81), Soc. of War of 1812. Republican. Episcopalian. Clubs: Union League Chgo.; Milw. Athletic. Home: 2433 N Wahl Ave Milwaukee WI 53211

RODECK, WILLIAM FRED, JR., mech. engr.; b. Chgo., Nov. 30, 1925; s. William Fred and Martha (Schultz) R.; B.S. in Mech. Engring., U. Ill., 1952; m. Virginia M. Springs, July 12, 1952; 1 son, Alan. Mech. engr. N.Y. Central R.R., Chgo., 1952-54; mech. engr. Schmidt, Garden & Erikson, Chgo., 1954—; dir. mech. engring. Schmidt, Garden & Erikson, Chgo., 1975—, dir. co-op. engring. edn., 1975—. Served with USAAF, 1943-45. Decorated Air medal with 1 oak leaf cluster. Registered profl. engr., Ill., Mich., Wis., Fla. Roman Catholic. Club: Elks. Home: 15230 Irving Ave Dolton IL 60419 Office: 104 S Michigan Ave Chicago IL 60603

RODENBERG, SIDNEY DAN, univ. adminstr.; b. St. Louis, Apr. 5, 1926; s. Martin and Etta (Goldfried) R.; A.B., Washington U., St. Louis, 1948, A.M., 1950, Ph.D., 1953; M.A. (hon.), U. Pa., 1971; m. Dolores Ann Knight, Dec. 21, 1950; children—Nancy Lee, Wendy Jane, Amy Marie. Research investigator Anheuser-Busch, St. Louis, 1950; lectr. in microbiology Washington U., 1951, instr., 1953-56, asst. prof. microbiology, 1956-61, asso. prof., 1961-69, prof., 1969-75; dean Sch. Allied Med. Professions, U. Pa., 1969-75; dean Coll. Health Related Professions, prof. microbiology and health sci. Wichita State U., 1976—; clin. prof. pathology U. Kans. Sch. Medicine, Wichita, 1981; mem. accreditation rev. bd. Nat. Accrediting Agy. for Clin. Lab. Scis., 1974-79; dir. Com. on Allied Health Edn. and Accreditation, 1980—. Bd. dirs. Upper Merion (Pa.) Student Loan Fund, 1960-64, chmn., 1962-64; mem. Upper Merion Area Sch. System Sch. Bd., 1969-75, pres., 1975; bd. dirs. Upper Merion San. Bd., 1965-66. Served with U.S. Army, 1944-46; Philippines. Recipient Lindback award U. Pa., 1964; NSF fellow, 1966-67. Mem. Am. Soc. Allied Health Professions (dir. 1973-79, pres. 1976-79, award for outstanding service 1979), AAUP, AAAS, N.Y. Acad. Scis, Phi Kappa Phi. Research on physiology devel., virus biosynthesis, bacterial growth, sporulation and germination. Home: 6710 E 10th St Wichita KS 67206 Office: Dean's Office Coll Health Related Professions Wichita State U Wichita KS 67208

RODES, JANICE ANSLINGER, dietitian; b. Milw.; d. Eugene L. and Margaret Ann (Feiner) Anslinger; B.S. in Nutrition and Chemistry, Milw.-Downer Coll., 1935; m. George P. Rodes, May 16, 1941; children—Robert A., Randie O. Dietetic intern U. Mich., 1936; food service dir. U. Mich. League, Ann Arbor, 1936-40; dietary dir. Battlecreek (Mich.) San., 1941; food service dir. Internat. House, U. Chgo., 1942-43; nutrition cons. Wis. Restaurant Assn., Milw., 1945-46; dir. dietetic dept. Zeller Mental Health Center, Peoria, Ill., 1965—; cons., lectr. nutrition and food service mgmt. Pres., Peoria Womens Civic Fedn., 1952-56; mem. Mayor's Adv. Council, Peoria, 1954-55; mem. Peoria County Bd. Suprs., 1953-57; pres. Broadway Theater League Peoria, 1959; mem. Peoria Sch. Lunch Adv. Com., 1978. Recipient Gov.'s Supporter Achievement award, 1972. Registered dietitian. Mem. Ill. Council on Nutrition (founding; sec. 1978), AAUW (dir. Peoria chpt. 1953-57), Am. Dietetic Assn. (Ill. del. 1978-81), Ill. Dietetic Assn. (pres. 1974), Peoria Dist. Dietetic Assn. (pres. 1971), Am. Soc. Hosp. Food Service Adminstrs., Ill. Nutrition Com. Appearances on radio and TV. Office: 5407 N University St Peoria IL 61614

RODGERS, ALICE LYNN, mktg. research corp. cons.; b. Mt. Clemens, Mich., Nov. 23, 1942; d. Albert William and Margaret Dorothy (Small) Kockentiet; B.S.C. magna cum laude, Rider Coll., 1975; m. Larry W. Rodgers, June 8, 1963. Prodn. mgr. Quar. Digest of Urban and Regional Research., Urbana, Ill., bus. mgr. Dept. Urban and Regional Planning, Urbana, 1968-73; mgr. Jour. Consumer Research and Jour. Am. Statis. Assn., Chgo., 1975-78; sr. cons. asso., dir. shopping research Mgmt. Horizons, Inc., Columbus, Ohio, 1978-81; pres. Mktg. Programs and Services, Worthington, Ohio, 1981—. Mem. Am. Mktg. Assn., Assn. for Consumer Research. Author articles in field. Address: 790 Maple Dr Worthington OH 43085

RODGERS, DENNIS BRUCE, lawyer; b. Decatur, Ill., Oct. 16, 1940; s. Richard Wilbur and Eleanor Frances (Cobb) R.; B.S., Trinity Coll., Hartford, Conn., 1962; J.D., Georgetown U., 1966; m. Marilynne Linda Wilson, Nov. 30, 1974; children—John, Andrew, Alainna, Aaron. Tchr., Bloomfield (Conn.) pub. schs., 1962-63; admitted to Ill. bar, 1966, since practiced in Decatur; mem. firm Denz, Lowe, Moore, Rodgers & See, 1966-77; legal planner Macon County Regional Plan Commn., 1970-76; part time prof. Richland Community Coll., 1976-79. Crusade chmn. Macon County unit Am. Cancer Soc., 1971-72, bd. dirs., 1972-77, chmn. bd., 1974-75; mem. Now and Tomorrow Council of Decatur Meml. Hosp., 1971-77; bd. dirs. Council Community Services, 1970-77, pres., 1975-77; pres. Sangamon Valley Assn., 1972-76; mem. Macon County Health Bd., 1981—; mem. Scholarships for Ill. Residents, 1970—; adminstrv. v.p. Decatur Jaycees, 1969-70; pres. Young Republican Orgn. Macon County, 1967-68. Recipient Disting. Service award Decatur Jaycees, 1971; named to Outstanding Young Men of Am., 1969-72. Mem. Ill., Decatur bar assns., Metro-Decatur C. of C. (chmn. transp. com. 1977—, dir. 1980—), Alpha Chi Rho, Phi Alpha Delta (cert. disting. service 1966). Kiwanian (bd. dirs. Decatur 1970-72). Co-author: Oakley Reservoir and Water Development for Central Illinois, 1968. Home: 90 John Dr Mount Zion IL 62549 Office: Suite 352 Milliken Ct 132 S Water St Decatur IL 62523

RODGERS, JAMES CHESTER, fluid power products mfg. co. exec.; b. Newark, Sept. 4, 1919; s. Chester Howard and Florence (O'Conner) R.; B.S., U. Cin., 1947, M.E., 1947; m. Rosemary V. Koenig, June 6, 1940; children—Rosemary F., Virginia C., Valarie A. Sales engr. to mgr. Ingersoll Rand Co., Chgo., 1947-62; dir. mktg. Scully Jones & Co., Chgo., 1962-63; v.p. Thor Power Tool Co., 1963-65; asst. to exec. v.p. Symington Wayne Corp., Chgo., 1965-69; v.p. API Industries, Inc., Elmhurst, Ill., 1969; v.p., gen. mgr. Tysaman Machine div. Carborundum Corp., Knoxville, Tenn., 1969-71; dir. mktg. BFF div. Whittaker Corp., Berwick, Pa., 1976-77; mgr. mktg. ops. Gen. Contracting Co., Saudi Arabia, 1978; founder, pres. Origa Corp., Elmhurst, 1978—; chief exec. officer MASTA. Served to lt. (j.g.) USN, 1940-43; with USAF, 1943-45. Mem. ASME, Soc. Mfg. Engrs., VFW. Republican. Roman Catholic. Contbr. articles to tech. jours. Office: Origa Corp 928 Oak Lawn Ave Elmhurst IL 60126

RODGERS, JAMES FOSTER, economist; b. Columbus, Ga., Jan. 15, 1951; s. Laban J. and Martha J. Rodgers; B.A. with honors in Econs. (Hohenberg fellow), U. Ala., 1973; Ph.D. in Econs., U. Iowa, 1980; m. Cynthia L. Bathurst, Aug. 20, 1975. Instr. econs. U. Iowa, 1978-79; research asso. Dept. Health Resource Analysis, Center Health Policy Research, AMA, Chgo., 1979-80, dir., 1980—. Pharm. Mfrs. Assn. dissertation grantee, 1978-80. Mem. Am. Econ. Assn., Am. Statis. Assn., Western Econ. Assn. Home: 2030 N Mohawk St Chicago IL 60614 Office: 535 N Dearborn St Chicago IL 60610

RODGERS, NORMAN GEORGE, state senator; b. Chatfield, Minn., Sept. 21, 1927; s. William and Rhoda R.; grad. high sch.; student Am. Inst. Bus.; m. Norma, Feb. 6, 1950; children—Pamela Kay, Michael Norman. Store mgr. Thriftway Stores, Inc., Creston, Iowa, 1950-51; Des Moines, 1952-54; field rep. Super Valu Stores, Inc., 1955-57; supermarket owner/operator, 1957—; dir. Adel Manor, Raccoon Valley State Bank. Mem. Iowa State Senate; bd. dirs. Adel Devel. Corp. Served in USN, 1944-46, 51, 52. Mem. Nat. Hist. Soc., Adel Hist. Soc., Urbandale C. of C., Am. Legion, VFW, Iowans for Tax Relief, Iowa Retail Food Dealers Assn., Farm Bur. Episcopalian. Clubs: Rotary, Elks. Office: State Capitol Des Moines IA 50319*

RODIER, DOLORES (DEE) MARICH, realty agy. exec.; b. Cleve., Sept. 18, 1932; d. George Joseph and Celeste Josephine (Kashuba) Marich; B.A., Ursuline Coll., 1978; m. Daniel G. Rodier, Apr. 11, 1953 (div.); children—Anne, Jane, Gregg, Jeffrey, Suzanne. Tchr., St. Ann's Sch., Cleveland Heights, Ohio, 1952-53; various library positions, Cleve. and Cleveland Heights, Ohio, John Carroll U., 1956-66; salesperson Taylor Sutliff Realtor, Cleve., 1969-76; salesperson Smythe Cramer Co., Pepper Pike, Ohio, 1976-79, dir. edn., 1979—. Pres. Assn. for Children with Learning Disabilities, Cleve., 1975-77, bd. dirs., 1977—. Recipient Mary Gillam Bardo award Assn. for Children with Learning Disabilities, 1977. Mem. Real Estate Trainers Assn. Internat., Real Estate Educators Assn., Am. Soc. Tng. and Devel. Republican. Roman Catholic. Club: Jr. League Cleve. Author in-house tng. manual. Office: 30650 Pine Tree Rd Pepper Pike OH 44124

RODKIN, HENRY HOLLISON, automotive parts co. exec.; b. Chgo., Oct. 22, 1935; s. Sidney and Laverne M. (Hollison) R.; B.S., Northwestern U., 1956; M.B.A., U. Chgo., 1966; m. Margaret Davidow, July 20, 1957; children—Nancy, Jill. Brand mgr. Procter & Gamble, Cin., 1961-63; gen. mktg. mgr. Chgo. Tribune, 1963-66; asst. to pres. A.C. Nielsen Co., Chgo., 1966-70; dir. mktg. Daubert Chem., Oakbrook, Ill., 1970-72; v.p. mktg. Maremont Corp. Chgo., 1972—; v.p. planning Alusuisse Am., N.Y.C., 1981—; dir. Equator Corp., Glencoe, Ill.; cons. IMS Research, N.Y.C., 1975-78. Served with U.S. Army, 1958-59. Mem. Am. Mktg. Assn., Am. Mgmt. Assn., Overseas Automotive Club. Home: 178 Lakeside Pl Highland Park IL 60035 Office: 200 E Randolph Dr Chicago IL 60601

RODOLFA, EMIL RAYMOND, psychologist; b. San Jose, Calif., Nov. 23, 1952; s. Joseph and Louise (Cava) R.; B.A., San Jose State U., 1976; M.S., Calif. State U., Hayward, 1977, 78; Ph.D., Tex. A&M U., 1981; m. Mary Jo Pyne, Jan. 6, 1979. Counselor, intern, child sexual abuse treatment program, San Jose, 1976-78; jr. staff psychologist U. Iowa Counseling Service, Iowa City, 1980—. Presidents scholar, 1975-76. Mem. Am. Psychol. Assn. (asso.), Am. Soc. Clin. Hypnosis, Am. Personnel and Guidance Assn., Am. Coll. Personnel Assn. Home: 608 Normandy Dr Iowa City IA 52240 Office: Counseling Service U Iowa Iowa City IA 52242

RODRIGUEZ, ELIZABETH, educator; b. Isabela, P.R., Aug. 13, 1946; d. Enrique and Luisa (Medina) Perez; B.A., Purdue U., 1976; M.S. (fellow), Ind. U. N.W., 1978, Ed.S. candidate; m. Samuel Rodriguez, Jan. 31, 1968; children—Nereida, John, Maria, Samuel. Substitute tchr., public schs., Gary, Ind., 1975-76, tchr. Spanish, 1976-77; exec. dir. Latin Am. Family Edn. Program, Gary, 1978; bilingual tchr. East Chicago (Ind.) Sch. System, 1979-81, Washington/McKinley/Franklin Schs., East Chicago, 1981—. Hostess, Miss Latin Am. Indiana Pageant, 1976; bd. dirs. Vol. Center, Lake Area United Way. Mem. Assn. Supervision and Curriculum Devel., Ind. U. Alumni Assn. Mem. Assemblies of God Ch.

RODRIGUEZ, SALLIE ANN, mfg. co. exec.; b. Highland Park, Mich., May 30, 1947; d. Robert Gilbert and Ruth Mary (Brown) Domke; B.S. in M.E., Marquette U., 1979; B.S. in Bus. Edn., Central Mich. U., 1970; M.B.A., U. Detroit, 1975; m. Reynel Rodriguez, Nov. 7, 1970; children—Heather, Holly. Instr., Detroit Bus. Inst., 1971-75; staff cons. Learson Asso., Detroit, 1975-76; compensation analyst, employment rep. Diamond Shamrock Corp., Cleve., 1976-78; mgr. salary and benefits adminstrn. Babcock & Wilcox, Bloomfield Hills, Mich., 1978-81; mgr. personnel adminstrn. Tractor div. Massey Ferguson, Inc., Detroit, 1981—. Mem. Parma Sch. Dist. bus. bd., 1977. Mem. Am. Soc. Personnel Adminstrn., Am. Soc. for Tng. and Devel., Am. Compensation Assn. (cert. compensation profl.), Assn. of M.B.A. Execs. Club: Cleve. Women's City. Home: 33970 Glouster Circle Farmington Hills MI 48018 Office: PO Box 322 Detroit MI 48232

RODRIGUEZ-ERDMANN, FRANZ, physician; b. Mexico City, Feb. 2, 1935; came to U.S., 1961; M.B., U. Heidelberg (Germany), 1958, M.D., 1960. Intern, Univ. Hosps., Heidelberg, 1958-61, Mercy Hosp., Detroit, 1962-63; research asso. Wayne State U., Detroit, 1961-62; jr. asst. resident in medicine Tufts New Eng. Med. Center, Boston, 1964-65, research fellow in hematology, 1964, clin. fellow in cardiology, 1965-66; resident in medicine Boston City Hosp., 1966-67; fellow in hematology Peter Bent Brigham Hosp., Boston, 1968-69, asso. in medicine, 1969-71; practice medicine specializing in internal medicine, Boston and Chgo.; attending physician Boston City Hosp.; instr. medicine Harvard U. Med. Sch., Boston, 1969-70, asst. prof. medicine, 1970-71; prof. medicine U. Ill., Chgo., 1971—; chief hematology sect. and hemostasis unit Edgewater Hosp., Chgo. Diplomate Am. Bd. Internal Medicine. Fellow A.C.P.; mem. Internat. Soc. Hematology, Am. Fedn. Clin. Research, Am. Soc. Hematology, Internat. Soc. Hemostasis and Thrombosis, Council on Thrombosis, World Fedn. Haemophilia, Brazilian Coll. Hematology, Mexican Nat. Acad. Medicine, Bolivian Soc. Internal Medicine, Colombian Soc. Hematology, Alpha Omega Alpha. Contbr. numerous articles in field to profl. jours. Office: Edgewater Hosp 5700 N Ashland Chicago IL 60660

ROEBER, EDWARD DEAN, ednl. adminstr.; b. St. Paul, Dec. 17, 1943; s. Edward Charles and Grace Belle (Raettig) R.; student Ohio Wesleyan U., 1962-63; B.A., U. Mich., 1966, M.A., 1967, Ph.D., 1970; m. Donna Lee Hildebrand, Sept. 10, 1977; children—Robert, Matthew. Cons., Nat. Assessment Ednl. Progress, Ann Arbor, Mich., Denver, 1969-72; cons. Mich. Dept. Edn., Lansing, 1972-74, coordinator, 1974-76, supr., 1976—; mem. part-time faculty Eastern Mich. U., 1973, 76. Mem. parent task force Community Mental Health Bd., 1979—; mem. parent adv. group Ingham Devel. Center, 1979—; bd. dirs. Lansing Area Soc. Autistic Children, 1980-81. Fellow Inst. Ednl. Leadership, George Washington U., 1979-80. Mem. Mich. Assn. Measurement and Evaluation in Guidance (pres.), Nat. Council Measurement and Evaluation, Mich. Personnel and Guidance Assn., Mich. Reading Assn., Phi Delta Kappa. Home: 1664 Algoma Dr Okemos MI 48864 Office: PO Box 30008 Lansing MI 48909

ROEBUCK, MARCIA VERONICA, mag. editor; b. Colon, Panama, Jan. 18, 1950; came to U.S., 1964; d. Ainsford Llewelyn and Daisy Viola (Briggs) Rowe; B.A. with honors, Nat. Coll. Edn., 1975, postgrad. 1975; 1 child, Turia Pilar. Textbook editor Scott, Foresman & Co., Glenview, Ill., 1976-79; quality control mgr. Scott, Foresman & Co., 1979-80; mng. editor Ebony Jr., Chgo., 1980—; lectr. in field. Exec. council Sta. WTTW-TV, Chgo., 1979—; bd. dirs. Chgo. UNICEF, 1980—, Reading is Fundamental, 198—. Ill. State scholar, 1975; Nat. Endowment for Arts fellow, 1977. Mem. Nat. Assn. Media Women, Ill. Black Writers Conf., Chgo. Assn. Black Journalists, Black Child Devel. Inst., Alpha Kappa Alpha. Roman Catholic. Office: 820 S Michigan Ave Chicago IL 60605

ROEING, RICHARD SVEN, mfg. co. exec.; b. Chgo., Dec. 29, 1926; s. Sven Eric and Grace Lydia (Hanson) R.; B.S. in Elec. Engring., U. Ill., 1948; M.B.A., No. Ill. U., 1972; m. Shirley Marie Walsh, Nov. 13, 1948; children—Richard Alan, Randall Robert,

Karen Marie. Asst. chief engr., dir. tech. mktg. C.E. Niehoff & Co., Chicago, 1953-68; plant mgr. Dixon div. Borg-Warner Corp. (Ill.), 1968-74; v.p., co-owner Mallard Mfg. Corp., Sterling, Ill., 1974—. Pres., Rock River Diabetes Assn., 1972—; bd. dirs. Martha Home for Girls, Dixon, 1970; v.p. Dixon C. of C., 1972; mem. council St. Paul's Ch. Served with USNR, 1944-48. Mem. Soc. Automotive Engrs. (chmn. tech. com. ignition mfg. inst. sect. 1964—), Internat. Materials Mgmt. Soc., Material Handling Inst. Republican. Clubs: Moose, Shriners, Rotary, Sterling Rock Falls Toastmaster, Rock River Country, Elks. Author: Automobile Engine Tune-up, 1968. Home: 3308 15th Ave Sterling IL 61081 Office: 101 Mallard Rd Sterling IL 61081

ROEMISCH, ROGER WILLIAM, automotive parts mfg. co. exec.; b. Cleve., Oct. 7, 1928; s. Lewis Harold and Lillian Ethyl (Coddington) R.; B.B.A. (Regent's Alumni Scholar), U. Mich., 1950; J.D., Wayne State U., 1960; m. Betty Joan Baldwin, Sept. 2, 1950; children—Jo Anne, John Burton, Jan Avis, Jill Lillian Louise. Employee service clk. Thompson Products Co., Detroit, 1950-53; personnel supr. Thompson Products, Inc., Detroit, 1953-60; admitted to Mich. bar, 1960; salaried personnel mgr. Thompson, Ramo, Wooldridge, Warren, Mich., 1960-68; asst. personnel dir. TRW Inc., Warren, 1968-73, personnel dir., 1973-81, dir. compliance mgmt., Cleve., 1981—, dir. labor relations, 1981—. Mem. Shelby Twp. Bldg Authority, 1967-73. Served with U.S. Army, 1950-52. Mem. Mich. Bar Assn., State Bar Mich., Macomb County Bar Assn., Warren/Sterling Heights C. of C., Indsl. Relations Assn. Detroit, Detroit Personnel Mgrs. Assn., Salary Adminstrn. Council. Home: 8591 Tanglewood Trail Chagrin Falls OH 44022

ROESEL, RUDOLPH WALTER, surgeon; b. Muenchen Bernsdorf, Germany, Mar. 3, 1924; s. Walter Hermann and Ida (Praessler) R.; came to U.S., 1952, naturalized, 1958; M.D., U. Zurich, 1952; m. Erica Erna Hirsig, Mar. 1, 1952; children—Thomas, Michael. Intern, Sioux Valley Hosp., Sioux Falls, S.D., 1952-53, resident in surgery Augustana Hosp., Chgo., Creighton U., Omaha, 1954-61; practice medicine specializing in surgery, S.D., 1952-54, Chgo., 1963—; mem. attending staffs Augustana Hosp., Ravenswoood Hosp., also mem. tumor bd., chmn. continuing edn. com. and Nelson M. Percy Research Com.; mem. vis. attending staff U. Ill., clin. asst . prof. surgery Abraham Lincoln Sch. Medicine. Diplomate Am. Bd. Surgery. Fellow ACS; mem. Chgo. Med. Soc., Chgo. Surg. Soc., AMA. Lutheran. Contbr. articles to profl. jours. Home: 1212 N Lake Shore Dr Chicago IL 60610 Office: 700 N Michigan Ave Chicago IL 60611

ROESENER, GERALD HOWARD, health services exec.; b. Indpls., May 9, 1945; s. Frederick H. and Helen Louise (Kespohl) R.; B.S. in Pharmacy, Butler U., 1968; M.B.A. candidate, Ind. U. Sch. Bus.; m. Karen Sue Alstott, Dec. 9, 1966; children—Daryn Kay, Derek Benton, Darcy Ann. Staff pharmacist Arlington Pharmacy, Indpls., 1961-72; staff pharmacist, cons., dir. ops., v.p. Mediply, Inc., Greenwood, Ind., 1972-78; v.p. ops. Med. Products, Inc., 1978—; v.p. Turtle Creek Convalescent Centres, Inc., Indpls., 1977-78; pres. Rehab. Health Services, Inc. div. Basic Am. Industries, Inc., Indpls., 1978-81. Exec. dir. Emmaus Luth. Ch., Indpls.; mem. subarea council Central Ind. Systems Agy. Served with U.S. Army, 1968-74. Fellow Am. Soc. Cons. Pharmacists; mem. Am. Pharm. Assn., Ind. Pharm. Assn., Am. Mgmt. Assn., Am. Geriatric Soc., Ind. Healthcare Assn. Republican. Clubs: El Dorado Country, Columbia (Indpls.). Office: PO Box 27249 Indianapolis IN 46227

ROESLER, JOSEPH FRANK, environ. engr.; b. Chgo., Dec. 15, 1930; s. Joseph Michael and Mary Teresa (Strobl) R.; B.S., Roosevelt U., 1954; M.S., Okla. State U., 1961; M.S. in Water Resources and San. Engring., U. Cin., 1970; m. Helen Anne Norris, Apr. 1, 1961; children—Joseph Robert, Helen Maria. Research chemist Ill. Inst. Tech., 1956-59; with Okla. State U., 1960-61, Rauland Corp., 1961-62; research chemist Air Pollution div. USPHS, Cin., 1962-67; san. engr., mgr. instrumentation and automation of waste water systems Nat. Environ. Research Center, EPA, Cin., 1967-78, environ. engr., regional liaison officer Office Research and Devel., Cin., 1978—. Served with USAF, 1952-56. Mem. Instrument Soc. Am. (asso. dir. water and wastewater industries div.), Water Pollution Control Fedn., ASCE. Roman Catholic. Club: Eastern Hills Cycle. Contbr. articles to profl. jours. Office: EPA 26 W St Clair Cincinnati OH 45268

ROESNER, KENDRA DOROTHY, rehab. specialist; b. Chgo., Aug. 6, 1949; d. George F. and Mary (Cavalenes) Hummel; B.A., So. Ill. U., 1972, postgrad., 1978—; m. William K. Roesner, June 2, 1978. Mgr. rehab. services Countryside Center for the Handicapped, Barrington, Ill., 1973-80; rehab. specialist Internat. Rehab. Assos., Inc., 1980-81, Midwest Rehab. Group, Inc., LaGrange, Ill., 1981—. Cert. rehab. counselor; registered social worker. Mem. Nat. Rehab. Assn., Ill. Rehab. Assn., Am. Personnel and Guidance Assn., Human Services Council of Lake County, Assn. Female Execs. Home: 269 Jackson Ct Bartlett IL 60103 Office: 1909 60th St LaGrange IL 60525

ROETHLE, JOHN DONALD, corp. exec.; b. Milw., Mar. 2, 1933; s. Rueben Henry and Helen Irene R.; B.A. in Econs., Loras Coll., 1958; M.B.A., Northwestern U., 1959; m. Janet Y. Zemlicka, Sept. 10, 1960; children—Elizabeth Ann, John Henry, Christopher Charles. Sales and adminstrv. asst. Rexnord, Milw., 1959-61; gen. mgr., treas. Wis. Capital Corp., Milw., 1961-62; v.p. fin. Romar Filter Corp., Milw., 1962-63; exec. v.p. Anderson/Roethle & Assos., Inc., Milw., 1963-70, pres., 1970—; Instr. fin., Marquette U., Milw., 1959-72; lectr. U. Wis., Madison, U. Wis., Milw., Milw. Sch. Engring., 1964-70. Commr., Milw. County Planning Commn., 1972—; fin. chmn. Milw. Tennis Classic, 1976—; bd. dirs. Sacred Heart Rehab. Hosp., 1979—, Friends of the Mus., 1979—; mem. Greater Milw. Com. Mem. Center for Venture Mgmt., Inc. (vice chmn., treas. 1967-75), Inst. Mgmt. Cons. (dir. 1980—), Assn. Mgmt. Cons. (trustee 1979-81). Republican. Episcopalian. Clubs: Univ., Rotary (dir. 1976-79, treas. 1978-79). Contbr. articles to profl. publs.; lectr. in field. Home: 6311 N Berkeley Blvd Whitefish Bay WI 53217 Office: 811 E Wisconsin Ave Milwaukee WI 53202

ROETTGER, KENNETH DAVID, chemist, educator; b. St. Louis, Sept. 24, 1925; s. William August and Tillie (Francis) R.; A.B., Washington U., 1949; M.S., St. Louis U., 1951; Ph.D., Worcester Poly. Inst., 1962; m. Sara Jo Montee, Mar. 3, 1951; children—Montie Jo, Hollie Ann, Vickie Rae, Kurt August, William Earl. Asst. instr. chemistry U. Kans., 1949; teaching fellow St. Louis U., 1949-51; research chemist DuPont Corp., Wilmington, Del., 1951-55; asst. prof. Worcester (Mass.) Poly. Inst., 1955-65; prof. Parsons Coll., 1965-73; vis. prof. St. Louis U., 1973; prof. Mt. Senario Coll., 1974; dir. chemistry Southeastern Coll., West Burlington, Iowa, 1975—. Trustee, Hubbardson (Mass.) Public, Library, 1958-65; mem. Hubbardson Town Council, 1964; police clk., Hubbardson, 1958-62; civil def. dir. Worcester County, Mass., 1962-65. Served with AUS, 1943-46. Decorated Bronze Star, Purple Heart; NSF grantee, 1959-62; HEW grantee, 1969-71; AEC grantee, 1978-80. Mem. Am. Chem. Soc., Am. Forensic Assn., Sigma Xi, Alpha Chi Sigma, Delta Phi Alpha, Phi Kappa Phi, Pi Mu Epsilon. Presbyterian. Clubs: Skeptical Chymists, Midwest Aviators, Beer Can Collectors of Am. Contbr. numerous articles to sci. jours. Home: 502 Bel Aire Fairfield IA 52556 Office: Southeastern Coll West Burlington IA 52655

ROGALSKI, LEONORE GENEVIEVE, chemist; b. Wheeling, Ill., June 28, 1926; d. Felix Joseph and Blanche Genevieve (Gogolewski) R.; B.S., Northwestern U., 1948, M.S., 1956. With Dr. Arnold Wagner Lab., Northwestern U. Med. Sch., 1944-48, IMC Corp., 1952-55; library supr. UOP, Inc., Des Plaines, Ill., 1955—. Mem. Am. Chem. Soc., Am. Inst. Chem. Engrs., Am. Petroleum Inst., Am. Soc. Info. Sci., AAAS. Roman Catholic. Home: 7422 N Claremont Chicago IL 60645 Office: 10 UOP Plaza Des Plaines IL 60016

ROGAN, JOHN BROCKWAY, chem. co. exec.; b. Kansas City, Kans., Sept. 3, 1930; s. John Bartholemew and Ellinor Grace (Ledyard) R.; B.S. with honors, U. Wyo., 1952; Ph.D., U. Calif., Berkeley, 1955; m. Winifred Jane Lytton, Apr. 5, 1966. Research chemist E.I. DuPont de Nemours, Inc., Wilmington, Del., 1955-59; asst. prof. chemistry Colo. State U., Ft. Collins, 1959-62; asso. prof. chemistry U. Nev., Reno., 1962-66; sr. project chemist Amoco Chems. Corp., Whiting, Ind., 1966-69, group leader research and devel., Naperville, Ill., 1969-72, research asso., 1972—. research asso., 1972—. Mem. asso. faculty Ind. U., Gary, 1968-70. Mem. adv. council DuPage area Vocat. Edn. Assn., (Ill.), 1968—. Fellow Calif., Berkeley, Ethyl Corp., U.S. Rubber Co., 1953-55; grantee NSF, 1960. Petroleum Research Fund Am. Chem. Soc., 1963, Desert Research Inst., 1964, U. Nev., 1964. Mem. Am. Chem. Soc., AAAS, Sigma Xi, Phi Kappa Phi, Sigma Tau, Gamma Sigma Epsilon. Contbr. articles to profl. publs. Patentee in field. Office: PO Box 400 Naperville IL 60540

ROGAN, PETER GEORGE, mgmt. cons.; b. Bronx, N.Y., Feb. 26, 1946; s. George Robert and Sarah (Cashman) R.; B.S., Niagara U., 1967; M.H.A., St. Louis U., 1970; Ph.D., U. Iowa, 1973; m. Judith Ann Koltunski, Apr. 5, 1975; children—Robert Cashman, Brian Peter. Asst. supt. St. Vincent Med. Center, N.Y.C., 1967-68; research asst. Center for Labor and Mgmt., Iowa City, 1971-72; instr. Med. Sch., U. Iowa, Iowa City, 1972-73; staff cons. Ernst & Ernst, Chgo., 1974-78; mgr. Ernst & Whinney, Chgo., 1978-81, prin., 1981—. Simmons Co. fellow, 1968. Mem. Am. Coll. Hosp. Adminstrs., Assn. Am. Med. Colls., Cath. Health Assn., Am. Hosp. Assn., Gamma Pi Epsilon. Roman Catholic. Clubs: Union League, Les Gourmets, Beefeater. Office: 150 S Wacker Dr Chicago IL 60606

ROGERS, BRYAN ALLEN, hosp. adminstr.; b. Akron, Ohio, Aug. 2, 1925; s. Jesse I. and Helen O. (Baker) R.; B.A., U. Akron, 1949; M.H.A., Washington U., St. Louis, 1954; m. Jean E. Hoffman, Dec. 29, 1950; children—Mark, Amy. Adminstrv. asst. Methodist Hosp., Indpls., 1954-57, asst. supt., 1957-60, asso. dir. 1960-66, asso. exec. dir., adminstr., 1966-71, exec. v.p., adminstr., 1971-72; adminstr. Toledo Hosp., 1972-77, pres., 1977—; dir. Toledo Trust Co.; charter mem. bus. adv. council U. Toledo Coll. Bus. Adminstrn.; adj. instr. health care adminstrn. Washington U., U. Toledo. Mem. Pub. Health Council, Ohio Dept. Health, 1978—; chmn. Task Force on Cost Effectiveness-Blue Cross, 1978—. Served with AUS, 1943-46. Fellow Am. Coll. Hosp. Adminstrs.; mem. Am. Hosp. Assn., Am. Pub. Health Assn., Toledo Area C. of C. (trustee). Presbyterian. Club: Rotary (Toledo). Home: 4626 Corey Rd Toledo OH 43623 Office: 2142 N Cove Blvd Toledo OH 43606

ROGERS, CHARLES THOMAS, mech. engr.; b. Grand Rapids, Mich., June 13, 1912; s. Charles Erwin and Helen Pearl (Smedley) R.; M.S., Detroit Inst. Tech., 1944; certificate completion engr. tech. orientation course U.S. Army Engr. Sch., 1960; m. Hilda Belle Busey, Aug. 17, 1944. Indsl. engr., Detroit Ordnance Dist., 1941-46; quality control analyst Cadillac Motor car div. Gen. Motors Corp., Detroit, 1948-54; mech. engr. U.S. Army Tank Auto. Command, Warren, Mich., 1954-80. Registered profl. engr., Mich.; recipient fallout shelter analysis certificate Dept. Def., 1968. Mem. Am. Def. Preparedness Assn. (life), Mich. Soc. Profl. Engrs., Nat. Soc. Profl. Engrs., Mich. Assn. Professions, Nat. Assn. Ret. Persons, Nat. Assn. Ret. Fed. Employees. Presbyterian. Clubs: Mason, Order Eastern Star. Home: 10622 Outer Dr W Detroit MI 48223

ROGERS, DANIEL JOHN, clergyman, educator; b. Calumet City, Ill., Feb. 8, 1927; s. Charles and Agnes (Ambrose) R.; B.A. with honors, Loras Coll., 1949; postgrad. St. Meinrad Sch. Theology, 1949-53; M.A. in English, U. Wis., Madison, 1957, Ph.D., 1964. Ordained priest Roman Catholic Ch., 1953; asst. pastor St. Patrick Ch., Cedar Rapids, Iowa, 1953-56, dir. guidance and counseling, 1953-56; mem. faculty Loras Coll., Dubuque, Iowa, 1956—, instr. English, 1957-60, 64-65, asst. prof., 1965-69, asso. prof., 1969-76, prof., 1976—, chmn. dept. English, 1977-80, dir. Center for Human Integration, 1978-79; vis. fellow Pain Clinic, Dept. Anesthesia, Coll. of Medicine, U. Iowa, 1980-81. Mem. Am. Assn. for Higher Edn., Assn. for Gen. and Liberal Studies, MLA, Assn. for Transpersonal Psychology, Am. Soc. Regional Anesthesia, Midwest Pain Soc., Inst. Noetic Scis., Center for Integral Medicine, Delta Epsilon Sigma. Contbr. poetry and articles to periodicals and anthologies.

ROGERS, EDMUND CHENAULT, patent lawyer; b. Louisville, June 8, 1908; s. Charlton Berbard and Linell (Chensulat) R.; B. Engring., Vanderbilt U., 1929; J.D., Georgetown U., 1933; m. Deane Hancock, May 16, 1936; children—Anne (Mrs. David F. Robinson), Eleanor (Mrs. E.R. Crittendon). Tchr., Wallace Sch., Nashville, 1928-29; admitted to D.C. bar, 1932, Mo. bar, 1935; examiner U.S. Patent Office, 1929-33; practice law, Cleve., 1934; asso. L.C. Kingsland, St. Louis, 1935-40; partner firm Rogers, Eilers & Howell and predecessors, St. Louis, 1941—; spl. asst. U.S. atty. gen., 1941. Mem. St. Louis County Human Rights Commn., 1964-70; bd. dirs. Legal Aid Soc., St. Louis; bd. dirs. Mid-County YMCA, 1955-70, chmn., 1960-61; bd. dirs. Grace Hill House, 1956-57; adv. council St. Louis U. Law Sch. Fellow Am. Coll. Trail Lawyers; mem. Am. Bar Assn., Mo. Bar Assn., St. Louis Bar Assn. (chmn. patent sect. 1946), Nat. Council Patent Law Assn., Pi Tau Beta, Beta Theta Pi. Episcopalian (lay reader). Clubs: Clayton Rotary (pres. 1961); Mo. Athletic; Bellerive Country (St. Louis). Home: 2 Bridle Creek Rd Saint Louis MO 63123 Office: 11 S Meramec Saint Louis MO 63105

ROGERS, GEORGE, III, educator; b. Chgo., Jan. 8, 1947; s. George and Gertrude R.; A.A., Wilson City Coll., 1967; B.S., Bethel Coll., 1969; M.Ed., Wichita State U., 1972; Ed.D. candidate U. Ark., 1979; m. Rita Faye Guhr, Aug. 14, 1976; children—Tara Marie, Bret Zachary. Dir. athletics, asst. prof. phys. edn., track coach Bethel Coll., North Newton, Kans., from 1969, now asso. prof. Mem. U.S. Track Coaches Assn., Collegiate Dirs. Athletics, AAHPER. Democrat. Office: Bethel Coll North Newton KS 67117

ROGERS, JOHN RUSSELL, engr.; b. St. Louis, May 12, 1929; s. John Flint and Faye (Russell) R.; A.B., Washington U., St. Louis, 1951; m. Lorraine Esther Klockenbrink, Sept. 15, 1951; children—John Oliver, Gail Joanne. Plant supt. Daybrite Lighting, Inc., Tupelo, Miss., 1959-64; plant mgr. White Rodgers Ltd., Markham, Ont., Can., 1964-66; ops. mgr. Metal Goods Corp., St. Louis, 1966-71; engr., v.p. Ross & Baruzzini, Inc., Cons. Engrs., St. Louis, 1971—. Dir. indsl. div. St. Louis Safety Council, 1968; leader Boy Scout Am., 1963-71, Girl Scouts U.S.A., 1972; dep. gen. conv. Protestant Episcopal Ch., 1976, 79, del. diocesan conv., 1967-79, pres. diocesan standing com., 1975; dir. Episc. Ednl. Center, St. Louis, 1974—; bd. dirs. Episc. Neighborhood Sch., St. Louis, 1974-80, Care and Counseling, 1975; bd. mgrs. Thompson Retreat House, St. Louis, 1975-80. Served to capt., inf. U.S. Army, 1951-54. Registered profl. engr., Mo, Ill. Mem. Assn. Profl. Material Hadling Cons., Internat. Materials Mgmt. Soc., Am. Inst. Indsl. Engrs., Am. Soc. Safety Engrs., Profl. Services Bus. Mgmt. Assn., Cons. Engrs. Council, Res. Officers Assn., Phi Delta Theta. Clubs: Downtown Rotary, Engrs. (St. Louis). Home: 10332 Richview Dr Saint Louis MO 63127 Office: 7912 Bonhomme Ave Saint Louis MO 63105

ROGERS, JOHN THOMAS, III, ins. exec.; b. Champaign County, Ohio, June 2, 1947; s. John Thomas and Leona Frances (Forbes) R.; B.A., Ohio No. U., 1973; student Bur. Criminal Investigation and Identification, London, Ohio, 1970. Dep. sheriff, field dep. Champaign County Sheriff Dept., 1970-72; carpenter Glenn Law, Builder, Urbana, Ohio, 1973-75; dep. sheriff, field dep. Champaign County Sheriff Dept., 1975-76; agt. Roger L. Johnson Ins. Co., Urbana, Ohio, 1976—. Served with USMC, 1973. Mem. Champaign County Ind. Ins. Agts. Assn. (pres.), Nat. Sheriff Assn., Buckeye State Sheriffs Assn., Nat. Rifle Assn., Ohio Gun Collectors Assn., Champaign County Range Officer Assn. Republican. Roman Catholic. Clubs: Optimists, K.C., Fraternal Order Police. Home: 788 Wooddale Dr Urbana OH 43078 Office: 776 Scioto St Urbana OH 43078

ROGERS, JOHN WILLARD, constrn. co. exec.; b. Oak Park, Ill., Dec. 20, 1908; s. Walter Alexander and Julia Margaret (Cushing) R.; student U. Wis., 1926-29; m. Ruth Woods Stiles, Apr. 16, 1933; 1 dau., Diane Rogers Carroll. With Bates & Rogers Constrn. Corp., 1929—; crane fireman, operator, carpenter, Ohio, 1929-31, civil engr., W.Va., 1931-32, foreman, Azusa, Calif., 1933-36, master mechanic, Dover, Ohio, 1936-37, supt., Villa Park, Ill., 1937-38, estimator, Chgo., 1939, tunnel supt., Chambersburg, Pa., 1939-40, div. supt. Kingsbury (Ind.) Ordinance Plant, 1940-41, project supt., Joliet, Ill., Duluth, Minn., 1941-42, Vicksburg, Miss., 1942, gen. supt. Alcan Hwy., Whitehorse, Yukon Ter., Alaska, 1943-45, dir., 1944—, sec., treas., Chgo., 1946-47, v.p., treas., 1948-61, exec. v.p., treas., 1961-67, pres., treas., 1968-79, chmn., chief exec. officer, 1979—, also dir. Bates & Rogers Found. Pres., trustee Glen Ellyn (Ill.) YMCA, 1937-58; mem. Glen Ellyn Sch. Bd., 1950-53; trustee George Williams Coll., 1956—; bd. dirs. Jr. Achievement Chgo.; mem. adv. bd. B.R. Ryall YMCA. Mem. ASCE, Western Soc. Engrs., Am. Inst. Constructors, Cons. Constructors Council, Ohio Contractors Assn. (Hall of Fame), Associated Gen. Contractors Am. (dir.), Asso. Gen. Contractors Ill. (dir.), Builders Assn. Chgo. (dir.), Ill. Legis. Network (chmn.), Nat. Assn. Gen. Contractors (regional chmn. legis. network), Beavers (founding mem.). Republican. Congregationalist. Clubs: Union League Chgo. (active Civic and Arts Found.), Execs., Econ.; Glen Oak Country (Glen Ellyn); Capitol Hill (Washington); Surf (Surfside, Fla.). Office: 600 W Jackson Blvd Chicago IL 60606

ROGERS, JOY JEANNE, psychologist; b. St. Joseph, Mich., Dec. 9, 1942; d. Harold John and Frieda (Ulmer) Rogers; B.A. in Psychology and English, Western Mich. U., 1964; M.A. in Sch. Psychology, 1966, Ed.S., 1966; Ph.D., U. Mich., 1970. Teaching asst. Western Mich. U., 1964-66, part-time instr., 1965-67; clin. psychologist Kalamazoo State Hosp., 1966-68; research asst. Center Research on Learning and Teaching, U. Mich., 1968-70; asst. prof. psychology Purdue U., 1970-73; asso. prof. psychology Loyola U., Chgo., 1972—; cons. in field. Recipient Purdue U. award for excellence in undergraduate teaching, 1971. Mem. Am. Psychol. Assn., Am. Ednl. Research Assn., Nat. Soc. for Programmed Instn., AAUP. Contbr. articles to profl. jours. Home: 520 Chase St Park Forest IL 60466 Office: Loyola Univ 820 N Michigan Ave Chicago IL 60611

ROGERS, JUDY ANN, accountant; b. Pontiac, Mich., May 25, 1948; d. Charles Michael and Virginia (Perna) Crickon; drug sci. scholar, U. Mich., 1965; B.A. summa cum laude, Oakland U., Rochester, Mich., 1978; postgrad. Wayne State U. Law Sch., 1978-79; m. Ronald Richard Rogers, Aug. 30, 1967; 1 dau., Anne Michelle. Office mgr. Holforty Assos. Inc., Rochester, 1970-76; adminstr. asst. to controller Perry Drug Stores, Inc., Pontiac, 1976-78; office mgr. Artcraft Blueprint Co., Pontiac, 1978-81; plant acct. Gates Rubber Co., Pontiac, 1981—. Mem. Orion Twp. Environ. Task Force; active local Republican Party. Walter Reuther Meml. Fund scholar, 1978. Mem. Nat. Assn. Exec. Females (v.p. programs univs. women 1981), Nat. Assn. Accts., Am. Bus. Women, Mich. Profl. Women's Network. Club: Deer Lake Racquet. Contbr. to The Poet and Our Twentieth Century's Greatest Poems. Home: 4383 Morgan Rd Pontiac MI 48055 Office: 3700 S Lapeer Rd Pontiac MI 48057

ROGERS, JUSTIN TOWNER, JR., utility co. exec.; b. Sandusky, O., Aug. 4, 1929; s. Justin Towner and Barbara Eloise (Larkin) R.; A.B. cum laude, Princeton, 1951; J.D., U. Mich., 1954; m. Virginia Logan Luscombe, May 6, 1955; children—Sarah Luscombe, Anne Larkin, Justin Towner, III. Admitted to Ohio bar, 1954; atty. Wright, Harlor. Purpus Morris & Arnold, Columbus, O., 1956-58; atty. Ohio Edison CO., Akron, 1958-61, gen. coordinator personnel relations, 1961-67, div. mgr. Springfield. (O.) div., 1967-70. v.p., 1970-78, exec. v.p., 1978-79, pres., 1980—, also dir.; chmn. bd., dir. Pa. Power Co., New Castle; dir. 1st Nat. Bank Akron. Past pres. and trustee Akron Child Guidance Center, Akron Community Trusts; past chmn. Akron Associated Health Agys.; trustee, v.p. Akron Regional Devel. Bd.; trustee Akron Gen. Med. Center; mem. adv. com. Coll. Arts and Scis., U. Akron; past chmn. U. Akron Assos.; dir. Akron Devel. Corp., Akron Priority Corp. Served with AUS, 1954-56. Mem. Am., Ohio bar assns. Ohio Electric Utility Inst. (dir.), Edison Electric Inst. (dir.), Phi Delta Phi, Beta Gamma Sigma (hon.). Clubs: Akron City, Portage Country, Mayflower (Akron); Princeton (N.Y.C.); Capitol Hill (Washington). Office: 76 S Main St Akron OH 44308

ROGERS, KELLY WALTER, internat. transp. co. exec.; b. Chgo., July 26, 1930; s. Kelly Howard and Sophie Dolores (Bednarczyk) R.; student Chgo. and Calvert City (Ky.) pub. schs., 1936-48; m. Celeste Fern Mykol, Oct. 4, 1962; children—Derrick, Karla, Blake. Truck driver various firms, 1957-61; regional mgr. northwestern states Republic Van Lines, Seattle, 1961-63; regional mgr., western area Greyhound Van Lines div. Greyhound, Corp., Los Angeles, 1964-71; exec. v.p., gen. mgr. Hawaiian Hauling Service, Honolulu, 1971-74; asst. gen. mgr. Atlas Van Lines Internat., Evansville, Ind., 1974, v.p. and gen. mgr., 1974-76, exec. v.p., 1976, pres., 1976—. Served with U.S. Army, 1948-53. Named Boss of Year, Internat. Secs. Assn., 1976; commd. Ky. Col., 1976. Mem. Nat. Def. Transp. Assn., Household Goods Forwarders Assn. Am., Inc. Republican. Baptist. Club: Oak Meadow Golf & Country. Home: 410 Kings Valley Rd Evansville IN 47711 Office: 1212 St George Rd Evansville IN 47711

ROGERS, LAWRENCE H., II, gen. mgmt. cons.; b. Trenton, N.J., Sept. 6, 1921; s. Norman Tallman and Nancy (Titus) R.; B.A., Princeton U., 1943; postgrad. Harvard U., 1963; m. Suzanne Long; children—Hallie, Suzanne, Lawrence H. III, Campbell, Natalie, Christian. Builder, Sta. WSAZ-TV Inc., 1949; with Taft Broadcasting Co., Cin., 1960-76, pres., 1963-76; pres., chief exec. officer Omega Communications, Inc., Sta. WOFL-TV 35, Orlando, Fla., 1977—; chmn. bd. Devel. Communications Inc., Cin., 1976—; dir. Tech. Service Corp., InterOcean Ins. Co., Cin., Oak Industries, Inc., Cin. Fin. Corp., Cardinal Fund, Inc., Cardinal Govt. Securites Fund,

Columbus, Ohio; chmn. bd. dirs. Cin. br. Fed. Res. Bank of Cleve. Past mem. TV Code Rev. Bd.; treas. TV Bur. Advt., then chmn. bd. dirs.; vice chmn. bd. NBC-TV Affiliates; v.p., dir. Assn. Maximum Service Telecaster, Washington; mem. info. com. Nat. Assn. Broadcasters, then editorial com.; mem. TV Code Rev. Bd. Chmn. trustees distbn. com. Greater Cin. Found.; former mem. W.Va. Econ. Devel. Agy.; bd. dirs. Cin. Council World Affairs, Theatre Devel. Fund; gen. chmn. Greater Cin. Fine Arts Fund. Served to capt. F.A., AUS, World War II; ETO. Recipient Disting. Service award U.S. Jaycees, 1956. Mem. Washington Broadcasting Club, Internat. Radio-TV Execs. Soc., Newcomen Soc. Clubs: Queen City (Cin.); Camargo; Brook (N.Y.C.); Rolling Rock (Ligonier, Pa.); Univ. (Orlando, Fla.).

ROGERS, MICHAEL K, state senator, coal co. exec.; b. Winchester, Ind., June 14, 1941; s. Robert E. and Margaret Pauline (Kennedy) R.; B.S. in Radio and TV, Ind. U., 1964; M.A. in Journalism, Ball State U., 1970; m. Nancy Ann Williams, May 17, 1964. News dir. Sta. WCTW, New Castle, Ind., 1964-67; asst. dir. radio and TV Ball State U., Muncie, Ind., 1967-71; v.p. Howard S. Wilcox, Inc., Indpls., 1971-75; dir. communications AMAX Coal Co., Indpls., 1975—; rep. Ind. Legislature, 1966-72; mem. Ind. State Senate, 1981—. Sec. New Castle Mayor's Human Rights Commn., 1964-67; chmn. Wilbur Wright State Birthplace Commn., 1970-73. Recipient Journalism award Ball State U., 1971; named Sagamore of the Wabash, 1974, Ky. col., 1977. Mem. Sigma Delta Chi. Republican. Quaker. Clubs: Elks (New Castle); Columbia (Indpls.). Contbr. articles on legis. secrecy to periodicals. Office: 105 S Meridian St Indianapolis IN 46206

ROGERS, PAUL W., chewing gum co. exec.; b. Toronto, Ont., Can., Jan. 20, 1926; s. John Franklyn and Elsie Mildred (Johnston) R.; ed. public schs.; m. Antonia Thompson, Mar. 6, 1965; children—Elyse, John, Mary. Div. gen. mgr. Alberto Culver Co., Melrose Park, Ill., 1961-72; v.p. Amurol Products Co., Naperville, Ill., 1972-73, pres., chief exec. officer, 1973-79, chmn., 1979—, also dir.; v.p. Wm. Wrigley Jr. Co., Chgo., 1979—, also dir.; chmn., dir. Wrigley Can., Inc., Toronto, 1980—; pres., chief exec. officer, dir. Zeno Mfg. Co., Chgo., 1981—; pres. Amurol Bldg. Corp., Chgo., 1981—. Served with RCAF, 1943-45. Home: 225D N Kenilworth Ave Oak Park IL 60302 Office: 410 N Michigan Ave Chicago IL 60611

ROGERS, RAYMOND EARL, mktg. exec.; b. St. Louis, Sept. 17, 1941; s. Ralph Raymond and Mary Louise (Wright) R.; B.J., U. Mo., 1963, M.A., 1973; m. Carolyn Jeanne Martines, Sept. 7, 1963; children—Mark, Kent. Asst. mgr. pub. info. and bank relations Fed. Res. Bank, St. Louis, 1966; mgr. advt. and pub. relations Credit Systems, Inc., St. Louis, 1968-70; dir. advt. and pub. relations Bank Bldg. Corp., St. Louis, 1970-80; v.p., account exec. Frank Block Assos., St. Louis, 1980—. Served to capt. U.S. Army, 1964-66. Mem. Bus. Profl. Advt. Assn. (pres. St. Louis 1975), Pub. Relations Soc., Advt. Club. Republican. Methodist. Office: 212 N Kingshighway Saint Louis MO 63108

ROGERS, ROBERT LEE, physician; b. Sabetha, Kans., Jan. 29, 1930; s. William Henry and Lora B. (Haynes) R.; B.A., Kans. U., 1952, M.D., 1955; m. Marjory Elaine Bauerle, Aug. 10, 1952; children—Clark William, Hugh Alan, Emily Sue. Intern, Mpls. Gen. Hosp., 1955-56; staff Gelvin-Haughey Clinic, Concordia, Kans., 1958-60; resident in ENT, Kans. U. Med. Center, Kansas City, 1960-63; practice medicine, specializing in otolaryngology Otolaryngic Med. Group, Kansas City, Mo., 1963—, v.p., 1968—; asso. clin. prof. ENT, Kans. U. Med. Center, 1964—; staff and chief ENT, Research Med. Center, Menorah, Bapt., St. Joseph hosps. Served with U.S. Army, 1956-58. Mem. Jackson County Med. Soc., Mo. Med. Soc., AMA, Kansas City Soc. Ophthalmology and Otolaryngology, Am. Soc. for Head and Neck Surgery, ACS, Am. Soc. Otology, Rhinology and Laryngology, Phi Beta Kappa, Alpha Omega Alpha. Republican. Lutheran. Club: Indian Hills Country. Contbr. articles in field to profl. jours. Office: 6724 Troost St Kansas City MO 64131

ROGERS, ROSENA P., educator; b. Chgo.; d. Joseph Everett and Sarah Ann (Ledford) R.; B.A. in Elem. Edn., Chgo. State U., 1969; M.A. in Ednl. Supervision and Adminstrn., Roosevelt U., 1979. Sec., VA Regional Office, Chgo., 1959-68; tchr. 3d grade Chgo. Bd. Edn., 1970—; tutor Austin Presbyterian Ch.; fin. sec. Chgo. chpt. Ledford, Williams, Rogers Family Reunion, Inc. Mem. Assn. Supervision and Curriculum Devel., Nat. Urban League, NAACP. Home: 314 N Waller Chicago IL 60644 Office: 214 N Lavergne Chicago IL 60644

ROGERS, THOMAS KAY, corporate ednl. adminstr.; b. Lorain, Ohio, May 4, 1933; s. Ralph Clark and Alice (Kay) R.; B.S. in Edn., Ohio U., 1957, M.Ed., 1958; postgrad. John Carrol U., 1962, Wayne State U., 1961; m. Betty Ann Kovacs, Apr. 24, 1954; children—Thomas K., David A., Robert D. Grad. asst. Ohio U., Athens, 1957-58; tchr., coach Warrensville (Ohio) Heights Schs., 1958-64; dist. sales mgr. Brodhead-Garrett Co., Cuyahoga Heights, Ohio, 1965-66, ednl. cons., 1967—; speaker, lectr. in field. Trustee Walsh Jesuit High Sch., 1975—. Served with U.S. Army, 1953-55. Mem. Am. Sch. Bus. Offcls., Am. Vocat. Assn., Am. Indsl. Arts Assn., Edn. Industry Assn. (pres. 1976), Ednl. Exhibitors Assn. (pres. 1977, 78), Epsilion Pi Tau, Phi Delta Kappan, Iota Lamba Sigma. Contbr. articles to profl. jours. Home: 130 Pickwick Dr Northfield OH 44067 Office: 4560 E 71st St Cleveland OH 44105

ROGERS, VAN RENSSELAER, adminstrv. and sales cons.; b. nr. Lexington, Ky., Jan. 9, 1914; s. Edgar Alfred and Nellie Estella (Burton) R.; grad. Cleve. Inst. Art, 1937; m. Ruth Charlotte Reichelt, Aug. 3, 1941; 1 son, Peter Van. Commd. sculptor Walt Disney Enterprises, Hollywood, Calif., 1937-38; co-founder Rogers Bennett Studios, Cleve., 1938; pres., owner Rogers Display Studios div. NESCO, Inc. (now Rogers Displays Inc.), Cleve., 1959—; profl. sculptor, artist, designer, painter. Asst. registrar John Huntington Poly. Inst., Cleve., 1938-41. Chmn. Zoning Commn., Russell Twp., Geauga County, Ohio, 1974. Served to lt. comdr. USNR, 1942-46. Mem. Exhibit Designers and Producers Assn., Nat. Trade Show Exhibitor Assn. (founder, citation as Godfather of orgn. 1977), Archaeol. Soc. Ohio, Dunham Tavern Soc. Collectors, Ohio Hist. Soc., Geauga County Hist. Soc., Russell Twp. Hist. Soc., Nat. Trust Hist. Preservation, Found. Ill. Archeology, North and South Skirmish Assn., Nat. Muzzle Loading Rifle Assn., Greater Cleve. Growth Assn., Western Reserve Hist. Soc., Nat. Hist. Soc., Ohio Acad. History, Imperial German Mil. Collectors Assn., Great Lakes Hist. Soc. Clubs: Hon. Order Ky. Cols.; Masons (32 deg.), K.T.; Advt. (Cleve.). Home: 8230 Fairmount Rd Box 147 Novelty OH 44072 Office: Rogers Displays Inc 26470 Lakeland Blvd Cleveland OH 44132

ROGERS, WALTER EUGENE, educator; b. Chgo., June 5, 1922; s. Walter Eugene and Olivette (Dougan) R.; A.B., Lincoln U., 1948; M.S.W., Loyola U., 1959; m. Alpha Spikner, Sept. 12, 1948; 1 dau., Pier Camille. Social worker Gary (Ind.) Public Schs., 1961-71, adminstr., 1973—; dir. Upward Bound Project Purdue U., W. Lafayette, Ind., 1971-73; asst. prof. dept. sociology Ind. U. and Valparaiso (Ind.) U.; cons. Midsouth Health Corp., 1974—. Vol. Am. Cancer Soc. program, 1976—. Served with U.S. Army, 1943-46. Decorated Bronze Star. Mem. Nat. Assn. Social Workers, Phi Delta Kappa. Presbyterian. Home: 37 Elm St Park Forest IL 60466 Office: North Lembke Hall #3 Valparaiso IN 46437

ROGNAN, LLOYD NORMAN, artist, illustrator; b. Chgo., June 14, 1923; s. John and Gertrude Sophia (Hagen) R.; student Am. Acad. Art, 1941, 50, 51; diploma Acad. de la grande Chamiere, 1949; m. Sylvia Marcella Erickson, July 18, 1953; children—Bruce Byron, Cindy Lou. Cover artist French edit. Ellery Queen, Paris, France, 1947-49; sci. fiction cover artist Greenleaf Publs., Evanston, Ill., 1956-58; with Meyer and Booth Studio, Chgo., 1958-61; biol. artist Golden Books Press, N.Y.C., 1961-63; cartoonist United Card Co., Rolling Meadows, Ill., 1966-71; art dir. Gallant Greetings, Chgo., 1972; calendar artist Brown & Bigelow, St. Paul, 1976-79, Baumgarth, Brown & Bigelow, 1979—; with Saga, Inc., ltd. edits. Western prints Albuquerque, 1977—; art dir., creative editor United Card Co., Arlington Hts., Ill., 1978—. Art counsellor Boy Scouts Am. Served with U.S. Army, 1943-46; ETO. Decorated Purple Heart. Home and studio: 3620 Linneman St Glenview IL 60025

ROGOL, HEIDI SCHNITMAN, cons. engring. co. ofcl.; b. New Haven, Jan. 17, 1955; d. Morton Everett and Florence (Niederman) Schnitman; B.S., So. Conn. State Coll., 1976; postgrad. Northeastern Ill. U., 1979—; m. Charles S. Rogol, July 4, 1976. Behavior disorders tchr. Spl. Edn. Dist. Lake County, Lake Zurich (Ill.) Jr. High Sch., 1977-79; office mgr. Storer Cable TV, Des Plaines, Ill., 1979-80; acctg. clk. Wiss, Janney, Elstner & Assos., Northbrook, Ill., 1980—. Sec., ednl. cons. Children's Channel TV Assn., 1980—. Mem. Council for Exceptional Children, Am. Council for Better Broadcasting, Hadassah. Jewish. Home: Apt 207 9374 Landings Ln Des Plaines IL 60016

ROGOSHESKE, WALTER F., justice Minn. Supreme Ct.; b. Sauk Rapids, Minn., July 12, 1914; student St. Cloud Tchrs. Coll., 1932-33, Valparaiso U., 1933-34; B.S., U. Minn., 1937, LL.B., 1939; LL.D. (hon.), William Mitchell Coll. Law; m. Dorothy Heywood, 1940; 5 children. Gen. practice law, Sauk Rapids, 1940-50; mem. Minn. Ho. of Reps., 1943-49; dist. judge, Minn., 1950-62; asso. justice Minn. Supreme Ct., 1962-80; adj. prof. U. Minn. Law Sch., 1981—. Former chmn. Mpls.-St. Paul Met. Airports Commn. Served in World War II. Fellow Am. Bar Found.; mem. Am. Bar Assn. (chmn. adv. com. on prosecution and def. functions, project on standards for criminal justice, council sect. criminal justice). Home: 138 Canabury Ct Saint Paul MN 55117 Office: Minn Supreme Ct Bldg State Capitol Saint Paul MN 55105

ROGUS, FRANCES AGNES (MRS. HENRY JOSEPH ROGUS), horse trainer, driver, breeder; b. Chgo., Jan. 11, 1922; d. Albert and Agnes (Murzyn) Wojnicki; student Triton Coll., 1968, 74, 78, 80, 81, Chgo. Conservatory of Music, 1950-52; m. Henry Joseph Rogus, June 6, 1942; children—Susan Barbara Rogus Swatek, William Henry, Nancy Rose Rogus Shields, Joseph Guy, Mary Jane Hope Rogus Kucia, Mark Andrew, Margot Ann. Code clk. War Dept., Q.M.C., Transp. Corp., Tracy, Calif., 1943-45; owner, tchr. ballet classes Sch. of Dance, Westchester, Ill., 1958; sec. to personnel dir. Alberto-Culver Co., Melrose Park, Ill., 1962; actress in Music Man, Temple Theatre, Westchester, 1961, Guys and Dolls, 1963, Pajama Game, 1964; sec. Oak Brook Sch. of Horsemanship, Oakbrook, Ill., 1967; owner harness horses, Westchester, 1964—, trainer harness horses, Chgo., 1968—, standardbred horse breeder, Harvard, Ill., 1968—. Patron, DuPage Ballet. Bd. dirs. Divine Infant Guild, 1961-63; ofcl. Ill. Girls High Sch. Assn. Mem. Hinsdale Community Artists, Bus. and Profl. Women's Club, U.S. Trotting Assn., Ill., Ky. harness horseman's assns., Internat. Platform Assn. Clubs: Variety, Polish Am. Cultural (constn. com.), Chgo. Zephers Track (dir.). Address: 1406 Gardner Rd Westchester IL 60153

ROGUS, JOSEPH FRANCIS, educator; b. N.Y.C., Dec. 31, 1938; s. Joseph Stanley and Margaret R.; B.S., U. Dayton, 1960; M.Ed., Miami U., Ohio, 1962; Ph.D., Ohio U., 1968; m. Grace Roberta Lerch, Aug. 22, 1959; children—Kevin, Christopher, Peter, Susan, Timothy, Daniel. Tchr., elem. schs., Dayton, Ohio, 1959-64; expeditor fed. programs Dayton Public Schs., 1964-65, tchr. cons., prin., 1966-69, asst. supt. instrn., 1969-72; asso. prof. edn. Cleve. State U., 1972-79, prof., 1979-81; Peter Kuntz prof. edn. U. Dayton, 1981—; cons. schs. systems. Recipient Sr. Disting. Faculty award Cleve. State U., 1976. Mem. Am. Assn. Sch. Adminstrs., Assn. Supervision and Curriculum Devel., Nat. Assn. Elem. Prins., Phi Delta Kappa. Contbr. articles to profl. jours. Home: 6854 Morrow Dr Dayton OH 45415 Office: Office Ednl Services Coll Edn U Dayton Dayton OH 45469

ROHAN, MICHAEL EDWARD, mfg. co. ofcl.; b. St. Louis, May 29, 1943; s. Edward John and Dorothy Vera (Bernhardt) R.; B.S., U. Mo., 1965; m. Patricia Ann Rickard, June 25, 1966; children—Jennifer Christine, Suzanne Elizabeth. Copywriter to account supr. Gen. Electric Co., N.Y.C., 1971-72; advt. projects mgr. Agrl. div. Monsanto Co., St. Louis, 1972, advt./sales promotion mgr., 1973-80, dir. corp. advt. programs, 1980—. Served with USAF, 1965-70. Decorated D.F.C., Air medals (8). Mem. Nat. Agri-Mktg. Assn. (advt. awards 1977, nat. award 1977), Assn. Nat. Advertisers, Am. Mgmt. Assn., Bus. Profl. Advt. Assn. Democrat. Episcopalian. Office: A3NA 800 N Lindbergh Blvd Saint Louis MO 63166

ROHLFER, CHARLES RANDOLPH, accountant; b. Medford, Oreg., Nov. 27, 1943; S. Charles William and Selma Lee (Kramer) R.; B.S., U. Evansville (Ind.), 1967; postgrad. Ind. U., 1967-68; m. Martha Louise Schroeder, Aug. 9, 1975. Acct., Arthur Andersen & Co., St. Louis, 1965-68; sr. acct. Gaither, Hortin & Kowler, Evansville, 1970-73; partner Gaither, Koewler, Rohlfer, Luckett & Co., Evansville, 1974—; dir. Complas Industries, Inc. Bd. dirs. Evansville chpt. A.R.C., 1972—; bd. dirs. Evansville Philharmonic Orch. Corp., 1974—, treas., 1976—; mem. fin. and budget com. Evansville Roman Catholic Diocese, 1976-77; bd. dirs. Ind. State U.-Evansville Campus Ministry, Inc., 1971—, treas., 1971-76, pres., 1976-78; mem. allocations com. United Way of Southwestern Ind., 1972-75, chmn. bus. div., 1979; mem. Newburgh (Ind.) Econ. Devel. Commn., 1974-77, v.p., 1976-77; participant Leadership Evansville, 1976; mem. adv. bd. St. Mary's Med. Center, 1979—. Served with AUS, 1968-70. Decorated Army Commendation medal. Mem. Am. Inst. C.P.A.'s, Ind. Assn. C.P.A.'s, Nat. Assn. Accts., Evansville C. of C. Republican. Clubs: Evansville Country, Petroleum. Home: 4200 Williamsburg Rd Evansville IN 47711 Office: 111 Main St Evansville IN 47708

ROHLFING, STEPHEN ROY, pharm. co. exec.; b. Toledo, July 25, 1936; s. Stephen Fredrick and Jennie (Stout) R.; B.S., Bowling Green U., 1958; M.S., Miami U., Ohio, 1960; Ph.D., Western Res. U., 1965; m. Janet Lois Geithman, Aug. 15, 1959; children—Valerie Jean, Curtice Andrew. Asst. prof. microbiology Chgo. Med. Sch., 1965-69; sr. microbiologist Minn. Mining & Mfg. Co., St. Paul, 1969-72, research specialist Riker Labs., 1972-75, supr., 1975-78, project leader, antiinfective drug research, 1978—; asst. prof. U. Minn., Mpls., 1973-81, asso. prof., 1981—. Mem. Am. Soc. for Microbiology, AAUP, Brit. Soc. for Antimicrobial Chemotherapy. Lutheran. Club: N. Star Ski Touring. Contbr. articles in field to profl. jours. Home: 1081 Cedarwood Dr Woodbury MN 55125 Office: Minnesota Mining & Mfg Bldg 270-2 Saint Paul MN 55144

ROHLING, PAUL VERNON, stainless steel utensils mfg. co. exec.; b. Kenosha, Wis., Mar. 6, 1917; s. Mads Lange and Anna Katrina (Egmose) R.; B.S. in Mech. Engring., U. Wis., 1944; m. Hazel Marie Sorensen, July 1, 1944; children—Paul, Joanne. Methods engr., Vollrath Co., Sheboygan, Wis., 1944-46, chief engr., 1947-51, asst. factory mgr., 1951-59, factory mgr., 1959-60, mfg. v.p., 1960-64, sr. v.p., 1964-65, exec. v.p., 1965-68, pres., 1968—, chmn. bd., chief exec. officer, 1976—. Registered profl. engr., Wis. Mem. Soc. Mfg. Engrs. (pres. 1952-53), Assn. Commerce (dir. 1966-68), Sheboygan Econ. Club. Lutheran (mem. council 1948-54, 56-60, 67-71). Club: Country (Sheboygan). Home: 1244 Riverview Dr Sheboygan WI 53081 Office: 1236 N 18th St Sheboygan WI 53081

ROHMANN, HERBERT KURT, sch. prin.; b. Chgo., May 31, 1935; s. Karl Theodore and Martha Helen (Betshowa) R.; B.Sc., Bob Jones U., 1961; M.Sc., No. Ill. U., 1965; cert. adv. studies Concordia Coll., 1979; Ph.D., Pacific Western U., 1981; m. Renate Irene Zilian, June 27, 1959; children—Heidi, Timothy, Karen, John, Mark. Tchr. elem. sch., Forest Park, Ill., 1962-64; Plymouth Brethren missionary, Nigeria, 1965-67, 70-72; tchr., elem. sch. Oak Park, Ill., 1967-79, asst. prin., 1969-70, prin., summer 1970, tchr. lang. arts, social studies, 1972-73, asst. prin., 1973-76, prin. Irving Sch., 1976—. Organizer Mansfield (Ohio) Christian Sch., 1961. Pres., Abundant Life Ministries, 1978—. Served with U.S. Army, 1954-56. Recipient award for excellence in adminstrn. Ill. Supt. Public Instrn., 1974. Mem. Oak Park Prins. Assn. (pres. 1980-81), Assn. Supervision and Curriculum Devel. Home: 124 Franklin St River Forest IL 60305 Office: 1125 Cuyler St Oak Park IL 60304

ROHRBACH, MAX SIDNEY, mfg. co. exec.; b. Heidenheim, Germany, July 10, 1914; s. Sigmund R. and Mathilde (Sachsendorfer) R.; came to U.S., 1936; naturalized, 1941; Abitur degree, Real & Handelschule, Marktbreit am Main, 1930; student Hoehere Preussische Textil Fachschule, Munchen-Gladbach-Rhein, Germany, 1931-33; m. Susan Bendheim, Apr. 11, 1954; children—Monica, Stuart. With Cohn-Hall-Marx, N.Y.C., 1938-67, nat. sales mgr.; pres., founder Fabric Distributers, Inc., Cin., 1968—, Fabric Merchants, Inc., Cin., 1968—, Fabric Circle U.S.A., Cin., 1968—; pres. Monique Fabric & Daytex Outlet Stores, Dayton, Ohio, 1976—. Bd. dirs. Jewish Welfare Fund, Cin., 1975-78; bd. dirs. Jewish Family Service, Cin., Jewish Nat. Fund; nat. bd. dirs. HIAS; bd. dirs. Bonds for Israel, Cin., 1975-77; founder cert. Center Internat. Security Studies, Am. Security Council Edn. Found. Served as spl. agent counter Intelligence Corps, U.S. Army, 1941-44. Decorated 2 Invasion Arrowheads, Battle Stars, etc. Mem. Internat. Council of Shopping Centers, Nat. Mass Retail Inst., Am. Security Council, Prime Ministers Club of Israel. Clubs: Capitol Hill of Washington, Crest Hills Country, New Hope Congregation. Home: 6673 E Farm Acres Rd Cincinnati OH 45237 Office: 8911 Rossash Rd Cincinnati OH 45236

ROHRBACHER, DAVID JONATHAN, lawyer; b. Toledo, Ohio, Jan. 8, 1949; s. Vernon Eugene and Hazel Jane R.; student U. Toledo, 1967-68; B.A., Manchester Coll., 1971; J.D., U. Toledo, 1974; m. Robin S. DeVries, Sept. 16, 1978. Admitted to Ohio bar, 1975, Supreme Ct. State of Ohio bar, U.S. Dist. Cts. of Ohio bar, 1975, U.S. Supreme Ct. bar, 1980; asso. firm Cobourn, Smith, Rohrbacher & Gibson, Toledo, 1975-76, partner, 1976—. Pres. bd. trustees Three Meadows Property Owners Assn. Mem. Am. Bar Assn., Ohio Bar Assn., Ohio Def. Assn., Am. Bar Found., Toledo Law Assn. (trustee), Def. Research Inst. Clubs: Toledo, Mich. Squash Raquets Assn. Home: 880 Sandalwood St W Perrysburg OH 43551 Office: 624 Adams St Toledo OH 43604

ROHRBOUGH, ROBERT PAUL, computer data service co. exec.; b. Omaha, June 25, 1946; s. Alexander Tully and Ethel Frances (Paxton) R.; B.S., Iowa State U., 1968; M.B.A., U. Nebr., 1980; m. Louise Ann Lewis, Aug. 12, 1978. With Control Data Corp., Mpls., 1968-72; mgr. computer services Henningson, Durham and Richardson Systems, Inc., Omaha, 1972-75; v.p. Systems Cons., Inc., Omaha, 1975-77; pres. Rohrbough System Design, Inc., 1977-78; systems mktg. rep. The Service Bur. Co., Omaha, 1978-80; sr. account exec. HDR Systems, Inc., Omaha, 1980—. Mem. Assn. Computing Machinery, Alpha Iota Delta. Republican. Presbyterian (deacon). Clubs: Omaha Sports, Calvin. Home: 9215 Dorcas St Omaha NE 68124 Office: 8404 Indian Hills Dr Omaha NE 68114

ROHRER, HAROLD HUGH, physician; b. Junction City, Kans., Sept. 19, 1934; s. Harold Adelbert and Helen Monica (Whitehair) R.; student St. Louis U., 1953-56, M.D., 1960; M.P.H., U. Mich., 1965; m. Barbara Marie Mobus, Sept. 24, 1960; children—Amy, Christopher, Mary Helen, Roger. Intern, Walter Reed Gen. Hosp., Washington, 1960-61; dir. Jackson County Health Dept., Murphysboro, Ill., 1965-68; resident in public health, DuPage County, Ill., 1968-69; dir. Comprehensive Health Center, San Luis, Colo., 1969-70; dir. El Paso County Health Dept., Colorado Springs, Colo., 1970-71; dir. Peoria City (Ill.)/County Health Dept., 1971—; asso. clin. prof. U. Ill. Coll. Medicine; lectr. U. Ill. Sch. Public Health. Served to capt. USAR, 1960-63. Decorated Army Commendation medal. Recipient Margaret D. Lewis Pioneer award Nat. Assn. Home Health Agencies, 1977. Diplomate Nat. Bd. Med. Examiners, Am. Bd. Preventive Medicine. Fellow Am. Coll. Preventive Medicine; mem. Am. Public Health Assn., AMA, Ill. Med. Soc., Peoria County Med. Soc., Roman Catholic. Home: 5632 N Isabell St Peoria IL 61614 Office: 2116 N Sheridan Rd Peoria IL 61604

ROHRMAN, DOUGLASS FREDERICK, lawyer; b. Chgo., Aug. 10, 1941; s. Frederick Alvin and Velma Elizabeth (Birdwell) R.; A.B., Duke U., 1963; J.D., Northwestern U., 1966. Admitted to Ill. bar, 1966; legal coordinator Nat. Communicable Disease Center, Altanta, 1966-68; asso. firm Keck, Mahin & Cate, Chgo., 1968-73, partner, 1973—; exec. v.p., dir. Kerogen Oil Co., 1967—. Vice chmn., commr. Ill. Food and Drug Commn., 1970-72. Served as lt. USPHS, 1966-68. Mem. Am., Chgo. (chmn. com. on food and drug law 1972-73), 7th Circuit bar assns., Am. Soc. Law and Medicine, Selden Soc. Democrat. Episcopalian. Clubs: Legal, Union League (Chgo.). Co-author: Commercial Liability Risk Management and Insurance, 2 vols., 1978. Contbr. articles on law to various profl. jours. Home: 2666 Prairie Ave Evanston IL 60201 Office: 8300 Sears Tower Chicago IL 60606

ROHRS, DENNIS KERLIN, educator; b. Johnson, Nebr., Nov. 26, 1929; s. Vernon Kerlin and Lena Ellen (Rademacher) R.; B.M.E., U. Nebr., 1951, Mus.M., 1952; Ph.D., U. Iowa, 1963; m. Margaret Ritchie Rohrs, Aug. 19, 1950; children—Roxann, Elaine, Rex. Research asst. U. Iowa, 1957-58; instr. music Midland Coll., Fremont, Nebr., 1954-57; asst. prof. music Ball State U., Muncie, Ind., 1958-59; asso. prof. music Manchester Coll., North Manchester, Ind., 1959-63; prof. music, dir. bands U. Wis., Whitewater, 1963-79, chmn. music dept., 1974-79; band clinician and adjudicator; guest condr. Regents Scholar, 1947-51. Mem. Music Educators Nat. Conf. (life), Phi Mu Alpha Sinfonia (gov. Province 29 1970-76). Home: Route 1 Oak Clay Rd Whitewater WI 53190 Office: Coll of Arts U Wis Whitewater 800 W Main St Whitewater WI 53190

ROHRS, DONALD LEE, portable lighting mfg. co. exec.; b. Omaha, Sept. 8, 1940; s. John Walter and Helen Virginia (Buck) R.; student U.S. Air Force Academy, 1959-62, Art Center Coll. of Design,

1962-63; B.F.A. in Indsl. Design, Kansas City Art Inst., 1971; m. Barbara Suzanne Clarke, June 4, 1977; children—Robert, Paul, Gretchen, Sara. Designer, Lear Jet Corp., Wichita, Kans., 1963; project supr. Jensen Engring. Co., Inc., Kansas City, Mo., 1963-73; dir. engring. Collins Industries, Inc., Hutchinson, Kans., 1973-76; dir. mktg. and product devel. Nicholl Bros., Inc., Kansas City, Mo., 1976—; instr. bus. mgmt. Hutchinson Jr. Coll., 1975-76; guest lectr. various univs. Mem. Soc. Automotive Engrs., Soc. Plastics Engrs., Indsl. Designers Soc. Am., Porsche Club Am. Republican. Home: 9913 Wedd Dr Overland Park KS 66212 Office: Nicholl Bros Inc 1204 W 27th St Kansas City MO 64108

ROITZ, EDWARD JOSEPH, petroleum distbg. co. exec., state senator; b. Joplin, Mo., Mar. 18, 1955; s. Anton F. and Mary F. (Fleming) R.; student acctg. Pittsburg (Kans.) State U., 1976; m. Carla J. Stovall, Dec. 1981. Pres., Roitz Oil Co., Inc., Pittsburg, 1972—; mem. Kans. Senate from 13th Dist., 1980—. Bd. dirs. Crawford County Heart Assn., 1982. Recipient Outstanding Young Kansan award Pittsburg Jaycees, 1982. Mem. Nat. Republican Legislators Assn., Kans. Oil Marketers Assn., Kans. Assn. Commerce and Industry, Pittsburg State U. Alumni Assn., Aircraft Owners and Pilots Assn., Smokey Hill Ry. Hist. Soc., Little Balkans Hist. Preservation Soc., Pittsburg Area C. of C. Roman Catholic. Clubs: Rotary (dir. Frontenac 1978-80), Elks, K.C. (4th deg.). Office: PO Box 1 1401 N Broadway Pittsburg KS 66762

ROJANASAKUL, PHADEJ, educator; b. Thailand, Jan. 9, 1952; s. Phol and Kim R.; student U. Wis., Milw. Teaching asst. U. Wis., Milw., 1977-80; asst. prof. dept. econs. St. Mary's Coll., Winona, Minn., 1980—, chmn. dept., 1981—. Mem. Am. Econ. Assn. Office: Dept Econs PO Box 1484 St Mary's Coll Winona MN 55987

ROJKIND, JAIME MIGUEL, export and ins. exec.; b. Buenos Aires, Argentina, Aug. 30, 1952; came to U.S., 1978; s. Gregory and Sara Leia (Rosenberg) R.; M.B.A., U. Buenos Aires, 1977. Sales rep. GIOL Winery and Can Products, 1974-76; asst. mgr. internat. sales Pirelli-Dunlop, Buenos Aires, 1976-77; advisor on fin. and ins. problems Techint Engring. Co., 1977-78; asst. prof. acctg. U. Buenos Aires, 1978; estate planner adv., ins. cons. Sun Life Assurance Co. of Can., 1978-80; pres. Lexar Corp., Chgo. 1979—; pres. Rolei Fin. Services, 1981—. Mem. Internat. Bus. Council, Chgo. Council Fgn. Relations, Nat. Assn. Life Underwriters, Nat. Assn. Public Notaries. Clubs: Exporters (Argentina); Lions. Author articles in field. Office: 3525 W Peterson Ave Suite 301-303 Chicago IL 60659

ROLEWICZ, THOMAS FRANCIS, pediatrician, pharmacologist, educator; b. Chgo., Nov. 27, 1939; s. Harry Joseph and Lucille Mary (Slomka) R.; B.S. summa cum laude, Coll. of St. Thomas, 1961; M.D., U. Minn., 1966, Ph.D. in Pharmacology, 1973; m. Patricia Anne Palon, Sept. 9, 1961; children—Thomas Francis, Christopher Palon, Paul Joseph. Intern, U. Minn. Hosp., Mpls., 1969-70, resident in pediatrics, 1970-72, chief resident, 1972; practice medicine specializing in pediatrics and clin. pharmacology, 1973—; staff pediatrician St. Paul Ramsey Med. Center, 1975—, chmn. pharmacy and therapeutics com., 1978—, dir. pediatric in-patient service and pediatric intensive care unit, 1975—, coordinator pediatric edn. of residents and med. students, 1978—; asst. prof. depts. pediatrics and pharmacology U. Minn., 1973-75, 75—. Mem. St. Matthew's Sch. Bd., St. Paul, 1967-77, chmn., 1973-76, mem., vice chmn. parish council, 1972-73; bd. dirs. Kaposia Developmental Learning Center, 1973-80, chmn., 1977-80; mem. corp. bd. Archbishop Brady High Sch., 1977—, chmn., 1979—. Recipient Faculty Devel. award Pharm. Mfrs. Assn. Found., 1973-75; named Tchr. of Year dept. Family Practice, St. Paul Ramsey Med. Center, 1979; U. Minn. research grantee, 1973; Minn. Med. Found. research grantee, 1974. Mem. NW Pediatric Soc., Am. Acad. Pediatrics, Ramsey County Med. Soc., Minn. Med. Assn., AMA, Sigma Xi, Delta Epsilon Sigma. Roman Catholic. Contbr. articles in field to profl. jours.; editor: (with Peter Parrish) The Doctors and Patients Handbook of Medicine and Drugs (Peter Parrish), 1977. Home: 703 Ottawa Ave Saint Paul MN 55107 Office: 640 Jackson St Saint Paul MN 55101

ROLF, FRANK PAUL, mech. engr.; b. Peekskill, N.Y., July 30, 1928; s. Frank and Paula (Hartman) R.; B.M.E., Clarkson Coll., 1954; m. Eleanor Gaines, Feb. 16, 1951; children—James E., John A., Jeffrey O., Cecilia A., Catharine L., Cristin M. Test engr. Aberdeen Proving Ground, 1954-55; design engr. New Departure div. Gen. Motors Corp., Bristol, Conn., 1955-56, applications engr., 1956-57, project engr., 1957-59, supr. auto testing, 1959-67; maintenance supr. Lane Constrn. Co., Fulton, N.Y., 1967; project engr. Lubrizol Corp., Wickliffe, Ohio, 1967-70, supr. fleet test, 1970—. Served with USN, 1946-48, 51-52. Mem. Soc. Automotive Engrs., Coordinating Research Council, Regular Common Carrier Conf. Republican. Roman Catholic. Club: Elks. Office: 29400 Lakeland Blvd Wickliffe OH 44092

ROLF, VERNON JOHN, ednl. adminstr.; b. Newport, Ky., Feb. 15, 1943; s. Henry Vernon and Rosemary Emily (Bradley) R.; B.A., Thomas More Coll., 1965; postgrad. Xavier U., 1978—; m. Grace Gwendolyn Kelsey, June 1, 1974; children—Bradley, Elizabeth, Brian. Fiscal asst. U. Cin. Med. Coll., 1966-67, bus. affairs asst., 1967-70, mgmt. and fin. officer, 1970-76, dir. mgmt. and fin., dept. family medicine, 1976—; trustee, treas. Univ. Family Medicine, Inc., Cin., 1981—. Active Big Bros., 1977—. Fellow, King Edwards Hosp. Fund, London, 1978. Mem. Med. Group Mgmt. Assn., Soc. Tchrs. Family Medicine, Hosp. Fin. Mgmt. Assn., Nat. Soc. Research Adminstrs. Republican. Roman Catholic. Club: Toastmasters (v.p. edn. 1979-81). Home: 50 Avenel Pl Fort Thomas KY 41075 Office: Dept Family Medicine Univ Cin Cincinnati OH 45267

ROLFE, MICHAEL N., mgmt. cons.; b. Chgo., Sept. 9, 1937; s. Mark Alexander and Antoinette (Wittgenstein) R.; A.B., U. Mich., 1959; postgrad. Grad. Sch. Bus., U. Chgo., 1962-64; m. Judith Mary Lewis, June 16, 1959; children—Andrew Jay, Lisa Kay, James Lewis. With Brunswick Corp., Chgo., 1962-68, mgr. systems and programming, 1966-68; with A.T. Kearney, Chgo., 1968—, v.p., 1979—. Mem. Sch. Dist. #113 Bd. Edn., Highland Park-Deerfield, Ill., 1977—, pres., 1979—. Served with USNR, 1959-61. Mem. Soc. Mgmt. Info. Systems, Common Computer Users Group (dir.). Clubs: Northmoor Country, Met. (Chgo.). Home: 1730 Overland Trail Deerfield IL 60015 Office: 222 S Riverside Plaza Chicago IL 60606

ROLFS, MARVIN EUGENE, mathematician; b. Geneseo, Kans., Feb. 15, 1913; s. Henry Rudolf and Clara Ruth (Schroeder) R.; B.S., Ottawa U., 1934; M.A., U. Kans., 1935; postgrad. U. Kans., 1935, 36, 37, U. Minn., summer 1939; m. Ardelle Lavinia Baker, July 27, 1938; children—Leland Eugene, Jane Ann, Kay Helen. Instr. Dodge City (Kans.) Jr. Coll., 1936-43, U. Kans., 1943-44; mathematician U. Iowa, Iowa City, 1945; instr. U. Kans., 1945-47; asso. prof. No. Mich. Coll. Edn., Marquette, 1947-51; analyst USAF, Forbes AFB, Topeka, 1951-61; instr. Fort Hays (Kans.) State Coll. (now U.), 1961-63, asst. prof., 1963-72, asso. prof., 1972—. Mem. Nat. Council Tchrs. Math., Math. Assn. Am., Kans. Assn. Tchrs. Math, Fort Hays (Kans.) State Coll. Faculty Assn., Fort Hays State Coll. Faculty Men, Nat., Topeka Audubon socs., Kans. Ornithol. Soc., Nat., Internat. wildlife fedns., Sigma Pi Sigma, Pi Mu Epsilon. Republican. Baptist. Home: 211 W 24th St Hays KS 67601 Office: Dept Math Fort Hays State U Hays KS 67601

ROLINSKI, EDMUND JOSEPH, chem. engr., educator; b. Bklyn., Jan. 3, 1935; s. Bronislaw F. and Anna Rolinski; B.Chem. Engring., CCNY, 1958; M.S., Ohio State U., 1966; Ph.D., U. Cin., 1970; m. Alberta A. Petkewitz, Nov. 17, 1964; children—Elizabeth, Adam, Richard, Marisha. Engr., Air Force Materials Lab., Wright Patterson AFB, Ohio, 1958-80; prof. chem. engring. U. Dayton (Ohio), 1980—, chmn. dept. chem. engring., 1979—. Recipient numerous awards Air Force, 1972-80. Fellow Am. Inst. Chemists; mem. Am. Inst. Chem. Engrs., Air Pollution Control Assn. Contbr. articles on thermodynamics and fluid mechanics to profl. jours.; patentee in field.

ROLLAND, IAN MCKENZIE, ins. co. exec.; b. Fort Wayne, Ind., June 3, 1933; s. David and Florence (Hunter) R.; B.A., DePauw U., 1955; M.A., U. Mich., 1956; m. Miriam Vee Flickinger, July 3, 1955; children—Cheri Lynn, Lawrence David, Robert Arthur, Carol Ann, Sara Kay. With Lincoln Nat. Life Ins. Co., Fort Wayne, 1956—, sr. v.p., 1973-77, pres., chief exec. officer, 1977—; pres., chief exec. officer Lincoln Nat. Corp., 1975—, dir. affiliate cos.; dir. Central Soya Co., No. Ind. Public Service Co., Gen. Telephone of Ind., Lincoln Fin. Corp. Chmn. citizens bd. St. Francis Coll.; bd. dirs. United Way, Neighborhood Care, Inc., Parkview Meml. Hosp., YMCA, Met. Bd. Mem. Am. Acad. Actuaries, Health Inst. Assn. Am. (dir.), Am. Council Life Ins. (dir.). Methodist. Home: 3825 Dalewood Dr Fort Wayne IN 46805 Office: 1300 S Clinton Fort Wayne IN 46801*

ROLLAND, PAUL, music educator; b. Budapest, Hungary, Nov. 21, 1911; grad. Franz Liszt Acad. Music, 1937; M.Mus., 1943; m. Clara Szekely, Dec. 24, 1940; children—Peter, John. First violist Budapest Symphony Orch., 1935-38; Pro Ideale Quartet, Budapest, 1936-38; fellow Westminster Choir Coll., Princeton, N.J., 1938-40; prof. U. Iowa, Iowa City, 1943-44, Simpson Coll., Indianola, Iowa, 1940-45, U. Ill., 1945-78; dir. Strings Nat. Acad. Arts, Champaign, Ill., 1974-78; dir. U. Ill. HEW String Research Project, 1967-70. Recipient Outstanding Tchr. of Year award U. Ill., 1976; Eugene Ysaye medal, Exeter, Eng., 1975; Dept. State Am. Specialist grantee, 1960-61. Mem. Am. String Tchrs. Assn. (founding mem., editor for 10 yrs., past pres., chmn. publs.; Disting. Service award 1973), Music Tchrs. Nat. Assn., Music Educators Nat. Conf., Nat. Sch. Orch. Assn. Author: Basic Principles of Violin Playing, 1960; Prelude to String Playing, Method, 1972; The Teaching of Action in String Playing (series 17 films, books, audio-visual aids), 1973. Home: 404 E Oregon St Urbana IL 61801 Died Nov. 9, 1978.

ROLLER, MAC C., physician; b. Ft. Wayne, Ind., Apr. 25, 1935; s. George Franklin and Dortha (Cottrell) R.; student Purdue U., 1953-56; M.D., Ind. U., 1960; m. Velva Ann Roller, Aug. 14, 1959; children—Douglas Alan, Gregory Lee, Brian Christopher. Intern St. Joseph's Hosp., Denver, 1960-61; practice medicine specializing in family practice, Chetek, Wis., 1961-62, Purdue U., 1964-66, Franklin, Ind., 1966—; mem. med. staff Johnson County (Ind.) Meml. Hosp. clin. instr. medicine dept. family practice Ind. U. Med. Center, 1976—. Served with U.S. Army, M.C., 1962-64. Diplomate Am. Bd. Family Practice. Mem. AMA, Ind. Med. Assn., Am. Acad. Family Practice. Contbr. articles to profl. jours. Home: 1260 E Adams St Franklin IN 46131 Office: 1551 N Main St Franklin IN 46131

ROLLINS, WILLIAM LYMAN, mfg. exec.; b. Lyman, Wyo., Dec. 30, 1909; s. William Clarence and Clara Rachel (Slade) R.; ed. Lyman public schs., Chgo. Music Coll.; m. Margaret Pratt, June 25, 1934; children—Mabel, Craig. Singer, 1930-33; with Utah Radio, 1933-35, Radio Speakers, Inc., 1935-36, Ariston Mfg., 1936-39, Crescent Industries, Inc., 1939-54; pres. Oaktron Industries, Inc., Monroe, Wis., 1954—, also gen. mgr.; dir. NTW Corp., Dallas, Tiberon Corp., Denver. Mem. Am. Loudspeakers Mfg. Assn. (past pres.), Electronics Industries Assn., NAM, Wis. Mfg. Assn. Republican. Mormon. Clubs: Monroe Country, Monroe Lions. Rec. album: I Love Life, 1978. Home: 1503 28th Ave Monroe WI 53566 Office: 1000 30th St Monroe WI 53566

ROLLISON, STEPHEN FRANK, broadcast co. exec.; b. Atlanta, July 19, 1948; s. Ellie Frank and Ruth (Brogden) R.; B.A., U. Ga., 1973; M.Ed., Columbus Coll., 1975; postgrad. Auburn U., 1976-77. Broadcast journalist, anchorman Sta. WTVM-TV, Inc., Columbus, Ga., 1973-75; anchorman, producer Sta. WRBL-TV. Columbus, 1977-78; sales exec. community relations and estate planning depts. Prudential Ins. Co. Am., Albany, Ga., 1978-79; assignment editor Sta. WQAD-TV, Moline, Ill., 1979-81; news dir. Sta. KAAL-TV, Austin, Minn., 1981—. Served with U.S. Army, 1968-71; to capt. Res., 1971-77. Decorated Bronze Star; Cross of Gallantry with bronze star, Silver Star (Republic of Vietnam). Mem. Radio and Television News Dirs. Assn., Am. Hist. Assn., Res. Officers Assn., U. Ga. Alumni Soc., Columbus Coll. Alumni Assn., Sigma Delta Chi, Phi Alpha Theta. Republican. Roman Catholic. Home: 409 13th Ave NE Austin MN 55912 Office: KAAL-TV PO Box 577 Austin MN 55912

ROLSTEN, ROBERT FRED, materials mech. engr.; b. Fort Wayne, Ind., Feb. 6, 1925; s. Chalice Lloyd and Nell Jane (Good) R.; B.Sc., Capital U., 1948; Ph.D., Ohio State U., 1955. Research scientist Battelle Meml. Inst., 1950-55, E. I. duPont deNemours & Co., 1955-59; research chemist, head tech. engring. service U.S. Borax Research Corp., 1959; engring. design specialist Gen. Dynamics, 1960-63; asso. prof. sci. dept. Calif. Western U., 1960-64; sect. mgr. Am. Machine & Foundry Co., 1964; sr. staff scientist Tech. Ops. Research, Lexington, Mass., 1964-65; pvt. practice as cons., Kettering, Ohio, 1965—; pres. The Wright Co., 1966-81, Biomechanics Internat., 1981—; prof. dept. engring. Wright State U., Dayton, Ohio, 1971—, acting chmn., 1974-75, asst. dean Coll. Continuing and Community Edn., 1975—, asst. dean Coll. Sci. and Engring., 1975—. Mem. AAAS, AAUP, Am. Chem. Soc., Am. Geophys. Union, Am. Inst. Aeros. and Astronautics, Am. Ordnance Assn. (life), Chem. Abstracts, Electrochem. Soc., Marine Tech. Soc., Ohio Acad. Scis., Sigma Xi, Phi Lambda Upsilon. Author: Iodide Metals and Metal Iodides, 1961; contbr. articles to profl. jours.; tech. adviser motion picture Overlords; patentee in field. Home: 1436 Adirondack Trial Kettering OH 45409 Office: Coll Sci Engring Wright State U Dayton OH 45431

ROLSTON, MARGARET ELIZABETH, realtor; b. Knox County, Mo., Mar. 10, 1910; d. Marvin and Beryl (Miller) Florea; B.S. in Music, North Mo. State Coll., 1932; m. Howard E. Rolston, Nov. 25, 1931 (dec.); children—Anna Sue Barlow, James M. Co-owner Rolston & Rolston Realtors, Kirksville, Mo., 1953—, also ins. agt. Organizer, 1st pres. state chpt. Womens Council, Mo. Real Estate Bd., 1957. Pres. Adair County Parents Assn., Washington Sch. P.T.A., 1947-48; organized Grey Lady Service, A.R.C., 1964, sec. Red Cross bd., 1951-62; mem. com. for Collegiate Nursing Program, North Mo. State Coll., 1972, adv. com. Child Devel. Program, adv. council Free Enterprise Inst., 1979; chmn. financial drive United Fund, 1975, 78. Bd. dirs. Adair County Center Exceptional Children; mem. governance com. Kirksville Coll. Osteo. Med., 1972—, chmn. governance com., 1976—, also trustee; bd. dirs., v.p. N.E. Mo. Health and Welfare Council, from 1978, now pres. Mem. Kirksville (dir. 1973—, treas. 1975—, pres. 1976—), Mo. chambers commerce, Adair County Credit Bur. (1st v.p. 1976), N.E. Central of Realtors (pres.), Mo. Real Estate Assn. (dir. 1976—), Nat. Bd. Realtors, Womens Council (past regional gov.), Omega Tau Rho. Republican. Mem. Christian Ch. Mem. Am. Bus. Woman's Assn., El Kadir Jewels (pres. 1975). Clubs: Sojourners, Kirksville Country, Life After Fifty (pres. 1976). Home: 804 Shannon Ln Kirksville MO 63501 Office: 208 S Franklin St Kirksville MO 63501

ROMANI, JOHN HENRY, polit. scientist; b. Milan, Italy, Mar. 6, 1925; s. Henry A. and Hazel (Pettengill) R. (parents Am. citizens); B.A. in Govt., U. N.H., 1949, M.A., 1949; Ph.D., U. Mich., 1955; children—David John, Paul Nichols. Instr. social scis. Leicester (Mass.) Jr. Coll., 1949-50, dept. govt. U. N.H., Durham, 1950-51; instr. dept. polit. sci. U. Mich., Ann Arbor, 1954-55, asso. prof. public health adminstrn. Sch. Public Health, 1961-65, prof. public health adminstrn., 1965-69, 71—, asso. v.p. acad. affairs, 1971-75, chmn. health planning and adminstrn., 1975-80; vice chancellor U. Wis.-Milw., 1969-71; research asso. Inst. Public Adminstrn., U. Philippines, 1953-54; asst. prof. dept. polit. sci. Western Res. Mich. U., Kalamazoo, 1956-57; asso. dir. Cleve. Met. Services Commn., 1957-59; asso. prof. Grad. Sch. Public and Internat. Affairs, U. Pitts., 1959-61; cons. public adminstrn. Ford Found., N.Y.C., 1965, Gov.'s Adv. Com. on Health Care in Prisons, Office of Med. and Health Affairs, Lansing, Mich., 1974; chmn. work group on adminstrn. Public Health Statue Revision Project, State of Mich., 1975-76, div. of population Economic and Social Commn. Asia and the Pacific, Thailand, 1974. Vestry, St. Andrew's Episcopal Ch., Ann Arbor, 1965-68, jr. warden, 1967-68, treas. 1971-73. Served with U.S. Army, 1943-46. Fellow Am. Public Health Assn. (pres. 1979-80), (hon.) Royal Soc. Health; mem. Am. Soc. Public Adminstrn. (sec., v.p. Cleve. chpt. 1958-59), Midwest Polit. Sci. Assn., Mich. Public Health Assn., Am. Acad. Polit. and Social Sci., Am. Acad. Health Adminstrn. (v.p. 1967), Acad. Polit. Sci., AAAS, AAUP (v.p. U. Mich. chpt. 1964-65), Soc. for Psychol. Study of Social Issues, Policy Studies Orgn., Wis. Public Health Assn., Am. Polit. Sci. Assn. Author: The Philippine Presidency, 1956; Post-Entry Training in the Local Public Service, 1963; contbr. numerous articles on public adminstrn. to profl. publs. Home: PO Box 7903 Ann Arbor MI 48107 Office: School of Public Health Univ Mich 109 S Observatory Ann Arbor MI 48109

ROMANOFF, EDWARD MARTIN, oil co. ofcl.; b. Pitts., Oct. 25, 1945; s. Erwin I. and Julia Ann (Gross) R.; B.A., Washington and Jefferson Coll., 1967; M.S., Northwestern U., 1968; m. Joyce Lynn Cummings, June 22, 1969; children—Derek, Joshua. News producer Sta. WIIC-TV, Pitts., 1968-70; news producer, editor Sta. KYW-TV-Radio, Phila., 1970-72; public affairs supr. E.I. du Pont de Nemours & Co., Inc., Wilmington, Del., 1972-78; asso. dir. public affairs Standard Oil Co. (Ohio), Cleve., 1978—. Trustee, LWV Ednl. Fund, 1982—. Served with USAR, 1969-75. Mem. Public Relations Soc. Am., Internat. Indsl. TV Assn. Office: Midland Bldg Cleveland OH 44115

ROMANOFF, MARJORIE REINWALD, educator; b. Chgo., Sept. 29, 1923; d. David Edward and Gertrude (Rosenfield) Reinwald; student Northwestern U., 1941-42, 43-45; B.Ed., U. Toledo, 1947, M.Ed., 1968, Ed.D., 1976; m. Milford M. Romanoff, Nov. 1, 1945; children—Bennett Sanford, Lawrence Michael, Janet Beth (dec.). Tchr., Old Orchard Elem. Sch., Toledo, 1946-47, McKinley Sch., Toledo, 1964-65; substitute tchr., Toledo, 1950-68; instr. Mary Manse Coll., Toledo, 1974; instr. children's lit. Sylvania (Ohio) Bd. Edn., 1977; supr. student tchrs. U. Toledo, 1968-73, researcher, 1973-74, instr. Am. Lang. Inst., 1978—; adj. prof. elem. edn. Bowling Green (Ohio) State U., 1978—. Trustee Children's Services Bd., 1974-76; pres. bd. Cummings Treatment Center for Adolescents, 1978-80; mem. Crosby Gardens Adv. Bd., 1976—, Community Planning Council, 1980—, Citizens Rev. Bd. of Juvenile Ct., 1980—; mem. allocations com. Mental Health and Retardation Bd., 1980—; mem. Bd. Jewish Edn., 1976—, Jewish Family Service, 1978—; bd. dirs. Temple Sisterhood, 1955-61. Mem. Tchrs. English to Speakers Other Langs., Am. Assn. Supervision and Curriculum Devel., Am. Edn. Research Assn., Nat. Soc. for Study Edn., Am. Assn. Colls. Tchr. Edn., Toledo Assn. Children's Lit., Nat. Council Jewish Women, Orgn. Rehab. and Tng., Hadassah (chpt. pres. regional bd. 1961-64), Northwestern U. Alumni Assn., Phi Kappa Phi, Phi Delta Kappa, Kappa Delta Pi (pres./faculty adv. 1971-75), Pi Lambda Theta (pres. nat. com. 1979—). Democrat. Home: 2514 Bexford Pl Toledo OH 43606 Office: U Toledo CEC 1006 Toledo OH 43606 also Coll Edn Bowling Green State U Bowling Green OH 43402

ROMANOFF, MILFORD MARTIN, bldg. contractor; b. Cleve., Aug. 21, 1921; s. Barney Sanford and Edythe Stolpher (Bort) R.; student Coll. Arch., U. Mich., 1939-42; B.B.A., U. Toledo, 1943; m. Marjorie Reinwald, Nov. 6, 1945; children—Bennett S., Lawrence M., Janet Beth (dec.). Pres., Glass City Constrn. Co., Toledo, 1951-55, Milford Romanoff Inc., Toledo, 1956—. Co-founder, Neighborhood Improvement Found. Toledo, 1960; mem. Lucas County Econ. Devel. Com., 1979—; mem. citizens adv. bd. Recreation Commn. Toledo, 1973—; mem. campus adv. com. Med. Coll. Ohio, 1980—; trustee Cummings Treatment Center for Adolescents, 1981—; mem. Children's Services Bd. of Lucas County, 1981—; pres. Ohio B'nai B'rith, 1959-60; bd. dirs. Anti-Defamtion League, 1955-60, Ohio Hillel Orgns.; chmn. Toledo Amateur Baseball and Softball Com., 1979-81; mem. Democratic Precinct Com., 1975-78; trustee Temple Brotherhood, 1956-58, 79—; pres. Cherry Hill Nursing Home: Mem. U. Toledo Alumni Assn., Toledo Mus. Art (asso.), U. Mich. Alumni Assn., Zeta Beta Tau. Clubs: Masons; B'nai B'rith (pres. Toledo lodge 1958-59). Address: 2514 Bexford Pl Toledo OH 43606

ROMANOFF, ROSTISLAV, JR., internat. banker; b. Chgo., Dec. 3, 1938; s. Rostislav and Alexandra Pavlovna (Galitzine) R.; B.A., Yale, 1961, M.B.A., U. Chgo., 1968; m. Stephena Verdel Cook, Sept. 9, 1960 (div. Jan. 1979); 1 dau. Stephena Alexandra; m. 2d, Christia A. Ipsen, Aug. 16, 1980. With No. Trust Co., Chgo., 1962-64, asst. cashier met. div. banking dept., 1964-68, 2d v.p. met. div., 1968-70, 2d v.p., dep. mgr. London br., 1970-71, v.p., dep. mgr. London br., 1971-75, v.p., div. head multinat. div., 1975-80, v.p., div. head internat. div. of trust dept., 1980—. Sec. bd. trustees Children's Meml. Hosp., 1967-70; trustee Hadley Sch. for Blind, 1975. Served with U.S. Army, 1961-62. Clubs: Buck's (London), Yale (N.Y.C.), Chgo., Shoreacres. Home: 650 E Northmoor Rd Lake Forest IL 60045 Office: 50 S LaSalle Street Chicago IL 60675

ROMANS, CHARLENE RAE, personnel exec.; b. Lorain, Ohio, Nov. 18, 1948; d. Charles Raymond and Pearl Rowena (Myers); A.A., Lorain County Community Coll., 1972; B.A., U. Akron, 1974; m. Melvin Orin Romans, Sept. 7, 1967; 1 dau., Melissa Maria. Store tng. mgr. The Higbee Co., Cleve., 1973, personnel mgr., Elyria, Ohio, 1974-76, personnel mgr., Cleve., 1976-77, dir. personnel services, 1977—. Mem. Vocat. Guidance Rehab. Services Affirmative Action Adv. Com., 1978—; mem. Corp. Safety Com. Cleve., 1979—. Club: Women's City. Office: 100 Public Square Cleveland OH 44113

ROMBS, VINCENT JOSEPH, accountant, lawyer; b. Newport, Ky., Mar. 8, 1918; s. John Thomas and Mathilda (Fromhold) R.; student Xavier U., 1936-37; B.S. with honor, Southeastern U., 1941; J.D., Loyola U., Chgo., 1952; m. Ruth Burns, Aug. 15, 1942; 1 dau., Ellen (Mrs. James P. Herman). Admitted to Ill. bar, 1952; tax partner with local and nat. pub. accounting firms, Chgo., 1952—; with firm

Laventhol & Horwath, Chgo., 1970-75; of counsel Edelman & Rappaport, Chartered, 1975—; officer Ostrow Reisin Berk & Abrams, Ltd., 1977—. Bd. dirs. Miller Found. Served to lt. comdr., USNR, 1941-46. Recipient Scholarship Key award Delta Theta Phi, 1953. C.P.A., Ill. Mem. Am. Inst. C.P.A.'s, Ill. Soc. C.P.A.'s. Home: 1400 N Elmhurst Rd Mount Prospect IL 60056 Office: 1 N LaSalle St Suite 1714 Chicago IL 60602 also 676 St Clair St Suite 2100 Chicago IL 60611

ROMEO, JAMES NICHOLAS, SR., data processing exec.; b. Chgo., Aug. 13, 1942; s. Frank Nicholas and Anne (Tuozzo) R.; student Wright Jr. Coll., 1960-62, Am. Mgmt. Assn., 1976—; m. Phyllis Pallone, Nov. 27, 1965; children—James Nicholas II, Christopher. Acctg. clk. Skil Corp., Chgo., 1963-64; acctg. supr. Fund Am. Ins. Co., Chgo., 1964-66; project leader Kraft Inc., Glenview, Ill., 1966-73; mgr. data processing center Joslyn Mfg. & Supply Co., Chgo., 1973-79, mgr. corporate systems, mgr. data processing Howe div., 1979—. Treas., Nat. Y Indian Guides, 1972-73; mgr. Little League, 1979; mem. bldg. com. Catholic Ch., 1976-78, mem. fin. com., 1977-78, mem. adv. com., 1978—. Mem. Soc. Mgmt. Info. Systems, Am. Mgmt. Assn., Nat. Microfilm Assn. Roman Catholic. Club: Lions (pres. local club 1976-77). Office: 2 N Riverside St Chicago IL 60606

ROMERO, JOSEFINO TABERNILLA, artist; b. Tayabas, Quezon, Philippines, Mar. 19, 1939; d. Melanio Romero and Teodorica Talavera (Tabernilla) R.; grad. nurse Quezon Meml. Hosp., 1961; grad. nurse anesthetist Mt. Carmel Hosp., Detroit, 1968. Psychiat. nurse Nat. Mental Hosp., Mandaluyong Rizal, Philippines, 1961-63; operating room nurse St. Vincent Hosp., Worcester, Mass., 1963-64, Michael Reese Hosp., Chgo., 1964-65, Sarnia (Ont., Can.) Gen. Hosp., 1965-66; nurse Quezon Meml. Hosp., Lucena City, Philippines, 1971-72; nurse anesthetist Mt. Carmel Hosp., Detroit, 1972-74, Brent Hosp., Detroit, 1974-76; one-man shows include: Ramada Inn, Southfield, Mich., 1975, Romero Art Gallery, 1976; group shows include: Scarab Club Art Show, Troy, Mich., 1975, 77, Keatington Antique Village Art Show, Lake Orion, Mich., 1975. Recipient Merit award Mich. Ann. Art Festival Show, Livonia, 1975; award Cambridge Village Assn., 1976. Mem. Am. Assn. Nurse Anesthetists, Internat. Soc. Artists, Mich. Watercolor Soc., Friends of Paris Am. Acad. Club: Scarab (Detroit). Home and Office: 27360 Lexington Pkwy Southfield MI 48076

ROMICK, JEROME MICHAEL, health care co. exec.; b. Houston, May 7, 1943; s. Arthur and Lillian Y. (Smolensky) R.; B.B.A., U. Tex., 1967; m. Ina Sue Hirsch, Aug. 8, 1971; 1 dau., Stephanie Alisha. With Procter & Gamble, Corpus Christi, 1967-68; self-employed, Victoria, Tex., 1968-69; with Drustar, Inc., Grove City, Ohio, 1969-72; pres. Artromick Internat., Inc., Columbus, Ohio, 1972—. Trustee, Citizens Research, Inc., Columbus, 1978-79. Served with U.S. Army, 1964-69. Recipient Small Bus. Person of Yr. award SBA, 1977. Mem. Am. Soc. Cons. Pharmacists (asso.), Am. Soc. Hosp. Pharmacists. Jewish. Patentee on unit dose medication handling system, 1974, visible file card system, 1977. Home: 170 N Drexel St Bexley OH 43209 Office: 2008 Zettler Rd Columbus OH 43227

ROMIG, JAMES LYLE, editor; b. Whittier, Calif., Oct. 19, 1938; s. Lawrence M. and Lois Jane (Morris) R.; A.B., Whittier Coll., 1960; Ed.D., U. So. Calif., 1972; m. Angela Carol LaBella, June 1, 1968; children—Teri Lyn, James Carl, Andrew John, Seth Joseph. Elementary tchr. East Whittier (Calif.) Schs., 1960-61, 64-65; instr. gen. studies Whittier Coll., 1961-64, dir. freshman English, 1967-70, dean of students, 1970-71, asst. prof. edn., 1971-74, asso. prof., 1974-75; editor field rep., asst. to nat. sales mgr. Scott Foresman & Co., Glenview, Ill., 1965-67, exec. editor, 1975-79; editor-in-chief U. Chgo. Press, 1979-80; with W. C. Brown Co., Dubuque, Iowa, 1981—. Mem. Am. Psychol. Assn., Am. Ednl. Research Assn.

ROMKEMA, ROBERT J., univ. adminstr.; b. Grand Rapids, Mich., Dec. 17, 1930; s. Joe and Violet E. Romkema; B.S., Mich. State U., 1952; m. Elizabeth J. Musser, June 28, 1952; chidlren—Linda, Sandra, Joe, Todd. Dir. phys. plant Grand Valley State Coll., Allendale, Mich., 1963-75; dir. phys. plant Eastern Mich. U., Ypsilanti, 1975-76, v.p. bus. and fin., 1976—. Registered profl. engr., Mich. Office: Eastern Mich U Ypsilanti MI 48197

RONFELDT, LEO LEONARD, sch. prin.; b. Anthon, Iowa, Oct. 24, 1927; s. Emil William and Margie Faye (Dawdy) R.; B.S., Morningside Coll., 1959; M.A., U. No. Colo., 1962; Ed.D. (teaching fellow 1968-69), U. S.D., 1969; m. Lily Mae Downing, Aug. 10, 1958. Tchr. public schs., Anthon, Iowa, 1946, College Corner, Iowa, 1947-48, Smithland, Iowa, 1948-50, Climbing Hill (Iowa) Community Sch., 1953-58; with Sioux City (Iowa) Community Schs., 1960—, elem. sch. prin., 1969—. Bd. dirs. ARC, 1974—; mem. exec. bd. Siouxland Chpt., 1981—. Served with AUS, 1950-52. Iowa State Edn. grantee, 1968-69; Izaak Walton League scholar, 1957. Mem. NEA (life), Nat. Elem. Prins. Assn. (life), Iowa Elem. Prins. Assn., Assn. Childhood Edn. Internat., Assn. Supervision and Curriculum Devel., Phi Delta Kappa. Methodist. Author: A Determination of Basic Urban Environmental Understandings. Home: 4416 Crown Point Ct Sioux City IA 51106 Office: 2700 S Maple St Sioux City IA 51106

RONINGEN, JEWEL EDGAR, stockyards exec.; b. Pelican Rapids, Minn., Jan. 15, 1922; s. James Marion and Effie Amanda (Holt) R.; B.S., N.D. State U., 1943; m. Grace Marlyn Carlen, Jan. 16, 1943; 1 son, Bruce Jewel. Instr. vocat. agr., Pelican Rapids, 1944-45; county extension agt., McIntosh, Minn., 1945-47; dist. supt. U.S. Dept. Agr., Packers & Stockyards Adminstrn., Sioux City, Iowa, 1948-58; pres., gen. mgr. Sioux Falls (S.D.) Stockyards Co., 1958-67; pres., gen. mgr. Union Stockyards Co. of Fargo, West Fargo, N.D., 1967—, also dir.; mem. N.D. Beef Commn., 1979—. Served with USMCR, 1943-44. Recipient Pilot Study Grant, EPA, 1970, Gamma Sigma Delta award, 1966. Mem. Fargo (chmn. N.D. hwy. users conf. 1973-77, chmn. N.D. Hwy. Hall of Honor com. 1974-77), West Fargo chambers commerce. Lutheran (mem. stewardship com. 1968—). Mason (Shriner), Elk, Rotarian. Home: 213 21st Ave N Fargo ND 58102 Office: Livestock Exchange Bldg West Fargo ND 58078

ROOBOL, NORMAN RICHARD, chemist; b. Grand Rapids, Mich., Aug. 19, 1934; s. Pleune and Henrietta (Sietsema) R.; B.S., Calvin Coll., 1958; Ph.D. in Organic Chemistry, Mich. State U., 1962; m. Joan Lois Ezinga, Aug. 15, 1957; children—Kerri Linda, Michael Eric, Victoria May, Sara Elizabeth Angelique. Research chemist Shell Oil Co., Emeryville, Calif., 1962-65; asst. prof. chemistry Gen. Motors Inst., Flint, Mich., 1965-68, asso. prof., 1968-72, prof., 1972—; Rodes prof. Rüsselsheim, W. Ger., 1980-81; tchr. short course on paint; cons. coatings application processes. Sr. adviser Sci. Fair, Flint. Served with Signal Corps, U.S. Army, 1954-56. Johnson fellow, 1957-58, NSF fellow, 1960-62; Dow fellow, 1961-62. Fellow Am. Inst. Chemists; mem. AAUP, Am. Sci. Affiliation, Soc. Mfg. Engrs. (dir. Asso. Finishings Proc., (v.p. profl. devel. council), Sigma Xi, Alpha Tau Omega, Pi Tau Sigma (sr. adviser chpt. 1979—). Lutheran. Contbr. numerous articles to profl. jours.; pub. Quar. Paint Newslaetter to Gen. Motors employees in U.S., 14 fgn. countries, 1976—; patentee in field. Office: 1700 W 3d Ave Flint MI 48502

ROOD, F. C. (JIM), greeting card co. exec.; b. Ridgway, Pa., Apr. 30, 1934; s. Nolan Waters and Helen D. (Hahn) R.; student Pa. State U., 1956-59; m. Marlene A. Sobkowiak, May 9, 1964; children—James, David, Jane, Jon. Supr., Ford Motor Co., 1959-67; controller Trailmobile div. Pullman Co., Chgo., 1967-70; corp. v.p., v.p., gen. mgr. Allis-Chalmers Credit Corp., West Allis, Wis., 1970-73; corp. v.p. fin. Hallmark Cards, Inc., Kansas City, Mo., 1973—; dir. David L. Babson Investment Fund, Inc., D.L. Babson Money Market Fund, Inc., David L. Babson Tax Free Income Fund, Inc. Served with USMC, 1953-56. Club: Mission Hills Country. Office: 25th and McGee Kansas City MO 64108

ROOKS, CHARLES SHELBY, clergyman: b. Beaufort, N.C., Oct. 19, 1924; s. Shelby A. and Maggie (Hawkins) R.; A.B., Va. State Coll., 1949; B.D., Union Theol. Sem., 1953; D.D., Coll. of Wooster, 1968, Interdenominational Theol. Center, 1979, Va. Union U., 1980; L.H.D. (hon.), Howard U., 1981; m. Adrienne Martinez, Aug. 7, 1946; children—Laurence Gaylord, Carol Ann. Ordained to ministry United Ch. of Christ, 1953; pastor Shanks Village Ch., Orangeburg, N.Y., 1951-53; pastor Lincoln Meml. Congl. Temple, Washington, 1953-60; asso. dir. Fund for Theol. Edn., Princeton, N.J., 1960-67, exec. dir., 1967-74; pres. Chgo. Theol. Sem., 1974—; mem. exec. bd. dept. ministry Nat. Council Chs., 1962-70; chmn. bd. Office of Communication, United Ch. of Christ, 1964-81, chmn. com. structure Central Atlantic Conf., 1970-72, mem. Union Theol. Sem. Alumni Council, 1968-70, Theol. Perspectives Commn. Nat. Com. Black Churchmen; now pres. Chgo. Theol. Sem.; vis. fellow Epis. Theol. Sem. Southwest, Austin, Tex., 1966; lectr. in field. Chmn. planning com. Nat. Consultation Negro in Christian Ministry, 1965. Mem. Princeton Regional Sch. Bd., 1969-70. Bd. dirs., chmn. housing com. Washington Urban League; chmn. ednl. adv. com. Chgo. Urban League, 1978—; trustee Bexley Hall Theol. Sem., Colgate Rochester Div. Sch., 1968-73, Lancaster Theol. Sem., 1969-74, Eastern Career Testing Center; pres. Communications Improvement, Inc., 1971-81. Served with U.S. Army, 1943-46; PTO. Recipient Elizabeth Taylor Byrd Fund award for outstanding community service, 1969. Mem. Va. State Coll. Nat. Alumni Assn. (pres. 1966-67), Soc. for Study Black Religion (pres. 1970-74, 80—), Assn. Theol. Schs. (cons. Black ch. studies 1970-71, mem. commn. on accrediting 1976-82, chmn., 1980-82). Editor: Toward a Better Ministry, 1965; mem. editorial bd. Theology Today, New Conversations; contbr. articles to religious jours. Address: 5757 University Ave Chicago IL 60637

ROONEY, EDWIN ANTHONY, chemist; b. Seneca, Ill., July 12, 1919; s. Michael James and Mary (Kelleher) R.; B.S., DePaul U., 1942; Mus.B., Am. Conservatory Music, 1958. Chemist F.E. Schundler & Co., Joliet, Ill., 1941, 42; with Apco Oil Corp., Chgo., 1945-78, lab. dir., 1964-78; lab. dir. Okla. Refining Co., Chgo., 1978—. Mem. Sheffield Neighborhood Assn., Chgo., 1964—; mem. Lincoln Park Conservation Assn., Chgo., 1966—. Served with AUS, 1942-45. Mem. Am. Chem. Soc., ASTM, Am. Indsl. Hygiene Assn., Nat. Paint and Lacquer Assn., Nat. Fedn. Paint Tech., Internat. Soc. Contemporary Music, Holy Name Soc., Phi Beta Epsilon. Roman Catholic. Home: 1248 W Norwood St Chicago IL 60660 Office: 3921 N Ravenswood Ave Chicago IL 60613

ROONEY, JAMES FRANCIS, state legislator; b. Racine, Wis., Sept. 29, 1935; s. Cornelius J. and Mabel A. (Behrend) R.; m. Nancy Lee Schulz, Jan. 1960; children—Erin Marie, James Connell, John Connell, Richard Connell. Bus. mgr. Nielson-Madsen Engring., Racine, 1956-72; mem. Racine County (Wis.) Bd., 1966—; mem. Wis. Ho. of Reps., Madison, 1972—. Served with U.S. Army, 1954-56. Democrat. Roman Catholic. Club: Racine Yacht. Home: 1500 Michigan Blvd Racine WI 53402 Office: 234N State Capitol Madison WI 53702

ROOP, JAMES JOHN, public relations exec.; b. Parkersburg, W.Va., Oct. 29, 1949; s. James Vaun and Mary Louise (McGinnis) R.; B.S., W.Va. U., 1971; m. Margaret Mary Ellen Kuneck, Dec. 30, 1972. Public relations account asst/asst. account exec. Ketchum, MacLeod & Grove, Pitts., 1972, account exec., 1973, account supr., 1975, v.p., 1977-79; client services mgr. Burson-Marsteller, Chgo., 1979, v.p., client services mgr., 1980—. Mem. Public Relations Soc. Am. (grantee 1972, mem. exec. com. 1979—), Nat. Investor Relations Inst. Club: Publicity of Chgo. Home: 1937 Hudson Ave Chicago IL 60614 Office: 1 E Wacker Dr Chicago IL 60601

ROOS, ALBERT DEVIN, engring. co. exec.; b. Glenwood, Minn., Sept. 1, 1946; s. Al and Pauline (Barnett) R.; B.S. in Mech. Engring., Tulsa U., 1969. Engr. U.S. Govt.-Rock Island (Ill.) Arsenal, 1969-75; engr.-salesman Benner Engring. Sales, Rock Island, 1975-76, engr., mgr., v.p., St. Louis, 1977-80; pres. Roos Engring. Sales, Inc., St. Louis, 1980—. Mem. ASME, Nat. Soc. Profl. Engrs., Okla. Soc. Profl. Engrs. Home and Office: 9466 W Milton Saint Louis MO 63114

ROOS, LAWRENCE K., banker; b. St. Louis, Feb. 1, 1918; s. Sol and Selma (Kalter) R.; B.A., Yale U., 1940; LL.D., U. Mo., 1974; m. Mary Watson, Apr. 30, 1955; children—Pamela, Mary Ellen, Jennifer, Lawrence K. Pres., Mound City Trust Co., 1950-62; chmn. bd. 1st Security Bank, Kirkwood, Mo., 1950-62; supr. St. Louis County, 1962-74; exec. v.p., dir. 1st Nat. Bank, St. Louis, 1975-76; pres. Fed. Res. Bank St. Louis, 1976—. Active Mo. Citizens for Eisenhower, 1952; mem. Mo. Ho. of Reps., 1946-50; Republican candidate for gov. Mo., 1968; chmn. Mo. Com. for Re-election of Pres., 1972; del. Rep. Nat. Conv., 1972; Mo. del. Rep. Nat. Com., 1973-74; active Radio Free Europe, 1954, U.S. Assay Commn., 1955; mem. U.S. Adv. Commn. on Intergovtl. Relations, 1969-74; mem. adv. com. Woodrow Wilson Internat. Center for Scholars, 1974; chmn. bd. East-West Gateway Coordinating Com., 1965-67, 73-75; chmn. Mo., Crusade for Freedom, 1954; mem. Pres.'s Commn. on Jobs for Vietnam Vets., 1971; pres. Wesley House Found., St. Louis, 1955-60; bd. dirs. St. Louis Jewish Hosp., 1975—, Central Inst. for Deaf, 1975—, Maryville Coll., St. Louis, 1975-78, United Way Greater St. Louis, 1955—, St. Louis Regional Commerce and Growth Assn., 1976—, Govtl. Research Inst., St. Louis, 1975—, Nat. Assn. Counties, 1963-72; chmn. St. Louis County Charter Revision Commn., 1979. Served to maj. U.S. Army, ETO. Decorated Bronze Star. Named Mo. Rep. of Year, 1972, Man of Year, St. Louis Globe-Democrat, 1974; recipient Torch of Liberty award Anti-Defamation League, 1974. Office: PO Box 442 Saint Louis MO 63166*

ROOS, LINDA PILLSBURY, sch. counselor; b. St. Louis, July 4, 1946; d. Fred Hobart and Anne (Larsen) Pillsbury; B.A. in Edn., William Jewell Coll., 1968; M.A. in Guidance and Counseling, U. Mo., St. Louis, 1974; m. Howard Norman Roos, Sept. 23, 1972; 1 son, Nelson Thomas. Tchr. phys. edn. public schs., St. Louis, 1968-73; tchr. phys. edn. Parkway East Jr. High Sch., St. Louis, 1974-75; counselor Parkway Central Sr. High Sch., St. Louis, 1975-76, Parkway South Sr. High Sch., Ballwin, Mo., 1976—; pvt. practice counseling, Kirkwood, Mo., 1981—. Mem. adv. bd. Met. Sch.; trustee 3d Baptist Ch., 1975-77. Mem. Am. Personnel and Guidance Assn., Mo. Guidance Assn., Am. Fedn. Musicians, NEA, Mo. Nat. Edn. Assn., Parkway Community Tchrs. Assn., AAUW, Sigma Alpha Iota. Home: 1199 Clayton Pl Town and Country MO 63131 Office: Parkway South Sr High Sch 801 Hanna Rd Ballwin MO 63011 also 10502 Manchester Rd Kirkwood MO 63122

ROOT, CARY MICHAEL, mgmt. cons. co. exec.; b. Chgo., Nov. 14, 1951; s. Sherman and Bernadine Violet (Waller) R.; B.S. in Indsl. Engring., Purdue U., 1973, M.S., 1973. Systems analyst Burroughs Corp., Detroit, 1973-76; mgmt. cons. Cleveland Cons. Assos., Lansing, Mich., 1976-78, Cleve., 1978-79, partner, dir., 1979—. Pres., chmn. bd. dirs. Nob Hill Condominium Assn., 1977—. Mem. Am. Inst. Indsl. Engrs., Assn. Systems Mgmt., Am. Prodn. and Inventory Control Soc. (chmn. Cleve. chpt., chmn. nat. distbn. spl. interest group), Nat. Council Phys. Distbn. Mgmt. Author articles. Home: 6000 Nob Hill Dr Chagrin Falls OH 44022 Office: 23925 Commerce Parte Rd Cleveland OH 44122

ROOT, DAVID LEIGH, outdoor advt. co. exec.; b. Toledo, Aug. 14, 1950; s. Robert William and Mary Josephine (Gardner) R.; B.A., Hillsdale Coll., 1972; m. Kay Fuhrman, July 15, 1972; children—Whitney, Jay. Real estate regional mgr. Root Outdoor Advt., Inc., Toledo, 1972-74, v.p. real estate, 1974-76, exec. v.p., 1976-81; v.p. R & B Investments, Inc., 1974—, Root Parking Systems, 1974—, Producers Exchange, Inc., 1974—; treas. Toledo Media, Inc., 1980—; pres. Pima Investment Group, Toledo, 1980—; mem. adv. bd. Mid-Am. Bank & Trust, 1980—. Mem. Nat. Fedn. Ind. Bus., Inst. Outdoor Advt., Outdoor Advt. Assn. Am., Outdoor Advt. Assn. Ohio, Toledo C. of C., Better Bus. Bur., Delta Tau Delta. Clubs: Belmont Country (Perrysburg, Ohio), Toledo, Rotary, Press, Advt. Office: Root Outdoor Advt Inc 21 S Erie St Toledo OH 43602

ROPER, ROY ERNEST, anthropologist; b. Prineville, Oreg., Oct. 12, 1948; s. Richard Elroy and Milred R.; B.A., Sophia U., Tokyo, 1973; M.A., U. Ill., 1978. Teaching and research asst. dept. anthropology U. Ill., Urbana, 1974-75, 76-79, project co-dir. Water Resources Center, Inst. Environ. Studies, 1979-81. Served with U.S. Army, 1967-71. Decorated Bronze Star; NDEA fellow, 1973-74, 75-76. Mem. Am. Anthrop. Assn., Central State Anthrop. Assn., Soc. Med. Anthropology, Soc. Applied Anthropology, Assn. Anthropologists in Gerontology, Gerontology Soc., Sigma Xi. Contbr. articles to profl. jours., chpts. to books. Home: 809 W Illinois #6 Urbana IL 61801

RORER, LEONARD GEORGE, psychologist; b. Dixon, Ill., Dec. 24, 1932; s. Leonard Gleason and Marion Emma (Geyer) R.; B.A., Swarthmore (Pa.) Coll., 1954; Ph.D., U. Minn., 1963; m. Gail Evans, Apr. 30, 1958; children—Liat, Eric Evans; m. 2d, Nancy McKimens, Jan. 9, 1969; 1 dau., Mya Noelani. Research asso., then asso. dir. Oreg. Research Inst., Eugene, 1963-75; prof. psychology Miami U., Oxford, Ohio, 1975—, dir. clin. psychology tng. program, 1976—; pres. Oreg. Psychol. Assn., 1973-75. NIMH spl. research fellow, 1967-68; fellow Netherlands Inst. Advanced Study, 1971-72. Mem. Am. Psychol. Assn. (council reps. 1968-72), Ohio Psychol. Assn., Midwestern Psychol. Assn., Assn. Advancement Behavior Therapy, Soc. Multivariate Exptl. Psychology. Author articles in field, mem. editorial bds. profl. jours. Home: 327 W Sycamore St Oxford OH 45056 Office: Psychology Dept Miami U Oxford OH 45056

RORIG, KURT JOACHIM, chemist; b. Bremerhaven, Germany, Dec. 1, 1920; s. Robert Herman and Martha (Grundke) R.; came to U.S., 1924; naturalized, 1929; B.S., U. Chgo., 1942; M.A., Carleton Coll.; Ph.D., U. Wis., 1947; m. Helen Yonan, Mar. 20, 1949; children—James, Elizabeth, Miriam. Lectr. Loyola U. Chgo., 1950-62; chemist to asso. dir. Chem. Research G.D. Searle & Co., Chgo., 1947—. Mem. Sch. Bd., Wilmette, Ill., 1969-71. Mem. Am. Chem. Soc. (dir. Chgo. sect.), N.Y. Acad. Sciences, AAAS, Chgo. Chemists Club (past pres.). Presbyterian. Patentee in field. Home: 337 Hager Ln Glenview IL 60025 Office: G D Searle & Co PO Box 5110 Chicago IL 60680

ROSANOVA, CAROLE ANN, psychiatrist; b. Hammond, Ind., Jan. 18, 1945; d. John Paul and Jennie (Hasara) Uhercik; student Northwestern U., 1963-66, M.D., 1970; student U. Miss. Med. Sch., 1966-68; m. Albert R. Rosanova, Jr., June 25, 1966 (div. 1981); children—Albert Ralph, John Paul, Christopher Robin, Benjamin Joshua, Daniel Jeremy. Resident in psychiatry, Ill. State Psychiat. Inst., 1970-73; attending physician dept. psychiatry Cook County Hosp., Chgo., 1974-75; psychiatrist boys' and girls' adolescent units Med. and Surg. Hosp., Chgo. Reed Mental Health Center, 1975-77; practice medicine specializing in psychiatry, Barrington, Ill., 1974—; instr. Abraham Lincoln Sch. Medicine, 1974-75. Den mother Northwestern Suburban council Boy Scouts Am., 1975-76, 79—. Diplomate Am. Bd. Psychiatry and Neurology. Mem. Am. Psychiat. Assn. Home: 21627 Andover Rd Kildeer IL 60047

ROSARIO, MAXIMA QUINTOS, tng. coordinator; b. Philippines, May 16, 1916; came to U.S., 1974, naturalized, 1979; d. Domingo and Petra Quintos; B.S. in Edn., U. Philippines, 1939, M.A. in Edn., 1959; children—Aurelio, Thelma, Danilo, Lourdes. Tchr., Philippines, 1958-65; librarian, Philippines, 1965-66; tng. asst. Devel. Bank of Philippines, 1966-68, chief tng. div., 1968-74; tchr. asst. Clayton High Sch., St. Louis, 1975-76; tng. coordinator St. Louis Agy. on Tng. and Employment, 1977—. Tng. Policy and Adminstrn., grantee, London, Eng., 1966, Am. U. grantee, 1970. Mem. Am. Soc. Tng. and Devel., Govt. Tng. Officers Assn. Philippines (pres. 1971-72). Home: 3002 Compton Saint Louis MO 63118 Office: St Louis Agy on Tng and Employment 5800 Lindell Blvd Saint Louis MO 63108

ROSCHEK, WILLIAM PAUL, paper co. ofcl.; b. Kalamazoo, Mar. 5, 1949; s. Urban Michael and Beverly (Jones) R., Jr.; B.B.A., Western Mich. U., 1972; m. Kathy A. Harrison, July 23, 1971; children—Lisa Rae, William Paul. With Ga.-Pacific Corp., 1967—, prodn. worker Kalamazoo Paper div., 1967-68, sales rep., 1972-75, sales rep., Kalamazoo Hopper div., 1975-76, account exec. print and splty. papers, Franklin Park, Ill., 1976-81; Western regional sales mgr. Finch, Pruyn & Co., Rolling Meadows, Ill., 1981—. Mem. Hackett High Sch. Alumni Assn., Western Mich. Alumni Assn. Home: 2504 Brook Ln Aurora IL 60505 Office: 1 Crossroads of Commerce Rolling Meadows IL 60008

ROSDAIL, JAMES RUSSELL, veterinarian; b. Norway, Iowa, Apr. 13, 1917; s. LeRoy and Mabel Olena (Olson) R.; m. Mildred Annetta Cruzen, July 3, 1948; children—Jay, Gail, Jan, Joy, Leanne, Tom, Jon. Pvt. practice vet. medicine specializing in large animals, Pomeroy, Iowa, 1951—; mem. Iowa State Bd. Med. Examiners, 1969-75, chmn., 1970-71; mem. Nat. Bd. Examiners in Vet. Medicine, 1972-78; mem. Ednl. Commn. for Fgn. Vet. Grads., 1971-78. Mem. Pomeroy Town Council, 1955-57, Pomeroy Community Sch. Bd. Edn., 1961-64; mem. Calhoun County Bd. Edn., 1965-71, 74-75. Bd. dirs. Iowa Vet. Med. Assn. Found., 1963-71, 79—, pres., 1965-71; bd. dirs. Ft. Dodge Trinity Regional Hosp., 1978—. Served to capt. AUS, 1942-46. Decorated Bronze Star medal; recipient Stange award for meritorious service Iowa State U., 1971. Mem. Iowa Vet. Med. Assn. (exec. bd. 1957-75, v.p. 1971, pres.-elect 1972, pres. 1973; Veterinarian of Year award 1976), Assn. Am. State Bds. Examiners in Vet. Medicine (v.p. 1970, pres. 1971), AVMA (exec. bd. 1978—). Republican. Lutheran (congregation pres. 1969-73). Club: Met. Dinner of Greater Fort Dodge (gov. 1975—, pres. 1976). Address: Pomeroy IA 50575

ROSE, BETTY ANN, editor, writer; b. Kenosha, Wis., May 17, 1934; d. Albert and Emily Albertine (Johnson) Rose; B.S. (Kemper K. Knapp scholar), U. Wis., 1955; postgrad. Northwestern U., 1959, Ind.

U., 1961. Tchr., Luxemburg (Wis.) High Sch., 1955-57; tchr., pub. relations dir. Ela-Vernon High Sch., Lake Zurich, Ill., 1957-63; Mid-west advt. mgr. Harcourt, Brace & World, Inc., Chgo., 1963-64; asst. editor Reuben H. Donnelley Corp., Chgo., 1964-68; presentation editor Scranton Pub. Co., Inc., Chgo., 1968-70; asst. to pres. Gurnham & Assos., Inc., Chgo., 1970-78; mng. editor Indsl. Finishing, Hitchcock Pub. Co. subs. ABC, 1978—. Mem. Am. Electroplaters Soc., Chgo. Indsl. Water, Waste and Sewage Group (chmn. 1974-76), Soc. Plastics Engrs. (dir. decorating div. 1979—), Constrn. Writers Assn. (dir., v.p., pres.), Sigma Epsilon Sigma, Phi Kappa Phi. Co-author chpt. in handbook, 1976. Contbr. articles on pollution control to profl. jours. Office: Hitchcock Bldg Wheaton IL 60187

ROSE, ERNST, dentist; b. Oldenburg, Germany, July 22, 1932; s. William and Elsie (Lowenbach) R.; came to U.S., 1940, naturalized, 1946; B.S., Georgetown U., 1955; D.D.S., Western Res. U., 1963; m. Shirley Mae Glassman, Dec. 24, 1960; children—Ruth Ellen, Michele Ann, Daniel Scot, Seth Joseph. Intern, Waterbury (Conn.) Hosp., 1964; pvt. practice dentistry, Hubbard, Ohio, 1964—; pres., treas. Dr. Ernst Rose, Inc. Lab. instr. Ohio State U., Columbus, 1956-57; dental adviser Asso. Neighborhood Center. Mem. Liberty Twp. Zoning Commn., 1967-74; chmn., 1970-74; chmn. Hubbard (Ohio) Urban Renewal Com., 1968-74. Served with AUS, 1957-59. Fellow Royal Soc. Health; mem. Chgo. Dental Soc., Am., Ohio dental assns., Corydon Palmer Dental Soc., Warren Dental Soc., Hubbard C. of C. (dir. 1973—), Jewish Chatauqua Soc. (life), Alpha Omega (council mem. 1968—, sec. 1970-71, v.p. 1971-72, pres. 1972-73). Jewish (mem. brotherhood bd. 1967—, treas. 1971-73, pres. 1975-77, temple bd. dirs. 1975—). Mem. B'nai B'rith (pres. 1970-71, trustee 1971—), Rotarian. Home: 418 Arbor Circle Youngstown OH 44505 Office: 30 N Main St Hubbard OH 44425

ROSE, HAROLD EUGENE, ednl. adminstr.; b. Pope County, Ill., Oct. 7, 1933; s. Cecil Truman and Dora Stacy R.; B.A. in Philosophy, Olivet Coll., 1957; M.Ed., Bowling Green State U., 1962; postgrad. in ednl. adminstrn. Mich. State U., 1962-68; student (Sch. scholar) Higgens Lake Sch. Conservation, 1965, (Sch. fellow) Meadowbrook Sch. Music, 1966; m. Miriam Ruth Hegle, Aug. 6, 1955; children—Stacey Eugene, Alita Ruth. Ordained to ministry, 1949; founder, pastor Dolton (Ill.) Community Ch., 1955-58; tchr., coach public schs., Ai, Ohio, 1958-60; tchr. public schs., Pontiac, Mich., 1960-62, 64-67, community sch. dist. Elem. and Jr. High Complex, 1967-71; owner, chef Julies Restaurant, Pontiac, 1962-64; dir. community edn. programs Whitmer Human Resources Center, Pontiac, 1971-72; regional community edn. dir. Pontiac High Sch., Oakland County Jail and Trustee Camp, St. Joseph and Gen. Hosp. Learning Centers, 1972-77; supr. CETA job tng., prin. Central Continuing Edn. Center, Pontiac, 1977—; dir. basic edn. Human Resource Center, Pontiac, 1979—; pres. Oak Grove Devel. Corp., through 1979; lectr. on youth, drugs, family and religion, 1955—; rec. artist Mark V Studios, Greenville, S.C., 1972—; nat. anthem soloist Pontiac Silverdome, 1979. Bd. dirs. Rose Twp. (Mich.) Republican Com., 1978—; treas. Holly (Mich.) Bd. Edn., 1979—; team mem. Spl. Olympics, Oakland U., 1979. Rochester (Mich.) Community Edn. Mott grantee, 1967. Mem. Nat. Community Sch. Edn. Assn. (charter), Nat. Assn. Sch. Adminstrs. Clubs: Civitan (pres. Pontiac club 1978-79); Tee Creek Hunt and Conservation (pres.). Home: 10563 Tamryn St Holly MI 48442 Office: 60 Parkhurst Pontiac MI 48058

ROSE, JEANNE KURRASCH, mfg. co. staff; b. Clinton, Minn., Aug. 28, 1925; d. Harry G. and Marie B. (Ossowskie) Kurrasch; B.A., U. Minn., 1951; postgrad. Orange Coast Coll./West Coast Coll., 1964-67; 1 dau., Sandra Jeanne. Public relations DuPont Corp., Wilmington, Del., 1952-57; advt. Hercules Powder Co., Wilmington, 1959-60; tech. writer, editor A.C. Sparkplug Corp., Milw., 1960-63; sr. systems analyst McDonnell Douglas Corp., Huntington Beach, Calif. and St. Louis, 1963-71; job shop Pa. Tech. Services, St. Louis, 1971-73; sr. procedures specialist Emerson Electric Co., St. Louis, 1973—; free lance writer/editor, 1957—. Mem. Assn. Systems Mgmt. Office: Emerson Electric Co 8100 W Florissant Saint Louis MO 63136

ROSE, JERRY KENT, TV sta. exec.; b. Terrell, Tex., July 31, 1941; s. William Flenoy and Jackie Velma (Humphreys) R.; student Paris (Tex.) Jr. Coll., 1960-62, N. Tex. State U., Denton, 1962-64; B.A. in Broadcast Communications, Northeastern Ill. U., Chgo., 1980; m. Shirley Jean Rider, Aug. 6, 1967; children—Jeffrey Todd, Trevor Lane, Vanessa Paige. Ordained to ministry Assemblies of God Ch., 1976; announcer KERA-TV, Dallas, 1963-65, KMAP-FM, Dallas, 1965-66; scenic designer WFAA-TV, Dallas, 1965-66; producer, dir. KDTV-TV, Dallas, 1966-70; program mgr. KROD-TV, El Paso, Tex., 1970-72; gen. mgr. KXTX-TV, Dallas, 1972-74; ops. mgr. Christian Broadcasting Network, Virginia Beach, Va., 1974-75; v.p., gen. mgr. WCFC-TV38, Chgo., 1975-79, pres., chmn. bd., 1979—; instr. Grad. Sch. Communications, Wheaton (Ill.) Coll.; cons. Internat. Corr. Inst. Served with USCG, 1962-68. Mem. Nat. Religious Broadcasters Assn. (2d v.p.), Nat. Assn. Broadcasters, Nat. Acad. TV Arts and Scis. (bd. govs.), Nat. Assn. Evangelicals. Contbr. articles to mags. and jours. Office: WCFC TV 38 20 N Wacker Dr Chicago IL 60606

ROSE, LEONARD GEORGE, credit agy. exec.; b. Highland Park, Mich., Mar. 6, 1927; s. Frank S. and Gladys (Piper) R.; B.A., Wayne State U., 1949; m. Rosemary M. Macaulay, Aug. 23, 1952; children—Martha L., Sheila E., Suzanne E. Exec. v.p. Creditors Service, Inc., Detroit, 1955-68; pres., chief exec. officer Nat. Account Systems, Inc. subs. Diners Club, Chgo., 1968-81; pres. Master Collectors, Inc., Hinsdale, Ill., 1981—; accredited instr. Am. Collectors Assn. Pres., Green Lake Village, Mich., 1964-68; mem. planning commn., W. Bloomfield Twp., Mich., 1966-67. Served with USNR, 1944-46, 50-52. Named Pres. of Year, Am. Collectors Assn., 1961-62; recipient Outstanding Achievement award Mich. Assn. Credit Agys., 1968. Mem. Am. Collectors Assn. (past pres.), Am. Inst. Mgmt. (pres.'s council 1969-70). Roman Catholic. Clubs: Lake Forest (Ill.); Execs., Met. (Chgo.); Racquet (Libertyville, Ill.). Contbr. articles to newspapers, trade jours.; numerous radio and tv. appearances on use of credit. Home: 150 W Onwentsia Lake Forest IL 60045 Office: 120 E Ogden Ave Hinsdale IL 60521

ROSE, RICHARD (RICK), chem. co. exec.; b. Chgo., Aug. 24, 1920; s. Joseph Samuel and Eudel (Bernstein) R.; student Northwestern U., 1937-39; grad. Freight Traffic Inst., 1952, Coll. Advance Traffic, 1954; postgrad. Rutgers U., 1955; m. Germaine Vander Louis, June 14, 1948; children—Ronald Gerald, Annette Jean. Vice pres. Coldway Express, Jersey City, 1954-57, Foodway Express, Jersey City, 1954-57; gen. ops. and traffic mgr. ABC Air Freight, N.Y.C., 1957-61; v.p. traffic, dir. J. Moyles & Asso., Elk Grove Village, Ill., 1970-72; pres. Rose Orgn., Downers Grove, Ill., 1965-76; mgr. Internat. Minerals & Chem. Corp., Mundelein, Ill., 1976—; condr. numerous seminars on hazardous materials; lectr. in field. Mem. adv. com. U. Wis.-Extension; scoutmaster Boy Scouts Am., Hazlet, N.J., 1960-65. Served with USN, 1942-45. Decorated Purple Heart, Legion of Merit; recipient Letters of Commendation, U. Wis., 1978, Wis. Police Dept., 1979, Am. Inst. Plant Engrs., 1979; lic. ICC, FMC, CAB. Mem. ICC Practitioners Assn., Nat. Indsl. Traffic League, Fertilizer Inst., Chem. Mfrs. Assn., Inst. Makers of Explosives, Hazardous Materials Adv. Council, Am. Soc. Traffic and Transp., Delta Nu Alpha. Club: Masons. Contbr. articles to profl. jours.; author: IMC Hazardous Materials Manual. Home: 920 Blanchard St Downers Grove IL 60515 Office: 421 E Hawley St Mundelein IL 60060

ROSE, ROSEMARY CATHERINE, printing co. exec.; b. Antigo, Wis., Jan. 2, 1931; d. Ernest J. and Rose F. Slizewski; secretarial cert. Bryant-Stratton Sch., Milw., 1953; real estate course Spencerian Sch., Milw., 1964-65; 1 son, Ted R. Adminstrv. asst. H. R. Salen, Waukesha, Wis., 1951-55; owner, operator motel, Brookfield, Wis., 1955-65, restaurant and dry cleaning plant, Lannon, Wis., 1960-65; exec. sec. E.P. Hoyer, New Berlin, Wis., 1967-70; owner, operator Sanitation Service Inc., Menomonee Falls, Wis., 1970-75, North Twin Supper Club, Phelps, Wis., 1975-79; v.p. systems O.L. Schilffarth Co. div. Crown Industries, Milw., 1979—; owner, operator R-Service Co., Germantown, Wis., 1980—; broker, prin Alrose Realty Co. Lic. real estate broker, Wis. Club: Elks. Office: 326 N Brown St Milwaukee WI 53212

ROSE, STANLEY JAY, newspaper exec.; b. Kansas City, Mo., June 3, 1918; s. Joseph and Mae (Lund) R.; A.A., Los Angeles City Coll., 1939; B.J., U. Mo., 1941; m. Shirley Mallin, Oct. 7, 1942; children—Roberta Susan (Mrs. Stephen Q. Small), Stephen F. Chmn. bd., pub. Sun Publs., Inc., Overland Park, Kans., 1950—; pub. Kansas City (Mo.) Jewish Chronicle, Inc., 1964—. Bd. dirs. Kaw Valley Heart Assn., Heart of Am. council Boy Scouts Am.; chmn. bd. trustees Suburban Med Center, also moderator bd. dirs.; mem. adv. council U. Kans. Med. Center. Served to lt. (j.g.) USNR, World War II; PTO. Recipient Sweepstakes, 1st place awards Kans. Better Newspaper Contest, 1968, 69, 70, 72, 73, William Allen White News Enterprise award, 1975; Bea Johnson award Am. Cancer Soc.; honoree Matrix Table, 1980; named hon. col. Kans. Cav. Mem. Overland Park C. of C. (dir.), Kans. Assn. Commerce and Industry (dir.), Sigma Delta Chi. Mason (Shriner), Rotarian. Clubs: Kansas City (Mo.) Press; Optimist (Prairie Village, Kans.). Home: 470 Navajo Ln W Lake Quivira KS 66106 Office: Sun Publs Bldg Overland Park KS 66212

ROSE, VIRGINIA LOU, educator; b. Indpls., July 18, 1940; d. John Rentschler and Bonnie Mae (Powell) Jones; B.S.Ed., Ind. Central U., 1966; M.S.Ed., Butler U., 1971; postgrad. Ball State U.; m. James W. Rose, Jr., Aug. 2, 1964. Primary tchr., remedial reading tchr. Indpls. Public Schs., 1966-72; pvt. tutor, 1972-74; adj. reading prof. urban/rural sch. devel. program Purdue U. and Indpls. Public Schs., 1974-77; remedial reading tchr. middle sch. Met. Sch. Dist. Pike Twp., Indpls., 1977-80; spl. reading tchr. Met. Sch. Dist. Washington Twp., Indpls., 1980—. Mem. Internat. Reading Assn., Nat. Orton Soc. (past dir. local chpt.), Assn. Supervision and Curriculum Devel., Delta Kappa Gamma. Presbyterian. Home: 10145 N Park Ave Indianapolis IN 46280 Office: 1750 W 64th St Indianapolis IN 46260

ROSE, WILLIAM, bus. service co. exec.; b. Waukegan, Ill., Nov. 7, 1919; s. Louis and Bertha (Rose) R.; student pub. schs.; m. Vivian May Gulledge, July 15, 1951; children—Whyland, Calvin, Marcia. Pres., dir. Jobs, Inc., Waukegan, 1951—. Mem. adv. com. bus. edn. dept. North Chicago Community High Sch., 1963-64, graphic arts dept. Waukegan High Sch., 1963-71, career program devel. Coll. Lake County, 1968-75; mem. Lake County Mental Health Adv. Com., 1971—. Justice of peace, Lake County, Ill., 1957-61, police magistrate, 1959-61; mem. Shields Twp. Bd. Auditors, 1957-61. Fin. chmn. Boy Scouts Am., 1959-60, bd. dirs., 1966-71; bd. dirs. Lake County Mental Health Clinic, 1957-68, United Community Services, 1964-71, Lake County Crime Commn., 1969-75; bd. dirs., v.p. Lake County Welfare Council, 1963. Served with Signal Corps, AUS, 1944-46. Mem. Ind. Office Services Inst. (pres. 1971-73), Nat. Assn. Temporary Services (dir. 1975-78), Am. Legion (comdr. 1951), Lake County Mental Health Soc. (pres. 1961), Waukegan-North Chicago C. of C. (dir. 1968-74, pres. 1973). Jewish (treas. congregation 1968-74, pres. 1976). Mem. B'nai B'rith. Clubs: Waukegan Exchange (pres. 1963-64), North Shore Craftsman (pres. 1965). Home: 2439 Dunlay Ct Waukegan IL 60085 Office: 1534 Washington St Waukegan IL 60085

ROSE, WILLIAM RICHARD, meat processing co. exec.; b. Corry, Pa., Feb. 20, 1927; s. William R. and Adeline (Clinkenbead) R.; student Mich. Coll. Mining and Tech., 1947-50; m. Barbara Cory Blanchard, June 19, 1948; children—Peter William, Susan Jo, Michael Charles. Vice pres. Rose Packing Co., Inc., Chgo., 1951—, now pres.; pres. Ashland Cold Storage, Barrington Constrn., Ridgeway Enterprises; dir. R.T.W. Corp., Chgo. pres. Bd. dirs. alumni Valley Forge Mil. Acad. Mem. Village Bd., South Barrington, 1959—. Served with USMCR, 1945-47. Mem. Chgo. Meat Packers Assn. (pres. 1960-63). Presbyterian (elder 1963-66). Home: 15 Mundhank Rd Barrington IL 60010 Office: 65 S Barrington Rd Barrington IL 60010

ROSEKRANS, JAMES MERLIN, architect; b. Denton, Nebr., Apr. 17, 1923; s. James Charles and Pearl Della (Hocking) R.; B.Arch., U. Nebr., 1949; m. M. Eileen Fox, June 2, 1946; children—Dee Wayne, Douglas Ray, Jama Lynn. Partner, J.C. Rosekrans & Son, constrn., Denton, 1950-55; archtl. designer Raymond H. Reed & Co., Columbus, Nebr., 1955-58; architect Reed, Veach, Wurdeman & Assos., Columbus, 1958—, sr. architect, exec. v.p., 1977—. Past mem. Denton Village Bd., Denton Public Sch. Bd.; mem. Columbus Bd. Adjustment, 1977—. Served as pilot USAAF, 1943-45. Mem. AIA, Constrn. Specifications Inst., Nebr. Soc. Architects. Republican. Mem. United Ch. Christ. Clubs: Columbus Rotary (past pres.), Skyroamers Flying (dir.), Masons. Home: 2421 22d St Columbus NE 68601 Office: 1370 31st Ave Columbus NE 68601

ROSELLE, WILLIAM CHARLES, librarian, educator; b. Vandergrift, Pa., June 30, 1936; s. William John and Suzanne Esther (Clever) R.; B.A., Thiel Coll., 1958; M.L.S., U. Pitts., 1963; m. Marsha Louise Lucas, Aug. 2, 1959; 1 son, Paul Lucas. Tchr., Milton Hershey Sch., Hershey, Pa., 1960-62; trainee Pa. State Library, 1962-63; asst. catalog librarian Pa. State U., 1963-65; engring., math. librarian U. Iowa, 1965-66, library adminstrv. asst., 1966-69, asst. dir. of libraries, 1969-71; prof., dir. library U. Wis.-Milw., 1971—; chmn. planning task force on computing U. Wis. System, 1973-74. Served with U.S. Army, 1958-60. Fellow Am. Geog. Soc. (hon.); mem. ALA (life), Spl. Libraries Assn., Iowa Library Assn. (chmn. audit com. 1968-70, chmn. intellectual freedom com. 1969-70), Wis. Library Assn., Midwest Acad. Librarians Conf. (chmn. 1969-71), Council Wis. Librarians (chmn. 1973-74), AAUP (treas. U. Iowa chpt. 1969-70), Phi Kappa Phi, Beta Beta Beta, Beta Phi Mu, Phi Alpha Theta, Phi Delta Kappa. Lutheran. Contbr. articles to profl. jours. Editorial cons. Current Geog. Publs., 1978—. Home: 324 Sunny Ln Thiensville WI 53092 Office: Univ of Wis-Milw Golda Meir Library PO Box 604 Milwaukee WI 53201

ROSEMAN, ARNOLD SAUL, food scientist; b. Boston, Mar. 15, 1930; s. O. Harry and Evelyn W. (Wasserman) R.; B.S., Northeastern U., 1952; M.S. (Glass Container Mfrs. Inst. fellow, 1952-54), U. Mass., 1954 Ph.D., 1956; m. Joan L. Lipman, Mar. 20, 1955; children—David J., Ann L. Research instr. dept. food teach. U. Mass., Amherst, 1954-56; biochemist So. Regional Research Lab., U.S. Dept. Agr., New Orleans, 1956-60; sr. research scientist, research and devel. div. Kraft Co., Glenview, Ill., 1960-68; research mgr. John Morrell & Co., Chgo., 1968-74; dir. research and devel. CFS Continental, Chgo., 1974—. Served with Army N.G., 1946-66, to col. Med. Service Corps, USAR, 1966—. Fellow Am. Inst. Chemists; mem. Am. Chem. Soc., Am. Assn. Cereal Chemists, Inst. Food Technologists, Nat. Guard Assn., Res. Officers Assn., Sigma Xi, Phi Tau Sigma. Contbr. articles in field to profl. jours.; holder 7 U.S. and fgn. patents. Office: CFS Continental 2550 N Clybourn Ave Chicago IL 60614

ROSEN, A. ABBOT, human relations agy. exec.; b. N.Y.C., June 7, 1915; s. Bernard Jules and Augusta (Carton) R.; B.A., Yale U., 1934; LL.B., Columbia U., 1937; m. Charlotte Zion, Sept. 27, 1949; children—B. Joshua, Julie Beth. Admitted to N.Y. bar, 1937; practiced in N.Y.C., 1937-42; atty. sabotage and espionage unit U.S. Dept. Justice, 1942-43, spl. asst. to atty. gen. in prosecution war fraud cases, 1946-47, chief civil rights sect., 1947-48; mem. U.S. Del. to UN, 1947-48; dir. Chgo. Exec. Offices, Anti-Defamation League of B'nai B'rith, 1948—. Served with Signal Corps, AUS, 1943-46. Recipient Thomas H. Wright award Chgo. Commn. on Human Relations, 1958; Founders' Day award Loyola U., Chgo., 1965. Jewish. Office: 222 W Adams St Suite 1449 Chicago IL 60606

ROSEN, CARL LEONARD, diamond account exec., Reiki healer; b. Mpls., June 9, 1930; s. Leonard Carl and Esther Matilda (Anderson) R.; B.A., St. John's U., 1954; postgrad. St. John's Sem., 1954-58; M.S., St. Cloud State U., 1972; postgrad. Moorhead State U., 1969-70, U. San Francisco, 1968, U. Minn., 1969, U. N.Mex., 1971; m. Natalie Ann Fish; children—Michael, Patrick, Edward, Joy. Mem. St. John's Abbey, Collegeville, Minn., 1951-70; ordained priest Roman Catholic Ch., 1958; asst. pastor St. Boniface Ch., Mpls., 1958-61, St. Bernard's Ch., St. Paul, 1961-63, Sts. Peter & Paul Ch., Richmond, Minn., 1963-65; dir. religious edn. St. Boniface High Sch., Cold Spring, Minn., 1965-68; dir. Newman Center, Moorhead State U., 1968-70; asst. dir. fin. aids St. Cloud State U., 1972-73; adminstr. fin. aids Minn. Higher Edn. Coordinating Bd., St. Paul, 1973-76; dir. Carl's House, St. Paul, 1974—; instr. continuing edn. Coll. St. Francis, St. Paul, 1976-78; communications cons. Norstan Inc., Plymouth, Minn., 1978-80; account exec. A.E. Internat. Diamond Corp., 1981—; cons. St. Cloud Sch. Nursing, 1972. Mem. Am., Minn. personnel and guidance assns., Am. Rehab. Assn. Mem. Democratic Farm Labor Party. Author: Since I Think, I Exist, 1975; Persons, 1976. Home: 4540 W Arm Rd Spring Park MN 55384

ROSEN, PHILIP TERRY, educator; b. Syracuse, N.Y., Mar. 22, 1946; s. Theodore and Martha (Mason) R.; student U. Philippines, 1966-67; B.A., Sterling Coll., 1968; postgrad. Universidad Indsl. de Santander (Colombia), 1970; M.A., Emporia State U., 1970; Ph.D., Wayne State U., 1975; m. Jackie McGillivray, May 2, 1970; 1 son, Philip Terry Mason. Instr. Am. history Wayne State U., 1970-73; fellow Smithsonian Instn., 1974-75; asst. prof. Am. history U. Md., 1975-77; asst. dir. council of continuing edn. Marygrove Coll., Detroit, 1977-78, dean div. continuing edn., 1978—. Liberty Fund fellow, 1977. Mem. Am. Hist. Assn., So. Hist. Assn., Orgn. Am. Historians, Council for Advancement of Exptl. Learning, S.E. Mich. Ednl. TV Consortium, Assn. Surg. Technologists. Author: The Treaty Navy, 1919-1937, 1979; Peace and War: U.S. Naval Policies, 1776-1979, 1979; The Modern Stentors: Radio Broadcasters and the Federal Government, 1920-34, 1980. Home: 17355 Quincy St Detroit MI 48221 Office: 8425 W McNichols Rd Detroit MI 48221

ROSENBAUM, GEORGE, market/survey research co. exec.; b. Vienna, Austria, Apr. 13, 1930; came to U.S., 1938, naturalized, 1943; s. Gustav and Margaret (Brand) R.; B.A., U. Chgo., 1949, M.A., 1953; m. Dorothy Seyfried, Mar. 25, 1956; children—David, Julie Ann, Larry. With Sci. Research Assos., Chgo., 1954-56; with Leo J. Shapiro & Assos., Inc., Chgo., 1956—, pres., 1970—; lectr. in field. Mem. Am. Sociol. Assn. Jewish. Office: 505 N Lake Shore Dr Chicago IL 60611

ROSENBAUM, IRA S., psychologist, educator; b. N.Y.C., May 18, 1931; s. Hirsch and Dora (Kahn) R.; B.A., U. Wis., 1953; M.S., Purdue U., 1957; Ph.D., N.Y. U., 1964; m. Marilyn J. Schuurmans, Oct. 7, 1967; children—David A., Peter H. Postdoctoral fellow Austen Riggs Center, Stockbridge, Mass., 1964-66; adj. attending psychologist, asst. prof. Montefiore Hosp. and Med. Center, Albert Einstein Coll. Medicine, N.Y.C., 1966-70; asso. prof. psychology Central Mich. U., Mt. Pleasant, 1970—; cons. Saginaw Community Mental Health Center, 1978—. Served with AUS, 1954-56. Diplomate Am. Bd. Profl. Psychology. Mem. Am. Psychol. Assn., Am. Group Psychotherapy Assn., Soc. Personality Assessment, Am. Orthopsychiat. Assn., Mich. Psychol. Assn. (v.p. acad. affairs). Office: Psychology Dept Central Michigan University Mount Pleasant MI 48859

ROSENBAUM, LINDA MAE, advt. agy. exec.; b. Sioux City, Iowa, June 20, 1950; d. Daryl E. and Joyce (Jensen) Williams; student public schs., South Sioux City, Iowa; 1 son by previous marriage, Chad. Continuity dir. Sta. KMNS-AM, Sioux City, 1968-70; copywriter Sta. KCAU-TV, Sioux City, 1970-72; copywriter, media buyer Fairall & Co., Advt., Sioux City, 1972-74; account exec. Sta. KBCM-FM, Sioux City, 1974-75; copywriter, media dir. Bass Magnuson Advt., Sioux City, 1975—. Dir. publicity March of Dimes, 1981; sec. Planned Parenthood, 1981; chmn. publicity PTA. Mem. Advt. Club Sioux Cities (editor newsletters 1980-81), Internat. Assn. Bus. Communicators, Am. Advt. Fedn. (3d lt. gov. 9th dist.). Republican. Lutheran. Home: 214 E 20th St South Sioux City NE 68776 Office: 815 Nebraska St Sioux City IA 51101

ROSENBERG, DALE HENRY, plastic and reconstructive surgeon; b. Belleville, Ill., Sept. 13, 1927; s. Henry and Evelyn (Miller) R.; student Springfield Jr. Coll., 1946-48; B.S., U. So. Calif., 1949; M.D., U. Ill., 1953; m. Nancy E. Biggs, July 1, 1950; children—Dirk, Jenny, Candra, Charles. Intern, Sacramento County Hosp., 1953-54; resident in plastic surgery Orange Meml. Hosp., Orlando, Fla., 1963-65; asso. Plastic Surgery Consultants, Ltd., Belleville, Ill., 1966—; pres. med. staff Belleville Meml. Hosp., 1974-75; exec. sec.-treas. So. Ill. Med. Assn. Served with USNR, 1944-46. Mem. AMA, Ill., St. Clair County med. socs., Midwestern Assn. Plastic Surgeons, Am. Assn. Plastic and Reconstructive Surgeons. Home: 303 Paddock Rd Belleville IL 62223 Office: Suite 3E 6401 W Main St Belleville IL 62223

ROSENBERG, DALE NORMAN, educator; b. St. Ansgar, Iowa, Dec. 12, 1928; s. Eddie Herman and Ella (Kirchgatter) R.; B.S., Mankato State Coll., 1956; M.Ed., U. S.D., 1959; postgrad. Ball State Tchrs. Coll., 1962, U. Nebr., 1961, Colo. State Coll., 1963-67; D.Arts, U. Central Ariz., 1978; m. Delrose Ann Hermanson, Sept. 10, 1950; children—Jean Marie, James Norman, Julie Ann, Lisa Jo. Tchr. public schs., Holstein, Iowa, 1956-60; prin., guidance dir., Crystal Lake, Iowa, 1960-62; prin. Grafton (Iowa) Jr. High Sch., 1962-66; psychol. tester Dept. Rehab., State of Iowa, 1960-66; prof. psychology North Iowa Area Community Coll., Mason City, 1966—. Served with USAF, 1949-53. Mem. NEA, Iowa Edn. Assn., Kappa Delta Pi, Phi Delta Kappa. Lutheran. Author multi-media curriculum for teaching disadvantaged introductory welding. Home: Rural Route 3 Mason City IA 50401 Office: North Iowa Area Community Coll Mason City IA 50401

ROSENBERG, HERMANN PAUL, lithographing co. exec., profl. basketball team exec.; b. Las Vegas, N.Mex., Aug. 25, 1924; s. Hermann Paul and Ruby Shell (Holland) R.; B.B.A., U. Tex., 1945; m. Barbara Rosenberg; children—Nita Rosenberg Levy, Paul, James. Pres. Midland Lithographing Co., Kansas City, Mo., 1961—; pres.

Kings Profl. Basketball Club, Inc., Kansas City, 1973—; dir. Traders Bank. Pres. Beth Shalom Congregation, 1973-75; pres. Jewish Fedn. Greater Kansas City, 1974-77; dir. Am. Joint Distribution Com; mem. exec. com. United Jewish Appeal; trustee United Israel Appeal, Community Alcohol Program. Recipient Herbert Lehman award Israel Bond Orgn. Mem. Soc. of Fellows Graphic Arts Tech. Found. (pres. 1971-72), Printing Industry Assn. Kansas City (pres. 1965-66), Graphic Arts Union Employers of Am. (pres. 1971-72), Graphic Arts Internat. Union (co-chmn. early retirement trust); mem. Nat. Basketball Assn. (gov.). Democrat. Jewish. Club: Oakwood Country. Office: care Kansas City Kings 1800 Genessee Suite 101 Kemper Arena Kansas City MO 64102

ROSENBERG, MARC JEFFREY, educator, tng. specialist; b. N.Y.C., Aug. 14, 1951; s. Ben and Sherry Rosenberg; B.S. in Bus. Adminstrn., SUNY, Albany, 1972, M.S. in Ednl. Communications, 1974; Ph.D. in Instructional Devel. (Phi Delta Kappa Dissertation award 1977), Kent (Ohio) State U., 1977; m. Harlene Zaretsky, Aug. 5, 1979. Grad. asst. SUNY, Albany, 1972-74; teaching fellow Kent State U., 1974-77, summer research fellow, 1977; asst. prof. edn., dir. teaching skills lab. So. Ill. U., Carbondale, 1977-80; asst. mgr. learning tech. Bell System Center Tech. Edn., Lisle, Ill., 1980—; speaker confs. and seminars. Judge 16th Chgo. Internat. Film Festival, 1980. Grantee So. Ill. U., 1978, 79. Mem. Assn. Ednl. Communications and Tech. (sec. div. telecommunications 1978-80, nat. del. 1980), Nat. Soc. Performance and Instrn., Am. Soc. Tng. and Devel., Phi Delta Kappa. Author articles, revs. in field. Home: 8901 Western Ave Apt 204 Des Plaines IL 60016 Office: Bell System Center Tech Edn 6200 Route 53 Lisle IL 60532

ROSENBERG, MICHAEL RAPHAEL, car rental exec.; b. Honolulu, June 21, 1949; s. Joseph Moses and Suzanne Esther (Solomon) R.; B.A., San Diego State U., 1971; M.A., U. Calif., 1975; M.A., U. Mich., 1977; m. Gayle Lynn Sosin, Feb. 22, 1974. Market research analyst Campbell-Ewald Co., advt., Detroit, 1976-79, account exec. subs. Ceco Pub. Co., Detroit, 1979, regional account exec. parent co., Chgo. Office, 1979-81; account exec. Nat. Car Rental Acct., Warren, Mich., 1981—. Mem. Am. Mktg. Assn., Adcraft Club Detroit, U. Mich. Alumni Assn., U. Calif. Alumni Assn., Mensa. Democrat. Jewish. Home: 1632 Dennett Ln Rochester MI 48063

ROSENBERG, STEVEN ALLAN, psychologist; b. N.Y.C., May 26, 1948; s. William and Mollie (Golfman) R.; B.A., U. Rochester, 1970; Ph.D., George Peabody Coll., 1977; m. Cordelia Robinson, May 10, 1945; 1 son, Daniel. Asst. prof. dept. psychiatry Creighton U., Omaha, 1978-79; dir. intensive services to families project U. Nebr. Med. Center, Omaha, 1979—; pvt. practice, 1981—. Bd. dirs. Head Start Child Devel. Corp., 1979-80. HHS grantee, 1977-81. Mem. Am. Psychol. Assn., Assn. Advancement of Psychology, Soc. Research in Child Devel., Am. Orthopsychiat. Assn., Am. Assn. Mental Deficiency. Jewish. Home: 5910 N 52d St Omaha NE 68104 Office: 5002 Dodge St Omaha NE 68131

ROSENBERG, YETTA SCHIFFMAN, sculptor; b. N.Y.C., Mar. 19, 1905; d. Samuel and Sara (Mattlin) Schiffman; grad. Cleve. Inst. Art; m. David V. Rosenberg, Sept. 2, 1927; children—JoAnn Plotkin, Mary Ann Rose. One-man shows: Mather Gallery, Cleve., 1976; group shows include: Toledo Mus., 1937, Cleve. Mus. Art, 1937, 41-59, 69, 77, Everson Mus., Syracuse, N.Y., 1940, 57, Butler Mus., Youngstown, Ohio, 1970, 72, Canton (Ohio) Mus., 1974, Patterson Art Gallery, Westfield, N.Y., 1975; represented in pvt. collections; designer bronze award for N. Ohio chpt. Am. Soc. Interior Designers, 1979; pvt. tchr. painting and sculpture. Recipient prizes and awards for sculpture from various orgns. and museums including: Nat. League Am. Penwomen, Cleve. Mus. Art. Mem. Allied Artista Am., Nova; Ohio State Fair Sculpture prize, 1974; included in book Outdoor Sculpture in Ohio (Richard Campen), 1981.

ROSENBERGER, HELEN MARIE, chemist; b. Toledo, Dec. 6, 1923; d. Ferdinand Anthony and Helen Barbara (Schmider) R.; B.S., Mary Manse Coll., 1945; postgrad. Northwestern U., 1949-50. Chemist, Monsanto Chem. Co., Dayton, Ohio, 1945-47; with A. B. Dick Co., Chgo., 1947—, research asso., 1969-72, mgr. analytical services, materials research, 1972-79, mgr. advanced tech. research, 1979—; tech. adviser Creative Products, 1970—. Mem. Am. Chem. Soc., Am. Inst. Chemists (past chmn. Ill. accreditation program), Photog. Soc. Am. Roman Catholic. Patentee reprographic processes and supplies. Contbr. articles to profl. jours. Home: 7643 Park Ave Skokie IL 60077 Office: 5700 Touhy Ave Niles IL 60648

ROSENBLATE, HOWARD JEROME, hepatologist; b. Chgo., July 1, 1936; s. Adolph Jon and Elizabeth (Bernstein) R.; B.A., Northwestern U., 1958; M.D., U. Ill., 1962; m. Karen Kohn, June 11, 1961; children—Elizabeth Ann, Robin Lynn, Adam Hunter. Intern, Presbyn. St. Lukes Hosp., Chgo., 1962-63, resident in internal medicine, 1965-67, attending physician, mem. sect. hepatology, 1969-73; chief sect. hepatology Luth. Gen. Hosp., Park Ridge, Ill., 1972-77; asst. prof. medicine Rush Med. Coll., also instr. U. Ill., 1972—. Served with M.C., AUS, 1963-65. Decorated Army Commendation Medal. USPHS fellow, 1967-69. Fellow A.C.P.; mem. Am. Assn. Study of Liver Disease, Internat. Acad. Pathology, Chgo. Soc. Gastroenterology, Am. Fedn. Clin. Research. Jewish. Research on the liver in sickle cell anemia, liver injury in heroin addiction, alcoholic liver disease. Home: 64 Woodley Rd Winnetka IL 60093 Office: 950 Northwest Hwy Park Ridge IL 60068

ROSENBLUM, MARTIN JACK, educator, writer; b. Appleton, Wis., Aug. 19, 1946; s. Sander and Esther Pearl R.; B.S., U. Wis., Madison, 1964, M.A., 1971, Ph.D., U. Wis., Milw., 1980; m. Maureen Rice, Sept. 6, 1970; 1 dau., Sarah Terez. Dir., instr. continuing edn. Marquette U., 1972; lectr. creative writing, lit. U. Wis., Milw., 1971-78, now acad. adv./admissions specialist dept. ednl. opportunity; exec. dir. Lawyers for Creative Arts, Chgo., 1980; editor, pub. Albatross Press and Lionhead Pub., 1969-76. Mem. MLA, Com. of Mag. Editors and Pubs. Author, editor: Albatross One: An Anthology of Poetry from Madison, 1970; Bright Blue Coats, 1970; Brewing: 20 Milwaukee Poets, 1972; The Werewolf Sequence, 1974; as i magic, 1976; Divisions/One, 1978, Divisions/Two, 1979. Contbr. articles and poetry to jours., mags. Home: 2521 E Stratford Ct Shorewood WI 53211 Office: PO Box 413 U Wis Milw Milwaukee WI 53201

ROSENBLUM, RAY HARRIS, communications exec.; b. Butler, Pa., Aug. 15, 1935; s. David H. and Sara E. (Borisky) R.; student Princeton U., 1956; m. Helen Faye Davis, Mar. 4, 1962; children—Joshua, Steven, Charles. News dir., co-owner Sta. WTIG, Massillon, Ohio, 1957-64; sales mgr. Sta. WKPA/WYDD, New Kensington, Pa., 1964-68; owner, pres., nat. news corr. Sta. WACB, Kittanning, Pa., 1964—, Sta. WMOA AM-FM, Marietta, Ohio, 1968—; pres. Larchmont Enterprises Advt. Agy.; guest lectr. Marietta Coll. Chmn. Ohio Program in Humanities; mem. Ohio Arts Council; chmn. Washington County ARC, 1970-72. Named Marietta Jaycee Boss of Yr., 1972. Mem. Marietta C. of C. (v.p., 1976-80), Soc. Profl. Journalists, CBS Radio Affiliates Assn. (dir.), NAACP. Clubs: Masons, Rotary, Elks; Pitts. Press, Harvard-Yale-Princeton (Pitts.). Office: 925 Lancaster St Marietta OH 45750

ROSENCRANZ, ROBERT, elec. engr.; b. Chgo., July 2, 1926; s. Bernard and Lillian (Greenstein) R.; B.S. in Elec. Engring., U. Ill., 1948; B.S. in Indsl. Engring., Ill. Inst. Tech., 1955, B.S. in Mech. and Aerospace Engring., 1969; M.B.A., Roosevelt U., 1977; m. Judith Diane Levey, June 29, 1952; children—Leslie Joyce, Holly Ann. Chief engr. Standard Stamping & Perforating Co., Chgo., 1948-58, also cons. engr.; research engr. Clearing Machine Corp. div. U.S. Industries, Chgo., 1958-60; sr. elec. engr. U.S. Industries Tech. Center, Pompano Beach, Fla., 1960-61; chief engr. Lumen Electronics div. Esterline Angus Instrument Co., Joliet, Ill., 1961-65, Zenith Electric Co., Chgo., 1965-66; mgr. electronic and optical engring. Sargent-Welch Sci. Co., 1966-73; sr. engr. Abbott Labs., North Chicago, 1973—. Served with USNR, 1944-46. Mem. IEEE, Soc. Photog. Scientists and Engrs. (pres. 1970-71; service award 1972), Instrument Soc. Am. (sr.), Beta Gamma Sigma. Clubs: Masons, Shriners. Contbr. articles to profl. jours. Patentee in field. Home: 1762 McCraren Rd Highland Park IL 60035

ROSENDALE, GEORGE WILLIAM, aircraft co. exec.; b. Keenan, Okla., Nov. 4, 1933; s. John Webster and Laura Lee (Schawo) R.; student Okla. Baptist U., 1957-58, U. Wichita, 1959-63; B.A. in English, Wichita State U., 1969, M.S. in Adminstrn., 1971; m. Penney Sue Tillotson, Dec. 27, 1964; children—James Christopher, Kathleen Marie, John Charles. Engring. draftsman Skyline Corp., Wichita, Kans., 1952, Boeing Aircraft Co., Wichita, Kans., 1953, O.A. Sutton Corp., Wichita, 1956, engring. checker, 1956-57; dept. clk. Cessna Aircraft Co., Wichita, 1958-59, bench hand, 1959-61, scheduling clk., 1961-62, mfg. scheduler, 1962-67, personnel rep., 1967-69, tng. supr., 1969-73, mgr. employee tng. and devel., 1973—; vocat. instr. evening sch. Wichita pub. schs., 1963. Area comdr. United Fund, Wichita, 1971; sec., Haysville Jr. Football League, Haysville, Kans., 1973-75; study com. chmn. Wichita Community Planning Council, 1972-73; mem. Haysville Planning Commn., 1976—, chmn., 1977-79, 80—; exec. com. Kans. State Employment and Tng. Council, 1979—, chmn. employment and tng. services com., 1981—; Sunday sch. tchr. Olivet Bapt. Ch., Wichita, 1951-53; children's choir dir. 2d Gen. Hosp. Chapel, Ger., 1955-56; music dir. Southside Bapt. Ch., Wichita, 1956-57; minister music Bapt. Ch., Hominy, Okla., 1957-60, youth dir., 1958-60; dir. tng. First Bapt. Ch., Mulvane, Kans., 1981—, numerous other ch. positions; bd. dirs. Christian Braile Found., 1971-74, Amigos de SER, Wichita, 1975-77. Am. Cancer Soc., Sedgwick County (Kans.) unit, 1977—, Ark-Valley Jr. Football League, 1974-75. Served with U.S. Army, 1953-56. Recipient Campaign award United Fund of Wichita, 1969, 70, 71, Outstanding Service plaque award Am. Cancer Soc., 1978, 79, 81, Individual Support award, 1979, others. Mem. Am. Mgmt. Assn., Am. Soc. Personnel Adminstrn. (pres. Wichita chpt. 1973-74, past president's plaque award 1975, chmn. nat. tng. and devel. com. 1979), Employee Devel. Assn., Psi Chi. Republican. Home: 424 Hollywood Dr Wichita KS 67217 Office: Cessna Wallace Div PO Box 7704 Wichita KS 67277

ROSENFELD, ARNOLD SOLOMON, editor; b. N.Y.C., Apr. 18, 1933; s. William and Sarah (Cohen) R.; student U. Houston, 1951; Profl. Journalism fellow Stanford, 1967; m. Ruth Doris Lilly, Sept. 30, 1956; children—William Bennett, Jonathan Andrew, Lauren Gay. Mem. staff Houston Post, 1953-67; asso. editor Detroit mag., Detroit Free Press, 1967; editor Detroit mag., 1968; mng. editor Dayton Daily News, 1968-76, editor, 1976—. Served with AUS, 1951-53. Recipient Editorial Writing award A.P. Mng. Editors Assn. Tex., 1966; Tex. Theta Sigma Phi award, 1969, 72; Media award Nat. Assn. Mental Health, 1976. Mem. Am. Soc. Newspaper Editors. Editor: A Thomason Sketchbook, 1969. Home: 563 E Dale Dr Dayton OH 45415 Office: Dayton Daily News Dayton OH 45401

ROSENFELD, MARTIN JEROME, hosp. adminstr.; b. Flint, Mich., Oct. 3, 1944; s. Israel Edward and Lillian Edith (Natchez) R.; B.A. (named Outstanding Sr. 1966), Mich. State U., 1968; M.H.A. with honors, Ind. No. U., 1978, M.B.A., 1979; 1 son, Joshua. Adminstr., Care Corp., Grand Rapids, Mich., 1969-70, Chandler Convalescent Center, Detroit, 1970-71, Grand Community Hosp., Detroit, 1971-73; exec. v.p., chief exec. officer Msgr. Clement Kern Hosp. Spl. Surgery, Warren, Mich., 1973—; instr. Marygrove Coll., 1975—; asso. prof. Mercy Coll., Detroit, 1978—. Vice pres. Detroit chpt. Jewish Nat. Fund, 1978—; pres. Cranbrook Village Homeowners Assn., 1977; chmn. Community Hosps. of Southeastern Mich.; mem. tech. work group Comprehensive Health Planning Council of Southeastern Mich.; mem. fin. mgmt. com., mem. hosp. affairs bd. Greater Detroit Area Hosp. Council. Mem. Am. Coll. Hosp. Adminstrs., Am. Acad. Med. Adminstrs. (state pres. 1978-79), Am. Hosp. Assn., Am. Pub. Health Assn., Mich. Hosp. Assn. (hosp. revenue resources com., adv. com. hosp. research and ednl. res.), Royal Soc. Health, Warren C. of C. (com. chmn. 1975). Author papers in field. Mem. editorial bd. The Human-Size Hosp.; mem. panel of experts The Health Care News. Home: 18917 Filmore Southfield MI 48075 Office: 21230 Dequindre Warren MI 48091

ROSENFELD, MARTIN SANFORD, physician; b. Des Moines, Jan. 11, 1946; s. Abraham S. and Beverly Lucille (Press) R.; B.S., U. Iowa, 1969; D.O., Coll. Osteo. Medicine and Surgery, Des Moines, 1971; m. Beverly Joseph, June 10, 1979; children—Sari Nicole, Amy Michelle, Jeremy Seth, Natalie Marin. Intern, Michael Reese Hosp., Chgo., 1971-72; resident in orthopedic surgery U. Tenn. Clin. Edn. Center-Baroness Erlanger Hosp., Chattanooga, 1972-76; practice medicine specializing in orthopedic surgery, Albuquerque, 1976-78, Des Moines, 1978—; mem. staff Des Moines Gen. Hosp., Iowa Meth. Med. Center, Mercy Med. Center, Luth. Hosp., N.W. Community Hosp.; clin. adj. prof. Coll. Osteo. Medicine and Surgery. Fellow Am. Acad. Orthopedic Surgeons; mem. Am. Osteo. Assn., Iowa Soc. Osteo. Physicians and Surgeons, Polk County Osteo. Med. Soc. Jewish. Club: Shriners. Home: 723 Foster Dr Des Moines IA 50312 Office: 1440 E Grand St Des Moines IA 50316

ROSENFELD, STEVEN ALAN, computer systems co. exec.; b. Queens, N.Y., Aug. 25, 1950; s. Morton and Carol Lois (Leibowitz) R.; B.A., Brandeis U., 1971; postgrad. Boston U., 1973-75, M.Data Processing, 1979; m. Gwendolyn Jane Kerstetter, June 22, 1974; 1 dau., Tiffany Amber. Asso. programmer Nixdorf Computer Inc., Wellesley, Mass., 1973, programmer, 1973-74, programmer, analyst, 1974, systems rep., 1974-75, systems mgr., 1975-78; pres. CMAC Systems & Software Co., Florissant, Mo., 1979—. Jewish. Home: 3463 Norberg Dr Florissant MO 63031 Office: PO Drawer T Florissant MO 63031

ROSENFIELD, DONALD ALLEN, psychologist; b. Buffalo, July 29, 1945; s. Lewis and Mildred Elizabeth (Allen) R.; B.A., U. Buffalo, 1965; M.S.W., U. Kans., 1972; Ph.D., U. Mo., 1981. Clin. dir. Catholic Charities of Kansas City-St. Joseph, Mo. Inc., Kansas City, Mo., 1974—. Mem. Am. Psychol. Assn., Mo. Psychol. Assn., Am. Assn. Marriage and Family Therapists (clin. mem.), Phi Delta Kappa. Home: 3726 Locust St Kansas City MO 64109 Office: 1112 Broadway Kansas City MO 64105

ROSENGARD, ABE BENJAMIN, wholesale furniture co. exec.; b. Chgo., Sept. 30, 1914; s. Charles L. and Anna (Braude) R.; grad. Morton Coll., 1936; m. Maeta Kaplan, June 23, 1946; children—Frances, Charles, Allen, Shelley, Sue. Sales mgr. Louisville Chair Co., Chgo., 1960—; pres. Abe Rosengard and Assos., Inc., Chgo., 1962—. Pres., Morton Parents' Swim Team Club, 1966—; precinct capt. Combined Jewish Appeals, 1965—. Bd. dirs. Dialogue Mag. for Blind. Served with inf., AUS, 1941-45. Mem. Mfrs. Agts. Club (pres., chmn. bd.), Furniture Club Am. (head com.), Nat. Wholesale Furniture Assn., Am. Legion (comdr. furniture mart post). Jewish religion (pres. temple). Mason (Shriner). Clubs: Village Field (dir.) (La Grange Park, Ill.); La Grange YMCA Bus. Men's. Home: 6858 Riverside Dr Berwyn IL 60402 Office: Pierce Industries Merchandise Mart Chicago IL 60654

ROSENKOETTER, GERALD EDWIN, engring. exec.; b. St. Louis, Mar. 16, 1927; s. Herbert Charles and Edna Mary (Englege) R.; B.C.E. (St. Louis Engrs. Club scholar), Washington U., St. Louis, 1951; M.C.E., Sever Inst., 1957; m. Ruth June Beekman, Sept. 10, 1949; children—Claudia Ruth, Carole Lee. Engr. and group leader Sverdrup & Parcel, Engrs. and Architects, St. Louis, 1951-58, project engr., 1959-63, project mgr., 1964-69, asst. chief engr., 1970-72, asst. v.p., chief engr. indsl. div., 1972-74, v.p., mgr. indsl. div., 1975-76, corp. v.p., corp. indsl. prin., 1977-80; pres. Sverdrup/CM, 1980—; mem. exec. bd. Sverdrup Corp., 1980—; lectr., cons. in field. Councilman, City of Berkeley (Mo.), 1957-59, councilman-at-large, 1959-60, mem. Zoning Bd. and Bd. Adjustment, 1957-64. Served with U.S. Army, 1945-46. Registered profl. engr., Mo., Colo., Ind., N.J., Tex., Wis., Pa., Del., Idaho, N.C., Ga., Fla., Kans. Mem. ASCE (Outstanding Sr. award 1951), Air Force Assn. Clubs: St. Louis Media, Forest Hills Country. Home: 42 Ballas Ct Town and Country MO 63131 Office: 801 N 11th St Saint Louis MO 63101

ROSENTHAL, HERBERT M., real estate exec.; b. Chgo., Oct. 1922; s. Nathan and Bess (Jacobson) R.; B.S. in Econs., U. Ill., 1947; m. Kaye L. Kimbro, June 27, 1950; children—Robert N., Richard M., Steven E., James D. Pres. Hyland Builders, 1949-55; pres. Dunbar Corp., Chgo., 1955—, chmn. bd., 1973—. Served in USAAF, 1943-47; ETO. Recipient Builder of Yr. award Home Builders Assn. Chgo., 1966; Recognition award Commonwealth Edison, 1971; Dunbar Day proclaimed by City of Chgo. to honor 25th anniversary of constrn. of nation's 1st condominium, July 31, 1981. Mem. Nat. Assn. Home Builders, Sigma Alpha Mu. Club: Mid-Am. Introduced condominium type dwelling to U.S., 1962. Home: 1353 Westmoor Trail Winnetka IL 60093 Office: 6033 N Sheridan Rd Chicago IL 60660

ROSENTHAL, LESLIE, commodity broker; b. Oradeamare, Romania, May 31, 1933; came to U.S., 1939, naturized, 1951; s. Alex and Elizabeth (Goldstein) R.; B.A., Roosevelt U., Chgo., 1955; m. Harriet Natalie Gross, June 19, 1955; children—David E., Arla Gail, Andrew Michael. Floor broker Chgo. Bd. Trade, 1959-60; nat. commodity mgr. Harris, Upham & Co., Chgo., 1960-65; partner S & R Commodities, Chgo., 1965-68, Peters & Co., Chgo., 1968-70; mng. partner Rosenthal & Co., Chgo., 1970—; dir. Chgo. Bd. Trade, 1973—, vice chmn., 1979-81, chmn., 1981—; bd. govs. Chgo. Bd. Trade Clearing Corp., 1974—, Chgo. Merc. Exchange, 1972—; served with AUS, 1956-58. Mem. Mid-Am. Exchange, Chgo. Bd. Options Exchange, Internat. Monetary Market. Office: 141 W Jackson Blvd Chicago IL 60604*

ROSENZWEIG, PETER MORRIS, clin. psychologist; b. Bklyn., May 1, 1949; s. Sidney and Judy (Nuszen) R.; B.A. magna cum laude, Yeshiva U., 1971; Ph.D., Northwestern U., 1975; m. Bobbie Sue Novetsky, June 20, 1971; children—Rivka, Joshua, Rena. Trainee in group therapy St. Luke Hosp., Day Hosp., Columbia U., N.Y.C., 1970; student intern Northwestern U. Outpatient Psychitric Clinic, Chgo., 1971-73; psychology resident U. Ill., Neuropsychiatric Inst., Chgo., 1974-75; pvt. practice clin. psychology, Niles, Ill., 1980—; pvt. practice psychology Behavioral Cons., Inc., Des Plaines, Ill., 1974-80; part-time asso. Asso. Psychotherapists of Chgo., Cathedral of St. James Counseling Center, 1975-77; mem. faculty div. psychology Northwestern U. Med. Center, Chgo., 1975—; mem. psychology staff Luth. Gen. Hosp., Park Ridge, Ill., 1975—, Old Orchard Hosp., Skokie, Ill., 1976—; staff psychologist The Ark, Chgo., 1976—. Mem. Am. Psychol. Assn., Ill. Psychol. Assn., Ill. Group Psychotherapy Soc., Assn. Labor-Mgmt. Adminstrs. and Cons. on Alcoholism, Delta Sigma Rho, Tau Kappa Alpha, Psi Chi. Jewish. Author: The Meaning of Egocentrism, 1975. Office: 228 Golf Mill Profl Bldg Niles IL 60648

ROSHEL, JOHN ALBERT, JR., orthodontist; b. Terre Haute, Ind., Apr. 7, 1941; s. John Albert and Mary M. (Griglione) R.; B.S., Ind. State U., 1963; D.D.S., Ind. U., 1966; M.S., U. Mich., 1968; children from previous marriage—John Albert III, James Livingston, Angela Kay. Individual practice dentistry, specializing in orthodontics Terre Haute, 1968—. Mem. Am. Dental Assn., Am. Assn. Orthodontists, Terre Haute C. of C., Lambda Chi Alpha, Delta Sigma Delta, Omicron Kappa Upsilon. Clubs: Terre Haute Country, Lions, Elks, K.C. Roman Catholic. Home: 1829 43d Dr Terre Haute IN 47802 Office: 4241 S 7th St Terre Haute IN 47802

ROSHELL, MARVIN J., state senator; b. Chippewa Falls, Wis., Oct. 27, 1932; ed. elec. trade sch.; married; 3 children. Elec. contractor; mem. Wis. Senate, 1978—. Sec.-treas., Chippewa Falls Indsl. Devel. Corp.; chmn. Chippewa Falls Fiscal Bd.; supr. Lafayette Town Bd., 1969—, chmn., 1975-79. Served with USAF, 1950-54. Mem. Am. Legion, VFW, AFL-CIO, Nat. Elec. Contractors Assn. (v.p. chpt.), Indianhead Towns Assn. Democrat. Clubs: Lions, Masons, Shriners, Elks. Address: Room 136 South State Capitol Madison WI 53702

ROSINGER, GEORGE, research psychologist; b. Prague, Czechoslovakia, Jan. 27, 1935; s. Julius and Anna (Lichtig) R.; m. Joyce Marlene Burger, Aug. 23, 1958; children—David Steven, Alan Scott, Julie Lynn; came to U.S., 1946, naturalized, 1951; student Hunter Coll., 1953-54; B.B.A., CCNY, 1957; M.A. (scholar), Lehigh U., 1959. Licensed psychologist, Ohio. Research psychologist Army Natick (Mass.) Labs., 1958-60; human factors specialist Martin Marietta Corp., Balt., 1961-65; project leader, sr. human factors engr. Rockwell Internat., Columbus, Ohio, 1965-67; mgr. Human Resources Research, Battelle-Columbus Labs., 1967—; participant, rev. panel NSF, 1977, 78; adv. com., gifted and talented sci. and math. project Columbus Public Schs., 1982. Mem. Am. Psychol. Assn., Soc. Applied Learning Tech., Am. Soc. for Tng. and Devel., Columbus C. of C. (sch. issues com. 1974-76, subcom. chmn. 1975), Psi Chi. Contbr. articles to profl. jours. Home: 2840 Berwick Blvd Columbus OH 43209 Office: Battelle-Columbus Labs 505 King Ave Columbus OH 43201

ROSKENS, RONALD WILLIAM, univ. system pres.; b. Spencer, Iowa, Dec. 11, 1932; s. William E. and Delores A.L. (Beving) R.; m. Lois Grace Lister, Aug. 22, 1954; children—Elizabeth, Barbara, Brenda, William; B.A., U. No. Iowa, 1953, M.A., 1955; Ph.D., State U. Iowa, 1958; LL.D., Creighton U., 1978, Huston-Tillotson Coll., 1981; Litt.D., Nebr. Wesleyan U., 1981, L.H.D., Hastings Coll., 1981. Tchr., Minburn (Iowa) High Sch., 1954, Woodward (Iowa) State Hosp., summer 1954; asst. counselor to men State U. Iowa, 1956-59; dean of men, asst. prof. spl. edn. Kent (Ohio) State U., 1959-63, asso. prof. spl. edn., 1963-68, prof., 1968-72, asst. to pres., 1963-66, dean for adminstrn., 1966-68, v.p. for adminstrn., 1968-71, exec. v.p., prof. ednl. adminstrn., 1971-72; chancellor, prof. ednl. adminstrn. U. Nebr. at Omaha, 1972-77, pres. U. Nebr. system, 1977—; dir. Omaha Nat. Bank, InterNorth, Inc., Guarantee Mut. Life Co., Art's Way Mfg. Co.; mem. Nat. Exec. Res. Corps. Mem. Kent City Planning Commn.

mem. bus.-higer edn. forum, chmn. govtl. relations, bd. dirs. Am. Council on Edn.; chmn. com. on financing higher edn. Nat. Assn. State Univs. and Land-grant Colls. bd. dirs. Found. Study Presdl. and Congl. Terms, Met. YMCA, Boy Scouts Am., Midlands United Community Services, NCCJ; mem. exec. bd. North Central Assn.; trustee Huston Tillotson Coll., Austin, Tex., chmn., 1976—; trustee Brownell-Talbott Sch., Joslyn Art Mus., 1970-73, Nebr. Meth. Hosp., 1974-77, Willa Cather Pioneer Meml. and Ednl. Found., 1979, Harry S Truman Inst. Named Nat. 4-H Alumnus, 1968, Outstanding Alumnus, U. No. Iowa, 1974; recipient NCCJ Brotherhood award, 1977, B'nai B'rith Americanism citation, 1978, others. Mem. AAAS, Am. Personnel and Guidance Assn., Am., Ohio coll. personnel assns., Assn. Urban Univs. (pres. 1976-77), AAUP, Am. Ednl. Research Assn., Am. Psychol. Assn., Kent Area C. of C. (pres. 1966), Young Pres.'s Orgn., Com. on Fgn. Relations, Phi Delta Kappa, Phi Eta Sigma, Sigma Tau Gamma (pres. grand council 1968-70, Disting. Achievement award 1980), Omicron Delta Kappa, Mason (32 deg.). Co-editor: Paradox, Process and Progress, 1968; Contbr. articles to profl. jours. Home: 5930 Norman Rd Lincoln NE 68512 Office: 3835 Holdrege St Lincoln NE 68583

ROSMANN, MICHAEL RAY, clin. psychologist, farmer; b. Harlan, Iowa, June 23, 1946; s. Raymond Joseph and Ellen (Mertens) R.; B.A., U. Colo., 1968; M.S., U. Utah, 1972; Ph.D., U. Utah, 1974; m. Marilyn Sanada, June 23, 1972; children—Shelby, Jon-Michael. Staff psychologist Granite Mental Health Center, Salt Lake City, 1971-72; teaching fellow U. Utah, Salt Lake City, 1972-74; asst. prof. dept. psychology U. Va., Charlottesville, 1974-79; pvt. practice clin. psychology, Harlan, 1979—; dir. Family Counseling Program, Charlottesville, 1975-79; instr. Iowa Western Community Coll.; farmer, Harlan. Chmn., Shelby County Democratic Platform Com. Recipient grants Div. Justice and Crime Prevention, 1976-79, Commonwealth of Va., 1976-79, U. Va., 1974-79; lic. psychologist, Iowa, Va. Mem. Am. Psychol. Assn. Roman Catholic. Contbr. chpt. to book, articles to sci. publs. Home and office: Box 164 Route 1 Harlan IA 51537

ROSS, ALVIN EUGENE, sales exec.; b. Minot, N.D., Apr. 4, 1923; s. Samuel and Goldie (Perlin) R.; B.A. in Bus. and Mktg., U. Wash., 1947; m. Barbie Wechsler, Apr. 14, 1946; children—Talby Wynne, Elyse Marie, Mark Wechsler. Territorial rep. Hat Corp. Am., 1960-63; territorial rep. H.D. Lee Co., Inc., 1963-65, dist. mgr., 1965-69, regional mgr., 1969-73; regional v.p. sales Wrangler Boyswear div. Blue Bell, Inc., Chgo., 1973—. Served with USAAF, 1942-45; PTO. Named Sales Mgr. of Year, Wrangler Sportswear, 1977, 81. Mem. Mid-Am. Menswear Assn. Clubs: Elks, B'nai B'rith (past pres. Salem, Oreg.). Home: 263 Club House Dr #216 Palatine IL 60067 Office: 8-102 Apparel Center Chicago IL 60654

ROSS, ANTHONY HARLAN, steel co. exec.; b. Kansas City, Mo., July 13, 1956; stepson Maurice S. and Florence Warshawsky; student No. Mich. U.; m. Kathleen Ann Dodge, June 18, 1976; 1 dau., Nicole Leigh. With Ishpeming Steel Corp. (Mich.), 1975—, v.p., 1977—. Sec.-treas. Temple Beth Sholom, Ishpeming, 1976, pres., 1977-78, dir., 1979; sec.-treas. Ishpeming Diplomats, 1977, v.p., 1978, pres., 1979. Clubs: Golden Wildcat (No. Mich. U.); Ishpeming Rotary (dir. 1977, sec. 1979); Wawonowin Country. Home: 1765 Rose St Ishpeming MI 49849 Office: PO Box 379 North Lake Location Ishpeming MI 49849

ROSS, BERNARD HARRIS, acct.; b. St. Louis, Mar. 30, 1927; s. Solomon and Anna (Goodman) R.; student U. Mich., 1944-45; B.S. in Acctg., U. Ill., 1949; D. Health Administrn. (hon.), U. Guayaquil, Ecuador, 1975; m. Marian Frager, June 15, 1952; children—Curtis Bennett, Debra Benita. Jr. acct. Touche, Niven, Bailey & Smart, Chgo., 1949; jr. acct. Chase Conover & Co., Chgo., 1949; staff acct. Robert Penn & Co., Chgo. and St. Louis, 1949-52; partner Curtis and Ross (now Laventhol & Horwath), Carbondale, Ill., 1952-77; exec. nat. services dir. health care Touche Ross & Co., Chgo., 1977—. Served with USAAF, 1944-46. C.P.A., Ill., La., N.C., Va. Mem. Am. Inst. C.P.A.'s, Ill. C.P.A. Soc., Nat. Assn. Accts., Hosp. Fin. Mgmt. Assn., Am. Hosp. Assn., Catholic Hosp. Assn., Fedn. Am. Hosps (hon. dir.), Am. Health Care Assn., Am. Coll. Nursing Home Adminstrs., Am. Public Health Assn. Home: 1853 Mission Hills Ln Northbrook IL 60062 Office: 111 E Wacker Dr Chicago IL 60601

ROSS, CHESTER WHEELER, clergyman; b. Evansville, Ind., Nov. 3, 1922; s. Mylo Wheeler and Irma (Berning) R.; A.B. cum laude, Kans. Wesleyan U., 1952; M.Div., Garrett Theol. Sem., 1954; D. Ministry, St. Paul Sch. Theology, 1979; m. Ruth Eulaine Briney, Aug. 30, 1949; children—James W., Deborah R., Judith K., Martha S., John W. Ordained to ministry United Meth. Ch., 1953; enlisted pvt. USAAF, 1942, advanced through grades to lt. col., 1968; chaplain, Africa, Europe, Alaska, Greenland, Taiwan; installation chaplain, Columbus AFB, Miss., 1972-75; ret., 1975; pastor Unity Parish, Iuka, Kans., 1975-80, Ness City (Kans.) United Meth. Ch., 1980. Instr. Parent Effectiveness Tng., 1st aid ARC; cubmaster, scoutmaster, dist. chmn. Boy Scouts Am., recipient Silver Beaver award, 1975; mem. parish devel. council Kans. area United Meth. Ch., 1975-81, mem. dist. council Hays dist., 1980-81, mem. Global Ministry Council, 1975-81. Decorated Air medal (2), Meritorious Service medal (2). Mem. Ness City Ministers Assn., Mil. Chaplains Assn., Acad. Parish Clergy, Ret. Officers Assn., Res. Officers Assn., Air Force Aid, Air Force Assn., Nat. Hist. Soc., Appalachian Trail Conf., Assn. Ret. Persons, Order Ky. Col., Am. Legion, VFW. W. Club: Rotary. Address: 417 N School Ness City KS 67560

ROSS, DAVID EUGENE, JR., physician; b. Lorain, Ohio, June 15, 1930; s. David Eugene and Linnie S. (Feazell) R.; A.B., Tougaloo Coll., Miss., 1950; M.D., Meharry Med. Coll., 1955; m. Ruthie Ellison, March 26, 1968; children—David, Karen, Anthony, Michael, Mildred, Nathaniel, Ruth, Rachael, Rebeccah. Intern, Madigan Army Hosp., Tacoma, 1955-56; practice medicine specializing in family practice, Gary, Ind., 1960—; dir. emergency dept. Meth. Hosp., Gary, 1970-76, dir. family residency program, 1975, med. dir. paramedic program, 1974-76; asso. prof. Ind. U.; pres. med. staff Meth. Hosp., 1974-75. Police civil service commr., Gary, 1972-74. Diplomate Am. Bd. Family Practice. Mem. Lake County Med. Soc. (v.p. 1975-76), Am. Acad. Family Physicians, Am. Acad. Emergency Physicians, AMA. Lutheran. Home: 433 Arthur St Gary IN 46404 Office: 2318 W 5th Ave Gary IN 46404

ROSS, EARL E., juvenile worker; b. St. Louis, July 3, 1942; s. Edward Earl and Ruth Randles (Loewen) R.; B.A. in Psychology, Central Mo. State U., 1965; M.A. in Corrections, Webster Coll., Webster Groves, Mo., 1976; m. Mary Donna Moore, May 31, 1964; 1 son, Damon Moore. Reporter, Warrensburg (Mo.) Daily Star-Jour., 1965; social worker St. Louis County Welfare Div., Maplewood, Mo., 1966-68; asso. dist. scout exec. Boy Scouts Am., St. Louis, 1968; dep. juvenile officer St. Louis County Juvenile Ct., Clayton, Mo., 1969-72; program dir. St. Louis County Detention Center, Clayton, 1972—; asst. supt. St. Louis County Detention Center, Clayton, 1978—; instr. tng. sessions. Mem. Am. Mgmt. Assn., Mo. Juvenile Officers Assn., St. Louis County Juvenile Justice Assn., Greater St. Louis Probation and Parole Assn., Am. Corrections Assn. Home: 15333 Appalachian Trail Chesterfield MO 63017 Office: 501 S Brentwood Blvd Clayton MO 63105

ROSS, EDWARD, physician; b. Fairfield, Ala., Oct. 10, 1937; s. Horace and Carrie Lee (Griggs) R.; B.S., Clark Coll., 1959; M.D., Ind. U., 1963; m. Catherine I. Webster, Jan. 19, 1974; children—Edward, Ronald, Cheryl, Anthony. Intern, Marion County Gen. Hosp., Indpls., 1963; resident in internal medicine Ind. U., 1964-66, 68, cardiology research fellowship, 1968-70, clin. asst. prof. medicine, 1970; cardiologist Capitol Med. Assn., Indpls., 1970-74; pvt. practice medicine, specializing in cardiology, Indpls., 1974—; staff cardiologist Winona Meml. Hosp., Indpls.; Methodist Hosp., Indpls. Mem. Central Ind. Health Planning Council, 1972-73; dir. Ind. chpt. Am. Heart Assn., 1973-74; dir. multiphasic screening East Side Clinic, Flanner Ho. of Indpls., 1968-71; med. dir. Nat. Center for Health Service Research and Devel., HEW, 1970; dir. hyptertensive screening State of Ind., 1974. Served to capt., MC, USAF, 1966-68. Woodrow Wilson fellow, 1959; Nat. Found. Health scholar, 1955. Diplomate Am. Bd. Internal Medicine. Fellow Royal Soc. Promotion of Health (Eng.), Am. Coll. Angiology, Am. Coll. Cardiology; mem. AMA, Ind. Med. Soc., Marion County Med. Soc., Am. Soc. Internal Medicine, Am. Heart Assn., Aesculapean Med. Soc., Hoosier State Med. Assn. (pres. 1980-82), NAACP, Urban League, Alpha Omega Alpha, Alpha Kappa Mu, Beta Kappa Chi, Omega Psi Phi. Baptist. Office: 3737 N Meridian St Indianapolis IN 46208

ROSS, EDWIN FRANCIS, hosp. adminstr.; b. Struthers, Ohio, June 19, 1917; s. Edwin Francis and Ehtel Marie (Wymer) R.; B.S., Mt. Union Coll., 1939; M.H.A., Washington U., St. Louis, 1949; m. Virginia Kerr, Apr. 26, 1941; children—Richard, David. Tchr., Public Schs. Struthers, 1940-42; adminstrv. resident Huron Rd. Hosp., East Cleveland, 1948-49; adminstr. Doctor's Hosp., Cleveland Heights, 1949-53; asst. dir. Univ. Hosp., Cleve., 1953-62; adminstr. Univ. Hosp., Omaha, 1962-66; pres. Fairview Gen. Hosp., Cleve., 1966—; faculty Coll. Medicine, U. Nebr., 1962-66; pres. Cleve. Area League Nursing, 1956. Mem. Greater Cleve. Hosp. Assn. (pres. 1972-74, chmn. exec. council 1974-75), Ohio Hosp. Assn., Am. Hosp. Assn., Am. Coll. Hosp. Adminstrs. Republican. Presbyterian. Clubs: Masons, Kiwanis. Office: 18101 Lorain Ave Cleveland OH 44111

ROSS, GEORGE EDWIN, social scientist; b. St. Louis, June 12, 1927; s. Isaac Felix and Emma Antoinette (Basola) R.; B.S., U. Ill., 1951, M.Ed., 1953, D.Ed., 1960. Tchr. pub. schs., Sandoval, Ill., 1949-50; prin., Centralia (Ill.) City Schs., 1950-56; prof. edn. Western Ill. U., Macomb, 1960-67; asst. dir. Ill. Office Edn., 1967-69; staff devel. coordinator Ill. Dept. Children and Family Services, E. St. Louis, Ill., 1969-74, child welfare adminstr. Salem area, 1974—. Chmn. Human Relations Com. City of Macomb, 1964-67, REgional Manpower Com., 1976—; mem. Gov.'s Com. on Spl. Edn., 1964-67. Mem. Western Ill. Higher Edn. Assn. (pres. 1966), Ill. Welfare Assn. (dir.), Child Care Assn. Ill., NEA, Ill. Edn. Assn. Republican. Mem. Ch. Disciples of Christ. Clubs: Elks (past state chmn), Odd Fellows (past dist. pres.), Moose. Contbr. articles to profl. jours. Home: 19 Orchard Dr Sandoval IL 62882 Office: 205 E Locust St Salem IL 62881

ROSS, GEORGE PAUL, educator; b. Galion, Ohio, June 1, 1943; s. George Edwin and Verna May (Bachelder) R.; B.A., Milligan Coll., 1966, postgrad., 1969-70; postgrad. Ozark Bible Coll., 1963-64, E. Tenn. State U., 1970; vocat. cert. Kent State U., 1979, Bowling Green U., 1980; m. Nancy Ellen Parke, Feb. 11, 1967; children—Timothy Paul, Matthew Peter. Ordained to ministry Christian Ch., 1966; with Ideal Electric Co., Mansfield, Ohio, 1966-69; instr. driving Ted Oakland Driving System, Akron, Ohio, 1970-72; adult probation officer Stark County, Canton, Ohio, 1972-73; security guard Babcock Wilcox, Canton, Ohio, 1973—; instr. auto body repair Indian River Sch., Massillon, 1979—, Stark County Jount Vocat. Sch., 1978-79; owner, mgr. Best Quality Auto Service, Canton, 1974-78. Mem. Aux. Police Force, Galion, 1967-69; jr. adviser 4-H Club, 1960-61; records keeper Cub Scouts, North Canton; elder, tchr. Sunday Sch., Jackson Christian Ch., Massillon. Mem. United Steel Workers Am., Ohio Educators Assn., Am. Vocat. Assn., Ohio Vocat. Assn., Amateur Radio Relay League, Ohio Sideband Assn. Home: 8492 Portage St NW Massillon OH 44646 Office: 2775 E Erie St Massillon OH 44646

ROSS, JACOB NATHAN, podiatrist; b. Molchad, Poland, Dec. 25, 1919; s. Bernard and Ida (Orjechowski) R.; came to U.S., 1923, naturalized, 1929; D.P.M., Ill. Coll. Podiatric Medicine, 1940; B.S., Chgo. State U., 1967; m. Raye Noven, June 4, 1944; children—Lewis, David, James. Podiatrist, Dr. Scholl Co., 1944-45, Ill. Foot Ambulatory, 1945; podiatrist Mandel Bros. Employees, 1945-47; pvt. practice podiatry, South Shore Area, Chgo., 1946-67, Homewood, Ill., 1967—; mem. staff various rest homes and pvt. hosps. Bd. dirs. South Suburban Adv. Council Health Services Adminstrn; chmn. Health Careers Work/Study High Sch. Program, 1980-81. Served with M.C., U.S. Army, 1941-44. Cert. in sports medicine N.Y. Coll. Podiatric Medicine, Calif. Coll. Podiatric Medicine. Mem. Am. Podiatry Assn. (Mennen award 1947), Acad. Ambulatory Foot Surgeons (charter), Mil. Assn. Podiatrists, Am. Med. Writers Assn., Am. Public Health Assn., Ill. Podiatry Soc. (continuing edn. awards 1976-80), Ill. Public Health Assn., Homewood C. of C. (dir. 1969-73). Clubs: Rotary (sec. 1979) (Homewood); Lapidary (Chgo.); Earth Sci. (Park FOrest, Ill.); B'nai B'rith. Office: 1916 Ridge Rd Homewood IL 60430

ROSS, LYNNE NANNEN, food service cons.; b. Pierson, Iowa, Sept. 10, 1936; d. Ben M. and Shirley Nannen; B.S., Iowa State U., 1958, M.S., 1966, Ph.D., 1978; children—Joyce, Brenda. Dietitian, Stouffer Corp., Cleve., 1958-59, Pitts., 1959-60; chief dietitian Meth. Hosp., Sioux City, Iowa, 1960-64; therapeutic dietitian Iowa Meth. Hosp., Des Moines, 1965-66; dietitian Friley Hall, Iowa State U., Ames, 1965-66; dietary cons. Iowa Dept. Health, Des Moines, 1966-70; coordinator instrn. dept. nutrition and dietetics U. Mo.-Columbia Med. Center, 1970-71; instr. food service programs Des Moines Area Community Coll., Ankeny, Iowa, 1971-72, dir. food services and food service programs, 1972-76; supr. bus. enterprises Iowa Commn. for Blind, Des Moines, 1976-78; asst. dir. dept. dietetics Iowa Meth. Med. Center, Des Moines, 1978-79; pres. Creative Concepts, Ankeny, 1979—; mem. food service adv. com. Des Moines Public Schs., 1975-76, adv. com. Des Moines Tech. High Sch., 1976-79, chmn. vocat. food service adv. com., 1974-81. Mem. Adminstrv. Mgmt. Soc., Am. Home Econs. Assn., Am. Hotel Motel Assn., Am. Sch. Food Service Assn., Am. Vocat. Assn., Des Moines Assn. Dietitians and Food Mgrs., Dietetic Educators Assn., Dietitians in Bus. and Industry (treas.) Greater Des Moines Hotel Motel Assn. (sec.), Iowa Chefs and Culinarians Club, Iowa Dietetic Assn. (pres.-elect), Iowa Health Care Assn., Iowa Home Econs. Assn., Iowa Hotel Motel Motor Inn Assn., Iowa Restaurant Assn., Iowa Sch. Food Service Assn., Iowa Vocat. Assn., Nat. Assn. Coll. and Univ. Food Services, Nat. Restaurant Assn., Nat. Assn. Postsecondary and Adult Vocat. Home Econs. Educators (treas.), River Valley Culinary Assn., Am. Dietetic Assn., Omicron Nu. Address: 814 SE Sherman Dr Ankeny IA 50021

ROSS, MARY ANN, statistician; b. Frankfort, Ind., June 2, 1946; d. Jack L. and Dorothy Irene R.; B.S., Purdue U., 1968, M.S., 1970, Ph.D., 1974. Research asst. Purdue U., West Lafayette, Ind., 1966-69, statis. cons. Computing Center, 1969-71, supr. statis. services, 1971—; cons., 1969—. NDEA fellow, 1968-70. Mem. Am. Statis. Assn., Multiple Linear Regression Spl. Interest Group, Info. Exchange for Users of Statis. Software. Contbr. articles to profl. jours. Home: 40 LaRosa Ct Lafayette IN 47905 Office: Computing Center Purdue U West Lafayette IN 47907

ROSS, MYRON DONALD, office adminstrn. cons.; b. Chgo., Sept. 30, 1909; s. Michael J. and Bertha (Krutch) R.; B.S., Northwestern U., 1934; m. Marie V. Manning, June 13, 1935; children—Donald R., Darlene M. With Jewel Tea Co., Inc. (name changed to Jewel Cos., Inc.), Melrose Park, Ill., 1932-70, mgr. inventory control, cost accounting depts., mgr. cash, payroll dept., store personnel mgr., office mgr., 1932-45, mgr. cash operating div., 1945-54, mgr. systems div., 1954-63, mgr. electronic data processing div., 1963-66, asst. controller Chicagoland Stores, 1966-67, asst. to exec. v.p., 1967-70; cons. office adminstrn., 1970—. Recipient Merit Award key Office Mgmt. Assn. Chgo., 1950, Leadership plaque Nat. Office Mgmt. Assn., 1951. Mem. Nat., Chgo. (pres. 1949-50) office mgmt. assns., Bus. Electronics Round Table Assn. (pres. 1964-65), S.W. Suburban Council on Aging (v.p. 1980—), Exec. Club Chgo. Home and Office: 10543 Dorchester Rd Westchester IL 60153

ROSS, NEIL L., ophthalmologist; b. Chgo., Dec. 5, 1948; s. John Gunther and Doris (Serrins) R.; B.S.E.E., B.S., M.I.T., 1971; M.D., Northwestern U., 1975; m. Lynn Elizabeth Hauser, June 20, 1975. Resident in ophthalmology Northwestern U. Med. Sch., 1975-79, fellow in retina, 1979-80; practice medicine specializing in ophthalmology, DeKalb, Ill., 1980—; mem. staff Kishwaukee Community Hosp., DeKalb, Sycamore Mcpl. Hosp.; instr. dept. ophthalmology Northwestern U. Med. Sch., 1980—. Diplomate Am. Bd. Ophthalmology. Mem. DeKalb County Med. Soc., Ill. State Med. Soc., AMA, Am. Acad. Ophthalmology, Chgo. Ophthal. Soc., Sigma Xi. Club: Rotary. Office: 8 Health Services Dr PO Box 968 DeKalb IL 60115

ROSS, NORMAN ALEXANDER, banker; b. Miami, Fla., Jan. 30, 1922; s. Norman DeMille and Beatrice (Dowsett) R.; A.B., Stanford U., 1946; postgrad. Trinity Coll., Oxford (Eng.) U., 1953; D.H.L., Lincoln (Ill.) Coll., 1959, Fisk U., 1978, Roosevelt U., 1979; Litt.D., Lake Forest Coll., 1967; children—Isabel, Susan Diana. Airport mgr. Pan Am. Airways, 1943; asst. to producer Metro-Goldwyn-Mayer, 1943-44; partner Norman Ross & Co., 1947-50; owner Norman Ross Record Club, 1951-52; radio-TV commentator NBC, ABC, Chgo., 1953-64, ABC, WGN and WBKB, Chgo., 1964-68; v.p. pub. affairs First Nat. Bank Chgo., 1968—, sr. v.p. communications dept., 1979—; pres. Ross-McElroy Prodns., Inc., 1962-68; former columnist Chgo. Daily News and Chgo. mag. Served with inf. AUS, World War II. Decorated cavaliere Dell Ordine Repubblica Italiana; U.S. Army Outstanding Civilian Service medal; officer and cross of chevalier Legion of Honor (France); recipient Peabody award for TV program Off the Cuff, 1964. Mem. Phi Gamma Delta. Clubs: Chgo., Racquet, Oxford, Mid Day, Econ. (Chgo.); Wayfares. Office: Communications Dept 1st Nat Bank Chgo One First Nat Plaza Chicago IL 60670

ROSS, PATRICK CONROY, rubber co. exec.; b. Iron River, Mich., Aug. 27, 1929; s. William D. and Elsie A. (Thompson) R.; A.B., U. Mich., 1951, M.A., 1976; grad. Advanced Mgmt. Program, Harvard U., 1969; m. Ann M. Groves, Feb. 2, 1952; children—Stewart C., Charles E., Nancy J. Merchandising mgr. WWJ-The Detroit News, 1956-57; sales mgr. Argus Cameras, 1957-62; area dir. Europe, B.F. Goodrich, pres. internat. div., 1962-70, pres. B.F. Goodrich Tire group, 1972—, exec. v.p. B.F. Goodrich Co., 1978—. Mem. Ohio Council on Econ. Edn.; bd. dirs. Akron Internat. Inst., Center for Econ. Edn., U. Akron; trustee Akron Children's Hosp. Served with USAF, 1951-55. Mem. Rubber Mfrs. Assn. Club: Portage Country. Office: 500 S Main St Akron OH 44318

ROSS, RAYMOND SAMUEL, educator, author; b. Milw.; s. Samuel and Agnes Tobina (Thorkildsen) R.; Ph.B., Marquette U., 1950, M.A., 1951; Ph.D., Purdue U., 1954; m. Ricky Reichmann, June 19, 1948; children—Mark, Scott. Instr., Marquette U., Milw., 1950-51; asst. prof. Ohio State U., Columbus, 1954-58; mem. faculty Wayne State U., Detroit, 1958—, prof. speech communication 1965—. Served with inf., U.S. Army, 1943-45. Decorated Purple Heart. Mem. Internat. Communication Assn., Am. Psychol. Assn., Speech Communication Assn. Author: Persuasion: Communication and Interpersonal Relations, 1974; Essentials of Speech Communication, 1979; Speech Communication, 5th edit., 1980; (with Mark Ross) Understanding Persuasion, 1981, Relating and Interacting, 1982. Home: 1714 Norfolk Dr Birmingham MI 48009 Office: Wayne State Univ 535 Manoogian Hall Detroit MI 48202

ROSS, RUSSELL MARION, educator; b. Washington, Iowa, June 2, 1921; s. Harold Ellis and Lucille Carrie (Dorris) R.; B.A., U. Iowa, 1942; certificate Harvard, 1945; M.A., U. Iowa, 1946, Ph.D., 1948; m. Shirley Arlene Jackson, June 1, 1944; children—Sheryl Ross, Jule. Instr. dept. polit. sci. U. Iowa, Iowa City, 1946-48, asst. prof., 1948-52, asso. prof., 1952-60, research prof., 1963-64, prof., 1965—, chmn. dept., 1970—; adminstrv. asst. to atty. gen. Iowa, 1960; exec. asst. to Gov. Iowa, 1961-62. Chmn., Regional Planning Commn., 1966-68; pres. Iowa City Community Sch. Bd., 1969-70; chmn. Iowa Campaign Finance Disclosure Commn., 1973-77. Mayor, University Heights, 1954-60. Bd. dirs. Goodwill Industries S.E. Iowa. Served to lt. USNR, 1942-45. Mem. Internat. City Mgrs. Assn. (hon.), Am. Pub. Adminstrn. Soc., AAUP, Am., Mid-West polit. sci. assns., Phi Beta Kappa, Phi Delta Kappa, Pi Sigma Alpha. Kiwanian. Author: Iowa Government and Administration, 1958; State and Local Government and Administration, 1966. Home: 315 Highland Dr Iowa City IA 52240

ROSS, WILLIAM D., chem. research corp. exec.; b. Eaton, Ohio, Jan. 9, 1930; s. Roy C. and Ramona Nannette (Bangs) R.; B.A., Earlham Coll., 1953; M.S., Miami U., 1974; m. Maralyn L. Clark, Nov. 1, 1957; 1 dau., Susan Anne William. With Monsanto Research Corp., 1957—, sr. research specialist, 1980—, project mgr., supr. biol. labs., Dayton, Ohio, 1975—. Mem. Sch. Bd., Dayton, 1970-74; precinct chmn. Democratic party, 1965-75; deacon United Ch. of Christ, 1978—. Served with AUS, 1954-56. Mem. Tissue Culture Assn. (vice chmn. regional chpt. 1978—), AAAS, Ohio Valley Chromatography Discussion Group, Sigma Xi. Contbr. numerous articles to profl. jours.; patentee in field. Home: 9060 Concord Rd Eaton OH 45320 Office: Monsanto Research Corp 1515 Nicholas Rd Dayton OH 45418

ROSS, WILLIAM EARL, JR., educator; b. Kansas City, Mo., May 23, 1935; s. William Earl and Katherine Greenlee (Holmes) R.; B.S. in Edn., U. Mo., 1957, M.A., 1969; m. Patricia Nichols, June 6, 1956; children—Debra, Cynthia, Katherine. Tchr., head basketball coach, intramural dir. Tarkio (Mo.) High Sch., 1957-58; tchr., head track and basketball coach Kansas City (Mo.) Westport High Sch., 1958-60; tchr., head basketball and golf coach Kansas City Paseo High Sch., 1960-68; men's and women's head basketball coach, men's and women's head golf coach U. Mo., Kansas City, 1968-73, prof. health and phys. edn., sports info. dir., 1973—; referee Nat. Football League, 1973—. Pres., Red Bridge Hills Homes Assn., Kansas City, 1978-79. Named Kansas City Interscholastic Coach of the Year, 1967-68; West Central Basketball Coach of the Year, 1968-69; referee Nat. Football League Hall of Fame Game, 1977. Mem. Kansas City Coaches Assn. (pres. 1967-68), Kansas City Ofcls. Assn. (pres. 1970-72, dir. 1981—), Nat. Assn. Intercollegiate Athletics (dist. chmn. 1972-73, Sports Info. Dir. of Yr. 1979), Nat. Collegiate Athletic Assn., Nat. Football League Ofcls. Assn., Mo. High Sch. Activities Assn. Christian Ch. Clubs: U. Mo. Kansas City Phys. Edn., U. Mo. Kansas City Booster. Inventor most original basketball uniform Naismith Basketball Hall of Fame, 1964; author: McCalls Rebounder Drills - Article and Drills, 1966. Home: 340 E 106th St Kansas City MO 64114 Office: 5100 Rockhill Rd Kansas City MO 64110

ROSSI, DAVID LEWIS, oil and gas co. ofcl.; b. Greensburg, Pa., Jan. 12, 1953; s. Achilles Victor and Mary (Scarpo) R.; B.S., Salem Coll., 1975; safety courses; m. Peggy L. Greene, Apr. 22, 1978. Tchr., Hempfield Area Sch. Dist., 1975-78; safety technician, Lebanon, Tenn., 1978-79; asst. safety supr. Tex. Eastern Transmission, Seymour, Ind., 1980—. Defensive driving instr. Nat. Safety Council; vol. fireman Carbon Vol. Fire Dept., Greensburg, 1970-78, capt., 1976-78. Cert. indsl. audiometric technician; cert. self-contained breathing apparatus instr.; recipient advanced safety cert. Nat. Safety Council. Mem. Am. Soc. Safety Engrs. Roman Catholic. Club: Moose. Office: PO Box 427 Seymour IN 47274

ROSSI, JEAN JOSEPH, clin. and social psychologist; b. Plainfield, N.J., Mar. 30, 1926; s. Jean and Margaret (Marra) R.; B.Sc., Seton Hall U., 1949; M.A., Cath. U. Am., 1954; Ph.D., U. Ottawa, 1957; m. Ilene Georgene Lindsoe, Dec. 31, 1956; children—Mary Beth, Anna Christine, Paula Jeanne, John Paul. Psychologist, Cath. U. Counseling Center, 1949-51, Nat. Tng. Sch. for Boys, 1950-51, Willmar State Hosp., 1951-61; clin. psychologist West Central Minn. Mental Health Center, 1958-61; pvt. practice, chief psychologist Luth. Gen. Hosp., Des Plaines, Ill., 1961-69, program dir. alcohol treatment center, 1968-74, dir. research and evaluation psychiatry, 1974, dir. personality lab., 1967—; pres. Behavioral Consultants, Inc., 1972—; mental health cons. Govt. of Can. Health and Welfare, Provinces of Alta. and Man., States of Ill., Ky., Iowa; invited faculty U. Alaska, Alaska Meth. U., U. Iowa, Northwestern U., U. Ala. Served with USNR, 1943-46; PTO. Recipient grants Hill Found., 1956-60, Am. Luth. Ch., 1976-77. Mem. Am., Ill. psychol. assns., AAAS, Assn. Advanced Behavior Therapy, Am., Ill. group psychotherapy socs., Internat. Council Alcoholism and Addictions, Alcohol and Drug Problems Assn. N.Am. Democrat. Roman Catholic. Author: Treatment Issues in Alcoholism, 1977. Editor: (with others) Therapeutic Community, 1975; Alcohol and Alcohol Problems, New Thinking and New Directions, 1976; Core Knowledge Package-Alcoholism Treatment, 1978; contbr. articles profl. jours. Office: 2474 Dempster St Suite 105 Des Plaines IL 60016

ROSSMAN, ELMER CHRIS, agronomist; b. Rawlins, Wyo., Nov. 17, 1919; s. Chris and Margreth (Knudsen) R.; B.S., Oreg. State U., 1941; M.S., Mich. State U., 1943; Ph.D., Iowa State U., 1948; m. Elizabeth Jean Schell, Aug. 8, 1942; children—Chris, Janet, David. Asst. prof. crop sci. Mich. State U., 1948-53, asso. prof., 1953-57, prof., 1957—. Fellow AAAS; mem. Am. Soc. Agronomy, Am. Soc. Plant Physiologists, Genetics Soc. Am., Genetics Soc. Can., Am. Genetics Assn., Sigma Xi, Phi Kappa Phi, Sigma Gamma Delta, Phi Kappa Psi (faculty adv. and dir. Mich. State U. chpt. 1954—). Republican. Contbr. numerous articles on corn hybrids, breeding and prodn. to profl. publs.; developer numerous inbred parents and hybrids for improved corn varieties, prodn. practices for improved corn. Home: 943 Lantern Hill Dr East Lansing MI 48823 Office: Dept Crop and Soil Scis Mich State U East Lansing MI 48824

ROSSMAN, MARGARET MARY DRYZ, search and cons. co. exec.; b. Chgo., July 6, 1939; d. Gregory T. and Margaret M. Dryz; B.A., Rosary Coll., River Forest, Ill., 1971; m. Donald L. Rossman, June 27, 1959; 1 dau., Theresa Lynn. Copywriter, Butler Bros. Co., Chgo., 1958-60; tchr. elementary schs., Chgo., 1960-68; with advt. sales dept. Paddock Crescent Newspapers, Downers Grove, Ill., 1971-73; co-founder, pres. Women's Inc., Hinsdale, Ill., 1973—, also dir.; instr. career devel. Harper Coll., Palatine, Ill. Mem. Woodridge (Ill.) Bd. Library Dirs., 1969-75; mem. Woodridge Youth Commn., 1970-71. Mem. Nat. Assn. Women Bus. Owners (pres.). Office: 15 Spinning Wheel Rd Suite 14 Hinsdale IL 60521

ROSSWAY, MELVIN WEAVER, r.r. exec.; b. Belle Plaine, Iowa, Sept. 7, 1918; s. Samuel W. and Edna (Weaver) R.; diploma in certified pub. accounting, Internat. Corr. Schs., 1953; m. Marian Ruth Morehead, Oct. 31, 1946; children—Ronald Alan, Rhonda Kay, Rita Jean. Agt. helper C. & N. W. Ry., 1937-38, telegraph, sta. agt., 1938-53, travelling accountant, Chgo., 1953-56; asst. controller, auditor Lake Superior & Ishpeming R.R. Co., Marquette, Mich., 1956-58, treas., controller, 1958-61, v.p., treas., controller, 1961-73, sr. v.p., 1973-79, exec. v.p., sec., treas., 1979—; pres., dir. Lasco Devel. Corp.; dir. 1st Nat. Bank & Trust Co., Mich. Fin. Corp. Treas. Marquette Hosp. Bond Authority. Served with AUS, 1944-46; dist. staff officer USCG Aux. Mem. Tax Execs. (Wis. chpt.), Am. Legion, Marquette Range Engrs., Marquette C. of C. Republican. Lutheran. Clubs: Masons, Lions, Elks. Home: 800 W Magnetic St Marquette MI 49855 Office: 105 E Washington St Marquette MI 49855

ROST, J. WALDO, accountant; b. Axtell, Nebr., June 21, 1927; s. John A. and Martha (Lonnquist) R.; A.A., Luther Coll., 1948; certificate in Accounting, LaSalle Extension U., 1955; m. Marcia V. Stohl, July 23, 1950; children—Genon Verlene, Monica Raye, Clendon Waldo. Office mgr. Grainger Bros. Wholesale 1949-50; pvt. practice pub. accounting J. Waldo Rost, Holdrege, Nebr., 1954—. Chmn. Phelps County chpt. ARC, 1960-61; mem. Bd. Edn. Holdrege Pub. Schs., 1968-72, v.p., 1968-72; trustee Found. of Nebr. Soc. C.P.A.'s. Served with AUS, 1951-53. C.P.A., Nebr. Mem. Nebr. Soc. C.P.A.'s (dir. 1976—), Am. Inst. C.P.A.'s, Am. Legion, Holdrege C. of C., Ak-Sar-Ben. Lutheran (mem. council). Elk, Rotarian (sec. Holdrege 1961-62, dir. 1962—, pres.). Club: Country (sec. Holdrege, 1955-57). Contbg. author: Portfolio of Accounting Systems for Small and Medium-Sized Businesses. Home: 1130 Sheridan St Holdrege NE 68949 Office: 709 4th Ave Holdrege NE 68949

ROST, WILLIAM JOSEPH, educator; b. Fargo, N.D., Dec. 8, 1926; s. William Melvin and Christine Ruth (Hamerlik) Rost; m. Rita Cincoski, Sept. 15, 1951; children—Kathryn, Patricia, Carol. B.S., U. Minn., 1948, Ph.D., 1952. Registered Pharmacist, Minn. Asst. prof. pharmaceut. chemistry Sch. Pharmacy, U. Kansas City, 1952-56, asso. prof., 1956-61, prof., 1961-63; prof. pharmaceut. chemistry Sch. Pharmacy, U. Mo. at Kansas City, 1963—. Mem. Am. Pharmaceut. Assn., Am. Chem. Soc., Kappa Psi, Rho Chi, Phi Lambda Upsilon, Sigma Xi. Recipient Wulling Club Key, U. Minn., 1948. Co-author (with William O. Foye et al): Principles of Medicinal Chemistry, 1974. Contbr. articles to profl. jours. Home: 10910 Washington St Kansas City MO 64114 Office: Sch Pharmacy U Mo Kansas City MO 64110

ROSTENKOWSKI, DAN, congressman; b. Chgo., Jan. 2, 1928; s. Joseph P. and Priscilla (Dombroski) R.; student St. John's Mil. Acad., 1942-46, Loyola U., 1948-51; m. LaVerne Pirkins, May 12, 1951; children—Dawn P., Kristie M., Gayle A., Stacy L. Mem. Ill. Gen. Assembly, 1952, Senate, 1954, 56; mem. 86th-97th Congresses, 8th Dist. Ill., chmn. ways and means com., chmn. joint com. on taxation; chmn. Democratic Caucus 90th, 91st Congresses; chief dep. majority whip 95th and 96th Congresses. Exec. dir. Automobile Assn., 1956-58. Chmn. Northwest Town Joint Appeal Fund, 1958; mem. mayor's youth adv. commn., Chgo.; mem. N.W. area redevel. commn., Chgo., 1952—. Served as cpl. 7th Inf. Div., AUS, 1946-48. Mem. YMCA, V.F.W. Democrat. K.C., Kiwanian. Home: 1372 W Evergreen St Chicago IL 60622 Office: House Office Bldg Washington DC 20515

ROTELLA, SALVATORE G., coll. pres.; b. Italy, July 24, 1934; came to U.S., 1951, naturalized, 1957; s. Sebastian and Maria (Maio) R.; B.A., Hunter Coll., N.Y.C., 1955; M.A., U. Chgo., 1956, Ph.D., 1971; doctorate U. Pavia (Italy), 1958; m. Pilar Vives, July 24, 1961; children—Sebastian, Carlo, Salvatore. Research asso. dept. econ. research AMA, Chgo., 1959-60; asst. prof. polit. sci. Wright Coll., Chgo., 1960-62; chairperson dept. social scis. Loop Coll., Chgo., 1962-67; asst. dean, dir. Public Service Inst., City Colls. Chgo., 1967-70, v.p. career and spl. programs Loop Coll. and dean Public Service Inst., City Colls. Chgo., 1971-74, asso. vice-chancellor Inst. City-Wide Programs, 1974-75, pres. Chgo. City-Wide Coll., 1976—; adj. prof. public adminstrn. Ill. Inst. Tech., Chgo.; mem. Ill. Gov's Grievance Panel; mem. exec. adv. com. youth services dept. Office Sheriff of Cook County. Mem. adv. bd. Servicemen's Opportunity Coll., Washington; trustee St. Xavier Coll., Chgo., 1975—. U. Chgo. scholar, 1956-57; Inst. Internat. Edn. fellow, 1957-58; Lawrence Coll. fellow, 1960; Ill. Bd. Vocat. Edn. grantee, 1966; Sears Found. grantee, 1967; recipient Italian Govt. award, 1958, Superior Public Service award cert. of recognition City of Chgo., 1969. Mem. Am. Polit. Sci. Assn., Am. Arbitration Assn. (panel of arbitrators), Am. Assn. Community and Jr. Colls. (task force on uses of mass media in learning), Nat. Assn. Schs. Public Adminstrn. and Public Affairs (task force on undergrad. programs), Am. Soc. Public Adminstrn. (chpt. pres., nat. council, chmn. com. public policy, gen. chmn. nat. conf. 1975), Am. Soc. Public Ofcls.. Democrat. Roman Catholic. Club: Exec. (Chgo.). Contbr. articles to scholarly jours. Home: 6918 S Euclid Ave Chicago IL 60649 Office: 185 N Wabash Ave Chicago IL 60601

ROTH, ALEDA VENDER, statistician; b. Cleve., Oct. 8, 1945; d. Joseph P. and Beatrice W. Vender; B.S. in Psychology, Ohio State U., 1968, M.S.P.H. in Biostats., U. N.C., 1970; m. George Douglas, Sept. 26, 1970; children—Brian, Lauren. Chief statistician Ark. Children's Colony, Conway, 1968-69; research asso. epidemiologic field sta. Greater Kansas City Mental Found., Mo., 1970-72; adj. faculty mem. dept. biostats. U. N.C., 1972-74; cons. statis. analysis, 1971—; dir. dept. stats. Am. Nurses Assn., Kansas City, Mo., 1972-79; teaching asso. faculty mgmt. sci. Ohio State U., Columbus, 1979—; mem. cooperative health stats. system adv. com. Nat. Center for Health Stats., HEW, 1974-75, 76-77; mem. data analysis com. collaborative study on mental health epidemiology NIMH, 1970-72. NIMH fellow, 1969-70. Mem. Am. Statis. Assn., Am. Public Health Assn. (mem. nominating com. stats. sect. 1976, mem. stats. sect. council 1978—), Am. Prodn. and Inventory Control Soc. Contbr. articles on psychol. and nursing stats. to profl. jours.; editor Facts About Nursing, 1972-73, 74-75, 80-81; LPN's—1974 Inventory of Licensed Practical Nurses, 1977; 1977 National Sample Survey of Registered Nurses, 1979. Home: 6066 Tulip Hill Ct Worthington OH 43085 Office: 424 Hagerty Hall Ohio State Univ Columbus OH 43210

ROTH, FREDERIC HULL, accountant; b. Cleve., Feb. 20, 1914; s. Stanley Edward and Myrtle (Hull) R.; A.B., Wooster Coll., 1935; M.B.A., Harvard U., 1937; m. Emmy Alice Braun, Aug. 17, 1936; children—Frederic Hull, Robert Allan. With Scovell, Wellington & Co., 1939-62; partner Lybrand, Ross Bros. & Montgomery, Cleve., 1962-73, Coopers & Lybrand, Cleve., 1973—; dir. Magnetics Internat., Inc. Paul Harris fellow, 1979; C.P.A., Ohio, La., Va., N.C. Mem. Nat. Assn. Accountants, Am. Inst. Mgmt., Inst. Internal Auditors (bd. govs. Cleve. chpt. 1972-75), Ohio Soc. C.P.A.'s (pres. 1967-68), Am. Inst. C.P.A.'s (council 1968-70), Tax Club of Cleve., Newcomen Soc. N.Am., Internat. Platform Assn., C. of C., Western Res. Hist. Soc., Ohio Hist. Soc., Gt. Lakes Hist. Soc., Early Settlers Assn., Nat. Trust for Hist. Preservation, S.A.R., Mil. Order Stars and Bars, S.C.V., Soc. War of 1812, others. Republican. Methodist. Clubs: Westwood Country, Masons, Shriners, Mid-Day, Harvard Bus. Sch., City, Rotary, others. Home: 20661 Avalon Dr Rocky River OH 44116 Office: Lybrand & Coopers 2800 National City Center 1900 E 9th St Cleveland OH 44114

ROTH, PHYLLIS SANDRA, mail order co. exec.; b. Cleve., Feb. 25, 1933; d. David and Adele (Greenfield) Swerdlow; A.S. in Nursing, Cuyahoga Community Coll., Cleve., 1967; B.A., Cleve. State U., 1977; M.A. in Med. Anthropology, Case Western Res. U., 1980; m. Arnold A. Roth, Dec. 30, 1951; children—Amy Rebecca, Barbara Lynn, Elizabeth Gwen. Staff nurse St. Luke's Hosp., Cleve., 1967-68, Kaiser Permanente Found., Cleve., 1972-73; sec.-treas., dir. Right-O Spltys. Co., Cleve., 1980—; nurse Salk Polio Vaccination Program, Cleve., 1971, Red Cross Blood Bank Program, Cleve., 1971-76; nurse coordinator Swine Flue Innoculation Program, Cleve., 1978; mem. Red Cross Disaster Action Team, Cleve., 1980—; vol. Mt. Sinai Hosp., Hypertension Clinic, Cleve., 1980-81; founding mem. Lake Erie Anthrop. Network, Cleve., 1980—. Democratic leader 3d Ward, Cleveland Heights, Ohio, 1967-70. Mem. Am. Anthrop. Assn., Soc. Advanced Anthropology, Am. Folklore Soc., Am. Ethnographical Soc., Soc. Med. Anthropology, Zionist Orgn. Am., Hadassah. Club: B'nai B'rith. Home: 2131 Waynoka Rd Euclid OH 44117 Office: 1123 Terminal Tower Cleveland OH 44113

ROTH, ROBERT A., ednl. adminstr.; b. Cleve., Jan. 26, 1943; B.A., Hiram Coll., 1964; M.Ed., Pa. State U., 1968; Ph.D., Kent State U., 1971; postgrad. Rutgers U., 1972-73; m. Doris Roth. 3 children. Tchr. Kirkland (Ohio) High Sch., 1965-67, Cuyahoga Heights High Sch., Cleve., 1968-69; teaching fellow, grad. asst. Kent State U., 1969-71; lectr. edn. Rutgers U., New Brunswick, N.J., 1971-73; coordinator performance evaluation project N.J. State Dept. Edn., 1971-72, dir. performance evaluation project, 1972-73; supr. tchr. preparation program Mich. Dept. Edn., Lansing, 1974-79, acting dir. tchr. preparation and cert. services, 1977-81, state dir. tchr. preparation and cert. services, 1981—; chmn. Interstate Cert. Compact, 1981—. Mem. Mich. Assn. Tchr. Educators (exec. bd. 1975—, pres. 1978-79), N.J. Assn. Tchr. Educators (treas. 1972-73), Assn. Tchr. Educators (pres.-elect, exec. bd. 1979—), Nat. Assn. State Dirs. Tchr. Edn. and Cert. (v.p. 1981—), Am. Soc. Tng. and Devel., Phi Delta Kappa. Author works in field. Office: Mich Dept Edn Lansing MI 48909

ROTH, STEVEN DONALD, health care exec.; b. Sandusky, Ohio, Feb. 10, 1952; s. Charles A. and Betty J. (Roth) R.; B.A. in Psychology, Bowling Green State U., 1974, M.Social Psychology, 1979; m. Gerilyn Sekela, Oct. 25, 1975; 1 dau., Lindsay. Foreman, Barr Rubber Co., Sandusky, 1974; caseworker Erie County Welfare Dept., Sandusky, 1974-78; work evaluator/procurement specialist Double S Industries, Sandusky, 1978-80; coordinator tng. programs, Williston, Ohio, 1980—. Mem. Am. Statis. Assn., Alpha Kappa Delta. Episcopalian. Club: Sandusky Sailing. Office: 5810 N Main St Williston OH 43648

ROTH, THOMAS CHARLES, advt. agy. exec.; b. Evanston, Ill., May 2, 1946; s. Charles Daniel and Ellen Margaret (Jordan) R.; B.A., De Pauw U., 1968; M.B.A., Ind. U., 1973; m. Karen Melissa Price, July 17, 1976; children—Brian Thomas, Charles Leonard. Trainee, Leo Burnett Co., Chgo., 1973-75; account exec., 1975-78; pres. Gilmore Advt., Kalamazoo, 1978—; Bd. dirs. Bronco Athletic Assn. Served with U.S. Army, 1969-72. Mem. Am. Mktg. Assn. (dir. West Mich. chpt.). Office: Gilmore Advt 200 Michigan Bldg Kalamazoo MI 49007

ROTH, TOBY, Congressman; b. Oct. 10, 1938; B.A., Marquette U., 1961; m. Barbara Fischer, 1964; children—Toby, Vicky, Barbie. Realtor; mem. Wis. Ho. of Reps., 1972-78; mem. 96th and 97th Congresses from 8th Dist. Wis., mem. Fgn. Affairs Com. Named Wis. Legislator of Yr., 1978. Mem. Northside Businessmen's Assn. (past pres.), Am. Legion. Republican. Office: 215 Cannon House Office Bldg Washington DC 20515

ROTHBLATT, STEPHEN HOWARD, chem. engr., lawyer; b. Chgo., Nov. 11, 1946; s. Bernard B. and Bertha (Guss) R.; B.S. in Chem. Engring., U. Ill., 1969; J.D., DePaul U., 1974; m. Jeanne Orgish, Nov. 21, 1976; children—David, Joanna. Plant engr. Inmont Corp., Chgo., 1969-70; engr. dept. environ. control City of Chgo., 1971-73; admitted to Ill. bar, 1974. engr. region V, U.S. EPA, Chgo., 1974-76, chief engring. investigation sect., 1976-78, chief air programs br., 1978—; guest lectr. U. Wis., Madison, 1977. Pres., Pierre Condominium Assn., 1981—. Recipient cert. of Appreciation, U. Wis., 1977; cert. of Commendation, CSC Cook County, 1977; Quality award EPA, 1976. Patentee in field. Home: 2100 Lincoln Park W Chicago IL 60614 Office: 230 S Dearborn St Chicago IL 60604

ROTHE, HAROLD FREDERICK, mgmt. cons.; b. Boston, Aug. 11, 1914; s. Albert Henry and Edythe Frances (Schlehuber) Roth; A.B. magna cum laude, Bates Coll., 1939; M.A., U. Minn., 1942, Ph.D., 1944; m. Jean Ellen Tyler, Nov. 4, 1944; children—Ingrid, Frederick, Kristin. Chief psychol. staff Stevenson, Jordan & Harrison, Inc., Chgo., 1944-51; mgr. personnel Fairbanks, Morse & Co., Beloit, Wis., 1953-61; corp. staff asst. Beloit Corp., 1961-75; pvt. practice mgmt. cons., Beloit, 1975—; lectr. U. Minn., 1941, U. Wis., Whitewater, 1976. Fellow Am. Psychol. Assn.; mem. Midwest Psychol. Assn., Indsl. Relations Research Assn. Cons. editor: Jour. Applied Psychology, 1952-70. Home: 2013 E Ridge Rd Beloit WI 53511

ROTHENBERG, ELLIOT CALVIN, lawyer, state ofcl.; b. Mpls., Nov. 12, 1939; s. Sam S. and Claire Sylvia (Feller) R.; B.A. summa cum laude, U. Minn., 1961; J.D., Harvard U. (Fulbright fellow), 1964. Asso. project dir. Brookings Inst., Washington, 1966-67; fgn. service officer, legal advisor U.S. Dept. State, Washington, 1968-73; nat. law dir. Anti-Defamation League, N.Y.C., 1973-74; legal dir. Minn. Public Interest Research Group, Mpls., 1974-77; admitted to Minn. bar, 1966; pvt. practice law, Mpls., 1977—. State bd. dirs. YMCA Youth in Govt. Program, 1981—; v.p. Twin Cities chpt. Am. Jewish Com., 1980—; mem. Minn. House of Reps., 1978—, asst. floor leader (whip), 1981—; mem. citizens adv. com. Voyageurs Nat. Park, 1979-81. Recipient Legis. Evaluation Assembly Legis. Excellence award, 1980; North Star award, U. Minn., 1961. Mem. Am. Bar Assn., Harvard Law Sch. Assn., Izaak Walton League, Minn. Bar Assn., Am. Legion, Mensa, Minn. Distance Runners Assn., Phi Beta Kappa. Republican. Jewish. Clubs: Rotary, B'nai B'rith. Contbr. articles to profl. jours.; author: (with Zelman Cowen) Sir John Latham and Other Papers, 1965. Home: 3901 W 25th St Saint Louis Park MN 55416 Office: 388 State Office Bldg Saint Paul MN 55155

ROTHENBERG, HAROLD JAY, II, pathologist; b. Chgo., Sept. 30, 1941; s. Harold J. and Florence (Light) R.; M.D., U. Ill., 1966. Rotating intern Cook County (Ill.) Hosp., 1966-67; resident pathology Passavant Meml. Hosp., Chgo., 1967-68, Presbyn. St. Luke's Hosp., 1970-72; clin. pathology fellow U. Ill. Hosp., Chgo., 1972-73, dir. blood bank, 1973-77; asst. dir. dept. pathology Abraham Lincoln Sch. Medicine, U. Ill., Chgo., 1976-79; dir. pathology curriculum Ill. Coll. Podiatric Medicine, Ill. Coll. Optometry, 1978-79; dir. Phys. and Surg. Labs., Waukegan, Ill., 1976-80; now chief Lab. Service, Augustana Hosp., Chgo. Served with USNR, 1968-70. Diplomate Am. Bd. Family Practice, Am. Bd. Pathology. Mem. AMA, Am. Soc. Clin. Pathologists, Coll. Am. Pathologists, Ill., Chgo. med. socs., Chgo. Pathol. Soc. Jewish. Address: Lab Service Augustana Hosp 411 W Dickens Ave Chicago IL 60614

ROTHFUS, JOHN ARDEN, chemist; b. Des Moines, Dec. 25, 1932; s. Truman Clinton and Beatrice (Keeney) R.; B.A., Drake U., 1955; Ph.D., U. Ill., 1960; m. Paula Kay Harris, Sept. 26, 1959; children—Lee Ellen, David Merrill. Asst. biochemistry U. Ill. at Urbana, 1955-59; instr. U. Utah Coll. Medicine, Salt Lake City, 1961-63; asst. prof. U. Calif. Med. Sch., Los Angeles, 1963-65; prin. research chemist U.S. Dept. Agr., Peoria, Ill., 1965-70, investigations head, 1970-74, research leader, 1974—. Proctor & Gamble Co. fellow, 1957-58; USPHS postdoctoral fellow, 1959-61. Mem. Am. Chem. Soc., AAAS, Am. Assn. Cereal Chemists, N.Y. Acad. Scis., Am. Oil Chemists Soc., Am. Soc. Plant Physiologists, Phi Beta Kappa, Sigma Xi, Phi Lambda Upsilon, Omicron Delta Kappa, Alpha Chi Sigma. Home: 5615 N Sherwood Ave Peoria IL 61614 Office: 1815 N University St Peoria IL 61604

ROTHHAAR, RAYMOND EUGENE, pedodontist; b. Muncie, Ind., Mar. 18, 1925; s. Raymond Charles and Estella Iva (Leininger) R.; student Ball State U., Muncie, 1946-48; D.D.S., Ind. U., 1952; postgrad. U. Pa., 1958; m. Frances Wynne Kimbrough, Aug. 12, 1949 (dec. 1966); children—Gayle, Karen, Gretchen, Karl, Kendra; m. 2d, Arlene Helen Campbell, Dec. 1, 1966; children—Eric Ray, Kirk Tyler. Practice dentistry, Muncie, 1952—; mem. pedodontics faculty Ind. U. Dental Sch., 1957-58; sr. class guest lectr. preventive dentistry, 1961-79. Mem. Ind. Bd. Dental Examiners, 1971-78; dental examiner Nat. Testing Service Bd., 1974-78. Mem. Muncie Community Bd. Sch. Trustee, 1964-72. Bd. dirs. local Am. Cancer Soc., Soc. Crippled Children and Adults, Boy Scouts Am.; mem. Ind. State Controlled Substance Adv. Bd., 1973-78. Served with USNR, 1943-46. Recipient Distinguished Service award Muncie Jaycees, 1958. Fellow Am. Acad. Pedodontics, Acad. Internal. Dentistry, Acad. Canadienne des Scis. Dentaires; mem. Ind. Soc. Dentistry Children (pres. 1963-64), E. Central (pres. 1957-58), Del. County (pres. 1953-54) dental socs. Methodist (trustee). Mason. Club: Delaware Country (Muncie, Ind.). Home: 2605 Wood-Bridge St Muncie IN 47304 Office: 610 S Tillotson St Muncie IN 47304

ROTHMAN, DAVID, physician; b. St. Louis, Apr. 30, 1911; s. Ben and Ida (Gidansky) R.; B.S., M.D., Washington U., 1935; m. Frances Strauss, June 14, 1934; children—Helen Jean Rothman Flegel, Elaine Pearl, Sally Ann. Intern, Jewish Hosp., St. Louis, 1935-36; resident St. Louis Maternity Hosp., 1936-37, Jewish Hosp., St. Louis, 1937-38; practice medicine specializing in obstetrics and gynecology, St. Louis, 1938—; staff mem. Jewish Hosp., Barnes, St. Louis Maternity, all St. Louis, 1938—; dir. dept. obstetrics and gynecology Jewish Hosp., St. Louis, 1956-72; pres. med. staff, 1959-61; asso. clin. prof. obstetrics and gynecology Washington U. Med. Sch., St. Louis, lectr. obstetrics Warren Brown Sch. Social Service, 1954—. Bd. dirs. Jewish Med. Social Service Bur., 1951-54, Jewish Childrens Home, 1956-57, St. Louis Psychoanalytic Found.; med. adv. bd. Salvation Army. Served to capt. M.C., USAF, 1942-45. Diplomate Am. Bd. Obstetrics and Gynecology. Mem. AMA, Am. Coll. Obstetrics and Gynecology, Central Assn. Obstetrics and Gynecology, St. Louis Gynecol. Soc., Internat. Soc. Psychosomatic Obstedrics and Gynecology, Acad. Psychosomatic Medicine, Am. Fertility Soc. Home: 8033 Davis Dr Clayton MO 63105 Office: 2821 N Ballas Rd St Louis MO 63131

ROTHMAN, KENNETH JOEL, lawyer, lt. gov. Mo.; b. St. Louis, Oct. 11, 1935; s. Herman and Anna (Ollanik) R.; A.B., then LL.B., Washington U., St. Louis; m. Geri Jaffe, Apr. 19, 1965; children—David Aaron, Sarah Ann, Rachel Eve, Daniel Joseph. Admitted to Mo. bar; individual practice law, Clayton, Mo., 1959—; asst. pros. atty., St. Louis, 1959-61; mem. Mo. Ho. of Reps., 1964-80, majority floor leader, 1973-76, speaker, 1976-80; lt. gov. Mo., 1981—. Served with Air N.G., 1953-62. Recipient Legis. award Mo. Assn. for Mental Health; Mo. Bar award; Mo. Assn. Counties award; Mo. Probation and Parole Officers Assn. award; Conv. and Visitors Bur. of Greater St. Louis award; St. Louis County Bar Assn. award; Mo. Assn. Realtors award; others. Mem. Phi Delta Phi, Eta Sigma Phi, Sigma Alpha Mu. Democrat. Jewish. Club: Masons. Home: 50 Overhills Ladue MO 63124 Office: Room 326 State Capitol Bldg Jefferson City MO 65101

ROTHMAN, STEPHEN J(ACK) M(ICHAEL), theatrical dir.; b. N.Y.C., Oct. 9, 1950; s. Leonard Leon and Helen Rita (Gendel) R.; B.S. in Theatre Edn. and Speech (Selby Found. fellow), Fla. State U., 1972, M.F.A. in Theatre Mgmt. (univ. fellow), 1974; m. Ilisa Potash, June 17, 1973. Publicity dir. Fla. Dept. Theatre, Tallahassee, 1972-73; asst. to mng. dir. Asolo State Theatre, Sarasota, Fal., 1973-74; dir. public relations Stage/West, Springfield, Mass., 1974-75; dir. audience devel. Hartman Theatre Co., Stamford, Conn., 1975-77; producing dir. Paramount Arts Centre, Aurora, Ill., 1977—; cons. in field; guest lectr. U. Wis., U. Bridgeport; theatre specialist Community Relations and Emotional Control Govt. Project. Mem. Assn. Theatrical Press Agts. and Mgrs., Internat. Assn. Auditorium Mgrs. Jewish. Dir.: Stag At Bay with Dick Shawn and Alfred Drake, 1976, with Ed Asner and Alfred Drake, 1978, Serenading Louie, Asolo State Theatre, 1977.

ROTHMANN, BRUCE FRANKLIN, pediatric surgeon; b. Akron, Ohio, July 11, 1924; s. Edwin Franklin and Mary Madelene (Policy) R.; student Western Res. U., 1942-43, Wesleyan U., 1943-44; M.D., N.Y.U., 1948; postgrad. surgery U. Pa., 1952-53; m. Lola Secor, June 14, 1947; children—Susan Ann, Pamela Jane Rothmann Perkins, Elizabeth May. Intern, Akron City Hosp., 1948-49, resident in surgery, 1949-50, gen. surg. resident, 1953, chief surg. resident, 1954-55; resident in pediatric surgery Children's Hosp., Akron, 1953-54, mem. staff, 1955—, chief of surgery, 1969-74, chief of staff, 1973-74; practice medicine specializing in surgery, Akron, 1955-68, practice limited to pediatric surgery, 1968—; asst. surgeon Univ. Hosps., Cleve., 1962—; clin. instr. pediatric surgery Case-Western Res. U., Cleve., 1962-64, sr. instr., 1964-67, asst. clin. prof., 1967—. Mem. adv. com. Coll. Fine and Applied Arts, U. Akron, 1972—, Blossom Music Center, 1973—, Children's Concert Soc. Akron, 1972—; bd. mgrs. Cuyahoga Falls Community YMCA, 1957-63; trustee 1st Congl. Ch., Akron, 1960-64, Performing Arts Hall Assn., 1974—, Akron Symphony Orch., 1958—. Served with USN, 1943-45, 50-52. Diplomate Nat. Bd. Med. Examiners, Am. Bd. Surgery (spl. competence in Pediatric Surgery). Fellow Am. Acad. Pediatrics, ACS; mem. Am. Pediatric Surg. Assn., Am. Burn Assn., Brit. Assn. Pediatric Surgeons, Am. Broncho-Esophagological Soc., AMA, Cleve. Surg. Soc., Summit County Med. Soc. Contbr. articles to med. jours. Clubs: Akron City, Silver Lake Country. Home: 3020 Kent Rd Silver Lake Cuyahoga Falls OH 44224 Office: 300 Locust St Akron OH 44302

ROTHNEM, MORRIS STANLEY, obstetrician, gynecologist; b. Fargo, N.D., Dec. 3, 1919; s. Thomas Peter and Ovidia (Rosten) R.; student St. Olaf Coll., 1937-40; B.S., U. Minn., 1942; M.S., 1944, M.D., 1944; m. Lorraine Elizabeth Englert, Oct. 5, 1948; children—Bradford Thomas, Susan Lorraine, Gregory Lambert. Intern, resident in obstetrics and gynecology St. Barnabas Hosp., Mpls., 1946-48; practice medicine specializing in obstetrics and gynecology Paul Larson Obstetrics and Gynecology Clinic, Mpls., 1950—; pres. Northwestern Hosp. Med. staff, Mpls., 1966, mem. hosp. bd. and corp., instr. in intern and residency tng. program in obstetrics and gynecological surgery; mem. med. staff Abbott-Northwestern Hosp., 1950—, Fairview Community Hosps., 1962—; clin. instr. dept. Ob-gyn U. Minn. Med. Sch., 1975—; med. dir. Planned Parenthood, Mpls., 1954-55; mem. com. for orgn. pub. health services Hennepin County (Minn.), 1973, 74; mem. Morse Twp. Planning and Zoning Commn., 1974—; active Physicians Met. Health Force, 1975—; mem. Hosp. and Physician Health Resource Advisory Com. to Met. Health Bd., 1975—. Served to capt. M.C., U.S. Army, 1944-46. Diplomate Am. Bd. Obstetrics and Gynecology. Mem. Am. Coll. Obstetrics and Gyncology, Mpls. Acad. Medicine, Mpls. Council Obstetrics and Gynecology, AMA, Minn. State, Hennepin County med. socs., Minn. State Obstetrics and Gynecology Soc. Lutheran. Club: Decathalon Athletic (Mpls.). Contbr. articles in field to med. jours. Home: 6566 France Ave S Apt 809 Minneapolis MN 55435 Office: 6517 Drew Ave S Edina MN 55436

ROTHSTEIN, DAVID ANTHONY, psychiatrist; b. Chgo., Jan. 14, 1935; s. Alexander and Lillian Alice (Spitler) R.; B.S., U. Ill., 1957, M.S., 1959, M.D. cum laude, 1959; m. Laila Usprich Cohen, June 30, 1957; children—Lisa Anne, Peter David. Intern, St. Francis Hosp., Evanston, Ill., 1959-60; resident Michael Reese Hosp., Chgo., 1960-63; pvt. practice psychiatry, Chgo., 1965—; attending physician Michael Reese Hosp. Psychosomatic and Psychiat. Inst., 1965—; attending psychiatrist Chgo. Lakeshore Hosp., 1972—, mem. governing bd., 1978-80; attending physician Ill. Masonic Hosp., 1979—; cons. psychiatrist Thorek Hosp., 1979—, Weiss Hosp., 1980—; asst. prof. psychiatry U. Chgo. Med. Sch., 1974—; sr. cons. Ill. State Psychiat. Inst., 1973-75; cons. Ill. Dept. Mental Health Inst. for Juvenile Research, 1964-66, community mental health program, 1972; psychiat. cons. Chgo. Public Schs., 1978—; cons. Warren Commn., 1964, Nat. Commn. on Causes and Prevention of Violence, 1968. Pres., Dist. 2 edn. council, Chgo. Bd. Edn., 1974-76; pres. Jamieson Sch. Community Council, 1972-73; mem. city-wide adv. com. to desegregate Chgo. Public Schs., 1977—; bd. mgrs. Montefiore-Motley Spl. Schs. PTA, 1976-80. Served to lt. comdr. USPHS, 1963-65. Diplomate Am. Bd. Psychiatry and Neurology. Fellow Am. Orthopsychiat. Assn., Am. Psychiat. Assn. (com. financing mental health care, public affairs rep., Editor of Yr. award 1980); mem. AMA (recipient Physicians Recognition award 1970, 73, 76, 79, Roche award 1957), Ill. Psychiat. Soc. (editor Psychiat. Examiner, sec. 1978-80, councillor 1980—, chmn. peer rev. com., legis. liaison com., chmn. malpractice subcom., com. on insanity def., residents research award 1963), Am., Chgo. (chmn. ad hoc com. desegregation, co-chmn. com. on revised mental health code, program chmn. 1979-80) socs. adolescent psychiatry, Ill. Group Psychotherapy Soc. (councillor 1977-78), Ill. Med. Soc. (ho. dels., task force on profl. liability, council affiliated socs.), Chgo. Med. Soc. (councillor, sec. North Shore br. 1979-80, v.p. 1980-81, pres. 1981-82, mem. resolutions com. 1979-80, mem. public affairs com. 1979—, chmn. 1981—), AAAS, ACLU, Center Study Dem. Instns., SANE, Ams. for Democratic Action, Ind. Voters Ill., Council for a Livable World, Amnesty Internat., Physicians for Social Responsibility, Alpha Omega Alpha. Contbr. chpts. to books, articles to profl. jours.; research on presdl. assassination and study of leaders, info. theory applications to psychiatry, study of diagnosis and treatment of deaf patients, econs. of health care, group process in community and profl. groups; Office: 55 E Washington St Chicago IL 60602 also 5419 N Sheridan Rd Chicago IL 60640

ROTHSTEIN, STANLEY HAROLD, mental health center exec.; b. Louisville, Mar. 10, 1926; s. Jack and Sara (Fine) R.; B.A., U. Louisville, 1948; M.A., U. Chgo., 1951, Ph.D., 1967; m. Linda Rae Smith, Feb. 13, 1960; children—Jan Stephen, Jason Joel. Dir. social service Loretto Hosp., Chgo., 1960-64; dir. S.E. Community Mental Health Center, Chgo., 1967—; exec. dir. S.E. Community Health Orgn. Alcoholism Treatment Program, 1976—; mem. faculty Stritch Sch. Medicine Loyola U., 1955-70, Chgo. City Coll., 1955-70; partner Tape Mate, rec. and distbn., Calumet City, Ill., 1981—; cons. in field. Mem. adv. council Olive-Harvey br. Chgo. City Coll. Served with AUS, 1943-45; ETO. Decorated Purple Heart. USPHS fellow gerontology, 1964-67. Mem. Am. Orthopsychiat. Assn., Nat. Assn. Social Workers. Home: 4748 S Kenwood Ave Chicago IL 60615 Office: 30 N Michigan Ave Chicago IL 60602 also 1461 Ring Rd Calumet City IL 60409

ROTTET, SUZANNE MARGUERITE, nursing educator; b. Chgo., Dec. 28, 1941; d. Richard Joseph Conrad and Evelyn Carolyn (Spring) R.; grad. Evanston Hosp. Sch. Nursing, 1962; B.S., U. Ill., Champaign-Urbana, 1975; M.S., No. Ill. U., DeKalb, 1976. Instr. nursing edn. N.W. Community Hosp., 1971-73, med.-surg. nurse clinician, 1973-74; health edn. coordinator Luth. Gen. Hosp., Park Ridge, Ill., 1977-78; dir. nursing edn. and research Mercy Hosp. and Med. Center, Chgo., 1978—; adj. prof. U. Ill. Coll. Edn., Champaign, summer 1977; ednl. cons. Continuing Edn. in Nursing, 1974-75; moderator radio program Focus on Diabetes, Arlington Heights, Ill., 1973; site coordinator community teaching program North Suburban Cook County Heart Assn., 1973. Mem. Chgo. Council on Fgn. Relations. Lutheran. Office: Stevenson Expressway at King Dr Chicago IL 60616

ROTTMANN, BETTY COOK (MRS. LEROY F. ROTTMANN), univ. ofcl.; b. Longton, Kans., Oct. 9, 1922; d. J. Fred and Ora Mae (Allen) Cook; A.A., Central Wesleyan Coll., 1940; B.J. (Benjamin Franklin scholar), U. Mo., 1958, postgrad., 1963—; postgrad. U. Denver, 1968, 69, 70; m. Leroy F. Rottmann, Apr. 4, 1942; children—Larry, Tina. Asst. librarian U.S. Spl. Services, Ft. Campbell, Ky., 1944-45; asst. librarian Columbia (Mo.) Public Library, 1945-48; exec. sec. ARC, Ste. Genevieve, Mo., 1950; substitute tchr., Mo., 1948-56; reporter, columnist Ste. Genevieve Herald, 1956-57; women's columnist Mo. Ruralist and Kans. Farmer, 1957-58; corr. Fairchild Publs., 1960-62; newswriter, info. specialist U. Mo.-Columbia Office Public Info., 1958-80, coordinator visitor and guest relations Office Univ. Relations, 1981—. Co-founder Mo. Women's Polit. Caucus, 1972, Mo. Equal Rights Coalition, 1973; mem. Internat. Women's Decade, Mid-Mo. Speakers Bur. on Status of Women, 1975-80; mem. coordinating com. Mo. Women's Meeting, 1976-77; co-founder Women's Register for Leadership in Mo., 1979; chmn. adv. bd. Columbia New Directions Center, 1981—; mem. Columbia Community Congress, 1970-72; mem. bldg. bd. Nora Stewart Nursery, 1966—. Research grantee Women in Communications, 1965. Mem. Adminstrv. Mgmt. Soc., Council Advancement and Support of Edn., AAUW (media topic chmn. 1973-75, pres. Mo. div. 1975-77 mem. cultural exchange study seminar to China 1977, v.p. SW Central Region 1979-81), Women in Communications (Award of Excellence as Columbia chpt. pres. 1961, adv. U. Mo.-Columbia student chpt. 1974-76), LWV, Internat. Fedn. Univ. Women (workshop leader), Mo. Press Women (pres. 1966, Woman of Achievement 1982), Mo. Writers Guild, Nat. Women's Studies Assn., Sigma Delta Chi, Kappa Tau Alpha. Home: 1200 Coats St Columbia MO 65201

ROTTSCHAFER, WALTER C., podiatrist; b. Grand Rapids, Mich., Mar. 25, 1946; s. Walter Cornelius and Janet R.; A.B., Calvin Coll., 1968; D.P.M., Ill. Coll. Podiatric Medicine, 1975; m. Eileen Joyce Albers, June 28, 1968; children—Julie Beth, Karen Elizabeth, Walter Christopher. Surg. resident, Northlake (Ill.) Community Hosp., 1975-76; practice podiatric medicine, Zeeland, Mich., 1976—. Counselor, Calvinist Cadet Corps, Bethel Christian Reformed Ch.; lectr. civic groups. Served with U.S. Army, 1968-70. Diplomate Am. Bd. Podiatric Surgery. Fellow Am. Coll. Foot Surgeons; mem. Mich. State Podiatry Assn. (bd. dirs., chmn. peer rev. com.), Kappa Tau Epsilon. Home: 258 Park Zeeland MI 49464 Office: 502 E Main Zeeland MI 49464

ROUDANÉ, CHARLES, metal products co. exec.; b. Los Angeles, July 16, 1927; s. Rudolph and Irene (Warner) R.; B.S., Tulane U., 1950; m. Orient Fox, Aug. 20, 1948; children—Mark, Matthew. Gen. mgr. Master div. Koehring Co., Chgo., 1955-67; gen. sales mgr. Wilton Corp., Schiller Park, Ill., 1967-70; dir. mktg. Flexonics div. UOP Inc., Bartlett, Ill., 1970-73, v.p., gen. mgr. Flexonics div., 1973—; dir. Center for Indsl. Mktg. Planning, Inc., Pow Rhouse Products, Inc. Served with U.S. Army, 1945-46. Mem. Am. Mgmt. Assn. (bd. dirs., chmn. mktg. council, Wall of Fame 1978), ASME (exec. affiliate), Pres.'s Assn., Newcomen Soc. Gt. Brit. Republican. Presbyterian. Office: 300 E Devon Ave Bartlett IL 60103

ROUSE, DONALD NELSON, fashion sales exec.; b. Kansas City, Mo., May 22, 1942; s. John Wilson, Sr., and Gail Agnes (Palmar) R.; B.S.E.E., U. Ill., 1964; m. Jennie Ella Petrarca, June 6, 1965; children—Wendy Marie, Bryan Keith. Foreman bar soap prodn. Procter & Gamble, Chgo., 1965, supr. synthetic packaging, 1966, prodn. and warehouse engr., 1967, plant liaison mgr., 1968; mgr. distbn. Beeline Fashions, Bensenville, Ill., 1969, asst. to mgr. EDP, 1970, systems analyst, 1971, asst. to v.p. sales adminstrn., 1972-74, dir. sales adminstrn., 1974-77, asst. to pres., 1977-79, dir. sales services, 1979-80, v.p. sales services, 1980—. Mem. citizens adv. com. Sch. Dist. 54; v.p. Sheffield Park Home Owners Assn.; former pres. Arlington Heights Jaycees, Jr. Chamber Internat. Sen., 1971. Mem. Direct Selling Assn., Am. Mgmt. Assn., Internat. Platform Assn., Mensa. Republican. Roman Catholic. Office: 100 Beeline Dr Bensenville IL 60106

ROUSE, JOHN EDWARD, JR., educator; b. Anderson, S.C., July 23, 1942; s. John Edward and Zana (Wilson) R.; B.A., Furman U., 1964; M.A., U. Md., 1967, Ph.D., 1974; postgrad. Boston U., 1969; m. Barbara B. Maves, May 24, 1981. Faculty research asst. Bur. Govtl. Research, U. Md., College Park, 1970-75; adj. prof. govt. and adminstrv. mgmt. U. Md., 1973-76, George Washington U., Washington, 1975-76; asst. prof. polit. sci. Ball State U., Muncie, Ind., 1976—, faculty advisor model UN del., 1981—; Ind. corres. Midwest Rev. Public Adminstrn., 1978—; moderator Public Affairs Roundtable, weekly news analysis program Sta. WBST-FM Muncie, 1979—, exec. producer and commentator, 1980—; Mem. Am. Soc. for Public Adminstrn., Ind. Soc. for Public Adminstrn., Am. Polit. Sci. Assn., Pi Sigma Alpha. Democrat. Methodist. Editor: Urban Housing: Public and Private, 1978; Public Administration in American Society, 1980; mng. editor Pi Sigma Alpha Newsletter, 1969-71; mem. editorial bd. News for Tchrs. Polit. Sci., 1981—. Office: 226 N Quadrangle Ball State U Muncie IN 47306

ROUSE, JOHN RATCLIFFE, art museum dir., curator; b. Cunningham, Kans., Aug. 27, 1917; s. John R. and Edith Belle (Cole) R.; B.A., Bethel Coll., Newton, Kans., 1939. With 4th Nat. Bank & Trust Co., Wichita, 1940-46; mgr. Commodore Hotel, Wichita, 1946-56; pvt. cons. antiques, 1955—; curator, dir. Wichita Art Assn. Galleries, Inc., 1973—. Mem. Wichita Hist. Mus. Assn. (trustee 1972-78), Wichita Art Assn. (trustee 1973—, pres., 1973-75), Wichita Art Mus. Mems. Found., Fine Arts Council Wichita, Am. Assn. Museums, Mountain Plains Mus. Conf., Kans. Mus. Assn., Am. Crafts Council. Republican. Christian Scientist. Home: 1400 N Woodlawn Ave Wichita KS 67208 Office: 9112 E Central St Wichita KS 67206

ROUSH, ALLAN NELSON, chemist; b. DeKalb, Ill., Mar. 21, 1939; s. Glenn William and Maryon Eleanor (Nelson) R., B.S., No. Ill. U., 1962, M.S., 1966; m. Patricia Rose Latham, Feb. 4, 1961; children—Allan Richard, Stephanie Lyn. Project leader Synthetic Aircraft Lubricant R & D Sinclair Research, Inc., Harvey, Ill., 1967-69; project mgr. Lubricants R & D Atlantic Richfield Co., Harvey, 1969-72, sr. product compliance specialist fuels, 1972-74; mgr. product research D-A Lubricant Co., Indpls., 1974-77, asst. v.p. research, 1977-81, v.p. research, 1981—. Dir. Home Owners Assn., Park Forest South, Ill., 1968; cub scout leader, Boy Scouts Am., 1972. Mem. Soc. Automotive Engrs., Am. Soc. Testing and Materials. Patentee stable synthetic ester lubricant composition. Home: 3406 Beech Dr Carmel IN 46032 Office: 1331 W 29th St Indianapolis IN 46208

ROUSH, MILDRED JESSIANNA, nutritionist; b. Bidwell, Ohio, Oct. 5, 1920; d. Lester Leroy and Ruth Florence (Shain) R.; student Ohio Wesleyan U., 1938-40; B.S., Ohio State U., 1942; M.A., Columbia U., 1947, profl. diploma, 1950. Research asst. Columbia U., 1948-50; asst. prof. Colo. State U., Ft. Collins, 1953-65; nutrition officer Food and Agr. of UN, Thailand, 1966-68; asst. prof. Ohio State U., 1969-74; nutritionist Columbus (Ohio) Bd. Edn., 1974—; cons. U. Peshawar, West Pakistan. Active, Clintonville Womens Club, ARC. Mem. Am. Dietetic Assn., Ohio Inst. Food Tech., Ohio Assn. Maternal and Child Health, Soc. for Nutrition Edn., Soc. for Internat. Devel., Pi Lambda Theta, Kappa Delta Pi, Phi Tau Sigma. Contbr. articles on food and nutrition to profl. jours. Home: 2889 Neil Ave Apt 411B Columbus OH 43202

ROUSSEAU, MARK OWEN, sociologist; b. Ft. Wayne, Ind., Apr. 5, 1940; s. Richard Jackson and Wilma (Combs) R.; B.A., Ind. U., 1962, M.A., 1966; Ph.D., U. N.C., Chapel Hill, 1971; cert. III Dégré, Alliance Francaise, Paris, 1972; m. Marion Frances Pruss, Aug. 18, 1973; 1 son, Mark Owen. Asst. instr. U. N.C., 1966-68; mem. faculty U. Nebr., Omaha, 1968—, asst. prof. sociology, 1971—. Nat. Endowment Humanities fellow, summer 1979. Mem. Am. Sociol. Assn., AAUP, Inst. Icarian Investigations (pres. 1976—), Midwest Sociol. Soc., Ind. U. Alumni Assn., Alpha Kappa Delta. Contbr. articles to profl. jours. Home: 5001 Izard St Omaha NE 68132 Office: Dept Sociology Univ Nebr Omaha NE 68182

ROVELSTAD, TRYGVE A., sculptor; b. Elgin, Ill., Sept. 27, 1903; s. Theador and Anna (Evensen) R.; student of Lorado Taft, 1922, Frederick Hibbard, Chgo., 1923, U. Wash., 1927; m. Gloria G. Michel, July 8, 1950; 1 dau., Gloria-Ann. Exhibited at Acad. Galleries, Elgin, Gallery of Pallette and Chisel Club, Chgo., 1938-39, Peabody Inst., Balt., 1959-60, Pub. Library, Washington, 1964, North Mississippi Valley Artists Exhbn., Ill. State Mus., 1964, Elgin Coin Club, 1966, Hudson Valley Art Assn., Inc., 1970, Am. Artists Profl. League, N.Y.C., 1971-78; in permanent collections Smithsonian Instn. Numis. Hall, Washington, Am. Meml. Chapel St. Paul's Cathedral, London, Eng., Crane Tech. High Sch., Chgo., Ill. State Capitol, Ill. State Office Bldg.; instr. sculpting U.S. Army U., Shrivenham, Eng., 1945-46; designed, executed Elgin Commemorative Half Dollar U.S. Mint, Phila., 1936; designer, editor Am. Roll Honor St. Paul's Cathedral, London, 1951; designer U.S. Army Occupation Germany medal, Roland Victor Libonati I Will medal-award, 1964; designer Senator Richard J. Barr statue Ill. State Capitol, 1953; designer Gov. William G. Stratton dedication plaque Stratton Bldg., Springfield, Ill., 1955, William G. Stratton portrait medallion, 1978; designer-sculptor Logan Hay Lincoln medal award of Abraham Lincoln 1967; Mark Twain medal Chase Commemorative Soc., 1967; Ill. Sesquicentennial medals, 1968; Chgo. Coin Club 50th Anniversary medal, 1969; Lincoln Heritage Trail medal, 1969; 101st Airborne Div. medal, 1969; Eisenhower Proclamation medal, 1969;

Chgo. Fire Centennial medal, 1971; Rovelstad Pioneer-I Will medal, 1971; heroic sculptures, 1971—; pres., bd. dirs. Pioneer Meml. Found. Ill.; pres., bd. govs. Asso. I Will Sculptors Chgo., 1964-75; pres., dir. Tryg's Sculpture Sch., 1963-72; pres., dir. Pathfinder Inc., 1973-75. Recipient silver Ill. Sesquicentennial medal Ill. Sesquicentennial Commn., 1968; ofcl. commemorative medal Lincoln Heritage Trail Found., 1969; silver CCC Golden Anniversary medal Chgo. Coin Club, 1969; Captive Nations Eisenhower Proclamation medals and certificate Captive Nations Friends Com., 1969; Charlotte Dunwiddie prize for heroic Pioneer Father bronze head Am. Artists Profl. League, 1971, Anna Hyatt Huntington Meml. award for heroic Pioneer Scout aluminum sculpture head, 1974; hon. mention for Pioneer Mother heroic aluminum head Hudson Valley Art Assn., 1972; Pioneer Mother heroic bronze head, 1979; Ill. Bicentennial Medal design prize Franklin Mint, 1972. Mem. Elgin Area Hist. Soc. (dir. 1966-67), Am. Artists Profl. League, Alumni Assn. Sch. Art Inst. Chgo., Chgo. Architecture Found., Ill. Hist. Soc., Elgin Coin Club (hon.). Address: 535 Ryerson Ave Elgin IL 60120

ROVNYAK, RICHARD MICHAEL, elec. engr.; b. Ford City, Pa., Feb. 24, 1935; s. Michael Frank and Elizabeth Mary (Maus) R.; B.S., Ind. Inst. Tech., 1961; m. Judith Ann Rucker; children—Elizabeth, Mark, Kathleen, Richard, Michael, Jennifer, Rebecca. With GTE Automatic Electric Lab., Northlake, Ill., 1961—, staff engr., 1963, sr. engr., 1968, supr. microcircuit design and testing, 1978—. Served with USAF, 1953-57. Fellow Coll. of Relay Engring.; mem. Internat. Soc. for Hybrid Microcircuits. Roman Catholic. Contbr. articles to profl. jours.; patentee in field. Home: 433 S Salem Dr Schaumburg IL 60193 Office: 400 N Wolf Rd Northlake IL 60164

ROWAN, JOHN FRANCIS, tng. and devel. cons.; b. Evergreen Park, Ill., Feb. 16, 1948; s. John Francis and Alice Marie (Trainor) R.; B.A., Loyola U., 1970, Ph.D., 1981; M.S., Chgo. State U., 1973; m. Mary Ann Hyland, June 13, 1969; children—Kevin, Daniel. Salesman, Trainor Glass Co., Alsip, Ill., 1969-71; tchr. Chgo. Bd. Edn., 1971-80; pres. John F. Rowan Ltd., Chgo., 1980—; instr. Chgo. State U., 1974-80. Mem. Am. Soc. Tng. and Devel., Ill. Tng. and Devel. Assn., Assn. Supervision and Curriculum Devel., Phi Delta Kappa. Club: Rotary. Home: 2907 Caroline St South Bend IN 46614

ROWAN, RICHARD JOHN, automotive equipment mfg. co. exec.; b. Cleve., Aug. 20, 1931; s. Rudolph George and Mary (Magdalene) R.; B.S. in Mech. Engring. (Am. Steel & Wire scholar), Case Inst. Tech., 1953; M.B.A. (univ. scholar), Syracuse U., 1967; m. Julia Park, Dec. 28, 1957; children—Carol, Kathleen, Richard, Robert. With Am. Steel & Wire div. U.S. Steel Corp., Cleve., 1953-62, indsl. engr., 1957-59, foreman, combustion control, maintenance engr., 1959-62; sr. system analyst Corning Glass Works, (N.Y.), 1962-63, supr. equipment engring., 1963-67; asst. plant mgr. Continental Can Co., N.Y.C., 1967-69; mgr. mfg. Rockwell Standard div. Rockwell Internat., Newark, Ohio, 1969-71, plant mgr., Tilbury, Ont., Can., 1971-72, New Castle, Pa., 1972-75; v.p., gen. mgr. O.E.M. div. Heavy Vehicle System Group, Bendix Corp., Elyria, Ohio, 1975-78; pres. Gen. Seating div. Lear Siegler, Livonia, Mich., 1978-79, v.p. Chesterfield Cyl. div., Eng., 1979—. Councilman-at-large, Heath, Ohio, 1970-71; mem. Greater New Castle Assn., 1972—; mem. Parents Tchrs. Orgn., New Castle; coach Poland (Ohio) Little League Football. Bd. dirs. Lawrence County (Pa.) United Fund. Served with USNR, 1953-57. Recipient outstanding adviser jr. achievement area award Am. Soc. Tng. Dirs., 1961. Mem. ASME, Am. Inst. Indsl. Engrs., Am. Mktg. Assn., Greater New Castle Assn., Canadian Mfg. Assn., Automotive Parts Mfg. Assn., Syracuse Alumni Assn., Rockwell Axle Club, Horse Heads Transp. Com. Author: Market Planning and Behavioral Concepts, 1963. Home: 5101 S Bunker Hill Brandywine Farms Brighton MI 48116

ROWAN, ROBERT DALE, mfg. co. exec.; b. Holland, Mich., Mar. 27, 1922; s. Henry and Mabel Barbara (Streur) R.; B.S., Mich. State U., 1947; m. Frieda A. Young, Apr. 2, 1945 (dec.); children—Richard Paul, Kristine Louise, Ruthanne Marie. Jr. acct. to audit supr. Touche, Niven, Bailey & Smart, Detroit, 1947-55; with Fruehauf Corp., Detroit, 1955—, beginning as controller, successively v.p. and controller, v.p. fin., exec. v.p. fin., pres. and chief operating officer, pres. and chief exec. officer, chmn, pres. and chief exec. officer, 1955-81, chmn., chief exec. officer, 1981—, dir., 1970—. Served to lt. AUS, 1942-46, to capt., 1950-52; Korea. Mem. Mich. Assn. C.P.A.s, Detroit C. of C., Nat. Def. Transp. Assn. Republican. Presbyterian. Clubs: Oakland Hills Country, Detroit, Detroit Athletic, Econ. of Detroit, Renaissance, Hundred (Detroit); Sky (N.Y.C.); Masons (Berkley, Mich.). Office: 10900 Harper Ave Detroit MI 48232*

ROWCLIFFE, DONALD HUGH, JR., pension fund exec., accountant; b. Aurora, Ill., Aug. 20, 1924; s. Donald Hugh and Valborg Elizabeth Hannah (Okerblad) R.; B.S. in Bus. Adminstrn., Aurora Coll., 1948; m. Frances Evlyn Peck, June 19, 1946; children—Wanda Lee, David Hugh. Instr. acctg. Aurora Coll., 1952, 66-70; lectr. acctg. Northwestern U., 1953-55; controller Globe Bldg. Materials Co., 1955-60; mgr. Podolak, Hooper, Kerr & Co., 1965-70 (both Aurora); asst. gen. controller Ill. Agrl. Assn., 1960-61, asst. comptroller Am. Dental Assn., 1961-65 (both Chgo.); adminstr. Chgo. Dist. Council Carpenters Welfare and Pension Funds, 1971-79; adminstrv. mgr. Carpenters Welfare and Pension Funds Ill., 1979—. Bd. dirs. Internat. Found. Employee Benefit Plans, Brookfield, Wis. Served to lt. (j.g.) USNR, 1943-45. Mem. Am. Inst. C.P.A.'s, Ill. Soc. C.P.A.'s (pres. Fox Valley chpt. 1971-72, chmn. chpt. operations com. 1973-74). Mason (Shriner), Odd Fellow. Home: 445 S Calumet Ave Aurora IL 60506 Office: 28 N 1st St Geneva IL 60134

ROWE, CLARENCE JOHN, psychiatrist; b. St. Paul, May 24, 1916; s. Clarence John and Sayde E. (Mabin) R.; B.A., Coll. St. Thomas, 1938; M.B., U. Minn., 1942, M.D., 1943, fellow in psychiatry, 1946-49; m. Patricia A. McNulty, Jan. 15, 1945; children—Padraic, Rory, Kelly Michael. Intern St. Joseph's Hosp., St. Paul, 1942-43; resident VA Hosp., Mpls., U. Minn. hosps., Mpls., 1946-49; instr., asst. prof. U. Minn., 1949-54; dir. Hamm Meml. Psychiat. Clinic, St. Paul, 1954-57; pvt. practice St. Paul, 1957—; cons. 3M Co., 1957-72, Ramsey County Mcpl. Ct., 1958—, Constance Bultman Wilson Center, Faribault, Minn., 1973—; clin. prof. psychiatry U. Minn. Med. Med. Sch., 1964—; adj. faculty mem. Antioch Coll., 1974—; cons. St. Thomas Acad., 1970—; chmn. Minn. Mental Health Planning Council, 1963-69; mem. Mayors Com. on Drug Use and Abuse, 1969-71, Govs. Council on Employment of Handicapped, 1954-65; mem. adv. bur. hearing and appeals Social Security Adminstrn., 1965—. Trustee St. Thomas Acad., 1970-76; bd. dirs. St. Johns U. Inst. Mental Health, Collegeville, Minn., 1954-78. Served with M.C., AUS, 1943-46. Fellow Am. Psychiat. Assn. (chmn. mental health in industry com., 1965-71); mem. AMA, Group for Advancement Psychiatry, Minn. Psychiat. Soc. (pres., 1973-75), Minn. Soc. Adolescent Psychiatry (pres. 1977-78), St. Paul Soc. Psychiatry and Neurology (pres., 1978—). Roman Catholic. Clubs: St. Paul Athletic, Town and Country, Informal. Author: An Outline of Psychiatry, 7th ed., 1980; The Mentally Ill Employee, 1965; (with Allan McLean) The Clergy and Pastoral Counselling, 1969. Home: 1770 Colvin Ave St Paul MN 55116 Office: 551 S Snelling St St Paul MN 55116

ROWE, ELISE MURPHY, ednl. adminstr.; b. Cedar Falls, Iowa, Sept. 30, 1929; d. Harold Edward and Eva Ruth (Webb) Murphy; B.A., U. N.D., 1951; M.A., Calif. State U., 1966; Ed.S., U. Mo., 1974; Ed.D., No. Ill. U., 1980; m. Bernard John Rowe, Nov. 26, 1976; children—Beth, Blair; stepchildren—John, David, Katherine. Tchr. lang. arts/social studies, Whittier, Calif., 1952-54; adminstrv. reading curriculum tchr., Saratoga, Calif., 1960-65; asst. prof. speech Calif. State U., San Jose, 1965-69; chmn. reading and speech, Kansas City, Mo., 1970-71; chmn. devel. reading Shawnee Mission, Kans., 1971-74; dir. reading Downers Grove (Ill.) South High Sch., 1974—; cons., lectr. in field. Active Hinsdale Village Caucus, Am. Field Service, Katherine Legge Meml. Aux. Sylvania Electronic Corp. grantee. Mem. AAUW, Am. Assn. Sch. Adminstrs., Assn. for Supervision and Curriculum Devel., Council for Basic Edn., Ill. Edn. Assn., Ill. Assn. Sch. Adminstrs., Ill. Assn. for Supervision and Curriculum Devel., Ill. Assn. Reading, Nat. Secondary Reading Interest Group, Nat. Assn. Tchrs. Speech, Nat. Council Tchrs. English, NEA, Sec. Reading League, Ill. Women in Adminstrn., P.E.O., Phi Delta Kappa, Pi Lambda Theta, Kappa Delta Pi, Alpha Phi. Republican. Presbyterian. Clubs: Holiday Dinner Dance, Jr. Women's. Contbr. articles to profl. jours. Home: PO Box 416 Hinsdale IL 60521 Office: Community High Sch Dist 99 S 1436 Norfolk St Downers Grove IL 60515

ROWE, FRED WERNER, mfg. co. exec.; b. Heilbronn, West Germany, Sept. 14, 1921; s. William A. and Irma (Rothschild) R.; came to U.S., 1939, naturalized, 1944; B.E.E. (Rackham Found. scholar), U. Detroit, 1944; m. Betty S. Shaffer, Aug. 16, 1947; children—Linda Ann, Steven Shelby. Elec. engr. Bulldog Electric Products Co., Detroit, 1941-44; research engr., fgn. tech. coordinator Bundy Tubing Co., Detroit, 1946-66; with Mich. Seamless Tube Co. (now Quanex Corp.), South Lyon, Mich., 1966—, corporate dir. research and devel., 1966—; dir. Commodity Corp., Ann Arbor. Bd. dirs. Am. Cancer Soc., 1976—, treas. Oakland and Wayne counties, 1980-81, dir. met. devel. bd., 1982-84; mem. West Bloomfield Planning Commn., 1981-84. Served with USNR, 1944-46. Fellow Am. Soc. Nondestructive Testing (dir. 1976-79); mem. Internat. Tube Assn., Am. Soc. Metals, IEEE, Engring. Soc. Detroit. Jewish. Club: Optimist (dir. 1970-74). Home: 7178 Heatherheath Ln West Bloomfield MI 48033 Office: Quanex Corp 400 McMunn St South Lyon MI 48178

ROWE, HARVEY JOHN, bldg. materials co. exec.; b. Oshkosh, Wis., Jan. 29, 1936; s. Harvey Jackson and Grace Linnea (Anderson) R.; B.A., U. Mo., 1959; m. Marjorie Susan Beckman, Feb. 28, 1959; children—Richard Edward, Renee Suzanne, Risa Lee. Mgmt. trainee, advt. merchandiser Walgreen Co., Chgo., 1954-63; buyer, asst. purchasing mgr. U.S. Gypsum Corp., Chgo., 1963-72, mktg. mgr. chems. div., 1972-79; gen. mgr. Arrowhead Drywall Supplies, Olathe, Kans., 1979—. Trustee Village of Deer Park, Ill., 1975-79; pres., co-founder Barrington (Ill.) Area Hockey League, 1973-74; pres. Kansas City Amateur Hockey League, 1981-82. Served as ensign USNR, 1958. Mem. Nat. Lime Assn., Kansas City Area C. of C., Olathe C. of C., Sigma Phi Epsilon. Republican. Christian Scientist. Club: Hillcrest Country (Kansas City, Mo.). Home: 10219 Catalina St Overland Park KS 66207 Office: Arrowhead Drywall Supplies 15660 S Keeler Terr Olathe KS 66062

ROWE, JOHN FREDERICK, JR., mfg. co. exec.; b. Hamden, Ohio, July 20, 1947; s. John Frederick and Ruth Evelyn (Lambert) R.; student Campbellsville (Ky.) Coll., 1965-67; A.B., Morehead State U., 1970; M.B.A., Ohio U., 1979; m. Carolee Walters, Feb. 1, 1969. Mgr. intern City of Ashland, Ky., 1970-71; asst. div. mgr. Woolco Dept. Stores, Columbus, Ohio, 1971-72; personnel mgr. N. Wasserstrom & Sons, Inc., Columbus, 1972-77; indsl. relations mgr. Glass div. Combustion Engring. Inc., Lancaster, Ohio, 1977-79; mgr. indsl. relations Dresser Transp. Services Inc., Worthington, Ohio, 1979—; mem. faculty adv. council for personnel and indsl. relations Ohio U. Mem. Order Ky. Cols. Office: 400 W Wilson Bridge Rd Worthington OH 43085

ROWE, NATHANIEL HAWTHORNE, dentist; b. Hibbing, Minn., May 26, 1931; s. Nathaniel Hawthorne and Edna (Bockler) R.; D.D.S., B.S., U. Minn., 1955, M.S.D., 1958; div.; children—Bradford Scott, Nathaniel Edwin, Lorna Michelle, Jonathan Alan. Teaching asst. dept. oral pathology Sch. Dentistry, U. Minn., 1955-56, research fellow, 1956-58, clin. instr., 1958-59; asst. prof. pathology Washington U. Sch. Dentistry, St. Louis, 1959-65, asso. prof., 1965-69, prof. Grad. Sch. Arts and Scis., 1966-69, vis. prof. pathology Sch. Dentistry, 1969-71, chmn. dept. gen. and oral pathology, 1959-68, coordinator oral cancer teaching, 1959-68; asso. research scientist Cancer Research Center, Columbia, Mo., 1967-71; asso. prof. pathology Sch. Medicine, U. Mich., Ann Arbor, 1969-76, prof. pathology, 1976—, prof. dentistry Sch. Dentistry, 1968—, asso. dir. Dental Research Inst., 1970—, sr. research scientist Virus Research Group, 1977-80; cons. staff Jewish Hosp., St. Louis, 1960-68; cons. Ellis Fischel State Cancer Hosp., Columbia, 1967—, sci. adv. bd. Cancer Research Center, 1975-79; cons. oral pathology U.S. VA Hosps., St. Louis, 1965-68, Ann Arbor, 1973—, Mo. Dental Assn., St. Louis, 1967-69; civilian profl. cons. Office of Surgeon, 5th U.S. Army, 1967—; cons. Bur. Medicine Adv. Panel System, HEW, dental agts. adv. com. FDA, 1968-70; mem. profl. adv. council on cancer Mich. Assn. Regional Med. Programs, 1969-73; mem. policy council Met. Detroit Cancer Control Program, 1976—; Recipient D.E. Listiac award, faculty U. Minn. Sch. Dentistry, 1955; award Mich. div. Am. Cancer Soc., 1979, Tiffany nat. divisional award, 1979; Outstanding Civilian Service medal Dept. Army, 1979; named Hon. Alumnus Washington U. Sch. Dentistry, 1966. Diplomate Am. Bd. Oral Pathology. Fellow Am. Acad. Oral Pathology (councillor 1971-74, v.p. 1975-76, pres.-elect 1976-77, pres. 1977-78), Am. Coll. Dentists, Internat. Coll. Dentists; mem. AAAS, N.Y. Acad. Scis., Am. Assn. Cancer Research, ADA (cons. Council on Dental Edn. 1971-72, 75—, mem. commn. on accreditation 1976-80, cons. com. on hosp. and instl. dental service 1979—), Mich. (cons. com. on cancer control 1971-77, chmn. com. on cancer control and hosp. dentistry 1977—), Dist. dental assns., Mich. Soc. Pathologists, Internat. Assn. Dental Research, Royal Soc. Health (Eng.), Fedn. Dentaire Internationale, Internat. Acad. Pathology, Am. Cancer Soc. (dir. St. Louis City and County unit 1964-68, chmn. profl. edn. com. 1967-68, v.p., 1967-68, dir. Mo. div. 1965-68, dir., mem. exec. com. Mich. div. 1970—, chmn. profl. edn. com. 1973-76, v.p. unit 1975-76, pres. 1976-78, v.p. Mich. div. 1977-78, pres. 1978-79), Sigma Xi, Xi Psi Phi, Omicron Kappa Upsilon. Editor Proc. of Symposium: Salivary Glands and Their Secretion, 1973; Proc. of Symposium: Dental Plaque: Interfaces, 1974; Proc. of Symposium: Oral and Perioral Ulcerations: Cause and Control, Emphasis on Herpes Simplex Virus, 1975; Proc. of Symposium: Research in Form and Function, 1976; Proc. of Symposium: The Sci. Basis for Evaluation of Peridontal Therapy, 1977; Proc. of Symposium: Incipient Caries of Enamel, 1978; Proc. of Symposium: Diet Nutrition and Dental Caries, 1979; mem. editorial bd. Jour. Mo. Dental Soc., 1963-69, Bull. Greater St. Louis Dental Soc., 1964-68, Cancer, 1967—, Oral Research Abstracts, 1967-77, Jour. Dental Research, 1971-73; contbr. articles to profl. jours.; also chpts. to books. Home: 1042 Greenhills Dr Ann Arbor MI 48105

ROWE, ROBERT BRADFORD, urologist; b. Binghamton, N.Y., Aug. 15, 1918; s. Charles Eckert and Ethel Alice (Quick) R.; A.B., Williams Coll., 1940; M.D., Syracuse U., 1943; m. Elizabeth Reed Spencer, Mar. 22, 1943; children—Linda H., Barbara S., Susan S., Robert B., Sarah H., Constance K. Intern, St. Joseph Hosp., Syracuse, N.Y., 1943-44; resident in gen. surgery Syracuse Med. Center, 1944-45; commd. 1st lt. U.S. Army, 1945, advanced through grades to lt. col., 1951; resident in urology Walter Reed Gen. Hosp., Washington, 1947-50; chief urology Valley Forge Gen. Hosp., Phoenixville, Pa., 1950-54; urologist Carle Clinic Assn., Urbana, Ill., 1954—, bd. govs., 1968-74, sec.-treas., 1968-69, chmn., 1971-73; mem. staff Carle Hosp., 1954—, chief of staff, 1966; trustee Carle Found., 1974-80; cons. Chanute Air Force Hosp., div. vocat. rehab. U. Ill. Chmn. Urbana Civic Center Com., 1966-72. Diplomate Am. Bd. Urology. Fellow ACS; mem. Am. Group Practice Assn. (credentials chmn. 1964-70, sec.-treas. 1970-74, v.p. 1974-76, pres. 1976-77), AMA, Midwest Surg. Soc. (founding mem.), Ill. State, Champaign County med. socs., Am. Assn. Med. Clinics (N. Central sect.), Group Practice Polit. Action Com. (chmn. 1979-80), Pan Am. Med. Assn., Am. Urol. Assn., Urbana Assn. Commerce (dir. 1961-64). Republican. Presbyterian. Club: Lions (pres. 1960-61). Contbr. articles to med. jours. Home: 1501 N Coler Ave Urbana IL 61801 Office: Carle Clinic Urbana IL 61801

ROWEN, EUGENE, engr., state ofcl.; b. Miller, S.D., July 6, 1935; s. Alexander and Francis (Lichty) R.; B.S. in Engring., S.D. State U., 1958; m. Joyce Ellen Duxbury, Sept. 2, 1956; children—Richard Eugene, Jodene Marie. Asst. engr. S.D. Dept. Hwys., 1958-62, res. engr., 1962-67; dep. sec. S.D. Dept. Transp., Pierre, 1967-79, sec., 1979—; dir. Am. State Bank. Mem. Pierre City Planning Commn.; elder Presbyterian Ch. Recipient Minute Man award ROTC. Mem. Am. Assn. State Hwy. and Transp. Ofcls. (nat. standing com. planning), S.D. Soc. Profl. Engrs. (past pres.), Nat. Soc. Profl. Engrs. Republican. Clubs: Toastmasters (dep. lt. gov.), Elks. Office: SD Dept Transp Transportation Bldg Pierre SD 57501*

ROWLAND, HOWARD RAY, ednl. adminstr.; b. Eddy County, N.Mex., Sept. 9, 1929; s. Lewis Marion and Ursula Lorene (Hunt) R.; B.Journalism, U. Mo., Columbia, 1950; M.S. in Journalism, So. Ill. U., Carbondale, 1959; Ph.D. in Higher Edn. (NDEA fellow, 1967-69), Mich. State U., 1969; m. Meredith June Lee, Apr. 19, 1951; children—Runay Ilene Rowland Smith, Rhonda Lee Rowland Solberg. Editor Seymour (Mo.) Citizen, 1950-51, Lamar (Mo.) Daily Jour., 1951; feature writer Springfield (Mo.) Newspapers, 1954; editor Monett (Mo.) Times, 1954-55; editorial writer So. Ill. U., Carbondale, 1955-59; dir. info. services St. Cloud (Minn.) State U., 1959—; prof. Denmark Studies Program, Aalborg, Denmark, 1976, 80. Served with U.S. Army, 1951-53. Mem. Council for Advancement and Support of Edn. (nat. trustee, 1977-79, chmn. Dist. V, 1977-78), St. Cloud Area C. of C. (chmn. All-Am. City com., 1973-74), Sigma Delta Chi (pres. Minn. profl. chpt., 1963-64), Phi Delta Kappa (pres. Mich. State U. chpt., 1968-69, St. Cloud State U. chpt., 1978-79). Presbyterian. Club: Rotary Internat. Editor: Effective Community Relations, 1980. Home: Route 2 Kraemer Lake Saint Joseph MN 56374 Office: St Cloud State University Saint Cloud MN 56301

ROWLAND, RAYMOND EDGAR, business exec.; b. Kansas, Ill., Dec. 8, 1902; s. William and Lula Pearl (Estes) R.; student U. Ill., 1921-23; B.S., U. Wis.; m. Connie Lou Melton, July 30, 1928; children—Raymond Edgar, Eleanor Frances and Doris Elaine (twins). Sales div. Ralston Purina Co., 1926-34, plant mgr., Circleville, Ohio, 1934-40, asst. v.p., St. Louis, 1940-43, v.p., 1943-56, pres., 1956-64, chmn. bd., chief exec. officer, 1964-68, dir., 1951-79; dir. Merc. Trust Co. Chmn. bd. Barnes Hosp., St. Louis, 1968—; bd. dirs. St. Louis Area council Boy Scouts Am., 1962—; trustee Wis. Alumni Research Assn., 1963—. Mem. Alpha Zeta (hon.), Phi Sigma (hon.). Presbyterian. Clubs: Noonday, Bellerive Country, Bogey, St. Louis, Eldorado Country, Crystal Downs Country, Bohemian. Home: 710 S Hanley Rd Clayton MO 63105 Office: 100 N Broadway Saint Louis MO 63102

ROWLANDS, ROBERT EDWARD, educator, engr.; b. Trail, B.C., Can., July 7, 1936; s. Edward Howel and Eda May (Randell) R.; B.A. Sc., U. B.C., Vancouver, 1959; M.S., U. Ill., 1964, Ph.D., 1967; m. Mary Roma Ranaghan, Nov. 14, 1959; children—Robert Philip, Edward Hugh. Mech. engr. MacMillan & Bloedel, Powell River, B.C., 1959-60; research engr. Ill. Inst. Tech. Research Inst., Chgo., 1967-71, sr. research engr., 1971-74; asst. prof. engring. U. Wis., 1974-76, asso. prof. engring., 1976-79, prof. engring., 1979—; lectr. in field; cons. to auto, food processing, instrumentation, equipment mfg. and wood-product industries. Am. rep. to USSR-U.S.A. Advanced Composite Materials Meeting, Riga, 1978; mem. U.S.A. organizational com. U.S.A.-USSR Composite Materials Meeting, 1980. Active boys program YMCA, Park Forest, Ill., 1970-74; active youth racing program Madison Ski Club, 1978—; mem. com. Boy Scouts Am., Madison, 1975—, Guardian mem. Mohawk Dist. council, 1976—. Registered profl. engr., Wis. Mem. Soc. Exptl. Stress Analysis (mem. papers rev. com. 1967—, mem. editorial com. 1976—, book rev. editor 1976—, chmn. composite com. 1977-79, tech. chmn. 1975, also chmn. various tech. sessions; Hetényi award 1970, 76), ASME, ASTM, N.Am. Photonics Assn. (past sec.-treas.), Am. Acad. Mechanics. Protestant-Roman Catholic. Author chpt. Handbook of Composite Materials. Contbr. numerous articles to profl. jours. Home: 5401 Russett Rd Madison WI 53711 Office: Dept Engineering Mechanics U Wisconsin 1415 Johnson Dr Madison WI 53706

ROWLETT, RUSSELL JOHNSTON, JR., pub. co. exec.; b. Richmond, Va., Sept. 19, 1920; s. Russell Johnston and Carmine Ercell (Smith) R.; B.S., U. Va., 1941, M.S., 1943, Ph.D., 1945; m. Lillian Frances German, June 18, 1943; children—Russell J., William H. Research chemist DuPont Co., Wilmington, Del., 1946; asso. editor Chem. Abstracts Service, Columbus, Ohio, 1947-52, editor, dir. publs. and services, 1967—; dir. research and devel. Va.-Carolina Chem. Corp., Richmond, 1952-60; asst. dir. Va. Inst. Sci. Research, Richmond, 1960-67; dir. Columbus Center of Sci. and Industry. Bd. dirs. Goodwill Industries, Columbus, 1973-78; chmn. adminstrv. bd. Maple Grove United Meth. Ch., 1977-78. Recipient Miles Conrad Lecture award Nat. Fedn. Abstracting and Indexing Services, 1981. Mem. Am. Chem. Soc., Va. Acad. Sci., AAAS, Sigma Xi. Republican. Club: Ohio State U. Golf. Contbr. articles to profl. jours. Office: 2540 Olentangy River Rd PO Box 3012 Columbus OH 43210

ROY, CHARLES PHILLIP, mfg. co. exec.; b. Tulsa, July 16, 1945; s. Eugene W. and Hertha V. (Hulett) R.; student Kansas City Coll. and Bible Coll., 1966; m. Becky E. Roy; children—Cyndee Lynn, Trina Annette, Phillip Todd. Owner, mgr. Royal Washette, Inc., Huntington, W.Va., 1968-75; with KEI, Chanute, Kans., 1970-78, sales mgr., 1973-75, dir. advt. and promotions, 1975-78; gen. mgr. Baldwin Piano & Organ Co., Chanute, 1979—; dir. R.W. Inc. Charlie Roy Day proclaimed by Nashville and State of Tenn., 1978. Mem. Nat. Assn. Music Mchts., Country Music Assn., Audio Engring. Soc., Adminstrv. Mgmt. Soc., Gospel Music Assn., Nat. Acad. Recording Arts and Scis., CAMEO (dir.), GAMA. Home: 1314 S 8th St Humboldt KS 66748 Office: 908 W Chestnut St Chanute KS 66720

ROY, ELMON HAROLD, clergyman; b. Russell Springs, Ky., Dec. 17, 1924; s. Leslie Combs and Olza Myrtle (Gosser) R.; B.A., So. Missionary Coll., 1953; M.A., Belin U., 1958; Ph.D., Colo. Coll. and Sem., 1966; postgrad. Spalding Coll., 1969-70, Andrews U., 1974; m. Retha Mae Adkins, Mar. 16, 1946; children—Joel, Michael. Ordained to ministry Seventh-day Adventist Ch., Mt. Vernon, Ohio, 1959; asso. pastor, Bucyrus, Ohio, 1955-56, Akron, Ohio, 1956-57; pastor East Liverpool (Ohio) Seventh-day Adventist Ch., 1957-60, Coudersport, Pa., 1960-64, St. Matthews Seventh-day Adventist Ch., Louisville, 1965-71; chaplain Seventh-day Adventist Hosp., Louisville, 1971-75; pastor Springfield (Ohio) Seventh-day Adventist Ch., 1975—; pres. South Oldham Ch. Council, 1971; mem. Ohio Conf. Ordination Com., 1980; mem. Ohio Conf. Bd. Edn., 1979—; chaplain Jefferson County Ct., 1975, Sons Am. Revolution, Louisville, 1974-75. Bd. dirs. Pleasant Grove Hosp., Louisville, 1971-76. Served with USN, 1943-46. Fellow Philos. Soc. Gt. Britain, Royal Geog. Soc., Royal Soc. Arts, Huguenot Soc. London; mem. Am. Acad. Religion, S.A.R., Ky. Hist. Soc. Author: Earth's Coming Events, 1968; Bible Promises, 1971; Courage for Hospital Days, 1973; Moments of Meditation, 1975. Home: 1541 Villa Rd Springfield OH 45503 Office: 151 S Bird Rd PO Box 1563 Springfield OH 45501

ROY, WILFRED ELMER (WILL), educator; b. Van Buren, Maine, Aug. 7, 1935; s. Leo and Isabel (Boudreau) R.; A.B. in English, Boston U., 1961; Ed.M., Salem State Coll., 1966; Ph.D. in Urban Edn., U. Wis., Milw., 1974; children—Denise, Patrice. Tchr., Amesbury (Mass.) High Sch., 1962-64, North Reading (Mass.) High Sch., 1964-67; asst. supt. schs., Windsor, Vt., 1967-69; Edn. Profl. Devel. Act fellow So. Ill. U., Edwardsville, 1969-70; asso. prof. curriculum and instrn. dept. U. Wis., Milw., 1972—; cons. Nat. Center for Gifted, 1978-81, Am. Inst. for Human Interaction, 1978-81, Good Apple Inc., 1979—; speaker at convs. and confs. Served with USAF, 1953-57. NDEA fellow, 1967; fellow Robert A. Taft Inst. Practical Politics, 1967. Mem. Am. Humanist Assn., Assn. for Tchrs. Edn., Assn. Sch. Curriculum Devel., ACLU, Wis. Council for Gifted and Talented. Democrat. Roman Catholic. Author: Creative Coping: Getting Along with Yourself and Others, 1980, 81; contbr. articles to profl. pubIs. Home: 706 W Rock Pl Milwaukee WI 53209 Office: PO Box 413 Dept Curriculum & Instrn Sch Edn U Wis Milwaukee WI 53201

ROYALTY, DENNIS MARION, material handling equipment co. exec.; b. Bloomington, Ind., Nov. 17, 1923; s. Henry Dennis and Lois Vivian (Malicote) R.; student King Coll., 1943; B.S., Ind. U., 1946-49; postgrad. Butler U., 1955, Youngstown U., 1957-58; m. Kathleen Hollis Barnhart, Aug. 26, 1946; children—Dennis Michael, David Alan. With RCA, 1949-54; personnel mgr. Mallory-Sharon Metals, Niles, O., 1955-58; chief plans and controls Martin-Marietta, Denver, 1958-64; personnel mgr. Fed.-Mogul Corp., Frankfort, Ind., 1964-70; dir. personnel Mallory Timers Co., Indpls., 1970-71; plant mgr. Delphi Body Works (Ind.), 1972-73; mgr. employee and community relations Stephens-Adamson div. Allis Chalmers, Aurora, Ill., 1974—. Bd. dirs. Jr. Achievement Aurora, 1976-80; div. chmn. Aurora Wayside Cross Rescue Mission Fund Dr., 1980—. Served with USAF, 1943-46. Recipient Award of Merit, U.S. Treasury Dept., 1964-70, Nat. Safety Council, 1953, 57. Mem. Valley Personnel Assn. (pres. 1977), Conveyor Equipment Mfrs. Assn. (chmn. IR conf. 1979-80), Greater Aurora C. of C. (chmn. congressional action com. 1977-81), Ind. U. Club of Clinton County (dir. 1966-69, pres. 1970). Clubs: Elks, Kiwanis (pres. 1981-82). Home: 378 Michigan Ave Aurora IL 60506 Office: Stephens-Adamson Ridgeway Ave at Woodlawn Aurora IL 60507

ROYHL, JOHN CHARLES, ins. agt.; b. Chgo., June 26, 1943; s. John Henry and Florence Adelaide (Miller) R.; B.A., Valparaiso U., 1966; M. Ed., Loyola U., Chgo., 1973; m. Marcia Ann Kniph, Feb. 1, 1969; children—Heather Renee, Annette Michele. Sales, customer service Pyramid Moulding Inc., Chgo., 1969-73; guidance counselor, tchr. Lisle (Ill.) Community Sch. Dist., 1973-77; spl. agt. Northwestern Mut. Life Ins. Co., Chgo., 1977—; systems cons. Norelco WPS, Philips Bus. Systems, sales mgr. micon data systems Chgo. br.; exec. v.p. Tomorrow's Office Products, Inc. Sponsor, Future Bus. Leaders Am., Lisle Sr. High Sch., 1973-75; sponsor Kiwanis Builders CLub, Lisle Jr. High Sch., 1977. Mem. Ill., Am. personnel and guidance assns. Lutheran. Club: YMCA Y's Men's (sec. 1969-70) (Elmhurst, Ill.). Home: 44 W Sunset St Lombard IL 60148 Office: 100 S Wacker Dr Chicago IL 60606

ROYKO, MIKE, newspaper columnist; b. Chgo., Sept. 19, 1932; s. Michael and Helen (Zak) R.; student Wright Jr. Coll., 1951-52; m. Carol Joyce Duckman, Nov. 7, 1954 (dec. 1979); children—M. David, Robert F. Reporter, Chgo. North Side Newspapers, 1956; reporter, asst. city editor Chgo. City News Bur., 1956-59; reporter, columnist Chgo. Daily News, 1959-78, Chgo. Sun Times, 1978—. Served with USAF, 1952-56. Recipient Heywood Brown award, 1968, Pulitzer prize for commentary, 1972. Mem. Chgo. Newspaper Reporters Assn. Club: LaSalle St. Rod and Gun. Author: Up Against It, 1967; I May Be Wrong but I Doubt It, 1968; Boss—Richard J. Daley of Chicago, 1971; Slats Grobnik and Some Other Friends, 1973. Office: Chgo Sun Times 401 N Wabash Ave Chicago IL 60611

ROZELLE, LEE THEODORE, phys. chemist; b. Rhinelander, Wis., Mar. 9, 1933; s. Theodore and Alice (Omholt) R.; B.S., U. Wis., 1955, Ph.D. (NIH fellow, 1958-60), 1960; m. Barbara J. Ingli, June 21, 1955; children—David, Steven, Carolyn, Ann, Kenneth. Research chemist DuPont Corp., Circleville, Ohio, 1960-63; prin. scientist-tech. coordinator Honeywell, Mpls., 1963-67; dir. chemistry div. North Star Research Inst., Mpls., 1967-74; v.p. research and devel. USCI div. C.R. Bard, Billerica, Mass., 1974-77; dir. engring. tech. div. Mellon Inst., Pitts., 1977-78; dir. research and devel. Permutit Co., Monmouth Junction, N.J., 1978-80; v.p. research and devel. Gelman Scis., Inc., Ann Arbor, Mich., 1980—; cons. Bd. dirs. Unitarian Ch., Andover, Mass., 1974-77. Fellow Am. Inst. Chemists; mem. Am. Chem. Soc., Am. Soc. Artificial Internal Organs, Health Industry Mfrs. Assn. (chmn. spl. activities com.), Water Pollution Control Fedn., Sigma Xi, Eta Phi Alpha, Phi Lambda Upsilon. Contbr. chpts. to books, numerous articles to profl. jours. Home: 3405 Brentwood Ct Ann Arbor MI 48104 Office: 600 S Wagner Rd Ann Arbor MI 48106

ROZICH, ILEENE SHAFFER, clubwoman; b. Greenville, Pa., Jan. 5, 1932; d. Charles Tennyson and Elizabeth Irene (McClimans) Welk; student Youngstown State U., 1950-51; m. John Henry Shaffer, Dec. 1, 1951 (dec.); children—Kathy Charlene Shaffer Spadin, Marybeth Dawn Shaffer Lang, Jon Mark; stepchildren—Kenneth Shaffer, Karen Shaffer Allen; m. 2d, William Steve Rozich, Feb. 14, 1975. With G.M. McKelvey, Youngstown, Ohio, 1948-51; with Livingston's, Youngstown, 1951-53; with Tippecanoe Country Club, Canfield, Ohio, 1965-73; pres. Girard Republican Club, 1979—; precinct committee person, Girard City, Ohio, 1965—; mem. exec. com. Trumbull County, Ohio, 1968—; mem. Dames of Malta, 1955—, Queen Esther, 1961; mem. Protectors Club, pres., 1971-75; mem. Mahoning chpt. DAR. Republican. Lutheran. Mem. Mercer County Geneal. Soc. (pres. 1980). Author: Welk Family History. Home: 362 Iowa Ave Girard OH 44420

ROZMAN, JOSEPH JOHN, JR., artist, educator; b. Milw., Dec. 26, 1944; s. Joseph J. and Julia Mary (Vicic) R.; B.F.A. with honors, U. Wis., 1967, M.F.A., 1969; m. Nicolee Teegarden, Dec. 26, 1973; children—Terri Nicole, Eric Todd. Instr. in art U. Wis., Milw., 1967-69, vis. lectr. in art, 1972-73, also vis. lectr. U. Wis. at Parkside, 1970-71; instr. in printmaking Milw. Art Center, 1968-76; instr. in art Carthage Coll., Kenosha, Wis., 1969-72; instr. design and printmaking Layton Sch. of Art and Design, Milw., 1973-74; asst. prof. art Mount Mary Coll., Milw., 1975—; juror for various art exhbns., 1969—; one man shows of Prints/paintings include: Southwest Tex. State Coll., San Marcos, 1969, U. Wis., Milw., 1969, Northern State Coll., Aberdeen, S.D., 1971, Carroll Coll., Waukesha, Wis., 1972, Milw. Art Center, 1973, Fanny Garver Gallery, Madison, Wis., 1973, Wustum Mus., Racine, Wis., 1975, U. Wis., Parkside, 1980, Joy Horwich Gallery, Chgo., 1980, others; group shows include: Chgo. and Vicinity Exhbn., Chgo. Art Inst., 1966, 68, 73, 77, 78, 81, Nat. Boston Printmakers Exhbn., Boston Mus. Fine Arts, 1967-69, Pratt Internat. Miniature Print Exhbn., N.Y.C., 1968, 71, 75, Tex. Tech. U., 1969-71, State Univ. N.Y., Oneonta, 1972, So. Ill. U., 1972, Okla. Art Center; represented in permanent collections: Milw. Art Center, Decordova Mus., Lincoln, Mass., U. Wis., Milw., SW Tex State Coll., San Marcos, Carthage Coll., Kenosha, 1st Wis. Center, Milw., Wis. State U., Stevens Point, Sears Tower, Chgo., others. Recipient numerous awards including: Wis. Salon of Art award, 1966; Logan award and prize Chgo. Art Inst., 1966, John G. Curtis, Jr. prize, 1981; Carthage Coll. Faculty Research grantee, 1970; Lakefront Festival of Arts award, 1977, 79, 81; Main award Watercolor Wis., 1977; Mt. Mary Coll. grantee, 1982. Mem. Boston Printmakers, Art Inst. Chgo., Milw. Art Center. Christian Scientist. Home: 4419 Lindermann Ave Racine WI 53405 Office: 2900 N Menomonee River Parkway Milwaukee WI 53222

RUBASH, ARLYN ROBERT, educator; b. East McKeesport, Pa., Mar. 23, 1941; s. Joseph Robert and Anna (Peckman) R.; B.S., Pa. State U., 1970, M.B.A., 1972, Ph.D., 1975; m. Marjorie Ann Shaffer, Aug. 29, 1964; children—Kevin Robert, Cindy Lee. Prodn. dept. Hercules, Inc., Washington, Pa., 1964-69; teaching asst. in finance Pa. State U., 1971-74; asso. prof. finance Bradley U., Peoria, Ill., 1974—; pres., dir. Cons. Resources for Mgmt., Peoria, 1978—. Mem. Am. Finance Assn., Financial Mgmt. Assn., Eastern Finance Assn., Midwest Finance Assn., Am. Inst. for Decision Scis., Am. Risk and Ins. Assn., Beta Gamma Sigma. Republican. Club: South-West Peoria Kiwanis. Author: A Measure of the Relationship Between Information and Commonstock Returns, 1975. Abstracter for ops. research Management Sci. Internat. Lit. Digest Periodical, 1977—. Home: 2908 W Brookside Dr Peoria IL 61615 Office: Baker Hall Bradley U Peoria IL 61625

RUBBO, ROD J., profl. arts adminstr.; b. Johnstown, Pa., July 1, 1948; s. Archie J. and Biece E. (Maples) R.; B.F.A., U. Okla., 1971; m. Kathy W. Widner, May 30, 1970. Lighting designer Southwest Repertory Theatre, Norman, Okla., 1970-71; prodn. stage mgr. Pitts. Ballet Theatre, 1971-72; co. mgr. PFH Ballet Theatre, Pitts., 1972-74; gen. mgr. NC Dance Theatre, Winston-Salem, N.C., 1974-76; gen. mgr. Ohio Ballet, Akron, 1976-79; exec. dir. Cultural Center for the Arts, Canton, Ohio, 1979—; chmn. dance panel Ohio Arts Council. Mem. Assn. Ohio Dance Cos. (treas. 1976-79, v.p. 1979—). Roman Catholic. Office: 1001 Market St N Canton OH 44702

RUBEL, JOAN GERTRUDE, radio sta. exec.; b. Hartford, Conn., Nov. 17, 1950; d. Herbert J. and Ruth (Bonyhadi) R.; B.A. in Sociology, U. Wis., 1972. Research asst. Equal Rights div. State of Wis., 1973-74; project dir. Dane County (Wis.) Project on Rape, Madison, 1974-77; sta. mgr. Sta. WORT, Madison, 1977—; pres. Back Porch Radio Broadcasting, Inc., 1977—, also dir.; partner whole Woman Newspaper, 1973-75. Co-founder Madison Rape Crisis Center, 1973-77; organizer Madison Women's Center, 1973-74; v.p. Dane County Mental Health Consortium, 1977. Wis. Humanities Com. grantee, 1979. Mem. Nat. Fedn. Community Broadcasters (mem. steering com.). Office: 2049 Winnebago St Madison WI 53704

RUBEN, JOSEPH S., newspaper ofcl.; b. N.Y.C., Apr. 18, 1933; s. Louis and Marcia (Pellman) R.; B.S., Purdue U., 1959; m. Rebecca S. Piech, Feb. 22, 1977; 1 dau., Leah Tracy. Dir. research Playboy Enterprises, Inc., Chgo., 1959-76; pres. JSR & Assos., Ltd., Chgo., 1976-80; advt. research mgr. Chgo. Sun-Times, 1980—. Served with AUS, 1954-55. Mem. Am. Mktg. Assn., Advt. Research Found., Newspaper Research Council. Home: 130 N Park St Glen Ellyn IL 60137 Office: 401 N Wabash Ave Chicago IL 60611

RUBENSTEIN, ALBERT IRWIN, fin. exec.; b. Chgo., Mar. 28, 1927; s. William D. and Regina (Ribaysen) R.; student Herzl City Coll., 1944-46, Roosevelt Coll., 1946-48; LL.B., J.D., John Marshall Law Sch., 1951; m. Joyce Shirley Leeman, June 12, 1954; children—Jeffrey, Lauren, Jan. Admitted to Ill. bar, 1951; individual practice law, Chgo., 1951-64; pres., chief exec. officer Fleetwood Realty Corp., Chgo., 1969—, also dir.; sr. partner Fleetwood Realty Co., Chgo., 1969—; dir. Exec. Bus. Center, Inc., Fleetwood Industries; lectr. in field. Mem. Am. Bar Assn., Ill. Bar Assn., Chgo. Bar Assn., Am. Trial Lawyers Assn., Chgo. Assn. Commerce and Industry, Nat. Real Estate Bd., Chgo. Real Estate Bd. (dir. 1980—), Decalogue Soc. Lawyers, Nat. Realty Com., Inc., Am. Arbitration Soc. Clubs: Covenant of Ill., B'nai B'rith. Contbr. articles in field to profl. jours. Office: 200 W Jackson Blvd Chicago IL 60606

RUBENSTEIN, BERNARD, conductor; grad. Yale U., Eastman Sch. Music. Former condr., music dir. orch. and opera Sch. Music, Northwestern U., Evanston, Ill.; now asso. condr. Cin. Symphony Orch.; guest condr. Berlin Radio Orch., Vienna Tonkuenstler Orch., Warsaw Philharmonic, Austrian Radio Orch., Vienna, Frankfurt Radio Orch., die reihe, Vienna, Stuttgart Opera, Frankfurt Opera, Milw. Symphony Orch., St. Paul Chamber Orch., Grant Park Orch., Chgo., St. Louis Little Symphony, Guadalajara Symphony; condr. U.S. premieres including: The Knot Garden, Requiem by Ligeti. Office: Cin Symphony Orch 1241 Elm St Cincinnati OH 45210*

RUBIE, JAMES STANLEY, JR., consulting actuary co. exec.; b. St. Louis, Mar. 16, 1944; s. James S. and Alma M. R.; A.B., Coll. Holy Cross, 1966; postgrad. (NDEA fellow), U. Kans., 1966-67; m. Kathleen E. Moran, June 25, 1966; children—Laura, Allison, Amy. Actuarial asst. Gen. Am. Life Ins. Co., St. Louis, 1967-71; v.p., prin. Tillinghast, Nelson & Warren, Inc., St. Louis, 1971—. Fellow Soc. Actuaries, Conf. Actuaries in Public Practice; mem. Am. Acad. Actuaries, Internat. Actuarial Assn. Club: Mo. Athletic. Home: 14522 Brittania Dr Chesterfield MO 63017 Office: 222 S Central Ave Saint Louis MO 63105

RUBIN, CARL BERNARD, fed. judge; b. Cin., Mar. 27, 1920; s. John I. and Ethel (Friedman) R.; B.A., U. Cin., 1942, J.D., 1944; m. Gloria Weiland, Sept. 23, 1945; children—Marc W., C. Barry, Pam G., Robert S. Admitted to Ohio bar, 1944; practiced in Cin., 1944-71; asst. pros. atty. Hamilton County (Ohio), Cin., 1950-60; judge U.S. Dist. Ct. So. Dist. Ohio, 1971—, chief judge, 1979—; instr. criminal law Chase Coll. Law, Cin., 1965-67; mem. com. on ct. adminstrn. fed. cts. U.S. Jud. Conf., 1975; adj. prof. law U. Dayton Coll. Law, 1976—. Mem. Cin. CSC, 1960-66, chmn., 1965-66; pres. S.W. Ohio Regional Transit Authority, 1971. Mem. Am. Contract Bridge League (dir. 1966-73, pres. 1970-71). Office: US Courthouse 5th and Walnut Sts Cincinnati OH 45202

RUBIN, STEPHEN DAVID, wholesale distributor; b. Milw., May 30, 1939; s. Ephraim I. and Ruth (Grodin) R.; B.B.A., U. Wis., 1961, LL.D., 1965; m. Marcia Rubin; children—Wendy Lynn, Michael Allen. Vice pres. Liberman & Gittlen Metal Co., Grand Rapids, Mich., 1965-74; pres. Graver-Dearborn Corp., Chgo., 1966-79, Mercil Plating Co., Chgo., 1968-74, Master Plating Co., Chgo., 1968-74; v.p. P.J. Gould Co., 1973-74, Odd 02 Amusements; pres. Donnell Co., Fla., Tex., Ga., 1975—; pres. Baker Rite Baking Co., Stevens Point, Wis., 1976-79, Am. Dynamics Corp., 1978—. Pres. Swiss Internat. Marketing Group. Mem. Young Men's Jewish Council (dir.), Young Presidents Orgn., Zeta Beta Tau. Home: 7314 N Lowell Ave Lincolnwood IL 60646 Office: 111 E Wacker Dr Suite 400 Chicago IL 60647

RUBINER, RAYMOND KOPEL, investment co. exec.; b. Detroit, Sept. 14, 1918; s. Abram Joseph and Dora (Presman) R.; student Wayne State U., 1934-36, McKinley Coll. Law, 1937-39; B.S., Great Lakes Coll., 1959; m. Elise Julia Cohen, Dec. 11, 1939; children—Lois Elaine, Joan Carol, Audrey Jane. With Cunningham Drug Corp., Detroit, 1933-40; real estate investor, Mich. and Fla., 1946-60; v.p. Hubbard Assos. Real Estate Investment Co., Detroit, 1961-70; pres. Gen. Properties Corp., Birmingham, Mich., 1970—; dir. Glades Hotel Properties, Redington Beach, Fla., Broderick Tower Properties, Detroit; cons. to Amber & Amber Devel. Co.; lectr. Oakland U., Rochester, Mich., 1964-68. Mem. Mayor's Detroit Tomorrow Com., 1952-55. Served with AUS, 1941-46. Mem. Am. Arbitration Assn., Am. Soc. Appraisers (sr. mem., dir. Detroit chpt.), Nat. Assn. Accountants, Nat. Assn. Pub. Accountants, Nat. Assn. Real Estate Bds., Birmingham-Bloomfield Bd. Realtors, Detroit Bd. Realtors. Club: Mason. Home: 2945 Woodward Ave Winter Bldg #88 Bloomfield Hills MI 48013 Office: 280 N Woodward Ave Suite 307 Birmingham MI 48011

RUBINIC, PAUL ROBERT, educator; b. Johnstown, Pa., Aug. 25, 1937; s. Louis and Mary (Mehall) R.; married, 2 children. B.A. in Secondary Edn. and Latin, Youngstown (Ohio) State U., 1962, M.S.Ed. in Elementary Adminstrn., 1971; Specialist in Learning Disabilities, Syracuse (N.Y.) U., 1965; postgrad. Kent State U.; m. Colleen; children—Patrick, Michael. Learning disabilities tchr. Montgomery County Schs., Rockville, Md., 1965-66; reading coordinator Mahoning Valley Vocat. Sch., Vienna, Ohio, 1966-70; dir. Head Start, Youngstown Area Community Action Council, 1970; cons., supr. for children with learning disabilities and/or behavior disorders, also autistic children Trumbull County Bd. Edn., Warren, Ohio, 1970-76; dir. Mid Eastern Ohio Spl. Edn. Regional Resource Center, Akron, 1976—. Author: Focus on Non Public Schools in Ohio; Handbook of Learning Disabilities; Teaching of Reading. Certified supt., prin., supr., tchr. Latin and spl. edn., Ohio. Home: 675 Rob's Rd Girard OH 44420 Office: 65 Steiner St Akron OH 44301

RUBINO, TONY MICHAEL, caterer; b. Akron, Ohio, Feb. 19, 1953; s. Uito and Lena (Massa) R.; student Akron U., 1972-74; m. Dona Gene Dugan, Mar. 28, 1981. Pres., Rubino Prodns., Akron, 1970—; owner Rubino Music Co., Akron and Cleve., 1974-79; pres. Party House Caterers, Inc., Cuyahoga Falls, Ohio, 1971—; owner Rubino's Village Pump-Nite Club, Cuyahoga Falls, 1981—. Recipient award as top pop organist Contemporary Keyboard Mag., 1976. Mem. Nat. Caterers Assn. (pres., bd. dirs.), Nat. Rifle Assn. Republican. Club: Cascade (Akron). Author: Lenny Oee, 1976; Contemporary Keyboard, 1976. Office: 2771 Front St Cuyahoga Falls OH 44221

RUBINOWICZ, ALYCE ANN (RUBY), food industry exec.; b. b. Meriden, Conn., Sept. 8, 1946; d. Edward Peter and Alyce Muriel (Harding) R.; student in Bus. Adminstrn., Butler U., 1974-77. Enlisted U.S. Air Force, 1965, advanced through grades to master sgt., 1979, served acctg. and fin., 1969-73, med. technician, 1965-69, ret., 1973; sr. bookkeeper, acctg. McDonald's Corp., Indpls., 1973-76, regional office services mgr., 1976—. Mem. Modern Office Procedures (research adv. com. 1980-81). Office: PO Box 50414 Indianapolis IN 46250

RUBINS, IRA MARC, ednl. adminstr.; b. Cleve., Nov. 4, 1947; s. Alex and Betty (Buller) R.; B.A., Miami U., Ohio, 1969, M.A., 1971; postgrad. Kent State U.; m. Sherry Ruth Weintraub, Aug. 24, 1969; children—Jennifer Sarah, Dana Reed. Producer of Radio Talk Music Show, sta. WIXY, Cleve., 1970-71; chmn. broadcast mgmt. dept. Jones Coll., Jacksonville, Fla., 1971-72; announcer Sta. WKTZ, Jacksonville, Fla., 1971-72; faculty coordinator WIXY Sch. Broadcast Technique, Cleve., 1973-75; dir. edn. Ohio Sch. Broadcast Technique, Cleve., 1975—; v.p. Ednl. Broadcast Services, Inc., Cleve., 1975—; v.p. Nashville Sch. Broadcasting Technique, 1980—. Dir. auctions Renaissance Fine Arts Gallery, Cleve., 1974—. Mem. Nat. Assn. of Trade and Tech. Schs. (public relations com. 1976-79, chmn. 1979-80), Nat. Assn. Ednl. Broadcasters (mem. broadcast edn. com. 1975-77), Radio TV Council Greater Cleve., Northeastern Ohio Chpt. Proprietary Schs. (sec. 1977-79, pres. 1979-80), Ohio Council Pvt. Colls. and Schs. (sec. 1977-80, dir. 1977-83). Jewish. Home: 16004 Fernway Rd Shaker Heights OH 44120 Office: 1737 Euclid Ave Cleveland OH 44115

RUBIO, ELENITA IGNACIO, physician; b. Cavite, Philippines, May 22, 1943; d. Pedro Ignacio and Francisca San Miguel (Reyes) Ignacio; A.A., U. St. Tomas, 1962, M.D., 1967; m. Nunilo G. Rubio, June 20, 1970; children—Nunilo, Noel, Nathaniel. Intern, Swedish Hosp., Mpls., 1968-69; resident in internal medicine Hines (Ill.) VA Hosp., 1970-72; attending physician, 1972—; practice medicine, specializing in internal medicine, Chgo. and Franklin Park, Ill., 1973—; co-owner Chgo. Hamlin Med. Center, 1974—; co-owner, treas. RVR Med. Splty. Group Ltd., 1974—; clin. instr. Loyola Stritch Sch. Medicine, 1972—. Mem. AMA, Ill., Chgo. med. socs., Philippine Med. Soc. Chgo. Club: Indianhead Park Village. Home: 6555 Cochise Dr Indianhead Park IL 60525 Office: 3758 W Chicago Ave Chicago IL 60651

RUBIO, NUNILO GUINTO, physician; b. Bacoor, Cavite, Oct. 22, 1943; came to U.S., 1967; s. Leopoldo Francisco Rubio and Emilia Guinto; M.D., Far Eastern U., 1967; m. Elenita R. Ignacio, June 20, 1970; children—Nunilo, Noel, Nathaniel. Intern, Grant Hosp., Chgo., 1967, cons. attending physician, 1970—; resident in internal medicine and endocrinology Hines VA Hosp., 1969-72, attending physician, 1970—, co-dir. metabolic sect., 1977—; pres. RVR Med. Splty. Group Ltd., Chgo., 1975—; asst. clin. prof. Loyola Stritch Med. Sch., Maywood, Ill., 1977—; chmn. dept. medicine St. Elizabeth's Hosp., Chgo., 1978—, mem. exec. com., 1978—, cons. attending physician, 1972—; attending physician Westlake Hosp., 1974—; cons. Bethany Garfield Hosp. Named Intern of Yr., St. Lukes Hosp., 1967; Caviteno of Yr., Cavite Assn. Am., 1977; Far Eastern U. Coll. Medicine scholar, 1964-65. Mem. Am. Soc. Internal Medicine, Am. Diabetes Assn., Am. Coll. Utilization Review Physicians, Ill. Soc. Internal Medicine, Ill. Med. Soc., Philippine Med. Assn. Chgo. (gov. 1977—), Chgo. Soc. Internal Medicine, Chgo. Found. Med. Care. Club: Cavite Assn. Am. (pres.). Editorial cons. Philippine Med. Bull., 1978—. Home: 6555 Cochise Dr Indianhead Park IL 60525 Office: 3758 W Chicago Ave Chicago IL 60651

RUBLE, BERNARD ROY, grocery chain exec.; b. Greensburg, Ind., Apr. 4, 1923; s. Jesse Emory and Marietta (Ward) R.; B.S., Ind. U., Bloomington, 1949; postgrad. transactional analysis Midwest Inst. Human Understanding, 1972-75; m. Mary Helen Rullman, Dec. 22, 1946; children—Barry Reece, Blane Rodney. Asst. mgr. Morris 5 and 10 Stores, Greensburg, 1941; store keeper Public Service Co. Ind., Greensburg, 1941-43; asst. mgr. personnel Kroger Co., Cin., 1949-51, mgr., personnel, Madison, Wis., 1951-56, Ft. Wayne, Ind., 1956-58, Cleve., 1958-73, mgr. labor relations Erie Mktg. Area, Solon, Ohio, 1973—; faculty Kroger Edn. Center, Cin., 1978—; trustee Meat Cutters Health and Welfare Fund, 1971-79, Retail Clks. Union Health and Welfare Fund, Akron, 1970—, No. Ohio Hospice Council, 1981—. Active United Appeal Greater Cleve., Community Chest Greater Cleve., Met. Health Planning Corp.; v.p., trustee Urban League Greater Cleve., 1968-75; adv. com. Family Health Care, Washington, 1977-78; trustee Community Health Found.; team rep. B.R. Ruble Racing, Chesterland, Ohio. Served with USAAF, 1943-45. Mem. Internat. Transactional Analysis Assn. (cert. clin), Photog. Soc. Am., Soc. for Advancement Mgmt. (trustee Madison chpt. 1952-55), Am. Soc. Personnel Adminstrn., Cleve. Personnel Assn., Indsl. Relations Research Assn. (pres.). Clubs: Masons, Sertoma (trustee Madison 1952-58) (charter). Lic. minister Disciples Christ, 1975. Home: 8644 Ranch Dr Chesterland OH 44026 Office: Erie Mktg Area Kroger Co 31000 Aurora Rd Solon OH 44139

RUBLE, RONALD ALVIN, educator; b. Los Angeles, Sept. 14, 1929; s. Ronald A. and Maria Alvina (Abeyta) R.; B.A., U. N.Mex., 1952, M.A., 1959, Ed.D., 1964; m. Angelina Garcia, June 28, 1952; 1 dau., Regina Christine. Tchr., Otero County (N.Mex.) Schs., 1952-53; tchr. mcpl. schs. Taos, N.Mex., 1954-56, counselor, 1956-57; counselor, asst. dir., dir. Lincoln Guidance Research Project, Albuquerque Pub. Schs., 1957-65; prof., counselor edn., chmn. div. counselor edn. St. Louis U., 1965—. Mem. Am. Personnel and Guidance Assn., Assn. Specialists in Group Work, Assn. Counselor Edn. and Supervision, Am. Psychol. Assn., Profl. Counselors' Assn., Nat. Tng. Labs. Home: 7605 Arlington Ave St Louis MO 63119 Office: 221 N Grand Blvd St Louis MO 63103

RUBLE, THOMAS JAMES, mfg. co. exec.; b. Toledo, Nov. 27, 1952; s. Eugene Leonard and Junita Ellen (Ferner) R.; B.M.E., Gen. Motors Inst., 1975; m. Jacquelyn Ann Deppen, Feb. 16, 1974; children—Brian Anthony, Craig Michael, Andrew Thomas. Prodn. engr. Delco Moraine div. Gen. Motors Corp., Dayton, Ohio, 1975-76, prodn. supr., 1976-77, prodn. gen. supr., 1977-79, project mgr., 1979—. Mem. Am. Mgmt. Assn., Soc. Mfg. Engrs., Theta Xi. Office: 1420 Wisconsin Blvd Dayton OH 45401

RUBLOFF, ARTHUR, real estate developer; m. Josephine Sheehan (dec.); m. 2d, Mary Taylor. Chmn., dir. Rubloff Devel. Corp., Chgo.; chmn., pres., dir. North Kansas City Devel. Co. (Mo.); developer Evergreen Park Shopping Plaza, Chgo.; developer, partner Bay Shore Properties, Sun Valley, Southland, Eastridge, San Francisco, Carl Sandburg Village, Chgo.; partner Interurban Devel. Corp., Chgo.; gen. partner Park Pl. Assos., Chgo.; partner real estate holdings with Charles and Herb Allen, Allen & Co., investment bankers, N.Y.C.; former real estate cons. Port N.Y. Authority-World Trade Center. Former mem. sr. council All Chgo. Citizens' Com.; former chmn., dir. Horatio Alger awards com.; former bd. dirs. Goodwill Industries; life mem., adv. bd., chmn. div. Chgo. Heart Assn.; bd. dirs., former exec. v.p. Chgo. Boys' Clubs; bd. dirs Lyric Opera, Chgo.; mem. pres.'s council Lincoln Park Zool. Soc.; former trustee Jr. Achievement, Chgo., Roosevelt U., Chgo., Hull House, Chgo., Chgo. Community Trust; former bd. dirs., citizens bd. Loyola U., Chgo.; former mem. bus. adv. council Chgo. Urban League; life mem. Art Inst. Chgo.; mem. steering com. United Negro Coll. Fund; former cons. Chgo. council Girl Scouts U.S.; former mem. com. econ. and cultural devel., past bd. dirs. Jewish Fedn. Met. Chgo.; chmn. bd. dirs. United Cerebral Palsy Chgo.; former dir. Mayor's Commn. for Sr. Citizens; former bd. dirs. Inst. Religion and Health, N.Y.C.; bd. govs. Med. Research Inst. Michael Reese Hosp.; former bd. dirs. Sr. Centers Met. Chgo., Civic Fedn.; vice-chmn. library bd. Northwestern U.; nat. bd. dirs., nat. co-chmn. NCCJ. Decorated Stella Della Solidarieta Italiana award; recipient Ann. Horatio Alger award Am. Schs. and Coll. Assn., 1955; named Man of Yr., Catholic War Vets., 1963, Outstanding Civic Leader, 1969, Chicagoan of Yr., 1971, Internat. Humanitarian award B'nai B'rith, 1974; Outstanding Bus. Leader award Northwood Inst., 1982. Mem. Internat. Real Estate Fedn. (dir. Am. chpt.), Chgo. Assn. Commerce and Industry (mem. sr. council), Chgo. Real Estate Bd., Nat. Assn. Real Estate Bds., Greater North Michigan Ave. Assn. (dir., past pres), Am. Soc. Real Estate Counselors, U.S. C. of C., Lambda Alpha. Kiwanian. Clubs: Variety Internat.; Harmoniy, Doubles (N.Y.C.); Standard, Execs., Oil Men's (hon.), Monroe, Arts, Mid-day, Econs., Mid-Am., Carlton, Plaza (Chgo.); Poinciana, Yacht (Palm Beach, Fla.); St. George's, Anabel's, Crockford (London). Pioneer major devel. areas including North Michigan Ave.'s Magnificient Mile Devel., North Loop Redevel., Ft. Dearborn Project, Old North Town Redevel. Project. Office: 69 W Washington St Chicago IL 60602

RUBLOFF, BURTON, real estate broker, appraiser; b. Chisholm, Minn., June 1, 1912; s. Solomon W. and Mary R.; grad. Northwestern U., 1940; m. Patricia F. Williams, July 17, 1943; 1 dau., Jenifer. Entire business career with Arthur Rubloff & Co., Chgo., 1930—, v.p., 1947-76, sr. v.p., 1976—. Bd. dirs. Municipal Art League of Chicago, West Central Assn. Chgo. Served as sgt. AUS, 36th Div., ETO, 1943-46. Mem. Am. Inst. Real Estate Appraisers, Nat., Ill., Chgo. assns. real estate bds., Bldg. Mgrs. Assn. Chgo., Wacker Dr. Assn. (dir.), Lambda Alpha. Clubs: City of Chgo. (gov.); The John Evans (Northwestern U.), Plaza. Home: 633 N Waukegan Rd Lake Forest IL 60045 Office: 69 W Washington St Chicago IL 60602

RUCK, CHARLES MITCHELL, veterinarian; b. Jeffersonville, Ind., Oct. 12, 1924; s. Charles Jacob and Nina Maude (Mitchell) R.; student Franklin Coll. Ind., 1941-42; D.V.M., Mich. State U., 1946; m. Annette Joyce Wolfe, Sept. 4, 1946; children—Carol Ann Ruck Cook, Patricia Jean Ruck, Charlene Diane, Ruck Jagger. Practice veterinary sci., Normal, Ill., 1947-50; veterinarian Ruck Animal Hosp., East St. Louis, Ill., 1950-65; owner, dir. Bel East Animal Hosp., Belleville, i Ill., 1965—; cons. veterinarian East Side Health Dept., East St. Louis, 1950-65. Pres. Belleville Humane Soc., 1970-75, bd. dirs., 1970-77. Served with U.S. Army, 1943-44. Mem. Greater St. Louis (past pres.), So. Ill. (past pres.), Ill. veterinary med. assns., AVMA, Lambda Chi Alpha. Republican. Mem. Christian Ch. (elder). Clubs: Masons, Shriners, Rotary. Home: 2013 Ruck Ln Jeffersonville IN 47130 Office: Rt 161 & Carson Rd Belleville IL 62223

RUDD, BERNARD J., ins. co. ofcl.; b. Louisville, Oct. 2, 1938; s. Leon and Effie R.; student public schs., Jeffersonville, Ind.; m. Linda Wolfe, Feb. 14, 1964; 1 son, Jason. With Prudential Ins. Co., 1961—, agt., New Albany, Ind., 1961-64, sales mgr., 1964-69, sales mgr., South Bend, Ind., 1969-71, agt., Lafayette, Ind., 1971, sales mgr., 1971-73, gen. mgr., Evansville, Ind., 1973—. Served with USAF, 1956-60. Recipient various sales awards. Mem. Nat. Assn. C.L.U.I.'s (dir.), Nat. Assn. Accts., Gen. Agts. and Mgrs. Assn. Methodist. Clubs: Old Time Car (v.p.), Optimists (pres.), Jaycees. Home: 300 Kingsvalley Rd Evansville IN 47711 Office: PO Box 888 Evansville IN 47706

RUDD, RALPH CORLIES, lawyer; b. Suifu (now Ipin), Szechuan, China, May 22, 1915 (parents Am. citizens); s. Herbert Finley and Anna (Corlies) R.; B.A., U. N.H., 1936; LL.B., Yale, 1942; postgrad. Columbia 1942-43; m. Mary Carolyn Clausen, June 17, 1941; children—Darnell (Mrs. David Mandelblatt), Herbert Finley II, Corlies Anna (Mrs. Gregory Delf), Rachel Clausen (Mrs. Eric Christensen). Admitted to Ohio bar, 1946, since practiced in Cleve., asso. firm Schaefer & Schaefer, 1946, Harrison, Thomas, Spangenberg & Hull, 1946-49; asso. firm Harrison, Spangenberg & Hull, 1949-54, partner, 1954-59; partner firm Rudd, Ober, Finley & Miller, 1959-61, Rudd, Ober & Miller, 1961-68, Rudd, Miller, Sheerer & Lybarger, 1968-71, Rudd, Karl, Sheerer & Lybarger, 1971-72; pres. Rudd, Karl, Sheerer, Lybarger & Campbell Co., L.P.A. and predecessor firm, 1972-76; adj. prof. law Cleve.-Marshall Coll. Law, Cleve. State U., 1975-76; atty. Legal Aid Soc., Cleve., 1977-79, Lake and Geauga Counties, 1979—. Adviser, Draft Counselling Assn., Cleve., 1968-73; hearing examiner Ohio Civil Rights Commn., 1972; mem. policy com. Friends Com. Nat. Legislation, 1968-76, 80—, mem. exec. com., 1974-80, chmn. gen. com., 1975-80. Mem. Ohio Ho. of Reps., 1959-62; mem. Lake County Democratic Exec. Com., 1966-78; trustee West Lake County Dem. Club; chmn. ACLU, Cleve., 1952-55, 74-76, chmn., Ohio, 1954-56, treas., Ohio, 1975-76. Mem. Lake County, Ohio bar assns. Mem. Soc. Friends. Kiwanian. Author: Syllabus on Selective Service Classification, 1968; Syllabus on Law of Conscientious Objection, 1968; Suggestions for Answering CO Questionnaire, 1970. Home: 4777 Wood St Willoughby OH 44094 Office: 8 N State St Painesville OH 44077

RUDDLE, JAMES FARRIS, TV newscaster; b. Oakhurst, Okla., May 20, 1932; s. George Lawrence and Evelyn Lucille (Baxter) R.; B.A., U. Tulsa, 1956, M.A., 1957; postgrad. (Univ. fellow), U. N.Mex., 1963; m. Patricia Anne Abbett, May 25, 1956; children—Kathryn, Blake, Valerie, Kristen. Newscaster, KOTV, Tulsa, 1955-58, XEAK, Tijuana, Mexico, 1958-59, WTVT, Tampa, Fla., 1963-65, WGN, Chgo., 1965-67, WMAQ, Chgo., 1967-75, sr. editor, corr. WTTW, Chgo., 1975-77, NBC News/WMAQ, Chgo., 1977—. Instr. U. N.Mex., 1959-62, U. South Fla., Tampa, 1963-65. Chmn. grand council Am. Indian Center, Chgo., 1976—. Served with USCGR, 1951-54. Recipient Silver Gavel award Am. Bar Assn., 1968, Emmy awards for investigative reporting, 1978, 79. Mem. Am. Studies Assn., Chgo. Council Fgn. Relations, Chgo. Com., Civil War Roundtable, Nat. Acad. TV Arts and Scis. (pres. 1973, nat. trustee 1974—). Home: Glenview IL Office: WMAQ-TV/NBC News Merchandise Mart Chicago IL 60654

RUDEN, VIOLET HOWARD (MRS. CHARLES VAN KIRK RUDEN), Christian Sci. tchr., practitioner; b. Dallas; d. Millard Fillmore and Henrietta Frederika (Kurth) Howard; B.J., U. Tex., 1931; C.S.B., Mass. Metaphys. Coll., 1946; m. Charles Van Kirk Ruden, Nov. 24, 1932. Radio continuity writer Home Mgmt. Club broadcast Sta. WHO, Des Moines, 1934; joined First Ch. of Christ Scientist, Boston, 1929; C.S. practitioner, Des Moines, 1934—; C.S. minister WAC, Ft. Des Moines, 1942-45; 1st reader 2d Ch. of Christ Scientist, Des Moines, 1952, Sunday sch. tchr., 1934—; instr. primary class in Christian Sci., 1947—. Trustee Asher Student Found. Drake U., Des Moines, 1973. Mem. Women in Communications, Mortar Bd., Orchesis, Cap and Gown. Republican. Club: Des Moines Women's. Home: 5808 Walnut Hill Dr Des Moines IA 50312 Office: 206 Kresge Bldg Des Moines IA 50309

RUDER, PHILLIP, concertmaster; b. Chgo.; grad. Hartt Coll. Music. Made recital debut, N.Y.C., 1963; former concertmaster New Orleans Philharm., Dallas Symphony Orch., Santa Fe Opera Co.; concertmaster Cin. Symphony Orch., 1973—; adj. prof. violin and orchestral repertoire U. Cin. Coll.-Conservatory of Music; condr. Cin. Symphony Orch. String Orch., 1974—; appeared with Casals Festival Orch., Spoleto, Italy, Salzburg Festival; performed in permiere season Chamber Music Festival, Elko, Nev.; concertmaster, soloist Summer Music Festival, Sunriver, Oreg. Office: Cin Symphony Orch 1241 Elm St Cincinnati OH 45210*

RUDICK, MILTON MARTIN, civil engr., contractor; b. Youngstown, Ohio, July 11, 1920; s. Ben and Dina (Greenblatt) R.; B.S., Carnegie Mellon U., 1946; m. Marie Taussig, June 28, 1945; children—Jerald David, Leonard Taussig, Lois. Engr., Truscon Steel Co., Youngstown, 1946-48; asst. chief engr. Ring Constrn. Co., Albany, N.Y., 1948-49; exec. v.p. Ben Rudick & Son, Inc., Youngstown, 1949-74, pres., 1974—; pres. Nat. Fire Repair, Inc., 1976—; bldg. damage cons., 1965—. Bd. dirs., treas. Rodef Sholom Temple. Served to 2d lt. C.E., AUS, 1943-45. Mem. ASCE (fire protection subcom.), Nat. Soc. Profl. Engrs., Builders Assn. Eastern Ohio and Western Pa. Clubs: Rotary, B'nai B'rith, Squaw Creek Country, Youngstown. Home: 532 Madera Ave Youngstown OH 44504 Office: 855 Tod Ave Youngstown OH 44502

RUDINEC, JOSEPH PAUL, photographer; b. New Eagle, Pa., July 26, 1947; s. Joseph Andrew and Anna (Karch) R.; B.E., Youngstown State U., 1970, M.S. in Engring., 1973. Photographer, Abey Studio, Youngstown, Ohio, 1965-70; engr. Comml. Shearing, Inc., Youngstown, 1970-75; prin. Joe Rudinec, Photography, Youngstown, 1975—; instr. mech. engring. Youngstown State U., 1973—. Registered profl. engr., Ohio. Mem. Bus. and Profl. Advt. Assn. (pres. Youngstown chpt. 1980), Profl. Photographers Am. (qualified studio, cert. prof. photographer), Youngstown Advt. Club, ASME (pres. Youngstown chpt. 1976). Home: 5781 Sheridan Rd Youngstown OH 44514 Office: 120 City Centre One Youngstown OH 44503

RUDMAN, DANIEL STEPHEN, cons. firm exec.; b. Galesburg, Ill., Nov. 15, 1945; s. Mitchell and Rose (Levy) R.; B.S., U. Ill., 1969; m. Susan B. Meyer, June 22, 1969; children—Deborah, Julie. Controller, Brown Splty. Co., Galesburg, Ill., 1969-75; pres. Rudman & Asso., cons., Galesburg, 1975—; cons., lectr. in field. Chmn. mayor's com. on swimming pool constrn., 1977-78. Mem. Am. Bus. Clubs U.S., Ill. Soc. C.P.A.'s, Am. Soc. Tng. and Devel., Galesburg C. of C., Beta Alpha Psi (regional Howard), Beta Gamma Sigma (award), Ill. Jaycees (named outstanding local pres. 1975, 1 of 10 outstanding persons in Ill. 1979), Alpha Kappa Psi. Republican. Jewish. Club: B'nai B'rith (past pres.). Office: PO Box 447 1320 N Henderson St Galesburg IL 61401

RUDNIK, SISTER MARY CHRYSANTHA, librarian; b. Winona, Minn., Dec. 2, 1929; d. Basil John and Sarah (Knopick) Rudnik; student Loyola U., 1951-52, Felician Coll., 1952-54, Cardinal Stritch Coll., 1954-57, Coll. St. Francis, 1957; Ph.B., DePaul U., 1958; postgrad. Mundelein Coll., 1959-60, Northeastern Ill. State U., 1964; M.A., Rosary Coll., 1962. Page, clk. Hill Reference Library, St. Paul, 1946-48; tchr. Holy Innocents Sch., Chgo., 1948-49, 50-54, St. Bruno Sch., Chgo., 1954-55, Holy Family Sch., Cudahy, Wis., 1955-57, Good Counsel High Sch., Chgo., 1958-67; instr. Felician Coll., Chgo., 1963—, librarian, 1957—, also dir. devel. and public relations. Organizer, coordinator Felician Library Service, 1966-74, Arts and Crafts Festival, 1972—; coordinator instl. self-study for accreditation North Central Assn.; mem. task force for study fo instl. research for Ill. Assn. Community and Jr. Colls., 1968; library cons. St. Clement Sch., 1969. Rev. Andrew Bowhuis meml. scholar Cath. Library Assn., 1960. Cert. fund raising exec. Nat. Soc. Fund Raising Execs. Mem. ALA, Ill. Library Assn., Cath. Library Assn. (life, chmn. No. Ill. unit 1968-69, exec. bd. 1981—), Art Inst. Chgo. (life), Council on Library Tech. (v.p. 1970, pres. 1971). Address: 3800 Peterson Ave Chicago IL 60659

RUDOLF, DAVID S., mgmt. cons.; b. St. Louis, Jan. 17, 1940; s. Walter Andrew and Mary Margaret (Walsh) R.; M.B.A., U. Chgo., 1978. With Nuclear Consultants Corp., St. Louis, 1960-64; owner, mgr. Pvt. Fleet Delivery, St. Louis, 1964-66; vending specialist Navy Ship's Store Office, Bklyn., 1966-69; services mgr. Navy Exchange, Great Lakes, Ill., 1969-81. Bd. dirs. Lake County Council on Alcoholism, 1981—. Mem. Assn. M.B.A. Execs., Photo Mktg. Assn., Nat. Automatic Merchandising Assn., U. Chgo. Alumni Assn., U. Chgo. Exec. Program Club. Republican. Roman Catholic. Home: 1430 Buena Rd Lake Forest IL 60045 Office: PO Box 745 Lake Forest IL 60045

RUDOLPH, JACK WALLACE, freelance writer; b. Ellsworth, Wis., Oct. 22, 1908; s. Solomon Francis and Mary (Casey) R.; student Lawrence Coll., 1926-29; B.S., U.S. Mil. Acad., 1933; m. Leora O. Calkins Quinn, Apr. 12, 1958; 1 step dau., Leora Jane (Mrs. Thomas Marshall). Commd. 2d lt. U.S. Army, 1933, advanced through grades to col., 1945-53, ret., 1953; served in War Dept. Mil. Intelligence div. during World War II, comdg. officer 38th Inf. Regt., 1949-50; music-drama critic, feature writer Green Bay (Wis.) Press-Gazette, 1954-71; news editor, music-drama critic Green Bay (Wis.) The Spirit, 1971-73; free lance writer, 1974—. Mem. Brown County Hist. Soc. (pres. 1961), Music Critics Assn., Assn. U.S. Army, Ret. Officers Assn. Republican. Roman Catholic. Club: Army and Navy (Washington). Home: 703 Glenwood Ave De Pere WI 54115

RUDOLPH, PEARLYE MARIETTA JESSIE, educator; b. Niagara Falls, N.Y., May 23, 1929; d. Willie and Beatrice (Smith) Jessie; B.S., Ala. State U., 1948; M.Ed., Wayne State U., 1960; Specialist Art, Eastern Mich. U., 1974; Ph.D., U. Mich., 1974; m. Timothy Rudolph, Sr., Sept. 14, 1947; children—Timothy, Gary C., Glenda, Marilynn, Marietta J. Prin., Battle Sch., Montgomery, Ala., 1948-50; dir. Detroit Assn. for Retarded Children, 1959-63; spl. edn. tchr. Detroit Bd. Edn., 1963-70; sci.-social studies tchr., Detroit, 1970—. Mem. com. United Negro Coll. Fund, 1970-81; mem. Sr. Citizens Com. Recipient awards Mich. State U., 1974-76, Mich. Diabetic Assn., 1980. Mem. NAACP (award), Top Ladies of Distinctions, Inc., Alpha Kappa Alpha, Phi Delta Kappa. Roman Catholic. Author: Phenylketournia: A Serious Type of Mental Deficiency, 1960; The Black Ghetto Child, 1970. Home: 17327 Birchcrest St Detroit MI 48221 Office: 13141 Rosa Park Blvd Detroit MI 48238

RUDRAPPA, GANGADHAR, pathologist; b. Bangalore, India, Apr. 8, 1945; came to U.S., 1971, naturalized, 1978; s. Rudrappa and Parvatamma (Puttappa) Basappa; P.U.C., St. Joseph's Coll., Bangalore, 1962; M.B., B.S., Bangalore Med. Coll., 1968; m. Meera G. Itigi, Sept. 10, 1973; children—Tara, Nidhi. Intern, Bangalore Med. Coll. Hosps., 1969-70; resident pathologist South Bend (Ind.) Med. Found., 1971-75; fellow immunohematology St. Luke's Hosp., Houston, 1975-76; asso. pathologist Fort Wayne (Ind.) Med. Lab., 1976—; lectr. immunohematology Sch. Med. Tech., Parkview Meml. Hosp., Fort Wayne, 1976. Bd. govs. ARC, 1977—. Mem. Coll. Am. Pathologists, Am. Soc. Clin. Pathologists, Am. Assn. Blood Banks, AMA. Home: 8427 Fantasia Way Fort Wayne IN 46815 Office: Fort Wayne Med Lab Box 268 Fort Wayne IN 46801

RUDY, DAVID ROBERT, physician; b. Columbus, Ohio, Oct. 19, 1934; s. Robert Sale and Lois May (Arthur) R.; B.Sc., Ohio State U.,1956, M.D., 1960; children by previous marriage—Douglas D., Steven W., Katharine L. Intern, Northwestern Meml. Hosp., Chgo., 1960-61; resident in internal medicine Ohio State U. Hosp., 1963-64; resident in pediatrics Children's Hosp., Columbus, Ohio, 1964; practice medicine specializing in family practice, Columbus, 1964-75; dir. Family Practice Center and residency program Riverside Meth. Hosp., Columbus, 1975—; clin. asso. prof. Ohio State U. Served as capt., Flight surgeon, M.C., USAF, 1961-63. Diplomate Am. Bd. Family Practice (charter). Fellow Am. Acad. Family Physicians; mem. AMA, Ohio Med. Assn., Central Ohio Acad. Family Practice (pres. 1979), Am. Mensa Soc., Columbus Maennerchor, Columbus Med. Symposium (pres. 1981). Republican. Contbr. articles to profl. jours. Home: 1633 Timberlake Dr Delaware OH 43015 Office: 797 Thomas Ln Columbus OH 43214

RUDY, JOEL SANFORD, coll. adminstr.; b. Bklyn., Jan. 20, 1941; s. Sidney T. and Selma (Rayvis) R.; B.S., Bethany Coll., 1962; M.A., Kent State U., 1964; m. Marlene Yourga, Nov. 24, 1965; children—Lisa Michele, Brian Scott. Dir. student activities, asst. dean, instr. Hunter Coll. in Bronx, 1964-67; asso. dir. housing, dir. resident student devel. U. Miami, Coral Gables, Fla., 1967-71; dean student residence life Kent (Ohio) State U., 1971-75, asst. v.p. for edn. and student services, 1975-76; dir. residence life Ohio U., Athens, 1976-78, asso. dean students, 1979—. Chmn. bd. dirs. Tallmadge Coop PreSchool, 1973-75; v.p. Athens City Elem. Sch. PTA, 1977-78, pres., 1979-81; vice chmn. Athens County Heart Fund, 1980-81; coordinator United Way, 1981-82. Recipient Outstanding Adminstr. award Ohio U., 1980-81. Mem. Am. Personnel and Guidance Assn., Ohio Coll. Personnel Assn., Nat. Assn. Student Personnel Adminstrs., Ohio Assn. Student Personnel Adminstrs., Assn. Coll. and Univ. Housing Officers, Internat. Narcotic Enforcement Officers Assn., Phi Delta Kappa, Beta Beta Beta, Alpha Phi Omega, Phi Kappa Tau. Pi Gamma Mu. Home: 19 Roxbury Dr Athens OH 45701 Office: 209 Cutler Hall Ohio Univ Athens OH 45701

RUEBEL, MARION ALBERT, educator, univ. adminstr.; b. Manson, Iowa, May 15, 1933; s. Charles F. and Ruth E. (Calmer) R.; B.A., U. No. Iowa, 1958, M.A., 1962; Ph.D., Iowa State U., 1969; m. Neoma Marie Horbach, Nov. 27, 1952; children—Vicki, Sherri, Joni, Tom. Tchr., coach Colo (Iowa) High Sch., 1953-55; tchr., coach Tripoli (Iowa) High Sch., 1959-61, Oskaloosa (Iowa) High Sch., 1961-64; prin. Jr. High Sch., Oskaloosa, 1964-67; adminstrv. asst. to dir. Midwestern State Ednl. Info. Project, Dept. Public Instrn., Des Moines, 1967-70; asst. prof. secondary edn. U. Akron, Ohio, 1970-71, acting head dept. secondary edn., 1971-72, head dept., 1973-74, asst. dean Coll. Edn., 1974-78, dean Univ. Coll., 1978—. Served with U.S. Army, 1953-55. Mem. NEA, Ohio Assn. Secondary Sch. Prins., Ohio State Edn. Assn., Nat. Assn. Secondary Sch. Prins., Phi Beta Beta. Republican. Roman Catholic. Office: University Coll U of Akron Akron OH 44325

RUEBSAMEN, NEIL NEWAYNE, indsl. relations exec.; b. Giltner, Nebr., June 8, 1929; s. Dean Henry and Lucille L. R.; student U. Colo., 1956; diploma Internat. Corr. Schs., 1959; m. Gail Virden; children—Cathleen, Rickey, Regina, Perry, Mina, Trey. Chem. technician Colo. Sch. Mines Research Found., Golden, 1957-58; safety engr. Cotter Corp., Canon City, Colo., 1958-61; safety engr. Amax Chem. Co., Vicksburg, Miss., 1961-64, personnel and safety supr., 1964-72; employee relations mgr. Amax Spec Metals, Parkersburg, W.Va., 1972; safety dir. Amax Zinc Co., Sauget, Ill., 1973-74, indsl. relations mgr., Sauget, 1974—. Pres., Warren County Safety Council, 1964-66; mem. curriculum adv. bd. So. Ill. U. Served to lt. col. U.S. Army, 1955-56. Cert. safety profl.; registered profl. engr., Calif. Mem. Am. Soc. Safety Engrs. (nat. dir. 1967-69), Am. Soc. Personnel Adminstrn., Indsl. Relations Assn. St. Louis, Am.

Water Ski Assn., Res. Officers Assn. Methodist. Clubs: Little Eqypt Water Ski (DuQuoin, Ill.); Holiday Shores Assn.; Kiwanis. Home: 111 Lou Rosa St Collinsville IL 62234 Office: PO Box 2347 East St Louis IL 62202

RUED, DAVID EVAN, state senator; b. Aitkin, Minn., May 17, 1932; student St. Cloud State Coll., 1955-56; B.S., U. Minn., 1956-59; postgrad., 1965; m. Ardella Rued; 3 children. Farmer, Aitkin, Minn.; extension agt. Aitkin County (Minn.) 1967-68; vocat. agr. instr. Aitkin High Sch., 1964-65, 1968—; mem. Minn. Senate, 1978—, serves senate coms. on Edn., Agr. and Nat. Resources, Fin., Local Gov. and Urban Affairs, Judiciary. Mem. Sch. Bd., Aitkin, 1967-68; mem. resources conservation and devel. com., 1967-68; vice chmn. Wild Rice Promotion Council, 1976-78; Served with USAF; Korea. Recipient hon. deg. state Farmer, 1982. Mem. Farm Bur., Wild Rice Growers Assn. (past chmn.), Iron Range Resources and Rehab. bd., 1981-82, Farmers Union, Minn. Vocat. Assn., Am. Vocat. Assn., Am. Legion, Aitkin County Agrl. Soc. Club: Lions. Office: 137 State Office Bldg St Paul MN 55155*

RUEF, JOHN S., clergyman, ednl. adminstr.; b. Chgo., Jan. 24, 1927; s. John E. and Leota A. (Rice) R.; D.B., U. Chgo., 1945; B.D., Seabury Western Sem., 1950, S.T.M, 1955, S.T.D. (hon.), 1966; Th.D., Harvard U., 1960; m. Jane Margraves Holt, Oct. 11, 1951; children—Marcus, Adam, Seth, Sarah. Ordained to ministry Episcopal Ch., 1950; faculty Berkeley Divinity Sch., New Haven, 1960-71; dir. continuing edn. Diocese of Western N.Y., 1972-74; pres. Nashotah (Wis.) House, 1974—. Fellow Ch. Soc. for Coll. Work, St. John's Parish, Lafayette Sq., Washington; mem. Soc. Bibl. Lit. Club: Rotary Internat. Author: The Gospels and Teachings of Jesus, 1967; The First Letter of Paul to Corinth, 1971. Office: Nashotah House Nashotah WI 53058

RUEGGE, RONALD DUNCAN, food processing and metal fabricating mfg. co. exec.; b. Washington, Mo., July 19, 1944; s. Russell Henry and Vivian Marceline (Duncan) R.; B.A., Westminster Coll., 1966; M.B.A., Washington U., St. Louis, 1968; m. Nancy A. Drobisch, June 10, 1967; children—Heather, Marcus. Mktg. research analyst Monsanto Co., St. Louis, 1967-68; sr. acct. mgr. Exxon Chem. USA, Houston, 1968-73; mktg. dir. Zero Mfg. Co., Washington, Mo., 1973—, v.p., 1976—, dir., 1972—. Mem. Food Processing and Machinery Assn., Dairy Industry and Food Supply Assn., Fertilizer and Equipment Assn., Master Brewers Assn., Parental Drug Assn., Delta Tau Delta. Republican. Methodist. Club: Forest Hills Country. Home: 15201 Isleview Dr Ballwin MO 63011 Office: Zero Mfg Co 811 Duncan Ave Washington MO 63090

RUEGSEGGER, DONALD RAY, JR., radiol. physicist; b. Detroit, May 29, 1942; s. Donald Ray and Margaret Arlene (Elliot) R.; B.S., Wheaton Coll., 1964; M.S., Ariz. State U., 1966, Ph.D. (NDEA fellow), 1969; m. Judith Ann Merrill, Aug. 20, 1965; children—Steven, Susan, Mark, Ann. Radiol. physicist Miami Valley Hosp., Dayton, Ohio, 1969—; physics cons. X-ray dept. VA Hosp., Dayton, 1970—; adj. asst. prof. physics Wright State U., Fairborn, Ohio, 1973—, clin. asst. prof. radiology, 1976-81, clin. asso. prof. radiology, 1981—, group leader in med. physics, dept. radiol. scis. Med. Sch., 1978—. Diplomate Am. Bd. Radiology. Mem. Am. Assn. Physicists in Medicine (pres.-elect chpt. 1981-82), Am. Coll. Radiology, Am. Phys. Soc., AAAS, Ohio Radiol. Soc., Health Physics Soc. Baptist. Home: 2018 Washington Creek Ln Centerville OH 45459 Office: Radiation Therapy Miami Valley Hospital 1 Wyoming St Dayton OH 45409

RUEGSEGGER, LOYAL, JR., elec. co. exec.; b. Canton, Ohio, June 19, 1920; s. Loyal and Dora (Leyman) R.; student Purdue U., 1945-46; B.S. in Elec. Engring., Ohio No. U., 1950; m. L. June Smith, May 20, 1944; children—Carol June, Loyal III. Test engr. Eureka Williams Corp., Bloomington, Ill., 1950-51; system relay engr. Ohio Power Co., Canton, 1951-54; coordinator field engrs. Ohio Valley Electric Corp., Gallipolis, Ohio, 1954-56, system meter engr. supr., Waverly, Ohio, 1956—; corr. Edison Electric Inst. Judge Jr. Sci. Fair, Ohio U., Athens. Served from pvt. to tech. sgt. USAAF, 1941-45. Decorated D.F.C., Air medal with 10 oak leaf clusters (Army). Mem. Mid-South Metermens Assn. (2d v.p. 1957-58), IEEE (sr.), Power Engring. Soc. (sr.), Nat., Ky. Socs. profl. engrs., Instrument Soc. Am. (sr.), VFW, Am. Legion. Clubs: Masons, Shriners, Order Eastern Star. Contbr. articles to profl. jours. Home: 1171 Star Route 552 Waverly OH 45690 Office: PO Box 468 Piketon OH 45661

RUETER, STEVEN WAYNE, health systems mgmt. cons.; b. Moline, Ill., Oct. 7, 1946; s. Donald Henry and Elaine Ruth (Seidel) R.; B.B.A., U. Iowa, 1969; M.H.A., Washington U., 1971. Adminstrv. asst. Rush-Presbyn.-St. Luke's Med. Center, Chgo., 1971-73; v.p. K & R Assoc., Inc., Shawnee Mission, Kans., 1973-75; sr. cons. for health services Lawrence-Leiter and Co., Kansas City, Mo., 1975-80, v.p. health services, 1980—; lectr. in field. Mem. Am. Coll. Hosp. Adminstrs., Am. Hosp. Assn. Home: 4304 Brookridge Dr Shawnee Mission KS 66205 Office: Lawrence-Leiter and Co 427 W 12th St Kansas City MO 64105

RUGH, MARTY FASONE, hosp. exec.; b. Williamson, W.Va., Mar. 29, 1945; d. William Joseph and Mary Jane (Smith) Gorman; B.A., Marian Coll., Indpls., 1967; M.S. in Edn., Ind. U., 1974; m. Thomas E. Rugh, June 11, 1978; 1 son from previous marriage, Rod Fasone; stepchildren—Charles Rugh, Michael Rugh, Peter Rugh, Beth Rugh. Graphic artist Calif. State U., Fresno, 1974-75; media specialist Calif. State U. and Colls., Long Beach, 1975-76; dir. communications Family Health Program, Long Beach, 1976-77; mgr. public relations St. Vincent Hosp., Indpls., 1977—. Vol., Nat. Found. March of Dimes. Mem. Nat. Assn. Female Execs., Alliance Indpls. Hosps. (pres. public relations div.), Ind. Bus. Communicators (recipient journalism awards), Women in Communications, Am. Soc. Hosp. Public Relations; Ind. Soc. Hosp. Public Relations (exec. com. 1980—). Author article in field. Home: 25 W 49th St Indianapolis IN 46208 Office: 2001 W 86th St Indianapolis IN 46260

RUGH, WILLIAM BATMAN, mech. engr.; b. Alton, Ill., Nov. 6, 1947; s. Robert Handlin and Elizabeth Lenore (Batman) R.; B.S. in Mech. Engring., Duke U., 1969; M.B.A., U. N.C., 1972. Mem. indsl. engring. staff Owens-Ill., Inc., North Bergen, N.J., 1972-74, engr. glass container div. engring. group, Toledo, 1974—. Dist. committeeman Boy Scouts Am., 1974-78. Recipient Eagle Scout award Boy Scouts Am., 1962. Mem. ASME, Nat. Soc. Profl. Engrs., Internat. Brotherhood Magicians, Toledo Soc. Magicians (treas.), Nat. Flag Found., Alpha Phi Omega (past nat. bd.), Beta Gamma Sigma. Home: 834 Maple Ln Waterville OH 43566 Office: 1 Seagate Toledo OH 43666

RULAU, RUSSELL, editor; b. Chgo., Sept. 21, 1926; s. Alphonse and Ruth (Thorsen) R.; student U. Wis., 1946-48; m. Hazel Darlene Grizzell, Feb. 1, 1968; children—(by former marriage) Lance Eric, Russell A.W., Marcia June, Scott Quentin, Roberta Ann, Kyle Christopher; 1 step-dau., Sharon Maria Modia. Entered U.S. Army, 1944-1950, served to master sgt. USAF, 1950-62; resigned active duty, 1962; asst. editor Coin World newspaper, Sidney, Ohio, 1962-74, editor World Coins mag., 1964-74, Numis. Scrapbook mag., 1968-74; editorial coordinator How to Order Fgn. Coins guidebook, 1966-74; mng. editor World Coin News newspaper, 1974—; fgn. editor Numis. News newspaper, 1974-77; editor-in-chief Standard Catalog of World Paper Money, 1975-81; contbg. editor Standard Catalog of World Coins, 1974-81. Mem. U.S. Assay Commn., 1973. Sec., Numismatic Terms Standardization Com., 1966-74; vice-chmn. Waupaca County Republican party, 1977-79, chmn., 1979—; chmn. county chairmen, 3d vice chmn. Wis. Rep. Party, 1981—; del. Rep. Nat. Conv., 1980. Fellow Royal Numis. Soc., Am. Numis. Soc. (asso.); mem. Token and Medal Soc. (editor 1962-63), Am. Numis. Assn., Canadian, S. African numis. assns., Mont. Hist. Soc., Am. Vecturist Assn., Numis. Lit. Guild (dir. 1974-78). Lutheran. Author: (with George Fuld) Spiel Marken, 1962-65, American Game Counters, 1972: World Mint Marks, 1966; Modern World Mint Marks, 1970; (with J. U. Rixen and Frovin Sieg) Seddelkatalog Slesvig Plebiscit Zone I og II, 1970; Numismatics of Old Alabama, 1971-73; Hard Times Tokens, 1980; Early American Tokens, 1981. Contbr. numis. articles to profl. jours. Home: Rt 2 Box 15-BA Iola WI 54945 Office: Krause Publications Iola WI 54990

RULIFFSON, HARMON WARREN, fraternal orgn. exec.; b. Lincoln, Nebr., Dec. 11, 1926; s. Warren Beach and Olga Louise (Waite) R.; B.A., U. Nebr., 1952; B.B.A., U. Minn., 1956; cert. indsl. engring. Iowa State U., 1958; m. Shirley June Kazmark, Sept. 2, 1950; 1 son, Harmon James. Ops. researcher Graphic Arts Engraving div. Brown & Bigelow, Mpls., 1952-55; prodn. control mgr. Pillsbury Mills, Inc., Mpls., 1955-56; med. service rep. Stuart Pharm. Co., 1956-58; exec. sec. Mpls. Scottish Rite Bodies, 1958—; exec. dir. Internat. Frat.-Sorority Hall of Fame, Evanston, Ill., 1972—; sec. Mpls. 33 deg. Council; mem. Minn. Scottish Rite Com. Childhood Aphasia; mem. faculty Big 10 Interfrat.-Panhellenic Conf.; past exec. sec. fgn. relations com. Supreme Council 33 deg., Ancient and Accepted Scottish Rite Freemasonry, So. Jurisdiction U.S.; treas. Devices Inc.; asso. Argentarius, investment cons.; past pres. Minn. Indsl. Mgmt. Assn. Bd. dirs. Groves Learning Center Children with Learning Disabilities, 1975—. Served with U.S. Army, 1945-46. Recipient numerous frat. orgn. awards, civic and service awards. Mem. Minn. Vet. Pharmacists, Assn. for Children with Learning Disabilities, Travellers Protective Assn., Minn. Interfraternity Alumni Assn. (past pres., past del. to Nat. Interfraternity Conf., sec. 1968—), Frat. Cerebrals (internat. sec., past internat. pres.), Soc. of Golden Key (internat. sec., past internat. pres.), Order of Omega (internat. awards com.), Epsilon Beta (internat. sec., past internat. pres.), Delta Sigma Phi (internat. scholarship commr., past internat. leadership commr.), Alpha Kappa Delta, Kappa Delta Pi, Omicron Delta Kappa, Sigma Mu Sigma. Republican. Methodist. Clubs: Masons, Shriners, KT, Order of DeMolay (hon. Legion of Honor). Editor: The Circle, 1968-78; contbr. articles to profl. publs. Office: 2011 Dupont Ave S Minneapolis MN 55416

RUMBAUGH, MAX ELDEN, motor vehicle component engring. co. exec.; b. Ada, Okla., Dec. 11, 1937; s. Max Elden and Gertrude Maude (Gulker) R.; B.S. in Engring., U.S. Mil. Acad., 1960; M.S. in Engring., Purdue U., 1965, M.B.A., 1972; m. Joan E. Brockway, Oct. 21, 1962; children—Maria, Max Elden III. Instr. engring. Purdue U., 1963-65; corp. officer Midwest Applied Sci. Corp., West Lafayette, Ind., 1965-72, also dir.; chief engr. Schwitzer, Wallace Murray Corp., Indpls., 1972-77, dir. research engring., 1977—; cons. small bus. fin. affairs, 1970-73. Chmn. Future Scientists and Engrs. Day, Indpls., 1977-81; chmn. Mr. and Miss Tech. Program for Central Ind., 1977-81; mem. deans indsl. adv. com. Indpls. campus Purdue U. Sch. Engring., 1978—, mem. Univ. Pres. Council, 1979—; sec.-treas. Central States Rotary Youth Exchange Program; bd. dirs. Ind. Sci. Edn. Fund, Ind. Acad. Sci. Served to lt. U.S. Army, 1960-63. Mem. Soc. Automotive Engrs., (regional sect. coordinator 1979—, chmn. Ind. sect. 1978-79), Soc. Research Adminstrs. (nat. pres. 1973-74), Indpls. Sci. and Engring. Found. (dir.), Indpls. Wine Soc. Club: Rotary (Indpls.). Editor: (with Harold DeGroff) Combustion and Propulsion: Energy Sources and Energy Conversion, 1967. Home: 10941 Timber Ln Carmel IN 46032 Office: 1125 Brookside Ave Indianapolis IN 46206

RUMELY, EMMET SCOTT, ret. automobile co. exec., banker; b. N.Y.C., Feb. 15, 1918; s. Edward A. and Fanny (Scott) R.; grad. Phillips Exeter Acad., 1935; B.S., Yale, 1939; postgrad. U. Mich., 1940-41; m. Elizabeth Hodges, July 5, 1947; children—Virginia H., Elizabeth Scott Visser, Scott Hodges. Mgr., Marenisco Farms, La Porte County, Ind., 1939-73; dir. La Porte Hotel Co., Inc., 1938-70, pres., 1965-70; pres., dir. Rumely Corp., 1970—; product planning mgr. tractor ops. Ford Motor Co., Birmingham, Mich., 1961-70, asst. to v.p., gen. mgr., 1970-75; dir., mem. exec. com. 1st Nat. Bank & Trust Co., La Porte. Mem. Detroit Inst. Arts Founders Soc., Am. Soc. Agrl. Engrs., Soc. Automotive Engrs., Am. Mktg. Assn. Clubs: Orchard Lake (Mich.) Country; Huron Mountain (Big Bay, Mich.); Yale (Detroit). Home: 207 Abbey Rd Birmingham MI 48008 Office: 800 Jefferson Ave La Porte IN 46350

RUMERY, MYRON G. A., state legislator; b. Julesburg, Colo., July 29, 1905; B.S., U. Nebr.; m. Mattie Ella Washburn, June 10, 1934; children—Myron Leslie, Margene Phares. Formerly worked in constrn., farming; high sch. tchr.; livestock and dairy research U. Nebr. N. Platte Sta., also supr.; mem. Nebr. Legislature, 1974—. Former leader Boy Scouts Am., 4-H Clubs. Mem. N. Platte C. of C., Am. Soc. Animal Sci., Dairy Sci. Assn., Nebr. Acad. Sci. Baptist. Clubs: Odd Fellows, Rotary. Address: North Platte NE *

RUND, DOUGLAS ANDREW, physician; b. Columbus, Ohio, July 20, 1945; s. Carl Andrew and Caroline Amelia (Row) R.; B.A., Yale U., 1967; M.D., Stanford U., 1971. Intern in medicine U. Calif., San Francisco-Moffett Hosp., 1971-72; resident in gen. surgery Stanford-Santa Clara Valley Med. Center, 1972-73, Stanford (Calif.) VA, 1973-74; Robert Wood Johnson Found. clin. scholar in medicine Stanford U., 1974-76; coordinator emergency panel physicians San Mateo County Hosp. Emergency Room, 1973-75; emergency physician Mills Meml. Hosp., San Mateo, 1974-76, Sequoia Hosp. Dist., Redwood City, Calif., 1974-76; med. dir. Mid-Peninsula Health Service, Palo Alto, Calif., 1975-76, med. dir. Hillhaven Convalescent Hosp., Palo Alto, 1975-76; clin. instr. dept. medicine and dept. family community and preventive medicine Stanford U. Med. Sch., 1975-76, asst. dir. early clin. experience in family medicine program, 1975-76; asst. prof., dir. div. emergency medicine Ohio State Coll. Medicine, 1977-80; dir. emergency med. services Ohio State U. Hosps., 1977-80, dir. emergency medicine residency program, asst. prof. dept. family medicine, 1976-80, asst. prof. dept. preventive medicine; attending staff Ohio State U. Hosps., 1976-80. Bd. dirs. Big Bros. Assn., Columbus, Ohio 1978-80. Lic. physician, Ohio, Calif.; diplomate Nat. Bd. Med. Examiners, Am. Bd. Family Practice, Am. Bd. Emergency Medicine. Mem. Soc. Tchrs. Emergency Medicine, Am. Coll. Emergency Physicians, Soc. for Health and Human Values, Univ. Assn. for Emergency Medicine, Alpha Omega Alpha. Author: Triage, 1981; contbr. chpt. to Family Medicine Principles and Practice, 1978; contbr. articles to profl. jours. Office: 450 W 10th Ave Columbus OH 43210

RUND, JOSEPH VICTOR, mfg. co. exec.; b. Chgo., Jan. 17, 1941; s. Joseph Victor and Betty (Potucek) R.; B.S. in Indsl. Mgmt., U. Ill., 1964; m. Patricia Darlene Condon, Feb. 2, 1964; children—Joseph Victor III, James Scott. Asst. salesman Appliance div. Sunbeam Corp., Phila., 1966-67, territorial mgr. Personal Care div., Mpls., 1967-68, dist. sales mgr. Appliance Group, Peoria, Ill., 1968-69, Detroit, 1969-73, market mgr. Sunbeam Appliance Co. div., Chgo., 1973-75, sr. account exec. Product Spltys., Inc. div., Chgo., 1975-77, product mgr. Home Comfort Group, Sunbeam Appliance Co., Chgo., 1977, dir. contract sales Sunbeam Outdoor Co. div., Chgo., 1977-78, v.p. contract sales, 1978—, v.p. contract sales Aircap Mfrs., Inc. div., Tuoelo, Miss., 1978—. Mgr., coach Wheaton (Ill.) Little League Baseball, 1974-78, Wheaton Youth Football, 1974-77; treas. Streams Homeowners Property Assn., 1977-78. Served to 1st lt. U.S. Army, 1964-66. Mem. Outdoor Power Equipment Assn., U. Ill. Alumni Assn., Phi Kappa Tau. Republican. Roman Catholic. Home: 1473 Sandy Hook Wheaton IL 60187 Office: 2001 S York Rd Oak Brook IL 60521

RUNKEL, FRANCIS JOHN, telephone op./engring. holding co. exec.; b. Arcadia, Wis., Aug. 6, 1949; s. John and Helen R.; B.A. in Acctg., Winona State U., 1971; m. Rhonda Jean Engelien, June 16, 1971; children—Angela Kay, Mark Gene. With Cencom Inc., Rushford, Minn., 1971—, treas., asst. corp. sec., 1980—. Mem. Am. Mgmt. Assn. Roman Catholic. Clubs: Ferndale Golf Course (dir. 1981-83), Rushford Area Flyers, Centerville Curling. Office: PO Box 606 Rushford MN 55971

RUNQUIST, ALFONSE WILLIAM, chemist, chem. co. exec.; b. Hibbing, Minn., Apr. 4, 1945; s. Henrik Alfonse and Eleanore Irene (Anderson) R.; B.S., Hamline U., 1967; Ph.D. (NIH fellow), Northwestern U., 1974; m. Jennifer Agnes Jackson, July 13, 1974. Instr. in organic chemistry Northwestern U., 1974; postdoctoral research asso. Johns Hopkins U., 1974-76; chemist devel. dept. Aldrich Chem. Co., Milw., 1976-79, mgr. tech. services, 1979—. Served with U.S. Army, 1969-71. Recipient Scholastic award Am. Inst. Chemists, 1967. Mem. Kenosha Hist. Soc., Am. Chem. Soc. Contbr. articles to profl. jours. Office: 940 W Saint Paul Ave Milwaukee WI 53233

RUNSER, DENNIS JOSEPH, chemist, educator; b. Chgo., Dec. 21, 1945; s. Robert Joseph and Sheli (Dally) R.; B.S., Ill. Benedictine Coll., 1967; Ph.D., U. Iowa, 1971; m. Judith Ann Vlazny, May 23, 1970. Chemist, Personal Care div. Gillette Co., Chgo., 1971-73; supr. analytical devel. G.D. Searle Co., Skokie, Ill., 1973-77, mgr. analytical control lab., 1977-79, mgr. quality control, 1979-80; dir. corp. chem. affairs Marion Labs., Inc., Kansas City, Mo., 1980—; instr. Roosevelt U., Chgo., part time 1976-77. Pres., St. Alexander Sch. Bd., Villa Park, Ill., 1976-78. Phillips Petroleum fellow, 1970-71; cert. profl. chemist. Fellow Am. Inst. Chemists; mem. Am. Chem. Soc. (alt. councilor div. profl. relations 1981—), Chgo. Chromatography Discussion Group, Soc. Applied Spectroscopy, Phi Lambda Upsilon, Alpha Chi Sigma. Author textbook on chromatography; contbr. articles to profl. jours. Office: 10236 Bunker Ridge Rd Kansas City MO 64137

RUNYAN, ROBERT WILLIAM, sales ofcl.; b. Middletown, Ohio, Jan. 4, 1951; s. Cecil William and Mary Ellen R.; B.A. in Mktg., Miami U., Oxford, Ohio, 1974; m. Deborah Roehll, Dec. 7, 1974; children—Brandon Roehll, Kiersten Brooke. Sales trainee Packaging Corp. Am., Rittman, Ohio, 1974-75, field sales rep. Ohio, Rittman, 1975, No. Ill., Wis., Evanston, Ill., 1976-78; field sales rep. Midwest region, Sonoco Products Co., West Chester, Ohio, 1978-79, sales mgr. Midwest region, Lancaster, Ohio, 1979—. Named salesman of year, paper div. Packaging Corp. Am., 1977. Mem. Composite Can and Tube Inst., Am. Paper Inst., Phi Gamma Delta. Office: PO Box 39 831 S Columbus Ave Lancaster OH 43130

RUOSCH, DOLORES MARY, univ. dean; b. Waukegan, Ill., Mar. 7, 1929; s. Carl Louis and Esther C. (Bruhn) R.; B.S., Valparaiso U., 1951; M.S., U. So. Calif., 1957; postgrad. Los Angeles State Coll., Long Beach State Coll., UCLA, Ind. U. Elem. tchr., Kouts, Ind., 1951-54, Norwalk-LaMirada, Calif., 1954-61; dir. sorority affairs, asst. to dean women Valparaiso (Ind.) U., 1961-63, dean women, 1963—, also asso. prof. edn., dir. Scheele Sorority Complex, dir. sorority affairs. Bd. dirs. United Way Porter County, 1972—, pres., 1977, mem. rev. com., 1981; mem. adv. bd. dirs. Salvation Army, 1978—. Mem. NEA, Nat. Assn. Women Deans, Adminstrs. and Counselors (recorder 1974-74), Nat. Council Tchrs. English, AAUW, Am. Personnel and Guidance Assn., Am. Assn. Higher Edn., Am. Acad. Polit. and Social Sci., Student Personnel Assn. Tchr. Edn., Coll. Student Personnel Assn., Ind. Tchrs. Assn., Ind. Assn. Women Deans, Counselors and Adminstrs. (historian 1978-79). Mem. editorial adv. bd. Gary Post Tribune, 1978—. Home and Office: Valparaiso U Box 32 Valparaiso IN 46383

RUPERT, JOHN EDWARD, savs. and loan exec.; b. Cleve., Oct. 19, 1927; s. Edward J. and Emma (Levegood) R.; B.A., Cornell U., 1949, LL.B., 1951; certificate Grad. Sch. Savs. & Loan, Ind. U., 1958; m. Virginia Carlson, Oct. 27, 1951; children—Kristen, Karen, David. With Broadview Savs. & Loan Co., Cleve., 1953—, v.p., 1964-74, mng. officer, 1965—, pres., chief exec. officer, 1974—, also dir.; mem. Cleve. Real Estate Bd., 1955—. Mem. Lakewood (Ohio) Bd. Edn., 1971-77, pres., 1975—; v.p., trustee Lakewood Hosp., 1966-71; trustee Cleve. Orch., WVIZ Ednl. TV, Cleve. Zool. Soc., Greater Cleve. Growth Assn., Ohio Motorists Assn., Neighborhood Housing Services; bd. dirs. West Side YMCA; mem. Lakewood Hosp. Found.; mem. Cornell U. Council, 1971—, pres., 1977. Served with USAF, 1951-53. Mem. Cleve. Interfaith Housing Corp. (pres. 1971—), Am. Savs. and Loan Inst. (pres. 1970), Cleve. Real Property Inventory (pres. 1976—), Am., Ohio, Cleve. bar assns., Bluecoats, Inc., Delta Kappa Epsilon, Phi Delta Phi, Sphinx Head Soc. Clubs: Westwood Country; Union; Midday, Cleve. Yachting, Cornell (trustee) (Cleve.). Home: 18129 W Clifton Rd Lakewood OH 44107 Office: 6000 Rockside Woods Blvd Cleveland OH 44131

RUPP, DOUGLAS ALAN, constrn. co. exec.; b. Slayton, Minn., July 1, 1944; s. Calvin A. and Norma A. (Koopman) R.; B.S. in Constrn., Ariz. State U., 1966; postgrad. in bus. U. S.D., 1966-67; m. Joan D. Phillips, Dec. 10, 1971, children—Lincoln Douglas, Tyson David, Rylan Mitchell, Landon Alan. Vice pres. Rupp Constrn. Co. Inc., Slayton, 1970-71, pres., 1971—; pres. D.A. Rupp Asphalt Co. Inc., 1972—, Rupp Contracting Corp., 1976—, Pipestone Bituminous Corp., 1976—, Lake Shelek Lodge, Inc., 1979—; chmn. bd. dirs. Peoples State Bank of Slayton 1979—; dir. Slayton Service Corp. Served with USNR, 1967-69. Mem. Am. Inst. Constructors, Associated Builders and Contractors, Minn. Asphalt Pavement Assn. Home: 3035 Queen Ave Slayton MN 56172 Office: Box 1 Slayton MN 56172

RUPP, JAMES H., state senator; ed. Monmouth Coll. Mayor, Decatur, Ill., 1977; mem. Ill. Senate, 1977—. Ruling elder Presbyn. Ch.; active civic orgns. Served with USNR, World War II, Korea. Mem. Ill. Mcpl. League (v.P.), Decatur Ins. Agts. Assn., Farm Bur. Republican. Clubs: Rotary, Decatur, Elks, Moose, Eagles, Shriners, Decatur Ski. Address: 1011 New State Office Bldg Springfield IL 62706*

RUPP, JAMES MAHLON, broadcasting exec.; b. Pocatello, Idaho, Nov. 7, 1935; s. Mahlon E. and Ila Grace (Burnham) R.; B.A., Idaho State U., 1957; M.A., Ohio State U., 1959; m. Sharon E. Enell, Aug. 28, 1955; children—Julene, Sandra, Steven. Group v.p., gen. mgr. Cox

Broadcasting Corp., Atlanta, 1965-76; pres., chief operating officer Midwest Radio-TV, Inc., Mpls., 1976—; mem. TV cooperation subcom. of U.S.-Japan Conf. of Cultural and Ednl. Interchange, 1979—. Bd. dirs. Minn. Safety Council, 1977—, Children's Theater, 1978-80, NCCJ, 1977—; trustee Nat. Found. for Ileitis and Colitis, 1970-81. Mem. Am. Women in Radio and TV (trustee), Nat. Assn. Broadcasters, Minn. Assn. Broadcasters. Clubs: Minneapolis, Wayzata. Office: 50 S 9th St Minneapolis MN 55402

RUPP, ROBERT GEORGE, mag. editor; b. Aurora, Nebr., Oct. 28, 1918; s. Laurin Everett and Cassie Ellen (Dean) R.; B.Sc., U. Nebr., 1941; postgrad. U. Minn., 1945-46; m. M. Dee Schill, 1942 (dec. 1961); children—Victoria Ann, Robert George II, Lorna Lee; m. 2d, Matilda Alice Towne, May 26, 1962. News editor Agr. Extension Service, Iowa State U., Ames, 1946-48; extension news editor Agrl. Extension Service, U. Minn., St. Paul, 1948-50; asso. editor The Farmer mag., St. Paul, 1950-59, mng. editor, 1959-69, editor, 1969—. Dir. farms Nat. Safety Council, 1970-77; mem. adv. council U. Minn. at Crookston and Waseca, Minn. Dept. Edn. vocat. agrl. div.; mem. Minn. Humanities Commn., 1976-80; bd. dirs., chmn. fin. com. Minn. Agrl. Interpretive Center, 1978—. Served to col. Minn. Army N.G.; ret. Named hon. state farmer Minn. Future Farmers Am.; recipient hon. Am. Farmer degree, 1979; Meritorious Service award 4H Fedn., 1961; Nat. Soil Builders award Nat. Plant Food Council, 1957; Communications award Nat. Assn. Conservation Dists., 1979, Exceptional Service award SSS, 1979. Mem. Internat. Fedn. Agrl. Journalists (U.S. dir. 1971—, jr. v.p., pres.'s medal Austria 1978), Minn. Assn. Commerce and Industry (v.p. agr. 1972-75, 78-80), Minn. Agri-Growth Council (dir. 1973—), Minn. Safety Council (chmn. agr. div. 1964-80, Meritorious Service award, 1966), Am. Agrl. Editors Assn. (pres. 1966-67). Rotarian. Home: 14906 50th St S Afton MN 55001 Office: 1999 Shepard Rd St Paul MN 55116

RUPPEL, HOWARD JAMES, JR., sociologist, sexologist; b. Orange, N.J., July 22, 1941; s. Howard J. and Lillian M. (Wordley) R.; B.A., St. Joseph's Coll., Ind., 1963; M.A., No. Ill. U., 1968; postgrad. U. Iowa, 1968—; m. Barbara Margaret Wiedemann, June 3, 1967. Instr. social sci. St. Francis High Sch., Wheaton, Ill., 1963-65, debate coach, 1963-65; instr. sociology St. Dominic Coll., St. Charles, Ill., 1966-67; instr. sociology Cornell Coll., Mt. Vernon, Iowa, 1969-70, asst. prof., 1970-72, lectr., 1972-73; research dir. Social Sci. Research Assos., Cedar Rapids, Iowa, 1973-80; founder, co-dir. Center for Sexual Growth and Devel., Mt. Vernon, 1980—; instr. Sch. Social Work, U. Iowa, 1976-78, adj. asst. prof., 1979-81, adj. asso. prof., 1981—; instr. continuing edn. program Mt. Mercy Coll., Cedar Rapids, 1976-77; cons. Iowa Dept. Social Services, Mankato (Minn.) State Coll., Ohio State Chiropractors Assn., Cath. U., Nijmegen, Holland, Sch. Social Work, U. Iowa, Kirkwood Community Coll., Cedar Rapids, Families Inc., West Branch, Iowa Hosp. Assn., Linn County (Iowa) Juvenile Probation Office. Bd. dirs. Hawkeye Area Community Action Program, Cedar Rapids, Iowa, 1970-71. NSF fellow, 1968. Cert. sexologist Am. Coll. Sexologists. Mem. Am. Sociol. Assn., Midwest Sociol. Soc., Nat., Iowa (dir. 1976-77) councils family relations, Assn. for Sociology of Religion, Soc. Sci. Study Religion, Soc. for Study of Social Problems, Soc. for Sci. Study Sex, Assn. Sexologists, Am. Assn. Sex Educators, Counselors and Therapists (cert. sex educator), Sex Info. and Edn. Council of U.S. (asso.), Soc. Sex Therapy and Research (research mem.), Nat. Forensic League, No. Ill. U. Alumni Assn., Alpha Kappa Delta. Democrat. Contbr. articles on complex orgns., marriage and the family, sexual attitudes and behavior, preadolescent sexuality, methodology and child care theory to profl. publs. Home: 608 5th Ave N Mount Vernon IA 52314 Office: Sch Social Work North Hall U Iowa Iowa City IA 52242

RUPPERT, RUPERT EARL, lawyer; b. Middletown, Ohio, Nov. 22, 1943; s. Paul Edward and Sarah Elizabeth (Morgan) R.; B.A., Ohio State U., 1968; J.D., Capital U., 1976; m. Candace E. Sheward, June 7, 1969; children—Jason, Ryan, Bradley, Matthew. Admitted to Ohio bar, 1976; asst. to gov. state of Ohio, Columbus, 1971-74, to atty. gen., 1974-77, spl. counsel to atty. gen. and to asst. atty. gen., 1977—; partner firm Ruppert, Bronson & Chicarelli, Franklin, Ohio, 1977—, also firm Riley & Ruppert, Franklin; legal counsel Miami Valley Bldg. & Loan Assn., Franklin, 1979—, also dir. Mem. Warren County Democratic Central Com., 1977—; chmn. Warren County Dem. Com., 1978-80; chmn. Warren County Brown for Atty. Gen., 1978; dep. campaign mgr. William J. Brown for Gov. Ohio, 1982; mem. Franklin City Charter Commn., 1978, Franklin CSC, 1978-79; v.p. Franklin City Schs. Bd. Edn., 1978—; mem. Warren County Bd. Elections, 1979—. Served with AUS, 1968-70; Vietnam. Decorated Bronze Star, Combat Infantryman Badge; recipient Presdl. award for outstanding civic achievement among Viet Nam vets, 1979. Mem. Am. Bar Assn., Ohio Bar Assn., Warren County Bar Assn., Ohio Trial Lawyers Assn., Nat. Rifle Assn., Am. Legion, VFW. Home: PO Box 70 Franklin OH 45005 Office: 1063 E 2d St Franklin OH 45005

RUPRECHT, MARY MARGARET WYANT, word processing, mgmt. cons.; b. O'Neill, Neb., Oct. 20, 1934; d. Charles Ellsworth and Mary Loretto (Cuddy) Wyant; student Coll. St. Benedict, 1952-54; certificate, Am. Inst. Banking, 1970; m. Gregory Earl Ruprecht, Sept. 24, 1955; children—Mary Debra, Sharie Marie. Dist. clk. U.S. Soil Conservation, Aitkin, Minn., 1956-68; comml. loan sec. No. City Nat. Bank, Duluth, Minn., 1965-71; office mgr. Fryberger, Buchanan Law Firm, Duluth, 1971-72; pvt. practice word processing and mgmt. consulting, Duluth, 1972-76; v.p., prin. Altman & Weil, Inc., mgmt. cons., 1976-79; pres. Mary M. Ruprecht & Assos., 1979—; tchr. Am. Inst. Banking. Mem. adv. council Minn. State Bd. Edn., Duluth Office Edn. Assn., Coll. Applied Scis. at Miami U., Oxford, Ohio. Finance dir. 8th Congl. Dist. Dem.-Farm Labor Party, 1972-73. Mem. Internat. Word Processing Assn. (internat. pres. 1974-75), Am. Inst. Banking (nat. chmn. women's com. 1970-71), Adminstrv. Mgmt. Soc., Am. Mgmt. Assn., Bus. and Profl. Women's Assn., Internat. Platform Assn. Contbr. articles to profl. jours. Home: 140 W Myrtle St Duluth MN 55811

RUPRECHT, THOMAS GEORGE, ins. co. exec.; b. Pitts., Nov. 29, 1941; s. George Edward and Catherine Barbara (Ivanovic) R.; B.S. in Bus., Ohio State U., 1967; m. Signe Larson; children—Michelle, Matthew. Group supr. personnel and public relations Bell Labs., 1967-73; dir. organizational planning J.C. Penney Ins. Co., Westerville, Ohio, 1973-74, asst. v.p. organizational planning and personnel, 1974-78, v.p. personnel, 1978—. Mem. career guidance com. Griffith Found. Served with U.S. Army, 1959-62. Accredited exec. in personnel. Mem. Am. Soc. for Personnel Adminstrn., Personnel Soc. Columbus (dir.), Ohio State Pace Setters, Beta Gamma Sigma, Alpha Kappa Psi. Club: Phoenix Flyers. Office: J C Penney Ins Co 800 Brooksedge Blvd Westerville OH 43081

RUSCH, CARROLL ERNEST, educator; b. Campbellsport, Wis., Oct. 16, 1914; s. Frederick Henry and Kathryn Rose (Scheid) R.; B.A., Lakeland Coll., Sheboyan, Wis., 1935; M.A., U. Wis., Madison, 1946, Ph.D., 1957; m. Marian Martha Beisser, June 28, 1939; children—Frederic, Sandra, Margaret, Kristine. Mem. math. faculty Lakeland Coll., 1936-55, U. Wis., Eau Claire, 1955-58; prof. math., chmn. dept. SUNY, Oneonta, 1958-62, Parsons Coll., Fairfield, Iowa, 1962-67, U. Wis., Superior, 1967-81; prof. math. U. Wis., Eau Claire, 1981—; vis. prof. U. Colo., U. Wis., Eau Claire.; cons. on math. textbooks. Recipient Outstanding Alumni award Lakeland Coll., 1981; NSF grantee, 1956-65. Mem. Am. Math. Soc., Math. Assn. Am., Nat. Council Tchrs. Math., Central Assn. Sci. and Math. Tchrs., AAAS. Presbyterian. Club: Elks. Home: 3338 Rudolph Rd Eau Claire WI 54701 Office: Dept Math U Wis Eau Claire WI

RUSCH, JOHN JAY, educator; b. Manitowoc, Wis., Apr. 8, 1942; s. Norbert John and Viola (Pleuss) R.; B.S., Carroll Coll., 1963; M.A.T. (NSF fellow), Ind. U., Bloomington, 1968, Ed.D. (Univ. fellow), 1970; m. Carole R. Vasey, Aug. 14, 1965; children—Karl Phillip, Hans Christoph. Tchr. sci., public schs., Elmhurst, Ill., 1963-65, Waukesha, Wis., 1965-67, asst. prof. earth sci. Okla. U., 1970-74; asst. prof. sci. edn. U. Wis., Superior, 1974-77, asso. prof., 1977-81, dir. numerous NSF edn. programs; cons. Wis. Dept. Public Instrn. Bd. dirs. Goodwill Industries Vocat. Enterprises, Duluth, Minn., 1977-80. Recipient Max Lavine award U. Wis., Superior, 1977, 78, 79. Fellow AAAS; mem. Nat. Sci. Tchrs. Assn. (Gustav Ohaus award 1977, 81), Nat. Assn. Geology Tchrs., Assn. Edn. Tchrs. Sci., Sch. Sci. and Math. Assn., Phi Delta Kappa. Democrat. Lutheran. Author books, the most recent being: Science and Societal Issues, 1981; Teaching Science in Grades 5 Through 9, 1982. Home: 3 Maple Ave Superior WI 54880 Office: 128 McCaskill U Wis Superior WI 54880

RUSE, WILLIAM ELLIOT, hosp. adminstr.; b. Cleve., Dec. 3, 1934; s. Ollie Owen and Mary V. R.; B.S. in Pharmacy, Ohio No. U., 1957; M.Bus., Xavier U., 1963; J.D., U. Toledo, 1972; m. Donna Lee Brown, June 23, 1956; children—William S., Rebecca Sue, Robert Scott. Chief pharmacist Lima (Ohio) Meml. Hosp., 1957-60; dir. pharmacy Blanchard Valley Hosp., Findlay, Ohio, 1960-63, asst. adminstr., 1963-64, adminstr., 1964-75, pres., 1975—; tchr. hosp. adminstrn. and/or hosp. law Xavier U., Cin., U. Toledo, Bowling Green (Ohio) State U.; admitted to Ohio bar, 1972. Scout master Boy Scouts Am., 1961-64; pres. Family Service Agy. Hancock County, 1968-69; campaign chmn. United Way Hancock County, 1970, pres., 1973; pres. Hancock County chpt. ARC, 1969, Hancock County Safety Council, 1966; chmn. adv. bd. Salvation Army, 1970-72. Recipient Disting. Service award Jr. C. of C., 1967; Service to Mankind award Sertoma Internat., 1972; L.D. Lucus award Baptist Missionary and Ednl. Conv. of Mich. Women's Aux., 1975. Mem. Am. Hosp. Assn., Am. Coll. Hosp. Adminstrs., Am. Bar Assn., Ohio Hosp. Assn., Western Ohio Hosp. Council, Northwestern Ohio Pharm. Assn., Findlay Area C. of C. (2d v.p. 1981). Republican. Roman Catholic. Clubs: Rotary, Elks (Findlay). Home: 201 Glendale Ave Findlay OH 45840 Office: Blanchard Valley Hosp 145 W Wallace St Findlay OH 45840

RUSE, WOODY NORMAN, shoe co. exec.; b. Big Rapids, Mich., Mar. 9, 1945; s. Norman E. and June (Carter) R.; m. Deborah Lee Holbrook, Nov. 8, 1975. With Bronson Shoe Co., Lowell, Mich., 1966—, sales mgr., 1978—. Served with U.S. Army, 1974-75. Mem. Nat. Small Bus. Assn. Address: 2097 Grand River SE Lowell MI 49331

RUSH, BOB, state senator; lawyer; b. Lake Forest, Ill., Oct. 30, 1944; B.A., Northwestern U., 1966; J.D., U. Iowa, 1970. Admitted to Iowa bar, D.C. bar; spl. asst. U.S. atty. for D.C., 1971-73; practice law, Cedar Rapids, 1973—; mem. Iowa State Senate, asst. minority leader. Bd. dirs. ARC. Mem. LWV, Iowa Civil Liberties Union, Cedar Rapids Law Club (past pres.). Methodist. Office: State Senate State Capitol Des Moines IA 50319*

RUSH, DAVID HARRY, lumber co. exec.; b. Cleve., Mar. 31, 1927; s. Harry John and Minnie (Schwarzer) R.; B.S. in M.E., Case Inst. Tech., 1951; m. Marjorie Lillian Couch, Mar. 31, 1951; children—Cynthia Lynn, Janet Lee. Application engr. Relianc Electric Corp., 1951-53, dist. mgr., Rochester, N.Y., 1954-55; v.p. Hilton & Rush Co., Cleve., 1956-59; pres., 1960—. Mem. forest products adv. com. Chgo. Merc. Exchange; bd. overseers Case Western Res. U. Served with USN, 1945-46. Mem. N. Am. Wholesale Lumber Assn. (pres. 1973-74), Nat. Assn. Wholesalers (dir. 1973-75), Econ. Council Forest Products Industries, Case Alumni Assn. (pres. 1976-77), Phi Delta Theta, Tau Beta Pi, Theta Tau, Pi Delta Epsilon. Home: 134 Lakeview Ln Chagrin Falls OH 44022 Office: PO Box 16430 Cleveland OH 44116

RUSH, GERALD ELMER, food service co. exec.; b. New Orleans, Aug. 5, 1930; s. Elmer H. and Alta (Billig) R.; B.S., Western Mich. U., 1953; M.S., U. Calif., San Fernando Valley, 1965; m. Audrey E. Hammond, Feb. 14, 1956; children—Diane E., Gerald E., Heidi E., David E. Designer, prodn. and executor nat. network TV shows for ABC, NBC, CBS, and ind. studios, including Dean Martin Show, Jack Benny Spl., Bob Hope Spls., Danny Thomas Spl., Laugh In, Bill Cosby Spl., Jonathon Winters Show, Let's Make a Deal, Hollywood, Calif., 1963-67; tchr. TV prodn. and stagecraft Pasadena Playhouse, Hollywood, Los Angeles, 1963-67; dir. tng. and personnel McDonald Corp., Los Angeles, 1967-73, Ky. Fried Chicken, Louisville and San Diego, 1973-77; dir. tng. Sportservice Corp., Buffalo, 1977-78, Interstate United Corp., Chgo., 1978-82, Hickory Farms of Ohio, Maumee, 1982—. Served with U.S. Army, 1953-63. Mem. Am. Soc. Tng. Dirs., Conf. Hotel and Restaurant Trainers, Nat. Restaurant Assn., Employment Mgmt. Assn., Nat. Audio-Visual Assn. Home: 206 W Hintz St Arlington Heights IL 60004 Office: 300 Holland Rd PO Box 219 Maumee OH 43537

RUSH, ISABEL ENDSLEY, educator; b. Cuyahoga Falls, Ohio, Sept. 7, 1914; d. Hugh Harper and Caroline M. Endsley; B.A., U. Akron, 1975, M.S., 1979; m. George Arthur Rush, Sept. 12, 1936; 1 son, David Lee (dec.). Cafeteria mgr. Cuyahoga Falls Bd. Edn., 1947-71; foods instr. Cuyahoga Valley Joint Vocat. Sch., Brecksville, Ohio, 1971-75, Cuyahoga Community Coll., Cleve., 1975-80, U. Akron (Ohio), 1980—. Named Food Service Employee of Year, N.E. Ohio Assn. Public Sch. Employees, 1971. Mem. Am. Vocational Assn., Am. Home Econs. Assn., Postsecondary and Adult Vocat. Assn., Am. Sch. Food Service Assn., Ohio Home Econs. Assn., Ohio Vocat. Assn., Ohio Council Hotel, Restaurant and Instl. Educators, Pi Lambda Theta. Mem. United Ch. of Christ. Clubs: Women's City, College, University (Akron); Order Eastern Star (Cuyahoga Falls); Order of Amaranth (Kent, Ohio). Home: 230 Wadsworth Ave Cuyahoga Falls OH 44221 Office: 224 Schrank Hall S U Akron Akron OH 44325

RUSH, JAMES RAYMOND, local govt. exec.; b. Chgo., Sept. 18, 1944; s. Clyde G. and Winifred M. (Campbell) R.; student So. Ill. U., Carbondale, 1965-68; m. Linda Boeser, Dec. 30, 1973; 1 dau., Amanda. With Greater Egypt Regional planning and Devel. Commn., Carbondale, Ill., 1967—, dir. spl. programs, 1978—; writer, lectr. in field. Mem. Am. Planning Assn. (dir. 1981—), Nat. Criminal Justice Planners Assn., Ill. Criminal Justice Planners Assn. (pres. 1974-77), Nat. Council Crime and Delinquency. Presbyterian. Office: PO Box 3160 Carbondale IL 62901

RUSH, JAMES RICHARD, cons. engr.; b. Minot, N.D., May 29, 1930; s. Ira L. and Eula (Brooks) R.; B.S., U. Minn., 1952, M.S., 1953; m. Virginia Cox, Nov. 20, 1954; children—Nancy, Barbara, James Robert. Draftsman, Cerny Assos., Mpls., architects, 1952; mech. engr. Bloom & Oftedal, Mpls., cons. engrs., 1955-59; pres. Schmit, Smith, & Rush, Minot, N.D., cons. engrs., 1959—; dir. Design Profl. Fin. Corp., San Francisco; nat. dir. from N.D., Cons. Engrs. Council/U.S., 1971—, v.p., 1974-75, sr. v.p., 1975—. Mem. Minot City Planning Commn., 1973—, chmn., 1976—; bd. dirs. YMCA, Minot, 1963-79. Served to 1st lt. U.S. Army, 1953-55. Mem. ASHRAE, Minot C. of C. Clubs: Elks, Minot (N.D.) Country (dir.). Home: 1500 Glacial Dr Box 593 Minot ND 58701 Office: Box 1802 Minot ND 58701

RUSH, ROBERT JOHN, ednl. cons.; b. St. Louis, Apr. 19, 1942; s. Robert E. and Louise L. Rush; student Northwestern U., 1960-61; B.A. in English and Psychology, MacMurray Coll., 1965; postgrad. U. Tours (France), summer, 1966, Washington U., St. Louis, 1966-67, U. Ill., 1970-72, LaVerne Coll., 1974, Nat. Coll. Edn., Evanston, Ill., 1975; M.A., Sangamon State U., 1979; postgrad. Western Ill. U., 1977. Tchr., Athens (Ill.) Public Sch. Dist. 213, 1965-66; tchr. Springfield (Ill.) Public Sch. Dist. 186, 1966-79; ednl. cons. for equal ednl. opportunity sect. Ill. State Bd. Edn., 1980—; supr. student tchrs. from State of Ill., 1968-79. Bd. dirs. Tchr. Centers for Sangamon County, Ill., 1978-80, chmn., 1979-80. Recipient Outstanding Service award Ill. State Bd. Edn., 1977, others. Mem. Assn. for Supervision and Curriculum Devel., Am. Fedn. State Educators, Nat. Council Social Studies, Ill. Council Social Studies, Springfield English Tchrs. Assn. (pres. 1970-71), Ill. Council for Exceptional Children (editorial bd. 1970-72), Springfield Edn. Assn. (exec. bd. 1969-70), Nat. Council Tchrs. English (English award 1978), Phi Delta Kappa. Home: 302 E Lawrence Ave Springfield IL 62703 Office: Ill State Bd Edn 100 N 1st St E-230 Springfield IL 62777

RUSHER, LYNN LESLIE, architect; b. Ft. Dodge, Iowa, Apr. 25, 1954; s. Delbert Charles and Dorothy Mae (Schmoker) R.; A.A., Iowa Central Community Coll., Ft. Dodge, 1974; postgrad. Iowa State U., Ames, 1976; m. Elizabeth Ann Amundson, June 9, 1979; 1 dau., Lanna Xylina. Draftsman/rodman Asso. Engrs., Inc., cons., Ft. Dodge, 1971-74, archtl. designer, 1975-77; archtl. designer, constrn. mgr. Landmark Constrn. Co., Ft. Dodge, 1974-75; co-owner Residential Constrn. Products Co., Fort Dodge, 1977, Sunspot Solar Devel. Co., Fort Dodge, 1981—; project architect MER Engring., Inc., cons., Rockwell City, Iowa, 1978—. Asso. mem. AIA. Republican. Baptist. Home: Route 3 Scenic Valley Fort Dodge IA 50501 Office: Route 3 N Twin Lakes Rockwell City IA 50579

RUSK, THOMAS JOSEPH, anesthesiologist; b. Cleve., Nov. 27, 1933; s. Martin Stanley and Mary Elizabeth (Czech) Rusnaczyk; B.S. in Natural Sci., John Carroll U., 1955; postgrad. Case-Western Res. U., 1956-57; D.O., Chgo. Coll. Osteo. Medicine, 1961; m. Patricia Ann Creed, May 27, 1967; children—Mary Elizabeth, Pamela Kathleen, Barbara Rebecca, Thomas Baird. Intern, then resident to chief resident in anesthesiology Detroit Osteo. Hosp., 1961-64; practice medicine specializing in anesthesiology, 1964—; with Ucchino & Rusk Anesthesia Assos., 1964-71; v.p., sec. Warren (Ohio) Anesthesia, Inc., 1971—; courtesy staff Youngstown, Sharon (Pa.) hosps; chief of staff Warren Gen. Hosp.; asst. clin. instr. Coll. Osteo. Medicine, Ohio U., W. Va. Coll. Osteo. Medicine. Trustee, NE Ohio Health Planning Commn. Served to 1st lt. M.S.C., USAR, 1955-67. Diplomate Am. Osteo. Bd. Anesthesiology. Mem. Ohio, N.E. Ohio (trustee), Trumbull County (pres. 1978, 79) heart assns., Am. (hosp. and physician inspection and exam. team 1972, 73), Ohio osteo. assns., 14 and 12 Dist. Acad. Osteo. Medicine (pres. 1974), Am. Osteo. Coll. Anesthesiology, Ohio (sec.-treas. 1971-75, pres. 1975—), Mich. socs. osteo. anesthesiology, Am. Coll. Osteo. Anesthesiologists (diplomate), Internat. Anesthesia Research Soc., Ohio Prevention of Blindness Assn., Am., Ohio thoracic socs., Ohio, Trumbull County med. socs. Republican. Roman Catholic. Home: 182 Marwood Dr Warren OH 44484 Office: 2838 Howland Wilson Rd Cortland OH 44410

RUSS, EDMOND VINCENT, JR., mktg. and distbn. co. exec.; b. Washington, Feb. 14, 1944; s. Edmond Vincent and Thayer Kennedy (Thompson) R.; B.A., Kent State U., 1966; M.B.A., U. Pitts., 1967; children—Jamie, Edmond, Christina, Cory. Asst. mgr. inventory control Automotive Parts div. Borg-Warner Corp., Chgo., 1967-70; dir. mktg. Borg Warner Ednl. Systems, Chgo., 1970-74; v.p. Rusty Jones Inc., Chgo., 1974—. Bd. dirs. Children's Theater of Winnetka (Ill.), Winnetka Community Theatre. Mem. Am. Mgmt. Assn., Assn. M.B.A. Execs. Episcopalian. Club: Porsche of Am. Home: 460 Cedar St Winnetka IL 60093 Office: 5757 N Lincoln Ave Chicago IL 60659

RUSS, KENNETH LANCE, psychologist; b. N.Y.C., Sept. 4, 1944; s. Benjamin Herbert and Marion (Stern) R.; A.B., U. Rochester, 1965; Ph.D. in Clin. Psychology, Grad. U. Pitts., 1970; postgrad. U. Colo. Sch. Medicine, 1971; m. Linda Terkel, Dec. 10, 1978; 1 dau., Jennifer Elana. VA trainee in clin. psychology 1966-70; asst. dir. psychology tng. Jewish Hosp. St. Louis, 1971-74, dir. biofeedback program, 1974-78; pvt. practice clin. psychology, Clayton, Mo., 1978—; instr. med. psychology Washington U. Sch. Medicine, St. Louis, 1976-78; lectr. on biofeedback. Recipient award for grad. study in psychology NIMH, 1965; N.Y. State Regents scholar 1961-65. Fellow Mo. Psychol. Assn. (pres. 1980-81); mem. Am. Psychol. Assn., Assn. Advancement Behavior Therapy, Biofeedback Soc. Am., Biofeedback Soc. Mo. (co-founder; pres. 1977-78). Contbr. numerous articles on biofeedback to profl. jours. Office: 200 S Hanley Rd Suite 311 Clayton MO 63105

RUSSELL, ANNE DORA, ednl. adminstr.; b. Daleville, Ala., Jan. 7, 1931; d. Curtis G. and Annie B. (Engram) Robinson; B.S., Ala. State Coll., 1958; M.S., U. Mich., 1969, postgrad., 1972-79; children by previous marriage—John, Shirley Jenkins. Tchr. English and bus. edn. public schs., Enterprise, Ala., 1958-62; substitute tchr. Pontiac (Mich.) Bd. Edn., 1962-63, tchr. English and bus. edn., 1965-71; sec. U. Mich. Med. Sch., Ann Arbor, 1963-64; dir. health edn. and welfare Pontiac Area Urban League, 1964-65; part-time instr. secretarial sci. Wayne Community Coll., Mich., 1977; asst. prin. Pontiac Central High Sch., 1971-80, Pontiac No. High Sch., 1980—. Del. 48th Precinct, Pontiac, 1974-76; bd. dirs. Newman Non-Profit Housing Corp., 1965—. Recipient cert. of award Jefferson Jr. High Sch., 1968, You Can award Pontiac Adult Edn., 1975, cert. of appreciation Mich. State U., 1974. Served with USAF, 1952-53. Mem. Nat. Assn. Secondary Sch. Prins., Pontiac Assn. Sch. Adminstrs. (cert. of appreciation 1976), NAACP, Ala. State U. Alumni Assn., U. Mich. Alumni Assn., Delta Kappa Gamma. Democrat. Methodist. Author: Blacks in Pontiac, 1975; Builders of Detroit, 1978. Home: 1158 Dudley St Pontiac MI 48057 Office: 1051 Arlene St Pontiac MI 48055

RUSSELL, DAVID LEE, educator; b. Louisville, May 9, 1947; s. Wendell and Elizabeth Noble R.; B.S., Eastern Ky. U., 1974, M.A., Western Ky. U., 1975; postgrad., So. Ill. U., 1976; m. Linda G. Keith, May 9, 1971; children—Heather Lenore, Sarah Elizabeth. Agr. tchr. Edwardsville (Ill.) Sr. High Sch., 1975-78, Brownstown (Ind.) Central High Sch., 1978-80, South Decatur High Sch., Greensburg, Ind., 1980—. Served with USAF, 1966-70. Cert. tchr., Ky., Ill., Ind. Mem. Decatur County Tchrs. Assn., Ind. Vocat. Assn., Ind. Vocat. Agr. Tchrs. Assn., NEA, Nat. Vocat. Agr. Tchrs. Assn., Future Farmers Am. (adv. 1975-81, numerous awards). Baptist. Club: Kiwanis. Home: PO Box 551 Westport IN 47283

RUSSELL, DAVID WARD, biologist; b. McCook, Nebr., Oct. 18, 1921; s. Samuel Henry and Teckla Adele (Westrin) R.; A.S., McCook Jr. Coll., 1941; B.A., U. Nebr., 1946, M.S., 1947; m. Gretchen Schroeder, Dec. 20, 1946; children—Jeanne Adele, David Minor, Sally Blanchard. Asst. and asso. research pharmacologist Parke Davis Co., Detroit, 1947-56, asso. control pharmacologist, 1956-68, sr. product planner, 1968-70, sr. control pharmacologist, 1970-77, acting mgr. pharmacol. control, 1977-78, sect. head biol. control, 1978—. Bd. dirs. Grosse Point Human Relations Council, 1960. Served with USN, 1942-44. Fellow AAAS; mem. Detroit Physiology Soc., Am. Assn Lab. Animal Sci., Sigma Xi. Episcopalian. Club: Golf. Contbr. articles to profl. jours. Home: 1228 Harvard Rd Grosse Pointe Park MI 48230 Office: GPO Box 118 Detroit MI 48232

RUSSELL, DAVID WILLIAMS, lawyer; b. Lockport, N.Y., Apr. 5, 1945; s. David Lawson and Jean Graves (Williams) R.; A.B. (Army ROTC scholar, Daniel Webster scholar), Dartmouth Coll., 1967, M.B.A., 1969; J.D. cum laude, Northwestern U., 1976; m. Frances Yung Chung Chen, May 23, 1970; children—Bayard Chen, Ming Rennick. English tchr. Talledega (Ala.) Coll., summer 1967; math. tchr. Lyndon Inst., Lyndonville, Vt., 1967-68; instr. econs. Royalton Coll., South Royalton, Vt., part-time 1968-69; asst. to pres. for planning Tougaloo (Miss.) Coll., 1969-71, bus. mgr., 1971-73; mgr. will and trust rev. project Continental Ill. Nat. Bank & Trust Co. Chgo., summer 1974; law clk. Montgomery, McCracken, Walker & Rhoads, Phila., summer 1975; admitted to Ill. bar, 1976; asso. firm Winston & Strawn, Chgo., 1976—; cons. Alfred P. Sloan Found., 1972-73. Mem. nat. selection com. Woodrow Wilson Found. Adminstrv. Internship Program, 1973-76; vol. Lawyers for Creative Arts, Chgo., 1977—. Woodrow Wilson Found. adminstrv. intern, 1969-72. Mem. Am., Ill., Chgo. bar assns., Chgo. Council Lawyers, ACLU, Chinese Music Soc., Zeta Psi. Presbyterian. Home: Apt 3A 1622 W Farwell Ave Chicago IL 60626 Office: Suite 5000 1 1st Nat Plaza Chicago IL 60603

RUSSELL, DESI RAKICH, mgmt. cons.; b. Ljubovo, Yugoslavia, Feb. 16, 1949; came to U.S., 1953; d. Milan S. and Milka M. Rakich; B.A., De Paul U., 1972; postgrad. Inst. Indsl. Relations, Loyola U., Chgo., 1973; m. John F. Russell, Dec. 18, 1976. Systems analyst, instr. Bowne Info. Systems, Chgo., 1971-74; mktg. rep., 1974-76, product mgr., N.Y.C., 1976-77; cons. Data Processing Staff Cons., Chgo., 1979-80; pres. SysteMethods, Inc., Schaumburg, Ill., 1980—. Mem. N.W. Suburban Assn. Commerce and Industry, Chgo. Sales Tng. Assn. (past pres.), Mensa. Club: Intertel. Home: 1314 S Fernandez Ct Arlington Heights IL 60005

RUSSELL, FRANK ASHBY, cons. co. exec.; b. Oakland, Calif., Feb. 14, 1950; s. George A. and Ruth A. R.; B.A., So. Ill. U., 1973; M.A., U. Ill., 1977; m. Christine J. Price, May 21, 1977; children—Angelic Dawn, Heather Melissa, Frank Kelly. Personnel adminstr. Control Data Corp., Mpls., 1976-77; mgr. edn. div. Batten, Batten, Hudson & Swab, Inc., Des Moines, 1977-79, v.p. mktg., 1980—; state tng. adminstr. State of Iowa, Des Moines, 1979-80. Bd. dirs. Batten Found., Des Moines, 1981—. Mem. Am. Soc. Tng. and Devel., Sales and Mktg. Execs. Assn., Phi Eta Sigma. Home: 416 Hillcrest St Polk City IA 50226 Office: Batten Batten Hudson & Swab Inc 820 Keoway Des Moines IA 50309

RUSSELL, GARTH SAMUEL, orthopaedic surgeon; b. Kingsland, Ark., Aug. 4, 1929; s. Lindsay W. and Nancy (Bussey) R.; student U. Ark., 1946; B.S., Kan. State U., 1953; M.D., U. Kans., 1959; m. Ruth Cristine Erwin, Dec. 19, 1948; children—David Garth, Kyle Erwin. Dir. health dept., Gt. Bend, Kans., 1953-55; intern Wesley Hosp., Wichita, Kans., 1959; resident in orthopaedic surgery U. Mo., 1960-65; practice medicine specializing in orthopaedic surgery, Columbia, Mo., 1965—; mem. staff Columbia Regional Hosp., Boone County (Mo.) Hosp.; asst. prof. orthopaedic surgery U. Mo. Sch. Medicine; dir. Med. Dental Co. of Am., trustee Columbia Regional Hosp., 1975—; vis. prof. orthopaedic surgery U. Mancipal, India, 1977. Served with AUS, 1946-49. Diplomate Am. Bd. Orthopaedic Surgery. Mem. Am. Acad. Orthopaedic Surgery, Mo. Orthopaedic Assn. (pres. 1976). Editorial cons. Jour. Continuing Edn., 1973—. Contbr. articles in field to profl. jours. Address: 3205 Lansing Ave Columbia MO 65201

RUSSELL, JOHN EDWARDS, mfg. co. exec.; b. Cin., Oct. 7, 1927; s. Richard Wilbur and Evelyn Louise R.; B.S.C., Ohio State U., 1950; m. Rosalyn Joan Bailey, May 8, 1954; 1 dau., Lisa Lynn. With Jeffrey Mfg. Co., Columbus, Ohio, 1950-71, buyer, 1955-64, purchasing agt., 1964-71; v.p. purchasing Columbus Auto Parts Co. (Ohio), 1972—. Bd. dirs. Family Counseling and Crittenton Services, 1968-79, pres., 1973-74; mem. Columbus Minority Purchasing Council, 1979—. Served with AUS, 1946-47. Nen. Nat. Assn. Purchasing Mgmt. (pres., dir. nat. affairs 6th dist. Columbia area), Ohio State U. Alumni Assn. Republican. Presbyterian. Clubs: Rotary, York Temple Country, Masons. Home: 4330 Ingham Ave Columbus OH 43214 Office: PO Box 2005 Columbus OH 43216

RUSSELL, JOHN T., state senator; b. Lebanon, Mo., Sept. 27, 1931; s. Aubrey F. and Velma F. (Johnson) R.; student Drury Coll.; LL.D., SW Bapt. Coll.; m. Margaret Ann Carr, Dec. 29, 1951; children—John Douglas, Georgia Jeanette, Sarah Melissa. Dir., officer Laclege Metal Products Co., Lebanon, 1957—, Detroit Tool & Engring. Co., Lebanon, 1957—, Gen. Aluminum Supply Co., Kansas City, 1959—, So. Mo. Transp. Co., Lebanon, 1960; partner Faith Leasing Co., Lebanon, 1969—; mem. Mo. Ho. of Reps., 1962-76, Mo. Senate, 1976—. Del. Republican Nat. Conv., 1972. Served with USAF, 1951-54. Mem. Lebanon C. of C. Baptist. Clubs: Masons, Scottish Rite. Office: State Capitol Jefferson City MO 65101*

RUSSELL, LUETTA, integrationist; b. Newton, Kans., July 1, 1926; d. Riley Warren and Annie May (Hamilton) Banks; student Wichita State U., 1972—; m. Dewitt Russell, Feb. 20, 1944; children—DeEtta, James, Martha, Tonya. With Boeing Co., Wichita, 1951-54; beautician, Wichita, 1954-66; with Beech Co., Wichita 1966-70, Community Devel., Flint, Mich., 1970-74, Child Devel. and Adminstrn., Wichita, 1974-76; with Nat. Minority Small Bus. Agy. of Community Ednl. Services, Wichita, 1978, integrationist Nat. Minority Bur., 1979—, now interim regional budget dir.; broker cons. Bd. dirs. 11th St. Golden Agers, Wichita, 1976; bus. mgr. Wichita Collegiate Sch., 1979-80. Mem. LWV, Nat. Small Bus. Assn., Urban Land Mgrs., Consumer Bank Assn. Mem. Ch. of Christ. Home: 1203 N Piatt St Wichita KS 67214 Office: PO Box 973 Wichita KS 67201

RUSSELL, NORMA JEAN, environ. scientist; b. Keokuk, Iowa, Mar. 14, 1952; d. Norman Eugene and Marilyn Maxine (Sebree) R.; B.S. in Gen. Sci., U. Iowa, 1974. Wastewater treatment plant operator III, City of Ft. Madison (Iowa), 1976-78; environ. specialist Iowa Dept. Environ. Quality, Des Moines, 1978—. Cert. water and wastewater treatment operator, Iowa. Mem. Am. Water Works Assn., Iowa Water Pollution Control Assn. Republican. Baptist. Office: DEQ Henry A Wallace Bldg 900 E Grand Ave Des Moines IA 50319

RUSSO, FRANK ANTHONY, safety engr.; b. Bklyn., Feb. 29, 1940; s. Frank B. and Jennie (Pellegrino) R.; B.S., St. Francis Coll., 1961; postgrad. U. W.Va., 1961-62, Va. Poly. Inst. and State U., 1970-71; m. Kathryn Ann Russo, Nov. 7, 1962; children—Frank Anthony, Dorothy JoAnn. Devel. chemist, quality control engr. Hercules Inc., Allegany Ballistics Lab., Cumberland, Md., 1961-67, prodn. supr., safety engr., Radford Ammunition Plant (Va.), 1967-72; product testing supr., quality assurance engr. Tech. Products div. Brunswick Corp., Sugar Grove, Va., 1972-74; process engr. hazards analysis Atlantic Research Corp., Gainesville, Va., 1974-75; safety engr./dir. Am. Cyanamid Co., Hannibal, Mo., 1975—. Troop com. chmn., chmn. dist. com. Boy Scouts Am., 1981—. Cert. safety profl. Mem. Am. Soc. Safety Engrs., Am. Chem. Soc., Quincy Area Indsl. Safety Council. Roman Catholic. Clubs: K.C., Elks, Optimist. Contbr. articles to profl. jours. Home: 6 Rutledge Pl Quincy IL 62301 Office: PO Box 817 Hannibal MO 63401

RUSSO, JOHN GEORGE, constrn. engr., educator; b. Sault Ste. Marie, Mich., May 5, 1944; s. James Joseph and Vera Marie (Siltala) R.; B.S., U. Wis., 1967; M.B.A., Mich. State U., 1970, Ph.D., Iowa State U., 1978; m. Susan Lynne Ranta, May 19, 1967; children—John Patrick, Lynne Eriika, Matthew Joseph. Dist. engr. Mobil Oil Corp., Mich., Ohio, 1967-70, div. constrn. engring. mgr., Chgo., 1971-72; hockey coach Iowa State U., 1972-76; v.p., partner Trico Investments, Inc., Ames, Iowa, 1976—; faculty Iowa State U., Ames, 1976—, now prof. in charge constrn. engring.; cons., lectr. in field. Mem. City of Ames Parks and Recreation Commn., 1977—, pres., 1979-81; bd. dirs. Ames-Cyclone Area Community Center, 1976-80; mem. Iowa State U. Center Commn., 1976-78; mem. U. No. Iowa Constrn. Adv. Council, 1978-81. Nominated Young Engr. of Yr., Nat. Soc. Profl. Engrs., 1978. Mem. Asso. Gen. Contractors of Am. (grantee), Sigma Xi, Sigma Lambda Chi. Roman Catholic. Club: Elks. Contbr. articles to profl. jours. Home: 1534 Meadowlane Ave Ames IA 50010 Office: 456 Town Engring Bldg Iowa State Univ Ames IA 50010

RUSSO, JOSE, pathologist; b. Mendoza, Argentina, Mar. 24, 1942; came to U.S., 1971; s. Felipe and Teresa (Pagano) R.; B.S., Agustin Alvarez Nat. Coll., 1959; M.D., U. Nat. Cuyo, 1967; m. Irma Haydee, Feb. 8, 1969. Instr., Inst. Gen. and Exptl. Pathology, Med. Sch., Mendoza, 1961-66, asst. prof. Inst. Histology and Embryology, 1967-71; Rockefeller Found. postdoctoral fellow Inst. Molecular and Cellular Evolution, U. Miami, 1971-73; chief exptl. pathology lab. Mich. Cancer Found., Detroit, 1973—; asso. clin. prof. pathology Wayne State U., Detroit, 1979—. USPHS grantee, 1978—; Am. Cancer Soc. grantee, 1982; NRC Argentina fellow, 1967-71. Mem. Am. Assn. Cancer Research, Am. Soc. Cell Biology, Soc. Exptl. Biology and Medicine, Tissue Culture Assn., Am. Soc. Clin. Pathology, Sigma Xi. Roman Catholic. Research on breast cancer. Office: 110 E Warren Ave Detroit MI 48201

RUSSO, KAREN BARTELL, interior designer; b. Detroit, Aug. 1, 1941; d. Clarence Carl and Dolores Rose (Bahs) Bartell; student Denison U., 1959-61; B.A. cum laude, Wayne State U., 1968; m. Anthony Russo, Aug. 22, 1964. Designer, J.L. Hudson Co., Detroit, 1968-72, sr. designer, 1972-74; sr. designer Contract Interiors Co., Detroit, 1974—, mktg. mgr., 1981—. Mem. Am. Soc. Interior Designers (dir. Mich. chpt. 1980—), AIA (profl. affiliate). Club: Catawba Island (Ohio). Home: 22700 Garrison St Dearborn MI 48124 Office: Contract Interiors Co 511 Woodward Ave Detroit MI 48226

RUSSO, MARTIN A., congressman; b. Chgo., Jan. 23, 1944; s. Anthony and Lucille R.; B.A., DePaul U., 1965, J.D., 1967; m. Karen Jorgensen; children—Tony, Dan. Admitted to Ill. bar, 1967, U.S. Supreme Ct. bar, 1974, D.C. bar, 1977; law clk. Judge John V. McCormack, Ill. Appellate Ct., 1967-68; asst. state's atty. Cook County (Ill.), 1971-73; practice in Chgo., 1973—; mem. 94th-97th congresses from 3d Dist. Ill., mem. Com. On Ways and Means, Select Com. Aging. Bd. dirs. St. Xavier Coll., Chgo.; mem. Joint Civic Com. of Italian-Ams.; mem. citizens bd. Ill. Masonic Med. Center. Recipient Disting. Service award Pinta Neri K.C.; named One of Roseland's Ten Outstanding Young Men, Gateway br. Chgo. Jr. Assn. Commerce and Industry, 1968; Man of Yr., Chgo. W. Suburban chpt. United Neighbors of Italy Community Orgns., 1975, Chog. chpt. Magen David Adom, 1977; Outstanding Legis. Leader, Soc. Little Flower, 1975; One of Ten Outstanding Young People, Harvey (Ill.) Jaycees, 1977. Mem. Am., Fed., Ill., D.C., S. Suburban bar assns., Justinian Soc. Lawyers (named Man of Yr. 1976), Alpha Phi Delta Alumni Assn. Roman Catholic. Clubs: K.C., Elks, Order Sons of Italy. Office: 206 Cannon House Office Bldg Washington DC 20515

RUSSO, MICHAEL EUGENE, pharm. corp. ofcl.; b. St. Louis, Aug. 5, 1939; s. Michael W. and Lyda Mae (Wooten) R.; A.B., Washington U., 1961, Ph.D. in Phys. Chemistry, 1970. With Mallinckrodt, Inc., St. Louis, 1967—, research investigator, 1967-72, research asso., 1972-74, group leader, 1974-75, research mgr. drug and cosmetic chem. div., 1975—; v.p., dir. Parkside Devel. Corp., St. Louis. NSF fellow, 1963, Shell fellow, 1964-65, NASA trainee, 1965-67. Mem. Am. Chem. Soc., Soc. Cosmetic Chemists, AAAS, Sigma Xi, Sigma Chi. Club: Washington U. (St. Louis). Home: 10 Kingsbury Pl Saint Louis MO 63112 Office: 3700 N Broadway St Saint Louis MO 63147

RUST, EDWARD BARRY, ins. exec.; b. Bloomington, Ill., Sept. 5, 1918; s. Adlai H. and Florence Fifer (Barry) R.; A.B. cum laude in Econs., Stanford U., 1940; m. Harriett B. Fuller, Aug. 7, 1940; children—Florence M., Harriet H., Edward B. Asst. sec. State Farm Mut. Automobile Ins. Co., 1942, dir. br. offices, 1946-51, v.p., 1951-58, pres., 1958—, also chief exec. officer, dir., exec. com.; pres., dir. State Farm Life Ins. Co.; pres., dir., exec. com. State Farm Fire & Casualty Co.; pres. State Farm Life & Accident Assurance Co., State Farm County Mut. Ins. Co. Tex., State Farm Gen. Ins. Co.; dir. Gen. Telephone Co. Ill. Trustee Ill. Wesleyan U. Served as lt. USNR, 1943-46. Mem. U.S. C. of C. (dir., pres. 1972-73), Phi Beta Kappa. Office: State Farm Life Ins Co One State Farm Plaza Bloomington IL 61701

RUSTAND, KEITH MARVIN, jeweler; b. Bismarck, N.D., Oct. 8, 1948; s. Leonard O. and Lillian (Nodland) R.; student Dickinson State Coll., 1967-68; student Gemological Inst. Am., 1971—, diamond cert., 1972; m. E. Lynnell Doppler, Feb. 14, 1969; children—DeRikki Kay, Mieka Nicole. With Scotty's Drive-In, Bismarck, 1965-66; glass cutter Hedahl's QG & R, Bismarck, 1966-67; with Kokkelers Jewelry, Bismarck, 1968-75; pres., owner Rustand Jewelers, Inc., Dickinson, N.D., 1975—, Williston, N.D., 1980—; owner, pres. Western Outpost, Inc., Dickinson, 1979—. Treas., Roughrider Festival Commn., Dickinson, 1977, 78; mem. nominating com. and stewardship chmn. St. John's Luth. Ch., 1977—; Sunday Sch. tchr. Good Shepard Luth. Ch., Bismarck, 1974-77. Served with USAR, 1968-74. Mem. Am. Legion, Am. Gem Soc. (registered), Retail Jewelers of Am., Jr. C. of C. Clubs: Capitol City Gun (dir. 1973-75), Rotary, Elks, Masons, German-Hungarian, Dickinson Country, Dickinson Gun. Home: 674 Surrey Heights Dickinson ND 58601 Office: 46 Sims St Dickinson ND 58601

RUSTEN, ELMER MATHEW, dermatologist; b. Pigeon Falls, Wis., Oct. 5, 1902; s. Ener E. and Clara L. (Benrud) R.; B.A., St. Olaf Coll., 1925; B.S., U. Minn., 1928, B.M., 1928, M.D., 1929, postgrad., 1929-31, U. Vienna, 1932; m. Helen Marthine Steidl, July 19, 1930; 1 son, Elmer Michael. Intern, Mpls. Gen. Hosp., 1929, resident, 1929-31; practice medicine specializing in dermatology, Mpls., 1933—; instr. dermatology U. Minn., Mpls., 1934-38, clin. instr., 1938-42, clin. asst. prof., 1942-71; mem. cons. staff Mpls. Gen. Hosp., 1933-40, 51-60, Glen Lake Sanatorium, Oak Terrace, Minn., 1936-60; mem. attending staff Methodist Hosp., St. Louis Park, Minn., 1959-77, Abbott Hosp., Mpls., 1935—, Asbury Hosp., Mpls., 1934-50. Del. to 14th Internat. Tb Conf., New Delhi, India, 1957. Mem. Minn. Citizens Council, 1963-66; bd. dirs. Correctional Service of Minn., pres., 1963-67; bd. dirs. Minn. Dermatol. Found., 1950-54, Central Luth. Found., 1952—. Diplomate Am. Bd. Dermatology. Mem. Am., Minn. med. assns., Mpls. Acad. Medicine (past pres.), Am. Acad. Dermatology, Soc. for Investigative Dermatology, Minn. (pres.), Chgo. dermatol. socs., Internat. Soc. Tropical Dermatology, Am. Acad. Allergy, Internat. Corrs. Soc. of Allergists, Hennepin County Med. Soc., Alaska Territorial Assn. (hon.). Republican. Lutheran. Clubs: Rotary (pres. 1961), Boone and Crockett (hon. life mem., chmn. Big Game Competition 1961, 64, v.p. 1965-74), Big Game (pres. 1940, dir. Spl. Projects Found. 1970—). Author: Wheat, Egg and Milk-Free Diets, 1932; contbr. to Ofcl. Scoring System for N. Am. Big Game, 1971. Home: 18420 D 8th Ave N Plymouth MN 55447 Office: 1645 Medical Arts Bldg Minneapolis MN 55402

RUSTERHOLTZ, WALLACE PALMER, historian; b. Erie, Pa., Mar. 21, 1909; s. Harper George and Blanche (Billings) R.; A.B., Dartmouth Coll., 1931; M.A., Harvard U., 1932; A.M., U. Chgo., 1956; Ph.D., U. Buffalo, 1949; m. Hazel Everitt, Sept. 14, 1946 (dec. 1959). Librarian, U. Buffalo, 1937-40; instr. So. Coll., 1940-42; instr. Case Inst. Tech., 1945-47; asst. prof. history Butler U., 1947-51; librarian U. Chgo., 1956-57; prof. Chgo. City Colls., 1962-74; Trustee, Chgo. Meml. Assn., Meadville-Lombard Theol. Sch., First Unitarian Ch. Chgo. Served with U.S. Army, 1942-45. Recipient Paul Cornell award Hyde Park Hist. Soc., 1981. Mem. Am. Hist. Assn. (life). Democrat. Author: American Heretics and Saints, 1938; The Swiss Family Rusterholtz in America, 1972; The First Unitarian Society of Chicago, 1980. Home: 1545 E 60th St Chicago IL 60637

RUSYNYK, DENNIS JOHN, indsl. exec.; b. Cleve., May 6, 1948; s. Sam and Victoria (Gluszik) R.; B.B.A., Ohio U., 1970. Laborer, Union Carbide Corp., Cleve., summers 1966-70; press operator Airco Welding Products, Cleve., 1971-73; indsl. engr. Lamson & Sessions Co., Cleve., 1973-75; supr. Gen. Industries, Elyria, Ohio, 1975-81, plant mgr., 1981—. Treas. Little League North, Elyria, 1977-78; advisor Jr. Achievement Assn., Cleve., 1974-75. Greek Catholic. Developer one resin formulations in bulk molding compounds. Home: 327 Canterbury Ct Elyria OH 44035 Office: Gen Industries Co Olive & Taylor Sts Elyria OH 44035

RUTENBERG-ROSENBERG, SHARON LESLIE, journalist; b. Chgo., May 23, 1951; d. Arthur and Bernice (Berman) Rutenberg; student Harvard U. Summer Sch., 1972; B.A., Northwestern U., 1973, M.S.J., Medill Grad. Sch. Journalism, 1975; m. Michael J. Rosenberg, Feb. 3, 1980. Bus. mgr. Northwestern U. Yearbook, 1971-72; reporter-photographer Lerner Home Newspapers, Chgo., 1973-74; corr. Medill News Service, Washington, 1975; reporter-newsperson UPI, Chgo., 1975—; mem. exec. bd. Northwestern U. Student Adv. Council, 1972-73. Vol. worker Chgo.-Read Mental Health Center. Recipient Peter Lisagor award exemplary journalism in print feature category; Golden Key award Nat. Adv. Bd. to Children's Oncology Services, Inc., 1981; Peter Lisagor award, 1980; cert. student pilot, cert. scuba diver. Mem. Hadassah, Sigma Delta Chi, Sigma Delta Tau. Covered Pres. of U.S., the Pope, prime minister of Israel. Home: 745 Marion Ave Highland Park IL 60035 Office: 360 N Michigan Ave Chicago IL 60601

RUTH, MICHAEL DAVID, chemist; b. Santa Monica, Calif., Apr. 6, 1948; s. Edward Appleton and Macel Grey (Mace) R.; B.S. in Chemistry, Calif. State U., Northridge, 1975; M.S. in Chemistry, U. Ill., Urbana, 1977, Ph.D., 1982; m. Jean Elizabeth Salyers, Mar. 8, 1969; children—David Michael (dec.), Paul Michael, John Michael, Suzanne Marie. Teaching asst. Calif. State U., Northridge, 1974-75, teaching asst. U. Ill., Urbana, 1975-77, research asst., 1976—, Union Carbide Research fellow, 1977-78. Served with USN, 1967-71. Mem. Am. Chem. Soc., Am. Assn. Clin. Chemistry, Soc. Applied Spectroscopy, AAAS. Republican. Baptist. Clubs: Mensa, Alpha Phi Omega. Office: Univ Ill Dept Chemistry Box 100 Roger Adams Lab Urbana IL 61801

RUTHERFORD, CECIL LEROY, broadcaster; b. Evarts, Ky., Oct. 19, 1943; s. Cecil Theopolus and Dorothy Virginia (Mattingly) R.; student Morehead State U., 1961, Crossroads Bible Coll., 1980; m. Carol Sue Powell, Apr. 4, 1964; children—Lee II, Christopher Todd, Myles Anthony. Announcer, Sta. WDRK, Greenville, Ohio, 1962-64; news dir. Sta. WLTH, Gary, Ind., 1964-67, Sta. WIFE, Indpls., 1967-71; owner, pres. Sta. WDRK, Greenville, 1971—; partner, pres. ColorSound, Inc.; owner, pres. Tower Sound & Communications, Inc. Pres Full Gospel Businessmen's Fellowship Internat., 1978-79. Recipient 3M Co. Top Dealership award, 1978, 1st place sales promotion award Nat. Assn. Radio Broadcasters, 1979. Mem. Nat. Assn. Broadcasters, Aircraft Owners and Pilots Assn., Radio Advt. Bur. Clubs: Lions, Optimists, Masons, Shriners. Home: Lakeview Estates Greenville OH 45331 Office: 1625 Dayton Rd Greenville OH 45331

RUTHERFORD, JAMES WILLIAM, mayor; b. Flint, Mich., Apr. 23, 1925; s. Harry Elwood and Isabelle Rachel (Leake) R.; B.S. in Police Adminstrn., Mich. State U., 1960, M.A., 1964; m. Dorothy Marie Petyak, May 17, 1947 (dec.); children—Marcia Rutherford Alvord, Michelle Marie, Michael James, James Andrew; m. 2d, Betty J. Merrell, 1975. Mem. Flint Police Dept., 1948—, line insp., 1967, chief police, 1967-75; dep. city mgr., City of Flint, 1963, mayor, 1975—; owner Rutherford & Assocs., Cons., Flint; tchr. Flint Community Coll.; guest lectr. in field. Chmn. Flint Anti-poverty Program, 1966; mem. Mich. Police Hall of Fame Com.; vice-chmn. Flint Manpower Devel. Com.; mem. citizens study com. Flint Bd. Edn.; mem. law enforcement adv. com. Ferris (Mich.) State Coll., 1970-71; chmn. Downtown Devel. Authority, Econ. Devel. Commn. Flint; mem. Flint Area Conf. Inc.; dir. Flint-Genesee Corp.; bd. dirs. Flint Renaissance, Inc. Served with USNR, 1945-47. Recipient Reverence for Law award, Fraternal Order Eagles, 1968; Golden Deeds award, Flint Exchange Club, 1969; J. Edgar Hoover award, Ridge Homes, 1973. Mem. Internat. (sgt. at arms, chmn. membership com. 1973; named 1 of 10 outstanding police officers 1966), Mich. (dir. 1969), Saginaw Valley, Genessee County (pres.) assns. chiefs police, U.S. Conf. Mayors, Pi Alpha, Phi Kappa Phi. Methodist. Club: Masons, K.P., Old Newsboys of Flint. Contbr. for manuals in field. Office: Office of Mayor City Hall 1101 S Saginaw St Flint MI 48502

RUTHMAN, THOMAS R., mfg. co. exec.; b. Cin., May 24, 1933; s. Alois H. and Catherine (Gies) R.; grad. LaSalle U., 1970; m. Audrey J. Schumaker, Mar. 17, 1979; children—Thomas G., Julia C., Theresa K. With Ruthman Machinery Co., Cin., 1953—, gen. mgr., 1964-70, v.p., 1970-74, pres., 1974—, pres., owner Ruthman Corp., 1981—. Served with U.S. Army, 1953-55. Mem. Cin. Council World Affairs, Navy League U.S. Club: Rotary. Home: 6858 Dimmick Rd West Chester OH 45067 Office: 1212 Streng St Cincinnati OH 45223

RUTIGLIANO, SAM, profl. football coach; b. Bklyn., July 1, 1932; B.S., U. Tulsa, 1956; M.S., Columbia U., 1959. High sch. football coach, N.Y. and Conn., 1956-63; asst. coach U. Conn., 1964-65, U.

Md., 1966, Denver AFL team, 1967-69, Denver NFL team, 1970, New Eng. Patriots, 1971-73, N.Y. Jets, 1974-75, New Orleans Saints, 1976-77; head coach Cleve. Browns, 1978—. Address: Cleve Browns Cleve Stadium Cleveland OH 44114*

RUTLEDGE, JERRY EUGENE, ins. co. exec.; b. Waseca, Minn., Jan. 20, 1936; s. Lyle Eugene and Virginia Alberta (Olsen) R.; B.B.A., U. Minn., 1958; student Carleton Coll., 1954-58; m. Carol Genevieve Greer, Dec. 21, 1957; children—Lisa Dianne, Thomas Scott, Rebecca Anne. Asst. mgr., v.p. Waseca Mut. Ins. Co. (Minn.), 1958-62, pres., gen. mgr., 1962—, also dir.; sec., mgr., dir. Clear Lake Mut. Ins. Co. (merger Waseca Mut. Ins.), Waseca, 1958-78; dir. First Bank, Waseca. Mem. Waseca Planning Commn., 1961-62; bd. dirs. So. Central Edn. Assn., 1970-71; pres. Waseca Sleigh and Cutter Festival Assn., 1959; sec., treas., bd. dirs. Who's He? Inc., 1963—; mem. Waseca Charter Commn., 1965-68, sec., 1967-68; trustee Waseca Area Meml. Hosp., 1970—, chmn. bd., 1974; bd. dirs. Waseca Players, 1972—, pres., 1973-75. Mem. Crop Ins. Research Bur. (mem. exec. com. 1976—), Nat. Assn. Mut. Ins. Cos., Minn. Assn. Farm Mut. Ins. Cos., Multiperil Crop Ins. Assn. (mem. exec. com. 1975-80), Alliance of Am. (mem. insurance adv. bd. 1977—), Statewide Reinsurance Underwriters (dir. 1976—), Minn. Assn. Windstorm Cos. (v.p. 1960—). Methodist (lay leader 1980). Clubs: Waseca Rotary (pres.); American Iris Soc. (dir.); Iris Society of Minnesota (dir. 1972); Waseca Lakeside (dir. 1980—). Home: 43 Timberlane St Waseca MN 56093 Office: 1000 W Elm Ave Waseca MN 56093

RUTLEDGE, VIRGINIA ALICE, bus. services co. exec.; b. Grant Tower, Ill., Dec. 15, 1919; d. Emora F. and Dora A. (Davis) Howe; children by former marriage—Walter, Patricia. Corporate pres. Gateway Account Service Inc., St. Louis, 1968—; lectr. in field. Pres. bd. trustees Mo. Consumer Credit Ednl. Found., 1979. Recipient exec. achievement award Asso. Credit Burs. Inc., 1976. Mem. Mo. (pres. 1974-75, credit exec. of yr. award 1973), Internat. (distinguished service award 1975) consumer credit assns., Mo. Collector Assn. (pres. 1973-74), Soc. Consumer Credit Execs., Asso. Credit Burs. Inc. Nat. leader in consumer credit. Office: 8460 Watson Rd St Louis MO 63119

RUTSHAW, ARTHUR JOSEPH, JR., mfrs. agt.; b. Chgo., June 19, 1919; s. Arthur Joseph and Mary Ellen (Burke) R.; student DePaul U., eves. 1937-40; m. Norine T. McElligott, Nov. 21, 1940; children—Mary, Noreen, Sally, Patti, Nancy. With Uarco Inc., Barrington, Ill., 1938-70, asst. dist. mgr., 1949-50, dist. sales mgr., 1951-57; accountant R.M. O'Brien & Co. Real Estate, Chgo., 1937-38; pres. Identification Specialists Inc., Cin., 1967—. Pres., Westwood Civic Assn., 1971, Mother of Mercy PTA, 1972; pres. Hamilton County Republican Club. Served with AUS, 1941-46, to lt. col. USAR, 1959-70. Decorated Bronze Star, Purple Heart; Croix de Guerre (France); Forregare (Belgium). Mem. Am. Legion (comdr. 1974), Res. Officers Assn., 3d Armored Div. Assn. (pres. 1948-49), Data Processing Mgmt. Assn. Roman Catholic. Clubs: K.C., Cincinnati, Elks, Kiwanis (dir.), Cuvier Press (v.p.).

RUUD, BETTY JUNE, health care adminstr.; b. Willmar, Minn., July 27, 1953; d. Royce Glendolan and Norma Alma (Hoyer) R.; B.A., Macalester Coll., 1975; cert. in long term health care adminstrn. U. Minn., 1975. Owner, mgr. Machiaada Rocker Co., St. Paul, 1975-78; dir. Renville County Community Residence, Inc., Bird Island, Minn., 1979-80, Kindlehope, Willmar, 1978—. Sec., Kandiyohi County Assn. Retarded Citizens, 1979-81. Mem. Willmar C. of C., Am. Coll. Nursing Home Adminstrs., Am. Forestry Assn., Assn. Residences for Retarded (inservice com.), Nat. Audubon Soc. Home: 411 N 10th St Willmar MN 56201 Office: 1217 SE 7th St Willmar MN 56201

RUZICKA, FRANCIS FREDERICK, JR., radiologist, educator; b. Balt., June 30, 1917; s. Francis Frederick and Anne (Kaspar) R.; A.B. cum laude, Holy Cross Coll., Worcester, Mass., 1939; M.D., Johns Hopkins, Balt., 1943; m. Margaret M. Kernan, May 31, 1941; children—Margaret M., Mary Frances, John F., Francis Frederick III, M. Therese, Joseph T. Intern, Univ. Hosp., Balt., 1943, resident in radiology, 1944-45; fellow Univ. Hosp., Mpls., 1948-49, instr. in radiology, 1949-50; dir. radiology St. Vincent's Hosp. and Med. Center, N.Y.C., 1950-73; prof. radiology U. Wis., Madison, 1973-76; prof. radiology U. Wis. Center for Health Scis., 1976—, chmn. dept., 1976-81; asso. clin. prof. to clin. prof. N.Y.U., 1950-73; acting chmn., clin. prof. radiology N.J. Coll., Jersey City, 1964-67; cons. Nat. Acad. Scis., 1975-76. Served with M.C., AUS, 1945-47. Diplomate Am. Bd. Radiology. Fellow Am. Coll. Radiology; mem. Am. Roentgen Ray Soc., Radiol. Soc. N.Am., AMA, Wis. Med. Soc., N.Y. Acad. Scis., Soc. Gatrointestinal Radiology, Soc. Cardiovascular Radiology, Cath. Physicians Guild, N.Y. Roentgen Soc. (past pres.). Editor: (with others) Vascular Roentgenology, 1964. Contbr. articles to profl. jours. Home: 5705 Cove Circle Monona WI 53716 Office: 600 Highland Ave Madison WI 53792

RYAN, CLARENCE EDWARD, JR., indsl. cons.; b. Moline, Ill., Jan. 27, 1919; s. Clarence Edward and Dorothy A. (Olson) R.; B.S., St. Ambrose Coll., 1943; LL.B., Blackstone Sch. Law, 1956; postgrad., Augustana Coll., U. Ill., U. Ala., Mich. State U., John Marshall Law Sch., U. Notre Dame, 1943-56; m. Josephine Ann Frankville, Sept. 22, 1941; 1 dau., Dorothy A. Lab. technician Ill. Dept. Pub. Welfare, East Moline, 1938-39; instr. U. Ill. Extension Div., 1946-47; chemist Aluminum Co. Am., Davenport, Iowa and Richmond, Ind., 1948-50; tech. dir., chief chemist Casper Tinplate Co. (now Ball Metal Decorating and Services Div.), Chgo., 1950-74; cons. various coal, petroleum, organic coating cos., 1974—; pres. C R Land Corp.; v.p., dir. Transcontinental Internat., Inc. Served with USNR, 1941-67; PTO. Fellow Am. Inst. Chemists; mem. Am. Chem. Soc., Am. Def. Preparedness Assn., Internat. Platform Assn., VFW, Ret. Officers Assn. Democrat. Roman Catholic. Contbr. articles in chem. field to profl. jours. Home: Rural Route 1 Box 32 Matteson IL 60443 Office: C R Land Corp PO Box 23 Oak Forest IL 60452

RYAN, DAVID MATHER, corp. exec.; b. Toledo, Jan. 19, 1933; s. Burt T. and Nathalie (Mather) R.; A.B., Colgate U., 1956; m. Ellen Moran, Aug. 24, 1963; children—David Mather, Ellen Marie, Richard Peter, Molly Moran. With H.H. Donnelly, Toledo, Ohio, 1958—, 1958-75, pres., 1975-80, owner, chief exec. officer, 1981—. Served with U.S. Army, 1956-58. Mem. Material Handling Equipment Soc., Soc. Packaging and Handling Engrs. Republican. Roman Catholic. Clubs: Toledo, Toledo Racquet. Home: 5342 Northbrook Ct Sylvania OH 43560 Office: 853 S Reynolds Rd Toledo OH 43615

RYAN, DONALD PATRICK, contractor; b. Janesville, Wis., July 13, 1930; s. William H. and Myrtle (Westrick) R.; B.S. in Civil Engring., U. Wis., 1953, B.S. in Naval Sci., 1953; m. Diana Houser, July 17, 1954; children—Patrick, Susannah, Nancy, David, Josephine, Rebecca, Polly, Adam. Partner, Ryan Bros. Co., Janesville, Wis., 1949—; dir. Ryan, Inc., Janesville; pres. Engring. Service Corp., Janesville, 1959—; pres. P. W. Ryan Sons, Inc., Janesville; dir. Bank of Wis., Janesville, Bankwis Corp. Bd. dirs. U. Wis. Found. Served with USNR, 1953-55. Registered profl. engr., Wis., Ill. Mem. Nat. Soc. Profl. Engrs., Wis. Meml. Union Bldg. Assn. (trustee), U. Wis. Alumni Assn., Chi Epsilon, Phi Delta Theta. Home: 703 St Lawrence Ave Janesville WI 53545 Office: PO Box 1079 Janesville WI 53545

RYAN, ELEANOR ABELL, educator; b. Mendota, Ill., Sept. 14, 1932; d. Otto Henry and Lelia Dorothy (Cradduck) Abell; B.A. in Spanish, No. Ill. U., 1967; M.A., Ill. State U., 1972; m. Glen Ryan, Jr., Sept. 14, 1950; children—Eileen Lorraine Ryan Martin, Colleen Lavonne Ryan Grafton. Tchr. Spanish, LaSalle (Ill.)-Peru Twp. High Sch., 1967—; legis. co-ordinator 45th dist. Ill. Fedn. Tchrs., 1977—; pres. No. LaSalle Bur. and Putnam Counties council AFL-CIO, 1976—; chmn. 15th congl. dist. com. on polit. edn. AFL-CIO, 1976—. Sec. overall econ. devel. com. LaSalle County Regional Planning Commn., 1976-78, mem., 1978—; mem. jobs div. Ill. Valley C. of C., 1976-77, mem. indsl. devel. com., 1977-78; mem. budget com. Ill. Valley United Fund, 1976. Mem. Am. Assn. Tchrs. Spanish and Portuguese (pres. chpt. 1974), Am. Fedn. Tchrs. (v.p. Local 1973), Ill. Council Central Bodies (sec.-treas. 1979—), Illinois Valley LWV, NOW, Phi Alpha Theta, Sigma Delta Pi. Democrat. Methodist. Home: 2517 Rock St Peru IL 61354 Office: 541 Chartes St LaSalle IL 61301

RYAN, FRANK JOSEPH, mgmt. cons.; b. Lake Forest, Ill., Sept. 9, 1931; s. Thomas F. and Frances M. (Cuffe) R.; B.A., Lake Forest Coll., 1959; M.S. in Psychology, No. Ill. U., 1965, postgrad., 1979-80; m. Alice Jane Smith, Oct. 18, 1952; children—Sheila Mary, Terance Francis, Ann Mary, Patrick J., Kevin R., Marion J. Mgr., Rolling Acres Farm, Tinley Park, Ill., 1952-55; plant mgr. evening div. Kleinschmidt Labs., Deerfield, Ill., 1955-59; tchr. Waukegan (Ill.) Sch. Dist., 1959-63; coordinator programs for educationally disadvantaged DeKalb (Ill.) Sch. Dist., 1964-68; co-dir. spl. edn. DeKalb County Spl. Edn. Co-op., 1968-69; exec. dir. Marion County Assn. for Retarded Children, Indpls., 1969-74, Harbor Regional Center, Torrance, Calif., 1974-76; instr. dept. pediatrics UCLA Sch. Medicine, 1974-76; asso. dir. Assn. for Disabled of Elkhart County, Bristol, Ind., 1976-78; mgmt. cons. Ind. Dept. Mental Health, Indpls., 1978—; mem. Ind. State Residential Study Com. for the Mentally Retarded, 1970-71. Recipient Presidential Citation, 1974. Mem. Am. Assn. on Mental Deficiency. Roman Catholic. Author: (manual) Uniform Client Information System, 1979. Address: 51229 Cr123 Bristol IN 46507

RYAN, GEORGE HOMER, pharmacist, state legislator; b. Maquoketa, Iowa, Feb. 24, 1934; s. Thomas J. and Jeanette (Bowman) R.; B.S. in Pharmacy, Ferris State Coll., Mich.; m. Lura Lynn Lowe, June 10, 1956; children—Nancy, Lynda, Julie, Joanne and Jeanette (triplets), George. Vice-pres., Ryan Pharmacies, Kankakee, Ill.; mem. Kankakee County Bd., 1966-72, chmn., 1970-72; mem. Ill. Ho. of Reps., 1972—, minority leader, 1977-81, speaker, 1981—. Active local polit. campaigns; mem. Pres.-elect Reagan's Ill. Adv. Com., 1980. Served in U.S. Army; Korea. Named Outstanding Pharmacist/Legislator, Am. Pharm. Assn., 1980; other awards. Mem. Am. Legion. Republican. Methodist. Clubs: Shriners, 100 (founder), Elks, Moose. Office: 300 State Capitol Bldg Springfield IL 62706

RYAN, HELEN LENORE, educator; b. Akron, Ohio, Oct. 20, 1943; d. Charles Bertrand and Helen Lenore (Maxwell) R.; B.A., Ohio Wesleyan U., 1965; M.A., Middlebury Coll., 1967, 73, Dr. Modern Langs., 1980. Instr. Spanish, Western Coll. for Women, Oxford, Ohio, 1967-68; asst. prof. modern langs. U. Akron, 1968—. Mem. Jr. League Akron, 1969—; trustee, pres. alumni assn. Old Trail Sch., 1972-74. Mem. Am. Assn. Tchrs. Spanish and Portuguese (pres. No. Ohio chpt. 1979-81), Ohio Program in the Humanities (dir. 1977—), MLA, Am. Council Teaching Fgn. Langs., Sigma Delta Pi, Pi Delta Phi. Author film, media prodn.; Spain - Years of Revolution, Champagne - A Blend of People and Tradition, Gaspe - The Isolated Counterpoint, 1977. Home: 684 Ridgecrest Rd Akron OH 44303 Office: Dept Modern Langs U Akron 302 E Buchtel Ave Akron OH 44325

RYAN, HOWARD CHRIS, chief justice Ill. Supreme Ct.; b. Tonica, Ill., June 17, 1916; s. John F. and Sarah (Egger) R.; B.A., U. Ill., 1940, LL.B., J.D., 1942; LL.D. (hon.), John Marshall Law Sch., 1978; m. Helen Cizek, Oct. 16, 1943; children—John F., Elizabeth Ellen, Howard Chris. Admitted to Ill. bar, 1942; practice in Decatur, 1946-47, Peru, 1947-57; asst. state's atty. LaSalle County, 1952-54; county judge LaSalle County, 1954-57, circuit judge, 1957-68, chief judge, 1964-68; judge Appellate Ct. 3d Jud. Dist. Ill., 1968-70; justice Ill. Supreme Ct., 1970—, chief justice, 1982—. Served with USAAF, 1942-45. Mem. Am., Ill., LaSalle County bar assns., Am. Judicature Soc., Am. Legion, Phi Alpha Delta. Republican. Methodist. Mason (33 deg.), Elk, Odd Fellow. Home: Box 53 Tonica IL 61370 Office: 111 E Jefferson St Ottawa IL 61350

RYAN, JAMES LEO, state supreme ct. justice; b. Detroit, Nov. 19, 1932; s. Leo Francis and Irene Agnes R.; LL.B., U. Detroit, 1956; LL.D., Madonna Coll., 1976; m. Mary Elizabeth Rogers, Oct. 12, 1957; children—Daniel P., James R., Colleen M., Kathleen A. Justice of peace, Redford Twp., Mich., 1963-66; circuit judge 3d Jud. Circuit Mich., 1966-75; justice Mich. Supreme Ct., 1975—; faculty U. Detroit Sch. Law, Nat. Jud. Coll., Reno, Am. Acad. Jud. Edn., Washington. Bd. dirs. Thomas M. Cooley Law Sch., Lansing, Mich., Donald M. Barton Found., Detroit, U. Detroit Law Sch. Alumni Assn. Served in USN, 1957-60, to comdr. JAGC, Res., 1960—. Mem. Am. Judicature Soc., Am., Detroit bar assns., Naval Res. Lawyers Assn., Nat. Conf. Appellate Ct. Judges, State Bar Mich. Roman Catholic. Club: KC. Contbr. article to legal jour. Office: care Supreme Ct Mich State Capitol Lansing MI 48024

RYAN, JOHN WILLIAM, univ. pres.; b. Chgo., Aug. 12, 1929; s. Leonard John and Maxine (Mitchell) R.; B.A., U. Utah, 1951; M.A., Ind. U., 1958, Ph.D., 1959; D.Litt. (hon.), Coll. St. Thomas, Minn., 1977; LL.D. (hon.), U. Notre Dame, 1968, Oakland City Coll., 1981, Coll. St. Joseph, 1981; m. D. Patricia Goodday, Mar. 20, 1949; children—Kathleen Elynne Ryan Acker, Kevin Dennis Mitchell, Kerrick Charles Casey. Research analyst Ky. Dept. Revenue, Frankfort, 1954-55; vis. research prof. Ind. U. project at U. Thammasat, Bangkok, Thailand, 1955-57; asst. dir. Inst. Tng. for Public Service, Ind. U., 1957-58; successively asst. prof., asso. prof. polit. sci., also asso. dir. Bur. Govt., U. Wis., 1958-62; exec. asst. to pres., sec. of univ. U. Mass., Amherst, 1962-63, chancellor, Boston, 1965-68; v.p. acad. affairs Ariz. State U., 1963-65; v.p., chancellor regional campuses Ind. U., Bloomington, 1968-71, pres. Ind. U., 1971—, also prof. polit. sci.; dir. Ind. Bell Telephone Co. Pres., Ind. Newman Found., 1969-71, bd. dirs., 1969—; pres. Ind. Conf. Higher Edn., 1977-78; bd. govs. Riley Meml. Assn., 1971—, Public Broadcasting Service, 1973—; bd. dirs. Corp. Community Council, 1976, Ind. Center for Advanced Research, 1977-80, Council for Fin. Aid to Edn., 1981; bd. govs. Am. U. Field Staff, 1971—, chmn. bd., 1972-77; chmn. bd. dirs. Ind. U. Found., 1972—; trustee Coll. St. Thomas, 1975—; bd. visitors Air U., 1974—, chmn. Air Force Inst. Tech. subcom., 1976—; mem. univ. adv. com. Council Am. Life Ins.; mem. White River Park Devel. Commn., 1979—; mem. council of pres. Midwest Univs. Consortium for Internat. Activities, 1971—, chmn., 1976-78; bd. dirs. Inst. Campus Ministries, Inc., 1975-78, mem. devel. com.; common instl. cooperation rep. to NCAA, Council of Ten, 1980—. Mem. Am. Soc. Public Adminstrn. (pres. Ind. chpt. 1969-70, pres. nat. chpt. 1972-73, nat. council 1970—), Indiana Soc. Chgo. (non-resident v.p. 1976—), Am. Polit. Sci. Assn., Assn. Asian Studies, Am. Council on Edn., Am. Judicature Soc., Assn. Am. Univs. (exec. com. 1978—, health edn. com. 1978—, chmn. 1981-82), Indiana Soc. N.Y., Indiana Soc. Washington, Indiana Acad., Nat. Acad. Public Adminstrn., Explorers Club, Adelphia (hon.), Phi Kappa Phi, Phi Alpha Theta, Pi Sigma Alpha, Kappa Sigma. Clubs: KC, Rotary, Elks. Author papers and reports in field. Home: Presidents House Indiana U Bloomington IN 47405

RYAN, LEO VINCENT, univ. dean; b. Waukon, Iowa, Apr. 6, 1927; s. John Joseph and Mary Irene (O'Brien) R.; B.S., Marquette U., 1949; M.B.A., DePaul U., 1954; Ph.D., St. Louis U., 1958; postgrad. Catholic U. Am., 1951-52, Bradley U., 1952-54, Northwestern U., 1950. Joined Order Clerics of St. Viator, Roman Catholic Ch., 1950; mem. faculty Marquette U., Milw., 1957-65, dir. continuing edn. summer sessions, coordinator evening divs., 1959-65, prof. indsl. mgmt., 1964; prof. mgmt. Loyola U., Chgo., 1965-66, adj. prof. mgmt., 1967-69; dir. Peace Corps, Lagos, Nigeria, 1966-67, Ibadan, Nigeria, 1967-68; asst. superior gen. and treas. gen. Clerics of St. Viator, Rome, 1968-69, dir. edn. Am. province, Arlington Heights, Ill., 1969-74; pres. St. Viator High Sch., 1972-74; dean Coll. Bus. Adminstrn. U. Notre Dame (Ind.), 1975-80, Coll. Commerce, DePaul U., Chgo., 1980—; dir. Peace Corps tng. program, 1962-65; adj. prof. human devel. St. Mary's Coll., Winona, Minn., 1972-74; mem. sch. bd. Archdiocese Chgo., 1972-75; mem. nat. edn. com. U.S. Cath. Conf., 1971-75, mem. exec. com., 1973-75; mem. nat. adv. bd. Benedictine Sisters of Nauvoo, 1973—; vis. prof. U. Ife, Ibadan, 1967, dir. Vilter Mfg. Co., Filbert Corp., Vilter Sales & Service, Vilter Internat., 1973—, 1st Bank System, Wis. div., 1977—, Haas Co., 1976—, McHugh, Freeman Assos., 1978—. Mem. Pres.'s Com. on Employment Handicapped, 1959-75, Wis. Gov.'s Com. on Employment Handicapped, 1959-65, Wis. Gov.'s Com. on UN, 1961-64; cons. Vatican Sec. of State, Pontifical Commn. on Justice and Peace, 1968-70. Served with inf. U.S. Army, 1945-47. Recipient Freedom award Berlin Commn., 1961; chieftaincy title Asoju Atoaja of Oshogbo, Oba Adenle I, Yorubaland, Nigeria, 1967; Brother Leo V. Ryan award created in his honor Cath. Bus. Edn. Assn., 1962; named Man of Year, Jr. C. of C. Milw., 1959, Marquette U. Bus. Adminstrn. Alumni Man of Year, 1974; recipient B'nai B'rith Interfaith award Milw., 1963; Distinguished Alumnus award DePaul U., 1976; Milw. Bd. Realtors travelling fellow, 1964; Nat. Assn. Purchasing Agts. faculty fellow, 1958. Mem. Nigeria Inst. Mgmt., Cath. Bus. Edn. Assn. (nat. pres. 1960-62, nat. exec. bd. 1960-64), Assn. Sch. Bus. Ofcls. (nat. com. chmn. 1965-67), Am. Assembly Collegiate Schs. Bus. (mem. com. internat. relations, program com.), Am. Fgn. Service Assn., Conf. Religious Dirs. Edn., Nat. Cath. Edn. Assn., Soc. Advancement Mgmt., Nigerian Inst. Mgmt., Pi Gamma Mu, Alpha Sigma Nu, Alpha Kappa Psi, Beta Alpha Psi (named Tchr. of Yr., U. Notre Dame 1980), Delta Mu Delta, Tau Kappa Epsilon, Beta Gamma Sigma (dir. 1978—, chmn. chpt. ops. 1980—). Club: K.C. Author: The Business Management of Central Catholic High School, 1958; Accounting Manual for Catholic Elementary and Secondary School, 1969; also articles. Home: 1212 E Euclid St Arlington Heights IL 60004 Office: Office of Dean Coll Commerce 25 E Jackson Blvd Chicago IL 60604

RYAN, PATRICK JAMES, original equipment mfg. co. exec.; b. St. Louis, July 26, 1945; s. Richard J. and Dorothy R. (Brewer) R.; cert. St. Louis County Vocat. Sch., 1963; grad. Forest Park Community Coll., 1970; B.S. in Mech. Engring., Washington U., St. Louis, 1971, B.S. in Indsl. Mgmt., 1973, postgrad., 1974; postgrad. Clarion (Pa.) State Coll., 1974; cert. Alexander Hamilton Inst., 1974; m. Cynthia L. Cain, Aug. 11, 1973; children—Bill, Kevin, Andy. Prodn. engr. Nooter Corp., St. Louis, 1969-70; purchasing inventory control mgr. and design engr. Multiplex Display Fixture Co., Fenton, Mo., 1968-69, 71-73; dir. purchasing, accounts payable mgr. Binkley Co., Warrenton, Mo., 1973-76; purchasing mgr. mcpl. and utilities div. Rockwell Internat., DuBois, Pa., 1976-77; group purchasing mgr. Outdoor Products Group, Roper Corp., Bradley, Ill., 1977-79; corp. dir. procurement Arctic Enterprises, Inc., Thief River Falls, Minn., 1979-81; div. purchasing mgr. Constrn. Machinery div. Clark Equipment Co., Benton Harbor, Mich., 1981—; lectr. Washington U., 1975, St. Louis U., 1976; mem. Modern Plastics Adv. Bd., 1977, 81. Chmn. exec. com., asst. packmaster, Weblo leader Rainbow council Cub Scouts Am., 1977-79; coach minor league baseball team, 1977-78; coach flag football and T-ball YMCA, 1975-76. Served to sgt. U.S. Army, 1965-68; Vietnam. Cert. purchasing mgr. Nat. Assn. Purchasing Mgmt. Mem. Soc. Mfg. Engrs., Am. Purchasing Soc. (cert. purchasing profl.), Am. Soc. Quality Control, Fiberglass Fabrication Assn., Am. Soc. Metals, Am. Powder Metal Inst., Am. Production and Inventory Control Soc., Twin City Purchasing Mgmt. Assn., Nat. Contract Mgmt. Assn., Sigma Phi Epsilon. Republican. Methodist. Club: Elks. Home: 2949 Bluffwood Terr Saint Joseph MI 49085 Office: 2303 Pipestone Rd Benton Harbor MI 49022

RYAN, ROBERT EMMETT, otolaryngologist; b. St. Louis, July 1, 1917; s. Linus M. and Corinne C. (Fuchs) R.; B.S., St. Louis U., 1938, M.D., 1943; M.S. in Otolaryngology, U. Minn., 1947; m. Eunice M. Burtt, Dec. 4, 1943; children—Robert Emmett, Ronald Emmett. Intern St. John's Hosp., St. Louis, 1943-44, Mayo Clinic, 1944-47; practice medicine specializing in otolaryngology, St. Louis, 1948—; chief dept. otolaryngolgoy St. John's Mercy Med. Center, 1968—; asso. otolargynology St. Louis U. Hosp., 1948—; prof. clin. otolaryngology St. Louis U. Med. Sch., 1968—. Bd. dirs. St. Louis U. High Sch., 1949-81, Khoury League, 1953-81; mem. lay adv. bd. Fontbonne Coll., 1959-64. Recipient Pres.'s award St. Louis U. High Sch. Sch., 1971; certificate of award St. Louis U., 1972, Man of Year award Khoury League, 1977. Diplomate Am. Bd. Otolaryngology. Fellow A.C.S.; mem. Am., Mo., So., Pan Am. med. assns., Am. Acad. Ophthalmology and Otolaryngology (certificate 1952, Honor award 1966), St. Louis Med. Soc., Mayo Clinic Alumni Assn., Am. Assn. Study Headache (pres. 1966-68; certificate appreciation 1970, 79), Am. Triological Soc., Am. Council Otolargynology, Royal Soc. Medicine, Sigma Xi. Clubs: Missouri Athletic (St. Louis); Stadium, Centurion. Author: The Nose in Health and Disease, 1968; Headache-Diagnosis and Treatment, 1954; Headache, 1957; Synopsis of Ear, Nose and Throat Diseases, 3d edit., 1970; Tratao and International de Alergia, 1957, Tratado De Prognostico y Therapeutica, 1972; Headache and Head Pain, 1978, also papers. Home: 1 West Point Lane St Louis MO 63131 Office: 621 S New Ballas Rd St Louis MO 63141

RYAN, ROBERT S., cons.; b. Columbus, Ohio, July 25, 1922; s. Howard L. and Jennie (McComis) R.; B.S. in Indsl. Engring., Ohio State U., 1947; m. Esther Lee Moore, Mar. 15, 1947; children—Phillip Craig, Lynda Joyce, Lois Jean. Maintenance foreman Internat. Harvester Co., Richmond, Ind., 1947-52; prin. welding engr. Battelle Meml. Inst., Columbus, 1952-55; dir. engring. Columbia Gas System, Columbus, 1955-67, sr. v.p., Pitts., 1967-73; sr. v.p., dir. Columbia Gas Distbn. Cos. in Ohio, Pa., Ky., W.Va., Md., Va., N.Y., 1973-75; dir. Columbia Gas of N.Y., Inc., Columbia Gas of Md., Inc., Columbia Gas Ky., Inc., Columbia Gas Ohio, Inc., Columbia Gas W.Va., Inc., Columbia Gas Va., Inc.; dir. Ohio Energy and Resource Devel. Agy., 1975—, Ohio Dept. Energy, 1976-80; mem. Gov.'s Cabinet, to 1980; pres. Robert S. Ryan & Assos., energy cons., Columbus, 1981—. Served to capt. AUS, 1944-47. Mem. Am., Pa. (pres., dir.), W.Va. (dir.) gas assns., Am. Mgmt. Assn., Am. Inst. Indsl. Engrs., Nat. C. of C. Methodist. Club: Duquesne (Pitts.). Contbr. articles profl. jours.

Home: 6566 Plesenton Dr S Worthington OH 43085 Office: 50 W Broad St Columbus OH 43215

RYAN, RONALD DALE, aviation corp. exec.; b. Burlington, Iowa, Jan. 17, 1939; s. Everett T. and Mildred M. Ryan; grad. Met. Jr. Coll., Kansas City, Mo., 1966; m. Raunda Robinson, July 30, 1977; children by previous marriage—Dale, Mark, Scott. Chief pilot Skyway Aviation, Ft. Leonard Wood, Mo., 1966-67; personal pilot for stockholders Mid-Continent Aviation and Midwest Lear Jet, Kansas City, Kans., 1967-68; chief pilot, v.p. DeBoer Aviation Corp., Wichita, Kans., 1968-76; pres., dir. Ryan Aviation Corp., Wichita, 1976—. Active, Quiet Birdmen, Sales and Mktg. Execs. Cert. pvt. pilot, comml./multi-engine/instrument pilot, flight instr., airline transport pilot. Mem. Aircraft Owners and Pilots Assn., Nat. Bus. Aircraft Assn., C. of C. Methodist. Clubs: Masons, Shriners, Flying Fezzes. Home: 820 Shadyway Wichita KS 67203 Office: 1600 Airport Rd Mid-Continent Airport Wichita KS 67209

RYAN, WILLIAM EDWARD, trade assn. exec.; b. Chgo., Apr. 11, 1922; s. John Michael and Lucy Kathleen (Burke) R.; m. Jean M. Schaid, Sept. 18, 1948; children—William Edward, Timothy J., Daniel T., Kevin D., Robert M.; B.A. in Philosophy, St. Mary's on the Lake Coll., Chgo., 1944. Rep., br. mgr., mgr. group promotion dept. Blue Cross/Blue Shield Plan, Chgo., 1946-60; v.p. enrollment, sr. v.p. mktg. Blue Shield Assn., Chgo., 1960-76, pres., 1976-77; sr. exec. v.p. Blue Cross Assn. and Blue Shield Assn., 1978—. sec. Med. Indemnity of Am., Inc.; council mem. Internat. Fedn. Vol. Health Service Funds; mem. AMA Commn. on Cost of Med. Care. Mem. Internat. Found. Employee Benefit Plans, Am. Soc. Assn. Execs., Am. Mgmt. Assn., Am. Pub. Health Assn. Club: International (Washington). Office: 676 N St Clair Chicago IL 60611

RYAN, WILLIAM EMMETT, veterinary products mfg. co. exec.; b. Midland, Tex., Mar. 7, 1927; s. William Emmett and Quincey Belle R.; student Hardin Simmons U., 1946, Abilene Christian Coll., 1946; D.V.M., Okla. State U., 1951; m. Joyce Leta Anderson, Apr. 14, 1962; children—Sharron Ann, Sheila Kay, Timberly, Erin, William Emmett, Michael Patrick, Gregory Shane. Cowboy, Midland, 1939-41; cowboy and sheepherder, Cheyenne, Wyo., 1942-43; farrier, Stillwater, Okla., 1947-51; vet. practitioner, Duncan, Okla., 1951-58; tech. supr. Agrl. Mktg. Service, U.S. Dept. Agr., Des Moines, 1958-60; advt. account exec., Kalamazoo, 1960-61; sales promotion mgr. Fort Dodge Labs. (Iowa), 1961-66, dir. advt., 1966—; public relations and advt. cons. vet. orgns. Vestryman, sr. warden local Episcopal ch.; Founder, pres. Children's Heart Found.; founder Midwest Pioneer Ednl. Inst. for Teaching the Pioneer Crafts; founder Fort Dodge Dragoons; pres. Fort Dodge Dragoon Corp.; founder Frontier Days ann. celebration, chmn. Frontier Days central com.; pres. Fort Dodge Hist. Found. and Fort Mus.; mem. central com. Webster County Republican party. Served with inf. U.S. Army, 1945-46. Recipient Community Devel. Leadership award Gov. Iowa, 1977; Service to Mankind Sertoma Internat., 1981. Mem. Greater Fort Dodge Area C. of C. (v.p. exec. com., dir., chmn. public relations com.), Am. Vet. Exhibitors Assn. (pres.), Internat. Vet. Acupuncture Soc. (dir.), Am. Vet. Hist. Soc. (founder, dir.), Am. Assn. Equine Practitioners (chmn. public relations com.), Iowa Vet. Med. Assn. (Veterinarian of Yr. 1979, dir.), Iowa Horse Industry Council (dir.), Iowa Paint Horse Assn. (co-founder, pres.), Am. Paint Horse Assn. (dir., chmn. public relations com.), AVMA, Okla. Vet. Med. Assn., Am. Assn. Avian Pathologists, Nat. Agrl. Mktg. Assn., Am. Horse Publs., Nat. Rifle Assn., Nat. Muzzleloading Rifle Assn. Club: Elks. Editor Biochemic Rev., 1964-78; contbr. articles to horse publs. Home: RFD 3 Fort Dodge IA 50501 Office: 800 5th St NW Fort Dodge IA 50501

RYAN, WILLIAM SCOTT, pediatrician; b. Emporia, Kans., Nov. 5, 1947; s. Edward Joseph and Helen Louise (Harvey) R.; B.A., U. Kans., 1969; M.D., U. Kans. Sch. Medicine, 1973; m. Vickie Ann Brown, Mar. 15, 1969; children—Jeffrey Scott, Bradley Curtis. Resident in pediatrics Good Samaritan Hosp., Phoenix, 1973-75; practice medicine specializing in gen. pediatrics, Emporia, Kans., 1976—; mem. staffs Newman Meml. Hosp., St. Mary's Hosp.; med. advisor Lyon County Health Dept., Emporia, 1977—; chmn. City-County Joint Bd. Health, Emporia, 1977-80. Diplomate Am. Bd. Pediatrics. Fellow Am. Acad. Pediatrics; mem. Flint Hills Med. Soc. (pres. 1981), AMA, Kans. Med. Soc. Methodist. Club: Rotary. Home: 1626 Trowman Way Emporia KS 66801 Office: 2510 W 15th Emporia KS 66801

RYBARCZYK, ROBERT L., real estate co. exec.; b. Wausau, Wis., Feb. 20, 1938; s. Henry and Helen (Letarski) R.; student Milw. Inst. Tech., 1963, U. Wis.-Stevens Point, 1973, U. Wis.-Marathon County, 1974; m. Gloria Oleson, June 24, 1961; children—Robert, Dawn. Pres., Action Realty, Inc., Schofield, Wis., 1970—; sec.-treas. Real Estate Buyers Inc., Wausau, Wis. Chmn., Marathon County (Wis.) Democratic Com., 1973—; sec. Wis. Dept or Regulation and Licensing, Real Estate Examining Bd., 1976-78; mem. Wis. State Dem. Adminstrv. Com.; chmn. Marathon County Dem. Party, 1981. Served with U.S. Army, 1955-58. Mem. South Area Businessmen's Assn. (pres. 1974), Wausau Bd. Realtors (pres. 1974), Wausau Area C. of C. (past dir.), Nat. Real Estate Bd., Wis. State Real Estate Bd. Methodist. Clubs: Elks, Wausau, Wausau Country. Home: 5211 Arrow St Schofield WI 54476 Office: 928 Grand Ave Schofield WI 54476

RYBARSKI, MICHAEL ANTON, pub. co. exec.; b. Chgo., Apr. 4, 1949; s. Walter Frank and Dorothy Grace (Zak) R.; A.B., Providence Coll., 1971; M.A., U. Chgo., 1972, M.B.A., 1981; m. Margaret M. Keating, Apr. 3, 1971. Asst. editor Scott, Foresman & Co., Glenview, Ill., 1972-74; asso. editor Open Court Pub. Co., La Salle, Ill., 1974-75, dir. planning and ops., 1975-77, asst. gen. mgr., 1977—. Mem. exec. bd. Big Bros., 1969-71; v.p. Providence Film Soc., 1970-71. Mem. Assn. Am. Pubs. (mem. fin. com.). Roman Catholic. Home: 38 Norfolk St Clarendon Hills IL 60514 Office: 1058 8th St La Salle IL 61301

RYBERG, ERICK LEONARD, clin. social worker; b. Detroit, Feb. 16, 1947; s. Leonard Erick and Sophie Mary R.; B.A., U. Mich., 1969, M.S.W., 1972; m. Amy Beth Fox, Dec. 23, 1969. Clin. social worker Downriver Guidance Clinic, Lincoln Park, Mich., 1972-74, dir. emergency psychiat. services, 1974-76; dir. social services Cottage Hosp., Grosse Pointe, Mich., 1976-79; pvt. practice psychotherapy Eastpoint Mental Health Center, P.C., Harper Woods, Mich., 1978—; clin. field instr. U. Mich. Grad. Sch. Social Work, 1974—. Mem. Nat. Assn. Social Workers, Acad. Cert. Social Workers, Am. Orthopsychiat. Assn., Mich. Soc. Clin. Social Work. Home: 30247 Overdale Ct Farmington Hills MI 48018 Office: 19959 Vernier Rd Harper Woods MI 48225

RYCKMAN, MARK DEVERE, environ. systems engr.; b. Lansing, Mich., July 8, 1951; s. DeVere Wellington and Betty Jane (Rendall) R.; B.A. in Math., DePauw U., 1974; B.S. in Civil Engring. with honors, Clemson U., 1974, M.S. in Environ. Systems Engring., 1975; m. Jean Diane Lorch, Aug. 3, 1974; 1 dau., Amanda Jean. Environ. technician St. Louis County Health Dept., summers 1970-71; engr. asst. Ryckman, Edgerley, Tomlinson & Assos., St. Louis, summer 1971; environ. cons. Town Hall, LaPlata, Md., 1971-72; asst. dir. Rome (Italy) operation Ryckman, Edgerley, Tomlinson & Assos., St. Louis, summer 1972; environ. engr. Ryckman, Edgerley, Tomlinson & Assos., St. Louis, summer 1973; research asst. dept. environ. systems engring. Clemson (S.C.) U., 1972-75; environ. engr. Environ. Triple S Co., St. Louis, 1974; v.p. D.W. Ryckman & Assos., Inc., St. Louis, 1975—, v.p., founder Ryckman's Emergency Action and Cons. Team, 1976—; v.p. D.W. Ryckman & Assos., Inc., 1978—. Jr. high youth sponsor Kirk of the Hills Presbyn. Ch., 1976-77; campaign solicitor United Way, 1976-79. Recipient Service award Rough Rock Demonstration Sch., Ariz., 1968; registered profl. engr., S.C., Mo., Ind. Mem. ASCE, Water Pollution Control Fedn., Air Pollution Control Assn., Am. Water Works Assn., Tau Beta Pi, Theta Chi Epsilon. Presbyterian. Clubs: St. Louis DePauw Alumni, Rotary, St. Louis Engrs. Author: Design Manual for Thickening of Biological Sludges in Seconday Settling Tanks, 1975; contbr. papers to confs. and jours. Home: 283 Oak Pass Ct Ballwin MO 63011 Office: 2208 Welsh Indsl Ct PO Box 27310 Saint Louis MO 63141

RYDSTEDT, MARIA LAGERVALL, educator; b. Detroit, Apr. 3, 1944; d. Lars Herman and Lillian (Mazark) Rydstedt; Ph.B., Monteith Coll., Wayne State U., 1965, elem. teaching cert., 1965; M.A., U. Mich., 1976, specialist in edn., 1981; 1 dau., Wendy Maria. Tchr., Fairlane Dist., Dearborn Heights, Mich., 1966-67, Valparaiso (Ind.) Community Schs., 1967-68, Duneland Pub. Schs., Chesterton, Ind., 1968-70, Grand Rapids (Mich.) Public Schs., 1970-72, 74-78, 79—, reading cons., 1974-76; tchr. asso. Social Sci. Edn. Consortium, Boulder, Colo., 1978-79. Mem. Nat. Council for Social Studies, Am. Ednl. Research Assn., NEA, Mich. Edn. Assn., Grand Rapids Edn. Assn., Alpha Gamma Delta. Author: Keeping Up: Looking At...International Education, 1978; Data Book: Social Studies Materials and Resources, vol. 4, vol. 5, 1979; contbr. articles to profl. jours. Address: 917 Lancashire Ct SE Grand Rapids MI 49508

RYHAL, JAMES LAWRENCE, JR., lawyer; b. Cleve., Dec. 24, 1924; s. James Lawrence and Eleta (Hoffman) R.; A.B. magna cum laude, Western Res. U., 1949, J.D., 1952. Admitted to Ohio bar, 1952, since practiced in Cleve.; partner firm Gallagher, Sharp, Fulton, Norman & Mollison, 1970—; lectr. law Cleve. Marshall Coll. Law; sec., dir. Stevenson Oil & Chem. Corp. Trustee, Cleve. Ballet. Served with AUS, 1944-46. Mem. Am., Ohio, Cleve. (chmn. speakers bur. 1960-65) bar assns., Cleve. Coll. Alumni Assn. (pres. 1952-56), Omicron Delta Kappa, Tau Delta Alpha, Phi Soc., Delta Theta Phi. Democrat. Episcopalian. Composer: Prelude in A Flat Minor, 1942. Home: 14724 Clifton Blvd Lakewood OH 44107 Office: 6th Floor Bulkley Bldg 1501 Euclid Ave Cleveland OH 44115

RYMAR, JULIAN W., mfg. co. exec.; b. Grand Rapids, Mich., June 29, 1919; student Grand Rapids Jr. Coll., 1937-39, U. Mich., 1939-41, Wayne U., 1948-52, Rockhurst Coll., 1952-53; m. Margaret Macon Van Brunt, Dec. 11, 1954; children—Margaret Gibson, Gracen Macon, Ann Mackall. Entered USN as aviation cadet, 1942, advanced through grades to capt., 1964; chmn. bd., chief exec. officer, dir. Grace Co., Belton, Mo., 1955—; chmn. bd. dirs. Shock & Vibration Research, Inc., 1956—; chmn. bd., chief exec. officer Bedtime Story Fashions; comdg. officer Naval Air Res. Squadron, 1957-60, staff air bn. comdr., 1960-64. Bd. dirs. Bros. of Mercy, St. Lukes Hosp.; adv. bd. dirs. St. Joseph Hosp.; trustee Missouri Valley Coll., 1969-74. Mem. Mil. Order World Wars, Navy League U.S. (pres. 1959-60, dir. 1960—), Rockhill Homes Assn. (v.p.) Friends of Art (pres., chmn. bd. govs. 1969-70, exec. bd. 1971—), Soc. of Fellows of Nelson Gallery Found. (exec. bd. 1972-77), Sigma Delta Chi. Episcopalian (dir., lay reader, lay chalice, vestryman, sr. warden, diocesan fin. bd., parish investment bd.). Clubs: Press, University of Mich. (Kansas City); Arts (Washington). Home: 1228 W 56th St Kansas City MO 64113 Office: Mill St Belton MO 64012 also 614 W Mill St Belton MO 64012

RYNIAK, GEORGE ALBERT, state ofcl.; b. Chgo., July 17, 1943; s. Chester R. and Jean D. R.; B.A., Ill. Benedictine Coll., 1965; m. Cheryl E. Ulrich, July 14, 1972; children—Keith Jason, Thad Joseph. Enforcement officer Ill. Commerce Commn., 1969-71; hearing officer Office of Sec. of State of Ill., Springfield, 1972-73, asst. dir. drivers license facility, 1974-77, dir. drivers license facility, Midlothian, 1977—. Trustee Village of Chicago Ridge (Ill.), 1975—, chmn. Police Com. Recipient civic service award VFW, Chicago Ridge. Mem. Ill. State Employee's Assn., Polish Nat. Alliance, Chicago Ridge Jr. C. of C. Democrat. Club: 14th Ward Polish. Home: 10800 McVicker St Chicago Ridge IL 60415 Office: 14424 S Pulaski St Midlothian IL 60445

RYTTER, DARREL JOHN, biochemist; b. Kenmare, N.D., Dec. 15, 1944; s. Viggo and Helen Ann (Hanson) R.; B.S. in Chemistry, U. N.D., 1966, M.S., 1969; postgrad. Mich. State U., 1973-75; spl. courses Technicon Ednl. Center, Tarrytown, N.Y., 1975. With quality control dept. Boeing Co., Seattle, 1966; research asst. biochemistry U. N.D., 1969-70; research biochemist Dow Chem. Co., Indpls., 1970-72, Midland, Mich., 1972-77, sr. research biochemist, Indpls., 1977—. Mem. Smithsonian Assos., Sigma Xi. Contbr. articles and abstracts to profl. jours. Home: 19042 N 1025 E Brownsburg IN 46112 Office: Dow Chemical Co PO Box 68511 Indianapolis IN 46268

RYU, JAI HYUN, scientist, educator; b. Ham-nam, Korea, Oct. 27, 1940; s. Chang Yul and Byung Sun (Park) R.; came to U.S., 1960, naturalized, 1973; B.S.E. in Aerospace Engring., U. Mich., 1966, M.S.E. in Bio-Mech. Engring., 1972; Ph.D. in Bio-Systems Engring., U. Iowa, 1979; m. Jacqueline Ellen Brisbin, June 16, 1973; children—Juliette Jaie, Jessica Jaie, Jennifer Jaie. Research asst. dept. otorhinolaryngology U. Mich., 1961-66; asso. research scientist dept. otolaryngology U. Iowa, 1966-74, research scientist, 1974-80, dir. vestibular research labs., 1974-80, asso. prof., dir. research, 1980—. Mem. Barany Soc., AIAA, Aerospace Med. Assn., Soc. Neurosci., Bioengring. Soc., Sigma Xi. Author: The Vestibular System, 1975; Vestibular Physiology in Understanding the Dizzy Patient, 1980; contbr. articles to profl. jours. Home: 1840 Kathlin Dr Iowa City IA 52240 Office: Med Research Center U Iowa Iowa City IA 52242

RZEMINSKI, PETER JOSEPH, personnel adminstr.; b. Chgo., Apr. 19, 1947; s. Casmir Stanley and Bertha Emma (Rudisill) R.; B.S., U. Ill., 1973; M.B.A., De Paul U., 1976; grad. U.S. Army Command and Gen. Staff Coll., 1981; m. Dorothy Morowczynski, Jan. 10, 1970; children—Peter Joseph II, Stacey Bobbe. Asst. dir. personnel St. Francis Hosp., Blue Island, Ill., 1974-78, asso. dir. personnel, 1979-80, dir. personnel, 1980— mem. Sauk Area Career Center Advisory Com., 1974-77, chmn. med. office program, 1980—. Served with U.S. Army, 1967-72, to maj. USAR, 1972—. Decorated D.F.C., Bronze Star, Air medal (22), Army Commendation medal, Purple Heart, Vietnam Cross of Gallantry with Palm, others. Mem. Southwest Area Hosp. Personnel Dirs. Assn. (sec. 1975-76, treas. 1979-80), Ill. Soc. Human Resource Adminstrn. in Health Care, Chgo. Hosp. Personnel Mgmt. Assn. (sec. 1976-77, chmn. survey com. 1980—), Am. Soc. for Personnel Adminstrn. (accredited), Young Adminstrs. Chgo. (program com. 1978), Res. Officers Assn. (sec. 1977-79), Am. Soc. Hosp. Personnel Adminstrs., Sisters of St. Mary Personnel Dirs. Assn., Hosp. Mgmt. Systems Soc., Interallied Confedn. Res. Officers, Chgo. Health Execs. Forum, 101st Airborne Div. Assn., Tippers Internat. Roman Catholic. Home: 13417 Medina Dr Orland Park IL 60462 Office: 12935 S Gregory St Blue Island IL 60406

SABALLUS, DONALD ERWIN, orgnl. devel./tng. cons. co. exec.; b. Chgo., Apr. 11, 1938; s. Erwin James and Madeline Hellen S.; B.A., DePaul U., 1961, M.A., 1963; postgrad. Ill. Inst. Tech., 1966; m. Susan Brown, June 3, 1977; children—Martin, Katy, Stacy, Donna, Tom. Human factors research ITT, Chgo., 1961-66; ind. cons. orgnl. devel., motivation devel. Motorola Inc., Schaumburg, Ill., 1966-71; researcher treatment evaluation Forest Hosp., Des Plaines, Ill., 1971-72; cons. communications Wilding div. Bell & Howell, Chgo., 1972-76; owner, prin. cons. specialist D.E. Saballus Assos., Winnetka, Ill., 1976—; lectr. in field. Bd. dirs. Winnetka Community Theatre-Children's Theatre. Mem. Am. Mgmt. Assn., Chgo. Sales Tng. Assn., Soc. for Advancement Mgmt., Internat. Work Simplification Inst. Clubs: Winnetka Yacht (dir.), Winnetka Tennis, Cherokee Village Country. Inventor computerized operant conditioning apparatus, sequentially dependent problem-solving equipment. Home: 571 Orchard Ln Winnetka IL 60093 Office: 807 Rosewood Ave Winnetka IL 60093

SABATINO, ANTHONY CARMEN, ins. co. exec.; b. Chgo., June 22, 1930; s. Russell Anthony and Isabel Fradinardo S.; B.S. in Accounting, Walton Sch. Commerce, 1968; m. Dolores M. Rito, May 5, 1951; children—Paul, Susan, Pamela. Office mgr., accountant Elgin Gravure Service (Ill.), 1956-57; sr. accountant Edward J. Hutchens, C.P.A., Chgo., 1957-69; treas. Casualty Ins. Co., Chgo., 1969—; treas. CIC Fin. Corp., Chgo., 1971—, asst. sec., 1978—; sec.-treas., dir. Walensa Direct Mail, Inc.; dir., treas. CIC Acceptance Corp., Walro Shoes Inc. Trustee, Lawrence Hall Sch. for Boys. Served with U.S. Army, 1951-53; ETO. Mem. Am. Accounting Assn., Ins. Accounting and Statis. Assn., Adminstrv. Mgmt. Soc., Am. Mgmt. Assn. Moose. Clubs: North Riverside (Ill.) Sportsman's (pres. 1970-71), Columbian (sec.). Home: 2225 S Burr Oak Ave North Riverside IL 60546 Office: 323 N Michigan Ave Chicago IL 60601

SABBAGH, HAROLD ABRAHAM, research engr.; b. Lafayette, Ind., Jan. 9, 1937; s. Elias Morshed and Waded Katharine (Corey) S.; B.S. in E.E., Purdue U., 1958, M.S. in E.E., 1958, Ph.D., 1964; m. Sandra Claire Abookire, June 18, 1966; children—Elias Harold, Kahlil George, Amira Ann. Prof. elec. engring. and physics Rose-Hulman Inst. Tech., Terre Haute, Ind., 1964-73; research engr. Naval Weapons Support Center, Crane, Ind., 1973-80; pres. Analytics, Inc., Bloomington, Ind., 1979—. Served with USN, 1958-61. NASA/Am. Soc. Engring. Edn. summer faculty fellow, 1965, 66. Mem. IEEE, Sigma Xi, Tau Beta Pi, Eta Kappa Nu, Sigma Pi Sigma, Pi Mu Epsilon, Phi Eta Sigma. Mem. Antiochian Orthodox Ch. Club: Masons. Editor: IEEE Council Oceanic Engring. Newsletter, 1978—; research in underwater acoustics, structural dynamics, electromagnetics, electroacoustics, computer modeling. Home: 2634 Round Hill Ln Bloomington IN 47401

SABBANN, ROBERT BRUCE, podiatrist; b. Monona, Iowa, Aug. 12, 1925; s. Ewald and Hilma M. (Klinge) S.; student Wartburg Coll., 1946-47; D.P.M. cum laude, Ill. Coll. Podiatric Medicine, 1951; m. Jean Pederson, Oct. 28, 1960; children—Mark, Kimberly, Michael, Bruce, Heidi. Pvt. practice podiatry, Red Wing, Minn., 1951-53, Rochester, Minn., 1953—; staff Olmsted Community Hosp., Rochester, 1962—; lectr. in field. Served with USN, 1943-46. Diplomate Am. Bd. Podiatric Surgery. Fellow Am. Coll. Foot Surgeons; mem. Minn. Hosp. Podiatrists (pres. 1971-81), Minn. Podiatry Assn. (pres. 1966-67). Republican. Lutheran. Clubs: Ducks Unltd. (nat. trustee 1981), Am. Kennel (lic. judge), Kiwanis (pres. 1966, dist. lt. gov. 1967). Contbr. articles to profl. jours. Home: 1823 18 1/2 NW Rochester MN 55901 Office: 915 3rd Ave SE Rochester MN 55901

SABIO, MORADA AQUIAS, anesthesiologist; b. Philippines, Apr. 21, 1934; d. Juan Tadeo and Mercedes (Balbuena) Aquias; student Manila Central U., 1950; M.D., U. Santo Tomas, 1957; m. Andres R. Sabio, June 4, 1959; children—John, Marguerite, Elaine, Andrew, Christine, Neysa, Morada, Victoria. Intern, Kanawha Valley Hosp., Charleston, W.Va.; resident in anesthesiology Marymount Hosp., Cleve., 1961-64; staff anesthesiologist Forest City Hosp., Cleve., 1964-75; chief anesthesia dept. Shaker Med. Center, Hosp., Cleve., 1976-77, now mem. staff; staff anesthesiologist Marymount Hosp., Garfield Heights, Ohio, 1978—; pres. Parkwood Anesthesia Group, Cleve., 1978—. Mem. Assn. Philippine Physicians Ohio (bd. govs. 1976—), Womens Aux. Assn. Philippine Practicing Physicians Am. (treas. 1977-78), Philippine Am. Soc. Ohio Womens Aux. (treas., 1976-78, pres. 1978-80), Am., Ohio, Cleve. socs. anesthesiologists, AMA, Philippine Am. Soc. (pres. women's aux. 1978—), Ohio Med. Assn., Cleve. Acad. Medicine, Internat. Anesthesia Research Soc. Republican. Roman Catholic. Home: 6900 Norvale Circle W Gates Mills OH 44040 Office: 11710 Shaker Blvd Cleveland OH 44120

SABO, JOHN BENJAMIN, pharmacist; b. Herminie, Pa., Nov. 11, 1927; s. Julius Louis and Lottie Belle (Eckenrod) S.; B.S. in Pharmacy, Purdue U., 1950; m. Helen Marie Calhoun, June 30, 1951; children—Cynthia Jean, Michael John. Mgr., Hook's Drugs, Gary, Ind., 1950-53; pharmacist Black Oak Pharmacy, Gary, 1953-58; owner Park Plaza Pharmacy, Merrillville, Ind., 1958-62; mem. staff Methodist Hosp., Gary, 1962-81, chief pharmacist, 1968-69, dir. pharmacy, 1969-75, dir. pharmacy services, 1975-81; dir. pharmacy services Broadway Meth. Hosp., Merrillville, 1975-81; pharmacy staff Our Lady of Mercy Hosp., Dyer, Ind., 1981—; cons. Norwich Lab., Eaton Lab.; clin. instr. Purdue U. Sch. Pharmacy. Served with USNR, 1945-46. Recipient service and recognition awards. Mem. Am. Soc. Hosp. Pharmacists, Ind. Soc. Hosp. Pharmacists (pres. 1968-69). Methodist. Home: 1830 Dale Dr Merrillville IN 46410

SABROSKY, DON EDWARD, state records ofcl.; b. Lansing, Mich., July 29, 1928; s. Edward F. and Lila E. (Case) B.S., Mich. State U., 1952; m. Beverly I. Piper, Jan. 14, 1946; children—Jill, Lore,

Kimberly. Prodn. foreman Oldsmobile Co., Lansing, 1954-55; asst. registrar Mich. State U., East Lansing, 1956-65; records mgr. State of Mich. Dept. Mgmt. and Budget, Lansing, 1966—; mgr. Mgmt. Info. Systems, 1966—. Served with USN, 1946-48. cert. Inst. Cert. Records Mgrs. Mem. Assn. Records Mgrs. and Adminstrs. (chpt. pres. 1975-76, Chpt. Mem. of Yr., 1977), Pi Kappa Phi (adv. 1958-62). Club: Mich. State Univ. Faculty. Author: Paperwork Management Microfilm Handbook, 1977, Office File Equipment Guide, 1978. Home: 1230 N Magnolia St Lansing MI 48912 Office: Dept Mgmt and Budget State of Mich PO Box 30026 Lansing MI 48909

SACCOMANNO, LOUISE ANN, retail co. advt. exec.; b. Chgo., Oct. 20, 1948; d. Guy G. and Mary (Casali) S.; B.A. in English, U. Dayton, 1970; postgrad. Northwestern U., 1971-72. Asst. copy chief Goldblatt's, Chgo., 1970-74; sr. writer Standard Rate & Data Service, Skokie, Ill., 1974-76; creative planner Enterprise Cos., Wheeling, Ill., 1976-78; pres., owner LS & Co., Dallas, 1978-79; advt. dir. McDade & Co., Carol Stream, Ill., 1979—. Mem. Jr. Women's Advt. Club Chgo.

SACHS, HERBERT L., educator, counselor, psychologist; b. Chgo., May 1; s. Morris and Esther (Ross) S.; B.Sc., Roosevelt U., Chgo., 1949; M.A. in Psychology, Loyola U., Chgo., 1951, M.Ed., 1953; postgrad. DePaul U., Northeastern Ill. U., Gov.'s State U.; m. Renee Goldfarb, Aug. 14, 1949; children—Michael, Kerry, Richard. Asst. prin., prin. Chgo. Public Schs., 1955-66; prof. psychology and counseling Truman Coll., City Colls. Chgo., 1965—, chmn. dept. social sci., 1970—; psychol. cons., pvt. clinician, lectr. Mem. Am., Midwestern, Ill. psychol. assns., AAUP, Am. Personnel and Guidance Assn., Ill. Personnel and Guidance Assn. Clubs: B'nai B'rith; George Howland Prins., Chgo. Prins. Author: Student Projects in Child Psychology, 1967; Dynamic General Psychology: An Introduction, 1971; Student Workbook to Accompany Dynamic General Psychology: An Introduction, 1971; Dynamic Personal Adjustment, 1974; Every Parent is a Tutor, 1982. Contbr. articles to profl. jours. Office: Social Scis Dept Harry S Truman Coll City Colls Chgo 1645 W Wilson Ave Chicago IL 60640

SACHS, MARJORIE BELL, vocat./ednl. counselor; b. Cleve., Aug. 16, 1926; d. Julius Mark and Molly Evelyn (Hascal) Bell; B.A., Western Res. U., 1948; M.Ed., Cleve. State U., 1975, cert. rehab. counselor, 1979; m. Sidney H. Sachs, Feb. 25, 1950; children—Wendie Elizabeth, Peter Bell. Research asso. Urban Reports Corp., Cleve., 1973-75; counselor Preterm Clinic, Cleve., 1974-76, Jewish Vocat. Service, Cleve., 1975-76, Resource, Cleve., 1975-76; vocat./ednl. counselor At-Home Rehab. project, The Cancer Center, Inc., Cleve., 1976-79, project dir. At-Home Rehab. Program, U. Hosps. Cancer Center, Cleve., 1979-80; dir. community services Jewish Community Center, 1980—. Undergrad. admission adviser Case Western Res. U., 1973—, mem. vis. com. of bd. overseers Sch. of Dentistry, 1977—. Bd. dirs. Mt. Sinai Med. Center Aux., 1950—. Mem. Am. Personnel and Guidance Assn., Nat. Rehab. Assn. Home: 3706 Sutherland Rd Shaker Heights OH 44122 Office: Jewish Community Center 3505 Mayfield Rd Cleveland Heights OH 44118

SACHS, ROBERT GREEN, physicist, educator, lab. adminstr.; b. Hagerstown, Md., May 4, 1916; s. Harry Maurice and Anna (Green) S.; Ph.D., Johns Hopkins U., 1939; D.Sc. (hon.), Purdue U., 1967, U. Ill., 1977; m. Selma Solomon, Aug. 28, 1941; m. 2d, Jean K. Woolf, Dec. 17, 1950; children—Rebecca, Jennifer, Jeffrey, Judith, Joel; m. 3d, Carolyn L. Wolf, Aug. 21, 1968; stepchildren—Thomas Wolf, Jacqueline Wolf, Katherine Wolf. Served as research fellow George Washington U., 1939-41; instr. physics Purdue U., 1941-43; on leave as lectr., research fellow U. Calif. at Berkeley, 1941; sect. chief Ballistic Research Lab., Aberdeen (Md.) Proving Ground, 1943-46; dir. theoretical physics div. Argonne Nat. Lab., 1946-47; asso. prof. physics U. Wis., 1947-48, prof., 1948-64; asso. dir. Argonne Nat. Lab., 1964-68; prof. physics U. Chgo., 1964—, dir. Enrico Fermi Inst. of U. Chgo., 1968-73; dir. Argonne Nat. Lab., 1973-78; Higgins vis. prof. Princeton U., 1955-56; vis. prof. U. Paris, 1959-60, Tohoku U., Japan, 1974; cons. Ballistic Research Labs., 1945-59, Argonne Nat. Lab., 1947-50, 60-64, radiation lab. U. Calif. at Berkeley, 1955-59; adv. panel physics NSF, 1958-61; mem. physics survey com., chmn. elem. particle physics panel Nat. Acad. Scis., 1969-72; high energy physics adv. panel div. research AEC, 1966-69; mem. steering com. A Five Yr. Outlook on Sci. and Tech., Nat. Acad. Scis., 1979. Research in theoretical nuclear and atomic physics, terminal ballistics, nuclear power reactors, theoretical particle physics. Guggenheim fellow, 1959-60. Fellow Am. Acad. Arts and Scis. (v.p., chmn. Midwest Center 1980—); mem. Nat. Acad. Scis. (chmn. physics sect. 1977-80, chmn. Class I math. and phys. scis. 1981—), Am. Phys. Soc. (council 1968-71, regional sec. Central States 1964-69), AAAS (v.p., chmn. physics sect. 1970-71), Am. Inst. Physics (mem. governing bd. 1969-71), Phi Beta Kappa, Sigma Xi. Author: Nuclear Theory, 1953. Chief editor: High Energy Nuclear Physics, 1957; editor: National Energy Issues: How Do We Decide?, 1979. Home: 5490 South Shore Dr Chicago IL 60615 Office: Enrico Fermi Inst U Chgo 5630 Ellis Ave Chicago IL 60637

SACHS, SAMUEL, mech. and elec. engr.; b. Chgo., Aug. 14, 1917; s. Benjamin and Gertrude (Soloducho) S.; student Wright Jr. Coll., 1934-36; B.S., U. Ill., 1939, M.S., 1942; m. Rita Chilow, Feb. 8, 1942; children—Barbara (Mrs. Charles Allen Linn), Laurie Ellen. With Skidmore, Owings & Merrill, Chgo., 1947—, asso. partner, 1955—, dir. of design, 1972—, sr. cons., 1979—; trustee dept. mech. and indsl. engrng. U. Ill.; vice pres. Automated Procedures for Engrng. Mem. Winnetka Caucus Com., 1964-65; mem. exec. bd. Anti-Defamation League, Chgo., 1969-77. Served with AUS, 1943-45. Named Distinguished Alumnus, Dept. Mech. and Indsl. Engrng., U. Ill., 1972. Fellow Am. Soc. Heating, Refrigerating and Air Conditioning Engrs.; mem. Nat. Soc. Fire Prevention Engrs., Nat. Soc. Profl. Engrs., Solar Energy Industries Assn., Art Inst. Chgo., Brain Research Found. Club: Standard. Engring. design projects include USAF, Colorado Springs, 1958, U. Ill. Chgo., 1965, 60" Solar Telescope, Kitt Peak Ariz., 1961, 150" Stellar Telescopes, Kitt Peak A and Cerro Tololo, Chile, 1972, Chgo. Civic Center, 1968. Home: 860 Burr Ave Winnetka IL 60093 Office: 33 W Monroe St Chicago IL 60603

SACHTLEBEN, BETTY JUNE, social worker; b. Centralia, Ill., Oct. 29, 1929; d. William Charles and Nellie Josephine (Winstead) Sissom; B.S., Washington U., 1962, M.S.W., 1966; m. Roland Sachtleben, Feb. 9, 1951; children—Stewart Gary, Cynthia Barbara, Sherwood Roland, Sanford Stanley, Kristin Charles. Psychiat. social worker Malcolm Bliss Mental Health Center, St. Louis, 1966-67; with div. pupil personnel St. Louis Public Schs., 1967-68; supr. social service dept. Parkway Sch. Dist., Chesterfield, Mo., 1969-72; social worker Family and Childrens Service, St. Louis, 1972-73; pvt. practice psychiat. social work, St. Louis, 1973-75; exec. dir. Mo. Counseling Service, Bridgeton, Mo., 1975-81; exec. dir. REACH, St. Louis, 1981—; adj. asst. prof. St. Louis U.; instr. Washington U. Bd. dirs. New Hope Found. for Retarded Children, 1972-73; dir., sec. Sunshine Found., 1973—; dir. Parents Without Partners, 1975—. Mem. Nat. Assn. Social Workers, Am. Assn. Marriage and Family Therapists. Lutheran. Home: 12669 Northwinds Dr Creve Coeur MO 63141 Office: PO Box 24546 Saint Louis MO 63141

SACK, RICHARD HENRY, publishing co. exec.; b. Chgo., Sept. 4, 1945; s. Herman A. and Mathilde (Gleass) S.; B.S. in Bus. Adminstrn., Roosevelt U., 1969; m. Kathleen F. Sack; children—Jane Margaret, Christopher John. Account exec. Campbel Mithun Advt. Co., Chgo., 1969-71; regional sales mgr. Outdoor Life Mag., Chgo., 1971-78; Chgo. mgr. Road and Track Mag., Chgo., 1978—; with NBC Radio Network, 1980—. Mem. Bd. Edn. Community Consol. Dist. #54, Schaumburg, Ill. Mem. Mag. Publs. Assn., Elk Grove Jaycees, Pi Sigma Epsilon. Methodist. Office: 303 E Ohio St Chicago IL 60611

SACKETT, LOIS MARILYN, med. clinic adminstr.; b. Kearney, Nebr., Apr. 23, 1939; d. Donald Reuben and Emma Leila (Duehn) Roker; R.N., Bryan Sch. Nursing, 1962; B.S., Westmar Coll., 1963; m. James Stanley Sackett, Mar. 28, 1964; children—Ashlyn Rae, Cheryl Lynn. Asst. supr. Bryan Meml. Hosp., Lincoln Nebr., 1963-65, 67-68, area dir., 1970-73; staff nurse Kearney (Nebr.) Clinic, 1966-67; office mgr. Internal Medicine Specialties, Lincoln, 1975—. Mem. Nebr. Med. Group Mgmt. Assn. (sec.-treas. 1976-78, v.p. 1978-79), Med. Group Mgmt. Assn. Home: 6700 Rexford Dr Lincoln NE 68506 Office: 2121 S 56th St Lincoln NE 68506

SACKS, GLORIA, interior designer; b. Chgo., May 4, 1931; d. Melvin Drachler and Dorothy (Pikowsky) Drachler Karlin; adopted dau. of Jules Karlin; student Wilson Jr. Coll., 1949-50; U. Ill., 1950-51; B.A., Sch. Art Inst. Chgo., 1956; m. Seymour Sacks, June 13, 1954; children—Paul, Jerrold, William, Joseph. Interior designer Royal Metal Mfg. Co., 1953-54; designer tie-dyed silk fabric Marshall Field & Co., 1972-76; mem. faculty dept. interior design Prairie State Coll., 1972-79; prin. Designs On Tomorrow, Chgo., 1972—. Sec., South Shore Valley Assn., 1968; program chairwoman Zahava group Chgo. chpt. Hadassah, Flossmoor, Ill., 1974-76, pres., 1977-79. Address: 1212 N Lake Shore Dr Chicago IL 60610

SADD, JOHN ROSWELL, plastic surgeon; b. Chgo., Apr. 18, 1933; s. Sumner Harry and Louise Elizabeth (Beardsley) S.; B.S., Purdue U., 1955; M.D., U. Rochester, 1959; m. Valerie Crim Lavery, June 23, 1956; children—Elizabeth, Katherine, Virginia, Dorothy. Intern, U. Wis., Madison, 1959-60, resident in plastic surgery, 1960-62, 64-67; practice medicine specializing in plastic surgery, Toledo, 1967—; chmn. dept. surgery Toledo (Ohio) Hosp., 1973—; asst. clin. prof. surgery Med. Coll. Ohio. Diplomate Am. Bd. Plastic Surgery. Fellow A.C.S.; mem. Ohio Med. Soc. (del.), Toledo Surg. Soc. (pres. 1975), SAR. Republican. Contbr. articles to med. jours. Office: 3939 Monroe St Toledo OH 43606

SADEK, SALAH EDLINE, pathologist; b. Cairo, Egypt, June 9, 1920; s. Ahmad A. and Zienab (Zahran) S.; D.V.M., U. Cairo, 1945; M.R.C.V.S., U. Edinburgh, 1948; M.S., Mich. State U., 1950; Ph.D., U. Ill., 1956; m. Helen Ann Phoenix, Apr. 12, 1952; children—Craig, Ramsay, Mark. Asst. prof. U. Cairo, 1945-48; asst. U. Ill., Urbana, 1953-55; pathologist Dow Chem. Co., Midland, Mich., 1956-67; head of pathology Hoffmann La Roche, Nutley, N.J., 1967—; clin. prof. pathology N.J. Coll. Medicine and Dentistry, Newark. Pres., Midland County Humane Soc., 1965-67. Diplomate Am. Bd. Indsl. Hygiene. Mem. Am. Vet. Med. Assn., N.Y. Acad. Sci., British Vet. Assn., Royal Coll. Veterinary Surgeons, Mich. Soc. Pathologists, N.Y. Pathol. Soc., Soc. Toxicology, Soc. Toxicologic Pathologists, Am. Acad. Indsl. Hygiene. Research in exptl. pathology and toxicology. Club: Midland Country. Home: 3910 Valley Dr Midland MI 48640 Office: Hoffmann La Roche Nutley NJ 07110

SADOVE, MAX SAMUEL, anesthesiologist; b. Balt., Mar. 8, 1914; s. Harry and Rebecca (Must) S.; B.S., Balt. City Coll., 1932; Pharm. B., U. Md., 1935, M.D., 1939; m. Ethel Segall, Apr. 6, 1941; children—Ellen Rose, Alan Michael, Richard Craig. Intern, St. Agnes Hosp., Balt., 1939-40; resident in anesthesiology Hines (Ill.) VA Hosp., 1946-47; dir. anesthesiology U. Ill. Med. Sch., Chgo., 1947-71, prof. anesthesiology, 1951-71, chmn. dept., 1949-71; head dept. U. Ill. Research and Ednl. Hosps., 1950-71; dir. anesthesiology West Side VA Hosp., Chgo., 1954-71, cons., 1971; dir. dept. Hines VA Hosp., 1954-71, cons., 1971—; prof. anesthesiology Rush Med. Coll., Chgo., 1971-81; chmn. dept. Presbyn.-St. Luke's Hosp., 1971-81; prof. anesthesiology, chmn. emeritus Rush-Presbyn. Med. Center, 1981—; adv. bd. Chgo. Narcotic Rehab. and Research Center; adv. Med. Council Civil Def., Chgo. Bd. Health; lectr. Gt. Lakes Naval Hosp., Somner Meml. lectr., 1963; hon. chmn. dept. anesthesia Coll. Medicine, U. Philippines, 1957—; cons. numerous area hosps. Mem. Oak Park (Ill.) Bd. Edn., 1962-66. Served to capt. M.C., AUS, 1941-46. Recipient award in anesthesiology U. Chgo., 1980; diplomate Am. Bd. Anesthesiologists. Fellow AAAS, Hines Surg. Assn., Soc. U. Profs., Am. Geriatrics Soc., Am. Soc. Anesthesiologists (chmn. subcom. motion pictures 1958-60), Am. Soc. Clin. Pharmacology and Chemotherapy; mem. Soc. Med. Cons. to Armed Forces, Internat. Coll. Surgeons (vice regent, chmn. U.S. anesthesiology sect. 1981), Chgo. Soc. Anesthesiologists (pres. 1950-51), Walter Reed Soc. (pres. 1954), Am. Soc. Inhalation Therapists (bd. govs., adv. bd. 1956-57), Am. Coll. Chest Physicians (chmn. sect. resuscitation 1957-59), Am. Fedn. Clin. Research, AMA, Ill. Med. Soc., Chgo. Med. Soc., Ill. Soc. Anesthesiologists (pres. 1963-64, 68-69), Warren H. Cole Soc., Soc. Med. History Chgo., Ill. Soc. Med. Research, Inst. Medicine Chgo., Am. Med. Authors, Am. Dental Soc. Anesthesiologists (hon.), Hollywood (Calif.) Acad. Medicine, Flint (Mich.) Acad. Medicine, Sigma Xi; corr. fellow Soc. Mexican Anesthesiology. Co-author: Recovery Room, 1956; Cardiovascular Collapse in the Operating Room, 1958; Halothane, 1962; Electroencephalography for Anesthesiologists and Surgeons, 1967; contbr. articles to med. jours., chpts. to books; cons. editor med. jours. Home: 1021 Lathrop Ave River Forest IL 60305 Office: 1753 W Congress Pkwy Chicago IL 60612

SAEGER, ARTHUR WILLIAM, real estate appraiser; b. St. Louis, Nov. 4, 1943; s. Kenneth Lloyd and Ethel Catherine (Donnelley) S.; B.S. in Bus. Adminstrn., Ind. U., 1972; m. Kathleen Anne Mathis, Aug. 17, 1968; children—Ashlie Anne, Heather Anne. Dir. adminstrn. mktg. dept. State Life Ins. Co., Indpls., 1968-71; with Fletcher Savs. and Loan Assn., Indpls., 1972-79, corp. officer, head mortgage loan ops., 1976-79; pvt. practice real estate appraising, Indpls., 1979—. Mem. Soc. Real Estate Appraisers, Republican. Roman Catholic. Clubs: Indpls. Sailing, Internat. Yacht Racing Union. Home: 8470 North Park Ave Indianapolis IN 46240 Office: 10000 Allisonville Rd Indianapolis IN 46220

SAENT-JOHNS, GERALDINE MCCORMICK, painter, miniaturist, sculptor; b. Montreal, Que., Can., Sept. 12, 1930; d. Alexander Gerald Makohoniac and Anne (Lubkowski) McCormick; came to U.S., 1952, naturalized, 1965; student McGill U., 1948-49. Artist, Ohio Bell Telephone Co., 1962-65; comml. tech. artist Jayme Orgn., 1965-69; freelance artist, 1969—; owner, operator Eden Mood Studios 1973—; lectr. animals in art; miniature painting on gemstone rep. in collection of 8th Duke of Wellington, Pres. and Mrs. Gerald Ford. Mem. Audubon Soc., East African Wild Life Soc. (pres. Ohio area chpt.), Nat. Wildlife Fedn., Aircraft Owners and Pilots Assn., Canadian Nature Fedn. Republican. Home: 4800 Lander Rd Orange Village OH 44022

SAGE, HAROLD EDWARD, auto center mgr.; b. Council Bluffs, Iowa, Jan. 27, 1932; s. Clyde Edward and Clara (Bock) S.; B.S. in Bus., U. Omaha, 1954; m. Betty Lou Coleman, Dec. 31, 1957; children—Scott, Kurt, Brett. With Sears Roebuck and Co., 1957—, mgmt. trainee, Omaha, 1957, div. mgr. men's furnishings, 1958-62, soft lines mdse. mgr., Belleview, Nebr., 1962-64, asst. mgr., Belleview, 1964, asst. mgr. Council Bluffs, Iowa, 1965, asst. mgr. St. Joseph, Mo., 1966-68, service mgr., Hutchinson, Kans., 1969-70, Springdale, Ark., 1971, auto center mgr., Omaha, 1972—. Scoutmaster troop 404 Covered Wagon council Boy Scouts Am., Omaha, 1975-76; mem. U. Omaha Alumni Council, 1959-60; pres. PTA, Ralston, Nebr., 1965, St. Joseph, 1967; exec. dir. drum corps Omaha Boys Club, 1976; mem. parents adv. council Westside High Sch., Omaha, 1975-80. Served to capt. USAF, 1954-57. Named Omaha Businessman of Day, 1965. Republican. Methodist. Home: 529 S 90th St Omaha NE 68114 Office: 7424 Dodge St Omaha NE 68114

SAGE, JOHN BERNARD, educator; b. Janesville, Wis., July 6, 1952; s. John F. and Virginia A. (Kasmarek) S.; B.S., U. Wis., 1974; M.A. in Edn., Ball State U., 1975; m. Jean A. Blumreich, May 14, 1977; children—William P., Paul J. Grad. asst. Ball State U., Muncie, Ind., 1974-75; tchr. Wisconsin Heights High Sch., Mazomanie, Wis., 1975-77; instr. Madison Area Tech. Coll., Watertown, Wis., 1977—. Pres., Village of Clyman (Wis.), 1979-81. Mem. Am. Vocat. Assn., Wis. Indsl. Edn. Assn. Home: PO Box 71 824 Main St Clyman WI 53016 Office: 1300 W Main St Watertown WI 53094

SAGE, MYRON ALVIN, heavy constrn. co. exec.; b. Cardington, Ohio, July 8, 1920; s. Walter J. and Inez (Caris) S.; student Marion Bus. Coll., 1939; m. Vivian Gaynell; children—Judith Ann Addis, Michael Allen, Cynthia Lynn Sage McCleese, James, Pamela Baumgarner. With Gledhill Road Machinery Co., Galion, Ohio, 1939-59, v.p., 1955-59; founder, pres. Iberia (Ohio) Earthmoving Service, Inc., 1950—; founder, sec.-treas. Cliffshire Estates, Inc., Galion, 1960—; founder, pres. Iberia Mining Corp., 1965—, Mylan Co., Iberia, 1965—, Sagler Realty Co., Iberia, 1966—; pres. Earthworm Constrn. Co.; founder, sec.-treas. Saber Equipment Corp.; dir. Peoples Bank, Mt. Gilead, Ohio. Pres., SSS Draft Bd., Mt. Gilead, 1952-70; bd. dirs. Harding Area council Boy Scouts Am., Galion Community Hosp.; adv. council Ohio State U., Marion. Served as staff sgt. AUS, World War II; ETO. Decorated Bronze Star. Named Ohio commodore. Mem. Ohio Contractors Assn. (dir.), Internat. Brotherhood of Magicians. Club: Masons (32 deg.). Home: Iberia OH 43325 Office: Iberia OH 43325

SAGE, ROBERT FLOYD, found. exec.; b. Battle Creek, Mich., Dec. 15; s. Charles Floyd and Effa Laurinda (Mooney) S.; student pub. schs., Hillsdale, Mich.; L.H.D. (hon.), Siena Heights Coll., 1973; m. Genevieve Ray Phillips, Nov. 30, 1946; children—Melissa Jane Sage Booth, Anne Elizabeth. Various positions in labor, 1933-42, 46-58; profl. pilot, owner-operator fixed base operation, Marion, Ohio, 1958-68; v.p., dir. Guest House Inc., Lake Orion, Mich., 1968-76, dir., 1963—; pres. Sage Found., Detroit, 1962—; trustee, chmn. student affairs com. Siena Heights Coll., Adrian, Mich., 1969—. Bd. dirs. Catholic Social Service, Adrian, 1976-79; mem. Franklyn Two. (Mich.) Planning Commn., 1976-78; mem. Congressman Dave Stockman's Indsl. Adv. Com., 1977-81; chmn. com. alcohol studies Mercy Coll., Detroit, 1977, trustee, 1974—; bd. assos. Adrian (Mich.) Coll., 1979; bd. visitors Mich. Cancer Found., 1979—. Served with USAAF, 1942-46. Recipient Lenawee County Citizen of Yr. award, 1979, Disting. Achievement award Hope Coll., 1979, cert. of recognition Nat. Aborist Assn., 1979, leadership award Cath. Charities, Diocese of Lansing (Mich.); (with Genevieve Sage) Works of Mercy medallion Mercy Coll., Detroit, 1980, President's Cabinet award Siena Heights Coll., Adrian, Mich., 1981; named to Order of Owl, Regis High Sch., N.Y.C., 1978. Republican. Roman Catholic. Office: 2500 Detroit Bank & Trust Bldg Detroit MI. *Be comfortable with yourself and you will be comfortable with most people and on most occasions.*

SAGER, DONALD JACK, library exec.; b. Milw., Mar. 3, 19 38; s. Alfred Herman and Sophia (Sagan) S.; B.S., U. Wis., Milw., 1963; M.S. L.S., U. Wis., Madison, 1964; m. Irene Lynn Sleeth, June 28, 1969. Sr. documentalist AC Electronics div. Gen. Motors Corp., Milw., 1958-63; teaching asst. U. Wis., 1963-64; dir. Kingston (N.Y.) Pub. Library, 1964-66, Elyria (Ohio) Pub. Library, 1966-71, Mobile (Ala.) Pub. Library, 1971-75, Pub. Library of Columbus and Franklin County (Ohio), 1975-78; commr. Chgo. Pub. Library, 1978-81; vis. scholar Online Computer Library Center, Dublin, Ohio, 1981—; bd. dirs. Ill. Regional Library Council, 1978-81, Chgo. Met. History Fair, 1981; mem. adv. council Ill. State Library, 1979—; instr. U. Ala. Grad. Library Sch., summer 1974; bd. dirs., sec. Ohio Coll. Library Center, 1976-78. Chmn., Columbus Area CATV Commn., 1976-78, Chgo. Ednl. and Cultural CATV Consortium, 1981—; bd. dirs. Options, Adult Edn. of Met. Columbus, 1977-78, Edgebrook Community Ch.; mem. Mus. Contemporary Art, Internat. Visitors Center, Balzekas Mus. Mem. Am. (chmn. legis. assembly 1980-81), Ill., Public (dir., chmn. legis. com. 1980-81, pres.-elect 1981—) library assns., Chgo. Library Club, Am. Soc. Public Adminstrn., Info. Sci. and Automation Assn. Club: Rotary. Author: Reference: A Programmed Instruction, 1970; Binders, Books and Budgets, 1971; Participatory Management, 1981; contbr. articles to profl. jours. Home: 6964 N Tonty Ave Chicago IL 60646 Office: 6565 Frantz Rd Dublin OH 43017

SAGER, ROBERT DAVID, dentist, lectr., cons.; b. Manhattan, Kans., May 17, 1950; s. Robert Frank and Betsy Jane (Otey) S.; B.S. cum laude in Biology, Kans. State U., 1972; D.M.D. with honors, Washington U., St. Louis, 1975. Mem. faculty Dental Sch., Washington U., St. Louis, 1975-76; gen. practice dentistry, St. Louis, 1975-76; outpatient clinic mgr., dept. dentistry Ill. Masonic Med. Center, Chgo., 1977-78, mem. staff, 1977—; hosp. gen. dentistry practice, Chgo., 1977—; clinician, lectr. hosp. dentistry, 1978—; pres. Dentcare Ltd., hosp. dentistry cons., Chgo., 1978—, Dentsystems, Inc., 1979—; mem. staff Swedish Am. Hosp., Rockford, Ill., 1979—, St. Mary's Hosp., Manhattan, 1980—; cons. Cook County Hosp., 1979—; guest instr. hosp. gen. practice residency U. Colo. Sch. Dentistry, 1980—. Bd. dirs. Riley County Heart Assn. br. Am. Heart Assn., 1980—. Lic. comml. pilot. Recipient Dentsply Internat. Prosthetic award Dentsply Internat., 1975; Edward R. Hart clin. dentistry award Washington U., 1975. Mem. ADA, Am. Acad. Dental Radiology, Flying Dentists Assn., Acad. Gen. Dentistry, Assn. Hosp. Dentists, Ill. Dental Soc., Chgo. Dental Soc., Acad. Dentistry for Handicapped (dir. 1980—, rep. to ADA Council on hosps. and instl. care 1980—). Clubs: Masons, Shriners. Author: Hospital Dentistry, 1979. Home: 1421 Normandy Pl Manhattan KS 66502 also 514 Humboldt Plaza Manhattan KS 66502

SAH, CHIH-TANG, educator; b. Peking, China, Nov. 10, 1932; s. Adam Peng-tung and Shushen (Huang) S.; B.S. in Physics, U. Ill., 1953, B.S. in Elec. Engring., 1953; M.S., Stanford, 1954, Ph.D., 1956; Dr. honoris causa, Catholic U. Leuven, 1975; m. Linda Chang, Nov. 29, 1959; children—Dinah, Robert. Research asst. Stanford Electronics Lab., 1954-56, asso., 1956; mem. tech. staff Shockley Semiconductor Lab., 1956-59; with Fairchild Semiconductor Lab., 1959-65, mgr., head physics dept., 1961-65; faculty U. Ill., Urbana, 1962—, prof. elec. engrng. and physics, 1963—; NSF Research Initiation Grant Panelist, 1973, Franklin Inst. award on MOS devices,

1975; mem. IEEE fields award com., 1970; committeeman Nat. Acad. Scis.-NRC, 1975-78, mem. Honeywell H.W. Sweaft engr.-scientist award com., 1977; cons. Fairchild Semicondr. Corp., 1964-65, Picatinny Arsenal, 1966, Zenith Radio Corp., 1966-69, U. Fla., 1966-82, IBM Corp., 1968-73, Micro-Bit Corp., 1969-78, Teletype Corp., 1971, Indsl. Research Products, inc., 1972-73, Harry Diamond Lab., 1974-75, Am. Micro Systems, Inc., 1975, Jet Propulsion Lab, 1975-82, Honeywell Corp., 1977, Control Data Corp., 1978. Recipient cert. of merit Franklin Inst. of Phila., 1975; named One of 1000 Most Cited Scientists of 1965-78, Current Comments, 1981. Fellow IEEE (Browder J. Thompson prize 1962, J.J. Ebers award 1981), Am. Phys. Soc.; mem. Electrochem. Soc., Sigma Xi, Phi Kappa Phi, Tau Beta Pi, Sigma Tau, Pi Mu Epsilon, Eta Kappa Nu, Phi Eta Sigma. Home: 403 Pond Ridge Ln Urbana IL 61801

SAHLSTROM, STANLEY DAVID, coll. adminstr.; b. Milaca, Minn., Apr. 15, 1921; s. David and Julia (Johnson) S.; B.S. with distinction, U. Mich., 1942, M.S., 1953, Ph.D., 1955; postgrad. U. Iowa, 1958, U. Mich., 1960, Pa. State U., 1969; m. Ludmilla K. Kasanezki, Oct. 5, 1946; children—Kristine, David, Stephen, Timothy. Vo-ag instr., high sch. coach, Marietta, Minn., 1942-43; high sch. instr., adminstr., Milaca, Minn., 1947-52; instr. U. Minn., St. Paul, 1952-55; asst. to pres., dir. field services St. Cloud (Minn.) State Coll., 1955-65; provost U. Minn. Tech. Coll., Crookston, 1965—; cons. UN, 1980—, Saudi Arabia, 1980; past pres. Minn. Assn. Community and Jr. Colls. Past pres. Minn. Citizens Com. on Public Edn. Fulbright scholar, Cyprus, 1963. Mem. NEA, Nat. Vocat. Assn., Nat. Agr. Tchrs. Assn., Am. Assn. Community and Jr. Colls., Minn. Coordinating Com. for Edn., Minn. Edn. Assn., Minn. Vocat. Assn., Minn. Vocat. Agrl. Instrs. Assn., Crookston Area C. of C. (past pres.), Am. Legion, V.F.W. Presbyterian. Clubs: Rotary (past pres., past dist. gov.), Elks, Masons. Contbr. articles to profl. jours. Home: 106 Golf Terr Crookston MN 56716 Office: U Minn Crookston MN 56716

SAHU, SAHEB, pediatrician; b. Mulbar, India, May 3, 1944; came to U.S., 1970, naturalized, 1972; s. Bidyadhar and Sakuntala Sahu; M.D., All-India Inst. Med. Scis., 1969; m. Krishna, June 8, 1970; 1 child, Raj. Resident in pediatrics Raymond Blank Meml. Hosp. for Children, Des Moines, 1970-72; fellow in neonatology Med. Coll. Wis., Milw., 1972-73; asst. prof. U. Osteopathic Medicine and Surgery, Des Moines, 1973-76, asso. prof., 1976-77, prof., 1978—; dir. neonatal ICU, Mercy Hosp. Med. Center, Des Moines, 1974—; cons. to sec. Dept. Health and Human Services, 1980. Sec.-treas. Children Health Care Fund Assn., Des Moines. Fellow Am. Acad. Pediatrics, Internat. Coll. Pediatrics; mem. Iowa Med. Soc., Polk County Med. Soc., Indo-Am. Assn. Des Moines (founding pres. 1975). Contbr. articles to med. jours. Office: 3200 Grand Ave Des Moines IA 50312

ST. CLAIR, KENNETH EDSON, historian; b. Appleton, Wis., July 3, 1908; s. Edson Willis and Margaret Elizabeth (Krull) St. C.; A.B., Lawrence U., 1931; A.M., U. Wis., 1933; Ph.D., Ohio State U., 1939; m. Miriam Wiley Preston, Sept. 2, 1938; children—Miriam Wiley, Kenneth Edson, Fairman Preston, Charles Ainsworth. mem. faculty, Lees Jr. Coll., Jackson, Ky., 1934-37; teaching asst. Ohio State U., 1937-39; mem. faculty dept. history Pikeville (Ky.) Coll., 1939-42; pres. Sayre Sch., Lexington, Ky., 1942-47; prof. history Ind. Central Coll., Indpls., 1947-64, also chmn. dept., chmn. div. social scis.; prof. history Tarkio (Mo.) Coll., 1964—, emeritus, 1978—; lectr. history Ind. U. Indpls. Center, 1947-60; vis. prof. history Transylvania Coll., 1945-46; vis. prof. history, govt. U. Ky., summers 1945, 47. Mem. Tarkio Community Betterment Com., 1978—, treas., 1980-81; mem. Tarkio Bi-Centennial Commn., 1975-76, Tarkio Centennial Commn., 1980. Recipient Lewis prize for scholarship Lawrence U., 1931; Social Sci. Research Council faculty grantee, 1951-53, Kansas City Regional Council for Higher Edn. faculty research grantee, 1969-71. Mem. Am. Hist. Assn., Orgn. Am. Historians, So. Hist. Assn., Atchison County Hist. Soc., AAUP, Civil War History Assn., Nat. Geog. Soc., Oceanic Soc., Smithsonian Instn., Mo. Citizens for Arts, Mid-Am, Masters Track and Field Assn., Phi Alpha Theta. Presbyterian. Clubs: Tarkio Golf, Tarkio Rotary (pres. 1973-74). Book reviewer, contbr. articles to various hist. jours. Home: 411 N 12th St Tarkio MO 64491 Office: Dept History Tarkio Coll Tarkio MO 64491

SAINT DENIS, BARBARA LOUISE DION, artist; b. Muskegon, Mich., Sept. 8, 1928; d. Halley Joseph and Helen Sophia (Johnson) Dion; grad. high sch.; m. Richard Breen Saint Denis, Sept. 20, 1947 (div. 1969); children—Peggy (Mrs. David Scouten), Michele (Mrs. Joseph Hecksel), Richard L. Advt. mgr. Muskegon Grocery Wholesale Co. Co-op. (Mich.), 1953-56; dir. Grand Haven (Mich.) Art Center, 1957-60; founder, pres. Custom Service Printers, 1959-60; account exec. Indsl. Advt. Agy., Muskegon, 1960-63; owner Saint Denis Fine Arts Studios, Muskegon, 1963—, Traverse City, Mich., 1975—; exhibited one-woman shows Grand Haven Art Center, 1960, Battle Creek (Mich.) Civic Art Center, 1969, Chgo. Uptown Savs. & Loan, 1967, Grand Haven Civic Center, 1968, Americana Hotel, N.Y.C., 1967, Jenny Wren Art Gallery, Pentwater, Mich., 1971; groups shows Hackley Art Gallery, Muskegon, 1962-66, Grand Rapids Art Museum, 1965, 67-69; represented in permanent collections Mus. Contemporary Crafts, N.Y.C., 1963, W.K. Kellogg Found., Battle Creek, Mich., 1970. Chmn. Seaway Art Festival, 1961-62, Am. Art Week, 1965, Muskegon Cultural Series, 1964-66; mem. bldg. com. St. Francis de Sales Ch., Muskegon, Mich., 1965-67; mem. exec. bd. Lakeside Community Devel. Council, 1979; mem. Liturgical Art Commn., Diocese Grand Rapids, Mich., 1969; mem. Muskegon Mayor's Art Commn., 1976; mem. Muskegon Citizens Dist. Council, 1978-79, Muskegon/Oceana Manpower Adv. Council, 1979, Muskegon Citizens Charter Rev. Com., 1979. Recipient Major Art award Hackley Art Gallery, 1965; named Muskegon Businesswoman of Year, 1978. Mem. Mich. Acad. Arts. Sci. and Letters, NAACP. Roman Catholic. Home: Route 2 Box 273 Suttons Bay MI 49682 Office: M-22 and Hilltop Rd Suttons Bay MI 49682

ST. JEAN, CHARLES ALBERT, veterinarian; b. Pawtucket, R.I., Apr. 15, 1945; s. Albert Henri and Emerica (Palagi) St. J.; B.S., Ohio State U., 1966, D.V.M., 1971; m. Kathryn Sue Starrett, July 5, 1975; 1 dau., Kristen Nicole. Partner, Chittenden Vet. Clinic, Columbus, Ohio, 1971—; tchr. Columbus Tech. Inst., 1971—, chmn. dept. animal health technology, 1972-74; owner, mgr. Yorkshire Pacers Stud Farm; mem. Columbus Vet. Emergency Service. Mem. AVMA, Ohio Vet. Med. Assn., Columbus Acad. Vet. Medicine, Am. Assn. Equine Practitioners, U.S. Trotting Assn., Ohio Horsemen Assn., 5th Dist. Equine Practitioners Assn., Internat. Vet. Acupuncture Soc. Democrat. Roman Catholic. Home: 1739 State Rt 61 Sunbury OH 43074 Office: 239 Chittenden Ave Columbus OH 43201

SAINT JOHN, CHARLES VIRGIL, pharm. co. exec.; b. Bryan, Ohio, Dec. 18, 1922; s. Clyde W. and Elsie V. (Kintner) St. J.; A.B., Manchester Coll., 1943; M.S., Purdue U., 1946; m. Ruth Ilene Wilson, Oct. 27, 1946; children—Janet St. John Amy, Debra St. John Mishler. Research chemist Manhattan Dist. atomic energy project, West Lafayette, Ind., 1944—46; chemist Eli Lilly & Co., Lafayette, Ind., 1946—; asst. gen. mgr., dir. ops. Clinton Labs., 1971-74, gen. mgr. Tippecanoe and Clinton Labs., Lafayette and Clinton, Ind., 1974-77, v.p. prodn. ops. div., 1977—; dir. Lafayette Life Ins. Co. Bd. dirs. Purdue Nat. Bank, Lafayette, Capital Funds Found. Greater Lafayette; chmn. lay adv. council St. Elizabeth Hosp., Lafayette; mem. pres.'s council Purdue U., also mem. research found.; mem. adminstrv. bd., treas., fin. com. 1st United Meth. Ch., Lafayette; trustee Manchester Coll., North Manchester, Ind. Mem. Am. Chem. Soc., Lafayette C. of C. Club: Lafayette Country. Contbr numerous articles in field to profl. jours. Home: 320 Overlook Dr W Lafayette IN 47906 Office: PO Box 685 Lafayette IN 47902

SAINT JOHN, PERRY JOE, broadcast co. exec.; b. Algona, Iowa, May 14, 1938; s. George Morris and Elizabeth (Caroll) Saint J.; student, Brown Inst., Mpls., 1956-58; m. Eleanor McKee, Dec. 31, 1969; children—Michael, Kelly, Lanae, Amy. Announcer, Sta. KCIM, Carroll, Iowa, 1959-62; announcer, prodn. mgr. Sta. WDGY, Mpls., 1962-68; announcer Sta. KSO, Des Moines, 1969-70, prodn. mgr., 1970-71, program dir., sta. mgr., 1971-76, on air personality, 1969-78; v.p. gen. mgr. Sta. KSO & KGGO, Des Moines, 1976—; tchr. broadcasting Des Moines Area Community Coll. Precinct committeeman City of Des Moines, 1972, 76; delegate of Republican State Conv., 1976. Mem. Nat. Assn. Broadcasters, Nat. Radio Broadcasters Assn., Country Mus. Assn. Roman Catholic. Club: Toastmasters. Recs. include You Lit the Fire, Now Fan the Flame, 1981. Office: 3900 NE Broadway St Des Moines IA 50317

ST. ONGE, HUBERT LOUIS, corp. and mktg. communications cons.; b. Sioux City, Iowa, Oct. 15, 1914; s. Joseph Abel and Marie Venus (Prarie) St. O.; B.S., U. Md., 1959; M.B.A., U. Chgo., 1970; m. Lorraine K. Frankenberg, Oct. 8, 1955; children—Lorraine E., Denise M. Mgr. merchandising promotion Walgreen Drug Co., Chgo., 1945-47; mgr. advt. sales promotion and public relations Martin Senour Co., Chgo., 1947-51, exec. asst. to pres., 1967-70; commd. maj., inf. U.S. Army, 1951, advanced through grades to lt. col., 1954, ret., 1967; asst. prof. Drexel U., Phila., 1964-67; mgr. corp. and mktg. communications Belden Corp., Geneva, Ill., 1970-81; corp. and mktg. communications cons., 1981—. Chmn. UN Mixed Armistice Commn., Israel/Jordan, 1962-64. Served with U.S. Army, 1942-45. Decorated Bronze Star; Croix de Guerre with 3 silver stars (France); recipient UN Peace medal and cert.; cert. bus. communicator Bus./Profl. Advt. Assn. Mem. Nat. Investor Relations Inst. (dir.), Automotive Advertisers Council, Phi Kappa Phi. Republican. Roman Catholic. Home: 3655 Red Bud Ct Downers Grove IL 60515

SAKALEY, JOHN ANDREW, III, toy mfg. co. exec.; b. Washington, Jan. 3, 1944; s. John Andrew and Mary Anne E. Sakaley; B.A., U. Notre Dame, 1965; m. Margo Ann Eup, May 1, 1976; children—Melissa Ann, Christina Marie. Asso. carpet buyer Burdine's Dept. Store, Miami, Fla., 1969-70, toy and bicycle buyer, 1970-75; v.p. retail merchandising Internat. Toy Corp., North Babylon, N.Y., 1975-76; dir. merchandising Kenner Products, Cin., 1976-80, dir. toy group merchandising, 1981—. Served with U.S. Army, 1965-68. Decorated Bronze Star, Air medal. Mem. Point-of-Purchase Advt. Inst., Am. Mktg. Assn. Republican. Clubs: K.C., Notre Dame Alumni Home: 630 Woodsway Dr Loveland OH 45140 Office: Kenner Products 1014 Vine St Cincinnati OH 45202

SAKHAII, MOHSEN, internist, cardiologist; b. Kashan, Iran, Mar. 10, 1944; came to U.S., 1971; s. Hosein and Tahereh (Mortazavi) S.; M.D., U. Tehran (Iran), 1969; m. Nina Tabatabai, Apr. 9, 1970; 1 dau., Houri. Intern, Tehran U. Hosp., 1968-69, Fairview Gen. Hosp., Cleve., 1971-72; resident in internal medicine Good Samaritan Hosp. and Health Center, Dayton, Ohio, 1973-75; fellow in cardiology Cleve. Clinic, 1975-77; resident in psychiatry Fairhill Hosp., Cleve., 1972-73; practice medicine, specializing in internal medicine, cardiology, Dayton, Ohio, 1978—; staff internist, cardiologist Good Samaritan Hosp., Dayton, 1979—, coordinator cardiology fellowship program, 1979—; cons. sr. cardiologist, lectr. Firoozgar Ednl. Hosp. and Research Inst., Tehran, 1978; asso. clin. prof. medicine Wright State U., Dayton, 1979—. Diplomate Am. Bd. Internal Medicine, supsplty. cardiovascular disease. Fellow Am. Coll. Cardiology; mem. A.C.P., Am. Soc. Internal Medicine, Am. Coll. Emergency Physicians, Montgomery County Med. Soc., AMA. Mem. editorial bd. Jour. Heart and Lung. Home: 1962 W Alexander Bell Rd Dayton OH 45459 Office: 33 W 1st St IBM Bldg Suite 500 Dayton OH 45402

SAKOWITZ, SIDNEY NATHAN, wholesale grocer; b. Indpls., July 8, 1925; s. Louis and Nesha (Marks) S.; student Purdue U., 1942-43; m. Sarah Frances Draizar, Aug. 3, 1947; children—Marcia Sakowitz Sklare, Anita Sakowitz Kramer, Jeffrey M. With Grocers Supply Co., Indpls., 1946—, partner in charge purchasing, sales and acctg., 1950-74, inc., 1974, exec. v.p., 1974—; cons. to small bus. Treas., bd. dirs. Hooverwood Home for Aged; former pres. Congregation B'nai Torah. Mem. Ind. Assn. Credit Mgmt., Nat. Am. Wholesale Grocers Assn. (gov.), Indpls. C. of C. Clubs: East Side Lions (v.p.), Masons, Shriners, B'nai B'rith. Home: 7233 N Illinois St Indianapolis IN 46260 Office: 1025 W Washington St PO Box 1846 Indianapolis IN 46206

SALANCIK, GERALD ROBERT, social psychologist; b. Chgo., Jan. 29, 1943; s. Andrew and Anne (Hanson) S.; B.S. in Journalism, Northwestern U., 1965, M.S., 1966; Ph.D., Yale U., 1970; m. Charytyna Helen Krupka, Dec. 27, 1969; 1 dau., Sofia Katerina. Research asso. Mktg. Control, Inc., N.Y.C., 1968-70, Inst. for Future, Middletown, Conn., 1970-71; mem. faculty U. Ill., Urbana, 1971—, prof. organizational behavior, dir. grad. studies, 1977—; mem. rev. panels Nat. Inst. Edn., Adminstr. Sci. Quar.; cons. to govt. and industry. Fellow Chgo. Advt. Club, 1965, Yale U., 1966-68, Stanford U., NIMH, 1975; grantee NATO Advanced Study Inst., 1972; hon. fellow U. Bradford (Eng.), 1976. Mem. Am. Psychol. Assn., Acad. Mgmt., Human Systems Mgmt. Circle, Phi Theta Kappa. Mem. Ukrainian Cath. Ch. Club: Yale (Chgo.). Author: The Interview, 1966; New Directions in Organizational Behavior, 1977; The External Control of Organizations, 1977; also articles. Home: 704 Park Lane Dr Champaign IL 61820 Office: 350 Commerce West Univ Ill Urbana IL 61801

SALATO, SALVATORE ROSARIO, ednl. adminstr.; b. Chgo., Jan. 12, 1925; s. Leopoldo and Rose Theresa (Salerno) S.; B.S., Drake U., 1950, M.S., Purdue U., 1962; m. Mary Lou Ann Rose, Aug. 13, 1949; children—Steven Michael, Patricia Ann, Rose Marie, Adelynn Rose. Tchr., coach St. Mel High Sch., Chgo., 1951-61; tchr. Thornridge High Sch., Dolton, Ill., 1961—, dean, 1965-68, asst. prin., 1968-76, prin., 1976—. Mem. Thornton Twp. Youth Com., 1973-79; trustee Elizabeth Seton High Sch., 1974-80; mem. adv. com. South Holland Park, 1977-79; bb. dirs., pres. Cath. Grade Sch. Conf., 1977—, South Inter-Conf. Assn., 1978-80. Served with USNR, 1943-46. Mem. Ill. Prins. Assn., Nat. Assn. Secondary Sch. Prins., Phi Delta Kappa. Roman Catholic. Clubs: Holy Ghost Sports, Nat. D. Home: 942 E 171st Pl South Holland IL 60473 Office: Thornridge High Sch Sibley Blvd and Cottage Grove Sts Dolton IL 60419

SALCEDO, RODOLFO NACINO, city ofcl.; b. Los Banos, Laguna, Philippines, Dec. 18, 1940; s. Felix Nacino, Sr. and Julita Agustin (Nacino) S.; came to U.S., 1965; B.S. in Agrl. Edn. magna cum laude (Coll. scholar), Visayas State Coll. Agr., 1960; M.S. (Univ. scholar), U. Philippines, 1962; Ph.D., Mich. State U., East Lansing, 1968; m. Conchita D'Bayan Yniguez-Salcedo, Feb. 22, 1964; children—Rudolph John Patrick, Cheryl Rosana. Research instr. U. Philippines, 1963-65; research asst. Mich. State U., 1966-68; dir. pesticides labeling study U. Ill., 1968-74; asst. prof. U. Ill., 1968-74; environ. scientist City of Milw., 1974—; curriculum cons. U.S. Office of Edn., 1968; coordinator Communication Sensitivity for Extension Agts. and Urban Planners, 1970-72; lectr. U. Wis., Milw., 1975; mem. four regional environ. planning tech. adv. coms.; coordinator Menomonee River Valley Generic Environ. Impact Model Tech. Adv. Com. Research fellow U. Philippines, 1961-62; recipient pesticide labeling study research grant U.S. Dept. Agr. and EPA, 1968-72; NSF grantee, 1976-81. Mem. Am. Statis. Assn., Am. Acad. Polit. and Social Scis., Nat. Assn. Environ. Profls., Nat. Assn. Environ. Edn., Rural Sociol. Soc., Alpha Tau Alpha, Gamma Sigma Delta. Roman Catholic. Author: (with J.F. Evans) Communications in Agriculture: the American Farm Press, 1974; reviewer Rural Sociology, 1970-72; contbr. articles to profl. jours. Home: 7644 W Palmetto Ct Milwaukee WI 53218 Office: Dept City Devel 734 N 9th St Milwaukee WI 53201

SALDIEN, KAREL FRANS, animal feed co. exec.; b. Brasschaat, Belgium, Aug. 31, 1931; came to U.S., 1975; s. Edgard and Antoinette Maria (Ruelens) S.; B.S. in Mechanics and Electronics, Hoger Instituut De Nayer Mechelen, 1955, M.S. in Civil Constrn., 1955; m. Agnes M. Baerts, Oct. 30, 1956; children—Jocelyne, Carl, Koenraad. Field engr. N.C. Econosto, Antwerp, Belgium, 1956; chief engr. Hens Voeders, Antwerp, 1956-66; asso. dir. engring. Ralston Purina Co., Brussels, Belgium, 1966-69; asst. prodn. mgr. Duquesne Purina, Rouen, France, 1969-72; nat. prodn. mgr. Provimi France, Paris, 1972-75; dir. internat. prodn. Central Soya Inc., Ft. Wayne, Ind., 1975—; mfg. cons., U.S. and abroad. Served to 1st lt. C.E., Belgian Army, 1955-57. Mem. Am. Feed Mfg. Assn. Patentee pelleting system for animal feed and concentrates. Home: 5024 Wapiti Ct Fort Wayne IN 46804 Office: Central Soya Internat Div 1300 Fort Wayne Nat Bank Bldg 17th Floor Fort Wayne IN 48802

SALEM, DOROTHY I., educator; b. Dayton, Ohio, Jan. 29, 1946; d. Donald Robert and Ethel A. (Carlson) Meyer; B.A., Cleve. State U., 1971, M.A., 1973; postgrad. Kent State U.; m. Thomas G. Salem, Sept. 4, 1971; children—Kelle Ann, Beth Marie, Jennifer Lynn. Teaching asst. Cleve. State U., 1971-73; teaching fellow Kent State U., 1975; mem. faculty dept. social sci.-history Cuyahoga Community Coll., Cleve., 1973—, asso. prof., 1980—. Mem. Cleve. Women Working, NOW, Nat. Women's Studies Assn., Higher Edn. Resources, Am. Hist. Assn., AAUP, AAUW, Womenspace, Women of Metro. Presbyterian. Home: 5673 Rock Point Circle N Ridgeville OH 44039 Office: Cuyahoga Community Coll 2900 Community College Ave Cleveland OH 44115

SALIBI, BAHIJ SULAYMAN, neurosurgeon; b. Omdurman, Sudan, May 16, 1922; s. Sleiman Khalil and Salva Ibrahim (Salibi) S.; came to U.S., 1946, naturalized, 1961; B.A., Am. U. Beirut (Lebanon), 1941, M.A., 1944; postgrad. U. Mich., 1946; M.D., Harvard, 1950; m. Margaret Elizabeth Beverley, May 16, 1954; children—Lillian Salwa, Charles Khalil, Ernest Kamal. Intern in pathology and clin. pathology Children's Hosp., Boston, 1950-51, research fellow in neurosurgery, 1956; intern in surgery Barnes Hosp., St. Louis, 1951-52, asst. resident in surgery, 1952-53; resident in neurosurgery St. Lukes Hosp., Chgo., 1953-54; resident in neurosurgery U. Ill. Neuropsychiat. Inst., Chgo., 1954-56, chief resident in neurosurgery, 1955-56; asst. in surgery (neurosurgery) Harvard Med. Sch., Boston, 1956; neurosurgeon Marshfield Clinic, Marshfield, Wis., 1958—; mem. staff St. Joseph's Hosp.; asso. clin. prof. neurol. surgery U. Wis. Med. Sch., Madison. Served as capt. MC, U.S. Army, 1956-58. Diplomate Am. Bd. Neurol. Surgery. Fellow A.C.S.; mem. AMA, Wis. State Med. Soc., Wood County Med. Soc., Chgo. Neurol. Soc., Congress Neurol. Surgeons, Central Neurosurg. Soc. (pres. 1968-69), Am. Assn. Neurol. Surgeons, Internat. Med. Soc. Paraplegia. Democrat. Episcopalian. Contbr. articles in field to profl. jours. Inventor artery clamp. Home: 1006 W 8th St Marshfield WI 54449 Office: Marshfield Clinic Marshfield WI 54449

SALISBURY, ALVIN BURTON, JR., physician; b. Rockford, Ill., Mar. 11, 1922; s. Alvin Burton and Mildred Elizabeth (Scott) S.; student Beloit Coll., 1941-43, Vanderbilt U., 1943-44; M.D., Ohio State U., 1949; m. Cecelia Mitchell, Aug. 26, 1944; m. 2d, Jane Jefford, Aug. 26, 1976; children—Jennifer Lee, Elizabeth Ann, Robert Alvin. Intern, White Cross Hosp., Columbus, Ohio, 1949-50; practice medicine, Fairborn, Ohio, 1952—, Piqua, Ohio, 1979-80; mem. staff Greene Meml. Hosp., Xenia, Ohio; courtesy staff Piqua Meml. Hosp., Miami Valley, St. Elizabeth's hosps., both Dayton, Ohio; founder, pres. Ankh Labs., Inc., Fairborn, 1955-69. Founder, Mus. of Old Northwest Frontier, Lockington, 1970. Served to capt. M.C., AUS, 1943-46, 51-52. Mem. AMA, Miami County Med. Soc., Ohio State Med. Assn. Patentee med. instruments. Editor, pub. Adventures of Col. Daniel Boone (John Filson), 1968. Address: Greater Miami Valley Health Plan 850 E Xenia Dr Fairborn OH

SALISBURY, DAVID JOSEPH, mech. engr.; b. Rome, N.Y., Sept. 11, 1954; s. John Irving and Constance Marguerite Salisbury; B.S. in Mech. and Ocean Engring., U. R.I., 1976, postgrad., 1979; postgrad. in engring. Purdue U., 1979—; m. Barbara J. Foreman, Oct. 14, 1978. Mech. engr., lead mech. engr. sonobuoy program Submarine Signal div. Raytheon Co., Portsmouth, R.I., 1976-79; prin. mech. engr. tech. staff in environ. engring. Magnavox Govt. and Indsl. Electronic Co., Ft. Wayne, Ind., 1979—. Roman Catholic. Home: 10015 Tiffany Dr Fort Wayne IN 46804 Office: 1313 Production Rd Fort Wayne IN 46808

SALITERMAN, LAURA SHRAGER, pediatrician; b. N.Y.C., June 26, 1946; d. Arthur M. and Ida (Wildman) Shrager; A.B. magna cum laude (Greenberg Sci. award 1967), Brandeis U., 1967; M.D. (med. scholarship for merit 1967), N.Y. U., 1971; m. Richard Arlen Saliterman, June 15, 1975. Intern, Montefiore Hosp. and Med. Center, Bronx, N.Y., 1971-72, resident in pediatrics, 1972-74; pediatrician Morrisania Family Care Center, N.Y.C., 1974-75; pediatrician Share Health Plan, St. Paul, 1975—, dir. pediatrics, 1976—; clin. asst. prof. U. Minn. Med. Sch. Mem. Am. Acad. Pediatrics, Phi Beta Kappa. Club: Oak Ridge. Home: 11911 Live Oak Dr Minnetonka MN 55343 Office: 555 Simpson St Saint Paul MN 55104

SALLEE, KENNETH HARVEY, soil scientist; b. Pawnee, Okla., Nov. 22, 1932; s. William Herman and Edna Mae (Hope) S.; B.S., Okla. State U., 1956; postgrad. Iowa State U., 1977; m. Betty Ann Lowery, Sept. 3, 1955; children—Robin Ann, Kenneth Scott, Shelley Sue. Soil scientist Dept. Agr., Syracuse, Kans., 1956-59, Scott City, Kans., 1959-61, Dighton, Kans., 1961-64, Garnett, Kans., 1964-73, Troy, Kans., 1973—. Coach, Little League Baseball, Garnett; leader County 4-H, 1970-73. 4H scholar, 1951-53. Recipient disting. service awards FFA, also hon. farmer award, 4-H alumni award, Anderson County (Kans.), 1973. Mem. Soil Conservation Soc. Am., Am. Soc. Agronomy, Soil Sci. Soc. Am. Baptist.

SALLIS, DOUGLAS ARNOLD, physician; b. Summerland, B.C., Can., Jan. 4, 1923; s. Arthur Roland and Beatrice Florence (White) S.; student U. B.C., 1947-49; M.D., Queen's U., 1955; m. Margaret Willms, Aug. 2, 1950 (dec. 1966); children—Friedemann, Christine; m. 2d, Carol Arbutus Anderson, June 15, 1967; children—Jennifer, Ronald. Intern, St. Joseph Hosp., Flint, Mich., 1955-56; gen. practice medicine, Smithville, Ont., Can., 1956-58, Stanley, Wis., 1958—; med. officer Govt. of Papua New Guinea, 1976-78; owner LaSalle Med. Service, Stanley. Served with Can. Mcht. Navy, 1942-46.

Diplomate Am. Bd. Family Practice. Fellow Am. Acad. Family Physicians; mem. AMA, Wis. Affiliate Am. Heart Assn., State Med. Soc. Wis., Chippewa County Med. Soc., Wis. Affiliate Am. Diabetes Assn. Republican. Home: 130 E 10th Ave Stanley WI 54768 Office: 305 E 1st Ave Stanley WI 54768

SALMON, OLIVER NORTON, phys. chemist; b. Syracuse, N.Y., Mar. 24, 1917; s. Oliver Jerome and Hazel (Norton) S.; A.B., Cornell U., 1940, Ph.D., 1946; m. Alma May Schwenk, Apr. 8, 1945; children—Pamela (Mrs. Michael T. Budion), Oliver N., Douglas, Julianne (Mrs. James C. Long). Chemist, Corning Glass Works (N.Y.), 1941-43; research asst. Cornell U., Ithaca, N.Y., 1943-45, research asso., 1946-47; phys. chemist Gen. Electric Co., Schenectady and Syracuse, N.Y., 1947-60; research chemist 3M Co., St. Paul, 1960-62, supr., 1962-64, mgr. solid state physics, 1964-72, mgr. basic and pioneering research, 1972-73, sr. research specialist, 1973—. Mem. Am. Chem. Soc., Am. Ceramic Soc., Minn. Acad. Sci., Internat. Solar Energy Soc. Phi Beta Kappa, Sigma Xi. Research on liquid metal coolants for nuclear reactors, hydrogen isotopes purification and separation; thermodynamics of solid state, solar energy. Home: 418 Glenwood Ave Saint Paul MN 55113 Office: 3M Center Saint Paul MN 55144

SALOCKER, RICK PAUL, podiatrist; b. Des Moines, Oct. 5, 1948; s. Andrew S. and Evelyn Bennett S.; B.S., U. S.D., 1971; D.P.M., Ill. Coll. Podiatry, 1977; m. Brenda M. Jensen, Oct. 21, 1972. Resident, Thorek Hosp. and Med. Center, Chgo., 1977-78; pvt. practice podiatric medicine, Ft. Dodge, Iowa, 1978—; mem. staff Trinity Regional Hosp., Ft. Dodge, Iowa, also mem. infectious control com.; mem. staff Humboldt County Hosp. Mem. Am. Podiatry Assn., Iowa Podiatry Assn. Republican. Lutheran. Clubs: Elks, Lions. Home: 3141 12th Ave N Fort Dodge IA 50501 Office: 1605 1st Ave N Fort Dodge IA 50501

SALONEN, JAMES JOHN, podiatrist; b. Hibbing, Minn., Sept. 14, 1945; s. John Gust and Rose (Selvo) S.; A.A., Hibbing Jr. Coll., 1965; B.A., U. Duluth, 1967; M.S., Mont. State U., 1969; D. Podiatric Medicine cum laude, Ill. Coll. Podiatric Medicine, 1976; m. Jean Ann Ferrell, Aug. 4, 1970. Podiatric asst. Dr. A. C. Larson, Hibbing, Minn., 1974; field worker public relations dept. Iron Range Resources Bd., State of Minn., Hibbing, 1975; podiatric resident Podiatric Medicine Surgery Residence Program, St. Francis Hosp., Shakopee, Minn., 1976-77; podiatrist, foot specialist, surgeon, Virginia, Minn., Duluth, Minn., 1977—; mem. Minn. Bd. Podiatry, 1979—, chmn., 1981; clin. instr. Calif. Coll. Podiatric Medicine, San Francisco, 1978-79. Mem. bd. Range Community Health Center, 1977—, chmn. bd., 1981; mem.-at-large Boy Scouts Am., 1982. Served with U.S. Army, 1969-72; Vietnam. Decorated Army Commendation medal, Joint Service Commendation medal. Fellow Am. Coll. Foot Orthopedists; mem. Am. Acad. Podiatric Sports Medicine, Minn. Podiatry Assn. Club: United No. Sportsman. Home: 1701 Dunedin Ave Duluth MN 55802 Office: 717 N 9th St Virginia MN 53792 also Medical Arts Bldg Suite 400 Duluth MN 55802

SALTER, EDWIN CARROLL, physician; b. Oklahoma City, Jan. 19, 1927; s. Leslie Ernest and Maud (Carroll) S.; B.A., DePauw U., 1947; M.D., Northwestern U., 1951; m. Ellen Gertrude Malone, June 30, 1962; children—Mary Susanna, David Patrick. Intern, Cook County Hosp., Chgo., 1951-53; resident in pediatrics Children's Meml. Hosp., Chgo. and Cook County Hosp., 1956-58; practice medicine specializing in pediatrics, Lake Forest, Ill., 1958—; attending physician Lake Forest Hosp., 1958—, pres. med. staff, 1981; attending physician Children's Meml. Hosp., Chgo.; clin. faculty mem. dept. pediatrics Northwestern U. Med. Sch. Served to capt. M.C., U.S. Army, 1954-56. Mem. AMA, Ill. State Med. Soc., Lake County Med. Soc., Phi Beta Kappa. Republican. Methodist. Home: 19 N Maywood Rd Lake Forest IL 60045 Office: 800 Westmoreland Rd Lake Forest IL 60045

SALTER, KWAME SAMUEL, ednl. adminstr.; b. Delhi, La., Jan. 31, 1946; s. Samuel Leon and Reva (Daniels) S.; B.Ed., U. Wis., Whitewater, 1968; M.A. in Ednl. Adminstrn. (Ford fellow), U. Wis., Madison, 1970, postgrad. (Advanced Opportunity fellow), 1980—; m. Connie S. Jones, June 3, 1967; children—Kevin Jamal, Keri Jamelda. Tchr., Francis Parkman Jr. High Sch., Milw., 1968-69; exec. dir. U. Wis. Afro-Am. Race Relations Cultural Center, Madison, 1970-73; corporate exec. officer Dane County Parent Council, Inc., Madison, 1976—. Mem. Madison Met. Sch. Dist. Bd. Edn., 1977, chmn. personnel com., 1977-80, v.p., 1980—, chmn. bldg. and grounds com., 1977—, chmn. budget and finance com., 1980. Named Outstanding Educator/Leader Wis. Omega Phi Psi, 1979. Mem. Parental Stress, Inc., Am. Assn. Sch. Adminstrn., Am. Mgmt. Soc., Phi Delta Kappa. Roman Catholic. Club: Optimists. Office: Dane County Parent Council Inc 802 Williamson St Madison WI 53703

SALTER, PAUL SANFORD, univ. dean.; b. Springfield, Mass., May 21, 1926; s. Leonard Austin and Clara Ann (Weary) S.; B.S.E., Mass. State Coll., 1950; M.A., Ind. U., 1951; Ph.D., U. N.C., 1965; m. Barbara Kirby, Sept. 9, 1950; children—Paul Sanford, Kim Ann, Nancy Eileen. Instr., critic-tchr. Mass. State Coll., Westfield, 1956-60; asso. dean undergrad. acad. affairs Coll. Arts and Scis., prof. geography U. Miami, Coral Gables, Fla., 1974-76; dean Coll. Arts and Scis., prof. geography U. Alaska, Fairbanks, 1976-79; dean Coll. Arts and Scis., prof. urban geography dept. sociology Washburn U., Topeka, Kans., 1979—. Served with USN, 1944-46. Mem. Am. Assn. Higher Edn., Assn. Am. Geographers, Council Colls. Arts and Scis., Gamma Theta Epsilon. Contbr. chpts. to books, articles to profl. jours. Home: 5518 W 15th Terrace Topeka KS 66604 Office: Washburn U Topeka KS 66621

SALTER, RICHARD MACKINTIRE, artist, photographer; b. Iowa City, May 7, 1940; s. John Randall and Josephine Senn (Heath) S.; B.A., No. Ariz. U., 1964; M.F.A., Instituto Allende, San Miguel Allende, Mex., 1968; m. Sonette E. Chanson, Dec. 22, 1968; children—Richard Mackintire, Michele, Robert, Mary. One-man shows U. Wis., Green Bay, 1977, Rockford (Ill.) Coll., 1974, Concordia Coll., Milw., 1977, Rock Valley Coll., Rockford, 1976, Ozaukee County Art Center, Cedarburg, Wis., 1977, DePaul U., Chgo., 1978, Western Ill. U., Macomb, 1979, West Bend (Wis.) Gallery Fine Arts, 1979, Eastern Ill. U., Charleston, 1979, U. Wis., Whitewater, 1980, Carroll Coll., 1981, Mitchell Mus., Mt. Vernon, Ill., 1981, Sioux Indian Mus., Rapid City, S.D., 1981; exhibited in group shows Gallery A., Taos, 1977, Elaine Horwitch Gallery, Scottsdale, Ariz., 1976, Wis. Gallery, Milw. Art Center, 1977, Turtle Mountain Gallery, Phila., 1977, Red Cloud Indian Art Show, Pine Ridge, S.D., 1978, 81, Heard Indian Arts/Crafts Show, Phoenix, 1978, 81; represented in permanent collections U.S. Dept. Interior, Bur. Indian Affairs, Washington, Phoenix Indian Sch., Will Harnsen Western Collection, Denver, No. Ariz. U., Arthur Adams Western Collection, Beloit State Bank, Pioneer Savs. & Loan, Walworth, Racine, Wis., Walworth State Bank, Lake Geneva Pub. Library, Red Cloud Indian Sch., Pine Ridge, S.D., Miller Brewing Corp., Milw., D.E.K. Industries, St. Charles, Ill., Western Ill. U., No. Ariz. U., Wis. Civil Liberties Union, Milw.; tchr. art Colinga Jr. Coll., 1967-68, Albuquerque Pub. Schs., 1967-68, Rockford Art Assn., 1968-69, U. Wis., Green Bay, 1973, Big Foot High Sch., Walworth, 1969-77, J.F. Kennedy Center for Performing Arts, 1982, Smithsonian Inst., 1982, Native Am. Center for the Living Arts, Niagara Falls, N.Y., 1982, Alverno Coll. (one person) Milw. Wis. 1982. Recipient 1st prize Red Cloud Indian Art Show, 1976, 80, 81, award Heard Mus. Indian Arts and Crafts Show, Phoenix, 1976, 80, 81. Mem. Coll. Art Assn. Am., Wis. Painters and Sculptors Assn.

SALTER, WILLIAM SIDNEY, banker; b. Washington, Oct. 30, 1932; s. William Sidney and Vivian Helen S.; B.S., Georgetown U., 1959; postgrad. exec. mgmt. program Columbia U., 1977; m. Iris Schachter, Jan. 14, 1956; children—Deborah, Kevin, Beth. Comml. lending officer Bank of Am., San Francisco, Hong Kong, 1959-71; sr. v.p., officer-in-charge internat. div. 1st Nat. Bank of St. Louis, 1971—; lectr. local coll. M.B.A. programs. Served with USNR, 1951-55. Mem. Council for Fgn. Affairs (dir.), UN Assn. St. Louis (dir.), Japan Am. Soc. (dir.), Am. Inst. Banking, Bankers Assn. for Fgn. Trade. Unitarian. Office: First Nat Bank of St Louis 515 Olive St Saint Louis MO 63166

SALTMAN, ELIAS ALLAN, mech. engr.; b. Chgo., Oct. 25, 1913; s. Isaac and Sarah S.; B.S., U. Mich., 1951; postgrad. seminars U. Wis.; m. Rochelle Annette Fried, May 30, 1953; children—Roberta Ina, Sharon June, Allan Jay. Design engr. Barber-Colman, Rockford, Ill., 1951-60; products mgr. Bartelt Engring. Co., Rockford, 1960-67; mgr. mech. devel. Packaging Corp. Am., Grand Rapids, Mich., 1967-69; sr. project engr. George J. Meyer Mfg. Co., Cudahy, Wis., 1969-78; project mgr., internat. engr., 1978—; packaging cons. Served with AUS, 1943-46; ETO. Decorated French Fourragere Colors of Croix de Guerre; registered profl. engr., Wis. Mem. ASME, Soc. Mfg. Engrs. Patentee in resistance welding heads, dynamometer, bacon wrapper, bag in box container. Home: 7444 N Lombardy Rd Milwaukee WI 53217 Office: 4751 S Meyer Pl Cudahy WI 53110

SALTZBERG, BERNARD G., devel disabilities agy. exec.; b. Chgo., May 3, 1932; s. Irving and Pauline (Carl) S.; B.A. in Bus., U. Ill., 1953; m. Alta Rothenberg, Sept. 20, 1953; children—Arthur Michael, Barry Mark, Gary Ried. Salesman, Herbert Metal Products, 1953-56; v.p. Abco Enterprises, Inc., Chgo., 1954-60; pres. Ascot Builders Supply, Inc., Skokie, Ill., 1960-66, Churchill Ins. Agy. Ltd., Chgo., 1967-70; exec. dir. Orchard Assn. for Retarded Orchard Village, Skokie, Ill., 1970—. Mem. Govs. Planning Council on Developmentally Disabled, 1974-80. Named Man of Yr., Inter-Village Mental Health Assn., 1975. Mem. Am. Assn. Mental Deficiency, Ill. Assn. for Retarded Citizens, Nat. Assn. for Retarded Citizens (President's Horizon Club), Council for Exceptional Children, Coordinating Council for Handicapped Children, Nat. Conf. Execs. of Assn. for Retarded Citizens, Nat. Downs Syndrome Assn., Found. for Exceptional Children, Autistic Assn., Community Living Facilities Dirs. Assn. Ill. (chmn. 1977-80), Epilepsy Found. Am., Skokie C. of C. Jewish. Clubs: Rotary (Skokie); B'nai B'rith. Home: 5302 W Jarvis St Skokie IL 60077

SALURI, JAYNE CHARLOTTE, dept. store ofcl.; b. Belle Plaine, Iowa, Feb. 2, 1952; d. Charles Walter and Anna Maria (Kucera) Bradford; A.A.S., Ellsworth Coll., 1972; B.A., Mt. Mercy U. Iowa, 1981, postgrad. in bus. adminstrn., 1981—; m. Thomas Ralph Saluri, Jr., Apr. 24, 1976; 1 son, Michael Thomas. Tng. dir. Younkers, Inc., Des Moines, 1972-75; asst. tng. dir. Armstrong's, Inc., Cedar Rapids, Iowa, 1975—. Mem. Am. Soc. for Tng. and Devel. (program chmn. Cedar Rapids chpt. 1979-80, 1st v.p. 1978-79, dir. 1980-81, pres. 1981-82, cert. of commendation and achievement 1979). Methodist. Club: Rainbow. Office: Armstrong's Inc 3d Ave and 3d St Cedar Rapids IA 52401

SALVA, VLADIMER MICHAEL, JR., accountant; b. Cleve., Nov. 21, 1948; s. Vladimer Michael and Concetta (Corrado) S.; student U. Dayton, 1967-68, Cuyahoga Community Coll., 1969, San Angelo State Coll., 1970, U. Md., 1971-72, U. Balt., 1972-73; B.B.A., Kent State U., 1976, postgrad. 1977—; m. Karen Ann Matyaszek, Nov. 19, 1969; children—Bradley Scott, Bryan Spencer, Allegra Samantha. Pvt. practice accounting, Balt., 1973-74, Cleve., 1974—; tax accountant, supr. Revco D.S. Inc., Cleve., 1974-76; pvt. practice, S. Euclid, Ohio, 1975—; tax accountant Cook United Inc., Maple Heights, Ohio, 1977-81; tax mgr. Automated Packaging Systems, Inc., Twinsburg, Ohio, 1981—. Served with USAF, 1969-73. Mem. Nat. Accounting Assn., Kent Accounting Assn., Am. Mgmt. Assn., Nat. Hist. Soc., Musical Arts Assn., Smithsonian Assn., South Euclid Lyndhurst Jr. C. of C. (sec. 1976-77, treas. 1981-82), Cleve. Orch. Assn., Sigma Pi, Sigma Phi Epsilon. Roman Catholic. Home: 1782 S Green Rd South Euclid OH 44121 Office: 8400 Darrow Rd Twinsburg OH 44087

SALVESON, DOUGLAS SHERMAN, artist, educator; b. Ada, Minn., Sept. 16, 1947; s. Sherman Clifford and Delores Marion S.; B.A., Moorhead State U., 1969; M.F.A. (Grad. fellow), U. Cin., 1971; m. Raye L. Vaule, Dec. 28, 1967; 1 dau., Stephanie Raye. Faculty, U. Cin., 1970-71; asso. prof. art Findlay (Ohio) Coll., 1971—; founder Salveson Collection; exhibited in numerous one man and group shows, 1968—; represented in numerous collections. Trustee, Findlay Area Arts Council. Scholar, Kent State U., Blossom Art Program, 1970, Faculty research grantee for study in Europe, Findlay Coll., 1977. Mem. Coll. Art Assn. Home: 1215 Hurd Ave Findlay OH 45840 Office: Findlay Coll Findlay OH 45840

SALYER, DONALD MORGAN, pharmacist; b. Texon, Tex., May 22, 1931; s. Wade David and Ava A. (Cox) S.; student Schreiner Inst., 1948-50; B.S. in Pharmacy, U. Tex., Austin, 1954; M.R.E., Southwestern Bapt. Theol. Sem., 1961; m. Lorene E. Wood, Mar. 23, 1957; children—Kimberly Sue, Glenn Edwin, Rodney Harold. With Ballard Drug, Beeville, Tex., 1954, 56, Cunningham Pharmacy, Port Lavaca, Tex., 1956-57, Victoria Pharmacy (Tex.), 1957-58, Harris Hosp., Ft. Worth, 1958-60, All Saints Hosp., Ft. Worth, 1960-63; with Kind div. Gray Drug, Warren, Ohio, 1963-65; dir. pharmacy Warren (Ohio) Gen. Hosp., 1965—; pharmacy preceptor Ohio No. U. Ednl. dir. Austin Village Baptist Ch., 1963-79; mem. Warren Bd. Health, 1979—; trustee Brookhaven Retirement Center, Mason, Ohio, 1978-80; mem. exec. bd. State Conv. Baptist in Ohio, 1974-76. Served with U.S. Army, 1954-56. Mem. Am. Soc. Hosp. Pharmacists, Ohio Soc. Hosp. Pharmacists, League of Intravenous Therapy Edn. Republican. Club: Kiwanis (pres. 1974-75) (Warren). Home: 2856 Northwest Blvd Warren OH 44485 Office: Warren Gen Hosp 667 Eastland Ave Warren OH 44484

SALYERS, DAVID BRUCE, pub. co. exec.; b. Lincoln, Ill., Sept. 3, 1940; s. Dewey and Josephine (Cox) S.; B.A., U. Ill., 1965. Mng. partner Sentinel Programming Assos., Champaign, Ill., 1965-68; asso. office mgr. Brintex Exhbns., London, 1968-69; feature editor Instns. mag., Chgo., 1969-72; dir. public relations Playboy mag., Chgo., 1972—; partner Athey-Salyers Properties, Chgo. Served with U.S. Army, 1959-62. Mem. Alpha Delta Phi. Republican. Methodist. Club: Canyon. Home: 1128 Wrightwood Ave Chicago IL 60614 Office: 919 N Michigan Ave Chicago IL 60611

SALZMAN, MARILYN B. WOLFSON, service co. exec.; b. Chgo., Dec. 25, 1943; d. Joseph and Sera (Krol) Wolfson; student U. Ill., Barat Coll., Lake Forest, Ill., 1961-64; 1 son, Lawrence Todd. Pres., MWS Assos., Chgo., and Highland Park, Ill., 1980—; exec. adminstrv. dir. Crystal Tips of No. Ill., Inc., 1980—; dir. adminstrn. Ice Dispensers, Inc., 1981—; dir. adminstrn. Sani-Serv of Ill., Inc., 1981—; adminstrv. and organizational cons. 1140 Corp., 1980—; adminstrv. dir. Iceman's Ice Co., Inc., 1980—; reporter Suburban Trib of Chgo. Tribune, 1979-80; adminstrv. project asst. Sci. Research Assos., Chgo., 1964-70. Active Friends of Highland Park (Ill.) Library, Highland Park Hosp. Found., Boy Scouts Am., Mid-West chpt. ARC, Chgo. Hort. Soc. Mem. Mgmt. Forum, Highland Park Hist. Soc., Women's Am. ORT. Contbr. articles to newspapers and indsl. jours. Home: 902 Marion Ave Highland Park IL 60035 Office: PO Box 5045 Chicago IL 60680

SAMARTANO, JAMES ANTHONY, structural engring. firm exec.; b. Chgo., Apr. 28, 1929; s. Martin and Mary (Giacalone) S.; B.S.C.E., U. Ill., 1951; children—Martin V., Catherine M. Bridge designer Pa. R.R., Chgo., 1951-52; structural engr. Abell-Howe Co., Forest Park, Ill., 1952, Johnson & Johnson, Chgo., 1952-53; project engr. Vern E. Alden Co., Chgo., 1955-59; pres., owner Samartano & Co., Chgo., 1959—. Served to 1st lt. USMC, 1953-55. Recipient award Chgo. chpt. AIA and Chgo. Assn. Commerce and Industry, 1964; Residential Design citation Progressive Arch. Mag., 1963, others. Mem. ASCE, Nat. Soc. Profl. Engrs., Am. Concrete Inst., Prestressed Concrete Inst., Structural Engrs. Assn. Ill., Internat. Assn. for Bridge and Structural Engrs. Clubs: Ill. Athletic, East Bank, Builders. Home: 505 N Lake Shore Dr Chicago IL 60611 Office: 221 N LaSalle St Chicago IL 60601

SAMET, ALLAN THOMAS, archaeologist; b. Chgo., Aug. 14, 1946; s. Walter Bryan and Marjorie Louise (Schwickrath) S.; B.S., U. Ill., Urbana, 1969; m. Sue Henslee, Sept. 21, 1979. Asst. curator museums anthropology U. Ill., 1977-81, staff archaeologist, 1981—; archaeology field supr. State of Ill., 1977—; resource investigation archaeologist Ill. Dept. Transp., 1977-81. Mem. Am. Anthrop. Assn., Ill. Archaeol. Survey. Author articles in field. Office: Dept Anthropology U Ill Urbana IL 61801

SAMMOND, PETER H., hosp. exec.; b. Milw., Jan. 16, 1933; s. Frederic and Marie (Freitag) S.; B.A., Williams Coll., 1955; M.B.A., U. Chgo., 1962; m. Mary Kay Zagaria, Aug. 6, 1976; children—Douglas, Karen, David. Lectr., U. Chgo. Grad. Sch. Bus., 1962-64; asst. supt. U. Chgo. Hosp. and Clinic, 1962-64; adminstrv. adv. U. Ill. Adv. Project to Govt. of Thailand, 1964-66; asso. dir. U. Minn. Hosps., Mpls., 1966-71, sr. asso. dir., 1971-73; asst. prof. Sch. Public Health, U. Minn., 1975—; asso. exec. dir. Mt. Sinai Hosp., Mpls., 1973-75; exec. dir. Mt. Sinai Hosp., Mpls., 1975—, pres., 1979—; founder, dir. North Star Mut. Assurance Com. of Bermuda; Hosp. div. chmn. United Way of Mpls., 1976, 78; class chmn. U. Chgo. 40th Anniversary Fund Drive, 1973; mem. adv. bd. Hennepin County Health and Social Services, 1975-76; bd. dirs. Affiliated Hosps. Services, 1973-78, pres., 1976-78; bd. dirs., exec. com. Found. for Health Care Evaluation, 1977—, Hennepin County Health Coalition, 1975-76, Mpls. War Meml. Blood Bank, 1975-80. Served with USMC, 1955-57. Mem. Am. Hosp. Assn., Minn. Hosp. Assn. (dir. 1978—, chmn. govt. relations com. 1978-80), Am. Coll. Hosp. Adminstrs., Council of Community Hosps. (mem. tech. advisory com. Asso. Univ. Programs in Health Adminstrn. internat. div.; bd. dirs. 1975—). Club: Minneapolis Athletic. Home: 1315 Spring Valley Rd Minneapolis MN 55422 Office: Mt Sinai Hosp 2215 Park Ave Minneapolis MN 55404

SAMMONS, DAVID GALE, clergyman; b. Chgo., Feb. 11, 1938; s. Joseph Albert and Helen Louise (Leonard) S.; A.B., Dartmouth Coll., 1960; student Meadville/Lombard Theol. Sch., 1961-62; M.Div., Starr King Sch. Ministry, 1965; D.Min., Pacific Sch. Religion, 1978; m. Janis E. Miller, Jan. 24, 1974; children—Donna, David Gale, Michal Ann, Benjamin, Matthew. Head order dept. Haggard & Marcusson Co., Chgo., 1960-61; asst. sales mgr. H&M div. U.S. Bedding Co., Chgo., 1962-63; ordained to ministry, Unitarian-Universalist Ch., 1965; asso. minister 1st Unitarian Ch., Rochester, N.Y., 1965-67; minister St. John's Unitarian Ch., Cin., 1967-68; sr. minister Unitarian Ch. of Evanston (Ill.), 1978—; also public speaker; dir. Beacon Press. Bd. dirs. Voters for Peace, 1965-67; pres. Cin. Action for Peace, 1968-70; adv. Parents Without Partners, 1968-72; bd. dirs. Ind. Voters of Ohio, 1968-76; chmn. Lake Geneva Summer Assn., 1977; sec., v.p. Met. Area Religious Coalition of Cin., 1976-78; mem. steering com. Evanston Ecumenical Action Council, 1978—; sec. N. Shore Peace Initiative, 1979-80, pres., 1981—; pres. Chgo. Area Liberal Ministers, 1980—; mem. Chgo. Peace Week Coalition, 1981, North Shore Ministers Conf., 1981—; sec. Unitarian Universalist CMD Inst., 1981—. Mem. Assn. Social Econs., Soc. Philosophy and Public Affairs, Unitarian Universalist Ministers Assn., Downtown Ministers Assn., Nat. Network for Ethics in Bus., Religious Ethics Inst., Phi Beta Kappa, Phi Kappa Psi. Democrat. Author: The Marriage Option, 1977. Contbr. articles to mags. Home: 811 Gaffield Pl Evanston IL 60201 Office: 1330 Ridge Ave Evanston IL 60201

SAMMONS, FREDDIE WILLIS, steel co. ofcl.; b. Firebrick, Ky., July 30, 1937; s. Earl Willis and Erma Helen (Miller) S.; student Internat. Corr. Schs.; m. Katherine Faye Cantrall, Dec. 2, 1955; children—Jeffrey, Rhonda, Melinda, Gregory, Barry. Electrician, Detroit Steel Corp., 1955-64, maintenance supr., 1964-68; elec. repair supr. Hennepin (Ill.) Works, Jones & Laughlin Steel Corp., 1968—. Club: Masons. Home: Rural Route 1 Hennepin IL 61327 Office: Box 325 Hennepin IL 61327

SAMMONS, JAMES HARRIS, assn. exec.; b. Montgomery, Ala., Mar. 13, 1928; s. Jesse Delmar and Sally Eulalia (Scroggins) S.; B.A., Washington and Lee U., Lexington, Va., 1947, M.D., St. Louis U., 1951; m. JoAnne Halloway, Oct. 14, 1971; children—James Harris, Patricia Sammons Sheets. Intern Alabama City/County Hosp., Mobile, 1951; gen. practice medicine, Baytown, Tex., 1952-74; pres. staff San Jacinto Methodist Hosp., Baytown, 1964, service chief in surgery and obstetrics, 1962-63; mem. faculty Baylor Coll. Medicine, 1972-76, clin. asst. prof. family medicine, 1972-75, vis. asso. prof. family practice, 1975-76; dep. med. examiner Harris County (Tex.), 1962-74; exec. v.p. AMA, Chgo., 1974—, chmn. trustees, 1973-74; chmn. Am. Med. Polit. Action Com., 1969-70; pres., chmn. bd. Houston Acad Medicine. Served with USNR, 1944-45. Mem. AMA, So. Med. Assn. (asst. councilor 1968-71), Tex. Med. Assn. (pres. 1971-72), Harris County Med. Soc. (v.p. 1962), Am. Acad. Gen. Practice, Tex. Acad. Gen. Practice, Harris County Acad. Gen. Practice, Am. Soc. Assn. Execs., Am. Med. Soc. Execs., Phi Chi, Kappa Alpha. Club: Economic (Chgo.). Address: AMA 535 N Dearborn St Chicago IL 60610

SAMORA, JULIAN, sociologist, educator; b. Pagosa Springs, Colo., Mar. 1, 1920; B.A. (Frederick G. Bonfile Found. scholar), Adams State Coll., Colo., 1942; M.S., Colo. State U., 1947; Ph.D. (Hermans fellow), Washington U., St. Louis, 1953; widowed. Tchr., Huerfano County High Sch., Walsenburg, Colo., 1942-43; research fellow Colo. State U., 1943-44; mem. faculty Adams State Coll., 1944-45; teaching asst. U. Wis., 1948-49, Washington U., 1949-50; asst. prof. preventive medicine and public health U. Colo. Sch. Medicine, Denver, 1955-57; asst. prof. sociology and anthropology Mich. State U., 1957-59; prof. sociology U. Notre Dame (Ind.), 1959—, head dept., 1963-66; vis. prof. U. N.Mex., 1954, U. Nacional de Colombia, Bogota, 1963, UCLA, 1964, U. Tex., Austin, 1971; fieldwork in Colo., N.Mex.,

Mich., Denver, Bogota, East Chicago, Ind., U.S.-Mex. border; program adv. in population Ford Found., Mex., C. Am.; cons. U.S. Commn. on Civil Rights, USPHS, Rosenberg Found., John Hay Whitney Found., Nat. Endowment for Humanities, NIMH, Weatherhead Found., U.S. Human Resources Corp., Harcorurt Brace Jovanovich, Inc., Bur. of Census, U.S. Dept. Labor, NSF; mem. President's Commn. on Rural Poverty, President's Commn. on Income Maintenance Program, Ind. Civil Rights Commn., Colo. Anti-Discrimination Commn.; past or present com. or bd. mem. Mexican-Am. Legal Def. and Edn. Fund, Nat. Assessment Ednl. Progress, Immigration and Naturalization Service, Am. Immigration and Citizenship Conf., U.S.-Mex. Border Research Program, Harvard Ency. of Am. Ethnic Groups, Council on Found. Recipient La Raza award Nat. Council of La Raza, 1979; Office Inter-Am. affairs scholar, 1943; Inst. Internat. Edn. scholar, 1943-44; John Hay Whitney Found. fellow, 1951-52; Am. Sociol. Assn. Sydney Spivack fellow, 1978; Nat. Endowment for Humanities Hispanic scholar in humanities, 1979; also recipient numerous grants. Author: (with E. Galarza and H. Gallegos) Mexican-Americans in the Southwest, 1969; (with P.V. Simon) A History of the Mexican American People, 1977; (with J. Bernal and A. Pena) Gunpowder Justice: A Reassessment of the Texas Rangers, 1979; editor: La Raza; Forgotten Americans, 1966; mem. editorial bd. Ethnicity: An Interdisciplinary Jour. of Study Ethnic Relations, Migration Today, Nuestro, Latin Am. Research Rev. Office: Dept Sociology U Notre Dame Notre Dame IN 46556

SAMOREK, ALEXANDER HENRY, elec. engr.; b. Detroit, Mich., Feb. 14, 1922; s. Walter and Gladys (Kurys) S.; B.S., Detroit Inst. Tech., 1961; m. Matilda Louise Dusincki, May 10, 1952; 1 son, David A. Electronic instr. Radio Electronic and TV Sch., Detroit, 1946-49; electronic insp. U.S. Air Force Procurement Office, Detroit, 1950-53; chief technician Wayne Engring. and Research Inst., Wayne U., Detroit, 1954-57; elec. engr. Control Engring. Co., Detroit, 1957-60; sr. research engr. Weltronic Co., Clare, Mich., 1960—; electronic instr. Redford High Sch., Mich., 1966. Served with USAAF, 1942-46. Mem. Soc. Automotive Engrs., IEEE, Am. Welding Soc. Lutheran. Home: 323 Markley St Clare MI 48617

SAMPAT, SUNDERDAS G., structural engr.; b. Khambhalia, India, July 29, 1934; s. Gordhandas B. and Gunvanti N. (Gajaria) S.; came to U.S., 1963, naturalized, 1971; B.Engring. with honors, Poona U., 1955; M.S. in Engring., Lehigh U., 1960; m. Rajni V. Kapadia, May 14, 1963; children—Manish, Piyush. Sr. civil engr. W.K. Shahaney & Co., Bombay, India, 1955-59; structural engr. in tng. McDowell-Wellman Co., Inc., Cleve., 1961-63; project engr. Jervis B. Webb Co., Detroit, 1964-73; sr. product engr. Chrysler Corp., Detroit, 1973-75; chief structural engr., project mgr., mgr. contracts Mid-West Conveyor Co., Inc., Kansas City, Kans., 1975—. Registered profl. engr., Kans., Ohio, Ind., Mich., Nebr. Mem. ASCE. Hindu. Research on plastic design for multistory frames. Home: 13209 W 82d St Lenexa KS 66215 Office: Mid-West Conveyor Co 450 E Donovan Rd Kansas City KS 66115

SAMPLES, ROBERT WAYNE, sales and mgmt. exec.; b. Los Angeles, Jan. 31, 1936; s. Victor Willis and Vida Opal (Prayther) S.; B.S., Ft. Hays (Kans.) State U., 1958; M.S., Kans. State U., 1966; m. Shirley Lee Conard, June 13, 1956; children—Mardi, Linda, Julie. Pres., Sales Incentives Plans, Inc., Belleville, Ill., 1970—; motivational speaker. Pres. St. Louis chpt. Fellowship of Christian Athletes, 1975-76; dir., former pres. Belleville Family YMCA; bd. dirs. Meml. Hosp., 1980—. Named Conf. Coach of Yr., Hutchinson (Kans.), 1965; nominee Young Man of Yr., Belleville Jaycees, 1970. Mem. Belleville Area C. of C., Ft. Hays U. Alumni Assn. (life). Republican. Presbyterian. Home: 213 Berkshire St Belleville IL 62223 Office: 112 E Main St Belleville IL 62220

SAMPSON, DONALD ROGER, heating and air conditioning contractor; b. Black River Falls, Wis., Mar. 8, 1936; s. Eldon Joseph and LaValice Olga (Burch) S.; student public schs., Taylor, Wis.; m. Sharon Helene Staff, Apr. 15, 1961; children—Diane, Dawn, Denise. Owner, operator Sampson Heating and Air Conditioning Hixton, Wis., 1959—. Served with USN, 1955-56. Recipient Nat. Dealer award Gen. Electric Co., 1975, 76, 77, 78, 79, 80. Mem. Small Businessman's Assn. Lutheran. Club: Rod and Gun. Home: 172 W Main St Hixton WI 54635 Office: Sampson Heating and Air Conditioning 126 W Main St Hixton WI 54635

SAMPSON, HERBERT MARTIN, JR., diversified energy co. exec.; b. Greeley, Nebr., July 23, 1925; s. Herbert Martin and Florence Marie (Harrahill) S.; B.S. in Bus. Adminstrn. cum laude, U. Notre Dame, 1950; m. Adelene V. Coad, Aug. 27, 1949; children—Herbert Martin, III, Steven J., Richard M., Mark C., Laura M., Nancy M. With No. Natural Gas Co., Omaha, 1951—, group v.p. corp. devel., 1979—. Mem. adv. council Coll. Bus. Adminstrn., U. Notre Dame; mem. president's council Creighton U., Omaha; bd. dirs. Father Flanagan's Boys' Home, Boys Town, Nebr. Served with USAAF, World War II. Mem. Ind. Natural Gas Assn., Am. Gas Assn., Mfg. Chemists Assn., Soc. Chem. Industry, Chemists Club N.Y.C. Roman Catholic. Club: Omaha Country. Home: Rural Route 1 Elkhorn NE 68022 Office: 2223 Dodge St Omaha NE 68102

SAMPSON, JOHN EUGENE, food co. exec.; b. Lincoln, Nebr., Feb. 25, 1941; s. Delbert John and Mary Etta (Dodrill) S.; A.B. with distinction, Nebr. Wesleyan U., 1963; M.B.A., Ind. U., 1964; m. Mary Margaret Treanor, Aug. 14, 1965; children—J. Mark, Sharon Marie. Mgmt. asst., exec. trainee Office Sec. Def., Washington, 1963-64; staff mem. Com. for Econ. Devel., Washington, 1964-69; coordinator environ. planning Gen. Mills, Inc., Mpls., 1969-72, mgr. devel. planning, 1972-74; dir. corp. planning Central Soya Co., Inc., Ft. Wayne, Ind., 1974-76, v.p. corp. planning, 1976-80, v.p. corp. planning and devel., 1980—; dir. O's Gold Seed Co., 1977—. Chmn. adminstrv. bd. St. Joseph United Methodist Ch., Ft. Wayne, 1979—; trustee Nebr. Wesleyan U.; lay mem. No. Ind. Conf., United Meth. Ch., 1980—. Mem. Ind. U. Alumni Assn. (life), Ind. U. Sch. Bus. Alumni Assn. (dir. 1979—). Home: 5212 W Arlington Park Blvd Fort Wayne IN 46815 Office: 1300 Fort Wayne Nat Bank Bldg Fort Wayne IN 46802

SAMPSON, PATSY HALLOCK, psychologist, educator; b. Picher, Okla., July 9, 1932; d. Daniel Webster and Mary Gladys (Whitehead) Hallock; B.A., U. Okla., 1961; Ph.D., Cornell U., 1966; children—Catherine, Jacquelyn, Rebecca. Asst. prof., psychology, dir. Child Study Center, Wellesley (Mass.) Coll., 1967-70; prof., chmn. dept. psychology Calif. State Coll., Bakersfield, 1970-73; coordinator adolescence research, exec. sec. maternal and child health research com. Nat. Inst. Child Health and Human Devel., Bethesda, Md., 1973-75; psychologist Nat. Inst. Alcohol Abuse and Alcoholism, Washington, 1975-77; dean of faculty, prof. Pitzer Coll., Claremont, Calif., 1977-80; dean Coll. Liberal Arts, prof. psychology Drake U., Des Moines, 1980—. Mem. Am. Psychol. Assn., AAUP, Am. Conf. Academic Deans, Am. Assn. Higher Edn., Assn. Am. Colls. (dir. 1981—), Phi Beta Kappa. Home: 1066 Woodland Park Dr West Des Moines IA 50265 Office: Drake University College of Liberal Arts Des Moines IA 50311

SAMPSON, SCOTT OSCAR, audio visual co. exec.; b. Mpls., June 26, 1952; s. Sigved Theodore and Elouise Olivia (Torkelson) S.; B.A., Augsburg Coll., 1974; m. Nancy Gayle Hagfors, Oct. 9, 1976. Salesman, Machine Tool Supply Co., Mpls., 1974-77; computer operator, salesman Computer Chrome, Inc., Mpls., 1977-79; mgr. Digi-Slide Div., Super Dupes, Inc., Mpls., 1979—. Volunteer, Friend-of-Child, Mpls. Mem. Jaycees. Lutheran. Home: 14015 38th Pl Plymouth MN 55441

SAMS, ROBERT EUGENE, psychiatrist; b. Parkersburg, W.Va., July 30, 1939; s. Robert James and Irene B. (Stonestreet) S.; A.B., W.Va. U., 1961, M.D., 1965; m. Judith Ann Starcher, Dec. 15, 1963; children—Robert Steven, Patricia Ann, Erik Jason. Intern, Bayfront Med. Center, St. Petersburg, Fla., 1965-66; resident psychiatry Rollman Psychiat. Inst., Cin., 1969-71; practice medicine specializing in psychiatry, Parkersburg, W.Va., 1971—; founder Psychiat. Assos.; developer mental health unit St. Josephs Hosp., Parkersburg; asst. clin. prof. psychiatry Marshall U.; cons. Western Dist. Guidance Clinic, 1971-75; clin. dir., cons., Nelsonville (Ohio) Children's Center, 1974-75. Served with USAF, 1966-68. Mem. AMA, Am., W.Va. psychiat. assns., Parkersburg Acad. Medicine. Clubs: Parkersburg Country, Blennerhasset Yacht (vice commodore), Masons, Shriners. Home: Route 1 Reedsville OH 45772 Office: 3211 Emerson Ave Parkersburg WV 26101

SAMSEN, MAYNARD RALPH, educator; b. Plymouth, Mich., July 15, 1914; s. Ralph G. and Ida C. (Olsaver) S.; B.F.A. in Drama, Carnegie Mellon U., 1939. Designer-technician, actor Barter Theater, 1934; designer, stage mgr., actor Ethel Barrymore Colt and the New Jitney Players, 1935-37; instr. Carnegie Mellon U., 1939; designer-technician, bd. ops. Erie Civic Theater, 1941-43; producer and dir. summer stock Rabbit Run Theater, Madison, Ohio, 1946-51; prodn. designer-technician Port Players, Oconomowoc, Wis., 1954-58; mem. faculty Wesleyan Coll., Macon, Ga., 1943-57; mem. faculty Mt. Mary Coll., Milw., 1957—, now asso. prof. theater arts/communications, drama and tech. dir. Served with U.S. Army, 1943-46. Mem. Book-fellows of Milw., Am. Soc. Theater Research. Home: 3456 N 84th St Milwaukee WI 53222 Office: Mt Mary Coll Milwaukee WI 53222

SAMUELSEN, JOHN DAVID, beverage wholesaler; b. Hettinger, N.D., Aug. 30, 1943; s. James Calvin and Shirley Marie (Howell) S.; B.A., Black Hills State Coll., 1967; m. Ruth Ann Duncan, Aug. 24, 1968; 1 son, John Christopher. Ins. adjuster Gen. Adjustment Bur., Bismarck, N.D., 1968-69; gen. mgr. Lakes Bldg. Corp., Rapid City, S.D., 1969-70; sales mgr. Rushmore Homes, Rapid City, 1970-71; salesman Highland Beverage Co., Rapid City, 1971-72, v.p., co-owner, 1972-78, pres., owner, 1978—. Bd. dirs. Girls Club of Rapid City, 1980—. Mem. Nat. Beer Wholesalers Assn., S.D. Beer Wholesalers Assn. (dir. 1974—, pres. 1975-76, legis. adv. 1975—), Rocky Mountain Beer Wholesalers (dir. 1972—), Rocky Mountain Conf. Beer Distbrs. Assn. (pres. 1979-81), Rapid City C. of C. (dir. 1979), S.D. C. of C. Republican. Clubs: Elks; Rapid City Sertoma. Home: 4531 S Glen Pl Rapid City SD 57701 Office: 802 E St Patrick St Rapid City SD 57701

SAMUELSON, DENNIS RAY, pathologist; b. Burlington, Iowa, Jan. 4, 1940; s. Norman Russell and Josephine Katherine (McQueen) S.; B.A., U. Iowa, 1962, M.D., 1965; m. Virginia Lea Matthews, Aug. 29, 1964; children—Erik Sven, Heidi Jo, Alek Justin. Intern Denver Gen. Hosp., 1967-70; practice medicine specializing in pathology and nuclear medicine, Denver, 1967-70, Wichita Falls, Tex., 1970-72; Macomb, Ill., Burlington, Iowa, 1972—; pathologist NuPath Profl. Corp., Macomb, 1972—; mem. staff Burlington Med. Center, 1972—, McDonough Dist. Hosp., Macomb, Community Meml. Hosp., Monmouth, Ill., Meml. Hosp., Carthage, Ill., all 1972—; dir. of labs. McDonough Dist. Hosp., Macomb, Ill., 1975—; asst. clin. prof. pathology Peoria Sch. Medicine. Mem. McDonough County Bd. Health. Served with USAF, 1970-72. Recipient Ewen Murchison MacEwen Meml. prize, 1965; diplomate Am. Bd. Pathology, Am. Bd. Nuclear Medicine, Am. Bd. Family Practice. Mem. Coll. of Am. Pathologists, Ill., McDonough County med. socs., Ill. Soc. of Pathologists, Am. Assn. of Physicians and Surgeons, Soc. of Nuclear Medicine, S. Central Assn. of Clin. Microbiology, Am. Coll. Nuclear Medicine, AMA. Methodist. Club: Elks. Contbr. articles in field to med. jours. Home: 1300 W Adams Macomb IL 61455 Office: 525 E Grant Macomb IL 61455

SAMUELSON, MARVIN L., veterinarian; b. Oketo, Kans., July 25, 1931; s. Eben R. and Mabel (Brown) S.; B.S., Kans. State U., 1956, D.V.M., 1956; m. Judith Ann Mooney, Aug. 13, 1973. Pvt. practice veterinary medicine, San Pedro, Calif., 1958-73; prof. veterinary medicine Kans. State U., 1973—. Mem. Los Angeles County Animal Control Com., 1971-73. Served with AUS, 1956-58. Recipient Norden Disting. Teaching award, 1978. Mem. Am., Kans., Calif., veterinary med. assns., Am. Animal Hosp. Assn., Am. Acad. Veterinary Dermatologists, Am. Assn. Veterinary Med. Eudcators. Democrat. United Methodist. Home: Route 1 Manhattan KS 66502 Office: Dept Surgery Medicine Kans State U Manhattan KS 66506

SAN, NGUYEN DUY, psychiatrist; b. Langson, Vietnam, Sept. 25, 1932; s. Nguyen Duy and Tran Tuyet (Trang) Quyen; came to Can., 1971, naturalized, 1977; M.D., U. Saigon, 1960; postgrad. U. Mich., 1970; m. Eddie Jean Ciesielski, Aug. 24, 1971; children—Megan Thuloan, Muriel Mylinh, Claire Kimlan, Robin Xuanlan, Baodan Edward. Intern, Cho Ray Hosp., Saigon, 1957-58; resident Univ. Hosp., Ann Arbor, Mich., 1968-70, Lafayette Clinic, Detroit, 1970-71, Clarke Inst. Psychiatry, Toronto, Ont., Can., 1971-72; chief of psychiatry South Vietnamese Army, 1964-68; staff psychiatrist Queen St. Mental Health Center, Toronto, 1972-74; unit dir. Homewood San., Guelph, Ont., 1974-80; cons. psychiatrist Guelph Gen. Hosp., St. Joseph's Hosp., Guelph; practice medicine specializing in psychiatry, Guelph, 1974-80; unit dir. Inpatient Service, Royal Ottawa (Ont., Can.) Hosp., 1980—; asst. prof. psychiatry U. Ottawa Med. Sch., 1980—. Served with Army Republic of Vietnam, 1953-68. Mem. Can. Med. Assn., Can., Am. psychiat. assns., Am. Soc. Clin. Hypnosis, Internat. Soc. Hypnosis. Buddhist. Author: Etude du Tetanos au Vietnam, 1960; (with others) The Psychology and Physiology of Stress, 1969. Home: 121 Sherwood Dr Ottawa ON K1Y 3V1 Canada Office: 1145 Carling Ave Ottawa ON K1Z 7K4 Canada

SANBORN, JAMES LEROY, mfg. plant mgr.; b. Faribault, Minn., Sept. 10, 1936; s. Edgar Percy and Sarah Etta (Richards) S.; diploma in gen. bus. adminstrn., Am. Tech. Soc., 1960; diploma, mgmt. of mgrs. program U. Mich., 1980; m. Beverly Jo Munsch, July 27, 1968; children—William J., Maria L., Daniel P., Melissa J., Tara R. Plant mgr. TubeCo, Inc., Owatonna, Minn., 1956-68; supr. J.R. Clark Co., Spring Park, Minn., 1968-69; supt. Continental Tube Co., Bellwood, Ill., 1969-70; asst. plant mgr. Mich. Tube Co., Eau Claire, 1970; plant mgr. Owatonna Mfg. Co., Mitchell, S.D., 1970—. Former chmn. Mitchell Vo-Tech Adv. Bd.; vice chmn. Davison/Hanson County ARC Bd.; mem. Dist. 3 Manpower Planning and Devel. Bd. Mem. Mitchell Area C. of C. Republican. Lutheran. Home: Box 237 Rt 4 Mitchell SD 57301 Office: Box 336 Ohlman Mitchell SD 57301

SANBORN, KENNETH EDWARD, automotive engr.; b. North Conway, N.H., Aug. 27, 1930; s. Leon Henry and Lillian May (Abbott) S.; student Tri-State Coll., 1956-59; children—Kathie, Cynthia, Lorraine. Flight instr. Tri-State Airport, Angola, Ind., 1959-60; chief pilot and flight instr. G.H. Bailey Co., Sturgis, Mich., 1960-61; automotive project test engr. Ford Motor Co., Romeo, Mich., 1962-72, design engr., Dearborn, Mich., 1972, sr. test engr., 1972—. Served with USN, 1947-56; PTO, ETO. Mem. Soc. of Automotive Engrs., Am. Security Council (dir. 1974—), Aircraft Owners and Pilots Assn. Republican. Lutheran. Home: 99 Stratford Ln Rochester MI 48063 Office: 4305 Mack Rd Romeo MI 48065

SAND, PAUL MEINRAD, justice N.D. Supreme Ct.; b. Balta, N.D., Oct. 21, 1914; s. Paul Alexius and Clara (Vetsch) S.; LL.B., U. N.D., 1941, J.D., 1969; m. Gloria L. Gray, Jan. 15, 1952; 1 dau., Sheila G. Admitted to N.D. bar, 1941; individual practice law, Rugby, N.D., 1948-49; asst. atty. gen. State of N.D., Bismarck, 1949-63, 1st asst. atty. gen., Bismarck, 1963-75; justice N.D. Supreme Ct., 1975—. Served to lt. col. U.S. Army, 1941-47. Hon. mem. Order of Coif, Phi Alpha Delta. Roman Catholic. Clubs: Lions, Elks. Office: Supreme Ct Capitol Bismarck ND 58505

SAND, RICHARD EUGENE, physician; b. Cin., Feb. 2, 1931; s. Harry Joseph and Lulu Louise (Schray) S.; B.S., U. Cin., 1953; M.D., 1957; m. Margaret Catanzaro, Feb. 21, 1975; children by previous marriage—Barbara Melissa, Jonathon Parker. Intern, U.S. Naval Hosp., Phila., 1957-58, resident, Portsmouth, Va., 1959-61; resident U. N.C. Hosp., Chapel Hill, 1959-61; chief dept. pediatrics U.S. Naval Hosp., Key West, Fla., 1961-63; practice medicine specializing in pediatrics and allergy, St. Paul, Minn., 1963—, mem. staff Children's Hosp., St. Paul, 1963—, chief of staff, 1974, co-dir. pediatric allergy clinic, 1974—; mem. staff St. Paul Allergy Clinic, 1963—, sec.-treas., 1963-76, v.p., 1976—; mem. staff St. Paul Ramsey Hosp., St. Joseph Hosp., United Hosp., Midway Hosp.; clin. asst. prof. pediatrics U. Minn. Sch. Medicine; med. corporate mem. Blue Cross and Blue Shield of Minn., 1974-77. Bd. dirs. Am. Lung Assn. Asthma Camp, Hennepin County, 1970—, People Inc., St. Paul. Served to lt. comdr. USN, 1957-63. Recipient awards Am. Acad. Family Physicians, 1975-80. Diplomate Am. Bd. Pediatrics, Am. Bd. Allergy and Immunology. Fellow Am. Acad. Pediatrics, Am. Coll. Allergists; mem. Am. Acad. Allergy, AMA, Northwestern Pediatric Soc., Minn. Med. Assn., Ramsey County Med. Soc., Minn., N. Central allergy socs. Lutheran. Home: 364 Summit Ave Saint Paul MN 55102 Office: 565 S Snelling Ave Saint Paul MN 55116

SANDAGE, ELIZABETH ANTHEA, educator; b. Larned, Kans., Oct. 13, 1930; d. Curtis Carl and Beulah Pauline (Knupp) Smith; student Okla. State U., 1963-65; B.S., U. Colo., 1967; M.A., 1970; postgrad. in communication U. Ill., 1970-71, 77—; m. Charles Harold Sandage, July 18, 1971; children by previous marriage—Diana Louise Danner (Mrs. Vern White), David Alan Danner. Pub. relations rep., editor Martin News, Martin Marietta Corp., Denver, 1960-63, 65-67; retail advt. salesperson Denver Post, 1967-70; instr. advt. U. Ill., 1970-71, vis. lectr. advt., 1977—. Mem. Women in Communications, Sigma Delta Chi, Kappa Tau Alpha. Republican. Presbyterian. Editor: Occasional Papers in Advertising, 1971; The Sandage Family Cookbook, 1976; The Inkling, Carle Hosp. Aux. Newsletter, 1975-76. Home: 106 The Meadows Urbana IL 61801

SANDEFUR, JOHN EVERETT, real estate co. exec.; b. Columbus, Ohio, Apr. 20, 1931; s. Everett and Ruth (Montgomery) S.; B.E.E., Ohio State U., 1954; m. Tana Vaseley, June 12, 1954; children—Debra Ann, Jane Ann. Partner, E&J Sandefur Builders, Columbus, 1950-60; v.p. Sandefur Builders, Inc., Columbus, 1960-67, pres., 1967—; pres. Sandefur Co., 1977—. Mem. Columbus Housing Adv. Bd., 1976; bd. dirs. Godman Guild Assn., 1980. Served to 1st lt. USAF, 1955-57. Mem. Nat. Apartment Assn. (v.p. 1979), Nat. Rehab. Assn., Ohio Home Builders Assn. (pres. 1968), Columbus Home Builders Assn. (pres. 1962), Tau Beta Pi. Methodist. Clubs: Shriners, Lions. Office: Sandefur Co 935 E Broad St Columbus OH 43205

SANDEMAN, THOMAS JOHN, food service and restaurant industry exec.; b. Dodgeville, Wis., Feb. 11, 1948; s. Albert Dean and Iola Celeste (Neff) S.; B.B.A., U. Wis., Whitewater, 1970; M.B.A., U. Wis., Madison, 1972; m. Barbara Jean, June 28, 1969; children—Todd, Elizabeth. Acct., Arthur Andersen & Co., Mpls., 1972-74; controller, comptroller ITT, Grinnell, Mpls., Evansville (Ind.), and Ft. Lauderdale (Fla.), 1974-77; v.p. internal audit/fin. planning Ponderosa System, Inc., Dayton, Ohio, 1977—. Asst. cubmaster Miami Valley Council Boy Scouts Am., Dayton, 1981; active St. Christopher's Ch.; basketball coach Cath. Youth Orgn., 1981-82. C.P.A., Minn. Mem. Nat. Assn. Accts., Planning Execs. Inst., Minn. Soc. C.P.A.s, Nat. Restaurant Assn. Office: 3371 Diamondback Dr Dayton OH 45414

SANDER, ESTHER ELAINE, nursing adminstr.; b. Creston, Nebr., July 11, 1928; d. Arthur S. and Mary M. (Hall) Anson; R.N., U. Nebr., Lincoln, 1947; B.S. in Nursing, U. Nebr. Hosp., Omaha, 1950; m. Dallas Sander, Jan. 14, 1950; children—Marcia Suzanne, Janice Marie, Judith Ann, Kathryn Louise. Staff nurse Luth. Hosp., Columbus, Nebr., 1950-63, pvt. duty nurse, 1963-68; pvt. duty nurse St. Mary Hosp., Columbus, 1963-68, charge nurse, 1968-69, dir. nursing, 1969-72; dir. nursing Columbus Community Hosp., 1972—. County ARC nurse, 1958. Mem. Orgn. Nursing Service Adminstrs. Democrat. Lutheran. Home: 4609 60th St Columbus NE 68601 Office: 3111 19th St Columbus NE 68601

SANDER, FREDERICK WILLIAM, multi-industry co. exec.; b. Chgo., May 9, 1926; s. Paul Frederick and Flossie Helen (Freese) S.; B.S. in Bus. Adminstrn., Northwestern U., 1949, M.B.A., 1958; m. Marilyn Joan Johnson, Feb. 18, 1950; children—James Frederick, Kurt William. Dist. sales mgr. Jewel Ridge Coal Sales Co., Cin., 1959-63; planning economist Gen. Am. Transp. Corp., Chgo., 1963-68; dir. corp. and fin. devel. IC Industries, Inc., Chgo., 1968—; dir. Dad's Root Beer Co., Bubble Up Co.; lectr. econs. Trinity Coll., Deerfield, Ill. Bd. dirs. Chgo. Tract Soc. Served with U.S. Navy, 1944-46. Mem. Assn. Corp. Growth, Am. Econ. Assn., Nat. Assn. Bus. Economists, Delta Mu Delta. Mem. Evang. Free Ch. Home: 1224 Blackthorn Pl Deerfield IL 60015 Office: 111 E Wacker Dr Chicago IL 60601

SANDER, LARRY DEAN, physician; b. Fargo, N.D., Mar. 24, 1948; s. Orville Ernest and Adele Bernice (Olson) S.; B.S., U. N.D., 1970; M.D., Case Western Res. U., 1974; m. Margaret Jean Parnell, June 13, 1970; 1 son, Jeremy Ray. Resident in family practice Hunterdon Med. Center, Flemington, N.J., 1974-77; family practice medicine, Orrville, Ohio, 1977—; mem. staff Dunlap Meml. Hosp., Orrville; sr. clin. instr. dept. community health, Case Western Res. Sch. Medicine; pres., med. dir. Wayne County Family Medicine, Inc. Bd. dirs. Health Planning and Devel. Council. Mem. AMA, Am. Acad. Family Physicians, Ohio Acad. Family Physicians, Ohio Med. Assn., Wayne County Med. Soc., Phi Beta Kappa. Home: 1503 W High St Orrville OH 44667 Office: 830 S Main St Orrville OH 44667

SANDERS, JACK FORD, physician; b. St. Louis, Mich., July 16, 1918; s. Ford and Viva (Marvin) S.; B.S. summa cum laude, Alma (Mich.) Coll., 1939; M.D., U. Mich., 1945; LL.D. (hon.), Northwood Inst.; m. Gretchen A. Jellema, Feb. 2, 1945; children—Karen Jean, Vicki Leigh, Mary Beth, Donald Curtis, Wendy Lynn. Intern, Henry Ford Hosp., 1945-46, resident internal medicine, 1947-50; practice medicine, specializing in internal medicine; sr. attending physician internal medicine Butterworth Hosp., Blodgett Hosp., Grand Rapids, Mich.; cons. St. Mary's Hosp., Grand Rapids, Ferguson-Droste-Ferguson Hosp.; med. dir. Mich. Masonic Hosp., Alma, 1960—; med. dir. rehab. div., chmn. dept. medicine, chief staff Gratiot Community Hosp.; chmn. dept. medicine Tri-County Hosp., Edmore, Mich.; asso. prof. medicine Coll. Human Medicine, Mich. State U. Chmn. Com. Aging; mem. adv. Gov.'s Council on Heart Disease, Cancer and Stroke; del. White House Conf. on Aging. Served as lt. (j.g.) M.C., USNR, World War II. Diplomate Am. Bd. Internal Medicine. Fellow Am. Geriatrics Soc., A.C.P.; mem. Am., Mich. med. assns., Wayne, Kent, Gratiot-Isabella-Clare County (pres. 1965) med. socs., Am. Diabetes Assn., Am. Heart Assn., Am. Multiple Sclerosis Soc., Mich. Crippled Children and Adults Soc., East Central Mich. Health Service Assn., Phi Sigma Pi. Basic sci. and clin. research. Clubs: Masons (33 deg.), Rotary. Home: 250 Purdy Dr Alma MI 48801 Office: Michigan Masonic Hosp Alma MI 48801

SANDERS, NORMAN O., lawyer; b. Kansas City, Mo., Jan. 22, 1931; s. William O. and Gertrude V. (Devine) S.; B.A., LL.B., U. Mo., Kansas City, 1958; m. Shirley Ann Stasi, May 9, 1953; children—Debra, Craig, Patrick, Brian, Stacy. Admitted to Mo. bar, 1957; practiced in Kansas City, 1957—; asso. firm Popham, Popham, Conway, Sweeny & Fremont, 1957-60, Pew, Taylor, Welch & Sheridan, 1960-61; partner firm Sheridan, Baty, Markey, Sanders & Edwards, 1961-66; sr. partner firm Sheridan, Sanders & Simpson, 1966—; cons., atty. Kansas City Area Transp. Authority, 1971—; legal adviser Kansas City Youth Ct., 1963-69. Pres., co-founder, chmn. bd. dirs. De La Salle Ednl. Center, 1971-77; chmn., pres. Kansas City Legal Aid and Defender Soc., 1971-72, bd. dirs., 1969—; pres. Bros. Boys Assn., 1964—; mem. Mayor's Prayer Breakfast Com., 1962—, pres., 1971; bd. dirs. U. Mo. at Kansas City Law Found., 1970—, pres., 1975-78; trustee U. Mo. at Kansas City, 1975-78. Recipient Lon O. Hocker Trial Lawyer award Mo. Bar, 1965; Outstanding Alumni award De La Salle Alumni Assn., 1972; named One of Outstanding Young Men Am., 1967; Hon. col. Gov. Warren Hearnes, 1964-72. Mem. U. Mo. at Kansas City Law Sch. Alumni Assn. (pres. 1971), Phi Alpha Delta. Roman Catholic. Club: Kansas City. Home: 9400 Jarboe St Kansas City MO 64114 Office: Traders Bank Bldg 1125 Grand Ave Kansas City MO 64106

SANDERS, RICHARD LEE, coll. pres.; b. Clintonville, Wis., Jan. 2, 1937; s. Claude Henry and Lucille Bernice (Wedde) S.; B.S., U. Wis., Eau Claire, 1959; M.S., U. Wis., Milw., 1966; Ed.D., Marquette U., Milw., 1971; m. Janice Mae Miles, Aug. 30, 1958; children—Scott Richard, Todd Mitchell, Zachary Lee, Nicolle Allisa, Jennifer Elizabeth (dec.). Research asso. Milw. Public Schs., 1966-67; asst. prof. edn., registrar Lakeland Coll., Sheboygan, Wis., 1967-71; successively dean community service, dean students, asso. dean instrn. Lakewood Community Coll., White Bear Lake, Minn., 1971-81; instr. Bemidji (Minn.) State U., 1975-81; pres. Lincoln Trail Coll., Robinson, Ill., 1981—. Bd. dirs. White Bear Cable TV, 1979-80, St. Paul N.E. YMCA, 1980-81, Met. Area Nursing Edn. Consortium, St. Paul, 1977-80. Mem. Nat. Council Staff, Program and Orgnl. Devel., Phi Delta Kappa. Club: Rotary (past dir. North St. Paul). Office: Lincoln Trail Coll Robinson IL 62454

SANDERS, WALLACE WOLFRED, JR., educator; b. Louisville, June 24, 1933; s. Wallace Wolfred and Mary Jane (Brownfield) S.; B.C.E., U. Louisville, 1955; M.S., U. Ill., Urbana, 1957, Ph.D., 1960; m. Julia B. Howard, June 9, 1956; children—Linda, David. Research asst. U. Ill., Urbana, 1955-59, research asso., 1959-60, asst. prof., 1960-64; asso. prof. civil engring. Iowa State U., Ames, 1964-70, prof., 1970—, asst. dir. Engring. Research Inst., 1980—; cons. in structural engring. to govt. and industry. Bd. dirs. Northcrest Retirement Community, Ames. Mem. ASCE (recipient R.C. Reece research prize 1978), Am. Welding Soc. (recipient Adams Meml. membership award 1971), Transp. Research Bd., Am. Ry. Engring. Assn., Nat. Soc. Profl. Engrs., Am. Soc. Engring. Edn. Baptist. Contbr. numerous tech. papers to profl. publs. Home: 1809 Maxwell Ave Ames IA 50010 Office: 104 Marston Hall Iowa State U Ames IA 50011

SANDERS, WAYNE LAWRENCE, broadcasting ofcl.; b. Glendive, Mont., June 15, 1954; s. Lawrence Arnold and Emma (Dvorak) S.; Broadcast Communications degree Brown Inst. Broadcasting, 1973; m. Lorna Willer, Sept. 8, 1974; 1 son, Scott Gregory. Disc jockey Sta. KDIX Radio & TV, Dickinson, N.D., 1970-72, TV account exec., 1973-74; account exec. KFYR-TV, Bismarck, N.D., 1974-80; sales mgr. KQCD-TV div. Meyer Broadcasting Co., Dickinson, 1980—. Roman Catholic. Clubs: K.C., Elks. Home: 1028 Dell Ave Dickinson ND 58601 Office: Box 1577 Dickinson ND 58601

SANDERS, WILLIAM HUGGINS, lawyer, rancher; b. Springfield, Mo., Nov. 24, 1922; s. J.W. and Helen Pipkin (Huggins) S.; A.B., U. Chgo., 1945; m. Nancy Jane Crane, Dec. 24, 1943; children—Christopher, Cynthia, William Huggins, Dan Crane. Admitted to Mo. bar, since practiced in Kansas City; partner firm Blackwell, Sanders, Matheny, Weary & Lombardi, 1953—. Recipient Lon O. Hocker Meml. Trial Lawyers award Mo. Bar Found., 1957. Clubs: University (Kansas City, Mo.); Lane Recreation Assn. Home: No 3002 San Francisco Tower 2510 Grand Ave Kansas City MO 64108 Office: 5 Crown Center Kansas City MO

SANDERSFELD, RUSSELL RUDOLPH, restauranteur; b. Homestead, Iowa, Apr. 17, 1932; s. Rudolph Henry and Dora Dorthea (Witte) S.; m. Mary Martinson, May 20, 1953; children—Randy, Vickie, Dan, Mike, Jay. Asst. mgr. Oxyoke Inn, Amana, Iowa, 1955-65; pres. Colony Village Corp., Williamsburg, Iowa, 1967—, Sandersfeld Food Services, 1976—; pres., gen. mgr. Colony Village Restaurants, 1967—. Pres., First Luth. Ch., 1977. Served with U.S. Army, 1953-55. Mem. Iowa Restaurant Assn., Nat. Restaurant Assn. Republican. Home: PO Box R-71 Amana IA 52203 Office: I-80 Williamsburg IA 52361

SANDERSON, EDWARD DONALD, hosp. ofcl.; b. Chgo., Mar. 21, 1946; s. Thomas James and Marygrace Ellen S.; student Ill. State U., Normal, 1964-67; B.A., Aurora (Ill.) Coll., 1977; m. Donna Jean Hendrickson, Nov. 4, 1967; children—Leslie Marie, Catherine Lavonne. Enlisted U.S. Air Force, 1967, advanced through grades to staff sgt., 1971; med. materiel specialist USAF Hosp., Scott AFB, Ill., 1967-69, USAF Acad. Hosp., Colo., 1969-73; dir. materials mgmt. Palos Community Hosp., Palos Heights, Ill., 1973-75; ret., 1975; dir. materials mgmt. Delnor Hosp., St. Charles, Ill., 1975-79, St. Francis Hosp., Blue Island, Ill., 1979—. Decorated USAF Commendation medal. Fellow Nat. Assn. Hosp. Purchasing Mgmt. (sr.); mem. Am. Soc. Hosp. Purchasing and Materials Mgmt., Tri-City Soccer Assn. Home: 517 N Van Buren St Batavia IL 60510 Office: 12935 S Gregory St Blue Island IL 60406

SANDERSON, ROBERT VINCENT, food co. exec.; b. Champaign, Ill., July 23, 1946; s. Ellis J. and Kathryn (Vincent) S.; B.S. in Chem. Engring. with high distinction, U. Ariz., 1968; M.S. in Chem. Engring., Washington U., 1973; M.B.A., Harvard U., 1975; m. Jacqueline Bromley, July 7, 1973; 1 dau., Kathryn Bromley. Engr., Shell Chem. Co., Los Angeles, 1968-70; sr. engr. Monsanto Co., St. Louis, 1970-73; bus. mgr. Ralston Purina Co., St. Louis, 1975—. Registered profl. engr., Mo. Mem. Am. Inst. Chem. Engrs. Republican. Club: Harvard Bus. (St. Louis). Home: 420 N Harrison Kirkwood MO 63122 Office: Checkerboard Sq Saint Louis MO 63188

SANDERSON, VIRGINIA KATHRYN, educator; b. Mpls., Dec. 2, 1943; d. Bruce Harvey and Jeanette Pauline (Dishington) Anderson; B.S. with distinction, U. Minn., 1966; M.S., St. Cloud State Coll., 1974; postgrad. San Francisco State U., U. Wis., St. Cloud U., U. Minn.; m. Wayne Arthur Sanderson, Aug. 16, 1980. Tchr., Columbia Heights (Minn.) Schs., 1966-81, North Park Sch., 1966-71, Valley View Sch., 1971-81. Mem., Fridley City Band, 1968-71. Mem. Nat. Assn. Gifted Children, AAUW (edn. com. 1980—, long range planning com. 1981—, state topic com. 1981—, chpt. topic chairperson 1981—), Minn. Assn. Ednl. Data Systems, Assn. Ednl. Data Systems, Edn. Futures, Sierra Club, Pi Lambda Theta. Lutheran. Clubs: North Star Ski Touring, Sierra. Home: 4217 Nancy Pl Shoreview MN 55112

SANDFORD, PHILLIP ARTHUR, engr.; b. Pontiac, Mich., May 17, 1927; s. Frederick Tom and Alice Ruth (Howland) S.; B.S. in Elec. Engring., U. Mich., 1950; postgrad. Gen. Electric Test Program, 1951; creative Engring. Program 1953; m. Joyce Elaine Wagner, Sept. 13, 1947; children—Harold, Kerry, Craig, Phyllis, Dale. Advance devel. engr. General Electric Co., Bridgeport, Conn., 1953-54, Asheboro, N.C., 1954-61, thermal electric engr., Schenectady, 1961-63; dir. advanced devel. engring. Norge div. Borg Warner Corp., Des Plaines, Ill., 1963-65; mgr. appliance advanced devel. Philco-Ford Corp., Phila., 1965-70, mgr. automotive climate control research and advanced engring, Connersville, Ind., 1970-72; mgr. engring. comfort products No. Electric Co., Chgo., 1972-78; sr. project engr. McDonald's Corp., Oak Brook, Ill., 1978-80, mgr. systems devel., 1980-81, staff dir. systems devel., 1981—. Elder Presbyn. Ch., Highland Park, Ill., 1973—; mem. Comprehensive Plan Task Force, Highland Park, 1975. Served with USNR, 1945-46. Registered profl. engr., N.C. Mem. IEEE. Holder 2 patents. Home: 310 Central Ave Highland Park IL 60035 Office: McDonald's Oak Brook IL

SANDIDGE, REX JOSEPH, broadcast products co. exec.; b. LaGrande, Oreg., Feb. 1, 1940; s. Joseph Luff and Muriel Helen S.; A.S., Mo. Inst. Tech., 1960; B.S., Central Mo. State U., 1966; M.S., So. Ill. U., 1982; m. Tran Thi Hai, June 2, 1970; children—Alan Roy, Susan Lynn. Test set technician Western Electric Co., Lee's Summit, Mo., 1960-62; chief technician Central Mo. State U., Warrensburg, 1966-67; electronic engr. NBC, N.Y.C., Vietnam, 1967-70; sr. technician, supr., systems engr. Page Communications Engrs., Vienna, Va., with duty in Vietnam, Libya, 1971-74; tech. instr. Ferris State Coll., Big Rapids, Mich., 1974-76; mgr. Broadcast Tech. Learning Center, Harris Corp. Broadcast Products div., Quincy, Ill., 1976—. Mem. Am. Vocat. Assn., Ill. Vocat. Assn., Soc. Broadcast Engrs. Mem. Reorganized Ch. Jesus Christ Latterday Saints. Home: 1740 Gayla Dr Quincy IL 62301 Office: 3200 Wismann Ln Quincy IL 62301

SANDLIN, WILLIAM DONALD, forest products mfg. co. exec.; b. Hamilton, Ohio, Sept. 9, 1934; s. William Henry and Barbra (Eleton) S.; Paper Tech. degree, Miami U., Oxford, Ohio, 1965; m. Betty Ray Ashlock, May 17, 1957; 1 son, Douglas William. Apprentice, Champion Papers Co., 1952-54; with Champion Internat. Corp., Hamilton, 1959—, mgr. printing and trade sampling services, 1978—; cons. in field. Republican precinct committeeman, 1976-78; alt. Ohio Rep. Conv., 1976; elder, trustee Ch. of Christ, Hamilton, 1975—; pres. N.W. Hamilton Neighborhood Assn., 1974. Served with USAF, 1954-58. Recipient numerous service awards. Mem. Inplant Printing Mgmt. Assn. Clubs: Kiwanis, Masons. Home: 344 Sherman Ave Hamilton OH 45013

SANDO, RODNEY WAYNE, forester; b. Independence, Iowa, May 30, 1941; s. Richard William and Leona (Hahn) S.; B.S., U. Minn., 1965, M.S., 1967, postgrad. 1971-77; m. Corinne L. Glader, Aug. 23, 1977; children—Susan Lee, Sara Beth, Erika Dawn. Research technician U.S. Forest Service, Grand Rapids, Minn., 1962-63, smokejumper, Missoula, Mont., 1965, research forester, St. Paul, 1967-71; research officer Can. Forestry Service, Winnipeg, Man., 1967; instr. Coll. Forestry, U. Minn., St. Paul, 1971-77; dir. Div. Forestry, Minn. Dept. Natural Resource, 1978-79, regional dir. Ruffed Grouse Soc. Am., Chisago City, Minn., 1979-80; land adminstr. Minn. Dept. Natural Resources, 1980—. Chosen and N.W. R.R. scholar, 1965; Caleb Doerr Found. grantee, 1964; Ober Family Found. grantee, 1974. Mem. Soc. Am. Foresters, Am. Forestry Assn., Wildlife Soc., Sigma Xi, Xi Sigma Pi. Contbr. articles to profl. jours. Home: Route 1 PO Box 771 Chisago City MN 55013

SANDO, THOMAS CORNELL, dairy co. exec.; b. Mpls., Mar. 12, 1944; s. Otto Melrose and Phyllis Elizabeth Sando; B.S., U. Minn., 1967; m. Lois Lynn Lundberg, June 12, 1965; children—Dana, Jeffrey, Jill. Sales rep. Midwest region Dairyland Products, Inc., Savage, Minn., 1968-71, nat. sales mgr., 1971-73, v.p. mktg. and new product devel., 1973-76, pres., chief exec. officer, 1976—; pres., dir. Profat Feeds, Inc., Savage, 1975—. Mem. Inst. Food Technologists, Am. Assn. Cereal Chemists, U. Minn. Alumni Assn. Republican. Mem. Covenant Ch. Am. Home: 7452 Shannon Dr Minneapolis MN 55435 Office: 5345 W 125th St Savage MN 55378

SANDRY, MARTIN EMANUEL, psychologist; b. Phila., Sept. 1, 1937; s. Benjamin Harris and Ida Sarah (Kravitz) S.; B.A., U. Pa., 1959, M.A., 1961, Ph.D., 1974; m. Nancy Louise Jerz, Aug. 18, 1974; children—Paul, Pamela. Research asso. dept. neurology U. Pa. Med. Sch., 1960; psychologist Childrens Seashore House, Atlantic City, 1961-62, chief psychologist, research dir., 1963; research asso. Assn. Rehab. Centers, Evanston, Ill., 1964-67; pvt. practice psychotherapy, Chgo., 1967—; adminstr. Zone 11, Ill. Dept. Mental Health, 1967-68; program evauator Chgo. Read Hosp., 1968-69, clin. psychologist, 1970-74; psychologist Ravenswood Community Mental Health Center, Chgo., 1974—; vis. asst. prof. clin. counseling program, dept. psychology Ill. Inst. Tech., 1978-79; dir. clin. services, mem. faculty Chgo. Inst. for Rational Living, Ltd., 1974—, also bd. dirs., 1974-80; clin. dir. Libra Sch., Riverdale, Ill., 1980—; staff mem. dept. allergy and clin. immunology Grant Hosp. of Chgo. Certified psychologist, Ill. Mem. Am., Eastern, Ill. psychol. assns., Nat. Alliance for Family Life (clinical), Acad. Psychologists in Marital and Family Therapy. Fellow Inst. for Advanced Study Rational Contbr. Psychotherapy. Author: Rational-emotive Theory: Relationship between Adjustment and Irrational Ideas, 1974. articles to profl. jours. Home and office: 2503 N Halsted St Chicago IL 60614

SANDS, ERNEST MONROE, state ofcl.; b. Pincher Creek, Alta., Can., Apr. 30, 1922; s. Monroe Edwin and Anna (Barr) S.; B.S. in Bus. Adminstrn., U. N.D., 1946; m. Ione Yeager, May 8, 1944; children—Nancy, William. Owner hardware and furniture store, 1947-62; owner Sands Dept. Store, 1961-81, Sands Funeral Home, 1947-81; lt. gov. State of N.D., Bismarck, 1981—. City commr., Velva, N.D., 1960-62, mayor, 1962-70; mem. N.D. Senate, 1967-69, 73-80; state pres. League of Cities, 1966. Served with USAAF, World War II; prisoner of war. Mem. Am. Legion, VFW, DAV. Republican. Methodist. Office: State Capitol Bismarck ND 58501

SANDSTEAD, HAROLD HILTON, physician, govt. nutrition research adminstr.; b. Omaha, May 25, 1932; s. Harold Russel and Florence (Hilton) S.; B.A., Ohio Wesleyan U., 1954; M.D., Vanderbilt U., 1958; m. Kathryn Gordon Brownlee, June 6, 1958; children—Eleanor, James, William. Intern, Barnes Hosp., Washington U., St. Louis, 1958-59; resident in internal medicine Barnes Hosp., 1959-60; resident in pathology Vanderbilt Hosp., Nashville, 1960-61; resident Thayer VA Hosp., Nashville, 1963-64, chief resident in medicine, 1964-65; asst. prof. biochemistry Vanderbilt U., 1965-70, asso. prof. nutrition, 1970-71, asst. prof. medicine, 1967-71; dir. Dept. Agr. Agrl. Research Service Human Nutrition Research Center, Grand Forks, N.D., 1971—; adj. prof. biochemistry, clin. prof. medicine U. N.D., 1971—. Served with USPHS, 1961-63. Recipient Future Leader award Nutrition Found., 1968. Fellow ACP; mem. Am. Soc. Clin. Nutrition, Am. Inst. Nutrition (Mead Johnson award in nutrition 1972), Central Soc. Clin. Research, So. Soc. Clin. Investigation, Am. Fedn. Clin. Research, Soc. Exptl. Biology and Medicine, Soc. Environ. Geochemistry and Health, Alpha Omega Alpha. Contbr. chpts., numerous articles, revs. to profl. publs.; editorial bd. Jour. Nutrition, 1972-76, 81—, Am. Jour. Clin. Nutrition, 1975-78, Ann. Rev. Nutrition Research, 1975—, Dialogue Infant Nutrition, 1976-81, Jour. Lab. Clin. Medicine, 1978—, Biol. Trace Element Research, 1979—, Nutrition Research, 1981—, Nutrition Report Internat., 1981—. Office: 2420 2d Ave N Grand Forks ND 58202

SANDWELL, JOHN ROBERT, broadcasting co. exec.; b. Marion, Kans., Apr. 17, 1949; s. Edmond Robert and Philomene (Shramek) S.; B.S., Fort Hays (Kans.) State U., 1972; m. Judy Ellen Smith, Aug. 22, 1970; children—Chad Michael, Sean Robert, Molly Elizabeth, Joshua Steven. Account exec. KAKE-TV, Wichita, Kans., 1972-76; account exec. WJAR-TV, Providence, 1976-78; local sales mgr. KBMT-TV, Beaumont, Tex., 1978-80; gen. sales mgr. WFIE-TV, Evansville, Ind., 1980—. Mem. blood donor recruitment com. Wichita Regional Red Cross, 1974-76. Mem. Evansville Advt. Club, Fort Hays State U. Alumni Assn. (life), Phi Sigma Epsilon (chmn. bd., nat. pres. 1978—). Republican. Roman Catholic. Club: K.C. (Knight of Year 1977-78). Home: 8413 Holly Ct Evansville IN 47710

SANDY, PAUL CLYDE, cons.; b. Milo, Iowa, June 24, 1918; s. Clyde Brown and Lela (Flesher) S.; student several Midwest schs. and colls., 1935-54. Engring. aide Warren County, Indianola, Iowa, 1941, asst. country engr., 1946-50, project engr., head hwy. design sect., 1951-55; project mgr. Stanley Consultants, Inc., Muscatine, Iowa, 1951-76; now cons. Mem. Muscatine Service Club. Served with AUS, 1941-46; Registered profl. engr., Iowa, Ill., Ohio, Nebr. Fellow ASCE; mem. Nat. Soc. Profl. Engrs., Soc. Am. Mil. Engrs. (past dir.), Iowa Engring. Soc. (acting dir. 1976; Disting. Service award 1976), Am. Road and Transp. Builders Assn., Iowa Good Roads Assn. (dir.), Muscatine County Mus. and Fine Arts Assn. Methodist. Elk. Club: Geneva Golf and Country. Home: 2103 Mulberry Ave Muscatine IA 52761

SANDY, WILLIAM HASKELL, tng. and communications systems co. exec.; b. N.Y.C., Apr. 28, 1929; s. Fred and Rose S.; A.B., U. Md., 1950, J.D., 1953; postgrad. Advanced Mgmt. Program, Harvard U., 1971; m. Marjorie Mazor, June 15, 1952; children—Alan, Lewis, Barbara. Admitted to Md. bar, 1953; planner-writer, account exec., account supr. Jam Handy Orgn., Detroit, 1963-64, v.p., 1964-69, sr. v.p., 1969-71; pres. Sandy Corp., Southfield, Mich., 1971—. Bd. govs. Northwood Inst., 1976-80. Mem. Am. Mktg. Assn. (pres. Detroit chpt. 1975), Am. Soc. Tng. and Devel., Adcraft Club, Nat. Assn. Ednl. Broadcasters. Clubs: Harvard Bus. Sch. (v.p., dir. Detroit club), The Hundred. Home: 596 Rudgate Bloomfield Hills MI 48013 Office: Sandy Corp 16025 Northland Dr Southfield MI 48075

SANE, DEAN MATTHEW, hosp. adminstr.; b. Sask., Can., Sept. 11, 1937; B.A. in Psychology, U. Sask., 1965; M.H.A., U. Ottawa, 1967; m. Olivia Sane, Aug. 13, 1960; children—Joette, Margot, Jodie. Adminstrv. resident Hamilton (Ont.) Civic Hosps., 1966-67; asst. adminstr., then adminstr. Victoria Union Hosp., Prince Albert, Sask., 1967-70; adminstrv. v.p. N. York Gen. Hosp., Willowdale, Ont., 1970-81; pres. Credit Valley Hosp., 1981—; pres. Centennial Hosp. Linen Services Corp., 1978—; lectr. in field, 1972—; bd. dirs. Toronto Inst. Med. Tech.; bd. dirs. lab. services adv. com. Hosp. Council Met. Toronto. Mem. Canadian Coll. Health Services Execs., Am. Coll. Hosp. Adminstrs., Am. Public Health Assn., Can. Hosp. Assn., Ont. Hosp. Assn., U. Sask. Alumni Assn., Assn. Grad. Students Hosp. Adminstrn. U. Ottawa. Club: Kinsmen (N.Y.C.). Home: 9 Rubicon Ct Willowdale ON M2M 3P7 Canada Office: Box 34 Streetsville Mississauga ON L5M 2B7 Canada

SANFORD, PAUL EVERETT, educator; b. Milford, Kans., Jan. 14, 1917; s. Charles Riley and Ina Bertha (Kneeland) S.; B.S., Kans. State U., 1941; M.S. (Quaker Oats fellow), Iowa State U., 1942, Ph.D., 1949; m. Helen Louise Crenshaw, Oct. 31, 1942; children—Paula Louise Sanford Schubert, Patricia Kathleen Sanford Banning, Carolyn Ruth Sanford Elmore. Sr. teaching fellow Iowa State U., Ames, 1946-47, grad. research asst., 1947-48, grad. asst., 1948-49; asso. prof. Kans. State U., Manhattan, 1949-60, prof. dept. animal scis. and industry, 1960—. Guest lectr. P.R., 1957, Japan, 1963. Treas., pres. PTA, Manhattan, 1963-64. Republican precinct committeeman, 1974—. Chmn. bd. trustees Hosp. Assn. Kans. State U., Manhattan, 1958-60. Served with AUS, 1943-46; PTO, ETO. Eli Lilly Co. grantee, 1959-60; Comml. Solvents Corp. grantee, 1960-61; Gulf Oil Co. grantee, 1967-68; U.S. Dept. Agr. grantee, 1965-69; Pfizers Co. grantee, 1971-72; Fellow AAAS; mem. Poultry Sci. Assn., World Poultry Sci. Assn., Am. Poultry Hist. Soc. (sec. 1967-70), Animal Nutrition Research Council, United Comml. Travelers (sr. counselor 1975-76), Poultry Sci. Club Kans. State U., Broiler Soc. Japan (hon.), Nat. Assn. Coll. Tchrs. Agr., Council Agrl. Sci. and Tech., Kans. Acad. Scis., Am. Registry Cert. Animal Scientists, Manhattan C. of C. Presbyterian (deacon 1954-60, elder 1960-66). Home: 343 N 14th St Manhattan KS 66502

SANFORD, RICHARD BRUCE, mgmt. and investment co. exec.; b. Battle Creek, Mich., Mar. 8, 1931; s. Elmer Hurley and Lucille Carolyne (Cummings) S.; student Ohio State U., 1952-53; m. Catherine Ann Ruble, Dec. 21, 1963; children—Robbin Ann, Tamara Lynn, Elizabeth Ann. With Abrams Aerial Survey Corp., Lansing, Mich., 1955-56; sales mgr. Capitol Bus. Services Corp., Lansing, 1957-59; instr. Dale Carnegie Courses, Lansing, 1959-69; mktg. exec. Fidelity Life & Income Mut., Benton Harbor, Mich., 1964-67; founder, pres., chmn. bd. RBSA Corp., Kalamazoo, 1967—; pres., founder Ind. Bus. Assn./Mich., 1969—, IBA Mut. Ins. Co., Kalamazoo, 1980—, IBA Life Ltd., Cayman Islands, B.W.I., 1980—. Vice chmn. commr. Kalamazoo Planning Bd., 1975-76; 1st chmn., mem. Mich. Gov.'s Small Bus. Adv. Bd., 1976—; chmn. Mich. Conf. on Small Bus., 1980-81; mem. U.S. Small Bus. Adminstrv. Adv. Bd., Detroit, 1976—; chmn. Mich. delegation White House Conf. on Small Bus., 1980; regional V chmn. Nat. Small Bus. Unity Council, 1980—. Served with USAF, 1951-55. Mem. Am. Soc. Assn. Execs., Nat. Small

Bus. Assn., Small Bus. Legis. Council, Mich. C. of C., Kalamazoo County C. of C. (bd. dirs. 1973-75, vice chmn. 1975, v.p. 1973-75), C. of C. of U.S., Ind. Bus. Assn. Mich. Congregationalist. Clubs: Rotary (dir. 1979-80), Kalamazoo Park, Mullett Lake Country. Home: 3320 Bronson Blvd Kalamazoo MI 49008 Office: 458 W South St Kalamazoo MI 49005

SANFORD, ROY LEON, pharm. co. exec.; b. Mpls., Nov. 5, 1946; s. Clement Edwin and Mabel Elvira (Telander) S.; B.A. magna cum laude (univ. scholar), U. Minn., 1968, M.S., 1970, Ph.D., 1973; M.B.A., Keller Grad. Sch. Mgmt., 1980; m. Mary Louise Carroll, Nov. 22, 1972; children—Miranda Carroll, Jeremy Edwin. Computer programmer, dept. chemistry U. Minn., Duluth, 1965-67; engring. asst. Cretex Cos., Inc., Elk River, Minn., summers 1966, 68; teaching asst. dept. math. U. Minn., Mpls., 1968-70; postdoctoral asso. U. Minn., St. Paul, 1973-74; dir. data mgmt. Normandeau Assos., Inc., Manchester, N.H., 1974-75; with Travenol Labs., 1975—, group mgr. stats., Morton Grove, Ill., 1978-79, asso. dir. stats., Deerfield, Ill., 1979—; cons., lectr. in field; a founder, treas. Midwest Biopharm. Stats. Workshop, 1978-80, co-chmn. 2d Ann. Midwest Biopharm. Stats. Workshop, 1979; mem. Expert Panel on Quality Assurance, Nat. Coordinating Com. for Large Vol. Parenterals, 1979-80. Baxter Travenol co-chmn. Crusade of Mercy, 1977. Recipient Duluth Arrowhead award U. Minn., 1968; USPHS trainee, 1970-74; Anderson fellow, 1971; stipend awardee Internat. Inst. Statis. Ecology, Pa. State U., 1972. Mem. Am. Mgmt. Assn., Am. Statis. Assn., Am. Soc. Quality Control, Ops. Research Soc. Am., Pharm. Mfrs. Assn. (chmn. biostats. subsect. 1980 ann. meeting), Nat. Trust Hist. Preservation, Recreational Equipment, Inc. Contbg. author: Statistics in the Pharmaceutical Industry (C.R. Buncher), 1981. Home: 1239 Cherrywood Ln Libertyville IL 60048 Office: Travenol Labs 1 Baxter Pkwy Deerfield IL 60015

SANFORD, WINFRED LEON, SR., mgmt. cons.; b. Steele, Mo., July 23, 1938; s. John William and Opal Geraldine (May) S.; B.S. in Acctg., St. Louis U., 1968, M.B.A., 1970; m. Arlene Julia Messenger, July 28, 1956; children-Winfred Leon, Jeffrey Alan, Tracy Ann. With Pet Inc., St. Louis, 1956-68, dir. mgmt. info. systems, 1963-68; sr. cons. Touche Ross & Co., St. Louis, 1968-77, mgr. cons., 1973-78; pres. Leon Sanford & Assos. Inc., Maryland Heights, Mo., 1977—; instr. St. Louis U. C.P.A., Mo.; cert. data processor; cert. mgmt. cons. Mem. Data Processing Mgmt. Assn. (exec. v.p.), Assn. for Systems Mgmt., Assn. for Computing Machinery. Democrat. Baptist. Club: Optimists. Home: 605 Agean Way Ballwin MO 63011 Office: 3A Worthington Dr Maryland Heights MO 63043

SANGAL, SATYA PRAKASH, educator; b. Roorkee, India, Oct. 21, 1931; came to U.S., 1978; d. Sant and Kesari (Devi) Lal; B.S.C., Agra U., India, 1950, M.S.C., 1952; Ph.D., Johns Hopkins U., 1971; m. Kusum Sangal, May 5, 1960; children—Sanjay, Shefali. Research scholar Indian Statis. Inst., Calcutta, 1955-60; statis. officer Durgapur Steel Plant, Bengal, India, 1960-62; chief statistician Narangwal, India, 1962-67; asst. prof. Med. Coll. Va., Richmond, 1971-72; asst. prof. U. Western Ont., London, Ont., Can., 1972-78; asso. prof. dept. community medicine Wright State U. Med. Sch., Dayton, Ohio, 1978—; cons. in field. Recipient Sr. Public Health Scientist award, Govt. of Can., 1972-78. Mem. Am. Public Health Assn., Am. Statis. Assn., Biometric Soc., Internat. Assn. Survey Statisticians. Author: (with Takulia, Alter, Taylor) Health Center Doctor, 1967; (with Taylor, Alter, Grover, Andrews) Doctors for Villages, 1976. Home: 1031 Hyde Park Dr Centerville OH 45429 Office: PO Box 927 Dept Community Medicine Wright State Med Sch Dayton OH 45401

SANGMEISTER, GEORGE EDWARD, lawyer, state senator; b. Joliet, Ill., Feb. 16, 1931; s. George Conrad and Rose Engaborg (Johnson) S.; B.A., Elmhurst Coll., 1957; LL.B., John Marshall Law Sch., 1960, J.D., 1970; m. Doris Marie Hinspeter, Dec. 1, 1951; children—George Kurt, Kimberly Ann. Admitted to Ill. bar, 1960, since practiced in Joliet; partner firm McKeown, Fitzgerald, Zollner, Buck, Sangmeister & Hutchison, 1969—; justice of peace, 1961-63; states atty. Will County, 1964-68; mem. Ill. Ho. of Reps., 1972-76, Ill. Senate, 1977—. Chmn. Will County chpt. Salvation Army; trustee Will County Family Service Agy.; bd. dirs. Joliet Jr. Coll. Found. Served with inf. AUS, 1951-53. Mem. Am., Ill., Will County bar assns., Am. Trial Lawyers Assn., Am. Legion, Frankfort (past pres.), Mokena chambers commerce, Old Timers Baseball Assn. Lion. Home: S Wolf Rd Mokena IL 60448 Office: 2455 Glenwood Ave Joliet IL 60431

SANKEY, BRANT BURDELL, physician; b. New Castle, Pa., Nov. 7, 1908; s. Brant Elder and Lillian Grace (Mosier) S.; B.S., Allegheny Coll., 1929; M.D., Hahnemann Med. Coll., 1933; m. Helen Patterson, May 25, 1935; children—Richard, Roger. Intern, Huron Rd. Hosp., Cleve., 1933-34, resident 1934-36; practice medicine, specializing in anesthesiology, Cleve., head dept anesthesiology St. Luke's Hosp., Cleve., 1943-80; staff anesthesiologist St. Vincent Charity Hosp., Cleve., 1981—; asst. clin. prof. anesthesiology Case Western Res. U. Sch. Medicine, Cleve., 1959—; cons. Cleve. Safety Dept. Trustee, Anesthesia Found., 1956—. Diplomate Am. Bd. Anesthesiology. Fellow Am. Coll. Anesthesiologists; mem. Am. (pres. 1955), Ohio, Cleve. socs. anesthesiologists, Acad. Anesthesiology (pres. 1968), AMA, Ohio Med. Assn., Internat. Anesthesia Research Soc. (trustee 1957—, exec. sec. 1965—), Aesculapean Soc., Med. Arts Club, Acad. Medicine Cleve. Rotarian. Club: The Country. Home: 31311 Trillium Trail Cleveland OH 44124 Office: 2351 E 22d St Cleveland OH 44115

SANSBURY, RUSSELL JOSEPH, lang. specialist, therapist; b. Warsaw, Ind., Oct. 30, 1934; s. James Ralph and Rose Marian (Huddleston) S.; B.A., Manchester Coll., 1957; postgrad. Eastern Mich. U., 1961; M.A., Mich. State U., 1969; M.A., Eastern Mich. U., 1972; Ph.D., U. Mich., 1977; m. Mary Alice Gilchrist, Sept. 3, 1960; children—Rosanne, Michelle, R. Gregory, Jill. Lang. therapist Hawthorn Center, Northville, Mich., 1958-66, dir. lang. clinic, 1966—; alumni bd. dirs., Manchester Coll., trustee, 1981—. Recipient Manchester Coll. Alumni Service award. Mem. Am. Speech and Hearing Assn., Mich. Speech and Hearing Assn., Internat. Reading Assn., Council for Exceptional Children, Concerned Citizens for Mental Health, Mich. Spl. Edn. Suprs., Nat. Alliance Black Sch. Educators, Mich. Assn. Learning Disabilities Educators, Mich. State Employees Assn. (pres.), Phi Delta Kappa. Roman Catholic. Contbr. articles to profl. jours. Home: 719 Sunset Rd Ann Arbor MI 48103 Office: Hawthorn Center Northville MI 48167

SANSOTERRA, JAMES ANTHONY, bank exec.; b. Grosse Pointe Farms, Mich., Mar. 31, 1942; s. Albert A. and Mary F. (Mobarak) S.; B.S., Wayne State U., 1966; M.A., U. Detroit, 1968; m. Jeanette Anne Leier, Sept. 3, 1966; children—Michael A., Mark L. Portfolio mgr., personal trust Detroit Bank & Trust Co., 1968-78, v.p., endowment mgmt., 1978—. Mem. Nat. Assn. Bus. Economists, Fin. Analysts Fedn., Am. Econ. Assn. Office: Detroit Bank & Trust Co 211 W Fort St Detroit MI 48231

SANSTEAD, WAYNE GODFREY, boys' ranch exec., former lt. gov. of N.D.; b. Hot Springs, Ark., Apr. 16, 1935; s. Godfrey A. and Clara (Buen) S.; B.A. in Speech and Polit. Sci., St. Olaf Coll., 1957; M.A. in Public Address, Northwestern U., 1966; Ed.D., U. N.D., 1974; m. Mary Jane Bober, June 16, 1957; children—Timothy Wayne, Jonathan Paul. Dir. debate, Luverne, Minn., 1959-60; dir. forensics Minot (N.D.) High Sch., 1960-69; mem. N.D. Ho. of Reps., 1965-70, N.D. Senate, 1971-73; lt. gov. of N.D., Bismarck, 1973-80; dir. devel. Dakota Boys Ranch, 1981—. Del. N.D. Constl. Conv., 1972. Served with AUS, 1957-59. Coe Family Found. scholar, 1963; Eagleton scholar Rutgers U., 1969; named N.D. Outstanding Freshman Senator, AP Survey, 1971; N.D. Outstanding Young Educator, N.D. Jaycees, 1967; Minot's Outstanding Young Man, Minot Jaycees, 1969; named Ark. Traveler. Mem. Am. Fedn. Tchrs. (past pres. local), N.D. Edn. Assn., NEA (mem. citizenship com. 1969-79), Central States Speech Assn., Am. Forensics Assn., Jaycees, ACLU, Phi Delta Kappa. Democrat. Lutheran (chmn. Western N.D. research and social action com. 1962-68). Elk, Toastmaster; mem. Sons of Norway. Office: Dakota Boys Ranch Box 396 Minot ND 58701

SANTANGELO, MARIO VINCENT, dentist, assn. exec., educator; b. Youngstown, Ohio, Oct. 5, 1931; s. Anthony and Maria (Zarlenga) S.; student U. Pitts., 1949-51; D.D.S., Loyola U. (Chgo.), 1955, M.S., 1960. Instr. Loyola U., Chgo., 1957-60, asst. prof., 1960-66, chmn. dpt. radiology, 1962-70, dir. dental aux. utilization program, 1963-70, asso. prof., 1966-70, chmn. dept. oral diagnosis, 1967-70, asst. dean, 1969-70; practice dentistry, Chgo., 1960-70; cons. Cert. Bd. Am. Dental Assts. Assn., 1967-76, VA Research Hosp., 1969-75, Chgo. Civil Service Commn., 1967-75; counselor Chgo. Dental Assts. Assn., 1966-69; mem. dental student tng. adv. com. Div. Dental Health USPHS, Dept. Health, Edn. and Welfare, 1969-71; cons. dental edn. rev. com. NIH, 1971-72; cons. USPHS, HEW, Region IV, Atlanta, 1973-76, Region V, Chgo., 1973-77. Bd. visitors Sch. Dental Medicine, Washington U., St. Louis, 1974-76. Served to capt. USAF, 1955-57. Fellow Am. Coll. Dentists; mem. Am. Assn. Dental Schs., Odontographic Soc. Chgo., Am. (asst. sec. council dental edn. 1971—, asst. sec. commn. on accreditation 1975—), Ill., Chgo. dental assns., Am. Acad. Oral Pathology, Am. Acad. Dental Radiology, Am. Acad. Oral Medicine, Omicron Kappa Upsilon (pres. 1967-68), Blue Key, Xi Psi Phi. Contbr. articles to profl. jours. Home: 1440 N Lake Shore Dr Chicago IL 60610 Office: 211 E Chicago Ave Chicago IL 60611

SANTEE, SHIRLEY ANN, food co. exec.; b. Sioux City, Iowa, Sept. 29, 1938; d. Jess and Violet Ida (Piper) Copple; student Western Iowa Tech. U., 1969-70, Internat. Corr. Schs., 1973-74; m. Carl Raymond Santee, Dec. 6, 1958; children—Bonnie Santee Baughman, Jack, Rick, Kim. Grocery checker, health and beauty aid clk. A & P Grocery, Sioux City, 1959-61; grocery checker, health and beauty aid clk. Am. Communities Stores, Omaha, 1961-63, gen. merchandise mgr., 1963-73; gen. merchandise supr. Am. Communities Corp., Omaha, 1973-79, territory mgr. Coca Cola foods div., 1979-82; owner, pres. Santee Food Mart, Inc., Springfield, Nebr., 1982—. Mem. Am. Bus. Womens Assn. Republican. Methodist. Clubs: Eagles, Toastmasters, Springfield Women's. Home: 12804 Cottonwood Ln Villa Springs Lake Springfield NE 68059 Office: 176 Main St Springfield NE 68059

SANTIAGO, ARTEMIO CAPILI, internist; b. Santa Maria, Philippines, Jan. 7, 1947; came to U.S., 1972; s. Pedro and Mercedes (Capili) S.; M.D., U. Santo Tomas, 1971; m. Josefina Mendoza, July 7, 1972; children—Artemio, Brian. Intern, St. Joseph Hosp., Lorain, Ohio, 1973-74; resident in gen. practice Kirkwood Gen. Hosp., Detroit, 1972-73; resident in internal medicine Wayne State U., Detroit, 1974-77; chief of medicine, dir. coronary care unit and respiratory dept. Ft. Madison (Iowa) Community Hosp., 1977—. Diplomate Am. Bd. Internal Medicine. Office: Dept Internal Medicine Valley Clinic Fort Madison IA 52627

SANYAL, NARENDRA NATH, tube mfg. co. exec.; b. Lucknow, India, Sept. 7, 1926; came to U.S., 1970, naturalized, 1976; s. Sailendra Nath and Sudha Rani S.; B.S., Lucknow U., 1946; B.S. in Elec. Engring., Rajasthan (India) U., 1951; M.B.A., Drexel U., 1974; m. Aparna Banerjee, May 7, 1956; children—Nirmalya, Mohua, Papiya. Mill engr. BR Group Industries, 1951-58; project mgr. Hindustan Steel Corp., Rourkela, Ind., 1958-61, gen. supr. rolling mills, 1962-68, mgr. power distbn., 1968-70; staff engr. A.W. Steel Co., Conshohocken, Pa., 1971-72, gen. supr. utilities, 1972-73, supt. maintenance and shop crafts, 1973-77; supt. maintenance Regal Tube Co., Chgo., 1977-81, mgr. engring. and maintenance, 1981—. Vice pres. Chgo. chpt. Assn. Indians in Am., 1980-81. Registered profl. engr., Pa., Ill. Fellow Instn. Engrs. (India); mem. IEEE, Assn. Iron and Steel Engrs. Democrat. Hindu. Club: Palos Hills (Ill.) Racquet. Contbr. articles to profl. jours. Home: 7701 Baker Ct Darien IL 60559 Office: 7401 S Linder Ave Chicago IL 60638

SAPPINGTON, JOHN MULLETT, oil co. exec.; b. West Branch, Mich., Feb. 28, 1937; s. Henry Ransom and Josephine (Duggan) S.; B.S., Petroleum Engr., Okla. U., 1960; B.A., Saginaw Valley State Coll., 1980; m. Carol Jane Bleumlien, Sept. 2, 1976; children by previous marriage—Julie, Christopher, Michael; stepchildren—Carrie Bachelder, Richard Bachelder, Michael Bachelder. Staff petroleum engr. Amerada Corp., Hobbs, N.Mex., 1960-62, reservoir and evaluation engr., Midland, Tex., 1962-64; petroleum engr., supt. Henry Sappington Oil Co., West Branch, Mich., 1964-75; pres. Sappington Crude Oil, Inc., West Branch, 1975—. City tax assessor City of West Branch, 1972-75. Registered profl. engr., Tex.; lic. real estate salesman. Mem. Ind. Producers Assn. Am., Soc. Petroleum Engrs., Mich. Oil and Gas Assn., Mich. Assn. Petroleum Landmen. Roman Catholic. Home: 4238 Lakeside Dr West Branch MI 48661 Office: PO Box 35 West Branch MI 48661

SARAPO, DONATO FRANK, physician; b. N.Y.C., July 2, 1925; s. Donato Frank and Theresa (Miglionico) S.; student Columbia U., 1949; M.D., N.Y. Med. Coll., 1952; married; children—Terry, Nora, Guy, David. Intern, Detroit Gen. and Va hosps., Dearborn, Mich., 1952-53, resident, 1953-56; pvt. practice specializing in internal medicine, Adrian, Mich., 1956—; chief of medicine, chief of staff Emma L. Bixby Hosp.; mem. Mich. State Bd. Med. Licensure, 1969-78; pres., dir. Adrian Profl. Bldgs.; dir. Comml. Savs. Bank of Adrian. Alt. del. Rep. Nat. Conv., 1968; mem. Lenawee County Rep. Exec. Com.; treas. Lenawee County Reps., 1969-70; bd. dirs., pres. Cath. Social Services; bd. dirs. Detroit Cath. Charities, Goodwill Industries; mem. lay adv. bd., vice chmn. Siena Heights Coll., 1966-68, chmn., 1968-69, bd. dirs., 1970—; v.p., bd. dirs. Lenawee County Social Services Found.; bd. dirs. Guest House, 1970—; trustee Mercy Coll., Detroit, 1976—. Served with U.S. Army, 1943-46. Mem. Mich. Med. Soc. (council mem. 1970—, del. 1960-70), Lenawee County Med. Soc., AMA, Mich. Soc. Internal Medicine, ACP, Mich. Assn. of Professions (dir. 1974-76), Adrian Area C. of C. Republican. Roman Catholic. Club: Rotary. Home: 4314 Evergreen Dr Adrian MI 49221 Office: Mill St Profl Bldg Adrian MI 49221

SARBER, GLENN SCOTT, environ. engr.; b. Continental, Ohio, Sept. 25, 1929; s. Glenn Scott and Olive Leola (Gott) S.; B.C.E., Ohio State U., 1954; children—David Scott, Anne Louise, Elizabeth. Sr. engr. Holmquist Engrs., Phoenix, 1955-60; owner Scott Sarber Engr., Casa Grande, Ariz., 1960-64; civil specialist Sverdrup & Parcel, St. Louis, 1964-69; asst. chief civil engr. Hok-Helmuth-Obata-Kassabaum, St. Louis, 1968-73; engring. specialist in environ. Monsanto Co., St. Louis, 1973—. Bd. dirs. Grace Hall Settlement House, St. Louis, 1972-80, pres., 1976-77, treas., 1978-79. Fellow ASCE; mem. Water Pollution Control Fedn. Episcopalian. Club: Masons. Address: 7466 Gannon Ave University City MO 63130

SARDEGNA, CHARLES JOHN, hosp. adminstr.; b. N.Y.C., Mar. 18, 1945; s. Leo and Rose Sardegna; B.S. in Nursing, Cornell U., 1971; M.A. in Health Care Adminstrn., Washington U., St. Louis, 1975; m. Ann Kathryn Pfeil, June 3, 1972; children—James, William. Public health nurse Westchester County (N.Y.) Dept. Public Health, 1971-73; adminstrv. asst., then asst. exec. dir. St. Mary's Health Center, St. Louis, 1974-78; exec. dir. St. Mary on the Mt. Hosp./Rehab. Center, St. Louis, 1978—; adv. com. Cardinal Ritter Inst. Home Health Services, 1976, chmn. adminstrv. com., 1978, mem. corp. subcom. action care elderly, 1978. Bd. govs. Cath. Charities St. Louis, 1977-78. N.Y. State Dept. Public Health grantee, 1970; recipient Leadership award Cornell U./N.Y. Hosp. Sch. Nursing, 1971. Mem. Am. Coll. Hosp. Adminstrs., St. Louis Young Adminstrs. Forum, Washington U. Alumni Assn., Cornell U. Alumni Assn., Sigma Theta Tau. Roman Catholic. Club: K.C. Home: 632 Dougherty Oaks Ct Manchester MO 63011 Office: 9101 S Broadway Saint Louis MO 63125

SARGENT, CHARLES LEE, sanitation systems and pollution control systems mfg. co. exec.; b. Flint, Mich., Mar. 22, 1937; s. Frank T. and Evelyn M. (Martinson) S.; B.M.E., Gen. Motors Inst., 1960; M.B.A., Harvard, 1962; m. Nancy Cook, June 9, 1962; children—Wendy L., Joy A., Candace L. Reliability engr. AC Spark Plug div. Gen. Motors Corp., Flint, 1962-63; with Thetford Corp., Ann Arbor, Mich., 1962—, pres., 1974—, chmn. bd., 1974—; pres., chmn. bd. Thermasan Corp., 1969-72; dir. Stirling Power Systems Corp., Ann Arbor Bank and Trust Co. Trustee, mem. bd. edn. Lincoln Consol. Schs., Ypsilanti, Mich., 1973-77; elder Presbyn. Ch., 1980—. Mem. Recreational Vehicle Industry Assn. (dir. 1978-80). Home: 747 Country Club Rd Ann Arbor MI 48105 Office: PO Box 1285 Ann Arbor MI 48106

SARGENT, DONALD VIRGIL, gynecologist; b. Bay City, Mich., Apr. 7, 1911; s. Edward Daniel and Nellie Ellen (Brady) S.; B.S., Loyola U., Chgo., 1932, M.D., 1936; m. Helen Marie Van Colen, Feb. 6, 1937; children—Saundra Donahue, Donald Virgil II, Michael, Pamela Richardson. Intern, St. Mary's Hosp., Saginaw, 1936-38, preceptorship, 1938-42, chmn. dept. obstetrics-gynecology, 1948-80; practice medicine specializing in gynecology, Saginaw, 1946—; cons. staff Saginaw Gen. Hosp., St. Luke's Hosp., 1948-81; mem. bd. Valley Obstetrics-Gynecology Clinic, 1965-81; asso. clin. prof. Mich. State U. Coll. Human Medicine, 1972-77. Served to lt. comdr., M.C., USNR, 1942-46. Diplomate Am. Bd. Obstetrics-Gynecology. Fellow ACS, Am. Coll. Obstetricians and Gynecologists; mem. AMA, Mich., Saginaw County med. socs., Mich. Soc. Obstetricians and Gynecologists (council). Roman Catholic. Clubs: Saginaw, Germania. Home: 6355 Weiss Saginaw MI 48603 Office: 926 N Michigan Ave PO Box 3216 Saginaw MI 48605

SARGENT, FRANK LYMAN, cons. elec. engr.; b. Vicksburg, Miss., Aug. 9, 1922; s. Harry B. and Hilah Estill (White) S.; B.E.E., Miss. State U., 1943; student U. Kans. City Law Sch., 1948-51; m. Margaret Jane Holland, Aug. 17, 1946; children—Stephen J., Sarah H. Sargent VanderLippe, David B., Nancy A. Elec. engr. Rural Electrification Adminstrn., Washington, 1946-47; elec. engr. Black & Veatch, Cons. Engrs., Kansas City, Mo., 1947—; cons.; engring. econ. specialist. Served with USAAF, 1943-46. Registered profl. engr., Mo. Mem. IEEE, (chmn. Kansas City sect. 1964-65), Mo. Soc. Profl. Engrs., Nat. Soc. Profl. Engrs. Episcopalian. Clubs: Leawood Country; Carnival Dance (past pres.). Home: 8009 Wenonga Rd Leawood KS 66206 Office: Box 8405 Kansas City MO 64114

SARGENT, THOMAS ANDREW, educator; b. Indpls., Apr. 24, 1933; s. Thomas Edward and Inez (Secrest) S.; B.A., DePauw U., Greencastle, Ind., 1955; M.A., Fletcher Sch. Law and Diplomacy, Tufts U., 1959, M.A. in Law and Diplomacy, 1968, Ph.D., 1969; m. Cecily Constance Fox-Williams, July 10, 1965; children—Sarah Beatrice, Andrew Fox. With First Nat. City Bank, N.Y.C., 1959-64, asst. accountant, 1963-64; asst. sec. Irving Trust Co., N.Y.C., 1964-66; mem. faculty Ball State U., Muncie, Ind., 1969—, prof. polit. sci., 1979—, asst. to dean Coll. Scis. and Humanities, 1981—, dir. London Center, 1973-74, chmn. dept. polit. sci., 1977-80, chmn. univ. senate, 1977-79; mem. Indpls. Com. Fgn. Relations, 1977—. Dir., exec. v.p. Eastern Ind. Community TV, Inc., Muncie, 1974-76, pres., 1976-77. Mem. nat. governing bd. Ripon Soc., Washington, 1976—; bd. dirs. Hist. Muncie, Inc., pres., 1980; bd. dirs. Muncie Civic Theatre Assn., 1st v.p., 1979-80, sec., 1980-81. Served to 1st lt. USAF, 1955-58. Mem. Am. Polit. Sci. Assn., Am. Soc. Internat. Law, Am. Acad. Polit. Sci., Sigma Delta Chi, Phi Delta Theta. Republican. Methodist. Clubs: Muncie; Columbia (Indpls.). Contbg. editor Ripon Forum, 1973-78. Home: 801 N Briar Rd Muncie IN 47304

SARKESIAN, SAM CHARLES, educator, polit. scientist; b. Chgo., Nov. 7, 1927; s. Charles and Khatoon (Babigian) S.; B.A., The Citadel, 1951; M.A., Columbia, 1962, Ph.D., 1969; certificate African studies, Syracuse U., 1962; m. Jeannette Minasian, May 7, 1955; children—Gary Charles, Joye Simone, Guy Samuel. Enlisted in AUS, 1945, commd. 2d lt., U.S. Army, 1951, advanced through grades to lt. col., 1967; service in Germany, Korea and Vietnam; asst. prof. U.S. Mil. Acad., 1962; vis. prof. Northwestern U., 1964, Buffalo State U., 1965; ret., 1968; mem. faculty Loyola U., Chgo., 1970—, prof. polit. scis., 1974—, chmn. dept., 1974—. Pres. Rosehill Citizens Council, 1971-74. Del. elector Democratic Party, 1974. Bd. dirs. Edgewater Community Council, 1973—. Decorated Legion of Merit, Bronze Star with 2 oak leaf clusters, Combat Inf. badge. Joint grantee Russell Sage Found., 1970; travel grantee Inter-Univ. Seminar, 1971; research grantee Army Research Inst., 1974. Mem. Am. Polit. Sci. Assn., African Studies Assn. (chmn. am. program 1974), Inter-Univ. Sem. in Armed Forces and Society (asso. chmn. 1973, exec. sec. 1968-72), Pi Sigma Alpha. Author: The Professional Army in a Changing Society, 1975; co-author: Politics and Power, 1975. Editor: The Military-Industrial Complex: A Reassessment, 1972; Revolutionary Guerrila Warfare, 1975; Defense Policy and the Presidency, 1979; Non-Nuclear Conflicts in the Nuclear Age, 1980.

SARKETT, JOHN ALLEN, mktg. and communications exec.; b. Cleve., Sept. 29, 1951; s. John Alexander and Helen S.; B.S., Ohio State U., 1973, M.S., 1973; m. Bonnie S. Beck, Sept. 17, 1975; 1 son, Franklin Sandor. Account exec. Burson-Marsteller, Chgo., 1973-75; dir. communications Farm and Indsl. Equipment Inst., Chgo., 1975-76; v.p. The John Volk Co., Chgo., 1976-79; pres. Sarkett & Assos., Inc., Chgo., 1979—. Recipient Founders Day award Agrl. Relations Council, 1978. Mem. Public Relations Soc. Am. (accredited), Agrl. Relations Council, Chgo. Press Club, Am. Agrl. Editors Assn., Nat. Assn. Farm Broadcasters. Office: 333 N Michigan Ave Chicago IL 60601

SARVAY, JOHN THOMAS, sales exec.; b. Weirton, W.Va., Apr. 29, 1937; s. George and Anna (Kasich) S.; B.S. in Design, U. Cin., 1961; postgrad. Case Western Res. U., 1963; m. Beth Ann Ogan, July 15, 1961; children—Margaret Louise, Anna Beth. Plant mgr., dir. design Altech div. Ravens Metals Products, Parkersburg, W.Va., 1960-63; mgr. applied research Ohio Rubber Co. div. Eagle-Pitcher Corp., Willoughby, Ohio, 1963-65; devel. mgr. Standard Products Co.,

Cleve., 1965-70; dir. tech. info. group Stirling Homex Corp., Avon, N.Y., 1970-72; dir. corporate design and mktg. services Schlegel Corp., Rochester, N.Y., 1972-77; v.p. mktg. Modernfold, an Am. Standard Co., New Castle, Ind., 1977-79; sr. sales rep. Computervision Corp., Bedford, Mass., 1979—; planning cons. Wirt County (W.Va.), 1962-63. Recipient awards for water color paintings. Mem. Am. Inst. Aeros. and Astronautics, ASTM, Soc. Automotive Engrs., Am. Soc. Metals, Aircraft Owners and Pilots Assn., Nat. Muzzle Loading Rifle Assn., Indsl. Designers Soc. Am., Brit. Airways Exec. Club. Byzantine Catholic. Clubs: Kiwanis (Cleve.); United Red Carpet. Contbr. articles to profl. jours. Patentee in field of archtl. wall and window systems (5). Home: 1200 Ivywood Ct New Castle IN 47362

SARVER, GARY STEVEN, clin. psychologist, educator; b. Boston, Nov. 20, 1946; s. Samuel and Judith Edith (Keesan) S.; B.A., Boston U., 1969; M.A., U. Fla., 1970, Ph.D., in Psychology, 1973; children—Andrea, Joshua. Asst. prof. psychology Ohio U., 1973—; partner Athens Psychology Clinic, Inc. Clin. Psychologists, Athens, Ohio, 1973—; cons. Athens City Schs., O'Bleness Hosp., Athens County Cts. Recipient award Ohio U., 1977; Ohio U. grantee, 1973. Mem. Am., Ohio, Southeast Ohio psychol. assns., Soc. Research Child Devel., Internat. Neurospsychol. Assn. Contbr. articles to, reviewer for profl. jours. Home and Office: Windy Hills Farm Rte 3 Box 163 Athens OH 45701

SARVER, JAMES MICHAEL, psychologist; b. Stephensburg, Ky., Oct. 28, 1948; s. James Calvin and Velma Lois (Nugent) S.; B.A., Columbia Coll., 1976; M.A. in Counseling Psychology, U. N.D., 1978; m. Mavis Elaine Sandvik, Aug. 12, 1972; 1 son, James Calvin. Enlisted, U.S. Air Force, 1966; staff psychologist, dep. dir. mental health services, USAF Hosp., Grand Forks AFB, N.D., 1978—; instr., dir. psychology program Park Coll. Extension Program, 1978—. Mem. Am. Psychol. Assn., Am. Assn. Sex Educators and Therapists, Biofeedback Assn. Am. Republican. Methodist. Home: 3415 20th Ave S Apt 101 Grand Forks ND 58201 Office: USAF Hosp Mental Health Clinic Grand Forks AFB ND 58205

SARYA, ARNOLD FRED, orthodontist; b. Allouez, Mich., May 16, 1934; s. Arne Edwin and Ethel Suzanne (Petaja) S.; M.S., U. Mo., Kansas City, 1959; D.D.S., U. Mich., 1958; m. Constance Mae Geranen, Sept. 24, 1955; children—Rebecca, Arne, Ann, John, David, Daniel. Orthodontist, Traverse City, Mich., 1960—; chmn. bd., pres. Acad. Dimension Systems, 1971-73; pres., chmn. bd. Glacier Dome, 1974—. Founder, bd. dirs. Traverse City Area Found., 1968—; bd. govs. Sch. Dentistry, U. Mich., 1970—. Recipient Others award Salvation Army, 1974, Alumni of Yr. award U. Mich., 1974; diplomate Am. Bd. Orthodontists. Fellow Internat. Coll. Dentists; mem. Mich. Soc. Orthodontists (pres.). Lutheran (past pres. ch.). Club: Kiwanis (pres. 1968, disting. lt. gov. Mich. div. 19, 1979-80, gov.-elect Mich. dist. 1981, gov. 1982-83). Home: 919 Allouez Trail Traverse City MI 49684 Office: 403 E State St Traverse City MI 49684

SASENICK, JOSEPH ANTHONY, health care co. exec.; b. Chgo., May 18, 1940; s. Anthony E. and Caroline E. (Smicklas) S.; B.A., DePaul U., 1962; M.A., U. Okla., 1963; m. Barbara Ellen Barr, Aug. 18, 1962; children—Richard Allen, Susan Marie, Michael Joseph. With Miles Labs., Inc., Elkhart, Ind., 1963-70, product mgr. Alka-Seltzer, 1966-68, dir. mktg. Grocery Products div., 1968-70; mktg. dir. for Braun AG, Gillette Corp., Kronberg, W. Ger., 1970-73, chmn., mng. dir. Braun Electric U.K., Ltd., 1973-77, dir. new products/new ventures Personal Care div., Boston, 1977, v.p. diversified cos. and pres. Jafra Cosmetics Worldwide, 1977-79; corp. v.p. Abbott Labs., North Chicago, Ill., 1979, pres. Consumer Products div., 1979—. Mem. Omicron Delta Epsilon. Club: Knollwood Country (Lake Forest, Ill.). Home: 555 Lakeland Dr Lake Bluff IL 60044 Office: Abbott Park North Chicago IL 60064

SASMAN, ROBERT THOMAS, hydrologist; b. Plattsburg, N.Y., July 23, 1923; s. Louis Milton and Nina Evalyn (Packard) S.; student U. Wis., Madison, 1940-43, B.S., 1947; hon. grad. U.S. Army Command and Gen. Staff Coll., 1966; m. Julia Ann Vos, May 13, 1951; children—Gary Robert, Dean Karl, Marcia Ann. Soil scientist U.S. Soil Conservation Service, Viroqua, Wis., 1947-48, geologist, Indpls., 1948-51; hydrologist Ill. Water Survey, Urbana, 1951-56, Warrenville, 1956—, supr. No. Regional Office, 1956—; lectr. 15 Ill. univs., colls., acads.; regular lectr. water plant operator short courses. Served with U.S. Army, 1943-46. Mem. Am. Water Works Assn. (bd. dirs. 1975-78, chmn. Ill. sect. 1974-75, newsletter editor 1965-68, Fuller award 1976, Diamond Pin club 1976, Ambassador award 1981), Nat. Water Well Assn. (pres.'s club 1978-81), Chgo. Public Health Engrs. Club (chmn. 1963-64), Mid-Central Water Works Assn. (charter), Chgo. Indsl. Water, Waste and Sewage Group (chmn. 1966-68). Methodist. Author, co-author numerous articles profl. publs. in field. Home: 1217 Sunset Rd Wheaton IL 60187 Office: 29 W 002 Main St PO Box 409 Warrenville IL 60555

SASSIN, CAROL PAMELA, banker; b. N.Y.C., July 22, 1947; d. Jerry A. and Estelle S.; B.A. in Fine Arts, Rutgers U., 1970. Sports feature writer Newark (N.J.) Star Ledger, 1970-73; public relations dir. N.J. Soccer Coaches Assn., 1970-73, Schaefer Soccer League, 1970-73; client services rep. Reddy Communications, Inc., Greenwich, Conn., 1973-76; client services coordinator Central Survey Inc., Shenandoah, Iowa, 1976-79; dir. communications QUESTER div. GMI, Ltd., Des Moines, 1979-81; market devel. mgr. card services div. Iowa-Des Moines Nat. Bank, 1981—. Named one of Outstanding Young Women of Am., 1978. Mem. Am. Mktg. Assn. Exhibited painting in statewide exhibition, N.J. Office: 7th and Walnut St Des Moines IA 50304

SATINOVER, TERRY KLIEMAN, lawyer; b. Chgo., Apr. 25, 1936; d. Charles D. and Mary (Klieman) Satinover; student Shimer Coll., 1952-54; B.A. cum laude, U. Chgo., 1955, J.D. magna cum laude (Weymouth Kirkland scholar), 1958; m. Richard Rees Fagen, June 15, 1958 (div. June 1970); children—Sharon, Ruth, Elizabeth, Michael. Admitted to Ill. bar, 1970; practice in Chicago, 1971—; partner firm Pope, Ballard, Shepard & Fowle, Chgo., 1971—; inquiry panel Ill. Atty. Registration and Disciplinary Commn. Bd. dirs. Congregation Rodfei Zedec, Charles Satinover Fund. Mem. Am. Friends Hebrew U. Order of Coif, Phi Beta Kappa. Jewish (v.p. congregation). Home: 155 N Harbor Dr Chicago IL 60601 Office: 69 W Washington St Suite 3200 Chicago IL 60602

SATO, SHOZO, artist; b. Kobe City, Japan, May 18, 1933; came to U.S., 1964; s. Takami and Midori Sato; Fine Arts degree, Bunka Gakuin Coll., 1955; diplomas in traditional arts; m. Alice Y. Ogura, June 19, 1975. Dir. Kamakura Ryusei Sch. Fine Arts, Japan, 1959-64; faculty U. Ill., Urbana, 1964-66, 68—, artist in residence, prof. art, 1968—, dir. Japan House, 1976—; vis. lectr. colls., univs., 1964—; dir. opera, theatre prodns., 1965—; faculty U. Wis., 1966-67. U. Ill. research grantee on Middle Eastern, South E. Asian performing arts, 1974. Mem. Am. Theatre Assn., Am. Guild Mus. Artists, AAUP. Author: The Art of Arranging Flowers, 1966, The Appreciation of Oriental Art, 1967. Office: 124 Fine Arts Bldg U Ill Champaign IL 61820

SATORY, JOHN JOSEPH, surgeon; b. Wabasha, Minn., Feb. 14, 1910; s. Marcus Cosmus and Josephine (Noll) S.; B.S., St. Mary's Coll., 1933, M.B., U. Minn., 1938, M.D., 1939; m. Mina C. Miencke, 1948; children—Christine Jean, John Joseph. Intern, Milw. County Gen. Hosp., 1938-39; resident Milw. County Gen. Hosp., 1939-42; practice medicine specializing in surgery, 1943—; mem. staffs Grandview Hosp., LaCrosse, Wis., chief staff, 1948-54, chief surgery, 1948-69; staff St. Francis Hosp., La Crosse, Wis.; founder, pres. dir. Grandview Clinic, LaCrosse, 1948-67; instr. surgical anatomy Marquette, U., 1940-42; preceptor U. Wis., 1960-65; instr. Mayo Sch. Med., Rochester, Minn., 1977-81; dir. Wis. Health Care Review, 1969-77; med. dir. LaCrosse Civil Defense, 1954-58; mem. Wis. Bd. Med. Examiners, 1968-72, pres., 1971-72; dir. LaCrosse Cancer Soc., 1952, pres., 1954; bd. dirs. U. Wis.-La Crosse Found., 1978—. Served to maj. U.S. Army, 1942-46. Diplomate Am. Bd. Surgery. Fellow Am. Coll. Surgeons, Internat. Coll. Surgeons (regent Wis. 1975-77), Internat. Acad. Proctology. Mem. Am., Wis., LaCrosse County (pres. 1953) med. assns., Optimists. Republican. Roman Catholic. Clubs: KC, Elks. Contbr. articles to med. jours. Home: 1404 Main St LaCrosse WI 54601 Office: 815 S 10th St LaCrosse WI 54601

SATTI, JOHN ANTHONY, mech. engr.; b. Pola, Italy, June 24, 1938; came to U.S., 1952, naturalized, 1957; m. Luciano and Antonia (Bartoli) S.; B.S. in Mech. Engring., U. Ill., 1963, M.S., 1964; m. Mary Louise Toborg, Aug. 17, 1963; children—Marie, John, Paul. Design engr. Fahralloy Co., Harvey, Ill., 1959-62; project engr. Lawrence Berkeley Lab., Berkeley, Calif., 1964-68; project engr., group leader Fermi Nat. Accelerator Lab., Batavia, Ill., 1968—. Chief youth orgn. YMCA, Naperville, Ill., 1977-80. Mem. ASME. Registered profl. engr., Ill. Roman Catholic. Contbr. articles in field to profl. jours.; patentee superconducting magnets. Office: PO Box 500 Batavia IL 60510

SATTLER, DALE ADAM, state ofcl.; b. Richardton, N.D., Sept. 13, 1941; s. Adam and Margaret Catherine (Miller) S.; B.S. in Edn., Dickinson State Coll., 1962; M.S. in Rehab., U. Ariz., 1975; children—Todd, Teri, Tracy, Wayne. Tchr. high sch., Scobey, Mont., 1962-65, Lusk, Wyo., 1965-66; instr. Job Corps, Dickinson, N.D., 1966-69; instr. phys. therapy, adult edn. Dickinson Pub. Schs., 1968—; regional adminstr. Dept. Vocat. Rehab., Dickinson, 1969—. Mem. Mayor's Com. on Employment of Handicapped; mem. N.D. Conf. on Social Welfare. Mem. Nat. Rehab. Assn. (pres. Gt. Plains region 1980), N.D. Rehab. Assn. (pres. 1978), Nat. Rehab. Adminstrn. Assn. (dir. 1981—), N.D. Adult Edn. Assn. Clubs: Eagles, K.C., Elks. Home: 1111 W 2d St Dickinson ND 58601 Office: Dept Vocat Rehab Pulver Hall Dickinson ND 58601

SATTLER, LEE ANTHONY, advt. agy. exec.; b. Regent, N.D., July 25, 1920; s. Leo Charles and Clara Marie (White) S.; student Northwestern U., 1942, Monmouth Coll., 1944, U. Ga., 1945; B.A., Fenn Coll., 1947; B.A. (hon.), Cleve. State U., 1964; m. Gertrude Louise Hoffman, June 2, 1949; children—Mary Claire, Neil Raymond, Laura Lee, Steven Charles. Gen. mgr. White Adv. Co., Cleve., 1946-53; pres. Ritchie & Sattler, Inc., Cleve., 1953—, Media Assistance Co., Cleve., 1971—. Mem. U.S. Senatorial Bus. Adv. Bd. Served with USNR, 1942-46. Decorated Purple Heart medals, D.F.C., Air medals. Mem. Cleve. Advt. Club, Indsl. Marketers. Club: K.C. Contbr. articles on electronic and metal working to profl. jours. Created microfilm cassette projector adopted by USN Tng. Command. Home: 3193 Rumson Rd Cleveland Heights OH 44118 Office: 1001 Euclid Bldg Suite 406 Cleveland OH 44115

SATTLER, RAYMOND LOUIS, neurosurgeon; b. Concord, Calif., July 16, 1944; s. Ernest Louis and Dorothy Alberta (Bright) S.; A.B., U. Calif., Berkeley, 1967; Pharm.D., U. Calif., San Francisco, 1971; M.D., Case Western Reserve U., Cleve., 1977. Spl. asst. to adminstr. Health Services and Mental Health Adminstrn., Dept. HEW, Rockville, Md., 1971-72; spl. asst. to dir. Bur. Health Manpower Edn., NIH, Dept. HEW, Bethesda, Md., 1972-73; planning asso. Devel. Planning Group, Office of Dean, Sch. Medicine, Case Western Reserve U., Cleve., 1973-74, research asso., Dept. Medicine, 1973-75, fellow gen. surgery, 1977-78, fellow neurol. surgery, 1978—; intern, asst. resident gen. surgery Univ. Hosp. Cleve., 1976-78, asst. resident neurol. surgery, 1978-81, resident, 1981-82. Served to lt. USPHS, 1971-73. Mem. Student Am. Pharm. Assn. (pres. 1970-71), Internat. Fedn. Med. Student Assns. (v.p. for N. Am. 1973-75), Am. Med. Student Assn. (treas., mem. exec. com. bd. trustees 1974-75), Am. Med. Student Assn. Found. (bd. trustees 1972-75), Nat. Coalition of Student Profl. Orgns. (chmn., co-founder 1969-71), AMA, Ohio Med. Assn., Am. Pharm. Assn., A.C.S. (participant candidate's group), Congress Neurologic Surgeons, Acad. Medicine Cleve., Alpha Omega Alpha. Republican. Address: 891 Yellowstone Rd Cleveland Heights OH 44121

SAUER, HERBERT IRVIN, epidemiologist-demographer; b. West Alexandria, Ohio, June 13, 1910; s. Irvin Lewis and Lucy (Pontius) S.; B.A., Ohio State U., 1932; M.S., U. Mo., 1965; postgrad. Stanford U., 1962; m. Esther Doris Johnson, Sept. 13, 1946; children—Charles H., Lucy H. Statistician-intake supr. Transient Bur., Columbus, Ohio, 1933-35; asst. city supr. consumer purchases study bur. Labor Statistics, Beaver Falls, Pa., 1936; dir. social studies Tb Assn., Los Angeles, 1937-44; med. analyst, supervisory statistician Tb program USPHS, Washington, 1944-56, supervisory statistician Heart Disease and Stroke Control Program, Washington and Columbia, Mo., 1956-70; dir. health demography and statistics, also asst. prof. community health, U. Mo., 1970-78, research asso., 1978—; cons., 1978—; cons. cardiovascular diseases and trace elements WHO, 1973. Served with U.S. Army, 1942-43. Fellow A.A.A.S., Am. Pub. Health Assn., Am. Heart Assn.; mem. Am. Statis. Assn., Population Assn. Am., Soc. Epidemiological Research, Gerontological Soc., Phi Beta Kappa, Sigma Xi, Alpha Kappa Delta. Contbr. articles in field to profl. jours. Home: 1635 Highridge Circle Columbia MO 65201

SAUER, HERMAN KARL, communications co. exec.; b. Ehrinshausen, Germany, Mar. 29, 1925; came to U.S., 1928, naturalized, 1935; s. Herman Carl and Emma (Halter) S.; B.S., Ursinus Coll., 1950; postgrad. Drexel U., 1950-51; m. Marie Grace MacNeill, Nov. 14, 1969; children—Erika, Mark. Mgr. product devel. RCA, Moorestown, N.J., 1961-68; v.p. engring. GTE Info. Systems, Mt. Laurel, N.J., 1968-73; pres. satellite communications AII Systems, Moorestown, 1973-76, chmn. bd., 1975-76; v.p. products, satellite communications Harris Corp., Melbourne, Fla., 1977; pres. CATV div. Oak Communications, Inc., Crystal Lake, Ill., 1977—. Served with USMC, 1943-46; PTO. Mem. Internat. Radio and TV Soc. Republican. Baptist. Club: Turnberry. Home: 7602 S Turnberry Rd Crystal Lake IL 60014 Office: South Main St Crystal Lake IL 60014

SAUER, MARY LOUISE, civic leader; b. Chillicothe, Ohio, June 26, 1923; d. Maurice Edward and Sarah Katherine (Kieffer) Steirhilber; B.A. in Edn., Northwestern U., 1945; postgrad. U. Mo., Kansas City, 1963-64, 70-71; m. Gordon Chenoweth Sauer, Dec. 28, 1944; children—Elisabeth Ruth, Gordon Chenoweth, Margaret Louise, Amy Kieffer. Co-chmn., Kansas City Chamber Choir, pres. Kansas City Philharmonic League, 1959-60; pres. women's com. Conservatory of Music, U. Mo., 1963-64; bd. dirs. regional auditions Met. Opera Guild, 1965-69; bd. dirs., program chmn. Nettleton Home, Kansas City, 1976-77; bd. dirs., women's council U. Mo., Kansas City, Univ. Assos.; co-chmn. assos. div. Kansas City Mus. Club. Recipient Distinguished Achievement Internat. Register Profiles award, 1976; Community Leaders and Noteworthy Americans award, Vol. Teaching Assn., 1970-74. Mem. AAUW, Am. Guild Organists, D.A.R., Northwestern U. Alumni Assn., Lyric Opera Guild, Rotary Wives Club, Kansas City Musical Club, Mu Phi Epsilon, Kappa Delta, Presbyterian. Clubs: Rockhill Tennis, Kansas City, Woman's City. Producer bicentennial pageant, Under the Liberty Tree, 1976. Home: 830 W 58th Terr Kansas City MO 64113

SAUER, PETER WILLIAM, elec. engr., educator; b. Winona, Minn., Sept. 20, 1946; s. Alfred Von Rohr and Eleanor Frances (Sawyer) S.; B.S.E.E., U. Mo., Rolla, 1969; M.S.E.E., Purdue U., 1974, Ph.D., 1977; m. Sylvia Louise Stenzel, Aug. 23, 1969; children—Katherine Dora, Daniel Alfred. Elec. design engr. USAF, Langley AFB, Va., 1969-73; research asst. Purdue U., West Lafayette, Ind., 1973-77; asst. prof. elec. engring. U. Ill., Urbana, 1977—; cons. U.S. Army Constrn. Engring. Research Lab., 1976—. Served with USAF, 1969-73. NSF grantee, 1978—. Registered profl. engr., Va., Ill. Mem. IEEE, Sigma Xi, Eta Kappa Nu, Phi Kappa Phi. Lutheran. Contbr. articles in field to profl. jours. Office: 155 EEB U Ill Urbana IL 61801

SAUER, SHARON, fin. co. exec.; b. Montrose, S.D., Apr. 2, 1938; d. George Leland and Oleta Marie (Baade) Johnson; B.A., U. S.D., 1973; M.B.A., U. Minn., 1981; m. Harold A. Sauer, Dec. 30, 1974; children—Elizabeth Jean, Clifford Leland, Richard LeRoy. With Investors Diversfied Services, Mpls., 1973—, mgr. adminstrn., budget and reports, 1980—; owner Sauer Acctg. Services, 1977—. Mem. Nat. Assn. Accountants, Nat. Assn. Female Execs. Republican. Home: 6495 Valley View Rd Corcoran MN 55340 Office: Investors Diversfied Services IDS Tower Minneapolis MN 55402

SAUL, JULIE MATHER, biomed. anthropologist; b. Indpls., May 23, 1941; d. William Green and Bertha Gladys (Williams) Mather; B.A., Pa. State U., 1963; cert. U. Salamanca (Spain), 1963; m. Frank P. Saul, Feb. 1, 1964; children—Joseph Mather, Jennifer Mather. Research technician in agronomy Pa. State U., University Park, 1960-61, research asso. in anthropology, 1964-69; research asso. in anatomy and biomed. anthropology Med. Coll. Ohio, Toledo, 1969—. Co-leader Maya Research Project, Nat. Geog. Soc., Mex., 1979; co-prin. investigator Maya Research Project, NSF, 1981. Mem. Am. Anthrop. Assn., Paleopathology Assn., Sigma Xi, Pi Gamma Mu, Alpha Kappa Delta. Contbr. writings to profl. publs. Home: 3518 E Lincolnshire Blvd Toledo OH 43606 Office: Dept Anatomy Med Coll Ohio C S 10008 Toledo OH 43699

SAUL, RICHARD CUSHMAN, pediatrician, allergist; b. Boston, Aug. 23, 1936; s. John Stanley and Shirley (Cushman) S.; A.B., Washington and Jefferson Coll., 1957, M.D., 1961; m. Yolanda Merdinger, Jan. 1, 1967; children—Bradley, Eric, Jason. Intern, Michael Reese Hosp., Chgo., 1961-62; resident Childrens Meml. Hosp., Chgo., 1962-64, mem. med. bd. dirs., 1969-77; pvt. practice medicine specializing in pediatrics and allergy, Northbrook, Ill., 1966-76; instr. Northwestern U. Sch. Medicine, Chgo., 1966-74; prof. pediatrics U. Health Scis., Chgo. Med. Sch., 1974, lectr., mem. dean's adv. group, 1975—; med. dir. Barwell Clinic, Waukegan, Ill., com. chmn., infant and preschool child, 1974-77; chmn. dept. pediatrics and adolescent medicine Highland Park (Ill.) Hosp., 1978-81, also chmn. child protection team; instr. devel. disabilities Am. Acad. Pediatrics, 1980—, med. cons. SEDOL, Lake County, Ill.; cons. pediatrics U.S. Navy, 1978—; cons. devel. disabities Lakemont Sch., Lake County, Ill., Mary Potter Sch., Lake County. Bd. dirs. Kane, Lake, Mc Henry Health Systems Agy., 1975—, v.p., 1980—; bd. dirs. Barwell Settlement, Waukegan, 1975—; lectr. in field to civic groups. Served to capt., pediatric cons., U.S. Army, 1964-66. Fellow Am. Assn. Clin. Immunology and Allergy, Chgo. Inst. Medicine, Am. Acad. Pediatrics (chmn. com. on child health 1978—), Am. Coll. Allergists; mem. AMA, Ill. Med. Soc., Internat. Coll. Allergology, Chgo. Med. Soc. Congretationalist. Developed scientific exhibit on infant feeding used by Am. Osteopathic Assn., 1972, AMA, 1973. Home: 1620 Spruce Rd Highland Park IL 60035 Office: 1500 Shermer Rd Northbrook IL 60076

SAUNDERS, ARTHUR, architect; b. Kansas City, Mo., June 12, 1920; s. Arthur and Beulah B. (Smith) S.; B.S., Kans. State U., Pittsburg, 1940; B.Arch., Kans. State U., Manhattan, 1951; 1 dau., Susan Dianne, Draftsman, Leavitt and Spieth Architects, Cleve., 1950-54, designer, 1954-55; prin. A. Saunders, Architect, Cleve., 1955—; mem. East Cleveland Architects Bd. Served with USAF, 1942-47. Mem. AIA, Nat. Council Archtl. Registration Bds. Episcopalian. Home: 1700 E 13th St Cleveland OH 44114 Office: 1220 Huron Rd Cleveland OH 44115

SAUNDERS, CARYLN LEE, counselor; b. Ottawa, Kans., Jan. 11, 1943; d. Caryl Newton and Mona Merle (Eaton) Saunders; B.A., U. Kans., 1965; M.A. (teaching asst.), U. Mo., Kansas City, 1969, Ph.D. (Jack C. Coffey scholar, teaching asst.), 1979; m. Clifford E. Chamney, May 3, 1980; children—Amy Christine Rhoads, Heather Eileen Rhoads. Office mgr. Operation Discovery Sch., Kansas City, 1971-72; psychometrist Center Behavioral Devel., Overland Park, Kans., 1973-76; counselor Meadowlake Counseling Center, Kansas City, 1976—; intern counselor S. Kansas City Mental Health Network, Mo., 1976-77; psychotherapist Gardner Community Med. Center (Kans.), 1977-80; project dir. Santa Fe Trail council Girl Scouts U.S., 1980-81; rep. on bd. dirs. Shawnee Mission Assn. Gifted, 1976-77; mem. Region VII Mental Health Evaluation Network Planning Com. Mem. Am. Personnel and Guidance Assn., Am. Assn. Mental Health Counselors, Nat. Vocat. Guidance Assn., Internat. Transactional Analysis Assn., Psi Chi, Pi Lambda Theta. Home: 5048 Reeds Rd Mission KS 66202 Office: 4706 Broadway Suite 115 Kansas City MO 64112

SAUNDERS, DAVID RAE, ednl. adminstr.; b. Danville, Ill., May 26, 1932; s. John David and Orena Gladys (Glick) S.; A.A.S., So. Ill. U., 1977; m. Helen Ruth Hughes, Sept. 1, 1973; 1 son, Benjamin Andrew. Free-lance reporter, corr. So. Illinoisan Carbondale, and editor Menard (Ill.) Time. 1950-61; editor-mgr. Carterville, (Ill.) Herald, 1961-64; writer Univ. News Service, So. Ill. U., Carbondale, 1964-71; info. officer So. Ill. U. Carbondale Vocat.-Tech. Inst., 1971-73, dir. office info. services Sch. Tech. Careers, 1973—; lectr. in field. Dir. civil def. City of Carterville, 1961-65; spl. dep. sheriff, Williamson County, Ill., 1963-68; commd. dep. sheriff Jackson County, Ill., 1972-74; judge Okla. Newspaper Contest, 1966, Am. Penal Press Contest, 1972-78, others. Served with Signal Corps, U.S. Army, 1949-50. Recipient Public Service award Ill. Press Assn., 1963; Excellence in Writing award Soc. Tech. Communication, 1980. Mem. Council for Advancement and Support of Edn. (citation of excellence 1977), Soc. Profl. Journalists, Nat. Assn. Vocat.-Tech. Edn. Communicators, Am. Vocat. Assn., Ill. Vocat. Assn., Sigma Delta Chi. Lutheran. Contbr. articles to newspapers, profl. jours. Home: 412 Elles Ave Carterville IL 62918 Office: Sch of Tech Careers So Ill Univ Carbondale IL 62901

SAUNDERS, KATHERINE (KIT), univ. adminstr.; b. Teaneck, N.J.; d. Alfred R. and Katherine M. (Krall) Saunders; B.A., Trenton State Coll., 1962; M.S., U. Wis., 1966, Ph.D., 1977. Teaching asst., women's phys. edn. U. Wis., Madison, 1964-66, instr., 1966-74, dir. women's intercollegiate athletics, 1974—; founder Wis. Women's Intercollegiate Athletic Conf., 1971, sec.-treas., 1971-73, pres., 1978-79; nat. v.p. for div. I univs. Assn. for Intercollegiate Athletics for Women, 1978—; mem. Wis. Gov.'s Commn. Sports and Phys. Fitness, 1975—, Wis. Gov.'s Commn. on Prevention and Wellness, 1978—; bd. dirs. Madison Met. YMCA, 1977—. Mem. Wis. Assn. Girls and Women's Sports (past pres.). Club: Madison Altrusa (1st v.p.). Office: U Wis Madison WI 53706

SAUNDERS, KENNETH D., ins. co. exec.; b. Chgo., Jan. 4, 1927; s. Maurice and Mildred (Cochrane) S.; A.B., Dartmouth Coll., 1949; m. Jean S. Davies, Dec. 17, 1949; children—Karen Leigh, William Thomas. With Continental Casualty Co., Chgo., 1949-59, asst. v.p., 1957-59; exec. asst. Standard Accident Ins. Co., Detroit, 1959-62; with Combined Ins. Co. Am., Chgo., 1962—, v.p., 1969-74, sr. v.p., 1974—. Served with USMCR, 1945-46. Mem. Health Ins. Assn. Am., Chgo. Group Ins. Assn. (past treas., dir.). Clubs: Economic, Tavern (Chgo.); Exmoor Country. Office: 5050 Broadway Chicago IL 60640

SAUNDERS, RICHARD GORDON, retail exec.; b. Dubuque, Iowa, Sept. 25, 1946; s. Wilson Joseph and Marie Rose (Ungs) S.; B.A., U. No. Iowa, 1972, M.A., 1974; m. Deborah Ann Shay, Dec. 28, 1974. Asst. store mgr. J.L. Brandeis, West Des Moines, Iowa, 1975-77, buyer, 1977, dir. personnel, Omaha, 1977-79, v.p. personnel, 1979—; mem. Nat. Bd. Exec. Compensation. Active Young Republicans, Nat. Alliance of Businessmen, Big Bros., Omaha Youth Council; adv. Nebr. Job Service. Served with AUS, 1968-71; Vietnam. Mem. Soc. Advancement Mgmt., Am. Assn. Personnel Adminstrs., Am. Mgmt. Assn. Roman Catholic. Club: Fontenelle Country. Research on effect of employment on coll. students' grades. Home: 402 MMK Dr Bellevue NE 68005 Office: 16th and Douglas Sts Omaha NE 68102

SAUNDERS-CARR, JUDITH ANN, social worker; b. Charleston, W.Va., Apr. 26, 1942; d. James Allen and Grace Ann (Revels) Saunders; B.S. in Social Work, Eastern Mich. U., 1975, M.Guidance and Counseling, 1979; M.S.W., U. Mich., 1977, cert. specialist in gerontology, 1979; children—Marcia Arlene, Martin Anthony. With Ann Arbor (Mich.) Community Center, Inc., 1966—, dir. sr. citizen program, 1977—; field instr. U. Mich.; dir. Washtenaw County Area Agy. on Aging. Mem. Nat. Assn. Social Workers, Huron Valley Assn. Social Workers, Nat. Council on Aging. Home: 2918 Verle Ave Ann Arbor MI 48104 Office: 625 N Main St Ann Arbor MI 48104

SAUTTER, BRUCE CHARLES, equipment mfg. co. exec.; b. Toledo, Nov. 24, 1953; s. LeRoy George and Geraldine Elizabeth Sautter; B.B.A., Toledo U., 1975; M.B.A., U. Maine, 1977. Staff asst. in fin. Hickory Farms of Ohio, Inc., Maumee, 1977-78, mgr. cash investments, 1978-79, mgr. risk and cash investments, 1979-80, asst. treas., 1980-81, sec./treas. subsidiaries Cheese Barn, Inc., Ross Freeberg, Inc., 1978-81; corp. cash mgr. Reliance Electric Co. subs. Exxon Corp., Cleve., 1981—. Advisor, Jr. Achievement, 1971-74, 79-80. Mem. Northeastern Ohio Cash Mgmt. Assn., Beta Gamma Sigma. Roman Catholic. Home: 31924 N Roundhead Dr Solon OH 44139 Office: 29325 Chagrin Blvd Cleveland OH 44122

SAUVEY, DONALD (ROBERT), musical instrument co. exec.; b. Green Bay, Wis., Mar. 15, 1924; s. Irving and Alice (LaBelle) S.; student Am. TV Lab., 1942-43; cert. electronic tech. Milw. Sch. Engring., 1947; m. Shirley Ann Capelle, Nov. 24, 1949. Sales mgr. Conn Organ Co., Elkhart, Ind., 1960-65; dir. mktg. Electro Music, Pasadena, Calif., 1965-70, v.p., gen. mgr., 1970-73; v.p., gen. mgr. Gulbransen Organ Co. subs. CBS, Chgo., 1973-75; pres., chief exec. officer Hammond Organ Chgo., 1975—; dir. Marmon Co. Mem. businessmen's adv. council Forty-Plus of Chgo., Inc., 1977—. Served with USAAF, 1943-46. Mem. Nat. Assn. Music Mchts. Republican. Roman Catholic. Patentee in field. Office: 4200 W Diversey Ave Chicago IL 60639

SAVAGE, BARRY EMERY, lawyer; b. Jackson, Mich., Apr. 19, 1940; s. Herbert E. and Marva V. (Schultz) S.; B.A. in Econ., U. Mich., 1962, J.D., 1965; m. Joyce A. Diaz, Oct. 6, 1977; 1 son by previous marriage, Steven Vincent. Admitted to Ohio bar, 1965, Mich. bar, 1966; practice in Toledo, 1965—; with firm Savage & Lindsley, P.A., Toledo; engaged in real estate investment, 1968—; rep. Oakland Fin. Group. Licensed real estate broker, Ohio. Mem. Mich. State Bar, Toledo Bar Assn. (chmn. unauthorized practice com. 1970-72), Am. Bar Assn. Clubs: Jolly Roger Sailing (Toledo); Indian Hills Boat (Maumee, Ohio). Home: 4009 River Rd Toledo OH 43614 Office: Savage & Lindsley 228 N Erie St Toledo OH 43624

SAVAGE, GEORGE ROLAND, microbiologist; b. Ft. Worth, Apr. 2, 1929; s. Benjamin Ford and Beatrice Dora (Byrd) S.; B.S., N. Tex. U., 1949; M.A., U. Tex., 1951; m. Helen Jeanne Riley, May 7, 1955; children—Mary, Carol, John, Phyllis. Research asst. Noble Research Found., Ardmore Okla., 1949-50; bacteriologist-serologist N.M. Dept. Public Health, Carslbad, 1951-52; chief med. technologist Meml. Hosp., Carlsbad, 1952-55; asst. dir. Carnegie Inst., Cleve., 1955-59; chief viral and rickettsial lab. br. Dept. U.S. Army, Pine BLuff Arsenal, Ark., 1959-67; sr. biologist Midwest Research Inst., Kansas City, Mo., 1967-73 environ. scientist Black & Veatch, Cons. Engrs., Kansas City, 1973—. Recipient Cert. of Achievement award Dept. Army, 1964. Mem. Am. Soc. Microbiology, Nat. Registry Microbiologists, N.Y. Acad. Sci., Air Pollution Control Assn., Sigma Xi, Beta Beta Beta. Club: Masons. Patentee gell diffusion column measuring device, 1967. Home: 9801 Bluejacket St Shawnee Mission KS 66214 Office: 1500 Meadow Lake Pkwy Kansas City MO 64114

SAVAGE, GERIANNE AGNEW, religious edn. trainer, cons.; b. Chgo., Nov. 14, 1941; d. Edward C. and Adelaide (Brost) Agnew; A.A., Mt. St. Clare Coll., 1961; B.A., Marycrest Coll., 1967; M.R.E., Notre Dame Sem., New Orleans, 1975; m. Frank X. Savage, Dec. 30, 1972; children—Clare, Mark. Tchr., Sacred Heart Sch., Clinton, Iowa, 1961-63; tchr. St. Patrick Sch., Maysville, Ky., 1964-66; tchr. St. Kieran Sch., El Cajon, Calif., 1966-70; tchr. Bridge City (La.) Elem. Sch., 1971-72; dir. total religious edn. Sacred Heart Sch., New Orleans, 1971-75; religious edn. cons. Cath. Diocese of Birmingham (Ala.), 1975-81; founder and dir., ENABLERS, Indpls., 1981—. Ind. ednl. cons. Paulist Press, Paramus, N.J., 1975; keynote speaker Catechist Enrichment Day, Rural Office Religious Edn., Archdiocese of Louisville, 1979; main speaker Ministries Weekend, Diocese of Jackson (Miss.), 1981. Mem. Mid-City Neighborhood Improvement Assn., New Orleans, 1973-75; mem. Mt. Ruffner Nature Coalition, Inc. Mem. Nat. Conf. Diocesan Dirs., Am. Soc. Tng. and Devel. Roman Catholic. Home: 275 W Westfield Blvd Indianapolis IN 46208

SAVAGE, GUS, congressman, newspaper columnist, editor and publisher; b. Detroit, Oct. 30, 1925; s. Thomas and Mollie (Wilder) S.; B.A. in Philosophy, Roosevelt U., 1951; postgrad. Chgo.-Kent Coll. Law, 1951-53; m. Eunice King, Aug. 4, 1946; children—Thomas James, Emma Mae. Editor, Am. Negro Mag., 1955-56, Woodlawn Booster, Chgo., 1961-65, Bull. Newspaper, 1963-65; asst. editor Ill. Beverage Jour., 1956-59; editor, pub. Westside Booster, Chgo., 1959-60; editor Citizen Newspapers, Chgo., 1965—; pub. The Chgo. Weekend Newspaper, 1974—; mem. 97th Congress from Ill. 2d Dist. Chmn., Protest at the Polls, 1963, Coalition for a Black Mayoral Candidate, 1977. Served with USAAF, 1943-46. Recipient Vol. Service award Steelworkers Ad Hoc Com., 1969; Citizenship award Operation PUSH, 1976; medal of Merit City of Chgo., 1976; Journalism award Nat. Newspaper Pubs. Assn., 1978; Disting. Achievement award Chatham Bus. Assn., 1979. Mem. Orgn. for S.W. Communities (pres. 1969-70), Chgo. League Negro Voters (founder, campaign mgr. 1958-59). Democrat. Author pamphlets. Home: 7447 South Shore Dr Chicago IL 60649 Office: 1743 E 87 St Chicago IL 60617 also 1233 Longworth House Office Bldg Washington DC 20515

SAVAGE, JAMES MARTIN, hosp. adminstr.; b. Anderson, Ind., June 17, 1950; s. Robert E. and Annabel S.; B.S. in Indsl. Engring., Purdue U., 1972; M. Mgmt. in Hosp. Adminstrn., Northwestern U., 1974; m. Mary Theresa Berry, July 15, 1978; children—Marcy, Michael, Justin Robert. Adminstrv. asst. Peninsula Gen. Hosp., Salisbury, Md., 1973; adminstrv. asst. E. W. Sparrow Hosp., Lansing, Mich., 1974-76, v.p., 1976—; pres. Physicians Health Plan of Sparrow, 1981—; bd. dirs. Central Mich. Med. Care Rev., Inc., 1978—. Mem. Am. Coll. Hosp. Adminstrs., Am. Hosp. Assn., Mich. Hosp. Assn., Lansing Jr. C. of C. Presbyterian. Home: 116 Feldspar Dr Williamston MI 48895 Office: E W Sparrow Hosp 1215 E Michigan Ave Lansing MI 48909

SAVAGE, JOHN PAUL, educator; b. Detroit, July 12, 1946; s. Neil Saxton and Josephine Alice (Ettinger) S.; B.A., U. Mich., 1968; M.Ed., Wayne State U., 1980; m. Mary Margaret Bermel, Nov. 27, 1971; 1 son, John Paul. Tchr., Public Schs. Lincoln Park (Mich.), 1968—, Carr Elem. Sch., 1979—. Asst. scoutmaster Boy Scouts Am., 1964-76, commr., 1972-74, asst. dist. commr., 1974-76, dist. dir. tng., 1977—, recipient Order of Arrow, 1974, Dist. Merit award, 1976. Served with AUS, 1970-71. Named Outstanding Young Educator, Lincoln Park Jaycees, 1976; Disting. Service award Lincoln Park PTA Council, 1977. Mem. Carr Sch. PTA (tchr. v.p.), Dearborn Jaycees (individual devel. v.p. 1981-82), Mich. Edn. Assn., NEA, Lincoln Park Edn. Assn., Mich. Council Tchrs. Math., Detroit Area Council Tchrs. Math, Mich. Sci. Tchrs. Assn., Met. Detroit Sci. Tchrs. Assn., Assn. Supervision and Curriculum Devel., Phi Delta Kappa. Home: 7840 Calhoun St Dearborn MI 48126 Office: 1545 Southfield St Lincoln Park MI 48146

SAVAGE, ROBERT ENGLEBERT, veterinarian; b. Spencer, Iowa, June 21, 1917; s. Guy David and Hattie Ruth (Knudson) S.; D.V.M., Iowa State U., 1943; m. Josephine May Ricklefs, June 11, 1943; children—David, Susan (Mrs. Larry Eilers), John. Practice veterinary medicine, Monticello, Iowa, 1946—; dist. veterinarian Iowa Dept. Agr., 1973-79. Councilman-at-large City of Monticello, 1968—; mem. adv. council Kirkwood Coll., 1977. Served to capt. AUS, 1943-46. Recipient Silver Beaver award Boy Scouts Am., 1959, Iowa Woodland Owner of Year award, 1976. Mem. Am., Iowa, E. Central Iowa (pres. 1950), Eastern Iowa (pres. 1957) vet. med. assns., Iowa Polled Shorthorn Cattle Assn. (pres. 1968-69), Am. Legion, Alpha Gamma Rho. Republican. Congregationalist. Mason, Rotarian. Contbr. articles to profl. publs. Address: 200 S Chestnut St Monticello IA 52310

SAVELKOUL, DONALD CHARLES, lawyer; b. Mpls., July 29, 1917; s. Theodore Charles and Edith (Lindgren) S.; B.A. magna cum laude, U. Minn., 1939; BS. cum laude, William Mitchell Coll. Law, 1950, J.D. cum laude, 1951; m. Mary Joan Holland, May 17, 1941; children—Jeffrey Charles, Jean Marie, Edward Joseph. Admitted to Minn. bar, 1951; adminstrv. work various U.S. govt. depts., including Commerce, War, Labor, Wage Stblzn. Bd., 1940-51; municipal judge, Fridley, Minn., 1952-54; law practice, Mpls. and Fridley, 1951—; chmn. bd. Fridley State Bank, 1962—, Blaine State Bank, 1972—; pres. Banrein, Inc., Blaine Bldg. Corp., Babbscha Co. Mem. faculty Wm. Mitchell Coll. Law, 1952-59, corp. mem., 1956—; sec. Fridley Recreation and Service Co., 1955—. Mem. Minn. Legislature, 1967-69. Mem. Gov.'s Com. Workers Compensation, 1965-67, Gov.'s Adv. Council on Employment Security, 1957-69. Chmn. Fridley Police Civil Service Commn., 1962-63. Served 1st lt. AUS, 1943-46. Decorated Bronze Star. Mem. Hennepin County, Minn., Am. bar assns., Am., Minn. trial lawyers assns., Justice William Mitchell Soc., Am. Legion, Phi Beta Kappa. Roman Catholic. K.C. (4 deg.). Clubs: Midland Hills Country, U. Minn. Pres.'s, Alexandria Country, U. Minn. Alumni. Home: 916 W Moore Lake Dr Fridley MN 55432 Office: Fridley State Bank Bldg 6315 University Ave NE Fridley MN 55432

SAVICKAS, FRANK DAVID, state senator, plumber; b. Chgo., May 14, 1935; s. Frank L. and Estelle (Ivaskevich) S.; student Wildon Jr. Coll.; m. Adrienne C. Shenoha, 1954; children—Michael David, Linda Diane, Sharon Eileen. Plumber, Chgo. Mem. Ill. State Senate, 1973—, Ill. Ho. of Reps., 1966-72; del. Democratic Nat. Conv., 1976. Mem. Chgo. Journeyman Plumbers Local Union 130, Lithuanian C. of C. Clubs: KC (4th deg.), Riano Social. Roman Catholic. Office: State Capitol Gen Assembly Springfield IL 62700*

SAVIN, SAMUEL M(ARVIN), geologist; b. Boston, Aug. 31, 1940; s. George and Sarah (Lewiton) S.; B.A., Colgate U., 1961; Ph.D., Calif. Inst. Tech., 1967; m. Norma Goulder, Nov. 4, 1978; children—Robert Goulder, Lisa Rebecca. Asst. prof. geol. scis. Case Western Res. U., 1967-73, asso. prof., 1973-76, prof., 1976—, chmn. dept. earth scis., 1977—; Industry fellow Marathon Oil Co., Denver, 1976; mem. NSF Adv. Panel for Earth Scis., 1978-81. Fellow AAAS; mem. Geol. Soc. Am., Am. Geophys. Union, Clay Minerals Soc. (councilor 1978—), Nat. Assn. Geology Tchrs., Am. Assn. Petroleum Geologists, Geochem. Soc., No. Ohio Geol. Soc. Contbr. articles to profl. jours.; asso. editor Geochimica et Cosmochimica Acta, 1976-79, Marine Micropaleontology, 1979—. Office: Dept Geol Scis Case Western Res U Cleveland OH 44106

SAVOIE, LEONARD NORMAN, transp. co. exec.; b. Manchester, N.H., Aug. 8, 1928; s. Joseph Peter and Angelina (Desmarais) S.; B.S., Queen's U., 1952; M.B.A., U. Detroit, 1955; m. Elsie Anne Berscht, June 9, 1951; children—Deborah Anne, Judith Lynn, Andrew Peter. Indsl. engr. Kelsey-Hayes Can. Ltd., Windsor, Ont., Can., 1952-60; mgmt. cons. P.S. Ross & Partners, Toronto, Ont., 1960-64; pres., gen. mgr. Kelsey-Hayes Can. Ltd., 1964-70; pres., chief exec. officer Algoma Central Ry., Sault Ste Marie, Ont., 1970—; dir. Algoma Steel Corp. Ltd., Great Lakes Power Ltd., Ont. Hydro, Empire Life Ins. Co., Thibodeau-Finch Express Ltd., Newaygo Forest Products Ltd., E-L Fin. Corp. Ltd. Bd. dirs. United Appeal. Mem. Profl. Engrs. Ont., Engring. Inst. Can., Canadian, Sault Ste Marie chambers commerce. Clubs: Toronto, Toronto Railway, Sault Ste Marie Golf. Home: 19 Atlas St Sault Ste Marie ON Canada Office: 289 Bay St Sault Ste Marie ON Canada

SAWYER, DWIGHT WESLEY, consumer products mfg. co. exec.; b. Los Angeles, Jan. 10, 1933; s. Dwight Hobson and Oma Zelma (Roundy) S.; B.S., UCLA, 1958; postgrad. U. So. Calif., 1959-62; m. Jacquolyn Asaro, July 1, 1955; children—Pamela Jo, Stacy Ann, Dwight Douglas. Mgr. personnel Firestone Tire & Rubber Co., South Gate, Calif., 1955-62, mgr. indsl. relations, Christchurch, New Zealand, 1962-65, Bombay, India, 1965-67, mgr. indsl. relations, Akron (Ohio) plants, 1967-73; v.p. human resources Amway Corp., Ada, Mich., 1973—. Dist. chmn. council Boy Scouts Am., Akron, 1968-73, Grand Rapids, Mich., 1975-79; bd. deacons Mayflower Ch., Grand Rapids, 1977-80, trustee, 1980—; trustee Davenport Coll. Served with U.S. Army, 1955-57. Mem. Mfrs. Assn. Akron (dir. 1968-73), NAM, Am. Assn. Personnel Adminstrs., Employers Assn. Grand Rapids (trustee indsl. relations group). Republican. Home: 3025 Mary St SE Grand Rapids MI 49506 Office: 7575 E Fulton Rd Ada MI 49355

SAWYER, HAROLD SAMUEL, congressman, lawyer; b. San Francisco, Mar. 21, 1920; s. Harold S. and Agnes (McGugan) S.; B.A., U. Calif. at Berkeley, 1940, LL.B., 1943; m. Marcia C. Steketee, Aug. 26, 1944; children—Stephen R., David H., Keary W., Mariya Sinclair. Admitted to Calif. bar, 1943, Mich. bar, 1946, D.C. bar, 1978; practiced in Grand Rapids, Mich.; mem. firm Warner, Norcross and Judd, 1950-76, chmn., 1969-75; pros. atty. Kent County (Mich.), 1975-76; mem. 95th-97th congresses from 5th Mich. dist. Vice pres., dir. Grand Hotel, Mackinac Island, 1957-76; chmn. bd. Citation Cos., Inc., Grand Rapids, 1953-77, Kysor Indsl. Corp., Cadillac, Mich., 1960-77. Spl. legal counsel Gov. Romney, 1962; mem. Mich. Law Revision Commn., 1967-76. Pres., bd. dirs. D. A. Blodgett Home for Children, 1950-61. Served to lt. (j.g.) USNR, 1941-45. Fellow Internat. Acad. Trial Lawyers (dir. 1964-72), Internat. Soc. Barristers, Am. Coll. Trial Lawyers, Am. Bar Found.; mem. Am. Law Inst. Home: 11195 Summit Ave Rockford MI 49341 Office: 166 Gerald R Ford Bldg Grand Rapids MI 49502

SAWYER, JOHN, profl. football team exec.; s. Charles Sawyer; m. Ruth Sawyer; children—Anne, Elizabeth, Catherine, Mary. Pres., part owner Cin. Bengals, NFL; pres. J. Sawyer Co., Ohio, Miss., Mont., Wyo. Home: Cincinnati OH Office: 8050 Hosbrook Ct Cincinnati OH 45236

SAWYER, ROBERT MCLARAN, educator; b. St. Louis, Nov. 12, 1929; s. Lee McLaran and Harrie (Alcock) S.; B.S., S.E. Mo. State Coll., 1952; M.A., U. Ill., 1953; Ph.D., U. Mo., 1966; m. Patricia Ann Covert, Nov. 23, 1955; children—Ann Marie, Lee McLaran, Gail Louise. Tchr., Rolla (Mo.) Public Schs., 1955; asst. prof. to asso. prof. U. Mo., Rolla, 1956-67; asso. prof. history of edn. U. Nebr., Lincoln, 1967-69, prof., 1969—, chmn. dept. history and philosophy of edn., 1975—, mem. council Coll. Arts and Scis.; vis. prof. Ark. State U., Jonesboro, summer 1966; proposal reviewer Nat. Endowment for Humanities. Served with U.S. Army, 1953-55. Mem. Orgn. Am. Historians, History of Edn. Soc., Am. Ednl. Studies Assn., Soc. Profs. Edn., Phi Alpha Theta, Phi Delta Kappa. Author: The History of the University of Nebraska 1929-1969, 1973; contbr. articles and revs. to profl. jours. Home: 2640 S 35th St Lincoln NE 68506 Office: 111 Tchrs Coll U Nebr Lincoln NE

SAWZIN, STEPHEN ALLEN, design engr.; b. Lorain, Ohio, Nov. 7, 1950; s. Steve and Julia Cecilia (Horvath) S.; A.A.S., Lorain County Community Coll., Elyria, Ohio, 1970; B.S. in Tech., Bowling Green State U., 1972, M.Ed., 1974; m. Dorothy Ann Gurtzweiler, Aug. 19, 1978. Draftsman, Lorain County Regional Planning Commn., Elyria, 1969, 70, James H. Schmidt, Registered Surveyor, Elyria, 1971; design draftsman Sanborn, Steketee, Otis & Evans, Inc., Toledo, 1973; instr. dept. indsl. edn. Wilmington (Ohio) Coll., 1975-77; instr. So. State Community Coll., Wilmington, 1977-80, asso. prof., 1980-81, chmn. dept. engring. tech., 1979-81; design engr., engring. trainer Cin. Milicron Corp., Wilmington, 1981—. Mem. Ohio Air N.G., 1972-78. Mem. ASTD, Am. Vocat. Assn., Ohio Vocat. Assn., Ohio Assn. Engring. Graphics (pres. 1980-81), Am. Tech. Edn. Assn., Nat. Assn. Indsl. Tchr. Educators. Contbr. articles to profl. jours. Roman Catholic. Office: Cin Milicron Corp Wilmington OH 45177

SAX, JANET BERMAN, pediatrician; b. Toledo, Feb. 6, 1924; d. Carl H. and Lillian (Shapiro) Berman; B.S., U. Mich., Ann Arbor, 1948; M.D., Western Res. U., 1953; div.; children—Steven, Richard, Leonard. Rotating intern Jefferson Davis Hosp., Houston, 1953-54; resident in pediatrics Children's Hosp., San Francisco, 1960-62; fellow in juvenile diabetes Babies and Children's Hosp., Cleve., 1963-64; practice medicine specializing in pediatrics, San Francisco, 1962-63; founding pediatrician Ohio Permanente Med. Group, Cleve., 1964—; mem. staff Kaiser Found. Hosps., 1964—; cons. Juvenile Diabetes Clinic, Rainbow Babies and Children's Hosp., 1965-80, asso. clin. prof. pediatrics, 1978; asso. vis. pediatrician Mt. Sinai Hosp., 1966; sr. clin. instr. dept. community health Sch. Medicine, Case Western Res. U., 1975. Active United Torch Services of Cleve.; mem. allocations com. Health Fund Greater Cleve., 1976—, priorities determination com., 1976-77; trustee Am. Jewish Com., 1976—; bd. govs. Temple men's club, 1978-79; bd. dirs. Jr. Welfare Fedn., 1979—; mem. child issues com. Fedn. Community Planning. Lic. pediatrician, Ohio, Tex., Calif. Diplomate Am. Bd. Pediatrics. Fellow Am. Acad. Pediatrics; mem. Cleve. Acad. Medicine (various coms. 1981—), Ohio State Med. Assn., No. Ohio Pediatric Soc. (pres. 1980-81), Mt. Sinai Med. Soc., Am. Diabetes Assn., Diabetes Assn. Greater Cleve. (sec. 1979—). Jewish. Contbr. article to New Eng. Jour. Medicine, Yearbook Pediatrics; med. editor Diabetes Newsletter Greater Cleve., until 1980. Home: 18128 Scottsdale Blvd Shaker Heights OH 44122 Office: Kaiser Health Found 50 Severance Circle Cleveland Heights OH 44118

SAX, MARY RANDOLPH, speech pathologist; b. Pontiac, Mich., July 13, 1925; d. Bernard Angus and Ada Lucile (Thurman) TePoorten; B.A. magna cum laude, Mich. State U., 1947; M.A., U. Mich., 1949; m. William Martin Sax, Feb. 7, 1948. Supr. speech correction dept. Waterford Twp. Schs., Pontiac, 1949-69; lectr. Marygrove Coll., Detroit, 1971-72; pvt. practice speech and lang. rehab., Wayne, Oakland Counties, Mich., 1973—; mem. sci. council stroke Am. Heart Assn. Grantee Inst. Articulation and Learning, 1969, others. Mem. Am. Speech-Lang.-Hearing Assn., Mich. Speech Pathologists in Clin. Practice, Mich. Speech and Hearing Assn. (com. community and hosp. services), Mich. Heart Assn. (stroke com. Oakland County), AAUW, Internat. Assn. Logopedics and Phoniatrics (Switzerland), Theta Alpha Phi, Phi Kappa Phi, Kappa Delta Pi. Contbr. articles to profl. jours. Home and Office: 31320 Woodside Franklin MI 48025

SAXENA, SWARAN LAL, marketing exec.; b. Haripur, Pakistan, Jan. 18, 1934; s. Beli Ram and Ram Kali (Nanda) S.; came to U.S., 1964, naturalized, 1972; B.A., Panjab U. (India), 1955; M.S., No. Ill. U., 1966; m. Shiv Kumari Seth, July 17, 1956; children—Gunita, Ursula, Meena. Taxation inspector Excise and Taxation Dept., India, 1956-64; account exec. Market Research Corp. Am., Chgo., 1966-69; dir. research planning Burgoyne Inc., Cin., 1970-71, dir. consumer research, 1972-73; mktg. research mgr. Peter Eckrich & Sons, Inc., Ft. Wayne, Ind., 1974—; part-time mktg. instr. St. Francis Coll., Ft. Wayne, 1977—; seminar dir. seminars on consumer research Am. Mktg. Assn., 1972, on sales mgmt., 1972, on product planning, 1973, on application marketing research, 1974, on usage of census data, 1976. Recipient Appreciation award Am. Mktg. Assn., 1972. Mem. India-Am. C. of C. (founder, chmn. 1967-74), Gita Soc. Greater Chgo. (pres. 1967-69), India Assn. Met. Chgo. (dir.-at-large 1968), Sikh Study Circle (exec. mem. 1967-68), Am. Mktg. Assn. (chpt. pres. 1977-78), Sangam Indian Assn. Club: Toastmasters. Contbr. articles in field to co. publs. Home: 3518 Springbrook Dr Fort Wayne IN 46815 Office: 3515 Hobson Rd Fort Wayne IN 46805

SAY, MARLYS MORTENSEN (MRS. JOHN THEODORE SAY), supt. schs.; b. Yankton, S.D., Mar. 11, 1924; d. Melvin A. and Edith L. (Fargo) Mortensen; B.A., U. Colo., 1949, M.Ed., 1953; adminstrv. specialist U. Nebr., 1973; m. John Theodore Say, June 21, 1951; children—Mary Louise, James Kenneth, John Melvin, Margaret Ann. Tchr. Huron (S.D.) Jr. High Sch., 1944-48, Lamar (Colo.) Jr. High Sch., 1950-52, Norfolk Pub. Sch., 1962-63; Madison County supt., Madison, Nebr., 1963—. Mem. N.E.A. (life), Am. Assn. Sch. Adminstrs., Dept. Rural Edn., Nebr. Assn. County Supts. (pres.), Nebr. Elementary Prins. Assn., AAUW (pres. Norfolk br.), N.E. Nebr. County Supts. Assn. (pres.), Assn. Sch. Bus. Ofcls., Nat. Orgn. Legal Problems in Edn., Assn. Supervision and Curriculum Devel., Nebr. Edn. Assn., Nebr. Sch. Adminstrs. Assn. Republican. Methodist. Home: 4805 S 13th St Norfolk NE 68701 Office: Courthouse Madison NE 68748

SAYLER, O(RVAL) DALE, holding co. exec.; b. Rapid City, S.D., June 13, 1922; s. Orval Mark and Millie Louisa (Edzards) S.; student Black Hills State Coll., 1941-42; B.C.S., Drake U., 1949; m. Lois Alma Jenkins, July 8, 1943; children—Susan Dayle Sayler Schneider, Larry Mark, Cheryl Ann. Acctg. clk. Mobil Oil Corp., 1949; internal revenue agt. U.S. Treasury, 1949-51; public accountant H.S. Heimes, C.P.A., 1951-54, S.S. Schouweiler, 1954-59; partner C.P.A. firm Sayler, Thorstenson & Co., Rapid City, 1981—; pres., chief exec. officer Dynamo G. Inc., Rapid City, 1981—; mem. S.D. Bd. Accountancy, 1960-68. Mem. Rapid City Mayor's Adv. Com. on City Regional Airport, 1980-81. Served with Signal Corps, AUS, 1942-46. C.P.A. Mem. S.D. Soc. C.P.A.'s, Am. Inst. C.P.A.'S, Nat. Assn. State Bds. Accountancy. Republican. Presbyterian. Clubs: Arrowhead Country, Cosmopolitan, Elks, Masons, Shriners. Home: 4610 Ridgewood St Rapid City SD 57701 Office: PO Box 2754 2426 E St Patrick St Rapid City SD 57709

SAYLOR, HOWARD LEROY, JR., physician; b. Cogswell, N.D., July 25, 1917; s. Howard L. and Claire I. (Lyken) S.; B.S., U. S.D., 1941; M.D., Northwestern U., 1943; m. Mary Ann Peterson, Apr. 9, 1943; children—Mary Diane, Howard LeRoy III, James C. Intern, Northwestern U. Hosp., Chgo., 1943; fellow in surgery Mayo Found., Rochester, Minn., 1947-50; practice medicine specializing in surgery, Huron, S.D., 1950—; clin. instr. surgery U. S.D. Med. Sch., 1976—; mem. med. adv. com. Crippled Children's Hosp., 1976—. Mem. Gov.'s Council on Emergency Med. Service, 1968—; chmn. S.D. Welfare Commn., 1968-72; trustee Huron Coll. Served to capt. M.C., AUS, 1943-46. Recipient Presdl. citation for employment of handicapped, 1970; diplomate Am. Bd. Surgery. Fellow A.C.S. (past pres. S.D. chpt.); mem. AMA, S.D. Med. Soc., Am. Trauma Soc., Priestley Soc., Huron C. of C., Am. Legion, VFW. Republican. Clubs: Huron Country, Ducks Ultd., Sertoma, Elks, Masons, Shriners. Home: 1360 Ohio St Huron SD 57350 Office: 530 Iowa St SE Huron SD 57350

SAYRE, ROBERT FREEMAN, educator; b. Columbus, Ohio, Nov. 6, 1933; s. Harrison M. and Mary (White) S.; B.A., Wesleyan U., Middletown, Conn., 1955; Ph.D., Yale U., 1962; divorced; children—Gordon, Nathan, Laura. Instr., U. Ill., Urbana, 1961-63; Fulbright lectr. Lund (Sweden) U., 1963-65; mem. faculty U. Iowa, 1965—, prof. lit., 1972—; dir. Nat. Endowment Humanities inter-profl. seminars, 1978, 79. Guggenheim fellow, 1973-74. Mem. MLA, Am. Studies Assn., Midwest Modern Lang. Assn. Author: The Examined Self: Benjamin Franklin, Henry Adams, Henry James, 1964, Adventures, Rhymes and Designs of Vachel Lindsay, 1968, Thoreau and the American Indians, 1977; also articles, revs. Office: English Dept Univ Iowa Iowa City IA 52242

SCAFONE, JOHN TRIPOLI, broadcasting co. exec.; b. Providence, July 25, 1939; s. John Tripoli and Alma G. (Quade) S.; B.S., U. Md., 1961; m. JoAnna L. Truskowski, Aug. 7, 1977; children—Scott, Samantha; stepchildren—Margo, Lyn, Chris, Tracy. Account exec. Stanley G. House & Asso., Washington, 1961-62; public info. specialist NIH, Bethesda, Md., 1962-64; asst. promotion mgr. air talent Sta. WWDC-AM/FM, Washington, 1967-68; creative service dir. Sta. WLW, Sta. WLWT-TV, Cin., 1968-70; creative service dir. Sta. WOAI-AM/TV, San Antonio, 1970-71; promotion mgr. Sta. WPHL-TV, Phila., 1971-73; dir. advt. and promotion Sta. WTCN-TV, Mpls., 1973-77, Sta. WBNS-TV, Columbus, Ohio, 1977—; guest lectr. U. Md., College Park, 1967-68, U. Minn., Mpls., 1974-76, Normandale Community Coll., 1974-76, Capitol U., 1980—; cons. in field. Served with USAF 1964-67. Decorated Silver Star, Air medals; recipient Merit awards, Broadcasters Promotion Assn., 1978, 79, 80, 81; Advt. Fedn. awards, 1978-81. Mem. Broadcasters Promotion Assn., Am. Advt. Fedn., Nat. Assn. TV Program Execs. Office: 770 Twin Rivers Dr Columbus OH 43216

SCALES, WENDELL PHILLIP, dentist; b. Detroit, Mar. 18, 1951; s. Erise and Esther (Hogan) S.; student Highland Park Coll., 1969-70, Wayne State U., 1970-73; D.D.S., U. Detroit, 1976; grad. Dale Carnegie Sch.; m. Lynda Joye Ashford, Aug. 5, 1972. Pvt. practice dentistry, Detroit, 1976—; mem. faculty U. Detroit Sch. Dentistry; tchr. Dale Carnegie Sch. Recipient Columbia Dentoform award U. Detroit Dental Sch., 1976, Dentsply Internat. Merit award, 1976, Francis Vedder Fixed Prosthodontic award, 1976, others. Mem. Nat., Am., Mich., Wolverine dental assns., Francis B. Vedder Soc. Fixed Prosthodontics, Acad. Gen. Dentistry, Detroit Dental Study Club, Delta Sigma Delta, Omicron Kappa Upsilon. Home: 23121 Thorncliff Southfield MI 48034 Office: 18241 Greenfield St Detroit MI 48221

SCANLON, JOHN CHARLES, physician; b. Cleve., Jan. 25, 1940; s. Charles Patrick and Mary Abigail (Dahm) S.; A.B., Xavier U., Cin., 1961; M.D., Loyola U., Chgo., 1965; m. Phyllis Catherine Steinker, May 8, 1965; children—Matthew, Lisa, Susan, Daniel. Intern, St. Vincent Charity Hosp., Cleve., 1965-66; fellow in internal medicine Cleve. Clinic, 1968-70, fellow in pulmonary disease, 1970-71; practice medicine specializing in pulmonary diseases, Lafayette, Ind., 1971-77; physician Arnett Clinic, Lafayette, Ind., 1971—; med. dir. respiratory services dept. Lafayette (Ind.) Home Hosp., 1971—; med. dir. respiratory services dept. St. Elizabeth Hosp., Lafayette, 1971—; med. dir. respiratory technician program Ind. Vocat. Coll., Lafayette, 1972—. Served to capt. M.C., U.S. Army, 1966-67. Diplomate Am. Bd. Internal Medicine. Fellow Am. Coll. Chest Physicians. Republican. Roman Catholic. Home: 4811 Homewood Dr West Lafayette IN 47906

SCANNELL, FRANCIS XAVIER, librarian; b. Boston, Dec. 15, 1917; s. William James and Helen Gertrude (Ahern) S.; A.B., Harvard U., 1942; B.S., Columbia U., 1943; m. Mary R. Donovan, Dec. 28, 1946; children—Chris, Joel, Elizabeth, Martha. Reference librarian Boston Pub. Library, 1943-46; gen. reference librarian Detroit Pub. Library, 1946-48, asst. chief reference, 1948-53; head reader services Mich. State Library, Lansing, 1953-65; reference librarian Mich. State U., 1965-68, state librarian Mich., 1968—; mem. library adv. com. Sch. Librarianship, Western Mich. U., Kalamazoo, 1968—; del. White House Conf. on Libraries, 1979. Recipient library service citation Mich. Constl. Conv., 1961. Mem. Mich. Library Assn., ALA, U. Mich. Library Sci. Alumni Assn. (hon.). Author: (pamphlet) Michigan Novelists, 1964. Home: 3627 Colchester Rd Lansing MI 48906 Office: 735 E Michigan Ave Lansing MI 48913

SCARBOROUGH, CURTISS CLINTON, communications exec.; b. West Frankfort, Ill., Dec. 10, 1935; s. Curtis Clinton and Olive Jane (Keith) S.; B.A., So. Ill. U., 1956; B.C.M., Southwestern Bapt. Sem., 1959, M.R.E., 1959; M.A., Evangelical Coll., 1961; Litt.D. (hon.), Stanton U., 1976; Ph.D., Columbia Pacific U., 1980; m. Ruth Ann Jent, Nov. 23, 1955; children—Karol Ruth, Keith Curtiss. Ordained to ministry Baptist Ch., 1964; minister First Bapt. Ch., Metropolis, Ill., 1959-61, Westview Bapt. Ch., Belleville, Ill., 1961-63, Water Tower Bapt. Ch., St. Louis, 1963-67, N. Side Bapt. Ch., Florissant, Mo., 1967-75; dir. communications Christian Civic Found., St. Louis, 1975—; pres. Paradox Enterprises, Inc., book pubs. Bd. dirs. Polit. Action for Christian Environment, Inc., 1980—; lectr. Drug-Alcohol-Tobacco-Edn., Inc., 1978—; mem. media com. St. Louis Bapt. Assn., 1979—; mem. Youth Adv. Commn., St. Louis County, Mo., 1981—. Mem. Internat. Platform Assn., Nat. Writer's Club, Nat. Assn. Prevention Professionals, Religious Public Relations Council, Mo. Prevention Network. Republican. Club: Optimists. Author: (with Cleveland R. Horne) Citizens, Under God, 1979; (with John D. King) An Ounce of Prevention, 1980; Basics on Abused Drugs, 1981; author, compiler (with Gerald Young) Choice Sermons from Missouri Pulpits, 1981; newspaper editor The Christian Citizen, 1975—, Dateline, 1975—; syndicated columnist Drug Quiz, 1979—. Home: 2476 Buttonwood Ct Florissant MO 63031 Office: 3426 Bridgeland Dr Bridgeton MO 63044

SCARBOROUGH, NEAFIE BURTON, JR., machinery co. exec.; b. Phila., May 29, 1935; s. Neafie Burton and Hilda M. (Brinsfield) S.; student Beacon Coll., 1954; m. Hilda Margaret Hennicke, Oct. 16, 1954; children—Dean Andrew, Brian David. Fed. agt. Sec. of Treasury for Law Enforcement, USCG, Gt. Lakes Area, 1959-63; with Prachar & Jenks Machinery Co., Cleve., 1963-67; pres., chief exec. officer Clipper Machinery Co., Inc., Cleve., 1967—. Mem. Am. Machine Tool Distbrs. Assn. (pres. 1980-81), Soc. Mfg. Engrs. Republican. Clubs: Masons, Hermits, Put-In-Bay Yacht, Cleve. Yacht. Home: 17894 Captain's Cove Lakewood OH 44107 Office: Clipper Machinery Co Inc 17008 Madison Ave Lakewood OH 44107

SCARBROUGH, ALVA WILLIAM, hosp. adminstr., state senator; b. Canova, S.D., Aug. 8, 1929; s. Walter Ray and Minnie Pauline (Laufmann) S.; B.A., Augustana Coll., Sioux Falls, S.D., 1951; postgrad U. Minn., 1954-60; m. Mary Lee Syverson, June 26, 1955; children—Mary Elisabeth, Susan Marie, Steven Edward, David Walter. Tchr., Public High Sch., Salem, S.D., 1954-55, Mitchell, S.D., 1955-57, Sioux Falls, S.D., 1957-60; tng. dir. John Morrell & Co., Sioux Falls, 1960-67; personnel dir., v.p. human resources Sioux Valley Hosp., Sioux Falls, from 1967; now mem. S.D. Senate, 1979—; faculty Sioux Falls Coll., 1979. Pres., Augustana Alumni Council, 1960-63; chmn. Sioux Falls Sch. Bd., 1972-73. Served with U.S. Navy, 1951-54, USNR, 1949-70. Recipient Bush Fellow award, 1975. Mem. Sioux Falls Personnel Assn., S.D. Hosp. Personnel Assn., Am. Soc. Personnel Adminstrn. (accredited), Am. Soc. Hosp. Personnel. Republican. Lutheran. Clubs: Kiwanis (pres. 1976-77), Am. Legion. Club: Toastmasters. Office: 1100 S Euclid Ave Sioux Falls SD 57105*

SCARLETT, HAROLD OWEN, retail exec.; b. Detroit; s. Howard O. and Irene J. (LaSprance) S.; B.S. in Mech. Engring., Purdue U., 1949; m. Helen L. Steigerwalt, Apr. 15, 1950. Design engr. Detroit Edison Co., 1949-52; with S.S. Kresge Co., Detroit, 1952-73, gen. mgr. constrn. dept., 1969-73; v.p. constrn. Kmart Corp., Troy, Mich., 1973—; pres. Huck Fixture Co., Quincy, Ill., 1969-79, chmn. bd., 1979—. Mem. corp. Merrill-Palmer Inst., Detroit. Served with AUS, 1942-45. Registered profl. engr., Mich. Mem. Engring. Soc. Detroit, Pi Tau Sigma, Tau Beta Pi. Office: 3100 W Big Beaver Rd Troy MI 48084

SCARPINO, PASQUALE VALENTINE, environ. microbiologist, educator; b. Utica, N.Y., Feb. 13, 1932; s. Antonio and Mary Ann (Lia) S.; B.A. magna cum laude, Utica Coll., Syracuse U., 1955; M.S., Rutgers U., 1958, Ph.D. (USPHS fellow), 1961; 1 dau., Andrea Lia. USPHS research asst. Rutgers U., New Brunswick, N.J., 1958-61; asst. prof. biol. scis. Fairleigh Dickinson U., Madison, N.J., 1961-63; asst. prof. san. engring. U. Cin. 1963-66, asso. prof. environ. health engring., 1966-70, prof. environ. engring., 1970—. Chmn. water subcom. of Environ. Task Force, City of Cin. 1972-73, chmn. Environ. Adv. Council, 1980-82, chmn. Citizen-Scientist Com. on Drinking Water Quality, 1975—, chmn. Nuclear Safety Com. Environ. Adv. Council, 1979—; mem. adv. council Cin. Experience, 1973-81. USPHS research grantee, 1965-68, Space Inst. grantee, 1967-69, EPA research grantee, 1969-82. Recipient Presdl. award for Excellence in Community Service, U. Cin., 1975, Tristate Air Com. award, 1977. Fellow Am. Acad. Microbiology; mem. Am. Soc. Microbiology (chmn. com. on edn. 1970-72, chmn. com. on role of microbiology in edn. of other disciplines 1972-73), AAAS, Water Pollution Control Fedn., Am. Water Works Assn., Internat. Assn. Water Pollution Research, Sigma Xi. Contbr. articles to profl. jours. Home: 3843 Middleton Ave Cincinnati OH 45220 Office: 721 Rhodes Hall Dept Civil and Environ Engineering U Cin Cincinnati OH

SCEARCE, WILLIAM CARROLL, retail exec., former city ofcl.; b. Moultrie, Ga., Aug. 19, 1941; s. James Boyd and Lois Audry (Harrell) S.; B.S., Ga. So. Coll., 1963; M.A., U. Ga., 1967; m. Penelope Ann Leffen, Apr. 3, 1976; children—Lois Shala, W. Carroll, Helen Patricia, Margaret Ann. Dir., Recreation Center, Winston-Salem, N.C., 1963-64, also dist. supr. Parks and Recreation Dept.; park and recreation dir. Decatur (Ga.), 1964-68, Joplin (Mo.), 1968-78; pres. Shank Army Surplus, Joplin, 1978—. Mem. City Beautiful Com., Joplin, 1968—; mem. Joplin Council for the Arts, 1968—; pres. Joplin Area Assn. for Retarded Citizens, 1972-74; sec. Joplin Boys Club; bd. dirs. Joplin Area Sheltered Workshop; chmn. mcpl. sect. Clean Community Systems of Joplin, 1980-81. Mem. Mo. Park and Recreation Assn. (v.p. 1975-76), Ga. Park and Recreation Soc. (dir. 1966-68), Am. Inst. Park Execs., Nat. Recreation and Park Assn., Nat. Parks and Conservation Assn., Nat. Audubon Soc., Am. Forestry Assn. Club: Kiwanis. Home: 626 Jaccard Pl Joplin MO 64801 Office: Shank Army Surplus 1312 Main St Joplin MO 64801

SCHAAF, ROBERT EDWARD, ins. co. exec.; b. Eau Claire, Wis., Oct. 25, 1935; s. N.A. and Lillian P. (Betz) S.; B.B.A., U. Wis., 1957; postgrad. Purdue U., 1962-63; m. Rosemary McCoy, July 26, 1958; children—Anne, Susan, Gregory, James, Douglas. Supr. treasury dept. Prudential Ins. Co. Am., Mpls., 1957-60; dir. planning, systems Farm Bur. Ins. Cos., Des Moines, 1960-66; sr. v.p., treas. Roosevelt Nat. Life Ins. Co. Am., Springfield, Ill., 1966-69; pres., dir. Country Convenience, Inc.; dir. Roosevelt Roosevelt Nat. Investment Co., Kirk Structures, Inc., Ill. Life & Health Guaranty Fund, Bldg. Material Distbrs., Inc.; instr. Des Moines Pub. Schs.; lectr. Drake U., Des Moines. Mem. Springfield Central Area Devel. Assn., 1967—, Salvation Army Assn., Springfield, 1973—; mem. adv. com. Lincoln Land Community Coll., 1972-75; bd. dirs. Springfield Urban League, 1974-77. Named Ky. col., N.Mex. col.; licensed ins., securities, real estate broker, Ill. Fellow Life Office Mgmt. Assn.; mem. Systems and Procedures Assn. (sec., v.p., pres. 1964-66), Health Ins. Assn. Am., Inst. Ins. Mktg., Ill. (dir., pres. 1976-78), Nat. assns. life cos., Am. Coll. Life Underwriters (dir., pres. local chpt.), Nat. Assn. Securities Dealers, Ill., Springfield chambers commerce. Republican. Roman Catholic. Clubs: Wisconsin W, Elks. Contbr. numerous articles in field. Home: 2613 Arlington Dr Springfield IL 62704 Office: PO Box 5147 Springfield IL 62705

SCHAAL, LOIS MARIE, dietitian; b. Delaware, Ohio, July 1, 1944; d. Ernest L. and Ruth (Eckert) S.; B.S., Ohio U., 1966. Dietetic intern Mass. Gen. Hosp., Boston, 1967; charge dietitian Hosp. U. Pa., Phila., 1967-70; regional supervising dietitian Servomation, Balt., 1970-72; v.p. Dietary Mgmt. Cons., Wayne, Pa., 1972-75; dir. food and nutrition services Hurley Med. Center, Flint, Mich., 1975-79; dir. dietary services U. Cin. Med. Center, 1979—; lectr. Montgomery County (Pa.) Community Coll., 1978, Pa. Nursing Home Adminstrs. Continuing Edn., 1974. Mem. Am. Dietetic Assn. (chmn. 3-yr. route to membership 1977-78), Cin. Dietetic Assn., Ohio Dietetic Assn., Am. Soc. Hosp. Food Service Adminstrs., Nutrition Today Soc. Office: U Cin Med Center 234 Goodman St Cincinnati OH 45267

SCHABEL, DONALD ALBERT, lawyer; b. Hammond, Ind., July 22, 1927; s. Francis William and Kathleen (Conroy) S.; A.B., Ind. U., 1948; J.D. cum laude, Harvard, 1951; m. Amelia Llana Agtarap, Oct. 7, 1967; children—Victoria Eileen, Donald Albert. Admitted to N.Y. bar, 1952, Ind. bar, 1954; asso. Milbank, Tweed, Hope & Hadley, N.Y.C., 1951-53; asso. Buschmann, Krieg, DeVault & Alexander, Indpls., 1954-57, partner, 1957-60; partner Buschmann, Carr & Schabel, 1961-75; individual practice law, 1976—. Mem. cts. div. Ind. Jud. Study Commn., 1973—. Served with USNR, 1945-46. Mem. Am., Ind., Indpls. bar assns., Bar Assn. 7th Fed. Circuit, Assn. Bar City N.Y. Roman Catholic. Club: Columbia (Indpls.). Home: 4455 Broadway Indianapolis IN 46205 Office: One Indiana Sq Suite 3300 Indianapolis IN 46204

SCHABEL, DONALD JACOB, librarian; b. Chgo., May 20, 1937; s. Frank Rudolph and Marie J. (Waszak) S.; B.S. in Edn., No. Ill. U., 1959; M.L.S., Rosary Coll., 1967; postgrad. U. Chgo. Grad. Library Sch., 1960; m. Patricia Mackey, June 18, 1960; children—Michael, Mary Jo, Christine. Librarian, tchr. Blue Island (Ill.) Public Schs., 1959-60, 61-66; librarian Thornton Twp. High Schs., Dolton, Ill., 1960-61; with Chgo. Public Library, 1967—, dir. tech. services, 1979—. Active Internat. Visitors Center. Mem. ALA, Ill. Library Assn., Library Adminstrs. Conf. No. Ill., Phi Mu Alpha Sinfonia. Contbr. articles to profl. jours. Office: 425 N Michigan Ave Chicago IL 60611

SCHACHT, HENRY BREWER, diesel engine mfg. co. exec.; b. Erie, Pa., Oct. 16, 1934; s. Henry Blass and Virginia (Brewer) S.; B.S., Yale U., 1956; M.B.A., Harvard U., 1962; m. Nancy Godfrey, Aug. 27, 1960; children—James, Laura, Jane, Mary. Sales trainee Am. Brake Shoe Co., N.Y.C., 1956-57; investment mgr. Irwin Mgmt. Co., Columbus, Ind., 1962-64; v.p. fin. Cummins Engine Co., Inc., Columbus, 1964-66, v.p., central area mgr. internat., London, Eng., 1966-67, group v.p. internat. and subsidiaries, 1967-69, pres., Columbus, 1969-77, chmn., chief exec. officer, 1977—; dir. CBS, ATT. Trustee Com. Econ. Devel., Urban Inst., Rockefeller Found., Conf. Bd. Served with USNR, 1957-60. Mem. Bus. Council, Council Fgn. Relations, Mgmt. Execs. Soc., Tau Beta Pi. Republican. Home: 4300 N Riverside Dr Columbus IN 47201 Office: 432 Washington St Columbus IN 47201

SCHADE, RUDOLF GOTTLIEB, JR., lawyer; b. N.Y.C., Sept. 26, 1941; s. Rudolf Gottlieb and Hanna Hilda (Krause) S.; A.B., Heidelberg Coll., 1963; J.D. with honors, John Marshall Law Sch., 1968; m. Lucinda Ann Webster, Mar. 24, 1962; children—Rudolf Gottlieb III, Paul, Ingrid. Admitted to Ill. bar, 1968; asso. firm Hinshaw, Culbertson, Moelmann, Hoban & Fuller, Chgo., 1968-74, partner, 1974-79; partner firm Cassiday, Schade & Gloor, Chgo., 1979—; instr. John Marshall Law Sch., 1969-72. Del., Consultation on Church Union, 1968-77; mem. Plan Commn., LaGrange, Ill., 1978—. Mem. Am. Bar Assn., Ill. Bar Assn., Chgo. Bar Assn., Am. Soc. Hosp. Attys., Ill. Soc. Hosp. Attys., Def. Research Inst., Ill. Def. Council (dir. 1975—), Evang. Hosp. Assn. (dir. 1972, chmn. 1975-78). Mem. United Ch. of Christ. Clubs: Trial Lawyers (dir. 1973—, v.p. 1979), Econ., Legal (Chgo.); LaGrange Country. Home: 317 S 7th St LaGrange IL 60525 Office: Cassiday Schade & Gloor 100 W Monroe St Chicago IL 60603

SCHADE, SYLVIA ZOTTU, biochemist; b. Middletown, Conn., June 2, 1933; d. Paul Demosthenes and Grace Fay (Fountain) Zottu; B.A. cum laude in chemistry, Mt. Holyoke Coll., 1955; Ph.D., U. Wis., 1967; m. Stanley Greinert Schade, Mar. 24, 1966; children—David Stanley, Robert Edward. Research asst. in biol. chemistry Harvard Med. Sch., Boston, 1955-59, research asst., 1960-62; research asst. NOVO Terapeutisk Laboratorium, Copenhagen, 1959-60; instr. biol. chemistry U. Ill. Med. Center, Chgo., 1970-72, research asso. biol. chemistry, 1978—. Mem. Assn. for Research in Vision and Optics, Assn. for Women in Sci., Phi Beta Kappa, Sigma Xi. Contbr. articles to profl. jours. Home: 189 N Delaplaine Rd Riverside IL 60546 Office: Dept Biol Chemistry Univ Ill Med Center 835 S Wolcott Ave Chicago IL 60612

SCHAEFER, JOSEPH ROBERT, JR., archtl. design co. exec.; b. Des Moines, Feb. 13, 1949; s. Joseph Robert and Janet Marie (Walker) S.; B.A., Drake U., 1980; m. Paula Janine Middleton, July 16, 1977. Sect. supr. Hygiene Lab. U. Iowa, 1971-79; owner, pres. Archtl. Graphic Services, Inc., Des Moines, 1978—; plan adminstr. Bankers Life Ins. Co., 1979-80; ins. employment cons. Snelling & Snelling, Inc., Des Moines, 1981—. Historian Sherman Hill Restoration Assn., Des Moines, 1978-80. Mem. Kappa Kappa Iota. Republican. Methodist. Home: 1319 23d St Des Moines IA 50311 Office: 606 Equitable Bldg Des Moines IA 50309

SCHAEFER, LAWRENCE VINCENT, educator; b. Bridgeport, Conn., July 3, 1931; s. William Joseph and Loretta Mary (Lawrence) S.; B.S., Fairfield U., 1953, M.A., 1954; M.A., Fordham U., 1961, Ph.D., 1976; diploma Internat. Inst. for Montessori Studies (Italy), 1970-71; m. Patricia Ann Scallen, Sept. 3, 1960; children—Anne L., Lawrence P., Mary J., Kristin A. Tchr., Fordham Prep. Sch., N.Y.C., 1960-67; asst. prof. European history Sacred Heart U., Bridgeport, Conn., 1967-70; headmaster Toronto Montessori Schs., Thornhill, Ont., Can., 1970-75, bd. dirs., 1974-75; adminstr. elementary sch. Montessori Found. of Minn., St. Paul, 1975-76; founder, prin. Lake Country Sch., Mpls., 1976—; lectr. Toronto Montessori Inst., 1971-75; cons. adminstrv. coordinator Milw. Montessori Sch., 1975-76; cons. Montessori Found. of Minn., 1975-76. Mem. Bishop's Commn. on Human Rights, Diocese of Bridgeport, 1968-70; mem. Norwalk Cath. Interracial Council, 1967-70; bd. dirs. The Child's Work Center, Norwalk, 1963-66, Lake Country Sch.. 1976—. Served with UsN, i955-58. Mem. Am. Hist. Assn., Assn. Montessori Internat., N. Am. Montessori Tchrs. Assn., Minn. Alliance of Montessorians, Smithsonian Assos., Minn. Soc. Fine Arts, Minn. Geol. Soc. Democrat. Roman Catholic. Contbr. articles in field to profl. jours; designer, creator in collaboration with Jodi Abssy, Montessori ednl. materials: Time Line of the History of the Holocene Period, 1973; Time Line of American Civilizations, 1974; The Language Tree, 1974. Home: 1630 W Skillman Ave Roseville MN 55113 Office: 3755 Pleasant Ave S Minneapolis MN 55409

SCHAEFFER, ROBERT FRANÇOIS, printing co. exec.; b. Esch/Alzette, Luxembourg, Nov. 7, 1930; came to U.S., 1953; s. Philippe Jean-Pierre and Marguerite Schaeffer; Diplome, Hautes Etudes Commerciales, Paris, 1953; postgrad. (Fulbright scholar), U. Kans., 1953-54; children—Jeanne M., Edward P. Researcher, Chambre des Métiers, Luxembourg, 1954-56; exec. v.p. Krug Litho Art Co., North Kansas City, Mo., 1956—. Pres., Kansas City Ballet, 1970; trustee Conservatory of Music, U. Mo., 1975—. Decorated chevalier Order of Merit (Luxembourg); recipient Elmer G. Voight award Ednl. Council Graphic Arts, 1969; named hon. consul of Luxembourg. Mem. Printing Industries Am. (Man of Yr. 1980), Nat. Assn. Printers and Lithographers, Nat. Assn. Litho Clubs (pres. 1966-67), Walter Soderstrom Soc. Contbr. articles to profl. jours. Office: 1429 Atlantic St North Kansas City MO 64116

SCHAEFFER, SARA SUE, counselor, cons.; b. Sturgis, Mich., June 10, 1947; d. Ernest Victor and Jessie S. (Eicholtz) S.; B.A., Albion Coll., 1969; student U. Grenoble (France), 1968; M.A., Western Mich. U., 1971, Ed.S., 1975. Tchr. high sch. French and English, White Cloud, Mich., 1969-70; counselor Marshall (Mich.) High Sch., 1971-75, English tchr. adult edn. program, 1973-74; counselor Lakeview High Sch., Battle Creek, Mich., 1975-80, dir. counseling program Lakeview Adult High Sch. Program, 1976-80; pres. Humanistic Assos., 1980—; asso. chief of staff for edn. VA Med. Center, Battle Creek, 1981—; chairperson Counselor Licensure Com., 1981—; cons. in field. Named Calhoun Area Counselor of Year, 1977; recipient George H. Hilliard award Western Mich. U., 1979. Mem. Am. Personnel and Guidance Assn., Mich. Personnel and Guidance Assn. (pres. 1980-81, Outstanding Leadership award 1981), Kalamazoo Personnel and Guidance Assn., Mich. Sch. Counselors Assn., Mich. Vocat. Guidance Assn. (treas. 1978-80), Mich. Assn. Specialists in Group Work, Calhoun Area Counselors Assn. (pres. 1977-78), Phi Beta Kappa. Episcopalian. Contbr. writings to book, articles in field. Home: 1534 Woodland Ave Portage MI 49081 Office: VA Med Center Battle Creek MI 49016

SCHAEPPI, JOSEPH JOHN, optometrist; b. St. Paul, Feb. 9, 1923; s. Joseph John and Barbara Jane (Childs) S.; student U. Minn., 1942-43, 46-49; O.D., Chgo. Coll. Optometry, 1951; m. Patricia Clair Shimek, Sept. 10, 1949; children—Dennis M., Thomas J., Patti C., Cheryl A., Lawrence J. Pvt. practice optometry, Mpls., 1951—. Served with USNR, 1943-46. Mem. Am., Minn., Mpls. optometric assns., Minn. Optometric Polit. Action Com. (treas.), Northside Comml. Club, Northside Businessmen's Assn., Am. Legion. Catholic. Clubs: Elks; Golden Valley Country (Minn.), Mardi Gras Dance. Home: 6000 Wolfberry Ln Golden Valley MN 55422 Office: 1014 W Broadway Minneapolis MN 55411

SCHAERER, JACQUES PAUL, neurosurgeon; b. Zurich, Switzerland, Aug. 14, 1917; s. Georg Paul and Anna (Hiestand) S.; came to U.S., 1948, naturalized, 1951; M.D., U. Zurich, 1942, Ph.D., 1944; m. Cheryl L. Pulis, Jan. 31, 1974; children—Ann Carol, Marguerite Janet, Elizabeth Eleanor, Maria Amy, Paul Jacques. Rotating intern Hosp. Waedenswil (Switzerland), 1942-43; asst. instr. Inst. Anatomy, U. Zurich, 1943-44, surg. intern Childrens Hosp., 1944-45; surg. resident Kantonsspital Winterthur Suval Winterthur, Switzerland, 1947-48; rotating intern Luth Hosp., St. Louis, 1948-49; resident in psychiatry Binghamton (N.Y.) State Hosp., 1949-51; resident in neurosurgery SUNY, Syracuse, 1951-54, instr. neurosurgery, 1954-55; acting chief neurosurgery VA Hosp., Syracuse, 1954-55; practice medicine, specializing in neurosurgery, St. Louis, 1957—; mem. acting staff Mo. Bapt. Hosp.; mem. courtesy staff Incarnate Word Hosp., Alexian Bros. Hosp., St. Joseph's Hosp., Kirkwood, Mo. Hon. consul Switzerland, 1973—; sec.-treas. St. Louis Consular Corps, 1978, v.p., 1979, pres., 1980. Served to 1st lt. M.C., Swiss Army, 1942-48; served to maj. M.C., U.S. Army, 1955-57. Diplomate Am. Bd. Neurol. Surgery, Am. Acad. Neurol. and Orthopaedic Surgeons. Fellow Internat. Coll. Surgeons, Internat. Coll. Angiology, Am. Geriatrics Soc.; mem. Congress Neurol. Surgeons, Neurosurg. Socs. Germany and Switzerland, Am. Soc. Stereotactic and Functional Neurosurgery, Assn. Research Nervous and Mental Diseases, AMA, Pan Am. Med. Assn., Swiss Neurol. Soc., Swiss Med. Soc., So. Med. Assn., Mo. State Med. Assn. Office: 777 S New Ballas Rd St Louis MO 63141

SCHAFER, ERNEST WENDELL, publisher; b. Corder, Mo., Jan. 10, 1932; s. Ernst and Anna (Nuttleman) S.; B.S., U. Mo., 1957; m. Helen Darlene Carter, May 23, 1954; children—Cynthia, Mark, Steven. Tchr. pub. schs., Wheaton, Ill., 1957-62; sci. editor Prentice-Hall, Inc., Englewood Cliffs, N.J., 1962-67, asst. v.p., 1966-67; editor-in-chief for sci. Houghton Mifflin Co., Boston, 1967-68; chief sci. editor Random House, N.Y.C., 1968-69; pres., pub. Pawnee Pub. Co., Inc., Corder, Mo. Served with USAF, 1951-54. NSF fellow, 1959-62. Mem. Nat. Council Tchrs. Math, Nat. Sci. Tchrs. Assn. Republican. Lutheran. Club: Optimist (past pres.), Author: The Story of Kansas. Editor: Life: A Question of Survival, 1972. Home: Rural Route 1 Box 130 Corder MO 64021 Office: PO Box 107 Corder MO 64021

SCHAFER, MICHAEL FREDERICK, orthopedic surgeon; b. Peoria, Ill., Aug. 17, 1942; s. Harold Martin and Frances May (Ward) S.; B.A., U. Iowa, 1964, M.D., 1967; m. Eileen M. Briggs, Jan. 8, 1966; children—Steven, Brian, Kathy, David, Daniel. Intern, Chgo. Wesley Meml. Hosp., 1967-68; resident in orthopedic surgery Cook County Program Northwestern U., Chgo., 1968-72; practice medicine specializing in orthopedic surgery, Chgo., 1974—; asst. prof. orthopedic surgery Northwestern U., 1977-80, prof., chmn. dept. orthopedic surgery, 1980—; attending orthopedic surgeon Northwestern Meml. Hosp., 1974—; adj. staff Children's Meml. Hosp., Chgo., 1974—; cons. VA Lakeside Hosp., 1974—; mem. advisroy bd. Center for Sports Medicine, Northwestern U., 1976—; panelist Bur. Health Manpower, HEW, 1976. Served to maj., U.S. Army, 1973-74. Am. Orthopaedic Assn. fellow, 1975. Diplomate Am. Bd. Orthopedic Surgery. Mem. Am. Acad. Orthopaedic Surgeons, Am. Med. Assn., Ill., Chgo. med. socs., Internat. Soc. Study Pain, Assn. Bone and Joint Surgeons. Roman Catholic. Contbr. articles to med. jours. Home: 1520 Executive Ln Glenview IL 60025 Office: 303 E Chicago Ave Chicago IL 60611

SCHAFERNAK, DALE EDWARD, indsl. designer; b. Chgo., Oct. 17, 1936; s. William and Martha Ruth (Berg) S.; B.F.A. in Indsl. Design, U. Ill., 1961; m. Judith Theresa Gron, Oct. 27, 1962; children—Krina Eden, Daria Allison, Melissa Thea, Kristian Theo. Jr. designer Montgomery Ward & Co., 1961; with Masonite Corp., St. Charles, Ill., 1962—, now staff designer in product devel. Served with US. Army, 1961-62. Mem. Indsl. Designers Soc. Am. Roman Catholic. Club: Men's Garden of Villa Park (past pres.). Patentee hardboard hardware. Home: 243 Hampton Ct Palatine IL 60067 Office: Powis Rd Saint Charles IL 60174

SCHAFFER, HARWOOD DAVID, clergyman; b. Dayton, Ohio, Oct. 15, 1944; s. Phillip David and H. Ruth (Scheid) S.; B.S. in Math., Ohio State U., 1965; M.Div., Hartford Sem. Found., 1969; m. Gail Corrine Poth, June 25, 1966; children—Rosita, Virginia, Chandra. Ordained to ministry United Ch. of Christ, 1969; chaplain, tchr. Austin Sch., Hartford, Conn., 1967-71; asst. pastor S. Congl. Ch., Middletown, Conn., 1967-71; pastor Trinity United Ch. of Christ, Hudson, Kans., 1971-79, Emma Lowery United Ch. of Christ, Luzerne, Mich., 1979—; area counselor 17/76 Achievement Fund of United Ch. of Christ, 1974-75; mem. Western Assn. council Kans.-Okla. Conf., United Ch. of Christ, 1971-74, 76-79, sec.-treas., 1971-74, chmn. ch. and ministry com., 1976-79; mem. various bds. Mich. Conf., United Ch. of Christ, 1979—; Am. camp mgr. Joint Archaeol. Expdn. to Tel Aphek/Antipatris, Israel, 1978, 80. Bd. govs. Austin Sch., Hartford, 1970-71; mem. Stafford County Democratic Central Com., 1976-79, Oscoda County Dem. Com., 1980—; mem. Stafford Council Overall Econ. Devel. Planning Com., 1976-79, chmn., 1977-79; mem. Oscoda County Housing Commn., 1979—. Home: 3621 Park Rd Luzerne MI 48636 Office: PO Box 170 Luzerne MI 48636

SCHAFFER, JACK RAYMOND, state senator; b. Chgo., Dec. 10, 1942; s. Raymond Paul and Frances (Barter) S.; B.S., No. Ill. U.; m. Linda L. Bellerud, 1969. Active Young Republican groups; dist. gov. 12th Congressional dist. Ill. Young Reps. Orgn., 1965, membership chmn., 1969; auditor McHenry County, 1968—; mem. Ill. Senate, 1973—. Served with U.S. Army, 1956-67. Mem. Ill. Assn. County Auditors (sec.-treas 1969—), Spring Beach Improvement Assn. (trustee), Am. Legion, Jaycees, Farm Bur. Office: 423 State Capitol Springfield IL 62706*

SCHALLERT, BARBARA ANN, food service ofcl.; b. Florissant, Mo., May 20, 1934; d. Raymond V. and Irma A. (Peters) Stroer; student St. Louis U., 1952-53, Washington U., St. Louis, 1970-72, Maryville Coll., St. Louis; A.A., Florissant Valley Community Coll., 1974; m. John G. Schallert, Aug. 21, 1954; children—Michelle, Joseph, Mary ELizabeth. Data technician McDonnell-Douglas, 1954-57; YWCA Center dir., Florissant, 1970-71; center sec. Boys Town of Mo., University City, 1974-76; gen. mgr. Mid-Am. Coffee Service, St. Louis, 1976-81; purchasing agt., mgr. Steelcote Mfg. Co., St. Louis, 1982—. Pres. St. Louis Civic Ballet, 1977; active Painting and Decorating Contractor's Aux., 1979-81; v.p. alumni bd. Florissant Valley Community Coll., 1981. Recipient Edna Fishel Gellhorn award, LWV, 1973; winner speech contest St. Louis Toastmistress Club, 1976. Mem. Adminstrv. Mgmt. Soc. Democrat. Roman Catholic. Home: 840 N Castello St Florissant MO 63031 Office: 3418 Gratiot St Saint Louis MO 63103

SCHAMBERGER, MARY KATHRYN, coll. ofcl.; b. Freeport, Ill., Oct. 15, 1942; d. Orville Thomas and Duane Rosetta (Haring) Bonjour; B.S., No. Ill. U., 1964; M.S. Ed., Western Ill. U., 1970; m. Dale Schamberger, Mar. 18, 1967. Tchr. math. Shannon (Ill.) High Sch., 1964-66, Stockton (Ill.) High Sch., 1966-67; tchr., math. and sci. Nauvoo (Ill.)-Colusa High Sch., 1967-68; tchr. math. Lab. Sch., Western Ill. U., Macomb, 1970-71; math. cons. Ill. Gifted Program, Carthage, 1971-72; instr. math. Carl Sandburg Community Coll., Carthage, part-time 1974-78, dir. Carthage and Fountain Green Extension Centers, 1978—. Tchr. Sunday sch., supt. Bible sch., mem. counsel Luth. Ch.; chmn. Carthage Interagy. Council; bd. dirs. Hancock County Mental Health Bd., 1981—; dir. Carthage Indsl. Devel. Corp., 1976—. Mem. Ill. Council Community Coll. Adminstrs., Assn. Supervision and Curriculum Devel., Bus. and Profl. Women (pres.), AAUW. Home: Rural Route 2 Carthage IL 62321 Office: PO Box 398 Carthage IL 62321

SCHANCK, JORDAN THOMAS, mfg. co. exec.; b. Portland, Oreg., Feb. 5, 1931; s. Francis R. and Catherine (Short) S.; B.A., Dartmouth, 1952; m. Barbara Burgoyne, Apr. 27, 1957; children—Karen, William, Rebecca. Field engr. Signode Corp, Glenview, Ill., 1954-56, packaging lab. tech., 1957, asst. to v.p. sales, 1958, sales rep., 1959, sales mgr. Paslode div., 1960-65, Eastern div., 1966, asst. to pres., 1967-69, v.p. corporate planning, 1970-71, exec. v.p., 1972, pres., chief operating officer, 1973-75, pres., chief exec. officer, 1975—; dir. Am. Nat. Bank, Maytag Co, Amsted Industries, Lindberg Corp, Signode Corp., Walter E. Heller Internat. Mem. advisory bd. YMCA Metro. Chgo., BUILD Chgo.; bd. govs. United Republican Fund; governing mem. Orchestral Assn. of Chgo. Symphony Orch.; trustee George Williams Coll.; mem. adv. council Kellogg Grad. Sch. Mgmt., Northwestern U.; mem. Northwestern U. Assos. Served with U.S. Army, 1952-54. Mem. Ill. Mfrs. Assn., Chgo. Assn. Commerce and Industry, Chgo. Council on Fgn. Relations, Presbyterian. Clubs: Chgo., Econ. (dir.), Chgo. Commonwealth, Commercial, Glen View, Mid-Am., Hinsdale Golf, Oak Brook Bath and Tennis. Office: 3600 W Lake Ave Glenview IL 60025

SCHANTZ, CURTIS MICHAEL, air force officer; b. Mountain Lakes, N.J., Mar. 12, 1938; s. Ernest Leslie and Ruth Catherine Schantz; B.S., U. So. Miss., 1971; M.B.A., U. N.D., 1979; m. Barbara Ann Iversen, Aug. 25, 1956; 1 son, Douglas Michael. Enlisted USAF, 1961, commd. 2d lt., 1971, advanced through grades to capt., 1975; nuclear safety officer, Grand Forks AFB, N.D., 1978-80, detachment comdr. Air Force Inst. Tech., Grand Forks AFB, 1980—; asst. prof. mgmt. U. N.D., 1980—. Pres., Ascension Luth. Ch., 1975-77, lay minister, 1975—. Mem. Am. Soc. Safety Engrs., Pi Gamma Mu, Phi Delta Kappa, Kappa Delta Pi. Republican. Contbr articles to profl. jours. Home: Rural Route 1 Box 95C Emerado ND 58228 Office: AFIT Det 12 Grand Forks AFB ND 58205

SCHAPAUGH, WILLIAM TAYLOR, agrl. seed co. exec.; b. Jamesport, Mo., Mar. 16, 1932; s. Earl R. and Frances Louise S.; student Ill. Inst. Tech., 1950-52; B.S., Iowa State U., 1959; m. Marjorie Nadine Doughty, June 15, 1952; children—William Taylor, Randal L. With, Asgrow Seed Co., Kalamazoo, Mich., 1959—, gen. mgr. internat. west., 1979—. Bd. dirs. Plant Variety Protection, 1980—. Served with U.S. Army, 1952-54. Mem. Am. Seed Trade Assn. (1st v.p. 1981-82, dir. 1980-82), Am. Assn. Ofcl. Seed Certifying Agencies (asso.), Nat. Rifle Assn. Republican. Methodist. Club: Mason. Home: 8119 West R Ave Kalamazoo MI 49009 Office: Asgrow Seed Co Gull Rd Kalamazoo MI 49001

SCHAPER, CHERYL PALACK, steel tank mfg. co. exec.; b. Fairview, Ohio, Feb. 20, 1945; d. Alvin J. and Eleanor S. (Scigay) Palack; B.S. in Bus. Edn./Adminstrn., Bowling Green State U., 1967; m. Richard P. Schaper, Aug. 6, 1967 (div. Mar. 1979). Tchr. bus. edn. Liberty-Benton High Sch., Findley, Ohio, 1967-70; office mgr. Rink's Bargain City, 1968-70; asst. controller Vacuform Corp., Columbus, Ohio, 1971-77; controller Airmark Corp., Kansas City Mo., 1977-78, v.p. fin., 1978—. Mem. Nat. Assn. Accountants, Am. Soc. Women Accountants, Nat. Assn. Credit Mgmt., Kansas City Womens C. fo C., Bowling Green State U. Alumni Assn., Kappa Delta. Home: 7005 Hallet St Shawnee KS 66216 Office: 1700 W 29th St Kansas City MO 64108

SCHARLEMANN, MARTIN HENRY, clergyman, theologian; b. Nashville, Ill., Dec. 28, 1910; s. Ernst Karl and Johanna Sophie (Harre) S.; M.Div., Concordia Sem., St. Louis, 1934; M.A., Washington U., 1936, Ph.D., 1938; Th.D., Union Theol. Sem., 1964; m. Dorothy Hoyer, June 18, 1938; children—Edith Louise Scharlemann Rehbein, Ernst Theodor, Martin George, John Paul. Ordained to ministry, Lutheran Ch.-Mo. Synod, 1934; asst. pastor St. Paul's Luth. Ch., St. Louis, 1935-38, St. John's Ch., Osseo, Minn., 1938-39; pastor Trinity Luth. Ch., Athens, Wis., 1939-41; chaplain U.S. Army, U.S. Air Force, 1941-52; prof. biblical interpretation Concordia Sem., St. Louis, 1952—, acting pres., 1974, dir. grad. studies, 1954-62. Mem. exec. com. Mo. Coalition for Peace Through Strength, 1980—. Served to brig. gen. USAFR. Mem. Luth. Acad. Scholarship (pres. 1946-72), Soc. Bibl. Lit., Cath. Bibl. Assn., Soc. New Testament Studies, Phi Beta Kappa. Republican. Clubs: Early Birds, Rotary (dist. gov.). Author works in field. Home: 17 Seminary Terr N Saint Louis MO 63105 Office: Concordia Sem 801 De Mun Ave Saint Louis MO 63105

SCHAUBEL, HOWARD JAMES, surgeon; b. Grand Rapids, Mich., May 20, 1916; s. Charles Theodore and Jennie (Slager) S.; Asso. Sci., Grand Rapids Jr. Coll., 1936; A.B., Hope Coll., 1938; M.D., U. Mich., 1942; certificate orthopedics Duke, 1946; m. Marjorie Faye Moody, June 19, 1943; children—Candice (Mrs. James M. Edwards), Janis (Mrs. Robert C. Timmons), Wendy (Mrs. Henry Dickinson), Gayla Sue (Mrs. Gary Klooster). Intern, Duke Hosp., Durham, N.C., 1942-43; resident N.C. Orthopedic Hosp., Gastonia, 1943-44, Duke Hosp., 1944-46; sr. orthopedic surgeon Butterworth Hosp., Grand Rapids, 1946-72, emeritus staff, 1973—; sr. orthopedic surgeon St. Mary's, Sunshine hosps., Grand Rapids, 1946-72, Mary Free Bed Vocational Instn., Grand Rapids, 1946-72; chief clin. surgeon Saladin Shrine Crippled Children's Unit, Grand Rapids, 1947-72; cons. Holland (Mich.) Municipal, North Ottawa Community, Zeeland Community, Pennock, Ionia Meml., Greenville Meml., Kelsey hosps., 1948-72; chief orthopedic surgery Ferguson Hosp., Grand Rapids, 1968-72, orthopedic cons., 1972—; practice medicine specializing in orthopedic surgery, Marathon, Fla., 1970-79; sr. orthopedic surgeon Fla. Keys Meml. Hosp., Key West, 1970-79, De Poo Hosp., Key West; cons. orthopaedic surgeon Upper Keys Community Hosp.; sr. orthopedic surgeon Fisherman's Hosp., Marathon, 1970-79, chief surgery, 1974-77; orthopedic cons. Saladin Shrine Orthopedic Clinic, Grand Rapids, 1972—; instr. orthopedic surgery Duke U. Bd. dirs. Camp Blodgett, Grand Rapids, v.p., 1971-72, pres., 1972-73. Served to maj. M.C., AUS, 1954. Recipient Disting. Alumni award Grand Rapids Jr. Coll., 1967; diplomate Am. Bd. Orthopedic Surgery. Fellow Internat. Coll. Surgeons, Am. Acad. Orthpaedic Surgeons, Am. Occupational Medicine Assn., Mich. Occupational Medicine Assn., Mich. Orthopaedic Soc.; mem. Eastern, Piedmont (chmn. 1963) orthopaedic socs., AMA, So. Med. Assn., Mich. Med. Soc., Ottawa County Med. Soc., Am. Fracture Assn., Monroe County Med. Soc. (sec.-treas. 1974, pres. elect 1975, pres. 1976), Galens. Hon. Med. Soc., Blue Key, Phi Rho Sigma. Mason (Shriner, Jester), Rotarian. Club: Century (Muskegon, Mich.). Contbr. articles to med. jours. Home: 10843 Lake Shore Dr Grand Haven MI 49460 Office: 456 Cherry St SE Grand Rapids MI 49503

SCHAUER, THOMAS ALFRED, ins. co. exec.; b. Canton, Ohio, Dec. 24, 1927; s. Alfred T. and Marie A. (Luthi) S.; B.Sc., Ohio State U., 1950; m. Joanne Alice Fay, Oct. 30, 1954; children—Alan, David, Susan, William. Ins. agt., Canton, 1951—; with Schauer & Reed Agy., 1951—, Kitzmiller, Tudor & Schauer, 1957—, Webb-Broda & Co., 1971—, Foglesong Agy., 1972—; pres. Ind. Ins. Service Corp. Akron and Canton, Canton, 1964—, Laurenson Agy., 1978—, Wells-Williams, 1978—, J.D. Craig Agy., 1981—; dir. Central Trust Co. NE Ohio (N.A.). Chmn., Joint Hosp. Blood Com., 1974; bd. dirs. Better Bus. Bur., Canton, 1970—, chmn., 1979-80; bd. dirs. Dist. YMCA, 1974, v.p., 1975—; bd. dirs. Hosp. Bur. Central Stark City, 1972-78; vice chmn. bd. Aultman Hosp., 1981—, JMS Found., 1968—; bd. dirs. United Way, 1974—, pres., 1976-78; mem. distbn. com. Stark County Found., 1977—; adv. bd. Malone Coll., 1979—; trustee Kent State U., 1980—. Served with USNR, 1946-48. C.L.U., C.P.C.U. Mem. Chartered Ins. Inst. London, Nat. Assn. Mfg., Am. Soc. C.P.C.U.'s, Am. Soc. C.L.U.'s, Am. Mgmt. Assn., Assn. Advanced Life Underwriters, Am. Risk and Ins. Assn., Am. Soc. Pension Actuaries. Clubs: Canton, Brookside Country, Atwood Yacht. Home: 3755 Eaton Dr NW Canton OH 44708 Office: 100 Cleve-Tusc Bldg Canton OH 44702

SCHEANWALD, MARJORIE DIANA, med. office adminstr.; b. Toledo, Sept. 27, 1926; d. August G. and Henrietta H. (Helbing) S.; student public schs., Saginaw, Mich. Bookkeeping machine operator Sugar Beet Products, Gen. Office, Saginaw, 1944-46; bookkeeping machiner operator Heavenrich's, Saginaw, 1946-53, sec. to pres., 1953-56; receptionist/sec. Dr. Sargent & Dr. Bruggers, Saginaw, 1956-72; office mgr., asst. corp. sec. Valley Ob-Gyn Clinic, Saginaw, 1972—, also dir. Mem. Med. Group Mgrs. Assn., Am. Assn. Med. Assts., Mich. Assn. Med. Group Mgrs., Republican. Presbyterian. Home: 311 S Wheeler St Saginaw MI 48602 Office: 926 N Michigan St Box 3216 Saginaw MI 48605

SCHECKELHOFF, DIANE SIEGLAFF, ednl. adminstr.; b. Cin., June 24, 1952; d. Charles Lewis and Shirley Marie (Fleming) Sieglaff; B.S., Bowling Green State U., 1974, M.Ed., 1977; m. George R. Scheckelhoff, Aug. 2, 1975. Exec. sec. Office of Vice Pres. and Pres., Bowling Green (Ohio) State U., 1974-75; tchr. coop. edn. Sandusky (Ohio) City Schs., 1975-77; tchr. intensive edn. Ehove Joint Vocat. Sch., Milan, Ohio, 1978-79; sch. adminstr., 1979—. Advisor, Girl Scouts U.S.A., 1976-78, Jr. Achievement, 1978-80. Mem. Office Edn. Assn. (advisor 1976—), Ohio Vocat. Assn., Am. Vocat. Assn., Nat. Bus. Edn. Assn. Republican. United Ch. of Christ. Office: 316 W Mason Rd Milan OH 44846

SCHEEL, EARL JENNINGS, engring. co. ofcl.; b. New Brighton, Pa., Feb. 25, 1929; s. John Hice and Lavina Viola (Leiper) S.; B.S., Geneva Coll., 1952; postgrad. U. Pitts., 1962-63; m. Waneta Jane Hoyt, Mar. 28, 1953; children—John, Constance, Margaret, Earl Jennings II. Sr. turn foreman Crucible Steel, Midland, Pa., 1955-62, indsl. engr., 1962-63; with Arthur G. McKee & Co., 1963-79; sr. sales rep. Davy McKee Corp., Cleve., 1979—. Active Boy Scouts Am., 1961-72. Served with USMC, 1952-54. Mem. AIME, Am. Inst. Steel Engrs., Eastern States Blast Furnace and Coke Oven Assn., Western States Blast Furnace and Coke Oven Assn. Republican. Presbyterian. Club: Masons. Home: 20859 Westway Blvd Rocky River OH 44116 Office: Davy McKee Corp 6200 Oak Tree Blvd Cleveland OH 44131

SCHEELE, RONALD VICTOR, radiation physicist; b. Sheboygan, Wis., Jan. 29, 1944; s. Victor H. and Hilda A. (Wesenberg) S.; B.S., Lakeland Coll., 1966; M.S., N.D. State U., 1969; m. Constance E. Wiesner, Dec. 28, 1968; children—Justin Elizabeth, Adam Victor. Instr. radiology U. Va., Charlottesville, 1969-72, asst. prof., 1972-75; radiation physicist St. Vincent Hosp., Green Bay, Wis., 1975—; cons. to numerous hosps. Co-dir. Smoking Withdrawal Clinic, 1975; bd. dirs. Am. Heart Assn., 1979—. Mem. Am. Assn. Physicists in Medicine, Health Physics Soc., AAAS. Author: Elements of Radiation Protection, 1975. Contbr. articles in field to profl. jours. Office: St Vincent Hosp 835 S Van Buren St Green Bay WI 54301

SCHEFFEL, KENNETH GEORGE, splty. chems. co. exec.; b. St. Louis, May 2, 1936; s. George and Katherine S.; A.B., U. Mo.; M.A., U. Calif.; m. Marilyn L. Hardy, June 7, 1959; children—Steven, Laurl, Sherri, Beth. Program mgr. UMC Industries, Phoenix, 1960-62; bus. devel. mgr. Dow Chem. Co., Midland, Mich., 1962-69; group product mgr. Ralston Purina Co., St. Louis, 1969-73; v.p., gen. mgr. splty. chems. C.J. Patterson Co., Kansas City, Mo., 1973-77, also dir.; pres., chief exec. officer Christian Hansens Lab., Inc., Milw., 1977-81; pres. Koch Sulfur Co., Wichita, Kans., 1981—. Com. dir. Daniel Boone council Boy Scouts Am., St. Louis; Mem. Am. Mgmt. Assn., Am. Mktg. Assn., Am. Chem. Soc., Inst. Food Tech., Phi Kappa Psi.

Republican. Methodist. Club: Rotary. Home: 2460 Greenleaf Ct Wichita KS 67226 Office: PO Box 2256 Wichita KS 67201

SCHEFFERS, JULIUS MERLE, indsl. psychologist; b. Grand Haven, Mich., July 12, 1942; s. Frank and Ione Ellen (Moore) S.; B.A., Albion (Mich.) Coll., 1964; M.A., U. Detroit, 1969; Ph.D., Bowling Green (Ohio) State U., 1975; m. Judy Lynne Brolin, Aug. 22, 1964; children—Todd Julius, Nichole Lynne. Mgr. recruitment and govt. programs Mich. Employment Security Commn., 1965-68; personnel research specialist, then mgr. personnel research Xerox Corp., Rochester, N.Y., 1972-77; asst. dir. tng. Inland Steel Co., East Chicago, Ind., 1977-79, dir. tng., 1979—, also corp. chmn. personnel selection procedures com.; mem. adj. faculty U. Rochester 1973, St. John Fisher Coll., Rochester, 1974-77. Bd. dirs. United Way Flossmoor (Ill.) and Olympia Fields, 1979—, Forest Ridge Assn., 1976-77; mem. New Detroit Com., 1967-68. Mem. Am. Mgmt. Assn., Am. Soc. Tng. and Devel., Ill. Tng. and Devel. Assn., Indsl. Relations Assn. Chgo., Calumet Area Personnel Assn., Exec. Study Conf. Mem. Flossmoor Community Ch. (governing bd.). Author papers in field. Home: 3024 Balmoral Crescent Flossmoor IL 60422 Office: 3210 Watling St East Chicago IN 46312

SCHEFTNER, GEROLD, dental radiology equipment mktg. co. exec.; b. Milw., June 1, 1937; s. Arthur Joseph and Alice Agnes (Gregory) S.; student Milw. Bus. Inst., 1953, Great Lakes Naval Acad. Sch. Dental-Med. Surgery, USAF, 1955-56, USAF Inst., 1959, Marquette U., 1959-60; m. Irene; children—Marc A., Margaret L., Mark A., Mary L., Scot P., Michael D., Natalie. Territorial rep. Mossey-Otto Co., dental retailers, Milw., 1960-63; with Den-Tal-Ez Mfg. Co., dental equipment mfg., Des Moines, 1963—, dir. foreign affairs, 1969-71, dir. far eastern affairs, 1971-72, exec. dir. internat. sales, marketing, 1973-74, v.p., gen. mgr. internat. ops., 1974—, also dir.; chmn. bd. Dentalez (Gt. Britain) Ltd., 1974—; pres. Seven Seas Ltd., gen. mktg. cons./Europe for Gen. Electric Med. Systems, Des Moines. Dir. Iowa Dist. Export Expansion Council, 1969-73; mem. Lake Panorama (Iowa) Devel. Assn., 1972-73; chmn. Iowa World Trade Council. Mem. adv. bd. St. Charles Boys Home Bldg. Program, Milw., 1963. Served with USAF, 1955-59. Recipient presdl. mgr. of the year award Den-Tal-Ez Co., 1967; Lecture award Faculdade de Odontologia, U. Ribeiro Preto, Brazil, 1974. Mem. Am. Dental Trade Assn., Am. Dental Mfrs. Assn., Greater Des Moines C. of C. (dir. dist. export council); hon. mem. Hong Kong Dental Trade Assn., Internat. Platform Assn. Republican. Lion. Clubs: TWA Ambassador; International (Frankfurt, Germany). Research in develop. equipment and apparatus for radiographic therapy. Office: 2516 SE 6 St Des Moines IA 50315

SCHEIB, ORVILLE DAVID, educator; b. Lisle, Mo., May 5, 1939; s. Orville Wilbur and Dorothy Evelyn (Neal) S.; B.S. in Math., Kans. State Coll., Pittsburg, 1961; M.S. in Edn., Central Mo. State U., 1972; M.S. in Psychology, Emporia State U., 1977; m. Oleita Jane Graham, Sept. 7, 1973; 1 son, David Neal; 1 dau. by previous marriage, Rhonda May. Tchr. math. Adrian (Mo.) High Sch., 1963-64; tchr. math., physics Drexel (Mo.) RIV Schs., 1964-65, Cass Midway Reorganized Dist. 1 Schs., Freeman, Mo., 1966-71; with M-S Aircraft Parts, San Antonio, 1965-66; tchr. spl. edn. math. Adolescent Sch., Osawatomie (Kans.) State Hosp., 1972—. Pres., PTA, Paola, Kans., 1976-78; dir. Christian edn. Drexel (Mo.) 1st Bapt. Ch., 1969-71; music dir. Pearl St. Bapt. Ch., Paola, 1976-78, 1st So. Bapt. Ch. (formerly Franklin Bapt. Chapel), Wellsville, Kans., 1978—; ordained dean So. Baptist Conv., 1978. Served with U.S. Army, 1961-63. Mem. Kans. Edn. Assn. (bldg. rep. 1977-78, 80-81), Osawatomie Edn. Assn. (treas. 1981-82). Republican. Home: Route 3 Paola KS 66071 Office: Adolescent Sch Osawatomie State Hospital Osawatomie KS 66064

SCHEID, BOBBY GENE, health care exec.; b. Springfield, Mo., Jan. 28, 1945; s. Arthur W. and Dale E. (Steele) S.; student S.W. Mo. State U., 1963-64, Drury Coll., Springfield, 1964-65; m. Sarah Cox. Asst. mgr. Plimmer Investment Co., Springfield, 1966-69; dept. mgr. K-Mart div. S.S. Kresge Co., Springfield, 1969-75; ins. agt., Springfield, 1975-76; div. mgr. Fidelity Union Life Ins. Co., Fargo, N.D., 1976-78; gen. mgr., treas. Central Health Care Centers, Inc., Springfield, 1978—; cons. nursing home ops., 1975—. Vice chmn. Springfield Personnel Bd., 1978—. Recipient Clarence H. Howard Meml. award U.S. Jaycees, 1976. Mem. Am. Health Care Assn., Mo. Health Care Assn., Springfield Jaycees (pres. found.; Harold A. Marks Meml. award 1976, internat. senator 1976—). Republican. Methodist. Club: Rotary. Author tng. manuals. Home: 3707 S Parklane Springfield MO 65807 Office: Suite 1-203 Number One Corporate Sq Springfield MO 65804

SCHEINFELD, JAMES DAVID, business service exec.; b. Milw., Nov. 11, 1926; s. Aaron and Sylvia (Rosenberg) S.; B.A. in Econs. magna cum laude, U. Wis., 1949; m. Mary Kathleen McGrew, Dec. 29, 1974; children by previous marriage—John Stephen, Nancy Ellen, Robert Alan. With Manpower, Inc., 1948-78, salesman, Chgo., 1949-51, br. mgr., 1951-53, nat. sales mgr., Milw., 1953-56, dir. sales, corp. sec., 1956-59, v.p. sales, 1959-62, v.p. marketing, 1962-65, exec. v.p., 1965-70, exec. v.p., chief ops. officer, 1970-76, cons., 1976—; dir., exec. v.p., mem. exec. com., Transpersonnel, Inc., 1959-76, Any Task, Inc., 1959-76, Manpower Argentina, Manpower Europe, Manpower Ltd. (U.K.), Manpower Australia, Manpower Japan, Manpower Germany GmbH, Manpower Norway, Manpower Denmark, Manpower Venezuela; pres. Aide Services, Inc., Tampa, Fla., 1976-81; pres., chief exec. officer Travel Power Inc., Inc., 1976—; dir. Heritage Bank of Whitefish Bay, Nat. Assn. Temporary Services, 1969-77. Chmn., Cancer Crusade Milw. County, 1970. Bd. dirs. Better Bus. Bur. Milw., Am. Cancer Soc. Milw., U. Wis.-Milw. Found., 1977—, Ballet Found. of Milw., Mount Sinai Med. Center, 1980—. Served with USNR, 1944-46. Mem. Sales Promotion Execs. Assn. (1st pres. Milw. chpt. 1965), Nat. Assn. Temporary Services (pres. 1975-76), Hickory Assn. (pres. 1979-81). Rotarian. Clubs: Coral Casino Swim (Santa Barbara, Calif.); University (Milw.). Contbr. articles to profl. jours. Home: 7210 N Beach Dr Milwaukee WI 53217 Office: 8911 N Port Washington Rd PO Box 17170 Milwaukee WI 53217.

SCHELHORN, MARGARETTE BRIZIUS, med. lab. adminstr.; b. Evansville, Ind., Feb. 28, 1915; d. Martin Carl and Eada (Collins) Brizius; R.N. cert. Deaconess Hosp. Sch. Nursing, Evansville, 1936; various courses in mgmt., tech.; m. Wilfred K. Schelhorn, Apr. 22, 1938 (dec.). Pvt. duty nurse, 1936-41; gen. duty nurse Union Hosp., Terre Haute, Ind., 1941-43; med. technologist dept. lab. Associated Physicians and Surgeons, Terre Haute, 1943-47; with Terre Haute Med. Lab., Inc., 1947—, corp. sec., 1957—, lab. adminstr., 1970—. Recipient Salute, Terre Haute C. of C., 1964; named Woman of Yr., Terre Haute Bus. and Profl. Women's Club, 1964. Mem. Ind. State Med. Technologists (past dir., past West Central chmn.), Am. Soc. Clin. Pathologists cert. in cytotechnology, asso.), Am. Soc. Med. Technologists, Union Hosp. Service League. Congregationlist. Home: 3700 Parkview Dr Terre Haute IN 47803 Office: PO Box 1468 Terre Haute IN 47808

SCHENK, BOYD FREDERICK, food co. exec.; b. Providence, Utah, July 23, 1922; s. Frederick Lyman and Mabel (Reddish) S.; student U. Utah, 1942, U. Idaho, 1940-43, also exec. program Columbia U., 1961; m. June Verlee Hansen, Aug. 21, 1942; children—Sandra Lee, Greg F., Brent J., Julie, Peggy. With Pet, Inc., 1947—, pres. frozen foods div., 1963-65, corp. v.p., 1964—, corp. group v.p., 1965—, exec. v.p. ops., 1968—, pres., chief exec. officer, 1969—, chmn. exec. com., 1969-75, chmn. bd., 1975—; dir. First Nat. Bank St. Louis, Gen. Steel Industries, Inc., St. Louis, Laclede Gas Co., St. Louis, Ill. Power Co., A.E. Staley Mfg. Co., Decatur, Ill., IC Industries, Inc., Chgo. Mem. exec. bd. St. Louis area council Boy Scouts Am.; mem. Civic Progress, St. Louis; mem. Mo. Cancer Research Center Devel. Council; mem. vis. com. Washington U., St. Louis. Served with inf. AUS, World War II. Office: PO Box 392 Pet Plaza 400 S 4th St Saint Louis MO 63166

SCHEPER, JACK LEE, radio sta. exec.; b. Chgo., Jan. 20, 1934; s. Ernest R. and Ruth Viola (Harrison) S.; student U. Mo. at Columbia, 1955-57; m. Jacqueline Jean Hays, Sept. 8, 1961; children—Linda Ruth, Jack Lee, John Leslie. With Irwin's Men Shop, Cape Girardeau, Mo., 1946; mem. mgr. tng. program J.C. Penny Co. Cape Girardeau, 1947-50; asst. mgr. Allen's Dept. Store, Wildwood, N.J., 1957; mgr. Gidding Dept. Store, Wildwood, 1957-59; gen. mgr. radio sta. WHCO, Sparta, Ill., 1959—, host program People Speak, 1961—; supr. radio sta. KFMO, Flat River, Mo., 1975—. Active Boy Scouts Am.; dir. Civil Def., Sparta, 1960—; chmn. Sparta Community Devel. Study with So. Ill. U., 1960-63, mem. Randolph County (Ill.) Devel. Study, 1959-63; treas. Sparta Municipal Bldg. Commn., 1969—; mem. policy bd. Sparta OEO, 1969-71; mem. adv. com. Dist. 140 Sch. Bd., 1974-76; sec. Ill. State Adv. Bd. on Emergency Communication and Transp., 1975—; chmn. adv. com. Sparta City Council, 1966-70; mem. Sparta Zoning Commn., 1967-71; mem. Regional Manpower CETA Program State of Ill., 1976. Served with USAF, 1950-54. Decorated Nat. Def. Service medal. recipient Community Devel. award So. Ill. U., 1963; U.S. Savings Bond Service award, 1973; Radio Talkathon award Carbondale chpt. Easter Seal Soc., 1974; Broadcast Service award Optimist Club, 1974; Be Counted Again award Am. Legion, 1974; Appreciation award VA, 1971; Neighborhood award Sparta OEO, 1972; Statuette award Boy Scouts Am., 1973; Thank You award Lions Club Internat., 1973; March of Dimes Merit award, Nat. Found., 1970; Ill. Sec. of State Minuteman 76 award; Devoted Service award Easter Seals Soc./Sparta Rotary, 1979. Mem. Nat., Ill. assns. broadcasters, U.S., Sparta (indsl. rep. 1961—, dir. 1959—, pres. 1960, 67-69, 74-75) chambers commerce. Presbyterian (deacon, Sunday Sch. tchr. and gen. supt.). Mason, Rotarian (pres. 1964, dir. 1959-65; Fellowship award 1964). Home: 208 S Dickey St Sparta IL 62286 Office: WHCO Box 255 Sparta IL 62286

SCHEPIS, MICHAEL EUGENE, ednl. adminstr.; b. Fort Worth, July 24, 1943; s. Michael Salvador and Marcella Lucille S.; B.S., Friends U., Wichita, 1965; M.Ed., Wichita State U., 1969; m. Nancy Joan Kroeker, July 30, 1965; children—Matthew, Andrea, Heidi. Instr., athletic coach Mahaska (Kans.) Public High Sch., 1965-66, Dexter (Kans.) Public High Sch., 1966-67, Cheney (Kans.) Public Schs., 1967-68; instr. phys. edn., athletic coach Wichita Pub. Sch. System, 1968-74; athletic dir., athletic coach Bapt. Bible Coll., Springfield, Mo., 1974-81. Ward committeeman Rep. Party, Greene County, Mo., 1978—. Mem. AAHPER, Fellowship of Christian Athletes, Nat. Assn. Intercoll. Athletics, Athletics Dirs., Assn., Ozark Coll. Conf. (treas.), Nat. Christian Coll. Athletic Assn. (Nat. Coach of Year in Div. II Basketball 1978, regional chmn. Div. II). Baptist.

SCHEPMAN, HENRY FREDERICK, lawyer; b. Lockwood, Mo., Sept. 26, 1898; s. William and Friedericke (Heuke) S.; student U. Chgo., 1921; A.B., U. Nebr., 1924, J.D., 1924; m. Sherlie Whitaker, Dec. 6, 1928; 1 son, John Henry. Admitted to Nebr. bar, 1924, since practiced in Falls City; sec. to Congressman Morehead 69th and 72d Congresses, county atty. Richardson County, Nebr., 1953-67, 71-75. Chmn. local unit Salvation Army, 1949-75; exec. bd. Cornhusker council Boy Scouts Am., 1959. Mem. Nebr. Ho. of Reps., 1925-27, Nebr. Senate, 1929-32. Bd. control Concordia Tchrs. Coll., Seward, Nebr., 1958-68. Served with inf., U.S. Army, World War I. Mem. Am. Legion (past adj.), Nebr. County Attys. Assn. (pres. 1959-60), S.E. Nebr. (pres. 1958), Nebr., Am. bar assns., Luth. Laymen's League (pres. Nebr., Wyo. 1957, 58), Delta Theta Phi. Mem. bd. of appeals Luth. Ch.-Mo. Synod, 1956-59. Rotarian (dist. gov. 1954-55). Home: 2302 Chase St Falls City NE 68355 Office: Richardson County Bank Bldg Falls City NE 68355

SCHERECK, WILLIAM JOHN, historian, cons.; b. Chgo., Dec. 22, 1913; s. Frank and Adele (Schubert) S.; student Wofford Coll., 1950-51; B.S. in Sociology, U. Wis., 1952, postgrad., 1952-53; m. Flora Blanche George, May 19, 1943; children—Linda, William John, Ralph, George. With Crawford County (Wis.) Welfare Dept., 1938-42; with State Hist. Soc. Wis., Madison, 1953-79, research asst., 1954-55, field services supr., 1956-59, head Office Local History, 1960-79, Wis. Council Local History, 1961—. Active Girls Scouts U.S.A., Spartanburg, S.C., 1947-48, Boy Scouts Am., Madison, 1956-58. Served to 2d lt. U.S. Army, 1942-45. Decorated Bronze star medal; recipient 1st place award S.C. State Coll. Press Assn., 1951, Crusade for Freedom awards, 1951, 1st place award for Sounds of Heritage, Am. Exhbn. Ednl. Radio and Television, 1955. Mem. Am. Legion, Ret. Officers Assn., Am. Fedn. State, County and Municipal Employees, Wis. Alumni Assn., Smithsonian Instn., Madison Civic Opera Guild, Costeau Soc., Field Mus. Natural History. Episcopalian. Author numerous publs. State Hist. Soc. Am. Contbr. articles to mags. and newspapers. Home: Route 3 4329 Harmony Dr Lodi WI 53555 Office: 816 State St Madison WI 53706

SCHERER, VICTOR RICHARD, physicist; b. Poland, Feb. 7, 1940; came to U.S., 1941, naturalized, 1951; s. Emanuel and Florence B. Scherer; B.S. magna cum laude, CCNY, 1960; M.A., Columbia U., 1962; Ph.D., U. Wis., Madison, 1974; m. Gail R. Dobrofsky, Aug. 11, 1963; children—Helena Cecille, Markus David. Health physics asst. Columbia U., N.Y.C., 1961-63; research asst. dept. physics U. Wis., Madison, 1967-74, project asso., project mgr. Inst. for Environ. Studies, World Climate-Food Research Group, 1974-78, specialist computer systems Acad. Computing Center, 1978—. AEC fellow, 1960-61. Mem. Am. Phys. Soc., Am. Meteorol. Soc., Am. Soc. Agronomy, Assn. Computing Machinery, Nat. Computer Graphics Assn., AAAS, Sigma Xi, Phi Beta Kappa. Researcher in particle physics, agriclimatology, soil-yield relationships and computer graphics. Office: Academic Computing Center U Wis Madison WI 53706

SCHERER, WILLIAM JAMES, educator; b. Ravenna, Ohio, Aug. 27, 1949; s. Donald C. and Florence M. (Johnson) S.; B.S., Kent State U., 1972, Ed.M., 1975, Ed.S., 1977; children—Matthew Donald, Elizabeth Marie. Tchr. elem. grades Stow (Ohio) City Schs., 1972-75, chmn. faculty adv. com. 1973-75; tchr. Shaker Heights (Ohio) City Schs., 1975—, mem. math. curriculum com., 1980—, mem. supt.'s adv. com., 1980-81. Mem. Kent (Ohio) Community Pool Com., 1976; mem. bd. deacons United Ch. Christ, 1978-80. Served with USN, 1967-69. Cert. tchr. and prin., Ohio. Mem. NEA, Ohio Edn. Assn. (state del. 1977-80), Shaker Heights Tchrs. Assn. (sec. 1980-81, exec. bd. 1980-81), Northeastern Ohio Tchrs. Assn., Assn. Supervision and Curriculum Devel., Council for Exceptional Children Ret. Tchrs. Assn., Phi Delta Kappa. Democrat. Club: Masons.

SCHERICH, ESTHER ANNE, editor; b. New Haven, Dec. 15, 1943; d. Millard and Esther (Petersen) Scherich; B.A., Oreg. State U., 1966; M.A., U. Oreg., 1970, D.Arts, 1973, Ph.D., 1975. Sec. dept. English, U. Oreg., Eugene, 1966-69, research asst., 1969-70, teaching fellow in English, 1970-75; manuscript editor Moody Bible Inst., 1977—. Mem. Women in Communications, Am. Bus. Women's Assn., MLA, Am. Soc. Eighteenth Century Studies, Kappa Delta. Republican. Episcopalian. Home: 821 N Washington Wheaton IL 60187 Office: Moody Bible Inst 820 N LaSalle St Chicago IL 60610

SCHERTZ, DAVID L., conservation agronomist; b. Bloomington, Ill., Jan. 27, 1945; s. Earl D. and Ladine V. Schertz; B.S. in Agronomy, Ill. State U., 1968; M.S. in Agronomy (scholar), U. Ill., 1970-71; postgrad. Purdue U., 1980—; m. Sharron L. Funk, Sept. 3, 1966; 1 dau., Stacey M. Soil conservationist Soil Conservation Service, U.S. Dept. Agr., Pekin, Ill., 1969-70, dist. conservationist, Decatur, Ill., 1971-72, Ill. state agronomist, Champaign, 1972-75, remote sensing staff agronomist, Washington, 1975-77, Calif. state agronomist, Davis, 1977-79, Ill. state resource cons., Champaign, 1979-80, agronomist detailed to erosion control research Agrl. Research Service, Purdue U., 1980—. Recipient cert. of merit U.S. Dept. Agr., also letters of appreciation and commendation. Mem. Am. Soc. Agronomy, Soil Conservation Soc. Am. Office: US Dept Agr Nat Soil Erosion Lab Purdue U West Lafayette IN 47907

SCHICK, HAROLD PHILIP, mfg. co. exec.; b. N.Y.C., Sept. 22, 1926; s. John Gustav and Frieda Elizabeth (Kaiser) S.; B.Chem. Engrng. cum laude, CCNY, 1949; M.S. in Engrng., Akron (Ohio) U., 1967; m. Joyce Ragna Ellsworth, Dec. 6, 1952; children—Lawrence, Gordon, Roland, Diana. With Gen. Tire & Rubber Co., 1957—, tech. mgr. chem.-plastics div., Akron, 1971-78, tech. dir. reinforced plastics div., Marion, Ind., 1978—; lectr. adult edn. Akron U., 1966-68. Scoutmaster Gt. Trail council Boy Scouts Am., 1964-77. Served with U.S. Army, 1944-46; ETO; to 1st lt., 1951-53; Korea. Decorated Bronze Star with oak leaf cluster; registered profl. engr., Ohio. Mem. Soc. Plastics Engrs. (pres. Akron sect. 1969-70), Am. Chem. Soc., Tau Beta Pi. Club: Meshingomesia Country (Marion). Author, patentee in field. Home: 3960 Woodbine Dr Marion IN 46952 Office: 1700 Factory Ave Marion IN 46952

SCHICK, JOSEPH SCHLUETER, educator; b. Davenport, Iowa, Mar. 23, 1910; s. Charles and Johannah (Schlueter) S.; grad. Browne and Nichols Sch., Cambridge, Mass., 1927; B.A., U. Iowa, 1931; M.A., U. Chgo., 1932, Ph.D., 1937. English instr. U. Iowa, 1935-36; prof. English, State Tchrs. Coll., Duluth, Minn., 1938-42, 45-46; lectr. Am. lit. Caserta Tech., Italy, 1945; Merit prof. English, Ind. State U., 1946-76. Served from pvt. to sgt. U.S. Army, 1942-45, cryptanalyst Signal Intelligence. Mem. Am. Assn. U. Profs., Modern Lang. Assn. Am., Iowa, Ind. hist. socs., Phi Sigma Iota, Blue Key. Author: The Early Theater in Eastern Iowa, 1939; also articles profl. jours. Exhibited paintings Swope Gallery, Terre Haute, 1953, 55. Patentee on cobber. Home: 248 S 26th St Dr Terre Haute IN 47803

SCHICK, ROY JOHN, trust co. exec.; b. St. Louis, May 5, 1917; s. John C. and Blanche A. S.; LL.B., Vanderbilt U., 1941, J.D., 1970; m. Else Lou Daniels, Sept. 2, 1950; children—Diane Louise, Carl Jay. With Travelers Ins. Co., St. Louis, 1941-42; admitted to Mo. bar, 1941; mem. firm Lamm and Barnett, Sedalia, Mo., 1946-48; with N.Y. Life Ins. Co., 1948-61; with St. Louis Union Trust Co., 1961—, v.p. estate planning 1977—. Served with USAAF, 1942-46. Mem. Am. Bar Assn., Mo. Bar Assn., C.L.U.'s, St. Louis Bar Assn., Life Underwriters Assn. St. Louis, Estate Planning Council St. Louis. Home: 449 Elm St Saint Louis MO 63122 Office: St Louis Union Trust Co 510 Locust St Saint Louis MO 63101

SCHIEFFER, GERALD WILLIAM, educator; b. Yankton, S.D., Apr. 23, 1948; s. Lawrence Henry and Helen Catherine (Goeden) S.; B.S. cum laude in Edn., U. S.D., Springfield, 1972; m. Carol Ann Ells, June 6, 1970. Profl. carpenter, Robert Burns Lumber Co., Mitchell, S.D., 1970-74, Mueller Lumber Co., Mitchell, 1976-78; instr. cabinetmaking U. S.D., Springfield, 1974-76, Mitchell Area Vocat.-Tech. Sch., 1977—. Mem. Mitchell Area Tech. Educators, S.D. Vocat. Assn., Am. Vocat. Assn. Republican. Roman Catholic. Club: Nat. Rifle Assn. Home: 996-2739 400 W 5th St Mitchell SD 57301 Office: 996-6671 821 N Capital St Mitchell SD 57301

SCHIFF, JOHN JEFFERSON, fin. corp. exec.; b. Cin., Apr. 19, 1916; s. John Jefferson and Marguerite (Cleveland) S.; B.Sc. in Commerce, Ohio State U., 1938; m. Mary Reid, July 26, 1941; children—John Jefferson, Suzanne, Thomas R. Vice chmn. Cin. Ins. Co., 1979—; chmn. Cin. Fin. Corp., 1979—; chmn. bd. Inter-Ocean Ins. Co., Cin., 1979—, Life Ins. Co. of Cin.; dir. Fifth Third Bancorp. Vice pres. Deaconess Hosp. of Cin., Griffith Found. for Ins. Edn.; pres. council Xavier U.; trustee Cin. Art Mus., Cin. Bus. Com. Served to lt. comdr. Supply Corps, USNR, 1942-46. Named Ins. Man of Year in Cin., Cin. Ins. Bd., 1977. Mem. Cin. C. of C. (v.p. 1972). Republican. Methodist. Clubs: Queen City, Western Hills Country, Cin., Ohio State U. Pres.'s. Home: 1926 Beech Grove Dr Cincinnati OH 45238 Office: PO Box 14567 Cincinnati OH 45214

SCHILLER, JAMES JOSEPH, lawyer; b. Cleve., July 1, 1933; s. Jacob Peter and Helen Elizabeth (Tosh) S.; B.S. in Mech. Engrng., Case Western Res. U., 1955; J.D., U. Mich., 1961; m. Sara Brooke Wilson, Oct. 24, 1964; children—Charles Alexander, Brooke VanGeem, Kristan Wilson. Admitted to Ohio bar, 1961, since practiced in Cleve.; mem. firm Weston, Hurd, Fallon, Paisley and Howley, and predecessor, 1973—. Co-chmn. John J. Gilligan Gubernatorial campaign, Cuyahoga County, 1970; campaign dir. U.S. Senator Howard Metzenbaum, 1974. mem. Ohio Democratic Exec. Com., 1970-74, Cuyahoga County Dem. Exec. Com., 1971—; del., mem. drafting com. Ohio Dem. Constl. Conv., 1971; dep. registrar motor vehicles Cuyahoga County, 1971-75. Served to lt. (j.g.) USNR, 1955-58. Mem. Am., Ohio, Cleve. bar assns. Clubs: Cleve. City; Shaker Heights Country. Home: 3311 Maynard Rd Shaker Heights OH 44122 Office: 2500 Terminal Tower Cleveland OH 44113

SCHILLING, JOHN IRVING, funeral dir.; b. Moline, Ill., Oct. 14, 1947; s. Richard Maurice and Olive Amolia (Lage) S.; student Blackhawk, Jr. Coll., Moline, 1965-66, Wis. Inst. Mortuary Sci., 1966-67; m. Sara Jo Enstrom, Aug. 14, 1970; children—John Paul, Mark Irving. Apprentice funeral dir., embalmer Sundberg Funeral Home, Rockford, Ill., 1967-68; mgr. Querhammer Funeral Home, Crystal Lake, Ill., 1968-72; founder Schilling's Wonder Lake (Ill.) Funeral Home, 1972-75; owner, operator Melvin-Schilling Funeral Home, Sterling, Ill., 1975—; partner Greenan, Reedy & Schilling Livery Service, Sterling, 1978—. Mem. Ill. Funeral Dirs. Assn., Nat. Funeral Dirs. Assn. Republican. Congregationalist. Clubs: Internat. Order Golden Rule, Elks, Moose, Masons, Shriners. Home and office: 702 1st Ave Sterling IL 61081

SCHILLING, KATHERINE LEE TRACY, educator; b. Mitchell, S.D., May 31, 1925; d. Ernest Benjamin and Mary Alice (Courier) Tracy; B.A., Dakota Wesleyan U., 1947; M.A., U. S.D., 1957; postgrad. U. Wyo., U. Nebr., Kearney State Coll.; m. Clarence R.

Schilling, Oct. 14, 1951; 1 dau., Keigh Leigh. Tchr. elem. and secondary schs., also colls., S.D. and Nebr.; now with specially funded project for disadvantaged children Winnebago Indian reservation, Nebr. Mem. staff S.D. Girls' State, 1950-51; mem. S.D. Gov.'s Com. on Library, Nebr. Gov.'s Com. on Right to Read. Recipient Outstanding Tchr. award S.D. High Sch. Speech Tchrs., 1966. Mem. NEA, Nebr., Thurston County (pres.) edn. assns., Winnebago Tchrs. Assn., Delta Kappa Gamma. Clubs: Internat. Toastmistress (internat. dir. 1963-65, Mitchell Toastmistress of Year 1959), Order Eastern Star. Contbr. articles to profl. jours., also poetry. Home: 39 S Harmon Dr Box 578 Mitchell SD 57301 Office: Winnebago Public Sch Nebr Indian Community Coll Winnebago NE 68071

SCHILLING, RONALD BARRY, med. equipment co. exec.; b. N.Y.C., Jan. 13, 1941; s. Nathan Francis and Ada (Steinhause) S.; B.S. in Elec. Engring., Coll. City N.Y., 1961; M.S., Princeton U., 1963; Ph.D., Poly. Inst. N.Y., 1967; m. Marilyn Goldstein, Dec. 24, 1961; children—Karen Robin, Lisa Joy, Robert David. Mem. tech. staff RCA Labs., Princeton, N.J., 1961-66; mgr. product engring. Solid State div. RCA, Somerville, N.J., 1966-71; mgr. mktg. Solid State div. Motorola Corp., Phoenix, 1971-76; mgr. mktg. Med. div. Gen. Electric Co., Milw., 1976-78, op. mgr. Far East, 1978-80, strategic planning mgr., 1980, gen. mgr., 1981—; adj. prof. Coll. City N.Y., 1968-71; adj. lectr. Poly. Inst. N.Y.; mem. U.S. Export Devel. Mission to Japan, 1978. Pres., Har Zion Congregation, 1975; v.p. Colonial Oaks Civic Assn., 1966. Recipient RCA doctoral study award, 1964. Mem. IEEE (sr.), Am. Mgmt. Assn., Sigma Xi, Tau Beta Pi, Eta Kappa Nu. Club: K.P. Author: Semiconductor Modeling for Computer Aided Design, 1972. Contbr. articles to profl. jours. Patentee electronic devices. Home: 9515 N Sequoia Dr Bayside WI 53217 Office: Box 414 Milwaukee WI 53201

SCHILLING, STUART ROBERT, podiatrist; b. Columbus, Ohio, Sept. 2, 1945; s. Jack Isaac and Anne Yetta (Hemmelstein) S.; student Ohio State U., 1963-66; D.P.M., Ohio Coll. Podiatric Medicine, 1970; m. Linda Sue Gross, Aug. 30, 1969; children—Richard, David. Preceptorship, Columbus, 1970-71; pvt. practice podiatry, Columbus, 1971—; surg. staff Grant Hosp., Columbus, 1981—. Trustee Ohio Coll. Podiatric Medicine, 1980-81. Recipient Past Pres.'s award, Ohio Podiatry Assn., 1981. Mem. Podiatry Referral Bur. (chmn. bd. 1972-74), Central Acad. Podiatry (pres. 1973-75), Ohio Podiatry Assn. (pres. 1980-81), Am. Public Health Assn., Am. Podiatry Assn. (mem. ho. of dels. 1980-81), Acad. Ambulatory Foot Surgery. Clubs: B'nai B'rith Men's Assn., F.O.P.A. Office: 2827 Cleveland Ave Columbus OH 43224

SCHINDLER, FREDERICK PERRY, food mfg. co. exec.; b. Pitts., Aug. 7, 1943; s. Frederick John and Alyce Perry S.; B.A. in Bus. Adminstrn., Grove City Coll., 1965; m. Susan L. Lammert, June 25, 1966; 1 dau., Heidi Lynn. Media supr. Ketchum, MacLeod & Grove, Pitts., 1968-74; media supr. Bloom Advt., Dallas, 1974-75; media supr. Tracy-Locke Advt., Dallas, 1975-76; advt. mgr. Consumer Products div. Borden Inc., Columbus, Ohio, 1978—. Served to capt. USAF, 1965-68. Mem. Am. Mktg. Assn., Columbus Advt. Fedn. (dir. 1978—). Republican. Presbyterian. Office: 180 E Broad St Columbus OH 43215

SCHINDLER, MARVIN SAMUEL, educator; b. Boston, Jan. 2, 1932; s. Edward Esau and Esther Marian (Wiseman) S.; B.A., U. Mass., 1953; M.A., Ohio State U., 1955, Ph.D., 1965; m. Roslyn Frances Abt, Aug. 11, 1974; children—Daniel Mark, Lore Elaine, Inge-Marie, Neal Elliott. Instr. German, Pa. State U., Pottsville, 1955-59; asst. prof. German, Ohio State U., 1965-67; asso. prof. German, asso. dean Grad. Sch. Arts and Scis., U. Va., Charlottesville, 1967-71; prof. German, chmn. fgn. lang. dept. No. Ill. U., DeKalb, 1971-74; prof. German, chmn. dept. Romance and Germanic langs. and lits. Wayne State U., Detroit, 1974—, dir. Jr. Year in Germany Programs, 1975—. Fulbright fellow, 1961-62; grantee DAAD, 1981, Am. Council Learned Socs., 1981. Mem. Am. Assn. Tchrs. of German (exec. council), Modern Lang. Assn. Am., Midwest Modern Lang. Assn., Am. Assn. Advancement Humanities, Assn. Depts. Fgn. Langs. (exec. com., pres. 1981). Author: The Sonnets of Andreas Gryphius, 1971; asso. editor The German Quarterly, 1971-78. Home: 26171 Burg St Warren MI 48089 Office: 487 Manoogian Hall Wayne State University Detroit MI 48202

SCHINDLER, ROBERT STANLEY, surgeon, med. missionary; b. Berne, Ind., Oct. 17, 1930; s. Vilas A. and Mary Ann (Depp) S.; student Wheaton Coll., 1948-50, 51-52; B.A., N.Y. U., 1954; M.D., N.Y. Med. Coll., 1958; m. Marian Ruth Wilson, May 30, 1954; children—Robert Stanley, John Wilson. Intern, Saginaw (Mich.) Gen. Hosp., 1958-59, resident, 1959-62; med. missionary to Liberia, W.Africa, Sudan Interior Mission, 1962-75; founder, med. dir. Elwa Hosp., Monrovia, Liberia, 1962-75; chief of staff Berrien Gen. Hosp., Berrien Center, Mich., 1975-77, chief of surgery, 1977—; surgeon Southwestern Med. Clinic, Berrien Center, 1975—. Decorated knight grand comdr. Humane Order of African Redemption, Govt. Liberia, 1969, knight gt. band, 1971. Diplomate Am. Bd. Surgery. Fellow A.C.S.; mem. AMA, Berrien County Med. Soc. (pres. 1982), Liberian Med. Assn., Christian Med. Soc. Baptist. Club: Lakeshore Rotary. Home: 2280 Shiawasee Ln Stevensville MI 49127 Office: 2 Hospital Dr Berrien Center MI 49102

SCHIPPERS, LILLIAN VOGT, educator; b. St. Louis; married. A.B. in Edn., Harris Tchrs. Coll., St. Louis; M.A. in English and Edn., Washington U., St. Louis, 1955; Ph.D. in Edn. Instruction, St. Louis U., 1974. Reading specialist St. Louis Bd. Edn., 1947-59; lang. arts dir. Affton Sch. Dist., St. Louis, 1959-74, dir. reading center, 1974—. Chairperson edn. com., pres. Southampton Neighborhood Assn., 1974—; pres. bd. dirs. Gravois Sr. Citizens, Inc.; bd. dirs. Gardenville Community Center. Mem. Internat. Reading Assn., Nat. Council Tchrs. of English, NEA, Mo. Edn. Assn. Author: Melvin, the Bashful Giraffe; Bluebell, the Skunk; many other children's books. Certified as elementary prin., reading specialist, English, social studies. Home: 5300 Sutherland St Saint Louis MO 63123 Office: 8903 Mackenzie Rd Saint Louis MO 63123

SCHIRM, HELMUT THEOBALD, petroleum co. exec.; b. Dussel dorf, Germany, Dec. 29, 1926; came to U.S., 1954, naturalized, 1958; s. Willy Hubert and Elisabeth (Wermund) S.; Mech.Eng., Coll. Engring., Wupperthal, Germany, 1948-52; B.M.E., U. Toledo, 1953; m. Beatrice M. Miles, June 18, 1955; children—Jeffery Michael, Gwen Susan. With Owens Ill. Glass Co., Toledo, 1957-69; with Sun Petroleum Products Co., 1969—, sr. refinery project engr., Toledo, 1971—. Served to lt. German Army, 1943-45. Fulbright scholar, 1952-53. Mem. Nat. Mgmt. Assn. (v.p.), Nat. Alliance Businessmen. Clubs: Torch, Toledo. Patentee, author in field. Home: 3637 Lauderdale St Toledo OH 43615 Office: Sun Petroleum Products Co PO Box 920 Toledo OH 43693

SCHIRMER, GARY JEROME, risk mgmt. cons. co. exec.; b. Dayton, Ohio, Sept. 1, 1946; s. Elmer William and Florence Helen (Kaminski) S.; B.S., Central Mo. State U., 1969, B.S., 1969, M.S., 1970; m. Linda Lee Tashler, Sept. 10, 1968; children—Kelley Lynn, Scott William Wendell. Safety engr. Aetna Ins. Co., St. Louis, 1970-72; loss control mgr., corp. dir. Reliance Ins. Co., Phila., 1972-76; adminstr. safety and health Anheuser Busch Inc., St. Louis, 1976-79; pres. Cannon Cockran Mgmt. Services Inc., Danville, Ill., 1979—, also dir., dir. Cannon Cochran Inc.; adj. prof. Mo. State U., Danville Are Community Coll. Vice-pres., Danville Area Safety Council, 1980-81. Certified safety profl.; cert. hazard control mgr. Mem. Am. Soc. Safety Engrs. Clubs: Elks, American Business Man's. Home: 1417 Wood Ridge Danville IL 61832 Office: 326 N Vermillion St Danville IL 61832

SCHIRN, JANET SUGERMAN, interior designer; b. Jersey City, N.J.; d. Oscar H. and Mary (Lustig) Sugerman; B.F.A., Pratt Inst., 1947; M.F.A., Columbia U., 1952; student U. Ill., Chgo., 1970—; m. Leonard H. Schirn, June 24, 1948; 1 dau., Mindy. Tchr., N.Y.C. Bd. Edn., 1948-52, Bd. Adult Edn., 1948-52; prin. Janet Schirn Interiors, N.Y.C., Chgo., 1950—; pres. Schirn Assos., Inc., Chgo., 1968—; mem. adv. bd. Masland Carpet Co., 1981—. Mem. adv. bd. interior architecture and design dept. Mundelein Coll., 1981—; bd. dirs. Chgo. Archtl. Assistance Center, 1975—, pres., 1982. Named Designer of Yr., Am. Soc. Interior Designers, 1978; award of Merit, Chgo. Lighting Inst., 1979; Nat. Endowment Arts grantee, 1981, 82. Mem. Am. Soc. Interior Designers (nat. dir. 1979—, pres. Ill. chpt. 1977, 78, regional v.p. 1981, 82; citation for excellence in interior design West Central region 1977, Ill. chpt. 1978, Presdl. citation, 1976, 80, citation for excellence in interior design 1978, Medal of Honor, Ill. chpt. 1980, 50th Anniversary award 1981), AIA (nat. urban planning and design com. 1981, 82), Am. Arbitration Assn. (arbitrator). Home: 220 E Walton Pl Apt 7E Chicago IL 60611 Office: 663 Fifth Ave New York NY 10022 also 919 N Michigan Ave Chicago IL 60611

SCHLEIFER, GREGORY SCOTT, psychologist, educator, univ. ofcl.; b. St. Paul, Sept. 3, 1947; s. Alfred Howard and Lorraine Elizabeth (Martinson) S.; B.A., U. Minn., 1969; postgrad. Mankato State U., 1969-70; M.A., Ball State U., 1972, Ed.D., 1976; m. Joyce Lynne Vander Werf, Sept. 22, 1973. Dir. assessment and tng. Can. Assn. for Mentally Retarded, Winnipeg, Man., Can., 1973-74; univ. fellow in psychology Ball State U., Muncie, Ind., 1974-76, asst. prof. psychology-counseling, also dir. Human Learning Center, Ball State U.-Europe, Wiesbaden, W. Ger., 1976-79; dir. student counseling service, asst. prof. U. Minn., Morris, 1979—; cons. in psychodramatic method dept. mental health U.S. Air Force Hosp., Wiesbaden, 1977-79, European div. U. Md., 1978; cons. in counselor tng., program devel. and direction Wiesbaden Women's Crisis Center, 1978-79; cons. Women's advocacy program 5th Corps, U.S. Army Europe, Frankfurt, 1978-79; research cons. and cons. in group dynamics Community Drug and Alcohol Assistance Center, U.S. Army, Wiesbaden, 1979; cons. in field. Mem. com. multiply handicapped Man. Dept. Health and Social Devel., 1974. Served with U.S. Army, 1970-72. Mem. Am. Psychol. Assn., Am. Personnel and Guidance Assn., Assn. Humanistic Psychology, Nat. Assn. Lit. and Arts, Phi Delta Kappa. Democrat. Club: Okinawah Shorin-Ji Kempo Assn. Home: 908 Colorado Ave Morris MN 56267 Office: Student Counseling Service U Minn Morris MN 56267

SCHLENKER, GEORGE JOHN, ops. research analyst; b. Fort Wayne, Ind., July 23, 1931; s. Carl George and Flora Louise (Boerger) S.; B.S. in Edn., Ind. U., 1953, postgrad., 1954; postgrad. U. Ill., 1957-60; M.S. in Indsl. Engring., U. Iowa, 1968; m. Emily Catherine Diehl, Apr. 28, 1962; children—Charles Eric, Lisa Anne. High sch. tchr., Fort Wayne, 1955-56; physicist Rock Island (Ill.) Arsenal, 1958-63; ops. research analyst U.S. Army Weapons Command, Rock Island, Ill., 1964-69, mech. engr., 1970-72, ops. research analyst Armaments Command, 1973-76, Armaments Readiness Command, 1976—. Served with U.S. Army, 1956-58. Recipient Meritorious Civilian Service award Dept. Army, 1977, Systems Analyst of Year award U.S. Army Devel. and Readiness Command, 1978-79, Am. Math. Soc. fellow U. Colo., 1960. Mem. AAAS, Am. Statis. Assn., Sigma Xi. Lutheran. Home: 3611 33d Ave Rock Island IL 61201 Office: US Army Armaments Readiness Command Rock Island IL 61299

SCHLEPPI, ROBERT FREDERICK, state govt. ofcl.; b. Sept. 11, 1945; s. Vernon Chester and Margaret Louise (Humphrey) S.; B.S. in Edn., Ohio State U., 1968; M.S. in Adminstrn., Xavier U., Cin., 1975; m. Leah Joan Blankenship, Apr. 6, 1968; children—Jennifer Lynn, Michelle Ann. Transp. specialist Ohio Exposition Commn., 1965; successively counselor, athletic instr., boys club dir., recreation center supr. Columbus (O.) Recreation Dept., 1963-68; mem. staff Ohio Youth Commn., 1970-80, asst. to dep. dir., Columbus, 1974-80; printing adminstr. State of Ohio, 1980—. Served to 1st lt. AUS, 1968-70; Vietnam. Decorated Army Commendation medal with 2 oak leaf clusters. Mem. In-Plant Printing Mgmt. Assn., Ohio State U. Varsity O Assn. Lutheran. Home: 2899 Castlewood Rd Columbus OH 43209 Office: 35 E Gay St Columbus OH 43215

SCHLERNITZAUER, DONALD ALLEN, ophthalmologist; b. Bellaire, Ohio, Jan. 5, 1942; s. Edward Anthony and Sara Elizabeth (Duvall) S.; A.B. with high honors, Cornell U., 1963, M.D., 1967; m. Pamela Joyce Trimbey, June 26, 1965; children—Amy Rose, Lori Jean. Intern, Mary Imogene Bassett Hosp., Cooperstown, N.Y., 1967-68; resident Wilmer Inst., Johns Hopkins Hosp., Balt., 1968-71; NIH spl. fellow in ophthalmic pathology Armed Forces Inst. Pathology, Washington, 1971-72; ophthalmologist Alliance (Ohio) Eye and Ear Clinic, 1974-78, Eye Clinic of Manitowoc (Wis.), 1978—; attending surgeon Meml. Hosp., Holy Family Hosp., Manitowoc; asst. clin. prof. ophthalmology Sch. Medicine, Case Western Res. U., 1975-79; lectr. George Washington U., 1972, 73. Served to lt. comdr. M.C., USNR, 1972-74; Recipient James Metcalf Polk prize Cornell U., 1967. Diplomate Am. Bd. Ophthalmology. Fellow Am. Acad. Ophthalmology and Otolaryngology; mem. AMA, Wis.-No. Mich. Ophthalmol. Soc., Wis. State, Manitowoc County med. assns., Alpha Omega Alpha. Republican. Mem. Evang. Free Ch. Club: Rotary. Co-author articles in tech. jours. Home: 6625 Hartlaub Lake Rd Manitowoc WI 54220 Office: 1119 Marshall St Manitowoc WI 54220

SCHLEUSENER, RICHARD AUGUST, engr., univ. dean; b. Oxford, Nebr., May 6, 1926; s. August William and Katherine C. (Albrecht) S.; B.S. in Agrl. Engring., U. Nebr., 1949; M.S. in Agrl. Engring., Kans. State U., 1956; Ph.D., Colo. State U., 1958; m. Elaine E. Wilhelm, June 12, 1949; children—Kathryn J. Schleusener Hanna, Richard D., Rand L., Debra S., Jeffrey T. Instr. agrl. engring. Kans. State U., 1949-50; asst. prof. to asso. prof. civil engring, exec. officer Colo. State U., 1958-64; dir. civil engring. sect. Inst. Atmos. Scis., S.D. Sch. Mines and Tech., Rapid City, S.D., 1964-74, v.p., dean engring., 1974-75, pres., 1975—; dir. 1st Nat. Bank Rapid City. Bd. dirs. Rapid City Regional Hosp.; co-chmn. S.D. Water Goals Conf. Served to maj., USAF, 1950-55; mem. Res., 1955-67. Mem. Am. Meteorol. Soc., ASCE, Am. Soc. Engring. Edn., Weather Modification Assn. Lutheran. Clubs: Rotary, Cosmopolitan. Office: 600 E Saint Joe St Rapid City SD 57701*

SCHLICHER, RAYMOND JOHN, univ. adminstr.; b. Centerville, Iowa, Dec. 5, 1911; s. Edward Jacob and Blanche Madelyn (Cosner) S.; B.A., Iowa Wesleyan Coll., 1935; M.A., U. Iowa, 1939, Ph.D., 1949; m. Genevieve Annetta Fowler, May 22, 1938; children—John Edward, Jenifer Rae, Mary Ann. Tchr. Iowa public schs., 1936-46; counselor U. Iowa, 1946-49; asst. prof. Iowa State Tchrs. Coll., 1949-59, dir. placement, 1950-56; asso. dir. extension State Coll. Iowa, 1954-75; dean extension and continuing edn. U. No. Iowa, Cedar Falls 1975-80, cons. div. continuing edn., 1980—; cons. Tchrs. Coll., Colombia, 1966. Pres. chpt. A.R.C., 1966-69. Recipient Alumni Service award Iowa Wesleyan Coll., 1966, U. No. Iowa, 1962; named to Hall of Fame, North Central Intercollegiate conf., 1974. Mem. Nat. Univ. Extension Assn. (fellow-in-extension), Assn. Continuing Profl. Edn., Cedar Falls C. of C. (pres. 1975-76), Sigma Phi Epsilon, Phi Delta Kappa. Republican. Methodist. Club: Kiwanis (pres. 1954). Home: 115 W 14th St Cedar Falls IA 50613 Office: 1222 W 27th St Cedar Falls IA 50614

SCHLOSS, NATHAN, real estate research corp. exec.; b. Balt., Jan. 14, 1927; s. Howard L. and Louise (Levi) S.; B.S. in Bus., Johns Hopkins U., 1950; m. Rosa Montalvo, Mar. 1, 1958; children—Nina L., Carolyn D. Buyer, Pacific coast merchandise office Sears Roebuck & Co., Los Angeles, 1955-60, staff asst. econ. research dept., Chgo., 1960-63; sr. market analyst corp. research dept. Montgomery Ward & Co., Chgo., 1963-65; research mgr. real estate dept. Walgreen Co., Chgo., 1970-72; v.p. research and planning Maron Properties Ltd., Montreal, Que., Can., 1972-74; fin. analyst Real Estate Research Corp., Chgo., 1974—, chief fin. officer, 1976—; cons. economist, since 1965—; mem. com. on price indexes and productivity Bus. Research Adv. Council of Bur. Labor Stats., Dept. Labor, 1979—. Mem. Plan Commn., Village of Wilmette, Ill., 1975-77, tech. adv. com. on employment and tng. data Ill. Employment and Tng. Council, 1979—. Mem. Am. Mktg. Assn., Lambda Alpha. Contbr. articles on fin. and market analysis of real estate to profl. jours. Home: 115 Hollywood Ct Wilmette IL 60091 Office: 72 W Adams St Chicago IL 60603

SCHLOSSMAN, JOHN ISAAC, architect; b. Chgo., Aug. 21, 1931; s. Norman Joseph and Carol (Rosenfeld) S.; student Grinnell Coll., 1949-50; B.A., U. Minn., 1953, B.Arch., 1955; M.Arch., Mass. Inst. Tech., 1956; m. Shirley Goulding Rhodes, Feb. 8, 1959; children—Marc N., Gail M., Peter C. Archtl. designer Architects Collaborative, Cambridge, Mass., 1956-57; architect Loebl, Schlossman & Bennett, Chgo., 1959-65; asso. Loebl, Schlossman, Bennett & Dart, Chgo., 1965-70, partner, 1970-75; prin. Loebl, Schlossman, Dart & Hackl, 1975-76, Loebl, Schlossman & Hackl, 1976—; vis. lectr. Boston Archtl. Center, 1955-57, U. Ill., Chgo., 1965. Bd. dirs. Young men's Jewish Council, Chgo., 1959-70, mem. exec. com., 1965-70, life dir., 1970—; trustee Chgo. Sch. Architecture Found., 1970-75; bd. dirs. Chgo. Archtl. Assistance Center, 1975-81; bd. dirs. Village of Glencoe Plan Commn., 1976—, chmn., 1977—; mem. archtl. adv. com. Oakton Community Coll., 1981—. Rotch Traveling scholar., 1957. Fellow AIA (v.p. Chgo. chpt. 1975, treas. chpt. 1979-80 chmn. nat. com. ins. 1974-75, mem. architects liability com. 1980—); mem. Alpha Rho Chi. Clubs: Tavern, Arts (Chgo.). Office: 845 N Michigan Ave Chicago IL 60611

SCHLUSSMAN, GILBERT MARTIN, plastic co. exec.; b. Bklyn., Sept. 2, 1926; s. David and Sarah (Malinsky) S.; B.Chem. Engring., Poly. Inst. Bklyn., 1949; m. Rona June Kotcher, Feb. 16, 1950; children—Peri, Sandford, Stefan. Plant mgr. Formed Container Corp., Orangeburg, N.Y., 1960-63, Union Carbide Corp., Fairlawn, N.J., 1963-69; v.p. Norprint div. No. Petrochem. Co., N.Y.C., 1969-74; v.p. Poly-Tech div. U.S. Industries, Mpls., 1976—. Bd. dirs. Jewish Family and Children's Service Inc., Adath Jeshuran Congregation; mem. aging panel Mpls. Fedn. for Jewish Services; mem. adv. bd. Internat. Order of DeMolay. Served with U.S. Army, 1945-46. Mem. Am. Mgmt. Assn. Clubs: Masons, Shriners. Patentee. Office: US Industries 1401 W 94th St Minneapolis MN 55431

SCHMAEDEKE, WAYNE WILLIAM, utility co. exec.; b. Mpls., May 30, 1931; s. Garfield W. and Alice Mae (Walker) S.; Ph.D., U. Minn., 1963; m. Ruth Henrietta Dahlberg, Sept. 1, 1956; children—Scott, Guy, Mary. Prof. math., U. Minn., 1964-68; cons. Univac Corp., 1964-68; prof. math. sci. Rice U., 1968-69; cons. Esso Research Co., 1967-70; dir. mgmt. info. servs. Minn. Gas Co., Mpls., 1977—; adj. prof. U. Minn., 1976—; pres. Ullr, Inc. Served with AUS, 1951-53. Decorated Purple Heart medal; Legion of Merit (Korea); recipient award Control Data Corp., 1977. Mem. Inst. Tech. Alumni Soc. U. Minn. (pres. 1977), Inst. Mgmt. Sci. Patentee in field. Home: 17511 Kilmer Ave Eden Prairie MN 55344 Office: Minnesota Gas Co 9525 Wayzata Blvd Minneapolis MN 55426

SCHMALHOLZ, DEBORAH LYNN, educator; b. Oak Park, Ill., Sept. 24, 1953; d. Edwin Peter and Dolores Irene (Drzewjecki) Wielgot; B.A. in Am. Studies (Ill. State scholar), Rosary Coll., River Forest, Ill., 1975; M.A. in Am. Studies, Northeastern Ill. U., 1981; m. Donald R. Schmalholz, July 1, 1978. Substitute tchr. Proviso Twp. High Schs., Maywood, Ill., 1975-76; tchr. English, Am. studies and contemporary humanities Proviso West High Sch., Hillside, Ill., 1976—. Mem. exec. bd. Proviso Council, 1977-80. Mem. Am. Studies Assn., Nat. Assn. Tchrs. English, Ill. Assn. Tchrs. English. Roman Catholic. Home: 2S771 Winchester Circle E4 Warrenville IL 60555 Office: Wolf and Harrison Sts Hillside IL 60162

SCHMELTER, RAYMOND FRANCIS, nuclear pharmacist; b. Crown Point, Ind., Dec. 16, 1944; s. Raymond Frank and Mildred Agnes (Gerlach) S.; B.S., Purdue U., 1967, M.S., 1969, Ph.D., 1978; m. Suzanne Lange, Sept. 6, 1970; children—Kristen, Jeffrey, Tedrick. Pharmacist, USPHS Indian Health Service, Phoenix, 1969-70; mfg. pharmacist Supply Service Centr, Perry Point, Md., 1970-71; pharmacist U.S. VA Hosp., Indpls., 1971-74, Dallas, 1974-75; asst. prof. pharmaceutics and radiology U. Nebr., 1978—. Mem. Am. Pharm. Assn., Am. Soc. Hosp. Pharmacists, Soc. Nuclear Medicine, AAAS, Omaha Jaycees (asst. public relations dir. 1979-80), Sigma Xi, Rho Chi. Contbr. articles in field to profl. jours. Office: U Nebr Med Center Dept Pharmaceutics Omaha NE 68105

SCHMERTZ, WILLIAM ERWIN, JR., advt. exec.; b. Ft. George G. Meade, Md., Sept. 6, 1945; s. William Erwin and Margaret (Gage) S.; B.F.A., Ohio U., 1967; 1 dau., Jessica Rande. Tech. artist and illustrator Advt. and Sales Promotion Operation, Gen. Electric Co., Schenectady, 1968-71; art dir. D. J. Moore Advt., Inc., Albany, N.Y., 1971-73; creative art dir. Burkholder Flint Nichols, Inc., Columbus, Ohio, 1973-77; dir. communications Gebhardt Assos./The Paper Mill, Columbus, 1977-78; advt. mgr. Wasserstrom Co., Columbus, 1978—. Group leader Children's Mental Health Services Franklin County-Big Sisters Program, 1975; judge Council Advancement and Support of Edn., 1981. Recipient recognition award Pulse Program, Columbus Central YMCA, 1977. Mem. Columbus Advt. Fedn., Columbus Soc. Communicating Arts (dir. 1979-81, President's award 1978), Phi Kappa Sigma. Editor: Central Ohio's Creative Directory, 1978. Home: 307 Tibet Rd Columbus OH 43202 Office: 477 S Front St Columbus OH 43215

SCHMIDT, ALBERT DANIEL, utilities co. exec.; b. Alpena, S.D., Nov. 16, 1925; s. Ernest Otto and Dorothea Marie Augusta S.; student Miami U., Oxford, Ohio, 1943-45; B.S. with honors in Elec. Engring., S.D. Sch. Mines and Tech., 1949; m. Joyce Bernice Anderson, Nov. 24, 1946; children—Roxanne Rae Schmidt Eisen, Janet Jaye Schmidt Foss. With Northwestern Public Service Co., 1949—, v.p. ops., Huron, S.D., 1958-65, pres., chief exec. officer, 1965-80, chmn., chief exec. officer, 1980—, dir.; mem. adv. bd. Huron br. Northwestern Nat. Bank. Trustee, Huron Coll., 1970-73; vice chmn., mem. exec. com. Mid-Continent Area Power Pool; trustee Nat. Electric Reliability

Council. Served with USNR, 1943-46. Named Man of Yr., S.D. Electric Council, 1979; Boss of Yr., Huron Jaycees, 1979. Mem. N. Central Electric Assn. (exec. com.), Food and Energy Council (dir., past chmn.), Nat. Assn. OTC Cos. (adv. council), U.S. Indsl. Council (dir.), S.D. C. of C. (dir.), S.D. Council Econ. Edn. (dir.), Nat. Assn. Electric Cos. (past dir.), Am Gas Assn. (past dir.), Midwest Gas Assn. (past pres.), S.D. Electric Council, S.D. Engring Soc., Huron C. of C. Republican. Lutheran. Clubs: Elks, Masons, Huron Country. Office: Northwestern Public Service Co Northwestern Nat Bank Bldg Huron SD 57350

SCHMIDT, ARTHUR IRWIN, steel fabricating co. exec.; b. Chgo., Sept. 9, 1927; s. Louis and Mary (Fliegel) S.; student Colo. A. and M. Coll., 1946-47; B.S. in Aero. Engring., U. Ill., 1950; m. Mae Rosman, July 25, 1950;children—Jerrold, Cynthia, Elizabeth, Richard. Sec. Rosman Iron Works, Inc., Franklin Park, Ill., 1950—. Served with USNR, 1944-46, 51-52. Mem. N.W. Suburban Mfrs. Assn., Iron League Chgo., Ill. Mfrs. Assn., U. Ill. Alumni Assn. Mem. B'nai B'rith (trustee, past pres. Lincolnwood). Home: 3601 Golf Rd Evanston IL 60203 Office: 9109 Fullerton Ave Franklin Park IL 60131

SCHMIDT, AUGUST ROBERT, III, athletic scientist, coach, educator; b. Chgo., Dec. 26, 1936; s. August Robert and Alice Dorthea (Lester) S.; B.S., Carthage Coll., 1962; M.S., Western Ill. U., 1964; m. Lisa Rose Thompson, July 15, 1978; 1 dau., Sunshine Rose; children by previous marriage—August Robert IV, Heather Shawn. Instr. phys. edn. Carthage Coll., Kenosha, Wis., 1961-63, asst. prof., 1964-75, asso. prof., 1976—, coach baseball, 1961-80, acting athletic dir., 1979—. Bd. dirs. Christer Youth Council, 1970—; pres. Holy Nativity Luth. Ch. Council, Kenosha, 1975—. Named coach of yr. Wis. Ind. Athletic Conf., 1971, 73. Mem. Nat. Baseball Coaches Assn., Fellowship of Christian Athletes. Home: 1723 25th St Kenosha WI 53140

SCHMIDT, C. OSCAR, JR., machinery mfg. co. exec.; b. Cin.; s. C. Oscar and Charlotte A. (Fritz) S.; Mech. Engring., U. Cin., also B.S. in Mech. Engring.; M.B.A., Harvard; postgrad. Rutgers U.; L.H.D., Sterling Coll.; m. Eugenia Hill Williams, June 29, 1944 (dec. June 22, 1975); children—Carl O., Christoph R., Milton W., Eugene H., Juliann R. Schmidt Hansen; m. 2d, Georgia Lee Schmidt, Aug. 9, 1977. Apprentice, Am. Can Co., Cin.; mem. engring. dept. Cin. Shaper; now with Cin. Butchers' Supply Co., successively asst. to pres., v.p. prodn., v.p., gen. mgr., exec. v.p., now pres., also dir.; dir. Boss Pack Co.; pres., dir. BEC, Inc., Trussville, Ala., Winger Boss Co., Ottumwa, Iowa; dir. Cin. Refrigerator & Fixture Works, Ky. Chem. Industries, Inc., Meat Packers Equipment, Inc. of Fla., Mille Lacs Products Co.; dir., chmn. bd., treas. LeFiell Co. Active Boy Scouts Am., past chmn. Valley dist.; chmn. finance com. Nat. United Cerebral Palsy Assn.; mem. review com. United Funds Cin. Mem. Pres.'s bd. assos. Rose Hulman Inst. Tech.; trustee, past pres. Hamilton County Soc. for Crippled Children, United Cerebral Palsy of Cin.; trustee Deaconess Hosp., also mem. sch. com. Served to capt. U.S. Army, 1940-45. Recipient Distinguished Engring. Alumnus award U. Cin., 1969; Silver Beaver award Boy Scouts Am., also Harman award. Registered profl. engr., Ohio. Mem. Am. Oil Chemists Soc. (life), Am. Ordnance Assn., Engrs. Soc. Cin., Am. Assn. Indsl. Mgmt. (dir.), Air Pollution Soc., Cin. Indsl. Inst., Cin. C. of C., Meat Industry Supply and Equipment Assn. (dir., past co-chmn.), N.A.M. Nat. Metal Trades Assn. (mem. dist. council), Meat Machinery Mfrs. Inst. (past pres.), Acacia (past sec.-treas.), Heroes of '76, Cin. Hist. Soc. (life), Cin. Natural History Mus., Audubon Soc., Ohio Hist. Soc., Nat. Parks Assn., Zool. Soc. Cin., Aircraft Owners and Pilot Assn., U. Cin. Alumni Assn., Cin. Harvard Bus. Sch. Alumni (past sec.-treas.), Harvard Alumni Assn., Harvard Bus. Sch. Assn., Kappa Sigma Pi (dir., nat. sec.). Presbyterian (ruling elder, past pres. adult class, ruling elder commr., mem. eccles. order com.). Mason (Shriner), Rotarian. Clubs: Cincinnati; Wyoming Golf. Contbr. articles in field to profl. jours. Patentee in field. Home: 405 Meadow Lane Cincinnati OH 45215 Office: Box 16098 5601 Helen St Elmwood Pl Cincinnati OH 45216

SCHMIDT, CHARLES EDWARD, JR., lawyer; b. Chgo., Nov. 7, 1937; s. Charles Edward and Dorothy Faris S.; B.S. cum laude, Fla. State U., 1960; J.D., Northwestern U., 1964; m. Virginia Hamilton, Dec. 16, 1978; children—Debora, Cathy, Kim, Julie, Ginger, Jennifer, Kiki. Admitted to Ill. bar, 1965; v.p. Community Centers, Chgo., 1961-67; tax shelter mgr. Merrill Lynch, Chgo., 1967-76; mem. firm Shaheen, Lundberg & Callahan, Chgo., 1964-67; chmn. Ill. Racing Bd., Chgo., 1977-82; owner Sunrise Farm Thoroughbreds. Pres., coach Northbrook (Ill.) Speed Skating Club, 1975-77. Served with U.S. Army, 1956-57. Mem. Nat. Assn. State Racings Commns. (pres.), Thoroughbred Breeders and Owners Assn. Republican. Clubs: Barrington Hills Country, Sunset Ridge Country. Office: 160 N LaSalle Chicago IL 60064

SCHMIDT, CHARLES MATHEW, cons. mech. engr.; b. Charles City, Iowa, Apr. 29, 1937; s. Earl Mathew and Amy Corien (Anderson) S.; B.S., State U. Iowa, 1960; m. Carolyn May Heath, Sept. 6, 1958 (div. 1977); children—John, Michael, Greta; m. Nancy Linder, Aug. 1978. Engr. chem. div. Pitts. Plate Glass, Barberton, Ohio, 1960-63; asst. chief engr. Karl R. Rohrer Assos., Akron, Ohio, 1963-65; chief engr. Noble W. Herzberg Assos., Cleve., 1965-67; pres. Schmidt Assos., 1968—; dir. Mahoning Assos., The Continental Bank; lectr. U. Wis. Coll. Engring., 1979, 80, 81, Pa. State U. Coll. Engring., 1980, U. Ky. Coll. Engring., 1976, U.S. Dept. Energy, 1978. Spl. cons. engr. Pa. State U., 1971-73, Ohio Dept. Pub. Works, 1973—; judge East Ohio Energy Conservation Award Program, 1974. Village engr., Boston Heights, O., 1967-71; councilman Village of Boston Heights, 1972—. Bd. dirs. Youth Enrichment Services for Retarded Children. Registered profl. engr., Ohio, Iowa, Ky., Ill., Ind., Mich., Pa. Mem. Nat., Ohio socs. profl. engrs., ASME. Patentee in field. Home: 458 Hines Hill St Hudson OH 44236 Office: 7333 Fair Oaks St Cleveland OH 44146

SCHMIDT, DAVID PATRICK, broadcaster; b. Berwyn, Ill., Feb. 22, 1945; s. Carl Arthur and Lucille Cathryn S.; student Ill. State U., 1963-65; m. Christine Perry, May 3, 1969; children—Sandra Kaye, Barbara Anne. FM program dir., prodn. mgr. Sta. WIZZ AM-FM, Streator, Ill., 1967-70; morning announcer Sta. WKAN, Kankakee, Ill., 1970-75; chief dep. treas. Kankakee County, 1975-77; sales mgr., morning announcer Sta. WBYG, Kankakee, 1977—; instr. continuing edn. Kankakee Community Coll. Entertainment com. 125th Anniversary of Kankakee, 1978; pres. Abraham Lincoln PTO, 1979-80. Served with AUS, 1965-67; Vietnam. Mem. Nat. Assn. Broadcasters, Kankakee Jaycees (v.p., dir., past sec., regional dir., Dirs. award 1978), Kankakee C. of C. Democrat. Clubs: Bradley Lions, Kankakee Elks. Home: 1888 Summit St Kankakee IL 60901 Office: PO Box 183 Kankakee IL 60901

SCHMIDT, GEORGE, engineer; b. Chicago Heights, Ill., Aug. 26, 1925; s. George and Evelyn Marie (LaVine) S.; student Concordia Theol. Sem., 1943-44, U.S. Merchant Marine Acad., 1944-45, Valparaiso U., 1947, Ray-Vogue Sch., 1950; m. Jean Ann VanBuren, Oct. 26, 1947; children—George Frederick, Paul Phillip, Gregory Joseph, Erick Charles. Draftsman Whiting Corp., Harvey, Ill., 1948-49; head methods engring. dept. Harris Hub Co., Harvey, 1949-59; chief engr. Superior Sleeprite Corp., Chgo., 1959-66; plant engr. Rheem Mfg. Co., Chgo., 1966—. V.P. South Shore Subdivision Improvement Assn., 1976-77. Served with U.S. Army, 1946-47. Mem. Am. Legion (historian post 261, 1978, 79). Roman Catholic. Home: 5019 Elm Circle Dr Oaklawn IL 60453 Office: 7600 S Kedzie Chicago IL 60652

SCHMIDT, JAKOB EDWARD, medical and medicolegal lexicographer, physician, author, inventor; b. Riga, Livonia, Latvia, June 16, 1906 (came to U.S. 1924, naturalized 1929); s. Michael E. and Rachel I. (Goldman) S.; grad. Balt. City Coll., 1929; Ph.G., U. Md., 1932, B.S. in Pharmacy, 1935, M.D., 1937; postgrad., 1939. Intern, Sinai Hosp., Balt.; engaged in pvt. med. practice, Balt., 1940-53; resident, Charlestown, Ind., 1953—; indsl. physician Ind. Ordnance Works, 1953-54; med., paramed., and medicolegal lexicographer, 1950—; columnist What's the Good Word (Balt. Sun); Sharpen Your Tongue (Am. Mercury); The Medical Lexicographer (Modern Medicine); Medical Semantics (Medical Science); Underworld English (Police); Medical Vocabulary Builder (Trauma); English Word Power and Culture (Charlestown Courier), also Understanding Med. Talk. Asso. med. editor, Trauma, 1959—; editor Medical Dictionary, 1959—; compiler 50,000-word vocabulary test, 1956; numerous articles in med. jours., lay press, Esquire, Playboy, others; contbr. articles to press services U.P.I., N.A.N.A., others; cons. JAMA (Jour. AMA); cons., med. and medicolegal terminology; also cons. in med. lexicography, med. tradenames and trademarks; pres. Sculptural Arts Jewelers, 1973—, Med. Sculpture Art Co., 1974—. Mem. revision com. U.S. Pharmacopeia XI. Mem. Am. Dialect Soc., Nat. Writers Club, Nat. Hist. Soc., Planetary Soc., Authors Guild, Authors League Am., Am. Name Soc., Am. Med. Writers' Assn., Internat. Soc. Gen. Semantics, AMA, Med. and Chirurgical Faculty of Md., Balt. City Med. Soc., Nat. Assn. Standard Med. Vocabulary (chmn. 1961-64), Nat. Soc. Lit. and Arts, Smithsonian Instn., Owl Club, Rho Chi. Inventor iodine-pentoxide-shunt method and apparatus for detection of carbon monoxide in oxygen, atmosphere, and medicinal gases; shock-proof electric fuse; magnetic needle finger ring; prosthetic papilla mammae; mammary hammock cum indwelling mammillary surrogates; cosmetic mammillary simulators; discovered effect of cesium and related metals on oxidation of organic matter in lakes, ponds and drinking water; the TV eye phenomenon; others. Recipient Owl gold medal Balt. City Coll., 1929; Rho Chi gold key U. Md. Sch. Pharmacy, 1932; gold medal for excellence in all subjects, 1932; certificate of honor U. Md. Sch. Medicine, 1937; award and citation Am. Med. Writers' Assn., N.Y. Met. chpt., 1959. Author: Dr. Schmidt's Sex Dictionary: Terminology of Sex and Related Emotions, 1954; Medical Terms Defined for the Layman, 1957; Reversicon, A Physician's Medical Word Finder, 1958; Medical Discoveries, Who and When, 1959; Dictionary of Medical Slang and Related Expressions, 1959; Narcotics, Lingo and Lore, 1959; Libido, Scientific, Lay, and Slang Terminology, 1960; Baby Name Finder—The Romance of Names, 1961; Attorneys' Dictionary of Medicine, 1962, 14th edit., 1978, 15th edit., 1979; Attorneys' Medical Word Finder, 1964; One Thousand Elegant Phrases, 1965; Supplement to Attorneys' Dictionary of Medicine and Word Finder, 1966, ann. revision, 1967—, also The Medical Lexicographer, 1966; Cyclopedic Lexicon of Sex Terminology, 1967; Police Medical Dictionary, 1968; Practical Nurse's Medical Dictionary, 1968; Paramedical Dictionary, 1969, 2d edit., 1973; Structural Units of Medical and Biological Terms, 1969; English Word Power for Physicians, 1971; English Idioms and Americanisms, 1972; English Speech for Foreign Students, 1973; Textbook of Medical Terminology, 1972; Visual Aids for Paramedical Vocabulary, 1973; Analyzer of Medical-Biological Words, 1973; Index of Medical-Paramedical Vocabulary, 1974; Diccionario para Auxiliares de la Medicina, 1976; Schmidt's Illustrated Attorneys' Dictionary of Medicine and Word Finder, 3 vols., 2d edit., 1982; Erotica Exotica-scholarly, colloquial and slang expressions of the libido. Home: Monroe nr Park St Charlestown IN 47111 Office: 934 Monroe St Charlestown IN 47111

SCHMIDT, JOHN DAVID, mktg. and devel. co. exec.; b. Williamsburg, Pa., Nov. 16, 1952; s. John David and Marjorie Wallace (Mckay) S.; student Geneva Coll., 1970-71; B.A., Nyack Coll., 1974; M.A., Wheaton Coll., 1977. Founder, pres. J. David Schmidt and Assos., Wheaton, 1977—; guest lectr. Wheaton Coll. Grad. Sch., 1978—; condr. various seminars in mktg. and fundraising, 1978—. Vol., Wheaton Bible Ch., 1978—. Club: Wheaton Sports. Office: 1415 Hill St Wheaton IL 60187

SCHMIDT, JOHN JOSEPH, holding co. exec.; b. Chgo., Jan. 13, 1928; s. William Fred and Mildred C. (Petrone) S.; B.S., DePaul U., 1951; J.D., Loyola U., Chgo., 1955; m. Gail Bormann, Oct. 8, 1955; children—Cathleen M., Karen B., Linda G. Admitted to Ill. bar, 1955; trial atty. The Atchison, Topeka and Santa Fe Ry., Chgo., 1955-69, asst. v.p. exec. dept., 1969-73; v.p. Santa Fe Industries, Inc., Chgo., 1969-73, exec. v.p., 1973-78, pres., 1978—, also dir.; dir. The Atchison, Topeka and Santa Fe Ry., Santa Fe Natural Resources, Inc., Santa Fe Pipelines, Inc., Harris Trust & Savs. Bank, Harris Bankcorp, Inc. Mem. Zoning Bd. Appeals, Planning Commn., Village of Burr Ridge, Ill., from 1973. Served with U.S. Army, 1945-47. Mem. Am., Ill., Chgo. bar assns., Soc. Trial Lawyers (past dir.), Ill. Def. Council (past pres.), Nat. Assn. R.R. Trial Counsel (past pres.). Clubs: Chgo. Athletic, Chgo. Economic. Office: Santa Fe Industries Inc 224 S Michigan Ave Chicago IL 60604

SCHMIDT, ROBERT, civil engr.; b. Ukraine, May 18, 1927; came to U.S., 1949, naturalized, 1956; s. Alfred and Aquilina (Konotop) S.; B.S., U. Colo., 1951, M.S., 1953; Ph.D., U. Ill., 1956; m. Irene Hubertine Bongartz, June 10, 1978; 1 son, Ingbert Robert. Engr., C.E., U.S. Army, Omaha, 1951-52; asst. prof. theoretical and applied mechanics U. Ill., Urbana, 1956-59; asso. prof. civil engring. U. Ariz., Tucson, 1959-63; prof. engring. mechanics U. Detroit, 1963—, chmn. dept. civil engring., 1978-80. Recipient 4 research grants NSF. Mem. ASCE, ASME (cert. of recognition), Am. Acad. Mechanics(founding mem.), Indsl. Math. Soc., Am. Soc. Engring. Edn., AAUP, Indsl. Math. Soc. (pres. 1966-67), Sigma Xi. Editor Indsl. Math., 1969—; contbr. 85 articles to tech. and sci. jours. Research on linear and nonlinear theory of elasticity and methods of analysis. Office: College of Engineering University of Detroit Detroit MI 48221

SCHMIDT, ROBERT THOMAS, JR., neurologist; b. Milw., July 25, 1944; s. Robert Thomas and Jane Beth (Sterling) S.; student Northwestern U., 1962-63; B.S., Marquette U., 1966; M.D., Med. Coll. Wis., 1970; m. Carol Ann O'Brien, Dec. 21, 1968; children—Paul, Joseph, Margaret. Intern, Thomas Jefferson U. Hosp., 1970-71; resident in neurology Northwestern U., Chgo., 1970-74; resident in pathology Mallory Inst. Pathology, Boston, 1974-75; practice medicine, specializing in neurology, Green Bay, Wis., 1975—; med. coordinator Curative Workshop Rehab. Center, Green Bay, 1977—; mem. staff St. Vincent Hosp., Bellin Meml. Hosp., St. Marys Hosp. Served with U.S. Army, 1970-79. Diplomate Am. Bd. Psychiatry and Neurology. Mem. AMA, Med. Soc. Wis. (chmn. neurology sect. 1980), Am. Acad. Neurology. Roman Catholic. Contbr. articles to profl. jours. Office: 704 S Webster Ave Green Bay WI 54301

SCHMIDT, TODD WARNER, architect; b. Dearborn, Mich., May 7, 1943; s. Howard Carl and Barbara Virginia (Warner) S.; B.Arch., Ohio U., 1966. Designer, Willis F. Griffin, Architect, El Paso, Tex., 1968, Richard L. Bowen & Assos., Cleve., 1969; project architect, designer Outcalt, Rode, Kaplan and Curtis, Cleve., 1970-72, Stephen J. Bucchieri, Architect, Cleve., 1972-73; partner Bucchieri and Schmidt, Architects, Cleve., 1973-74; pres. and treas. Todd Schmidt and Assos., Inc., Architects, Landscape Architects and Planners, Cleve., 1973—. Bd. dirs. YMCA Camp Fitch, Youngstown, Ohio, 1976, 79; chmn. landscape com. Rapid Recovery, Inc., Cleve., 1978-79. Served with U.S. Army, 1966-68. Registered architect, Ohio, Mich., Pa., N.Y., N.J. Mem. AIA, Architects Soc. Ohio, Constrn. Specifications Inst. Home: 12900 Lake Ave Lakewood OH 44107 Office: 1360 W 9th St Cleveland OH 44113

SCHMIDT, WILLIAM ALBERT, retail bldg. materials co. exec.; b. Romeo, Mich., May 10, 1937; s. Albert William and Lorena Martha-Marie (Sieger) S.; m. Nancy Jean Martell, July 28, 1956; children—Timothy William, Mary Jo, Patricia Janet. Gen. supt. Frank Rewold & Son, Rochester, Mich., 1956-61; sales rep. The Wickes Corp., Romeo, Mich., 1962-64, asst. mgr., Norwalk, Ohio, 1964-65, mgr., Owesso, Mich., 1965-66, Lawrence, Kans., 1966-71; owner, mgr., pres. Topeka Lumber Inc., 1971—; owner, pres. Central Wholesale Distbrs., Topeka, 1980—. Mem. Republican Nat. Com., 1976. Mem. Fedn. Ind. Bus., Topeka Home Bldrs. Assn., Nat. Home Builders Assn., Mid-Am. Lumbermens Assn. Republican. Lutheran. Club: Moose. Home: 2922 NE Knoll Rd Topeka KS 66617 Office: 721 N Kansas Ave Topeka KS 66608

SCHMIT, LORAN, state senator, helicopter service exec., farmer; b. Butler County, Nebr., Aug. 13, 1929; B.S., U. Nebr., 1950; m. Irene JoAnn Squire, 1950; children—Marcia, Steven, Mary, Jullie, John, Michele, Susan, Jeanie, Lori, Mike. Pres., Mid-Am. Helicopter Service, Inc.; farmer, Butler County. Mem. Nebr. State Senate, 1969—; chmn. Butler County Republican party. Roman Catholic. Office: State Senate State Capitol Lincoln NE 68509*

SCHMITT, EDWARD HENRY, fast food chain exec.; b. Chgo., Aug. 26, 1925; s. Henry Peter and Anne (Kemp) S.; B.S., DePaul U., 1952; m. Marie Clare Collins, Aug. 23, 1952; children—Edward Henry, Richard C. Self-employed, 1952-64; with McDonald's Corp., Oak Brook, Ill., 1964—, exec. v.p., chief operating officer, 1970-77, pres., chief adminstrv. officer, 1977—, also dir. Served to 1st lt. AUS. Decorated Purple Heart, Silver Star, Bronze Star, Croix de Guerre, Presdl. Citation. Club: Aurora (Ill.) Country. Office: 1 McDonald's Plaza Oak Brook IL 60521*

SCHMITT, GERALDINE ANN, advt. agy. exec.; b. St. Paul, July 14, 1947; s. Peter J. and Lois H. (Budewitz) S.; B.A., U. Minn., 1969. Writer, Dayton/Hudson Advt., 1969-71, Sielaff-Grawert Advt., 1972-74; TV writer Gray Advt., 1974-75; sr. writer Bozell & Jacobs, 1976-77, BBDO Advt., 1978-79; owner, partner Schmitt Anderson Ekdahl Advt., Mpls., 1979—. Mem. Minn. Advt. Fedn., Nat. Assn. Women Bus. Owners, Art Dirs.-Writers Club. Office: 1030 Lumber Exchange Bldg 10 S 5th St Minneapolis MN 55401

SCHMITT, MARK, bishop; b. Algoma, Wis., Feb. 14, 1923; ed. Salvatorian Sem., St. Nazianz, Wis., St. John's Sem., Collegeville, Minn. Ordained priest Roman Catholic Ch., 1948; titular bishop of Ceanannus Mor, aux. bishop of Green Bay (Wis.), 1970-78; bishop of Marquette (Mich.), 1978—. Address: Chancery Office PO Box 550 444 S 4th St Marquette MI 49855*

SCHMITZ, CHARLES JOHN, appliance control mfg. co. exec.; b. Lafayette, Ind., Mar. 7, 1946; s. Harold J. and Rose J.; B.S. in Physics, U. Mo., 1968; M.B.A., Ill. Inst. Tech., 1973. Devel. engr. Frequency Components div. Motorola Corp., Chgo., 1968-71, engring. group leader Products div., Schaumburg, Ill., 1971-74, engring. mgr. Internat. div., 1974-79; dir. engring. Harper-Wyman Co., Hinsdale, Ill., 1979—. Recipient Cert. of Meritorious Service, Am. Blind Skiing Found., 1977. Mem. Am. Mgmt. Assn., Nat. Elec. Mfrs. Assn., IEEE, Chgo. Assn. Commerce and Industry. Patentee in field. Office: 930 N York Rd Hinsdale IL 60521

SCHMITZ, SISTER MARY VERONE, speech pathologist; b. Alexander, N.D., Nov. 24, 1914; d. Peter and Hedwig (Hackenburg) Schmitz; B.A., Avila Coll., 1960; M.S. (Rehab. Service grantee), Marquette U., 1970. Tchr. elementary schs., Devils Lake, N.D., 1939-41, 53-54, Kansas City, Mo., 1941-52, Williston, N.D., 1952-53, Kansas City, Mo., 1954-58, Omaha, 1958-63, Kansas City, 1963-68; prin. St. Wenceslaus Sch., Omaha, 1961-63; speech pathologist, dir. Our Lady of Mercy Speech and Hearing Center, Kansas City, Mo., 1970—. Lic. speech pathologist, Mo. Mem. Am., Mo., Greater Kansas City speech and hearing assns. Home: 134 N Hardesty St Kansas City MO 64123 Office: PO Box 6679 Kansas City MO 64123

SCHMITZ, PAUL ARTHUR, utilities exec.; b. Wadesville, Ind., Jan. 24, 1936; s. Moses and Lorena Elizabeth (Hoell) S.; B.S., Evansville Coll., 1958; M.B.A., U. Evansville, 1972; m. Clara Ethel Reimann, June 8, 1962; children—Eric Earl, Eva Emily. With So. Ind. Gas and Electric Co., Evansville, 1961-68, mgr. taxes and ins., 1969-74, asst. comptrller, 1974-75, asst. comptroller, asst. treas., 1975-76; vice gen. mgr. fin. Big Rivers Electric Corp., Henderson, Ky., 1976-81, asst. gen. mgr., 1981—. Vice chmn. allocations com. Southwestern Ind. United Way, 1975-76. Served with U.S. Army, 1959-60. Mem. Ind. Electric Assn. (vice chmn. joint acctg. com. 1976), Am. Inst. C.P.A.'s, Ky. Soc. C.P.A.'s, Ind. Soc. C.P.A.'s, Nat. Assn. Accts. Mem. United Ch. of Christ. Club: Petroleum. Home: Rural Route 1 Box 232 Wadesville IN 47638 Office: Big Rivers Electric Corp 201 3d St Henderson KY 42420

SCHMITZ, ROBERT JOSEPH, state senator; b. Jordan, Minn., Apr. 23, 1921; student public schs.; m. Grace Savage; children—Murray, Susan Schmitz Seifert, Kris Schmitz Beuch, Robin, Karen. Owner, operator farm St. Lawrence Twp., Minn.; owner Schmitz Farm Equipment, Inc., Jordan; mem. Ind. Senate from Dist. 36, 1974—, chmn. vets. affairs com.; chmn. subcom. gen. policy transp. com.; dir. Northwestern State Bank, Jordan; pres. New Prague Mut. Fire Ins. Co. Supr. Scott Soil and Water Conservation Dist.; pres. Jordan Devel. Corp., Scott County Farms Union; bd. dirs. St. Francis Hosp., Shakopee, Minn. Named Outstanding Soil Conservation Farmer Scott County. Mem. Minn. Safety Council (dir.), Minn. Good Roads Assn. (dir.). Address: Rural Route 1 Box 186 Jordan MN 55352

SCHMITZ, STANLEY JOSEPH, retail jewelry chain supr.; b. Bklyn., Jan. 16, 1948; s. Albert J. and Adeline E. Schmitz; student Ind. Inst. Tech., 1966-70; splty. courses Gemological Inst. Am., Retail Jewelers Am.; B.A. in Bus. Adminstrn., SUNY, Albany, 1982; postgrad. in bus. adminstrn. Syracuse U., 1982—. Research and devel. technician Peter Eckrich and Sons, Inc., Ft. Wayne, Ind., 1969-73, process and smokehouse foreman, 1973-75; regional supr. Zale Corp., Decatur, Ill., 1973—; bd. dirs., mem. promotional com. Hickory Point Mall, Decatur. Served to staff sgt. USAR, 1976-81. Decorated Achievement medal; recipient Eagle Scout award Boy Scouts Am., 1963, Ad Alter Dei award, 1964, Order of Arrow award, 1965; Citizenship award Am. Legion, 1965; Meritorious Service award Ind.

Inst. Tech., 1968, Dizmond Z award Zale Corp., annually 1976-81. Registered gemologist Gemological Inst. Am. Mem. Retail Jewelers Am., Acad. Diamond Profls., Diamond Council Am. (registered diamondologist). Home: 4280 Forest Creek Ct Apt 202 Grand Rapids MI 49808 Office: Zales Woodland Mall Grand Rapids MI 49808

SCHMOLZI, RUSSELL WILLIAM, indsl. engr.; b. California, Mo., Oct. 25, 1953; s. John William and Nedra Ann (Strickfaden) S.; B.S. in Indsl. Tech., S.W. Mo. State U., Springfield, 1975; m. Brenda Kay Russell, Jan. 4, 1975; 1 son, Ross William. With Neosho Products Co. (Mo.), 1975—, design engr., 1977-78, indsl. engr., 1978—; mfg. data processing cons. Home: Route 3 Box 182 Neosho MO 64850 Office: Box 622 Neosho MO 64850

SCHMUCKER, RUBY ELVY LADRACH, nurse, educator; b. Sugarcreek, Ohio, Nov. 17, 1923; d. Walter F. and Carrie M. (Mizer) Ladrach; R.N., Aultman Hosp., Canton, Ohio, 1945; B.S. in Nursing, U. Akron, 1970, M.S. in Edn., 1973; children—Gary, David, Barbara, Steven. Gen. duty nurse, head nurse Aultman Hosp., 1945-47, part-time, 1950-62, instr. nursing, 1962-64, 69-74; instr. nursing Coll. Nursing, U. Akron (Ohio), 1974-76; instr. div. nursing edn. Children's Hosp., Akron, 1976-78; psychiat. nurse and supr. Massillon (Ohio) State Hosp., 1978—, cons. to nursing dept., 1980—, dir. nursing edn., 1981—; cons. Stark-Tuscarawas Counties Student Nurses Assn., 1973-74. Health chmn. Avondale Sch. PTA, Canton, 1956, mem. coms., 1954-70; vol. instr. home nursing courses ARC, 1959-62. Cert. psychiat. nurse. Mem. Aultman Hosp. Sch. Nursing Alumni Assn., Am. Nurses' Assn., Nat. League Nursing, Am. Personnel and Guidance Assn., Am. Coll. Personnel Assn., U. Akron Alumni Assn., Alpha Sigma Lambda. Mem. Ch. of Christ. Home: 4214 Bellwood Dr NW Canton OH 44708 Office: 3000 Erie St Massillon OH

SCHMULBACH, CHARLES DAVID, chemist, educator; b. New Athens, Ill., Feb. 2, 1929; s. Charles Joseph and Helen Virginia (Carter) S.; B.S., U. Ill., 1951, Ph.D., 1958; m. Barbara Ellen Williamson, June 11, 1955; children—Angela Leigh, Eric David, Andrea Ellen. Research chemist Monsanto Chem. Co., St. Louis, summer 1958, E. I. duPont de Nemours & Co., Wilmington, Del., summers 1959, 60; vis. prof. U.S. Naval Postgrad. Sch., 1963-64; mem. faculty Pa. State U., 1958-63, 64-65; mem. faculty So. Ill. U., Carbondale, Ill., 1965—, prof., 1970—, chmn. dept. chemistry and biochemistry, 1975—; cons. Nat. Lead Co., 1965-66, Ill. Power Co., 1974-77. Served in USN, 1951-54. Eastman Kodak fellow, 1956-58; Deutsche Forschungsgemeinschaft vis. prof., 1980-81; NSF grantee, 1964-67, 69-71, others. Mem. Am. Chem. Soc., Chem. Soc. (London), Sigma Xi, Phi Lambda Upsilon, Alpha Chi Sigma. Republican. Club: Rotary. Office: So Ill U Carbondale IL 62901

SCHNABL, FRANK JOSEPH, educator; b. Nichols, Wis., June 3, 1927; s. Frank Joseph and Hazel Ann (O'Brien) S.; B.S., U. Wis., Oshkosh, 1952, M.S., U. Wis., Eau Claire, 1965. Tchr. sci-math. Orfordville (Wis.) High Sch., 1952-54; research asso. Inst. Paper Chemistry, Appleton, Wis., 1954-58; tchr. sci. and math. Kewaunee (Wis.) High Sch., 1958-66, tchr. chemistry and physics, 1971—; instr. chemistry U. Wis., Fox Valley Campus, Menasha, 1966-68, Green Bay-Menasha campus, 1968-70. Kewaunee County radiol. def. officer, 1960-66; chmn. Kewaunee County United Way, 1981—, Kewaunee County Republican Com. 1977—. Served with U.S. Army, 1944-46; ETO. Gen. Electric fellow Purdue U., 1960; Wis. Public Service scholar Pa. State U., 1981. Mem. AAUP, Am. Chem. Soc., Exptl. Aircraft Assn., VFW, Am. Legion, Am. Vets. Republican. Roman Catholic. Club: Lions. Home: 722 Center St Kewaunee WI 54216 Office: 911 3d St Kewaunee WI 54216

SCHNAKE, BETTY BERNIECE, nurse; b. Centralia, Ill., Nov. 30, 1930; d. Charles E. and Gladys O. (Myers) Talbott; Asso. Degree in Nursing, Kaskaskia Coll., 1976; m. Eugene R. Schnake, Apr. 1, 1949; children—Pamela Sue, Robert Eugene, Jeffrey Harlan. Nurse intensive and coronary care, Good Samaritan Hosp., Mt. Vernon, Ill., 1976; pvt. duty nurse, Washington County Hosp., Nashville, Ill., 1976-77; pvt. duty nurse, St. Mary's Hosp., Centralia, Ill., 1976-77, staff nurse, 1977-79; instr. LPN program Kaskaskia Coll., Centralia, Ill., 1980—. Bd. dirs. Washington County Cancer Soc. Mem. Am., Ill. Nurses Assns., Ill. Heart Assn., St. Mary's Hosp. Aux., Phi Theta Kappa. Methodist. Home: Rural Route Box 94 Hoyleton IL 62803

SCHNEGELBERGER, ELIZABETH CARTER, librarian; b. Humphreys, Mo., Nov. 30, 1920; d. Duffy and Helen (Clelland) Carter; B.S. in Edn. in Music and Bus., N.E. Mo. Coll., Kirksville, 1946; m. Leonard E. Schnegelberger. Tchr., Duffield Dist., Sullivan County; band, vocal and bus. tchr. Craig (Mo.) High Sch., 1944-49, Humphreys High Sch., 1949-51, Craig Reorganized Sch. Dist. III, 1951-69; sch. librarian Maysville (Mo.) Reorganized-I Sch., 1970—. Mem. Mo., local tchrs. assns., Mo. Music Educators Assn., Mo. Bandmasters Assn. (charter), Mo. Library Assn., Mo. Assn. Sch. Librarians, Alpha Delta Kappa (rec. sec. chpt., pres.-elect). Certified in library sci., Mo. Home: Box 2 Craig MO 64437 Office: Maysville R-I Jr/Sr Library PO Box 68 Maysville MO 64469

SCHNEIDER, ALEXANDER WILLIAM, JR., elec. engr.; b. Kalamazoo, Nov. 25, 1945; s. Alexander William and Jennylouise Standish (Lockwood-White) S.; B.S. in Elec. Engring., Northwestern U., 1967, M.S., 1968; M.B.A., U. Chgo., 1972; m. Lauretta Ann Gerretse, Sept. 18, 1971; children—Alexander William III, James Albert. With Commonwealth Edison Co., Chgo., 1968—, sr. engr. system planning, 1980—. Registered profl. engr., Ill. Mem. IEEE, Tau Beta Pi, Eta Kappa Nu. Presbyterian. Home: 610 Belmont Ave Addison IL 60101 Office: Box 767 Chicago IL 60611

SCHNEIDER, BENJAMIN, educator; b. N.Y.C., Aug. 11, 1938; s. Leo and Rose (Cohen) S.; B.A., Alfred U., 1960; M.B.A., City U. N.Y., 1962; Ph.D., U. Md., 1967; m. H. Brenda Jacobson, Jan. 29, 1961; children—Lee Andrew, Rhody Yve. Asst. prof. adminstrv. sci. and psychology Yale U., New Haven, 1967-71; asso. prof. U. Md., College Park, 1971-75, prof. psychology and bus., 1975-79; Fulbright prof. psychology Bar-Ilan U., Israel, 1973-74; John A. Hannah prof. orgnl. behavior in psychology and mgmt. Mich. State U., East Lansing, 1979—; cons. Am. Tel. & Tel., Chase Manhattan Bank, Citibank, J.C. Penney Co. Served with U.S. Army, 1962-64. Recipient James McKeen Catell award, Am. Psychol. Assn., Div. 14, 1966; Naval Research grantee, 1971-74, 75-78, 79-82; lic. psychologist, Md. Mem. Am. Psychol. Assn., AAAS, Acad. of Mgmt. Author: Organizational Climates and Careers (with D.T. Hall), 1973; Staffing Organizations, 1976. Home: 3905 Hemmingway Dr Okemos MI 48864 Office: Dept Psychology Mich State U East Lansing MI 48824

SCHNEIDER, DAVID MURRAY, educator, anthropologist; b. N.Y.C., Nov. 11, 1918; B.S., Cornell U., 1940, M.A., 1941; Ph.D., Harvard, 1949. Field trips to Yap Island, Trust Terr. Pacific, 1947-48, Mescalero Apache, N. Mex., 1955-58; lectr. London Sch. Econs., 1949-51; asst. prof. Harvard, 1951-55; prof. anthropology U. Calif. at Berkeley, 1956-60; prof. anthropology U. Chgo., 1960—, William B. Ogden disting. service prof. anthropology, 1978—, chmn. dept. anthropology, 1963-66. Cons. behavioral sci. study sect., NIH, 1960-64; mem. com. personnel Social Sci. Research Council, 1960-62; rep. Am. Anthrop. Assn. to div. anthrop. and psychol. NRC-Nat. Acad. Scis., 1962-64; bd. dirs. Founds. Fund Research Psychiatry, 1963-66. Fellow Center Advanced Study in Behavioral Scis., 1955-56, 66-67. Fellow Am. Anthropology Assn. (exec. bd. 1968-70), Am. Acad. Arts and Scis., Royal Anthrop. Inst. Great Britain, Assn. Social Anthropologists, AAAS. Author: (with Homans) Marriage, Authority and Final Causes, 1955; (with Gough) Matrilineal Kinship, 1961; American Kinship, 1968; (with Smith) Class Differences and Sex Role in American Kinship and Family Structure, 1973; (with Cottrell) The American Kin Universe, 1975. (with Dolgin and Kemnitzer) Symbolic Anthropology, 1977; A Critique of the Study of Kinship, 1982. Office: Dept Anthropology University of Chicago 1126 E 59th St Chicago IL 60637

SCHNEIDER, HAROLD WILLIAM, educator, editor; b. Redwood County, Minn., Feb. 26, 1926; s. William Theofeld and Bertha Augusta (Mell) S.; B.A., U. Minn., 1950, postgrad., 1952-56; m. Mary Bell Willis, July 7, 1956. Teaching asst. U. Minn., 1954-56, instr. English, 1956-61; instr. English, Kans. State U., Manhattan, 1961-68, asst. prof. English, 1969—. Mem. creative writing adv. panel Kans. Cultural Arts Commn., 1969-81, film adv. panel, 1971-76; mem. Manhattan Library Bd., 1981—. Served to master sgt. U.S. Army, 1950-52. Mem. MLA (rep. del. assembly 1979-82), AAUP, ACLU, Phi Beta Kappa (v.p. Alpha assn. Kans. 1971-72, pres. 1973-74), Lambda Alpha Psi. Lutheran. Mng. editor Critique: Studies in Modern Fiction, 1956-61, adv. editor, 1961-64; editor Kans. Mag., 1967-68, Kans. Quar., 1968—. Contbr. articles to profl. jours. Home: 1405 Nichols St Manhattan KS 66502

SCHNEIDER, HARVEY EARL, lawyer, human services cons.; b. Detroit, Oct. 6, 1941; s. Marvin William and Ruth Katherine (Schefges) S.; B.A., Western Mich. U., 1963; M.A., Wayne State U., 1968; J.D. with distinction, U. Ky., 1973; seminars/workshops Ohio State U., Oakland U., Peabody Coll., U. Nebr., N.Y. U., U. Ariz.; m. Martha Jane Alexander, July 18, 1970; children—William Alexander, Elizabeth Anne. With Parks and Recreation Dept., City of Detroit, 1961-64; tchr. Highland Park (Mich.) Bd. Edn., 1964-65; faculty Project Upward Bound, Wayne State U., Detroit, 1965-69; tchr. Oak Park (Mich.) Bd. Edn., 1963-67, Lamphere High Sch., Madison Heights, Mich., 1967-69; faculty Regional Spl. Edn. Instrn. Materials Center, U. Ky., Lexington, 1969-73; exec. dir. developmental disabilities Dept. Human Resources, State of Ky., Frankfort, 1973-74; coordinator specialized residential services Eastern Nebr. Human Services Agy./Eastern Nebr. Community Office of Retardation, Omaha, 1974-76; exec. dir. for comprehensive, pvt., non-profit rehab. Skyline Center, Inc., Clinton, Iowa, 1976-79; exec. dir. Iowa Assn. for Retarded Citizens, 1979-81; legal service cons. in handicapped law, 1972—; cons. community based services; surveyor Commn. Accreditation of Rehab. Facilities. Mem. Nebr. Bar Assn., Ky. Bar Assn., Am. Bar Assn., Am. Judicature Soc., Council for Exceptional Children, Am. Assn. Mental Deficiency, Assn. for Ednl. Communication and Tech., Nat. Assn. for Retarded Citizens, Iowa Assn. of Rehab. Facilities, Delta Theta Phi. Club: Kiwanis. Contbr. articles in field to profl. jours. Office: 6717 Holcomb Urbandale IA 50322

SCHNEIDER, JOHN DURBIN, state senator; b. St. Louis, Mar. 1, 1937; s. John S. and Kathleen (Durbin) S.; B.S., St. Louis U., J.D., 1960; m. Mary Joan Steppan, Nov. 4, 1961; 4 children. Atty. Transit Casualty Co., 1960-65, chief trial atty., 1965-70; former instr. Sanford-Brown Bus. Coll., St. Louis; mem. Mo. Ho. of Reps., 1968-70, Mo. Senate, 1970—, majority floor leader, 1976-80. Served with U.S. Army. Mem. St. Louis Bar Assn. Democrat. Roman Catholic. Office: State Capitol Jefferson City MO 65101*

SCHNEIDER, LEONARD MORTON, ednl. film maker; b. N.Y.C., Mar. 19, 1932; s. Samuel and Evelyn (Siegelbaum) S.; B.A., Coll. William and Mary, 1954; M.A., U. Kans., 1967; m. JoAnna March, May 10, 1959; children—Paul Miles, John March. Freelance motion picture cameraman, N.Y., 1962-66; motion picture dir. Centron Corp., Lawrence, Kans., 1967-69; ind. ednl. film-maker, Lawrence, 1972—; artist-painter, 1961—; one-man shows: U. Kans., Lawrence, 1970, Atlanta (Ga.) Artists Club Nat. Exhbn. I, 1970, Washington and Jefferson (Pa.) U. 3rd Nat. Exhbn., 1971, 9th Nat. Exhbn., 1977, touring exhbn. Wichita Art Mus., 1981, statewide exhbn. Kans. Arts Commn., 1981. Served with Signal Corps, U.S. Army, 1954-56. Recipient Chris award Columbus (Ohio) Film Festival, 1972, Bronze plaque, 1973, 74, 76, Chris Statuette, 1973; Creative Excellence certificate U.S. Indsl. Film Festival, 1972, 75, Golden Eagle CINE Film Festival, Washington, 1975, Gold award IFPA Film Festival, Hollywood, 1976, Gold award Greater Chicagoland Film Festival, 1976; finalist Nat. Ednl. Film Festival, 1977. Ednl. films include: Rainy Day Story, 1972; Me, 1972; They, 1972; You, 1973; The American Phoenix (screenplay), 1975; Captain Dinosaur, 1975. Home: 945 Lawrence Ave Lawrence KS 66044

SCHNEIDER, MARLIN DALE, state legislator Wis.; b. La Crosse, Wis., Nov. 16, 1942; s. Donald M. and Elva M. (Peterson) S.; B.S., Wis. State U., La Crosse, 1965; M.S., U. Wis., Stevens Point, 1976; M.S., U. Wis., Madison, 1979; m. Georgia Jean Johansen, July 14, 1973; 1 dau., Jeanine Marie. Tchr. social sci. Wisconsin Rapids and Lomira pub. schs., 1965-70; mem. Wis. Ho. of Reps., 1971—, chmn. Com. on Revenue, 1977—, majority caucus vice-chmn. Chmn. Nat. Brotherhood Week, South Wood County, 1967; mem. Bldg. Commn., 1977—; mem. com. on rural devel. Nat. Conf. State Legislatures, 1979-80. NSF grantee in sociology La. State U., Baton Rouge, 1970. Mem. Wisconsin Rapids Edn. Assn. (pres. elect), Am. Fedn. Musicians. Democrat. Lutheran. Author: (poem) Since Revere, 1976. Home: 3820 S Brook Ln Wisconsin Rapids WI 54494 Office: 8 North Capitol Madison WI 53702

SCHNEIDER, NORMAN RICHARD, veterinarian, educator; b. Ellsworth, Kans., Mar. 28, 1943; s. Henry C. and Irene C. (Ney) S.; B.S., Kans. State U., 1967, D.V.M., 1968; M.S. (Air Force Inst. Tech. fellow), Ohio State U., 1972; m. Karen Marjorie Nelson, July 1, 1968; 1 son, Nelson R. Commd. capt. U.S. Air Force, 1968, advanced through grades to maj., 1976; base veterinarian Goose AB, Labrador, Can., 1968-70; veterinary scientist/toxicologist Armed Forces Radiobiology Research Inst., Bethesda, Md., 1972-76; vet. toxicologist Aerospace Med. Research Lab., Wright-Patterson AFB, Dayton, Ohio, 1976-79; asso. prof./vet. toxicologist dept. vet. sci. Univ. Nebr., Lincoln, 1979—; chief vet. services 155th Tactical Reconnaissance Group, Nebr. Air Nat. Guard, Lincoln, 1979—. Decorated Joint Services Commendation medal; diplomate Am. Bd. Vet. Toxicology. Mem. Am. Coll. Vet. Toxicologists, Am. Vet. Med. Assn., Nebr. Vet. Med. Assn., Kans. Vet. Med. Assn., Alliance Air Nat. Guard Veterinarians, Assn. Mil. Surgeons U.S., N.Y. Acad. Scis., Council Agrl. Sci. and Tech., Alpha Zeta, Phi Zeta, Am. Legion, Nat. Rifle Assn., Farmhouse Fraternity. Roman Catholic. Home: Route 1 Box 70 Ceresco NE 68017 Office: Vet Center Lincoln NE 68583

SCHNEIDER, RALPH WILLIAM, automobile mfg. co. exec.; b. Iroquois County, Ill., June 7, 1926; s. William F. and Louise (Wickboldt) S.; B.A. in Bus. Adminstrn., Mich. State U., 1949; m. Virginia A. Murnane, July 2, 1977; children—Steven R., Debra J., Carol L. Mgmt. trainee Chrysler Corp., Detroit, 1949-50; supr. budgets Kaiser Frazer/Kaiser Jeep Corp., Toledo, 1950-57, mgr. govt. sales and govt. products div. Kaiser Jeep Corp., 1957-67; dir. contract adminstrn. Kaiser Jeep Corp./AM Gen. Corp., South Bend, Ind., 1967-77, gen. mgr. truck div., 1977-79; v.p. govt. Contracts A. M. Gen. Corp., 1979—. Past pres., Redeemer Lutheran Ch. Served with U.S. Army, 1944-45. Decorated Purple Heart, Bronze Star. Certified profl. contracts mgr., Ind. Mem. Assn. U.S. Army, Am. Def. Preparedness Assn., Nat. Security Indsl. Assn., Nat. Contract Mgmt. Assn. Home: 15349 Lakeside Pl Plymouth MI 48170 Office: 14250 Plymouth Rd Detroit MI 48232

SCHNIEDERJANS, JILL MARLENE, educator; b. St. Louis, Oct. 19, 1950; d. Herman Jerome and Wanda Lee (Russell) Goehler; B.S. magna cum laude (Univ. scholar), U. Mo., St. Louis, 1972; M.A., St. Louis U., 1978; m. Schniederjans, Aug. 13, 1971. Tchr., Gateway Elem. Sch., St. Louis, 1972-75; elem. math. specialist Maplewood (Mo.)-Richmond Heights Sch. Dist., 1976, University City (Mo.) Sch. Dist., 1976-77; title I supr. nonpublic schs. City of St. Louis, 1977-80; Title I reading tchr. Hawaii Dept. Edn., Hilo, 1980; dissemination specialist Central Midwest Regional Ednl. Lab., Math. and Sci. Group, St. Louis, 1981—. Mem. Nat. Council Tchrs. Math., Assn. Supervision and Curriculum Devel., Internat. Reading Assn., Kappa Delta Pi. Home: 3122 La Vista Dr Saint Ann MO 63074 Office: 3120 59th St Saint Louis MO 63139

SCHNIPKE, RITA JANE, engring. research center exec.; b. Lima, Ohio, May 25, 1952; d. Joseph Clement and Agnes Rose (Faeth) S.; B.S., Heidelberg Coll., 1974; B.S magna cum laude, U. Toledo, 1978, M.S., 1979. Tchr. heat transfer lab. U. Toledo, 1978-79; sr. engr. Alliance (Ohio) Research Center, Babcock & Wilcox, 1979—. Registered profl. engr., Ohio. Mem. Nat. Soc. Profl. Engrs., ASME, Ohio Soc. Profl. Engrs., Sigma Xi, Pi Tau Sigma. Home: 5825 Daisy St NE Louisville OH 44641 Office: Alliance Research Center Babcock & Wilcox 1562 Beeson St Alliance OH 44601

SCHNOES, ROBERT FREDERICK, diversified co. exec.; b. Mt. Lebanon, Pa., Apr. 4, 1926; s. Sebastian J. and Henrietta C. (Schertler) S.; B.S. in Indsl. Mgmt., U. Pitts., 1949; m. Dolores K. Hewston, Aug. 13, 1949; children—Carolyn S. Schnoes Black, Christine P. Schnoes Rost, Nancy E. Schnoes Anderson, Judith A. Schnoes Thompson. With Midwest sales div. Autographic Register Co., Hoboken, N.J., 1949-50; with quality control dept. Fisher body div., Gen. Motors Corp., Pitts., 1950-51; buyer, supervisory buyer, asst. purchasing agt., asst. to surface ship project mgr., Bettis Atomic Power div. Westinghouse Electric Corp., Pitts., 1951-59; dir. material and facilities dept. Am. Standard Mil. Products Div., Norwood, Mass., 1959-62; exec. v.p. Hamill Mfg. Co., Monroeville, Pa., 1962-63; gen. mgr. aero-research instrument dept. Am. Standard Corp., Chgo., 1963-65, pres. controls div., 1965-68; pres. Dresser indsl. valve and instrument div. Dresser Industries, Inc., Stratford, Conn., 1968-70, pres. Indsl. Spltys. Group, Stratford, 1970-71, v.p. ops., Dallas, 1971-74, sr. v.p. ops. office of pres., 1975-77; pres., chief operating officer, dir. IC Industries, Inc., Chgo., 1977—; dir. Abex Corp., Ill. Central Gulf R.R., Pepsi-Cola Gen. Bottlers, Inc., Pet Inc., Midas Internat. Corp., Am. Nat. Bank and Trust Co. Chgo., Walter E. Heller Internat. Corp. Mem. council Grad. Sch. Bus., U. Chgo.; bd. visitors U. Pitts.; mem. Chgo. Com. Served with USN, 1944-46. Mem. Engring. Soc. Detroit, Northwestern U. Assos., Chgo. Assn. Commerce and Industry (dir.). Clubs: Chicago, Mid-Am., Executives (Chgo.); Indian Hill (Winnetka, Ill.). Office: IC Industries Inc 111 E Wacker Drive Chicago IL 60601

SCHOBER, CHARLES COLEMAN, III, psychiatrist, psychoanalyst; b. Shreveport, La., Nov. 30, 1924; s. Charles Coleman and Mabel Lee (Welsh) S.; B.S., La. State U., 1946, M.D., 1949; m. Martha Elizabeth Welsh, Dec. 27, 1947 (dec.); children—Irene Lee, Ann Welsh; m. 2d, Argeree Maburl Stiles, Feb. 4, 1972; 1 son, Charles Coleman. Intern, Phila. Gen. Hosp., 1949-51; resident psychiatry Norristown (Pa.) State Hosp., 1953-56; asso. clin. dir. Pa. Hosp. Inst., Phila., 1957-59; practice medicine, specializing in psychiatry and psychoanalysis, Phila., 1960-71, St. Louis, 1973—; attending psychiatrist Pa. Hosp. Inst., Phila., 1963-68, sr. attending psychiatrist, 1968-71; staff St. Louis U. Hosp., 1973—; instr. psychiatry U. Pa. Med. Sch., Phila., 1958-62, asso. in psychiatry, 1962-70, asst. prof., 1965-71; prof., chmn. psychiatry La. State U. Med. Sch., Shreveport, 1971-73; psychiatrist in chief Confederate Meml. Med. Center and VA Hosp., Shreveport, 1971-73; prof. psychiatry St. Louis U. Med. Sch., 1973—; cons. psychiatry VA Hosp., St. Louis, 1973—; faculty Phila. Psychoanalytic Inst., 1966-71, New Orleans Psychoanalytic Inst., 1972-73, St. Louis Psychoanalytic Inst., 1973—. Served to capt. USAF, 1951-53. Decorated Air Force Commendation medal. Fellow Am. Coll. Psychiatrists, Am., Mo. psychiat. assns.; mem. ACLU, AMA, Mo., St. Louis med. socs., Am. Psychoanalytic Assn., St. Louis Psychoanalytic Soc. Contbr. articles to profl. jours. Home: 7232 Greenway Ave Saint Louis MO 63130 Office: 4524 Forest Park Saint Louis MO 63108

SCHOCKE, HAROLD EDWIN, chem. co. exec.; b. Frankfort, Ind., Jan. 7, 1937; s. Frank J. and Helen (Hibbard) S.; B.S., Purdue U., 1960; postgrad. in indsl. engring Ind. U./Purdue U., Indpls., 1975; m. Winona Jean Westbrook, June 28, 1974; 1 dau., Dayna Laurel. Owner, mgr. Schocke Farms, Inc., Frankfort, 1970-74, Schocke Farm Supply Inc., Frankfort, 1970-74; indsl. engr. Nat. R.R. Transp. Corp., Indpls., 1974-76; area mgr. nat. accounts Occidental Chem. Co., Indpls., 1976-78; regional mgr. C. F. Industries, Long Grove, Ill., from 1978, now regional mgr. Mem. County Extension exec. bd., 1960-68, County Council, 1964-68; pres. bd. County Fair, 1968-72. Mem. Am. Mgmt. Assn., Fla. Agrl. Research Inst., Ga. Plant Food Ednl. Soc., Nat. Fertilizer Solutions Assn. Republican. Mem. United Pentecostal Ch. Club: Killearn Country. Home: 3425 Brandywine Rd Barrington IL 60010 Office: CF Industries Inc Salem Lake Dr Long Grove IL 60047

SCHOCKLING, LINDA SUE, banker; b. Pitts., Aug. 9, 1948; d. Leonard August and Susan (Odlivak) S.; B.S., Edinboro State Coll., 1970; postgrad. U. Pitts. Trainer data processing Rockwell Internat., Pitts., 1976-77; cost and systems analyst Koppers Co., Inc., Pitts., 1975-76; programmer PPG Industries, Pitts., 1971-75; bus. systems planning officer No. Trust Co., Chgo., 1977—; instr. Am. Inst. Banking, 1979—. Bd. dirs. Easter Seals, 1978-81. Mem. Assn. Systems Mgmt. (officer Pitts. 1972-77), Chgo. Data Processing Edn. Council (sec. 1977-80). Home: 558 Woodfield Trail Roselle IL 60172 Office: 125 S Wacker Dr Chicago IL 60675

SCHOEDEL, VICKI L. (MRS. JOHN F. SCHOEDEL), telephone co. exec.; b. Fort Worth, Aug. 20, 1949; d. Lawrence B. and Floyce L. (Haney) Vaughn; B.A. in Psychology, Tex. Christian U., 1971; m. John F. Schoedel, Apr. 3, 1976. With Southwestern Bell Telephone Co., St. Louis, 1967—, supr. course devel., 1974-77, asst. staff mgr. gen. marketing dept., 1977-79, staff specialist staffing, 1979—. Vice pres. Aid Assn. for Luths., 1979—; bd. chmn. adult nurture bd. Concordia Luth. Ch., 1979—, mem. ch. council, 1979—; vol. Arthritis Found. Mem. Nat. Assn. Exec. Women, Tex. Christian U. Alumni Assn., AAUW. Club: Tex. Christian U. Century. Home: 678 Dougherty Estates Dr Manchester MO 63011 Office: 112 N 4th St Room 410 St Louis MO 63102

SCHOELLHORN, ROBERT ALBERT, pharms. co. exec.; b. Phila., 1928; grad. Phila. Coll. Textiles and Sci., 1955. With Am. Cyanamid Co., 1947-73; pres. Lederle Labs.; with Abbott Labs., North Chicago,

Ill., 1973—, exec. v.p. hosp. group, 1976-79, pres., chief operating officer, 1979—, also dir. Office: Abbott Labs Abbott Park North Chicago IL 60064*

SCHOEMEHL, VINCENT CHARLES, JR., mayor St. Louis; b. St. Louis, Oct. 30, 1946; s. Vincent Charles and Lucille Mary (Miller) S.; B.A. in History, U. Mo., St. Louis, 1972; m. Lois Brockmeier, Sept. 18, 1971; children—Timothy, Joseph. Alderman, City of St. Louis, 1975-81, mayor, 1981—. Clubs: Lions, Ancient Order Hibernians. Democrat. Roman Catholic. Office: City Hall Saint Louis MO 63103

SCHOENBECK, ROBERT JOSEPH, advt. agy. exec.; b. Evanston, Ill., July 27, 1947; s. Joseph C. and Frances R. (Zrazik) S.; B.S., U. Ill., 1969; M.B.A., Loyola U., Chgo., 1971; m. Allison M. McCall, Oct. 2, 1976. Research coordinator Masonite Corp., Chgo., 1971; product mgr. Booth Fisheries, Consol. Foods, Chgo., 1971-74; group product mgr. Barton Brands, Chgo., 1974-76; account exec. Leo Burnett USA, Chgo., 1976-79, v.p., account supr., 1979—. Mem. Am. Mktg. Assn. Home: 1520 Forest Evanston IL 60201 Office: Leo Burnett USA 1 Prudential Plaza Chicago IL 60601

SCHOENEBERGER, BARBARA ALICE, cons.; b. St. Louis, Nov. 23, 1945; d. Vincent Henry and Virginia Alice (Mattox) S.; A.B., Washington U., 1970; M.A., Webster Coll., 1975. Counselor, Mo. Dept. Labor, St. Louis, 1970-76; orgn. devel. cons. United Van Lines, St. Louis, 1976-77, Internorth, Inc., Omaha, 1978—; cons. to bus. in field of human resource devel., planning and productivity, 1978—. Mem. bd. Omaha Area Council Alcoholism, 1980—, chmn. edn. com., 1980; mem. adv. bd. Center Stage, 1981—. Mem. Nat. Orgn. Devel. Network, Am. Soc. Personnel Adminstrs., Am. Soc. Tng. and Devel. Roman Catholic. Office: 2223 Dodge St Omaha NE 68102

SCHOENMANN, LINDA JANE, marketing exec.; b. San Diego, Oct. 19, 1951; d. Marvin Edward and Margaret Fern (Phillips) Sprecher; B.S. in Mktg., No. Ill. U., 1973. Mktg. analyst Kohler Co., Kohler, Wis., 1973-80; project dir. William C. Brown Co., pubs., 1980-81; mng. sr. distbr. SASCO, 1981—. Advisor, Jr. Achievement, Kohler. Mem. Am. Mktg. Assn., Wis. State Hist. Soc. Roman Catholic. Home: Route 1 Box 271 Arena WI 53503

SCHOENOFF, ARTHUR WILLIAM, ednl. adminstr./cons.; b. Waverly, Iowa, Apr. 24, 1930; s. Arthur Frederick and Evelyn Madeline (Stahl) S.; B.A., U. No. Iowa, 1952, M.A., 1959; M.F.A., U. Iowa, 1970, Ph.D., 1972; m. Ann Louise Lane, Feb. 24, 1952; children—Jon Frederic, Joanna Louise, Ellen Elisabeth. Tchr. vocal, instrumental, gen. music, public schs., Kans., Iowa, Wis., 1952-67; asst. prof. music Carthage Coll., Kenosha, Wis., 1967-73; asso. prof. music Mercer U., Macon, Ga., 1973-77; adj. asst. prof. Ga. Coll., Milledgeville, 1974-77; adminstr. music edn. Anoka-Hennepin Sch. Dist., Coon Rapids, Minn., 1977—; pvt. instr. music, 1950—; instrumental/vocal soloist. Bd. dirs. Racine (Wis.) Symphony Orch., 1965-72, personnel mgr., 1965-69, 65-71, pres., 1970-71; dir. Anoka-Ramsey Community Chorus, 1978-79; minister of music Luth. Chs. in Iowa, Wis., Ga., Minn., 1953—. Served with USAF, 1953-57. Luth. Ch. Am. doctoral study fellow, 1969; Iowa Research grantee, 1972; recipient Alpha Psi Omega Cert. of Recognition, 1971; Mercer Spirit award, 1975. Mem. Music Educators Nat. Conf., Minn. Music Educators Assn., Soc. for Research in Music Edn., Nat. String Orch. Assn., Nat. Assn. Jazz Educators, Am. Choral Dirs. Assn., Internat. Horn Soc., Nat. Assn. Coll. Wind and Percussion Instrs., Coll. Music Soc., Am. Fedn. Musicians, Nat. Ret. Tchrs. Assn., Found. for Christian Living. Republican. Lutheran. Clubs: Kogudus, Kiwanis. Composer, arranger instrumental music for use in worship, 1953—. Home: 1203 Norwood Ln Anoka MN 55303 Office: 11299 Hanson Blvd NW Coon Rapids MN 55433

SCHOETTGER, RICHARD AARON, fishery biologist; b. Arlington, Nebr., Oct. 24, 1932; s. George Emmet and Nelda Elizabeth (Bender) S.; B.S., Colo. State U., 1954, M.S., 1959, Ph.D. (NIH grantee), 1966; m. Lorraine Louise Nelson, June 20, 1954; children—David Scott, Lisa Marie. Fishery research biologist toxicology and physiology U.S. Fish and Wildlife Service, Fish Control Lab., LaCrosse, Wis., 1962-67, asst. dir., 1967-69; dir. Columbia (Mo.) Nat. Fisheries Research Lab., U.S. Fish and Wildlife Service, 1969—; research asso. U. Mo., 1970—; project leader U.S./USSR Environ. Exchange Program, 1978—. Served to capt. USAF, 1954-57. Mem. Am. Fisheries Soc., Soc. Environ. Toxicology and Chemistry, Am. Inst. Fishery Research Biologists, Nat. Wildlife Fedn., Sigma Xi. Contbr. articles to profl. jours. Patentee in field. Office: Route 1 Columbia MO 65201

SCHOETTLIN, SHIRLEY ANN, Realtor; b. Piggott, Ark., May 3, 1938; d. Raymond Andrew and Sylvia Virginia (Hughes) Wright; student public schs., Piggott; children—Melissa Leigh, Phillip Andrew. Property mgr. Charles F. Curry Co., Kansas City, Mo., 1970-73, project mgr., sales asso., 1973-77; sales asso. TMI Realtors, Lee's Summit, Mo., 1977-78, broker, 1978—, v.p., 1978—; owner, prin. Schoettlin Realtors, 1981—; chmn. real estate coms. Mem. bd. dirs. Met. March of Dimes. Mem. Real Estate Bd. Lee's Summit (dir.), Real Estate Bd. Kansas City, Nat. Assn. Realtors, Mo. Assn. Realtors (dir.), Womens Council Realtors (governing bd.). Club: Million Dollar. Contbr. articles to profl. jours. Home: 3741 Woodland Ct Lakewood Lee's Summit MO 64063 Office: 606 W 3d St Lee's Summit MO 64063

SCHOLES, GENE WASHINGTON, univ. adminstr.; b. Detroit, Sept. 5, 1933; s. Sam and Amye Lillian (Taylor) S.; B.S., Murray State U., 1956, M.A., 1960; Ed.S., U. Ill., 1965; Ph.D., So. Ill. U., 1972; m. Shirley Ann Hughes, May 30, 1959; children—Steven, Greg, Emily. Tchr., Mayfield (Ky.) High Sch., 1956-60; dir. pupil personnel Trigg County (Ky.) Schs., 1960-62; asst. prin. Unity High Sch., Tolono, Ill., 1962-63; prin. Ele Jr. High Sch., Shelbyville, Ill., 1963-66; coordinator campus services Audio Visual Center, Eastern Ill. U., Charleston, 1966-72, chmn. dept. instructional media, 1972-76, dir. Audio Visual Center, 1972-—; asst. dir. learning resource services So. Ill. U., Carbondale, 1971-72. Served with U.S. Army, 1956-57. Mem. Assn. Ednl. Communications and Tech. (mem. com. on program consultation and evaluation 1979—, mem. certification com. 1980-83), Ill. Assn. Ednl. Communications and Tech. (Pres. award 1978, Cert. of Appreciation 1980, pres. elect 1980-82, dir. 1980—). Repubublican. Baptist. Club: Masons (Mayfield, Ky.). Home: 815 6th St Charleston IL 61920 Office: Eastern Ill U Charleston IL 61920

SCHOLL, RALPH HERMAN, chem. co. exec.; b. Chgo., May 13, 1945; s. Herman and Serena Edna S.; B.S. in Bus. Adminstrn., Valparaiso U., 1967; M.B.A. in Mktg., Mich. State U., 1968. Mktg. rep. Mobil Oil Corp., Quincy, Ill., 1971-72; personnel councilor Snelling & Snelling, Des Plaines, Ill., 1973; merchandising analyst Chemetron Corp., Chgo., 1974-77; market services mgr. Vesicol Chem. Corp., Chgo., 1977—. Local community campaign chmn. People's Party, 1979, publicity chmn., 1981; founder, chmn. Elmhurst Pres.'s Council, 1976-78; mem. Elmhurst Community Theater, 1978—, treas., 1979; mem. Track of Elmhurst Com., 1979-81, Elmhurst Zoning and Planning Commn., 1979—. Served with USNR, 1968-70; Vietnam. Mem. Am. Mktg. Assn., Nat. Pest Control Assn., Bensonville Jaycees (charter), Elmhurst Jaycees (pres. 1976-77, v.p. 1975-76, dir. 1974-75, Jaycee of Yr. award 1976), Ill. Jaycees (dist. dir. N.E. region 1977-78, Outstanding Dist. Dir. award 1978). Republican. Lutheran. Home: 184 Willow St Elmhurst IL 60126 Office: 341 E Ohio St Chicago IL 60611

SCHOMERS, DIANE MARIE, occupational therapist; b. Ransonville, N.Y., Oct. 28, 1954; d. William Joseph and Margaret Mary (Lardner) S.; B.S., SUNY, Buffalo, 1976; postgrad Grad. Med. Sch. Northwestern U., 1980-81. Occupational therapist Braintree (Mass.) Hosp., 1976-77; occupational and phys. therapist Peace Corps, 1977-80; orthotist Wis. Orthopedic Co., Green Bay, Wis., 1980-81; dir. occupational therapy St. Vincent's Hosp., Green Bay, 1981—; nursing home cons., 1980—. HEW grantee, 1974-76. Mem. Am. Occupational Therapy Assn. Orthotics Prothetics Assn. Home: 624 E Allovez Ave Green Bay WI 54301 also 4 Roosevelt Dr Lockport NY 14094

SCHOONOVER, SARAH MOREHART (MRS. DONALD JOHN SCHOONOVER), psychologist; b. Syracuse, N.Y., Mar. 27, 1925; d. Grover Cleveland and Clara Caroline (Keesecker) Morehart; A.B., Syracuse U., 1946, A.M., 1949; Ph.D., U. Mich., 1953; m. Donald John Schoonover, Aug. 19, 1950; children—John Morehart, Charles Philip, Suzanne Rebecca. Personnel trainee Sears, Roebuck & Co., Syracuse, 1946-48; asst. psychometrican U. Mich. Elementary Sch., Ann Arbor, 1948-49, chief psychometrican, 1949-51; supr. employee testing program GTE Sylvania Electric Products, Inc., Ottawa, Ohio, 1951-52; lectr. child devel. Ohio No. U., Ada, 1957-58; staff psychologist Northwest Guidance Center, Inc., Lima, Ohio, 1958-62, chief psychologist, 1962-63, psychologist dir., 1969-71; psychologist dir. Hancock County Mental Health Clinic, Findlay, Ohio, 1963-69; psychologist Putnam County Schs., Ottawa, 1969-70; clinic dir. Putnam County Mental Health Clinic, Inc., Ottawa, 1970-79; psychotherapist, staff psychologist Toledo Mental Health Center, 1979-81; pvt. practice, 1979—. Mem. Am., Ohio, Northwest Ohio psychol. assns., Mich. Alumni Assn., Alumni Assn. of Syracuse U., D.A.R., Lima Power Squadron, Psi Chi, Alpha Kappa Delta, Theta Beta Phi, Kappa Delta Pi, Pi Lambda Theta, Phi Kappa Phi, Alpha Chi Omega. Clubs: Tawa Bridgette, Kildaire Country. Home: 550 North Thomas St Ottawa OH 45875

SCHOPP, NORMAN RAY, product engr.; b. Moberly, Mo., July 12, 1952; s. Selby Ray and Edris Anna (Swackhammer) S.; Asso. in Applied Sci., Moberly Jr. Coll., 1972. Draftsman, Orscheln Co., Moberly, 1973-76, engr. technician, 1976-78, product engr., 1978—. Mem. Jr. C. of C. (external v.p. 1978—). Home: 212 Lotter St Moberly MO 65270 Office: Orscheln Co PO Box 280 Moberly MO 65270

SCHOTTELKOTTE, ALBERT JOSEPH, broadcasting exec.; b. Cheviot, Ohio, Mar. 19, 1927; s. Albert William and Venetta (Mentrup) S.; student pub. and parochial schs.; m. Virginia Louise Gleason, July 2, 1951; children—Paul J., Carol Ann, Linda Louise, Joseph G., Matthew, Louis A., Martha Jane, Amy Marie, Mary Jo, Ellen Elizabeth, William H., Michael E. Wtih Cin. Enquirer, 1943-61, successively copy boy, city-wide reporter, columnist, 1953-61; news broadcaster WSAI radio, Cin., 1953-59; news broadcaster WCPO radio-TV, 1959—, dir. news-spl. events, 1961—; gen. mgr. news div. Scripps-Howard Broadcasting Co., 1969—, v.p. for news, 1971—, sr. v.p., 1981—; mem. broadcast bd. UPI. Trustee, Scripps-Howard Found. Served with AUS, 1950-52. Recipient Nat. CD award for reporting on subject, 1958. Mem. Radio-TV News Dirs. Assn. Roman Catholic. Clubs: Maketewah Country, Cin. Home: 7647 Pineglen Dr Cincinnati OH 45224 Office: 500 Central Ave Cincinnati OH 45202

SCHOTTENSTEIN, HAROLD, ret. soft drink co. exec.; b. Columbus, O., Aug. 18, 1910; s. Jacob Meyer and Gertrude (Goldberg) S.; B.Sc. in Pharmacy, Ohio State U., 1931; m. Regene Gloria Wides, Apr. 7, 1946; children—James Mark, Terri Lynn, Edwin Michael. Owner, Eagle Drug Store, Columbus, 1933-36; partner Pepsi Cola Bottling Co., Columbus, 1936-62; pres., Schott Enterprises, Inc., Columbus, 1962—; sec. Niam Corp., Columbus, 1969—; pres. De Long Devel. Co., So. Devel. Co., Columbus, 1969—, Clinic Pharmacies Inc., Columbus, 1978-81. Chmn., Israel Bond, 1961, 62, big gifts United Jewish Fund and Council, 1962, 63, campaign, 1964, jubilee dinner Friends of Yeshiva U., 1962; asst. treas. Heritage House, 1967—; pres. Jacob and Gussie Schottenstein Found. Served with M.C., AUS, 1942-45; ETO. Mem. Ohio Bottlers Assn. (pres. 1956), Zionist Orgn. Am., Rho Pi Phi. Jewish religion (pres. synagogue 1962-63, hon. trustee congregation 1963). Mem. B'nai B'rith. Clubs: Whitehall Bexley Rotary (pres. 1979-80); Winding Hollow (Columbus). Home: 544 Noe Bixby Rd Columbus OH 43213

SCHOTZ, LARRY ALLEN, elec. engr.; b. Milw., Dec. 26, 1949; s. Alex M. and Ruth (Barland) S.; A.A., Milw. Sch. Engring., 1973, B.S. in Elec. Engring., 1973. Project engr. Sherwood Electronic Labs., Chgo., 1973-74; chief engr. Lynn Industries, Chgo., 1974-75; pres. Draco Labs., Inc., Milw., 1975-80, LS Research, Inc., Thiensville, Wis., 1980—; instr. U. Wis. Mil. Extension. Mem. indsl. adv. com. Milw. Sch. Engring. Mem. IEEE, Audio Engring. Soc., Sales Mktg. Execs. Milw. Recipient Hon. mention Am. Soc. Engring. Edn., 1972; Patentee vehicle intrusion alarm, solid state echo producing systems, radio control circuit with microprocesser. Home: 183 Green Bay Rd Thiensville WI 53092 Office: 118 Green Bay Rd Thiensville WI 53092

SCHOWALTER, LUKE ABRAHAM, clin. social worker; b. Scott County, Kans., June 21, 1941; s. William Peter and Agnes Elizabeth (Miller) S.; diploma Christian edn. Moody Bible Inst., Chgo., 1962; B.A. in Religious Edn., Ft. Wayne (Ind.) Bible Coll., 1965; M.S.W., Wayne State U., Detroit, 1970; m. Millicent Ruth Palmquist, July 25, 1964; children—Daniel William, Lisa Marie. Dir. Christian edn. Royal Oak (Mich.) Missionary Ch., 1965-66; intake worker Family Service Agy. Detroit, 1967-68; adult day center coordinator Kalamazoo State Hosp., 1970-73, clin. social worker outpatient dept., 1973-77; sr. clin. social worker inpatient program Kalamazoo Regional Psychiat. Hosp., 1977—; field placement supr. grad. students Western Mich. U. Sch. Social Work. Trustee Concerned Landlords Assn., Kalamazoo, 1978; deacon, clk., mem. ofcl. bd., Sunday sch. tchr., adult choir dir. Calvary Bible Ch., Kalamazoo. Mem. Acad. Cert. Social Workers, Nat. Assn. Social Workers, Christian Assn. Psychol. Studies, Kalamazoo Oratorio Soc. Home: 675 South Shore Dr Portage MI 49002 Office: Kalamazoo Regional Psychiat Hosp Box A Kalamazoo MI 49001

SCHOWENGERDT, ROWLAND EASLEY, hosp. engr.; b. Topeka, Mar. 18, 1932; s. Theodore L. and Winston H. (Easley) S.; student Kans. State U., 1950-51; m. Dixie C. Breymeyer, Feb. 17, 1952; children—Joan Lee, Jean Marie, Jan Laurie, Ted Louis, Julie Ann, Jill Elaine, Tim Allen. Farmer, Hamlin, Kans., 1952-68; sales rep. Hiawatha (Kans.) Daily World, 1968; soil conservation technician Soil Conservation Service, Hiawatha, 1968-70; chief engr. Hiawatha Community Hosp., 1971—. Mem. Kans. Hosp. Engrs. Assn. (pres. 1980-81). Republican. Methodist. Home: Rural Route 3 Hiawatha KS 66434 Office: 300 Utah St Hiawatha KS 66434

SCHRADER, LAWRENCE FREDRICK, JR., fluid power component mfg. co. exec.; b. Port Clinton, Ohio, Sept. 16, 1946; s. Lawrence Fredrick and Sylvia Eileen S.; Asso. in Electronic Tech., Community Coll. Elyria, 1968; B.A., U. Akron, 1971, post-secondary tech. student, 1976; m. Linda Casini, July 25, 1975. Tchr. math. Columbia Middle Sch., Columbia Station, Ohio, 1971-73, Oberlin (Ohio) Sr. High Sch., 1973-76; tng. specialist Parker Hannifin Corp., Cleve., 1976-78, dir. tng., 1978—; guest lectr. Milw. Sch. Engring.; instr. Lakeland Community Coll., Cleve. State U. Served with USAR, 1970-71. Mem. Fluid Power Soc. (v.p. elect), Am. Soc. Tng. and Devel., Soc. Lubrication Engrs. Contbr. articles to jours., textbooks. Office: 17325 Euclid Ave Cleveland OH 44112

SCHRADIE, JOSEPH, educator; b. Los Angeles, July 19, 1933; s. Norbert and Katherine (Nielsen) S.; A.A., Pasadena City Coll., 1953; PharmD., U. So. Calif., 1957, M.S. in Pharmacy, 1961, Ph.D. in Pharm. Chemistry, 1966; postgrad. UCLA, 1960, 63; m. Marjorie Jane Thiele, June 18, 1960; children—Cynthia Christine, Kathleen Jane, Jennifer Anne, Heidi Lynn. Lectr. Sch. Pharmacy, U. So. Calif., 1962-65; asst. prof. pharmacognosy U. Toledo, 1966-70, asso. prof., 1970-77, 78—, chmn. dept. medicinal chemistry and pharmacognosy, 1981—; vis. prof. pharmacognosy U. Mich., Ann Arbor, 1977-78; cons. to poison control center and toxicology dept. Med. Coll. Toledo; dir. medicinal plant collection R.A. Stranahan Arboretum of U. Toledo. Bd. trustees Met. YMCA, Toledo, 1969; charter mem. adv. bd. Crosby Gardens of Toledo, 1968—, vice chmn. hort., 1977-78; pres. Commn. on Theology and Ch. Relations, Lutheran Ch.-Mo. Synod, 1972-77, 77-81. Served with AUS, 1957-58, USAR, 1958-63. Recipient Lundsford Richardson award for grad. research Richardson-Merrell Co., 1962, Mead Johnson grant, 1967-68, HEW Title VI grant, 1968, Lederle grant, 1974-77; U. Toledo Research grantee, 1977, Am. Cancer Soc. grant, 1978-81; registered pharmacist, Calif. Mem. AAAS, Am. Chem. Soc., Am. Pharm. Assn., Acad. Pharm. Scis. (sec. sect. pharmacognosy and natural products), Am. Soc. Pharmacognosy, N.Y. Acad. Scis., Am. Assn. Colls. Pharmacy, Hunt Bot. Library, Ohio Acad. Sci., Rho Chi, Sigma Xi, Phi Kappa Phi. Republican. Contbg. editor Pharmacognosy Titles, 1970-75; contbr. articles research jours. Inventor extractor-flash evaporator. Home: 3323 Gallatin Rd Ottawa Hills Toledo OH 43606 Office: College of Pharmacy University of Toledo Toledo OH 43606

SCHRAFFENBERGER, LUELLA KATHERINE, nurse; b. Monticello, Iowa, Jan. 15, 1914; d. Lou A. and Matilda (Jacobs) Oltman; R.N., South Shore Hosp., Chgo., 1936; cert. in nursing adminstrn. Baylor U., 1938; m. Howard Edward Schraffenberger, Apr. 30, 1949; 1 dau., Lou Ann. Operating room supr. Mahaska County Hosp., Oskaloosa, Iowa, 1938-40, Ottumwa (Iowa) Gen. Hosp., 1940-41, Moline (Ill.) Public Hosp., 1941-42, Swedish Hosp. of Mpls., 1942-43; operating room supr., clin. instr. Sch. Nursing, South Shore Hosp., Chgo., 1943-52, asst. dir. nurses, 1953-64, dir. nursing service, 1965—. Blood drive vol. ARC, Homewood and Flossmoor, Ill., 1971—. Recipient 35 Years of Service award South Shore Hosp., 1978. Mem. Am. Nurses Assn. (cert. nursing adminstr.), Am. Soc. Nursing Service Adminstrs., Am. Hosp. Assn., Ill. Nurses Assn., Chgo. and Suburban Dirs. Council, South Shore Hosp. Sch. Nursing Alumni Assn. (past pres.). Republican. Lutheran. Club: Dixie Oaks Bus. and Profl. Women's (rec. sec. 1978-79, Woman of Achievement 1978). Office: 8015 S Luella Ave Chicago IL 60617

SCHRAG, MERVIN WAYNE, mfg. co. exec.; b. McPherson, Kans., Jan. 12, 1938; s. Peter J.P. and Esther Schrag; student public schs., McPherson; m. Shirley Martha Schrag, Aug. 10, 1956; children—Rick Rene, Randy Jaye, Russell Denae, Rynnell Raye. Welder, plant supt. Moridge Mfg. Co., Moundridge, Kans., 1958-64; engring. supr. Hesston Corp. (Kans.), 1964-67, qualtiy assurance supr., 1967-69, qualtiy insp. mgr., 1969-75, mgr. quality control, 1975—. Mem. Am. Soc. Metals, Am. Soc. Quality Control, Am. Foundrymans Soc. Mennonite. Office: Lincoln Blvd Hesston KS 67062

SCHRAMM, DAVID NORMAN, educator, astrophysicist; b. St. Louis, Oct. 25, 1945; s. Marvin and Betty (Math) S.; S.B. in Physics, MIT, 1967; Ph.D. in Physics, Calif. Inst. Tech., 1971; m. Melinda Holzhauer, 1963 (div. 1980); children—Cary, Brett. Research fellow in physics Calif. Inst. Tech., Pasadena, 1971-72; asst. prof. astronomy and physics U. Tex. at Austin, 1972-74; asso. prof. astronomy, astrophysics and physics Enrico Fermi Inst. and the Coll., U. Chgo., 1974-77, prof., 1977—, chmn. dept. astronomy and astrophysics, 1978—; vis. fellow Inst. Theoretical Astronomy, Cambridge, Eng., 1972; vis. prof. Stanford U., 1977; Philips lectr. Haverford (Pa.) Coll., 1977; vis. fellow Japan Soc. for Promotion of Sci., 1979; lectr. Adler Planetarium, 1976—; cons. and lectr. in field; investigator grants NSF, NASA, Smithsonian Instn., Dept. Energy. Sloan Found. scholar, 1963-67; NDEA fellow, 1967-71; NSF fellow, 1970-71. Fellow Am. Phys. Soc.; mem. Am. Astron. Soc. (exec. com. 1977-78, sec.-treas. 1979—; Helen B. Warner prize 1978), Astron. Soc. Pacific (Robert J. Trumpler award 1974), Meteoritical Soc., Internat. Astron. Union (various commns.), Sigma Xi. Contbr. articles to profl. jours.; co-editor: Explosive Nucleosynthesis, 1973, Physical Cosmology, 1980, Essays in Nuclear Astrophysics, 1981, Fundamental Problems in the Theory of Stellar Evolution; editor: Supernovae, 1977, Theoretical Astrophysics Series; co-author: Advanced States of Stellar Evolution, 1977; editorial com. Ann. Rev. Nuclear Sci., 1976-80; asso. editor Am. Jour. Physics, 1978—. Clubs: Am. Alpine, Quadrangle, X, Austrian Alpine. Home: 4923 S Kimbark St Chicago IL 60615 Office: Astronomy and Astrophysics Center U Chgo 5640 S Ellis Ave Chicago IL 60637

SCHRAMM, PAUL HOWARD, lawyer; b. St. Louis, Oct. 6, 1933; s. Benjamin Jacob and Frieda Sylvia (Goruch) S.; A.B., U. Mo., 1955, J.D., 1958; m. Susan Ann Susman, June 6, 1959; children—Scott Lyon, Dean Andrew, Thomas Edward. Admitted to Mo. bar, 1958, practiced in Clayton, also St. Louis, 1958—; mem. firm Schramm and Schramm, 1959-61, Schramm and Morganstern, 1970-76, Schramm, Pines & Marshall, 1977-79, Schramm, Newman, Pines & Freyman, 1979—; judge City of Ellisville (Mo.) Mcpl. Div., St. Louis County Circuit Ct., 1977—. Mem. Estate Planning Council, St. Louis, 1968—. Mem. U. Mo. Law Sch. Found., 1969—; mem. music adv. com. Mo. State Council on Arts, 1971-77; pres. Kirkwood Symphony Soc., 1961; mem. Ladue Sch. Dist. Council, 1970-74; bd. dirs. Young Audiences, Inc., 1972-78, pres. elect, 1974-75, pres., 1975-76; bd. dirs. St. Louis Dance Concert Soc., 1969-74, sec., 1969; bd. dirs. St. Louis Jewish Family and Children's Service, 1975-77; mem. Ladue Sch. Dist. Council, 1970-74; mem. exec. com. East Ladue Jr. High Sch. Assn., 1975-76. Mem. Am., St. Louis County (chmn. lawyer reference service 1971, chmn. circuit ct. judiciary com.), Mo. bar assns., Bar Assn. Met. St. Louis (exec. com. 1976-77, chmn. St. Louis County sect. 1976-77), Am. Judicature Soc., Reed Sch. Assn. (pres. 1970-71), Phi Delta Phi, Psi Chi, Sigma Alpha Mu. Home: 2 Cedar Crest Ladue MO 63132 Office: 120 S Central Ave Clayton MO 63105

SCHRAYER, MAX ROBERT, ins. exec.; b. Chgo., Nov. 17, 1902; s. Robert Max and Jennie (Weber) S.; B.S., U. Mich., 1923; m. Mildred Mayer, July 3, 1925; children—Helaine (Mrs. A.A. Freeman), Jean (Mrs. Robert L. Adler), Robert Max. Propr., Max Robert Schrayer & Assos., Chgo., 1933-42, now pres.; v.p. Asso. Agys., Inc., 1942-64, pres., 1965-75, chmn. bd., 1975—; dir. Allied Tube & Conduit Co. Gen. chmn. Combined Jewish Appeal, 1964-65, pres., 1966. Past pres. Better Govt. Assn.; bd. dirs. Jewish Telegraphic Agy.; vice chmn. bd. trustees Roosevelt U.; gen. chmn. Jewish United Drive Met. Chgo., 1964-65, 79; bd. dirs. Am. Joint Distbn. Com.

Home: 4950 Chicago Beach Dr Chicago IL 60615 Office: 223 W Jackson Blvd Chicago IL 60606

SCHREEN, ROBERT RAY, food co. exec.; b. Ft. Wayne, Ind., Dec. 1, 1945; s. Herbert Lee and Mary Ellen S.; student Ind. U., 1970-72; m. Jacqueline Sue Stickney, Mar. 1, 1980. With Accountronics Systems Inc., Ft. Wayne, 1969-77, H.K. Porter Co., Inc., Huntington, Ind., 1977-78; supr. data processing ops. Mohawk Tools Inc., Montpelier, Ohio, 1978-81; cost system exec. Weaver Popcorn Co., Van Buren, Ind., 1981—. Served with U.S. Army, 1966-69. Home: 1719 Mayflower Rd Fort Wayne IN 46813 Office: 911 Main St Montpelier OH 43506

SCHREIBER, HELMUT, surgeon; b. Novi-Sad, Yugoslavia, Aug. 6, 1942; came to U.S., 1956, naturalized, 1967; s. Julius and Kathy (Bechtler) S.; B.A., Kent State U., 1966; M.D., Ohio State U., 1970; m. Helen Kusznir, Aug. 17, 1967; children—Katrina, Ingrid, Richard. Surg. intern Case Western Res. Med. Sch., 1970-71, resident, 1971-75, instr., 1975, sr. instr., 1976, asst. prof. surgery, 1975—; mem. attending surg. staff Cleve. Met. Gen. Hosp., Univ. Hosp. Cleve., 1978—; dir. surgery Huron Rd. Hosp., Cleve., 1981—. Diplomate Am. Bd. Surgery. Fellow A.C.S.; mem. Assn. Acad. Surgery, Am. Fedn. Clin. Research, Am. Soc. Gastrointestinal Endoscopy, Ohio State Med. Assn., Am. Coll. Gastroenterology, Am. Gastroent. Assn., Cleve. Surg. Soc., Eastern Coop. Oncology Group, Internat. Soc. Lymphology, Alpha Omega Alpha. Lutheran. Home: 2947 Torrington Rd Shaker Heights OH 44122 Office: 13951 Terrace Rd Cleveland OH 44112

SCHREIBER, JOAN EMELIA, educator; b. La Porte City, Iowa, Feb. 24, 1928; d. Louie and Dorathea Magdalena (Lange) Schreiber; student U. Iowa, 1945-46; B.A., Iowa State Tchrs. Coll., 1949; M.A., State Coll. Iowa, 1960; Specialist in Edn., U. No. Iowa, 1963; Ph.D., U. Iowa, 1967. Tchr. Cedar Rapids (Iowa) public schs., 1949-59; ednl. cons. Cass County, Atlantic, Iowa, 1961-63; asst. prof. Edn. Augustana Coll., Rock Island, Ill., 1963-65; asst. prof. history Ball State U., Muncie, Ind., 1966-69, asso. prof., 1969-74, prof., 1974—, coordinator social studies methods, 1968—, pres. univ. senate, 1979-80; social studies program developer for Scott, Foresman. Mem. Ind. State Social Studies Adv. Com., 1974—, Ind. State Tchr. Edn. Adv. Council, 1974-75. Mem. Nat., Ind. (pres. 1974-75) councils social studies, AAUP, Ind. Acad. Social Scis., AAUW, Del. County (Ind.) Hist. Soc., Pi Lambda Theta, Pi Gamma Mu, Phi Delta Kappa. Author: (with Lloyd L. Smith) Social Studies K-6: A Guide for Curriculum Revision, 1971; also social studies textbook for kindergarten, grades 1 and 2. Contbr. articles to profl. jours. Home: 30 Eucalyptus Dr Route 12 Muncie IN 47302 Office: E Quadrangle 308D Ball State U Muncie IN 47306

SCHREIBER, ROBERT JOHN, JR., state govt. ofcl.; b. Granite City, Ill., Nov. 10, 1950; s. Robert John and Muriel H. Schreiber; B.S. in Chem. Engring., U. Mo., Columbia, 1972; m. Patricia A. Raymond, May 12, 1973. Environ. engr. Ill. Environ. Protection Agy., 1972-74; with Mo. Dept. Natural Resources, 1974—, dir. div. environ. quality, 1980—; instr. U. Mo., Columbia, 1979. EPA fellow, 1977—; registered profl. engr., Mo. Mem. Air Pollution Control Assn., State and Terr. Air Pollution Program Adminstrs., Am. Water Works Assn., Conf. State San. Engrs. Author papers in field. Office: PO Box 1368 2010 Missouri Blvd Jefferson City MO 65102

SCHREIER, JOHN FRANK, labor exec.; b. Cleve., Oct. 24, 1905; s. Frank Michael and Katherine (Bauman) S.; student Chgo. Tech. Coll., 1924; Spencerian Bus. Coll., 1926; m. Elizabeth Ethel May, May 27, 1933; children—Jeanne (Mrs. Kelly Heffner, Jr.) and Joyce (Mrs. Kenneth Roberts)(twins), John Frank. Sec., Arch Metal Workers AFL, 1933-37; AFL staff rep. Ohio-Ill.-Ind.-Iowa-N.Y., 1936-53, area dir., Buffalo, 1946-53, dir. Mich., 1953-56; asst. nat. dir. AFL-CIO North Central States, 1956-66, dir. Mich., 1966-67, dir. Region XI Mich.-Wis., 1968-74, asst. dir. Region I, Mich.-Ind.-Ill.-Iowa-Wis.-Minn., 1974-77; v.p. labor prodns. Video One, Inc., 1977—. Chmn., AFL Optical Council, 1944-50; mem. exec. bd. Mich. Council AFL-CIO; mem. labor adv. com. Inst. Labor and Indsl. Relations, Wayne State U. and U. Mich. Vice pres. Labors Internat. Found. and Hall of Fame; mem. bd. N.Y. State, Ams. for Democratic Action, 1948-53; trustee Cleve. Metal Trades Council (AFL); mem. exec. bd. Labor's Com. to Combat Intolerance Buffalo. Mem. Assn. Registered Pharmacists (past local bus. mgr.). Home: 10770 Blaine Rd Brighton MI 48116

SCHREIER, LEONARD, allergist, immunologist; b. Detroit, June 3, 1934; s. Alexander and Fanny (Wayne) S.; M.D., U. Mich., 1959, M.S. in Internal Medicine, 1965; m. Barbara Gay Hirsch, Aug. 11, 1956 (div. 1980); children—Eric Marvin, Jordan Scott, Barry Andrew. Intern, Sinai Hosp., Detroit, 1959-60, resident in internal medicine, 1960-63; fellow in allergy and immunology U. Mich., 1963-65; practice medicine specializing in allergy and immunology, Detroit, 1965-66, Pontiac, Mich., 1968—; staff St. Joseph Mercy Hosp., Pontiac, acting chmn. dept. medicine, 1980-81; asst. clin. prof. medicine Wayne State Coll. Medicine, 1976—. Served with M.C., U.S. Army, 1966-68. Diplomate Am. Bd. Internal Medicine, Am. Bd. Allergy and Immunology. Fellow Am. Acad. Allergy. Jewish. Contbr. articles to med. jours. Office: 909 S Woodward Ave Suite 16 Pontiac MI 48053

SCHREINER, DAVID ALLAN, planning agy. exec.; b. Wayne, Nebr., Dec. 7, 1943; s. Raymond Allan and Mildred Ila (Vaughn) S.; B.S.C.E., U. Nebr., 1966; postgrad. Kans. State U.; m. Linda Lee Muff, July 6, 1968; children—Jeffrey, Andrew. Engr., Kans. Hwy. Commn., Topeka, 1966-70, 72-74; instr. Kans. State U., 1970-72; dir. trans. planning, asst. exec. dir. Omaha-Council Bluffs Met. Area Planning Agy., Omaha, 1974-75, exec. dir., 1975—. Chmn. deacons Dundee Presbyterian Ch., 1979. Mem. ASCE, Am. Planning Assn., Nat. Soc. Profl. Engrs., Omaha Engrs. Club. Club: Optimists (dir. 1976). Office: 7000 W Center Rd Omaha NE 68106

SCHRENK, LORENZ PHILIP, human resource planner; b. Utica, N.Y., Feb. 8, 1932; s. Matthew Henry and Katheryn Charlotte (Hess) S.; B.A., George Washington U., 1954; M.A., Ohio State U., 1962, Ph.D., 1964; m. Ann Reed Sweeney, Apr. 28, 1956; children—Janet, Stephen, Lisa. Mgr. life scis. research Honeywell Systems and Research Center, Mpls., 1967-77, mgr. tng. systems programs, 1977-80, mgr. human resources planning Honeywell, Inc., Mpls., 1980—; cons. human factors NATO, 1974; cons. Naval Research Adv. Com., 1979—. Served with USNR, 1954-56. Mem. Nat. Security Indsl. Assn. (chmn. tng. systems sub-com. 1979—), Am. Psychol. Assn., Human Factors Soc., U.S. Naval Inst., Human Resource Planning Soc. Office: Honeywell Plaza MN 12-3174 Minneapolis MN 55408

SCHRIER, ARNOLD, historian, educator; b. Bronx, N.Y., May 30, 1925; s. Samuel and Yetta (Levine) S.; student Bethany Coll., 1943-44, Ohio Wesleyan U., 1944-45; B.S., Northwestern U., 1949, M.A., 1950, Ph.D. (Social Sci. Research Council fellow), 1956; postgrad. (Learned Socs. Fgn. Area fellow), Ind. U., 1963-64; m. Sondra Weinshelbaum, June 12, 1949; children—Susan Lynn, Jay Alan, Linda Lee, Paula Kay. Asst. prof. history U. Cin., 1956-61, asso. prof., 1961-66, prof., 1966, dir. grad. studies in history, 1969-78, Walter C. Langsam prof. modern history, 1972—; vis. asst. prof. history Northwestern U., summer 1960; vis. lectr. in Russian history Duke U., summer 1966; vis. asso. prof. history Ind. U., 1965-66; dir. NDEA Inst. in World History for Secondary Tchrs., 1965. Served with USNR, 1943-46, to lt. USNR, 1952-54. Taft Faculty grantee, 1964, 67, 70. Mem. Am. Hist. Assn., Am. Assn. Advancement Slavic Studies, AAUP (pres. U. Cin. chpt. 1970-71), Midwest Slavic Conf. (pres. 1980), So. Slavic Conf., Ohio Acad. History (pres. 1973-74), Immigration History Soc., Soc. Hist. Edn., Nat. Council Social Studies, Phi Alpha Theta. Jewish. Author: Ireland and the American Emigration, 1958, 2d edit., 1970; The Development of Civilization, 2 vols., 1962, rev. edit., 1969; Modern European Civilization, 1963; Living World History, 1964, rev. edit., 1982; Twentieth Century World, 1974; History and Life: The World and Its People, 1977, rev. edit., 1982; A Russian Looks at America, 1979. Home: 9155 Peachblossom Ct Cincinnati OH 45231 Office: History Dept Univ of Cincinnati Cincinnati OH 45221

SCHRIEVER, PAUL GRADY, county ofcl.; b. Lowell, Mass., Nov. 13, 1936; s. Louis Edwin and Helen Ivers (Grady) S.; student Northwestern U., 1954-56; B.A., U. Tex., 1958, M.A., 1961; m. Patricia Alice Kraeplin, Apr. 27, 1963; children—Christopher Arnold, Catherina Marie. Adminstrv. asst. City of San Antonio, 1960-62; staff asst. Internat. City Mgmt. Assn., Chgo., 1962-64; asst. county mgr. Forsyth County, N.C., Winston-Salem, 1964-66; city mgr. Moberly, Mo., 1966-69, Texarkana, Ark., 1969-72, Winona, Minn., 1972-74; village adminstr. Bensenville, Ill., 1974-79; county adminstr. County of Winnebago, Rockford, Ill., 1980—. Served to 1st lt. USAR, 1958-66. Mem. Nat. Assn. County Adminstrs., Ill. City Mgmt. Assn. Internat. City Mgmt. Assn., Met. City Mgrs. Assn., Nat. Mcpl. League. Episcopalian. Author space utilization studies for two cities and counties. Home: 4313 Easton Dr Rockford IL 61111 Office: Courthouse 400 W State St Suite 806 Rockford IL 61101

SCHROEDER, ALFRED GUSTAV, justice Kans. Supreme Ct.; b. Newton, Kans., June 5, 1916; s. Gustav D. and Grete (Janzen) S.; student Bethel Coll., Newton, 1933-35; B.S. with high honors, Kans. State Coll., 1937; LL.B., Harvard U., 1940; m. Katheryn Marie Diel, Aug. 8, 1942; children—John Scott, Hedy Marie, Marilyn Sue. Admitted to Kans. bar, 1940; individual practice law, Newton, 1940-42, also farm mgr.; judge Probate and County Ct., Harvey County, Kans., 1947-53, 9th Jud. Dist. Ct. Kans., 1953-57; justice Kans. Supreme Ct., 1957—, chief justice, 1977—; chmn. Kans. Jud. Council, 1963-79. Bd. dirs. Kans. Council Chs., 1962-66; mem. Freedoms award Jury Freedoms Found., 1959, 68; mem. So. Assn. Conglist Chs. Kans., moderator 1956. Served to capt. USAAF, 1942-46. Mem. Am., Kans. bar assns., Phi Kappa Phi, Alpha Zeta. Republican. Home: 825 Buchanan St Topeka KS 66606 Office: State House Topeka KS 66612

SCHROEDER, CHARLES EDGAR, business exec.; b. Chgo., Nov. 17, 1935; s. William Edward and Lelia Lorraine (Anderson) S.; B.A. in Econs., Dartmouth Coll., 1957; M.B.A., Amos Tuck Coll., 1958; m. Martha Elizabeth Runnette, Dec. 30, 1958; children—Charles Edgar, Timothy Creighton, Elizabeth Linton. Security analyst Miami Corp., Chgo., 1960, treas., 1969-77, dir., 1969—, pres., 1978—; security analyst Cutler Oil & Gas Corp., Chgo., 1960, treas., 1969-77, dir., 1969—, pres., 1978—; dir. Nat. Blvd. Bank of Chgo., 1969, chmn. bd., dir., 1981—; dir. Nat. Standard Co., Niles, Mich. Asso., Northwestern U., Evanston, Ill., 1975—; trustee 1st Presbyn. Ch., Evanston, 1968—. Served with to lt. (j.g.) USN, 1958-60. Mem. Fin. Analysts Soc. Chgo., Casque and Gauntlet, Beta Theta Pi. Clubs: Chicago, Glen View, Mid-Am., Mich. Shores. Office: 410 N Michigan Ave Chicago IL 60611

SCHROEDER, DAVID J. DEAN, psychologist; b. Hutchinson, Kans., Mar. 21, 1942; s. David John and Louise (Wedel) S.; B.A., Tabor Coll., 1964; M.S., Kans. State Tchrs. Coll. of Emporia, 1967; Ph.D., U. Okla., 1971; m. Nevonna Joyce Thomas, May 24, 1964; children—Taryn Dee, Anita Joy. Psychology technician Civil Aeromed. Inst. FAA, Oklahoma City, 1967-70, research psychologist, 1970-72; postdoctoral clin. psychology intern Norfolk (Nebr.) Regional Center and NE Mental Health Clinic, 1972-73; clin. psychologist VA Hosp., Murfreesboro, Tenn., 1973-75; clin. psychologist VA Med. Center, Topeka, 1975-80, chmn. research com., 1979-80; chief clin. psychology research unit Aviation Psychology Lab., FAA, Oklahoma City, 1980—; adj. asst. prof. psychology Middle Tenn. State U., 1974-75, Washburn U., 1975—. Co-chmn. steering com. Madison County (Nebr.) Alcohol Safety Action Project, Norfolk, 1973. Recipient Outstanding Performance award FAA, 1972. Asso. fellow Aerospace Med. Assn. (mem. membership and registration coms.); mem. Southwestern, Midwestern psychol. assns., Am. Psychol. Assn., Psychonomic Soc., Assn. Aviation Psychology, Topeka Tennis Assn. (bd. govs. 1979), Sigma Xi. Contbr. articles to profl. jours. Home: 13731 Woodthrush Choctau OK 73020 Office: Aero Center PO Box 25082 Oklahoma City OK 73020

SCHROEDER, GARY KEITH, furniture co. exec.; b. Rileyville, Pa., Aug. 1, 1935; s. George Herbert and Florence (Kilgallen) S.; B.S., Susquehanna U., 1957; m. Analee Clendenin Cisco, July 3, 1969; children from previous marriage—George Scott, Leslie Ann; stepchildren—Kim and Zachary Cisco. Buyer, Joseph Horne Co., Pitts., 1957-62; v.p. sales, dir. Canterbury House, Inc., Peru, Ind., 1962-64; dir. new product planning and marketing La-Z-Boy Chair Co., Monroe, Mich., 1964-68, v.p. sales, 1968-72, exec. v.p. sales and marketing, 1972-77, also dir., v.p. sales Kroehler Mfg. Co., Naperville, Ill., 1977—. Bd. dirs. Brand Names Found., 1972—, YMCA, Monroe; bd. dirs. Father's Day Council, Inc., N.Y.C., 1968—, v.p., 1971—. Mem. Nat. Assn. Furniture Mfrs. (dir. 1970—, pres. 1975—), Home Furnishings Council (exec. com. 1973—), Theta Chi. Lutheran. Home: 21 W 361 Crescent Glen Ellyn IL 60137 Office: Kroehler Mfg Co 222 E 5th St Naperville IL 60540

SCHROEDER, LEONARD WILLIAM, chiropractor; b. Oak Park, Ill., June 10, 1921; s. Paul C. and Anna (Berndt) S.; student Valparaiso U., 1952-53; Dr. Chiropractic, Nat. Coll. Chiropractic, 1948; m. Elaine Klank, Nov. 19, 1960. Asst. instr. X-ray, Nat. Coll. Chiropractic, Chgo., 1962-75, asso. prof. dept. clin. scis., 1962—; resident dr. Chgo. Gen. Health Service, 1948-49; physician Nat. Roller Derby, 1950-52, dept. phys. medicine Hines (Ill.) VA Hosp., 1952-55; team physician Luther High Sch. N., Chgo., 1953—; asst. trainer Chgo. Cardinal Football Club, 1958-60; pvt. practice chiropractic medicine, Oak Park, Ill., 1961—. Served with M.C. AUS, 1941-46. Fellow Internat. Chiropractic Coll.; mem. Ill. Chiropractic Soc. (dir. 1963-70, chmn. bd. 1965-70), Council on Sport Injuries (pres. 1972—), Am. Chiropractic Assn., Am. Coll. Sports Medicine, Chi Rho Sigma, Delta Tau Alpha. Lutheran (sec. ch. 1947-48, v.p. ch. 1949-50, mem. bd. edn., 1963-65, deacon 1977, bd. dirs. No. Ill. Dist., Mo. Synod 1980—, pres. St. Paul's Luth. Ch.). Contbr. articles to profl. jours. Home and office: 6601 W North Ave Oak Park IL 60302

SCHROEDER, LEROY JOHN, pharm. co. exec.; b. Hooper, Nebr., Nov. 13, 1928; s. John A. and Alma M. (Osterloh) S.; A.B., Midland Coll., Fremont, Nebr., 1945-48, U. Nebr., 1947; m. Betty L. Christiansen, Aug. 8, 1948; children—Steven, Marcia, Kent, Mary. Tchr., Fullerton (Nebr.) Public Sch., 1949; sales rep. Armour Labs., 1953; with Dorsey Labs., Lincoln, Nebr., 1960—, gen. sales mgr., 1972, v.p., gen. mgr., 1974—; pres. Wander Found. Med. Research, 1974; dir. 1st Nat. Bank, Lincoln, Lincoln Mut. Life Ins. Co. Trustee, Bryan Meml. Hosp., Lincoln; bd. govs. Wesleyan U., Lincoln; past chmn. Lincoln-Lancaster County Savs. Bond Drive, Lancaster County Cancer Soc.; past bd. dirs. Lincoln C. of C. Recipient Disting. Service award U. Nebr. Coll. Pharmacy, 1978. Mem. Pharm. Mfrs. Assn., Am. Mgmt. Assn., An. Legion. Lutheran. Clubs: Univ., Nebr., Lincoln Country, Shriners. Author articles in field. Home: 3541 Calvert St Lincoln NE 68506 Office: Dorsey Labs US 6 and Interstate 80 Lincoln NE 68501

SCHROEDER, RAYMOND ERNEST, educator; b. South Bend, Ind., Dec. 8, 1949; s. Marvin Klopsch and Jean Edna (Hirsch) S.; A.B., Augustana Coll., 1970; M.S., U. Ill., 1972; m. Gail Arnsdorf, Mar. 5, 1977; 1 dau., Geneva Marie. News dir. WVIK-FM, Rock Island, Ill., 1968, program dir., 1969, gen. mgr., 1970; news photographer WAND-TV, Decatur, Ill., part time 1974-77; reporter, producer WILL-AM-FM, Urbana, Ill., part time 1971-75; instr. radio-TV, U. Ill., Urbana, 1971-77; asst. prof. communication Sangamon State U., Springfield, Ill., 1977—; producer video documentary Season of the Sangamon, 1981; dir. Illini Pub. Co., 1976-77. Mem. Urbana City Human Relations Commn., 1976-77. Mem. Ill. News Broadcasters Assn. (dir.), Soc. Profl. Journalists, Broadcast Edn. Assn., Radio-TV News Dirs. Assn., Alpha Epsilon Rho (faculty adv., profl. mem.). Editor newsletter Ill. News Broadcasters Assn., 1974—. Home: PO Box 937 Riverton IL 62561 Office: Dept Communication Sangamon State Univ Springfield IL 62708

SCHROEDER, ROBERT ANTHONY, lawyer; b. Bendena, Kans., May 19, 1912; s. Anthony and Nanon (Bagby) S.; LL.B. cum laude, U. Kans., 1937; m. Janet Manning, Nov. 21, 1936; 1 son, Robert Breathitt. Admitted to Mo. bar 1937; atty. Allstate Ins. Co., Chgo., 1937-38; asso. firm Madden, Freeman, Madden & Burke, Kansas City, Mo., 1938-48; partner firm Swofford, Schroeder & Shankland, Kansas City, 1948-59; owner law offices Robert A. Schroeder, 1959-67; partner firm Schroeder & Schroeder, 1967—; chmn. 16th Circuit Bar Com., 1972-80; commr. 16th Jud. Selection Com., 1974-80; commr. Appellate Jud. Selection Com. of Mo., 1980—; v.p. Roxbury State Bank (Kans.), 1954-72, pres., 1972-77, chmn. bd., 1977—, also dir.; pres., dir. Douglas County Investment Co.; chmn. bd., dir. Hub State Bank, Independence, Mo. Vice pres. Mo. Found., 1965-70; pres. Mo. Bar Found., 1970-73; trustee Kans. U. Law Sch. Soc.; hon. trustee Kansas City Art Inst. Fellow Am. Bar Found., Am. Coll. Probate Counsel, Kans. U. Law Soc., Harry S. Truman Library Inst. (hon.); mem. Nat. Legal Aid, Defenders Soc., Mo. Bar (co-chmn. continuing legal edn. com. 1958-59, chmn. fin. planning subcom. 1958-59, gov. 1959-67, chmn. public edn. com. 1965-66, pres. 1965-66, chmn. cts. and jud. com. 1971-72, Pres.'s award 1972), Am. (state chmn. standing com. on membership 1961-62, mem. lawyer referral com. 1966-70, Ho. of Dels. 1967-71, vice chmn. Mo. bench and bar com. 1968-71, mem. bench and bar com. 1971—), Kans. (hon. life), Kansas City (pres. 1957-58, chmn. exec. com. 1957-58, judicial recommendations com. 1957-58, 69-70, public relations com. 1958-60, medico-legal com. 1962-64, law day com. 1964-65, lawyer welfare and placement com. 1966-72, program com. 1969-70, pre-paid legal services 1975-77, Achievement award 1976) bar assns., Am. Judicature Soc. (dir. 1967-69), Greater Kansas City Kans. U. Law Sch. Alumni Assn. (pres. 1963-64), Delta Tau Delta, Phi Delta Phi (pres. 1936-37), Order of Coif. Clubs: Executives, Chancellor's (U. Kans.); Masons. Author: Twenty-Five Years Under the Missouri Plan; Twenty-Five Years Experience with Merit Judicial Selection in Missouri. Asso. editor Kans. Law Jour., 1935-37. Office: Lathrop Bldg Kansas City MO 64106

SCHROEDER, WILLIAM CHRISTOPHER MARTIN, ret. auto supply co. exec.; b. Chgo., Jan. 8, 1897; s. John Adolph and Corena Fredericka (Hildebrandt) S.; B.S., U. Ill., 1923; LL.B., Chgo. Law Sch., 1929; m. Olga Elizabeth Leutnegger, June 6, 1938. Accountant, Ill. Bell Telephone Co., Chgo., 1923-29, Duttine & Young, 1929-30; asso. firm Norcross & Norcross, Chgo., 1930-31; asst. comptroller Allied Motors Corp., Chgo., 1931-32; salesman central, western states B.F. Goodrich Co., Akron, Ohio, 1932-57; owner, operator Schroeder Supply Co., Galesburg, Ill., from 1958, now ret. Finance adviser Muscatine (Iowa) Luth. Homes, 1971—, bd. dirs., exec. bd., 1975—. Recipient Nat. Republican Congressional award, 1978. Mem. Sierra Club, Audubon Soc., Internat. Platform Assn., Alpha Kappa Psi, Phi Alpha Delta, Tau Kappa Epsilon. Republican. Lutheran. Clubs: Cosmopolitan, Internat. Cultures, Masons, Shriners, K.T. Home and office: 256 Phillips St Galesburg IL 61401

SCHROEDER, WILLIAM ROBERT, county govt. ofcl.; b. Chgo., May 7, 1945; s. William August and Anna Marie (Aufmuth) S.; B.S., Loyola U., Chgo., 1967; student John Marshall Law Sch., Chgo., 1967-69; m. Margaret Mary Bray, June 22, 1968; children—William Robert, Jennifer Anne. With firm Peterson, Bogucki and Beck, Chgo., 1967-69, Commerce Clearing House, Chgo., 1969-71; with Cook County (Ill.) Bur. Adminstrn., 1971—, tng. dir. dept. personnel, 1976—; mem. adv. council masters program in adminstrv. sci./public agy. adminstrn. program U. Ill., Chgo., 1980—. Bd. dirs. Leaning Tower YMCA, 1975—, vice chmn., 1978-81, chmn., 1981—; chmn. fund raising St. Constance Roman Cath. Ch., Chgo., 1977-78; coach Norwood Park Boys Baseball, 1979—; bd. dirs. 45th Ward Regular Democratic Orgn., 1968—. Recipient various service certs. Mem. Intergovtl. Tng. Assn. Chgo. (v.p. 1978), Am. Soc. Public Adminstrn. (sec. Chgo. chpt. 1980-81, pres. 1981), Ill. Correctional Assn. (dir. 1979-80; cert. commendation 1981), Am. Soc. Tng. and Devel., Gentlemen Sportsmen Striders, Polish Nat. Alliance (dir. Chgo. chpt. 1980-81), Chgo. Soc. Club: Moose. Office: 118 N Clark St Room 834 Chicago IL 60602

SCHROER, EDMUND ARMIN, utility co. exec.; b. Hammond, Ind. Feb. 14, 1928; s. Edmund Henry and Florence Evelyn (Schmidt) S.; B.A., Valparaiso U., 1949; J.D., Northwestern U., 1952; children—James, Fredrik, Amy, Lisa, Timothy, Suzanne. Admitted to Ind. bar, 1952; practiced in Hammond, Ind., 1952-77; asso. Crumpacker & Friedrich, 1952; partner Crumpacker & Schroer, 1954-56; asso., then partner Friedrich, Petrie & Tweedle, 1957-62; partner Schroer & Eichhorn, 1963-66; partner Schroer, Eichhorn & Morrow, Hammond, 1967-77; gen. counsel No. Ind. Public Service Co., 1967-77, pres., chief exec. officer, chmn., 1977—; asst. dist. atty. No. Ind., 1954-56. Sch. bd. trustee, Munster, Ind., 1969-71, pres., 1971; Republican finance chmn., Hammond, 1958-62; del. to Ind. Rep. Conv., 1958, 60, 64, 66, 68. Mem. Am., Fed., Fed. Power, Ind. (bd. mgrs. 1969-71), Hammond (pres. 1966-67) bar assns., Am. Judicature Soc. Lutheran. Rotarian (pres. Hammond chpt. 1968). Office: 5265 Hohman Ave Hammond IN 46320

SCHROTT, JANET ANN, social worker; b. Cleve., Dec. 11, 1941; d. Louis Vincent and Amelia Jane (Lauko) Cupolo; B.A., Flora Stone Mather Coll. of Case Western Res. U., 1963, M.S. in Social Adminstrn., 1974; m. Norman Schrott, July 25, 1964. Research asst. Aging Baseline Study, HEW Grant, Miami, Fla., 1964-65; caseworker Div. Social Services, Cuyahoga County Welfare Dept., Cleve., 1965-72, protective services supr., 1974-78; dir. social services Luth. Housing Corp., Cleve., 1973-74; dir. travelers aid services Center for Human Services, Cleve., 1978—. Bd. Dirs. adv. council Adult Rehab.

Services, Salvation Army, 1978—. Cuyahoga County Welfare Dept. grantee, 1972-74. Mem. Acad. Cert. Social Workers, Nat. Assn. Social Workers, Am. Humane Soc., Brookings Inst., Nat. Geographic Soc., Theta Phi Omega. Home: 25925 Lake Rd Bay Village OH 44140 Office: 1005 Huron Rd Cleveland OH 44115

SCHROTT, NORMAN, social worker; b. N.Y.C., Jan. 26, 1938; s. Walter Quido Otto and Anna (Klein) S.; B.A. in Sociology, Cleve. State U., 1972; M.S. in Social Planning and Adminstrn. (grantee State of Ohio 1974-76), Case Western Res. U., 1976; m. Janet Ann Cupolo, July 25, 1964. Adminstrv. specialist div. social services Cuyahoga County Welfare Dept., Cleve., 1972-74, foster care specialist, 1976-79, child abuse supr., 1979—. Served with U.S. Army, 1962-65. Mem. Acad. Cert. Social Workers, Nat. Assn. Social Workers, Nat. Conf. Social Welfare, Am. Public Welfare Assn., Am. Acad. Polit. and Social Scis., Nat. Audubon Soc., Am. Orchid Soc. Home: 25925 Lake Rd Bay Village OH 44140 Office: 2925 Euclid Ave Cleveland OH 44115

SCHROY, JERRY MICHAEL, chem. engr.; b. Dayton, Ohio, Nov. 6, 1939; s. Lloyd Felton and Georgia (Kostoff) S.; Ch.E., U. Cin., 1963; postgrad. Bklyn. Poly. Inst., 1970-71, Washington U., St. Louis, 1974-75; m. Barbara Ann Meyrose, Jan. 11, 1969; children—Catherine Marie, David Michael, Mark Alan. Process engr. Monsanto Co., St. Louis, 1963-67, supr. tech. service, Columbia, Tenn., 1967-69, process engring. specialist Monsanto Biodize Systems Inc. and Monsanto Enviro-Chem System Inc., L.I. and Chgo., 1969-72, mgr. process engring. Monsanto Enviro-Chem System Inc., Chgo., 1972, process engring. specialist, St. Louis, 1973-75, engring. specialist Monsanto Co., St. Louis, 1975-76, prin. engring. specialist, 1976-80, Monsanto fellow, 1981—. Registered profl. engr., Ohio, N.Y., Ill., Iowa, Mo. Mem. Am. Inst. Chem. Engrs., Water Pollution Control Fedn., Am. Chem. Soc., AAAS, Alpha Chi Sigma. Home: 5 Springlake Ct Ballwin MO 63011 Office: Monsanto Co 800 N Lindbergh Blvd Saint Louis MO 63166

SCHUBERT, ALBERT WILLIAM GUSTAVE, ret. dentist; b. nr. Abilene, Kans., Mar. 6, 1910; s. Albert Franz Gustave and Auguste (Bentz) S.; student Kans. State Tchrs. Coll. Emporia, 1933-35; D.D.S., Kansas City (Mo.) Western Dental Coll., 1940; m. Hazel Ann Pagenkopf, Mar. 16, 1941; children—Phyllis Ann (Mrs. Dale Wayne Marsh), Albert William Gustave. Practice dentistry, Wichita, Kans., 1940-41, Herington, Kans., 1945-47, Great Bend, Kans., 1947-80, ret., 1980; chief dental services, mem. planning bd. Central Kans. Med. Center; chief dental services St. Rose Hosp. Pres., Morrison Sch. P.T.A., Great Bend, 1954. Served from 1st lt. to maj. Dental Corps, AUS, 1940-46; PTO. Recipient citation for meritorious service for rehab. Corregidor POWs and Bataan Death March at Fitzsimons Gen. Hosp., Denver, 1944-45. Fellow Am. Coll. Dentists; mem. Am., Kans. dental assns., Central Dist. Dental Soc. (pres. 1965, Honored guest 1974), Pierre Fauchard Acad., VFW, DAV, Psi Omega. Democrat. Lutheran (elder, chmn. bd. edn.). Lion. Home: 2501 Cheyenne Dr Great Bend KS 67530

SCHUBERT, ELIZABETH M(AY), paralegal adminstrv. asst.; b. Hamilton, Ohio, Sept. 10, 1913; d. A(ndreas) Gordon and Grace Symmes (Laxford) S.; B.S. in Edn. cum laude, Miami U., 1933. Sec., Beta Kappa Nat. Frat., Oxford, Ohio, 1931-38; adminstrv. asst. to dir. Ohio State Employment Service, Columbus, 1938-45, supr. procedures, 1945-47; adminstrv. asst. to pres. Schaible Co., Cin., 1948-50; paralegal adminstrv. asst. to Gordon H. Scherer, Atty.-at-Law, mem. U.S. Congress, U.S. del. to UN, U.S. rep. to exec. bd. UNESCO, Paris, 1950—. Mem. Phi Beta Kappa. Republican. Presbyn. Home: 1071 Celestial St Apt 1701 Cincinnati OH 45202 Office: 1700 Carew Tower Cincinnati OH 45202

SCHUBERT, HELEN CELIA, pub. relations cons.; b. Washington County, Wis., May 30, 1930; d. Paul H. and Edna W. (Schmidt) S.; B.S., U. Wis., Madison, 1952. Dir. publicity United Cerebral Palsy Assn., Chgo.; writer Philip Lesly Co., public relations agy., Chgo., 1958-61; dir. dept. consumer interest, dir. Nat. Design Center, Chgo., 1963-67. Fellow Nat. Home Fashions League (dir.); mem. Women in Communications (pres. Chgo. chpt. 1969-70, regional v.p. 1970-71, Disting. Service award 1972, dir.), Am. Women in Radio-TV, Publicity Club Chgo. (Disting. Service award 1966), Public Relations Soc. Am., Am. Soc. Interior Designers (public relations affiliate), Fashion Group Chgo., Women's Advt. Club Chgo. (pres. 1981-82), Art Inst. Chgo. (life). Lutheran. Clubs: U. Wis. Alumni (life), Chgo. Press. Contbr. articles to profl. jours. Home: 1400 N Lake Shore Dr Chicago IL 60610

SCHUBERT, WILLIAM HENRY, educator; b. Garrett, Ind., July 6, 1944; s. Walter William and Mary Madeline (Grube) S.; B.S., Manchester Coll., 1966; M.S., Ind. U., 1967; Ph.D., U. Ill., 1975; m. Ann Lynn Lopez, Dec. 3, 1977; children by previous marriage—Ellen Elaine, Karen Margaret. Tchr., Fairmount, El Sierra and Herrick Schs., Downers Grove, Ill., 1967-75; clin. instr. U. Wis., Madison, 1969-73; teaching asst., univ. fellow U. Ill., Urbana, 1973-75; asst. prof. U. Ill., Chgo., 1975-80, asso. prof., 1981—, coordinator secondary edn., 1979—, coordinator instructional leadership, 1979—; vis. asso. prof. U. Victoria (B.C., Can.), summer 1981. Mem. Profs. of Curriculum, Soc. for Study of Curriculum History (founding mem., sec.-treas. 1981-82, pres. 1982-83), Am. Ednl. Research Assn. (chmn. creation and utilization of curriculum knowledge 1980-82, program chmn. curriculum studies div. 1982-83), John Dewey Soc., Assn. for Supervision and Curriculum Devel. (steering com. of curriculum com. 1980-83), Am. Ednl. Studies Assn., Soc. for Profs. of Edn., Nat. Soc. for Study of Edn., Phi Delta Kappa, Phi Kappa Phi (pres. U. Ill.-Chgo. chpt. 1981-82). Clubs: Masons, Scottish Rite. Author: Curriculum Books: The First Eighty Years, 1980; contbr. articles to profl. publs. Home: 607 W Wrightwood St Chicago IL 60614 Office: Univ Ill Coll Edn Box 4348 Chicago IL 60680

SCHUBERT, WILLIAM KUENNETH, pediatrician; b. Cin., July 12, 1926; s. Wilfred S.; B.S., U. Cin., 1949, M.D., 1952; m. Mary Jane; children—Carol, Joanne, Barbara, Nancy. Intern, Ind. U. Med. Center, 1952-53; resident in pediatrics Children's Hosp. Med. Center, Cin., 1953-55. USPHS research fellow div. hematology, 1955-56, now mem. staff, physician exec. dir.; practice medicine specializing in pediatrics, Cin., 1956-63; mem. faculty U. Cin. Med. Sch., now prof. pediatrics, chmn. dept.; attending pediatrician Cin. Gen. Hosp.; cons. Christ, Good Samaritan hosps. Served with USNR, 1944-46. Diplomate Am. Bd. Pediatrics. Fellow Am. Acad. Pediatrics; mem. Soc. Pediatric Research, Am. Fedn. Clin. Research (councilor Midwestern sect. 1963-66), Electron Microscope Soc. Am., Am. Pediatric Soc., Am. Assn. Study Liver Diseases, Am. Gastroent. Assn., Assn. Med. Sch. Pediatric Dept. Chairmen, Internat. Assn. Study Liver Disease, AMA, Nat. Reye's Syndrome Found. (med. dir.), Midwestern Soc. Pediatric Research, Central Soc. Clin. Research, Cin. Acad. Medicine, Phi Beta Kappa, Alpha Omega Alpha. Author numerous papers in field. Office: Children's Hosp Med Center Elland and Bethesda Aves Cincinnati OH 45220*

SCHUCHART, JOHN ALBERT, JR., utility co. exec.; b. Omaha, Nov. 13, 1929; s. John A. and Mildred Vera (Kessler) S.; B.S. in Bus., U. Nebr., 1950; grad. Stanford U. Exec. Program, 1968; m. Ruth Joyce Schock, Dec. 2, 1950; children—Deborah J. Kelley, Susan K. Felton. With No. Natural Gas Co., Omaha, 1950-71, asst. sec., 1957-60, mgr. accounting, 1960-65, adminstrv. mgr., 1965-71; v.p., treas. Intermountain Gas Co., Boise, Idaho, 1972-75, chief fin. officer, 1973-75; fin. v.p. and treas., chief fin. officer Montana-Dakota Utilities Co., Bismarck, N.D., 1976-77, pres. and chief operating officer, 1978-80, pres., chief exec. officer, 1980—, also dir.; dir. 1st Bank, Bismarck. Mem. budget com. of United Way, Omaha, 1969-70; bd. dirs. Girl Scouts U.S., Boise, 1975; trustee Bismarck YMCA, 1980. Served with U.S. Army, 1951-53. Recipient Scroll and Merit award Adminstrv. Mgmt. Soc., 1972. Mem. Am. (Merit award 1968), Midwest gas assns., Edison Electric Inst., N. Central Electric Assn., Fin. Execs. Inst., Delta Sigma Pi. Republican. Methodist. Clubs: Elks, Apple Creek Country. Contbr. articles on accounting to profl. jours. Home: 1014 Cottage Dr Bismarck ND 58501 Office: 400 N 4th St Bismarck ND 58501

SCHUENKE, DONALD JOHN, ins. co. exec.; b. Milw., Jan. 12, 1929; s. Ray H. and Josephine P. (Maciolek) S.; Ph.B., Marquette U., 1950, LL.B., 1958; m. Joyce A. Wetzel, July 19, 1952; children—Ann, Mary. Admitted to Wis. bar, 1958; spl. agt. Nat. Life of Vt., 1958-59; real estate rep. Standard Oil Co. of Ind., Milw., 1959-63; asst. gen. counsel Northwestern Mut. Life Ins. Co., Milw., 1963-65, v.p., gen. counsel, sec., 1974-76, sr. v.p. investments, 1976-80, pres., 1980—; chmn., trustee Northwestern Mut. Life Mortgage and Realty Investors. Bd. dirs. Milw. Symphony Orch., Milw. Art Mus., Curative Workshop, Greater Milw. Com., U. Wis. Milw. Found., Wis. Taxpayers Alliance; mem. adv. council Am. Heart Assn.; mem. pres.'s adv. council Cardinal Stritch Coll.; mem. Milw. Area Task Force, St. Norbert Coll.; mem. adv. bd. YWCA Milw. Mem. Wis. Bar Assn., Am. Council Life Ins. Office: 720 E Wisconsin Ave Milwaukee WI 53202

SCHUERMAN, JOHN RICHARD, educator; b. Scotts Bluff, Nebr., Feb. 27, 1938; s. Lawrence and Mildred Jeanette (France) S.; B.S., U. Chgo., 1960, M.A., 1963, Ph.D., 1970; m. Charlotte Kavaloski, Sept. 12, 1964; children—Gabrielle Ann, Matthew Lawrence. Social worker Ill. Dept. Mental Health, Chgo., 1963-65; faculty sch. social service adminstrn. U. Chgo., 1968—, prof., 1978—, asso. dean, 1970-79; cons. various Chgo. social agencies on research design. Mem. Ill. Mental Health Planning Bd., 1971-73. Mem. Nat. Assn. Social Workers, Council on Social Work Edn. Condr. research on psychiat. rehab.; contbr. papers in field to profl. publs. Home: 1229 E 50th St Chicago IL 60615 Office: 969 E 60th St Chicago IL 60637

SCHUETZE, ARMIN WILLIAM, clergyman, sem. pres.; b. Litchfield, Minn., Apr. 25, 1917; s. Martin and Wilhelmina (Albrecht) S.; student Martin Luther Acad., New Ulm, Minn., 1930-33; B.A., Northwestern Coll., Watertown, Wis., 1933-37; grad. Wis. Luth. Sem., Mequon, 1937-40; M.A., Marquette U., 1969; m. Esther Lucille Waidelich, Sept. 20, 1941; children—Virginia Weiderhold, Beth Gabb, Barbara Otto, Frederick, Kristine Learman, Katherine Lotito, John. Ordained to ministry Evang. Lutheran Synod, 1941; instr. Mich. Luth. Sem., Saginaw, 1940-41; pastor St. Paul's Ch., Timber Lake, S.D. and Peace Ch., Isabel, S.D., 1941-43, Calvary Luth. Ch., Thiensville, Wis., 1943-48; prof. Northwestern Luth. Acad., Mobridge, S.D., 1948-56; pastor Divine Peace Luth. Ch., Milw., 1956-58; pres. Wis. Luth. Sem., Mequon, 1978—, prof., 1958-78. Author: Family Life under Christ, 1971; Guidance from God's Word, 1967; Shepherd under Christ, 1974; Basic Doctrines of the Bible, 1969. Home: 11844 N Luther Ln Mequon WI 53092 Office: 11831 N Seminary Dr Mequon WI 53092

SCHUH, JANICE SUE, mfg. co. mgr.; b. Marysville, Kans., Dec. 14, 1942; d. Fredrick J.W. and Violet Clara (Yaussi) Millenbruch; B.S., Kans. State U., 1966; m. Dec. 31, 1970; 1 son, Jeffrey Scott. Reporter, Racine (Wis.) Jour. Times, 1966-68; asst. women's editor Pioneer Publs., Wilmette, Ill., 1968-69; food reporter Chgo. Daily News, 1969; editorial home economist Kitchens of Sara Lee, Deerfield, Ill., 1969-70; supr. public relations Ekco Products Inc., Wheeling, Ill., 1971-81, mgr. advt., sales promotion, public relations and design, mgr. mktg. communications, 1981—. Mem. Chgo. Advt. Club, Women in Mgmt. Club, Internat. Orgn. Women Execs., Women's Advt. Assn. Methodist. Home: 1013 Duxbury St Schaumburg IL 60193 Office: 777 Wheeling Rd Wheeling IL 60090

SCHUL, BILL DEAN, psychol. adminstr., author; b. Winfield, Kans., Mar. 16, 1928; s. Fred M. and Martha Mildred (Miles) S.; B.A., Southwestern Coll., 1952; M.A., U. Denver, 1954; Ph.D., Am. Internat. U., 1977; m. Virginia Louise Duboise, Aug. 3, 1952; children—Robert Dean, Deva Elizabeth. Reporter and columnist Augusta (Kans.) Daily Gazette, 1954-58, Wichita (Kans.) Eagle-Beacon, 1958-61; Kans. youth dir. under auspices of Kans. Atty. Gen., 1961-65; Kans. state dir. Seventh Step Found., Topeka, 1965-66; mem. staff Dept. Preventive Psychiatry, Menninger Found., Topeka, Kans., 1966-71; dir. cons. Center Improvement Human Functioning, Wichita, 1975—; author: (with Edward Greenwood) Mental Health in Kansas Schools, 1965; Let Me Do This Thing, 1969; (with Bill Larson) Hear Me, Barabbas, 1969; How to Be An Effective Group Leader, 1975; The Secret Power of Pyramids, 1975; (with Ed Pettit) The Psychic Power of Pyramids, 1976, Pyramids: The Second Reality, 1979; The Psychic Power of Animals, 1977; Psychic Frontiers of Medicine, 1977. Bd. dirs. Recreation Commn., Topeka, Kans., United Funds, Topeka. Served with USN, 1945-46. Recipient John H. McGinnis Meml. award for Nonfiction, 1972, Am. Freedom Found. award, 1966, Spl. Appreciation award Kans. State Penitentiary, 1967. Mem. Acad. of Parapsychology and Medicine, Kans. Council for Children and Youth (pres. 1965-66), Assn. for Strenghtening the Higher Realities and Aspirations of Man (pres. 1970-71), Smithsonian Inst. Club: Lions (pres. 1957). Address: Rural Route 3 Winfield KS 67156

SCHULD, DONALD JOHN, sch. psychologist; b. Dickinson, N.D., May 27, 1953; s. John Francis and Alvera Margaret (Brilz) S.; B.S. cum laude, St. John's U., 1974; M.S., Eastern Mich. U., 1976; m. Charlotte Ann Marquart, Aug. 4, 1973; children—Eric John, Sarah Marie. Psychologist, Faribault County Human Service, Blue Earth, Minn., 1977-79; sch. psychologist Martin County Spl. Edn. Coop., Fairmont, Minn., 1979—; pvt. practice clin. psychology, Blue Earth, 1980—. St. John's U. edn. grantee, 1977-79. Mem. Am. Psychol. Assn., Minn. Psychol. Assn., Minn. Sch. Psychologists Assn., Psi Chi. Roman Catholic. Contbr. articles to profl. jours. Home: 427 E 9th St Blue Earth MN 56013 Office: 115 S Park St Fairmont MN 56031

SCHULER, ERIC L., nursing center exec.; b. Detroit, Sept. 28, 1957; s. Richard and Katherine L. (Goran) S., Jr.; Asso. in Acctg., Davenport Coll. Bus., 1977; student Grand Valley State Colls., 1977-79. Asst. office mgr. Multi-Cut Tool, Inc., Kentwood, Mich., 1972-76; bus. mgr. Aspen Distbg., Inc., Wyoming, Mich., 1976-79; owner, operator V.I.P. Enterprises, Grand Rapids, Mich., 1979; comptroller Grand Valley Nursing Centre, Grand Rapids, 1979—. Co chmn. United Way Kent County. Mem. Nat. Assn. Accts., Hosp. Fin. Mgmt. Assn., Am. Ski Assn., Grand Rapids Council Stutters. Club: S.E. Grand Rapids Lions (treas.). Home: 4244-8 Stonebridge SW Wyoming MI 49509 Office: 4118 Kalamazoo St SE Grand Rapids MI 49508

SCHULER, RICHARD JOSEPH, accountant; b. Pitts., Feb. 22, 1947; s. Richard Valentine and Jeannette Craig (Kirkpatrick) S.; B.S. in B.A., Duquesne U., 1969, M.B.A., 1973; m. Nancy Patricia Sippos, Nov. 11, 1972. Computer programmer, analyst Duquesne U., Pitts., 1966-70; sr. accountant ACF Industries, St. Charles, Mo., 1975-76; internal auditor Monsanto Co., St. Louis, 1976-78, supr. cost acctg., St. Peters, Mo., 1978-81, supr. acctg. policies, St. Louis, 1982—. Served with USAF, 1971-75. USAF Fin. Assistance grantee, 1967-69. C.P.A., Mo.; cert. mgmt. acct., cert. internal auditor. Mem. Am. Inst. C.P.A.'s, Nat. Assn. Accts., Assn. M.B.A. Execs., Mo. Soc. C.P.A.'s, Inst. Mgmt. Acctg., Inst. Internal Auditors, Beta Gamma Sigma, Beta Alpha Phi. Republican. Roman Catholic. Home: 9 Park Charles Blvd N Saint Peters MO 63376 Office: PO Box 8 Saint Peters MO 63376

SCHULMAN, MELVIN LOUIS, food co. exec.; b. Balt., Nov. 5, 1921; s. Louis and Rose (Kasoff) S.; B.A., U. Cin., 1947; m. Zelma Sharff, Jan. 18, 1953; children—Stuart, Karen, Alan, H. Glenn. With Food Spltys. Co., Inc., Cin., 1947—, now pres. Mem. Cin. Summer Opera Bd., 1967—; sec. Big Bros. Assn., 1970-72, Jewish Community Center, 1972—; nat. campaign policies bd. United Jewish Appeal; bd. dirs. Cin. Jewish Fedn., Cin. chpt. Am. Jewish Com. mem. bd. U. Cin. Found., 1979—. Served with AUS, 1943-46. Mem. U. Cin. Alumni Assn. (bd. govs.). Home: 7201 Fair Oaks Dr Cincinnati OH 45237 Office: 12 E Sunnybrook Dr Cincinnati OH 45237

SCHULTZ, ALLEN H., lawyer; b. Chgo., Mar. 15, 1911; s. Hyman and Minnie (Goldman) S.; J.D., DePaul U., 1932; m. Ida A. Greenberg, Oct. 13, 1940; children—Jay, Edward. Admitted to Ill. bar, 1932, since practiced in Chgo.; mem. firm Schultz & Schwartz, 1945-51, Schultz & Biro, 1954-57, Schultz, Biro & Karmel, 1957-71, Schultz & Schultz, 1973—. Mem. Am., Ill., Chgo. bar assns., Chgo. Law Inst., Decalogue Soc. of Lawyers, Pi Gamma Mu (scholastic honor soc.). Jewish. Clubs: Covenant, City. Home: 405 N Wabash Ave Chicago IL 60611 Office: 221 N La Salle St Chicago IL 60601

SCHULTZ, ARTHUR WARREN, communications co. exec.; b. N.Y.C., Jan. 13, 1922; s. Milton Warren and Genevieve (Dann) S.; A.B., U. Chgo., 1967; m. Elizabeth Carroll Mahan, Apr. 23, 1949; children—Arthur Warren, John Carroll (dec.), Julia Schultz Hollingsworth. With, Foote, Cone & Belding, Chgo., 1948—, v.p., 1957-63, sr. v.p., dir., 1963-69, exec. v.p., 1969, chmn. bd., 1970-81, chmn. exec. com., 1981—; dir. Paxall Co., Spring Mills Inc. Trustee, Art Inst. Chgo., 1975—, Chgo. Council Fgn. Relations, 1977—, U. Chgo., 1977—, Chgo. Public TV, 1978—, Chgo. Central Area Com., 1978—; bd. dirs. Chgo. Crime Commn., 1965-71, Community Fund, 1966-67, Better Bus. Bur., 1970-78; pres. Cook County Sch. Nursing, 1963-64, Welfare Council Met. Chgo., 1965-67. Served with USAAF, 1943-45. Mem. Am. Assn. Advt. Agys. (dir. 1968-71, 74-76, chmn. Central region 1970-71), Delta Kappa Epsilon. Clubs: Barrington Hills Country, Racquet, Commonwealth, Chgo., Econ., Execs., Comml., Old Elm. Home: Route 2 Meadow Hill Rd Barrington IL 60010 Office: Foote Cone & Belding 401 N Michigan Ave Chicago IL 60611

SCHULTZ, DONALD RAYMOND, chemist; b. North Tonawanda, N.Y., Nov. 2, 1918; s. Helmuth William and Eda (Kurkowski) S.; B.S., U. Mich., 1940, M.S., 1952, Ph.D., 1954; postgrad. Case Sch. Applied Sci., Cleve., 1941-42; m. Sarah Emma Toth, Sept. 25, 1942 (dec. Apr. 1967); children—Donna Schultz Friedrich, Thomas, Winifred Schultz Krohn, Nancy; m. 2d, Eleanor Augusta Anderson, Aug. 23, 1968. Analytic chemist Penn Salt Mfg. Co., Wyandotte, Mich., 1940, McGean Chem. Co., Cleve., 1940-41; research engr. Trojan Powder Co., Sandusky, Ohio, 1942-44, Mich. Chem. Corp., St. Louis, Mich., 1946-50; teaching fellow, research fellow U. Mich., Ann Arbor, 1950-54; sr. research chemist 3M Co., St. Paul, 1954-68, sr. patent liaison, 1968—; prof. chemistry Bethel Coll., St. Paul, 1965-66. Adult leader Boy Scouts Am., 1955—, recipient numerous adult scouter awards, 1958-80; Served with USNR, 1944-46. Recipient Outstanding Citizen citation Sta. WTCN, Mpls.-St. Paul, 1964. Mem. Am. Chem. Soc., Am. Inst. Chemists, A.A.A.S., Am. Legion, Sigma Xi, Phi Lambda Upsilon, Phi Kappa Phi. Lutheran (youth counselor Mo. Synod 1954-68, chmn. 1948-50, 70-72, 76-81). Lion. Contbr. articles to profl. jours. Patentee boron chemistry. Home: 2592 Sumac Ridge White Bear Lake MN 55110 Office: 3M Co Research Center St Paul MN 55101

SCHULTZ, FREDERICK MARSHALL, educator; b. Vincennes, Ind., Nov. 21, 1936; s. James Robert and Virginia (Hamilton) S.; student Asbury Coll., Wilmore, Ky., 1955-56; B.S., Ind. U., Bloomington, 1962, M.S., 1966, Ph.D. (NDEA fellow), 1969; m. Aug. 14, 1964 (div. 1975); children—Heidi, Frederick; m. 2d May 14, 1976; 1 dau., Susan Meredith. Tchr. history and English, Franklin Sr. High Sch., Baltimore County, Md., 1962-65; prof. hist., philos. and cultural founds. of edn. Akron U., 1969—. Bd. dirs., treas. Friends of Akron-Summit County Library; chairperson ecumenical and community projects of Episcopal Ch., Diocese of Ohio, 1977—. Served with U.S. Army, 1959-61. Fellow Philosophy of Edn. Soc., John Dewey Soc. Study Edn. and Culture; mem. Am. Ednl. Research Assn., Am. Ednl. Studies Assn., Am. Studies Assn., Soc. Study of Am. Civilization, NEA, Ohio Edn. Assn., Ohio Valley Philosophy of Edn. Soc. (pres. 1976), Comparative and Internat. Edn. Soc. Club: Montrose Swim and Tennis (Akron). Author: Social-Philosophical Foundations of Education, 1974, 2d edit., 1977; Education in America (with James Monroe Hughes), 1976; contbr. articles to profl. jours. Home: 2804 Chamberlain Rd Akron OH 44313 Office: Dept of Ednl Founds Coll of Edn U Akron Akron OH 44325

SCHULTZ, JILL MARLA, banker; b. Warren, Ohio, July 2, 1947; d. Dwight W. and Mildred M. (Brooks) Roudebush; B.S. in Edn., Bowling Green State U., 1969; postgrad. Laverne Coll., 1973; 1 son, Zachary. Head Start tchr. Warren, Ohio, 1969; tchr. kindergarten Montesorri, Reading City Schs., Cin., 1969-70, Big Walnut Sch. Dist., Columbus, Ohio, 1970-73; with Ind. Soc. Prevention of Blindness, Indpls., 1975-76; tchr. Montessori Activities Center, Indpls., 1975-76; br./ops. communications coordinator Bank One of Columbus, 1976-79, tng. dir., 1979—. Named Outstanding Young Woman of Yr., 1978-79, Bank One Moneybag, 1978—. Mem. Am. Bus. Women's Assn., Am. Inst. Banking (bd. govs. 1979-82), Bus. and Profl. Women, Am. Soc. Tng. and Devel. Clubs: Columbus Metropolitan. Met. Women's Center. Office: 100 E Broad St 6th Floor Columbus OH 43215

SCHULTZ, JOHN LEO, univ. adminstr.; b. Cape Girardeau, Mo., Feb. 1, 1931; s. Louis J. and Norma E. (Shivelbine) S.; B.S. magna cum laude, Southeast Mo. State Coll., 1954, B.S. in Edn. magna cum laude, 1957; M.S. in Edn., So. Ill. U., 1959, Ed.S., 1965; Ph.D. Open U., 1977; postgrad. U. Chgo., 1960-63, U. Tenn., 1954, Louisville Sem., 1953, U. Mo., 1977; m. Carole Nelle Sparks, Aug. 19, 1959; children—Elizabeth Ann (dec.), Deborah Lorraine. Asst. in guidance and counseling Community High Sch., Downers Grove, Ill., 1959-60; dir. curriculum research Sch. Dists. 58 and 59, Downers Grove, 1960-64; adminstrv. supr. student employment program So. Ill. U., Carbondale, 1964-65; adminstrv. asst. and prof. psychology Jefferson Coll., Hillsboro, Mo., 1965-66; registrar Cornell Coll., Mt. Vernon, Iowa, 1966-67, asst. prof. edn., 1966-67; registrar, sec. to exec. faculty Sch. Medicine, Washington U., St. Louis, 1967—, asst. prof., 1967—, asst. dean acad. adminstrn., 1976—, registrar Barnes Hosp. Med. Staff, 1967—, lectr. resident program in orthodontics Sch. Dental Medicine,

1970—; cons. Fed. Aid Coordinating Services, Inc., Chgo., 1965-67, Washington, 1966-67; dist. rep. to sch. improvement program U. Chgo., 1960-63. Pres. Internat. Forum, Open U., 1977-79. Served with U.S. Army, 1954-56. Mem. Am. Ednl. Research Assn., Am. Assn. Coll. Registrars and Admissions Officers (chmn. profl. schs. com. 1975-76), Midwestern Psychol. Assn., Mo. State Tchrs. Assn., NEA, Nat. Soc. for Study Edn., Am. Assn. U. Adminstrs., Am. Assn. Higher Edn., Assn. Am. Med. Colls., Phi Kappa Phi, Kappa Delta Pi, Phi Delta Kappa. Lutheran. Author: (with George J. Fuka) New Education Interaction Curriculum Model, 1966; author curriculum studies; contbr. articles to profl. publs. Office: Washington Univ School Medicine 660 S Euclid Ave Saint Louis MO 63110

SCHULTZ, LOUIS MICHAEL, advt. agy. exec.; b. Detroit, Aug. 24, 1944; s. Henry Richard and Genevieve S.; B.A., Mich. State U., 1967; M.B.A., Wayne State U., m. Susan K. Hammel, Sept. 10, 1966; children—Christian David, Kimberly Anne. With Campbell-Ewald Co., Warren, Mich., 1967—, v.p., group dir., 1975-77, sr. v.p., asso. media dir., 1977—; guest lectr. U. Mich., Mich. State U. Served with U.S. Army, 1968-74. Mem. Am. Mktg. Assn., Detroit Advt. Assn., Detroit Jaycees, Adcraft Club, Nat. Acad. TV Arts and Scis. Democrat. Roman Catholic. Club: Great Oakes Country (Rochester, Mich.). Office: 30400 Van Dyke Warren MI 48093

SCHULTZ, MARTHA ANN, hosp. ofcl.; b. Galesburg, Ill., Dec. 9, 1941; d. John Wilbur and Laura Naomi (Johnson) Asplund; B.A., Augustana Coll., Rock Island, Ill., 1964; cert. Mt. Sinai Hosp. Sch. Med. Tech., 1965; student Central Mich. U. Inst. for Personal and Career Devel., 1973-77; m. Michael J. Schultz, Apr. 20, 1968; children—Michael John, Mark Douglas, David Ryan. Med. technologist hematology Mt. Sinai Hosp. Med. Center, Chgo., 1965-67, lab. supr., ednl. coordinator, 1967-70, adminstrv. asst. dept. pathology, 1970-78, lab. adminstr., 1978—; instr. dept. med. tech. U. Health Scis./Chgo. Med. Sch., 1973-74; on-site survey team mem. Coll. Am. Pathologists Inspection and Accreditation Program, 1972—. Recipient Leadership cert. YMCA Met. Chgo., 1977, 78. Mem. Am. Soc. for Med. Tech., Am. Soc. Clin. Pathologists (registered med. technologist). Republican. Lutheran. Home: 7440 Prescott Ln LaGrange IL 60525 Office: Mount Sinai Hosp Med Center 2750 W 15th Pl Chicago IL 60608

SCHULTZ, RICHARD DEWYL, zoo dir.; b. Jefferson City, Mo., Jan. 19, 1917; s. Carl Frederick and Molly Mabel (Cruzen) S.; B.S. in Bus. Adminstrn., Washington U., St. Louis, 1938; M.B.A., U. Chgo., 1943; m. Jean Crowder, June 18, 1959. C.P.A., Price Waterhouse & Co., St. Louis, 1938-56; controller Petrolite Corp., St. Louis, 1956-64, financial v.p., 1964-72, dir., 1969-72; dir. finance St. Louis Zool. Park, 1973-75, dir., 1975—. C.P.A., Mo. Mem. Internat. Union Dirs. Zool. Gardens, Fin. Execs. Inst., Am. Inst. C.P.A.'s, Am. Assn. Zool. Parks and Aquariums, Explorers Club, Beta Gamma Sigma, Phi Delta Theta. Episcopalian. Club: University (St. Louis). Home: 425 Breeze Wood Dr Ballwin MO 63011 Office: St Louis Zoo Park Forest Park Saint Louis MO 63110

SCHULTZ, ROBERT HARRY, sch. prin.; b. Chgo., Aug. 9, 1921; s. Henry and Lorrene (Hajck) S.; B.S.S., St. Marys Coll., Winona, Minn., 1947; M.Ed., DePaul U., 1956; m. Alice M. Evans, Aug. 19, 1950; children—Kevin, MaryLee, Gerald, Robert. Tchr., coach Easton (Kans.) High Sch., 1947-49, St. Rita High Sch., Chgo., 1949-53; coach Weber High Sch., Chog., 1953-56; tchr., coach Roosevelt Jr. High Sch., 1956-63, Bellwood Schs., asst. prin., McKinley High Sch., 1963-65, prin. Grant Elem. Sch., 1966-79, Wilson Sch., 1979—. Coach, Little League Baseball, Pony League Baseball, 1975-81. Served with AUS, 1942-45: PTO. Mem. Prins. Assn. (treas. Region 1 sect. 209 1980—), Nat. Assn. Elem. Sch. Prins., Assn. Supervision and Curriculum Devel. Roman Catholic. Club: Lions. Home: 2724 W Pope John Paul II St Chicago IL 60632 Office: 2723 W 43d St Chicago IL 60632

SCHULTZ, THEODORE WILLIAM, ret. educator, economist; b. Arlington, S.D., Apr. 30, 1902; s. Henry Edwward and Anna Elizabeth (Weiss) S.; grad. Sch. fo Agr., Brookings, S.D., 1924; B.S., S.D. State Coll., 1927, D.Sc. (hon.), 1959; M.S., U. Wis., 1928, Ph.D., 1930; LL.D., Grinnell Coll. 1949, Mich. State U., in 1962, U. Ill., 1968, U. Wis., 1968, Cath. U. Chile, 1979; m. Esther Florence Werth; children—Elaine, Margaret T. Paul. Mem. faculty Ia. State Coll., Ames, 1930-43, prof., head dept. econs. and sociology, 1934-43; prof. econs. U. Chgo., 1943-72, chmn. dept. econs., 1946-61. Charles L. Hutchinson Distinguished Service prof., 1952-72, now emeritus. Econ. adviser, occasional cons. Com. Econ. Devel., U.S. Dept. Agr., Dept. of State Fed. Res. Bd., various congl. coms., U.S. Dept. of Commerce, FAO, U.S. Dept. of Def. (in Germany 1948), Fgn. Econ. Adminstrn. (in U.K. and Germany 1945), Internat. Bank for Reconstrn. and Development, Resources for the Future, Twentieth Century Fund, Nat. Farm Inst., and others. Dir. Nat. Bur. Econ. Research, 1949-67; research dir. Studies of Tech. Assistance in Latin Am., also bd. mem. Nat. Planning Assn.; chmn. Am. Famine Mission to India, 1946; studies of agrl. developments in central Europe and Russia, 1929, Scandinavian countries and Scotland, 1936, Brazil, Uruguay and Argentina, 1941, Western Europe, 1955; research fellow Center Advanced Study in Behavioral Sci., 1956-57. Recipient Nobel Prize in Econs., 1979. Fellow Am. Acad. Arts and Scis., Am. Farm Econs. Assn., Nat. Acad. Scis.; mem. Am. Farm Assn., Am. Econ. Assn. (pres. 1960, Walker medal 1972), Royal Econ. Soc., Am. Philos. Soc., also others. Author: Redirecting Farm Policy, 1943; Food for the World, 1945; Agriculture in an Unstable Economy, 1945; Production and Welfare in Agriculture, 1950; The Economic Organization of Agriculture, 1953; Economic Test in Latin America, 1956; Transforming Traditional Agriculture, 1964; The Economic Value of Education, 1963; Economic Crises in World Agriculture, 1965; Economic Growth and Agriculture, 1968; Investment in Human Capital: The Role of Education And of Research, 1971; Human Resources, 1972; Economics of the Family; Marriage, Children, and Human Capital, 1974; Distortions of Agricultural Incentives, 1978; Investing in People: The Economics of Population Quality, 1981; co-author: Measures for Economic Development of Under-Developed Countries, 1951. Editor: Distortions of Agricultural Incentives, 1978; editor Jour. of Farm Economics, 1939-42. Contbr. articles to profl. jours. Home: 5620 Kimbark Av Chicago IL 60637

SCHULTZ, WALTER, sch. prin.; b. Chgo., Feb. 17, 1941; s. Walter August and Elizabeth (Liebert) S.; B.S., St. Joseph's Coll., Ind., 1963; M.S.Ed., Purdue U., 1969; postgrad., 1970—; m. Kathleen Boyle, Nov. 26, 1966. Tchr., elem. sch. Diocese of Gary (Ind.), 1962-63; tchr., St. Francis de Sales High Sch., Chgo., 1963—, chmn. dept. social studies, 1969-79, dir. curriculum, 1970—, dir. public relations, 1977-80, asst. prin. in charge curriculum and public relations, 1979-80, co-prin. curriculum, 1980—. Mem. Nat. Council Social Studies, Founds. of Social Studies Spl. Interest Group (pres.), Purdue Alumni Assn., John Purdue Club, Assn. Supervision and Currculum Devel., Ind. Council for Social Studies, Phi Delta Kappa. Office: 10155 S Ewing Ave Chicago IL 60617

SCHULTZ, WALTER ARTHUR, ch. agy. exec.; b. Winnipeg, Man., Can., Jan. 16, 1928; s. Ludwig and Matilda (Hoffman) S.; Chartered Acct., U. Man., 1955; m. Dorothea Marie Brethauer, Aug. 8, 1952; children—Laurie Ann, Walter David, Brenda Marie, Mark Douglas. Audit group head taxation div. Revenue Can., 1955-63; treas. Can. sect. Luth. Ch. Am., 1963—; exec. sec. div. info. service Can. Luth. Council, 1963-67; exec. sec. div. info. services Luth. Council Can., 1967-76, exec. dir., 1976—; dir. Luth. Life Ins. Soc. Can.; mem. fin. com. Can. Council Chs., 1971—; vice chmn. world hunger appeal Luth. Ch. Am., 1972—; mem. commn. world service Luth. World Fedn., Geneva, 1977—. Mem. allocation com. United Way Winnipeg, 1963-69; chmn. bd. Sr. Citizen Day Centres, Winnipeg, 1963-69. Recipient Disting. Service award Luth. Brotherhood Ins. Co., 1967. Mem. World Assn. Christian Communicators, Inst. Chartered Accts. Man., Religious Public Relations Council. Office: 500-365 Hargrave St Winnipeg MB R3B 2K3 Canada

SCHULZ, FLORENCE HELEN ZEALLEAR (FLO), owner secretarial and bridal service; b. Columbus, Ohio, June 25, 1913; d. Frederick J. and Clara Marie (Weber) Zeallear; student Bliss Bus. Coll., 1932-33; m. May 9, 1936. Secretarial position Curtiss Wright Co., Columbus, 1941-43, 47-57; with Masonic Temple, Columbus, 1957-68; mgr. Office Res., Columbus, 1968-69; sec., personnel counselor Ohio State U., Columbus, 1959-69; secretarial position Columbus Police Dept. Tng. Acad., 1969—; owner, operator Flo Schulz Agy., Columbus, 1969—, dep. registrar, 1975—. Mem. Hilltop Bus. Assn. (pres. 1979—), Women's Internat. Bowling Congress (permanent), Columbus Woman's Bowling Assn. (sec. 1948-60). Republican. Presbyterian. Clubs: Order of Eastern Star, Order of Amaranth. Home: 53 N Brinker Ave Columbus OH 43204 Office: Flo Schulz Agy 3253 W Broad St Columbus OH 43204

SCHULZ, VALDYN, retail exec.; b. 1929; married. With Red Owl Stores, Inc., 1959-73; exec. v.p. Nat. Tea Co., Rosemont, Ill., 1973-76, pres., chief exec. officer, 1976—. Office: Nat Tea Co 9701 W Higgins Rd Rosemont IL 60018*

SCHULZE, ARTHUR ROBERT, JR., food co. exec.; b. La Crosse, Wis., Jan. 31, 1931; s. Arthur Robert and Elizabeth Margaret (Showers) S.; B.A., Carleton Coll., 1952; M.B.A. with distinction, Harvard U., 1958; m. Joan M. Hanifan, June 25, 1955; children—Brett, Mark, David, Anne. Sales trainee to product mgr. Procter & Gamble Co., Cin., 1959-62; with Gen. Mills, Inc., Mpls., 1962—, v.p., gen. mgr. Golden Valley div., 1970-73, group v.p. consumer foods, 1973-80, exec. v.p. consumer foods, 1981—. Trustee, Carleton Coll.; bd. govs. Meth. Hosp., Mpls.; active Civic League Mpls., United Way Mpls.; bd. dirs. Family and Children's Service Mpls. Served with CIC, U.S. Army, 1953-58. Recipient Merit award United Way Mpls. Republican. Clubs: Harvard Bus. Sch., Interlachen Country. Home: 14 Paddock Rd Edina MN 55436 Office: 9200 Wayzata Blvd Minneapolis MN 55440

SCHULZE, FREDERICK KILLIAN, welding power supply mfg. co. exec.; b. Waukesha, Wis., June 21, 1932; s. Frederick Carl and Dorothea Margaret S.; B.S., U. Wis., Milw., 1958; M.S., Northwestern U., 1959; m. Judy Beth O'Donnell, Dec. 28, 1954; children—Frederick James, Elizabeth Anne, Mary Leigh, Daniel Killian. Instr., grad. asst. Northwestern U., 1958-61; sales engr. Internat. Rectifier, El Segundo, Calif., 1962-63, v.p. sales, 1972-76, sales mgr., dir. internat. sales, v.p./gen. mgr. Crydom Controls div., 1967-72; power specialist Welding Products div. A.O. Smith, Milw., 1963-67; v.p. domestic sales Miller Electric Mfg. Co., Appleton, Wis., 1976-77, exec. v.p. ops., 1977—, also dir. Served with U.S. Army, 1951-55. Mem. Fox Cities C. of C. (dir. 1980—, treas. 1981—), Am. Welding Soc., Nat. Elec. Mfrs. Assn. Republican. Roman Catholic. Clubs: Am. Legion, Elks. Office: 718 S Bounds St Appleton WI 54911

SCHULZE, PEGGY MARIE HUGHES, psychologist; b. Chgo., Mar. 30, 1939; d. George Ingersoll and Rose M. (Reed) Hughes; student U. Ill., 1957-59; A.A., Belleville (Ill.) Area Coll., 1970; B.A., So. Ill. U., Edwardsville, 1973, M.A., 1976; Ph.D., St. Louis U., 1980; m. Edward Thomas Schulze, Sept. 5, 1959; children—Mary Katherine, Theresa Gail, Susan Elizabeth. Research and teaching asst. So. Ill. U., 1974; psychologist Belleville Mental Health Center, 1974; instr. psychology Belleville Area Coll., 1977; instr. psychology for law enforcement div. McKendree Coll., Lebanon, Ill., 1977-78; instr. psychology and child care services Lewis and Clark Coll., Godfrey, Ill., 1978-79; dir. mental health services Washington County Community Counseling, 1979—; pvt. practice, 1981—; staff Washington County Hosp., St. Elizabeth Hosp., Meml. Hosp. Vol. group leader LaLeche League Internat., 1962-68, nat. conv. del., 1964, 65, sec. Met. East chpt., 1965, pres. Met. East chpt., 1966; mem. Citizens Are Responsible for Edn., 1973; bd. dirs. comprehensive Mental Health Center of St. Clair County; leader Girl Scouts U.S.A., 1967-69, athletic dir. camp, 1968, 69. Nominee for outstanding grad. student in psychology So. Ill. U., 1975. Mem. Am. Personnel and Guidance Assn., Rural Mental Health Assn., Am. Assn. Marriage and Family Therapy, Am. Assn. Sex Educators, Counselors and Therapists, Am. Psychol. Assn., Midwestern Psychol. Assn., Ill. Psychol. Assn., Am. Soc. for Clin. Hypnosis, Internat. Platform Assn., Psi Chi (v.p. 1972, editor newsletter 1972), Pi Lambda Theta. Home: 9 W E St Belleville IL 62221

SCHUM, MARY LOUISE, interior designer; b. Billings, Mont., Aug. 13, 1917; d. Ellsworth F.J. and Marie (Doyle) Reilly; student Mount Mary Coll., 1935-37; B.F.A., Art Inst. Chgo., 1942; m. Eugene Charles Schum, Aug. 8, 1942; children—Jane, Martha, Marie, Sara, Reilly. Interior designer Mary Gertrude Condon Interiors, Kansas City, Mo., 1947-48; founded Mary Louise Schum Interiors, Hamilton, Ohio, 1948, pres., 1948-79; interior designer, v.p. Asso. Design Planning & Art, Los Angeles, 1972-77, Hamilton, 1972-77; interior designer, pres. Asso. Contract Design & Art, div. Mary Louise Interiors, Inc., Hamilton, 1977-79; owner, operator Mary Louise Schum Interiors, Inc., 1979—; guest lectr. trade shows, univs., profl. groups, 1948—; cons. design to major industries, 1955—. Recipient numerous awards, latest being: Design award Burlington House, 1974, Award of Merit, Illuminating Engring. Soc., 1976, Design award Ohio Hosp. Assn., 1978. Mem. Am. Soc. Interior Designers, Hamilton-Fairfield Arts Council (dir. 1978-81). Contbr. articles on interior design to profl. pubs. Address: Mary Louise Schum Interiors Inc 723 Dayton St Hamilton OH 45011

SCHUMACHER, BROCKMAN, educator; b. St. Louis, Aug. 26, 1924; adopted s. Dorothea Louise Brockman; B.A., U. Iowa, 1948; M.Ed., Washington U., St. Louis, 1952, Ph.D., 1969; m. Doris Goodman, July 20, 1948; children—Brockman, Andrew Jason, Douglass William. Dir. rehab. services St. Louis State Hosp., 1957-66; dir. comprehensive manpower programs Human Devel. Corp., St. Louis, 1966-68; coordinator, prof. Rehab. Counselor Tng. Program Rehab. Inst. So. Ill. U. at Carbondale, 1968—; dir. research, demonstration Halfway House Psychiat. Patients, St. Louis, 1959-62; asst. prof. social scis. Webster Coll., Webster Groves, Mo., 1966-67. Mem. Ill. Mental Health Planning Bd., 1970-73, Ill. Bd. Mental Health Commrs., 1974—; pres. Nat. Council Rehab. Edn., 1971—. Served with USAAF, 1943-46. Recipient citation St. Louis Mental Health Assn., 1963; Services award Human Devel. Corp., 1968. Mem. Am. Rehab. Counselor Assn. (chmn. accreditation rehab. counselor tng. program 1972—), Nat. Rehab. Assn. (dir. 1971—), Nat. Assn. Non-White Rehab. Workers, Am. Psychol. Assn. Author: (with H. Dunlap) Intensive Services for the Disadvantaged, 1972; (with H. Allen) Five Vest Pocket Books on Severe Handicaps, The Physical Disabilities: A Resource Package for Counselors, Practitioners and Trainers, 1976; (with E. Bender) Medical Aspects of Disabilities, 1976. Editor: Problems Unique to the Rehabilitation of Psychiatric Patients, 1963. Home: 609 Skyline Dr Carbondale IL 62901

SCHUMACHER, GEBHARD FRIEDERICH BERNHARD, physician; b. Osnabrueck, West Germany, June 13, 1924; s. Kaspar and Magarete (Pommer) S.; M.D., U. Goettingen and Tuebingen, 1951; Sc.D. equivalent in obstetrics and gynecology, U. Tuebingen, 1962; m. Anne Rose Zanker, Oct. 24, 1958; children—Michael A., Marc M. Came to U.S., 1962. Intern, U. Tuebingen Med. Sch., 1951-52; tng. biochemistry Max Planck Inst. for Biochemistry, Tuebingen, 1952-53; tng. biochemistry and immunology Max Planck Inst. for Virus Research, 1953-54; resident obstetrics and gynecology U. Tuebingen, 1954-59, tng. internal medicine, 1959, asst. scientist in obstetrics and gynecology and biochem. research, 1959-62, dozent in obstetrics and gynecology, 1964-65; research asso. immunology Inst. Tb Research U. Ill. Coll. Medicine, 1962-63; research asso., asst. prof., dept. obstetrics and gynecology U. Chgo., 1963-64; asso. prof. dept. obstetrics and gynecology, asst. prof. dept. biochemistry Albany Med. Coll. of Union U., 1965-67; research physician, div. labs. and research N.Y. State Dept. Health, Albany, 1965-67; asso. prof. obstetrics and gynecology U. Chgo.-Chgo. Lying-In Hosp., 1967-71, chief sect. reproductive biology, 1971—, prof., 1973—. Cons. WHO, Nat. Inst. Health, other nat. and internat. orgns. Fellow Am. Coll. Obstetricians and Gynecologists; mem. Soc. Gynecologic Investigation, Am. Fertility Soc., Soc. for Study of Reprodn., Am. Acad. Reproductive Medicine, Am. Soc. Cytology, Am. Assn. Pathologists, N.Y. Acad. Sci., Deutsche Gesellschaft fur Gynakologie and Geburtshilfe, Gesellschaft für Biologische Chemie, Gesellschaft für Immunologie, Deutsche Gesellschaft für Bluttransfusion, Gesellschaft Deutscher Naturforscher and Ärzte. Author: (with F.K. Beller) The Biology of the Fluids of the Female Genital Tract, 1979; (with D.S. Dhindsa) Immunological Aspects of Infertility and Fertility Regulation, 1980; (with R. Kaiser) Human Reproduction-Fertility-Sterility-Contraception, 1981. Contbr. articles to profl. jours. Home: 557 Hamilton Wood Homewood IL 60430 Office: 5841 S Maryland Ave Chicago IL 60637

SCHUMACHER, JOSEPH STUART, foundry cons.; b. Hillsboro, Ohio, June 7, 1912; s. Ernest W. and Helen H. (Hussey) S.; student Denison U., 1930-32; B.S., Ohio State U., 1935; m. Dorothy Jene Lamb, July 24, 1936; 1 son, Joseph Stuart. Metallurgist, Cin. Milacron, Cin., 1935-44; tech. dir., v.p. The Hill & Griffith Co., Cin., 1944-69; pres. J. Schumacher & Co., Cin., 1969-72, 77—; tech. dir. Internat. Minerals & Chem. Corp., Libertyville, Ill., 1972-77; former dir. H.W. Dietert Co., Detroit; v.p. Exec. Cons. Assn., 1978—; cons., speaker to industry, 1944—. Registered profl. engr., Ohio. Fellow Inst. Brit. Foundrymen; mem. Am. Foundrymen's Soc. (chpt. chmn. 1949, award of Sci. Merit 1967, Gold medal 1974), Sigma Chi. Club: Masons. Patentee in field. Contbr. articles to profl. jours.; cons. editor The Foundry Mag., 1968—. Home: 1262 Briarwood Ln Libertyville IL 60048

SCHUMACHER, PAULA RUTH, journalist; b. Hays, Kans., Dec. 17, 1938; d. Henry Andrew and Pauline (Dreiling) Schumacher; B.A., Fort Hays State Coll., 1960; M.S., Kans. State U., 1974; 1 son by previous marriage, Mitchell Roy. Tchr., Stockton (Kans.) Jr. High Sch., 1960-61, Valley Center (Kans.) High Sch., 1961-68, Campus High Sch., Wichita, Kans., 1968-72, public schs., Wichita, 1972-75, public schs., Leavenworth, Kans., 1975-77; arts and entertainment, design editor Sun Publs., Overland Park, Kans., 1977-79; owner, pres. Paula Schumacher & Assos., public relations and advt., 1979—; editor Platte County Gazette; journalism coordinator Park Coll.; instr. Summer Sch. Journalism, Blair Acad., Blairstown, N.J., 1977. Recipient Disting. Journalism Tchr. of Yr. award, 1968. Mem. Kans. Orgn. Publs. Advs. (sec. treas. 1963-65, pres. 1968-72), Journalism Edn. Assn. (pres. 1977—; Disting. Journalist award 1979), Women in Communications, Platte County Bus. and Profl. Assn., Press Women, Kansas City Press Club, Sigma Delta Chi. Roman Catholic. Contbr. articles to profl. jours. Home: 6415 N Pennsylvania Kansas City MO 64118 Office: 5930 Barton St Shawnee KS 66203

SCHUMAKER, DALE HOWARD, chem. engr.; b. Red Wing, Minn., Aug. 25, 1933; s. Berlyn I. and Marie G. (Raphael) S.; B.S. in Chem. Engring., U. Wis., 1955; m. Lois J. Wildenberg, Sept. 13, 1958; children—Howard, Brian, Stacey. With research and devel. dept. Marathon Corp., Menasha, Wis., 1955-57; with research and devel. dept. Am. Can Co., Neenah, Wis., 1958-62, prodn. supt., 1962-65; asst. mgr. Appleton Coated Paper (Wis.), 1965-68, prodn. mgr., 1968-71, mill mgr., 1971-78, v.p. mfg., 1978—; dir. Appleton Papers, Inc. Mem. Appleton Police and Fire Commn.; vol. in probation Outagamie County, Appleton YMCA. Mem. Paper Industry Mgmt. Assn., Tau Beta Pi. Lutheran. Clubs: Masons, Rotary. Home: 701 E McArthur St Appleton WI 54911 Office: 825 E Wisconsin St Appleton WI 54911

SCHUPP, PAUL EUGENE, educator; b. Cleve., Mar. 12, 1937; s. Paul Eugene and Venna Marie (Shinn) S.; B.A., Western Res. U., 1959; M.A., U. Mich., 1961, Ph.D., 1966; m. Elva Ruth Stewart, Aug. 25, 1966. Asst. prof. U. Wis., 1966—67; asst. prof. math. U. Ill., Urbana, 1967—71, asso. prof., 1971—75, prof., 1975—, asso. mem. Center Advanced Study, 1973-74; vis. mem. Courant Inst. Math. Scis., N.Y. U., 1969-70. John Simon Guggenheim Meml. fellow, 1977—78. Mem. Am., London math. socs., AAUP. Author: (with R. C. Lyndon) Combinatorial Group Theory, 1977. Contbr. articles to math. jours. Home: 1010 W Church St Champaign IL 61820 Office: Dept Mathematics U Ill Urbana IL 61801

SCHURDELL, THEODORE ARTHUR, advt. agy. exec.; b. Cleve., Mar. 27, 1933; s. Arthur Gustave and Lucille Elanor (Jones) S.; student Butler U.; m. Karel Ann Kingham, Feb. 15, 1958; 1 son, Theodore Arthur. Account exec. La Grange & Garrison, 1954-60; pres. Bell & Schurdell, 1960-62; project supr. Anaconda Co., 1962-65; v.p., account mgr. Griswold-Eshleman, Cleve., 1965-73, Meldrum & Fewsmith, Cleve., 1973-76; pres. Mills Hall Walborn, Inc., Cleve., 1976-80, Swink & Schurdell, 1981—. Trustee, Arthritis Found. Mem. Sales and Mktg. Execs. Clubs: Cleve. Advt. (sec.-treas.); Shaker Heights Country (past dir.), Cleve. Athletic. Home: 22849 Holmwood St Shaker Heights OH 44122

SCHURMEIER, L. JON, hosp. adminstr.; b. Elgin, Ill., Feb. 17, 1937; s. LeRoy H. and June (Zorn) S.; B.A., DePauw U., Greencastle, Ind., 1959; M.B.A., U. Pitts., 1960, M.H.A., 1970; m. Donna Kay Cunningham, Apr. 1, 1961; children—Kristin, Darla, Steffany. From merchandiser to mgr. Carson, Pirie, Scott & Co., Chgo., 1963-67; adminstrv. extern Presbyn.-St. Luke's Hosp., Chgo., 1967-68; adminstrv. resident, then asst. adminstr. Cin. Gen. Hosp., 1969-72; asso. adminstr. S.W. Gen. Hosp., Middleburg Heights, Ohio, 1972-81, adminstr., 1981—; adminstrv. preceptor U. Pitts.; dir. Ohio Hosp. Mgmt. Services; mem. Hudson (Ohio) Com. Emergency Health Care. Pres. Olde Towne Colony Homeowners Assn., 1979; ch. lay leader, Hudson, 1973-76, trustee, 1981-84; bd. dirs. Hudson Girls Softball League, 1980-82. Served with U.S. Army, 1961-63. Recipient recognition award Seven Hills Neighborhood Houses, Cin., 1972. Fellow Am. Coll. Hosp. Adminstrs.; mem. Hosp. Fin. Mgmt. Assn.,

Am. Public Health Assn., Health Care Adminstrs. N.E. Ohio, DePauw U. Alumni Assn., U. Pitts. Alumni Assn. Health Adminstrn. (pres. 1976), Middleburg C. of C. Clubs: Hudson, Western Res. Tennis. Author articles in field. Home: 49 Keswick Dr Hudson OH 44236 Office: 18697 E Bagley Rd Middleburg Heights OH 44130

SCHUSTER, EUGENE IVAN, art gallery exec.; b. St. Louis, Dec. 8, 1936; s. David Theodore and Anne (Kalisher) S.; B.A., Wayne State U., 1959, M.A., 1962; postgrad. U. Mich., 1959-62, (Fulbright scholar) Warburg Inst., U. London, 1962-65, Courtauld Inst., U. London and London Sch. Econs., 1962-65; m. Barbara Zelmon, June 22, 1958 (div.); children—Joseph, Sarah, Adam. Lectr. art history Wayne State U., Detroit, 1959-62, Eastern Mich. U., Ypsilanti, 1960, Rackham extension U. Mich., 1961, Nat. Gallery, London, 1962-65; owner London Art Gallery, Detroit, 1965—; pres. Nanny's Soup Kettle, Inc., Dearborn, Mich., Cherry Creek Drilling Co. Recipient Distinguished Alumni award Wayne State U., 1968. Mem. Founders Soc., Detroit Inst. Arts, Detroit Art Dealers Assn., Art Appraisers Assn. Am. Home: 25425 Dennison Franklin MI 48025 Office: London Art Gallery 321 Fisher Bldg Detroit MI 48202

SCHUSTER, MONROE GARY, med. technologist; b. Gary, Ind., Dec. 4, 1935; s. Monroe Goeble and Lucille (Ingram) S.; B.S., Ball State U., 1961, postgrad., 1962-63; postgrad. Central Mich. U., U. Ky.; div.; children—Monroe Gary, Richard Kent, Tonya Louise. Modelmaker, Delco-Remy div. Gen. Motors Corp., Anderson, Ind., 1953—; med. technologist St. John's Hosp., Anderson, 1962-65, edn. coordinator Sch. Med. Tech., 1965—. Mem. Am. Soc. Allied Health Professions, Am. Soc. Med. Tech., Am. Assn. Clin. Chemistry, Am. Soc. Clin. Pathologists, Internat. Soc. Clin. Lab. Tech. Disciple of Christ. Office: 2015 Jackson St Anderson IN 46014

SCHUSTER, WILLIAM BURT, electronics engr.; b. Cuyahoga County, Ohio, Apr. 7, 1939; s. Alfred and Thelma Marie (Jacobsen) S.; B.S.E.E., M.I.T., 1962. Mktg. rep. W.B.S. Hi-Fi Co., Cleve., 1966-70; designing engr. E.E.E. Enterprises, Toledo, 1970-72; systems analyst W. R. S. Data Services, Detroit, 1972-76; design engr., pres. W.B.S. Electronics, Toledo, 1976—. Active campaign Ronald Reagan for Pres. Served with USN, 1962-66. Mem. Greater Toledo Area Model Engrs., Am. Radio Relay League. Mem. Tabernacle of God Ch. Clubs: Maumee Valley Model Boat, Elks. Author: Communications Receiver Construction, 1968. Office: PO Box 522 Toledo OH 43601

SCHUSTER, WILLIAM CRAIG, architect; b. Rock Island, Ill., July 13, 1950; s. Gerald Glen and Nell Amelia S.; student Ind. U., 1968-69; B.A. in Architecture, Iowa State U., 1975; m. Karen Lynn McLennan, Aug. 28, 1971; children—Theodore M., Tsinial. With Bossenberger-Reitz Cons. Engrs., Ames, Iowa, 1975-76, Lynch-Payne-Champion-Bernabe Architects, Des Moines, 1976-78; pvt. practice architecture, freelance cons. Better Homes and Gardens Books and Mags., Cedar Rapids, Iowa, 1978—; designer passive and active solar homes and bus. bldgs.; job capt. Brown-Healey-Bock Architects; archtl. cons.; pvt. pilot. Served with Air N.G., 1971-78. Decorated Meritorious Service ribbon with oak leaf cluster. Mem. AIA (asso.), Cedar Rapids Architecture Council. Mem. Conservative Evangelical Christian Ch. 4-time All-Am. swimmer. Home: 3208 14th Ave SE Cedar Rapids IA 52403 Office: 1035 3d Ave SE Cedar Rapids IA 52403

SCHWAB, PAUL JOSIAH, psychiatrist; b. Waxahachie, Tex., Jan. 14, 1932; s. Paul Josiah and Anna (Baeuerle) S.; B.A. with honors, North Central Coll., 1953; M.D. with honors, Baylor U., 1957; m. Martha Anne Beed, June 8, 1953; children—Paul Josiah, John Conrad, Mark Whitney. Intern Phila. Gen. Hosp., 1957-58; clin. asso. metabolism service Gen. Medicine br. Nat. Cancer Inst., NIH, Bethesda, Md., 1958-60; resident dept. medicine U. Chgo., 1960-62, dept. psychiatry, 1962-65, chief resident, instr. dept. psychiatry, 1964-65, lectr., 1968-74, asso. prof., 1974-79, chief inpatient psychiat. service, 1975-79, clin. asso. prof., 1980—, dir. psychiat. residency tng., 1976-79; practice medicine, specializing in psychiatry, 1965—; sr. attending staff Forest Hosp., 1966—. Trustee, N. Central Coll., 1980—. Served as sr. asst. surgeon, USPHS, 1958-60. Diplomate Am. Bd. Psychiatry and Neurology. Fellow Am. Psychiat. Assn.; mem. Ill. Psychiat. Soc., AMA, DuPage County Med. Soc., Am. Acad. Clin. Psychiatrists, Alpha Omega Alpha. Contbr. articles to profl. jours. Home: 725 E Highland Ave Naperville IL 60540 Office: 720 Brom Dr Naperville IL 60540

SCHWABEROW, EDWARD LEWIS, village mgr.; b. Dayton, Ohio, Jan. 13, 1946; s. Orville Christian and Naomi Gertrude (Bender) S.; B.A. in Public Adminstrn., Capital U., 1968; M.B.A., U. Dayton, 1973; m. Lynne Diane Hyde, Sept. 1, 1968; children—Chad Michael, James Edward, Andrea Lynne. Intern, Ohio Dept. Finance, Columbus, 1968-69; cost accountant Master div. Koehring, Dayton, 1971-73; adminstrv. asst. City of Lebanon (Ohio), 1973-76; village mgr. Village of Pickerington (Ohio), 1976—. Commr. Fairfield County Regional Park Dist., 1981—. Served with U.S. Army, 1969-71. Mem. Internat. City Mgmt. Assn. Lutheran. Home: 571 Pickerington Hills Dr Pickerington OH 43147 Office: 500 Hereford Dr Pickerington OH 43147

SCHWAMB, DONALD FREDERICK, cons. agy. exec.; b. West Bend, Wis., July 21, 1952; s. Franklin Harold and Maxine Ida (Oechsner) S.; A.S., U. Wis., Washington County, 1972; B.S. in Indsl. and Mfg. Engring., U. Wis., Milw., 1975. Mem. mfg., process and design engring. staff West Bend Co. (Wis.), 1969-73, indsl. and mfg. engr., 1973-76; mem. appraisal and project staff Valuation Research Corp., Milw., 1976-77, dir. research, 1977—, mgr. corp. adminstrn., 1979—; mgr. adminstrv. reorgn. Am. Valuation Consultants subs. Valuation Research Corp., Des Plaines, Ill., 1979-80. State orgn. dir. and adminstrv. asst. Democratic Youth Party, 1966-73; active local and nat. hist. preservation socs. Mem. Am. Inst. Indsl. Engrs., Am. Assn. Cost Engrs., Nat. Assn. Rev. Appraisers, Soc. for Advancement Mgmt. (a founder, 1st v.p. West Bend Co. chpt.), Nat. Assn. Rev. Appraisers (cert.). Office: Valuation Research Corp 250 E Wisconsin Milwaukee WI 53202

SCHWAN, LEROY BERNARD, artist; b. Somerset, Wis., Dec. 8, 1932; s. Joseph L. and Dorothy (Papenfuss) S.; student Wis. State U., River Falls, 1951-53, Southeastern Signal Sch., Ga., 1954; B.S., U. Minn., 1958, M.Ed., 1960, postgrad., 1961-64; postgrad. No. Mich. U., 1965, Tex. Tech. U., 1970, So. Ill. U., 1978, U. Iowa, 1980; children—David A., Mark J., William R., Catherine L., Maria E. Head art dept. Unity Pub. Schs., Milltown, Wis., 1958-61; instr. art Fridley Pub. Schs., Mpls., 1961-64; asst. prof. art No. Mich. U., Marquette, 1964-66; asst. prof. art Mankato (Minn.) State Coll., 1966-71, asso. prof., 1971-74, tchr. off-campus grad. classes Northeast Mo. State U., John Wood Community Coll.; dir. Art Workshop Educultural Center, 1968; dir. art edn. Quincy (Ill.) Pub. Schs., 1974-78, now art tchr.; tchr. art to mentally retarded children, Faribault, Minn., Owatonna, Minn., Mankato, Lake Owasso Children's Home, St. Paul; dir. art workshops, Mankato, 1970, St. Paul, 1972, 73, 74, 75; dir. workshops tchrs. mentally retarded Mankato, 1971, Faribault, 1972, Omaha, 1972-73, Quincy, 1974; asst. adj. Ill. VA Home, 1980—; one-man shows: Estherville Jr. Coll., 1968, Mankato State Coll., 1968, 71, 73, Farmington, Wis., 1970, 71, Good Thunder, Minn., 1972, Quincy, 1975, 77, Mankato, Minn., 1975, Western Ill. U., 1979; exhibited in group shows: Pentagon, Washington, 1955, U. Minn., 1958, No. Mich. U., 1965, St. Cloud State Coll., 1967, Moorhead State Coll., 1967, Bemidji (Minn.) State Coll., 1967, MacNider Mus., Mason City, Iowa, 1969, 72, 73, 74, Gallery 500, Mankato, Minn., 1970, Rochester, Minn., 1972, Minn. Mus., St. Paul, 1973, Hannibal, Mo., 1976, 77-78, Quincy, Ill., 1976-77; producer ednl. TV series, 1964-65, also 2 shows Kids Komments, Sta. WGEM, Quincy; mural commd. Gem City Coll., 1977. Webelos leader Twin Valley council Boy Scouts Am., 1968-69. Served with Signal Corps, AUS, 1954-56. Recipient certificate of accomplishment Sec. Army, 1955. Mem. Nat. Art Edn. Assn., Ill. Art Edn. Assn., Cath. Order Foresters, Am. Legion, Phi Delta Kappa. Author: Art Curriculum Guide Unity Public Schs., 1961; Portrait of Jean, 1974; co-author: Bryant-Schwan Design Test, 1971, Bryant-Schwan Art Guide, 1973; contbr. articles to profl. jours. Home: 1826 N 24th St Quincy IL 62301

SCHWARK, HOWARD EDWARD, civil engr.; b. Bonfield, Ill., Aug. 31, 1917; s. Edward F. and Florence M. (Schultz) S.; student St. Viators Coll., Bourbonnias, Ill., 1935-37; B.S., U. Ill., 1942; m. Arlene M. Highbarger, Sept. 28, 1940. Asst. to county supt. hwys. Ford County (Ill.), 1941-43; engr. E. I. DuPont de Nemours Co., 1942; asst. county supt. hwys. Kankakee County (Ill.), 1946-52, county supt. hwys., 1952—; dir. 1st Bank of Meadowview, Kankakee Devel. Corp.; adviser county rds. FHWA. Co-chmn., Republican Finance Com., 1962-66; pres. Kankakee Park Dist., 1959-70; mem. tech. adv. com. to Ill. Transp. Study Commn., 1975—; trustee, pres. Azariah Buck Old People's Home; mem. exec. bd. Rainbow council Boy Scouts Am.; bd. dirs. Soil and Water Conservation Service, 1967-74. Served with AUS, 1943-46. Recipient Disting. Alumnus award Civil Engring. Alumni Assn. U. Ill., 1975. Mem. Nat. Assn. County Engrs. (v.p. North Central region 1979-81), Ill. Soc. Profl. Engrs., Ill. Assn. County Supts. Hwys. (pres. 1970), Ill. Engring. Council (pres. 1971-72), Am. Road and Transp. Builders Assn. (dir. county div. 1969-75, dir. 1975-81, pres. county div. 1975; Outstanding Service award transp. ofcls. div. 1981), Kankakee Area C. of C. (dir. 1960-74), Am. Soc. Profl. Engrs., Western Soc. Engrs., Twp. Ofcls. Ill., Freelance Photographers Assn., Ill. Wildlife Fedn. Lutheran. Rotarian. Club: South Wilmington Sportsman. Home: 1051 W Vanmeter Kankakee IL 60901 Office: 750 S East Ave Kankakee IL 60901

SCHWARTAU, NEAL WILLIAM, pharmacist; b. Red Wing, Minn., Oct. 26, 1922; s. Adolph William and Edith Cornelia (Erickson) S.; B.S. in Pharmacy, U. Minn., 1943; m. Margaret Jane Peterson, July 19, 1947; children—Linda, William, Julie. Asst. chief pharmacist VA Hosp., Mpls., 1946-53; partner R & S Pharmacy, Red Wing, 1953-54; chief pharmacist Rochester (Minn.) Meth. Hosp., 1954-66, dir. pharmacy-central supply, 1967—; dir., treas. Southeastern Minn. Health Planning Council. Bd. dirs. YMCA. Served with USNR, 1944-46; PTO. Recipient Hallie Bruce Meml. Lecture award Minn. Soc. Hosp. Pharmacists, 1965; Harold R. Popp award Minn. State Pharm. Assn., 1978. Mem. Am. Soc. Hosp. Pharmacists, Am. Pharm. Assn., Fedn. Internat. Pharmaceutique, Minn. Soc. Hosp. Pharmacists (dir. 1977-81, pres. 1982), Minn. Pharm. Assn. (dir. 1969-73), AMA (affiliate). Republican. Lutheran. Club: Elks. Home: 2053 Carriage Dr SW Rochester MN 55901 Office: 201 W Center St Rochester MN 55901

SCHWARTZ, A(LBERT) TRUMAN, chemist, educator; b. Freeman, S.D., May 8, 1934; s. Albert and Edna (Kaufman) S.; A.B., U. S.D., 1956; B.A., Oxford U., 1958, M.A., 1960; Ph.D., M.I.T., 1963; m. Beverly Joan Beatty, Aug. 12, 1958; children—Ronald Eric, Katherine Marie. Teaching and research asst. M.I.T., Cambridge, 1958-63; research chemist Procter & Gamble Co., Cin., 1963-66; asst. prof. Macalester Coll., St. Paul, 1966-72, asso. prof., 1972-78, dean faculty, 1974-76, prof., 1978—, chmn. dept., 1980—; Arthur Lee Haines lectr., vis. scientist U. S.D., 1965; vis. prof. U. Wis., Madison, 1979-80; mem. state and regional coms. for selection of Rhodes scholars, 1963—. Rhodes scholar, 1956; NSF summer fellow, 1959; Macalester fgn. fellow, 1968; NSF-COSIP fellow, 1967, 72, 73; NSF grantee, 1979. Mem. Am. Chem. Soc. (mem. various coms. div. chem. edn.), AAAS, Assn. Am. Rhodes Scholars, Phi Beta Kappa, Sigma Xi. Author: Chemistry: Imagination and Implication, 1973; contbr. articles to profl. jours. Home: 68 Otis Ave Saint Paul MN 55104 Office: Dept Chemistry Macalester Coll Saint Paul MN 55105

SCHWARTZ, FRANKLIN DAVID, nephrologist, educator; b. Balt., May 16, 1933; s. George Henry and Anna (Snyder) S.; B.S. cum laude, U. Md., 1953, M.D. summa cum laude, 1957; m. Harriet Joan Mohline, May 25, 1972; children—Michael Howard, Ellen Sue. Intern U. Hosp., Balt., 1957-58, asst. resident in medicine, 1958-60; USPHS research fellow, U. Md., 1960-61; practice medicine specializing in nephrology, Balt., 1957-60, Washington, 1960-64, Chgo., 1964—; asso. dir. sect. nephrology U. Ill. Hosp., Chgo., 1970-71, acting chief, 1971-72, asso. chief, 1972—, attending physician U. Ill. Hosp., 1972—; attending physician St. Joseph Hosp., Chgo., 1971—, dir. sect. nephrology, 1971—, chief dept. medicine, 1974-77; adj. physician Rush-Presbyn.-St. Luke's Med. Center, 1964-65, asst. attending physician, 1965-67, asso. attending physician, 1967-70, dir. hemodialysis unit, 1968-70, cons. physician in medicine, 1970-71; asso. chief sect. nephrology Columbus-Cuneo Carbini Med. Center, 1971—; asst. prof. medicine Abraham Lincoln Sch. of Medicine, Chgo., 1964-69, asso. prof., 1969-75, clin. prof., 1975-76, prof. clin. medicine, 1976—; mem. cons. staff Ill. Masonic Med. Center, 1970-79, Augustana Hosp., Martha Washington Hosp., Ravenswood Hosp., Resurrection Hosp., South Chgo. Community Hosp., Northwest Community Hosp., Ill. Central Hosp.; mem. Renal Disease Advisory Com., State of Ill. Dept. Pub. Health, 1972—; mem. Sci. Advisory Bd., Kidney Found. of Ill., 1972—; co-dir. of hepatitis project Walter Reed Army Inst. of Research, 1962; cons. physician VA West Side Hosp., Chgo., 1972—. Diplomate Am. Bd. Internal Medicine, Am. Bd. Nephrology. Mem. Ill., Chgo. med. socs., Am., Ill., Chgo. socs. of internal medicine, World Med. Assn., Pan Am. Med. Assn., Am. Mgrs. Assn., Pres.'s Assn., Internat. Platform Assn., Am. Soc. Law and Medicine, A.C.P., Internat. Soc. Nephrology, Am. Soc. Nephrology, Am. Fedn. Clin. Research, AMA, Sigma Xi. Contbr. numerous articles in field to med. jours. and chpts. in field to med. books., Home: 1110 N Lake Shore Dr Chicago IL 60611 Office: 450 E Ohio St Chicago IL 60611

SCHWARTZ, HAROLD SIDNEY, ophthalmologist; b. Chgo., Nov. 2, 1950; s. William and Pearl (Landis) S.; B.S., U. Ill., 1972, M.D., M.S., 1976, Ph.D., 1980; m. Susan Kaplan, Apr. 13, 1978. Intern, U. Ill. Hosp., Chgo., 1976-77, resident in ophthalmology, 1976-80 resident in ophthalmology Ill. Eye and Ear Infirmary, Chgo., 1977-80; ophthalmologist Ophthalmology N.W., Chgo., 1980—; clin. asst. prof. U. Ill., Chgo., 1980—. Active ARC. Mem. AMA, Research to Prevent Blindness, Chgo. Med. Soc. (chmn. physician recruitment 1981), N.Y. Acad. Sci., Sigma Xi, Alpha Omega Alpha, Phi Kappa Phi. Democrat. Jewish. Club: Lions.

SCHWARTZ, JACOB JACK, cons.; b. Bklyn., May 8, 1918; s. Abraham and Gussie (Steigman) S.; B.B.A., St. John's U., Bklyn., 1939; m. Jenette Shorr, Mar. 18, 1945; children—Robin, Stanley, Alan. Sr. cost accountant Kay Mfg. Corp., Bklyn., 1939-42; mgr., comptroller Shores Cafe, Dearborn, Mich., 1946-55; owner, operator Jack's Food Box, Oak Park, Mich., 1955-58; accountant, line supr. Detroit Ordinance Dist. (now Detroit Procurement Dist.), 1958-60, from contract price analyst to supervisory price analyst Fin. Services Div., 1960-72, acting chief, 1972-73, pricing and fin. officer, dir. contract adminstrn. directorage, 1973-75, dir. contract adminstrn., chief fin. services div., 1975-77; asst. dist. dir. SBA of Mich., Detroit, 1976-78; cons. Cadillac Gage Co. subs. Excello Corp., Mich., 1979—. Vice-pres., Louis Stone Found., 1965-76. Served with USAAF, 1942-46. Recipient numerous awards, including awards Louis Stone Found., 1950-76, Govt. Contracts Assn., 1960-76, City of Detroit, 1961-62, State of Mich., 1962, U.S. Def. Supply Agy., 1964-75, Detroit Pub. Schs., 1966, Fed. Bar Assn., 1972. Mem. Govt. Contracts Assn. (v.p. 1969-71, treas., 1972-77), Engring. Soc. Detroit, Am. Def. Preparedness Assn., Allied Vets. Council (Gold award 1970), Am. Legion, Jewish War Vets. (mem. nat. exec. com. 1976-77, Man of Year 1966). Home: 27405 Fairfax St Southfield MI 48076

SCHWARTZ, LARRY JAY, bus. exec.; b. Chgo., July 2, 1936; s. Martin William and Rae (Kalchiem) S.; B.S., Purdue U., 1958; M.B.A., Cornell U., 1960; postgrad. Northwestern U., 1960-62; m. Lynne C. Mavon, Jan. 21, 1966; children—Jennifer Lynne, Jay Edward. Asst. prof. fin. DePaul U., Chgo., 1962-63; pres. Markstone Mfg. Co., Chgo., 1963-78; mem. Chgo. Bd. Trade and Chgo. Bd. Options, 1978—; with Morgan Stanley & Co., 1981—. Bd. dirs. Chgo. Boys' Clubs Summer Camp. Mem. Am. Mgmt. Assn., Illuminating Engrs. Soc. Club: Saddle and Cycle (Chgo.). Home: 819 Roslyn Pl Evanston IL 60201 Office: 115 S LaSalle St Chicago IL 60603

SCHWARTZ, MARSHA HEDY, educator; b. Berkeley, Calif., Oct. 19, 1943; d. Lawrence Jackson and Thelma Ruth S.; Cert., Joliet Jr. Coll., 1963; B.A., U. Ill., 1965, M.A. (Univ. fellow), 1967; Piano Teaching Cert., Joliet Conservatory of Music, 1963. Teaching asst. U. Ill., 1966-67, research asst., 1967; Spanish tchr. Lyons Twp. High Sch., La Grange, Ill., 1967—, sub-chmn. Spanish dept., 1973—, audiovisual coordinator fgn. lang. dept., 1967—. Mem. Am. Assn. Tchrs. Spanish and Portuguese, Am. Council Tchrs. Fgn. Langs., Spanish Heritage Assn., Ill. Fgn. Lang. Tchrs. Assn., Assn. for Ednl. Communications and Tech., NEA, Ill. Edn. Assn., Phi Beta Kappa. Jewish. Club: Joliet Bus. and Profl. Women's. Contbr. articles to profl. jours. Office: 100 S Brainard Ave La Grange IL 60525

SCHWARTZ, ROBERT, automotive mfg. co. exec.; b. Atlantic City, Mar. 9, 1939; s. Robert A. and Irene V. (Davis) S.; B.S. in Bus. Adminstrn., Drexel U., Phila., 1961; M.B.A., U. Pa.-Wash. State U., 1962; m. Judith H. Amole, Apr. 30, 1961. With Ford Motor Co., 1964-70; with Am. Motors Corp., 1971—, Eastern regional mgr., Detroit, 1975-76, gen. mgr. U.S. sales, also pres. Am. Motors Sales Corp., Detroit, 1976-80, mng. dir. N.Am. ops., 1980—. Mem. Republican Nat. Com., 1978—. Mem. Soc. Automotive Engrs., Sales Execs. Club N.Y. Office: 27777 Franklin Rd Southfield MI 48034

SCHWARTZ, RONALD ELMER, elec. engr.; b. Ann Arbor, Mich., May 4, 1934; s. Elmer G. and Esther C. (Eisele) S.; B.S. in Elec. Engring., U. Mich., 1957; postgrad. U. Conn., 1958; M.S. in Elec. Engring., Wayne State U., 1963; m. Ellen Shirley Eckwall, Aug. 25, 1957; children—Steven, Bradley, George. Engr., Hamilton Standard Co., Broadbrook, Conn., 1957, Chrysler Missile, Sterling Heights, Mich., 1958-60; engr. mfg. devel. Gen. Motors Tech. Center, Warren, Mich., 1960—; tchr. (part-time) Lawrence Inst. Tech., Southfield, Mich., 1967. Fellow Am. Soc. Nondestructive Testing; mem. Classic Guitar Soc. of Mich., Warren Power Squadron. Lutheran. Clubs: Sierra, Tech. Center Ski, Detroit Navigators. Contbr. articles on testing methods in mfg. to profl. publs. Home: 5589 Streefkerk Warren MI 48092 Office: Mfg Devel GM Tech Center Warren MI 48090

SCHWARTZ, (ELLEN) SHIRLEY ECKWALL, chemist; b. Detroit, Aug. 26, 1935; d. Emil Victor and Jessie Grace (Galbraith) Eckwall; B.S., U. Mich., 1957; M.S., Wayne State U., 1962, Ph.D., 1970; B.S., Detroit Inst. Tech., 1978; m. Ronald Elmer Schwartz, Aug. 25, 1957; children—Steven Dennis, Bradley Allen, George Byron. Asst. prof. Detroit Inst. Tech., 1973-78, head div. math. sci., 1976-78; research staff mem. BASF Wyandotte Corp., Wyandotte, Mich., 1978-81, head sect. functional fluids, 1981; staff research scientist Gen. Motors Corp., Warren, Mich., 1981—. Corr. sec. Childbirth Without Pain Edn. Assn., 1962, Warren-Centerline Human Relations Council, 1968. Mem. Am. Soc. Lubrication Engrs. (treas. Detroit sect. 1981, v.p. sect. 1981-82), Am. Chem. Soc., Tissue Culture Assn., Mensa, Sigma Xi. Lutheran. Club: Warren Adult Tennis. Contbr. articles to profl. jours.; patentee in field. Office: Gen Motors Research Labs Warren MI 48090

SCHWARTZ, WILLIAM THOMAS, banker; b. Kansas City, Mo., Apr. 2, 1940; s. Lawrence Michael and Nadine Lois (Weber) S.; A.B., Harvard U., 1962; M.A., U. So. Calif., 1972; M.B.A., U. Pa., 1970; m. Catherine E. Marx, Nov. 25, 1977; 1 son, William F.W. With Coldwell Banker & Co., San Francisco, 1967-69; banking officer Bankers Trust Co., N.Y.C., 1971-75; area treas. Abbott Labs., North Chicago, Ill., 1975-76; mgr. treasury services Sunbeam Corp., Oak Brook, Ill., 1976-81; v.p., gen. mgr. Security Pacific Internat. Bank, Chgo., 1981—; lectr. in real estate. Served with USN, 1962-66. Mem. Nat. Wharton Alumni Assn. (bd. dirs. 1978-81). Clubs: Hasty Pudding Inst. of 1770, Wharton Alumni of Chgo. (pres. 1978-81). Home: 1306 Rosalie St Evanston IL 60201 Office: 55 W Monroe St Chicago IL 60603

SCHWARZ, CATHERINE ELIZABETH, educator; b. Flint, Mich., May 1, 1928; d. Anthony S. and Margaret Ellen (McAlindon) Gatza; B.A., Marygrove Coll., Detroit, 1957; M.A. in History, U. Detroit, 1963; M.A. in Guidance and Counseling, U. Mich., 1977; m. John C. Schwarz, Jan. 30, 1971. High sch. tchr., 1950—; tchr. English/humanities and career planning Howell (Mich.) High Sch., 1969-81, counselor, 1981—; founder, dir. Career Planning Services, Ann Arbor, Mich., 1978; cons. in field; tchr. cons. Office Career Edn., U.S. Office Edn., 1975. NDEA grantee, 1967, 68. Mem. Am. Personnel and Guidance Assn., Nat. Employment Counselors Assn., Mich. Employment Counselors Assn., NEA, Mich. Edn. Assn., Howell Edn. Assn. Mem. Christian Ch. Address: 2777 Colony Rd Ann Arbor MI 48104

SCHWARZ, KENNETH (PAUL), control equipment mfg. co. exec.; b. Charter Oak, Iowa, May 26, 1938; s. Paul C. and Aletha C. Schwarz; B.S.E.E., Iowa State U., 1965; M.S.E.E., U. Iowa, 1969; m. Joleen H. Bahnsen, Aug. 6, 1960; children—Traci, Guy, Michael, Tanis. Sr. devel. engr. Dupont Co., Clinton, Iowa, 1965-71; with Fisher Control Inc., Marshalltown, Iowa, 1971—, mktg. mgr., 1977-79, dir. sales, 1979-81, dir. mktg., 1981—; instr. Clinton Community Coll. Served with USAF, 1956-60. Mem. Instrument Soc. Am. (sr.), Tau Beta Pi. Republican. Lutheran. Patentee web transfer. Home: 1711 W Lincolnway Marshalltown IA 50158 Office: 205 S Center St Marshalltown IA 50158

SCHWARZROCK, SHIRLEY PRATT, author, lectr., educator; b. Mpls., Feb. 27, 1914; d. Theodore Ray and Myrtle Pearl (Westphal) Pratt; B.S., U. Minn., 1935, M.A., 1942, Ph.D., 1974; m. Loren H. Schwarzrock, Oct. 19, 1945 (dec. 1966); children—Kay Linda, Ted Kenneth, Lorraine V. Sec. to chmn. speech dept., U. Minn., Mpls., 1935, instr. in speech, 1946, team tchr. in creative arts workshops for tchrs., 1955-56, guest lectr. Dental Sch., 1967-72, asst. prof. (part-time) of practice adminstrn. Sch. Dentistry, 1972—; tchr. speech, drama and English, Preston (Minn.) High Sch., 1935-37; tchr. speech, drama and English, Owatonna (Minn.) High Sch., 1937-39, also dir. dramatics, 1937-39; tchr. creative dramatics and English, tchr.-counselor Webster Groves (Mo.) Jr. High Sch., 1939-40; dir. dramatics and tchr.-counselor Webster Groves Sr. High Sch., 1940-43; exec. sec. bus. and profl. dept. YWCA, Mpls., 1943-45; tchr. speech and drama Covent of the Visitation, St. Paul, 1958; editor pro-tem Am. Acad. Dental Practice Adminstrn., 1966-68; guest tchr. Coll. St. Catherine, St. Paul, 1969; vol. mgr. Gift Shop, Eitel Hosp., Mpls., 1981—; cons. for dental med. programs Normandale Community Coll., Bloomington, Minn., 1968; cons. on pub. relations to dentists, 1954—; guest lectr. to various dental groups, 1966—; lectr. Internat. Congress on Arts and Communication, 1980, Am. Inst. Banking, 1981. Author of books on dental assisting, including: (with J.R. Jensen) Effective Dental Assisting, 1954, 6th edit., 1982; (with Lorraine Schwarzrock) Workbook for Effective Dental Assisting, 1979, 6th edit., 1982, Manual for Effective Dental Assisting, 1978, 6th edit., 1982; (with Donovan F. Ward) Effective Medical Assisting, 1969, 1976; Workbook for Effective Medical Assisting, 1969, 76; Manual for Effective Med. Assisting, 1969, 2d edit., 1976; author: (with C.G. Wrenn) The Coping With series of books for high sch. students, 1970, 73, The Coping With Series Manual, 1973, Contemporary Concerns of Youth, 1980. Pres. University Elementary Sch. PTA, 1955-56. Fellow Internat. Biog. Assn.; mem. Minn. (hon.) Acad. Dental Practice Adminstrn., Internat. Platform Assn. Zeta Phi Eta (pres. 1948-49), Eta Sigma Upsilon. Presbyterian. Home: 7448 W Shore Dr Minneapolis MN 55435

SCHWARZWALDER, MICHAEL, state senator, lawyer; b. San Diego, Oct. 30, 1943; s. Alan Enright and Caroline (Burch) S.; student Ohio U., 1961-63; B.A., Ohio State U., 1965, J.D., 1970; m. Karen E. Rounds, Mar. 21, 1965; children—Elizabeth, Abigail. Admitted to Ohio bar, 1970; mem. staff Legal Aid and Defender Soc. Columbus (Ohio), 1969-72; asso. partner firm Campbell, Boyland & Schwarzwalder, and successors, Columbus, 1972—; Sanford, Fisher, Fahey, Boyland & Schwarzwalder, 1980—; mem. Ohio State Senate, 1977—. Bd. dirs. various non-profit service agys. Served with U.S. Peace Corps, 1965-67. Recipient Disting. Service award Columbus Jaycees, 1978; Found. award ACLU Ohio, 1981. Mem. Am. Bar Assn., Columbus Bar Assn., Nat. Conf. State Legislatures. Democrat. Episcopalian. Office: Statehouse Columbus OH 43215

SCHWEGLER, JOHN FREDERICK, indsl. engr.; b. Rock Island, Ill., Aug. 24, 1931; s. Fred Herman and Susie (Forgy) S.; student Augustana Coll., 1950-51; B.S.I.E., U. Ill., 1958; M.S., U. Iowa, 1964, postgrad. 1968-73; m. Nancy Kathryn Knosher, July 3, 1960; children—Thomas Mark, William John. With Internat. Harvester Co., Rock Island, 1949-64, plant equipment designer, 1960-64; indsl. engr. U.S. Army Mgmt. Engring. Tng. Activity, Rock Island, 1964-73, chief process engring. div. Rock Island (Ill.) Arsenal, 1973-79, indsl. engr. Armament Readiness Command, 1979—; instr. value engring. Dept. Def., 1967-73. Served with U.S. Army, 1952-53. Registered profl. engr., Ill. Mem. Am. Inst. Indsl. Engrs., Nat. Soc. Profl. Engrs., Am. Def. Preparedness Assn., U. Ill. Alumni Assn., Nat. Rifle Assn. Methodist. Author: Drumheller and Godden) Systems Engineering Process, 1971. Home: 2339 46 St Rock Island IL 61201 Office: Commander Armament Readiness Command attn DRSAR LEW A Rock Island IL 61299

SCHWEITZER, ARTHUR, economist; b. Pirmasens, Germany, Nov. 27, 1905; came to U.S., 1938, naturalized, 1945; s. Heinrich and Louise (Haarlos) S.; student U. Berlin, 1930-32, U. Basel, 1933-36, Harvard U., 1938, Columbia U., 1938, U. Chgo., 1939; m. Elfriede L. Zimmermann, Oct. 20, 1937; children—Linda, Eric A. Lectr., U. Basel, 1937-38; Rockefeller fellow, 1938-39, 66-67; asst. prof. U. Wyo., 1939-45; vis. asst. prof. U. Chgo., 1945-47; asso. prof. econs. Ind. U., 1947-51, prof., 1951-76, prof. emeritus, 1976—; Fulbright prof., Berlin, 1961-62, 70. Recipient Newcomen award Harvard Bus. Rev., 1965; Social Sci. Research Council grantee, 1951, 57, 60. Mem. Am. Econ. Assn., Econ. History Assn., Assn. Revolutionary Econs., Assn. Social Econs., Assn. Comparative Econs. (pres. 1965). Unitarian. Author: Spiethoffs Konjunkturlehre, 1938; Big Business in the Third Teich, 1964; Nazifizierung des Mittelstandes, 1970; Age of Charisma; contbr. articles to profl. jours. Home: 925 Ballantine Rd Bloomington IN 47401 Office: Dept of Economics Indiana University Bloomington IN 47405

SCHWEITZER, MARY-ELIOT SMITH, electronic engring. technician, civic worker; b. San Jose, Calif., July 7, 1927; d. Julius Avery and Elise (Peyton) Smith; A.A., Marymount Coll., 1948; grad. Normandale Community Coll., Bloomington, Minn., 1981; m. Robert Schweitzer, Jr., Sept. 18, 1952; children—Mary-Eliot, James-Peyton, Mary-Neale. Sec., Teen-age Jr.'s Stanford Convalescent Home, Palo Alto, Calif., 1944-45; receptionist, driver ARC, Palo Alto, 1947-51; unit mgr. Magnetic Peripherals, Inc., Control Data Corp., Bloomington, Minn., 1981—. Leader, Girl Scouts U.S.A., Mpls., 1966-69; mem. Citizens Com. for Public Edn., Mpls., 1968-76, Citizens League, Mpls., 1968-80; docent Mpls. Inst. Arts, 1965-66, Hennepin County Hist. Soc., 1965-66; pres. Douglas Elem. Sch. PTA, 1968-70; v.p. West High Sch. PTA, 1970-71, pres., 1971-73; bd. dirs. Womens UN Rally, 1966-72, Friends Mpls. Inst. Arts, 1968-73; bd. dirs. Asso. James Ford Bell Library, 1968—, pres., 1972-75; bd. dirs. Mpls. Council PTAs, 1969-76, treas., 1974-76; bd. dirs. Minn. World Affairs Center, 1969-76, UN Assn. Minn., 1970-76; mem. adv. bd. Childrens Theatre Co., Mpls., 1969-72, house mgr., 1971-72; vice chmn. Hennepin Lowry Council, 1972-74; chmn. bd. Jr. League Thrift Shop, 1966-67; mem. citywide adv. com. for ednl. facilities and plant planning Mpls. Public Schs., 1975-76. Mem. DAR, Mpls. Soc. Fine Arts, Womens Assn. Minn. Symphony Orch., Mpls. League Catholic Women (dir. 1974-80), LWV, English Speaking Union, West Dist. Schs. Assn. (vice chmn. 1972-73, chmn. 1974-75), Peyton Soc. Va., Minn. Zool. Soc. Club: Jr. League (dir. Mpls. 1966-67). Home: 5140 W 102d St Bloomington MN 55437 Office: Magnetic Peripherals Inc Bloomington MN

SCHWENDEMANN, DONALD EUGENE, mfg. exec.; b. Otho, Iowa, May 21, 1919; s. Francis and Mildred (Lundgren) S.; student Ft. Dodge Jr. Coll., 1936-37; B.S., Iowa State U., 1941; postgrad. Pa. State Coll., 1942; m. Barbara M. Brueck, Nov. 13, 1948; children—Sandra Kay, Sheryl Lee. With Detroit Diesel Engine div. Gen. Motors Corp., 1946-68, successively sales engr., zone sales rep., zone sales mgr., sales promotion mgr., 1946-56, regional mgr., Chgo., 1956-57, mgr. market research, Detroit, 1958-59, mgr. orgn. and bus. mgmt., 1957-68; v.p., gen. mgr. Baker div., Marine City, Mich., 1968-80, exec. v.p., 1980-81; pres. Reef-Baker Corp., Mt. Clemens, Mich., 1981—, also dir. Bd. dirs. Down Pines Community Services, Algonac, Mich., 1979—. Served to lt. Reef-Baker Corp., USNR, 1941-46. Mem. Alpha Gamma Rho. Republican. Presbyterian. Clubs: Masons; Optimist; Chgo. Athletic Assn.; University, Economic (Detroit). Home: 2444 St Clair River Dr Algonac MI 48001 Office: 5664 N River Rd Marine City MI 48039

SCHWENGELS, FORREST V., state senator; b. Sheffield, Iowa, Aug. 27, 1915; s. Gerhardt and Grace (Stover) S.; B.A., Parsons Coll., 1950; M.A., Georgetown U.; m. Betty Pickett, 1943; children—Forrest Victor, Paul F., Suzanne K. Real estate salesman; commd. cadet USAF, 1942, advanced through grades to lt. col.; served with SAC, 1942-63; ret., 1963; mem. Iowa State Senate, 1973—, chmn. appropriations subcom., natural resources com., state govt. com.; chmn. appropriations energy policy council. Elder, First Presbyterian Ch.; mem. Indian Hills Community Coll. Devel. Corp. Decorated comdr. Order of Phoenix (Greece). Mem. Farm Bur., Ret. Officers Assn., Air Force Assn., Am. Legion, VFW, C. of C., Soil Conservation Soc. Am., Phi Sigma Epsilon. Clubs: Lions, Elks, Masons, Shriners. Office: State Senate State Capitol Des Moines IA 50319*

SCHWENSEN, JOHN CHRISTIAN, funeral dir.; b. Corpus Christi, Tex., June 7, 1954; s. Mert Harvey and Julia Patricia (Johnson) S.; B.S., Kans. State U., 1979; A.A. in Mortuary Sci., San Francisco Coll. Mortuary Sci., 1977; postgrad. U. Kans., 1977—, La. State U., 1979; m. Cynthia Renee Pesha, May 22, 1976. Mortuary staff Conroy Funeral Home, Manhattan, Kans., 1972-76, Parkview Funeral Home, Manhattan, 1972-76; apprentice embalmer, mortuary staff McNary & Morgan Chapel, Berkeley, Calif., 1976-77; apprentice embalmer, funeral dir. W. L. Frye & Son Funeral Home, Olathe, Kans., 1977-78; mortuary staff, embalmer, funeral dir. Elliott Mortuary, Inc., Hutchinson, Kans., 1978-79; asso. Neill-Schwensen Funeral Home, Clay Center, Kans., 1980—; lectr. in field. Mem. Jr. C. of C. (dir. 1977-78), Kans. Embalmers Assn., Kans. Embalmers Eye Enucleation Assn., Nat. Assn. Skin Diving Schs., Beta Theta Pi. Republican. Episcopalian. Clubs: Masons, Rotary. Home: 708 Clark St Clay Center KS 67432 Office: 918 7th St Clay Center KS 67432

SCHWERIN, KURT, emeritus educator, librarian; b. Beuthen, Germany, Apr. 17, 1902; came to U.S., 1938, naturalized, 1946; s. Louis and Jenny (Freund) S.; grad. U. Breslau, 1934; M.S.Sc., New Sch. Social Research, 1940; B.S.L.S., Columbia U., 1943, Ph.D., 1955; m. Herta Bernstein, July 1, 1937 (dec.); m. 2d, Gertrude Dosenheimer, Mar. 27, 1950. Research asst. U. Breslau, 1931-32; cataloger Columbia U. Libraries, 1942-46; head cataloger U. Va. Law Library, 1946-48; head fgn. and internat. law sects. Northwestern U. Law Library, 1948-64, asst. librarian, 1953-64, librarian, 1964-70, 72-73, research asso. internat. and comparative law, 1957-58, asso. prof. law, 1958-63, prof., 1963-70, prof. emeritus, 1970—; lectr. U. Va., 1947, DePaul U., 1956-58; mem. Com. on Index to Fgn. Legal Periodicals, 1960-74. Bd. dirs. Selfhelp of Chgo., Inc. Research grantee Conf. Jewish Material Claims Against Germany, 1955; Ford Found. grantee, 1957-58, German Research Council, 1972, 75; decorated Officers Cross, Order of Merit, Fed. Rep. Ger., 1965. Mem. Internat. Assn. Law Libraries (dir. 1965-71), Am. Hist. Assn., Am. Soc. Internat. Law, Am. Assn. Law Libraries, Am. Fgn. Law Assn., Chgo. Assn. Law Libraries (past pres.), Chgo. Council Fgn. Relations, Leo Baeck Inst. N.Y. (dir., chmn. Chgo. br.). Jewish. Author: Classification for International Law and Relations, 1947, 3d edit., 1969; (with J.A. Rahl) Northwestern University School of Law: A Short History, 1960; German Compensation for Victims of Nazi Persecution, 1972; Bibliography of German Language Legal Monograph Series, 1978; The German-Jewish Emigration of the 1930's and its Impact on Chicago: Individuals in Science and Culture, 1980; editorial bd. Jour. Criminal Law, 1949-70, Excerpta Criminologica, 1961-64; contbr. articles to profl. jours. Home: 6007 N Sheridan Rd Chicago IL 60660 Office: 357 E Chicago Ave Chicago IL 60611

SCHWINN, EDWARD R., JR., bicycle mfg. co. exec.; B.A., U. Denver, 1972. Adminstrv. asst. to exec. v.p. Schwinn Bicycle Co., Chgo., 1972-79, v.p. corp. devel., 1974-79, pres., chief operating officer, 1979—, dir. 1974—. Office: Schwinn Sales Inc 1856 N Kostner Ave Chicago IL 60639

SCIAKY, ALBERT MARLO, welding equipment mfg. co. exec.; b. Paris, Mar. 20, 1929; came to U.S., 1941, naturalized, 1947; s. Sam Samuel and Linette (Miranda) S.; Ph.B., U. Chgo., 1949; B.S.E.E., Ill. Inst. Tech., 1955; m. Fritzi Kurtz, Sept. 9, 1957; children—Alexandra, Dolsa, Juliette, David, Ada. Project engr. Admiral Corp., Chgo., 1955-56; with Sciaky Bros., Inc., Chgo., 1956—, v.p. engring., 1970-75, exec. v.p., 1975-81, pres., 1981—, dir., 1974-78, also dir. Mem. IEEE, Am. Welding Soc. Democrat. Jewish. Clubs: Whitehall, Executives. Patentee in field. Office: Sciaky Bros Inc W 67th St Bedford Park IL 60638

SCIARA, JOSEPH FRANK, real estate broker; b. Chgo., Mar. 7, 1920; s. Antonino and Grace S.; B.A., Ill. Coll. Commerce; m. Amanda Sturgill, Dec. 20, 1948. Pub., exec. officer Post-Tribune newspaper, Chgo., 1952-65; pres. Post Tax Service, Chgo., 1965; real estate broker House of Sciara Realty, Niles, Ill., 1979—. Active Little League. Served with U.S. Army, 1942-47; ETO. Mem. Am. Mgmt. Assn., Am. Ind. Businessmen, Ind. Accts. Assn., Fed. Tax Assn., DAV, VFW, Am.-Italian Vets. Roman Catholic. Home: 9222 Courtland Dr Niles IL 60648

SCIESZINSKI, MARY LOUISE, ednl. dir., nun; b. Mason City, Iowa, July 25, 1938; d. Patrick Joseph and Mary (Donahue) S.; B.A., Clarke Coll., 1959, M.A., 1968; postgrad. Middlebury Coll., summers 1965-67, Clarke Coll., Loras Coll., summers. Joined Order Sisters of Presentation of Blessed Virgin Mary, Roman Catholic Ch., 1954; tchr. elem. schs., Dubuque, Iowa, 1959-67; prin. St. Columbkille Sch., Dubuque, 1968-75; dir. elem. curriculum Archdiocese of Dubuque, 1971—; instr. Clarke Coll., part-time, 1971—. Experienced Tchr. fellow, 1967-68. Mem. Internat. Reading Assn., Iowa Assn. Non-Public Sch. Adminstrs., Assn. for Supervision and Curriculum Devel., Nat. Cath. Edn. Assn., Nat. Council Social Studies. Home: 2360 Carter Rd Dubuque IA 52001 Office: 1229 Mt Loretta Ave Dubuque IA 52001

SCIMECA, DOMINIC JOSEPH, tool box mfg. co. exec.; b. Chgo., Aug. 29, 1942; s. Steve J. and Muriel E. Siemeca; B.S. in Bus. Adminstrn., Roosevelt U., 1965; M.B.A., DePaul U., 1978; m. Elaine J. Baird, Oct. 25, 1974; children—Kathleen, Karen, Jessica, Sara. Plant controller Eclipse div. Ill. Tool Works Inc., Detroit, 1967-72, controller Illitron div., 1972-76; controller Pioneer Screw & Nut, Elk Gove Village, Ill., 1976-77, Ogden Steel Co., Chgo., 1977-78, Chgo. Dial Co., 1978-79; v.p., gen. mgr. Model Industries, Yorkville, Ill., 1981—, also dir. Mem. Fin. Execs. Inst., Nat. Assn. Accts. Office: Route 47 and Cannonball Trail Yorkville IL 60560

SCOFIELD, GARY LEE, banker; b. Brookings, S.D., Dec. 19, 1944; s. Alonzo Emerson and Mabel Josephine (Jensen) S.; B.S., S.D. State U., 1972; student U. S.D., 1962-63, 64-65; m. Susan Lee Chamberlin, July 6, 1967; children—Charles C., Thomas. Agrl. loan officer Nat. Bank S.D., Huron, 1973, v.p. and mng. officer, Sioux Falls, 1981—; asst. cashier Aberdeen (S.D.) Nat. Bank, 1974-76; liaison credit officer 1st Bank System, Inc., Mpls., 1976-78; pres. 1st State Bank Park River (N.D.), 1978-81. Chmn. S.D., Nat. FFA Found., 1976; mem. long range planning com. St. Ansgar's Hosp., Park River, 1979. Served with AUS, 1965-69. Decorated D.F.C. (2), Air medal (22), Combat Medics Badge. Mem. Park River C. of C., Bank Adminstrn. Inst., Am. Bankers Assn., N.D. Bankers Assn., Upper Midwest Council, Greater N.D. Assn., Alpha Tau Omega. Republican. Club: Lions (dir.). Office: 141 N Main Ave Sioux Falls SD 57101

SCOFIELD, GORDON LLOYD, mech. engr., univ. ofcl.; b. Huron, S.D., Sept. 29, 1925; s. Perry Lee and Zella Frederica (Reese) S.; B.S. in Mech. Engring., Purdue U., 1946; M.S. in Mech. Engring., U. Mo. at Rolla, 1949; Ph.D. (NSF fellow), U. Okla., 1968; m. Nancy Lou Cooney, Dec. 27, 1947; children—Cathy Lynn, Terrence Lee. Instr. in mech. engring. S.D. State Coll., Brookings, 1946-47; instr. Sch. of Mines and Metallurgy, U. Mo., Rolla, 1947-50, asst. prof., 1950-53, asso. prof., 1953-57, prof., 1957-69; prof., head mech. engring., engring. mechanics Mich. Tech. U., Houghton, 1969-80; disting. prof. mech. engring., asst. to v.p. for acad. affairs S.D. Sch. Mines and Tech., Rapid City, 1981—; cons. to U.S. Naval Ordnance Test Sta., China Lake, Calif., 1956-71, Gen. Electric Co., summer, 1954, Douglas Aircraft Co., summer, 1962. Served with USN, 1943-46. Recipient Alumni Achievement award U. Mo., Rolla, 1975. Registered profl. engr., Mo. Mem. Soc. Automotive Engrs. (pres. 1977), ASME, Am. Soc. for Engring. Edn., Am. Inst. Aeros. and Astronautics, Sigma Xi, Phi Kappa Phi, Tau Beta Pi, Pi Tau Sigma. Clubs: Rotary. Contbr. articles on thermal radiation and engring. edn. to profl. jours. Address: PO Box 1085 Rapid City SD 57709

SCOFIELD, W. RICKARD, mfg. co. exec.; b. Ann Arbor, Mich., May 13, 1952; s. William and Joy S.; B.A. cum laude in Bus., Albion (Mich.) Coll., 1974; m. Susan Rockey, June 28, 1974. Vice pres. May & Scofield, Inc., Howell, Mich., 1974—. Sec., Howell Community Chest, 1976; 1st treas. Livingston County United Way, 1977-81, v.p., 1981—; mem. Howell Planning Commn., 1976—. Mem. Howell C. of C. (past treas., past v.p., pres. 1979—). Clubs: Rotary, Jaycees. Office: 627 S Dearborn Howell MI 48843

SCOGGINS, SHIRLEY LOIS, computer mfg. co. exec.; b. Dearborn, Mich., Mar. 27, 1929; d. Frederick August Andrew and Anna Marie Elizabeth (Pletz) Morris; student Slippery Rock Tchrs. Coll., 1948, Ind. State Tchrs. Coll., 1949-50; children—Bruce Edward, Michael Albert. Detailer, atomic power div. Westinghouse, Pitts., 1956-64, detailer, research, 1961-64; designer Computer Peripherals, Inc., Rochester, Mich., 1964-78, mgr. documentation control, 1978—. Mem. Am. Soc. Profl. and Exec. Women, Am. Mgmt. Assn. Republican. Lutheran. Home: 30134 Fink St Farmington Hills MI 48024 Office: Computer Peripherals Inc 1480 N Rochester Rd Rochester MI 48063

SCONCE, EVA MAE, theatre exec., former educator; b. Danville, Ill., May 9, 1905; d. William E. and Elizabeth L. (Strawser) Lynch; A.B. magna cum laude, Ind. Central U., 1928; A.M., U. Ill., 1931; postgrad. in computer sci. U. So. Calif., 1963; m. Joseph Byce Sconce, Feb. 15, 1941; children—William Joseph, David Reid (dec.). Tchr. math. public high schs., Ind., Ill., 1929-33; partner Sconce Theatres, Indpls., 1943-81; asst. prof. engring. math. and computer sci. Purdue U., 1960-70, prof. emeritus, 1970—. Mem. Edinburgh (Ind.) Sch. Bd., 1950-55; pres. Ind. Sch. Bds. Assn., 1952-53. Mem. Sigma Xi, Epsilon Sigma Alpha. Presbyterian. Club: Propylaeum (Indpls.). Author: (with Ruth Hutchison and Jean Denk) Rest Haven Cemetery—150 Years, 1972. Office: PO Box 98 Edinburgh IN 46124

SCOTT, ALICE FEATHERSTONE, ednl. adminstr.; b. Toledo; d. Harold Milton and Dorothy Marie (Bolton) Featherstone; B.A., U. Toledo, 1981; m. Milton Arthur Scott, June 8, 1940 (dec.); children—Jeffrey Milton and Jonathan Arthur (twins). Asst. dir. public relations ARC, Toledo, 1945-47, 61-62; feature editor The Percolator, 1960-61; editor Toledo Club newsletter, 1960-65; chief copywriter Tiedtke's Dept. Store, 1962-66; mgr. public relations Lighting Products div. Lear Siegler Inc., Toledo, 1966-69; supr. info. services Toledo Public Schs., 1969—; freelance asst. to comic strip writer Allen Saunders, 1950-70. Co-chmn. publicity fund drives United Appeal Crusade Mercy, 1967-69, U.S. Savs. Bonds drives, 1967-69. Recipient 1st place grand award Internat. Council Indsl. Editors, 1967, Silver medal Womens Advt. Club/Printers Ink Mag., 1968. Mem. Womens Advt. Club Toledo (pres. 1972-74), Am. Advt. Fedn., Public Relations Soc. Am., Nat. Public Relations Soc. Am., Nat. Sch. Public Relations Assn., U. Toledo Alumni Assn. (past sec.), Women in Communications, Internat. Council Indsl. Editors, Psi Chi Phi, Alpha Phi Gamma. Presbyterian. Club: Press (Toledo). Home: 2313 Oak Grove Pl Toledo OH 43613 Office: Adminstrn Bldg Manhattan and Elm Sts Toledo OH 43608

SCOTT, BETTY ANN, advt. agy. exec.; b. Canton, Ohio, May 23, 1949; d. Charles M. and Betty M. (Barthel) Scott; student Kent State U., 1967-75. Asst. art dir. Goodway Pub., Ft. Lauderdale, Fla., 1968-69; layout and design artist Creative Universal, Detroit, 1969-70; owner, pres., account exec. Scott & Assos., Canton, 1971—. Chmn. enshrinee com. Pro Football Hall of Fame, 1979-81, active display com., 1971-81. Recipient Public Service award Mayor Stanley Cmich, Canton, 1980. Mem. Indsl. Marketers of Cleve., Network of Akron/Canton, Canton C. of C. Republican. Club: Advt. Home: 3990 Townhouse Ln Uniontown OH 44685 Office: 4041 Batton Dr NW Suite 215 North Canton OH 44720

SCOTT, CARMEN LYNN, planning exec.; b. West Liberty, Ohio, Jan. 9, 1940; s. Oliver Pearl and Winnie Margaret S.; student Wittenberg U., 1968, 77. Tech. asst. to dist. dept. dir. Dept. Transp. State of Ohio, Sidney, Ohio, 1958-68; exec. dir. Logan-Union-Champaign Regional Planning Commn., East Liberty, Ohio, 1968—. Chmn. budget com. United Fund of Logan County, Ohio, 1966; chief counselor Buckeye Boys' State. Served with Signal Corps U.S. Army, 1963-65. Mem. County Planning Dirs. Assn. Ohio, Am. Planning Assn., Logan County Community Improvement Corp., Ohio Planning Conf., Top of Ohio Resource, Conservation and Devel. Council. Am. Legion. Republican. Methodist. Club: Elks. Office: PO Box 141 East Liberty OH 43319

SCOTT, CRAIG LINDSAY, info. systems specialist; b. Flint, Mich., May 1, 1952; s. Ronald Marshall and Shirley Ann S.; B.A., Mich. State U., 1974; A.M.L.S., U. Mich., 1975; postgrad. Mich. State U., 1975-76; m. Jane Marie Setla, June 17, 1977. Jr. librarian Mich. State U., East Lansing, 1975-76; archtl. reporter McGraw-Hill, Inc., Lansing, Mich., 1976-78; info. systems and bus. communications specialist F.W. Dodge div. McGraw-Hill, Inc., Lansing, 1978-79; nat. accounts rep. F.W. Dodge div. McGraw-Hill, Inc., Detroit, 1979-80, Chgo., 1980—. Mem. Am. Mktg. Assn., Delta Chi. Home: 984 Hyacinth Dr Bartlett IL 60103 Office: 230 W Monroe St Chicago IL 60606

SCOTT, DANIEL ELLIS, mfg. co. exec.; b. Saginaw, Mich., Sept. 28, 1941; s. Benjamin Arturo and Lizzell (Perkins) S.; A.A., Flint (Mich.) Community Jr. Coll., 1968; B.A., U. Mich., 1971; M.B.A., Mich. State U., 1978. Operator electronic acctg. machine, computer programmer Buick Motor div. Gen. Motors Corp., 1963-72; systems analyst Kelsey Hayes Corp., Romulus, Mich., 1972-74; with Rockwell Internat., Troy, Mich., 1974—, mgr. fin., personnel and mktg. systems, 1976—. Served with U.S. Army, 1960-63. Mem. Engring. Soc. Detroit, Assn. Systems Mgmt. Contbg. author: Common Manufacturing Systems, 1978. Home: 2727 Renshaw Dr Troy MI 48098 Office: 2135 W Maple Rd Troy MI 48084

SCOTT, DAVID C., mfg. co. exec.; b. Akron, Ohio, 1915; B.Sc. in Chem. Engring., U. Ky., 1940, D.Sc. (hon.), 1974; J.D. (hon.), Marquette U., 1980. Owner engring. cons. firm. Inst. Tech. Research,

1940-45; exec. Gen. Electric Co., 1945-63, mgr. power tube plant, Schenectady, 1954-60, gen. mgr. cathode ray tube dept., Syracuse, 1960-63; v.p., group exec. several subs. Colt Industries Inc., 1963-68, exec. v.p., dir., 1965-68; pres. Allis-Chalmers Corp., Milw., 1968-69, chmn. bd., pres., chief exec. officer, 1969-81, chmn. bd., chief exec. officer, 1981—; dir. First Wis. Corp., Am. Can Co., Martin Marietta Corp., Travelers Corp., Humana, Inc., Harris Corp., Royal Crown Cos. Founding mem. Rockefeller U. Council; mem. exec. com. U.S. sect. Egypt-U.S. Bus. Council; mem. German Dem. Republic-U.S. Bus. Council; bd. dirs. U.S.-USSR Trade and Econ. Council; mem. exec. com., vice chmn. Nat. Council for U.S.-China Trade. Mem. U.S. C. of C. (internat. policy com.). Office: Allis-Chalmers Corp 1205 S 70th St PO Box 512 Milwaukee WI 53201

SCOTT, DON, chem. co. exec.; b. Bklyn., July 8, 1925; s. Joseph and Ruth (Dobenko) Scochman; B.S., Cornell U., 1944, M.S., 1945; postgrad. U. Mich., 1945, U. Chgo., 1945-46, M.B.A., 1970; Ph.D., Ill. Inst. Tech., 1950; m. Beverley Lorraine Tepper, Oct. 28, 1946 (dec. 1972); children—Rickie Deborah, Keith Wesley, Wendy Sue; m. 2d, Patricia Louise Marshall, May 13, 1978; 1 stepson, Greg Marshall. Bacteriologist, Vitazyme Labs., Chgo., 1945-46, tech. dir., 1951-54; instr. Ill. Inst. Tech., Chgo., 1947-50; research bacteriologist E. I. du Pont de Nemours & Co., Inc., 1950-51; v.p. Fermco Labs., Chgo., 1954-66; v.p., gen. mgr. Fermco div. G. D. Searle & Co., Skokie, Ill., 1966-71, v.p., gen. mgr. Searle Biochemics div., 1972-73, pres. div., 1973-75, tech. dir. New Venture div., 1973-75; pres. Fermco Biochemics, 1975—. Mem. Am. Chem. Soc., Inst. Food Technologists, Soc. Soft Drink Technologists, Am. Assn. Clin. Chemists, Am. Inst. Chem. Engrs., Sigma Xi, Phi Lambda Upsilon. Contbr. articles to sci. jours. Patentee on enzyme purification, food processing, med. diagnostic reagents in U.S. and fgn. countries. Office: 2638 Delta Lane Elk Grove Village IL 60007

SCOTT, DOROTHY ALLENE, travel counselor; b. Detroit, July 20, 1922; d. James Russel and Allene Frances (Griffin) Bily; student public schs.; m. Elmer Francis Scott, Jr., July 26, 1944; children—Christine Frances, Richard Allen, Lawrence James, Edward Francis. With art dept. Mosstype Corp., Elk Grove, Ill., 1968-77; travel counselor Da Prato Travel, Itasca, Ill., 1973-78; drop-ship specialist Long Fleet, Elmhurst, Ill., 1978—. Recipient Blue Ribbons, Ill. Regional Town and Country Art Show, 1972, 73, 74, 76. Cert. travel counselor. Mem. Inst. Cert. Travel Agts., Oceanic Soc. Roman Catholic. Home: 429 S Cherry St Itasca IL 60143 Office: 388 Carol Ln Elmhurst IL 60126

SCOTT, ERIC ANSIL, editor, publisher; b. Sandusky, Ind., Apr. 12, 1899; s. William Henry and Florida (Fleetwood) S.; student pub. schs., Sandusky; m. Cleo Arvillia Faulkner, June 20, 1923. Masonry supt. Michael Kinder & Sons, engrs., contractors, Ft. Wayne, Ind., 1935-61; editor, pub. The Pioneer, 6th Regt. Engrs. bi-monthly mag., Ft. Wayne, 1958—. Founder Gen. Edmund L. Daley Meml. Hall and Mus., Ft. Wayne; pres. War Vets. Meml. Shrine Am. History; hon. comdr. Garrison at Ft. Wayne, 1979—. Served with U.S. Army, 1917-19; AEF in France. Recipient Verdun medal, 1953; Veterans Council Americanism award, 1966; Spl. Merit citation Nat. Navy Club Aux., 1974; Community Service award Lincoln Post 82, Am. Legion, 1974; Nat. Comdrs. award Disabled Am. Vets., 1977. Mem. V.F.W. (life, cited by dept. Ind. 1970, Allen County 1972), Am. Legion (hon. life), Smithsonian Instn., Soc. 3d Inf. Div. (nat. v.p. 1960-61, Ind. pres. 1958—, Audie Murphy award 1972; life), Vets. 6th U.S. Engrs. (nat. sec.-treas. 1958—, hon. col.), World War I Vets. (adj. dept. Ind. 1978-79, judge advocate Ft. Wayne barracks 1963, comdr. Anthony Wayne barracks 30, 1965, 4th dist. legis. officer, 1965, comdr. 4th dist. Ind. 1967-68, nat. dep. chief of staff 1969—, historian Ind. dept. 1972-73), Allen County Vets. Council (vice-comdr. 1965, comdr. 1966-67, Patriotic award 1973), Naval Hist. Found. Republican. Address: Elrico Gardens 2122 O'Day Rd Fort Wayne IN 46818

SCOTT, GEORGE MATTHEW, state supreme ct. justice; b. Clark, N.J., Sept. 14, 1922; s. Francis Patrick and Harriet Ann (O'Donnell) S.; B.S., U. Minn.; J.D., William Mitchell Coll. Law; m. Joyce E. Hughes, July 26, 1947; children—Dan, Neil, Brian, George Matthew, Sheila. Admitted to Minn. bar; practice law, 1951-55; dep. atty. gen. State of Minn., 1955; atty. Hennepin County, Mpls., 1955-73; justice Minn. Supreme Ct., St. Paul, 1973—. Trustee William Mitchell Coll. Del. Democratic Nat. Conv., 1960; campaign chmn. Hubert H. Humphrey for Senator, 1960. Served with AUS, 1942-45. Mem. Am., Minn. bar assns., Nat. Dist. Atty's. Assn. (pres. 1964-65), Am. Legion. Roman Catholic. Club: Optimists. Contbr. articles to profl. jours. Office: 228 Minnesota State Capitol Saint Paul MN 55155*

SCOTT, HAROLD JOSEPH, state senator; b. Flint, Mich. Oct. 5, 1938; s. Harold Leroy and Irene (Archambault) S.; B.A., U. Mich., 1960; M.A., Wayne State U., 1964; m. Jacqueline I. Dombrosky, 1960; children—Harold Anthony, John Charles, Anne Marie, Michael Andrew. Mem. Mich. Ho. of Reps., 1972-76; mem. Mich. State Senate, 1977—, mem. appropriations com.; tchr. Wyandotte (Mich.) Schs., 1961-67, Indian River Jr. Coll., Ft. Pierce, Fla., 1967-68, Grand Blanc (Mich.) Schs., 1968-69, Mt. Morris (Mich.) Schs., 1969-72. Clubs: KC, Croatian Slovene, Eagles. Roman Catholic. Office: Mich Senate Capital Bldg Lansing MI 48933*

SCOTT, IRENA MCCAMMON, biologist; b. Delaware, Ohio, July 31, 1942; d. James Robert and Gay (Nuzum) McCammon; B.Sc., Ohio State U., Columbus, 1965; M.S., U. Nev., Las Vegas, 1972; Ph.D., U. Mo., Columbia, 1976; m. John Watson Scott, Dec. 6, 1969. Teaching and research asst. U. Nev., 1970-72; research asst. U. Mo., 1972-76; researcher Cornell U., 1977-78; asst. prof. biology St. Bonaventure (N.Y.) U., 1978-79; researcher Ohio State U., 1979—, Batelle Meml. Inst., 1980—. Grantee St. Bonaventure U. Mem. AAAS, Am. Physiol. Soc., Am. Dairy Sci. Assn., Mo. Acad. Sci., Ohio State U. Astronomy Club, Verse Writers Guild Ohio, Olentangy Poets, Mensa, Sigma Xi, Gamma Sigma Delta. Contbr. articles to profl. jours. Home: 6520 Bale Kenyon St Galena OH 43021 Office: 130 Hamilton Hall Ohio State U Columbus OH 43210

SCOTT, JAMES VICTOR, veterinarian; b. Chrisman, Ill., Dec. 25, 1930; s. Victor and Mabel Gertrude (Miller) S.; student James Millikin U., 1948-50; B.S., U. Ill., 1952, M.S. in Physiology, 1957, B.S. in Vet Medicine, 1957, D.V.M., 1959; postgrad. Columbia U., 1954, CCNY, 1955; m. Patricia Ruth Millsap, Aug. 7, 1959; 1 son James Victor II. Research asso. U. Ill., Urbana, 1956-61; pvt. practice vet. medicine, Philo, Ill., 1959—; owner Triple S Farms, Camargo, Ill., 1963—; research dir. Eureka (Ill.) Mineral Co., Inc., 1970-75; owner, dir. Triple S Bull Stud, Camargo, Ill., 1974—. Served with U.S. Army, 1953-55. Mem. Am. Vet. Medicine Assn., Ill. Vet. Med. Assn., Eastern. Ill. Vet. Med. Assn., AAAS, Embryo Transfer Soc., Sigma Xi, Gamma Sigma Delta, Phi Zeta. Clubs: Masons, Shriners. Home: Univ of Ill Trail Philo IL 61864

SCOTT, JAMES WALTER, metall. engr.; b. Rolla, Mo., Feb. 2, 1899; s. John Walter and Stella Aurora (Sappenfield) S.; B.S. in Metallurgy, U. Mo., Rolla, 1919, Met.E., 1925; M.S. in Metallurgy, U.Nev., 1923; postgrad. in bus. adminsrn. Northwestern U., 1930-31; m. Catherine Alice Culbertson, Aug. 12, 1919; children—Anne Estelle, James Walter. Resident engr. Ill. Hwy. Constrn. Springfield, summer 1917; asst. instr. in metallurgy, U. Mo., Rolla, 1918-19; metall. chemist Ducktown Sulphur Copper and Iron Co., Isabella, Tenn., 1919; mining engr. La Democrata Mine, Cananea, Sonora, Mexico, 1920; metallurgist Rare and Precious Metals Sta., U.S. Bur. Mines, Rolla and Reno, Nev., 1920-23; metall. engr. Western Electric Co., Chgo., from 1923, later asst. supt. devel. engring., until 1964, ret., 1964; cons. metall. engring., Downers Grove, Ill., 1964—; instr. in metallurgy Lewis Inst. Evening Sch., 1929-36; Am. del. World Metall. Congress, Eng., Germany, France, 1955, Chgo., 1957. Mem. Downers Grove High Sch. Dist. 99 Bd. Edn., 1939-42; trustee Downers Grove Methodist Ch., 1945-63; pres. Downers Grove Village Forum, 1948. Served with U.S. Army, World War I. Lic. profl. engr., Ill.; lic. registered pharmacist, Mo. Mem. AIME (life; sec. Chgo. sect. 1932), Am. Soc. Metals (life; chmn. Chgo. chpt. 1944), Tau Beta Pi. Republican. Contbr. articles to profl. publs. Home: 4629 Highland Ave Downers Grove IL 60515

SCOTT, JANE NICHOLSON, educator; b. Lexington, Ky., Nov. 24, 1944; d. Horace and Ruby (Wells) N.; B.A., Transylvania U., 1966; M.S., U. Ky., 1968, Ph.D., 1971; m. Robert James Scott, Dec. 18, 1971. Postdoctoral fellow, U. Ky., Lexington, 1971-72; asst. prof. Eastern Ky. U., Richmond, 1972-73; lectr. Ahmadu Bello U., Nigeria, 1973-75; asst. prof. Wright State U. Sch. of Medicine, Dayton, Ohio, 1975-81, asso. prof., 1981—. Mem. Ohio Acad. Sci., Soc. for Study of Reprodn., Am. Assn. Anatomists, Assn. Women in Sci. Office: Dept Anatomy Wright State Sch of Medicine Dayton OH 45435

SCOTT, JOHN E., state senator; b. Charleston, Mo., July 24, 1939; grad. high sch.; m. Patricia Ann Crowe, 1957; 3 children. Real estate investor; mem. Mo. Ho. of Reps., 1970-76, Mo. Senate, 1976—. Served with Mo. N.G. Recipient award St. Louis Globe Democrat. Democrat. Office: State Capitol Jefferson City MO 65101*

SCOTT, JOHNIE THOMAS, nutritionist; b. Shamrock, Tex., June 21, 1950; s. John Thomas and Alta Mae (Austin) S.; B.S., Tex. A. and M. U., 1972, M.S., 1974, Ph.D., 1976; m. Helen Charlene Mundy, July 17, 1970. Teaching asst. nutrition Tex. A. and M. U., College Station, 1973-76; mgr. Tech. Service Bur., Diamond Shamrock, Cleve., 1976-78, mgr. nutritional services, 1979—; head poultry research Swift & Co., Chgo., 1979; nutritional cons. Recipient Am. Farmer award, 1969. Mem. Poultry Sci. Assn., Assn. Feed Microscopy, Nat. Feed Ingredients Assn., Am. Feed Mfrs. Assn., Sigma Xi. Ch. of Christ. Contbr. articles to profl. jours. Home: 6610 Orchard St Parma OH 44129 Office: 1100 Superior St Cleveland OH 44114

SCOTT, JULES FRANKLIN, horticulture firm advt. ofcl.; b. Chgo., May 22, 1920; s. Jules Franklin and Helen Veronica (Kasmer) S.; B.S., Northwestern U., 1942; postgrad. U.S. Naval Acad., 1941; 1 son, Mark S. Copywriter, Montgomery Ward & Co., 1946-47, catalog advt. mgr., 1947-56; creative dir. Carter & Galantin Advt. Agy., 1956-59; creative dir., account supr. Hammett & Gillespie Advt. Agy., 1964-68; corp. dir. advt., sales promotion, and public relations Vaughan-Jacklin Corp., Downers Grove, Ill., 1968—. Former scoutmaster Boy Scouts Am.; former treas. P.T.A.; pres. Homeowner Assn. Served to lt. comdr., USNR, 1941-45; ETO, PTO. Writer short stories; contbr. articles to hort. trade publs. Home: 946 Dartmouth Dr Wheaton IL 60187 Office: 5300 Katrine Ave Downers Grove IL 60187

SCOTT, RALPH C., physician, educator; b. Bethel, Ohio, June 7, 1921; s. John Carey and Leona (Laycock) S.; B.S., U. Cin., 1942, M.D., 1945; m. Rosemary Ann Schultz, June 26, 1945; children—Susan Ann, Barbara Lynne, Marianne. Intern Univ. Hosps., U. Iowa, 1945-46; resident, asst. dept. pathology U. Cin. Coll. Medicine, 1948-49, fellow internal medicine, 1949-53, fellow cardiology, 1953-57, mem. faculty, 1950—, prof. medicine, 1968—; staff clinics Cin. Gen. Hosp., 1950-75, clinician in internal medicine, 1952-75, dir. cardiac clinics, 1965-75, attending physician med. service, 1958—; staff VA Hosp., Cin., 1954—, cons., 1961—; attending physician Med. Service, Christian R. Holmes Hosp., Cin., 1957—; attending staff USAF Hosp., Wright Patterson AFB, 1960—; staff Good Samaritan Hosp., Cin., 1961—, cons., 1967—; staff Jewish Hosp., Cin., 1957—, cons., 1968—; cons. Children's Hosp., Cin., 1968—; attending physician Providence Hosp., Cin., 1971—. Served from 1st lt. to capt., AUS, 1946-48. Nat. Heart Inst. grantee, 1964-68, 67-74, 76—. Diplomate Am. Bd. Internal Medicine (subspecialty cardiovascular disease). Fellow A.C.P. Am. Coll. Cardiology, Am. Coll. Chest Physicians; mem. AMA, Ohio State Med. Assn., Cin. Acad. Medicine, Central Soc. Clin. Research, Am. Heart Assn. (fellow council clin. cardiology), Cin. Soc. Internal Medicine, Heart Assn. Southwestern Ohio, Am. Fedn. for Clin. Research, Internat. Cardiovascular Soc., Sigma Xi, Alpha Omega Alpha, Phi Eta Sigma, Phi Chi. Contbr. articles to med. jours. Editorial bd. Am. Heart Jour., 1967-79, Jour. Electrocardiology, 1967—; editor Electrocardiographic-Pathologic Conf., Jour. Electrocardiology, 1967—, Clin. Cardiology and Diabetes, Vols. I, II, III, 1980-81. Home: 2955 Alpine Terr Cincinnati OH 45208 Office: Room 7157 Med Scis Bldg Univ Cincinnati Med Center 231 Bethesda Ave Cincinnati OH 45267

SCOTT, RALPH KENNETH, indsl. edn. co. exec.; b. Detroit, Aug. 23, 1936; s. Virgil and Ora S.; M.A., Wayne State U., 1961; postgrad. Harvard U., 1978; Ph.D., Columbia U., 1979; m. Diane Pasny, May 20, 1978; children—Sean, Stephanie. Asst. prof. Detroit Coll. Bus., 1962-65; sr. sales trainer Mich. Blue Cross, 1965-67; sr. acct. exec. Jam Handy Ongn., Detroit, 1967-71; v.p. mktg. Sandy Corp., Southfield, Mich., 1971—, also dir. Mem. Am. Soc. Tng. and Devel., Harvard Bus. Sch. Assn. Detroit. Club: Great Oaks Country (Rochester, Mich.). Home: 2765 Bolingbroke Troy MI 48084 Office: 16025 Northland Dr Southfield MI 48074

SCOTT, ROBERT ALLYN, ednl. adminstr.; b. Englewood, N.J., Apr. 16, 1939; s. William D. and Ann. F. (Waterman) S.; B.A., Bucknell U., 1961; Ph.D., Cornell U., 1975; m. Phyllis Virginia Brice, Mar. 23, 1963; children—Ryan Keith, Kira Elizabeth. Mgmt. trainee Procter & Gamble Co., Phila., 1961-63; asst. dir. admissions Bucknell U., Lewisburg, Pa., 1965-67; asst. dean Coll. Arts and Scis., Cornell U., Ithaca, N.Y., 1967-69, asso. dean, 1969-79, prof. anthropology, 1978-79; dir. acad. affairs Ind. Commn. for Higher Edn., Indpls., 1979—; lectr. U. Philippines, 1964-65; cons. to Sta. WSKG Public TV and Radio, 1977-79; cons. to various colls. and univs., 1966—. Trustee, Bucknell U., 1976-78, First Unitarian Ch., Ithaca, 1970-73, 78-79, chmn., 1971-73. Served with USNR, 1963-65. Spencer Found. research grantee, 1972, Exxon Edn. Found. research grantee, 1977. Fellow Am. Anthrop. Assn.; mem. Assn. Study Higher Edn., Am. Sociol. Assn., Am. Assn. Higher Edn., Higher Edn. Colloquium, Bucknell U. Alumni Assn. (dir. 1971-80, pres. 1976-78), Indpls. Com. on Fgn. Relations, Phi Kappa Psi, Phi Kappa Phi. Clubs: Ithaca Yacht; Econs. of Indpls. Contbr. articles to sociol., ednl. and popular publs.; author books and mongraphs; editorial bd. Cornell Rev., 1976-79; book rev. editor Coll. and Univ., 1974-78; cons. editor Change mag. Office: 143 W Market St Indianapolis IN 46204

SCOTT, ROBERT CLINTON, banker; b. Bayonne, N.J., Dec. 13, 1932; s. William James and Marion Josephine (White) S.; A.B., U. Miss., 1954; J.D., U. Mich., 1959; m. Josephine W. Garner, May 31, 1954; children—Marion C., Robin W. Admitted to Ill. bar, 1960; pvt. practice law, Chgo., 1959-67; officer Chgo. Title and Trust Co., 1967-70; sr. v.p. Security Nat. Bank, Battle Creek, Mich., 1970-72; group v.p. Mich. Nat. Bank, Detroit, 1972-77, sr. v.p., 1977—; faculty trust and estates John Marshall Law Sch., Chgo., 1963-67. Served with USMC, 1954-57. Mem. Am. Bar Assn., Detroit Estate Planners Assn. Episcopalian. Clubs: Univ., Forest Lake Country. Home: 7225 Deer Hill Rd Clarkston MI 48016 Office: 1000 W Maple St Troy MI 48099

SCOTT, SHERIDAN, educator; b. Sioux Falls, S.D., June 28, 1942; d. Dale Stuart and Betty Jane (Bowman) Burgum; student Portland State Coll., 1960-62; Glassboro Coll., 1967-68; B.S.Ed., Wright State U., 1970, M.A., 1971, postgrad., 1973. m. Aug. 22, 1979; children—Kasie, Mark. Stewardess, United Airlines, 1962-66; tchr. Glouster Twp. (N.J.) Schs., 1966-69; tchr. Centerville (Ohio) City Schs., 1971—; adj. instr. Wright State U., 1972-79. Mem. edn. comn. Friends of Dayton Ballet, 1980, vol. coordinator, 1981. Mem. Nat. Middle Sch. Assn. (v.p. 1977-79, pres. 1980-81), Ohio Middle Sch. Assn. (dir. 1975-80, chmn. state conf. 1976), Assn. Supervision and Curriculum Devel., NEA, Ohio Edn. Assn., Centerville Classroom Tchrs. Assn., Phi Delta Kappa. Republican. Methodist. Home: 6699 Statesboro St Centerville OH 45459 Office: 5900 Hithergreen Dr Dayton OH 45429

SCOTT, SIDNEY WILLIAM, media corp. exec.; b. Galesburg, Ill., Dec. 8, 1942; s. Ralph Eldrich and Helen Laverne (Bean) S.; B.S., Ill. State U., 1968; M.B.A., Bradley U., 1977; m. Janice Elaine Smith, Aug. 20, 1966; children—Britain, Erin, Ryan Andrew. Creative coordinator Peoria (Ill.) Jour. Star, 1968-76; customer service mgr. Tazewell Pub. Co., Morton, Ill., 1976-77; public relations and art dir. Telegraph Herald, Dubuque, Iowa, 1977-79, dir. devel. and promotion, 1979-80, dir. organizational devel., 1980-81; corp. dir. human resources Woodward Communications Inc., Dubuque, 1982—. Vice chmn. Dubuque County chpt. ARC, 1972—; bd. dirs. Dubuque Symphony, 1980—; trustee United Way of Dubuque, 1981—; mem. devel. council Clarke Coll., 1981—, U. Dubuque, 1982—. Served with Army N.G., 1964-70. Mem. Newspaper Personnel Relations Assn., Am. Soc. Personnel Adminstrs., Am. Soc. Tng. and Devel., Assn. M.B.A. Execs., Internat. Registry of Orgn. Devel. Profls., Mensa. Club: Dubuque Golf and Country. Office: Woodward Communications Inc 801 Bluff St Dubuque IA 52001

SCOTT, THEODORE R., lawyer; b. Mt. Vernon, Ill., Dec. 7, 1924; s. Theodore R. and Beulah (Flannigan) S.; A.B., U. Ill., 1947, J.D., 1949; m. Virginia Scott, June 1, 1947; children—Anne, Sarah, Daniel, Barbara. Admitted to Ill. bar, 1950: law clk. to Judge Walter C. Lindley, U.S. Ct. Appeals, 1949-51; asso. Spaulding Glass, 1951-53, Loftus, Lucas & Hammand, 1953-58, Ooms, McDougall, Williams & Hersh, 1958-60; partner McDougall, Hersh, & Scott and predecessor, 1960— (all Chgo.). Served to 2d lt. USAAF, 1943-45; ETO. Decorated Air medal. Mem. Am., Ill., Chgo., 7th Circuit bar assns., Am. Coll. Trial Lawyers, Legal Club Chgo., Law Club Chgo., Patent Law Assn. Chgo. (past pres.), Phi Beta Kappa. Club: Union League (Chgo.); Exmoor Country (Highland Park, Ill.). Home: 1569 Woodvale Ave Deerfield IL 60015 Office: 135 S LaSalle St Chicago IL 60603

SCOTT, THOMAS RICHARD, educator; b. Alta., Can., Nov. 12, 1929; s. Ira Elwood and Vera Geraldine (Murphy) S.; B.S., George Williams Coll., 1961, M.S., 1963; Ed.D., No. Ill. U., 1975; CAS, U. Chgo., 1967; m. Shirley Ann Klein, June 10, 1961. Dir. continuing edn. Central YMCA Community Coll., Chgo., 1958-75, dean continuing edn., 1975-78; asst. dean Coll. Continuing Edn., No. Ill. U., DeKalb, 1975-78, also prof. edn.; dir. Center Extended Programs, George Williams Coll., Downers Grove, Ill., 1980—, also prof. Mott fellow, 1967; named Outstanding New Citizen of Yr., Citizenship Council Greater Chgo., 1970. Mem. Ill. Adult Edn. Assn. (pres. 1976-77), Adult Edn. Assn. Am., Profs. Adult Continuing Edn., Ill. Public Adult Continuing Adult Edn. Assn. Home: 2S474 Beechwood Ln Glen Ellyn IL 60137 Office: George Williams Coll Center Extended Programs Downers Grove IL 60515

SCOTT, TIMOTHY RALPH, internist; b. Champaign, Ill., Jan. 7, 1948; s. Ralph Leslie and Crystal Maxine (Snider) S.; B.S. in Biology, U. Ill., 1970; M.D., St. Louis U., 1974; m. Joan Lucille Wikoff, Dec. 30, 1972; children—Brian, Melissa. Intern, Northwestern U., Chgo., 1974-75, resident in internal medicine, 1975-77; practice medicine, specializing in internal medicine Carle Clinic, Urbana, Ill., 1977—, head dept. gen. internal medicine, 1978—; med. dir. Clark-Lindsey Nursing Home and Retirement Village, Urbana; clin. asst. prof. medicine U. Ill. Sch. Medicine, Urbana, 1978—. Active various charitable orgns. Recipient Physicians Recognition award AMA, 1977-80, 81. Fellow A.C.P.; mem. AMA, Ill. Soc. Internal Medicine, Am. Soc. Internal Medicine, Champaign County Med. Soc., AAAS, Phi Beta Pi, Alpha Epsilon Delta. Presbyterian. Home: 2205 S Pond St Urbana IL 61801 Office: Carle Clinic 602 W University St Urbana IL 61801

SCOTT, WALTER DILL, fin. services exec.; b. Chgo., Oct. 27, 1931; s. John Marcy and Mary Louise (Gent) S.; student Williams Coll., 1949-51; B.S., Northwestern U., 1953; M.S., Columbia, 1958; m. Barbara Ann Stein, Sept. 9, 1961; children—Timothy Walter, David Frederick, Gordon Charles. Cons. Booz, Allen & Hamilton, N.Y.C., 1956-58; asso. Glore, Forgan & Co., N.Y.C., 1958-63, partner, Chgo., 1963-65; partner Lehman Bros., Chgo., 1965-72, sr. partner, 1972-73, also dir.; asso. dir. econs. and govt. Office Mgmt. and Budget, Washington, 1973-75; sr. v.p. internat. and fin. Pillsbury Co., Mpls., 1975-78, exec. v.p., 1978-80, also dir.; pres., chief exec. officer Investors Diversified Services, Inc., Mpls., 1980—; dir. Investors Group of Funds, Jostens, Inc. Mem. adv. council Kellogg Grad. Sch. Mgmt., Northwestern U.; mem. bd. overseers Sch. Mgmt., U. Minn.; trustee Mpls. Soc. Fine Arts; bd. dirs. Urban Coalition of Mpls., Guthrie Theater Found. Served to lt. (j.g.) USN, 1953-56. Clubs: Woodhill; Minneapolis. Home: 2520 Cedar Ridge Rd Wayzata MN 55391 Office: 2900 IDS Tower Minneapolis MN 55402

SCOTT, WALTER EDWIN, ret. state ofcl.; b. Milw., Feb. 27, 1911; s. James Wylock and Ida (Fisher) S.; B.A., Kalamazoo Coll., 1933, M.A., 1955; M.S., U. Wis., 1965; m. Gertrude May Cox, Apr. 15, 1941. Warden, Wis. Dept. Natural Resources, Madison, 1934-36, game mgmt. supr., 1936-48, editor info. edn. div., 1948-50, asst. to dir., sec., 1950-75. Sec., Wis. Natural Resources Council State Agys., 1968-75; co-founder, past pres., sec. Wis. Natural Resources Found., 1957-77. Served with inf. CIC, AUS, 1943-46. Recipient citation Am. Motors Conservation award, 1967, citations U.S. Geol. Survey, also EPA, 1975, Outstanding Environmentalist award U. Wis., 1976; Disting. Service award Wis. Natural Resources Council, 1975. Fellow AAAS; mem. Wis. Soc. Ornithology (co-founder, past pres., custodian, spl. recognition award 1964), Citizens Natural Resources Assn. Wis. (citation 1964, co-founder), Historic Madison (co-founder, past pres., Spl. Recognition award 1976), Wildlife Soc. (charter), Am. Soc. Pub. Adminstrn. (co-founder, past pres. Wis. Capital chpt.), Wildfowl Trust Eng. (life), Wis. Writers Council (life), Wis. Acad. Scis., Arts and Letters (hon.; councilor 1954-76, librarian 1959-61, pres. 1964-65, citation 1966, Centennial award 1970), U. Wis.-Madison Friends of Library (past pres.; hon.), Izaak Walton League Am. (citation Wis. div. 1966), Wis. Wildlife Fedn.

(Conservationist of Year 1975, hon. v.p.), Dane County Conservation League (Distinguished Service award), Nature Conservancy, Assn. Midwest Fish and Game Commrs. (past sec.-treas., recognition citation), Internat. Assn. Fish and Wildlife Agencies (past sec.-treas., citation 1973), Wis. Hist. Soc., Wis. Outdoor Communicators Assn. (hon. life). Author: Poems to Trudi, 1950; Water Policy Evolution in Wisconsin, 1965; Conservation's First Century in Wisconsin, 1967; Our Oldest Oaks-a Living Heritage, 1976; Wisconsin Conservation Law Enforcement-A Centennial Chronology, 1979; A Wisconsin Deer Management Chronology 1836-1980; Bibliography of Wisconsin Birds, 1980; editor: Silent Wings — A Memorial to the Passenger Pigeon, 1947; The Passenger Pigeon, 1939-43, Wis. Acad. Rev., 1954-63; Wis. cons. Activities Progress Report, 1947-52; The Hickory Hill Herald, 1941-78. Home: 1721 Hickory Dr Madison WI 53705

SCOTT, WILLIAM PAUL, lawyer; b. Staples, Minn., Nov. 8, 1928; A.L.A., U. Minn., 1949; B.S.L., St. Paul Coll. Law, 1952, J.D., 1954; m. Elsie Elaine Anderson, Feb. 7, 1968; 1 son, Jason Lee; children by previous marriage—William P., Mark D., Bryan D., Scott; stepchildren—Thomas J., Terri L. Berg. Admitted to Minn. bar, 1954: atty. right of way div. Minn. Hwy. Dept., 1945-52, civil engr. traffic and safety div., 1953-55; practice law Arlington, Minn., 1955-61, Gaylord, Minn., 1963-67; sr. partner firm Scott Law Offices and predecessors, Minn., 1967—; probate, juvenile judge Sibley County, Minn., 1956-61; Minn. pub. examiner, 1961-63; county atty. Sibley County, 1963-68, city atty., Pipestone, 1978—. Formerly nat. committeeman Young Rep. League; Sibley County Rep. chmn., 1961. Served with USMCR, 1946-50; from 2d lt. to lt. col. USAF Res., 1950-77; liaison officer USAF Acad.; ret. Recipient George Washington Honor medal Freedoms Found., 1970, 72. Mem. Am., Minn. bar assns., Mensa, V.F.W., Am. Legion, Air Force Assn., Res. Officers Assn., U.S. Supreme Ct. Bar Assn. Mason (32 deg., Shriner). Home: Box 704 Pipestone MN 56164 Office: Park Plaza Offices Pipestone MN 56164

SCOTT, WINFIELD JAMES, mktg. exec.; b. Worcester, Mass., Jan. 4, 1933; s. Gherald Dean and Helen L. S.; B.A., Norwich U., 1955; postgrad. Marquette U., 1961-62; m. Betty Joan Price, June 29, 1957; children—Mary Jo, Susan Elizabeth. With sales dept. Norton Co., Worcester, 1956, sales rep. Chgo. dist., 1957, sales supr. Wis. dist., 1960-71; founder, pres. The Abrasive Group, Wauwatosa, Wis., 1971—; ad hoc prof. mktg. U. Wis. Extension. Mem. Abrasive Engrng. Soc. (co-gen. chmn. internat. conf.), Nat. Small Bus. Assn., Wis. Mfrs. and Commerce, Ind. Bus. Assn. Wis., Met. Milw. Assn. Commerce, Nat. Fedn. Ind. Bus. Republican. Episcopalian. Author: Modern Machine Shop, 1967. Home: 11037 W Derby Ave Wauwatosa WI 53225 Office: PO Box 13244 Wauwatosa WI 53213

SCOTT, WINIFRED ELEANOR PHILLIPS, occupational therapist; b. Chgo., May 11, 1934; d. Alfred and Doesrous (Thurman) Phillips; B.S., U. Ill., 1957; M.A., Howard U., 1977; Ph.D. (Univ. fellow, So. Fellowships Fund grantee) U. Chgo., 1981; children—Lynn Alison, Stephanie Anne. Staff and supr. occupational therapists VA Hosp., Hines, Ill., 1957-58; staff therapist Westside VA Hosp., Chgo., 1958-61; instr., supr. occupational therapy in medicine and surgery U. Ill. Hosp., Chgo., 1963-66, asst. prof., supr. occupational therapy in psychiatry, 1969-70; Vocat. Rehab. Adminstrn. trainee, 1967-68; asst. clin. tng. supr. dept. occupational therapy St. Elizabeths Hosp., Washington, 1968-69; group activities coordinator, child psychiatry div. Children's Meml. Hosp., Chgo., 1971-74; asst. prof. family practice U. Ill. Abraham Lincoln Sch. Medicine, part-time, 1976-77; individual practice orgn. devel. cons., 1974—; head dept. occupational therapy U. Ill., Chgo., 1981—. Mem. Am. Occupational Therapy Assn. (program chmn. ann. conf. Chgo., 1973), Ill. Occupational Therapy Assn., Am. Ednl. Research Assn., World Fedn. Occupational Therapy, Nat. Soc. Study Edn., Nat. Tng. Lab. Inst., Chgo. Forum, Pi Lambda Theta. Unitarian. Home: 3634 S Rhodes Ave Chicago IL 60653 Office: Dept Occupational Therapy U Ill 1919 W Taylor St Chicago IL 60612

SCOTTI, MARGARET HUNT, former market research co. exec., civic worker; b. Bushnell, Ill., June 2, 1904; d. Clarence Aller and Ora May (Wolff) Hunt; B.S., Stetson U., 1928; postgrad. Western Ill. U., 1928-29, Bradley U., 1947; m. Nestore Armondo Scotti, May 24, 1932 (div. 1936). Field rep., lectr. on nutrition edn. dept. Knox Gelatin Co., Chgo., 1928-29, El Paso Tex., 1929-30, Los Angeles, 1930-39; asst. dir. Peoria (Ill.) dist. WPA Sch. Lunch Program, 1940; dir. Ill. WPA Sch. Lunch Test Kitchen, Peoria, 1941-43; nutritionist Peoria Mfg. Assn., 1943; price asst. Office Price Adminstrn., Peoria, 1943-45, vol. specialist, 1945-46; owner, founder, prin. Scotti Bur. Mktg. Research, Peoria, 1947-78, chmn. bd., 1978-81; mem. public relation com. Central Ill. chpt. ARC, Peoria, 1975—; mem. state legis. com. Peoria C. of C., 1978-81. Mem. Mktg. Research Assn. (nat. v.p. 1963-64, dir. 1964-65), Am. Mktg. Assn. (bd. mem. 1971-72 Central Ill. chpt. Pioneer award 1978). Republican. Presbyterian. Clubs: Altrusa (v.p. 1978-79), Bus. and Profl. Women's (Peoria dist. chmn. 1959-60, pres. 1960-61, Ill. state legis. chmn. 1962-68); P.E.O. Sisterhood (pres. 1963-65), Pi Beta Phi Alumni. Home: 116 N North St Peoria IL 61606 Office: 1120 N North St Peoria IL 61606

SCOTT-LEWIS, DIANE, personnel cons.; b. Chgo., Jan. 24, 1936; d. George W. and Kathryn (McKinnen) Walker; B.S., U. Ill., 1957; children—William Brosius, Dwight Scott. Founding dir., exec. officer Interviewing Technicians, Inc., Chgo., 1959-69, Interviewing Dynamics, Inc., Chgo., Atlanta and Houston, 1969—, London, 1980—; owner I.D. Mgmt., 1981—. Mem. Aircraft Owners and Pilots Assn., Am. Mgmt. Assn., Ill. Employment Assn., Am. Horse Show Assn., Ill. Hunters and Jumpers Assn. Home: 1560 N Sandburg Apt 3705 Chicago IL 60610 Office: 444 N Michigan Ave Chicago IL 60611

SCOVILLE, MARY SYDNEY BRANCH (MRS. MERRILL SCOVILLE), social worker; b. Fulton, Mo., May 14, 1909; d. Raymond Sydney and Marian (Marquess) Branch; B.A., Western Coll. Women, 1930; M.A., U. Chgo., 1934, postgrad., 1940-41; postgrad. U. N.C., 1937, U. Cin., 1930-31; m. Merrill Scoville, Sept. 13, 1947; 1 son, Raymond Merrill. Asst. prof. econs. and sociology Western Coll., 1932-38; instr. econs. and sociology Wellesley Coll., 1938-40; asst. prof. social service adminstrn. U. Chgo., 1941-50; dir. research Edwin Shields Hewitt & Assos., Chgo., 1950-51; psychiat. caseworker Mental Health Clinic, Will County Health Dept., Joliet, 1958-59; caseworker Family Service Agy. of Will County, Joliet, 1959-70. Mem. adv. com. Consumers Union, 1940-50. Pres., Will County Community Services Council, 1962-64, mem. exec. com., 1960-70, 73-76; mem. Commn. on Christian Social Concerns, 1958-68, 72-77; Ill. Com. for 1970, White House Conf. Children and Youth.; mem. adv. com. Foster Grandparents, 1972-74. Bd. dirs. Sr. Service Center of Will County, 1971-78. Cited by bd. dirs. Family Service Agy. of Will County, 1970, U. Chgo. Sch. Social Service Adminstrn., 1970. Mem. Nat. Assn. Social Workers, Acad. Certified Social Workers, Ill. Welfare Assn., League Women Voters (dir. 1955-58, 71-74), A.C.L.U., Will Grundy Mental Health Assn. (dir. 1971-74), UN Assn. U.S.A., United Meth. Women, Ch. Women United, Art Inst. Chgo., Joliet Artists League, Nat. Wildlife Fedn., Am. Assn. Ret. Persons, Nat. Ret. Tchrs. Assn., Western Coll., U. Cin., U. Chgo. alumni assns. Methodist. Author: Women and Wealth, 1934. Contbr. articles to profl. jours. Home: 925 Oakland Ave Joliet IL 60435

SCRAPER, ROBERT DALE, grain moisture tester service exec.; b. Beloit, Kans., July 31, 1923; s. Joseph Franklin and Bessie Ruth Melton Dickie; ed. Asherville public schs., service schs.; m. Vida Lee Davis, May 17, 1942; children—R. David, Larry Eugene, Randy Lee. Farmer, Beloit, 1946-49; dirt contractor, Beloit, 1949-52; grain elevator mgr. B.C. Christopher, Scranton, Kans., 1952-54; salesman Daffin Mfg. Co., Maryville, Kans., 1954-58; gen. mgr. Brown County Coop., Hiawatha, Kans., 1958-59; salesman, builder, 1959-63; pres. Mid Am. Testing Service, Inc., 1963—; auctioneer; square dance caller, instr. Cub Scout master, 1956-58; founder Hiawatha Men's Prayer Breakfast, pres., 1967, 74; organizer, pres. Hiawatha Maple Leaf Squares, 1977. Served with AUS, 1943-46; PTO. Mem. Kans. Grain and Feed Assn. (asso.), Kans. Sq. Dance Callers Assn. Democrat. Methodist. Clubs: Masons, Elks. Composer songs, poems; patentee automatic grain scale. Home: 409 N 7th St Hiawatha KS 66434 Office: 106 N 6th St Hiawatha KS 66434

SCRIBNER, GILBERT HILTON, JR., real estate broker; b. Milw., June 1, 1918; s. Gilbert Hilton and Nancy (Van Dyke) S.; B.S., Yale U., 1939; m. Helen Shoemaker, Mar. 22, 1941; children—Helen Eaton (Mrs. Gregory E. Euston), Nancy Van Dyke (Mrs. David W. Clarke, Jr.), William Van Dyke, II. Chmn. bd. Scribner & Co.; dir. No. Trust Co., No. Trust Corp., Quaker Oats Co., Gen. Electric Co. Pres., Civic Fedn., 1955-57; bd. dirs. Mid-Am. chpt. ARC, 1952-57, 67-73, Northwestern Meml. Hosp.; chmn. Ill. Commn. for Constnl. Revision, 1959-61; chmn. adv. com. to bd. commrs. Forest Preserve Dist. Cook County (Ill.); trustee Northwestern U., Com. Econ. Devel., 1967-73. Served as lt. comdr. USNR, 1941-45. Republican. Episcopalian. Clubs: Mid-Day, Chgo., Univ., Comml. (Chgo.); Indian Hill (Winnetka); Links (N.Y.C.); Shoreacres (Lake Bluff); Old Elm (Highland Park). Home: 17 Meadowview Dr Northfield IL 60093 Office: 1 First Nat Plaza Chicago IL 60603

SCRIMGEOUR, GARY JAMES, writer, educator; b. Auckland, N. Z., Jan. 15, 1934; s. Colin Graham and Caroline Lenna (Hardie) S.; came to U.S., 1957; B.A. with honors, U. Sydney (Australia), 1954; M.A. in English, Washington U., 1959; Ph.D. (Jane E. Procter fellow), Princeton U., 1968. Asst. personnel officer Dexion Ltd., London, 1956-57; mem. faculty English dept. Fla. U., Gainesville, 1959-61, Rutgers U., New Brunswick, N.J., 1963-64, Ind. U., Bloomington, 1964-69; editor and writer for Benjamin Blom, Inc., N.Y.C., 1969-70; chief of social systems div. and head editorial office Sch. of Public and Environ. Affairs, Ind. U., Bloomington, 1970-74; dir. Profl. Studies Assos., Bloomington, 1973—; cons. for research in alcoholism, ct. systems, hwy. safety and design of seminars to various govt. agys., schs. and social orgns., 1970—. Mem. Am. Judges Assn., Am. Bar Assn., Am. Soc. for Theatre Research, ACLU, Women's Equity Action League. Contbr. numerous manuals on ct. systems and alcohol safety to profl. publs. and articles on lit. criticism to lit. jours. Office: PO Box 464 Bloomington IN 47402

SCRIPTER, FRANK C., mfg. co. exec.; b. Dansville, Mich., June 21, 1918; s. Edgar and Maggie Alice (Havens) S.; student Warren's Sch. of Cam Design, 1946; m. Dora Maebelle Smalley, Nov. 2, 1940 (dec. Sept. 1945); 1 dau., Karen (Mrs. Dee Allen); m. 2d, Elvira Elaine Taylor, Aug. 6, 1951; children—James Michael, Mark Lee, Anita Elaine, Warren Arthur, Charles Edward. Apprentice, Lundberg Screw Products Co., 1940-41; set up man Reo Motors, Inc., 1942-43; night supt. Manning Bros. Metal Products Co., 1943; with McClaren Screw Products Co., 1946-47; partner Dansville Screw Products Co., 1946-54, pres., dir. Scripco Mfg. Co., Laingsburg, Mich., 1954—. Chmn., Citizens Com. Laingsburg, 1956-58; mem. Laingsburg Community Schs. Bd. Edn., 1971—, sec., 1973-74, pres., 1974-75. Served with USNR, 1944-45. Mem. Nat. Rifle Assn. (life). Republican. Methodist. Patentee in field. Home: 9701 E Round Lake Rd Laingsburg MI 48848 Office: 9805 E Round Lake Rd Laingsburg MI 48848

SCRUTTON, KEITH ROBERT, mfg. co. exec.; b. Detroit, Feb. 3, 1932; s. Robert and Myrtle M. S.; student Lawrence Inst., 1956-57, Henry Ford Community Coll., 1957-62; m. Joan M. McGray, June 25, 1960; children—Suzanne J., Jennifer J. With Am. Standards Co., Dearborn, Mich., 1950-64, personnel mgr., 1959-64; with Jervis B. Webb Co., Detroit, 1964—, dir. personnel and indsl. relations, 1970-72, v.p. personnel, officer, 1972—. Served with USN, 1952-56. Mem. Employers Assn. Detroit, Indsl. Relations Assn. Detroit, Conveyor Equipment Mfrs. Assn., Am. Soc. Personnel Adminstrn. Clubs: Western Golf and Country, Alpena Country, Elks. Office: Jervis B Webb Co Webb Dr Farmington Hills MI 48018

SCUDIERO, DOMINIC JAMES, accountant, educator; b. Melrose Park, Ill., Apr. 8, 1929; s. Dominick and Maria (Buonauro) S.; C.P.A., U. Ill., 1954; M.B.A., DePaul U., 1955, B.S., 1951; postgrad. Ill. C.P.A. Found., 1975-81; m. Anne Marie Stafford, Sept. 4, 1954; children—John Jude, Joseph Anthony. Sr. acct., supr. Busby and Qury, Chgo., 1952-61; cons., sr. acct., supr. George Bagley and Co., Chgo., 1961-64; asst. controller, controller, chief acct. Vance Pub. Co., Chgo., 1964-66; asst. prof. bus. adminstrn. Elmhurst (Ill.) Coll., 1966-79, asso. prof., 1980—, acting chairperson dept. bus. adminstrn., 1970-72, chairperson, 1972-75, coordinator bus. adminstrn. majors, 1975—, coodinator small bus. inst. program, 1974—; cons. in field. Mem. Am. Acctg. Assn., Ill. Soc. C.P.A.s, Ill. Tchrs. Acctg., Midwest Bus. Adminstrn. Assn., Delta Mu Delta. Democrat. Roman Catholic. Home: 3825 Van Buren St Bellwood IL 60104 Office: Elmhurst College 190 Prospect St Elmhurst IL 60126

SCULLY, MICHAEL EDWARD, univ. adminstr.; b. Detroit, Sept. 12, 1942; s. Robert Edward and Jean Lenore (Carmichael) S.; B.A., Parsons Coll., 1967; M.S., Ind. U., 1970; Ph.D., So. Ill. U., 1981. Head resident adviser/area coordinator U. Wis., Oshkosh, 1970-73 head resident adviser Western Ill. U., Macomb, 1973-76; asst. dir. housing for residence life So. Ill. U., Carbondale, 1976-80. Recipient Disting. Service award St. Jude Children's Research Hosp., 1977, 78, 79. Mem. Nat. Assn. Student Personnel Adminstrs., Am. Assn. Coll. and Univ. Housing Officers (editorial bd.), Ill. Assn. Coll. and Univ. Housing Officers, Gt. Lakes Assn. Coll. and Univ. Housing Officers, Am. Coll. Personnel Assn., Am. Personnel and Guidance Assn., Delta Sigma Phi (life). Methodist. Home: 6234 238th Ave Salem WI 53168

SCUSSEL, JAMES ALLEN, occupational therapist; b. Detroit, May 12, 1951; s. Harold Chester and Bertha Elizabeth (LaForte) S.; B.S., Eastern Mich. U., 1973; M.A., U. Mich., 1980; m. Sandra Krass, June 28, 1975. Occupational therapist Lafayette Neuro-Psychiat. Clinic, Detroit, 1974-75, Saginaw (Mich.) Public Schs., 1975-78; occupational therapist, coordinator health personnel Bay Arenac Intermediate Sch. Dist., Bay City, Mich., 1978—; part-time instr. Delta Coll., University Center, Mich. Mem. Am. Occupational Therapy Assn. (mem. Council State Assn. Pres.'s 1981-83), Mich. Occupational Therapy Assn. (Disting. Service award 1979, chmn. Council on Public Info. 1979-80, pres. 1981-83), Saginaw Valley Occupational Therapy Assn. (chmn. 1977-79, Founding Fathers award 1977). Democrat. Roman Catholic. Home: 2257 N Carolina Saginaw MI 48602

SEARCY, MARY DENISE, broadcasting sales exec.; b. Champaign, Ill., Feb. 24, 1955; d. Ronald Eugene and Gertrude Anna (Buerkle) Dailey; B.J., U. Mo., Columbia, 1977; m. Dean Lloyd Searcy, July 21, 1977. Loan supr. Sta. KQTV affiliate ABC, St. Joseph, Mo., 1977, sales coordinator, 1977-78, regional sales mgr. for Kansas City (Mo.), St. Louis, and Omaha, 1978—. Mem. Kansas City Advt. Club, Am. Women in Radio and TV (local chpt. publicity chmn. and dir.). Office: KQTV 40th and Faraon Saint Joseph MO 64506

SEARLE, DANIEL CROW, med. and health services co. exec.; b. Evanston, Ill., May 6, 1926; s. John Gideon and Frances Louise (Crow) S.; B.S., Yale, 1950; M.B.A., Harvard, 1952; m. Dain Depew Fuller, Sept. 2, 1950; children—Anne Searle Meers, Daniel Gideon, Michael Dain. With G.D. Searle & Co., Chgo., 1938—, successively staff asst. to v.p. charge fin. and mfg., asst. sec., sec., 1952-59, v.p., 1961-63, exec. v.p., 1963-66, pres., chief ops. officer 1966-70, pres., chief exec. officer, 1970-72, chmn. exec. com., from 1972, chmn. bd., 1977—, dir., 1964—; dir. Atlanta/LaSalle Corp., Chgo., Harris Trust & Savs. Bank, Chgo., Utilities Inc., Maynard Oil Co., Jim Walter Corp. Bd. dirs. Evanston Hosp.; trustee Northwestern U., Com. for Econ. Devel., Better Govt. Assn.; mem. exec. com. Yale Devel. Bd.; mem. at large Yale Alumni Bd.; bd. dirs. Pharm. Mfrs. Assn. Found. Served with USNR, World War II. Mem. Pharm. Mfrs. Assn. (dir.). Republican. Episcopalian (vestry). Clubs: Glen View (Golf, Ill.); Indian Hill (Winnetka, Ill.); Shoreacres (Lake Bluff, Ill.); Chicago, Chicago Commonwealth, Mid-America (Chgo.); Seminole Golf; Augusta Nat. Golf; Old Elm (Highland Park, Ill.); Jupiter Island (Fla.). Home: 33 Woodley Rd Winnetka IL 60093 Office: GD Searle & Co PO Box 1045 4711 Golf Rd Skokie IL 60076

SEARLES, JERRY LEE, television exec., fin. cons., philanthropist; b. Chgo., July 6, 1931; s. Leo Keith and Mary Rosalynne (Pendy) S. Pres., owner Minn. Buyers Service, St. Paul, 1953-60, Progressive Industries, Diversified, St. Paul, 1953—, Midwest Tele-Prodns., Inc., St. Paul, 1958—; creator TV shows Jeopardy, Let's Make a Deal and Treasure Chest, others; cons. to Pres. Jimmy Carter, Pres. Ronald Reagan; cons. vets. affairs, TV programs, creative writing. Bd. dirs. Minn. Handicapped Recreational Assn., Human Rights Commn.; state comdr. Mil. Order Purple Heart, 1976-77, nat. jr. vice comdr., 1978-79, nat. sr. vice comdr., 1979-80, nat. comdr., 1980-81, nat. fin. committeeman, 1977—, chmn. nat. cemetery program, 1977; pres. Meml. Day Assn., 1980-81; rep. Nat. VA Hosp. Vol. Services, 1977—; mem. awards jury Freedoms Found. at Valley Forge, 1980. Served with AUS, 1951-52; Korea. Decorated Purple Heart, Bronze Star medal, others; recipient WCCO-Radio Good Neighbor award, Midwest Writers Assn. award, Internat. Man of Achievement award Cambridge U., 1981, Humanitarian award Minn. Handicapped Assn., Employment of Vets. award, Mem. Writer's Guild Am., Ind. Producers in Television, Am. Businessmen's Alliance, United Vets. Council, Am. Assn. Parliamentarians, Am. Legion (Outstanding award 1973), VFW, Amvets, DAV, 40 and 8, Cooties, Internat. War Vets. Alliance. Clubs: Masons (32 deg.), Shriners, Athletic, Univ., Millionaires, others. Author mag. articles, procedural advt. formats, bus. promotions, books. Home: 1704 Maryland Ave Saint Paul MN 55106

SEARS, CARROLL DWIGHT, lumber co. exec.; b. Jacksonville, Ill., July 18, 1929; s. John Ogden and Jessie Beulah (Hart) S.; student Ill. Coll., 1947, Western Ill. U., 1948-50; m. Mary Louise Miller, Dec. 11, 1952; children—Rita Gail, John Kelly. Owner, mgr. Sears Lumber Co., Bluffs, Ill., 1954—; farmer nr. Bluffs, 1976—. Mem. Ill. Evaluation Bd. for Vocat. and Tech. Edn., 1977-78. Served with U.S. Army, 1950-53. Decorated Bronze Star. Mem. Nat. Bus. Assn., Ill. Lumber and Material Dealer Assn., U.S. C. of C., Am. Legion. Methodist. Club: Odd Fellows. Home and Office: PO Box 77 Bluffs IL 62621

SEARS, ROBERT WILLIAM, JR., fiberglas co. exec.; b. Bloomington, Ind., Aug. 27, 1940; s. Robert William and Wilma Jean Sears; B.S. in Mgmt., Ind. U., 1963; m. Constance Joe Sweet, Nov. 4, 1960; 1 dau., Susan Michele. With Owens Corning Fiberglas Co., 1963—, process supr., Newark, Ohio, 1963-65, personnel asst., Barrington, N.J., 1965-66, personnel dir., Huntingdon, Pa., 1966-68, personnel dir., Jackson, Tenn., 1968-72, fabrication supt., 1972-73, personnel dir., Barrington, 1973-77, personnel mgr., Toledo, 1977-79, personnel mgr. corp. staff sci. and tech., 1979—. Loaned exec. Toledo United Way, 1978. Named Outstanding Young Man, Jaycees, 1968. Mem. Am. Mgmt. Assn., Am. Soc. Personnel Adminstrn. (pres. local chpt. 1972, regional dir. Tenn. 1973), Toledo Personnel Assn. (social chmn. 1979). Republican. Home: 845 Yargerville Rd Ida MI 48140 Office: Owens Corning Fiberglas Fiberglas Tower Toledo OH 43659

SEARS, STUART EUGENE, coll. adminstr.; b. Nashua, Iowa, Apr. 27, 1926; s. Warner Russell and Gladice L. (Noble) S.; A.A., Mason City Jr. Coll., 1949; B.S., Upper Iowa U., 1951; M.A., U. No. Iowa, 1963; m. M. Jeanne Swartz, Feb. 8, 1948; children—Jeffry Stuart, Suellen Mary. Acct., office mgr. Escherich Refrigeration Co., Mason City, Iowa, 1948-51; bus. tchr. West Union (Iowa) High Sch., 1951; faculty Gates Coll., Waterloo, Iowa, 1951-73, pres., 1968-73; dept. head Hawkeye Inst. Tech., Waterloo, Iowa, 1973-76; chief adminstrv. officer, chmn. bd. Madison (Wis.) Bus. Coll., 1977—. Nat. chmn. Accrediting Commn. for Bus. Schs., 1966. Served with U.S. Army, 1944-46. Mem. Nat. Bus. Edn. Assn., Central Comml. Tchrs. Assn., Wis. Council for Ind. Edn. (dir. 1977—), Midwestern Bus. Coll. Assn., Phi Delta Kappa, Delta Pi Epsilon, Am. Legion, Amvets. Republican. Methodist. Clubs: Rotary, Elks. Office: Madison Business Coll 1110 Spring Harbor Dr Madison WI 53705

SEAS, SHIRLEY WILLIAM, dairy scientist; b. White, S.D., Mar. 13, 1928; s. Carl William and Blanche Gertrude (Murphy) S.; B.S., S.D. State U., 1955, M.S., 1959; m. Arlene Opal Barenklau, Aug. 16, 1950; children—Cheryl, Bradley, Blake. Buttermaker, Farmers' Coop. Creamery, Canton, S.D., 1949-50; technician S.D. State U. Dairy Plant, Brookings, 1950-51, mgr., 1953—, asso. prof. dairy sci., 1955—. Mem. Brookings City Planning Commn., 1977—. Served with U.S. Army, 1945-47; PTO. Winner, Nat. Dairy Products Judging Contest, 1968, 69, 74, 76, 78, 79; named Coach of Year, Nat. Dairy Products Judging Contest, 1968, 74, 76, 78, 79; recipient Disting. Service award Jr. C. of C., Brookings, 1968. Mem. Am. Dairy Sci. Assn., S.D. State Dairy Assn., V.F.W., Brookings Jaycees (pres. 1960), Alpha Zeta, Gamma Sigma Delta, Alpha Gamma Rho. Republican. Roman Catholic. Clubs: Elks, K.C., Brookings Country (pres. 1968). Author research papers in field. Home: 403 Dakota Ave Brookings SD 57006 Office: Dairy Sci Dept SD State U Brookings SD 57007

SEATON, GEORGE LELAND, former utility co. exec., civic worker; b. Sunny South, Calif., Feb. 9, 1901; s. Frank H. and Charity Jane (Lee) S.; B.S.E.E., Iowa State U., 1923; A.A. (hon.), Coll. DuPage; m. Mildred Irene Sandall, Aug. 14, 1926; children—Robert Lee, James Mann, Mary Seaton Martin. Engr., Gen. Electric Co., Ft. Wayne, Ind., 1923; with Ill. Bell Telephone Co., Chgo., 1923-66, asst. v.p., 1952-64, v.p., 1964-66, ret., 1966. Mem. Hinsdale (Ill.) Bd. Edn., 1941-47; chmn. Chgo. council Boy Scouts Am., 1958-63; chmn. exec. com. Gt. Books Found., Chgo., 1965—; treas. Disciples Div. House, U. Chgo., 1945—, mem. vis. com. U. Chgo. Div. Sch., 1977—; mem. Ill. Fair Employment Com., 1961-69; chmn. Coll. DuPage, 1966-72. Served to 2d lt. C.E., USAR, 1923-28. Recipient Silver Beaver award

Boy Scouts Am., Silver Antelope award. Mem. Western Soc. Engrs., Am. Statis. Assn. Republican. Mem. Christian Ch. (Disciples of Christ). Clubs: Union League (Chgo.); Hinsdale Golf, Econ. Home: 6110 S County Line Burr Ridge IL 60521

SEATON, RICHARD MELVIN, pub., broadcaster; b. Washington, Jan. 25, 1913; s. Fay Noble and Dorothea Elizabeth (Schmidt) S.; B.S. in Journalism, Kans. State U., 1934; m. Mary Holton, June 1, 1936; children—Richard H., Frederick D., Elizabeth, Edward L. Sec.-treas. Seaton Pub. Co., Manhattan, Kans., 1937-47, pres., 1952—; pres. Coffeyville (Kans.) Pub. Co., 1947-79, Midwest Broadcasting Co., 1947—, Manhattan (Kans.) Broadcasting Co., 1954—, Winfield (Kans.) Pub. Co., 1974—, Alliance (Nebr.) Pub. Co., 1974—, Seaton Pub. Co., Lead, S.D., 1974—, Sheridan (Wyo.) Newspapers, Inc., 1974—; chmn. bd. South Plains Broadcasting Co., 1979—; dir. numerous cos. Trustee William Allen White Found., Kans. State U. Found.; endower R.M. Seaton Profl. Journalist Chair, Kans. State U.; mem. Kans. State Water Resources Bd., 1954-61; mem. Kans. Cultural Arts Commn., 1965-67; founder Coffeyville Hist. Mus. Mem. Kans. Press Assn. (pres. 1949), Kans. A.P. (chmn. 1953), Am. Soc. Newspaper Editors, Internat. Press Inst., Kans. State Hist. Soc. (dir. 1979—), Sigma Delta Chi, Beta Theta Pi, Phi Kappa Phi. Republican. Unitarian. Clubs: Coffeyville Country; American (Paris, France); Kansas City Press, Sportsman's (Deerwood, Minn.). Author syndicated book rev. column, 1971—. Home: 1700 Seaton Rd Coffeyville KS 67337 Office: 218 W 8th Coffeyville KS 67337

SEAVER, JAMES EVERETT, historian; b. Los Angeles, Oct. 4, 1918; s. Everett Herbert and Gertrude Lillian (Sharp) S.; A.B., Stanford U., 1940; Ph.D., Cornell U., 1946; m. Virginia Stevens, Dec. 20, 1940; children—Richard Everett, William Merrill, Robert Edward. Asst. instr. Cornell U., 1940-42, 44-46; instr. Mich. State U., 1946-47; asst. prof. history U. Kans., Lawrence, 1947-52, asso. prof., 1952-60, prof., 1960—. Pres., Old West Lawrence Assn., 1972. Recipient Fulbright Hayes grant, Italy, 1953-54, Israel, 1963-64; Carnegie grantee, Costa Rica, 1966-67. Mem. Am. Hist. Assn., Am. Philol. Assn., Archeol. Inst. Am., Am. Numis. Soc., AAUP, Am. Acad. Rome, U.S. Archives of Recorded Sound. Republican. Episcopalian. Clubs: Alvamar Tennis, Alvamar Country. Author: The Persecution of the Jews in the Roman Empire, 313-438 A.D., 1952. Contbr. articles to profl. jours. Home: 600 Louisiana St Lawrence KS 66044 Office: Dept History Univ Kansas Lawrence KS 66045

SEAY, JAMES ALLEN, individual, marriage, and family counselor; b. Hot Springs, Ark., Aug. 24, 1946; s. James David and Bonnie Lou Ledwidge (Allen) S.; B.A., U. Mo., Kansas City, 1975, M.A., 1978. Counselor, Community Treatment Center, Bur. of Prisons, Kansas City, Mo., 1977-78, Univ. Counseling Center, U. Mo., Kansas City, 1978-81, Cath. Charities, 1979—. Served with USMC, 1968-69. Decorated Purple Heart; Victor Wilson scholar, 1979-80. Mem. Am. Psychol. Assn., Mo. Psychol. Assn., Am. Personnel and Guidance Assn., Mo. Personnel and Guidance Assn., Assn. Specialists in Group Work, Am. Mental Health Counselors Assn., Assn. Counselor Edn. Students, Assn. Humanistic Psychology, Assn. Transpersonal Psychology, Psi Chi. Roman Catholic. Home: 4324 Mercier St Kansas City MO 64111 Office: 1112 Broadway Kansas City MO 64105

SEBASTIAN, JAMES JOSEPH, real estate devel. co. exec.; b. Warren, Ohio, Apr. 20, 1947; s. James V. and Julie M. S.; B.S., Ohio State U., 1969; M.B.A., Western Colo. U., 1977; m. Molly M. Moline, June 14, 1975. Mgr. sales/engring. Werner Constrn. Co., Columbus, Ohio, 1971-77; dir. adminstrv. services Red Roof Inns, Columbus, Ohio, 1977-78; pres. James J. Sebastian Co., Inc., real estate developers, cons. and brokers, Columbus, 1978—. Mem. Nat. Republican Com. Mem. Am. Mgmt. Assn., Assn. M.B.A. Execs., Columbus Builders Exchange. Clubs: Columbus Athletic; Little Turtle Country; Amateur Radio Relay League. Home: 103 Nob Hill Dr Gahanna OH 43230 Office: Borden Bldg PO Box 30245 Columbus OH 43230

SEBASTIAN, STUART, choreographer; b. Dayton, Ohio, July 26, 1950; s. Virginia (Lorah) S.; B.A. magna cum laude, Am. U., 1976. Profl. dancer, 1965—; prin. dancer Nat. Ballet of Washington, 1972-73; choreographer Met. Opera, Royal Winnipeg Ballet, Washington Ballet, others; speaker for USIA in Russia and Eastern Europe; now dir./prin. choreographer Dayton Ballet, 1980—; choreographer operas, off-Broadway musicals, ballets. Mem. dance panel Ohio Arts Council. U.S.-U.K. grantee, 1977; Ford Found. scholar 1963-68 scholar Tex. Christian U., 1968-70. Mem. Assn. Ohio Dance Cos. (dir.), Nat. Assn. Regional Ballet (dir.), Am. Guild Mus. Artists. Office: 140 N Main St Dayton OH 45402

SEBELIUS, KEITH GEORGE, lawyer; b. Almena, Kans., Sept. 10, 1916; s. Carl E. and Minnie (Peak) S.; A.B., Ft. Hays (Kans.) State U., 1941; J.D., George Washington U., 1939; m. Bette A. Roberts, Mar. 5, 1949; children—Keith Gary, Ralph Douglas. Investigator, U.S. Civil Service Commn., N.Y.C., 1939-41; admitted to Kans. bar, 1941; practiced in Norton, 1945—; city atty. Norton, 1953-68; mem. Kans. Senate, 1962-68; mem. 91st-96th congresses from 1st Dist. Kans. Served from pvt. to maj., AUS, 1941-45, 51-52. Mem. Am. Legion (state comdr. Kans.), D.A.V., V.F.W., Pi Kappa Delta, Pi Gamma Mu, Phi Kappa Phi. Methodist. Mason (33 deg.). Home: 602 W Wilberforce Norton KS 67654 Office: PO Box 10 Norton KS 67654

SEBEOK, THOMAS A., linguist, author, educator; b. Budapest, Hungary, 1920; came to U.S., 1937, naturalized, 1944; B.A., U. Chgo., 1941; M.A., Princeton U., 1943, Ph.D. (fellow), 1945. Mem. faculty Ind. U., Bloomington, 1943—, Disting. prof. linguistics, 1967-78, Disting. prof. linguistics and semiotics, 1978—, former prof. anthropology, founder dept. Uralic and Altaic studies, prof. Uralic and Altaic studies, dir. Uralic and Altaic Lang. and Area Center, dir. Air Force lang. tng. program; vis. prof. various univs. in U.S. and Europe, 1946—; lectr. English, French, German or Hungarian on linguistics to various univs. and acads. in U.S., Can., Europe and Asia; cons. to Ford Found., Guggenheim Found., U.S. Office Edn., NSF, Found. for Anthrop. Research; mem. council of consultants Hungarian Research Center, 1975—; mem. com. on linguistics and psychology Social Sci. Research Council, com. on sociolinguistics, 1963-64; U.S. mem. internat. organizing com. Internat. Congress of Fenno-Ugrists, 1965—; founder and chmn. Com. on Linguistic Info. Numerous fellowships and grants including: Fulbright grant, 1966, 71, NSF fellow, 1966-67; Nat. Endowment for Humanities fellow; Johns Hopkins Centennial scholar, 1975; Exchange prof. of Nat. Acad. Scis. with Acad. Scis. of USSR, 1973. Fellow Am. Folklore Soc., AAAS, Am. Anthrop. Assn., Culture Learning Inst., Netherlands Inst. for Advanced Study, N.Y. Acad. Scis., Linguistic Soc. Am. (pres. 1975, dir. Linguistic Inst. 1964); mem. Toronto Semiotic Circle (hon.), Deutsche Gesellschaft fur Semiotik, Assn. for Philosophy of Sci., Psychotherapy and Ethics, Fedn. Am. Scientists, Internat. Soc. for History Rhetoric, Central States Anthrop. Soc. (past pres.), Semiotic Soc. Am. (exec. dir. 1976—, editorial bd. 1976—), Indpls. Zool. Soc. (edn. adv. com.), Am. Assn. for Machine Translation and Computational Linguistics (exec. bd. 1964-66), Animal Behavior Soc., Internat. House of Japan, Internat. Brotherhood Magicians, Sigma Xi. Clubs: Cosmos, University (Chgo.); Bloomington Country. Home: 1104 Covenanter Dr Bloomington IN 47401 Office: Patton House PO Box 10 Ind U 516 E 6th St Bloomington IN 47402

SECREST, RICHARD PHILLIP, printing co. exec.; b. Westerville, O., Sept. 17, 1937; s. Laurence Clark and Elizabeth Jackson (Fickel) S.; B.S., No. Ill. U., 1959; m. Brigitte Jutta Sack, Jan. 12, 1966. Exec. v.p. D.C. Lithographers, 1959-61; prodn. supr. Duplex Products, Inc., 1961-63; cons. Precision Forms, Milw., 1963-64; mgr. systems quality control Star Forms, Bettendorf, Iowa, 1964-66; exec. v.p. DeKalb County Press, Inc., (Ill.), 1966-79; owner, Tri-Hobbies, Inc., 1968-71, Secrest Engring., 1977—, Sch. & Library Pub. Co., 1978—. Served with U.S. Army, 1961. Mem. CAP, Exptl. Aircraft Assn., Confederate Air Force (col.), Internat. House Printing Craftsmen, Printing Industries Am., Sigma Pi, Epsilon Pi Tau. Elk. Club: Country (Kishwaukee, Ill.). Home: 134 Mattek Ave DeKalb IL 60115 Office: 110 N Sacramento St Sycamore IL 60178

SECRIST, ROBERT HEROLD, II, educator; b. Blawnox, Pa., Feb. 26, 1935; s. Robert Herold and Carolyn Elizabeth (Shawfield) S.; A.B. cum laude, Harvard U., 1957; M.A., N.Y. U., 1959; postgrad. U. Amsterdam, 1957-58; Ph.D., N.Y. U., 1965; postgrad. U. Ibero-Americana, Mexico City, 1966. Chmn. fgn. langs. East Rockaway High Sch. (N.Y.), 1959-64; head modern lang. dept. Kingsborough Community Coll. (N.Y.), 1964-68; vis. asso. prof. English linguistics U. Vt., Burlington, 1968; prof. English and linguistics Youngstown (Ohio) State U., 1968—. Vice-pres. Youngstown Ballet Guild, 1976-77. Fulbright fellow U. Amsterdam, 1957; NDEA grantee Pace Coll., N.Y.C., 1963; recipient Founders Day award N.Y. U., 1966. Mem. Modern Lang. Assn., Linguistic Soc. Am., Internat. Linguistic Assn., Coll. English Assn., Dictionary Soc. N.Am., Am. Name Soc., Cleve. Linguistic Circle. Home: 264 Madison Ave Youngstown OH 44504 Office: English Dept Youngstown State U Youngstown OH 44555

SEDDON, JAMES ARNOLD, clergyman; b. Evansville, Ind., Jan. 31, 1944; s. Hassel Leroy and Eileen (Porter) S.; B.A., Oakland City Coll., 1974; m. Sharon Ann Piper, Aug. 7, 1966; children—James Brian, Sherry Jo. Orderly, St. Josephs Hosp., Huntingburg, Ind., 1971-73; announcer Sta.-WRAY-AM-FM, Princeton, Ind., 1973-74; ordained to ministry American Baptist Ch., 1973; pastor First Bapt. Ch., Cannelton, Ind., 1974-76, 1st Bapt. Ch., Spencer, Ind., 1976-80, 1st Bapt. Ch., Galveston, Ind., 1980—; clin. pastoral trainee Deaconess Hosp., Evansville, Ind., 1975-76; v.p. bd. dirs., chmn. program planning and evaluation com. South Central Mental Health Found., 1977-80; vol. chaplain Ind. State Police, 1978—. Served with USAF, 1962-66. Office: Box 626 Galveston IN 46932

SEDELBAUER, NORMAN JOHN, mfg. co. exec.; b. Grand Rapids, Mich., Aug. 23, 1934; s. Norman Elmer and Edna May S.; B.S., Mich. State U., 1956; postgrad. Pa. State U., 1957-58; m. Susan Kay White, May 3, 1957; children—Kathy Sue, Norman Jay, Scott Kevin, John Steven. With Bauer Products, Inc., Grand Rapids, 1959—, salesman, 1962-70, sales mgr., 1970-75, treas., 1975—, also v.p. Served to capt., USAF, 1956-59. Republican. Presbyterian. Home: 700 Crahen St Grand Rapids MI 49506 Office: 702 Evergreen St SE Grand Rapids MI 49507

SEDELOW, WALTER ALFRED, JR., scientist, educator; b. Ludlow, Mass., Apr. 17, 1928; s. Walter Alfred and Una M. (Roberts) S.; A.B. summa cum laude, Amherst Coll., 1947; M.A., Harvard U., 1951, Ph.D., 1957; m. Sally Ann Yeates, June 14, 1958. Master, Milton (Mass.) Acad., 1947-48; instr. history Williams Coll., 1948-50; instr., asst. prof. history Amherst Coll., 1954-56, 57-60; asso. prof. history and sociology, chmn. dept. sociology Parsons (Iowa) Coll., 1960-61; Jane Addams asso. prof. sociology and history, chmn. dept. sociology Rockford (Ill.) Coll., 1961-62; human factors scientist System Devel. Corp., 1962-64; asso. prof. sociology and anthropology, chmn. dept., dir. health orgn. research program St. Louis U., 1964-66; mem. faculty U. N.C., 1966-70, research asso. Inst. Research Social Scis., 1966-68, asso. prof. sociology and info. sci., 1966-68, research prof. Inst. for Research Social Scis., 1968-70, dean Sch. Library Sci., 1967-70, prof. sociology, computer and info. sci., 1968-70; prof. sociology and computer sci. and program in history and philosophy of sci. U. Kans., Lawrence, 1970—, also program in Soviet and East European Studies, 1979—; dir. Networking-for-Sci. and staff asso. Computers and Society project, div. math. and computer scis. NSF, Washington, 1974-77; vis. faculty mem. Menninger Sch. Psychiatry, Topeka Inst. for Psychoanalysis, 1981—; cons. in field, 1964—; mem. com. info. tech. Am. Council Learned Socs., 1968-70; mem. evaluation panel project INTREX, NSF, 1968; U.S. Office Edn. grantee, 1968-70; prin. investigator NASA project, 1968-70, NSF project, 1971-73; vis. scientist NSF/Assn. for Computing Machinery Vis. Scientist Program, 1969-70; fellow interdisciplinary studies Menninger Found., Topeka, 1977—; cons. Coll. Human Ecology, Mich. State U., 1973; lectr. NSF Summer Inst., Computers in Behavioral Sci., U. Colo., 1973; mem. oversight com. info. networks tech. assessment project Battelle-Columbus Lab., 1975-76; mem. adv. panel (computer applications) Nat. Endowment for Humanities, 1975—; mem. adv. panel Western Behavioral Scis. Inst., 1976-77; mem. adv. panel for computer sci. Fulbright-Hays Act, 1977—; trustee Internat. Social Sci. Inst., Santa Barbara, Calif., 1966-73, Taos Alpine Acad., 1980-81; trustee, mem. corp. Porter-Phelps-Huntington Found., 1957-60; v.p. Taos Book Shop, Inc., 1975-80, treas., 1980—; chmn. Fulbright Selection Panel in Computer Sci., 1979-80. Served to lt. USAF, 1952-54, to capt. Res., 1956-68. Recipient Woods prize, Travis prize Amherst Coll., 1948; Charles Smith scholar Harvard, 1951-52; Henry P. Field fellow, 1956-57; Amherst Meml. fellow, 1956-57. Fellow Am. Sociol. Assn.; mem. Assn. Computing Machinery, Soc. Gen. Systems Research, Human Factors Soc., AAAS, Am. Hist. Assn., Assn. Computational Linguistics, Am. Fedn. Info. Processing Socs. (mem. electronic funds transfer com. 1976-79), Soc. for History of Tech., Phi Beta Kappa. Club: Cosmos (Washington). Co-author: Language Research and the Computer, 1972; author: Bibliography for a Science of Language, 1975; also articles. Contbr. chpts. to books. Asso. editor Social Forces, 1966-70; co-editor, contbg. author: Formal Methods: Computers in Language Research, 1979; Computers in Language Research: Formalization in Literature and Discourse Analysis, 1982; bd. editors Computer Studies in Humanities and Verbal Behavior, 1966-75; series editor Free Press, 1968-70; bd. editors Hist. Abstracts, 1973—. Home: 1401 Engel Rd Lawrence KS 66044 Office: Dept Computer Sci U Kans 18 Strong Hall Lawrence KS 66045 also Taos Book Shop Inc PO Box 827 Taos NM 87571

SEDER, ARTHUR RAYMOND, JR., utility exec.; b. Oak Park, Ill., Apr. 20, 1920; s. Arthur Raymond and Mary Aline (Grantham) S.; student U. Minn., 1938-39; B.S.L., Northwestern U., 1946, LL.B., 1947; m. Marion Frances Heltzel, Feb. 28, 1942; children—James A., Susan J., Elizabeth A. Admitted to Ill. bar, 1948, Mich. bar, 1961; law clk. Supreme Ct. Justice Vinson, 1948-50, mem. firm Sidley & Austin, Chgo., 1950-72; pres., Am. Natural Resources Co., Detroit, 1973-76, chmn., chief exec. officer, dir., 1976—, also dir. certain subsidiaries; dir. NBD Bancorp., Burroughs Corp. Bd. dirs. Detroit Symphony Orchestra, Detroit Grand Opera; trustee St. John Hosp., Detroit, Northwestern U., Evanston, Ill. Mem. Am., Ill., Mich. bar assns. Clubs: Links (N.Y.C.); Detroit, Detroit Athletic, Country of Detroit. Home: 96 Vendome Grosse Pointe Farms MI 48236 Office: 1 Woodward Ave Detroit MI 48226

SEDERBURG, WILLIAM A., state ofcl.; b. Chadron, Nebr., Aug. 1, 1947; s. Marion E. and Viola A. S.; B.S., Mankato State Coll., 1969; M.A., Mich. State U., 1972, Ph.D., 1974; m. Joyce Sederburg, July 29, 1972; children—Matthew E., Kari. Research specialist dept. polit. sci. Mich. State U., 1973-75; edn. specialist Republican staff Ho. of Reps., Lansing, Mich., 1975-77, exec. dir., 1977-78; mem. Mich. Senate, 1978—. Trustee Mich. Lung Assn., 1976-79; Ingham County commr. Mich. Bd. Edn., 1976-78; bd. dirs. Mich. Multiple Sclorosis, 1979—. Mem. Kappa Delta Pi. Lutheran. Author: Education and the State: Decision Making on the Reform of Educational Finances in Michigan, 1971; Planning and Changing, 1974; Implementing Educational Accountability: The Michigan Experience, 1974. Office: 802 Senate Office Bldg Lansing MI 48909

SEE, GARY GLENN, mech. engr., microcomputer mfg. co. exec.; b. Erie, Pa., Feb. 21, 1943; s. Gaylord Glenn and Helen May See; B.S.M.E., U. Cin., 1966; M.S.M.E., Cleve. State U., 1970; m. Sandra L. Turner, Sept. 11, 1965; children—Courtney, Lindsay. With Addressograph-Multigraph Corp., Cleve., 1962-72, sr. design engr., devel. and product engring. dept., 1966-68, mech. engr., 1968-69, mech. engr., advanced devel. engring. dept., 1969-71, sr. mech. engr., magnetic and telecommunication systems devel. dept., 1971-72; research engr. Bus. Equipment Research Center, Harris-Intertype Corp., Cleve., 1972-73; program mgr. Life Systems, Inc., Cleve., 1973-77; v.p. engring. Telxon Corp., Bath, Ohio, 1977-80; co-founder, pres., bus. mgr. Tellog Systems, Inc., Streetsboro, Ohio, 1980—. Advisor, Jr. Achievement, 1970; pres. Lake Louise Lake Assn., 1978-79. Registered profl. engr., Ohio. Mem. ASME. Contbr. articles to profl. publs.; patentee in field in U.S. and fgn. countries. Office: 9307 SR43 Streetsboro OH 44240

SEEBERT, KATHLEEN ANNE, commodity brokerage co. exec.; b. Chgo., Sept. 5, 1949; d. Harold Earl and Marie Anne (Lowery) S.; M.A., U. Notre Dame, 1976; postgrad. Northwestern U. Publications dir. Mother McAuley High Sch., Chgo., 1976-77; publications editor ContiCommodity Services, Inc., Chgo., 1977-79, supr. mktg., 1979—; guest lectr. U. Notre Dame, Publicity Club Chgo. Registered commodity rep. Mem. Public Relations Soc. Am. Republican. Roman Catholic. Club: Notre Dame of Chgo. Office: 1800 Board of Trade Bldg Chicago IL 60604

SEEFLUTH, AUGUST RAYMOND, bus. cons.; b. Geridge, Ark., Aug. 7, 1922; s. August Theodore and Clara Eunice (Dunham) S.; student Air Force tech. and flying schs., 1943, 48, 52, Wright State U., 1961-65; m. Nan. L. Morgan, Oct. 3, 1942; children—Nancy, Ted, Karen, Scott. Served as 2d lt. U.S. Army Air Force, 1942-45, to maj. U.S. Air Force, 1947-65; electronic warfare instr. Keesler AFB, Miss., 1952-57; service in W. Ger. and Eng., 1958-61, group leader Aero. System Div., Wright-Patterson AFB, Ohio, 1961-65; ret., 1965; mgr. new bus. devel. TRACOR, Inc., Austin, Tex., 1965-70; regional mktg. mgr. Lundy Electronics & Systems, Pompano Beach, Fla., 1970-73; prin. Seefluth & Assos., Dayton, Ohio, 1973—. Tchr. adult classes 1st United Meth. Ch., Troy, Ohio. Decorated Air medal; recipient commendation U.S. Army, 1957, RAF, 1960, Luftwaffe, 1959, NATO, 1960. Mem. Air Force Assn., Am. Def. Preparedness Assn., Assn. Old Crows. Author various tech. studies, reports, primarily on USAF electronic ops. Home: 102 Finsbury Ln Troy OH 45373 Office: 4130 Linden Ave Dayton OH 45432

SEELEY, MARK, agronomist; b. Gary, Ind., May 3, 1942; s. Clayton Barron and Margaret Louise (Cook) S.; B.S., Purdue U., 1967; M.A. in Edn., Austin Peay State U., 1971. Staff asst. Purdue U., 1962; sci. tchr. Lake Central Sch. Corp., St. John, Ind., 1967-78; sci. tchr., Gary, Ind., 1972-73; mgr. agronomic crops R. L. Schultz Farms, Hobart, Ind., 1973—, dir. Lupin introduction and devel., 1980—. Mem. Lake Area United Way Vol. Service, Lake County Health Fair, 1974. Mem. Am. Soc. Agrl. Engrs. (mem. president's club 1980-81), AAAS, Am. Inst. Biol. Scis., Am. Soc. Hort. Sci., Am. Soc. Hort. Sci. Food Quality and Nutrition Working Group, Am. Soc. Agrl. Engrs., Am. Soc. Agronomy, Am. Soc. Plant Physiologists, Council Agrl. Sci. and Tech., Crop Sci. Soc. Am., Fedn. Am. Scientists, Internat. Soc. Hort. Sci., Soil Sci. Soc. Am., Lake Michigan Flyers Assn., U.S. Hang Gliding Assn. Address: 6126 Sykes Rd Route 1 Hobart IN 46342

SEELEY, MARY LYNN, educator; b. Gregory, S.D., Oct. 20, 1947; d. Marvin Joseph and Eileen Doris (Wilkinson) Drees; B.S. in Edn., U. S.D., 1969; M.S., S.D. State U., 1976; m. Gregory Eugene Seeley, June 19, 1970; 1 dau., Erin Marie. Distributive edn. tchr. Lincoln Sr. High Sch., Sioux Falls, S.D., 1969—, night supr. community edn. services, 1980—, chmn. vocat. dept., 1974—; speaker in field. Named Outstanding Young Educator, Sioux Falls Jaycees, 1977; Lincoln Sr. High Sch. Outstanding Tchr., 1976. Mem. Distributive Edn. Clubs Am., Nat. Assn. Distributive Edn. Tchrs., NEA, S.D. Assn. Distributive Edn. Tchrs. (Distributive Edn. Tchr. of Yr. 1980), S.D. Edn. Assn., Sioux Falls Edn. Assn., Chi Omega Alumnae (chpt. pres. 1974-75). Democrat. Roman Catholic. Author handbook, curriculum materials. Home: 2401 E 52d St Sioux Falls SD 57103 Office: 2900 S Cliff St Sioux Falls SD 57105

SEELY, STEVEN WELLMAN, bank ofcl.; b. Lansing, Mich., Jan. 20, 1951; s. William Charles and Virginia Marian (Wellman) S.; B.A., Mich. State U., 1973; M.B.A., Central Mich. U., 1979; m. Catherine Marie Sheets, Feb. 19, 1970; children—Christopher Steven, Patrick Michael. Lending mgmt. ofcl. Am. Bankcorp Inc., Lansing, 1973-75, dir. advt., 1975-77; dir. mktg. services BancOhio Nat. Bank, Columbus, 1977—; speaker, cons. Sales trainer United Way, Lansing, 1973-77, solicitor, Columbus, 1977-79; active Salesian Center/Boys Club, 1978-80. Recipient numerous advt. and mktg. awards, including: Addy award, 1978; Gold Key award Incentive Mfrs. Rep. Assn., 1978; Bank Mktg. Assn. Best of TV award, 1979; Buckeye Mktg. award, 1980. Mem. Am. Mktg. Assn., Columbus Advt. Fedn., Columbus Sales Exec. Club, Mich. State U., Central Mich. U. alumni assns., U.S. Golf Assn., Porsche Club Am., Volkswagen Club Am. Republican. Roman Catholic. Home: 1845 Ashland Ave Upper Arlington OH 43212 Office: 155 E Broad St Columbus OH 43265

SEEMUTH, PAUL DOUGLAS, chemist; b. Tiffin, Ohio, Feb. 19, 1951; s. Jack Richard and Helen Mae (Rumschlag) S.; B.S., Bowling Green State U., 1973; M.S., Purdue U., 1975; Ph.D., U. Cin., 1978; m. Marilou Elise Moyer, July 25, 1973. Quality control technician Martin Mareitta Corp., Woodville, Ohio, 1969-73; postdoctoral fellow Schering Plough Corp., Bloomfield, N.J., 1978-79; chemist Ethyl Corp., Detroit, 1979—. Congl. sci. counselor, 1980—. NIH fellow, 1976-78; U. Cin. fellow, 1977. Mem. Am. Chem. Soc. (exec. com., chmn. public relations com.), Chem. Soc. London, Nat. Acad. Sci., Sigma Xi, Phi Lambda Upsilon. Contbr. articles to profl. jours. Roman Catholic. Home: 24856 Rensselaer St Oak Park MI 48237 Office: 1600 W 8 Mile Rd Ferndale MI 48220

SEGA, NANCY RUTH, telecommunications exec.; b. Bakersfield, Calif., Dec. 4, 1939; d. Bruce Argyle and Edna Mae (Corbeil) Campbell; student public schs., Van Nuys, Calif.; m. Armando Joseph Sega, Jan. 7, 1975; children by previous marriage—Debra Bobo Ringler, Michael Bobo. With Gen. Telephone Co. of Calif., Santa Monica, 1957-68; telecommunications research mgr. Communications Mgmt., Inc., Los Angeles, 1970-73; owner Tech. Communications Services, El Segundo, Calif., 1973-78;

telecommunications analyst Computer Scis. Corp., El Segundo, 1978-79; mgr. corp. telecommunications Diebold, Inc., Canton, Ohio, 1979—. Mem. Internat. Communications Assn., Mich.-Ohio Telecommunications Assn. Office: 818 Mulberry Rd SE Canton OH 44711

SEGALL, STEWART ROGER, personnel, tng. exec.; b. Cleve., Sept. 6, 1946; s. Erwin I. and Bessie B. S.; B.B.A., U. Toledo, 1968; M.B.A., Case Western Res. U., 1973; m. Alyce Goldman, Mar. 22, 1969; children—Charles, Melissa. Gen. mgr. Segall Foods Co., Cleve., 1969-72, asst. personnel dir. Curtis Industries div., Eastlake, Ohio, 1972-75; owner, cons. Cuyahoga Cons. Services, Cleve., 1975—, part-time, 1976—; employment mgr. U. Hosps. of Cleve., 1976-79; internal cons. MCI Telecommunications, Cleve., 1979—; mem. faculty Kent (Ohio) State U., 1976—, Cuyahoga (Ohio) Community Coll., 1972—, Garfield Sr. Coll., 1978—. Mem. bus. adv. council Kent State U., 1976—, Garfield Coll., 1981—. Served with USAR, 1966-68. Mem. Am. Soc. Personnel Adminstrn., Am. Soc. Tng. and Devel., Am. Mgmt. Assn., Nat. Collegiate Athletic Assn., Ohio High Sch. Athletic Assn. Clubs: Masons, Shriners. Contbr. chpts. to mgmt. textbooks. Office: 1621 Euclid Ave Suite 1414 Cleveland OH 44115

SEGATTO, BERNARD GORDON, lawyer; b. Joliet, Ill., July 27, 1931; s. Bernard Gordon and Rose Mary (Fracaro) S.; B.A., Beloit Coll., 1953; J.D. (Univ. scholar), U. Ill., 1958; m. Nancy L. Grady, May 2, 1959; children—Bernard Gordon III, Randall Wayne, Amy Margot. Admitted to Ill. bar, 1958; since practiced in Springfield; partner Barber, Hall, Segatto & Hoffee, and predecessor firm, 1958—; dir. Rochester State Bank (Ill.). Pres., Little Flower Sch. P.T.A., Springfield, 1971-73; chmn. adv. bd. Griffin High Sch., Springfield, 1974—. Nat. judge adv. Daus. Union Vets. of Civil War 1861-65, 1972-73, 75—. Served with AUS, 1953-55. Recipient Real Estate award Lawyers Title Ins. Co. of Richmond (Va.), 1958. Mem. Am., Ill. (chmn. sch. law com. 1965-66, v.p. jud. adv. polls com. 1974—), Sangamon County bar assns., Am. Arbitration Assn. (arbitrator 1977—), Order of Coif, Phi Delta Phi, Sigma Chi. Roman Catholic. Rotarian. Club: Sangamo, Island Bay Yacht (Springfield). Contbr. articles to profl. jours. Home: 2600 W Lakeshore Dr Springfield IL 62707 Office: PO Box 79 Springfield IL 62705

SEGHI, PHILLIP DOMENIC, profl. baseball team exec.; b. Cedar Point, Ill., 1918; student Northwestern U., 1931-34. Former infielder profl. baseball teams; mgr. minor league teams Pitts. Pirates, 1946-48; with Cleve. Indians Am. League baseball team, 1949-55, 71—, mgr. minor league teams Fargo-Moorhead, Green Bay, 1949-55, v.p., dir. player personnel, 1971-72, v.p., gen. mgr., 1973—; scout Cin. Reds, 1956-58, farm dir., 1958-68; farm dir. Oakland A's, 1968-71. Office: Cleveland Stadium Cleveland OH 44114*

SEGUIN, DONALD ROLAND, distillery exec.; b. Windsor, Ont., Can., Nov. 27, 1941; s. John Roland and Rose Marie (Racine) S.; student Wayne State U., 1964-65, U. Toronto, 1975, Rochester Inst. Tech., 1978, St. Clair Coll., 1970-75; m. Shirley Ann Beneteau, July 6, 1963; children—Anita, Katherine, Donald, Christopher. Quality control technician Hiram Walker & Sons, Inc., Detroit, 1962-65, package design staff asst., 1967-76, asst. dir. package design, 1976—. Mem. Packaging Inst., Great Lakes Packaging Assn. Roman Catholic. Home: 405 Elmstead Rd Rural Route 1 Tecumseh ON N8N 2L9 Canada Office: PO Box 33006 Detroit MI 48232

SEIBERLING, JOHN FREDERICK, congressman; b. Akron, Ohio, Sept. 8, 1918; s. Fred and Henrietta S.; student Staunton (Va.) Mil. Acad.; grad. with honors Harvard U., 1941; LL.B., Columbia U., 1949; m. Elizabeth Behr, 1949; children—John B., David P., Stephen M. Admitted to N.Y. bar, 1950, Ohio bar, 1955; asso. firm, N.Y.C., 1949-54; specialist antitrust law Goodyear Tire & Rubber Co., Akron, 1954-70; mem. 92d-97th congresses from 14th Ohio dist. Served to maj. AUS, 1942-46. Decorated Legion of Merit, Bronze Star; also decorations France, Belgium. Mem. Akron Bar Assn. Democrat. Address: 1225 Longworth House Office Bldg Washington DC 20515

SEIDEL, RICHARD MAURICE, life ins. co. exec.; b. Chgo., May 21, 1926; s. Alexander and Maree (Moss) S.; student U. Ill.; m. Judith Jaffe, Apr. 11, 1948; children—Jan, Karen, Laurie, Richard. Owner, R. M. Seidel, Chgo., 1948-54, Rapid Mailing & Advt., Chgo., 1950-57; v.p., sec. Guarantee Reserve Life Ins. Co., Hammond, Ind., 1958-63, v.p., treas., 1964-70, sr. v.p., treas., 1970-71, exec. v.p., 1971-72, pres., 1973—. Mem. Med. Research Inst. Council, Michael Reese Hosp., 1970-75. Jewish. Clubs: Standard (Chgo.); Ravisloe Country (Homewood, Ill.). Home: 2226 Carroll Pkwy Flosshoor IL 60422 Office: 530 River Oaks W Calumet City IL 60409

SEIFERT, GEORGE G., educator; b. Bklyn., Dec. 15, 1926; B.A. in Psychology, Antioch Coll., 1952; M.A. in Edn., Western Res. U., 1956, Ph.D. in Edn., 1965; married. Asso. examiner Ednl. Testing Service, Princeton, N.J., 1965-67; asst. prof. to prof. edn. Bowling Green State U., 1967—. Fulbright scholar, cons. Ministry of Edn., Sri Lanka, 1977-78; mem. com. of examiners in advanced edn. Grad. Record Exam., 1974—, chmn., 1980—. Mem. Am. Ednl. Research Assn., Am. Psychol. Assn., Nat. Soc. Study Edn., Nat. Council Measurement in Edn., Instrumental in devel. of new tests. Author: Applying Statistical Concepts, 1977. Certified as psychologist, pupil personnel adminstr., tchr., adminstr., Ohio; specialist in devel. of achievement examinations. Home: 1308 Brownwood Dr Bowling Green OH 43402 Office: Dept of Ednl Founds and Inquiry Bowling Green State U Bowling Green OH 43403

SEILER, CHARLOTTE WOODY, ret. educator; b. Thorntown, Ind., Jan. 20, 1915; d. Clark and Lois Merle (Long) Woody; A.A., Ind. State U., 1933; A.B., U. Mich., 1941; M.A., Central Mich. U., 1968; m. Wallace Urban Seiler, Oct. 10, 1942; children—Patricia Anne Bootzin, Janet Alice Seiler. Tchr. elementary schs., Whitestown, Ind., 1933-34, Thorntown, Ind., 1934-37, Kokomo, Ind., 1937-40, Ann Arbor, Mich., 1941-44, Willow Run, Mich., 1944-46; instr. English div. Delta Coll., University Center, Mich., 1964-69, asst. prof., 1969-77, ret., 1977; organizer, dir. Delta Coll. Puppeteers, 1972-77. Treas., Friends of Grace A. Dow Meml. Library, 1974-75, 77-79, corr. sec., 1975-77; mem. Midland Art Assn.; adv. bd. Salvation Army, 1980-81. Mem. Internat. Reading Assn., Am., Mich. library assns., AAUW (fellowship honoree 1979), Midland Symphony League, Pi Lambda Theta, Chi Omega, Midland Panhellenic. Presbyterian. Clubs: Tuesday Review (pres. 1979-80), Midland Garden, Seed and Sod Garden. Home: 5002 Sturgeon Creek Pkwy Midland MI 48640

SEILER, ROBERT ELDRIDGE, state supreme ct. justice; b. Kansas City, Kans., Dec. 5, 1912; s. Walter Albert and Maude Virginia (Eldridge) S.; A.B., U. Mo., 1933, LL.B., 1935; m. Faye Poore, Apr. 2, 1942; children—Sunny (Mrs. Frederick F. Dupree), Lu (Mrs. David Fahrland), Robert Poore. Admitted to Mo. bar, 1934; practiced in Joplin, Mo., 1935-66; city atty. of Joplin, 1950-54; judge Supreme Ct. Mo., 1967—, chief justice, 1975-77. Sec. Joplin Home Rule Charter Commn., 1953-54; mem. Mo. Bd. Law Examiners, 1948-65, sec., 1950-63, pres., 1963-65. Fellow Am. Coll. Trial Lawyers; mem. Am., Jasper County, Kansas City bar assns., Am. Judicature Soc., Inst. Jud. Adminstrn., Mo. Bar, Mo. Law Sch. Alumni Assn., Nat. Conf. Bar Examiners (chmn. 1967-68), Order of Coif, Kappa Sigma. Club: Jefferson City Country. Office: Supreme Ct Bldg Jefferson City MO 65101

SEILER, WALLACE URBAN, chem. engr.; b. Evansville, Ind., Aug. 31, 1914; s. Samuel Alfred and Anna Beatrice (Grossman) S.; student U. Evansville, 1932-34; B.S., Purdue U., 1937; postgrad. U. Mich., 1945-46; m. Charlotte Woody, Oct. 10, 1942; children—Patricia Anne, Janet Alice. With Dow Chem. Co., 1937-80, engr., Midland, Mich., 1937-39, cons. research engr., Ann Arbor, Mich., 1939-49, tech. service engr., Midland, 1950-55, mgr. solvents field service, 1955-64, contract research and devel. specialist, 1964-80. Mem. Am. Chem. Soc., AAAS, Am. Inst. Chemists, Sigma Xi, Tau Beta Pi, Phi Lambda Upsilon. Home: 5002 Sturgeon Creek Pkwy Midland MI 48640

SEILING, ALFRED WILLIAM, chem. co. exec.; b. Watseka, Ill., May 28, 1936; s. Alfred William and Edith M. (Miller) S.; B.A., Blackburn Coll., 1957; Ph.D., Ind. U., 1962; postgrad. Stanford U., 1979; m. Patricia A. Whelan, Sept. 7, 1957; children—David A., Sheryl A., Brad W., Bryan K. Research chemist Morton Chem. Co., Chgo., 1961-64, research supr., 1964-67, tech. service supr., 1967-72, tech. mgr. electronics, 1973-75, group mgr. electronics, 1975-77, gen. mgr. electronics, 1977-79, v.p. electronics materials, 1979—. Vice-pres. Lake Region YMCA, 1964-65, pres., 1966-67. Mem. Soc. Plastics Engrs., Semiconductor Equipment and Materials Inst., Am. Chem. Soc., Sigma Xi, Phi Lambda Upsilon. Methodist. Club: Lake Region Y Men's. Home: 6312 Walkup Ln Crystal Lake IL 60014 Office: 2 N Riverside Plaza Chicago IL 60606

SEIPEL, RICHARD ALAN, educator, state extension service ofcl.; b. Columbus, Ohio, Mar. 11, 1953; s. William J. and Mary J. (Tompkins) S.; B.S. in Agr., Ohio State U., 1975, M.S. in Agr., 1980; m. Debra Sue Hand, June 9, 1973; 1 son, Joseph. Vocat. agr. tchr., Future Farmers Am. advisor Greenville (Ohio) High Sch., 1976-81; 4-H agt. Darke County, Ohio Coop. Extension Service, 1981—; tchr. adult hort. classes, Youth Employment Tng. Program. Parliamentarian Village of Wayne Lakes, Ohio, also mem. rules com., 1981—; bd. dirs. Darke Econ. Found.; initiated neighborhood watch program. Named one of 8 Outstanding Young Agr. Tchrs., State of Ohio, 1980; recipient awards for publs. Ohio Vocat. Agr. Tchrs. 30 Minute Club, 1978-80. Mem. Ohio Vocat. Agr. Tchrs. Assn., Nat. Vocat. Agr. Tchrs. Assn., Ohio Vocat. Assn., Am. Vocat. Assn., Nat. Edn. Assn., Ohio Edn. Assn., Western Ohio Edn. Assn., Greenville Edn. Assn., Ohio Coop. Extension Agts. Assn., Future Farmers Am. Alumni Assn., Ohio State Alumni Assn. (life), Greenville C. of C. Roman Catholic. Clubs: Rotary, Young Farmers, K.C. Home: 3612 Scenic Dr Greenville OH 45331 Office: 700 Wayne St Greenville OH 45331

SEITZ, DAVID FREDERICK, tech. co. exec.; b. Buffalo, Nov. 17, 1944; s. Carlton Herman and Jane Carolyn (Gibbs) S.; B.S. in Civil Engring., U. Cin., 1970; m. Judith Lynn Moore, July 6, 1968; children—Lisa Carolyn, Brian David, Eric William. Structural designer, draftsman KZF Inc., Cin., 1966-73; project structural engr. McClurg, Smith & Assos., Cin., 1973-75; ops. officer, project mgr. A-E Design Assos., Cin., 1975—, also dir. Chmn. membership New Eng. Hills Homeowners Assn., 1977, pres., 1978, 79; spokesman Fairfield (Ohio) Neighborhood Council, 1978-81; mem. City of Fairfield Masterplan Com., 1979, 80; mem. City of Fairfield Bd. Zoning Appeals, 1980-81, vice chmn., 1980, chmn., 1981; bd. dirs. Greentrust, sec., 1981—; mem. Fairfield Bd. Edn., 1982—. N.Y. State Regents Coll. scholar, 1961-62. Registered profl. engr., Ohio. Mem. ASCE (corr. sec. 1974-75, sec. nat. conv. 1974), Chi Epsilon, Sigma Nu (steward, lt. comdr.). Home: 3292 Greenwich Dr Fairfield OH 45014 Office: A-E Design Assos 11499 Chester Rd Cincinnati OH 45246

SEITZ, JACOB NICHOLAS, fin. co. exec.; b. Krissesszell, Germany, Sept. 19, 1945; came to U.S., 1955, naturalized, 1965; s. Nicholas and Katharine (Uitz) S.; student Northwestern Bus. Coll., 1966-67; student Am. Savs. and Loan Assn., 1964-65; m. July 11, 1965; children—Michelle Andrea, Nicole Marie. Appraiser trainee and mortgage loan servicer Apollo Savs., Chgo., 1964-67, litigation coordinator, 1968-69, property mgr. and appraiser, 1968; property mgr. Fed. Savs. and Loan Ins. Corp., Chgo., 1968-69; staff appraiser Clyde Savs. and Loan Assn., N. Riverside, Ill., 1969-71; with Nat. Mortgage Corp., Norridge, Ill., 1971-73; asst. to v.p. mortgage dept. Unity Savs. Assn., Norridge, 1973-74; mgr. condominium homeowner assns. Midwest Assn. Mgmt. Corp.; Des Plaines, Ill., 1974-75; loan officer Chgo. Fed. Savs. & Loan Assn., 1975-76; with Continental Mortgage Ins., Inc., Madison, Wis., 1976-77; bus. devel. officer Public Savs. & Loan Assn., Chgo., 1977—, security officer, 1977—. Served with U.S. Army, 1967. Mem. Home Builders Assn. of Chicagoland, Northwest Builders Assn. Democrat. Roman Catholic. Home: 3636 N Bell Ave Chicago IL 60618 Office: 6422 W Archer Ave Chicago IL 60638

SEITZ, JAMES EUGENE, coll. pres.; b. Columbia, Pa., July 27, 1927; s. Joseph Stoner and Minnie (Frey) S.; B.S., Millersville (Pa.) State Coll., 1950; M.Ed., Pa. State U., 1952; Ph.D., So. Ill. U., 1971; m. Florence Arlene Dutcher, Apr. 5, 1950; children—Diane Louise, Ellen Kay, Linda Marie, Karl Steven. Lectr., Temple U., Phila., 1956-62; asst. prof. engring. tech. Kans. State U., Pittsburg, 1962-66; dean Mineral Area Coll., Flat River, Mo., 1965-69, Coll. Lake County, Grayslakes, Ill., 1969-73; pres. Edison State Community Coll., Piqua, Ohio, 1973—; cons. in field. Bd. dirs. Family Service Agy. Lake County, 1970-73. Served with USNR, 1944-45. Mem. AAUP, Am. Tech. Edn. Assn., Council for Occupational Edn., Am. Vocat. Assn., Ohio Tech. Transfer Orgn. (dir.), Ohio Tech. and Community Coll. Assn. (dir.), Dayton-Miami Valley Consortium of Colls. and Univs. (dir.), Piqua C. of C., VFW, Sidney Epicurean Soc. (pres. 1978-79). Clubs: Rotary, Exchange of Grayslake (Ill.) (founding pres. 1970). Author articles in field. Office: 1973 Edison Dr Piqua OH 45356

SEITZ, PETER, graphic designer, educator; b. Augsburg, Germany, Aug. 15, 1931; s. Georg and Olga (Kirschenhofer) S.; ed. Acad. Art, Germany, 1945-55; diploma Ulm (Germany) Sch. Design, 1959; M.F.A., Yale U., 1961; m. Patricia Susan Umholtz, Aug. 26, 1963; children—Christopher Jon, Bryan Alexander, Mandy Tai Soon. Graphic designer I.M. Pei Assos., N.Y.C., 1961-62; chmn. graphic design dept. Md. Inst. Art, Balt., 1962-64; designer, design curator, editor Walker Art Center, Mpls., 1964-68; co-founder, prin. InterDesign Inc., Mpls., 1968-79, graphic designer, 1968-79; pres. Seitz Graphic Direction Inc., 1979—; now asso. prof. Mpls. Coll. Art and Design; mem. project asst. panel Minn. State Arts Bd., 1976-79; co-founder Community Design Center. Mem. Com. Urban Environment, 1968-73. Recipient Honor award Environ. Graphics Soc., 1978; N.Y. Type Dirs. Club award, 1979, others. Mem. Am. Inst. Graphic Art, Univ. and Coll. Designers Assn., Mpls. Arts Dirs. Club, Yale U. Art Assn. (exec. com.). Contbr. articles to profl. publs. Home: 4401 E Lake Harriet Blvd Minneapolis MN 55409 Office: 4402 E Lake Harriet Blvd Minneapolis MN 55409

SEITZINGER, EDWARD FRANCIS, lawyer; b. Mapleton, Iowa, Apr. 3, 1916; s. John and Catherine Emma (Griffin) S.; student Iowa State U., 1935-36, 37-38; B.S., S.D. State U., 1943; J.D. with distinction, U. Iowa, 1947; m. Marian Bernice Westerberg, June 27, 1943; 1 dau., Pam K. Admitted to Iowa bar, 1947, since practiced in Des Moines; partner firm Seitzinger, Morain & Catterall; asst. gen. counsel Farm Bur. Fedn. and Affiliated Cos., 1958-78, gen. counsel, 1978—; dir. Legal Aid Soc., Polk County, 1970-73. Mem. exec. com. Polk County Republican Central Com. Trustee, Luth. Home for Aging, 1967-75; bd. dirs. Izaak Walton League, United Campaign for Polk County Lawyers. Served with inf., AUS, World War II. Recipient award Iowa Farm Safety Council, 1961. Mem. Iowa Def. Counsel Assn. (pres. 1964-65, dir. 1964—), Am., Iowa (gov. 1973-75), Polk County (pres. 1969-70) bar assns., Iowa Conf. Bar Assn. Pres.'s (pres. 1974-79), Fedn. Ins. Counsel (v.p. 1968-69, 74-75, gov. 1970-72), Internat. Assn. Ins. Counsel, Def. Research Inst. (dir. 1968-75, pres. 1973-74, chmn. bd. 1974-75, hon. chmn. bd. 1975-76), Des Moines C. of C. (agrl. com.), Lincoln Inne (pres. 1968-69). Mason (Shriner). Club: Des Moines Golf and Country. Contbr. articles to profl. jours. Home: 1223 Cummins Pkwy Des Moines IA 50311 Office: 5400 University Ave West Des Moines IA 50265

SEKELY, JOSEPH DALE, III, architect; b. Canton, Ohio, Mar. 13, 1941; s. Joseph and Anna Catherine (Wiley) S.; B. Arch., Kent State U., 1969; m. Valerie L. Descutner, Aug. 28, 1965; children—Anita Dawn, Debora Kay. Staff, Union Metal Mfg. Co., Canton, 1963-67; staff Lawrence, Dykes, Goodenberger & Bower, Architects, Canton, 1967-69; staff Marr, Knapp & Crawfis, Architects, New Philadelphia, Ohio, 1969-73; architect Gibbons-Grable Co., Canton, 1973-75; prin. Joseph D. Sekely III, Architect, Carrollton, Ohio, 1975—. Mem. adv. bd. Tuscarawas campus Kent State U., 1978—, pres. adv. bd., 1981; chmn. Carroll County (Ohio) Salvation Army, 1979—; pres. Carroll County Improvement Corp., 1979—; mem. Eight County Health Planning and Devel. Council, 1979—. Registered architect, Ohio, Fla., W.Va. Mem. AIA (v.p. 1981), Carroll County C. of C. (dir. 1979—), Nat. Council Architect and Registration Bds., Kent State U. Alumni Assn., Sigma Nu. Presbyterian. Clubs: Rotary (pres. Carrollton 1979), Atwood Yacht, Eagles, Moose. Home: 2034 Fargo Rd SW Sherrodsville OH 44675 Office: Joseph D Sekely III Architect 65 W Main St Carrollton OH 44615

SEKIGUCHI, YOSHI, graphic designer, visual communicator; b. Yokosuka, Japan, Apr. 15, 1931; came to U.S., 1964; s. Tatsuji and Ume (Fukuda) S.; diploma with honors, Tamagawa Comml. Art Coll., 1953; postgrad. Art Inst. Chgo., 1965-66; m. Yoshiko Nakajima, Dec. 19, 1959; children—Risa, Chika, Juri. Art dir. Staff, Inc., Tokyo, 1955-64, Medalist Publs., Chgo., 1964-65; asst. prodn. dir. Nobart, Inc., Chgo., 1965-69; art dir. Cahners Pub. Co., Chgo., 1969-71, Playboy Clubs Internat., Chgo., 1971-75; pres., owner Rising Sun Design, Chgo., 1975—; cons. graphic dir. Conflict Resolution Movement. Recipient Internat. Calendar Design award, 1964; Nat. Christmas Seal design award, 1967; Jesse H. Neal Editorial Achievement awards, 1970, 80; Soc. Publ. Designers ann. awards, 1971, 72; Communication Art Mag. ann. award, 1975, 81; N.Y. One Show award, 1976; Type Dirs. Club ann. awards, 1976, 77; N.Y. Art Dirs. Club ann. award, 1978. Mem. Artists Guild Chgo., Japanese C. of C. and Industry Chgo. Contbr. articles to U.S. and Japanese profl. jours. Home: 437 Marshman St Highland Park IL 60035 Office: 166 E Superior St Chicago IL 60611

SEKSARIA, DINESH CHAND, mech. engr.; b. Agra, India, Apr. 20, 1944; came to U.S., 1963, naturalized, 1977; s. Gopaldas and Krishnadevi Seksaria; B.S., Agra U., 1962; B.S. in Mech. Engring., Chgo. Inst. Tech., 1964; M.S., U. Mich., 1966; m. Madhuri Raniwala, June 2, 1971; children—Shikha, Priti. Jr. designer M.P.L. Inc., Chgo., 1965; stress analyst Nat. Water Lift Co., Kalamazoo, 1967-70; with Clark Equipment Co., Inc., 1971—, chief engr. structures and materials, Lima, Ohio, until 1978, analytical services mgr. truck div., Battle Creek, Mich., 1979—. Organizer, bd. govs. India Assn., Kalamazoo, 1968-70. Registered profl. engr., Ohio. Mem. ASME (past pres. Lima), Soc. Automotive Engrs. Democrat. Hindu. Office: 525 N 24th St Battle Creek MI 49015

SELBE, JANE ELLEN WILLIAMS, dentist; b. Rocky Ford, Colo., Mar. 16, 1926; d. Arthur R. and Mabel (Baxter) Williams; student U. Colo., 1944-47; postgrad. U. Nebr. Coll. Dentistry, 1947-48; D.D.S., Northwestern U., 1951; m. Rexford L. Selbe, Sept. 5, 1948 (div. 1971); children—Susan Lynn Katz, Scott Dow, Cynthia Kay. Gen. practice dentistry, Evanston, Ill., 1952-54, Skokie, Ill., 1954-60, Glenview, Ill., 1960—. Dental intern teaching program Michael Reese Hosp., 1961-63. Fellow Am. Coll. Dentists; mem. Am. (com. chmn. 1967), Ill. (pres. 1960-61, exec. council 1961-67, sec. 1981-82) socs. dentistry for children, Ill. (nat. children's dental health week chmn. 1975-77), Chgo. (clinican, chmn. various coms., public relations commn. 1975—) dental socs., Am. Assn. Women Dentists (dist. chmn. 1966-69, sec.-treas. 1971-73, v.p. 1973-74, treas. 1979-80, pres. 1975-76), ADA (chmn. pedo sect. sci. session 1976, cons. video continuing edn. com.), Am. Acad. Pedodontics, Odontographic Soc. Chgo., Northwestern U. Dental Sch. Alumni (pres. 1972-73, alumni council 1972-74), Alpha Chi Omega, Upsilon Alpha (grand treas. 1968-72; past chpt. pres.). Presbyterian (elder). Address: 938 Kenilworth Ln Glenview IL 60025

SELBY, JOHN DOUGLAS, utility exec.; b. Odebolt, Iowa, Oct. 12, 1921; s. John Hanna and Della Anna (Nelson) S.; B.S. in Gen. Engring., Iowa State U., 1946; postgrad. in advanced mgmt. Harvard U. Bus. Sch., 1971; m. Marion Elizabeth Harrison, Oct. 23, 1944; children—Elizabeth Selby Beckingham, Marcia Selby Cubeck, John Douglas, Michael Paul. Mem. staff light mil. electronics dept. Gen. Electric Co., Utica, N.Y., 1965-67, aerospace electronics dept., 1967-71, nuclear energy dept., San Jose, Calif., 1971-75; pres., chief exec. officer Consumers Power Co., Jackson, Mich., 1975—, chmn., 1979—; dir. No. Mich. Exploration Co., Plateau Resources Ltd.; dir., officer Mich. Gas Storage Co. Bd. dirs. Atomic Indsl. Forum, 1979; bd. dirs. Inst. Nuclear Power Ops. Served with USN 1942-46. Mem. ASME, Profl. Engrs. Assn., Edison Electric Inst. (dir., mem. com. on nuclear power), Detroit Econ. Club, Mich., Greater Jackson chambers of commerce. Republican. Clubs: Jackson Country, Jackson Town. Office: Consumers Power Co 212 W Michigan Ave Jackson MI 49201

SELBY, ROY CLIFTON, JR., neurosurgeon; b. Little Rock, Sept. 28, 1930; s. Roy and Ann (Bular) S.; B.Sc., La. State U., 1952; M.D., U. Ark., 1956; m. Marilyn Triffler, May 15, 1960; children—Brian Manfred, Bretta Lorraine. Intern, Montreal (Can.) Gen. Hosp., 1956-57; resident in neurosurgery U. Ill., Chgo., 1958-61; sr. fellow in neurosurgery Lahey Clinic, Boston, 1961-62; neurosurgeon Ministry Health, Malaysia, 1963-70; chmn. dept. neurosurgery Cook County Hosp., Chgo., 1970-74; practice medicine specializing in neurosurgery, Wheaton, Ill., 1974—; vis. asso. prof. neurosurgery Rush-Presbyn. St Luke's Med. Center, Chgo., 1972—. Bd. dirs. Chgo. Foundlings Home, 1972—; mem. pres.'s adv. com. Coll. DuPage, Glen Ellyn, Ill., 1979—. Named comdr. defender realm King Govt. Malaysia, 1970. Diplomate Am. Bd. Neurol. Surgery. Fellow A.C.S., Internat. Coll. Surgeons (Fedn. sec. N. Central Am. 1970-74); mem. Société Neurochirurgie de langue française (hon.), Central Neuropsychiat. Soc., Pan Am. Med. Assn., Société Internationale de Chirurgie (titulaire), Internat. Leprosy Assn. Editorial bd. Internat. Surgery; contbr. articles and editorials to profl. publs.; novelist. Home: 1303 S Elizabeth St Lombard IL 60148

SELDEN, EDWARD H(ARVEY), educator; b. Duluth, Minn., Sept. 15, 1915; s. William W. and Lylan M. (Scott) S.; B.S. in Chemistry and Biology, U. Wis., Superior, 1940; M.A. in Ednl. Psychology, U. Minn., 1947, Ph.D. in Ednl. Psychology, 1960; m. Mary Coughlin; children—Mary C., Frances E., Margaret J. Dir. student personnel Moorhead (Minn.) State U., 1947-48; chief clin. psychologist Dept. Ct. Services, Mpls., 1950-59; asst. prof. child study service St. Cloud (Minn.) State U., 1959-61; prof. psychology U. Wis., River Falls, 1961—, chmn. dept., 1964-79. Mem. Am. Psychol. Assn. Certified sch. psychologist, Wis.; specialist in abnormal behavior, self-theory, goal-setting behavior, behavior assessment. Home: Route 3 Box 274 Hudson WI 54016 Office: Dept Psychology U Wis River Falls WI 54022

SELDERS, GEORGE EVANS, editorial service co. exec.; b. Kansas City, Mo., Apr. 2, 1952; s. David Victor and Dorothy Louise (Evans) S.; B.S.J. in Advt., Monmouth (Ill.) Coll., 1971; postgrad. U. Kans., Lawrence, 1971-74; m. Barbara Ann Steadman, Feb. 28, 1976; children—Lindsay Ann, Brent Steadman, Collin Michael. Pres., co-founder Family Features Editorial Services, Inc., Shawnee Mission, Kans., 1974—. Active United Way, Kansas City Chiefs Coaches Club; bd. dirs. First Stringers Club, Kansas City Chiefs Football Club. Mem. Kansas City Press Club, Kansas City C. of C., Sigma Delta Chi, Phi Gamma Delta. Presbyterian. Club: Rockhill Tennis (Kansas City). Home: 3707 W 73d St Prairie Village KS 66208 Office: 3500 W 75th St Prairie Village KS 66208

SELEKMAN, SAMUEL TYLER, social worker; b. Pitts., Nov. 17, 1928; s. Max and Ruth (Tyler) S.; B.S., U. Pitts., 1950; M.S.W., Carnegie Mellon U., 1952; m. Carolyn Schutte, Mar. 18, 1951; 1 son, Matthew. Family caseworker Jewish Family and Children's Service, Pitts., 1954-57; chief psychiat. social worker Beaver County Mental Hygiene Clinic, Rochester, Pa., 1957-61; child therapist Bellefaire, Cleve., 1961-64; dir. social service Sagamore Hills Children's Psychiat. Hosp., Northfield, Ohio, 1964-66; with Beech Brook, Pepper Pike, Ohio, 1966—, coordinator student tng. and vol. sers., 1976—; pvt. practice counciling, Mayfield Heights, Ohio; coordinator student tng. serving univs. N.E. Ohio; instr. parent effectiveness tng., adj. instr. Case Western Reserve U.; pvt. practitioner. Served with AUS, 1952-54. Mem. Nat. Assn. Social Workers, Acad. Cert. Social Workers. Home: 3469 Green Rd Beechwood OH 44122 Office: 3737 Lander Rd Pepper Pike OH 44124 also 6801 Mayfield Rd Hillcrest Med Bldg Mayfield Heights OH

SELFRIDGE, CALVIN, lawyer; b. Evanston, Ill., Dec. 20, 1933; s. Calvin Frederick and Violet Luella (Bradley) S.; B.A., Northwestern U., 1956; J.D., U. Chgo., 1960. Admitted to Ill. bar, 1961; trust officer Continental Ill. Nat. Bank & Trust Co. Chgo., 1961-71; individual practice law, Chgo., 1972-76; mem. firm Howington, Elworth, Osswald & Hough, Chgo., 1976-79; individual practice law, 1979—; pres., dir. Des Plaines Pub. Co., Northwest Newspapers Corp., Ozark Woodworking Corp. Pres., bd. dirs. Scholarship Fund Found., 1965—; trustee Lawrence Hall Sch. for Boys, 1982—. Served with AUS, 1959. Mem. Chgo., Am., Ill. bar assns., Law Club Chgo., Legal Club Chgo., Chi Psi, Phi Delta Phi. Republican. Congregationalist. Clubs: Attic, Univ. (past dir.), Racquet (treas., gov.) (Chgo.); Balboa (Mazatlan); Indian Hill Country. Home: 1340 N Astor St Chicago IL 60610 Office: 135 S LaSalle St Suite 2012 Chicago IL 60603

SELIG, ALLAN H. (BUD), profl. baseball team exec.; b. Milw., July 30, 1934; s. Ben and Marie Selig; grad. U. Wis. at Madison, 1956. With Selig Ford, West Allis, Wis., 1959—, pres., 1966—; part owner Milw. Braves became Atlanta Braves 1965), 1963-65; co-founder Teams, Inc., 1964; co-founder Milw. Brewers Am. League baseball team, 1965, owner, pres., 1970—. Served with AUS, 1956-58. Address: care Milwaukee Brewers Milwaukee County Stadium Milwaukee WI 53214

SELK, JAMES DOUGLAS, mag. pub.; b. Marshfield, Wis., July 31, 1934; s. August Fred and Lillian Louise (Albrecht) S.; B.S. in Journalism, U. Wis., 1958; m. Gale B. Volck, June 21, 1969; children—Michelle E., Jennifer M. Editor Tomah (Wis.) Jour. and Monitor Herald, 1958-59; reporter Racine (Wis.) Jour. Times, 1959-61, Wis. State Jour., Madison, 1961-73; editor editorial page Wis. State Jour., Madison, 1973-77; editor, pub. Madison Mag., 1977—. Served with U.S. Army, 1953-55. Mem. U. Wis. Alumni Assn., Greater Madison C. of C. Club: Madison Press. Home: 414 N Livingston St Madison WI 53703 Office: 123 E Doty St Madison WI 53703

SELLE, STANLEY JOHN, mech. engr.; b. Crosby, N.D., Mar. 21, 1945; s. John L. and Stella (Struxness) S.; B.S.E.E. (Maxwell Upson scholar 1963-67, Sigma Tau scholar 1964-65), U. N.D., 1968, M.S.M.E., 1970; m. Constance Marie Dubbert, Apr. 16, 1970; children—Karen, Leslie, Michael. Mech. engr. Grand Forks (N.D.) Energy Tech. Center, U.S. Dept. Energy, 1970-79; pres. N.W. Research, Inc., Grand Forks, 1979—; cons. in field. Recipient Eta Kappa Nu award, 1964. Mem. ASTM, ASME, Phi Eta Sigma, Grey Gowns, Delta Upsilon. Lutheran. Contbr. articles to profl. jours. Home: Rural Route 3 East Grand Forks MN 56721 Office: PO Box 1153 Grand Forks ND 58201

SELLERS, MARGARET REGULAR, personnel adminstr.; b. Pendleton, S.C., Sept. 28, 1935; d. Daniel and Annie Mae (Morris) Regular; B. Gen. Studies, Wayne State U.; m. Thomas James Sellers, Jan. 22, 1955; children—Loren Sellers Jackson, Sharon Elizabeth. Various positions Detroit Public Library, 1951-72, asst. dir. personnel, 1972-74, asso. dir. personnel, 1974-77; dir. personnel Wayne County Community Coll., Detroit, 1977-80; dir. personnel Mich. Dept. Natural Resources, 1980—; chmn. Mich. Personnel Dirs. Council, 1981; mem. adv. com. Classified Exec. Service, State of Mich.; lectr. in field. Trustee, Rehab. Inst., 1980-81; mem. exec. com. Wayne County Dist. 1, Vols. for Re-election of Gov. William G. Milliken, 1978. U. Md. fellow, 1973. Mem. Internat. Personnel Mgmt. Assn. U.S. (exec. bd. Mich. chpt. 1977—, pres. Mich. chpt. 1978, v.p. central region 1980-81, pres. region 1981), ALA (adv. office library personnel resources), Mich. Public Employer Labor Relations Assn. (exec. bd. 1977, program com. 1980). Baptist. Office: Dept Natural Resources PO Box 30028 Lansing MI 48909

SELLERS, MARJORIE SCOTT, bookseller, former librarian; b. Decatur, Ala., Apr. 18, 1925; d. Clyde R. and Eula W. (Lewis) Scott; student Kansas City Met. Jr. Coll., Park Coll.; m. Leonard S. Sellers, Nov. 25, 1943; children—Carol, Steve, Mark. Substitute and library asst. Oak Park Sr. High Sch., North Kansas City, Mo., 1968-71; periodicals bank coordinator Kansas City Regional Council for Higher Edn., 1971-74; co-founder, dir. Mid-Am. inter library services, interlibrary loans librarian Park Coll., Parkville, Mo., 1974-81; owner Bell Rd. Barn Books, Parkville, 1981—; mem. N. Central Evaluation Com. Mem. ALA, Mo. Library Assn., Kans. Library Assn., Mo. Assn. Coll. and Research Libraries, Mountain Plains Library Assn., Am. Assn. for Higher Edn., Oral History Assn., Kansas City Women's C. of C. Mem. Assembly of God Ch. Editor: The Loaner newsletter, 1974-81, Mid-Am. Shelflist, 1981—. Office: Bell Rd Barn Books 6008 NW Bell Rd Parkville MO 64152

SELLINGER, FRANCIS JOHN, brewing co. exec.; b. Phila., July 8, 1914; s. Frank and L. Caroline (Wiseman) S.; B.S. in Biochemistry St. Joseph's Coll., Phila., 1936; postgrad. Drexel Inst., 1936-37, E.A. Siebel Inst. Tech., Chgo., 1938; m. Helen Brown, Feb. 22, 1941; children—Frank, Mary, Joseph, Helen, Dorothy, John, Patricia, Elizabeth, James. Chief chemist, asst. brewmaster Esslinger Brewing Co., Phila., 1936-41; chief chemist, purchasing agt., Hudepohl Brewing Co., Cin., 1941-46; asst. to gen. mgr. August Wagner Breweries, Columbus, Ohio, 1946-50; owner, pres. Hi-State Beverage Co., 1950-52; supr. packaging and purchasing agt. Burger Brewing Co., 1952, v.p., gen. mgr., 1956-64; asst. to pres. and v.p. and gen. mgr. Anheuser-Busch Inc., St. Louis, 1964, tech. dir. ops., 1964-66, v.p. engring., 1966-74, group v.p., 1974-76, exec. v.p. mgmt. and industry affairs, 1976-77; pres. Jos. Schlitz Brewing Co., Milw., 1977-80, vice chmn., chief exec. officer, 1980—, dir., 1979—; dir. Marine Nat. Exchange Bank, Milw. Mem. Master Brewers Assn. Am. Clubs: Milw. Athletic, Milw. Country. Office: Jos Schlitz Brewing Co 235 W Galena St Milwaukee WI 53201

SELLMAN, RICHARD LEE, steel co. exec.; b. Dayton, Oct. 29, 1948; s. John Richard and Neva Margaret (Simpson) S.; B.S., Eastern Ky. U., 1970; postgrad. Central Mich. U., 1972-73, U. Dayton, 1973-74; m. Rebecca Ann Linebaugh, Apr. 4, 1970; children—Bret Richard, Jeff Eugene. Tchr. biology, chemistry and physics Henry Clay High Sch., Lexington, Ky., Centerville (Ohio) High Sch., 1970-73; indsl. engr. Dayton Walther Corp., 1973-78; supr. indsl. engring. Duiron Co., Inc., Dayton, 1978-79, mgr. mfg. services, 1979—; lectr. Miami Jacobs Jr. Coll. Mem. Am. Inst. Indsl. Engring., Kappa Alpha. Presbyterian. Home: 3251 Claar Ave Kettering OH 45429 Office: PO Box 1145 Dayton OH 45401

SELMAN, NEAL ALLEN, copywriter; b. Birmingham, Ala., Mar. 6, 1950; s. William Jack and Christine (Dixon) S.; B.A. in Communications and History, U. Ala., 1977; m. Vickie Ann Moseley, Jan. 19, 1969; children—Stacey Carlene, Jamie Renee. Feature writer Birmingham Reporter, 1974-75; creative dir. Advt. and Art Council, Birmingham, 1975-78; free-lance writer, photographer, Hollywood, Calif., 1978-79; copywriter McDonald & Little Advt., Atlanta, 1979-80, Leo Burnett Advt., Chgo., 1980—. Recipient Internat. Photography award Kodak Co., 1975, Collegiate Press Assn. award, 1974, 75, Addy award, 1978, 79. Mem. Writer's Group Chgo., Playwright's Center Chgo., Omicron Delta Kappa. Republican. Home: 2253 N Burling St Chicago IL 60614 Office: Leo Burnett Advt Prudential Plaza Chicago IL 60601

SELTZER, PHILIP ALAN, physician; b. Bronx, N.Y., Oct. 17, 1944; s. Irving Joseph and Elsie Marilyn (Greenhut) S.; B.S., City U. N.Y., 1965; D.C., Columbia Coll. Chiropractic, N.Y.C., 1969; M.S. in Pharmacology, St. John's U., N.Y.C., 1971; B.S. in Practice Mgmt., Upper Iowa U., Fayette, 1979; M.D., U. Santo Domingo, 1981; m. Anita Nancy Samek, Nov. 1, 1970; children—Sean Reid, Bret Jay. Practice chiropractic, Mass., 1969, Lansing, Mich., 1971, Ann Arbor, Mich., 1971—. Mem. Mich. Task Force on Health Personnel Licensure and Certification, 1973—; mem. Washtenaw County (Mich.) Comprehensive Health Planning Commn., 1974—; mem. Mich. Council on Roentgenology, 1971—. Bd. dirs. Huron Valley Humane Soc. Recipient Vinton F. Logan Meml. award Columbia Coll. Chiropractic, 1969, Frank E. Dean Meml. award, 1969, Distinguished Service award, 1969; D. D. Palmer Meml. award Acad. Chiropractic, 1969; Acad. Key scholar, 1965-69. Diplomate Nat. Bd. Chiropractic Examiners. Fellow Am. Coll. Chiropractors; mem. Columbia Coll. Physicians and Surgeons, Am. (council diagnosis and internal disorders 1970—, council on roentgenology 1970—; award 1969), Mich. chiropractic assns., Washtenaw County Soc. Chiropractic Physicians (pres. 1974—), Am. Assn. Chiropractic Medicine, Beta Omega Chi. Jewish. Home: 3895 Waldenwood Dr Ann Arbor MI 48105 Office: 825 Packard St Ann Arbor MI 48104

SELZER, CHARLES LOUIS, supt. schs.; b. Homestead, Iowa, Dec. 21, 1914; s. Louis Carl and Caroline (Shoup) S.; B.A. cum laude, Coe Coll., 1935; M.A., State U. Iowa, 1950, postgrad., 1951—; m. Louis Kippenhan, Mar. 9, 1935; 1 dau., Patricia Madelyn (Mrs. Robert Carstensen). Tchr., prin., coach Amana (Iowa) High Sch., 1935-50; supt. Amana Community Schs., 1950—; mem. Grant Wood Spl. Edn. Commn.; guest lectr. U. Iowa, 1978, 79, 80; past dir. Amana Telephone Co., Amana Woolens, Inc.; dir. Title V Area X Edn. TV and Media. Mem. Iowa County Bd. Narcotics and Drug Edn.; mem. Area X Iowa Agy. on Aging; bd. dirs. Amana Hist. Preservation Com.; bd. dirs. Amana Travel Council; mem. Iowa County Info. and Referral Center; pres. Amana Community Chest, 1951-53; mem. adv. bd. Kirkwood Coll.; mem. Iowa County Crime Commn.; former justice of peace Iowa County. Cited by Iowa Legislature for service to edn., charitable and civic activities, 1980. Mem. Nat. Assn. Sch. Adminstrs., Associated Sch. Adminstrs. (mem. European study tour 1976), Iowa Assn. Sch. Adminstrs. (past pres., chmn. ethics bd.), NEA, Iowa Edn. Assn., Iowa County Supt.'s Assn., Joint County Area X Supts. Assn. (legis. com.), Iowa Peace Officers Assn., Iowa Hist. Soc. (pres. 1965-67), Iowa County Schoolmasters Assn. (past pres.), Phi Beta Kappa. Mem. Amana Ch. Soc. (trustee, elder, pres. 1971—). Clubs: Homestead Welfare (past pres., sec.), Cedar Rapids Toastmasters (hon.), Elks, Masons (32 deg., Shriner), El Kahir. Translator Amana documents, catechism and testimonies; columnist Amana News Bulletin; author Amana Coop. plan. Home: Homestead IA 52236 Office: Middle IA 52307

SEMB, GEORGE, psychologist, educator; b. West Chester, Pa., Dec. 4, 1943; s. Balwen A. and Katherine (Argo) S.; B.S. with honors, U. Wash., 1966; M.Sc. in Psychology, Brown U., 1968; Ph.D., U. Kans., 1972. Research and teaching asst. dept. psychology Brown U., Providence, 1967-68; instr. dept. psychology Adirondack Community Coll., Glens Falls, N.Y., 1969, Keuka Coll., Keuka Park, N.Y., 1969-70, project dir. reading study skills program for coll. students, summer, 1970; teaching asst. dept. human devel. and family life U. Kans., Lawrence, 1970-71, asst. instr., 1971-72, asst. prof., 1972-75, asso. prof., 1975-79, prof., 1980—; vis. prof. dept. psychology Georgetown U., Washington, 1976, research asso. Center for Personalized Instrn., 1975-79; cons. to various colls. and ednl. orgns., 1973—; exec. dir. Internat. Soc. Individualized Instrn., 1982—. Bd. dirs. Ind. Learning Sch., Larkspur, Calif., 1982—. U. Kans. higher edn. teaching research grantee, 1972-77. Mem. Am. Psychol. Assn., Assn. for Behavior Analysis, Nat. Council Tchrs. of English, Inst. of Chartered Fin. Analysts, Kans. Acad. Sci., Phi Beta Kappa, Aviation Hall of Fame. Author: Of Children: A Study Guide, 1974; Study Guide for Of Children, 1977, 3d edit., 1980; (with D.M. Glick) Biology-The Unity and Diversity of Life: A Study Guide, 1978; Study Guide for Psychology, 1980; Test-item File for Psychology, 1980; Study Guide for Marriage and Families, 1981, Test-item File for Marriage and Family, 1981; Workbook for an Invitation to Fly, 1982; contbr. numerous articles on research in edn. to profl. jours.; guest reviewer Jour. Applied Behavior Analysis, 1970-74, mem. editorial bd. 1976-79; mem. editorial bd. Jour. Personalized Instruction, 1975—. Home: 2412 Atchison Lawrence KS 66044 Office: Univ of Kansas Lawrence KS 66045

SEMKOW, JERZY GEORG, conductor; b. Radomsko, Poland, Oct. 12, 1928; s. Aleksander and Waleria (Sienczak) S.; came to U.S., 1975; student U. Cracow (Poland), 1946-50; grad. Leningrad Mus. Conservatoire (USSR), 1951-55. Asst. condr. Leningrad Philharmonic Orch., 1954-56, Bolshoi Opera and Ballet Theater, Moscow, 1956-58; artistic dir., prin. condr. Warsaw (Poland) Nat. Opera, 1959-62; permanent condr. Danish Royal Opera, Copenhagen, 1966—; music dir., prin. condr. St. Louis Symphony Orch., 1975-79; prin. condr. Orch. Sinfonica della Radiotelevisione Italiana, Rome, 1979—; guest condr. Vienna (Austria) Symphony Orch., Suisse Romande Orch., Orchestre de Paris, London Philharm., Madrid Symphony Orch., orchs. in Berlin, Milan and Rome, Italy, and others in Europe, also N.Y. Philharm., Boston Symphony, Chgo. Symphony, Cleve. Symphony Orch. and others in U.S.; condr. at numerous festivals. Decorated Great Order Commandoria Polonia Restituta; recipient Polish Radio award, 1965. Mem. Respighi Soc. Bologne (hon.). Address: care St Louis Symphony Orch 718 N Grand Blvd Saint Louis MO 63103

SEMLER, JERRY D., ins. co. exec.; b. Indpls., Mar. 5, 1937; B.S. in Indsl. Econs., Purdue U., 1958. With Am. United Life Ins. Co., Indpls., 1959—, pres., dir., 1980—, also mem. exec. com. Bd. dirs. Mus. Indian Heritage, 500 Festival Assos., Indpls. Conv. and Vistors Bur.; v.p. Ind. Sports Corp. Mem. Million Dollar Round Table (life), Ind. C. of C., Indpls. C. of C., Am. Coll. Life Underwriters, Gen. Agts. and Mgrs. Assn., Alpha Tau Omega. Office: Am United Life Ins Co One W 26th St Indianapolis IN 46206*

SEMPLE, EDWARD EUGENE, JR., educator; b. Youngstown, Ohio, Oct. 15, 1946; s. Edward Eugene and Alma Agnes (Haas) S.; B.A. magna cum laude, Hiram Coll., 1972; M.S., Youngstown State U., 1974, 77; Ph.D., U. Akron, 1982; m. Patrice Mary Thedka, Aug. 1, 1970; children—Hans Brent, Jonathan Spencer, Matthew Todd. Tchr. elem. schs. Hubbard Village, Ohio, 1972-73, Girard (Ohio) City Schs., 1973-81; asst. prin. James A. Garfield Elem. Sch., Garrettsville, Ohio, 1982—. Mem. Girard City Council, 1980—; chmn. utilities com., 1980—; mem. Girard Bd. Zoning Appeals, 1978-79, vice chmn., 1979; trustee Girard Hist. Soc., 1979; pres. Friends of McKinley Meml. Library and Mus., 1972-73. Served with USN, 1966-70. Named Girard-Liberty Rotary Tchr. of Month, 1975; Jennings fellow, 1975-76. Mem. Phi Delta Kappa (chpt. treas. 1979-81, chpt. 2d v.p. 1981-82). Democrat. Roman Catholic. Home: 1571 Oak St Girard OH 44420 Office: 10207 State Route 88 Garrettsville OH 44231

SEMPROCH, GERALD HENRY, educator, biologist; b. Cleve., May 20, 1947; s. Henry Leo and Amy (Konikowski) S.; B.S.Ed., Kent State U., 1969; M.Ed., 1979. Head sci. dept., dir. athletics Waterloo High Sch., Atwater, Ohio, also dir. Portage County Sci. Fair, 1969-71; tchr. Walsh Jesuit High Sch., Cuyahoga Falls, Ohio, 1971-73; tchr. biology Ravenna (Ohio) High Sch., 1973-75; tchr. biology, head sci. dept. Stow (Ohio) City Schs., 1975—. Mem. NEA, Ohio Ednl. Assn., Assn. Curriculum and Supervision, Am. Chem. Soc. Tchrs. Affiliate, Phi Delta Kappa. Democrat. Roman Catholic. Club: K.C. (4th degree). Active in gaining 8 million dollars in scholarship funds for students, 1969—. Home: 2036 Valleybrook Rd Streetsboro OH 44240 Office: 3732 Darrow Rd Stow OH 44224

SEN, ASHISH KUMAR, urban scientist, educator; b. Delhi, India, June 8, 1942; came to U.S., 1967; s. Asoka Kumar and Arati S.; B.S. with honors, Calcutta U., 1962; M.A., U. Toronto, 1964, Ph.D., 1971; m. Colleen Taylor, Apr. 7, 1972. Research asso., lectr. geography Northwestern U., Evanston, Ill., 1967-69; asst. prof. Coll. Urban Scis., U. Ill., Chgo. Circle, 1969-73, asso. prof., 1973-78, prof., 1978—, acting dean coll. urban scis., 1977, dir. Sch. Urban Scis. 1977-78; pres. Ashish Sen and Assos., Chgo., 1977—. Mem. Transp. Research Bd. Transp. Research Forum, Am. Statis. Assn., Inst. Math. Statistics, Am. Soc. Planning Ofcls., Regional Sci. Assn. Hindu. Contbr. articles to profl. publs. statistics, transp. Home: 1949 W Granville Ave Chicago IL 60660 Office: Sch Urban Scis U Ill Chicago IL 60680

SENA, PATRICK, JR., priest, educator; b. Detroit, Mar. 9, 1939; s. Pasquale and Margaret (Tartaglia) S.; student St. Joseph Coll., Rensselaer, Ind., 1957-59, St. Charles Sem., Carthagena, Ohio, 1960-66; B.A., U. Dayton, 1962, M.A., 1965; S.T.L., Pontifical Lateran U., Rome, 1968; S.S.L., Pontifical Bibl. Inst., Rome, 1971. Ordained priest Roman Catholic Ch., 1966; asst. prof. scripture St. Charles Sem., 1966-67; asso. prof. bibl. theology Mt. St. Mary's Sem., Cin., 1971—; retreat dir. throughout U.S. and Can., 1972—; pres. Acad. for Evangelism in Theol. Edn.; dir. continuing edn. Soc. Precious Blood, Cin. Province, 1980—. Mem. Cath. Bibl. Assn., Eastern Great Lakes Bibl. Assn. Contbr. articles to profl. jours. Home and Office: Mt St Mary's Seminary 6616 Beechmont Ave Cincinnati OH 45230

SENDAK, THEODORE LORRAINE, legal and polit. commentator; b. Chgo., Mar. 16, 1918; s. Jack and Annette (Frankel) S.; A.B., Harvard U., 1940; LL.B., Valparaiso U., 1958, J.D., 1970; m. Tennessee Read, Sept. 13, 1942; children—Theodore Tipton, Timothy Read, Cynthia Louise. Admitted Ind. bar, 1959; gen. practice law, Crown Point, Ind., 1959-68; atty. gen. Ind., Indpls., 1969-81; legal and polit. commentator, 1981—. Served with U.S. Army, World War II; col. Res. ret. Recipient Freedoms Found. award, 1973, 77. Mem. Nat. Assn. Atty. Gens. (pres. 1977-78). Home: PO Box 359 Crown Point IN 46307 Office: 219 State House Indianapolis IN 46204

SENEKER, DONALD LEE, criminologist, coll. adminstr.; b. Mt. Vernon, Mo., July 5, 1935; s. Dwight and Elizabeth (Orr) S.; B.S., Central Mo. State U., 1970, M.S., 1978; m. Rosemary M. Allen. Chief police City of Riverside (Mo.), 1956-59; lt. Clay County (Mo.) Sheriff's Office, Liberty, 1959-67; chief of police City of Lee's Summit (Mo.), 1967-69; dir. criminal justice programs Mo. So. State Coll., Joplin, 1971—; vis. faculty Drury Coll., Springfield, Mo., 1973, 74; cons. U.S. Office Edn., HEW. Chmn. bd. Mt. Vernon Ambulance Dist., 1975—; active Boy Scouts Am. Mem. Mo. Acad. Sci., Mo. Tchrs. Assn. Author: Nuclear Transportation Security Training. Home: 434 E College St Mount Vernon MO 65712 Office: Police Acad Mo So State Coll Joplin MO 64801

SENGPIEHL, PAUL MARVIN, state ofcl.; b. Stuart, Nebr., Oct. 10, 1937; s. Arthur Paul and Anne Marie (Andersen) S.; B.A., Wheaton (Ill.) Coll., 1959; M.A. in Pub. Adminstrn., Mich. State U., 1961; J.D., Ill. Inst. Tech.-Chgo. Kent Coll. Law, 1970; m. June S. Cline, June 29, 1963; children—Jeffrey D., Chrystal M. Adminstrv. asst. Chgo. Dept. Urban Renewal, 1962-65; supr. Ill. Municipal Retirement Fund, Chgo., 1966-71; admitted to Ill. bar, 1971; mgmt. officer Ill. Dept. Local Govt. Affairs, Springfield, 1971-72, legal counsel, Chgo., 1972-73; spl. asst. atty. gen. Ill. Dept. Labor, Chgo., 1973-76; asst. atty. gen. Ct. of Claims div. Atty. Gen. of Ill., 1976—; local govt. law columnist Chgo. Daily Law Bull., 1975—; instr. polit. sci. Judson Coll., Elgin, Ill., 1963. Mem. Ill. Bar Assn. (local govt. law sect. council 1973-79, vice chmn. 1976-77, co-editor local govt. newsletter 1976-77, chmn. 1977-78, editor newsletter 1977-78, state tax sect. council 1979—), Chgo. Bar Assn. (local govt. com., chmn. legis. subcom. 1978-79, sec. 1979-80, vice chmn. 1980-81, chmn. 1981-82, state and mcpl. tax com.), Am. Judicature Soc., Am. Soc. Public Adminstrn., Internat. Platform Assn. Republican. Baptist (vice chmn. deacons 1973-76, 79-80). Home: 727 N Ridgeland Ave Oak Park IL 60302 Office: 188 W Randolph St Chicago IL 60601

SENGSTACKE, JOHN HERMAN HENRY, pub. co. exec.; b. Savannah, Ga., Nov. 25, 1912; s. Herman Alexander and Rosa Mae (Davis) S.; B.S., Hampton (Va.) Inst., 1933; postgrad. Ohio State U., 1933; children—Robert Abbott, Lewis Willis. With Robert S. Abbott Pub. Co., publishers Chgo. Defender, Tri-State Defender, 1934—, v.p., gen. mgr., 1934-40, pres., gen. mgr., 1940—; chmn. bd. Mich. Chronicle (Detroit), Louisville Defender; pres. Tri-State Defender, Defender Publs., Amalgamated Pubs., Inc.; pub. Daily Defender; pres. Sengstacke Enterprises, Inc., Sengstacke Publs., Pitts. Courier Newspaper Chain; dir. Ill. Fed. Savs. & Loan Assn., Golden State Mut. Life Ins. Co. Mem. exec. bd. Nat. Alliance Businessmen; bd. govs. USO; mem. Ill. Sesquicentennial Commn., Pres.'s Com. on Equal Opportunity in Armed Services; mem. pub. affairs adv. com. Air Force Acad.; trustee Bethune-Cookman Coll., Daytona Beach, Fla., Hampton Inst.; bd. dirs. Washington Park YMCA; chmn. bd. Provident Hosp. Recipient Two Friends award Nat. Urban League, 1950; Hampton Alumni award, 1954; 1st Mass. Media award Am. Jewish Com. Mem. Negro Newspaper Pubs. Assn. (founder), Nat. (founder, pres.), Am. newspaper pubs. assn., Am. Soc. Newspaper Editors (dir.). Congregationalist. Clubs: Royal Order of Snakes, Masons, Elks, Rotary, Econs., Chgo. Press. Address: 2400 S Michigan Ave Chicago IL 60616

SENHAUSER, DONALD A(LBERT), pathologist; b. Dover, Ohio, Jan.30, 1927; s. Albert Carl and Maude Anne (Snyder) S.; student U. Chgo., 1944-45; B.S., Columbia U., 1947, M.D., 1951; grad. with honors U.S. Naval Sch. Aviation Medicine, 1953; m. Helen Brown, July 22, 1961; children—William, Norman. Intern, Roosevelt Hosp., N.Y.C., 1951-52; resident Columbia-Presbyn. Hosp., N.Y.C., 1955-56, Cleve. Clinic, 1956-60; instr. in pathology Columbia U., 1955-56; fellow in immuno-pathology Middlesex Hosp. Med. Sch., London, 1960-61; mem. dept. pathology Cleve. Clinic Found, 1961-63; asso. prof. pathology U. Mo., 1963-65, prof., asst. dean Sch. Medicine, 1969-70, dir. teaching labs., 1968-70, prof., vice-chmn. dept. pathology, 1965-75; prof. pathology, chmn. dept. pathology, Ohio State U. Coll. Medicine, 1975—, prof. Sch. Allied Med. Professions, 1975—; dir. labs. Ohio State U. Hosps., 1975—; bd. dirs. Columbus area chpt. ARC, 1978—; cons. in field; WHO-AMA Vietnam med. edn. project mem. U. Saigon Med. Sch., 1967-72; vis. scientist HEW, 1972-73; acting dir. Central Ohio Regional Blood Center, 1976-79. Served as capt. M.C., USNR, 1944-45, 52-55; China, Korea. Recipient Lower award Bunts Ednl. Found., 1960; diplomate Am. Bd. Pathology. Mem. Coll. Am. Pathologists (chmn. com. edn. resources 1977-78, gov. 1980—), Am. Soc. Clin. Pathologists, Assn. Pathology Chairmen, Am. Assn. Pathology, Internat. Acad. Pathology, Assn. Am. Med. Colls., Am. Assn. Blood Banks, Ohio Soc. Pathologists (gov. 1979—), AAAS, Ohio Hist. Soc., Columbus Art League, Sigma Xi. Lutheran. Club: Masons Co-editor: Proc. 2d Midwest Conf. on the Thyroid, 1967, 3d, 1968, 5th, 1970; mem. editorial bd. Am. Jour. Clin. Pathology, 1965-76; contbr. articles to profl. jours. Office: 333 W 10th Ave Columbus OH 43210

SENIOR, RICHARD JOHN LANE, textile rental services exec.; b. Datchet, Eng., July 6, 1940; came to U.S., 1972, naturalized, 1977; s. Harold Denis and Jane Lane Dorothy (Chadwick) S.; B.A., Oxford U., 1962; M.I.A., Yale U., 1964; m. Diana Morgan, Dec. 19, 1966; children—Alden, Alicia, Amanda. Mgmt. cons. McKinsey & Co., Inc., London and Chgo., 1967-74; pres., chief exec. officer Morgan Services, Inc., Chgo., 1974—. Pres. bd. trustees Latin Sch., Chgo. Mem. Textile Rental Services Assn. Am. (pres.-elect). Clubs: Racquet, Chicago, Glen View, Econ. Home: 1420 Lake Shore Dr Chicago IL 60610 Office: Morgan Services Inc 222 N Michigan Ave Chicago IL 60601

SENSENBRENNER, FRANK JAMES, JR., congressman; b. Chgo., June 14, 1943; s. Frank James and Margaret Anita (Luedke) S.; B.A. in Polit. Sci., Stanford U., 1965; J.D., U. Wis., 1968; m. Cheryl Warren, 1977. Admitted to Wis. bar, 1968, U.S. Supreme Ct. bar, 1972; mem. firm McKay & Martin, Cedarburg, Wis., 1970-75; asst. to Congressman J. Arthur Younger of Calif., 1965, to majority leader Wis. Senate, 1966-68; mem. WIs. Assembly, 1969-75; mem. Wis. Senate, 1975-79, asst. minority leader 1977-79; mem. 96th-97th Congresses from 9th Dist. Wis. Mem. Riveredge Nature Center, 1970—. Mem. North Shore Republican Club, 1964—, Wis. Fedn. Young Reps., 1957-79. Recipient Robert Taft award Midwest Fedn. Coll. Rep. Clubs, 1969. Mem. Am. Inst. Parliamentarians, Phi Alpha Delta. Episcopalian. Club: Shorewood (Wis.) Men's. Office: 315 Cannon House Office Bldg Washington DC 20515

SENTURIA, RICHARD HARRY, fin. planning co. exec.; b. West Frankfort, Ill., Aug. 14, 1938; s. Irwin J. and Frances (Persow) S.; student So. Ill. U., 1956-57; student Bus. Sch., Washington U., St. Louis, 1957-59, 60-61, Law Sch., 1959-60; m. Ilene M. Bluestein, Dec. 24, 1961; children—Beth, Philip, Laura. From registered rep. to asst. mgr. Dempsey-Tegeler & Co., Inc., St. Louis, 1961-70; asst. mgr. E.F. Hutton & Co., Inc., St. Louis, 1970; sales promotion, research analyst Stix & Co., St. Louis, 1970-74; v.p. in charge sales promotion, tng., seminars, product acquisition, br. mktg. for tax shelter dept. R. Rowland & Co., St. Louis, 1976-79; pres., chief exec. officer Investment Capital Assos., Creve Coeur, Mo., 1979—; structuring and mktg. cons. to Meridian Co., Equity Programs Investment Corp., Cardinal Resources, Bishop Investments, Weinrich, Zitzman & Whitehead, JEV Income Fund, Inc., 1979—; mem. faculty continuing edn. seminar U. Kansas City Dental Sch., 1978; gen. partner Downtown Devel. Assos., Ltd., 1980—, Riverside Hotel Investments, Ltd., 1981—; v.p. Wharfside Devel. Co., Riverside Landing Parking Systems, Inc.; pres. Dunn Venture, Inc.; tchr. numerous adult evening schs., St. Louis area, 1961—. Founding mem., dir. Traditional Congregation of Creve Coeur, 1964-72; bd. dirs. Forsyth Sch., 1977—, B'nai Amoona Congregation, 1980, St. Louis chpt. Am. Jewish Congress, 1981. Served with U.S. Army, 1961-62. Mem. Internat. Assn. Fin. Planners, Am. Assn. Registered Reps. Home: 425 Shadybrook Dr Creve Coeur MO 63141 Office: Suite 200 707 N 2d St Saint Louis MO 63102

SENTY, CAROL LYNNE, clin. psychologist; b. Rockford, Ill., Dec. 16, 1935; d. Samuel Harold and Dolores (Milkwick) Dorsey; B.A., Drake U., Des Moines, 1959, student Law Sch.; R.N., Iowa Methodist Hosp., Des Moines, 1958; M.S. in Clin. Psychology, Coll. Osteop. Medicine and Surgery, Des Moines, 1975; m. Roger F. Senty, Dec. 20, 1954; children—Lynne Marie, Kristin Lee. Clin. instr. obstet. nursing Iowa Meth. Hosp., 1958-59; prof. obstet. nursing Mt. Carmel Hosp., Columbus, Ohio, 1959-61; cons. Iowa Dept. Vocat. Rehab. Deaf, 1973-75; clin. psychologist, health cons., W. Des Moines, 1975—. Mem. W. Des Moines Council Schs., 1972-74; vice chmn. bd. Elizabeth Ahern Sch. for Deaf. Am. Cancer Soc. scholar, 1954. Mem. Am. Nurses Assn., AAUW, Am. Personnel and Guidance Assn., Am. Osteop. Aux., AMA Aux., Iowa State Registry Interpreters for Deaf. Author articles in field. Home: 1511 Buffalo Rd West Des Moines IA 50265 Office: 1440 E Grand St Des Moines IA

SEPPALA, KATHERINE SEAMAN, business exec., clubwoman; b. Detroit, Aug. 22, 1919; d. Willard D. and Elizabeth (Miller) Seaman; B.A., Wayne State U., 1941; m. Leslie W. Seppala, Aug. 15, 1941; children—Sandra Kay, William Leslie. Mgr. women's bldg. and student activities adviser Wayne State U., 1941-43; pres. Harper Sports Shops, Inc., 1947—; partner Seppala Bldg. Co., 1971—. Mich. service chmn. women grads. Wayne State U., 1962—, 1st v.p., fund bd., active Mich. Assn. Community Health Services, Inc., Girl and Cub Scouts; mem. Citizen's adv. com. on sch. needs Detroit Bd. Edn., 1957—, mem. high sch. study com., 1966—; chmn., mem. loan fund bd. Denby High Sch. Parents Scholarship; bd. dirs., sec. Wayne State U. Fund; precinct del. Rep. Party, 14th dist., 1956—, del. convs. Recipient Ann. Women's Service award Wayne State U., 1963. Recipient Alumni award Wayne State U., 1971. Mem. Intercollegiate Assn. Women Students (regional rep. 1941-45), Women Wayne State U. Alumni (past pres.), Wayne State U. Alumni Assn. (dir., past v.p.), AAUW (dir. past officer), Council Women as Public Policy Makers (editor High lights) Denby Community Ednl. Orgn. (sec.), Met. Detroit Program Planning Inst. (pres.), Internat. Platform Assn., Detroit Met. Book and Author Soc. (treas.), Mortar Bd. (past pres.), Karyatides (past pres.), Anthony Wayne Soc., Alpha Chi Alpha, Alpha Kappa Delta, Delta Gamma Chi, Kappa Delta (chmn. chpt. alumnae adv. bd.). Baptist. Clubs: Zonta (v.p., dir.); Detroit Boat; Les Cheneaux. Home: 22771 Worthington Saint Clair Shores MI 48081 Office: 17157 Harper Detroit MI 48224

SEREDA, JOHN WALTER, lawyer; b. Chgo., June 27, 1918; s. Francis X. and Louise (Moson) S.; J.D., De Paul U., 1944; m. Theresa Mary Karlowicz, June 26, 1948; children—Ann Marie, John Walter, Amelia Louise. Admitted to Ill. bar, 1945; to practice Fed. Dist. Ct., U.S. Supreme Ct.; practice Chgo., 1945—, Govt. appeal agt. local bd. 66, Chgo., 1953—. Fellow Am. Acad. Matrimonial Lawyers; mem. Am., Ill., Chgo., Fed. bar assns., Advs. Soc., Judicature Soc., 7th Circuit Fed. Bar Assn., Polish Nat. Alliance, Delta Theta Phi. Elk. K.C. (4 degree). Home: 1 Cottage Lane Midlothian Country Club Grounds Midlothian IL 60445 Office: 11732 S Western Ave Chicago IL 60643 also 3728 S Paulina St Chicago IL 60609

SERGIOVANNI, THOMAS JOSEPH, educator; b. New Rochelle, N.Y., Apr. 18, 1937; s. Frank A. and Rose (LaBabara) S.; B.S., SUNY, Geneseo, 1958; M.A., Columbia U., 1959; Ed.D., U. Rochester, 1966; m. Elizabeth Ann Kinney, June 18, 1960; children—Susan, John, Steven. Elem. sch. tchr., Mamaroneck, N.Y., 1958-59, Bath, N.Y., 1959-62; instr. dept. edn. SUNY, Buffalo, 1962-64, supr. student tchrs., 1962-64; research asst. dept. ednl. adminstrn. U. Rochester (N.Y.), 1964-66; asst. prof. dept. ednl. adminstrn. and supervision U. Ill., Urbana, 1966-68, asso. prof., 1968-72, prof., 1972-77, chmn. dept. adminstr., higher and continuing edn., 1977—, prof. ednl. adminstrn. and supervision, 1977—; cons. various sch. dists., 1966—. Served to sgt. USAR, 1958-62. U.S. Office Edn. grantee, 1966, 68. Mem. Am. Ednl. Research Assn., Assn. for Supervision and Curriculum Devel. (editor 1982 Yearbook). Author books on ednl. adminstrn., 1969—, latest being: (with Robert J. Starratt) Supervision: Human Perspectives, 2d edit., 1979; (with Fred D. Carver) The New School Executive, 1980; (with Martin Burlingame, Fred D. Coombs and Paul Thurston) Educational Governance and Administration, 1980; Some Theoretical Issues in Educational Organization and Administration, 1981; contbr. articles on ednl. adminstrn. to profl. publs. Home: 1109 Harrington Champaign IL 61820 Office: 333 Education U Ill Urbana IL 61801

SERNETT, RICHARD PATRICK, pub. co. exec., lawyer; b. Mason City, Iowa, Sept. 8, 1938; s. Edward Frank and Loretta M. (Cavanaugh) S.; B.B.A., U. Iowa, 1960, J.D., 1963; m. Janet Ellen Ward, Apr. 20, 1963; children—Susan Ellen, Thomas Ward, Stephen Edward, Katherine Anne. Admitted to Ill. bar, 1965; with Scott, Foresman & Co., Glenview, Ill., 1963-80, house counsel, asst. sec., 1967-70, sec., legal officer, 1970-80; v.p. law, sec. SFN Cos., Inc., Glenview, Ill., 1980—; mem. adv. panel on internat. copyright U.S. State Dept., 1972-75. Mem. Am. (chmn. copyright div. sect. patent, trademark and copyright law 1972-73), Ill. (chmn. copyright law com. 1978-79), Chgo., bar assns., Am. Patent Law Assn. (chmn. copyright matters com. 1972-73, bd. mgrs. 1981—), Patent Law Assn. Chgo. (chmn. copyright com. 1972-73, 77-78, bd. mgrs. 1979-81), Copyright Soc. U.S.A. (trustee 1972-75, 77-80), Am. Judicature Soc., Am. Soc. Corporate Secs., Assn. Am. Pubs. (chmn. copyright com. 1972-73, vice chmn. 1973-75), Phi Delta Phi, Phi Kappa Theta. Home: 2071 Glendale Ave Northbrook IL 60062 Office: 1900 E Lake Ave Glenview IL 60025

SERNKA, THOMAS JOHN, physiologist, educator; b. Cleve., July 26, 1941; s. Valerian Frank and Eugenia Agnes (Arcipowski) S.; B.A. in Biology and Chemistry, Oberlin Coll., 1963; M.A., Harvard U., 1966; Ph.D. in Physiology, U. Iowa, 1969; m. Molly Phelps, Apr. 26, 1969; 1 dau. Heather Marie. Instr. physiology U. Tex. Med. Sch., Houston, 1971-72, asst. prof., 1972-74; asst. prof. physiology La. State U. Med. Center, Shreveport, 1974-75, asso. prof., 1975-76; asso. prof. physiology Wright State U. Coll. Sci. and Engring., Sch. Medicine, Dayton, Ohio, 1976—. Recipient Best Physiology Tchr. award La. State U. Med. Center, Shreveport, 1975. Mem. Am. Physiol. Soc., Soc. for Exptl. Biology and Medicine, Biophys. Soc., Ohio Acad. Sci., Sigma Xi. Democrat. Episcopalian. Club: Ohio River Road Runners. Contbr. chpts. on gastrointestinal physiology to books on med. sci.; contbr. articles on gastroenterology to profl. jours. Home: 426 Towncrest Dr Beavercreek OH 45385 Office: 140 Bio Sci II Wright State Univ Dayton OH 45435

SERSTOCK, DORIS SHAY, microbiologist, club woman; b. Mitchell, S.D., June 13, 1926; d. Elmer Howard and Hattie (Christopher) Shay; B.A., Augustana Coll., 1947; Blood Bank tng. course, Washington, 1963; postgrad. U. Minn., 1966-67, Duke, summer 1969, mycology tng. Communicable Disease Center, Atlanta, 1972; m. Ellsworth I. Serstock, Aug. 30, 1952; children—Barbara Anne, Robert E., Mark D. Bacteriologist, civil service positions, S.D., Colo., Mo., 1947-52; research bacteriologist U. Minn., 1952-53; clin. bacteriologist Dr. Lufkin's Lab., 1954-55; chief technologist St. Paul Regional Blood Center of A.R.C., 1959-65; microbiologist, then microbiologist in charge mycology lab. VA Hosp., Mpls., 1968—. Instr., Coll. Med. Scis., U. Minn., 1970-79, asst. prof. Coll. Lab. Medicine and Pathology, 1979—. Mem. Richfield Planning Commn., 1965-71. Recipient scholarship Am. Assn. U. Women, 1966; Ann. Distinctive Alumni medallion award Augustana Coll., 1977; Superior Performance cert. Mpls. VA Med. Center, 1978; named to Exec. and Profl. Hall of Fame, 1966; fellow Augustana Coll., Sioux Falls, S.D. Mem. Minn. Planning Assn., Am. Soc. Microbiology, Minn. Inter Lab. Microbiol. Assn. Republican Lutheran. Clubs: Richfield Women's Garden (pres. 1959), Wild Flower Garden (chmn. 1961). Author articles in field. Home: 7201 Portland Ave Richfield MN 55423 Office: VA Hospital Minneapolis MN 55417

SESLAR, BURL LYNN, advt. agy. exec.; b. Bryan, Ohio, July 18, 1949; s. Luther Merlen and Marie M. (Lyons) S.; B.F.A., Sch. Visual Art, N.Y.C., 1975; student Ft. Wayne Art Inst., 1971-73; m. Gail Lynn Winter, Feb. 4, 1979. Vice pres. design Ft. Wayne Poster (Ind.), 1969-71; art dir. Dinosaur Prodns., N.Y.C., 1976-77; art dir. Lauer Advt., Ft. Wayne, 1978-79; v.p., creative dir. Seslar, Commorato Inc., Ft. Wayne, 1979—; guest prof. Valparaiso (Ind.) U.; cons. Japan's productivity techniques. Recipient various Addy awards. Mem. N.Y. Art Dirs. Club. Office: 622 S Calhoun St Fort Wayne IN 46802

SESTRIC, ANTHONY JAMES, lawyer; b. St. Louis, June 27, 1940; s. Anton and Marie (Gasparovic) S.; B.A., Georgetown U., 1962; J.D., Mo. U., 1965; m. Carol F. Bowman, Nov. 24, 1966; children—Laura Antonette, Holly Nicole, Michael Anthony. Admitted to Mo. bar, 1965, U.S. Tax Ct., 1969, U.S. Supreme Ct., 1970; law clk. U.S. Dist. Ct., St. Louis, 1965-66; partner firm Sestric, McGhee & Miller, St. Louis, 1966-77, Fordyce & Mayne, 1977-78; spl. asst. to Mo. atty. gen., St. Louis, 1968. Mem. St. Louis Air Pollution Bd. Appeals and Varience Rev., 1966-73, chmn., 1968-73; mem. St. Louis Airport Commn., 1975-76; dist. vice chmn. Boy Scouts Am., 1970—. Bd. dirs. Full Achievement, Inc., 1970-77, pres., 1972-77; bd. dirs. Legal Aid Soc. of St. Louis, 1976-77, Law Library Assn. St. Louis, 1976-78. Mem. Am. Bar Assn. (state chmn. judiciary com. 1973-75), Lawyers Assn., Am. Judicature Soc., Mo. Bar (vice chmn. young lawyers sect. 1973-76, bd. govs. 1974-77), Bar Assn. Met. St. Louis (chmn. young lawyers sect. 1974-75, exec. com. 1974—, pres. 1981—). Club: Mo. Athletic. Home: 3967 Holly Hills Blvd Saint Louis MO 63116 Office: 1015 Locust St Saint Louis MO 63101

SESVOLD, RONALD LOUIS, bus. service co. exec.; b. Clarkston, Mich., Jan. 14, 1941; s. William and Thelma Yvonne (Mou Feis) S.; B.B.A., Eastern Mich. U., 1967; B.S. in Bus. Adminstrn., Cleary Coll., also D.Sc. in Bus. Adminstrn. (hon.); children—Mark Joel, Terry Scott, Chad Louis. Faculty and student affairs dir. Eastern Mich. U., Ypsilanti, 1966-68; mgr. retail advt. Oakland (Mich.) Press, 1968-71; gen. mgr. Tel-Twelve Mall, Southfield, Mich., 1971-78; dir. shopping centers and public affairs Ramco-Gershenson, Inc., Farmington Hills, Mich., 1979—; mem. faculty Internat. Council of Shopping Centers, chmn. Mich. conv., 1972, mem. admissions com., governing bd. Bd. dirs., pres. Southfield Arts Council, 1974; bd. dirs. Oakway Symphony, 1974—, West Bloomfield Symphony, 1976-78; v.p. Union Lake Shore Assn., 1973—; bd. dirs. Union Lake Subdiv. Property Owners Assn., 1973—, pres., 1974, 76, 79; bd. dirs. Oakland County Traffic Improvement Assn., 1973—; trustee Cleary Coll., 1975-77, treas., 1976; founder, chmn. Oakland County Cultural Council, 1976; chmn. Oakland County Mich. Week, 1975—; bd. govs. Greater Mich. Found., 1977—; founder Greater West Bloomfield Council for Arts, 1977, Lakes Area Council for Arts, 1977-79; chmn. Southeastern Mich. Week, 1977—; mem. career, vocat. and placement adv. council Southfield Public Schs., 1980-81; chmn. adv. council LWV, 1979-81; bd. dirs. Lake Orion Stadium Elem. Sch., 1980-81, pres., 1981—; vice chmn. United Fund North Oakland County, 1969-70; Mich. Week chmn. State of Mich., 1982. Recipient Outstanding Young Alumnus award Eastern Mich. U., 1972. Mem. Eastern Mich. U. Alumni Assn. (pres. 1976), Southfield C. of C. (dir. 1973-76, v.p. 1974), Spirit of Detroit Assn. (commodore 1978). Club: Civitan. Contbr. articles to trade publs. Home: 7860 Barnsbury St Union Lake MI 48085 Office: 31313 Northwestern Hwy Suite 201 Farmington Hills MI 48018

SETH, OLIVER, judge; b. Albuquerque, May 39, 1915; s. Julien Orem and Bernice (Grefe) S.; A.B., Stanford U., 1937; LL.B., Yale U., 1940; m. Jean MacGilivray, Sept. 25, 1946; children—Sandra Bernice, Laurel Jean. Admitted to N.Mex. bar, 1940; practice law, Santa Fe, 1940, 46-62; judge U.S. Ct. Appeals for 10th Circuit, 1962—, chief judge, 1976—; dir. Santa Fe Nat. Bank, 1949-62; chmn. legal com. N.Mex. Oil and Gas Assn., 1956-59, mem. regulatory practices com., 1960-62; counsel N.Mex. Cattlegrowers Assn., 1950-62, N.Mex. Bankers Assn., 1952-62; govt. appeal agent SSS, 1948-52, mem. bd. regents Mus. of N.Mex., 1956-60. Bd. dirs. Boys Club, Santa Fe, 1948-49; New Mex. Land Resources Assn., 1956-60, Ghost Ranch Mus., 1962—; mng. bd. Sch. Am. Research, 1950—. Served from pvt. to maj. AUS, 1940-45; ETO. Decorated Croix de Guerre (France.). Mem. Santa Fe C. of C. (dir.), N.Mex., Santa Fe County bar assns., Phi Beta Kappa. Presbyterian. Office: US Ct Appeals PO Drawer 1 Santa Fe NM 87501*

SETHI, VIJAY KUMAR, architect, planner, govtl. adminstr.; b. Balaghat, India, June 1, 1945; came to U.S., 1970; s. Vidya Prakash and Bimla Rani S.; B.Arch. (Sch. Architecture Merit scholar), U. Delhi, New Delhi, 1969; M.Arch., U. Ill., Urbana, 1974; M.Up., 1975; m. Mary Clare Walsh, Dec. 29, 1973; children—Kiran Marie, Arjun David. Asst. architect Powar & Powar, Architects, New Delhi, 1969-70; archtl. designer, draftsman Trossen, Wright and Assos., St. Paul, 1970-71; archtl. job capt. Thorsen & Thorsov, Architects & Planners, Mpls., 1972-73; teaching asst. U. Ill., Urbana, 1973, adminstrv. asst., 1974; community planner Fargo-Moorhead Met. Council Govts., Moorhead, Minn., 1975-76, exec. dir., 1976—; chmn. Fargo-Moorhead Met. Transp. Tech. Com. Mem. Minn. Planning Assn., Am. Planning Assn. Hindu. Office: 44 Foss Ln Moorhead MN 56560

SETHNA, NARI P., engr., assn. exec.; b. Karachi, Pakistan, Sept. 12, 1926; came to U.S., 1962, naturalized, 1970; s. Perozeshaw Burjorji and Meher Rustomji (Vakil) S.; ed. Victoria Jubilee Tech. Inst., Bombay, India. Engr., Textile Mills Bombay Dyeing and Mfg. (India), 1949-52; engr. Bombay Electric Supply and Transport Undertaking, 1952-62; instr. Greer Tech. Inst., Chgo., 1963-67; tng. coordinator, dir. Refrigeration Service Engrs. Soc., Des Plaines, Ill., 1967-78, exec. mgr., 1978—. Mem. ASHRAE, Am. Vocat. Assn. Office: 960 Rand Rd Des Plaines IL 60016*

SETTERQUIST, ALLEN JOHN, machine tool mfg. co. exec.; b. Rockford, Ill., Aug. 17, 1947; s. Donald and Virginia Grace S.; B.S., No. Ill. U., DeKalb, 1974; M.B.A., Saginaw Valley State Coll.; m. Paula Diane Wheat, July 26, 1969; children—Michelle Diane, Matthew Allen, Allyson Jennifer. Inside sales Gen. Electric Supply Co., Rockford, Ill., 1970-73; gen. acctg. mgr. ITT Holub Industries, Sycamore, Ill., 1974-76, mgr. mktg. services, 1976-78, mgr. fin. controls, 1978-80; acctg. mgr. Universal Engring. div. Houdaille Industries, Inc., Frankenmuth, Mich., 1980-81, cost acctg. mgr., 1981—; lectr. in field. Served with USNR, 1967-69; Vietnam. Lutheran. Home: 148 Frank Rd Frankenmuth MI 48734 Office: 126 N Main St Frankenmuth MI 48734

SETZEPFANDT, ALVIN O. H., II, state senator; b. Bird Island, Minn., Feb. 7, 1924; s. Alvin O.H. and Louis D. Setzepfandt; D.V.M., Iowa State U., 1945; m. Carol Wilson, Feb. 7, 1924; 4 children. Pvt. practice vet. medicine, Bird Island, 1945—; mayor City of Bird Island, 1952-69; mem. Minn. Ho. of Reps., 1975-76, mem. Minn. Senate, 1977—. Pres., Minn. Livestock San. Bd., 1970-74; mem. Minn. Health Planning Bd.; mem. Renville County Commn., 1971-74, chmn., 1974. Served with U.S. Army, 1942-43. Mem. Am. Vet. Medicine Assn., Minn. Vet. Medicine Assn. Office: 23 Capitol Bldg Saint Paul MN

SEVCIK, JOHN GEORGE, business exec.; b. Chgo., May 15, 1909; s. Joseph and Rose (Kostal) S.; J.D., DePaul U., 1939, LL.D., 1958; B.S.C., Central YMCA Coll., 1945; M.B.A., U. Chgo., 1947; M.P.L., John Marshall Law Sch., 1950, LL.M., 1954; LL.D., St. Mary's Coll., Ill. Benedictine Coll., 1960; m. Rose Vanek, Mar. 27, 1934; children—Joanne, John Wayne. Asso., Burton Dixie Co., 1925—, dir., 1942—, pres., 1949-72, vice chmn. bd., 1972—; admitted to Ill. bar, 1940, since practiced law; chmn. bd. Financial Marketing Services Inc., 1971—; gen. mgr. McCormick Pl., Chgo., 1971—; dir. Central Nat. Bank Chgo., Brunswick Corp., Bus. Capitol Corp. Mem. bd. govs. Chgo. Furniture Mart; dir. Nat. Cotton Batting Inst.; mem. editorial bd. Bedding mag. Commr., Pub. Bldgs. Commn. Chgo.; chmn. adv. bd. Chgo. Youth Commn.; mem. adv. com. Chief Justice Municipal Ct. Chgo.; active work Boy Scouts; gen. finance chmn. Chgo. Cerebral Palsy Assn., 1956; mem. exec. bd. Nat. Conf. Christians and Jews; mem. Bd. Edn. Berwyn, Ill. Vice chmn. bd. trustees St. Procopius

Coll.; mem., chmn. lay bd. trustees, mem. legal bd. trustees DePaul U.; mem. lay bd. trustees Rosary Coll., chmn. bd., 1966-70; asso. mem. lay bd. St. Xavier Coll., mem. adv. council Sch. of Bus.; citizens bd. U. Chgo.; adv. bd. St. Mary's Coll.; bd. dirs. MacNeal Meml. Hosp.; vice chmn. bd. Ill. Coll. Podiatric Medicine, 1968—; trustee John Marshall Law Sch. Chgo. Mem. Am. Judicature Soc., Am., Ill. bar assns., Nat. Assn. Bedding Mfrs. (pres. 1959-60), Ill. Mfrs. Assn., Furniture Club Am., AAUP, Internat. Assn. Auditorium Mgrs., DePaul U., John Marshall (pres. 1968-71) alumni assns. Phi Alpha Delta, Beta Gamma Sigma. Clubs: Executives, Economic, Union League. Address: McCormick Place Chicago IL 60616

SEVERINO, THOMAS JOSEPH, radio sta. exec.; b. Cleve., Oct. 30, 1951; s. Joseph Anthony and Rose (Foliano) S.; B.S., Murray (Ky.) State U., 1973; m. Linda A. Regets, June 17, 1977; 1 son, Thomas Ryan. Announcer, news dir. Sta. WRWR-FM, Port Clinton Ohio, 1973-75; account exec. Sta. WRIF, Detroit, 1975-77, retail sales mgr., 1977-78; retail sales mgr. Sta. WDAI, Chgo., 1978-79; station mgr. Sta. WXTZ, Indpls., 1979—, dir. ops. Mid-Am. Beautiful Music Stas., Indpls., 1981—. Bd. dirs. Indpls. Art League. Mem. Radio Advt. Bur., Nat. Assn. Broadcasters. Office: 4560 Knollton Rd Indianapolis IN 46208

SEVERS, EUGENE RYALS, oil co. exec.; b. Des Moines, Oct. 2, 1923; s. Shafter David and Martha Miriam (Ryals) S.; B.A., Drake U., 1949, postgrad., 1949-50; m. Barbara Jean Swanson, June 25, 1949; children—Mary, Robert, Cynthia, John, Steven, Donald. Staff accountant Arthur Andersen & Co., Chgo., 1950-51; staff accountant James C. Addison Co., Des Moines, 1951-52, partner, 1952-53; pres. Macmillan Oil Co. Inc., Des Moines, 1953—; v.p. Kinderhook Oil & Gas, Inc. Served with U.S. Army, 1943-46; ETO. C.P.A., Iowa. Mem. Des Moines Oilmen's Club, Toastmasters Internat., Iowa Ind. Oil Jobbers, New Pioneer Gun Club, YMCA, Highland Park Businessmen's Club, Des Moines Musicians Assn., Iowa, Nat. liquid petroleum gas assns., Asso. Gen. Contractors, Aircraft Owners Pilots Assn., Phi Beta Kappa, Phi Sigma Iota. Episcopalian (treas. 1951-53). Club: Des Moines. Home: 4013 29th St Des Moines IA 50310 Office: PO Box 4968 4306 2d Ave Des Moines IA 50306

SEWARD, JOHN EDWARD, JR., ins. co. exec.; b. Kirksville, Mo., June 12, 1943; s. John Edward and Ruth Carol (Connell) S.; B.S. in Fin., St. Joseph's Coll., 1968; children—Mitch, J.J. Mgr. acctg. services Guarantee Res. Life Ins. Co., Hammond, Ind., 1964-69; asst. controller Gambles Ins. Group, Mpls., 1969-71, N. Am. Cos., Chgo., 1971-73; pres. Home & Auto. Ins. Co., Chgo., 1975—, also v.p. fin., dir.; dir. Guarantee Res. Life Ins. Co. Bd. dirs. Calumet Council, Boy Scouts Am., 1979—, Teddy Bear Club for Shriners Hosp., 1979—, Chgo. Baseball Cancer Com., 1981—. Designated C.L.U., 1976, Chartered Property and Casualty Underwriter, 1979. Fellow Life Mgmt. Inst. Home: 1240 Camellia Dr Munster IN 46321 Office: 111 W Jackson Blvd Chicago IL 60604

SEXSON, WILLIAM ROBERT, neonatologist, educator; b. Washington, Dec. 3, 1945; s. Julius Calvin and Coyla Jeane (Fields) S.; B.S., U.S. Air Force Acad., 1967; M.D., U. Miss., 1971; m. Sandra Griffin Bishop, June 24, 1972; 1 dau., S. Kristen. Resident in pediatrics Wilford Hall Med. Center, San Antonio, 1971-74; fellow in neonatology U. Miss. Sch. Medicine, Jackson, 1975, Vanderbilt U., Nashville, 1975-76; commd. 2d lt. USAF, 1967, advanced through grades to lt. col., 1977—; teaching staff Scott Air Force Med. Center, 1976-78, Wright Patterson USAF Med. Center, also Dept. Pediatrics, Wright State U. Sch. Medicine, 1978—; asst. prof. pediatrics, 1978—; chief newborn nurseries Wright Patterson Air Force Med. Center, 1978—; cons. in field. Recipient Outstanding Tchr. Pediatric Residency award, 1980-81; Am. Heart Assn. grantee, 1981-82. Mem. Am. Acad. Pediatrics, Air Acad. Assn. of Grads. Mem. Christian Ch. Contbr. articles to profl. jours. Home: 1949 Zink Rd Fairborn OH 45324 Office: Childrens Med Center 1 Childrens Plaza Dayton OH 45404

SEXTON, DELORES MAE, surg. technologist; b. Buffalo, Minn., Aug. 19, 1934; d. Roy Martin and Amelia Bettha (Drawert) Cochran; student public schs.; m. Erwin John Sexton, Sept. 27, 1952; children—Phil, Becky, Jo, Craig, Julie, Laurie, Dean, Terri, Trudi, Jackie, Allen, Luke. Mem. staff St. Mary's Hosp. and Home, Winsted, Minn., 1969—, supr., surg. technologist, 1972—; instr. CPR, 1976—. Mem. Assn. Surg. Technologists. Roman Catholic. Address: St Mary's Hosp and Home 551 4th St N Winsted MN 55395

SEXTON, JOHN JOSEPH, mfr.; b. N.Y.C., Sept. 18, 1925; s. John Joseph and Anna Marie (Siedler) S.; B.E.E., Poly. Inst. Bklyn., 1951; M.B.A., L.I. U., 1967; postgrad. N.Y. U., 1969-73; m. Elfriede Turrek, Oct. 15, 1960; children—John Joseph, James Gottfried, Kimberley. Adminstr. ops., various positions engring. mgmt. Arma div. Ambac Industries, Garden City, N.Y., 1951-71; subcontract project mgr. Grumman Aerospace Corp., Bethpage, N.Y., 1971-73; pres., dir. Thermotron Corp., Holland, Mich., 1973—, Thermotron Industries, 1977—; pres. Thermotron Industries Internat., Inc., Holland, 1979—; chmn. bd. Thermotron (U.K.) Ltd., Chatham, Kent, Eng., 1979—; pres., chief exec. officer Sexton Industries, Inc., Zeeland, Mich., 1981—. Trustee Holland Community Found. Served with USNR, 1943-46. Fellow Inst. Environ. Scis.; mem. Instrument Soc. Am., Delta Mu Delta. Roman Catholic. Home: 958 S Shore Dr Holland MI 49423 Office: 131 Harrison Ave Zeeland MI 49464

SEYMOUR, DEBORAH TROTTER, speech pathologist; b. Ft. McPherson, Ga., Jan. 12, 1952; d. Hartwell Thomas and Georgia Francis (Maddox) Trotter; B.A., Columbus (Ga.) Coll., 1974; M.A., Vanderbilt U., 1976; m. Jack Deason Seymour, Apr. 1, 1972. Speech pathologist VA Hosp., Birmingham, Ala., 1976-77; speech pathologist cons. VA Hosp., Prescott, Ariz., also speech pathologist Chino Valley (Ariz.) Sch. System, 1977-78; speech pathologist Meade Sch. Dist. 46-1, Sturgis, S.D., 1978-79, VA Med. Center, Fort Lyon, Colo., 1981—; cons. VA Hosp., Ft. Meade, S.D., Sturgis Community Hosp., Sturgis Nursing Home, Child Devel. Center, Boces, Ark. Valley of Colo. Founder, coordinator Citizens for a Better Bradley Library, Columbus, 1970. Mem. Am. Speech and Hearing Assn., Colo. Speech and Hearing Assn., Ga. Speech and Hearing Assn., S.D. Speech and Hearing Assn. Baptist. Author: Clues: Speechreading for Children, 1981. Office: VA Med Center Fort Lyon CO 81038

SEYMOUR, KEITH GOLDIN, chem. products co. scientist; b. Fairfax, Mo., Jan. 25, 1922; s. Vern V. and Esther Althea (Goldin) S.; A.S., Kemper Mil. Sch., 1941; B.S., Iowa State U., 1943, M.S., 1950; Ph.D., Tex. A. and M. U., 1954; m. Wanda Allegra Cox, Dec. 2, 1943; children—John Kirk, Janette Ann. Farmer, Fairfax, 1946-49; chemist Dow Chem. Co., Freeport, Tex., 1953-59, research specialist, 1959-65, group leader, Midland, Mich., 1965-71, research mgr. agrl. products dept., 1971—. Chmn. Brazosport (Tex.) Area Planning Commn., 1962-64; mem. Lake Jackson (Tex.) City Council, 1964-65. Served with U.S. Army, 1943-46. Decorated Bronze Star. Fellow AAAS; mem. Am. Chem. Soc., N.Y. Acad. Sci., ASTM, Am. Inst. Chemists, Sigma Xi, Phi Kappa Phi. Club: Elks. Research and devel. in agrl. chem. formulations. Home: 6003 Sturgeon Creek Pkwy Midland MI 48640 Office: PO Box 1706 Midland MI 48640

SFIKAS, PETER MICHAEL, lawyer; b. Gary, Ind., Aug. 9, 1937; s. Michael and Helen (Thureanos) S.; B.S., Ind. U., 1959; J.D., Northwestern U., 1962; m. Freida Platon, Apr. 24, 1966; children—Ellen Michelle, Pamela Christine, Sandra Nicole. Admitted to Ill. bar, 1962; atty. Legal Aid Bur., United Charities of Chgo., 1962-63; asso. firm Peterson, Ross, Rall, Barber & Seidel, Chgo., 1963-70; sr. partner firm Peterson, Ross, Schloerb & Seidel, 1970—; adj. prof. Sch. Law, Loyola U., Chgo., 1977—; mem. com. on rules Ill. Supreme Ct., 1975—; arbitrator Nat. Panel of Arbitrators, 1972—; writer, lectr. program on in-house counsel practice Ill. Inst. Continuing Legal Edn., 1975, author program on counseling corps., 1979, writer, lectr. program on profl. assns. and antitrust laws, 1976; village prosecutor Village of LaGrange Park (Ill.), 1969-74. Bd. dirs. Northwestern U. Law Sch., 1981—. Recipient Maurice Weigle award Chgo. Bar Found., 1973. Fellow Am. Bar Found.; mem. ADA (hon.), Ill. Bar Found. (dir. 1975-77), Am. (chmn. publs. com. of sect. ins., negligence and compensation law 1973-75), Ill. (gov. 1970-76, mem. assembly 1972-76, council antitrust law 1978-79, 81—), Chgo. (vice chmn. spl. task force on appointive selection 1977-78, nominating com. 1979) bar assns., Bar Assn. 7th Fed. Circuit (chmn. com. on meetings 1973-75), Law Club Chgo., Legal Club Chgo. Mem. Greek Orthodox Ch. (council Holy Apostles 1978—). Contbr. articles to profl. jours. Home: 17 Sharron Ct Hinsdale IL 60521 Office: 200 E Randolph Dr Suite 7300 Chicago IL 60601

SHAARI, WANIS ALI, elec. engr.; b. Benghazi, Libya, Dec. 28, 1950; s. Ali Ahmad and Saida Ibrahim (Fellah) S.; B.Sc.E.E., U. Tripoli, 1973; M.S.E.E., Ohio State U., 1978; m. Hamida M. Legnain, Aug. 19, 1979. Projects and planning engr. Air Defense Command, Libya, 1973-75; grad. research asso. Ohio State U., Columbus, 1977—. Recipient Outstanding Master Thesis of Yr. award Ohio State U., 1978. Mem. Sigma Xi (asso.). Moslem. Home: 1161 Bunker Hill Blvd Columbus OH 43220 Office: 1320 Kinnear Rd Columbus OH 43212

SHABAZZ, ABDULALIM, educator; b. Bessemer, Ala., May 22, 1927; s. Lewis and Mary (Roberson) Cross; A.B., Lincoln U. of Pa., 1949; M.S., M.I.T., 1951; Ph.D., Cornell U., 1955; m. Della Café, Feb. 22, 1968; children—Markus, Suad. Mathematician, Cornell Aero. Lab., Buffalo, 1952-53; instr., teaching fellow Cornell U., 1953-55; mathematician metals research lab. Electro Metall. Co., Niagara Falls, N.Y., 1955; asst. prof. math. Tuskegee Inst., 1956-57; asso. prof., chmn. dept. math. Atlanta U., 1957-63; minister Muhammad Mosque 4, dir. edn. Muhammad U. Islam 4, Washington, 1963-75; dir. edn. World Community of Al-Islam in West, 1975, dir. adult edn., 1975—; mem. Imam Consultation Bd., Masjid Elijah Muhammad, 1976-77; resident Imam Masjid Wali Muhammad, Detroit, 1979—; mem. Council of Imams Am. Muslim Mission, 1979—, Midwest regional Imam, 1979—; adj. prof. math. Union Grad. Sch., Yellow Springs, Ohio, 1975—; ednl. columnist Bilalian News, Chgo., 1975—. Mem. Census Advisory Com. on Black Population for 1980 Census, 1973—. Served with USAAF, 1946-47. Mem. Am. Math. Soc., Math. Assn. Am., Am. Soc. Engring. Edn., Nat. Inst. Sci., AAAS, Nat. Alliance of Black Sch. Educators, Sigma Xi. Home: 18264 Birchcrest Detroit MI 48221 Office: 11529 Linwood Detroit MI 48206

SHABLESKY, MARTHA PONTIUS (MRS. PETER PAUL SHABLESKY), real estate investment co. exec.; b. Orrville, Ohio, June 29, 1918; d. Howard Taggart and Nova (Mead) Pontius; B.S., Miami U., Oxford, Ohio, 1940; m. Peter Paul Shablesky, Nov. 1, 1947; Exec. dir. Temple Israel, Dayton, Ohio, 1953-58; accountant-adminstr. Anchor Rubber Co., Dayton, 1958-63; controller-gen. mgr. Jos. Patterson & Assos., Dayton, 1963—; sec., asst. treas., dir. Wabash Plaza, Inc., Barlo, Inc., Haa-Guar, Inc., Augusta Plaza, Inc., Anderson Southdale, Inc., Bedford Plaza, Inc., Noblesville Shopping Center, Inc., Richmond Shopping Center, Inc. Asst. treas. Montgomery County chpt. Nat. Arthritis Found., 1970-71. C.P.S. Mem. Internat. Council Shopping Centers, Alpha Omicron Pi. Presbyn. Home: 3660 Briar Pl Dayton OH 45405 Office: 38 Woodsdale Rd Dayton OH 45404

SHACKELFORD, DOUGLAS ANDREW, indsl. contracting and distbg. co. exec.; b. Columbus, Ohio, Jan. 13, 1948; s. Joseph Andrew and Juanita Belle (Welling) S.; B.A. in Biology and Chemistry, Ohio Dominican Coll., 1973; m. Mary Jo Hatem, Dec. 14, 1968; children—Joseph Jonathan, Andrew. Maintainance mgr. Allen Refractories Co., Columbus, 1970-74, job forman, 1974-76; tech. adv. refractories CE Cast Indsl. Products, Inc., Oak Park, Ill., 1976-78, sales rep., Wis., 1978-80; br. mgr. Jay L. Angel, Inc., Lima, Ohio, 1980—, corp. sales mgr., 1981—. Bd. dirs. St. Vincent's Children's Center, Columbus, 1976-78, St. Francis Children's Activity and Achievement Center, Milw., 1978-80. Mem. Am. Foundrymen's Soc. (chmn. apprenticeship com. Southeastern Wis. chpt. 1979-80).

SHACKLEFORD, COVINGTON, container mfg. co. exec.; b. Louisville, July 2, 1924; s. William Nelson and Margaret Steele (Covington) S.; B.S. in Commerce, U. Va., 1950, J.D., 1954; m. Helen Julia Sterner, Dec. 27, 1950; children—Margaret, Covington, Elizabeth, Julia Ann. Admitted to Va. bar, 1954; arbitration proceedings rep. Ford Motor Co., Dearborn, Mich., 1954-57; mgr. indsl. relations Allied Chem. Corp., N.Y.C., 1958-61; dir. personnel Wallace & Tierman Inc., E. Orange, N.J., 1962-66; v.p. personnel PepsiCola Inc., Purchase, N.Y., 1966-76; v.p. indsl. relations Stone Container Corp., Chgo., 1976—; dir. Stanwick Corp., Washington. Served with inf., U.S. Army, 1943-46, 51-52. Mem. Am. Bar Assn., Va. State Bar. Episcopalian. Home: 691 Forest Hill Rd Lake Forest IL 60045 Office: Stone Container Corp 360 N Michigan Ave Chicago IL 60601

SHADE, JOYCE ELIZABETH, chemist; b. Louisville, Oct. 30, 1953; d. Joseph Edwin and Ruth Antoinette (Hubbuch) S.; B.A., U. Louisville, 1975, Ph.D. in Inorganic Chemistry, 1980. Salesperson, Greenups Belles & Brides, Louisville, 1969-75; grad. teaching asst. U. Louisville, 1975-80; postdoctoral researcher, fellow, dept. chemistry Ohio State U., Columbus, 1980—; physics tchr. part-time Presentation Acad., 1977-79. Rias summer fellow, 1978; Research Corp. fellow, 1979. Mem. Am. Chem. Soc., Smithsonian Instn. (asso.), Sigma Xi (research grantee, 1978), Gamma Sigma Sigma (pres., U. Louisville, 1974). Roman Catholic. Contbr. articles to profl. publs. Office: Ohio State U Dept Chemistry 140 W 18th Ave Box 106 Columbus OH 43210

SHAFER, DONALD MARION, educator; b. Bellefontaine, Ohio, Nov. 11, 1940; s. Marion Reilly and Ethel Mae (Kindle) S.; B.A. (Univ. grantee), Bowling Green State U., 1967; M.Ed. in Edn.-Curriculum, Wright State U., 1971; m. Kathry Ellen Dickson, Sept. 23, 1967. Caseworker Ohio Welfare Agy., Logan and Shelby Counties, 1967-68; tchr.-coordinator lang. arts Sidney (Ohio) City Schs., 1968-74; tchr., chmn. dept. English Fairview Park (Ohio) Schs., 1974—; tchr. human relations seminars. Pres., Homeowners Assn. North Ridgeville (Ohio), 1975-76. Served with U.S. Army, 1960-63. Mem. Fairview Park Tchrs. Assn. (pres. 1976-78), NEA, Ohio Edn. Assn., Nat. Council Tchrs. English, Assn. Supervision and Curriculum Devel. Methodist. Club: Moose (Sidney). Author curriculum guides. Office: 4507 W 213th St Cleveland OH 44126

SHAFER, EVERETT EARL, educator; b. Oelwein, Iowa, Apr. 19, 1925; s. Paul Emerson and Maude Blanche (Lovell) S.; B.S., Iowa State U., 1948; J.D., U. Iowa, 1951; M.B.A., U. Chgo., 1960; m. Kathryn Elaine Rose, Sept. 4, 1949. Admitted to Iowa bar, 1951, Ill. bar, 1952; mem. legal staff Motorola, Inc., Chgo., 1951-54, fin. adminstr. Motorola Fin. Corp., Chgo., 1954-60, asst. treas., credit mgr. Motorola Consumer Products, Inc., Chgo., 1960-68; asso. prof. bus. adminstrn. Buena Vista Coll., Storm Lake, Iowa, 1968-72, chmn. faculty senate, 1970-71; treas. Admiral Corp., Chgo., 1972-74; asst. treas. Addressograph Multigraph Corp., Cleve., 1975-76; pres., treas. AM Internat. Leasing Corp., 1976-80; prof. bus. adminstrn. Buena Vista Coll., Storm Lake, Iowa, 1981—. Served with USAAF, 1943-45. Decorated D.F.C., Air medal; recipient Outstanding Tchr. award Buena Vista Coll., 1972. Methodist. Home: 36W934 Middlecreek Ln St Charles IL 60174 Office: Buena Vista Coll Storm Lake IA 50588

SHAFER, ROBERT REX, ins. co. exec.; b. Creston, Iowa, Jan. 24, 1950; s. John William and Naomi Ruth (Searles) S.; student Iowa State U., 1968-69, Des Moines Area Community Coll., 1969-70; m. Sheila Mary Wiese, Oct. 6, 1972; children—Michael John, Amy Catherine. With Cyclone Motors, Ames, Iowa, 1969-75, ser. mgr., 1973-75; sec.-mgr. Ringgold Mut. Ins. Assn., Mount Ayr, Iowa, 1975—. Mem. public relations com. Nat. Assn. Mut. Ins. Cos., 1981—. Mem. Mut. Ins. Assn. Iowa (chmn. pub. relations com. 1979-80, dir. 1981—), Southwest Iowa County Mut. Secs. Assn. (pres. 1976-78). Lutheran (dir. 1976-80, chmn. stewardship 1976-80). Clubs: Mount Ayr Community Improvement (past pres.), Mount Ayr Golf and Country. Home: 206 E Adams St Mount Ayr IA 50854 Office: 102 N Fillmore St Mount Ayr IA 50854

SHAFFER, DAVID ALAN, project engr.; b. Mansfield, Ohio, Nov. 10, 1946; s. Kenneth Paul and Mary Elizabeth (Wehinger) S.; student U.S. Naval Acad., 1964-67; B.S.M.E., Ohio State U., 1970; m. Linda Marie Young, June 14, 1969; children—Amy Lee, Carolinne Elizabeth, Gregory Kenneth. Design engr. Hixson, Inc., Cin., 1970-77; project engr. A.M. Kinney Inc., Cin., 1977—; instr. U. Cin. Mem. ASHRAE (pres. Cin. chpt. 1979-80, gov. 1975—). Democrat. Roman Catholic. Home: 7266 Deaconsbench Ct Cincinnati OH 45244 Office: 2900 Vernon Pl Cincinnati OH 45219

SHAFFER, HERBERT, JR., business exec.; b. Cin., Aug. 21, 1925; s. Herbert and Dorothy Sybil (Guckenberger) S.; B.A., Yale U., 1948; m. Mary Ann Hinsch, Apr. 27, 1957; children—Gregory, Pamela, Geoffrey. Asst. mgr. First Nat. City Bank, Tokyo, 1949-52; asst. nat. div. Citibank, N.Y.C., 1952-55; asst. v.p. Central Bancorp., Cin., 1956-64; partner Harrison & Co., Cin., 1964-77; exec. v.p. Riverbend Group, Inc., Cin., radio and TV brokers and cons., 1977—; v.p., dir. Vail Mountain Broadcasters, Inc., Vail Colo., 1979—; partner Town View Properties, Cin., 1981—. Vice chmn. allocations com. Community Chest, 1968-71; bd. dirs. Cancer Control Council, 1956—, chmn., 1976-79; chmn. parish council St. Francis de Sales Ch., 1977-79; bd. dirs. United Cerebral Palsy Cin., 1975-79, Cin. May Festival, 1978—. Served with U.S. Army, 1943-45. Republican. Roman Catholic. Clubs: Cin. Country, Cin. Racquet (treas. 1981—), Cin. Tennis, Miami. Home: 2546 Perkins Ln Cincinnati OH 45208 Office: KVMT Vail CO

SHAFFER, JAMES GRANT, educator; b. Washington, Kans., Jan. 17, 1913; s. Bowen Ross and Myrtle Katherine (Worley) S.; B.S., Manchester Coll., 1935, D.Sc., 1973; D.Sc., Johns Hopkins, 1940; m. Esther Elizabeth Willard, Sept. 3, 1939; children—Carol (Mrs. Wesley Stieg), Susan (Mrs. John Willard), Janet (Mrs. Gregory Harsha), Nancy (Mrs. James Lanier). Tchr., Jackson Twp. High Sch., Flint, Ind., 1935-36, Jefferson Twp. High Sch., Ossian, Ind., 1936-37; student instr. immunology and filterable viruses Johns Hopkins, Balt., 1937-40, instr., 1940-42; med. research biologist Am. Cyanamid Co., Stamford, Conn., 1942-43; asst. prof. preventive medicine Vanderbilt U. Sch. Medicine, Nashville, 1946-48, vis. prof. bacteriology, dept. biology, 1947-48; asso. prof. bacteriology and virology, U. Louisville Sch. Medicine, 1948-52; dir. labs. Louisville Children's Hosp., 1948-50, microbiologist, 1950-52; prof., chmn. dept. microbiology and pub. health Chgo. Med. Sch., 1952-60, asso. dean, prof. microbiology, 1967-74; dir. microbiology and hosp. epidemiology Luth. Gen. Hosp., Park Ridge, Ill., 1960-67, cons. hosp. epidemiology, 1967-74; dir. ednl. and profl. programs Mt. Sinai Hosp. Med. Center of Chgo., 1974—; prof. microbiology Rush U., Chgo., 1975—. Professorial lectr. microbiology U. Chgo., 1965-68; cons. VA Hosp., Hines, Ill., 1972—; coordinator devel. of projected urban-oriented med. sch. Mt. Sinai Hosp. Med. Center and Roosevelt U., 1974—. Pres. P.T.A., Lincoln Sch., Elmhurst, Ill., 1956-57. Mem. sch. bd. dist. 46 Elmhurst Elementary Sch., 1958-67. Served to maj. AUS, 1943-46. Recipient Outstanding Alumni award Manchester Coll., 1945, Award of Merit, Chgo. Tech. Socs. Council, 1969. Fellow Am. Pub. Health Assn. (mem. action bd. 1972—), Am. Inst. Chemists, Am. Acad. Microbiology; mem. Am. Soc. Microbiology, A.A.A.S., Am. Soc. Tropical Medicine and Hygiene, Soc. Ill. Bacteriologists, Ill. Pub. Health Assn., Assn. Tchrs. Preventive Medicine, Royal Soc. Health, Alumni Assn. Manchester Coll. (pres. 1962-63), Sigma Xi, Alpha Omega Alpha, Delta Omega. Author: Amebiasis: A Biomedical Problem, 1965. Contbr. to publs. in field. Home: 605 Swain Av Elmhurst IL 60126 Office: 15th St and California Av Chicago IL 60608

SHAFFER, JANE REGINA, assn. exec.; b. Peoria, Ill., June 4, 1933; d. Archie Henry and Ethel Rose (Pedreyra) Hall; student public schs., Peoria; m. Roy Alvin Shaffer, Jan. 31, 1955; children—Jamie Shaffer Hinson, Roy Michael, Shawn Rene. Sec.-treas. Diverco Corp., Winter Haven, Fla., 1957-70; sec.-treas. Mansyco Corp., Peoria, 1971; adminstrv. dir. Profl. Photographers Am., Des Plaines, Ill., 1972—. Chmn. Beautification Com. Fla., 1968-69. Recipient Honor certs. Indsl. div. Questioned Document Examiners, Inc., 1977, Am. Soc. Photographers, 1978; Nat. award Profl. Photographers Am., 1981. Mem. Evidence Photographers Internat. Council (hon.; Honor cert. 1976), Am. Photog. Artisans Guild (hon.; Honor cert. 1977). Home: 530 Springside Ln Buffalo Grove IL 60090 Office: Profl Photographers Am 1090 Executive Way Des Plaines IL 60018

SHAH, RAMESH M., chem. co. exec.; b. Baroda, India, Mar. 11, 1936; s. Mohanlal B. and Dahiben M. (Sheth) S.; B.Sc., M.S. U., Baroda (India), 1958; M.S., U. Cin., 1962; m. Saroj C. Mehta, Nov. 19, 1966. Research and teaching asst. U. Cin., 1959-61; inspection chemist Sarabhai Chems., Baroda, 1958-59; research asso. U. Mich. Med. Center, Ann Arbor, 1962-65; biochemist Eli Lilly Research Labs., Indpls., 1965-77; chmn. bd., pres., chief exec. officer Medico Electronics, Inc., Indpls., 1977-79; chmn. bd., pres., chief exec. officer DataChem, Inc., Indpls., 1979—. Mem. Dist. Export Council, Ind., 1980—. Fellow Am. Inst. Chemists; mem. Am. Assn. Clin. Chemists. Patentee in field. Office: 5763 W 85th St Indianapolis IN 46278

SHAH, SURESH, indsl. supply co. exec.; b. Vishwamitri, India; s. Maneklal and Manorama S.; came to U.S., 1969, naturalized, 1978; B.S.M.E., M.S. Univ., Baroda, India, 1960; M.B.A., Northwestern U., 1974; m. Vanlila, Feb. 10, 1965; children—Sagar, Manish. Project engr. Indequip Engring., India, 1964-67; engring. supr. Continental Can Co., Chgo., 1968-76; mdse. mgr. McMaster-Carr Supply Co., Chgo., 1976—. Mem. Assn. M.B.A. Execs. Contbr. articles to profl.

jours. Home: 9947 S Leavitt Chicago IL 60643 Office: 600 County Line Rd Elmhurst IL 60126

SHAIKH, ALI NAWAZ, physician; b. Pakistan, Oct. 16, 1935; came to U.S., 1964, naturalized, 1976; s. Din Mohammed and Rochan (Kimat) S.; M.B., B.S., Liaquat Med. Coll., 1958; D.M.R.D. with honors, King Edward Med. Coll., 1964; m. Leah N. Gary, Apr. 2, 1975; children—Michael Nazir, Sarah Elizabeth. With Pakistan Dept. Health, 1958-64; intern Euclid (Ohio) Gen. Hosp., 1964-65; intern Fairview Gen. Hosp., Cleve., 1965-66, resident in internal medicine, 1966-70; house physician St. Vincent Charity Hosp., Cleve., 1970-71; fellow in cardiology St. Luke's Hosp., Kansas City, Mo., 1971-72; practice medicine specializing in internal medicine and cardiology, Cleve., 1972—; chief dept. medicine Southwest Gen. Hosp.; asso. chief cardiology Fairview Gen. Hosp.; pres. Ali N. Shaikh, M.D., Inc. Fellow Am. Coll. Cardiology; mem. Am. Heart Assn., Acad. Medicine Cleve. Author articles in field. Home: 17010 Amber St Cleveland OH 44111 Office: 18099 Lorain St Cleveland OH 44111

SHAIN, IRVING, univ. adminstr.; b. Seattle, Jan. 2, 1926; s. Samuel and Selma S.; B.S. in Chemistry, U. Wash., 1949, Ph.D., 1952; m. Mildred R. Udell, Aug. 31, 1947; children—Kathryn A., Steven T., John R., Paul S. Instr. dept. chemistry U. Wis., Madison, 1952-54, asst. prof., 1954-59, asso. prof., 1959-61, prof., 1961—, vice chancellor, 1970-75, chancellor, 1977—, provost, v.p. for acad. affairs U. Wash., Seattle, 1975-77. Served with U.S. Army, 1943-46. Fellow AAAS; mem. Am. Chem. Soc., Internat. Soc. Electrochemistry, Electrochem. Soc., Sigma Xi, Phi Beta Kappa, Phi Kappa Phi, Phi Lambda Upsilon. Office: 158 Bascom Hall Univ Wis Madison WI 53706

SHAIN, MARK WARREN, beverage co. exec.; b. Bridgeport, Conn., Mar. 29, 1950; s. George and Shirley (Landau) S.; B.A. with distinction, U. Wis., 1972, M.A., 1975; m. Bonnie Kay Norin, Sept. 3, 1978. Editorial and public relations asst. Reiman Asso., Milw., part-time, 1974-75; account exec. Harshe Rotman & Druck, Chgo., 1975-76; public relations dir. Creamer Dickson Basford, Chgo., 1976-77; asst. advt. and public relations dir. Dad's Root Beer Co., Chgo., 1977—. Mem. Public Relations Soc. Am. Clubs: Chgo. Advt., Pub. of Chgo. Home: 5048 N Marine Dr Chicago IL 60640 Office: 2800 N Talman Ave Chicago IL 60618

SHAKESPEAR, HORACIO, auto engr.; b. Rosario, Argentina, May 26, 1922; s. Valentin and Julia (Carbajo) S.; came to U.S., 1956, naturalized, 1962; C.E., Universidad del Litoral, Rosario, 1945; m. Mary Rita Gonzalez, Feb. 12, 1947; children—Ann Mary, Paul, Michael, George, Julie Rose, Daniel. Partner civil engring. firm, Rio Negro, Argentina, 1946-47; asst. chief vehicle maintenance Public Works Dept. Buenos Aires, 1948-53; asst. gen. mgr. Crisoldinie steel co., Quilmes, Argentina, 1953-55; chief explt. engr. Industrias Kaiser Argentina, 1956; sr. designer Chevrolet Engring., Gen. Motors Tech. Center, 1956-57, engr., 1957-65, asst. staff engr., 1965-69, staff engr., engring. staff advanced products, 1970—. Served as 1st lt. Argentinian Air Force, 1948. Mem. Soc. Auto Engrs., Societe des Ingenieurs de l'Automobile. Roman Catholic. Patentee in automotive chassis and body systems and components. Home: 4141 Wendell Rd West Bloomfield MI 48033 Office: GM Tech Center 12 Mile and Mound Rd Warren MI 48090

SHAMANSKY, ROBERT NORTON, lawyer, Congressman; b. Bexley, Ohio, Apr. 18, 1927; s. Harry S. and Sarah (Greenberg) S.; B.A., Ohio State U., 1947; J.D., Harvard U., 1950. Admitted to Ohio bar, 1950; founding partner firm Feibel, Feibel, Shamansky and Rogovin (name now Guren, Merritt, Feibel, Sogg & Cohen), Columbus, Ohio, 1970; partner Saramin Realty Co., Columbus, 1954; mem. 97th Congress from 12th Dist. of Ohio; commentator news program Sta. WBNS-TV, Columbus, 1977-80; a founder, pres. Legal Aid and Defenders Soc. Columbus, 1954. Pres., Columbus Assn. for Performing Arts, 1980, Columbus Mus. Art; bd. dirs. Columbus Urban League. Served with CIC, U.S. Army, 1950-52. Mem. Am. Bar Assn., Ohio Bar Assn., Columbus Bar Assn., Harvard U. Law Sch. Alumni Assn., Ohio State U. Alumni Assn. Democrat. Jewish. Clubs: President's (Ohio State U.), B'nai B'rith; University Columbus; Harvard (N.Y.C.). Office: 200 N High St Columbus OH 43215 also 308 Cannon House Office Bldg Washington DC 20515

SHAMBAUGH, GEORGE ELMER, III, internist; b. Boston, Dec. 21, 1931; s. George Elmer and Marietta Susan (Moss) S.; B.A., Oberlin Coll., 1954; M.D., Cornell U., 1958; m. Katherine Margaret Matthews, Dec. 29, 1956; children—George, Benjamin, Daniel, James, Elizabeth. Gen. med. intern Denver Gen. Hosp., 1958-59; research fellow physiologic chemistry U. Wis., Madison, 1967-69; asst. prof. medicine Northwestern U. Med. Sch., Chgo., 1969-74, asso. prof., 1974-81, prof., 1981—; mem. Center for Endocrinology, Metabolism and Nutrition, 1969—; chief endocrinology and metabolism VA Lakeside Med. Center, Chgo., 1974—; attending physician Northwestern Meml. Hosp., Chgo., 1969—. Served with M.C., U.S. Army, 1959-67. NIH spl. postdoctoral fellow, 1967-69; Schweppe Found. fellow, 1972-75; diplomate Am. Bd. Internal Medicine. Fellow ACP; mem. Am. Fedn. Clin. Research, Sci. Research Soc. Am., Endocrine Soc., Am. Thyroid Assn., Am. Inst. Nutrition, Am. Soc. Clin. Nutrition (vice chmn. nat. com. on clin. nutrition issues), Central Soc. Clin. Research, Inst. Medicine Chgo., Taipei Internat. Med. Soc. (pres. 1960), Sigma Xi. Episcopalian. Contbr. articles to text books and profl. jours. Home: 530 S Stone Ave LaGrange IL 60525 Office: VA Lakeside Med Center 333 E Huron St Chicago IL 60611

SHANAFIELD, HAROLD ARTHUR, educator; b. South Bend, Ind., Nov. 26, 1912; s. Harry Bacon and Anna (Paulsen) S.; B.A., U. Notre Dame; M.S.J., M.A., Northwestern U.; M.Ed., Chgo. State U.; m. Margaret Ann Goodman, Nov. 23, 1939; 1 son, Harold A. Copy editor Chgo. Herald Am., 1945-46; night picture editor Chgo. Sun-Times, 1946-47; mng. editor Elec. Dealer, Chgo., 1947-52; editor, mgr. Florists' Telegraph Delivery News, Detroit, 1952-61; asst. mng. editor AMA Jour., Chgo., 1961-62; asst. dean Northwestern U., Chgo.-Evanston campus, evening divs., 1962-73; with Chgo. Bd. Edn., 1973—. Vice chmn., bd. visitors Freedoms Found. at Valley Forge. Served to capt. USCG, 1945—. Bd. dirs. Northwestern U. and Alumni Council, Am. Bus. Writing Assn., Assn. Evening Univs., Quill and Scroll (lifetime faculty mem.), Nat. Sojourners (pres. Chgo. chpt. 1971), Ind. Soc. Chgo. (resident v.p. 1975—), Delta Mu Delta, Phi Chi Theta, Delta Sigma Pi, Sigma Delta Chi, Iota Sigma Epsilon. Clubs: Masons, Shriners, Chgo. Press, North Shore Shrine (pres. 1970), Chgo. Headline; Star Craft of Ill. (sec. 1972-77, pres. 1977-78). Editor Scottish Rite publs., 1976—. Home: 2515 Marcy Ave Evanston IL 60201

SHANAHAN, MICHAEL FRANCIS, computer co. exec.; b. St. Louis, Oct. 29, 1939; s. James John and Mary Agnes (Foley) S.; B.S., St. Louis U., 1961; postgrad. Washington U., St. Louis, 1964; m. Mary Ann Barrett, Aug. 24, 1963; children—Megan Elizabeth, Michael Francis, Maureen Patricia. With McDonnell Douglas Automation Co., St. Louis, 1962-73, sales mgr., 1969-71, br. mgr., 1971-72, area mgr. Southwestern area, 1972-73; v.p. mktg. Numerical Control, Inc., St. Louis, 1973-74, pres., 1974-79, also dir.; v.p.-gen. mgr. computers div. Cleve. Pneumatic Co., 1979—; dir. Biomed. Systems, Inc., St. Louis. Trustee, Whispering Hills, 1969, 70. Served with U.S. Army, 1961. Mem. Data Processing Mgmt. Assn., Sales and Marketing Execs. St. Louis (Distinguished Salesman award 1967), Phi Kappa Theta Alumni Assn. K.C. Home: 12058 Carberry Pl Town and Country MO 63131 Office: Cleve Pneumatic Co 12115 Lackland Rd Saint Louis MO 63141

SHANAHAN, PATRICIA MAYER, gerontologist, occupational therapist; b. Wilmington, Del., Nov. 28, 1937; d. Kenneth Frank and Ina Julia (Mead) Mayer; B.A., U. Iowa, 1960; M.A., N.Y. U., 1965; postgrad. Miami U., Oxford, Ohio, 1977—; m. William Joseph Shanahan, Jan. 16, 1972. Staff therapist Norwich (Conn.) Hosp., 1960-61, N.Y. State Psychiat. Inst., N.Y.C., 1961-65; asst. prof. U. Ill. Med. Center, Chgo., 1965-68; community coordinator Ill. Psychiat. Inst., Chgo., 1968-70, dir. activity therapies, 1970-72; project dir. Am. Occupational Therapy Assn., Inc., N.Y.C., 1972, cons., 1965-67, 75; asst. prof., asso. chmn. Occupational Therapy Sch., State U. N.Y. at Downstate Med. Center, Bklyn., 1972-73; asst. prof. Ohio State U., Columbus, 1973-77; exec. dir. Office Geriatric Medicine/Gerontology, dept. medicine Med. Coll. Ohio, Toledo; mem. faculty Lourdes Coll., Sylvania, Ohio, 1979-80; cons. Drexel Home for Aged, Chgo., 1968-72; adj. asst. prof. Hunter Coll., City U. N.Y., 1972; participant Inst. for Potential Educators, Gerontol. Soc., 1971. Active, Jefferson Twp. Civic Assn., 1973-76; bd. dirs. Trinity House, Hamilton, Ohio, 1977-79. Fellow Am. Occupational Therapy Assn.; mem. Gerontol. Soc., N.W. Ohio Gerontol. Assn., Ohio Occupational Therapy Assn., Am. Geriatrics Soc., Phi Lambda Theta. Contbr. articles to profl. jours.

SHANARD, GEORGE H., state senator; b. Bridgewater, S.D., July 30, 1926; s. Jacob H. and Martha E. (Findahl) S.; B.S., U. S.D., 1950; m. Iris L. Achenbach, 1952; children—George H., Laurie Jean, Keri E., Heidi Ann. Pres., Shanard, Inc., 1964—; v.p. Ramkota, Inc., 1968—; mem. S.D. Seante, 1975—, majority whip, 1977—. Pres. S.D. Gov.'s Task Force Rail Abandonment, 1972-75; del. Republican Nat. Conv., 1980. Served with USN, 1943-46; PTO. Named Alumnus of Yr. S.D. U., 1968. Mem. Am. Legion. Clubs: Masons, Shriners. Office: State Capitol Pierre SD 57501*

SHANDLER, DONALD DAVID, coll. adminstr.; b. Newark, Dec. 1, 1940; s. Nathan and Tillie (Barash) S.; B.A., Montclair State Coll., 1963, M.A., 1968; Ph.D., Ohio State U., 1972; m. Judy Ann Christiano, June 6, 1969; children—Joshua David, Eve Rebekah. Asst. prof., staff cons. communication and theatre Boston Coll., 1971-77; staff cons. New Eng. Telephone Co., Marlboro, Mass., 1974-77; dir. continuing edn. McKendree Coll., Lebanon, Ill., 1977-79, So. Ill. U., Edwardsville, 1979—. Bd. dirs. Adult Edn. Council Greater St. Louis, 1977—. Mem. Nat. Univ. Continuing Edn. Assn., Am. Soc. Tng. and Devel., Ill. Council Continuing Higher Edn. (mem. exec. bd. 1979—), Ill. Univ. Extension Council. Democrat. Jewish. Home: 1720 Duke St Edwardsville IL 62025 Office: So Illinois U Office Continuing Edn Edwardsville IL 62026

SHANK, RICHARD EUGENE, state senator; b. North Lima, Ohio, Oct. 26, 1932; s. Lauren J. and Mary (Yoder) S.; ed. Hesston Coll., 1950-51; m. Eileen A., 1957; children—Larry J., David L., Sharon K. Sec., Concord Twyp. Adv. Bd., 1964-66; vice chmn. Ind. Gov.'s Traffic Safety Adv. Com., 1967—; mem. Ind. State Senate. Mem. Elkhart County Homebuilders, Goshen Realtors, Farm Bur. Methodist. Clubs: Moose, Toastmasters. Office: Ind Capitol Indianapolis IN 46204*

SHANKAR, SRINIVASAN, materials scientist; b. Srirangam, Tiruchy, T. Nadu, India, Nov. 20, 1950; came to U.S., 1973; s. Panchapakesan and Savithri S.; B.Tech. Metallurgy, Indian Inst. Tech., Madras, 1973; Ph.D. in Materials Sci., SUNY, Stony Brook, 1977; m. Padmini Thyagarajan, Aug. 30, 1979. Sr. project engr. Howmet Turbine Components Corp., Whitehall, Mich., 1977-79, supr. coating devel., 1979-80, mgr. materials devel., 1980—; instr. materials sci. courses SUNY. Mem. Assn. Profl. Engrs. Ont., Can., Am. Soc. Metals, AIME, Electrochem. Soc., Indian Inst. Metals. Club: Tennis. Patents, publs. in field. Office: Howmet Turbine Components Corp 699 Benston Rd Whitehall MI 49461

SHANKER, RAMAN, anesthesiologist; b. Kanpur, India, Dec. 27, 1936; came to U.S., 1967, naturalized, 1977; s. Bhavani Venkat and Seethalakshmi (Narayan) Raman; M.B.B.S., U. Madras (India), 1966; m Meena Ramaswami, Apr. 30, 1967; children—Priya, Vidhya, Vijay. Intern, Vassar Bros. Hosp., Poughkeepsie, N.Y., 1967-68; resident St. Elizabeth Hosp., Youngstown, Ohio, 1968-69, Youngstown Hosp. Assn., 1969-72; anesthesiologist St. Anthony Hosp., Columbus, Ohio, 1972—, chief anesthesiologist, 1977—; anesthesiologist Mercy Hosp., Columbus, 1973—, Mt. Carmel Hosp., Columbus, 1976—; v.p. Allied Anesthesia, Inc., Columbus, 1976—; clin. asst. prof. Sch. Allied Health Professions, Ohio State U., 1980—. Diplomate Am. Bd. Anesthesiology, Fellow Am. Coll. Anesthesiologists; mem. Acad. Medicine Columbus, Columbus Soc. Anesthesiologists, Ohio Med. Assn., Ohio Soc. Anesthesiologists, Am. Soc. Anesthesiologists, Internat. Soc. Anesthesiologists. Home: 4572 Ravine Dr Westerville OH 43081 Office: 1450 Hawthorne Ave Columbus OH 43203

SHANKS, DAVID L., mfg. co. exec.; b. Chgo., Apr. 25, 1927; s. Edwin H. and Katherine Florence (Ingalls) S.; B.S. in Mech. Engring., Northwestern U., 1951; m. Lucille P. Ennis, June 11, 1949; children—Kent, Todd, Jennifer, Ellen, Lori, Scott. Vice-pres. mktg. Hanna Co., Chgo., 1961-63; v.p. cylinder div. Rexnord Inc., Chgo., 1963-65, dir. mktg. services, mgr. corp. planning, 1966-69, dir. corp. public relations and advt., Milw., 1969-79, v.p. corp. relations, 1979—. Pres., bd. dirs. YMCA. Served with USAF, 1945-46. Mem. Public Relations Soc., World Future Soc., Bus.-Profl. Advt. Assn., Nat. Planning Assn., Sales and Mktg. Execs. Club, Pi Sigma Epsilon. Episcopalian. Office: Box 2022 Milwaukee WI 53201

SHANKS, MARY ELMA WINDIATE, hosp. exec.; b. Pontiac, Mich., Aug. 2, 1911; d. William Alfred and Rosa (Nelsey) Windiate; student U. Ill., 1931; m. Leslie Talbot Shanks, Dec. 23, 1933; children—Nancy Sue (Mrs. John T. Kennedy), William L. With Community Nat. Bank, Pontiac, 1933-51; supr. warrent squad IRS, Pontiac, 1951-55; dir. reimbursement Oakland County Bd. Auditors, Pontiac, 1955-76; reimbursement officer Northville (Mich.) State Hosp., 1976-77, Muskegon (Mich.) Developmental Center, 1977-78, Western region Mich. Dept. Mental Health, 1978-81. Mem. adv. group mental health code implementation project Mich. Dept. Mental Health, 1974; treas., bd. dirs. Every Woman's Place, 1979—. Mem. Nat. (v.p. 1966-67, pres. 1967-68, chmn. site com. 1974-75, ability to pay chmn. 1976-79), Mich. (chmn. 1970—) reimbursement officers assns., Greater Detroit Area Hosp. Credit Assn. (mem. inst. com. 1970—, chmn. 1971-72, pres. 1972-73, history chmn. 1974-75), Muskegon C. of C. (dir.). Presbyn. Club: Altrusa (local past pres., dir., dist. treas. 1964-67, internat. membership chmn. 1967—, dist. gov. 1970-72, dist. dir. 1972—, internat. resolutions com. 1973—, chmn. fund-raising 1975-76). Address: 740 Wendover Blvd Muskegon MI 49441

SHANLEY, MICHAEL ROY, plant geneticist; b. Pratt, Kans., June 18, 1951; s. William F. and Lola G. Shanley; A.A. in Life Sci., Hutchinson Community Coll., 1971; B.S. in Biology, Kans. State U., 1973; m. Becky S. Bailey, Dec. 24, 1976. With Farm Bur., 1972-73; research asst. Kans. State U., Manhattan, 1973, teaching and research asst. horticulture and forestry dept., 1973-74; research plant geneticist (hybrid wheat) Pioneer Hi-Bred Internat., Hutchinson, Kans., 1974—. Mem. Am. Soc. Agronomy, Crop Sci. Soc. Am., Council for Agrl. Sci. and Tech., Wheat Quality Adv. Council. Mem. Christian Ch. (Disciples of Christ). Home: 209 Hyde Park St Hutchinson KS 67501 Office: Pioneer Hi-Bred Internat Rural Route 2 Hutchinson KS 67501

SHANNON, ALBERT JOSEPH, educator; b. Pitts., Apr. 12, 1949; s. William Park and Dorothea B. (Brown) S.; B.A. summa cum laude, Marquette U., 1971; M.Ed., Boston U., 1972; Ph.D., Marquette U., 1978; m. Mary Jean Boblick, May 22, 1971; children—Erica Lynne, Sean Paul. Tchr. reading North Division High Sch., Milw., 1972-76; reading cons. sch. dists. Wis., 1976-78; mem. faculty Saint Mary's Coll., Notre Dame, Ind., 1978—, asst. prof. dept. edn., 1978—; cons. reading edn. State of Ind., 1978—; profl. reading cons., various cities in midwest, 1976—. Mem. sch. bd. edn. St. Joseph Sch., South Bend, Ind., 1979—; pres. neighborhood study help program Saint Mary's Coll., Notre Dame, Ind., 1981—; chmn. Students Assisting Students Shoplifting Prevention Clinic, South Bend, 1980—. Recipient Outstanding Secondary Teaching award, 1975. Mem. Internat. Reading Assn., Assn. Supervision and Curriculum Devel., AAUP, Phi Beta Kappa, Phi Delta Kappa. Roman Catholic. Contbr. articles to profl. jours. Home: 208 Sylvan Glen Dr South Bend IN 46615 Office: 338 Madeleva Hall Dept of Education Saint Mary's College Notre Dame IN 46556

SHANNON, CYRIL GEORGE, JR., newspaper exec.; b. Evanston, Ill., Aug. 7, 1926; s. Cyril George and Ann (Van Arsdale) S.; B.S. in Bus. Adminstrn., Northwestern U., 1949; m. Margaret Priscilla Elg, Aug. 6, 1949; children—Margaret Ann, Gregory George, Jeffrey Cort. With Lorenzen & Thompson Inc., Chgo., 1949-50; with Shannon & Assos., Inc., Chgo., 1950-65, v.p., 1954-60, pres., 1960-65, Shannon & Cullen, Inc., Chgo., 1965-69; sr. v.p. Mathews, Shannon & Cullen, Inc., Chgo., 1969-76, Landon Assos., Inc., Chgo., 1976—; dir. Pubs. Assos., Shannon-Whitehead Co. Adv. com. cardiac resuscitation Boy Scouts Am.; active Community Chest, Western Springs Republican Com. Served with USN, 1944-46. Mem. Inland Daily Press Assn., Internat. Newspaper Advt. Execs., Suburban Press-Suburban Newspapers Am. Clubs: University (Chgo.); La Grange (Ill.) Country. Office: 435 N Michigan Ave Chicago IL 60611

SHANNON, DONALD SUTHERLIN, ecducator; b. Tacoma Park, Md., Dec. 28, 1935; s. Raymond Corbett and Elnora Pettit (Sutherlin) S.; B.A., Duke, 1957; M.B.A., U. Chgo., 1964; Ph.D., U. N.C., 1972; m. Virginia Ann Lloyd, June 24, 1961 (div.); children—Stacey Eileen, Gail Allison, Michael Corbett; m. 2d, Kay Powe, Dec. 30, 1977; stepchildren—Christopher, Bonnie Bertelson, Mem. auditing staff Price Waterhouse & Co., N.Y.C., 1957-61; sr. accountant Price Waterhouse, Chgo., 1964-65; instr. Duke U., Durham, N.C., 1964-69; asst. prof. bus. adminstrn. U. Ky., Lexington, 1969-76, asso. prof., 1976-81; asso. prof. acct. Depaul U., Chgo., Ill., 1981—. Served with AUS, 1958-59, 61-62. Mem. Ky. Soc. C.P.A.'s, Am. Inst. C.P.A.'s, Western Finance Assn., Am. Finance Assn., Beta Gamma Sigma. Office: DePaul U Acct Dept Chicago IL 60604

SHANNON, EDWARD LEO, food scientist; b. Keota, Iowa, June 9, 1939; s. William Ireneaus and Veronica Catherine (Peiffer) S.; B.S., Iowa State U., 1962, M.S., 1964; Ph.D., U. Wis., 1969; m. Christine Tucker, July 23, 1966; 1 son, Gerald. Food scientist Quaker Oats Research and Devel. Center, Barrington, Ill., 1968—. Home: 632 Prospect St Barrington IL 60010 Office: 617 W Main St Barrington IL 60010

SHANNON, LYLE WILLIAM, sociologist; b. Storm Lake, Iowa, Sept. 19, 1920; s. Bert Book and Amy Irene (Sivits) S.; B.A., Cornell Coll., Iowa, 1942; M.A., U. Wash., 1947, Ph.D., 1951; m. Magdaline W. Shannon, Feb. 27, 1943; children—Mary Shannon Will, Robert William, John Thomas, Susan Michelle. Acting instr. U. Wash., 1950-52; mem. faculty dept. sociology U. Wis.-Madison, 1952-62, asso. prof., 1958-62; prof. sociology U. Iowa, Iowa City, 1962—, chmn. dept. sociology and anthropology, 1962-70, dir. Iowa Urban Community Research Center, 1970—; vis. prof. Portland State U., Wayne State U., U. Wyo., U. Colo. Served with USNR, 1942-46. Mem. Am. Sociol. Assn., AAAS, Pacific Sociol. Assn., Evaluation Research Soc., Southwestern Social Sci. Assn., Population Assn. Am., Soc. Applied Anthropology, Am. Soc. for Criminology, Phi Beta Kappa. Democrat. Club: Kiwanis. Author: Underdeveloped Areas, 1957; Minority Migrants in the Urban Community, 1973. Editor: Social Ecology of the Community series, 1974-76, Social Organization of the Community series, 1977—. Home: River Heights Iowa City IA 52240 Office: 117 Macbride Hall Univ of Iowa Iowa City IA 52242

SHANNON, STIRLEY ALTON, educator; b. St. Louis, Feb. 15, 1935; s. Charles Henry and Gladys Pearl S.; A.B. in Elementary Edn., Harris U., St. Louis; M.A. in Elementary Adminstrn., Washington U., St. Louis; Ph.D. in Supervision and Gen. Adminstrn., St. Louis U., 1975; m. Barbara Sue Shannon; children—Susan Lee, Stacey Ann, Steven Michael. Prin. City of St. Louis, 1963-65, Mehlville Sch. Dist., St. Louis, 1965-71, dir. personnel, 1971-75, asst. supt., 1975-79, asso. supt., 1979—. Mem. Am. Assn. Sch. Adminstrs., Am. Assn. Sch. Personnel Adminstrs., Phi Delta Kappa. Cert. tchr., prin., supt., Mo. Home: 5091 Flametree Ct Saint Louis MO 63129 Office: 3120 Lemay Ferry Rd Saint Louis MO 63125

SHANOWER, DONALD THOMAS, educator; b. Canton, Ohio, Dec. 15, 1921; s. Merle F. and Ella (Baughman) S.; A.B., Kent State U., 1947, M.A., 1949; Ph.D., U. Mich., 1960; m. Patricia Ann Gibbs, June 28, 1951; children—Victoria Ann Shanower Wike, Paula Winnifred Shanower Coleman, Thomas Gibbs, Dan Fredric, Jonathan Blake. Steel worker Superior Sheet Steel Co., Ohio, 1939-42; instr. Coll. Wooster, Ohio, 1949-53; asst. prof. speech and theatre North Central Coll., Naperville, Ill., 1955-65, asso. prof., 1965-70, prof., 1970—; mng. dir. The Summer Place, Naperville, 1967—. Served with inf., U.S. Army, 1942-46. Mem. Ill. Speech and Theatre Assn. Club: Rotary (pres. 1971). Office: North Central College Naperville IL 60540

SHAPIN, JOHN LAWRENCE, direct mail advt. co. exec.; b. Chgo., Aug. 8, 1934; s. Tom Leon and Lucile (Rosenbush) S.; B.A. in Journalism, U. Ala., 1957; m. Margaret Ellen Levy, Apr. 10, 1960; children—Jean Ellen, Patricia Ann, Andrew John. Mgr. Midwest sales Bay State Thread Co., Chgo., 1960-63; v.p. Adams of Chgo., Inc., 1964-70, exec. v.p., 1970-79; pres. Shapes Mktg., 1979—. Served with U.S. Navy, 1957-60. Mem. Chgo. Assn. Direct Mktg. (dir. 1971-74, v.p. 1973-74). Club: Standard (Chgo.).

SHAPIRO, DAVID CHARLES, dentist, state senator; b. Mendota, Ill., Feb. 16, 1925; s. Hymen and Minnie (Sprizer) S.; student Stanford, 1943-44; B.S., U. Ill. at Chgo., 1950, D.D.S., 1952; m. Norma Jean Hall, Sept. 15, 1947; children—Sarah Beth Shapiro Hurley, Deborah Leah Shapiro Pontarelli, Margaret Sue, Edward Henry, Michael Andrew, Elizabeth Ann, Daniel Hall. Pvt. practice dentistry, Amboy, Ill., 1952—; pres. Farmer's Telephone Co., Franklin Grove, Ill., 1963; dir. First Nat. Bank, Amboy. City alderman, Amboy, 1961-69; pres. Lee County Bd. Health, Dixon, Ill., 1960-69; bd. mem. Sch. Dist. 272, 1961-69; mem. Ill. Ho. of Reps. from 35th Dist., 1969-73, mem. coms. county and twp. affairs, hwys. and traffic safety, edn., chmn. sub-com. twp. affairs, vice chmn. elementary and secondary edn. com., mem. toll road adv. com., interim com. on gov.'s appointments to state toll hwy. authority, narcotic adv. council; mem. Ill. Senate, 1973—, vice chmn. edn. com., chmn. pub. employees pension laws commn., minority leader, 1977—. Dir. Amboy Pub. Hosp. Served with AUS, 1943-46. Decorated Bronze Star; named Outstanding Freshman Legislator of 76th Gen. Assembly, Outstanding Freshman Senator of 78th Gen. Assembly; recipient Outstanding Legislator award Ill. Community Coll. Trustees Assn., award of recognition Ill. Police Assn. Mem. Am., Ill. (Distinguished Mem. award 1976), Whiteside-Lee (pres. 1962—) dental socs., Ill. Assn. Bds. Health (pres. 1964), Amboy C. of C., Am. Legion. Republican. Clubs: Masons, Shriners, Elks. Home: 32 N Jefferson St Amboy IL 61310 Office: 4 S Jones St Amboy IL 61310

SHAPIRO, HAROLD TAFLER, univ. pres.; b. Montreal, Que., Can., June 8, 1935; s. Maxwell and Mary (Tafler) S.; B. Comm., McGill U., 1956; M.A. and Ph.D. in Econs. (Harold Helm fellow 1961-64, Harold Dodd sr. fellow 1963-64), Princeton U., 1964; m. Vivian Bernice Rapoport, May 19, 1957; children—Anne, Marilyn, Janet, Karen. Asst. prof. econs. U. Mich., Ann Arbor, 1964-67, asso. prof., 1967-70, prof., 1970-76, chmn. dept. econs., 1974-77, prof. econs. and public policy, 1977—, v.p. for acad. affairs, 1977-79, pres. U. Mich., 1979—; research advisor Bank of Can., 1965-72; cons. U.S. Treasury, 1965-68. Mem. divisional bd. St. Joseph Mercy Hosp., Ann Arbor. Recipient Lt. Gov.'s medal in commerce McGill U., 1956. Mem. Mich. Soc. Fellows (sr. fellow), Council Am. Statis. Assn. Office: 2068 Adminstrn Bldg U Mich Ann Arbor MI 48109

SHAPIRO, MAYNARD IRWIN, physician, educator; b. Chgo., Dec. 18, 1914; B.S., U. Ill., 1937, C.M., 1939, M.D., 1940; 1 dau., Juli Ann. Intern, Mt. Sinai Hosp., Chgo., 1939-40, resident, 1940-41; practice medicine specializing in family practice, Chgo., 1946—; active staff dept. gen. practice Jackson Park Hosp., dir. dept. phys. medicine and rehab., pres. med. staff, 1975-77, also v.p. acad. affairs; past clin. asst. surgery, Mt. Sinai Hosp.; clin. prof. family medicine Chgo. Med. Sch. Past bd. dirs. Family Health Found. Am., Inst. Sex Edn.; past mem. regional adv. group Ill. Regional Med. Program; past chmn. profl. adv. council Nat. Easter Seal Soc.; bd. dirs. Citizens Alliance for VD Awareness, Jackson Park Hosp. Found. Fellow Am Occupational Med. Assn., Acad. Psychosomatic Medicine, Am. Geriatrics Soc., Central States Soc. Indsl. Medicine and Surgery, Inst. Medicine Chgo.; mem. AMA (ho. of dels.), Ill. (ho. of dels., 2d v.p.), Chgo. (council) med. socs., Chgo. Found. Med. Care (pres.), Am. (pres. 1968-69), Ill. (past pres.) acads. family physicians, Pan Am. Med. Assn., Am. Congress Rehab. Medicine, Assn. Hosp. Med. Edn., Am. Acad. Med. Adminstrs., Assn. Am. Med. Colls., Soc. Tchrs. Family Medicine, Ill. Soc. Phys. Medicine and Rehab., Chgo. Soc. Indsl. Medicine and Surgery (past pres.), Nat. Med. Vets. Soc. Home: 1700 E 56 St # 3609 Chicago IL 60637 Office: 7531 Stony Island Ave Chicago IL 60649

SHAPIRO, ROBERT DONALD, actuary; b. Milw., Sept. 11, 1942; s. Leonard Samuel and Adeline Ruth (Arnovitz) S.; B.S. with honors, U. Wis., 1964; m. Karen Jean Hubert, Apr. 14, 1979; children—Lee Evan, Stacy Ellen, Jenifer Erin, Tracy Elizabeth. Actuarial trainee Northwestern Mut. Life Ins., Milw., 1964-65; cons. actuary Milliman & Robertson, Inc., Milw., 1965-80; dir. Nat. Life Cons., Milw. C.L.U. Fellow Soc. Actuaries, Conf. Actuaries in Public Practice; mem. Am. Acad. Actuaries. Contbr. articles to profl. lit. Home: 4923 N Oakland Ave Milwaukee WI 53217 Office: First Wis Center 777 E Wisconsin Ave Milwaukee WI 53202

SHAPS, CELE, real estate exec., civic worker; b. Chgo., Feb. 14, 1914; d. Samuel and Golda (Barlade) Larman; student pub. schs., Terre Haute, Ind.; m. George Alpert, 1938 (dec. 1961); children—Gale Suzanne Alpert Facktor, Heather Judith Alpert Jackowski; m. 2d, Morris C. Shaps, July 9, 1964. Mgr. dress dept. A. Herz Dept. Store, Terre Haute, 1931-35; realtor, 1952; pres. Harbours Realty. Pres. women's aux. Decalogue Soc. Lawyers, Chgo., 1971-73; chmn. ann. fund raising Temple Sholom Sisterhood, 1970; pres. Children's Aid of La Rabida, also trustee LaRabida Hosp. Mem. Women's Am. O.R.T., Hadassah. Mem. Chgo. C. of C. (mem. environ. com., crime prevention com., comml. devel. com., indsl. devel. com.). Republican.

SHARKEY, JAMES ARTHUR, TV exec.; b. Royal Oak, Mich., Mar. 26, 1951; s. Raloh E. and Barbara J. Sharkey; B.A. cum laude, Mich. State U., 1974. Polit. reporter Sta. WITL, Lansing, Mich., 1974-75; sales rep. Sta. WSGW, Saginaw, Mich., 1975-76; account exec. DBG&H Advt., Dallas, 1976-78; regional mgr. Home Box Office, Inc., Dallas, 1978—. *

SHARMA, ASHOK KUMAR, polymer chemist; b. Uttar Pradesh, India, Mar. 1, 1951; came to U.S., 1976; s. Ramesh Chand and Ramkali Devi S.; B.S. with honors in Chemistry, U. Delhi, 1970, M.S. in Chemistry, 1972; M.Tech. in Chemistry, Indian Inst. Tech., 1974; Ph.D. in Chemistry, U. Mo.-Kansas City, 1979; m. Shashi Rani, Mar. 6, 1975; children—Anurag, Deepika. Research trainee Hindustan Lever Research Center, Bombay, India, 1973; sr. research officer Chem. Mfg. Co., Ghaziabad, India, 1974-75, head research and devel. div., 1977, 79; post-doctoral fellow Grad. Center for Materials Research U. Mo.-Rolla, 1979-80, research asst. prof., 1980-81; sr. chemist, head div. Applied Membrane Tech., Inc., Mpls., 1981—; research cons. chem. mfg. cos., India. Mem. Am. Chem. Soc. (polymer div.). Contbr. articles to profl. jours. Office: Applied Membrane Tech Inc Minneapolis MN 55435

SHARMA, MAHINDAR NATH, environ. engr.; b. India, Dec. 6, 1935; came to U.S., 1969, naturalized, 1981; s. Tejram and Rukmani Devi (Magotra) S.; B.A., Kashmir U., 1954; B.Chem. Engring., Jadavpur U., 1959; M.S., Northwestern U., 1972; m. Premlata, Jan. 30, 1967; 1 son, Manik. Dir. research and devel. Filters Internat., Inc., Chgo., 1972—. USPHS fellow, 1970-71; registered profl. engr., Ill. Mem. Nat. Soc. Profl. Engrs., Am. Inst. Chem. Engrs., Internat. Assn. Pollution Control. Patentee in field. Home: 230 Old Mill Grove Rd Lake Zurich IL 60047 Office: Filters International Inc 7130 Sears Tower Chicago IL 60606

SHARMA, SURYA KUMAR, pediatrician; b. Gaur, Nepal, Sept. 9, 1939; came to U.S., 1969, naturalized, 1977; s. Pashupati Nath and Subhalaxmi Kumari (Paudel) S.; M.B.B.S., Med. Coll. and Hosp., Nagpur, India, 1963; m. Kamala Kumari Gyawali, Nov. 12, 1965; children—Surit K., Bandana. Med. officer Br. of Pediatrics, Govt. of Nepal, 1966-69; intern Miriam Hosp., Providence, 1970-71; resident Children's Hosp., Chattanooga, 1972-74; practice medicine specializing in pediatrics, Albion, Mich., 1974-76, Moline, Ill., 1976—; staff, Luth. Hosp., Moline Public Hosp., Illini Franciscan Hosp., Quad Cities, Ill. Diplomate Am. Bd. Pediatrics. Fellow Am. Acad. Pediatricians; mem. AMA, Acad. Pediatrics, Ill. d. Assn. Address: 3637 23rd Ave Moline IL 61265

SHARP, BOBBY EARL, JR., computer co. exec.; b. Walnut Ridge, Ark., Aug. 30, 1949; s. Bobby Earl and Sammie Roberta S.; A.A. in Bus. Adminstrn., Grossmont Coll., 1972; B.S. in Info. Systems, San Diego State U., 1973; B.S. in Acctg., U. Evansville, 1977; m. Rebecca Lyn Groves, June 21, 1970; children—Sarah Lyn, Rachel Ann. With ops. Bank of Am., Spring Valley, Calif., 1971-73; programmer Babcock & Wilcox, Mt. Vernon, Ind., 1973-74; sr. programmer Anaconda Co., Sebree, Ky., 1974-76; gen. mgr. Plycom Services, Inc., Plymouth, Ind., 1976—; lectr. Ancilla Coll.; tax cons. Household Fin. Corp. Foster parent for Marshall County. Served with USMC, 1968-70. Cert. in data processing Inst. for Cert. of Computer Profls.; lic. broker, Ind. Real Estate Commn. Mem. Digital Equipment Computer Users Soc. Republican. Mem. Ch. of Christ. Home: 600 N Liberty Plymouth IN 46563 Office: PO Box 160 Plymouth IN 46563

SHARP, CARL EDWIN, podiatrist; b. Findlay, Ohio, Aug. 15, 1942; s. Roscoe William and Donna Delores (Schade) S.; student Bowling Green State U., 1960-62; B.S. in Anatomy, Ohio State U., 1965, B.S. in Pharmacy, 1970; D.P.M., Ohio Coll. Podiatric Medicine, 1975; m. Kathleen Blanche O'Connell, Dec. 28, 1968; children—Geoffrey Alan, Ryan Devon, Cameron Grannon. Med. and surg. resident Foot Clinic, Youngstown, Ohio, 1975-76; pvt. practice podiatric medicine, Worthington, Ohio, 1976—; mem. surg. staff Doctors Hosp., Columbus, Ohio, 1980-81; cons. Norworth, Worthington, Alum Crest, Friendship Village. Trustee Central Ohio Diabetes Assn., chmn. constitution com. Mem. Am. Podiatry Assn., Am. Acad. Podiatric Sports Medicine, Am. Pharm. Assn., Ohio Podiatry Assn. (chmn. public edn. and info. com. 1979-81, pres. central acad. 1980-81), Alpha Epsilon Delta. Republican. Clubs: Sawmill Athletic, Arlington Court, Breakfast Sertoma. Home: 2392 Sovron Ct Dublin OH 43017 Office: 37 E Wilson Bridge Rd Worthington OH 43085

SHARP, HOMER GLEN, dept. store exec.; b. Cleve., July 3, 1927; s. Homer David and Kathleen (Hawkins) S.; diploma Parsons Sch. Design, 1945; student Am. Acad. Art, 1947; m. JoAnn Harbour, Aug. 29, 1947; children—David Lee, Terry Glen. Trimmer window display Marshall Field & Co., Chgo., 1946-55, mgr. interior display, 1955-68, display dir., 1968-70, store design and display dir., 1970—, v.p. design and display div., 1971—. Served with USMCR, 1945-46. Recipient Nat. Assn. Display Industries award outstanding achievements, 1973. Mem. Chgo. Assn. Commerce and Industry, Chgo. Council Fgn. Relations, Chgo. Athletic Assn. Methodist (trustee). Office: Marshall Field & Co 111 N State St Chicago IL 60690

SHARP, MARY LUCILLE PEDEN, ednl. adminstr.; b. Kansas City, Mo., May 29, 1929; d. Clarence Allen and Laura Winifred (Henley) Peden; B.S., Missouri Valley Coll., 1950; M.Ed., Central Mo. State U., 1970; m. Richard Calvin Sharp, June 23, 1951; children—Richard Calvin, Robert Parker, Allen Russell Howland. Classroom tchr., Kans., Mo. and Wash., 1950-69; reading specialist Kansas City (Mo.) Public Schs., 1969-74, adminstr. remedial reading program, 1974-66, cons. K-6 grades, 1976-77, instr. facilitator, 1977-80, prin. E.C. Meservey Elem. Sch., 1980-81, prin. Graceland Elem. Sch., 1982—; speaker in field. Active local Boy Scouts Am., 1960-68, PTA, 1950-81; precinct capt. Clay County Republican Com., 1952-55. Mem. Internat. Reading Assn. (treas. Kansas City chpt. 1975), Nat. Assn. Elem. Sch. Prins., Mo. Assn. Elem. Sch. Prins., Kansas City Assn. Elem. Sch. Prins., Assn. Supervision and Curriculum Devel., Kansas City Sch. Adminstrs. Assn., Phi Delta Kappa, Delta Kappa Gamma (editor 1978-80, chmn. chpt. profl. affairs com. 1980-82). Episcopalian.

SHARP, PHILIP R., congressman: b. Balt., July 15, 1942; s. Riley and Florence Sharp; B.S. cum laude, Sch. Fgn. Service, Georgetown U., 1964, Ph.D. in Govt., 1974; postgrad. Exeter Coll., Oxford (Eng.) U., summer 1966; m. Marilyn Kay Augburn, 1972; 1 son, Jeremy Beck. Legis. aide to Senator Vance Hartke of Ind., 1964-69: asst. to asso. prof. polit. sci. Ball State U., Muncie, Ind., 1969-74; mem. 94th-97th Congresses from 10th Ind. Dist.; mem. Com. Energy and Commerce, Com. Interior and Insular Affairs. Democrat. Methodist. Office: 2542 Rayburn House Office Bldg Washington DC 20515

SHASSERE, JUNE KNIGHT, public relations cons.; b. Chgo., Apr. 22, 1940; d. John and Mary Alice (Rudisel) Knight; B.S., Ind. State U., 1962; M.A., Ball State U., 1976; m. William Glenn Shassere, July 27, 1963. Tchr. high sch. journalism and English in Ind., 1962-64; newspaper reporter, Plymouth, Ind., 1964-66; editor U. Notre Dame, 1966-68; dir. public relations and devel. Culver Mil. Acad., St. Mary's Acad., also Ladywood-St. Agnes Sch., Goodwill Industries Found., 1968—; dir. public info. Ind. Office Manpower Devel., 1974-76; ind. public relations cons., 1972—; staff asso. Ind. U., 1977-80, dir. women in politics project, 1977—, asso. faculty, 1981—; vis. lectr. communications Purdue U., 1978-80; mem. Ind. Gov.'s Commn. Status Women, 1973-75; program leader, tng. cons. in field. Active fund raising local Am. Cancer Soc. Named Outstanding Woman, Ind. Women's Polit. Caucus, 1979. Mem. Public Relations Soc. Am., Nat. Assn. Govt. Communicators, LWV, Ind. Soc. Public Adminstrn. (chmn. conf. 1979), Sigma Delta Chi (dir.). Author tng. guides in field; editor: Women in Politics: Practical Hints for Candidates and Campaigners, 1978, Development of Downtown Terre Haute, Indiana: A Feasible Strategy, 1977, The Role of Women on Indiana Newspapers 1876-1976, 1977, Running Winning Leading: Public Leadership Development for Women, 1980. Home: 4491 Washington Blvd Indianapolis IN 46205

SHATILA, AHMAD HUSSEIN, physician; b. Beirut, Lebanon, Apr. 1, 1942; s. Hussein Ahmad and Ysir Omar Shatila; B.S., Am. U. Beirut, 1965, M.D., 1970; m. Bonnye Lynn Oliver, June 24, 1972; children—Suzanne Lynn, Sarah Elizabeth, David Ahmad. Intern, Am. Univ. Hosp., Beirut, 1969-70; resident in surgery U. Louisville, 1970-72; asst. resident in surgery SUNY Upstate Med. Center, Syracuse, 1972-74, chief resident in surgery, 1974-75; fellow in surg. oncology Luth. Med. Center, and Cleve. Met. Gen. Hosp., 1975-76; practice medicine specializing in surgery, Cleve., 1976—; sr. clin. instr. surgery Case-Western Res. U. Sch. Medicine, Cleve. Diplomate Am. Bd. Surgery. Mem. Cleve. Acad. Medicine, Cleve. Surg. Soc., N.E. Ohio Soc. Clin. Oncology, Am. Soc. Clin. Oncology, Eastern Coop. Oncology Group. Office: 18660 E Bagley Rd Cleveland OH 44130

SHAUF, ANNE MARILYN, educator; b. Chattanooga, Jan. 7, 1958; d. Jack Allen and Marilyn (McMillan) S.; B.S. magna cum laude, Tenn. Tech. U., 1980. High sch. tchr. Am. and world history, geography St. Francis (S.D.) Indian Sch., 1980—, sponsor sr. class and pep club, 1980—; Mission Service Corps worker So. Bapt. Ch., 1980—. Mem. S.D. Indian Counselors Assn., Kappa Delta Pi, Alpha Delta Pi, Phi Lambda Theta, Phi Alpha Theta. Republican. Home: PO Box 458 Saint Francis SD 57572 Office: St Francis Indian Sch Saint Francis SD 57572

SHAUGHNESSY, CHARLES MICHAEL, architect; b. Westphalia, Kans., June 11, 1939; s. Lawrence Mark and Margaret Shaughnessy; B.Arch., Kans. State U., 1962. Architect in tng. Voskamp & Slezak Architects, Kansas City, Mo., 1963-65; architect in tng. Kivett & Myers Architects, Kansas City, Mo., 1965-67, architect, 1967-73; architect Midgley Shaughnessy Fickel and Scott Architects, Inc., Kansas City, Mo., 1973—, treas., 1979—, also dir. Chmn. arts and environ. com. Liturgical Arts Commn., Diocese of Kansas City/St. Joseph, 1978-79. Served with U.S. Army, 1962-63. Registered architect, Kans., Mo.; cert. Nat. Council Archtl. Registration Bds. Mem. AIA, Internat. Solar Energy Soc. Roman Catholic. Designer comml. bldgs. utilizing active solar energy systems. Office: Midgley Shaughnessy Fickel and Scott Architects Inc 20 W 9th St Kansas City MO 64105

SHAUGHNESSY, RITA ANN, psychologist; b. Chgo., May 21, 1948; d. Michael John and Mary Lee (Newman) S.; student Loyola U., Chgo., 1966-68; B.A., Govs. State U., 1974; M.A., U. Ill., Chgo., 1978, Ph.D., 1980. Teaching and research asst. U. Ill., Chgo., 1974-76; research scientist Ill. State Psychiat. Inst., Chgo., 1976-79; research asso. dept. psychiatry U. Chgo., 1979—. NIMH grantee, 1981—. Mem. AAAS, Soc. Biol. Psychiatry, N.Y. Acad. Scis., Sigma Xi. Research, publs. in field. Home: 644 S Cuyler Ave Oak Park IL 60304 Office: Ill State Psychiat Inst 1601 W Taylor St Chicago IL 60612

SHAUGHNESSY, WINSLOW MORSE, nature center dir.; b. Springfield, Ill., Oct. 27, 1935; s. Howard John and Grace (Heck) S.; student N. Central Coll., 1953-55; B.S. in Botany, U. Wis. at Madison, 1957; postgrad. zoology So. Ill. U., 1957-58; m. Judith Smith, June 15, 1957; children—Anne, Geoffrey, Susan. Naturalist, Forest Preserve Cook County (Ill.), 1958-59; ornithologist Ida Cason Callaway Gardens, Pine Mountain, Ga., 1959-60; instr. Biology dept. La Grange (Ga.) Coll., 1960; curator natural sci. Pa. State Mus., Harrisburg, 1961-67; mus. adminstr. Acad. Natural Scis. Phila., 1967-71; dir. Cumberland Mus. and Sci. Center, Nashville, 1971-77; dir. Chippewa Nature Center, Midland, Mich., 1978—; dir. Muse-Hopper, Inc., University Center, Mich., 1980-81, v.p., 1981. Recipient Elsie M.B. Naumburg award Natural Sci. for Youth Found., 1976. Mem. Am. Birding Assn., Am. Assn. Museums (Tenn. rep. 1974-76), Mich. Museums Assn. (dir. 1978-81), Bot. Club Wis., Hawk Mountain Sanctuary Assn., Midland Nature Club, Assn. Interpretive Naturalists, Mich. Nature Assn. Office: 400 S Badour Route 9 Midland MI 48640

SHAUL, PATRICK ANTHONY, mfg. co. exec.; b. Lincoln Park, Mich., Nov. 27, 1949; s. Harry George and Jmae Dorothy (Weaver) S.; B.S., U. Mich., 1971; m. Margaret Louise Mc Keown, Apr. 10, 1976. Systems programmer Mich. Blue Cross, Detroit, 1972-73; lead systems analyst Ex-Cell-O Corp., Walled Lake, Mich., 1973-80; systems analyst Guardian Industries, Northville, Mich., 1980—. Mem. Mich. Datapoint Users Group (dir. 1980—). Home: 224 Aqueduct Walled Lake MI 48088 Office: 43043 W Nine Mile Rd Northville MI 48167

SHAVER, JOSEPH MILTON PEARL, jewelry mfg. co. exec.; b. Rapid City, S.D., Apr. 2, 1920; s. Joseph Pearl and Nannie Minnie (Green) S.; ed. S.D. Sch. Mines, 1938; m. Inez Lenore Hofer, July 9, 1943; children—Nancy Jo, Marcia Jean, Peggy Ann. Clk. Buckingham Transp. Co., Rapid City and Denver, 1939-40; asst. mgr. N. Western Warehouse Co., Rapid City, 1940-45; mgr. Black Hills Jewelry Mfg. Co., Rapid City, 1945—. Pres. council Central PTA, 1951; committeeman Republican Precint, 1952; trustee, chmn. bd. Congregational Ch. Recipient Hire the Handicapped award, 1974. Mem. Mfg. Jewelers and Silversmiths Am (dir.), Rapid City C. of C. (dir.). Mem. United Ch. Christ. Clubs: Lions (dir.), Elks, Masons. Home: 4131 Park Ridge Pl Rapid City SD 57701 Office: 405 Canal St Rapid City SD 57701

SHAW, DONALD HARDY, public utility exec.; b. Oelwein, Iowa, June 1, 1922; s. John Hardy and Minnie (Brown) S.; B.S., Harvard U., 1942; J.D., U. Iowa, 1948; m. Elizabeth Jean Orr, Aug. 16, 1946; children—Elizabeth Ann, Andrew, Anthony. Admitted to Iowa bar, 1948, Ill. bar, 1949; lawyer firm Sidley, Austin, Burgess and Smith, Chgo., 1948-55; v.p. fin., dir. Iowa-Ill. Gas and Electric Co., Davenport, Iowa, 1956—; dir. First Nat. Bank Davenport. Mem. Iowa State Bd. Regents, 1969—; bd. dirs. Iowa Radio-TV, 1976—; trustee St. Luke's Hosp., 1967—. Served to capt. USAAF, 1942-45. Mem. Iowa, Ill. bar assns., Edison Electric Inst., Am. Gas Assn., Delta Theta Phi. Democrat. Conglist. Clubs: Davenport, Outing (Davenport, Iowa); Rock Island (Ill.) Arsenal Golf; Harvard (N.Y.C.). Home: 29 Hillcrest St Davenport IA 52803 Office: 206 E 2d St Davenport IA 52808

SHAW, EDWARD JAMES, physician; b. N.Y.C., Oct. 22, 1914; s. Samuel Johnson and Adele (Herndon) S.; B.A., Columbia, 1934; M.D., Yale U., 1937; m. Huguette Adele Herman, Apr. 19, 1965; children—Edward James, Emily K., Barbara A. Intern Bellevue Hosp., N.Y.C., 1937-38, resident surgery, 1938-39; resident surgery N.Y. Post Grad. Sch. and Hosp., N.Y.C., 1939-41; chief surg. services U.S. Army Sta. Hosp., Plattsburg Barracks, N.Y., 1941-42, chief gen. surg. sect. 69th Sta. Hosp., North Africa, 1942-44, comdg. officer and chief surgeon 16th Sta. Hosp., Wiesbaden, Germany, 1945-46; chief resident surgery New Rochelle (N.Y.) Hosp., 1946-47; practice medicine specializing in gen. surgery, New Rochelle, 1947-52; chief resident surgery Lawrence and Meml. Hosp., New London, Conn., 1952-53; chief resident and surgery resident Doctors Hosp., N.Y.C., 1953-54, attending surgeon, 1954-65; practice medicine specializing in gen. surgery, N.Y.C., 1954-65, St. Louis, 1965-67; chief surgeon Sutter Clinic, St. Louis, 1967-71; practice medicine specializing in surgery and occupational medicine, St. Louis and Granite City, Ill., 1971—; mem. surg. staffs Luth. Hosp., St. Louis, Incarnate Word Hosp., St. Louis, Alexian Bros. Hosp., St. Louis, St. Elizabeth Hosp., Granite City; asst. clin. prof. N.Y. Med. Coll., N.Y.C., 1954-65; asst. attending surgeon Flower Fifth Ave. Hosp., N.Y.C., 1954-65; asso. attending surgeon Met. and Bird S. Coler hosps., N.Y.C., 1954-65; pres. Shaw Surg. Clinic, St. Louis and Granite City, 1975—; med. dir. Am. Steel Foundries, Conalco. Bd. dirs. Western Ill. Found. Med. Care. Served with AUS, 1941-44, U.S. Army, 1944-46. Diplomate Am. Bd. Surgery, Am. Bd. Abdominal Surgery. Fellow Southwestern Surg. Congress, Internat. Coll. Surgeons, St. Louis Soc. Colon and Rectal Surgeons, A.C.S. (N.Y. and Bklyn. regional com. on trauma 1955-68), N.Y. Acad. Medicine; mem. Am. Soc. Colon and Rectal Surgeons, Am. Occupational Med. Assn., Am. Geriatrics Soc., Central States Soc. Occupational Medicine, Royal Soc. Medicine, Aerospace, Pan Am., St. Louis Met. (del. to Mo. Med. Assn. 1978-81), Mo., Madison County (Ill.), Ill., Am. med. assns., Mo. Surg. Soc., Assn. Mil. Surgeons of U.S., Am. Soc. Contemporary Medicine and Surgery, N.Y. Acad. Gastroenterology, Tri-Cities C. of C. Club: Yale of St. Louis. Home: 3105 Longfellow Blvd Saint Louis MO 63104 Office: 3654 S Grand Blvd Saint Louis MO 63118 and 1821 Edison Ave Granite City IL 62040

SHAW, JOHN ARTHUR, ins. co. exec.; b. San Antonio, June 6, 1922; s. Samuel Arthur and Ellen Agnes (Lawless) S.; student Loyola U., 1940-41, U. N.C., 1943-44; J.D., St. Louis U., 1948; m. Margaret Louise Strudell, June 9, 1951; children—John Richard, Barbara Ann, David William. Admitted to Mo. bar, 1948, since practiced in St. Louis; mem. firm Pollock, Tenney, & Dahman, 1948-51; with legal dept. Probate Ct., 1951-53; partner Pollock, Ward, Klobasa, & Shaw, 1953-63; with Reliable Life Ins. Co., Webster Groves, Mo., 1964—, asso. gen counsel, 1964-67, gen. counsel, 1967—, sr. v.p. 1969-80, sec., 1980—, also dir.; dir., gen. counsel Old Reliable Fire Ins. Co., 1967—; pres., dir. Reliable Life Corp., 1974-78. Active Boy Scouts Am., Glendale, Mo. Bd. dirs. Tatman Found., 1967—. Served as lt.

U.S. Army, 1943-46; maj. Res. (ret.). Mem. Am. Bar Assn., Am. Judicature Soc., Mo. Bar, Bar Assn. Met. St. Louis, Cath. Lawyers Guild St. Louis, Assn. Life Ins. Counsel, Am. Council of Life Ins., Alpha Sigma Nu, Delta Theta Phi. Cath. Contbg. author: Basic Estate Planning, 1957. Editor: Missouri Probate Law and Practice, 1960. Home: 306 Luther Ln Glendale MO 63122 Office: 231 W Lockwood Ave Webster Groves MO 63119

SHAW, KENNETH ALAN, univ. pres.; b. Granite City, Ill., Jan. 31, 1939; s. Kenneth W. and Clara H. (Lange) S.; B.S., Ill. State U.; Ed.M., U. Ill.; Ph.D. in Counseling, Purdue U.; L.H.D. (hon.), Towson (Md.) State U., 1978; m. Mary Ann Byrne, Aug. 18, 1962; children—Kenneth W., Susan L., Sara A. Tchr., coach Rich Twp. High Sch., Park Forest, Ill., 1961-63; residence hall dir. Ill. State U., 1963-64, instr. edn., lectr. sociology; asso. prof. sociology Towson State U., acting dean, dean; pres. So. Ill. U., Edwardsville, 1977-79, chancellor So. Ill. U. System, 1979—. Chairperson edn. com. Balt. chpt. NCCJ, 1973-77; mem. Baltimore County Citizens Adv. Com. on Racial and Cultural Concerns, 1974-77; vice chairperson Baltimore County Task Force on Edn., 1975-77; mem. Bloomington-Normal (Ill.) Town Meeting Com., 1967-69; chairperson United Community Services, McLean County, Ill., 1969; bd. dirs. St. Louis Symphony Soc., 1977-78, Balt. Urban Obs., 1972-73, St. Louis Regional Commerce and Growth Assn., 1977—. Mem. Am. Assn. Higher Edn. (chairperson Mid-Atlantic regional conf. 1974), Sociol. Assn., Ill. Council on Econ. Edn. (mem. governing bd. 1977—), Higher Edn. Coordinating Council (dir. 1977—), Assn. Am. Colls., Phi Delta Kappa, Pi Gamma Mu. Author: A Guide to Independent Study in Social Problems, 1975; contbr. articles on problems in higher edn. and ednl. adminstrn. to profl. jours. Office: Office of Chancellor Southern Illinois Univ Edwardsville IL 62901

SHAW, KENNETH W., sand and gravel co. exec.; b. Albion, Ill., July 10, 1910; s. William and Idella May (Severns) S.; student Lockyears Bus. Coll., 1931; m. Berneice Ellis, Apr. 9, 1932; children—Gary, Neale, James, William. Pres., Lawrenceville Ready-Mix Co. (Ill.), Mount Carmel Sand & Gravel Co., Inc. (Ill.), Wabash Asphalt Co., Inc., Mt. Carmel; dir. First Nat. Bank, Allendale, Ill. Mem. Asso. Gen. Contractors Assn., Ill. Asphalt Paving Assn. (past pres.), So. Ill. Builders' Assn., Wabash Valley Contractors' Assn. (pres.). Republican. Methodist. Clubs: Elks. Home: 1 Kingsway St Mount Carmel IL 62863 Office: Riverfront Mount Carmel IL 62863

SHAW, KIM DONALD, lawyer; b. Flint, Mich., Oct. 9, 1955; s. Donald William and Patricia Elizabeth (Robinson) S.; B.A., U. Mich., Flint, 1977; J.D., Wayne State U., 1980. Admitted to Mich. bar, 1980; individual practice law, Flint, 1980—. Del., Genesee County Republican Conv., 1976-80, Mich. Rep. Conv., 1976, 78. Mem. Am. Bar Assn., State Bar Mich., Genesee County Bar Assn., Assn. Am. Trial Lawyers, Mich. Trial Lawyers Assn., Am. Hist. Assn., Phi Alpha Theta. Roman Catholic. Home: 3814 Larchmont St Flint MI 48504 Office: 1161 N Ballenger Hwy Suite 4 Flint MI 48504

SHAW, ORENA MARGIE, nursing adminstr.; b. Levasy, Mo., Sept. 9, 1923; d. Herbert C. and Orena M. (Schroer) S.; diploma St. Luke's Hosp. Sch. Nursing, 1945; B.S. in Nursing, U. Mo., 1955; M.S. in Nursing Adminstrn., Frances Payne Bolton Sch. Nursing, Western Res. U., 1959. Staff nurse St. Luke's Hosp., Kansas City, Mo., 1946; staff nurse, instr., supr. Kennedy VA Hosp., Memphis, 1947-52; staff nurse Kansas City (Mo.) VA Hosp., 1952-53, surg. supr., 1953-54, asst. chief evening nursing service, 1955-57, asst. chief nursing service, 1959-61; chief nursing service trainee VA Hosp., Oklahoma City, 1961-62; chief nursing service VA Hosp., Shreveport, La., 1962-65, VA Hosp., Atlanta, Ga., 1965-68, VA Med. Center, St. Louis, 1968—; asst. prof. nursing Emory U., Atlanta, 1966-68; cons. to chief med. dir. adv. com. of hosp. dirs., 1971-72; mem. adv. bd. St. Louis Mcpl. Sch. Nursing, 1972-76; clin. instr. St. Louis U. Sch. of Nursing, 1975—; chmn. com. of VA chiefs of nursing service Med. Dist. 21, 1972-76; chmn. ad hoc com. chiefs nursing service VA Central Office, 1975-76. Served with Nurses Corps, U.S. Army, 1945-46. Named Boss of Yr., Am. Bus. Women's Assn., 1965; recipient Asst. Chief Med. Dir.'s Commendation, VA, 1977. Mem. Am. Nurses Assn., Nat. League of Nursing, St. Louis Council of Dirs. of Nursing Service, U. Mo. Alumni Assn., Frances Payne Bolton Sch. Nursing Alumni Assn. Mem. United Ch. Christ. Home: 2590 Cedar Knoll St Saint Louis MO 63031 Office: VA Medical Center Saint Louis MO 63125

SHAW, PATRICK, architect; b. Chgo., June 29, 1933; s. Alfred Phillips and Rue (Winterbotham) S.; student Middlesex Sch., Concord, Mass., 1947-51; A.B., Harvard U., 1958, postgrad., 1958-61; m. Joanne Nagel, Jan. 19, 1968 (div. Jan. 1978); children—Sophia Neoma, Alfred Michel. With various archtl. firms, 1960-65; pres. Shaw & Assos., architects, Chgo., 1965—. Bd. dirs., sec. Greater N. Michigan Ave. Assn. Chgo., chmn. zoning com.; trustee, sec. Poetry Mag. Served with U.S. Army, 1952-54. Mem. A.I.A., Chgo. Hist. Soc. Clubs: Univ., Arts (Chgo.), Tavern. Prin. works include Campus Center and Residence Hall at Loyola U., Chgo., Main P.O. Bldg., Springfield, Ill., Mid-Continental Plaza office bldg., Chgo., Commerce Plaza Office Bldgs., Oak Brook, Ill., Truman Coll. Multi-Use Facility, Chgo., Drake Hotel and office bldg., Oak Brook, Ill., Chgo. Bd. Trade addition, Presidents Plaza Office Bldgs, others. Home: 1450 N Astor St Chicago IL 60610 Office: 55 E Monroe St Chicago IL 60603

SHAW, ROBERT JOSEPH, ins. co. exec.; b. Vienna, Austria, Nov. 21, 1931; came to U.S., 1940, naturalized, 1945; s. Sigmund and Alice (DeMajo) S.; B.A., U. Ill., 1953; M.B.A., U. Pa., 1958; m. Sharon Reva Walner, Oct. 20, 1973; children—Leonora, Jonathan, Leslie, Nicole. Audit mgr. Arthur Young & Co., Chgo., 1958-67; asst. controller, asst. treas. Combined Ins. Co. of Am., Chgo., 1967-78; v.p., controller Nat.-Ben Franklin Life Ins. Corp., Chgo., 1978—. Served as lt. U.S. Army, 1953-55. C.P.A., Ill. Fellow Life Mgmt. Inst.; mem. Am. Inst. C.P.A.'s, Am. Mgmt. Assn., Planning Execs. Inst. (pres. Chgo. chpt. 1979-80), Ins. Acctg. and Statis. Assn. (sec. Greater Chgo. chpt.). Jewish. Office: 200 S Wacker Dr Chicago IL 60606

SHAW, ROBERT REED, advt. agy. exec.; b. Wilkinson, Ind., Sept. 1, 1922; s. Clyde J. and Effie J. (Reed) S.; grad. high sch.; m. Shirley Riha, July 13, 1972; children—Robert Reed, Nona Jane. With advt. div. Sportservice Corp., 1947-50; dir. advt. S.E. U.S., Midwest Advt. Co., Kansas City, Mo., 1950-54; v.p., account exec. Litman, Stevens & Margolis Advt., Kansas City, 1954-55; v.p., account exec. Christenson, Barclay & Shaw, Inc., Kansas City, 1955-81, exec. v.p., to 1981; pres. Mission Advt., Inc. (Kans.), 1981—; v.p. Musical Prodns. Inc.; v.p., treas. Broadway Enterprises, Mater Dei Prodns.; dir. Met. Bank, 1967-70. Pres. Civic Safety Assn., 1960-64; bd. dirs. CB & S Profit Sharing Trust. Served with USNR, 1940-44. Decorated Purple Heart. Mem. Advt. and Exec. Club, United Theatre Owners Assn., Nat. Agrl. Advt. and Mktg. Assn., Internat. Platform Assn. Mason. Clubs: Kansas Century (Topeka); Lake Ozark (Mo.) Yacht Assn. (mem. election bd. 1963-70). Home: 11004 W 96th Terr Overland Park KS 66214 Office: Mission Advt Inc 5700 Broadmoor Suite 115 Mission KS 66202

SHAW, RUSSELL CLYDE, lawyer; b. Cleve., Mar. 19, 1940; s. Clyde Leland and Ruth Arminta (Williams) S.; B.S., Ohio State U., 1962; J.D., Ohio State U., 1965; m. Jane Ann Mohler, Feb. 15, 1969; children—Christopher Scott, Robin Nicole, Curtis Russell. Admitted to Ohio bar, 1965, U.S. Supreme Ct. bar, 1968; asso. mem. firm Thompson, Hine & Flory, Cleve., 1965, 69-74, partner, 1974—. Mem. Geauga United Way Services Council, 1980—; trustee Geauga Humane Soc., 1981—. Served to capt. AUS, 1965-69. Mem. Am. Bar Assn., Fed. Bar Assn., Ohio Bar Assn., Nat. Lawyers Club, Old English Sheepdog Club Am. (nat. officer 1972-74), Fedn. Ohio Dog Clubs (pres. 1978—), Sugarbush Kennel Club (pres. 1975-78, 81), Midwest Pension Conf., Delta Sigma Phi (nat. officer 1975—), Presidents Club Ohio State U. Office: 1100 National City Bank Bldg Cleveland OH 44114

SHAW, THOMAS JOSEPH, ins. co. ofcl.; b. Pittsburg, Kans., Oct. 30, 1948; s. Fred H. and Margaret M. (Houser) S.; student S.E. Mo. State U., Cape Girardeau, 1968, Mo. So. State Coll., Joplin, 1977; m. Brenda Jo Meinz, Nov. 30, 1968; children—Aaron D., Nathan J. Trainee, property ins. co. mgmt. Barton County Mut. Ins. Co., Liberal, Mo., 1972-74, asst. mgr. ops., 1974—, claims mgr., 1975—; rep. Property Loss Research Bur., Chgo.; instr. seminars. City clk. Liberal, 1972-75. Served with U.S. Army, 1969-71. Mem. Am. Assn. Ins. Services, Nat. Assn. Mut. Ins. Cos. (claims edn. com., Merit award 1974), Mo. Assn. Mut. Ins. Cos. (policy forms com., dir.). Clubs: U.S. Jaycees, Mo. Jaycees (charter pres., 1977, dist. dir. 1979, Outstanding House Debater, Mock Legislature 1979), K.C. Home: 302 Walser Liberal MO 64762 Office: 120 S Main Liberal MO 64762

SHAW, WILFRID GARSIDE, chemist; b. Cleve., May 30, 1929; s. Wilfrid and Louise Clara Shaw; B.A., Oberlin Coll., 1951; M.S. (Rohm and Haas fellow 1951-53), U. Cin., 1953, Ph.D. (Dreyer fellow 1954-56), 1957; m. Joanne Elaine Morsfield, Aug. 22, 1953; children—Lorene Ann, Karen Lynn. With Standard Oil Co., Cleve., 1956—, research asso., 1971-74, sr. research asso., 1975—. Mem. Am. Chem. Soc., Catalysis Soc., Am. Fencers League Am., Sigma Xi. Presbyterian. Patentee in catalysts, chems., petroleum and chem. processes. Home: 1028 Linden Ln Lyndhurst OH 44124 Office: 4440 Warrensville Center Cleveland OH 44128

SHAWCHUCK, NORMAN L., clergyman, educator; b. Elgin, N.D., May 13, 1935; s. Alexander Nikita and Ava Marie (Brown) S.; Diploma in Theology, Lakewood Park Bible Sch., Devils Lake, N.D., 1957; B.A. cum laude, Jamestown (N.D.) Coll., 1967; M.Div., Garrett Theol. Sem., Evanston, Ill., 1969; Ph.D., Northwestern U., 1974; m. Verna Mae Dalin, Jan. 19, 1956; children—Carita, Melody Shawchuck Anderson, Kay Marie. Ordained to ministry, United Meth. Ch., 1959; founder, dir. Urban Missions, N.Y.C., 1962-65; founding dir. Turtle Mountain Counseling and Rehab. Center, Turtle Mountain Indian Reservation, Belcourt, N.D., 1970-72; dir. Parish Devel. Project, Chgo., 1973-75; asso. dir. Dakotas area program staff United Meth. Ch., Mitchell, S.D., 1975-80; minister spiritual formation Ind. area United Meth. Ch.; Indpls., 1981—; adj. faculty McCormick Theol. Sem., Chgo., 1974—, Trinity-Evang. Div. Sch., Deerfield, Ill., 1974—; cons. in field. Mem. Indian alcohol program rev. com. HEW, 1971-73. mem. Assn. Creative Change in Religious and Other Systems, Religious Research Assn., Soc. Sci. Study of Religion. Author: Taking a Look at Your Leadership Styles, 1977; How To Be A More Effective Church Leader, 1981; co-author: Management for your Church, 1977; Experiences in Activating Congregations, 1978; Let My People Go: Empowering Laity for Ministry, 1980; Revitalizing the Twentieth Century Church, 1982; contbg. editor Leadership.

SHAWHAN, STANLEY DEAN, educator; b. Mpls., Feb. 7, 1941; s. Elbert Neil and Ena Maxine (Burdine) S.; B.A., Ohio Wesleyan U., 1963; M.S., U. Iowa, 1965, Ph.D., 1966; m. Susan Jenkins, June 20, 1964; children—Peter Sven, Daniel Lloyd. Summer student engr. Sun Oil Co., Marcus Hook, Pa., 1961-62; student engr. United Aircraft Corp., E. Hartford, Conn., summer 1963; NASA grad. trainee U. Iowa, Iowa City, 1963-66, research asso., 1966-68, asst. prof., 1969-74, asso. prof., 1974-78, prof. physics, 1978—; vis. scientist div. plasma physics Royal Inst. Tech., Stockholm, Sweden, 1968-69, 76-77, Danish Space Research Inst., Lyngby, summer 1969, 76; vis. asst. scientist Nat. Radio Astronomy Obs., Green Bank, W.Va., summer 1970; cons. to NASA, 1974—, S.W. Research Inst., 1977—; mem. working group on ray tracing Internat. Sci. Radio Union-Internat. Assn. Geomagnetism and Aeronomy, 1976—; mem. joint bd. for radio sci. Am. Geophys. Union-Internat. Sci. Radio Union, 1976-78; mem. space sci. bd., panel on plasma processes Nat. Acad. Sci., 1976-77; mem. subcom. on space sci. com. on radio frequencies NRC, 1977—; mem. subsatellite working group of atmospheric, magnetospheric and plasmas in space program Goddard Space Flight Center/NASA, 1978-79, mem. steering com. for dynamics explorer mission, 1976—; U.S. del. to XIXth Gen. Assembly of Internat. Sci. Radio Union, 1978; payload specialist selection com. for Spacelab 2 Mission, MSFC/NASA, 1978. NSF grantee, 1972—, NASA grantee, 1975—. Mem. Am. Geophys. Union, Internat. Astron. Union, Am. Astron. Soc., Internat. Sci. Radio Union, Sigma Xi, Phi Beta Kappa, Pi Mu Epsilon, Chi Gamma Nu. Contbr. articles in field to profl. jours. Home: 1147 E Court St Iowa City IA 52240 Office: Univ of Iowa Dept of Physics and Astronomy Iowa City IA 52242

SHEA, DOROTHY MAXINE, coll. adminstr.; b. Kansas City, Mo., Aug. 26, 1926; d. Robert John and Loma Ellen (Westhoff) Hill; B.A., Benedictine Coll., 1947; m. David Joseph Shea, June 21, 1947. Mgr. exec. placement and devel. R. H. Macy & Co., Inc., Kansas City, Mo., 1949-75; dir. career planning and placement Rockhurst Coll., Kansas City, 1975—, also dir. Career Center; cons. in field. Recruiter, selection judge for internships Coro Found.; bd. dirs. United Campaign, Kansas City, Guadalupe Center, Mental Health Assn. Mem. Am. Soc. Personnel Adminstrn., Personnel Mgmt. Assn. Greater Kansas City, Coll. Placement Council, Midwest Coll. Placement Assn., Internat. Personnel Women's Assn., Am. Soc. Tng. Dirs. Roman Catholic. Home: 7924 Cambridge Dr Prairie Village KS 66208 Office: 5225 Troost Ave Kansas City MO 64110

SHEA, FRANCIS RAYMOND, bishop; b. Knoxville, Tenn., Dec. 4, 1913; s. John Fenton and Harriet (Holford) S.; A.B., St. Mary's Sem., Balt., 1935; B.S.T., N. Am. Coll.-Gregorian U., Rome, Italy, 1939; M.A., Peabody Coll., Nashville, 1942; D.D., 1969. Ordained pries Roman Cath. Ch., 1939; tchr. Christian Bros. Coll. and Siena Coll., Memphis, 1940-45; prin. Father Ryan High Sch., Nashville, 1945-46; pastor Immaculate Conception Ch., Knoxville, 1956-69; named bishop Evansville, Ind., 1969, consecrated, 1970. Mem. planning bd. United Fund Agys., Knoxville, 1968-69. Bd. dirs. Buffalo Trace council Boy Scouts Am., Evansville, Child and Family Services, Knoxville. Office: 219 NW 3d St Evansville IN 47708*

SHEAR, WALTER LEWIS, educator; b. Hillsboro, Wis., Sept. 24, 1932; s. Edwin Welland and Hilda (Christine) S.; B.A., U. Wis., Madison, 1954, Ph.D., 1961; M.A., U. Iowa, 1957; 1 dau., Stephanie Jeanne. Instr. to prof. English, Pittsburg (Kans.) State U., 1960—, prof. Am. lit., 1968—. Served with AUS, 1954-56. Mem. Modern Lang. Assn., Am. Studies Assn., Nat. Council Tchrs. of English, AAUP (pres. Pittsburg chpt. 1968, 71-75), NEA, Kans. Edn. Assn., Pittsburg State/Kans. Higher Edn. Assn. Contbr. chpt. to book, numerous articles to profl. jours. Home: 1915 S Taylor St Pittsburg KS 66762 Office: Pittsburg State University Pittsburg KS 66762

SHEARER, RODERICK CLINTON, univ. adminstr.; b. Saginaw, Mich., Aug. 7, 1933; s. Martin and Jule (Annabel) S.; A.B., U. Detroit, 1959; M.A., Mich. State U., 1961; m. Beverly Ann Flemming, Aug. 12, 1961. Dir. residence life U. Detroit, 1961-63; asst. dean students Eastern Mich. U., 1963-67; dean students Loyola Coll., Montreal, Que., Can., 1967-70; v.p., dean students Xavier U., Cin., 1970—. Served with U.S. Army, 1953-56. Can. Govt. grantee, 1968-69. Mem. Ohio Student Personnel Assn. (pres. 1978-79), Nat. Assn. Student Personnel Adminstrs., Assn. Jesuit Personnel Adminstrs. (v.p. 1976-78, 1981-83). Roman Catholic. Office: Xavier U Victory Pkwy Cincinnati OH 45207

SHEARMAN, WILLIAM MORGAN, educator; b. Bowling Green, Ohio, Apr. 8, 1924; s. Spicer Douglas and Hazel Lucile (Barkalow) S.; grad. Am. Acad. Art, 1950; B.S., Defiance Coll., 1967; M.A., Ball State U., 1969; M.F.A., Kent State U., 1975; m. Frances Marian Bunting, July 26, 1946; children—Sharon Leone, Michael Willam. Instr., Am. Acad. Art, Chgo., 1949-51; owner, operator W.M. Shearman and Assos., advt., Bryan, Ohio, 1951-54; comml. artist Gorny Winzeler, Inc., Bryan, 1954-65; prof. art, chmn. art dept. Defiance (Ohio) Coll., 1957—. Served with USNR, 1942-44. Recipient various local, state and nat. exhbn. awards. Mem. Ariz. Hist. Soc., N.W. Watercolor Soc., Ohio Crafts Council. Republican. Episcopalian. Clubs: Bryan Service, Moose. Author: Metal Alloys and Patinas for Castings, 1976. Home: 420 S Cherry St Bryan OH 43506 Office: Defiance Coll 701 N Clinton St Defiance OH 43512

SHEEHAN, DANIEL EUGENE, bishop; b. Emerson, Nebr., May 14, 1917; s. Daniel F. and Mary Helen (Crahan) S.; student Creighton U., 1934-36, LL.D. (hon.), 1964; student Kenrick Sem., St. Louis, 1936-42; J.C.D., Cath. U. Am., 1949. Ordained priest Roman Cath. Ch., 1942; asst. pastor, Omaha, 1942-46; chancellor Archdiocese Omaha, 1949-69, aux. bishop Omaha, 1964-69, archbishop, 1969—. Pres. Canon Law Soc. Am., 1953; del. 3d-4th sessions Ecumenical Council, Rome, Italy, 1964; chaplain Omaha club Serra Internat., 1950-66. Home: 6605 Farnam St Omaha NE 68132 Office: 100 N 62d St Omaha NE 68132*

SHEESLEY, JOHN HENRY, statistician; b. Harrisburg, Pa., May 26, 1944; s. Norman Austin and Helen Kirkpatrick (Brown) S.; B.S. in Math. Lafayette Coll., 1966; M.S. in Stats., Rutgers U., 1968; m. Lynn Thomas, June 1, 1968; children—Samantha, Emily Corinn, Amanda Lorin. Teaching asst. Rutgers U., New Brunswick, N.J., 1966-68; quality control engr. Western Electric Co., Allentown, Pa., 1968-73; sr. statistician Gen. Electric Co., East Cleveland, Ohio, 1973—; tchr. courses stats. and quality control. Registered profl. engr., Calif. Mem. Am. Soc. Quality Control (cert., Brumbaugh award 1978), Am. Statis. Assn., Phi Beta Kappa. Republican. Presbyterian. Club: TRW Rod and Gun. Contbr. articles to Jour. Quality Tech. Home: 8939 Jackson St Mentor OH 44060 Office: Nela Park East Cleveland OH 44112

SHEETS, DENNIS DEAN, elec. designer; b. Lebanon, Ind., June 8, 1946; s. Lloyd Richard and Cleo Mae (Miller) S.; student Purdue U., 1972-76; m. Cheryl Rae Smith, Nov. 7, 1975; children—Jennifer Kay, Christopher Jay. Elec. designer Bevington, Taggart & Fowler, Indpls., 1969-72; chief elec. designer James Assos., Indpls., 1972-75; project mgr. Long Electric Co., Inc., Indpls., 1975-79; mng. partner Smith Elec. Contractors, Inc., Indpls., 1979—; owner D.C. Enterprises. Bd. dirs. Greater Indpls. Progress Com. Served with USAF, 1966-69. Mem. Electric League Ind., Indpls. Jaycees (project chmn. 1978-79, pres. 1980-81), Illuminating Engring. Soc., Indpls. C. of C. (bd. govs., hon. dir.), Ind. Sub Contractors Assn., Nat. Fedn. Ind. Bus., Indpls. Jaycees (chmn. bd. 1981-82). Home: 1345 Wolf Ct Indianapolis IN 46229 Office: 410 S Franklin Rd Indianapolis IN 46219

SHEETS, LINDA SCHEU VETTER, advt. exec.; b. Oak Park, Ill., Nov. 6, 1948; d. George Charles and Betty Louise (Morrow) Scheu; B.F.A. in Fine Arts cum laude, U. Ill., 1970, M.F.A. in Art and Design, 1975; m. Richard Marshall Sheets, May 7, 1977; children—Jason Erik Vetter, Sally Alexandra, John Marshall. Cons. design, 1969-79; teaching fellow in art and design U. Ill., Urbana, 1974-75; with G.T. Hardwick Architects, Champaign, Ill., 1976-77; francise advt. coordinator Eisner Foods div. Jewel Cos., Champaign, 1977-79; corp. advt. dir. Flying Tomato, Inc. (doing bus. as Garcia's Pizza in a Pan), Champaign, 1979—; instr. Parkland Coll., 1970-71; exhibited in numerous shows and museums, 1969-76, including Chgo. Art Inst., 1975; represented in permanent collection So. Ill. U. Recipient 7 Chaamps awards, 16 certs. of merit Champaign County Ad Club, 1979-80. Mem. Women in Communications (pres. Champaign chpt. 1981-82), Champaign-Urbana Ad Club (dir. 1981-82), Bus. and Profl. Women. Office: 707 S Wright St Champaign IL 61820

SHEETS, RICHARD MARSHALL, land reclamation, waste mgmt. co. exec.; b. Urbana, Ill., Mar. 21, 1940; s. Robert Marshall and Verna Louise (Hollingsworth) S.; student U. Ill., 1958-61, U. Philippines, 1963; m. Linda Scheu Vetter, May 7, 1977; children—Sally A., John Marshall; 1 stepson, Jason Erik Vetter. Supervisory and asso. scientist Ill. State Natural History Survey, 1967-71; state mktg. dir. Diener Stereo, Inc., 1971-72; mktg. dir. Illini Union U. Ill., 1972-74; project dir., site mgr. C-V Solid Waste Mgmt. Group, 1974-76; owner, mgr. R.M. Sheets Devel. Co., Champaign, Ill., 1976—; chmn., pres. Western Lion Co., Inc., 1981—; dir. Abana Press, Inc., I'm Your Type, Inc. Coordinator George Bush for Pres., Champaign, 1980. Served with U.S. Army, 1961-64. Mem. Ill. Land Improvement Contractors, Am. Security Council, Am. Def. Preparedness Assn., Nat. Audubon Soc., Mensa. Illustrator in field. Home and Office: 1609 Parkhaven Dr Champaign IL 61820

SHEFFER, HAROLD VERMONT, coll. pres.; b. Nickleville, Pa., Feb. 25, 1921; s. George Peter and Theressa Marie S.; B.A., Allegheny Coll., 1950; M.Div. cum laude, Drew U., 1954, M.A., 1962; m. Joycelyn Shirley Fitzke, Mar. 30, 1976; children—Eric, Lynda, Suzanne, Robert, Johanna, David. Ordained to ministry Methodist Ch., 1950, Episcopal Ch., 1956; cleric Meth. Ch., Pa. and N.Y., 1947-55; cleric and canon to ordinary Episcopal Diocese of Calif., 1956-60; asst. nat. field dir. Multiple Sclerosis Soc., N.Y.C., 1960-63; self-employed, 1963-67; instr., dean of instrn., pres. Glen Oaks Community Coll., Centerville, Mich., 1967-72; pres. Jackson (Mich.) Community Coll., 1972—; mem. adv. bd. Midwest Bank, Jackson. Past pres., bd. dirs. Ella Sharp Mus., Jackson. Served with USN, 1944-45. Ezra Squier Tipple fellow Drew U., 1954-55. Mem. Am. Assn. Jr. and Community Colls., North Central Assn., Mich. Community Coll. Assn. (pres.), Jackson C. of C. (dir.). Republican. Roman Catholic. Clubs: Rotary; Elks. Home: 1135 Wickwire Rd Jackson MI 49201 Office: 2111 Emmons Rd Jackson MI 49201

SHEFFERT, MARK WARREN, JR., ins. co. exec.; b. Lincoln, Nebr., May 17, 1947; s. Mark Warren and Neneen Marcell (Maxey) S.; student U. Minn., 1965-69, grad. Exec. Program, Grad. Sch. Bus.; m. Danya Ann Spencer, Apr. 23, 1973; children—Mark Warren, Christopher Douglas, Brandon Spencer. Varous mgmt. positions Prudential Life Ins. Co., Mpls. and Detroit, 1970-77; div. v.p. N.Central Life Ins. Co., St. Paul, 1977-78, sr. v.p. mktg., 1978-79, exec. v.p., chief mktg. officer, 1979-80, sr. exec. v.p., chief operating officer, dir., 1980—. Active, Republican Party, YMCA; chmn. Needy

Children's Christmas Party, St. Paul. Recipient nat. mgrs. award Gen. Agts. and Mgrs. Assn., 1976, various industry and co. awards. Mem. Nat. Assn. Life Underwriters, S. Oakland County Life Underwriters (pres. 1973), Coll. Life Underwriters, Gold Key Soc. Lutheran. Club: St. Paul Athletic, Normandale Tennis. Home: 5600 Woodcrest Dr Edina MN 55434 Office: 445 Minnesota St Saint Paul MN 55164

SHEFFIELD, GARY ROBERT, hosp. supply co. exec.; b. Queens Village, N.Y., June 24, 1943; s. Robert G. and Marjorie P. (Evans) S.; B.A., Brown U., 1965; m. Kathleen Elizabeth Doherty, Nov. 2, 1969; children—Vanessa Anne, Erin Elizabeth, Glenn Christian. Sales rep. dietary products Am. Dietary Products div. Am. Hosp. Supply Corp., L.I., N.Y., 1967-70, product mgr. gen. offices, Evanston, Ill., 1970-71, sales mgr. SE area, Atlanta; 1971; v.p., SE area mgr., 1971-74, pres., 1974-80; pres. American V. Mueller div. Am. Hosp. Supply Corp., Niles; Ill., 1980—; tchr. and mgr. Am. Dietary Products mgmt. seminars, McGaw Park, Ill., 1977-80. Served to lt. (j.g.), USN, 1965-67; Vietnam. Recipient Top Area Mgr. award Am. Hosp. Supply Corp., 1973-74, Plan Achievement award, 1977, 79. Republican. Lutheran. Club: Tennaqua Tennis and Swim. Home: 1419 Wincanton Dr Deerfield IL 60015 Office: 7280 N Caldwell Ave Niles IL 60648

SHEFFIELD, LESLIE FLOYD, agrl. educator; b. Orafino, Nebr., Apr. 13, 1925; s. Floyd L. and Edith A. (Presler) S.; B.S. with high distinction in Agronomy, U. Nebr., 1950, M.S., 1964; postgrad. U. Minn., summer 1965; Ph.D., U. Nebr., 1971; m. Doris Fay Fenimore, Aug. 20, 1947; children—Larry Wayne, Linda Faye (Mrs. Bernard Eric Hempelman), Susan Elaine. County extension agt. Lexington and Schuyler, Nebr., 1951-52; exec. sec. Nebr. Grain Improvement Assn., 1952-56; chief Nebr. Wheat Commn., Lincoln, 1956-59; exec. sec. Great Plains Wheat, Inc., market devel., Garden City, Kans., 1959-61; asst. to dean Coll. Agr., U. Nebr. at Lincoln, 1961-66, supt. North Platte Expt. Sta., 1966-71, asst. dir. Nebr. Coop. Extension Service, Nebr. Agrl. Expt. Sta., Lincoln, 1971-75, asst. to vice chancellor Inst. Agr. and Natural Resources, also extension farm mgmt. specialist and asso. prof. agrl. econs., 1975—; sec.-treas. Circle 4S-L Acres, Wallace, Nebr., 1973—. Cons. econs. of irrigation in N.D., Minn., S.D. and Brazil, 1975, Sudan, Kuwait and Iran, 1976, People's Republic of China, 1977, 81, Can., 1977, 78, 79, 80, Mex., 1978, 79, Argentina, 1978, Hong Kong, 1981, Japan, 1981. Served with U.S. Army, 1944-46; ETO. Recipient Hon. State Farmer award Future Farmers Am., 1955, Hon. Chpt. Farmer award, North Platte chpt., 1973; fellowship grad. award Chgo. Bd. Trade, 1964; Agrl. Achievement award Ak-Sar-Ben, 1969. NASA research grantee, 1972-77. Mem. Am. Agrl. Econs. Assn., Am., Nat., Nebr. (Pres.'s award 1979) water resources assns., Nebr. Irrigation Assn., Nebr. Assn. Resource Dists., Am. Soc. Farm Mgrs. Rural Appraisers, Orgn. Profl. Employees of U.S. Dept. Agr., Lincoln C. of C. (chmn. agrl. com. 1974-77), Gamma Sigma Delta, Alpha Zeta. Rotarian (dir. 1965-66). Editor: Procs. of Nebr. Water Resources and Irrigation Devel. for 1970's, 1972; contbg. editor Irrigation Age Mag., St. Paul, 1974—. Contbr. articles to various publs. Home: 3800 Loveland Dr Lincoln NE 68506 Office: 223 Filley Hall U Nebraska-Lincoln Lincoln NE 68583

SHEGRUD, DONALD MAURICE, mech. engr.; b. Dubuque, Iowa, Sept. 15, 1935; s. Maurice S. and Evelyn Rose (Howes) S.; B.S. in Mech. Engring., Finlay Engring. Coll., 1960; m. Eva Jeanne Milburn, Oct. 8, 1960; 1 dau., Sonya Sue. Customer estimating engr. Ladish Co., Cudahy, Wis., 1960-61; mech. designer J.F. Pritchard Co., Kansas City, Mo., 1961-62; new products engr. in research and devel. dept. Gustin-Bacon Mfg. Co., Kansas City, Mo., 1962-65; sales engr. Black, Sivalls, and Bryson Co., Kansas City, 1965-68; sales mgr. Continental Disc Corp., Kansas City, 1968-74, v.p. and gen. mgr., 1974-79, sr. v.p., 1979—. Served with USAF, 1954-58. Registered profl. engr., Mo. Mem. ASME, Am. Mgmt. Assn., Nat., Mo. socs. of profl. engrs., Platte County Bus. and Profl. Assn., Northland C. of C. Roman Catholic. Clubs: North Kansas City Breakfast. Patentee in field. Home: 3407 NW 58th Terr Kansas City MO 64151 Office: 4103 Riverside NW Kansas City MO 64150

SHELDON, ANN WORKMAN, sociologist; b. Des Moines, Dec. 14, 1925; d. Charles Noel and Florence Marjorie (Knapp) Workman; B.A., U. Mich., 1948; M.A., Wayne State U., 1971; Ph.D., Mich. State U., 1975; m. Horace Earl Sheldon, May 31, 1952; children—Robert H., Catherine F., Joanne R. Elem. tchr. Willow Run (Mich.) Public Schs., 1948-50; asst. prof. dept. sociology Wayne State U., Detroit, 1974—; cons. in field. Mem. Bloomfield Twp. (Mich.) Library Bd., 1964-66; treas., vice-chmn. Oakland County OEO, 1963-69; chmn. Oakland planning com. United Community Services of Detroit, 1966-70; v.p. Camp Fire Girls of Detroit, 1977—. Named Ford Citizen of the Year, 1963; NIMH grantee, 1979—. Mem. N. Central Sociol. Soc., Midwest Sociol. Soc., Am. Sociol. Soc., Soc. for Study of Social Problems, Internat. Sociol. Assn., League of Women Voters. Democrat. Unitarian. Office: Wayne State U 118 Library Ct Detroit MI 48202

SHELLENBERGER, JOHN ALFRED, cereal chemist; b. Moline, Ill., Jan. 8, 1900; s. Wilbur Francis and Jennie Alice (Johnston) S.; B.S., U. Wash., 1930; M.S., Kans. State U., 1931; Ph.D. (Rockefeller fellow), U. Minn., 1935; m. Annabel Gangnath, June 3, 1939; children—Karen Shellenberger Stearns, Joan Shellenberger Black, Margo Shellenberger Caley. Asst. prof. U. Idaho, 1931-32; instr. biochemistry U. Minn., 1932-35; head products control Mennel Milling Co., Fostoria, Ohio, 1935-40; head biochemistry div. Rohm & Haas Co., Phila., 1940-42; cons. Argentine Govt., Buenos Aires, 1942-44; head grain sci. dept. Kans. State U., Manhattan, 1944-71, disting. prof. emeritus, 1971—; cons. Dept. Agr., Dept. State, UN. Served with Tank Corps, U.S. Army, World War I. Recipient Disting. Alumni Gold medal U. Minn., 1966, Neumann medal, 1967, C.H. Bailey gold medal, 1976. Mem. AAAS, Am. Chem. Soc., Inst. Food Technologists, Internat. Assn. Cereal Chemistry (pres. 1967-68), Am. Assn. Cereal Chemistry (pres. 1950-51). Republican. Episcopalian. Clubs: Rotary, Univ., Manhattan Country, Masons. Author: Bread Science and Technology, 1971; contbr. numerous articles to tech. jours. Home: 1715 Fairview St Manhattan KS 66502 Office: Shellenberger Hall Kansas State University Manhattan KS 66506

SHELTON, HERMAN THOMAS, hosp. adminstr.; b. Detroit, Jan. 14, 1932; s. Herman Moses and Leora (Thomas) S.; B.S. in Phys. Therapy, Ohio State U., 1957; M.B.A., Mich. State U., 1977; m. Leah Thompson, June 9, 1962; children—Sybil, Stephanie, Herman, Rebecca. Staff phys. therapist Detroit Gen. Hosp., 1957-60, chief phys. therapist, 1960-67; dir. phys. therapy Kirwood Gen. Hosp., Detroit, 1967—, adminstrv. asst. for ancillary services, 1975—; guest lectr. Wayne State U. Sch. Nursing, Detroit, 1963-72, others; cons. in field. Served with U.S. Army, 1952-54. Named Employee of the Month, Kirwood Gen. Hosp., 1973; Nat. Elks Found. grantee, 1957—; named Bachelor of the Year, Alpha Kappa Alpha, 1956. Mem. Am. Phys. Therapy Assn., Mich. Heart Assn., Mich. Multiple Sclerosis Soc., Nat. Soc. for Autistic Children, Kappa Alpha Psi. Baptist. Home: 18254 San Juan St Detroit MI 48221 Office: 4059 W Davison Ave Detroit MI 48238

SHELTON, ROBERT WALLACE, adminstrv. chem. engr.; b. St. Louis, Dec. 28, 1936; s. Lee William and Frances Wallace (Bulkley) S.; m. Elizabeth Becklenberg, Nov. 19, 1966; children—Trudy, Katherine, Angela; B.S. in Chem. Engring., Washington U., St. Louis, 1961, postgrad. Sever Inst. Tech., 1961-63; postgrad. Exec. Tng. Inst., Earlham Coll., 1975-76. Project engr., missiles space div. Emerson Electric Co., St. Louis, 1961-66; research engr. Linde div. Union Carbide Corp., Speedway, Ind., 1966-69, supt. labs., 1969-73, mgr. quality control, investment casting ops., 1973-75; mgr. analytical services Stellite div. Cabot Corp., Kokomo, Ind., 1975-77, div. mgr. quality control, 1977—. Mem. Am. Soc. Metals, Am. Soc. Quality Control, Internat. Standards Orgn., ASTM, Tau Beta Pi. Home: 1504 Green Acres Dr Kokomo IN 46901

SHEMORRY, CORINNE JOYNES, mktg. exec.; b. Rolla, N.D., Jan. 24, 1920; d. William H. and Edna Ruth (Conn) Joynes; children—Gay, Jan. Publisher, Williston (N.D.) Plains Reporter, 1953-78; mktg. dir. Williston Credit Union, 1979—; journalist, lectr., cons., author, reporter. Recipient numerous awards in journalism on state and nat. level, including being named Outstanding Woman in Journalism in N.D., 1975. Mem. N.D. Press Assn., N.D. Press Women (past pres.), Nat. Press Women, Williston C. of C., Sigma Delta Chi. Mem. United Ch. Club: Bus. and Profl. Women's (past pres.). Home: 210 E 14th St Williston ND 58801

SHEN, LINUS LIANG-NENE, biochemist; b. China, Aug. 28, 1941; s. K.H. and D.J. (Yu Shen) S.; came to U.S., 1965, naturalized, 1973; M.A., N.C. State U., 1969; Ph.D., U. N.C., Chapel Hill, 1972; m. Alice Ping-Lu, Apr. 11, 1968; children—Sandra, Jennifer. Research asso. U. N.C., Chapel Hill, 1972-73, instr., 1973-74, asst. prof., 1974-75; sr. scientist Abbott Labs., North Chicago, Ill., 1975—. Mem. Am. Heart Assn., Sigma Xi. Patentee in biochem. instrumentation and methods; contbr. articles to profl. jours. Home: 516 Fairlawn Ave Libertyville IL 60048 Office: Dept 474 Abbott Labs North Chicago IL 60064

SHENKER, LILLIAN ROSE KOPLAR (MRS. MORRIS A. SHENKER), lawyer; b. St. Louis, May 8, 1913; d. Sam and Jeannette (Grollnek) Koplar; B.S., B.A., Washington U., St. Louis, 1934, LL.B., 1939; m. Morris A. Shenker, Dec. 23, 1939; children—Morris Arthur, Patricia Ann. Admitted to Mo. bar, 1939; provisional judge St. Louis Municipal Ct., 1949, St. Louis Ct. Criminal Correction, 1949-53; pres. Park Plaza Drug Co., St. Louis, 1935-68, sec., 1968—; v.p. 220 TV Inc., St. Louis, 1953—; sec. Hotel Mgmt. Co., St. Louis, 1964—; exec. cons. design and planning Dunes Hotel & Casino Inc., Las Vegas, 1975-78, v.p. corp. expansion, 1978—. Chmn. ann. Inst. Human Rights, St. Louis, 1951-54; vice chmn. St. Louis Council Human Relations, 1950-53, chmn., 1953; chmn. Jewish Welfare Dr., 1957; co-chmn. St. Louis Bd. State Israel Bonds, 1960-65, nat. bd. dirs., 1963—; mem. citizens adv. com. St. Louis Juvenile Ct., 1962-63; mem. Mo. adv. com. U.S. Commn. on Civil Rights, 1965-67; mem. Nat. Small Bus. Adv. Council, 1965-67; chmn. Bus. and Profl. Women Mo. for Johnson-Humphrey, 1964; mem. adv. bd. Dismas Clark Found., 1960—; bd. dirs. Jewish Fedn. women's div., 1950—, pres. bd., 1955-57, life mem., 1965—; bd. dirs. Am.-Israel Cultural Found., Am. Friends Hebrew U., Jerusalem; bd. dirs. St. Vincent's Hosp. Aux., chmn. ann. Christmas prelude, 1971-72. Recipient Nat. Humanitarian award Am. Jewish Com., 1979. Mem. Mo. Bar Assn., AAUW, Mo. Assn. Social Welfare, Adult Edn. Council Greater St. Louis, League Women Voters, Nat. Council Jewish Women, Hadassah, Mo. Hist. Soc. Jewish religion (trustee temple 1965-68). Club: Westwood Country. Home: 1230 Topping Rd Saint Louis MO 63131 Office: 408 Olive St Saint Louis MO 63102 also Dunes Hotel and Country Club 3650 Las Vegas Blvd S Las Vegas NV 89109

SHEPARD, RANDALL TERRY, judge; b. Lafayette, Ind., Dec. 24, 1946; s. Richard S. and Dorothy I. (Donlen) S.; B.A. cum laude, Princeton U., 1969; J.D., Yale U., 1972. Admitted to Ind. bar, 1972, U.S. Dist. Ct. for So. Dist. Ind., 1972; spl. asst. to under sec. U.S. Dept. Transp., Washington, 1972-74; exec. asst. to mayor City of Evansville (Ind.), 1974-79; judge Vanderburgh Superior Ct., Evansville, 1980—; instr. U. Evansville, 1975-78; cons. Marston Robling, Inc., Evansville, 1980-81. Regional vice chmn. bd. advs. Nat. Trust for Historic Preservation, 1980—; chmn. State Student Assistance Commn. of Ind., 1980—; vice chmn. Vanderburgh County Republican Central Com., 1977-80. Recipient Friend of Media award Cardinal States chpt. Sigma Delta Chi, 1979. Mem. Fed. Bar Assn., Ind. Bar Assn., Ind. Judges Assn. Republican. Methodist. Clubs: Princeton (N.Y.); Capitol Hill (Washington); Evansville Petroleum. Author: Preservation Rules and Regulations, 1980; contbr. articles to profl. pubs. Home: 120 S Frederick St Evansville IN 47714 Office: 218 Courts Bldg Evansville IN 47708

SHEPHERD, DONALD HENRY, psychologist, educator; b. Clarksburg, W.Va., Apr. 3, 1951; s. Donald E. and Elsie Kathryn (Palmer) S.; B.A., W.Va. U., 1973; M.A., U. Notre Dame, 1976, Ph.D., 1978. Part-time instr. Fairmont State Coll., 1978-79; asst. prof. psychology St. Ambrose Coll., 1979—. Mem. Central Dist. Mental Health Citizens Adv. Bd., Clarksburg, 1978-79. Mem. Am. Psychol. Assn., AAAS, AAUP, Sigma Xi, Psi Chi. Unitarian Universalist. Office: St Ambrose Coll 518 W Locust St Davenport IA 52803

SHEPPARD, RONALD JOHN, automobile mfg. exec.; b. New Rochelle, N.Y., Apr. 13, 1939; s. Lester John and Louise Marie (Cox) S.; B.S., Rensselaer Poly. Inst., 1961; M.S., Howard U., 1962, Ph.D., 1965; M.B.A., Rochester Inst. Tech., 1974; student Detroit Coll. Law; m. Shirly Christine Saddler, June 8, 1963; children—Jeffrey Brandon, Mark Justin. Systems analyst RCA, Moorestown, N.J., 1965-66; mgr. strategic planning Booz Allen Hamilton, Inc., Washington, 1966-69; program mgr. space research Teledyne Brown Engring. Co., Huntsville, Ala., 1969-71; planning mgr., asst. group program mgr. Xerox Corp., Rochester, N.Y., 1971-77; now with Gen. Motors Corp., Warren, Mich.; cons. Rensselaer Human Dimensions Center, 1975—; coll. student adviser Keuka Coll., 1975--; vis. faculty So. U., 1975, Empire State Coll., 1975-76, Rochester Inst. Tech., 1974-75. Pres., Rochester Montessori Sch. Bd., 1975-76; bd. dirs. Easter Seal Soc., Rochester Better Contractors Bur. NDEA fellow, 1962-64, Howard U. Trustee fellow, 1964-65, NATO fellow U. Newcastle, Eng., 1964; recipient K.B. Weissman Meml. Found. Human Relations award, 1957. Mem. Am. Mktg. Assn., Assn. Masters in Bus. Adminstrn. Execs., Nat. Black Masters Bus. Adminstrn. Assn. Democrat. Methodist. Clubs: Rensselaer Alumni, Rotary, Univ. of Rochester, Cornell of N.Y., Shriners. Home: 19521 Burlington Dr Detroit MI 48203 Office: Gen Motors Corp Warren MI

SHEPPARD, SAMUEL EUGENE, graphic designer; b. Cin., Dec. 17, 1953; s. Hulon Eugene and Jacqueline Lee (Hilkebrand) S.; student Gable Advt. Art Sch., 1973-75. Paste-up artist Goyert Group, 1976; prodn. artist Lipson & Assos., 1976-78; graphic designer Campbell & Assos., 1978-79; designer, owner Sheppard Graphics & Assos., Cin., 1979—; art instr. Acad. Communicative Arts. Recipient various design awards; cert. comml. artist. Mem. Greater Cin. Indoor Tennis Assn., U.S. Parachute Assn. Club: U. Cin. Flying. Office: 2179 Gilbert St Cincinnati OH 45206

SHERAN, ROBERT JOSEPH, chief justice Minn. Supreme Ct.; b. Waseca, Minn., Jan. 2, 1916; s. Michael J. and Eleanor (Bowe) S.; B.A., Coll. St. Thomas, St. Paul, 1936; LL.B., U. Minn., 1939; m. Jean Marie Brown, Feb. 3, 1940; children—Michael, Thomas, Kathleen, John, Daniel. Admitted to Minn. bar, 1939; practice in Glencoe, 1939-42, Mankato, 1945-63; sec. to chief justice Minn. Supreme Ct., 1938-40, asso. justice, now chief justice; spl. agt. FBI, 1942-45. Mem. Minn. Bd. Law Examiners, 1956-62, 70-73, Minn. Bd. Tax Appeals, 1961-63. Mem. Minn. Ho. of Reps., 1945-49; trustee Coll. St. Thomas, 1964-73. Fellow Am. Coll. Trial Law Lawyers, Internat. Coll. Trial Lawyers, Am. Bar Found.; mem. Am., Minn. bar assns., Am. Judicature Soc., Inst. Jud. Adminstrn., Conf. Chief Justices U.S. (chmn. 1980-81), U. Minn. Alumni Assn. (pres. 1979-80). Office: Minn Supreme Ct 230 State Capitol Saint Paul MN 55155

SHERE, DENNIS, publisher; b. Cleve., Nov. 29, 1940; s. William and Susan (Luskay) S.; B.S. in Journalism, Ohio U., 1963, M.S. in Journalism 1964; m. Maureen Jones, Sept. 4, 1965; children—Rebecca Lynn, David Matthew, Stephen Andrew. Staff writer Dayton (Ohio) Daily News, 1966-69; asst. prof. Sch. Journalism Bowling Green (Ohio) State U., 1969-70; fin. editor Detroit News, 1970-72, city editor, 1973-75; editor Dayton Jour. Herald, 1975-80; publisher, Springfield Newspapers Inc., 1980—. Served with AUS, 1964-66. Mem. Sigma Alpha Epsilon, Omicron Delta Kappa. Home: 606 Westchester Pk Dr Springfield OH 45504

SHERIDAN, KIM ALAN, computer software co. exec.; b. Lima, Ohio, Jan. 24, 1948; s. Charles Joseph and Jayn Elizabeth (Kassner) S.; B.S. in Mktg., U. Ariz., 1970; M.B.A. in Quantitative Analysis, U. Cin., 1971; m. Mary Margaret Gray, July 17, 1970; children—Nathan, Ben, Siovhan, Otto, Stephanie. Salesman, Sears, Roebuck and Co., 1969-70; mem. customer service staff Sheridan Assos., Cin., 1970-73, div. v.p., 1973-76; pres. Interactive Info. Systems Inc., Cin., 1976—. Bd. dirs. Cath. Big Bros., 1973-79. Mem. Am. Inst. Decision Scis., Assn. Data Processing Services Orgn. Roman Catholic. Home: 9475 Fallson Ct Cincinnati OH 45242 Office: IIS Inc 10 Knollcrest Dr Cincinnati OH 45237

SHERIDAN, SISTER MARY FLORIANNE, nursing sch. adminstr.; b. Hymera, Ind., Dec. 27, 1908; d. William Sherman and Della May (Bledsoe) Sheridan; R.N., St. Anthony Hosp. Sch. Nursing, Terre Haute, Ind., 1938; certificate primary edn. Ind. State Tchrs. Coll., 1928, B.S., 1941; postgrad. DePaul U., 1948-49, M.S., 1954; postgrad. St. Louis U., summers 1953, 54. Elementary tchr. Terre Haute, Ind., 1929-35; nursing arts instr. St. Anthony Hosp. Sch. Nursing, Terre Haute, 1939-42; clin. instr. med., surg. nursing St. Francis Sch. Nursing, Evanston, Ill., 1942-44; joined Order of St. Francis, 1944; dir. nursing, dir. Sch. Nursing, St. Margaret Hosp., Hammond, Ind., 1946-58; dir. Sch. Nursing, St. Elizabeth Hosp., Lafayette, Ind., 1958—. Trustee St. Francis Coll., Fort Wayne, Ind., 1957—. Mem. Am., Ind. nurses assns., Nat., Ind. (v.p. 1957-60) leagues for nursing, Ind. Conf. Cath. Schs. Nursing (pres. 1964—), Nat. Council Cath. Nurses, Cath. Audio-Visual Edn. Assn., Ind. Cath. Hosp. Assn. (pres. 1965-66). Home: St Francis Convent Mount Alverno Mishawaka IN 46544 Office: 1508 Tippecanoe St Lafayette IN 47904 also St Francis Hosp Center 1600 Albany St Beech Grove IN 46107

SHERIDAN, WILLIAM COCKBURN RUSSELL, bishop; b. N.Y.C., Mar. 25, 1917; s. John Russell Fortesque and Gertrude Magdalene (Hurley) S.; A.B., Carroll Coll., 1939; M.Div., Nashotah House Theol. Sem., 1942, D.D., 1966; certificate St. Mary's Grad. Sch. Theology, 1966; S.T.M., Nashotah House Theol. Sem., 1968; m. Rudith Treder, Nov. 13, 1943; children—Elizabeth Sheridan Beeler, Margaret Sheridan Wilson, Mary Sheridan Janda, Peter, Stephen. Ordained deacon and priest Episcopal Ch., 1943; asst. priest St. Paul's Ch., Chgo., 1943-44; rector Gethsemane Ch., Marion, Ind., 1944-47, St. Thomas's Ch., Plymouth, Ind., 1947-72; bishop of Episcopal Diocese of No. Ind., 1972—. Vice pres. bd. trustees Nashotah House Theol. Sem.; pres. bd. trustees Howe (Ind.) Mil. Sch. Author: Journey to Priesthood, 1952; Between Catholics, 1966. Home: 2502 S Twyckenham Dr South Bend IN 46614 Office: 117 N Lafayette Blvd South Bend IN 46601

SHERIFF, ALFRED PEARSON, III, assn. exec.; b. Cadiz, O., July 2, 1927; s. Alfred P. and Edyth (Aiken) S.; B.A., Washington and Jefferson Coll., 1949; LL.B., Western Res. U., 1955; J.D., Case-Western Res. U., 1968; m. Margaret Ann Edwards, Aug. 2, 1967; children—Richard A., Thomas E., David G., Nancy G. Admitted to Ohio bar, 1956; with trust devel. div. Central Nat. Bank, Cleve., 1955-61; asst. to exec. v.p. Delta Tau Delta, Indpls., 1961-65, exec. v.p., 1965—. Bd. govs. Western Res. Sch. Law, 1960; mem. Washington and Jefferson Coll. Devel. Council, 1968-70; mem. Bd. Police Commrs., 1975-78; v.p. bd. dirs. Symphony Orch., 1981-82. Mem. Am., Ohio, Cleve. bar assns., Am. Soc. Assn. Execs., Frat. Execs. Assn. (pres. 1975-76), Newcomen Soc., Summit Soc. N. Am., Delta Tau Delta, Phi Alpha Delta. Republican. Presbyn. Mason (K.T., Shriner), Rotarian. Club: Indianapolis Athletic. Contbr. articles to mags. Home: 11825 Rolling Springs Dr Carmel IN 46032 Office: Suite 110 4740 Kingsway Dr Indianapolis IN 46205

SHERMAN, DAVID SOLTZ, JR., wholesale liquor and wine exec.; b. Little Rock, June 8, 1928; s. David Soltz and Dorothy (Cone) S.; B.B.A. in Mktg., Tulane U., 1951; children—David Soltz, III, Richard Keil. With Strauss Distbrs., Inc., Little Rock, to 1946; pres. Mid Continent Distbrs., Kansas City, Mo., 1951—, Paramount Liquor Co., St. Louis, 1955—, St. Louis Liquor Co., 1967—; chmn. bd. David Sherman Corp., 1974—. Active City of Hope. Named Disting. Wholesaler of Year, Time mag., 1980; recipient Spirit of Life award City of Hope, 1981. Mem. Mo. Wine and Spirits Assn. (pres.), Wine and Spirits Wholesalers Am., St. Louis Regional Commerce and Growth Assn. Jewish. Clubs: Westwood Country; Frontenac Racquet. Office: 5050 Kemper Ave Saint Louis MO 63139

SHERMAN, EVERETT GEORGE, mfg. co. exec.; b. Mpls., Oct. 14, 1918; s. Everett Benner and Esther Natalie (Swanson) S.; B.B.A., U. Minn., 1941; m. Evelyn I. Dahl, Oct. 21, 1944; children—James, Christie. Compensation and employee benefits mgr. Gen. Mills Inc., Mpls., 1946-60; mgr. compensation planning Honeywell Inc., Mpls., 1960-68, mgr. employee benefits, 1968-76, mgr. benefit adminstrn., 1976—. Bd. dirs. Abbott-Northwestern Hosp., Sister Kenny Inst.; sr. warden Episcopal Ch.; fund raising chmn. YMCA, Mpls. Served with AUS, 1941-46. Decorated Purple Heart, Silver Star. Mem. Nat. Council Employee Benefits (pres.), NAM (chmn. employee benefits steering com.); Alpha Delta Phi. Republican. Contbr. chpt. to Handbook of Modern Personnel Administration. Home: 16401 Canterbury Dr Minnetonka MN 55343 Office: Honeywell Plaza Minneapolis MN 55408

SHERMAN, HUNTER B., coll. dean; b. Long Beach, Calif., Aug. 30, 1943; s. Hunter B. and Mary Rawls (French) S.; B.A., Calif. State U., Long Beach, 1965; postgrad. Bapt. Bible Coll., 1965-66; M.Div., Talbot Theol. Sem., 1970; Ph.D., Calif. Grad. Sch. Theology, 1976; m. Louisa Ann Stahl, June 27, 1964; children—Whitnae Nicolle, Garrett Hunter. Prof., Bapt. Bible Coll., Springfield, Mo., 1970-75, chmn. Bible dept., 1975-78, acad. dean, 1979—. Mem. Soc. Bibl. Lit., Am. Assn. Collegiate Registrars, Am. Schs. Oriental Research, Israel Exploration Soc., Oriental Inst. U. Chgo. Author: Must Babylon Be Rebuilt, 1970; The Biblical Concept of Babylon, 1976. Recipient Audrey Talbot Meml. award Talbot Theol. Sem., 1970. Office: 628 E Kearney St Springfield MO 65802

SHERMAN, KENNETH IRA, elec. engr.; b. Festus, Mo., Apr. 29, 1917; s. Russell Ira and Vergie Ellen (Davis) S.; B.S.E.E., Mo. Sch. Mines and Metallurgy, 1942; postgrad. Harvard U., Mass. Inst. Tech., 1943, St. Louis U., 1958; m. Icie Roberta Gautney, Mar. 20, 1959; children—Randall Dean, Lynden Craig. Asst. research engr. McDonnell Aircraft Co., St. Louis, 1946-48, sr. electronics group engr., 1959-70; radar engr. Emerson Electric Co., St. Louis, 1948-59; elec. engr. River Cement Co., Festus, 1970-79, St. Joe Lead Co., Herculaneum, Mo., 1979—. Served to lt. (s.g.) USNR, 1943-46. Mem. IEEE (sr. mem.), Instrument Soc. Am. (sr. mem.). Republican. Baptist. Co-author chpt. on pulse generators in electronics book. Home: Route 2 Box 38 Abbey Rd Pevely MO 63070 Office: Saint Joe Lead Co Herculaneum MO

SHERMAN, PATRICIA ANN, educator; b. Winona, Minn., Oct. 3, 1942; d. Frederick D. and Joye E. (Baylon) S.; B.S. (Josephene Flagg scholar), Winona State U., 1964; M.A., U. Iowa, 1968, Ph.D., 1972. Asst. tennis instr. Winona Park Recreation Dept., summer, 1957, tennis instr., 1958-66; instr. girls phys. edn., health and first aid North High Sch., Sheboygan, Wis., 1964-65, chairperson women's dept. phys. edn., 1965-66; grad. asst. U. Iowa, Iowa City, 1966-67, instr. phys. edn., 1967-72, coach women's tennis, 1967-72; asst. prof. phys. edn. Gustavus Adolphus Coll., St. Peter, Minn., 1972-73, coach tennis, volleyball and basketball, 1972-73; asst. prof. phys. Edn. U. Wis., River Falls, 1973-79, coach tennis, basketball, 1973-79, coach volleyball, 1973-76; asst. prof. phys. edn., coach basketball and tennis Winona State U., 1979-81; clinician tennis workshops, Iowa, Minn., 1967-77. Mem. AAHPER and Dance, Minn. Assn. for Health, Phys. Edn., Recreation and Dance, AAUP, Nat. Assn. Girls and Women in Sport (chairperson tennis guide com. 1974-76, asso. guide coordinator 1976-77, guide coordinator 1977-78), U.S. Tennis Assn., NEA, Minn. Edn. Assn., Winona State U. Alumni Assn., Iowa Alumni Assn., Kappa Delta Pi, Pi Lambda Theta. Roman Catholic. Contbr. articles on tennis to profl. publs.; ranked 2d in women's singles and doubles right-handed Northwestern Women's Tennis Assn., 1968, 69, ranked 1st in women's 35 left-handed; singles and doubles in Northwestern Tennis Assn. for 1978 and singles in 1980 season, undefeated in women's 35 singles and doubles. Home: 675 W Sarnia St Apt 308 Winona MN 55987

SHERMAN, RALPH H., JR., mktg. exec.; b. St. Louis, July 26, 1949; s. Ralph H. and Maureen L. (Downey) S.; B.Journalism, U. Mo., 1971. Regional advt. mgr., creative services mgr. The 7UP Co., world hdqrs., St. Louis, 1971-76; account exec., account supr. Gardner Advt. Co., St. Louis, 1976-79; group mktg. mgr. Citicorp Person to Person, Creve Coeur, Mo., 1979—, staff v.p. asset products, 1980—. Recipient Ad Age Merit award for strategic mktg., 1976; Merit award Addy Competition, 1977; TV-Clio award, 1978. Mem. Am. Mktg. Assn. Club: Direct Mktg. Home: 7200 Stanford Saint Louis MO 63130 Office: 11475 Olde Cabin Rd Saint Louis MO 63141

SHERMAN, ROGER WALTER, city ofcl.; b. Watertown, Wis., July 10, 1943; s. Ralph Walter and Florence Josephine (Krahn) S.; student Calif. State U., 1976; m. Beverly Ann Rauber, Oct. 6, 1962; children—Tricia Lyn, Ryan Wade. Asst. supt. Ft. Atkinson (Wis.) Water Dept., 1966-74; supt. Ft. Atkinson Water Pollution Control Center, 1974—. Vol., Ft. Atkinson Fire Dept., 1968—, pres., 1974; dir., v.p. Wis. Wastewater Works Conf., 1977—, pres.-elect, 1981, pres., 1982; bd. mem. vocat. tech. adult edn. and operator apprentice tng. Mem. sch. bd. Ft. Atkinson Sch. Dist., 1980—, treas., 1981. Named Jefferson County Employer of the Year, Assn. Retarded Citizens of Wis., 1976; Wis. Wastewater Operator of the Year, Wis. Wastewater Operators Conf., 1977; cert. emergency med. tech. Mem. Nat. Water Pollution Control Fedn., Central States Water Pollution Control Fedn., Wis. Wastewater Operators Conf. (membership award 1979, 80), Am. Waterworks Assn. Inventor sludge judge sampler, 1976. Home: 715 W Sherman Ave Fort Atkinson WI 53538 Office: 101 N Main St Fort Atkinson WI 53538

SHERMAN, WILLIAM SCOTT, constrn. co. exec.; b. Camp Crook, S.D., June 3, 1921; s. Henry William and Martha Cinderella (Scott) S.; student N.D. State U., 1943-44; B.S., U. N.D., 1947; m. Mildred Lorraine Quam, Mar. 20, 1948; children—Douglas, Gerald, Roger, David. Owner, Sherman Plumbing & Heating, West Fargo, N.D., 1947-61; partner S.W. Fargo Excavating Co., West Fargo, 1950-53; owner Sheyenne Valley Farm, West Fargo, 1960—; pres. Sherman, Inc., Fargo, 1961—, also dir.; pres. Tourismo De Las Montaãnas, Monterrrey, Mex., 1980—; dir., v.p. West Fargo Holding Co. Served with U.S. Army, 1940-43. Mem. Nat. Plumbing and Heating Contractors, N.D. Master Plumbers Assn., N.D. Plumbing, Heating and Cooling Contractors, Am. Legion, V.F.W., DAV, Blue Key. Republican. Lutheran. Clubs: Elks, Eagles, Lions. Home: Route 2 Fargo ND 58102 Office: Sherman Inc 1005 Main Ave E West Fargo ND 58078

SHERRY, SCOTT ALLAN, cable industry cons.; b. Canton, Ohio, Apr. 13, 1948; s. Henry Allan and Betty Louise (Burris) S.; student Muskingum Coll., 1966-69; B.A., Ohio U., 1974; m. Candice Elaine Burcham, Oct. 14, 1977; 1 dau., Alexandra. Ednl. researcher Pa. Advancement Sch., Phila., 1970-71; supr. social services Ohio Youth Commn., 1972-76; sr. copywriter Angeletti, Winkler & Heller, Columbus, Ohio, 1976-77; research asso. Celeste for Gov., 1978; dir. Sherry & Assos., Columbus, 1979-80; dir. mktg. Cable Mktg. Mgmt., Columbus, 1980—; film critic Columbus Dispatch, 1977-78. Cons. Nat. Right-to-Life. Mem. Columbus Advt. Fedn. Home: 332 E Plum St Westerville OH 43081 Office: 5900 Roche Dr Columbus OH 43229

SHERWAN, ROY GLENN, travel agy. exec.; b. St. Louis, Aug. 19, 1930; s. August Carl and Florence (Worth) S.; student Spencerian Coll., Milw., 1949; m. Carol Lee Sorenson, Nov. 10, 1951; children—Scott, Kimberly. Adminstrv. asst. Wis. N.G., Whitefish Bay, 1949-50; teller Home Savs. Bank, Milw., 1951-52; sales corr. Centralab div. Globe Union Co., Milw., 1952-54; sales rep. Am. Airlines, Milw. and Chgo., 1954-70; pres. 1st Maine Travel Agy., Des Plaines, Ill., 1970—. Mem. United Air Lines Travel Agts. Council, Eastern Air Lines Travel Agts. Adv. Bd., Norwegian Caribbean Lines Agts. Council. Served to capt. U.S. Army, 1951-52, 61-62. Mem. Des Plaines C. of C., Am. Soc. Travel Agts., Assn. Bank Travel Burs., Chgo. Bon Vivants, Pacific Area Travel Assn., Chinese Passenger Club Chgo. Presbyterian. Clubs: Elks, Bus. Breakfast (pres. 1976), Rotary (dir. Des Plaines 1978, 79-80). Home: 837 Munroe Circle Des Plaines IL 60016 Office: 728 Lee St Des Plaines IL 60016

SHERWIN, LARRY EDWARD, chiropractor; b. White Hall, Ill., May 9, 1945; s. Perry Edward and Mabel Louise (Parks) S.; D.C., Nat. Coll. Chiropractic, Lombard, Ill., 1967; postgrad. Minn. Basci Sci. Inst., 1971; m. Debra Jean Scoggins, Oct. 2, 1971; children—Jonathan Lawrence, Michelle Renee, Jeffrey Matthew, Jennifer Lynette. Practice chiropractics, Winchester, Ill., 1967—. Real estate broker, Winchester, 1975—; owner farm, White Hall, Ill., 1966—. Served with AUS, 1969-70; Vietnam. Mem. Mo., Ky. State, Am. chiropractic assns., Ill. Chiropractic Soc., Ill. Pure Water Soc., Soil and Health Found., Nat. Health Fedn., Greene County Health Improvement Assn., Sigma Phi Kappa. Baptist. Clubs: Kiwanis, Elks. Home: Rural Route 2 Whitehall IL 62092 Office: 32 1/2 S Main St Winchester IL 62694

SHERWOOD, JAMES MICHAEL, tool mfg. co. exec.; b. New Castle, Ind., Sept. 27, 1948; s. Everett Russell and Dorothy Jean (Jackson) S.; m. Nanette Faye Harris, Jan. 5, 1980; 1 stepson, Kyle Dennis. Sports editor Kettering-Oakwood Times, Kettering, Ohio, 1968-69; asst. sports editor Palladium-Item, Richmond, Ind., 1970-71, Courier Tribune, Bloomington, Ind., 1971-72; editor, co-publisher Graphic Publications, Greenville, Ohio, 1972-75; mgr. mktg. services, mgr. sales promotion, nat. sales mgr., div. mgr., dir. sales devel. Shopsmith, Inc., Vandalia, Ohio, 1975-81; dir. mktg. BenchMark Tool Co., Jefferson City, Mo., 1981—. Office: 2601 Industrial Dr Jefferson City MO 65101

SHERWOOD, ORVAL RAY, mortician; b. Tower Hill, Ill., Mar. 21, 1916; s. Ben R. and Ocla Dell (Finks) S.; student Ill. Wesleyan U., Bloomington, 1935; grad. Coll. Mortuary Sci., St. Louis, 1939; m. Irene C. Cranmer, Dec. 24, 1937; 1 dau., Orva Jeanne Sherwood Christian. Mem. staff Donnell Funeral Home, Greenville, Ill., 1942-54, Williamson Funeral Home, Jacksonville, Ill., 1954-59; propr. Sherwood Funeral Home (name now Sherwood-Seitz Funeral Homes), Assumption, Ill., 1959-80, Moweaqua, Ill., 1970-80, asso., 1980—. Mem. Ill. Funeral Dirs. Assn. (past dist. pres.). Democrat. Methodist. Clubs: Christian County Shriners (past pres.); Assumption Rotary (past pres.; Paul Harris fellow 1977, gov. dist. 649). Home: 207 N Locust St Assumption IL 62510 Office: 101 S Walnut St Assumption IL 62510

SHERWOOD, STEPHANIE JAN WANNER, banker; b. Berwyn, Ill., July 7, 1944; d. Thomas Lewis and Janet Mae (Grissinger) Wanner; B.J., U. Mo., 1967; children—Leslie Christine, Jennifer Lynn, Stuart Miles. Staff writer Springfield (Mo.) Newspapers, Inc., 1974-78; exec. dir. Downtown Springfield Assn., 1978-79; exec. editor Springfield mag., 1979; mktg.-communications officer Boatmen's Union Nat. Bank, Springfield, 1979—. Bd. dirs. Downtown Springfield Assn.; mem. Citizens Adv. Com. for Fed. Community Devel. Funding, 1979-80; charter mem. Springfield Council of Arts; mem. Springfield Sesquicentennial Com., 1979; judge Springfield Sesquicentennial Parade, 1979; bd. dirs., chmn. public relations Dogwood Trails council Girl Scouts U.S.A., 1978—. Mem. Nat. Assn. Bank Women, Bank Mktg. Assn., Nat. Fedn. Press Women, Mo. Press Women, LWV, C. of C. (bd. dirs. women's div.). Home: 910 E University Springfield MO 65807 Office: Boatmen's Union Nat Bank 117 Park Central Square Springfield MO 65805

SHETH, JASHWANTLAL S., cosmetics co. exec.; b. Padra, India, July 30, 1939; s. Shankerlal P. and Champaben S. (Shah) S.; came to U.S., 1970; B.S. with honors, M.S. U., Baroda, India, 1960, M.S., 1962; diploma in business La Salle Extension U., 1973; m. Hasumati P. Parikh, May 10, 1963; children—Trusha, Gopali and Shefali (twins). Sr. chemist Sara Merck, Ltd., Baroda, India, 1963-70; various supervisory-mgmt. positions with drugs and cosmetics firms, U.S., 1970-73; quality assurance mgr. Johnson Products Co., Chgo., 1973-79, dir. tech. ops., 1975—. Mem. Am. Inst. Chemists, Am. Soc. Cosmetic Chemists. Office: 8522 S Lafayette St Chicago IL 60620

SHEVERBUSH, ROBERT L., univ. adminstr.; b. Wray, Colo., Aug. 5, 1935; s. Robert L. and Emma V. (Gerber) S.; B.A., U. Colo., 1957; M.A., U. No. Colo., 1960, Ed.D., 1967; m. Gladys Joan Kremers, Aug. 22, 1964; children—Robert L., William A., John James. Dir. research, head counseling dept. Colorado Springs (Colo.) Pub. Schs., 1960-68; asst. prof. Central Mo. State U., Warrensburg, 1968-70; asso. dean counseling services U. Ill. Med. Center, Chgo., 1970-76; prof. psychology, chmn. dept. psychology and counseling Pittsburg (Kans.) State U., 1976—; Fulbright exchange prof., 1979-80. Mem. Am., Kans. psychol. assns. Home: Route 4 Box 161B Pittsburg KS 66762 Office: Room 112 Hughes Hall Pittsburg State U Pittsburg KS 66762

SHEWARD, CLARENCE WILLIAM, gaseous diffusion co. exec.; b. Jackson County, Ohio, Feb. 6, 1942; s. Delmar Jay and Mildred Alice (Rapp) S.; B.S., U.S. Air Force Acad., 1964; M.B.A., Capital U., 1980; m. Ann Carlisle, June 4, 1965; children—Heather Lynn, Bethany Dawn. Commd. 2d lt. U.S. Air Force, 1960, advanced through grades to capt., 1972, resigned, 1972; plant engr. Jackson Corp. (Ohio), 1972-76; div. safety coordinator Goodyear Atomic Corp., Piketon, Ohio, 1976-78, supr. maint. services, 1979—; tchr. Rio Grande (Ohio) Community Coll., 1980—; mem. adv. bd., Buckeye Hills Vocational Center, 1976-78; deacon local Presbyterian Ch. Decorated D.F.C. with 2 oak leaf clusters, Air medal with 9 oak leaf clusters. Mem. Improvement Inst., Am. Assn. M.B.A. Execs., Assn. Grads. U.S. Air Force Acad. Republican. Club: Lions. Home: Route 3 Box 52B Jackson OH 45640 Office: PO Box 628 Piketon OH 45331

SHIBLEY, FREDERIC JAMILE, glass co. mgr.; b. Copperhill, Tenn., May 7, 1946; s. George Toufic and Adele (George) S.; B.S. cum laude in Marketing, U. Tenn., 1968; m. Andrea Mannal Haug, Sept. 27, 1969; 1 son, Robert Liggett. Sales trainee Owens Corning Fiberglas, Raleigh, N.C., Miami, Fla., 1968-69, salesman, Cleve., 1969-72, salesman, Chgo., 1973-74, nat. marketing mgr., Toledo, 1974-77, mgr. shingle mktg. sect., 1977-78, product line mgr. residential roofing, 1978-79, product and facilities devel. mgr. residential roofing, 1979-80, product and market mgr., residential roofing, 1980—; asst. mgr. Shibley's Fabric Center, Dayton, Tenn., 1972-73. Scoutmaster, Boy Scouts Am., Dayton Tenn., 1973; advisor Jr. Achievement, Toledo, 1978-80. Mem. Asphalt Roofing Mfrs. Assn. (residential roofing com. 1980—), Phi Sigma Kappa, Phi Kappa Phi, Delta Sigma Pi, Beta Gamma Sigma. Home: 4624 Kathy Lane Toledo OH 43623 Office: Owens Corning Fiberglas Corp 1 Levis Sq Toledo OH 43659

SHIDELER, SHIRLEY ANN WILLIAMS, lawyer; b. Mishawaka, Ind., July 9, 1930; d. William Harmon and Lois Wilma (Koch) Williams; LL.B., Ind. U., 1964; 1 dau., Gail Shideler Frye. Legal sec. Barnes, Hickam, Pantzer & Boyd, Indpls., 1953-63; admitted to Ind. bar, 1964; practiced in Indpls., 1964—; asso. firm Barnes, Hickam, Pantzer, & Boyd, 1963-70, partner, 1971—. Active fund drives Indpls. Symphony, 1968—, Indpls. Mus. Art, 1969-79; bd. dirs. bus. unit gals Indpls. Mus. Art, 1973-80. Fellow Am. Coll. Probate Council; mem. Am., Ind. (sec. 1975-76, chmn. probate, trust and real property sect.), Indpls. (bd. mgrs. 1968-72, v.p. charge affairs 1972), 7th Circuit bar assns., Ind. Bar Found. (bd. mgrs. 1980—, sec. 1981-82), Indpls. Bar Found. (bd. mgrs. 1970—, sec. 1972-77), Estate Planning Council. Club: Woman's Rotary (pres. 1969-71, dir. 1968-79) (Indpls.). Home: 5150 Hawthorne Dr Indianapolis IN 46226 Office: 1313 Merchants Bank Bldg Indianapolis IN 46204

SHIDLER, JON AULDIN, advt. exec.; b. Chgo., Mar. 29, 1940; s. Glenn Auldin and Ethel Helena (Salchow) S.; B.S. in Journalism, So. Ill. U., 1962, postgrad., 1962-63; M.S.M.C. with honors, Roosevelt U., 1979; m. Lynne Susan Porter, Apr. 18, 1964; 1 dau., Julie Eileen. Retail advt. copywriter Sears Co., Chgo., 1964-65, copywriter trainer/spl. assignments, 1966, staff asst., 1967, TV prodn. mgr., 1968-70, asst. dir. nat. broadcast services, 1970-80; account supr. Ross Roy, Inc., advt. agy., Detroit, 1980—; Sears rep. Radio Advt. Bur. Panel, Washington, 1976; Sears advt. rep. Olympics, Munich, 1972, Montreal, 1976; Sears dir. AAU-Sears Jr. Olympics TV Program, 1977-79. Active Gen. Woods Boys Club, 1965-66, Heart Fund, 1967, Sears YMCA, 1964-66, Crusade of Mercy, 1977, others. Mem. Chgo. Advt. Club, Jaycees (pres. Glen Ellyn 1974-75, chief ambassador Ill. 1977-78, senator 1978), Beta Gamma Sigma. Presbyterian. Office: Ross Roy Inc 2751 E Jefferson Ave Detroit MI 48207

SHIELDS, JAMES CRAIG, ins. co. exec.; b. Noblesville, Ind., June 1, 1942; s. Woodrow Wilson and Margert Ann (Driver) S.; student Taylor U., 1960-62; B.A., Anderson Coll., 1966; m. Linda R. Roudebush, June 14, 1963; children—Michael Todd, Kelly Ann, Christina Michelle. Jr. cost acct. Buehler Corp., Indpls., 1966-68, sr. cost acct., 1968-70; staff auditor Peat, Marwick & Mitchell & Co., Indpls., 1970-71; staff acct. Am. United Life Ins. Co., Indpls., 1971, supr. treasury dept., 1971-77, asst. treas., 1977—; exec. adv. for Jr. Achievement Cos. sponsored by Am. United Life Ins. Co., 1976-78. Treas., Forest Hill Sch. Parent-Tchr. Orgn., Noblesville, Ind., 1977-79; mem. enterprise fundraising team United Way Greater Indpls., 1979; mem. acctg. curriculum adv. Com. J. Everett Light Career Center Vocat. Sch., 1979—; trustee Noblesville Public Sch. Bd., 1980—; state judge speech contestants Office Edn. Assn. Ind., 1980. Named to Outstanding Young Men Am., U.S. Jaycees, 1977. Mem. Ind. C.P.A. Soc., Am. Inst. C.P.A.'s, Ind. Sch. Bds. Assn., Noblesville Jaycees (treas. 1969-70, Outstanding Jaycee 1970). Republican. Club: Sertoma (dir. club 1977-78). Home: 103 Charliewood Ct Noblesville IN 46060 Office: 1 W 26th St Indianapolis IN 46208

SHIELDS, JAMES JOSEPH, broadcasting co. exec.; b. Omaha, Jan. 20, 1949; s. Glenn Anthony and Henrietta Marie (Cordova) S.; B.S., U. Nebr., 1971; m. Treca Ann Johnston, July 1, 1978; children—John S., Chadwick Bartholomew. Regional sales mgr. Sta. WOW, Omaha, 1971-78; v.p., gen. mgr. stas. KMNS/KSEZ, Sioux City, Iowa, 1978—; v.p., gen. mgr. Radio Sentry Broadcasting, Inc., 1978—. Bd. dirs. Downtown Mchts. Assn., 1980-81. Mem. Nat. Assn. Broadcasters, Radio Advt. Bur., Sioux City C. of C. Roman Catholic. Club: Sioux City Ad (pres. 1980—). Home: 3717 Lindenwood Sioux City IA 51104 Office: Sentry Broadcasting Inc 901 Stueben St Sioux City IA 51101

SHIELDS, JAMES WESLEY, sch. counselor; b. Evansville, Ind., Dec. 18, 1940; s. James West and Dora Buelah (Griffin) S.; B.S., Ind. State U., 1965, M.S., 1967; guidance counselor certification U. Evansville, 1971; m. Lee Ann Sturgeon, Mar. 26, 1965; 1 son, Matthew James. Tchr. social studies Evansville-Vanderburgh Sch. Corp., 1965-71, tchr.-counselor, 1971-73, spl. concerns counselor, 1974—; real estate broker, 1977—. Mem. Evansville Elem. Social Studies Adv. Council, 1967-69. Bd. dirs. Evansville Assn. for Retarded Citizens, 1978—, 4th Ann. Leadership Evansville Class, 1979-80; study group facilitator Leadership Evansville, 1980-81; mem. adminstrv. bd. Trinity Methodist Ch., 1982—. Served with U.S. Army, 1958-61. Recipient Ind. Disting. Sec. award Ind. State Optimist Clubs, 1973. Mem. Counselor Caucus of Evansville, NEA, Am. Personnel and Guidance Assn., Ind. Tchrs. Assn., Evansville Tchrs. Assn., Southwestern Ind. Personnel and Guidance Assn. (pres. 1981-82), Ind. Personnel and Guidance Assn. (exec. council 1981-82), Pari-Mutuel Clks. Union Ky., Leadership Evansville Alumni Assn. (1st v.p. 1980-81), Phi Delta Kappa, Ind. State U. Alumni Assn. Clubs: Masons, Shriners, Scottish Rite, Optimist (dir. 1973-74) (Evansville). Home: 6600 E Chestnut St Evansville IN 47715 Office: 800 S Evans Ave Evansville IN 47713

SHIELDS, JOHN AUGUSTUS, retail food co. exec.; b. Atlanta, May 19, 1943; s. John Augustus and Christine (Thiesen) S.; B.B.A. with distinction, Emory U., 1964; M.B.A. (Love fellow), Harvard U., 1966; m. Laura Watts DeCamp, Sept. 25, 1975; 1 dau., Lisa Alden. With Jewel Co., Inc., 1966—, v.p. store ops. Midwest region Jewel Food Stores, Melrose Park, Ill., 1975-78, v.p. produce and floral, 1978-80, v.p. sales and advt., 1980—. Dir., Community Renewal Soc. Mem. Produce Mktg. Assn. (dir., div. chmn.). Clubs: Econ., Racquet, Glen View, Anglers, Trout Unlimited (dir.). Office: 1955 W North Ave Melrose Park IL 60160

SHIER, WALTER LEE, oil co. exec.; b. Amlin, Ohio, Dec. 2, 1937; s. Carl Henry and Helen Marie (Schacherbauer) S.; student Fla. Profl. Acad., 1973-75; m. Carol Ann Bausch, Nov. 14, 1958; children—Timothy, Deborah, Leann. Foreman, Westinghouse Corp., Columbus, Ohio, 1962-63; agt. Bankers Life Ins. Co., Columbus, 1963-64; asst. store mgr. Zayre Corp., 1964-71, Topps & Rinks Dept. Store, Columbus, 1971-72; truck driver to sec.-treas., stock holder Rowling & Michaels, Inc., Plain City, Ohio, 1972—. Served with USNR, 1955-57. Recipient cert. of achievement Columbus Jr. C. of C., 1953, Service award Zayre Corp., 1969, cert. of service Little League Baseball, 1965. Mem. Ohio Petroleum Marketers Assn. Lutheran. Home: 7353 Wells Rd Plain City OH 43064 Office: 9279 Railroad St Plain City OH 43064

SHIFFLETT, JAMES EDWARD, JR., technol. engr.; b. Charlottesville, Va., July 23, 1950; s. James Edward and Joyce Lee (Sites) S.; B.S., U. Va., 1972; M.S., Princeton U., 1974; postgrad. student Purdue U., 1974-75; M.B.A., Washington U., 1980. Research asst. U. Va., summer 1971; research asst. Princeton U., 1972-74; teaching asst. Purdue U., 1974-75; engr. in tech. McDonnell Aircraft Co., McDonnell Douglas Corp., St. Louis, 1975—. Mem. Am. Mgmt. Assn., Common Cause (coordinator 1976); Inst. Mgmt. Scis., Soc. Logistics Engrs., Ops. Research Soc. Am. Baptist. Club: Toastmasters. Home: 605 US Route 250 By-Pass Charlottesville VA 22901 also 1616 Fairview Saint Louis MO 63132 Office: PO Box 516 Saint Louis MO 63044

SHIH, CHIA HSIN, elec. power engr., plasma physicist; b. Peking, China, Mar. 8, 1941; s. Shao and Hen Feng (Wen) S.; came to U.S., 1966, naturalized, 1977; B.S., Nat. Taiwan U., 1963; M.S., U. Toronto, 1966; Ph.D., Poly Inst. Bklyn., 1970; m. Grendy P. Wang, Oct. 10, 1970; children—Willard C., Loren C. Asst. engr. Stanford Linear Accelerator Center, summer 1967; engr., sr. engr. Am. Electric Power Service Corp., 1970, 75-78, head elec. research, N.Y.C., now Columbus, Ohio, 1978—; lectr. math. dept. Chinese Naval Acad.; adj. lectr. elec. engring. dept. CCNY; Nat. Research Council Can. research asst. Mem. IEEE (sr.), Sigma Xi. Contbr. chpts. to Handbook of Electrical and Computer Engineering, articles to engring. jours. Office: AEP 180 E Broad St Columbus OH 43215

SHIMMENS, PATRICIA MARIE, fed. govt. ofcl.; b. Sault Ste. Marie, Mich., Sept. 25, 1947; d. Rexford Alexander and Theresa Marie (Pretty) Briggs; student Lake Superior Coll., part-time 1967-68, 76-77, 79-80; m. Robert J. Shimmens, Sept. 23, 1977; children by previous marriage—Christinia M. Peltier, Robert A. Peltier II. Stenographer, State's Atty.'s Office for Prince George County, Md., 1968-70; legal sec. Richard W. Sterling, Belleville, Ill., 1971-72, Coates & Kline, Sault Ste. Marie, 1972-73; exec. sec. City of Sault Ste. Marie, 1973-75; Title VI coordinator Eastern Upper Peninsula Employment and Tng. Consortium, CETA, Sault Ste Marie, 1975, employment specialist, 1975-76, employment and tng. counselor, 1976-77, intake dept. head, 1977-79, ind. monitor, 1979—; mem. Job Devel. Council, Sault Ste. Marie, 1978-79. Baptist. Club: Bowating Bus. and Profl. Women (co-chmn. Bay Cliff auction 1981, 82, sec. 1982). Home: 422 Carrie St Sault Sault Sainte Marie MI 49783 Office: Eastern Upper Peninsula Employment and Tng Consortium PO Box 717 Sault Sainte Marie MI 49783

SHINDLE, WILLIAM RICHARD, musicologist; b. Van Orin, Ill., Nov. 2, 1930; s. Ira William and Elsie Virginia (Showalter) S.; Mus.B., Ill. Wesleyan U., 1959; Mus.M., Ind. U., 1963, dissertation year fellow, 1965-66, Ph.D., 1970. Music librarian State U. N.Y., Binghamton, 1964-65; mem. faculty Sch. Music, Kent (Ohio) State U., 1966—, asso. prof. musicology, 1972—, summer fellow, 1974. Served with USN, 1951-55. Mem. Am. Musicol. Soc., Renaissance Soc. Am., Pa. German Soc. Author articles; editor, transcriber keyboard works. Home: 2020 Hastings Kent OH 44240 Office: School Music Kent State Univ Kent OH 44242

SHINE, BARBARA ANNETTE, advt. exec.; b. Mpls., July 22, 1938; d. Monroe J. and Charlotte K. Shine; Ph.B. in Commerce, Northwestern U., 1982; A.A., U. Minn., 1960. With Dow Jones & Co., Inc., Wall St. Jour., Denver, Los Angeles, Silver Spring, Md. and Chgo., 1962—. Midwest advt. coordinator Travel for Bus. and Pleasure, office mgr. classified advt. sales, 1980—. Com. mem. Mental Health Assn. Montgomery County, Kensington, Md., 1973-77; mem. mental health edn. adv. com. State Md., Balt., 1975-77; com. mem. Mental Health Assn. Greater Chgo., 1977-78; mem. leadership com. U. Minn. Alumni Assn., Chgo., 1980—. Recipient Crystal Prism award Advt. Club, 1974. Mem. Am. Advt. Fedn. (Citations for Meritorious Service 1972, 74, dir. 2d dist. 1971-76), Advt. Club Met. Washington (com. mem., dir. 1974—, pres. 1973-74). Office: 200 W Monroe St Chicago IL 60606

SHINEDLING, MARTIN MYRON, psychologist, adminstr.; b. Pateron, N.J., Oct. 13, 1936; s. Archie Edward and Ruth (Potash) S.; B.A., Calif. State U., 1965, M.A., 1967; Ph.D. (NDEA fellow, Univ. fellow), Brigham Young U., 1971; m. Mary Annette Self, Nov. 29, 1958 (div.); children—Michelle, Dorothy, Michael, Brian. Staff psychologist CIA, Washington, 1971-72; adminstr. Gladwin (Mich.) Mental Health Clinic, 1972-75; asso. prof. Saginaw Valley Coll., Saginaw, Mich., 1973-76; dir. Planning for Living, 1976—. Served with U.S. Army, 1955-64. Mem. Am., Mid-Mich. (pres. 1975-76) psychol. assns. Mem. Ch. Jesus Christ of Latter-day Saints. Contbr. articles to profl. jours. Home: 9111 Waterman Rd Vassar MI 48768 Office: 2355 Delta Rd Bay City MI 48706

SHINN, LARRY LEE, educator; b. Winchester, Ind., May 31, 1937; s. Everett D. and Ethel P. (Million) S.; B.S., Ball State U., 1958, M.S., 1959, vocat. certificate, 1968. Bus. edn. tchr. Lincoln High Sch., Cambridge City, Ind., 1959—, dept. chmn., 1959—. Recipient Disting. Service citation, Office Edn. Assn., 1978; Jr. C. of C. Outstanding Young Educator award, 1966; Ind. Vocat. Assn. Award of Merit, 1974. Mem. Nat. Assn. Classroom Educators in Bus. and Office Edn. (pres. 1978-82), NEA, Nat. Bus. Edn. Assn., Am. Vocat. Assn., Ind. Vocat. Assn., Ind. State Tchrs. Assn., Office Edn. Assn., N. Central Bus. Edn. Assn., Ind. Bus. Educators Assn., Council Vocat. Educators, Western Wayne Edn. Assn., Ind. Bus. Educators Club, Delta Phi Epsilon. Contbr. articles to profl. jours. Home: Route 2 Cambridge City IN 47327 Office: Lincoln High Sch East Parkway Dr Cambridge City IN 47327

SHIPLEY, DAVID GEORGE, ceramic engr.; b. Clarksburg, W. Va., Apr. 26, 1954; s. Edward Woodruff and Mary Ellen (Hetrich) S.; B.S. in Ceramic Engring., Alfred U., 1977; m. Linda Lee Williamson, Nov. 14, 1981. Engr. maintenance Harbison-Walker Refractories, Balt., 1977-78; plant engr., Hammond, Ind., 1978-81, asst. plant mgr. engring., Windham, Ohio, 1981—. Mem. Am. Ceramic Soc., Nat. Inst. Ceramic Engrs. Presbyterian. Home: 259 Perkinswood Blvd NE Apt C-15 Warren OH 44483 Office: E Center St Windham OH 44288

SHIPLEY, JAMES LEE, hosp. pub. relations exec.; b. New Philadelphia, Ohio, Sept. 27, 1935; s. Melvin McKinley and Sarah Ann (Smith) S.; student U.S. Army Guided Missile Sch., 1956-57, Republic Indsl. Edn. Inst., 1968, Kent State U., 1971-73. Staff announcer Sta.-WJER, Dover, Ohio, 1951-53; with Sta. WSOM-AM-FM, Salem, Ohio, 1953-66, sta. and sales mgr., 1959-66, news commentator, 1960-66; mgr. advt.-pub. relations Lyle Pub. Co., Salem, 1966-68; dir. pub. relations-communications, editor co. employee publ. Copperweld Steel Co., Warren, Ohio, 1968-73; dir. dept. community relations St. Joseph Riverside Hosp., Warren, 1973—; pub. relations adviser Trumbull County (Ohio) YMCA; bd. dirs. for pub. info. Vis. Nurses Assn.; mem. pub. relations com. Trumbull County United Way; mem. Ohio TV Steering Com.; mem. Mahoning-Shenango Area Health Edn. Network. Pres. bd. trustees Trumbull County Council on Alcoholism; bd. dirs. Trumbull County chpt. ARC; bd. dirs., chmn. scholarship com. Western Res. chpt. March of Dimes; mem. com. Western Res. council Boy Scouts Am. Served with U.S. Army, 1950-60. Recipient award of Appreciation for community service Columbiana County (Ohio) Med. Soc., 1962, citation for pub. service Muscular Dystrophy Assn., 1968, 70, 1st award for excellence in patient staff and community edn. Sylvania Comml. Electronics Corp., 1976. Mem. Northeastern Ohio Hosp. Pub. Relations Assn., Pub. Relations Soc. Am. (pres. Western Res. chpt., charter mem. sect. health), Greater Cleve. Hosp. Assn. (Achievement award 1976), Amateur Trap Shooters Assn., Eastern Ohio Conservation Club. Episcopalian. Clubs: Rotary (co-chmn. info. com. local club), Elks. Home: 3190 Dunstan Dr Warren OH 44485 Office: 1400 Tod Ave Warren OH 44485

SHIPMAN, DEAN J., judge; b. Charlotte, Mich., Oct. 8, 1931; B.S., Coll. of Holy Cross, 1953; J.D., U. Mich., 1960; Instr., Bay de Noc Community Coll.; dir. Office Community Services and Family Life, Inc., Diocese of Marquette; judge dist. 94th Mich. Dist. Ct., Escanaba, 1969—; mem. dist. ct. com. Mich. Supreme Ct.; mem. Jud. Council Mich. Mem. Mich. Commn. on Criminal Justice, Mich. Gov.'s Emergency Preparedness Adv. Council. Served with USN; capt. Res. Mem. Mich. Dist. Judges Assn., Am. Bar Assn., State Bar Mich., Delta County Bar Assn., Lake Michigan Yachting Assn. Club: Escanaba Yacht. Office: 310 Ludington St Escanaba MI 49829

SHIPP, MAURINE SARAH HARSTON (MRS. LEVI ARNOLD SHIPP), realtor; b. Holiday, Mo., Mar. 6, 1913; d. Paul Edward and Sarah Jane (Mitchell) Harston; grad. Ill. Bus. Coll., 1945; student real estate Springfield Jr. Coll., 1962; student law LaSalle Extension U., 1959-62; m. Levi Arnold Shipp, Jan. 30, 1941; children—Jerome Reynolds, Patricia (Mrs. Rodney W. England). With Ill. Dept. Agr., Springfield, 1941-65, supr. livestock industry Brucellosis sect.; saleswoman Morgan-Hamilton Real Estate Co., Springfield, 1962-64; owner, mgr. Shipp Real Estate Agy., Springfield, 1965—. Prin. appraiser urban renewal Dept. Housing and Urban Devel., 1971-72; mem. Springfield Pub. Bldg. Commn. Bd. dirs. Springfield Travelers Aid, 1971—. Mem. Springfield Bd. Realtors, Nat., Ill. assns. real estate bds., N.A.A.C.P., Urban League, Iota Phi Lambda. Episcopalian. Mem. Order Eastern Star. Club: Bridge. Home: 31 Bellerive Rd Springfield IL 62704 Office: 2200 E Cook St Springfield IL 62703

SHIRAEF, JOHN DRAGON, educator; b. Phila., Apr. 18, 1912; s. John and Rose (Kret) S. Tchr., Cass Tech. High Sch., Detroit, 1936-43; newspaperman Detroit Times, 1943-47; tchr.-lectr. on Russia, Europe, 1947—. Served with U.S. Army, 1943-44. Decorated battle star. Mem. Internat. Platform Assn. Republican. First Am. lectr. to travel to Russian villages off-limits to foreigners; 12 trips to iron curtain countries; innovator compressed method of speech for sch. lectures. Office: PO Box 451 Owosso MI 48867

SHIREMAN, JOAN FOSTER, educator; b. Cleve., Oct. 28, 1933; d. Louis Omar and Genevieve (Duguid) Foster; B.A., Radcliffe Coll., 1956; M.A., U. Chgo., 1959, Ph.D., 1968; m. Charles Howard Shireman, Mar. 18, 1967; 1 son, David Louis. Caseworker, N.H. Children's Aid Soc., 1959-61; caseworker Chgo. Child Care Soc., 1961-63, dir. research, 1968-74; research asso., lectr. U. Chgo., 1964-68; asso. prof. Jane Addams Coll. Social Work, U. Ill., Chgo., 1974—, acting asso. dean, 1979-80. Mem. Nat. Assn. Social Workers, Ill. Child Care Assn., Council on Social Work Edn., AAUP, Phi Beta Kappa. Co-author monographs; contbr. articles to profl. jours. Home: 2058 Maple St Homewood IL 60430 Office: Box 4348 Chicago IL 60680

SHIVELY, BARBARA JEAN, advt. exec.; b. St. Louis, May 14, 1943; d. Robert Carl and Mary Jean (Lilly) Ausbeck; B.A., Northwestern U., 1965; M.A., Ind. U., 1968; m. James Robert Shively, Aug. 28, 1965; children—Erin Suzanne, James Douglas. Writer, Ind. U. News Bur., 1965-68; free-lance journalist, adult edn. tchr. creative writing; dir. career devel. Jr. League, Birmingham, Mich., 1973-75; program dir. Car Care Council, Detroit, 1975-77; account exec. public relations J. Walter Thompson Advt., Dearborn, Mich., 1977-79; account supr. public relations Kenyon & Eckhardt Advt., Birmingham, 1979-80, account. exec., 1980—; free-lance public relations, advt., mktg. communications for women's market; cons. women's market to Chrysler Corp. Mem. Detroit Press Club, Adcraft Club of Detroit, Women in Communications, Inc. (pres. Detroit chpt. 1981). Home: 2677 Somerset Troy MI 48084 Office: Kenyon & Eckhardt 30600 Telegraph Birmingham MI 48010

SHIVELY, LAWRENCE ALVIN, mfg. co. exec.; b. Dayton, Ohio; s. Alvin E. and Carolyn (Kippenburger) S.; B.S., U. Dayton, 1952; m. Betty Jeane Lilly, Aug. 12, 1957; children—Randy A., Rodney A., Joshua A. (dec.). Vice pres. engring. Globe Tool & Engring. Co., Dayton, 1952-68, v.p. planning and devel., 1977-78, v.p. mfg., 1978—, also dir.; pres. Mechaneer Inc., Dayton, 1968-77; dir. Stature Industries, Anchor Tool Co. Scoutmaster, Boy Scouts Am. Served with USN, World War II; PTO. Mem. Eagle Scout Assn., Nat. Mgmt. Assn. Republican. Mem. Assembly of God. Clubs: Masons, Full Gospel Businessmen Fellowship (dir. Dayton). Holder 5 patents, U.S. and U.K. Address: Globe Tool Co 5051 Kitridge Rd Dayton OH 45424

SHOAF, FRANCIS ARISTA, steel casting co. exec.; b. Kokomo, Ind., Apr. 20, 1918; s. Francis Arista and Nellie Lucile (McCarty) S.; A.B., Duke U., 1940; postgrad. Columbia U., 1940-41; m. Patricia Jane Harrison, July 17, 1942; children—Candace Anne, John Lester. With Harrison Steel Castings Co., Attica, Ind., 1945—, asst. works. mgr., 1945-60, asst. sec., 1960-66, v.p., 1966-68, exec. v.p., 1968-80, chmn. bd., 1980—. Served with USN, 1941-45. Mem. Am. Foundrymen's Soc., Steel Founders Soc. Republican. Methodist. Clubs: Columbia, Card Sound Golf, Ocean Reef, Elks, Masons. Home: 601 E Pike St Attica IN 47918 Office: PO Box 60 Attica IN 47918

SHOCH, DAVID EUGENE, physician, educator; b. Warsaw, Poland, June 10, 1918; s. Henry and Hannah (Dembina) S.; B.S., CCNY, 1938; M.S., Northwestern U., 1939, Ph.D., 1943, M.D., 1946; m. Gertrude Amelia Weinstock, June 10, 1945; children—James, John. Intern Cook County Hosp., Chgo., 1945-46, resident ophthalmology, 1948-52; practice medicine, specializing in ophthalmology, Chgo., 1952—; asst. prof. ophthalmology dept. Northwestern U., Chgo., 1952-66, prof., head ophthalmology dept., 1966—; head ophthalmology dept. Northwestern Meml. Hosp., Children's Meml. Hosp., VA Research Hosp.; trustee Assn. Univ. Profs. Opthalmology, pres., 1973. Bd. dirs., sec. Heed Ophthalmic Found. Served to capt., M.C., AUS, 1946-48. Diplomate Am. Bd. Ophthalmology (dir., vice chmn. 1978, chmn. 1979). Fellow ACS; mem. AMA, AAAS, Am. Acad. Ophthalmology (sec. for instrn. 1972-78, pres. 1981), Assn. Research in Vision and Ophthalmology, Inst. Medicine Chgo., Chgo. (past pres.), Am., Pan-Am., French ophthalmol. socs., Sigma Xi. Editorial cons. in ophthalmology Postgrad. Med.; abstract editor Am. Jour. Ophthalmology. Home: 1070 Hohlfelder Rd Glencoe IL 60022 Office: 303 E Chicago Ave Chicago IL 60611

SHOCKEY, WILLIAM LEE, research animal scientist; b. Frostburg, Md., Apr. 7, 1953; s. Robert Franklin and Rebecca Irene (Mazer) S.; A.B., W.Va. U., 1975, Ph.D., 1979; m. Alcinda Kathryn Trickett, June 16, 1979. Grad. asst. W.Va. U., 1975-79; postdoctoral research scientist Ohio Agrl. Research and Devel. Center, Wooster, Ohio, 1979-81; research animal scientist Agrl. Research Service, U.S. Dept. Agr., U.S. Dairy Forage Research Center, Ohio Cluster Program, Wooster, Ohio, 1981—. Served with AUS, 1976. Mem. Am. Soc. Animal Sci., Am. Dairy Sci. Assn., Am. Chem. Soc., Am. Soc. Agronomy. Lion. Home: 318 Nold Ave Wooster OH 44691 Office: US Dept Agr Agrl Research Service Dept Dairy Sci Ohio Agrl Research and Devel Center Wooster OH 44691

SHOCKLEY, DEBORAH LEIGH, human resources planner; b. Jefferson City, Mo., Jan. 26, 1953; d. Arthur Warren and Mary Alice (Keller) Shockley; B.S. in Edn., S.W. Mo. State U., 1975, M.S. in Guidance and Counseling (fellow), 1977. Aid counselor, research asst. Financial Aids Office, S.W. Mo. State U., 1975-77, also vol. workers various social service orgns.; psychiat. technician Springfield (Mo.) Park Central Hosp., 1977; youth counselor Springfield Dept. Human Resources, 1977-79, spl. programs coordinator, 1979, human resources planner, 1979—. Mem. Am. Personnel and Guidance Assn., Am. Coll. Personnel Assn. Address: 1156 E Loren Springfield MO 65807

SHOEMACK, HARVEY RAYMOND, mktg. center exec.; b. Cleve., Oct. 1, 1942; s. Ted and Lilian (Covitt) S.; B.S.J., Ohio U., 1965; postgrad. in communications U. Ill., 1966-67; m. Geraldine Bragman, Mar. 20, 1966; children—Todd, Brian. Publicity dir. Sta. WILL-TV, U. Ill., Urbana, 1966-67; v.p. Pub. Relations Bd., Inc., Chgo., 1967-76; pres. Internat. Mktg. Center, Ltd., Chgo., 1976—; editor, pub. Internat. Bus. Digest, 1981—; internat. trade cons.; lectr. U.S.-Japan trade and econ. relationship. Mem. Ill. Dist. Export Council, 1978-79, 80-81. Recipient Golden Trumpet award (3) Publicity Club Chgo., 1969-70. Mem. Japan-Am. Soc. Chgo. (dir.), Internat. Trade Club Chgo. (dir. 1975—), Chgo. Council Fgn. Relations, Internat. Visitors Center, Sigma Delta Chi. Contbr. articles to profl. jours. Home: 2854 Twin Oaks Highland Park IL 60035 Office: 166 E Superior St Chicago IL 60611

SHOEMAKER, MORRELL MCKENZIE, JR., architect; b. Granville, Ohio, Aug. 25, 1923; s. Morrell McKenzie and Ruth (Doehleman) S.; B.Arch., Cornell U., 1945. Archtl. designer Mundie, Jensen & McClurg, Chgo., 1946-49; chief architect Laramore & Douglass, Chgo., 1949-53; partner McClurg, Shoemaker & McClurg, Chgo., 1953-67, McClurg, Shoemaker, Chgo., 1967-74; pvt. investor, 1975—. Registered architect, Ill. Mem. AIA, Soc. Am. Registered Architects, Nat. Council Archtl. Registration Bds., Nat. Soc. Archtl. Hist. (life), Landmark Preservation Council, Nat. Trust for Historic Preservation, Chgo. Assn. Commerce and Industry, Chgo. Natural History Mus. (life), Chgo. Hist. Soc. (life), Chgo. Orch. Assn. (life), Ill. Soc. Architects, Art Inst. Chgo. (life), Ill. St. Andrews Soc., Victorian Soc. Republican. Presbyn. (elder, trustee). Clubs: Cornell of Chicago; The Cliff Dwellers. Author: Five Walks In and Around Chicago's Famous Buildings, 1969. Editor: The Building Estimator's Reference Book, 20th edit., 1980. Home: 1310 N LaSalle St Chicago IL 60610

SHOEMAKER, RICHARD WAYNE, assn. exec.; b. Westerville, Ohio, June 19, 1925; s. Ross Welling and Lois Margaret (Tracht) S.; student Denison U., 1943-44; A.B., Otterbein Coll., 1948; M.E., Ohio State U., 1953; m. Marion Bryant Daniels, Aug. 7, 1948; children—Mark David, Jane Ellen, Carol Ann. Public relations dir. Columbus (Ohio) Goodwill Industries, 1948-49, Columbus Recreation Dept., 1950; floor mgr., producer/dir., public affairs dir. Sta. WBNS-TV, Columbus, 1953-63; field sec., exec. sec. Ohio Info. Com., Columbus, 1963-69; exec. dir., v.p. Assn. Ind. Colls. and Univs. Ohio, Columbus, 1969—. Scoutmaster, Boy Scouts Am., 1953-54; public affairs/info. dir. Columbus-Franklin County CD, 1958-74; CD chmn. Indian Springs PTA, 1959-64; state chmn. Project Freedom POW/MIA, 1970-71; public awareness cons. POW/MIA's, 1973—. Served with USN, 1943-46, 50-52. Recipient Sabin on Sun. award of Excellence, 1963; Columbus-Franklin County CD Meritorious award, 1963; cert. of appreciation U.S. Navy League, 1971; Golden Mike award Ohio Am. Legion Aux., 1976; honor cert. Freedoms Found. at Valley Forge, 1977. Mem. Public Relations Soc. Am., State Assns. Exec. Council. Baptist. Writer, narrator, recorder Audiovisual Report on Our POW-MIA's, 1974; writer, producer, narrator, recorder America-One Nation under God, 1976. Office: 50 W Broad St Suite 711 Columbus OH 43215

SHOEMAKER, ROBERT LOUIS, audio visual co. exec.; b. Independence, Kans., Sept. 30, 1907; s. Walter Ellsworth and Blanch (Hawley) S.; A.B. in English Lit., U. Ill., 1930; student architecture Armour Inst., 1927-28; m. Helen Margaret Gerard, Oct. 9, 1942; 1 son, Theodore Merrill. Archtl. draftsman Zook & McCaughey, Chgo., 1927-28; baker Hampshire Restaurant, Hollywood, Calif., 1932; waiter Old Heidelberg Inn, Chgo., 1933-35; service mgr. Gas Appliances, Inc., Miami, Fla., 1935-37; owner The Home Appliance Store, West Palm Beach, Fla., 1937-41; mgr. aviation radio sales Lear, Inc., 1946-47; div. mgr. DuKane Corp., 1947-56; mgr. Salesmate div. Charles Beseler Co., 1957-62; v.p., co-owner Double Sixteen Co., film prodns., 1962-63; pres., owner AVACO, mfrs. reps. audio visual supplies, Winnetka, Ill., 1962—; regional mgr. LaBelle Industries, Inc., 1963—; mem. com. to establish bldg. code for sch. constrn. for audio visual use Ind. Dept. Edn., 1954-55; founder, chmn. bd. govs., mem. faculty Nat. Inst. Audio-Visual Selling, 1949-57; founder, chmn. Nat. Sound Slidefilm Contest, 1954-56; bd. dirs., mem. faculty Audio Visual Inst. Effective Communications, 1966; exec. bd., adviser archtl. com., dept. audio visual and broadcast edn. Nat. Council Chs., 1954-60. Chmn. art-antique auction Hadley Sch. Blind, 1975. Served to lt. comdr. USNR, World War II; liaison officer Office Sci. Devel./Nat. Def. Research Council, 1944. Recipient 2 awards for films The Ugly Duckling, 1955, Masha and the Bear, 1956. Mem. Soc. Motion Picture and TV Engrs. (life), NEA (ofcl. adviser bd. dirs., dept. audio visual instruction 1953), Nat. (dir. 1953-56, Meritorious Service award 1973, Past Service award 1977; life), Ill. audio visual assns., Audio Engring. Soc. (life), Am. Soc. Tng. and Devel., Sales-Mktg. Execs. Internat., Aircraft Owners and Pilots Assn., Assn. Ednl. Communication and Tech., Internat. Waiters Union, Phi Delta Theta. Club: Lions (pres. Winnetka). Producer over 100 sound slide films; 1st ednl. sound filmstrips, 1955. Author: Theory of Automated Selling, 1962; Psychology of Selling with Audio-Visual, 1969; Get the Job You Want, 1981; contbr. articles to periodicals. Home: 1017 Elm St Winnetka IL 60093 Office: PO Box 45 Winnetka IL 60093

SHONS, ALAN RANCE, plastic surgeon; b. Freeport, Ill., Jan. 10, 1938; s. Ferral Caldwell and Margaret (Zimmerman) S.; A.B., Dartmouth Coll., 1960; M.D., Case Western Res. U., 1965; Ph.D. in Surgery, U. Minn., 1976; m. Mary Ella Misamore, Aug. 5, 1961; children—Lesley, Susan. Intern, U. Hosp., Cleve., 1965-66, resident in surgery, 1966-67; research fellow transplantation immunology U. Minn., 1969-72; resident in surgery U. Minn. Hosp., 1972-74; resident in plastic surgery N.Y. U., 1974-76; asst. prof. plastic surgery U. Minn., Mpls., 1976-79, asso. prof., 1979—; dir. div. plastic and reconstructive surgery U. Minn. Hosp., St. Paul Ramsey Hosp., Mpls. VA Hosp., 1976—; cons. plastic surgery St. Louis Park Med. Center, 1980—. Served to capt. USAF, 1967-69. Diplomate Am. Bd. Surgery, Am. Bd. Plastic Surgery. Fellow ACS (chmn. Minn. com. on trauma); mem. Am. Soc. Plastic and Reconstructive Surgeons, Minn. Acad. Plastic Surgeons (pres.), AMA, Soc. Head and Neck Surgeons, Am. Assn. Surgery Trauma, Transplantation Soc., Am. Assn. Immunologists, Soc. Exptl. Pathology, Am. Burn Assn., Am. Cleft Palate Assn., Am. Soc. Nephrology, Assn. Acad. Surgery, Pan Am. Med. Assn., Central Surg. Assn., Minn. Med. Assn., Mpls. Surg. Soc., Ramsey County Med. Soc., Sigma Xi. Office: U Minn Hosps Minneapolis MN 55455

SHOOK, DONALD D., coll. adminstr.; b. Marshfield, Mo., Feb. 26, 1932; s. Perry John and Etolia Vivian S.; B.S., SW Mo. State U., 1954; M.S., U. Mo., 1960, Ed.D., 1962; m. June Illene Davis, Dec. 16, 1954; children—Gregory Dean, John William. Dean, Mineral Area Coll., Flat River, Mo., 1962-64; pres. Crowder Coll., Neosho, Mo., 1964-68; pres. East Central Coll., Union, Mo., 1968—. Served with U.S. Army, 1954-56. Mem. Mo. Assn. Community Jr. Colls. (pres. 1969-70), Phi Delta Kappa. Mem. United Ch. of Christ. Club: Franklin County Country. Office: East Central Coll Hwy 50 and Prairie Dell Rd Union MO 63084

SHOOK, GWEN LEBOST, educator; b. Detroit; d. Paul and Betty Viola (Gilman) LeBost; diploma Bryant and Stratton Bus. Coll., 1947; B.A. in Elementary Edn., Roosevelt Coll., 1951; A.M., U. Chgo., Reading Specialist, 1955; 1 son, Jeffrey Max. Classroom tchr., Oak Park, Ill., 1951-55, Oak Park, Mich., 1955—. Leader, Am. Youth Hostels, Girl Scouts Served with USNR, 1944-46. Mem. Nat., Mich., Oak Park edn. assns., Assn. Childhood Edn. Internat., Mich. Assn. Supervision and Curriculum Devel., Mich. Assn. on Open Edn., Mich. Assn. for Children with Learning Disabilities, Mich. Assn. for Emotionally Disturbed Children, Mich. Assn. Sci. Edn. Specialists, Mich. Assn. for Academically Talented, Mich. Council Tchrs. English, Detroit Area Council Tchrs. Math., Wayne Ednl. Options, Oakland County Reading Council, Oakland Assn. Gifted and Talented, Internat. Platform Assn., NOW, Nat. Audubon Soc., Center Sci. in Public Interest, Union Concerned Scientists, Common Cause, Detroit Audubon Soc., Founders Soc. Detroit Inst. Arts, Action for Children's TV, Met. Detroit Com. for Children's TV, Pi Lambda Theta. Home: 1653 Taunton Rd Birmingham MI 48008

SHOPHER, WILLIAM EUGENE, mfg. co. exec.; b. St. Louis, Jan. 22, 1926; s. Joseph E. and Tuna (Blakeburn) S.; student St. Louis U., 1946-47, Washington U., 1955-56, Harvard Grad. Sch. Bus., 1965; m. Emogean J. Smith, Feb. 3, 1946; children—Patricia Ann, Jacqulyn Marie. Dir. purchasing Cherry-Burrell, Cedar Rapids, Iowa and Chgo., 1963-68; with Weyerhaeuser Co., 1968-74, mgr. purchasing systems and training, Tacoma, Wash., 1968-72; dir. purchasing Lockwood Corp., Gering, Nebr., 1974—; lectr. U. Wis. Mgmt. Extension Div., Madison, 1966—. Pres. bd. dirs. Scottsbluff/Gering United Way, 1979-80, bd. dirs., 1979—; bd. dirs. Western Nebr. unit Am. Cancer Soc., 1980—; mem. Scottsbluff/Gering Clean Communities Commn., 1981—. Served with USNR, 1944-46, 51-52.

Mem. Nat. Assn. Purchasing Mgrs. (steel exec. com. 1979—), Scottsbluff/Gering C. of C. (chmn. edn. com. 1977-78). Contbr. articles to profl. jours. Office: PO Box 160 Gering NE 69341

SHOPNECK, GEORGE, dentist; b. Boston, Oct. 23, 1919; s. Hyman and Rebecca (Paul) S.; B.S., Toledo U., 1941; D.D.S., Ohio State U., 1943; m. Hannah Offner, Dec. 3, 1944; children—Marlene Maniloff, Daryl, Craig, Jill. Pvt. practice dentistry, Toledo, 1947—; dental cons. Collingwood Park, St. Theresa's nursing homes, 1965-77; instr. Whitney Sch. Dental Assts., Toledo, 1954-56; mem. dental staff St. Vincent's Hosp. Med. Center, 1974—. Vice-pres. Community Center Players, 1956-59; mem. Jewish Community Relations Com., 1966-67; bd. dirs. Jewish Community Center, 1959-61; bd. dirs., vice chaplain Toledo Meml. Assn., 1959-63; bd. dirs. Toledo Repertoire Theater, 1964, Toledo Children's Theater, 1972-73, Toledo Village Players, 1965-79. Served to capt., Dental Corps, AUS, 1943-46. Recipient Cert. of Merit, Toledo Jewish Family Service, 1974; WDHO-TV TV award, 1976. Mem. ADA, Ohio State, Toledo dental assns., Am. Legion (chaplain 1967—), Vedder and Bunning Dental Socs., Alpha Epsilon Pi, Alpha Omega (pres. Toledo chpt. 1956-57). Clubs: Masons, B'nai B'rith, Twin Oaks Country, Tennis, Racquet (Toledo). Home: 3652 Indian Rd Toledo OH 43606 Office: 3100 W Central Ave Toledo OH 43606

SHORB, EUGENE MURRAY, utility exec.; b. Cleve., Mar. 6, 1920; s. Charles F. and Beth (Murray) S.; B.S. in M.E., Purdue U., 1949; m. Harriet Elizabeth Colman, July 14, 1951; children—Janet E., William M., Thomas C. Engr. gas utilization dept. NIPSCO, East Chicago, Ind., 1949-52, mgr. tng. and utilization, Michigan City, Ind., 1952-63, adminstrv. asst., Hammond, Ind., 1963-74, v.p. gas ops. and fuel procurement, 1974-77, sr. v.p. ops., 1977-79, 1st v.p., 1979-81, exec. v.p., chief operating officer, 1981—; dir. Merc. Nat. Bank of Ind. Served with USNR, 1942-45. Mem. Am. Gas Assn., Ind. Gas Assn. (dir.), Ind. Electric Assn., Am. Mgmt. Assn. Methodist. Home: 1401 Fran-Lin Pkwy Munster IN 46321 Office: 5265 Hohman Ave Hammond IN 46325

SHORNEY, GEORGE HERBERT, music pub.; b. Oak Park, Ill., Dec. 16, 1931; s. George Herbert and Mary Louise (Wallace) S.; B.A., Denison U., 1954; m. Nancy Leith, Aug. 27, 1955; children—Cynthia Ann, George Herbert, John Leith, Scott Alfred. Asst. mgr. adjusting service Marshall Field & Co., Chgo., 1956-58; office mgr. Hope Pub. Co., Carol Stream, Ill., 1959-62, v.p., 1962-70, pres., 1970—. Chmn., Wheaton Bd. Fire and Police Commrs.; nat. donor com. Nat. Council Chs.; mem. Nat. UN Day Com.; bd. dirs. Central DuPage Hosp., Winfield, Ill. Served with USNR, 1953-55. Mem. Ch. Music Pubs. Assn. (past pres.). Presbyterian (trustee). Clubs: Univ. (Chgo.); Soc. Alumni Denison U. (past pres.); Anvil (Dundee, Ill.). Home: 160 W Elm St Wheaton IL 60187 Office: Carol Stream IL 60187

SHORS, CLAYTON MARION, cardiologist; b. Beemer, Nebr., June 10, 1925; s. Joseph Albert and Morva Edith (Clayton) S.; B.S., U. Nebr., 1950, M.D., 1952; m. Arlene Towle, June 6, 1948; children—Susan Debra, Clayton Robert, Scott Towle. Intern, Detroit Receiving Hosp., 1952-53, resident, 1953-56; practice medicine specializing in cardiology, Detroit; mem. staff St. John Hosp. Served with U.S. Army, 1943-46. Diplomate Am. Bd. Internal Medicine. Fellow Am. Coll. Cardiology, Internat. Coll. Angiology, Am. Heart Assn. Council on Clin. Cardiology; mem. Alpha Omega Alpha. Home: 19950 Norton Ct Grosse Pointe Woods MI 48236 Office: 22151 Moross Rd Detroit MI 48236

SHORT, BARBARA JOAN, ednl. cons.; b. St. Clair County, Mich., Aug. 8, 1934; d. Herman M. and Beulah (Lashbrook) S.; B.S. cum laude, Mich. State U., 1956; postgrad. Central Mich. U., 1973—; children—Richard, Katrina, Graydon, Melissa. With U.S. Dept. Agr., 1956-57, 64-66; tchr. public schs., Capac, Mich., 1958-62, New Haven, Mich., 1962-63, Grand Ledge, Mich., 1963-64, Reese, Mich., 1966-67, Caro, Mich., 1967-71, 77-79; womens editor WKYO, Caro, 1968-69; instr. Mich. Tech. U., 1968-71; mgr. Indianfields Park, Caro, 1977-78; disaster mgmt. cons. Fed. Emergency Mgmt. Agy., Battle Creek, Mich., 1978—. Chmn. bd. Creative Child Care, 1972; bd. dirs. Thumb Area Econ. Opportunity Commn., 1965-67. Named Woman of Yr., Tuscola County Bus. and Profl. Women, 1965. Mem. Nat. Assn. Female Execs. Contbr. articles to Better Homes and Gardens, Parents, Sci. News, Farm Jour., others. Home: 1222 111th Ave Martin MI 49070 Office: Region V Federal Bldg Battle Creek MI 49016

SHORT, JAMES EDWARD, JR., chem. engr.; b. Gary, Ind., Apr. 6, 1940; s. James E. and Lorraine L. Short; B.S. in Chem. Engring., Purdue U., 1963; m. Susan G. Benjamin, Dec. 18, 1976; 1 dau., Amanda Rei. Chem. engr. No. Ind. Public Service, 1963; chem. engr. U.S. Navy, Naval Weapons Support Center, Crane, Ind., 1966—, program mgr. research and devel. dept., 1966-70, program mgr. applied scis. dept., 1971—; cons. (part-time) to industry, 1969—. Served with Chem. Corps, U.S. Army, 1963-66. Mem. Am. Def. Preparedness Assn., Internat. Pyrotechnics Soc., Am. Legion. Patentee in field. Home: Rural Route 1 Switz City IN 47465 Office: Code 505 NWSC Crane IN 47522

SHORTER, KATIE MARIE, sch. prin.; b. Pine Bluff, Ark., June 6; d. Lewis and Jessie Bennett; B.Ed., U. Toledo, 1963; M.Ed., Cleve. State U., 1973; postgrad U. Akron, 1977—. Tchr., Toledo Bd. Edn., 1963-65; tchr. Cleve. Bd. Edn., 1965-69, adminstrv. intern, 1970-73, reading specialist Diagnostic Reading Center, 1973-74; prin. Canterbury Elem. Sch., Cleveland Heights, Ohio, 1975—; ednl. cons. Carolyn Morris & Assos. Sears Roebuck Found. summer fellow, 1978. Mem. Nat. Assn. Elem. Sch. Prins., Assn. Supervision and Curriculum Devel., Ohio Assn. Elem. Sch. Prins., Nat. Alliance Black Sch. Educators, Urban League (dir.), Phi Delta Kappa, Delta Sigma Theta. Clubs: Women's City of Cleve., Karamu Women. Office: 2530 Canterbury St Cleveland Heights OH 44118

SHORTRIDGE, DOUGLASS RONALD, lawyer; b. Indpls., July 3, 1931; s. Norman Howard and Lillian (Painter) S.; B.S., Purdue U., 1953; LL.B., Ind. U., 1959; divorced; 1 dau., Sylvia. Admitted to Ind. bar, 1959; dep. atty. gen. State of Ind., 1959-60; practice in Indpls., 1960—; propr. Douglass R. Shortridge P.C., 1972—. Served as officer U.S. Army, 1953-56. Mem. Am. Bar Assn., Am. Judicature Soc., 7th Fed. Circuit Bar Assn., Ind. Bar Assn., Indpls. Bar Assn. (pres. 1974), Iron Key, Sigma Delta Chi, Tau Kappa Alpha, Phi Gamma Delta. Republican. Episcopalian. Clubs: Woodstock, Univ., Traders Point Hunt, Crooked Stick Golf. Home: 1473 Prestwick Ln Carmel IN 46032 Office: 1 Indiana Sq Suite 1960 Indianapolis IN 46204

SHOUP, PAUL CONNELLY, banker; b. El Paso, Tex., May 24, 1938; s. Paul Leo and Laura Mary (Pendleton) S.; B.B.A., U. Detroit, 1973; M.B.A., Mich. State U., 1976. Asst. cashier Public Bank, Detroit, 1966; asst. v.p. Bank of the Commonwealth, Detroit, 1966-71, v.p., 1971—; lectr. Am. Mgmt. Assn., 1970-71. Cert. purchasing agt. Mem. U. Detroit Nat. Alumni Assn. (alumni rep. 1976-79, dir. 1976-79), Nat. Assn. Purchasing Agts., Bus. Owners and Mgrs. Assn. (cert. real property adminstr.), Delta Sigma Pi. Republican. Roman Catholic. Clubs: Grosse Pointe Sail (sec.-treas. 1965-71), Kiwanis (pres., sec.-treas. 1968-71). Home: 101 Shore Club Dr Saint Clair Shores MI 48080 Office: 719 Griswold St Detroit MI 48226

SHOWALTER, MONIQUE GONCZY, mktg. communications mgr.; b. Chgo., May 21, 1953; d. Stephen Istvan and Doris (Eberhardt) Gonczy; B.S. in Communications, U. Ill., 1976; m. Kenneth Alton Showalter, Apr. 22, 1978; 1 stepdau., Kelly Renee. Sales rep. Dictaphone Corp., Chgo., 1976; account exec. USA Chgo., advt. agy., Chgo., 1976-78, Kachlik & Linka Assos., advt. agy., Rolling Meadows, Ill., 1978-80; communications coordinator EMI Med. Inc., Northbrook, Ill., 1978; mgr. mktg. communications MARPAC unit Mark Controls Corp., Evanston, Ill., 1980—; dir. communications for non-profit orgns., 1980—. Vestrywoman, St. Alban's Episcopal Ch., Chgo. Mem. TAPPI, Am. Contract Bridge League. Home: 1155A Peterson St Park Ridge IL 60068 Office: 1900 Dempster Ave Evanston IL 60204

SHOWALTER, STAN, criminologist; b. Syracuse, N.Y., Apr. 12, 1936; s. William Edward and Beulah Vae (Williamson) S.; B.A., Andrews U., 1962, M.A., 1966, M.A., 1974, Ed.D., 1976; m. Jeannine Wittschiebe, June 9, 1963. Teacher, Dowagiac (Mich.) Pub. Schs., 1962-66; instr. psychology Southwestern Mich. Coll., 1966-67; caseload counselor, staff psychologist, dir. psychol. services, adminstrv. asst. to warden, spl. asst. to dir. adult authority Ind. Dept. Corrections, 1967-76; lectr. criminology and criminal justice Lake Mich. Coll., 1971—, Purdue U., 1976—, Western Mich. U., 1977—; pres. Criminal Justice Assos., Inc., New Buffalo, Mich., 1977—; bd. commrs. Berrien County Juvenile Detention Center, 1975—; mem. Chikaming Twp. Pub. Safety Commn., 1977, Berrien County Mental Health Bd.; mem. U.S. Contingent, 5th UN Congress on Crime, Geneva, 1975. Fellow Menninger Found.; mem. Am. Soc. Criminology, Am. Psychol. Assn., Am. Correctional Assn., Soc. Police and Criminal Psychologists, Am. Personnel and Guidance Assn., Internat. Assn. Chiefs Police, Fraternal Order Police, Nat. Council Crime Delinquency, Phi Delta Kappa. Seventh-day Adventist. Clubs: Am. Philatelic Soc., Soc. Philataelic Americans. Office: PO Drawer 130 New Buffalo MI 49117

SHRADER, DOUGLAS EDMUND, chemist; b. Ewing, Nebr., Sept. 2, 1943; s. Willie Louis and Leah Frances (Fry) S.; B.S.E., Wayne State Coll., 1965; Ph.D. (NASA and NDEA fellow 1969-73), Mont. State U., Bozeman, 1973; postgrad. (Climax Molybdenum Indstry scholar) U. Colo., 1966, (NSF In-service Inst. scholar) Colo. Sch. Mines, 1966-67, (NSF Acad. Yr. Inst. fellow) U. S.D., 1968-69; m. Mary Angala Bauer, Feb. 23, 1963; children—Douglas Bradley, Michael Scott, Trevor Lee. Chemistry tchr. Douglas County Sch. Dist., Castle Rock, Colo., 1965-68; field application chemist Varian Instrument Group, Park Ridge, Ill., 1973-80, mgr. atomic absorption resource center, 1980—; participant seminars in field. Committeeman, Cub Scouts, Boy Scouts Am., Bozeman, 1971-73. Mem. Am. Chem. Soc., Soc. for Applied Spectroscopy, Sigma Xi. Condr. research, contbr. papers to sci. publs. in field. Home: 274 Trowbridge Elk Grove IL 60007 Office: 205 W Touhy Ave Park Ridge IL 60068

SHREVE, ROBERT PRYOR, sch. ofcl.; b. Cambridge, Ohio, May 22, 1928; s. Raymond G. and Gladys O. (Pryor) S.; A.B., Youngstown State U., 1949; B.S. in Edn., Kent State U., 1950, M.Ed., 1958; Ed.D., Case Western Res. U., 1964; postgrad. U. Colo., 1964; m. Dolores M. Harrison, June 16, 1951; children—David Harrison, Charles Raymond, Paul Robert. Indsl. engr. U.S. Steel Co., Youngstown, Ohio, 1951; tchr. Austintown Schs., Youngstown, 1951-52, 55-58; prin. Lynn-Kirk Sch., Austintown, 1958-60; dir. edn. Niles (Ohio) Schs., 1960-62; supr. sci. and math. Youngstown Schs., 1962-66; supr., Mahoning County Schs., 1966-69, supt., 1969—; supt. Mahoning County Joint Vocat. Sch., Canfield, Ohio, 1969-73. Mem. vis. faculty Kent State U., 1965, Youngstown State U., 1972, 78-80. Mem. Ohio State Adv. Council, Elementary Secondary Edn. Act, Title III, 1971-74; mem. Ohio Assessment Adv. Com., 1974—, chmn., 1979; mem. Ohio Inservice Edn. Adv. Council, 1979—, chmn., 1980-81. Bd. dirs. Mahoning County Red Cross, 1967-80, Mahoning County Mental Health Assn., 1967-73, Youngstown Area Cystic Fibrosis Found., 1969—, Youngstown Players, Inc., 1968-71, 73—, pres., 1977-79; pres. Child and Adult Mental Health Center, 1981; bd. dirs. Canfield Fair Bd., 1969—. Served as lt. USNR, 1952-55. Mem. Am. Assn. Sch. Adminstrs., N.E. County Supt. Assn. (pres. 1971), Phi Delta Kappa, Kappa Delta Pi. Mem. Ch. of Christ. Home: 4209 Claridge Dr Youngstown OH 44511 Office: 25 E Boardman St Youngstown OH 44503

SHREWSBURY, GEORGE SCHROEDER, earth moving and compaction mfg. co. exec.; b. St. Louis, Nov. 8, 1930; s. Augustus George and Ella Jane (Pelke) Schroeder; B.S., Carthage Coll., 1954; cert. bus. mgmt. So. Ill. U., 1962; m. H. Luise Bonrath, Aug. 15, 1953; children—Kathryn, Kimberly, Kelly-Jo, Karen. Trainee, A.O. Smith Corp., Milw., 1956, jr. buyer central purchasing, 1957, coordinator manpower/benefits, Granite City, Ill., 1957-65; supr. employment/safety Sheller-Globe Corp., Keokuk, Iowa, 1965-67; mgr. indsl. relations Constrn. Equipment div. J.I. Case Co., Wichita, Kans., 1967—; loaned exec. Nat. Alliance Businessmen, 1969. Gen. chmn. Air Capital Mgmt. Conf., 1970-71; pres. Sedgwick County (Kans.) chpt. Am. Cancer Soc., 1977-78; active Jr. Achievement, United Way. Served with U.S. Army, 1954-56. Recipient Max H. Miller award Jr. Achievement, 1976-77. Mem. Wichita Indsl. Relations Council (chmn. 1980), Am. Soc. Personnel Adminstrn. (pres. Wichita chpt. 1971-72, Superior Merit award 1972) (cert. accredited exec. personnel), Am. Soc. Safety Engrs. (pres. Wichita chpt. 1971-72, Superior Merit award 1972). Republican. Lutheran. Clubs: Constrn. Equipment Div. Employees (mgmt. rep. 1968—), Masons. Office: PO Box 9228 Wichita KS 67277

SHRIVER, PAUL LESTER, psychologist; b. Mattoon, Ill., Jan. 19, 1941; s. Paul Leslie and Vivian Winifred (Roberts) S.; A.B., Bradley U., Peoria, Ill., 1963, M.A., 1964; Ed.D., Ind. U., 1978; m. Karen K. Teaters, May 28, 1972; children—Cindy Sue, Elizabeth Ann, Patricia Lynn. Psychologist, Galesburg (Ill.) Research Hosp., 1964, Eastern Ill. Spl. Edn. Coop., 1965-68, Coles County Mental Health Clinic, Mattoon, Ill., 1969; instr. Eastern Ill. U., 1970-76; psychologist Ind. U. Devel. Tng. Center, 1976, Ind. U. Counselling Center, 1976-77, Ind. Women's Prison, Indpls., 1977—, Indpls. Southside Youth Council, 1978—; asso. prof. Ind. U., 1977—; instr. Ivy Tech.; founder Well-Being of Ind., 1981—; cons. in field. Mem. Am. Psychol. Assn. (cert. in pvt. practice), Am. Personnel and Guidance Assn., Biofeedback Soc. Am., Soc. Psychophysiol. Research, Ind. Psychol. Assn., Ind. Personnel and Guidance Assn., Ind. Biofeedback Soc., Phi Eta Sigma, Omicron Delta Kappa. Republican. Methodist. Author papers in field. Home: 206 S Heritage St Bloomington IN 47401 Office: 401 N Randolph St Indianapolis IN 46201

SHRIVER, PHILLIP RAYMOND, univ. pres.; b. Cleve., Aug. 16, 1922; s. Raymond Scott and Corinna Ruth (Smith) S.; B.A., Yale U., 1943; M.A., Harvard U., 1946; Ph.D., Columbia U., 1954; Litt.D., U. Cin., 1966; LL.D., Heidelberg Coll., 1966, Eastern Mich. U., 1972, Ohio State U., 1973; D.H., McKendree Coll., 1973; D.P.S., Albion Coll., 1974; L.H.D., Central State U., 1976, No. Ky. U., 1980; m. Martha Damaris Nye, Apr. 15, 1944; children—Carolyn Shriver Helwig, Susan Shriver La Vine, Melinda Shriver Williams, Darcy, Raymond Scott. Mem. faculty Kent (Ohio) State U., 1947-65, prof. Am. history, 1960-65, asst. dean Coll. Arts and Scis., 1959-63, dean., 1963-65; pres. Miami U., Oxford, Ohio, 1965-81, pres. emeritus, 1981—, prof. history, 1965—; dir. Cin. br. Fed. Res. Bank Cleve., 1968-75, chmn., 1975. Chmn. bd. Univ. Regional Broadcasting, Inc., 1978-79; chmn. council of pres.'s Nat. Assn. State Univs. and Land Grant Colls., 1975-76; trustee Ohio Coll. Library Center, 1968-74; chmn. Mid-Am. Conf., 1971-77; pres. Ohio Coll. Assn., 1974-75. Served with USN, 1943-46; PTO. Recipient Most Disting. Faculty Mem. award Kent State U., 1961; Disting. Acad. Service award AAUP, 1965, Gov.'s award, 1968, A.K. Morris award, 1974. Mem. Orgn. Am. Historians, Ohio Acad. History, Ohio Hist. Soc., Mortar Bd., Phi Beta Kappa, Omicron Delta Kappa, Phi Alpha Theta, Alpha Kappa Psi, Kappa Delta Pi, Phi Eta Sigma, Phi Kappa Phi, Kappa Kappa Psi, Beta Gamma Sigma, Alpha Lambda Delta, Sigma Delta Pi, Alpha Phi Omega, Delta Upsilon. Presbyterian. Author: The Years of Youth, 1960; George A. Bowman: The Biography of an Educator, 1963; (with Donald J. Breen) Ohio's Military Prisons of the Civil War, 1964. Office: 214 Irvin Hall Miami U Oxford OH 45046

SHROCK, STEPHEN ELLSWORTH, univ. adminstr.; b. Indpls., Dec. 22, 1951; s. Ethan Ellsworth and Julia Emogene (Tucker) S.; B.S. in Bus. Adminstrn./Gen. Mgmt., Ind. U., 1974. Bus. rep. Schs. Engring., Purdue U., West Lafayette (Ind.) Campus, 1974-77, bus. adminstr., 1977-79, mgr. univ. stores, 1979-81, mgr. stores and service ops., 1981—. Mem. Nat. Assn. Purchasing Mgmt., Delta Chi. Quaker. Club: Optimists. Home: 3809 Rome Dr Lafayette IN 47905 Office: Service Bldg Purdue U West Lafayette IN 47907

SHROPSHIRE, WILLIAM WALLACE, JR., non-ferrous metals co. exec.; b. Lexington, Ky., Nov. 26, 1936; s. William Wallace and Nell Davis (Humphreys) S.; B.S. in Metall. Engring., Purdue U., 1959; M.B.A., U. Chgo., 1960; m. V. Harlan Wilson, Sept. 3, 1960; children—Virginia Nell, William Harlan. Mem. sales staff Huntington Alloys div. Inco Ltd. (W.Va.), 1961-70, sales mgr. New. Eng., Natick, Mass., 1970-73; mgr. ventures planning and devel. Inco, Ltd., N.Y.C., 1973-76; pres. Am. Chemet Corp., Deerfield, Ill., 1976—; dir. Columbia Paint Co., Spokane, Wash., 1972—; instr. mktg. Marshall U., Huntington, W.Va., 1968-70. Served to capt. U.S. Army, 1961-62. Mem. AIME, Am. Soc. Metals, Am. Powder Metall. Inst., Copper Club. Republican. Episcopalian. Clubs: Skokie Country (Glencoe, Ill.); Montana (Helena, Mont.); Ill. Tennis Assn. (dir. chpt.). Home: 560 Sheridan Rd Winnetka IL 60093 Office: 400 County Line Rd Box 165 Deerfield IL 60015

SHROTE, ROBERT ALLWIN, food co. exec.; b. Morganfield, Ky., Oct. 4, 1924; s. Allwin Dixon and Cora Elizabeth (Jones) S.; student DePauw U., 1942-44; B.S., U. Ill., 1947; m. Paula Esther Anslinger, Sept. 12, 1953; children—Kevin Allwin, Jennifer Sue, Curtis Kent. Sales trainee Standard Oil Co. (Ind.), Rockford, Ill., 1946-47; asst. to plant auditor Swift & Co., Evansville, Ind., 1947-56; systems engr. IBM, Indpls., 1956-59; mgr. programming and computer ops. Am. States Ins. Co., Indpls., 1959-62; mgr. systems devel. Peoples-Home Life Ins. Co., Frankfort, Ind., 1962; data processing mgr. Stokely-Van Camp, Inc., Indpls., 1962-68, asst. dir. info. systems, data processing mgr., 1968-73, staff v.p. info. systems, 1973—. Served to lt. USNR, 1943-46, 50-51. Certified data processor Data Processing Mgmt. Assn. Mem. Grocery Mfrs. Assn. (sec. adminstrv. systems com.), Assn. for Computing Machinery, Phi Gamma Delta. Methodist. Club: Masons. Home: 7139 Creekside Ln Indianapolis IN 46250 Office: 941 N Meridian St Indianapolis IN 46206

SHTOHRYN, DMYTRO M., librarian; b. Zvyniach, Ukraine, Nov. 9, 1923; came to U.S., 1950, naturalized, 1955; m. Mykhailo and Kateryna (Figol) S.; student Ukrainian Free U., Munich, W. Ger., 1947-48; M.A. in Slavic Studies, U. Ottawa (Can.), 1958, B.L.S. summa cum laude, 1959, Ph.D. in Ukrainian Lit., 1970; m. Eustachia Barwinska, Sept. 3, 1955; children—Bohdar O., Liudoslava V. Slavic cataloger U. Ottawa, 1959; cataloger Can. Nat. Research Council Library, 1959-60; mem. faculty U. Ill., Champaign-Urbana, 1960—, prof. library adminstrn., 1975—, head Slavic cataloging, 1964—, lectr. Ukrainian lit., 1969—; vis. prof. U. Ottawa, summer 1974, Ukrainian Free U., 1977; asso. prof. Ukrainian Catholic U., Rome, 1978. Recipient Silver medal Can. Parliament, 1959, Glorier Soc. Can. award, 1959. Mem. Am. Assn. Advancement Slavic Studies, Assn. Advancement Ukrainian Studies (charter, pres. 1981—), ALA, Shevchenko Sci. Soc. (exec. com. 1977—), Ukrainian Library Assn. Am. (pres. 1972-76, pres. elect 1980—), Ukrainian Acad. Arts and Scis. in U.S., Ukrainian Hist. Assn. (exec. com. 1981—), Internat. I. Franko Soc. (pres. 1978-80), Permanent Conf. Ukrainian Studies (chmn. 1979-80), Am.-Ukrainian Assn. U. Profs. (exec. com. 1977—), Ukrainian Writers Soc., Delta Tau Kappa. Mem. Ukrainian Catholic Ch. Compiler: (biographical directory) Ukrainians in North America), 1975; author articles. Editor: Catalogue of Publications of the Ukrainian Academy of Sciences 1918-1930, 1966; newsletter Slavic sect. ALA, 1969. Office: Slavic and East European Dept U Ill Library 1408 W Gregory Dr Urbana IL 61801

SHUGAN, STEVEN MARK, educator; b. Chgo., Apr. 21, 1952; s. David Lester and Charlotte Rose Shugan; B.S. in Chemistry, So. Ill. U., 1973, M.B.A., 1974; Ph.D. in Managerial Econs. and Decision Scis. (fellow), Northwestern U., 1978; m. Irene H. Ginter, Dec. 16, 1973; 1 son, Adam Joshua. Lectr. Grad. Sch. Mgmt., Northwestern U., Evanston, Ill., 1976-77; asst. prof. bus. adminstrn. Grad. Sch. Mgmt., U. Rochester (N.Y.), 1977-79; asst. prof. mktg. Grad. Sch. Bus., U. Chgo., 1979—; chmn., organizer sessions numerous nat. confs., 1979—; cons. various cos., 1976—. Mem. Am. Mktg. Assn., Ops. Research Soc. Am., Assn. for Consumer Research, Inst. Mgmt. Scis., Am. Statis. Assn. Contbr. articles and revs. to profl. jours., chpts. to books. Office: 1101 E 58th St Chicago IL 60637

SHUGAR, SAMUEL ROBERT, communications exec.; b. Houtzdale, Pa., July 18, 1935; s. Orville and Bernice Henrietta (Kramp) S.; A.B. in Math., Wilkes Coll., Wilkes-Barre, Pa., 1956; postgrad. Poly. Inst. Bklyn., 1965-66, M.S. in Mktg., No. Ill. U., 1980; m. Edwardeen Shirley Penhallick, Sept. 3, 1960; children—Dana Renée, Tracy D'Anne, Kristin Kyle. Engring. supr. Western Elec. various locations in U.S., 1956-66; computer prins. instr. AT & T Long Lines, Cooperstown, N.Y., 1966-68; asst. mgr. staff Western Electric Co., Met. N.Y.C., 1968-73, field support mgr., Montgomery, Ill., 1973-78; gen. sales mgr. Teletype Corp., Skokie, Ill., 1978—; teaching cons. computer prins. Cooperstown Sch. Dist., Mary Imogene Bassett Hosp., 1966-68; guest lectr. Am. Mgmt. Assn., 1968-70; discussant Soc. Mgmt. Info. Systems Conf., 1970. Mem. Bound Brook (N.J.) Sch. Bd., 1971-72, v.p., 1972-73; elder, deacon Fox Valley Presbyn. Ch., Geneva, Ill.; bd. dirs. Assn. for Individual Devel., Aurora, Ill. Mem. Am. Mktg. Assn., Telephone Pioneers Am., Beta Gamma Sigma, Alpha Mu Alpha. Clubs: Montgomery Amateur Radio, Masons. Contbg. author to The Burning Bush, 1974—, Western Electric Engr., 1958, 70.

SHULER, FRANK F., dentist; b. Janesville, Wis., Apr. 1, 1926; s. Frank F. and Ruth K. Shuler; ed. U. Wis., 1946-48; D.D.S., Marquette U., 1952; m. Jean Brann; children—Charles, Kathryn, Andrew, Kristine. Gen. practice dentistry, Clinton, Wis.; mem. Wis. Bd. Dental Examiners, 1980—. Mem. Rock County Dept. Pub. Welfare; village trustee; mem. Wis. Gov.'s Com. Brotherhood Week; mem. planning com. Rock County Library. Recipient Five Outstanding Young Men of Wis. award, 1960; Seldon Waldo award U.S. Jaycees, 1962; Disting. Alumnus award Marquette U. Sch. Dentistry, 1973. Fellow Internat. Coll. Dentists, Am. Coll. Dentists; mem. ADA (pres. 1976-77), Wis. Dental Assn. (pres. 1970-71, Disting. Service award 1973), Rock County Dental Soc., Wis. Assn. Professions (pres. 1968-69), Acad. Gen. Dentistry (pres. Wis. chpt. 1970), Chgo. Dental Soc., Am. Soc. Dentistry for Children, Fedn. Dentaire Internationale (del. 1976-79), Pierre Fauchard Acad., Am. Legion, Kappa Sigma, Omicron Kappa Upsilon. Lutheran. Office: 714 Milwaukee Rd Clinton WI 53525

SHULMAN, ARTHUR DAVID, psychologist; b. Port Jervis, N.Y., June 28, 1942; s. William E. and Rose (Albert) S.; B.A., Alfred U., 1964; M.A., McMaster U., 1966; Ph.D. in Distinction, State U. N.Y., 1969; children—Shanna, Joanna. Vocat. and rehab. counselor Jewish Vocat. Service, Toronto, Ont., Can., 1966; asst. prof. psychology Washington U., St. Louis, 1968-74; research psychologist Inst. Black Studies, St. Louis, 1973-77; asso. prof. psychology Washington U., St. Louis, 1974—, dir. social psychology program, 1974—; vis. scholar Communications Studies Group, U. Coll., U. London (Eng.), 1975; vis. sr. research fellow dept. psychology U. Melbourne (Australia), 1977, Ashworth scholar in sociology and psychology, 1979-80, sr. research asso., 1981—. HEW grantee, 1974-75, 77—; Telecom Australia contractee, 1979-81. Mem. Am., Australian, Midwestern psychol. assns., Soc. Exptl. Social Psychology, Soc. Psychol. Study of Social Issues, AAAS, Am. Sociol. Assn., Gerontology Soc., Sigma Xi, Psi Chi. Contbr. articles on communication processes, tech., coping strategies across the life span and social psychology to profl. jours. and books. Office: PO Box 1125 Dept Psychology Washington U Saint Louis MO 63130

SHULTIS, JAMES MICHAEL, advt. co. exec.; b. Mpls., Mar. 16, 1944; s. James Edward and Muriel Helen S.; B.A., U. Minn., 1971; m. Lizabeth. Asst. store mgr. Sears, Roebuck & Co., Coon Rapids, Minn., 1965-69; prodn. mgr. U. Minn. Newspaper, Mpls., 1970-71; v.p., co-owner Advt. Communications, Inc., Mpls., 1971—. Served with U.S. Army, 1965-71. Mem. N.W. Council Advt. Agencies, Advt. Fedn. Minn., Eden Prairie C. of C. Roman Catholic. Home: 12346 Oxbow Dr Eden Prairie MN 55344 Office: Advertising Communications Inc 10800 Lyndale Ave S Minneapolis MN 55420

SHULTS, EUGENE CHARLES, computer software co. exec.; b. Detroit, Mar. 22, 1930; s. Nathan Charles and Florence Theresa (Busch) S.; B.A., Wayne State U., 1953, M.S., 1962; m. Carol Joy Staton, July 16, 1960; children—Patty, Doreen, Chuck, Kim, Mark, Eric, Chris. Systems engr. IBM, Santa Barbara, Calif., 1962-67; mem. systems staff U. Calif., Santa Barbara, 1967-69; pres. Jefferson Fin. Systems, Chgo., 1969—. Served with USN, 1953-57. cert. data processor. Home: 25465 N Oakwood Dr E Barrington IL 60010 Office: Jefferson Financial Systems 5245 W Lawrence Ave Chicago IL 60630

SHUMATE, PATRICIA EAST, educator; b. Chgo., Aug. 28, 1952; d. Dwight Irving and Elsie East; B.S., U. Ill., 1974, M.Ed., 1977, adminstrv. cert., 1980; m. Mack Harrice Shumate, Jr., June 14, 1975. Tchr. home econs. Proviso East High Sch., Maywood, Ill., 1974-76, York Community High Sch., Elmhurst, Ill., 1976—; cons. Ill. State U., 1980-81; adv. mem. Nat. Coll. Edn.-Job Creation Project, 1979—; nat. cons. FHA/HERO youth orgn. Mem. Am. Vocat. Assn., Am. Home Econs. Assn., Ill. Coop. Vocat. Edn. Coordinators (dir.), Ill. Vocat. Assn., Ill. Vocat. Home Econs. Tchrs. Assn. (regional dir.), Ill. Home Econs. Assn. (dir.), Chgo. Suburban Work Coordinators, Alpha Phi. Office: 355 W St Charles Rd Elmhurst IL 60162

SIBILSKY, ROBERT L., univ. adminstr.; b. Hancock, Mich., Oct. 4, 1943; s. Elmer E. and Arbutus (Hearn) S.; A.A., Suomi Coll., 1963; B.S., No. Mich. U., 1975; m. Darlene M. Krym, Dec. 21, 1963; children—Jim, Donald, Joan. Asst. purchasing agt. Mich. Tech. U., 1963-65, acting dir. purchasing, 1965-67; buyer No. Mich. U., Marquette, 1967-77, asst. dir. purchasing, 1977—; sec.-treas. Sanderson, Sibilsky & Sibilsky, Inc.; former pres. County Plumbing & Heating Co., Sibilsky & Sibilsky, Inc., LTASC Corp. Trustee, 1st United Meth. Ch., 1970. Mem. Mich. Assn. Coll. and Univ. Purchasing Agts., Nat. Assn. Ednl. Buyers, Home Builders Assn., Upper Peninsula Sch. Bus. Ofcls., Air Force Assn., Nat. Fedn. Ind. Businessmen. Clubs: Golden Wildcat (exec. bd.), Elks. Home: 1038 Ortman Rd Marquette MI 49855 Office: No Mich Univ Adminstrn Bldg Marquette MI 49855

SICAT, LUZVIMINDA FRANCISCO, radiologist; b. Manila, Philippines, Aug. 24, 1941; came to U.S., 1966; d. Victoriano and Priscilla (Desiderio) Francisco; M.D., U. St. Tomas, 1964; m. Alfonso V. Sicat, Aug. 22, 1965; children—Hans, Eric. Intern, Trinity Lutheran Hosp., Kansas City, Mo., 1966-67, resident, 1968-69; resident in internal medicine Menorah Med. Center, Kansas City, Mo., 1969-70, resident in diagnostic radiology, 1970-73; practice medicine specializing in radiology, Jefferson City, Mo., 1973-75, Warrensburg, Mo., 1975-77; staff radiologist Children's Mercy Hosp., Kansas City, Mo., 1977-79, VA Med. Center, Kansas City, 1979—. Recipient Physicians Recognition award AMA, 1979; diplomate Am. Bd. Radiology. Mem. Mo. Med. Soc., Jackson County Med. Soc., Am. Coll. Radiology, Radiol. Soc. N.Am., Mo. Radiol. Soc., Kansas City Radiol. Soc. Home: Route 4 Warrensburg MO 64093 Office: 510 E Gay St Warrensburg MO 64093

SICHLAU, JAMES HAROLD, assn. exec.; b. Vineland, N.J., Mar. 27, 1945; s. Harry William and Gertrude Penny S.; B.A., Ill. Coll., 1967; M.S., Western Ill. U., 1970; m. Linda Ring, Dec. 31, 1975; 1 son by previous marriage, Michael James; 3 stepchildren. Social work trainee Jacksonville (Ill.) State Hosp., 1967-68, mental health program worker, 1968-69, psychologist intern, 1970-71; staff psychologist, dir. children's programs Hancock County Mental Health Clinic, Carthage, Ill., 1971-73; exec. dir. Cass County Mental Health Assn., Beardstown, Ill., 1973—; part-time instr. Lincoln Land Community Coll.; asso. in psychiatry So. Ill. U. Sch. Medicine. Lay leader First United Meth. Ch., 1978-80; team coordinator World Wide Marriage Encounter Meth. Expression, Ill., 1979-80, presenting couple, 1979—; charter mem. Campus Jaycees, Jacksonville State Hosp., 1968-69. Clubs: K.T., Lions (sec. Beardstown 1976-77), Masons, Elks. Home: 900 Adams Beardstown IL 62618 Office: 101 W 15th Beardstown IL 62618

SICK, MELVIN JOHN, educator; b. Avoca, Iowa, Oct. 1, 1934; s. Alfred and Freda Johanna (Schmidt) S.; B.S. in Gen. Scis., Dana Coll., 1958; M.A. in Gen. Scis., U. No. Iowa, 1969; postgrad. (NSF grantee) Iowa State U., 1960, Nebr. Wesleyan U., 1961, Temple U., 1962, Drake U., 1964; m. Patsy Jo Crees, June 16, 1957; children—David Jon, Connie Jo. Tchr. sci. Tri Center Community Sch., Neola and Persia, Iowa, 1958-59, Elk Horn-Kimballton Community Sch., Elk Horn, Iowa, 1959-61, Stuart (Iowa) Community Sch., 1961-68; asst. prof. sci. Iowa Central Community Coll., Ft. Dodge, 1969—; salesman Radio Shack, 1975—; participant various NSF Summer Insts.; mem. Gov.'s Sci. Adv. Com., State of Iowa. Mem. NEA (life), Iowa State Edn. Assn., Iowa Acad. Sci. (life), Am. Assn. Physics Tchrs., Am. Radio Relay League, Iowa Higher Edn. Assn. Democrat. Presbyterian. Clubs: Amateur Radio (pres. club 1977-79), Computer (pres. 1980-81); Lions (pres. 1976-77, dir. 1975-78, dist. zone chmn. 1977-79, dist. chmn. convention 1979-80, dist. chmn. environment 1979—) Ft. Dodge. Research in x-ray crystallography, electronic circuitry. Home: 2640 16th Ave N Fort Dodge IA 50501 Office: 330 Ave M Fort Dodge IA 50501

SIDDENS, JANE, psychologist; b. Eldorado, Ill., Oct. 17, 1927; d. Charles Edward and Elsie Lorraine (Kelly) Proctor; B.S., U. So. Miss., Hattiesburg, 1974, M.A., 1976; Ph.D., Ind. U., 1978, Clayton U., 1978; divorced; children—David P., William C. Social worker Ill. Dept. Public Welfare, 1965-66; mem. faculty Vincennes (Ind.) U., 1966-67; owner wholesale supply co., Amarillo, Tex., 1968-73; frat. housemother U. So. Miss., 1974; psychologist, dir. residential services Martin Luther Home, Beatrice, Nebr., 1976; asst. dir. intake, screening and referral Amarillo State Center, 1977-78; dir. vocat. services Knox County Assn. Retarded Citizens, Vincennes, Ind., 1978, dir. children's and psychol. services, 1979—; pvt. practice psychology, 1981—; bd. dirs. Vols. for Youth on Probation, 1978—; speaker in field. Bd. dirs. Christian Edn. for Retarded Citizens, 1978—, Lawrence County (Ill.) Blood Program, 1965; treas. Lawrence County Young Republicans, 1965. Mem. Nat. Soc. Autistic Children, Nebr. Psychol. Assn., Tex. Psychol. Assn., Am. Assn. Marriage and Family Therapists (clin.), U. So. Miss. Grad. Assn. Students in Psychology (past pres.), Mensa, Psi Chi. Presbyterian. Office: 2322 Marshall St Mattoon IL 61938

SIDHU, AMARJIT SINGH, architect, planner; b. Lyall Pur, India, Apr. 13, 1935; came to U.S., 1962, naturalized, 1975; s. Pal Singh and Dalip (Kaur) S.; B.Arch., Indian Inst. Tech., 1961; M.Arch., M.S. in City Planning, U. Pa., 1964; m. Jaswinder Kaur, June 15, 1969; children—Navreet K., Kavanjit S. Asst. architect Corbusier's Office, Chandigarh, India, 1961-62; planner Wallce and McHarg, Architects-Planners, Phila., 1963-64; prin. A.S. Sidhu, Architect-Planner, New Delhi, India, 1967-69; asso. firm Shaw and Assos., Chgo., 1969—. Mem. AIA, Am. Inst. Planners. Home: 2207 Greenview Rd Northbrook IL 60062 Office: 55 E Monroe St Chicago IL 60603

SIDHU, KIRPAL SINGH, public health scientist; b. Rani Majra, India, Sept. 12, 1938; naturalized, 1977; s. Joginder Singh and Bachan Kaur S.; B.V.Sc., Panjab U., India, 1959; M.S., U. Mo., 1966; Ph.D., Okla. State U., 1969; m. Narvinder Kaur Hira; children—Jasvinder S., Sarbjit S. Vet. asst. surgeon Palampur Regional Nutrition Research Center, India, 1961-62; grad. asst. U. Mo., 1963-66, Okla. State U., 1966-69; asst. prof. Ohio Coll. Podiatric Medicine, 1969-70; research asso. Mich. State U., 1970-72; research instr. U. Miami, 1972-74; public health scientist Mich. Dept. Public Health, Lansing, 1974—; research scientist dept. pharmacology and toxicology Coll. Human Medicine, Mich. State U., East Lansing, 1975—. Mem. lang. devel. com. East Lansing Public Schs., 1977-78. Mem. AAAS, Soc. Toxicology, Am. Inst. Biol. Sci., Am. Soc. Animal Sci., Am. Dairy Sci. Assn., Am. Conf. Govtl. Indsl. Hygienists, Am. Registry Cert. Animal Scientists, Sigma Xi. Club: Sikh Cultural Assn. Contbr. articles to profl. jours. Home: 1989 Pinecrest Dr East Lansing MI 48823 Office: Mich Dept Public Health 3500 N Logan St PO Box 30035 Lansing MI 48909

SIDOTI, DANIEL ROBERT, beverage co. exec.; b. North Bergen, N.J., Jan. 17, 1921; s. John and Dora (Disposti) S.; student N.Y. U., 1939-42; B.S., Union Coll., 1947; M.S. in Indsl. Engring., Stevens Inst. Tech., 1959; m. Gloria Virginia Ebaugh, Mar. 24, 1951; 1 dau., L. Stephanie. Group leader, asst. to research mgr. Gen. Foods Corp., Tarrytown. N.Y., 1947-66; prodn. mgr. Frenchette div. Carter Wallace Corp., Cranbury, N.J., 1969; sect. head Monsanto Co., St. Louis, 1966-69; research mgr. Anheuser Busch Companies, Inc., St. Louis, 1969-80, brand devel. mgr., 1980—. Served with USN, 1943-46; PTO. Mem. Inst. Food Technologists (chmn. St. Louis 1972-73, nat. council 1974—), Am. Assn. Cereal Chemists, Am. Soc. Brewing Chemists. Patentee in field. Home: 500 Wellshire Ct Ballwin MO 63011 Office: 1 Busch Pl Saint Louis MO 63118

SIDWELL, STEPHEN RICHARD, mfg. co. exec.; b. Santa Ana, Calif., July 31, 1948; s. Max R. and Goldie S. (Hanson) S.; student Kearney State Coll., 1966-67; B.S., U. Nebr., 1975; m. Lynn K. Kinzer, May 24, 1969; 1 dau., Tiffany L. Receiving insp. Dale Electronics, Columbus, Nebr., 1968-69; quality control supr. Square D Co., Lincoln, Nebr., 1972-76; sr. quality engr. Black & Decker Mfg. Co., Tarboro, N.C., 1976-78; quality assurance mgr. Amerock Corp., Rockford, Ill., 1978-80, mgr. prodn. and inventory control, 1980—. Mem. quality assurance adv. bd. Rock Valley Coll., Rockford. Served with U.S. Army, 1969-71. Mem. Am. Soc. Quality Control (treas. chpt. 1979-80, vice chmn. 1980-81), Nat. Mgmt. Assn., Am. Mgmt. Assn., Am. Prodn. and Inventory Control Soc. Republican. Home: 10314 Chris Dr Roscoe IL 61073 Office: 4000 Auburn St Rockford IL 61101

SIEBEN, HARRY ALBERT, JR., state legislator; b. Hastings, Minn., Nov. 24, 1943; s. Harry A. and Mary S. (Luger) S.; B.A., Winona (Minn.) State Coll., 1965; J.D., U. Minn., 1968; m. Wanda Alphin, Aug. 21, 1971; children—Jeffrey, Thomas. Admitted to Minn. bar, 1968; partner firm Grose, Von Holtum, Sieben & Schmidt, Mpls., 1969—; mem. Minn. Ho. of Reps. from 52d Dist., 1971—. Served with U.S. Army, 1968-69. Mem. Democrat-Farm-Labor Party. Roman Catholic. Office: 900 Midwest Plaza E Minneapolis MN 55402

SIEBEN, IVAN HENDRIK, energy saving products mfg. co. exec.; b. Antwerp, Belgium, Aug. 27, 1932; came to U.S., 1978; s. Jan Jozef and Theodora Maria (Hurkens) S.; Lic. Econ. Scis., U. Gent (Belgium), 1954; m. Gilberte Hermus, July 31, 1958; children—Inez M., Patrick M. Dir. sales AGFA Gevaert do Brasil, 1967-72; div. mgr. BASF Can. Ltd., 1973-76; dir. comml. BASF Indonesia Magnetics, 1976-78, also dir.; dir. mktg. BASF Systems, Bedford, Mass., 1978-80; pres., mng. dir. Enertec Systems, Inc., Thermodecor Wallcovering Industries Inc., Barrington, Ill., 1980—. Mem. Am. Mktg. Assn. Roman Catholic.

SIEBEN, JAMES GEORGE, adj. gen. Minn.; b. Hastings, Minn., Apr. 19, 1924; s. Harry A. and Irene H. (Buckley) S.; student U. Minn., Stanford U.; m. Charlotte Jean Gove, July 10, 1954; children—James, Lisa, Terrance. Served as enlisted man AUS, 1942-45; commd. 2d lt. N.G., advanced through grades to maj. gen.; served as 1st lt. U.S. Army, 1951-52; comdt. Minn. Mil. Acad.; now adj. gen. Minn. Mem. NG Assn. of U.S., Adj. Gen's Assn., Am. Legion, VFW. Decorated Silver Star medal with oak leaf cluster, Purple Heart, Bronze Star medal, Combat Inf. badge, Minn. Commendation medal, Minn. medal for merit, others. Office: Veterans Service Bldg Saint Paul MN 55155

SIEBENMORGEN, PAUL, physician; b. Terre Haute, Ind., Sept. 16, 1920; s. Louis and Ruby E. (Curtis) S.; B.S. in Edn., Ind. State U., 1941; M.D., Ind. U., 1944; m. Jane Maxine Waggoner, June 20, 1948; children—Paul Stephen, Elizabeth Ann, Susan Lynn. Intern, Meth. Hosp., Indpls., 1944-45; practice medicine, Terre Haute, 1947—; mem. staff St. Anthony Hosp., Terre Haute, pres. staff, 1975, instr. Hosp. Sch. Nursing, 1948-58, mem. adv. council, 1959-60; asso. clin. faculty Terre Haute center for med. edn. Sch. Medicine, Ind. U., 1973—. Pres., Vigo County Heart Assn., 1965, 66; chmn. profl. div. United Fund, Terre Haute, 1960; pres. Med. Edn. Found. Terre Haute, 1976, Vigo County Bd. Health, 1967-71, 73-75, 81; mem. Ind. Health Coordinating Council, 1977—, sec., 1981; bd. dirs. So. Ind. Health Systems Agy., 1976-79; trustee Ind. State U., 1975—, v.p., 1979-80; trustee Terre Haute Regional Hosp., 1975-81, staff pres., 1975. Served to capt. M.C., AUS, 1945-47. Mem. AMA, Am. (charter fellow), Ind. (dist. pres. 1971; state dir. 1973-80, pres. 1980) acads. family physicians, Ind. State Med. Assn. (trustee 1978—) Terre Haute Acad. Medicine (pres. 1974-75), Vigo County Med. Soc. (pres. 1970), Aesculapian Soc. Wabash Valley, Ind. State U. Alumni Assn. (pres. 1971-73), Vigo County Comprehensive Health Planning Council (sec. 1975, charter mem.), Blue Key, Alpha Phi Omega, Sigma Alpha Epsilon, Phi Rho Sigma, Kappa Delta Pi. Mem. Christian Ch. (bd. mem. Ind. region 1966-76, gen. bd. 1969-75, 77-81, moderator Ind. region 1974-76). Clubs: Masons, Elks, Wabash Valley Lecture (pres. 1959-60). Home: 2515 N 7th St Terre Haute IN 47804 Office: 501 Hospital Ln Terre Haute IN 47802

SIEBERT, DONALD EDWARD, mktg. research exec.; b. Cin., Jan. 20, 1941; s. Edward Stephan and Marion Ruth (Carroll) S.; B.S. in Psychology, Xavier U., Cin., 1964; M.B.A. in Mgmt., U. Cin., 1967; m. Diane L. Mazur, Aug. 16, 1980; children—Michael Sean, David Edward. Project dir. Burke Mktg. Research Inc., Cin., 1967-69, sr. project dir., 1969-72, account exec., 1972-75, asso. dir. copy research, 1975-76, mktg. mgr., 1976-78, v.p., 1978—. Adviser, Cin. Jr. Achievement; judge, com. mem. U.S. Figure Skating Assn. Mem. Am. Mktg. Assn. Club: Queen City Figure Skating (pres. Cin. 1972-74). Home: 7706 Glenover Dr Cincinnati OH 45236 Office: 2600 Victory Pkwy Cincinnati OH 45206

SIECK, HAROLD F., state legislator; b. Pleasant Dale, Nebr., Dec. 29, 1916; ed. public schs.; m. Elise Meinberg, Feb. 8, 1942; children—Thomas, Barbara, Roger, Gerald, Annette. Farmer; mem. Nebr. Legislature, 1978—. Bd. dirs. Seward County (Nebr.) Rural Power Dist.; chmn. Lower Platte S. NRD; Democratic precinct committeeman. Lutheran. *

SIECZKA, EDWARD STANLEY, engr.; b. Detroit, May 24, 1924; s. Dominic and Blanche (Rotffan) S.; grad. Gen. Motors Inst., 1948; A.A.S., South Macomb Community Coll., 1974; B.S. in Mfg. Engring., Detroit Inst. Tech., 1976; postgrad. U. Wis., 1980—; m. Dolores Kroly, May 1, 1948; children—Colette, Charmain. Asst. automotive zone service mgr. Packard Motor Car Co., Detroit, 1948-50; major proposal engr. Ex-Cell-O Corp., Detroit, 1950-56, major machine designer and checker, 1956-65; mfg. research and devel. design checker Bower Roller Bearing div. Federal-Mogul Corp., Southfield, Mich., 1965-66, research and devel. project engr., 1966-71, product design leader, 1971-72, sr. mfg. engr., 1972-74; chief engr. Enterprise Machine Products Corp., Madison Heights, Mich., 1974-75; sr. project engr. Kelsey-Hayes Co., Romulus, Mich., 1975-77, mfg. engring. mgr., 1977-79, sr. project engr., 1979-80. Served with USAAF, 1942-46. Registered profl. engr., Calif., Can. Cert. mfg. engr. Mem. Nat. Soc. Profl. Engrs., ASME, Soc. Mfg. Engrs. Democrat. Roman Catholic. Club: K. of C. Home: 47683 Westlake Dr Utica MI 48087

SIEFKER, DONALD L(EON), librarian; b. Seymour, Ind., Jan. 4, 1935; s. Louis A. and Gertrude M. (Stahl) S.; A.B., Wabash Coll., 1957; M.A., Ind. U., 1961; m. Barbara L. Marshall, June 4, 1961; children—Lynn, Scott, Lori. Reference and catalog librarian Earlham Coll., 1961-64; asst. librarian, instr. Tri-State U., 1964-66; head div. library service, asst. prof. library ser. Ball State U., 1966—. Served with U.S. Army, 1958. Recipient award for appreciation of loyal support Ind. U. Alumni Assn., 1976, cert. in archives and records mgmt. Ohio Hist. Soc., 1971. Mem. ALA, Assn. Coll. and Research Libraries, Ind. Library Assn., Steinbeck Soc. (dir. 1978-80, spl. asst. to pres. 1981—), Tri-State Gas Engine and Tractor Assn., Ind. U. Grad. Sch. Library and Info. Sci. Alumni Assn. (pres. 1975-76, dir. 1972-77). Mem. United Church of Christ. Indexer 4 books on Steinbeck; compiler 2 cumulative indexes to jours.; contbr. articles to profl. jours.; asst. editor: Steinbeck Monograph Series, 1971-79; mng. editor Steinbeck Quar., 1970-81, editorial bd., 1981—. Office: Ball State U Bracken Library Muncie IN 47306

SIEG, CAROLYN, nun, ednl. adminstr.; b. Des Plaines, Ill., July 4, 1939; d. Joseph Frank and Catherine Elizabeth (Stanke) S.; B.A., St. Mary of the Woods Coll.; M.A., Coll. St. Thomas; Joined Benedictine Community, Roman Catholic Ch., 1956; tchr. pariochial elem. schs., Tex., Ill., 1958-67; tchr. St. Joan of Arc Sch., Lisle, Ill., 1964-66, prin., 1967—, also bd. dirs. Mem. religious edn. bd., parish council Roman Cath. Ch.; bd. dirs. Benedictine Sisters, 1978-81. Mem. Joliet Diocesan Prins. Club. Address: Saint Joan of Arc Sch 4913 Columbia Ave Lisle IL 60532

SIEGAL, BURTON LEE, product designer cons.; b. Chgo., Sept. 27, 1931; s. Norman A. and Sylvia (Vitz) S.; B.S. in Mech. Engring., U. Ill., 1953; m. Rita Goran, Apr. 11, 1954; children—Norman, Laurence Scott. Torpedo designer U.S. Naval Ordnance, Forest Park, Ill., 1953-54; chief engr. Gen. Aluminum Corp., Chgo., 1954-55; product designer Chgo. Aerial Industries, Melrose Park, Ill., 1955-58; chief designer Emil J. Paidar Co., Chgo., 1958-59; founder, pres. Budd Engring. Corp., Chgo., 1959—; dir. Dur-A-Case Corp., Chgo.; cons. in field. Mem. math., sci. and English adv. bds. Skokie High Sch., 1975-79; electronic cons. Chgo. Police Dept., 1964. Winner Internat. Extrusion Design Competition, 1975. Mem. Soc. Automotive Engrs. Jewish. Contbr. articles to tech. publs.; holder 84 patents. Office: 8707 Skokie Blvd Skokie IL 60077

SIEGAL, RITA GORAN, engring. co. exec.; b. Chgo., July 16, 1934; d. Leonard and Anabelle (Soloway) Goran; student U. Ill., 1951-53, Roosevelt U., 1953-54; B.A., DePaul U., 1956; m. Burton L. Siegal, Apr. 11, 1954; children—Norman, Laurence Scott. Tchr. elementary schs. Chgo. Public Schs., 1956-58; v.p. Easy Living Products Co., Chgo., 1960-62; free-lance interior designer, Chgo., 1968-73; dist. sales mgr. Super Girls, Chgo., 1976; v.p. Budd Engring., Skokie, Ill., 1974—; pres. Easy Living Products, 1979—. Mem. adv. council Skokie High Schs., 1975-79; adv. Cub Scouts Skokie council Boy Scouts Am. Recipient Cub Scout awards Boy Scouts Am., 1971-72, Sales award Super Girls, 1976. Mem. Buten Museum, Nutrition for Optimal Health Assn. (dir., bus. mgr. 1980-81), Women in Mgmt., North Shore Art League. Club: Profit Plus Investment (founder 1970). Office: 8707 Skokie Blvd Skokie IL 60077

SIEGEL, LESTER E., public relations cons.; b. Chgo., May 9, 1919; s. Emanuel and Bessie (Bass) S.; student U. Ill., 1937-41, Northwestern U., 1946-47; children—Paul, Steven. With Ruder & Finn, N.Y.C., 1951-61; dir. bus. devel. Martin E. Janis, Chgo., 1962-69; freelance bus. and public relations cons., Chgo., 1946—; cons. to Golda Meir, 1952, 73-74. Served with USAAF, 1943-45. Mem. No. Ill. Indsl. Assn., Greater O'Hare Assn., Sales-Mktg. Execs. Club, Nat. Automatic Merchandising Assn. Clubs: Lake Point Tower Duplicate Bridge, B'nai B'rith. Home and Office: 5225 N Kenmore Chicago IL 60640

SIEGEL, MARGOT MARJORIE (MRS. HAROLD SIEGEL), public relations exec., author, journalist; b. St. Paul, Apr. 2, 1923; d. William and Jeanne (Braunschweig) Auerbacher; B.A., U. Minn., 1944; m. Harold Siegel, Oct. 26, 1956; children—William Joseph,

Sandra Marguerite. Editor, corr. Fairchild Publs., N.Y.C., also Europe, 1946-60; pub. relations dir. Walker Art Center, Mpls., 1962-66; free lance book reviewer, travel writer Mpls. Star and Tribune, 1969-72; partner Siegel-Hogan Enterprise, Mpls., 1970—; columnist Mpls. Star, 1976-77, Twin Cities Woman, until 1978; columnist Twin Cities mag. Founder, bd. dirs., pres. Friends of Goldstein Gallery, U. Minn. Mem. Mpls. Fashion Group (dir. 1967-68), Women in Communications, Pub. Relations Soc. Am., U. Minn. Alumni Assn. (dir.). Clubs: Overseas Press Am., Minn. Press; President's (U. Minn.). Author: Look Forward to a Career: Fashion, 1970, 3d printing, 1977. Columnist, Corp. Report mag., 1973-81. Home: 25 Park Ln Minneapolis MN 55416 Office: 920 Nicollet Mall Minneapolis MN 55402

SIEGEL, SAUL MARSHALL, psychiatrist, psychoanalyst; b. Chgo., July 16, 1921; s. Morris and Lena (Adler) S.; B.A., U. Chgo., 1942, Ph.D., 1951, M.D., 1955; m. Janis Fey, Dec. 25, 1969; children—Cara, Stephen, Matthew, Amie. Intern, U. Chgo. Clinics, 1955-56, resident, 1956-59; dir. adult psychiatry clinic Michael Reese Hosp., Chgo., 1959-74, dir. psychiatry clinic, 1974-78, sr. cons., 1978—; pvt. practice psychiatry, Chgo., 1959—; clin. asso. prof. U. Chgo., 1972—; instr. Chgo. Inst. Psychoanalysis, 1977—. Served with USAAF, 1943-46. Fund for Psychoanalytic Research grantee, 1981—. Mem. Am. Psychiatric Assn., Am. Psychol. Assn., Am. Psychoanalytic Assn., Phi Beta Kappa. Contbr. articles to profl. jours. Office: 151 N Michigan Ave Chicago IL 60601

SIEGEL, SHELDON LLOYD, coll. dean; b. Chgo., Sept. 18, 1932; s. Oscar and Min S.; B.S., U. Ill., 1954, M.S., 1956; postgrad. U. Chgo., 1960, Northeastern Ill. U., 1971-73; M.Ed., Loyola U., Chgo., 1976, Ed.D., 1980. Producer-dir. childrens program WILL-TV, 1954-60; writer Coronet Instructional Films, 1960-64; writer-editor/project supr. sales promotion Field Enterprises Ednl. Corp., 1964-68; registrar, dean students, tchr. Columbia Coll. of Chgo., 1968-72; dean students, dir. admissions Ill. Coll. Optometry, Chgo., 1972; with Spertus Coll. Judaica, 1979; lectr. student personnel work Loyola U. Active, Ravenswood YMCA, Leadership awards, 1973, 74. Mem. Am., Ill. assns. collegiate registrars and admissions officer, Am. Personnel and Guidance Assn., Ill. Assn. Student Financial Aid Officers, U. Ill., Loyola U. (life) alumni assns., Phi Delta Kappa, Sigma Delta Chi, Century Club. Recipient Sr. Class award for excellence in guidance and teaching Columbia Coll., 1971; Social Sci. Research Council fellow, 1957; writer numerous films in in edn., 1960-64; contbr. articles to profl. jours. Office: 618 S Michigan Ave Chicago IL 60616

SIEGFRIED, S(AMUEL) CEDRIC, lawyer; b. Independence, Mo., July 31, 1914; s. Mark Harrison and Madge May (Craig) S.; A.B., Mo. U., 1938, J.D., 1939; student Kirksville State U., 1932, Central Mo. State Coll., 1934; children—Mary Elizabeth, Martha Jane, Cedric Mark. Admitted to Mo. bar, 1939, Fed. bar, 1939, Fed. Communications bar, 1949; asst. pros. atty. Jackson County (Mo.), 1948-50; gen. counsel Jackson County Zoning and Planning Commn., 1950-52; city counselor City of Independence (Mo.), 1966-67; individual practice law Cedric Siegfried, Atty. At Law and Assos., Inc., P.C., Independence, 1939—; incorporator, gen. legal counsel, dir. Noland Rd. Bank, Independence, 1964—, White Tractor Parts, 1954—, L.S.B. Corp., 1974—, Turner Contracting Co., 1955—, M.H. Siegfried & Co., 1952—, Sterling Corp., 1962—, Isokinetic Corp., 1976—; founder 1st Citibank, Olathe, Kans., 1977-78, now gen. counsel, treas.; trial examiner Midwest region CAB, 1950-55. Founder, Independence Area Devel. Corp., 1952, Midcontinent Devel. Council, 1960; mem. U. Mo. Law Sch. Found.; bd. dirs. Kansas City Heart Assn., 1955-69, Mo. Heart Assn., 1960-65, Am. Heart Assn., 1965. Served as flight instr. USAF, 1942-45. Hon. fellow Harry S Truman Library, U. Mo. Mem. C. of C., Independence Bar Assn., Mo. Bar Assn., Am. Bar Assn., Jackson County Bar Assn. (pres. 1958-60), SAR, Phi Delta Phi. Democrat. Mem. Reorganized Ch. of Jesus Christ of Latter Day Saints. Clubs: Rotary, Jefferson (U. Mo.). Office: 308 W Maple Bldg Suite 200 Independence MO 64050

SIEGLER, ROBERT STUART, psychologist, educator; b. Chgo., May 12, 1949; s. Allen and Ilse Siegler; B.A., U. Ill., 1970; M.A., SUNY, Stony Brook, 1972, Ph.D., 1974; m. Alice G. Rysdon, Aug. 21, 1972; children—Todd Michael, Beth Ann, Aaron Julius. Asst. prof. psychology Carnegie Mellon U., Pitts., 1974-78, asso. prof., 1978-80; asso. prof. U. Chgo., 1980—. Spencer fellow Nat. Acad. Edn., 1978. Mem. Am. Psychol. Assn. (disting. young developmental psychologist award 1979), Am. Ednl. Research Assn., Soc. Research in Child Devel., Psychonomic Soc. Editor: Children's Thinking: What Develops?, 1978; mem. editorial bd. Child Devel., 1976—, Devel. Psychology, 1977—; contbr. articles to profl. jours. Home: 724 Gardner Rd Flossmoor IL 60422 Office: Dept Edn U Chicago Chicago IL 60637

SIEH, MAURINE KAY, nurse; b. Leon, Iowa, Sept. 28, 1950; d. Vernon Charles and Dorothy Maxine (Akes) Dobson; B.S. in Nursing, N.E. Mo. State U., 1972; m. Robert Hans Sieh, Nov. 18, 1972; children—Robert Carter, Jennifer Clarissa. Charge nurse psychiat. unit St. John's Hosp., Springfield, Mo., 1972-74; public health nurse Will County Health Dept., Joliet, Ill., 1974-75; unit nurse Mental Health Inst. Mentally Retarded Children, Park Forest, Ill., 1977-79; instr. Lamaze method childbirth, Topeka, Kans., 1981; staff nurse, co-chmn. nursing standards com. Menninger Found., Topeka, 1980-81; fund raiser local chpts. Am. Cancer Soc., Mental Health Assn. Mem. Nat. Assn. Female Execs., Am. Soc. Psychoprophylaxis in Obstetrics. Mem. Brethren Ch. Home: 4953 Oak Leaf Dr Jackson MS 39212

SIEKMANN, SHIRLEY JEANNE, arts adminstr.; b. South Bend, Ind., Aug. 31, 1928; d. George F. and Clarice B. (Rapp) Burdick; student St. Mary's Coll., 1946-47; B.A., DePauw U., 1950; postgrad. Ind. U., South Bend, 1951; m. Max R. Siekmann, June 23, 1951; children—Sheryl, Pamela, David. Tchr. public schs., St. Joseph County, Ind., 1950-51, Greencastle, Ind., 1951-52, Ft. Lauderdale, Fla., 1952-53; exec. dir. Michiana Arts and Scis. Council, Inc., South Bend, Ind., 1973—; tech. asst. cons., adv. panelist Ind. Arts Commn.; v.p. Ind. Alliance Arts Councils Steering Com., 1979, treas., 1981. Mem. St. Joseph County Parks and Recreation Bd., 1971—; pres. Mental Health Assn. of St. Joseph County, 1972; bd. dirs. Century Center Found., South Bend, 1974—, St. Joseph County Scholarship Found., 1977—; pres., bd. dirs. United Way St. Joseph County. Recipient Community Service award Michiana Arts and Scis. Council, 1968. Mem. Ind. Arts Advs., Ind. Alliance Arts Councils, Nat. Assn. Arts Councils. Club: Jr. League South Bend (pres. 1968). Producer 13 week TV series: Inside Our Schools (Jr. League of South Bend Outstanding Community Service award 1964), 1963. Office: 120 S St Joseph St South Bend IN 46601

SIELOFF, RONALD BRUCE, state senator; b. Thief River Falls, Minn., May 30, 1944; s. Marvin W. and Betty (Knutson) S.; B.S., William Mitchell Coll. Law, 1968, J.D. cum laude, 1970; m. Mary M. Sorenson, Oct. 16, 1969; children—Ryan T., Melissa L. Tax mgr. Fiduciary Counseling, Inc., St. Paul, 1972-74; admitted to Minn. bar, 1970; practiced in St. Paul, 1974—; mem. Minn. Ho. of Reps., 1975-76, Minn. Senate, 1977—. Mem. Am., Minn., Ramsey County bar assns. Lutheran. Office: 9th Floor Commerce Bldg St Paul MN 55101

SIEMION, ARTHUR THADDEUS, stockbroker; b. Chgo., Jan. 25, 1946; s. Thaddeus John and Florence Theresa (Gadowski) S.; student Buena Vista Coll., 1964-66; B.S., Ill. State U., 1971; m. Dorothea Elizabeth Jackel, Feb. 8, 1965; children—Gayle, Heather, Courtney. Stockbroker, Blunt Ellis & Loewi, Oak Brook, Ill., 1975—; faculty William Rainey Harper Coll., Palatine, Ill., 1975-77. Pres., Golfview Hills Homes, Hinsdale, 1976-77; co-founder and adv. council Heritage Council of DuPage County Republicans, 1978—, del. Caucus 86, 1977-78, 81, chmn. nominating com., 1977—; dir. community relations com. Polish Am. Congress, 1977-79. Clubs: Chgo. Soc. (dir. 1978—), Polish-Am. Cultural (pres. 1979—), Polish Am. Exhibition (exec. com. 1977-80). Asso. editor Polish-Am. Jour., 1979—. Home: 5333 S Quincy St Hinsdale IL 60521 Office: 2000 Spring Rd Oak Brook IL 60521

SIERADSKI, LEONARD MICHAEL, solar energy co. exec., inventor, cons.; b. Detroit, Jan. 31, 1938; s. Leonard M. and Eleanore M. (Sobkowski) S.; B.S. in Math. and Physics, U. Dayton, 1959; M.S. in Physics, Purdue U., 1964; m. Floral Anne Schnurr, Oct. 5, 1968; children—Diana Lynn, Michael Allan, Lisa Marie, Angela Mary. Physicist Bendix Research Labs., Southfield, Mich., 1962-64; sr. scientist NASA Jet Propulsion Labs., Calif. Inst. Tech., Pasadena, 1965-77; pres. Sunrise Energy Products, Inc., Pellston, Mich., 1977-80, also dir.; asst. dir. analysis and assessment Mid-Am. Solar Energy Center, 1980—; cons. Venture Tech., 1978—; tech. cons. solar heating-systems, 1977—; mem. Mich. Solar Resources Adv. Panel, 1979—. U.S. Dept. Energy grantee, 1977. Mem. ASHRAE, Solar Energy Industries Assn., Mich. Solar Energy Assn., Pasadena Artists Assn. (pres. 1975-76). Patentee Air solar heating system, Viking Mars atmosphere mass spectrometer, computer device. Home: 5115 Woodland Rd Minnetonka MN 55343

SIERLES, FREDERICK STEPHEN, psychiatrist, educator; b. Bklyn., Nov. 9, 1942; s. Samuel and Elizabeth (Meiselman) S.; A.B., Columbia, 1963; M.D., Chgo. Med. Sch., 1967; m. Laurene Harriet Cohn, Oct. 25, 1970; children—Hannah Beth, Joshua Caleb. Intern, Cook County Hosp., Chgo., 1967-68; resident in psychiatry Mt. Sinai Hosp., N.Y.C., 1968-69, Mt. Sinai Hosp., Chgo., 1969-71; staff psychiatrist U.S. Reynolds Army Hosp., Ft. Sill, Okla., 1971-73; asso. attending psychiatrist Mt. Sinai Hosp., Chgo., 1973-74; instr. psychiatry Chgo. Med. Sch., 1973-74, dir. undergrad. edn. in psychiatry, 1974—, asst. prof., 1974-78, asso. prof., 1978—; cons. in psychiatry Cook County Hosp., North Chicago (Ill.) VA Hosp., St. Mary of Nazareth Hosp. Served to maj., M.C., U.S. Army, 1971-73. Recipient Ganser Meml. award Mt. Sinai Hosp., 1970; Prof. of Year award Chgo. Med. Sch., 1977, 80; N.Y. State Regents scholar, 1959-63; NIMH grantee, 1974—. Diplomate Am. Bd. Psychiatry and Neurology. Mem. Am. Psychiat. Assn., AMA, Assn. Interns and Residents Cook County Hosp., Assn. Dirs. Med. Student Edn. in Psychiatry, Alpha Omega Alpha, Phi Epsilon Pi. Editor textbook series Clinical Behavioral Science, 1982. Contbr. articles to profl. jours. Office: Chicago Medical School 3333 Green Bay Rd North Chicago IL 60064

SIEVERT, JAMES MICHAEL, safety engr.; b. Norristown, Pa., Sept. 2, 1951; s. Myron Herman and Yolanda Marie (Falone) S.; student Villanova U., 1973-74; grad. Wash. Tech. Coll., 1977; m. Karen Gantz, Apr. 3, 1970; children—Elisabeth, Todd. Contract adminstr. United Engrs. & Constructors, Inc., Marietta, Ohio, 1980-82, safety engr., 1974-80. Vice pres. Elderly Corp. Marietta; former v.p., pres. Marietta Jaycees, also dist. dir., regional dir. Served with AUS, 1971-73. Cert. safety profl. Bd. Cert. Safety Profls. Mem. Am. Soc. Safety Engrs., Tchrs. Assn. Republican. Roman Catholic. Club: Toastmasters. Home: 106 Sunnyhill Dr Marietta OH 45750 Office: PO Box 9 Willow Island WV 26190

SIEVERT, ROBERT ALBERT, clergyman, secondary sch. adminstr.; b. Watertown, Wis., May 20, 1935; s. Hubert A. and Ada L. (Frey) S.; B.A., Northwestern Coll., 1958; Div.M., Wis. Lutheran Sem., 1963; M.A., Coll. of St. Thomas, 1980; m. Jean Ann Ihde, Oct. 11, 1964; children—Julie Ann, Sharyn Jean, Scott Robert, Deanne Lyn. Instr., Northwestern Luth. Acad., Mobridge, S.D., 1960-61; ordained to ministry Wis. Evang. Luth. Synod, 1964; pastor Luth. chs. Montrose, Minn., 1964-68, Onalaska, Wis., 1968-71; prin. Saint Croix Luth. High Sch., West St. Paul, Minn., 1971—; mem. Minn. Dept. Edn. Nonpublic Sch. Study Com., 1972—; dir. public relations Western Wis. Dist., Wis. Evang. Luth. Synod, 1969-71. Mem. bd. control Luther High, Onalaska, Wis., 1969-71, chmn., 1970-71; mem. Minn. Dist. Bd. for Info. and Stewardship, Wis. Evang. Luth. Synod, 1965-68. Mem. Nat. Assn. Secondary Sch. Prins., Minn. Assn. Pvt. Sch. Adminstrs., Assn. Luth. High Schs. (pres. 1976-78), Assn. for Supervision and Curriculum Devel.

SIEVERT, VERNON ESTRES, state dept. conservation adminstr.; b. Truxton, Mo., Mar. 29, 1920; s. Gustave Henry and Ada Christina (Bahr) S.; B.P.A., U. Mo., 1948; m. June Faye Hawkins, Apr. 6, 1944; 1 dau., Margery June Sievert Detring. Univ. cashier U. Mo., Columbia, 1948-52; mgmt. analyst Gen. Motors Corp., Kansas City, Kans., 1952-54; mgmt. and procedures engr. Westinghouse Electric, Kansas City, Mo., 1954-57; budget analyst Mo. State Div. Budget & Comptroller, 1957-61; personnel and fiscal officer Coll. Agr., U. Mo., Columbia, 1961-62; fiscal officer Mo. Dept. Conservation, Jefferson City, 1963-77, departmental internal auditor, 1977—. Div. chmn. Jefferson City United Fund, 1973-77; mem. fin. com. Heart of Am. council Girl Scouts U.S.A., 1957-60; adult advisor Ashland (Mo.) 4-H Club, 1960-69. Served with USAAF, 1943-45; ETO. Decorated Air medal with two oak leaf clusters. Mem. Conservation Bus. Mgmt. Assn. (pres. 1970), Adminstrv. Mgmt. Soc. (past pres. Mid-Mo. chpt.), Assn. Govt. Accountants (pres. Mid-Mo. chpt. 1976-77), Am. Legion. Baptist. Clubs: Masons, Shriners. Home: Route 1 Box 16 Ashland MO 65010 Office: PO Box 180 Jefferson City MO 65102

SIGAL, KASS F., psychiat. social worker; b. Ft. Lewis, Wash., Feb. 7, 1943; d. Edward Michael and Gertrude Lavinia (McNeill) Flaherty; B.A., U. Colo., 1965; postgrad. Roosevelt U., Chgo., 1966-68; M.S.W., U. Ill., 1970; m. Michael S. Sigal, May 16, 1971. Research asst. dept. genetics Fels Research Inst., Antioch Coll., Yellow Springs, Ohio, 1965-66; social worker Cook County Dept. Public Aid, Chgo., 1966-68; psychiat. social worker Northwestern Meml. Hosp., Chgo., 1970-74, cons., 1974—; instr. Northwestern U. Med. Sch., 1971-75, asso., 1975—; pvt. practice family therapy, Chgo., 1974—. Cert. social worker, Ill. Mem. Nat. Assn. Social Workers, Acad. Cert. Social Workers, Lincoln Park Zool. Soc., U. Ill. Alumni Assn., U. Colo. Alumni Assn., Alpha Chi Omega. Home: 2821 N Pine Grove Ave Chicago IL 60657 Office: 251 E Chicago Ave Chicago IL 60611

SIGEL, BERNARD, surgeon, educator; b. Wilno, Poland, May 14, 1930; came to U.S., 1937, naturalized, 1945; s. Zundel and Hinda (Lubetska) S.; student So. Meth. U., 1947-49; M.D., U. Tex., 1953; m. Lois Savitch, Dec. 1, 1956; children—Paul, Carin, Gwynne, Ellen, Adam. Intern, Grad. Hosp. U. Pa., Phila., 1953-54, resident, 1954-58; resident VA Hosp., Coral Gables, Fla., 1958-59; instr. gen. surgery U. Miami (Fla.) Sch. Medicine, 1959-60; asso. Med. Coll. Pa., Phila., 1960-62, asst. prof., 1962-64, asso. prof., 1964-69, prof., 1969-74, dean, 1969-74, acting pres., 1971-74; prof. surgery Abraham Lincoln Sch., U. Ill. Coll. Medicine, Chgo., 1974—, dean Abraham Lincoln Sch., 1974-78; practice medicine specializing in surgery, Chgo., 1978—; mem. staff U. Ill. Hosp. Recipient USPHS research career devel. award, 1963; diplomate Am. Bd. Surgery. Mem. A.C.S., Soc. Univ. Surgeons, Am. Assn. Pathologists, Soc. for Surgery of Alimentary Tract, Am. Gastroent. Assn., IEEE, Am. Heart Assn., Internat. Soc. Thrombosis and Hemostasis, Am. Inst. Ultrasound in Medicine. Author: Clinical Simulations in Surgery, 1981; contbr. articles to med. jours. Office: 840 S Wood St Room 518-J Chicago IL 60612

SIGLE, JOHN RAYMOND, univ. adminstr., ry. products co. exec.; b. Chgo., July 8, 1950; s. Carl and LaVerne E. S.; B.S. in Polit. Sci. (Ill. State Tchrs. scholar), Ill. State U., 1972; M.A. in Public Adminstrn., Sangamon State U., 1973; m. Kathleen Ann Buechner, June 26, 1976; children—John Michael, Kara Brook. Grad. asst. to v.p. planning Sangamon State U., 1972-73, dir. office space utilization and capital planning Div. Bus. and Adminstrv. Services, 1976—, staff senator, 1978-80; intern to asst. city mgr. City of Peoria (Ill.), 1973; urban planner Chgo. Dept. Devel. and Planning, 1974-76; exec. dir. Tie Collar Assos., Pawnee, Ill., 1975—; mem. Springfield (Ill.) Project Bike Path, 1972-73; mem. Ill. Inst. Natural Resources Bicycle Transp. Task Force, 1979; adv. mem. Springfield Area Transp. Study Tech. Com., 1978—. Mem. Soc. Coll. and Univ. Planners (instl.). Club: Elks (Springfield). Patentee ry. tie collar. Home: Rural Route 1 Pawnee IL 62558 Office: Sangamon State U Springfield IL 62708

SIKKENGA, STEVE ROBERT, mfg. co. exec.; b. Detroit, June 24, 1952; s. Louis Robert and Dickey Marie (Dunville) S.; B.S., Eastern Mich. U., 1974, postgrad., 1974-75; m. Theresa Marie Neumann, May 18, 1974; children—Caroline Anne, Katherine Marie. Office mgr. Dearborn Fabricating & Engring. Co., Detroit, 1971; supr. mfg. Sullivan Equipment Co., Detroit, 1974-75; supr. infra-red mfg. div. Solaronics, Inc., Rochester, Mich., 1970-71, 72-73, 74-76; v.p., gen. mgr. Am. Infra-Red, Inc., Detroit, 1976—; instr. infra-red heating seminars Macomb Community Coll., 1976—. Republican. Roman Catholic. Contbr. articles to profl. jours. Home: 26039 Fordson Hwy Detroit MI 48239 Office: 11840 Edlie St Detroit MI 48214

SIKORSKI, GERRY, state senator; b. Breckenridge, Minn., Apr. 26, 1948; s. Elroy J. and Helen (Voit) S.; B.A. summa cum laude, U. Minn., 1970, J.D. magna cum laude, 1973; m. Susan Erkel, 1974; 1 dau., Anne. Practice law, Stillwater, Minn.; pres. Washington County Legal Assistance, 1975-76; treas. Legal Assistance of Minn., 1975-76; mem. Minn. Senate, 1977—. Chmn. Minn. Young Democrats, 1968-69; chmn. legis. com. Minn. Gov.'s Council Aging, 1975-76; former pres. River Town Restoration, Inc. Washington County Bar Assn. Roman Catholic. Club: Jaycees. Office: State Capitol St Paul MN 55155*

SIKULA, JOHN PAUL, educator; b. Akron, Ohio, Oct. 7, 1944; s. John and Anna Marie S.; B.A. with honors, Hiram Coll., 1966; M.A. (NDEA fellow), Case Western Res. U., 1967, Ph.D. (NDEA fellow), 1969; m. Roberta Rae Rutan, Aug. 20, 1966; children—Michelle Marie, Nicole Rae, Adam John, Danielle Renee. Asst. prof. edn. Bloomsburg State Coll., 1969-70; asst. prof. edn. U. Toledo, 1970-73, asso. prof., 1973-76, tchr. corps instr., 1971-72, dir. univ. accountability study, 1971-72, asso. dir. Center Ednl. Research and Services, 1975-76; prof., chmn. div. edn. Ind. U. N.W., Gary, 1976—. Recipient Outstanding Teaching award U. Toledo, 1976, award and cert. for excellence in ednl. journalism for disting. achievement Ednl. Press Assn. Am., 1971. Mem. Assn. Tchr. Educators (editor Action in Tchr. Edn. 1978—), Am. Ednl. Research Assn., Assn. Individually Guided Edn., Ind. Assn. Colls. Tchr. Edn., Ind. Assn. Founds in Tchrs. Edn., Phi Delta Kappa (pres. Toledo chpt. 1975-76). Roman Catholic. Author: Accountability in Schools, 1972; Sociological Foundations of Education in an Urban Society, 1975; contbr. articles to profl. jours.; editor: (with others) Idols and Ideals: Educational Encounters, 1970; Teacher Education for an Urban Setting, 1973. Home: Rural Route 2 Randolph St Hobart IN 46342 Office: 3400 Broadway Gary IN 46408

SILBERMAN, ALLEN, psychologist; b. Houston, Mar. 28, 1943; s. Morris and Sylvia (Bellebroff) S.; B.A., Troy State Coll., 1964; M.A., Ball State U., 1973; Ed.D., U. S.D., 1974; m. Lillian Link, Mar. 9, 1968; 1 dau., Leslie. Social worker, City of N.Y., 1965; pvt. practice psychology, Des Moines, 1975—. Served to capt. USAF, 1965-73; Vietnam. Decorated Bronze Star; Vietnamese Honor medal 1st class. Mem. Am., Iowa psychol. assns., Assn. Counselor Edn. Supervision, Am. Personnel Guidance Assn., Soc. Pediatric Psychology, Soc. Clin. Exptl. Hypnosis, Iowa Acad. Sci. Jewish. Contbr. articles to profl. jours. Home: 225 Foster Dr Des Moines IA 50312 Office: 1454 30 St Suite 209 West Des Moines IA 50265

SILBERMAN, CARL MORRIS, physician; b. Phila., Aug. 7, 1946; s. Emanuel Harry and Sylvia (Cohen) S.; B.A., Temple U., 1968; M.D., Jefferson Med. Coll., 1972. Resident, Cooper Med. Center, Camden, N.J., 1974-76; fellow in cardiology Northwestern U. Hosp., Chgo., 1977-79; practice medicine specializing in cardiology, Chgo., 1979—; asst. prof. medicine dept. cardiology Chgo. Med. Sch., 1979—; dir. cardiology unit Naval Regional Med. Center, North Chicago, Ill.; cons. in cardiology 11th Naval Dist., Cook County Hosp. Diplomate Am. Bd. Internal Medicine, Sub-bd. Cardiovasular Disease. Fellow Am. Coll. Chest Physicians, Am. Coll. Cardiology; mem. AMA, Chgo. Med. Assn., Ill. Med. Assn., A.C.P. Home: 1344 N Dearborn Pkwy Chicago IL 60618 Office: Chgo Med Sch VA Hosp Bldg 50 North Chicago IL 60064

SILIGER, AGNES ISABELLE, psychologist; b. Memphis, Feb. 21, 1921; d. Claude Jefferson and Zulee (Dancy) Brantley; B.A., Roosevelt U., 1949; M.A., U. No. Colo., 1956; m. Fred Joseph Siliger, Feb. 19, 1966; 1 adopted son, Fred Joseph. Tchr., Chgo. Bd. Edn., 1950; psychologist, 1958; psychology instr. Phillips Evening Sch., Chgo., 1961-62; sr. psychologist Chgo. Sch. Dist. 16, 1967—; supr. interns sch. psychology, Ill., 1965—; pres. Area A Psychologists, Chgo. Pub. Schs., 1971-72. Certified Ill. sch. psychologist, 1958, registered psychologist, Ill., 1963. Mem. Am., Ill. (chmn. com. minority concerns 1974-75) psychol. assns., Nat. Assn. Sch. Psychologists (chmn. com. minority concerns rap session Las Vegas Conv. 1974), Chgo. Assn. Sch. Psychologists (pres.), Chgo. Psychol. Club (council), Alpha Kappa Alpha, Kappa Delta Pi, Pi Lambda Theta. Office: 10115 S Prairie St Chicago IL 60628

SILJANDER, MARK DELI, congressman; b. Chgo., June 11, 1951; s. William A. and Evelyn (Deli) S.; B.S., Western Mich. U., Kalamazoo, 1972, M.A., 1973. Distbr., dealer Rustic Homes, Timber Lodge Redwood Homes, also Chalet Homes, Three Rivers, Mich., from 1973; trustee Fabius Twp. (Mich.), 1972-76; mem. Mich. Ho. of Reps. from 42d Dist., 1976-80; mem. 97th Congress from 4th Dist. Mich. Mem. Nat. Assn. Towns and Twps., Mich. Conf. Polit. Scientists, Mich. Twps. Assn. (past dir.), Christian Fellowships, Jaycees, Grange. Republican. Office: US Ho of Reps Washington DC 20515*

SILK, STUART M., pub. co. exec.; b. St. Louis, Mar. 12, 1943; s. Louis H. and Gussie (Press) S.; B.S. in Bus. Adminstrn., U. Mo.; m. Kae Hammond, Apr. 21, 1979; children by previous marriage—Clifton Robert, Douglas Matthew. Account exec. CBS Woman's Day mag., Chgo., 1971-79; Midwest sales mgr. N.Y. mag., Chgo., 1979; v.p., nat. sales mgr. The Mother Earth News, Chgo., 1979—. Served with USAR, 1961. Clubs: Chgo. Agate, Chgo. Advt. Office: 405 N Wabash St Suite 5109 Chicago IL 60611

SILLERS, DOUGLAS HUGH, former state senator, farmer; b. Calvin, N.D., Feb. 9, 1915; s. Archie and Mabel (Tuthill) S.; B.A., Concordia Coll., 1939; m. Margaret Rose Baller, Aug. 2, 1941; children—Jean M. Sillers Bardwell, D. Hal, Cynthia B., Heather P. Instr. social sci. high sch., Menahga, Minn., 1939-42; fieldman Fed. Land Bank, Washburn, N.D., 1942; owner, operator farm, Moorhead, Minn., 1946—; mem. Minn. Ho. of Reps., 1963-72, Minn. Senate, 1972-81; dir. Minn. F.B. Service Co., St. Paul; pres., sec. Clay County F.B. Service Co., Moorhead, 1949-68; mem. State Planning Commn., 1967—; com. mem. Upper Midwest Research & Devel., 1960—; instr. polit. sci. Concordia Coll. Bd. dirs. Future Farmers Am. Minn.; mem. exec. bd. Tri Coll., 1978; mem. Minn. Higher Edn. Coordinating Bd. Served to lt. (j.g.) USNR, 1942-45; ETO. Recipient Goodyear Conservation award, 1956, Agr. award N.D. State U., 1974; named Minn. Soil Saver, Clay County Soil Conservation Soc., 1956. Mem. N.W. Farm Mgrs. (pres. 1961), Farm Bur., Am. Legion, VFW, Moorhead C. of C. Clubs: Masons, Rod and Gun.

SILVER, DAVID MAYER, coll. adminstr., historian; b. West Pittston, Pa., July 16, 1915; s. Morris J. and Florence (Mayer) S.; A.B., Butler U., 1937; M.A. (Univ. scholar), U. Ill., Urbana, 1938, Ph.D. (Univ. scholar), 1940; m. Anita Cohen, May 10, 1942; children—Gregory K., Terence A. Instr. in history Butler U., 1940-42, asst. prof. history, 1942-48, asso. prof., 1948-54, prof., 1954—, dean Coll. Liberal Arts and Scis., 1963—; research dir. Ind. Democratic Com., 1943-45; cons.-evaluator North Central Assn.; mem. Ind. Conf. Acad. Deans, 1963—. Pres. Indpls. Bd. Public Safety, 1956-63; bd. dirs. Indpls. Hebrew Congregation, 1961-67, pres., 1965-67; mem. youth study commn. Ohio Valley Council Hebrew Congregations, 1963-65. Recipient J. I. Holcomb award Butler U., 1956. Mem. Am. Hist. Assn., Orgn. Am. Historians, Ind. Hist. Soc., AAUP. Democrat. Author: Lincoln's Supreme Court, 1956. Office: Room 108 Jordan Hall Butler U 4600 Sunset Ave Indianapolis IN 46208

SILVER, GERALD, coll. dean; b. N.Y., Feb. 19, 1939; s. Harry and Freida (Cohen) S.; B.A., Queens Coll., 1961; M.B-A.. Columbia U., 1963, Ed.D., 1974. Fin. analyst Hotel Corp. Am., Washington, 1963-64; prof. mgmt. Fairleigh Dickinson U., Rutherford, N.J., 1966-73, acting dean Coll. Bus. Adminstrn., 1974-76; dean Coll. Bus. Adminstrn., Ohio U., Athens, 1976—; cons. Served with U.S. Army Res., 1963. Recipient Outstanding Service award Bergen County (N.J.) C. of C. Mem. Am. Assn. Univ. Adminstrs., Assn. Continuing Higher Edn., Am. Assn. Higher Edn., Acad. of Mgmt., Ohio Council Econ. Edn. (trustee 1976—), Beta Gamma Sigma. Jewish. Clubs: Rotary, Athens Country. Office: Coll Bus Adminstrn Ohio U Athens OH 45701

SILVER, MICHAEL, ednl. adminstr.; b. Landsberg, Germany, Jan. 30, 1948; s. Norman and Esther (Kleiner) S.; B.A., Washington U., St. Louis, 1970, M.A., 1973, Ph.D., 1982; m. Beverley Ann Moss, May 16, 1971; children—Sabina Lynn, Joseph Elliot. Came to U.S., 1949, naturalized, 1955. Tchr. Social Studies Normandy Sch. Dist., St. Louis, 1970-72; tchr., chmn. dept. social studies Parkway Sch. Dist., St. Louis, 1972-75; asst. prin. Central Jr. High Sch., Parkway Sch. Dist., St. Louis, 1976-79; adminstrv. asst. to supt. Parkway Sch. Dist., 1979—; grad. asst., supr. student teaching, lectr. Washington U. Mem. St. Louis Conf. Edn., 1976-82; Campaign chmn. United Way Greater St. Louis, Parkway Sch. Dist., 1979-81. Served with USAR, 1971. Recipient Title VI fellowship award, Washington U., 1971-73; IDEA fellow, 1978; Campaign award for outstanding achievement United Way Greater St. Louis, 1979, 80, 81. Mem. Am. Assn. Sch. Adminstrs., Am. Ednl. Research Assn., Assn. Supervision and Curriculum Devel., Nat. Assn. Secondary Sch. Prins., Nat. Soc. Study Edn., Phi Delta Kappa. Jewish. Club: Kiwanis. Author: Facing Issues of Life and Death, 1976; Values Education, 1976. Home: 402 Glen Cove Dr St Louis MO 63017 Office: Parkway Sch Dist 455 N Woods Mill Rd Chesterfield MO 63017

SILVER, SANDRA, ednl. adminstr.; b. Boston, Jan. 27, 1953; d. Aaron Alexander and Marcia (Rosenbaum) S.; B.S., Boston U., 1974; M.Ed., Fitchburg (Mass.) State Coll., 1975; cert. advanced grad. study, Northeastern U., 1978. Spl. needs resource tchr. Methuen (Mass.) Middle Sch., 1974-77; learning disabilities specialist Pembroke Acad., Suncook, N.H., 1977-78; tchr. children with moderate spl. needs Chelsea (Mass.) Public Schs., 1978-79; child study coordinator SW and West Central Ednl. Coop. Service Unity, Windom, Minn., 1979—; part-time faculty, human services div. Worthington (Minn.) Community Coll. Cottonwood County rep. for Camp SOS, ARC, 1979—. Mem. Nat. Assn. State Dirs. of Spl. Edn., Council for Exceptional Children, Am. Assn. on Mental Deficiency, Assn. for Children with Learning Disabilities, Assn. for Sch. Dirs., Pi Lambda Theta. Office: 1045 4th Ave Windom MN 56101

SILVER, TERRY MARK, physician; b. N.Y.C., May 2, 1944; s. Ralph K. and Bertha (Phillips) S.; B.S. with distinction, U. Mich., 1966; M.D. cum laude, SUNY Downstate Coll. Medicine, 1970; m. Sarajane Serwin, Dec. 24, 1967; children—Jill Laurie, David Adam. Intern in internal medicine SUNY, Kings County Hosp. Center, 1970; resident in diagnostic radiology Univ. Hosp., Ann Arbor, Mich., 1971-74, instr. radiology, 1974-75, asst. prof., 1975-77, asso. prof., 1977-81, prof., 1981—, dir. diagnostic ultrasound, Univ. Hosp., U. Mich. Med. Center, 1981—; cons. ultrasound VA Hosp., Ann Arbor, Wayne County Gen. Hosp., Eloise, Mich. Diplomate Am. Bd. Radiology, Nat. Bd. Med. Examiners. Mem. Assn. Univ. Radiologists, Am. Coll. Radiology, Radiol. Soc. N. Am., Soc. Uroradiology, Am. Inst. Ultrasound in Medicine, Mich. Radiol. Soc., Mich. State, Washtenaw County Med. Socs., U. Mich. Alumni Assn., State U. N.Y. Downstate Med. Center Alumni Assn. Club: Univ. Mich. of Ann Arbor. Asso. editor Yearbook of Radiology, 1977—; editorial cons. Am. Jour. Roentgenology and Radiology 1976. Contbr. articles to med., sci. jours. Home: 3050 Foxcroft Ann Arbor MI 48104 Office: Univ Hosp 1405 E Ann St Ann Arbor MI 48109

SILVERMAN, FRANKLIN HAROLD, educator; b. Providence, Aug. 16, 1933; s. Meyer and Reba (Sack) S.; B.S. in Speech, Emerson Coll., 1960; M.A., Northwestern U., 1961; Ph.D., U. Iowa, 1966; m. Ellen-Marie Loebel, Feb. 5, 1967 (div. Feb. 1981); 1 dau., Catherine. Research asso. U. Iowa, 1965-68; asst. prof. U. Ill., Urbana, 1968-71; asso. prof. Marquette U., Milw., 1971-77, prof., 1977—. Fellow Am. Speech Lang. and Hearing Assn.; mem. Author's Guild, Psychometric Soc., Inst. Gen. Semantics, Sigma Xi. Author: Research Design in Speech Pathology and Audiology, 1977; Communication for the Speechless, 1980; asso. editor Jour. Speech and Hearing Research, 1977-80; contbr. articles to profl. jours. Home: 823 N 2d St Milwaukee WI 53203 Office: Marquette U Milwaukee WI 53233

SILVERMAN, HOWARD BURTON, banker; b. Chgo., July 20, 1938; s. Jack B. and Pearl (Solomon) S.; B.S., Northwestern U., 1959, M.B.A., 1970; m. Sharon Shanoff, June 4, 1967; children—Julie, Jill. Internal auditor Toni Co. div. Gillette Co., Chgo., 1959-60; gen. acct. Apeco Corp., Evanston, Ill., 1960-62; acctg. officer Continental Ill. Nat. Bank and Trust Co., Chgo., 1964-70; with First Nat. Bank & Trust Co. Evanston, 1970—, pres., dir., 1975—; pres., dir. First Ill. Corp. and affiliates. Bd. dirs. St. Francis Hosp., Evanston, Child Care Center, Evanston. Served with AUS, 1962-64. C.P.A., Ill. Mem. Evanston, Am.-Israel chambers commerce, Ill. C.P.A. Soc., Clubs: Bankers, Economic, Covenant (Chgo.); Rotary; Ravinia Green Country. Contbr. articles to profl. jours. Office: 800 Davis St Evanston IL 60204

SILVERMAN, PERRY RAYNARD, lawyer; b. N.Y.C., Nov. 5, 1950; s. Harry and Mary Sheila (Diamond) S.; B.A., SUNY, Albany, 1971; J.D., Boston U., 1974; M.A., Ohio State U., 1981; m. Ruth Ann Klarin, Oct. 7, 1979. Admitted to N.Y. State bar, 1975, Ohio bar, 1976, U.S. Dist. Ct. bar, 1976, U.S. Ct. Claims bar, 1977, U.S. Supreme Ct. bar, 1978; research asso. Polimetrics Lab., Ohio State U., 1974-75, Behavioral Scis. Lab., 1975; asst. atty. gen. State of Ohio, Columbus, 1975—; adj. prof. Capital U., Columbus, 1978. Mem. Am. Bar Assn., Ohio State Bar Assn., Am. Polit. Sci. Assn., Midwest Polit. Sci. Assn. Office: 30 E Broad St Columbus OH 43215

SILVERMAN, ROBIN LANDEW, retail advt. exec.; b. Newark, Apr. 27, 1954; d. Melvin and Marion (Zabarsky) Landew; B.A. in English, U. Pa., 1975; m. Stephen Mayer Silverman, Aug. 18, 1974; 1 dau., Amanda Gail. Coll. services mgr. All-Star Forum, Phila., 1975-76; dir. public relations Balch Inst., Phila., 1976-77, Market Place, Phila., 1977-79; v.p. advt. Silverman's, Inc., Grand Forks, N.D., 1979—; guest lectr. U. N.D. Bd. dirs. Greater Grand Forks Regional Assn. for Arts and Humanities. Recipient Sol Feinstone award, U. Pa., 1975, Ten Best award, Internat. Newspaper Advt. Execs., 1978. Mem. Valley Advt. and Mktg. Fedn. (sec., 1979-80, bd. dirs., 1979—), Am. Advt. Fedn. Theatre and film critic, 1976-79; featured writer Phila. Inquirer Today mag.; contbr. articles to publs. including Bucks County Courier Times, Suburban Newspaper Group. Office: 11 City Center Mall Grand Forks ND 58201

SILVERMAN, WILLIAM JOSEPH, hosp. adminstr.; b. Mpls., Sept. 4, 1916; s. Maurice and Dora (Berkuvitz) S.; m. Lynne Helen Houts, 1950; children—Sandra Lynne, Pamela Ann, James Laurence, Deborah Marie; B.A., U. Minn., 1939, M.S. in Psychometrics, 1942. Psychometrist, Minn. Civil Service, 1939-42; cons. pub. adminstrn. Pub. Adminstrn. Service, Chgo., 1946-50; adminstr. Guam Meml. Hosp., Island of Guam, 1950-52; asso. dir. Michael Reese Hosp., Chgo., 1952-59, exec. dir., 1960-70; dir. health services and facilities div. Comprehensive Health Planning, Inc., 1970-72; asst. dir. Chgo. Hosp. Council, 1970-72; dir. Cook County Hosp., Chgo., 1972-80; ret., 1981. Mem. Southside Planning Bd., Chgo., 1960-70; chmn. emergency med. services Commn. Met. Chgo., 1974-76; bd. dirs., mem. exec. com. Chgo. Community Fund, 1962-68; bd. dirs. Video Nursing, Inc., 1968-73, Hosp. Service Corp. (Blue Cross), 1970-71, Mid South Side Health Planning Orgn., 1970-71; vice chmn. bd. dirs. Ill. Regional Med. Program, 1969-70. Fellow Am. Coll. Hosp. Adminstrs.; mem. Am., Ill. hosp. assns., Chgo. Hosp. Council (pres. 1964).

SILVERNAIL, JAY THOMAS, ednl. adminstr.; b. Morganfield, Ky., Jan. 18, 1944; s. Jack F. and Helen (Carter) S.; B.S., U. Wis., Platteville, 1966, M.S., 1973; postgrad. in adminstrn. U. Wis., Madison, 1975; m. Judith Ann Jones, Nov. 26, 1966; 1 son, Jon Carter. Field technician Wis. Elec. Power Co., Ft. Atkinson, 1966; tchr. indsl. arts, Palmyra, Wis., 1966-68, Elkhorn, Wis., 1968-74; vocat. edn. coordinator Elkhorn Area Schs., 1974—; instr. solar energy Gateway Tech. Inst.; participant solar energy workshop Dept. Energy, 1980. Mem. Whitewater Fire Dept., 1971—. Mem. Coop. Ednl. Service Agy. 18 Assn. Vocat. Edn. (pres.), Am. Vocat. Assn. (life), Nat. Assn. Secondary Sch. Prins., Assn. Wis. Sch. Adminstrs., Wis. Assn. Vocat. and Adult Edn. Club: Rotary (sec. 1977—) (Elkhorn). Home: 983 South St Whitewater WI 53190 Office: Elkhorn Area Schs 482 E Geneva St Elkhorn WI 53121

SILVESTRI, JOHN HENRY, broadcasting co. exec.; b. Detroit, July 3, 1935; s. John Angelo and Lucille (Grace) S.; B.A., Wyane State U., 1960; m. Judy Kay Strick, May 8, 1969; children—Kimberly Ann, Christopher John, Steven Michael. Advt. specialist Chrysler Corp., Detroit, 1961-64; mgr. advt. and public relations UniRoyal Inc., Detroit, 1964-68; mgr. nat. sales WWJ-AM-TV, Detroit, 1968-71; mgr. central radio network sales, dir. network TV sales Central div. NBC, Chgo., 1971—. Served with AUS, 1955-57. Mem. Nat. Acad. Arts and Scis., Broadcast Advt. Club. Republican. Home: 1765 Maple Ln Wheaton IL 60187 Office: NBC Merchandise Mart Chicago IL 60654

SILVEY, ORAN ALLEN, elec. engr.; b. Nacogdoches, Tex., Apr. 15, 1939; s. Orin Elwood and Allie Maye (Ewell) S.; A.S.B.A., Mt. Wachusett Coll., 1967; B.S.E.E., Boston Coll., 1969; M.B.A., U. Md., 1976. Joined U.S. Army, 1956, served in Far East, 1956-63, N.Africa 1964-67, Middle East, 1970-73; ret., 1976; sr. mem. tech. staff Litton Industries, College Park, Md., 1976-77; system engr. staff Corvus Systems Inc., Vienna, Va., 1977-78, dir. Corvus Dayton Field Services div., Fairborn, Ohio, 1978-80; scientist Computer Tech. div. Internat. Computing Co., Fairborn, 1980—. Pres., Green County Republican Club; mem. Univ., Student and Community Relations Commn. for Green County. Mem. Assn. Old Crows, Dayton Ind. Bus. Council, C. of C. (v.p.). Presbyterian. Club: Rotary. Home: 3049 Blue Green Dr Beavercreek OH 45431 Office: 3150 Presidential Dr Fairborn OH 45324

SIMACEK, MILO JAMES, woodcrafter; b. Montgomery, Minn., June 6, 1930; s. Matt and Emma (Koldin) S.; B.S., Mankato State U., 1952; M.S., Eastern Ky. U., 1969; postgrad. St. Cloud State U., Winona State U., River Falls State U.; m. Lois Mae Davis, Dec. 26, 1955; children—Michele, Mark, David, Scott. Tchr., St. Anns Sch., Wabasso, Minn., 1955-56; tchr. indsl. arts, chmn. dept. Hastings (Minn.) High Sch., 1956—; owner, mgr. Artistry With Wood, Hastings, 1960—; also designer, builder houses. Mem. Hastings City Planning Commn., 1979—; founding pres. Hastings United Fund. Served with M.C. AUS, 1952-54. Silver Beaver award Boy Scouts Am., 1980, Minn. Indsl. Arts Tchr. of Yr. award, 1981. Mem. Am. Legion (comdr. 1976), Jaycees (senator), Minn. Indsl. Arts Assn., Am. Indsl. Arts Assn., Minn. Edn. Assn., NEA, Internat. Wood Collectors Soc., DAV. Roman Catholic. Clubs: Lions, Hastings Snowmobile, Snow Patrol. Home: 1041 W 4th St Hastings MN 55033 Office: 11th and Pine Sts Hastings MN 55033

SIMCOX, EDWIN JESSE, state ofcl.; b. LaPorte, Ind., Jan. 12, 1945; s. J. Willard and Rachel (Gibbs) S.; A.B. in Govt. and Econs., Ind. U., 1967, J.D., 1971; m. Sandra Sue Stephenson, Aug. 30, 1970; 1 son, Edwin Jesse. Sec., Ind. Hwy. Commn., 1969-71, Public Service Commn. Ind., 1971; chief dept. Office Reporter Supreme Cts. and Jud. Ct. Appeals Ind., 1973-78; sec. of state State of Ind., Indpls., 1978—. Sec., Ind. Republican Central Com., 1972-77; chmn. Ind. Rep. Platform Com., 1980; chmn. adminstrv. bd. White Harvest United Methodist Ch., 1975-76, 80-81. Mem. Am. Bar Assn., Ind. Bar Assn., Indpls. Bar Assn., Nat. Assn. Secs. State (sec. 1981-82). Clubs: Kiwanis, Masons, Shriners. Author man. for conduct mcpl. campaigns, 1975, Republican precinct man., 1975. Office: 201 State House Indianapolis IN 46204

SIME, CHARLES JOHN, accountant; b. Prairie du Chien, Wis., June 15, 1905; s. Peter J. and Tourina (Sorem) S.; diploma in commerce Northwestern U., 1946; m. Mary M. Neault, July 23, 1927 (dec.); children—Mary Ada Sime Krahe, Charles John. With Acme Steel Co., Chgo., 1927-62, sales personnel adminstr., 1962; self-employed as accounting and tax practitioner, Orland Park, Ill., 1962—. Bd. dirs. Duncan Med. Center YMCA, Chgo., 1949—. Mem. Ind. Accountants Assn. Ill. (South Cook County pres. 1968-69, 1974-75, state dir. 1970—), Northwestern U. Alumni Assn. Club: Glenwood Lions (pres. 1977—). Home: 222 Brentwood Dr Chicago Heights IL 60411 Office: 14620 La Grange Rd Orland Park IL 60462

SIMERS, RONALD EARL, estate planner; b. Akron, Ohio, Oct. 14, 1954; s. Robert Earl and Gladys Emma (Beougher) S.; B.S. in Bus. Adminstrn., U. Akron, 1976; m. Jo Ann Morris, June 26, 1976; 1 dau., Marla Kay. Estate planner Gen. Bd. of Ch. of Nazarene, Kansas City, Mo., 1976—; treas. Overland Park (Kans.) Ch. of Nazarene, 1980—. Home: 8146 Walmer Ln Overland Park KS 66204 Office: 6401 The Paseo Kansas City MO 64131

SIMKINS, CHARLES ABRAHAM, soil scientist; b. Reading, Kans., Nov. 3, 1923; s. Stanley Abehue and Mamie Eugene (Fuller) S.; student Kans. State Tchrs. Coll., Bowling Green State U., Kans. State U.; B.S. in Sci., B.S. in Agr., 1948; M.S. in Agronomy, 1950; Ph.D. in Agronomy, 1958; hon. degree U. Keszthely (Hungary); m. Marylouise Walker, Aug. 10, 1945; children—Mary Sue, John James, George Stanley, Joann Louise, Patricia Jane, Sara Elizabeth. Instr. soils Kansas State U., Manhattan, 1948-49; asst. agronomist U. Idaho, Aberdeen, 1949-51; asst. prof. U. Minn., St. Paul, 1953-58, chief of party, Santiago, Chile, 1964-70, prof. soils and extension, 1970-73, 76-80; chief of soils Khueztan Devel. Corp., Ahwaz, Iran, 1958-62; soil scientist FAO, Nicosia, Cyprus, 1963-64; project mgr. UN, Lebanon and Pakistan, 1974-76; chief div. natural resources Bur. Tech. and Sci., AID, Washington, 1981—. Served with USMC, 1942-45. Mem. Am. Soc. Agronomy, Soil Sci. Soc. Am., Soil Conservation Soc., Sigma Xi, Gamma Sigma Delta. Home: 4305 Brigadoon Dr Saint Paul MN 55112

SIMMONS, CARL KENNETH, coop. exec.; b. Kingman, Ind., Dec. 5, 1914; s. Claud Elmer and Sylvia Ethyl (Myers) S.; grad. exec. devel. program Ind. U., 1959; m. Allice Lucille Weaver, Dec. 16, 1939; 1 dau., Erma Jane (Mrs. Thomas Stephen Barlow). Petroleum dept. mgr. Fountain County Coop., Veedersburg, Ind., 1936-40; dist. mgr. Ind. Farm Bur. Coop., Indpls., 1946-47; treas., mgr. Delaware County Coop., Muncie, 1940-46, 48—. Mem. Mayor's Citizens Com. Muncie, 1962. Bd. dirs. Delaware County Airport Authority, 1972—. Mem. Ind. Flying Farmers. Clubs: Masons (32 deg.), Muncie Rifle. Home: 225 E Centennial St Muncie IN 47303 Office: 901 Granville Ave Muncie IN 47305

SIMMONS, CLARA SMITH, educator; b. Washington, Apr. 7, 1935; d. William Arthur and Lelia Bernice (Chase) Smith; B.A., U. Ill., 1957; M.S.W., Howard U., 1959; m. David Earl Simmons, Sept. 9, 1956; children—Steven, Cheryl, Spencer. Cons. cystic fibrosis Dept. Health and Welfare, Concord, N.H., 1968-69; dir. spl. programs Smith Coll., 1970-72, coordinator Spl. Undergrad. programs, 1971-72; asst. prof. social work Case Western Res. U., 1972—. Pres. bd. trustees Parents Anonymous of Northeast Ohio, Inc.; pres. League of Women Voters, 1970. NIMH fellow, 1958-59. Mem. Nat. Assn. Social Workers, Acad. Cert. Social Workers, Council Social Work Edn., Assn. Black Social Workers. Democrat. Mem. Ch. of Christ. Club: The Clevelanders. Producer videotape Who's Watching the Children?, 1979; author: Child Welfare Supervision, 1981; contbr. in field. Home: 3315 Daleford Rd Shaker Heights OH 44120 Office: 2035 Abington Rd Cleveland OH 44106

SIMMONS, DAVID EARL, hosp. admnstr.; b. Water Valley, Miss., Feb. 25, 1929; s. Walter Bernard and Mary (Moss) S.; B.S., U. Ill., 1956; M.A., U. Iowa, 1958; Ph.D., St. Andrew U., 1960; diploma Command and Gen. Staff Coll., U.S. Army, 1973; grad. Fed. Exec. Inst., 1977; m. Clara Smith, Sept. 9, 1956; children—Steven, Cheryl, Spencer. Admnstrv. asst. Mercy-Douglass Hosp., Phila. 1958-61; mgmt. analyst VA Hosp., Tuskegee, Ala., 1961-63; mgmt. specialist VA Central Office, Washington, 1963-64, staff asst. to chief med. dir., 1964-65; asst. dir. trainee VA Hosp., Richmond, Va., 1965-67; asst. dir. VA Hosp., Manchester, N.H., 1967-69, VA Hosp., Northampton, Mass., 1969-72, Cleve., 1972-75; dir. VA Hosp., Erie, Pa., 1975-79; dir. Health Systems Inc., Northwestern Pa., Erie, 1975-79; dir. VA Med. Center Southfield and Outer Allen Park, Mich., 1979-80, VA Med. Center, Butler, Pa., 1980—. Bd. dirs. Erie Area United Way program, 1975-79, Community Blood Bank of Erie, 1975-79; chmn. Erie County Hosp. Authority 1975-79; v.p. Erie chpt. NAACP, 1976-79; pres. Booker T. Washington Center, Erie 1977-79. Served with U.S. Army, 1948-54. Recipient commendation VA Hosp., Cleve., 1974, 75, City of Cleve. 1975, Cleve. Fed. Exec. Bd., 1974; Outstanding Service award VACO, Washington, 1972, 74. Fellow Royal Soc. Health, Am. Coll. Hosp. Admnstrs.; mem. Am. Hosp. Assn., Assn. Mil. Surgeons, Forest City Hosp. Assn. (pres. 1975), Sigma Iota Epsilon (U. Ill. chpt. 1954-56), Alpha Delta Mu (charter, 1st pres. 1956-58), Kappa Alpha Psi. Democrat. Congregational. Club: Urban League. Home: 3315 Daleford Rd Shaker Heights OH 44120 Office: VA Med Center Butler PA 16001

SIMMONS, DONALD DUANE, psychiatrist, farmer; b. Lee's Summit, Mo., June 30, 1930; s. Herbert A. and Margaret (Larson) S.; B.S., U. Mo., 1958, M.D., 1962; m. Sherry Sue Eastin, June 2, 1962; children—Donald Steven, Morgan W. (adopted). Intern, Orange County (Calif.) Gen. Hosp., 1962-63, resident in internal medicine, 1964-65; resident in psychiatry Western Mo. Mental Health Center, Kansas City, 1963-64, 65-67, staff psychiatrist, 1967-71; staff psychiatrist Kansas City VA Hosp., 1971—, acting chief mental clinic, 1972—; practice medicine specializing in psychiatry, Kansas City, 1971—; farmer Caldwell County, Mo. Served with M.C., AUS, 1952-53. Diplomate Am. Bd. Psychiatry and Nuerology. Mem. AMA, Mo., Jackson County med. socs., Am., Mo., Kansas City psychiat. assns., Alpha Omega Alpha. Home: 3826 S Delaware St Independence MO 64055 Office: 4301 Main St Kansas City MO 64111

SIMMONS, IVAN VIRGIL, educator; b. Chiona, Mo., Aug. 12, 1938; s. Arthur Thomas and Ada Justina (Meyers) S.; B.S., Ind. State U., 1970, M.S., 1971; Ph.D., Tex. A&M U., 1975; m. Shirley Mitchell, Oct. 4, 1959; children—Kimberly Kristi, Thomas Mitchell, John Glen. Grad. asst. Ind. State U., 1970, Tex. A&M U., 1971-72; tchr. Proviso (Ill.) Twp. Public Schs., 1972-73; research asso. Tex. Transp. Inst., Tex. A&M U., 1973-74; tchr. Bryan (Tex.) Ind. Sch. Dist., 1974-75; tchr. educator, chmn. dept. vocat. edn. State Tech. Inst., Memphis, 1975, 77; vocat. tchr. educator Valdosta (Ga.) State Coll., 1975-77; dir. Curriculum Materials Center, Ind. State U., Terre Haute, 1977-79, tchr. educator 1979—. Mem. Am. Vocat. Assn., Phi Delta Kappa, Epsilon Pi Tau. Home: 915 S 34th St Terre Haute IN 47803 Office: Sch Tech Ind State U Terre Haute IN 47809

SIMMONS, MERLE EDWIN, educator; b. Kansas City, Kans., Sept. 27, 1918; s. Walter Earl and Mabel Sophronia (Shoemaker) S.; A.B., U. Kans., 1939, M.A., 1941; Ph.D., U. Mich., 1952; postgrad. Harvard U., 1946-47, U. Mexico, 1945; m. Concepcion Rojas, Sept. 8, 1948; children—Martha Irene Simmons Hunt, Mary Alice. Faculty, Ind. U. at Bloomington, 1942—, prof. Spanish, 1962—, dir. grad. studies dept. Spanish and Portuguese, 1967-76, chairperson dept., 1976—; teaching fellow Harvard U., Cambridge, Mass., 1946-47. Am. Philos. Soc. grantee, 1955, 76; Am. Council Learned Socs. grantee, 1962. Mem. AAUP, Am. Folklore Soc., Am. Assn. Tchrs. Spanish and Portuguese, Conf. on Latin Am. History, MLA, Midwest MLA, Midwest Assn. Latin Am. Studies, Phi Beta Kappa, Phi Sigma Iota. Author: The Mexican Corrido, 1957; A Bibliography of the Romance and Related Forms in Spanish America, 1963; Folklore Bibliography for 1974, 1977; Folklore Bibliography for 1975, 1979; Santiago F. Puglia, An Early Philadelphia Propagandist for Spanish American Independence, 1977; U.S. Political Ideas in Spanish America before 1830: A Bibliographical Study, 1977; contbr. articles to profl. jours. Home: 4233 Saratoga Dr Bloomington IN 47401 Office: Ballantine Hall 844 Ind U Bloomington IN 47405

SIMMONS, RICHARD KNIGHT, weapon research, devel. and mfg. co. exec.; b. Bisbee, Ariz., Mar. 14, 1928; s. Warren Arthur and Marie Helen (Moon) S.; B.S.M.E., U. Colo., 1954; m. Margaret I. Roome, Aug. 20, 1949; children—Stephen (dec.), Michael, Candace. Program mgr. aeronutronic div. Ford Motor Co., Newport Beach, Calif., 1964-74; dir. tactical systems PDA Inc., Costa Mesa, Calif., 1974-76; mgr. new product devel. Gould CID Co., Glen Byrnie, Md., 1977; dir. devel. ARES, Inc., Port Clinton, Ohio, 1977—. Served with USAAF, 1946-49, USAF, 1950-51. Mem. Am. Def. Preparedness Assn., Pi Tau Sigma, Sigma Tau. Republican. Office: 818 Front St Erie Indsl Park Port Clinton OH 43452

SIMMONS, VIRGINIA LEE COWAN, ednl. adminstr.; b. Ft. Wayne, Ind., May 17, 1921; d. James Clarence and Julia (Webster) Cowan; A.B., Ind. U., 1942, Ed.S., 1970; M.S., Butler U., 1957; postgrad. U. Wis., 1964-67, Ball State U., 1981—; m. Eric L. Simmons, Apr. 25, 1943 (div. 1948); children—Nancy Lee Simmons Green, Eric Leslie. Market research analyst McCann-Erickson, Chgo., 1944-48; retail mcht. Aquatic Galleries, Cin., 1949-52; sales alvt. Empire Tropical Fish Import Co., N.Y.C., 1952-53, Direct Mail Advt., Halvin Products, Bklyn., 1953-55; tchr. Indpls. Sch. 76, 1955-60; asst. prin. Sch. 61, 1960-61, prin. Sch. 101, 1962-63; prin. Law Wallace Sch. 107, Indpls., 1964-72, Frances Bellamy Sch. 102, Indpls., 1972-74, William H. Evans Sch., Indpls., 1974-80, George B. Loomis Sch., Indpls., 1980-82; cons. prin. Indpls. Public Schs., 1982—; program supr. audio-visual center Ind. U., Bloomington, 1961-62; lectr. Butler U., summer 1965; cons. Ind. U., summer 1969. Contbg. mem. Children's Mus.; mem. Indpls. Mus. Art, Indpls. chpt. Project HOPE; sponsoring mem. Met. Indpls. TV Assn., Inc., 1969-73; coordinator Christmas gift and hobby show Indpls. Public Schs., 1969-75; bd. dirs. Young Audiences of Ind., 1969-80, co-chmn., 1976-78, chmn., 1977-78; bd. dirs. Indpls. Women's chpt. Freedoms Found. at Valley Forge, 1st v.p., 1971-73, 75-77, pres., 1973-75, v.p., 1977—, also awards, 1977—. Recipient Am. Educators Medal award Freedoms Found., 1972. Mem. NEA (life), Ind. U. Alumni Assn. (life), Indpls. Zool. Soc. (charter), Ind. Tchrs. Assn., Bus. and Profl. Women's Clubs, Inc., Indpls. Council Adminstrv. Women Edn., (dir.), Nat. Soc. Study Edn., Nat. Congress Parents and Tchrs., Butler U. Alumni Assn., Nat. Elem. Prins. Assn., Ind. Edn. Art Assn., Hoosier Salon, Assn. Supervision and Curriculum Devel., Internat. Reading Assn., Indpls. Art League, Brown County Art Gallery Assn., AAUW, Izaak Walton League Am., DAR, Alpha Chi Omega, Delta Kappa Gamma, Phi Delta Kappa (hon.), Pi Lambda Theta. Methodist. Clubs: Ind. Schoolwomens; Century, Indpls. Propylaeum, Indpls. Athletic. Author monographs. Home: PO Box 689005 Indianapolis IN 46268

SIMMONS-WILLIS, BEVERLEY, social worker; b. Chgo., Sept. 30, 1941; d. Ward and Louise (Baskin) Simmons; A.A., Wilson Jr. Coll., 1962; B.A., Roosevelt U., Chgo., 1964; A.M., U. Chgo., 1970; m. Johnnie E. Willis, Oct. 8, 1966. Caseworker, supervising caseworker Cook County (Ill.) Dept. Public Aid, Chgo., 1964-72; caseworker, program coordinator Family Service Bur., United Charities Chgo., 1972-78; coordinator children and adolescent services Chgo. Health Dept., Mental Health Div., 1978—; cons. parent effectiveness tng. and family therapy. Cert. social worker, Ill. Mem. Acad. Cert. Social Workers, Nat. Assn. Social Workers, Nat. Assn. Black Social Workers. Office: 1971 W 111 St Chicago IL 60643

SIMMS, W. TIMOTHY, state senator, funeral home dir.; b. Morrison, Ill., Apr. 9, 1943; s. Donald and Elizabeth (Whistler) S.; ed. Worsham Coll. Mortuary Sci., 1964, Parsons Coll., 1968; m. Karen S. Locarno, 1965; 1 son, Timothy W. Funeral dir. Long-Klontz Funeral Home, 1964-65, Julian-Poorman Funeral Home, 1965-67, Sundberg Funeral Home, Rockford, 1967—. Alderman and Republican committeeman, Rockford, 1967-71; majority leader Rockford City Council, 1970-71; former mem. Ill. Ho. of Reps.; mem. Ill. State Senate; del. Rep. Nat. Conv., 1980. Recipient State Govt. award Ill. Jaycees. Presbyterian. Office: State Capitol Room 2003 Springfield IL 62706*

SIMON, GEORGIANNA, educator, nun; b. St. Johns, Mich.; d. Alfred J. and Eva A. (Thelen) S.; A.B. in Sociology, Nazareth Coll., 1965; M.A., Eastern Mich. U., 1970; Ph.D., U. Mich., 1977. Joined Sisters of St. Joseph, 1954; tchr. elem. grades Cath. schs. in Mich., 1957-68; prin. St. Joseph Sch., Watervliet, Mich., 1968-69; tchr. Our Lady of Good Country Sch., Plymouth, Mich., 1969-71; asso. supt. schs. Saginaw (Mich.) Schs., 1972-74, 76-77; asso. prof. edn. Marygrove Coll., Detroit, 1977—; tchr. asso. Social Sci. Ednl. Consortium, Boulder, Colo., 1974-75; tchr. asso. S.W. Research Lab., Austin, Tex., 1976; cons. various sch. dists. in Mich., 1972—; textbook reviewer State Dept. Mich., 1976, 79; social sci. cons. San Bernadino County, Calif., 1975. Recipient Outstanding Service to Edn. award Prins. Assn. of Diocese of Saginaw, 1977. Mem. NEA, Mich. Assn. for Suprs. of Curriculum, Nat. Council for Social Studies (curriculum com.), Mich. Council Social Studies (exec. bd. 1978—), Nat. Council Tchrs. Math., Mich. Council Tchrs. Math., Mich. Assn. Tchr. Edn., Cath. Edn. Assn., Nat. Council for Reading, Mich. Council for Reading. Co-author, co-editor: Michigan Social Studies Textbooks, Vols. I and II, 1980; co-author: So You Want to Revise Social Studies, 1981; contbr. articles on social sci. edn. to profl. publs. Home: 8500 Marygrove Dr Detroit MI 48221 Office: 8425 W McNichols St Detroit MI 48221

SIMON, MARILYN (LYNN) MAE, dietitian; b. Buffalo, May 28, 1941; d. Mathew and Lucille Irene (Markisen) S.; B.S., Mundelein Coll., 1966; R.D., U. Iowa, 1969, M.S., 1975. Corp. dietitian Am. Healthcare Corp., Monticello, Ill., 1976—. Mem. Am. Dietetic Assn., Am. Home Econs. Assn., Am. Soc. Hosp. Food Service Adminstrs., Am. Hosp. Assn. Home: PO Box 187 Monticello IL 61856 Office: 105 S State St Monticello IL 61856

SIMON, MORDECAI, rabbi; b. St. Louis, July 19, 1925; s. Abraham M. and Rose (Solomon) S.; B.A., St. Louis U., 1947; M.A., Washington U., 1952; M.H.L., Jewish Theol. Sem. Am., 1952, D.D. (hon.), 1977; m. Maxine R. Abrams, July 4, 1954; children—Ora, Eve, Avrom. Rabbi, 1952; rabbi Beth El Synagogue, Mpls., 1952-56, Sons of Jacob Synagogue, Waterloo, Iowa, 1956-63; exec. dir. Chgo. Bd. Rabbis, 1963-80, exec. v.p., 1980—. Mem. Chgo. Conf. on Religion and Race, 1963—, Com. on Urban Opportunity, 1964-75. Served with U.S. Army, 1943-46. Honored by Jewish War Vets., 1966, Jewish Com. on Scouting, 1968, 74, Am. Jewish Congress, 1973, Chgo. Com. on Urban Opportunity, 1973, Chgo. Conf. Religion and Race, 1976, Chgo. Bd. Rabbis, 1973, others. Mem. Rabbinical Assembly. Home: 621 County Line Rd Highland Park IL 60035 Office: 618 S Michigan Ave Chicago IL 60605

SIMON, NEIL STUART, former state senator, meat co. sales mgr.; b. Omaha, Aug. 5, 1946; s. Ervin Ross and Miriam (Rubnitz) S.; student U. Iowa, 1964-66; B.A., U. Nebr., Omaha, 1970. Planner, Greater Omaha Community Action, 1971-72; salesman Simon Meats, Omaha, 1973-80, sales mgr., 1981—; mem. Nebr. State Senate, 1977-80; mem. nat. urban affairs com. Nat. Conf. State Legislators, 1978-80, mem. Midwest region energy com., 1979-80; mem. Nat. Assn. Jewish Legislators, 1977; Pres., Orgns. United to Contain Healthcosts, 1981—; mem. exec. bd. Health Planning Council of Midlands, 1980—, chmn. plan devel. com., 1980—, bd. dirs., 1979—; mem. Legis. Coalition for Children, 1981—; vice-chmn. staff tng. com. Nebr. Correctional Improvement Program, 1977-80; del. Douglas County Democratic Conv., 1980, Nebr. Dem. Conv., 1980; mem. Urban League, 1976—, bd. dirs., 1978; bd. dirs. Nebr. chpt. ACLU, 1977; mem. adv. bd. Nebr. Town meeting Assn., 1977; mem. GOCA Winterization Com., 1976-77. Recipient cert. of appreciation Franklin Community Credit Union, 1981, Nat. Sudden Infant Death Syndrome Found., 1978; Friend of Edn. award Nebr. Edn. Assn., 1980. Mem. Omaha Jaycees (dir. membership 1977, chmn. Pull Together program 1976, Internat. Senator 1977). Home: 2810 S 162 Plaza Omaha NE 68130 Office: 5934 S 25th St Omaha NE 68130

SIMON, PAUL, congressman; b. Eugene, Oreg., Nov. 29, 1928; s. Martin Paul and Ruth (Troemel) S.; student U. Oreg., 1945-46; student Dana Coll., Blair, Nebr., 1946-48, LL.D., 1965; D.Litt., McKendree Coll. (Ill.), 1965; D.C.L., Greenville Coll., 1968; LL.D., Concordia Coll., 1969, Lincoln Coll., 1969, Loyola U., Valparaiso U., 1976; m. Jeanne Hurley, Apr. 21, 1960; children—Sheila, Martin. Pub., Troy (Ill.) Tribune, 1948-66; mem. Ill. Ho. of Reps., 1955-63, Ill. Senate, 1963-69; lt. gov. Ill., 1969-73; mem. faculty Sangamon State U., 1972-73; lectr. John F. Kennedy Inst. Politics, Harvard U., 1973; mem. 94th-97th Congresses from 24th Dist. Ill. Bd. dirs. Wheatridge Found., McKendree Coll. Served with CIC, U.S. Army, 1951-53. Recipient Am. Polit. Sci. Assn. award, 1957; named Best Legislator 7 times. Mem. Luth. Human Relations Assn., Am. Legion, V.F.W., NAACP, Urban League, Sigma Delta Chi. Lutheran. Lion. Author: Lovejoy: Martyr to Freedom, 1964, Lincoln's Preparation for Greatness, 1966, A Hungry World, 1966; (with Jeanne Hurley Simon) Protestant-Catholic Marriages Can Succeed, 1967; You Want to Change the World? So Change It, 1971; (with Arthur Simon) The Politics of World Hunger, 1973; writer weekly column Sidelights from Springfield, 1955-72, P. S/Washington, 1975—; contbr. articles to periodicals, including Saturday Rev., Harper's, The New Republic. Home: Carbondale IL 62901 Office: 227 Cannon House Office Bldg Washington DC 20515*

SIMON, SAMUEL, JR., fin. exec.; b. Lakewood, Ohio, Oct. 30, 1927; s. Samuel and Mamie (Elzeer) S.; B.B.A., Dyke Coll., 1951; m. Mary Louise Pallotta, Oct. 10, 1953; children—Mary Louise, Samuel James, Larry J., Timothy David. With The Telephone Credit Union, Inc., Cleve., 1951—, treas., chief exec. officer, gen. mgr., 1968—; treas., dir. Cubanc Corp.-Bank Holding Co., Columbus, Ohio, 1976-81; vice-chmn. bd. Ohio Central Credit Union, Inc., Columbus, 1975-81. Served with USN, 1946-47. Mem. Credit Union Exec. Soc., Adminstrv. Mgmt. Soc. (past pres. Cleve. chpt.). Republican. Lebanese Orthodox. Clubs: Masons, Shriners. Home: 2055 Radcliffe Rd Westlake OH 44145 Office: 921 Huron Rd Cleveland OH 44115

SIMON, SEYMOUR F., justice Supreme Ct. Ill.; b. Chgo., Aug. 10, 1915; s. Ben and Gertrude (Rusky) S.; B.S., Northwestern U., 1935, J.D., 1938; m. Roslyn Schultz Biel, May 26, 1954; children—John B., Nancy Harris, Anthony Biel. Admitted to Ill. bar, 1938; spl. atty. Dept. Justice, 1938-42; practice law, Chgo., 1946-74; judge Ill. Appellate Ct., Chgo., 1974-80, presiding justice 1st Dist., 3d Div., 1977-79; justice Ill. Supreme Ct., 1980—. Mem. Bd. Commrs. Cook County, 1961-66, pres., 1962-66; pres. Cook County Forest Preserve Dist., 1962-66; mem. Pub. Bldg. Commn., City Chgo., 1962-67. Alderman, 40th ward, Chgo., 1955-61, 67-74, Democratic ward committeeman, Chgo., 1960-74. Bd. dirs. Schwab Rehab. Hosp., 1961-71, Swedish Covenant Hosp., 1969-75. Served with USNR, 1942-45. Decorated Legion of Merit; recipient citation for distinguished service North Park Coll., Chgo., 1967, 9th Ann. Pub. Service award Tau Epsilon Rho, 1963. Mem. Ill., Chgo. bar assns., Chgo. Hist. Soc., Izaak Walton League, Chgo. Hort. Soc., Phi Beta Kappa, Order of Coif. Clubs: Standard, Variety (Chgo.). Home: 1555 N Astor St Chicago IL 60610

SIMON, SHIRLEY SCHWARTZ (MRS. EDGAR H. SIMON), author; b. Cleve., Mar. 21, 1921; d. Bernard H. and Sylvia (Silverman) Schwartz; student Western Res. U., 1938-40; B.A., Goddard Coll., 1973; m. Edgar H. Simon, Mar. 1, 1942; children—Allen Harold, Ruth Esther. Tchr. juvenile writing div. gen. studies Western Res. U., Cleve., 1965-68, Shaker Heights (Ohio) Adult Edn. Program, Cleve., 1968-70, John Carroll U., 1969—; instr. creative writing extended learning program Ohio U., 1972-74; chairperson English dept. Glen Oak Sch., Gates Mills, Ohio, 1973—; speaker Cleve. Book Fair, 1963-68, Dayton (Ohio) Book Fair, 1965. Author: Molly's Cottage, 1959; Molly and the Rooftop Mystery, 1961; Cousins at Camm Corners, 1963; Best Friend, 1964, paperback edit., 1968; Libby's Stepfamily, 1966. Contbr. stories, serials and plays to Jack and Jill, Child Life, The Writer, and other nat. juvenile and tchrs. publs. Home: 3630 Cedarbrook Rd Cleveland OH 44118

SIMONETT, JOHN EDWARD, justice Minn. Supreme Ct.; b. Mankato, Minn., July 12, 1924; s. Edward J. and Veronica M. Simonett; B.A., St. John's U., Collegeville, Minn., 1948; LL.B., U. Minn., 1951; m. Doris M. Bogut, Oct. 1951; children—Anne, John, Mary, Martha, Paul, Luke. Admitted to Minn. bar, 1951; partner firm Rosenmeier & Simonette, Little Falls, Minn., 1951-80; asso. justice Minn. Supreme Ct., 1980—. Served in U.S. Army, 1943-46. Mem. Am. Bar Found., Am. Coll. Trial Lawyers. Roman Catholic. Office: 230 State Capitol Saint Paul MN 55155

SIMONS, HELEN, psychologist; b. Chgo., Feb. 13, 1930; d. Leo and Sarah (Prohov) Pomper; student U. Ill., 1947-50; B.A. in Biology, Lake Forest Coll., 1951; M.A. in Clin. Psychology, Roosevelt U., 1972; Psy.D., Ill. Sch. Profl. Psychology, 1980; children—Larry, Sheri. Sch. psychologist Chgo. Bd. Edn., 1974—; intern in clin. psychology Cook County (Ill.) Hosp., Chgo., 1979-80. Mem. Am. Psychol. Assn., Ill. Psychol. Assn., Nat. Assn. Sch. Psychologists, Ill. Sch. Psychologists Assn., Chgo. Assn. Sch. Psychologists, Am. Mental Health Assos. for Israel. Jewish. Club: Haddasah. Home: 6145 N Sheridan Rd Chicago IL 60660 Office: 211 S Kildare Chicago IL 60624

SIMONS, RICHARD STUART, journalist, retailer; b. Marion, Ind., July 26, 1920; s. Erwin Philip and Tillie Ethel (Bernstein) S.; A.B., Ind. U., 1942; m. Rosmarie Roeschli, Mar. 5, 1957; 1 dau., Charlotte. Editor, Winchester (Ind.) News, 1942-44, Tipton (Ind.) Daily Tribune, 1944-48; feature writer Sunday mag. Indpls. Star, 1949—; partner Richard Clothing Co., Marion, 1954-63, owner, 1963—; lectr. journalism Ind. U., 1952. Pres. Mississinewa Arts Council, 1971-72, Marion Philharmonic Orch., 1974-75; mem. Ind. Ty. Sesquicentennial Commn., 1950; mem. New Harmony Commn., 1978—; mem. adv. com. Ind. Statehood Sesquicentennial, Ind. Hist. Bur., 1980—; bd. dirs. Marion Gen. Hosp. Authority, 1974—, pres., 1981—; bd. dirs. Marion Gen. Hosp., 1955-64, pres., 1963-64; trustee Marion Pub. Library, 1976-80, pres., 1977. Recipient award of merit Am. Assn. State and Local History, 1972. Mem. Ind. Hist. Soc. (trustee), Nat. Ry. Hist. Soc. Clubs: Elks, Kiwanis (Disting. Service award). Contbg. editor: Popular Mechanics Picture History of Am. Transp., 1952; contbg. author: Indiana in World War II, 1952. Contbr. articles to profl. jours. Office: 326 S Washington St Marion IN 46952

SIMONS, ROBERT MARVIN, health agy. exec.; b. Buckhannon, W.Va., June 20, 1927; s. Henry Gilbert and Jessie Catherine (Wagner) S.; A.B., W. Va. Wesleyan U., 1952; M.P.H., U. Mich., 1958; postgrad. Ind. U., 1964, Marquette U., 1966; m. Mary K. Smallridge, July 9, 1949; children—Robert Brian, Scott Alan. Sanitarian, Clarksburg (W. Va.) Health Dept., 1952-57; health educator Fla. Dept. Health, St. Petersburg, 1958-59; dir. Div. Health Edn., W. Va. State Health Dept., Charleston, 1959-61; exec. dir. Heart Assn. W. Va., 1961-64, Heart Assn. Iowa, 1964-68, North Central Region, Chgo., 1968-73; exec. dir. Mich. Heart Assn., Southfield, 1973—. Served with USN, 1944-45. USPHS grantee, 1957-58. Fellow Am. Public Health Assn.; mem. Mich. Public Health Assn., Am. Mgmt. Assn., Am. Soc. Assn. Execs., Soc. Heart Assn. Profl. Staff, Royal Soc. Health. Republican. Methodist. Clubs: Elks, Masons, Engring., Shriners. Home: 30855 Lincolnshire St Birmingham MI 48010 Office: 16310 W 12 Mile St Southfield MI 48076

SIMONSON, DAVID C., publishing co. exec.; b. N.Y.C., May 9, 1927; s. Simon and Rebecca (Coolman) S.; A.B., Hamilton Coll., 1947; postgrad U. Vt., 1948, Art Students League of N.Y., 1948; m. Lois Sneider, Nov. 1, 1952; children—Peter, Eric, John Frederick. Copy writer Forwell Advt., N.Y.C., 1950; editor Croton (N.Y.)-Cortlandt News, 1950-52; gen. mgr. Colony Publications, N.Y.C., 1952-54; advt. sales, promotion mgr., asst. publisher Patent Trader, Mt. Kisco, N.Y., 1955-72, publisher, 1972-77; pres., publisher Pioneer Press, Inc. Div. Time, Inc., Wilmette, Ill., 1977—; 2d v.p. Suburban Newspapers of Am. Chmn. planning bd. City of Croton-on-Hudson, N.Y., 1960-67, trustee, 1968, mayor, 1969. Served with U.S. Navy, 1944-45. Recipient Nat. Newspaper Assn. Promotion award, 1960. Mem. Ill. Press. Assn. (dir.), Cook County Publishers Assn. (pres., dir. 1980—), Am. Mgmt. Assn., Am. Newspaper Publishers Assn., Am. Press Inst. Author numerous articles in field. Office: 1232 Central Ave Wilmette IL 60091

SIMONSON, LARRY SIMON, coll. adminstr.; b. Viroqua, Wis., Sept. 26, 1946; s. Everett C. and Orla M. (Jones) S.; B.S., U. Wis., 1968, M.S., 1973; m. Jan. 13, 1968; children—Mary Ellen, Michael Larry. Tchr. bus. edn. Ithaca Public Schs., Richland Center, Wis., 1968-69, Richland Public Schs., Richland Center, 1969-77; bus. mgr. Lincoln (Ill.) Christian Coll., 1978—, faculty, 1979—; pvt. counselor on family fin. and budgeting, 1980—. Volunteer coach girls basketball Dept. Recreation, Lincoln, 1980-81; broadcaster high sch. basketball games, Sta. WPRC, Lincoln, 1979-81. Recipient cert. of completion, Dale Carnegie Course 1978. Mem. Assn. Bus. Adminstrs. of Christian Colls., Nat. Assn. Coll. Aux. Services. Home: 275 Institute St Lincoln IL 62656 Office: PO Box 178 Lincoln IL 62656

SIMOWITZ, FREDRIC MALCOLM, neurologist; b. Augusta, Ga., Oct. 4, 1937; s. Joseph and Thelma Dorothy (Levy) S.; M.D., Med. Coll. Ga., 1962; m. Beverly Ann Seigal, Jan. 29, 1966; children—Lynn, Mark. Intern, Ohio State U. Hosp., Columbus, 1962-63; resident Sinai Hosp., Balt., 1965-66; resident in neurology U. Mich. Med. Ann Arbor, 1966-68, chief resident, 1969; instr. in neurology St. Louis U., 1969-71, sr. instr., 1971-73, clin. asst. prof. neurology, 1973—; practice medicine specializing in neurology, St. Louis, 1969—; cons. U.S. VA, 1972—, Sandoz Pharms., 1973—. Served with USN, 1963-65. Diplomate Bd. Psychiatry and Neurology, Am. Bd. Electroencephalography. Fellow Am.-Israel Physicians, Am. Acad. Neurology; mem. AMA (Physician's Recognition award 1970—), Am. Electroencephalographic Soc., Pan-Am. Med. Assn. Jewish. Contbr. articles to med. jours. Home: 538 Chalet Ct Saint Louis MO 63141 Office: 224 S Woods Mill Rd Saint Louis MO 63131

SIMPKINS, JOSEPH ALBERT, mfg. co. exec.; b. St. Louis, Sept. 15, 1905; s. Leo and Ella (Friedkin) S.; grad. high sch.; m. Florence Putnam, Oct. 2, 1978; 1 dau. by previous marriage, Linda (Mrs. Farrell Kahn). Self-employed auto dealer, St. Louis, 1929-47; chmn. bd., pres. Tiffany Industries, St. Louis, 1968—; owner Joe Simpkins Oil Co., 1944—. Vice pres. Herbert Hoover Boys Club, 1969—. Bd. dirs. Jewish Hosp., Child Center Our Lady of Grace, Dismas House. Mem. Independent Men's Assn. Club: Variety (pres. 1969-71) (St. Louis). Home: 2220 Warson Rd St Louis MO 63124 Office: 1055 Corporate Square Dr Saint Louis MO 63132

SIMPKINS, WINIFRED JOAN, nurse; b. Chgo., July 18, 1931; d. James Frank and Mildred Jane (Heilman) Kamba; R.N., Englewood Hosp., Chgo., 1954; B.S., Coll. St. Francis, 1979; m. S.A. Simpkins, July 25, 1953; children—Kathryn, Mark, Karen, Michael. Emergency room nurse Englewood Hosp., 1954-61; operating room nurse Our Lady of Mercy Hosp., Dyer, Ind., 1961-64; operating room supr. Starke Meml. Hosp., Knox, Ind., 1964—; nurse, CPR instr. ARC; camp nurse Girl Scouts U.S.A., 1965-69. Den mother Boy Scouts

Am., 1965-68. Mem. Am. Nurses Assn., Assn. Operating Room Nurses, Dare Soc. Methodist Women. Republican. Clubs: Women of the Moose, Ladies Aux. Eagles. Home: Route 3 Box 967 Knox IN 46534 Office: 102 E Culver Rd Knox IN 46534

SIMPSON, CALVIN, JR., recording co. exec.; b. Birmingham, Ala., Aug. 24, 1948; s. Calvin and Dorothy Ree (Binion) S.; student Port Huron Coll., 1965-66; A.S., Highland Park Jr. Coll., 1970; student U. Mich., 1970-73; m. Barbara Desmangles, Sept. 4, 1977; 1 son, Calvin. Mgr. trainee Frank's Nursery Sales, Detroit, 1960-64; asst. mgr. Lindy's Supermarket, Detroit, 1964-67; mgr. Simpson's Record Shop, Detroit, 1967-71; founder, pres. Simpson's Wholesale, Inc., Detroit, 1971—. Mem. Black Music Assn. (v.p. mktg. and merchandising), Nat. Assn. Rec. Merchandisers, Detroit C. of C., People United to Save Humanity. Club: Detroit Optimist. Office: 845 Livernois Ferndale MI 48220

SIMPSON, DAVID, mfg. co. exec.; b. Ceres, Fife, Scotland, 1926; ed. Dundee Wireless Coll., 1943, Dundee Tech. Coll., London U.; Grad. Exec. Program, Stanford U. Sch. Bus., 1966. Gen. mgr. Hughes Aircraft Co., 1960-61; mng. dir. Hewlett-Packard Ltd., 1962-69; group ops. dir. George Kent Ltd., 1969-75; mng. dir. Cambridge Instrument Co., 1975-76; mng. dir. Gould Advance Ltd. subs. Gould Inc., 1976-78, v.p. and gen. mgr. instruments div. Gould Inc., Rolling Meadows, Ill., 1978-79, group v.p.-elec., 1979-80, pres., chief operating officer, 1980—. Served with Royal Signals, 1945-48. Office: Gould Inc Gould Center Rolling Meadows IL 60008*

SIMPSON, DONALD BRUCE, librarian; b. Ithaca, N.Y., Dec. 13, 1942; s. Francis Alfred and Drusilla Lucille (Dickson) S.; B.A., Alfred (N.Y.) U., 1964; M.S. in L.S., Syracuse (N.Y.) U., 1970; postgrad. in public adminstrn. Ohio State U., Columbus, 1971-74; m. Lupe M. Rodriguez, Nov. 10, 1977; 1 son, Michael John. Asst. librarian Keuka (N.Y.) Coll., 1970-71, head catalog center State Library Ohio, Columbus, 1971-75; exec. dir. Bibliog. Center Research, Rocky Mountain Region, Denver, 1975-80; del., mem. fin. com., v.p. OCLC, Inc. Users Council, Columbus, 1978-80; dir. center for Research Libraries, Chicago, 1980—; mem. bd. Satellite Library Network, 1975-77, Telefax Library Network, 1978—; mem. network adv. com. Library of Congress, 1978-80; cons. in field. Served to capt. USAF, 1965-69. Decorated Air Force Commendation medal. Mem. Assn. State Library Agencies (pres. 1977-78), Assn. Specialized and Coop. Library Agencies, ALA (editor State Library Agencies 1973-79, councilor-at-large 1979—), Am. Mgmt. Assn., Am. Soc. Info. Sci., Assn. Research Libraries, Internat. Fed. of Library Assn. (UAP Adv. Com., 1980—), Spl. Libraries Assn., Beta Phi Mu. Author articles, papers in field. Office: 5721 Cottage Crove Ave Chicago IL 60637

SIMPSON, DONALD ROY, apparel mfg. co. exec.; b. Hydro, Okla., Apr. 3, 1937; s. George W. and Luella J. S.; m. Sherry, May 20, 1977; 1 son, David Roy II. Chief engr. Don Stohlman & Assos., Louisville, 1959-68; exec. v.p. 10X-Mfg. Co., Des Moines, 1969-74; v.p. mfg. Boss Mfg. Co., Kewanee, Ill., 1979--. Mem. Ill. Mfrs. Soc. Home: 445 E McClure Kewanee IL 61443 Office: 221 W 1st St Kewanee IL 61443

SIMPSON, DOUGLAS, hosp. products co. exec.; b. Utica, N.Y., June 8, 1931; s. Reginal Filmore and Grace S.; B.S., Bowling Green State U., 1958; m. Sylvia Kopko, July 30, 1955; 1 son, John David. Salesman, Pfizer Labs., Pitts., 1958-60, Corning Glass Works, Pitts., 1960-64, Perkin Elmer, Chgo., 1964-68; midwest sales mgr. Cahn Inst., Chgo., 1968-72; midwest regional mgr. Ivac, Chgo., 1972-75; nat. sales mgr. Filac Corp., Villa Park, Ill., 1975-80, internat. market mgr., 1980-81, mgr. N.Am. Chesebrough Ponds sales, 1981—. Served with USN, 1951-55. Episcopalian. Home and Office: 102 Leslie Lane Villa Park IL 60181

SIMPSON, EDWIN KERSHAW, III, educator, researcher, editor; b. N.Y.C., Apr. 24, 1935; s. Edwin Kershaw II and Hedwig Elizabeth (Schacht) S.; B.A., Rutgers U., 1965; M.B.A., U. Dayton, 1968; Ph.D., U. Cin., 1976; m. Geraldine Winifred Macfarlane, Feb. 15, 1958; children—Eric Malcolm, Craig Kershaw. Dist. sales rep. Gen. Analine & Film, 1963-69; instr. Miami U., Oxford, Ohio, 1972-76, asst. prof. mktg., 1976-79, asso. prof., 1979—; adj. asso. prof. Wright State U., summer 1977; editor Jour. Personal Selling and Sales Mgmt.; cons. to industry; prin. Delphi Group, cons. Served with AUS, 1957-59. Mem. Am. Marketing Assn. (pres. Dayton chpt. 1975-76, now bd. dirs., Outstanding Achievement award 1976, Nat. award for outstanding service to marketing 1976), AAUP, Beta Gamma Sigma, Pi Sigma Epsilon (educator v.p.), Mu Kappa Tau (nat. bd. dirs.). Democrat. Presbyterian. Clubs: Dayton MBA, Dayton Sales and Mktg. Execs. (v.p.). Engaged in source credibility research. Home: 418 Aberdeen Ave Dayton OH 45419 Office: Laws Hall Miami University Oxford OH 45056

SIMPSON, EVERETT JAMES, architect; b. Fairbury, Nebr., Sept. 16, 1922; s. Ralph A. and Frances A. (Chorn) S.; student Inst. Design (now Ill. Inst. Tech.), 1946; m. Sally S. Shaw, Jan. 16, 1945; children—James, Robert, Sue, Jan. Drapery salesman, window trimmer J.M. McDonald Co., Norfolk, Nebr., 1949-52; draftsman Watson & Strong, Architects, Norfolk, 1952; chief designer Howard J. Strong & Assos., Norfolk, 1953-63; partner Simpson & Strong, Architects, Norfolk, 1964-67; owner E.J. Simpson & Assos., Architects, Inc., Norfolk, 1968-74; pres. Architects Inc., Lincoln, Nebr., 1974—; project architect Hosp. Bldg. and Equipment, St. Louis, 1978-79, archtl. project mgr., 1979—. Bd. dirs. Norfolk YMCA. Served with USNR, 1942-45. Decorated Purple Heart. Mem. AIA (pres. Western Nebr. sect. 1973-74), Norfolk C. of C. (chmn. legislative affairs com. 1968-70). Methodist (supt. ch. sch. 1960-66, trustee 1967-70, chmn. 1969-70). Clubs: Rotary (pres. Norfolk 1968-69), Odd Fellows (grand master Nebr. 1974-75). Home: 756 Foxwick Dr Manchester MO 63011 Office: 5610 Colby St Lincoln NE 68505

SIMPSON, GENEVIEVE EILEEN, mfg. co. exec.; b. Lewistown, Ill., Oct. 3, 1924; d. James Howard and Eathel Mae (Richardson) Huff; student MidState Coll., Peoria, Ill., 1944, 52-54; children—Stephen, Michael, David. Office mgr. Brown's Peoria Sch. Bus., 1953-59, also vets. coordinator; exec. sec. to chmn. bd. Keystone Consol. Industries, Inc., Peoria, 1960-69, adminstr. corp. records, 1969-71, asst. corp. sec., 1971—. Mem. Assn. Records Mgrs. and Adminstrs., Soc. Am. Archivists, Corp. Shareholders Systems User Group. Republican. Home: 412 W Columbia Terr Peoria IL 61606 Office: 7000 SW Adams St Peoria IL 61641

SIMPSON, JACK BENJAMIN, med. technologist, mng. exec.; b. Tompkinsville, Ky., Oct. 30, 1937; s. Benjamin Harrison and Verda Mae (Woods) S.; student Western Ky. U., 1954-57; grad. Norton Infirmary Sch. Med. Tech., 1958; m. Winona Clara Walden, Mar. 21, 1957; children—Janet Lazann, Richard Benjamin, Randall Walden, Angela Elizabeth. Asst. chief med. technologist Jackson County Hosp., Seymour, Ind., 1958-61; chief med. technologist, bus. mgr. Mershon Med. Labs., Indpls., 1962-66; founder, dir., officer Am. Monitor Corp., Indpls., 1966—; mng. partner Astroland Enterprises, Indpls., 1968—, 106th St. Assos., Indpls., 1969-72, Keystone Asso., Ltd., Indpls., 1972—, Delray Rd. Asso., Ltd., Indpls., 1970-71, Allisonville Asso., Ltd., Indpls., 1972—, Rucker Asso., Ltd., Indpls., 1974—; mng. partner Raintree Assos., Ltd., Indpls., 1979—, Westgate Assos., Ltd., Indpls., 1978—; dir. Topps Constrn. Co., Bradenton, Fla., Indpls. Broadcasting, Inc. Mem. Am. Soc. Med. Technologists (cert.), Indpls. Soc. Med. Technologists, Ind. Soc. Med. Technologists, Am. Soc. Clin. Pathologists, Royal Soc. Health (London). Republican. Baptist. Clubs: Columbia of Indpls., Harbor Beach Surf, Fishing of Am., Elks. Office: 7729 Rucker Rd Indianapolis IN 46250

SIMPSON, LYLE LEE, lawyer; b. Des Moines, Oct. 15, 1937; s. R. Clair and Martha B. (Accola) S.; B.A., Drake U., 1960, J.D., LL.B., 1963; m. Marci T. Simpson; children—Sondra Sue, Donald Scott. Asst. to dean students Drake U., 1960-62; admitted to Iowa bar, 1963; prin. Lyle L. Simpson, atty., Des Moines, 1963-64; mem. firm Beving & Swanson, 1964-68, Peddicord, Simpson & Sutphin, 1968—. Instr. mil. leadership Iowa Mil. Acad., 1965-68. Treas., Mental Health Coordinating Commn., 1975—. Mem. exec. bd. Polk County Republican Central Com., 1964-68. Bd. counselors Drake U. Law Sch., 1969-72; bd. dirs. Polk County Health Service Corp., 1976—, Polk County Mental Health Center, 1976-79; trustee, chmn. bd. Broadlawns Med. Center, 1973-80; bd. dirs. Homes, Inc., 1981—, The Batten Found., 1981—. Served to capt. Signal Corps, U.S. Army, 1955-68; comdr. USNR, 1968—. Recipient Class of 1915 award Drake U., 1960, Oren E. Scott award, 1960. Mem. Am. Humanist Assn. (humanist counselor 1974—, gen. counsel 1975-80, dir. 1976—, nat. pres. 1980—), Naval Res. Lawyers Assn., Res. Officers Assn., Am. (coms. recent devels. real estate, condominiums, mil. lawyers and probate 1970—), Iowa (chmn. coms. mil. affairs 1968-80, prison reform 1968-69, public info. 1980—), Polk County (coms. ethics and grievance 1963-69) bar assns., Delta Theta Phi, Omicron Delta Kappa, Psi Chi, Tau Kappa Epsilon, Phi Eta Sigma. Clubs: Masons, Shriners, Scottish Rite, York Rite; Des Moines, Des Moines Golf and Country; Embassy; Morning (pres. 1964). Home: 3901 SW 28th Pl Des Moines IA 50321 Office: Suite 300 Fleming Bldg Des Moines IA 50309

SIMPSON, ROBERT OTIS, social worker; b. Kalamazoo, Mich., Jan. 15, 1937; s. Thurman John and Margaret Helen (Pratt) S.; B.S., Western Mich. U., 1967, M.S.W., 1971; m. Pamela Kay Greenawalt, Aug. 23, 1968; children—Robin C.F., Robert Otis, John T., Charles F., William D. Delinquency worker Calhoun County Dept. Social Services, Battle Creek, Mich., 1971-73, child welfare supr., 1973-77, family and youth supr., 1977-78, youth services supr., 1978-79; adult foster care licensing cons., 1979—; tchr. foster parent effectiveness Eastern Mich. U.; field instr. Western Mich. U. Mem. citizens adv. com. Supt. Schs. Comstock Sch. Dist., 1978—. Served with USN, 1954-57. Mem. Nat. Assn. Social Workers. Baptist. Home: 2623 Texel Dr Kalamazoo MI 49001 Office: 322 Stockbridge Kalamazoo MI 49001

SIMPSON, WILLIAM STEWART, psychiatrist, psychoanalyst; b. Edmonton, Alta., Can., Apr. 11, 1924; s. William Edward and Ethel Lillian (Stewart) S.; came to U.S., 1950, naturalized, 1963; B.Sc., U. Alta., 1946, M.D., 1948; m. Eleanor Elizabeth Whitbread, June 17, 1950; children—David Kenneth, Ian Stewart, James William, Bert Edward. Rotating intern U. Alta. Hosp., 1948-49, resident internal medicine, 1949-50; resident psychiatry Topeka State Hosp., fellow Menninger Sch. Psychiatry, 1950-53; asst. sect. chief Topeka State Hosp., 1953-54, clin. dir., 1954-59; chief C. F. Menninger Meml. Hosp., 1959-66, dir. edn., 1963-66; asso. dir. Menninger Sch. Psychiatry, 1966-68; clin. dir. Topeka State Hosp., 1968-72; dir. field services Menninger Found., 1972-74, sr. staff psychiatrist, adult outpatient dept., 1977—; chief psychiatry service, psychiat. residency tng. program Topeka VA Hosp., 1974-77; faculty mem. Menninger Sch. Psychiatry, 1953—, mem. exec. com., 1954-59, 63-72, mem. mgmt. com., 1974-77; mem. dean's com. Topeka VA Hosp., 1976-77; mem. faculty Ann. Seminar Inst. on Alcoholism, U. Wis., 1973-74; cons. Topeka State Hosp., 1967-68, Osawatomie State Hosp., 1954-68; mem. staffs Stomont-Vail, Meml., St. Francis hosps., Topeka. Bd. dirs. Topeka Civic Symphony Soc., 1953-55, Topeka People to People Council, 1963-66; mem. Kans. Citizen's Adv. Com. on Alcoholism, 1973-78; founder Topeka Affiliate Nat. Council on Alcoholism, 1964, pres., dir., 1964, dir. N.Y.C., 1967, v.p., 1971-73, pres., 1973-75, mem. exec. com., 1967, Bronze Key award, 1972, Silver Key award, 1975. Cert. Am. Psychoanalytic Assn. Diplomate Am. Bd. Psychiatry and Neurology, Topeka Inst. Psychoanalysis. Recipient Achievement award U. Alta. Med. Alumni Assn., 1975. Fellow Am. Psychiat. Assn.; mem. Am. Psychoanalytic Assn., AMA, Kans. Psychiat. Soc., Kans., Shawnee County med. socs., Topeka Psychoanalytic Soc., Menninger Sch. Psychiatry Alumni Assn. (pres. 1979-80). Presbyterian. Club: Rotary (Topeka). Asso. editor Bull. Menninger Clinic, 1963-70. Office: PO Box 829 Topeka KS 66601

SIMS, GARY WILLIAM, air force officer; b. Hollywood, Calif., Jan. 23, 1944; s. Jack Cole and Betty Faye (Harvey) S.; B.S. with highest distinction, Ariz. State U., 1967; M.S., Leland Stanford Jr. U., 1971; m. Cindy Rae Goodsell, Aug. 17, 1962; children—Tammi Joann, Diana Sue. Enlisted U.S. Air Force, 1963, commd. 2d lt., 1967, advanced through grades to maj., 1979; chief engr. digital applications div. Aero. Systems Div. Computer Center, Wright-Patterson AFB, Ohio, 1980—. Decorated Meritorious Service medal, Commendation medal (2). Mem. Am. Def. Preparedness Assn., Air Force Assn., Assn. for Computing Machinery, Aircraft Owners and Pilots Assn., Exptl. Aircraft Assn., Mensa. Office: ASD Computer Center Digital Applications Div Wright-Patterson AFB OH 45433

SIMS, GREGORY LEE, minister; b. Moline, Ill., Apr. 8, 1952; s. Roy Leon and Betty Jo (Dawson) S.; B.A., Harding U., Searcy, Ark., 1974; M.A., Sangamon State U., Springfield, Ill., 1978; m. Karen Jane Farrar, Dec. 23, 1972; children—Jason Gregory, Lucas Wade, Clayton Lee. Salesman, Gate City Steel Co., Davenport, Iowa, 1974-75; ordained to ministry Ch. of Christ, 1975; minister Sunnyside Rd Ch. of Christ, Decatur, Ill., 1975-79; prin. 20th St. Christian Sch., Rockford, Ill., 1979-80; minister edn. and outreach East Park Ch. of Christ, Danville, Ill., 1980—. Bd. dirs. Wabash Valley Christian Camp, 1980—. Mem. Am. Personnel and Guidance Assn., Am. Rehab. Counseling Assn. Home: 921 Blue Ridge Danville IL 61832 Office: 1224 E Voorhees St Danville IL 61832

SIMS, KENNETH J., JR., chem. co. exec.; b. Cleve., Dec. 13, 1935; s. Kenneth J. and Ella (Gibbons) S.; B.S., Thiel Coll., 1958; m. Gail McKelvey, June 30, 1962; children—Kelly, Lori. Tchr. history, English public schs., Aurora, Ohio, 1959-62; tchr. history, asst. basketball coach public schs., Wickliffe, Ohio, 1962-63; tchr. govt., head basketball coach public schs., Aurora, 1963-69; with Detrex Chem. Industries, Inc., 1969—, field sales mgr. chem. div., 1976-78, sales mgr., Ashtabula, Ohio, 1978—. Sec., City Status Commn., Aurora, 1966; vice chmn. Aurora Planning Commn., 1967-71. Served with U.S. Army, 1958-59. Mem. Cleve. Chem. Assn., Columbus Chem. Assn., St. Louis Chem. Assn. Episcopalian. Home: 33840 Country View Ln Solon OH 44139 Office: PO Box 623 Ashtabula OH 44004

SIMS, KEVIN FRANCIS, educator; b. Waterloo, Iowa, May 16, 1952; s. William Francis and Dorothy Lorain (Campbell) S.; B.A., Cedarville (Ohio) Coll., 1974; M.A., U. No. Iowa, 1978; m. Cheryl Lynn Cole, July 14, 1979. Personnel asst. Cedarville Coll., 1972-74; grad. asst. dept. history U. No. Iowa, 1976-77; prof. history Pillsbury Baptist Bible Coll., Owatonna, Minn., 1978—, chmn. dept. history, since 1979—. Del. county and dist. convs. Ind.-Republican Party Minn., 1980. Mem. Am. Hist. Assn., Minn. Hist. Soc., Conservative Historians Forum. Baptist. Home: 536 E Main St Owatonna MN 55060 Office: 315 S Grove St Owatonna MN 55060

SIMS, RICHARD LEE, hosp. adminstr.; b. Columbus, Ohio, Jan. 6, 1929; s. Dorwin Delos and Christine Anna (Hanstein) S.; B.S., Ohio State U., 1951; m. Marilyn Lou Atkinson, June 2, 1951; children—John Christopher, Steven Paul. Adminstr., Doctors Hosp., Columbus; preceptor faculty Ohio State U. Coll. Health Care Adminstrn.; past bd. dirs. Mid Ohio Health Planning Fedn.; adminstr. Sattelite Hosp.-Doctors Hosp. West, Columbus; chmn. bd. trustees Doctors' Hosp., Nelsonville, Ohio; hosp. adv. com. Blue Cross of Central Ohio; mem. Statewide Health Coordinating Council; chmn. Hosp. Shared Service Inc. Past pres. Franklin County Crippled Childrens Soc.; pres. Franklin County chpt. ARC, 1978-80; past chmn. 1st Community Village Bd.; past chmn. adv. bd. Ohio U. Coll. Osteo. Medicine. Served with Med. Service, AUS, 1953-56; to maj. Ohio N.G., 1956-74. Recipient Distinguished Service award Columbus Jr. C. of C., 1960-63. Mem. Am. Hosp. Assn. (ho. of dels.), Am. Osteo. Hosp. Assn. (trustee), Am. Coll. Hosp. Adminstrs., Am. Coll. Osteo. Hosp. Adminstrs., Ohio Trade Assn. Execs. (past pres.), Ohio Hosp. Assn. (past chmn. bd.), Ohio Osteo. Hosp. Assn. (past pres.), Am. Legion (past post comdr.), Sigma Chi. Clubs: University, Rotary (pres. 1978-79) (Columbus). Home: 2431 Southway Dr Columbus OH 43221 Office: 1087 Dennison Ave Columbus OH 43201

SIMS, THOMAS ELWOOD, judge; b. Independence, Mo., Dec. 15, 1931; s. Thomas Harold and Francis (Taylor) S.; B.B.A., U. Kansas City, 1958, LL.B., 1961; postgrad. U. Utah, summer 1972, U. Nev., 1973; m. Beverly J. McCroskie, July 23, 1955; children—Thomas Elwood, Shelby Anne, Stephen Angus. Teaching fellow Sch. Bus., U. Kansas City, 1957-61; claim rep. State Farm Mutual Ins. Co., 1959-61; admitted to Mo. bar, 1961; asso. firm Rogers, Field and Gentry, Kansas City, Mo., 1961-67, partner firm Rogers, Field, Gentry, Benjamin and Robertson, 1968-70; mcpl. judge, Kansas City, Mo., 1970-78; judge Kansas City mcpl. div. 16th Jud. Circuit Ct. Mo., 1979—; vice chmn. assistance com. Clay County (Mo.) Juvenile Ct., 1970; mem. faculty Nat. Coll. for State Trial Judges, U. Nev., Reno, 1974-75; instr. Mcpl. Judges Statewide Tng. Seminars, 1976; mem. Statewide Jud. Planning Com., Mo., 1977—; mem. bd. Criminal Justice Coordinating Council, Regional, Mo.; chmn. bd. dirs. Retel, Inc., Now Showing, Inc. Troop com. chmn. Heart of Am. council Boy Scouts Am., 1978-80; chmn. audit com. community staff North Kansas City (Mo.) Meml. Hosp., 1979-80; pres. Southwest Clay Republican Assn., 1969-70; elder First Presbyn. Ch., N. Kansas City, Mo., 1971—; bd. dirs. Regional Center for Criminal Justice, 1970-71, chmn., 1971; bd. dirs. Sober House, Inc., 1971-74, chmn., 1971-74; bd. dirs. Spl. Offenders Counsel, 1976-77, Alternative Opportunities, Inc., 1975-76, trustee U. Mo. Kansas City Law Found., 1971-77, sec., 1973-77. Served with USN, 1950-54; Korea. Mem. Am. Bar Assn., Mo. Bar Assn., Kansas City Bar Assn. (chmn. mcpl. cts. com. 1966-69), Clay County Bar Assn., Am. Judges Assn., Am. Judicature Soc. (dir. 1974-78), Mo. Inst. for Justice (dir. 1973—, pres. 1976—), Mo. Mpcl. and Magistrate Judges Assn. (dir. 1976-78, pres. 1977), Mo. Mcpl. and Asso. Circuit Judges Assn. (dir. 1978—), Am. Soc. Hosp. Attys., St. Andrew's Soc., U. Mo. Kansas City Alumni Assn. (Service award 1974), U. Mo. Kansas City Sch. Bus. Alumni Assn. (Service award 1966), Phi Alpha Delta. Co-author: Local Court Rules, 1971; co-author proposed Mo. Supreme Ct. rules for Mcpl. and Asso. Circuit Ct., 1982; producer 5 ednl. films on Mo. courts; introduced closed circuit TV into nation's courts for receipt of evidence, 1973. Home: 126 NE 43d Kansas City MO 64116 Office: 1101 Locust St Kansas City MO 64106

SINCLAIR, WARREN KEITH, physicist; b. Dunedin, N.Z., Mar. 9, 1924; s. Ernest W. and Jessie E. (Craig) S.; came to U.S., 1954, naturalized, 1959; B.Sc., U. Otago (N.Z.), 1944, M.Sc., 1945; Ph.D., U. London, 1950; m. Elizabeth J. Edwards, Mar. 19, 1948; children—Bruce W., Roslyn E., Allen. Radiol. physicist U. Otago, 1945-47; radiol. physicist U. London, Royal Marsden Hosp., 1947-54; prof., chmn. dept. physics U. Tex., M.D. Anderson Hosp., 1954-60; sr. biophysicist Argonne (Ill.) Nat. Lab., 1960—, div. dir., 1970-74, asso. lab. dir., 1974—; prof. radiation biology U. Chgo., 1964—; mem. Internat. Commn. on Radiation Units and Measurements, 1969—, Internat. Commn. on Radiol. Protection, 1977—; dir. Nat. Council on Radiation Protection and Measurements, 1967—, pres., 1977—; sec. gen. 5th Internat. Congress Radiation Research, 1974; U.S. alt. del. to UN Sci. Com. on Effects Atomic Radiation, 1976—. Served with N.Z. Army, 1942-43. Nat. N.Z. scholar, 1942-45. Fellow Inst. Physics; mem. Am. Assn. Physicists in Medicine (pres. 1961-62), Radiation Research Soc. (council 1964-67, pres. 1978-79), Brit. Inst. Radiology (council 1953-54), Internat. Assn. Radiation Research (council 1966-70, 74—), Radiol. Soc. N.Am., Biophys. Soc., Soc. Nuclear Medicine. Club: Innominates (U. Chgo.). Contbr. numerous articles to profl. jours., also chpts. to books. Office: 9700 S Cass Ave Argonne IL 60439

SINDERMAN, ROGER WILLIAM, health physicist; b. West Olive, Mich., May 4, 1942; s. William August and Marta Marie (Beck) S.; B.S. in Engring. (Dupont fellow), U. Mich., 1964; M.S. in Health Physics (USPHS fellow), 1965; M.P.H. in Radiation Biology (USPHS fellow), 1966; m. Christine Kubiak, May 30, 1964; children—Christian, Heidi. Asso. engr., gen. engr. nuclear ops. dept. Consumers Power Co. Big Rock Nuclear Plant, Charlevoix, Mich., 1966-68, health physicist, plant health physicist, environ. health physicist, Jackson, Mich., 1968-80, dir. radiol. services, Jackson, 1980—. Mem. Health Physics Soc. Author tech. papers in field. Home: 4403 Maple Lane Rd Rives Junction MI 49277 Office: 1945 W Parnall Rd Jackson MI 49201

SINENENG, ROLANDO SUNPONGCO, physician; b. Philippines, May 3, 1943; s. Felipe T. and Estella T. (Sunpongco) S.; came to U.S., 1967; A.A., U. Philippines, 1961, M.D., 1967; m. Leda J. Laureta, June 25, 1971; children—Rolando L., Philip B. Intern, St. Michael Hosp., Milw., 1967-68; resident in medicine and liver diseases N.J. Coll. Medicine Hosp., 1968-72; fellow gastroenterology Bridgeport (Conn.) Hosp., 1972-73; staff gastroenterologist VA Hosp., Dayton, Ohio, 1974; practice medicine specializing in gastroenterology, Dayton, 1975—; mem. staff Miami Valley Hosp., Good Samaritan Hosp.; clin. asso. prof. medicine Wright State U. Med. Sch., Dayton. Diplomate Am. Bd. Internal Medicine. Mem. Ohio, Montgomery County med. socs., Am. Soc. Gastrointestinal Endoscopy, Philippine Med. Assn. Roman Catholic. Home: 5700 Price Hill Pl Dayton OH 45459 Office: 3535 Salem Ave Dayton OH 45406

SINGER, STEPHEN GERALD, actuary; b. Boston, Jan. 21, 1944; s. Samuel and Helen Esther (Ackerman) S.; B.A. cum laude, Harvard U., 1965; m. Janet Bell, Apr. 17, 1970; children—Scott, Eric. Actuarial trainee Equitable Life Assurance Soc. N.Y., 1965-67;

actuarial mgr. A.S. Hansen, Inc., N.Y.C., 1967-69, cons., Boston, 1969-72, mgr. profl. support, Lake Bluff, Ill., 1972-76, dir. actuarial services, 1976-78, v.p., dir. actuarial services, dir., 1978—; pres. Hansen Employees Fed. Credit Union, 1978—. Fellow Soc. Actuaries, Canadian Inst. Actuaries, Conf. Actuaries in Public Practice; mem. Am. Acad. Actuaries, Mensa. Clubs: Harvard (N.Y.C. and Chgo.). Home: 824 Ellen Way Libertyville IL 60048 Office: 1080 Green Bay Rd Lake Bluff IL 60044

SINGH, BIRENDRA BIKRAM, agronomist; b. Indamau, Unnao, India, Jan. 12, 1946; came to U.S., 1972; s. Chandra B. and Shanti D. Singh; B.Sc., Agra U., India, 1965; M.S. (Nat. Merit scholar), Kanpur U., India, 1968; M.Sc. (Can. Nat. Research Council scholar), U. Man., Can., 1971; Ph.D., U. Idaho, 1974; m. Asha Singh, June 16, 1967; children—Nitish, Harish Paul, Angela. Lectr., Azad Agrl. and Tech. U., India, 1968-69; teaching asst. in soil chemistry and plant physiology U. Idaho, 1973-74; soil scientist Soil Conservation Service, U.S. Dept. Agr., Pocatello, Idaho, 1975; research soil scientist dept. agronomy Iowa State U.; agronomist and state coordinator Agronomic Services, State of Nebr., 1977—; participant Internat. Symposium on Salt Affected Soils, Karnal, India, 1980. Recipient Top Agronomist award Inter-Am. Agrl. Cons. Corp., 1979-80. Mem. Am. Soc. Agronomy, Soil Sci. Soc. Am., Internat. Soc. Soil Sci., Western Soc. Soil Sci., Nebr. Ind. Crop Cons. Assn. (pres. 1979-80), Council of Agrl. Sci. and Tech., Nat. Alliance of Ind. Crop Consultants, U. Idaho Alumni Assn., Gamma Sigma Delta. Contbr. articles on soil sci. and agronomy to Am. and European profl. jours. Home: 619 North Shore Dr Hastings NE 68901 Office: PO Box 844 Hastings NE 68901

SINGH, DARSHAN, psychologist; b. Punjab, India, Apr. 15, 1938; came to U.S., 1963, naturalized, 1971; m. Amar and Kartar K. (Samra) S.; B.S., U. Punjab, 1958, B. Teaching, 1960; M.S., Ind. State U., 1964; postgrad. Ball State U., 1967, Drake U., 1979—; m. Jasvinder K. Grewal, June 14, 1971; children—Rupinder K., Sangeeta K. Tchr. math., sci. Punjab schs., 1958-61; tchr. math. Dudley (Eng.) schs., 1962-63, Lewisville (Ind.) schs., 1964-65, New Castle (Ind.) schs., 1965-67; psychologist Des Moines Public Schs., 1967-77, coordinator psychol. services, 1977—. Mem. Am. Psychol. Assn., Iowa Psychol. Assn., Nat. Assn. Sch. Psychologists, Iowa Sch. Psychologists Assn., Council Exceptional Children, Internat. Assn. Children with Learning Disabilities, Iowa Talented and Gifted Children. Democrat. Sikhism. Club: Indo Am. Assn. (pres. 1980). Office: 1800 Grand Ave Des Moines IA 50307

SINGH, GYANENDRA, consumer products co. exec.; b. Lansdowne, India, July 15, 1946; came to U.S., 1968; s. Dhyan Pal and Raj S.; B.Ch.E., Birla Inst. Tech. and Sci. (India), 1968; M.S. in Chem. Engring., U. Ill., Urbana-Champaign, 1970, M.B.A., 1971; m. Suman Singh, Aug. 8, 1969; children—Amitabh, Ajit. Project engr. Procter & Gamble Co., Cin., 1971-72, group leader, 1972-75, food process devel., sales trainee case food sales, St. Louis, 1975-76, asst. brand mgr. food products advt., 1976-77, sect. head food products research, 1977-80, sect. head bar soap and household cleaning product devel., 1980-81, sect. mgr. mgmt. systems div., 1981-82, systems mgr. Buckeye Cellulose, 1982—. Named Outstanding Univ. Student India, 1967. Mem. Am. Inst. Chem. Engring., Am. Mgmt. Assn., Am. Oil Chemists Assn., Inst. Food Technologists, Assn. M.B.A.'s. Contbr. articles to profl. jours.; patentee in field. Office: B2510 SWTC Reed Hartman Hwy Cincinnati OH 45241

SINGH, JASWANT, educator; b. Jagraon, Punjab, India, May 20, 1932; came to U.S., 1970, naturalized, 1976; s. Anunt and Bhagwanti Ram; B.Sc. with honours, Punjab U., 1953; M.Sc. (Govt. W. Bengal scholar 1958), Calcutta U., 1959; B.Ed., U. Alta. (Can.), 1965, M.A., 1968; M.L.S. (univ. fellow 1977-78), Western Mich. U., 1971, Ed.D., 1982; m. Jasjit Kaur, Dec. 30, 1968; 1 dau., Amardeep Kaur Hoonjan. Tchr. schs. in India and Can., 1953-70; head librarian Ontonagon (Mich.) Area Sch. Dist., 1971-74; media dir. Regional Ednl. Media Center, Copper County Intermediate Sch. Dist., Hancock, Mich., 1975—. Mem. NEA, Assn. Ednl. Communication and Tech., Assn. for Supervision and Curriculum Devel., Nat. Assn. Regional Media Centers, ALA, Mich. Intermediate Media Assn. (pres. 1980-81), Mich. Edn. Assn., Indian Library Assn., Indian Adult Edn. Assn. Democrat. Club: Lions. Office: 600 Hecle St Hancock MI 49930

SINGH, RAJENDRA, engr.; b. Dhampur, India, Feb. 13, 1950; s. Raghubir and Ishawar (Kali) S.; came to U.S., 1973; B.S., Birla Inst. Tech. and Sci., 1971; M.S., U. Roorkee, 1973; Ph.D., Purdue U., 1975; m. Veena, June 24, 1979; 1 child, Rohit. Grad. instr. Purdue U., 1973-75; sr. acoustics, dynamics engr. Carrier Corp., Syracuse, N.Y., 1975-79; asst. prof. mech. engring. Ohio State U., 1979—; adj. lectr. Syracuse U., 1977-79; cons. in field. Mem. Acoustical Soc. Am., Am. Soc. Engring. Edn., Inst. Noise Control Engring., ASHRAE, ASME, Soc. Computer Simulation, Am. Acad. Mechanics, Phi Kappa Phi. Contbr. articles to profl. jours. Home: 3108 Aullwood Ct Dublin OH 43017 Office: 206 W 18th Ave Columbus OH 43210

SINGHAL, ASHOK KUMAR, cons. civil engr.; b. Gwalior, India, Apr. 8, 1946; came to U.S., 1967, naturalized, 1980; s. Uma Shanker and Shri Kumari Singhal; B.Tech.Civil (Govt. India Merit scholar 1962-67), Indian Inst. Tech., Kanpur, 1967; M.S. in Civil Engring. (Univ. Research fellow 1967-68, U. Calif., Berkeley; M.B.A. in Fin., Eastern Mich. U., 1979; m. Veena Gupta, July 17, 1975; children—Neha, Nihar. Environ. engr., then project mgr. Ayres, Lewis, Norris & May, Inc., Ann Arbor, Mich., 1969-75, head systems and studies dept., 1975-80, v.p., 1980—. Sec. Indian Students Assn., 1970. Registered profl. engr., Mich. Mem. Am. Water Works Assn., Mich. Soc. Profl. Engrs. Author papers in field. Home: 7889 Poppy Ln Saline MI 48176 Office: 3983 Research Park Dr Ann Arbor MI 48104

SINGHAL, VIVEK K., corp. exec.; b. New Delhi, India, May 15, 1949; came to U.S., 1970, natrualized, 1975; s. Swami Om and Kirti Prakash; B.S., Indian Inst. Tech., 1970; M.S., U. Mich., 1971, M.B.A., 1973; m. Asha, May 29, 1975; children—Ritu, Vikas. Internat. fin. analyst Rockwell Internat., Troy, Mich., 1973-74, mgr. fin., Newark, Ohio, 1974-75, mgr. cost and pricing, Troy, 1976-77; dir. spl. projects Consol. Foods, Chgo., 1977-79, corporate dir. strategic planning, 1979—. Mem. Am. Mgmt. Assn., Midwest Planning Assn., Planning Execs. Inst., Beta Gamma Sigma, Eta Kappa Nu. Home: 6104 Washington St Downers Grove IL 60516 Office: Consolidated Foods 135 S LaSalle St Chicago IL 60603

SINGLETON, HERBERT, data processing mgr.; b. Jacksonville, Fla., July 21, 1947; s. Henry Baker and Henrietta Singleton; B.A., Morris Brown Coll., 1969; M.B.A., St. Francis Coll., 1978, M.B.A., 1979; m. Brenda Ann Oliver, Nov. 7, 1970; children—Wanda Yvette, Chanté Lynette. Programmer, Lincoln Nat. Life Ins. Co., Ft. Wayne, Ind., 1974-76, programmer analyst, 1976, data processing tng. cons., 1976-78, mgr. profl. devel. and tng., 1978-80, data processing devel. mgr., 1980—. Served with USAF, 1970-74. Cert. computer programmer; cert. tchr. Calif. community colls. Mem. Assn. M.B.A. Execs., Alpha Phi Alpha. Methodist. Office: 1300 S Clinton St Fort Wayne IN 46801

SINGLETON, MARVIN AYERS, physician, real estate broker, bus. exec.; b. Baytown, Tex., Oct. 7, 1939; s. Henry Marvin and Mary Ruth (Mitchell) S.; B.A., U. of the South, 1962; M.D., U. Tenn., 1966. Intern, City of Memphis Hosps., 1966-67; resident in surgery Highland Alameda City Hosp., Oakland, Calif., 1967-68, resident in otolaryngology U. Tenn. Hosp., Memphis, 1968-71; Am. Acad. Otolaryngology and Ophthalmology fellow in otolaryngic pathology Armed Forces Inst. Pathology, Washington, 1971; fellow in otologic surgery U. Colo. at Gallup (N.Mex.) Indian Med. Center, 1972; practice medicine specializing in otolaryngology and allergies, Joplin, Mo., 1972—; founder, operator Home and Farm Investments, Joplin, 1975—, Video Systems, Joplin, 1977—; staff mem. Freeman Hosp., St. John's Hosp., Joplin; cons. in otolaryngology Parsons (Kans.) State Hosp. and Tng. Center, Mo. Crippled Children's Service, Santa Fe R.R.; pres. Ozark Mfg. Co., Inc., Joplin. Served with USNG, 1966-72. Diplomate Am. Bd. Otolaryngology. Fellow A.C.S., Am. Acad. Otolaryngology and Ophthalmology, Am. Acad. Ophthalmologic and Otolaryngologic Allergy, Am. Assn. Clin. Immunology and Allergy; mem. AMA (Mo. del.), Mo. State, So., Jasper County med. assns., Council of Otolaryngology, Mo. State Allergy Assn., Ear, Nose and Throat Soc. Mo. (past pres.), Joplin C. of C., Sigma Alpha Epsilon, Phi Theta Kappa, Phi Chi. Episcopalian. Club: Elks. Contbr. articles to profl. jours. Home: Five Mile Ranch Route 2 Box 138 Seneca MO 64856 Office: 114 W 32d St Joplin MO 64801

SINGSIME, GRACE SMOCK, catering co. exec.; b. Chgo., Nov. 22, 1924; d. Albert William and Martha Krueger (Manke) Smid; m. Alvin E. Singsime, Apr. 16, 1966; 1 dau., Stacey G. Smock, stepchildren—Delores Singsime De Lellis, Mardi Singsime Schlondrop, Deane A. With Athey Truss Wheel Co., Chgo., 1942-43, J.J. Collins' Sons, Inc., Chgo., 1943-46, Kellogg Switchboard and Supply, Chgo., 1946-48, Lane Drafting Coll., Evansville, Ind., 1949, City Dressed Beef, Milw., 1949-53; owner, mgr. Smock's Yankee Doodle Restaurant-Gracious Catering, Milw., 1953-59, Grace Smock-Gracious Catering, Milw., 1959-70, Off-Premise Catering, Elm Grove, Wis., 1970—. Mem. Internat. Food Service Exec. Assn. (Food Service Exec. of Yr. Milw. br. 1978), Elm Grove Bus. Assn., Waukesha Old Car Club. Mem. Order Eastern Star. Home: S 36 W 26579 Velma Dr Waukesha WI 53186 Office: Grace Smock Gracious Catering 890 Elm Grove Rd Elm Grove WI 53122

SINK, ALVA GORDON (MRS. CHARLES A. SINK), civic worker; b. Rose Twp., Mich.; d. Nathaniel J. and Ella M. (Highfield) Gordon; student Eastern Mich. U., summers 1914, 18; A.B., U. Mich., 1923; m. Charles A. Sink, June 18, 1923 (dec.). Tchr. public schs., Rose Center, Mich., 1914-17, Hickory Ridge, Mich., 1917-18, Holly, Mich., 1918-19, Canfield Pvt. Sch., Ann Arbor, Mich., 1919-22. Bd. dirs. Faculty Women's Club, 1940-42; dir. Washtenaw County chpt. ARC, 1943-48, 53-59, in charge First Aid and Accident Prevention, 1941-61; pres. Mich. House and Senate Club, 1929-30, U. Mich. Alumnae Club, 1931-33, Sara Browne Smith Group Alumnae Club, 1957-59, Woman's Soc. Congl. Ch., 1946-48; trustee Women's City Club, 1954-57; regent Sarah Caswell Angell chpt. DAR, 1955-57. Recipient Red Cross citation, 1959; Alumnae Council award U. Mich., 1971; Alva Gordon Sink Group of U. Mich. Alumnae named in her honor. Recipient Disting. Alumni Service award U. Mich., 1978. Mem. French Huguenots, AAUW, Ann Arbor Art Assn., PEO. Clubs: Art Study, Garden, Faculty Women, Women's Republican (Ann Arbor); Presidents, Emeritus (pres. 1975-76), Henry P. Tappan Soc. (U. Mich.) Home: 1325 Olivia Ave Ann Arbor MI 48104

SINK, DAVID MICHAEL, editor; b. Omaha, Nov. 29, 1948; s. Calvin E. and Anna Mae (Hansen) S.; B.S., U. Nebr., Omaha, 1978. Reporter, Sun Newspapers of Omaha, 1974-79, asst. editor, 1979—. Office: 4875 F St Omaha NE 68117

SINKS, JOHN R., state senator; B.S., Ball State U., 1955, M.A., 1957; m. Mary Louis S., 1952; 1 son, John Robert. Guidance counselor Elmhurst High Sch., Ft. Wayne, Ind.; mem. Ind. Ho. of Reps., 1965-76, Ind. State Senate, 1977—. Served with USAAF; Korea. Mem. NEA, Ind. State Tchrs. Assn. Episcopalian. Office: Ind State Senate State Capitol Indianapolis IN 46204*

SINOR, DENIS, orientalist; b. Kolozsvar, Hungary, Apr. 17, 1916; s. Miklos and Marguerite (Weitzenfeld) S.; B.A., U. Budapest, 1938; M.A., U. Cambridge (Eng.), 1948; D. hon. causa, U. Szeged, 1971. Asst., Institut des Hautes Études Chinoises, U. Paris, 1941-45; attaché de recherches Centre de la Recherche Scientifique, Paris, 1946-48; lectr. Cambridge U., 1948-62; prof. Uralic and Altaic studies and history Ind. U., Bloomington, 1962—, disting. prof., 1975—, chmn. dept. Uralic and Altaic studies, 1963-81; dir. U.S. Office of Edn. Uralic and Inner Asian Nat. Resource Center, 1963—; dir. Asian Studies Research Inst., 1967-79, dir. Research Inst. Inner Asian Studies, 1979-81; v.p. UNESCO Commn. for Preparation History of Civilizations of Central Asia, 1981—. Guggenheim fellow, 1968-69, 81-82; scholar-in-residence Rockefeller Found. Study Center, Villa Serbelloni, Bellagio, 1975; recipient grants Am. Council Learned Socs., 1962, Am. Philos. Soc., 1963, U.S. Office Edn., 1969-70; Nat. Endowment for Humanities, 1980-82. Fellow Korosi Csoma Soc. (hon.); mem. Am. Oriental Soc. (pres. 1975-76, chmn. Inner Asian regional com. 1968—), Permanent Internat. Altaistic Conf. (sec. gen. 1960—), Royal Asiatic Soc. Gt. Britain and Ireland (hon. sec. 1952-62), Societas Uralo Altaica (v.p. 1964—), Assn. Asian Studies (chmn. devel. com. Inner Asian studies 1973-79), Explorers Club, Tibet Soc. (pres. 1967-69), Mongolia Soc. (chmn. bd. 1964—), Internat. Union Orientalists (past sec.), Am. Hist. Assn., Société Asiatique, Société de Linguistique, Deutsche Morgenlandische Gesellschaft, Hungarian Acad. Scis. (hon.). Clubs: United Oxford and Cambridge U. (London); Cosmos (Washington), Explorers (New York). Served with Forces Françaises de l'Interieur, 1943-44, French Army, 1944-45. Author: Introduction a l'étude de l'Eurasie Centrale, 1963; History of Hungary, 1959; Inner Asia, 1969; Modern Hungary, 1977; Inner Asia and Its Contact with Medieval Europe, 1977; contbr. articles to profl. jours.; editor Jour. Asian History, 1967—. Office: Uralic Altaic Studies Dept Ind Univ Bloomington IN 47405

SINQUEFIELD, REX A(NDREW), bank exec.; b. St. Louis, Sept. 7, 1944; B.S., St. Louis U., 1967; M.B.A. in Fin., U. Chgo., 1972; m. Jeanne Cairns, Dec. 31, 1971; 1 son, Randolph. With Am. Nat. Bank & Trust Co., Chgo., 1972—, head trust investment dept., 1976-78, sr. v.p., head trust dept., 1978, exec. v.p., head trust dept., 1978—. Mem. Com. on Fgn. Affairs, Chgo. Council. Served with U.S. Army, 1968-70. Mem. Cosmopolitan C. of C. Author: (with Roger Ibbotson) Stocks, Bonds, Bills, Inflation: The Past (1926-1976) and the Future (1977-2000), 1978. Office: 33 N La Salle St Chicago IL 60602

SIPIERA, PAUL PETER, JR., scientist, educator; b. Chgo., Nov. 30, 1948; s. Paul P. and Frances A. (Blazejack) S.; B.A., Northeastern Ill. U., 1971, M.S., 1975. Instr. geology and astronomy Aurora (Ill.) Coll., part-time 1974-77; research asso. Center for Meteorite Studies, Ariz. State U., Tempe, summers 1974, 75, 76; asst. prof. geology and phys. sci. Harper Coll., Palatine, Ill., 1974—, also dir. meteorite research group; instr. earth sci. Northeastern Ill. U., adj. faculty, 1979-80; research asso. Field Mus. Natural History, Chgo., 1976—; adj. faculty Wayland Coll., 1979; sci. cons. Young Peoples Sic. Ency. for Children's Press, 1977-78; research proposal reviewer NSF, 1978-80. Recipient Research award Ill. State Acad. Sci., 1975, 77; Nininger Meteorite Research award, 1975; AAAS/NASA Research award, 1978; Harper Coll. grantee, 1976-77. Mem. Geol. Soc. Am., Meteoritical Soc., Ill. State Acad. Sci., Chgo. Acad. Sci., Explorers Club, Sigma Xi (Research award 1979), Phi Alpha Theta. Roman Catholic. Contbr. 14 articles to profl. jours. Home: 766 Windsor Dr Crystal Lake IL 60014 Office: William Rainey Harper Coll Dept Geology and Phys Sci Algonquin and Roselle Rds Palatine IL 60067

SIPPY, JOHN CORE, educator; b. Richland Center, Wis., Jan. 19, 1938; s. Scott Ambrose and Iva Beatrice (Core) S. B.A., N. Central Coll., 1960; M.S.Edn., No. Ill. U., 1967, postgrad. 1980—; children—Sarah Elizabeth, Karin Ruth, Paula Jane. Tchr. social studies Central Jr. High Sch., Zion, Ill., 1960-61, O'Neill Jr. High Sch., Downers Grove, Ill., 1961-67; tchr. social studies Downers Grove South High Sch., 1967—, asst. coach golf, 1968-70, asst. coach basketball, 1968-70, asst. dean students, 1970-72, dir. student activities, 1970-76, head dept. social studies, 1976—, head coach girls track and field, 1977-80. Mem. grad. council No. Ill. U., 1980-81, mem. grad. fellowship com., 1980-81, mem. grad. student adv. com. for elem. edn., 1981-82. Mem. NEA, Ill. Edn. Assn., Downers Grove Edn. Assn., Nat. Council for Social Studies, Ill. Council for Social Studies, Assn. for Supervision and Curriculum Devel., Chgo. Suburban Social Studies Suprs., West Suburban Council Social Studies, World Future Soc., ACLU, Phi Delta Kappa. Democrat. Methodist. Home: 5623 Brookbank Rd Downers Grove IL 60516 Office: 1436 Norfolk St Downers Grove IL 60516

SIPPY, RODNEY EDWARD, dentist; b. Chgo., Feb. 2, 1934; s. Everett Tunis and Helen Marie (Rydell) S.; student Purdue U., 1952-54; B.S., U. Ill., 1956, D.D.S., 1960; m. Marilyn Joyce Landis, June 13, 1954 (dec. June 1971); children—Deborah Lynn, Linda Darlene; m. 2d, Polly Palmer Lloyd, Apr. 13, 1974; children—Joseph William, Mellisa Palmer. Practice dentistry, LaGrange, Ill., 1960—; mem. attending staff Community Meml. Gen. Hosp., 1966—, sec. dental staff, 1962-65, chmn. dental staff, 1965-77; mem. staff Hinsdale San., 1968-70; chief dental service Suburban Cook County Tb Sanatorium, 1961-70; clin. instr. dept. prosthetics U. Ill. Coll. Dentistry, 1960-61; adviser Tri-County Dental Assts. Soc., Oak Brook, Ill., 1968-69, 73-74, dental asst. program Morton Coll., 1974-77; Fellow Royal Soc. Health, Am. Coll. Dentists, Am. Acad. Gen. Dentistry, Internat. Coll. Dentistry; prin. RPS Industries; owner La Grange Prosthetic Lab.; cons. Manor Care Nursing Center, Hinsdale, Ill.; chief dentist med. staff Medinah Temple, 1978-80. mem. Am. Dental Assn., Ill., Chgo., West Suburban (pres. 1977-78) dental socs., Am. Acad. Dental Group Practice, Am. Assn. Hosp. Dental Chiefs, Am. Orthodontic Soc., Internat. Acad. Orthodontics (dir. central sect. 1966-68), Pierre Fauchard Acad., Am. Soc. Preventive Dentistry, Fedn. Dentaire Internationale, U. Ill. Alumni Assn. (dir. 1967-71, pres. 1974-75), Far West Study Club, West Suburban C. of C., Art Inst. Chgo., Mus. Contemporary Art, Delta Sigma Delta. Republican. Clubs: Mason (32 deg.), Shriners, Illini, Progressive (sec. 1970-71, treas. 1968-69, pres. 1974-75); Plaza (Chgo.). Home: 1324 Laurie Lane Burr Ridge IL 60521 Office: 4727 Willow Springs Rd LaGrange IL 60525

SIRACUSA, ANTHONY JOHN, psychologist; b. N.Y.C., Feb. 10, 1948; s. Vito and Angelina (Scalia) S.; B.A. in Psychology, L.I. U., 1971; M.S. in Psychology, SUNY, 1975; postgrad. Ind. U., 1976—; m. Susan Hillman, Mar. 20, 1981; children—Jessica, Amy. Youth counselor specialist Youth Counsel Bur., Bklyn., 1973-74; clin. psychologist, project dir. Queensboro Soc. for Prevention Cruelty to Children, Queens, N.Y., 1974-76; psychotherapist S. Central Community Mental Health Center, Bloomington, Ind., 1978—; clin. supr. Mental Health Center, Bloomington, 1978—; cons. program devel. and obstetrics, Bloomington Hosp., 1979-81. Chmn. direct services com. Monroe County Task Force on Child Abuse, 1978-80. Recipient Dr. Richard Runyon research potential award in psychology, L.I. U., 1971; Disting. Achievement award Ind. chpt. Nat. Commn. for Prevention Child Abuse, 1979; Community Service award State of Ind., 1979. Mem. Am. Psychol. Assn., Soc. Pediatric Psychology, Soc. Research in Child Devel. Quaker. Home: 309 N Fairview St Bloomington IN 47401 Office: 631 S Rogers St Bloomington IN 47401

SIRMANS, DAN LAMAR, personnel adminstr.; b. Durham, N.C., July 13, 1941; s. Horace Lamar and Juanita (Fort) S.; B.B.A., Ga. State U., 1967; m. Sandra Elaine Bridges, Dec. 27, 1962; children—Todd Anthony, Elizabeth Anne. Asso. engr. Western Electric Co., Inc., Atlanta, 1962-67, sr. tng. specialist, St. Louis, 1968-74; dir. tng. and devel. ITT Aetna Corp., Denver, 1975-77; dir. personnel ITT Fin. Corp., St. Louis, 1978-79, dir. adminstrn., 1979-81; dir. employment Gen. Dynamics Communications, St. Louis, 1981— Mem. Am. Soc. for Tng. and Devel., Am. Soc. Personnel Adminstrn. Methodist.

SISLER, MAYNARD LEE, physician, ret. naval officer; b. Massillon, Ohio, Aug. 12, 1923; s. George Turner and Audrey Augusta (Athey) S.; student Washington Missionary Coll., 1939-40, Shepherd State Tchrs. Coll., 1941, U. So. Calif., 1950-51, Long Beach (Calif.) City Coll., 1948-50; B.S., Northwestern U., 1953, M.D., 1956; m. Sandra Ellen Byrd, Mar. 24, 1977; children by previous marriage—Suzanne, Judith, Kathleen, Mary Elizabeth, Maynard Lee, Leandra; 1 stepdau., Kim Wilburn. Intern, Passavant Meml. Hosp., Chgo., 1956-57; resident U.S. Naval Hosp., St. Albans, N.Y., 1958-61; practice medicine specializing in internal medicine, 1957—; commd. lt. M.C., U.S. Navy, 1957, advanced through grades to comdr., 1968; gen. med. officer U.S. Naval Acad., 1957-58; mem. staff U.S. Naval Hosp., Memphis, 1961-63; head gen. medicine U.S. Naval Hosp., San Diego, 1963-66, head sick officer quarters, 1968-69; chief of medicine U.S. Naval Hosp., Corpus Christi, 1966-68; ret., 1969; asso. with Med. Group, Internal Medicine Assos., Palm Springs, Calif., 1969-70, Dunmire-Cash Clinic, Kennett, Mo., 1970-73; dir. Saturday Clinic, Parma, Mo., 1973-74; pvt. practice internal medicine, Kennett, 1973—. Served with USN, 1941-50. Recipient Freedoms Found. award, 1963, 66, 67; Stitt award U.S. Naval Hosp., San Diego, 1966. Diplomate Am. Bd. Internal Medicine. Fellow A.C.P.; mem. Mo. State, Dunklin County med. socs., Royal Soc. Medicine (London). Author: A Large Slice of Life, Carved Into Poetry, 1974; contbr. numerous poems and essays to various newspapers and mags.; editorial editor Dunklin County Press, 1974—. Home: 217 College Ave Kennett MO 63857

SISSON, EVERETT ARNOLD, diversified industry exec.; b. Chgo., Oct. 24, 1920; s. Emmett B. and Norma (Merbitz) S.; A.B., Valparaiso U., 1942; postgrad. Yale, 1944; m. Roberta E. Blauman, Mar. 20, 1943; children—Nancy Lee Genz, Elizabeth Anne Levy. Sales mgr. Ferrotherm Co., Cleve., 1946-51, Osborn Mfg. Co., Cleve., 1951-56; dir. sales Patterson Foundry & Machine Co., East Liverpool, Ohio, 1956-58; mgr. sonic energy products Bendix Corp., Davenport, Iowa, 1958-60; pres., chief exec. officer, dir. Lamb Industries, Inc., Toledo, 1960-65, Lehigh Valley Industries, Inc., N.Y.C., 1965-66, Am. Growth Industries, Inc., Chgo., 1966—, Workman Mfg. Co., Chgo., 1966-69, Am. Growth Devel. Corp., Chgo., 1968—, Am. Growth Mgmt. Corp., Oak Brook, Ill., 1970—, Oak Brook Club Co., 1969—; chmn. Hausske Harlen Furniture Mfg. Co., Peru, Ind., 1976—, Deutsch Furniture Mfg. Co., Chicago, 1981—; chmn. bd. Luth. Mut. Life Ins. Co., Waverly, Iowa; dir. Telco Mktg. Services, Inc., Chgo., Wis. Real Estate Investment Trust, Milw., The Ross Orgn., Orlando, Fla., Hickory (N.C.) Furniture Co. Pres., City Council Mayfield Heights, Ohio, 1952-57. Adviser to bd. trustees Valparaiso U., 1960-69; bd. regents Calif. Luth. Coll. Served to capt. USAAF,

1943-46. Fellow Calif. Luth. Coll.; mem. Am. Mgmt. Assn., Cleve. Engring. Soc., President's Assn., Tau Kappa Epsilon. Clubs: Mich. City Yacht, Chicago Power Squadron. Home: 1405 Burr Ridge Club Burr Ridge IL 60521 Office: 1550 Spring Rd Oak Brook IL 60521

SISSON, PAULA SPURLIN, ednl. adminstr.; b. Rule, Tex., Jan. 1, 1939; d. Otto Swinney Spurlin and Artie Harriet (Roberts) Spurlin Price; B.S., McMurry Coll., 1961; M.Ed., Abilene Christian U., 1965; postgrad. Ohio State U., 1978-80, Colo. U., 1968-73; m. Lavere C. Wilson, Mar. 4, 1961; children—Kimberly Dain Wilson Kirk, Jana Lynn Wilson; m. 2d, Charles M. Sisson, June 4, 1976. Tchr. public schs., Odessa, Tex., 1961-62, Abilene, Tex., 1962-65; tchr., lang. arts coordinator Boulder Valley Schs., Boulder, Colo., 1965-76; ednl. cons. III, Ohio Dept. Edn., 1976-79; elem. prin. Westerville (Ohio) Schs., 1979—; cons. in field; workshop, ednl. TV presentor; Ohio basic skills commr. and area chmn. Active campaigns on sch. issues; vol. Am. Cancer Soc. Recipient Freedom's Found. award, 1976. Mem. Ohio Assn. Elem. Sch. Adminstrs., Westerville Prins. Assn., Assn. Supervision and Curriculum Devel., Ohio Assn. Supervision and Curriculum Devel. Republican. Methodist. Home: 4863 Powderhorn Ln Westerville OH 43081 Office: 120 Hiawatha Ave Westerville OH 43081

SISSON, THOMAS OREN, packaging containers co. exec.; b. Boise, Idaho, May 4, 1936; s. George Arnold and Marjorie Elvira (Palmer) S.; student public schs., Boise; m. Pamela Jeanne Marshall, July 9, 1971; children—Bradford Ray, Sherrie Leigh. Surveyor, Morrison Knudsen Co., Timothy Meadows Dam, Oreg., Taft, Oreg. and Selleck, Wash., 1954-56; logger, powderman, catskinner Jones Logging Co., Ocean Lake, Oreg., 1957; field service rep. Sealright Co., Inc., Los Angeles and Kansas City, Kans., 1963—, field engr., mgr. Ultrakan Systems, Kansas City, Mo., now central div. service mgr., Kansas City, Kans. Served with USAF, 1957-61. Republican. Mem. Evangelical Ch. Developer aircraft dock stock parts; inventor in field. Home: 5868 N Oakley St Kansas City MO 64119 Office: 2925 Fairfax Rd Kansas City KS 66115

SITTE, DAVID WERNER, educator; b. Crookston, Minn., Aug. 16, 1942; s. Werner Wilhelm and Hazel Adeline (Schroeder) S.; B.S., N.D. State U., 1964, M.A., 1967; m. Margaret Anne Ulmen, June 11, 1976; 1 son, Benjamin. Tchr., asst. prin. Max (N.D.) High Sch., 1964-66; grad. asst. history and polit. sci. N.D. State U., Fargo, 1966-67; prof. polit. sci. Bismarck (N.D.) Jr. Coll., 1967—. Mem. NEA, Missouri Valley Adult Edn. Assn., Nat. Community Coll. Social Sci. Assn., N.D. Edn. Assn. Democrat. Roman Catholic. Club: Elks, K.C. Home: 710 N 13th St Bismarck ND 58501 Office: Bismarck Jr College Bismarck ND 58501

SITZMANN, GENE EARL, clergyman, social worker, family therapist; b. LeMars, Iowa, June 13, 1935; s. Edwin Joseph and Irene Earle (Nugent) S.; B.A., Benedictine Coll., Atchison, Kans., 1958; M.A., U. Louvain (Belgium), 1962; M.S.W., U. Iowa, 1976. Ordained priest Roman Catholic Ch., 1962; asso. pastor St. Joseph Ch., Sioux City, Iowa, 1962-63, Corpus Christi Ch., Ft. Dodge, Iowa, 1963-68, St. Rose of Lima Ch., Denison, Iowa, 1968-69, Holy Spirit Ch., Carroll, Iowa, 1969-70; instr. Am. history Kuemper High Sch., Carroll, 1969-70; instr. social studies Immaculate Conception Sch., Cherokee, Iowa, 1970-72; pastor Visitation Ch., Cherokee, 1970—; chaplain-intern Mental Health Inst., Cherokee, 1972-73, chaplain-educator, 1974—; pastor St. John's, Quimby, Iowa, 1974-76; lectr. in field. Mem. Task Force on Battered Women (Family Violence), Cherokee, 1978—. Recipient Disting. Service award Ft. Dodge Jaycees, 1967; permanent profl. teaching cert, Iowa. Mem. Am. Assn. Sex Educators, Counselors and Therapists (cert. sex counselor), Nat. Assn. Catholic Chaplains (cert chaplain-supr.), Iowa Chaplains Assn. (pres. chpt. 1979-80), Nat. Assn. Social Workers, Acad. Cert. Social Workers, Am. Assn. for Marriage and Family Therapy (clin. mem., approved supr.; dir. Iowa div. 1978-80), Nat. Council Family Relations, Mental Health Assn. Iowa (past dir.), Internat. Platform Assn. Democrat. Club: K. C. Contbr. poetry and articles on ecumenism and psychotherapy to periodicals. Home: Route 3 Box 63 Cherokee IA 51012 Office: 1200 W Cedar St Cherokee IA 51012

SIU, KENNETH KWONG CHEE, surgeon; b. Hong Kong, Sept. 7, 1928; s. Hon Kit and Kam Ching (Choy) S.; came to U.S., 1953, naturalized, 1970; M.B., B.S., U. Hong Kong, 1952; m. Mary Elizabeth Faber, Aug. 22, 1956; children—Ravenna Kay, Stephen Marcus, Deborah Jean, Rebecca Mary, Yvette Elizabeth. House surgeon Queen Mary Hosp., Hong Kong, 1952; clin. asst. in medicine U. Hong Kong, 1953; rotating intern St. Thomas Hosp., Akron, Ohio, 1953-54; resident in surgery Md. Gen. Hosp., Balt., 1954-57, chief resident in surgery, 1957-58, resident in pathology Women's Hosp., Balt., 1958-59; acting sr. surgeon Nethersole Hosp., Hong Kong, 19S9-61, asst. surgeon, 1964-66, sr. surgeon, head dept. surgery, 1966-68; practice medicine specializing in surgery, Balt., 1962-64, Jefferson City, Mo., 1970—; active staff Meml. and St. Mary's Hosps., 1970—, pres. med. staff, 1978-79. Bd. dirs. Jefferson City Family YMCA, 1969-76, pres., 1975-76, trustee, 1977—; adminstrv. bd. First United Methodist Ch., 1975—, chmn., 1977; chmn. Five Rivers dist. Boy Scouts Am., 1974-76; mem. exec. bd. Great Rivers council, 1974— v.p. membership, 1978-80, commr., 1980—. Recipient Scouter's award Boy Scouts Am., 1972, Scouter's Key, 1973, Wood Badge, 1974, Dist. award of Merit, 1977, Silver Beaver, 1978. Diplomate Am. Bd. Surgery. Fellow Internat. Coll. Surgeons, A.C.S., Royal Coll. Surgeons of Edinburgh (Scotland); mem. Cole County (Mo.) Med. Soc. (pres. 1973-74), Mo. State, Am., So., Brit. med. assns., Mo. Surg. Soc., Christian Med. Soc. Clubs: Rotary, Shriners; Masons (Jefferson City). Home: 1009 Fairmount Blvd Jefferson City MO 65101 Office: 915A Leslie Blvd Jefferson City MO 65101

SIVE, REBECCA ANNE, educator; b. N.Y.C., Jan. 29, 1950; d. David and Mary (Robinson) Sive; B.A., Carleton Coll., 1972; M.A. in Am. History, U. Ill., 1975; m. Clark Steven Tomashefsky, June 18, 1972. Asst. to librarian Am. Hosp. Assn., Chgo., 1973; researcher Jane Addams Hull House, Chgo., 1974; instr. Loop Coll., Chgo., 1975, Columbia Coll., Chgo., 1975-76; cons. Am. Jewish Com., Chgo., 1975, Center for Urban Affairs, Northwestern U., Evanston, Ill., 1977, Ill. Consultation on Ethnicity in Edn., 1976, Modern Lang. Assn., 1977; dir. Ill. Women's History Project, 1975-76; guest speaker at various ednl. orgns., 1972—; exec. dir. and founder Midwest Women's Center, Chgo., 1977-81; exec. dir. Playboy Found., 1981—; instr. Roosevelt U., Chgo., 1977-78; dir. spl. projects Inst. on Pluralism and Group Identity, Am. Jewish Com., Chgo., 1975-77; cons. Nat. Women's Polit. Caucus, 1978-80; trainer Midwest Acad.; adv. bd. urban studies program Asso. Colls. Midwest; proposal reviewer Nat. Endowment Humanities. Mem. steering com. Ill. Commn. on Human Relations, 1976; mem. structure com. Nat. Women's Agenda Coalition, 1976-77; del.-at large Nat. Women's Conf., 1977; mem. Ill. Gov.'s Com. on Displaced Homemakers, 1979-81; mem. Ill. coordinating com. Internat. Women's Year; coordinator Ill. Internat. Women's Year Photg. Exhbn., 1977; mem. Ill. Employment and Tng. Council; mem. employment com. Ill. Com. Status Women; mem. Ill. Human Rights Commn., 1980—; bd. dirs. Nat. Abortion Rights Action League and NARAL Found., Ill div. ACLU, Midwest Women's Center. Recipient award for outstanding community leadership YWCA of Met. Chgo., 1979. Mem. ACLU, Women's Inst. for Freedom of Press (asso.). Contbr. articles on women in Am. history to profl. publs.; editor Ill. Women's Agenda Newsletter, 1975-79. Office: 919 N Michigan Ave Chicago IL 60611

SIVERS, CORA RUDE, educator; b. Brookings, S.D., Aug. 13, 1914; d. Bert T. and Clara Marie (Knutson) Rude; R.N., St. Luke's Hosp., Chgo., 1939; B.S. in Nursing Edn., S.D. State U., Brookings, 1940, B.S. in Home Econs. Edn., 1960, M.S. in Home Econs., Textiles and Clothing, 1961; student textile design Alfred (N.Y.) U., 1949-50. Asst. dir. nursing Rockford (Ill.) Hosp., 1940-42; instr. nursing Swedish Hosp. Sch. Nursing, Mpls., 1954-57; grad. asst., then lab. asst. S.D. State U., 1959-61, mem. faculty, 1963—, asso. prof. textile research, curator Marghab Linen Gallery, 1970—; asst. prof. textiles Central Wash. State Coll., 1961-63. Served to lt. (j.g.) Navy Nurse Corps, 1942-44. Mem. Internat. Fedn. Home Econs., Am. Home Econs. Assn., Assn. Coll. Profs. Textiles and Clothing, Am. Assn. Textile Chemists and Colorists, Am. Assn. Testing and Materials, S.D. Home Econs. Assn., Sigma Xi, Phi Upsilon Omicron, Delta Kappa Gamma. Author articles in field. Home: 727 N Main Ave Brookings SD 57006 Office: Meml Art Center SD State Univ Brookings SD 57007

SIXTA, JANE ANNE WATERS, security co. exec.; b. Bklyn., May 13, 1951; d. Frank Theodore and Irene Regina (Huyck) Waters; B.A., Aurora Coll., 1973; m. Lorrin Lee Sixta, Aug. 19, 1977. Chief of security Fermilab, Batavia, Ill., 1975-77; br. mgr. Advance Security, Inc. subs. Figgie Internat., Inc., Kansas City, Mo., 1978—; chmn. mgmt. steering com. for pres. Advance Security, Inc. Corp. hdqrs., 1981—. Cert. protection profl. Mem. Am. Soc. Indsl. Security (chmn. membership com. Kansas City chpt. 1982), AAUW, Humane Soc. Greater Kansas City (pres. bd. dirs. 1981—). Home: 9813 Aberdeen Leawood KS 66206 Office: 3515 Broadway St Suite 100 Kansas City MO 64111

SKAFF, DUANE LEE, telephone co. mgr.; b. Sioux City, Iowa, Mar. 14, 1939; s. George A. and Delia B.S.; B.A., Morningside Coll., 1962; m. Wanda A. George, Aug. 28, 1966; children—Vince, Matt, Suzanne. With Northwestern Bell Telephone Co., Omaha, 1965—, mgr., 1979—. Sec.-treas. Fire Dist. 10, 1978-79, 80-81; troop leader Boy Scouts Am. Served with USMC, 1962-64. Recipient cert. United Way, 1977, 78, 79, 80, 81, Omaha/Douglas County Bicentennial Commn., 1975-76. Mem. Internat. Assn. Mgrs., Am. Legion. Eastern Orthodox. Clubs: Phoenician of Omaha (pres.), Masons, Shriners, Toastmasters (Able Toastmaster award). Home: 8624 N 57th St Omaha NE 68152 Office: 100 S 19th St Omaha NE 68102

SKAFTE, MARJORIE DORIS WESTEGARD, mag. editor, pub.; b. Ossee, Wis., Aug. 1, 1921; d. Nels E. and Rena B. (Severson) Westegard; student St. Olaf Coll., 1939-41, U. Minn. at Duluth, 1965-66; m. Lloyd A. Skafte, Feb. 14, 1942; children—Merilee (Mrs. James Main), Patricia, Linwood, Robert. Editorial asst. Ojibway Press (became publs. div. Harcourt Brace Jovanovich Publs., Inc., 1971), Duluth, 1964-67, mng. editor, 1967-68, editor, 1968—, pub./editor The Hearing Instruments, 1971—. Sec., Better Hearing Inst., 1973-74; active Girl Scouts U.S.A., Duluth, 1952-57, Boy Scouts Am., Duluth, 1959-61. Mem. Hearing Industries Assn. (sec., chairperson market devel. com.). Lutheran. Clubs: Order Eastern Star. Home: 4311 Tioga St Duluth MN 55804 Office: 131 W 1st St Duluth MN 55802

SKAGGS, WILLIAM T., chem. engr.; b. Centralia, Mo., Apr. 10, 1949; s. Lory T. and Betty (Wade) S.; B.S. in Chem. Engring., Auburn U., 1971; M.B.A., Washington U., St. Louis, 1978; m. Darlene L. Wallis, Aug. 31, 1974. Environ. engr., group leader Research 900 div. Ralston Purina Co., St. Louis, 1971-74, environ., microscopy lab. supr., 1975-76, mgr., 1976-80, mgr. mktg./client service Raltech Sci. Services, 1981—. Mem. Am. Inst. Chem. Engrs., Water Pollution Control Fedn., Air Pollution Control Assn., Am. Water Works Assn. (asso. referee), Assn. Ofcl. Analytical Chemists. Mem. Christian Ch. Home: 1847 Winegard Dr Manchester MO 63011 Office: 900 Checkerboard Sq Saint Louis MO 63188

SKALLE, HANS JORGEN, restaurant exec.; b. Lunde-Sogne, Norway, Jan. 27, 1919; came to U.S., 1949, naturalized, 1959; s. Wilhelm and Hansine (Hansen) S.; grad. Hotelfagskole, Norway, 1948; m. Mavis Schubert, May 29, 1954; children—Hans Jorgen, II, Heidi Mavis. Food and beverage mgr. Norsk Hotelcompagnie, 1946-49; mgr. Cavalier Room, Mpls. Athletic Club, 1949-50; supervisory trainee Waldorf-Astoria Hotel, N.Y.C., 1950-54; gen. mgr. Interlachen Country Club, Edina, Minn., 1954-64; pres., owner Camelot, Inc., Bloomington, Minn., 1964-80, Skalco, Inc., Mpls., 1975—; adv. bd. Hennepin County Vocat. Sch.; exec. council Greater Mpls. Area Hospitality Assn.; pres. Upper Midwest chpt. Club Mgrs. Assn., 1960. Adv. bd. Mpls. Boys' Club. Served with Norwegian Navy, 1940-46. Recipient Venture mag. award, 1969; Hospitality Hall of Fame award, 1967; Ivy award, 1975; Epicurean award, 1977; Meritorious Service award Minn. Air/Army N.G., 1979; Recognition award Norwegian Home Guard, 1979; Holiday mag. award, 1966, 80; named hon. knight of St. James (Spain), 1971. Mem. Nat. Restaurant Assn., Norwegian Am. C. of C., Confrerie de la Chaine des Rotisseurs (chpt. co-founder 1968). Lutheran. Clubs: Rotary (Merit award), Masons, Torske Klubben, Sagaklubben. Home: 5021 Ridge Rd Edina MN 55436

SKAMSER, ERIK BENDIK, clin. social worker; b. Chgo., Sept. 22, 1947; s. Bruce Robb and Mary K. (Kwiek) S.; B.S. in Edn., No. Ill. U., DeKalb, 1970; M.S.W., U. Ill., Urbana-Champaign, 1976. Ward adminstr. Elgin (Ill.) State Hosp., 1970-73; cons. Ill. Dept. Children and Family Services, summer 1975; sch. social worker Danville (Ill.) public schs., 1975-76, Union Ridge Sch., Harwood Heights, Ill., 1976-78; clin. supr. Hull House Assn., Des Plaines Valley Community Center, Summit, Ill., 1978—; clin. social worker Child Sexual Abuse Treatment and Tng. Center Ill., Inc., 1980—; field instr. Sch. Social Service Adminstrn., U. Chgo., 1980—, Jane Addams Coll. Social Work, U. Ill., Chgo., 1981—. Cert. social worker, Ill. Mem. Acad. Cert. Social Workers, Nat. Assn. Social Workers. Office: 6125 S Archer Rd Summit IL 60501

SKATZES, DAWERANCE HORACE, ret. educator; b. Delaware, Ohio, Aug. 21, 1914; s. Carl Henry and Eulalia (Strickler) S.; B.S., Ohio U., 1951, M.Ed., 1954; postgrad. Ohio State U., 1958-59, 67-73, Muskingum Coll., 1965-66; m. Ruth Helen Jones, Apr. 1, 1941 (div. June 1949); children—Thelma Ruth Skatzes Moore, Elta Anne Skatzes Hower, Carl Alvin, Neatha Elaine Skatzes Bostic, August Brent; m. 2d, Mildred M. Stillion, Feb. 18, 1975. Transient laborer, 1932-36; enrollee Civilian Conservation Corps, Price, Utah, 1936-37; unit clk. Soil Conservation Service, Price, 1938-41; field office mgr. Hunt & Frandsen, Gen. Contractors, Elko, Nev., 1942-44; boiler operator, supt. bldgs. and property Delaware (Ohio) City Schs., 1946-49; tchr. South Zanesville (Ohio) High Sch., 1951-54, 58-59; supt. Wills Local Sch. Dist., Old Washington, Ohio, 1954-58, Somerset (Ohio) Sch., 1959-60; prin. Adamsville (Ohio) Elementary Sch., 1960-61; supt. Quaker City (Ohio) Sch. Dist., 1961-62; prin. Valley High and Elementary Sch., Buffalo, Ohio, 1962-66; tchr. Columbus City Schs., 1967-74. Mayor, Old Washington, Ohio, 1975-79; Democratic candidate state rep., 1960-74. Served with U.S. Army, 1945. Mem. Nat. Soc. Study of Edn., Am. Assn. Sch Adminstrs., Nat. Council Tchrs. of Math., Acad. Polit. and Social Sci., Ohio Hist. Soc., Am. Legion, Am. Def. Preparedness Assn., 37th Div. Vets. Assn., Ohio Def. Corps, Kappa Delta Pi. Clubs: Eagles, Elks, Moose, Masons, Shriners. Home: Old Washington OH 43768

SKELTON, ISAAC NEWTON, IV, Congressman; b. Lexington, Mo., Dec. 20, 1931; s. Isaac Newton and Carolyn (Boone) S.; A.B., U. Mo., 1953, LL.B., 1956; m. Susan B. Anding, July 22, 1961; children—Ike, Jim, Page. Admitted to Mo. bar, 1956; practiced in Lexington; pros. atty. Lafayette County, Mo., 1957-60; spl. asst. atty. gen. Mo., 1962-65; mem. Mo. Senate from 28th dist., 1970-76; mem. 95th-97th Congresses from 4th Mo. Dist., 1977—. Chmn., Lafayette County Tom Eagleton for Senator campaign, 1968. Active Cub Scouts. Mem. Phi Beta Kappa, Sigma Chi. Democrat. Mem. Christian Ch. Clubs: Masons, Shriners, Elks. Office: 1404 Longworth House Office Bldg Washington DC 20515

SKIDMORE, ORA LEE MAE, nurse; b. Oakland, Nebr., Mar. 23, 1927; d. Arvid W. and Rachel O. (Carlson) Fredstrom; R.N., Immanuel Med. Center, Omaha, 1948; B.S., Morningside Coll., 1972; M.A., U. S.D., 1974; children—Jayne, Diane, B. William. Staff, head nurse Onawa (Iowa) Hosp., 1948-56, nurse supr., 1957-62; staff nurse VA Hosp., Lincoln, Nebr., 1956-57; dir. nurses Elmwood Home for Aged, Onawa, 1962-65; nurse Whiting (Iowa) Community Sch., 1965-72; instr. St. Lukes Sch. Nursing, Sioux City, Iowa, 1972-75, dir. Sch. Nursing, St. Lukes Med. Center, 1978—; asst. prof. nursing edn. dept. Morningside Coll., Sioux City, 1975-78; mem. adv. com. for nursing edn. Briar Cliff Coll., Sioux City, 1978—. Mem. Am. Nurses Assn., Iowa Nurses Assn. (dir.), Nat. League for Nursing, Dirs. Diploma Schs. Nursing in Iowa, Gt. Plains Consortium of Schs. Nursing. Clubs: Treble Clef Singers, Community Women. Home: 3616 Court St Sioux City IA 51104 Office: St Lukes Sch Nursing St Lukes Med Center 2720 Stone Park Blvd Sioux City IA 51104

SKIFTON, RUSSELL DEAN, hosp. adminstr.; b. LaCrosse, Wis., Sept. 7, 1948; s. Howard Alfred and Mary Jean (Otto) S.; diploma St. Francis Sch. Radiologic Tech., LaCrosse, Wis., 1968; B.S., U. Wis., 1972; m. Margaret M. DuMond, June 27, 1970; children—Russell, Kristin, Stephanie. With St. Francis Hosp., 1968—, adminstrv. radiologic technologist, 1974—. Chmn. Crucificion Elementary Sch. Bd., LaCrescent, Minn., 1976-79; Served with USAR, 1972. Mem. Am. Soc. Radiologic Technologists, Am. Hosp. Radiology Adminstrs., Wis. Soc. Radiologic Technologists (pres. dist. 6 1970-71), Minn. Citizens Concerned for Life, Am. Legion. Roman Catholic. Club: K.C. Home: 609 S 3d St LaCrescent MN 55947 Office: 700 West Ave South LaCrosse WI 54601

SKILES, KRISTIE KAY, accountant; b. Beatrice, Nebr., Feb. 25, 1953; d. Arthur A. and Darlene Jeanette Bauers; B.S., Kearney State Coll., 1975; postgrad U. Nebr., 1981—. Acct., Rockwell Internat., Kearney, Nebr., 1975—. Fund raiser Nat. Arthritis Found., Nebr. Assn. Retarded Citizens, Diabetic Children, Good Samaritan Hosp. Mem. Women in Mgmt. Assn., Kearney C. of C., Rockwell Ladies Assn., Alpha Omicron Pi. Mem. Christian Ch. Home: 1910 W 35th St Kearney NE 68847 Office: Box 424 Kearney NE 68847

SKILLAS, CHARLES WILLIAM, cons. co. exec.; b. Youngstown, Ohio, Mar. 22, 1930; s. Charles William and Margaret Mary (Nagy) S.; B.S.M.E., U. Detroit, 1953; M.S.E., UCLA, 1956; Ph.D., Calif. Western U., 1980; m. Laura Alice James, Mar. 11, 1972; children—Kathleen, Michelle, Charles. Project engr. U.S. Naval Air Missile Test Center, Point Mugu, Calif., 1953-56; chief engr. Bendix Missiles, Mishawaka, Ind., 1956-60; dir. mktg. Sanders Assos., Nashua, N.H., 1960-68; v.p. mktg. Sparton Electronics, Jackson, Mich., 1968-80; pres. Skillas Assos., Atlanta, 1981—; cons. to Sec. of Navy, House and Senate Armed Services Com., 1978-80. Chmn., N.H./Maine Bistate Commn. on Oceanography, 1965-68. Recipient Navy Meritorious Public Service award, 1978. Mem. IEEE, AIAA, Nat. Security Indsl. Assn., Marine Tech. Soc., Am. Def. Preparedness Assn. Home: 3072 Rockaway Rd Chamblee GA 30341 Office: 5241 New Peachtree Rd Atlanta GA 30341

SKILLINGS, RALPH E., counseling psychologist; b. Troy, Ohio, Sept. 4, 1946; s. Charles Lewis and Helen Esther S.; B.S., Owosso Coll., 1968; M.A., Ball State U., 1971; Ph.D., U. Pitts., 1977; m. Karen L. Bowie, June 22, 1973. Grad. asst. secondary, adult and higher edn. Ball State U., Muncie, Ind., 1970-71; instr. psychology State U. N.Y. Agrl. Tech. at Alfred, Olean extension, 1972-73, asst. prof., 1973-74; instr. psychology Houghton (N.Y.) Coll., 1971-73; asst. prof., 1973-74; counseling intern U. Pitts. Counseling Center, 1975; staff psychologist Newaygo County Mental Health Center, White Cloud, Mich., 1977-79; asso. dir. clin. services Scioto Paint Valley Mental Health Center, Chillicothe, Ohio, 1979-80; pvt. practice as counseling psychologist, 1980—. Bd. dirs. Congregational Homes, Pitts., 1976-77; treas. Newaygo County Interagy. Council, 1977-78, pres., 1978-79; mem. citizens adv. bd. Portsmouth Psychiat. Hosp. Owens fellow, 1975-76; lic. psychologist, Mich., Ohio. Mem. Houghton Coll. Alumni Assn. (pres. Pitts. chpt. 1975-76), Am. Psychol. Assn. Republican. Home: 46 Coventry Dr Chillicothe OH 45601 Office: 88 1/2 W 2d St Chillicothe OH 45601

SKINNER, CHARLES MATHER, III, resort complex developer, operator; b. Webster Groves, Mo., Aug. 30, 1933; s. Charles Mather and Eleanor (Whiting) S.; B.S.L., U. Minn., 1956, LL.B. cum laude, 1959; m. Sara Catherine McIntire, Dec. 31, 1970; children—Charles, Ann, Mary. Asst. to dean Law Sch., U. Minn., Mpls., 1959; admitted to Minn. bar, 1959; partner law firm Anderson & Skinner, Grand Rapids, Minn., 1959-62; v.p. Skylark, Inc., Waterville, Maine, 1970-71, pres., 1971-73; pres. Squaw Mountain Resort, Greenville, Maine, 1970-73; pres. Sugarloaf Mountain Corp., Kingfield, Maine, 1973-76; founder, pres., owner Sugar Hills Lodge, Grand Rapids, Minn., 1962—, Lutsen (Minn.) Mountain Resort, 1980—; cons. engring. various ski resort developments; instr. ski area and resort seminars; lectr. in field. Chmn. 8th Dist. Young Republicans, 1960; mem. econ. policy com. Arrowhead Regional Devel. Commn., 1977-80; chmn. Itasca County Planning Commn., 1977-80. Served with USN, 1950-54. Decorated Air medal (2). Recipient Jr. C. of C. Community Service award, 1963. Mem. Midwest Ski Areas Assn. (pres. 1964-65), Minn. Bar Assn. Patentee snowmaking systems, 1971. Home: Sugar Hills Resort Grand Rapids MN 55744 Office: PO Box 369 Grand Rapids MN 55744 or PO Box 86 Lutsen MN 55612

SKINNER, CLEMENTINE ANNA MCCONICO, sch. adminstr.; b. Birmingham, Ala., Feb. 9, 1916; d. John F.A. and Alice (Burnett) McConico; B.E., Chgo. State U., 1961, M.E., 1963; Ed.D., Nova U., 1976; m. Herbert Skinner, Dec. 9, 1947; children—Herbert, Kenneth Charles. Sales clk., mgr. Woolworth Co., Chgo., 1934-43; with War Assets Adminstrn. U.S., 1946-47; with Ill. Dept. Labor, 1945-46; sch. library clk. Chgo. Bd. Edn., 1950-53, elem. tchr., librarian, 1960-69, high sch. tchr., librarian, 1969-70, spl. asst. prin. in charge curriculum, 1970—. Sec., Lake Grove Village Housing Devel., 1970—; chmn. Woodlawn Adv. Council, Dept. Human Services, 1978—; mem. Mayor Byrne's Community Devel. Adv. Com., 1980—; chmn. bd. dirs. Plano Child Devel. Center, 1975—; bd. dirs. Harris YWCA; elder, Presbyterian Ch. Served with WAC, 1943-45. Recipient Dedicated Tchr. award Chgo. Citizens Schs. Com., 1972, Ralph Metcalfe Humanitarian award Plano, 1980, and others. Mem. Chgo. Area Reading Assn. (award 1972), Assn. Supervision and Curriculum Devel., Assn. Study Afro Am. Life and History (pres. Chgo.), Nat.

Geog. Soc., Chgo. High Sch. Asst. Prins. Assn., High Sch. Librarians Assn., Kappa Delta Pi (nat pres. 1976-78), Alpha Gamma Pi (pres.), Phi Delta Kappa. Club: Westminster. Author: Motifs in African Folklore, 1962. Home: 8245 S Champlain Ave Chicago IL 60619 Office: 7529 S Constance Ave Chicago IL 60649

SKINNER, DAVID BERNT, surgeon; b. Joliet, Ill., Apr. 28, 1935; s. James Madden and Bertha Elinor (Tapper) S.; B.A. with high honors, U. Rochester (N.Y.), 1958, D.Sc. (hon.), 1980; M.D. cum laude, Yale U., 1959; m. May Elinor Tischer, Aug. 25, 1956; children—Linda Elinor, Kristin Anne, Carise Berntine, Margaret Leigh. Intern, then resident in surgery Mass. Gen. Hosp., Boston, 1959-65; sr. registrar thoracic surgery Frenchay Hosp., Bristol, Eng., 1963-64; teaching fellow Harvard U. Med. Sch., 1965; from asst. prof. surgery to prof. Johns Hopkins U. Med. Sch., also surgeon Johns Hopkins Hosp., 1968-72; Dallas B. Phemister prof. surgery, chmn. dept. U. Chgo. Hosps. and Clinics, 1972—; mem. President's Biomed. Research Panel, 1975-76; past cons. USPHS, Office Surgeon Gen. U.S. Navy. Elder, Fourth Presbyn. Ch., Chgo., 1976—. Served to maj. M.C., USAF, 1966-68. Grantee NIH, 1968—; John and Mary Markle scholar acad. medicine, 1969-74. Diplomate Am. Bd. Surgery (dir. 1974-80), Am. Bd. Thoracic Surgery. Fellow A.C.S.; mem. Am., Western, So. surg. assns., Soc. Univ. Surgeons (pres. 1978-79), Am. Soc. Artificial Internal Organs (pres. 1977), Soc. Surg. Chmn. (pres. 1980-82), Am. Assn. Thoracic Surgery, Soc. Vascular Surgery, Soc. Thoracic Surgery, Soc. Surgery Alimentary Tract, Am. Coll. Chest Physicians, Central Surg. Soc., Assn. Acad. Surgery, Halsted Soc., Soc. Clin. Surgery, Phi Beta Kappa, Alpha Omega Alpha. Clubs: Quadrangle (Chgo.); Cosmos (Washington). Co-author: Gastroesophageal Reflux and Hiatal Hernia, 1972. Editor Jour. Surg. Research, 1972—, Current Topics in Surg. Research, 1969-71. Contbr. profl. jours., chpts. in books. Home: 5490 South Shore Dr Chicago IL 60615 Office: 950 E 59th St Chicago IL 60637

SKINNER, JAMES C., mech. engr.; b. Indpls., Dec. 28, 1910; s. Oramel H. Skinner; B.M.E., Rose-Hulman Inst. Tech., 1933; m. Martha Mott, 1954; children—Nancy, Charles, Paul A., Daniel C., James S., Mary N. With Wheeling Steel Corp., Steubenville, Ohio, 1933; with Pa. R.R., Harrisburg and Phila., 1934-38; with Thomas & Skinner, Inc., Indpls., 1938-78, v.p., gen. mgr., 1946-47, pres., 1947-68, chmn. bd., 1968-78; cons., 1978—; chmn. Tesla Magnetic Holdings, Inc.; chmn. Coreco, Inc. Active Crossroads of Am. council Boy Scouts Am.; bd. mgrs. Rose-Hulman Inst. Tech., 1959—, also sec. bd.; pres. Ind. Sci. Edn. Fund, 1979—. Served with USAF, 1941-46. Recipient Community Service award Indpls. Sci. and Engring. Found., 1974. Mem. Am. Assn. Indsl. Mgmt. (v.p., dir.), ASME (chmn. exec. com.), Magnetic Material Producers Assn. (pres. 1971-72, treas.), Scientech Club of Indpls. Inc. (dir.), Indpls. Scientific & Engring. Found. Inc. (dir.). Republican. Club: Kiwanis (chpt. pres. 1974-75). Home: 1025 W 52d St Indianapolis IN 46208 Office: 1120 E 23d St Indianapolis IN 46206

SKINNER, JASPER DALE, II, prototype equipment co. exec.; b. Ainsworth, Nebr., July 11, 1947; s. Jasper Dale and Marilyn Fawn (Thompson) S.; B.A., U. Nebr., Lincoln, 1969, M.S., 1971, Ph.D., 1974; m. Ethel Marie Baysinger, Oct. 30, 1966; 1 dau., Cliti Eleta Nokomis. Extension entomology technician U. Nebr., Lincoln, 1969-70, research asso. agronomy dept., 1974-75; asst. entomologist Internat. Crops Research Inst. for Semi-arrid Tropics, Hyderabad, India, 1975-76; dir., chief designer Slatem & Tunlaw, Lincoln, 1976—. Regent's scholar, 1964-65; NDEA Title IV fellow, 1970-73. Fellow Internat. Biog. Assn.; mem. Nat. Rifle Assn., Sigma Xi, Phi Eta Sigma. Democrat. Lutheran. Office: PO Box 94993 Lincoln NE 68509

SKINNER, WILLIAM LANGDON, forging co. exec.; b. Oneida, N.Y., Nov. 19, 1937; s. Joseph Langdon and Marion Josephine (Rich) S.; student U.S. Air Force Acad.; B.S.C.E. (Sr. Honor Soc.), U. Mich., 1961; m. Julie Ann Kempf, June 28, 1962; children—Eric William, Michael Joseph, John Craigin. Sales corr. Armco Steel Corp., Indpls., 1961-62, sales engr., Chgo., 1962-63; sales engr. Ontario Corp., Muncie, Ind., 1964-67, plant mgr., 1967-70, sales mgr., 1970-73, v.p. mktg., 1973-79, mng. dir. Welsh Forging div., 1979—. Personnel dir. Child Guidance Clinic, 1966-72; troop com. Boy Scouts Am.; sr. warden, treas. Grace Episcopal Ch., 1969-76. Served with USAF, 1956. Registered profl. engr., Mich.; recipient Gold medal Canadian Gymnastic Championships, 1958; named All-American Gymnast, 1959. Mem. Am. Soc. for Metals, Forging Industry Assn. (chmn. sales promotion com.), Alliance of Metalworking Industries, Muncie-Delaware County C. of C., Am. Mktg. Assn. (dir. Ind. chpt. 1975). Republican. Episcopalian. Clubs: Delaware Country, Muncie Tennis, Ambassador, 1,000,000 Mile, Alpha Tau Omega. Exec. producer Forging the Pivotal Industry, 1976. Home: 301 Winthrop St Muncie IN 47304 Office: Salt's Lodge Monmouth Gwent UK

SKOGLUND, WESLEY JOHN, state legislator; b. Mpls., June 9, 1945; s. John Paul and Edith C. (Peterson) S.; B.A., U. Minn., 1967; married. Sr. personnel adminstr. Control Data Corp., Mpls., 1967—; commr. Hennepin County Park Res., 1974; mem. Minn. Ho. of Reps., 1974—. Minn. rep. Bicentennial Commn., 1976. Recipient Service award Mpls. YMCA, 1973, 74, Hennepin County, 1974. Mem. Am. Swedish Inst., Am. Legion. Democratic-Farm-Labor Party. Home: 4915 31st Ave S Minneapolis MN 55417 Office: State Capitol St Paul MN 55155

SKOOG, DONALD PAUL, physician; b. Sioux City, Iowa, Sept. 29, 1931; s. Paul R. and Mary Ann (Francisco) S.; B.A. magna cum laude, Midland Coll., 1953; M.D. cum laude, U. Nebr., 1958; m. Mary Ann Bunn, 1955; children—Robert Eugene, David Alan (dec.), Kristin Marie. Intern, Bishop Clarkson Meml. Hosp., Omaha, 1958-59, resident in pathology, 1959-62; resident in pathology Parkland Meml. Hosp., Dallas, 1962-63; fellow in pathology U. Tex. Southwestern Med. Sch., 1962-63; practice medicine specializing in pathology, Omaha, 1963—; pathologist Bishop Clarkson Meml. Hosp., 1963—, chmn. radioisotope and radiation safety, 1976-78, chmn. dept. pathology, 1978-80, chmn. med. edn. com., 1980—; prof. pathology U. Nebr. Coll. Medicine, 1977—, mem. dean's faculty adv. council, 1977-79, grad. and continuing edn. com., 1980—; mem. regional med. adv. com. Omaha Red Cross Blood Program, 1968—. Ch. councilman Luther Meml. Lutheran Ch., 1966-72; trustee Midland Luth. Coll., Fremont, Nebr., 1968—, chmn., 1973-75. Recipient Alumni Achievement award Midland Luth. Coll., 1972; diplomate Am. Bd. Pathology. Fellow Am. Soc. Clin. Pathologists (mem. adv. council 1972-78, mem. hematology profl. self-assessment examination com. 1972—; mem. council hematology 1975-81, chmn. 1978-81), Coll. Am. Pathologists (hematology resource com. 1981—); mem. Nebr. Assn. Pathologists, Nebr. Med. Assn., Met. Omaha Med. Soc., AMA, Am. Assn. Blood Banks, Omaha Midwest Clin. Soc., Midland Luth. Coll. Alumni Assn. (pres. 1969-70), Alpha Omega Alpha (chpt. pres. 1976-77), Omaha C. of C. Contbr. articles on clin. pathology and hematology to profl. jours.; editorial bd. Laboratory Medicine, 1979—. Office: Bishop Clarkson Meml Hosp Box 3328 Omaha NE 68103

SKORNICKA, JOEL L., city ofcl.; b. Green Bay, Wis., Jan. 29, 1937; s. Lester A. and Jean U. (Hanson) S.; B.S. in Polit. Sci., U. Wis., 1959, M.S., 1964; m. Carol Nechrony, Feb. 2, 1962; children—Christopher, Jennifer. Asst. bus. mgr., program advisor Wis. Union, U. Wis., Madison, 1960-63, asst. dir. Office of Student Orgn. Advisors, 1963-65, asso. dir., 1965-68, asst. dir. Adminstrn.-Acad. Computing Center, 1968-70, asst. to vice chancellor, 1970-72, asst. vice chancellor, 1972-77, asst. chancellor, 1977-79; mayor City of Madison, 1979—; mem. transp. com. U.S. Conf. Mayors. Bd. dirs. Madison Civic Music Assn., pres., 1974-77; bd. dirs. Greater Madison Found. for Arts, Wis. Arts Bd.; mem. correction industries adv. bd. Central Madison Council; mem. Dane County Public Affairs Council; mem. adv. com. Dane County Regional Airport Commn. Served to 2d lt. U.S. Army, 1959-60. Mem. State Hist. Soc. Wis., Madison Art Assn. Office: 210 Monona Ave Madison WI 53709

SKOV, LEONARD CLIFTON, coll. adminstr.; b. Riverdale, Nebr., Feb. 10, 1935; s. Jens Christian and Edith Louetta (Johnson) S.; B.A., Kearney State Coll., 1956, M.A., 1960; Ed.D., U. Nebr., 1967; m. Dolores June McConnel, June 6, 1954; children—Steven, Randall, Jeffrey, Michael. Tchr., prin. Red Cloud (Nebr.) Public Schs., 1956-59; supt. schs. Wilcox (Nebr.) Public Schs., 1959-62; dir. tchr. edn. Nebr. State Dept. Edn., Lincoln, 1962-68; dean Sch. Edn., Kearney (Nebr.) State Coll., 1968—. Chmn. Kearney Municipal Airport Adv. Bd., 1979, mem. 1979—. Recipient Nebr. DAV Appreciation award, 1976. Mem. NEA, Nebr. State Edn. Assn., Council Ednl. Facility Planners, Am. Assn. Sch. Adminstrs., Nebr. Council Sch. Adminstrs., Phi Delta Kappa. Republican. Baptist. Home: 1602 W 36th St Kearney NE 68847 Office: Kearney NE 68847

SKOWRONSKI, GEORGE VICTOR, mfg. co. exec.; b. Poznan, Poland, Sept. 29, 1928; came to U.S., 1949, naturalized, 1954; s. Marian Wladyslaw and Elzbieta (Rosenbaum) S.; B.S., U. Wis., 1956, M.B.A., 1973; m. Nancy Blanche Andrews, June 16, 1956; children—Victoria Elizabeth, Constance Ann Maria, Deborah Nan Christina, Timothy George. Conservation aide State of Wis. Conservation Dept., Madison, 1957; detail man US Vitamin Co., N.Y.C., 1958; with Am. Can. Co., Neenah, Wis., 1958—, research asso., 1975—. Liaison officer U.S. Mil. Acad., Neenah, 1973—. Served with U.S. Army from 1955. Mem. TAPPI, Am. Mgmt. Assns. Republican. Episcopalian. Home: 113 Sugar Tree Ln Neenah WI 54956 Office: American Can Co 1915 Marathon Ave Neenah WI 54956

SKOZEK, STANLEY, office supply co. exec.; b. Chgo., Dec. 25, 1918; s. John and Anna (Mroz) S.; student, Northwestern U., 1951-54, De Paul U., 1954; m. Irene Gulczynski, Oct. 12, 1946. With Lindberg Corp., Chgo., 1946-74, asst. sec., 1960-74; owner, mgr. Grove Office Supply, Chgo., 1974—; dir. Century Savs. & Loan Assn., Chgo. Bd. dirs. Chgo. Midwest Credit Mgmt. Assn., 1967-68. Served with U.S. Army, 1942-46. Decorated Purple Heart, Bronze Star. Mem. Nat. Office Products Assn., Brighton Park C. of C. Office: Grove Office Supply 3801 S Kedzie Ave Chicago IL 60632

SKRAMSTAD, HAROLD KENNETH, JR., inst. exec.; b. Takoma Park, Md., June 3, 1941; s. Harold Kenneth and Sarah Catherine (Shroat) S.; A.B., George Washington U., 1963, Ph.D., 1971; m. Susan Edith Chappelear, Dec. 28, 1963; children—Robert Christopher, Elizabeth Ann. Instr., Am. lit. and Am. civilization George Washington U., 1966-67; project dir. in community devel. Peace Corps, 1966-67; research fellow in material culture Smithsonian Instn., Washington, 1967-68, acting dir. office Am. studies, 1968-69, asst. dir. office Am. studies, 1969-71, spl. asst. to dir. Nat. Mus. History and Tech., 1971, chief spl. projects, 1971-72, chief exhibit programs, 1972-74; dir. Chgo. Hist. Soc., 1974-81; pres. Edison Inst., Dearborn, Mich., 1981—; cons., lectr., condr. seminars in field; served on various NEA and Nat. Endowment for Humanities rev. panels; founding v.p. Don't Tear It Down, Inc.; mem. Joint Com. on Landmarks of Nat. Capital, 1972—, vice chmn., 1978—; mem. Chgo. Commn. on Hist. and Archtl. Landmarks, 1975-80; mem. Ill. Hist. Sites Adv. Council, 1975-78; mem. Ill. Hist. Records Adv. Bd., 1976-78; mem. Am. Issues Forum, Chgo. Com., 1975-76. Trustee Chgo. Chamber Orch. Assn., 1974-77, Chgo. Sch. Architecture Found., 1975-77, Kendall Coll., 1976-80. Mem. Am. Assn. Museums (council 1976—), Am. Assn. State and Local History, Am. Hist. Assn. Clubs: Arts, Tavern, Econ. of Chgo., Caxton. Contbr. articles, revs. to profl. jours. Office: The Edison Inst Dearborn MI 48121

SKRIBA, STEPHEN JOSEPH, III, savs. and loan exec.; b. Chgo., Aug. 7, 1947; s. Stephen J. and Evelyn S.; B.A., U. Ill., 1969; M.A., Roosevelt U., 1976; m. Andrea Lynn LeCompte, Feb. 14, 1970; children—Brian J., Bryce J. With Clyde Fed. Savs. & Loan Assn., North Riverside, Ill., 1972—, personnel mgr., 1974-75, asst. v.p., 1975-78, v.p., personnel mgr., 1979—. Served with AUS, 1969-70; Vietnam. Mem. Am. Soc. Personnel Adminstrn., Inst. Fin. Edn. (pres., dir.). Republican. Roman Catholic. Office: 7222 W Cermak Rd North Riverside IL 60546

SKROWACZEWSKI, STANISLAW, condr., composer; b. Lwow, Poland, Oct. 3, 1923; s. Pawel and Zofia (Karszniewicz) S.; diploma faculty philosophy U. Lwow, 1945; diploma faculties composition and conducting Acad. Music Lwow, 1945, Conservatory at Krakow (Poland), 1946; L.H.D., Hamline U., 1963, Macalaster Coll., 1973; Dr.h.c., U. Minn., 1979; m. Krystyna Jarosz, Sept. 6, 1956. Came to U.S., 1960. Composer, 1931—; first symphony and overture for orch. written at age 8, played by Lwow Philharmonic Orch., 1931; pianist, 1928—, violinist, 1934—, conductor, 1939—; permanent conductor and music dir. Wroclaw (Poland) Philharmonic, 1946-47, Katowice (Poland) Nat. Philharmonic, 1949-54, Krakow Philharmonic, 1955-56, Warsaw Nat. Philharmonic Orch., 1957-59, Minn. Orch., 1960-79; guest conductor, Europe, S. Am., U.S., Japan, Israel, Australia, Can., 1947—. Recipient nat. prize for artistic activity, Poland, 1953; first prize Santa Cecilia Internat. Concours for Conductors, Rome, 1956; Ricercari Notturni award Kennedy Center, 1977; Condr's. award Columbia U., 1973; Mahler-Bruckner gold medal of honor, 1969; 4 awards for programming Minn. Orch., ASCAP, 1961-79. Mem. Union Polish Composers, Internat. Soc. Modern Music, Nat. Assn. Am. Composers-Conductors, Am. Music Center, Nat. Soc. Lit. and Arts. Composer: 4 symphonies; Prelude and Fugue for Orchestra (conducted 1st performance Paris), 1948; Overture 1947 (2d prize Symanowski Concours, Warsaw 1947), 1947; Cantiques des Cantiques, 1951; String Quartet (2d prize Internat. Concours Composers, Belgium 1953), 1953; Suite Symphonique (first prize gold medal Composers Competition Moscow, 1957), 1954; Music at Night, 1954; English Horn Concerto, 1969; also music for theatre, motion pictures, songs and piano sonatas. Address: PO Box 700 Wayzata MN 55391

SKRZYPEK, MICHAEL ALLEN, service engr.; b. Chgo., June 3, 1948; s. Albert and Julia (Biela) S.; B.A., Northeastern U., 1974; m. Judith Anne Rosen, Aug. 18, 1974. Field service engr. Datagraphix, San Diego, 1971-72; prodn. mgr. Container Corp. Am., Chgo., 1974-75; sr. field service engr. Datapoint, Chgo., 1975-77; regional field service mgr. Dymo Retail Systems, Boston and Westchester, Ill., 1977-78; product support mgr. Memorex Corp., Lombard, Ill., 1978-81; mktg. and adminstrv. mgr. MCI Communications Corp., Chgo., 1982—. Served with USNR, 1967-71. Home: 1424 Richards Ave Downers Grove IL 60516 Office: MCI Communications Corp John Hancock Bldg Chicago IL 60601

SKUBIC, PAUL RICHARD, accountant; b. Chgo., July 19, 1948; s. Robert Lee and Albina Ursula (Raczek) S.; B.B.A. (Athletic scholar 1966-68), U. N.Mex., 1970; M.B.A., Northwestern U., 1971; m. Pamela Lynn Smith, Oct. 28, 1967; children—Sandra Lynn, Robert Paul. Mgr., Arthur Andersen & Co., C.P.A.'s, Chgo., 1971—. C.P.A., Ill. Mem. Am. Inst. C.P.A.'s, Ill. Soc. C.P.A.'s. Roman Catholic. Clubs: Anderson Sch. Alumni, Oak Lawn Racquet, Wimbledon Tennis. First place in pentathlon Midwest AAU Masters Tournament, 1979, 80. Home: 15625 Linden Dr Oak Forest IL 60452 Office: 33 W Monroe St Chicago IL 60602

SKUBIZ, JOHN JOSEPH, former lumber co. exec.; b. St. Louis, Dec. 4, 1913; s. John and Mary (Premrn) S.; B.B.A., Washington U., St. Louis, 1939; m. Grace Ethel Treece, Nov. 20, 1940; children—Carol Ann Savidge, John Joseph, Jr. Pub. accountant Price, Waterhouse & Co., St. Louis, 1939-44; with Monarch Hardwood Lumber Co., Chgo., 1945-76, acct., 1945-46, treas., 1946-76, pres., 1965-69, bd. chmn., 1969-76; ret., 1976. Active various community drives; pres. Glenbrook High Sch. Caucus, 1956. Served with USNR, 1944-45. C.P.A., Mo. Mem. Nat. Hardwood Lumber Assn. (bd. mgrs. 1963-69, v.p. 1970-76, hon. dir. 1976—), Lumber Trade Assn. (pres. 1973, v.p. 1971-72), Washington U. Alumni Assn. Chgo. (pres. 1950). Clubs: North Shore Country; Oro Valley Country (Tucson). Home: 1451 Estate Ln Glenview IL 60025

SKULINA, THOMAS RAYMOND, lawyer; b. Cleve., Sept. 14, 1933; s. John J. and Mary B. (Vesely) S.; A.B., John Carroll U., 1955; J.D., Case Western Res. U., 1959, LL.M., 1962. Admitted to Ohio bar, 1959, U.S. Supreme Ct. bar, 1964, ICC bar, 1965; mem. firm Skulina & Stringer, Cleve., 1967-72, Riemer Oberdank and Skulina, 1978-81, Skulina, Fillo, Walters & Negrelli, 1981—; atty. Penn Central Transp. Co., Cleve., 1960-65, asst. gen. atty., 1965-78, trial counsel, 1965-76; with Consol. Rail Corp., 1976-78; dir. High Temperature Systems, Inc., Active Chem. Systems, Inc.; tchr. comml. law Practicing Law Inst., N.Y.C., 1970. Income tax and fed. fund coordinator Warrensville Heights, Ohio, 1970-77; spl. counsel City of N. Olmstead (Ohio), 1971-75; pres. Civil Service Commn., Cleve., 1977—. Served with U.S. Army, 1959. Mem. Nat. Assn. R.R. Trial Counsel, Internat. Assn. Law and Sci., Am. bar assn., Cleve. bar assn., Cuyahoga bar assn., Ohio bar assn., Fed. Bar Assn. Democrat. Roman Catholic. Club: River Run Racquet. Contbr. articles to legal jours. Home: 5870 Cable Ave Cleveland OH 44127 Office: 1520 Standard Bldg Cleveland OH 44113

SKUTT, VESTOR JOSEPH, ins. exec.; b. Deadwood, S.D., Feb. 24; s. Roy N. and Catherine (Gorman) S.; ed. public and pvt. schs., S.D.; LL.B., Creighton U., 1923, LL.D. (hon.), 1971; hon. degree U. Nebr., Omaha, U. Nebr. Coll. Medicine, U. S.D.; m. Angela Anderson; children—Donald Joseph, Thomas James, Sally Jane (Mrs. John G. Desmond, Jr.). Joined legal dept. Mut. of Omaha Ins. Co., advanced to chmn. bd., chief exec. officer; chmn. bd., chief exec. officer United of Omaha, Companion Life of N.Y.; chmn. bd. Mut. of Omaha Fund Mgmt. Co.; dir. Omaha Nat. Bank, 1954-71, adv. council, 1971—; dir. Fairmont Foods Co., 1958-73, H.F. Ahmanson & Co., 1972-73. Mem. Pres.'s Com. on Employment of Handicapped; bd. dirs. World Rehab. Fund, Inc.; mem. Nat. Bus. Council Consumer Affairs; founding pres. Nebr. Wildlife Fedn., 1970-72, chmn. bd., 1972-74; nat. brotherhood chmn. NCCJ, 1966, Cath. co-chmn., 1978—, vice chmn. nat. bd. trustees; nat. crusade chmn. Am. Cancer Soc., 1967; chmn. Jr. Achievement Omaha, 1974; nat. chmn. Explorer Scouts Bicentennial Exhbn., 1975-76; Nebr. chmn. United Negro Coll. Fund, 1975; dir., mem. exec. com., chmn. Region VII, Nat. Alliance Businessmen, nat. chmn., 1976-77; mem. Nat. 4-H Adv. Council; bd. regents Mcpl. U. Omaha, 1944-50; bd. dirs. Health Ins. Inst., 1972-75, Nat. Arthritis Found., 1972-74; mem.-at-large nat. council Boy Scouts Am.; chmn. communications com. North Central region Boy Scouts Am.; past trustee-at-large Nebr. Ind. Coll. Found.; bd. govs. Boys' Clubs Omaha; trustee Nat. Little League Found., 1976—; hon. chmn. Boys Republic ann. Della Robia wreath program, 1978. Recipient Harold R. Gordon Meml. award, 1950; Air Force Exceptional Service medal, 1963; Golden Sword of Hope, Am. Cancer Soc., 1966; Can Do award Omaha C. of C., 1968; named Internat. Boss of Year, Nat. Secs. Assn., 1964, Nebraskan of Year, Nebr. Broadcasters Assn., 1964, Scouting Man of Year, 1971, Man of Year, Fedn. Ins. Counsel, 1971; Nat. Salesman of Yr. award Nat. Sales and Mktg. Execs., 1972; Nat. Disting. Service award United Negro Coll. Fund, 1975; Golden Plate award Am. Acad. Achievement, 1976; Silver Beaver award Mid-Am. council Boy Scouts Am., 1976. Mem. Am. Life Conv. (chmn. legal sect. 1947), Nebr., Tex., Okla. bar. assns., Internat. Assn. Health Underwriters, Ins. Fedn. Nebr. (exec. council), Ins. Econs. Soc. Am., Health Ins. Assn. Am. (charter dir., pres. 1959), Fedn. Ins. Counsel, Creighton U. Alumni (nat. pres. 1935), Newcomen Soc. N.Am., Delta Theta Phi, Ak Sar-Ben (Omaha) (bd. govs.). Clubs: Omaha Country, Omaha; Marco Polo. Home: 400 N 62d St Omaha NE 68132 Office: Mut of Omaha Plaza Omaha NE 68175

SKWERES, THOMAS WALTER, sales and marketing exec.; b. Chgo., May 11, 1929; s. Marion John and Sophie (Rataiczyk) S.; student Wright City Coll., 1947-49, Northwestern, 1949-55; m. Charmaine Liska, Oct. 28, 1950; children—Thomas Allan, Pamela Charmaine, Patricie Ann. Prodn. mgr. Reincke Meyer & Finn, 1953-55; v.p. account exec. Hanson & Stevens, 1955-62; v.p. sales Ross & White Co., 1962—. Marketing and advt. cons., pub. relations writer, 1962—. Served with U.S. Army, 1951-53. Mem. Eta Iota Psi. Home: 5613 Snowdrop Lisle IL 60532 Office: 50 W Dundee Wheeling IL 60090

SLAATEN, DORIS ADELE, educator; b. Charlson, N.D., Oct. 5, 1920; d. Alfred O. and Maude L. (Dukette) S.; B.S., Minot State Coll., 1949; M.A., Northwestern U., 1957; Ph.D., Colo. State U., 1975. Tchr. public schs., N.D., Mont., 1942-57; faculty Minot (N.D.) State Coll., Div. Bus., 1957—, prof. bus., 1976—. N.D. rep. to bd. dirs. Mountain Plains Bus. Edn. Assn., 1977—; mem. Minot State Coll. Devel. Bd., 1977—, bd. regents, 1977—; bd. dirs. Minot Chamber Chorale, 1979-82. Recipient Sigma Sigma Sigma Outstanding Alumni Recognition award, 1970; Alumni Golden award Minot State Coll., 1979; Nat. Bus. Edn. Meritorious Service award, 1979; 25-Yr. Profl. award Minot C. of C., 1979. Mem. N.D. Office Edn. Assn. (pres. 1969-70), Nat. Bus. Edn. Assn., N.D. Bus. Edn. Assn., NEA, Profl. Secs. Internat., Am. Vocat. Assn., Bus. and Profl. Women (Woman of Yr. 1979), Phi Beta Lambda, Pi Omega Pi, Pi Lambda Theta, Delta Pi Epsilon, Delta Kappa Gamma. Lutheran. Club: M1000. Author: Office Education for Tomorrow's World, 1972; manual for N.D. office edn. coordinators, 1980. Address: 1000 20th Ave NW Apt B4 Minot ND 58701

SLADE, ROY, art mus. adminstr., artist; b. Cardiff, Wales, Apr. 14, 1933; came to U.S., 1967, naturalized, 1975; s. Trevor and Millicent (Roberts) S.; art tchrs. diploma U. Wales, 1954; nat. diploma of design Cardiff Coll. Art, 1954; m. Susan Shifley, June 6, 1974. Head arts and crafts dept. Heolgam Sch., Wales, 1956-60; lectr. art Claredon Coll., Nottingham, Eng., 1960-64; lectr. painting Leeds Coll. Art, Eng., 1964-65, dir. post-diploma studies, 1965-67; prof. painting Corcoran Sch. Art, Washington, 1967-68, asso. dean, 1969-70, dean, 1970-77, dir. Corcoran Gallery Art, 1972-77; pres. Cranbrook Acad. Art, Bloomfield Hills, Mich., 1977—; one-man shows include: U. Birmingham (Eng.), 1969, Jefferson Pl. Gallery, Washington, 1970,

72, Madison Coll., 1971, Hood Coll., Frederick, Md., 1972, Pyramid Gallery, Washington, 1976-77, Robert Kidd Gallery, Birmingham, Mich., 1981; group exhbns. include: Corcoran Gallery Art, 1971, SUNY, Albany, 1971, Art in Washington, Phillips Collection, Washington, 1972, Gallerie Allen, Vancouver, Can., 1974, Marion Locks Gallery, Phila., 1975; represented inpermanent collections: Corcoran Gallery Art, Cranbrook Acad. Art, Arts Council Gt. Brit., Nuffield Found., Brit. Overseas Airways Corp., U. Birmingham, Westinghouse Corp., Brit. Embassy, Washington, numerous pvt. collections; mem. architecture and environ. arts panel Nat. Endowment Arts, 1977, mem. mus. panel and visual arts panel, 1974; chmn. design Mich. Advt. Council, 1978—; arts cons. St. Francis Hosp., Tulsa, 1978, City of Southfield, (Mich.), 1980, 1st Fed. Savs. and Loan Assn., Detroit, 1980. Bd. dirs. Artists for Environ. Found., 1974; mem. D.C. Commn. on Arts, 1972-74; visitor Boston Mus. Sch. Fine Arts, 1971-74; mem. numerous accreditation teams N. Central Assn., Nat. Assn. Schs. Art. Served with Brit. Army, 1954-56. Fulbright-Hayes scholar, 1967-68; recipient award Welsh Soc. Phila., 1974. Mem. Nat. Council Art Adminstrs. (Sec.-treas. 1980, chmn. 1981, dir.), Nat. Assn. Schs. Art (commr. on accreditation 1978—), Nat. Soc. Lit. and the Arts, Nat. Soc. Arts and Letters (adv. council 1973), Am. Art Mus. Conf., Assn. Art Mus. Dirs. Organizer, numerous exbhns., author exbhn. catalogues. Office: 500 Lone Pine Rd PO Box 801 Bloomfield Hills MI 48013

SLADOJE, GEORGE, commodity future exchange exec.; b. Duncanwood, Ohio, Apr. 19, 1942; s. Marko and Jovanka S.; B.S., Ohio State U., 1965; M.B.A., Northwestern U., 1973; m. Susan Jane Mueller, July 20, 1968; children—Steven Thomas, Julie Anne, Kathryn Jane. Cost acctg. mgr. Am. Hosp. Supply Corp., Evanston, Ill., 1967-69; audit supr., cons. Peat, Marwick, Mitchell & Co., Chgo., 1969-76; div. controller, audit supr. McGraw-Edison Co., Elgin, Ill., 1976-78; exec. v.p., treas. Chgo. Bd. Trade, 1978—. Mem. Sch. Dist. 34 Caucus, 1977—, Citizens Action Com. Dist. 34, 1976—; bd. dirs. Better Bus. Bur. Met. Chgo., 1981—; active local Cub Scouts, Indian Guides. Served with AUS, 1965-67; Vietnam. C.P.A., Ill. Mem. Am. Inst. C.P.A.'s, Fin. Execs. Inst. (dir. Chgo. chpt.), Inst. Internal Auditors, Ill. Soc. C.P.A.'s. Office: Chgo Bd Trade LaSalle and Jackson Sts Chicago IL 60604

SLAGER, RONALD DALE, wholesale-retail co. exec.; b. Kalamazoo, Mich., Oct. 16, 1952; s. Robert Peter and Ruth M. Slager; student Western Mich. U., 1970, Mich. State U., 1971; m. Janeen K. Walters, May 4, 1974. Sales rep. Investors Diversified Services, Mpls., 1971-73; sales rep., sales mgr. Dykema Office Supply, Kalamazoo, 1973-77; owner, mgr. Stage Lighting Distbrs., Kalamazoo, 1974-75; co-founder The Hearing Aid Center of Kalamazoo, 1976-78; v.p., dir. Hearing Aid Centers of Am., Inc., Kalamazoo, 1978—; treas., MLR Inc., Kalamazoo, 1980—; mem. Mich. State Bd. Hearing Aid Licensing, 1981—. Bd. dirs. Kalamazoo Youth for Christ, 1973, Youth Opportunities Unltd. Kalamazoo, Inc., 1980—; advisor Jr. Achievement, Kalamazoo, 1978-79. Mem. Ad Club Kalamazoo, Sales and Mktg. Execs., Kalamazoo C. of C., Ind. Businessmen Assn., A.G. Bell Assn. for Deaf. Reformed Ch. Club: Sertoma (pres. 1976-77, chmn. 1977-78, dist. gov. N.W. Ohio-Mich. dist. 1978-79). Home: 6481 East S Ave Scotts MI 49088 Office: 3130 Portage Rd Kalamazoo MI 49003

SLANKARD, J(AMES) EDWARD, obstetrician and gynecologist; b. Pittsburg, Kans., Oct. 11, 1928; s. James Alfred and Hazel Rachel (Nimmo) S.; B.A., U. Kans., 1953, M.D., 1958; m. Camille Cheryl Marsh, Mar. 8, 1975; children by previous marriage—James Andrew, Myra Kay, Carrie Elizabeth. Rotating intern Bethany Hosp., 1958-59; gen. practice medicine, Kansas City, Kans., 1959-60; fellow in gen. surgery Alton Ochsner Med. Found., New Orleans, 1960-61, in obstetrics and gynecology, 1961-64; Am. Cancer Soc. fellow M.D. Anderson Hosp. and Tumor Inst., Houston, 1968; practice medicine specializing in obstetrics and gynecology, Kansas City, Mo., 1964—; staff St. Luke's Hosp., Suburban Med. Center; courtesy staff Research Hosp.; cons. Kansas City Gen. Hosp., U. Mo. (Kansas City). Med. dir. Planned Parenthood of Western Mo., 1965-69; bd. dirs. Jackson County unit Am. Cancer Soc., 1969-80. Served with AUS, 1946-49. Diplomate Am. Bd. Obstetrics and Gynecology. Fellow ACS; mem. Am. Coll. Obstetrics and Gynecology, Kansas City, Continental gynecol. socs., AMA, Mo., So. med. assns., Jackson County Med. Soc., Kansas City S.W. Clin. Soc., Central Assn. Obstetrics and Gynecology, Royal Soc. Medicine, Pan Pacific Surg. Assn. Episcopalian. Clubs: Masons, Saddle and Sirloin, Carriage. Office: Plaza Medical Bldg 4320 Wornall Rd Kansas City MO 64111

SLASH, JOSEPH ALEXANDER, city ofcl.; b. Huntington, W.Va., Aug. 25, 1943; s. Joseph A. and Clare P. (Rose) S.; B.B.A. in Acctg., Marshall U., 1966; m. Meredith Dawson, Jan. 21, 1967. Staff acct. to audit mgr. Arthur Young & Co., Indpls., 1968-78; dep. mayor City of Indpls., 1978—; condr. audit seminars for staff accts. Bd. dirs. Indpls. Bus. Devel. Found.; trustee YWCA. Served to lt. U.S. Army, 1966-68. Decorated Army Commendation medal; C.P.A., Ind. Mem. Am. Inst. C.P.A.'s, Ind. Soc. C.P.A.'s, Nat. Assn. Black Accts., Indpls. Urban League (dir.), Kappa Alpha Psi. Republican. Baptist. Office: 2501 City County Bldg Indianapolis IN 46204

SLASIENSKI, BRUCE EDWARD, air force officer; b. Westfield, Mass., Oct. 30, 1947; s. Edward Domonick and Frances Ann (Brezezinski) S.; B.S., Northrop Inst. Tech., Los Angeles, 1970; M.S. in Safety, U. So. Calif., 1979; m. Marsha Gail Naten, Feb. 14, 1970; children—Lori Ann, Scott Edward. Commd. 2d lt. USAF, 1970, advanced through grades to capt., 1974; service in Vietnam; flying safety officer Ellsworth AFB, S.D., 1979—. Decorated Air Force Commendation medal. Mem. Soc. Safety Engrs., Assn. Old Crows. Lutheran. Home: 615 Fairlawn Dr Rapid City SD 57701 Office: 28 BMW SE Ellsworth AFB SD 57706

SLATER, RAYMOND E.O., mfg. co. exec., cons. engr.; b. Springfield, Mo., June 27, 1913; s. Edgar Otis and Rosa S. (Mosser) S.; B.S., Iowa State Coll., 1936; postgrad. LaSalle Extension U., 1937-41; degree in Indsl. Engring., Iowa State U., 1942; m. Eleanor Johnson, Jan. 30, 1937; children—Janet Rae Slater Darwin, Marian Joan Slater Swaine. Asst. prodn. mgr. Chgo. Vitreous Enamel Co., 1936-37; asst. mgr. spl. services div. Ernst & Ernst, Chgo., 1938-42, mgr. mgmt. services, 1943-50; pres. Asso. Bus. Services, Inc., St. Louis, 1946-50; owner Slater Engring. Assos., St. Louis, 1950—; comptroller Hawthorn Co., New Haven and Glasgow, Mo. and St. George, Utah, 1960-64, v.p., comptroller, 1964-73; comptroller H. Wenzel Tent & Duck Co., St. Louis, 1959-72; controller New Haven (Mo.) Mfg. Co., 1960-73, also dir.; pres., dir. REOS, Inc., 1969—; controller Am. Waterproofing Co., New Haven, 1959-73, Judson Group, 1970-73; dir. bus. devel. recreation groups Kellwood Co., New Haven, 1973-75; sec. First Mo. Devel. Fin. Corp., 1969-70, pres., 1971—, also dir.; chmn. bd., chief exec. officer Zero Mfg. Co., Washington, Mo., 1974-77. C.P.A., Ill., Mo.; registered profl. engr., Ill., Iowa, Mo. Mem. Fin. Execs. Inst., Ill. Soc. Profl. Engrs., ASME, Am. Inst. C.P.A.'s, Am. Mgmt. Assn., Adminstrn. Mgmt. Soc. (chpt. sec. 1947-50), Nat. Assn. Accountants, Ill. Soc. C.P.A.'s, Nat. Assn. Registered Profl. Engrs., Mo. Soc. Registered Profl. Engrs. Home: 18 York Dr Saint Louis MO 63144

SLATER, TOM LEON, state senator, public relations counsel; b. Templeton, Iowa, Nov. 5, 1945; s. Donald T. and Geraldin (Trecker) S.; B.A., Washburn U., 1967; postgrad. Iowa State U., 1975-76; 1 dau., Angela. Partner public relations firm, Council Bluffs, Iowa, 1974—; recreation supr. City of Omaha, 1967-68; dir. recreation City of York (Nebr.), 1968-69; dir. parks, recreation and public property City of Council Bluffs, 1969-74; mem. Iowa State Senate, 1977—; instr. Coll. St. Mary, Omaha, 1976-77; mem. Regional Transp. Council, Pottawattomie County Women's Polit. Caucus. Mem. Common Cause, Iowa Civil Liberties Union. Roman Catholic. Office: State Senate State Capitol Des Moines IA 50319*

SLATKIN, LEONARD, conductor; b. Sept. 1; s. Felix Slatkin and Eleanor Aller; began violin study, 1947, piano study with Victor Aller and Selma Cramer, 1955, composition study with Castelnuovo-Tedesco, 1958, viola study with Sol Schoenbach, 1959; conducting study with Felix Slatkin, Amerigo Marino and Ingolf Dahl; attended Ind. U., 1962, Los Angeles City Coll., 1963, Juilliard Sch. (Irving Berlin fellow in musical direction), beginning 1964; student of Jean Morel and Walter Susskind. Conducting debut as asst. condr. Youth Symphony of N.Y., Carnegie Hall, 1966; asst. condr. Juilliard Opera Theater and Dance Dept., 1967; asst. condr. St. Louis Symphony Orch., 1968-71, asso. condr., 1971-74, prin. condr., 1979—; founder, music dir. and comdr. St. Louis Symphony Youth Orch., beginning 1969; debut with Chgo. Symphony Orch., 1974, N.Y. Philharmonic, 1974, Phila. Orch., 1974; European debut with Royal Philharmonic Orch., 1974; debut with USSR orchs., 1976-77; prin. guest condr. Minn. Orch., beginning 1974, summer artistic dir., 1979-80; music dir. New Orleans Philharmonic Symphony Orch., 1977-78, musical adv., 1979-80; guest condr. orchs. throughout world; former vis. asst. prof. music Washington U., St. Louis; initiated Friday afternoon lecture series; hosted weekly radio program. Office: care Mariedi Anders Artist Mgmt 535 El Camino Del Mar San Francisco CA 94121 also St Louis Symphony Orch Powell Symphony Hall 718 N Grand Blvd Saint Louis MO 63103*

SLAUGHTER, ROBERT LESLIE, advt. exec.; b. Cleve., Feb. 19, 1933; s. Edwin M. and Florence L. (Black) S.; ed. Wayne State U., 1951-53, 57-58, U. Mich., 1971; m. Jean E. Little, June 1, 1968; children—Robert Leslie, Susan, Laurie, James. Asso. dir., then dir. Mich. Republican Com. and affiliates, 1960-64; account exec. N.W. Ayer & Son, Detroit and San Francisco, 1965—; pres. Slaughter & Assos., Inc., Dearborn, Mich., 1966—. Mem. Dearborn (Mich.) City Beautiful Commn.; citizens adv. com., past pres. Players Guild of Dearborn; presdl. elector, 1976, 80; bd. dirs. Dearborn Police Res. Served with USAF, 1953-57. Mem. Am. Arbitration Assn., Bus. and Profl. Advt. Assn., Mich. Advt. Agy. Council (chmn. 16th dist. Mich.). Republican. Methodist. Home: 441 S Melborn St Dearborn MI 48124

SLAVEN, W(ILLIAM) CHARLES, mgmt. cons.; b. Oneida, Tenn., Aug. 17, 1950; s. Charles Linden and Phyllis Doren (Foster) S.; B.S., Miami U., Oxford, Ohio, 1972, M.B.A., 1974; m. Diana Jean Herth, Sept. 2, 1972; children—Brian Charles, Kevin William. Fin. aid counselor Miami U., 1973-74; staff auditor Arthur Young & Co., Cin., 1974-75, computer auditor, 1975-78, computer audit mgr., mgmt. cons., 1978-79; dir. planning and corp. devel. Pizza Hut of Ohio, 1979-81; vis. lectr. Ohio U., Athens, 1980-81; sr. mgmt. cons. Main Hurdman, Cin., 1981—. C.P.A., Ohio. Mem. Am. Inst. C.P.A.'s, Ohio Soc. C.P.A.'s, Nat. Accts. Assn., Am. Acctg. Assn., Soc. Advancement of Mgmt. (past dir.), Data Processing Mgmt. Assn., Am. Mgmt. Assn. Mem. Disciples of Christ Ch. Home: 125 Joyce Ave Harrison OH 45030 Office: First Nat Bank Center Cincinnati OH 45202

SLAVIN, WILLIAM STEPHEN, psychologist; b. Howell, Mich., Oct. 12, 1949; s. William Joseph and Frances Imogene (Haire) S.; B.S. cum laude, Mich. State U., 1971; M.A., Western Mich. U., 1976; m. Marianne Edwards, Oct. 14, 1977; children—Bryan Dare, Nathan Christian, Emily Elizabeth. Staff therapist/client services mgr. North Central Mich. Community Mental Health Services, Cadillac, 1976—. Mem. adv. bd. Community, Family and Children's Services, 1979—. Mem. Assn. Advancement Behavior Therapy, Mich. Assn. Profl. Psychologists. Home: 8528 Finkle Rd McBain MI 49657 Office: 401 Lake St Cadillac MI 49601

SLAYTON, RANSOM DUNN, elec. products co. engr.; b. Salem, Nebr., Mar. 10, 1917; s. Laurel Wayland and Martha Ellen (Fisher) S.; B.S. with distinction, U. Nebr., 1938; postgrad. Ill. Inst. Tech., 1942, DePaul U., 1945-46; m. Margaret Marie Ang, Sept. 25, 1938; children—R. Duane, David L., Sharon J. Slayton Manz, Karla M. Slayton Fogel, Paul L. With Western Union Telegraph Co., Lincoln, Nebr., 1937-38, St. Paul, 1938-40, Omaha, 1940, Chgo., 1940-45; asst. prof. elec. engring. Chgo. Tech. Coll., 1945-46; with Teletype Corp., Chgo. and Skokie, Ill., 1946-82, elec. engr., dept. chief, 1950-59, project supr., sr. engr. research and devel., 1959-82; lectr., China and Japan, 1978, 79, 80. Active vol. civic orgns., numerous ch. offices. Mem. IEEE (sr.; numerous coms.), IEEE Communications Soc. (parliamentarian 1972-80, 82—, vice chmn. terminals com. 1980—). Editor: IEEE mag. Trans. on Communication Tech., 1964-69; contbr. articles to profl. publs. Patentee in field. Home: 1530 Hawthorne Ln Glenview IL 60025 Office: 5555 Touhy Ave Skokie IL 60077

SLEDGE, BARNETT JENKINS, mech. engr.; b. Memphis, Aug. 1, 1914; s. Turner Elmore and Ethel Elizabeth (Jenkins) S.; B.S. in Mech. Engring., U. Tenn., 1936, postgrad. in structrual engring., 1950; m. Rachael Pauline Davis, May 28, 1928; children—Barnett Jenkins, Thomas Davis, Elizabeth Ann. With Champion Papers, Canton, N.C., and Hamilton, Ohio, 1936—, supt. maintenance engr. and construction, 1945-60, chief engr., 1966-80, dir. internat. engring., 1968-80, ret., 1980. Served to col. USAR, 1936-40, 45-66, C.E. U.S. Army, 1940-45. Mem. ASME, Paper Industry Mgmt. Assn., TAPPI. Episcopalian. Home: 985 Sunview Dr W Hamilton OH 45013

SLEGER, PAUL HARVEY, ins. co. exec.; b. Green Bay, Wis., Sept. 15, 1924; s. Joseph J. and Rose E. (Herrick) S.; B.S., in Acctg., Marquette U., 1949; m. Doris A. Quade, June 18, 1949; children—Paul, Lynn Marie, Alan Dale, Laura Lee, Richard Dennis, Deborah Sue. With Allstate Ins. Co., 1949—, sr. systems mgr. home office, 1972-76, ops. mgr. Tech-Cor, Inc., Allstate subs., Wheeling, Ill., 1976-77, asst. v.p., 1977—. Bd. dirs. Omni House. Served with U.S. Army, 1943-45. Decorated Bronze Star. Mem. Nat. Assn. Accts., 11th Armored Div. Assn., Delta Sigma Pi. Roman Catholic. Office: 100 E Palatine Rd Wheeling IL 60090

SLEIGHT, NORMAN REED, ins. co. exec.; b. Clinton County, Mich., Feb. 15, 1920; s. Rolan W. and Bernice G. (Beckwith) S.; A.B., Albion Coll., 1940; postgrad. Iowa State Coll., Ohio State U.; m. Alethea E. Paul, June 3, 1942; children—Douglas R., Susanne (Mrs. Gary Fuller). Group leader Manhattan Project, Iowa State Coll., 1942-46; agt. State Farm Ins. Cos., St. Johns, Mich., 1946-53, Ohio dir., Columbus, 1953-60, Ohio dep. regional v.p., Newark, 1960-61, regional v.p., 1961—. Pres., Griffith Found. for Ins., 1971-73, chmn., 1973—. Past pres., bd. dirs. United Appeal Licking County; trustee Licking County Meml. Hosp., 1965-71, pres., 1968-70; trustee Mid-Ohio Health Planning Fedn., 1970—, v.p., 1974, 78-81, pres., 1981-82; bus. adv. council Coll. Adminstrv. Sci., Ohio State U., 1976—, chmn. adv. council Newark campus, 1977—; bd. dirs. YMCA Newark; mem. Licking County Bd., 1976—. C.L.U. Mem. Assn. C.L.U. (pres. Columbus chpt. 1957-58), Gen. Agts. and Mgrs. Assn. (dir. 1955-58), Newark Area C. of C. (exec. bd. 1962-65. 68-71, pres. 1972-73), Gamma Iota Sigma, Omicron Delta Kappa, Phi Lambda Upsilon, Alpha Chi Sigma, Kappa Mu Epsilon. Presbyn. (elder). Rotarian (dir. Newark 1965-72, pres. 1972). Home: 685 Snowdon Dr Newark OH 43055 Office: 1440 Granville Rd Newark OH 43055

SLEMMONS, ROBERT HOOPER, health planning exec.; b. Kalamazoo, Mich., Mar. 29, 1944; s. Robert Holt and Dorothy Jean S.; B.A., Western Mich. U., Kalamazoo, 1966; M.P.A., Wayne State U., Detroit, 1968; postgrad. Oxford U., Eng., 1966; m. Susan Annette Slemmons, June 23, 1968; children—Elizabeth Anne, Sarah Lynne. Asst. dir. med. records U. Md. Hosp., Balt., 1972-73; health facility planner Charleston (S.C.) Area Comprehensive Health Planning, 1973-76; health planner project rev. West Central Ill. Health Systems Agy., Springfield, 1976-78, asst. dir. data mgmt., 1978-81; sr. planner Ill. Dept. of Aging, Springfield, 1981—. Served to capt. M.S.C., AUS, 1968-71; Vietnam. Decorated Bronze Star, Army Commendation medal, Dept. of Def. medal; recipient Achievement award Dept. of Def., 1971. Mem. Am. Hosp. Assn., Am. Health Planning Assn., Gerontol. Soc., Sigma Alpha Epsilon. Methodist. Club: Optimist. Author: Trident Area Long Term Care Plan, 1974; Hospital Laboratory and Cost Study, 1974; Trident Area Hospital and Health Care Cost Report, 1975; Trident Area Acute Care Plan, 1976; Area Data Profile: West Central Illinois Health Systems Agency, 1979. Home: 2829 Trenton Ct Springfield IL 62704 Office: 421 E Capitol St Springfield IL 62701

SLEMMONS, ROBERT SHELDON, architect; b. Mitchell, Nebr., Mar. 12, 1922; s. M. Garvin and K. Fern (Borland) S.; B.A., U. Nebr., 1948; m. Dorothy Virginia Herrick, Dec. 16, 1945; children—David (dec.), Claire, Jennifer, Robert, Timothy. Draftsman, Davis & Wilson, architects, Lincoln, Nebr., 1947-48; chief designer, project architect Office of Kans. State Architect, Topeka, 1948-54; asso. John A. Brown, architect, Topeka, 1954-56; partner Brown & Slemmons, architect, Topeka, 1956-69; v.p. Brown-Slemmons-Kreuger, architects, Topeka, 1969-73; owner Robert S. Slemmons, A.I.A. & Assos., architects, Topeka, 1973—. Cons. Kans. State Office Bldg. Commn., 1956-57; lectr. in design U. Kans., 1961. Bd. dirs. Topeka Civic Symphony Soc., 1950-60. Served with USNR, 1942-48. Mem. A.I.A. (Topeka pres. 1955-56, Kans. dir. 1957-58), Topeka Art Guild (pres. 1950), Kans. Council Chs. (dir. 1961-62), Greater Topeka C. of C., Downtown Topeka, Inc. Presbyn. (elder, chmn. trustees). Kiwanian (pres. 1966-67). Prin. archtl. works include: Kans. State Office Bldg., 1954, Topeka Presbyn. Manor, 1960-74, Meadowlark Hills Retirement Community, 1979. Office: 1515 1 Townsite Plaza Topeka KS 66603

SLICHTER, CHARLES PENCE, physicist, educator; b. Ithaca, N.Y., Jan. 21, 1924; s. Sumner Huber and Ada (Pence) S.; A.B., Harvard U., 1946, M.A., 1947, Ph.D., 1949; m. Anne FitzGerald, June 7, 1980; children—Sumner Pence, William Almy, Jacob Huber, Ann Thayer. Research asst. Underwater Explosives Research Lab., Woods Hole, Mass., 1943-46; mem. faculty U. Ill. at Urbana, 1949—, prof. physics, 1955—, prof. physics Center for Advanced Study, 1980—; Morris Loeb lectr. Harvard U., 1961; dir. Polaroid Corp., 1975—; mem. Nat. Sci. Bd., 1975—; mem. Pres. Sci. Adv. Com., 1964-69, Com. on Nat. Medal Sci., 1969-74. Mem. corp. Harvard U. Recipient Langmuir award Am. Phys. Soc., 1969; Alfred P. Sloan fellow, 1955-61. Mem. Nat. Acad. Scis., Am. Acad. Arts and Scis., Am. Philos. Soc. Author: Principles of Magnetic Resonance, 1963, 2d rev. edit., 1978; contbr. articles to profl. jours. Office: Dept Physics U Ill 1110 W Green St Urbana IL 61801

SLICKO, THOMAS MICHAEL, retail exec.; b. Highland, Ind., Apr. 19, 1951; s. Ancietas Frank and Ruth Ann S.; B.S. in Indsl. Mgmt., Purdue U., 1973, M.S. in Mgmt., 1979; m. Marlene Ann Sklanka, Aug. 12, 1972. Salesman, dept. mgr. J.C. Penney Co., Hammond, Ind. and Harvey, Ill., 1971-73; raw materials mgr. Rand McNally Co., Hammond, 1974; gen. mgr. Hyland Corp., Highland, Ind., 1974-75; mgr. sales adminstrn. Dreis & Krump Mfg. Co., Chgo., 1975-78; dir. adminstrv. ops. Maremont Corp., Chgo., 1976-78; v.p. adminstrn., sec.-treas. Lee Enterprises, Inc., Prospect Heights, Ill., 1978-79; dist. mgr. Southland Corp., Hammond, 1979—. Mem. Amateur Golfers Assn., Highland Jr. C. of C. (founder, pres.), Purdue Alumni Assn., Phi Sigma Kappa, Alpha Mu Omega. Home: 7415 McCook St Hammond IN 46323 Office: 3700 179th St Hammond IN 46323

SLINGERLAND, CHARMAINE KINSLEY, librarian; b. Albany, N.Y., Aug. 2, 1930; d. Reginald Pardon and Luella Mary (Woodhull) Kinsley; B.A., Bates Coll., 1953; M.L.S., SUNY, Albany, 1972; m. Claude William Slingerland, Oct. 15, 1955; children—Stuart, Douglas. Plant adminstrv. clk. N.Y. Telephone Co., Albany, 1953-58; tech. asst., library Rensselaer Poly. Inst., Troy, N.Y., 1966-68; periodicals/documents librarian SUNY, Albany, 1967-72; head serials librarian Miami U., Oxford, Ohio, 1972-80, head circulation librarian, 1980—; cons. library Preble County Hist. Soc., 1976-80. Mem. AAUP, AAUW, ALA, Acad. Library Assn. Ohio, Am. Mgmt. Assn., Nat. Fedn. Bus. and Profl. Women, Ohio Library Assn., Ohio Valley Group Tech. Service Librarians Assn. (sec. 1977), Preble County Hist. Soc., Bus. and Profl. Women (Hwy. Safety Program award 1978, club treas. Eaton, Ohio 1978-80), Delta Kappa Gamma. Republican. Club: Univ. Women's. Home: 2841 Camden-College Corner Rd Camden OH 45311 Office: King Library Miami U Oxford OH 45056

SLJIVIC-SIMSIC, BILJANA, educator; b. Belgrade, Yugoslavia, Jan. 20, 1933; s. Branko and Radoyka (Pesic) Sljivic; came to U.S., 1962, naturalized, 1977; diploma U. Belgrade, 1955; A.M., Harvard U., 1963, Ph.D., 1966; m. Branko Simsic, Jan. 24, 1953 (div. 1963); 1 dau., Violet Ljubica. Instr. U. Belgrade, 1957-62; vis. exchange lectr. U. Clermont-Ferrand, France, 1959-61; acting instr., acting asst. prof. UCLA, 1964-66; asst. prof. U. Ky., Lexington, 1966-67, U. Pa., Phila., 1967-73; vis. lectr. Princeton U., 1967-68, 68-69; asso. prof., head Serbian studies program U. Ill. Chicago Circle, Chgo., 1973-81, asso. prof., head dept. slavic langs. and lits., 1981—. Radcliffe Fund scholar, 1962-63, Harvard grad. fellow, 1963-64. Mem. N.Am. Soc. Serbian Studies (founding mem., sec.-treas., 1978—), Am. Assn. Advancement Slavic Studies. Mem. Serbian Orthodox Ch. Clubs: Serbian Acad., Harvard and Radcliffe (Chgo.). Author: (with Morton Benson) Serbo-Croatian-English Dictionary, 1972; (with S. Armistead and J. Silverman) Judeo-Spanish Ballads from Boshia, 1972; contbr. articles to profl. jours. Office: Dept Slavic Langs and Lit UH 1228 U Ill at Chicago Circle Box 4348 Chicago IL 60680

SLOAN, BRUCE DANIEL, food ingredients mfg. co. exec.; b. Milw., Dec. 2, 1946; s. Norman Jacob and Elizabeth Louise (Soderland) S.; B.S. in Journalism, U. Kans., 1969; M.A. in Mass Communications, Central Mo. State U., 1980; m. Laura L. Batty, June 23, 1972; children—David Jeffrey, Emily Alyce. Dir. public relations Kansas City Kings Profl. Basketball Club, 1972-77; advt. and promotion mgr. ITT Paniplus, Olathe, Kans., 1977, adminstrv. promotion mgr., 1978-79, mgr. nat. programs, regional sales mgr., 1979—. Served with U.S. Army, 1969-71. Republican. Roman Catholic. Home: 7604 Overton St Raytown MO 64138

SLOAN, ELMER WESTON, furniture mfg. co. exec.; b. Corydon, Iowa, Feb. 15, 1922; s. David Lewis and Jessie Alice (Mitchell) S.; B.C.S., Drake U., 1950; m. Mary Agnes Delles, Aug. 19, 1950; children—Mark Weston, Craig Paul, Timothy Dale, Kathryn Suanne, Jennifer Lynn, Brian Alan. Office mgr. Goodyear Tire & Rubber Co., Clinton, Iowa, 1952-54; indsl. engr. Maytag Co., Newton, Iowa, 1954-56; v.p. mfg. Schnadig Corp., Rushville, Ind., 1956—; dir. Rushville Nat. Bank. Cubmaster Richmond (Ind.) council Boy Scouts Am., 1959-60; mem. Rush County (Ind.) Aviation Bd., 1969; pres. Babe Ruth League, Rushville, 1969; chmn. fund-raising drive St. Mary's Catholic Ch., 1971. Served with USN, 1942-46, 50-52. Mem. Indsl. Mgmt. Soc., Nat. Assn. Furniture Mfrs. (dir. prodn. div. 1977—), Am. Legion, VFW, 45th Naval Seabee Assn. Democrat. Roman Catholic. Clubs: K.C., Elks. Home: RFD 3 Box 266 Rushville IN 46173 Office: PO Box 397 Rushville IN 46173

SLOCUM, ARTHUR FONDA, JR., mfg. co. exec.; b. Phila., Aug. 4, 1946; s. Arthur Fonda and Jane (Sigman) S.; student U. Richmond, 1964-68, Syracuse U., 1971-72, U. Va., 1978; m. Lynne Colville Seidel, June 28, 1969; children—Kristin Seidel, Arthur Fonda. Regional accts. mgr. Lea Industries, Richmond, Va., 1972-77; southeastern sales mgr. Stanley Furniture Co., Stanleytown, Va., 1977-79; nat. accts. sales mgr. La-Z-Boy Chair Co., Monroe, Mich., 1979—. Elder, deacon Westminster Presbyterian Ch., Richmond. Served with U.S. Army, 1969-70; Vietnam. Decorated Bronze Star. Mem. Nat. Accts. Mktg. Assn., So. Furniture Mfrs. Assn., Nat. Furniture Mfrs. Assn. Club: Detroit Beach Boat. Home: 471 Hollywood Dr Monroe MI 48161 Office: 1284 N Telegraph St Monroe MI 48161

SLONIM, ARNOLD ROBERT, biochemist, physiologist; b. Springfield, Mass., Feb. 15, 1926; s. Sam and Esther (Kantor) S.; B.S., Tufts Coll., 1947; A.M., Boston U., 1948; postgrad. (NIH grantee), George Washington U. Med. Sch., 1949-50; Ph.D., Johns Hopkins U., 1953; m. Kathe Mueller, 1951 (div. 1973); children—Charles Bard, Susan Harlyn, Elyse Gail. Research asst. nutrition Sterling-Winthrop Research Inst., Rensselaer, N.Y., 1948-49; research asst. pharmacology George Washington U., Washington, 1949-50; research asst., jr. instr. biology Johns Hopkins U., Balt., 1950-53; research asso. chemotherapy Children's Cancer Research Found., Harvard Med. Sch., Boston, 1953-54; head chem. lab. Lynn (Mass.) Hosp., 1955-56; research physiologist Aerospace Med. Research Lab., Wright-Patterson AFB, Ohio, 1956-60, chief applied ecology sect., 1960-62, research biochemist, group leader biotech. and environ. pollution, 1962—; lectr. Mass. Sch. Physiotherapy, Boston, 1955-56; mem. Internat. Bioastronautics Com. (Life Support Group) of Internat. Bioastronautical Fedn., 1966-70, Com. on Biol. Handbooks of Fedn. Am. Socs. for Exptl. Biology, 1966-71. Served with USN, 1944-46. Mem. AAAS, Aerospace Med. Assn., Am. Soc. Biol. Chemists, Am. Physiol. Soc., N.Y. Acad. Scis., Sigma Xi. Club: Masons. Editorial bd. Aerospace Medicine, 1967-71; contbr. articles to profl. jours. Office: Aerospace Med Research Lab Wright-Patterson AFB OH 45433

SLOTT, MICHAEL PAUL, advt. sales promotion exec.; b. South Bend, Feb. 4, 1950; s. Casimir B. and Gene Theresa (Kush) S.; B.B.A., U. Notre Dame, 1972; M.B.A., DePaul U., 1976. Sales and mktg. asso. Eli Lilly & Co., Indpls. and Chgo., 1973-77; brand planning mgr., nat. sales promotion mgr. Helen Curtis Industries, Inc., Chgo., 1977-78; account supr. K-Promotions, Inc., Schiller Park, Ill., and Milw., 1978-79; account supr. Columbian Advt., Inc., Chgo., 1979—. Mem. U. Notre Dame Alumni Assn. Home: 1201B Central St Evanston IL 60201 Office: 201 E Ohio St Chicago IL 60611

SLOVER, WILLIAM GODFREY, educator, city ofcl.; b. Trenton, N.J., June 15, 1938; s. H. Edwin and Marian B. (Beans) Stockwell; B.S. in Edn., Miami U., Oxford, Ohio, 1967, M.Ed., 1970; grad. Inst. Ednl. Mgmt., Harvard U., 1977. Clk., Johnson and Johnson, 1960-61; mgmt. trainee Morgan Guaranty Trust Co., 1961-65; asst. registrar Miami U., Oxford, Ohio, 1967-69, sec. of univ., 1969—, affirmative action officer. Mem. CSC Oxford, 1974—, chmn., 1975, 76, vice chmn., 1977, 78; mem. Tax Equalization Bd. Oxford, 1973-75. Served with USMCR, 1959-64. Mem. Am. Assn. Higher Edn., Newcomen Soc. N.Am., Beta Gamma Sigma, Omicron Delta Kappa, Beta Theta Pi, Phi Delta Kappa. Presbyterian. Home: 505 Brookview Ct Oxford OH 45056 Office: 204 Roudebush Hall Miami U Oxford OH 45056

SLOWINSKI, FRANK ANTHONY, JR., hosp. exec.; b. Toledo, Aug. 30, 1947; s. Frank Anthony and Virginia S.; A.A., U. Toledo, 1972; m. Elsene Komenda, Nov. 20, 1976; children—Melanie, Norman. Buyer, Am. Standard Co., Toledo, 1969-72; mgr. data processing Samborn, Steketee, Otis & Evans, Toledo, 1972-78; dir. data processing Mercy Hosp. Toledo, 1978—. Mem. parish council Immaculate Conception Ch. Served with USAF, 1965-69. Mem. Data Processing Mgmt. Assn. Club: K.C. Home: 9106 W Bancroft St Holland OH 43528 Office: 2200 Jefferson Ave Toledo OH 43625

SLOWINSKI, WALLACE JOHN, communications co. exec.; b. Austin, Minn., Dec. 14, 1946; s. Wallace James and Manetta Lorain (Halverson) S.; A.A.S., Austin State Jr. Coll., 1967; B.A., Winona State U., 1978; M.B.A., Mankato State U., 1981; children—Tawnya Dawn, Laura Lee. Meat cutter/union rep. George Hormel Co., Austin, 1967-76; pres. N. Am. Mgmt., Maple Grove, Minn., 1976—; personnel cons. United and Children's Hosps., St. Paul, 1978-80; v.p. adminstrn. Norstan Communications, Plymouth, Minn., 1980—. Dir. edn. Ind. Sch. Dist. 492, Austin, Minn., 1974-76; del. Minn. State High Sch. Legis., Dist. 492, 1974-76; dept. chmn. AFL-CIO, Amalgamated Meat Cutters and Butcher Workmen local P-9, Austin, 1970-75. Mem. Am. Soc. Personnel Adminstrn., Twin Cities Personnel Assn., Am. Soc. Tng. and Devel., Am. Electronics Assn., Am. Mgmt. Assn. Republican. Roman Catholic. Clubs: Masons, Eagles. Home: 14693 94th Pl Maple Grove MN 55369 Office: 15755 32d Ave N Plymouth MN 55447

SLUSS, LAWRENCE MALONE, data processor; b. Indpls., Aug. 25, 1937; s. Ellis and Dorothy Mae (McGail) S.; student Purdue U., 1955-57; m. Wanda Annette Smith, Oct. 5, 1957; children—Deborah, Jay, Rebeccah, David. Data processing specialist U.S. Army Fin. Center, Ft. Harrison, Inc., 1964-67; mgr. systems support Community Hosp. of Indpls., 1967—. Bd. dirs., sec. Ind. Christian Retirement Park, Zionsville. Recipient Dept. Army award, 1967. Mem. Ind. Christian Benevolent Assn. (dir. 1972-80, sec. 1975-79). Republican. Home: 3937 Della Ct Indianapolis IN 46236 Office: 1500 N Ritter Ave Indianapolis IN 46219

SMALE, JOHN GRAY, mfg. exec.; b. Listowel, Ont., Can., Aug. 1, 1927; s. Peter J. and Vera Gladys (Gray) S.; B.S. in Bus., Miami U. (Ohio), 1949, LL.D. (hon.), 1979; LL.D. (hon.), Kenyon Coll. (Ohio), 1974; m. Phyllis Anne Weaver, Sept. 2, 1950; children—John Gray, Catherine Anne, Lisa Beth, Peter McKee. With Vick Chem. Co., N.Y.C., 1949-51, Bio-Research Inc., N.Y.C., 1952-52; pres., dir. Procter & Gamble Co., Cin., 1952—, chief exec. officer, 1981—; dir. Eastman Kodak Co. Chmn. bd. trustees Kenyon Coll.; trustee Cin. Mus. Assn.; mem. Bus. Com. for Arts; bd. dirs. United Negro Coll. Fund, Inc.; mem. bus.-higher edn. forum Am. Council on Edn. Served with USNR, 1945-46. Mem. Grocery Mfrs. Am. (dir.). Clubs: Commercial, Commonwealth Cin. Country, Queen City (Cin.); Zanesfield Rod and Gun. Office: Procter and Gamble Co PO Box 599 Cincinnati OH 45201

SMALL, ARTHUR A., JR., state senator; b. Brunswick, Maine, Oct. 14, 1933; B.A., Bowdoin Coll.; M.A., U. Iowa; m. Mary Jo O'Callaghan, Nov. 26, 1960; children—Peter, Martha, Arthur. Mem. faculty St. Ambrose Coll.; legis. asst. U.S. Congressman John R. Schmidhauser; former mem. Iowa Ho. of Reps.; now mem. Iowa State Senate. Office: State Capitol Des Moines IA 50319*

SMALL, DONALD DAVID, educator; b. Hammond, Ind., Dec. 30, 1932; s. Victor Peter and Wanda (Rubinska) S.; M.S., Ind., U., 1963, Ed.D., 1967; m. Sergine Anne Oliver, June 6, 1970 (dec. 1974); children—(by previous marriage)—David Arthur, Elaine Diane. Asso. prof. Coll. Edn., Western Ky. U., 1967-68; asso. prof. edn. U. Toledo, 1968-77, prof., 1977—, dir. honors programs in edn., chief instr. karate programs, 1969-75. Chmn., nat. com. on English methods, conf. on English edn., 1967—; cons. in grammar and linguistics to numerous Ohio sch. dists. under Title III Elementary and Secondary Edn. Act. Mem. steering com. Students of Toledo Organized for Peace, 1970—; bd. dirs. Toledo Mental Hygiene Center, 1977—; mem. Ohio Council Mental Health Centers, 1979—. Served with AUS, 1955-57. Mem. AAUP, Am. Fedn. Tchrs., Nat. Council Tchrs. English, Western Lake Erie Hist. Soc., Am. Ednl. Studies Assn., Assn. Supervision and Curriculum Devel., English Assn. Ohio, Toledo Power Squadron (comdg. officer 1981), U.S. Power Squadrons, Am. Karate System (charter), AAU (exec. com. Karate nat. com. 1973—). Club: Bayview Yacht. Author numerous books and articles on edn. Home: 2807 Goddard Rd Toledo OH 43606

SMALL, HELEN FRANCIS, nun, behavioral scientist; b. Chgo., June 9, 1920; d. Francis Joseph and Florence Helen (Lawson) S.; B.A., Mt. Mary Coll., Milw., 1950; M.A., Loyola U., Chgo., 1963; Ph.D., McMaster U., Can., 1973. Joined Congregation Sch. Sisters of Notre Dame, Roman Catholic Ch., 1940; tchr. jr. and sr. high schs., Wis. and Ill.; mem. faculty Mt. Mary Coll., Milw., 1963—, prof. behavioral scis., 1973—, chmn. dept., 1975—. Ont. Grad. fellow, 1968-73. Mem. Am. Sociol. Assn., Assn. Sociology of Religion, Midwest Sociol. Soc., Religious Research Assn., Soc. Sci. Study of Religion, Wis. Sociol. Assn., Alpha Kappa Delta. Home and Office: 2900 N Menonomee Pky Milwaukee WI 53222

SMALL, JEROME KUHN, clin. psychologist; b. Nashville, Dec. 6, 1947; s. Jerome Kuhn and Eleanor Klein (Bloch) S.; B.A., U. Va., 1969; M.A., U. Ga., 1970, Ph.D., 1972; m. Holly Lynn Cohen, Sept. 4, 1977. Postdoctoral fellow in clin. psychology Med. U. S.C. and VA Hosp., Charleston, 1972-73; clin. psychologist psychiatry service VA Center, Hampton, Va., 1973-74; asst. prof. community psychology, dept. psychiatry and behavioral scis. Eastern Va. Med. Sch., Norfolk, 1973-74; postdoctoral fellow in community and clin. psychology U. S.Fla., 1974-75; asst. prof. psychology U. Tenn., Martin, 1975-76; asst. prof. psychology Youngstown (Ohio) State U., 1976—; pvt. practice clin. psychology, Youngstown. NDEA fellow, 1969-72. Mem. Am. Psychol. Assn., Ohio Edn. Assn., Midwestern Psychol. Assn., Southeastern Psychol. Assn., Psi Chi. Jewish. Home: 2529 Elm St Youngstown OH 44505 Office: Dept Psychology Youngstown State U Youngstown OH 44555

SMALL, RICHARD DONALD, travel co. exec.; b. West Orange, N.J., May 24, 1929; s. Joseph George and Elizabeth (McGarry) S.; A.B. cum laude, U. Notre Dame, 1951; m. Arlene P. Small; children—Colleen P., Richard Donald, Joseph W., Mark G., Brian P. With Union-Camp Corp., N.Y.C., Chgo., 1952-62; pres. Alumni Holidays, Inc., Studentaire Travel, Inc., Chgo., 1962—, AHI Internat. Corp., Chgo. Mem. Chgo. Assn. Commerce and Industry (edn., visitors bur., transp. coms.). Club: University (Chgo.). Home: 17 Park Ln Park Ridge IL 60068 also 1111 Crandon Blvd Apt B-905 Key Biscayne FL 33149 Office: 1st Nat Bank Bldg 701 Lee St Des Plaines IL 60016

SMALLER, VICTORIA VARON, assn. exec., mental health profl.; b. Chgo., Nov. 10, 1920; d. Samuel A. and Estella (Hasson) Varon; B.S., U. Chgo., 1945; B.A., Mundelein Coll., 1967; M.A. with honors, U. Chgo., 1970; m. Bernard Smaller, Oct. 11, 1941 (dec. 1972); children—Dana, Shelley, Scott; m. 2d, Manuel Finkelstein, July 15, 1973 (dec. 1980). Dir. clin. lab. Rest Haven Rehab. Center, Chgo., 1953-55; research technologist dept. medicine U. Chgo., 1950-52; project dir. Inst. for Tb Research, 1963-65; psychiat. social worker Michael Reese Hosp., Chgo., Incentives Psychol. Treatment Center, Des Plaines, Ill.; asst. to dir. State of Ill. Dept. Mental Health, Chgo., 1971-73; sr. staff specialist, dir. mental health, psychiat. services sect. Am. Hosp. Assn., Chgo., 1973—; field cons. U. Ill.; mental health cons. to various nursing homes, 1973—. Bd. dirs. Theodoron Found. Mem. Acad. Certified Social Workers, Assn. Mental Health Adminstrs., Nat. Assn. Social Workers, Am. Assn. BioFeedback Clinicians, Am. Soc. Clin. Pathologists (affiliate). Contbr. foreward to book, book revs. to profl. jours., papers to profl. confs. Home: 6033 N Sheridan Rd Chicago IL 60660 Office: 840 N Lake Shore Dr Chicago IL 60611

SMALLEY, DOYTE MARVIN, state police officer; b. Marion, Ind., Nov. 17, 1936; s. James Everett and Margaret Pauline (Davis) S.; A.S., Ind. U., 1978, B.S., 1981; m. Kathryn E. Drischel, Jan. 1, 1980; 1 son, David Michael. Trooper, Ind. State Police, Indpls., 1960, sgt., 1968, lt., 1974, capt., 1978, comdr. Pub. Info. Office, 1980—; instr. Ind. Law Enforcement Acad., Plainfield, Ind., 1967-81. Served with USAF, 1955-58. Mem. FBI Nat. Acad. Assos., Northwestern U. Traffic Inst. Assn. Club: Masons, Shriners, Scottish Rite. Contbr. articles to profl. jours. Home: 1418 Hornaday Rd Brownsburg IN 46112 Office: 100 N Senate St Indianapolis IN 46204

SMALLEY, JAMES ADDISON, Realtor; b. Mt. Auburn, Iowa, Apr. 26, 1930; s. Edwin Royal and Florence Iva (Willson) S.; student Oakland U., 1965—; m. Lillie Kathryn Ledbetter, Aug. 6, 1955; 1 son, Edwin Royal. Served as enlisted man U.S. Army, 1948-51, now lt. col., C.E., U.S. Army Res.; pres. Smalley Inc., Realtors, Rochester, Mich., 1955—; pres. The J.E.L. Corp.; tchr. real estate investments Oakland U.; instr. Real Estate Investments and Taxation U. Mich., Ann Arbor. Trustee, mem. adminstrv. bd. St. Paul's United Meth. Ch., 1955—. Mem. Nat. Assn. Realtors, Mich. (pres. Exchange Comml. Group 1969-73) Assn. Realtors, Rochester Bd. Realtors (pres. 1961-65, Realtor of Year 1965), Soc. Exchange Counselors (bd. govs.), Ind. Fee Appraisers, C. of C. (v.p. 1965-74), Am. Legion Res. Officers Assn. (life). Clubs: Masons (32 deg.), Moslem Temple Shrine (pres. 1961), Rochester Shrine, Elks, Gt. Oaks County. Office: 2660 S Rochester St Rochester MI 48063

SMEDVIG, MAGNE, real estate developer; b. Stavanger, Norway, Feb. 24, 1920; s. Erling and Henny (Ness) S.; student U. Seattle, 1945, 49, U. Minn., 1951, So. Meth. U., 1959; m. Esther W. Tralnes, Oct. 24, 1942; children—Erling S., Mark S. Surburban agt. Seattle Post Intelligence, 1934-41; gen. mgr. Sons of Norway, Mpls., 1949-75, also pres.; v.p. S/N Found.; dir. Torske Klubben; real estate developer, Minn., Brit. V.I., 1975—. Bd. dirs., exec. com. Nat. Fraternal Congress Am. Served with USAAF, 1942-45; ETO. Decorated by King Olav V Norway for promotion of cultural relations and arts between U.S., Can. and Norway, 1966. Mem. Minn. Fraternal Congress (past pres.), Sons of Norway, Mpls. Bd. Realtors, Minn. Bd. Realtors, Nat. Bd. Realtors. Lutheran. Clubs: Norwegian Glee, Minneapolis Six O'Clock, Minneapolis Athletic. Office: 3910 W 50th St Edina MN 55408

SMELLER, PAUL JOSEPH, ins. co. exec.; b. Barberton, Ohio, Aug. 31, 1941; s. Lloyd F. and Magdalene (Juszli) S.; B.A., Purdue U., 1964; m. Ellen Weidner, Feb. 2, 1963; children—Carl Patrick, Christina Marie, Matthew Christopher Michael. Agt., sales mgr. Met. Life Ins. Co., Akron, Ohio, 1964-70; br. mgr. Montgomery Ward Life Ins. Co., Akron, 1970-71; sales mgr. Union Central Life Ins. Co., Akron, 1971-72, Met. Life Ins., 1972-76; gen. agt. Am. United Life Ins. Co., Akron, 1976-80, Central Res. Life, Akron, 1978-80, Westfield Life, Akron, 1978-80; asst. v.p., mgr. life mktg. Westfield Life Ins. Co., Westfield Center, Ohio, 1980—; instr. bus. ins. Life Underwriters Tng. Council, 1972—; instr. Am. Coll., Bryn Mawr, Pa. and Akron. Treas., Great Trails council Boy Scouts Am., 1972-74; basketball coach Cath Youth Orgn., 1965—. C.L.U. Mem. Nat. Assn. Life Underwriters (com. chmn., 7 nat. quality awards), Am. Soc. C.L.U.'s (com. chmn., pres. Akron chpt. 1981—), Gen. Agts. and Mgrs. Assn., Akron Estate Planning Council, Phi Sigma Kappa. Roman Catholic. Home: 383 Allen Dr Wadsworth OH 44281 Office: 341 White Pond Dr Akron OH 44320 also 1 West Park Circle Westfield Center OH 44251

SMET, RONALD JAMES, pharmacist; b. Superior, Wis., June 19, 1938; s. Edward Aloyius and Leah Mary (Lagae) S.; B.S., Creighton U., Omaha, 1962; m. Diane L. DeRiemaker, Aug. 5, 1961; children—Steven, Craig, Scott. Staff pharmacist Lane Drug Store, Omaha, 1962-63; asst. mgr. Greys Drug Store, St. Paul, 1963-64; staff pharmacist Gags Drug Store, Marshall, Minn., 1964-68; dir. pharmacy St. Marys Hosp. and Nursing Center, Detroit Lakes, Minn., 1969-79, Axtell Christian Hosp., Newton, Kans., 1979—; cons. pharmacist Frazer Retirement Center; former mem. Minn. Med. Drug Utilization Com.; area coordinator for continuing edn. for pharmacists; cons. Sisters of St. Joseph's Coordinated Services for Hosps. Mem. Holy Rosary Sch. Bd., 1976-77; bd. dirs. Detroit Lakes chpt. Birthright, 1976-78. Mem. Am. Soc. Hosp. Pharmacists, Am. Pharm. Assn., Minn. Soc. Hosp. Pharmacists (dir. 1976-78, candidate Hallie Bruce award 1979), Minn.-Dak. Soc. Hosp. Pharmacists, Kans. Soc. Hosp. Pharmacists Am. Contract Bridge League, Alpha Sigma Nu. Roman Catholic. Clubs: K.C.; Elks (chaplain 1981). Office: Axtell Christian Hosp 209 E Broadway Newton KS 67114

SMITH, ADELL EDDIE, mgmt. tng. cons. co. exec.; b. Memphis, May 14, 1945; s. Dan Edward and Annie Bell (Slayton) S.; B.A. in Psychology, U. Mo., 1974; M.B.A., Washington U.; m. Bertha Jean Newman, Sept. 8, 1963; 1 dau., Toni Michele. Teaching asst. U. Mo., St. Louis, 1970-74; mgmt. tng. supr. APC Skills Co., Palm Beach, Fla., 1975-77; pres. A. Edward Smith and Assos., St. Louis, 1977—; mem. faculty St. Louis Community Coll., 1981—; cons. on upward mobility tng. for women and minorities to bus. and industry, 1977—. Pres. consumer products and services Northwoods-1st Ward Civic Assn., 1980; chmn. edn. and tng. com. Minority Bus. Forum Assn., 1980, pres., 1981; treas. Youth Employment Coalition; mem. St. Louis EEO Group. Served with USAF, 1963-67. Recipient Outstanding Community Service award St. Louis Agy. on Tng. and Employment, 1980, St. Louis Leadership Program Participant award Danforth Found., 1980. Mem. Am. Soc. for Tng. and Devel., Ind. Cons. Am., Am. Inst. Profl. Cons., Am. Entrepreneurs Assn., Community C. of C., St. Louis Black Leadership Roundtable, Christian Athletic Assn. (pres.). Home: 4435 Crestland Dr Saint Louis MO 63121 Office: 3466 Bridgeland Dr Bridgeton MO 63044

SMITH, ANDREW WARREN, educator; b. Johnstown, Pa., May 16, 1932; s. Andrew W. and Agnes Blair (Cranston) S.; B.S., Ind. State Coll., 1954; M.Mus., U. Mich., 1961, Ph.D., 1970; student Internat. Summer Academie, Mozarteum, Salzburg, Austria, 1961, 63, U. Innsbruck, 1963-64, U. Vienna, State Acad. Music, Vienna, 1964-65; m. Nancy Jane Kroehl, Aug. 14, 1965; children—Andrew Thomas, David Howard. Organist, choirmaster various chs., 1948—, also organ cons.; supr. elementary music, Ford City, Pa., 1958-62; high sch. choral dir., Ford City, 1962-63; asso. prof., coordinator music edn. Moorhead (Minn.) State U., 1968—; organist Gethsemane Epis. Cathedral, Fargo. Served with U.S. Army, 1954-57. Mem. Music Educators Nat. Conf., Am. Guild Organists. Mason (Shriner). Organist for 1964 Winter Olympic Games, Protestant Chapel, Innsbruck, Austria. Home: 1020 1st St N Fargo ND 58102

SMITH, ARTHUR APPLEBY, physician and surgeon; b. Springfield, Mo., Sept. 16, 1931; s. Harold Byron and Lucille Helen (Appleby) S.; B.A., S.W. Mo. U., 1952; M.S. in Biochemistry, U. Ark., 1954; M.D., St. Louis U., 1958; m. Stella Elizabeth Baber, May 30, 1952; children—Michael Arthur, Barbara Ann, James Edward, Cynthia Sue. Intern, St. Louis City Hosp., 1958-59, resident in obstetrics and gynecology, 1959-62; practice medicine specializing in obstetrics and gynecology, Belleville, Ill., 1962—; pres. Arthur A. Smith M.D. Service Corp.; mem. Ill. State Maternal Mortality Com., 1971—. Diplomate Am. Bd. Obstetrics and Gynecology. Fellow A.C.S., Am. Coll. Obstetrics and Gynecology; mem. St. Clair County, St. Louis, Ill. med. socs., AMA. Methodist. Home: 25 Oak Hill Belleville IL 62273 Office: 800 E 8th St O'Fallon IL 62269

SMITH, BARNELL GEORGE, ednl. adminstr.; b. Chgo., Dec. 15, 1944; s. LeMoyne and Lazora (Shelton) S.; B.S., Loyola U. Chgo., 1967, M.S., 1969, Ed.D., 1977; children—Christine, Barnell George. Exec. dir. Marcy Center, Chgo., 1963-65; tchr St. Willibrord Sch., Chgo., 1965-66, asst. prin., 1966-67; founder, chief adminstr. Acad. of St. James Coll. Prep., Chgo., 1966—, instr. psychology, sociology, interpersonal relations, 1967—. Active Boy Scouts Am.; advisor Key Club, 1967-78; active Operation Push, U. Ill. Minority Affairs. Recipient Soc. Disting. Am. Students Nat. Approval award, 1980, 81; Malcom X Coll. Citation of Merit, 1973; Award of Merit, E. Garfield Park Citizen Com., 1969; Humanitarian award African Meth. Episcopal Ch., 1977; Community Service award City of Chgo., 1976. Mem. NAACP, Nat. Assn. Sec. Sch. Prins., Nat. Cath. Edn. Assn., Chgo. Council Exceptional Children, Phi Delta Kappa. Clubs: Wellington Phi Esses Frat., Kiwanis (internat. adv. com. S.E. Area). Address: 7550 S Phillips St Chicago IL 60649

SMITH, BETTY MURNAN, educator; b. Indpls., Sept. 11, 1921; d. Carl J. and Helene Alice (Stephens) Murnan; B.A. (cum laude) in English, Butler U., 1944; M.A. in English, State U. Iowa, 1950; m. Richard Norman Smith, Oct. 21, 1951; children—Allegra Louise

Smith Jrolf, Timothy Dwight and Michael Murnan (twins). Tchr. Kingsford (Mich.) High Sch., 1944-46, Bosse High Sch. Evansville, Ind., 1946-48; instr. English, Ely (Minn.) Jr. Coll., 1950-51; acting instr. English, U. Wis. at Milw., 1961-66; instr. English, U. Wis. Center-Waukesha County, 1966-70, asst. prof., 1970-81, asso. prof., 1981—, mem. faculty senate, 1981—; lectr. in field. Co-prin. Hdqrs. Freedom Mil. Sch. Boycott, 1963; bd. dirs. Waukesha Symphony Orch., 1969-72; sec. Waukesha Equal Opportunity Commn., 1970-73; bd. dirs. Waukesha Civic Theatre, 1973-74. Recipient Community Service award U. Wis., Waukesha, 1979. Mem. AAUP (pres. chpt. 1969-70), Modern Lang. Assn., Midwest Modern Lang. Assn., Nat., Wis. councils tchrs. English, Am. Fedn. Tchrs. (treas. Milw. chpt. 1962-66), Assn. Univ. Wis. faculties, Kappa Delta Pi, Sigma Tau Delta. Presbyterian. Contbr. poetry to mags. Home: 1128 Oxford Rd Waukesha WI 53186 Office: Univ Wis Waukesha County 1500 University Dr Waukesha WI 53186

SMITH, CAMILLE DOMBROWSKI, ednl. adminstr.; b. Buffalo; d. Eugene Anthony and Anna Victoria (Sliwinska) Dombrowski; B.A., Syracuse U.; M.A., Boston U.; Ed. Specialist, Mich. State U., 1971, Ph.D., 1978; children—Thomas Dan, Cynthia Camille, Pamela Susan. Dir. music Port Byron (N.Y.) Central Sch., Michaelangelo Sch., Boston, Orchard Park (N.Y.) Sch.; piano tchr., Orchard Park; acad. advisor Mich. State U., East Lansing, 1966-70, dir. Career Center, 1970-81, counseling psychologist Counseling Center, 1981—; presdl. appointee, mem. Career Planning and Placement Council; career devel. cons. high schs. and colls.; pres. Priam Publs. Inc. Pres. Planned Parenthood Greater Lansing, 1966-68; membership chmn. Opera Assn. Greater Lansing, 1980-81; active Friends of Kresge Art Gallery, Women's Symphony Assn. (Lansing). Ednl. devel. grantee, 1975; career planning and placement grantee, 1979, 80. Mem. Am. Personnel and Guidance Assn., Am. Coll. Personnel Assn., Nat. Vocat. Guidance Assn. Club: University (Mich. State U.). Editor The Gracious Reader, Mich. State U. Counseling Center Referral Directory, CAM Report. Office: Counseling Center Michigan State Univ East Lansing MI 48824

SMITH, CARL EDWIN, electronics co. exec.; b. Eldon, Iowa, Nov. 18, 1906; s. Seldon L. and Myra (Hutton) S.; B.S. in E.E., Iowa State U., Ames, 1930; M.S. in E.E., Ohio State U., 1932, E.E., 1936; m. Hannah B. McGuire, Sept. 3, 1932; children—Larc A., Darvin W., Barbadeen Jo, Margene Sue, Ada Kay, Ramona Lee. Draftsman, Iowa Electric Co., Fairfield, summer 1929; student engr. RCA Victor Co., Camden, N.J., 1930-31; engr. Radio Air Service Corp., Cleve., 1932; radio operator WGAR, Cleve., 1933; engr. United Broadcasting Corp., Cleve., 1933-36, asst. chief engr., 1936-41, chief engr., 1941-45, v.p., 1946-53; owner, mgr. Carl E. Smith Consulting Radio Engrs., Cleve., 1953-80; pres. Smith Electronics, Cleve., 1956—; founder Cleve. Inst. Electronics Inc., 1934, chmn. ednl. com., 1970—. Recipient Dist. Achievement citation Iowa State U., 1980. Served with Office of Chief Signal Officer, U.S. Army, World War II. Registered profl. engr., Ohio. Fellow IEEE (life), Radio Club Am.; mem. Cleve. Engring. Soc., Brecksville C. of C. Republican. Reformed Presbyterian. Evang. Author 49 books including: Directional Antenna Patterns, Theory and Design of Directional Antennas, Applied Mathematics, Communications Circuit Fundamentals; Contbr. articles to tech. jours. Patentee electromech. calculators; elliptical polarization electromagnetic energy radiation systems; slotted cylindrical antenna; three-slot cylindrical antenna; spiral slot antenna; low loss antenna system. Home: 8704 Snowville Rd Cleveland OH 44141 Office: 8200 Snowville Rd Cleveland OH 44141

SMITH, CARLYLE SHREEVE, anthropologist; b. Great Neck, N.Y., Mar. 8, 1915; s. Harold William and Lulu (Allen) S.; B.A., Columbia U., 1938, Ph.D., 1949; Litt.D. (hon.), U. S.D., 1979; m. Judith Eva Pogany, May 2, 1942; children—Evan Shreeve, Pamela Anne Smith Baxter. Unit supr. archaeol. survey W.P.A. of Nebr. and La., 1939, 40-41; asst. Hudson Valley Archeol. Survey, Vassar Coll., 1940; curator div. anthropology Mus. Natural History, U. Kans., Lawrence, 1947-68, prof. anthropology, 1947-80, prof. and curator emeritus, 1981—; archaeologist Norwegian Archaeol. Expdn. to Easter Island and East Pacific, 1955-56; participant internat. anthrop. congresses, N.Y.C., 1949, San Jose de Costa Rica, 1958, Vienna, 1960, Paris, 1960, Honolulu, 1961, Moscow, 1964, Barcelona, Madrid, Seville, 1964; cons. to Lindblad Travel, Inc., 1967—. Mem. Kans. Hist. Sites Bd. of Rev., Topeka, 1970—; mem. div. behavioral scis. NRC, 1961-64. Served with USAF, 1943-46. NSF grantee, 1960-67; Nat. Park Service grantee, 1950-76; Am. Philos. Soc. grantee, 1960, 64. Fellow Am. Anthrop. Assn., Co. Mil. Historians; mem. Soc. for Am. Archaeology (1st. v.p. 1954-55), Soc. for Hist. Archaeology, Am. Ethnol. Soc., Explorers Club, Sigma Xi. Editor: U. Kans. Publs. in Anthropology, 1969-73; adv. editor N.Am. Archaeologist, 1979—; contbr. articles and revs. to scholarly jours.; the Carlyle S. Smith Archaeol. Labs. named in his honor at Nassau County Mus. Natural History, Glen Cove, N.Y., 1967. Home: 2719 Harvard Rd Lawrence KS 66044

SMITH, CHARLES ROGER, JR., veterinarian; b. Hartville, Ohio, Mar. 31, 1918; s. Charles Roger and Ethel Olive (Seeman) S.; student Ohio U., 1936-38, 40-41; D.V.M., Ohio State U., 1944, M.S., 1946, Ph.D., 1953; m. Genevieve Lorraine Taylor, Aug. 9, 1946; children—Ronald Roger, Debra Smith Beckstett, Eric William. Instr. dept. vet. physiology and pharmacology Ohio State U., Columbus, 1944-53, asst. prof., 1953-55, asso. prof., chmn. dept., 1955-57, prof., chmn. dept., 1957-69, research prof., chmn., 1969-71, acting dean Coll. Vet. Medicine, 1972-73, dean, 1973-80, dean emeritus and prof., 1980—. Recipient Gamma award Omega Tau Sigma, 1964; diplomate Am. Coll. Vet. Internal Medicine. Fellow Am. Coll. Vet. Pharmacology and Therapeutics; mem. Am. Vet. Med. Assn., Ohio Vet. Med. Assn. (Veterinarian of Yr. 1979), AAAS, Am. Physiol. Soc., N.Y. Acad. Sci., Am. Assn. Vet. Med. Colls. Republican. Methodist. Clubs: Faculty Ohio State U., Masons, Maennerchor (Columbus). Contbr. to Dukes Physiology of Domestic Animals, also articles. Address: Ohio State U 1900 Coffey Rd Columbus OH 43210

SMITH, CHARLES TIMOTHY (TIM), youth adv. adminstr.; b. Chgo., Feb. 22, 1944; s. Richard G. and Jeanne E. S.; student Bowling Green State U., 1962-64; m. Brenda Rucker, Feb. 12, 1977. Dir., Initial Youth Drop-in Center, Cleve., 1968; dir. Community Ednl. Services Center, Cleve., 1971-74; fundraiser job search program Cuyahoga Community Coll., Cleve., 1968-70; dir. Operation Salvage Youth Services Program, Cleve., 1974—; exec. dir. Cleve. Jaycees Found. Fund-raising cons., vol. worker 21st Congl. Caucus; trustee Hough Multi-Service Center; trustee, sec. Spanish Am. Com.; co-chmn. adv. council Cleve. Am. Indian Center. Recipient Martin Luther King Outstanding Citizen award Martin Luther King Mchts. Assn., 1977; Human Relations award City of Cleve.; Outstanding Community Services award Community Guidance for Human Services; named Outstanding New Jaycee, Cleve. chpt. Jaycees, 1977, Outstanding Jaycee of Yr., 1980; One of 10 Outstanding Citizens of Cleve., Cleve. C. of C., 1978. Mem. Cleve. Jaycees (pres. 1980-81, chmn. bd. 1981-82). Democrat. Christian Scientist. Club: Kiwanis (Cleve.). Home: 1707 W 31st Pl Apt 1 Cleveland OH 44113 Office: 1925 St Clair Ave Cleveland OH 44115

SMITH, CHARLES WARREN, educator; b. Palmerton, Pa., Sept. 5, 1936; s. Stanley Aquilla and Luella Mae (Ziegenfus) S.; B.M. with honors, U. Wyo., 1958; M.A., N.Y. U., 1965; postgrad. Eastman Sch. Music, 1967-68, U. N.C., 1970; D.Mus. Arts, George Peabody Coll., 1974; m. Janet Lucille Bass, Aug. 24, 1957; children—Randall Allan, Bradley Taylor, Bryan Keith, Roger Andrew. Music tchr., supr. pub. schs., Wyo., Mont., N.J., N.Y., 1957-68; asst. prof. music Madison Coll., Harrisonburg, Va., 1968-69; asst. prof. Wake Forest U., Winston-Salem, N.C., 1969-75; prof. Southeast Mo. State U., Cape Girardeau, 1975—; prin. flutist in numerous symphony orchs. Recipient Prize winning award certificate Am. Guild Musical Artists, 1958; Academia award Wake Forest Univ. Students, 1974. Mem. Am. Fedn. Musicians, ASCAP, Music Educators Nat. Conf., Nat. Music Theory Soc., Am. Soc. Univ. Composers, Phi Mu Alpha Sinfonia. Composer numerous published and commd. music. Home: Route 1 Gordonville MO 63752 Office: Dept Music Southeast Mo State Univ Cape Girardeau MO 63701

SMITH, CRAIG ALAN, lawyer; b. Valparaiso, Fla., May 1, 1953; s. George Alan and Sara S.; B.A. cum laude (Anthony R. Rollins scholar), U. Mo., Columbia, 1975, J.D., 1978; m. Linda Susan Drummond, June 5, 1976. Admitted to Mo. bar, 1978; partner firm Hindman, Vollers & Smith, Columbia, 1981—. Mem. Mo. Bar Assn. (council young lawyers sect. 1980—), Am. Bar Assn., Boone County Bar Assn., Columbia Jaycees (dir. 1979-81, v.p. 1980, pres. 1981, Disting. Service award 1981), Phi Beta Kappa. Republican. Home: 407 Bourn St Columbia MO 65201 Office: 1001 E Walnut St Suite 300 Columbia MO 65201

SMITH, DANIEL SCOTT, historian; b. Galesburg, Ill., Sept. 24, 1942; s. Charles Edward and Mildred (McCloud) S.; B.A., U. Fla., 1963; M.A. (Woodrow Wilson fellow), U. Calif., Berkeley, 1965, Ph.D., 1973; certificate in demography (Population Council fellow 1973-74) Princeton U., 1974; m. Yvonne, Neu, Mar. 24, 1967; children—Jason Scott, Sarah Elizabeth. Asst. prof. U. Conn., Storrs, 1971-73; asst. prof. history U. Ill., Chgo., 1974-77, asso. prof., 1977—; asso. dir. Family and Community History Center, Newberry Library, Chgo., 1974—; mem. grants rev. panel NIH, 1980; participant profl. confs. Am. Council Learned Socs. fellow, 1977-78. Mem. Am. Hist. Assn. (exchange scholar USSR 1981), Population Assn. Am., Social Sci. History Assn., Econ. History Assn. Editor: Historical Methods, 1979—; editorial bd. Social Sci. History, 1977—; contbr. articles to profl. jours. Office: U Ill Dept History Chicago IL 60680 also Newberry Library 60 W Walton Chicago IL 60610

SMITH, DARWIN EATNA, paper mfg. co. exec.; b. Garrett, Ind., Apr. 16, 1926; s. K. Bryant and Hazel (Sherman) S.; B.S. in Bus. with distinction, Ind. U., 1950; LL.B. cum laude, Harvard, 1955; m. Lois Claire Archbold, Aug. 19, 1950; children—Steven, Pamela, Valerie, Blair. Admitted Ill. bar, 1955, Wis. bar, 1958; asso. firm Sidley, Austin, Burgess & Smith, Chgo., 1955-58; with Kimberly-Clark Corp., Neenah, Wis., 1958—, gen. atty., 1960—, v.p., 1962-67, v.p. fin. and law, 1967-70, pres., 1970—, chmn., chief exec. officer, 1971—. Served with AUS, 1944-46. Mem. Am., Wis. bar assns., Am. Legion. Presbyn. Mason (32). Home: Rural Route 1 Box 211 Menasha WI 54952 Office: Kimberly-Clark Corp Neenah WI 54957

SMITH, DAVID WESLEY, orthopedic surgeon; b. Piqua, Ohio, Sept. 21, 1937; s. Richard and Harriet Smith; student Ohio Wesleyan U., 1958; D.O., Kirksville Coll. Osteo. Medicine, 1962; m. Tanzy J. Smith, May 21, 1962; children—Douglas M., Dyanna. Intern, Doctors Hosp., Columbus, Ohio, 1962-63, resident in orthopedic and traumatic surgery, 1963-66; practice medicine specializing in orthopedic surgery, Columbus, 1966-67, Massillon, Ohio, 1967—; mem. staff Doctors Hosp.; clin. asso. prof. orthopedics Ohio U. Diplomate Am. Osteo. Bd. Surgery. Fellow Am. Coll. Osteo. Surgeons, Am. Osteo. Acad. Orthopedics (pres.); mem. Eighth Dist. Acad. Osteo. Medicine. Office: 3244 Bailey St NW Massillon OH 44646

SMITH, DILLON, TV sta. exec.; b. Pitts., June 30, 1941; s. Robert M. and Mary Cecelia (Dillon) S.; B.J., Northwestern U., 1963, M.S., 1964, J.D., 1967; m. Loretta Bowler, Jan. 28, 1967 (div. 1980); children—Kevin, Lisa, Colleen, Kerry. Admitted to Ill. bar, 1967; news reporter, producer WTIC-TV-Radio, Hartford, Conn., 1967-69; newswriter, producer NBC News, Chgo., 1969; asst. editorial dir. WMAQ-TV, Chgo., 1970-72, editorial dir., 1972-80, program dir., 1980—; chmn. Nat. Broadcast Editorial Conf., 1972; faculty Medill Sch. Journalism, Northwestern U., 1974—. Recipient Silver Gavel award Am. Bar Assn., 1976; Nat. Headliner award, 1972, 73, Broadcast Media awards, 1972, 73, Chgo. Emmy awards, 1975, 76, 77, 78, 79. Mem. Nat. Broadcast Editorial Assn. (v.p. 1976-77, pres. 1977-78), Nat. Assn. TV Arts and Scis. (v.p. Chgo. chpt.), Am., Chgo. bar assns. Office: WMAQ-TV Merchandise Mart Chicago IL 60654

SMITH, DONALD CALLISTUS, computer services exec.; b. New Albany, Ind., May 26, 1942; s. Callistus John and Geneva Margaret (Buechler) S.; B.A., Ind. U., 1964; m. Mary Katherine Russell, Jan. 4, 1963; children—David, Matthew, Christopher. Mgr. info. Services Bus. Div., Gen. Electric, Louisville, 1966-74; regional v.p. Compuserve Network, Louisville, 1974-76; v.p. Sheldon Enterprises, Louisville, 1976-79, also dir. Fulton Data Joint Venture, Atlanta, 1976-79; corp. v.p. S.I. Computer Services, 1979—; dir. Louisville Trust Bank; cons., dir. Fulton Nat. Bank (Atlanta). Com. dir. United Way, 1971. Served with USAF, 1960-66. Recipient Paladin award, 1968; Gen. Electric Outstanding Achievement award, 1973-74; Marion Kellogg award, 1974. Mem. Am. Mktg. Assn. (v.p. 1975-77), Data Processing Mgmt. Assn., Printing Industries Assn. of South, Econ. Resource Mgmt. Assos. Democrat. Roman Catholic. Clubs: Louisville Bonsai (pres. 1975), Kiwanis (v.p. 1970-73). Landscape designer for several maj. archtl. works, Ind., Ky., Ga. Home: Scottsville Rd Pinecliffe Floyds Knobs IN 47119 Office: 110 N Indiana Ave Sellersburg IN 47172

SMITH, DONALD CAMERON, physician, educator; b. Peterborough, Ont., Can., Feb. 2, 1922; s. James Cameron and Clarice (Leighton) S.; came to U.S., 1952, naturalized, 1960; M.D., Queen's U., Kingston, Ont., 1945; M.Sc., U. Toronto (Ont.), 1948; m. Jean Ida Morningstar, Sept. 11, 1946; children—Douglas Frazer, Scot Earle, Donald Ian. Intern, Victoria Hosp., London, Ont., 1944-45; fellow in physiology U. Toronto, 1947-48; asst. med. dir. East York-Leaside (Ont.) Health Dept., 1949-50; exec. dir. Kent County (Ont.) Health Dept., 1950-52; Commonwealth Fund fellow in pediatrics U. Mich., 1952-55, asst. prof. maternal and child health, research asso. in pediatrics, 1955-57, asso. prof. maternal and child health, asso. prof. pediatrics, 1957-61, prof. maternal and child health, prof. pediatrics, 1961—, dir. Child Health Center, 1955-62, 64-72, chmn. dept. health devel., 1964-72; chmn. health policy bd. Mich. Dept. Corrections, 1975—; prin. adviser on health and med. affairs Gov. Mich., 1972-78; dir. Mich. Dept. Mental Health, Lansing, 1974-78; prof. psychiatry and behavioral scis. Northwestern U., Chgo., 1979—; sr. med. advisor Sisters of Mercy Health Corp., 1978—; chmn. med. assistance adv. council Sec. HEW, 1969-72; v.p. for accreditation Joint Commn. on Accreditation of Hosps., 1979-81. Chmn. Ann Arbor (Mich.) Youth Commn., 1965-68; mem. Barton Hills (Mich.) Village Council, 1974-78. Served to lt. Royal Canadian Navy, 1945-47. Diplomate Am. Bd. Pediatrics, Am. Bd. Preventive Medicine. Fellow Royal Coll. Physicians (Can.) Am. Acad. Pediatrics (chmn. com. legislation 1966-72), Am. Pub. Health Assn. (chmn. sect. maternal and child health 1968-70); mem. AMA, Mich. State Med. Soc., Assn. Tchrs. Preventive Medicine, Midwest Soc. Pediatric Research, Ambulatory Pediatric Assn., Delta Omega (nat. pres. 1966-68). Contbr. articles to profl. publs. Office: 28550 Eleven Mile Rd Farmington Hills MI 48018

SMITH, DONALD DEAN, bus. exec.; b. Lewistown, Ill., June 25, 1926; s. Donald Mansfield and Gladys (Dawson) S.; B.S., Bradley U., Peoria, Ill., 1954; m. Priscilla Dean Wightman, Apr. 1, 1954; children—Todd Morrison, Susan Kimberly, Debra Dean. Rep., ICS, 1954-57, dist. sales mgr., 1958-65; nat. sales mgr. Britannica Inst., 1966-68, Chgo. Tech. Coll., 1969-71; owner, pres. Shaklee Center, Lombard, Ill., 1972—; dir. I.B. Systems, Hasco, Inc.; lectr. motivation and tng. Served with U.S. Army, World War II; PTO. Named to Bradley U. Hall of Fame, 1979. Mem. U.S. Masters Track and Field Assn., AAU, Steel Plate Fabricators Assn, Sigma Chi. Unitarian. Current nat. and world champion in masters 800 meter run, joint world record holder 4 by 400 relay, nat. record holder 1500 meter run. Office: 1113 S Main St Lombard IL 60148

SMITH, DONALD ROY, state ofcl.; b. Elmhurst, Ill., Nov. 13, 1926; s. George C. and Florence (Straus) S.; student Loyola U., 1946-49, John Marshall Law Sch., 1949-50; m. Dorothy J. Covington, May 17, 1952; children—Brian, Marilyn, Virginia, Kevin, Karen. Mem. DuPage County Bd. Rev., Wheaton, Ill., 1950-54, chief dep. treas., 1954-58, treas., 1958-61, supr., 1961-64; chief fin. officer State of Ill., Springfield, 1964-77, state treas., 1977-79, chief fiscal officer, 1979—. Served with USNR, 1944-46. Mem. Mcpl. Fin. Officers Assn., Am. Soc. for Public Adminstrn., Nat. Assn. State Treasurers. Roman Catholic. Club: K.C. Home: 2313 Black Hawk St Springfield IL 62702 Office: Capital Bldg Springfield IL 62706

SMITH, DONNA MAE, nurse, businesswoman; b. Indianola, Iowa, Oct. 15, 1926; d. Donald Roger and Bessie Laura (Merriam) Squire; grad. Iowa Luth. Hosp. Sch. Nursing, 1948; m. Roy Alvin Smith, Apr. 5, 1950; children—Bonita Elaine, Leslie Rae. Nurse, U.S. Indian Health Service, 1947-50; partner Smith Amusement Co., 1956-81; partner Stateline Wholesale Co., Whiteclay, Nebr., 1963—; part time nurse USPHS, Pine Ridge, S.D., 1976-81. Mem. Nat. Automatic Merchandise Assn., Nat. Assn. Female Execs., Midwest Amusement Assn. Republican. Address: PO Box 85 Whiteclay NE 69365

SMITH, DUDREY CRAIG, computer engr.; b. Weatherford, Tex., Aug. 7, 1945; s. Richard Farmer and Alice Jean (Gebo) S.; student Grand Rapids Jr. Coll., 1963-66; B.S., Grand Valley State Coll., 1973; M.S. in Math., U. Mich., 1974, M.S. in Computer Info. and Control Engring., 1976; m. Martha Joanne Tuthill, Dec. 16, 1972. Software engr. Lear Siegler, Inc., Grand Rapids, 1976—; guest lectr. Aquinas Coll., Grand Valley State Coll., 1976, 79. Served with U.S. Army, 1967-71. Decorated Bronze Star; academic scholar Grand Valley State Colls., 1971-73; Rackham scholar U. Mich., 1973-74; Rackham teaching fellow U. Mich., 1975-76. Mem. Math. Assn. Am., IEEE, Assn. Computing Machinery. Home: 417 Alger SE Grand Rapids MI 49507 Office: 4141 Eastern SE Grand Rapids MI 49508

SMITH, EDWARD BYRON, bank exec.; b. Chgo., 1909; student Yale U., 1932; married. With No. Trust Co., Chgo., 1932—, exec. v.p., 1949-57, pres., 1957-63, chmn. bd., chief exec. officer, 1963-78, chmn. Nortrust Corp., Chgo., 1978—, chmn. exec. com. No. Trust Corp., 1979-80, hon. chmn. bd., 1981—, also dir.; mem. war savs. staff Office of Procurement Material, U.S. Dept. Treasury, 1942-43; dir. Ill. Tool Works. Served to lt. USN, 1943-45. Office: No Trust Co 50 S LaSalle St Chicago IL 60675

SMITH, EDWARD TOWNSLEY, pub. constrn. exec.; b. Cin., Sept. 27, 1930; s. Edward M. and Linna P. (Townsley) S.; B.S. B.A. cum laude, Xavier U., 1956; m. Shirley Anne Caldwell, Apr. 27, 1957; 1 son, Edward C. Office mgr. Crane Supply Co., Cin., 1962-66; pres., chief exec. officer Servomation Corp., SVM Western Mo., Kansas City, 1966-72; v.p. adminstrn. Capitol Plumbing & Heating, Springfield, Ill., 1972-74; dir. adminstrn. Capital Devel. Bd., Springfield, 1974—. Served with USN, 1950-54. Named Outstanding Jaycee, 1960-61, Jaycee of Year, 1961. Mem. Am. Mgmt. Assn. Roman Catholic. Club: K.C. Home: 38 Hazel Dell Springfield IL 62707 Office: 401 S Spring St Springfield IL 62706

SMITH, ELIZABETH LAWALL, advt. agy. exec.; b. Syracuse, N.Y.; d. Paul Helsel and Jean D. (Lawall) S.; B.A., Smith Coll.; postgrad. Wayne State U. Reference librarian Campbell-Ewald Advt. Agy., Detroit, 1949-53, asst. librarian, 1953-57, librarian, 1958-71, mgr. reference center, 1971-75, v.p., mgr. reference center, 1975—. Mem. Spl. Libraries Assn. (consultation officer Mich. chpt. 1968-77, pres. chpt. 1978-79, chmn. advt./mktg. div. 1964-65). Republican. Lutheran. Contbg. editor: A Handbook for the Advertising Agency Account Executive, 1969; contbr. chpt. to Special Librarianship: A New Reader, 1980. Home: 911 Henrietta St Birmingham MI 48009 Office: 30400 Van Dyke Warren MI 48093

SMITH, ERIC CRAIG, constrn. co. exec.; b. Washington, Nov. 27, 1945; s. Craig Champney and Mary Elizabeth (Leinen) S.; B.A., Brown U., 1967; M.B.A., Wharton Sch., U. Pa., 1971; m. Nancy Mercer Bishop, Feb. 10, 1973; children—Jordan Leinen, Ian Eric, Edward Clark. Acct., Arthur Young & Co., C.P.A.'s, N.Y.C., 1971-74; partner, cons. Fails & Assos., Ltd., Raleigh, N.C., 1974-79; v.p., dir. Fishel Co., Columbus, Ohio, 1979—; dir. V.O.G., Inc., Tractor Parts & Equipment Co.; instr. Fails Mgmt. Inst., Raleigh. Served with USN, 1967-70; Vietnam. C.P.A., N.Y. State. Mem. Am. Inst. C.P.A.'s, N.Y. State Soc. C.P.A.'s, Builders Exchange Columbus. Republican. Clubs: Swim and Racquet (Columbus); Brown. Editor, contbr. Contractor's Digest, 1974-79. Home: 2636 Berwyn Rd Columbus OH 43221 Office: 1170 Kinnear Rd Columbus OH 43212

SMITH, EUGENE VALENTINE, chem. co. exec.; b. Ossian, Ind., Jan. 7, 1924; s. Keith R. and Clona M. (Valentine) S.; B.S. in Mech. Engring., Purdue U., 1948; s. Maxine Louise Byerly, May 19, 1945; children—Penelope Ann Smith Scheidt, Rebecca Jo Smith Schinderle. Mech. engr., plant engr. Stanolind Oil and Gas Co., Midwest, Wyo., 1948-54; sr. project engr. Amoco Chems. Corp., Brownsville, Tex., 1954-57, asst. chief plant engr., Texas City, Tex., 1957-61, ops. supr., 1961-65, supt. ops., Joliet, Ill., 1965-71, tech. dir., 1972—. Trustee Jesse Walker United Meth. Ch., 1968—, pres. trustees, 1972-74, v.p. bd., 1978—; mem. Will-Grundy Mfg. Environ. Control Commn., 1965—; dir. Homeowners Assn., 1971-74. Served with USAAF, 1943-45. Mem. ASME (past pres. Texas City chpt.), Am. Inst. Chem. Engrs. (dir. Joliet sect. 1976—), Three Rivers Mfg. Assn., Joliet C. of C., Pi Tau Sigma, Tau Beta Pi. Republican. Home: 2504 Chevy Chase Dr Joliet IL 60435 Office: PO Box 941 Joliet IL 60434

SMITH, EVANGELINE CHRISMAN DAVEY (MRS. ALEXANDER MUNRO SMITH), civic worker; b. Kent, Ohio, May 30, 1911; d. Martin Luther and Berenice Murl (Chrisman) Davey; A.B. (Scholar), Wellesley Coll., 1933; postgrad. Akron U., 1933-34; m. Alexander Munro Smith, Oct. 5, 1935; children—Berenice Jessie Smith Hardy, Diantha Barret Smith Harris, Letitia Amy Smith Manley. Sec., Davey Tree Expert Co., Kent, 1934, dir., 1962-73, mem. dirs. adv. com., 1973-76. Trustee, Kent Free Library, 1957-77, pres., 1961-63; trustee Patton House, 1966-68, 79-81, historian, 1981—; mem. women's assn. Robinson Meml. Hosp., 1947—, mem. women's assn. governing bd., 1947-68; co-founder Kent council Girl Scouts U.S.A., sec., 1941-45; mem. Kent State U. Pres's. Club, 1976—, Kent State U. Chestnut Soc., 1977—. Mem. Am. Legion Aux., D.A.R. (chpt. regent, 1966-68, registrar, 1973—), Daus. Am. Colonists (regent, 1978-80, registrar 1980—), Colonial Dames XVII Century (librarian), Kappa Kappa Gamma, Phi Sigma Soc. Congregationalist. Clubs: Akron Area Wellesley, Akron Woman's City. Home: 260 Whittier Ave Kent OH 44240

SMITH, F. JOSEPH, musicologist, composer, educator; b. Superior, Wis., Mar. 19, 1925; s. Robert Glen and Clare (Farrell) S.; B.A., Quincy Coll., 1953; M.A., Catholic U., 1955; Ph.D., U. Freiburg (Ger.), 1960; m. Gertrude Ann Kass, 1966; children—Adrienne Ruth, Laurel Elizabeth, Ian Edward (dec.). Vis. prof. Duquesne U., Pitts., 1963-64; researcher U. Freiburg, 1964-65; asso. prof. philosophy Emory U., Atlanta, 1965-67; prof. music Kent (Ohio) State U., 1967; vis. prof. Conservatory Music, U. Bucharest (Romania), 1978-79; editor Jour. Musicological Research, Gordon and Breach, N.Y.C.-London, Paris, 1979; keyboard recitalist; mgr. Musica Nova series, Chgo.; composer; cons. fine arts, music therapy. Mem. Am. Musicological Soc., Am. Husserl Conf. (hon.), Internat. Musicology Soc., Phi Beta. Author: A Triptych in Sound, 1981; In Search of Musical Method, 1976; Experiencing of Musical Sound, 1979; Commentary on Speculum Musicae, 3 vols., 1966, 70, 81; numerous other books in field; contbr. articles in music, philosophy, religion to profl. jours. Home: 6134 N Maplewood Ave Chicago IL 60659

SMITH, FRANCIS THOMAS, III, health center adminstr.; b. Detroit, June 14, 1934; s. Francis Thomas, Jr. and Maxine (Greene) S.; A.B., Hope Coll., Holland, Mich., 1960; M.H.A. (Nat. Tb Assn. grad. fellow 1960), Wayne State U., Detroit, 1961; m. Barbara Elvera Reuss, June 27, 1959; children—Thomas John, Karen Marie. Program devel. cons., dir. patient service programs Ill. Tb Assn., Springfield, 1961-63; exec. dir. Peoria (Ill.)-Stark County Tb Assn., 1963-66; adminstrs. Allied Agencies Center-Peoria County Bd. Care and Treatment Mentally Deficient Persons, Peoria, 1966—; cons. exec. dir. Ill. Assn. Maternal and Child Health; cons. exec. sec. Downstate Ill. Pediatric Soc.; mem. tri-county project rev. com. Ill. Health Systems Agy. Mem. program and budget com. Heart of Ill. United Way, 1970-78; mem. Forest Park Found., 1971—; bd. dirs. Tower Park, Inc., 1975, Council Responsible Driving, 1976—; lay leader First United Meth. Ch., Peoria, 1979—, chmn. adminstrv. bd., 1981—. Served with USNR, 1953-57. Mem. Am. Soc. Public Adminstrn. (chpt. charter mem., past chpt. pres.), Am. Assn. Mental Deficiency, Nat. Rehab. Counseling Assn., Bldg. Owners and Mgrs. Assn., Nat. Rehab. Assn., Ill. Rehab. Assn., Ill. Public Health Assn. Republican. Clubs: Peoria Rotary, Masons, Shriners. Contbr. articles to profl. jours. Office: 320 E Armstrong Ave Peoria IL 61603

SMITH, FRANK RAY, aerospace mfg. co. exec.; b. Waco, Tex., Aug. 18, 1924; s. Frank Carruthers and Osie Helen (Womack) S.; B.A. in English with honors, U. Tex., 1948, M.A. in English, 1949, Ph.D. in English, 1956; m. Patricia Mattingly, Oct. 1, 1948; children—Patricia Kathleen, Ramona Louise, Rebecca Jo. Instr. English U. Tex., 1949-50, 52-53; asst. prof. dept. humanities Air Force Inst. Tech., Dayton, Ohio, 1953-56, asso. prof., 1956-59, prof., head dept., 1959-62; editor Douglas Aircraft Co., Santa Monica, Calif., 1962, sect. head, 1962-64, br. mgr., 1964-65, mgr., 1965-69; corporate mgr., tech. info. McDonnell Douglas Corp., St. Louis, 1969—; cons. in field. Served with U.S. Army, 1943-46. Fellow Soc. Tech. Communication (past pres.), Am. Soc. Engring. Edn. Contbr. articles in field to profl. jours. Editor in chief: Technical Communication, 1977—. Home: 910 Milldale Dr Ballwin MO 63011 Office: PO Box 516 Saint Louis MO 63166

SMITH, FRANKLIN DEWEY, mktg. exec.; b. Lincoln, Nebr., Apr. 3, 1939; s. Charles H. and Dorothy D. (Franklin) S.; B.S. in Law, U. Nebr., Lincoln, 1960; B.A. in Mgmt. Systems and Personnel, Buena Vista Coll., 1981; m. Susan Mary Crosby, Sept. 5, 1959; children—Douglas, Robert, Shari. Vice-pres. sales S & S Products Co., Omaha, 1968-70; regional mktg. coordinator Peoples Natural Gas Co., Council Bluffs, Iowa, 1970-73, sales mgr., 1973-75, mktg. services supr., 1975-81, area mktg. specialist, 1981—. County chmn. Thone for Gov., 1978, 82; Sarpy Republican candidate recruitment chmn., 1980. Served with USMC, 1955-61. Mem. Nebr. Indsl. Developers Assn., ASHRAE, Omaha Indsl. Assn., Sales and Mktg. Execs. (dir.), Papillion C. of C. (v.p. econ. div.), Nebr. Jaycees (past pres.). Republican. Presbyterian. Home: 810 Sherman St Papillion NE 68046 Office: 1246 Golden Gate Dr Papillion NE 68046

SMITH, GARY WILLARD, coll. adminstr.; b. Harrisville, W.Va., Sept. 14, 1945; s. Willard Kester and Freda Arlene S.; B.S., Fairmont State Coll., 1980; m. Elaine Smith, May 31, 1968; children—Christopher, Whitney. Exec., Boy Scouts Am., Clarksburg, W.Va., Boston and Pitts., 1967-70, 71-75; mgr. sales and service Continental Can Co., Clarksburg, 1970-71; mgr. corp. support W.Va. U. Found., 1975-76; dir. devel. Wheeling (W.Va.) Coll., 1977-79; v.p. devel. McKendree Coll., Lebanon, Ill., 19—. Mem. Council Advancement and Support of Edn. Republican. Methodist. Clubs: Kiwanis, Toastmasters (dir.). Office: McKendree College Lebanon IL 62254

SMITH, GEORGE SHERMAN, musician; b. Indpls., Jan. 28, 1934; s. William Lloyd and Edna Esther (Smith) S.; student Butler U., 1952-53; m. Norma Jean Ooten, July 1, 1956; children—Lonnie, Scott, Eric. Profl. musician; organ, piano tchr., Anderson, 1959—; owner George Smith's Kimball Music, Anderson and New Castle, Ind., 1966—; performances for Mrs. Pat Nixon, 1970, Pres. Jimmy Carter, 1979; organist/pianist Internat. Assn. Lions Clubs, 1979—, Ind. Lions Clubs, 1973-80; organist Masons of Indpls., 1978—; rec. artist Amron Records; star TV and radio shows, 1969—. Served with U.S. Army, 1956-58. Recipient Internat. Lions Pres.'s award, 1980; winner Ind. State Fair Organ Contest (2). Mem. Internat. Platform Assn., Musicians Union Local #32, Am. Theatre Organ Soc., Amateur Organists Assn. Internat. Republican. Clubs: Lions, Elks, Masons. Home: 929 Cardinal Way Anderson IN 46011 Office: 2030 Raible Ave PO Box 2501 Anderson IN 46018 also PO Box 2501 Anderson IN 46018

SMITH, GEORGE WOLFRAM, physicist, educator; b. Des Plaines, Ill., Sept. 19, 1932; s. Murray Sawyer and Alice Lucile (Wolfram) S.; B.A., Knox Coll., 1954; M.A., Rice U., 1956, Ph.D., 1958; m. Mary Lee Sackett, Sept. 7, 1956; children—Dean, Grant. Welch Found. fellow Rice U., 1958-59; sr. research physicist Gen. Motors Research Labs., Warren, Mich., 1959-76, deptl. research scientist, 1976—; lectr. physics and astronomy Cranbrook Inst. Sci., Bloomfield Hills, Mich., 1963—; tchr. Lawrence Inst. Tech., 1963-65; vice chmn. Gordon Research Conf. on Orientational Disorder in Crystals, 1976, chmn., 1978; co-chmn. internat. symposium on particulate carbon, 1980. Mem. Mich. Regtl. Civil War Roundtable, 1965-77, pres., 1971-72; active Boy Scouts Am., Sci.-Engring. Fair Met. Detroit. Recipient Knox Coll. Achievement award, 1977, John M. Campbell Research award, 1980. Fellow Am. Phys. Soc.; mem. Am. Carbon Soc., Phi Beta Kappa, Sigma Xi (chpt. pres. 1980-81), Phi Delta Theta, Alpha Delta. Contbr. articles to sci., tech. jours. Co-editor: Particulate Carbon: Formation During Combustion, 1981. Patentee temperature measuring device, liquid crystal device technology. Home: 1882 Melbourne St Birmingham MI 48009 Office: Physics Dept Gen Motors Research Warren MI 48090

SMITH, GERALD JAMES, clin. psychologist; b. Chgo., Feb. 4, 1943; s. Edward James and Josephine Marie (Strenk) S.; B.S., Loyola U., Chgo., 1966, Ph.D., 1974; postgrad. Marquette U., 1966-68; postdoctoral student psychotherapy Chgo. Med. Sch., 1974-76; m. Denise Marie Dahl, July 27, 1968; children—Edward Dahl, Lisa Marie. Program dir. youth care program Children and Family Services, Lockport, Ill., 1974; asso. prof., chmn. dept. psychology Lewis U., Lockport, 1968-76; pvt. practice, Calumet City, Ill., 1976-79; clin. dir. Southlake Center Mental Health, 1979-81; adminstrv. dir. mental health Dept. Health, City of Chgo., 1981—; co-founder, 1974, past pres. Ill. Sch. Profl. Psychology, Chgo.; chmn. task force on mental health manpower devel. Ind. Dept. Mental Health; lectr. Chgo. Coll. Osteo. Medicine. Bd. dirs. NW Ind. Symphony Soc. Mem. Am. Psychol. Assn., Midwestern, Ind., Ill. psychol. assns., Assn. Advancement Psychology, Am. Soc. Psychologists in Pvt. Practice, Blue Key, Psi Chi, Phi Kappa Theta. Roman Catholic. Home: 6227 N Oak Park Ave Chicago IL 60631

SMITH, GERALD RALPH, educator; b. Schenectady, Oct. 26, 1929; s. Albert R. and Alice J. (Enos) S.; A.A., Concordia Coll. Inst., 1951; B.A., SUNY, Albany, 1955, M.A., 1956; Ed.D., Tchrs. Coll., Columbia U., 1964; m. Betty Louise Dickheuer, Nov. 27, 1954; children—Linda Louise, Paul David. Tchr. English, Elwood Union Free Sch. Dist., L.I., N.Y., 1956-59; adminstrv. asst. Cooperative Research program, U.S. Office Edn., Washington, 1959-60, research asso., 1960-62, research coordinator, 1962-64; asso. prof. Coll. Edn. and Maxwell Grad. Sch. Citizenship and Public Affairs, Syracuse (N.Y.) U., 1964-68; prof. edn. Ind. U., Bloomington, 1968—; cons. to public and pvt. schs., colls., univs., state edn. depts., U.S. govt. agys. Mem. adv. bd. Work Release Center, Bloomington, 1972-75, Harmony Sch., Bloomington, 1972-79; chmn. Outdoor Ministries Task Force, Ind.-Ky. Synod, Luth. Ch. Am., 1980; telephone activist Common Cause; pres. ch. council St. Thomas Luth. Ch., Bloomington, 1980. Recipient numerous grants, 1966-81. Mem. Assn. Supervision and Curriculum Devel., Am. Ednl. Research Assn., Nat. Soc. Study Edn., NEA, Am. Fedn. Tchrs. Lutheran. Contbr. articles to various publs. Home: 411 Audubon Dr Bloomington IN 47401 Office: 337 Sch of Education Ind U Bloomington IN 47405

SMITH, GLENN LEE, chem. co. exec.; b. St. Louis, Apr. 7, 1929; s. Clifford Edward Peter and Genevieve Mary (Heesen) S.; B.M.E., U. Cin., 1952; M.B.A., Am. Internat. Coll., 1962; m. Elaine Rose Radloff, June 4, 1949; children—Richard Erwin, Barbara Ann. With Aeroproducts div. Gen. Motors Corp., Vandalia, Ohio, 1947-51; constrn. engr. Monsanto Co., Addyston, Ohio, 1952-53, devel. engr., Dayton, Ohio, 1953-54, sr. engr., engring. supr., Springfield, Mass., 1957-62, gen. mfg. supt., plant engr., Addyston, 1962-69, mgr. dist., product adminstr., dir. mfg., Resin Products div., St. Louis, 1969—, now engring. dir. environ. and energy systems. Elder, Bonhomme Presbyn. Ch., Chesterfield, Mo., 1973-76; pres. Glan Tai Homeowners Assn., Manchester, Mo., 1973-74, trustee, 1973-76; com. chmn., scoutmaster, unit commr., asst. dist. commr. Boy Scouts Am., 1972-81. Served to lt. USNR, 1954-57. Named Distinguished Engring. Alumnus, U. Cin., 1976; registered profl. engr., Ohio, Mass. Mem. ASME. Republican. Presbyn. Home: 13 Swindon Ct Manchester MO 63011 Office: 800 N Lindbergh Blvd Saint Louis MO 63167

SMITH, GLENN WILLIAM, pub. accountant; b. Major County, Okla., Dec. 10, 1908; s. Frank Henry and Pearl V. (Brown) S.; student Oklahoma City U., Hills U., 1927-30, Internat. Accounting Soc., 1930; m. Billie Jeanne Redman, Apr. 2, 1944; children—Richard G., Timothy W. Jr. accountant Bonicamp & Young, Enid, Okla., 1930-33; treas., chief accountant Central Appliance Co., also controller Midwest Maytag Co., Enid, 1933-35; sr. accountant John P. Bonicamp, Wichita, 1935-42; civilian chief accountant USAAF, Air Transport Command, 1942-45; gen. partner Bonicamp, Keolling & Smith, C.P.A.'s, Wichita, 1945-63, Bonicamp, Koelling, Smith & Farrow, 1964-69; partner Peat Marwick Mitchell & Co., 1969-71; individual C.P.A. practitioner, 1971-73; partner Smith & Russell, 1973—. Chmn., Wichita Cancer Campaign Com., 1956-58; treas., chmn. Cloudridge Community Center, 1956-66; chmn. explorer post Boy Scouts Am., 1957-58; treas. K-9 patrol Wichita Police Dept., 1956-69; treas. Wichita Crime Commn., 1969-72; mem. Tony Manhardt Inst. Speech Tng.; mem. awards jury Freedoms Found., Valley Forge, 1961. C.P.A., Kans.; hon. adm. Nebr. Navy, 1961; hon. citizen Tex., 1961; hon. mayor San Antonio, Ft. Worth, 1961; recipient Cosmopolitan Club awards, 1951, 63; others. Mem. Kans. Soc. C.P.A.'s (dir. 1957-59, pres. 1960-61, chmn. bd. 1962-64, chmn. nominating com. 1963-64, co-chmn. audit procedures com. 1969-70), Am. Inst. C.P.A.'s (mem. council 1961-62, auditing procedures com. 1965-66), Am. Assn. Oil Well Drilling Contractors, Am. Inst. Accountants (mem. council), Wichita Tennis Assn. (past treas.), C. of C., Kans. Ind., Mid-Continent oil and gas assns., Am. Accounting Assn. Methodist (auditor 1948—). Clubs: Petroleum, Toastmasters (chpt. sec.-treas. 1958, pres. 1959—), Crest View Country, Cosmopolitan Internat. (gov. Mo.-Kans. fedn. 1956-57, internat. pres. 1960-61, chmn. bd. 1962-63, chmn. past pres.'s council 1962-64); Air Capitol Cosmopolitan (past hon. pres.). Contbr. articles to profl. mags. Home: 8234 Limerick St Wichita KS 67206 Office: 1425 Vickers KSB&T Bldg Wichita KS 67202

SMITH, GLENN WILLIS, univ. adminstr.; b. Lincoln, Nebr., Feb. 6, 1931; s. Russell Blair and Mabel Luella (Combellic) S.; B.Sc., U. Nebr., 1955, M.A., 1968; m. Janet Irene Tiekotter, June 18, 1953; children—H. Bradley, David G. Staff accountant Ernst & Ernst, Chgo., 1955-57; sr. accoumtant Peat, Marwick, Mitchell & Co., Lincoln, Nebr., 1957-61; controller, sec. Benner Tea Co.. Burlington, Iowa, 1961-63; with U. Nebr., 1963-77, asst. v.p. adminstrn. Lincoln, 1972-77, vis. asst. prof. mgmt., 1973-75, vis. asst. prof. accounting, 1976-77; controller U. Minn., Mpls., 1977—. Del., Lancaster County (Nebr.) Republican. Conv., 1974, 76; bd. dirs. United Way of Lincoln/Lancaster County, 1976; bd. dirs., asst. treas. Cornhusker council Boy Scouts Am., 1977. Served with USMC, 1949-50, 51-52. C.P.A., Nebr., Minn. Mem. Soc. Advancement Mgmt. (dir., v.p. Mpls. chpt., treas. Twin City chpt. 1980-81), Minn. Soc. C.P.A.'s, Am. Inst. C.P.A.'s (discussion leader profl. devel. course), Am. Mgmt. Assn., Nebr. Soc. C.P.A.'s, Delta Sigma Pi. Presbyterian. Club: Lions (dir. Mpls. chpt. Found.). Home: 6805 Indian Hills Rd Edina MN 55435 Office: Univ Minnesota 335 Morrill Hall 100 Church St SE Minneapolis MN 55455

SMITH, GORDON CLYDE, health agy. exec.; b. Alma, Mich., Feb. 25, 1934; s. James George and Lucinda Ellen (Godwin) S.; B.A., Alma Coll., 1957; M.P.H., U. Mich., 1963; children—Steven, Patrick, Michael. Dir., Bur. of Hosp. and Community Health Services, Mich. Tech. U., Houghton, 1964-68; dir. Ohio Valley Health Services Found., Ohio U., Athens, 1968-69; exec. dir. Health Planning Council of Western Ohio, Lima, 1969-72; exec. dir. SE Tenn. Area Health Edn. Center, Chattanooga, 1972-76; exec. dir. Mich. Mid-South Health Systems Agy., Mason, 1976—; pres. Smith, Blackshear & Assos., Chattanooga, 1976—; asst. prof. Mich. State U., Coll. of Human Medicine, 1976—; chmn. bd. dirs. Clearwater Pub., Ltd., 1979—. Fellow Am. Public Health Assn., Am. Health Planning Assn., AAUP. Contbr. articles to profl. jours. Address: 528 Mason Plaza Mason MI 48854

SMITH, HAROLD FREDERICK, librarian; b. Kansas City, Mo., July 9, 1923; s. Lee Clarence and Georgia Irene (Hauptmann) S.; A.B., Park Coll., Parkville, Mo., 1944; A.M., U. Kans., 1946; A.M. in L.S., U. Denver, 1950; Ph.D., So. Ill. U., 1963; m. Carolyn Douglas, Aug. 9, 1947; children—Douglas, Gregory, Alan. Mem. library staff Kansas City Star, 1946-48, U. Denver, 1950-51, U. Nebr., 1951-52, U. No. Colo., Greeley, 1952-57, So. Ill. U., 1957-64; librarian Park Coll., 1964—; program dir. Kansas City Regional Council Higher Edn., 1970-74; project dir. Mid Am. Inter Library Services, 1974-81; cons. in field. Sec. Parkville Human Rights Commn., 1968-72; mem. bd. Presbyn. Credit Union, 1966—; mem. nominations com. Kansas City Union Presbytery, 1968-79, 81—, chmn., 1970-73. Mem. ALA, Mountain Plains Library Assn., Mo. Library Assn., Platte County Hist. Soc. (pres. 1972-73), Mo. Hist. Soc., Oral History Assn., Am. Assn. Higher Edn. Democrat. Author: American Travellers Abroad, 1969; also articles. Office: Park College Parkville MO 64152

SMITH, HARRY MORGAN, anthropologist; b. Orlando, Fla., Dec. 31, 1926; s. Claude Earle and Pearl Adelaide (Morgan) S.; B.S., Fla. State U., 1953; postgrad. Troy State U.; div.; 1 son, Charles Michael Moras. Research asso. dept. anthropology, field research Caribbean and Central Am., Fla. State U., 1952-53; supervisory research scientist USAF, Maxwell AFB, Ala., 1954-81; ret., 1981; founding v.p. Family Survival, Inc., 1981—; tchr., lectr. emergency survival, cross-cultural communications and environ. utilization planning, 1966—; dir. Fla. State U.'s Panama Archeol. and Bot. Expdn., 1952, participant Cuba Expdn., 1953; dir. Zundapp Mid-Am. Expdn., 1953-54, Peruvian Amazon River Basin Expdn., 1963; dir. family survey Ethnol. Research Expdn. Panama, Choco Indians, 1981. Served with USCG, 1944-46; PTO. Recipient Air Force decoration for exceptional civilian service, 1967, Air Force certificate of honor for outstanding service Am. MIA of PWs in S.E. Asia, 1970; named Civilian of Year, USAF, 1967, Hon. Air Commando, 1st Air Commando Wing, 1962. Mem. Soc. Applied Anthropology, Am. Polar Soc., Explorers Club, Ala. Acad. Sci., Assn. Tropical Biology, Nat. Audubon Soc., Isthmian Anthropology Soc. Author: Family Survival Shelters; Terrorism and Crime: Practical Security Measures; contbr. articles to profl. jours. Home: PO Box 2748 Ann Arbor MI 48106 Office: PO Box 344292 Coral Gables FL 33114

SMITH, HOWARD WESLEY, engr.; b. N.Y.C., Nov. 24, 1929; s. Albert Edwin and Rose Maria (Fabri) S.; B.S., Wichita State U., 1951, M.S., 1958; Ph.D., Okla. State U., 1968. Registered profl. engr., Kans. Jr. engr. Boeing Co., Wichita, Kans., 1950-52, stress analyst, 1952-55, structures engr., 1956-58, group supr., 1959-63, structures res. mgr., 1965-68, staff engr., Seattle hdqrs., 1969-70; asso. prof. U. Kans., Lawrence, 1970-74, asso. dean, 1974-76, prof., 1977—. Rocketry leader Douglas County (Kans.) 4-H Club, 1976-77. Asso. fellow Am. Inst. Aeros. and Astronautics; mem. Soc. Exptl. Stress Analysis, Air Force Hist. Found., Mid-Am. Engring. Guidance Council, Soc. Am. Mil. Engrs., Kans. Acad. Sci., Am. Soc. Engring. Edn. (chmn. aero div. 1978-79), Phi Kappa Phi. Named Outstanding Faculty Advisor of Year, Am. Inst. Aeros. and Astronautics, 1973; Outstanding Campus Activity Coordinator, Am. Soc. Engring. Edn., 1973-74; Tasker Howard Bliss medal Soc. Am. Mil. Engrs., 1974. Author: Loads, 1979; Materials & Processes, 1979; Structural Design, 1980. Contbr. articles to profl. jours. Home: 1612 Crescent Rd Lawrence KS 66044 Office: Aerospace Engring Dept U Kans Lawrence KS 66045

SMITH, HUESTON MERRIAM, cons. forensic engr.; b. Almeta, Tex., Dec. 19, 1912; s. Harry Merriam and Ruth Alice (Vasconcellos) S.; B.S. in Elec. Engring., U. Mo., Rolla, 1938; m. Edith Adele Fort, Dec. 12, 1970; 1 son, Joseph Hueston. Asst. engr., Mo. Pub. Service Commn., 1938-40; indsl. engr. Union Electric Co., St. Louis, 1947-50; chief engr. Fruin-Colnon Co., St. Louis, 1950-54; pres., Smith-Zurhelde & Associates, Inc., cons. engrs., St. Louis, 1954-65; sr. v.p. Thatcher & Patient, Inc., St. Louis, 1965-69; exec. v.p. Milling Design, Inc., St. Louis, 1955-69; prin. Hueston M. Smith & Associates, Inc., cons. engrs., St. Louis, 1969—; mem. editorial advisory bd. Cons. Engr. Mag., 1958-77; city engr. Frontenac, Mo., 1957-59. Chief of police, City of Frontenac, 1952-54. Served to col. C.E., U.S. Army, 1940-46; PTO. Decorated Bronze Star; named Hon. Asst. Dist. Engr., St. Louis Engring. Dist., U.S. Army; registered profl. engr., Mo., Tex., Kans., Ark. Mem. Cons. Engrs. Council of U.S. (pres. 1960-61, dir. 1963-64), Cons. Engrs. Mo. (pres. 1956-57, dir. 1962-63), Mo. Soc. Profl. Engrs. (Outstanding Achievement award 1962), Soc. of Am. Mil. Engrs., Res. Officers Assn. of U.S., Ret. Officers Assn., Mil. Order of World Wars, Mo. Real Estate Assn., Nat. Rifle Assn., U. Mo.-Rolla Alumni Assn., Acad. Elec. Engrs. of U. Mo., Rolla; Eta Kappa Nu. Clubs: Masons, Mo. Athletic. Editorial bd. Building Construction Mag., 1960-74. Home: 711 E Monroe Ave Saint Louis MO 63122 Office: 8460 Watson Rd Saint Louis MO 63119

SMITH, IAN MURRAY, oral surgeon; b. Toronto, Ont., Can., Mar. 11, 1924 (parents Am. citizens); s. Percy Thomas and Margaretta (Carrigan) S.; student DePaul U., 1942, U. Chgo., 1942-44, U. Ill., 1944-46; B.S., U. Detroit, 1948, D.D.S., 1952, M.S., 1955; postgrad. U. Mich., Wayne State U., 1952-55; m. Barbara Jean Moran, Aug. 15, 1953; children—Kathleen, Karen, Ian Murray, Patrick. Resident oral surgery Detroit Receiving Hosp., 1952-55; chief oral surgery Wright Patterson AFB, 1955-57; practice dentistry specializing in oral surgery, Wyandotte, Mich., 1957—; staff oral surgeon Wyandotte Gen. Hosp., Seaway Hosp., Trenton, Mich., Outer Dr. Hosp., Allen Park, Mich.; mem. teaching staff Detroit Gen. Hosp. Dir. Sailmasters of Mich.; instr. U.S. Power Squadron, 1960—, U.S. Coast Guard Aux., 1975—; pres. Sacred Heart Sch. Parent Tchrs. Orgn., 1970-71; mem. Sacred Heart-Grosse Ile Parish Council, 1972; pres. Down River br. Mich. Cancer Soc., 1977-79. Served with U.S. Army, 1942-45; to capt. USAF, 1955-57. Mem. Detroit Acad. Oral and Maxillofacial Surgeons (pres.), ADA, AMA, Wayne County Med. Soc., Internat., Am., Gt. Lakes, Mich. socs. oral and maxillofacial surgeons, Southwestern Dental Club, Blue Key, Psi Omega, Nu Sigma Nu. Clubs: Grosse Ile Yacht (dir. 1966-69), Grosse Ile Golf and Country, Grosse Ile Tennis; Offshore Racing of Detroit, River Isles Yachting, Detroit River Yachting, Grosse Ile Islanders; Great Lakes Cruising (Chgo.). Home: 28315 Elba Island Dr Grosse Ile MI 48138 Office: 1811 Fort St Wyandotte MI 48192

SMITH, JAMES DOUGLAS, architect; b. Chgo., May 14, 1943; s. Lyman Douglas and Hallie Marie (Sanders) S.; B.Arch. with honors (Lydia Bates scholar 1964-66, Schlaeder Meml. scholar 1966-67, Deeter-Ritchey-Sipple fellow 1967, A. Epstein meml. scholar 1967-68), U. Ill., 1968; certificate with honors Ecole des Beaux Arts, Fontainbleau, France, 1967; m. Anita Louise Metzger, June 24, 1967; 1 dau., Elisa Marie. Planner, Northeastern Ill. Planning Commn., Chgo., 1966, Dept. Devel. and Planning, Chgo., 1968-69; archtl. designer A. Epstein Internat., Chgo., 1969-72; architect-planner, partner Smith-Kureghian & Assos., Chgo., 1972-77; city architect City of Gary (Ind.), 1977-79; v.p. H. Seay Cantrell Assos., Inc., Architects, 1979—; planning dir. Indsl. Council/N.W. Community,

Chgo., 1972; urban planning cons. Nathan-Barnes & Assos., Chgo., 1972—; prin. works include Sheraton Hotel, Gary, Gary Hotel Renovation, Pub. Safety Bldg., Gary, Multi-Modal Transp. Center, Gary; co-designer Hyatt Regency Hotel, Chgo.; other city and comml. rehab. plans; co-author bldg. code; bd. dirs. Ind. Archtl. Found., 1981—. Precinct del. 44th Ward Assembly, Chgo., 1973—, chmn. services com., 1973-74, chmn. steering com., 1974—, campaign area chmn., 1974-76. Named an Outstanding Young Man Am., 1974; registered architect, Ill., Ind., Mich., Mo.; lic. real estate broker, Ind. Mem. AIA (sec. planning com. 1972-75), Internat. Platform Assn., Prestressed Concrete Inst., Constrn. Specifications Inst., Nat. Council Archtl. Registration Bds., Chgo. Assn. Commerce and Industry, Gargoyle Soc. (membership chmn. 1968), Scarab, Sigma Tau. Home: 1215 W Wellington St Chicago IL 60657 Office: 522 Broadway Suite 212 Gary IN 46402

SMITH, JAMES EDWIN, former retail chain exec.; b. Austin, Tex., June 10, 1916; s. James Edwin and Hattie Lee (Campbell) S.; B.S., Springfield Coll., 1939; postgrad. Tex. A&M Coll., 1943, U. Wis., Madison, 1945; Litt.D. (hon.), King Meml. Coll., 1977; m. Anita Lain, June 27, 1940; children—James Edwin III, Adrien Yvonne Smith Arnold, Lee Stanley, Annette Louise Smith Washington. Asst. dir. S.E. Settlement House, Washington, 1940; social case worker Dept. Pub. Welfare, Dallas, 1941-42; mgr. Frazier Cts., Housing Authority City of Dallas, 1942-52; owner, mgr. J.E. Smith and Co. Fire and Casualty Ins. Agy., Dallas, 1947-57; supr. mgmt. Housing Authority City of Dallas, 1952-64; merchandising and personnel exec. Sears, Roebuck and Co., Chgo., 1964-66, asst. dir. civic affairs, nat. pub. relations exec. staff, 1966-67, manpower specialist, nat. personnel hdqrs., 1967-73, dir. minority affairs and asst. dir. corp. affirmative action programs, 1973-81; ret., 1981. Com. mem. Dallas Area council Boy Scouts Am., 1944-64, dist. chmn. Chgo. Area council, 1967-72; mem. John F. Kennedy Citizens Meml. Com., Dallas, 1963-64; bd. dirs. Dallas County Community Fund, 1961-64, ARC, Chgo., 1978-81; trustee Provident Hosp., Chgo., 1972-76; bd. dirs. St. Philip's Episcopal Ch. Community Center, Dallas, 1960-64; mem. vestry St. Philip's Episcopal Ch., Dallas, 1955-64, Episcopal Ch. of Messiah, Chgo., 1978—. Served with USNR, 1945-46. Recipient commendation Disaster Shelter Com., ARC, Dallas, 1950; Disting. Achievement commendation Housing Authority City of Dallas, 1964; Disting. Citizen award Negro C. of C., Dallas, 1966. Mem. Nat. Negro Bus. League, Nat. Urban League, Nat. Assn. Market Developers, NAACP (life), Nat. Newspaper Pubs. Assn., Alpha Phi Alpha (life).

SMITH, JAMES FRANKLIN, educator; b. Ishpheming, Mich., Sept. 11, 1923; s. Claude and Tiami (Mitchell) S.; B.S., No. Mich. U., 1950; M.A., U. Mich., 1951, postgrad., 1953, 56, 57, 62; specialist in Edn. degree U. Mich., 1966; m. Elizabeth Ann Buswell, Sept. 6, 1947; children—Peggy, Barbara, Joan, Rebecca. Tchr., Madison Heights (Mich.) pub. schs., 1951-52, 56-57; tchr., dir. adult edn., coordinator coop. occupational tng. Lake Shore Pub. Schs., St. Clair Shores, Mich., 1952-56, vis. tchr. sch. social work, 1957—, now dir. spl. ednl. services. v.p. 1968-69. Served with AUS, 1943-46; ETO. Mem. Mich. Assn. Vis. Tchrs., Macomb County Vis. Tchrs. Assn. (pres. 1958-59), Mich., Macomb County (pres. 1972-73, 78-79) assns. adminstrs. spl. edn., Lake Shore Am., (treas. 1973-74) assns. sch. adminstrs., Mich. Assn. Professions. Rotarian (pres. St. Clair Shores 1962-63). Home: 23030 Euclid St St Clair Shores MI 48082 Office: 23100 Thirteen Mile Rd St Clair Shores MI 48082

SMITH, JAMES FREDRICK, broadcasting exec.; b. Joplin, Mo., Apr. 7, 1942; s. Fred W. and Margie I. (McQuality) S.; B.S., Northwestern U., 1964; m. Janet Binder, Oct. 17, 1967; children—Judson, Jeremy. Producer, dir. Sta. WGN-TV, Chgo., 1964-69; dir. adminstrn. ABC-FM, N.Y.C., 1969-72; gen. sales mgr. Sta. WDAI, Chgo., 1972-76; nat. sales mgr. ABC Radio Spot Sales, N.Y.C., 1976-78; group v.p. FM Stas., Mariner Communications, Cin., 1978-81; v.p., gen. mgr. Sta. WKQX, NBC, Chgo., 1981—. Mem. Ill. Broadcasters Assn., Radio Broadcasters Chicagoland. Office: 1700 Merchandise Mart Plaza Chicago IL 60054

SMITH, JAMES GILBERT, elec. engr., educator; b. Benton, Ill., May 1, 1930; s. Jesse and Ruby Frances Smith; B.S. in Elec. Engring., U. Mo., Rolla, 1957, M.S., 1959, Ph.D., 1967; m. Barbara Ann Smothers, July 29, 1955; 1 dau., Julie. Instr., then asst. prof. U. Mo., Rolla, 1958-66; mem. faculty So. Ill. U., Carbondale, 1966—, prof. elec. engring., 1972—, chmn. dept. elec. scis. and systems engring., 1971-80, dir. Lighting Research Lab., 1980—. Served with AUS, 1951-53; Korea. Decorated Bronze Star. Mem. IEEE, Am. Soc. Engring. Edn., AAAS. Club: Rotary. Office: Coll Engring So Ill Univ Carbondale IL 62901

SMITH, JANIETTA, univ. adminstr.; b. Little Rock, Sept. 3, 1938; d. Cecil Homer and Janietta (Ellis) Robinson; Mus.B., Lincoln U., Mo., 1960; children—Michael Lamar, Eva Lynette. Employment counselor U. Okla. Health Scis. Center, Oklahoma City, 1974-75, employment mgr., 1975-77, tng. coordinator, 1977-78; tng. mgr. U. Cin., Med. Center, 1978-80, mgr. employment and tng., 1980—, mgr. profl. recruitment, 1981—, mem. adv. com. Secretarial studies div., 1980-81. Bd. dirs. YMCA. Mem. Am. Soc. Tng. and Devel., Intergovt. Tng. Council, Cin. Personnel Assn., Alpha Kappa Kappa. Home: 605 Dewdrop Circle Apt E Cincinnati OH 45240 Office: Health Professions Bldg Eden and Bethesda Aves Cincinnati OH 45267

SMITH, JAY ALAN, educator; b. Aurora, Ill., May 2, 1952; s. Arthur Ashe and Clare (Magram) S.; B.S. in Theater Arts, Beloit Coll., 1974; M.S. in Ednl. Adminstrn., Peabody Coll., Vanderbilt U., 1979; m. Sherry Mogy, June 17, 1979. Tchr., Woodrow Wilson Sch., Niles, Ill., 1977-78, Washington Sch., Glenview, Ill., 1979, Nelson Sch., Niles, 1980, Mark Twain Sch., Des Plaines, Ill., 1981; tchr. elem. sch. E. Maine Sch. Dist. 63, Des Plaines, Ill., 1981—, Adlai E. Stevenson Sch., Des Plaines, 1981-82. Dir., E. Maine Players Theatre Group, 1976-80; dir. B.J.B.E. Judaica Youth Theatre. Mem. Assn. Supervision and Curriculum Devel., Ill. Assn. Sch. Adminstrs. Home: 8880 W Golf Rd Des Plaines IL 60016 Office: 9000 Capitol Des Plaines IL 60016

SMITH, JEANNE KELLENBERGER, speech pathologist; b. Park Ridge, Ill., Sept. 23, 1910; d. William Gaild and Georgia Mae (Esmond) Kellenberger; B.A., U. Iowa, 1933, M.A., 1937; m. Clyde H. Smith, Apr. 18, 1941; 1 dau., Mary Jeanne. Speech clinician pub. schs., Mankato, Minn., 1934-35, Beaver Dam, Wis., 1935-36; dir. speech and hearing program, Racine, Wis., 1937-39, Davenport, Iowa, 1939-41; speech and hearing cons. dept. otolaryngology Univ. Hosp., Iowa City, 1953—, asso. prof. U. Iowa, 1966—; cons. Augustana Coll. summer program, 1973—. Fellow Am. Speech and Hearing Assn.; mem. Am. Cleft Palate Assn. (mem. council 1972-75, mem. parent edn. com. 1973, edn. found. pub. edn. com. 1974-75, honors and awards com. 1975), Iowa Speech and Hearing Assn. (edn. com. 1977—), Council Speech, Hearing and Lang. Disorders Iowa (mem. council 1974-77). Alexander Graham Bell Assn., Am. Audiology Soc., Kappa Kappa Gamma. Roman Catholic. Contbr. articles to profl. jours. Office: Dept Otolaryngology Univ Hosp Iowa City IA 52242

SMITH, JEROME MICHAEL, fed. govt. ofcl.; b. Chgo., Feb. 22, 1942; s. Stanley Julian and Charlotte (Warzon) S.; B.S. in Pub. Adminstrn., Roosevelt U., 1977; Certificates in Contract Law, Adminstrn., Air Force Inst. Tech., 1970; m. Bonnie Auble, Oct. 26, 1963. Tchr. public schs., Chgo., 1962-68; def. property adminstr. Dept. Def., Indpls., 1968-72, dir. employee devel., Chgo., 1972-80, Columbus, Ohio, 1980, dep. dir. personnel, Columbus, 1981—; adj. faculty Sch. Mgmt., Columbus Inst. Tech., 1980—. Recipient Outstanding Performance award Dept. Def., 1974, 75, 76, 77, 78, 79, 81. Mem. Am. Soc. Tng. and Devel., Ill. Tng. Dirs. Assn. Republican. Roman Catholic. Contbr. articles to various publs. Office: 3990 E Broad St Columbus OH 43215

SMITH, JESSE JOHNSON, JR., acctg. and mgmt. cons. co. exec.; b. St. Louis, Dec. 31, 1954; s. Jessie Johnson and Susan (Edmondson) S.; B.S. cum laude in Bus. Adminstrn., Georgetown U., 1977. Tech. supr. H & R Block, Washington, 1977; fin. analyst Nationwide Fin. Service, St. Louis, 1977; mgr. data systems Southwestern Bell Telephone, St. Louis, 1978-80; chief exec. officer Jessie and Susan Mgmt., St. Louis, 1980—; dir., fin. chmn. Kingdom House; dir. Union Meml. Credit Union, St. Louis. Mem. Regional Commerce and Growth Assn., Nat. Assn. Black Accts., Ind. Computer Cons.'s Assn., Met. Bus. and Econ. Council, NAACP. Methodist. Club: Chez Se' Coir. Home: 2816 Abner Pl Saint Louis MO 63120 Office: 214 Morgan Laclede's Landing Saint Louis MO 63101

SMITH, JESSOP, mech. products mfg. co. exec.; b. Cleve., Oct. 23, 1933; s. Vincent Kinsman and Anne Thomas (Jessop) S.; B.S., Kent State U., 1960; m. June Evelyn Dickinson, Sept. 7, 1956; children—Kimberly Jessop, Scott Vincent. Vice pres. mfg. Aquarium Systems, Inc., Eastlake, Ohio, 1964-68, dir., 1964-68; v.p. Marine-Electro-Mech., Inc., Wickliffe, Ohio, 1968-71; pres. Triple-S Devel. Co., Inc., Wickliffe, 1976-79, Speed Sport Inc., Wickliffe. Bd. dirs. Cleve. Center on Alcoholism, 1975—; trustee Cleve. Zoo, 1977, Big Bros. Greater Cleve., 1978—. Served with AUS, 1956-58. Mem. ASME, English Speaking Union (dir. Cleve. br. 1974—, v.p. 1977-79), Great Lakes Offshore Powerboat Racing Assn. (trustee 1975—, treas. 1977—), Internat. Wine and Food Soc. (dir. Cleve. br. 1975—, pres. 1977, chmn. bd. 1978-81), Gt. Lakes Hist. Soc. (trustee 1980—), Am. Power Boat Assn. (offshore com. 1980—, offshore chmn. region VI, 1981—), Alpha Tau Omega. Republican. Episcopalian. Clubs: Kirtland Country, Union (Cleve.), Chagrin Valley Hunt, Mentor Harbor Yachting. Patentee in field. Home: Rd Gates Mills Address: County Line Rd Box 268 Gates Mills OH 44040 Office: 1450 E 289th St Wickliffe OH 44092

SMITH, JOAN KAREN, educator; b. Oak Park, Ill., Mar. 17, 1939; d. Raymond D. and Mildred D. Johnsos; B.S., U. Ill., 1961; M.S., Iowa State U., 1970, Ph.D., 1976; m. L. Glenn Smith, Aug. 7, 1971; 1 son, Jeffrey Robert. Tchr. public schs., Champaign, Ill., 1961-64, Ames, Iowa, 1964-65; instr. Des Moines Area Community Coll., 1969-70, counselor, 1970-71; teaching asst., instr. Iowa State U., 1973-76, postdoctoral fellow, 1976-78; asst. prof. founds. of edn. Ill. State U., Normal, 1978-81; asst. prof. Loyola U., Chgo., 1981—. Mem. Am. Edn]. Studies Assn. (mem. ex-officio exec. council 1977—), Orgn. Am. Historians, Comparative and Internat. Edn. Soc., Delta Kappa Gamma (pres. chpt. 1976-78). Club: Lakeside Country (Bloomington, Ill.). Editor: (with L. Glenn Smith) The Development of American Education: Selected Readings, 1976; Ella Flagg Young: Portrait of a Leader, 1979. Mng. editor Ednl. Studies, 1977-79, editor, 1979-81. Office: Water Tower Campus Loyola U 820 N Michigan Ave Chicago IL 60611

SMITH, JOHN WILLIAM, polit. scientist; b. Jamestown, N.D., Oct. 31, 1938; s. John William and Lena R. (Jordheim) S.; A.A., U. N.D., 1958; B.A., Northwestern U., 1960; M.A., U. Mich., 1963; m. Therese AL Hout, Nov. 22, 1980. Instr., U. Detroit, 1962-63, No. Mich. U., 1965-67; asst. prof. Indiana (Pa.) U., 1967-69; adj. prof. U. Detroit, 1970—; vis. lectr. U. Mich., Dearborn, 1975-80; instr. polit. sci. Henry Ford Community Coll., Dearborn, 1969—; pres. Aquatic Environ. Consultants, Inc., Southfield, Mich., 1981—. Mem. Am. Polit. Sci. Assn., So. Polit. Sci. Assn., Western Polit. Sci. Assn., Assn. for Asian Studies, Mich. Conf. Polit. Sci. Contbr. chpts. to Riot in the Cities, 1970; City-Surburban Relations, 1979. Contbr. articles to profl. jours. Home: 21652 N Riverview Ct Birmingham MI 48010 Office: Henry Ford Community Coll Dearborn MI 48128 also PO Box 2407 Southfield MI 48034

SMITH, JOSEPH WAYNE, automotive aftermarket co. exec.; b. Lamar, Mo., Oct. 16, 1935; s. Joseph Preston and Kathryn (Hastings) S.; student S.W. Mo. State U., 1954-56, Dallas Inst., Gupton Jones Coll. Mortuary Sci., 1957-58; m. Mary Jo Inbody, Nov. 21, 1959; children—Connie Lynne, Elizabeth Ann. Apprentice embalmer Blackman Funeral Home, 1959-60; staff embalmer and funeral dir. Speaks Funeral Home, Independence, Mo., 1960-65; sales rep. Jones & Herald Office Equipment, Independence, 1965-70; v.p., gen. Midwest Rebuilders, Inc., Kansas City, Mo., 1970—. Club: Sunrise Optimist. Office: 1402 Winchester Kansas City MO 64126

SMITH, KENNETH GAYLE, govt. ofcl.; b. Newport News, Va., Apr. 28, 1944; s. John Thomas and Lucille Mae (Oaks) S.; B.S. in Bus. Adminstrn., Old Dominion U., Norfolk, Va., 1970; m. Diane L. Reid, June 26, 1971; children—Pamela Lynn, Kathleen Gayle. With VA, 1970—, liaison officer N.Y. region, 1976-77, chief field ops. Ill. region, Chgo., 1977—. Treas., Logewhego Nation of Indian Princesses, 1981-82. Served with U.S. Army, 1965-68; Vietnam. Decorated Army Commendation medal; recipient U.S. Govt. Public Service medal, 1971. Mem. Glendale Heights Jaycees (pres. 1979-80). Home: 283 Hillside Ave Glen Ellyn IL 60137 Office: 536 S Clark St Chicago IL 60611

SMITH, KENNETH LELAND, clergyman, social worker; b. Hong Kong, China, Apr. 21, 1924; s. Albert Ray and Verona Martha (Kreider) S.; A.B., Denison U., 1949; postgrad. U. Chgo., 1950-51; M.Div., Colgate Rochester Div. Sch., 1956; M.S. in Social Work, U. Wis., 1965; m. Phyllis Grace Vander Plaats, Aug. 16, 1952; children—Cheri, Grantley, Andrew, Kermit. Ordained to ministry, Bapt. Ch., 1956; pastor asst. First Bapt. Ch., Weirton, W.Va., 1951-52, Greece Bapt. Ch., Rochester, N.Y., 1955-56; chaplain, social worker Weirton Christian Center, 1951-52; pastor Mumford First Bapt. Ch., N.Y., 1953-54, Hulburt Bapt. Ch., Milw., 1958-61; exec. dir. Milw. Christian Center, 1958—. Founder, Inner City Youth Service Agys., United Community Center; founder Southeast Community Center, 1968—, mem. council, 1977-79; mem. Neighborhood Centers Council, Milw., 1968-79, Neighborhood Improvement Project Council, 1976-79; chmn. Walkers Point Improvement Council, 1958-61, Joint Drug Program Council, 1975-79; founder Centro de la Comunidad Unida and Latin Am. Union for Civil Rights; active United Way Speakers Bur., 1960-70. Served with U.S. Army, 1943-46. NIMH grantee, 1964-65. Mem. Nat. Assn. Social Workers, Nat. Conf. Social Welfare, Common Cause, Greater Milw. Clergy, Southside Clergy, South Community Orgn., Denison Commons Club, Alpha Delta Phi. Democrat. Home: 1230 S 29th St Milwaukee WI 53215 Office: 2137 W Greenfield Ave Milwaukee WI 53204

SMITH, LAWRENCE EDWARD, ednl. adminstr.; b. Detroit, May 1, 1928; s. Harry Lawrence and Vergual Charllote (Freer) S.; B.S., Eastern Mich. U., 1954; M.A., U. Mich., 1957; postgrad. Mich. State U., 1970-72, Central Mich. U., 1968-81; m. Agnes Ann Patterson, July 11, 1953; children—John Lawrence, David Wendell, Margaret Ann. Classroom tchr. Royal Oak (Mich.) Public Sch., 1954-60; elem. sch. prin. Brighton (Mich.) Area Sch., 1960-68; dep. sec. Mich. Assn. Sch. Bds., East Lansing, Mich., 1966-68; elem. sch. prin. Mount Pleasant (Mich.) Public Schs., 1968—; asso. prof. ednl. adminstrn. Central Mich. U., Mount Pleasant, 1971—. Mem. dist. council Boy Scouts Am., 1970-72. Served with USN, 1946-47, 50-52. Mem. Nat. Assn. Elem. Prins., Nat. Assn. Curriculum Developers, Nat. Assn. Tchr. Trainers, Mich. Assn. Middle Sch. and Elem. Prins., Mich. Assn. Curriculum Developers, Mich. Assn. Tchr. Trainers, Isabella County Child Devel. Assn. (v.p.), Ducks Unltd. (treas. 1979—), Phi Delta Kappa. Methodist. Clubs: Rotary East (pres. 1979), (Mount Pleasant, Mich.); Isabella County 4-H, Masons. Editor Mich. Sch. Bd. Jour., 1966-68. Office: 101 S Adams St Mount Pleasant MI 48858

SMITH, LAWRENCE NORVAL, former meat packing co. exec.; b. Alden, Kans., Sept. 12, 1920; s. Chris Clark and Eleanor Susan (Colwell) S.; m. Helen Geneva Fox, Aug. 5, 1939; children—Geneva Ferne Smith Barrington, Lawrence Allie, Steven Craig, Eddie Lee. With Winchester Packing Co., Hutchinson, Kans., 1940-81, supt., 1950-72, v.p., plant mgr., 1972-81, also dir.; ret., 1981. Bd. dirs. Hutchingson Safety Council, 1958-63. Served with AUS, 1945-46. Mem. Hutchinson C. of C. Republican. Home: 708 W 22d St Hutchinson KS 67501

SMITH, LINDA, fed. govt. ofcl.; b. Tachikawa, Japan, July 23, 1952; d. Howard Ira and Michiko (Yostaki) S. (father Am. citizen); B.S. (Cook's Trust scholar), Ball State U., 1975, M.Public Adminstrn., 1978. Community devel. specialist Region 6 Planning and Devel. Commn., Indpls., 1975-77; social worker div. for handicapped Ind. Bd. Health, 1977-78; presdl. mgmt. intern Army Fin. and Acctg. Center, Indpls., 1978-80; computer systems analyst, regional office U.S. Dept. Agr. Forest Service, Indpls., 1980—. Active Muncie-Delaware Community Services council, 1975, Wayne County Community Welfare Council, 1978. Mem. Am. Soc. Public Adminstrn., Acad. Polit. Sci. Democrat. Home: 3408 Alsuda Ct Apt G Indianapolis IN 46205

SMITH, LOREN MITCHELL, wire mfg. co. exec.; b. Cleve., Jan. 30, 1943; s. Robert H. and Janet (Lebby) S.; B.S., Miami U., Ohio, 1964; M.B.A., Northeastern U., 1974; m. Gloria Goetze, June 15, 1976; children—Bradley, David. Sales engr., Standard Pressed Steel, 1964-66; with Texas Instruments, Attleboro, Mass., 1966-75, product mgr., 1972-73, div. gen. mgr., 1973-75; v.p., gen. mgr. Augat Co., Attleboro, 1975-76; pres. Monona Wire Corp. (Iowa), 1976—. Home: 812 Maple St Decorah IA 52101 Office: Monona Wire Corp Old State Rd Decorah IA 52101

SMITH, LOUIS ADRIAN, lawyer; b. Lansing, Mich., Apr. 22, 1939; s. John Paul and Marjorie (Christmas) S.; B.A. in Communication Arts cum laude, Mich. State U., 1962; J.D. (univ. scholar), U. Mich., 1965; m. Karen Terry Emens, Feb. 5, 1966; children—Timothy Paul, Patrick Louis, Elizabeth Karen. Mem. labor relations staff Gen. Motors Corp., Detroit, 1963-65; admitted to Mich. bar, 1965; practiced in Lansing, 1965-75, Traverse City, Mich., 1975—; partner firm Fowler & Smith, 1965-67; partner firm, Doyle, Smith, Whitmer & Carruthers, 1967-75, pres., 1970-75; partner firm Smith & Johnson, Traverse City, 1975—; part-owner Estes Furniture Co., Lansing; co-founder Thomas M. Cooley Sch. Law, Lansing, 1st v.p., sec., 1972-75, pres., 1975—. Bd. dirs., also a founder Mich. Montessori Internat. Sch., Okemos, Mich. Mem. Am., D.C., Ingham County (dir. 1972—), Fed. bar assns., Am. Judicature Soc., Am. Trial Lawyers Assn., State Bar of Mich., Nat. Assn. Accountants, Phi Delta Phi. K.C. Office: 607 Bay St Traverse City MI 49684

SMITH, LUCILLE ELEANOR, educator; b. Osterdock, Iowa, Mar. 5, 1918; d. Harry J. and Lucille (Nolte) Hansel; R.N., Moline (Ill.) Public Hosp. Sch. Nursing, 1941; B.S. in Nursing, Marycrest Coll., 1965; grad. student U. No. Iowa, 1978-80. Nurse, Med. Div., Rock Island (Ill.) Arsenal, 1941-45; staff nurse Moline Public Hosp., 1958-61; head nurse St. Anthony's Hosp., Rock Island, Ill., 1961-67; instr. Northeast Iowa Tech. Inst., Calmar, 1968—; instr. Practical nurse and A.S. degree nursing, 1965—; nurse cons. Community Colls., Ithaca, N.Y., Pitts. Sec. bd. trustees Palmer Meml. Hosp., West Union, Iowa. Mem. Iowa Nurses Assn. (pres. Dist. 14 1969-73), Am. Nurses Assn., Am. Vocat. Assn., Iowa Vocat. Assn., Iowa Higher Edn. Assn. Methodist. Clubs: Order Eastern Star, West Union Country. Home: 103 1/2 N Vine St West Union IA 52175 Office: Northeast Iowa Tech Inst Box 400 Calmar IA 52132

SMITH, LYNN HOWARD, mfg. co. exec.; b. Ft. Wayne, Ind., Mar. 9, 1936; s. Lester Earl and Catherine Lois (McCurdy) S.; student Ind.-Purdue U. Extension, Ft. Wayne, 1956-57; grad. Internat. Harvester Tech. Sch., 1961; m. Jean Marie Bauman, Sept. 2, 1955; children—Julie, Linnett, Jeffery, Lisa. Methods engr. Jervis Corp., Grandville, Mich., 1964-67; project engr. Twigg Industries, Martinsville, Ind., 1967-70; project engr. Tri Industries, Terre Haute, Ind., 1970-74; tool and mfg. engr. Berko Electric Mfg. Co., Peru, Ind., 1974-77, fabrication supt., 1977-78, mgr. mfg. engring., 1978-79, plant supr., 1979; chief project engr. Tube Processing Corp., Indpls., 1979—; cons. Groteness Machine Works, Chgo. Pres. Harlan (Ind.) Days Assn., 1962; adv. Jr. Achievement, Terre Haute, Ind., 1972-73. Named Jr. Achievement Adv. of Yr., Terre Haute Jr. Achievement, 1973. Methodist. Clubs: Berko Mgmt., Masons (Harlan lodge master 1964), Shriners. Developed proprietary spot welding process and equipment, 1966, proprietary high temperature brazing process, 1970-74; developer, editor Berko Electric Mfg. Procedures Man., 1975-79. Home: Rural Route 1 Box 269-A Peru IN 46970 Office: 1401 S Harding St Indianapolis IN

SMITH, LYNWOOD HERBERT, JR., physician; b. Kansas City, Mo., Aug. 2, 1929; s. Lynwood H. and Arline Estel (Chandler) S.; B.S. in Bus., U. Kans., 1951, M.D., 1960; m. Margery Davis Waddell, Dec. 15, 1951; children—Michael Chandler, Katherine Ann, Phillip Waddell, Martha Lynn. Intern, Met. Gen. Hosp., Cleve., 1960-61; resident in medicine Mayo Grad. Sch., Rochester, Minn., 1961-64; research fellow in medicine Johns Hopkins Sch. Medicine, Balt., 1964-65; fellow in nephrology Mayo Grad. Sch. Medicine, 1965, instr. in medicine, 1968-70, asst. prof. internal medicine, 1970-73; practice medicine specializing in internal medicine, Rochester, 1965—; dir. Stone Clinic, Mayo Clinic, 1966-74, mem. mineral research unit, 1972—; asso. prof. internal medicine Mayo Med. Sch., 1974-77, prof. internal medicine, 1977—; dir. Urolithiasis Research Lab., Mayo Clinic, 1966—, asst. chmn. nephrology research com., 1972—, mem. clin. study unit com., 1975—, mem. research com., 1977—; cons. internal medicine and nephrology Mayo Clinic and Mayo Found., 1965—; chmn. 4th Internat. Symposium on Urolithiasis Research, Williamsburg, Va., 1980; sec. sci. adv. bd. Nat. Kidney Found., 1979—. Served with USN, 1952-56. Recipient Postgrad. Travel award Mayo Grad. Sch., 1965; NIH grantee, 1968—. Mem. Internat. Soc. Nephrology, Am. Soc. Nephrology, A.C.P., Central Soc. Clin. Research, Am. Fedn. Clin. Research, N.Y. Acad. Scis., Sigma Xi, Alpha Omega Alpha, U. Kans. Alumni Assn., Mayo Alumni Assn.

Republican. Episcopalian. Author: (with others) Urolithiasis: Physical Aspects, 1972, Urolithiasis Research, 1976; contbr. numerous articles in nephrology to profl. jours. and chpts. to med. texts. Home: 4912 Weatherhill Dr Rochester MN 55901 Office: 200 1st St Southwest Rochester MN 55901

SMITH, MARION LEIGH, hosp. ofcl.; b. Pontiac, Mich., June 9, 1928; d. Guy Chester and Anna Louise (Griffith) S.; student Garland Jr. Coll., 1946-47, Wayne U., 1950. Asst. buyer, buyer, store mgr. J.L. Hudson Co., Detroit, 1948-54, Bullock's, Inc., Los Angeles, 1954-60, Malcolm Brock Co., Bakersfield, Calif., 1960-66, Holman's, Pacific Grove, Calif., 1967-68, Vegod Corp., Hayward, Calif., 1968-73; field rep., office coordinator of vols. Am. Cancer Soc., Pasadena, 1973-74; dir. vol. services Flower Hosp.-Crestview Center, Sylvania, Ohio, 1976—. Vol. aide Orthopedic Hosp., Detroit, 1943-46; mem. Jr. League, 1948—; vol. interviewer and trainer Community Hosp., Monterey, Calif., 1967-68; crusade chmn. publicity chmn., bd. dirs. Am. Cancer Soc., Merced, Calif., 1971-73; vol. worker Hollywood Presbyn. Med. Center, Los Angeles, 1974-76; mem. com. Hospice N.W. Ohio, 1979—; mem. health occupations adv. bd. Bedford-Mason Schs., 1978—; mem. exec. bd. Ret. Sr. Vol. Program, Toledo, 1979; stewardship chmn. Epworth United Meth. Ch., 1981. Mem. Am. Hosp. Assn., Women Involved in Toledo, Ohio Hosp. Assn., Sigma Gamma. Club: Toledo Woman's. Home: 3913 Sheffield Ct Toledo OH 43623 Office: Flower Hosp-Crestview Center 5200 Harroun Rd Sylvania OH 43560

SMITH, MARLENE ANN, mfg. co. exec.; b. St. Paul, Oct. 6, 1935; d. Edgar Leonard and Luella Johanna (Rahn) Johnson; widow; children—Rick, Debora, Ronald, Lori, Carlson. Bookkeeper Jeans Implement Co., Forest Lake, Minn., 1952-53, part-time bookkeeper, 1953-57; bookkeeper Great Plains Supply, St. Paul, 1960-62; bookkeeper Plastic Products Co., Inc., Lindstrom, Minn., 1962-75, pres., chief exec. officer, 1975—. Bookkeeper, Trinity Lutheran Ch., Lindstrom, 1976—. Mem. Nat. Assn. Women Bus. Owners, Soc. Plastic Engrs. Home: 28940 Olinda Trail Lindstrom MN 55045 Office: 30355 Akerson St Lindstrom MN 55045

SMITH, MARY ANN E., social worker; b. Chgo., Jan. 28, 1940; d. Frank J. and Alice Chuman; M.S.W., Loyola U., Chgo., 1968. Asso. prof. social sci. Ottumwa Heights Coll., 1962-65; asso. prof. social sci. Marycrest Coll., 1965-66; social work supr. Mercy Hosp. and Med. Center, Chgo., 1968-71, dir. dept. patient and family counseling, 1971—. Recipient Nat. Inst. Mental Health grant, 1966-67, 67-68. Mem. Nat. Soc. Hosp. Social Work Dirs., No. Ill. Hosp. Social Work Dirs., Southwest Hosp. Social Work Dirs., Internat. Soc. Prevention of Child Abuse, Acad. Cert. Social Workers (cert.), Nat. Registry Clin. Social Workers, Kappa Gamma Pi. Office: Dept Patient and Family Counseling Mercy Med Center Stevenson Expressway at King Dr Chicago IL 60616

SMITH, MARY LUCY, educator; b. Richland, Ga., Dec. 12, 1940; d. Charles and Odessa Lucille (Mathis) Martin; B.A., St. Xavier Coll., 1973; postgrad. Governor State U., 1973-75. Tchr., Crispus Attucks Elementary Sch., Chgo., 1973—. Mem. profl. women aux. Provident Hosp., 1973-77, corr. sec., 1975-76, installation chmn., 1977; mem. civic aux. Planned Parenthood, Chgo., 1975—, social chmn., 1976-77, corr sec., 1977; mem. Parish Council Bd., St. Thaddeus Ch., 1978—; mem. nomination com. Women of 21st Ward Democratic Orgn., 1979. Address: 9722 S Yale Ave Chicago IL 60628

SMITH, MAUREEN SHEILA MOSIER, ednl. adminstr.; b. Albuquerque, Jan. 4, 1950; d. Donald Maxwell and Grace Elizabeth (McCarthy) M.; B.S., U. N.Mex., Albuquerque, 1972, M.A., 1976; Ed.S., Va. Poly. Inst. and State U., 1979; m. Clifton Lee Smith, Aug. 7, 1976. Reservationist, Sheraton Western Skies, Albuquerque, 1968-70; asst. front office mgr. Hilton Inn, Albuquerque, 1970-73; tchr. bus. Albuquerque Public Schs., 1972-76; adminstrv. asst. to dir. curriculum and instrn. div. Va. Poly. Inst. and State U., Blacksburg, 1976-77; tchr. bus. Pulaski County Schs., Dublin, Va., 1977-79. Named Adviser of Yr., Jr. Achievement, 1973. Mem. Columbia C. of C. program coordinator adult edn. Columbia (Mo.) Public Schs. 1979—. Mem. Am. Soc. Tng. and Devel., Am. Bus. Women's Assn., Mo. Vocat. Assn., Mo. Assn. Adult and Continuing Edn., Am. Vocat. Assn. Home: 4503 Georgetown Dr Columbia MO 65201 Office: 1104 N Providence St Columbia MO 65201

SMITH, MICHAEL, univ. dean; b. St. Joseph, Mo., Jan. 30, 1941; s. Walton J. and Margaret D. (Chubb) S.; A.S. in Bus., Mo. Western Community Coll., 1960; B.S.Ed., N.E. Mo. State U., 1967; M.A. candidate Mankato State U., 1969; Ph.D., U. Nebr., 1975; m. Connie I. Smith, Nov. 27, 1965; children—Jeffrey, Timothy. Mgmt. specialist U.S. Army, 1960-63; ins. investigator Retail Credit Co., St. Joseph and Trenton, Mo., 1963-65; tchr., Ill. and Iowa, 1967-69; prof. English, Albany (Ga.) Jr. Coll., 1975-78; chmn. Arts and Scis. Div., U. Minn., Crookston, 1978-80; dean N.D. State U., Bottineau, 1980—; cons., project evaluator Minn. Humanities Commn., 1979-80; evaluator AID, 1979-80. Served with U.S. Army, 1960-63. Nat. Endowment Humanities grantee, 1979-80; Minn. Humanities Commn., N.W. Regional Commn. grantee, 1979-80; U. Minn. Internat. Devel. grantee, 1980. Mem. Am. Assn. Higher Edn., C. of C. Clubs: Lions, Logrollers, Quarterback. Home: Route 1 Bottineau ND 58318 Office: ND State U Bottineau ND 58318

SMITH, MICHAEL ROLAND, engring. co. exec.; b. Grantsburg, Wis., Oct. 23, 1938; s. Charles D. and Bernice Ann (Hjort) S.; B.A., U. Minn., 1960. Dist. sales mgr. trainee Rose Chem. Products Co., Columbus, Ohio, 1965-66; co-founder, co-operater Chardon Labs., Inc., Columbus, 1966—, also Weatherator Engring. Co. div., 1976—. Chmn. coordinator Jr. Achievement, 1976-77; fin. chmn. Boy Scouts Am., 1978-79. Served with USCG, 1960-64. Recipient Contbns. award Distbv. Edn. Clubs Am., 1976-77. Mem. Chem. Splty. Mfg. Assn., Internat. San. Supply Assn., Aircraft Owners and Pilots Assn., Pi Sigma Epsilon. Republican. Lutheran. Clubs: Sales Exec. Columbus (dir.), Masons, Highlands Golf, Hideway Hills, Flying Nobles. Home: 8948 Chevington Chase St Pikerington OH 43147 Office: 539 Stimmel Rd PO Box 1004 Columbus OH 43216

SMITH, MILDRED TAYLOR, psychologist; b. Arcadia, Kans., Nov. 22, 1911; d. James Newton and Nora Ellen (Rollen) Taylor; A.A., Horner Conservatory Music, Kansas City, Mo., 1926-28; B.S., Kans. State Coll., Salina, 1928-32; A.B., Marymount Coll., 1958; M.Ed., Xavier U., Cin., 1962; postgrad. U. Kans., U. Cin., U. Ill.; m. Linus B. Smith, Apr. 1, 1932 (dec.); 1 dau., Mildred A. Ednl. asso. Social Hygiene Soc., Cin., 1958-61; dean, headmistress Fairfax Hall, Waynesboro, Va., 1961-65; project dir. William A. Mitchell Center, Cin., 1965-68, exec. dir., psychologist, 1968—. Mem. personnel com. Cin. Metropolitan YWCA, 1976—; mem. mgmt. bd. and adv. bd. Edgecliff Coll., Cin., 1976—; mem. Women's State Com. Ohio, Jewish Community Center Forum. Fellow Royal Soc. Health (London), Am. Orthopsychiat. Assn., Am. Public Health Assn., Soc. Public Health Educators; mem. Internat. Union Health Edn., Am. Psychol. Assn., Nat. Rehab. Counseling Assn., Southwestern Psychol. Assn., Southwestern Ohio Rehab. Assn., Ohio Public Health Assn., Ohio Rehab. Counseling Assn., Ohio Psychol. Assn., Ohio Assn. Community Mental Health Adminstrs., Delta Kappa Gamma, Nat. Fedn. Music Clubs (life), Kans. Congress Parents and Tchrs. (life), DAR (past regent Indian Hill chpt.). Clubs: Women's City (Cin.), Cincinnati, Medi-Club, Inc. Home: 1410 Springfield Pike 53D Cincinnati OH 45215 Office: 2517 Burnet Ave Cincinnati OH 45219

SMITH, MURRAY EUGENE, tool engr.; b. Ann Arbor, Mich., Sept. 5, 1933; s. Murray J.A. and Juliette J. (Wines) S.; student Mich. State U., 1955-56, U. Mich., 1956-57, Eastern Mich. U., 1957-58, Detroit Coll. Applied Sci., 1958-59; m. Gertrude E. Wente; children—Bradley E., Leslie E. Plant mgr. Ann Arbor (Mich.) Machinery Co., 1956-73; pres. Pinnacle Engring. Co., Inc., Manchester, Mich., 1973—; co-chmn. bd. dirs. Ultraspherics, Inc., 1979—. Served with U.S. Army, 1951-53; Korea. Mem. Soc. Mfg. Engrs. Office: 617 City Rd Manchester MI 48158

SMITH, NEAL EDWARD, congressman; b. Hedrick, Iowa, Mar 23, 1920; s. James N. and Margaret M. (Walling) S.; student U. Mo., 1945-46, Syracuse U., 1946-47; LL.B., Drake U., 1950; m. Beatrix Havens, Mar. 23, 1945; children—Douglas, Sharon. Farmer, Iowa, 1937—; admitted to Iowa bar, 1950; practiced in Des Moines, 1950—; atty. 50 sch. bds. in Iowa, 1953—; asst. county atty. Polk County, Iowa, 1951; mem. 86th-92d Congresses from 5th Dist. Iowa, 93d-97th Congresses from 4th Dist. Iowa. Chmn. Polk County Bd. Social Welfare, 1954-56; pres. Young Democratic Clubs Am., 1953-55. Served with AUS, World War II. Decorated Air medal with 4 oak leaf clusters, Purple Heart. Mem. Am. Bar Assn., Farm Bur., Farmers Union., DAV. Club: Masons. Office: 2373 Rayburn House Office Bldg Washington DC 20515

SMITH, NORMAN JOHN, educator; b. Chgo., Sept. 26, 1945; s. John Henry and Nona Louise (Bateman) S.; B.S., Ill. State U., 1968; M.S., Eastern Ill. U., 1971; M.S., No. Ill. U.; m. Etta Hall, June 26, 1968; children—Renae and Genae (twins). Tchr., Forrestville High Sch., Chgo. Public Schs., 1968-70; tchr. computer sci. Larkin Sr. High Sch., Elgin, Ill., 1971-79; asst. prof. info. systems and computer programming dept. Purdue U.-Calumet, Hammond, Ind., 1979—. Mem. Assn. Computing Machinery, Ill. Assn. Ednl. Data Systems, AAUP, Sigma Pi Sigma. Democrat. Baptist. Home: 809 Academy Ave Matteson IL 60443 Office: Purdue U Calumet 2233 171st St Hammond IN 46323

SMITH, PAULINE ROSALEE, ednl. adminstr.; b. Lawton, Okla., July 16, 1928; d. Robert Paul and Elsie (Tahkofper) Chaat; A.A., Cameron State U., 1948; B.S., Okla. State U., 1950, M.S., 1960; m. Clodus R. Smith, June 25, 1950; children—Martha Lynn, William Paul, Paula Diane. Tchr., public schs., Bradley, Okla., 1950-52, Booker, Tex., 1953-54, Candor, N.Y., 1957-59, Silver Spring Md., Burtonsville, Md., 1961-74; project mgr. Indian Edn. Services, Cleveland City Schs., 1977—; vis. instr. Cleve. State U., 1978—. Bd. dirs. Women Space, 1977-81, Council Econ. Opportunity, Cleve., 1981—; mem. ACCESS bd. Cuyahoga Community Coll.; chmn. Lau Adv. Task Force Cleve. City Schs., 1979-80. Recipient Career Woman of Achievement award Cleve. YWCA, 1979. Mem. AAUW (pres. Cleve. 1981), Indian Edn. Assn. Ohio (pres. 1981), Nat. Indian Edn. Assn., Citizens League Cleve., Assn. Childhood Edn., Assn. Supervision and Curriculum Devel., Phi Delta Kappa. Democrat. Methodist. Clubs: Zonta, Womens City Home: 3174 Onaway Rd Shaker Heights OH 44120 Office: 4200 Bailey Ave Cleveland OH 44113

SMITH, PETER LANG, aviation co. exec.; b. Paterson, N.J., Mar. 25, 1930; s. Peter and Louise (Lang) S.; B.Ed. with honors U. Nebr., 1965, M.S., U. So. Calif., 1968; m. Vera Marie Elkins, Nov. 2, 1954; 1 son, Dana Lang. Enlisted U.S. Air Force, 1951, commd. 2d. lt., 1953, advanced through grades to col., 1974; ret., 1979; aircraft comdr. SAC KC-97 and KC-135, Castle AFB, Calif., 1962-63, instr. SAC combat crew tng. crew, 1963-70, ops. officer, also comdr. rescue helicopter unit Korea, 1971-72; comdr. SAC air refueling squadron, Westover AFB, 1972-73; dep. comdr. ops. 384th. Air Refueling Wing, McConnell AFB, Kans., 1973-79; v.p., gen. mgr. Midwest Piper Flight, Inc., Wichita, 1979—. Decorated Air medal. Mem. Am. Mgmt. Assn., Am. Def. Preparedness Assn., Mensa. Clubs: Masons, Shriners. Home: 2483 N Belmont St Wichita KS 67220 Office: PO Box 8067 Munger Sta Wichita KS 67208

SMITH, PHILLIP, banker; b. English, Ind., Nov. 11, 1934; s. Gerald M. and Lucille (Tucker) S.; B.S. in Mktg., Ind. U., 1956; m. Joan Bennett, Dec. 23, 1955; children—Phillip Samuel, Stephanie Smith Scott. Sec.-treas. Smith Motors Corp., 1956-66; asst. cashier Orange County Bank, 1966-73; organizer 1st Nat. Bank of Paoli (Ind.), 1973-76, chmn. bd., pres., 1976—. Trustee Town of Paoli, 1959; mem. Paoli Community Schs. Bd. Edn., 1969—, pres., 1972-73; pres. Paoli Econ. Devel. Commn., 1977—; mem. Paoli Library Bd., 1969-73; elder Paoli Christian Ch., 1963—. Named Ky. col., 1976. Mem. Ind. Bankers Assn. (exec. com. 1978), Paoli C. of C. (pres. 1967-68, 77-78). Club: Masons. Home: 238 E Thornton St Paoli IN 47454 Office: 215 W Main St Paoli IN 47454

SMITH, PHYLLIS ALYSE, edn. coordinator; b. Dayton, Ohio, Jan. 7, 1926; d. Harold Hamlin and Georgia Alice (Williams) Shaw; B.Ed., U. Dayton, 1960; m. Lee Wilford Smith, May 5, 1947, (dec.); children—Patricia Antoinette, Christi Collette. Clk., Wright-Patterson AFB, Ohio, 1947-54; sec., bookkeeper Atlantic Bldrs., Inc., Dayton, 1954-58; tchr. Dayton Bd. Edn., 1960-73; edn. coordinator Dayton Newspapers, Inc., 1973—, mem. Jour. Herald Newspaper in Edn. Program; mem. Area XI Right to Read Com., Mem. Nat. Council Tchrs. English, Nat. Council Social Studies Ohio, Assn. of Supervision and Curriculum Devel., Career Guidance Inst., NAACP, Urban League, Alpha Kappa Alpha. Episcopalian. Clubs: Order Eastern Star, Nat. Epicureans Inc. Home: 1505 Bryn Mawr Dr Dayton OH 45406 Office: Dayton Newspapers Inc 37 S Ludlow St Dayton OH 45402

SMITH, PRISCILLA DEAN, constrn. co. exec.; b. Hammond, Ind., Nov. 25, 1935; d. David Dean and Mary Eleanor (Morrison) Wightman; ed. Shimer Coll., Mt. Carroll, Ill., 1953; m. Donald Dean Smith, Apr. 1, 1954; children—Todd Morrison, Susan Kimberly, Debra Dean. Trainee, Todd Co., Peoria, Ill., 1959-64, v.p., Lombard, Ill., 1965-71; asst. to pres. Hasco Tank Erectors, Inc., Lombard, 1971-72, pres., 1972—, chmn. bd., 1976—; dir. I.B. Systems, Inc., Hinsdale, Ill. Mem. Steel Plate Fabricators Assn. Unitarian. Home: 1061 Daniel Ct Lombard IL 60148 Office: 20 W 603 Glen Ct Lombard IL 60148

SMITH, RANDY PAUL, savs. and loan assn. exec.; b. La Porte, Ind., Oct. 27, 1950; s. Paul F. and Ferne R. S.; B.S., Ind. State U., 1973; M.B.A., U. Wis., 1979. Regional indsl. relations mgr. Rich Products, Buffalo, 1975-78; v.p. personnel First Savs. Assn. of Wis., Milw., 1979—. Mem. adv. bd. Milw. Area Schs. Bus. Edn. Com. Mem. Am. Soc. Personnel Adminstrs., Am. Soc. Tng. and Devel., Personnel and Indsl. Relations Assn., Human Resource Planning Soc. Office: 250 E Wisconsin Ave Milwaukee WI 53202

SMITH, RAYMOND GARFIELD, ins. co. exec.; b. Columbus, Ohio, Nov. 20, 1916; s. Raymond Garfield and Nelle Dorbert (Richie) S.; student Ohio State U., Franklin U., Columbus, Ohio, Case Inst. Tech.; m. Louise Lenora Patton, Nov. 3, 1939; children—David R., Donald R., Barbara Louise Smith Belknap. With Nationwide Ins. Cos., Columbus, 1937—, sr. v.p. fin. Nationwide Mut. Ins. Co., Nationwide Mut. Fire Ins. Co., Nationwide Gen. Ins. Co., Nationwide Life Ins. Co., Nationwide Property and Casualty Ins. Co., Nationwide Variable Life Ins. Co., Automotive Recycling Center, Inc., Nationwide Found., Nationwide Premium Accounts, Inc., Nationwide Profl. Services, Inc., Nationwide Transport, Inc. Served with U.S. Army, 1943-46. Recipient Outstanding Alumnus of Year award Franklin U., 1978. Mem. Am. Mgmt. Assn., Fin. Exec. Inst., Treasurers Club of Columbus Area C. of C. Methodist. Home: 1280 Fountaine Dr Columbus OH 43221 Office: 1 Nationwide Plaza Columbus OH 43216

SMITH, RICHARD BUTLER, clergyman, educator; b. Laurel, Miss., Sept. 26, 1923; s. George Washington and Winnie Mae (Sellers) S.; diploma Clarke Coll., 1945; B.A., Miss. Coll., 1947; B.D., New Orleans Bapt. Theol. Sem., 1960, Th.D., 1968; m. Nina Lucile Hutchison, Mar. 1, 1942; children—Peggy Ann (Mrs. Donnie Lee Collins), Carol (Mrs. Roy David Ambrose), George Richard, John Wayne, Warren Butler. With Memphis Union Sta., 1942-44; ordained to ministry Bapt. Ch., 1942; pastor Leesburg Ch., Morton, Miss., 1944-47, Hardy (Miss.) Ch., 1947-59, Fairview Ch., Indianola, Miss., 1959-61; Inner-City Parish, New Orleans, 1962-64, First Ch., Winslow, Ariz., 1964-72; asso. prof. philosophy and theology Oakland City (Ind.) Coll., 1972-79, prof., 1979—, dean students, 1975—, dir. MANPOWER, 1975-78, chmn. div. religious studies, 1976—; lectr., counselor; curriculum writer Sunday Sch. Bd., So. Bapt. Conv., Nashville, 1969; exec. bd. Ariz. So. Bapt. Conv., Phoenix, 1968-71; curriculum writer Gen. Assn. Gen. Bapt. Ch., 1973, 81. Chmn. personnel Office Econ. Opportunity, Winslow, 1969-70. Chmn. bd. dirs. Navajo County Guidance and Counseling Clinic, Winslow, 1965-72, No. Ariz. Comprehensive Guidance and Counseling, 1969-72; trustee Ariz. Bapt. Children's Home, Phoenix, 1968-71. Mason (32 deg.). Home: 431 W Oak St Oakland City IN 47660

SMITH, ROBERT BROWN, indsl. lab. ofcl.; b. Newark, Ohio, Oct. 20, 1923; s. Walter G. and Hattye (Brown) S.; student Ohio State U., 1941-43, B.M.E., 1948; m. Lucille Alice Taintor, Dec. 20, 1947; children—Marc T., Laurie. Coordinator research Columbia Gas System Service Corp., Columbus, Ohio and N.Y.C., 1948-57; asst. dir. research Am. Gas Assn., N.Y.C., 1957-66; mgr. gas industry programs Battelle Columbus (Ohio) Labs., 1966—; chmn. confs. and symposia; speaker in field. Mgr. Little League, 1960-65; coach Pony League basketball, 1961-63; asst. leader cub scouts Hudson River council Boy Scouts Am., 1961-63; ch. sch. tchr. Presbyn. Ch., supt., 1963-66, deacon, 1961-63, elder, 1963—, mem. various coms. Served with USAF, 1943-46. Mem. ASME, Am. Soc. Gas Engrs., Am. Gas Assn., Slurry Transport Assn. (tech. com.), Ohio State U. Alumni Assn., U.S. Tennis Assn. Republican. Clubs: Village Squares; Racquet (Columbus). Contbr. chpt. to handbook in field, articles to sci. jours. Home: 3139 Leeds Rd Columbus OH 43221 Office: 505 King Ave Columbus OH 43201

SMITH, ROBERT DRAKE, transp. co. exec.; b. Ft. Worth, Oct. 26, 1944; s. Kermit Rudebeck and Lynne Grace (Harris) S.; B.A. with honors in Econs., U. Puget Sound, 1966; M.B.A., U. Pa., 1968. Planning analyst C.&N.W. Transp. Co., Chgo., 1968, supr. program planning, 1969, mgr. program planning, 1970-73, corp. sec., 1973—; dir. Western R.R. Properties, Inc., Des Moines & Central Iowa Ry., Ft. Dodge, Des Moines & So. Ry., Mpls. Indsl. Ry., Northwestern Communications Co., Ry. Transfer Mpls., Oshkosh Transp. Co. Vol., Cook County Juvenile Ct., 1970-78; mem. jr. gov. bd. Chgo. Symphony. Mem. Am. Soc. Corp. Secs., Assn. Am. R.R.'s, Nat. Investor Relations Inst., Wharton Sch. Alumni Assn. Clubs: Tower, Union League, Barclay, Bd. Room (N.Y.C.). Home: 535 N Michigan Ave #3208 Chicago IL 60611 Office: C &N W Transp Co 165 N Canal St Room 800 Chicago IL 60606

SMITH, ROBERT EARL, coll. adminstr.; b. Dallas, May 15, 1936; s. Robert A. and Lillie (Harrell) S.; A.A., Central Coll., McPherson, Kans., 1955; B.S., Greenville Coll., 1957; M.S. (Univ. fellow), So. Ill. U., 1958; Ph.D., Fla. State U., 1973; m. Joanna M. Riggs, Aug. 30, 1957; children—Charles Edward, Cynthia Kay. Prof. phys. edn., baseball coach Taylor U., Upland, Ind., 1958-61; dir. phys. edn., coach Greenville (Ill.) Coll., 1961-69, dir. phys. edn., coach, asst. to pres., 1974-77, v.p. instl. advancement, 1977—; asst. baseball coach Fla. State U., Tallahassee, 1969-71. Mem. exec. bd. U.S. Olympic Com., 1980-84. Named Coach of Yr., Nat. Assn. Intercollegiate Athletics, 1969. Mem. U.S. Baseball Fedn. (sec.-treas. 1974-78, chmn. bd. 1978—, pres. 1980), Nat. Assn. Intercollegiate Athletics (pres. baseball coaches assn. 1976-78), Am. Assn. Coll. Baseball Coaches (research com. 1974, clinic com. 1974), Internat. Assn. Amateur Baseball (1st v.p. 1980, acting pres. 1981-84), Ill. Assn. Health, Phys. Edn. and Recreation, Greenville Coll. Alumni Assn. (pres. 1965-68). Kiwanian. Home: 503 Shannon Dr Greenville IL 62246

SMITH, ROBERT JAMES, designer, pub.; b. Chgo., Oct. 23, 1918; s. Edward W. and Emma (Olson) S.; student Chgo. Tech. Coll., 1936, U. Ill., 1937-39, U. Chgo., 1943, Elmhurst Coll., 1949; m. Ruth Marion Hall, Feb. 8, 1942; children—Gregory Hall, Gerald Edward, Marilyn Emily Smith Lovett, Brian Woodly. Partner, designer Craft Patterns internat. home workshop newspaper feature, Elmhurst, Ill., 1947—; pres. Crafts Products Co., Elmhurst and St. Charles, Ill., 1965—; owner Craft Clocks & Gifts, Elmhurst, 1967—. Committeeman Republican party Addison Twp., 1965-72; pres. bd. York High Sch., Elmhurst, 1955-61. Served with Manhattan Dist. Engrs., 1943-46. Mem. Delta Kappa Epsilon. Methodist. Designed and invented instruments for AEC pioneering modern, quick-reading, portable Geiger counter and deep hole probe. Office: 2200 Dean Saint Charles IL 60147

SMITH, ROBERT JAMES, immunopharmacologist; b. Bklyn., May 30, 1944; s. James and Mollie Smith; B.S., St. John's U., Jamaica, N.Y., 1966; M.S., U. Md., 1970, Ph.D. (dissertation fellow), 1971; m. Florence Christine Varrone, Aug. 8, 1970; 1 son, James Michael. USPHS postdoctoral research fellow Tulane U. Med. Sch., 1972-74; sr. scientist Schering Corp., Bloomfield, N.J., 1974-78; research scientist hypersensitivity diseases Upjohn Co., Kalamazoo, 1978—; guest lectr. various local univs. Chesapeake Bay research fellow, 1971; NSF fellow, 1970. Mem. Am. Soc. Pharmacology and Exptl. Therapeutics, Am. Rheumatism Assn., Am. Soc. Hematology, Am. Soc. Cell Biology, Soc. Exptl. Biology and Medicine, Reticuloendothelial Soc., AAAS, Inflammation Research Assn., N.Y. Acad. Scis., Sigma Xi, Phi Sigma. Author numerous papers on imunoinflammatory diseases. Office: Upjohn Co Henrietta St Kalamazoo MI 49001

SMITH, ROBERT JOHN, office equipment co. exec.; b. Indpls. Feb. 4, 1927; s. Samuel R. and Rosemary (Berry) S.; B.S. in Bus., Butler U., 1950; M.S., U. Pitts., 1951; m. Arlene Ann Sondgerath, Aug. 19, 1950; children—Pat and Michael (twins), Kathleen, Daniel, Timothy, Robert. Sales agt. Marchant Calculating, Lafayette, Ind., 1951-54; founder, pres. Smith Office Equip. Co., Lafayette, 1955—. Mem. St. Thomas Ch. adv. bd., Lafayette, 1960-63; pres. Lafayette Area Parochial Fund dr., 1968. Served with U.S. Army, 1945-47. Decorated Army Commendation medal. Named Man of the Yr., Marchant Calculators, 1953; Gestetner Outstanding Dist. Dealer, 1968. Mem. Lafayette C. of C., Nat. Office Machine Assn., Nat. Office

Products Assn. Democrat. Roman Catholic. Clubs: K.C., Lafayette Country. Home: 3521 S 100 St E Lafayette IN 47905 Office: 311 Sagamore Pkwy N Lafayette IN 47904

SMITH, ROBERT LYNWOOD, mktg. exec.; b. Lansing, Mich., Sept. 11, 1934; s. Frank Seth and Vera May (Spangler) S.; B.S.I.E., Gen. Motors Inst., 1957; m. Judith Karen Jerome, Apr. 2, 1955; children—Kevin Robert, Kerri Lynn, Mark Jerome. Student engr. Chevrolet div. Gen. Motors Corp., 1952-57, prodn. engr., quality rep. Fisher Body div., 1957-66; sales and mktg. exec. Dow Corning Corp., Farmington Hills, Mich., 1966—, also automotive market devel. mgr. Mem. Soc. Automotive Engrs., Engring. Soc. Detroit. Republican. Home: 9127 Frome Dr Brighton MI 48116 Office: 32969 Hamilton Ct Farmington Hills MI 48024

SMITH, ROBERT OWEN, environ. engr.; b. Jasper, Ind., Feb. 17, 1955; s. Francis J. and Martha J. (Gates) S.; B.S. in Biology and Chemistry, U. Evansville, Ind., 1977; postgrad. Ind. State U., 1977-78, U. Louisville, 1980—. Chemist, So. Ind. Gas & Electric Co., Evansville, 1977; environ. engr. Big Rivers Electric Co., Henderson, Ky., 1978-80, sr. environ. engr., 1980-81, supr. environ. quality, 1981—; cons. in field; chief advisor Evansville C. of C. Air Pollution Task Force, 1980. U.S. Dept. Energy grantee, 1979-80. Mem. Am. Chem. Soc., Am. Phys. Soc., Am. Inst. Physics, Inst. Environ. Scis., Am. Soc. Quality Control, Water Pollution Control Fedn., Hon. Order Ky. Cols. Club: YMCA (Henderson). Contbr. articles to profl. jours. Patentee in field. Home: 1258 S Weinbach Ave Evansville IN 47714 Office: 201 3d St Henderson KY 42420

SMITH, ROGER PERRY, physician, educator; b. Tucson, Jan. 31, 1949; B.S., Purdue U., 1968; B.S.M., Northwestern U., 1969, M.D., 1972; m. Barbara Ann Nason, May 25, 1974; 1 son, Scott Andrew. Intern, Chgo. Wesley Meml. Hosp., 1972-73; resident in Ob-Gyn, Northwestern Meml. Hosp.-McGaw Med. Center, 1973-76, Prentice Women's Hosp. and Maternity Center, Chgo., 1973-76; clin. asst. prof. Sch. Clin. Medicine, U. Ill., Champaign-Urbana, 1979—; attending staff Carle Found. Hosp., Urbana, 1976—; mem. courtesy staff Burnham City Hosp., Mercy Hosp., McKinley Hosp., Paris (Ill.) Community Hosp. Fellow Am. Coll. Obstetricians and Gynecologists; mem. Central Assn. Ob-Gyn (Community Hosp. award 1979), Am. Inst. Ultrasound in Medicine, Assn. Advancement of Med. Instrumentation, Ill. Obstetrical and Gynecol. Soc. (asst. sec. 1976-79, sec., 1979—), Ill. Assn. Maternal and Child Health, AMA, Ill. State Med. Soc., Chgo. Med. Soc., Champaign County Med. Soc., Mensa. Contbr. articles to profl. jours. Home: 2204 Galen Dr Champaign IL 61820 Office: Dept Obstetrics and Gynecology Carle Clinic Assn 603 W University Ave Urbana IL 61801

SMITH, ROLAND EMERSON, accountant; b. Kalkaska, Mich., Jan. 9, 1918; s. Ernest C. and Sybil M. (Planck) S.; student Mich. State U., 1935-36; B.A., Olivet Coll., 1939; certificate Walsh Coll., 1942; m. Lois F. Frontjes, Feb. 11, 1950; 1 son, Richard. Accountant, Coopers & Lybrand, Detroit, 1942-46, Chgo., 1946-52; partner, accountant Moore, Smith & Dale, Detroit and Southfield, Mich., 1952—. C.P.A., Mich., Ill. Mem. Am. Inst. C.P.A.'s, Mich. Assn. C.P.A.'s. Mem. Ch. of Jesus Christ of Latter day Saints. Clubs: Franklin Racquet, Torch Lake Yacht. Home: Piety Hill Pl 600 W Brown St Apt 110 Birmingham MI 48009 Office: 24700 Northwestern Hwy 206 Southfield MI 48075

SMITH, ROY L., farmer, agrl. constrn. co. exec.; b. Omaha, Aug. 2, 1940; s. Royal P. and Clara M. (Gobelman) S.; B.Sc. with distinction, U. Nebr., 1961, M.Sc., 1968; m. Sharon Ilene Ramge, June 8, 1961; children—Kristine Lynn, Laura Kay. Tchr. vocat. agr. Filley (Nebr.) High Sch., 1963-68; farmer, Plattsmouth, Nebr., 1968—; owner, mgr. Smith-Ag Systems Inc., agrl. constrn. co., Plattsmouth, 1973—. Mem. Cass County Planning Commn., 1975—. Served with M.I., U.S. Army, 1961-63. Mem. Nebr. Soybean Assn. (pres. 1980-81), Farm Bur. Republican. Methodist. Club: Masons (past master).

SMITH, SHARLEEN ROSE, educator; b. Chgo., Aug. 28, 1950; d. Richard Randolph and Rose Mary (Gordeychuk) S.; B.S., Elmhurst Coll., 1972; M.S., DePaul U., 1974; postgrad. Chgo. State U., 1975-79, U. Ill., Chgo., 1978-80, Nat. Coll. Edn., 1980; m. Robert Haas, May 8, 1981. Math. tchr. Carl Sandburg High Sch., Orland Park, Ill., 1973—, tchr. alternative edn. program, mem. curriculum com., resource person alternative edn. program; coach Mathletes. Vol., Christ Hosp., 1972—; youth counselor Meth. Ch., mem. edn. and stewardship coms. Mem. NEA, Ill. Edn. Assn., Nat. Council Tchrs. of Math., Ill. Council Tchrs. of Math. (speaker state conv. 1979, 80, 82), Assn. Supervision and Curriculum Devel., Ill. Assn. Supervision and Curriculum Devel., Council Exceptional Children (pres. Div. Children with Learning Disabilities 1979-80), Ill. Council Exceptional Children, Wildlife Com., Audubon Soc., Am. Mus. Natural History, Cousteau Soc. Home: 1738 Lawrence Lockport IL 60441 Office: 133d St and LaGrange Rd Orland Park IL 60462

SMITH, SHARON ILENE, home economist; b. Plattsmouth, Nebr., June 6, 1939; d. Maynard S. and Ruth M. (Holcomb) Ramge; B.S. with high distinction, U. Nebr., 1961, M.S., 1967; m. Roy L. Smith, June 8, 1961; children—Kristine, Laura. Tchr. home econs., West Jr. High Sch., Colorado Springs, Colo., 1962-63; tchr. Filley (Nebr.) Consol. Schs., 1963-68; tchr. home econs. Murray (Nebr.) Public Sch., 1972-76; tchr. home econs. Plattsmouth (Nebr.) Community Schs., 1976—; v.p. Smith Ag-Systems, Inc. Mem. Am. Home Econs. Assn., Nebr. Home Econs. Assn., Am. Vocat. Assn., Nebr. Vocat. Assn., Nebr. State Edn. Assn., NEA, Nebr. Vocat. Home Econs. Assn., Alpha Delta Kappa. Republican. Methodist. Clubs: Toastmasters (adminstrv. v.p.), Order Eastern Star, Jobs Daus. (council). Office: 1724 8th Ave Plattsmouth NE 68048

SMITH, SHIRLEY C., hosp. adminstr.; b. Lethbridge, Alta., Can., Dec. 1, 1932; came to U.S., 1963; d. Earl Duncan and Annie Armour; ed. Copley Meml. Sch. Nursing, 1970; B.S.N., No. Ill. U., 1974, M.S., 1975; m. William T. Smith, July 20, 1930; children—Dean, Earl, Glen. Nurse, U. Ill. Hosp., Chgo., 1970, Central DuPage Hosp., Winfield, Ill., 1971-74; instr. No. Ill. U., 1976; clin. specialist Good Samaritan Hosp., Downers Grove, Ill., 1976; operating room coordinator Elmhurst (Ill.) Hosp., 1977-78; dir. nursing service Delnor Hosp., St. Charles, Ill., 1979—. Mem. adv. bd. Elgin Community Coll. Dept. Nursing; v.p. Two Rivers Council Boy Scouts Am., 1977-80. Served with Royal Can. Air Force, 1951-53. Mem. Am. Nurses Assn., Ill. Nurses Assn., Fox Valley Nursing Adminstrs., Am. Soc. Nursing Service Adminstrs. Unitarian. Office: 975 N 5th Ave St Charles IL 60174

SMITH, STEVEN DICKINSON, electronics co. exec.; b. Indpls., Sept. 13, 1953; s. Gerald Dickinson and Dorothy Jane Smith; B.S. in Bus., Ind. U., 1976. Mech. engr., ops. mgr. Mouron & Co., Indpls., 1972-74; mech. engr. Carson Mfg. Co., Indpls., 1974-75; mfg. mgr. Internat. Energy Mgmt. Corp., Indpls., 1975-78; pres., 1978, since pres. Manutek, Inc., Indpls. Mem. IEEE, Indpls. C. of C., Sports Car Club Am. Republican. Presbyterian. Office: 8108 Zionsville Rd Indianapolis IN 46268

SMITH, STEWART GENE, retail drug co. exec.; b. Wyandotte, Mich., Feb. 5, 1926; s. William Melvin and Margaret Nichols (Cameron) S.; B.A., U. Mich., 1949, J.D., 1952; m. Veronica Lucille Latta, Apr. 12, 1952; children—Stewart Gregory, Patrick Allen, Paul Donald, Alison Veronica, Alisa Margaret, Glenn Laurence. Admitted to Mich. bar, 1952; tax atty. Detroit Trust Co., 1952; with Cunningham Drug Stores, Inc., Detroit, 1952—, v.p. charge real estate, 1959-62, sr. v.p. adminstrn., 1969-81, pres., 1981—, also dir., mem. exec. com. Chmn. Grosse Isle (Mich.) Municipal Airport Commn., 1971-72. Served with USNR, 1944-46. Mem. Am. Bar Assn., State Bar Mich., Internat. Council Shopping Centers, Am. Legion. Clubs: Detroit Athletic; Grosse Isle Golf and Country. Home: 22225 Balmoral Dr Grosse Ile MI 48138 Office: 1927 12th St Detroit MI 48216

SMITH, TEMPEL JEAN, JR. (TIM), steel co. exec.; b. Chgo., May 25, 1950; s. Tempel Jean and Esther (VanderLaan) S.; B.S. in Bus. Adminstrn., St. Louis U., 1972; postgrad. Imede Sch., Lausanne, Switzerland, 1978; M.B.A., U. Chgo., 1979. Personnel mgr. Tempel Steel Co., Chgo., 1976-77, asst. to pres., 1977—, trustee Pension Plan; pres., founder Prodn. Machinery Leasing Co., Park Ridge, Ill., 1975—. Dir. tent fest Young Republicans, 1976. Founder pres. Timco (Tempel Investment Mgt. Co.). Mem. Am. Soc. Mfg. Engrs. Presbyterian. Clubs: Tavern (vice chmn. jr. com.), Big Sand Lake. Home: 1236 N Dearborn Chicago IL 60610 and 17405 Simpson Rd Wadsworth IL 60083 Office: Tempel Steel Co 1939 Bryn Mawr Ave Chicago IL 60626

SMITH, THEODORE CHARLES, electronics co. exec.; b. Port Huron, Mich.; s. Clarence George and Lucy Agatha (Lewandowski) S.; B.Econs., U. Detroit, 1957; M.B.A., Syracuse U., 1974; m. Jane Guze, Nov. 13, 1971; children—Kent A., Keith A., L. David, Laura J. Sales mgr. Pegasus Labs. Inc., Troy, Mich., 1958-61, Renwell Industries, South Hadley Falls, Mass., 1961-65; mktg. mgr. Ferrand Industries, Valhalla, N.Y., 1965-71, Umac div. Sperry Rand Corp., Burlington, Vt., 1971-76; exec. v.p. Gen. Numeric Corp., Elk Grove Village, Ill., 1976-80; pres. Yasnac Am., Northbrook, Ill., 1981—; mem. numerically controlled machine tools tech. adv. com. Bur. East West Trade, Dept. Commerce, 1974-76. Served with 11th airborne div. U.S. Army, 1954-56. Mem. Numerical Control Soc., Computer and Automated Systems Assn., Soc. Mfg. Engrs. Clubs: Ethan Allen (Burlington, Vt.); Lake Point Tower (Chgo.); Itasca (Ill.) Country; Lake Forest (Ill.). Contbr. articles to profl. and trade jours. Office: 305 Era Dr Northbrook IL 60062

SMITH, TRENT WHITMER, plastic surgeon; b. Columbus, Ohio, Apr. 7, 1913; s. Harvey H. and Almetta W. S.; A.B., Ohio State U., 1933, M.D., 1937; postgrad. Washington U., 1946-47; m. Eileen Marie Ebert, Sept. 29, 1939; children—T. Wynn, Muguet Smith Jones. Intern, St. Luke Hosp., Cleve., 1937-38; resident White Cross Hosp., Columbus, 1938-39, Ohio State U. Hosp., Columbus, 1947-48; practice medicine, Loveland, Ohio, 1939-40, Cin., 1940-42; practice medicine specializing in plastic surgery, 1948—; clin. prof. Coll. Medicine, Ohio State U., 1947—; pres. staff Children's Hosp., Columbus, 1957-58. Served to maj. USAF, 1942-46. Diplomate Am. Bd. Otolaryngology. Fellow Am. Acad. Facial, Plastic and Reconstructive Surgery (pres. 1973-74), A.C.S., Am. Acad. Otolaryngology and Head and Neck Surgery mem. AMA, Ohio State Med. Assn., Columbus Acad. Medicine, Am. Assn. Cosmetic Surgeons (pres. 1976-77), Columbus Surg. Soc., Columbus Eng. Soc. Republican. Episcopalian. Clubs: Rocky Fork Headley Hunt (master fox hounds 1971-81), Columbus Country, Faculty, Univ. Contbr. articles to med. jours. Home: 46 N Parkview Ave Columbus OH 43209 Office: St Anthony Towers 1450 Hawthorne Ave Columbus OH 43203

SMITH, VANITA RAE, producer, dir.; b. Lebanon, Mo., Feb. 1, 1944; d. Ray and Esther Asilee (Chastain) S.; B.A., Anderson (Ind.) Coll., 1967. Civilian asst. post entertainment dir. Ft. Leonard Wood, Mo., 1967-69, dinner theatre dir., 1972-75; asst. command entertain dir. U.S. Army, Hawaii, 1969-72; chief army music and theatre, Ft. Knox, Ky., 1975-79; freelance producer, dir., 1979—. Recipient 4 commendations Dept. Army, 3 comdr.'s certs. Ft. Knox, 1 spl. award Air Force, Hawaii. Mem. Am. Theatre Assn., Southeastern Theatre Conf., Army Theatre Arts Assn. (4 spl. awards), Ky. Theatre Assn. Mem. Ch. of God. Address: 3035 S Dayton St Springfield MO 65807

SMITH, VIRGINIA DODD (MRS. HAVEN SMITH), congresswoman; b. Randolph, Iowa, June 30, 1911; d. Clifton Clark and Erville (Reeves) Dodd; A.B., U. Nebr., 1936; m. Haven N. Smith, Aug. 27, 1931. Nat. pres. Am. Country Life Assn., 1951-54; nat. chmn. Am. Farm Bur. Women, 1954-74; dir. Am. Farm Bur. Fedn., 1954-74, country Women's Council; world dep. pres. Assn. Country Women of World, 1962-68; mem. Dept. Agr. Nat. Home Econs. Research adv. com., 1960-65; mem. Crusade for Freedom European Inspection tour, 1958; del. Republican Nat. Conv., 1956, 72; bd. govs. Agrl. Hall of Fame, 1959—; mem. Nat. Livestock and Meat Bd., 1955-58, Nat. Commn. Community Health Services, 1963-66; adv. mem. Nebr. Sch. Bds. Assns., 1949; mem. Nebr. Territorial Centennial Commn., 1953, Gov.'s Commn. Status of Women, 1964-66; chmn. Presdl. Task Force on Rural Devel., 1969-70; mem. 94th-97th Congresses from 3d Dist. Nebr., mem. appropriations com., agr., energy and water subcoms., ranking mem. minority agr. appropriations com. Vice pres. Farm Film Found., 1964-74. Recipient award of Merit, D.A.R., 1956; Disting. Service award U. Nebr., 1956, 60; award for best public address on freedom Freedom Found., 1966; Eyes on Nebr. award Nebr. Optometric Assn., 1970; Internat. Service award Midwest Conf. World Affairs, 1970; Woman of Achievement award Nebr. Bus. and Profl. Women, 1971; selected as 1 of 6 U.S. women Govt. France for 3 week goodwill mission to France, 1969; Outstanding 4H Alumni award Iowa State U., 1973, 74. Mem. AAUW, Delta Kappa Gamma (state hon. mem.), Beta Sigma Phi (internat. hon. mem.), Chi Omega, P.E.O. (past pres.). Methodist. Clubs: Bus. and Profl. Women, Order of Eastern Star. Good Will ambassador to Switzerland, 1950. Office: 2202 Rayburn House Office Bldg Washington DC 20515

SMITH, WALLACE PAUL, educator; b. Cleve., July 10, 1923; s. Paul C. and Helen (Poland) S.; B.A., Baldwin-Wallace Coll., 1948; M.A., Northwestern U., 1952. Tchr. drama Medina (Ohio) High Sch., 1948-52, Lakewood (Ohio) High Sch., 1952-57; dir. auditorium activities Evanston (Ill.) Twp. High Sch., 1957-81, coordinator program for gifted, 1972-81, coordinator research and curriculum devel., 1973-75, dir. urban arts program, 1976-80, dir. program planning and implementation, 1980-81; cons. HEW; v.p. Evanston Symphony Orch., 1964-68; dir. Secondary Sch. Theatre Conf., 1963-65, Ill. Demonstration Center for Gifted Arts Students; mem. Ill. Sesquicentennial Com. on Arts, 1968; mem. artists-in-sch. panel Nat. Endowment for Arts, 1974; treas. Ill. Alliance for Arts Edn., 1974-75; pres. Am. Council on Arts in Edn., 1976-79. Trustee, Am. Council on Arts in Edn., 1975. Served with AUS, 1943-45; PTO. Recipient regional award of excellence Am. Coll. Theatre Festival, 1973, nat. award excellence, 1973; Founders award Secondary Sch. Theatre Assn., 1979; Walter Peck award Secondary Sch. Theatre Conf., 1967. Fellow Am. Ednl. Theatre Assn.; mem. Am. Theatre Assn. (v.p. 1969-70, pres. 1971, chief regional officer Gt. Lake Region 1979-81), Ill. Theatre Assn. (award of Honor 1981), Ill. Art Edn. Assn. (Outstanding Contbn. award 1976), Phi Delta Kappa, Alpha Sigma Phi, Pi Kappa Delta, Theta Alpha Phi. Contbr. articles to profl. jours. Home: 111 E Chestnut St Chicago IL 60611

SMITH, WALTER REXFORD, utility co. exec.; b. Pleasant Hill, Ill., Aug. 2, 1916; s. Walter Cash and Arlie Ruth (Gregory) S.; B.S. in E.E., U. Ill., 1947; m. Marjorie Rose Havens, June 20, 1942; children—Kathy Lynn Smith Nowlin, David Bruce, Gregory Havens, Michael Rexford; m. 2d Jade Bishop Jones, July 1, 1977. Systems engr. Illini Electric Cooperative, Champaign, 1947-60, gen. mgr., 1960-75, exec. v.p., gen. mgr., 1975—; pres. bd. Soyland Power Coop., Inc. Instl. rep. Arrowhead council Boy Scouts Am., Champaign, 1961-65. Served with U.S. Army, 1943-46. Mem. Champaign C. of C. Republican. Clubs: Rotary, Mason. Home: 1211 W Healey St Champaign IL 61820 Office: PO Box 637 Champaign IL 61820

SMITH, WARD, mfg. co. exec., lawyer; b. Buffalo, Sept. 13, 1930; s. Andrew Leslie and Georgia (Ward) S.; student Georgetown U., 1948-49; A.B., Harvard, 1952; LLB., J.D., U. Buffalo, 1955; m. Gretchen Keller Diefendorf, Oct. 29, 1960; children—Jennifer Hood, Meredith Ward, Jonathan Andrew, Sarah Katherine. Admitted to N.Y. bar, 1955, Mass. bar, 1962, Ohio bar, 1977; asso. firm Lawler & Rockwood, N.Y.C., 1959-62; sec., gen. counsel Whitin Machine Works, Whitinsville, Mass., 1962-66; sec., White Consol. Industries, Inc., Cleve., 1966-69, v.p., 1967-69; sr. v.p. 1969-72, exec. v.p., 1972-76, pres., chief adminstrv. officer, 1976—, also dir.; sec., dir. Blaw-Knox Co.; dir. Centran Corp. Trustee Case-Western Res. U., Cleve. Orch., Cleve. Music Sch. Settlement; bd. advs. Notre Dame Coll., Cleve. Served to lt. USNR, 1955-59. Mem. Am., N.Y. State bar assns. Clubs: Pepper Pike, Country (Pepper Pike, Ohio); Union (Cleve.). Home: 2706 Landon Rd Shaker Heights OH 44122 Office: 11770 Berea Rd Cleveland OH 44111

SMITH, WARREN EDWIN, city ofcl.; b. Findlay, Ohio, Oct. 18, 1946; s. Walter Franklin and Helen O. (Hill) S.; student Toledo U., 1975-76; m. Linda Susan Proudfoot, Mar. 22, 1967; children—Christopher Lynn, Heather Lynne. Mem. staff sewer dept. Village of North Baltimore (Ohio), 1965-66; supt. sewage Village of Payne (Ohio), 1969-70; water plant supt. Village of Paulding (Ohio), 1970-71, village adminstr., 1971-75, tech. supr., 1975-78; village adminstr. Village of Delta (Ohio), 1975—. Chmn., Delta Happy Hearts Recreation Council, 1977-79; treas. Maumee Valley Resource, Conservation and Devel. and Planning Orgn. Served with U.S. Army, 1966-69; Vietnam. Decorated Bronze Star (2). Mem. Am. Water Works Assn., Water Pollution Control Fedn., Ohio Water Pollution Control Conf., Internat. City Mgrs. Assn., Ohio City Mgrs. Assn., Delta C. of C. Republican. Club: Kiwanis. Home: 404 Maplewood St Delta OH 43515 Office: 401 Main St Delta OH 43515

SMITH, WAVERLY GRAVES, ins. co. exec.; b. Durham, N.C., Jan. 21, 1924; s. George W. and Lyla (Graves) S.; m. Anne Kathleen Williamson, July 30, 1943; children—Cheryl, Allen, Carolyn. With St. Paul Fire & Marine Ins. Co., 1949—, head mktg. div., 1966-69, exec. v.p., 1969-73, pres., 1973-77; pres., chief operating officer St. Paul Cos., Inc., 1978—; dir. Gen. Mills, Mpls. Trustee, vice chmn. Sta. KTCA-TV; bd. dirs. Bush Found. Served with USMCR, 1943-46. Mem. Nat. Assn. Property Casualty Execs. (pres.). Home: 11 Evergreen Rd Saint Paul MN 55110 Office: St Paul Cos Inc 385 Washington St Saint Paul MN 55102

SMITH, WILBERT LEE, hosp. adminstr.; b. Jackson, Miss., Oct. 13, 1934; s. James and Sallie Mae (Chrismon) S.; B.S., Tougaloo Coll., 1957; M.A., Governors State U., 1976; children—Jennifer M., Nicole C. Tchr., Marshall High Sch., Chgo., 1958-63; ins. cons. Mut. of N.Y., 1963-68; sales rep. Humble Oil Co., 1968-69; fin. analyst Atlanta Richfield, 1969-70; tchr. Calumet High Sch., Chgo., 1971-72; dir. coop. edn. Malcolm X Coll., Chgo., 1972-76; dir. community relations South Shore Hosp., Chgo., 1977—. Bd. dirs. Community Mental Health Council, 1979—; mem. adv. bus. council William Dawson Skill Center, 1981—; mem. adv. com. Chgo. Bd. Edn. Drop-Out Prevention Program, 1979—; mem. steering com. 4th Dist. Chgo. Police Dept., 1979—. Recipient award of merit Chgo. Assn. Commerce and Industry, 1979, 80, 81; named Alumnus of Yr., Tougaloo Coll., 1980. Mem. Ill. Hosp. Public Relations Soc. (pres.), Chgo. Hosp. Public Relations Soc., South Shore C. of C. (dir.), Am. Soc. Dirs. of Vols. Services, Am. Soc. Hosp. Public Relations, Chgo. Inter-Alumni Council Negro Coll. Fund, Chgo. Tougaloo Alumni Club, Alpha Phi Alpha. Home: 7808 S Colfax Ave Chicago IL 60649 Office: 8015 S Luella Ave Chicago IL 60617

SMITH, WILLIAM JACOB, II, bank examiner; b. Huntington, W. Va., May 15, 1946; s. William Jacob and Opal (Cyrus) S.; student Ohio State U., 1964-65; B.B.A., Morehead State U., 1969; certificate Am. Inst. Banking, 1973; grad. Stonier Grad. Sch. Banking, Rutgers U., 1980; m. Patricia Rose Ball, June 16, 1973; children—Stephanie Suzanne, William Jacob III. Law enforcement officer Village of Chesapeake (Ohio), 1967-69; trainee examiner FDIC, Columbus, 1969-70, jr. asst. examiner, 1970-71, sr. asst. examiner, 1971-73, examiner, 1974-78, bank examiner (EDP), 1978—. Mem. Chesapeake Vol. Fire Dept., 1959-70. Republican. Methodist. Club: Masons. Home: 11282 Bridgeview Dr NW Pickerington OH 43147 Office: Suite 2600 One Nationwide Plaza Columbus OH 43215

SMITH, WILLIAM ROBERT, utility co. exec.; b. Mount Clemens, Mich., Nov. 11, 1916; s. Robert L. and Elsie (Chamberlain) S.; B.S., Detroit Inst. Tech., 1947; postgrad. Detroit Coll. Law, U. Mich. Grad. Sch. Bus. Adminstrn.; m. Ann Sheridan; children—William R., Laura Ann. Indsl. engr. Detroit Edison Co., 1934-60; mgr. econ. devel. East Ohio Gas Co., Cleve., 1960-80; mgr. nat. accounts Consol. Natural Gas Co., Cleve., 1980—; pres. T.S.T. Corp. Vice pres. Cleve. Ballet; bd. dirs. No. Ohio Research Info. Center; councilman City of Pepper Pike (Ohio); bd. dirs. Animal Protective League; mem. trustees' devel. council St. Luke's Hosp. Served with USAAF, 1942-45. Registered profl. engr., Mich., Ohio. Fellow Am. Econ. Devel. Council; mem. Ohio, Cleve. chambers of commerce, Assn. Ohio Commodores, Nat. Assn. Corp. Real Estate Execs., Soc. Indsl. Realtors, Citizens League Greater Cleve., Delta Theta Tau. Presbyn. Clubs: Mid-Day, Shaker Heights (Ohio) Country. Home: 27750 Fairmount Blvd Pepper Pike OH 44124 Office: 1717 E 9th Cleveland OH 44114

SMITH, WORTHINGTON LEHURAY, ry. exec.; b. Tacoma, Feb. 12, 1925; s. Worthington C. and Doris (LeHuray) S.; B.A., Yale, 1950; M.A., U. Minn., 1953; postgrad. Harvard Bus. Sch., 1967; m. Elizabeth Ann Getzoff, June 30, 1950; children—Worthington R., Scott, Nancy. With Great No. R.R., 1954-70; with Burlington No., Inc., Seattle and St. Paul, 1970-72; pres. Chgo., Milw., St. Paul & Pacific R.R., Chgo., 1972-79, pres., chief exec. officer, 1979—, also dir. Trustee, Farm Found., Chgo., 1973—. Served with AUS, 1943-46, 51-52. Mem. Nat. Freight Traffic Assn., Am. Soc. Traffic and Transp., Traffic Club Chgo., Western Ry. Club. Club: Met. (Chgo.). Office: 516 W Jackson Blvd Chicago IL 60606*

SMITHBURG, WILLIAM DEAN, food mfg. co. exec.; b. Chgo., July 9, 1938; s. Pearl L. and Margaret L. (Savage) S.; B.S., DePaul U., 1960; M.B.A., Northwestern U., 1961; m. Alberta Hap, May 25, 1963; children—Susan, Thomas. Research analyst Leo Burnett Co., 1961-63; sr. account exec. McCann-Erickson, Inc., 1963-66; with

Quaker Oats Co., Chgo., 1966—, v.p., 1971, pres. foods div., 1975, corp. exec. v.p., 1976-79, pres., chief operating officer, 1979—, also dir. Served with USAR, 1959-60. Roman Catholic. Office: Quaker Oats Co 345 Merchandise Mart Plaza Chicago IL 60654*

SMITHSON, GEORGE RAYMOND, JR., environ. research exec.; b. New Vienna, Ohio, Mar. 2, 1926; s. George Raymond and Lola Clarice (Runk) S.; B.S. in Chemistry, Wilmington Coll., 1949; M.S. in Chemistry, Miami U., Oxford, Ohio, 1950; m. Isla Jean Shaw, July 24, 1950; children—Vicki Rae, Holly Jean, Bonnie Lou. Instr. phys. scis. Rio Grande (Ohio) Coll., 1950-52; prin. chemist extractive metallurgy Battelle Meml. Inst., Columbus (Ohio) Labs., 1952-61, project leader, 1961-62, sr. scientist, 1962-65, asso. div. chief minerals and metall. processing, 1965-68, div. chief minerals and metall. waste tech., 1968-70, div. chief waste control and process tech., 1970-72, asst. dept. mgr. environ. systems and processes, 1972-74, asst. program office mgr. energy/environ. programs, 1974-76, program office mgr. environ. tech., 1976—; head tech. activity team for exchange environ. info. with USSR, 1974-80; mem. com. on sulfur dioxide control NRC, 1976-79. Served with Signal Corps, U.S. Army, 1944-46; PTO. Fellow AAAS, Am. Inst. Chemists; mem. Ohio Water Pollution Control Conf., Ohio Acad. Sci., Sigma Xi. Methodist (ordained deacon 1975). Contbr. articles to profl. jours. Patentee in field. Home: 3068 Kingston Ave Grove City OH 43123 Office: 505 King Ave Columbus OH 43201

SMITHSON, ORLA DALE, oil co. exec.; b. Flint, Mich., Nov. 24, 1921; s. Orla C. and Mable (Downey) S.; student public schs., Clio, Mich.; m. Beverly J. Morse, Mar. 11, 1967; children—Debra Lee (dec.), Jeannine; stepchildren—James, Michael, Helen, Edward, Christopher, Mary Ann, Jeanette. With Smithson Petroleum Co., Clio, 1957-68, pres., 1962-66; founder, pres. Crest Petroleum Co., Flint, 1968, Time Gulf Inc., Lansing, Mich., 1972-74; founder, pres. ODS Energy, Inc., Flint, 1974—. Served with AUS, 1942-46. Mem. Genesee County Power House Assn. (v.p. 1978-79), Ky. Coal Assn., Detroit Coal and Oil Assn. Roman Catholic. Clubs: Elks (Elk of Yr. 1970), U. Mich., 100 of Flint (Mich.). Home: 5510 Broadmoor St Grand Blanc MI 48439 Office: 3425 W Pierson Rd Flint MI 48504

SMITHWICK, FRED, JR., hosp. cons.; b. Washington, June 24, 1934; s. Fred and Genevieve (Davis) S.; A.A., Montgomery Coll., 1953; B.A., George Washington U., 1955, M.A., 1974. Asst. to pres. Dwoskin, Inc., Atlanta, 1956-63; dir. mktg. Moderncote, Inc., New Castle, Ind., 1963-70; v.p. Riverside Meth. Hosp., Columbus, Ohio, 1973-81, also sec. found.; pres. Physicians Profl. Mgmt. Corp., Columbus, 1981—; dir. Washington Wallcoverings, Inc.; lectr. health care adminstrn. Ohio State U., George Washington U.; chmn. adv. com. Sch. Licensed Practical Nurses, Columbus Pub. Schs.; chmn. Health Resource Mgmt., Inc., Boca Raton, Fla. Fellow Royal Soc. Health (Gt. Britain), Am. Hosp. Assn.; mem. Am. Coll. Hosp. Adminstrs., Ohio Hosp. Assn., Delta Tau Delta. Methodist. Clubs: Touchdown (Washington), Masons; Porta Bella Yacht and Racquet (Boca Raton); Tower (Ft Lauderdale, Fla.). Home: 289 E Beck St Columbus OH 43206

SMOCK, MARTHA FLORENCE (MRS. CARL FRANCIS SMOCK), mag. editor; b. Kansas City, Mo., Nov. 3, 1913; d. James Vincent and Maybelle Frances (Snell) McNamara; student Kansas City Jr. Coll.; m. Carl Francis Smock, Jan. 25, 1935; children—Stephanie Smock Thomas, Katherine Smock Wales. With Unity Sch. of Christianity, Unity Village, Mo., 1933—, editor Daily Word, non-sectarian devotional mag., 1944—. Author: Meet It With Faith, 1966; Halfway Up The Mountain, 1971; Turning Points, 1976; Listen Beloved, 1980. Home: 6408 High Dr Shawnee Mission KS 66208 Office: Unity Village MO 64065

SMOLAREK, ZENON MARION, mgr. engr.; b. Racine, Wis., Apr. 25, 1918; s. Walter and Lucy Barbara (Plonska) S.; student U. Wis. Extension, Racine, 1950-58, U. Wis., Madison, 1974-77; m. Agnes Lucille Habeck, July 13, 1940; 1 son, Zenon Theodore. Machine operator Famco Machine Co., Racine, 1936, J.I. Case Co., Racine, 1937; machine operator Whitney Tool Co., Rockford, Ill., 1940; tool and diemaker Dumore Corp., Racine, 1941-53, toolroom and plant maintenance supr., 1953-80, ret., 1980; instr. dept. trades and industry Gateway Tech. Inst., Racine, 1981—; owner Holdur Co., Racine; partner, co-owner Kurzan Co., Racine. Registered profl. engr., Calif., Wis. Mem. Nat. Soc. Profl. Engrs., Wis. Soc. Profl. Engrs. (Southeastern chpt.), Soc. Mfg. Engrs. (chpt. 2, Racine, cert.). Republican. Lutheran. Patentee ice skate sharpening device; designer, builder various mfg. products. Home: 3828 Saratoga Ct Racine WI 53405 Office: 1001 Main St Racine WI 53403

SMOLDT, CHARLES ELDON, farmer; b. Indpls., Nov. 5, 1937; s. Eldon Charles and Frances (Willoughby) S.; B.S., Iowa State U., 1959; m. Darlene Ann Willms, Dec. 7, 1958; children—Cynthia L., David C. Farm mgr. Henderson Investment Co., Cedar Rapids, Iowa, 1959-63; mortgage loan appraiser Prudential Ins. Co., Monticello, Iowa, 1963-66; engaged in farming, custom feeding, Grundy Center, Iowa, 1966—. Dir. Grundy Center Schs., 1976—; dir. Area Edn. Agency, 1975—; trustee First Baptist Ch., Grundy Center, 1971-80. Mem. Agrl. Council Am., Profl. Farmers Am., Am. Farm Bureau Fedn., Alpha Zeta. Home: Route 1 Box 51 Grundy Center IA 50638

SMOLICH, PAULINE ANNA, ednl. adminstr.; b. Bloomington, Ill., Nov. 6, 1933; d. Harvey Raymond and Helen Louise (Devore) Storm; B.Mus., Bradley U., 1955; M.S., Western Ill. U., 1976, postgrad., 1977—; m. Robert S. Smolich; children—Sherri, Mark, Berkley. Dir. Matthews Music Co. Studio, 1955-72; musician, hostess Channel 19, Peoria, Ill., 1970-74; dir. student services Graham Hosp. Sch. Nursing, Canton, Ill., 1972-77; developmental edn. coordinator Community Workshop Training Centers, Inc., Canton, 1977—; cons. in field; mem. adv. bd. Spoon River Coll., 1974-77; exec. bd. Multiple Sclerosis of Peoria, 1970-81; coordinator sch. services Sch. Nursing, Meth. Med. Center Ill., Peoria, 1979—; mem. faculty, coordinator research early childhood handicapped program Western Ill. U., 1979, also mem. adv. bd. 0-3 early childhood handicapped outreach project; mem. Fulton County Bd. Citizens for Mental Health, 1974-77, Fulton County Assn. Mental Retarded and Handicapped, 1977—; mem. bd. United Way, also v.p.; mem. bd. Friendship Festival, Canton. Bradley U. scholar, 1952-55. Mem. Am., Ill. personnel and guidance assns., Ill. Assn. Student Fin. Aid Adminstrs., Midwest Assn. Student Fin. Aid Adminstrs., Nat. Assn. Student Fin. Adminstrs., Council for Exceptional Children, AAUW, Ill. Assn. Nonpublic Sch. Adminstrs., Federated Bus. and Profl. Womans Assn. (membership chmn.), Altrusa Internat. (pres. Canton), Lambda Chi Omega, Sigma Alpha Iota, Sigma Kappa. Contbr. articles to profl. jours. Home: 12 N C Ave Canton IL 61520 Office: Meth Med Center Ill 221 NE Glen Oak St Peoria IL 61636

SMOLIN, ROBERT I., cons. engring. co. exec.; b. N.Y.C., Feb. 11, 1942; s. Jack and Claire S.; B.S. in Chem. Engring., Poly. Inst. Bklyn., 1962; M.S., U. Cin., 1965; M.S.C.E., Miami U., Ohio, 1966-67; m. Gerry Daum, Nov. 23, 1969; 1 dau., Tamara Lynne. Process devel. engr. Formica Corp., Evendale, Ohio, 1964-68; plant mgr. Elco Corp., Hooven, Ohio, 1968-70; project and fire protection engr. Panacon Corp., Cin., 1970-72; with Monsanto, Miamisburg, Ohio, 1972-73; with Pedco, Inc., Cin., 1973—, sr. project engr., 1979—. Mem. Am. Inst. Chem. Engrs., Aircraft Owners and Pilots Assn. Office: Pedco Inc Chester Towers Chester Rd Cincinnati OH 45246

SMOLINSKI, LEONA MARIE, nurse, educator; b. Chgo., Dec. 8, 1924; d. Michael and Rose (Sands) S.; grad. Cook County Sch. Nursing, 1946; B.S. in Nursing Edn., Loyola U., Chgo., 1952; M.A., U. Chgo., 1957; D.N.Sci., Cath. U. Am., 1975. Staff nurse Cook County Hosp., U. Ill. Hosp., 1946-48; instr. Hurley Hosp. Sch. Nursing, Flint, Mich., 1951-53; staff nurse U. Chgo. Billings Hosp., 1956-57; asst. prof. Sch. Nursing, U. Oreg., Portland, 1957-59; asst. prof. Sch. Nursing, Loyola U., Chgo., 1959-62, asso. prof., 1962—, chmn. dept. med.-surg. nursing, 1968-71, acting dean Sch. Nursing, 1969, dir. grad. program in nursing, 1976-78; cons. in field. Treas., Adelante, Inc., 1978-79; mem. Edgewater Community Council, Chgo. Recipient Pres.'s medallion Loyola U., Chgo., 1970; Loyal and Disting. Service award Loyola U. Med. Center, 1979. Mem. Am. Nurses Assn., Ill. Nurses Assn. (commr. human rights 1977-79), Midwest Alliance Nursing, AAAS, Nurse Faculty Devel. in Midwest, Sigma Theta Tau (pres. Alpha Beta chpt. 1980-82). Roman Catholic. Home: 5855 N Sheridan Rd Chicago IL 60660 Office: 6525 N Sheridan Rd Chicago IL 60626

SMOLKA, HORST, machine corp. exec.; b. Hamburg, Germany, July 13, 1920; came to U.S., 1953, naturalized, 1962; s. Carl and Elisabeth (Schwendel) S.; Master's degree, Trade Coll. Hamburg, 1953; m. Anita Marianne Adermann, May 16, 1953; 1 son, Ronald. Tool maker apprentice Max Rentsch, Hamburg, Germany, 1937-40; tool maker machinist Hamburg Electric Works, 1949-53; machinist V & S Grinding, Chgo., 1953-54; model maker machinist Decker & Klingberg Co., Chgo., 1954-65, name changed Decker-Smolka Corp., 1965, pres., 1965—. Served with German Army, 1940-45. Prisoner of war USSR, 1945-48. Home: 3031 N Nashville Ave Chicago IL 60634 Office: 5157 W Homer St Chicago IL 60639

SMOOT, THURLOW BERGEN, lawyer; b. Glendive, Mont., Dec. 30, 1910; s. Marvin A. and Ivah (Cook) S.; J.D., U. Colo., 1933. Admitted to Ohio bar, 1933; practice in Cleve., 1933-37, 47—; atty., later trial examiner NLRB, 1937-47. Served with U.S. Army, 1942-45; ETO. Mem. Am. (chmn. labor relations law sec. 1967, sect. del. to Ho. Dels. 1970-71), Cleve., Ohio, Cuyahoga County bar assns., Nat. Trial Lawyers Assn., Ohio Acad. Trial Lawyers. Home: 12700 Lake Ave Lakewood OH 44107 Office: 806 Mall Bldg Cleveland OH 44114

SMUCKLER, RALPH HERBERT, univ. dean; b. Milw., Apr. 10, 1926; s. Robert H. and Celia (Berliand) S.; B.A., U. Wis., 1948, M.A., 1949, Ph.D., 1952; m. Lillian Zembrosky, July 6, 1946; children—Gary, Sandra, Harold. Mem. faculty Mich. State U., East Lansing, 1951—, prof. polit. sci., 1963—, dean internat. studies and programs, 1968—; v.p. Edn. and World Affairs, Inc., N.Y.C., 1963-64; rep. Ford Found. in Pakistan, 1967-69; dir. planning office Inst. for Sci. and Technol. Cooperation, Washington, 1978-79; mem. research adv. com. AID, 1971—, chmn. 1973—; bd. dirs. Midwest Univs. Consortium for Internat. Activities, 1965-67, 69—; trustee Inst. Internat. Edn., N.Y.C., 1974—; bd. dirs. Mich. Internat. Council, 1974—, Mich. Partners of Americas, 1970—. Mich. chmn. UN Day, 1960; mem. internat. affairs com. Nat. Assn. State Univs. and Land Grant Colls., 1970—. Served with inf. U.S. Army, 1944-46; ETO. Recipient Disting. Citizen award Steuben Jr. High Sch., Milw., 1965; John Gilbert Winant humanitarian award, Marine City, Mich., 1976. Mem. Am. Polit. Sci. Assn., Am. Soc. for Public Adminstrn., Soc. for Internat. Devel., Internat. Studies Assn., Mich. UN Assn. (v.p. 1972-76). Jewish. Club: Univ. (Mich. State U.). Author: (with Leroy Ferguson) Politics in the Press, 1953; (With George Belknap) Leadership and Participation in Urban Political Affairs, 1956; contbr. articles to profl. jours. Office: Internat Studies and Programs Mich State U East Lansing MI 48824

SMULYAN, SAMUEL WILLIAM, hotel/motel corp. exec.; b. Princeton, Ind., June 1, 1920; s. Calvin A. and Fannie R. (Gross) S.; student Ind. U., 1937-39; m. Natalie Jean Stolkin, Dec. 27, 1942; children—Dale Marlene, Jeffrey, James. Partner, C.A. Smulyan & Son Wholesale Poultry Distributors, 1945-47; pres. Ind. Fin. Corp., Indpls., 1948—; pres. Howard Johnson's Motor Lodges, Downtown, East and Speedway, Indpls., 1978—; partner Northampton Village Apts., Indpls., 1965-79; chmn. bd., pres. S & M Broadcasting Co., Inc., Sta. WNTS, Indpls., 1973—, Sta. KCRO, Omaha, 1979—. Served with USAAF, 1942-45. Pres. Beth-El Zedeck Congregation, Indpls., 1967-69; vice pres. Jewish Welfare Fedn., Indpls., 1966-68. Mem. Indpls. Bd. Realtors, Indpls. Hotel and Motel Assn. Clubs: Broadmoor Country (v.p. 1966-67), Columbia, Mason, Beth-El Zedeck Men's (pres. 1962-64).

SMUTNY, JOAN FRANKLIN (MRS. HERBERT PAUL SMUTNY), educator; b. Chgo.; d. Eugene and Mabel (Lind) Franklin; B.S. Northwestern U., M.A.; m. Herbert Paul Smutny; 1 dau., Cheryl Anne. Tchr., New Trier High Sch., Winnetka, Ill.; mem. faculty, founder, dir. Nat. High Sch. Inst., Northwestern U. Sch. Edn., Chgo., 1958-67; mem. faculty, founder dir. high sch. workshop in critical thinking and edn., chmn. dept. communications Nat. Coll. Edn., Evanston, Ill., 1967—, exec. dir. high sch. workshops, 1970—, founder, dir. Woman Power Through Edn. Seminar, 1969—, dir. Right to Read seminar in critical reading, 1973—, seminar gifted high sch. students, 1973, dir. of Gifted Programs for 6, 7 and 8th graders pub. schs., Evanston, 1978-79, 1st-8th graders, Glenview (both Ill.) 1979—, Nat. Coll. of Edn., Evanston, 1980-82, dir. Job Creation Project, 1980-82; dir. new dimensions for women, 1973, dir. Thinking for Action in Career Edn. project, 1974—, dir. Individualized Career Edn. Program, 1976-79, dir. TACE, dir. Humanities Program for Verbally Precocious Youth, 1978-79; co-dir., instr. seminars in critical thinking Ill. Family Service, 1972—. Writer ednl. filmstrips in Lang. arts and Lit. Soc. for Visual Edn., 1960—; mem. speakers bur. Council Fgn. Relations, 1968—; mem. adv. com. edn. professions devel. act U.S. Office Edn., 1969—; mem. state team for gifted, IOE, Office of Gifted, Springfield, Ill., 1977; writer, cons. Radiant Ednl. Corp., 1969—; cons. A.L.A., 1969—, cons., workshop leader and speaker in area of gifted edn., 1971—, coordinator of career edn. Nat. Coll. Edn., 1976—; dir. Future Tchrs. Am. Seminar in Coll. and Career, 1970—; cons. for research and devel. Ill. Dept. Vocat. Edn., 1973—; cons. in career edn. U.S. Office Edn., 1976—; evaluation cons. DAVTE, IOE, Springfield, Ill., 1977, mem. Leadership Tng. Inst. for Gifted, U.S. Office Edn., 1973-74; dir. workshops for high sch. students; dir. Gifted Young Writer's and Young Writer's conferences, 1978, 79. Mem. Soc. Arts and Letters (1st v.p. Evanston chap.), A.A.U.P., Mortar Bd., Outstanding Educators of Am. 1974, Pi Lambda Theta, Phi Delta Kappa (chpt. v.p.). Editor, contbr. Maturity in Teaching, 1962. Writer ednl. filmstrips The Brother's Grimm, 1960, How the West Was Won, 1960, Mutiny on the Bounty, 1960, Dr. Zhivago, 1964, Space Odessey 2001, 1969, Christmas Around the World, 1973. Author of numerous books in field. Editor, Ill. Gifted Jour., 1982—. Contributing editor of numerous books in field. Contbr. articles to profl. jours. Reviewer of Programs for Gifted and Talented, U.S. Office of Edn., 1976-78. Home: 633 Forest Ave Wilmette IL 60091

SMUTZ, DOROTHY DRING, pianist, music educator; b. Kansas City, Mo.; d. Johnson and Emma L. (Mack) Dring; studied with Walter Goff, Sterling, Colo., Dr. Ernest R. Kroeger, St. Louis, E. Robert Schmitz, San Francisco, Paul Badura-Skoda, U. Wis.; postgrad. Kroeger Sch. Music, 1926-28; m. Harold Turk Smutz, Oct. 27, 1930 (dec. Sept. 1976); 1 son, Robert Allen. Radio, TV appearances, also concerts, recitals; soloist St. Louis Philharmonic, St. Louis Little Symphony, St. Louis Symphony orchs.; harpsichordist St. Louis Bach Soc., 1940-44; piano, clavichord, seminars and master classes for tchrs., 1946—; debut Town Hall, N.Y.C., 1949; guest artist, forum leader Okla. Music Tchrs. Assn., 1950; guest artist, workshop cons. Okla., Nebr., Kans. music tchrs. assns.; mem. faculty, adjudicator Nat. Guild Piano Tchrs.; artist-in-residence recital and master classes Concordia Coll., Bronxville, N.Y., 1979, Jefferson Coll., Hillsboro, Mo., 1981; vis. artist in piano Webster Coll., St. Louis, 1981—; lectr., guest artist various assns. convs.; dir. tchrs. clinic and workshop, So. Ill. U., 1963; guest artist, condr. workshop music dept. Coll. William and Mary, 1973; mem. piano faculty St. Louis Conservatory Music, 1974-80; analyst J.S. Bach Seminars, also lecture recitals. Mem. Nat. Music Tchrs. Assn. (cert.) Mo. (cert.; exec. bd., Bach lectr., recital 1980), Nat. (mus. theory com. 1962-64, adjudicator West Central div. 1979) music tchrs. assns., St. Louis Piano Tchrs. Round Table, Suburban Community Concerts Assn. (exec. bd. 1951-57), Mu Phi Epsilon. Presbyterian. Home: 619 Hollywood Pl Webster Groves MO 63119

SMYKOWSKI, JAMES, farmer, auctioneer, former state legislator; b. Cayuga, N.D., July 9, 1934; s. George and Kathryn (Kacynski) S.; student public schs.; m. Annette Olson, May 3, 1956; children—Ken, Kevin, Dennis, Bob, Candy, Tony, Pat. Owner, operator farm, Cayuga, 1955—; auctioneer Smykowski Auction Service, 1957—; real estate broker Smykowski Realty, 1965—; mem. N.D. Senate, 1972-80; sec.-treas. Genesco Grain & Seed Co.; dir. First Bank Lidgerwood (N.D.). Mem. Lidgerwood Sch. Bd., 1963-69, pres., 1964-69; Republican candidate for U.S. Congress, 1980. Republican. Roman Catholic. Clubs: K.C., Masons, Elks, Eagles.

SMYTH, DAVID JOHN, economist; b. Twickenham, Eng., Apr. 19, 1936; s. John Richard and Ena Caryle (Stuart) S.; B.Econs., U. Queensland (Australia), 1957, M.Econs., 1960; Ph.D., U. Birmingham (Eng.), 1968; came to U.S., 1967; m. Jane Mair, July 19, 1969; 1 son, Seamus John. Lectr. econs. U. Queensland (Australia), 1957-60; U. Queensland research scholar London Sch. Econs., 1960-63; lectr. econs. U. Birmingham (Eng.), 1963-65, sr. lectr. math. econs., 1965-67; prof. econs. State U. N.Y., Buffalo, 1967-70; prof. econs. Claremont (Calif.) Grad. Sch., 1971-76, chmn. econs. dept., 1973-76; prof. econs., chmn. dept. econs. Wayne State U., Detroit, 1976—. Recipient Ann. Faculty Recognition award Bd. Govs. Wayne State U., 1980. Mem. Am. Economic Assn., Econometric Soc., Royal Economic Soc., Am. Fin. Assn., Econ. Soc. Australia and New Zealand, Western Econ. Assn., Am. Agrl. Econ. Assn., AAUP (pres. Claremont Coll. chpt. 1975-76), Economic Club Detroit. Author: The Demand for Farm Machinery, 1970, Forecasting the United Kingdom Economy, 1973; Size, Growth, Profits and Executive Compensation in the Large Corporation, 1975; editor: Jour. of Macro-econs., 1977—; contbr. articles in field to profl. jours. Home: 1955 Wellesley Dr Detroit MI 48203 Office: Dept Econs Wayne State U Mackenzie Hall Detroit MI 48202

SMYTH, JOHN MCDONNELL, retail furniture exec.; b. Chgo., 1915; B.A., Princeton U., 1937; J.D., Northwestern U., 1940. Admitted to Ill. bar, 1940; pres., dir. John M. Smyth & Co., Chgo.; pres. Jaymesco, Inc.; pres., dir. Homemakers Furniture, Inc., dir. Smyth Properties, Inc. Address: 12 N Michigan Ave Chicago IL 60602

SMYTH, MARY ELLEN, medical supply co. exec.; b. Lander, Wyo., July 2, 1935; d. Fred and Mary (Kosanovich) Savage; B.A. with honors, U. Wyo., 1956, M.A., 1960; m. W. Patrick Smyth, June 20, 1964; children—Timothy Murphy and Kevin Anthony (twins). Tchr. secondary schs. in Colo., 1956-59; instr. U. Wyo., 1959-60, 63-64; instr. speech Pa. State U., 1960-63; tchr. high sch. in Ill., 1964-70; owner Med. Mgmt. Services Co., 1981—. Summer theatre stock appearances, 1959-70; TV show hostess, 1962; speech cons., 1974—. Mem. Ill. Com. on Media. Vice pres. aux. MacNeal Hosp., 1973-74; program dir. aux. Oak Park Hosp., 1973-74, pres., 1976-78; mem. Ill. Adv. Com. on Edn. governing mem. Chgo. Symphony Orch., Chgo. Zool. Soc., Oak Park-River Forest Community Chest. Mem. Speech Communication Assn., Ill. Speech Assn., Chgo. Council Fgn. Relations, Common Cause, AAUW (dir. Ill. div., pres. Riverside br. 1972-74, del. nat. conv. 1973, 75, 77, 81; mem. AAUW-LWV del. to China 1976), Phi Beta Kappa, Pi Beta Phi (pres. Chgo. West Suburban chpt. 1973-74), Phi Kappa Phi, Kappa Delta Pi, Theta Alpha Phi. Contbr. articles to publs. Address: 7600 Augusta St River Forest IL 60305

SNADER, JACK ROSS, cons. and edn. co. exec.; b. Athens, Ohio, Feb. 25, 1938; s. Daniel Webster and Mae Estella (Miller) S.; B.S., U. Ill., 1959; m. Sharon Genevieve Perschnick, Apr. 4, 1959; children—Susan Mae, Brian Ross. Salesman, Wm. S. Merrell div. Richardson-Merrell, Cin., 1959-61, product mgr., 1961-63, asst. tng. mgr., 1963-64, sales promotion mgr. 1964-65; nat. account mgr. Xerox Corp., N.Y.C., 1965-66, product mgr., 1966-67; gen. mgr. Profl. Communications Assos. div. Sieber & McIntyre Inc., Chgo., 1967-69; pres. Systema Corp., cons. in sales and mktg. mgmt., specializing in high tech. learning systems, Chgo., 1969—. Cert. mgmt. cons. Mem. Nat. Soc. Performance and Instrn., Am. Soc. Tng. and Devel., Assn. Mgmt. Consultants (regional v.p.), Soc. for Applied Learning Tech., Instructional Systems Assn., Inst. Mgmt. Consultants, Chgo. Assn. Commerce and Industry. Clubs: Masons, Shriners, Rotary, Exmoor Country, Tower. Home: 647 Ambleside Dr Deerfield IL 60015 Office: 150 N Wacker Dr Chicago IL 60606

SNAGE, ALEXANDER MICHAEL, II, chem. engr.; b. Detroit, June 18, 1948; s. Edward and Helen Louise (Ammar) S.; B.S. in Chem. Engring., Wayne State U., 1970; m. Loretta Strenk, May 2, 1970; 1 son, Bryan Alexander. Asst. chemist Nelson Chems., Detroit, 1965-69; process chem. engr. Monsanto Co., Trenton, Mich., 1970-74, mfg. chem. process supr., Augusta, Ga., 1974-78, process chem. engring. supr., Trenton, 1978—, also chmn. supervisory com. Monsanto Fed. Employees Credit Union. Mem. Am. Inst. Chem. Engrs., Tau Beta Pi. Roman Catholic. Home: 22111 Irongate Dr Woodhaven MI 48183 Office: Monsanto Co 5045 W Jefferson St Trenton MI 48183

SNAWDER, KENNETH DAVID, dentist; b. Valley Station, Ky., Dec. 5, 1934; s. Nelson Edward and Carrie Elizabeth (Hibbs) S.; B.S., Georgetown Coll., 1962; D.M.D., U. Ky., 1967; m. Carolyn Virginia Marshall, July 26, 1957; children—Lisa Anne, Kenneth David. Intern, James Whitcomb Riley Children's Hosp., Indpls., 1967-68, resident, 1968-69; chmn. dept. pedodontics U. Louisville, 1969-76; part-time practice dentistry specializing in pedodontics, Jeffersonville, Ind., 1969-76, full-time practice, 1976—; cons. to hosps., rehab. centers; lectr. in field. Lic. dentist, Ky., Ind., Ga., Ill., New South Wales, Australia. Diplomate Am. Bd. Pedodontics. Mem. ADA, Internat., Am., SE, Ind., Ky. socs. dentistry for children, Ky. Dental Soc., Ind. Dental Assn. Contbr. articles to profl. jours. Home: 200 N Howard St Clarksville IN 47130 Office: 207 Sparks Ave Jeffersonville IN 47130

SNEAD, THOMAS WESLEY, JR., controls mfg. co. exec.; b. New Eagle, Pa., Dec. 22, 1952; s. Thomas Wesley and Audrey Bernice (Craft) S.; B.S. in Mech. Engring., Bucknell U., 1975, B.A. in Econs., 1975; M.B.A., Rensselaer Poly. Inst., Troy, N.Y., 1977; m. Janis Elaine Ross, Feb. 18, 1978; 1 dau., Heather Lynn. Project engr. Monsanto Co., South Windsor, Conn., 1975-77; sales engr. Fisher Controls Co., Marshalltown, Iowa, 1977, market analyst, 1977-80, mgr. mktg. services, 1980—. Adv., Jr. Achievement, Marshalltown, 1978-79; mem. Marshalltown Community Concert Assn., 1978-79; sponsor Christian Childrens Fund. Mem. ASME, Am. Mktg. Assn., Omicron Delta Epsilon, Omicron Delta Kappa. Republican. Methodist. Club: Iowa Valley Bicycle, Sigma Phi Epsilon. Home: 310 Wauconda Rd Marshalltown IA 50158 Office: PO Box 190 205 S Center St Marshalltown IA 50158

SNEATHEN, JAMES PAUL, mech. engr.; b. Petoskey, Mich., Jan. 19, 1943; s. Lee E. and Helen M.S.; student North Central Mich. Coll., 1961-63; B.S. in Mech. Engring., Mich. State U., 1967; m. Maurine E. Sanford, June 15, 1963; children—Todd, Mark. Designer, HVAC systems and utilities Phys. Plant div. Mich. State U., 1969, power plant maintenance and operations engr., 1970, developer preventive maintenance program, 1971-75, gen. supr. mech. operations, 1976-79, sr. engr. charge energy mgmt. program, 1979; dir. maintenance and ops. Grand Rapids (Mich.) Public Schs., 1979—; condr. workshops and seminars on energy mgmt. Mem. Williamston (Mich.) City Council, 1971-79; mayor City of Williamston, 1977-79; mem. Williamston Planning Commn., Zoning and Bldg. Code Bd. Appeals; chief negotiator for labor contracts. Mem. Nat. Soc. Profl. Engrs. (Young Engr. of Year 1977), Nat. Assn. Energy Engrs., Mich. Sch. Bus. Ofcls., Council Ednl. Facilities Planners, Assn. Phys. Plant Adminstrs. Mem. United Ch. of Christ. Home: 1804 S Hampton SE Grand Rapids MI 49508 Office: 900 Union NE Grand Rapids MI

SNELL, JOSEPH WARREN, assn. exec.; b. Topeka, Mar. 21, 1928; s. Loren Orval and Mabel Lovejoy (Jones) S.; B.A., Washburn U., Topeka, 1955; M.A., U. Kans., 1962; m. Ruth Maria Lassiter, Aug. 28, 1955; children—Bruce Loren, Michael Charles. Mem. staff Kans. Hist. Soc., Topeka, 1957—, dep. dir., 1977, sec., exec. dir., 1977—; author, seminar instr., archival cons. Served to 2d lt. AUS, 1950-53. Mem. Am. Assn. State and Local History, Kans. Hist. Soc., Western History Assn., Kans. Corral Westerners, Pi Gamma Mu, Tau Delta Pi. Congregationalist. Author: Why The West Was Wild, 1963; Great Gunfighters of the Kansas Cowtowns, 1967; Painted Ladies of the Cowtown Frontier, 1964. Editor: The Prairie Scout, 3 vols., 1974, 75, 76; Kansas and the West, 1976. Office: 120 W 10th St Topeka KS 66612

SNELL, JUNE BUENDGEN, educator; b. Chgo., Sept. 27, 1917; d. William George and Julia Marie (Moran) Buendgen; A.A., Wilbur Wright TV Coll., 1966; B.S. in Bus. Adminstrn., Roosevelt U., 1966-69; m. Ralph William Snell, June 7, 1941; children—John Thomas, Juil Thea. Sec. to bus. mgr. U. Ill., Chgo., 1941-44; sec. to v.p. Hall Printing Co., Chgo., 1944-46; owner letter-press bus., 1950-56; office supr., sec. to supt. Dist. 80 Schs., Norridge, Ill., 1957-65; elem., gym, vocat. tchr., librarian, Gt. Books counselor Chgo. Sch. System, 1968-73, tchr. computer sci. and bus. high schs., 1973—; part-time bus. instr., counselor Triton Coll., River Grove, Ill., 1970-80. Mem. exec. council Coll. Edn., Roosevelt U., 1975—; Sunday sch. tchr., supt. St. James Luth. Ch., Chgo., 1955-69, recipient Service to Youth award, 1958, missionary sec. Ladies Guild, 1952-53, counselor Camp Augustana, 1957-58; mem. curriculum planning bd. United Luth. Chs. Am., 1959-60, area instr. Sunday sch. tchrs., 1960-61; transp. coordinator Pennoyer Sch. PTA, Harwood Hts., Ill., 1953-66, sec., 1959, pres., 1960, program chmn., 1963, recipient citation for service, 1957; active Goodman Theatre Guild, 1970—; life mem. Bethesda Sr. Citizen Home, 1945—, tag day chmn., 1954-55; area chmn., publicity worker Cancer Soc., 1945-50; drama coach Chgo. Park Dist., 1940-43; counselor Spectrum Youth Service, Schaumburg, Ill., 1981. Life mem. AAUW, Soc. for Advancement Mgmt. (hon. mem.; sec. Chgo. sr. chpt. 1976), Roosevelt U. Alumni Assn.; mem. Chgo. Bus. Tchrs. Assn., Adult and Continuing Educators Assn., Nat. Fedn. Republican Women, Ill. Fedn. Rep. Women, Public Adult and Continuing Educators (charter mem., hon. award 1965), Luth. Welfare Assn. (Life; tag day chmn. 1955-58), Ill. Assn. Bus. Tchrs., Chgo. Zool. Soc., Chi Sigma Beta (nat. pres. 1943), Phi Gamma Mu (alumni pres. 1972, editor 1973-75). Clubs: Portage Park Players Drama (sec. 1937), Lady Elks, Order Eastern Star, Dau. of Nile, Republican. Bus. Women Chgo. (pres. 1979-80). Home: 1532 W Bates Ln Schaumburg IL 60193

SNELL, KATHRYNE ELIZABETH, public relations exec.; b. Bicknell, Ind., Dec. 16, 1922; d. Homer Hugh and Lima Blanche (Wagstaff) Cargal; student Lansing Community Coll., 1979—; m. Elwyn Snell, Apr. 4, 1944; children—Kathryne Ann Snell Nuveman, Edward Franklin. Cashier/bookkeeper, agt. Indian Trails Bus Line, Owosso, Mich., 1941-45; personnel clk. Universal Electric Co., Owosso, 1947-51, sec. to v.p./dir. indsl. relations, 1951-55, exec. sec. to chmn. bd., 1955-78, dir. public relations, 1972—. Sec., Washington Sch. P.T.A., 1958-60; sec. Shiawassee dist. exec. bd. Girl Scouts Am., 1960-61; sec. Mother's Club, troop and post 85 Boy Scouts Am., 1963-65; bd. dirs. Com. on Alcohol and Drug Abuse, Shiawassee area, 1974-76; trustee First Bapt. Ch., 1979—, chmn., 1981; mem. Bicentennial Com., Owosso area, 1976-77; mem. indsl. com., spl. gifts com. Shiawassee Area United Way, 1974-79; mem. Shiawassee dist. Boy Scouts Am., 1976—; v.p. Ambassadors, 1977-80; chmn. bd. Christian Edn., First Bapt. Ch., 1967-69. Mem. Profl. Secretaries Internat. (Sec. of Year Shiawassee Valley chpt. 1969, pres. Mich. div. 1975-77), Owosso-Corunna Area C. of C. (mem. exec. bd., Internat. Woman of Year in Bus. and Industry 1975, dir. 1973—, v.p. 1979-80, pres. 1981—). Clubs: Zonta (dir. 1979-81, 1st v.p. 1981—), Order Eastern Star. Home: 2509 Vandekarr Rd Owosso MI 48867 Office: 300 E Main St Owosso MI 48867

SNELL, LUKE MURRAY, materials engr., educator; b. Potsdam, N.Y., June 17, 1945; s. Murray Dean and Pauline Emmajean (Leonard) S.; B.S.C.E., M.S., Okla. U., 1970; m. Wilma Gene Williams, Aug. 20, 1966; children—Diana Marie, Valarie Anne. Materials engr. Law Engring. Testing Co., Birmingham, Ala., Nashville and Louisville, 1974-79; soils and materials engr./constrn. services mgr. Soils and Materials Engrs., TriCities, Tenn., 1979; asso. prof. constrn. So. Ill. U., Edwardsville, 1979—; adj. lectr. Vanderbilt U., 1975-78; spl. instr. Nashville State Tech. Inst., 1977, TriCities State Tech. Inst., 1979. Served in U.S. Army, 1970-71. Registered profl. engr., Tenn., Ky., Ala., W.Va., Ill. Mem. ASCE, Am. Concrete Inst. (6 coms.), Sigma Xi, Chi Epsilon, Assn. Nazarene Bldg. Profls., Engring. Assn. Nashville. Mem. Ch. of Nazarene (chmn. bd. trustees). Contbr. articles to profl. jours. Home: 218 4th Ave Edwardsville IL 62025 Office: Dept Engring and Tech Edwardsville IL 62026

SNIDER, EVANGELINE RUTH, nurse; b. Pontiac, Ill., July 2, 1933; d. John Robert and Helen Bernice (Shroyer) S.; grad. Grace Hosp. Sch. Nursing, Hutchinson, Kans., 1968; A.A., Hutchinson Community Jr. Coll., 1969; B.S.N., Marymount Coll., 1970; M.S.N., Ohio State U., 1971. Staff nurse Grace Hosp., Hutchinson, 1968-69; coll. nurse Marymount Coll., Salina, Kans., 1970; dir. Sch. for Practical Nurse Edn., William Booth Meml. Hosp., Covington, Ky., 1971-73, acting dir., 1977-78, coordinator nursing staff edn., 1974-79; asst. prof. nursing Olivet Nazarene Coll., Kankakee, Ill., 1973; instr. Kankakee Community Coll., 1974; clin. instr. Allied Health Edn., U. Ky., 1974-75; instr. nursing adminstrn. John Wood Community Coll., Quincy, Ill., 1979-81; with dept. nursing VA Med. Center, Cin., 1981—. Mem. Am. Nurses Assn., Ill. Nurses Assn. (commn. on edn.). Home: 2101 Grandin Rd Cincinnati OH 45208 Office: VA Med Center Cincinnati OH

SNIDER, HAROLD FRANCIS, mech. engr.; b. Somerset, Ohio, Dec. 2, 1923; s. Edward Joseph and Mildred Irene (Beaver) S.; B.S. in Mech. Engring., Ohio State U., 1947, M.S. in Mech. Engring., 1948; m. JoAnn Sirockman Winkler, July 19, 1975; children by previous marriage—Janet Snider Samet, Philip Lynn (dec.), Betsy Kay. Project engr. Ohio State U., Columbus, 1948-50; design engr. Ranco Inc., Columbus and Fort Lauderdale, Fla., 1950-61; asst. engring. mgr. Robertshaw Controls Co., Milford, Conn., 1961-65; engring. mgr. Therm-O-Disc Inc., Mansfield, Ohio, 1965-81, dir. engring., 1981, v.p. engring., 1981—; instr. Ohio State U., mem. industry ednl. adv. com.; adv. N. Central Tech. Coll., Mansfield. Served with AUS, 1943-46; PTO. Mem. ASME, Ohio State U. Alumni Assn. Republican. Congregationalist. Patentee electromech. control devices. Home: 57 Yoha Dr Mansfield OH 44907 Office: 1320 S Main St Mansfield OH 44907

SNIDER, JOANNE HOLTZMAN, computing systems co. exec.; b. Johnstown, Pa., Nov. 10, 1943; d. C. Joseph and Kathleen (Welch) Holtzman; A.B. cum laude in Math., U. Mich., Flint, 1970; postgrad. U. Detroit, 1975; children—Christine Marie Snider, Cathy Ann Snider. Tchr. elem. grades Holy Rosary Sch., Flint, Mich., 1965-66; research programmer and analyst U. Mich., Flint, 1968-71; computer cons., Flint, Mich., 1971-72; sr. computer systems analyst dept. EDP, City of Detroit, 1972-73; marketing rep. Xerox computer div., Southfield, Mich., 1973-74; corp. mgr. mgmt. info. systems Bendix Corp., Southfield, 1974-77; marketing cons. Infonetics, Southfield, 1977-78; pres. Citation Computing Systems, Inc., Southfield, 1978—. Named Oakland County Employer of Year, 1980. Mem. Data Processing Mgmt. Assn., NOW. Home: 549 Rolling Rock Bloomfield Hills MI 48013 Office: Citation Computing Systems Inc 25100 Evergreen Rd Southfield MI 48075

SNIDER, KENNETH C., state senator; b. Vincennes, Ind., Jan. 24, 1946; s. Charles A. and Mildred M. (Elhaney) S.; A.S. in Agr., Vincennes U., 1966; B.S., Purdue U., 1968; m. Gwendlolyn S. Mueller, 1968 (div.); 1 son, John. Farmer, auctioneer, Knox County, Ind., 1962—; mem. Ind. State Senate, 1969—. Del. Dem. State Conv., 1968, 70, 72. Served with U.S. Army, 1968-69. Mem. Am. Legion, VFW, Harmony Soc. Methodist. Clubs: Moose, Bincennes Gun. Ind. Golden Gloves boxing champion, 1968, 70. Office: Ind State Senate State Capitol Indianapolis IN 46204*

SNIPE, RONALD HOLLOWAY, publishing co. exec.; b. Berkeley, Calif., Mar. 6, 1944; s. James Roger and Margery Elaine (Holloway) S.; B.S., Utah State U., 1968; M.S., U. Utah, 1969, Ph.D., 1975; m. Elizabeth Jean Norris, June 16, 1968. Teaching fellow in geography U. Utah, 1968-69; dir. Snipe Internat., Lawrence, Kans., 1969—; tchr. civil-criminal law, track coach Air Acad. High Sch., Colorado Springs, Colo., 1976-78; tour guide to Europe, S.Am., Mex., 1971, 77, 78, 79; dep. supt. Colegio Americano de Guayaquil (Ecuador), 1975-76; Dept. State grantee, Bolivia, 1979. Served with USN, 1962-65; Vietnam. Mem. Internat. Reading Assn., Nat. Council Social Studies, Assn. Supervision and Curriculum Devel., Assn. Am. Geographers, U. Hawaii East-West Center, Nat. Geog. Soc., Oceanic Soc., Smithsonian Inst., Nat. Hist. Soc., Phi Delta Kappa, Phi Kappa Phi. Democrat. Episcopalian. Club: Elks (Lawrence). Publisher various Snipes indexes. Home: 2635 Missouri Lawrence KS 66044

SNITZER, MARTIN HARRY, advt. agy. exec.; b. Chgo., Oct. 24, 1925; s. Louis A. and Lillian (Councilbaum) S.; B.S., U. Ill., 1948; postgrad. Northwestern U., 1949; m. Rosalie Ruth Lichtenstien, Mar. 30, 1952; 1 son, Thomas A. With Young & Rubicam, Inc., Chgo., 1948-52; account exec., Earle Ludgin & Co., Chgo., 1952-58; chmn. exec. com. Leo Burnett USA, Chgo., dir., 1970-81; dir. Continental Ill. Venture Corp. Bd. dirs. Chgo. Easter Seal Soc., 1958-62. Served with USAAF, 1943-46. Clubs: Standard (Chgo.); Mid-Am.; Northmoor (Ill.) Country. Office: Prudential Plaza Chicago IL 60601

SNOOK, SYLPHA MAE HIBBS, author, dir.; b. Polk County, Iowa; d. William and Olive (Hibbs) S.; grad. in drama Drake U., 1923; m. Norman Dale Spencer, Sept. 6, 1949. Dir. drama Earlham (Iowa) High Sch. and Jr. Coll., 1928-30; instr. Univ. Forum, Des Moines, 1929-30; dir. drama Ankeny (Iowa) High Sch., 1931-42, St. Augustins Sch., Des Moines, 1948-69, propr. Snook Studios of Singing and Drama, Des Moines, 1940-76; dir. drama and singing Des Moines Jewish Community Center, 1924-70, Salvation Army Community Center, 1945-81, Met. Community Centers, 1945-47; author plays: Corn, 1923, Red Flannels, 1935, Roses on Her Table, 1937, Gold Swords and Silver Buckles, 1939, Women of the Storm, 1936, Stage Business, 1936, Dr. Arthur Beauty Surgeon, 1927, Skunk at the Ladies Aid, 1927, Union Station, 1932, Balcony of Kings, 1942, Up the Valient Road, 1973, Historic Moments, 1976; published Hibbs geneology, 1950; dir. E. Des Moines Kiwanis Spotlight Parade, 1948-65, Iowa State Fair Shows, Living Masterpieces, 1964-81, Iowa Fedn. Music Clubs Prodn., 1963-76; judge talent contests; as actress toured U.S., Can., Peg O' My Heart, 1923, Pays to Advertise, 1924, Across the Street, 1925, Patsy, 1927. Republican precinct committee woman, 1966; Rep. county and state del., 1968. Recipient certificate of appreciation Rep. Party, 1966, Salvation Army, 1974, trophy for play corn, 1946, Pub.'s prize for play Red Flannels, 1937, Best Actress award Iowa Fedn. Women's Clubs, Iowa U., 1936; 1st prize for story Jasper County Heritage Trail, 1980. Fellow Nat. Assn. Tchrs. of Singing; mem. Des Moines Council Allied Arts (pres. 1944-45, 55-59, 69-71), Jr. Counselors Club Des Moines (charter; pres. 1960), Alpha Alpha Alpha. Quaker. Clubs: Des Moines Women's (lit. chmn. 1973-76, drama chmn. 1976-81), Poetry Soc. Des Moines (v.p. 1975-79), Rep. Women's. Home and Office: 1122 6th Ave Des Moines IA 50314

SNORTLAND, HOWARD J., supt. public instrn. State of N.D. Office: State Capitol Bismarck ND 58505

SNOWDEN, GENE, state senator; b. Huntington, Ind., Apr. 7, 1928; s. Ben W. and Anna L. (Orr) S.; student Olivet Nazarene Coll., Kankakee, Ill., 1948-49; m. Carol J. Replogle, Aug. 26, 1949; children—Connie J., Barbara J. and Beverly J. (twins), Jodi Ann. Office mgr. Weaver Popcorn Co., Huntington, 1949-50; operator grocery store, Huntington, 1951; dept. mgr. Montgomery Ward & Co., Huntington, 1951-54; appliance and TV dept. mgr. Wolf & Dessauer Dept. Store, Huntington, 1954-58; life ins. underwriter, Huntington, 1958—; mem. Ind. Ho. of Reps. from 10th Dist., 1964-66, Ind. Senate from 17th Dist., 1966—, pres. pro tem, 1979-80, asst. pres. pro tem, 1981-82; mem. Huntington County Council, 1962-64. Trustee Olivet Coll., 1968—. Huntington Coll., 1965. Recipient Disting. Service award Ind. Jaycees, 1960. Mem. Nat. Soc. State Legislators (past pres., chmn. bd. govs.). Republican. Mem. Nazarene Ch. Club: Huntington Optimists (charter pres.). Office: 18 W Washington St Huntington IN 46750

SNOWDEN, PHILLIP H., state senator; b. St. Joseph, Mo., Oct. 14, 1938; s. Leonard A. and Lillian Pauline (Phillips) S.; B.A., U. Mo., Columbia, 1960, LL.B., 1964; m. Jane Ellen Armstrong, 1961; children—Sharon Lyn, Kristen Gai, Stephanie Mill. Mem. firm Snowden, Crain & DeCruyper; mem. Mo. Ho. of Reps., 1967-77, Mo. Senate, 1977—. Mem. Greater Kansas City Sports Commn., trustee YMCA; adv. bd. Fedn. Christian Athletes; past pres., trustee Meth. Ch. Mem. Phi Delta Theta. Office: State Capitol Jefferson City MO 65101*

SNYDER, BROCK ROBERT, lawyer; b. Topeka, Kans., Sept. 18, 1935; s. Ralph Ernest and Helen Dorothy (Fritze) S.; B.S., U. Kans., 1957; J.D., Washburn U., 1964; m. Carol Lee Cunningham, June 5, 1957; children—Lori, Holli, Staci. Admitted to Kans. bar, 1964; since practiced in Topeka; partner firm Edison, Lewis, Porter Haynes, Topeka. Lectr. Kans. Bar Rev., Nat. Assn. Sch. Execs.; adj. faculty Washburn U. Bd. dirs. Campfire Girls, Topeka Legal Aid Soc., Kans. Legal Services. Served with USMC, 1957-61. Mem. Am., Topeka (chmn. pub. relations com.) bar assns., Bar Assn. State of Kans., Phi Alpha Delta. Clubs: Counselors, Topeka. Home: Route 2 Box 76 Berryton KS 66409 Office: 1300 Merchants National Bank Topeka KS 66612

SNYDER, CHARLES ROYCE, sociologist, educator; b. Haverford, Pa., Dec. 28, 1924; s. Edward D. and Edith (Royce) S.; B.A., Yale U., 1944, M.A., 1949, Ph.D., 1954; m. Patricia Hanson, June 30, 1951; children—Stephen Hoyt, Christiana Marie, Constance Patricia, Daniel Edward. Mem. staff Yale Center Alcohol Studies, 1950-60; asst. prof. sociology Yale U., 1956-60; prof. sociology So. Ill. U., Carbondale, 1960—, chmn. dept., 1964-75, 81—; vis. prof. human genetics Sackler Sch. Medicine, Tel Aviv U., 1980; cons. behavioral scis. tng. com. Nat. Inst. Gen. Med. Scis., NIH, 1962-64; mem. planning com., chmn. program 28th Internat. Congress Alcohol and Alcoholism, 1964. Mem. theol. commn. United Ch. of Christ, 1964—. Served with USNR, World War II. Fellow Am. Sociol. Assn.; mem. Soc. Study of Social Problems (v.p. 1963-64, rep. to council Am. Sociol. Assn. 1964-66), Midwest Sociol. Soc. (dir. 1970—), AAUP. Author: Alcohol and the Jews, 1958; editor: (with D. J. Pittman) Society, Culture and Drinking Patterns, 1962; editorial bd. Quar. Jour. Studies on Alcohol, 1957—; asso. editor Sociol. Quar., 1960-63. Home: 705 Taylor Dr Carbondale IL 62901

SNYDER, DONALD WILLIAM, assn. exec.; b. Nebr., Dec. 17, 1920; s. Christian U. and Mary E. (Kauffman) S.; B.A. in Commerce, Goshen Coll., 1959; M.S. in Hosp. Adminstrn., Northwestern U., 1961; m. Leta, Sept. 9, 1945; children—Donna, JoAnne, Catherine. Adminstrv. resident Riverside Meth. Hosp., Columbus, Ohio, 1960-61; asst. adminstr. N.W. Community Hosp., Arlington Heights, Ill., 1961-63; asst. adminstr. Hackley Hosp., Muskegon, Mich., 1963-66, pres., 1967-75; adminstr. Tawas St. Joseph Hosp., Tawas City, Mich., 1976-79; v.p. Mich. Hosp. Assn. Service Corp., Lansing, 1979—. Fellow Am. Coll. Hosp. Adminstrs.; mem. Am. Hosp. Assn. Office: 6215 W St Joseph Hwy Lansing MI 48917

SNYDER, GARY RONALD, hosp. planner; b. Akron, Ohio, May 7, 1946; s. Harry H. and Zola S.; B.A., Calif. State Coll., Northridge, 1969; M.P.H., U. Mich., 1972; m. Francine Susan Snyder, Sept. 2, 1972; children—Mark Kenneth, Joel Martin. USPHS trainee, 1970-72; cons. HEW, Chgo., 1976-78; mem. Chgo. Bd. Trade, 1976-78; dir. plan devel. and coordination Comprehensive Health Planning Council, Detroit, 1978—. Chmn., Am. Cancer Soc., Detroit, 1973-76; del. Mich. Public Health Assn. Recipient Exceptional Service citation Calif. State Colls., 1970. Mem. Am. Public Health Assn., Mich. Public Health Assn., Am. Mgmt. Assn., Am. Hosp. Assn. Home: 5522 Beauchamp Pl Dr West Bloomfield MI 48033 Office: 1200 Book Bldg Detroit MI 48226

SNYDER, HARRY COOPER, JR., state senator, mcht.; b. Blanchester, Ohio, July 10, 1928; s. Harry Cooper and Marion Elizbeth (Sprague) S.; student Ohio U., 1946-47, Wilmington Coll., 1947-48; m. Dorothy Bacot Blakeney, July 7, 1949; children—Maryanne, Phillip, Emily, Harry, Elizabeth. Vice-pres., treas. family hardware bus., Blanchester. Mem. Ohio State Senate, 1979—; originating dir. Citizens United for Responsible Edn., to 1979, Ohio Retail Polit. Action Com., to 1979; mem. Clinton County Bd. Edn., 1965-79. Mem. Ohio Hardware Assn. (trustee 1975-77), S.W. Region Sch. Bds. Assn. (pres. 1969-79), Ohio Sch. Bds. Assn. (past pres., trustee 1970-79). Republican. Methodist. Clubs: Rotary, Masons. Office: Statehouse Columbus OH 43216*

SNYDER, JACK FREDERICK, educator; b. York, Nebr., May 3, 1930; s. George Frederick and Anna Louise (Barth) S.; B.M.E., U. Nebr., 1953, M.M., 1956, Ed.D. (fellow), 1961; m. Bilva Darlin Stuhr, Mar. 22, 1951; children—William F., Theresa L. Tchr. public schs., Deshler, Nebr., 1956-59; tchr., supr. public schs., Aurora, Nebr., 1959-60; mem. faculty Ball State U., Muncie, Ind., 1961—, prof. ednl. adminstrn., 1971—, dir. advanced grad. programs, 1973—. Served to 1st lt. Adj. Gen. Corps, U.S. Army, 1953-55; Korea. Mem. Am. Assn. Sch. Adminstrs., Assn. for Supervision and Curriculum Devel., Nat. Middle Sch. Assn., Ind. Middle Sch. Assn. (exec. sec., editor jour.), Phi Delta Kappa. Lutheran. Clubs: Muncie Camera; Elks. Home: Rural Route 12 Box 8 Muncie IN 47302 Office: TC 915 Ball State U Muncie IN 47306

SNYDER, MERLE LAVERNE, elec. engr.; b. Anthony, Kans., Mar. 21, 1917; s. Don Richard and Florence (Ford) S.; student Kans. State Tchrs. Coll., 1946-47, Kans. State Engring. Coll., 1947-48; m. Paula Mae McDaniel, Nov. 23, 1941; children—Jeanne Ann (Mrs. Johnnie W. Breckenridge), Kent Edward. Gen. engr., scientist U.S. Bur. Mines, Amarillo, Tex., 1953-56; elec. engr. Litwin Engring. Refinery & Petrochem. Design Co., Wichita, Kans., 1956-60; elec. engr. USAF, McConnell AFB, Wichita, 1960-69; indsl. engr. Def. Contracts Adminstrn., 1969—; pres., chmn. bd. 5B Plastics, Inc.; pres. Plastics Machinery Research, Inc., Ezel Craft Co., Wichita; process cons. Wichita Plastics, Inc. Bd. examiners CSC, 1964-68. Served with USNR, 1942-45. Registered profl. engr., Kans. Mem. Am. Inst. Plant Engrs. Mason. Home: 100 E Lincoln St Derby KS 67037 Office: Mid Continent Airport Wichita KS 67209

SNYDER, MICHAEL ALAN, health services agy. exec.; b. Ft. Wayne, Ind., Aug. 8, 1953; s. Raymond Nicholas and Mary Marceil (Isenbarger) S.; B.A. in English, Ind. U., 1975, B.A. in Media Communications, 1975. Editor, art dir. Univ. Publs., Ft. Wayne, 1974-76; asso. pub. Times Group Newspapers, New Haven, 1976-78; editor, creative dir. Ft. Wayne and Metro Mags., 1978-80; dir. Office of Public Affairs, ARC Regional Hdqrs., Ft. Wayne, 1980—; instr. Ind. U.; cons. United Way, N.E. Ind. Emergency Med. Service. Mem. task force on minorities and media Urban League, 1980—; bd. dirs. Tara Neighborhood Assn., 1977—; mem. Mayor's Govt. Reorgn. Study Com., 1975; bd. dirs. Ft. Wayne Ednl. TV Found.; chmn. arts and letters com. Ind. U. Recipient Fourth Estate award Am. Legion, 1976, 11 awards for writing, editing, photography and art Ind. Collegiate Press Assn. Mem. Ind. U. Alumni Assn. (dir.), Internat. Assn. Bus. Communicators. Roman Catholic. Editor: Return to Learning, 1977; composer: Who Will Roll Away the Stone, 1972; The Writer, To Your Side and A Song for Rhonda, all 1979. Home: 136

E Essex Ln Fort Wayne IN 46825 Office: 1212 E California Rd Fort Wayne IN 46825

SNYDER, MICHAEL DENNIS, EDP exec., clergyman; b. Iowa City, Iowa, Nov. 9, 1942; s. Dennis George O'Brien and Catherine Irene (Brown) S.; B.S. magna cum laude, Mankato State U., 1970; m. Rose Marie Kasper, May 17, 1969; 1 son, Patrick Michael. Accounting clk. Peavey Co., Omaha, 1965-66, programmer, Mpls., 1966-67; tech. cons. data processing Jostens, Owatonna, Minn., 1967-71, systems mgr. corp. finance, 1971-76, group systems mgr., 1977-78; v.p., gen. mgr. Key Mgmt., Inc., Mpls., 1978—; ordained deacon Episcopal Ch., 1976; clergyman, several mission congregations, 1976-78; asst. rector St. John's Ch., Mpls., 1978-80; ordained priest Anglican Catholic Ch., 1981; rector St. Dunstan's Ch., Mpls., 1981—. Served with USAF, 1961-65. Mem. Minn. Honeywell Users Group (pres. 1974-75, dir. 1973-76). Republican. Home: 1550 E 83d St Minneapolis MN 55420 Office: 5201 Eden Circle Minneapolis MN 55436

SNYDER, NATALIE JOYCE, florist; b. Elberfeld, Ind., Feb. 14, 1929; d. Elmer F. and Lydia L. (Ahrens) Thene; student Lockyear's Bus. Coll., 1949; m. James P. Snyder, Apr. 8, 1951; children—James Phillip, James David. With Jim Snyder Florist Greenhouses, Princeton, Ind., 1953—, partner, 1953, sole prop., 1961—. Recipient Florists Transworld Delivery Assn. Disting. award, 1979. Mem. Florists Transworld Delivery Assn., Florafax Internat., Soc. Am. Florists, State Florists Assn. Ind., Ohio Florists Assn., Ky. Florists Assn. Jehovah's Witnesses. Home: 619 S Gibson St Princeton IN 47670

SNYDER, RALPH HOWARD, automotive repair co. exec.; b. Manly, Iowa, July 16, 1923; s. Ralph Harnden and Gertrude Francis (Wendt) S.; student Iowa State U., 1941-43, 46; Brigham Young U., 1943-44; m. Opal Dorothy Peterson, Jan. 19, 1947; children—Donald Carleton, Douglas Eugene, Steven Leroy (dec.). Shop foreman Olds-Cadillac Agy., Estherville, Iowa, 1946-50; exptl. engr. Boeing Aircraft Co., Wichita, Kans., 1950-53; founder Snyder's Garage, Wichita, 1953—. Cons. with instrs. of local auto vocational classes in various high schs. Active Boy Scouts Am., 1959-68. Chmn. Democratic precinct com., 1969-71. Served with USAAF, 1943-46. Mem. Automotive Service Council. Presbyn. (trustee 1971-73). Clubs: Masons, Shriners, Lions. Club: Bella Vista (Ark.) Country. Home: Route 3 Box K 147 Augusta KS 67010 Office: 3419 E Harry St Wichita KS 67218

SNYDER, ROBERT EDWARD, engring. co. exec.; b. Bloomsburg, Pa., Oct. 7, 1929; s. Allen Russel and Florence Elenore (Heddings) S.; A.A.S. in Food Tech., State U. N.Y., Morrisville, 1955; Mech. Engr., Pa. State U., 1970; m. Frances V. Eiholzer, July 21, 1956; children—Robert E., Karl A., David J. Lab. technician new product devel. and research Libby McNeill & Libby, 1955-56, supr. indsl. engr., 1956-59, plant engr., 1959-63, supr. prodn., 1963-64, plant supt., 1964-65; cons. engr. low temperature refrigeration and cryogenics St. Onge, Ruff & Assos., York, Pa., 1966-69; plant supt. Hanover Brands, Bloomsburg, Pa., 1969-70, corp. dir. engr., 1970-72; pvt. practice consulting to food industry, 1972-76; staff process cons. Arthur G. McKee, Chgo., 1974-76; staff food process cons. Ellerbe Assos., Inc., Bloomington, Minn., 1976-79; sr. staff specialists Brown & Root, Houston, 1979—. Pres. Houston (Del.) Vol. Fire Co.; sec. Shiloh (Pa.) Vol. Fire Co.; v.p. Shiloh Vol. Fire Police. Served with USN, 1948-52. Mem. Inst. Food Technologists, Assn. Operative Miller, Am. Soc. Heating and Refrigeration Engrs., Grain Elevator and Processing Soc. Democrat. Roman Catholic. Home: 2919 Holly Green Dr Kingwood TX 77339 Office: 4100 Clinton Dr Houston TX 77001

SNYDER, RONALD WARREN, mktg. research and devel. co. exec.; b. Phila., Feb. 6, 1947; s. Ronald Clark and Bertha Elizabeth S.; A.A.S., Gloucester County Coll., Sewell, N.J., 1972. Owner, operator Eagle Advt., Inc., Springfield, Mo., 1973-74; profl. adventurer, 1974-78; chmn. bd., chief exec. officer Overseas Research & Devel. Inc., Springfield, 1978—; Mo. coordinator Vietnam Vets. in Bus., 1979-80; mem. U.S. Senatorial Bus. Adv. Bd. Served with USAR, 1966-69; Vietnam. Decorated Purple Heart, Combat Inf. badge. Mem. Am. Mgmt. Assns., Solar Lobby, Am. Assn. Small Research Cos., Internat. Shooters Devel. Fund, Nat. Rifle Assn., Springfield Area C. of C. Republican. Lutheran. Editor Vanguard mag., 1971-72. Office: Box 267 Jewell Sta Springfield MO 65801

SNYDER, SONYA RUTH MCGINNIS, hosp. personnel adminstr.; b. Ft. Leavenworth, Kans., Jan. 30, 1936; d. Velmer Wayne and Ruth Maxine (Babbitt) McGinnis; B.A., Northwestern U., 1957; M.S. in Indsl. Relations, Loyola U., Chgo., 1967; m. Daniel W. Snyder, Jr., Nov. 29, 1968. Personnel dir. Luth. Deaconess Hosp., Chgo., 1961-68; dir. personnel policies and procedures Rush Presbyn.-St. Lukes Med. Center, Chgo., 1968-71; personnel dir. Schwab Rehab. Hosp., Chgo., 1971-73, Copley Meml. Hosp., Aurora, Ill., 1973-79, Palos Community Hosp., Palos Heights, Ill., 1979—. Mem. adult edn. com., evening lay acad. Palos Park (Ill.) Presbyterian Community Ch., 1976-81, chmn., 1978—; mem. Palos Park Bicentennial Com., 1975-76. Mem. Am. Soc. Personnel Adminstrs. (accredited exec. in personnel), Am. Soc. Hosp. Personnel Adminstrs., Chgo. Hosp. Personnel Mgmt. Assn. (pres. 1975-76), Chgo. Hosp. Council. Office: Palos Community Hosp 80th Ave and McCarthy Rd Palos Heights IL 60463

SNYDER, TIMOTHY LEE, educator; b. Canton, Ohio, June 27, 1956; s. Robert William and Betty Ann (Christman) S.; B.S. in Organizational Communication, Ohio U., 1978, M.A. in Human Resource Devel., 1981. Dir. communications O'Neil's, Akron, Ohio, 1978-80; instr. interpersonal communication Ohio U., Athens, 1980—, pre-coll. counselor, 1981—; cons. Ohio U. Alumni Assn. Office trainer Careline Inc. vol. service Southeastern Ohio Crisis Intervention Center, 1978, 80-81, bd. dirs., 1981—. Mem. Internat. Assn. Bus. Communicators, Am. Soc. for Tng. and Devel., Omicron Delta Kappa. Office: 107 Kantner Hall Ohio U Athens OH 45701

SNYDER, WILLIAM EDWARD, librarian; b. Johnsonburg, Pa., Nov. 12, 1930; s. William Penn and Margaret (Stewart) S.; B.A., Pa. State U., 1952; M.L.S., U. Pitts., 1969. Control teller Pitts. Nat. Bank, 1952-63; tchr., librarian Turkeyfoot Valley Area Schs., Confluence, Pa., 1963-68; reference library Ohio State U., Lima, 1969-70, head librarian, Mansfield, 1970-72, Newark, 1976—; head library adminstrv. services SUNY, Albany, 1972-76; cons. Agrl./Tech. Inst. Library, Wooster, Ohio, 1979. Mem. ALA, Acad. Library Assn. Ohio, Alpha Kappa Delta, Beta Phi Mu. Club: Faculty. Home: 327 Union St I-22 Newark OH 43055 Office: Founders Hall University Dr Newark OH 43055

SNYDER, WILLIAM JUNIOR, hosp. adminstr.; b. Meyersdale, Pa., Apr. 6, 1926; s. William Roy and Fannie (Miller) S.; student Bethany (W.Va.) Coll., 1943-44, U. N.C., 1944-45, Harvard U., 1945, George Washington U., 1948-49; M.S. in Mgmt., U.S. Naval Postgrad. Sch., 1964; m. Anna Philip, Aug. 23, 1947; children—Robbyn, Cheryl, Carol. Commd. ensign U.S. Navy, 1945, advanced through grades to comdr., 1963; chief acct., Luke AFB, 1954-55; comdr. Supply Corps, 1955-70; ret., 1970; coordinator mgmt. Supervision Program, San Jose, Calif., 1970-71; asso. prof. W.Va. U. and Frostburg (Md.) State Tchrs. Coll., 1971-72; materiel mgr. Univ. Hosps. of Cleve., 1973—; instr. Case Western Res. U., Cuyahoga Community Coll. Pres., Indian Wells Valley Council for Retarded Children, 1965-67; mem. Speakers Bur., Potomac State Coll. of W.Va. U., 1971-72. Decorated Joint Services Commendation medal; recipient Jr. Coll. Teaching certs., Calif., Ariz. Mem. Am. Soc. Hosp. Purchasing and Materiel Mgmt., N.E. Ohio Soc. Health Care Materiel Mgmt. (past pres.), Internat. Material Mgmt. Soc. (cert. profl. in health care material mgmt.), Ret. Officers Assn. Clubs: Orchard Hills Golf and Country; Lander Haven Country. Author: Bookkeeping for the Small Businessman, 1969; (with Bruce Moritz) Four Functions of Management, 1970. Home: 4016 Ellison Rd South Euclid OH 44121 Office: Univ Hosps 2065 Adelbert St Cleveland OH 44106

SNYDLE, FRANK EMIL, physician, educator; b. Chgo., Jan. 11, 1945; s. Frank and Emily (Capek) S.; B.A., So. Ill. U., 1968, M.S., 1971; Ph.D., U. South Fla., 1975; postgrad. (Ford Found. fellow), Wayne State U., 1975-76; M.D., U. Fla., 1980. NSF fellow, instr. dept. obstetrics and gynecology and anatomy, U. Fla., Gainesville, 1976-77, dir. semen analysis unit, 1976-77, asst. prof. dept. obstetrics and gynecology, 1977-78, instr. and clin. asso. dept. obstetrics and gynecology and div. urology, dept. surgery, 1978-80; lectr., cons. in field. Rasmussen scholar, 1979; Eva H. Wheat scholar, 1978; Mobile Chem. Grad. research grantee, 1974; Biol. Stain Commn. fellow, 1968; So. Ill. U. scholar, 1968. Mem. Pan Am. Andrology Assn., Am. Assn. Sex Educators, Counselors and Therapists (cert.), AMA, Sigma Xi, Phi Sigma. Democrat. Contbr. articles to profl. jours. Office: Dept Obstetrics and Gynecology Oakwood Hospital 18101 Oakwood Blvd Dearborn MI 48124

SOBEL, BURTON ELIAS, educator, physician; b. N.Y.C., Oct. 21, 1937; s. Lawrence J. and Ruth (Schoen) S.; A.B., Cornell U., 1958; M.D. magna cum laude, Harvard U., 1962; m. Susan Konheim, June 19, 1958; children—Jonathan, Elizabeth. Intern Peter Bent Brigham Hosp., Boston, 1962-63, resident, 1964-66; clin. asso., cardiology br. NIH, Bethesda Md., 1968-71; asst. prof. med., U. Cal. at San Diego, La Jolla, 1971-72, asso. prof. med., also dir. Myocardial Infarction Research Unit, also dir. Coronary Care, 1972-73; asso. prof. medicine Washington U.-Barnes Hosp., St. Louis, 1973-75, prof., 1975—, adj. prof. chemistry, 1979—, dir. cardiovascular div., 1973—, program dir. Specialized Center Research in Ischemic Heart Disease, 1975—, Principles in Cardiovascular Research, 1975—. Cons. U.S. Naval Hosp., San Diego, 1971-73, Geomet Inc., Los Angeles, 1972-73; mem. renal adv. com. Nat. Heart, Lung and Blood Inst., 1975-79; prin. investigator Multicenter Investigation of Limitation of Infarct Size, 1978—. Served to lt. comdr. USPHS, 1964-68. Recipient Research Career and Devel. award, USPHS, 1972; Internat. Recognition award Heart Research Found., 1981. Fellow ACP; mem. Am. Heart Assn. (pub. com., 1970-73, clin. and basic sci. councils), Am. Coll. Cardiology (pub. com., 1972-73), Assn. Univ. Cardiologists, Am. Soc. Clin. Investigation (councillor 1978-81), Assn. Am. Physicians, Am. Physiol. Soc., Cardiac Muscle Soc., Western Soc. for Clin. Research, Soc. for Exptl. Biology and Medicine, Am. Fedn. for Clin. Research (councillor 1972—), Alpha Omega Alpha. Asso. med. editor The Heart Bull., 1971-72; editor Clin. Cardiology, 1971-74; editorial bd. Circulation, 1971-78, Am. Jour. Cardiology, 1976—; editorial bd., asso. editor Jour. Clin. Investigation, 1977—; editorial bd. Circulation Research, 1974—, Annals of Internal Medicine, 1976—; asso. editor Am. Jour. Physiology, 1978-81. Home: 444 Baker Ave Webster Groves MO 63119 Office: Barnes Hosp 660 S Euclid Av St Louis MO 63110

SOBRERO, AQUILES JOSE, physician; b. Santa Fe, Argentina, Jan. 7, 1922; came to U.S., 1957; s. Aquiles R. and Angela (Gonzalez) S.; M.A., Nat. Coll. Simon de Iriondo, Argentina, 1938; M.D., Universidad Nacional del Litoral, Argentina, 1949; m. Adela Hortensia Mai, Aug. 19, 1954; children—Maria Ines, Aquiles Carlos, Raul Javier. Extern, Police Med. Service, Rosario, Argentina, 1945-49; gen. surgery service Hosp. Roque Saenz Pena, Rosario, 1947-48; intern gen. surgery service Hosp. Central Marcelino Freyre, Rosario, 1947-49, Central Emergency and Surgery Service, Mun. of Rosario, 1948-49; asst. surgeon Hosp. Central Marcelino Freyre, 1949-50; 1st surg. asst. physician Service of Women's Gen. Surgery, 1949-51, outpatient dept. gynecology and sterility Hosp. Italiano Caribaldi, Rosario, 1949-51; sr. coroner Police Med. Service, State Police Santa Fe, 1950-57; chief gynecol. sect., radiotherapy dept. Instituto de Oncologia, Santa Fe, 1950-57; tech. sec. Ministerio de Salud Publicay Bienester Social, Provincia de Santa Fe, 1956-57; med. fellow, chief resident, research dir. M. Sanger Research Bur., N.Y.C., 1957-62, dir., 1962-73;

SODERBERG, FREDERICK ALEXANDER, mfg. co. exec.; b. Braham, Minn., Dec. 28, 1915; s. Fred and Sallie Victoria (Monson) S.; A.A., U. Minn., 1938; m. Virginia Mae Wilson, May 29, 1940; children—Thomas Frederick, Gloria Lynn. Pres., Northwest Optical Service, St. Paul, 1945-58, Soderberg Optical Service, St. Paul, 1958-74; chmn. bd. dirs. Soderberg, Inc., St. Paul, 1974—; dir. Aquarius Contact Lens Co., Indpls. Chmn. St. Paul Police Study Commn., 1964-65; bd. dirs. St. Paul Goodwill Industries; trustee House of Hope Ch., St. Paul. Mem. Nat. Assn. Ind. Optical Wholsalers (pres. 1958), Optical Labs. Assn., Contact Lens Mfg. Assn., Better Vision Inst., Upper Midwest Council for Better Vision. Republican. Presbyterian. Clubs: Town and Country, Northoaks Country, Decathalon, Pools Yacht, Royal Order of Jesters. Home: 6 Evergreen Rd Saint Paul MN 55110 Office: 230 Eva St Saint Paul MN 55107

SODERLUND, HAROLD ARTHUR, radio TV advt. rep. co. exec.; b. Lincoln, Nebr., Jan. 23, 1913; s. Axel D. and Anna E. (Johnson) S.; A.B., U. Nebr., 1935; m. Ethel Bash Perkins, Nov. 3, 1936; children—Sandra (Mrs. Arthur Soons), Jan Allen, Janis B. (Mrs. Robert Kruse), Cecily (Mrs. Michael Frazier). Partner, Universal Advt. Co., Lincoln, 1933-37, Outdoor Display Advt., Omaha, 1947-49; advt. mgr. Sheridan County Star, Rushville, Nebr., 1937, Nebr. Hardware Mcht., Lincoln, 1937; salesman Von Hoffman Corp., 1938-41, Burroughs, 1941-42; civilian moblzn. adviser Office Civilian Def., Omaha, 1942-44; account exec. Buchanan Thomas Advt. Agy., 1944; sales mgr. KFAB Broadcasting Co., 1944-57; owner, mgr. K000 Radio Sta., 1957-58; pres. The Soderlund Co., radio TV representation, Omaha, 1957—. Sunday sch. supt. Congl. Ch., 1952; publicity chmn. Community Chest, Omaha, 1952; instl. rep. Boy Scouts Am., Omaha. Mem. Nat. Assn. Broadcasters (sales mfrs. exec. com. 1947, Broadcast Hall of Fame 1979), Omaha Advt. Club (pres. 1952), Omaha Better Bus. Bur. (dir. 1952), Delta Sigma Rho, Alpha Tau Omega, Masons (32 deg.), Omaha Club, Happy Hollow Club. Recipient certificate meritorious service U.S. Office Civlian Def., 1944, Silver medal award Am. Advt. Fedn., 1971; named Omaha Advt. Man of Year, 1961, 9th dist. Advt. Man, 1962; named to Nebr. Broadcast Hall of Fame, 1979. Home: 2502 Garden Rd Omaha NE 68124 Office: Suite 241 Terrace Plaza 11414 Center St Omaha NE 68144

SOFTLEY, DONALD WESLEY, agronomist; b. Grant, Nebr., Oct. 27, 1953; s. Dwight Wesley and Ruth Luella (Reams) S.; B.S. in Agr., U. Nebr., Lincoln, 1976; m. Cynthia Sue Nelson, June 8, 1974; children—Chad Alan, Craig Wesley. Agriculturist, Agrl. Tech. Co., McCook, Nebr., 1976-78; pres. Farmers Ag Services, Inc., Grant, 1978—. Sr. deacon Grant Congregational Ch., 1980—; pres. Grant Area Jaycees, 1980; past sec., past rescue capt. Grant Vol. Fire Dept., fire capt., 1981. Recipient various Jaycee awards; cert. profl. agronomist Am. Registry Cert. Profls. in Agronomy, Crops, and Soils. Mem. Agronomy Soc. Am., Crop Sci. Soc. Am., Soil Sci. Soc. Am., Nebr. Fertilizer and Agr-Chem. Inst., Nat. Alliance Ind. Crop Cons., Nebr. State Vol. Firefighters Assn., Nebr. Soc. Fire Service Instrs., Nebr. Emergency Care and Rescue Assn., Nat. Assn. Emergency Med. Technicians, Future Farmers Am. Alumni Assn., Grant C. of C., U. Nebr. Alumni Assn. (life), Alpha Zeta. Mem. United Ch. Christ. Club: Elks. Home: Box 703 Grant NE 69140 Office: 332 Central St Suite 2 Grant NE 69140

SOGNEFEST, PETER WILLIAM, mfg. co. exec.; b. Melrose Park, Ill., Feb. 4, 1941; s. Peter and Alvera E. Sognefest; B.S. in E.E., U. Ill., 1964, M.S., in E.E., 1967; m. Margaret Brunkow, Aug. 15, 1964; children—Scott, Brian, Jennifer. Elec. engr. Magnavox Corp., Urbana, Ill., 1964-67; sr. fellow, mgr. research, United Techs. fellow Mellon Inst., Pitts., 1967-71; gen. mgr. for semicondr. ops. United Techs., Pitts., 1971-77; v.p. instruments and controls bus. unit Motorola Inc., Schaumburg, Ill., 1977—; dir. Two-Six Inc. Mem. IEEE. Republican. Presbyterian. Clubs: Univ., Longue Vue, Forest Grove Tennis. Patentee in field. Home: 4 Back Bay Rd Barrington IL 60010 Office: 1299 E Algonquin Rd Schaumburg IL 60196

SOHL, STANLEY DUANE, former museum dir.; b. Naperville, Ill., Nov. 5, 1924; s. Aaron W. and Mable E. (Fauss) S.; B.F.A., U. Nebr., 1949, postgrad.; m. Norma Jean Fischer, Aug. 19, 1949; children—Duane, Jeanine, Glen, Martha, Mark. Instr. art and journalism depts. U. Nebr., Lincoln, 1948-54; mem. staff Nebr. State Hist. Soc., 1949-54; dir. Kans. State Hist. Soc., Topeka, 1954-79, ret., 1979; cons. Truman, Eisenhower museums, Wichita Hist. Assn., Fort Leavenworth Mil. Mus., West Tex. State Mus.; past pres. Mountains-Plains Mus. Conf.; past chmn. Mid-Am. Mus. Conf. Mem. adv. council Menninger Found. Served with USAF. Mem. Kans. Mus. Assn., Am. Assn. State and Local History, Am. Assn. Museums (exec. bd., regional rep., council mem.), Photog. Soc. Am. (asso.), Westerners (Kans. Corral), Kappa Alpha Mu. Editor Mountains-Plains Mus. Conf. Ann. Proc., 1969—; contbr. numerous articles to profl. and popular mags. Home: PO Box 528 Lawrence KS 66044

SOHN, HERBERT, physician; b. N.Y.C., May 23, 1927; s. Maurice I. and Anna (Perlman) S.; B.A., U. Va., 1950; M.D., Chgo. Med. Sch., 1955; m. Rayna Barbara Mayer, June 23, 1971; children—Andy, Douglas, Marc, Tracy, Dana. Intern, Bellevue Med. Center, N.Y.C., 1955-56; resident in urology Univ. Hosp., Cleve., 1956-60; physician Strauss Surg. Group, Chgo., 1960—, chief urology, 1968—; asso. prof. surgery U. Ill., 1978—; mem. staff Louis A. Weiss Hosp., Chgo., Cook County (Ill.) Hosp. Trustee, Chgo. Med. Sch., also sec. bd. trustees; bd. govs. Am. Cancer Soc. Chgo. Served with USN, 1945-46. Am. Urol. Soc. traveling fellow, 1956. Mem. Chgo. Urol. Soc. (past pres.), Chgo. Med. Soc., Ill. Med. Soc. (chmn. polit. action com.), Alumni Assn. Chgo. Med. Sch. (past nat. pres.), AMA, Am. Urol. Assn. Jewish. Splty. editor Chgo. Medicine, 1976—. Office: 4640 N Marine Dr Chicago IL 60640

SOKOL, ROBERT JAMES, obstetrician, gynecologist, educator; b. Rochester, N.Y., Nov. 18, 1941; s. Eli and Mildred (Levine) S.; B.A. with highest distinction in Philosophy, U. Rochester, 1963, M.D. with honors, 1966; m. Roberta Sue Kahn, July 26, 1964; children—Melissa Anne, Eric Russell, Andrew Ian. Intern, Barnes Hosp., Washington U., St. Louis, 1966-67, resident in obstetrics and gynecology, 1967-70, asst. in obstetrics and gynecology, 1966-70, research asst., 1967-68, instr. clin. obstetrics and gynecology, 1970; Buswell fellow in maternal fetal medicine Strong Meml. Hosp., U. Rochester, 1972-73, asst. prof., asso. obstetrician and gynecologist, 1972-73; fellow in maternal fetal medicine Cleve. Met. Gen. Hosp., Case Western Res. U., Cleve., 1974-75, asso. obstetrician and gynecologist, 1973-81, asst. prof. obstetrics and gynecology, 1973-77, asst. program dir. Perinatal Clin. Research Center, 1973-78, co-program dir., 1978—, acting dir. obstetrics, 1974-75, co-dir., 1977—, asso. prof., 1977-81, prof., 1981—, asso. dir. dept. ob-gyn, 1981—; pres. med. staff Cuyahoga County Hosps.; mem. profl. adv. bd. Educated Childbirth, Inc., 1976-80; cons. NIH task forces and Nat. Clearinghouse for Alcohol Info. Mem. pres.'s leadership council U. Rochester, 1976—. Served from capt. to maj. M.C., USAF, 1970-72. Diplomate Nat. Bd. Med. Examiners, Am. Bd. Obstetrics and Gynecology, Sub-Bd. Maternal-Fetal Medicine. Mem. Am. Coll. Obstetricians and Gynecologists, Soc. Gynecologic Investigation, Perinatal Research Soc., Assn. Profs. Ob-Gyn, AMA, Royal, Cleve. acads. medicine, Cleve. Ob-Gyn Soc., Soc. Perinatal Obstetricians, Phi Beta Kappa Alpha Omega Alpha. Republican. Jewish. Contbr. articles and chpts. to med. jours. and books; reviewer several med. jours.; researcher computer applications in perinatal medicine, fetal alcohol effects, cardiac and neuro-physiology. Home: 20120 Scottsdale Blvd Shaker Heights OH 44122 Office: Cleve Met Gen Hosp Perinatal Clin Research Center 3395 Scranton Rd Cleveland OH 44109

SOLAND, EUGENE FREDERICK, clergyman; b. Decorah, Iowa, Jan. 8, 1936; s. Embret G. and Louise Gunhilda (Arness) S.; A.B., Luther Coll., 1950, B.D., 1967; postgrad. St. Mary's U., 1962-63; m. Wanda Mae Gish, Nov. 4, 1961; children—Robert Glen, Ronald Gene, Brenda K. Brain chemistry researcher, Glenwood City, Wis., 1966-69; ordained to ministry Lutheran Ch., 1967; postor Immanuel Luth. Ch., Sioux Center, Iowa, 1969-76, Peace and Our Savior's Luth. Ch., 1969-76, Elk Horn Luth. Ch., Iowa, 1976—. Mem. council Boy Scouts Am., 1970—; bd. dirs. Salem Nursing Homes, 1976—, Okoboji Bible Camp, 1970-76; mem. Rock Valley Betterment Council, 1974-75. Served with USAF, 1960-63. Republican. Lutheran. Home: 4405 Bornholm St Elk Horn IA 51531 Office: 4313 Main St Elk Horn IA 51531

SOLBERG, INGVALD (ESKY), state senator; b. Minot, N.D., Sept. 18, 1905; s. Bert and Lena (Hilden) S.; B.A., Minot State Coll., 1930; M.S., U. N.D., 1940; m. Nellie Florence Coad, Aug. 24, 1930; children—Jeanne Solberg Unruh, Kay Solberg Link, Walter J. Supr. schs., Lansford, Des Lacs and Rolette, N.D., 1939-42; with OPA, 1942-47; fuel tax adminstr., N.D., 1947-48; head dept. econs. Bismarck (N.D.) Jr. Coll., 1948-67; mgr. N.D. Motor Carriers Assn., 1967-73; mem. N.D. Senate from 32d Dist., 1972-75, from 49th Dist., 1975—, vice chmn. transp. com., 1973-75, chmn., 1975—, mem. state and fed. govt. com., employment com., 1975—. Chmn. N.D. Hwy. Users Conf., 1949-73; chmn. bd. dirs. Bismarck Hosp., 1959-67; bd. dirs. Nat. Hwy. Users Fedn., 1958—; del. N.D. Constl. Conv., 1972. Named to N.D. Hwy. Dept. Hall of Honor, 1975. Fellow U. Wis., 1956. Mem. Bismarck Art Assn. (pres. 1954-56), Soc. for Preservation of Gov.'s Mansion, Bismarck C. of C. (chmn. transp. com. 1973-75). Republican. Presbyterian. (elder). Author column Esky Comments in Rolling Along mag., 1967—. Address: 925 N 6th St Bismarck ND 58501

SOLBERG, NELLIE FLORENCE COAD, artist; b. Sault Ste. Marie, Mich.; d. Sanford and Mary (McDonald) Coad; B.A., Minot State Tchrs. Coll., 1930; M.A., N.D. State U., 1963; postgrad. Wash.

State U., 1960, Wyo. U., 1964, St. Cloud (Minn.) Coll., 1971; m. Ingvald Solberg, Aug. 24, 1930; children—Jeanne Elaine (Mrs. Clarence Unruh), Walter Eugene, Kay Louise (Mrs. Arthur Link). Tchr., Bismarck (N.D.) Elementary Schs., 1954-63, art dir. high sch., 1963-72; art instr. Bismarck Jr. Coll., 1964-67; one-woman shows: Minot State Coll., 1963, Dickinson State Coll., 1964, Jamestown Coll., 1964, U. N.D., Valley City State Coll., Bismarck Jr. Coll., 1963, 65, 68, 69, N.D. State U., 1970, 74, Linha Gallery, Minot, N.D., 1972, 74-77, Bank of N.D., 1972-74, 76-77; group shows Gov. John Davis Mansion, 1960, Concordia Coll., Moorhead, Minn., 1965, N.D. Capitol, 1968, 69, Gov. William Guy Mansion, 1971, Internat. Peace Gardens, 1969; mem. Indian Culture Found., 1964—, numerous others; cons. Bismarck Art Assn. Gallery, 1973—, State Capitol Galleries, 1973—; dir. N.D. Petroleum Art Show, 1962, 64, Statewide Religious Arts Festival, Bismarck, 1969—; dir. State Treas.'s Gallery, 1977, N.D. State Capitol, Bismarck, 1973—; co-dir. Indian Art Show, Nat. Congress Am. Indians, Bismarck, 1963. Mem. Civic Music Assn., 1942—; religious arts com. Conf. Chs., 1973; bd. dirs. Citizens for Arts, 1978—. Recipient 3d pl. graphics Five State Show, Pierre, S.D., 1968; Purchase award S.D. Arts Council, 1968, Gov.'s award for arts, 1977; named N.D. Woman Artist of Yr., 1974. Mem. Bismarck (charter, Honor award 1960, pres. 1963-64, 71-72), Jamestown art assns., Linha Gallery (Minot), Nat. League Am. Pen Women (pres. N.D. 1964-66, pres. Medora br. 1972—), Mpls. Soc. Fine Arts, Am. Crafts Council, AAUW, P.E.O. (chpt. pres. 1967-69), Order Eastern Star, Zonta, Bismarck Vets, Meml. Library (life), Soc. Preservation Gov.'s Mansion (charter), Republican Wives Club, Republican Women 1st Ladies Club, Sigma Sigma Sigma. Presbyn. Home: 925 N 6th St Bismarck ND 58501 Studio: 1021 N 6th St Bismarck ND 58501

SOLBRIG, INGEBORG HILDEGARD, educator; b. Weissenfels, Germany, July 31, 1923; came to U.S., 1961, naturalized, 1966; d. Reinhold Johannes and Hildegard (Ferchland) Solbrig; dipl. chem., U. Halle (Germany); B.A. summa cum laude, San Francisco State U., 1964; M.A., Stanford U., 1966, Ph.D., 1969. Chemist, Schoeller Co., Osnabrück, Ger., 1951-58, Stazione Zoologica and Ditta Mercedes, Naples, Italy, 1958-61; asst. prof. German, U. R.I., Kingston, 1969-70, U. Tenn., Chattanooga, 1970-72, U. Ky., Lexington, 1972-75; asso. prof. German U. Iowa, Iowa City, 1975-81, prof. German, 1981—. Recipient Gold medal Austrian Hammer-Purgstall Soc. Cultural and Econ. Relations with Near and Middle East, 1974; Old Gold fellow, 1977; fellow Austrian Ministry Edn., 1976-80; Am. Council Learned Socs. grantee, 1979, German Acad. Exchange Service grantee, 1980; tuition grantee, dissertation fellow Stanford U., other research grants. Mem. Internat. Assn. German Studies, Modern Lang. Assn., Am. Assn. Tchrs. German, Am. Soc. German Lit. in 16th-17th Centuries, Am. Soc. 18th Century Studies, Am. Council Study Austrian Lit., Am. Goethe Soc. (founding mem.), Deutsche Schillergesellschaft, Arthur Schnitzler Soc. Author: Hammer-Purgstall und Goethe, 1973. Prin. editor; Rilke Heute, 1975; editor, translator: Reinhard Goering, Seabattle/Seeschlacht, 1977. Author poems, articles, revs. Home: 1126 Pine St Iowa City IA 52240 Office: Dept German Univ Iowa Iowa City IA 52242

SOLBRIG, NANA SHINEFLUG, dancer, choreographer; b. Chgo., Dec. 21, 1935; d. Otto Ernst and Angelina (Ryan) Strohmeier; B.A. in Math., Northwestern U., 1957; children—Lisa Ann, Otto John. Dancer, Phyllis Sabold Dance Co., 1963-69, Chgo. Contemporary Dance Theatre, 1968-71, Felix Fibich Dance Co., 1971-72; dancer, choreographer, artistic dir. Chgo. Moving Co., 1972—; tchr. Kieth Allison Sch. Ballet, 1968-70, Giordano Sch. Dance, 1971-74, Chgo. Dance Center, from 1971, Columbia Coll., 1974-77; mem. dance panel Ill. Arts Council. Mem. Am. Assn. Dance Cos., Ill. Assn. Dance Cos. Office: Chgo Moving Co 2433 N Lincoln Ave Chicago IL 60614*

SOLEM, MAIZIE ROGNESS, educator; b. Hendricks, Minn., Nov. 8, 1920; d. John A. and Nora Adeline (Engelstad) Rogness; B.A., Augustana Coll., 1942; postgrad. George Washington U., 1955-57, Wright State U., 1970-71; M.Ed., Miami U., Oxford, Ohio, 1970-71; Ed.D., U. S.D., 1976; postgrad. U. Calif., 1978. Tchr., LeMars, Iowa, 1942-43, Internat. Children's Centre, Bangkok, Thailand, 1952-53, George Washington U., Washington, 1957, Fairfax (Va.) schs., 1956-58, Maxwell AFB Sch., Montgomery, Ala., 1963-66; tchr., librarian Central High Sch., Madison, S.D., 1943; dir., tchr., supr. remedial reading tchrs. City schs., Fairborn, Ohio, 1966-71; Title I resource tchr. L.B. Anderson Elem. Sch., Sioux Falls, S.D., 1971-73; primary coordinator Instructional Planning Center, Sioux Falls, 1973-77; curriculum coordinator Sioux Falls public schs., 1973—. Mem. adv. bd. Ret. Sr. Vol. Program, 1974-78, publicity chmn., 1975-78; mem. adv. bd. Vol. Action Center, 1976-78, mem. service com., 1974-78; chmn. exec. bd. Augustana Fellows, 1979-81; scholarship chmn. LaSertoma, 1979-80; active various drives including Heart Fund, Muscular Dystrophy, Cancer Fund. Mem. AAUW, Sch. Adminsrs. S.D. (v.p. 1977-78), Assn. Supervision Curriculum Devel. (pres. 1976-78, nat. exec. council 1979-82), Nat. Assn. Supervision Curriculum Devel. (bd. dirs. 1977-79; mem. nat. selection com. 1977-78), Assn. Childhood Edn. Internat., S.D. Assn. Elem. Prins., Elem., Kindergarten, Nursery Sch. Edn., Nat. Assn. Edn. Young Children, Sioux Land Assn. for Edn. Young Children, NEA, S.D. Edn. Assn., Nat. Council Social Studies, Internat. Reading Assn., S.D. Tchrs. Maths. Orgn., S.D. Assn. Supervision and Curriculum Devel., Orton Soc. Republican. Lutheran. Home: 1600 North Dr Box 911 Sioux Falls SD 57101 Office: 201 E 38th St Sioux Falls SD 57102

SOLES, G. EDWARD, electronics co. exec.; b. Columbus, Ohio, Oct. 29, 1939; s. Clode Mox and Bessie V. (Burdett) S.; student Capital U., 1961; Ph.D. (hon.), Grace Bible Inst., 1973; m. Karen Lee Scott, Aug. 12, 1966; children—Susan Kay, Karie Sue. Installation and service mgr. Boller Electronics, Columbus, 1958-68; pres. Music Man Sound Co., Columbus, 1967—; nat. bus. mgr. Bible Study League Am., Columbus, 1978—. Cable TV commr. City of Columbus, 1975—; mem. arbitration com. Better Bus. Bur., 1976—; sec. Karmel Civic Assn., 1973—; lay minister Methodist Ch., 1976—, chmn. bd. trustees, chmn. adminstrv. bd. Mem. Gospel Music Assn. (life), Columbus C. of C., Jr. C. of C. (Exec. and Pres. award), Fraternal Order Police Assos. (state and local pres., life). Republican. Methodist. Clubs: Capital Men's (past pres.), Electronic VIP (life), Sertoma. Home: 1306 Belden Rd Columbus OH 43229 Office: 3242 N High St Columbus OH 43202

SOLIE, O. B., designer; b. Thorp, Wis., Oct. 29, 1925; s. Henry H. and Jennie (Dahl) S.; B.S., U. Wis., 1950, M.S. with honors, 1951; m. Lorraine M. Ormson, May 24, 1952; 1 dau., Susan Lori. Freelance furniture, housewares designer for firms as Counselor Products, West Mich. Flair, Selig, Dunbar, Ello, Stav-Oak, Dearborn Borg-Warner Health Products, Electrohome Ltd. (Can.), Rockford, Ill., 1951—. Served with USNR, 1944-46. Recipient Product Design award Resources Council Inc., 1976; Walnut Classics award, 1965, 68. Mem. Am. Legion. Republican. Lutheran. Home: 2626 Starkweather Rd Rockford IL 61107 Office: 913 N Main St Rockford IL 61103

SOLOMON, BERNARD, educator; b. Brownsville, Pa., Nov. 19, 1942; s. Nathan and Mary (Leon) S.; B.S. in Elem. Edn. and History, California (Pa.) State Coll., 1965, M.Ed. (grad. fellow) in Spl. Edn., 1969, Ed.S., 1973. Spl. edn. tchr. Avella (Pa.) Area Schs., 1965-66, Uniontown (Pa.) Sr. High Sch., 1966-71; prof., chmn. spl. edn. dept. St. Francis Coll., Ft. Wayne, Ind., 1972—; cons. Head Start, 1973-79; condr. community workshops in community and pvt. schs.; mem. ednl. assessment team Head Start, 1978-79, affirmative action com., 1978-79, now evaluator, trainer, Garrett and Ft. Wayne. Bd. dirs. Allen County Econ. Opportunity Council, 1978-79, Coordinating Council for Handicapped, 1977-79; state advisor Student Council Exceptional Children, 1977-79; co-developer theatre for exceptional children, 1979; mem. ednl. adv. com. Ft. Wayne Head Start, 1981-82; mem. Ft. Wayne Magnet Sch. Com., 1981-82. active Girl Scouts U.S.A., recipient award 1977. Recipient Profl. Service award Allen County Retarded Citizens, 1977; Rotarian fellow to N.Z., 1982—. Mem. Council Exceptional Children (pres.-elect Ind. fedn. 1981-82), Am. Assn. Spl. Educators (dir. 1978-79). Clubs: Masons, Shriners. Contbr. articles to newspapers. Home: 3904 W Taylor Rd Apt 26 Fort Wayne IN 46804 Office: 2701 Spring St Saint Francis College Fort Wayne IN 46804

SOLOMON, CHESTER DOUGLAS, steel co. exec.; b. Monticello, Iowa, Dec. 6, 1924; s. David Sol and Dora (Marmis) S.; student U. Dubuque, 1942-43, U. Iowa, 1946-47; m. Charlotte Lynn Schwartz, Mar. 23, 1947; children—Mark Jay, Steven Lee, Cynthia Kay. Pres., sec., Dubuque Gases and Steel Co. (Iowa), 1954—, dir. Chmn. Dubuque Transit Bd., 1973—; mem. Clarke Coll. Devel. Council, Dubuque, 1975—; trustee Finley Hosp., Dubuque, 1974—; bd. dirs. Dubuque Symphony Orch.; mem. policy bd. Dubuque Met. Area Transit Study, 1973. Served with AUS, 1943-46. Recipient Philanthropic Service award Nat. Jewish Hosp., 1971. Mem. Assn. Steel Distributors (vice chmn. govt. relations com., mem. small bus. legisl council, chmn. Midwest region 1978, nat. dir. 1978, 80-81, pres.'s award for outstanding service 1979). Republican. Jewish. Clubs: Dubuque Golf and Country, B'Nai Brith (past pres.). Home: 1030 Arrowhead Dr Dubuque IA 52001 Office: 120 Railroad Ave Dubuque IA 52001

SOLOMON, DONALD WILLIAM, educator; b. Detroit, Feb. 6, 1944; s. Sidney C. and Bertha C. (Chaiken) S.; B.S. with distinction, Wayne State U., 1961, B.Medicine, 1961, M.S., 1963, Ph.D., 1966, M.D., 1968. Instr. math. Wayne State U., Detroit, 1966; asst. prof. math. U. Wis., Milw., 1966-68, asso. prof. math., 1970-74, asso. chmn. dept. math., 1975-78, chmn. div. natural scis., 1976-78, prof. math. scis., 1974—. NSF fellow, 1962, 63, 64-65; U. Wis. Grad. Sch. research grantee, 1967-68, 73-74; NSF research grantee, 1968-73. Mem. Am. Math. Soc., Math. Assn. Am., N.Y. Acad. Scis. Home: 924 E Juneau St Milwaukee WI 53202 Office: Dept Math Scis Univ of Wis Milwaukee WI 53201

SOLOMON, MICHAEL, civil engr., univ. ofcl., cons.; b. Youngstown, Ohio, Oct. 27, 1921; s. Steve and Maria (Kulynch) S.; B.E., Youngstown U., 1957; M.S., U. Akron, 1962; m. Myrtle M. Chapman, July 7, 1957. Various positions constrn., also press operator Youngstown plant Chrysler Corp., 1946-50; hwy. insp. Ohio Hwy. Dept., Youngstown, 1953; engr.-surveyor Mahoning Valley San. Dist., Youngstown, summers 1954, 57; designer Mahoning County San. Engring. Dept., Youngstown, 1957-67; asst. prof. civil engring. Youngstown U. (now Youngstown State U.), 1957-67; project mgr. san. engring., municipal engring. Mosure & Syrakis Co., Ltd., Youngstown, 1967-80; dir. phys. plant Youngstown State U., 1980—. Served with US Army, 1942-46, to capt. C.E., 1942-53. Registered profl. engr., Ohio. Decorated Bronze Star. Mem. ASCE, Sigma Tau.

SOLOMON, RICHARD HUMPHREY, fire protection engr.; b. Bloomington, Ill., June 2, 1933; s. Robert Clinton and Mildred Marie (Clark) S.; B.S., Ill. Inst. Tech., 1955; m. Jane Joanne Henderson, Oct. 9, 1955; children—Karen, Diane. Asst. chief engr. Ins. Services Office Ill., Chgo., 1955-66; owner, operator Richard H. Solomon & Assos., cons. fire protection engring., 1967—; dir. bldg. and zoning City of Naperville (Ill.), 1971; lectr. in field. Mem. Ill. Fire Commn., 1972-77, chmn., 1975-77; chmn. City of Naperville Bldg. Rev. Bd., 1974-76; adv. bd. Ill. Supt. Pub. Instrn., 1964-70; tech. adv. bd. DuPage County (Ill.), 1966—, fire marshall, 1977—. Served with USNR, 1956-57. Western Actuarial Bur. scholar, 1951-55. Registered profl. engr. Ill., Calif., Ky. Mem. Wis.-No. Ill. Firemen's Assn. (hon.), Nat. Fire Protection Assn. (chmn. bldg. heights and areas 1976—), Ill. (chmn. ethics and practice com. 1968), Nat. socs. profl. engrs., Internat. Assn. Fire Chiefs, Bldg. Ofcls. and Code Adminstrs., Internat. Soc. Fire Protection Engrs. (chmn. engring. edn. com. 1972—). Republican. Congregationalist. Moose. Home: 356 S Loomis St Naperville IL 60540

SOLON, SAM GEORGE, state senator, educator; b. Duluth, Minn., June 25, 1931; s. Nicholas and Demitra (Stasinopoulos) S.; B.S., U. Minn., Duluth, 1958; m. Paula Tool, Nov. 22, 1974; children—John, Nick, Chris, Dina, Vicki, Tracy. Tchr., Duluth Sch. Dist., 1959—, then Morgan Park High Sch.; mem. Minn. Ho. of Reps., 1971-72, Minn. Senate, 1973—. Chmn. Duluth Alcoholic Beverage Adv. Bd., 1967-70; active United Cerebral Palsy. Served with AUS, 1952-54. Recipient awards Minn. Epilepsy League, Western Lake Superior Sanitary Dist., Lake Superior Steelhead Assn. Mem. Nat. Fedn. Tchrs., Minn. Fedn. Tchrs., Duluth Fedn. Tchrs., NEA, Minn. Edn. Assn., Duluth Edn. Assn., YMCA, Am. Legion, VFW. Mem. Democratic-Farmer-Labor Party. Greek Orthodox. Clubs: Moose, Eagles, GIVE, United Comml. Travelers, Am. Hellenic Ednl. Progressive Assn. Office: State Capitol Saint Paul MN 55155

SOLTI, SIR GEORG, conductor; b. Budapest, Hungary, Oct. 21, 1912; s. More and Theres (Rosenbaum) S.; ed. Budapest Music High Sch.; m. Hedi Oechsli, October 29, 1946; m. 2d, Anne Valerie Pitts, Nov. 11, 1967. Musical asst. Budapest Opera House, 1930-33, condr., 1934-39; pianist (refugee), Switzerland, 1939-45; gen. music dir. Bavarian State Opera, Munich, Germany, 1946-52, Frankfurt (Germany) Staatstheater, 1952-60; mus. dir. Royal Opera House Covent Garden, London, 1961-71, Chgo. Symphony Orch. 1969—; pianist Concours Internat., Geneva, 1942; guest condr. various orchs.; condr. Salzburg Festival, Edinburgh and Glyndebourne festivals, Vienna State Opera, Paris Opera, Vienna Philharmonic, Berlin, London, N.Y. Philharmonic orchs., Amsterdam, Concertgebouw, orchs. in San Francisco, Hollywood, Los Angeles, St. Louis, Ravinia (Ill.) Park, Chgo., Chgo. Lyric Opera. Decorated Great Cross of German Republic; comdr. Order Brit. Empire; knight Order Brit. Empire, comdr. Legion Honor (France); recipient grand prix du Disque Mondiale, 1959, 62, 63, 64, 66, 70, 77. Address: Chgo Symphony Orch 220 S Michigan Ave Chicago IL 60604

SOMERS, JAMES LAVAUGHN, tool mfg. co. exec.; b. Portland, Ind., Jan. 19, 1944; s. Ralph Lavaughn and Matilda Fay (Van Trees) S.; B.S., Purdue U., 1967, M.S., 1968, Ph.D., 1972; m. Carol Sue Zorn, Jan. 25, 1964; children—Michael, Jeffrey, Gregory, Daniel. Material handling expediter Armstrong Cork Co., Dunkirk, Ind., 1963-65; prodn. control coordinator, prodn. control supr., sr. staff indsl. engr., mgr. materials mgmt. Collin's Radio Co., Cedar Rapids, Iowa, 1969-73; mgr. inventory mgmt. Snap-on-Tools Corp., Kenosha, Wis., 1973-77, dir. phys. distbn., 1977—. Bd. dirs. Gateway Vocat., Tech. and Adult Edn. Dist., 1978—, Gateway Tech. Inst. Found., 1980—. Mem. Nat. Council Phys. Distbn. Mgmt., Am. Prodn. and Inventory Control Soc., Am. Inst. Indsl. Engrs., Am. Vocat. Assn., Wis. Assn. Vocat. and Adult Edn., Wis. Vocat., Tech. and Adult Edn. Bds. Assn., Sigma Xi, Alpha Pi Mu, Tau Beta Pi. Lutheran. Contbr. articles in field to profl. jours. Home: 1903 89th Place Kenosha WI 53140 Office: Snap-on-Tools Corp 2801 80th St Kenosha WI 53140

SOMERS, ORVILLE HAROLD, hosp. data processor; b. S. Lyon, Mich., Feb. 17, 1937; s. Harold and Mina Pearl (Bariger) S.; B.S., Ferris State Coll., 1959; m. Deloris Ann Wade, Mar. 25, 1961; children—Jeffrey, Michelle. Sr. programmer Fisher Body div. Gen. Motors Corp., Warren, Mich., 1959-66; data processing mgr. Evans Products Co., Plymouth, Mich., 1966-68; dir. info. systems St. Joseph Mercy Hosp., Ann Arbor, Mich., 1968—. Active Little League, South Lyon, Mich., 1971-75. Mem. Am. Hosp. Assn., Electronic Computing Hosp. Orgn., Am. Accounting Assn., Hosp. Info. Systems Assn. (pres. 1974, trustee 1973, 75), Assn. for Computing Machinery, Assn. Record Mgrs. and Adminstrs., Spl. Interest Groups on Bus. Data Processing, Biomed. Computing, Data Communications, Delta Sigma Pi. Baptist. Home: 9555 Rushton South Lyon MI 48178 Office: 5301 E Huron Dr Ann Arbor MI 48106

SOMERS, PATRICIA ANN, ednl. adminstr.; b. Lansing, Mich., Apr. 22, 1949; d. Arthur John and Stella Rose (Hendges) Somers; B.A. with honors, Mich. State U., 1971; M.A. with high honors, U. Ill., 1973; Ph.D. candidate Ohio State U.; m. Mark M. Willett, June 5, 1969; 1 dau., Susan B. Anthony. Recruiter ACTION: Peace Corps/VISTA, 1972; research asso. U. Ill., 1972-73; teaching asso. Ohio State U., 1973; state compliance coordinator NOW, Ohio, 1973-75; personnel specialist women's unit Ohio Dept. Adminstrv. Services, 1974; research coordinator Women's Resource and Policy Devel. Center, Columbus, Ohio, 1975-76; dir. career and life/work planning Denison U., Granville, Ohio, 1976—; tchr. workshops, cons. in field. Democratic candidate city and county offices, Champaign, Ill., 1972, 73; mem. Columbus Area Leadership Program; past chmn. Licking County (Ohio) Fair Housing Commn.; chmn. Coll. Intergovtl. Council Ohio; chmn. govt. affairs com. Midwest Coll. Placement Assn. v.p. Newark (Ohio) chpt. United Ostomy Assn., also mem. Ho. of Dels., 1981. Wodrow Wilson instr., 1977. Mem. NOW (Susan B. Anthony Sisterhood award Ohio chpts. 1975), Am. Soc. Personnel Adminstrn., Midwest Coll. Placement Assn., Columbus Area Coll. Placement Consortium, Am. Coll. Personnel Assn., Am. Personnel and Guidance Assn. Unitarian. Office: Slayter Hall Denison Univ Granville OH 43023

SOMMER, ROGER A., state senator; b. Tazawell County, Ill., Nov. 6, 1943; B.A., Bradley U.; LL.B., U. Va. Admitted to Va. bar, Ill. bar; asst. atty. gen. Ill.; individual practice law, Pekin and Morton, Ill.; mem. Ill. Senate, 1972—. Mem. Am. Legion, Farm Bur. Republican. Address: State Capitol Springfield IL 62706*

SOMMERS, PAUL ALLEN, health care exec.; b. Marshfield, Wis., Apr. 9, 1945; s. Frank Albert and Rosalie Bertha (Steffen) S.; B.S., U. Wis., 1967; M.S., So. Ill. U., 1969, PH.D., 1971; m. Carol Ann Newsom, June 10, 1967; children—Eric Paul, Marc Allen. Instr. health/phys. edn. Wisconsin Rapids (Wis.) public schs., 1967-68; instr. dept. health/phys. edn. So. Ill. U., Carbondale, 1968-69, research asso. dept. spl. edn., 1969-70, instr., 1970-71; evaluation cons. Minn. State Dept. Edn., St. Paul, 1971-72; dir. Spl. Edn. Services-Coop. Edn. Service Agy. 4, Cumberland, Wis., 1972-73; dir. spl. edn. services Wausau (Wis.) Dist. public schs., 1973-75; dir. liaison edn. affairs Comprehensive Child Care Center, Marshfield (Wis.) Clinic and Med. Found., 1975-80; instr. exeptional children U. Wis., Stevens Point, 1973-79, Milton (Wis.) Coll., 1973-79; exec. dir. Comprehensive Child Care Center, Gundersen Clinic and Med. Found., LaCrosse, Wis., 1980—. Bd. dirs. Midstate Epilepsy Chpt., 1976-78, Neurodevel. Inst. for Cerebral Palsy, Wausau Med. Center, 1973-80; bd. dirs., mem. edn. policy com. Sunburst Youth Homes for Emotionally Disturbed, 1975-80, Wis. Assn. Perinatal Centers, 1976-79. Recipient Disting. Service award Epilepsy Assn., 1980; Nat. Doctoral Honors fellow, 1970-71; State of Ill. Masters Honors fellow, 1969-70; State of Wis. scholar, 1966-67, many grants. Mem. Am. Public Health Assn., Nat. Council Adminstrs. of Spl. Edn., Wis. Council Adminstrs. of Spl. Edn. (exec. officer 1975-76), Council for Exceptional Children, Am. Assn. on Mental Deficiency, United Cerebral Palsy Assn. Am., United Cerebral Palsy Assn. Wis., Nat. Epilepsy Assn., Wis. Epilepsy Assn. (pres. Midstate chpt. 1978-80), Easter Seal Soc. Wis. (v.p. 1978-79), Wis. Assn. Perinatal Centers. Lutheran. Contbr. articles to profl. jours. and books. Home: 221 13th Ave S Onalaska WI 54650 Office: 1836 South Ave LaCrosse WI 54601

SOMOGYI, LEL FERENC, info. systems cons.; b. Cleve., July 20, 1954; s. Ferenc and Sarolta Bonaventura (Varga) S.; B.S. in Computer Engring., Case Inst. Tech., Case Western Res. U., 1976, M.S. in Mgmt. Info. Systems, Sch. Mgmt., 1977. Info. systems cons. Ernst & Whinney, Cleve., 1977—, sr. info. systems cons., 1977—; instr. review courses mgmt. actg. Co-chmn. Hungarian Holy Crown Com., 1978. Recipient 1st place award for Engring. and Sci. Rev., Engring. Coll. Mags. Asso., 1975. Mem. Assn. for Systems Mgmt., IEEE, Assn. for Computing Machinery, Cleve. Engring. Soc., Hungarian Assn. (public relations dir. 1979-81, pres. youth com. 1976-79), Arpad Acad. Artists, Scientists, and Writers. Republican. Hungarian Catholic. Club: Sigma Nu Alumni. Co-author: Faith and Fate: A Short Cultural History of the Hungarian People Through a Millenium, 1976 (silver medal Arpad Acad.); editor Engring. and Sci. Rev., 1975-76, Insights—A Hungarian School Publ., 1980—. Home: 19608 Thornridge Ave Cleveland OH 44135 Office: Ernst & Whinney 1300 Union Commerce Bldg Cleveland OH 44115

SOMS, ANDREW PETER, educator; b. Riga, Latvia, Mar. 7, 1938; came to U.S., 1950, naturalized, 1956; s. Peter and Elsa S.; B.S. with high honors in Math. (Disting. Alumni fellow 1956-60), Mich. State U., 1960; M.S. in Math. (Woodrow Wilson fellow 1960-61), U. Wis., Madison, 1961, M.S. in Statistics (Wis. Alumni Research Found. fellow 1968-70), 1970, Ph.D. in Statistics (fellow 1970-71), 1972. Statistician, Mich. State Dept. Health, Lansing, 1961-62, Delco Electronics, Milw., 1962-68; computer scientist Burroughs, Wayne, Pa., 1973; sr. statistician G.D. Searle & Co., Skokie, Ill., 1973-75; asso. prof. dept. math., U. Wis., Milw., 1975—; vis. asst. prof. Math. Research Center, summer 1978, fall 1979; cons. pharm. firms. Research grantee U. Wis., Milw., 1976-77, 77-78; Office Naval

Research co-grantee, 1979-81. Mem. Am. Statis. Assn., Biometrics Soc., Inst. Math. Stats. Contbr. papers in field to sci. publs. Home: 401 N Eau Claire Madison WI 53705 Office: Dept Math U Wis Milwaukee WI 53201

SON, SUNG WON, banker; b. Seoul, Korea, Nov. 11, 1944; s. Suk Ryong and Chum Soon (Park) S.; student Harvard Bus. Sch., 1968; Ph.D., U. Pitts., 1972; children—Anne Marie, Rebecca Jill. Asso. prof. Slippery Rock (Pa.) State Coll., 1973-74, asst. prof., 1969-73; sr. economist President's Council Econ. Advisers, Washington, 1973-74; adj. prof. fin. Bethel Coll., Arden Hills, Minn., 1979-80; v.p. Northwestern Nat. Bank, Mpls., 1974-77, sr. v.p., 1977—. Bd. dirs. Minn. State Community Coll. System, 1980—, Children's Theatre Co. and Sch., 1979—; Mem. Bank Adminstrn. Inst. (council 1980—), Nat. Assn. Bus. Economists, Western Econ. Assn., So. Econ. Assn., Atlantic Econ. Assn., Minn. Econ. Assn. (pres. 1979-81). Club: Minneapolis. Office: 7th and Marquette Sts Minneapolis MN 55479

SONKSEN, LARRY LYNN, clin. social worker; b. Marshalltown, Iowa, Sept. 28, 1944; s. Erwin Nicholas and Ardella Winnifred (Petitt) S.; B.A., Calvin Coll., 1968; M.S.W. (fellow 1971-73), Western Mich. U., 1973; m. Joanne Elaine Nienoord, Sept. 3, 1966; children—Andrea Lynne, Derek James, Chad Nicholas. Caseworker, Bethany Christian Services, Grand Rapids, Mich., 1970-71, child welfare supr., 1975-78; family and marriage counselor Family Sers. Assn., Grand Rapids, 1973-75; coordinator, short-term Crisis Unit, clin. social worker Pine Rest Christian Hosp., Grand Rapids, 1978—; clin. instr. dept. psychiatry Coll. Human Medicine, Mich. State U., 1981—; pvt. practice as marriage and family counselor; bd. dirs., pres. Suspected Child Abuse and Neglect, Inc. Sponsor young adults Kelloggsville Christian Reformed Ch. Served with U.S. Army, 1968-70. Cert. social worker, marriage counselor, Mich. Mem. Nat. Assn. Social Workers (Mich. del. assembly coordinator, 1977-79, alt. to del. assembly, 1975, del., 1977), Acad. Certified Social Workers. Club: Grand Rapids Bus. and Profl. Couples (chmn.). Home: 1761 52nd St Kentwood MI 49508 Office: 6850 S Division St Grand Rapids MI 49508

SONNHALTER, MARTHA JEAN, tire and rubber co. public relations exec.; b. Barberton, Ohio, Nov. 20, 1926; d. Karl Frederick and May Rose (Bartel) S.; B.A., U. Akron, 1949. Advt. mgr. Marshall's Dept. Store, Barberton, 1949-50; with Firestone Tire & Rubber Co., Akron, Ohio, 1950—, public relations specialist—ednl. materials, 1961-67, Sr. public relations specialist—corp. publs. and films, 1967—; guest speaker Kent State U. Sch. Journalism. Trustee, Akron Family and Children's Services, 1961-72; mem. public relations com. United Fund, Akron, 1970-71; trustee Associated Health Agys., 1972—; pres. Akron area chpt. Arthritis Found., 1974-76; mem. adv. com. N.E. Ohio Arthritis Center, Cleve., 1979—. Recipient Nat. Vol. Service citation Arthritis Found., 1976. Mem. Bus. Editors Assn. (pres. Akron area chpt. 1957-58), Public Relations Soc. Am. (eligibility chmn. Akron chpt.), Alpha Delta Pi. Author numerous co. booklets, articles. Office: 1200 Firestone Pkwy Akron OH 44317

SONNINO, CARLO BENVENUTO, mfg. co. exec.; b. Torino, Italy, May 12, 1904; s. Moise and Amelia S.; Ph.D., U. Milano (Italy), 1927, LL.B., 1928; m. Mathilde Girodat, Jan. 21, 1949; children—Patricia, Frederic, Bruno. Dir. research Italian Aluminum Co., Milan, 1928-34; pres. Laesa Cons. Firm, Milano, 1934-43; tech. adviser Boxal, Fribourg, Switzerland, 1944-52, Thompson Brand, Rouen, France, 1972-76; materials engring. mgr. Emerson Electric Co., St. Louis, 1956-72, sr. staff scientist, 1972—; prof. metall. engring. Washington U., St. Louis, 1960-68, U. Mo. at Rolla, 1968—; cons. Monsanto Chem. Co., other major firms U.S., Europe. Decorated knight comdr. Italian Republic. Fellow Am. Soc. Metals, ASTM, Sigma Xi, Alpha Sigma Mu (hon.). Patentee process for synthetic cryolite; mfr. 1st aluminum cans in world, 1940; patentee in field metallurgy corrosion. Home: 7206 Kingsbury Blvd Saint Louis MO 63130 Office: Emerson E and S div Emerson Electric Co 8100 W Florissant St Saint Louis MO 63136

SONS, LESTER GEORGE, newspaper exec.; b. Harvey, Ill., June 7, 1931; s. William Henry and Gladys Lydia (Steinko) S.; B.A., U. Mich., 1954; M.A., No. Ill. U., 1979; m. Meya H. Arosemena, Aug. 19, 1961. Reporter, S. Bend (Ind.) Tribune, 1956-57; with Chgo. Heights (Ill.) Star Publs., 1957—, editor, 1974-75, exec. editor, 1975—. Served with AUS, 1954-56. Recipient various profl. awards Nat., No. Ill. Newspaper assns., Ill. Press Assn. Mem. U. Mich. Alumni Assn., Sigma Delta Chi, Kappa Tau Alpha. Club: Chgo. Headline. Roman Catholic. Contbr. to instructional textbooks. Home: 17806 Larkspur Ln Homewood IL 60430 Office: 1526 Otto Blvd Chicago Heights IL 60411

SOOD, JAGDISH CHAND, elec. engr.; b. Amritsar, India, June 30, 1942; s. Fateh Chand and Indra S.; m. Suman Mohindra, Aug. 30, 1970; children—Serena, Neeta, Jiten; came to U.S., 1969, naturalized, 1974; B.E.E., Jadavpur U. India, 1968; M.S. in Indsl. Engring., Ill. Inst. Tech., 1973, M.B.A., 1976. Registered profl. engr., Ill. Sectional officer elec. Central Pub. Works Dept., Govt. of India, Nagpur, 1963-64, Calcutta, 1964-68; asst. lectr. Kenya Poly. Inst., Nairobi, 1969; plant engr. Western Electric Co., Chgo., 1969-78, 79-80, sr. engr., 1981—; power engr. Am. Bell Internat., Inc., Tehran, Iran, 1978-79. Mem. IEEE. Home: 3935 Elm St Downers Grove IL 60515 Office: Western Electric Co Hawthorne Works Dept 4931 Chicago IL 60623

SOPER, HENRY VICTOR, neuroscientist; b. Glen Ridge, N.J., Mar. 10, 1945; s. Kenneth L. and Sylvia (Caldwell) S.; B.A., Yale U., 1966; M.A., U. Conn., 1972, Ph.D., 1974. Neurophysiologist, Brain Research Inst., UCLA, 1974-76, NIH fellow dept. psychology, 1976-78; asst. prof. psychology Calif. State U., Northridge, 1980; research neuroanatomist U. Ill. Coll. Medicine, Chgo., 1978-80, neuroscientist clin. psychology U. Ill., Chgo., 1980—. Served with C.E., U.S. Army, 1966-68. Decorated Bronze Star; Nat. Inst. Neurol. and Communicative Disease and Stroke grantee, 1974-76, NIMH grantee, 1976-78. Mem. Am. Psychol. Assn., AAAS, Psychonomic Sci., Soc. Neurosci., N.Y. Acad. Sci., Am. Assn. Primatologists, Internat. Primatological Soc., Sigma Xi. Episcopalian. Club: Chgo. Griffins Rugby Football. Contbr. articles in field to profl. jours. Home: 1008 S Wisconsin Ave Oak Park IL 60304 Office: Dept Psychology U Ill Chicago Circle Box 4348 Chicago IL 60680

SOPER, MARLEY HUBER, librarian; b. Leslie, Mich., Nov. 11, 1934; s. Wynton Huber and Ruth Anne Mae (Jones) S.; B.A., Andrews U., Berrien Springs, Mich., 1958, M.A. in History, 1978; M.A. in L.S., U. Wis., 1965; m. Beverly Jeanne Jorgensen, Aug. 18, 1957; children—Scott Allen, Sheila Rae. Tchr., librarian Stanton (Mich.) public schs., 1958-61, Wis. Acad., Columbus, 1961-67; acquisitions librarian, then circulation librarian Andrews U., 1961-81, dir. James White Library, 1981—, chmn. dept. library sci., 1979—; treas. Berrien Library Consortium, 1977—. Officer, deacon Seventh-day Adventist Ch., Berrien Springs, 1967—. Mem. ALA, Mich. Library Assn. Office: Room 205 James White Library Andrews Univ Berrien Springs MI 49104

SOPER, QUENTIN FRANCIS, chemist; b. Buhl, Minn., Dec. 3, 1919; s. Claude E. and Dessie E. (Zern) S.; B.Chem., U. Minn., 1940; Ph.D. in Organic Chemistry, U. Ill., 1943; m. Genevieve Landreth, Oct. 5, 1946; children—John, Julia, Dan, Jean. Sr. organic chemist Eli Lilly & Co., Indpls., 1944-62; research scientist, 1962-66, head agrl. organic chemistry research, Greenfield, Ind., 1965-72, sr. agrl. asso., 1972-76, research advisor, 1976—. Recipient Outstanding Achievement award U. Minn., 1977, John Scott award City of Phila., 1980, Pioneer award Am. Inst. Chemists, 1981. Mem. Am. Chem. Soc., Weed Sci. Soc. Presbyterian. Co-inventor Penicillin V; inventor herbicides Treflan, Balan, Paarlan, Surflan, Sonalan, Dipan. Home: 2120 W 38th St Indianapolis IN 46208 Office: Eli Lilly & Co Greenfield IN 46140

SOQUEL, JOHN ALBERT, physician; b. Elyria, Ohio, May 31, 1928; s. John Albert and Mary Ellen (Mills) S.; B.A. in Anatomy, Ohio State U., 1950, M.D., 1954; m. Patricia Ann Graham, Sept. 9, 1950; children—Kay Ellen Soquel Hilton, Lynn Marie. Intern, Akron (Ohio) City Hosp., 1954-55; resident Jefferson Davis Hosp., Houston, 1956-57; public health control officer State N.C., 1955, City of Houston, 1956-57; practice medicine specializing in family medicine, Cuyahoga Falls, Ohio, 1957—; mem. staff Akron City Hosp., 1957—, chief family practice service, 1971-73, hon. mem. staff, 1974—. Bd. dirs. Family Ser., Cuyahoga Falls, 1961-65. Served with USPHS, 1955-57. Diplomate Am. Bd. Family Practice. Fellow Am. Acad. Family Practice; mem. Summit County Med. Assn., Summit County Acad. Family Practice, Ohio State Med. Assn., Ohi State Acad. Family Practice, Interlake Yacht Racing Assn. Lutheran. Clubs: Ohio Republican., Portage Lake Yacht; Masons (Barberton, Ohio). Office: 2695 N Haven Blvd Cuyahoga Falls OH 44223

SORAH, BAXTER LEE, JR., labor union exec.; b. Lee County, Va., June 9, 1920; s. Baxter Lee and Laura Mae (Tignor) S.; degree McClungs' Bus. Coll., Greensboro, N.C., 1942; postgrad. Detroit Inst. Tech., 1950-52; certificate trade union program Harvard U., 1949; m. Eunice G. Gabel, Aug. 19, 1944; children—Sandra, Terry, Janice, Dian, Margaret, Charles, John Scott. Trackman, So. Ry. System, St. Charles, Va., 1940; chief clk.-organizer So. System div. Brotherhood Maintenance of Way Employees, Greensboro, 1940-47, administrtv. asst to pres. Grand Lodge, 1948-70, internat. sec.-treas., 1970—; mem. R.R. Retirement Bd., 1970—; treas. Maintenance of Way Polit. League, 1970—. Served as flight officer USAF, 1942-45; PTO. Decorated Bronze Star. Mem. AFL-CIO Sec.-Treas.'s Assn. Club: Lions. Office: 12050 Woodward St Detroit MI 48203

SORENSON, CATHERINE ADA, mathematician; b. Mt. Vernon, Ohio, Nov. 1, 1949; d. Gus William and Eulaylah (Craig) S.; B.S., U. Ill., Chgo., 1974, M.A., 1978. Lectr. math U. Ill., Chgo., 1979-80, asst. in math., 1980—; lectr. math DePaul U., Chgo., part-time, 1980—. Mem. Ill. Acad. Sci., Nat. Council Tchrs. Math, Ill. Council Tchrs. Math. Methodist. Office: 601 S Morgan St Chicago IL 60635

SORENSON, PAUL MORRIS, farmer, farm orgn. exec.; b. Kennedy, Minn., Feb. 12, 1912; s. Olof Nels and Anna (Helseth) S.; grad. N.W. Sch. Agr., 1932; m. Dorothy Marie McIlraith, Apr. 18, 1936; children—Janice Sorenson Stroom, Alice Sorenson Sedenquist, Betty Sorenson Treumer, Paula. Farmer, Hallock, 1930—; pres.; mem. Kittson County Agr. Soc., 1950—. Chmn. bd. supr. Thompson Twp. Kittson County; bd. dirs. Kittson County Meml. Hosp. Recipient Valley Farmer and Homemaker award Red River Valley Winter Show, Crookston, Minn., 1967, Premier Seed Grower award State of Minn., 1978. Mem. Kittson County (dir.), Minn. crop improvement assns., Kittson County Twp. Officers Assn. (dir., pres.), Internat. Platform Assn. Lutheran (deacon 1941-48). Clubs: Masons, Shriners, Lions (pres. 1965-66). Address: Hallock MN 56728

SORIANO, DANILO BUENAFLOR, neurosurgeon; b. Manila, P.I., May 15, 1938; s. Restituto F. and Leonisa (Buenaflor) S.; B.S., U. Phillippines, 1957, M.D., 1962; m. Lydianila S. San Pedro, Sept. 5, 1964; children—Brian, Perry, Jennifer. Intern, St. Francis Hosp., Pitts., 1962-63; teaching fellow, resident in neurosurgery U. Pitts., 1964-66; asst. instr. neoranatomy Albert Einstein Coll. Medicine, 1966-67, neurosurgery, 1968-69, instr. neurosurgery, 1969-70; chief of neurosurgery Queens Hosp. Center, N.Y., 1970-73; asst. prof. neurosurgery State U. N.Y., Stony Brook, 1972; asst. prof. neurosurgery Rush Med. Coll., Chgo., 1976—; chief of neurosurgery Hempstead Gen. Hosp., 1972-74; cons. neurosurgeon Palos Community, Holy Cross, Central Community, Christ hosps. Recipient William C. Menninger award; NIH research fellow. Diplomate Am. Bd. Neurosurgery. Fellow ACS; mem. Am. Assn. Neurol. Surgeons, Congress Neurol. Surgeons, Internat. Coll. Surgeons, AMA, Chgo., Ill. med. socs., Central Neurosurg. Soc., Soc. Functional Neurosurgery, Mensa, U.S. Chess Fedn., Phi Kappa Phi, Phi Sigma. Republican. Roman Catholic. Contbr. articles profl. jours. Research on spinal cord physiology, spasticity, pain. Composer: I Endure (Voice and Piano), 1960; Silangan Quartet (2 Violins, Viola, Cello), 1976. 1st violinist SW Symphony Orch.; mem. Chamber Music Players. Office: 6600 W College Dr Palos Heights IL 60463

SORKIN, ALEX, optometrist; b. Chgo., Aug. 6, 1937; s. Sidney and Nettie (Horwitz) S.; B.S., Ill. Coll. Optometry, 1963, Dr. Optometry, 1964. Mem. faculty Ill. Coll. Optometry, 1964-66; gen. practice optometry, Chgo., 1964-66, Champaign, Ill., 1972—; researcher and lectr. contact lens design and fitting; supr. research clinic Wesley-Jessen, Inc., Chgo., 1969-72; attending staff dept. ophthalmology Cook County Hosp., Chgo., 1971-72; optometry officer med. service corps U.S. Army, U.S. Army Hosp., Nurnberg, Bavaria, Germany, 1966-68; preceptor Pa. Coll. Optometry, 1979—; Judge Chgo. Pub. Schs. Sci. Fair, 1965, 66; classical music annotator Sta. WTWC-FM, 1973-76; chmn. sect. on eye photography Nat. Eye Research Found., 1969-72, traveling lectr., 1969—, vice chmn. sect. keratoscopy, 1973—; bd. dirs. Cancer Coop., 1977—, pres., 1978-81. Bd. dirs. Champaign-Urbana Symphony, 1980—. Recipient service award Cancer Coop., 1981; cert. in contact lenses Nat. Eye Research Found. Mem. Am. Optometric Assn., Ill. Optometric Assn. (exec. council 1978—, v.p. edn. 1980—, chmn. membership task force 1979—), East Central Ill. Optometric Assn. (pres. 1978-80). Contbr. articles to profl. jours. Home: 1210 W Union St Champaign IL 61820 Office: 605 S Wright St Champaign IL 61820

SOROKAC, JOSEPH ANTHONY, psychologist; b. Wilkes-Barre, Pa., May 21, 1940; s. Joseph Anthony and Anna (Vasilko) S.; B.S., Villanova U., 1963; M.A., U. Detroit, 1965; postgrad. Wayne State U., 1967-68; m. Cheri Lynn Sado, July 12, 1969; children—Elizabeth Marie, Matthew Joseph. Teaching fellow U. Detroit, 1963-65; clin. psychologist Wayne County Gen. Hosp., Eloise, Mich., 1965-77, Walter Reuther Psychiat. Hosp., Westland, Mich., 1977—; lectr. social sci. Lawrence Inst. Tech., Southfield, Mich., 1972-75; instr. psychology U. Windsor (Ont., Can.), 1969-70, Henry Ford Community Coll., Dearborn, Mich., 1976—; part time teaching Wayne County Community Coll., Providence Hosp. Sch. Nursing, Oakland Community Coll., Marygrove Coll., 1971-73; vocat. rehab. tester State of Mich., Livonia, 1972-76; vol. abstractor Psychol. Abstracts, 1971—. Mem. Am. (asso.), Midwestern (asso.), Mich., Pa. psychol. assns., Internat. Psychohist. Assn., Sociedad Interamericana de Psicologia. Roman Catholic. Home: 30109 Lyndon Ave Livonia MI 48154 Office: Walter Reuther Psychiat Hosp Westland MI 48185

SOSEBEE, ALLEN LOUIE, univ. adminstr.; b. Atlanta, Apr. 20, 1921; s. Arbelia and Mary Agusta (Bell) S.; A.B., Cin. Bible Coll., 1949; M.A., Jackson Coll., Honolulu, 1956, B.D., 1958; Ed.D., Ind. U., 1963; m. Doris Yvonne Vester, Aug. 7, 1946; children—Linda Sue, Allen Louie, Craig Elliott. Ordained to ministry Christian Ch. 1947; minister/missionary, 1947-60; teaching asso. Ind. U., 1961-63; dean students Valdosta State Coll., 1963-67; asst. prof. edn. Central Mo. State U., 1967, prof., 1975—, dean admissions and records, 1970—. Mem. Warrensburg (Mo.) exec. bd. Community Betterment Assn., 1974-79. Served with USN, 1942-45. Mem. Mo. Assn. Coll. Registrar and Admissions Officers (pres. 1973-74), Am. Assn. Coll. Registrar and Admissions Officers (regional rep. 1974-76), Am. Legion, Phi Delta Kappa. Club: Rotary (pres. local club 1972-73, dist. govt. 1979-80). Office: Central Mo State U Warrensburg MO 64093

SOSTROM, SHIRLEY ANNE, written communications cons. co. exec., educator; b. Billings, Mont., Dec. 22, 1933; d. Jack Kenneth and Edith Ester (Bates) Thompson; student U. Wyo., 1951-59; B.Sc., No. Ill. U., 1966; M.A., Central State U., 1970; Ph.D., Ohio State U., 1976; m. John Philip Sostrom, July 11, 1950; children—John David, Kristen Ingrid, Edith May. Tchr. various high schs., Ohio, Mont., 1966-74; with Carroll Coll., Helena, Mont., 1972-74; lectr. linguistics and writing Sinclair Coll., 1976-78; program coordinator Sch. Public Adminstrn., Ohio State U., Columbus, 1978-80; lectr. English and journalism Muskingum Coll., 1980-81; pres. Sostrom Assos., Columbus, 1979—; prof. Grad. Sch. Adminstrn., Capital U., Columbus, 1980—. Bd. dirs. Seven Days of Creation, 1980. Mem. Women's Poetry Workshop, Columbus Women's Network, Am. Assn. for Tng. and Devel., Internat. Assn. Bus. Communicators, NEA, Am. Soc. Public Adminstrn., Ohio State U. Alumni Assn., Phi Delta Kappa. Republican. Conglist. Contbr. articles and poetry to mags. Home: 99 E Weber St Columbus OH 43202 Office: 2199 E Main St Columbus OH 43209

SOTER, CONTANTINE SOTIRIOS, radiologist; b. Rachova, Greece, June 30, 1922; s. Sotirios K. and Evangeline (Angeletopoulos) Soteropoulos; came to U.S., 1952, naturalized, 1956; M.D., U. Athens (Greece), 1948; m. Constance Trampas, May 2, 1954; children—Susan, Desirée. Intern, Ill. Masonic Hosp., Chgo., 1952-53, resident in radiology, 1953-56; mem. staff Ill. Masonic Hosp.; chmn. dept. radiology and nuclear medicine NW Community Hosp., Arlington Heights, Ill.; pres. O'Hare Indsl. Clinic. Mem. councilor bd. St. John the Baptist Greek Orthodox Ch., Des Plaines, Ill. Served with Nat. Greek. Army, 1948-51. Diplomate Am. Bd. Radiology, Am. Bd. Nuclear Medicine, Fellow Am. Coll. Radiology; mem. AMA, Radiol. Soc. N.Am., Soc. Nuclear Medicine, Chgo. Radiol. Soc. (sec., pres. 1978-79), Chgo., Ill. med. socs., Hellenic Med. Soc. (pres. Chgo. chpt.). Contbr. articles on radiology to med. jours. Home: 3455 Whirlaway Dr Northbrook IL 60062 Office: 800 W Central Rd Arlington Heights IL 60005

SOUDER, MARK EDWARD, retail furniture exec.; b. Ft. Wayne, Ind., July 18, 1950; s. Edward Getz and Irma (Fahling) S.; B.S., Ind. U., Ft. Wayne, 1972; M.B.A., U. Notre Dame, 1974; m. Diane Kay Zimmer, July 28; children—Brooke Diane, Nathan Elias. Mgmt. trainee Crossroads Furniture Co., Houston, 1974; mktg. mgr. Gabberts Furniture & Studio, Mpls., 1974-76; mktg. mgr., exec. v.p. Souder's Furniture & Studio, Grabill, Ind., 1976-80, pres., 1981—. Publicity chmn. Grabill County Fair, 1977-81; chmn. Quayle for Congress Com., 2d Ward, Ft. Wayne, 1976; adv. Dan Coats for Congress Com., 1980-81; vice chmn. Historic River Cruises of Ft. Wayne. Mem. Midwest Home Furnishings Assn. (dir.), Ft. Wayne, Grabill (dir., sec.) chambers commerce, Allen County Hist. Soc., Alumni Assn. Ind. U. at Ft. Wayne (pres.), Alumni Assn. U. Notre Dame, Ft. Wayne C. of C. (chmn. congressional action com.). Republican. Mem. Apostolic Christian Ch. Home: 13733 Ridgeview Ct Grabill IN 46741 Office: State at Main Grabill IN 46741

SOUDER, PAUL CLAYTON, banker; b. Greencastle, Ind., Dec. 2, 1920; s. Dewey C. and Julia (Dowell) S.; B.A., DePauw U., 1941; grad. Harvard Grad. Sch. Bus. Adminstrn., 1943, Grad. Sch. Banking, Rutgers U., 1951; m. Doris E. Elliott, Sept. 27, 1941; children—Douglas Paul, Julie Jan. Office mgr. Comml. Credit Corp., 1941; credit mgr. Mich. Nat. Bank, 1946, asst. v.p., 1947-52, v.p. Saginaw bd. dirs., 1952-61, sr. v.p., dir., 1961-71, exec. v.p., 1970-72, pres., dir., 1972-80, vice chmn., 1980—; chmn. Mich. Nat. Corp. Outstate Banks, 1980—; chmn. bd., dir. MNB-Valley, MNB-Michiana, MNB-Huron; vice chmn., dir. MNB-Mid Mich.; dir. MNB-Midland, MNB West, MNB of Detroit, Auto-Owners Ins. Co., Wickes Co., Property-Owners Ins., Mich. Nat. Bank, Mich. Nat. Corp., Eisenhour Constrn. Co., Detroit & Mackinac R.R. Co., Jameson Corp., Lake Huron Broadcasting Corp., Homeowners Mut. Ins. Co., Auto Owners Life Ins. Co., Owners Ins. Co., W.F. McNally Co., Inc. Trustee Mich. Wildlife Found., Mich. Week, Delta Wesley Found., Mich. State U. Devel. Fund; bd. dirs., v.p. Frank N. Andersen Found.; bd. dirs. Woldumar Nature Center; co-gen. chmn. devel. fund Saginaw Valley Coll.; mem. Lansing Bicentennial Exec. Com.; past dir. Saginaw Symphony Assn. Served from ensign to lt. comdr. USNR, 1942-46. Recipient Distinguished Service awards; named Saginaw's Outstanding Young Man. Mem. Robert Morris Assos., Am., Mich. bankers assns., Ind. Petroleum Assn. Am., Mich. Oil and Gas Assn., Greater Saginaw C. of C. (past dir.). Methodist. Clubs: Saginaw; Detroit Bankers, Econ. (Detroit); Otsego Ski; Country of Lansing. Author: Financing Oil Production in Michigan, 1951. Home: 2800 Maurer Rd Charlotte MI 48813 Office: Mich Nat Bank Lansing MI 48901

SOUGHERS, RICHARD KEITH, veterinarian; b. Sullivan County, Ind., Jan. 27, 1934; s. Harry Archie and Donna (Gouckenour) S.; student Ind. State U., 1952-54, Ohio State U., 1954-55; D.V.M., Ohio State U., 1961; m. Peggy Sue Angleton, Nov. 14, 1954; children—K. Richard, Tara Kathleen. Practice vet. medicine and surgery, Mooresville, Ind., 1961—. Agrl. subcom. of Haiti Com., Episcopal Diocese of Indpls., 1972-76; vestryman, former jr. and sr. warden St. Mark's Episcopal Ch.; trustee Rural Outreach Opportunity to Serve. Served with U.S. Army, 1954-57. Mem. Central Ind., Ind., Am. vet. med. assns., Phi Zeta. Democrat. Club: Elks. Home: 30 West St Mooresville IN 46158 Office: PO Box 171 Mooresville IN 46158

SOUGSTAD, GREGG EDWARD, chem. engr.; b. Rapid City, S.D., Feb. 11, 1953; s. Edward Eldon and Margaret Venoy (Glendenning) S.; B.Chem. Engring., U. Minn., 1976. Prodn. supr. Corn Sweeteners div. Archer Daniels Midland Corp., Cedar Rapids, Iowa and Decatur, Ill., 1976-79; project engr. Henkel Corp., Mpls., 1979—. Mem. Am. Inst. Chem. Engrs. (asso.). Home: 5212 Beard Ave S Minneapolis MN 55410 Office: 4620 W 77th St Minneapolis MN 55435

SOUKUP, ELOUISE MARILISS, assn. exec.; b. Hastings, Nebr., Oct. 15, 1926; d. Robert George and Gretchen Eloise (Guildner) Hoff; student U. So. Calif., 1945-48; B.A., U. Nebr., 1973; m. Leo Soukup, Jr., Mar. 22, 1948; Children—Leo III, Mariliss Suzanne Soukup Erickson. Bus. mgr., co-owner Leo Soukup Cleaners, Beatrice, Nebr., 1955-78; controller C.D. Hoff, Inc., Hastings, Nebr., 1976—; curator edn. Nebr. State Hist. Soc., Lincoln, 1974-77. Vice chmn. Gage County Republican Party, 1964; bd. dirs. Beatrice (Nebr.) YWCA, 1965-67; bd. dirs. Nebr. Commn. Status of Women, 1977—. Mem. Hastings C. of C., U. Nebr. at Lincoln Alumni Assn. (women's adv. bd. 1974-77), Internat. Fabricare Inst., Women in Laundry and Drycleaning, Nebr. Writers Guild, AAUW, DAR, Pi Alpha Theta, Kappa Delta. Conglist. Clubs: Lockland Country, Soroptimist. Home: Route 1 Doniphan NE 68832 Office: 834 W 2d St Hastings NE 68901

SOULAK, JOSEPH HAROLD, publishing co. exec.; b. Adams, Wis., Mar. 25, 1932; s. Harold Joseph and Mary I. (Turski) S.; A.B., Providence Coll., 1960; postgrad. Boston U., 1960, Roosevelt U., 1969; m. Leanora Galante, Sept. 1, 1956 (div. Oct. 1971); 1 dau., Deborah; m. 2d, Judith A. Sharpe, Oct. 1975. Sports editor Lakeland Pubs., Grayslake, Ill., 1960-62, news editor, 1962-64, mng. editor, 1964-65; news editor Pawtuxet Valley Times, West Warwick, R.I., 1964; mgr. pub. relations Bastian-Blessing Co., Chgo., 1966-68; publs. mgr. Ryerson Steel, Chgo., 1969; dir. news services Ency. Brit., Inc., Chgo., 1969-75; pub., editor South Milw. Voice-Jour., Cudahy Free-Press, The Bay Viewer, Suburbanite (all South Milw.), 1975—; editor PR/Chicago, 1969-75; sec. Wis. Spectacle of Music, Inc., 1977; columnist, writer Waukegan (Ill.) News Sun, 1969-75. Mem. Lake County Safety Commn., 1961-65; mgr. pub. relations for Ill. Senator, 1964-75. Served with USN, 1952-56; Korea. Mem. Nat. Newspaper Assn., Wis. Press Assn., S. Milw. Assn. Commerce (dir., pres. 1976—); Chgo. Press Club. Home: 1332 Manitoba South Milwaukee WI 53172 Office: 723 Milwaukee Ave South Milwaukee WI 53179

SOURS, CALVIN DEAN, veterinarian; b. Marble Rock, Iowa, May 7, 1919; s. Clifton Eugene and Vera Mabel (Bower) S.; D.V.M., Iowa State U., 1941; m. Wanda Charlotte Cooper, Mar. 7, 1942; children—Carol Frances, Roy Cooper. Gen. practice veterinary medicine, Brooklyn, Iowa, 1941-42, Nora Springs, Iowa, 1943, 46-73, Rockford, Iowa, 1973—. Mem. Soldiers and Sailors Relief Commn., 1948-56; school bd. Nora Springs, 1948-51, councilman, Nora Springs, 1954-58; pres. N. Iowa Area Community Coll. Found., Mason City, 1970—. Served with Veterinary Corps, U.S. Army, 1943-46. Mem. Am. Vet. Medicine Assn., Upper Iowa Vet. Medicine Assn. (program chmn. 1978-79, sec., treas. 1958-59, pres. 1979-80), Iowa Vet. Medicine Assn. (meat inspection com., life mem. award, 1976). Republican. Club: Rockford Country. Home: 502 Riverview Dr Rockford IA 50468 Office: 106 E Main St Rockford IA 50468

SOUTHWELL, EUGENE ALLEN, psychologist; b. San Diego, Apr. 9, 1928; s. Daniel and Nora (Valleroy) S.; A.B., Coll. of Pacific, 1951; M.A., U. Iowa, 1961, Ph.D., 1961; children—William Glen, Kim Marlene, Kirk Daniel. Asst. prof. psychology U. Chgo., 1961-64; asso. prof. psychology, chmn. dept. Ind. U., Gary, 1964—; practice clin. psychology, Olympia Fields, 1961—. Served with USAAF, 1945-47. Mem. Ill. Psychol. Assn., N.Y. Acad. Scis., AAUP, Sigma Xi. Author: (with M. Merbaum) Personality: Readings in Theory and Research, 1964, 3d edit., 1978; (with H. Feldman) Abnormal Psychology; Readings in Theory and Research, 1969. Office: 2555 W Lincoln Hwy Olympia Fields IL 60461

SOUTHWELL, HELEN, mental health clinic exec.; b. Gary, Ind., Mar. 9, 1933; d. Louis and Evangeline (Christos) Kremizes; B.A. in English, Ind. U., 1981; m. Eugene A. Southwell; children—Jeffrey, Patricia, Evangeline. Sec., The Anderson Co., Gary, 1951-52, Allied Ins. Agy. Gary, 1952-56; exec. sec. Ind. U., Gary, 1963-69; exec. dir. Southwell Inst., Olympia Field, Ill., 1969—. Vice precinct committeewoman, Gary, 1960-64. Mem. St. Helen's Philoptochos Soc. (dir., membership com. 1975-77), Sigma Kappa Pi (pres. 1951). Mem. Greek Orthodox Ch. Home: 5330 Delaware St Merrillville IN 46410 Office: 2601 W Lincoln Hwy Olympia Fields IL 60461

SOWER, CHRISTOPHER ELIAS, sociologist, educator; b. Ludington, Mich., June 1, 1912; s. David E. and Dorothy (Shafford) S.; B.S., Ashland Coll., 1934; M.A., Ohio State U., 1936, Ph.D., 1948; m. Virginia Judy, Oct. 2, 1937; children—Charles, John, Margaret, William. Sociologist, U.S. Govt., 1941-46; club supr. ARC, Europe, 1943-45; asst. prof. to prof. sociology Mich. State U., East Lansing, 1946—; cons. in field; coordinator seminar on devel. orgns., Colombo, Sri Lanka, 1980. Fulbright scholar, Ceylon, 1955-56; mem. UN Mission on Community Devel. to Ceylon, 1961-62. Mem. Mich. Gov.'s Conservation Study Com., 1963. Mem. Am., Rural, Mich. sociol. assns. Author: (with others) Community Involvement, 1957; contbr. articles profl. jours. Home: 4330 Hulett Rd Okemos MI 48864 Office: Dept Sociology Michigan State Univ East Lansing MI 48824

SOWERS, WESLEY HOYT, lawyer, mgmt. counsel, state senator; b. Whiting, Ind., Aug. 26, 1905; s. Samuel Walter and Bertha E. (Spurrier) S.; B.S., Purdue U., 1926, M.S., 1927; J.D., DePaul U., 1941; grad. Advanced Mgmt. Program, Harvard U., 1960; m. Gladys Krueger, Jan. 21, 1929; children—Penny Sowers Buxton, Wesley Hoyt. Chemist, Shell Oil Co., East Chicago, Ind., 1927-29; sales engr. Nat. Lead Co., St. Louis, 1929-31; admitted to Ill. bar, 1940; lab. supr., patent atty. Pure Oil Co., Chgo., 1932-42; v.p. Bay Chem. Co., New Orleans, 1942-50; v.p. Frontier Chem. Co., Wichita, Kans., 1950-57, pres., 1958-65; mgmt. counsel, Wichita, 1965—; former chmn. bd. Archer Taylor Drug Co., Hershberger Explorations, Inc., Community Antenna TV Wichita, Inc., First Worth Corp.; dir. Fourth Nat. Bank, Coleman Co., Wichita, Gt. Lakes Chem. Co., West Lafayette, Ind.; mem. Kans. State Senate, 1970-80. Past chmn. Met. Planning Commn., Wichita and Sedgwick County, 1958; commr. Kans. Econ. Devel. Bd.; chmn. Kans. Com. for Constl. Revision; chmn. Sedgwick County U.S. Savs. Bonds Sales; past chmn. Kans. Radio Free Europe; meme mem. adv. com. Kans. Geol. Survey; former mem. engring. adv. council Sch. Engring. and Architecture, Kans. State U.; bd. regents Wichita U.; trustee Wichita State U., Wesley Med. Center, Wichita; bd. dirs. Inst. Logopedics, Quivira council Boy Scouts Am., YMCA; trustee M.W. Research Inst.; former mem. adv. bd. Kans. U. Bus. Sch.; mem. Statewide Health Coordinating Council. Registered patent atty. and practitioner ICC. Mem. AAAS, Kans. C. of C. (past pres., past dir.), Wichita C. of C. (pres. 1959, past dir.), Kans. Assn. Commerce and Industry (past pres., dir.), Am. Chem. Soc., Soc. Chem. Industry, Health Systems Agy. Southwest Kans., Ill. Bar Assn., Wichita Bar Assn., Phi Delta Theta. Republican. Club: Rotary. Patentee petroleum tech. Office: 1010 Union Center Wichita KS 67202

SOYUGENC, RAHMI, mfg. co. exec.; b. Pazarcik, Turkey, May 5, 1931; s. Ismail and Ayse S.; came to U.S., 1954, naturalized, 1965; B.S. in Indsl. Engring., U. Evansville, 1959; M.S. in Indsl. Engring., Ill. Inst. Tech., 1964; m. Marjori Zurstadt, Sept. 10, 1960; children—Altay Yakup, Perihan Ayla. Systems analyst Am. Nat. Bank & Trust Co., Chgo., 1960-63; chief of ops. Chgo. Bd. Health, 1963-70; pres. Evansville Metal Products Co. (Ind.), 1970—, Keller St. Corp., Evansville, 1973—. Founder, dir. The Chicago Mosque. Recipient Meritorious Service award Chgo. Heart Assn., 1963, 66. Mem. Ops. Research Soc. Am., Am. Soc. Quality Control (chpt. pres.), Tri-State Council Sci. and Engring. (region pres.), Turkish Am. Cultural Alliance (charter). Moslem. Clubs: Petroleum, Evansville Country. Home: 119 LaDonna Ct Evansville IN 47711 Office: Evansville Metal Inc 2100 N 6th Ave Evansville IN 47710

SPACKMAN, JAMES ROBERT, city planner; b. Bridgeport, Conn., Oct. 28, 1941; s. Paul Eugene and Marion Frances (Biddle) S.; B.S. in Urban Planning, Mich. State U., 1965, M.S. in Resource Devel., 1981; m. Brenda Ann Sabins, Sept. 5, 1964; children—Renate Jill, Kurt Jeffery. Community planner, planning dept. City of Lansing (Mich.), 1967-71; chief planner Model Cities Program, Lansing, 1971-72, dep. planning dir., 1972—. Merit badge counselor Chief Okemos council Boy Scouts Am., 1965-67; bd. dirs. Lansing Swim Assn. Served with C.E., U.S. Army, 1966-67; maj. Mich. Army N.G. Mem. Am. Planning Assn., Am. Inst. Cert. Planners, Nat. Guard Assn., Old Newsboys Assn., Smithsonian Assos. Methodist. Club: Elks. Home: 2931 Pleasant Grove Lansing MI 48910 Office: 119 N Washington Sq Lansing MI 48933

SPADEMAN, ROB A., advt. exec.; b. Lorain, Ohio, Nov. 22, 1954; s. Richard N. and Mary B. (Kozarec) S.; B.S., Kent (Ohio) State U., 1977, postgrad. 1982—. Advt. mgr. Ohio Sci. Inc., Aurora, Ohio, 1977-78; advt. coordinator Gen. Tire Internat., Akron, Ohio, 1978—; instr. public relations Kent State U., 1980-81. Mem. Internat. Assn. Bus. Communicators (1st v.p. 1981), Lake Erie Indsl. Mktg. Assn. Republican. Roman Catholic. Office: 1 General St Akron OH 44329

SPADY, RICHARD JAY, agrl. co. exec.; b. Hastings, Nebr., July 18, 1929; s. John and Alberta Elaine (Perkins) S.; B.S., U. Nebr., 1956, M.A. in Agrl. Econs., 1958; m. Norma Eilene Wolf, June 14, 1958; children—Sarah, John, Stephen, Thomas. Profl. baseball player, Bklyn. Dodgers System, 1948-56; land mgr. Nebr. Game and Parks Commn., Lincoln, 1958-59, area mgr., 1959-63, acquisition agt., 1962-63, chief land mgmt., 1963-69, asst. dir., 1969-74; mgr. farm and trust McKinley & Lanning Co., Hastings, 1974-75, partner, 1975—; dir. First Nat. Bank Hastings. Gov.'s rep. Fed. Pub. Land Law Rev. Commn., 1965-70. Trustee Hastings Coll., 1972—, Mary Lanning Meml. Hosp., Hastings, 1975—. Mem. Soil Conservation Soc. Am., Wildlife Soc., Wildlife Fedn., Soc. Farm Mgmt. and Rural Appraisers, Assn. Profl. Ballplayers. Clubs: Elks, Rotary. Home: 1330 Heritage Dr Hastings NE 68901 Office: 122 N Hastings Ave Hastings NE 68901

SPAETH, DANIEL ROBERT, mfg. co. exec.; b. Cin., Mar. 29, 1946; s. Robert George and Helen Catherine (Jansen) S.; B.A. in Econs. (Western Golf Assn. Evans scholar), Ohio State U., 1968; M.B.A. in Mgmt., Xavier U., Cin., 1972; m. Patricia Ellen, June 24, 1978. With Clopay Corp., Cin., 1972—, product mgr. folding doors div. homewares, 1977-78, mktg. mgr. div. doors, 1978—. Served with U.S. Army, 1968-70. Decorated Army Commendation medal. Mem. Evans Scholars Alumni Assn. Roman Catholic. Home: 7271 Gungadin Dr Cincinnati OH 45230 Office: 101 E 4th St Suite Cincinnati OH 45202

SPAETH, HERBERT HELLMUT, internat. mktg. specialist; b. Bandjermasin, Indonesia, Aug. 28, 1930; came to U.S., 1956, naturalized, 1970; s. Erwin Alfred and Elisabeth (Fanderl) S.; Diploma in Indsl. Mgmt., Bus. Coll., Nuernberg (W. Ger.) 1952. Exec. asst. Acme Mfg. Co., Detroit, 1958-72; internat. relations dir. Acme-Murray Way Internat., Detroit, 1973-75; dir. internat. mktg. Fraser Automation, Sterling Heights, Mich., 1977-78; asso. H.M. Seldon Co., investment realtors, Detroit, 1979—; cons. to indsl., legal and investment firms, 1975—. Mem. Am. Mgmt. Assn., Detroit Bd. Realtors, Christian Bus. Men's Com. U.S.A. Club: Rotary. Home: 770 Withington St Ferndale MI 48220 Office: HM Seldon Co 500 City Nat Bank Bldg Detroit MI 48226

SPALDING, AL, realtor; b. Akron, Ohio, July 30, 1928; s. F. Ross and Margaret (Younker) S.; student Kent State U., 1950-53, Cleve. Coll., 1955-57; m. Mary H. Pickett, Mar. 21, 1952; children—Lisa Anne, Laura Jean, Anne Renee. Real estate appraiser Summit County Auditor's office, 1953-59; sec. Frank Krause, Inc., Akron, 1959-62; pres. Spalding Realty Co., Akron, 1962—; Instr. Am. Inst. Savs. and Loans, 1962-63, Soc. Real Estate Appraisers, 1965—; guest lectr. U. Akron Community Coll., Kent State U., U. Okla., U. Rochester (N.Y.), U. Conn., Malone Coll., Canton, Ohio. Trustee Loyola of Lakes; sec. Akron Area Regional Devel. Bd. Served with USMCR, 1946-49, 50-52. Mem. Am. Soc. Appraisers (sr.; chpt. pres. 1962-63), Akron Area Bd. Realtors (pres. 1970), Nat., Ohio assns. real estate bds., Soc. Real Estate Appraisers (past chpt. pres.; sr. real estate analyst), Am. Soc. Real Estate Appraisers (state dir. 1963-65), Soc. Indsl. Realtors. Clubs: Athletic, Akron City. Home: 594 Upper Merriman Dr Akron OH 44303 Office: 207 Ohio Bldg Akron OH 44308

SPALTER, JON ARTHUR, fin. analyst; b. Cin., Apr. 2, 1953; s. Ben and Bettyann S.; student architecture, U. Cin., 1971-73; archtl. asso., London, 1974; B.Ed. in Architecture (Kinnaird Found. scholar), Miami U., Ohio, 1975; M.B.A. in Fin. and Mgmt., 1977. Surveyors asst. I. Lazarus & Assos., Cin., 1970-72; draftsman Benjamin Dombar, AIA & Assos., Cin., 1969-72; designer Huber Welding and Fabrication, Cin., 1972-74; mgmt. cons. Arthur Andersen & Co., Chgo., 1977-79; fin. methods and controls analyst M&M/Mars, Chgo., 1979—. Home: 621 S Maple Ave 206 Oak Park IL 60304 Office: 2019 N Oak Park Ave Chicago IL 60635

SPANGLER, PAUL LEON, organic chemist, chem. mfg. co. exec.; b. Garnett, Kans., Jan. 5, 1941; s. Donald James and Elma (Pinneo) S.; B.A., Kans. State Coll., 1963, M.S., 1965; m. Mary Jon Hall, June 6, 1965; children—Jennifer Anne, Jeffery Noel. Synthesis chemist Chemagro Corp., Kansas City, Mo., 1965-68; operations mgr. Mallinckrodt, Inc., St. Louis, 1968-74; with Pathfinder Labs., Inc., Maryland Heights, Mo., 1974—, now pres. Mem. Am. Chem. Soc. Methodist. Office: 11542 Fort Mims Dr Saint Louis MO 63141

SPANGLER, RODNEY ZANE, safe co. mgr.; b. Massillon, Ohio, Mar. 27, 1946; s. Zane Franklin and Katherine Florence (Eby) S.; B.S. in Bus. Adminstrn., Franklin U., 1971; M.B.A. candidate Fairleigh Dickinson U., 1976; m. Carmel Anne Massone, June 8, 1974; children—Kimberly Marie, Kara Anne. Tax agt. State of Ohio, Columbus, 1971-73; property tax mgr. MAI, N.Y.C., 1973-76; sales rep. Best Foods, Inc., Cleve., 1976-78; sales engr. Forgings div. Portec, Inc., Canton, Ohio, 1978-79; sales engr. Columbia Tool Steel Co., 1979-81; nat. sales mgr. Herring-Hall-Marvin Safe Co., Canton, 1981—. Served with AUS, 1966-69; Vietnam. Decorated Army Commendation medal, Vietnamese Commendation medal. Mem. Canton Jaycees. Club: Elks. Home: 157 Calico Dr Dover OH 44622 Office: 818 Mulberry Rd Canton OH 44711

SPANN, BETTYE JEAN, ednl. adminstr.; b. East St. Louis, Ill., Nov. 16, 1930; d. LeRoy H. and Minnie P. (Ford) Patterson; B.S., U. Ark., 1952; M.A., U. Mo., 1967; m. Patric N. Spann, June 25, 1952; children—Derrick LeRoy, Monique Renata. Tchr. primary and secondary grades Sch. Dist. 189, East St. Louis, 1952-65, supr. reading clinics, 1966, reading supr., 1967-69, dir. Project Conquest (reading clinics), 1969-82; cons. to Ill. Office Edn., 1972—, RMC Research, Palo Alto, Calif., 1977-78, Learning Achievement Corp., Calif., 1975-77. Active United Fund, East St. Louis, 1968-70, March of Dimes, East St. Louis, 1979—. Mem. Ill. Edn. Assn., Ill. Reading Assn., Internat. Reading Assn., Assn. for Supervision and Curriculum Devel., Ill. Women's Assn. Democrat. Baptist. Home: 632 N 24th St East Saint Louis IL 62205 Office: 2700 Henrietta St East Saint Louis IL 62205

SPANN, CHARLES WARNER, fin. co. exec.; b. Riceville, Iowa, Oct. 4, 1913; s. Charles Frederick and Mary Lucille (Jackson) S.; student Central Coll., 1934, Friends U., 1937-38; B.A. hon. magna cum laude, Greenville Coll., 1939; m. Beulah Mae Devore, Feb. 25, 1956; children—Frederick W., Richard W., David W. Insp., Cessna Aircraft Co., Wichita, Kans., 1940; various positions Wichita Police Dept., 1941-63, lt. col. staff div., 1963-70; dir. security 1st. Data Resources Co., Omaha, 1970—; security bd. Interbank, N.Y.C., 1978—: asst. treas. Mid-Am. Bankcard Assn. lectr. in field. Bd. dirs. Wichita Police and Fire Pension Bd., 1968-70, pres., 1969; bd. dirs. Wichita Municipal Credit Union, 1965-70, pres., 1969. Mem. Am. Soc. Indsl. Security, Met. Law Enforcement Agencies, Internat. Assn. Credit Card Investigators, Nat. Assn. Chiefs Police. Republican. Methodist. Club: Lions (dir. Wichita Downtown 1968-69). Home: 1401 S Kansas Wichita KS 67211 Office: 1st Data Resources Co 7301 Pacific St Omaha NE 68114

SPANNAUS, WARREN RICHARD, atty. gen. Minn.; b. St. Paul, Dec. 5, 1930; s. Albert and Anna S.; ed. U. Minn., U. Minn. Law Sch.; m. Marjorie Clarkson; children—Christine Ann, David, Laura. Admitted to Minn. bar; spl. asst. atty. gen. State of Minn., 1963-65, now atty. gen.; mem. staff Senator Walter F. Mondale, 1965-66, campaign dir., 1966; finance dir. Minn. Democratic-Farmer-Labor State Central Com., 1967, state chmn., 1967-69, chmn. Midwestern Regional Conf. Attys. Gen., 1972-73. Bd. dirs. Sch. Social Devel., Mpls., United Cerebral Palsy Greater St. Paul. Served with USNR, 1951-54. Mem. Hennepin County Bar Assn., Ramsey County Bar Assn., Minn. Bar Assn., Nat. Assn. Attys. Gen., Am. Judicature Soc. Office: State Capitol St Paul MN 55155*

SPANSKY, ROBERT ALAN, systems analyst; b. Hamtramck, Mich., July 29, 1942; s. Harry J. and Alice E. (Kossak) S.; B.S., U. Detroit, 1964, M.B.A., 1967. Asst. br. mgr. Nat. Bank Detroit, 1965-67, sr. asst. br. mgr., 1969-71; computer programmer Ford Motor Co., Dearborn, Mich., 1972-76, systems analyst, project leader, 1976—. Served with U.S. Army, 1967-69; Vietnam. Decorated Army Commendation medal. Mem. Assn. M.B.A.'s, Alpha Kappa Psi (dist. dir. 1970-74, program chmn. Motor City alumni chpt. 1981-82, Nat. Pres.'s Service and Achievement cert. 1977). Club: Econ. (Detroit). Home: 5574 Haverhill St Detroit MI 48224

SPARBERG, MARSHALL STUART, gastroenterologist; b. Chgo., May 20, 1936; s. Max Shane and Mildred Rose (Haffron) S.; B.A., Northwestern U., 1957, M.D., 1960; m. Nancy Carol Zimmerman, Dec. 27, 1958 (div.). Intern, Evanston (Ill.) Hosp., 1960-61; resident in internal medicine Barnes Hosp., St. Louis, 1961-63; fellow U. Chgo., 1963-65; practice medicine specializing in gastroenterology, Chgo., 1967—; asst. prof. medicine Northwestern U. Med. Sch., 1967-72, asso. prof., 1972-80, prof. clin. medicine, 1980—; instr. Washington U., St. Louis, 1961-63, U. Chgo., 1963-65. Pres. Fine Arts Music Found., 1974-76; bd. dirs. Lyric Opera Guild, 1974—. Served with USAF, 1965-67. Named Outstanding Tchr. Northwestern U. Med. Sch., 1972. Mem. AMA, A.C.P., Am. Gastroent. Assn., Chgo. Med. Soc., Chgo. Soc. Internal Medicine, Chgo. Soc. Gastroenterology (pres.), Chgo. Soc. Gastrointestinal Endoscopy (sec.-treas.). Democrat. Jewish. Author: Ileostomy Care, 1969; Primer of Clinical Diagnosis, 1972; Ulcerative Colitis, 1978; contbr. numerous articles to profl. jours. Office: 233 E Erie St Chicago IL 60611

SPARBOE, ROBERT DUANE, agrl. and food co. exec.; b. Roland, Iowa, June 3, 1931; s. Carl John and Carrie (Quam) S.; student bus. adminstrn. U. Minn., 1955-61, advanced exec. devel. program, 1980; m. Shirley Ann Monson, Mar. 31, 1956; children—Garth David, Beth Ann, Mark Damon, Craig Duane. Founder, Sparboe Chick Co., 1954-61; pres., chmn. bd. Sparboe Agrl. Corp., Litchfield, Minn., 1963—, Sparboe Summit Farms, 1972—; sec., dir. Egg Clearinghouse, Inc. (Durham, N.H.); dir. 1st State Bank of Litchfield; mem. White House Conf. Small Bus., 1980. Mem. U. Minn. Found.; mem. Litchfield City Council, 1968-71. Served with inf. AUS, 1951-54; Korea. Decorated Army Commendation medal. Mem. Am. Mktg. Assn., Am. Mgmt. Assn., Midwest Egg Producers Assn. (past dir.). Republican. Clubs: Mpls. Athletic, Masons, Shriners. Home: 420 Golf Terr Litchfield MN 55355 Office: 125 E Commercial St Litchfield MN 55355

SPARGER, CHARLES FORREST, physician and surgeon; b. Goree, Tex., Sept. 25, 1924; s. Marvin Wheeler and Rosa Nell (Perrien) S.; student N. Tex. U., 1941-43; B.S., Tex. Christian U., 1945; M.D. cum laude, Southwestern Med. Coll., Tex. U., 1947; Intern, St. Elizabeth's and Gallinger hosps., Washington, 1947-48; gen. practice resident All Saints Episcopal Hosp., Ft. Worth, Tex., 1948-49, resident in surgery USPHS Hosp., New Orleans, 1953-56, resident in thoracic surgery USPHS Hosp., S.I., N.Y., 1956-58; fellow in cardiovascular surgery Bailey Clinic and Hahnemann Hosp., Phila., 1958-59; asst. chief surgery USPHS Hosp., S.I., N.Y., 1956-58, 59-62; chief thoracic surgery USPHS Hosp., S.I., N.Y., 1959-62; chief gen. and thoracic surgery USPHS Hosp., Gallup, N. Mex., 1962-66; asst. chief Emergency Health Services, USPHS, Washington, 1967-68; chief surgery and vascular surgery VA Hosp., Butler, Pa., 1968-69; instr. coronary care Frank Phillips Coll., 1975-76; practice medicine specializing in endoscopy, thoracic and gen. surgery, Poplar Bluff, Mo., 1977—; dep. chief of staff Poplar Bluff Hosp.; dep. chief of surgery Lucy Lee Hosp.; chief of staff Ripley County Meml. Hosp., Donphan, Mo., 1981—, also chief of surgery, 1981—. Served with USNR, 1943-45, USPHS, 1947-68. Diplomate Am. Bd. Gen. Surgery. Fellow Am. Coll. Surgeons, Am. Coll. Chest Physicians, Am. Coll. Angiology. Democrat. Baptist. Clubs: Rotary, Toastmasters Internat. Home: Box 1130 Poplar Bluff MO 63901 Office: 117 W Jefferson St Donphan MO 63935

SPARKS, BILLY SCHLEY, lawyer; b. Marshall, Mo., Oct. 1, 1923; s. John and Clarinda (Schley) S.; A.B., Harvard, 1945, LL.B., 1949; student Mass. Inst. Tech., 1943-44; m. Dorothy O. Stone, May 14, 1946; children—Stephen Stone, Susan Lee, John David. Admitted to Mo. bar, 1949; partner Langworthy, Matz & Linde, Kansas City, Mo., 1949-62, firm Linde, Thomson, Fairchild Langworthy & Kohn, 1962—. Mem. Mission (Kans.) Planning Council, 1954-63; mem. Kans. Civil Service Commn., 1975—. Mem. dist. 110 Sch. Bd., 1964-69, pres., 1967-69; mem. Dist. 512 Sch. Bd., 1969-73, pres., 1971-72; del. Dem. Nat. Conv., 1964; candidate for representative 10th Dist., Kans., 1956, 3d district, 1962; treas. Johnson County (Kans.) Dem. Central com., 1958-64. Served to lt. USAAF, 1944-46. Mem. Kansas City C. of C. (legis. com. 1956—), Am., Kansas City bar assns., Mo. Bar, Law Assn. Kansas City, Harvard Law Sch. Assn. Mo. (past dir.), Nat. Assn. Sch. Bds. (mem. legislative com. 1968-73), St. Andrews Soc. Mem. Christian Ch. (trustee). Clubs: Harvard (v.p. 1953-54) (Kansas City, Mo.); Milburn Golf and Country. Home: 8517 W 90th Terr Shawnee Mission KS 66212 Office: City Center Sq 12th and Baltimore Sts Kansas City MO 64196

SPARKS, EARL CHESTER, III, chem. co. exec.; b. Phila., Nov. 9, 1943; s. Earl Chester and Beatrice Elizabeth (Harrison) S.; B.S., Worcester Poly. Inst., 1966, M.S., 1969; M.B.A., SUNY, Buffalo, 1974; m. Janet Ann Wiggins, Aug. 14, 1965; children—Susan Elizabeth, Earl Chester IV, Carol Ann. Process engr. Hooker Chem. Corp., Niagara Falls, N.Y., 1968-74, project engr., 1974-75; project engr. IMC Chem. Group, Ashtabula, Ohio, 1975-76, project mgr., 1976-77, plant supt., 1977-80; sr. project engr. IMC Fertilizer Group, Mundelein, Ill., 1980—. Com. chmn. Boy Scouts of Am., 1979-80. Served to capt. U.S. Army, 1969-71. Mem. Am. Inst. Chem. Engrs., Cleve. Engrng. Soc. Home: 27805 N Orchard Dr Wauconda IL 60084 Office: IMC Fertilizer Group 421 E Hawley St Mundelein IL 60060

SPARKS, MARVIN DAVID, broadcasting co. exec.; b. Dayton, Ohio, Nov. 2, 1948; s. Travis E. and Nanie M. S.; B.D., Arlington Baptist Coll., 1971; postgrad. Wright State U. Announcer, feature personality Sta. WBAP-AM-FM-TV, Ft. Worth-Dallas, 1968-71; pres. M.D. Sparks and Assos., public relations, real estate investment counseling, comml. voice talent, Dayton, 1971-74; v.p., gen. mgr. Sta. WFCJ-FM, Dayton, 1974-80; v.p., gen. mgr. Sta. WTJC-TV, Channel 26, Springfield, Ohio, 1980—. Mem. Ohio Assn. Broadcasters, Nat. Assn. Broadcasters, Nat. Religious Broadcasters, Dayton Area Bd. Realtors, Aircraft Owners and Pilots Assn., Am. Radio Relay League, Nat. Rifle Assn. Republican. Office: PO Box 26 Dayton OH 45401

SPARKS, ROBERT DEAN, gastroentologist, found. exec.; b. Newton, Iowa, May 6, 1932; B.A., U. Iowa, 1955, M.D., Coll. of Medicine, 1957; Dr. (h.c.), Creighton U., 1978; m. Shirley L. Nichols, Sept. 5, 1954; children—Steven, Ann, John. Intern, Charity Hosp. La., New Orleans, 1957-58; resident Charity Hosp. La. in New Orleans Tulane U. Service, 1958-59, fellow in internal medicine, 1959-62; asst. in medicine Tulane U., 1958-59, instr. in medicine, 1959-63, asst. prof. medicine, 1963-64; asso. prof., 1964-68, prof., 1968-72, asst. dean curricular and hosp. affairs, 1964-66, coordinator regional and affiliated clin. programs, 1966-67, dir. of div. grad. and postgrad. med. studies, 1967-68, acting dean, 1967-68, vice dean, 1968-69, chief section gastroentology dept. medicine, 1968-72, dean, 1969-72; vice pres. U. Nebr. and chancellor U. Nebr. Med. Center, 1972-76, prof. medicine Coll. of Medicine, 1972-76; program dir. W.K. Kellogg Found., Battle Creek, Mich., 1977—; asst. vis. physician Charity Hosp. of New Orleans, 1959-63, vis. physician, 1963-70, head Tulane U. Service, 1968-72, sr. vis. physician, 1970-72; asso. internist Ill. Central R.R. Hosp., 1959-72; asso. staff internist DePaul Hosp., New Orleans, 1961-72, chief gastroentology service VA Hosp., New Orleans, 1966-68; mem. med. staff Bishop Clarkson Meml. Hosp., Omaha, 1972-76; med. staff U. Hosp., Omaha, 1972-76; cons. staff Community Hosp., Battle Creek, 1977—; nat. asso. Nat. Center Faculty Devel., U. Miami Sch. Medicine, 1979-80. Mem. interagy. adv. com. New Orleans Area Health Planning Council, 1967-72; vice chmn., 1967-70, chmn., 1970-72, bd. dirs., 1970-72; asst. dir. La. Regional Med. Program, 1967-68, mem. regional adv. group, 1970-72; mem. Mich. Public Health Adv. Council, 1978—; trustee Lakeview Sch. Dist. Bd. Edn., Battle Creek, 1979—, sec., 1980-81. Diplomate Am. Bd. Internal Medicine. Fellow Am. Coll. of Physicians; mem. AAAS, Am., Calhoun County, Mich. med. socs., Health Edn. Media Assn. (bd. dirs., chmn. of the bd. emeritus), Am. Fedn. for Clin. Research, Am. Assn. Med. Colls. (adv. com. for feasibility study on multimedia in health edn., 1973-74, Distinguished mem. 1974—), Am. Gastroenterology Assn., Am. Soc. Internal Medicine, Am. Med. Soc. on Alcoholism (co-chmn. region VI 1973-75), Assn. Acad. Health Center, La. Heart Assn. (student research com. 1964-70, chmn. 1966-70, govt. relations com. 1968-70, bd. dirs. 1968-71), Am. Cancer Soc. (La. div., service com. 1967-72, bd. dirs. 1968-72, sec. 1969-71, chmn. 1971-72, exec. com. 1969-72), Am. Coll. Ob-Gyn (pub. adv. com. 1978—), Cancer Assn. of Greater New Orleans (research adv. com. 1968-72), La., Orleans Parish med. socs., Nu Sigma Nu, Omaha C. of C. (mem. adv. bd. 1976). Contbg. editor Biomed. Communications, 1975—, editorial advisory bd., 1977—; editorial advisory com. Preventive Medicine, 1977—; contbr. numerous articles to profl. jours. Home: 144 Waupakisco Beach Battle Creek MI 49015 Office: WK Kellogg Found 400 North Ave Battle Creek MI 49016

SPARKS, YVONNE STALLARD, vocat. counseling and rehab. center exec.; b. St. Louis, Dec. 31, 1954; d. Fred Homer Stallard and Dorothy June (Hudson) Harris; student St. Louis U., 1973-75; B.S. in Adminstrn. of Justice cum laude, U. Mo., St. Louis, 1977. Sec., New Town/St. Louis, Inc., 1974-75, office mgr., 1975-76; adminstrv. coordinator St. Louis Agy. on Tng. and Employment, 1976-77, adminstrv. asst. to dir.-mgr. adminstrv. support, 1977-80; exec. dir. Vocat. Counseling and Rehab. Services, Inc., St. Louis, 1980—, mem. adv. council, 1980—; mem. employment-edn. com. Urban League St. Louis; mem. service agy. council United Way Greater St. Louis. Bd. dirs. St. Louis Office on Resources for Mentally Retarded/Developmentally Disabled, Midtown Community Corp., 1975-76. Recipient Community Achievement award Iota Phi Lambda, 1980. Mem. Am. Personnel and Guidance Assn., Nat. Employment and Tng. Assn., Am. Mgmt. Assn., Nat. Assn. Rehab. Facilities, Mo. Vocat. Assn., Mo. Assn. Rehab. Facilities. Office: 4000 Laclede Ave Saint Louis MO 63106

SPARR, JAMES EVERHART, fire chief; b. El Dorado, Kans., Oct. 14, 1946; s. James Monroe and Ora Ray Sparr; B.A. in Edn., Wichita State U., 1974, M.P.A., 1981. Mem. Wichita Fire Dept., 1967—, fire chief, 1980—; tchr. fire sci. courses Wichita State U., 1974-76; mem. Nat. Arson Task Force. Mem. Internat. Assn. Fire Chiefs, Met. Fire Chiefs Assn. Office: 455 N Main St 12th Floor Wichita KS 67202

SPATARO, JOSEPH MICHAEL, architect; b. New Brunswick, N.J., Jan. 6, 1948; s. Frederick Carl and Yolanda (Inzano) S.; student Buena Vista Coll., Storm Lake, Iowa, 1967-68; B. Arch., Kent State U., 1974; m. Janet Lee Hughes, July 22, 1972; 1 son, Joseph Edward. Draftsman, Edward W. Prusak, Architect, Ravenna, Ohio, 1971-74; resident designer Walden Co., Aurora, Ohio, 1974-76; architect for David L. Rockman, Warren, Ohio, 1976—; pres. Joseph M. Spataro, Architects, Inc., Ravenna, Ohio, 1976—. Chmn. Ravenna Planning Commn., 1976-77; vice-chmn. Portage County Met. Housing Authority, 1977-78. Recipient Energy Design award Ohio Edison Co., 1972. Mem. Ravenna C. of C., AIA (corp. mem.), Architects Soc. Ohio, Italian Am. Soc. Clubs: Rotary (dir. 1977—), Elks (Ravenna). Architect 1st. Fed. Savs. & Loan Assn., Ravenna, 1977, New Ravenna Safety Complex, 1977, Hudson (Ohio) Common Condominiums, 1978-79, new office bldg. for John Flynn and Robert Paoloni, Kent, Ohio, 1979, New Kent br. Bank One of Ravenna, 1979. Home: 1140 E Riddle Ave Ravenna OH 44266 Office: 222 W Main St Ravenna OH 44266

SPAUN, WILLIAM BECKER, lawyer; b. Atchison, Kans., Aug. 22, 1913; s. Floyd and Bertha (Becker) S.; J.D., U. Mo., Kansas City, 1936; m. Sidney Clyde Collins, Sept. 13, 1930 (dec.); 1 dau., Theon Spaun Martin; m. 2d, Mary Louise Robinson, Aug. 5, 1948; children—William Becker, Mary Lou Spaun Montgomery, Robert R., Sarah Jean Fletcher, Shirley Anne. Admitted to Mo. bar, 1937; U.S. Supreme Ct., 1960; practice law, Hannibal, 1937—; charter mem. World Peace Through Law Center, participant Washington conf., 1965. Regional fund chmn. ARC, 1961, nat. staff mem., 1943-44, nat. vice chmn. fund campaigns, 1963-64, local chpt. chmn., 1977—; govt. appeal agt. SSS, 1968-72, chmn., 1972—. Recipient award for meritorious personal service WW II from ARC. Fellow Am. Coll. Probate Counsel, Harry S. Truman Library Inst. (hon.); mem. Am., Tenth Jud. Circuit (pres. 1958-60) bar assns., Mo. Bar (chmn. Law Day 1961, asso. editor jour. 1942-43), Am. Judicature Soc., Scribes. Republican. Home: 2929 McKinley St Hannibal MO 63401 Office: 617A Broadway Hannibal MO 63401 also PO Box 1169 Hannibal MO 63401

SPEAR, ALLAN HENRY, state legislator; b. Michigan City, Ind., June 24, 1937; s. Irving Seesholtz and Esther Marion (Lieber) S.; B.A., Oberlin Coll., 1958; M.A., Yale U., 1960, Ph.D., 1965. Lectr. in history U. Minn., Mpls., 1964-65, asst. prof. history, 1965-67, asso. prof., 1967—; vis. asso. prof. Carleton Coll., 1970, Stanford U., 1970; mem. Minn. Senate, 1973—, chmn. com. on public employees and pensions, 1981—. Mem. Minn. Hist. Soc.; mem. Democratic Central Com. Minn., 1970-72, del. state conv., 1972; mem. state exec. com. Minnesotans for McGovern, 1971-72. Social Sci. Research Council grantee, 1962-63, Nat. Endowment for Humanities grantee, 1968. Mem. Orgn. Am. Historians, Minn. Edn. Assn. Author: Black Chicago: The Making of a Negro Ghetto, 1890-1920, 1967; contbg. author: Key Issues in the Afro-American Experience, 1971. Office: 323 State Capitol Saint Paul MN 55155

SPECHT, FREDERICK LOUIS, internat. ins. brokerage co. exec.; b. Chgo., Jan. 27, 1939; s. Fred R. and Ida P. (Marini) S.; B.B.A. in Acctg., Loyola U., 1962; postgrad. in acctg. U. Ill., 1963; J.D., John Marshall Law Sch., 1968; m. Signe M. Bellande, Sept. 10, 1960; children—Suzanne M., Lisa, Frederick Matthew. Auditor, J.H. Gilby & Co., Chgo., 1961-63; sr. tax accountant Interlake, Inc., Chgo., 1963-65; tax mgr. Union Spl. Corp., Chgo., 1965-69; admitted to Ill. bar, 1968; spl. atty. gen. for antitrust, taxation and condemnation litigation State of Ill., Chgo., 1969-72; asso. firm Moses, McGarr, Gibbons, Abramson & Fox, Chgo., 1969-72; tax mgr. A.B. Dick Co., Chgo., 1972-74; mgr. internat. taxes FMC Corp., Chgo., 1974-75; v.p. taxes, dir. corp. tax Gould, Inc., Rolling Meadows, Ill., 1975-78; v.p. fin. and adminstrn. Gould-Brown Boveri, Rolling Meadows, 1979-80; v.p. fin. Arthur J. Gallagher & Co., Rolling Meadows, 1980—; profl. speaker Am. Mgmt. Assn., Panel Publishers, World Trade Inst., Tax Exec. Inst.; teaching asst. John Marshall Law Sch., Chgo., 1972-73. Pres. Pierce Sch. Adv. Council, Chgo., 1972-73, Edgewater Community Council, Chgo., 1971-72. Mem. Am. Bar Assn., Am. Inst. C.P.A.s, Chgo. Assn. Commerce and Industry, Chgo. Bar Assn., Ill. Inst. C.P.A.s, Internat. Fiscal Assn., Tax Execs. Inst. Home: 113 Rose Terrace Tower Lakes Barrington IL 60010 Office: 10 Gould Center Rolling Meadows IL 60008

SPECK, SAMUEL WALLACE, JR., state senator; b. Canton, Ohio, Jan. 31, 1937; s. Samuel Wallace and Lois I. (Snyder) S.; B.A. summa cum laude, Muskingum Coll., 1959; M.A., (Danforth fellow, Woodrow Wilson fellow), Harvard U., 1963, Ph.D., 1968; postgrad. U. Rhodesia and Nyasaland (Rotary fellow), 1961; m. Sharon Jane Anderson, Jan. 20, 1962; children—Sammy, Derek. Asso. prof. polit. sci. Muskingum Coll., New Concord, Ohio, 1964—, chmn. dept., 1968-71; mem. Ohio Ho. of Reps., 1971-77, mem. fin. and appropriations, environ. and natural resources, health and welfare coms., 1971-77; mem. Ohio Senate, 1977—. Mem. African adv. council State Dept., 1972, Ohio Constl. Revision Commn., 1973-74. Precinct committeeman, chmn. Guernsey County Republican central com., 1971-75, Guernsey County Young Reps., 1969; chmn. polit. edn. Ohio League Young Reps., 1969-70. Named Outstanding Legislator, Ohio Conservation Soc., 1971. Fellow African Studies Assn.; mem. Am., Midwest polit. sci. assns., Ohio Assn. Economists and Polit. Scientists (pres. 1970-71). Methodist. Contbr. articles on African politics to profl. jours. Address: RD 2 Box 79 New Concord OH 43762

SPECTER, MELVIN H., lawyer; b. E. Chicago, Ind., July 12, 1903; s. Moses and Sadie (Rossuck) S.; A.B., U. Mich., 1925; J.D., U. Chicago, 1928; m. Nellie Rubenstein, Feb. 1, 1927; children—Lois, Michael Joseph. Admitted to Ind. bar, 1928; individual practice law, East Chicago, Ind. 1928—. Bd. dirs. ARC (chpt. chmn. 1940-46), Community Chest Assn., Salvation Army Adv. Bd., pres., 1930-35; bd. dirs. Vis. Nurse Assn., pres., 1943-44; bd. dirs. East Chgo. Boys Club, 1958-65; trustee East Chicago Pub. Library, 1956-80, pres., 1957-67; pres. Anselm Forum, 1957-58; chmn. Brotherhood Week NCCJ, East Chicago, 1958-61; exec. bd. Twin City council Boy Scouts Am.; city chmn. U. Chgo. Alumni Found. Fund, 1951-55. Awarded James Couzen Medal for Inter-collegiate debate, U. Mich., 1924; citation for distinguished pub. service, U. Chgo. Alumni Assn., 1958. Citizenship award Community Chest Assn., 1965. Mem. Am. Ind. (del.), East Chicago (pres. 1942-44) bar assns., Am. Judicature Soc., Comml. Law League Am., Community Concert Assn. (dir. 1950-55), Wig and Robe Frat., Phi Beta Kappa, Delta Sigma Rho. Elk (exalted ruler 1945), K.P., Kiwanian (dir. 1946, 49-51, 52-55, pres. 1961); mem. B'nai B'rith. Home: 4213 Baring Ave East Chicago IN 46312 Office: 815 W Chicago Ave East Chicago IN 46312

SPECTOR, RICHARD JACOB, chem. co. exec.; b. N.Y.C., Mar. 6, 1949; s. David and Doris (Danenbaum) S.; B.S. in Chemistry, Carnegie-Mellon U., 1973, M.S., 1977; m. Karla Marie Salvi, Apr. 24, 1976. Research and devel. chemist Mooney Chems., Inc., Cleve., 1977-79, dir. research and devel., 1979—; surface chemistry-defoamer cons. Eastman Kodak fellow, 1974-75; Am. Chem. Soc. award in analytical chemistry, 1969; Warner prize in chemistry Carnegie-Mellon U., 1968. Mem. Cleve. Soc. for Coatings Tech., Akron Rubber Group, Phi Kappa Phi, Tau Beta Pi. Democrat. Jewish. Patentee in field. Home: 631 Prior Park Dr Cuyahoga Falls OH 44223 Office: 2301 Scranton Rd Cleveland OH 44113

SPEECE, SUANNE KAYE, hosp. adminstr.; b. Dayton, Ohio, Apr. 27, 1938; d. Kenneth Russell and Sue Elizabeth (Coulter) Boyd; B.S.N., U. Dayton, 1963; R.N., Christ Hosp. Sch. Nursing, 1959; m. Terry S. Speece, June 25, 1960; children—Noel Steven, Jennifer Sue. Staff nurse surgery, maternity instr. Miami Valley Hosp., 1959-61; tchr. pre-nursing Dayton Bd. Edn., 1962-64; charge nurse Good Samaritan Hosp., 1965; float nurse, asst. head nurse Kettering (Ohio) Med. Center, 1968-70, home care coordinator 1970-75; dir. patient services dept. Good Samaritan Hosp. and Health Center, Dayton, 1975—; vol. asst. prof. medicine in soc. Wright State Med. Sch., 1977—; mem. spl. edn. com. Oakwood High Sch., 1979. Mem. parent adv. com. Title I funds Oakwood Sch. System, 1978-79; chmn. task force coms. Dayton Area Hosp. Council, 1976-77; vol. ARC in Xenia (Ohio) tornado, 1974. Mem. Nat. Mgmt. Assn. Hosps., Nat. Assn. Quality Assurance Profls. (bd. mem. 1978-80), Soc. Social Work Dirs. of Am. Hosp. Assn., Area Wide Utilization Review Nurse Coordinators Region II, S.W. Ohio-No. Ky. Social Work Dirs. Assn., Greater Miami Valley Nurse Discharge Planners, Ohio Council Home Health Agys., Quality Rev. Coordinators Ohio (dir. 1978-81), Ohio Hosp. Assn. (com. mem. 1977-78), Kettering Assn. Children with Learning Disabilities. Republican. Baptist. Club: Order Eastern Star. Home: 214 Dellwood Ave Dayton OH 45419 Office: 2222 Philadelphia Dr Dayton OH 45406

SPEER, BILLY LEE, architect; b. Syracuse, Kans., Dec. 24, 1947; s. John L. and Margaret Jo. (Heiland) S.; B.Arch., Kans. State U., 1973; m. Connie Louise Hampton, Jan. 25, 1969; 1 son, William Eric. Draftsman, Marshall and Brown, Kansas City, Mo., 1968-70, Kan. State U., Planning Office, Manhattan, 1970-72, Prickett and Onek, Topeka, 1972, Rodney S. Davis, Denver, 1973; architect Marvin Knedler & Assos., Lakewood, Colo., 1973-74, Flickinger & Assos., Denver, 1974; owner/architect Design Dimensions, Lakewood, 1974-75, Dodge City, Kans., 1975-78; owner/architect Bill Speer, Environ. Architect, Lee's Summit, Mo., 1978—; asst. sec.-treas. Monterra Devel. Corp., Breckenridge, Colo., 1979—; architect Environ. Design Assn., Lee's Summit, 1977-79; developer, Breckenridge, Colo., 1978—; architect Marshall & Brown, Kansas City, Mo., 1981—; part-time instr. Dodge City Community Coll., 1976-77; v.p. Prairie Glenn Townhouses, Inc., Manhattan, Kans., 1972-73. Lic. architect, Colo., Kans.; cert. Nat. Council Archtl. Registration Bds. Mem. Alpha Phi Omega. Designer solar generator. Home: 1615 NE Ridgeview Lee's Summit MO 64063

SPEER, KATHRYN ELIZABETH, advt. exec.; b. Racine, Wis., Nov. 16, 1942; d. Edward Louis and Mary Elizabeth (Rowlands) S.; B.A., U. Wis., 1964. Pres., Clark & Co., Madison, Wis., 1976-80, merged with John Robertson & Assos., 1979, account exec. John Robertson & Assos., 1979-82; owner, mgr. Speer Creative Advt., Madison, 1982—. Bd. dirs. United Way; bd. dirs., past pres. Family Service Soc. Dane County. Recipient local, regional and nat. creative advt. awards. Mem. Madison Advt. Fedn. (past pres., dir.), Am. Advt. Fedn. Home and Office: 17 Sunfish Ct Madison WI 53713

SPEH, ALBERT JOHN, JR., data processing exec.; b. Chgo., May 29, 1919; s. Albert J. and Rose S.; student Northwestern U., U. Ga.; m. Claire DeRudder, Aug. 23, 1941; children—Kathleen, Albert, Lawrence. Data processing mgr. Gen. Fin. Corp., 1939-41, Ency. Britannica, 1946-47; pres., chmn. bd. May & Speh Data Processing Center, Inc., Oak Brook Terrace, Ill., 1947—; dir. various banks and corps. Served with U.S. Army, 1941-46. Decorated Legion of Merit. Roman Catholic. Clubs: Medinah Country, Itasca Country, Elks (Chgo.), Tamarac Country (Fla.). Home: 21W 380 Par Ln Itasca IL 60143 also 5300 NE 32d Ave Fort Lauderdale FL Office: 18 W 100 22d St Oak Brook Terrace IL 60181

SPEIGHT, PAUL L., ednl. adminstr., cons.; b. Iowa City, Iowa, Feb. 7, 1924; s. Glenn A. and Mildred (Wetherall) S.; student Grinnell Coll., 1941-43; B.Ed., Northwestern U., 1949, M.Mus. Edn., 1949; postgrad. (vocat. edn. fellow), U. Wis., 1973—; m. Charlotte Wells, Jan. 26, 1946; children—Leslie Ann, Kent W., Mary Beth. Tchr., Edgerton (Wis.) public schs., 1949-51; operating dept. mgr., personnel mgr. merchandising Marshall Field & Co., Chgo., 1951-60; dist. sales mgr. Bissell Corp., Grand Rapids, Mich., 1960-61; dir. research and devel., product mgr. E.R. Wagner Mfg. Co., Milw., 1961-70; vocat. edn. dir. Coop. Ednl. Service Agy. No. 10, Plymouth, Wis., 1970-73; dir. spl. projects and high sch. equivalency GED, Wis. Dept. Public Instruction, Madison, 1973—; mem. Gov's Youth Council, task force on edn. Gov.'s Conf. on Small Bus., Wis. Council for Occupational Info., Vice Pres.'s Council on Youth Employment; mem. adv. coms. to schs., univs., ednl. orgns. Active sch. bd. Barrington (Ill.) public schs., 1955-61; mem. Nicolet High Sch. bd., Milw., 1965-71, pres. bd., 1968-70. Served with Signal Corps U.S. Army, 1943-45. Recipient citations for service sch. bds. and univ. adv. coms. Mem. Am. Vocat. Assn., Wis. Assn. Vocat. and Adult Edn., Wis. Assn. Secondary Vocat. Adminstrs., Nat. Assn. for Industry and Edn. Cooperation, Wis. Ednl. Research Assn., Midwest Ednl. Research Assn., Future Farmers Am. Alumni Assn., Phi Delta Kappa. Club: Wis. Meml. Union Assn. Originator Wis. in-sch. job placement program; contbr. articles in field to pubis. Home: 3101 Nottingham Way Madison WI 53713 Office: 125 S Webster St Madison WI 53702

SPEIKER, CHARLES ARTHUR, ednl. adminstr.; b. St. Paul, Nov. 27, 1943; s. Joseph A. and Phyllis M. (Unze) S.; B.A., St. Thomas Coll., 1965; M.A., Mich. State U., 1970; Ed.D. U. Minn., 1974, m. Gloria M. Schmid, June 10, 1967; children—Marc Josef, Rebecca Ann, Matthew John. Tchr. public schs., Mich., 1967-70; adj. prof. U. Minn., Mpls., 1970-74; dir. curriculum North schs., St. Paul, 1970-74; asso. dir. Assn. for Supervision and Curriculum Devel., Washington, 1974-77, dir. secondary edn. Millard Public Schs., Omaha, 1977-80, dir. planning and evaluation, 1980—; cons. in field. Advisor, S.E. Community Action, Minn., 1966; dir., treas. Rehab. Complex, VA., 1974-77; bd. dirs. YMCA, Nebr., 1978-81; scoutmaster Cub Scouts Am. Recipient Disting. Edn. award Tenn. Assn. for Supervision and Curriculum Devel., 1976. Mem. Assn. for Supervision and Curriculum Devel., Nebr. Assn. for Supervision and Curriculum Devel., Assn. for Ednl. Data Systems, Nebr. Assn. for Ednl. Data Systems, Am. Ednl. Research Assn., D.C. Assn. for Supervision and Curriculum Devel. (hon. life), Phi Delta Kappa. Contbr. articles to profl. jours. Home: 427 S 150 Circle Omaha NE 68154 Office: 12801 L St Omaha NE 68137

SPEIR, KENNETH GUINTY, lawyer; b. Peabody, Kans., June 22, 1908; s. John and Bessie (Guinty) S.; student Colo. Coll., 1926-28; LL.B., Kans. U., 1931; children—Helen Ann, Patricia Jane, Elizabeth Eve; m. 2d, Shirley Whittemore. Admitted to Kans. bar, 1931, N.Mex. bar, 1932, U.S. Supreme Ct. bar, 1943; practiced in Albuquerque, 1932-34, Newton, Kans., 1934—; county atty. Harvey County (Kans.), 1939-41; Judge 9th Jud. Dist. Kans., 1941-44; dir., gen. counsel Central Securities, Inc., Acra-Plant, Inc., 1st Fed. Savs. & Loan Assn. of Newton, Legg Co., Inc.; counsel Hesston Corp., Midland Nat. Bank, Newton. Mem. Kans. Bd. Health, 1950-51. Served as lt. col. USMCR, 1942-46, Res. ret. Mem. Am., N.Mex., Kans., Harvey County bar assns., Am. Legion, VFW. Republican. Lutheran. Home: 1411 Hillcrest Rd Newton KS 67114 Office: PO Box 546 809 Main St Newton KS 67114

SPEISMAN, JOYCE ELLIS, spl. edn. cons.; b. Chgo., June 4, 1949; d. Samuel and Sylvia (Akwa) E.; B.A., Clark U., 1971; M.Ed., Northeastern U., 1972; postgrad. Northwestern U., 1978—; m. Albert Speisman, Mar. 19, 1977. Tchr. spl. edn. Wilmette (Ill.) public schs., 1972-75; spl. edn. cons. No. Suburban Spl. Edn. Dist., Highland Park, Ill., 1975—. Mem. Council Exceptional Children, Council Children with Behavioral Disorders, Council Adminstrs. Spl. Edn., Assn. Supervision and Curriculum Devel., Phi Delta Kappa. Jewish. Home: 2979 Lexington Ln Highland Park IL 60035 Office: 760 Red Oak Ln Highland Park IL 60035

SPELLER, EUGENE THURLEY, coll. pres.; b. Charleston, Mo., Jan. 25, 1928; s. Oliver William and Nicula Luvenia (McElvaine) S.; B.S. in Engring., Mich. State U., 1955, M.A. in Edn., 1967; Ph.D. in Ednl. Adminstrn., Union Grad. Sch., 1975; m. Thelma Mae Wilson, Sept. 4, 1955; children—Barry Eugene, Bernnine Elaine, Michelle Annette. Engr., Sundstrand Hydro-Transmission Co., LaSalle, Ill., 1967-71; fellow Nat. Program for Ednl. Leadership, Ohio State U.; dean Austin Community Coll., 1973-75; now pres. Olive-Harvey Coll., Chgo. Bd. dirs. Roseland Hosp., Chgo., 111th YMCA, Chgo., COMPRAND; mem. Calumet Indsl. Commn. Served with F.A., U.S. Army, 1956-58. Recipient Disting. Citizenship award Ill. Valley C. of C., 1971. Mem. Soc. Automotive Engrs., Am. Assn. Univ. Adminstrs., Am. Assn. Community and Jr. Colls., Chgo. South C. of C. (ednl. achievement award 1978), Phi Delta Kappa. Methodist. Office: Olive-Harvey Coll 10001 S Woodlawn Ave Chicago IL 60628

SPELLMAN, GEORGE GENESER, SR., internist; b. Woodward, Iowa, Sept. 11, 1920; s. Martin Edward and Corinne (Geneser) S.; B.S., St. Ambrose Coll., 1940; M.D., State U. Iowa, 1943; m. Mary Carolyn Dwight, Aug. 26, 1942; children—Carolyn Anne Spellman Rambow, George G., Mary Alice Spellman Gross, Elizabeth Marie, John Martin, Loretta Suzanne. Intern, Providence Hosp., Detroit,

1944; resident in internal medicine State U. Iowa, Iowa City, 1944-46; practice specializing in internal medicine, Mitchell, S.D., 1948-50, Sioux City, Iowa, 1950—; instr. Coll. Medicine U. S.D., 1975-77, now clin. asso. prof. medicine; mem. staff St. Joseph Mercy Hosp., 1950—, chief of staff, 1963; mem. staff St. Vincent Hosp., 1950—, chief of staff, 1954, 77, also bd. dirs.; mem. staff St. Luke's Med. Center; clin. asso. prof. medicine State U. Iowa; instr. schs. nursing St. Vincent Hosp., Luth. Hosp.; co-founder, pres. Siouxland Mental Health Assn., 1968-75; bd. dirs. Marian Health Center, also co-founder, 1st pres. chem. dependency unit. Served to capt., M.C., U.S. Army, 1946-48. Decorated knight of St. Gregory (Vatican); diplomate Am. Bd. Internal Medicine. Fellow A.C.P.; mem. AMA, Am. Acad. Scis., Iowa State, Woodbury med. socs., Am., Iowa socs. internal medicine, Am., Iowa thoracic socs., Am., Iowa heart assns., Am. Geriatric Soc., Alpha Omega Alpha. Contbr. articles to med. jours. Home: 3849 Jones St Sioux City IA 51104 Office: 505 Badgerow Bldg 4th and Jackson Sts Sioux City IA 51101

SPELTZ, GEORGE HENRY, bishop; b. Altura, Minn., May 29, 1912; s. Henry and Josephine (Jung) S.; B.S., St. Mary's Coll., Winona, Minn., 1932, LL.D., 1963; student theorlogy St. Paul Sem., 1936-40; M.A., Cath. U. Am., 1942, Ph.D., 1944; D.D., Holy See, Rome, 1963. Ordained priest Roman Catholic Ch., 1940, now bishop; vice chancellor Diocese of Winona (Minn.), 1944-47, supt. schs., 1946-49, aux. bishop, 1963-66; pastor St. May's Ch., Minneiska, Minn., 1946-47; tchr. Mary's Coll., 1947-63; rector Immaculate Heart of Mary Sem., Winona, 1948-63; co-adjutor bishop, St. Cloud, Minn., 1966-68, bishop, 1968—; pres. Nat. Cath. Rural Life Conf., 1970-72. Address: 214 S 3d Ave Saint Cloud MN 56301

SPENCE, DYNSDALE OLDFIELD, youth services agy. ofcl.; b. Welcome, Jamaica, West Indies, Mar. 22, 1933; came to U.S., 1970, naturalized, 1976; s. George Adolphus and Imogene Matilda (Spencer) S.; B.Th., West Indies Coll., 1970; M.A. in Edn., Andrews U., 1972; postgrad. Mich. State U., 1975-78; m. Gloria Elaine Levy, Apr. 26, 1959; 1 son, Richard Donovan Oldfield. Religious and ednl. dir. West Jamaica Conf., Jamaica, 1954-70; caseworker Dept. Social and Health Services, Seattle, 1970-71; sr. counselor Berrien County Youth Service Bur., Benton Harbor, Mich., 1973-76, dir., 1976—; adj. faculty Lake Mich. Coll. Vice chmn. exec. bd. Berrien Opportunities Industrialization Center, 1979-81, pres. Crofts Hill Citizens Assn., 1956-57, Balaclava Citizens' Assn., 1960-63; mem. Juvenile Justice Com. Mich., 1976—. Mem. Am. Mgmt. Assn., Mich. Assn. Youth Service Burs. (pres. 1977-78), Assn. Supervision and Curriculum Devel., Phi Delta Kappa (pres. Andrews U. 1979-80). Seventh Day Adventist. Author Handbook for Secondary Schools, 1972; contbr. article to profl. jour. Home: 1100 Centerfield Dr Berrien Springs MI 49103 Office: 72 W Main St Suite 10 Benton Harbor MI 49022

SPENCE, HOWARD TEE DEVON, lawyer; b. Corinth, Miss., Sept. 29, 1949; s. Tee P. and Dorothy M. (Bowers) S.; B.A., Mich. State U., 1970, M.S., 1975, M.L.I.R., 1980; J.D., U. Mich., 1976, M.P.A., 1977; m. Diane Earl; children—Derek T., Tina Denise, Steven D. Admitted to Mich. bar, 1976, U.S. Dist. Ct. bar, 1976, U.S. Circuit Ct. of Appeals bar, 1976, U.S. Supreme Ct. bar, 1980; prison counselor/unit mgr. Mich. Dept. Corrections, Jackson, 1971-76; personnel adminstr. Mich. Dept. Commerce, Lansing, 1976-77, asst. dir. policy Mich. Public Service Commn., 1977-78; asst. ins. commr. Mich. Ins. Bur., Lansing, 1978—; instr. U. Mich., Ann Arbor, 1975, Jackson (Mich.) Community Coll., 1977; adj. prof. law Thomas M. Cooley Law Sch., Lansing, 1977—, pvt. practice law, Lansing, 1976—. Bd. dirs., City of Lansing Econ. Devel. Corp., 1980—; dist. commr. Boy Scouts Am., 1980—. Presdl. scholar, 1967; Nat. Merit scholar, 1967-70; recipient Award for Outstanding Contbns. to Human Rights, Frontiers Clubs Internat. of Decatur (Ill.), 1967. Mem. State Bar of Mich., Am. Bar Assn., Wolverine Bar Assn., Ingham County Bar Assn., Fed. Bar Assn., Indsl. Relations Research Assn., Am. Arbitration Assn. (community disputes panel), Am. Mgmt. Assn., Am. Soc. Personnel Adminstrn., Assn. Am. Law Schs., Am. Soc. for Public Adminstrn., Assn. for Public Policy Analysis and Mgmt., Am. Correctional Assn., Mich. State U. Alumni Assn., NAACP, U. Mich. Alumni Assn., Greater Lansing Regional C. of C., Alpha Phi Alpha. Ch. of Christ. Clubs: Renaissance of Detroit, Econ. of Detroit, Lawyers of U. Mich. Law Sch., Masons. Home: 4462 Seneca Dr Okemos MI 48864 Office: 1048 Pierpont St Lansing MI 48909

SPENCE, JOHN D(ANIEL), cons., former univ. ofcl.; b. Lethbridge, Alta., Can., May 18, 1915; s. Benjamin Abner and Clara May (Fullerton) S.; came to U.S., 1915, naturalized, 1943; A.B., Grinnell Coll., 1938; LL.D. (hon.), Rockford Coll., 1979; m. Phyllis Saxton Johnson, Feb. 4, 1939; children—Susan Kathleen Spence Horton, John-Daniel. With Container Corp. Am., 1938-54, v.p., 1949-54; Lanzit Corrugated Box Co., 1954-64; dir. devel. Rockford (Ill.) Coll., 1964-65, v.p. devel., 1965-77, acting pres., 1977-79; bus. and edn. cons., 1980—. Mem. adv. bd. Forest Preserve Commn., 1974—; mem. land adv. council Winnebago County Forest Preserve, 1975—; chmn. Severson Dells Adv. Council, 1976—; mem. community adv. bd. WNIU-FM, No. Ill. U., 1981—; trustee Keith Country Day Sch.; former trustee Children's Home Rockford, until 1976; bd. dirs. John Howard Assn., until 1974, Pecatonica Prairie Path, 1975—; trustee Rockford Art Assn., 1980—. Recipient Karl C. Williams award Rockford Coll. Alumni Assn., 1980; Sci. above Self award Rockford Rotary, 1980. Mem. Ill. (com. for respect law enforcement 1967-72), Rockford (dir. 1966-72) chambers commerce. Republican. Presbyterian. Clubs: Univ. (Chgo.); Lions. Home and Office: 6710 Woodcrest Pkwy Rockford IL 61109

SPENCE, ROBERT HERMAN, coll. exec.; b. McComb, Miss., Sept. 13, 1935; s. Thomas Herman and Lucille A. (Everett) S.; B.S., U. Ala., M.A., 1959; D.D., Southeastern Coll. of Assemblies of God, 1975; m. Margaret Anne Tindol, Aug. 11, 1956; children—Jennifer, Thomas Joseph, Jonathan Claude, David Timothy, Stephen Robert. Tchr. public schs., Tuscaloosa, Ala., 1956-57; sch. prin. Tuscaloosa County Schs., 1958-61; ordained to ministry Assemblies of God Ch., 1958; pastor Pineview Assembly of God Ch., Marion, Ala., 1954-57, First Assembly of God Ch., Tuscaloosa, 1957-68, Crichton Assembly of God Ch., Mobile, Ala., 1968-74; pres. Evangel Coll., Springfield, Mo., 1974—. Bd. dirs. Cox Med. Center, Springfield. Mem. Springfield C. of C. (dir.), Phi Delta Kappa. Club: Rotary. Office: 1111 N Glenstone St Springfield MO 65802

SPENCER, BRENDA LOU, indsl. engr.; b. Youngstown, Ohio, July 7, 1951; d. Walter J. and Flonerra (Thompson) Henry; B.S. in Indsl. Engring., Kent State U., 1978; m. Herbert Edwin Spencer, Jr., Mar. 20, 1976. Lab. technician South Side Hosp., Youngstown, 1969-73; with Gen. Motors Corp., Warren, Ohio, 1973-76; indsl. engr. Rep. Steel Corp., Youngstown, 1976—. Mem. Mahoning County Selective Service Bd.; nat. bd. dirs. Big Bros./Sisters Am. Mem. Speakers Bur., Nat. Assn. Negro Bus. and Profl. Women's Clubs (dir. youth and young adult affairs, pres. Ohio Valley club), Am. Inst. Indsl. Engrs. Home: PO Box 5814 Youngstown OH 44504

SPENCER, CHARLES T., educator; b. Grenada, Miss., Oct. 8, 1923; s. Eugene and Johnnie Spencer; A.B., Rust Coll.; M.S., Wayne State U., 1971; M.A., Central Mich. U., 1977; Ph.D., So. Ill. U., 1980; m. Apr. 30, 1945; children—Mary Ellen, Charlynn, Iris. Chief med. tech. and ednl. coordinator Meml. Hosp., Springfield, Ill., 1955-69; chief med. tech. Meml. Hosp. Detroit, 1969-71; asso. prof. med. tech. Ill. State U., 1972—, chmn. dept. health scis., 1972—. Served with U.S. Navy, 1943-46. HEW fellow, 1970. Mem. NAACP (life), Am. Soc. Med. Technologists, Am. Soc. Allied Health Professions. Baptist. Home: 932 S Wheeler St Springfield IL 62703 Office: Illinois State University Normal IL 61761

SPENCER, DONALD ROY, aero. engr.; b. Carlinville, Ill., Feb. 2, 1925; s. Roy Frederick and Lois Wilda (Cochran) S.; B.S. in Aero. Engring., Tri-State Coll., 1945; M.B.A., Mich. State U., 1965; m. Helen Mabel Hinrichsen, Oct. 11, 1947; children—David Roy, Nancy Lois Spencer Crull. Aero. design engr. Chance Vought Aircraft, Dallas, 1948-50; project engr. Bendix Corp., Mishawaka, Ind., 1950-55, chief design engr., 1955-58, chief project engr., 1958-64; engr. adminstrv. mgr. McDonnell Douglas, St. Louis, 1964-70, mgr. F-15 Configuration and Data Control, 1970-76, mgr. Israel Air Force F-15 program, 1976—. Vice chmn. Jersey County (Ill.) Planning Commn.; trustee Rosedale Methodist Ch.; sec. Jersey County Zoning Commn.; pres. U. Ill. County Extension Council. Mem. Am. Def. Preparedness Assn., Aerospace Industries Assn. Republican. Club: Masons.

SPENCER, EDSON WHITE, mfg. co. exec.; b. Chgo., June 4, 1926; s. William M. and Gertrude (White) S.; student Princeton U., 1943, Northwestern U., U. Mich., 1944; B.A., Williams Coll., 1948; B.A., Oxford (Eng.) U., 1950, M.A., 1950. With Sears, Roebuck & Co., 1951-54, Venezuela and Mpls., 1954; with Honeywell, Inc., 1954—, dir. exports, 1964-65, v.p. fgn. ops., 1965-69, exec. v.p., 1969-74, pres., chief exec. officer, 1974-78, chmn. bd., chmn. exec. com., 1978—. Mem. Mpls. C. of C., St. Paul Com. Fgn. Relations, Mpls. Citizens League, Phi Beta Kappa. Office: Honeywell Inc 2701 4th Ave S Minneapolis MN 55408*

SPENCER, HARRY ARTHUR, project adminstr. Nebr. Supreme Ct.; b. Bishops Walton, Eng., Sept. 16, 1903; s. Richard and Mary (Richardson) S.; A.B., U. Nebr., 1929, LL.B. cum laude, 1930; m. Leona Maria Eggenberg, June 28, 1925; children—Pegean Marie Spencer Carter, Harry Arthur, Marlene Dell Spencer Mansfield, Leone Lorraine Spencer Harlan, Terry Lee, Victor Richard. Admitted to Nebr. bar, 1929; practiced law, Lincoln, Nebr., 1929-44; judge Lancaster County (Nebr.) Ct., 1945-51, 3d Jud. Dist. Ct. Nebr., 1952-60; justice Supreme Ct. Nebr., 1960-79, dir. Pre-argument Settlement Project, 1979—; lectr. U. Nebr., 1942-61; chmn. Nebr. Jud. Council, 1972-79; chmn. continuing edn. com., project dir. continuing legal edn. Appellate Judges' Conf. Past commr. local council Boy Scouts Am.; past dir. N.E. br. YMCA; chmn. traffic commn., Lincoln, 1951-62; chmn. Lancaster County Republican Central Com., 1936-40, del. nat. conv., 1936, 40; pres. Young Rep. Orgn. Nebr., 1937, v.p. nat. orgn., 1940; trustee Nebr. Masonic Home, 1941—. Recipient Good Govt. award Lincoln Jr. C. of C., 1959, Herbert Hartley award Am. Judicature Soc., 1980. Mem. Am. Bar Assn. (past chmn., mem. exec. com. appellate judges conf. sect. jud. adminstrn., mem. council jud. adminstrn. div. 1972—, ho. of dels. 1972-80), Nebr. Bar Assn. (v.p. 1948, exec. com. 1947-61), Lincoln Bar Assn. (pres. 1946), Lincoln Council Chs. (pres. 1957), Acacia, Delta Theta Phi. Methodist. Clubs: Masons, Shriners (grand master Nebr. 1965), Kiwanis (past gov., past internat. chmn.), Order Eastern Star. Office: Pre-argument Settlement Project Nebr Supreme Ct Lincoln NE 68509

SPENCER, JOSEPH STEWART, mfg. co. exec.; b. Kilbirnie, Scotland, Apr. 26, 1922; s. Hugh Morrison and Mary (MacInnes) S.; A.B., Harvard, 1948; M.B.A., Columbia, 1950. Tax accountant, asst. to treas., asst. treas., sec.-treas. Union Spl. Corp., 1950-78, v.p., sec., 1978—. Served with AUS, 1942-45. Mem. Am. Soc. Corp. Secs., Ill. C. of C., Ill. St. Andrew Soc., Chgo. Assn. Commerce and Industry. Presbyn. Home: 1450 Astor St Chicago IL 60610 Office: 400 N Franklin St Chicago IL 60610

SPENCER, MERLIN CLIFFORD, educator; b. Lake City, Iowa, Sept. 10, 1938; s. Clifford Cecil and Alice Mildred (Deuel) S.; B.S., Iowa State U., 1960; M.B.A., Ind. U., 1961, D.B.A., 1964; m. Jacqueline Bell, Jan. 8, 1972; children—Heather Sabrina, Ansley Monique. Asst. prof. marketing U. Kans., 1964-67; U. Mo., Kansas City, 1967-71, asso. prof., 1972-79; pres. Spencer Profl. Cons., Kansas City, Mo., 1966; univ. assoc. Lawrence-Leiter & Co., Kansas City, 1966-78; v.p. corp. devel. Topsy's Internat., 1971-72; exec. dir. Nat. Educators Found., 1971-72; pres. Constituency Response, Inc., Kansas 1977—, Spencer & Assos., Inc., 1978—; v.p. Lawrence-Leiter & Co., 1980—; cons. in field. Bd. dirs. Prime Health of Kansas City, 1975-77; chmn. Mo. State Environment Improvement Authority, 1974-78; cons. Clay County Devel. Commn., 1977-79. Mem. Citizens Assn. Kansas City, Mo. (bd. dirs. 1977-81), Am. Marketing Assn., Sales and Marketing Execs. Kansas City, Nat. Platform Speakers Assn., Internat. Relations Club, Friends of Art, Philharmonic Men's Club, Kansas City Hist. Soc. Republican. Episcopalian. Home: 8800 Ensley Ct Leawood KS 66206 Office: 8800 Ensley Ct Leawood KS 66206

SPENCER, ROBERT LEE, soil conservationist, govt. ofcl.; b. Hardeman County, Tenn., Dec. 25, 1952; s. Daniel and Estella (McClellan) S.; B.S. in Agronomy, Tenn. State U., 1974, M.S. in Agr. Sci., 1976. Soil conservation aide Soil Conservation Service, U.S. Dept. Agr., Bolivar, Tenn., 1970, Springfield, Ill., 1971, trainee, Springfield, 1972, Lincoln, Ill., 1973, soil conservationist, Murphysboro, Ill., 1976-77, dist. conservationist, Pinckneyville, Ill., 1977—. Coach, Optimist Little League Baseball, Pinckneyville. Recipient hon. farmer award Pinckneyville chpt. Future Farmers Am., 1980. Mem. Soil Conservation Soc. Am. (treas.-sect. area 7), Agronomy Soc. Am. (pres. chpt. 1972-74). Methodist. Club: Pinckneyville Optimist (dir.). Home: 609 S Mill St Pinckneyville IL 62274 Office: 907 S Main St Pinckneyville IL 62274

SPENCER, THOMAS LEE, JR., sch. adminstr.; b. Cleve., Mar. 16, 1943; s. Thomas L. and Irene J. (Harvey) S.; B.S. (univ. scholar), So. Ill. U., 1967, M.S., 1974; Ph.D., St. Louis U., 1978; m. Carolyn J. Stanley, Sept. 10, 1966; 1 dau., Stephanie. Tchr., University City (Mo.) Sch. Dist., 1970-75; mathematics specialist CEMREL, Nat. Ednl. Research Lab., St. Louis, 1975-76; dir. fed. programs, dir. family sch. program University City Sch. Dist., 1976-79, asst. prin. University City High Sch., 1979-80, asst. prin. 12th grade, 1980—; pres. Psychol. Research Assos., Creve Coeur, Mo., 1979—; corp. vice chmn. bd. Bus. Opportunity Leadership Corp., St. Louis, 1981—. Mem. MO. Senator Harriett Woods' adv. com., 1978—; facilitator U.S. Dept. Justice, 1978; presenter Conf. on Edn., St. Louis, 1978; hon. dir., bd. dirs. Rockhurst Coll., 1979—; mem. University City Sch. Dist. steering com. for tax levy, 1977-78, others. Recipient Project Milestone award, Columbia U., 1981, named to Nat. Orgn. Outstanding Elem. Tchrs. of Am., 1974. Mem. Mo. Assn. Supervision and Curriculum Devel. Assn. Supervision and Curriculum Devel., Mo. State Tchrs. Assn., University City Edn. Assn., World Council for Curriculum and Instruction, Phi Delta Kappa (named an Outstanding Young Ednl. Leader of Am., 1980). Contbr. articles to profl. jours. Home: 12648 Villa Hill Ln Creve Coeur MO 63141 Office: 7401 Balson Ave University City MO 63130

SPENCER, WILLIAM EDWIN, telephone co. exec., engr.; b. Kansas City, Mo., Mar. 22, 1926; s. Irwin Blanc and Edith Marie (Peterson) S.; student U. Kansas City, 1942; A.S., Kansas City Jr. Coll., 1945; B.S. in E.E., U. Mo., 1948; postgrad. Iowa State U., 1969; m. Ferne Arlene Nieder, Nov. 14, 1952; children—Elizabeth Ann, Gary William, James Richard, Catherine Sue. With Southwestern Bell Telephone Co., Kansas City, Mo., 1948-50, Topeka, 1952-61, sr. engr., 1966-69, equipment maintenance engr., 1969-76, engring. ops. mgr., 1976-79, dist. mgr., 1979—; mem. tech. staff Bell Telephone Labs., N.Y.C., 1961-62, Holmdel, N.J., 1962-66. Served with AUS, 1950-52. Recipient Best Kans. Idea award Southwestern Bell Telephone Co., 1972. Mem. Kans. Engring. Soc., Nat. Soc. Profl. Engrs., IEEE, Topeka Engrs. Club. Registered profl. engr., Kans. Republican. Patentee in field. Home: 3201 MacVicar Ct Topeka KS 66611 Office: 220 E 6th St Topeka KS 66603

SPENGLER, DONALD EDWIN, oral and maxillofacial surgeon; b. Bay City, Mich., Mar. 3, 1931; s. Carl August and Elsie Frieda (Loehne) S.; student Bay City Jr. Coll., 1949-51; D.D.S., U. Mich., 1956, M.S., 1962; m. Barbara Joy Maxwell, June 20, 1953; children—Stephen M., Suzanne M. Teaching fellow oral surgery U. Mich., Ann Arbor, 1959-60; intern Univ. Hosp., Ann Arbor, 1960-61, resident oral surgery, 1961-62; individual practice oral surgery, Saginaw, Mich., 1962—; active staffs St. Luke's Hosp., Saginaw Gen. Hosp., St. Mary's Hosp. (all Saginaw); asso. clin. prof. surgery Mich. State U. Sch. Human Medicine at Saginaw Coop. Hosps., 1974—. Bd. dirs. Saginaw County chpt. Am. Cancer Soc., 1964-67, pres., 1967; dir. Saginaw Cleft Palate Clinic Team, 1977—. Served with USAF, 1956-59. Fellow Am. Coll. Dentists; mem. ADA, Mich. Dental Assn. (trustee 1981—), Saginaw Valley Dist. Dental Soc. (pres. 1976-77), Am. Bd. Oral Surgery, Am. Assn. Oral and Maxillofacial Surgery, Mich. Soc. Oral and Maxillofacial Surgery (pres. 1979-81), Saginaw County Dental Soc. (pres. 1974), others. Republican. Lutheran. Club: Saginaw. Office: 4291 State St Saginaw MI 48603

SPENGLER, VERNE CHAMPNEY, educator; b. Grand Forks, N.D., July 11, 1932; s. Verne Clifton and Elizabeth (Sanfacon) S.; B.S., N.D. State U., 1955; M.A., U. Minn., 1965; m. Catherine Muir, Sept. 29, 1956; children—Keith (dec.), Susan, David. Tchr. agr. Elgin (N.D.) High Sch., 1957-58, Minto (N.D.) High Sch., 1958-64, Lincoln High Sch., Thief River Falls, Minn., 1964-66; tchr. farm mgmt. Area Vocat. Tech. Inst., Thief River Falls, 1966—. Served with U.S. Army, 1955-57. Mem. Minn. Vocat. Agr. Instrs. Assn. (state sec. 1978-79, v.p. 1979-80, pres.-elect 1981-82), Minn. Edn. Assn., NEA, Minn. Vocat. Assn., Am. Vocat. Assn., Nat. Vocat. Agr. Tchrs. Assn., Am. Legion. Republican. Methodist. Home: Rural Route 4 Thief River Falls MN 56701 Office: Area VocTech Inst Thief River Falls MN 56701

SPENSLEY, GEORGE THOMAS, lawyer; b. Chgo., Mar. 29, 1905; s. Walter Franklin and Charlotte (Dechert) S.; LL.B., DePaul U., 1927; m. Irene Mungovan, Dec. 18, 1936. Admitted to Ill. bar, 1927, since practiced in Chgo. Mem. Am., Ill., Chgo. bar assns., Am. Judicature Soc., Sigma Delta Kappa. Home: 810 Vine Ave Park Ridge IL 60068 Office: 105 W Madison Chicago IL 60602

SPERO, KEITH ERWIN, lawyer; b. Cleve., Aug. 21, 1933; s. Milton D. and Yetta (Silverstein) S.; B.A., Western Res. U., 1954, LL.B., 1956; m. Carol Kohn, July 4, 1957 (div. 1974); children—Alana, Scott, Susan; m. 2d, Karen Weaver, Dec. 28, 1975. Admitted to Ohio bar, 1956; asso. firm Sindell, Sindell & Bourne, Cleve., 1956-57; asso. firm Sindell, Sindell, Bourne, Markus, Cleve., 1960-64; partner firm Sindell, Sindell, Bourne, Stern & Spero, 1964-74, firm Spero & Rosenfield, Cleve., 1974-76; pres. firm Spero, Rosenfeld & Bourne Co., P.A., Cleve., 1977—; tchr. bus. law U. Md. Overseas div., Eng., 1958-59; lectr. Case-Western Res. U., 1965-69; instr. Cleve. Marshall Law Sch. of Cleve State U., 1968—; mem. nat. panel arbitrators Am. Arbitration Assn. Served as 1st lt., JAGC, USAF, 1957-60; capt. Res., 1960-70. Mem. Am., Ohio, Cleve., Cuyahoga bar assns., Ohio (pres. 1970-71), Am. acads. trial lawyers, Order of Coif, Assn. Trial Lawyers Am. (state committeeman Ohio 1971-75, bd. govs. 1975—, sec. family law litigation sect. 1975-76, vice chmn. 1976-77, chmn. 1977-79), Phi Beta Kappa, Zeta Beta Tau, Tau Epsilon Rho. Jewish (trustee, v.p. congregation). Club: Masons. Author: The Spero Divorce Folio, 1966. Home: 2 Bratenahl Pl Bratenahl OH 44108 Office: Terminal Tower Cleveland OH 44113

SPERRY, FREDERICK EDWARD, univ. adminstr.; b. Milw., Aug. 11, 1936; s. Edward Joseph and Victoria Rose (Korek) S.; B.S., Marquette U., 1958; M.S., U. Wis., Milw., 1979; m. Barbara Jean Rhody, Nov. 18, 1961; children—Frederick J., Kathryn E., Robert J. With U. Wis., Milw., 1960—, asso. dir. admissions and records, 1969-75, dir. admissions, 1975-78, exec. asso., 1978—, registrar, dir. admissions, 1979—. Recipient Disting. Service award Nat. Micrographics Assn., 1975, Outstanding Service award Serbian Orthodox Community of Milw., 1981. Mem. Wis. Assn. Collegiate Registrars and Admissions Officers (past pres.), Wis. Micrographics Assn. (past pres.), Am. Assn. Collegiate Registrars and Admissions Officers, Phi Kappa Phi. Roman Catholic. Lectr. on microfilming, U.S., Can. Home: 1519 Lake Bluff Blvd E Shorewood WI 53211 Office: PO Box 749 Milwaukee WI 53201

SPERRY, JAMES EDWARD, anthropologist, hist. soc. exec.; b. Weeping Water, Nebr., May 17, 1936; s. John Edward and Augusta Anea (Frandsen) S.; student Bethany Coll., Lindsborg, Kans., 1953-55; A.B. in Art and Anthropology, 1962, M.A. in Anthropology, U. Nebr., Lincoln, 1965; m. Gail Louise Killen, Sept. 26, 1964; 1 son, Patrick Reuben. Teaching asst. dept. anthropology U. Nebr., Lincoln, 1961-63, instr., 1964-65; research archeologist State Hist. Soc. N.D., Bismarck, 1965-69, supr., 1969—; sec. N.D. Heritage Found., 1973-76; mem. N.D. Lewis and Clark Trail Council, 1969—, sec., 1970, chmn., 1971; N.D. historic preservation officer, 1969—; N.D. state records coordinator, 1975—. Mem. Theodore Roosevelt Rough Rider Award Com., 1969—, N.D. Natural Resources Council, 1969—. Served with USAF, 1956-59. Am. Assn. for State and Local History fellow, 1967. Mem. Sigma Xi, Delta Phi Delta, Sigma Gamma Epsilon. Methodist. Editor: N.D. History: Jour. of No. Plains, 1969-73; contbr. numerous articles and reports to profl. publs. Office: ND Heritage Center Bismarck ND 58505

SPETCH, DORIS EDNA JACKSON, educator; b. Hudson, S.D., Mar. 2, 1920; d. Olin DeBuhr and Edna Anna (Hanson) Jackson; B.A., Hamline U., St. Paul, 1942; M.A., Northeastern Ill. U., 1970; m. William B. Spetch, Dec. 23, 1942; children—Barbara Spetch Mader, John. Tchr. schs. in Minn. and Ohio, 1942-45; newswriter Richfield Messenger, Mpls., 1945-46; tchr., choir dir., Appleton, Wis., 1958-66; tchr., Oak Lawn, Ill., 1966-74; with alumni dept. Lawrence U., Appleton, 1956-58; tchr. English and Communications Alan B. Shepard High Sch., Palos Heights, Ill., 1966—; lectr. speech dept. Moraine Valley Coll., 1976—; cons. workshops, coach forensics teams. Pres. Winona (Minn.) YWCA, 1955. Named Woman of Year, Winona Bus. and Profl. Women, 1955; Ill. Coach of Year, Northeastern Ill. U., 1976; recipient degree of distinction Nat. Forensic League; 1976. Mem. NEA, Ill. Edn. Assn., Ill. Speech and Theatre Assn., Ill. Tchrs. English, AAUW (pres. Winona 1954, mem. Minn. bd. 1953-55), Speech Communications Assn., Nat. Reading Assn.

SPETHMAN, DOROTHY MARIE, educator; b. Hillhead, S.D., Apr. 7, 1935; d. John L. and Josephine Haggerty; student U. Dallas, 1963, U. Detroit, 1957; B.S.Ed., Villanova U., 1960; M.A.Ed., U. S.D., Vermillion, 1975; m. Robert Spethmann, May 30, 1970; 1 dau., Mary Jo. Tchr. elementary schs., Pa., Tex., Mich., S.D., N.D., 1953-69; pvt. tutor spl. edn. students Madison, S.D., 1969-74; instr. elementary and spl. edn. methods Dakota State Coll., Madison, 1974-81, asst. prof., 1978—; cons. spl. edn. S.D. Dept. Edn. Bd. dirs. Every Citizens Counts Orgn. handicapped program, 1975-78, acad. adviser, 1975-79; supr. tutoring program Newman Center, team mem. marriage classes; mem. Franciscan order Roman Catholic Ch., 1952-69. Mem. AAUW, Dakota State Women, S.D. Council Tchrs. Math., Nat. Council Tchrs. Math., Delta Kappa Gamma. Republican. Home: 904 NW 5th St Madison SD 57042 Office: Sch Edn Dakota State Coll Madison SD 57042

SPEYER, FRED B., scientist; b. Kalamazoo, Feb. 28, 1916; s. Alfred and Cora (Burow) S.; B.A., Kalamazoo Coll., 1939, M.S., 1940; Ph.D., Internat. U., 1964; children—Alfred W. (dec.), Kip. With Dow Chem. Co., 1934-35, 40-41; chemist Upjohn Co., 1939-40; chief chemist Shellmar div. Continental Can Co., 1943-45, Am. Resinous Chem. Co., 1945-49; product devel. specialist Gen. Mills Chem. Div., 1949-53; supr. Splty. Coatings Pierce & Stevens Co., 1953-55; Union Oil Co. of Calif., 1955-59; supr. materials engring. Bendix Corp., 1959-62; Supr. plastics pilot plant Avco Corp., Lowell, Mass., 1962-65; prin. engr. TRW, Inc., Cleve., 1965-78; dir. Cons. Research Assos. Upjohn fellow, 1939; Purdue Research fellow, 1942-43, teaching asst., 1943-44; recipient engring. award Manhattan Atomic Energy Project; St. Andrews ecumenical research fellow, London, 1964; life fellow Internat. U., 1970. Mem. Am. Chem. Soc., Soc. Plastics Engrs., Sigma Xi. Republican. Christian Scientist. Patentee in field. Home: 24101 Lake Shore Blvd Euclid OH 44123

SPHIRE, RAYMOND DANIEL, anesthesiologist; b. Detroit, Feb. 12, 1927; s. Samuel Raymond and Nora Mae (Allen) S.; B.S., U. Detroit, 1948; M.D., Loyola U., Chgo., 1952; m. Joan Lois Baker, Sept. 5, 1953; children—Suzanne M., Raymond Daniel, Catherine J. Intern, Grace Hosp., Detroit, 1952-53, Harvard Anesthesia Lab., Mass. Gen. Hosp., 1953-55; attending anesthesiologist Grace Hosp., 1955-72, dir. dept. inhalation therapy, 1968-70; sr. attending anesthesiologist, dir. dept., dir. dept. respiratory therapy Detroit-Macomb Hosps. Assn., 1970—, trustee, 1978—, chief of staff, 1980—; clin. asst. prof. Wayne State U. Sch. Medicine, 1967—; clin. prof. respiratory therapy Macomb County Community Coll., Mt. Clemens, Mich., 1971—. Examiner, Am. Registry Respiratory Therapists, 1972—; insp. Joint Rev. Com. Respiratory Therapy Edn., 1972—; Served with AUS, 1944-45; as 1st lt. M.C., USAF, 1952. Diplomate Am. Bd. Anesthesiology. Fellow Am. Coll. Anesthesiologists, Am. Coll. Chest Physicians; mem. AMA, Am., Wayne County (pres. 1967-69), socs. anesthesiologists, Am. Assn. Respiratory Therapists, Soc. Critical Care Medicine. Clubs: Detroit Athletic, Country of Detroit, Otsego Ski, Severance Lodge. Co-author: Operative Neurosurgery, 1970; First Aid Guide for the Small Business or Industry, 1978. Home: 281 Lake Shore Rd Grosse Pointe Farms MI 48236 Office: 119 Kercheval St Grosse Pointe Farms MI 48236

SPICER, CLARENCE MARTIN, advt. co. exec.; b. Cin., Sept. 24, 1913; s. Clarence Everett and Vina Winefred (McDermott) S.; B.Indsl. Engring., U. Cin., 1939; student radar theory Harvard U., 1942, elec. engring. course M.I.T., 1942; m. Helen P. Feist, Dec. 28, 1940; children—Barbara J., Lynn A., Timothy M. Design engr., advt. mgr. Lodge & Shipley Machine Tool, Cin., 1939-41, 45-47; mktg. and advt. mgr. Keleket X-Ray Co., Cin., 1947-49; indsl. agency account exec., v.p. S.C. Baer Co., Cin., 1949-55; agy. pres. Baer, Kemble & Spicer, Inc., Cin., 1955-79, chmn. bd., 1979—; pres. C.M. Spicer & Asso., 1979—; partner Campbell-Turner, Inc., 1968-75. Mem. econ. research com. City of Cin., 1970-78; v.p. bd. dirs. Cin. Ballet Co., 1976-80; bd. dirs. Cin. chpt. ARC, 1964-67. Served to maj. U.S. Army, 1941-46; PTO. Mem. Am. Mktg. Assn., Am. Advt. Fedn., Advertisers Club Cin. Republican. Roman Catholic. Clubs: Cin., Western Hills Country. Office: Baer Kemble & Spicer Inc 2260 Francis Ln Cincinnati OH 45206

SPICER, HAROLD OTIS, educator; b. Gosport, Ind., Dec. 10, 1921; s. Otis R. and Hattie Grace (Wampler) S.; A.B., DePauw U., 1947, M.A., 1949; Ph.D., Ind. U., 1962; m. Hilda Jane Templeton, June 21, 1946; children—Sheryl Lynne Spicer Ecenbarger, Sylvia Jean, Stephen Michael. Teaching asst. DePauw U., 1947-49, asst. prof., 1957-63; instr. Western Ill. U., 1949-55, asst. prof., 1955-57; asso. prof. English, Ind. State U., Terre Haute, 1963-73, prof., 1973—; lectr. English, Ind. U. Extension Center at Indpls., 1960-63; news dir. Sta. WWKS-FM, Macomb, Ill., 1955-57; editorial dir., office pub. relations DePauw U., 1957-60. Publicity man Community Concerts Assn., Macomb, Ill., 1952-56, Crippled Children's Soc., Greencastle, Ind., 1957-60; pres. Putnam County Com. on Child Abuse, 1979-81. Served with USNR, 1942-46. Recipient Danforth Tchr. award 1959-60, Disting. Contbn. to Journalism award Ind. State U., 1977. Ind. U. fellow, 1955, 60. Mem. Am. Fedn. Tchrs., Modern Lang. Assn., Assn. Edn. and Journalism, Modern Humanities Research Assn., Ind. Coll. English Assn., Nat. Council Coll. Publs. Advisers (nat. head dist. chmn. 1964-65; editor Coll. Press Rev. 1965-67), Soc. Profl. Journalists, Lambda Chi Alpha, Sigma Delta Chi (Man of Year award 1968). Christian Scientist. Author: News Writing, 1964; contbr. to 3d edit. Halkett and Lang Dictionary Anonymous and Pseudonymous Literature; asso. editor Ind. English Jour., 1974—. Home: 706 Highwood Ave Greencastle IN 46135 Office: 206 Parsons Hall Ind State U Terre Haute IN 47809

SPICER, S. GARY, lawyer; b. Dickson, Tenn., Jan. 8, 1942; s. Clark and E. Maybelle (Hogin) S.; A.B., Adrian Coll., 1964; M.B.A., Wayne State U., 1965; J.D., Detroit Coll. of Law, 1969; m. Katherine Stettner, May 12, 1972; children—Victoria, S. Gary, Matthew, Katherine Anne, Mark. Admitted to Tenn. bar, 1969, Mich. bar, 1969; with personnel dept. Gen. Motors Corp., Pontiac, Mich., 1964-66; with trust dept. Nat. Bank of Detroit, 1966-69; accountant Price Waterhouse and Co., Detroit, 1969-71; sr. partner Spicer and Littman, P.C., Detroit; dir. PMH, Inc., Clarklift of Detroit Inc., Self Psych, Inc., Tayler Internat. Inc., Ronan & Kunzl Inc., KTC Industries Inc., Bob Owens Sales Inc., Bob Owens Datsun Inc., Clodell Enterprises, Inc., Mark Wallace Assos., Inc. Elder Fort St. Presbyn. Ch.; trustee Don Smith Found. Served with USAR, 1966-72. Mem. Mich., Tenn., Detroit bar assns. Clubs: Detroit Athletic, Adrian Coll. Alumni (dir.). Home: 15 Elmsleish Ln Grosse Pointe MI 48230 Office: 200 Renaissance Center Suite 2930 Detroit MI 48243

SPIEGEL, ROBERT HARTER, newspaper editor; b. Odebolt, Iowa, Feb. 20, 1922; s. Harvey H. and Ada B. (Harter) S.; B.A., Drake U., 1943; m. Dorothy Kilbourne Kerr, Aug. 3, 1946; children—Ronald, Richard, Craig. With Des Moines (Iowa) Register and Tribune, 1939-43, 1946-63; editor Mason City (Iowa) Globe-Gazette, 1963-74, Wis. State Jour., Madison, 1974—; lectr. Am. Press Inst. Served with U.S. Army, 1943-46. Recipient Headliner award, 1951; Sidney Hillman award, 1956; AP news writing sweepstakes awards, Iowa 1953, 56, 59, 61; Iowa Edn. Assn. award for edn. reporting, 1961. Mem. Am. Soc. Newspaper Editors, Wis. Newspaper Assn. Methodist. Home: 1109 Woodland Way Madison WI 53711 Office: 1901 Fish Hatchery Rd PO Box 8058 Madison WI 53708

SPIER, ANTHONY SAMUEL, tool mfg. co. exec.; b. London, Jan. 27, 1944; came to U.S., 1966, naturalized, 1975; s. David and Freda Francis (Albert) S.; B.Sc., U. London, 1966; M.B.A., U. Pa., 1968; m. Lauren Blondis, June 8, 1968; 1 son, Peter Curtis. Controller direct selling div. Helene Curtis Industries, Chgo., 1974-75; v.p., controller Am. Hosp. Supply Corp., Evanston, Ill., 1975-81; v.p. fin. Skil Corp., Chgo., 1981—; chmn. audit com., bd. dirs. Guardian Savs. and Loan Assn., Chgo. Trustee, Mt. Sinai Hosp. and Med. Center, Chgo. Mem. Am. Inst. C.P.A.'s, Ill. Soc. C.P.A.'s. Office: 4801 W Peterson Ave Chicago IL 60646

SPIESS, WILLIAM JOE, educator; b. Napoleon, Ohio, Nov. 9, 1951; s. Royce Grandville and Carolyn Grace (James) S.; B.S. in Agr., Ohio State U., 1974, postgrad., 1975—; postgrad. Toledo U., 1978—; m. Debbra Sue Emahiser, Nov. 10, 1972; children—Stephanie Lynn, Jamie Rae. Tchr., Four County Joint Vocat. Sch., Archbold, Ohio, 1974—, sr. tchr. horticulture, 1974—. Mem. Liberty Center (Ohio) Local Sch. Bd., 1975-79, pres., 1979; mem. Washington Twp. (Ohio) Zoning Bd., 1980—. Recipient Teaching award Ohio Vocat. Agr. Tchrs. Assn. 1980. Mem. Ohio Vocat. Assn., Am. Vocat. Assn., Ohio Sch. Bds. Assn., Future Farmers Am. (hon. chpt. farmer). Home: Box 242-A Route 2 Liberty Center OH 43532 Office: Box 245-A Route 1 Archbold OH 43502

SPILBERG, ISAIAS, physician; b. Trujillo, Peru, July 18, 1936; s. Salik and Rosa (Kolker) Shpilberg; came to U.S., 1963, naturalized, 1970; M.D., U. San Marcos, Lima, Peru, 1963; m. Fradi Goldstein, July 14, 1962; 1 son, Mark. Intern, U. Louisville Med. Sch., 1963-64, resident, 1964-66; fellow in rheumatology N.Y. U. Sch. Medicine, 1966-68; instr. Washington U. Sch. Medicine, St. Louis, 1968-70, asst. prof., 1970-77, asso. prof. medicine, 1978—; head rheumatology sect. Washington U. Med. Service-St. Louis City Hosp., 1970-77; dir. rheumatology unit VA Med. Center, St. Louis, 1977—. Mem. med. and sci. com. Arthritis Found., 1976—. USPHS fellow, 1966-68; NIH grantee, 1976—; Nat. Arthritis Found. grantee, 1976—. Mem. Am. Rheumatism Assn., Am. Fedn. Clin. Research, Central Soc. Clin. Research, N.Y. Acad. Scis., Am. Soc. Cell Biology, Am. Assn. Immunologists, Am. Soc. Clin. Investigation. Contbr. articles toprofl. jours. Office: 915 N Grand Ave Saint Louis MO 63125

SPILLANE, RICHARD JEROME, utility co. mgr., alcoholism cons.; b. Chgo., Nov. 13, 1935; s. Jerry and Helen (Kelly) S.; B.S.C., Loyola U., Chgo., 1957, postgrad., 1959; student in alcoholism counseling Central States Inst. on Addiction, 1975; advanced safety cert. Nat. Safety Council, 1976; m. Annette Busse, Feb. 11, 1961; children—Mary Ellen, Patrick, John, Joseph, Kathleen, Susan, Daniel, Michael, William, Mary Anne, David. Steel salesman A. M. Castle, Franklin Park, Ill., 1959-62; with Ill. Bell Telephone Co., 1962—, employment mgr., Oak Brook, 1971-73, personnel mgr., 1973-75, mgmt. tng. mgr., Hinsdale, 1977—; cons. occupational alcoholism, Oak Park, 1975—; guest lectr. numerous colls., hosps., agys.; bd. govs. Ill. Alcoholism Cert. Bd.; counselor/lectr. Driving While Intoxicated Program, Suburban Cook County, Ill., 1975; mem. Ill. Task Force on Cert., 1976-80; chmn. profl. coms. Served to 1st lt. U.S. Army, 1957-59. Recipient Presdl. award Ill. Bell Telephone, 1979, Community Leadership-Alex award, 1979; Ill. Combined House/Senate commendation, 1978, Ill. Task Force on Cert. award, 1980; cert. alcoholism counselor, Ill. Mem. Assn. Labor Mgmt. Cons. on Alcoholism (pres.), Ill. Alcoholism Counselor Alliance (gov.), Nat. Alcoholism Counselors Assn., Am. Soc. Safety Engrs., Ill. Alcoholism and Drug Dependence Assn., Antique Airplane Assn. Roman Catholic. Research in interpersonal aspects of human behavior. Home: 320 Wisconsin Oak Park IL 60302 Office: 12 Salt Creek Ln Hinsdale IL 60521

SPINDLER, EUGENE LAVERNE, accountant, soc. adminstr.; b. Marshfield, Wis., Mar. 31, 1945; s. Norbert LaVerne and Delores Elizabeth (Bell) S.; B.B.A. in Acctg., U. Wis., 1968; m. Bonnie Lynne Rusch, June 10, 1967; children—Sean, Ryan, Tyler. Acct. dept. research adminstrn. U. Wis., Madison, 1970, acct. Fin. Reporting, 1970-76; chief of fiscal services State Hist. Soc. Wis., Madison, 1976—. Cub master Four Lakes council Boy Scouts Am., Middleton, Wis., 1980—; mem. fin. com. Friends of Channel 21, 1981—. Served with U.S. Army, 1968-70. Home: 3460 Hickory Hill Rd Verona WI 53593 Office: 816 State St Madison WI 53706

SPIRER, EDWIN SHEV, social worker, hosp. adminstr.; b. N.Y.C., Feb. 15, 1947; s. Aaron Maurice and Naomi (Werblowsky) S.; B.A., C.W. Post Coll., 1968; cert. environ. planning, Victoria U., Manchester, Eng., 1971; M.S.W., Fordham U., 1972; M.P.H., Harvard U., 1980; m. Arlene Weber, June 27, 1974; children—Judith Ann, David Jacob. Groupworker, N.Y.C. Dept. Social Services, 1968-70, caseworker, 1972-73; social groupworker Bronx (N.Y.) House, 1970-71; community organizer Flushing Ave. Sr. Center, Bklyn., 1971-72; commd. lt. USPHS, 1973, advanced through grades to lt. comdr., 1980; staff social worker USPHS Hosp., S.I., N.Y., 1973-76; asst. asso. dir. for ambulatory care USPHS Hosp., Boston, 1976-80; spl. asst. to dir. USPHS Outpatient Clinic, Chgo., 1980—; pvt. practice social work; cons. social work. Served with USAF, 1967-72. Cert. social worker, N.Y. State. Mem. Nat. Assn. Public Adminstrs., Nat. Assn. Social Workers, Am. Public Health Assn., Aircraft Owners and Pilots Assn., Commd. Officers Assn. USPHS, Nat. Acad. Cert. Social Workers. Club: Flying. Home: 538 N Grant St Hinsdale IL 60521 Office: USPHS Outpatient Clinic 1439 S Michigan Ave Chicago IL 60605

SPITZ, LINDA PACKER, radio sales reps. mgr.; b. Chgo., Nov. 16, 1951; d. Jack and Layle Rochelle Packer; B.S.B.A., Roosevelt U., 1973; m. Edward Spitz, Aug. 17, 1980. Researcher traffic dept. Sta. WLS-TV, Chgo., 1973-75; account exec. Sta. WFLD-TV, Chgo., 1975-77; nat. account exec. Field Communications, 1977; account exec. RKO Radio Sales Reps., Chgo., 1977-80, mgr., 1980—; dir. La Petite Maison. Active Muscular Dystrophy Assn., Spl. Children's Charities. Recipient radio sales awards. Mem. Women in Broadcasting. Office: 401 N Michigan Ave Chicago IL 60611

SPITZER, ROBERT RALPH, engring. sch. pres., food and agrl. cons.; b. Waukesha, Wis., May 4, 1922; s. John and Ruth (St.George) S.; B.S. in Agr., U. Wis., 1943, M.S. in Animal Nutrition and Biochemistry, 1945, Ph.D., 1947; L.H.D. (hon.), Milton Coll., 1978; m. Marie Lilian Woerfel, June 22, 1946; children—John, Jeff, Susan. Dir. research Murphy Products Co., Inc., Burlington, Wis., 1947-53, v.p. research and promotion, 1953-57, exec. v.p., 1957-58, pres., 1958-74, chief exec. officer, 1958-74, chmn. bd., 1974-75; coordinator Food for Peace, 1975-76; citizen adv. World Food Program, Rome, Italy, 1972, U.S. del., 1975, 76; pres. Milw. Sch. Engring., 1977—; world food lectr. Iowa State U., 1977; lectr. various univs., profl. groups, service clubs and bus. convs. in U.S., 1950—; sr. adv. food and agr. Allis-Chalmers Corp., 1976—; dir. Mirro Aluminun Co.; dir. Tracy & Son, Inc., 1976—, adv., 1976—; dir. Larsen Co., Unishelter, Inc.; mem. adv. bd. U.S. Commodity Credit Corp., 1969-70. Chmn. adv. com. Milw. Billy Graham Crusade, 1979; nat. food and agr. chmn. Republican Party, 1968; warden St. John the Divine Episcopal Ch., Burlington, Wis., 1965-66; bd. dirs. Kearney & Trecker Found., Inc., Milw., 1978-79, Sci. and Tech. Center, Milw. Public Mus., 1979; trustee The Nutrition Found., 1979, Farm Found., 1975-79; mem. vocat. industries bd. for handicapped Walworth County, Wis., 1978-79. Recipient Coll. of Agr. award U. Wis., 1971, Disting. Ser. award U. Wis., 1972, Disting. Lectr. award Mich. State U., 1976, Businessman of Wis. award, 1969. Mem. Am. Dairy Sci. Assn., Am. Chem. Soc., Am. Poultry Sci. Assn., Am. Soc. of Animal Production, Am. Inst. Chemists, Wis. Mfrs. Assn. (pres. 1970-72), U. Wis. Internat. Alumni Assn. (pres. 1964-65), Sigma Xi, Phi Eta Sigma, Phi Lambda Upsilon, Alpha Zeta, Delta Theta Sigma, Gamma Sigma Delta, Phi Kappa Phi, Delta Phi Zeta, Phi Sigma. Republican. Clubs: University (Washington); Rotary (hon. mem.); Milw. Athletic, Milwaukee; Lake Geneva Country. Author: The Family Organizer, 1977; The American Challenge, 1980; contbr. articles on nutrition, agr. and business to various publs. Home: 1134 North Rd Burlington WI 53105 Office: 1025 N Milwaukee St Milwaukee WI 53202

SPITZNAGEL, WILLIAM F., transp. co. exec.; b. Fairfield, Ala., July 15, 1926; B.A., Auburn (Ala.) U., 1949. With Roadway Express, Inc., 1950—, v.p. N.E. div., 1967, v.p. ops., 1973, exec. v.p., 1974-78, chmn. bd., pres., Akron, Ohio, 1978—, also dir. Address: Roadway Express Inc 1077 Gorge Blvd Akron OH 44309

SPLANE, BEVERLY J., commodity exchange exec.; b. Santa Monica, Calif., Dec. 5, 1943; d. Donald Ernest and Eleanor Anne (McInnes) S.; A.B., U. Chgo., 1967, M.B.A., 1969. Mgmt. cons. Boston Cons. Group, 1969-73; dir. career devel. Harvard Bus. Sch., 1973-74; asso. dir. presdl. personnel office White House, 1974-75; acting exec. dir. Commodity Futures Trading Commn., Washington, 1975; exec. v.p. Chgo. Mercantile Exchange, 1975—. Mem. U. Chgo. Alumni Assn. (exec. com. 1978-79, pres. 1980—). Clubs: Econs of Chgo., Met. Office: 444 W Jackson Blvd Chicago IL 60606

SPLITT, THEODORE BERNARD, JR., mech. engr.; b. Warrenton, Mo., Aug. 19, 1934; s. Theodore and Julia Margaret (Lammers) S.; student U. Mo., Columbia, 1953-54, Rolla, 1970; Asso. in Liberal Arts, St. Mary's Coll., 1975, Asso. in Adminstrn. Justice, 1977; B.A. in Adminstrn. of Justice, Lindenwood Coll., 1981; m. Lorna Lulu Smith, Nov. 12, 1955; 1 son, Kenneth Bernard. Draftsman, Binkley Co., Warrenton, 1954-56; tool designer Ritepoint, Inc., Hermann, Mo., 1956; tool designer McDonnell Douglas Co., St. Louis, 1956-57, 1958-60, Carr Lane Co., St. Louis, 1960-61; jr. engr. Binkley Co., Warrenton, 1961-70, project engr., supr. data base, 1971—; owner, operator farm, 1969—. Dep. sheriff Warren County, 1976—; mcpl. judge City of Warrenton, 1968-76; spl. agt. Mo. Nat. Guard, 1972—. Served with AUS, 1957-58. Cert. profl. police officer Mo. Dept. Public Safety. Mem. U.S. Army Warrant Officers Assn., Nat. Guard Assn. U.S., Mo. Nat. Guard Assn., Am. Def. Preparedness Assn., Air Force Assn., Nat. Sheriffs Assn., Am. Prodn. and Inventory Control Soc., Am. Law Enforcement Officers Assn., Mo. Sheriffs Assn., Nat. Rifle Assn., U. Mo. Alumni Assn., St. Mary's Coll. of O'Fallon Alumni Assn., Lindenwood Coll. Alumni Assn., Alpha Sigma Tau. Roman Catholic. Patentee in mini-fifth wheel for gooseneck trailers. Home: 410 McKinley Ave Warrenton MO 63383 Office: Main and Elm Sts Binkley Co Warrenton MO 63383

SPLITTSTOESSER, WALTER EMIL, educator; b. Claremont, Minn., Aug. 27, 1937; s. Waldemar Theodore and Opal Mae (Young) S.; B.S. with distinction (univ. fellow), U. Minn., 1958; M.S., S.D. State U., 1960; Ph.D., Purdue U., 1963; m. Shirley Anne O'Connor, July 2, 1960; children—Pamela, Sheryl, Riley. Plant breeder U. Minn., 1956-58; weed scientist S.D. State U., 1958-60; plant physiologist Purdue U., Lafayette, Ind., 1960-63, Shell Oil, Modesto, Calif., 1963-64; biochemist U. Calif., Davis, 1964-65; prof., head, vegetable crops div. U. Ill., Urbana, 1965—; vis. prof. Univ. Coll., London, Eng., 1972; biologist Parkland Coll., Champaign, Ill., 1974; research asso. Rothamsted Exptl. Sta., Harpenden, Eng., 1980. NIH fellow, 1964-65. Recipient J.H. Gourley award Am. Fruit Grower and Am. Soc. Hort. Sci., 1974. Mem. Weed Sci. Soc. Am., Am. Soc. Hort. Sci. (rev. editor Jour. 1969—), Am., Japanese, Scandinavian socs. plant physiologists, Sigma Xi, Alpha Zeta, Gamma Sigma Delta, Delta Theta Sigma, Phi Kappa Phi. Author: Vegetable Growing Handbook, 1979. Rev. editor Hort. Sci., 1969—, Analytical Biochemistry, 1969-78, NSF, 1978-79; contbr. articles to profl. jours. Home: 2006 Cureton Urbana IL 61801 Office: 201 Vegetable Crops Bldg U Ill 1103 W Dorner Dr Urbana IL 61801

SPOHN, JOHN EDWARD, meat co. exec.; b. Madison, Wis., July 24, 1928; s. William H. and Ethel M. (Crowley) S.; B.S., U. Wis., 1951; m. Mary T. Fauerbach, Nov. 23, 1950; children—William, Peter, Ann, Kathryn, Thomas, Michael, Patricia, Sue. With Oscar Mayer & Co., Inc., Madison, 1953—, automotive supr., 1953-60, transp. mgr., 1960-66, gen. fleet and transp. mgr., 1966-71, gen. distbn. mgr., 1971-73, mgr. Madison plant ops., 1973-74, plant mgr., 1974—, v.p., 1979—; dir. Edward Kraemer & Sons, Inc., Plain, Wis. Past pres. Village of Maple Bluff, Wis.; asst. chief Maple Bluff Vol. Fire Dept. Mem. Wis. Mfrs. and Commerce (dir.), Greater Madison C. of C. (dir.), Wis. Motor Carrier Assn. (dir., past pres.). Republican. Roman Catholic. Clubs: Madison; Maple Bluff Country. Home: 209 Lakewood Blvd Madison MI 53704 Office: PO Box 7188 Madison WI 53707

SPOONER, WILLIAM AUSTIN, mgmt. cons.; b. Madison, S.D., Mar. 20, 1918; s. William Tracy and Abigail Pauline (Connell) S.; B.S., Calif. Inst. Tech., 1940; M.B.A., Harvard U., 1956; m. Rita Therese Nicholson, Sept. 7, 1946; children—William Austin, Eileen T. Spooner O'Brien. Commd. ensign U.S. Navy, advanced through grades to comdr., 1956; ret., 1963; bus. operations mgr. F-111 Systems programs Litton Industries, Inc., 1963-65; controller Rocket Research Corp., Seattle, 1966; supr. missiles mgmt. systems Columbus div. Rockwell Corp., 1965-70; pres., chief exec. officer William A. Spooner Assos., Inc., Columbus, Ohio, 1970—; dir. Superior Plating Co.; speaker on mgmt. planning to community and trade assns. Mem. Ind. Profl. Cons. Assn., Planning Execs. Inst. Roman Catholic. Home: 1746 Pin Oak Dr Columbus OH 43229 Office: 1900 E Dublin Granville Rd Columbus OH 43229

SPOOR, WILLIAM HOWARD, food mfg. co. exec.; b. Pueblo, Colo., Jan. 16, 1923; s. Charles H. and Doris Field (Slaughter) S.; B.A. in History, Dartmouth Coll., 1949; m. Janet Spain; children—Melanie, Cynthia, Lincoln. With Pillsbury Co., 1949—, v.p., gen. mgr. Pillsbury Internat., Mpls., 1968-73, chmn. bd., chief exec. officer, 1973—; dir. Honeywell, Inc., Dayton Hudson Corp. Bd. dirs. United Negro Coll. Fund, Found. Mgmt. Edn. in C. Am. Served with U.S. Army, 1943-46. Mem. Minn. Orchestral Assn. (dir.), Minn. Bus. Partnership. Office: Pillsbury Center Minneapolis MN 55402

SPRAGUE, BERNARD, judge; b. Hastings, Nebr., May 1, 1932; s. Leon A. and Helen M. (McNeny) S.; B.S., U. Denver, 1956, LL.B. cum laude, 1958; m. Barbara Mary Flanagan Aug. 6, 1955; children—Michael, Kathleen, Patrick, Ann. Admitted to Nebr. bar, 1958; practice in Red Cloud, 1958-60, 63-72; asst. U.S. atty., 1960-63; atty. Webster County, 1966-72; dist. county judge, 1972-77; dist. judge 10th Jud. Dist. Nebr., 1977—. Mem. Nebr. Democratic Central Com., 1958-60; del. Nebr. Dem. Conv., 1958-62; mem. Red Cloud High Sch. System, 1965-66. Served with USMC, 1952-55. Mem. Nebr. Dist. County Judges Assn. (pres. 1975-76), Am. Legion, VFW, DAV, Order St. Ives, Omicron Kappa Delta, Delta Tau Delta, Phi Delta Phi. Roman Catholic. Home: 840 W 7th St Red Cloud NE 68970 Office: Webster County Ct House Red Cloud NE 68970

SPRIGGS, GARRY LEE, coll. adminstr.; b. Portsmouth, Ohio, May 19, 1940; s. Harvey Carl and Marie Ellen (Dawson) S.; student Frankfort Pilgrim Coll., 1959-61; B.A., Hobe Sound Bible Coll., 1977; m. Eunice Junice Williams, Jan. 16, 1960; children—Kevin, Debbie, Phillip, Timmy. Ordained to ministry Pilgrim Holiness Ch. Am., 1966; pastor Pilgrim Holiness Ch., Afton, Ohio, 1961-63, Syracuse, N.Y., 1968-73; field mgr. for Ohio and Ind., Furst McNess Co., 1963-64; gen. evangelist Pilgrim Holiness Ch. of America (now Wesleyan Ch.), Marion, Ind., 1964-68; Christian service dir. Hobe Sound Bible Coll., 1973-81; dir. Youth and evangelism Ch. of God (Holiness), Overland Park, Kans., 1981—; v.p. external affairs Kansas City Coll. and Bible Sch., Overland Park, 1981—. Republican. Home: 7401 Metcalf Ave Overland Park KS 66204 Office: 7407 Metcalf Ave Overland Park KS 66204

SPRINGER, BILL, publisher; b. Detroit, Feb. 6, 1945; s. William and Cornelia Seagraves (Hartsell) S.; grad. high sch. With New Center News, Detroit, 1959, owner, 1973—; founder Tech Center News, Warren, Mich., 1976; pub. Monday Morning Newspapers, Detroit, 1973—. Named Eagle scout Boy Scouts Am., 1958. Episcopalian. Home: 4100 Hill Dr Utica MI 48087 Office: 1-218 General Motors Bldg Detroit MI 48202

SPRINGER, GEORGE ERBIN, JR., hotel devel. co. exec.; b. Augusta, Ga., Jan. 23, 1918; s. George Erbin and Marguerite M. (Latimer) S.; B.S. in Hotel Adminstrn., Cornell U., 1940; m. Marjorie Gundersen, Aug. 23, 1945; children—Jeffrey Judd, Mark Leonard. Various exec. positions with New Yorker Hotel, N.Y.C., 1938-42, Secor Hotel, Toledo, 1942-48; founder, v.p. Bates & Spring, Inc., Cleve., 1948-68; founder, pres. G.E. Springer Inc., Cleve., 1970—; dir. Capital Nat. Bank. Mem. Urban Land Inst., Apt. Owners Assn., Am. Hotel Assn., Cleve. Apt. Assn. (pres.). Clubs: Cornell (pres.), Trails and Riding (pres.), Rotary (Cleve.); Chagrin Valley Hunt (Gates Mills, Ohio); Acacia Country (Lyndhurst, Ohio); Camelback Country (Scottsdale, Ariz.). Office: G E Springer Inc 28001 Chagrin Blvd Cleveland OH 44122

SPRINGER, HAROLD EUGENE, hosp. adminstr.; b. Lima, Ohio, Aug. 20, 1920; s. Clarence W. and Edith (Reed) S.; A.B., Taylor U., 1943; B.D., Hamma Div. Sch., Wittenberg Coll., 1946; M.S. in Hosp. Adminstrn. Northwestern U., 1956; m. Kathryn L. Smith, Aug. 22, 1941; children—Paul Edwin, Robert Earl. Ordained to ministry Meth. Ch., 1947; minister United Meth. Ch., East Liberty, Ohio, 1946-49; asst. adminstr. White Cross Hosp., Columbus, Ohio, 1949-54; purchasing agt. Rush-Presbyn.-St. Lukes Med. Center, Chgo., 1954-58; adminstr. Meml. Community Hosp., Edgerton, Wis., 1958-59; bus. adminstr. Peoria (Ill.) State Hosp., 1959-65; bus. mgr. Alaska Meth. U., Anchorage, 1965-68; exec. dir. Emanuel Hosp., Turlock, Calif., 1968-75; exec. dir. Swedish Covenant Hosp., Chgo., 1975—. Fellow Am. Coll. Hosp. Adminstrs.; mem. Nat. Assn. Purchasing Mgmt. (pres. 1958-59), Ill. Hosp. Assn., Chgo. Hosp. Council. Contbr. articles in field to profl. jours. Office: 5145 N California Ave Chicago IL 60625

SPRINGER, JAMES JEROME, ins. co. exec.; b. Chgo., Apr. 19, 1932; s. Anton Andrew and Alice Agnes (Hahn) S.; B.S. in Bus. Adminstrn. (scholar), Lewis U., 1954. Actuarial clk. Sterling/Constitution Ins. Co., Chgo., 1954-56; key clk. Bankers Life & Casualty Co., Chgo., 1956-60; statis. supr. Fed. Life Ins. Co., Chgo., 1960-67, records mgr., home office, 1967-81; speaker Inst. for Graphic Communications, 1977, ARMA Nat. Conf., 1979, 81, numerous others. Mem. adv. com. DuPage Area Ednl. Vocat. Authority, 1979-80; active Crusade of Mercy, 1977-79. Cert. records mgr. Fellow Life Ins. Mgmt. Assn.; mem. Assn. of Records Mgrs. and Adminstrs. (chpt. mem. of year 1974, 77, Regional award of merit 1977, editor bull. 1968-72, pres. 1973-74, adv. bd.), Nat. Micrographics Assn. (chpt. dir., Service award 1979). Contbr. articles on bus. mgmt. to profl. jours.

SPRINGER, NINFA SATURNINO, nutritionist; b. Cadiz, Negros Occidental, Philippines, Oct. 22, 1928; d. Juan Duldulao and Estrella (Aguilar) Saturnino; came to U.S., 1955, naturalized, 1967; B.S. in Nutrition and Dietetics cum laude, U. Philippines, 1952, M.S., 1957; Ph.D. in Nutrition (Dept. State scholar), U. Iowa, 1959; m. Robert Earl Springer, Jr., Sept. 1, 1958; children—Robert Earl, Pamela Stellene. Administrv. dietitian Philippine Gen. Hosp., Manila, 1953-55; asst. prof. U. South Philippines, 1959-60, U. Philippines, 1960-63; project dir. Nat. Sci. Devel. Bd.-U. Philippines research project, 1961-63; lectr. Wayne State U., Detroit, 1965, Marygrove Coll., Detroit, 1965-67; program dir. nutrition Inst. Study Mental Retardation and Related Disabilities, 1969-81; asst. prof. Sch. Public Health, U. Mich., Ann Arbor, 1969-77, asso. prof., 1978—; cons. in field. Bd. dirs. YWCA, Cebu City, Philippines, 1959-60; sec. Filipino Women's Club Detroit, 1967-69. Fulbright travel grantee, 1955-59; named Most Outstanding Filipino Woman, Philippine-Am. Assn., 1975; named "Balik Scientist", Nat. Sci. Devel. Bd., Philippine Govt., 1977; recipient Most Outstanding Alumni award U. Philippines, 1978; Appreciation plaque Nutritionists-Dietitians Assn. Philippines, 1980. Mem. Am. Dietetic Assn., Am. Public Health Assn., Am. Assn. Mental Deficiency, Ann Arbor Dietetic Assn. Contbr. articles profl. publs. Home: 1405 Hewett St Ann Arbor MI 48103

SPROUL, STEVEN EDWARD, lawyer; b. Dixon, Ill., Mar. 24, 1948; s. Gerald and Dorothy J. (Book) S.; B.S., Bradley U., 1970; J.D., Coll. William and Mary, 1974; m. Jan Lee Schuttler, Feb. 20, 1971. Staff acct. Price Waterhouse & Co., Peoria, Ill., 1970-71; admitted to Ill. bar, 1974; partner firm Reno, Zahm, Folgate, Lindberg & Powell, Rockford, Ill., 1974—; dir. JSM Industries, Inc., 1976—. Chmn. com. for today and tomorrow Rockford Meml. Hosp., 1980-81, trustee hosp., 1980-81. Mem. Winnebago County, Ill. bar assns. Republican. Club: Rockford YMCA. Home: 225 Calvin Park Blvd Rockford IL 61107 Office: Reno Zahm et al Suite 900 1415 E State St Rockford IL 61108

SPROUSE, GARY LEE, mfg. co. sales exec.; b. St. Louis, Dec. 22, 1938; s. Grady Louise and Eleanor May S.; student (working scholar 1959-61), Central Meth. Coll., 1959-61; B.S.B.A., Washington U., St. Louis, 1963; M.B.A., Central Mich. U., 1968; m. Donna Sue Green, July 27, 1963; children—Anne Elizabeth, Gregory Herbert. Staff mgmt. asst. Western Electric Co., St. Louis, 1963-65; with Dow Corning Corp., 1965—, regional sales mgr., Englewood Cliffs, N.J., 1972-74, gen. mgr. SE Asia, Hong Kong, 1974-78, regional sales mgr., Chgo., 1978—. Served with U.S. Army, 1957-58. Republican. Episcopalian. Clubs: Bull Valley Hunt, Am. Hardware, Elks. Home: 30W 235 Bellingham Bartlett IL 60103 Office: 4825 N Scott St Schiller Park IL 60176

SPROWL, CHARLES RIGGS, lawyer; b. Lansing, Mich., Aug. 22, 1910; s. Charles Orr and Hazel (Allen) S.; A.B., U. Mich., 1932, J.D., 1934; m. Virginia Lee Graham, Jan. 15, 1938; children—Charles R., Robert A., Susan G., Sandra D. Admitted to Ill. bar, 1935, pvt. practice, 1934—; practice as partner in firm of Taylor, Miller, Magner, Sprowl & Hutchings; dir. Paul F. Beich Co., Busch & Schmitt, Inc., Petersen Aluminum Corp., A.H. Ross & Sons Co. Mem. Bd. Edn. New Trier Township High Sch., 1959-65, pres., 1963-65; chmn. Glencoe Zoning Bd. of Appls., 1965-76; bd. dirs. Glencoe Public Library, 1953-65, pres., 1955-56; bd. dirs. Northwestern U. Settlement Assn., pres., 1963-70; bd. dirs. Cradle Soc., Juvenile Protective Assn., 1943-53; trustee Highland Park Hosp., 1959-69. Mem. Chgo. (mem. bd. mgrs. 1949-51), Ill., Am. bar assns., Am. Coll. Trial Lawyers, Soc. Trial Lawyers. Delta Theta Phi, Alpha Chi Rho. Presbyn. Clubs: Law (pres. 1969-70), Legal (pres. 1953-54), University, Monroe, Skokie Country. Home: 558 Washington Ave Glencoe IL 60022 Office: 120 S LaSalle St Chicago IL 60603

SQUILLACE, ALEXANDER PAUL, investment adviser; b. Missoula, Mont., Feb. 25, 1945; s. Dominick Paul and Kathleen Marie S.; B.S. in Bus. Adminstrn., Ohio State U., 1967; m. Miriam Palmer Patterson, June 17, 1967; children—Sandra, Scott, Brian, Susan. Investment analyst Nationwide Ins. Cos., Columbus, Ohio, 1967-69; instl. bond rep. Hornblower & Weeks-Hemphill, Noyes, Columbus, 1969-71, mgr. fixed income securities, Indpls., 1971-74; v.p. United Nat. Bank-United Nat. Corp., Sioux Falls, S.D., 1974-79; pres. Investment Mgmt. Group, Sioux Falls, S.D., 1979—, Farmers State Bank, Stickney, S.D., 1979—, Bormann Ins. Agy., Stickney, 1979—; vice chmn. S.D. Investment Council; instr. Am. Inst. Banking. Named hon. citizen of Indpls., 1974; chartered fin. analyst. Fellow Fin. Analysts Fedn.; mem. Am. Inst. Banking, S.D. Bankers Assn., S.D. Investment Soc., Twin Cities Soc. Security Analysts, Ohio State Alumni Assn. Home: 2009 E 52d St Sioux Falls SD 57103 Office: 301 S Garfield St Suite 6 Sioux Falls SD 57104

SREDL, DARLENE RITA MAJKA, nurse; b. Chgo., Feb. 20, 1943; d. Joseph Harry and Bernice Charlotte (Pacyna) Majka; B.S. in Nursing, Loyola U., Chgo., 1964; M.A. in Hosp. Adminstrn., Webster Coll., St. Louis, 1979; m. Frederick H. Sredl, Oct. 17, 1964; children—Steven, Michael, Stacy Jolie, Thomas. Nurse epidemiologist DuPage County, Ill., 1964-65; mem. faculty asso. degree nursing program Lincoln U., Jefferson City, Mo., also dir. nurses Regency Nursing Inn, St. Louis, 1974; dir. service, dir. profl. edn. Am. Cancer Soc., St. Louis, 1975-76; edn. asso. Washington U. Sch. Medicine, St. Louis, 1977; dir. nurses Clayton-on-the-Green Extended Care Facility, St. Louis, 1978, St. Joseph Hosp., Alton, Ill., 1978-79; founder, pres. AV-Nurse, Ltd., aviation nursing cons., Ballwin, Mo., 1977—; bd. dirs. Madison County (Ill.) unit Am. Cancer Soc., 1978; CPR coordinator Ill. Heart Assn., 1978. Named Outstanding Alumna, Loyola U., 1978. Mem. Soc. Nursing Service Adminstrs., Aerospace Med. Assn., Oncology Soc., Am. Nurses Assn., Mo. Nurses Assn. (council nursing research), Mo. Nurses for Life (co-founder), Alpha Tau Delta. Roman Catholic. Author numerous articles in aviation nursing field. Office: Box 1247 Ballwin MO 63011

SRODE, WALTER EDWARD, JR., computer mfg. co. ofcl.; b. Dayton, Ohio, June 13, 1939; s. Walter Edward and Marcella Eleanor (Osterfeld) S.; B.S. E.E., U. Dayton, 1962; M.S.E.E., Wayne State U., 1969; m. Elizabeth M. Winefer, Aug. 18, 1962; children—Ladonna, Tina, Kenneth. Elec. engr. Honeywell, St. Petersburg, Fla., 1963-65; reliability test engr. Gen. Electric, Huntsville, Ala., 1965; system engr. Ling Tempco Vought, Detroit, 1965-68; project leader, engring. mgr. Nat. Cash Register, Dayton and Cambridge, Ohio, 1968-77, dir. quality assurance, Cambridge, 1977—. Served with USMCR, 1957-58. Mem. C. of C. (dir.). Office: PO Box 728 Cambridge OH 43725

SROKA, STEPHEN ROLAND, II, educator; b. Cleve., June 17, 1943; s. Stephen Roland and June Virginia (Icke) S.; B.A., Cleve. State U., 1967, M.Ed., 1974; Ph.D., Case Western Res. U., 1978; 1 dau., Laura Ann. Chem. lab. technician Glidden Co., Cleve., 1962-67, polymer chemist, 1967-69; supr. student tchrs. Case Western Res. U., Cleve., 1976-78; health tchr. Cleve. Public Schs., 1969—; adj. asst. prof. health edn. Cleve. State U., 1976—; cons. Ohio Dept. Edn., 1979—, Ohio Dept. Health, 1976-79. Chmn. sch. subcom. public edn. Cuyahoga County unit Am. Cancer Soc., 1973—; sec., v.p. Youth Outreach Services, Cleve., 1973—; pres. Northeastern Ohio Health Edn. Assn., 1978—. Named Health Tchr. of Year, Cleve. Public Schs., 1976. Mem. Am. Public Health Assn., Am. Sch. Health Assn., Assn. Advancement Health Edn., Northeastern Ohio Health Edn. Assn., Phi Delta Kappa (named Young Ednl. Leader of Am. 1981). Author: Health Textbook Series, 1979—; reviewer Jour. Sch. Health, 1977—. Home: 7002 Detroit Ave 2 Cleveland OH 44102 Office: Dept Health Phys Edn and Recreation Room PE 215 Cleveland State U Cleveland OH 44115

STAAS, JOHN WILLIAM, psychologist, educator; b. Freeport, Ill., July 28, 1942; s. William Franklin and Lucille Ann (Harney) S.; A.A., Cerritos Jr. Coll., 1962; student Calif. State U., Fullerton, 1962-63; B.S., No. Ill. U., 1964; M.A., U. Mo., Kansas City, 1966; postgrad. in Psychology, Bowling Green State U., 1966-67, Wayne State U., 1969-71; m. Zee L. Kinman, children—Laura Christine, Kevin Gregory. Research asst. Kansas City Mental Health Found., 1965-66; asst. psychologist Peace Corps., U. Mo., Kansas City, 1966; research asso. Kans. U. Med. Center, 1965; staff psychologist Kansas City Found. for Exceptional Children, 1965-66; asst. prof. psychology Mary Manse Coll., Toledo, 1967-70; asso. prof. psychology Monroe County (Mich.) Community Coll., Monroe, 1970—; pvt. practice clin. psychology, Toledo, 1968—; cons. psychologist Rescue, Inc., 1968-71, Holy Spirit Sem. and Vocat. Office Toledo Cath. Charities, 1971-77, Dr. S.N. Petas, Med. Clinic, Toledo, 1972-76; cons. clin. psychologist Toledo Mental Hygiene Clinic, 1967-74; clin. psychologist, adj. med. staff St. Charles Hosp., Oregon, Ohio, 1977—; cons., workshops on non-verbal communication and psychology of multiple personalities, 1968—. Named Tchr. of Year, Monroe County Community Coll., 1975-76, 78-79; registered psychologist; lic. psychologist, Ill., Ohio; cert. hypnotist. Mem. Am. Psychol. Assn., Assn. for Advancement of Psychology, Ill. Psychol. Assn., Assn. for Advancement of Behavior Therapy, N.W. Ohio Psychol. Assn., N.W. Ohio Clin. Hypnosis Assn., NEA, Mich. Edn. Assn., Phi Theta Kappa (spl. tchr.'s award 1973, hon. mem.). Roman Catholic. Club: Heatherdowns Country (Toledo). Author script Voice of Am. Radio. Home: 4125 Greenglen Rd Toledo OH 43614 Office: 1455 S Raisinville Rd Dept Psychology Monroe MI 48161 also 5321 Southwyck Blvd Suite L Briarwood Medical Center Toledo OH 43614

STACHOWIAK, ROBERT EDWARD, mfg. co. exec.; b. South Bend, Ind., Mar. 29, 1951; s. Edward Joseph and Irene Elizabeth S.; B.S., Ind. U., South Bend, 1973; postgrad. N.Y. U., 1976; m. Cathy L. Cukrowicz, Mar. 6, 1976; children—Mark Allan, Matthew Robert. With Nat. Bank & Trust Co., South Bend, 1968-73, asst. cashier in ops., 1971-73; staff acct. Coopers & Lybrand, South Bend, 1973-75, in-charge acct., 1975-76; controller Lock Joint Tube Co., Inc., South Bend, 1976—. Mem. South Bend Area C. of C. Mem. Ind. U. Alumni Assn., Am. Mfrs. Assn., Ind. Mfrs. Assn., Sigma Rho. Roman Catholic. Home: 18100 Brightlingsea Pl South Bend IN 46637 Office: 1400 Riverside Dr South Bend IN 46624

STACKELBERG, OLAF PATRICK, mathematician, acad. adminstr.; b. Munich, Germany, Aug. 2, 1932; s. Curt F. and Ellen (Biddle) vonStackelberg; B.S., Mass. Inst. Tech. ,1955; Ph.D., U. Minn., 1963; m. Cora E. Sleighter, Sept. 4, 1954; children—John S., Peter O., Paul E. Asst. prof. math. Duke U., Durham, N.C., 1963-68, asso. prof., 1968-76; prof., chmn. math. dept. Kent (Ohio) State U., 1976—; Alexander von Humboldt fellow U. Stuttgart (Germany), 1965-66; vis. asso. prof. math. U. Ill., Urbana, 1969-70, London (Eng.) U., 1974; mem. vis. staff math. Wesleyan U., Middletown, Conn., summers 1965-76. Served with Chem. Corps, U.S. Army, 1956-58. Editor, Duke Math. Jour., 1971-74; contbr. articles to math. jours. Home: 5924 Horning Rd Kent OH 44240

STACKHOUSE, DAVID WILLIAM, JR., furniture systems installation contractor; b. Cumberland, Ind., Aug. 29, 1926; s. David William and Dorothy Frances (Snider) S.; B.S., Lawrence Coll., Appleton, Wis., 1950; m. Shirley Pat Smith, Dec. 23, 1950; 1 son, Stefan Brent. Indsl. designer Globe Am. Co., Kokomo, Ind., 1951-53; product designer, chief engr. L.A. Darling Co., Bronson, Mich., 1954-66; contract mgr. Brass Office Products, Indpls., 1966-73; mfrs. rep., Nashville, Ind., 1973-78; mktg. exec. Brass Office Products, Inc., Indpls., 1978-80; office furniture systems installation contractor, 1980—. Precinct committeeman Republican Party. Served with USNR, 1944-46; PTO. Mem. Bldg. Owners and Mfrs. Assn. (past pres. Indpls. chpt.), Brown County Bd. Realtors, Beta Theta Pi. Anglican. Clubs: Lions, Kiwanis (past v.p.), Masons, Shriners. Patentee interior structural systems. Home: Rural Route 3 Box 324 Nashville IN 47448

STACY, BILL W., coll. pres.; b. Bristol, Va., July 26, 1938; s. Charles Frank and Louise Nelson (Altwater) S.; B.S., SE Mo. State U., 1960; M.S., So. Ill. U., 1965, Ph.D., 1968; m. Jane Cooper, July 26, 1958; children—Mark, Sara, James. Tchr., Malden (Mo.) High Sch., 1960-64; grad. asst. So. Ill. U., 1964-65, instr., 1965-67; mem. faculty dept. speech communication SE Mo. State U., Cape Girardeau, 1967—, prof., from 1974, asst. to pres., 1972-76, dean Grad. Sch., 1976-79, interim pres., 1979, pres., 1980—; dir. First Nat. Bank. Mem. Am. Assn. State Colls. and Univs., Am. Assn. Higher Edn., Cape Girardeau C. of C. (chmn.). Democrat. Baptist. Club: Optimist. Office: SE Mo State U Cape Girardeau MO 63701

STACY, DENNIS WILLIAM, architect; b. Council Bluffs, Iowa, Sept. 22, 1945; s. William L. and Mildred Glee (Carlsen) S.; B.Arch., Iowa State U., 1969; postgrad. U. Nebr., Omaha Grad. Coll., 1972; m. Judy Annette Long, Dec. 28, 1968. Designer Troy & Stalder Architects, Omaha, 1967, Architects Assos., Des Moines, 1968-69, Logsdon & Voelter Architects, Temple, Tex., 1970; project architect Roger Schutte & Assos., Omaha, 1972-73; architect, asso. Robert H. Burgin & Assos., Council Bluffs, 1973-75, Neil Astle & Assos., Omaha, 1975-78; owner, prin. Dennis W. Stacy, AIA, Architect, Glenwood, Iowa, 1978—. Chmn., Glenwood Zoning Bd. Adjustment, 1980-81; chmn. Mills County Plant Iowa Program, 1980-81; mem. Southwest Iowa Citizen's Adv. Com., Iowa State Dept. Transp., 1977-81. Served with U.S. Army, 1969-71. Decorated Nat. Def. Service medal, Vietnam Service medal, Vietnam Campaign medal, Army Commendation medal. Mem. AIA, Nat. Council Archtl. Registration Bds. Clubs: Glenwood Optimist; Masons. Archtl. works include Davies Amphitheater, 1980; Maher Law Office, 1981; Rogers Law Bldg., 1980; Cheyney Ins. Office, 1979; Frysek Med. Office, 1979. Home: 708 N Locust St Glenwood IA 51534 Office: 12 1/2 N Walnut St Glenwood IA 51534

STACY, TIMOTHY JAMES, SR., newspaper exec.; b. Chgo., Apr. 7, 1947; s. Frank Joseph and Margaret L. (Murray) S.; student U. Dayton, 1965-66; B.S. in Psychology, Loyola U., Chgo., 1969; m. Carla M. Zimmermann, Nov. 12, 1966; children—Timothy James, Michele, Darren. With Chgo. Tribune/Chgo. Today, 1969-73, Westinghouse Broadcasting, 1973-74; with Tribune Co., Hinsdale, Ill., 1974—, now display advt. mgr. Mem. NW Assn. Commerce and Industry, Western Advertisers Assn., Broadcast Ad Club, Chgo. Clubs: K.C. (Schaumburg, Ill.). Home: 716 Sand Pebble Dr Schaumburg IL 60193 Office: Tribune Co 765 N York Rd Hinsdale IL 60521

STACZEK, JAMES JOHN, indsl. distbn. co. exec.; b. Rossford, Ohio, Feb. 7, 1937; s. John Walter and Phyllis Frances Staczek; B.S. in Indsl. Tech., U. Toledo, 1960; m. Helen L. Crossen, June 17, 1960; children—Gerald, Patricia, Michael. Technician, nuclear fuel rods and ceramic insulators Electric Auto-Lite Co., Fostoria, Ohio, 1960; bottle designer plastic products div. Owens Ill. Inc., Toledo, 1961-62, mold designer, 1962-63, machine designer, 1963-65, standards and project engr., 1965-66; with J.N. Fauver Co., Northwood, Ohio, 1966—, product mgr., 1975—, dir. tng., 1976—, advt. mgr., 1978—, mktg. mgr., 1979-81, internat. mktg. mgr., 1981—; cons., 1971—. Rossford rep. Toledo Area Council Govt., 1973. Served with USNR, 1957-63. Mem. Am. Soc. Tng. and Devel., Fluid Power Soc., Am. Foundrymen's Assn. Democrat. Roman Catholic. Home: 417 Forest Dr Rossford OH 43460 Office: J N Fauver Co 1500 E Avis Dr Madison Heights MI 48071 also 6979 Wales Rd Northwood OH 43619

STADE, CHARLES EDWARD, archtl. co. exec.; b. Des Plaines, Ill., June 28, 1923; s. Chris E. and Martha (Drexler) S.; B.S., U. Ill., 1946; M.F.A., Princeton, 1948; certificate Beaux Art Inst. Design, N.Y.C., 1948; French Govt. traveling scholar, 1948; 1 dau., Ramsey. With W.J. McCaughey, architect, Park Ridge, Ill., 1945-48, K. Kessler, architect, Princeton, N.J., 1948; owner Charles Edward Stade & Assos., architects, Park Ridge, 1948—; various designs in permanent exhibit Am. Soc. Ch. Architecture. Served with USAAF, 1942-43. Recipient numerous AIA awards, 1956, 57, 61-63, 65, gold cup for excellence in masonry architecture, 1972, award of merit in outstanding lighting design, 1973; Crosby Butler prize, 1948; medal Prix-de-Emulation, Groupe Am., 1948; Nat. award for excellence in design GRA, 1974; 4 projects selected for permanent records Chgo. Archtl. Archives, 1977. Palmer fellow, 1946; Princeton fellow, 1947. Fellow Am. Soc. Ch. Architecture (past pres.); mem. Constrn. Specifications Inst., Gargoyle, Alpha Rho Chi. Past archtl. editor Your Church Mag., from 1956. Contbr. articles to mags., newspapers. Important works include Valparaiso (Ind.) U. Chapel. Home: 1020 S Knight St Park Ridge IL 60068 Office: 819 Busse Hwy Park Ridge IL 60068

STADNICKI, JERZY STANISLAW, chemist; b. Poznan, Poland, Oct. 11, 1927; came to U.S., 1967; s. Gustaw Maria and Helena (Czechowska) S.; M.S. with honors in Phys. Chemistry, U. Warsaw, 1952, Ph.D. cum magna laude, 1962. Asst. prof. research and devel. Inst. Phys. Chemistry, Polish Acad. Scis., Warsaw, 1955-63; dir. research labs. for methods and measures State Inst. Rubber Industries, Warsaw, 1963-67; research and devel. chemist Howmet Corp., Chgo., 1967-74; dir. research Harry J. Bosworth Co., Chgo., 1974-75; chemist III, City of Chgo. Dept. Health, Labs. Testing and Analysis, 1978—. Mem. Polish Chem. Assn.

STAEHR, CONNIE KAY, educator; b. York, Nebr., Mar. 22, 1950; d. Lavern Darrel and Evelyn Darlene (Dinkelman) S.; student Concordia Tchrs. Coll., 1968-69; A.S., Med. Inst. Minn., 1970; B.S., U. Nebr., 1977, M.Ed., 1978. Med. sec., lab. asst. Physicians Pathology Lab., 1970-72; salesperson-catering Villager Motel Conv. Center, 1972-74; sec. to dean acad. services U. Nebr., Lincoln, 1974-76, grad. research asst. mktg. and distributive edn., 1977-78, instr. mktg. tchr. edn., 1977—; mktg. and distributive edn. tchr.-coordinator SE High Sch., Lincoln, 1977-80; instr. mktg. and mgmt. SE Community Coll., Lincoln, 1980—; cons. Southwestern Pub. Co., 1978, 79. Mem. Am. Vocat. Assn., Nat. Assn. Distributive Edn. Tchrs. (v.p. central region 1980-81), NEA, Assn. Women Entrepreneurs, Nebr. Vocat. Assn. (legis. chmn. mktg. and distributive edn., 1978—), Distributive Edn. Assn. Nebr. (sec.-treas. 1979-80), Council for Distributive Tchr. Educators, Distributive Edn. Clubs Am. (mem. exec. council Nebr. 1979-80), Nebr. State Edn. Assn., Lincoln Edn. Assn. (mem. steering com. community action program 1979-80), Phi Delta Kappa. Lutheran. Home: 3300 Carnelian Ct 8 Lincoln NE 68516 Office: 311 Tchrs Coll U Nebr Lincoln NE 68588

STAFFORD, WILLA M., med. center exec.; b. Long Lane, Mo., Nov. 28, 1948; d. Lewey and Mary Elizabeth (Harrison) S.; B.S., Central Mo. State U., 1972, postgrad., 1978-81. Bus. edn. tchr. Sacred Heart High Sch., Sedalia, Mo., 1972-74; sec. N. Kansas City (Mo.) Meml. Hosp., 1974-76, adminstrv. sec., 1976-78, legal/adminstrv. asst., 1978-79; benefits and compensation mgr. Providence-St. Margaret Health Center, Kansas City, Kans., 1979-81, Bethany Med. Center, Kansas City, Kansas, 1981—. Mem. Am. Compensation Assn., Health Care and Personnel Mgrs. Assn. Home: 10411 E 41st St Kansas City MO 64133 Office: Bethany Med Center 51 N 12th St Kansas City KS 66102

STAGEMAN, PAUL JEROME, biochemist; b. Persia, Iowa, June 21, 1916; s. John Frederick and Vesta (Laing) S.; B.A., U. Omaha, 1939; M.S., State U. Iowa, 1950; Ph.D., U. Nebr., 1963; m. Mary Jane Holmes, Sept. 5, 1937; 1 son, Paul Jon. Tchr., Flagler (Colo.) Public Schs., 1939-40; chemist Cudahy Packing Co., Omaha, 1940-41; instr. chemistry U. Omaha, 1941-65; prof. chemistry U. Nebr., Omaha, 1965—; vis. prof. NSF Rocky Mountain Chem. Conf., 1963, 65. Fellow Am. Inst. Chemists, AAAS; mem. Am. Chem. Soc. Home: 308 W Oak St Council Bluffs IA 51501 Office: U Nebr 60th and Dodge Sts Omaha NE 68182

STAGL, JOHN MATTHEW, hosp. adminstr.; b. Chgo., Aug. 1, 1915; s. John and Marie (Schoenherr) S.; student Northwestern U. Sch. Commerce, 1936-41; m. Bernice Lowery, Aug. 14, 1943; children—John, Barry, Thomas, Richard. Exec. positions Passavant Meml. Hosp., Chgo., 1947-61, dir., pres., 1961-72; pres. Northwestern Meml. Hosp., Chgo., 1972-76; exec. v.p. McGaw Med. Center, Northwestern U., Chgo., 1974-76, pres., 1976-80. Mem. Inst. Medicine, Chgo., 1962-76, Ill. Health Facilities Planning Bd., 1974-79, Joint Commn. on Accreditation of Hosps., 1979; bd. dirs. Community Fund, 1966-68. Served to capt. AUS, 1943-46. Recipient Frederick Morgan award Hosp. Financial Mgmt. Assn., 1960. Fellow Am. Coll. Hosp. Adminstrs.; mem. Am. Hosp. Assn. (chmn. 1977), Assn. Am. Med. Colls. (exec. council 1976), Ill. Hosp. Assn. (trustee 1965-68, Disting. Ser. award 1977). Roman Catholic.

STAHL, CLAUD LAWRENCE, screen co. exec.; b. Pierceton, Ind., Feb. 4, 1928; s. Lawrence Nay and Minnie Alice (Bareham) S.; student Internat. Corr. Sch., 1948-52, Purdue U., 1967-71; grad. Ind. Coll. Auctioneering, 1975; m. Betty Rose Nichols, Oct. 23, 1948; children—Bradley Rene, Belinda Jane. With Gatke Corp., Warsaw, Ind., 1946-55, R. T. Brower Co., Pierceton, Ind., 1955-57; with Da-Lite Screen Co., Inc., Warsaw, 1957—, personnel mgr., 1976—. Interim bd. mem. Whitko Community Sch., 1966-68, treas., 1967; active Boy Scouts Am., Warsaw, 1946-49, Jr. Achievement, 1976-79; bd. dirs. Kosciusko Community Hosp., Warsaw, 1967-81; trustee Washington Twp., 1963-71. Served with Ind. N.G., 1948-52. Mem. Kosciusko County Hist. Soc. (1st pres. 1965-66), Ind. Auctioneers Assn., Ind. Personnel Mgrs. Assn. Democrat. Methodist. Clubs: Lions, Masons, Shriners, Order Eastern Star. Inventor reversible boat oars. Home: 207 W Elm St Pierceton IN 46562

STAHL, DAVID, condr.; b. N.Y.C., Nov. 4, 1949; s. Frank L. and Edith (Cosmann) S.; B.M., Queens Coll., 1972, M.A., 1974; m. Ellen Weiss, Nov. 26, 1970. Music dir. Doctors' Orchestral Soc. N.Y., 1973-76; asst. condr. N.Y. Philharmonic, N.Y.C., 1976, Cin. Symphony Orch., 1976-79; music dir. St. Louis Philharmonic, 1976—; guest condr. various symphony orchs., including: Pitts., Dallas, Atlanta, Buffalo Philharmonic, St. Louis, Nat., Am., N.J.; guest condr. Cin. Opera, Opera Omaha, also opera in Italy, concerts in France; music dir. West Side Story on Broadway, 1981 and on internat. tour, 1981. Mem. Am. Symphony Orch. League. Office: PO Box 591 Saint Louis MO 63188

STAHL, JOEL SAUL, plastic-chem. engr.; b. Youngstown, Ohio, June 10, 1918; s. John Charles and Anna (Nadler) S.; B.Chem. Engring., Ohio State U., 1939; postgrad. Alexander Hamilton Inst., 1946-48; m. Jane Elizabeth Anglin, June 23, 1950; 1 son, John Arthur. With Ashland Oil & Refining Co. (Ky.), 1939-50, mgr. spl. products, 1946-50; pres. Cool Ray Co., Youngstown, 1950-51, Stahl Industries, Inc., Youngstown, 1951—, Stahl Internat., Inc., Youngstown, 1969—, Stahl Bldg. Systems, Inc., Youngstown, 1973—. Active Boardman Civic Assn., Boy Scouts Am., Community Chest, ARC. Named Ky. col., 1967. Mem. Regional Export Expansion Council, Soc. Plastics Engr., Soc. Plastics Industry, Internat. Platform Assn., Ohio Soc. N.Y., Tau Kappa Epsilon, Phi Eta Sigma, Phi Lambda Upsilon. Republican. Christian Scientist. Mason (Shriner), Rotarian. Clubs: Toastmasters (pres. 1949); Berlin Yacht (North Benton, O.); Circumnavigators. Patentee insulated core walls, plastic plumbing wall. housing in continous process. Contbr. articles to profl. jours. Home: 746 Golf View Ave Youngstown OH 44512 Office: Dollar Bank Bldg 9th Floor Youngstown OH 44503

STAHL, RAYMOND EARL, research chemist; b. Chgo., Feb. 21, 1936; s. Arthur Daniel and Gladys Hazel (Lockwood) S.; Ph.B., Northwestern U., 1971. Technician-coatings formulator DeSoto Inc., Chgo., 1956-62, sr. chemist, research chemist, sr. research chemist, research asso., 1967-73; group leader metal finishes Adcote div. Morton Chem. Co., Chgo., 1962-66; tech. dir., cons. Am. Indsl. Finishes Co., Chgo., 1966-67; staff scientist, research asso. Dexter-Midland Co., Waukegan, Ill., 1973—. Served with U.S. Army, 1954-56; PTO. Fellow Am. Inst. Chemists; mem. Société de Chimie Industrielle, Am. Chem. Soc., Am. Inst. Physics, Am. Phys. Soc., AAAS, Ill. Acad. Sci., Am. Statis. Assn., Am. Math. Assn., Fedn. Socs. Paint Tech., Am. Mgmt. Assn., Am. Platform Assn., Nat., Ill. rifle assns. Republican. Inventor chem. coatings. Home: 2207 Rolling Ridge Ln Lindenhurst IL 60046 Office: Dexter-Midland Co E Water St Waukegan IL 60085

STAHMANN, FRED SOEFFNER, educator, physician; b. Spanish Fork, Utah, Aug. 24, 1909; s. Benjamin Robert and Lydia Ann (Soeffner) S.; B.A., U. Utah, 1931; M.D., Northwestern U., 1935; m. Mary Emma Thompson, Dec. 17, 1938; children—Robert, Fred, Mary. Intern, St. Lukes Hosp., Chgo., 1934-35; resident in obstetrics-gynecology, 1935-37; practice medicine specializing in obstetrics-gynecology, Peoria, Ill., 1937-42, Sioux Falls, S.D., 1946-74; staff Sioux Valley Hosp., 1946—, chief of staff, 1949-50; staff McKennan Hosp., Sioux Falls, 1946—; cons. VA Hosp., Sioux Falls, 1950-74; faculty Sch. Medicine, U. S.D., Sioux Falls, 1955—, asso. prof. obstetrics-gynecology, 1955—. Mem. dist. council Boy Scouts Am., 1949-51; service chmn. Am. Cancer Soc., Minnehaha County, 1971-73. Served to maj. M.C., AUS, 1942-46. Diplomate Am. Bd. Obstetrics and Gynecology. Mem. Central Assn. Obstetricians and Gynecologists, Am. Coll. Obstetricians and Gynecologists (founding mem.), S.D. Soc. Obstetrics and Gynecology (pres. 1954). Republican. Presbyterian. Clubs: Rotary, Masons, Shriners. Contbr. articles to profl. jours. Address: 401 E 27th St Sioux Falls SD 57105

STAHR, HENRY M., analytical chemist; b. White, S.D., Dec. 10, 1931; s. George C. and Kathryn E. (Smith) S.; B.S., S.D. State U., 1956; M.S., Union Coll., 1961; Ph.D., Iowa State U., 1976; m. Irene F. Sondey, July 27, 1952; children—Michael, John, Mary, Patrick, Matthew. Analytical chemist Gen. Elec. Co., Hudson Falls, N.Y., 1956-64; sr. scientist Philip Morris Research, Richmond, Va., 1964-69; asso. prof. Iowa State U., 1969—. Bd. dirs. Isaac Walton League, Ames, Iowa, 1969-71; pres. K.C., Ogden, Iowa, 1978-79; comdr. Am. Legion, Ogden, 1975-81; bd. dirs. Ogden Community Sch. Dist., 1976-81; active Boy Scouts Am. Mem. Am. Chem. Soc., Electro-chem. Soc., Instrument Soc. Am., Soc. Applied Spectroscopy, Am. Microchem. Soc., Nat. Safety Council, Assn. Ofcl. Analytical Chemists, Soc. Thinlayer Chromatography, Veterinary Toxicologists, Am. Assn. Vet. Lab. Diagnosis, Inst. Food Tech., Nutrition Council, Soc. for Mass Spectroscopy, Iowa Acad. Sci., Gov.'s Sci. Council, Am. Legion, Sigma Xi, Gamma Sigma Delta. Asso. referee analysis Chlorinated Hydrocarbons in Whole Blood, 1972-77, also Sodium Flouroacetate, 1975-79. Managerial Award for Outstanding Patent, Gen. Electric Co., 1961; co-developer Thinlayer Chromatography Symposia, 1974-82; participant in World Food Conf., Iowa State U., 1976. Clubs: Lions, K.C. Home: 802 Locust St Ogden IA 50212 Office: Room 1636 Veterinary Coll Iowa State U Ames IA 50011

STAIB, WILLIAM HENRY, JR., ins. co. exec.; b. Balt., Oct. 25, 1944; s. William Henry and Lorraine Marie S.; A.A., Essex Coll., 1964; B.S., U. Nev., 1967; m. Melinda Sue Miller, Feb. 22, 1980; 1 dau., Mindee Miller. Mech. design engr. Warren & Assos., Balt., 1968-74; mktg. tng. mgr. Nationwide Ins. Co., Columbus, Ohio, 1974—. Pres., Neighborhood Assn., 1975-77. Served with USAF, 1964-68. Decorated Purple Heart. Mem. Nat. Assn. Life Underwriters (sec. 1978), Nat. Assn. Health Underwriters, Am. Soc. Tng. and Devel. Republican. Lutheran. Home: 2552 Sawmill Meadows Dublin OH 43017 Office: 1 Nationwide Plaza Columbus OH 43216

STALEY, C.W., minister; b. Kansas City, Mo., July 24, 1917; s. Arthur F. and Cassie Ella (Barton) S.; B.S., Okla. Bapt. U., 1953; M.Ed., Kans. State Tchrs. Coll., 1965; m. Ann Marie McGlauglin, Dec. 26, 1944; 1 dau., Carol Ann. Ordained to ministry Bapt. Ch., 1940; pastor, Glasgow, Mo., 1939-41, Brunswick, Mo., 1941-44, Kansas City, Mo., 1944-45, Wichita, Kans., 1945-48, Stroud, Okla., 1948, Healdton, Okla., 1948-52, Larned, Kans., 1954-58; asso. chaplain Larned State Hosp., 1954-58; dist. staff mem. N.W. Kans. Bapt. Conv., Topeka, 1958-62; instl. chaplain Norton (Kans.) State Hosp., 1963-66; pastor, Phillipsburg, Kans., 1961-66, First Bapt. Ch., Vinton, Iowa, 1966-74; prof. Coe Coll., Cedar Rapids, Iowa, 1975; founder The Bapt. Preacher, nat. jour. for Bapt. ministers, Kansas City, Mo., 1943, The Career-Work Service Group, 1975, Iowa 40 Plus, 1975; founder, pres. Nat. Football Ladies, Inc., 1978—. Recipient Communicators award Syracuse U., 1973; Disting. Service to Community citation Internat. Biog. Centre, Cambridge, Eng., 1976. Mem. Internat. Platform Assn., Ministerial Assn., Media Assn. Ch. Communicators (dir. 1975-76). Democrat. Contbr. articles to profl. jours.; patentee football target hoop, CheeReceiver, Football Showplace, Miss Football inventions. Home: 807 W 15th St Vinton IA 52349 Office: Box 543 Vinton IA

STALEY, JOHN HARLAN, hosp. adminstr.; b. Tulsa, Nov. 4, 1943; s. Harlan Granger and Margaret Jocye S.; B.A., Cornell (Iowa) Coll., 1966; M.A., in Econs., U. Iowa, 1969, Ph.D. in Hosp. and Health Adminstrn. (USPHS predoctoral research fellow), 1974; m. Sally Jeanette Cross, Aug. 15, 1970; children—Kenneth William, Thomas Walter, Robert Harlan. Research asst. Iowa Regional Med. Program, Iowa City, 1967-69; instr. hosp. adminstrn. U. Iowa, 1973; adminstrv. asst. to U. Iowa Hosps. and Clinics, Iowa City, 1973-74, asst. dir., 1974-81, sr. asst. dir., 1981—; adj. asst. prof. U. Iowa, 1977—. Bd. dirs., sec.-treas. Prairie Region Affiliated Blood Services. Served with M.S.C., AUS, 1972-73. Named Disting. Mil. Grad., Army ROTC, 1968. Mem. Am. Hosp. Assn., Am. Coll. Hosp. Adminstrs., Hosp. Fin. Mgmt. Assn., Am. Public Health Assn., Omicron Delta Epsilon. Presbyterian. Clubs: Toastmasters, Masons. Home: 314 Beldon Ave Iowa City IA 52240 Office: University of Iowa Hospitals and Clinics Newton Rd Iowa City IA 52242

STALEY, KENNETH ALVIN, coll. adminstr.; b. Campbellsville, Ky., Jan. 5, 1943; s. Morris Alvin and Mae (Ratcliffe) S.; B.A., McKendree Coll., Lebanon, Ill., 1976; M.S., Ind. State U., Terre Haute, 1978; m. Jeanne Buck, Jan. 29, 1965; 1 son, Kenneth Darren. Adminstrv. asst. Ind. Vocat. Tech. Coll., Sellersburg, 1971-73, dir. student services, 1973-79, dir. Occupational Devel. Center, CETA, 1979-81; dir. instrn. Ind. Vocat. Tech. Coll., Sellersburg, Ind., 1981—; cons. in field. Served with U.S. Army, 1963-70. Named Ky. col. Mem. Am. Vocat. Assn., Ind. Vocat. Assn., Ind. Post-Secondary Vocat. Edn. Assn., Ind. Assn. Coll. Admissions Counselors, Ind. Student Fin. Aid Assn., Nat. Council Community Relations, Nat. Assn. Vets. Program Adminstrs., Ind. Council-Advancement and Support Edn. Baptist. Office: 8204 Hwy 311 Sellersburg IN 47172

STALEY, WALTER GOODWIN, JR., materials scientist; b. St. Louis, Oct. 20, 1932; s. Walter Goodwin and Martha McHenry (Green) S.; B.A., U. Mo., 1956; B.S., Washington U., St. Louis, 1962, M.A., 1963; Ph.D., Pa. State U., 1968; m. Katherine Walton, June 17, 1961; children—Walter Goodwin III, Katherine Waggoner, Franklin Edward Walton. Research mineralogist A.P. Green Refractories Co., Mexico, Mo., 1968-69, research engr., 1969-74, research mgr., 1974-76, research cons., 1976—; instr. horsemanship Stephens Coll., Columbia, Mo., 1953-54; mem. U.S. equestrian team Olympic Games, 1952, 56, 60. Bd. dirs. Allen P. and Josephine B. Green Found., 1968—, v.p., 1972-80, pres., 1980—; cubmaster Boy Scouts Am., Mexico, 1971-73; bd. dirs. Audrain County Cerebral Palsy Assn., 1972-76; chmn. horsemanship com. Audrain County 4-H Club, 1978-80; elder 1st Presbyn. Ch., Mexico, 1975—. Served with U.S. Army, 1956-57. Recipient Golden Circle 4-H Leadership award, 1979. Mem. Am. Ceramic Soc. (editor Ann. Refractories Symposium, St. Louis sect. 1972—, chmn. St. Louis sect. 1980), ASTM, Sigma Xi. Club: Mexico Country. Home: RFD 3 Apple Tree Ln Mexico MO 65265 Office: AP Green Refractories Co Mexico MO 65265

STALLARD, RICHARD ELGIN, dentist, health adminstr.; b. Eau Claire, Wis., May 30, 1934; s. Elgin Gale and Caroline Francis (Betz) S.; B.S., U. Minn., 1956, D.D.S., 1958, M.S., 1959, Ph.D., 1962; m. Norma Ann Woock, Oct. 15, 1956 (dec. 1973); children—Rondi Lynn, Alison Judith; m. 2d, Jaxon Shirley Sandlin, May 2, 1974; 1 son, Elgin Sandlin. Co-dir. periodontal research Eastman Dental Center, Rochester, N.Y., 1962-65; prof., head dept. periodontology Sch. Dentistry, U. Minn., Mpls., 1965-68, adj. prof. public health, 1976—; asst. dir. Eastman Dental Center, 1968-70; prof. anatomy, asst. dean Sch. Grad. Dentistry, dir. clin. research center Boston U. Sch. Grad. Dentistry, 1970-74; dental dir., head dept. periodontology Group Health Plan, Inc., St. Paul, 1974-79; sec. Minndent, Inc., Mpls., 1980—; dental dir. Horizon Dental Assos., P.A., Mpls., 1981—; cons. U.S. Air Force, 1968—, U.S. Navy, 1971-75; mem. tng. grant com. NIH/Nat. Inst. Dental Research, 1969-72; edn. cons. Project Vietnam, AID, Saigon, 1969-74; mem. grants and allocations com. Am. Fund for Dental Health, 1976-81. Recipient Meritorious Achievement citation for dental research and edn. Boston U., 1970. Fellow Am., Internat. colls. dentists, Internat. Congress Oral Implantologists (diplomate, pres. 1980-81); mem. Am. Acad. Periodontology (pres. 1974), Am. Acad. Dental Spltys. (pres. 1971-75), Am. Public Health Assn., Omicron Kappa Upsilon, Sigma Xi. Club: Alumni (Mpls.). Author preventive dentistry textbook; contbr. articles to profl. jours.; editor The Implantologist, Jour. Mktg./Mgmt. for Professions. Home: 4200 W 44th St Edina MN 55424 Office: 7645 Metro Blvd Minneapolis MN 55435

STALLARD, WAYNE MINOR, lawyer; b. Onaga, Kans., Aug. 23, 1927; s. Minor Regan and Lydia Faye (Randall) S.; B.S., Kans. State Tchrs. Coll., Emporia, 1949; J.D., Washburn U., 1952; m. Wanda Sue Bacon, Aug. 22, 1948; children—Deborah Sue, Carol Jean, Bruce Wayne. Admitted to Kans. bar, 1952 pvt. practice Onaga, Kans., 1952—; atty. Community Hosp. Dist. No. 1, Pottawatomie and Jackson Counties, Kans., 1955—; Pottawatomie County atty., 1955-59; city atty. Onaga, 1953-79; atty Unified School Dist. 322, Pottawatomie County, Kans., 1966—. Bd. dirs. N. Central Kans. Guidance Center, Manhattan, 1974-78; atty. Rural Water Dist. No. 3, Pottawatomie County, Kans., 1974—. Fund dr. chmn. Pottawatomie County chpt. Nat. Found. for Infantile Paralysis, 1953-54. Served from pvt. to sgt., 8th Army, AUS, 1946 to 47. Mem. Am., Pottawatomie County, Kans. bar assns., Onaga Businessmen's Assn., Am. Judicature Soc., City Attys. Assn. Kan. (dir. 1963-66), Phi Gamma Mu, Kappa Delta Pi, Delta Theta Phi, Sigma Tau Gamma. Conglist. Mason (Shriner); mem. Order Eastern Star. Address: Onaga KS 66521

STALLARD, WAYNE REX, mfr.; b. Lawrence, Kans., Nov. 17, 1926; s. Clarence N. and Nora E. (Herd) S.; B.S. in Bus., U. Kans., 1948; m. Florence A. Schutte, Sept. 6, 1952; children—Rebecca Anne, Melanie Kay, Jennifer Elaine. Acct., Haskins & Sells, 1948-55; v.p., controller to pres. Pitman Mfg. Co., 1955-67; v.p., treas. A.B. Chance Co., 1967-70; pres. Stelco, Inc., Kansas City, Kans., 1970—. Treas., City of Westwood Hills (Kans.); v.p., bd. dirs. Westwood View Sch. Dist. Served to 2d lt. USAAF, 1944-45. C.P.A., Kans. Mem. Farm Indsl. Equipment Inst. (dir.), Nat. Fedn. Ind. Bus. Methodist. Clubs: Carriage, Masons, Shriners. Home: 6107 W 64th Terr Mission KS 66202 Office: 5500 Kansas Ave Kansas City KS 66106

STALLINGS, EDWARD SYKES, chem. co. adminstr.; b. Starkville, Miss., Feb. 10, 1945; s. Allen Jerome, Sr., and Marion Justine (Sykes) S.; A.S., Triton Coll., 1971; student Roosevelt U., 1971-73; m. Rustica Tapao, Aug. 18, 1967; children—Agustin, Paulita, Rosemarie, Edward Sykes. With research dept. Borg Warner Corp., Bellwood, Ill., 1967-68, chem. group leader research and devel., 1968—. Served with USAF, 1963-67; Vietnam. Mem. Am. Legion. Democrat. Baptist. Research on pultrusion prodn. of reinforced friction material. Home: 153 S 18th St Maywood IL 60153 Office: 700 S 25th Ave Bellwood IL 60104

STALLINGS, JAMES OTIS, III, plastic surgeon; b. Memphis, Jan. 11, 1938; s. James Otis, II and Mabel R. (Haygood) S.; B.S., Miss. Coll., 1958; M.D., U. Pa., 1962; M.S. (NIH fellow), U. Iowa, 1968; m. Sandra Marie Stallings. Diplomate Am. Bd. Otolaryngology, Am. Bd. Plastic Surgery. Intern, U. Pa. Hosp., 1962-63; resident gen. surgery VA Hosp., Iowa City, Iowa, 1963-64, Mercy Hosp., Mason City, Iowa, 1964-65; resident otolaryngology Univ. Hosp., Iowa City, 1965-68; resident plastic surgery Inst. Reconstructive Plastic Surgery, N.Y. U. Med. Center, 1970-72; practice medicine, specializing in otolaryngology and plastic surgery, West Des Moines, Iowa, 1972—; dir. Plastic Surgery Inst., 1972—; chmn. dept. plastic and reconstructive surgery Mercy Hosp. Med. Center, Des Moines; teaching asst. plastic surgery N.Y. U. Sch. Medicine, 1970-72. Mem. AMA, Iowa, Polk County med. socs. Author: A New You: How Plastic Surgery Can Change Your Life, 1977; contbr. articles to med. jours. Home: 5447 NW 72d Pl Des Moines IA 50323 Office: 1025 Ashworth Rd 528 Univac Bldg West Des Moines IA 50265

STALNAKER, ARMAND CARL, ins. co. exec.; b. Weston, W.Va., Apr. 24, 1916; s. Thomas Carl and Alta (Hinzman) S.; B.B.A., U. Cin., 1941; M.A., U. Pa., 1945; Ph.D., Ohio State U., 1952; m. Rachel Pickett, Apr. 26, 1946; children—Timothy L., Thomas A. Asst. prof. bus. Ohio State U., Columbus, 1946-50; asst. regional mgr., exec. gen. mgr. Prudential Ins. Co., Newark, 1950-63; adminstrv. v.p. Gen. Am. Life Ins. Co., St. Louis, 1963-65, exec. v.p., 1965-69, pres., 1969-79, chmn., 1974—; dir. Anheuser-Busch Cos., Inc., St. Louis, Brown Group, Inc., St. Louis, Fed. Res. Bank St Louis. Bd. dirs. Washington U., Barnes Hosp., United Way Greater St. Louis, St. Louis Area council Boy Scouts Am., YMCA, Civic Center Redevel. Corp. Recipient Man of Year award St. Louis Globe-Democrat, 1978; Right Arm of St. Louis award, 1981. Mem. Am. Coll. Life Underwriters. Quaker. Clubs: Bogey, N.Y. Yacht, Noonday, Round Table, St. Louis. Author: Life Insurance Agency Financial Management, 1965; contbr. articles to profl. jours. Home: 8027 Kingsbury Blvd Saint Louis MO 63105 Office: PO Box 396 Saint Louis MO 63166

STALOCH, JAMES EDWARD, JR., vocat. educator; b. Worthington, Minn., Aug. 14, 1946; s. James Edward and Cecil Ilo (Rist) S.; B.S., Moorhead (Minn.) State U., 1971; m. Susan Kay Schroeder, June 8, 1968; children—Paul, Jennifer, Michael. Asst. constrn. engr. Ford Motor Co., Dearborn, Mich., 1968-69; tchr. St. Paul Public Schs., 1971-72; mgr. litho shop, Mpls., 1972-74; trade and indsl. supr. Dakota County Vocat. Sch., Rosemount, Minn., 1974—. Sr. mem. CAP. Served with AUS, 1966-68; Vietnam. Decorated Air Medal, Army Cdmmendation medal; cert. flight instr., corp. pilot. Mem. Am. Legion. Roman Catholic. Office: PO Box K Rosemount MN 55068

STALON, CHARLES GARY, economist, govt. ofcl.; b. Cape Girardeau, Mo., Oct. 26, 1929; s. Charles Douglas and Lucy Idell (Row) S.; B.A., Butler U., 1959; M.S., Purdue U., 1963, Ph.D., 1966; m. Marie Alene Hitt, Mar. 15, 1952; children—Connie Lucille, Donna

Jean. Asso. prof. econs. So. Ill. U., Carbondale, 1963-77; research economist FPC, Washington, 1969-70; vis. asso. prof. Washington U., St. Louis, 1972; commr. Ill. Commerce Commn., Springfield, 1977—. Served in USN, 1948-49, 52-54. Mem. Am. Econ. Assn., Missouri Valley Econs. Assn., Ill. Econs. Assn. Democrat. Contbg. author: Papers in Quantitative Economics, 1968. Office: 527 E Capitol St Springfield IL 62706

STAMBERGER, EDWIN HENRY, farmer, civic leader; b. Mendota, Ill., Feb. 16, 1916; s. Edwin Nicolaus and Emilie Anna Marie (Yost) S.; grad. high sch.; m. Mabel Edith Gordon, Oct. 6, 1937; 1 son, Larry Allan. Farmer seed corn and livestock, machinery devel., nr. Mendota, 1939; dir. Mendota Co-op. & Supply Co., 1949-67, pres., 1958-67. Mem. Mendota Watershed Com., 1966-73, 77—; asst. in devel. Mendota Hosp., Mendota Lake; bd. dirs. LaSalle County Mental Health Bd., 1969-74; chmn. bldg. com. Mendota Luth. Home, 1972-73; mem. revue and comment com., subregion and region Ill. Central Comprehensive Health Planning Agy., 1974-76; bd. dirs. U. Ill. County Extension, 1963-67, chmn., 1966-67; bd. dirs. Soil and Water Dist., 1968-73, vice-chmn., 1971-73. Mem. Soil Soc. Am., Ill. Council Watersheds (founder), Smithsonian Assos., Mental Health Assn., People to People, Internat. Platform Assn., Mendota C. of C. (Honor award 1974). Lutheran (mem. ch. council 1958-64, chmn. 1964, treas. N.W. Conf. men, 1966-68, trustee bible camp). Clubs: Mendota Sportsman's, Lions (dir. 1965-67, honor award 1981). Goodwill farm tours, Europe, Africa, Australia and New Zealand, Central and S.Am., Russia, Hungary, NATO countries, India, Scandinavia, Mainland China. Address: Rural Route 1 Sabine Farm Mendota IL 61342

STAMETS, WILLIAM, mech. engr.; b. Bellevue, Pa., May 24, 1919; s. William Kerr and Lillie Mae (Smith) S.; B.M.E., Cornell U., 1942, M.M.E., 1949; m. Ramona Hinton, June 12, 1975; children—Lillian, John, William, C. North, Paul. Vice pres., dir. William K. Stamets Co., Pitts., 1942-59; cons. engr., Columbiana, Ohio, 1959-70; engring. cons. Sperry Rand Corp., Huntsville, Ala., 1971-72; prin. engr. Babcock & Wilcox Co., Mt. Vernon, Ind., 1972-78; sales engr. oilwell div. U.S. Steel Corp., Evansville, Ind., 1978-79; chief engr. Bucyrus-Erie Co., South Milwaukee, Wis., 1979—; instr. Cornell U., 1947-49; asso. prof. Jefferson County Tech. Inst., Steubenville, Ohio, 1970; lectr. engring. U. Evansville (Ind.), 1973—; mem. indsl. adv. bd. Ind. State U. Div. Engring. Tech., Evansville, 1975—. Served to lt. USNR, 1943-46. Recipient Appreciation certificate Design Engring. Conf., Chgo., 1974, 76; registered profl. engr., N.Y., Ohio, Ind., Wis. Mem. ASME, Am. Acad. Mechanics, Soc. Exptl. Stress Analysis. Republican. Methodist. Club: Petroleum. Designer nuclear reactors, pressure vessels, sawmills and steel mill equipment; contbr. articles to profl. jours. Home: 5206 Roberts Dr Greendale WI 53129

STAMM, GERALD LEE, gas co. exec.; b. Lincoln, Nebr., Mar. 22, 1936; s. WalterG. and Maxine S.; B.S. in Bus. Adminstrn., S.D. State U., 1961; m. Marilyn C. Comer, Nov. 18, 1965; children—Cindy, Terry, Larry. With Inter North Co., various locations, 1961—, controller Peoples Natural Gas Co. div., Council Bluffs, Iowa, 1977-80, v.p. adminstrn., 1980—. Treas., Escalanete Hills Property Owners Assn.; sec. bd. dirs. Ashland Recreation Assn. Served with U.S. Army, 1955-58. Mem. Am. Gas Assn., Midwest Gas Assn., Nebr. Blue Flame Assn., Am. Legion, VFW. Republican. Lutheran. Clubs: Masons, Shriners, Omana Ski. Home: 4827 N 109th St Omaha NE 68164 Office: 25 Main Pl Council Bluffs IA 51501

STAMOS, SUSAN ANNE, corporate planner; b. Harvey, Ill., Apr. 12, 1948; d. William Leonard and Anita Kathryn (Bruhn) L.; student Univ. Oslo, Norway, 1968; B.A., U. Ill., 1971; M.B.A. in Finance, DePaul U., 1978; m. Richard F. McCloskey, Sept. 9, 1978; 1 son, William. Corporate planning cons. Nat. Assn. Blue Cross/Blue Shield Plans, Chgo., 1976-78; mgr. budgeting and analysis Am. Reserve Corp., Chgo., 1978-79; dir. budgeting Ben Franklin div. City Products Corp., Des Plaines, Ill., 1979—. Recipient scholarship Univ. Oslo's Internat. program, 1968. Mem. Midwest Planning Assn., Council Fgn. Relations. Contbr. articles to Consumer Digest, Chgo. Tribune Mag. Home: 5247 W Berenice St Chicago IL 60641 Office: 1700 S Wolf Rd Des Plaines IL 60018

STAMOS, THEODORE JAMES, psychiat. social worker; b. Oskaloosa, Iowa, May 1, 1933; s. James and Sophia (Zaffiras) S.; student Ball State Coll., 1951-52, N.Y.U., 1952-53; B.A., U. Iowa, 1957, M.S.W., 1959; m. Sally Jane Stamos; children—Theodore, Sara, Jacqueline, James. Staff Hastings (Minn.) State Hosp., 1959-61, Mental Hygiene Outpatient Clinic of VA Center, St. Paul, 1961-63; exec. dir. Dakota County Mental Health Center, South St. Paul, Minn., 1963-73, 78—; pvt. practice, 1973-78; guest lectr. group psychotherapy U. Minn., 1963, clin. faculty instr., 1965—; chmn. east Met. Regional Mental Health-Mental Retardation coordinating com., 1968-70; sec. Minn. Assn. of Mental Health Programs, 1968-70. Mem. mental health adv. com. to Gov. of Minn., 1963-65, Gov.'s State Com. on Study Suicide, 1967. Served with USAF, 1953-55. Mem. Am. Group Psychotherapy Assn., Am. Assn. Marriage counselors, Nat. Assn. Social Workers, Minn. Group Psychotherapy Soc. (pres.), Acad. Cert. Social Workers. Independent. Mem. United Ch. of Christ. Club: Masons. Home: 4423 Ardenview Ct St Paul MN 55112 Office: Dakota County Mental Health Center South St Paul MN 55075

STAMP, DAVID LEE, agronomist; b. Clinton, Iowa, July 21, 1936; s. Henry and Evelyn Vera S.; B.S., Iowa State U., 1964, M.S., 1968, Ph.D., 1971; m. Sandra Maxwell, Feb. 23, 1963; children—Elizabeth, Matthew, Mark, Sarah, Rebekah. Asst. prof. agronomy Oreg. State U., Corvallis, 1971-73; asso. prof. agronomy Texx Tech. U., Lubbock, 1974-75; mgr. pest devel. north Central region Stauffer Chem. Co., Westport, Conn., 1975-78; dir. research and devel. Circle Seed Hybrids, Albion, Nebr., 1978—. Served with U.S. Army, 1959-61. Mem. Am. Soc. Agronomy (chmn. edn. div. 1973-76), Crop Sci. Soc. Am. Republican. Roman Catholic. Home: 637 4th St Albion NE 68620 Office: 355 Church Albion NE 68620

STAMP, JAMES ALLEN, fin. cons., accountant; b. Salem, Ohio, Nov. 3, 1942; s. Elmer Richard and Fae L. (Andre) S.; B.A., Mt. Union Coll., Alliance, Ohio, 1966; postgrad. in acctg. U. Akron, 1967-68; m. Margaret Jane Boski, June 19, 1966; children—Shawn R., Heather L., Eric L. Telegrapher, CB&Q R.R., Chgo., 1960-62; draftsman Sterling-Salem Corp., Salem, 1962-63; credit mgr. Sears, Roebuck & Co., Alliance, 1964-66; acct. Ernst & Ernst, Akron, Ohio, 1966-70; area sales coordinator Bestline Products, Akron, 1970-73; budget dir. Timken Mercy Hosp., Canton, Ohio, 1973-76; dir. fin. Green Cross Gen. Hosp., Cuyahoga Falls, Ohio, 1977-78; practice public acctg., Norton, Ohio, 1978—; dir. Community World, Inc., Agriworld, Inc., Master Machine Corp., No. Fish Co., Inc., Mac R&D Inc., Ashtabula Fish & Chips Inc., Tech Pow'r Inc., Shema, Inc., All Cleve. Podiatry Group, Inc.; founder Boardroom Exchange Assn. Sponsor, mgr. Norton Nat. Little League Baseball; mem. Senatorial Bus. Adv. Bd. C.P.A., Ohio. Mem. Nat. Assn. Accts. (Mem. of Yr., 1980, dir. 1978-81), Ohio Soc. C.P.A.'s, Internat. Platform Assn., Hosp. Fin. Mgmt. Assn., Am. Mortgage Brokers Assn. Republican. Methodist. Home: 3405 Mark Ln Norton OH 44203 Office: PO Box 1216 Norton OH 44203

STANBERY, ROBERT CHARLES, veterinarian; b. Conneaut, Ohio, Apr. 5, 1947; s. Robert James and Ruth Virginia S.; student Miami U., Oxford, Ohio, 1965-67; D.V.M., Ohio State U., 1971; m. Constance Ann Coutts, July 24, 1971; 1 son, Scott Andrew. Veterinarian, Lexington (Mass.) Animal Hosp., 1971-74, Avon Lake Animal Clinic Inc. (Ohio), 1974-76; pres., treas. Bay Village Animal Clinic Inc. (Ohio), 1976—. Mem. AVMA, Ohio Vet. Med. Assn., Animal Hosp. Assn. Cleve. Acad. Vet. Medicine, Lorain County Vet. Assn. Internat. Platform Assn., Bay Village C. of C. (bd. dirs.), U.S. Jaycees. Fundamentalist Christian. Home: 309 Timberlane Dr Avon Lake OH 44012 Office: 627 Clague Rd Bay Village OH 44140

STANCILL, MAYNA ANNE, ins. co. exec.; b. Madison, N.J., Nov. 15, 1946; d. Sherwood Haywood and Christine (Weems) S.; B.A. in Home Econs., Marycrest Coll., Davenport, Iowa, 1968. Audiovisual dir. Marycrest Coll., 1968-70; utility home economist No. State Power Co., Mpls., 1970-73; editorial writer 3M, St. Paul, 1973, program adminstr., career devel., 1973-79, mktg. research analyst, 1979-80; dir. affirmative action personnel programs St. Paul Fire & Marine Ins. Co., 1981—. Bd. dirs. St. Paul YWCA, 1980—. Mem. Minn. Women's Network (dir.), St. Paul C. of C. (exec. com. 1981). Club: Marycrest Coll. Century. Office: 385 Washington St Saint Paul MN 55102

STANDER, JOSEPH WILLIAM, univ. adminstr.; b. Covington, Ky., Dec. 2, 1928; s. Charles G. and Rosa (Kerner) S.; B.S., U. Dayton, 1949; M.S., Catholic U. Am., 1957, Ph.D. in Math., 1959. Joined Soc. of Mary, Roman Cath. Ch., 1946; tchr. Hamilton Cath. High Sch., 1949-50, Colegio Ponceno, Ponce, P.R., 1950-55; mem. faculty dept. math. U. Dayton, 1960-68, dean Grad. Sch., 1968-74, v.p. acad. affairs, 1974—. Mem. Math. Assn. Am., Sigma Xi. Office: U Dayton Dayton OH 45469

STANDISH, NORMAN WESTON, oil co. exec.; b. Marion, Iowa, Apr. 4, 1930; s. Fred Weston and Mary Caroline (Cooley) S.; B.S., Beloit Coll., 1952; M.S., Purdue U., 1957, Ph.D., 1960; m. Ingrid Charlotte Jueschke, Aug. 11, 1956; children—Robin Standish Hicks, Christopher Brian, Hillary Ann. Research chemist Pitts. Plate Glass Co., Milw., 1952-53; research chemist Standard Oil Co. (Ohio), Cleve., 1960-65, mgr. tech. service, 1967-81, lab. dir. exploration and prodn., 1981—; tech. dir. Pro Brush Co., Florence, Mass., 1965-67. Scoutmaster, Cleve. council Boy Scouts Am., 1971-79; active Jr. Achievement, Cleve., 1967-69; tchr. Student Instrument Course, Cleve., 1971-72, Student Environ. Camp, Cleve., 1976-77. Served with U.S. Army, 1953-55. Recipient Order of Merit, Boy Scouts Am., 1978, Wood badge, 1978; Comml. Solvents fellow, 1957-59. Mem. Cleve. Tech. Soc. (chmn. council 1976-77), Am. Chem. Soc. (chmn. Cleve. sect. 1968-69, nat. councilor 1973—), Soc. Plastic Engrs., Soc. Plastic Industries, Cleve. Engring. Soc. (elector), Soc. Mayflower Descs. (treas., lt. gov., rec. sec. Ohio), Cleve. Council World Affairs, Sigma Xi. Episcopalian (vestry). Contbr. articles to profl. jours.; patentee in field. Home: 3098 Huntington Rd Shaker Heights OH 44120 Office: 4440 Warrensville Center Rd Cleveland OH 44128

STANDLEY, MARVIN MORRIS, telephone co. exec.; b. Kansas City, Mo., Mar. 15, 1939; s. Lee E. and Nellie E. (Smith) S.; B.S., Central Mo. State U., 1961; M.S., St. Louis U., 1968; m. Suzanne Jane Wedler, July 31, 1970; children—Todd, Scott, Craig. Comml. staff asst. Southwestern Bell Telephone Co., St. Louis, 1961-63, mgr., Fulton, Mo., 1963-64, unit mgr., 1964-66, exchange rate engr., 1966-68, rate engr., 1968-69, supr. personnel devel., 1969-71, dist. mgr., Ferguson, Mo., 1971-80, div. staff mgr., seminar dir., St. Louis, 1980—; dir. United Mo. Bank of Ferguson. Pres., St. Louis County League of C. of C., 1976; chmn. St. Louis County Planning Commn., 1978—; pres. Florissant Fine Arts Council, 1974-77; v.p. Am. Cancer Soc., 1978; bd. mgrs. YMCA. Recipient Disting. Service award St. Louis County League chambers commerce, Florissant Valley Jaycees, 1975, 76. Mem. Florissant (Mo.) C. of C. (pres. 1974). Clubs: Rotary (pres. Ferguson 1976-77, dist. gov. elect), Mo. Athletic, Norwood Hills Country. Home: 6630 Lakeside Hills Dr Florissant MO 63033 Office: Southwestern Bell Telephone Co 1335 S Lindbergh St Saint Louis MO 63141

STANDRIDGE, LARRY ALLEN, ednl. adminstr.; b. Chickasha, Okla., May 17, 1935; s. Russell Allie and Rubie Dale (Cunningham) S.; B.A., Baylor U., 1956; M.R.E., Southwestern Bapt. Theol. Sem., 1965; Ph.D., Ohio State U., 1971; m. Betty June Ellis, Nov. 7, 1980; children—Kay Annette, Brent Alan, Sheri Dawn. Indsl. arts tchr. Columbus (Ohio) Public Schs., 1970-72; dir. continuing edn. John Wesley Coll., Owosso, Mich., 1972-78, Lansing (Mich.) Coll., 1978—. Adv. council, adult and continuing edn. Lansing Public Schs., 1978, sec., 1980-81; sec. Baylor Michigan Club, 1979—. Mem. Adult Edn. Assn. (dir.), Capital Area Continuing and Community Edn. Assn. (sec. 1978—). Author monograph: Continuing Education: Blueprint for Excellence, 1980. Home: 4516 Wildflower Way Lansing MI 48917 Office: Lansing Community Coll PO Box 40010 Lansing MI 48901

STANELUIS, JAMES MICHAEL, indsl. tape mfg. co. exec.; b. Cleve., Feb. 18, 1943; s. Michael Leo and Mary (Nolan) S.; B.Chem. Engring., U. Dayton, 1964; M.B.A., Case Western Res. U., 1968; m. Kim Ely Peck, May 20, 1978; children—Mark Nolan, Christian Nolan. Process mgr. Uniroyal, Painesville, Ohio, 1964-66; product devel. engr. B. F. Goodrich, Cleve., 1966-68; mgr. corp. devel. PPG Industries, Pitts., 1968-74, devel. analyst corp. devel., 1970-72, dir. mktg. and corp. devel. Pitts. Corning, 1972-74; gen. mgr. Archwood Tobacco Co., Cleve., 1974-77; tech. dir. indsl. div. Avery Internat., Painesville, 1978—. Mem. Cleve. Engring. Soc. Home: 2516 Norfolk Rd Cleveland Heights OH 44106 Office: 250 Chester St Painesville OH 44022

STANFORD, JOHN DAVID, food processing equipment mfg. co. exec.; b. Salem, Ill., Sept. 12, 1946; s. William Thomas and Melba (Hagar) S.; B.S., Georgetown Coll., 1969; cert. AMA Mgmt. Internship Program; m. Donna Maxine Green, Aug. 14, 1971; children—Shane, Matthew. With Bettendorf Stanford Inc. Salem, 1969—, pres., 1970—, owner, 1973—; dir. Best Sales Co., Community State Bank. Past trustee Kaskaskia Coll. Named Hon. Farmer, Future Farmers Am. Mem. Georgetown Coll. Assos. (vice chmn.), Am. Soc. Bakery Engrs., Bakery Equipment Mfg. Assn. Baptist. Clubs: Mo. Athletic, Rotary (past pres.). Office: PO Box 90 Salem IL 62881

STANGELAND, ARLAN INGHART, Congressman; b. Fargo, N.D., Feb. 8, 1930; s. Inghart and Pearle (Olson) S.; student pub. schs., Moorhead, Minn.; m. Virginia Grace Trowbridge, June 24, 1950; children—David, Beth, Brian, Jean, Todd, Jeffrey, Stuart. Farmer, Barnesville, Minn., 1951—; mem. Minn. Ho. of Reps., 1966; mem. 95th-97th Congresses from 7th Minn. Dist. Pres., Barnesville PTA, 1965-66; sec. Republican Party of Wilkin County (Minn.), 1960-65, pres., 1965-66. Recipient N.D. State U. Agriculturalist award for community service, 1976. Mem. Minn. Shorthorn Assn. (dir.). Lutheran. Office: 1519 Longworth House Office Bldg Washington DC 20515

STANGLE, PATRICIA ANN, educator; b. Mt. Pleasant Mich., Mar. 13, 1949; d. Albert George and Marie Cecila (Judge) S.; B.S. in Edn., Central Mich. U., 1971, M.A., 1972, postgrad. in info. systems analysis, personnel mgmt. and labor relations. Dir. alt. ednl. programming Crawford-Ogemaw-Ostego-Roscommon Intermediate Sch. Dist., Roscommon, Mich., 1972-73; tchr., cons. for reading Mr. Pleasant High Sch., 1973—; reading tchr. Summer Remedial Clinics, Central Mich. U., 1972-73, instr. secondary edn. Sch. Grad. Studies, 1974-76; statis. researcher Mich. Felony Sentencing Project, State Ct. Adminstrv. Office, Lansing, 1978; cons. in reading; cons., examiner for reading Mich. Vocat. Rehab. Div. Mem. Assn. Supervision and Curriculum Devel., Nat. Council Tchrs. English, Internat. Reading Assn., Mich. Reading Assn., Mt. Pleasant Edn. Assn., Mich. Edn. Assn., NEA. Democrat. Roman Catholic. Home: 617 E Broadway Mount Pleasant MI 48858 Office: 155 S Elizabeth Mount Pleasant MI 48858

STANICK, WALTER JOHN, dentist; b. St. Louis, Oct. 8, 1927; s. Stanley and Rose S.; student U. Wyo., 1946; A.B., Washington U., St. Louis, 1950, D.M.D., 1956; postgrad. Tufts U., Temple U.; m. Patricia Jean Hazelwood, Dec. 18, 1965; 1 dau., Nancy Marie. Pvt. practice dnetistry, St. Louis, 1958—; faculty Washington U. Sch. Dental Medicine, 1977—. Bd. dirs. Greater St. Louis Council Boy Scouts Am., St. Louis County YMCA. Served to capt. AUS, 1956-58. Mem. Am., Mo. dental assns., Greater St. Louis Dental Soc., Fedn. Dentaire Internationale, St. Louis Dental Research Group. Clubs: Masons, Shriners, Rotary, Elks, Castle Oak. Home: 16 Muirfield Ln St Louis MO 63141 Office: 777 S New Ballas Rd St Louis MO 63141

STANISIC, MILOMIR MIRKOV, mathematician, educator; b. Bujacic, Serbia, Aug. 19, 1914; s. Mirko Vule and Ana Milovana (Bujisic) S.; came to U.S., 1949, naturalized, 1955; Diploma Ing., Tech. U., Hannover, Ger., 1946, Dr. Ing., 1949; Ph.D. in Math., Ill. Inst. Tech., 1958; m. Oct. 2, 1954; children—Ana, Michael, Susana. Researcher, faculty mem. dept. mechanics Tech. U., Hannover, 1949-50; research scientist Armour Research Found. of Ill. Inst. Tech., Chgo., 1950-56; prof. engring. scis. Purdue U., West Lafayette, Ind., 1956-66, prof. aeros. and astronautics, 1967—; vis. prof. Johns Hopkins U., Balt., 1966-67; cons. scientist Gen. Electric Co., Boeing Aircraft Co., Lockheed Co., Picatinny Arsenal. Served with Yugoslavian Army, 1934-45. Mem. Am. Math. Soc., Am. Physics Soc., Soc. Natural Philosophy, AAUP. Mem. Free Serbian Orthodox Ch. Research in wing in supersonic flow, thermoelasticity, magnetic flow, turbulence, motion of heavy masses, nonlinear phenomena. Office: 801 Princess Dr West Lafayette IN 47906

STANKO, IVAN, neurologist; b. Topolcany, Czechoslovakia, Mar. 28, 1939; came to U.S., 1968, naturalized, 1976; s. Andrej and Ella (Bachnerova) S.; M.D., Komensky U., Bratislava, Czechoslovakia, 1962; m. Anna Pancakova, July 24, 1965; children—Susan, Peter. Intern gen. practice and neurology County Hosp., Michalovce, Czechoslovakia, 1962-68; house staff St. Ann's Hosp. for Women, Columbus, Ohio, 1969-70; resident in neurology U. Ariz. Hosp., Tucson, 1970-73; neurologist Wausau (Wis.) Med. Center, 1973—; mem. dir. Muscular Dystrophy Clinic, Electroneurophysiology Lab., Wausau Hosp. North, Mem. AMA, Am. Acad. Neurology, Wis. Neurol. Soc. Home: 9114 Reed Rd Rothschild WI 54474 Office: Wausau Medical Center 2727 Plaza Dr Wausau WI 54401

STANLEY, C. MAXWELL, cons. engr.; b. Corning, Iowa, June 16, 1904; s. Claude Maxwell Stanley, Sr. and Laura Esther (Stephenson) S.; B.S. in Gen. Engring., U. Iowa, 1926, M.S. in Hydraulic Engring., 1930; L.H.D., Iowa Wesleyan Coll., 1961, Augustana Coll., 1978; H.H.D. (hon.), U. Manila, 1970; m. Elizabeth M. Holthues, Nov. 11, 1927; children—David M., Richard H., Jane S. Buckles. Structural designer Byllesby Engring. and Mgmt. Corp., Chgo., 1926-27; with dept. grounds and bldgs. U. Iowa, 1927-28; hydraulic engr. Mgmt. & Engring. Corp., Dubuque, Iowa and Chgo., 1928-32; cons. engr. Young & Stanley, Inc., 1932-39; partner, pres. Stanley Engring. Co. 1939-66; pres. Stanley Consultants, Inc., Muscatine, Iowa, 1966-71, chmn. bd., 1971—; pres. HON Industries, Muscatine, 1944-64, chmn. bd., 1964—; pres. Stanley Cons., Ltd., Liberia, 1959-71, dir., 1971—; mng. dir. Stanley Cons., Ltd., Nigeria, 1960-67, dir., 1967—; pres. World Press Rev., 1975—. Chmn. Strategy for Peace Confs., 1962—, Confs. on UN of Next Decade, 1965—; pres. Stanley Found., 1956—; trustee Iowa Wesleyan Coll., 1951—, chmn., 1963-65; bd. dirs. U. Iowa Found., 1966—, pres., 1971-75. Recipient Disting. Service award U. Iowa, 1967, Hancher-Finkbine medallion, 1971, 1st Iowa Bus. Leadership award, 1980. Fellow ASCE (Alfred Noble prize 1933, Collingwood prize 1935), IEEE, ASME, Am. Cons. Engrs. Council (chmn. com. fellows 1975); mem. Iowa Engrs. Soc. (hon. mem., pres. 1949; John Dunlap prize 1943, Marston award 1947, Disting. Service award 1962, Herbert Hoover Humanitarian award 1979), Nat. Soc. Profl. Engrs. (award for outstanding service 1965, PEPP award 1975), World Federalists U.S.A. (council 1947—, pres. 1954-56, 64-66), New Directions (dir. 1976—), Assn. World Federalists (chmn. council 1958-65). Republican. Methodist. Rotarian (Paul Harris award 1976). Author: Waging Peace 1956; The Consulting Engineer, 1961, 2d edit., 1981; Managing Global Problems, 1979; also articles in profl. jours. Home: 115 Sunset Dr Muscatine IA 52761 Office: Stanley Bldg Muscatine IA 52761

STANLEY, JERRY LYNN, social worker; b. Cherokee, Okla., May 26, 1940; s. William Herbert and Frances L. (Nelson) S.; student Northwestern Okla. State U., 1958-59, 63-67, George Williams Coll., 1967-69; doctoral candidate Kans. State U.; m. Ruth Ann Fuson, Sept. 30, 1961; children—Shecky Lynn, Jalyn Chad. Recreation supr. Boys Tng. Sch., Helena, Okla., 1964-67; social work supr., 1969-70, program supr., 1970-71; social worker Bur. Indian Affairs, Ketchikan, Alaska, 1971-72; rehab. dir. drug and alcohol program Ft. Riley, Kans., 1975—; instr. classes on alcoholism. Served with USAF, 1959-63, with U.S. Army, 1972-75. Mem. Kans. Council on Drug Abuse, Nat. Assn. Social Workers, Acad. Cert. Social Workers, Adult Edn. Assn. Democrat. Methodist. Home: 2215 McDowell Ave Manhattan KS 66502 Office: Bldg 92 Holbrook Ave Fort Riley KS 66442

STANLEY, MARGARET DURETA SEXTON, speech therapist; b. Wells County, Ind., Aug. 7, 1931; d. James Helmuth and Bertha Anna (Kizer) Roberts; B.S., Ball State U., 1952, M.A., 1963; m. Gale Sexton, Nov. 21, 1950; children—Cregg Alan, Donna Sue, Sheila Rene; m. 2d, Charles Stanley, Mar. 24, 1979. Speech and hearing clinician Hamilton (Ohio) City Schs., 1955-59, Kettering (Ohio) Pub. Schs., 1959-60; speech, lang. and hearing clinician Muncie (Ind.) Community Schs., 1960—; dir. Psi Iota Xi Summer Clinic, Decatur, Ind., 1964; Psi Iota Xi summer clinician Ball State U., 1965-77; supervising clinician Tri-County Hearing Impaired Assn., summer 1978, 79, 80, 81. Mem. Muncie, Ind. tchrs. assns., NEA, Ind., Am. (cert. clin. competency in speech pathology) speech and hearing assns., Ind. Council Suprs. Speech and Hearing, Adminstrv. Women's Club, Delta Kappa Gamma. Republican. Methodist. Club: Women of Moose. Compiler, editor curriculum for speech, lang. and hearing clinicians of Muncie Community Schs. Home: 3609 N New York Ave Muncie IN 47304 Office: 3201 S Macedonia St Muncie IN 47302

STANLEY, SANDRA ORNECIA, ednl. adminstr.; b. Jersey City, July 6, 1950; d. McKinley and Thelma Louise (Newberry) S.; B.A., Ottawa U., 1972; postgrad. Jersey City State Coll., 1973; M.S.Ed., U. Kans., 1975, Ph.D. (fellow), 1980. Dir., head tchr. Salem Baptist Accredited Nursery Sch., Jersey City, 1972-73; spl. edn. instr. Joan Davis Sch. Spl. Edn., Kansas City, Mo., 1975-76; instructional media/materials trainee U. Kans. Med. Center, Kansas City, 1976-77; research asst., 1977-79; research asst. U. Kans., Lawrence, 1979; dir., coordinator tng. and observation Juniper Gardens Children's Project, Bur. Child Research, U. Kans., Kansas City, 1979—, co-adv. master students, 1977—, doctoral students, 1980—, ednl. tutor specialized services, 1980—; cons. YWCA, 1980, Dept. Spl. Edn. and Inst. Research in Learning Disabilities, U. Minn., 1980—. Recipient plaque Salem Bapt. Nursery Sch., 1973; Easter Seal Scholarship grantee, 1975. Mem. Council Exceptional Children, Div. Children with Learning Disabilities, Black Caucus - Minority Exceptional Children, Assn. Supervision and Curriculum Devel., Women's Ednl. Network, Coll. Women Inc., Nat. Assn. Female Execs., Easter Seal Soc. Crippled Children and Adults Mo. Democrat. Baptist. Author: The Relationship Between Learning Disabilities and Juvenile Delinquency: A Link Based on Family and School, 1980, also instructional manuals. Home: 5305 Oak Leaf Dr Apt 14 Kansas City MO 64129 Office: 1980 N 2d St Kansas City KS 66101

STANSELL, RONALD BRUCE, investment banker; b. Hammond, Ind., Apr. 9, 1945; s. Herman Bruce and Helen Rose S.; B.A., Wittenberg U., 1967; M.A., Miami U., Oxford, Ohio, 1969; m. Kathie Van Atta, Oct. 2, 1976; 1 dau., Kelsey. Investment officer First Nat. Bank, Chgo., 1969-73; mgr. investments Chrysler Corp., Detroit, 1973; asst. v.p. A.G. Becker, Chgo., 1973-76; v.p. Blyth Eastman Dillon, Chgo., 1976-79; v.p. Dean Witter Reynolds Inc., Chgo., 1979—. Mem. Mettawa (Ill.) Zoning Bd., 1978-81; trustee Village of Mettawa, 1981—. Served with USMCR, 1968-74. Named to Pres.'s Club, Blyth Eastman Dillon, 1977, 78, 79. Mem. Bond Club Chgo., Investment Analyst Soc., Fixed Income Group. Club: Exmoor Country. Home: Route #1 Box 49 Old School Rd Mettawa IL 60048

STANSFIELD, ROGER ELLIS, organic chemist; b. Sanford, Maine, July 16, 1926; s. Ernest and Eva (Ellis) S.; B.S., Northwestern U., 1950; M.S., Carnegie Inst. Tech., 1953; Ph.D., 1955; m. Audrey May Hasselbacher, June 16, 1951; children—Samuel Ernest, Harold William. With Baldwin-Wallace Coll., Berea, Ohio, 1956—, prof. chemistry, 1966—; vis. prof. Forman Christian Coll., Lahore, Pakistan, 1964-66. Ruling elder United Presbyterian Ch. U.S.A. Served with USN, 1944-46. Recipient Bechberger award Baldwin-Wallace Coll., 1973. Mem. Am. Chem. Soc. (chmn. Cleve. sect. 1974), AAAS, Danforth Assos. (chmn. Ohio 1971), Ohio Acad. Sci., Sigma Xi. Democrat. Research on nucleophilic substitution reactions, reactions in non-aqueous systems. Home: 145 Beech St Berea OH 44017 Office: Baldwin Wallace College Berea OH 44017

STANTON, JEANNE FRANCES, lawyer; b. Vicksburg, Miss., Jan. 22, 1920; d. John Francis and Hazel (Mitchell) S.; student George Washington U., 1938-39; B.A., U. Cin., 1940; J.D., Salmon P. Chase Coll. Law, 1954. Admitted to Ohio bar, 1954; chief clk. Selective Service Bd., Cin., 1940-43; instr. USAAF Tech. Schs., Biloxi, Miss., 1943-44; with Procter & Gamble, Cin., 1945—, legal asst., 1952-54, head advt. services sect. legal div., trade practices dept., 1954-73, mgr. advt. services, legal div., 1973—. Team capt. Community Chest Cin., 1953. Mem. AAAS, Am., Ohio (chmn. uniform state laws com. 1968-70), Cin. (sec. law day com. 1965-66, chmn. com. on preservation hist. documents 1968-71) bar assns., Vicksburg and Warren County, Cin. hist. socs., Internat. Oceanographic Found., Otago Early Settlers Assn. (asso.), Intercontinental Biog. Assn., Cin. Lawyers, Cin. Women Lawyers (treas. 1958-59, nominating com. 1976). Clubs: Terrace Park Country; Cincinnati, Lawyers of Cin. (exec. com. 1978—, sec. 1980—, 1st v.p. 1982). Home: 2302 E Hill Ave Cincinnati OH 45208 Office: 301 E 6th St Cincinnati OH 45202

STANTON, JOHN WILLIAM, congressman; b. Painesville, Ohio, Feb. 20, 1924; s. Frank M. and Mary (Callinan) S.; B.A., Georgetown U., 1949; m. Margaret Smeeton, Dec. 3, 1966; 1 dau., Kelly Marie. Pres. J. W. Stanton, Inc., Painesville, 1949-63; commr. Lake County, Ohio, 1956-64; mem. 89th-97th Congresses 11th Dist. Ohio. Served to capt. AUS, 1942-46. Decorated Bronze Star medal with 1 oak leaf cluster, Purple Heart. Mem. Painesville Jr. (charter), Painesville (pres. 1952-55) chambers commerce, Am. Legion, Elk, K.C. (4 deg.). Republican. Roman Catholic. Club: Painesville Exchange (pres. 1951). Office: 2466 Rayburn Bldg Washington DC 20515*

STAPLER, HARRY BASCOM, educator, pub.; b. N.Y.C., Mar. 10, 1919; s. Henry Bascom and Gertrude (Haupert) S.; B.A., Coll. Wooster (Ohio), 1950; M.A., Central Mich. U., 1981; m. Normalee Waggoner, May 16, 1961. Reporter, Daily Record, Wooster, 1940-41, 47-50, also photographer; reporter AP, Detroit, 1950, regional sports editor, 1951-53; sports reporter Detroit News, 1953-58; editor Fostoria (Ohio) Rev. Times, 1958-60; bus. reporter Lansing (Mich.) State Jour., 1960-62; pub., editor, founder East Lansing (Mich.) Towne Courier, 1962-73, pres., 1966-73; pub., editor, founder Meridian Towne Courier, Okemos, Mich., 1965-73; pub., editor Williamston (Mich.) Enterprise, 1966-73; instr. journalism Ferris State Coll., 1974-79, dir. journalism program, 1977-79; instr., asst. chmn. Sch. Journalism, Mich. State U., 1979—; mng. editor Competency Forum, 1977-79; v.p. Suburban Newspapers of Mich., 1969-73. Served with USNR, 1941-46. Recipient John Field Journalism Edn. award Mich. Interscholastic Press Assn., 1973. Mem. East Lansing C. of C. (dir. 1973), Gladwin Blue Lake and Emerald Valley Assn. (pres. 1971-73), Univ. Internat. (v.p. 1970-72). Presbyterian. Author: The Student Journalist and Sportswriting, 1974; Exploring Pro Sports, 1982. Home: 803-105 Cherry Ln East Lansing MI 48824

STAPLES, EMILY ANNE, state legislator; b. Mpls., May 3, 1929; d. Frank A. R. and Emily (Dunn) Mayer; B.A., U. Minn., 1950; m. Loring M. Staples, Sept. 10, 1954; children—Mary, Thomas, Gregory, Kathryn. Chmn. Hennepin County (Minn.) Bicentennial Planning Commn., 1974-76; mem. Minn. Senate, 1976—; del. White House Conf. on Balanced Nat. Growth; mem. HEW Com. on Nat. Health Ins. Pres. Mpls. Jr. League, 1965-67; bd. dirs. Assn. Jr. Leagues Am., N.Y.C., 1967-69; Minn. adv. Nat. Trust Hist. Preservation; bd. dirs. Minn. Hist. Soc., 1974-76, Minn. Public Radio, 1974-76, Breck Sch., Mpls., 1973-76, Minn. Council on Founds.; v.p. United Way of Greater Mpls., 1980—; mem. govt. relations com. United Way of Am., 1981—; v.p. Minn. Women's Econ. Roundtable. Bush Found. Leadership grantee, 1981. Mem. Minn. Women's Polit. Caucus, U. Minn. Alumni Assn. (bd. dirs. 1980—), Democratic Farm Labor Feminist Caucus, NOW, Women's Equity Action League, League Women Voters, U. Minn. Alumni, Minn. Press Council (dir. 1979-81). Mem. Democratic Farm Labor Party. Roman Catholic.

STAPLES, JAMES ALAN, state ofcl.; b. Lafayette, Ind., May 4, 1938; s. William Layman and Vera Opal (Garrett) S.; A.B., Franklin Coll. of Ind., 1963; postgrad. Purdue U., 1964, Ind. U., 1967—. Asso. faculty English, Ind. U., Indpls., 1966-79; writing and lit. instr. Franklin Coll. of Ind., 1968-71; staff Ind. State Senate, Indpls., 1977-78, Ind. House of Reps., Indpls., 1976, 79—. Precinct committeeman, Greenwood, Ind., 1972—; 6th Congressional Dist. coordinator for 1972 presdl. campaign; del. Ind. Democratic State Conv., 1974, 76, 78, 80; chmn. Greenwood Dem. Central Com., 1975; alt. del. Dem. Nat. Conv., 1976, 80; Johnson County Dem. Party chmn., 1977—; del. Dem. Nat. Party Conf., 1978; mem. from Ind., Dem. Nat. Platform Com., 1980. Served with USAF, 1962. Lutheran. Home: 50 W Main St Greenwood IN 46142 Office: House of Representatives Rm 4A2 State House Indianapolis IN 46204

STAPLES, LAURANCE STARR, JR., mfg. co. exec.; b. Kansas City, Mo., Jan. 31, 1931; s. Laurance Starr and Bertha Marie (Schaefer) S.; B.S. in Gen. Engring., U. Ill., 1956; m. Barbara Ruth Hazard, Oct. 5, 1957; children—Laurance Starr, III, Mary Ruth. Mgr. applied products Marley Co., Kansas City, Mo., 1957-69; dir. customer service Tempmaster Corp., Kansas City, 1969-71; sales rep. Kansas City Equipment Co., Kansas City, 1971; sales mgr. Havens Cooling Towers div. Havens Steel Co., Kansas City, 1971-73; with L.S. Staples Co., Kansas City, 1974-81, pres., 1974-81; sales adminstrv. asst. Marley Cooling Tower Co., Mission, Kans., 1981—; cons. Butler Mfg. Co., Kansas City, 1971. Superwalk chmn. safety and communications March of Dimes, Kansas City, Mo., 1972—, mem. gen. bd., 1977, 79; bd. dirs. Heart of Am. Radio Club, Kansas City, 1978-80; Master of servers St. Paul's Episcopal Ch., Kansas City, 1959-65, vestryman, 1967-73, treas., 1975-81; stewardship officer Episc. Diocese W. Mo., 1980—. Served with U.S. Army, 1953-55. Mem. ASHRAE (chpt. pres. 1980-81, vice chmn. energy mgmt. Region IX), Am. Inst. Plant Engrs., Am. Soc. Plumbing Engrs., Am. Soc. Mech. Engrs., Kansas City Engrs. Club, Refrigeration Engring. and Tech. Assn., Tau Kappa Epsilon. Episcopalian. Clubs: Heart of America Radio; Kansas City Association for Blind Amateur Radio; MoKan Repeater; Kansas City VHF (pres. 1961-62, corp. agt., trustee). Home: 425 W 49th Terr Kansas City MO 64112 Office: 5800 Foxridge Dr Mission KS 66201

STAPLETON, CHRISTOPHER GEORGE, ednl. adminstr.; b. Pasadena, Calif., Dec. 23, 1919; s. Christopher Charles and Elizabeth Hannah (Dubberly) S.; B.A. in Psychology, Lewis and Clark Coll., 1949, M.Ed., 1956; Ph.D. in Ednl. Adminstrn., U. Minn., 1981; m. Rosemary Norris, Mar. 15, 1947; children—Linda Elizabeth, Sally Ann Stapleton Clapp, Christopher Joseph. Tchr. Russellville Sch., Portland, 1949-52; prin. Sunnyside Sch., Milwaukee, Oreg., 1952-56; tchr. gen. sci. Oregon City Jr. High Sch., 1956-57; asst. prin. Clackamas (Oreg.) Sch., 1957-58; tchr. Portland Schs., 1958-62; asst. editor Am. Printing House for Blind, Louisville, 1962-65; cons. dept. edn. St. Paul, Minn., 1965-66; dir. spl. edn. Rochester (Minn.) schs., 1966-80, asst. for fin. and acctg., 1980—. Served with U.S. Navy, 1940-46. Fellow AAAS; mem. NEA, Phi Delta Kappa. Presbyterian. Club: Rotary. Home: 1336 NW 20th St Rochester MN 55901 Office: 334 SE 16th St Rochester MN 55901

STAPLETON, JAMES WILLIAM, editor; b. Chgo., Nov. 26, 1932; s. Patrick John and Marion Elizabeth (Boland) S.; student public and pvt. schs., Chgo. m. Winifred T. Manning, Sept. 26, 1954; children—Michael, Steven, James, Diane, Theresa, Karen, John. Mechanic, Capital Airlines, 1949-57; research technician Ford Motor Co., 1957-60; regional sales mgr. Allen Electric Co., Kalamazoo, 1960-63, Simpson Electric Co., Elgin, Ill., 1963-65; mng. editor Super Service mag. Irving-Cloud Pub. Co., Lincolnwood, Ill., 1965-68, mng. editor Jobber Topics mag., 1968-80, editor Hardware Merchandiser mag., 1980—. Served with USAF, 1952-56; Korea. Mem. Am. Soc. Bus. Press Editors. Roman Catholic. Office: 7300 N Cicero Lincolnwood IL 60646

STAPLETON, ROBERT J., indsl. devel. exec.; b. Ft. Wayne, Ind., Jan. 9, 1922; s. Clarence Albert and Eva Elizabeth (Grashoff) S.; A.B., Valparaiso U., 1946; M.S., U. Wis., 1947; postgrad., U. Mich., 1943; m. Marilyn Jeane Stinchfield, Sept. 7, 1946; children—Jan Elizabeth, Jill Leigh, Robert Guy. Indsl. devel. rep. Commonwealth Edison Co., Chgo., 1947-55; mng. dir., sec. Clinton Devel. Co. (Iowa), 1955-63; mgr. Cordova (Ill.) Indsl. Park, No. Natural Gas Co., 1963-69; exec. dir. Elgin (Ill.) Econ. Devel. Commn., 1969-71; exec. dir. Jobs div. IVAC, LaSalle, Ill., 1971-77; pres. Scioto Econ. Devel. Corp., Portsmouth, Ohio, 1977—; pvt. practice as indsl. devel. cons., 1955—. Past pres., dir. Ill. Devel. Council. Served to lt (j.g.), USNR, 1942-46; capt. Res. ret. Certified indsl. developer. Mem. Res. Officers Assn., Naval Res., Assn. Am. Soc. Planning Ofcls., Am. (dir.), Gt. Lakes States Area (past v.p., dir.) devel. councils, Nat. Assn. Corp. Real Estate Execs., Urban Land Inst., Indsl. Devel. Research Council (past chmn., dir.), Ohio Devel. Assn. (dir.), Council Urban Econ. Devel., Portsmouth C. of C., Valparaiso U. Lettermen's Assn., Wis. Alumni Assn. Republican. Lutheran. Clubs: Rotary, Elks Country. Home: 3219 Old Post Rd Portsmouth OH 45662 Office: 6th and Court Sts Portsmouth OH 45662

STARK, BETTY WALKER, mktg. exec.; b. Manitowoc, Wis., Sept. 18, 1940; d. Woodrow Nelson and Mary Ann (Sieracki) Walker; B.A., U. Wis., 1962, M.S.W., 1971; m. Richard Paul Stark, Apr. 20, 1974. Social worker, pub. info. officer Dane County (Wis.) Social Services, Madison, 1962-72; sales asso. and mgr., cons. Stark Co., Madison, 1972-75; account exec., media dir., v.p. ops. Stephan & Brady Advt., Madison, 1975-78; pres. B.W. Stark Cons., Madison, 1978—; prin. Sahr Seminars Inc., 1978-80; v.p. Condominium Ventures, Inc., Madison, 1980—. Bd. dirs. Wis. Arthritis Found.; bd. dirs. Jonah House, Madison, 1974—; adv. Madison Civic Repertory Theatre. Lic. salesperson, Wis. Real Estate Bd. Mem. Meeting Planners Internat., Nat. Assn. Social Workers, Wis. Public Welfare Assn., Madison Advt. Fedn. (chairperson 1978 Addys awards). Home: 12 Blue Spruce Trail Madison WI 53717 Office: 111 N Pinckney St Madison WI 53703

STARK, CHESTER ARTHUR, architect; b. Chgo., Apr. 27, 1905; s. Arthur Frank and Hulda Marie (Fritz) S.; student Marquette Inst., 1920-24; Architect, Chgo. Beaux Arts Inst. of Design, 1924-27; m. Eleanor Emma Schuster, Dec. 30, 1944; children—Sandra, Sonja, Sharon. Archtl. draftsman Mundie and Jensen, Chgo., 1924-32; archtl. designer Perkins & Will, architects, Chgo., 1933-36; chief draftsman Shaw, Metz, architects, Chgo., 1937-38; architect constrn. dept. Montgomery Ward Co., Chgo., 1938-46; prin. Chester A. Stark, architect, Glenview, Ill., 1948—; architect Cook County, Ill., 1967-69; mem. faculty Oakton Coll., Niles, Ill., 1950-65. Deacon Holy Trinity Luth. Ch., Glenview, 1950-55, supt. Sunday sch., 1950-55; mem. fin. com. Luth. Ch. of St. Philip, Glenview; pres. Glenview Countryside Civic Assn. 1950-55. Fellow Soc. of Am. Registered Architects (Gold Medal award 1962, nat. v.p. 1959-61, regent for Ill., Wis., Minn. 1959-65, Ill. council pres. 1966-67); mem. Ill. Soc. Architects (dir. 1960-70), Glenview C. of C. (dir. 1955-56), Constrn. Specification Inst., Nat. Archivist Soc. Am. Registered Architects. Club: Masons, Shriners. Designer first high rise in Oak Park (Ill.) with post tension concrete in floor and roof slabs. Address: 915 Glendale Rd Glenview IL 60025

STARK, JACK ALAN, psychologist; b. Hastings, Nebr., Sept. 20, 1946; s. Arlen O. and Virginia (Dryden) S.; B.A., St. Francis Coll., 1968; M.A., U. Nebr., 1970, Ph.D., 1973; m. Shirley Theis, Aug. 1, 1970; children—John, Nicholas, Suzanne. Counseling psychologist, pub. schs. Lincoln, Nebr., 1970-73; asso. prof. psychology U. Nebr., Omaha, 1973—, asst. prof. med. psychology Med. Sch., 1973—; instr. Creighton U., 1975—. Lic. and cert. psychologist, Nebr.; NDEA fellow, 1968-70. Fellow Acad. Psychologists in Marital, Sex and Family Therapy; mem. Nebr. Psychol. Assn., Nat. Assn. Retarded Citizens, Internat. Neuropsychiat. Assn., Am. Assn. Mental Deficiency, Assn. Advancement Community Services, Assn. of Severely Handicapped. Democrat. Roman Catholic. Contbr. articles to profl. jours.; also editor books, jours. Home: 306 Heavenly Dr Omaha NE 68154 Office: Dept Psychiatry Med Center Univ Nebr 42d and Dewey Ave Omaha NE 68501

STARK, PATRICIA ANN, psychologist; b. Ames, Iowa, Apr. 21, 1937; s. Keith Curtis and Mary Louise (Johnston) Moore; B.S., So. Ill. U., Edwardsville, 1970, M.S. (fellow 1970-72), 1972; Ph.D., St. Louis U., 1976; m. Edward Milton Stark, June 12, 1959. Counselor alcoholics Bapt. Rescue Mission, East St. Louis, Ill., 1969; Gateway Rehab. Center, 1972; intern. sch. psychologist Henry Stark Counties Spl. Edn. Dist., Kewanee, Ill., 1972-73; instr. psychology Lewis and Clark Community Coll., Godfrey, Ill., 1973-74, (developer complete child care degree program), coordinator child care services, 1974—, asst. prof., 1976—; group clin. pvt. practice, dir. child services Collinsville Counseling Center, 1978-81; dir. Complete Family Psychol. and Hypnosis Services, 1982—. Mem. Am. Soc. Clin. Hypnosis, Ill., Midwestern psychol. assns., Nat. Assn. Sch. Psychologists, Am. Psychol. Assn., Assn. Specialists in Group Work, Am. Personnel and Guidance Assn., Nat. Honor Soc. in Psychology, Psi Chi. Contbr. articles to profl. jours., producer, director videotape presentations. Home: 202 Bill Lou Collinsville IL 62234 Office: Lewis and Clark Community Coll Godfrey IL 62035 also Complete Family Psychol and Hypnosis Services 407 E Main St Collinsville IL 62234

STARK, ROBERT JAMES, JR., packing co. exec.; b. N.Y.C., Apr. 11, 1920; s. Robert James and Lucia (Rhyne) S.; B.A., Amherst Coll., 1941; m. Martha K. Lamb, Aug. 5, 1944 (dec. 1976); children—Martha Louise (Mrs. R. W. Clifford), Lucia Burnham (Mrs. C.W. Scott), Polly Robertson (Mrs. T. Wilson), Robert Bruce; m. 2d, Stella X. Gilbert, Feb. 5, 1977. Salesman, Graybar Electric Co., N.Y.C., 1941, 45-50; with John Crane-Houdaille (formerly Crane Packing Co.), Morton Grove, Ill., 1952—, asst. sales mgr. seal div., 1952-57, asst. to pres., 1954-57, sales mgr. seal div., 1957-63, asst. v.p. seal sales, 1963-65, v.p. 1965—. Active Northbrook (Ill.) United Fund, 1955-60, pres., 1959; mem. Dist. 28 Sch. Bd. Northbrook, 1961-68. Served to lt. USNR, 1941-45, lt. comdr., 1950-52; PTO. Mem. Am. Mgmt. Assn., Research Inst. Am., Am. Inst. Mgmt., Ill. C. of C., No. Ill. Ind. Assn. (pres. 1973), Phi Kappa Psi. Republican. Episcopalian. Clubs: Marshwood at the Landings (Savannah, Ga.); Sunset Ridge Country (pres. 1981—) (Northbrook). Home: 1854 Somerset Ln Northbrook IL 60062 Office: 6400 W Oakton St Morton Grove IL 60053

STARKE, RALPH ELBERT, rubber co. exec.; b. Cleve., Apr. 15, 1930; s. George H. and Elsie (Semler) S.; student geology Miami U., 1949-51; m. Margery C. Hardin, June 11, 1955; children—Cynthia, Roy, Rod, Ron. With Gates Rubber Co., 1953—, asst. dist. mgr., Cleve., 1964-65, dist. mgr., Milw., 1966—. Republican. Lutheran. Mason (Shriner), Lion. Home: 345 Crescent Ln Thiensville WI 53092 Office: Gates Rubber Co PO Box 18610 Milwaukee WI 53218

STARKEY, JUDITH ANN, oil co. exec.; b. Indpls.; d. Charles Lester and Frances Lorraine (Scott) Middleton; student Ind. U., 1955-58; Ph.B., Northwestern U., 1973; postgrad. bus. adminstrn. U. Chgo., 1978. Exec. sec., CBS, N.Y.C., 1958-63; office mgr. Radio Free Europe, Munich, 1963-65; exec. aide, cons. firm, Chgo., 1965-67, C&NW Ry. Co., Chgo., 1967-70; mgr. personnel systems, EEO, Chemetron Corp., Chgo., 1970-79; sr. employee relations rep. Standard Oil Co. (Ind.), Chgo., 1979—. Named hon. Ky. col. Mem. Young Execs. Club Chgo. (editor newsletter 1976-77, v.p. programs 1977-78), Indsl. Relations Assn. Chgo., Chgo. Council Fgn. Relations, Alpha Sigma Lambda. Office: 200 E Randolph St Chicago IL 60601

STARKEY, ROBERTA NEIL JOHNSTON (MRS. JOHN DOW STARKEY), educator; b. Eskota, Tex., June 13, 1921; d. Clarence Beaman and Fannie Irene (Hassell) Johnston; B.S., Tex. Technol. Coll., 1942, Ed.D., 1961; M.A., Eastern N.Mex. U., 1956; m. John Dow Starkey, Nov. 3, 1943; children—David Joe, Bill Clarence, Marilyn Elaine. Tchr. various schs., 1942-44; tchr. Clovis (N.M.) Lincoln-Jackson Elementary Sch., 1956-59; tchr. Mil. Heights Elementary Sch., prof. Roswell Community Coll., 1961-63; asst. prof. U. Wyo., Laramie, 1964-67; asso. prof. elementary edn. No. Ill. U., DeKalb, 1967-70, now prof. Mem. summer faculty Eastern N.Mex. U., 1961-63. Active Girl Scouts U.S.A. Mem. AAUW (Laramie pres. 1965-67, editor state bulletin 1958-60), N.E.A. (sectional chmn. 1959), Internat. Reading Assn. (state chmn. 1966-67), Am. Personnel and Guidance Assn. (exec. bd. 1975-76), Assn. Humanistic Edn. and Devel. (nat. pres. 1974-75), Student Personnel Assn. for Tchr. Edn. (nat. editor newsnotes 1968-72, pres. 1974-75), Nat. Soc. Coll. Tchrs. Edn., Ill., N.Mex. ednl. assns., Ill. Assn. for Study of Perception (v.p. 1975-76), Delta Kappa Gamma (pres. 1966-67, Phi Lambda Theta (pres. Beta Delta chpt.), Democrat. Methodist (chmn. bd. edn. 1959-61). Editor: Assn. Study of Perception newsletter. Home: Route 2 DeKalb IL 60115

STARKEY, WALTER LEROY, mech. engr.; b. Mpls., Oct. 5, 1920; s. Harry N. and Rena B. (Towne) S.; B.M.E., U. Louisville, 1943; M.S., Ohio State U., 1947, Ph.D., 1950; m. Bonna B. Preston, Dec. 17, 1949; children—David Harry, John Mark. Instr., U. Louisville, 1943-46; instr. Ohio State U., Columbus, 1947-49, asst. prof., 1950-54, asso. prof., 1954-58, prof. mech. engring., 1958-78, prof. emeritus, 1978—; cons. to attys.; ind. design cons., 1978—; chmn. bd. Jadco, Inc. Fellow ASME (Machine Design award 1976); mem. Am. Soc. Engring. Edn. Author: Motorhome Facts, 1973; contbr. tech. articles to profl. jours. Home: 7000 Coffman Rd Dublin OH 43017 Office: Mech Engring Dept Ohio State U Columbus OH 43210

STARKS, JUDITH ANN, ednl. adminstr.; b. Chgo., May 10, 1947; d. Willis Bland and Harriet Lorraine (Hanson) Minor; B.A., Cornell U., 1968; M.A., Roosevelt U., Chgo., 1970; postgrad. No. Ill. U., 1971-72; m. Robert Terry Starks, Aug. 21, 1971; children—Kenya Mariam, Robert Willis. Library asst. Cornell U., 1964-67; tchr. aide headstart program Walter Scott Sch., summer, 1967; tchr. Chgo. Bd. Edn., 1968-71; career edn. specialist and cons. Able Model program No. Ill. U., De Kalb, 1971-72; part-time instr. dept. inner city studies Northeastern Ill. U., Chgo., 1973—, program cons. for cultural linguistic approach, 1973-79, program dir. cultural linguistic approach, 1979—; cons. early childhood and career edn., 1971-81. Mem. Ednl. Task Force, 1st Congressional Dist., Ill., 1981—; mem. community adv. bd. Edward Wilmot Blyden Center for Creative Devel., 1976-78. Recipient service award Concerned Students Orgn., Northeastern Ill. U., 1980. Mem. Assn. for Supervision and Curriculum Devel., Internat. Reading Assn. (multi-literacy in multi-cultural settings com. 1981-82), Nat. Black Child Devel. Inst., Nat. Alliance Black Sch. Educators, Chgo. Alliance of Black Sch. Educators, Jack and Jill of Am. (parliamentarian 1980). Democrat. Episcopalian. Home: 5030 South Ellis Ave Chicago IL 60615 Office: 700 E Oakwood Blvd Chicago IL 60653

STARNES, JAMES WRIGHT, lawyer; b. East St. Louis, Ill., Apr. 3, 1933; s. James Adron and Nell (Short) S.; student St. Louis U., 1951-53; LL.B., Washington U., St. Louis, 1957; m. Helen Woods Mitchell, Mar. 29, 1958; children—James Wright, Mitchell A., William B. II. Admitted to Mo., Ill. bars, 1957; asso. Stinson, Mag & Fizzell, Kansas City, Mo., 1957-60, partner, 1960—; partner Mid-Continent Properties Co., 1959—, Fairview Investment Co., Kansas City, 1971-76, Monticello Land Co., 1973—; sec. Packaging Products Corp., Mission, Kans., 1972—. Bd. dirs. Mo. Assn. Mental

Health, 1968-69; bd. dirs. Kansas City Assn. Mental Health, 1966-78, pres., 1969-70; bd. dirs. Heed, 1965-73, 78—, pres., 1966-67, finance chmn. 1967-68; bd. dirs. Kansas City Halfway House Found., exec. com., 1966-69, pres., 1966; bd. dirs. Joan Davis Sch. for Spl. Edn., 1972—, v.p., 1972-73, 79—, pres., 1979—; bd. dirs. Sherwood Center for Exceptional Child, 1977-79, v.p., 1978-79. Served with arty. AUS, 1957. Mem. Am., Mo., Kansas City bar assns., Kansas City Lawyers Assn. Presbyterian (deacon). Mem. adv. bd. Washington U. Law Quar., 1957—. Home: 3715 W 63d St Shawnee Mission KS 66208 Office: 2100 Charter Bank Center Kansas City MO 64105

STARR, BRYAN BARTLETT, profl. football coach; b. Montgomery, Ala., Jan. 9, 1934; s. Benjamin B. and Lula I. (Tucker) S.; B.S., U. Ala., 1956; m. Cherry Morton, May 8, 1954; children—Bart, Bret. Quarterback, Green Bay Packers, Nat. Football League, 1956-71, asst. coach, 1972, gen. mgr., head coach, 1975—; owner, operator Bart Starr Lincoln-Mercury automobile dealership, Birmingham, Ala. Active in fundraising for numerous charities. Played in NFL Pro-Bowl after 1960, 61, 62, 66 seasons; NFL Passing Leader, 1962, 64, 66; NFL Player of Yr., 1966; Super Bowl Most Valuable Player, 1967, 68; named to Nat. Profl. Football Hall of Fame, 1977. Methodist. Co-author: Quarterbacking, 1967; Perspective on Victory, 1972. Office: Green Bay Packers 1265 Lombardi Ave Green Bay WI 54303

STARR, EDWARD CARYL, librarian; b. Yonkers, N.Y., Jan. 9, 1911; s. Edward Charles and Mary Hamilton (Reid) S.; A.B. cum laude, Colgate U., 1933; B.S., Columbia Univ. Sch. Library Service, 1939; M.Div., Colgate-Rochester Div. Sch., 1940; m. Hilda Ruth Thomforde, Aug. 31, 1940; children—Caroline May (Mrs. Norman C. Wehmer), E(dward) Jonathan. Curator, Samuel Colgate Baptist Hist. Collection, Colgate U., 1935-48; librarian Crozer Theol. Sem., Chester, Pa., 1948-54; curator Am. Baptist Hist. Soc., 1948-55; ordained to ministry Bapt. Ch., 1952; curator combined Samuel Colgate Bapt. Hist. Collection and Am. Bapt. Hist. Soc., Colgate Rochester Div. Sch., 1955-76. Archivist, Am. Bapt. Chs. in U.S.A., Colgate Rochester Bexley-Crozer Theol. Sem. Mem. Am. Soc. Ch. History, Am. Archivists, Am. Assn. Theol. Librarians, Phi Beta Kappa. Republican. Editor, compiler A Baptist Bibliography, 1947-76. Contbr. articles to periodicals. Home: 3215 Brookshire Dr Florissant MO 63033

STARR, GEORGE A., coll. adminstr.; b. Eldora, Iowa, Oct. 5, 1950; s. John Phillip and Virginia Lee (Saltzman) S.; B.A., U. Iowa, 1975; m. Mary Kathryn Keeley, July 18, 1981. Asst. mgr. Ben Franklin Store, Tucson, 1972-73; TV technician U. Iowa, 1974-75, ednl. media coordinator, 1975—; co-owner Apple Assos., personal care products distbn. firm. Asst. leader Tall Corn Area council Boy Scouts Am., Eldora. Photographer of cover photo for Jour. Am. Dentistry, 1979. Office: University Hospital School University of Iowa Iowa City IA 52242

STARR, MAURICE KENNETH, museum dir.; b. Libertytown, Md., Apr. 28, 1922; s. Maurice Scott and Nellie Gray (Fisher) S.; B.A., Duke U., 1945; M.A., Yale U., 1947, Ph.D. (Jr. Sterling fellow 1952, Sr. Sterling fellow 1953), 1957; m. Betty Jane Leslie, Dec. 23, 1943; children—Leslie Gray, Maurice Winfield. Prin., Tsingtao (China) Am. Sch., 1947-49; curator Asiatic archeology and ethnology Field Mus. Natural History, Chgo., 1953-70; dir. Milw. Public Mus., 1970—; lectr. Asian prehistory, dept. anthropology U. Chgo., 1958-73; Am. Council Learned Soc.-Social Sci. Research Council research grantee for China ink-rubbings, Taiwan, 1960. Mem. Am. Assn. Mus. (v.p. 1975-78, pres. 1978-80, exec. com. 1975-82, chmn. future objectives com. 1976-78, council 1975-82, chmn. honors com. 1980-82, legis. com. 1978—, commn. on mus. for new century 1981—, leader del. to People's Republic of China 1980, map policy panel 1981—), Internat. Council Mus. (exec. bd., 1976—, chmn. 1978-80), Assn. Sci. Mus. Dirs. (pres. 1974-76), Assn. Sci.-Tech. Centers (dir. 1975-77), Midwest Mus. Conf. (pres. 1974-76, Disting. Service award 1979), Wis. Fedn. Mus., Nat. Endowment for Arts (mus. policy panel 1981—), Phi Beta Kappa, Sigma Xi. Clubs: Caxton (Chgo.); Univ. (Milw.); Rotary. Translator, annotator: Ch'eng-tzu-yai: the Black Pottery Culture Site at Lung-shan-chen in Li-ch'eng-hsien, Shantung Province, 1956; co-author Catalogue of Chinese Rubbings from Field Mus., 1981; contbr. articles, revs. to profl. jours. Office: 800 E Wells St Milwaukee WI 53233

STARR, RONALD LEE, indsl. engr.; b. Keokuk, Iowa, Dec. 3, 1938; s. Floyd Lester and Izola Marie (Bryant) S.; A.A., Keokuk Community Coll., 1959; B.S., Iowa State U., 1961; m. Evelyn LaVonne Lewis, Aug. 17, 1963; children—Randall Lee, Gregory Warren. Acctg. mgr. Internat. Harvester Co., 1963-66; tool engr. Sheller Globe, Keokuk, 1966-68; indsl. engring. mgr. Champion Internat., Clinton, Iowa, 1968-73; indsl. engr. Chesebrough Ponds, Jefferson City, Mo., 1973-79; owner, mgr. M.R.S. Co., Eugene, Mo., 1974—. Scoutmaster Great Rivers council Boy Scouts Am., Russellville, Mo., 1976-78; pres. Russellville Band Boosters, 1978-80; v.p. Russellville Athletic Boosters, 1979-80. Served with U.S. Army, 1962-63. Recipient Key Man award Jaycees, 1970. Mem. Jefferson City C. of C., Am. Inst. Indsl. Engrs. Republican. Mem. United Ch. of Christ. Club: Jefferson City Racquet. Home: Rural Route 1 Eugene MO 65032 Office: 610 Mulberry St Jefferson City MO 65101

STASZAK, LAWRENCE ROBERT, electronics co. exec.; b. Toledo, June 25, 1941; s. Zigmond Robert and Ann Irene (Mioduzewski) S.; B.S. in Elec. Engring., U. Toledo, 1966; postgrad Mich. State U., 1966-67, Wharton Sch., U. Pa., 1979; m. Gloria R. Frey, Mar. 22, 1969; children—Terasa Marie, Todd Michael. With Sparton Electronics Div., Jackson, Mich., from 1966, project engr., 1969-74, mktg. rep., 1974-75, mgr. advanced programs and product devel., from 1975; now v.p., gen. mgr. Sparton of Can. Ltd. Mem. IEEE, Naval Helicopter Assn., Am. Radio Relay League, Assn. Old Crows, Cricket Soc., Am. Soc. Indsl. Security, Am. Def. Preparedness Assn. Republican. Roman Catholic. Home: 34 Farmington Crescent London ON N6K 3J3 Canada Office: 100 Elm St London ON N6A 4N2 Canada

STATLAND, HARRY, internist; b. St. Louis, Dec. 16, 1917; s. Samuel V. and Ida (Chalk) S.; M.D., U. Kans., 1939; m. Suzanne T. Ginsberg, Feb. 26, 1957. Intern, U. Kans. Hosp., Kansas City, 1939-40; resident Boston City Hosp., 1941-42, Mass. Gen. Hosp., Boston, 1949-50; practice medicine specializing in internal medicine, Kansas City, Mo., 1946—; asst. medicine Peter Bent Brigham Hosp., Boston, 1968-69; mem. staffs Menorah Med. Center and Research Hosp., Kansas City; asso. prof. medicine U. Kans. Sch. Medicine, 1951—, U. Mo. Med. Sch. at Kansas City, 1972—. Served with U.S. Army, 1942-46. Decorated Legion of Merit. Diplomate Am. Bd. Internal Medicine. Fellow ACP; mem. AMA, Am. Internist Soc., Am. Diabetes Assn., Jackson County Med. Soc. (pres. 1965-66), Civic Health Found. (pres. 1979-82), Wild Life Assn., Alpha Omega Alpha. Jewish. Club: B'nai B'rith. Author: Fluids and Electrolytes in Practice, 1954, 3d edit., 1963. Contbr. articles to profl. jours. Home: 648 E 45th St Kansas City MO 64110 Office: 6724 Troost St Kansas City MO 64131

STAUB, E. NORMAN, banker; b. Newark, Mar. 13, 1916; s. Walter Adolph and Ida (Flury) S.; A.B., Princeton U., 1937; M.B.A., Harvard U., 1939; m. Mary Ann Dilley, Dec. 28, 1940; children—Susan D., Sandra L. (Mrs. Richard F. Bradbury), Stephen R. Jr. accountant Lybrand Ross Bros. & Montgomery, Boston, 1939-41; treas. Nat. Research Corp., Cambridge, Mass., 1942-53; with No. Trust Co., Chgo., 1953-81, pres., 1972-81, chmn. bd., chief exec. officer, 1978-81; dir. U.S. Gypsum Co., Rollins, Burdick & Hunter. Bd. dirs. Chgo. Nursery and Half Orphan Asylum, 1963—; trustee Northwestern U., Better Govt. Assn., Mus. Sci. and Industry, Rush-Presbyn.-St. Luke's Med. Center; trustee, pres., chief exec. officer Orchestral Assn. Chgo.; mem. citizens bd. U. Chgo. Mem. Assn. Res. City Bankers, Chgo. Council on Fgn. Relations (vice chmn. bd.). Republican. Mem. Glencoe Union Ch. (treas., dir. 1964-67). Clubs: Princeton (N.Y.C.); Chicago, Econ., Comml., Mid-Am. (Chgo.); Indian Hill (Winnetka, Ill.); Old Elm (Ft. Sheridan). Home: 135 Sheridan N Winnetka IL 60093

STAUB, JAMES RICHARD, chiropractor; b. Peoria, Ill., Apr. 22, 1938; s. John and Dorothy Christine (Benson) S.; student Bradley U., 1956-60, U. Wis., 1972; D.Chiropractic, Palmer Coll. Chiropractic, 1972; B.A., Columbia Coll., 1977; m. Sandra Lee Herman, Dec. 21, 1958 (div. July 1979); children—Gary James, Gregory Alan; m. 2d, Sheryl Ann Vander Velde, Nov. 17, 1979. Asst. to mgr. A & J Lumber Co., Peoria Hts., Ill., 1956-60; with Central Ill. Light Co., Peoria, 1961-69; pvt. practice chiropractic, Valparaiso, Ind., 1972—. Recipient certificate of merit Palmer Coll. Chiropractic Clinic, 1972. Mem. Valpariaso Bus. and Profl. Couples Club (chmn. 1974-75), Internat., Am., Ky., Ind., Porter County (v.p. 1975-76), N.W. Dist. Ind. (sec. 1975-76), Christian chiropractic assns., Palmer Coll. Alumni Assn. (Ind. pres. 1974-79), Internat. Acad. Preventive Medicine, N.W. Ind. Comprehensive Health Planning Council, Phi Mu Alpha. Home: 811 E Chicago St Valparaiso IN 46383 Office: 1402 Evans Ave Valparaiso IN 46383

STAUFFACHER, DEAN WORTHING, ret. feed ingredient mfg. exec.; b. Waterloo, Iowa, Jan. 11, 1910; s. Charles Henry and Madge Ruth (Worthing) S.; B.A., Case-Western Res. U., 1931; J.D., U. Iowa, 1934; m. Barbara Bloomhall, Sept. 7, 1940; children—Stevan C., Scott Marr. Admitted to Iowa bar, 1934, Philippines bar, 1946; individual practice law, Cedar Rapids, Iowa, 1934-43; with Diamond V Mills, Inc., Cedar Rapids, 1946-81, salesman, 1946-50, dir., 1947—, v.p., sec., 1947-49, sales mgr., 1950-80, pres., 1974-81, ret., 1981; mem. feed adv. com. Iowa Sec. Agr., 1961-63. Served with AUS, 1943-46. Mem. Nat. Feed Ingredients Assn. (Distinguished Service award 1970, pres. 1960-61, dir. 1954-68, legal advisor, mem. exec. com. 1968-76, Spl. Service award 1976), Am. Feed Mfrs. Assn., Midwest Feed Mfrs. (assos. council 1970-75), Cedar Rapids Agribus. Execs. Forum (co-founder 1969), U.S., Cedar Rapids chambers commerce, Phi Delta Phi, Sigma Nu. Republican. Methodist. Clubs: Rotary, Cedar Rapids Country, Pickwick, Masons, Shriners. Home: 177 Braybrook SE Cedar Rapids IA 52403

STAUFFER, DAVID LEE, mfg. co. ofcl.; b. Rochester, N.Y., Oct. 27, 1941; s. Donald Scranton and Margaret Jane (Webster) S.; student Cleve. Inst. Art, 1960-61; B.A. in Edn., Ariz. State U., 1968, B.F.A., 1968; 1 child, Shannon Lee. Night mgr. Airways Rent-A-Car, Phoenix, 1965-68; sales rep. Maxwell House div. Gen. Foods Corp., Tucson and Phoenix, 1968-69, account mgr., 1969-70; ter. mgr. Facelle Royal div. Internat. Paper Co., Phoenix, 1970-71; asst. gen. mgr. Consol. Metal Products div. Schott Industries, Phoenix, 1971; sales mgr. Winlongdin Co., Phoenix, 1972; Western states sales mgr. Cuckler Steel Bldg. Systems div. LSI, Monticello, Iowa, 1972-79, dir. tng., 1979—; cons. in field. Mem. proposed recreation facility program and bldg. City of Monticello, 1981—. Mem. Monticello C. of C. (steering com. 1980-81), Am. Soc. Tng. and Devel., Pi Kappa Alpha. Contbr. articles to profl. jours. Home: 1615 Park Towne Ct NE S-6 Cedar Rapids IA 52402 Office: PO Box 438 Monticello IA 52310

STAUFFER, OSCAR STANLEY, editor, pub.; b. Hope, Kans., Nov. 26, 1886; s. Solomon Engle and Elizabeth (Conrad) S.; student U. Kans., 1908-10; m. Ethel Lucille Stone, Sept. 7, 1914 (dec. July 1964); children—Betty Stauffer Collinson, Stanley Howard, John Herbert; m. 2d, Cornelia Hardcastle, Conwell, July 15, 1965 (dec. July 1973). Reporter, Emporia Gazette, 1906-08, Kansas City (Mo.) Star, 1910-15; editor, owner Peabody (Kans.) Gazette, 1915-24; editor Arkansas City (Kans.) Traveler, 1924-40; editor, pub. Topeka State Jour. and Topeka Daily Capital; chmn. bd., exec. head Stauffer Publs., pubs. Ark. City Daily Traveler, Pittsburg (Kans.) Morning Sun, Grand Island (Nebr.) Daily Ind., Beatrice (Nebr.) Daily Sun, Maryville (Mo.) Daily Forum, Shawnee (Okla.) News & Star, Nevada (Mo.) Daily Mail, York (Nebr.) News Times, Newton (Kans.) Kans., Independence (Mo.) Examiner, Capper's Weekly, Marshall (Mo.) Democrat News, Brookings (S.D.) Register, Glenwood Springs (Colo.) Post, Hillsdale (Mich.) Daily News, Hannibal (Mo.) Courier-Post; pres. KGFF Broadcasting Co., Shawnee, Okla., WIBW-TV, AM-FM, Topeka, KGNC AM-FM, Amarillo, Tex., KSOK Broadcasting Co., Arkansas City, KRNT-AM-FM, Des Moines; former v.p. A.P. Trustee Washburn U., Menninger Found. Former chmn. Kans. Indsl. Devel. Commn., Kans. State Bd. Regents; past pres. Inland Daily Press Assn. Mem. Am. Soc. Newspaper Editors, Beta Theta Pi, Sigma Delta Chi. Republican. Presbyterian. Clubs: Topeka Country, Scottsdale (Ariz.) Villa Monterey, Rotary. Home: 1320 W 27th St Apt 6-44 Topeka KS 66611 Office: 6th and Jefferson Topeka KS 66607

STAUFFER, RICHARD GARY, ednl. adminstr.; b. Vestaburg, Mich., July 15, 1927; s. Clair C. and Mildred (Tupper) S.; B.S., Central Mich. U., 1948; M.A., U. Mich., 1954; Hu.D. (hon.), Am. Coll. Quito (Ecuador), 1970; m. Willa M. Kirkendall, Feb. 25, 1949; children—Christine Lee, Robin Shelley, Jeffrey Todd, Jonathan Clair. Tchr., athletic dir. coach, Vicksburg (Mich.) Community Schs., 1948-54; asst. prof. phys. edn., coach, asso. dir. admissions Alma (Mich.) Coll., 1954-59; co-founder, trustee, exec. v.p. Northwood Inst., Midland, Mich., 1959-74, vice chmn., 1974-78, pres., chief exec. officer, 1978-79, chmn., chief exec. officer, 1979—; mem. Devel. Coop. Ednl. Programs Mgmt., 1959—; dir. devel. First Nat. Automotive Edn. Center Northwood, 1971-73. Clubs: Mid County, Detroit Athletic. Mem. Christian Ch. (elder). Office: Northwood Inst Midland MI 48640

STAVRAKAS, DEAN, textile service co. exec.; b. Chgo., Dec. 6, 1943; s. Sam Gus and Helene (Lazaris) S.; B.A., MacMurray Coll., 1964; grad. Supervisory Devel. Inst., Purdue U., 1976; m. Joanne Stavrakas, Jan. 11, 1970; 1 son, Symeon Dean. With Cosmopolitan Textile Rental Service, Inc., Chgo., 1964—, v.p., gen. mgr., 1970—, mgr. semi-profl. baseball, Chgo. Invited del. 1st Pan Hellenic World Conf., Athens, Greece. Mem. Ill. Commn. for Bus. and Econ. Devel., 1976-77. Mem. Am. Mgmt. Assn., Textile Rental Services Assn. Am., Textile Maintenance Inst. (dir.), Chgo. Conv. and Tourism Bur., Am. Hellenic Ednl. Progressive Assn. (past dist. govt.). Greek Orthodox. Club: Union League (Chgo.). Home: 2961 W Gregory St Chicago IL 60625 Office: Cosmopolitan Textile Rental Service Inc 5730 S Halsted St Chicago IL 60621

STAVROPOULOS, D(IONYSOS) JOHN, banker; b. Vicksburg, Miss., Jan. 19, 1933; s. John D. and Olga Stavropoulos; B.S., Miss. State U., 1955; M.B.A., Northwestern U., 1956; m. Alexandra Gatzoyanni, Jan. 10, 1976; children—John, Theodore, Mark, Olga, Katerina. Various adminstrv. positions trust dept. First Nat. Bank of Chgo., 1956-69, v.p., 1966-75; 1st v.p., dir. research Bache & Co., N.Y.C., 1969-70; various positions in internat. banking dept. First Nat. Bank of Chgo., 1970-76, sr. v.p., 1975, sr. v.p. real estate dept., 1976-79, exec. v.p. comml. banking dept., 1979-80, chmn. credit policy com., 1981—; instr. Northwestern U., Chgo., 1962-68; dir. Central Ill. Public Service, 1974. Served with U.S. Army, 1951-53. Mem. Assn. Res. City Bankers, Chartered Fin. Analysts, Investment Analysts Soc. Chgo., Mortgage Bankers Assn. Am., Robert Morris Assos., Council Fgn. Relations (Chgo. com.). Club: Economic (Chgo.). Office: First National Bank of Chicago One First National Plaza Chicago IL 60670

STAVROS, DENNY, ednl. researcher; b. Wooster, Ohio, Nov. 2, 1929; s. Speros D. and Demetra (Syriopoulou) S.; B.A., Wayne State U., 1952, M.A., 1956, Ph.D., 1972; m. Gwen McFerran, Nov. 9, 1957; children—Jack, Margo. Tchr., Detroit Public Schs., 1954-64, research coordinator Spl. Edn. Vocation Rehab. project, 1964-67, research asso., 1966—, project dir. Quad County, 1975; instr. Wayne State U., 1957, 62-63; research affiliate Center for Mental Health and Research, Athens, Greece, 1967-68. Mem. exec. bd. Am. Hellenic Congress, 1974—, chmn., 1976; bd. advs. Wayne State Press, 1976—; co-chmn. Armenians and Greeks for Carl Levin, Mich., 1978. Found. Fund for Research in Psychiatry grantee, 1967; recipient Conf. Ethnic Communities of Greater Detroit Recognition award, 1970. Mem. Am. Sociol. Assn., Modern Greek Studies Assn., Orgn. Sch. Adminstrs. and Suprs. Greek Orthodox. Home: 2010 Hawthorne Blvd Dearborn MI 48128 Office: 10100 Grand River Rd Detroit MI 48204

STAZEN, PAUL JOSEPH, periodontist; b. Barberton, Ohio, Oct. 19, 1946; s. Paul and Frances Katherine (Guyris) S.; B.A., Kent State U., 1967; D.D.S., Ohio State U., 1971, M.S., 1975; Resident in periodontics Dwight Eisenhower Gen. Hosp., Augusta, Ga., 1971-73, Ohio State U., 1973-75; pvt. practice periodontics, Warren, Ohio, 1975—; asst. prof. periodontics Case Western Res. U., Cleve., 1973—, also Youngstown State U., Trumbell Hosp. Sch. of Nursing. Served with AUS, 1971-73. Mem. Am., Ohio dental assns., Corydon-Palmer Dental Assn., Am., Ohio acads. periodontics, Midwest Soc. Periodontics (bd. dirs.), Am. Assn. Prevention Oral Disease, Ohio State U. Alumni Assn. (mem. bd. govs. 1975—), Beta Beta Beta, Psi Chi, Blue Key. Home: 770 Shadowood Ln Warren OH 44484 Office: 3915 E Market St Warren OH 44484

STEAD, JAMES JOSEPH, JR., securities co. exec.; b. Chgo., Sept. 13, 1930; s. James Joseph and Irene (Jennings) S.; B.S., DePaul U., 1955, M.B.A., 1957; m. Edith Pearson, Feb. 13, 1954; children—James, Diane, Robert, Caroline. Asst. sec. C. F. Childs & Co., Chgo., 1955-62; exec. v.p., sec. Koenig, Keating & Stead, Inc., Chgo., 1962-66; 2d v.p., mgr. midwest municipal bond dept. Hayden, Stone Inc., Chgo., 1966-69; sr. v.p., nat. sales mgr. Ill. Co. Inc., 1969-70; mgr. instl. sales dept. Reynolds and Co., Chgo., 1970-72; partner Edwards & Hanly, 1972-74; v.p., instnl. sales mgr. Paine, Webber, Jackson & Curtis, 1974-76; v.p., regional instl. sales mgr. Reynolds Securities, Inc., 1976-78; v.p., regional mgr. Oppenheimer & Co., Inc., 1978—; instr. Mcpl. Bond Sch., Chgo., 1967—. Served with AUS, 1951-53. Mem. Security Traders Assn. Chgo., Nat. Security Traders Assn., Am. Mgmt. Assn., Municipal Finance Forum Washington. Clubs: Executives, Union League, Municipal Bond, Bond (Chgo.); Olympia Fields Country (Ill.); Wall Street (N.Y.C.). Home: 20721 Brookwood Dr Olympia Fields IL 60461 Office: 208 S LaSalle St Chicago IL 60604

STEADMAN, JACK W., profl. football exec.; b. Warrenville, Ill., Sept. 14, 1928; s. Walter Angus and Vera Ruth (Burkholder) S.; B.A., So. Methodist U., 1950; m. Martha Cudworth Steinhoff, Nov. 24, 1949; children—Thomas Edward, Barbara Ann, Donald Wayne. Accountant, Hunt Oil Co., Dallas, 1950-54; chief's acct. W.H. Hunt, Dallas, 1954-58; chief acct. Penrod Drilling Co., Dallas, 1958-60; gen. mgr. Dallas Texans Football Club, 1960-63; gen. mgr. Kansas City Chiefs Football Club, 1963-76, exec. v.p., 1966-76, pres., 1976—; pres. Mid-Am. Enterprises (Worlds of Fun), Kansas City, 1972—; v.p. First Fidelity Investment Trust, Kansas City; dir. Ct. Council; exec. com., bd. dirs. Starlight Theatre Assn., Kansas City; bd. dirs. Kansas City chpt. Fellowship Christian Athletes, 1976, chmn. finance com., 1977; bd. dirs. YMCA, Am. Royal Assn.; mem. exec. com., bd. dirs. Heart of Am. United Way, campaign chmn., 1979; adv. trustee Research Med. Center, Kansas City; deacon Leawood Bapt. Ch. Mem. Greater Kansas City C. of C. (dir. 1976—, chmn. world's fair com. 1976, v.p. membership 1978). Clubs: Kansas City Downtown Rotary, Kansas City, 711 Inner, Brookridge Country (Kansas City). Office: Kansas City Chiefs 1 Arrowhead Dr Kansas City MO 64129*

STEARMAN, SAMUEL WINFREY, mfg. co. exec.; b. Campbellsville, Ky., Apr. 30, 1940; s. Thomas Milton and Annie Lizzie (Berry) S.; B.S. with honors, U. Louisville, 1962; M.B.A., Drake U., 1970; m. Patricia Irene Phelps, May 26, 1973; children—Sheri, Scott, Diane, Sean, Eric. Sr. auditor Arthur Young, Chgo., 1962-66; asst. controller Gen. Box Co., Des Plaines, Ill., 1966-67; fin. mgr. Massey Ferguson, Inc., Des Moines, 1967-70; corporate controller Internat. Dairy Queen, Mpls., 1970-72; mgr. acctg. Youngstown Sheet and Tube Co. (Ohio), Lykes Corp., 1972-74; controller Van Huffel Tube Corp., Warren, Ohio, 1974-76, Essex group Telecommunication Products div. United Technologies, Decatur, Ill., 1976—. Bd. dirs. Jr. Achievement of Decatur, 1978—, pres., 1980—. C.P.A., Ill. Mem. Am. Inst. C.P.A.'s. Republican. Methodist. Home: 2610 Forrest Green Dr Decatur IL 62521 Office: 800 E Garfield Ave Decatur IL 62525

STEARNS, DAN HUNTER, curator; b. Lawrence County, Mo., July 13, 1909; s. Udell and Pernie Otis (Hunter) S.; student Joplin Bus. Coll., 1929-30; m. Thelma Lucille Duke, May 26, 1940; children—Lana Stearns Kern, Michael A., Linden G., Brent, Jan D. Operator, mgr. Stearns Food Store, Mt. Vernon, Mo., 1932-36; bookkeeper Lawrence County Treas. Office, 1938; asst. to mortician, salesman Fossett Funeral Home, Mt. Vernon, 1939-42; mgr., operator farm, Mt. Vernon, 1942-46; owner, operator Stearns Elec. Contracting Service, Mt. Vernon, 1946-67; electrician Mo. State Chest Hosp., Mount Vernon, 1967-75; accountant Yellowstone Nat. Park, 1975; curator, dir. Lawrence County Hist. Soc. Mus., Mt. Vernon, 1976-81. 4-H Club leader, counsel mem., 1937-40. Mem. Lawrence County Hist. Soc. (pres. 1969-77). Democrat. Presbyn. (elder 1942-77). Author: (with others) A Brief History of Lawrence County Mo. 1845-1970, 1970; (with others) A History of Lawrence County Missouri, 1975. Home: 210 N Main St Mount Vernon MO 65712

STEBBINS, ROBERT JOE, univ. alumni adminstr.; b. Mishawaka, Ind., Dec. 27, 1926; s. Lyle Ralph and Rena Idell (Buckland) S.; B.S., Ind. U., 1951; m. Carolyn Ann Warner, June 13, 1953; children—Elizabeth Ann, Annette Marie, Robert Joe, Lara Lynn. Instr. phys. edn., athletic coach DePauw U., 1952-53; with Ind. U. Alumni Assn., Bloomington, 1953-70, club dir., asst., then asso. alumni sec., also exec. asso. capital fund drive campaigns Ind. U., 1970-71, now adminstr. alumni office, program dir., exec. asso. Ind. U. Found, Bloomington, 1970-78. Active United Fund, 1965-74, City and County Planning and Zoning Commn., 1974-81; pres. County Plan Commn., 1975-78; chmn. United Fund, 1973, Hwy. Task Force, 1965; county dir. CD, 1960-64; precinct chmn. Republican Party,

1970-73. Served with AUS, 1945-46, USAF, 1951-52. Mem. Am. Soc. Assn. Execs., Council for Advancement and Support of Edn. Methodist. Clubs: University, Kiwanis. Home: 8101 S Victor Pike Bloomington IN 47401 Office: Ind Univ Alumni Assn IMU M-17 Bloomington IN 47405

STEBBINS, RODNEY JEROME, epoxy mfg. co. exec.; b. Klamath Falls, Oreg., July 2, 1936; s. Lester Siral and Volna Grace S.; B.S. in Constrn. Mgmt. and Engring., S.D. Sch. Mines and Tech., 1975; m. Kyong Suk Kim, Nov. 25, 1978; 1 son, Rodney Jerome. Contract adminstr. Premier Waterproofing Co., Denver, 1973-75; project mgr. Harrison Western Corp., Denver, 1975; program mgr. Foster-Miller & Assos., Waltham, Mass., 1978; v.p. adminstrn. Grain Spouting & Elevators of Kans., Inc., Hutchingson, 1979; v.p. Splty. Applications Corp., Reston, Va., 1980-81, Thermal-Chem, Inc., Elk Grove Village, Ill., 1981—; research coms. Urban and Mass Transp. Authority, Washington, 1977-78; cons., speaker, lectr., author in field. Served with USMC, 1953-56; Korea. Named to Hon. Order Ky. Cols., 1978. Mem. Am. Concrete Inst. (coms.), Transp. Research Bd. (coms.). Republican. Club: Rotary. Home: 1596 Manchester Rd Hoffman Estates IL 60195 Office: 1400 Louis Ave Elk Grove Village IL 60007

STEBEN, RAYMOND HENRY, JR., fluid transfer components mfg. co.; b. Elmhurst, Ill., Nov. 14, 1938; s. Raymond Henry and Emily S.; B.S., Iowa State U., 1961; M.B.A., U. Pa., 1965; m. Ann Candor Walby, Oct. 6, 1962; children—Tyler, Amy. Sr. systems analyst, subs. planning dir. Cummins Engine Co., 1965-69; v.p. Agrl. Computing Co., 1969-70; sr. cons. Internat. Research & Ventures Co., 1970-71; cons. McKinsey & Co., 1971-76; v.p. planning, controller Bundy Corp., Detroit, 1976-81, v.p. fin., chief fin. officer, 1981—. Served with USAR, 1961-63. C.P.A., Tex. Mem. Am. Inst. C.P.A.'s, Fin. Execs. Inst. (chpt. dir.). Club: Detroit Athletic. Office: 12345 E 9 Mile Rd Warren MI 48090

STECKLER, WILLIAM ELWOOD, judge; b. Mt. Vernon, Ind., Oct. 18, 1913; s. William Herman and Lena (Menikheim) S.; LL.B., Ind. Law Sch., 1936; J.D., 1937; LL.D., Wittenberg U., Springfield, Ohio, 1958; H.H.D., Ind. Central Coll., 1969; m. Vitallas Alting, Oct. 15, 1938; children—William Rudolph, David Alan. Admitted to Ind. bar, 1936, practiced in Indpls., 1937-50, mem. firm Key & Steckler; pub. counselor Pub. Service Commn., State Ind., 1949-50; judge U.S. Dist. Ct. So. Dist. Ind., 1950—, now chief judge. Served as seaman USN, 1943. Mem. Am., Fed., Ind., Indpls. bar assns., Am. Judicature Soc., Nat. Lawyers Club, Jud. Conf. U.S., Am. Legion, Order of Coif, Sigma Delta Kappa. Democrat. Lutheran. Mason (33 deg., Shriner). Club: Indianapolis Athletic. Home: 30 Jurist Ln Lamb Lake Trafalgar IN 46181 Office: US Courthouse 46 E Ohio Indianapolis IN 46204

STEDMAN, ERVIN FRANK, info. processing cons. co. exec.; b. St. Louis, July 27, 1937; s. E. Frank and Lydia Ella (Vogt) S.; A.A., Harris Tchrs. Coll., 1958; B.S., U. Mo., 1972; m. Patricia Sue Williams, Aug. 23, 1958; children—Beth, David, Daniel, Dean. With Maritz Motivation Co. div. Maritz Inc., Fenton, Mo., 1963-80, asst. mgr., 1965-66, mgr., 1967-69, dir., 1969-72, v.p. adminstrn., 1972-75, v.p. ops., 1975-78, corp. v.p., 1978-80; pres. Erv Stedman & Assos., info. processing cons., Chesterfield, Mo., 1980—; dir. Glenn Meadows Ltd. Served with U.S. Army, 1960-63. Mem. Adminstrv. Mgmt. Soc. (dir. systems), Internat. Word Processing Assn. (pres. St. Louis chpt. 1977, internat. dir. 1976, 77, internat. pres. 1978), U. Mo. St. Louis Alumni Assn., Creve Coeur Khoury League. Office: 15438 Harrisburg Ct Chesterfield MO 63017

STEELE, CLEMENT JOSEPH, computer cons.; b. Waukon, Iowa, June 16, 1937; s. Burnill William and Susan Lois (Stubstad) S.; student Marquette U., 1955-56; B.A., Loras Coll., 1961; postgrad. Ill. Inst. Tech., 1964, Lawrence U., 1966, U. Wyo., 1971, U. Iowa, 1972, U. Wis., 1973-76; M.S., Rutgers U., 1968; m. Mary Jane Valley, Aug. 11, 1962; children—Maureen, Teresa, Daniel. Tchr. math. Jefferson Jr. High Sch., Dubuque, 1961-63, Lake Forest (Ill.) High Sch., 1963-67, Campion Acad., Prairie du Chien, Wis., 1968-73; math. supervisory intern Milw. public schs., 1973-74; teaching asst., research asst. U. Wis., Madison, 1974-76; research and evaluation cons. Keystone Area Edn. Agy., Dubuque, 1976-77; instructional computer cons., computer center dir. Keystone Area Edn. Agy., 1977—; guest lectr. in research Clarke Coll., 1978-81; instr. Loras Coll., 1979-81. Served with U.S. Army, 1961. Named Outstanding Young Educator, Wis. Jaycees, 1972; NSF grantee, 1973-74. Mem. Iowa Assn. for Ednl. Data Systems (bd. dirs. 1980-82), Nat. Council Tchrs. Math., Nat. Council Suprs. Math., Iowa Council Tchrs. Math., Tri-State Data Processing Assn., Phi Delta Kappa. Roman Catholic. Club: Lions. Contbr. articles to profl. jours. Home: 2371 Carter Rd Dubuque IA 52001 Office: 1473 Central Ave Dubuque IA 52001

STEELE, DANIEL LEE, computer programmer; b. Wenatchee, Wash., Jan. 1, 1941; s. Danton Gibbs and Blanche Marion (Wynhoff) S.; B.S., U. Mo., 1962, M.A., 1969. Computer programmer, engring. sect. Mo. Hwy. Dept., Jefferson City, 1969-81. Served with USN, 1962-66. Mem. Math. Assn. Am., Am. Contract Bridge League, VFW, Mensa. Methodist. Home: 416 Brooks St Jefferson City MO 65101

STEELE, DARRELL STANLEY, veterinarian; b. Treynor, Iowa, Sept. 30, 1917; s. Carroll Chester and Hazel Lydia (Redman) S.; D.V.M., Kans. State U., 1939; m. Betty Jean Guyot, Feb. 1, 1936; children—Richard, Suzanne. Dir. small animal biol. products Pitman Moore Co., Zionsville, Ind., 1939-41; practice veterinary medicine specializing in small animals, Mpls., 1947—; pres. Minn. Veterinary Exam. Bd. Trustee North Methodist Ch., Mpls., 1959-63, chmn. ofcl. bd., 1961-63. Served to lt. col. U.S. Army, 1941-47; col. USAF, Res. Mem. Am., Minn. veterinary med. assns., Am., Met. (pres. 1956-57), animal hosp. assns., Midwest Small Animal Assn. (pres. 1958-59, Distinguished Service award 1960), Kans. State U. Vet. Alumni Assn. (pres. 1970), Res. Officers Assn. Clubs: Minn. 100 (v.p. 1978-79, pres. 1980-81), Midland Hills Country (pres. 1959-60), Masons, Jesters, Shriners. Home: 584 Westwood Village Saint Paul MN 55113 Office: 1332 Marshall St NE Minneapolis MN 55413

STEELE, EMMETT MITCHELE, music educator, condr.; b. Waverly, Iowa; s. Emmett M. and Mildred D. (McInroy) S.; B.A., U. of No. Iowa, 1949; student Juilliard Sch. Music, 1950; M.M., Eastman Sch. Music, 1953; further studies Sorbonne, Mozarteum; pvt. studies Pierre Monteux, Andre de Ribaupierre, Walter Hendl, Lorvo von Matacic, Leon Barzin, Milton Preves. Faculty Kemper Mil. Coll., 1953-54, North Central Coll., 1954-57, Cosmopolitan Sch. Music, Chgo., 1957-64, U. Ill., 1959-65, Park Forest (Ill.) Conservatory, 1960—, Inst. Musica Viva Lausanne, Switzerland, 1965—; mem. faculty Chgo. Conservatory Coll. 1967—, now dean, v.p. bd. trustees, head music history and lit. dept.; string adviser North Chicago (Ill.) Schs., 1957-59; string supr. Nat. Music Camp; condr., founder Concerts Symphoniques; condr. Chgo. Suburban Symphony, Emmett Steele Chorale, Handel Choral Soc.; officer Inter-Continental Records and Musica Viva Records; organizer, dir. Brush Hill Music Theatre; violist in Quintet Musica Viva-resident quintet Chgo. Conservatory Coll., 1967—; concert mgmt. Gosta Schwark, Copenhagen, Denmark; owner, pres. Internat. Art Assos., Ltd.; dir. Emmett Steele Gallery, Inc. Named nat. patron, Phi Beta, 1963. Mem. Condrs. Club N.Y., AAUP, Soc. Am. Musicians, Phi Mu Alpha, Alpha Phi Omega. Author: The Materials of Music. Home: 1439 Brassie Ave Flossmoor IL 60422

STEELE, HILDA HODGSON, home economist; b. Wilmington, Ohio, Mar. 24, 1911; d. George and Mary Jane (Rolston) Hodgson; A.A., Wilmington Coll., 1931, B.S., 1935; M.A. in Home Econs. Edn., Ohio State U., 1941; postgrad. Ohio U., 1954, Miami U., 1959; m. John C. Steele (dec. Jan. 1973). Tchr., Brookville (Ohio) Elementary Sch., 1932-37; tchr. home econs. Lincoln Jr. High Sch., Dayton (Ohio) Pub. Schs., 1937-40, coordinator home econs. dept., traveling exptl. home econs. tchr., 1940-45, supr. home econs., 1945-81, cons., 1981—; program dir. Family Life Adult Disadvantaged Program, 1969—. Mem. Ohio Farm Electrification Com., 1964-66. Mem. town and country br. career com. Miami Valley br. YMCA, 1948-59. Adv. bd. Dayton Sch. Practical Nursing, 1951—; adv. com. Dayton Miami Valley Hosp. Sch. Nursing, 1951-63; jr. adv. com. Montgomery County chpt. ARC, 1940-80; mem. com. United Appeal, 1970—; bd. dirs. (Ohio) FHA-HERO, 1979-81. Mem. Dayton area Nutrition Council, Am. (del. 1961), Ohio (chmn. elementary and secondary edn. com. 1947-51, co-chmn. ann. conv. 1961-77, mem. housing and equipment coms. 1965-68, chmn. found. com. 1981—), Dayton Met. (pres. 1949-50, 60-61) home econ. assns., Nat., Ohio edn. assns., Ohio Council Local Adminstrs., Dayton Sch. Adminstrs. Assn. (pres. 1960-61), Elec. Women's Round Table, Dayton City Sch. Mgmt. Assn. (charter), Ohio Vocat. Assn. (Disting. Service award 1981), Am. Vocat. Edn. Assn., Ohio Vocat. Edn. Assn. Mem. Ch. of Christ. Mem. Order Eastern Star. Club: Zonta (pres. Dayton 1950-52). Research in pub. sch. food habits, 1957. Home: 1443 State Route 380 Xenia OH 45385 Office: 348 W 1st St Dayton OH 45402

STEELE, IRA MAI, ednl. adminstr.; b. Cleve., June 24, 1952; s. Ira Jefferson and Audria Mai Steele; student Cuyahoga Community Coll., Cleve., 1969-71; B.S. in Elem. Edn., Tenn. State U., 1973; M.S. in Elem. Edn., Ind. U.-Purdue U., Indpls., 1977; supervision and adminstrn. cert. Butler U., 1982. Tchr. elem. sch., Danville, Ill., 1973-74, Columbia, Tenn., 1974-75; facilitator Center for Leadership Devel., Indpls., 1977-79; tchr. elem. schs. Indpls. Public Schs., 1975-80, Title VII multicultural tng. specialist dept. human relations, 1980-81, Title VI in-service tng. cons., 1981—; del. Ind. Tchrs. Conf., 1977-79. Vice precinct committeeman Indpls. Democratic Com., 1976—; mem. youth adv. council Center for Leadership Devel., 1975-81; vice chmn. Indpls. Polit. Action Com., 1977-78; senate coordinator Sch. 81, Operation P.U.S.H., Indpls., 1980; vol. cons. Center Twp. Young Citizens, Indpls., 1980-81. Named hon. sheriff and bailiff Marion County, Indpls., 1978; recipient recognition award Indpls. Public Schs. Bd. Sch. Commrs., 1980, plaque of appreciation Center for Leadership Devel., 1981. Mem. Assn. for Supervision and Curriculum Devel., Soc. for Intensified Edn. (Outstanding Classroom Tchr. award 1980), Ind. Tchrs. Assn. (music multicultural com. 1980-82), Tenn. State U. Alumni (v.p., scholarship chmn. Indpls. chpt. 1979-82), Indpls. Edn. Assn. (profl. relations chmn. 1978-79). Methodist. Clubs: The Committee, Elks. Home: 818 W 27th St Indianapolis IN 46208 Office: 120 E Walnut St Room 704-H Indianapolis IN 46202

STEELE, OLIVER LEON, seed co. exec.; b. Ill., Apr. 8, 1915; s. Blondee Wood and Mary (Eagle) S.; student Ill. State Normal U., 1934-35; B.S., Ill. Wesleyan U., 1940; postgrad. U. Ill., 1945-48; D.Sc. (hon.), Ill. Wesleyan U., 1967; m. Ruth Marie Holbert, June 21, 1941; children—David, Dennis, Nancy. Research asso. Michael-Leonard Seed Co., 1936-40; mgr. research dept. Funk Seeds Internat., 1940-52, asso. research dir., 1952-57, research dir., 1957-78, v.p., 1963-78, research cons., 1978—. Mem. AAAS, Soc. Agronomy, Bot. Soc., Genetics Soc., Genetic Assn. Presbyn. (elder). Rotarian. Home: 804 Broadway St Normal IL 61761 Office: 1300 W Washington St Bloomington IL 61701

STEELEY, CHARLES BEAUMONT, toy mfg. co. exec.; b. Phila., Dec. 18, 1931; s. George Tindall and Florence Ruth S.; B.A., Pa. State U., 1953; m. Mary Ann Simon, July 9, 1955; children—Susan Christine, William Charles. Sales and mktg. mgr. Solar Products Corp., 1955-66; nat. sales mgr. Dialogue Mktg., Inc. subs. Time, Inc., 1967-72; v.p. mktg. Athena Communications Corp. div. Gulf & Western Industries, 1972-74; gen. mgr. Skilcraft div. Western Pub. Co., Inc., Racine, Wis., 1974—. Served with AUS, 1953-55. Club: Llanerch Country (Havertown, Pa.). Home: 4340 Lighthouse Dr Racine WI 53402 Office: PO Box 705 Racine WI 53404

STEEMER, ALMETA DANIELS, health care exec.; b. Montgomery, Ala., Mar. 30, 1924; d. Roosevelt and Marie (Glenn) Daniels; student Ala. Tchrs. Coll., 1940-41, Clark Coll., Atlanta, 1941-42; grad. Homer G. Phillips Hosp. Sch. Med. Record Sci., St. Louis, 1960; B.A., Roosevelt U., 1974, M.P.A., 1980; m. Herbert Smith, Feb. 12, 1944 (div.); children—Michele Adrian Smith Johnson, Michael Julian Smith, Marcia Juanyta Smith Lanier; m. 2d, Elwood Steemer, Dec. 23, 1961 (dec. 1968). Dir. med. record dept. U. Nebr. Hosp., Omaha, 1960-63, Nat. Jewish Hosp., Denver, 1963-66; dir. med. record dept. Fitzsimmons Army Hosp., Denver, 1966-69, grievance examiner, 1968-69; dir. med. record dept. Wright Patterson AFB Hosp., Dayton, Ohio, 1969-71; dir. med. records systems Charles R. Drew Neighborhood Health Center, Dayton, 1969-72; med. record cons. HEW Regional Office, Chgo., 1972—; evaluator State Health Dept. Survey Agys., EEO counselor, 1972-74. Mem. Am. Med. Record Assn., Nebr., Omaha (pres. 1963), No. Colo. (pres. 1965-66), Colo. (pres. 1968) assns. med. record adminstrs., Eta Phi Beta (pres. 1980—), Nat. Assn. Health Service Execs. Unity. Contbr. articles to profl. publs. Home: 9252 S Michigan Ave Chicago IL 60619 Office: 175 W Jackson St Chicago IL 60604

STEEN, EDWIN BENZEL, biologist, author; b. Wheeling, Ind., July 23, 1901; s. Henry Wylie and Lora May (Benzel) S.; student Mo. Valley Coll., 1919-20; A.B., Wabash Coll., 1923; A.M., Columbia U., 1926; Ph.D., Purdue U., 1938; m. Harriet Ellen Lewis, July 23, 1927; children—Marjorie Alice (Mrs. Dayton D. Dickinson), Philip Lewis. Instr. zoology Wabash Coll., Crawfordsville, Ind., 1923-25, acting head dept., 1926-27; grad. asst. N.Y. U., 1926; instr. zoology U. Cin., 1927-31; instr., also asst. in agrl. expt. sta. Purdue U., 1931-38; instr. biology Coll. City N.Y., 1938-41; asst. prof. Western Mich. U., Kalamazoo, 1941-46, asso. prof., 1946-52, prof. biology, 1952-72, prof. emeritus, 1972—, head dept., 1963-65. Mem. Mich. Bd. Examiners in Basic Scis., 1960-63. Bd. dirs. Kalamazoo chpt. Mich. Soc. Mental Health, 1958-65. Mem. AAAS, Am. Inst. Biol. Scis., N.Y. Acad. Sci., Mich. Acad. Sci., Arts and Letters, Sigma Xi. Author: (with Ashley Montagu) Anatomy and Physiology, 1959; Dictionary of Abbreviations in Medicine, 1960; Dictionary of Biology, 1971; (with J.H. Price) Human Sex and Sexuality, 1977; also lab. manuals in anatomy and physiology. Contbg. editor: Taber's Cyclopedic Medical Dictionary, 1973, Acronyms, Initialisms and Abbreviations Dictionary, 1978. Home: 2011 Greenlawn Ave Kalamazoo MI 49007 Office: Western Michigan University Kalamazoo MI 49008

STEEN, JAN PHAFF, banker; b. Frederiksberg, Denmark, Jan. 31, 1935; s. Thomas Lais and Else Steen; B.A., Copenhagen State Coll., 1954; M.B.A., Copenhagen Comml. U., 1956; m. Diana Adelaide Buffington. Trainee, East Asiatic Co., Copenhagen, 1954; adminstrv. asst. USAF Base Exchange, Sondrestrom AFB, Greenland, 1959-60; purchase sales mgr., Royal Greenland Trade Dept., Copenhagen, 1960-63; comml. attache Royal Danish Consulate Gen., Kuwait, 1964-65; asst. v.p., mgr. Privatbanken Copenhagen, 1966-69; internt. mgr. Winters Nat. Bank & Trust Co., Dayton, Ohio, 1969-71, asst. v.p., 1971-73, v.p., div. mgr., 1973-77, sr. v.p., 1977—. Pres., Dayton Council World Affairs, 1977-79; gov. Ohio Adv. Council Internat. Trade, 1974-78; treas. So. Ohio Dist. Export Council, 1975; bd. dirs. Dayton Opera Assn. Served with Royal Danish Army, 1956-58. Danish Dept. Commerce Export fellow, 1964. Mem. Dayton C. of C. (chmn. world trade council 1974-75), Bankers Assn. Fgn. Trade, Robert Morris Assos., Res. Officers Assn. (hon.), Assn. U.S. Army. Club: Dayton Racquet. Contbr. articles to profl. jours. Office: Winters Nat Bank & Trust Co Winters Bank Tower Dayton OH 45401

STEEN, LOWELL HARRISON, physician; b. Kenosha, Wis., Nov. 27, 1923; s. Joseph Arthur and Camilla Marie (Henriksen) S.; B.S., Ind. U., 1945, M.D., 1948; m. Cheryl Ann Rectanus, Nov. 20, 1969; children—Linda C., Laura A., Lowell Harrison, Heather J., Kirsten M. Intern, Mercy Hosp.-Loyola U. Clinics, Chgo., 1948-49; resident in internal medicine VA Hosp., Hines, Ill., 1950-53; practice medicine specializing in internal medicine, Hammond, Ind., 1953—; pres., chief exec. officer Whiting Clinic; mem. sr. staff St. Catherine Hosp., E. Chicago, Ind.; bd. commrs. Joint Commn. Accreditation of Hosps. Served with M.C., AUS, 1949-50, 55-56. Fellow Am. Geriatric Soc., A.C.P.; mem. AMA (trustee 1975, chmn. bd. trustees 1979-81), Ind. Med. Assn. (pres. 1970, chmn. bd. 1968-69), World Med. Assn. (dir. 1978—, chmn. bd. dirs. council 1980—, del. World Assembly), Ind. Soc. Internal Medicine (pres. 1963), Lake County Med. Soc. Methodist. Home: 8800 Parkway Dr Highland IN 46322 Office: 2450 169th St Hammond IN 46323

STEFANOVICH, ROBERT JAMES, child day care cons.; b. Stambaugh, Mich., June 23, 1945; s. Albin John and Beryl Jean (Dallifior) S.; B.A. in Social Psychology, Oakland U., 1968, M.A.T., 1970; Ed.D., Wayne State U., 1981. Asst. elementary coordinator St. Andrews Elem. Sch., Rochester, Mich., 1968-71; tchr., dir. recreation and pre-sch. programs Avondale Sch. Dist., Auburn Heights, Mich., 1971-75; child day care licensing cons. State Mich., Lansing, 1975—; co-chmn. Sch. Dist. Spelling Com., 1973-75. Mem. com. Enrollment Study Commn., Avondale Sch. Dist., 1974-75, mem. planning com. community edn. 1975-75. Chrysler Corp. Fellowship grantee, 1964-68. Mem. Oakland Univ. Alumni Assn., Edn. Alumni Assn., NEA, Mich. State Employees Assn., Assn. Supervision and Curriculum Devel., Nat. Assn. Edn. Young Children, Mich. Assn. Edn. Young Children, Metro Detroit Assn. Edn. Young Children (area co-chmn.), Phi Delta Kappa. Republican. Roman Catholic. Home: 314 Lesdale St Troy MI 48098 Office: 1010 W Maple St Walled Lake MI 48088

STEFFAN, LLOYD JOHN, physician; b. Fond du Lac, Wis., Apr. 7, 1918; s. John L. and Frances A. (Kalt) S.; student Lawrence U., 1938-40, Northwestern U., 1940-41; M.D., George Washington U., 1944; m. Sirley J. Hafemeister, Apr. 25, 1947; children—John, Mary (Mrs. Alfred Harney), Michael, Ann Kathryn (Mrs. Michael Baumgartner), Peter. Intern, U.S. Naval Hosp., Great Lakes, Ill., 1944-45; gen. practice medicine, Plymouth, Wis., 1946—; partner Plymouth Clinic, 1946—; chief of staff Plymouth Hosp. Health officer City of Plymouth, 1952—. Vice pres., dir. Dairy State Bank, Plymouth, 1959—. Served with USNR, 1942-46. Mem. AMA, Am. Acad. Family Practitioners, Wis. Med. Soc., Wis. Soc. Obstetrics and Gynecology. Roman Catholic. Club: Sheboygan Country. Home: 824 Riverview Dr Plymouth WI 53073 Office: 1000 Eastern Ave Plymouth WI 53073

STEFFEL, PATRICIA EILEEN STEADMAN, nurse; b. Youngstown, Ohio, Apr. 21, 1924; d. Patrick and Mary Elizabeth (Farrell) Steadman; diploma St. Elizabeth Hosp. Sch. Nursing, Youngstown, 1945; cert. public health Case Western Res. U., 1946, B.S. in Nursing, 1948, M.S. in Nursing, 1964; m. George L. Steffel, Apr. 30, 1949; children—Patrick, Kevin (dec.), Charles, Gerry. Staff nurse St. Elizabeth Hosp., Youngstown, 1945; staff nurse, supr./instr. Vis. Nurse Assn., Cleve., 1946-50, 55-56; research asst. Tchrs. Coll., Columbia U., 1958-59; patient instr., coordinator patient teaching and continuity of care Cleve. Met. Gen. Hosp., 1959-62, acting dir. Sch. Nursing, 1976; med. supr. Univ. Hosps., Cleve., 1964-67; dir. nursing Health Hill Hosp. for Children, Cleve., 1967-70, Highland View Hosp., Cleve., 1970—, Sunny Acres Skilled Nursing Facility, 1975—; asst. clin. prof. med. surg. nursing Case Western Res. U., Cleve., 1965-67, 74—; adj. asst. prof. nursing Kent State U., 1981. Recipient Greater Cleve. Nurse Assn. Nurse Adminstr. award, 1980; Mindwendam Found. grantee, 1977. Mem. Am. Nurses Assn., Ohio Nurses Assn., Greater Cleve. Nurses Assn. (dir. 1972-77), Am. Hosp. Assn., Assn. Advancement Nursing Practice, Am. Soc. Hosp. Nursing Service Adminstrs. (charter), Nat. League Nursing, Cleve. Area Citizen League Nursing, Nat. Rehab. Assn., Ohio Rehab. Assn., N.E. Ohio Rehab. Assn., Nat. Spinal Cord Injury Found., Am. Congress Rehab. Medicine, Ohio Assn. Rehab. Nurses (charter), Assn. Rehab. Nurses, Ohio Hosp. Assn., Ohio Soc. Hosp. Nursing Service Adminstrs., Fedn. Community Planning. Home: 910 Colony Dr Highland Heights OH 44143 Office: 3395 Scranton Rd Cleveland OH 44109

STEFFENSEN, POUL VILHELM, adminstrv. mech. engr.; b. Copenhagen, Denmark, Mar. 26, 1922; s. Carl Christian Vilhelm Frederik and Anna (Svenson) S.; came to U.S., 1951, naturalized, 1955; B.S. in Mech. Engring., Marine Engring. Acad., Copenhagen, 1944; m. Elie Pedersen, July 18, 1951; children—Paul, Carl. Mech. engr. Sumner Sollitt Co., Chgo., 1957-63; mech. engr. Mid-Am. Engrs. Inc., Chgo., 1963-65; mgr. design engring. Commonwealth Assn., Chgo., 1965-71; sr. mech. engr. Consoer Townsend & Assos., Chgo., 1971-75; sr. environ. engr. P & W Engrs. Inc., Chgo., 1975-78; project mgr. Henningson, Durham & Richardson, Omaha, 1978—. Mem. bd. Danish Old People's Home, Chgo., 1964-78, pres., 1970-73; dir. Danish Am. Lang. Found. Decorated knight Order of Dannebrog (Denmark). Mem. Am. Soc. Mech. Engrs., Tech. Assn. Pulp Paper Industry, Am. Scandinavian Found., Rebild Nat. Park Soc., Smithsonian Nat. Assn., Danish Am. Athletic Club (hon., pres. 1960-65), Dansk Samvirke. Home: 10308 P St Omaha NE 68127 Office: 8404 Indian Hills Dr Omaha NE 68114

STEFFEY, WILLIAM GARNETT, city mgr.; b. Albion, Neb., Jan. 17, 1914; s. Irvin Harvey and Mary (Horne) S.; B.S. in Engring., U. Tenn., 1937; postgrad. N.Y. U., 1950; M.A. in Govt. Adminstrn., George Washington U., 1962; postgrad. Am. U., 1962—; m. Barbara Hennigan, Nov. 29, 1957; 1 dau., Melinda Mary. Commd. 2d lt. C.E., U.S. Army, 1937, advanced through grades to lt. col., 1950; tchr. advanced engring. Engr. Sch., Ft. Belvior, Va., 1947-50; tchr. engring. Paraguayan Nat. War Coll., Asuncion, 1954-57, engring. cons. to minister pub. works Paraguay, 1954-57; ret., 1961; city mgr. Tazewell, Va., 1961-65, Lewiston, Ida., 1965-71; Addison, Ill., 1971—. Tchr. higher math. Bluefield (W.Va.) State Coll., 1963-64. Decorated Grand Master Nat. Order of Merit. Pres. of Paraguay, 1957; recipient certificate appreciation for civic responsibility Gov. Va., 1963; named hon. citizen Lexington, Ky., 1968, hon. citizen, Lewiston, 1971. Mem. Internat. City Mgrs. Assn., Am. Pub. Works Assn., Permanent Internat. Assn. Nav. Congresses, Soc. Am. Mil. Engrs., Nat. Municipal League, Nat. League Cities, Ill. Municipal League, Assn.

Ida. Cities, Acad. Polit. Sci., Am. Acad. Arts and Scis., Am. Acad. Polit. and Social Scis., Am. Soc. Pub. Adminstrn., Ret. Officers Assn., Pub. Personnel Assn., Internat. Platform Assn., Lambda Chi Alpha, Alpha Chi Sigma. Mason (32 deg., Shriner). Rotarian. Clubs: Wayfarers (N.Y.C.); Lehigh Acres (Fla.) Country. Home: 231 Wood Dale Rd Addison IL 60101 Office: City Hall 130 Army Trail Rd Addison IL 60101

STEFKA, RICHARD STEPHAN, corp. exec.; b. Cleve., Apr. 22, 1951; s. Steve Joseph and Grace Ann (Gedgaud) S.; B.B.A. in Mktg., Cleve. State U., 1973, M.B.A. in Fin., 1979; m. Brigitte G. Pietzonka, Aug. 28, 1971. Asst. to pres. Juno Inc., Cleve., 24 1973-74; mktg. asst., acting mktg. mgr. Automatic Sprinkler Corp. div. ATO Inc., Broadview Heights, Ohio, 1974-76; mktg. analyst Ameritrust Corp., 1976-78, corp. planning officer, 1978-81, asst. v.p., 1981—. Mem. N.Am. Soc. Corp. Planning (chpt. dir.), Nat. Assn. of Bus. Economists. Clubs: U.S. Power Squadrons (asst. edn. officer). Home: 10769 Waterfall Rd Strongsville OH 44136 Office: 900 Euclid Ave Cleveland OH 44101

STEIDL, RICHARD MEREDITH, pathologist; b. Marion, N.D., Jan. 5, 1927; s. Martin Terence and Tressie (Keller) S.; B.S., N.D. State U., 1949; B.A., U. N.D., 1950, B.S., 1951; M.D., Albany Med. Coll., 1953; m. Virginia Whitley, Sept. 25, 1954; children—Scott Meredith, James Douglas. Intern, Presbyn.-St. Luke's Hosp., Chgo., 1953-54; resident in anatomic pathology U. Minn., 1957-59, in clin. pathology, 1959-61; practice medicine specializing in pathology, Mpls., 1963-82, Dayton, Ohio, 1982—; former mem. staffs Mercy, Unity, Glenwood Hills hosps.; chief lab. services VA Med. Center, Dayton, 1982—; instr. clin. pathology and phys. medicine and rehab. U. Minn., 1961-62, asst. prof., 1962-63; dir. labs. Glenwood Hills Hosp., Mpls., 1963-65, Mercy Hosp., Anoka, 1965-74; pres. Doctors Diagnostic Labs., Mpls., 1974-77. Bd. dirs. Met. Youth Symphonies, 1971-74, pres. bd. dirs., 1973-74. Served with USNR, 1944-46. Recipient Merit award City of Mpls. Com. on Urban Environment, 1976. Diplomate Am. Bd. Pathology. Mem. Coll. Am. Pathologists, Am. Soc. Clin. Pathologists, Am. Soc. Cytology, Internat. Acad. Cytology, Am. Coll. Nuclear Medicine, Minn. Med. Soc., AMA. Democrat. Conglist. Inventor microbiol. incubator. Home: 4924 Woodman Park Dr Apt 6 Dayton OH 45432 Office: VA Med Center 4100 W 3d St Dayton OH 45428

STEIN, ADLYN ROBINSON (MRS. HERBERT ALFRED STEIN), jewelry co. exec.; b. Pitts., May 8, 1908; d. Robert Stewart and Pearl (Geiger) Robinson; Mus.B., Pitts. Mus. Inst., U. Pitts., 1928; m. F. J. Hollearn, Nov. 14, 1929 (dec.); children—Adlyn (Mrs. Brandon J. Hickey), Frances (Mrs. Ralph A. Gleim); m. 2d, Allen Burnett Williams, Dec. 5, 1955 (dec.); m. 3d, Herbert Alfred Stein, Nov. 28, 1963 (dec. Oct. 1980); 1 dau., Rachel Lynn (Mrs. Stephen M. Kampfer). Treas., R. S. Robinson, Inc., Pitts., 1947—. Mem. Pitts. Symphony Soc., Tuesday Musical Club, Pitts.; mem. women's com. Cleve. Orch. Mem. DAR. Republican. Episcopalian. Clubs: Duquesne, University, South Hills Country (Pitts.); Lakewood Country, Clifton (Cleve.). Home: 22200 Lake Rd Cleveland OH 44116 Office: Clark Bldg Pittsburgh PA 15222

STEIN, DALE F., univ. pres.; b. Kingston, Minn., Dec. 24, 1935; s. David Frank and Zelda Jane (Petty) S.; B.S. in Metallurgy, U. Minn., 1958; Ph.D. in Metallurgy, Rensselaer Poly. Inst., 1963; m. June 7, 1958; children—Pam, Derek. Trainee, Gen. Electric Co., Schenectady, 1958-60; research metallurgist, Schenectady, 1960-67; asso. prof. U. Minn., Mpls., 1967-71, prof., 1971; prof., head dept. metall. engring. Mich. Technol. U., Houghton, 1971-77, v.p. acad. affairs, 1977-79, pres., 1979—. Mem. AIME (Hardy Gold medal 1965, dir., pres. Metall. Soc. 1980), Am. Soc. Metals, AAAS, Sigma Xi, Alpha Sigma Mu, Phi Kappa Phi, Tau Beta Pi. Club: Rotary. Contbr. articles to profl. jours. Office: Mich Technol U College Ave Houghton MI 49931

STEIN, DAVID JEROME, fin. co. exec., fin. cons.; b. Fairbury, Ill., Aug. 10, 1934; s. Frank F. and Doris Eleanor (Elliott) S.; B.S. in Agrl. Econs., U. Ill., 1959; grad. degree in credit and fin. mgmt. Dartmouth Coll., 1968; m. Roberta Frieda Riecks, June 5, 1955; children—Cheryl Ann, Dennis Ray, David Jay, Cindy Lou, Sandra Sue. Field credit mgr. Internat. Harvester Credit Corp., Dixon, Ill., 1959-61, credit supr., Lansing, Mich., 1961-64; retail credit dir. F.S. Services, Inc., Bloomington, Ill., 1964-67; regional fin. services mgr. Monsanto Co., St. Louis, 1967-69, dist. sales mgr., Kansas City, 1969-71; asst. regional mgr. farm mortgages Mut. of N.Y. Life Ins. Co., Kansas City, Mo., 1971-72, asst. to v.p., N.Y.C., 1972-74; fin. cons. and comml. mortgage broker, Peoria, Ill., 1974—; pres. Med. Condominiums, Inc., Peoria, 1975-78; propr., mgr. Karmelkorn Shoppe, Peoria, 1975—, Galesburg, Ill., 1975—; pres. Stein Enterprises, Inc., 1978—; propr., mgr. 8 Swiss Colony stores, 2 Karmelkorn stores, D & R Mktg., 1981—; trustee Doris Stein Land Trust, 1976—; exec. v.p., gen. mgr. Roy Demanes Industries, Inc., Peoria, 1977-78; sec. Ill. Valley Savs. & Loan Assn., 1977-78; pres. Med. Park Physician's Center Condominium Assn., 1975-78. Elder of ch. council First English Lutheran Ch., Peoria, 1974—, chmn. evangelism and worship com., 1974-78, tchr. adult edn., 1973-77, ch. treas., 1978-81, ch. v.p., 1981—. Served with U.S. Army, 1953-55. Recipient Exec. award Grad. Sch. fin. Mmgt., 1968. Republican. Club: Willow Knolls Country. Home: 906 W Kensington Dr Peoria IL 61614 Office: 906 W Kensington Dr Peoria IL 61614

STEIN, EDWARD HAROLD, physician; b. Tampa, Fla., Jan. 10, 1936; s. Maurice and Florence L. (Adelson) S.; B.S., Vanderbilt U., 1956, summa cum laude; M.D., Johns Hopkins U., 1962; m. Sheryl Paula Brookner, May 7, 1978; children—Letitia Emilie, Daniel Brookner. Intern, Johns Hopkins Hosp., Balt., 1962-63, asst. resident internal medicine, 1963-64; fellow in internal medicine Johns Hopkins U. Sch. Medicine, 1962-64; resident in psychiatry U. Cin. Sch. Medicine, 1964-67, chief resident, 1966-67, fellow dept. psychiatry, 1964-67; psychoanalytic tng. Chgo. Inst. Psychoanalysis, 1969—; practice medicine specializing in psychiatry, Chgo., 1969—; sr. cons., disting. teaching cons. in psychiatry Ill. State Psychiat. Inst., Chgo.; sr. cons. U. Chgo. Pritzker Sch. of Medicine, 1969—; faculty, staff psychiatry U. Chgo., 1969-74, asst. prof., 1971-74; asst. chief Adult Outpatient Clinic, U. Chgo. Hosps. and Clinics, 1969-74; asst. prof. psychiatry Rush U. Med. Sch., Chgo., 1974—. Served to maj., M.C., U.S. Army, 1967-69. Diplomate Am. Bd. Psychiatry and Neurology. Mem. Am. Psychiat. Assn., Ill. Psychiat. Assn., Chgo. Psychoanalytic Assn., Am. Psychoanalytic Assn., Am. Psychosomatic Assn., Alpha Omega Alpha. Contbr. articles on psychotherapy and psychosomatic medicine to profl. jours. Office: 111 N Wabash Ave Suite 1221 Chicago IL 60602

STEIN, ERIC SEDWICK, tng. and devel. mgmt. cons., educator; b. Wiesbaden, Germany, July 15, 1930; came to U.S., 1939, naturalized, 1951; s. Julius and Hilde B. (Kessler) S.; B.S., N.Y. U., 1952, M.A., 1956; postgrad. U. Chgo., 1957-58, Northwestern U., 1958-59; D.D. (hon.), Universal Life Ch., 1977; m. Christel Grabow, Feb. 24, 1969; children by previous marriage—T. Martin, Gabrielle, Peter. Floor supr. Alexander's Dept. Store, N.Y.C., 1955-56; asst. credit mgr. Bamberger's Dept. Store, Paramus, N.J., 1956-57; personnel dir. Hardy-Herp. Dept. Store, Muskegon, Mich., 1957-58; instr. retailing Wilkes Coll., Wilkes-Barre, Pa., 1958-59; prof. mgmt. and mktg. City Colls. Chgo., 1958—, chmn. bus. dept., 1965-70, tchr. mktg. and personnel courses over TV, 1964-79, over FM Radio WNIB, Chgo., 1981—; Fulbright-Hays guest prof. mgmt. and mktg. U. Munich (Ger.), 1969-70; part-time lectr. mktg. various univs. in Chgo., 1959—, including U. Ill., 1970-79; propr., chief cons. Devel. and Tng. Assos., 1962—; reviewer coll. texts Houghton Mifflin Co., Prentice Hall Inc., West Pub. Co., others, 1971—; speaker to various profl. orgns. Chmn. Ill. Patients Rights Com., 1977—; program chmn. Palos Heights Bicentennial Commn., 1975-76; bd. dirs. Safer Found., Chgo., 1975-80, Assn. Health Care Consumers, Chgo., 1977-79, Chgo. dist. ARC. Served with adj. br. U.S. Army, 1953-55. Mem. Acad. Mgmt., Am. Mktg. Assn. (chmn. 1970-71), Am. Soc. Tng. and Devel., Nat. Assn. Mgmt. Educators (pres. 1975-76). Author: Teleclass Study Guide for Personnel Management, 3d edit., 1979; contbr. numerous articles on marketing and mgmt. to jours. in bus., textbooks. Home: 13008 S 71st Ave Palos Heights IL 60463 Office: 10001 S Woodlawn Ave Chicago IL 60628

STEIN, GERTRUDE EMILIE, educator, soprano, pianist; b. Ironton, Ohio; d. S.A. and Emilie M. (Pollach) Stein; Mus.B., Capitol Coll., 1927; B.A., Wittenberg Coll., 1929, M.A., 1931, B.S. in Edn., 1945; Ph.D., U. Mich., 1948; piano and voice student Cin. Coll. Conservatory Music. Music supr. Centralized County Schs. Ohio, Williamsburg, 1932-37; dir. jr. high sch. music, 1937-68; mem. faculty Adult Evening Sch. Springfield (Ohio) Public Schs., 1951-68; head dept. music, asso. prof. piano and music edn. Tex. Lutheran Coll., Seguin, 1948-49. Donor, founder Rev. Dr. and Mrs. S.A. Stein Meml. Funds, 1955—. Mem. AAUW, Am. Symphony Orch. League, NEA, Ohio Edn. Assn., assns., Asso. Council Arts, Met. Opera Guild, Assn. Educators, Am. Film Inst., Ohio Music Tchrs. Assn., Nat. Story League, Music Tchrs. Nat. Assn., Music Educators Nat. Conf., N.Y. Writers' Guild (Local pres.), Nat. Assn. Ednl. Broadcasters, Nat. Assn. Schs. Music, Nat. Fedn. Music Clubs (spl. mem. Ohio, Tex.), Amateur Chamber Music Players, Nat. Fedn. Bus. and Profl. Women, Zonta Internat., Phi Kappa Phi, Pi Lambda Theta. Lutheran. Contbr. articles to profl. jours.; research in field. Home: 133 N Lowry Ave Springfield OH 45504

STEIN, HENRY CARL, mfg. co. mgr.; b. Chgo., Feb. 9, 1948; s. Joseph and Gertrude S.; B.A., Parsons Coll., 1970; m. Rosalie Eve Pozofsky, July 19, 1970; children—Michelle Lynn, Audrey Carol. Manpower programming counselor City of Chgo., 1971-76; dir. Trainco Truck Driving Sch., Trainco, Inc. Vocat. Schs., Chgo., 1976-78, dir. Trainco Admissions, 1978-80, dir. spl. programs, 1980-81; tng. and devel. mgr. Stone Container Corp., Chgo., 1981—. Mem. Am. Soc. Tng. and Devel., Am. Mgmt. Assn., Nat. Safety Council, Am. Vocat. Assn. Office: Stone Container Corp 360 N Michigan Ave Chicago IL 60601

STEIN, HERMAN DAVID, educator; b. N.Y.C., Aug. 13, 1917; s. Charles and Emma (Rosenblum) S.; B.S.S., Coll. City N.Y., 1939; M.S., Columbia U., 1941, postgrad. Sch. Social Work, 1945-47, D.S.W., 1958; m. Charmion Kerr, Sept. 15, 1946; children—Karen Gelender, Susan Deborah, Naomi Elizabeth. Case worker, dir. pub. relations, Jewish Family Services, N.Y.C., 1941-45; mem. faculty Columbia U. Sch. Social Work, N.Y.C., 1945-47, 50-64, prof., 1958-64, dir. research center, 1959-62; dean sch. applied social scis., Case Western Reserve U., Cleve., 1964-68, provost social and behavioral scis., 1967-71, provost of Univ., 1969-72, v.p., 1970-71, John Reynolds Harkness prof. social adminstrn. and Univ. prof., 1972—; vis. prof. U. Hawaii, 1971-72; fellow Center Advanced Study Behavioral Scis., Palo Alto, Calif., 1974-75, 78-79; mem. com. human resources Nat. Acad. Scis., 1972-74; mem., chmn. adv. coms. NIMH, 1958-71; lectr. Sch. Social Work, Smith Coll., Northampton, Mass., 1950-63; chmn. Mayor's Commn. Crisis in Welfare, Cleve., 1968; cons. UN Children's Fund, 1962—, also sr. adv. to exec. dir., 1974—. Commonwealth fellow 1941; recipient Disting. Service award Council Social Work Edn., 1970. Mem. Council Social Work Edn. (pres. 1966-69), Internat. Assn. Schs. Social Work (pres. 1968-76), Nat. Assn. Social Workers (chmn. commn. internat. social welfare, 1964-66), Internat. Council Social Welfare (exec. com. 1976—). Mem. editorial bd. Adminstration in Social Work, 1976—; author Curriculum Study of Columbia U. Sch. Social Work, 1960; editor (with Richard A. Cloward) Social Perspectives on Behavior, 1958; Planning for the Needs of Children in Developing Countries, 1965; Social Theory and Social Invention, 1968; The Crisis in Welfare in Cleveland, 1969; Organization and the Human Services, 1981; co-author: The Characteristics of American Jews, 1965; contbr. articles to profl. jours. Office: 436 Pardee Hall Case Western Reserve U Cleveland OH 44106

STEIN, KATHARINE ANNE BRZEZINSKI, psychol. counselor; b. Chgo., May 30, 1947; d. Casimir Frank and Anna Maria (Para) Brzezinski; B.A., So. Ill. U., 1970, M.A., 1973; Ph.D., U. Nebr., Lincoln, 1981; m. Michael Carl Stein, Nov. 18, 1967. Counselor Univ. Counseling Center, So. Ill. U., Carbondale, 1972-73; counseling psychologist, instr. psychology James Madison U., Harrisonburg, Va., 1973-75; counseling psychologist U. Nebr., Lincoln, 1975—. Mem. Am. Personnel and Guidance Assn., Am. Coll. Personnel Assn. Author: A Referral Service for Aid to Transient Women, 1972; Is There Life After Graduation, 1981. Home: 902 N 29th St Lincoln NE 68503 Office: Counseling Center 1310 Seaton Hall Univ Nebr Lincoln NE 68588

STEIN, MICHAEL JAY, osteopath; b. Bklyn., Apr. 25, 1941; s. Bernard and Ruth S.; B.S., Bklyn. Coll. Pharmacy, L.I. U., 1958-62; D.O., Coll. Osteo. Medicine and Surgery, 1966; m. Simma Rose, June 27, 1963; children—Stephen, Laura, Benjamin. Intern, Art Center Osteo. Hosp., Detroit, 1966-67; resident in neurology Detroit Osteo. Hosp., 1967-70, U. Wis. Med. Center, 1970-74; asso. prof. clin. sci. Coll. Osteo. Medicine and Surgery, Des Moines, 1974-78, prof. neuropsychiatry, 1978—, chmn. dept., 1974-78; chmn. dept. medicine Des Moines Gen. Hosp., 1977-78, chief of staff, 1978-80; moderator, lectr. Upper Midwest Osteo. Health Conf., 1979; adv. Des Moines chpt. Central Iowa affiliate Epilepsy Soc.; adv. Des Moines chpt. Multiple Sclerosis Soc. Chmn. sr. adult program coordinating com. Jewish Fedn. Greater Des Moines. Served with M.C., U.S. Army, 1967-69. Recipient Erwin Merlin award 1966. Mem. Nat. Bd. Examiners for Osteo. Physicians and Surgeons, Neurology and Psychiatry, Am. Osteo. Assn., Polk County Med. Soc., Iowa Med. Soc., Am. Assn. Neuropsychiatry, Acad. Neurology. Jewish. Contbr. osteo. med. articles to profl. jours. Home: 611 S 28th St West Des Moines IA 50265 Office: 1440 E Grand Suite 2-C Des Moines IA 50316

STEIN, MICHAEL JOHN, health care cons.; b. Chgo., Mar. 26, 1942; s. James R. and Helen E. (Waterhouse) S.; B.A. in Math., DePaul U., 1964; M.S. in Mgmt., Northwestern U., 1976. Chief mgmt. research sect. Def. Atomic Support Agy., Albuquerque, 1966-67, dir. edn. and tng. programs, 1967-68; mgr. med. assistance program Cook County, Chgo., 1969-72; dir. med. services program No. Cook County, 1972-73; dir. med. services City of Chgo. Programs, 1973-74; spl. cons. for health care Ill. State Legislature, Markham, Ill., 1974-79, dir. health programs Ill. Legis. Adv. Com., Chgo., 1980; fin. cons. Hyatt Med. Mgmt. Services, Inc., Chgo., 1981—; cons. in mgmt. Recipient disting. service award for uncovering fraud in fed. med. care programs Chgo. Assn. Commerce and Industry, 1977. Mem. Am. Hosp. Assn., Grad. Mgmt. Assn., Northwestern U., DePaul U. alumni assns., Chgo. Council Fgn. Relations, Beta Alpha Psi. Club: Century. Home: 3044 W Addison St Chicago IL 60618 Office: 1900 W Polk Chicago IL 60612

STEIN, PAUL DAVID, cardiologist; b. Cin., Apr. 13, 1934; s. Simon and Sadie (Friedman) S.; B.S., U. Cin., 1955, M.D., 1959; m. Janet Louise Tucker, Aug. 14, 1966; children—Simon, Douglas, Rebecca. Intern, Jewish Hosp., Cin., 1959-60, med. resident, 1961-62; med. resident Gorgas Hosp., C.Z., 1960-61; fellow in cardiology U. Cin., 1962-63, Mt. Sinai Hosp., N.Y.C., 1963-64; research fellow in medicine Harvard Med. Sch., Boston, 1964-66; asst. dir. cardiac lab. Baylor U. Med. Center, Dallas, 1966-67; asst. prof. medicine Creighton U., Omaha, 1967-69; asso. prof. medicine U. Okla., Oklahoma City, 1969-73; prof. research medicine U. Okla. Coll. Medicine, Oklahoma City, 1973-76; dir. cardiovascular research Henry Ford Hosp., Detroit, 1976—. Am. Heart Assn. Council on Clin. Cardiology fellow, 1971, Council on Circulation fellow, 1972. Fellow Am. Coll. Cardiology, Am. Coll. Chest Physicians; mem. Am. Physiol. Soc., Central Soc. Clin. Research, ASME. Author: A Physical and Physiological Basis for the Interpretation of Cardiac Auscultation: Evaluations Based Primarily on Second Sound and Ejection Murmurs, 1981; contbr. articles to profl. jours. Office: 2799 W Grand Blvd Detroit MI 48202

STEINBERGER, ROBERT, orthopedic surgeon; b. Detroit, July 17, 1938; s. Eugene and Fannie (Raskin) S.; B.S., Wayne State U., Detroit, 1960, M.D., 1966; m. Barbara F., June 26, 1981; children—Brita Ilene, Robert Anders. Intern, Henry Ford Hosp., Detroit, 1966-67, resident in orthopedic surgery, 1967-71; practice medicine specializing in orthopedic surgery, Jackson, Mich., 1974-77, McHenry, Ill., 1977—; partner Danville Orthopedic Clinic, Ltd. (Ill.), 1981—; mem. staff McHenry, Good Shepherd, Sherman, Lakeview, St. Elizabeth hosps. Served to maj., M.C., USAF, 1971-74. Diplomate Nat. Bd. Med. Examiners, Am. Bd. Orthopaedic Surgery. Fellow Am. Acad. Orthopaedic Surgeons, ACS; mem. AMA, Am. Assn. Hand Surgery, Ill., Vermilion County med. socs. Home: 3 Lincolnshire Danville IL 61832 Office: 917 Walnut St Danville IL 61832

STEINBERGER, ROBERT HERMAN, cons. engr.; b. Englewood, N.J., Sept. 28, 1940; s. C. Herman and Linda R. (Doelle) S.; B.S.E.E., Lafayette Coll., 1962; M.B.A. in Fin. Mgmt., U. Santa Clara, 1968; m. Nancy O. Clarke, Dec. 23, 1967; children—Kurt R., Susan C. Sales engr. Gen. Electric Co., Phila. and Millburn, N.J., 1969-73; sales mgr. Gas Turbine div. Gen. Electric Co., Greenville, S.C., 1973-76; gen. mgr. Laramore, Douglass & Popham, Inc., Boston, 1976-79, v.p., dir. exec. com., Chgo., 1979-81. Served with AUS, 1963-65. Mem. Chgo. Assn. Commerce and Industry (mem. small bus. com.), Western Soc. Engrs., Execs. Club Chgo.

STEINBRINK, JOHN PAUL, author, editor; b. Chgo.; s. Paul Ralph and Christine (Wolter) S.; M.B.A., U. Chgo., 1960; student Northwestern U., 1941-42; m. Myra G. Gold, 1947; children—Diane, Roger, Jill. Art and prodn. mgr. Sci. Research Assos., Chgo., 1947-52, asst. sales mgr., 1953-60, dir. field services, 1960-61, marketing cons., 1961-62; editor Dartnell Corp., Chgo., 1962-65, editorial dir., 1965-80, v.p., 1980—. Served to 1st lt. USAAF, 1942-45. Mem. Sales Mktg. Execs. Internat. (internat. dir. 1980—), Am. Mgmt. Assn., Am. Compensation Assn., Sales/Mktg. Execs. Chgo. (dir., sec. 1965-71, v.p. 1979, pres. 1981), Ill. Found. for Distributive Edn. (bd. govs. 1973—), Niles Art Guild, Pi Sigma Epsilon. Author: Selling Success, 1961; (with Walter C. Lane) DuPont Marketing Training, 1969; Compensation of Salesman, 1976, 78, 80. Author, editor: Dartnell Sales/Marketing Newsletter, 1962-79; Executive Compensation, 1979, 81; Dartnell Sales and Mktg. Exec. Report. Editor: Dynamic Sales Leadership (J.V. Fort), 1964; How to Comply with the Equal Employment Opportunity Act (Joseph Lawson), 1966; Collective Bargaining Guide for School Adminstrators (Hill & Quinn), 1970; How to Conduct Successful Sales Meetings (Jack Kielty), 1969; How to Plan and Manage Sales Territories (Charles C. Schlom), 1973; Dartnell 10-Point Sales Training Program (Charles C. Schlom), 1973; How to Make Sales Meetings Come Alive (George B. Anderson), 1974; How to Increase Sales and Profits Through Salesman Performance Evaluation (Frank Eby), 1975; How to Participate Profitably in Trade Shows (Konikow), 1976; Technical Marketing to the Government, 1980; Dartnell's Sales Training Kit, 1981; bd. advisers and contbrs. Jour. Acctg., Auditing & Fin.; contbr. article to Harvard Bus. Rev. Home: 8510 Shermer Rd Niles IL 60648 Office: 4660 Ravenswood Ave Chicago IL 60640

STEINDLER, MARTIN JOSEPH, chemist; b. Vienna, Jan. 3, 1928; Ph.B., U. Chgo., 1947, B.S., 1948, M.S., 1949, Ph.D., 1952; married; 2 children. Research asso. U. Chgo., 1952-53; with Argonne (Ill.) Nat. Lab., 1953—, sr. chemist, 1974—, asso. dir. chem. engring. div., 1978—; cons. advisory com. on reactor safeguards Nuclear Regulatory Commn., Livermore Lab.; mem. Atomic Safety and Licensing Bd. Panel. Mem. Royal Chem. Soc., Am. Chem. Soc., Am. Inst. Chem. Engrs., AAAS, Am. Nuclear Soc., Sigma Xi. Author numerous articles, reports on nuclear science, chemistry, safety, reprocessing, waste mgmt. Patentee. Office: Argonne Nat Lab 9700 S Cass Ave Argonne IL 60439

STEINEGER, JOHN FRANCIS, lawyer, state senator; b. Kansas City, Kans., Sept. 13, 1924; s. John F. and June (Wear) S.; A.B., U. Kans., 1947, J.D., 1949; m. Margaret Leisy, Dec. 2, 1949; children—John Francis, III, Cynthia, Melissa, Christian. Admitted to Kans. bar, 1949, Fed. bar, 1949; with solicitors office U.S. Dept. Labor, Washington, 1949-50; legal advisor U.S. Dept. State, Europe and Middle East, 1950-55, pub. affairs officer Middle East, 1955-57; probate judge protem, Kansas City, 1957-58; practice law, Kansas City, Kans., 1960—; chief dep. county atty., Kansas City, 1958-60; sr. mem. firm Steineger & Assos.; mem. Kans. Senate, 1964—, now minority leader. chmn. Gov.'s Prairie Park Commn., Spl. Ecology Commn. of Legislature. Mem. Gov.'s Com on Exec. Reorgn. Bd. dirs. Kansas City Ballet. Served to lt. USNR, 1943-46. Named One of Twenty Five Outstanding State Senators, Eagleton Inst. Politics Rutgers, 1972; Conservation Senator of Yr., Kans. Wildlife Fedn. Mem. Am. Bar Assn., Bar Assn. Kans., Nat. Council State Govts. (state and fed. assemblies), Midwestern Conf. of Commn. on Interstate Coop. (labor and commerce com.), Nat. Housing Conf., Phi Delta Theta, Phi Delta Phi. Democrat. Episcopalian. Home: 6400 Valley View Rd Kansas City KS 66111 Office: 2 Gateway Plaza Kansas City KS 66101

STEINER, BRADFORD EZRA, physician; b. Calcutta, India, Nov. 28, 1917; s. Ezra Bradford and Elizabeth (Geiger) S.; B.S., Wheaton Coll., 1939; M.D., U. Ill., 1943; m. Martha Ellen Milbourn, Dec. 25, 1942; children—Natalie A., Cheryl E. (dec.), Douglas M., Suzanne E., Mark E. Intern, Cook County Hosp., Chgo., 1943-44; resident Evang. Hosp., Chgo., 1946; med. missionary Evang. Alliance Mission, North India, 1947-58, med. supt. Almora Tb San.; med. supt. Landour Community Hosp.; resident surgeon VA Hosp., Hines, Ill., 1952-53, 57-58; practice medicine specializing in family practice, 1958—; mem. staff Meml. Hosp., Elmhurst, 1958—; sch. physician Dist. 87 Cook County, 1958—. Served with USN, 1944-46. Diplomate Am. Bd. Family Practice; licentiate Med. Council Can. Fellow Internat. Coll. Surgeons, Am. Acad. Family Physicians, Am. Soc. Abdominal

Surgeons; mem. AMA, Ill., DuPage County med. socs., Assn. Surgeons India, Am. Soc. Tropical Medicine and Hygiene, Am. Geriatrics Soc., Christian Med. Soc., Am. Sci. Affiliation. Home: Elmhurst IL 60126 Office: 240 E North Ave Northlake IL 60164

STEINER, CORKY PHILIP HARRY, toy mfg. exec.; b. Cin., Feb. 9, 1943; s. Philip and Desireé H. (Harris) S.; B.A., Tulane U., 1965; M.B.A., U. Chgo., 1967. With Kenner Products Co. div. Gen. Mills, Inc., Cin., 1967—, sr. product mgr., 1976, dir. spl. sales, 1977, dir. dept. store and supermarket sales, 1977—, Latin and S. Am. sales, 1979—, rep. Gen. Mills toy group sales C. and S. Am. Pres. Camp Livingston, 1974-79; bd. dirs. Boy Scouts Am., chmn. Cub-O-Rama; bd. dirs. Jewish Fedn. Cin., Jewish Vocat. Service. Recipient Kovod award for disting. service Jewish Center; named to Tulane U. Hall of Fame. Mem. Walnut Hills Alumni Assn. (pres.), Omicron Delta Kappa. Club: Losantiville Country (pres. LTD. bd. 1970-74, 77-79). Home: 1112 Fort View Pl Cincinnati OH 45202 Office: Kenner Products Co 1014 Vine St Cincinnati OH 45202

STEINER, IVAN, JR.; b. Ossining, N.Y., Jan. 1, 1912; s. Ivan and Merle (Holter) S.; B.A., Coll. Wooster, 1933; m. Lillian C. Gisinger, Dec. 27, 1939; children—Amy L. (Mrs. Anthony J. Pryor), Michael S., Sara A. (Mrs. William M. Marks), Deborah (Mrs. Martin T. Weber, Jr.), Jeffrey, Andrew. With W. C. Myers & Co., gen. ins. agy., Wooster, Ohio, 1936—, successively solicitor, jr. partner, 1940, mng. partner, 1948-70; merged with W.G. Whitaker & Son, 1970, pres. Whitaker-Myers Ins. Agy. Inc., 1970-76, chmn. bd., 1977, ret., 1978; v.p., dir. Wayne Recreation, Inc.; dir. Central Trust Co., Medal Brick & Tile Co.; instr. ins. Community Coll., U. Akron, 1956-57. Mem. Govs. Ins. adv. com. Fire and Casualty Ins. Bd., 1960-63; vice chmn. all-industry com. for revision agts. licensing manual Ohio Ins. Dept., 1960-61. Mem. Wooster Municipal Civil Service Commn., 1967-73. Chmn. bd. trustees Wooster YMCA, recipient Red Triangle award, 1978; trustee Greater Wayne County Found. Served from pvt. to 1st sgt. AUS, 1943-46; ETO. Chartered Property Casualty Underwriter, 1955. Mem. Wayne County Ind. Ins. Agts. Assn. (pres. 1957), Ind. Ins. Agts. Ohio (pres. 1959, chmn. legis. policy com. 1960-61, exec. com., 1965—, chmn. edn. com. 1957, 65, 66, chmn. long range planning team 1973, dir.; Paul Revere Trophy 1965), Ind. Ins. Agts. Assn. Am. (chmn. spl. acquisition cost allowance com. 1959-60), Nat. Soc. Chartered Property Casualty Underwriters (mem. seminar bd., pres. Akron-Canton chpt., regional v.p. N. Central dist. 1965-68, nat. v.p. 1968, chmn. com. revise soc.'s constn. and by laws, mem. long range planning bd. 1970-74, chmn. 1973-74), Am. Risk and Ins. Assn., Ins. Inst. Am. (diploma-asso. risk mgmt.), Ins. Soc. Phila., Wooster C. of C. (pres. 1954-55), Internat. Platform Assn., 8th Armored Div. Assn., SAR, Am. Legion, VFW. Democrat. Zion Lutheran (ch. council 1946-66, chmn. endowment com.). Clubs: Masons (32 deg.), Shriners, Elks, Rotary (pres. Wooster 1968-69), Century, Julie Fe Country. Contbr. to trade jours. Home: 257 W Henrietta St Wooster OH 44691

STEINER, KARL HANS, educator; b. Hamburg, Ger., July 10, 1915; naturalized U.S. citizen, 1963; s. Karl and Klara (Hasel) S.; Master degree, Tech. Coll., Linz, Austria, 1936; Eng. Dipl., Tech. Coll., Vienna, 1952; Ps.D., Ind. U., 1961; Ph.D., Walden U., 1974; m. Renee Sobotka, July 10, 1979. Mem. faculty Purdue U., West Lafayette, Ind., 1963—, prof. elec. engring. tech., 1966-81, prof. emeritus, 1981—; cons. City of Hamburg (Ger.), 1969—. Registered profl. engr., Wash., Oreg., Ill., B.C. Mem. Illuminating Soc. (award of merit 1959), Engring. Inst. Can., Wash. Soc. Profl. Engrs., Nat. Soc. Profl. Engrs., Assn. Profl. Engrs. of Province of B.C., AAUP, IEEE, Epsilon Delta Chi. Author: Deas Island Tunnel, 1959; Pocket Dictionary of Technical Terms, 1964; Technology and Education, 1973; Computer-Assisted Instruction, 1974; contbr. articles to profl. jours. Address: 1541 Melbrook Dr Munster IN 46321

STEINER, PAUL ANDREW, ins. co. exec.; b. Woodburn, Ind., Feb. 17, 1929; s. Eli G. and Emma M. Steiner; A.B. in Psychology, Taylor U., Upland, Ind., 1950; postgrad. Bluffton (Ohio) Coll.; m. Ruth E. Henry, Sept. 1, 1950; children—Mark, Nancy, Jonathan, David. Social worker Grant County (Ind.), 1950-51; engaged in feed, grain, lumber and constrn. bus., 1951-64; with Brotherhood Mut. Ins. Co., 1964—, v.p., treas., Ft. Wayne, Ind., 1968-71, pres., 1971—, chmn. bd., 1974—. Mem. Bluffton Bd. Edn., 1962-64; bd. dirs. Ft. Wayne Better Bus. Bur., 1979—; vice chmn. bd. Ft. Wayne Bible Coll., 1978—. C.P.C.U., 1972. Mem. Nat. Assn. Mut. Ins. Cos. (dir., Merit award 1973), Soc. C.P.C.U.'s, Conf. Casualty Ins. Cos. (dir., past pres.), Mut. Ins. Cos. Assn. Ind. (dir., past pres.), Greater Ft. Wayne C. of C., Nat. Assn. Evangelicals (treas., Layman of Year award 1977), Am. Bible Soc. (dir.), Christian Bus. Men's Com. Republican. Mem. Evang. Protestant Christian Ch. Club: Rotary. Office: PO Box 2227 Fort Wayne IN 46801

STEINFELD, MANFRED, furniture mfg. co. exec.; b. Josbach, Germany, Apr. 29, 1924; s. Abraham and Paula (Katten) S.; student U. Ill., 1942; B.S. Commerce, Roosevelt U., 1948; m. Fern Goldman, Nov. 13, 1949; children—Michael, Paul, Jill. Research analyst State Ill., 1948-50; v.p. Shelby Williams Industries, Inc., Chgo., 1954-63, pres., 1964-72, chmn. bd., 1973—; dir. Amalgamated Trust & Savs. Bank, Met. Bank of Addison (Ill.), Albany Bank & Trust. Trustee, Roosevelt U., Chgo.; pres. Roosevelt U. Bus. Sch. Alumni Council. Served to 1st lt. AUS, 1942-45, 50-52. Decorated Bronze Star, Purple Heart; named Small Bus. Man of Year Central Region, 1967; recipient Horatio Alger award, 1981. Mem. Beta Gamma Sigma. Clubs: Standard, Bryn Mawr Country. Home: 1300 Lake Shore Dr Apt 34D Chicago IL 60610 Office: Mdse Mart Room 1348 Chicago IL 60654

STEINIGER, (IRENE) MIRIAM LARMI, child devel. specialist; b. Weirton, W.Va., Dec. 20, 1916; d. (Kustaa) Edward and Aune Ellen (Raitanen) Larmi; B.S. in Edn., Ohio State U., 1936; M.A., Miami U. (Ohio), 1964; Ed.D., U. Cin., 1975; m. Erich W. Steiniger, June 6, 1941; children—Erika, Fredrik, Anthony, Karsten, Theron. Tchr., Ohio Sch. for Deaf, Columbus, 1937-41, 44-46; tchr. English and lit. Mason (Ohio) High Sch., 1955-56; tchr. elementary schs., Hamilton, Ohio, 1956-59, tchr. of deaf, Hamilton Pub. Schs., 1959-63, speech and hearing therapist, 1963-70; tchr.-cons. for neurologically handicapped, Hamilton, 1970-72; cooperating tchr. Tchr. Tng. Program, Miami U., Hamilton, 1970-72; vis. asst. prof., adj. vis. prof. U. Cin., 1972-75, asst. prof., 1975-79; asst. dir. presch. programs Cin. Center for Devel. Disorders, 1975-79; dir. Children's Diagnostic Center, Inc., Butler County, Ohio, 1979—; teaching cons. Perceptual Motor Workshops, Miami U., 1970, 71; dir., planner tchr. tng. projects and workshops Hamilton City Schs., 1965, 68, 69, 71. Vice pres. Talawonda Bd. Edn., Oxford, Ohio, 1968-72; pres., chmn. coms. LWV, Oxford; ednl. com. Butler County Mental Hygiene Assn.; leader Girl Scouts U.S.A., Dan Beard council Boy Scouts Am.; chmn. Early Childhood Edn. Task Force, SW Ohio Early Childhood Coalition Task Force on Certification; Sunday sch. tchr. Lutheran Ch.; mem. CORVA. Martha Holden Jennings Found. grantee, 1968; grantee Ohio Dept. MR/DD and Ohio DD Planning Council, 1981-82. Mem. Butler County (pres. 1969, legis. chmn. 1964—, dir. 1964—), Ohio, Nat. councils exceptional children, Am. (cert.), Cin., Ohio, Nat. speech and hearing assns., Tri-County (certificate of appreciation 1974), Ohio, Nat. assns. for children with learning disabilities, Nat., Ohio, Cin. assns. for edn. of young children, Day Care and Child Devel. Council Am., Inter-Univ. Council for Exceptional Children, AAUP, Delta Kappa Gamma. Democrat. Contbr. to Piagetian research book. Home: 208 Beechpoint Dr Oxford OH 45056 Office: Children's Diagnostic Center Inc 42 N 7th St Hamilton OH 45011

STEINKE, PAUL KARL WILLI, microbiologist; b. Friedeberg, Germany, July 13, 1921; came to U.S., 1925, naturalized, 1932; s. George Willey and Selma Ida (Hartel) S.; student Purdue U., 1943; B.S., U. Wis., 1947, M.S., 1948, Ph.D., 1951; m. Alma Louise Winkler, Aug. 17, 1944; children—Kristine, Lynda, Mark. Research asst. U. Wis., 1947-49, teaching asst., 1949-50; food bacteriologist Chain Belt Co., Milw., 1951-56; dir. microbiol. lab. Paul-Lewis Co., Milw., 1956-62; mgr. tech. services Pfizer Inc., N.Y.C., 1962-64, mgr. market devel., 1964-72, tech. dir., Milw., 1972—. Served with USNR, 1943-46. Mem. Master Brewers Assn. Ams., Am. Soc. Brewing Chemists, Am. Soc. Microbiology, Sigma Xi. Lutheran. Home: 6060 N Kent Ave Milwaukee WI 53217 Office: 4215 N Port Washington Ave Milwaukee WI 53212

STEINKE, WILLIAM FREDERICK, transp. co. exec.; b. Bellevue, Ohio, Nov. 19, 1948; s. John Everett and Helen Frances (Prokop) S.; B.A., Miami U., 1971; postgrad. (Univ. scholar) Ohio State U., 1972; m. Peggy Lynn Thorpe, Jan. 24, 1975; children—Stacey Lynn, Kimberly Sue, Michelle Frances. With Norfolk & Western Ry. Co., Bellevue, Ohio, 1967-69, Whirlpool Corp., Clyde, Ohio, 1970-71; regional dir. Consolidated Chem. Corp., Houston, 1972; with Norfolk & Western Ry. Co., various locations, 1973-77; mgr. intermodal equipment Trailer Train Co., Chgo., 1977—; lectr. in field. Mem. Nat. R.R. Intermodal Assn., Piggyback Assn. Chgo., Nat. Def. Transp. Assn., Assn. Am. R.R. Supts., Am. Short Line R.R. Assn. Republican. Lutheran. Clubs: Western Ry., Traffic. Office: 101 N Wacker Dr Chicago IL 60606

STEINMETZ, DONALD WALTER, asso. justice Wis. Supreme Ct.; b. Milw., Sept. 19, 1924; B.A., U. Wis., 1949, J.D., 1951. Admitted to Wis. bar, 1951; individual practice law, Milw., 1951-58; asst. city atty. Milw., 1958-60; 1st asst. dist. atty. Milwaukee County, 1960-65; asst. atty. gen. Wis., 1965-66; judge Milwaukee County Ct., 1966-79; asso. justice Wis. Supreme Ct., 1980—; chmn. Wis. Bd. County Judges; sec.-treas. Wis. Bd. Criminal Ct. Judges; mem. State Adminstrv. Commn. Cts., Chief Judge Study Com., Fin. Reporting Com., Study Com. TV and Radio Coverage in Courtroom. Pres., Sunday Morning Breakfast Club, South div. High Sch. Old Timers, Milw. W Club. Mem. Am. Bar Assn., Wis. Bar Assn., Am. Judicature Soc. Office: Supreme Ct Wis State Capitol Madison WI 53702

STEINMETZ, MANNING LOUIS, III, fin. co. exec.; b. Glasgow, Mo., Aug. 17, 1942; s. Manning Louis and Stella Marie (Fehling) S.; B.S., N.E. Mo. State U., 1964; m. Karen Suzanne Cockriel, July 18, 1970; children—Melissa Leigh, Suzanne Monique. Casualty ins. underwriter MFA Ins. Co., Columbia, Mo., 1965-67, systems analyst, 1967-70; systems analyst Kirksville (Mo.) Coll. Osteo. Medicine, 1970-72, dir. personnel, 1972-73, dir. devel., 1973-75; broker Edward D. Jones & Co., Maryland Heights, Mo., 1975-78, partner, 1978—; allied mem. N.Y. Stock Exchange. Active Council on Public Higher Edn. Served with U.S. Army, 1964-65. Mem. Nat. Assn. Security Dealers, Sigma Tau Gamma. Democrat. Roman Catholic. Clubs: Masons, Bogey Hills Country, Shriners, Kiwanis. Home: 2928 W Adams St Saint Charles MO 63301 Office: Edward D Jones & Co 201 Progress Pkwy Maryland Heights MO 63043

STEINMILLER, JOHN F., profl. basketball team exec.; b. Evanston, Ill., Nov. 26, 1948; s. Fred J. and Marynell Steinmiller; B.S. in Journalism, Marquette U., 1970; m. Corinne M. Nierman, Mar. 17, 1979. Public relations dir. Milw. Bucks, NBA, 1972-77, dir. bus. ops., 1977-80, v.p. bus. ops., 1980—; public speaker on profl. sports in Am. and public image improvement, 1976—. Sec., Midwest Athletes Against Childhood Cancer; mem. Milw. chpt. Big Bros. Recipient award Big Bros., 1980, Milwaukee County Vets. Orgn., 1976. Mem. Sales and Mktg. Execs. Roman Catholic. Clubs: Milw. Press, Ville du Parc Country. Office: 901 N 4th St Milwaukee WI 53203

STEINREICH, OTTO SELICK, surgeon; b. N.Y.C., Mar. 13, 1914; s. George and Ida (Mayer) S.; A.B., U. N.C., 1934; M.D., Med. Coll. Va., 1938; m. Helen Natalie Bane, June 19, 1938; children—Michael Martin, Steven Carl. Intern, Newark City Hosp., 1939-41; resident surgery St. Thomas Hosp., Akron, Ohio, 1946-48; practice medicine specializing in surgery, Akron, 1948—; med. staff St. Thomas Hosp., dir. med. edn.; mem. staff Akron Gen. Hosp., Akron City Hosp., Akron Children's Hosp. Bd. dirs. Jewish Welfare Fund, Jewish Family Service, Akron Jewish Center; trustee Summit Portage Area Health Edn. Network, Region Six Peer Rev. Orgn. Served to capt. M.C. AUS, 1941-46. Diplomate Am. Bd. Surgery. Fellow A.C.S., Internat. Coll. Surgeons; mem. AMA, Council of Deans (asso. dean clin. scis.), Northeastern Ohio Univs. Coll. Medicine, Zeta Beta Tau, Phi Lambda Kappa. Jewish (pres. congregation). Contbr. articles to profl. jours. Home: 433 Delaware Ave Akron OH 44303 Office: Saint Thomas Hosp Akron OH 44310

STELLER, ARTHUR WAYNE, ednl. adminstr.; b. Columbus, Ohio, Apr. 12, 1947; s. Fredrick and Bonnie Jean (Clark) S.; B.S., Ohio U., 1969, M.A., 1970, Ph.D., 1973. Tchr., Athens (Ohio) City Schs., 1969-71; curriculum coordinator, tchr. Belpre (Ohio) City Schs., 1971-72; prin. elem. schs., head tchr. learning disabilities South-Western City Schs., Grove City, Ohio, 1972-76; dir. elem. edn. Beverly (Mass.) Public Schs., 1976-78; adj. prof. Lesley Coll., Cambridge, Mass., 1976-78; coordinator spl. projects and systemwide planning Montgomery County Public Schs., Rockville, Md., 1978-80; asst. supt. elem. edn. Shaker Heights (Ohio), 1980—. Charles Kettering Found., IDEA fellow, 1976, 78, 80; Nat. Endowment Humanities fellow; 1977. Mem. Am. Assn. Sch. Adminstrs., Nat. Assn. Elem. Sch. Prins., Nat. Assn. Edn. Young Children, Nat. Sch. Public Relations Assn., Assn. Supervision and Curriculum Devel., Internat. Soc. Ednl. Planning, Nat. Soc. Study Edn., Nat. Planning Assn., Council Basic Edn. Northeastern U., Ohio Assn. Elem. Sch. Adminstrs., Buckeye Assn. Sch. Adminstrs., Ohio Assn. Supervision and Curriculum Devel., Ohio U. Alumni Assn. (nat. dir. 1975-78, pres. Central Ohio chpt. 1975-76, pres. Mass. chpt. 1976-78, life mem. trustee's acad.), World Future Soc., Tau Kappa Epsilon Alumni Assn. (regional officer Mass. 1976-78), Kappa Delta Pi (life), Phi Delta Kappa (life). Methodist. Contbr. articles to profl. jours. Office: 15600 Parkland Dr Shaker Heights OH 44120

STEMAN, ROBERT E., lawyer; b. Cin., Apr. 12, 1908; s. Louis J. and Lillie (Trarbach) S.; A.B., Miami U., Oxford, Ohio, 1931; J.D., U. Cin., 1933; m. Josephine Lambert, Oct. 28, 1944; children—Sara S. (Mrs. David A. Whittaker), Susan (Mrs. Ethan B. Stanley), E. Conrad, Sharon Steman Earl. Admitted to Ohio bar, 1933; practice law, Cin., 1933-41, 46—; chief trial counsel City of Cin., 1946-48, spl. counsel, 1965—; spl. counsel Cin. Bd. Edn., 1949—, city North College Hill, 1955-61; mem. firm Peck, Shaffer & Williams. Pres. bd. trustees Thomas Hughes Wills Fund. Served to lt. comdr. USNR, 1942-45. Recipient Freedoms Found. George Washington honor medal, 1972. Mem. Am., Ohio, Cin. bar assns., Mil. Order World Wars (judge adv. gen. 1965-69, comdr.-in-chief, 1970-71), Navy League, English Speaking Union. Mem. Mil. Hospitaler Order St. Lazarus of Jerusalem. Clubs: Queen City, Cin. Tennis (Cin.). Home: 2200 Victory Pkwy Cincinnati OH 45206 also 13 Bull Run Dr Oxford OH 45056 Office: First Nat Bank Center 425 Walnut St Cincinnati OH 45202

STEMPEL, GUIDO HERMANN, III, educator; b. Bloomington, Ind., Aug. 13, 1928; s. Guido Hermann and Alice Margaret (Menninger) S.; A.B., Ind. U., 1949, M.A., 1951; Ph.D., U. Wis., 1954; m. Anne Louise Elliott, Aug. 30, 1952; children—Ralph, Carl, Jane. Sports editor Frankfort (Ind.) Morning Times, 1949-50; copy editor Wis. State Jour., Madison, 1952-53; instr. Pa. State U., University Park, 1955-57, asst. prof., 1957; asso. prof. Central Mich. U., 1957-63, prof., 1963-65; asso. prof. Ohio U. Sch. Journalism, Athens, 1965-68, prof., 1968-72, prof., dir., 1972-79, prof. journalism, dir. Bush Research Endowment, 1979—. Served with U.S. Army, 1954-55. Recipient Chancellor's award, U. Wis., 1977; 20th Century Fund grantee, 1970; Am. Newspaper Pubs. Assn. grantee, 1973, 77, 79. Mem. Assn. Edn. in Journalism (chmn. com. on research 1968-71), Nat. Council Coll. Publs. Advs., Sigma Delta Chi. Democrat. Methodist. Club: Rotary. Asso. editor Journalism Quar., 1970-72, editor, 1972—; co-editor, Research Methods in Mass Communication, 1981. Home: 7 Lamar Dr Athens OH 45701 Office: Sch Journalism Ohio Univ Athens OH 45701

STEMPEL, JOHN EMMERT, educator, journalist; b. Bloomington, Ind., May 6, 1903; s. Guido Hermann and Myrtle (Emmert) S.; A.B., Ind. U., 1923, postgrad., 1926-27; M.S. in Journalism, Columbia U., 1928; m. Mary Roberts Farmer, Aug. 30, 1928; children—John Dallas, Thomas Ritter. Reporter, Bloomington Evening World, 1917-19; instr. journalism, dir. publicity, Lafayette Coll., Easton, Pa., 1923-26; part time instr. journalism, Ind. U., 1926-27; asso. editor Bloomington Star, 1926-27; news editor Columbia U. Alumni News, 1927-30; staff N.Y. Sun, 1929-36; news and mng. editor Easton Express, 1936-38; prof. journalism, chmn. dept. Ind. U., 1938-68, prof. emeritus, 1968—; acting ednl. adviser Def. Information Sch., 1968-69. Recipient Bronze medal Columbia Sch. Journalism; Distinguished Alumni Service award Ind. U., 1972; named Ind. Newspaper Man of Yr., 1968; named to Ind. Journalism Hall of Fame, 1970. Mem. Assn. Edn. for Journalism, Internat. Typog. Union, Greater Bloomington C. of C. (acting exec. v.p. 1977), Phi Kappa Psi, Sigma Delta Chi (past nat. pres.). Democrat. Episcopalian. Mason. Clubs: Rotary (past dist. gov., ex-chmn. Rotary Internat. Mag. com., publ. com.); Indpls. Press; University (Ind. U.). Compiled (with N.P. Poynter) The Indiana Daily Student Style Book, 1923 (revised several times). Author textbook. Contbr. to journalism publs. Home: 924 Atwater Ave Bloomington IN 47401

STEN, DOUGLAS LEROY, constrn. ofcl.; b. Washington, Pa., May 22, 1949; s. Leroy B. and Gerry P. Sten; student West Liberty State Coll., 1967-69; B.S. in Edn., California (Pa.) State Coll., 1973; M.S. in Safety Mgmt., West Va. U., 1977; m. Lori T. Swope, May 6, 1978; 1 son, Ryan Douglas. Secondary tchr. Washington (Pa.) Area High Schs., 1973-74; steelworker Jessop Steel Co., Washington, 1974-77; field safety supr. Koppers Co., Inc., Pitts., 1977-79; corp. safety edn. dir. Rieth-Riley Constrn. Co., Goshen, Ind., 1979—. Program chmn. Washington Jaycees, 1973-77. Mem. Am. Soc. Safety Engrs., Nat. Safety Mgmt. Soc., Ind. Constructors, Nat. Asphalt Pavement Assn., Ind. Motor Truck Assn. Democrat. Lutheran. Clubs: Elks. Home: 512 S 5th St Goshen IN 46526 Office: 311 W Madison St Goshen IN 46526

STEN, SABINA SCHUETTE, banker; b. Bussum, Netherlands, Oct. 26, 1936; came to U.S., 1962; d. Herbert Gustaf and Therese Henriette (Sprick) Schuette; student Dr. Paul Schmidt, Sprachen und Dolmetscherinstitut, 1961; Interpreter's Degree, U. Munich, 1961; m. John Paul Sten, June 16, 1962; children—Nikolas, Anika, Eike. Exec. sec. First Nat. Bank, Mpls., 1973-76, internat. credit analyst, 1976, mgr. internat. credit dept., 1977-79, comml. banking trainee, 1979, comml. banking officer, 1979—. Mem. Citizens League. Mem. Am. Inst. Banking, Minn. World Trade Assn. Office: 120 S 6th St Minneapolis MN 55402

STENE, DENNIS CARTER, podiatrist; b. Elgin, Ill., Aug. 1, 1944; s. Arvin and Erna Wanda (Loechelt) S.; D.P.M., Ill. Coll. Podiatric Medicine, 1967; m. Carol Jean Gray, May 25, 1974. Pvt. practice podiatry, Bensenville, Ill., 1967-69, Rockford, Ill., 1969-70, Elgin, Ill., 1969—. Active Norwegian Lutheran Bethesda Home Assn. Mem. Am. Podiatry Assn., Ill. Podiatry Soc., Alumni Assn. Ill. Coll. Podiatric Medicine. Republican. Clubs: Masons (worshipful master 1973), Shriners. Home: 1785 Joseph Ct Elgin IL 60120 Office: 100 E Chicago St Elgin IL 60120

STENEHJEM, WAYNE KEVIN, state senator; b. Mohall, N.D., Feb. 5, 1953; s. Martin Edward and Marguerite Mae (McMaster) S.; B.A., U. N.D., 1974, J.D., 1977; m. Tama Lou Smith, June 16, 1978; 1 son, Andrew. Admitted to N.D. bar, 1977; partner firm Kuchera, Stenehjem & Wills, Grand Forks, 1977—; mem. N.D. Ho. of Reps. from 42d Dist., 1976-80, N.D. Senate from 42d Dist., 1980—; mem. Gov. N.D. Spl. Com. Student Loans. Bd. dirs. Christus Rex Lutheran Ch., Grand Forks, United Hosp., Grand Forks, Agissiz Enterprises, Amigos de las Americas; mem. human rights com. Grafton State Sch.; mem. N.D. atty. standards com. Supreme Ct. Mem. Am. Bar Assn., N.D. Bar Assn., N.D. Trial Lawyers Assn., Indigent Def. Delivery Project, Phi Delta Phi, Sigma Delta Chi. Republican. Club: Elks. Sr. editor N.D. Law Rev., 1976-77. Office: PO Box 52 212 S 4th St Grand Forks ND 58201

STENGER, GLENN JOSEPH, computer co. exec.; b. Columbus, Nebr., Mar. 4, 1944; s. William Leo and Angela Ann (Borer) S.; student acctg. G.E. Bus. Coll., 1962-64; m. Dee C. Pfeifer, May 1, 1965; children—Denise, Jeffrey, Kevin, Jennifer. Jr. acct. public acctg. firm, 1964-67; asst. controller Darling Transfer Inc., 1967-69; office mgr., asst. controller Herman Bros. Inc., 1969-74; chmn. bd., treas. C.D. Systems, Inc., Omaha, 1974—. Mem. Nat. Assn. Accts. Republican. Roman Catholic. Home: 14917 L St Omaha NE 68137 Office: 14614 Grover St Omaha NE 68144

STENSETH, DAVID LOMEN, indsl. devel. found. exec.; b. Crookston, Minn., Dec. 22, 1936; s. Adolph Karl and Oral Blache (Lomen) S.; B.A. in Econs., St. Olaf Coll., 1958; postgrad. U. Okla., 1971-74; m. Shirley Ann Stolz, Sept. 6, 1958; children—Lynne, Maren, David. Adminstrv. asst. to Congressman Odin Langen, Washington, 1958-61; dir. fin. Minn. Republican Com., Mpls., 1961-64; dir. devel. Augustana Coll., Sioux Falls, S.D., 1964-70, acting v.p. for devel., 1968-70; pres. Sioux Falls Devel. Found., 1970—; dir. Brookings Internat. Life Ins. Co. (S.D.), N.Am. Nat. Corp., Columbus, Ohio. Fin. chmn. Sioux council Boy Scouts Am., 1975—; mem. S.D. Gov.'s Com. for Juvenile Delinquency, 1969-70, Private Industries Council; bd. dirs. S.E. Area Vocat. Sch., 1970-74, Fellows-Augustana Coll., 1964—, Parkview Nursing Home, 1968—; bd. dirs. Vis. Nurses Assn., pres., 1974-76; bd. dirs. Sioux Falls Boys Club, v.p., 1970-76; bd. dirs. Nordland Heritage Assn.; Mem. Nat. Alliance of Bus. (dir. 1974—), S.D. Mfrs. and Processors Assn. (dir. 1977), Am. Econ. Devel. Council, Nat. Assn. Indsl. Parks, S.D. Alcohol Fuels Assn. (dir.), Nat. Assn. Rev. Appraisers, Nat. Assn. Corp. Real Estate Execs., Com. Econ. Growth (vice-chmn.), Sioux Falls Area C. of C. Republican. Lutheran. Clubs: Rotary, Sons of

Norway, Elk, Westward Ho Country (dir. 1970-74). Office: 131 E 10th St Sioux Falls SD 57102

STEPAN, ALFRED CHARLES, JR., chem. mfg. exec.; b. N.Y.C., Apr. 17, 1909; s. Alfred Charles and Charlotte (Corbett) S.; B.A., U. Notre Dame, 1931, LL.D., 1963; postgrad. Northwestern U., 1931-33, Armour Inst. Tech., 1933-34; m. Mary Louise Quinn, Feb. 10, 1934; children—Marilee (Mrs. Richard Wehman), Alfred III, Quinn, Stratford, Charlotte (Mrs. Joseph Flanagan), Paul, John. Founder, Stepan Chem. Co., 1932, pres., 1932-73, chmn., chief exec. officer, 1973—; dir. 1st Nat. Bank of Winnetka. Bd. dirs. Ravinia Festival Assn., Lyric Opera of Chgo.; pres. Lyric Opera Sch. Chgo.; vis. com. humanities U. Chgo.; trustee Chgo. Orchestral Assn. Republican. Clubs: Chicago, Commercial (Chgo.); Glen View (Golf, Ill.); Bob O'Link Golf (Highland Park, Ill.); Everglades, Bath and Tennis, Seminole Golf (Palm Beach, Fla.). Home: 76 Woodley Rd Winnetka IL 60093 also 212 Via Palma Palm Beach FL Office: Edens and Winnetka Northfield IL 60093

STEPAN, FRANK QUINN, chem. co. exec.; b. Chgo., Oct. 24, 1937; s. Alfred Charles and Mary Louise (Quinn) S.; A.B., U. Notre Dame, 1959; M.B.A., U. Chgo., 1963; m. Jean Finn, Aug. 23, 1958; children—Jeanne, Frank Quinn, Todd, Jennifer, Lisa, Colleen, Alfred, Richard. Salesman Indsl. Chems. div. Stepan Chem. Co., Northfield, Ill., 1961-63, mgr. internat. dept., 1964-66, v.p. corporate planning, 1967-69, v.p., gen. mgr. Indsl. Chems. div., 1970-73, pres., 1974—, also dir.; dir. Kona Communications, Inc. Trustee, Loyola Acad.; mem. liberal arts council Notre Dame U., South Bend, Ind., 1972—. Served to 1st lt. AUS, 1959-61. Clubs: Economic (Chgo.); Exmoor (Highland Park, Ill.). Home: 200 Linden St Winnetka IL 60093 Office: Stepan Chem Co Edens and Winnetka Sts Northfield IL 60093

STEPANSKI, RAYMOND RICHARD, mfg. co. exec.; b. Alpena, Mich., June 13, 1931; s. Leonard and Eva (Greene) S.; student Alpena Community Coll., 1966-67, Wittenberg U., 1967, U. Wis., Madison, 1973-78; m. Marie Caroline Schliska, July 12, 1952; children—Kathleen, Nancy, Ryan, Rodney. With Abitibi Price Corp., Alpena, Mich., 1957—, mgr. mfg., 1973-81, mgr. tech. services, 1981—. Bd. dirs. Little League and Babe Ruth Baseball, Blue Line Club Hockey. Served with AUS, 1953-55. Mem. Am. Hardboard Assn., Pulp Industry Mgmt. Assn., Tech. Assn. Pulp and Paper Industry. Roman Catholic. Clubs: Exchange, Elks. Home: 1124 Hinckley St Alpena MI 49707 Office: 416 Ford Ave Alpena MI 49707

STEPHAN, DAVID GEORGE, environ. engr.; b. Columbus, Ohio, Feb. 8, 1930; s. Paul Raymond and Bess (Long) S.; B.Chem. Engring., Ohio State U., 1952, M.Sc. (Battelle Meml. Inst. fellow), 1952, Ph.D., 1955; m. Dorothy Virginia Spetnagel, June 10, 1951; children—Douglas King, Donn Paul, Dean David. Research asso. Battelle Meml. Inst., Columbus, 1952-55; dep. chief advanced waste treatment research program USPHS, Cin., 1964-65; dir. research Fed. Water Pollution Control Adminstrn., Washington, 1966-68; asst. commr. research and devel. Fed. Water Quality Adminstrn., Washington, 1968-70; dir. research program mgmt. EPA, Washington, 1971-75; dir. indsl. environ. research lab. EPA, Cin., 1975—, sr. ofcl. research and devel. A.W. Breidenbach Environ. Research Center, 1975—; adj. prof. chem. engring. U. Cin., 1976—. Served with USPHS, 1955-64. Registered profl. engr., Ohio; recipient Bronze medal EPA, 1980, Superior Service medal HEW, 1965. Fellow Am. Inst. Chem. Engring.; mem. Internat. Assn. Water Pollution Research (bd. govs.), Am. Inst. Chem. Engrs., Water Pollution Control Fedn., Am. Chem. Soc., Sr. Execs. Assn. (Cin. fed. exec. bd.), Sigma Xi, Texnikoi, Tau Beta Pi, Phi Lambda Upsilon. Elder, Anderson Hills Christian Ch. Contbr. articles to profl. jours. Home: 6435 Stirrup Rd Cincinnati OH 45244 Office: 5555 Ridge Rd Cincinnati OH 45268

STEPHAN, ROBERT T., atty. gen. Kans.; b. Wichita, Kans., 1933; B.A., J.D., Washburn U.; married; 1 son, 3 daus. Admitted to Kans. bar, 1957; judge Wichita Mcpl. Ct., 1963-65; judge Sedgwick County Dist. Ct., 1965-78; atty. gen. State of Kans., 1979—. Bd. dirs. state and county Am. Cancer Soc., hon. crusade chmn. state div., 1979-81; mem. adv. bd. Big Bros.-Big Sisters, Cath. Social Services; trustee Kans. chpt. Am. Leukemia Soc.; bd. dirs. Parents Against Leukemia and Malignancies Soc., Accent on Kids, Kans. Day Club. Named Kans. Trial Judge of Year, Kans. Trial Lawyers Assn., 1977. Mem. Am. Judges Assn., Am. Judicature Soc., Am. Bar Assn., Kans. Bar Assn., Nat. Assn. Attys. Gen. (exec. com., chmn. Midwest region), Kans. Dist. Judges Assn. (pres. 1977-78), Kans. Jud. Conf. (chmn. 1977). Republican. Clubs: Wagonmasters, Elks, Moose, Scottish Rite. Office: Office of Atty Gen Judicial Center Topeka KS 66612

STEPHANI, SYLVAN EARL, office equip. co. exec.; b. Austin, Minn., Sept. 23, 1939; s. Alfred J. and Florence C. (Vogt) S.; A.A., U. Minn., 1960; m. Kathleen P. Scheiber, Aug. 5, 1961; children—Julienne, Robert, Cheryl. With Sperry Univac, various locations, 1961-69, 71-73; mgr. pacific systems and tech. support Internat. Computers Ltd., Sydney, Australia, 1973-74, dir. worldwide tech. support, London, 1974-76, dir. European Space Agy. program, Darmstadt, W. Ger., 1976-77, dir. quality assurance div., London, 1977-79; v.p. spl. projects A.B. Dick Co., Chgo., 1979—. Served with USAR, 1961. Republican. Roman Catholic. Contbr. articles to profl. jours. Home: 4109 Avondale St Minnetonka MN 55343 Office: 5700 Touhy Ave Chicago IL 60648

STEPHEN, JOHN ERLE, lawyer, diversified mfg. cos. exec.; b. Eagle Lake, Tex., Sept. 24, 1918; s. John Earnest and Vida Thrall (Klein) S.; J.D., U. Tex., 1941; postgrad. Northwestern U., 1942, U.S. Naval Acad. Postgrad. Sch., 1945, Naval War Coll., 1946; m. Gloria Yzaguirre-Skidmore, May 16, 1942; children—Vida Leslie, John Lauro Kurt. Admitted to Tex. bar, 1946, D.C. bar, 1957, Mich. bar, 1981; gen. mgr. Sta. KOPY, Houston, 1946; gen. atty., exec.-asst. to pres. Tex. Star Corp., Houston, 1947-50; partner firm Hofheinz & Stephen, Houston, 1950-57; v.p., gen. counsel TV Broadcasting Co., Tex. Radio Corp., Gulf Coast Network, Houston, 1953-57; spl. counsel, exec.-asst. to Mayor, City of Houston, 1953-56; v.p., gen. counsel Air Transport Assn. Am., Washington, 1958-71; gen. counsel Amway Corp., Ada, Mich., 1972—; advisor U.S. dels. to diplomatic confs.: Warsaw Treaty, Hague Protocal, Bermuda Agreement, Tokyo Crimes Treaty, Montreal Liability Agreement; vis. lectr. Harvard Grad. Bus. Sch., Washington Fgn. Law Soc., Pacific Agribus. Conf.; advisor Consulates-Gen. of Mex. in U.S., 1956-66. Chief of protocol City of Houston, 1953-56; bd. dirs. Contemporary Arts Assn., 1953-57. Served to comdr. U.S. Navy, 1941-46. Mem. Am. Bar Assn. (past chmn., council sect. public utility law), Standing Com. on Aero. Law. Past chmn., Internat. Aviation Law Com.), World Peace Through Law Center. Mem. Fed. Bar Assn., D.C. Bar, State Bar Tex., State Bar Mich., Fed. Communications Bar Assn., Assn. ICC Practitioners, Am. Judicature Soc., Japanese Air Law Soc. (hon.), Venezuelan Soc. Air and Space Law (hon.). Clubs: Explorers, Houston Polo, Internat., Lakeshore, Saddle and Cycle, Breakfast, Nat. Aviation. U.S. editor: Year Book of International Aviation, 1965-71; asso. editor: Air Laws and Treaties of the World, 1966; bd. advisors Jour. Air Law and Commerce, 1964-71; contbr. articles to profl. jours. Office: 7575 E Fulton Rd Ada MI 49355

STEPHENS, ANNE ELIZABETH, sch. adminstr.; b. Erwin, Tenn., May 29, 1947; d. Gerald Andrew and Elizabeth Ellen (Lundy) Jelinek; B.A., West Liberty State Coll., 1968; M.A., W.Va. U., 1972; postgrad. Dayton U., Akron U.; m. Daniel Stephens, Aug. 2, 1969. With Buckeye Local Sch. Dist., Rayland, Ohio, 1968—, coordinator elem. edn. and spl. programs, now adminstrv. asst. to supt. Coordinator Spl. Olympics. Recipient Ohio PTA Educator of Yr. award, 1979. Mem. Eastern Ohio Coordinators Assn. (treas.), Internat. Reading Assn., Nat. Assn. Curriculum Devel., Assn. Children with Learning Disabilities, Ohio Suprs. Assn., Northeastern Ohio Sch. Supt. Assn., Am. Assn. Sch. Adminstrs. Presbyterian. Home: RD #1 Dillonvale OH 43917 Office: PO Box 300 Rayland OH 43943

STEPHENS, HERBERT MURRAY, real estate exec.; b. Lakeview, Mich., Oct. 17, 1940; s. Russell William and Mary Gilman (Thomson) S.; B.A., Western Mich. U., 1973; postgrad. U. Mich., 1975-76; m. Barbara Kay Quist, June 16, 1962; children—Todd Herbert, Herbert Murray II, Nathan Douglas, Kristen Lee, Terri Lynn, Kimberly Kay, Holly Michelle, Timothy Scott. Pres., Herb Stephens Investment Co., Flint, Mich., 1964—, White House Motor Lodges, Inc., Ann Arbor, Mich., 1971—, Pine Shores, Inc., Grayling, Mich., 1972—. Author: (investment guide) Green Tomorrows, 1980. Home: 1440 Briarcliffe Dr Flint MI 48504 Office: 3615 Clio Rd Flint MI 48504

STEPHENS, JAMES W., utility co. exec.; b. Pleasant Green, Mo., Mar. 8, 1920; s. James Wilbur and Mary Elizabeth (Parrish) S.; B.S.E.E., U. Mo., Rolla, 1947, Elec. Engr., 1957, Dr.Engring. (hon.), 1971; m. Sarah Maxine Dump, May 10, 1942; children—James Michael, John Robert. With Mo. Public Service Co., 1940-42, 47—, asst. to pres. Kansas City, Mo., 1960-64, v.p. community services, 1964-76, sr. v.p., 1976—; dir. Boatman's Baytown Bank (Mo.). Pres., Met. Jr. Coll. Bd. of Kansas City, 1966-69; chmn. 4-H Found. Trustees, 1966-67; pres. U. Mo. Alumni Alliance, 1968-70. Served with USNR, 1942-45. Mem. Associated Industries of Mo. (chmn. bd. dirs. 1980-82), Greater Kansas City C. of C. (pres. 1970-71), Nat. Soc. Profl. Engrs., Mo. Soc. Profl. Engrs., Am. Econ. Devel. Council (pres. 1972), So. Indsl. Devel. Council, Soc. Indsl. Realtors. Democrat. Methodist. Clubs: Masons, Scottish Rite, Shriners. Office: PO Box 11739 Kansas City MO 64138

STEPHENS, KATHERINE LEANN, occupational therapist; b. Ames, Iowa, July 7, 1946; d. Leo Bartle and Sarah Armina (Wilson) Mathison; student U. No. Iowa, 1964-66; B.S. in Occupational Therapy, U. Iowa, 1968; postgrad. Butler U., 1971, Kent State U., 1979—; m. Robert E. Stephens, Sept. 3, 1980. Staff therapist Cerebral Palsy Clinic, Ind. U. Med. Center, Indpls., 1969-71; learning specialist, occupational therapy cons. Marion County Assn. for Retarded Citizens, Indpls., 1971-74; statewide coordinator for handicapped Head Start, State of Iowa, 1974-77; therapist early childhood program Grantwood Area Edn. Agy., Cedar Rapids, Iowa, 1977; cons. in occupational therapy, ednl. assessment project Mid-Eastern Ohio Spl. Edn. Regional Resource Center, Akron, 1977—; mem. gov.'s com. Early Childhood Task Force Iowa, 1975; adv. com. for regional access projects Head Start, Kansas City, Mo., 1976-77. Mem. Am. Occupational Therapy Assn. (faculty nat. tng. program), Ohio Occupational Therapy Assn., Nat. Council for Exceptional Children, Ohio Council for Exceptional Children, Assn. for Severely Handicapped, Akron Dist. Occupational Therapy Assn., Center for Study of Sensory Integrative Dysfunction. Author tng. materials for teachers in field, handbooks for vols., curriculum guides, activity books. Home: 3030 Saybrooke Blvd Stow OH 44224 Office: 65 Steiner Ave Akron OH 44301

STEPHENS, MICHAEL JON, automobile mfg. co. exec.; b. Alpena, Mich., Aug. 30, 1948; s. Byron L. and Jeanne E. (Hackett) S.; B.S. in Indsl. Engring., Gen. Motors Inst., 1972; M.B.A., Wayne State U., Detroit, 1976. With Gen. Motors Corp., 1967-77, 79—, sr. quality control analyst/engr., Detroit, 1973-77, sr. staff asst. corp. mktg. staff, 1979—; market planning analyst Toyota Motor Sales Co., Torrance, Calif., 1977-78; nat. market and product mgr. Brit. Leyland Inc., Leonia, N.J., 1978-79; adj. prof. bus. Bergen (N.J.) Community Coll., 1978-79. Home: PO Box 1304 Troy MI 48099 Office: GM Bldg Room 9-230 Detroit MI 48202

STEPHENS, PAUL ALFRED, dentist; b. Muskogee, Okla., Feb. 28, 1921; s. Lonny and Maudie Janie (Wynn) S.; B.S. cum laude, Howard U., 1942, D.D.S., 1945; m. Lola Helena Byrd, May 7, 1950; children—Marsha Stephens Wilson, Paul Alfred, Derek M. Instr. dentistry Howard U., Washington, 1945-46; gen. practice dentistry, Gary, Ind., 1947—, also Indpls.; chmn. bd. Assos. Med. Center, Inc., Gary. Sec., Gary Ind. Sch. Bldg. Corp., 1967—; pres. Bd. Health, 1973—, Ind. State Bd. Dental Examiners, 1979—. Mem. adv. bd. Ind. U.-Purdue U. Calumet campus, 1973. Bd. dirs. Urban League N.W. Ind. Served with AUS, 1942-44. Fellow Internat. Coll. Dentists, Acad. Dentistry Internat., Acad. Gen. Dentistry (pres. chpt. 1973, nat. chmn. dental care com. 1977, Midwestern v.p.), Am. Coll. Dentists; mem. ADA, C. of C., Nat., N.W. Ind. (dir., pres. 1976-77) dental assns., Am. Soc. Anesthesia in Dentistry, Am. Acad. Radiology, Alpha Phi Alpha. Baptist. Home: 1901 Taft St Gary IN 46404 Office: 2200 Grant St Gary IN 46404

STEPHENS, ROBERT ALLAN, service agy. exec.; b. St. Louis County, Mo., Jan. 15, 1937; s. Charles Franklin and L. Pearl (Cales) Stephens; B.A., Mo. Valley Coll., 1958; postgrad Nova U., 1980—; m. Carolyn Beth Hurst, Aug. 26, 1956; children—Shari Lee, Beth Ann. Claims supr. Gen. Am. Life Ins. Co., Pitts., 1958-61, underwriting mgr., St. Louis, 1961-67, dist. sales mgr., Oklahoma City and St. Louis, 1967-69; dist. sales mgr. New Eng. Life, Dallas, 1969-71; exec. dir. Goodland Presbyn. Children's Home, Hugo, Okla., 1971-74; exec. dir. Beech Acres, Cin., 1974—. Mem. Hamilton County Juvenile Ct. Rev. Bd., 1975-81; mem. coordinating council Hamilton County Youth Services, 1980-81; legis. bd., Southeastern Ecumenical Ministries Manor, 1976-81, bd. dirs., 1980-81; mem. Clermont County Mental Health Bd., 1980-81, vice chmn., 1981; mem. Clermont County Youth Service Coordinating Council, 1980-81, Clermont County Juvenile Ct. Adv. Bd., 1980-81. Named Nat. United Presbyterian Man of Mission, 1978. Mem. Nat. Assn. Homes for Children (dir. 1975-80), Ohio Assn. Child Caring Agys. (dir. 1975-80, pres., 1978-79). Presbyterian. Club: Exchange (pres. 1980-81). Home: 1258 Maplecrest St Amelia OH 45102 Office: 6881 Beechmont Ave Cinncinnati OH 45230

STEPHENS, WILLIAM RICHARD, coll. pres.; b. Ashburn, Mo., Jan. 2, 1932; s. George Lewis and Helen Stephens; B.S., Greenville Coll., 1953; M.Ed., U. Mo., 1957; Ed.D., Washington U., St. Louis, 1964; m. Arlene Greer, June 28, 1952; children—Richard, Kendell, Kelli. Tchr., Sturgeon (Mo.) High Sch., 1955-57; asst. prof. to asso. prof. edn. Greenville (Ill.) Coll., 1957-61, v.p. acad. affairs and dean of faculty, 1971-77, acting pres., 1972, pres., 1977—; spl. instr. founds. of edn., supr. student tchrs. Washington U., St. Louis, 1961-64; asst. prof. to asso. prof. edn. Ind. State U., Terre Haute, 1964-70; vis. prof. Ind. U., Bloomington, summer, 1967, 69-70, prof. history and philosophy of edn., 1970-71, coordinator ednl. founds. and grad. council of coordinators, 1965-69, dir. doctoral program in history of Am. edn., 1970-71. Vice chmn. Kingsbury Park Dist., 1972-77; mem. edn. com. Bond County Mental Health Assn., 1974. Served with U.S. Army, 1953-55. Recipient award of merit Nat. Vocat. Guidance Assn., 1973. Mem. History of Edn. Soc. (chmn. nominating com. 1969), Midwest History of Edn. Soc. (pres. 1971-72), Philosophy of Edn. Soc., Ohio Valley Philosophy of Edn. Soc. (sec.-treas. 1967-70), Soc. Profs. of Edn. (asso. editor publs. 1968-70), Central States Faculty Colloquim (chmn. 1969—), John Dewey Soc. for Study of Edn. and Culture (chmn. 1973-78), North Central Assn. Commn. on Insts. of Higher Edn., Assn. Free Meth. Ednl. Insts. (v.p. 1978-80). Democrat. Methodist. Author: The Teacher Education Guide, 1961; (with William Van Til) Education in American Life, 1972; mem. rev. bd. Ednl. Theory, 1972—; editor: Proc. of Ohio Valley Philosophy of Edn. Soc. Ann. Meeting, 1968, 69, 70; Insights, 1973-78. Office: 315 E College St Greenville IL 62246

STEPHENSON, JAMES BLAKE, research chemist; b. Alton, Kans., Aug. 10, 1942; s. John Henry and Amanda Belle (Dibble) S.; B.S., Ft. Hays State U., 1964; postgrad. U. Mo., Rolla, 1968-69; m. Maxine F. King, Dec. 15, 1973; children—Mark, Jennifer, John, Julia, Aimee, Jessica. Phys. chemist Bur. Mines, Rolla, Mo., 1964-65, analytical chemist, 1965-67, chemist, 1967-72, research chemist, 1972-80, research chemist, tech. transfer officer, research chemist, 1980—. EEO adv. com. Rolla Research Center; CPR instr.; mem. Mental Health Assn. Phelps County, Rolla Bulldog Booster Club. NSF secondary sci. orientation fellow, 1959; recipient spl. achievement research awards U.S. Bur. Mines, 1974, 75. Mem. AIME, Metall. Soc., Electrochem. Soc., Am. Soc. Metals (formulating com. for 8th internat. chem. vapor deposition conf.), Am. Soc. Engring. Mgmt., AAAS, ASTM (coms. on erosion and wear, resource recovery), Colo. Mining Assn., Sigma Xi, Delta Epsilon, Sigma Pi Sigma. Methodist. Clubs: Rolla Lions, Odd Fellows, Ft. Hays State U. Alumni Assn. Contbr. chpt. to book, articles to profl. publs. Office: PO Box 280 Rolla MO 65401

STEPHENSON, PHILLIP ANTHONY, ednl. adminstr.; b. Mineral, Ohio, Oct. 11, 1937; s. David Lott and Elsie (Spencer) S.; B.S. Edn. in Secondary Edn., Ohio U., 1959, M.Edn. in Adminstrn., 1961; M.L.S., Ind. U., 1968; m. Bernice Frantz; children—Greg, Lynn, Richard. Jr. high social studies tchr. Tipp City (Ohio) Schs., 1959-65; English tchr. librarian Vandalia-Butler City Schs., Vandalia, Ohio, 1965-67, dir. instrn. media and program evaluation, 1968-80, dir. secondary edn., 1980—; instr. library sci. Wright State U., Dayton, Ohio, part time, 1969-75. Pres. Mason chpt. Am. Field Services, 1978-79; pres. choir Dayton Grace United Meth. Ch., 1978-80. Mem. Buckeye Assn. Sch. Adminstrs., Assn. for Supervision and Curriculum Devel., Ohio Assn. for Supervision and Curriculum Devel., ALA, Internat. Reading Assn., Ohio Assn. Sch. Librarians. Certified supt., high sch. prin., ednl. adminstrv. specialist, Ohio. Home: 4070 Stitt Rd Mason OH 45040 Office: 306 S Dixie Dr Vandalia OH 45377

STEPTO, HERMAN PEDRO, ednl. adminstr.; s. Robert Louis and Grace Elvie (Williams) S.; B.S., Morgan State Coll., Balt., 1951; M.Ed. in Ednl. Adminstrn. and Supervision, DePaul U., 1961; m. Marjorie L. Brown, July 4, 1954; 1 son, Steven Glen; m. 2d, Barbara N. Rosemond, Oct. 26, 1970; 1 dau., Kelly. Dir. vocat. guidance program St. Dorothy Sch., Chgo., 1962-64; asst. prin. Guggenheim Sch., Chgo., 1962-69; adminstrv. coordinator Sch. Dist. 20, Chgo., 1968-69; dir. area programs Chgo. Pub. Schs., 1969-76, dist. adminstr., 1976-79; coordinator staff devel., career guidance and counseling Chgo. Bd. Edn., 1979-80, mgmt. specialist alternate edn. program, govt. funded programs, 1981—. Mem. Community Fund, Chgo., 1970-71; cons. conf. Met. C. of C., 1971-72. Mem. Am. Personnel and Guidance Assn., AAHPER, Nat. Alliance Black Sch. Educators, Edn. Dir. Assn. (Chgo.). Office: 4815 S Karlov St Chicago IL 60632

STERLING, GEORGE ALBERT, ednl. adminstr.; b. Cadiz, Ohio, Dec. 9, 1929; s. Clarence George and Amanda L. (Nichols) S.; B.Bus. Edn., Kent State U., 1961, M.Bus. Edn., 1966, postgrad., 1966; postgrad. in econs. U. Pitts., 1963-64; postgrad. Ohio State U., summer 1964; m. Norma Jean Glenn, Sept. 16, 1950; children—Connie, Cindy, John. Tchr., Ravenna (Ohio) City Bd. Edn., 1958-69; intern vocat. edn. dir. Salem (Ohio) City Bd. Edn., 1969-70; state supr. Ohio Research Coordinating Unit, Columbus, 1970—; coordinator Ohio Gov.'s study of high sch. dropouts, 1980-81. Sunday Sch. tchr., Ch. of Christ, 1966—; v.p., treas. Ravenna Edn. Assn., 1960's; pres. Kent State U. Future Tchrs. Assn., 1954; active Boy Scouts Am. Served with USAF, 1952-55. Mem. Am. Vocat. Assn., Ohio Vocat. Assn., Ohio Edn. Assn. (life), Iota Lambda Sigma. Club: Green Chips Investment. Condr. research, contbr. annuals System for Analyzing Cost of Operating Vocat. Edn. Programs, 1973-74. Home: 4830 Georgesville Wrightsville Rd Grove City OH 43123 Office: 65 S Front St Room 904 Columbus OH 43215

STERN, CLARENCE AMES, historian, educator; b. McCluskey, N.D., Jan. 6, 1913; s. Adam M. and Minnie (Krieger) S.; A.B. (salutatorian), Eastern Mich. U., 1934; M.A., Wayne State U., 1938; postgrad. LaSalle Extension U., 1947-49; Ph.D., U. Nebr., 1958; m. Kathleen Gober, Feb. 20, 1946. Tchr. social sci. Ecorse (Mich.) Pub. Schs., 1934-37; tchr. history and social sci. Detroit Pub. Schs., 1937-42, River Rouge (Mich.) Pub. Schs., 1954-55; asst. prof. history and polit. sci. Coll. Engring., Lawrence Inst. Tech., Detroit, 1946-50; asst. dept. history U. Nebr., 1951-53; asso. prof. history polit. sci. Wayne (Nebr.) State Coll., 1958-65; asso. prof. constl. and polit. party history U.S. and Europe, U. Wis., Oshkosh, 1965—, asso. prof. history U. Wis., Fond du Lac, 1975—, chmn. history dept., 1977—, chmn. div. social scis., 1979-80; grant proposal reviewer Nat. Endowment Humanities, 1978—; polit. sci. expert Nat. Council Social Studies. Served with USAAF, 1942-46; ETO. Ford Found. Am. Polit. Sci. Assn. grantee U. Ind., 1962; hon. fellow Harry S. Truman Library Inst. Fellow Intercontinental Biog. Assn., Anglo-Am. Acad. (hon.), Internat. Inst. Community Service; mem. AAUP (pres. chpt. 1964-65), Am. Hist. Assn., Nat. Trust Historic Preservation, Smithsonian Instn. (nat. asso.), Orgn. Am. Historians, Am. Polit. Sci. Assn., ACLU, Wis. Civil Liberties Union (acad. freedom com.), Phi Alpha Theta, Pi Gamma Mu, Kappa Delta Pi. Author: Republican Heyday: Republicanism Through the McKinley Years, 1962, 69; Resurgent Republicanism: The Handiwork of Hanna, 1963, 68; Golden Republicanism: The Crusade for Hard Money, 1964, 70; Protectionist Republicanism: Republican Tariff Policy in the McKinley Period, 1971. Home: 1625 Elmwood Ave Oshkosh WI 54901 PO Box 2294 Oshkosh WI 54903

STERN, IRVING M., state senator; b. Nov. 6, 1928; student Roosevelt U.; m. Louise Gordon. Mem. Minn. Senate, 1979—; mayor, St. Louis Park, Minn., 1976-79. Mem. Democratic-Farmer-Labor party. Office: 309 State Capitol St Paul MN 55155*

STERN, RUSSELL THURSTON, JR., fin. services co. exec.; b. Chgo., Apr. 2, 1927; s. Russell T. and Eleanor J. S.; B.A., Princeton U., 1949; m. Carol Larson Stern, July 6, 1949; children—Russell Thurston, William Carl, K. Patricia, Darrell S. With Merrill Lynch Pierce Fenner & Smith Inc., Chgo., 1949-81, office mgr., 1969-72, regional v.p., 1972-78, mng. dir. mktg., 1979-81; sr. v.p. Smith Barney Harris Upham, Chgo., 1981—. Republican. Episcopalian. Clubs: Econs., Exec. Home: 46 Fox Lan Winnetka IL 60093 Office: Suite 4400 One First Nat Plaza Chicago IL 60603

STERN, SAMUEL NIESON, psychologist; b. Bklyn., Jan. 11, 1948; s. Louis and Gladys Shirley (Berman) S.; student L.I. U., 1965-67; B.A., Clark U., 1969; M.A., U. Ala., 1972, Ph.D., 1974; m. Renee Getzler, June 4, 1977. Chief unit psychologist Bryce Hosp., Tuscaloosa, Ala., 1973-74; psychologist Coney Island Hosp., Bklyn., 1974-75; psychologist, team leader Kingsboro Psychiat. Center, Bklyn., 1975-79; chief psychology service VA Med. Center, Saginaw, Mich., 1979—; part-time lectr. psychology Saginaw Valley State Coll., 1980—; pvt. practice clin. psychology, Saginaw, 1979—; player clarinet in band Saginaw Valley State Coll., 1980, Pit Orch., Pit and Balcony Playhouse, Saginaw, 1981, Kingsboro Community Coll., 1974-79, Am. Legion Band, 1974-79, Bklyn. Drs. Symphony, 1974-79. USPHS grantee, 1969-74. Mem. Am. Psychol. Assn., Assn. Advancement Psychology, Nat. Register Health Service Providers in Psychology, Psychologists for Legis. Action Now, Mich. Soc. Lic. Psychologists, Mich. Psychol. Assn., Mid-Mich. Psychologists, Assn. of VA Chief Psychologists, Psi Chi. Democrat. Jewish. Contbr. articles to profl. jours. Office: 1500 Weiss St Saginaw MI 48602

STERNBERGER, STEPHEN JEFFREY, ins. cons.; b. Indpls., May 26, 1949; s. Robert Sidney and Sandra Sue (Knoy) S.; B.S.Ed., Ind. U., 1971; m. Valerie Dale Garbrecht, July 31, 1971. Tchr., coach, Pike Twp. (Ind.) Schs., 1971-74; agt. Mass. Mut. Ins. Co., Indpls., 1974-75; dir. adminstrn. Compensation Systems, Inc., Indpls., 1975; author, cons. Pictorial Publishers, Inc., Indpls., 1975—; v.p. Ind. Assn. Health Underwriters, Indpls., 1974-75. Registered health underwriter (R.H.U.), C.L.U.; recipient Heart Fund Solicitors award, 1979. Mem. Indpls. Assn. Life Underwriters, Indpls. Assn. Health Underwriters, Nat. Assn. Life and Health Underwriters, Estate Planning Council Indpls., Am. Soc. C.L.U.'s, Am. Soc. Tng. and Devel., Assn. for Advanced Life Underwriting, Ind. U. Alumni Assn., Pi Kappa Alpha. Republican. Unitarian. Club: Ind. U. Varsity. Author: Advanced Underwriting Training Course, 1978; Estate Planning Training Course, 1979; Pension Planning Training Course, 1981; contbr. articles to profl. jours. Home: 9210 N Tacoma Ave Indianapolis IN 46240 Office: 8081 Zionsville Rd Indianapolis IN 46268

STERTMEYER, RANDALL LEE, insulation corp. exec.; b. Cin., Dec. 10, 1942; s. Harold Henry and Paula Charlotta (Theobald) S.; B.S. in Edn., Miami U., Oxford, Ohio, 1964; M.A., Xavier U., Cin., 1976; postgrad. Sch. Bus., U. Cin., 1977-78; m. Gail Lynn Murphy, Apr. 4, 1968; children—Scott Christopher, Allison Paige. Social worker Hamilton County (Ohio) Welfare Dept., 1965-68; diagnostic social worker Cin. Bd. Edn., 1968-70; pres. Lyran Homes, Inc., Cin., 1970-73; Cin. br. mgr. Mooney and Moses of Ohio, Inc., 1973-77, v.p., Cin., 1977—. Ward chmn. Dem. Com. City of Madeira, Ohio, 1973-78; candidate for city councilman, Madeira, 1975; del. State of Ohio Dem. State Conv., 1975; mem. Cin. Energy Policy Com., 1981-82. Served with USAR, 1965-71. Named citizen of the day Sta. WLW, 1978; mem. Tribe Miami, Miami U., 1964. Mem. Nat. Home Builders Assn., Ohio Home Builders Assn., Greater Cin. Home Builders Assn., No. Ky. Home Builders Assn., Greater Cin. Insulation Contractors Assn. (founding chmn. 1978). Home: 9577 Loveland-Maderia Rd Loveland OH 45140 Office: 207 Donald Dr Fairfield OH 45014

STETSON, JOHN BENJAMIN BLANK, anesthesiologist, educator; b. Chgo., Mar. 18, 1927; s. Louis Blank and Dorothy (Cohen) S.; student U. Chgo., 1942-44, 46-47; M.D., Harvard U., 1951; m. Gwyneth Evans, Dec. 22, 1966; children—Diana S., Dana L., Jonathan O. Intern, U. Utah Hosp., 1951-52; resident Mass. Gen. Hosp., Lowell Gen. Hosp., 1952-54; instr. anesthesiology U. Mich., 1954-57; practice medicine specializing in anesthesiology, Johnson City, Tenn., 1957-59; instr. anesthesiology Harvard Med. Sch., Children's Hosp., 1959-65; asst. prof., dir. vital function lab. U. Ind. Med. Sch., 1965-67; asso. prof., asso. dir. dept. anesthesiology Ohio State U. Sch. Medicine, 1967-68; dir. clin. pharmacology, acting med. dir. Strasenburgh Labs., Rochester, N.Y., 1968-70; asso. anesthesiologist Strong Meml. Hosp., U. Rochester (N.Y.), 1970-76; dir. clin. research Arnar Stone Labs., Inc., Mt. Prospect, Ill., 1976-77; prof. Rush Med. Coll., 1977—; cons. Roswell Park Meml. Inst., Buffalo, 1968—. Served with USNR, 1944-46. FDA grantee, 1973-76, Jackson Johnson research fellow in biochemistry Washington U., St. Louis, 1947—; diplomate Am. Bd. Anesthesiologists. Fellow Am. Coll. Anesthesiologists; mem. Canadian Anaesthetists Soc., Assn. Anaesthetists Gt. Britain and Ireland, Internat. Anesthesia Research Soc., Soc. Critical Care Medicine, Pan Am. Med. Assn., Am. Soc. Anesthesiologists (past chmn. history and archives com.). Republican. Unitarian. Editor: Cardiovascular Problems, 1963; Ventilation in Anesthesiology, 1965; Metabolism In Anesthesiology, 1967; Prolonged Tracheal Intubation, 1970; (with P. R. Swyer) Neonatal Intensive Care, 1976; contbr. articles to profl. jours. Office: Rush-Presbyterian-St Lukes Med Center Chicago IL 60612

STETSON, LAVERNE ELLIS, agrl. engr.; b. Crawford, Nebr., Aug. 26, 1933; s. Orville E. and Anna H. (Soester) S.; B.S., U. Nebr., 1962, M.S., 1968; m. Shirley R. Wasserburger, Mar. 3, 1956; children—Patricia, Erwin, Ronald, Helen. Research agrl. engr. Agrl. Research Service, Dept. Agr., U. Nebr., Lincoln, 1962—. Recipient Sustained Outstanding Performance award Dept. Agr., 1967, Spl. Merit award, 1972, 76; Disting. Service award Food and Energy Council, 1979; registered profl. engr., Nebr. Mem. Am. Soc. Agrl. Engrs. (Tech. Paper award 1965), IEEE, Soil Conservation Soc. Am., Irrigation Assn. (Man of Yr. award 1980), Sigma Xi, Tau Beta Pi, Sigma Tau, Gamma Sigma Delta, Alpha Epsilon. Republican. Roman Catholic. Author papers on electrically related agrl. engring. Home: 740 E Avon St Lincoln NE 68505 Office: Agrl Engring Dept Univ Nebr Lincoln NE 68583

STEVENS, CHARLES THOMAS, counseling psychologist; b. Nevada, Mo., Oct. 25, 1932; s. Glenn Monroe and Edna Estelle (Thomas) S.; B.S. in Agr., S.W. Mo. State U., 1955, B.S. in Psychology, 1974, M.S. in Guidance and Counseling, 1974; Ph.D. candidate, U. Mo., Columbia; m. Helen Louise Utterback, Dec. 27, 1953; children—Mark Thomas, Diana Lynn, Eric Allen. Served as enlisted man U.S. Army N.G., 1954-55; commd. 2d lt., 1955, advanced through grades to lt. col. inf., 1969; ret., 1971; vets. benefits counselor U. Mo., Columbia, Counseling Center, 1977-79; dir. Bur. for Blind, State of Mo., Jefferson City, 1979—; cons., counselor visually impaired coll. students, 1975-78; guest lectr. on blindness; state pres. Nat. Fedn. of the Blind, 1977-79. Decorated Legion of Merit, Bronze Star with V, Army Commendation Medal with V, 2 Purple Hearts, Combat Inf. Badge; Cross of Galantry (Vietnam); grantee Handicapped Manpower Availability Survey. Mem. Am. Personnel and Guidance Assn., Am. Psychol. Assn. Mem. Christian Ch. Club: Lions. Home: 1203 Fairview Rd Columbia MO 65201 Office: 619 E Capitol St Jefferson City MO 65101

STEVENS, HAROLD RUSSELL, physician; b. Detroit, Nov. 18, 1930; s. Harold Russell and Etheleen Mae (Stone) S.; A.B., Albion Coll., 1951; M.D., U. Mich., 1955; m. Shirley Ann Sias, Sept. 30, 1950; children—Kirk Russell, Martha Lee. Intern Toledo Hosp., 1955-56, resident in anesthesiology 1960-62, attending anesthesiologist, 1962—, med. dir. respiratory therapy, 1966—, research asso. Inst. Med. Research, 1965-70; practice medicine specializing in anesthesiology, respiratory therapy, Toledo, 1962—; med. dir. respiratory therapy U. Toledo, 1971—, prof. respiratory therapy, 1974—; asst. clin. prof. Med. Coll. Ohio, Toledo, 77-79. dir. anesthesiology Mercy Hosp., Toledo, 1968-79, med. co-dir. respiratory therapy, 1969—; dir. intensive care unit Toledo Hosp., 1975—. Health councilor Community Planning Council Northwestern Ohio, 1970-71. Trustee Maumee Valley Found. Served to capt. M.C., USAF, 1957-59. Diplomate Am. Bd. Anesthesiology. Mem. Acad. Medicine Toledo and Lucas County (councilor 1970-71), Am., Ohio med. assns., Am. Assn. Respiratory Therapy, Internat. Anesthesia Research Soc., Am., Ohio, Toledo (pres. 1971) socs. anesthesiologists, Phi Beta Kappa, Alpha Omega Alpha. Clubs: Masons (32 deg.), Shriners; Inverness, Toledo. Contbr. articles to profl. jours. Home: 2149 Emkay Dr Toledo OH 43606 Office: 3939 Monroe St Toledo OH 43606

STEVENS, JOANNE, guidance counselor; b. Indpls., Ind., Nov. 4, 1939; s. Asa Neiley and Elizabeth (Boyd) Stevens; B.S. (Hanover fellow), Hanover Coll., 1961; M.S., Ind. U., 1965; postgrad. U. Edinburgh, 1970. Instr. Indpls. Pub. Schs., 1961-63, 65-67; asst. dean of women Nat. Music Camp, 1963-68; asst. program office, 1971-76; guidance counselor, dir. Arlington Heights (Ill.) Pub. Schs., 1967-69; guidance counselor Palatine High Sch. Dist. 211, 1969—. Active Best Off Broadway Community Theatre Group, 1976—; dir. chancel choir St. Mark's Lutheran Ch., Mount Prospect, 1976-79; mem. adv. bd. Interlochen Center for Arts, 1971-72, 77-79. Recipient William C. Mc Cormack award Indpls. 2d Presbyn. Ch., 1957. Mem. Am. Choral Dirs. Assn., P.E.O., Ill. Guidance and Personnel Assn., Nat., Ill. edn. assns., Am. Sch. Counselors Assn., Am. Coll. Personnel Assn., Ill. Guidance Personnel Assn., Ind. U. Alumni Assn., Hanover Coll. Alumni Assn., Am. Personnel and Guidance Assn. Presbyterian. Home: 320 Whidah Ct Schaumburg IL 60194 Office: 1100 W Schaamburg Rd Schaumburg IL 60194

STEVENS, MILDRED JULIUS (MRS. ROBERT LOUIS STEVENS), physician; b. Burdick, Kans., Apr. 21, 1923; d. Carl Anderson and Sene (Nelson) Julius; student Bethany Coll., 1941-42; B.S., Kans. U., 1945, M.D., 1947; m. Robert Louis Stevens, Apr. 4, 1947; children—Laura Bea, Victor Louis, Rhoads Elliott, Leah Jane, James David. Intern, St. Margaret's Hosp., Kansas City, Kans., 1947-48; pvt. practice, Garnett, Kans., 1948—; mem. staff Anderson County Hosp., chief of staff, 1961, 65, 73. Mem. Kans., Anderson County (pres. 1961, 65, 73) med. socs., AMA, World Med. Assn., Alpha Omega Alpha. Republican. Presbyterian. Author: Memories of Salem, 1974; Memories of Hebron, 1974; This I Believe, 1975; From Now On . . . (pen and ink sketches), 1977. Home: 346 W 4th St Garnett KS 66032 Office: 202 W 4th St Garnett KS 66032

STEVENS, PATRICIA CAROL, univ. adminstr.; b. St. Louis, Jan. 11, 1946; d. Carroll and Juanita Donohue; A.B., Duke U., 1966; M.A., U. Mo., Kansas City, 1974, postgrad., 1974—; m. James H. Stevens, Jr., Aug. 27, 1966; children—James H. III, Carol Janet. Tchr. math, secondary schs., Balt., St. Louis, Shawnee Mission, Kans., 1966-71; lectr. U. Mo., Kansas City, 1975-76, research asst. affirmative action, 1976-79, coordinator affirmative action, 1979—. Bd. dirs., v.p. Am. Cancer Soc. Jackson County, 1973-80; bd. dirs. PTA, 1975-77. Recipient Outstanding Service and Achievement award U. Mo. Kansas City, 1976; Jack C. Coffey grantee, 1978; Cream Rose Outstanding Service award Delta Gamma, 1970. Mem. Nat. Council Tchrs. Math, Assn. Supervision and Curriculum Devel., Women's Equity Project, Nat. Assn. Student Personnel Adminstrs., Women's Network, Phi Delta Kappa, (pres.), Phi Kappa Phi, Delta Gamma (v.p.). Home: 5040 W 97th St Overland Park KS 66207 Office: 5100 Rockhill Rd Kansas City MO 64110

STEVENS, ROBERT GENE, fin. coms.; b. Marion, Ill., Jan. 4, 1930; s. Robert Bryan and Nellie Mae (Isaacs) S.; B.S., So. Ill. U., 1951; M.S., U. Ill., 1954, Ph.D., 1958; LL.D. (hon.), Mt. St. Joseph Coll., 1974; m. Susan Anne Krejci, Aug. 6, 1955; children—David R., Craig R., Brain R. Auditor, Arthur Anderson & Co., St. Louis, 1954; instr. accountancy U. Ill., 1953-58; partner Touche, Ross & Co., N.Y.C., 1958-68; v.p. planning and control 1st Nat. City Bank, N.Y.C., 1968-70; pres., chief exec. officer Old Stone Corp. and Old Stone Bank, Providence, 1970-76; chmn., pres., chief exec. officer BancOhio Corp., Columbus, also chmn., chief exec. officer BancOhio Nat. Bank, Columbus, 1976-81; prin. Stevens Planning Cons., Columbus, 1981—; dir. Student Loan Mktg. Assn., Washington, 1980—. Trustee, St. Anthony Hosp.; trustee, treas. Columbus Acad. Served to 1st lt. USAF, 1951-53. Named Disting. Alumnus, So. Ill. U., 1977; C.P.A., Ill., N.Y., Calif. Mem. Am. Inst. C.P.A.s, Ohio Soc. C.P.A.s, R.I. Soc. C.P.A.s. Presbyterian. Club: Rocky Fork Hunt and Country. Home: 363 Westland Ave Columbus OH 43209

STEVENS, ROBERT JAY, editor; b. Detroit, July 25, 1945; s. Jay Benjamin and Louise Ann (Beyreuther) S.; student Huron (S.D.) Coll., 1963-66, Wayne State U., 1968-72; m. Dahlia Jean Conger, Aug. 15, 1970; children—Sandra Lee, Julie Ann. Staff writer Automotive News, Detroit, 1968-71; editor Excavating Contractor Mag., Cummins Pub., Oak Park, Mich., 1971-78; editor Pro Journal, Sandy Corp., Southfield, Mich., 1978-79; editor Cars & Parts Mag., Amos Press, Sidney, Ohio, 1979—. Served with U.S. Army, 1966-68. Decorated Bronze Star. Recipient Robert F. Boger Meml. award Constrn. Writers Assn., 1975; Spl. award Am. Public Works Assn., 1978; Community Service award City of St. Ignace (Mich.), 1981. Mem. Soc. Automotive Historians, Detroit Auto Writers, Antique Automobile Club Am., Vintage Chevrolet Club Am. Republican. Presbyterian. Home: 653 Ridgeway Dr Sidney OH 43365 Office: PO Box 482 Sidney OH 45367

STEVENSON, ADLAI EWING, III, lawyer, former U.S. senator; b. Chgo., Oct. 10, 1930; s. Adlai Ewing and Ellen (Borden) S.; A.B., Harvard U., 1952, LL.B., 1957; m. Nancy L. Anderson, June 25, 1955; children—Adlai Ewing IV, Lucy W., Katherine R., Warwick L. Admitted to Ill. bar, 1957; law clk. Ill. Supreme Ct., 1957-58; asso. firm Mayer, Brown & Platt, Chgo., 1958-66, partner, 1966-67, Washington office, 1981; mem. Ill. Ho. of Reps., 1965-67; treas. State of Ill., Springfield, 1967-70; U.S. senator from Ill., 1970-81; Democratic candidate for gov. Ill., 1982. Served to capt. USMCR, 1952-54. Mem. Am., Ill., Chgo. bar assns., other assns. Office: Mayer Brown and Platt 888 17th St NW Washington DC 20037

STEVENSON, FORREST CAMP, JR., psychologist, marriage counselor; b. Deming, N.Mex., July 4, 1922; s. Forrest Camp and Fern (Norris) S.; A.B., Park Coll., 1945; M.A., U. Detroit, 1964; M.R.E., Central Bapt. Sem., 1949, B.D., 1950, D.R.E., 1959; m. Bernice Freda Wells, June 3, 1952; children—Rita Fern, Paul Forrest, Eric Jon. Dean, Calvary Coll., Kansas City, Mo., 1955-64; pvt. practice marriage counseling, Allen Park, Mich., 1964-74; pres. Personality Dynamics, Inc., Southfield, Mich., 1974—. Served with U.S. Army, 1952-55. Decorated Bronze Star medal. Mem. Am. Assn. Marriage and Family Counselors, Am. Psychol. Assn. Home: 11349 Culver Rd Brighton MI 48116

STEVENSON, GEORGE ALFRED, II, cons. engr.; b. Parkersburg, W.Va., Apr. 9, 1933; s. George Alfred and Kathrine (O'Brien) S.; student Bethany Coll., 1951-54; B.S.M.E., Ohio U., 1956; m. Barbara Russ, June 27, 1958; children—Eric, Peter. Instrument engr. E.I. duPont De Nemours & Co., 1956-58; project and sr. engr. Monsanto Chem. Co., 1958-60; research engr. Dixie Cup, 1961-62; chief design engr. Heil Process Equipment, 1962-66; chief facilities engr. Foseco, Inc., 1966-70; engr. Stevenson Engring. Co., 1970-78; cons. engr., br. office mgr. Clark-Trombley, Traverse City, Mich., 1980-81; owner Bay Engring. Co., Suttons Bay, Mich., 1981—; dir. Parkersburg Nat. Bank. Mem. Mishicot (Wis.) Sch. Adv. Com., 1974-77, Leeland (Mich.) Sch. Adv. Com., 1980-81; mem. heating adv. com. Northwestern Mich. Coll.; nat. bd. fellows Bethany Coll. Registered profl. engrs., Wis., Mich.; recipient Recon 5 award ASME, 1956. Mem. ASHRAE. Presbyterian. Club: Lions. Patentee in field. Home: Box 306 Rural Route 1 Lake Leelanau MI 49653 Office: Millside Bldg Suttons Bay MI 49682

STEVENSON, GERALD LEE, engring. contracting co. exec.; b. Salem, Ill., Jan. 16, 1937; s. Russell Claude and Oneta (Mills) S.; B.Ch.E., U. Mo., 1959, M.Ch.E., 1963, hon. profl. degree, 1981; student St. Louis U., 1959-61; postgrad. European Inst. Bus. Adminstrn.; grad. A.M.P., Harvard Bus. Sch., 1981; m. Eugenia Adele Bradford, Aug. 7, 1963; children—Lynne Anne, Laura Jean. Technologist, Shell Oil Co., Wood River, Ill., 1959-61; project/prodn. engr. Internat. Minerals, v.p. D. J. Stark Group of Cos., N.Y.C. and Toronto, Ont., 1967-70; sr. v.p. Davy McKee Corp., Cleve., 1970—, also dir., v.p., dir. subs. cos.; dir. Acres Davy McKee Ltd. (Can.). Served with U.S. Army, 1960. NSF fellow, 1962; Monsanto Chem. Co. scholar, 1958. Mem. Am. Inst. Chem. Engrs., Am. Chem. Soc., Ont. Soc. Profl. Engrs., Fertiliser Soc., Alpha Chi Sigma, Tau Beta Pi. Republican. Episcopalian. Clubs: Lone Palm Golf, Imperial Lakes Golf, Lakeland Yacht and Country, Directors, Chagrin Valley Country. Home: 511 N Main St Chagrin Falls OH 44022 Office: 6200 Oak Tree Blvd Cleveland OH 44131

STEVENSON, JOANNE SABOL, nurse, educator; b. Steubenville, Ohio, June 8, 1939; d. Joseph Andrew and Susan (Ploskunak) S.; B.S. in Nursing, Ohio State U., 1963, M.S., 1964, Ph.D., 1970; m. Robert James Stevenson, Aug. 6, 1966; children—James Joseph, Michael Joseph. With Ohio State U. Sch. Nursing, 1970—, prof., asst. dir. research, dir. Center for Nursing Research, 1972—. NIH Predoctoral fellow, 1967-70; Am. Jour. of Nursing Book of Year award, 1977; Women's Health Research Program grantee, 1980—; Biomed. Research Devel. grantee NIH, 1979-82. Fellow Am. Acad. Nursing; mem. AAUP, AAAS, Am. Nurses' Assn., Alpha Tau Delta (chpt. pres. 1962-63), Sigma Theta Tau. Roman Catholic. Club: Little Turtle Golf Assn. Author: Issues and Crises During Middlescence, 1977; (with N. A. Brunner, J. Larabee) A Plan for Nurse Staffing in Hospital Emergency Services, 1978. Office: Ohio State U Sch Nursing 1585 Neil Ave Columbus OH 43210

STEVENSON, RICHARD MARSHALL, chemist; b. Detroit, July 2, 1923; s. Richard Ambrose and Jeanne Margaret (Marshall) S.; B.S. cum laude, Detroit Inst. Tech., 1947; postgrad Wayne State U.; m. Marion Ignatius, Feb. 13, 1944; children—Michael Richard, Mark Alan. Chemist, Udylite Corp. div. Ocy Metal Industries, Warren, Mich., 1959-76; pres. Richard M. Stevenson & Co., Cons. Chemists, Grosse Pointe, Mich., 1976—; research dir. Detroit Plastic Molding Co., Sterling Heights, Mich., 1978—. Served with USN, 1944-46. Mem. Am. Chem. Soc., Am. Electroplaters Soc., Am. Contract Bridge League. Patentee in electrodisposition of metals. Home: 2179 Allard Ave Grosse Pointe MI 48236 Office: 6600 E 15 Mile Rd Sterling Heights MI 48077

STEWART, DONALD EUGENE, mech. engr.; b. Wyandotte County, Kans., Apr. 29, 1924; s. Thomas Jefferson and Minnie Sophia (Heinrichs) S.; B.A. in Math., U. Mo., Kansas City, 1960; B.S. in Engring. Scis., Calif. Christian U., Los Angeles, 1974, M.S. in Engring. Mgmt., 1976; m. Marjorie Jean Bloomfield, Oct. 5, 1946; 1 dau., Eileen Cheryl. Project engr. Colgate Palmolive Co., Kansas City, Kans., 1948-62; sales and field engr. Bublitz Machinery Co., North Kansas City, Mo., 1962-66; materials handling engr. Allis Chalmers Co., Independence, Mo., 1966-74; sr. engr. plant layout and materials handling John Deere Co., Dubuque, Iowa, 1974—. Advisor, Jr. Achievement, 1974-77. Served with U.S. Army, 1943-45; ETO. Recipient Diamond Achievement award Heart of Am. Engring. and Sci. Club, 1958; ann. engring. award Midwest Maintenance Inst., 1960; plaque and citation Tri-States Jr. Achievement Programs, Inc., 1975. Mem. ASME, Am. Inst. Plant Engrs., Soc. Mfg. Engrs. (spl. award Region VI, Zone II, Chpt. 175, 1979, programming award 1981, chmn.'s service pin 1981), Nat. Soc. Profl. Engrs., Iowa Engring. Soc. (Order of Engrs. 1981; pres./chmn. profl. engrs. in industry div. 1981—), Nat. Mgmt. Assn., Alpha Phi Omega (life mem.). Episcopalian. Club: Masons. Contbr. articles to profl. publs. Home: 170 Copper Kettle Ln East Dubuque IA 61025 Office: John Deere Co Hwy 386 Dubuque IA 52001

STEWART, DOUGLAS A., packaging co. exec.; b. Bronx, N.Y., Sept. 12, 1940; s. Arnold J. and Dorothy G.; B.B.A. in Finance, Manhattan Coll., 1962; m. Linda G. Sahagian, May 8, 1971; children—Debra Arlene, Phillip Douglas, Gregory Lynn. Sales rep. Hazel Atlas Glass subs. Continental Can Co., N.Y.C., 1962-64, Brockway Glass Co., N.Y.C., 1964-65; purchasing agent Chesebrough-Pond's, Inc., N.Y.C., 1965-68; sales mgr. Sheffield Tube Corp., N.Y.C., 1968-71, mgr. Western ops., Chgo., 1971-73, v.p. mktg., Broadview, Ill., 1973—. Mem. Am. Mktg. Assn., Metal Tube Pkg. Council of N. Am., Pkg. Inst. (Chgo. chpt.), Drug, Chemical & Allied Trades Assn., Chgo. Drug & Chemical Assn., Cosmetic Toiletry and Fragrance Assn. Clubs: City (Chgo.); Merchandising Execs.; Oak Park Country. Home: 1001 N Fair Oaks Ave Oak Park IL 60302 Office: 2850 Eisenhower Expwy Broadview IL 60153

STEWART, EDNA MAE, nurse; b. Liberty Twp., Ill., Jan. 16, 1915; d. Samuel Francis and Letah W. (Coats) McBride; diploma Parkview Hosp., Pueblo, Colo., 1944. Head nurse Meml. Hosp., Topeka, 1951-80, critical care nurse. Vol. ARC, from 1945; life trustee Cedars Home for Children, Lincoln. Served as 1st lt. Nurse Corps, U.S. Army, 1945-49. Registered nurse, Colo., Kans. Mem. Am., Kans. nurses assns., Nat. Audubon Soc., Am. Legion, St. Francis Hosp. Aux. (life), Nat. Wildlife Fedn. (life). Democrat. Roman Catholic. Home: 1255 Topeka Ave Topeka KS 66612 Office: Meml Hosp 600 Madison St Topeka KS 66606

STEWART, KAY CAROLE, univ. adminstr.; b. Oak Hill, W.Va., Aug. 29, 1944; d. Arthur P. and Eva Mae (Fry) Gilliam; B.S., W.Va. Inst. Tech., 1966; M.S., Ft. Hays State U., 1971; postgrad. Kans. State U., 1979-80; m. A. David Stewart, Dec. 25, 1965; children—Jeffrey, Shawn, Aaron. Sec., Am. Bapt. Chs., Valley Forge, Pa., 1966-67; tchr. Orange County (N.C.) Schs., 1967-68; instr. Ft. Hays State U., Kans., 1971-72; instr. Coll. Bus. Adminstrn., Kans. State U., Manhattan, 1972-75, asst. to dean, 1975—. Trustee, Am. Bapt. Ch., 1974-77; program chmn. LWV, 1967. Mem. Nat. Assn. Women Deans, Adminstrs. and Counselors, Nat. Acad. Adv. Assn. Democrat. Home: 3452 Chimney Rock Manhattan KS 66502 Office: Coll Bus Adminstrn Kans State U Manhattan KS 66506

STEWART, MAC ARTHUR, coll. ofcl.; b. Forsyth, Ga., July 7, 1942; s. Alonzo and Zillia (Watson) S.; B.A., Morehouse Coll., 1963; M.A. in Counseling and Guidance, Atlanta U., 1965; Ph.D., Ohio State U., 1973; m. Ernestine Clemons, June 4, 1967; children—Bruce Kifle, Justin Ché. Tchr. social sci. Jasper County Tng. Sch., Monticello, Ga., 1963-64, Crispus Attucks High Sch., Indpls., 1965-66; dir. student fin.

aid Morehouse Coll., Atlanta, 1966-70, dir. project upward bound, 1967-70, counselor, summer, 1965, 66, 67; dir. residence hall Ohio State U., Columbus, 1970-71, grad. adminstrv. asso., 1971-73, asst. dean U. Coll., 1973-75, asso. dean, 1975—, adj. asst. prof. Coll. Edn., 1975—; cons. Columbus Met. Area Community Action Orgn., 1974, Dayton (Ohio) Public Schs., 1976. Sec. vestry St. James Episcopal Ch., 1977-78; trustee Buckeye Boys Ranch, 1978—. Recipient Ohio Union Service award, 1977, Earl Anderson Meml. award Ohio State U. Coll. Edn., 1972. Mem. Am. Coll. Personnel Assn., Nat. Assn. Student Personnel Adminstrs., Am. Personnel and Guidance Assn., Mid-Western Assn. Student Fin. Aid Adminstrs., Alpha Kappa Delta, Phi Delta Kappa, Phi Kappa Phi. Episcopalian. Club: Lions (dir. 1976-78). Home: 6358 Stonebridge St Columbus OH 43229 Office: 1050 Carmack Rd Columbus OH 43210

STEWART, MARY AMANDA, social worker; b. Kansas City, Mo., Oct. 22, 1947; d. George Griffis and Mary Eugenie (Voorhis) Fowler; student Colo. State U., 1966-69; B.S., Okla. State U., 1972; M.S.W., Ind. U., 1977; children—Corin Justine, Benjamin George. Adminstrv. asst. Ind. Family Health Council, Indpls., 1977—; social worker Koala Center Alcohol Treatment Center, Lebanon, Ind., 1977; team dir. Crisis Unit, Midtown Community Mental Health Center, Indpls., 1977—, case mgr. inpatient services, 1980—; now also asso. clinician (part-time) Brashear Center; tng. faculty Marion County Mental Health Assn. Crisis & Suicide Intervention Service, 1972-80, mem. crisis and suicide intervention com., 1976-80, chmn., 1980. Recipient 2000 hr. award, Vol., Marion County Mental Health Assn., 1979. Mem. Ind. Crisis Resource Fedn. (treas. 1979-81, dir. 1979-81), Nat. Assn. Social Workers. Democrat. Roman Catholic. Home: 5929 Deerwood Ct Indianapolis IN 46254 Office: 1001 W 10th St Indianapolis IN 46202

STEWART, ROBERT GUY, editor; b. St. Joseph, Mo., May 26, 1955; s. Robert Gross and Jeanne Lucille (Robertson) S.; B.S. in Public Relations, Central Mo. State U., 1977. Employee publs. editor Mut. Benefit Life Ins. Co., Kansas City, Mo., 1978—. Recipient award of merit Kansas City Bus. Communicators, 1979. Mem. Public Relations Soc. Am. (sec. Kansas City chpt. 1982), Internat. Assn. Bus. Communicators. Mem. Christian Ch. (Disciples of Christ). Home: 7681 N Garfield Ave Gladstone MO 64118 Office: 2345 Grand Ave Kansas City MO 64108

STEWART, SUSAN, advt. agy. exec.; b. Detroit, Apr. 10, 1948; d. Eugene Norbert and Eleanor (Mirek) Biernat; B.S., U. Mich., 1970; m. Norman William Stewart, Aug. 9, 1968; 1 son, Corey William. Art. dir. intern Campbell-Ewald Advt. Co., Detroit, 1969; advt. asst. Fair St. Mktg. Services Div., Devlieg Machine Co., Royal Oak, Mich., 1970-71; sr. artist K-Mart Corp., Detroit and Troy, 1971-74; free-lance advt. designer, Birmingham, Mich., 1974-77; prin. Stewart & Stewart Advt. Design Cons., Birmingham, 1977—. Mem. Cranbrook Acad. of Art Mus., Detroit Inst. of Arts Founders Soc. & Drawing/Print Club, Mich. Assn. Gifted and Talented. Unitarian. Clubs: Adcraft, Econ. of Detroit. Office: 6785 Telegraph Rd Birmingham MI 48010

STEWART, VIRGINIA KAMPP (MIMI), hosp. pub. relations exec.; b. Oak Park, Ill., Dec. 12, 1939; d. Hubert Eugene and Virginia (Dalton) Kampp; student Northwestern U., 1957-59, Rosary Coll., 1959-60; m. Henry Lawrence Stewart III, Apr. 7, 1961; children—John Hubert, Peter David, Michael Edward. Asst. editor Internat. Altrusan, 1961-64; free-lance writer, 1964-71; editor Wheaton (Ill.) Leader, 1971-73; asso. dir. pub. relations Central DuPage Hosp., Winfield, Ill., 1973-78, dir. pub. relations, 1978—. Founder The Art Fair, Pitts., 1970; chmn. judges Daily Jour. Ad Craft, 1975—; chmn. Wheaton City Council Nominating Assembly, 1976; bd. dirs. Community Nursing Service DuPage County, 1976—; mem. Wheaton Plan Commn., 1979—. Named Editor of Yr., Ill. Press Assn., 1972; Profl. Woman of Yr., Bank of Wheaton, 1976. Mem. Am. Soc. for Hosp. Pub. Relations, Acad. Hosp. Pub. Relations (sec. 1979-80, dir. 1980—), Ill. Hosp. Pub. Relations Soc., Chgo. Hosp. Pub. Relations Soc., Greater Wheaton C. of C. (dir. 1973—). Republican. Clubs: Service (Chgo.), Altrusa. Home: 1103 N President St Wheaton IL 60187 Office: Central DuPage Hosp O N 025 Winfield Rd Winfield IL 60190

STEWART, W. RODERICK, mfg. co. exec.; b. Norwood, Ohio, Mar. 22, 1916; s. Raymond Forrest and Estelle Marie (Keller) S.; B.B.A., U. Cin., 1939; m. Dolores Faye Doll., Apr. 15, 1944; 1 dau., Sharon Marie. Owner, dir. Music by Roderick Orch., 1934-49; v.p. Cin. Lithographing Co., 1949-63; owner, pres. Concrete Surfacing Machinery Co., Cin., 1963-71, Bossert Machine Co., Cin., 1963-71, R & C Tool & Mfg., Amelia, Ohio, 1970-71, Bourbon Copper & Brass, Cin., 1968-71; pres. Stewart Industries, Inc., Cin., 1971-80, chmn. bd., chief exec. officer, 1980—; pres. Printing Machinery Co., Cin., 1976—; pres. Stewart Safety Systems, Inc., 1981—. Chmn., dir. Greater Cin. & Ky. chpt. Nat. Hemophilia Found., 1976-80; del. White House Conf. Small Bus., 1980. Served with USNR, 1942-45. Mem. Cin. C. of C. (Small Businessman of Yr. 1980), Engring. Soc. Cin., Sales and Mktg. Execs., Assn. Equipment Distbrs., Lambda Chi Alpha. Republican. Presbyterian. Clubs: Rotary, Masons (Shriner), Royal Jesters, Maketewah Country, Beckett Ridge Country, Northport Point Golf, Cin. (Man of Yr. 1979), Officers of World Wars. Home: 220 Linden Dr Cincinnati OH 45215 Office: Stewart Industries Inc 7234 Blue Ash Rd Cincinnati OH 45236

STEWART, WILLIAM ROBERT, profl. golfer; b. Chgo., Apr. 14, 1925; s. Albert R. and Hazel (Bakely) S.; m. Kathleen Joan Wilt, Sept. 20, 1975; children—Charles, Tina, Lisa, Anne, Kathleen, Amy, Emily, Angela. Profl. golfer Paw Paw Lake Golf Club, Watervliet, Mich., 1948—, owner club, 1965—. Mem. bd. Mich. sect. Boy Scouts Am.; bd. dirs. Humane Soc. S.W. Mich., 1970—, v.p., 1970—; mem. Verlon Walker Leukemia Center exec. com. Northwestern Meml. Hosp., Chgo. Mem. Profl. Golfers Assn. Am. (class A mem.), Watervliet C. of C. (past v.p.). Republican. Club: Rotary (Benton Harbor, Mich.). Home: Beechwood Circle Watervliet MI 49098 Office: 751 Paw Paw Ave Watervliet MI 49098

STEYER, RAYMOND JAMES, II, computer programmer; b. Downers Grove, Ill., Aug. 11, 1950; s. Raymond James and Jeane Olga (Wensch) S.; B.A. in Math. and Physics, Beloit (Wis.) Coll., 1972. Sr. programmer No. Trust Co., Chgo., 1972-75; v.p. software dept. Child Inc., Lawrence, Kans., 1975-77, also dir, 1976; sr. analyst/programmer Zurich Ins. Co., Chgo., 1977; programmer technician Montgomery Ward, Chgo., 1977-78; sr. systems engr. Econorex Systems, Kansas City, Mo., 1978-81; system engr. Electronic Data Systems, Kansas City, Mo., 1981—; cons., 1980—. Mem. Math. Assn. Am., Assn. Computing Machinery. Home: 4517 E 112th St Kansas City MO 64137 Office: 10950 Grandview St Bldg 34 Suite 540 Overland Park KS 66210

STICH, JOANNE MILDRED TETENS, hosp. ofcl.; b. Henning, Minn., Dec. 8, 1933; d. John Christian and Eva Marie (Person) Tetens; student pub. schs., Henning, Minn., 1939-51; grad. Dale Carnegie Course, 1978; m. Thomas Frank Stich, Aug. 2, 1958; children—Nancy Jo Stich Adams, Jeffrey Thomas, Gregory John. Secretarial positions Mpls.-Honeywell Co., 1951-58, Otter Tail Power Co., 1958-59; admitting officer Lake Region Hosp., Fergus Falls, Minn., 1959-60, comml. ins. clk., payroll clk., med. transcriptionist, 1960-66, personnel-payroll mgr., 1966—. Pres. local unit Am. Cancer Soc., 1981-82; mem. bd. nominating com., mem. stewardship com., mem. ch. council Augustana Lutheran Ch.; mem. Community Coll. Adv. Com.; bd. dirs. Fergus Falls Community Fed. Credit Union. Mem. Am. Soc. for Hosp. Personnel Adminstrn., Health Care Personnel Assn. Minn., Bus. and Profl. Women. Home: 613 S Peck St Fergus Falls MN 56537 Office: Lake Region Hosp 712 S Cascade St Fergus Falls MN 56537

STICHA, SUSAN ELIZABETH, occupational therapist; b. Sauk Centre, Minn., Jan. 8, 1956; d. Milo Stanley and LaVerne Anne (Remer) S.; B.A. in Occupational Therapy, Coll. of St. Catherine, 1978; postgrad. U. Minn., summer 1980. Dept. head geriatric phys.-psychosocial disabilities Lynwood Health Care Center, Fridley, Minn., 1978-79; staff therapist adult psyche Mercy Med. Center, Coon Rapids, Minn., 1979-80; dept. head geriatric phys.-psychosocial disabilities, occupatonal therapy cons. Westwood Nursing Home, St. Louis Park, Minn., 1980—; mem. allied health professions sect. Minn. Arthritis Found. Mem. World Fedn. Occupational Therapists, Am. Occupational Therapy Assn. (registered), Minn. Occupational Therapy Assn., Arthritis Found., Western Fraternal Life Assn. Roman Catholic. Club: Blaisdell Place. Office: 7500 W 22d St Saint Louis Park MN 55426

STICKLE, DAVID WALTER, state ofcl.; b. Boston, Apr. 18, 1933; s. Harold Edwards and Lucille Margaret (Magee) S.; B.S., Tufts U., 1955; M.S., Northeastern U., Boston, 1968; M.P.H., U. N.C., 1969, Dr.P.H., 1971; m. Mary DeLong, July 29, 1972. Chem. technician Nat. Research Corp., Boston, 1957-58; med. technician U.S. Dept. Agr., Boston, 1958-59; bacteriologist Mass. Dept. Pub. Health, Boston, 1959-63, bacteriologist in charge of spl. serology, 1963-68; chief clin. lab. improvement program Minn. Dept. Health, Mpls., 1971—, asst. dir. div. med. labs., 1975-76, acting dir., 1976—; adj. asst. prof. U. Minn., 1977—. Mem. Am. Soc. Microbiology, Am. Pub. Health Assn., Conf. Pub. Health Lab. Dirs., Minn. Assn. Blood Banks. Contbr. articles to profl. jours. Office: 717 Delaware St Minneapolis MN 55440

STIEHL, CHARLES WILLIAM, surgeon; b. South Milwaukee, Wis., Apr. 23, 1924; s. Carl Ernst and Marjorie (Simon) S.; B.S., Northwestern U., 1942, B.M., M.D., 1947; m. Sarah D. Harding, Dec. 20, 1945 (div. Oct. 1957); children—Patti (Mrs. Michael Boris), Carl Harding, Sarah Ann; m. 2d, Edith Ann Mauer, Nov., 1967; 1 dau., Edith Ann. Intern, Columbia Hosp., Milw., 1947-48; resident St. Mary's Hosp., Milw., 1948-49; physician and surgeon Algoma (Wis.) Clinic, 1950-66; chief surgery Algoma Meml. Hosp., 1964—; med. dir. Heil Co., Milw. owner Von Stiel Wine, Inc., Algoma, 1961—; pres. S & M Real Estate Corp., Algoma, 1958—. Mem. Sch. Bd., 1954-58. Served with USNR, 1942. Mem. Wis., Kewaunee County (past pres.) med. socs., Wis. Coll. Emergency Physicians (pres.), Acad. Indsl. Medicine, Beta Theta Pi, Nu Sigma Nu. Lutheran. Originator Von Stiehl natural cherry wine, stabilization natural cherry wine, aging wrap. Home: 2740 W Forest Home Ave Milwaukee WI 53215 Office: 2740 W Forest Home Milwaukee WI

STIER, RONALD LEE, elec. wire and cable mfg. co. exec.; b. Richmond, Ind., Aug. 6, 1937; s. Robert Lawrence and Mary Mildred (Cunningham) S.; student St. Meinrad Coll., 1955-61; student elec. engring. Internat. Corr. Schs., 1970-74; B.S. in Indsl. Mgmt., Aurora Coll., 1974; m. Donna Jean Foltz, Apr. 4, 1964; children—Kimberly, Denise, Ronald. Product engr. Belden Corp., Richmond, Ind., 1964-68, product devel. engr. Tech. Research Center, 1968-71, mktg. specialist, 1971-74, mktg. mgr., 1974-79, long range market and planning mgr., 1979—. Mem. St Andrews Parish Council, Richmond, 1975—; dist. chmn. Old Trails council Boy Scouts Am., bd. dirs. Crossroad council. Served with AUS, 1961-64. Mem. Electronics Industry Assn. (past co-chmn. Young Exec. group Central div.), Richmond Amateur Radio Assn. (pres.), Nat. Cable TV Assn., Security Equipment Industry Assn. (past dir.), Electronics Internat. Adv. Panel, Amateur Radio Relay League. Republican. Roman Catholic. Club: K.C., Elks, Knights of St. John. Contbr. articles electronics jours. Patentee in field. Home: 3605 Backmeyer Rd Richmond IN 47374 Office: PO Box 1327 Richmond IN 47374

STIER, WILLIAM FREDERICK, JR., educator; b. St. Louis, Feb. 22, 1943; s. William Frederick and Neoma (White) S.; B.A., St. Ambrose Coll., 1965; M.A., Temple U., 1966; Ph.D., U. S.D., 1972; postgrad. Marquette U., 1976, U. Wis., 1977; m. Veronica Ann Martin, Sept. 25, 1965; children—Mark, Veronica, Michael, Patrick, William III. Chmn. health, phys. edn. and recreation, athletic dir. St. Agnes High Sch., Springfield, Mo., 1966-67, Aquin High Sch., Cascade, Iowa, 1967-68, Briar Cliff Coll., Sioux City, Iowa, 1968-71; asst. prof., athletic dir. Shepherd State Coll., Shepherdstown, W.Va., 1972-73, St. Mary's Coll., Winona, Minn., 1973-74; pres., chief exec. officer Creative Children's Child Care Centers, Inc., Largo, Fla. and Milw., 1974—; pres. Fla. Breeders, Inc., Largo, 1974-77; adminstrv. asst. to v.p., dir. admissions, asso. prof., athletic dir., basketball coach Cardinal Stritch Coll., Milw., 1976-80; prof., chmn. dept. health and phys. edn. Ohio No. U., Ada, 1980—; dir. CFI Lands, Inc., Charolais of Fla., Inc., others. Active ARC, Boy Scouts Am.; judge Jr. Wis. Miss. Mem. Sch. Masters, AAHPER, Nat. Assn. Coll. Admissions Counselors, Am. Assn. Coll. Registrar and Admissions Officers, NEA, Assn. Higher Edn., Nat. Assn. Coll. Dirs. Athletics, Wis. Coll. Personnel Assn., Fla. Jaycees, Phi Delta Kappa (chpt. pres. 1979-80), Delta Epsilon Sigma, Kappa Delta Pi. Roman Catholic. Clubs: Elks, Lions, K.C., Milw. Pen and Mike, Rotary. Mem. nat. adv. bd. Coach and Athlete, 1976—; contbr. numerous articles to profl. jours.; author 10 books. Office: Ohio Northern U Ada OH 45810

STIKA, ELAINE ANNA, advt. exec.; b. Kenosha, Wis., July 3, 1924; d. Alexander and Paulina L. (Janota) Stika; student Kenosha Coll. Commerce, 1943, Mgmt. Center Marquette U., Milw., 1960, Kenosha Center U. Wis., DePaul U., 1963, Kenosha Tech. Inst., 1970. Asst. to mgr. market list div. sales dept. Macwhyte Wire Rope Co., Kenosha, 1943-49, asst. to advt., sales promotion, pub. relations, mktg. mgr., 1949-65, advt. and sales services adminstr., 1966-73, adminstr. marketing services, 1974—. Sec., treas. Kenosha Civic Council, 1955—; mem. Kenosha County Coordinated Plan and Budget Com., 1977-79; mem. Kenosha County Health Planning Commn., 1969—; loaned exec. United Way, 1976-79, mem. citizens panel, 1980—. Bd. dirs. Kenosha County United Fund, 1966-72, Kenosha County council Girl Scouts U.S.A., 1962-68, Kenosha Taxpayers, 1978—; bd. dirs. Kenosha County Blood Bank, 1964—, v.p., 1968-70, pres., 1971-74; br. adv. bd. Wis. Tb and Respiratory Disease Assn., 1970-79. Mem. Milw. Assn. Indsl. Advertisers, Constrn. Equipment Advertisers, Kenosha Bradford Alumni Assn. (bd. dirs. 1968-75, v.p. 1970-71, pres. 1971-73), Kenosha Advt. Club (dir. 1959-70, v.p. 1961-62, pres. 1963-64), Sigma Alpha Sigma (dir. 1953—, v.p. 1960-62, pres., 1962-64), Kenosha County Hist. Soc. Home: 926 48th St Kenosha WI 53140 Office: Macwhyte Wire Rope Co 2906 14th Ave Kenosha WI 53141

STILES, JAMES RICHARD, guidance counselor; b. Lowell, Mich., Mar. 2, 1938; s. Arthur H. and Marian Elizabeth (Everhart) S.; B.S., Central Mich. U., 1962; M.A., Western Mich. U., 1965; Ed.S., Mich. State U., 1971; children—Katherine, Daniel, Mark, Kari Sue. Instr. Battle Creek (Mich.) Central High Sch., 1962-66, coach wrestling and cross country, 1962-66; counselor, tchr. Lansing (Mich.) Everett High Sch., 1966-71, coach wrestling, 1966-71; counselor, guidance dir. Lansing Hill High Sch., 1971—; cons. in field; mem. Mich. Career Edn. Adv. Commn. Served with USNR, 1956-58. Recipient Outstanding Counselor Mich. award Mich. Sch. Counselors Assn., 1976. Mem. Am., Mich. personnel and guidance assns., Nat. Mich. vocat. guidance assns., Am. (pres. 1981—), Mich. sch. counselors assns., Nat. Mich., Lansing edn. assns., Nat. Jogging Assn., BMW Owners Assn. Methodist. Home: 3313 W Mount Hope Ave Apt 34 Lansing MI 48910 Office: 2 Skyline Pl Suite 400 5203 Leesburg Pl Falls Church VA 22041

STILL, RONALD DEAN, utilities exec.; b. Ida Grove, Iowa, Mar. 19, 1940; s. Robert Lee and Nellie Opal (Hawn) S.; cert. water mgmt. Iowa State U., 1975, U. Iowa, 1978, Iowa State U., 1978; m. Jean Marie Thies, June 20, 1959; children—Steven, Scott, Sandra, Shawn. Farmer, Arthur, Iowa, 1959-70; tilemaker Roetman Tile Co., Sheldon, Iowa, 1970; mechanic Verschoor Motor Co., Sheldon, 1970-73; insp., mgr. Rural Water System #1, Hospers, Iowa, 1973-74, mgr., operator, 1974—. Mem. Iowa Rural Water Assn., Am. Water Works Assn. (chmn. region 3). Democrat. Roman Catholic. Home: Rural Route 3 Box 308 Sheldon IA 51201 Office: Rural Water System 1 Rural Route 1 Hospers IA 51238

STILLMAN, MIKELE GARFIELD, city ofcl.; b. Cleve., Aug. 14, 1938; d. Howard R. and Dorothy L. (Garfield) Rome; A.A., William Woods Coll., 1958; postgrad. Edgewood Coll., 1970, U. Wis., Madison, 1974—; children—Eva, Eric, Amea, Sarah. Spl. events dir. H.S. Manchester's, Inc., Madison, 1962-66; public service dir. WISC-TV, Madison, 1966-72; placement services dir. Goodwill Industries, Madison, 1974-80; instr. mktg. Madison Area Tech. Coll., 1963-73; clin. asso. Vocat. Rehab. Program, U. Wis., 1977-80; events coordinator Concourse/Mall, City of Madison, Dept. Public Works, 1980—; cons., trainer Dane County Affirmative Action Office; cons. employee tng. State of Wis., 1980—; chairperson Dane County Sect. 504 Team; adv. council Women's Resource Center; mem. contract compliance com. State Wis., 1979-80. Developer spl. program for juvenile offenders, 1963-70; bd. dirs. United Way, 1968; city rep. to coordinate Swiss Festival with Swiss Govt., Zurich, 1965; appted. by Gov. to document renovation of exec. residence on film, 1968; bd. dirs. YWCA, 1979-81; publicity chmn. Internat. Yr. of Disabled, 1981. Recipient Outstanding Service award for public broadcasting, 1971. Mem. Nat. Rehab. Assn., Wis. Rehab. Assn., Job Placement for Handicapped Assn., Wis. Assn. Vocat. and Adult Edn., Phi Beta. Editor WIRE Rehab. Newsletter for Wis., 1977-78; contbr. articles to newspapers, poetry to Jewish Heritage, Wis. State Jour., Capital Times. Office: 510 Ciemons Ave Madison WI 53704

STIMPSON, CLINTON FRANK, III, mfg. co. exec.; b. Detroit, Nov. 14, 1936; s. Clinton Frank and Rachel S.; B.S.E., U. Mich., 1959, M.B.A., 1960; m. Catherine Elizabeth Corey, Sept. 17, 1966; children—Marguerite Rachel, Robert Clinton. Engr., Vickers div. Sperry Rand, Troy, Mich., 1960-64; sales engr. Bin Dicator Co., Detroit, 1964-68, project engr., Port Sanilac, Mich., 1968-71; gen. mgr. Conveyor Components Co., Croswell, Mich., 1971—, corporate sec. parent co. Material Control Inc. Mem. Instruments Soc. Am. Home: 5626 Lakeshore Rd Port Huron MI 48060 Office: 130 Seltzer St Croswell MI 48422

STINE, GORDON WAYNE, physician; b. Washington, Apr. 21, 1947; s. Gordon Edward and Vera Phyllis (Legge) S.; B.S., Purdue U., 1969; M.D., St. Louis U. Med. Center, 1972; m. Kathleen Lynn Vinson; children—Coy Randall, Gregory Guyer, Jennifer Erin. Intern, St. John's Mercy Med. Center, St. Louis, 1972-73; practice family medicine, Washington, Mo., 1977—; mem. staff Wesley Med. Center, Wichita, Kans., 1973-77; mem. staff St. Francis Mercy Hosp., Washington, 1977—; preceptor nurse practitioner program Wichita State U. br. Kansas U. Sch. Medicine, 1975-76, clin. asso. prof., 1974-77. Mem., Wichita Citizens Participation Orgn., 1975-77, del. Neighborhood and Central Council, 1975-77; med. dir. Wichita Model Cities Health Center, 1974-75; med. dir. Kans. Alcoholic Rehab. Center, 1975-77; med. dir. Profl. Home Health Services, New Haven, Mo., 1977—. Diplomate Nat. Bd. Med. Examiners, Am. Bd. Family Practice. Mem. Franklin Warren Gasconade Med. Soc. (sec. 1977—), Mo. Acad. Family Physicians, Am. Acad. Family Physicians, Soc. Tchrs. Family Medicine, Mo. Med. Soc., Washington (Mo.) C. of C. Club: Lions. Home: Route 1 Box 189R Washington MO 63090 Office: 205 Elm St Washington MO 63090

STINE, ROBERT HOWARD, physician; b. Bethlehem, Pa., Nov. 1, 1929; s. Harry Raymond and Mabel E. (Newhard) S.; B.S., Moravian Coll., Bethlehem, 1952; M.D., Jefferson Med. Coll., Phila., 1960; m. Lois Elaine Kihlgren, Oct. 22, 1960; children—Robert E., Karen E., Jonathan N. Intern, St. Luke's Hosp., Bethlehem, 1960-61, resident in surgery, 1961-62; resident in pediatrics State U. N.Y. Hosp., Syracuse, 1962-64; resident in allergy Robert A. Cooke Inst. Allergy, N.Y.C., 1964-65; practice medicine specializing in allergy, Peoria, Ill., 1965—; mem. staff St. Francis, Proctor Community hosps., Meth. Med. Center; pres. Robert H. Stine, M.D., S.C., 1972—; instr. U. Ill. Coll. Medicine, 1965-71, Rush-Presbyn.-St. Luke's Hosp., 1971—; asst. prof. Rush Med. Coll., 1979—; mem. teaching staff medicine and pediatrics St. Francis Hosp.; cons. staff Meth. Hosp. Served as officer USNR, 1952-56. Fellow Am. Acad. Allergy, Am. Assn. Certified Allergists, Am. Acad. Pediatrics; mem. AMA, Chgo., Peoria med. socs., Chgo. Allergy Soc., Christian Med. Soc. Republican. Presbyterian. Home: 105 Hollands Grove Ln Washington IL 61571 Office: 710 E Archer Ave Peoria IL 61603

STINSON, PATRICK BERNARD, assn. exec.; b. Oak Park, Ill., May 2, 1952; s. Paris Bernard and Gladys (Bond) S.; B.S. in Recreation and Park Adminstrn., Western Ill. U., 1974. Dir. membership Nat. Employee Services and Recreation Assn., Chgo., 1974, asst. exec. dir., 1975-77, exec. dir., 1977—; mem. adv. council, recreation and park adminstrn. dept. Western Ill. U. Recipient Outstanding Alumni award Western Ill. U., 1981. Mem. Am. Soc. Assn. Execs., Chgo. Soc. Assn. Execs. Republican. Roman Catholic. Home: 650 Stratford Rd Elmhurst IL 60126 Office: 20 N Wacker Dr Chicago IL 60606

STIPHER, KARL JOSEPH, lawyer; b. Indpls., Oct. 23, 1912; s. Josiah C. and Clara (Fuerst) S.; B.S., Butler U., 1935; student Harvard Law Sch., 1935-36; LL.B., Ind. U., 1938; m. Jean Houghteling, June 22, 1939; children—Richard, Karen (Mrs. John Irby), Stephen. Admitted to Ind. bar, 1938; asso. firm Gilliom & Gilliom, Indpls., 1938-45; dep. atty. gen. Ind., 1945-47; asso. firm Baker & Daniels, Indpls., 1948-50, partner, 1950—. Mem. Ind. Civil Code Study Commn., 1968-71. Bd. dirs. Catholic Social Services, 1968-78, Alcoholic Rehab. Center, Our Lady Grace Acad.; pres., bd. dirs. Domestic Relations Counseling Service; bd. visitors Ind. U. Law Sch., 1974-78; chmn. Indpls. Mayor's Task Force on Public Safety and Criminal Justice; mem. citizens Ct. Adv. Com.; pres. Ind. Lawyers Commn. Mem. Indpls. (pres. 1973), Ind. (pres. 1975-76), Am., 7th Fed. Circuit Ct. (pres. 1968-69), Inter-Am., Internat. bar assns., Am. Bar Found., Am. Coll. Trial Lawyers, Ind. Soc. Chgo., Nat. Assn. R.R. Trial Counsel. Clubs: Variety, Mud Creek Players, Indpls. Athletic,

Indpls. Columbia, Indpls. Lit. Home: 7111 Fremont Ct Indianapolis IN 46256 Office: Fletcher Trust Bldg Indianapolis IN 46204

STIRDIVANT, MICHAEL THOMAS, assn. exec.; b. Milw., Mar. 31, 1945; s. Aaron Lester and Gertrude (Mares) S.; B.A., St. Joseph's Coll., Rensselaer, Ind., 1968. Exec. dir. United Community Center Inc., Milw., 1973-81; exec. dir., chief operating officer Milw. Boys Club, 1981—; cons. mgmt., devel. Mem. State of Wis. Gov.'s Task Force on Youth, 1975-76; mem. Hist. Walkers Point (Wis.) Devel. Bd., 1976—; chmn. Wis. Electric Consumer Adv. Council, 1980—; mem. Bicentennial Com. Milw., 1976. Recipient El Centro Credit Union award, 1975; YMCA Outstanding Service award, 1975, Bus./Mgmt. award, 1975; award Bicentennial Com. Milw., 1976; Inner City Youth Serving Agys. award, 1977. Mem. Milw. Council for Adult Learning (pres.-elect 1979—), Milw. Mgmt. Support Orgn. (charter; dir. 1977—), Future Milw. (dir. 1977—). Roman Catholic. Home: 4666 N Woodburn St Whitefish Bay WI 53211 Office: Milw Boys Club 1437 N Prospect Ave Milwaukee WI 53202

STITT, ROSCOE DAVID, counselor; b. St. Louis, June 24, 1943; s. Roscoe Thomas and Mildred Iola (McCord) S.; B.A., William Jewell Coll., 1969; M.A., U. Mo., 1972, postgrad. 1973-80; m. Danielle K. Kenney, Sept. 11, 1964; children—Spencer David, Susan Danielle. With Am. Republic Ins. Co., Springfield, Ill., 1963; interviewer Kans. State Employment Service, Kansas City, 1970; dir. Prairie Village, Kans. Youth Center, Prairie Village, 1971-72; counselor Project Outreach, Pioneer Community Coll., Kansas City, Mo., 1972—, project coordinator, 1976—, chmn. counseling service, 1980—; cons. in human relations and career planning; mem. Acad. Senate, Met. Community Coll., Kansas City, Mo., 1978—. Served with USN, 1963-67. Recipient Outstanding Achievement award Mo. Handicapped Disadvantaged Assn., 1979; cert. counselor and coll. faculty, Dept. Edn., State of Mo. Mem. Pioneer Community Coll. Faculty Assn. (pres. 1977-79), Mo. Vocat. Spl. Needs Assn. (v.p. for community colls. 1978-80), Am. Personnel and Guidance Assn., Am. Vocat. Assn., Mo. Assn. for Community and Jr. Colls., Nat. Assn. for Vocat. Spl. Needs Personnel. Mem. Emmissaries of Divine Light Ch. Contbr. articles to profl. jours. Address: 6434 Baltimore St Kansas City MO 64113

STIVER, MYRTLE PEARL, nurse, bus. exec.; b. Osprey Twp., Ont., Can., Nov. 9, 1908; d. Henry and Abbie Olga (Smith) Stiver; R.N., Toronto Western Hosp., 1932; certificate Pub. Health Nursing, U. Toronto, 1940; B.S. in Nursing, Columbia, 1947. Individual practice nursing, Toronto, Ont., 1932-39; staff nurse Victorian Order Nursing, Toronto, 1940-41; staff nurse Toronto Dept. Health, 1941-43; nurse cons. Ont. Dept. Health, 1943-48; dir. pub. health nursing Ottawa Dept. Health, 1948-52; gen. sec.-treas. Canadian Nurses Assn., Montreal, 1952-60, hon. life mem., 1966—, exec. dir., Ottawa, 1960-63; exec. sec.-treas. Canadian Nurses' Found., 1963-64; co-owner Croft, Canadian handcraft shop, Baysville, Muskoka, Ont., 1963-75. Mem. nat. nursing adv. com. Victorian Order Nurses Can., 1952-63, Can. Civil Def., 1952-62; mem. dental med. services adv. bd. Canadian govt., 1955-62; mem. vocational adv. com. Dist. Muskoka Bd. Edn., 1969—. Bd. dirs. Canadian Citizenship Council. Recipient Centennial medal Govt. Can., 1968. Fellow Am. Pub. Health Assn.; mem. Bus. and Profl. Women's Club (v.p. Bracebridge 1969-71, pres. 1971-73), Zonta Internat. (pres. Ottawa 1961-63), Venerable Order St. John Jerusalem (comdr. sister), Ont. Pub. Health Assn. (hon. life mem.). Baptist (deacon). Club: University Women's (Toronto, Montreal). Author: (with Christine Livingston) Patient Care in the Home, 1965. Address: 360 Wellington St N Box 2112 Bracebridge ON P0B 1C0 Canada

STIVLEN, SYLVIA MILDRED, nurse; b. Lakota, N.D., Aug. 27, 1921; d. Sigurd Mathison and Marie Elsie (Ellefson) S.; B.S. in Nursing, Incarnate Word Coll., San Antonio, 1966; M.S. in Nursing Adminstrn., U. Md., 1972. Commd. nurse Nurse Corps, U.S. Army, 1943, advanced through grades to maj., 1958; service in Europe Korea and Hawaii; nursing methods analyst Brooke Gen. Hosp., Fort Sam Houston, Tex., 1961-64; ret., 1964; med. supr. Trinity Hosp., Minot, N.D., 1966-69; surg. supr. Sinai Hosp., Balt., 1972-76; surg. nursing dir. Methodist Med. Center, Peoria, 1977—. Decorated Army Commendation medal. Mem. Am. Nurses Assn., Ret. Army Nurse Corps Assn., Ret. Officers Assn., Ill. Soc. Nurse Adminstrs. Republican. Lutheran. Home: 5601 N Humboldt Ave Peoria IL 61614 Office: 221 NE Glen Oak Ave Peoria IL 61636

STOCK, GREGG FRANCIS, museum adminstr.; b. Kansas City, Mo., Jan. 30, 1925; s. Arthur Robert and Verna Marie (Prawitz) S.; student Rockhurst Coll., 1942, Central Mo. State Coll., 1942-43; B.S. in Journalism, U. Kans., 1948, B.S. in Advt., 1948; m. Sarah Ellen Smart, Nov. 8, 1947; children—Gregg Francis, Heidi Frances, Peter Huston. Pres., Wayne-Fastock Equipment Co., Kansas City, 1953-65; nat. dir. employee relations Automatique, Inc., Kansas City, 1965-71; dir. Kansas City (Mo.) Mus. History and Sci., 1971—; cons. in field; mem. adv. bd. Explorer Mag. Mem. adv. bd. Hist. Kansas City Found.; bd. dirs. Native Sons of Greater Kansas City; mem. Kansas City Mayor's Corps of Progress. Served to lt.(j.g.) USNR, 1943-46; PTO. Fellow Explorers Club; mem. Mo. Mus. Assos. (pres.), Midwest Mus. Conf., Am. Assn. Museums, Assn. Sci.-Tech. Centers, Assn. Sci. Mus. Dirs., Kansas City Archaeology Soc. (J. Mett Shippee award 1976, v.p. 1973—), Mo. Archaeology Soc. (v.p.). Clubs: Mercury, Rockhill; Rotary. Author: (film) Line Creek Man, 1976; Story Line for a Kansas City Regional History museum, 1973. Office: 3218 Gladstone Blvd Kansas City MO 64123

STOCK, KENNETH RICHARD, architect, structural engr.; b. Indpls., Dec. 21, 1948; s. Paul William and Mary (Lieland) S.; B.Arch., U. Ill., 1972, M.S. with honors in Archtl. Engring., 1973; m. Mary Kay McCloskey, July 8, 1972. Architect, engr. David G. Champ Assos., De Pere Wis., 1974-77, Py-Vavra Architects-Engrs., Inc., Milw., 1977-78, Oliver Constrn. Co., Oconomowoc, Wis., 1978—; pres. A/E Cons., Inc., Delafield, Wis., 1979—; mem. Wis. Solar Resource Adv. Panel, 1978-80. Recipient 1st Plym prize in grad. structures U. Ill. Sch. Architecture, 1974; registered architect, Wis.; registered profl. engr., Wis.; certified soil tester, Wis. Designer, constructor personal, earth-sheltered residence, featuring solar-heating design. Home: S14 W32155 Boys School Rd Delafield WI 53018 Office: Oliver Constrn Co 1311 W Wisconsin Ave Oconomowoc WI 53066 also A/E Cons Inc S14 W32155 Boys School Rd WI 53018

STOCK, RICHARD PAUL, mgmt. cons.; b. Canton, Ohio, Jan. 25, 1947; s. Carl V. and Naomi F. S.; B.A., Kent State U., 1970; postgrad. LaVerne U., 1978; m. Sandra Rose Keen, Apr. 17, 1971; children—Stacy Lynn, Shannon Nicole. Juvenile probation officer Stark County Family Ct., Canton, 1971-73; ins. investigator Retail Credit, West Palm Beach, Fla., 1973; probation officer State of Fla., 1973-74; fed. probation officer U.S. Govt., Orlando, Fla., 1974-79; mgmt. cons., pres. The Success Store, North Canton, Ohio, 1979—. Bd. dirs., sec. Community Outreach Services, Daytona Beach, Fla., 1976-78; vol. Am. Cancer Soc., 1979—. Mem. Am. Soc. Tng. and Devel., Am. Mgmt. Assn., Assn. Humanistic Psychology, Am. Personnel and Guidance Assn., Personal Dynamics Assn., Human Potential Assn., Am. Entrepreneurs Assn. Clubs: Toastmasters (past pres. Daytona Beach, Fla.), Jaycees. Home: 330 Lincoln St Hartville OH 44632 Office: 1407 Portage NW North Canton OH 44720

STOCKMAN, HERBERT ERECH, hosp. ofcl.; b. Eau Claire, Mich., Mar. 18, 1934; s. Edward John and Hedwig (Karog) S.; B.S., U. Nebr., Omaha, 1969; M.S., Mich. State U., East Lansing, 1973; m. Hilde Schauer, Sept. 22, 1956; children—Werner, Herbert Edward. Commd. 2d. lt., U.S. Army, 1961, advanced through grades to maj., 1968; dir. tng. and security 15th M.P. Brigade, 1969-72; dir. field ops. Criminal Investigation Commn., 1973-75; ret., 1975; asst. prof. U. Evansville (Ind.), 1975-77; dir. staff devel. Evansville State Hosp., 1977—. Decorated Bronze Star, Meritorious Service medal, Army Commendation medal, Vietnamese Honor medal. Mem. Acad. Criminal Justice Scis. (regional rep. 1979-80), Ind. Soc. Hosp. Edn. and Tng., Internat. Asn. Chiefs of Police, Am. Soc. Tng. and Devel., Ind. Intergovtl. Tng. Council. Home: 10588 Williamsburg Dr Newburgh IN 47630 Office: 3200 Outer Lincoln Ave Evansville IN 47704

STOCKMAN, RICHARD OWEN, mfg. co. ofcl.; b. Plymouth, Ind., Oct. 9, 1930; s. Samuel Seth and Emma Gail (Amones) S.; student public schs.; children—Gary Blake, Roxanne, John Jay. Field service specialist Worthington Corp., Harrison, N.J., 1955-63; service mgr., product engr. Haskon, Inc., Warsaw, Ind., 1963-70; mgr. customer service DePuy div. Bio Dynamics Co., Warsaw, 1970-80; dir. ops. Kellogg Industries, Jackson, Mich., 1981—; instr. Ind. Vocat. Tech. Coll. Served with USN, 1948-52. Clubs: Masons, Shriners. Home: 2315 Maple Dr Jackson MI 49203 Office: 159 W Pearl St Jackson MI 49201

STOCKTON, M. J., JR., educator; b. Houston, Nov. 5, 1939; s. Miles Jefferson and Erma Louise (Warren) S.; B.A. (Presdl. scholar), Baylor U., 1962; M.A., Sam Houston State U., 1967; Ed.D. (teaching fellow, Sparkman scholar), Baylor U., 1971; m. Carol Ann Christesson; children—Michael Warren, Carolyn Sue, Ronald Allan, Lisa Kaye. Tchr., Galena Park (Tex.) Public Schs., 1962-63, choral dir., 1963-68; instr. Baylor U., Waco, Tex., 1968-71; program coordinator Edn. Service Center, Waco, 1971-72; prof. edn., chmn. dept. William Jewell Coll., Liberty, Mo., 1972—; mem. State of Mo. Ednl. Conf.; cons. tchr. edn. and instrnl. design. Mem. Democratic Central Com. of Clay County (Mo.), 1975; mem. Fine Arts Chorale, 1972—, bd. dirs., 1974-78, pres., 1974, 75, 77. Mem. Mo. Psychol. Assn., Mo. Unit Assn. Tchr. Edn., Assn. Ednl. Communications and Tech., Assn. Supervision and Curriculum Devel., Tex. Music Educators Assn., Tex. Tchrs. Assn., Phi Delta Kappa, Phi Mu Alpha Sinfonia, Alpha Chi. Democrat. Baptist. Author: Study Guide for Educational Psychology, 1976; Study Guide for Instructional Methodology, 1975. Home: 1528 NE 51st Terr Kansas City MO 64118 Office: 1 College Hill Liberty MO 64068

STODDARD, CHARLES HATCH, conservation cons.; b. Milw., Apr. 28, 1912; s. Charles Hatch and Eloise (Jackson) S.; B.S. in Forestry, U. Mich., 1934, M.S., 1938; postgrad. U. Wis., 1941; m. Patricia Coulter, June 30, 1956; children—Charles Hatch, Abby Weed, Paul Christopher, Glenn McDonald, Jeffrey Jackson. Economist, U.S. Forest Service, 1934-40, Bur. Land Econs., 1941-43, Resources for the Future, 1955-61; cons. in resources, 1946-55; dir. resources program staff Dept. Interior, 1961-63, dir. Bur. Land Mgmt., 1963-66; exec. dir. Citizens Adv. Com. on Environment, 1966-68; conservation cons. Conservation Found., 1968-72. Chmn. Public Intervenor Adv. Com. on Environment, State of Wis., 1978—; mem. Pres.'s Quetico Superior Adv. Com., 1963-66; adviser on resources to Pres. Kennedy, 1960-61; chmn. U.S. Army C.E. Environmental Adv. Bd., 1970-72. Fellow Charles Lathrop Forestry Found., 1937-38, 46-48. Served as lt. USNR, 1942-46. Recipient Distinguished Service award Nat. Assn. Conservation Dists., 1964. Sr. mem. Soc. Am. Foresters; mem. Wilderness Soc. (pres. 1977-78), Ecol. Soc. Am., Wis. Acad. Sci., Sigma Xi, Beta Theta Pi. Unitarian. Club: Cosmos (Washington). Author: Forest Farming and Rural Employment, 1949; Essentials of Forestry Practice, 1958; (with Clawson, Held) Land for the Future, 1960; The Small Forest, 1961; Looking Forward, 1982. Home: Wolf Springs Forest Minong WI 54859.

STODDARD, STANFORD C., banker; b. Salt Lake City, 1930; student Grad. Sch. Bus. Adminstrn., U. Mich., 1952. Pres., dir. Mich. Nat. Corp., Bloomfield Hills; chmn. bd. Mich. Nat. Bank, Mich. Nat. Bank Detroit; dir. Chatham Super Markets, Inc., Dayco Corp., Fed. Home Life Ins. Co., PHF Life Ins. Co., Wolverine Ins. Co., Riverside Ins. Co. Office: Mich Nat Corp PO Box 589 Bloomfield Hills MI 48013*

STOELTING, JOHN ALBERT, advt. agy. exec.; b. Vincennes, Ind., Sept. 11, 1936; s. Floyd William and Virginia Marie (Weiler) S.; B.B.A., U. Cin., 1959. Dist. group mgr. Ohio Nat. Life Ins. Co., Washington and Cin., 1959-63, life ins. agt., 1963-65; service and fund dir. Am. Cancer Soc., Cin., 1965-68; account exec. Shulman Advt., Cin., 1968-71; pres. Advt. Mgmt. Inc., Cin., 1971-80; dir. mktg. services Dektas & Eger Advt., Cin., 1980-81, v.p., 1981—; career resource advisor U. Cin., 1977—. Mem. Greater Cin. exec. council City of Hope, 1975—; trustee Cin. Ednl. and Charitable Found., 1976—; mem. U. Cin. Greek Affairs Council. Mem. Am. Advt. Fedn., Delta Sigma Pi, Pi Delta Epsilon, Pi Kappa Alpha (dist. pres. 1960-66, Pres.'s Service award 1978, Outstanding Alumnus award Cin. chpt. 1979, dir. alumni assn. 1959-67, 74—, sec. 1979-80). Roman Catholic. Clubs: Cincinnatus, Advt. of Cin. (treas. 1978—). Editor, Pi Kappa Alpha Newsletter, 1957-60, contbr., 1962-66, 75—. Home: 2800 Temple Ave Cincinnati OH 45211 Office: 1077 Celestial St Cincinnati OH 45202

STOETZER, GERALD LOUIS, lawyer; b. Detroit, Apr. 6, 1914; s. Albin August and Ida (Kuhlman) S.; A.B., Valparaiso U., 1935; J.D., U. Mich., 1938; m. Helen Muriel Simons, Aug. 16, 1941; children—Gerald Louis, James Brian, Susan Hart (Mrs. Ronald J. Bockelman). Admitted to Mich. bar, Fed. bar, 1938, U.S. Supreme Ct., 1955; partner firm Clark, Klein, Brucker & Waples, Detroit, 1938-60, Clark, Klein, Winter, Parsons & Prewitt, Detroit, 1961-79, Clark, Klein & Beaumont, 1979—; lectr. U. Mich. Law Sch. Inst. of Continuing Legal Edn., 1964—. Sec., 14th Congl. Dist. (Mich.) Republican Party, 1950-54. Mem. Grosse Pointe Symphony Orch., pres. support orgn. Served with AUS, 1942-46. Decorated Bronze Star. Mem. Judge Advs. Assn., Mich. Assn. Professions, State Bar of Mich. (chmn. corp., fin. and bus. law sect. 1965-68), Am., Detroit bar assns., Fine Arts Soc. Detroit (pres.), Order of Coif, Lawyers Club, Pi Gamma Mu. Delta Theta Phi, Phi Delta Theta. Lutheran. Clubs: University; Hidden Valley (Gaylord, Mich.); Lochmoor (Grosse Pointe Woods, Mich.); The Players. Home: 1949 Littlestone Rd Grosse Pointe Woods MI 48236 Office: First Fed Bldg Detroit MI 48226

STOFFEL, THOMAS JOHN, radiation oncologist; b. Menasha, Wis., July 10, 1943; s. John Wenzel and Ethel Susan (Landig) S.; B.S. magna cum laude, Marquette U., 1965; M.D., Med. Coll. Wis., 1969; m. Mary Ann M. Smith, Dec. 30, 1967; children—Christine Marie, John Thomas, David Scott. Intern, Hennepin County Gen. Hosp., Mpls., 1969-70; resident in radiation oncology U. Minn., Mpls., 1970-73, chief resident, 1974; pres. Quint Cities Radiation Oncology, Ltd., Moline, Ill., 1977—; dir. radiation therapy dept. Walter Reed Army Hosp., Washington, 1975-76, Quad City Cancer Therapy Center, Luth. Hosp., Moline, 1977-82; asst. clin. prof. radiation oncology Georgetown U., 1975-76, Howard U., 1976, U. Iowa, 1977-82; chmn. cancer com. Quad City Cancer Center, 1978-80. Exec. bd. Rock Island County br. Am. Cancer Soc., 1978-82. Served to maj., AUS, 1975-77. Diplomate Am. Bd. Radiology, Nat. Bd. Med. Examiners. Mem. AMA, Am. Coll. Radiology, Am. Soc. Therapeutic Radiology, Central Ill. Soc. Radiation Therapists, Radiol. Soc. N.Am., Illowa Med. Club, Rock Island County Med. Soc. Roman Catholic. Contbr. articles to med. jours. Home: 5324 36th Ave Ct Moline IL 61265 Office: Lutheran Hospital Moline IL 61265

STOHR, EDMUND PAUL CONRAD, airline exec.; b. Elgin, Ill., Feb. 5, 1918; s. Edmund Paul Conrad and Magdalene L. (Seiger) S.; B.S. in Mktg., U. Ill., 1941; B.S. in Mktg., Advanced Mgmt., U. Calif., Berkeley, 1959; m. Charmaine Nauert, Nov. 28, 1952. Asst. credit mgr. United Airlines, Chgo., 1946-50, asst. to v.p. traffic, 1950-55, mgr. internat. sales, 1956, European dir., London, 1956-70, mgr. industry affairs, Chgo., 1970-75, v.p. industry affairs, 1975—. Served to capt. USAF, 1941-46. Mem. Internat. Air Transport Assn., Air Transport Assn. Am., Air Traffic Conf. (pres. 1979—). Republican. Clubs: Wentworth (London); Execs.' (Chgo.); Am. (London). Home: 420 Whitehall Dr Whytecliffe Palatine IL 60067 Office: United Airlines PO Box 66100 Chicago IL 60666

STOKES, LOUIS, congressman; b. Cleve., Feb. 23, 1925; s. Charles and Louise (Stone) S.; student Western Res. U., 1946-48; J.D., Marshall Law Sch., Cleve., 1953; LL.D. (hon.), Wilberforce U., 1969; Shaw U., 1971, Morehouse Coll., Meharry Coll. Medicine, Oberlin Coll.; m. Jeanette Francis, Aug. 21, 1960; children—Shelley, Louis C., Angela, Lorene. Admitted to Ohio bar, 1954, practiced in Cleve.; mem. firm Stokes, Character, Terry and Perry, 1966—; mem. 91st-97th Congresses from 21st Dist. Ohio, mem. Budget Com., Appropriations Com.; chmn. Select Com. King/Kennedy Assassinations, House Ethics Com.; dean Ohio Dem. del.; lectr. in field. Mem. internat. adv. council African Am. Inst. Served with AUS, 1943-46. Recipient numerous awards for civic activities. Mem. Am., Ohio (past chmn. criminal justice com.) bar assns., Nat. Assn. Def. Lawyers Criminal Cases (dir.), Fair Housing (dir.), Urban League, Citizens League, John Harlan Law Club, ACLU, Kappa Alpha Psi. Democrat. Clubs: Plus (Cleve.), Masons (33 deg.). Office: 2465 Rayburn House Office Bldg Washington DC 20515

STOKES, RICHARD HARPER, mfg. co. exec.; b. Greenville, Tex., Aug. 5, 1943; s. Richard Lloyd and Glenna Faye (Stooksberry) S.; B.S., Tex. A. and M. U., 1966; M.S., U. Mo.; m. Betty Claire Barnett, June 27, 1970; 1 son, Douglas Lee. With McDonnell Douglas Co., St. Louis and Titusville, Fla., 1966-74; mgr. quality compliance Norcliff Thayer Inc., St. Louis, 1975—. Registered profl. engr., Mo.; cert. quality engr., Am. Soc. for Quality Control. Mem. Nat. Soc. Profl. Engrs., Am. Soc. for Quality Control, Packaging Inst. Am., Am. Soc. Engring. Mgmt., Internat. Assn. Quality Circles (dir.). Home: 900 N Taylor Ave Kirkwood MO 63122 Office: 319 S 4 St Saint Louis MO 63102

STOKOWSKI, ANNE, state senator; children—Barbara, Steven, Laura, Robert, Jean Anne. Mem. Minn. Senate, 1979—. Bd. dirs. Mpls. Council Camp Fire, former sec., v.p. Recipient Luther Halsey Gullick award Nat. Camp Fire. Mem. Democratic-Farmer-Labor party. Clubs: Dome, Senate. Office: 29 State Capitol St Paul MN 55155*

STOLL, DONALD HAROLD, elec. mfg. co. engr.; b. Lincoln, Ill., Nov. 23, 1937; s. Harold Eugene and Eda Anna (Boerger) S.; B.S., U. Ill., 1959; postgrad. Union Coll., Schenectady, 1975-76; m. Doris Irene Henrichsmeyer, June 8, 1958; children—Donald Harold, Diane Carol. With Gen. Electric Co., Morrison, Ill., 1959—, sr. design engr., 1969-72, mgr. product engring., 1972-75, sr. application engr., 1975-82, sr. design engr., 1980—; co-founder Products Unltd. Corp. Cleve. Air Soc. scholar, 1958. Mem. Fort Wayne Assn. Gen. Electric Engrs., Engrs. and Suprs. Assn., Elfun Assn. Lutheran. Patentee in field. Home: Route 2 Morrison IL 61270 Office: West Wall St Morrison IL 61270

STOLL, JAMES ARTHUR, supermarket exec.; b. Canton, Ohio, Mar. 8, 1940; s. Otis Chester and Betty May (Mericle) S.; student Mt. Union Coll., 1959-60, Internat. Accountants Soc., 1962-64; m. Cynthia Louise Ross, Aug. 30, 1959; children—Vickie Lynn, Teresa Joy, Lisa Ann, Sharon Leann, Elizabeth Ann. Asst. mgr. White Cottage Food Center, Inc., Canton, 1955-65, v.p., gen. mgr., 1965-71; founder Stoll's Food, Inc., New Philadelphia, Ohio, 1972, pres., chmn. bd., 1972—. Active United Way. Mem. Asso. Grocers Inc. (bd. dirs. 1972—, chmn. bd. 1975-77, Meritorious Service award 1977), Nat. Assn. Retail Grocers U.S. (bd. dirs. 1977—. chmn. nat. conv. 1980, chmn. 1981—), Twin Cities United Retail Mchts. (bd. dirs. 1973), East Central Ohio Food Dealers Assn. (bd. dirs., pres. 1970-72), Ohio Retail Food Dealers Assn. (Grocers Spotlight award 1980), East Canton Jaycees, Tuscarawas County C. of C. Republican. Methodist. Club: Elks. Home: 5355 Woodlynn NE East Canton OH 44730 Office: 504 Bowers Ave NW New Philadelphia OH 44663

STOLL, WILLARD LEWIS, engr.; b. Corning, N.Y., Apr. 13, 1922; s. Willard Frank and Hazel Mildred (Stanton) S.; student Elmira Coll. Veterans Extension Center, 1946-47; B. Ae.E., U. Detroit, 1951; m. Cecelia Mary Syzdek, May 3, 1946; children—James Lewis, Susan Katherine, Daniel Willard. Stock expediter Ingersoll-Rand Co., Painted Post, N.Y., 1940-42; pre-engring. student asst. Elmira (N.Y.) Coll., 1946-47; engring. asst. Drake-Groves-Winkelman Constrn. Co., Elmira, 1947; coop engring. student U. Detroit, 1948-52; gen. foreman, staff asst. Kaiser Motors, Willow Run, Mich., 1952-53; process engr. Huron Engring. Corp., Roseville, Mich., 1953; material rev. engr. Continental Aviation and Engring. Co., Detroit, 1953-57; project engr. Teledyne-CAE, Toledo, 1956—. Scoutmaster, chmn. troop com., instl. rep. Boy Scouts Am., 1958—; cadet squadron advisor Civil Air Patrol, 1976-78. Served with USN, 1942-46. Mem. Soc. Automotive Engrs. (mem. com.), AIAA, Am. Def. Preparedness Assn. Roman Catholic. Clubs: Monroe Rod and Gun, Mgmt.

STOLNITZ, GEORGE JOSEPH, economist; b. N.Y.C., Apr. 4, 1920; s. Isidore and Julia (Jurman) S.; B.A., CCNY, 1939; M.A., Princeton U., 1942, Ph.D., 1952; m. Monique J. Delley, Aug. 26, 1976; children—Cindy, Wendy, Dia. Statistician, U.S. Bur. Census, 1940-41; research asso. Office Population Research, Princeton U., 1948-56; asst. prof. econs. Princeton U., 1953-56; prof. econs. Ind. U., Bloomington, 1956—; vis. research scholar Resources for the Future, 1965-67; dir. Ind. U. Internat. Devel. Research Center, 1967-72; prin. officer population and econ. devel. UN, N.Y.C., 1976-78; cons. Ford Found., Rockefeller Found., UN, U.S. Congress, U.S. Dept. Energy, Dept. Commerce, Dept. State, HEW; vis. lectr. univs.; cons. to pvt.

industry. Served to capt. USAF, 1942-46. NSF fellow, 1959-60. Mem. Am. Econ. Assn., Am. Statis. Assn., Econometric Soc., Population Assn. Am. (pres.-elect 1982, pres. 1983), Internat. Union for Sci. Study Population, Phi Beta Kappa. Club: Cosmos (Washington). Author: Life Tables from Limited Data: A Demographic Approach, 1956; editor: World Population: The Look Ahead, 1968; Concise Report on World Population: New Beginnings and Uncertain Ends, 1979; contbr. articles to profl. jours. Home: 2636 Covenanter Ct Bloomington IN 47401 Office: Dept Econs Ind Univ Bloomington IN 47405

STOLPIN, WILLIAM ROGER, mech. engr., artist; b. Flint, Mich., June 25, 1942; s. William and Dorothy Florence (Mitchell) S.; B.M.E., Gen. Motors Inst., 1965; m. Kathleen Diane Poyner, Aug. 14, 1970; children—Krishna Ann, James Mitchell. Project engr. Buick Motor div. Gen. Motors Corp., Flint, 1969-73, reliability engr., 1973-81, sr. reliability engr., 1981—; exhibited Left Bank Gallery, 1977, 79, 81; represented in permanent collection Nat. Air and Space Mus., Washington. Community mem. bd. edn. ad hoc com. on adult edn., 1975-77; bd. dirs. Flint Community Players, 1969-76, Friends of WFBE, Pub. Radio, Flint, 1978-81; vice chmn. Greater Flint Arts Council, 1976-77; exec. bd. Friends of Modern Art, 1973; active Flint Inst. Art, 1972—. Named first in graphics Internat. Platform Assn. Art Show, 1969, hon. mention, 1976. Asso. fellow Brit. Interplanetary Soc.; mem. Am. Fedn. Arts, Internat. Platform Assn. (bd. govs.), Soc. Automotive Engrs., AIAA, Left Bank Gallery, Flint Artists Market, Nat. Space Inst., Soc. for Creative Anachronism, World Future Soc. Home: 12201 Gage Rd Holly MI 48442 Office: Buick Motor Div Gen Motors Corp Flint MI 48550

STOLTE, LARRY GENE, computer processing co. exec.; b. Cedar Rapids, Iowa, Sept. 17, 1945; s. Ed August and Emma Wilhelmena (Tank) S.; B.B.A. with highest distinction (FS Services scholar), U. Iowa, 1971; m. Rebecca Jane Tappmeyer, June 13, 1970; children—Scott Edward, Ryan Gene. Tax and auditing acct. McGladrey Hendrickson & Co., Cedar Rapids, 1971-73; v.p. TLS Co., Cedar Rapids, 1973—, also dir. Served to sgt. USMC, 1964-67. C.P.A., Iowa, Ill., Mo., Minn., Wis.; cert. mgmt. acct. Mem. Nat. Assn. Computerized Tax Processors (pres.), Nat. Assn. Accts., Am. Inst. C.P.A.'s, Am. Mgmt. Assn. Republican. Methodist. Home: Rural Route 4 Box 215-E Solon IA 52333 Office: TLS Co 810 1st Ave NE PO Box 1686 Cedar Rapids IA 52406

STOLTZ, DANIEL LEWIS, metall. engr.; b. Princeton, Ind., Dec. 9, 1937; s. Eurus Vernon and Marjory (Mowe) S.; B.S., U. Ill., 1961; M.S., U. Fla., 1970, Ph.D., 1972; m. Orleen Faye Corn, Oct. 2, 1965; children—Daniel Lee, David Lewis, Douglas Lyle. Metall. engr. Delco Moraine div. Gen. Motors Corp., Dayton, Ohio, 1961-62; research metall. engr. Battelle Meml. Inst., Columbus, Ohio, 1962-66; grad. research asst., predoctoral asst. U. Fla., 1966-72; project engr., sr. supr. metall. and finishes sect. Materials Engring. dept. Bendix Corp., Kansas City, Mo., 1972-81, project engr. sr. metal products sect. Mech. Engring. dept., 1981—. Basketball and soccer coach St. John LaLande Sch., 1974—; pres. Athletic Assn.; v.p. St John LaLande Sch. PTA, 1975-76; asst. mgr. Little League Baseball, Blue Springs, Mo., 1974-75, asst. coach Pop Warner Football League, 1976—. Registered profl. engr.; registered high sch. ofcl. basketball and football, Mo. Mem. Am. Soc. Metals (mem. exec. com. 1974-76, vice-chmn. 1976-77, chmn. 1977, yearbook chmn. 1978—), Am. Vacuum Soc., ASTM, AAAS, Microbean Analysis Soc., U. Fla. Alumni Assn., Sigma Xi, Omicron Delta Kappa, Alpha Sigma Mu (pres. 1971-72), Epsilon Lambda Chi. Contbr. articles to profl. jours.; patentee in field. Home: 506 Wedgewood Dr Blue Springs MO 64015 Office: 2000 E Bannister Rd PO Box 1159 Kansas City MO 64141

STOLTZMANN, DAVID EUGENE, optical research scientist; b. St. Paul, Nov. 9, 1949; s. Allen Harvey and Norma Marie (Baumeister) S.; student (Elks scholar) Iowa State U., 1967-69; B.S. with high distinction in Physics, U. Minn., 1971; M.S. (Univ. scholar), U. Rochester, Inst. of Optics, 1972; m. Joy Lynn Peterson, Sept. 11, 1971; children—Carolyn Marie, Brock David. Sr. optical engr. Microfilm Products div. 3M Co., St. Paul, 1975-78; sr. optical research scientist Honeywell Systems & Research Center, Mpls., 1979—. Chmn. deacons, bd. elders Evangelical Lutheran Ch., St. Paul, 1979—. Served to 1st lt., USAF, 1972-75. Recipient Honeywell Alpha award, 1979, 80; N.W. Post Ordinance award, USAF-ROTC, 1971; Kiwi award, 1970; Outstanding Sr. Cadet award, 1971; Bausch & Lomb Sci. award, 1967. Mem. Optical Soc. Am., Soc. Photo-Optical Instrumentation Engrs., Assn. of Evang. Luth. Chs. Contributing editor Telescope Making Mag., 1980—; contbr. articles to profl. jours. Home: 368 N 9th St Bayport MN 55003 Office: 2600 Ridgway Pkwy Minneapolis MN 55003

STONE, DONALD D., investment co. and sales agy. exec.; b. Chgo., June 25, 1924; s. Frank J. and Mary N. (Miller) Diamondstone; student U. Ill., 1942-43; B.S., DePaul U., 1949; m. Catherine Mauro, Dec. 20, 1970; children—Richard, Jeffrey. Pres., Poster Bros., Inc., Chgo., 1950-71, Revere Leather Goods, Inc., Chgo., 1953-71; owner Don Stone Enterprises, Chgo., 1954—; v.p. Horton & Hubbard Mfg. Co., Inc. div. Brown Group, Nashua, N.H., 1969-71, Neevel Mfg. Co., Kansas City, Mo., 1969-71. Mem. exec. bd. Chgo. Area council Boy Scouts Am. Served with U.S. Army, 1943-46. Clubs: Bryn Mawr Country (dir.), Carlton. Home: 209 E Lake Shore Dr Chicago IL 60611 Office: 875 N Michigan Ave Suite 4020 Chicago IL 60611

STONE, DONNA JESSIE, found. exec.; b. Evanston, Ill., May 23, 1935; d. W. Clement and Jessie V. (Tarson) S.; student Northwestern U., 1954-56; Baldwin-Wallace Coll., 1956-58; children by previous marriage—Christopher Kneifel, Linda Kneifel; m. 3d, LeRoy A. Pesch, Dec. 28, 1975; step-children—Christopher Pesch, Brian Pesch, Daniel Pesch. Pres., W. Clement and Jessie V. Stone Found., Chgo., 1970—; founder Nat. Com. for Prevention of Child Abuse, Chgo., pres., 1972-78. Chmn., John F. Kennedy Center for Performing Arts, Washington, 1972—; Alliance for Arts Edn., 1976-78; sec. Child Welfare League Am.; chmn. Internat. Standing Com. on Child Abuse, Geneva, 1981; life mem. bd. govs. Art Inst. Chgo., 1966. Republican. Presbyterian. Clubs: Mich. Shores Country, Chgo. Yacht, Capital Hill, La Concha, Club de Yates, MidAm. Home: 333 N Mayflower Rd Lake Forest IL 60045 Office: 111 E Wacker Dr Suite 510 Chicago IL 60601

STONE, GERALD LEE, psychologist, educator; b. Glendale, Calif., Aug. 25, 1941; s. Jack C. and Edith B. (Alexander) S.; B.A. in Psychology, UCLA, 1963; B.D., Princeton Theol. Sem., 1966; M.A., Mich. State U., 1970, Ph.D., 1972; m. Cheryl A. Montgomery, Sept. 6, 1963; children—Corbin Lee, Carrie Leeanne. Ordained to ministry Presbyterian Ch., 1969; asst. minister College Park Presbyn. Ch., San Diego, 1966-69; chaplain Juvenile Hall, San Diego, 1967-68, The Cloisters-Convalescent Hosp., San Diego, 1967-68; teaching asst. Sch. of Tchr. Edn., Mich. State U., East Lansing, 1969-71, research asst. Human Learning Inst., 1969-70, supr. Sch. of Tchr. Edn., 1970-71, research asst. dept. counseling, 1970-71, research asst. dept. psychiatry, 1971-72; psychologist St. Thomas (Ont.) Psychiat. Hosp., Can., summer, 1972; asst. prof. dept. psychology U. Western Ont., London, 1972-76, asso. prof., 1977, chmn. counseling psychology program, 1975-77; asso. prof. Coll. Edn., U. Iowa, Iowa City, 1979-81, prof., 1981—, coordinator counseling psychology, 1979—; cons. to various hosps., 1972—; appraiser grant applications Can. Council, 1974-79. Old Gold Summer fellow, 1980, 81. Mem. Am. Psychol. Assn., Am. Ednl. Research Assn. Democrat. Author: Cognitive-behavioral counseling: Implications for practice, research and professional development, 1980; contbr. articles to jours. in psychology; editorial bd. Jour. of Counseling Psychology, 1977—. Office: Counseling Psychology Lindquist Center Univ Iowa Iowa City IA 52242

STONE, J. W., sch. adminstr.; b. Fortescue, Mo., Nov. 6, 1927; s. Perry Allen and May (Murrah) S.; B.S., NW Mo. State Coll., 1956; M.A., U. Mo., Kansas City, 1957, also postgrad. Farmer, Fortescue, Mo., 1944—; instr. Craig (Mo.) R-III High Sch., 1957-59; supt. schs., Holt County, Oregon, Mo., 1959-61, Craig R-III Sch. Dist., 1961—; del. to Hungary, USSR, Internat. Edn. Soc., 1968. Dist. dir. ARC, 1954—, bd. dirs. Midland Empire region, 1979—; bd. dirs. Heart Assn., Crippled Children's, March of Dimes, Tb Soc., 1954—; mem. Town Bd., Fotescue, Mo., 1962-78; mayor City of Fortescue, 1968-78; chmn. Holt County Citizens Council, 1979—; vice chmn. Wesley Found., NW Mo. State U., 1970—; mem. regional empire com. bd. Girl Scouts, 1973-75; mem. com. Mo. Council Public Higher Edn., 1973; regional dir. Mo. Vocat. Rehab., 1967—; chmn. bd. NW Mo. Community Services, 1980—. Mem. 6th Congressional Dist., 1960—, 6th Congressional Legis. Dist., 1960—, Mo. Republican State Com., 1960—; chmn. Holt County Rep. Central Com., 1954—; state com. del. to inauguration Pres. Reagan, 1981; mem. Balance of State Planning Council, State of Mo., 1981—. dir. OEO Corp.; sec.-treas. NW Mo. Econ. Opportunity Corp., Maryville, Mo., chmn. bd., 1969-79; v.p. Mo. Council Chs., 1948-50; dir. Camps and Conf., W. Mo. Conf., United Meth. Ch., 1965—, mem. bd. adminstrv. fin., 1972—; U.S. del. World Meth. Council Meeting, Dublin, 1976, Honolulu, 1981; Maryville dist. trustee Meth. Ch., 1960—. World del. Meth. Conf., Oslo, Norway, 1961; del. United Meth. Ch. Mo. West Conf. to World Meth. Council Evangelism, Jerusalem, 1974; world del. representing U.S. on Christian Edn., Tokyo, 1958; U.S. del. Comparative and Internat. Edn. Soc., Round-the-World, 1970, S. Am., 1971. Served with AUS, 1950-52. Mem. NEA, Nat., Mo. State assns. sch. adminstrs., Mo. State, Holt County (past pres.) tchrs. assns., Pi Omega Pi, Kappa Delta Pi, Tau Kappa Epsilon. Methodist (dist. lay leader 1968—). Clubs: Masons (32 deg., Shriner), Order Eastern Star. Home: Fortescue MO 64452 Office: Craig MO 64437

STONE, JOHN TIMOTHY, JR., author; b. Denver, July 13, 1933; s. John Timothy and Marie Elizabeth (Briggs) S.; student Amherst Coll., 1951-52, U. Mex., 1952; B.A., U. Miami, 1955; m. Judith Bosworth Stone, June 22, 1955; children—John Timothy, George William. Sales mgr. Atlas Tag, Chgo., 1955-57; br. mgr. Household Fin. Corp., Chgo., 1952-62; pres. Janeff Credit Corp., Madison, Wis., 1962-72; pres. Recreation Internat., Mpls., 1972-74; pres. Continental Royal Services, N.Y.C., 1973-74; author: Mark, 1973; Going for Broke, 1976; The Minnesota Connection, 1978; Debby Boone So Far, 1980; (with John Dallas McPherson) He Calls Himself "An Ordinary Man", 1981; Satiacum, The Chief Who's Winning Back the West, 1981; dir. Madison Credit Bur., Wis. Lenders' Exchange. Served with CIC, U.S. Army, 1957-59. Mem. Sigma Alpha Epsilon. Republican. Presbyterian. Clubs: Minarani, African First Shotters. Home: 5508 Williamsburg Way Madison WI 53719 Office: Lit Resources Inc 2005 N Central Ave Suite 603 Phoenix AZ 85004

STONE, KENNETH ANDREW, mfg. co. exec.; b. Detroit, May 2, 1948; s. Ralph and Rosalyn R. S.; B.B.A., Eastern Mich. U., 1970; m. Helen S. Schwarzberg, June 14, 1970; children—Richard, Allison. Vice pres., gen. mgr. Stone Soap Co., Inc., Detroit, 1970—, also dir. Mem. Internat. Carwash Assn., Nat. Carwash Assn., Mich. Carwash Assn. (merit award 1978), Mich. Lodging Assn., Greater Detroit Motel and Hotel Assn., Internat. San. Supply Assn., Mich. Restaurant Assn. Clubs: Franklin Racquet, Southfield Athletic. Office: 1490 Franklin St Detroit MI 48207

STONE, PAUL DOUGLAS, research and devel. exec.; b. Ottawa, Kans., Feb. 7, 1940; s. Paul Edwin and Ollie Francis (Zook) S.; B.S. in Chem. Engring., U. Kans., 1963; M.S. in Chem. Engring., U. Fla., 1967; postgrad. Mich. State U., U. Mich.; m. Betty Jane Hardage, Aug. 12, 1961; children—Deborah Jane, Trisha Denise. With Dow Chem. Co., Midland, Mich., 1968—, beginning as sr. materials engr., successively sr. pilot plant project leader, sr. area engr. maintenance tech. center, group leader materials and corrosion research and devel., 1968-76, group leader Halogens Research Lab., 1976-78, research mgr. process devel., 1978-81, lab. dir., functional products and systems tech. service and devel., 1981—. Loaned exec. United Community Fund; pres. Adams Grade Sch. Parent Tchr. Orgn., 1974-76; sec. fin. com. St. John's Episcopal Ch., Midland, 1980-81. Served to capt. USAF, 1963-68. Registered profl. engr., Mich. Mem. Am. Inst. Chem. Engrs. (chmn. Mid-Mich. sect., cert. profl. devel. recognition 1980), Nat. Assn. Corrosion Engrs., Am. Chem. Soc., Exptl. Aircraft Assn., Aircraft Owners and Pilots Assn., Nat. Eagle Scout Assn. Democrat. Episcopalian. Home: 5613 Whitehall St Midland MI 48640 Office: Larkin Lab Dow Chem Co Midland MI 48640

STONE, TERENCE FREDERICK, regional planning agy. exec.; b. Hanska, Minn., Jan. 16, 1934; s. Ivan Brude and Esther Bernice (Heagle) S.; B.S. in Agrl. Edn., U. Minn.; m. Colette Carrell, Sept. 15, 1956; children—Colleen, Mark, Paul, Alan, Maureen, Karin, Beth, Jon, Timothy. Tchr. public sch., Little Falls, Minn., 1959; with poultry service and sales Peavey Co., Mpls., 1960-67; owner, mgr. Stone Bros. Inc., Madelia, Minn., 1967-76; exec. dir. Region Nine Devel. Commn., Mankato, Minn., 1976—. Mayor City of Madelia, 1970-78; co-chmn. Watonwan County (Minn.) Republicans. Served with U.S. Army, 1953-55. Mem. Minn. Planning Assn., Am. Planning Assn., Public Adminstrn. Soc. Roman Catholic. Clubs: Am. Legion, K.C. Office: PO Box 2367 Mankato MN 56001

STONE, W. CLEMENT, ins. exec.; b. Chgo., May 4, 1902: s. Louis and Anna M. (Gunn) S.; student Detroit Coll. Law, 1920, Northwestern U., 1930-32; LL.D., Monmouth Coll., 1963; H.H.D., Interlochen Arts Acad., 1964; Litt.D., Coll. Chiropractic, Lombard, 1969; H.H.D. (hon.), Whitworth Coll., 1969, S.W. Baptist Coll., 1970, Lincoln Coll., 1970; LL.D., Whittier Coll., 1973; D. Pub. Service, Salem Coll., 1974; m. Jessie Verna Tarson; children—Clement, Donna, Norman. Chmn. bd., dir. Combined Am. Ins. Co., Dallas; chmn. bd. Combined Ins. Co. Am., Chgo.; chmn., dir. Combined Life Ins. Co. N.Y., Albany; chmn. bd. Combined Opportunities, Inc., Chgo.; chmn. bd., chief exec. officer, dir. Combined Ins. Co. Wis., Fond du Lac; organizer Combined Mut. Casualty Co., 1940, pres. 1940-47; dir. Alberto-Culver Co.; chmn. bd. Success Unltd., Chgo. Hon. chmn. bd. Chgo. Boys' Club, named Chicagoan of Yr., 1980; mem. nat. exec. com. Boys Club Am.; chmn. bd. W. Clement and Jessie V. Stone Found. chmn. bd. trustees Internat. Council on Edn. for Teaching; trustee George Williams Coll.; bd. govs. Chgo. Heart Assn.; bd. dirs., mem. Lyric Guild, Lyric Opera Chgo.; pres., trustee Religious Heritage Am.; mem. exec. com. Internat. Fedn. Keystone Youth Orgns.; hon. trustee So. Baptist Coll.; trustee Urol. Research Found., Coll. Medicine U. Utah; chmn. trustees Interlochen Arts Acad. and Nat. Music Camp. Recipient Horatio Alger award, 1963; Church Layman of the Year award, 1968; nominee Nobel Peace Prize, 1981. Mem. Chgo. Planetarium Soc., Chgo. Assn. Health Underwriters Chgo., Am. Life Ins. Assn., Soc. Midland Authors, United Shareholders Am. (mem. nat. policy adv. com.), Art Inst. Chgo. (life), Northwestern U. Alumni Assn., Ill. C. of C., Chgo. Ednl. TV Assn. (trustee), Insts. Religion and Health (chmn. bd.), Alpha Kappa Psi. Presbyn. Mason. Clubs: Chicago Press, John Evans, Executives, Michigan Shores Country. Author: (with Napoleon Hill) Success Through a Positive Mental Attitude; (with Norma Lee Browning) The Other Side of the Mind: The Success System that Never Fails. Chmn., Success Unltd. mag. Office: 707 Combined Centre Northbrook IL 60062

STONE, WILLIAM BRUHN, educator; b. Milw., May 31, 1929; s. William Herbert and Martha Emily (Bruhn) S.; B.A. with gen. honors, U. Chgo., 1948, M.A., 1957; m. Jane Bergman, Mar. 13, 1953; children—David, Daniel, Joyce. Instr. English, U. Ky., Lexington, 1958-61, Wis. State U., LaCrosse, 1961-62; lectr. English, Ind. U. N.W., Gary, 1962-71, 80—; asst. dir. composition U. Ill., Chgo., 1976-80; editorial cons. various pubs. Active member Amnesty Internat. U.S.A. Served with AUS, 1952-54; Korea. Mem. AAUP, Am. Bus. Communication Assn., Assn. Tchrs. Advanced Composition, Conf. Coll. Composition and Communication, Midwest Modern Lang. Assn., MLA, Nat. Council Tchrs. of English, Rhetoric Soc. Am., U.S. Chess Fedn. Editor: Anthony Powell Communications, 1977-79; editorial bd. Jour. Advanced Composition, 1979—; contbr. articles, revs. and poetry to profl. jours., articles to ency. Home: 5704 S Kenwood Ave Chicago IL 60637 Office: Indiana University Gary IN 46408

STONE, WILLIAM HAROLD, geneticist, educator; b. Boston, Dec. 15, 1924; s. Robert and Rita (Scheinberg) S.; A.B., Brown U., 1947; M.S., U. Maine, 1948; Ph.D., U. Wis., 1953; m. Carmen Maqueda, Dec. 22, 1971; children—Susan Stone Vansicklen, Debra Stone Bissinger, Alexander R. Research asst. Jackson Lab., Bar Harbor, Maine, 1947-48; instr. U. Wis., Madison, 1948-53, asst. prof. genetics, 1953-56, asso. prof., 1957-60, prof., 1965—; mem. Nat. Research Council, 1978—; cons. Wis. Alumni Research Fedn., Warner Bros. Film, Govt. of Spain. Served with USNR, 1942-45. Recipient Ivanov medal USSR, 1972. Mem. AAAS, Am. Primate Soc., Genetics Soc. Am., Am. Assn. Immunologists, Internat. Assn. Blood Group Research, Am. Genetics Assn., Am. Assn. Aging, Transplantation Soc. Democrat. Contbr. articles to profl. jours. Home: 3411 Stony Crest Dr McFarland WI 53558 Office: Lab of Genetics Univ of Wis Madison WI 53706

STONE, WILLIAM ROBERT, mgmt. cons.; b. Smith Center, Kans., July 28, 1921; s. Edward VanBuren and Daisy (Achenbach) S.; S.B., Harvard U., 1943; postgrad. Harvard-Mass. Inst. Tech. Radar Sch., 1944, N.Y. U., 1947-48, Bklyn. Poly. Inst., 1948-51; m. Vivian Adele Dowie, Jan. 31, 1948; children—Pamela Gail, Linda Janise, Wendy Carol. Engr., sect. mgr. Hazeltine Corp., N.Y.C., 1946-56; project controller Gen. Electric Co., 1956-58, specialist mgmt. sci., 1958-60, orgn. cons., 1960-63; gen. mgr., dir. Hunt Electronics, Dallas, 1963-65; cons. mgmt. systems IBM Armonk, N.Y., 1967-69; v.p. A.B. Dick Co., Chgo., 1969-74; exec. v.p. E.F. Johnson Co., Waseca, Minn., 1974-76; partner Brown/Ferrisco, Mgmt. Cons.'s, Wayzata, Minn., 1977-79; pres. Stone, Howard, Nowill & Kouwenhoven, Inc., 1979—; chmn. Kinetics Measurement Corp.; dir. Tachtronic Instruments, Inc.; mem. Nat. TV Systems Com., 1951-53; mgmt. cons., 1965-66; cons. U.S. Dept. Commerce, 1973—. Served to lt., Signal Corps, U.S. Army, 1943-46. Mem. IEEE. Republican. Clubs: Radio, Electronic-VIP, Harvard of N.Y., Harvard of Minn. Home: 1009 E Elm Ave Waseca MN 56093 Office: 250 N Central Ave Wayzata MN 55391

STONE, WINIFRED ODELL, univ. dean; b. Pax, W.Va., July 28, 1935; s. Otis O. and Flora D. Stone; A.B. in Psychology, W.Va. State Coll., 1957; M.Ed. in Counseling and Guidance, U. Toledo, 1963; Ph.D. in Counselor Edn. (Ford Found. fellow 1969), Fla. State U., 1971; m. Marva Vertell Turner, Oct. 14, 1961; children—Mark, Maya. Dir. Upward Bound, Fla. A&M U., Tallahassee, 1967-69; counseling psychologist Fla. State U., 1970-71; asst. provost minority affairs Bowling Green (Ohio) State U., 1971-73, asst. dean, dir. grad. admissions, 1973-81, asso. dean Grad. Coll., 1982—, asso. prof. ethnic studies, 1978—, dir. grad. and profl. opportunities program grant, 1978—; cons. in field; mem. services com. Grad. Record Exam. Bd., 1979-82. Pres. Conneaut Elementary Sch. PTA, Bowling Green, 1976-77; vice chmn. Bowling Green Human Relations Commn., 1976. Served as 1st lt. Med. Service Corps, U.S. Army, 1957-60. Recipient Spl. Achievement award Bowling Green State U., 1975, citation African Student Assn. Bowling Green State U., 1977. Mem. Am. Personnel and Guidance Assn., Soc. Spl. Emerging Programs in Higher Edn., Am. Assn. Collegiate Registrars and Admissions Officers, Mid-Am. Assn. Ednl. Opportunity Programs, Ohio Personnel and Guidance Assn., NAACP, Phi Delta Kappa, Alpha Phi Alpha. Presbyterian. Sr. editor: Black Gold, 1974; contbr. articles to profl. publs. Home: 934 Ferndale Ct Bowling Green OH 43402 Office: Grad Coll 120 McFall Center Bowling Green State Univ Bowling Green OH 43403

STONEKING, RANDALL IRWIN, ins. co. exec.; b. Sioux Falls, S.D., Sept. 20, 1946; s. Joseph Giles and Dorothy (Whyte) S.; B.A. magna cum laude, Morningside Coll., Sioux City, Iowa, 1968; m. Olivia Jeanne Gilbertson, July 10, 1966; children—Matthew Randall, Margaret Ann. Agt., Minn. Mut. Life Ins. Co., 1968-69; with Mut. Service Ins., St. Paul, 1969—, tng. specialist, 1970-71, sales supr., 1972-73, tng. specialist, 1973-74, sales tng. mgr., 1975-81, dir. mktg. services, 1981—; tng. specialist Sentry Ins., 1974-75; instr. Life Office Mgmt. Assn. C.L.U. Fellow Life Mgmt. Inst.; mem. Nat. Assn. Life Underwriters, Minn. Assn. Life Underwriters, St. Paul Assn. Life Underwriters, Am. Soc. C.L.U.s, Nat. Assn. Health Underwriters, Minn. Assn. Health Underwriters, Am. Soc. Tng. and Devel., Ins. Co. Edn. Dirs. Soc., North Central Tng. Dirs. Assn. Republican. Lutheran. Club: Arden Hills Tennis-Racquet. Home: 8434 Pleasant View Dr Mounds View MN 55432 Office: Two Pine Tree Dr Arden Hills MN 55112

STONEMAN, WILLIAM, III, univ. dean; b. Kansas City, Mo., Sept. 8, 1927; s. William and Helen Louise (Bloom) S.; B.S. in Biology, St. Louis U., 1948, M.D., 1952; m. Elizabeth Johanna Wilson, May 19, 1951; children—William Laurence, Sidney Camdon, Cecily Anne, Elizabeth Wilson, John Spalding. Intern, Kansas City (Mo.) Gen. Hosp., 1952-53; resident in surgery, then resident in plastic surgery St. Louis U. Hosp., 1953-59; mem. faculty St. Louis U. Med. Sch., 1959—, asso. prof. surgery, 1975—, exec. asso. dean, 1976—; mem. faculty Washington U. Med. Sch., 1969-74; dir. Univ. Learning Resources Center, 1977—; mem. Mo. Blue Shield Adv. Group, 1969—; mem. evaluation com. Inter Soc. Commn. Heart Disease Resources, 1971-72; mem. Gov. Mo. Com. Comprehensive Health Planning, 1969-72, Mo. Health Manpower Planning Task Force, 1974-77. Served with AUS, 1946-47. Diplomate Am. Bd. Surgery, Am. Bd. Plastic Surgery. Mem. AMA, Am. Soc. Plastic and Reconstructive Surgery, Assn. Am. Med. Coll., Midwest Assn. Plastic Surgeons, Mo. Med. Assn., St. Louis Met. Med. Soc., St. Louis Surg. Soc. Roman Catholic. Club: Racquet (St. Louis). Author papers in field; asso. editor Parameters, 1976-79. Office: 1402 S Grand St Saint Louis MO 63104

STONER, M. DOYLE, accountant; b. West Unity, Ohio, Mar. 26, 1927; s. Beryl Vincent and Francis Ruth (Davis) S.; B.S., Ohio State U., 1950; m. Joyce A. Miller, Apr. 26, 1980; children by previous marriage—Michael D., Susan Stoner Ells, Diane C.; stepchildren—Rodney, Karen, Julie. Salesman telephone Farm Bur. Coop., Columbus, Ohio, 1950; trainee City Nat. Bank, Columbus, 1950-51; accountant Brandt & Lee Co., Columbus, 1952-64; practice accounting, Worthington, Ohio, 1964—; pres. J. Plaza Inc., Worthington, 1966—. Treas., King Ave. United Methodist Ch., 1964-80; fin. adviser Childhood League Inc. Served with USNR, 1946-47, 51-52. C.P.A., Ohio. Mem. Columbus, Worthington chambers commerce, Ohio Soc. C.P.A.'s. Republican. Clubs: Univ. Columbus, Masons. Home: 1040 Melinda Dr Westerville OH 43081 Office: 6902 N High St Worthington OH 43085

STONEY, LARRY D., state legislator; b. Omaha, Nov. 12, 1937; student U. Nebr., Omaha, 1964; m. Janice E. Dunkle; 1 son, Todd Dunkle. Spl. service dept. Mut. of Omaha; mem. Nebr. Legislature, 1974—. Bd. dirs. Nebr. Kidney Found.; mem. Douglas-Sarpy County unit Am. Cancer Soc. Mem. Gideons Internat. Address: Omaha NE *

STORCE, FRANK ROBERT, optical exec.; b. Chgo., Apr. 2, 1938; s. Stanley Stephen and Pauline Anna (Szacik) S.; B.A., U. of Ill., 1960. Various positions Wesley-Jessen, Inc., Chgo., 1963-76; div. mgr. House of Vision Instrument Co., Chgo., 1976; mgr. Wesley-Jessen, Inc., 1977—. Served with U.S. Army, 1960-62. Mem. Nat. Eye Research Found., Nat. Pvt. Pilots Assn. Roman Catholic. Clubs: St. Peter's Social. Home: 1312 N Bosworth St Chicago IL 60622 Office: 37 S Wabash Ave Chicago IL 60603

STOTT, ALFRED FRANK, aero. engr., coll. pres.; b. Grand Rapids, Mich., Oct. 4, 1911; s. Tally F. and Louise (Fouts) S.; B.S. in Aero. Engring., Hancock Coll., 1932; D.Sc. (hon.), Ind. No. U., 1969; m. Martha Jane Allyn, June 26, 1937; children—James Lee, Allyn T., Carol Lynn Stott Conroy, Laura Louise Stott Otto. Asst. chief engr., Milw. Parts Corp., 1932-35; v.p., dean engring. Aero U., Chgo., 1935-59; asst. dir. tng. U.S. Army Air Corps Tech. Tng. Command, 1939-44; founder aero. engring and aviation adminstrn. sch. Aero-Space Inst., Chgo., 1959, pres., 1959—; cons. to airframe industry, 1958—; cons. to various tech. schs., 1958—. Registered profl. engr., Ill. Fellow Am. Inst. Aeros. and Astronautics (sec. Chgo. sect. 1948-53), Soc. Licensed Aircraft and Engine Technologists; mem. Profl. Racing Piolts Assn., Air Force Assn., Ill. Jr. Acad. Sci. (sec. 1968-70, chmn. aviation div. 1957-71), Am. Assn. of Specialized Colls. (vice chmn. 1970-71), Chgo. Assn. of Commerce and Industry (mem. edn. and aviation com. 1968—). Club: Masons. Home: 4044 Woodland Ave Western Springs IL 60558 Office: 57 W Grand Ave Chicago IL 60610

STOTTER, JAMES S., economist; b. Cleve., Feb. 13, 1941; s. Morton M. and Ruth B. (Biskind) S.; B.S., Miami U., Oxford, Ohio, 1965; M.A. in Econs., Case Western Res. U., 1972. Instr. econs., fin., statistics Cleve. State U., 1966-72; bus. devel. coordinator City of East Cleveland, Ohio, 1975-77; research analyst Predicasts, Inc., Cleve., 1978; sr. economist RAA, Inc., Cleve., 1978-79; mgr. bus. devel. Greater Cleve. Growth Assn., 1979-81; exec. dir. Cleve. Regional Minority Purchasing Council, Inc., 1979—; adj. prof. econs. and bus. Cuyahoga Community Coll., 1972—; cons. doing bus. as Busimetrics. Served with U.S. Army, 1960-61, 61-62. Mem. Am. Econ. Assn., Nat. Assn. Bus. Economists., Mktg. Research Assn. Author, co-author class materials in field, industry studies.

STOUDER, GREGORY DALE, optometrist; b. Ft. Wayne, Ind., Dec. 4, 1928; s. Herbert Albion and Maude Esther (Powell) S.; student Ind. U., 1950; B.S. in Optometry, No. Ill. Coll. Optometry, 1953, D. Optometry, 1954; m. Susan Brown McNabb, Dec. 29, 1954; children—Deborah, David, Ann, Amy. Individual practice optometry, Ft. Wayne, 1956—. Organizing dir., v.p. Ft. Wayne Fed. Savs. & Loan Assn.; v.p. S.W. Investment Corp. Donor, Ind. U. Found. Served with AUS, 1954-56. Mem. Am., Ind., North Eastern Ind. (past pres.) optometric assns., Ft. Wayne C. of C., United Comml. Travelers, Izaac Walton League, Ind. U. Alumni Assn., Tomb and Key Frat., Demolay (life). Republican. Baptist. Mason (Shriner), Lion. Home: 715 Nightfall Rd Fort Wayne IN 46819 Office: 2811 Lower Huntington Rd Fort Wayne IN 46809

STOUP, ARTHUR HARRY, lawyer; b. Kansas City, Mo., Aug. 30, 1925; s. Isadore and Dorothy (Rankle) S.; student Kansas City (Mo.) Jr. Coll., 1942-43; B.A., J.D., U. Mo., 1950; m. Kathryn Jolliff, July 30, 1948; children—David C., Daniel P., Rebecca Ann, Deborah E. Admitted to Mo. bar, 1950, D.C. bar, 1979; pvt. practice law, Kansas City, Mo., 1950—; mem. firm Stoup Thompson & Wohlner; mem. Lawyer to Lawyer Consultation Panel-Litigation, 1976—; chmn. U.S. Merit Selection Com. for Western Dist. Mo., 1981—. Chmn. com. to rev. continuing edn. U. Mo., 1978-79; trustee, pres. U. Mo. at Kansas City Law Found., 1979—; trustee U. Kansas City, 1979—. Served with USNR, 1942-45. Recipient Alumni Achievement award U. Mo.-Kansas City Alumni Assn., 1975. Fellow Internat. Soc. Barristers; mem. Kansas City (pres. 1966-67), Mo. (bd. govs. 1967-76, v.p. 1972-73, pres. 1974-75), Am. (ho. of dels. 1976-80) bar assns., Lawyers Assn. Kansas City, Mo. Assn. Trial Attys., Assn. Trial Lawyers Am. (dir. 1973—, pres. 1978—), So. Conf. Bar Pres.'s (life), Mobar Research Inc. (pres. 1978—), Phi Alpha Delta Alumni (justice Kansas City area 1955-56, William H. Pittman hon. award Lawson chpt. 1974), Tau Kappa Epsilon. Mem. B'nai B'rith. Clubs: Optimists (pres. Ward Pkwy. 1961-62, lt. gov. Mo. dist. internat. 1963-64); Sertoma. Home: 9002 Western Hills Dr Kansas City MO 64114 Office: Home Savs Bldg Kansas City MO 64106

STOUT, CHESTER BERNARD, librarian, curator; b. Jacksonville, Tex., May 31, 1918; s. Chester Bernard and Besse (Smith) S.; student W. Tenn. Bus. Coll., 1936-37, Tulane U., 1952-54; B.S., Auburn U., 1960; M.S., La. State U., 1963; M.A., Central Mo. State U., 1967; Ph.D., Case Western Res. U., 1976; m. Shirley Mae Carradine, June 13, 1953; children—Chester, Wayne (dec.), Sandra. Enlisted USN, 1937; librarian U.S. Submarine Base, Pearl Harbor, 1940; asst. library services U.S. Antarctic Expdn., 1955-57; instr. Naval R.O.T.C., Auburn U., 1957-61; ret., 1961; instr., asst. librarian Central Mo. State U., 1963-68; librarian, curator McKinley Meml. Library, Niles, Ohio, 1969—; micrographics cons. Active Boy Scouts Am., YMCA. Mem. ALA, Ohio, Northeastern Ohio (sec.) library assns, NEA, Fleet Res. Assn., Am. Legion, Vets. Fgn. Wars, Phi Delta Kappa, Omicron Delta Epsilon. Clubs: Kiwanis, Masons, Shriners; Order Eastern Star. Contbr. articles to profl. jours. Home: 67 Helen St Niles OH 44446 Office: 40 N Main St Niles OH 44446

STOUT, DONALD EVERETT, real estate developer and appraiser; b. Dayton, Ohio, Mar. 16, 1926; s. Thorne Franklin and Lovella Marie (Sweeney) S.; B.S., Miami U., 1950; m. Gloria B. McCormick, Apr. 10, 1948; children—Holly Sue, Scott Kenneth. Mgr. comml.-indsl. div. G.P. Huffman Realty, Dayton, 1954-58; leasing agt., mgr. Forest Park Plaza, Dayton, 1959-71; developer 1st transp. center for trucking in Ohio; pres. devel. cos. Sunderland Falls Estates, Wright Gate Indsl. Mall, Edglo Land Recycle, Grande Tierra Corp., Dayton and Eastwood Lake Lodge/Marina; pres. Donald E. Stout, Inc. Served with AUS, 1944-45, USN, 1945-46. Named Outstanding Real Estate Salesman in Dayton, Dayton Area Bd. Realtors, in Ohio, Ohio Bd. Realtors, 1961. Licensed real estate broker, Ohio, U.S. Virgin Islands. Mem. Dayton Area Bd. Realtors (founder; 1st pres. salesman div. 1959, dir. 1959-60), Nat. Assn. Real Estate Bds., Soc. Real Estate Appraisers (sr. real estate appraiser, dir. chpt. 1959-60, pres. chpt. 1964), Am. Inst. Real Estate Appraisers, Nat. Assn. Rev. Appraisers (charter), Soc. Indsl. Realtors, Appraisal Inst., Res. Officers Assn., C. of C., Phi Delta Theta. Clubs: Masons (32 deg.), Shrine, Dayton Racquet. Contbr. articles to profl. jours. Home: 759 Plantation Ln Dayton OH 45419 Office: 1340 Woodman Dr Dayton OH 45432

STOUT, GLENN EMANUEL, meteorologist, educator; b. Fostoria, Ohio, Mar. 23, 1920; s. Glen Hosler and Eva Mrytle (Barkley) S.; B.S., Findlay (Ohio) Coll., 1942, D.Sc., 1973; cert. U. Chgo., 1942, 46; m. Helen Lucille Beery, Nov. 15, 1942; children—Bonnie Gywnn, Steven Owen. Instr., U. Chgo., 1943; head atmospheric sci. sect. Ill. State Water Survey, Urbana, Ill., 1947-69, 71-73; sci. coordinator NSF, 1969-71; prof. environ. studies U. Ill., 1973—, dir. Water Resources Center, 1973—. Mem. Ill. Gov.'s Task Force on State Water Plan, 1980—. Served with USNR, 1942-52. Mem. Am. Meteorol. Soc., Am. Geophys. Union, Am. Water Resources Assn., Internat. Water Resources Assn. (pres. U.S. geog. com. 1979—), AAAS, Ill. Acad. Sci. Methodist. Club: Kiwanis (pres. Champaign-Urbana 1979-80). Editor in chief: Water Internat., 1981—. Office: University of Illinois 205 N Romine St Urbana IL 61801

STOUT, WALTER HOWARD, mfg. co. exec.; b. Grand Junction, Colo., Jan. 12, 1938; s. Walter A. and Millicent M. (Younger) S.; B.S. in Aero. Engring., B.S. in Bus. Mktg., Colo. U., 1961; m. Joyce Tupper, Aug. 21, 1960; children—Ann, Amy, Mark (dec.). With Dow Chem. Co., 1961-64; v.p. sales Sinclair Mfg. Co., Sylvania, Ohio, 1964-77, pres., 1977—. Home: 5915 Winslow Rd Whitehouse OH 43571 Office: 5644 Monroe St Sylvania OH 43560

STOVALL, EMMETT LUSTER, airline co. exec.; b. Seale, Ala., June 24, 1926; s. Felder and Iberta (Grier) S.; B.S., Roosevelt U.; m. Orlee Stovall, Dec. 22, 1945; 1 dau., Gloria Jean. Blueprint welder Internat. Harvester Co., Chgo., 1943-65; founder, chmn., chief exec. officer, capt. Nat. Air Commuter Inc., minority cargo airline, Chgo., 1965—. Served with U.S. Army, 1942-43. Recipient CORE award, 1975. Mem. Chgo. Assn. Commerce and Industry, Aircraft Owners and Pilots Assn., Nat. Small Bus. Assn. Author: The Face in the Sun, 1969. Office: Nat Air Commuter Inc Midway Airport 6200 S Cicero St Chicago IL 60638

STOVALL, JACK TERRANCE, ins. co. exec.; b. Omaha, June 20, 1945; s. George Clinton and Laura Goldy (Skalak) S.; B.B.A., U. Nebr., Omaha, 1967; M.B.A., U. Ark., 1969; m. Kathleen Ann Eilbeck, May 1, 1971; children—Laura, Aaron, Susan. Asst. dir. personnel Postal Finance, Sioux City, 1969-70; placement counselor Snelling & Snelling, Omaha, 1970-71; asst. dir. personnel Immanuel Med. Center, Omaha, 1971-72; dir. personnel Eastern Nebr. Human Services Agy., Omaha, 1973-75; human resource dir., corp. planning dir. Blue Cross of Western Iowa & S.D., Sioux City, 1975—; instr. U. Nebr. Bus. Coll., Omaha. Mem. Greater Omaha Assn. for Retarded Citizens, 1973-75. Mem. Am. Soc. Personnel Adminstrn., Am. Soc. Tng. and Devel. Republican. Presbyterian. Home: 3320 Jennings St Sioux City IA 51104 Office: I-29 and Hamilton Blvd Sioux City IA 51102

STOVER, DENNIS WAYNE, san. engr.; b. Centralia, Ill., Oct. 27, 1942; s. Paul Willis and Alvera Louise (Sprehe) S.; B.S. in Civil Engring., U. Mo. at Rolla, 1966, M.S. in San. Engring., 1967; m. Sharon Lee Conrad, Aug. 26, 1965; children—Teresa L., Cynthia L., Jennifer R. Engr., Ill. Dept. Pub. Health, Carbondale, 1967-70; regional mgr. regulatory and service work div. water supplies Ill. EPA, Marion, 1970—; mem. advisory bd. water and wastewater programs Southeastern Ill. Coll. Registered profl. engr., land surveyor, sanitarian, Ill. Mem. Am. Water Works Assn. (dist. rep.), ASCE, Nat. Soc. Profl. Engrs. Ill. Soc. Profl. Engrs. (rep., past chpt. pres., co-chmn. water quality com.), So. Ill. Water Works Operators Assn., Dist. Assn. County Supts. Hwys., Am. Acad. Environ. Engrs. (diplomate). Presbyn. Home: 1711 Julianne Dr Marion IL 62959 Office: 2209 W Main St Marion IL 62959

STOVER, JAMES R., mfg. co. exec.; b. Marion, Ind., 1927; B.M.E., Cath. U. Am., 1950; LL.B., George Washington U., 1955; married. Project engr. Eisenhauer Mfg. Co., 1950-51; patent examiner U.S. Patent Office, Washington, 1951-55; with Eaton Corp., Cleve., 1955—, hydrostatics program coordinator, Marshall, Mich., 1968-69, plant mgr., 1969-71, gen. mgr., 1971-73, gen. mgr. engineered fasteners div., 1973-74, group v.p. indsl. and security products, 1974-77, corp. exec. v.p. ops., 1977-78, vice-chmn., chief operating officer transp. products, 1978-79, pres., chief operating officer, 1979—, also dir.; dir. Nat. City Corp., Nat. City Bank, White Consol. Industries. Office: Eaton Corp 100 Erieview Plaza Cleveland OH 44114*

STOWELL, CHANNING, III, mktg. research corp. exec.; b. Baton Rouge, Dec. 3, 1943; s. Channing and Miriam Werner S.; S.B., M.I.T., 1965; m. Margaret Walker Cross, Aug. 19, 1967; children—Julia Nash, Channing Werner. Project leader Decision Tech., Inc., N.Y.C., 1967-69; mgr. corp. mktg. info. services Pillsbury Co., Mpls., 1970-74; mktg. dir. NPD, Schaumburg, Ill., 1974-75; group account exec. Mktg. Research Corp. Am., Northbrook, Ill., 1975-76, v.p. mktg., 1976—; v.p. Menu Census Services, 1980—. Deacon, Wayzata Community Ch., 1973-74. Mem. Am. Mktg. Assn., Inst. Mgmt. Sci. Republican. Home: 5 Tioga Trail Barrington IL 60010 Office: 2215 Sanders Northbrook IL 60062

STRACHAN, DONALD M., chem. co. exec.; b. Cleve., June 24, 1923; s. Harry Morris and Eva (Maffett) S.; student St. Catherine's Coll., Cambridge (Eng.) U., 1945; B.S. in Econs., U. Pa., 1947; m. Suzanne Merion, June 27, 1953; children—William, Paul. With Ernst & Ernst, C.P.A.'s, 1947-70, staff accountant to mgr., Cleve., 1947-63, partner, Charleston, W.Va., 1964-70; v.p. finance, treas. Cleve. Electronics, Inc., 1970-74; with Barnes, Wendling & Cook, Cleve., 1974-77; treas. McGean Chem. Co. Inc., Cleve., 1977—. Served with AUS, World War II. C.P.A., Ohio, W.Va. Mem. Delta Kappa Epsilon. Mem. United Ch. of Christ. Club: Chagrin Valley Country. Home: 135 Mill Creek Ln Moreland Hills OH 44022 Office: 1250 Terminal Tower Cleveland OH 44113

STRADER, JOHN JACOB, former co-owner radio sta.; b. Cin., Dec. 4, 1923; s. John Jacob and Jean Morton (Abbott) S.; student Coll. Music Cin., 1939-40; m. Joan Ganne, Oct. 20, 1944; 1 dau., Jacqueline. With Sta. WLW, Cin., 1939-40, WKRC, Cin., 1942-43, WCPO, Cin., 1943-45, WCKY, Cin., 1946; co-owner WVAW-FM, Cheviot, Ohio, 1947-48; now prin. Jack Strader Voice of Radio-TV-Film, Cin. Mem. Am. Theatre Organ Soc. (chpt. chmn. 1961-63), Sons and Daus. Pioneer Rivermen, Cin. Music Hall Assn. Home: 3650 Clifton Ave Cincinnati OH 45220

STRAFFON, RALPH ATWOOD, urologist; b. Croswell, Mich., Jan. 4, 1928; s. Lloyd Atwood and Verle R. (Rice) S.; M.D., U. Mich., 1953; m. Cary Arden Higley, Feb. 13, 1954; children—David, Daniel, Jonathan, Peter, Andrew. Intern, Univ. Hosp., Ann Arbor, 1953-54, resident in surgery, 1954-56, urology, resident, 1956-59; staff mem. dept. urology Cleve. Clinic, 1956-63, head dept. urology, 1963—; practice medicine specializing in urology Cleve., 1959—. Served with U.S. Army, 1946-48. Diplomate Am. Bd. Urology. Fellow A.C.S.; mem. Am. Assn. Genitourinary Surgeons, AMA, Cleve. Acad. Medicine, Am., Cleve. urol. assns., Clin. Soc. Genitourinary Surgeons, Soc. Univ. Urologists, Frederick A. Coller Surg. Soc., Am. Soc. Nephrology, Transplantaion Soc., Soc. Pelvic Surgeons, Soc. Pediatric Urology, Am. Fertility Soc., Am. Assn. Clin. Urologists, Société Internationale d'Urologie. Contbr. articles to med. jours. Home: 14200 Shaker Blvd Shaker Heights OH 44120 Office: 9500 Euclid Ave Cleveland OH 44106

STRAHLER, CLYTLE EVELYN, librarian, educator; b. Dayton, Ohio, June 17, 1907; d. Ezra Frederick and Bertha (Daniels) Strahler; A.B., Wittenberg Coll., 1934; B.S. in L.S., U. Ill., 1938. Asst. children's dept., high sch. dept., sch. br. asst. Dayton and Montgomery County Pub. Library, 1925-31, br. librarian, sch. librarian, 1932-49, head, tng. class activities and 1st asst. reference dept., 1949-56, coordinator personnel services, 1956-62; asst. head librarian Wittenberg U., Springfield, Ohio, 1962-64, chief reader services, 1964-66, asst. dir. univ. libraries, 1967, asso. dir. libraries, 1968-75, asso. prof., 1962-70, prof., 1971-75, prof., asso. dir. univ. libraries emerita, 1975—. Mem. ALA, Ohio Library Assn., Dayton Council on World Affairs, AAUP, AAUW, Springfield Art Assn., Springfield Urban League, Beta Phi Mu. Home: 5340 Brendonwood Ln Dayton OH 45415

STRAIN, EDWARD RICHARD, psychologist; b. Indpls., Apr. 12, 1925; s. Edward Richard and Ernestine (Kidd) S.; student DePauw U., 1943-44; A.B., Butler U., 1948; Ph.D., Duke, 1952; m. Marsha Ellen Beeler, 1972; children—Douglas MacDonald, Chadwick Edward, Sarah Abigail, Zachary Richard. Clin. psychologist Ohio State Med. Center, Columbus, 1952-53, Ind. U. Med. Center, Indpls., 1953-56; pvt. practice cons. psychology, Indpls., 1956—. Lectr. dept. psychology Butler U., Indpls., 1958-68. Pres. Marion County (Ind.) Mental Health Assn., 1967-69; 500 Festival asso., Indpls., 1961—; pres. Perry Twp. (Ind.) Rep. Club, 1968-69. Founder, bd. dirs. Downtown Sr. Citizens Center, Indpls., 1958-62. Served with USNR, 1943-46. Mem. Lambda Chi Alpha. Methodist. Clubs: Masons, Rotary, Indpls. Athletic. Home: 911 Briarpatch Ln Greenwood IN 46142 Office: 517-19 Illinois Bldg 17 W Market St Indianapolis IN 46204

STRALEY, HOWARD SCOTT, advt. and communications agy. exec.; b. Marietta, Ohio, Nov. 22, 1940; s. Howard Clifton and Doris Dosia (MacIntire) S.; B.S. in Journalism, Ohio U., 1966; m. Barbara Ann Koch, Sept. 2, 1967; 1 dau., Kristen Ann. Advt. asst. Brockway Glass Co., 1966-69; advt. and sales promotion mgr. Babcock & Wilcox, Diamond Power, Ohio, 1969-73; creative supr. Zylke & Affiliates, Chgo., 1973-75; dir. mktg. services Bell & Howell, Chgo., 1975-76; pres. H.S. Straley & Assos., Chgo., 1976—. Served with USN, 1958-62. Mem. Assn. Indsl. Advertisers, Nat. Mgmt. Assn. Republican. Home: 926 E Baldwin St Palatine IL 60067 Office: 540 Frontage Rd Northfield IL 60093

STRAND, ALAN LAWRENCE, mgmt. psychologist; b. Chgo.; s. Axel E. and Ruth (Tyler) S.; B.S., U. Ill., also M.A. in Psychology; Ph.D., Ill. Inst. Tech.; m. Anita Charlene Bray; children—Tyler, Lauren, Mark, Ruth. Instr., asst. research scientist Ill. Inst. Tech., Chgo.; mgmt. cons. Booz, Allen & Hamilton, Chgo.; mgr. planning Packaging div. Union Carbide Corp., Chgo.; v.p. Roy Doty & Assos., Inc., psychol. cons., Chgo.; now pres. Strand, Gill & Assos., Inc. Police commr. Evergreen Park, Ill. Bd. dirs. Mental Health Society Greater Chicago. Served to lt. (j.g.) USNR; PTO, MTO. Mem. Am., Ill. psychol. assns., S.A.R., Sigma Xi. Research in personnel assessment and devel.; test developer and pub. Address: 1301 W 22d St Oakbrook IL 60521

STRAND, JOHN ARTHUR, III, mfg. co. exec.; b. LaCrosse, Wis., Feb. 18, 1950; s. John A. and Grace S.; B.A., U. Wis., LaCrosse, 1972; m. Laurie R. Gibson, Aug. 7, 1971; children—Kathryn, John IV. With Seven-Up Bottling of LaCrosse, 1972—, v.p., 1978-81, pres., 1981—; pres. Route Acctg. Mgmt. Systems. cons. data processing. Mem. Nat. Soft Drink Assn., Wis. Soft Drink Assn., Nat. Seven-Up Developers Assn., LaCrosse Jaycees. Clubs: Masons, Shriners. Office: 2041 Avon St LaCrosse WI 54601

STRANG, DONALD WILLIAM, JR., hotel, restaurant exec.; b. Lakewood, Ohio, Jan. 5, 1938; s. Donald William and Jeannette (Canfield) S.; B.S., Cornell U., Ithaca, N.Y., 1960; m. Karen Kline, Apr. 20, 1957; children—Donald William III, David Eugene, Peter Wayne, Allison Jeanette. Pres., Strang Mgmt. Corp., 1960—; pres. Dr. Don's Inc., Don-Clar Corp.; pres., owner Howard Johnson Motor Lodge, Skokie, Ill., Don's Lighthouse Inn, Don's Butcherblock, Don's Fishmarket; dir. Nat. Franchise Council, Howard Johnson Co., Abramson Hemilfarb, Inc. Past trustee West Shore Concert series Cleve. Orch.; bd. dirs. Cleve. Opera Co. Mem. Greater Chgo. Hotel-Motel Assn. (dir.), N.E. Ohio Restaurant Assn. (dir.), Young Presidents Orgn., Skokie C. of C. (past pres., dir.), Beta Theta Pi. Clubs: Rotary, Cleve. Yacht (trustee). Home: 17820 Lake Rd Lakewood OH 44107 Office: 8905 Lake Ave Cleveland OH 44102

STRANG, WILLIAM CHARLES, psychiatrist; b. Bedford, Ind., Nov. 26, 1912; s. Howard Arthur and Rowenna Catherine (Kauffman) S.; B.S., Ind. U., 1935, M.D., 1937; m. Janet Rea Martin, Jan. 23, 1941; children—William, Joyce, Thomas, Priscilla. Intern, Ind. U. Med. Center, Indpls., 1937-38, resident in psychiatry, 1954-57; staff physician Evansville (Ind.) State Hosp., 1938-40; med. officer to asst. med. dir. U.S. Civil Service, Med. Div., Washington, 1940-54; chief of men's service LaRue Carter Meml. Hosp., Indpls., 1957-60, asst. supt., 1960-63; individual practice medicine, specializing in psychiatry, Indpls., 1963—; asst. prof. psychiatry Ind. U., Indpls., 1962—. Bd. dirs. Marion County Child Guidance Clinics, 1971-74. Diplomate Am. Bd. Psychiatry and Neurology. Mem. Marion County Med. Soc., Ind., Am. med. assns., Ind., Am. psychiat. assns. Republican. Methodist. Clubs: Riviera, Masons. Home: 7760 Cree Trail Indianapolis IN 46250 Office: 1815 N Capitol Ave Suite 407 Indianapolis IN 46202

STRANK, GALE BENJAMIN, market research exec.; b. Middletown, Mo., Jan. 28, 1918; s. Milton B. and Lillian (Gibson) S.; B.S., Mo. U., 1949; postgrad. Columbia U., 1968; m. Margie Delene Admire, Jan. 1, 1944; children—Gale B. II, Melinda Ann. Market analyst Deere & Co., Moline, Ill., 1949-54, corp. mgr. market research, 1959—; mgr. market research John Deere Ltd., Winnipeg, Man., Can., 1955-58. Served to 1st lt. USAAF, 1942-46. Decorated D.F.C., Air medal. Mem. Am. Mktg. Assn., Conf. Bd. (market research council), Delta Sigma Pi. Lutheran. Club: Outing (dir., officer) (Davenport). Home: 244 Hillcrest Ave Davenport IA 52803 Office: John Deere Rd Moline IL 61265

STRASSHEIM, DALE STEPHEN, hosp. adminstr.; b. Burlington, Iowa, Sept. 27, 1946; s. Fred G., Jr. and Mayme E. (Heiniger) S.; B.B.A., U. Iowa, 1968; M.S. in Health Care Adminstrn., Trinity U., San Antonio, 1973; m. Carol B. Rinkenberger, Aug. 3, 1968;

children—Angela, Brian, Eric, Alison. Adminstrv. resident Methodist Hosp., Indpls., 1971-72; mem. adminstrv. staff Elkhart (Ind.) Gen. Hosp., 1972—, v.p. adminstrn., 1974-76, pres., 1976—; bd. dirs. Assn. Disabled Elkhart County; bd. dirs. Lighthouse Inc., 1981—; mem. Gov. Ind. Com. Study Mental Health Laws; bd. dirs., exec. com. N. Central Ind. Med. Edn. Found.; chmn. med. services/transp. subcom. Elkhart County Emergency Planning Com.; mem. N. Central sub-area council No. Ind. Health Systems Agy. Adv. bd. Salvation Army Elkhart. Served with USAR, 1968-70. Recipient Disting. Service award Elkhart Jaycees, 1977. Mem. Am. Coll. Hosp. Adminstrs., Ind. Hosp. Assn. (dir., rep. 3d dist. fed. relations actions com.). Club: Elkhart Rotary (chmn. coms.). Office: 600 East Blvd Elkhart IN 46514

STRASSHOFER, ROLAND HENRY, JR., lawyer; b. Cleve., May 21, 1924; s. Roland Henry and Margaret Avis (Norris) S.; student Univ. Coll., Eng., 1949; A.B., Case Western Res. U., 1948, LL.B., 1950; m. Mary Jane Jewitt; children—Craig Thomas, Lesley Ann, Heidi Lynn, Carol Rae. Admitted to Ohio bar, 1950, U.S. Supreme Ct., 1957; atty. SEC, 1950-51, Goodyear Tire & Rubber Co., 1951-53, Pennell, Carlson & Rees, 1953-63, Brown & Strasshofer, 1963-67, Ford, Whitney & Haase, 1970-75, Bremer, Thompson, Morhard & Strasshofer, 1975—; mem. nat. labor panel Am. Arbitration Assn., Nat. Acad. Arbitrators, Fed. Mediation and Conciliation Service. Republican candidate Ohio Legislature, 1958. Trustee Hillcrest Hosp., Mayfield Heights, Ohio, 1967—; pres. Cleve. Meml. Med. Found., 1966-69, trustee, 1963—; asso. in law Am. Coll. Legal Medicine. Served with USCG, 1943-46; ETO. Mem. Am. Soc. Hosp. Attys., Am. Soc. Law and Medicine, Nat. Health Lawyers Assn., Am., Fed., Ohio, Cleve. (trustee 1973-77) bar assns., Phi Delta Phi, Delta Kappa Epsilon. Episcopalian (vestryman 1975-79). Clubs: Singers (pres. 1962-64), Cleve. Skating, City. Home: 2520 Stratford Rd Cleveland Heights OH 44118 Office: East Ohio Bldg Cleveland OH 44114

STRATTON, OLIN WILLMER, supt. schs.; b. Hettick, Ill., Feb. 21, 1921; s. Joseph W. and Bessie (Stewart) S.; B.S., So. Ill. U., 1947, M.S., 1949; m. Elaine Miller, Dec. 25, 1947; children—Candace Lou, Jeffrey William, John Noel. Tchr., prin. Shipman (Ill.) Elementary Sch., 1941-42; tchr., coach Highland (Ill.) High Sch., 1947-56, tchr., asst. prin., 1956-58; supt. Highland Community Schs., 1958—. Mem. Ill. Gov.'s Task Force on Edn., Adv. Com. State Supts. of Pub. Instns., Com. on Internat. Edn.; past pres. Southwestern Supts. Forum. Mem. Latzer Meml. Library Bd., State Life Safety Code Com.; past pres. Weinheimer Meml. Bd. Served with USAAF, 1942-45. Mem. Nat., Ill. edn. assns., Am. Assn. Sch. Adminstrs. (exec. com., v.p., pres. 1979, mem. Found. fund), Ill. Assn. Sch. Adminstrs. (past pres., dir.), Ill. Guidance and Personnel Assn., Highland C. of C. (past pres.). Conglist. Mason. Club: Optimist. Home: 800 Dolphin Dr East Highland IL 62249 Office: 1800 Lindenthal St Highland IL 62249

STRATTON, WILLIAM GRANT, food and vending service exec.; b. Ingleside, Ill., Feb. 26, 1914; s. William J. and Zula (Van Wormer) S.; B.A., U. Ariz., 1934; hon. degrees John Marshall Law Sch., N. Central Coll., Shurtleff Coll., 1954, Bradley U., Lincoln Coll., 1955, Elmhurst Coll., 1956, Lincoln Meml. U., 1957, So. Ill. U., U. Ariz., 1958; Mem. U.S. Congress from Ill., 1941-43, 47-49; treas. State of Ill., 1943-45, 51-53, gov., 1953-61; livestock farmer, Cantrell, Ill., 1954-70; ins. bus., Chgo., 1965-68; asst. to pres. Canteen Corp., Chgo., 1968, v.p. corporate relations, 1968—, dir., 1981—; dir. Dartnell Corp. Chmn., Interstate Oil Compact Commn., 1955, Nat. Gov.'s Conf., 1957; pres. Council State Govts., 1958; mem. Lincoln Sesquicentennial Commn., 1958, Fed. Adv. Commn. Intergovtl. Relations, 1959, Ill. Task Force on Higher Edn., 1970-71, Ill. Legis. Reapportionment Commn., 1971; regent Lincoln Acad. of Ill., 1966—; del. Rep. Nat. Conv., 1952, 56, 60, 76; former chmn. bd. trustees Robert Morris Coll., Carthage, Ill.; bd. dirs. Chgo. Conv. and Tourism Bur., 1980—, Better Bus. Bur. Chgo., 1981—, Chgo. Crime Commn., 1980—; bd. dirs. Mundelein Coll., Chgo., 1976—, Davenport Coll., Grand Rapids, Mich., 1976—; bd. dirs. Nat. Inst. Foodservice Industry, 1975—, pres., 1979—. Served to lt. (j.g.) USNR, 1945-46; PTO. Mem. Chgo. and Ill. Restaurant Assn. (chmn. 1977—), Ill. Automatic Merchandising Council (v.p. 1981—), Ill. C. of C. (dir. 1976—), Am. Legion, Amvets, Mil. Order World Wars (comdr. Chgo. chpt. 1971-72), Delta Chi. Methodist. Clubs: Masons (33 deg.), Rotary (pres. Chgo. 1979-80). Home: 3240 N Lake Shore Dr Chicago IL 60657 Office: 1430 Mdse Mart Chicago IL 60654

STRAUSS, ALFRED CARMICHAEL, cement co. exec.; b. N.Y.C., Oct. 13, 1932; s. Alfred Amiel and Lorraine (Carmichael) S.; B.S., U. N.C., 1954; J.D., U. Mich. Law Sch., 1959; m. Barbara Elizabeth Scully, Apr. 12, 1958; children—Patricia, Michael, Christopher. With Lehigh Portland Cement Co., 1959—, v.p. adminstrn., 1969-71, v.p. N. Central region, Mpls., 1971—. Bd. dirs. Indsl. Devel. Corp. Lehigh Valley. Served with USMCR, 1954-56. Mem. N.Y. State Bar Assn., Pi Kappa Phi, Delta Theta Phi. Presbyterian. Home: 1566 Rhode Island St Golden Valley MN 55427 Office: 12300 DuPont Ave S Burnsville MN 55337

STRAUSS, FRED, assn. exec.; b. Germany, Mar. 30, 1925; came to U.S., 1938, naturalized, 1944; s. Solly and Fanny (Wertheim) S.; student Purdue U., 1943-44, DePaul U., 1950-51; student in English and psychology Western Res. U., 1953; children—Scott, Jonathan, Daniel, Craig. Owner, Fred Strauss Agy., Cleve., 1953-58; pres. Talent Corp., N.Y.C., 1958-60; exec. producer Communications Corp. Am., Chgo., 1960-67; public info. dir. Am. Cancer Soc., Chgo., 1967—; lectr. public relations, Campfire Girls, Columbia Coll., 1980; tchr. practical public relations course, 1978-81. Served with M.I., U.S. Army, 1944-48. Decorated Purple Heart, Bronze Star. Recipient Chris award Columbus Film Festival, 1964, N.Y. Film Festival, 1964; Helen Cody Baker awards, 1976, 77; nat. award Am. Cancer Soc., 1970, honor citation, 1977. Mem. Publicity Club of Chgo. (disting. service award, 1973-75, pres., 1979-80), Social Service Communicators (Chgo.), Internat. Assn. Bus. Communicators (Chgo.). Producer TV film: The Last Full Measure of Devotion, 1964, nationally syndicated TV talk show: Telling a Child About Death, 1965-66. Office: Suite 400 American Cancer Society 37 S Wabash Ave Chicago IL 60603

STRAYER, GORDON BYERS, pub. relations exec.; b. Moose Jaw, Sask., Can., June 23, 1923; s. Carl J. and Nina Naomi (Carr) S.; student Bradley Poly. Inst., 1942, U. Chgo., 1943-44; B.A., Iowa State Tchrs. Coll., 1949; M.A., U. Iowa, 1951; m. Faye Adel Hyde, June 4, 1948; children—Hilary, Scott. News editor U. Iowa, Iowa City, 1950-53, editor, 1953-57, asst. dir., exec. editor, 1957-62, acting dir., 1962-64, dir. pub. information univ. relations, 1964-75, dir. health center information and communication, 1975—. Served with AUS, 1943-46; ETO. Mem. Am. Coll. Pub. Relations Assn. (dist. dir. 1963-64, nat. trustee 1966-71, nat. sec. 1969-71), Public Relations Soc. Am. (dir. Midwest dist. 1980), Argonne Univs. Assn. (info. com. 1968-71), Assn. Am. Med. Colls. Group on Public Relations (chmn. Midwest region 1979), N. Central Assn. Coll. and Secondary Schs. (publs. com. 1969-72), Iowa-Ill. Pub. Relations Council, Iowa City C. of C., Sigma Delta Chi, Phi Delta Kappa, Omicron Delta Kappa. Unitarian. Mason, Kiwanian. Clubs: Triangle, University Athletic (Iowa City). Contbr. articles to profl. jours. Home: 1 Forest Glen Iowa City IA 52240

STRECKER, IGNATIUS J., archbishop; b. Spearville, Kans., Nov. 23, 1917; ed. St. Benedict's Coll., Atchison, Kans., Kenrick Sem., Webster Groves, Mo., Catholic U. Am. Ordained priest Roman Cath. Ch., 1942; bishop of Springfield-Cape Girardeau (Mo.), 1962-69; archbishop of Kansas City (Kans.), 1969—. Address: Chancery Office PO Box 2328 2220 Central Ave Kansas City KS 66110*

STRECKER, LAWRENCE ALAN, mfg. co. exec.; b. St. Louis, May 23, 1930; s. John Charles and Mabel Margaret (Miller) S.; B.Sc. in Pharmacy, St. Louis Coll. Pharmacy, 1953; B.S. in Sci. with honors, Washington U., St. Louis, 1964; m. Mary Ann Mallmann, Oct. 25, 1952; children—Lawrence Alan, Michael. Mgr. devel. SAR div. Inmont Corp. subs. Carrier Corp., St. Louis, 1956-63, supr. new product devel., 1963-68, tech. dir., 1968—. Served with AUS, 1953-55; Korea. Mem. Sealant and Adhesive Council (chmn. tech. com.), Am. Chem. Soc., Sealed Insulating Glass Mfg. Assn., ASTM, Alpha Sigma Lambda. Mem. Disciples of Christ. Clubs: Harmony Lions, Carondolet Toastmasters, Masons, Shriners. Contbr. articles to Adhesive Age Mag., Glass Digest, Rubber Age, Chem. Week, Elastoplastics Jour. Home: 4510 Wigwam Dr Saint Louis MO 63123 Office: 1218 Central Industrial Dr Saint Louis MO 63110

STREETER, ROBERT DAVENPORT, elec. engr.; b. Springfield, Mass., Sept. 17, 1941; s. William Allen and Muriel Ethel (Davenport) S.; B.E.E., Ohio State U., 1964; M.S., Purdue U., 1968; m. Carole Janet Riley, Mar. 21, 1970; children—John, Susan. Engr., Research Found. Ohio State U., Columbus, 1960-64, Sta. WBNS-AM-FM-TV, Columbus, 1960-65; sr. staff engr. Magnavox Govt. and Indsl. Electronics Co., Fort Wayne, 1965-75, program engr. Magnavox Consumer Electric Co., 1975-81; cons., 1981—; lectr. Ind. U./Purdue U., Fort Wayne campus, 1969. Registered profl. engr., Ind. Mem. IEEE, Eta Kappa Nu. Patentee in error control and AM stereo. Home: 3424 Casselwood Dr Fort Wayne IN 46816 Office: PO Box 6217 Diplomat Plaza Fort Wayne IN 46896

STREETMAN, LENORA ANN (ANN MUSIC STREETMAN), author, editor; b. Grand Saline, Tex., Sept. 11, 1939; d. Rondo William and Madeline Callie (Hanson) Music; B.J., U. Tex., Austin, 1962; m. Ben Garland Streetman, Sept. 9, 1961; children—Paul Blake, Scott Richard. From editorial asst. to asso. editor Tex. Game and Fish, Austin, 1961-64; asst. editor Ill. Water Survey, Champaign, 1967; devel. editor Profl. Cosmetologist, West Pub. Co., St. Paul, 1976; free-lance manuscript editor Research Press, Champaign, 1976—; author poems, short stories, 1971—; speaker workshop Young Authors Conf., Urbana, Ill., 1979. Elder, chair congregational bd. University Pl. Christian Ch. (Disciples of Christ), Champaign, 1980—. Mem. Women in Communications, Nat. League Am. Pen Women, AAUW (creative writers group), Bread for the World, IMPACT. Democrat. Address: 2901 Rolling Acres Dr Route 2 Champaign IL 61820

STREIBICH, RONALD LELAND, coll. adminstr.; b. Peoria, Ill., May 5, 1936; s. Leland Roy and Evelyn (Moffatt) S.; B.A., Knox Coll., 1958; m. Donna Matthews, Sept. 14, 1958 (div.); children—John, James; m. 2d, Pamela McClure, Apr. 5, 1980. Mem. public relations mgmt. staff Gen. Electric Co., Schenectady, 1959-65; dir. devel. Northwestern U., Evanston, Ill., 1965-74, chief fund-raising officer Northwestern Med. Center, Chgo., 1974-76; chief exec. officer Meth. Med. Center Found., Peoria, 1976-79; v.p. devel., sec. Knox Coll., Galesburg, Ill., 1979—. Chmn. Evanston United Fund, 1972-73; bd. dirs. Galesburg United Way, Galesburg Symphony. Club: Soangetaha Country. Home: 1513 N Prairie St Galesburg IL 61401 Office: Knox Coll Galesburg IL 61401

STREICH, ARTHUR HAROLD, business exec.; b. Mpls., Apr. 22, 1925; s. Herman Henry and Rose (Anderson) S.; B.A. in Journalism, Macalester Coll., 1952; m. Arlene June Ostlund, Aug. 30, 1947; children—Jennifer Streich Hallam, Jack, Paula Jo. Partner, S&E Publs., St. Paul, 1952-55; asst. sec. Northwestern Lumbermans Assn., 1955-57; gen. mgr. Nat. Electronics Conf., 1957-59; public relations exec. Mullen & Assos., Inc., Mpls., 1959-60; investment adviser Dempsey Tegeler & Co., Inc., Mpls., 1960-63; regional sales mgr. Dreyfus Corp., 1963-68; regional v.p. Anchor Corp., Chgo., 1968-69; regional v.p. wholesale sales and mgmt. Dreyfus Sales Corp., Chgo., 1969-72; regional v.p. Crosby Corp., Chgo., 1972-73; regional sales mgr. John Nuveen & Co., Chgo., 1973-74; owner Fin. Planning Services Co., Lake Zurich, Ill., 1974—. Republican candidate for mayor St. Paul, 1952. Served with USN, 1942-46. Mem. Nat. Assn. Security Dealers (registered prin.). Republican. Mem. Evang. Free Ch. Address: 1201 Geneva Ln Lake Zurich IL 60047

STREIN, CHARLES THORVALD, economist; b. Iowa City, Iowa, Feb. 17, 1937; B.A., U. No. Iowa, 1961; M.A.T. in Econs., Purdue U., 1968; M.S., U. Ill., 1975, Ph.D., 1977; m. Janice A. Martinson, July 29, 1955; children—Craig, Mary, Carol. High sch. tchr. social studies, 1960-68; asst. prof. econs. Eastern Ill. U., Charleston, 1968-70; asst. prof. econs. U. No. Iowa, Cedar Falls, 1970—; cons., writer. Newspaper Fund fellow, NSF fellow, summer 1972; Gen Electric Co. fellow, summer 1964; Experienced Tchr. fellow, 1967-68. Mem. NEA, AAUP, Am. Econ. Assn., Midwest Econs. Assn., Mo. Valley Econs. Assn., Omicron Delta Epsilon. Club: Odd Fellows. Home: 1122 W 2d St Cedar Falls IA 50613 Office: University of Northern Iowa Cedar Falls IA 50614

STRENGER, JAN ELIZABETH, social worker; b. Lake Forest, Ill., Jan. 6, 1954; d. Donald Sell and Mona Elizabeth (Benson) S.; B.A., Yankton Coll., 1976. Supr., counselor Lewis/Clark Mental Health Center, Yankton, S.D., 1976-78, acting program adminstr., 1978; case mgr. Yankton Area Adjustment Tng. Center, 1978-80, program dir., 1980—. Cert. in behavior mgmt. techniques, U. S.D.; cert. mental retardation profl., S.D. State Adjustment Tng. Services. Mem. Am. Assn. Mental Deficiency, Nat. Rehab. Assn., Assn. for Retarded Citizens, S.D. Coast Guard Aux. Republican. Presbyterian. Home: 416 E 16th St Yankton SD 57078 Office: Yankton Area Adjustment Tng Center 229 Broadway Yankton SD 57078

STRENGTH, ROBERT SAMUEL, mfg. co. exec.; b. Tullos, La., May 14, 1929; s. Houston Orion and Gurcie Dean (Cousins) S.; B.S. in Indsl. Mgmt., Auburn U., 1956; M.S., Washington U., 1979; m. Janis Lynette Grace, Sept. 12, 1954; children—Robert David (dec.), James Steven (dec.), Stewart Alan, James Houston (dec.). Engr., supr. plant safety Monsanto Co., 1956-74, engring. standards mgr. Corporate Fire Safety Center, St. Louis, 1974-78, mgr. product safety and acceptability Plastics & Resins Co., St. Louis, 1978—. Pres. Greenwood (S.C.) Citizens Safety Council, 1966-68. Served with USAF, 1948-52. Recipient Outstanding Service to Safety award Nat. Safety Council, 1968; registered profl. engr., Calif.; cert. safety profl. Mem. Am. Soc. Safety Engrs., So. Bldg. Code Congress, Internat. Conf. of Bldg. Ofcls., Bldg. Ofcls. and Code Adminstrs. Internat., Nat. Fire Protection Assn., ASTM, Nat. Inst. Bldg. Scis., Plastic Pipe and Fittings Assn. Republican. Methodist. Club: Cherry Hills Country. Editor textile sect. newsletter Nat. Safety Council, 1961-62. Home: 56 High Valley St Chesterfield MO 63017 Office: 800 N Lindbergh Blvd Saint Louis MO 63166

STRESEN-REUTER, FREDERICK ARTHUR, II, mining co. exec.; b. Oak Park, Ill., July 31, 1942; s. Alfred Procter and Carol Frances (von Pohek) S.-R.; cert. in German, U. Vienna, 1963; cert. in polymer chemistry U. Mo., Rolla, 1967; B.A., Lake Forest Coll., 1967. Mgr. advt. Stresen-Reuter Internat., Bensenville, Ill., 1965-70; mgr. animal products mktg. Internat. Minerals & Chem. Corp., Mundelein, Ill., 1971-79, dir. animal products mktg., 1979—; lectr. mktg. U. Ill., 1977, Am. Mgmt. Assn., 1978; cons. mktg. to numerous agrl. cos., 1973—; cons., writer Wis. Vocat. Tech. and Adult Edn. System, 1976—; lectr. Trustee, governing mem. Library Internat. Relations, Chgo. Recipient cert. of excellence Chgo. 77 Vision Show, 1977; Silver Aggy award, 1977; spl. jury gold medal V.I., N.Y. Internat. film festival awards, 1977; CINE Golden Eagle, 1980; Bronze medal N.Y. Internat. Film Festival, 1981; Silver Screen award U.S. Indsl. Film Festival, 1981. Mem. Nat. Feed Ingredients Assn. (chmn. publicity and publs. 1976), Nat. Agrl. Mktg. Assn., Chgo. Paint and Coatings Assn. (chmn. publicity com., nat. exec. com. 1966-71), Chgo. Soc. Paint Tech. (chmn. publicity com. 1967-71), Chgo. Printing Ink Prodn. Club (sec. and officer 1969-71), Am. Feed Mfrs. Assn. (citation 1976, public relations com., conv. com.), Nat. Agrl. Mktg. Assn., World Expeditionary Assn. (London), USCG Aux. (9th Dist. public relations officer), U.S. Naval Inst., Am. Film Inst. Episcopalian. Contbr. articles to profl. jours. Home: Thaxmeade Farm 2500 W Everett Rd Lake Forest IL 60045 Office: 421 E Hawley St Mundelein IL 60060

STRETCH, JOHN JOSEPH, educator; b. St. Louis, Feb. 24, 1935; s. John Joseph and Theresa Carmelita (Fleming) S.; A.B., Maryknoll Coll., 1958; M.S.W., Washington U., 1961; Ph.D., Tulane U., 1967; M.B.A., St. Louis U., 1980; m. Marilee Sharon Milroy, Nov. 21, 1959; children—Paul, Leonmarie, Sylvan, Adrienne, Sharonalice. Dir. research Social Welfare Planning Council of Met. New Orleans, 1962-69; asso. prof. St. Louis U., 1969-72, prof., 1972—, asst. dean, 1976—, dir. doctoral studies, 1976—; cons. in field. Mem. alumni bd. George Warren Brown Sch. Social Work, Washington U. Served with M.C., U.S. Army, 1958-60. NIMH Career Leadership Devel. fellow, 1965-67. Mem. AAUP, AAAS, Nat. Assn. Social Workers, Council Social Work Edn., Mo. Assn. Social Welfare. Democrat. Roman Catholic. Mem. editorial bd. Social Work, 1968-74; manuscript referee Jour. Social Service Research, 1977—. Contbr. articles to profl. jours. Home: 1160 Arroya Trail Ellisville MO 63011 Office: 3550 Lindell St Saint Louis MO 63103

STRICKLAND, NORMALIE CATHERINE RICHARDS (MRS. JOSEPH HUBERT STRICKLAND), librarian; b. Effingham, Ill., Jan. 12, 1938; d. Leo J. and Josephine Gertrude (Lidy) Richards; B.A. in History, Marian Coll., 1960; M.L.S., U. Ill., 1961; m. Joseph Hubert Strickland, Mar. 20, 1965. Library asst. sci. dept. Enoch Pratt Free Library, Balt., 1961-62; library asst. sci. dept. Phoenix Pub. Library, 1962-63, acting head sci. dept., 1963-65; asst. acquisitions dept. U. Okla., Norman, 1965-66; library asst. St. Anthony High, Effingham, 1966-67; head Helen Matthes Library, Effingham, 1967—. Library Sch. scholar Enoch Pratt Free Library, 1960-61. Mem. ALA, Ill. Library Assn. (exec. bd. pub. libraries sect. 1976). Roman Catholic (rec. sec. 1970). Home: Rural Route 1 Box 176 Effingham IL 62401 Office: 100 E Market Ave Effingham IL 62401

STRICKLAND, REUBEN WILSON, public relations cons.; b. Marshall, Tex., Dec. 9, 1927; s. Holman Taylor and Flora Ann (Fort) S.; student Southwestern U., 1944-46, Mo. Sch. Mines, 1948; B.J., U. Tex., Austin, 1950; m. Joan Alice Mudlaff, May 14, 1954; children—Steven Marshall, Lawrence Jay, Nancy Jo. Asst. public relations dir. Ft. Worth C. of C., 1950-52; editor Internat. Minerals & Chem. Corp., Chgo., 1952-54; mem. public relations staff Link-Belt Co., Chgo., 1954-59; account exec. Burson-Marsteller Assos., Chgo., 1959-62; v.p., dir. public relations div. Robertson Advt., Inc., Chgo., 1962-72; mgr. public relations div. Hoffman-York, Inc., Chgo., 1972-74; prin. Strickland & Assos., Palatine, Ill., 1974—. Hunter safety instr. Ill. Dept. Conservation. Served with U.S. Army, 1946-48. Mem. Public Relations Soc. Am. (accredited mem., treas. Counselor's Acad., Chgo. chpt.), Chgo. Headline Club, Sigma Delta Chi. Republican. Methodist. Clubs: Chgo. Press, Richmond (Ill.) Hunting. Home and Office: 900 W Hillside St Palatine IL 60067

STRIETER, JAMES FREDERICK, optometrist; b. Hinsdale, Ill., Sept. 26, 1929; s. Theophilus William and Martha Augusta (Henn) S.; student Valparaiso U., 1948-51; B.S., Ill. Coll. Optometry, 1953, O.D., 1954; m. Margaretha Katharina Demling, Jan. 16, 1956; children—Barbara, Mark, Christopher. Pvt. practice optometry, Collinsville, Ill., 1956—; founder, pres. Ophthalmos, Inc., mfr. visual sci. products, Collinsville, Ill., 1967-79; founder Strieter Labs., hydrophilic contact lenses, 1979. Mem. Planning Commn. Collinsville, 1971-72. Served with AUS, 1954-56; now lt. col. Res. Diplomate Contact Lens Practice. Fellow Am. Acad. Optometry, Royal Soc. Health; mem. Mil. Optometrists Assn., Am., Ill. (v.p. 1963-67, 69-71, Distinguished Service award 1972, Optometrist of Year 1975) optometric assns., S.W. Ill. Optometric Soc. (pres. 1961-63), Collinsville C. of C. (dir., v.p. 1968-73). Lutheran (dist. bd. dirs. 1968-76, elder 1960-63, 72— sec. congregation 1969-70). Club: Lions (pres. 1970-71). Patentee in visual sci. field. Home: 537 E Lake Dr Edwardsville IL 62025 Office: 724 Saint Louis Rd Collinsville IL 62234

STRIGLOS, NICK G., office equipment co. exec.; b. DeKalb, Ill., July 21, 1935; s. Gus and Jean (Mitchell) S.; B.A., Northwestern U., 1958; m. Patricia Joan Grant, June 25, 1959; children—Scott G., Jamie D., Patricia E. Pres. Striglos Office Equipment Co., Decatur, Ill., 1960—, Contemporary Properties, Inc., Decatur, 1973—; v.p. Community Research, Decatur, 1968-71; dir. DCDF, Inc., 1980—. Mem. zoning bd. appeals City of Decatur, 1971—, city councilman, 1980—, mem. bd. local improvements, 1980—; bd. dirs. Decatur Macon County Opportunities, Inc., 1979—; pres. Decatur (Ill.) Merchant St. Mall Assn., 1969—. Episcopalian. Clubs: Decatur; Decatur Country. Home: 26 S Shores Dr Decatur IL 62521 Office: 124 E Prairie St Decatur IL 62523

STRIZEK, JAN, graphic designer; b. Berwyn, Ill., June 11, 1947; d. William J. and Rose F. (Jana) S.; B.F.A., No. Ill. U., 1969. Designer, Paper Play Creations, Chgo., 1969-72, Interthink, Chgo., 1973-75; design mgr. Jim Lienhart Design, Chgo., 1978-80; prin. Jan Strizek Design, Chgo., 1980—; com. mem. Soc. Typographic Arts, 1980, 81. Recipient awards for design excellence N.Y. Art Dirs. Club and Soc. Typographic Arts. Mem. Women in Design (treas. Chgo. 1980-81), Soc. Typographic Arts (v.p., treas. 1980-82). Research and prodn. textiles and flat pattern design for archtl. and interior installations. Office: 535 N Michigan Ave Chicago IL 60611

STROBECK, CHARLES LEROY, real estate exec.; b. Chgo., June 27, 1928; s. Roy Alfred and Alice Rebecca (Stenberg) S.; A.B., Wheaton Coll., 1949; m. Janet Louise Halverson, June 2, 1951; children—Carol, Nancy, Beth, Jane, Jean. Asso., Sudler & Co., real estate, Chgo., 1949-63, partner, 1959-63; pres. Strobeck, Reiss & Co., real estate, Chgo., 1964—. Pres., South Loop Devel. Co., 1970-75. Trustee, Wheaton Christian High Sch., 1968—, pres. bd., 1970-78; bd. dirs. Chgo. Youth Centers, pres., 1980—; trustee, pres. Wheaton San. Dist., 1975—. Served with AUS, 1950-51. Mem. Inst. Real Estate Mgmt. (chpt. pres. 1969) nat. pres. 1970), Am. Soc. Real Estate

Counselors, Chgo. Real Estate Bd. (1st v.p. 1966, chmn. admissions com. 1969-71), Nat. Assn. Christians Schs. (dir., treas. 1970-79), Union League Club Chgo. (dir. 1968-71, treas. 1972-73, 2d v.p. 1973-74, 1st v.p. 1974-75, pres. 1975-76), Chgo. Bldg. Owners and Mgrs. Assn. (past dir.), Lambda Alpha. Mem. Coll. Ch. Wheaton (chmn. bd. elders 1971-72, mem. bd. 1979—). Clubs: Chgo., Chgo. Golf, Mid-Am., Union League, Realtors Forty, Realty. Home: Hawthorne Ln Wheaton IL 60187 Office: 134 S La Salle St Chicago IL 60603

STROBEL, GEROLD CARL, state hwy. dept. exec.; b. Jefferson County, Nebr., Sept. 12, 1921; s. John George and Minnie Louise (Weishahn) S.; B.S. in Civil Engring., U. Nebr., 1947; m. Florence M. Bock, Jan. 9, 1945; children—Cory Thomas, James Carl, Debra Lynelle Strobel Fischer. Bridge structural designer Nebr. Dept. Roads, Lincoln, 1947-53, bridge engr., 1953-59, roadway design engr., 1959-60, dep. state engr. designs, ops., devel., 1960-72, dep. state engr. ops., 1972—. Served to capt. C.E. U.S. Army, 1942-46. Recipient Certificate of award James F. Lincoln Arc Welding Found., 1970; registered profl. engr., Nebr. Mem. ASCE, Am. Assn. State Hwy. and Transp. Ofcls. (25 Yr. award of Merit), Am. Rd. and Transp. Builders Assn. Lutheran. Home: 1164 S 47th St Lincoln NE 68510

STROHL, JOSEPH A., state legislator; b. Evanston, Ill., Mar. 19, 1946; B.S., No. Mich. U., 1968; postgrad. U. Wis., Milw., 1968. Legis. aide to Congressman Les Aspin, 1971-78; tchr., Washington Jr. High Sch., Racine, Wis., 1968-70, mem. Wis. Senate, 1978—. Mem. LWV, Preservation Racine Inc., Racine County Hist. Soc., NAACP, Urban League, Sierra Club, Jaycees, Citizens Utility Bd., Root River Restoration Council. Democrat. Address: Room 334 South State Capitol Madison WI 53702

STROMBACK, DURAY E., mfg. co. exec.; b. Phila., 1921; B.M.E., Drexel Inst., 1943; M.M.E., U. Pa., 1950. With Burroughs Corp., Detroit, 1949—, mgr. engring. services research center, Paoli, Pa., 1953-58, plant mgr., Plymouth, Mich., 1958-64, mgr. Pasadena (Calif.) plant, 1964-67, v.p. mfg. bus. machines group, 1967-70, v.p. and group exec. systems mfg. and engring. group, 1970-74, v.p. and group exec. fed. and spl. systems group, 1974-77, v.p. and group exec. internat. group, 1977-79, exec. v.p. planning, from 1979, now pres., chief operating officer, dir. Office: Burroughs Corp Burroughs Pl Detroit MI 48232*

STROMER, DELWYN DEAN, farmer, state legislator; b. Garner, Iowa, Apr. 22, 1930; s. Aaron and Ruby (Goll) S.; grad. high sch.; m. Harriet Ostendorf, Aug. 26, 1950; children—Linda, Randall (dec.), Pamela, David. Mem. Iowa Ho. of Reps., 1966—, speaker pro tem, 1980, speaker, 1981-82; vice-chmn. Iowa Legis. Council; mem. edn. task force Nat. Conf. State Legislatures, 1974-78, mem. exec. com., 1979-81, chmn. advanced legis. program seminars, 1981-82; farmer, Garner, Iowa. Served in Armed Forces, 1953-55, Res., 1951-53, 55-58; Far East. Mem. Farm Bur., People United for Rural Edn. Republican. Mem. United Ch. of Christ. Club: Lions. *

STROMQUIST, PETER S., broadcasting co. exec.; b. Duluth, Minn., Nov. 14, 1952; s. John W. and Janet E. (Stubbee) S.; B.A., St. Olaf Coll., 1974; m. Jane E. Phleger. Former account exec. Sta. WIZM, LaCrosse, Wis., agy. account exec. Sta. KSTP, Mpls., sr. account exec. Plough Broadcasting, Chgo., gen. sales mgr. Sta. KIRL, St. Louis; pres., chmn. bd. Stromquist Broadcast Services, Mpls., 1979—. Mem. Am. Film Inst., Minn. Broadcasters Assn., Iowa Broadcasters Assn., N.D. Broadcasters Assn., S.D. Broadcasters Assn. Episcopalian. Office: 7201 York Ave S Suite 912 Edina MN 55435

STRONG, DOROTHY MAE, ednl. adminstr.; b. Memphis, Feb. 3, 1934; d. John Harrison and Willie Beatrice (Hawkins) Swearengen; B.S. in Edn., Chgo. State U., 1958; M.A. in Math. Edn., 1964; m. Joseph Nathaniel Strong, Mar. 19, 1953; 1 dau., Joronda Ramette. Elem. and secondary tchr. Chgo. Public Schs., 1958-65, dir. math., 1976—; cons. math, 1965-76; instr. Chgo. State U., 1969-71; mem. Commn. on Tchr. Edn., Task Force on Math. in Urban Centers; Ill. Basic Skills Adv. Council, Nat. Inst. Edn. Conf. on Basic Skills; bd. dirs. Allendale Sch. for Boys, 1974—. Pres. youth dept. Midwest dist. United Pentecostal Council, Assemblies of God Inc., 1979—. Recipient Edn. PaceSetter award President's Nat. Adv. Council on Supplementary Centers, 1973. Mem. Assn. Supervision and Curriculum Devel., Nat. Council Tchrs. Math., Nat. Council Suprs. Math. (sec. chpt. 1973-75, pres. chpt. 1977-79), Elem. Sch. Math. Advs. Chgo. Area, Met. Math. Club, Math. Club Chgo. and Vicinity, Nat. Alliance Black Sch. Educators, Ill. Council Tchrs. Math., Delta Sigma Theta, Kappa Delta Pi, Kappa Mu Epsilon. Author: Modern Mathematics Structure and Use-Spirit Masters, 1977; author Chgo. Public Schs. curriculum materials; contbr. articles to profl. publs.; coordinator devel. numerous curriculum guides. Home: 2820 Paris Rd Olympia Fields IL 60461 Office: 228 N LaSalle St Chicago IL 60601

STRONG, MARK LAVON, civil engr., land surveyor; b. Garrett, Ind., July 26, 1950; s. Harry Leslie and Lois Jean (Tomlinson) S.; B.C.E., Tri-State Coll., 1972; m. Melanie Lou Carnahan, June 14, 1970; children—Nathan, Ryan, Eric. Jr. engr. Turnbell-Green & Assos., Fort Wayne, Ind., 1973, project mgr., 1973-76, sec.-treas., 1976-77, v.p., sec.-treas., 1977—, also dir.; v.p. Turnbell Engring. Co., Inc., 1978-81, sr. v.p., 1981—. Registered profl. engr. and land surveyor, Ind.; registered profl. engr., Mich. Mem. ASCE, Nat., Ind. socs. profl. engrs., Chi Epsilon. Republican. Mem. Ch. of Christ. Home: 6593 SR 1 Spencerville IN 46788 Office: 519 Tennessee Ave Fort Wayne IN 46805

STRONG, RICHARD ALLEN, safety engr., writer; b. Detroit, Apr. 11, 1930; s. Winfred and Jane Liddle (Cleveland) Gilbert; B.Sc. in Aero. and Astro. Engring., U. Mich., 1964; M.A., Central Mich. U., 1975; m. Rosa Maria Amaya, Aug. 18, 1957; children—Harold Allen, Edward Gilbert, Randall Ethan, Marisa Ann. Aircraft mechanic Mich. Flyers, Detroit, 1948, Naval Air Res., 1948-54; clk. Cadillac Motors, Detroit, 1948-54; enlisted in USAF, 1955, advanced through grades to maj., 1974; instr. pilot, 1957, nav. tng. pilot, 1958-61, project officer USAF Space Systems Div., 1964-65, foward air controller, 1966, engr. System Safety Engr. Space and Missile Systems div., 1967-69, aero engr., 1969-71, br. chief, Aero. Systems div. Wright-Patterson AFB, 1973-74, ret., 1974; sr. system safety engr. Global Graphics, Fort Worth, Lockheed Missile and Space Co., Sunnyvale, Calif., 1975; propr. Star-Tchr. Systems, Strongmobile Systems, Safety Analysis Systems, Sychic Sci. Systems, Dayton, Ohio, 1974—; lectr., cons. in field. Decorated Silver Star, D.F.C., Air medal Mem. System Safety Soc., Soc. Flight Test Engrs., Am. Soc. Psychical Research, Mensa (pres. psychic sci. spl. interest group), Air Force Assn. Roman Catholic. Editor Jour. Psychic Sci., 1977—. Home: 7514 Belle Plain Dr Dayton OH 45424 Office: 4950th Test Wing Safety Office Wright Patterson AFB OH 45433

STROTZ, ROBERT HENRY, univ. pres.; b. Aurora, Ill., Sept. 26, 1922; s. John Marc and Olga (koerfer) S.; student Duke U., 1939-41; B.A., U. Chgo., 1942, Ph.D., 1951; LL.D. (hon.), Ill. Wesleyan U., 1976, Millikin U., 1979; m. Margaret L. Hanley; children by previous marriage—Vicki, Michael, Frances, Ellen, Ann. Mem. faculty Northwestern U., Evanston, Ill., 1947—, prof. econs., 1958—, dean Coll. Arts and Scis., 1966-70, pres. univ., 1970—; vice-chmn., dir. Nat. Merit Scholarship Corp.; past chmn., dir. Fed. Res. Bank Chgo.; dir. Ill. Tool Works Inc., Norfolk & Western Ry. Co., MidCon Corp., U.S. Gypsum Co., Mark Controls Corp., 1st Nat. Bank & Trust Co., Evanston. Bd. dirs. McGaw Med. Center of Northwestern U., Northwestern Meml. Hosp.; trustee Mus. Sci. and Industry, Field Mus. Nat. History. Served with U.S. Army, 1943-45. Fellow Econometric Soc.; mem. Am. Econ. Assn., Econometric Soc. (council 1961-67), Royal Econ. Soc. Clubs: Old Elm (Ft. Sheridan, Ill.); Chicago, Commercial, Economic, University, Standard, Tavern (Chgo.); Glen View (Ill.); Bohemian (San Francisco). Mng. editor Econometrica, 1953-68; econometrics editor Internat. Ency. Social Scis., 1962-68; editor Contbns. to Econ. Analysis, 1955-70. Office: 633 Clark St Evanston IL 60201

STROUD, JERRY LEE, publishing, real estate sales exec.; b. Dale, Ind., June 26, 1938; s. Roland E. and Ruth (Herr) S.; B.S. in Spl. Edn., Ind. State U., 1960, M.S. in Psychology, 1964, M.S. in Counseling and Guidance, 1964; postgrad. Columbia U., 1964-65. Instr., Rockford (Ill.) Coll., 1960; tchr. Roberts Sch., Indpls., 1960-64; mem. sales staff Doubleday & Co., N.Y.C., 1964-65; sales mgr., v.p. Praeger & Co., N.Y.C., 1965-71; owner, pres. Fujii Assos., Chgo., 1971—; pres. K.S. Realty, Chgo., 1978—; v.p. S & S Leasing Corp.; cons. in field. Mem. Am. Booksellers Assn., Midwest Book Travelers, N.Y. Bookmen, Art Inst. Chgo., Mus. Contemporary Art, Chgo., Mensa, Sigma Phi Epsilon (past pres. Ind. Delta alumni). Club: Players. Office: 215 W Ohio St Chicago IL 60610

STROUD, JOE HINTON, newspaper editor; b. McGehee, Ark., June 18, 1936; s. Joseph Hilliard and Marion Rebecca (McKinney) S.; B.A., Hendrix Coll., Conway, Ark., 1957; M.A., Tulane U., 1959; LL.D. (hon.), Eastern Mich. U., 1977; m. Janis Mizell, Aug. 21, 1957; children—Rebecca McKinney, Joseph Scott, Alexandra Jane. Reporter, then editor editorial page Pine Bluff (Ark.) Comml., 1959-60; editorial writer Ark. Gazette, Little Rock, 1960-64; editorial writer then editor editorial page Winston-Salem (N.C.) Jour.-Sentinel, 1964-68; asso. editor Detroit Free Press, 1968-73, editor, 1973—, sr. v.p., 1978—; corp. mem. Merrill Palmer Inst., 1975—. Mem. gen. bd. publns. United Methodist Ch., 1975-76; adv. bd. Mich. Christian Advocate, 1975-79; bd. govs. Cranbrook Inst. Sci., 1978—; bd. dirs. S.E. Mich. chpt. A.R.C., 1972—, Detroit Symphony, 1978—; chmn. adv. com. Service to Mil. Families, 1974-77, chmn. program evaluation com., 1978-80. Recipient N.C. Sch. Bell award, 1967; Mich. Sch. Bell award, 1973; William Allen White award Inland Daily Press Assn., 1973, 76, 77; citation Overseas Press Club, 1974; Paul Tobenkin award Columbia U., 1976. Mem. Am. Soc. Newspaper Editors, Nat. Conf. Editorial Writers (program chmn. 1978), Detroit Econ. Club, Detroit Com. Fgn. Relations, Sigma Delta Chi. Clubs: Detroit, Renaissance, Pine Lake Country; Nat. Press. Home: 1614 Keller Ln Bloomfield Hills MI 48013 Office: 321 W Lafayette St Detroit MI 48231*

STRUBE, WILLIAM CURTIS, coll. adminstr.; b. St. Louis, Sept. 9, 1940; s. William Henry and Irene Louise (Bergmann) S.; B.A., Monmouth (Ill.) Coll., 1962; M.B.A., U. Ariz., 1965; Ph.D., U. Ark., 1972; m. Janet Grace Hoetker, June 18, 1966; children—Kim Janette, Randall William. Instr., Buena Vista Coll., Storm Lake, Iowa, 1966-67; asst. prof. Florissant Valley Community Coll., St. Louis County, 1967-68; instr. U. Ark., Fayetteville, 1968-69; faculty Drury Coll., Springfield, Mo., 1969—, prof., 1978—, asst. dean coll., fall 1973, dean students, 1973-75, dir. Breech Sch. Bus. Adminstrn., 1975—; leader mgmt. tng. programs, 1971—. Moderator, 1st Congl. Ch., United Ch. of Christ, Springfield, 1976—; faculty mem. Am. Youth Found. Christian Leadership Camp, 1977, 78; mem. Manpower Planning Council, 1977-78; bd. dirs. Springfield Boys Club, 1976—, Springfield council Girl Scouts U.S.A., 1979—. Danforth asso., 1978—; Title I, IPA grantee, 1977-78. Mem. Acad. Mgmt., S.W. Fedn. Adminstrv. Disciplines, Ozark Econs. Assn., Midwest Bus. Adminstrn. Assn., Midwest Econs. Assn., Theta Chi, Omicron Delta Kappa, Phi Eta Sigma. Home: 3709 Sugar Hill Springfield MO 65804 Office: Drury Coll 900 N Benton Ave Springfield MO 65802

STRUBLE, JAMES ROBERT, mech. engr.; b. Salina, Kans., June 2, 1935; s. James Lester and Kathryn L. (Brick) S.; student Kans. State U., 1953; B.S. in M.E., Wichita State U., 1963; postgrad. Tex. Christian U., 1965; m. Sue Jean Wallace, Oct. 30, 1954 (div. June 1967); children—Jennifer K., Stephanie L., Julienne J.; m. 2d, Earletta K. (Ditto) Divelbess, June 18, 1971. Pvt. practice as mech., elec. and structural engr. Struble & Co., cons. engrs., Salina, Kans., 1965—; contact engr. Boeing Co., Wichita, Kans., 1956-63; design and lead engr. McDonnell Aircraft, St. Louis, 1963-64, Gen. Dynamics Corp., Fort Worth, 1964-65; research and devel. engr. Salina Mfg. Co., 1965-66; project engr. Shaver & Co., Salina, 1966-68; group engr., asst. project engr. Beech Aircraft Co., Salina, 1968-72; mgr. engring. Certainteed Machinery Corp. McPherson, 1974-77; mech./elec. engr. Bucher & Willis Cons. Engrs., Architects & Planners, Salina, 1977-79; prin. Struble Engring., Salina, 1979—. Republican precinct committeeman, 1968-70. Registered profl. engr., Colo., Kans., Tex., Mo. Mem. ASHRAE, Nat. Soc. Profl. Engrs., Kans. Engring. Soc., Illuminating Engring. Soc., Assn. Energy Engrs. Clubs: Masons, Shriners. Home: 2169 Nottingham Salina KS 67401 Office: 421 N Ohio St Salina KS 67401

STRUCK, RICHARD CHARLES, univ. adminstr.; b. Beaver Dam, Wis., Dec. 20, 1938; s. Kenneth Maynard and Viola Minnie (Hartwig) S.; B.A., U. Minn., 1968; M.A., Western Ill. U., 1976; m. Peggy Pennington Lenix, Dec. 20, 1958; children—Robert M., Bonnie E., Matthew T. Publicist, Gen. Electric Co., Louisville, 1969-71; communications coordinator Halvorson, Inc., Duluth, Minn., 1971-73; account exec. Westmoreland, Larson, & Hill, Duluth, 1973-74; dir. public relations Kona Kai Club, San Diego, 1974; instr. mktg. Western Ill. U., 1977-78; press relations supr. Gen. Electric Co., Chgo., 1977; dir. annual fund, devel. office, asst. dir. Western Ill. U. Found., Western Ill. U., Macomb, 1978—. Active Boy Scouts Am., recipient Dist. award of merit. Served with U.S. Army, 1959-62. Mem. Public Relations Soc. Am. (accredited mem., chmn. profl. devel. Quad Cities chpt.), Council Advancement and Support Edn., Nat. Wildlife Fedn. Home: PO Box 328 La Harpe IL 61450 Office: 200 Sherman Hall Western Ill U Macomb IL 61455

STRUNK, RICHARD DEAN, mech. engr.; b. Burlington, Iowa, July 23, 1935; s. Frank Ray and Faye Elizabeth (Miller) S.; B.S.M.E., Iowa State U., 1958; M.S.M.E., U. Ill., 1964, Ph.D., 1969; m. Karole J. Silbaugh, Sept. 16, 1962 (div. Dec. 1975); children—Michael Dean, Susan Jane. With Deere & Co., Waterloo, Iowa, 1955-67, engr., 1960-63, sr. engr., Moline, Ill., 1964-67; staff engr. IBM, East Fishkill, N.Y., 1969-70; regional mgr. Bolt, Beranek & Newman, Chgo., 1970-73; mgr. acoustics Borg-Warner Research, Des Plaines, Ill., 1973-78; group leader controls Deere & Co. Tech. Center, Moline, Ill., 1978-80, mgr. engring. sci., 1980—. Served with U.S. Army, 1958-60. Ford intern fellow U. Ill., 1963-64, Univ. fellow, 1967-69. Mem. ASME, Soc. Automotive Engrs., Sigma Xi, Pi Tau Sigma, Tau Beta Pi. Home: 1800 7th St Apt 5C East Moline IL 61244 Office: 3300 River Dr Moline IL 61265

STUART, JAMES FORTIER, music educator; b. Baton Rouge, Dec. 22, 1928; s. Evander Morgan and Jeanne (Fortier) S.; Mus.B., La. State U., 1950, B. Music Edn., 1950, Mus.M., 1954; Mus.D., U. Rochester, 1968. Soloist with major opera cos. and symphonies, N.Y.C., Boston, Phila., Atlanta, New Orleans, 1950-70; leading tenor Am. Savoyards, 1957-60, Martyn Green Gilbert & Sullivan Co., 1961-67; asst. prof. voice, dir. opera Boston U. and Boston Conservatory, 1964-68; prof. music, dir. opera Kent (Ohio) State U., 1968—, founder, artistic dir. Kent Light Opera Co., 1969—, Nat. Light Opera Co., 1977—; artistic dir. Ohio Light Opera Co., Wooster, 1979—; pres. Stuart Prodns., Ltd., Cleve., 1974—. Musical cons. Internat. Hospitality Mgmt., Inc., Cleve., 1974; musical dir., cons. Brazilian Court Hotel, Palm Beach, Fla., 1981. Home: 135 Forest Dr Kent OH 44240

STUART, JOSEPH MARTIN, art center adminstr.; b. Seminole, Okla., Nov. 9, 1932; s. Arch William and Lillian (Lindsey) S.; B.F.A. in Art, U. N.Mex., 1959, M.A. in Art, 1962; m. Signe Margaret Nelson, June 18, 1960; 1 dau., Lise Nelson. Dir., Roswell (N.Mex.) Museum and Art Center, 1960-62; curator U. Oreg. Mus. Art, 1962-63; dir. Boise (Idaho) Gallery Art, 1964-68, Salt Lake (City) Art Center, 1968-71, S.D. Meml. Art Center, Brookings, 1971—; asso. prof. art S.D. State U., 1971—; represented in permanent collections: Coll. Idaho, Eureka Coll., Salt Lake Art Center, Sioux City (Iowa) Art Center, U. N.Mex. Art Mus. Served with USN, 1951-55. Mem. Am. Assn. Museums, Am. Fedn. Arts, Assn. S.D. Museums, Artists Equity, S.D. Coll. Art Assn., Phi Kappa Phi. Democrat. Unitarian. Club: Rotary. Author: Index of South Dakota Artists, 1974; Art of South Dakota, 1974; author numerous exhbn. catalogs. Office: SD Meml Art Center Brookings SD 57007

STUART, ROBERT, metal container mfg. exec.; b. Chgo., Aug. 3, 1921; s. Robert S. and Marie (Vavra) Solinsky; B.S., U. Ill., 1943; m. Lillian Constance Kondelik, Dec. 5, 1962 (dec. May 1978). Sec.-treas., gen. mgr. Warren Metal Decorating Co., 1947-49; asst. to gen. mgr. Cans, Inc., 1950-52; asst. to v.p. Nat. Can Corp., 1953-59, sr. v.p., 1959-62, exec. v.p., 1962-63, pres., 1963-69, chmn. bd., chief exec. officer, 1965-72, chmn. bd., 1972—, chmn. fin. com., also dir.; dir. LaSalle Nat. Bank, Chgo. Community Ventures. Mem. Midwest adv. council The Conf. Bd.; mem. past chmn. businessman's adv. council for Coll. Bus. Adminstrn., U. Ill. Chgo. Circle; mem. trustees' devel. council Elmhurst Coll.; mem. citizens bd. U. Chgo., also vis. com. Div. Sch.; past chmn. Nat. Minority Purchasing Council; mem. bus. adv. council Chgo. Urban League; trustee Provident Hosp., Ill. Masonic Med. Center; mem. citizens bd. Loyola U., Chgo.; mem., asso. Rehab. Inst. Chgo.; mem. grand council Am. Indian Center Chgo., adv. bd. Broader Urban Involvement and Leadership Devel.; past pres. Chgo. Crime Commn.; dir., vice chmn. Nat. Council Crime and Delinquency; dir., mem. Pres.'s council U. Ill. Found. Bd. dirs., v.p. Lloyd Morey Scholarship Fund; bd. dirs. Protestant Found. Greater Chgo., Chgo. Community Ventures, Inc.; chmn. World Federalists Assn.; trustee emeritus Nat. Jewish Hosp. at Denver. Served from sgt. to capt. AUS, 1943-46. Mem. Can Mfrs. Inst. (past chmn.), Newcomen Soc. N.Am., Alpha Kappa Lambda (past nat. pres.). Republican. Congregationalist. Mason (32 deg., K.T.). Rotarian (past commodore internat. yachting fellowship). Clubs: Rotary (past pres. Chgo., dist. gov.), Chicago, Chicago Yacht, Comml., Econ., Met. (Chgo.), Capitol Hill (Washington); Little Ship (Eng.). Home: 400 E Randolph St Chicago IL 60601 Office: 8101 W Higgins Rd Chicago IL 60631

STUART, ROBERT DOUGLAS, JR., food co. exec.; b. Hubbard Woods, Ill., Apr. 26, 1916; s. Robert Douglas and Harriet (McClure) S.; B.A., Princeton U., 1937; J.D., Yale U., 1946; m. Barbara McMath Edwards, May 21, 1938; children—Robert Douglas III, James McClure, Marian Pillsbury, Alexander Douglas. With Quaker Oats Co., Chgo., 1947—, v.p., 1955, pres., 1962-66, chief exec. officer, pres., 1966, chmn. bd., chief exec. officer, 1976—, also dir.; dir. United Airlines, Inc., 1st Nat. Bank Chgo., Deere & Co. Served to maj. AUS, 1942-45. Mem. Grocery Mfrs. Am. (dir.), Bus. Council. Office: Quaker Oats Co Merchandise Mart Chicago IL 60654

STUART, WALTER STANLEY, JR., mfg. co. exec.; b. St. Louis, Sept. 18, 1939; s. Walter Stanley and Barbara (Osborne) S.; student Beloit Coll., 1957-59; B.S., Ind. U., 1962, M.B.A. with honors, 1965; m. Judith M. Anderson, May 18, 1963; children—Michael Carl, Matthew David, Mark Stephen. Mem. product mgmt. staff Gen. Foods Corp., White Plains, N.Y., 1965-67; project dir. advanced methods group N.W. Ayer Co., Phila., 1968-69, v.p., mgmt. supr., Chgo., 1970-73; v.p. corp. mktg. devel. Ball Corp., Muncie, Ind., 1973-74, v.p., gen. mgr. consumer products div., 1974-78; v.p. mktg. service U.S. Gypsum Co., 1978—, pres., dir. subs. Marstrat, Inc., Chgo., 1978-79; instr. mktg. Roosevelt U., Chgo., 1968, Rutgers U., 1969; instr. Northwestern U. Grad. Sch. Mgmt., 1979. Pres., Indian guide program YMCA, Delaware County, Ind., 1974-75; bd. dirs. Delaware County Jr. Achievement, 1976-78; mem. legis. council Ind. U. Alumni Assn., 1975-78; past treas., bd. dirs. Lincolnshire Community Christian Ch., elder, 1979—; mem. Ind. U. Dean's Assos. Devel. Cabinet, 1978—, nat. chmn., 1979-81. Mem. Am. Mktg. Assn. (nat. dir. 1978-79, v.p. mktg.-mgmt. 1980-81), Ind. U. Sch. Bus. Alumni Assn. (past pres., mem. exec. council 1973-78), Ill. St. Andrew Soc. Chgo., Assn. Nat. Advertisers (advt. mgmt. policy com. 1978—), Ind. Soc. Chgo., Art Inst. Chgo., Chaine des Rotisseurs, Les Amis du Vin, Beta Gamma Sigma, Phi Delta Theta, Alpha Delta Sigma, Delta Sigma Pi. Clubs: Econ., Univ., Tavern, Arts, Exec. (dir. 1979—, 1st vice chmn. 1981—), Rotary, Sales and Mktg. (Chgo.); Delaware Country, Muncie (Muncie); Columbia (Indpls.); Sales Exec. (N.Y.C.). Author: Guidelines for Successful New Product Test Marketing, 1976. Home: 40 Fox Trail Deerfield IL 60015 Office: 101 S Wacker Dr Chicago IL 60606

STUART, WILLIAM CORWIN, fed. judge; b. Knoxville, Iowa, Apr. 28, 1920; s. George C. and Edith (Abram) S.; student Chariton Jr. Coll., 1937-38; A.B., U. Iowa, also J.D., 1942; m. Mary Elgin Cleaver, Oct. 20, 1946; children—William Corwin, Robert Cullen, Melanie Rae, Valerie Jo. Admitted to Iowa bar, practiced law, Chariton, 1946-62; city atty., Chariton, 1946-47; justice Iowa Supreme Ct., 1962-71; U.S. dist. judge So. Dist. Iowa, 1971—. Mem. Iowa Senate, 1953-61. Served with USNR, 1943-45. Mem. Am. Legion, Am., Iowa bar Assns., Am. Judicature Soc., Phi Kappa Psi, Phi Delta Phi, Omicron Delta Kappa. Presbyterian (elder). Clubs: Masons, Shriners. Office: US Dist Ct E 1st and Walnut Sts Des Moines IA 52818

STUBBLEBINE, WARREN, foundry and machine co. exec.; b. Reading, Pa., Jan. 18, 1917; s. William Edgar and Rebecca Dorothy (Reber) S.; B.S. in Chem. Engring., Pa. State Coll., 1938, M.S., 1940, Ph.D., 1942; m. Jane Elizabeth Kemmerling, Aug. 20, 1938; children—Warren, James Michael, Judith Elizabeth, Margaret Anne, Scott David. Grad. asst. Pa. State Coll., 1938-42; head flooring devel. Armstrong Cork Co., Lancaster, Pa., 1942-47; research dir. Office Q.M. Gen., Washington, 1947-52; v.p. Stowe-Woodward Co., Newton, Mass., 1952-63, Sandusky Foundry & Machine Co. (Ohio), 1963—. Mem. Medfield (Mass.) Sch. Com., 1961-63; scoutmaster Boy Scouts Am., 1957-63, 70-73. Registered profl. engr., D.C. Mem. Am. Chem. Soc., AAAS, Am. Nuclear Soc., TAPPI, Norwalk Conservation League, Sigma Xi, Phi Lambda Upsilon. Republican. Clubs: Lions, Plum Brook Country, Catawba Island, Elkhorn Lake

Shooting Park. Patentee in field. Office: Sandusky Foundry & Machine Co 615 W Market St Sandusky OH 44870

STUBBS, EUGENE ALVIN, micrographic specialist; b. Chgo., Mar. 25, 1952; s. Richard Frank and Vivian Lorraine (Bowie) S.; student public schs., Chgo.; m. Patricia Lampkin, Oct. 18, 1979; stepchildren—Major, Katrina, Reginald. Micrographic technician AT&T, Chgo., 1977-78; stores asst. mgr. Southland Corp., Chgo., 1979; micrographic specialist Montgomery Ward & Co., Chgo., 1980—; micrographic cons. Recipient Am. Mgmt. Assn. award for microfilm in records mgmt., 1980; CMR Assos. award, 1980. Mem. Nat. Microfilm Assn., Time Mgmt. Assn. Home: 5730 N Winthrop St Chicago IL 60660 Office: 1400 W Greenleaf St Chicago IL 60626

STUBER, BETTIE JEAN, chiropractor; b. Harrisonville, Mo., June 26, 1929; d. Arthur Vernon and Mary Betty (Brown) Barker; Dr. Chiropractics summa cum laude, Cleve. Chiropractic Coll., 1967; postgrad. Tex. Chiropractic Coll., 1973-74, Nat. Chiropractic Coll., 1973, 76, Logan Chiropractic Coll., Columbia (Mo.) Coll.; B.A., Columbia (Mo.) Coll., 1977; m. George Edgar Stuber, Sept. 4, 1948; children—Dennis, Debra Stuber Rearick, Diana. Clk., typist, stenographer, nurses aid IRS, 1948-52; gen. practice chiropractics, Kansas City, Mo., 1967—. Mem. Am. (council roentgenology, chiropractic council on sports injuries, council on chiropractic technique, council on chiropractic physiotherapy, council on nutrition, council on chiropractic neurology), Mo. (past treas., v.p., pres. dist. 2), Chiropractic Assn., Kans. Chiropractic Assn., Am. Chiropractic Council Diagnosis and Internal Disorders, Am. Council Women Chiropractors, Assn. for Research and Enlightenment (asso.). Home: 8910 Western Hills Dr Kansas City MO 64114

STUCKEY, RICHARD JORIAN, acctg. co. exec.; b. Reading, Eng., Jan. 6, 1943; came to U.S., 1965; s. Derek Richard and Gladys Muriel (Saunders) S.; B.Sc. with gen. honors, U. London, 1965; M.B.A., Stanford U., 1967; m. Lois Ilene Engel, July 3, 1976. Cons., Arthur Andersen & Co., San Francisco, 1967-76, world hdqrs. mgr. advanced practices, Chgo., 1976-81, partner, 1981—; lectr. Golden Gate U., San Francisco, 1974-76. Mem. Am. Mgmt. Assn., Assn. for Computing Machinery, Stanford Grad. Sch. Assn., King's Coll. London Assn. Contbr. articles in field to profl. publs. Home: 429-C Grant Pl Chicago IL 60614 Office: Arthur Andersen & Co 33 W Monroe St Chicago IL 60603

STUDENROTH, CARL WILSON, union ofcl.; b. Columbia, Pa., Apr. 14, 1915; s. Frederick Melvin and Priscilla Mary (Crist) S.; student Pa. State Coll., 1932-33; m. Helen Ardell Spence, Apr. 10, 1937; childrenanda Faye, Donna Marie. Laborer, Stehli Silk Co., Lancaster, Pa., 1932; laborer, sorter, molder Pa. R.R., Columbia, 1932-33; molder Grinnell Corp., Columbia, 1933-44; organizer Molders Union Eastern Pa., 1945-46, dist. rep., 1946-55, v.p. internat. union, 1955-76; pres. Internat. Molders and Allied Workers Union, Cin., 1976—; mem. exec. council AFL-CIO Metal Trades, Indsl. Union dept. AFL-CIO; labor mem. U.S. Trade Negotiations Com.; mem. OSHA heat stress com. U.S. Dept. Labor. Democrat. Lutheran. Office: 1225 E McMillan St Cincinnati OH 45206

STUDLEY, HELEN MARGARET, rancher; b. Herman, Nebr., May 2, 1930; d. Lester and Anna J. (Frankum) Rowson; student Mid Plains Community Coll., 1968; m. Dale H. Studley, May 27, 1951 (dec. 1971); children—Al (dec.), Ronald, Mark, Mary, Dan. Bookkeeper, First Nat. Bank, North Platte, Nebr., 1947-52, E. H. Evans, Atty., North Platte 1952-62; bookkeeper Rosedale Ranch, Inc., North Platte, 1971—, pres., treas., 1971—. Mem. Am. Legion, Cow Bells, Am. Simmental Assn. Republican. Methodist. Clubs: Elks, Does. Home: PO Box 244 North Platte NE 69101 Office: Route 3 Box 240 North Platte NE 69101

STUDY, MARY MARGARET (TELLER), print service center exec.; b. Oklahoma City, Dec. 3, 1945; d. Ernest Leonard and Mary Ann Teller; B.A., U. No. Colo., 1967; M.A. in Public Relations, M.A. in Journalism, Ball State U., 1970; m. Larry Lee Study, Jan. 3, 1970; 1 son, Darren Boyd. Report specialist, adminstrv. specialist, Avionics Research, Ohio U., Athens, 1971-73, exec. sec. dean coll. engring. and tech., 1973-74; instr.-lectr. public relations sch. mass communications, Mara Inst. Tech., Shah Alam, Malaysia, 1974-76; owner-mgr. Alpha Graphics Ltd., Print Media Service Center, Muncie, 1976—; free lance public relations writer, cons., Athens, 1970-74; free-lance writer, pub. periodicals on small bus., graphics, advt.; lectr. hands-on graphics workshops, 1980—. Chmn., Oktoberfest, 1979—; mem. Downtown Bus. Council Retail Promotions and Spl. Events Com., 1978—, chmn., 1979—; mem. Public Relations Task Force, 1972. Mem. Women in Communications (advisor Ball State U. chpt. 1969), C. of C. Muncie-Delaware County (small bus. council 1979), Alpha Gamma Delta. Editor, pub. Muncie Marketeer, 1978. Office: 111 E Adams Muncie IN 47305

STUEBE, DAVID CHARLES, mfg. co. exec.; b. Racine, Wis., May 29, 1940; s. Edwin Charles and Henrietta Alfreda (Dryanski) S.; B.B.A., U. Notre Dame, 1962; C.P.A., U. Ill., 1968; m. Ann E. McMahon, Aug. 11, 1962; children—David Charles, Kelly Ann. Auditor, Arthur Andersen & Co., Chgo., 1962-64, sr. auditor, 1964-68; audit mgr., 1968-75; controller Scholl, Inc., Chgo., 1975-76; pres. Arno Adhesive Tapes, Inc., Michigan City, Ind., 1976-80; v.p. Carpetland U.S.A. Inc., Merrillville, Ind., 1980—, MSL Industries, Inc., Lincolnwood, Ill., 1981—; dir. Lakeshore Bank & Trust Co. C.P.A., Ill. Mem. Am. Inst. C.P.A.'s, C. of C. Michigan City (v.p.). Home: 5 Fern Ln Dune Acres Chesterton IN 46302 Office: 7373 Lincoln Ave Lincolnwood IL 60646

STUELAND, DEAN THEODORE, physician, clinic adminstr.; b. Viroqua, Wis., June 24, 1950; s. Theodore Andrew and Hazel Thelma (Oftedahl) S.; B.S.E.E., U. Wis., 1972, M.S.E.E., 1973; M.D., 1977; m. Marlene Ann McClurg, Dec. 30, 1972; children—Jeffrey Dean, Michael Andrew. Cons. stats., computers U. Wis.-Regional Rehab. Research Inst.; intern St. Joseph's Hosp., Marshfield, Wis., 1977-78; intern Marshfield Clinic, 1977-78, resident, 1978-80, dir. emergency services, 1981—; emergency physician Riverview Hosp., Wisconsin Rapids, Wis., 1980-81. Diplomate Am. Bd. Internal Medicine. Mem. A.C.P., Am. Coll. Emergency Physicians, Biomed. Engring. Soc. (sr.), N.Y. Acad. Sci. Home: 7623 McLean Dr Hewitt WI 54441 Office: 1000 N Oak Marshfield WI 54449

STUERMANN, LEONARD HENRY, coll. adminstr.; b. Washington, Mar. 4, 1926; s. Leonard Henry and Augusta Margaret (Nau) S.; B.C.S., Benjamin Franklin U., 1949; postgrad. Boston U., 1955, U. Ky., 1963, U. Omaha, 1964-65, U. Wis., 1969-70; m. Doris C. Schmidt, June 25, 1955. Accountant, Marinus Koster, C.P.A., Washington, 1945-54; auditor GAO, Chgo., 1954-55; office mgr. Laborers Health and Welfare Adminstrn., Boston, 1955-56; auditor Dept. Army, Chgo., 1956-57; comptroller Milw. Area Tech. Coll., 1957—. Mem. Assn. Sch. Bus. Ofcls. U.S. and Can. (registered sch. bus. ofcl.), Wis. Assn. Sch. Bus. Ofcls., Am. Vocat. Assn., Wis. Assn. Vocat., Tech. and Adult Edn., Student Fin. Aid Adminstrs., Nat. Assn. Coll. and Univ. Bus. Officers, Central Assn. Coll. and Univ. Bus. Officers, Am. Mgmt. Assn., Am. Mgmt. Soc. Clubs: Masons, Shriners. Home: 7318 Wellauer Dr Wauwatosa WI 53213 Office: 1015 N 6th St Milwaukee WI 53203

STUHLMAN, ROBERT AUGUST, veterinarian; b. Cin., Apr. 9, 1939; s. Robert A. and Marion June (Hannig) S.; student U. Cin., 1962-63; D.V.M., Ohio State U., 1968; M.S. in Lab. Animal Medicine, U. Mo., 1971; m. Liliane Jeannine Pierre, Nov. 12, 1960; children—Robert A., Michael A., Lisa M. Research asso., dept. vet. medicine and surgery U. Mo., Columbia, 1968-71, asst. dir. dept. lab. animal medicine, 1971-75, instr. dept. pathology, 1971-75; vet. med. officer Research Service VA Hosp., Columbia, Mo., 1972-75; dir. Lab. Animal Resources Wright State U., Dayton, Ohio, 1975—, asso. prof. dept. pathology Sch. Medicine, 1975—, mem. dean's staff, 1975—; cons. in lab. animal care Research Service VA Center, Dayton, Ohio, 1975—, Central State U., Wilberforce, Ohio, 1980—; participant 3rd Brooklodge Workshop on Spontaneous Diabetes in Lab. Animals, 1974. Served with USAF, 1957-62. Nominated for Established Investigator award Am. Diabetes Assn., 1974; U.S. Public Health grantee, 1974—. Mem. Am. Assn. for Lab. Animal Sci., Am. Coll. Lab. Animal Medicine, AVMA, Am. Soc. Lab. Animal Practitioners, Phi Zeta. Contbr. articles on diabetes in lab. animals to profl. jours. Home: 780 Wilkerson Rd Fairborn OH 45324 Office: Wright State U Office Lab Animal Resources Dayton OH 45435

STUHR, ROBERT LEWIS, pub. relations cons.; b. Tabor, Iowa, Oct. 10, 1917; s. John R. and Elsa J. (Strange) S.; B.A., Drake U., 1939; M.A., U. Iowa, 1940; Ph.D., Northwestern U., 1961; m. Ruth P. Jones, Sept. 21, 1946; children—John, Margaret. Dir. pub. relations and devel. Drake U., Des Moines, 1947-59; partner Gonser Gerber Tinker Stuhr, devel. cons., Chgo., 1959—; asso. dir. Econ. Club Chgo., 1959-68, exec. dir., 1968—, mem. exec. com., 1968—. Served to capt., inf., AUS, 1941-46. Decorated Bronze Star medal; recipient Distinguished Alumni award Drake U., 1960. Mem. Pub. Relations Soc. Am., Internat. Pub. Relations Soc., Council Advancement and Support Edn., S.A.R., Phi Beta Kappa, Sigma Delta Chi, Sigma Alpha Epsilon, Omicron Delta Kappa, Phi Eta Sigma. Clubs: Univ. (Chgo.); Westmoreland Country (Wilmette, Ill.). Editor Bull. on Pub. Relations and Devel. for Colls., 1959—, Bull. on Pub. Relations and Devel. for Prep Schs., 1959—, Bull. on Pub. Relations and Devel. for Hosps., 1959—. Contbr. to various mags. Home: 3033 Iroquois Rd Wilmette IL 60091 Office: 105 W Madison St Chicago IL 60602

STUKEL, JAMES JOSEPH, engineer, educator; b. Joliet, Ill., Mar. 30, 1937; s. Philip and Julia (Mattivi) S.; B.S. in Mech. Engring., Purdue U., 1959; M.S., U. Ill., Champaign-Urbana, 1963, Ph.D., 1968; m. Mary Joan Helpling, Nov. 27, 1958; children—Catherine, James, David, Paul. Research engr. W. Va. Pulp and Paper Co., Covington, Va., 1959-61; asst. prof. U. Ill., Urbana, 1968-71, asso. prof., 1971-75, prof., 1975—, dir. office coal research and utilization, 1974-76, dir. office energy research, 1976-80, dir. public policy program Coll. of Engring., 1980—; exec. sec. MW Consortium on Air Pollution, 1972-73; chmn. bd. dirs., 1973-75; mem. adv. bd. regional studies program Argonne (Ill.) Nat. Lab., 1975-76; mem. adv. com. Energy Resources Center, U. Ill., Chgo., 1975-76; mem. coal study panel Energy Resources Commn., State of Ill., 1976; cons. in field. Pres. parish council Holy Cross Ch., Urbana, Ill., 1967-68. Mem. ASCE (State-of-the-Art of Civil Engring. award 1975), ASME, AAAS, Sigma Xi, Phi Kappa Phi, Pi Tau Sigma. Contbr. articles to profl. jours. Home: 2504 Bedford Champaign IL 61820 Office: 3219 CEB Univ Ill Urbana IL 61801

STULTS, ALLEN PARKER, banker; b. Chgo., June 13, 1913; s. Elmer E. and Minnie (Parker) S.; student U. Ill., 1931-32; diploma Northwestern U., 1941; student Loyola U., 1941-42; cert. Rutgers Grad. Sch. Banking, 1945; m. Elizabeth Van Horne, Aug. 19, 1939; children—Laurence, Shirley, John, James. With Fed. Res. Bank, 1933; asst. cashier Am. Nat. Bank & Trust Co., Chgo., 1942-45, asst. v.p., 1946-48, v.p., 1949-56, exec. v.p., 1956-63, pres., 1963-69, chmn. bd., 1969-78, chmn. exec. com., 1978-80, hon. chmn., 1980—, dir., 1957—; dir. McDonald's Corp., Health-Mor, Inc., Verson Allsteel Press Co. Pub. adviser Midwest Stock Exchange, 1964-65. Mem. adv. bd. Chgo. Area council, Nat. council Boy Scouts Am.; bus. adv. council Chgo. Uroan League; exec. com. Gateway Houses Found.; chmn. bd. Businessman's Council NCCJ; nat. corp. gifts com. United Negro Coll. Fund; adv. bd. YMCA; bus. adv. council Chgo. Urban League; trustee Alice Lloyd Coll. Mem. Am. (pres. 1971-72), Ill. (past pres.) bankers assns., Phi Gamma Delta, Skull and Crescent. Congregationalist. Clubs: Bankers, Chgo., Econ., Execs. (dir. 1956), Robert Morris Assos. (pres. 1952-53), Comml., Mid-Am.; Sunset Ridge Country (pres. 1956-57) (Winnetka, Ill.); Tucson Nat. Golf. Home: 1420 Sheridan Rd Wilmette IL 60091 Office: 33 N LaSalle St Room 1616 Chicago IL 60602

STUMP, JOHN EDWARD, veterinary anatomist and ethologist; b. Galion, Ohio, June 3, 1934; s. Clarence Willard and Mabel Katherine (Pfeifer) S.; D.V.M. summa cum laude, Ohio State U., 1958; Ph.D., Purdue U., 1966; m. Patricia Anne Auer, Aug. 7, 1955; children—Karen, James. Pvt. practice veterinary medicine, Bucyrus, Ohio, 1958-61; instr. veterinary anatomy Purdue U., W. Lafayette, Ind., 1961-66, asst. prof., 1966-70, asso. prof., 1970-76, prof., 1976—; vis. prof. dept. physiol. scis. Sch. Vet. Medicine, U. Calif., Davis, fall 1980; vis. prof. dept. vet. anatomy Coll. Vet. Medicine, Tex. A&M U., spring 1981; anatomy cons. Nat. Bd. Veterinary Med. Examiners. Mem. Lafayette (Ind.) Bd. Health, 1973—, Lafayette Animal Control Commn., 1976—. Recipient Borden award for highest academic average in veterinary medicine Ohio State U., 1958; Autotutorial Excellence award Student AVMA, 1974; Norden Distinguished Tchr. (in veterinary medicine) award Purdue U., 1977, Outstanding Teacher award Purdue Alumni Found., 1978, Amoco Found. Undergrad. Teaching award, 1979. Mem. Am., Ind. veterinary med. assns., Ind. Acad. Veterinary Medicine, World, Am. (pres. 1977-78) assns. veterinary anatomists, Am. Assn. Anatomists, Assn. Am. Vet. Med. Colls., Ind. Acad. Sci., Animal Behavior Soc., Am. Soc. Vet. Ethology, Sigma Xi, Phi Zeta, Gamma Sigma Delta. Republican. Presbyterian. Club: Kiwanis (pres. Lafayette chpt. 1972). Home: 2515 Oswego Ln Lafayette IN 47905 Office: Dept Anatomy Sch Veterinary Medicine Purdue U West Lafayette IN 47907

STUMPE, RICHARD ALLAN, ednl. adminstr.; b. St. Louis, Jan. 21, 1930; s. Carl George and Madeline Elsa (Zirnheld) S.; B.A., Harris Tchrs. Coll., 1951; M.S., Wash. U., 1955, B.S., 1960; Ph.D., St. Louis U., 1967; m. Janice Marie Sasse; 1 son, David. Elem. tchr. St. Louis Public Schs., 1951-61, elem. prin., 1961-63, supr. research, 1963-67, asst. to dep. supt. instrn., 1979—; pres. Harris-Stowe Coll., St.Louis, 1967-79. Mem. Higher Edn. Coordinating Council, 1968-79, St. Louis City-County White House Conf. on Edn., 1970-76; mem. adv. council to Mo. Coordinating Bd. Higher Edn., 1975-79. Served with USAF, 1951-52. Recipient; Top Tau award Sigma Tau Gamma, 1970; Outstanding Service as Pres. award Harris-Stowe Coll., 1979. Mem. Am. Assn. Sch. Adminstrs., Am. Ednl. Research Assn., Assn. Supervision & Curriculum Devel., Phi Delta Kappa, Kappa Delta Pi. Presbyterian. Office: 911 Locust St Saint Louis MO 63101

STUMPE, WARREN ROBERT, mfg. co. exec.; b. Bronx, N.Y., July 15, 1925; s. William A. and Emma J. (Mann) S.; B.S., U.S. Mil. Acad., 1945; M.S., Cornell U., 1949; M.S. in Indsl. Engring., N.Y. U., 1965; grad. Command and Gen. Staff Coll., 1972, Army War Coll., 1976; m. Jean Marie Mannion, June 5, 1952; children—Jeffrey R., Kathy, William E. Commd. 2d lt. C.E., U.S. Army, 1945, advanced through grades to capt., 1954; with 65th Engr. Bn., 1945-48; asst. prof. mechanics U.S. Mil. Acad., 1951-54; resigned, 1954; col. Res. assigned to dep. chief of staff for research and devel. Dept. Army, Washington, 1974-79; apptd. civilian aide to sec. Army for State of Wis., 1981—; dep. gen. mgr., gen. engring. div. AMF, Stamford, Conn., 1954-63; exec. v.p. Dortech, Inc., Stamford, 1963-69; dir. systems mgmt. group Mathews Conveyor div. REX, Darien, Conn., 1969-71; dir. research and devel. Rexnord, Milw., 1971-73, v.p. corp. research and tech., 1973-81, v.p. bus. devel. sector, 1981—. Founder, pres. No. Little League, Stamford, 1965-69; pres. Turn of River Jr. High Sch. PTA, Stamford, 1967-68; vice-chmn. Wis., Dept. Def. Nat. Com. Employer Support Guard and Res.; bd. regents Milw. Sch. Engring.; mem. liaison council Coll. Engring., U. Wis., mem. indsl. adv. council; mem. Wis. Gov.'s Task Force on Energy. Registered profl. engr., N.Y., Fla., Wis. Mem. Am. Mgmt. Assn., Soc. Am. Mil. Engrs., Am. Water Pollution Control Fedn., Process Equipment Mfrs. Assn., Indsl. Research Inst., West Point Soc. N.Y. (career adv. bd.), West Point Soc. Wis., Tau Beta Pi, Phi Kappa Phi. Clubs: Wis., Ozaukee Country. Contbr. articles to profl. jours. Home: 2555 W Hemlock Rd Glendale WI 53209 Office: PO Box 2022 Milwaukee WI 53201

STUMPF, LOWELL C(LINTON), artist-designer; b. Canton, Ill., Dec. 8, 1917; s. Oral Baxter and Marie (Dawson) S.; grad. Chgo. Acad. Fine Arts; student L'Ecole de Beaux Arts, Marseille, France, 1945; m. Jacqueline Jeanne Charlotte Andree Lucas, Sept. 5, 1945; children—Eric Clinton, Roderick Lowell. Staff artist Internat. Harvester Co., Chgo., 1939-42, Nugent-Graham Studios, Chgo., 1945-47; free lance artist, designer, Chgo., 1947—. Served with AUS, 1942-45; NATO USA, ETO. Mem. Artist Guild Chgo., Internat. Platform Assn. Contbr. sci. and tech. illustrations, maps to Compton's Pictured Ency., Rand McNally & Co., Macmillan Co., Scott, Foresman & Co., Ginn & Co. textbooks, World Book Year Book, Field Enterprises Sci. Yearbooks, Childcraft Ann. and Library, World Book Dictionary. Home: 7N161 Medinah Rd Medinah IL 60157 Office: 203 N Wabash Ave Chicago IL 60601 also PO Box 25 Medinah IL 60157

STUMPF, PETER PHILIP, state senator; b. St. Paul, Mar. 2, 1948; s. Peter P. and Helen Elizabeth (Berchem) S.; B.A., Coll. St. Thomas, 1971; postgrad. U. Minn., 1972. Mem. Minn. Senate, 1975—. Chmn. dist. Democratic-Farmer-Labor party, 1974-75; mem. Ramsey County Study Commn., 1973-74; active numerous civic orgns. Office: 235 State Capitol St Paul MN 55155

STUMPF, WILLIAM EUGENE, indsl. designer; b. St. Louis, Mar. 1, 1936; s. William G. and Ann J. (Kinzler) S.; B.F.A. in Indsl. Design, U. Ill., 1959; M.S. in Environ. Design (fellow), U. Wis., Madison, 1968; m. Sharon Rose Ford, Sept. 7, 1957; children—Jon, David, Carol, Karl, William. Designer, Peter Muller-Munk Assos., Pitts., 1959-62; research mgr. Franklin div. Studebaker Industries, 1962-66; asst. prof. design U. Wis., 1968-70, Inst. of Design, Ill. Inst. Tech., Chgo., 1970-72; v.p. Herman Miller Research Corp., Ann Arbor, Mich., 1970-72; owner, mgr. William Stumpf & Assos., Winona, Minn., 1972—; lectr., cons. on design. Mem. Zeeland (Mich.) Planning Commn., 1970-72. Served with USNR, 1955-60. Recipient Alcoa design award, 1959, award for furniture design Am. Soc. Interior Designers, 1976, Recource Council award, 1976, Design Mich. award, 1977. Mem. Indsl. Design Soc. Am. Author: Julia Child's Kitchen, 1977; contbr. articles to profl. jours. Home and Office: Pleasant Valley Route 3 Winona MN 55987

STUNARD, EUGENE WALTER, real estate appraiser; b. Chgo., Mar. 7, 1933; s. Louis and Harriet (Kurdas) S.; B.S., U. Ill., 1955; m. Joan Ann Stabach, June 22, 1955; children—Laura, Vicki, Walter. Regional appraiser Prudential Ins. Co. Am., Chgo., 1957-68; partner Real Estate Appraisal Corp., Oak Brook, Land Econ. Research Corp., Oak Brook, Ill., 1968; owner Real Estate Appraisal Co., Chgo., 1968—, pres. Appraisal Research Counselors, Ltd., Chgo., 1974—; instr. real estate appraisal Triton Coll., River Grove, Ill., 1966—; Am. Inst. Real Estate Appraisers, Chgo., 1974—. Village commr. Oak Park (Ill.) Plan Commn., 1973-76. Mem. real estate adv. com. Triton Coll., 1967—. Served with AUS, 1955-57. Mem. Am. Inst. Real Estate Appraisers, Appraisal Inst. Can., Soc. Real Estate Appraisers, Chgo. Real Estate Bd., Chgo. Mortgage Bankers and Chgo. Assn. Commerce and Industry, Lambda Alpha, Phi Eta Sigma, Delta Upsilon. Home: 155 Harbor Dr Chicago IL 60601 Office: 400 E Randolph Dr Chicago IL 60601

STURDEVANT, JAMES MICHAEL, mfg. co. exec.; b. Portsmouth, Va., Dec. 20, 1949; s. Glenn Wilson and Mamie Elizabeth (Foit) S.; A.B., Atlantic Christian Coll., 1972; children—Elizabeth, Jason, Seth. Expediter, Adams Concrete Products Co., Raleigh, N.C., 1972; plant supr. Mallinckrodt, Inc., St. Louis, 1974, customer service rep., 1975, sales rep., 1976, asst. product mgr., 1977, sales rep., 1978, sales mgr. Midwest region, 1981—. Recipient Top Producer of Yr. award Mallinckrodt, Inc., 1978, Salesman of Yr. award, 1979. Mem. Jaycees. Republican. Baptist. Office: PO Box 5840 Saint Louis MO 63134

STURGES, ALLAN WILLIAM, educator; b. Red Willow, Alta., Can., Oct. 23, 1927; s. William F. and Laura (Johnson) S.; B.A., N.W. Nazarene Coll., 1950; M.Ed., U. S.D., 1955; Ph.D., U. Iowa, 1959; children—Denyse Kim, Allan William II, Durwood D. Tchr., rural schs. Alta., 1945-46, secondary schs., S.D., 1951-52; prin., high sch., Iowa, 1956-58; prof. Winona (Minn.) State Coll., 1956-61; prof., head dept. edn. U. N.D., Grand Forks, 1964-71; prof., head dept. edn. U. Mo., Columbia, 1971—, also dir. edn. field experiences; adviser UNESCO, Thailand, 1967-68, 79, Pakistan, 1981. Ford travel grantee, Balkans, USSR, 1971. Mem. Assn. Supervision and Curriculum Devel., Phi Delta Kappa, Pi Lambda Theta. Contbr. articles to profl. jours. Office: Coll Edn U Mo Columbia MO 65211

STURM, BYRON DEWITT, regional planning exec.; b. Akron, Ohio, Sept. 6, 1937; s. Conrad and Edna Allrutz; student Case Western Res. U., 1978-80; B.S.C.E., Akron U., 1981; m. Beverly Joann Moss, Feb. 11, 1961; children—Mark, David, Adam, Matthew, Melissa. Tech. dir. Akron Met. Area Transp. Authority, 1961-68, city urban renewal mgr., 1968-72; asst. planning dir. Md. Dept. Transp., Balt., 1972-73; project mgr. Dalton, Dalton, Little and Newport, Warrensville Heights, Ohio, 1973-75; exec. dir. N.E. Ohio Four County Regional Planning and Devel. Orgn., Akron, 1975—; lectr. in urban planning U. Akron, 1965. Mem. planning and priorities com. United Way Summit County (Ohio), 1969-70. Registered profl. engr., cert. planner-in-charge, Ohio. Mem. Am. Planning Assn., Nat. Assn. Devel. Orgns. Club: Hoban High Sch. Booster. Author profl. reports. Office: 137 S Main St Akron OH 44308

STURM, HOWARD HERBERT, property mgmt. co. exec.; b. Amery, Wis., July 3, 1943; s. Herbert and Ethel Sturm; grad. public schs.; m. Mary Ellen Evenson, June 10, 1977; children—Angelique, Monique. With Turtlelake Creamery, Turtle Lake, Wis., 1963-65; with Anderson Window Corp., Bayport, Minn., 1965-69; owner, mgr. Sturm's Grocery & Sporting Goods, Range, Wis., 1969-71; salesman Coleman Co., Iowa and Minn., 1971-73; salesman Artic Cat, Minn., 1973-74; mgr. Farm and Ranch div. Lincoln Properties, Inc., Lakeville, Minn., 1974-79; gen. mgr. Realty Market Inc., 1979-80. Mem. Farm and Land Inst. (bd. dirs.), Am. Soc. Farm Mgrs. and Rural Appraisers. Congregationalist. Home: Box 282 Rural Route 2 Cannon

Falls MN 55009 Office: Box 68 Cannon Plaza S Cannon Falls MN 55009

STURM, MARK ALBERT, agronomist; b. Aurora, Ill., Apr. 6, 1957; s. William Herbert and Patricia C. Sturm; B.S., So. Ill. U., 1979; m. Vickie Lee Richmond, Jan. 10, 1981. Agronomist, Brandt Fertilizer & Chem. Co., Pleasant Plains, Ill., 1979—; research dir. Brandt Chem. Co., Inc.; participant So. Ill. Fertilizer and Herbicide Conf.; mem. Ill. Pesticide Waste Disposal Task Force. Mem. Am. Soc. Agronomy, Soil Sci. Soc. Am. Home: Rt 1 Pleasant Plains IL 62677 Office: Box 277 Pleasant Plains IL 62677

STURM, WILLIAM JAMES, adminstrv. nuclear physicist; b. Marshfield, Wis., Sept. 10, 1917; s. Jacob and Catherine (Coughlin) S.; B.S., Marquette U., Milw., 1940; M.S., U. Chgo., 1942; Ph.D. (AEC fellow and Univ. fellow), U. Wis., 1949; m. Arleen L. Weide, Aug. 20, 1951; children—Diana Patrice, Elissa Monique. Research asst. Metall. Lab., Manhattan Project U. Chgo., 1942-43; jr. physicist Argonne (Ill.) Nat. Lab., 1943-46, group leader, 1945-47, asso. physicist, 1946-47, cons. physicist, 1949-51, asso. physicist, 1956-59, mem. faculty Internat. Sch. Nuclear Sci. & Engring., Argonne Nat. Lab., 1960-66; mem. staff Office Coll. and Univ. Cooperation, 1965-66, asst. dir. applied physics div., 1967—; physicist Oak Ridge (Tenn.) Nat. Lab., 1951-53, sr. physicist, 1953-56; participating physicist, first self-sustaining nuclear chain reaction, U. Chgo. Recipient Commemorative medal Am. Nuclear Soc., 1962; Nuclear Pioneer award Soc. Nuclear Medicine, 1977. Contbr. articles to profl. jours. Home: 5400 Woodland Ave Western Springs IL 60558 Office: Argonne National Lab 9700 S Cass Ave Argonne IL 60439

STURTZ, CHARLES FREDERICK, univ. adminstr.; b. Bucyrus, Ohio, Aug. 26, 1936; s. Frederick Freeman and Jemima (Scott) S.; B.A., Wittenberg U., 1958; M.A. in Public Adminstrn. (Upson/Volker Citizens Research Council fellow), Wayne State U., 1961; m. Judith Elsie Flook, June 13, 1959; children—Michael, Mark, Matthew, Christopher, Karen. Research asso. Citizens Research Council Mich., Lansing, 1959-64; state budget analyst to dir. Office of Gov., Mich. Dept. Mgmt. and Budget, Lansing, 1964-75; v.p. for bus., fin., treas. Wayne State U., 1975-79, sr. v.p. adminstrn. and fin., 1979-81, exec. v.p., treas., 1981—; adj. prof. polit. sci. Mich. State U., spring 1975. Mem. dist-wide study com. (3) Lansing Public Schs., 1964-75; bd. dirs., mem. exec. com., chmn. budget steering Capitol Area United Way, Lansing, 1974-75; trustee, mem. exec. com. Detroit Receiving Hosp. and Univ. Health Center, 1980—; mem. fin. com. Lutheran Social Services of Mich., 1980—. Mem. Nat. Assn. Coll. and Univ. Bus. Officers, Nat. Assn. State Univs. and Land Grant Colls. (council on bus. affairs), Am. Soc. Public Adminstrn. Lutheran. Office: 1150 Mackenzie Hall Wayne State U Detroit MI 48202

STUTSMAN, WARREN EARL, asso. realtor; b. Deputy, Ind., Sept. 27, 1940; s. W. Warren and M. Marie (Howell) S.; B.S., Bob Jones U., 1966; m. Joy Ann Robinson, Aug. 18, 1962; children—Jennifer Lynn, Janelle Ann. Auditor, Arthur Andersen & Co., Indpls., 1966-69, dir. of office adminstrn., 1969-72; dir. fin. Indpls. Baptist Temple & Indpls. Baptist Schs., Inc., 1972-77; asso. realtor F.C. Tucker Co., Inc., Indpls., 1977—. Sec. Indpls. Bapt. Schs., Inc., 1971-77, treas., 1971-77; deacon Indpls. Bapt. Temple, 1968-70, 72, chmn. bd. trustees, 1972, jr. high dept. Sunday sch. supt., 1969-77. Mem. Met. Indpls. Bd. Realtors, Farm and Land Inst., Bob Jones U. Alumni Assn., Econ. Club of Indpls. Home: 2210 Brewer Dr Indianapolis IN 46227 Office: 2152 E S County Line Rd Indianapolis IN 46227

STUTZMAN, JACOB WILLIAM, pharm. co. exec.; b. Berlin, Pa., Jan. 17, 1917; s. Jacob Keener and Dora Mae (Felton) S.; B.S., Franklin and Marshall Coll., 1937; Ph.D., U. Wis., 1941, M.D., 1943; m. Geraldine Knepper Johnson, Aug. 6, 1946; 1 son, Walter Jacob. Asst. prof. physiology U. Wis. Med. Sch., 1946-47; asso. prof. pharmacology Boston U. Sch. Medicine, 1947-50; dir. pharmacology Smith Kline & French Labs., 1950-52; dir. biol. scis. Riker Labs. Inc. (became subs. Minn. Mining and Mfg. Co. 1970), St. Paul, 1952-53, v.p. research and devel., 1953-62, pres., 1962-66, 70—; chmn. ethical drug group Dart Industries, Los Angeles, 1966-70, dir. 1972-80. Trustee Franklin and Marshall Coll. Served with M.C., USNR, 1944-46. Fellow AAAS, Am. Physiol. Soc., Am. Soc. for Pharmacology and Clin. Research, Soc. for Exptl. Biology and Medicine, Am. Soc. for Pharmacology and Exptl. Therapeutics. Office: Riker Labs Inc 3M Center Bldg 225-5S Saint Paul MN 55144

STYKA, EDWARD JOHN, lawyer, acct.; b. Benald, Ill., Oct. 12, 1923; s. John and Catherine (Sapa) S.; B.S., DePaul U., 1948; postgrad. Northwestern U., 1948-56; J.D., DePaul U., 1960; m. Mildred Ann Holland, Oct. 14, 1945; children—David, Phillip, Linda, Sylvia. Asst. comptroller Individual Towel Co., 1948-50; chief fin. officer Calumet Index, 1950-56; sr. acct. John E. Burke, C.P.A.'s, Chgo., 1956-57; admitted to Ill. bar, 1962; chief fin. officer Robbins Co., 1957-63; chief fin. officer, gen. counsel Plastic Contact Lens Co., Inc., Chgo., 1963-67; counsel tax, ins. and benefits Scholl, Inc., Chgo., 1967-79, Elkay Mfg. Inc., Broadview, Ill., 1979—; treas., dir. Scholl Employee Credit Co. Served with USAAF, 1943. C.P.A., Ill. Mem. Ill. Bar Assn., Am. Bar Assn., Chgo. Bar Assn., Advocate Soc., Ill. Soc. C.P.A.'s, Chgo. Tax Club, Ill. C. of C. (mem. tax com.), Greater N. Michigan Ave Assn. (past dir.). Roman Catholic. Home: 17 W 731 Riordon Rd Villa Park IL 60181 Office: Elkay Mfg Co 2700 S 17th Ave Broadview IL 60153

STYLES, DOROTHY GENEVA, musician, educator, artist; b. Eldorado, Ark., Dec. 13, 1922; d. Alfred Alexander and Minnie Amy (Shelnut) Styles; diploma Detroit Inst. Mus. Art, 1945; Mus.B., U. Detroit, 1947; B.S. in Math., Columbia, 1954; M.A. in Lit., Eastern Mich. U., 1970, M.A. in Edn., U. Mich., 1970. Pvt. tchr. piano, Hazel Park, Mich., 1934—; organist Hazel Park Bapt. Tabernacle, 1932-43, 1st United Meth. Ch., Wayne, Mich., 1975—; organist, choir dir. First Bethany United Ch. of Christ, 1979—; choir dir. St. Timothy's Evang. Luth. Ch., Oak Park, Mich., 1970-71. Mem. Ruth Giese Com. for Needy Children, Hazel Park, 1971—. Mem. Mich. Festival Tchrs. Assn., Am. Coll. Musicians (certified), Am. Guild Organists, Nat. Assn. Organ Tchrs., Nat. Guild Piano Tchrs. (Hall of Fame), Detroit Musicians League (licentiate), Delta Omicron, Mensa. Composer: Lullaby, 1966; I Sing a Song, 1975; The Pledge of Allegiance to the Flag, 1976; Mrs. Santa Claus Loves Mr. Santa Claus, 1976; Mother, Tell Me, 1977. Author: (poetry) Young Verses for the Early Old; An Extension of the Idea of Countability as Applied to Real Numbers, 1966; A Prime Number Theorem, 1971; Projections of the Natural Harmonic Series: Some Implications, 1978; A Prime Number Sketchbook, 1979. Home and office: 443 W Evelyn St Hazel Park MI 48030

SUBA, ANTONIO RONQUILLO, surgeon; b. Philippines, Apr. 25, 1927; s. Antonio Mesina and Valentina Cabais (Ronquillo) S.; came to U.S., 1952, naturalized, 1961; M.D., U. St. Thomas, Philippines, 1952; m. Sylvia Marie Karl, June 16, 1956; children—Steven Antonio, Eric John, Laurinda Ann, Gregory Karl, Timothy Mark, Sylvia Kathleen. Intern, St. Anthony's Hosp., St. Louis, 1952-53; resident St. Louis County Hosp., St. Louis, 1953-57; trainee Nat. Cancer Inst., Ellis Fischel State Cancer Hosp., Columbia, Mo., 1957-59; chief surg. services U.S. Army, Bremerhaven, Germany, 1959-61; practice medicine specializing in gen. and hand surgery, St. Louis, 1961—; pres., prin. ARS, P.C., 1971—. Diplomate Am. Bd. Surgery. Fellow A.C.S.; mem. AMA, Pan-Pacific, Mo. State surg. assns., St. Louis Surg. Soc., Am. Assn. Hand Surgery. Club: K.C. Contbr. articles to med. jours. Home: 12085 Heatherdane Saint Louis MO 63131 Office: 141 N Meramec St Clayton MO 63105

SUBLETTE, RICHARD HORACE, newspaper exec.; b. Chgo., Apr. 3, 1934; s. Horace A. and Genevieve A. (McCormick) S.; B.S. in Broadcasting-Journalism, U. Ill., 1957, M.S. in Communications, 1962; m. Doris Lucille Moore, Jan. 27, 1957; children—April Jeanne, Melody Sue, Dawn Lucille. Mgr. Lowe's Discount Record, Champaign, Ill., 1957-62; account exec. WCHU-TV, Champaign, 1962; newspaper display advt. rep. Champaign-Urbana Courier, 1962-66; dir. advt. The Daily Illini, Champaign, 1966-70, pub., 1970—; gen. mgr. Illini Pub. Co., Champaign, 1970—. Sec. 6th Dist. Am. Advt. Fedn., 1968-70; v.p. Nat. Council Coll. Publs. Adviers, Inc., 1979-81; research coordinator Western Assn. Univ. Publs. Mgrs., 1978-82; bd. dirs. Champaign-Urbana Symphony Orch., 1980—, Cosmopolitan Frat., 1966-70; bd. dirs. Champaign-Urbana Fair Housing Bur., 1962-64, Campus Bus. and Mchts. Assn., 1970—. Mem. Am. Newspaper Publishers Assn., Internat. Newspaper Advt. Execs., Inland Daily Press Assn., Ill. Press Assn., Asso. Press Rep. for Daily Illini, Ill. Newspaper Adviser Group, Campus Bus. and Mchts. Assn., Campus Round Table, Univ. Ill. Alumni Assn., Western Assn. Univ. Publs. Mgrs., Champaign-Urbana Advt. Club, Champaign C. of C. Democrat. Methodist. Office: Illini Pub Co 620 E John St Champaign IL 61820

SUBTIRELU, MONICA PETRONELA, designer/architect; b. Romania, Sept. 22, 1945; d. Peter and Silvia S.; student Monterey Peninsula Coll., 1964-65, Ariz. State U., 1965-67, Pratt Inst., 1967-68, Kellogg Center for Continuing Edn., 1973, Columbus Tech. Inst., 1976-77, Wharton Sch. U. Pa., 1977. Archtl. designer Champion Bldg. Products Co., N.Y.C., 1967-72; dir. archtl. design Leisure Homes Inc., Youngstown, Ohio, 1972-73, Recreational Systems, Inc., Gainesville, Fla., 1973; archtl./engring. designer IBM, Poughkeepsie, N.Y., 1974; dir. archtl. design Cardinal Industries, Inc., Columbus, Ohio, 1974—; instr. visual arts, 1968-74; cons. interior design, 1967-74. Mem. AIA, Am. Mgmt. Assn., ASHRAE, Nat. Assn. Female Execs., Ohio Theater, Columbus Mus. Art. Club: Windsong Tennis. Office: 2040 S Hamilton Rd Columbus OH 43227

SUCCARI, OWAIS RIKKABI, internat. bus. cons., educator; b. Damascus, Syria, May 30, 1939; s. Bachir R. and Salwa A. (Murabet) S.; came to U.S., 1972, naturalized, 1975; B.A. with high honors, Damascus U., 1961; Ph.D., Louvain (Belgium) U., 1968; div.; 1 son, Alan. Officer, Syrian Ministry of Planning, Damascus, 1961-64; asst. prof. bus. Louvanium U., Kinshasha, Zaire, 1968-71; prof. mgmt. dept. DePaul U., Chgo., 1972—; exec. dir. Mid-Am. Arab C. of C., Chgo., 1974—. Mem. Acad. Mgmt., Acad. Internat. Bus., Chgo. Assn. Commerce and Industry, Chgo. Council Foreign Relations. Author: International Petroleum Market, Policy Confrontation of the Common Market and the Arab Countries, 1968. Home: 400 Main St Evanston IL 60202 Office: Mid-Am Arab Chamber of Commerce 135 S LaSalle St Chicago IL 60603

SUCHY, GREGORIA KARIDES (MRS. RAYMOND WILLIAM SUCHY), composer, educator; b. Milw.; d. George Peter and Maruly Alexander (Stratigos) Karides; B.S., Milw. State Tchrs. Coll., 1945; M. Music. Northwestern U., 1951, postgrad, summer 1957, 59, 60, DePaul U., 1959-60, 60-61, Roosevelt U., 1961-66, U. Chgo., 1967-69; m. Raymond William Suchy, Dec. 28, 1947; children—Jessica, Mara. Tchr. instrumental music Milw. Pub. Schs., 1943-44; tchr. piano and instrumental Northwestern Conservatory of Music, 1944-47; tchr. theory, instrumental teaching Carroll Music Studios, Milw., 1945; mem. faculty U. Wis., Milw., 1946—, prof. theory and composition dept. music Sch. Fine Arts, 1969—. Recipient Star award Delta Omicron, 1957, certificate of recognition Greek Orthodox Archidiocese of North and South Am., 1967, Univ. of Wis.-Milw. award for Excellence in Teaching 1979-80. Research grant Grad. Sch. U. Wis., 1960, 63, 65, 69, numerous prizes and awards including 1st prize Musicians Club of Women, Chgo., 1960, UWM grad sch. Faculty Computer-Assisted Music Composition 1979-80; grant for computer Graphics for Music by UWM Computer Center 1978-79, Central Adminstrn. U. Wis. for Teaching Improvement, Dean's Research Grant (Sch. of Fine Arts, UWM) 1976-77. Nat. Fedn. Music Clubs, 1973, Milw. Profl. Panhellenic Achievement award, 1973; Faculty fellow U. Wis., 1967. Mem. Am. Music Center, Inc., Delta Omicron, Internat. Soc. Comtemporary Music, Wis. Fedn. Music Clubs, Wis. Contemporary Composers Forum, Milw. Civic Concert Assn. (dir. 1948-59, pres. 1956-57, pres. ex officio, 1959). Am. Soc. of Univ. Composers, Am. Women Composers Inc., Civic Music Assn. of Milw., MacDowell Club of Milw., Nat. Assn. of Composers USA, Phi Hellenic Soc. of Wis., Soc. for Music Theory, Univ of Wis.-Milw. Com. on the Status of Women, Kappa Delta Pi. Mem. Greek Orthodox Ch. Home: 2601 E Newton Ave Milwaukee WI 53211 Office: Sch of Fine Arts Dept of Music U Wis Milwaukee WI 53201

SUDHEIMER, BARBARA LOUISE, educator; b. Rochester, Minn., June 13, 1932; d. Harold Clyde and Alberta Eva (Farley) Bowman; B.S. cum laude, U. Minn., Duluth, 1954; m. Richard H. Sudheimer, Nov. 30, 1957. Tchr. English, St. Louis Park (Minn.) Public Schs., 1955-57, Brookville (Ohio) Public Schs., 1958-63, Fairmont East High Sch., Kettering, Ohio, 1963—. Mem. NEA, Ohio Edn. Assn., Kettering Classroom Tchrs. Assn., Nat. Council Tchrs. English, Delta Kappa Gamma (pres. chpt. 1974-76), Assn. for Supervision and Curriculum Devel.). Home: 4358 Carlo Dr Kettering OH 45429 Office: Fairmont East High Sch 3000 Glengarry Dr Kettering OH 45420

SUDHEIMER, RICHARD HAROLD, systems engr.; b. Waconia, Minn., Sept. 16, 1933; s. Edward Andrew and Lydia Martha (Zeman) S.; B. Aero. Engring., U. Minn., 1956; postgrad. Ohio State U., 1964-68; m. Barbara Louise Bowman, Nov. 30, 1957. Asso. devel. engr. Honeywell Corp., Mpls., 1956-57; aerospace engr. U.S. Air Force, Wright Patterson AFB, Ohio, 1960-67, supv. aerospace engr., 1967-70, ops. research analyst, 1970-76, systems study engr., 1976—. Served with USAF, 1957-60. Registered profl. engr., Ohio; Stanford Sloan fellow, 1970-71. Mem. Am. Inst. Aeros. and Astronautics, Am. Def. Preparedness Assn., Air Force Assn., Assn. Old Crows, Toastmasters Internat. Lutheran. Contbr. articles to profl. jours. Home: 4358 Carlo Dr Kettering OH 45429 Office: ASD/XRM Wright Patterson AFB OH 45433

SUDILOVSKY, OSCAR, physician, educator; b. Rosario, Argentina, Nov. 8, 1933; s. Malquiel and Esther (Busel) S.; B.S., Nat. Coll., Tucuman, Argentina, 1949; M.D., U. Littoral, Argentina, 1959; Ph.D., Case Western Res. U., 1972. Licensed Argentina, 1959, Ohio, 1976; m. 1961; 4 children. Intern, Hosp. Nacional del Centenario, Rosario, 1957-58; resident Mt. Sinai Hosp., Cleve., 1962-64; USPHS fellow in pathology and oncology U. Kans. Med. Center, 1964-67; with dept. pathology U. Littoral, 1959-62, also chief tissue culture lab.; instr. dept. pathology Case Western Res. U., 1967-70, asst. prof., 1970-76, dir. autopsy service, 1971-76, asso. prof., 1976—, dir. Tissue Culture lab., 1976—; fellow McArdle Lab. for Cancer Research, 1969-71; mem. Pathology B study sect. NIH, 1980; adj. staff cons. in pathology div. research Cleve. Clinic, 1975-78. NIH Spl. Research fellow, 1967-69, 69-71; recipient Gold Medal award Nat. Coll., Tucuman, 1949. Mem. Am. Assn. Cancer Research, Am. Assn. Pathologists, Am. Soc. Clin. Pathologists, Internat. Acad. Pathology, N.Y. Acad. Sci., Tissue Culture Assn., Sigma Xi. Contbr. articles in field to profl. jours. including Science, Cancer Research, Analytical Biochemistry and others. Address: 2085 Adelbert Rd Cleveland OH 44106

SUDIMACK, JOSEPH, JR., physician; b. Bayonne, N.J., May 15, 1928; s. Joseph H. and Miriam (Tarasevick) S.; B.A., Ohio State U., 1949, M.Sc., 1952, M.D., 1956; children—Joseph III, James M., Jeffrey S., Miriam J., John R., Amy Jo, Jennifer Jo; m. Linda M. Sudimack, Dec. 22, 1973. Intern, Lankenau Hosp., Phila., 1956-57; practice medicine specializing in occupational medicine, Warren, Ohio, 1959—; past pres. staff Trumbull Meml. Hosp.; mem. staff St. Joseph's Hosp., Warren; med. dir. Republic Steel Corp., Mahoning Valley Dist., Ohio, 1980—; coroner Trumbull County, 1960—. Bd. dirs. Trumbull County Heart Assn.; trustee Trumbull County Community Chest, 1979—, Health Systems Agy. Eastern Ohio, 1980—. Served with USNR, 1957-59. Fellow Indsl. Med. Assn., Am. Occupational Med. Assn.; mem. Ohio Med. Assn. (del.), Trumbull County Med. Soc. (past pres.), Trumbull County Acad. Gen. Practice (past pres.), Ohio Coroners Assn. (pres. 1981-82), Nat. Football Found., Ohio State U. Alumni Assn. (past pres. Trumbull County), Warren Area C. of C. Republican Congl. Club, Sigma Xi, Sigma Nu. Republican. Clubs: Elks, Presidents, Faculty (Ohio State U.); Buckeye, Trumbull Country. Home: 8625 Deer Creek Ln Warren OH 44484 Office: 121 Center St W Warren OH 44481

SUEDHOFF, CARL JOHN, JR., lawyer; b. Fort Wayne, Ind., Apr. 22, 1925; s. Carl John and Helen (Lau) S.; B.S., U. Pa., 1948; J.D., U. Mich., 1951; m. Carol Mulqueeney, Apr. 10, 1954; children—Thomas Lau, Robert Marshall, Mark Mulqueeney. Admitted to Ind. bar, 1951; asso. mem. firm Hunt & Mountz, Fort Wayne, 1951-54; partner Hunt, Suedhoff, Borrorr & Eilbacher, and predecessors, 1955—; officer, dir. Inland Chem. Corp., Fort Wayne, 1952—; pres., dir. Lau Bldg. Co., Fort Wayne, 1951—, S.H.S. Realty Corp., Toledo, 1960—; officer, dir. Inland Chem. P.R., Inc., San Juan, P.R., 1972—; others. Mem. Allen County Council, 1972-76, pres., 1974-76; mem. Allen County Tax Adjustment Bd., 1973-74, N.E. Ind. Regional Coordinating Council, 1975-76; bd. dirs. YMCA, Fort Wayne, 1961-63. Served with AUS, 1943-45. Mem. VFW (comdr. 1958-59), Am., Ind., Allen County bar assns., Beta Gamma Sigma, Phi Delta Phi, Psi Upsilon. Republican. Lutheran. Clubs: Univ. Michigan (pres. 1965-66), Friars, Fort Wayne Country. Office: 900 Inland Bldg Fort Wayne IN 46802

SUELTER, DENNIS DEE, printing co. exec.; b. Salina, Kans., Oct. 22, 1948; s. Lorenz H. and Edna J.S.; B.S., Ft. Hays Kans. State U., 1970; m. Therese Anne Schmidtberger, Sept. 25, 1971; children—Jason Lorenz, Emily Elizabeth. Retail advt. assn. mgr. Dave Cook Sporting Goods, Denver, 1971-73; account exec., direct mail and mail order art dir. Holubar Mountaineering Ltd. subs. Johnson Wax Co., Boulder, Colo., 1973-78; account exec. advt. mgr. Arrow Printing Co., Salina, 1979—. Served with U.S. N.G., 1970-72. Roman Catholic. Home: Gen Delivery Beverly KS 67423 Office: Arrow Printing Co 119 S 7th St Salina KS 67401

SUELZLE, H. MARIJEAN, sociologist; b. Winnipeg, Man., Can., Feb. 23, 1940; d. John and Winnifred Mary (Ward) Ferguson; came to U.S., 1968; B.A., U. Alta., (Edmonton, Can.), 1966, M.A., 1969; Ph.D., U. Calif., Berkeley, 1977; m. William Kevin O'Connell, Sept. 23, 1972; 1 dau., Kimberly Ann. Instr. sociology U. Alta., Edmonton, Can., 1970; lectr. Calif. State U., San Francisco, 1971-72; acting asst. prof. U. Calif., Berkeley, 1972-74; asst. prof. Northwestern U., Evanston, Ill., 1974—. Danforth asso., 1976-82; grantee Ill. Dept. Mental Health and Devel. Disabilities, Russell Sage Found. Mem. Am. Assn. Public Opinion Research, Midwest Assn. Public Opinion Research (sec. treas. 1979-80), Soc. Study Social Problems, Am. Acad. Mental Retardation, Am. Assn. Mental Deficiencies, Am. Sociol. Assn., Nat. Assn. Edn. Young Children, Chgo. Assn. Edn. Young Children, Nat. Council Family Relations, Nat. Fedn. Bus. and Profl. Women's Clubs, Vanier Inst. of Family. Author: Child Care and Children's Social Development, 1976; Early Childhood Socialization in Great Britain, 1977; The World of the Developmentally Disabled Child, 1979. Home: 1926 Morse Ave Chicago IL 60626 Office: Dept Sociology Northwestern U Evanston IL 60201

SUEN, LAI-CHERNG, computer engr.; b. Taipei, Taiwan, Apr. 20, 1948; s. Ping-Haung and Hsueh-Yeh (Huang) S.; M.S., U. Notre Dame, 1974, Ph.D., 1977; came to U.S., 1972; m. Cheing-Mei Wang, July 26, 1977; 1 son, Robert. Mem. tech. staff Bell Labs., Naperville, Ill., 1977—. Mem. IEEE, Sigma Xi. Author: An Introduction to Fourier Analysis 1972; Boolean Algebra and Its Applications, 1972; Electronic Computer, vols. I and II, 1973; contbr. articles to profl. jours. Home: 210 Ketten Dr Naperville IL 60540 Office: Bell Labs Naperville-Wheaton Rd Naperville IL 60566

SUHADOLNIK, GARY C., state senator, indsl. engr.; b. Cleve., Apr. 20, 1950; s. John F. and Eleanor D. (Vorthman) S.; B.I.E., Cleve. State U., 1973; m. Nancy C. Davis, Aug. 2, 1969; children—Timothy, Jena. Foreman, Jones & Laughlin Steel Corp., 1969-71; mfg. engr. Gen. Electric Co., Cleve., 1971-74; indsl. engr. Republic Steel Corp., Cleve., 1974—; mem. Ohio Senate, 1981—. Mem. Parma Heights (Ohio) City Council, 1978-80. Mem. Parma Heights Jaycees, Friends of Library, Greenbrier Theatre Guild. Republican. Presbyterian. Office: State House Annex Columbus OH 43215

SUITER, JAMES PATRICK, ins. co. exec.; b. Indianola, Nebr., Apr. 27, 1930; s. Charles Francis and Mary M. (Ryan) S.; m. Audrey Mary Anderjaska, Oct. 23, 1954; children—Timothy, Shawn, Brian, Chad, Angela. Lab. technician McCook (Nebr.) Dental Lab., 1953-65; exec. v.p. McCook C. of C., 1966-74; dist. mgr. Blue Cross-Blue Shield of Nebr., 1974—. Vice mayor City of McCook, 1968-69, mem. city council, 1976—. Served with U.S. Army, 1951-52. Decorated Bronze Star, Purple Heart. Mem. Jaycees (v.p. Nebr. 1963-64), Nebr. C. of C. Execs. (pres. 1973-74). Republican. Roman Catholic. Address: 916 E 7th St McCook NE 69001

SUJECKI, JOY MARY, hosp. med. service adminstr.; b. Milw., Nov. 29, 1935; d. John Henry and Helen Eleanor (Bronikowski) Jakubowski; B.S. in Med. Tech., Marquette U., 1957; M.A. in Mgmt., Central Mich. U., 1979; children—Ellen, Michael, Laura, Paul, Carol, Nancy, Thomas. Med. technologist Milw. Luth. Hosp., 1957; med. technologist in physicians office, Milw., 1958-59; med. technologist St. Luke's Hosp., Milw., 1961-62; med. technologist Trinity Meml. Hosp., Cudahy, Wis., 1969-75, lab. mgr. and supr., 1975—; moderator Milw. Regional Med. Tech. Student Bowl, 1976, 77, 78, Wis. Med. Tech. Student Bowl, 1978, 79. Den leader Cub Scouts Am., Milw., 1968-79; mem. lab. purchasing adv. com. Wis. Hosp. Council, 1975—; bd. dirs. Trinity Meml. Hosp. Aux., 1979—, pres., 1982—. Mem. Am. Soc. Clin. Pathology, Wis. Assn. Med. Technologists (edn. chmn. 1976-77), Clin. Lab. Mgmt. Assn., Am. Cancer Soc. (dir. south unit 1975-79). Roman Catholic. Asso. editor Our Lady of Lourdes News, 1974-75. Office: 5900 S Lake Dr Cudahy WI 53110

SUKHWAL, BHERU LAL, educator; b. Palana Kalan, Udaipur, India, June 18, 1929; s. Bhuri Lal and Narayani Bai (Upadhyay) S.; came to U.S., 1964; B.A., Agra U., 1957; B.Ed., U. Rajasthan, Jaipur, India, 1958, M.A. in Geography, 1960; M.A. (Fgn. student scholar), U. Oreg., 1966; Ph.D., U. Okla., 1969; m. Lilawati Sharma, Mar. 10, 1955; children—Aditya, Archna. Tchr., dir. edn., Ajmer, Rajasthan, 1954-60, sr. tchr. geography, dir. edn., 1960-64; map librarian univs. Oreg., Okla., 1964-69; asso. prof. geography U. Wis.-Platteville, from 1969, now prof., Faculty research grantee, 1971; vis. prof. U. Rajasthan, Jaipur, India, 1975, U. Madras, 1977; sr. research fellow Am. Inst. Indian Studies; NEDA grantee, 1968-69. Life mem. Am. Geog. Soc., Assn. Geography Tchrs. India, Geog. Soc. India; mem. Assn. Am. Geographers, Internat. Geog. Union, Wis., Nat. councils geog. edn., Gamma Theta Upsilon. Author: India: A Political Geography, 1971; A Systematic Geographic Bibliography on Bangladesh, 1973; Theses and Dissertations in Geography of South Asia, 1973; South Asia: A Systematic Geographic Bibliography, 1974. Contbr. articles to profl. jours. Home: 630 W Madison St Platteville WI 53818

SUKSI, JAMES MATTHEW, indsl. arts educator; b. Sault Ste. Marie, Mich.; s. William R. and Lillian S. Suksi; B.S. in Indsl. Edn., U. Wis., 1963, M.S. in Vocat. Edn., 1969; Ph.D. in Edn., So. Ill. U., 1977; m. Karen Lee Ketterl, Apr. 5, 1969; 1 son, Matthew Anders. Jr. high tchr. indsl. arts Los Angeles City Sch. System, 1963-65; instr. indsl. arts Bayport High Sch., Green Bay, Wis., 1965-66; supr. apprenticeship tng. Am. Motors Corp., Kenosha, Wis., 1966-67; tech. program instr. Gateway Tech. Inst., Kenosha, 1967-69, apprentice program coordinator, 1967-68, instructional resources specialist, 1968-69; instr. constrn. tech. programs Coll. of Lake County, Grayslake, Ill., 1969-75, coordinator engring./tech., 1971-76, dean career programs, 1976-77, dean career and program devel., 1977-80; fire sci. services program coordinator So. Ill. U., Carbondale, 1975-78, vis. asst. prof. Div. Baccalaureate Studies, 1976—, adminstrv. intern, 1976, vis. asst. prof. dept. indsl. tech., 1976—, vis. asst. prof. dept. vocat. edn. studies, 1979; head dept. engring. tech. Lake Superior State Coll., Sault Ste. Marie, Mich., 1980—, asso. prof. dept. engring. tech., 1980—; cons. to various community colls. and fire depts. of cities in Ill., 1975-81; chmn. Chgo. Suburban Council Career Deans, 1978-79. Bd. visitors Nat. Registry Examination System for Fire Protection Personnel, 1978—; bd. control Lake County Area Vocat. Center, 1976-80. Served with USMC, 1957-60. Recipient Outstanding Tchr. of Indsl Arts award Robert Fulton Jr. High Sch., 1965, Meritorious Service award Gateway Tech. Inst., 1968, Meritorious Teaching award Coll. of Lake County, 1973. Mem. Am. Vocat. Assn., Am. Tech. Edn. Assn., Am. Soc. Engring. Edn., Council Occupational Edn., Soc. Mfg. Engrs., Coop. Edn. Assn., Nat. Council Local Adminstrs., Nat. Fire Protection Assn., Nat. Assn. Indsl. Tech., Soc. Am. Mil. Engrs., Iota Lambda Sigma, Phi Kappa Phi, Phi Delta Kappa. Contbr. reports on indsl. edn. programs to profl. publs.; editor The Quar. Report, 1977. Home: 409 W Easterday Sault Ste Marie MI 49783 Office: Lake Superior State Coll Sault Ste Marie MI 49783

SUKUMARAN, KIZHAKEPAT PISHAROTH, anesthesiologist; b. Kollengode, India, Oct. 10, 1938; s. Chakrapani Pisharoth and Kochu (Pisharasyar) Pisharoty; came to U.S., 1972; M.D., U. Kerala (India), 1964; m. Kamala Sukumaran; children—Harry S., Suma. Intern, Calicut Med. Coll., Hosp., Kerala, 1954-65; resident in anesthesiology Epsom (Surrey, Eng.) Dist. Hosp., United Liverpool (Eng.) Hosps., Walton and Wiston Hosp., Liverpool, 1967-70; med. officer govt. service, India, 1965-67, house officer, 1967-70; sr. registrar Nat. Health Service, Liverpool, 1970-71; staff anesthesiologist Kristinehamn (Sweden) Hosp., 1972; fellow Mt. Sinai Sch. Medicine, N.Y.C., 1972, Dalhousie U., Halifax, N.S., Can., 1972-74; staff, chief dept. anesthesia St. Mary's Hosp., Saginaw, Mich., 1977—; cons. staff St. Luke's Hosp., Saginaw, 1975—; clin. asst. prof. surgery Mich. State U.; practice medicine specializing in anesthesiology and critical care, Saginaw. Diplomate Royal Coll. Surgeons, Royal Coll. Physicians, Am. Bd. Anesthesiology. Fellow Royal Coll. Surgeons Ireland; mem. AMA, Am. Soc. Anesthesiologists. Home: 3590 Hickory Ln Saginaw MI 48603 Office: St Mary's Hosp S Jefferson Ave Saginaw MI 48603

SUKUP, EUGENE GEORGE, mfg. exec.; b. Venus, Nebr., May 11, 1929; s. Louis and Dorothy Amelia (Buerkley) S.; student pub. schs.; m. Mary Elizabeth Bielefeld, Feb. 24, 1952; children—Charles Eugene, Steven Eugene. Farmer, Hampton, Iowa, 1946-51; owner, farm mgr., Dougherty, Iowa, 1951—; pres. Sukup Mfg. Co., Sheffield, Iowa, 1963—, Sukup Enterprises Inc., Sheffield, 1968—. Mem. Sheffield-Chapin Community Sch. Bd., 1967—; mem. County Extension Council, 1962-65; pres. Sheffield Community Club, 1972; bd. regents Waldorf Coll., Forest City, Iowa, 1977—; bd. dirs., pres. Sheffield Health Care Center. Mem. Iowa Mfrs. Assn., Farm Bur. Republican. Lutheran (ch. council 1970-72, pres. 1971). Patentee in field. Home: Dougherty IA 50433 Office: North Rd Sheffield IA 50475

SULAYMAN, RABI FUAD, physician; b. Fih, Lebanon, Apr. 18, 1942; came to U.S., 1971, naturalized, 1979; s. Fuad K. and Josephine K. (Khouri) S.; B.S., Am. U. of Beirut, Lebanon, 1964, M.D., 1968; m. Aida Nassif, June 12, 1971; children—Fuad Christopher, Karim Nicholas. Resident in pediatrics Am. U. Med. Center, Beirut, 1968-70, chief resident in pediatrics, 1970-71; sr. resident in pediatrics Children's Hosp. Med. Center, Harvard Med. Sch., Boston, 1971-72; fellow in pediatric cardiology U. Chgo., 1972-75; practice medicine specializing in pediatrics Beirut, 1975-76, Chgo., 1976—; asst. prof. pediatrics and pediatric cardiology Am. U. Med. Sch., Beirut, 1975-76; mem. staff Am. U. Med. Center, Beirut, 1975-76; asst. prof. pediatrics Rush Med. Coll., Chgo., 1976—, coordinator core clerkship program, 1979—; dir. pediatric residency program dir., Christ Hosp., Oak Lawn, Ill., 1979—, sect. head pediatric ambulatory services, 1976—, sect. head devel. pediatrics and human resources, 1977—, med. dir. and cons. child and family protective services, 1977—; mem. adj. attending staff Rush-Presbyn.-St. Luke's Med. Center, Chgo., 1976—; cons. pediatric cardiology Little Company of Mary Hosp., Evergreen Park, Ill., 1977—; lectr. pediatric cardiology U. Chgo., 1977—; mem. treatment services adv. com. Easter Seal Soc., Chgo., 1980—; mem. Nat. Adv. Com. on Pre-Sch. and Early Intervention Devel. Programs, 1981—. Bd. dirs. YMCA, Chgo., 1978—. Diplomate Am. Bd. Pediatrics. Fellow Am. Acad. Pediatrics; mem. Ill. State Med. Soc., Chgo. Med. Soc., Chgo. Assn. for Children with Learning Disabilities (dir. 1979—), Chgo. Heart Assn. (mem. com. on hypertension 1978—). Contbr. articles on pediatrics to med. jours. Home: 5825 S Dorchester Ave Chicago IL 60637 Office: 4440 W 95th St Oak Lawn IL 60453

SULEIMAN, LOUISE FRANCES, nurse, educator; b. Auburn, July 24; d. Thomas P. and Anna (Pilote) Wailus; B.S.N., Boston U., 1958, M.S.N., 1961, Ed.D., 1974; children by previous marriage—Ann, Carolyn. Asso. prof. nursing Boston U., 1962-68, Quinsigamond Community Coll., Worcester, Mass., 1969-74; asso. prof. nursing, also chairperson div. nursing Ind. U. S.E., New Albany, 1975-80, asst. dean baccalaureate nursing Sch. Nursing, 1979—; cons. in field. Ednl. dir. So. Ind. Health Systems Agy., 1975-78, sec., 1978—; USPHS nursing capitation grantee, 1975-79. Mem. Am. Nurses Assn., Ind. Nurses Assn., Nursing Coalition for Action in Politics, Sigma Theta Tau. Office: Ind U SE Sch Nursing 4201 Grant Line Rd New Albany IN 47150

SULLIVAN, BARRY FRANCIS, banker; b. Bronx, N.Y., Dec. 21, 1930; s. John J. and Marion V. (Dwyer) S.; student Georgetown U., 1949-52; B.A., Columbia U., 1955; M.B.A., U. Chgo., 1957; m. Audrey M. Villeneuve, Apr. 14, 1956; children—Barry, Gerald, Mariellen, Scott, John. With Inland Steel Co., Chgo., 1955-56; with Chase Manhattan Bank, N.A., N.Y.C., 1957-80, exec. v.p., mem. mgmt. com., 1974-80; chmn. bd. 1st Chgo. Corp./1st Nat. Bank of Chgo., 1980—. Trustee, U. Chgo.; mem. adv. council Coll. Bus. Adminstrn., U. Notre Dame; bd. visitors Sch. Bus. Adminstrn., Georgetown U.; mem. governing bd., trustee Art Inst. Chgo.; mem. devel. council Regis High Sch., N.Y.C.; mem. President's Club, Loyola U., Chgo. Clubs: Chicago, Commercial, Mid-Am., Mid-Day (Chgo.); Glen View. Office: One 1st Nat Plaza Chicago IL 60670

SULLIVAN, CHARMAINE WISNIEWSKI, bus. exec.; b. Chgo., May 19, 1952; d. Edmund Henry and Regina Anna (Trzybinski) Wisniewski; B.S. in Engring. Physics, U. Ill., 1974; M.B.A. in Mktg., Xavier U., 1978—; m. Stephan C. Sullivan, Apr. 4, 1981. Mfg. supr. Procter & Gamble, Chgo., 1974-76, project eng., Cin., 1976, asst. tech. brand mgr., 1976-77, tech. brand mgr., 1978-79, group leader process devel., 1979-80, group leader internat. product devel., 1980—. Mem. Soc. of Women Engrs., Internat. Microwave Power Inst. Club: Cin. Ski; Up Downtowners. Home: 15 N Applewood Ct Fairfield OH 45014 Office: 6060 Center Hill Rd Cincinnati OH 45224

SULLIVAN, DANIEL EDWARD, environ. engr.; b. Syracuse, June 10, 1949; s. Francis Joseph and Irene Marie (Kolts) S.; B.S. in C.E., U. Maine, 1971; M.S., Environ. and Water Resources Engring., Vanderbilt U., 1974, Ph.D., 1979; m. Charlotta Christina Thylen, Jan. 1, 1978; 1 son, Jacob Kristofer. Instr. chem. engring. Vanderbilt U., Nashville, 1978-79; staff engr., human and environ. safety div. Procter & Gamble Co., Cin., 1979—. Vol. reader Nashville Sch. for Blind, 1975-76. Mem. Am. Inst. Chem. Engrs. (asso.), Sigma Xi. Club: YMCA. Home: 12010 Deerhorn Dr Cincinnati OH 45240 Office: 5299 Spring Grove Ave Cincinnati OH 45217

SULLIVAN, DAVID STAFFORD, clin. psychologist; b. Oak Park, Ill., Dec. 11, 1943; s. Orville A. and Voris A. (Stafford) S.; B.A., No. Ill. U., 1965, M.A., 1968, Ph.D., 1974; m. Sharon Eenigenburg, May 30, 1964; 1 son, David. Asso. prof. psychology Wheaton (Ill.) Coll., 1969-75; pvt. practice clin. psychology N. Park Clinic, Park Ridge, Ill., 1974-81, Bklyn., 1981—; chief psychol. cons. Comprehensive Acctg. Co., Aurora, Ill., 1975-78; pres. Winners Sports Service, Bklyn., 1972—; pres. Stafford Pub. Co., Bklyn., 1973—. Chmn. bd. mgrs. Ryall YMCA-DuPage Club, Glen Ellyn, Ill., 1975-78. Certified clin. psychologist, Ill. Mem. Am., Ill. psychol. assns., Nat. Register Mental Health Service Providers, Am. Assn. Marriage and Family Counselors, Acad. Psychologists in Marriage and Family Therapy, Sigma Xi. Author (under pen name Donald Sullivan): (with Hank Adams) Thoroughbred Racing: Predicting the Outcome, 1974, The S/A Advanced Method for Throughbred Handicapping, 1975, Harness Racing: Predicting the Outcome, 1975, The S/A Advanced Method for Harness Handicapping, 1976; editor, author (under pen name Donald Sullivan): Winners Sports Service Football Newsletter, 1971—; contbg. editor (under pen name Donald Sullivan): The Sullivan-Adams Racing Newsletter, 1976—; contbr. articles in field to profl. psychol. jours.

SULLIVAN, GERARD, psychodramatist, psychotheologist; b. Yonkers, N.Y., Oct. 31, 1927; s. Simon Joseph and Julia Agnes (McCaffery) S.; student Capuchin Sem., 1949, 54, Moreno Acad., 1972; m. Sheila Lynn Miller, Mar. 12, 1977. Ordained priest Roman Catholic Ch., 1953; asst. pastor Our Lady of Sorrows Ch., N.Y.C., 1954-60; staff psychodramatist Southdown Inst., Aurora, Can., 1973-74; coordinator personal growth systems St. Anthony Hosp., Columbus, Ohio, 1974—; asst. mgr. med. dept. counseling services Ohio Bell Telephone Co. Served with U.S. Army, 1970. Mem. Am. Soc. Psychodrama and Group Psychotherapy, Am. Persônnel and Guidance Assn., Spiritual Serenity Soc. (pres. 1978). Home: 9074 Mink St Pataskala OH 43062 Office: 150 E Gay St Columbus OH

SULLIVAN, JAMES ROBERT, educator; b. Saginaw, Mich., Oct. 1, 1947; s. Daniel Robert and Ethelyn (Smith) S.; B.A., Mich. State U., 1971; M.A., Ball State U., 1973; Ed.S., Central Mich. U., 1977; M.A., U. Mich., 1980, postgrad. Javariana U. (Colombia), summer 1974, Harvard U., summer 1977; m. Vera Virginia Loomis, July 25, 1973. Asso. v.p./Mid-West regional rep. for U.S., Student Nat. Edn. Assn., Washington, 1971-72; teaching asst. Mich. State U., East Lansing, 1970-71; intern Mich. Edn. Assn., 1970-71; grad. teaching asst. Ball State U., Muncie, Ind., 1971-73; tchr. sociology N. Coll. Hill High Sch., Cin., 1973-74; tchr. Houghton Lake High Sch., 1976-77, chmn. social sci. dept., 1975-78; research asso. Project CHOICE, U. Mich., 1978-80; instr. Kirtland Community Coll., Roscommon, Mich., 1976-78; lectr. in field. Vice chmn. N.E. Mich. Profl. Devel. Adv. Council and Tchr. Center, 1977-78. Recipient Gov. of Mich. award Mich. Internat. Council, 1976. Mem. Houghton Lake Edn. Assn. (pres. 1976-78, chief negotiator 1975-77), Mich. Edn. Assn. (mem. internat. understanding commn. 1976—), NEA (nat. exec. com. 1971-72), Mich. Assn. for Supervision and Curriculum Devel., UN Assn. (speakers bur.), Ohio Edn. Assn., Nat. Council Social Studies, AAUP, Mich. Assn. Student Tchrs., Am. Assn. for Higher Edn., Am. Ednl. Research Assn., Am. Psychol. Assn., Houghton Lake Jr. C. of C. (dir. 1976-78), Kappa Delta Pi, Phi Delta Kappa. Address: 825 E University Apt 1 Ann Arbor MI 48104

SULLIVAN, JOHN JOSEPH, bishop; b. Horton, Kans., July 5, 1920; s. Walter P. and Mary (Berney) S.; student Kenrick Sem., St. Louis, 1941-44. Ordained priest Roman Cath. Ch., 1944; parish priest Archdiocese of Oklahoma City, 1944-61; nat. dir. extension lay vols. Extension Soc., Chgo., 1961-68; parish priest, Tulsa, 1968-72; bishop Diocese of Grand Island (Nebr.), 1972-77, of Kansas City-St. Joseph, Mo., 1977—. Vice pres. Extension Soc., Chgo. Address: PO Box 1037 Kansas City MO 64141*

SULLIVAN, JOHN LEONARD, public utility exec.; b. Kansas City, Kans., Aug. 29, 1923; s. Leonard Riley and Katherine Bell (Singleton) S.; corr. student Internat. Accts. Soc., 1951-57; m. Mary Jane Sechrest, Apr. 13, 1947; children—Kay Cheryl, Patricia Lee, John Michael. Acct., Kansas City, Suburban Water Co., Inc., 1947-57; acct. Water Dist. 1 of Johnson County, Mission, Kans., 1957-60, chief acct., office mgr., 1960-69, asst. controller, 1970, dir. fin., 1970—; acctg., fin. mgmt. cons. for small businesses, 1962—. Served with USNR, 1942-46. Mem. Adminstrv. Mgmt. Soc. (pres. Kansas City chpt. 1971-72, asst. area dir. 1972-73, Diamond Merit award 1975), Am. Water Works Assn., Nat. Assn. Accts., Overland Park (Kans.) C. of C. Presbyterian. Club: Sertoma (life, steering com. Theater in Park project 1976-78). Contbr. articles to Adminstrv. Mgmt., Public Works. Home: 9618 Nieman Pl Overland Park KS 66214 Office: Water Dist 1 Johnson County 5930 Beverly St Mission KS 66202

SULLIVAN, JOSEPH FRANCIS, JR., car rental exec.; b. Sioux City, Iowa, Sept. 15, 1932; s. Joseph Francis and Martha (Wade) S.; B.A., U. Minn., 1954; m. Monica Lenz, May 21, 1955; children—Dennis, Richard, Theresa, Michael, Ann. Asst. product mgr. Gen. Mills, Mpls., 1957-58; media mgr. Hamm Brewing Co., St. Paul, 1958-59, point-of-sale advt. mgr., 1959-60, dir. advt. 1963-68, dir. public relations, 1968-69; v.p., dir. public relations Kaufmann Spicer Co., Mpls., 1969-72; dir. advt. and public relations Nat. Car Rental Systems, Inc., Mpls., 1972-80, v.p. mktg. 1980—. Served with USAF, 1955-57. Mem. Assn. Travel Mktg. Execs., Public Relations Soc. Am., Minn. Press Club. Republican. Roman Catholic. Home: 5133 Duggan Plaza Edina MN 55435 Office: 7700 France Ave South Edina MN 55435

SULLIVAN, PATRICK FLORENCE, clin. psychologist; b. Freeport, Ill., Nov. 26, 1942; s. Florence Leo and Magdalene Anne (Heinl) S.; student St. Benedict's Coll., 1960-63; B.A., U. Iowa, 1965, M.A., 1967; Ph.D., U. Vt., 1972; m. Jeanne Margaret Hildebrandt, Aug. 22, 1964; children—Suzanne Colleen, Daniel Florence, Sarah Elizabeth. Clin. psychology intern Des Moines Child Guidance Center, VA Hosp., 1967-68; instr., counselor Albion (Mich.) Coll., 1968-70; instr. U. Vt., 1971-72; clin. psychologist, program mgr. Polk County Mental Health Center, Des Moines, 1972-75; asst. prof. Grand View Coll., Des Moines, 1975-79; dir. criminal justice treatment unit Adapt, Inc., Des Moines, 1975-76; pvt. practice clin. psychology, Des Moines, 1975—; cons. Des Moines Police Dept.; cons., v.p. Polk County Rape-Sexual Assault Care Center. Commr. West Des Moines Park Bd., 1976-79, chmn., 1977-79; mem. City of West Des Moines Comprehensive Plan Com., 1978. Mem. Am. Psychol. Assn., Iowa Psychol. Assn. (pres. 1980-81, mem. exec. council 1978-82), Midwestern Psychol. Assn., Central Iowa Psychol. Assn., Am. Soc. Psychologists in Pvt. Practice, Assn. Advancement Psychology. Contbr. articles to profl. jours. Office: 1601 22d St Suite 210 West Des Moines IA 50265

SULLIVAN, PEGGY (ANNE), librarian, ednl. adminstr.; b. Kansas City, Mo., Aug. 12, 1929; d. Michael C. and Ella P. S.; A.B., Clarke Coll., 1950; M.S. in L.S., Catholic U. Am., 1953; Ph.D. (Tangley Oaks fellow 1968, Higher Edn. Act Title II fellow 1968-71), U. Chgo., 1972. Librarian in sch. and public libraries in Mo., Md. and Va., 1952-63; dir. Knapp Sch. Libraries Project, Chgo., 1963-68; asst. prof. Grad. Sch. Library and Info. Scis., U. Pitts., 1971-73; dir. Office for Library Personnel Resources, ALA, Chgo., 1973-74; asso. prof., dean students Grad. Library Sch., U. Chgo., 1974-77; asst. commr. Chgo. Public Library, 1977-81; prof., dean Coll. Profl. Studies, No. Ill. U., 1981—; UNESCO cons. on sch. libraries, Australia, 1970. Trustee, Clarke Coll., 1969-72. Mem. ALA (pres. 1980-81), Ill. Library Assn., Assn. Am. Library Schs., Chgo. Library Club. Roman Catholic. Author: Problems in School Media Management, 1971; Carl H. Milam and the American Library Association, 1976; Opportunities in Library and Information Science, 1977. Office: 218 Williston Hall No Ill U De Kalb IL 60115

SULLIVAN, WARREN GERALD, diversified industry exec.; b. Chgo., Sept. 8, 1923; s. Gerald Joseph and Marie (Fairrington) S.; student U. Wis., 1943; A.B., U. Ill., 1947; J.D., Northwestern U., 1950; m. Helen Ruth Young, Aug. 21, 1948 (div. May 1974); children—Janet Marie, Warren Douglas, William Carroll; m. 2d, H. Louise Curtis, July 27, 1974. Admitted to Ill. bar, 1950, Conn. bar, 1971, Mo. bar, 1981; lawyer Ill. Dept. Revenue, Chgo., 1950-52; mem. firm Naphin, Sullivan & Banta, Chgo., 1952-60; asst. gen. counsel labor Avco Corp., Greenwich, Conn., 1969-70, v.p. adminstrn. and personnel 1971-75; v.p. indsl. relations Gen. Dynamics Corp., St. Louis, 1975—; dir. Asbestos Corp. Ltd., Stromberg Carlson Corp. Bd. dirs. United Way, St. Louis YMCA. Served with AUS, Mil. Intelligence Service, 1942-45; ETO. Mem. Am., Conn., Chgo. (vice chmn. labor law com. 1964-65, chmn. 1966-69) Bar assns., Am. Judicature Soc., Indsl. Relations Soc., Am. Soc. Personnel Adminstrs., Aerospace Industries Assn. (indsl. relations com.), Nat. Mgmt. Assn. (chmn. exec. adv. com. 1978), Econ. Club Chgo., Delta Tau Delta, Phi Delta Phi. Clubs: St. Louis; Bellerive Country. Contbr. articles to profl. jours. Home: 2482 Indian Tree Run Glencoe MO 63038 Office: Pierre Laclede Center Saint Louis MO 63105

SULLIVANT, ROBERT SCOTT, univ. adminstr., educator; b. Williams, Ariz., Jan. 23, 1925; s. Alexander Scott and Gladys (Hackett) S.; A.B., UCLA, 1947, M.A., 1948; Ph.D., U. Chgo., 1958; postdoctoral exchange scholar, Moscow State U., 1961; m. Enid Marie Olsen, Dec. 27, 1952; children—Wayne Arthur, Stephen Scott, Barbara Kay, Cynthia Lynn. Instr. polit. sci. U. S.D., 1951-54; sr. research analyst, research project Georgetown U., 1954-59; asso. prof. polit. sci. DePauw U., 1959-65; vis. asso. prof. U. Chgo., 1962-63; asso. prof., chmn. polit. sci. dept. U. Mo.-St. Louis, 1965-69, prof. polit. sci., dean Grad. Sch., dir. research, 1969-73; prof. polit. sci., exec. v.p. U. Toledo, 1973—; cons. Atlantic Research Corp., 1967-68. Served with USAAF, 1943-46. Fellow Am. Council Learned Socs., 1969; Samuel MacClintock fellow, 1948-49; fellow U. Chgo., 1949-50; NDEA fellow, 1960; fellow Russian Research Center, Harvard, 1969, Inst. Ednl. Mgmt., 1972; recipient award Inter-Univ. Com. Travel Grants, 1960, Social Sci. Research Council, 1961. Mem. Am., Midwest, Mo. (pres. 1969-70) polit. sci. assns., AAUP, Am. Assn. Advancement Slavic Studies, Phi Beta Kappa, Pi Sigma Alpha, Phi Kappa Phi. Author: Soviet Politics and the Ukraine, 1917-57, 1962. Office: 2801 W Bancroft St Toledo OH 43605*

SULTAN, MICHAEL JAY, salesman; b. Chgo., June 13, 1947; s. Leonard H. and Edna F. S.; B.S. in Bus. Adminstrn., Woodbury Coll., Los Angeles, 1971; m. Karon L. Komiss, Apr. 21, 1974 (div.); 1 son, Sean Michael. With Montgomery Ward Co., Los Angeles, 1971-74; acct. rep. Reliable Corp., Chgo., 1975—. Co-founder Northwest Big Bros.-Big Sisters, Hoffman Estates, Ill.; mem. Schumburg Twp. Com. on Youth, 1977—; mem. Schumburg Twp. Republican Com., 1978—, Hoffman Estates Youth Commn., 1979-81. Mem. Jaycees (internal v.p., 1978—). Club: Kiwanis (dir. 1975-78). Home: 2038 Parkview Circle W Hoffman Estates IL 60195 Office: 1001 W Van Buren St Chicago IL 60607

SULTAN, WILLIAM WOODROW, JR., indsl. and med. diagnostic cons.; b. Cleveland, Miss., Sept. 26, 1943; s. William Woodrow and Mary Helen (Burdine) S.; B.S. in Biology/Chemistry, Delta State U., 1964; M.S. in Microbiology/Biochemistry, Miss. State U., 1966; M.B.A., Lake Forest Sch. Mgmt. (Ill.), 1979; m. Gloria Herbison, Dec. 19, 1965; children—William Woodrow III, Jennifer Rebecca. Commd. 2d lt. USAF, 1966, advanced through grades to capt., 1968; chief of microbiology 5th Epidemiol. Lab., Manila, 1967-70; chief microbiology lab. Wright-Patterson AFB, Ohio, 1970-71; resigned, 1971; microbiologist Abbott Labs., North Chicago, Ill., 1971-72, sr. microbiologist, 1973-75, group leader, 1975-77, mgr. tech. support, 1978, mgr. mfg., 1978-81; pres. ME-DI-CO, Inc., med. diagnostic cons., Waukegan, Ill., 1981—. Vice-chairperson, Waukegan Housing Authority, 1977—; mem. Community Action Council, 1980-82; active local United Methodist ch., 1970—. NASA fellow, 1964-66; recipient Presdl. award Abbott Labs., 1975, 77, 78. Mem. Am. Soc. Microbiology, Am. Prodn. and Inventory Control Soc., Am. Mgmt. Assn., Res. Officers Assn., Phi Mu Alpha Sinfonia, Delta State U. Alumni Assn. Democrat. Contbr. articles to profl. jours. Home: 314 Douglas Ave Waukegan IL 60085 Office: 901 Grand Ave Waukegan IL 60085

SUMERFORD, KENNETH SCOTT, chemist; b. Springfield, Mo., Jan. 10, 1948; s. Milton Scott and Martha Lucille (Orr) S.; B.S., S.W. Mo. State U., 1970; M.B.A., 1973; m. Donna Elaine Copelin, Jan. 29, 1972; 1 dau., Angela. Mgr. toy dept. Venture Stores, 1974; chemist Caterpillar Tractor Co., East Peoria, Ill., 1974-80, chem. technician,

Mossville, Ill., 1980—; pres. Sumerford Assos., Inc. Mem. Mensa. Republican. Baptist. Home: 6102 N Idlewhile Peoria IL 61615

SUMMERS, CHARLES L., physicist, engr.; b. Kansas City, Kans., Feb. 24, 1933; s. Samuel and Sarah (Karo) S.; B.S., M.I.T., 1954; M.A., Columbia U., 1958. Research asst. Columbia U., 1959-62; space scientist Geophys. Corp. Am., Bedford, Mass., 1963-64; mem. tech. staff TRW Systems, Houston, 1966-70; mem. program staff AT&T, Kansas City, Mo., 1970-78; engr. Remington Arms, Independence, Mo., 1978—; instr. physics CCNY, 1962, U. Kans., 1965. Mem. Am. Phys. Soc., Sigma Pi Sigma. Club: Masons. Home: 1307 W 85th St Kansas City MO 64114

SUMMERS, CHRISTINE MARY, fin. exec.; b. Chgo., Nov. 28, 1951; d. John T. and Helen W. (Ambrozik) Soch; B.S.C., DePaul U., 1973, M.B.A., 1975; m. Patrick J. Summers, June 3, 1979. Staff acct. Continental Ill. Nat. Bank, Chgo., 1973, sr. corporate acct., 1975, sr. acct., 1976, acctg. officer, 1977, mgr. corp. reporting, 1979—, interviewer Coll. Relations Bd., 1978-79, mem. acctg. policy com., 1981. Mem. Nat. Assn. Bank Women, Am. Soc. Women Accts. (pres.). Office: 231 S LaSalle St Chicago IL 60693

SUMMERS, DAVID ARCHIBOLD, mining engr., educator; b. Newcastle-on-Tyne, Eng., Feb. 2, 1944; came to U.S., 1968; s. William Archibald and Margaret Kilpatrick (Little) S.; B.Sc., U. Leeds, 1965, Ph.D., 1968; m. Barbara Lois Muchnick, July 30, 1972; children—Daniel Archibald, Joseph Andrew. Asst. prof. U. Mo., Rolla, 1968-74, asso. prof., 1974-77, dir. rock mechanics and explosives research, 1976—, prof., 1977-80, Curators prof., 1980—; cons. high pressure water jet tech., mining engring. Recipient Brit. Ropes Mining prize, 1965, Alumni Merit award for research, 1974, G.C. Greenwell medal, 1978, NASA cert. of recognition, 1980. Fellow Instn. Mining Engrs.; mem. Instn. Mining and Metallurgy, AIME, ASME, Am. Soc. Engring. Edn., Rolla C. of C., Tau Beta Pi. Anglican. Research on use of high pressure water jets for use in excavating material. Home: 808 Cypress Dr Rolla MO 65401 Office: Dept Rock Mechanics University of Missouri Rolla MO 65401

SUMMERS, FRANK LESLIE, psychologist; b. Chgo., May 19, 1945; s. Paul and Lillian Summers; student U. Ill., 1962-64; B.A. in Philosophy, U. Calif., 1966; M.A. in Ednl. Psychology, Columbia Tchrs. Coll., 1969; M.A. in Clin. Psychology, U. Chgo., 1972, Ph.D., 1975; m. Aug. 23, 1966 (div.); 1 dau., Kristen. Staff psychologist dept. psychiatry Cook County Hosp., Chgo., 1974-75; asso. dept. psychiatry Northwestern U., 1976-79, asst. prof., 1979—; psychologist Sustaining Care Program, Inst. Psychiatry Northwestern Meml. Hosp., Chgo., 1976-79, dir. research and tng. Extended Ambulatory Care, 1979—; pvt. practice individual psychotherapy and psychol. testing, Chgo., 1977—. USPHS fellow, 1970-73; Northwestern U. grantee, 1979-80; grantee Dept. Mental Health, State of Ill., 1981. Mem. Am. Psychol. Assn., Am. Orthopsychiat. Assn., Chgo. Assn. for Psychoanalytic Psychology (founding mem.). Contbr. articles in field to profl. jours. Office: 259 E Erie St Chicago IL 60611

SUMMERS, H. MEADE, JR., lawyer; b. St. Louis, Mar. 12, 1936; s. H. Meade and Josephine Elizabeth (Hicks) S.; A.B., Brown U., 1958; J.D., U. Mich., 1961; m. Bonnie Barton, Sept. 2, 1960; children—H. Meade III, Elizabeth Barton. Admitted to Mo. bar, 1961, U.S. Supreme Ct. bar; practiced in St. Louis, 1961—; asso. firm Thompson & Mitchell, St. Louis, 1960-67. Chmn., Mo. Adv. Council on Hist. Preservation, 1973-78; mem. exec. com. Am. Revolution Bicentennial Commn. of Mo., 1973-76; mem. Thomas Hart Benton Meml. Homestead Commn., 1976-77, co-founder, v.p., bd. dirs. Mo. Heritage Trust, Inc., 1976-79; mem. Estate Planning Council St. Louis; mem. Old Post Office Landmark Com., St. Louis, 1969—; mem. exec. com. St. Louis-St. Louis County Commn. on Equal Ednl. Opportunities, 1968-74; chmn. legis. com. City of Ladue (Mo.), 1976—; bd. dirs. Landmarks Assn. St. Louis, 1969—, pres., 1972-73, counselor, 1973—; mem. St. Louis County Hist. Bldgs. Commn., 1971—; bd. advisers Churchill Sch., St. Louis, 1977—; mem. Preservation Task Force of East-West Gateway Coordinating Council, 1976-80, Gateway Preservation Com., 1981—. Mem. Am., Mo., St. Louis County, St. Louis Met. (spl. com. on jud. refrom 1975-76) bar assns., Nat. Trust Historic Preservation, Preservation Action, State Hist. Soc. Mo., Mo. Hist. Soc. (trustee 1978—), St. Louis Met. C. of C. (edn. com. 1964-74, chmn. com. 1972-74), Beta Theta Pi, Phi Delta Phi. Clubs: Rotary, Clayton Twp. Republican Club (vice chmn. 1970-73). Home: 42 Woodcliffe Rd Ladue MO 63124 Office: 7777 Bonhomme Ave Saint Louis MO 63105

SUMMERS, JACKIE LEO, urologist; b. Clarksburg, W.Va., Feb. 18, 1939; s. Leo George and Margaret Eva (Snyder) S.; A.B., W.Va. U., 1962, M.D., 1966; m. Patricia Ann Walrond, Sept. 12, 1964; children—Scott Alan, Marcia Lynn. Intern, Akron (Ohio) City Hosp., 1966-67, resident in surgery, 1967-68, resident in urology, 1970-73; staff Akron Urol. Assos. (Ohio), 1973-79; chmn. dept. urology, mem. teaching staff Akron City Hosp.; prof. urology N.E. Ohio U. Coll. Medicine; clin. prof. W.Va. U. Served with USNR, 1968-71. Recipient Thirlby award, 1978, research award Arthritis Found., 1972, research award Kidney Found., 1973; diplomate Am. Bd. Urology. Fellow A.C.S.; mem. Am. Urol. Assn., Am. Fertility Soc., Am. Assn. Clin. Urologists, AMA, Ohio Med. Assn., Summit County Med. Soc. Methodist. Contbr. articles to profl. jours. Office: 75 Arch St Akron OH 44304

SUMMERS, JAMES EDWARD, aluminum co. adminstr.; b. Jackson, Tenn., Dec. 27, 1944; s. Leon Edward and Grace Kathryn (Brock) S.; B.A. in Econs. and Bus. Adminstrn., North Park Coll., 1974; m. Huong Le Thi, Oct. 19, 1965. Office mgr. Sunkist Growers Product Sales Co., Berwyn, Ill., 1970-72; asst. customer service mgr. Follet Pub. Co., Chgo., 1972-76; distbr. specialist, adminstrv. asst. Alumax Mill Products Inc., Westmont, Ill., 1976, advt. mgr., adminstrv. asst. to v.p. sales and mktg., 1976—. Served with U.S. Army, 1961-65; Vietnam. Decorated Army Commendation medal. Mem. Adminstrv. Mgmt. Soc. (asso.), Am. Numis. Assn., Delta Mu Delta, Alpha Nu. Methodist. Office: Alumax Mill Products Inc 700 E Ogden Ave Westmont IL 60559

SUMMERS, R. KIM, telephone co. ofcl.; b. Gaylord, Mich., Mar. 4, 1956; s. Leonard J. and Betty A. (Farrand) S.; B.S., Central Mich. U., 1978. Info. systems asst. Gen. Telephone Co. of Mich., Muskegon, 1978-79, info. systems analyst, 1979-80, sr. info. systems analyst, 1980—. Co-chmn. campaign United Way of Muskegon County. Mem. Central Mich. U. Alumni Assn. Club: Central Mich. U. Century. Office: 455 E Ellis Rd RC-3520 Muskegon MI 49443

SUMMERS, ROBERT CHARLES, mfg. co. ofcl.; b. Lakewood, Ohio, June 11, 1937; s. Homer V. and Irma (Truman) S.; B.A. in Labor Econs., Kans. State U., 1965; postgrad. U. Mich., 1975; m. Linda Webber, July 27, 1974; children—Kevin, Brian. With personnel dept. RCA, Bloomington, Ind. and Findlay, Ohio, 1969-73, McCall Pattern Co., Manhattan, Kans., 1974-76, Bear Mfg. Co., Rock Island, Ill., 1976; personnel mgr. Kawasaki Motors Corp. U.S.A., Lincoln, Nebr., 1976—; instr. labor relations Scott Community Coll., Eastern Iowa; speaker before ednl. and profl. groups. Chmn. bus. com. Great Teaching Program, Nebr. Wesleyan U. Mem. Lincoln C. of C. (past chmn. indsl. com.), Nat. Assn. Commerce and Industry, Adminstrv. Mgmt. Soc. Republican. Methodist. Home: 7600 Otoe St Lincoln NE 68506 Office: Kawasaki Motors Corp 6600 NW 27th St Lincoln NE 68524

SUMMERSETT, KENNETH GEORGE, psychiatric social worker, educator; b. Marquette, Mich., Mar. 9, 1922; s. Frank Elger and Ruth H. (Fairbanks) S.; B.S., No. Mich. U., 1948, M.A. in Sociology, 1964; M.S.W., Wayne State U., 1951; student U. Puget Sound, 1942-43; m. Vivian M. Wampler, June 17, 1950; children—Nancy M., Kenneth R., Mark G. With Mich. Dept. Mental Health, 1950—, Marquette (Mich.) Child Guidance Clinic, 1950-52; chief psychiat. social worker Battle Creek (Mich.) Child Guidance, 1952-54; dir. social services Newberry (Mich.) State Hosp., 1954-66, dir., cons. social services, 1966-73, adminstrv. dir. community psychiatry, 1973—, mental health exec., 1975—, dir. community services div., 1975—; extension prof. sociology dept. No. Mich. U., 1962-70; lectr. sociology Lake Superior State Coll., 1968—. Mem. Upper Peninsula Mental Health Planning Com., 1964-65, Mich. Task Force Com. Mentally Retarded, 1964-65, Upper Peninsula Mental Health Com. for Comprehensive Health Planning, 1972-75, Mich. Dept. Mental Health Legis. Planning Com. Release Planning, 1975—. Bd. dirs. Eastern Upper Penninsula Mental Health Clinic, v.p., 1970-72; bd. dirs. Luce County Extension Program, sec. bd., 1972-75. Served with AUS, 1943-46. Certified marriage counselor. Mem. Nat. Assn. Social Workers (chmn. upper Peninsula chpt. 1957-59, 64-65, vice chmn. 1972-73), Acad. Certified Social Workers, Theta Omicron Rho. Clubs: Lions (pres. 1959-60), Elks (maj. projects chmn. 1968-70). Author various articles pub. in profl. jours. Home: 217 W Truman Blvd Newberry MI 49868 Office: Newberry Regional Mental Health Center Newberry MI 49868

SUMMERVILLE, JANE ELEANOR SCHNEIDER, public relations exec.; b. Dayton, Ohio, Aug. 26, 1942; d. Robert Charles and Mildred Eleanor (McManaman) Schneider; B.A. in Journalism, Ohio State U., 1964; postgrad. Xavier U., 1967-68; m. Ward Summerville, Aug. 4, 1979. Asst. to pres. Paul Werth Assos., Columbus, Ohio, 1967-68; dir. publs. Cin. Symphony Orch., 1967-70; asst. supr. mktg. First Nat. Bank of Commerce, New Orleans, 1970-73; mktg. officer Kans. State Bank & Trust Co., Wichita, 1973-74; dir. public relations The Toledo (Ohio) Hosp., 1975—. Mem. Internat. Assn. Bus. Communicators, Women in Communications (pres. Toledo chpt. 1977-79), Am. Hosp. Assn., Ohio Hosp. Assn., Am. Soc. for Hosp. Public Relations, Ohio Soc. Hosp. Public Relations, Public Relations Soc. Am., Hosp. Council of N.W. Ohio, Jr. League of Toledo, Toledo Hosp. Aux. Club: Zonta Internat. Home: 2673 Goddard Rd Toledo OH 43606 Office: 2142 N Cove Blvd Toledo OH 43606

SUMMY, GARY ALAN, electric co. exec.; b. Bremen, Ind., Mar. 13, 1950; s. Russell Duward and Mary (Underwood) S.; B.A., DePauw U., 1972. Supr., Reith Riley Constrn. Co., Goshen, Ind., 1972-73; sales engr. Reliance Electric Co., Cleve., 1973-77, tng. dir., 1977-79, supr. sales tng., 1979—; cons. in field. Mem. Am. Soc. Tng. and Devel., Am. Mgmt. Assn. Designer, writer 2 video programs, 1978. Home: 7428 Essex Dr Mentor OH 44060 Office: 35000 Curtis Blvd Eastlake OH 44094

SUMNER, LESTER FRANCIS, brewery exec.; b. Washington, Aug. 2, 1948; s. Robert S. and Dorothy Irene (Bambick) S.; B.S. in C.E., U.S. Mil. Acad., 1970; m. Patricia Ann McConville, Feb. 7, 1981. Product mgr. Richardson Merrell Inc., Wilton, Conn., 1977-79, Gulf & Western, N.Y.C., 1979-80, Anheuser Busch, St. Louis, 1980—. Served to capt. U.S. Army, 1970-77. Mem. Assn. Grads. U.S. Mil. Acad., Am. Mgmt. Assn. Roman Catholic. Clubs: Mo. Athletic, Rambler Rugby Football. Home: 7570 Oxford Dr Saint Louis MO 63105 Office: 2800 S 9th St Saint Louis MO 63118

SUMNER, WILLIAM GRAHAM, newspaper editor; b. Palo Alto, Calif., May 9, 1921; s. Jonathon Henry and Ruth Elizabeth S.; B.A., Stanford U., 1943; m. Mildred Pearl Rivers, May 3, 1946; children—Gregory, Sally, Ann, William, Wendolyn. With Pasadena (Calif.) Star-News, Los Angeles Times and Los Angeles Daily News; successively reporter, sports editor, mng. editor, editor Pasadena Ind. Star-News; corr. Washington bur. Pasadena Ind. Star-News and Ridder newspapers, 1961-64; asso. editor, columnist St. Paul Pioneer Press Dispatch, 1964—. Served with USNR, 1943-46; PTO. Recipient awards St. Paul Bar Assn., Minn. Architects Assn. Mem. Am. Soc. Newspaper Editors, Nat. Conf. Editorial Writers. Clubs: Informal, Minn., North Oaks Golf. Office: 55 E 4th St Saint Paul MN 55101*

SUMNICHT, FRANCIS HENRY, learning innovation center exec.; b. Appleton, Wis., Dec. 25, 1921; s. Henry August and Rose Marie (Honeck) S.; B.S., Marquette U., 1948; m. Patricia Beth Gambsky, Feb. 4, 1964; children—Nancy Lee, Vern, Christopher, Shawn, Eric, Heidi. Advt. and display mgr. Sears Roebuck, Appleton, 1948-51; sec., founder Advance Industries Inc., electronics, Appleton, 1951-70; postmaster, Appleton, 1956-72; sec., founder A-1 Builders, Inc., Appleton, 1954—; partner Sumnicht Supply Co., Appleton, 1951-71; pres., dir. Children's Learning Innovation Center, Inc., Appleton, 1973; distbr. Amway, 1975—. Mem. E. Central Wis. Regional Planning Commn., 1974-75; treas. History Alive Inc., hist. mus. found., 1973—; co-founder nat. Pray for Peace movement, 1948. Sec., Outagamie County Republican Com., 1951-55; Wis. chmn. Young Republicans, 1952. Bd. dirs. Sumnicht Charitable Found., 1968—, Outagamie County Hist. Soc., 1948—. Served with USCGR, 1942-46. Mem. Am. Mgmt. Assn., Soc. Advancement Mgmt. (regional v.p. 1971-74, 77-79), Am. Soc. Personnel Adminstrn., V.F.W., Am. Legion, Catholic War Vets. K.C., Nat. Accountants Assn. Clubs: Butte des Morts Country. Home: 325 W Michigan St Appleton WI 54911 Office: 325 W Michigan St Appleton WI 54911

SUMRALL, LESTER F., missionary-evangelist; b. New Orleans, Feb. 15, 1913; s. George William and Betty (Chandler) S.; D.D., Berean Bible Coll.; Litt. D., Ind. Christian U.; postgrad. U. Chgo.; m. Louise Margaret Layman, Sept. 30, 1944; children—Frank Lester, Stephen Philip, Peter Andrew. Ordained to ministry Christian Ch. (Disciples of Christ); pastor Christian Center, South Bend, Ind.; missionary to numerous nations, built chs. in Philippines, Hong Kong, Brazil, U.S.; pres. Sta. WHMB-TV, Indpls., Sta. WHME-TV-FM, South Bend; prin. on TV program Today With Lester Sumrall. Editor: World Harvest Mag., 1962—.

SUN, ALBERT YUNG-KWANG, neurochemist; b. Amoy, China, Oct. 13, 1932; s. Peh-Cheng and Sui-Ho Kao W.; came to U.S., 1959, naturalized, 1972; B.S., Nat. Taiwan U., 1957; M.S., Oreg. State U., Ph.D., 1967; m. Grace Yan-Chi Cheung, May 9, 1964; 1 dau., Aggie Yee-Chun. Postdoctoral research asso. biochemistry Case Western Res. U., Cleve., 1967-68; sr. research scientist Lab. Neurochemistry, Cleve. Psychiat. Inst., 1968-74; research prof. biochemistry Sinclair Comparative Medicine Research Farm, U. Mo., Columbia, 1974—, asso. prof. biochemistry dept., 1977—. Grantee Nat. Inst. Alcohol Abuse and Alcoholism, 1974—, Nat. Inst. Neurol. and Communicative Disease and Stroke, 1975—, Nat. Cancer Inst., 1979—. Mem. A.A.A.S., A.C.S., Biochem. Soc., Am. Soc. Neurochemistry, Am. Soc. Neurosci., Am. Gerontol. Soc., N.Y. Acad. Sci., Internat. Soc. Neurochemists, Am. Soc. Biol. Chemists, Internat. Soc. Study of Pain, Phi Sigma, Phi Lambda Upsilon. Research on structure and function of membranes, roles of phospholipids in membrane function. Home: Box 335 Route 12 Columbia MO 65201 Office: Sinclair Comparative Medicine Research Farm U Mo Route 3 Columbia MO 65201

SUN, PAUL LUN-FANG, plant breeder; b. China, Feb. 15, 1934; came to U.S., 1959, naturalized, 1972; s. Pei Chien and Ton Shing (Wang) S.; Ph.D., U. Wis., Madison, 1969; m. Yun-Teh Han, Aug. 1, 1964; children—Hans, Ming-Ming. Alfalfa breeder Teweles Seed Co., Clinton, Wis., 1969-74; research dir. Americana Seed Co., Muscatin, Iowa, 1974-76; soybean research sta. mgr. Pfixer Genetics, Inc., Beaman, Iowa, 1976—. Mem. Am. Soc. Agronomy. Baptist. Patentee in field. Home: 1901 Edgebrook Dr Marshalltown IA 50158 Office: PO Box 99 Beaman IA 50609

SUN, TAMIN, safety engr.; b. Taiwan, Republic of China, Jan. 3, 1952; came to U.S., 1976, naturalized, 1979; s. Wunan and Shi-Shou (Chow) S.; B.E. in Indsl. Engring., Feng Chia U., 1974; M.S. in Occupational Safety and Health, Ill. State U., 1977. Loss prevention and audit rep. St. Paul Ins. Co., Chgo., 1978-79; safety engr. Rauland div. Zenith Radio Corp., Melrose Park, Ill., 1979—. Pres., Chinese Student Assn., Ill. State U., 1977. Served with Chinese Engring. Troops, Taiwan, 1974-76. Cert. asso. safety profl. asso. in risk mgmt. Mem. Am. Soc. Safety Engrs., Chinese Students and Alumni Assn. Chgo. (v.p.). Home: 18W 126 14th St Villa Park IL 60181 Office: 2407 North Ave Melrose Park IL 60160

SUNDARAM, SHANMUGHA K., surgeon; b. Kottayam, India, July 21, 1938; s. Kanniah P.C. and Saraswathi Chettiar; came to U.S., 1964; I.S.C., Kerala U. (India), 1956, M.D., 1961; m. Padma Sarada Pillai, May 4, 1964; children—Kannan, Anand, Ravi. Intern, Med. Coll. Hosp., Trivandrum, India, 1961-72, Mac Neal Meml. Hosp., Berwyn, Ill., 1964-65; resident Trumbull Meml. Hosp., Ohio, 1965-66, Mt. Sinai Hosp., Chgo., 1966-70; practice medicine, specializing in surgery, Bolingbrook, Ill., 1972—; mem. staff Hinsdale (Ill.) Sanitorium and Hosp., Good Samaritan Hosp., Downers Grove, Ill.; mem. staff, chmn. dept. surgery Loretto Hosp., Chgo.; instr. anatomy Med. Coll. Trivandrum (India), 1963-64; clin. instr. Mt. Sinai Hosp., Chgo., 1969-70. Fellow A.C.S., Internat. Coll. Surgeons. Office: 402 W Boughton Rd Bolingbrook IL 60439

SUNDBERG, COLLINS YNGVE, funeral dir.; b. DeKalb, Ill., May 29, 1911; s. Axel and Sophia (Collin) S.; student Worsham Coll. Mortuary Sci., 1937-38; m. Norma E. Johnson, June 20, 1942. Partner, Sundberg Funeral Home, Rockford, Ill., 1952—; pres. Col-Nor Corp., Rockford, 1961—. Pres. Winnebago County Humane Soc.; active Goldie B. Flaberg Center for Children. Served with USNR, 1942-45. Mem. Nat., Ill., No. Ill. funeral dirs. assns., Am. Vets. (comdr. Rockford post), Rockford C. of C., Rockford Hist. Soc., Swedish Hist. Soc. Am. Legion, VFW. Republican. Lutheran. Clubs: Masons, Shriners, Moose, Odd Fellows, Navy of U.S.A., Pyramid, John Ericsson (past pres.), Rock River Kennel (past pres., dir.) (Rockford); Forest Hills Country. Home: 5431 Einor Ave Rockford IL 61108 Office: 215 N 6th St Rockford IL 61107

SUNDBERG, NORMA ELIZABETH JOHNSON (MRS. COLLINS Y. SUNDBERG), funeral dir.; b. Rockford, Ill.; d. Conrad Walfred and Olga (Pierson) Johnson; student Brown's Bus. Coll., 1928-30; m. Collins Y. Sundberg, June 20, 1942. Partner Sundberg Funeral Home, Rockford, Ill., 1952—; sec.-treas. ColNor Corp., Rockford, 1961—. Mem. Winnebago County Women's Republican Club, 1948—, v.p., 1956, 57; active Goldie B. Flaberg Center for Children. Mem. Nat., Ill. funeral dirs. assns., Swedish Hist. Soc., Jenny Lind Soc., Am. Legion Aux., Humane Soc. Aux., Humane Soc., Women of Moose. Lutheran. Mem. Order Eastern Star, Order White Shrine of Jerusalem, Daus. of the Nile. Clubs: Zonta (bd. dirs. 1962-64), Rockford Woman's; Forest Hills Country. Home: 5431 Einor Ave Rockford IL 61108 Office: 215 N 6th St Rockford IL 61107

SUNDBERG, R. DOROTHY, hematopathologist, educator; b. Chgo., July 29, 1915; d. Carl William and Ruth Antoinette (Chalbeck) S.; student U. Chgo., 1932-34; B.S., U. Minn., 1937, M.A., 1939, Ph.D., 1943, M.D., 1953; m. Robert H. Reiff, Dec. 24, 1941 (div. 1945). Instr., Wayne State U., Detroit, 1939-41; instr., then asst. prof. anatomy U. Minn. Med. Sch., Mpls., 1939-53, asso. prof., 1953-60, prof., 1960-63, prof. lab. medicine and anatomy, 1963-73, prof. lab. medicine, pathology and anatomy, 1973—, dir. hematology labs., 1945-74, co-dir. hematology labs., 1974—. Diplomate Am. Bd. Pathology. Recipient Lucretia Wilder award, 1943. Mem. Am. Assn. Anatomists, Internat. Soc. Hematology, Am. Soc. Hematology, Soc. Exptl. Biology and Medicine, Minn. Soc. Clin. Pathologists, Am. Assn. Pathologists, Am. Soc. Cell Biology, Acad. Clin. Lab. Physicians and Scientists, Sigma Xi. Presbyterian. Club: Quota (Mpls.). Editorial bd. Blood, 1960-67, asso. editor, 1967-69; editorial bd. Procs. Soc. Exptl. Biology and Medicine, to 1975; contbr. articles to med. jours. Office: Mayo Bldg B275 U Minn Minneapolis MN 55455

SUNDLOF, WILLIAM ADOLPH, civil engr.; b. Chgo., Jan. 22, 1915; s. Sven Adolph and Jennie (Swanson) S.; B.S., U.S. Mil. Acad., 1938; M.S. in Civil Engring., Iowa State U., 1949; m. Mary Evelyn Cleary, Oct. 17, 1942; children—Mary Christina. Bridget Ann Sundlof McWilliams, John William. Commd. lt., U.S. Army, 1938, advanced through grades to col. C.E., 1952; served in World War II, Korea, 1950-52; engr. VII Corps, Engrs., U.S. Army, Stuttgart, W. Ger., 1956-59; ret., 1962; civil engr. Am. Wood Preservers Inst., Chgo., 1962-64; Chgo. rep. Am. Creosote Works, Inc., 1964-73; sr. design engr. City of Troy (Mich.), 1973-76; prin. William A. Sundlof P.E., Long Grove, Ill., 1976—; dir. Palatine Savs. & Loan Assn. (Ill.). Decorated Legion of Merit (2), Bronze Star (5); registered profl. engr., Ill., Mich., D.C. Mem. ASCE, ASTM, Nat. Soc. Profl. Engrs., Soc. Am. Mil. Engrs., Assn. U.S. Army, Mil. Order World Wars, North Shore Choral Soc., U.S. Mil. Acad. Alumni Soc., Iowa State U. Alumni Soc. Roman Catholic. Club: Univ. (Chgo.). Address: Box 212 Old McHenry Rd Long Grove IL 60047

SUNSTEIN, MICHAEL ALLEN, constrn. co. exec.; b. Chgo., June 4, 1942; s. Cass Herman and Shirley Jeanne (Blum) S.; B.A., Shimer Coll., 1964; m. Dennet Ann Sheridan, Sept. 30, 1961; children—Lisa, Robert, Julie, Vicki, Jason, Megan. Salesman, Vinco Industries Inc., Chgo., 1965-66, v.p. mktg., 1966-68; salesman Kaufman & Broad Homes Inc., Chgo., 1968-69, sales mgr., 1969-70, v.p. mktg. and sales, Freehold, N.J., 1970-72, asst. div. mgr., 1972-74, pres. div., chief exec. officer, Detroit, 1974-76; pres. Sunstein & Krull Homes Inc., Bloomfield Hills, Mich., 1976—, Power Disc Inc., 1980—; instr. mktg. Monmouth County (N.J.) Coll., Toms River, 1973-74. Recipient plaque Coventry Square Homeowners Assn., 1973. Mem. Home Builders Assn. (dir. state). Rotarian (hon.). Home: 5715 Andover Rd Troy MI 48084 Office: 300 E Long Lake Rd Bloomfield Hills MI 48013

SURACE, GENE ALLEN, telephone co. ofcl.; b. Lorain, Ohio, Dec. 7, 1946; s. Dominic and Helen (Balint) S.; B.S. in Social Studies, Kent (Ohio) State U., 1970; M.S. in Personnel Counseling, Jacksonville (Ala.) State U., 1974. Substitute tchr. Lorain city schs., 1970-71; econ. devel. coordinator Lorain City Hall, 1975; acting dir. Lorain County Econ. Devel. Com., 1975-78; planning staff adminstr. CENTEL,

Lorain Telephone Co., 1978—. Served with U.S. Army, 1971-73. Mem. Am. Personnel and Guidance Assn. Nat. Employment Counselors Assn., Nat. Vocat. Guidance Assn., Greater Lorain C. of C., Italian Am. War Vets., Fraternal Order Police Assos. Ohio. Democrat. Roman Catholic. Home: 193 Woodhill Dr Amherst OH 44001 Office: 203 W 9 St Lorain OH 44052

SURANYI, PETER, physicist; b. Budapest, Hungary, Jan. 31, 1935; came to U.S., 1969, naturalized, 1976; s. Joseph and Elizabeth (Szenes) Stern; physics diploma Lorand Eotvos U., 1958; candidate of physics Joint Inst. Nuclear Research, Dubna, USSR, 1965; m. Theresa Gal, May 24, 1960; children—Anna, Agnes. Jr. research fellow Central Research Inst. for Physics, Budapest, 1958-61, sr. research fellow, 1965-69; research fellow Joint Inst. Nuclear Physics, Dubna, USSR, 1961-65; vis. lectr. Johns Hopkins U., Balt., 1969-71; asso. prof. physics U. Cin., 1971-74, prof., 1974—, fellow Grad. Sch., 1977; sr. vis. fellow Imperial Coll., London, 1978-79. Recipient Schmidt award Hungarian Phys. Soc.; NSF grantee, 1974; Dept. Energy research grantee, 1976—. Mem. Am. Phys. Soc., Sigma Xi. Office: Dept Physics U Cin Cincinnati OH 45221

SURATH, VASANTH MADHAV, physician; b. Kakinada, India, May 3, 1948; came to U.S., 1972; s. Madhava Rao and Rathnavathi S.; M.B., B.S., Andhra U., Guntur, 1970. Intern, resident St. Joseph Hosp., Chgo., 1972-76, attending physician dept. internal medicine, 1976—, med. dir. emergency room, 1976—; practice medicine specializing in internal medicine, Chgo., 1976—; pres. Commonwealth Med. Assos. Diplomate Am. Bd. Internal Medicine. Mem. A.C.P., Am. Coll. Emergency Physicians, Am. Soc. for Study of Headache, AMA. Hindu. Office: 2913 N Commonwealth Ave Chicago IL 60657

SURBER, JOHN MAYNARD, animal nutritionist; b. Wilmington, Ohio, Sept. 4, 1953; s. Maynard R. and America I. (Donohoo) S.; grad. Ohio State U., 1975; m. Connie E. Ross, Dec. 1, 1975; children—Shawn, Shannon, Traci. Tchr., Bright Local Sch. Dist., Mowrystown, Ohio, 1975; salesman Sabina (Ohio) Farmers Exchange, Inc., 1975-79, sales mgr., 1981—, animal nutritionist, 1979—; owner, farm broadcaster Today's Farm Info. Radio Network, Sabina, 1979—; farm mgr.; cons. crop mgmt. Mem. Am. Registry of Cert. Animal Scientists, Clinton County Farm Bur., Future Farmers Am. (hon.). Club: Toastmasters (pres., charter mem. 3-C club). Home: 1471 Hornbeam Sabina OH 45169 Office: 292 N Howard Sabina OH 45169

SURDAM, ROBERT MCCLELLAN, banker; b. Albany, N.Y., Oct. 28, 1917; s. I. Burke and LeMoyne (McClellan) S.; grad. Deerfield (Mass.) Acad., 1935; B.A., Williams Coll., 1939; m. Mary Caroline Buhl, July 8, 1946; children—Peter Buhl, Robert McClellan, Mary Caroline. With Nat. Bank of Detroit, 1947—, v.p., 1954-60, sr. v.p., 1960-64, exec. v.p., 1964-66, pres., chief exec. officer, dir., 1966-72, chmn., chief exec. officer, 1972—; dir. Bundy Corp., Burroughs Corp., Bank of Tokyo Internat. Ltd., Internat. Bank Detroit. Mem. Assn. Res. City Bankers. Office: PO Box 116 RPA Detroit MI 48232

SURRELL, MATTHEW ANTHONY, hosp. adminstr., physician; b. Newberry, Mich., Aug. 21, 1910; s. Matthew A. and Alvina M. (Beaulieu) S.; A.B., Olivet Coll., 1931; M.D., U. Mich., 1935; grad. Army Command and Gen. Staff Sch., Ft. Leavenworth, Kans.; m. Agnes Grace Costello, July 2, 1932; children—Stephen E., Matthew J., James A. Intern Henry Ford Hosp., Detroit, 1935-36; practice medicine, Newberry, Mich., 1936-40, 50-66; clin. dir. Newberry State Hosp., 1947-50, med. dir. mentally retarded service, Served from lt. to col. M.C., AUS, 1941-46. Decorated Legion of Merit, Bronze Star medal, Army commendation medal; Croix de Guerre with gold star (France). Mem. Ret. Officers Assn., Am. Legion, VFW. Elk. Home: 416 W Ave B Newberry MI 49868 Office: Newberry State Hospital Newberry MI 49868

SUSSMAN, SHIRLEY IRENE, educator; b. St. Louis, Aug. 19, 1929; d. Nathan and Anna (Bermi) Hartstein; B.S. in Edn., Washington U., St. Louis, 1951; M.A. in Edn., U. Mo., 1980; m. Carl Horst Sussman, Dec. 27, 1953; children—David Michael, Barbara Jo, Frederic Andrew, Judith Faye. Tchr., Weber Sch., Creve Coeur, Mo., 1951-54, Fulton Sch., Evansville, Ind., 1957-58; tchr. St. Louis Public Schs., 1959-80, reading specialist, 1980—. Mem. St. Louis Tchrs. Assn., Mo.-Nat. Edn. Assn., NEA, Internat. Reading Assn. Jewish.

SUTCLIFFE, GRENVILLE GEORGE, mfg. co. exec.; b. St. Louis, May 27, 1944; s. Eugene Grenville DeCantwell and Hazel Louise (Duffendack) S.; B.S. in Bus. Adminstrn., U. Mo., 1971; m. Dianne E. Steed, Nov. 25, 1972; 1 dau., Katherine Mae. Vice pres. Husky Corp., Pacific, Mo., 1962-65, v.p., 1971—; dir. Am. Security Bank, Pacific, Mo., Petroleum Equipment Inst. Served with Spl. Forces U.S. Army, 1965-68. Decorated Purple Heart. Mem. Soc. Automotive Engrs., Exptl. Aircraft Inst., Am. Petroleum Inst., Nat. Assn. Petroleum Equipment Rebuilders (pres. 1972-77). Patentee pollution control devices. Home: Route 2 Box 189A Village Ridge MO 63089 Office: 1 Dailey Industrial Park Pacific MO 63069

SUTCLIFFE, TODD RAYMOND, chem. spltys. co. exec.; b. Washington, Feb. 27, 1944; s. Raymond Leroy and Bertha Helen (Barwis) S.; grad. Abington Sch., 1962; B.S., Drexel U., 1968; m. Pauline Theresea Wagner, Oct. 14, 1967; 1 son, Graham Todd. Research chemist Rohm & Haas Labs., Maple Glen, Pa., 1968-71; tech. service rep. E.F. Houghton & Co., Valley Forge, Pa., 1971-76, product mgr. metal cutting dept., 1976-79, asst. sales mgr., Detroit, 1979-80, sales mgr., 1980—. Mem. Soc. Mfg. Engrs. (chmn. tech. session 1980 nat. conf.), Am. Soc. Lubrication Engrs., Fluid Power Soc., Soc. Die Casting Engrs., Am. Soc. for Metals, Greater Detroit C. of C. Republican. Presbyterian. Club: Grosse Pointe Woods Boat. Contbr. articles in field to profl. jours. Office: E F Houghton & Co 14275 Lumpkin St Detroit MI 48212

SUTHERLAND, CRAIG DE LANO, lumber co. exec.; b. Kansas City, Mo., Oct. 25, 1949; s. Herman R. and Helen De Lano S.; student Colo. Coll., 1967-69; m. Laura Sifers, Oct. 11, 1975. Bldg. contractor, Aspen, Colo., 1971-75; partner Sutherland Lumber Co., Kansas City, Mo.; dir. United Mo. Bank, United Kans. Bancshares. Bd. dirs. St. Luke Hosp. Republican. Episcopalian. Office: Sutherland Lumber Co 4000 Main St Kansas City MO 64111

SUTHERLAND, DELMAR PAUL, journalist; b. Elm Creek, Nebr., Jan. 22, 1930; s. James McCullough and Emma (Larson) S.; B.S., Kearney State Coll., 1956; m. Joyce Ardelle Metzgor, Feb. 9, 1956; children—Paula, Quinten, Leah, Sherman. Sports and city editor Falls City (Nebr.) Journal, 1963—. Mem. Falls City Council, 1979—. Served with U.S. Army, 1950-53. Mem. Nebr. Sportswriters and Sportscasters Assn. (v.p. 1981—). Methodist. Clubs: Lions, Elks, Masons. Home: 2003 Barada St Falls City NE 68355 Office: Falls City Journal Falls City NE 68355

SUTHERLAND, GEORGE HENRY, mech. engr.; b. Edmonton, Alta., Can., Nov. 25, 1947; s. James Robert and Norah Margaret (Hutton) S.; came to U.S., 1970, naturalized, 1977; B.Sc., U. Alta., 1969; M.Eng., McMaster U., 1970; Ph.D., Stanford U., 1973; m. Judy Carlene Johnson, Aug. 30, 1969; 1 son, Eric John. Asst. prof. mech. engring. Ohio State U., Columbus, 1973-78, asso. prof., 1978-79; dir. Advanced Design Methods Lab., 1977-79; mgr. mech. devel. lab. Gen. Electric Co., East Cleveland, Ohio, 1979—. Registered profl. engr., Ohio; recipient various scholarships, fellowships and awards, 1964-73; recipient Ronald W. Thompson Meritorious Service award Ohio State U., 1975. Mem. Am. Soc. Engring. Edn. (local chpt. chmn. 1974-75; Outstanding Young Faculty award 1979), ASME (newsletter editor 1977-78), Lambda Chi Alpha (bd. trustees). Presbyterian. Contbr. tech. articles on machine design to profl. jours. Home: 698 Anthony St Richmond Heights OH 44143 Office: Gen Electric Co Nela Park East Cleveland OH 44112

SUTHERLAND, LESLIE EUGENE, mech. engr.; b. Parsons, Kans., Jan. 3, 1944; s. Luther Wendell and Virginia Mae (Whitacre) S.; student public schs., Altamount, Kans. Adminstrv. asst. Day & Zimmerman, Inc., Parsons, Kans., 1972-75, sr. indsl. engr., 1975-77, maintenance control engr., 1977-80, gen. mech. engr., 1980—. Mem. Methods Time Mgmt. Assn. Democrat. Mem. Christian Ch. Home: 714 W Maple Columbus KS 66725 Office: Day and Zimmerman Parsons KS 67357

SUTPHEN, DUNCAN DUNBAR, III, mfg. co. exec.; b. N.Y.C., May 3, 1933; s. Duncan Dunbar and Celeste Knox (Proctor) S.; A.B. cum laude in Geology, Princeton U., 1955; m. Barbara Ann Hoggson, June 17, 1955; children—John Duncan, William Wyckoff, Bruce Fraser. Works mgr. Dresser Indsl. Instrument Ops., Stratford, Conn., 1965-69, v.p. mfg., 1969-74, v.p. mfg. Dresser Europe, Brussels, 1974-78, v.p. planning Tool Group, Chgo., 1978-81, pres. hand tool div., 1981—. Bd. dirs., treas. Bridgeport (Conn.) Rehab. Center, 1968-71. Served with USN, 1955-57. Republican. Home: 454 Cedar St Winnetka IL 60093 Office: 3201 N Wolf Rd Franklin Park IL 60131

SUTTER, ELIZABETH HENBY (MRS. RICHARD A. SUTTER), civic leader; b. St. Louis, May 15, 1912; d. William Hastings and Alvina (Steinbreder) Henby; A.B., Washington U., 1931; m. Richard A. Sutter, June 15, 1935; children—John Richard, Jane Elizabeth, Judith Ann (Mrs. William Hinrichs). Nat. chmn. com. on mental health AMA Aux., 1960-62, v.p., 1962-63, 64-64, pres., 1965-66, editor Direct Line newsletter, 1967-74, now life mem.; asso. editor Facet's, 1973-80; mem. adv. bd. Deaconess Hosp. Sch. of Nursing, St. Louis; trustee John Burroughs Sch., 1958-61, v.p. 1959, devel. commn., 1960-61; mem. Historic Bldgs. Commn. St. Louis County, 1959—, chmn., 1973—; sec., treas. Sutter Clinic, Inc., St. Louis, Sutter Mgmt., Inc., Downtown Med. Bldg., Inc.; bd. dirs. Conv. and Visitors Bur. Greater St. Louis, 1976—, sec. bd., 1979-81; mem. planning bd. Health, Hosp. Health, Welfare Council Met. St. Louis, 1955-64; pres. Aux. Central States Soc. Indsl. Medicine and Surgery, 1960-61, St. Louis County Med. Soc. Aux., 1948-49, Mo. Med. Soc. Aux., 1952-53; sec. St. Louis County Health and Hosp. Bd., 1956-60, chmn., 1961; bd. dirs. Tb Soc. St. Louis, exec. com., 1956—, v.p., 1960-61; pres. Tb and Health Soc. of St. Louis, 1962-65; former mem. adv. council vol. services Nat. Assn. Mental Health; bd. dirs. Am. Cancer Soc., St. Louis, exec. com., 1954-64; bd. dirs. Mental Health Assn. St. Louis, 1960-61; mem. Practical Nursing Edn. Council, chmn. exec. com., 1959-60; mem. Nat. Def. Adv. Com. Women in Services, 1969-71, vice chmn., 1971; mem. bd. govs. Washington U. Alumni, 1970-71, 74-82, vice-chmn., 1979-80, chmn., 1980-81; trustee Washington U., 1979-81; mem. bd. Health Systems Agy. Greater St. Louis, 1976—; mem. East-West Gateway Coordinating Council Task Force on Historic Preservation, 1975-79; mem. University City Historic Preservation Com., 1977-81; mem. adv. bd. Mo. Heritage Trust, 1980—. Named one of 10 Women of Achievement in good citizen category St. Louis Globe-Democrat, 1961; recipient St. Louis County Med. Soc. award of merit, 1964; Alumna of Yr. award Gamma Phi Beta St. Louis, 1966; Disting. Alumni citation Washington U., St. Louis, 1968, Disting. Alumni Service citation, 1977. Mem. Mo. Hist. Soc., St. Louis Symphony Soc., AMA Aux. (hon. life), Mo. State Med. Assn. Woman's Aux. (hon. life), St. Louis Met. Med. Aux. (life). Presbyterian. Contbr. articles to med. publs. Home: 7215 Greenway Dr Saint Louis MO 63130

SUTTER, RICHARD ANTHONY, surgeon; b. St. Louis, July 20, 1909; s. John Henry and Molly (Schuchman) S.; A.B., Washington U., 1931, M.D., 1935; m. Elizabeth Henby, June 15, 1935; children—John Richard, Jane Elizabeth, Judith Ann Sutter Hinrichs. Intern, St. Louis City Hosp., 1935-36; preceptor, Otto Sutter, M.D., St. Louis; founder, dir. Sutter Clinic, Inc., St. Louis, 1946—; lectr. in indsl. medicine and rehab. in preventive medicine Sch. Medicine, Washington U.; med. dir. St. Louis Internat. Airport; med. advisor Union Electric Co., St. Louis Globe Democrat. Bd. dirs. Downtown St. Louis, Inc., Herbert Hoover Boys Club Ill.; elder, bd. trustees First Presbyn. Ch. of St. Louis. Served to lt. col. U.S. Army, 1941-45. Decorated Bronze Star. Diplomate Am. Bd. Preventive Medicine. Mem. AMA, Mo. State, So. Med. Assns., St. Louis Met. Med. Soc. (hon.), Royal Soc. Health, Pan Am. Med. Assn., Permanent Commn. and Internat. Assn. Occupational Health, Am. Acad. Occupational Medicine, Am. (Health Achievement in Industry award 1978), Central States occupational medicine assns., Am. Coll. Preventive Medicine, Am. Pub. Health Assn., Am. Assn. Ry. Surgeons, Aerospace Med. Assn., Air Medics Med. Assn., Nat., Mo. rehab. assns., Aircraft Owners and Pilots Assn. Clubs: Mo. Athletic, St. Louis, St. Louis Beta Theta Pi (Man of Year, 1974), Faculty of Washington U., Washington U. Club, Rotary (St. Louis), Am. Legion (hon. surgeon Fred W. Stockham Post). Advanced aviation med. examiner FAA; contbr. articles in field of occupational medicine and geriatrics to profl. jours. Home: 7215 Greenway Ave Saint Louis MO 63130 Office: Downtown Med Bldg 819 Locust St Saint Louis MO 63101

SUTTER, WILLIAM PAUL, lawyer; b. Chgo., Jan. 15, 1924; s. Harry Blair and Elsie (Paul) S.; A.B., Yale U., 1947; J.D., U. Mich., 1950; m. Helen Yvonne Stebbins, Nov. 13, 1954; children—William Paul, Helen Blair. Admitted to Ill. bar, 1950, Fla. bar, 1977, U.S. Supreme Ct. bar, 1981; asso. firm Hopkins & Sutter, and predecessor firm, Chgo., 1950-57, partner, 1957—; mem. Ill. Supreme Ct. Atty. Registration Commn., 1975—. Precinct capt. New Trier Twp. (Ill.) Rep. Party, 1960-68; asst. area chmn. New Trier Rep. Orgn., 1968-72. Chmn. Winnetka Caucus Committee, 1966-67. Trustee Gads Hill Center, pres., 1962-70, chmn., 1971-80. Served to 1st lt. AUS, 1943-46. Fellow Am. Bar Found., Am. Coll. Probate Counsel (bd. regents 1977—, exec. com. 1981—), Internat. Acad. Estate and Trust Law; mem. Am. (ho. dels. 1972-81, chmn. com. on income estates and trusts, taxation sect. 1973-75), Ill. (bd. govs. 1964-75, pres. 1973-74), Chgo. (chmn. probate practice com. 1963-64), bar assns., Am. Law Inst., Am. Judicature Soc., Ill. LAWPAC (pres. 1977—), Chgo. Assn. Commerce and Industry (govt. affairs div.), Am. Arbitration Assn., Order of the Coif, Phi Beta Kappa, Phi Delta Phi, Chi Psi. Episcopalian. Clubs: Law, Legal, Economic (Chgo.). Contbr. articles on estate planning and taxation to profl. jours. Home: 96 Woodley Rd Winnetka IL 60093 Office: 1 First National Plaza Chicago IL 60603

SUTTLE, DAVID DALE, architect/designer; b. San Antonio, Aug. 20, 1939; s. Ray and Mabel Lucille (Sargent) S.; student U. Kansas City, 1957-58; B.Arch., U. Kans., 1962; m. Joyce Stringfield, Sept. 9, 1960; children—Bethenny Brooke, Holly Camylle. Archtl. designer Hellmuth, Obata & Kassabaum, Inc., architects, St. Louis, 1962-66, asso., v.p., project designer, 1968-76, dir. for interior design, 1976-80, sr. v.p., prin. for architecture, mem. corp. design bd., 1980—; head archtl. designer The Drake Partnership, architects, St. Louis, 1966-68; mem. archtl. juries; co-designer Product Environ. traveling mus. exhbn. furniture, 1970; lectr. in field. Mem. University City (Mo.) Park Commn., 1977—; bd. dirs. New Music Circle, St. Louis, 1972-78; ordained elder Presbyn. Ch., 1970—. Recipient nat. awards for architecture and interior design. Prin. works include E.R. Squibb & Sons Corp. Hdqrs., Lawrenceville, N.J., 1971, Sheraton Washington Hotel, 1980, Galleria 2, Houston, 1976. Office: 100 N Broadway Saint Louis MO 63102

SUTTLES, RAYMOND HERSCHEL, bus. cons., real estate co. ofcl.; b. Indpls., May 31, 1923; s. Raymond H. and Maude (Thompson) S.; student Occidental Coll., 1943-44; B.S., U. So. Calif., 1946, postgrad., 1954-55; m. Patricia Ann Horkheimer, Oct. 19, 1955 (div. Mar. 1979); children—Steven Arthur, Kathleen Mary Suttles Nehmer, Nancy Lynn. Customer service engr. Douglas Aircraft Co., Santa Monica, Calif., 1955-59; missile service engr. Gen. Dynamics/Astronautics, San Diego, 1959-60; mktg. analyst Kintel div. Cohu Electronics, San Diego, 1960-61; co-owner Ednl. Materials Service, La Jolla, Calif., 1962-69; promotion dir. Educators Progress Service, Inc., Randolph, Wis., 1969-74, pres., 1974-77; bus. cons., St. Louis, 1978—; salesman Alice Hunter Realtors, St. Louis, 1980—. Asst. dist. commr. San Diego County council Boy Scouts Am., 1966-69, inst. rep., 1969—; treas. St. Gabriels's Ch. Corp., Randolph, 1970-78; pres. Randolph Centennial Corp. Served to lt. (j.g.) USN, 1941-54. Mem. Phi Kappa Tau. Clubs: Kiwanis (lt. gov. 1971-72, pres. 1976, v.p. 1980-81); Fox Lake Golf (sec. treas.) (Wis.). Editor: Supplement to Educators Grade Guide to Free Teaching Aids, 1959-76, Educators Guide to Free Tapes, Scripts and Transcriptions, 1970-75. Home: 910 Morrison LaSalle Sq Saint Louis MO 63104 Office: Alice Hunter Realtors 11720 Manchester Rd Saint Louis MO 63131

SUTTON, DAVID FEICKS, music co. exec.; b. Lorain, Ohio, June 19, 1934; s. David and Marion (Feicks) S.; B.A., Oberlin (Ohio) Coll., 1956; m. Arlyn Thora Anderson; 1 son, David Anderson. With Procter & Gamble Co., 1956-74, new products mgr. instn. and indsl., Cin., 1971-74; Gibson mktg. mgr., then product group dir. Norlin Music Inc., Lincolnwood, Ill., 1974-77, dir. mktg., 1978-79, v.p. mktg., 1979-80, v.p. planning and internat. sales, 1980-81, v.p. sales and mktg., 1981—; dir. DGI Inc., Cin.; mktg. fine arts Court Galleries, Cin. Regional fund drive mgr. Oberlin Coll., 1972-73; eagle scout; active local Boy Scouts Am., United Appeal. Served to capt. USAF, 1957-59. Mem. Guitar and Accessory Mfrs. Assn. (pres., dir.), Music Industry Mfrs. Assn. (chmn.), Am. Music Conf. (dir.), Council Industry Assn. Presidents. Home: 2411 Greenwood Ave Wilmette IL 60091 Office: 666 Dundee Rd Suite 707 Northbrook IL 60062

SUTTON, FRED CRAWFORD, educator, coll. dean; b. Minerva, Ohio, Jan. 3, 1925; s. Lester L. and Helen Leola (Nixon) S.; Ph.B., U. Chgo., 1948; B.A., State U. Iowa, 1949; M.Ed., U. Pitts., 1950; D.Ed., Wayne State U., 1962; m. Dorothy V. Warner, Dec. 18, 1948; children—Kathryn, James, Richard, Scott. Tchr. mentally retarded, Flint, Mich., 1950-51; employment counselor Mich. State Employment, Flint and Detroit, 1951-52; personnel supr. Chrysler Corp., Detroit, 1952-55; coordinator mgmt. tng. dean Henry Ford Community Coll., Dearborn, Mich., 1955-63; dean, acting campus pres. and asst. dean, dept. head, engring. technologies Cuyahoga Community Coll., Cleve., 1963—; accreditation cons. N. Central Coll., 1969—. Mem. council Triune Evang. Luth. Ch., Broadview Heights, Ohio, 1965-68; mem. Sch. Bd. Citizens Com., Brecksville, 1973-74. Served with U.S. Army, 1943-46. Decorated Bronze Star medal with oak leaf cluster; recipient Found. for Econ. Edn. award, 1957. Mem. N. Central Assn. Schs. & Colls. (exec. bd. 1970-74). Home: 8410 Sunnydale Dr Brecksville OH 44141 Office: Cuyahoga Community Coll Metro Campus Cleveland OH 44115

SUTTON, RICHARD OTTO, JR., orthopaedic surgeon; b. Little Rock, June 30, 1938; s. Richard Otto and Martha Elizabeth (Blaylock) S.; B.S., U.S. Mil. Acad., 1960; M.D., U. Tenn., Memphis, 1967; m. Dianne Waldon, Oct. 21, 1962; children—Richard Otto III, Jefferson Davis, Suzanne, Jennifer. Intern, William Beaumont Gen. Hosp., El Paso, Tex., 1967-68; resident Reynolds Army Hosp., Ft. Sill, Okla., 1968-69, William Beaumont Army Med. Center, El Paso, Tex., 1971-73, Carrie Tingley Hosp. for Crippled Children, Truth or Consequences, N.Mex., 1974, Irwin Army Hosp., Ft. Riley, Kans., 1974-76, Orthopaedic Clinic of Topeka, 1976-79; practice medicine specializing in orthopaedic surgery, Topeka, 1979—; mem. staffs Stormont-Vail Hosp., St. Francis Hosp., Meml. Hosp.; cons. Capper Found. for Crippled Children, Topeka. Second v.p. So. Baptist Convention, 1977; trustee So. Bapt. Theol. Sem., Louisville, 1979—. Served with M.C., U.S. Army, 1960-67; Vietnam. Diplomate Am. Bd. Orthopaedic Surgery. Fellow A.C.S.; mem. AMA, Mid-Central States Orthopaedic Soc., Kans. Orthopaedic Soc., Shawnee County Med. Soc. Club: Masons (Memphis). Home: 2135 SW Arvonia St Topeka KS 66614 Office: 1706 W 10th St Topeka KS 66604

SUZUKI, JON BYRON, microbiologist, dentist, educator; b. San Antonio, July 22, 1946; s. George K. and Ruby (Kanaya) S.; B.A. in Biology, Ill. Wesleyan U., 1968; Ph.D. magna cum laude in Microbiology, Ill. Inst. Tech., 1971; D.D.S. magna cum laude, Loyola U., 1978. Med. technologist Ill. Masonic Hosp. and Med. Center, Chgo., 1966-67; instr. of lab. in histology and parasitology Ill. Wesleyan U., Bloomington, 1967-68; med. technologist Augustana Hosp., Chgo., 1968-69; research asso. and instr. microbiology Ill. Inst. Tech., Chgo., 1968-71; clin. research asso. U. Chgo. Hosps., 1970-71; clin. microbiologist St. Luke's Hosp. Center, Columbia Coll. Physicians and Surgeons, N.Y.C., 1971-73; asso. med. dir. Paramed. Tng. and Registry, Vancouver, B.C., Can., 1973-74; dir. clin. labs. Registry of Hawaii, 1973-74; chmn. clin. lab. edn. Kapiolani Community Coll., U. Hawaii, Honolulu, 1974; lectr. periodontics Loyola U. Med. Center, Maywood, Ill., 1974—; NIH research fellow depts. pathology and periodontics Center for Research in Oral Biology, U. Wash., Seattle, 1978-80; asst. prof. dept. periodontics U. Md. Coll. Dental Surgery, Balt., 1980—; vis. scientist to Moscow (USSR) State U., summer 1972; lectr. Internat. Congress Allergology, Tokyo, 1973; lab. dir. Hawaii Dept. Health. Water safety instr. ARC, Honolulu, 1973—. Recipient pres.'s medallion Loyola U. Chgo., 1977; named Alumnus of Year, Wesleyan U., 1977. Mem. Am. Inst. Biol. Scis., Internat. Soc. Biophysicists, Internat. Soc. Endocrinologists, Ill. Acad. Sci. (chmn. microbiology session of 65th ann. meeting 1972), AAAS, ADA, Am., Internat. assns. dental research, Am. Acad. Microbiology, Am. Acad. Periodontology, NASA Bd., Am. Soc. Microbiology, Soc. Indsl. Microbiology, AAUP, N.Y. Acad. Scis., Sigma Xi, Omicron Kappa Upsilon, Beta Beta Beta, Blue Key. Author: Clinical Laboratory Methods for the Medical Assistant, 1974; contbr. numerous articles on research in microbiology, immunology and dentistry to sci. jours. Home: 6007 N Sheridan Rd Suite 30-J Chicago IL 60660 Office: Dept Periodontics/Oral Pathology Loyola U Sch Dentistry Maywood IL 60153 also Dept Periodontics/Microbiology U Md Coll Dental Surgery Baltimore MD 21201

SVEBAKKEN, GENE LEROY, social worker; b. Waukon, Iowa, Jan. 18, 1940; s. Roy Nelson and Ester (Colsch) S.; B.A., Luther Coll., 1961; M.S.W., U. Mo., 1964; m. Kathleen Adel Amundson, June 8,

1963 (div. 1980); children—Kristine, Peter, Hans. Social worker Howard County Dept. Social Welfare, Cresco, Iowa, 1961-62, Clayton County Dept. Social Welfare, Elkader, Iowa, 1964-65; social work supr. State of Iowa, Elkader, 1965-66; dir. dept. social services Story County, Nevada, Iowa, 1966-69; tng. specialist State Dept. Social Services, Des Moines, 1969-79; dir. social service Iowa Annie Wittenmeyer Home; field instr. U. Iowa Sch. Social Work; part time faculty Marycrest Coll., Davenport, Concordia Coll., River Forest, Ill.; exec. dir. Bethany Home, Moline, Ill., to 1979; exec. dir. Lutheran Child and Family Services Ill., River Forest, 1979—; pres. Rock Island County Community Services Council; adv. bd. Luth. Welfare Western Ill.; chmn. Alternatives to Detention Adv. Bd. of Rock Island County Probation Office; mem. bd. Service Info. Systems, Mpls.; mem. refugee resettlement standards task force Council on Accreditation for Family and Childrens Services, N.Y.C.; mem. accreditation team leader Council on Accreditation. Mem. Nat. Assn. Social Workers (pres. Quad City chpt., Social Worker of Yr., Quad City chpt. 1976), Ill. Child Care Assn. (dir.). Lutheran. Club: Rotary. Home: Lutherbrook Apt H 324 W Lake St Addison IL

SVOBODA, MARIE AGNES, museum educator; b. Chgo., Sept. 21, 1923; d. Charles J. and Marie C. (Cibery) Svoboda; student Chgo. Tchrs. Coll., 1942-44; B.S., Northwestern U., 1946, M.S., 1953; m. Robert O. Feltus, Mar. 19, 1977. Lectr. biology Field Museum Natural History, Chgo., 1946-68, supr. instruction, 1968-75, sr. instr. biology, 1976—. Mem. Juliette Low Interna. Friendship Com., 1970; vol. ARC, 1946-56. Mem. Am. Assn. Museums, Midwest Museums Conf., Delta Kappa Gamma. Author: Bible Plants, 1956; Plants That the American Indians Used, 1958; Spices, 1961; Trees, 1961. Home: 1401 Burr Oak Rd Hinsdale IL 60521 Office: Roosevelt Rd at Lake Shore Dr Field Museum Chicago IL 60605

SWAIMAN, KENNETH FRED, pediatric neurologist, educator; b. St. Paul, Nov. 19, 1931; s. Lester J. and Shirley (Ryan) S.; B.A. magna cum laude, U. Minn., 1952, B.S., 1953, M.D., 1955, postgrad., 1956-58, (fellow pediatric neurology) Nat. Inst. Neurologic Deseases and Blindness, 1960-63; m. Sheila Hershfield, 1973; children by previous marriage—Lisa, Jerrold, Barbara, Dana. Intern, Mpls. Gen. Hosp., 1955-56; resident pediatrics U. Minn., 1956-58, neurology, 1960-63; asst. prof. pediatrics, neurology U. Minn. Med. Sch., Mpls., 1963-66, asso. prof., 1966-69, prof., dir. pediatric neurology, 1969—, exec. officer, dept. neurology, 1977—, mem. internship adv. council exec. faculty, 1966-70. Cons. pediatric neurology Hennepin County Gen. Hosp., Mpls., St. Paul-Ramsey Hosp., St. Paul Children's Hosp. Chmn. Minn. Gov.'s Bd. for Handicapped, Exceptional and Gifted Children, 1972—; mem. human devel. study sect. NIH, 1976-79, guest worker NIH, 1978-81. Served to capt. M.C., U.S. Army, 1958-60. Diplomate Am. Bd. Psychiatry and Neurology, Am. Bd. Pediatrics. Fellow Am. Acad. Pediatrics, Am. Acad. Neurology (rep. to nat. council Nat. Soc. Med. Research); mem. Soc. Pediatric Research, Central Soc. Clin. Research, Central Soc. Neurol. Research, Internat. Soc. Neurochemistry, Am. Neurol. Assn., Minn. Neurol. Soc., AAAS, Midwest Pediatric Soc., Am. Soc. Neurochemistry, Child Neurology Soc. (1st pres. 1972-73, Hower award 1981), Internat. Assn. Child Neurologists (exec. com. 1975-79), Profs. of Child Neurology (pres. 1978—), Phi Beta Kappa, Sigma Xi. Author (with Francis S. Wright) Neuromuscular Diseases in Infancy and Childhood, 1969, Pediatric Neuromuscular Diseases, 1979; (with Stephen Ashwal) Pediatric Neurology Case Studies, 1978. Editor: (with John A. Anderson) Phenylketonuria and Allied Metabolic Diseases, 1966; (with Francis S. Wright) Practice Pediatric Neurology, 1975, 2d edit., 1982; mem. editorial bd. Annals of Neurology, 1977—, Neurology Update, 1977-81, Pediatric Update, 1977—. Contbr. articles to sci. jours. Home: 420 Delaware St SE Minneapolis MN 55455 Office: U Minn Med Sch Dept Pediatric Neurology Minneapolis MN 55455

SWAIN, TIMOTHY WHITZEL, II, lawyer; b. Peoria, Ill., Mar. 13, 1939; s. Timothy Whitsel and Katherine Cynthia (Altorfer) S.; A.B., U. Ill., 1961, J.D., 1963; m. Avalyn Berry, May 9, 1965; children—Devan Elizabeth, Kathryn Alicia, Timothy Whitzel III, Kristan Melissa. Admitted to Ill. bar, 1963; mem. firm Swain, Johnson & Gard, Peoria, 1965—. Spl. asst. atty. gen., 1969—. Campaign coordinator Senator Percy, Peoria County, 1972. Trustee Lakeview Center for Arts and Scis., Neighborhood Settlement House, Peoria; bd. dirs. Peoria Jr. Achievement. Mem. Senator Percy's Service Acad. Selection Bd., 1973—. Mem. Ill. Def. Counsel. Served with 101st Airborne Div., AUS, 1963-65. Decorated Combat Infantryman's badge, Bronze Star. Mem. Peoria County (chmn. legislative com., 1972-73), Ill., Am. bar assns., Am., Ill. trial lawyers assns., Am. Right of Way Assn., U. Ill. Alumni Assn. (life), Skull and Crescent, Toastmasters (pres. 1967), 101st Airborne Div. Assn. (life). Baptist (deacon). Clubs: Peoria Country, Peoria Illini. Home: 111 E Morningside Dr Peoria IL 61614 Office: Savings Center Tower Peoria IL 61602

SWAIN, WAYLAND ROGER, environ. research adminstr.; b. Boone, Iowa, Jan. 13, 1938; s. E. R. and E. Theo (Swain) S.; B.A. (Charles Stewart Brewster scholar), Ottawa (Kans.) U., 1960; M.S. (Regents scholar 1961-63, USPHS trainee 1963-64), U. Minn., 1965, Ph.D., 1969; m. Nancilee Davis, Sept. 3, 1960; 1 son, John R. Research fellow U. Minn., Mpls., 1964-65, instr., 1965-69, asst. prof. preventive medicine and biology, dir. Research and Edn. Center, Duluth campus, 1969-71, head dept. preventive medicine, asst. dean Med. Sch., Duluth campus, 1972-73, dir. Lake Superior Studies Center, Duluth campus, 1973-75, asso. prof. preventive medicine and biology, Duluth campus, 1975-76; dir. Large Lakes Research Lab., EPA, Grosse Ile, Mich., 1976—; U.S. chmn. water pollution control sect. US-USSR Joint Agreement on Environ. Protection; U.S. sci. adv. Inst. for Environ. Studies, U. Windsor (Ont.); chmn. research and devel. com. Gt. Lakes Basin Commn., 1978-80; Fgn. Study Award grantee Scottish Marine Biol. Assn., Edinburgh and Isle of Cumbrae, 1967. Bd. dirs. Area Mental Health Bd., Duluth, 1972-76, chmn. chem. dependency program, 1974-76, mem. regional med. programs adv. com., 1972-74. Served with USAR, 1957-61. Fellow Royal Soc. Health (London); mem. Internat. Assn. Gt. Lakes Research (organizational sec.), Am. Soc. Limnology and Oceanography, Entomol. Soc. Can. Contbr. numerous articles on large lake ecosystems and human health effects to profl. publs.; editor numerous vols. jointly published in English and Russian; translator sci. articles for gen. audiences. Office: EPA 9311 Groh Rd Grosse Ile MI 48138

SWALES, WILLIAM EDWARD, oil co. exec.; b. Parkersburg, W.Va., May 15, 1925; s. John Richard and Ellen (South) S.; B.A. in Geology, W.Va. U., 1949, M.S. in Geology, 1951; grad. advanced mgmt. program Stanford U., 1968; m. Lydia Eugena Mills, Dec. 26, 1948; children—Joseph V., Susan Eugena, David Lee. With Marathon Oil Co., 1954-70, 74—, spl. asst. to sr. v.p. prodn., internat., Findlay, Ohio, 1974, v.p. prodn., internat., 1974-77, sr. v.p. prodn. internat., 1977—, also dir.; exec. v.p. Oasis Oil Co. of Libya, Inc., Tripoli, 1970-72, pres., 1972-74. Served with USN, 1943-45. Mem. Am. Petroleum Inst., Am. Assn. Petroleum Geologists, Soc. Petroleum Engrs., Am. Geol. Inst. Clubs: Findlay Country, Muirfield Village Golf. Office: 539 S Main St Findlay OH 45840

SWAN, GEORGE SAMUEL, independent oil producer; b. Balt., Aug. 9, 1914; s. William R. and Carolyn E. (Lamp) S.; grad. McDonogh (Md.) Sch., 1932; student U. Md., Johns Hopkins, U. Va.; m. Pauline E. Womack, 1937; children—Nancy (Mrs. David S. Williams), Patricia (Mrs. Van Sandstrom), Susan (Mrs. Andrew R. Spence), George S. Asst. office mgr., plant cashier Chevrolet Motor Co., 1932-36; oil scout Tex-Jersey Oil Corp., Tyler, Tex., 1937-39; ind. oil producer, Saginaw, Michigan, 1939—. Past mem. bd. dirs. Saginaw div. ARC; bd. dirs. Cancer Soc. Mem. Mich. Oil and Gas Assn. (dir.), Ind. Petroleum Assn. Am. (pub. info. com.), Pi Kappa Alpha. Episcopalian (past sr. warden. vestryman). Clubs: Saginaw (past pres.), Kiwanis (past pres.) (Saginaw); Detroit; Otsego Ski (Gaylord, Mich.); Lost Tree (North Palm Beach, Fla.); Everglades (Palm Beach, Fla.). Home: Cottage Grove Route 1 Roscommon MI 48653 also 11701 Turtle Beach Rd Lost Tree Village North Palm Beach FL 33408 Office: 712 Second Nat Bank Bldg Saginaw MI 48607

SWAN, HERBERT SIEGFRIED, communications mfg. exec.; b. Montclair, N.J., Jan. 2, 1928; s. Herbert S. and Alma (Oswald) S.; grad. Phillips Exeter Acad., 1945; A.B. in Econs. and Bus. Adminstrn., Lafayette Coll., 1949; m. Roberta J. Whitmire, July 2, 1960; 1 dau., Roberta Allyson. Advt. supr. TV receiver dept. Gen. Electric Co., Syracuse, N.Y., 1954-55; copywriter Bresnick Co. advt. agy., Boston, 1955-58; sr. copywriter J.T. Chirurg Advt. Agy., Boston, 1958-59; advt. mgr. agrl. chems., indsl. minerals div. Internat. Minerals & Chem. Corp., Skokie, Ill., 1959-61; editor Motorola Newsgram, direct indsl. advt. mgr. Motorola, Chgo., 1962-68; dir. pub. info. Motorola Communications & Electronics, Schaumburg, Ill., 1968-71, mgr. indsl. advt. and sales, 1971-73, mgr. field merchandising, 1973—. Served with USAF, 1950-54. Mem. Community Radio Watch (nat. coordinator 1967-68). Home: 48 Little Cahill Rd Cary IL 60013 Office: 1300 E Algonquin Rd Schaumburg IL 60172

SWAN, PATRICIA BRINTNALL, nutritionist; b. Hickory, N.C., Oct. 21, 1937; d. Philip Earle and Lucille (Farmer) Brintnall; B.S., U. N.C., 1959; M.S., U. Wis., 1961, Ph.D., 1964; m. James Byron Swan, Apr. 23, 1962; children—Kathryn Ann, Deborah Lee. Research asst., research fellow U. Wis., 1959-64; research fellow U. Minn., 1964-65; asst. prof. nutrition, 1965-69, asso. prof., 1969-73, prof., 1973—. Mem. Am. Inst. Nutrition, British Nutrition Soc., Soc. Nutrition Edn. Home: 1525 Berne Rd Minneapolis MN 55421 Office: U Minn Dept Food Science St Paul MN 55108

SWAN, WALLACE KENT, govt. ofcl.; b. Kearney, Nebr., June 13, 1942; s. Kenneth Dean and Regina Joy (Young) S.; B.A., U. Idaho, 1964; M.A.P.A., U. Minn., 1969; M.P.A., Nova U., 1978, D.P.A., 1979; m. Alice Ramona Kyvig, Sept. 24, 1967; children—Gregory Dean, Eric William. Intern, Village of Edina, Minn., 1966-67; research fellow U. Minn., Mpls., 1967; adminstrv. analyst Minn. Dept. Pub. Welfare, St. Paul, 1967-72, planner, 1972-74, dir. regional devel., 1974; planning/evaluation dir. Hennepin County Welfare Dept., Mpls., 1975-78; adminstrv. support supr. Hennepin County Community Service Dept., Mpls., 1978—; dir. doctoral program in public affairs for Twin Cities, Nova U., Ft. Lauderdale, Fla. Nat. Endowment Humanities grantee program pub. adminstrs. Princeton U., 1976. Mem. Citizens League. Mem. Am. Soc. Public Adminstrn. (sec. Twin Cities chpt. 1974-75, pres. 1976-77, dir. 1977—, pres. 1978-79, dir. 1980-81), Am. Polit. Sci. Assn., Am. Public Welfare Assn., Minn. Social Service Assn., Am. Soc. Performance Improvement, Phi Beta Kappa, Pi Gamma Mu, Phi Kappa Phi. Contbr. articles to profl. jours. Home: 583 W Shryer Roseville MN 55113

SWANK, ROBERT L., assn. exec.; b. Green Bay, Wis., June 30, 1922; s. Orville M. and Mary M. (Steele) S.; B.S., Northwestern U., 1946; m. Karyl Komarek, Sept. 11, 1948; children—Marcy, Anne. With sales and mgmt. U.S. Steel, Chgo., Detroit and Pitts., 1946-72; dir. Midwest, Am. Mgmt. Assn., Chgo., 1974—; adv. bd. 40 Plus of Chicago. Mem. U.S. Senatorial Bus. Adv. Bd. Alt. mil. service War Shipping Adminstrn., 1944-45. Mem. Sales Mgrs. and Mktg. Assn. Chgo., Northwestern Grad. Sch. Mgmt. Alumni Assn., Delta Tau Delta. Office: 8655 W Higgins Rd Chicago IL 60631

SWANSON, ALICE MAY, educator; b. Bloomington, Ill., July 31, 1937; d. Charles Victor and Agnes (Funk) S.; student Ill. State U., summers 1957-58, 61; B.A., Eureka Coll., 1959, postgrad., 1978-79; M.Ed., U. Ill., 1964, postgrad., 1976-77; postgrad. Ind. U., 1979-80. Elem. tchr., public schs., Rossville, Ill., 1958-61; elem. tchr. Rantoul (Ill.) City Schs., 1961-72, reading specialist, 1972—, yearbook coordinator, 1968—; mem. tchr. liaison council Center for Study Reading, U. Ill., Champaign, 1977—. Choir dir. Evangelical Covenant Chs. Am., Paxton, Ill., 1976—. Mem. Internat. Reading Assn. (nat. conv. del. 1978), Assn. Supervision and Curriculum Devel., Orton Soc. (nat. del. 1979), Ill. Reading Council. Republican. Music arranger. Home: Rural Route 1 Paxton IL 60957 Office: 400 E Wabash Ave Rantoul IL 61866

SWANSON, ARTHUR P., architect; b. Chgo., Nov. 25, 1906; s. Paul William and Ida (Mord) S.; B.S., Ill. Inst. Tech., 1929; m. Jean M. Lillyquist, Feb. 4, 1939; children—Paul W., Lynn Virginia (Mrs. Thomas Wilson), Carol Jean (Mrs. David Robbin), Christine Mary, Carl John. With N. Max Dunning Co., Chgo., 1929-32, Douglas Aircraft Co., Chgo., 1941-42; pvt. practice architecture, Des Plaines, Ill., 1932-41, Chgo., 1943-59, Skokie, Ill., 1959-66, Rosemont, Ill., 1966—; v.p. O'Hare Inn, Chgo., 1959-71. Registered architect, Ill. Mem. AIA, Am. Srs. Golf Assn., Western Srs. Golf Assn. (dir.). Clubs: Architects (past pres.) (Chgo.); Bobolink Golf; Quail Ridge (Fla.). Prin. works include O'Hare Inn, Des Plaines, 1959, Win Schuler Restaurants, Mich., 1960—, O'Hare East Office Bldg., Rosemont, 1966, Gen. Mills Office Bldg., Internat. Harvester, Ft. Wayne, O'Hare Internat. Transp. Center Office Bldg., Rosemont, 1968, Nat. Assn. Ind. Insurers Office Bldg., Des Plaines, 1971. Home: 1454 Estate Ln Glenview IL 60025 Office: 9501 W Devon Ave Rosemont IL 60018

SWANSON, CHARLES ELROY, pub. co. exec.; b. Elgin, Ill., Nov. 14, 1927; s. Clarence E. and Florence T. (Nitchman) S.; B.S. in Indsl. Engring., Northwestern U., 1951; M.B.A., U. Chgo., 1956; m. Barbara J. Loveday, Mar. 31, 1955; children—Mark, Kimberly, Bradford. Mgr. econ. and fin. research Elgin Nat. Watch Co., 1951-57; mgr. estimating pricing Curtiss-Wright Corp., 1957-58; prin. Arthur Young & Co., Chgo., 1958-62; with Ency. Brit., Inc., Chgo., 1962—, exec. v.p., 1966-67, pres., 1967—, also chief exec. officer, dir. Bd. dirs. Chgo. Better Bus. Bur., from 1967. Served with AUS, 1946-47. Mem. Assn. Am. Pubs. (dir. 1970), Young Pres.'s Orgn., Direct Sell Assn. (dir.), Sigma Chi. Clubs: Mid Am., Chicago, Econ. (Chgo.); Knollwood. Office: Encyclopaedia Brittanica Inc 425 N Michigan Ave Chicago IL 60611

SWANSON, DAVID H(ENRY), economist; b. Anoka, Minn., Nov. 1, 1930; s. Henry Otto and Louise Isabell (Holiday) S.; B.A., St. Cloud State Coll., 1953; M.A., U. Minn., 1955; m. Suzanne Nash, Jan. 19, 1952; children—Matthew David, Christopher James. Economist area devel. dept. No. States Power Co., Mpls., 1955-56, staff asst., v.p. sales, 1956-57, economist indsl. devel. dept., 1957-63; dir. area devel. dept. Iowa So. Utilities Co., Centerville, 1963-67, dir. econ. devel. and research, 1967-70; dir. New Orleans Econ. Devel. Council, 1970-72; div. mgr. Kaiser Aetna Texas, New Orleans, 1972-73; dir. corporate research United Services Automobile Assn., San Antonio, 1973-76; pres. Lantern Corp., 1974-79; adminstr. bus. devel. State of Wis., Madison, 1976-78; dir. Center Indsl. Research and Service, Iowa State U., Ames, 1978—, mem. mktg. faculty Sch. of Bus. Adminstrn., 1979—. Vice chmn. Planning Commn. Roseville (Minn.), 1961; mem. Iowa Airport Planning Council, 1968-70; mem. adv. council office Comprehensive Health Planning, 1967-70; mem. adv. com. Center for Indsl. Research and Service, 1967-70, New Orleans Met. Area Com., 1972-73; mem. Dist. Export Council, 1978—; mem. region 7 adv. council SBA, 1978—; dir. Mid-Continent Research and Devel. Council, 1980—; chmn. Iowa del. White House Conf. on Small Bus., 1980. adv. com. U. New Orleans. County finance chmn. Republican Party, 1966-67; bd. dirs. Greater New Orleans Urban League, 1970-73. Served with USAF, 1951-52. C.P.C.U. Mem. Small Bus. Inst. Assn., Soc. Ins. Research, Iowa Profl. Developers, Nat. Assn. Mgmt. Tng. Adv. Centers. Republican. Episcopalian. Clubs: Rotary, Toastmasters (past pres.). Home: 1007 Kennedy Dr Ames IA 50010 Office: Iowa State U Ames IA 50011

SWANSON, DONALD WARREN, bicycle co. exec.; b. Wasco, Ill., Mar. 20, 1933; s. Wallace Austin and Louise Martha (Gerdau) S.; B.S., U. Ill., Urbana, 1960; m. JoAnne F. Gricunas, Oct. 14, 1956; children—Deanne Marie, Jill Louise. Sr. auditor Peat, Marwick, Mitchell & Co., Chgo., 1960-65; accountant Schwinn Bicycle Co., Chgo., 1965-66, office mgr. Midwest div., Elk Grove Village, Ill., 1966-68, controller div., 1968—, asst. sec.-treas. div., 1970—; pres. D.J.S. Investment Group, Geneva, Ill., 1973—; treas. Geneva Investment Group, 1976—. Chmn. finance com. Geneva Meth. Ch., 1972—, Geneva Meml. Community Center, 1974—, chmn. finance com. Geneva Bd. Edn. Dist. 304, 1977—. Served with U.S. Army, 1954-56. Mem. U. Ill. Alumni Assn., Nat. Assn. Accts., Am. Acctg. Assn., Fin. Execs. Inst. Club: Executives (Chgo.). Home: 119 Nebraska St Geneva IL 60134 Office: 2101 Arthur Ave Elk Grove Village IL 60007

SWANSON, EDWARD WILLIAM, JR., pen mfg. co. exec.; b. Cleve., Oct. 24, 1935; s. Edward William and Margaret Nellie (Kirkpatrick) S.; B.A. cum laude in Econs., Miami U., Oxford, Ohio, 1957; M.B.A., Carnegie Inst. Tech., 1967; m. Lois R. Ladley, May 20, 1961; children—Edward William III, David, Kristen, Jonathon. Data processing sales rep. IBM, Cin., 1960-65; cons., dir. corp. info. services Booz, Allen & Hamilton, Chgo., 1967-68; mgr. corp. acquisitions, dir. corp. analysis, dir. internat. protein Gen. Mills Co., Mpls., 1968-72; corp. v.p., mng. dir. Smiths Food Group (UK), Gen. Mills London Corp., 1972-75; gen. mgr. leisure group Parker Pen Co., Janesville, Wis., 1975-76, exec. v.p., 1976-77, pres., chief operating officer, 1977-80, pres., chief exec. officer, 1980—, dir., 1977—; dir. Manpower Inc., BANCWIS Corp., Warner Electric Brake & Clutch Co. Trustee Beloit Coll., 1977-80; bd. dirs. United Way North Rock County, 1979—, Janesville Found. Served to lt. USN, 1957-60. Clubs: Univ. (Milw.); Janesville (Wis.) Country. Office: Parker Pen Co Court and Division Sts Janesville WI 53545

SWANSON, FERN ROSE (MRS. WALTER E. SWANSON), educator; b. Kalmar Twp., Olmsted County, Minn., July 5, 1900; d. Henry E. and Susie (Hastings) Rose; student Winona (Minn.) Normal Coll., 1918-20; B.S., St. Cloud (Minn.) State Coll., 1955, M.S., 1958; m. Walter E. Swanson, June 24, 1928. Tchr. high sch. English, Latin, Eyota, Minn., 1920-21; tchr. jr. high sch. English, Appleton, Minn., 1921-22; tchr. elementary schs., Harmony, Minn., 1922-23; tchr. high sch. English, Latin, Augusta, Wis., 1923-24, South Haven, Minn., 1924-26; tchr. elementary, high sch. dramatics, Waterville, 1926-27; tchr. elementary schs., South Haven, 1927-41, 43-51, Silver Creek, Minn., 1941-43; tchr. elementary schs., Annandale, Minn., 1951-53, prin., 1953-67; tchr. elementary reading, Belgrade, Minn., 1967-71. Organizer, South Haven council Girl Scouts U.S.A., 1927, leader, 1927-30. Mem. Minn. Elementary Sch. Prins. Assn. 25 Year Club, NEA, Minn. Edn. Assn., Nat. Council Tchrs. English, Central Minn. Reading Council (past dir.), Internat., Minn. reading assns., D.A.R., Ladies of Grand Army Republic (pres. Minn. dept. 1974-77, nat. pres. Betsy Ross Club 1978, nat. patriotic instr. 1981-82), Minn. Hist. Soc., Delta Kappa Gamma (past pres. Upsilon chpt.). Club: Rebekahs. Home: 541 Fairhaven Ave South Haven MN 55382

SWANSON, FRANK WILLIAM, controls mfg. mgr.; b. Chgo., Dec. 28, 1946; s. Arthur B. and Alice M. (Balles) S.; B.S.E.E., No. Ill. U., 1968; m. Grace Palmenco, May 10, 1974; children—Edsel, Gemma, Jewelia, Maricel, Dawn, Kristin. Mgr., C.E. Niehoff, Chgo., 1977-79; materials mgr. Raymond Control Systems, St. Charles, Ill., 1979—; instr. Harper Coll. Served with AUS, 1968-70. Mem. Am. Prodn. and Inventory Control Soc. (cert. inventory mgr., pres. Fox River chpt.), Fox Valley Purchasing Soc., Am. Materials Mgmt. Soc. Republican. Lutheran. Home: 1100 Hermitage Ln Hoffman Estates IL 60195 Office: 315 Kirk Rd Saint Charles IL 60174

SWANSON, KENNETH EDWARD, mfg. co. exec.; b. La Porte, Ind., June 5, 1920; s. Edward O. and Dora A. (Schallow) S.; student Western Ky. U., 1938-41, Yale U., 1944, Ill. Inst. Tech. Evening Sch., 1946-49; m. Betty Lou Hightower, Feb. 27, 1943 (dec.); children—Peggy Lou, Kenneth Edward II; m. 2d, Charlotte L. Sullivan, Apr. 12, 1975. Indsl. engr., 1946-53; mgmt. cons., 1953-57; v.p. charge mfg. Crane Packing Co., Morton Grove, Ill., 1957—. Served to capt., USAAF, 1944-46. Mem. No. Ill. Indsl. Assn. (dir.), Indsl. Mgmt. Soc. Republican. Methodist. Clubs: Svithiod Singing (Chgo.), Masons, Shriners, Elks. Home: 615 Charlemagne Dr Northbrook IL 60062 Office: 6400 Oakton St Morton Grove IL 60053

SWANSON, KIMBERLY, mktg. and market research co. exec.; b. St. Paul, Jan. 23, 1952; d. Gunnar Iver and Arline Mary (Bowes) S.; A.A., Lakewood State Coll., 1972; B.A. in Communications (Univ. scholar), Hamline U., 1974, law student (Univ. scholar), 1975-77; m. Doran Jay Levy, Aug. 6, 1977. Free-lance market researcher, 1972-76; law clk. Kuehn Law Firm, St. Paul, 1976-78; v.p., owner Market Structure Insights, Inc., Mpls., 1978—. Vol. probation officer, St. Paul, 1975-77; del. Democratic Farm Labor Party, Mpls., 1979; bd. dirs. Minn. chpt. Lupus Found. Am. Recipient 2d pl. award Parliamentary Procedure Contest, Vocat. Indsl. Clubs Am., 1970, 2d pl. State Impromptu Speech Contest, 1970. Mem. Am. Mktg. Assn., Nat. Assn. Woman Bus. Owners, Phi Alpha Delta. Lutheran. Club: Good Old Girls. Home: 3928 Washburn Ave S Minneapolis MN 55410 Office: 305 Foshay Tower Minneapolis MN 55402

SWANSON, LAWRENCE CLIFFORD, ednl. adminstr.; b. Attica, Ind., Dec. 24, 1921; s. Albert Edward and Sarah Etta (Tyler) S.; B.S., Ind. State U., 1943; M.S., Butler U., 1946; postgrad. U. Mich., 1950, U. Colo., 1968; m. Rosanne Rehfuss, Aug. 3, 1946; children—Marvin Lawrence, Dale Clifford. Acct., Allison div. Gen. Motors Co., 1943; high sch. tchr., Greenfield, Ind., 1943-46; dept. head Ind. Bus. Coll., Indpls., 1945-47; instr. Gen. Motors Inst., Flint, Mich., 1947-63, asso. prof., 1963-66, adminstr. program devel., 1966-75, asso. dean acad. affairs, 1975-77, adminstrv. asst. to pres., 1977—. Recipient Authors award Nat. Assn. Accts., 1966. Mem. Am. Accounting Assn., Am. Soc. Engring. Edn., Flint Indsl. Mgmt. Assn. Methodist. Club: Masons. Home: 205 Cedarwood Dr Flushing MI 48433 Office: 1700 W 3d Ave Flint MI 48502

SWANSON, PAUL JOHN, JR., educator; b. Crawfordsville, Ind., May 10, 1934; s. Paul John and Helen (Bath) S.; student DePauw U., 1952; B.S. in Accountancy, U. Ill., 1959, B.S. in Econ. and Fin., 1960, M.S. in Fin., 1962, Ph.D., 1966. Grad. teaching asst. U. Ill., Urbana, 1960-65, grad. research asst., 1964-65; asst. prof. finance U. Cin., 1965-67, asso. prof., 1967—, prof.-in-charge dept. quantitative analysis, 1967-68. Cons. local bus. and govt. agencies. Served with AUS, 1956-58. Mem. Nat. Def. Exec. Res., Inst. Mgmt. Scis. (past pres. Miami Valley chpt.), Ops. Research Soc. Am., Am., Midwest finance assns., Fin. Analysts Soc., Inst. Chartered Fin. Analysts, Am. Statis. Assn., Delta Chi, Delta Sigma Pi. Republican. Presbyterian. Home: 3441 Telford St Cincinnati OH 45220

SWANSON, ROBERT MARTIN, univ. ofcl.; b. Bell, Calif., Oct. 14, 1940; s. Harold M. and Elsie Lorraine (Allison) S.; A.B., Long Beach (Calif.) State Coll., 1963; M.A., U. Iowa, 1965; Ph.D., U. Calif., Los Angeles, 1970; m. Patricia Ann Roberts, Dec. 20, 1962. Dir., Office of Mental Health Research, U. Iowa, Iowa City, 1966-70; research dir. Health Planning Council, St. Paul, 1970-73; exec. dir. Kansas City (Mo.) Health Plan, 1973-76; asst. dir. St. Louis U. Hosps., 1976-80; asst. v.p. St. Louis U. Med. Center, 1981—; dir. Organizational Research & Devel. Corp., Kansas City, Group Health Plan Greater St. Louis; clin. prof. St. Louis U. Grad. Program in Health and Hosp. Adminstrn., 1980—; adj. prof. Webster Coll., St. Louis, 1975—; spl. cons. to Kansas City (Mo.) Health Dept., 1975-76; tech. cons. Health Services Adminstrn., HEW, 1973-75; coordinator St. Louis Community-Univ. Conf., 1977-80; mem. health affairs task force Mo. Catholic Conf., 1977. Named Adm. in Nebr. Navy, 1971; State of Iowa grantee, 1969. Mem. Nat. Assn. Hosp. Devel. (cert.), Am. Mgmt. Assn., Soc. for Advancement Mgmt., N.Am. Soc. Corp. Planners, Internat. Platform Assn., Advt. Club Greater St. Louis, Zeta Beta Tau. Republican. Roman Catholic. Contbr. articles on health services to profl. jours. Home: Route 1 Box 338A Hillsboro MO 63050 Office: 3556 Caroline St Saint Louis MO 63104

SWANSON, ROBERT PAUL, real estate and investment co. exec.; b. Monmouth, Ill., Jan. 25, 1946; s. Ronald Louis and Jeanne Bunniff (McIntyre) S.; B.A., Western Ill. U., 1968, M.A., 1971; m. Debra L. Berg, Aug. 18, 1979. Instr. speech communication, dir. forensics Maine East High Sch., Park Ridge, Ill., 1968-72; instr. communications, asso. dir. forensics, dir. speech edn. Augustana Coll., Rock Island, Ill., 1972-74; sales asso. David M. Weiner & Assos., Inc., Moline, Ill., 1974-76, sales mgr., 1976-77, gen. mgr., 1977-80, v.p., 1980—; writer, announcer Sta. WKAI, 1964-68; writer, actor, dir. sta. WWIU, 1966-68; pres. United Enterprises HomeBuilders, 1977—. Mem. Rock Island County Rep. Central Com., 1976—, chmn., 1978—; mem. platform com. Ill. Rep. Party, 1978; candidate for Ill. Legislature, 1976; bd. dirs. Rock River Valley Assn., 1976—; mem. Bi-State Citizens Adv. Com. Named Ill. Debate Coach of Year, 1971; recipient Outstanding Young Tchr. award Central States Speech Assn., 1970. Lic. real estate broker, notary public, Ill. Mem. Nat. Assn. Realtors, Ill. Assn. Realtors (legis. steering com., chmn. comml. div.), Rock Island County Bd. Realtors (legis. chmn. 1975-78), Realtors Nat. Mktg. Inst., Quad City Homebuilders Assn., Nat. Assn. Homebuilders, Rock Island Jaycees (bd. dirs), Ill. Notaries Assn., Pi Kappa Delta. Clubs: Exchange (pres.), Internat. Order Vikings, Ready Riders Saddle (pres.), Rock Valley Racquet. Author: Pollution: Opinion and Evidence, 1969; Pollution: The Facts, 1969; Wage-Price Controls: What Policy?, 1969; Wage-Price Controls: The Facts, 1969. Home: 2207 44th St Rock Island IL 61201 Office: 1570 Blackhawk Rd Moline IL 61265

SWANSON, ROGER ARLISS, coll. dean; b. Luck, Wis., Dec. 29, 1939; s. Arthur C. and Alice Swanson; B.S., U. Wis., River Falls, 1963; M.S., S.D. State U., 1965; Ph.D., U. Ariz., 1968; m. Sally Erickson, May 30, 1969; stepchildren—David, Charles, Jon; children—Jodie, Karlyn. Extension soils specialist U. Wis., River Falls, 1973—, prof. soil sci., 1975—, dean Coll. Agr., 1980—, dir. W.K. Kellogg grant, 1978-81. Mem. Soil Conservation Soc. Am. (pres. Wis. chpt. 1981; Commendation award 1980), Am. Soc. Agronomy, Soil Sci. Soc. Am., Am. Water Resources Assn., Nat. Assn. Colls. and Tchrs. Agr., Gamma Sigma Delta, Alpha Zeta. Republican. Lutheran. Author articles in field. Office: Coll Agr U Wis River Falls WI 54022

SWANSTROM, KATHRYN RAYMOND, conv. mgmt. exec.; b. Milw., Sept. 5, 1907; d. William Hyland and Jessie Viola (Bliss) Raymond; student Bryant and Stratton Bus. Coll., 1927-28; m. Luther D. Swanstrom, Aug. 27, 1937; 1 son, William Hyland Raymond. Caterer, Racine, Wis., 1926; field rep., asst. mgr. Master Reporting Co., 1936-52; dir., sec. Diesel-Ritter Corp., 1942-46; pres. Kay C. Raymond Assos., 1952—; v.p., treas. Kenneth G. MacKenzie Assos., 1954—. Asst. sec. nat. com. U.S.A. 3d World Petroleum Congress, 1950-51. Sec. Ridge Civic Council, 1940-60; sec. Police Traffic Safety Com., Mayor's Com. Keeping Chgo. Clean. State chmn. legislation Ill. Congress Parents and Tchrs. Rep. state central committeewoman, 1938-44, asst. ofcl. reporter Rep. Nat. Conv., 1940-48. Mem. Anti-Cruelty Soc., AIM, Soc. Mayflower Descs., DAR (dep. gov. gen.), Nat. Geog. Soc., ASTM, Ladies Oriental Shrine N. Am., Founders, Patriots (nat. councillor), Aux. Ancient Honorable Arty. Co. of Boston (nat. pres. 1977-80), John Alden Kindred, Internat. Platform Assn., Hugenot Soc. (pres.), Pi Omicron (nat. pres. 1950-54). Republican. Episcopalian. Clubs: Beverly Hills Woman's, Crescendo. Address: 9027 S Damen Ave Chicago IL 60620 also 3 Old Hill Farms Rd Westport CT 06880

SWART, HANNAH WERWATH, museum curator; b. Milw., Mar. 21, 1913; d. Oscar and Hannah (Seelhorst) Werwath; student Milw. Downer Coll., part-time 1931-34, U. Wis., 1933-36, Milw. Sch. Engring., 1933-46; m. George Jerry Swart, Oct. 7, 1937; children—Greta Toni, JoHannah Werwath Nicholai, George Jerry Jr., Paul Oscar. Head dept. records, registrar coll. engring. Milw. Sch. Engring., 1931-51, mem. corp., 1952—, also cons. dept. alumni affairs; curator Hoard Hist. Mus., Fort Atkinson, Wis., 1967—. Mem. Wis. Gov.'s Bicentennial Commn. Bd. dirs. Girl Scouts Am. Recipient Bronze Statue, Girl Scouts U.S.A., Nat. Thanks badge, 1967. Mem. State Hist. Soc. Wis. (past pres. women's aux., life mem.), Watertown (hon. life), Fort Atkinson (program chmn.) hist. socs., Wis. Acad. Scis., Arts and Letters (councilor-at-large). Clubs: Tuesday, Quarter Century, Woman's of Wis. Author: Footsteps of our Founding Fathers, 1963; Biography of General Henry Atkinson, 1964; Margarethe Meyer Schurz, 1967; Koshkonong Country: A History of Jefferson County. Home: Rural Route 3 Box 27 Fort Atkinson WI 53538 Office: Hoard Historical Museum Merchants Ave Fort Atkinson WI 53538

SWARTZ, ALLAN ERNEST, engineer; b. Muskegon, Mich., Dec. 21, 1924; s. Ernest E. and Freda A. S.; student Bob Jones Coll., Cleveland, Tenn., 1946-47; B.S. in Mech. Engring., U. Mich., 1950; m. Wilma Jeanne Wilson, Sept. 2, 1950; children—Theodore, Dawn, Timothy, Bonnie. Project engr. Fisher Body Div. Gen. Motors Corp., Detroit, 1950-51; project engr. Muskegon (Mich.) Piston Ring Co., 1951-52, test engr., 1952-56, chief product engr., 1956-70, dir. engring., 1970-79, head engring. and research dept.; chmn. tech. com. Piston Ring Mfrs. Group. Bd. dirs. City Rescue Mission, Muskegon, 1972-79; chmn. bd. Evangel. Covenant Ch., Muskegon, 1967-69; pres. Band and Orchestra Parents, Muskegon High Sch., 1972-73. Served with U.S. Army, 1943-46. Certified profl. engr., Mich. Mem. Soc. Automotive Engrs., ASME. Republican. Clubs: Toastmasters, Christian Bus. Mens Com. Patentee reverse twist piston ring. Home: 3070 Sherwood Ct Muskegon MI 49441 Office: Muskegon Piston Ring Co Muskegon MI 49443

SWARTZ, B(ENJAMIN) K(INSELL), JR., archaeologist; b. Los Angeles, June 23, 1931; s. Benjamin Kinsell and Maxine Marietta (Pearce) S.; A.A. summa cum laude Los Angeles City Coll., 1952; B.A., UCLA, 1954, M.A., 1958; Ph.D., U. Ariz., 1964; m. Cyrilla Casillas, Oct. 23, 1966; children—Benjamin Kinsell III, Frank Casillas. Curator, Klamath County (Oreg.) Mus., 1959-61, research asso., 1961-62; asst. prof. anthropology Ball State U., Muncie, Ind., 1964-68, asso. prof., 1968-72, prof., 1972—; vis. sr. lectr. U. Ghana, 1970-71; exec. bd., ad hoc pres. Am. Com. to Advance Study of Petroglyphs and Pictographs; dir. Council Conservation Ind. Archaeology. Klamath County chmn. Oreg. Statehood Centennial, 1959. Served with USN, 1954-56. Fellow AAAS, Am. Anthrop. Assn., Royal Anthrop. Inst., Ind. Acad. Sci.; mem. Current Anthropology (asso.), Soc. Am. Archaeology, Soc. African Archaeologists in Am., Prehistoric Soc., Am. Quaternary Assn., Soc. Profl. Archaeologists, Sigma Xi, Lambda Alpha (nat. council). Editor: Archaeol. Reports; contbr. revs. and articles to profl. jours.; author monographs in field. Home: 3600 Brook Dr Muncie IN 47304 Office: Ball State U Muncie IN 47306

SWARTZ, EDWARD MORTON, dentist; b. Chgo., June 11, 1938; s. Aaron and Frances (Marc) S.; B.S., U. Chgo., 1960; D.D.S., U. Ill., 1963; m. Doreen Minus, Aug. 11, 1962; children—Arden, Alan, Heidi. Practice dentistry, Niles, Ill., 1965—; cons. Triton Coll. Served with AUS, 1963-65. Mem. Am. Dental Assn., Am. Analgesia Soc., N.W. Acad. Applied Dental Econs., Acad. Gen. Dentistry (past editor Ill. Pulse), Niles C. of C. Club: Rotary (pres. Niles-Morton Grove 1979-80). Contbg. author: Bloom's Textbook Histology. Contbr. articles profl. publs.; author lectrs. relative analgesia in modern dentistry. Home: 818 Prairie Lawn Rd Glenview IL 60025 Office: 7942 W Oakton St Niles IL 60648

SWARTZ, RICHARD RONALD, educator; b. Grosse Pointe, Mich., Feb. 28, 1946; s. Gordon George and Shirley Jean (Harris) S.; B.S. in Indsl. Edn., Eastern Mich. U., 1979; postgrad. in vocat. adminstrn. Central Mich. U., 1981—; m. Charlotte Brook Hanes, Jan. 2, 1978; children—Jodie, Jeff. Tchr. graphics Ypsilanti (Mich.) High Sch., 1972-74; foreman in printing industry, 1974-78; tchr. graphics Petoskey (Mich.) High Sch., 1979—; intern, vocat. dir. U. Mich. Leadership Devel. Program, 1980-81. Served with USN, 1967-68; Vietnam. Mem. Mich. Edn. Assn., No. Mich. Edn. Assn., Mich. Occupational Assn., Am. Vocat. Assn., Graphic Arts Tech. Found., Vocat. Indsl. Clubs Am. Lutheran. Club: Masons. Home: 1031 Jefferson St Petoskey MI 49770 Office: Petoskey High Sch East Mitchell St Petoskey MI 49770

SWARTZ, ROBERT DALE, newspaper pub.; b. Flint, Mich., Dec. 2, 1925; s. Harry C. and Mattie B. (Jespersep) S.; student Flint Jr. Coll., 1946-48; m. Idamae K. Stiehl, Nov. 2, 1946; children—Timothy J., Mary Swartz Smith, Kathleen Swartz Tupper, Dale R. With Flint Jour., 1949-58, controller, 1960-63, pub., 1979—; with Grand Rapids (Mich.) Press, 1958-60, mgr., 1963-79. Trustee Butterworth Hosp., Grand Rapids, 1972-78, McLaren Gen. Hosp., Flint, 1979—, Flint Area Conf. Bd., 1978—; pres. bd. dirs. Salvation Army, Grand Rapids, 1964-78, trustee, 1979—; pres. Jr. Achievement, Grand Rapids, 1966-78; mem. Health Systems Agy. for Western Mich., 1976-78; bd. dirs. Kent Med. Found., 1973-78, YMCA, 1972-78. Served with U.S. Army, 1944-46. Recipient Salvation Army Others award, 1978; Jr. Achievement award, 1976; Am. Legion 4th Estate award, 1972. Mem. Flint Area C. of C. (trustee 1979—), Am. Newspapers Pubs. Assn., Mich. Press Assn., Inland Press Assn. Clubs: Flint City, Flint Golf, Univ., Rotary. Home: 1603 Apple Creek Trail Flint MI 48507 Office: 200 E First St Flint MI 48502

SWARTZ, STANLEY L., educator; b. Fostoria, Ohio, Apr. 9, 1947; s. Roy Stanley and Lucille Winifred (Hoffman) S.; A.B., Findlay Coll., 1970; M.Ed., Bowling Green State U., 1972, Ph.D., 1976; postdoctoral study Rutgers U. Med. Sch.; m. Janet Ann Maule, Aug. 15, 1970; children—Stanley Neil, Philip Hemming, Daniel Pearson. Tchr. spl. edn. Ottawa (Ohio) Public Schs., 1970-72; adminstr. Allen County (Ohio) Schs., 1972-74; instr. spl. edn. Bowling Green State U., 1975-76; asso. prof. spl. edn. Union Coll. Ky., Barbourville, 1976-77; asso. prof. spl. edn. Western Ill. U., Macomb, 1977—, chmn. grad. studies program, 1980—; dir. Bethany Home/Residential Sch. and Treatment Program, Moline, Ill., 1979-81. Mem. Macomb Bd. Edn., 1979—. Recipient Presdl. Merit award Western Ill. U., 1980; U.S. Office Edn. fellow, 1971-72. Mem. Am. Ednl. Research Assn., Am. Assn. Mental Deficiency, Am. Orthopsychiat. Assn., Council Exceptional Children, Nat. Soc. Autistic Children, Nat. Assn. Retarded Children, Assn. Children with Learning Disabilities (Profl. Service award 1979), Internat. Assn. Sci. Study Mental Deficiency, Soc. for Pediatric Psychology, Phi Delta Kappa (Research in Edn. award 1977). Methodist (deacon). Contbr. articles to profl. jours., chpts. to books, monographs; editor: ICEC Quar., 1979-80; edit. bd. Mental Retardation, 1977-81. Office: Dept Spl Edn Western Ill U Macomb IL 61455

SWARTZBAUGH, JULIANA CRILEY, interior designer; b. Ottumwa, Iowa, Oct. 22, 1938; d. John Fry and Priscilla (Pedrick) Criley; B.S., Iowa State U., 1960; m. Robert Franklin Swartzbaugh, Apr. 1, 1960; children—Carrie, Kirk Criley. Tchr., Des Moines Pub. Schs., 1960-61; tchr. Westside High Sch., Omaha, 1961-64; instr. interior design U. Nebr., Omaha, 1964-77; pvt. practice interior design, Omaha, 1964—. Leader, Gt. Plains council Girl Scouts U.S.A., 1974-77. Mem. Am. Soc. Interior Designers, Kappa Kappa Gamma. Republican. Methodist. Home and office: 2512 S 126th St Omaha NE 68144

SWARTZLANDER, GARELD WILLIAM, electronics engr.; b. Milan, Ohio, Jan. 4, 1908; s. Clarence Henry and Mary Amelia (Paul) S.; student, Tri-State Bus. U., Toledo, 1926, Port Arthur (Tex.) Radio Coll., 1935; m. Iva Lucille Rafferty, July 1, 1930; children—David Lee, Janet Arlene Swartzlander Althoff. With Wabash R.R. Ann Arbor div., 1926-33; self-employed radio engr., Gibsonburg, Ohio, 1935-37, police radio constrn. engr., chief engr., various cities, 1937-57; chief engr., cons. engring., WFRO radio station, Fremont, Ohio, 1945-48; chief engr. Swartzlander Radio Ltd., Fremont, 1957—; cons. in field. Dir. United Fund, Fremont, 1977—. Mem. Assod. Police Communications Officers (mem. Frequency Allocations Com.), Amateur Radio Relay League, Sandusky Valley Amateur Radio Club (trustee), IEEE (life). Lutheran. Clubs: Rotary, Hi Twelve, Shriners (Fremont, pres. 1969), Fraternal Order Police. Office: 1524 Oak Harbor Road Fremont OH 43420

SWAYNE, MARLYN RAY, chiropractor; b. Burlington, Colo., June 28, 1955; s. Theodore Harold and Gertrude Leona (Schritter) S.; D.Chiropractic, Cleve. Chiropractic Coll., 1976; postgrad. Columbia Coll., 1976-77, Butler Community Coll., 1978. Pvt. practice chiropractic medicine, Eureka, Kans., 1977—. Mem. Kans. Chiropractic Assn., Parker Chiropractic Research Found., Cleve. Chiropractic Alumni Assn., Eureka Jaycees. Clubs: Elks, Kiwanis. Address: 201 N Main St Eureka KS 67045

SWEARINGEN, JOHN ELDRED, oil exec.; b. Columbia, S.C., Sept. 7, 1918; s. John Eldred and Mary (Hough) S.; B.S., U. S.C., 1938, LL.C. (hon.), 1965; M.S., Carnegie-Mellon U., 1939, D.Eng. (hon.), 1981; other hon. degrees; m. Bonnie L. Bolding, May 18, 1969; children (by previous marriage)—Marica Lynn (Mrs. F.G. Pfleeger), Sarah Kathryn (Mrs. T.E. Origer), Linda Sue (Mrs. Bradford Evans). Chem. engr. research dept. Standard Oil Co. (Ind.), Whiting, 1939-47; various positions Amoco Prodn. Co., 1947-51; gen. mgr. prodn. Standard Oil Co. (Ind.), Chgo., 1951, dir., 1952—, v.p. prodn., 1954-56, exec. v.p., 1956-58, pres., 1958-65, chmn. bd., 1965—, chief exec. officer, 1960—; dir. Chase Manhattan Corp., N.Y.C., Lockheed Corp.; chmn. Am. Petroleum Inst., 1978-79, Nat. Petroleum Council, 1974-76. Bd. dirs. Northwestern Meml. Hosp., 1965—; bd. dirs. Automotive Safety Found., 1959-69, chmn., 1962-64; bd. dirs. Hwy. Users Fedn. for Safety and Mobility, 1969-75, McGraw Wildlife Found., 1964-75; trustee Carnegie-Mellon U., 1960—, Depauw U., 1966-81, Orchestral Assn. Chgo., 1973-79; mem. adv. bd. Hoover Inst. War, Revolution and Peace, 1967—. Decorated Order of Taj (Iran); commendatore Dell'Ordine del Merito della Repubblica Italiana; Order of the Republic (Egypt); recipient Washington award Western Soc. Engrs., 1981; Charles F. Rand Meml. Gold medal AIME, 1980; Herbert Hoover Humanitarian award Boys' Clubs Am., 1980. Fellow Am. Inst. Chem. Engrs.; mem. Nat. Acad. Engring., AIME, Am. Chem. Soc., Phi Beta Kappa, Sigma Xi, Omicron Delta Kappa, Tau Beta Pi. Clubs: Chicago, Racquet, Mid-America (Chgo.); Glen View (Golf, Ill.); Old Elm (Lake Forest, Ill.); Links (N.Y.C.); Bohemian (San Francisco); Eldorado (Palm Springs, Calif.). Office: 200 E Randolph Dr Chicago IL 60601

SWEDBURG, WILMA ADELINE, educator, author; b. Nora Springs, Iowa; d. Lee Henry and Laura (Ellingson) Swedburg; B.S., U. Minn., 1954, M.A., 1956, specialist in edn., 1962. Supt., nursery classes, Edina Bapt. Ch., Mpls., 1952-62; tchr. kindergarten Mpls. Pub. Schs., 1954-58, 1st grade, 1958—. Adult tchr. for tng. nursery sch. classes Council Chs., Mpls., 1959-60, 62-64; workshop tchr. Nat. Ch. Confs., Columbus, Ohio, summers 1960—; asst. prof. edn. Augsburg Coll., Mpls., 1969—; asst. prin. Irving, Clinton and Greeley Elementary Schs., Mpls., 1972-73, reading specialist, resource tchr., 1973—; reading tchr. Andersen Sch., 1974-77; resource tchr., culturally disadvantaged children program, Mpls., summer 1965; free-lance writer. Mem. N.E.A., Minn., Mpls. edn. assns., Assn. for Childhood Edn., Internat. Platform Assn., Writers Guild, AAUW. Club: Rotary. Author: Christmas Donkey, 1962; Jeannie Goes to Sunday School, 1962; Just Like Me, 1962; The World Around Johnnie, 1966; The World Around Me, 1969; also packet materials for use by pre-sch. and head start programs Cook Pub. Co., Chgo.; mag. articles. Home: 5720 27th Ave S Minneapolis MN 55417 Office: 2727 10th Ave S Minneapolis MN 55417

SWEDO, DENNIS ALLEN, lamp mfg. co. ofcl.; b. Chgo., May 19, 1943; s. Louis and Roberta S.; student McHenry Jr. Coll., 1971, Coll. of DuPage, 1981; m. Carolyn M. Gibson, Mar. 10, 1962; children—Kelly Ann, Denise Lynn. Chief electro-plater Williams Mfg. Co., Elgin, Ill., 1963-66; chief electro-plater A.B. Dick Co., Niles, Ill., 1966-68, leadman plating, 1968-69, finishing foreman tech., 1969-79; prodn. mgr. Lindberg Heat Treating Co., Melrose Park, Ill., 1979-81; finishing supt. Stiffel Lamp Co., Chgo., 1981—. Cert. metal finishing technician. Mem. Am. Electro-Platers Soc., Am. Soc. Metals. Clubs: Northwood Sportsmans (past pres.), McHenry Lions (dir. 1975-76, pres. 1978-79, Pres.'s award 1979). Home: 1919 N Lakewood St McHenry IL 60050 Office: 700 N Kingsbury St Chicago IL 60610

SWEEN, EARL A., food co. exec.; b. Mpls., Jan. 4, 1921; s. August E. and Florence E. Sween; student U. Minn., 1938-42; m. Shirley Ann Ogin, Feb. 14, 1942; children—Deborah Ann, Thomas Earl. Gen. mgr. Sween Bros. Dairy Farms, Inc., Chanhassen and Wayzata, Minn., 1938-53; route supr. Franklin Dairy Co., Mpls., 1953-55; propr., mgr. Stewart Sandwiches, Eden Prairie, Minn., 1955—, chmn. bd. dirs., chief exec. officer, 1978—; pres. Nat. Stewart Infrared Assn., Fontana, Wis., 1965-66. Mem. Republican Nat. Com.; sustaining mem. Boy Scouts Am. Mem. U.S. Power Squadron. Mem. Wayzata Community Ch. Clubs: Lafayette Country, Decathlon Athletic, Port Royal, Masons, Shriners, Jesters. Home: 2440 Old Beach Rd Wayzata MN 55391 also 1400 Spyglass Ln Naples FL 33940 Office: 16101 W 78th St Eden Prairie MN 55344

SWEENEY, ASHER WILLIAM, state justice; b. Canfield, Ohio, Dec. 11, 1920; s. Walter W. and Jessie K. S.; student Youngstown Coll., 1939-42; LL.B., Duke U., 1948; m. Bertha Englert, May 21, 1945; children—Randall, Ronald, Gary, Karen. Commd. 2d lt. U.S. Army, 1950, advanced through grades to col., 1965; ret., 1968; admitted to Ohio bar, 1949; chief Fed. Contracting Agy., Cin., 1965-68; corp. lawyer, 1968-76; justice Ohio Supreme Ct., 1977—. Active Boy Scouts Am. Decorated Bronze Star, Legion of Merit; named to U.S. Army Hall of Fame, Ft. Benning, Ga., 1981. Mem. Ohio Bar Assn., Am. Legion Phi Delta Phi. Democrat. Roman Catholic. Office: 30 E Broad St Columbus OH 43215

SWEENEY, CHARLES HENRY, JR., state govt. ofcl.; b. Muncie, Ind., June 26, 1934; s. Charles Henry and Rosanna Barbara (Winters) S.; B.G.E., U. Nebr., 1964; postgrad. Mgmt. Inst., U. Ala., 1979; m. Mary Frances French, May 16, 1959; children—Scott, Todd. Field bus. mgr. Honeywell, Inc., Louisville and Milw., 1964-69; asst. supt. Ednl. Service Region Cook County, Chgo., 1969-70; dep. dir., gen. services adminstr. Ill. Dept. Children and Family Services, 1971-74; dist. adminstr. Iowa Dept. Social Services, Sioux City, 1974-76, dir. div. mgmt. and planning, Des Moines, 1976-79, dir. div. ops. control, 1980, insp. gen., 1981—. Pres., Friendly Hills Civic Assn., Louisville, 1964-65, Clark Elementary Sch. PTA, Springfield, Ill., 1973-74; active local Boy and Cub Scouts Am., Indian Guides, 1967-74. Served with AUS, 1954-56, 58-64. Mem. Human Resources Assn. Iowa (dir. 1974-76, pres. 1977-78), Nat. Welfare Fraud Assn., Mensa. Clubs: Masons, Shriners. Home: 1576 NW 96th St Des Moines IA 50322 Office: Hoover State Office Bldg Des Moines IA 50319

SWEENEY, JAMES LEE, govt. def. supply center ofcl.; b. Rocky River, Ohio, Mar. 23, 1930; s. John H. and Mary J. (Walkinshaw) S.; B.B.A., Case-Western Reserve, 1959; m. Marion J. Ridley, Oct. 4, 1958; children—John A., James L. Cost accountant AFB, Dayton, Ohio, 1959-62; accountant Defense Electronics Supply Center, Dayton, 1962-64, budget analyst, 1964-67, budget officer, 1967-74, supervisory budget analyst, 1974—; pres. 3001 Hoover Inc.; Mem. tax adv. com. Dayton-Montgomery County, 1967-70; bd. dirs. Dayton Human Relations Commn., 1970-74, Model Cities Housing Corp., 1972-74, M & M Broadcasting Co., Ohio Valley Broadcasting Co., 1979-81. Served with U.S. Army, 1952-54. Recipient Public Service award Def. Electronics Supply Center, 1972; Meritorious Civilian Service award, 1981. Mem. Alpha Phi Alpha. Episcopalian. Producer, commentator Spl. Community Report Sta. WHIO-TV, twice weekly 1970-76, daily, 1976—. Home: 743 Argonne Dr Dayton OH 45408 Office: DESC-CBO Dayton OH 45444

SWEENEY, JAMES RUSSELL, realtor; b. Indpls., July 2, 1929; s. Russell Thomas and Mildred (McCardle) S.; student Hanover Coll., 1947-48; B.S., Butler U., 1956; m. Rita A. McCann, 1958; children—Kathleen, James, Terrance, Kevin. Founder, owner

Sweeney Realty Co., Indpls., 1956—, Sweeney Ins. Agy., Indpls., 1956—. Served with USAF, 1951-54. Mem. Nat. Assn. Real Estate Bds., Ind. Real Estate Assn., Indpls. Real Estate Bd., Profl. Ins. Agts. of Am., Am. Legion, D.A.V. Roman Catholic. Clubs: Highland Country, Indpls. Athletic, Econ. of Indpls. Home: 444 Spring Mill Ln Indianapolis IN 46260 Office: 836 E 64 St Indianapolis IN 46220

SWEENEY, JOSEPH PATRICK, broadcasting co. exec.; b. Kokomo, Ind., Apr. 20, 1925; s. James B. and Anna (Cunningham) S.; student Sprayberry Acad. Radio, 1950-52; m. Patricia A. Smith, July 4, 1959; children—Cheryl, Michael, Maureen. With Delco Radio div. Gen. Motors Corp., Kokomo, 1952-62, electronics products trouble shooter, 1952-56, reliability engring. tester, 1956-62; founding pres. Fidelity Broadcasting Co., Inc., Rochester, Ind., 1962—, also subs. stations WFKO, Kokomo, WVTL, Monticello, Ind., WFDT, Columbia City, Ind., WROI, Rochester; established Tasty Q Restaurant, Rochester, 1981—. Elk, Kiwanian. Home: Rural Route 6 Box 100 Rochester IN 46975 Office: 116 W 9th St Rochester IN 46975

SWEENEY, RICHARD LESTER, mgmt. and cons. co. exec.; b. Des Moines, Oct. 23, 1936; s. Richard White and Lois Sara (Nickle) S.; B.A., Iowa State U., 1959; M.A., Colo. State Coll., 1963; Ed.S., Drake U., 1972, Ed.D., 1974; m. Melavie Joy Brendel, July 7, 1962; 1 dau., Alicia Joy. Tchr., chmn. sci. dept. public schs., Des Moines, 1967-71; exec. dir. Iowa Assn. Classroom Tchrs., 1971-72; instrn. and profl. devel. specialist Iowa Edn. Assn., Des Moines, 1972-81; pres. Sweeney Mgmt. & Cons. Service, Carlisle, Iowa, 1981—; lectr., adj. prof. Drake U., Upper Iowa U., U. No. Iowa, Lesley Coll. Grad. Sch. Asst. dir. Iowa Hawkeye Sci. Fair, 12 yrs.; bd. dirs. Carlisle Alumni Adv. Com., 1979-81. Mem. NEA, Iowa Acad. Sci., Assn. Supervision and Curriculum Devel., Am. Soc. Tng. and Devel., Phi Delta Kappa, Alpha Phi Omega. Mem. Disciples of Christ Ch. Home and office: Rural Route 1 Carlisle IA 50047

SWEENEY, RICHARD THOMAS, librarian; b. Atlantic City, Jan. 22, 1946; s. Harry A. and Margaret (McArdle) S.; B.A., Villanova U., 1967; M.A., Glassboro State Coll., 1970; M.L.S., Drexel U., 1972; m. Virginia Beschen, Aug. 26, 1967; children—Meghan, Moira, Thomas, Maureen. Tchr., Holy Spirit High Sch., Absecon, N.J., 1967-69; librarian Central Jr. High Sch., Atlantic City, 1969-70; dir. Atlantic City Free Public Library, 1971-76; mem. faculty Glassboro State Coll. Grad. Sch. Library Sci., 1973-74; dir. Genesee County Library, Flint, Mich., 1976-79; exec. dir. Public Library of Columbus and Franklin County, Columbus, Ohio, 1979—. Mem. adv. bd. Atlantic Community Coll.; chmn. personnel com. Thomas A. Edison Coll.; mem. Columbus Area Cable TV Adv. Com., CALICO; mem. adv. bd. Kent State U. Mem. ALA, Ohio Library Assn., Met. Library Dirs., Franklin County Dirs. Club: Rotary. Office: 28 S Hamilton Rd Columbus OH 43213

SWEENEY-RADKE, KATHLEEN ANN, clin. social worker; b. Spring Valley, Wis., May 27, 1947; d. Leo M. and Florence E. (Blegen) Sweeney; student U. Wis., Madison, 1965-69; B.S. in Labor Econs., U. Wis., Parkside, 1974; M.S.W., U. Wis., Milw., 1980; m. Ronald E. Radke, Oct. 15, 1977. Vocat. counselor Gateway Tech. Inst., Racine, Wis., 1975-78; clin. social work cons. Milw. Psychiat. Hosp., Wauwatosa, Wis., 1980—; psychiat. social worker Washington County Mental Health Center, West Bend, Wis., 1980—. Mem. planning and workshop coms. ann. Woman to Woman Conf., 1980; chmn. directory com. Woman's Resource Network, 1980. Gen. Mills Nat. scholar, 1965. Mem. Nat. Assn. Social Workers (dir. Wis. chpt.), Am. Assn. Marriage and Family Therapy (asso. affiliate), Phi Kappa Phi, Alpha Delta Mu. Author monograph. Home: 3153 S 25th St Milwaukee WI 53215 Office: Milw Psychiat Hosp 1220 Dewey Ave Wauwatosa WI 53223 also Washington County Mental Health Center West Bend WI 53095

SWEENY, ALLEN NEIL, machine tool mfg. co. exec.; b. Detroit, May 1, 1924; s. Donald Neil and Avis Marie (Allen) S.; B.S., Washington and Jefferson U., 1945; B.S. in Mech. Engring., M.I.T., 1947; m. Virginia Ann Bennett, July 17, 1948; 1 son, Allen Neil. With De Vlieg Machine Co., Royal Oak, Mich., 1947—, corp. v.p., dir., 1959—. Mem. Soc. Mfg. Engrs., Phi Gamma Delta. Republican. Episcopalian. Clubs: Detroit Country; Wianno (Mass.), Copt Heath Golf (Solihull, Eng.). Home: 63 Cambridge Rd Grosse Pointe Farms MI 48236 Office: DeVlieg Machine Co Fair St Royal Oak MI 48068

SWEET, BERNARD, airline exec.; b. Cin., Dec. 6, 1923; s. William B. and Elizabeth (Krent) S.; B.A., U. Wis., 1947; m. Betty Sweet, May 29, 1946; 1 dau., Laurie. Chief accountant Madison (Wis.) VA Hosp., 1948; with Republic Airlines, Inc., Mpls., 1948—, exec. v.p., 1967-69, pres., dir., 1969—, chief exec. officer, 1976—, vice chmn. bd., 1980—; dir. G & K Services, Inc., S.E. Rykoff & Co., Republic Energy, Inc. Mem. Minn. Bus. Partnership, Inc. Served with USAAF, 1943-46. Recipient State of Wis. Aerospace Man of Year award, 1972. Mem. Air Transport Assn. Am. (dir.), Assn. Local Transport Airlines (dir.). Office: 7500 Airline Dr Minneapolis MN 55450

SWEET, JAMES RILEY, printing co. exec.; b. Newton, Iowa, Sept. 27, 1944; s. Arthur Eugene and Dorothy (Mulinaux) S.; B.S. in Psychology, U. Iowa, 1968, M.A., 1969; m. Tannis Jeanne Reeves, Apr. 28, 1962; children—Michelle, Robert, Christine. Staff asst. indsl. relations Moore Bus. Forms, Inc., Glenview, Ill., 1969-74, mgr. human resource planning and devel., 1974-76, mgr. orgn. devel., 1976-78, mgr. human resources systems, 1978-79; mgr. corporate manpower devel. Moore Corp. Ltd., Toronto, Ont., Can., 1979—; instr. psychology Malcolm X Community Coll., 1970-72. Mem. Am. Soc. Tng. and Devel., Indsl. Relations Assn. Chgo., Nat. Tng. Lab. Orgn. Devel. Inst. Home: 470 Dorland Dr Oakville ON L6J 6B1 Canada Office: 1 First Canadian Pl Toronto ON M5X 1G5 Canada

SWEET, JEFFREY WARREN, playwright/journalist, educator, songwriter; b. Boston, May 3, 1950; s. James Stouder and Vivian Rita (Roe) S.; B.F.A. in Film, N.Y. U., 1971; m. Ruth Sheridan Sellers, July 28, 1980; 1 son, Jonathan Brian. Reporter/essayist, contbg. editor Dramatists Guild Quarterly, N.Y.C., 1970—; lectr., Goodman Theatre, Chgo., 1979—, O'Neill Center, Waterford, Conn., 1979—, Victory Gardens Theatre, 1979-80, Dramatists Guild, 1980—. Nat. Endowment for Arts lit. fellow, 1979; Office for Advanced Drama Research playwriting grantee, 1970. Mem. Dramatists Guild, Eugene O'Neill Theatre Center, New Drama Forum, Ensemble Studio Theater, N.Y. Writers' Bloc, Soc. Midland Authors (award for best drama 1978). Democrat. Author: Porch, 1976; Hard Feelings, 1979; After the Fact, 1980; Stops Along the Way, 1980; Ties, 1981; Holding Patterns, 1981; Routed, 1981 (plays); Something Wonderful Right Away (book), 1978.

SWEET, PHILIP WHITFORD KIRKLAND, JR., banker; b. Mt. Vernon, N.Y., Dec. 31, 1927; s. Philip Whitford Kirkland and Katharine (Buhl) S.; A.B., Harvard U., 1950; M.B.A., U. Chgo., 1957; m. Nancy Frederick, July 23, 1950; children—Sandra Harkness, Philip Whitford Kirkland, III, David A.F. With No. Trust Co., Chgo., 1953—, sr. v.p. bond dept., 1968-74, exec. v.p. bank, 1974-75, pres., dir., 1975-81, chmn., chief exec. officer, dir., 1981—; pres., dir. No. Trust Corp., 1975-81, chmn., chief exec. officer, 1981—. Vestryman, Ch. of Holy Spirit, Lake Forest, Ill., 1971-74; chmn. Ill. com. United Negro Coll. Fund, Northwestern Assos.; alderman, Lake Forest, 1972-74; bd. dirs. Johnston R. Bowman Health Center for Elderly, Lake Forest Hosp., U. Chgo. Council on Grad. Sch. Bus.; trustee Lake Forest Improvement Trust, Rush-Presbyn.-St. Luke's Med. Center; bd. dirs., treas. Protestant Found. Greater Chgo. Mem. Assn. Res. City Bankers. Clubs: Bankers, Econ., Chgo. Sunday Evening (treas., trustee), Attic, Bond, Chgo., Comml., Commonwealth (Chgo.); Onwentsia, Shoreacres, Old Elm. Home: 990 Ringwood Rd Lake Forest IL 60045 Office: 50 S LaSalle St Chicago IL 60675

SWEEZY, JOHN WILLIAM, polit. mgr.; b. Indpls., Nov. 14, 1932; s. William Charles and Zuma Frances (McNew) S.; B.S. in Mech. Engring., Purdue U., 1956; M.B.A., Ind. U., 1958; student Butler U., 1953-54, U. Ga., 1954-55, Ind. Central Coll., 1959; m. Carole Suzanne Harman, July 14, 1956; children—John William, Bradley E. Design, test engr. Allison div. Gen. Motors Corp., Indpls., 1953-57; power sales engr. Indpls. Power & Light Co., 1958-69; dir. pub. works City of Indpls., 1970-72; chmn. Marion County Republican Central Com., 1972—; mng. partner MCLB Co., Indpls., 1972—; dir. Lorco Engring., Indpls. Bd. dirs. Indpls. Humane Soc.; chmn. 11th Dist. Rep. Com., 1970, 73—; chmn. Rep. Congress of Urban Counties; alt. del. Rep. Nat. Conv., 1968, del., 1972, 76, 80; mem. credentials com., 1980; mem. Warren Schs. Citizens Screening Com., 1958-72. Served with AUS, 1953-55. Mem. Mensa, Sigma Iota Epsilon. Home: 166 N Gibson Indianapolis IN 46219 Office: 14 N Delaware St Indianapolis IN 46204

SWENGROSH, MARY JO, nursing home adminstr.; b. Alton, Ill., Oct. 22, 1946; d. Marion Joe and Freda (Smith) Walker; A.S. in Sci., Lewis and Clark Community Coll., Godfrey, Ill., 1981; children—Roger Lee Hicks, David Joe Hicks. Prodn. clk. Olin Corp., 1966-68; vol. local mental facility, 1964-73; adminstr. Burt Sheltered Care Home, Alton, 1973—, owner, 1975—. Mem. Ill. Health Care Assn. (chmn. residential/shelter care conf.), Beta Sigma Phi (past chpt. pres.). Home: PO Box 383 Godfrey IL 62035 Office: 1414 Milton Rd Alton IL 62002

SWENSEN, CLIFFORD HENRIK, JR., psychologist, educator; b. Welch, W.Va., Nov. 25, 1926; s. Clifford Henrik and Cora Edith (Clovis) S.; B.S., U. Pitts., 1949, M.S., 1950, Ph.D., 1952; m. Doris Ann Gaines, June 6, 1948; children—Betsy, Susan, Lisa, Timothy, Barbara. Instr., U. Pitts., 1951-52; clin. psychologist VA, 1952-54; from asst. to asso. prof. U. Tenn., Knoxville, 1954-62; asso. prof. psychology Purdue U., West Lafayette, Ind., 1962-65, prof., 1965—, dir. clin. tng., 1975—; vis. prof. U. Fla., 1968-69, U. Bergen (Norway), 1976-77; cons. VA, 1981 White House Conf. on Aging, others. Served with USN, 1944-46. Diplomate Am. Bd. Profl. Psychology; Am. Psychol. Assn./NSF Disting. Sci. lectr., 1968-69; Fulbright-Hays lectr., Norway, 1976-77. Fellow Am. Psychol. Assn. (pres. div. cons. psychology 1976-77), Soc. Personality Assessment; mem. Midwestern Psychol. Assn., Southeastern Psychol. Assn., Ind. Psychol. Assn., Gerontol. Soc., Sigma Xi, Psi Chi. Republican. Mem. Ch. of Christ. Author: An Approach to Case Conceptualization, 1968; Introduction to Interpersonal Relations, 1973; contbr. chpts. to books, articles to profl. jours. Home: 611 Hillcrest Rd West Lafayette IN 47906 Office: Purdue U West Lafayette IN 47907

SWENSEN, RICHARD DAVID, coll. dean, educator; b. Waverly, Iowa, Nov. 10, 1930; s. Alf Waldemar and Alice Mildred (Wilharm) S.; B.A. magna cum laude, Wartburg Coll., 1952; postgrad. Iowa State U., 1952-54; Ph.D. in Phys. Chemistry, State U. Iowa, 1961; m. Grace Marie Hartman, Aug. 3, 1952; children—David, Stephen, Linda, Jane, Daniel, Carolyn. Mem. faculty U. Wis., River Falls, 1955—, prof. dept. chemistry, 1961—, chmn. dept. chemistry, 1968-69, chmn. univ. faculty council, 1965-67, dean Coll. Arts and Scis., 1969—; dir. cultural exchange programs,cons. Internat. Cultural Exchange Programs, 1972—; guest lectr. to various orgns. in Far East, Scandinavia, Poland, 1975—. Bd. dirs., v.p. River Falls Sch. Dist., 1963-71; chmn. bd. deacons Ezekiel Luth. Ch., 1957-59, v.p., 1963-65; mem. State Wis. Adv. Council Future Edn. Professions, 1977-79; mem. Univ. Found. Bd., 1977—. Recipient Johnson Found. award, 1970; Alumni award Wartburg Coll., 1978; Univ. Insts. Health Research fellow, 1960-61. Mem. Am. Chem. Soc., AAAS, Council Colls. Arts and Scis. Lutheran. Home: Route 2 Box 354 River Falls WI 54022 Office: 172 Fine Arts Univ of Wisconsin River Falls WI 54022

SWENSON, DANIEL HART, educator; b. Balt., Aug. 26, 1935; s. Elmer Hart and Ethel Virginia (Moore) S.; B.S. in Bus. Mktg., Calif. State U., Chico, 1960, M.S. in Bus. Adminstrn., 1962; Ed.D. in Bus. Edn., Utah State U., 1976. Dir. admissions Kinman Bus. U., Spokane, 197—74; mktg. dir. Trend Bus. Colls., Vancouver, Wash., 1974; asso. prof. bus. edn. Govs. State U., Park Forest South, Ill., 1976-79, Western Mich. U., Kalamazoo, 1979—; participant North Central Assn. Accrediting Teams; cons. Hedman Co., Chgo. Served with USN, 1953-56. Recipient Delta Pi Epsilon Leadership award, 1976, scholarship award, 1975; Utah State U. summer fellow, 1976. Mem. Nat. Bus. Edn. Assn., Am. Soc. Tng. and Devel., Am. Bus. Communication Assn., North-Central Bus. Edn. Assn., Butte-Shasta Council Social Studies (pres., v.p. 1966-68), Delta Pi Epsilon. Club: Elks.

SWERHONE, PETER EDWARD, hosp. exec.; b. Canora, Sask., Can., May 30, 1931; s. Daniel and Marie (Zabinsky) S.; B.A., B. Commerce, U. Sask., 1953; diploma hosp. adminstrn., U. Toronto, 1955; m. Genevieve Miller, Dec. 27, 1956; children—Lorna M., Danielle K., Michelle A., Edward D.P., Patricia M. Adminstrv. asst. Calgary Gen. Hosp., 1953-56; asst. adminstr. Notre Dame Hosp., North Battleford, Sask., 1957-58; asst. adminstr. Winnipeg Gen. Hosp., 1958-63, adminstr., 1963-67, exec. dir., 1967-72; pres. Health Scis. Centre, Winnipeg, 1972—; asso. prof. pub. health U. Man., 1967—; vis. prof. U. Alta., 1967—; mem. survey team Canadian Council Hosp. Accreditation, 1970—. Bd. dirs. Man. Blue Cross, Winnipeg, 1970—, vice-chmn., 1979—, mem. exec. bd., 1973—; bd. dirs. Med. Products Inst., Inc., Man., 1973—. Dir., pres. Red River Exbn., Winnipeg, 1960-67. Bd. dirs. Holy Family Nursing Home, Winnipeg, chmn. bd., 1976-79; asso. mem. United Way Winnipeg, 1979—. Fellow Am. Coll. Hosp. Adminstrs. (bd. govs. 1972—, regent 1968-72, 76—, gold medal for excellence in hosp. adminstrn. 1976); mem. Canadian (dir. 1968—, pres. elect 1972-73), Man. (pres. 1966-67, dir. 1962-66) hosp. assns., Assn. Canadian Teaching Hosps. (pres. 1971), Hosp. Research and Devel. Inst. (dir. 1967—). Home: 306 Laidlaw Blvd Winnipeg MB R3P 0K5 Canada Office: Health Scis Centre 800 Sherbrook St Winnipeg MB R3A 1M4 Canada

SWETT, DANIEL ROBERT, lawyer; b. Chgo., Sept. 17, 1936; s. Israel and Rose (Crocker) S.; A.B., Harvard U., 1958, LL.B., 1961; m. Susan Kay Mann, Sept. 18, 1965; children—Karen Michelle, Brian Israel. Admitted to Ill. bar, 1962; asso. firm Sonnenschein Carlin Nath & Rosenthal, Chgo., 1962-69, partner, 1970—; asst. sec. Michael Reese Hosp. and Med. Center, Chgo., 1977—. Legal adv., bd. dirs. Planned Parenthood Assn. Chgo. Area, 1969—; bd. dirs. Jewish Fedn. Met. Chgo., 1979—. Mem. Am. Bar Assn., Ill. Bar Assn., Chgo. Bar Assn., Chgo. Council Lawyers. Democrat. Jewish. Clubs: Standard (Chgo.); Lake Shore Country (Glencoe). Home: 516 Sheridan Rd Glencoe IL 60022 Office: 8000 Sears Tower Chicago IL 60606

SWICK, MYRA AGNES, accountant; b. Chgo., Dec. 5, 1945; d. Arthur T. and Marcella M. (Pankiewicz) Swick; B.B.A. cum laude, Loyola U., Chgo., 1967. Mem. audit staff Ernst & Ernst, Chgo., 1967-72; controller Shorr Paper Products Co., Aurora, Ill., 1972-73; mgr. Otto Hillsman & Co., Ltd., Chgo., 1973-81, Walton, Joplin, Langer & Co., Chgo., 1981—. C.P.A., Ill. Mem. Am. Inst. C.P.A.'s, Nat. Assn. Accountants, Ill. Soc. C.P.A.'s, Am. Woman's Soc. C.P.A.'s (pres. 1976-77), Am. Soc. Women Accountants (pres. Chgo. chpt. 1974-75), Chgo. Soc. Women C.P.A.'s (founder 1977), Beta Alpha Psi, Beta Gamma Sigma. Contbr. accounting articles to profl. publs. Office: 55 E Jackson Blvd Chicago IL 60604

SWICKERT, MARYLEE GOLZ, psychotherapist; b. Aurora, Ill., Aug. 26, 1942; d. Wilbur Carl and Arlie Mary (Parker) Golz; B.A., Aurora Coll., 1971; M.Ed., Nat. Coll. Edn., Evanston, Ill., 1977; m. David C. Heywood; children—John Gerald, Heidi Mary. Learning disabilities tchr. Oswego (Ill.) Sch. Dist. 308, 1972-76; coordinator gifted program W. Northfield Sch. Dist. 31, Northbrook, Ill., 1977-78; outreach dir. Family Counseling Service, Aurora, 1978—; cons. in field. Cert. sex counselor Am. Soc. Sex Educators, Counselors and Therapists. Mem. Am. Personnel and Guidance Assn., NEA, AAUW (chmn. art study group 1975), Ill. Council Tchrs. Math. (rep. 1973-75), Oswego Edn. Assn., Phi Mu. Unitarian-Universalist. Office: 411 W Galena Blvd Aurora IL 60506

SWIFT, DOLORES MONICA MARCINKEVICH (MRS. MORDEN LEIB SWIFT), pub. relations exec.; b. Hazleton, Pa., Apr. 3, 1936; d. Adam Martin and Anna Frances (Lizbinski) Marcinkevich; student McCann Coll., 1954-56; m. Morden Leib Swift, Dec. 18, 1966. Pub. relations coordinator Internat. Council Shopping Centers, N.Y.C., 1957-59, Wendell P. Colton Advt. Agy., N.Y.C., 1959-61, Sydney S. Baron Pub. Relations Corp., N.Y.C., 1961-65, Robert S. Taplinger Pub. Relations, N.Y.C., 1965-66; prin. Dolores M. Swift, Pub. Relations, Chgo., 1966—. Bd. dirs. Welfare Pub. Relations Forum, 1971-79, treas., 1975-77; mem. pub. relations adv. com. Mid-Am. chpt. A.R.C., 1973—; mem. women's com. Mark Twain Meml., 1968-69; pub. relations dir. N.J. Symphony, Bergen County, 1969-70, mem. pub. relations/promotion com.; mem. Wadsworth Atheneum, 1968-69; bd. dirs. Youth Guidance, 1972-75; mem. NCCJ Labor, Mgmt. and Pub. Interest Conf., 1977—; mem. pub. relations com. United Way/Crusade of Mercy, 1979-80. Mem. Pub. Relations Soc. Am. (accredited, chmn. subcom. Nat. Center for Vol. Action 1971-72, pub. service com. Chgo. chpt. 1971-72, dir. 1975—, chmn. counselors sect. 1976-77, assembly del. 1976, 79-81, sec. 1977-78, v.p. 1978-79, pres.-elect 1979-80, pres. 1980-81, host chpt. chmn. 1981 conf.). Clubs: Women's (publs. chmn. Englewood, N.J., 1970-71); Publicity (chmn. pub. info. com. 1975-76) (Chgo.). Editorial bd. Pub. Relations Jour., 1978. Address: 525 Hawthorne Pl Chicago IL 60657

SWIFT, JONATHAN, educator, tenor; b. Glasgow, Scotland, Apr. 26, 1932; came to U.S., 1948, naturalized, 1954; s. John Francis and Catherine Little (McGowan) S.; M.A., Wayne State U., 1957; postgrad. (Fulbright scholar), Ecole Normale Superieure de St. Cloud, Paris, 1954-55; cert. Conservatoire Nat. de Musique (France), 1955; postgrad. U. Mich., 1959, Cambridge U., 1981, Mich. State U., 1981. On-camera tchr. French, Sta. WTVS, Detroit, 1955-56, Am. lit., 1960-62; instr. French, Wayne State U., Detroit, 1955-60; tchr. English, French and social studies Detroit Public Schs., 1957-64; tchr. English and history Glasgow Corp. Schs., 1967; tchr. English and French, Livonia (Mich.) Public Schs., 1967; chmn. English dept. Stevenson High Sch., Livonia, 1970-78, dir. Sch. Global Edn., 1978—; cons. to U.S. Dept. Edn., 1979, NEA pub. dept., 1979, Mich. State Dept. Edn., 1978, Gale Research Co., 1981; test writer Am. Coll. Testing Program, 1975-76. Debut in opera as Alfredo in La Traviata, 1961; leading tenor with Detroit Piccolo Opera Co., 1961-81, Detroit Grand Opera Assn., 1965, Mich. Opera Co., 1961-64; concert soloist with major symphonies in U.S., Can., Europe, Australia, 1961-81; appeared as tenor soloist in various radio and TV programs, 1961-81; rec. artist with Scotia and Andis (U.K.). Recipient French Govt. medal, 1954. Mem. NEA, Internat. Reading Assn., Nat. Council Tchrs. English (chmn. secondary sect. 1980-82), Assn. Tchr. Educators, Am. Assn. for Advancement of the Humanities, AAAS, Mich. Council for Social Studies, Assn. Supervision and Curriculum Devel., Mich. Council Tchrs. Fgn. Langs., Myasthenia Gravis Assn. (pres. 1968-69), Alliance Française, U.S./China Peoples Friendship Assn., Assn. of World Edn., Cousteau Soc., World Future Soc., Econ. Club of Detroit, Soc. Friends of St. George, Descs. of Knights of Garter. Roman Catholic. Contbr. articles and poems to profl. and lit. jours. Home: 6225 Golfview Dr Birmingham MI 48010 Office: 33500 W Six Mile Rd Livonia MI 48152

SWIFT, MORDEN L., telephone co. ofcl.; b. Chgo., Oct. 9, 1924; s. Jack and Reah (Leib) Steinberg; B.S., DePaul U., 1949; m. Dolores Monica Marcin, Dec. 18, 1966. Buyer Spiegel, Inc., Chgo., 1949-64; v.p. Ekco Products Import Co., N.Y.C., 1964-66; v.p. J & H Internat. Corp., Chgo., 1966-67; pres. Grinold Auto Parts, Inc., Hartford, Conn., 1968-69; div. dir. Topco Asso., 1970-79, Excello Ltd., Chgo., 1979-80; account exec. Ill. Bell Telephone Co., Chgo., 1980—. Mem. fund raising com. Community Chest, Chgo., 1962-63, ARC, 1961-62. Served with AUS, 1943-46. Mem. Housewares Clubs Chgo., N.Y., Furniture Club Am., Wadsworth Athenaeum, Hartt Opera Guild, Mark Twain Meml. Jewish. Home: 525 Hawthorne Pl Chicago IL 60657

SWIFT, ROBERT FILLION, automotive supply co. exec.; b. New Haven, Apr. 7, 1933; s. Franklin Robert and Loret (Fillion) S.; B.A., Yale U., 1958; student U. Paris, 1954-55; m. Monique Barbet, Nov. 17, 1956; children—Marc Franklin, Gregory Robert. Dir. internat. automotive ops. The Budd Co., 1958-64; cons. Spencer Stuart & Assos., N.Y.C., 1964-65; prin. McKinsey & Co., N.Y.C. and Paris, 1965-78; v.p. strategic planning and internat., automotive ops. Rockwell Internat., Troy, Mich., 1979—. Served with U.S. Army, 1955-57. Home: 3652 Erie Dr Orchard Lake MI 48033 Office: 2135 W Maple Rd Troy MI 48084

SWIGERT, THOMAS CRESAP, mgmt. cons.; b. Evanston, Ill., Apr. 17, 1948; s. Verne Wilson and Marjorie (Helm) S.; B.A. in History, U. Ill., 1970, M.B.A., 1975; m. Sue Anthone Pilger, May 26, 1974. Partner, fin. officer S.T. & W., Ltd., Urbana, Ill., 1970-74; gen. bus. cons. Swigert Enterprises, Urbana, 1970-75; mgr. and credit analyst, credit dept. Lake View Trust & Savs. Bank, Chgo., 1975-77; mgmt. cons. Deloitte, Haskins & Sells, C.P.A.'s, Chgo., 1977-78; sr. asso. Swigert & Assos., Inc., mgmt. and fin. cons., Evanston, 1978-81, pres., sr. asso., 1981—; sec., dir. Mark & Assos., Inc., Evanston, 1981—; instr. Am. Inst. Banking, 1978—. Cert. tax consultant (1981). Mem. Inst. Mgmt. Cons.'s, Inst. Tax Cons.'s, Nat. Assn. Income Tax Practitioners, U. Ill. Alumni Assn. (life), U. Ill. Commerce Coll. Alumni Assn., S.A.R. (bd. mgrs. Ill. soc.), Sigma Iota Epsilon (treas. 1971). Clubs: Univ. (Evanston); Union League (Chgo.). Home: 29 Salem Ln Evanston IL 60203 Office: 1603 Orrington Ave Suite 1200 Evanston IL 60201

SWINDLER, STEPHEN FRANCIS, sales exec.; b. Indpls., Jan. 27, 1942; s. Frank J. and Greta M. (Gormley) S.; student Purdue U., 1960-63; B.S., Ball State U., 1970; m. Sally Simpson, Feb. 6, 1971; children—Lori, Scott. Sales devel. rep. Merck & Co., Inc., Rahway,

N.J., 1970, sales rep., 1971-72, mgr. sales ops., 1973-74, mgr. N.Central region Health Div., 1975-76; nat. sales mgr. Bayvet div. Cutter Labs., Shawnee, Kans., 1976-81, dir. mktg., 1981—; speaker Animal Health Inst., 1974-75. Group leader United Fund, 1976; vol. football coach Muncie (Ind.) Schs., 1968-69; counselor Jr. Achievement, 1973-74; Republican committeeman, Westfield, N.J., 1973-74. Served with USN, 1964-67. Named Rookie of the Yr., Merck & Co., Inc., 1971; winner Toastmasters Speech Contest, 1973, 81. Mem. Am. Feed Mfrs. Assn., Nat. Cattleman's Assn., Am. Mgmt. Assn., Tex. Cattle Feeders Assn., Colo. Cattle Feeders Assn. Roman Catholic. Club: Toastmasters (v.p.). Home: 9506 Knox Dr Shawnee Mission KS 66212 Office: 12707 W 63rd St Shawnee KS 66201

SWINEHART, DAVID PARMER, educator; b. Ft. Wayne, Ind., Oct. 13, 1940; s. Harold Orlo and Celeste Amber (Gladieux) S.; B.S. in Humanities (Gen. Motors Coll. scholar), Loyola U., Chgo., 1962; M.S. in Bus. Adminstrn., Ind. U., 1975; m. Sheila Ann McVey, June 16, 1962; children—John, Mary, Margaret, David, Susan, Thomas, Cecilia. Writer, Bonsib Public Relations Co., Ft. Wayne, 1965-68; editor Lincoln Nat. Life Ins. Co., Ft. Wayne, 1968-69; communications specialist Gen. Electric Co., Ft. Wayne, 1969-71; personnel dir. St. Joseph's Hosp., Ft. Wayne, 1971-72, City of Ft. Wayne-City Utilities, 1972-76; dir. tng. and devel. Parkview Meml. Hosp., Ft. Wayne, 1976-79; asst. prof. bus. St. Francis Coll., 1979-80; asst. prof. personnel adminstrn. Purdue U. Sch. Supervision, 1980—; personnel cons. to local govt., 1980—. Bd. dirs. Neighbors, Inc., 1966-69, Family and Children's Service, 1975; mem. adv. bd. jobs program Nat. Alliance of Businessmen, 1971-73; mem. adv. bd. CETA, Ft. Wayne, 1974-76; chmn. exec. bd. Ft. Wayne Area Plan, 1974-76. Served to capt. inf. U.S. Army, 1963-65. Named Outstanding Ft. Wayne Bus. Editor, Ft. Wayne Bus. Editors Club, 1968. Mem. Am. Soc. for Tng. and Devel. (v.p. area chpt.), Am. Soc. Personnel Adminstrn., Am. Soc. for Hosp. Edn. and Tng. Democrat. Roman Catholic. Club: Kiwanis. Home: 3630 Burrwood Terr Fort Wayne IN 46815 Office: Ind-Purdue U 2701 Colliseum Blvd Fort Wayne IN 46805

SWING, GAEL DUANE, coll. pres.; b. LaPorte County, Ind., Mar. 13, 1932; s. William Edward and Dorothy Ruth (Jessup) S.; A.B., Franklin (Ind.) Coll., 1954; M.S., Ind. U., 1963; m. Sandra Sue Scott, Apr. 13, 1957; children—Scott, Kristie, Janet. Sales rep. Burroughs Corp., Indpls., 1954; successively dir. placement and admission counselor, dir. admissions, bus. mgr., v.p. devel. Franklin Coll., 1954-69; dir. spl. program services Office Devel., Washington U., St. Louis, 1969-73; exec. v.p. North Central Coll., Naperville, Ill., 1973-75, pres., 1975—; mem. Ill. Bd. Higher Edn. Non-Pub. Adv. Com. Recipient Alumni citation Franklin Coll., 1975. Mem. Fedn. Ind. Ill. Colls. and Univs. (exec. com.), Council West Suburban Colls. (dir.), United Methodist Found. (dir.), Asso. Colls. Ill. (pres., exec. com.), Council Advancement and Support of Edn. Methodist. Club: Naperville Country. Home: 329 S Brainard St Naperville IL 60540 Office: North Central Coll Naperville IL 60540

SWINTON, LEE VERTIS, state senator; b. Dadanelle, Ark., Aug. 9, 1922; B.A., Pittsburg State Coll.; J.D., U. Mo., Kansas City; m. Grace Thompson, Nov. 11, 1950; 1 child. Mem. Mo. Senate, 1980—. Former asst. county counselor; former chmn., mem. Jackson County Legislature. Mem. NAACP, Kappa Alpha Psi. Democrat. Mem. Christian Ch. Office: State Capitol Jefferson City MO 65101*

SWISHER, LOUISE DUNCAN, hosp. adminstr.; b. New Castle, Ind., Dec. 5, 1917; d. Paul Joseph and Dollie (Downey) Duncan; student Ind. Bus. Coll., 1936-37, Ind. U.-Purdue U., Indpls., 1972-73; m. Paul W. Swisher, Jan. 24, 1937; children—Janet Mackenzie, Charles Duncan, Paula Schelm. Clk.-treas. Town of Mooresville (Ind.), 1942-53; mgr. bus. officer Comer Hosp., Mooresville, 1953-61; asst. adminstr. Comer-Kendrick Hosp., Mooresville, 1961-72; adminstr. Kendrick Meml. Hosp. Inc., Mooresville, 1972—. Vice chmn. Republican Party, Morgan County, Ind., 1956—; sec. 6th Dist. Ind. Republicans, 1972—. Mem. Adminstrv. Mgmt. Soc., Am. Coll. Hosp. Adminstrs., Am. Bus. Women's Assn., Am. Med. Record Librarians Assn., Am. Hosp. Assn., Nat. Assn. Physicians Nurses. Quaker. Clubs: State Assembly Women's, Order of Eastern Star. Home: Rural Route 2 Box 1 Mooresville IN 46158 Office: Kendrick Meml Hosp Inc 1201 Hadley Rd Mooresville IN 46158

SWISHER, WILLIAM PORTER, physician; b. Mendota, Ill., Oct. 17, 1913; s. Ray and Ella (Skiles) S.; B.S., Beloit Coll., 1935; M.D., U. Ill., 1939; m. Pauline Hope Mills, June 19, 1939; children—Laura Hope, Corinne Sue, William Porter, Dwight Mills. Intern, U. Ill. Hosp., 1939-41, resident in internal medicine, 1941-43; gen. practice internal medicine, Evanston, Ill., 1946—; attending physician Hines VA Hosp., Maywood, Ill., 1947-53; asso. attending physician Cook County Hosp., Chgo., 1953-58, attending physician, 1958-70; attending physician Evanston Hosp., 1970—; asst. prof. dept. medicine Northwestern U. Sch. physician to parochial schs., Evanston, 1948-53; chmn. edn. com., mem. music com., tchr. Sunday sch. 1st Meth. Ch., Evanston, 1952-56; commr., public health adviser Boy Scouts Am., Evanston, 1950's; mem. Dist. 65 Bd. Edn., Evanston, 1956-62, pres., 1961-62, mem. com. for integration; caucus del. Dist. 202 Bd. Edn., Evanston; chmn. med. adv. com. Vis. Nurse Assn.; bd. dirs. Family Planning Clinic, Evanston, Youth Orgn. Umbrella, Evanston. Served as capt. M.C., U.S. Army, 1943-46. Diplomate Am. Bd. Internal Medicine. Fellow A.C.P.; mem. AMA, Chgo. Soc. Internal Medicine. Republican. Home: 1416 Hinman Ave Evanston IL 60201 Office: 636 Church St Evanston IL 60201 also 723 Elm Winnetka IL 60093

SWITT, KAREN JAY, librarian; b. Chgo., Sept. 2, 1952; d. Sydney Harold and Mary Switt Bender (Weinstein); B.A. in History (Ill. State scholar), Fla. Internat. U., 1974; M.A. in Library Sci., Rosary Coll., 1978; archeology fellow Tel Aviv U., 1972; honor scholar Roosevelt U., 1971-72. Bi-lingual classifier Spertus Coll., Chgo., 1975; librarian Paul Weir Co., Chgo., 1975-78; ref. librarian 1st Nat. Bank of Chgo., 1978; info. specialist Technomic Consultants, Chgo., mgr. info. services, 1980—. Mem. Spl. Libraries Assn. (hospitality chmn.), Small Spl. Libraries Assn., Chgo. On-Line Users Group (vice chmn.), Chgo. Assn. Law Librarians, Am. Soc. Info. Scientists (co-editor newsletter). Jewish. Clubs: Jewish Community Center of Rodgers Park, Yavnch. Author: Evaluation of a Mining Library, 1977. Home: 17944 Los Angeles Ave Homewood IL 60430 Office: Technomic Consultants One N Wacker Dr Chicago IL 60606

SWITZER, COLLEEN JOAN, mfg. co. exec.; b. Ames, Iowa, June 14, 1943; d. Lloyd K. and Anna Olava (Hia) Buckels; student Iowa State U., 1961-64; children—Shane S., Brett C. Recruiter, compensation and benefits specialist Shopsmith Inc., Vandalia, Ohio, 1976-80; personnel mgr. Bench Mark Tool, Jefferson City, Mo., 1980—. Mem. Am. Compensation Assn., Miami Valley Personnel Assn., Jefferson City Personnel Assn., Jefferson City C. of C. Home: 1013 Cimmaron St Jefferson City MO 65101 Office: 2601 Industrial Dr Jefferson City MO 65101

SWITZER, SUSAN MAHE, public relations exec.; b. St. Louis, Nov. 15, 1945; d. George Argeanton and Nadine (Schiller) Mahe; B.A., Manhattanville Coll., Purchase, N.Y., 1967; m. Thomas Switzer, May 23, 1969 (div. 1974); 1 dau., Sara. Sr. cons. fiscal unit Human Resources Adminstrn., N.Y.C., 1967; computer programmer McDonnell Automation Co., St. Louis, 1968-69; asst. dir. public relations St. Louis Symphony Orchestra, 1969-71, dir., 1974-77, mktg. dir., 1979-81; mgr. corp/orate relations Kellwood Co., St. Louis, 1977-79; dir. communications Peat, Marwick, Mitchell & Co., St. Louis, 1981—; Mem. adv. bd. Emergency Childrens Home, United Way, St. Louis. Mem. Public Relations Soc. Am., Women in Communications. Office: 720 Olive St Saint Louis MO 63101

SWOVICK, MELVIN JOSEPH, chemist; b. Altoona, Pa., Jan. 20, 1926; s. Walter Joseph and Magdalen Mary (Krish) S.; student U. Detroit, 1943-45, Med. Sch., Marquette U., 1945-47, Lawrence Inst. Tech., 1971-72; B.S. with honors in Chemistry, Detroit Inst. Tech., 1974; m. Maria Elizabeth Galatz, Nov. 23, 1968; 1 son, Michael Wayne. Med. technician, histopathy technician VA Hosp., Altoona, Pa., 1954-55; technician Allied Chem. Corp., Buffalo, 1955-60; devel. chemist Nopco Chem. Co., Linden, N.J., 1960-64; analytical chemist Schwarz Bio Research, Orangeburg, N.Y., 1964-65; analytical chemist, tech. service rep. Reichhold Chemicals Inc., Elizabeth, N.J. and Ferndale, Mich., 1966-80; tchr. clin. medicine Bon Secours Hosp., Grosse Pointe, Mich., 1975-79; tchr. Austin Cath. Prep. Sch., Detroit, 1975-78; forensic chemist, dep. sheriff Oakland County Sheriff Dept., Pontiac, Mich., 1980—. Active Boy Scouts Am., 1969-73. Mem. Am. Chem. Soc. Democrat. Roman Catholic. Clubs: Verein der Oesterreicher, Carpathia. Home: 345 Folkstone Ct Troy MI 48098 Office: Crime Lab Oakland County Sheriff Dept 1201 N Telegraph Rd Pontiac MI 48053

SYDOR, DARIA DOROTHY, accountant; b. Germany, May 22, 1946; came to U.S., 1949, naturalized, 1956; d. Michael and Maria (Stadnyk) S.; student Spencerian Bus. Coll., 1965-68, No. Mich. U., 1970-72, Milw. Area Tech. Coll.; children—Angela Marie, Chad Michael. Acct., Diocensan Office of Edn., Marquette, Mich., 1971-78; service rep. Kramer Machinery, Marquette, 1978-79; acct. Rexnord, Milw., 1979—. Lic. real estate broker, Wis.; lic. tax cons. Mem. Beta Sigma Phi. Ukrainian Catholic. Clubs: Ukrainian Dance Group, Ukrainian Lang. Home: 3811 S 94th St Milwaukee WI 53228 Office: 4800 W Mitchell St Milwaukee WI 53214

SYED, ALI TAJ, mfg. engr.; b. Karachi, Pakistan, Aug. 15, 1952; came to U.S., 1974, naturalized, 1979; s. Syed Jafar and Takreem Ali; B.S. in Mech. Engring., Engring. U. Lahore (Pakistan), 1973; M.S. in Indsl. Engring., Ill. Inst. Tech., 1975. Asso. cons. Dr. M.Z. Hassan, Chgo., 1974-75; indsl. engr. Johnson Products Co., Inc., Chgo., 1975-76; indsl. engr. Rego Co., Marmon Group, Chgo., 1976-80, sr. mfg. engr., 1981—; cons. GRI Corp., Chgo., 1974-75, Computer Peripherals, Inc., Rochester, Mich., 1975-76, Charlotte Charles, Inc., Chgo., 1977-78. Mem. Am. Inst. Indsl. Engrs. Club: Chgo. Falcons, Cricket (Chgo.). Home: 5445 N Sheridan Rd Chicago IL 60640 Office: 4201 W Peterson Ave Chicago IL 60646

SYED, SALAM ABDUS, microbiologist; b. Hyderabad Deccan, India, May 17, 1939; came to U.S., 1964, naturalized, 1974; s. Ghafoor Abdul and Jehangir (Begum) S.; B.S., D.J. Govt. Sci. Coll., Karachi, Pakistan, 1959; M.S., U. Karachi, 1961; Ph.D., Jefferson Med. Coll., 1968; m. Badar Zarina, Aug. 26, 1973; children—Jameel Abdul, Qadeer Abdul. Asst. lectr. U. Karachi, 1961-64; research fellow dept. microbiology, USPHS predoctoral trainee, Jefferson Med. Coll., Phila., 1964-67; research asso. dept. microbiology Med. Sch., U. Mich., Ann Arbor, 1968-70, Dental Sch., 1970-72, instr., 1972-73; sr. research asso. dept. oral biology Sch. Dentistry, U. Mich., 1973-74, asst. research scientist, 1974-78, asso. research scientist, 1978—, asst. prof. dept. oral biology, 1981—. Mem. AAAS, Am. Soc. Microbiology, Internat. Assn. Dental Research, Nat. Inst. Dental Research (spl. grants rev. com. 1979-81), N.Y. Acad. Scis., Sigma Xi. Muslim. Contbr. articles to profl. publs. Office: 3205 Dental Bldg School Dentistry U Mich Ann Arbor MI 48109

SYFERT, SAMUEL RAY, librarian; b. Beecher City, Ill., July 20, 1928; s. Fred and LaVonne Mildred (High) S.; B.S. in Edn., Eastern Ill. U., 1957, M.S., 1961; M.S. in Edn., Calif. Christian U., 1979. Tchr. bus. Geneseo (Ill.) Community Unit schs., 1957-59; tchr. English, Bethany (Ill.) Community Unit schs., 1961-77, sch. librarian, 1977—; extension coordinator Lake Land Coll., Mattoon, Ill.; bd. dirs., treas. Marrowbone Twp. Library, Bethany, 1978—. Served with AUS, 1950-52. Named Tchr. of Yr. in Moultrie County (Ill.), 1975. Mem. NEA, ALA, Ill. Edn. Assn., Ill. Library Assn., Bethany C. of C. (sec. 1977—), Am. Legion. Republican. Mem. Christian Ch. (Disciples of Christ). Home: Box 402 Bethany IL 61914 Office: Box 97 Bethany IL 61914

SYKES, CATHERINE, educator; b. Bowman, S.C., Feb. 19, 1942; d. Martha (Jones) S.; B.S., Clarion State Coll., 1964; M.A.T., Oakland U., 1973; Ed.S., Wayne State U., 1981; m. Barry Sykes, Dec. 23, 1966; 1 son, Barry Jabbar. Tchr., Freedom (Pa.) High Sch., 1964-67; reading specialist Pontiac (Mich.) Schs., 1967-75, curriculum analyst, 1975-78, staff devel. specialist, 1978—; human resource devel. trainer; cons. Tide Project, Wayne State U. Trustee Macedonia Missionary Baptist Ch., 1978—, also young adult usher, bd. divs. Project for Equal Ednl. Rights, Urban League. Mem. Nat. Assn. Negro Bus. and Profl. Women's Clubs (nat. 2d v.p.), Mich. Council Tchrs. English, Assn. Supervision and Curriculum Devel., Mich. Assn. Supervision and Curriculum Devel., NEA, Mich. Edn. Assn., Pontiac Edn. Assn., Mich. Ednl. Research Assn., Assn. Tchrs. English, Mich. Reading Assn., Mich. Assn. Middle Sch. Educators, Nat. Alliance Black Sch. Educators, Mich. Alliance Black Educators, Alpha Kappa Alpha. Home: 1172 Eckman St Pontiac MI 48057 Office: 25 S Sanford St Pontiac MI 48058

SYLORA, HERME O., urologist; b. Dumaguete City, Philippines, Apr. 13, 1936; s. Pin Liong and Che Tee (Ong) Sy; came to U.S., 1971; M.D., U. Santo Tomas, Manila, 1960; m. Mary T. Libi, Feb. 14, 1962; children—James, John, Roxanne. Rotating intern Mercy Hosp., Buffalo, 1961-62; resident in surgery Sisters Charity Hosp., Buffalo, 1962-66; hosp. dir. Holy Child Hosp., Dumaguete, 1966-71; resident in urology U. Chgo. Hosps. Clinics, 1971-74; practice medicine specializing in urology, Palos Heights, Ill., 1974-75, Evergreen Park, Ill., 1975—. Diplomate Am. Bd. Surgery, Am. Bd. Urology. Fellow A.C.S. Contbr. articles to med. jours. Home: 608 Prestwick Dr Frankfort IL 60423 Office: 9450 S Francisco Ave Evergreen Park IL 60642

SYLVESTER, GLEN MORRIS, tree service co. exec.; b. Goshen, Ind., Apr. 5, 1944; s. Clarence F. and Marjorie (Briggs) S.; B.S., Ind. U., 1970; m. Walda L. Estrup, Dec. 18, 1971; children—Tasha, Carolyn, Eleanor, Charles. Tel. salesman Richardson Homes Corp., Elkhart, Ind., 1970-73; salesman Steury Corp., Goshen, 1973-74, v.p. mktg., 1974-77, nat. sales mgr., 1974-77; pres. Goshen Tree Expert Service, 1977—. Served with USAF, 1964-67. Home: 54705 Holly Dr Elkhart IN 46514 Office: 17406 US 20 Goshen IN 46526

SYLVESTER, TERRY LEE, real estate devel. exec.; b. Cin., June 12, 1949; s. Wilbert Fairbanks and Jewell S.; B.S. in Bus. Accounting, Miami U., Oxford, Ohio, 1972; m. Janet Lynn Brigger, Nov. 29, 1975; children—Carisa, Laura, Jason. Staff accountant Alexander Grant & Co., C.P.A.'s, Cin., 1972; treas., controller Imperial Community Developers, Inc., Cin., subs. of Chelsea Moore Devel. Corp., 1972—; controller home bldg. div. Chelsea Moore Devel. Corp., 1978—; controller, chief fin. officer Armstrong Cos., apt. mgmt., 1978-79, Dorger Investments, Cin., 1979-81, Delta Mechanical Constructors, Inc., Fairfield, Ohio, 1981—. Home: 31 Woodmont Ct Fairfield OH 45014 Office: 8731 N Gilmore Rd Fairfield OH 45014

SYMONDS, BRUCE KNIGHT, mgmt. cons. services co. exec.; b. Contoocook, N.H., Mar. 20, 1923; s. Arthur George and Winnifred (Chase) S.; A.B. cum laude, Dartmouth Coll., 1950; m. Jane Balderston Cadbury, June 15, 1950; children—William C., Ann F., Robert B. With Ralston Purina Co., St. Louis, 1950-68, dir. market devel. Ralston Purina Internat., 1963-68; dir. mktg. Hubbard Milling Co., Mankato, Minn., 1968-74; v.p. mktg. Murphy Products Co., Burlington, Wis., 1974-75; pres. Bruce K. Symonds & Co., Waukesha, Wis., 1975—; dir. Doane Agrl. Services, Inc. Served with U.S. Army, 1948-50. Mem. Am. Mktg. Assn., Nat. Agri-Marketing Assn., Am. Feed Mfrs. Assn., Nat Feed Ingredients Assn. Methodist. Contbr. articles in field to profl. jours. Office: W288 S5023 Rockwood Trail Waukesha WI 53186

SYMONS, CLAYTON HAROLD, ednl. adminstr.; b. Detroit, Oct. 16, 1925; s. Harold S. and Ella M. S.; B.S., No. Mich. U., 1949; M.A., U. Mich., 1952, Edn. Specialist, 1972; m. C. Jean DeCaire, June 19, 1945; children—James, William, Mary, Michael, Patricia. Math. tchr. Onaway (Mich.) Pub. Schs., 1949-50, high sch. prin., 1950-52; supt. Merritt (Mich.) Consol. Schs., 1952-56; high sch. prin. LeRoy (Mich.) Community Schs., 1956-57, supt., 1957-62; supt. Covert (Mich.) Pub. Schs., 1962-64, Milan (Mich.) Area Schs., 1964—; participant IDEA fellows program Kettering Found., 1975, 76, 77, 78, 79. Pres. council local Roman Catholic Ch., 1972-74, treas. council, 1974-76, lector, 1966—, lay minister, 1970—. Served in USN, 1943-46. Recipient Community Service award Milan Jaycees, 1969. Mem. Am., Mich. (region pres. 1968-69, 78-79, state council 1968-71, 77-79, mem. edn. program com. 1973-74, legis. com. 1974-77), Washtenaw (pres. 1976-78, chmn. legis. com. 1975-76) assns. sch. adminstrs., Wayne County Bus. Ofcls., Mich. Congress Sch. Adminstrs. (pres. 1979-80), Washtenaw County Sch. Officers Assn. Club: Rotary (past dir.; mem. dist. found. scholarship com. 1971-77). Home: 123 E Michigan St Milan MI 48160 Office: 920 North St Milan MI 48160

SYNCHEF, RICHARD MICHAEL, lawyer; b. Chgo., Jan. 12, 1950; s. Barry Maurice and Rena Ruth (Jacobson) S.; B.A. with honors, U. Wis., 1972; J.D., Northwestern U., 1975. Admitted to Ill. bar, 1975; mng. partner firm Synchef & Synchef, Chgo., 1975—. Active Democratic gubernatorial campaigns, 1972, 76, candidate for del Dem. Nat. Conv., 1976. Mem. Am. (adminstrv. law sect. communications com.), Ill. (civil practice sect.), Chgo. bar assns., ACLU, Sierra Club, Ind. Voters Ill., Ams. for Dem. Action, Shorin Ryu Karate Assn., Phi Eta Sigma. Contbr. to U. San Francisco Law Rev. Office: Suite 1664 221 N LaSalle St Chicago IL 60601

SYNOVITZ, ROBERT JOSEPH, educator; b. Milw., Feb. 3, 1931; s. Francis Joseph and Estelle (Sibilski) S.; B.S., U. Wis., LaCrosse, 1953; H.S.D., Ind. U., 1959; m. Jane Lanier, Nov. 8, 1957 (dec.); children—Steven, Ronald, Catherine, Mark. Tchr., Webster Groves (Mo.) Public Schs., 1956-58; asst. prof. health edn. Eastern Ky. U., 1959-62; asso. prof. physiology and health scis. Ball State U., 1962-68; prof., chmn. dept. health scis. Western Ill. U., Macomb, 1968—. Mem. Fulton-McDonough County Mental Health Bd., 1977-78, Ill. Central Health Systems Agy. Bd., 1976-77, Western Counties Health Systems Agy. Adv. Council, 1976-79, Western Counties Comprehensive Health Planning Bd., 1972-75. Served with J.A.G.C., AUS, 1953-55. Creative Teaching grantee Ball State U., 1966-67; Emergency Med. Technician Tng. grantee Ill. Dept. Transp., 1975-77. Mem. Am. Sch. Health Assn. (pres.; Disting. Service award), AAHPER, Am. Alliance Health Edn., Eta Sigma Gamma (nat. v.p.). Democrat. Roman Catholic. Author: (with J. Schiefferes) Healthier Living, 4th ed., 1979; (with Schaller, Bock and Carrol) Critical Issues in Health, 1965. Office: Dept of Health Sciences Western Illinois University Macomb IL 61455

SYPRAZAK, JEANETTE GENEVIEVE, designer, illustrator; b. Chgo., Dec. 23, 1948; d. Eugene and Genevieve (Janisczewski) S.; B.S. in Plastic and Graphic Arts, U. Ill., 1970; postgrad. Art Inst. Chgo., 1967-71. Caseworker, State of Ill., 1971-74; TV graphic designer Sta. WFLD-TV, Chgo., 1974-78; owner, operator Bicycle Graphic, design, illustration, Chgo., 1978—; pres. Ventura, Inc. Mem. Artists' Guild Chgo. (chair-person social com. 1978-81, Design Show award of Excellence 1979), Women in Design, Chgo. Advt. Club, Air Force Art Program, Nat. Assn. Women Bus. Owners, Art Dirs. and Artists Club. Club: Metro. Office: 11 E Superior St Chicago IL 60611

SYVERSON, LESLIE ARTHUR, physician; b. Emmons, Minn., May 24, 1927; s. John Melvin and Minnie Theodore (Berkvam) S.; B.A., U. Minn., 1950, M.D., 1955; m. Lela M. Pertl, June 30, 1950; children—Patti J., Bonnie L., Ann R. Intern, St. Mary's Hosp., Duluth, Minn., 1955-56; practice medicine specializing in family practice, Fergus Falls (Minn.) Clinic (name now Fergus Falls Med. Group), 1958—; past mem. bd. dirs. Min-Dak Health Service Agy., Minn. Health Coordinating Council; asst. clin. prof. dept. family practice community health U. Minn. Med. Sch.; area cons. Minn. Dept. Vocat. Rehab.; dir. Western Minn. Savs. & Loan. Served with M.C., USAF, 1956-58. Diplomate Am. Bd. Family Practice. Mem. Minn. Acad. Family Practice (pres. Park Region chpt.). Republican. Mem. United Ch. Christ. Home: 628 W Maple Ave Fergus Falls MN 56537 Office: 615 S Mill St Fergus Falls MN 56537

SZAMBECKI, ANTHONY EDWARD, restaurant exec.; b. Wichita, Kans., Apr. 24, 1947; s. Edward A. and Frances Vivian (Beatty) S.; student Wichita State U., 1965-69, Youngstown State U., 1969-70; m. Diana K. Barton, June 6, 1970; children—Edward Aaron, Lee Barton, Shea Beatty. With Pizza Hut, Inc., Wichita, 1966-68, asst. gen. mgr., Ohio, 1968-74; owner, area gen. mgr. Hallrich Co., Youngstown and Kent, Ohio, 1974-78, dir. ops., 1976, v.p., dir. personnel and tng., 1979, v.p. restaurant operation, Kent, 1979—. Mem. Kent Hist. Soc., Am. Mgmt. Assn. Republican. Roman Catholic. Club: Kappa Sigma. Home: 1168 Norwood St Kent OH 44240 Office: PO Box 671 Kent OH 44240

SZEBEDINSZKY, JANOS EMIL, publisher; b. Budapest, Hungary, July 11, 1942; s. Jenö and Amalia (Krause) S.; came to U.S., 1949, naturalized, 1965; B.S. in Chemistry, Indiana U. of Pa., 1968; postgrad. anthropology Brandeis U., 1969, State U. N.Y. at Binghamton, 1970-74. Research chemist Jones & Laughlin Steel Corp., Pitts., 1963-68, pub., editor, 1972—; mng. editor Triad Mag., Chgo., 1973-74; pub. Around Publishing, Mentone, Ind., 1974—, And Books, South Bend, Ind., 1980—; geochem. cons., 1968-71; linguistic analyst, 1970-73. NSF grantee, 1968-69. Mem. Marshall County (Ind.) Graphic Design Council. Socialist. Lutheran. Home: PO Box 541 Mentone IN 46539 Office: 702 S Michigan Suite 836 South Bend IN 46618

SZERENYI, BELA JOSEPH, librarian; b. Budapest, Hungary, Nov. 13, 1914; s. Alajos and Ilona (Farkas) S.; came to U.S., 1956, naturalized, 1961; M.A. in Polit. Sci., Pazmany Peter U., Budapest, 1938; Ph.D. in Plit. Sci., Elizabeth U., Pecs, Hungary, 1940; M.S.L.S., Syracuse U., 1962; m. Irene Pornyeczy, Mar. 6, 1952;

children—Laszlo, Peter, Miklos. Atty. various govt. cos., Hungary, 1946-56; bookstack supr. Syracuse U., 1960-62; asst. librarian Cornell U., 1962-64; dir. library Tri-State Coll., 1964-67; dir. library sers. Eastern Ill. U., 1967—. Mem. ALA, Beta Phi Mu, Pi Sigma Alpha, Alpha Beta Alpha. Author: Investment Laws of Hungary, 1950. Office: Eastern Ill U Charleston IL 61920

SZMANT, HERMAN HARRY, chemist; b. Kalisz, Poland, May 18, 1918; came to U.S., 1936, naturalized, 1944; s. Leon and Teofila S.; B.A., Ohio State U., 1940; Ph.D., Purdue U., 1944; m. Adelina Mesa Avila, Aug. 16, 1941; children—Alina Margarita, Joseph Michael. Research chemist, Monsanto, 1944-46; mem. faculty Duquesne U., 1946-56; founder Center Chem. Research, U. Oriente, Santiago de Cuba, 1956-60; prof. U. P.R., head phys. scis. div. P.R. Nuclear Center, 1961-68; adv. AID mission, Dominican Republic, 1968; prof., chmn. dept. chemistry and chem. engring. U. Detroit, 1968—; cons. in field. Eli Lilly fellow, 1942-44. Recipient Leonardo Jgaravidez award P.R. sect. Am. Chem. Soc., 1976. Mem. Am. Chem. Soc. (chmn. P.R. sect. 1964, chmn. Detroit sect. 1973), AAAS, Mich. Orchid Soc. (pres. 1977-78). Author: Organic Chemistry, 1957. Contbr. chpts. to books, articles to profl. jours. Office: 4001 W McNichols Detroit MI 48221

SZOKA, EDMUND CASIMIR, bishop; b. Grand Rapids, Mich., Sept. 14, 1927; s. Casimir and Mary (Wolgat) S.; B.A., Sacred Heart Sem., 1950; J.C.B., Pontifical Lateran U., 1958, J.C.L., 1959. Ordained priest Roman Cath. Ch., 1954; asst. pastor St. Francis Parish, Manistique, Mich., 1954-55; sec. to bishop, Marquette, Mich., 1955-57, 59-62; chaplain St. Mary's Hosp., Marquette, 1955-57; tribunal, notary, defender of bond, Marquette, 1960-71; asst. chancellor Diocese of Marquette, 1962-69, chancellor, 1970-71; pastor St. Pius X Ch., Ishpeming, Mich., 1962-63, St. Christopher Ch., Marquette, 1963-71; bishop Diocese of Gaylord (Mich.), 1971-81; bishop Diocese of Detroit, 1981—; sec.-treas. Mich. Cath. Conf., Lansing, 1972-77; chmn. region VI, Nat. Conf. Cath. Bishops, 1972-77, now mem. nat. adminstrv. com.; mem. adminstrv. bd. U.S. Cath. Conf.; mem. budget and fin. com. Nat. Conf. Cath. Bishops/U.S. Cath. Conf. Mem. Canon Law Soc. Am. Office: 1234 Washington Blvd Detroit MI 48226

SZPADZINSKI, RAYMOND STANLEY, psychologist, marriage counselor; b. Hamtramck, Mich., June 10, 1941; s. Stanley and Stella (Wleklinski) S.; B.A., St. Mary's Coll., 1963; M.A., U. Detroit, 1973; M.Ed., Marygrove Coll., 1979; M.Div., St. John's Sem., 1981. Ordained priest Roman Catholic Church, 1967; asso. pastor Archdiocese of Detroit, Oak Park, Mich., 1967-69; hosp. chaplain Archdiocese of Detroit, Warren, and Detroit, 1970-78; pvt. practice psychology Center for Pastoral Growth and Devel., Detroit, 1975-77; pvt. practice psychology North Point Mental Health Assos., Farmington Hills, Mich., 1977—; in-service trainer Sacred Heart Alcoholic Rehab. Center, 1974-77. Mem. Am. Psychol. Assn. (asso.), Mich. Psychol. Assn., Am. Assn. Marriage and Family Therapy, Mich. Assn. Profl. Psychologists. Democrat. Home: 19701 Hilton Southfield MI 48075 Office: 30840 Northwestern Hwy Suite 100 Farmington Hills MI 48018

SZURA, THOMAS BRUNO, sch. adminstr.; b. Chgo., Sept. 20, 1946; s. Bruno Paul and Cecilia (Cichy) S.; B.A., Loyola U., Chgo., 1968, M.Ed., 1971; certificate in Adminstrn. Chgo. State U., 1976; m. Lucille Marie Bliss, June 7, 1969; children—Nicole Marie, Petra Ann. Tchr. French and English, counselor Leo High Sch., Chgo., 1968-73; vocat. counselor Amos Alonzo Stagg High Sch., Palos Hills, Ill., 1973-77, dir. guidance, 1977—, also summer coordinator Title I; guest advisor Office Extension, Short Courses and Confs., U. Ill., Chgo.; guest lectr. counselor workshop Ill. Assn. Coll. Admissions, 1979. Mem. Am. Personnel and Guidance Assn., Ill. Guidance and Personnel Assn., Assn., Ill. Sch. Counselors Assn., Phi Delta Kappa. Roman Catholic. Home: 6437 Fairfield St Berwyn IL 60402 Office: 111th and Roberts Rd Palos Hills IL 60465

SZWEDA, JOHN ALEXANDER, cardiologist, internist; b. Chgo., Nov. 19, 1926; s. John B. and Aleksa (Rozanski) S.; Pre-med. degree, Loyola U., Chgo., 1948, M.D., 1952; m. Alice Jean Osberg, Sept. 6, 1952; children—Barbara M., Alice M., Theresa M., John D., Luke I., Margaret M., Matthew B., Bridget M. Intern, Milwaukee County Hosp., 1952-53; gen. practice medicine, Beaver Dam, Wis., 1953-57; resident in internal medicine and cardiology, Henry Ford Hosp., Detroit, 1957-60; practice medicine specializing in cardiology, Beaver Dam, 1960—; chief of staff St. Joseph's Hosp., Beaver Dam, 1965, chief of medicine various years 1960-72; chief of staff Lutheran Hosp., Beaver Dam, 1970, chief of medicine various years 1960-72; chief of medicine Community Hosp., Beaver Dam, various years 1972—; cons. in field; participant preceptee and summer student programs Beaver Dam; cons. Waupun Meml. Hosp. Active Family Life Movement; bd. dirs. St. Peters Sch., 1967, religion and ethics tchr., various years 1960-70. Served with U.S. Army, 1945-47. Diplomate Am. Bd. Internal Medicine. Fellow A.C.P.; mem. AMA, Madison Acad. Internal Medicine, Am. Soc. Internal Medicine, Wis. (bd. dirs. 1971-73, speakers bur.), Am. heart assns., Dodge County Med. Soc. Roman Catholic. Contbr. research papers to med. jours. Home: 1300 N Center St Beaver Dam WI 53916 Office: 130 Warren St Beaver Dam WI 53916

TABER, MARGARET RUTH STEVENS (MRS. WILLIAM J. TABER), educator, engr.; b. St. Louis, Apr. 29, 1935; d. Wynn Orr and Margaret (Feldman) Stevens; B. Elec. Engring., Fenn Coll (now Cleve. State U.) 1958, B. Engring. Sci., 1958; postgrad. Western Res. U., 1959-64; M.S. in Engring., U. Akron, 1967; Ed.D., Nova U., 1976; m. William J. Taber, Sept. 6, 1958. Engring. trainee Ohio Crankshaft Co., Cleve., 1954-57, devel. engr., 1958-64, tng. dir., 1963-64; instr. elec.-electronic engring. tech. Cuyahoga Community Coll., Cleve. 1964-67, asst. prof., 1967-69, asso. prof., 1969-72, prof., 1972-79, acad. unit leader engring. tech., 1977-79; asso. prof. elec. engring. tech. Purdue U., West Lafayette, Ind., 1979—; lectr. Cleve. State U., 1963-64. Bd. dirs. West Blvd. Christian Ch., deaconess, 1974-77, elder, 1977-79; deacon Federated Ch., 1981-84. NSF grantee, 1970, 71, 72, 73, 78. Registered profl. engr., Ohio. Mem. IEEE, Soc. Women Engrs. (sr.), Am. Bus. Women's Assn. (ednl. chmn. 1964-66), Nat. Rifle Assn., Am. Soc. Engring. Edn., Am. Tech. Edn. Assn., Audio-Tutorial Congress, Tau Beta Pi (hon.). Author: (with Frank P. Tedeschi) Solid State Electronics, 1976; (with Eugene M. Silgalis) Electric Circuit Analysis, 1980; (with Jerry L. Casebeer) Registers, (with Kenneth Rosenow) Arithmetic Logic Units, Timing and Control, Memory Units, 1980. Home: 3036 W State Rd 26 West Lafayette IN 47906 Office: Michael Golden Engring Lab West Lafayette IN 47907

TABOREK, JOSEPH WILLIAM, ins. exec.; b. Ft. Benton, Mont., Oct. 29, 1942; s. Frank Joseph and Frances Anne (Dostal) T.; B.S. in Acctg., Coll. of Great Falls, 1967; m. Myra K. O'Connor, Aug. 10, 1968; children—Joseph W., Thomas F., Michelle Lynn, Philip Joseph. Payroll auditor Employers Group Ins. Co., Chgo., 1967-68; ins. accountant Allstate Ins. Co., Northbrook, Ill., 1968-70, Kemper Ins. Co., Chgo., 1970-72; ins. mgr. Borg-Warner Acceptance Corp., Chgo., 1972-78; dir. adminstrn. Borg-Warner Ins. Services, Chgo., 1978-80, Arcadia Ins. Co. & Arcadia Nat. Life Ins. Co., 1978-80, Centaur Ins. Co., Centaur Internat. Ins. Co. Ltd. and Creon Ins. Agy., Inc., 1978-80; treas. Creon Ins. Agy. Inc., Chgo., 1975-80, BWAC Ins., Chgo., 1975-80; founder Credit Ins. Markets, 1980—. Served with Mont. Air N.G., 1965-68. Roman Catholic. Home and Office: 1314 N Haddow Ave Arlington Heights IL 60004

TABRI, ADIB FARID, phys. scientist; b. Jerusalem, Palestine, July 24, 1928; s. Farid Farah and Theodora (Moubarak) T.; came to U.S., 1949, naturalized, 1959; B.S., Wilmington Coll., 1953; postgrad. Miami U., Oxford, Ohio, 1953-54, U. Cin., 1954-55, Xavier U., 1969-70; m. Valentina Bokatsch, Feb. 1954; children—Carmen Olivia, Edward Adib, Charles Farid. Research chemist The Christ Hosp., Cin., 1953-56; analytical chemist The Dow Chemical Co., Midland, Mich., 1956-57; research biochemist, The Christ Hosp., Inst. Med. Research, 1957-61; research chemist USPHS, Cin., 1961-70; research chemist Office of Enforcement, U.S. EPA, Cin., 1970-77, phys. scientist Environ. Research Info. Center, 1977—; mem. exec. devel. program U.S. E.P.A., 1975—. Vice pres. Arab-Am. Assn., Cin., 1967-73. Mem. Am. Chem. Soc., Am. Water Works Assn. (com. standard methods for exam. of water and waste water). Republican. Presbyterian. Contbr. articles to profl. jours. and guidelines to environ. regulations. Home: 10672 Indian Woods Dr Cincinnati OH 45242 Office: 26 W St Clair Cincinnati OH 45268

TACKE, ARTHUR WILLIAM, ophthalmologist; b. Milw., Sept. 27, 1921; s. Arthur Bernard and Esther Emily (Jeske) T.; B.A., Valparaiso U., 1942; M.D., Marquette U., 1946; m. Roberta Jean Hines, Sept. 9, 1950; children—David, Margret. Intern U.S. Naval Hosp., Bethesda, Md., 1946-47; resident Presbyn. Hosp., Chgo., 1949-51; pvt. practice ophthalmology, Milw., 1951—; mem. staff St. Joseph's, Milw. Children's, Milwaukee County hosps.; med. dir. Lumano Med. Dispensary, Zambia, 1958-65; instr. U. Ill. Med. Sch., 1949-51; asst. clin. prof. ophthalmology Med. Coll. Wis. 1956—. Sec. bd. Wis. Luth. High Sch. Assn., 1963; mem. exec. com. for N. Rhodesia, Wis. Evang. Luth. Synod, 1956-66. Served with USNR, 1943-49. Mem. Am. Acad. Ophthalmology, Am., Pan Am. assns. ophthalmology, Soc. Eye Surgeons, AMA, Milwaukee County, Wis. med. socs., Milw. Ophthalmic Soc. (past pres.), Chgo. Ophthal. Soc., Am. Assn. Ophthalmology, State Med. Soc. Wis. (co-chmn. sect. ophthalmology), Ferrari Club Am., Phi Chi. Home: 2205 W Greenwood Rd Milwaukee WI 53209 Office: 777 Glencoe Pl Milwaukee WI 53217

TAECKENS, DOUGLAS RICHARD, plastics mfg. co. exec.; b. Flint, Mich., May 9, 1950; s. Richard Ernst and Shirley Joanne (Currie) T.; B.B.A., U. Mich., 1972; children—James, April. Mem. sales dept. Helmac Products Corp., Flint, 1972-74, Southwest regional mgr., Dallas, 1974-76, nat. sales mgr., Flint, 1976-78, v.p. sales and mktg., 1978—. Mem. Sales and Mktg. Execs. Club, Nat. Assn. Service Merchandising, U. Mich. Alumni Assn. Republican. Office: PO Box 73 Flint MI 48501

TAEGE, MARLYS SCHMIDT, human services adminstr.; b. Milbank, S.D., Mar. 21, 1928; d. Daniel A. and L. Irene (Hoy) Schmidt; Ph.B. in Journalism, Marquette U., Milw., 1950; m. Jack F. Taege, Sept. 6, 1952 (dec. 1973); children—Linda, Lauren, James. Tchr. journalism and sr. English, Barron (Wis.) High Sch., 1950-51; asst. to editor Badger Luth. Newspaper, Milw., 1951-53, editor, 1971-74; corr. Waukesha (Wis.) Daily Freeman, 1957-59, editor home sect., 1968-71; editor-in-chief Luth. Women's Quar., 1966-77; public relations dir. Bethesda Luth. Home, Watertown, Wis., 1974-81, devel. dir., 1981—; mem. editorial commn. ofcl. periodicals Luth. Ch.-Mo. Synod, 1976—. Bd. dirs. Hawks Inn Hist. Soc., 1964-69, Kettle Moraine Ednl. Found., 1972-78, Concordia Coll. Century Club, 1979—; Republican precinct commiteewoman, Delafield, Wis., 1964-68. Recipient award of honor Hawks Inn, 1969, Gold Quill award in films Internat. Assn. Bus. Communicators, 1980. Mem. Women in Communications (Clarion award 1980), Public Relations Soc. Am., Luth. Public Relations and Devel. Guild, Assn. Luth. Devel. Execs., Milw. Press Club, Religious Public Relations Council, Luth. Women's Missionary League, Alpha Sigma Nu, Kappa Tau Alpha, Sigma Delta Pi, Delta Zeta. Author: And God Gave Women Talents, 1978; Why Are They So Happy, 1979. Home: N5W29116 Venture Hill Rd Waukesha WI 53186 Office: 700 Hoffmann Dr Watertown WI 53094

TAFLOVE, ALLEN, electronics engr.; b. Chgo., June 14, 1949; s. Harry and Leah Taflove; B.S., Northwestern U., 1971, M.S., 1972, Ph.D. (Cabell fellow Northwestern U. Tech. Inst. 1974-75), 1975. Asso. engr. IIT Research Inst., Chgo., 1975-77, research engr., 1978-80, sr. engr., 1981—. Mem. AAAS, IEEE, Sigma Xi, Eta Kappa Nu, Tau Beta Pi. Co-inventor radio frequency in situ process for oil shale and tar sands; patentee in field. Office: 10 W 35 St Chicago IL 60616

TAFT, ROBERT, JR., lawyer, former U.S. senator; b. Cin., Feb. 26, 1917; s. Robert A. and Martha (Bowers) T.; B.A., Yale U., 1939; LL.B., Harvard U., 1942; m. Blanca Noel, 1939 (dec.); children—Robert A., Sarah B. Taft Jones, Deborah, Jonathan D.; m. 3d, Joan M. Warner, 1978. Admitted to Ohio bar; asso. firm Taft, Stettinius & Hollister, Cin., 1946-51, partner, 1951-63, 77—; mem. Ohio Ho. of Reps., 1955-62, majority floor leader, 1961-62; mem. 88th Congress at-large from Ohio; mem. 90th-91th Congresses from 1st Ohio Dist.; U.S. senator from Ohio, 1971-76; practice law in Washington and Cin., 1976—. Trustee Children's Home Cin., Inst. Fine Arts. Served with USNR, 1942-46. Mem. Am., Ohio, Cin. bar assns. Republican. Clubs: Camargo, Racquet, Lit., Queen City (Cin.); Alibi; Burning Tree. Home: 4300 Drake Rd Cincinnati OH 45243 Office: 1800 Massachusetts Ave NW Washington DC 20036 also 1800 First Nat Bank Center Cincinnati OH 45202

TAGATZ, GEORGE ELMO, obstetrician, gynecologist, educator; b. Milw., Sept. 21, 1935; s. George Herman and Beth Elinore (Blain) T.; A.B., Oberlin Coll., 1957; M.D., U. Chgo., 1961; m. Susan Trunnell, Oct. 28, 1967; children—Jennifer Lynn, Kirsten Susan, Kathryn Elizabeth. Rotating intern Univ. Hosps. of Cleve., 1961-62, resident in internal medicine, 1962-63; resident in obstetrics and gynecology State U. Iowa, 1965-68; sr. research fellow in endocrinology U. Wash. dept. obstetrics and gynecology, 1968-70; asst. prof. obstetrics and gynecology U. Minn. Med. Sch., 1970-73, asso. prof., 1973-76, prof., 1976—, asst. prof. internal medicine, 1970-73, dir. div. reproductive endocrinology, 1974—. Served with M.C., U.S. Army, 1963-65. Diplomate Am. Bd. Obstetricians and Gynecologists (lectr. endocrinology postgrad. course 1975-76, examiner subsplty. bd. reproductive endocrinology 1976-79). Mem. Minn. Obstetrical and Gynecol. Soc., Am. Coll. Ob-Gyn (subcom. on reproductive endocrinology), Hennepin County (Minn.), Minn. State med. socs., AMA, Endocrine Soc., Internat. Soc. Advancement Humanistic Studies in Gynecology, Am. Fertility Soc., Central Assn. Obstetricians and Gynecologists, U. Iowa Obstetric and Gynecologic Alumni Soc. Contbr. articles to profl. publs.; ad hoc editor Am. Jour. Obstetrics and Gynecology, Obstetrics and Gynecology, Fertility and Sterility. Home: 6708 Sioux Tr Edina MN 55435 Office: PO Box 395 Mayo 420 Delaware St SE Minneapolis MN 55455

TAGATZ, GLENN EDWIN, educator; b. Milw., Jan. 27, 1934; s. Edwin Chistian and Sidonia Adelaide (Friedrichs) T.; B.S., Wis. State U., 1956; M.S., U. Wis., Milw., 1959; Ph.D., U. Wis., Madison, 1963; 1 son, Bradford Glenn Christian. Tchr. public schs. Milw., 1956-60; asst. prof. ednl. psychology Wis. State U., Oshkosh, 1963-65; asso. prof. psychology Ind. State U., Terre Haute, 1965-68; prof. edn. Marquette U., Milw., 1968—; pres. Internat. Personnel Services, Inc. Served with U.S. Army, 1961-62. Postdoctoral fellow U. Wis., Madison, 1966-67; recipient various grants including NSF, HEW. Mem. Am. Psychol. Assn., Am. Ednl. Research Assn., Phi Delta Kappa. Author profl. books and articles. Home: Route 2 Neshkoro WI 54960 Office: Marquette U Milwaukee WI 53233

TAGGART, PETER WILLIAM, retirement housing devel. co. exec.; b. Des Moines, May 7, 1946; s. Hans Robert and Bernadine (Williams) T.; B.A., Coe Coll., 1968; M.A., Drake U., 1978; m. Carol Meyer, Sept. 6, 1969; children—Elisabeth, Colin. Mgr. new product devel. Morton Salt Co., Chgo., 1968-72; dir. basic inventory control Younker Bros., Des Moines, 1972-79; dir. market research and property acquisition Life Care Services Corp., Des Moines, 1979—; instr. Am. Inst. Bus. Committeeman, Republican Party, Polk County, Iowa; trustee Des Moines Choral Soc. Mem. Am. Statis. Assn., Population Assn. Am., Assn. Public Data Users, Nat. Assn. Realtors. Episcopalian. Home: 201 Jordan Dr West Des Moines IA 50265 Office: 800 2d Ave Des Moines IA 50309

TAGLIA, PETER JOSEPH, accountant; b. Chgo., Apr. 1, 1947; s. Anthony Peter and Carolyn Mary (Meola) T.; B.S. in Acctg., U. Ill., 1969; m. Carol Ann Schmidt, Oct. 10, 1968; children—Meribeth, Carrie Ann, Peter Jay. Auditor, then supr. Coopers & Lybrand, C.P.A.'s, Chgo., 1969-73; controller Ceisel-McGuire Industries, Northbrook, Ill., 1973-75; treas., dir. McElvain Reynolds Co., Chgo., 1975-78, adv., 1978—, dir., 1974—; acct. Kulovsek and Taglia, C.P.A.'s, Crystal Lake, Ill., 1978—; vol. tax instr. Cary (Ill.) Park Dist., McHenry County Coll., 1981. Trustee, Village of Cary, 1977—; treas., dir. Marriage Encounter Fox Valley (Ill.), 1978—. Recipient Cary Disting. Citizen award, 1980. C.P.A., Ill. Mem. Am. Inst. C.P.A.'s, Ill. Soc. C.P.A.'s, Ill. Mortgage Bankers Assn., McHenry County Estate Planning Council, Cary-Grove Jaycees (Outstanding Young Man of Am. award 1975). Republican. Home: 219 Leath Way Cary IL 60013 Office: 95 Grant St Crystal Lake IL 60013

TAIT, JAMES M., corp. exec.; b. 1920; married. With Butler Bros., 1938-60; with Household Merchandising (formerly City Products Corp.), 1960—, pres. Ben Franklin Stores div., 1967-70, exec. v.p., 1970, pres., chief operating officer, 1971, pres., chief exec. officer, 1971—; dir. Household Internat., Snap-On Tools Corp. Office: 1700 S Wolf Rd Des Plaines IL 60018

TAKACS, ANDREW JOSEPH, mfg. corp. exec.; b. Toledo, July 20, 1933; s. Andrew Joseph and Ann Marie (Masney) T.; B.B.A. in Journalism and Bus. Adminstrn., U. Toledo, 1956, B.E. in Social Sci., 1957, M.E. in Polit. Sci., 1961; m. Anne Louise Schlicher, Nov. 10, 1956; children—Michael, David, Karen. Publicity dir. City of Toledo, 1954-56; reporter Toledo Times, 1954-56; asso. news dir. Sta. WSPD Radio-TV, Toledo; public relations Toledo Scale, 1957-59; with Whirlpool Corp., 1959—, mgr. community relations Clyde (Ohio) Div., 1959-61, public relations asst., Benton Harbor, Mich., 1962-63, mgr. public affairs, 1963-66, mgr. legis. affairs, 1966-67, dir. govt. affairs, 1967-70, dir. govt. and urban affairs, 1970-73, dir. public affairs, 1973-78, v.p. public and govt. relations, 1978—; trustee Whirlpool Found.; chmn., dir. Whirlpool Opportunities, Inc. Trustee, Twin Cities Area Cath. Sch. Fund, Inc. Served with U.S. Army, 1957, 61-62. Mem. Assn. of Home Appliance Mfrs. (chmn. energy coordinating com., leadership award 1980), Nat. Assn. Mfrs. (govtl. issues com.), U.S. C. of C. (public affairs com.), Public Relations Soc. Am., Twin Cities C. of C. (dir.). Roman Catholic. Clubs: Berrien Hills Country, Chgo. Press, Capitol Hill. Office: 200 US 33 N Benton Harbor MI 49022

TAKANO, MASAHARU, phys. chemist; b. Tainan, Taiwan, Jan. 20, 1935; s. Shuzo and Misao (Rengakuji) T.; B.S., Hokkaido U., 1957; M.S., U. Tokyo, 1959, D.Sc., 1963; m. Hiroko Takenoshita, Aug. 28, 1965; children—Kentaro, Jojiro, Miwako. Postdoctoral fellow McGill U., Montreal, 1963-67; with Monsanto Co., St. Louis, 1967—, sr. research specialist, 1979—. Fellow Am. Inst. Chemists; mem. Am. Chem. Soc., Am. Phys. Soc., AAAS, Soc. Rheology, Fine Particle Soc., Japan Soc. Polymer Sci., Japan Soc. Materials Sci., Sigma Xi. Buddhist. Contbr. articles to profl. jours. Home: 13146 Roundstone Ct St Louis MO 63141 Office: 800 N Lindbergh Blvd St Louis MO 63166

TAKEKAWA, THOMAS TSUYOSHI, social worker; b. Seattle, Nov. 5, 1933; s. Yasuhei and Kaneji Takekawa; B.A. in Sociology, U. Minn., 1956; M.S. in Social Adminstrn., Case Western Res. U., 1964; m. Kiyomi Komuta, May 24, 1966; children—Lisa Mari, Michael Thomas. Caseworker I, Olmsted County Welfare Dept., Rochester, Minn., 1959-62, caseworker III, 1964-66; social welfare supr. I, Olmsted County Dept. Social Services, Rochester, 1966—; cons. in field. Mem. Rochester Symphony Chorale, 1960—, Joint Religious Legis. Coalition Minn., 1975—. Served with AUS, 1957-58; Korea. Minn. Dept. Public Welfare grantee, 1962. Mem. Acad. Cert. Social Workers, Nat. Assn. Social Workers, Pacific-Asian Am. Mental Health Research Center, Minn. Social Service Assn. Democrat. Presbyterian. Home: 1361 8 1/2 Ave SE Rochester MN 55901

TAKEMORI, AKIRA EDDIE, pharmacologist; b. Stockton, Calif., Dec. 9, 1929; s. Matsutaro and Haruko (Teshima) T.; A.B., U. Calif. at Berkeley, 1951; M.S., U. Calif. at San Francisco, 1953; Ph.D., U. Wis., 1958; m. Valerie Williams, June 22, 1958; children—Tensho, Rima. Instr., State U. N.Y. at Syracuse, 1959-61; asst. prof., 1961-63; asst. prof. U. Minn., 1963-65, asso. prof., 1965-69, prof. pharmacology, 1969—; cons. NIH; review panel new drug regulation HEW, 1970-74. Served with AUS, 1953-55. Recipient Am. Cancer Soc. Postdoctoral fellowship, 1958-59; Alan Gregg fellowship, 1971; Nat. Acad. Scis. Internat. Travel award, 1962-65. Mem. Am. Soc. Pharmacology and Exptl. Therapeutics, AAAS, AAUP, Am. Chem. Soc., Soc. Exptl. Biology and Medicine, Sigma Xi. Buddhist. Contbr. numerous articles to sci. jours. Home: 5237 Wooddale Ave S Minneapolis MN 55424 Office: 3-260 Millard Hall 435 Delaware St SE U Minn Minneapolis MN 55455

TALBOT, BARBARA STANTON, communications specialist; b. Los Angeles, July 19, 1936; d. Robert Hulings and Inis Berniece (Egan) Stanton; student U. Utah, 1954-57; m. Peter Michal Talbot, Nov. 22, 1966 (div.); children—Tristen Michael, Heather Caress. Wendy Ward with Montgomery Ward, Los Angeles, 1964-65; fashion coordinator Bon Marche Dept. Store, Ogden, Utah, 1966-67; head instr. Patricia Stephens Career Coll., Dallas, 1968-70; dir. Barbizon Sch. Modeling, Dallas, 1970-71; mfr.'s rep. Continental Label Co., Atlanta, 1973-76; communications coordinator, nat. field trainer Bell & Howell Edn. Group, Chgo., 1977—. Republican. Mormon. Office: 2201 W Howard Evanston IL 60202

TALBOTT, LINDA HOOD, found. exec., educator, author; b. Kansas City, Mo., Dec. 29, 1940; d. Henry H. and Helen E. (Hamrick) Hood; B.A. in English with highest distinction, U. Mo., Kansas City, 1962, M.A. (fellow), 1964, Ph.D., 1973; postgrad. (fellow) Harvard U., 1974; m. Thomas H. Talbott, Mar. 5, 1965. Prof. English, Met. Jr. Coll., Kansas City, Mo., 1963-67, Queensborough Community Coll., Bayside, N.Y., 1967-68; prof. Nassau Community Coll., Garden City,

N.Y., 1968-69, also editor Nassau Review; prof. English, adminstr. Lesley Coll., Cambridge, Mass., 1969; founding editor Tempo mag., publs. dir. U. Mo., Kansas City, 1969-75, devel. officer, 1969-76; adj. prof. edn. U. Mo., 1975—, dir. spl. projects Office of Chancellor, 1976—; pres. Talbott and Assos., Kansas City, Mo., 1975—; exec. dir. Clearinghouse for Midcontinent Founds., Kansas City, Mo., 1975—; lectr., cons. in field. Bd. dirs. Dimensions Unlimited, Kansas City, 1973-77, United Community Services/Heart of Am. United Way, 1974—; chmn. Internat. Women's Year in Mid-Am. Symposium, 1975; del. Nat. Women's Conf., Houston, 1977; hon. fellow Harry S. Truman Inst., 1977—; hon. dir. Rockhurst Coll., 1977—; hon. trustee Truman Med. Center Found., 1980—; bd. dirs. exec. com. The Central Exchange, 1978—; mem. Kansas City Regional Commn. on Status of Women, 1978—; adminstrv. dir. Mid-Am. Assembly on Future of Performing Arts, 1979; bd. advisors Kansas City Arts Council, 1980—, Greater Kansas City Community Found., 1978—; bd. dirs. Greater Kansas City Mental Health Found., 1980—, Starlight Theatre Assn., 1980—. Recipient Higher Edn. Outstanding Achievement award U. Mo., Kansas City, 1973; Tomorrow Leadership award City Council Kansas City, 1979. Mem. AAUW, Am. Assn. Higher Edn. (Midwest coordinator 1973-76), Council Advancement and Support of Edn., Council on Founds., Women and Found./Corp. Philanthropy, Inc., Phi Delta Kappa, Pi Lambda Theta, Delta Kappa Gamma, Phi Kappa Phi, Phi Theta Kappa, Chi Omega. Presbyterian. Clubs: Univ. Womens, Woodside Racquet, Kansas City, Soroptimist Internat. (dir. 1977-80). Author: The Community College in Community Service: A Description Analysis of the Impact Program of the Higher Education Act, Title I, 1973; Grantmaking in Greater Kansas City: The Philanthropic Impact of Foundations, 1976, rev. edit., 1980; editor: The University of Kansas City: Prologue to an Urban University, 1976; A Brief History of Philanthropy in Kansas City, 1980; A Critical Difference: Philanthropy in Mid-America, 1982; pub., editor The Foundation Exchange, 1976—; contbr. articles to profl. jours. Home: 411 W 60th Terr Kansas City MO 64113 Office: PO Box 7215 Kansas City MO 64113

TALBOTT, THOMAS HOWARD, mfg. co. exec.; b. Kansas City, Mo., Mar. 4, 1940; s. William B. and June K. (Boyce) T.; B.A. in Econs., U. Mo., Kansas City, 1963, M.B.A. (fellow), 1965; m. Linda E. Hood, Mar. 5, 1965. With Mobil Oil Corp., 1965-73, staff analyst, N.Y., 1967-68, asst. to div. controller, Boston, 1968-69, div. supr. systems and indsl. engring., 1969, div. mgr. planning, systems and controls, Kansas City, Mo., 1969-73; project mgr. bus. planning and devel. C.J. Patterson Co., Kansas City, Mo., 1973-74, dir. fine food ops., 1974-75, asst. to pres., 1975-76, v.p. adminstrn., 1976—, dir., 1977—. Hon. fellow Harry S. Truman Library Inst., 1976; active United Fund, 1969, Friends of Art, Univ. Assos., Philharmonic Assos.; adviser Jr. Achievement, 1973. Victor Wilson Scholar, 1958-62. Mem. U. Mo. Kansas City Alumni Assn., Omicron Delta Kappa, Phi Kappa Phi, Tau Kappa Epsilon. Presbyterian. Clubs: Univ., Woodside Racquet. Home: 411 W 60th Terrace Kansas City MO 64113 Office: 3947 Broadway Kansas City MO 64111

TALBOTT, VERNON GLENN, labor relations educator; b. Keokuk, Iowa, Jan. 16, 1930; s. Vernon G. and Maxine (King) T.; B.A., U. Ill., 1951, postgrad., 1951-53; m. Nancy Inman Freeland, Sept. 8, 1957; 1 dau., Melissa. Quality control engr. Decatur Pump Co. (Ill.), 1968; with York div. Borg-Warner Corp., Decatur, 1960-68, 68-73, personnel dir., 1968-73. Instr. quality control courses; lectr. Inst. Labor and Indsl. Relations, U. Ill. at Champaign, 1973-77, asst. prof., 1977—; project dir. labor-mgmt. com. implementation project, 1974—; arbitrator, cons. in collective bargaining, cons. local govt. personnel adminstrn., 1974—. Mem. bd. Decatur Pub. Sch., 1969—; chmn. steering com. Prairie Jr. Coll., Decatur, 1966-69, Maconland Jr. Coll. 1971; Served with AUS, 1953-55. Mem. Am. Soc. Quality Control, Indsl. Relations Research Assn., Indsl. and Personnel Relations Assn., U. Ill. Alumni Assn. Home: 505 Fielding Ct Decatur IL 62522 Office: 504 E Armory Ave Champaign IL 61820

TALEH, MOHAMMAD BADR, educator; b. Rasht, Iran, Jan. 17, 1946; s. Taghi Badr and Hamideh Mirzaee T.; came to U.S., 1974; B.S. in Accounting, Accounting Coll., Tehran, 1967, M.S. in Accounting, 1968; M.S. in Mgmt., West Coast U., 1975; postgrad. (Univ. fellow) St. Louis U., 1976—. Fin. analyst Plan Orgn. of Iran, 1967-68; instr. Tehran Bus. Coll., 1971-74; teaching asst. St. Louis U., 1977-78; instr. U. Mo., St. Louis, 1978—; v.p. Internat. Student Council, 1976-78. Served to lt. Iranian Navy, 1969-71. Mem. Nat. Assn. Accountants, Acad. Polit. Sci., Smithsonian Assos. Moslem. Contbr. articles in Persian lang. to Iranian jours. Home: 3658 W Pine St Saint Louis MO 63108

TALENFELD, FRANK, pipe co. exec.; b. Pitts., Feb. 19, 1943; s. Leonard and Rae (Cardiff) T.; B.F.A. in Music, Carnegie Inst. Tech., 1965, B.F.A. in Music Edn., 1965; m. Myra Jean Lebow, Oct. 26, 1975. Music tchr. Matilija Jr. High Sch., Ojai, Calif., 1970-74, Warren High Sch., Downey, Calif., 1974-79; corp. sec., dir. purchasing, sales mgr. Tri-State Pipe Co., Bellaire, Ohio, 1979—. Dir. Downey Youth Symphony Orch., 1975-76, Downey City Youth Band, 1976-79. Served with USN, 1966-70. Recipient Tchr. of Yr. award Matilija Jr. High Sch., 1971-72; PTA Hon. Service award, 1978; Prin.'s Excellence in Teaching award Warren High Sch., 1979. Home: 167 S Park St Wheeling WV 26003 Office: Tri-State Pipe Co 31st and Guernsey Sts Bellaire OH 43906

TALIANA, LAWRENCE EDWIN, educator; b. Mt. Vernon, Ill., Feb. 27, 1929; s. Paul Thomas and Anastasia (Ulrich) T.; B.S., So. Ill. U., 1951, M.S., 1952; Ph.D., Purdue U., 1958; m. Phyllis Owen, Sept. 21, 1953; children—Lawrence Owen, Lisa Ellen. Counselor, chief counselor Purdue U. Counseling and Testing Center, 1954-57; surp. testing service So. Ill. U. at Carbondale, 1957-59, asso. prof. psychology and guidance So. Ill. U. at Edwardsville, 1959-67, prof. psychology and psychol. services, 1967—, coordinator acad. student counseling, 1962-65, acting chmn. dept. psychology, guidance and spl. edn., 1965, asst. to chancellor for acad. affairs, 1969-71, asst. v.p. planning and devel., 1971-72. Vis. prof. Ore. System Higher Edn., 1965-66. Cons., Social Security div. U.S. Dept. Health, Edn. and Welfare, 1962-66. Ill. Div. Vocational Rehab., 1959—, Ill. Dept. Guidance Services, 1961-66, State Supt. Pub. Instrn. Title III, 1970-75, 3d Circuit Ct. Ill., 1973—. Mem. Edwardsville Human Relations Commn., 1963-64, Ill. Mental Health Planning Bd., Council Univs., 1972-75. Served with M.C., AUS, 1952-54. Mem. A.A.A.S., Am., Midwestern, Ill. (chmn. acad. sect., mem. ethics com. 1976—) psychol. assns., Am., Ill. (past treas.) personnel and guidance assns., Soc. Personality Assessment, Nat. Register Health Service Providers in Psychology, Am. Ednl. Research Assn., Edwardsville C. of C. (dir. 1971-75), Sigma Xi. Home: 1312 Randle St Edwardsville IL 62025

TALKINGTON, ROBERT VAN, state senator; b. nr. Patrick, Tex., Aug. 23, 1929; s. William Henry and Nannie J. (Patrick) T.; A.A., Tyler Jr. Coll., 1949; B.S., U. Kans., 1951, LL.B., 1954, J.D., 1971; m. Donna Jill Schmaus, Mar. 25, 1951; children—Jill Talkington McCaskill, Jacki, James, Thomas, Lisa. Admitted to Kans. bar, 1954; county atty., Allen County, 1957-63; city atty., Moran, 1968; mem. Kans. Ho. of Reps. from 10th Dist., 1969-73; mem. Kans. Senate from 12th Dist., 1973—, v.p., 1977-81, majority leader, 1981—. Chmn. Republican Party, Allen County, 1964-68, state treas., 1964-66. Trustee, Iola Pub. Library, 1962-70; mem. adv. bd. Greater U. Fund, U. Kans., 1967-72. Served with CIC, AUS, 1954-56. Mem. Am. Legion, Sigma Alpha Epsilon, Phi Delta Phi. Clubs: Masons, Shriners, Elks. Home: 20 W Buchanan St Iola KS 66749 Office: 20 N Washington St Iola KS 66749

TALLACKSON, HARVEY DEAN, state senator; b. Grafton, N.D., May 15, 1925; s. Arthur J. and Mabel R. (McDougald) T.; student public schs.; m. Glenna M. Walstad, Aug. 4, 1946; children—Lynda, Thomas, Debra, Amy, Laura. Engaged in farming, Grafton, 1946—; N.D. rep. potato adv. com. to Dept. Agr., 1961-64; bd. dirs. Nodak Rural Electric Coop., 1965—, pres., 1969-70, 74-75; bd. dirs., v.p. Minnkota Power Coop., Grand Forks, N.D., 1975—; ins. agt., 1968—; propr. Harvey Tallackson Ins. Agy., Grafton, 1976—; mem. N.D. Senate from Dist. 16, 1976—, mem. edn. and agr. com., 1977, appropriations com., 1979—. Pres. Walsh County Baseball Assn., 1945-52, Walsh County Fair Assn., 1955-56. Recipient various sales awards; named Outstanding Young Farmer in Walsh and Pembina Counties, 1956. Mem. Ind. Ins. Agts. Assn., Grafton C. of C. Democrat. Lutheran. Clubs: Lions, Eagles, Shriners. Office: 53W5 Box 288 Grafton ND 58237

TALLCHIEF, MARIA, ballerina; b. Fairfax, Okla., Jan. 24, 1925; d. Alexander Joseph and Ruth Mary (Porter) T.; student pub. schs., Calif.; A.F.D. (hon.), Lake Forest Coll., Colby Coll., 1968, Ripon Coll., 1973, Boston Coll.; D.F.A. (hon.), Smith Coll., 1981; m. Henry Paschen, Jr., June 3, 1957; 1 dau., Elise. Joined Ballet Russe de Monte Carlo, 1942; prima ballerina N.Y.C. Ballet, 1947-60; guest star Paris Opera, 1947; prima ballerina Am. Ballet Theater, 1960; with N.Y.C. Ballet Co., until 1965; now artistic dir. Lyric Opera Ballet Chgo. Recipient Achievement award Women's Nat. Press Club, 1953; Dance mag. award, 1960; Capezio award, 1965; named Hon. Princess Osage Indian Tribe, 1953; Disting. Service award U. Okla., 1972; Jane Addams Humanitarian award Rockford Coll., 1973; award Dance Educators Am., 1956. Mem. Nat. Soc. Arts and Letters.

TALLEY, JUDITH ANN GOTTMANN, social worker; b. Hannibal, Mo., Feb. 27, 1942; d. Charles Lilburn and Grace Kathryn (Heckman) Gottmann; B.S. in Bus. Edn., Manchester Coll., 1964; M.S. in Counseling and Guidance, Ind. U., 1979; children—Christine Suzanne, Douglas Charles. Elem. tchr., Roann, Ind., 1964-65; med. social worker Bloomington (Ind.) Hosp., 1974-77, dir. med. social service, 1977—; mem. Child Protection Team Monroe County; chmn. Community Task Force on Adult Domestic Violence; mem. Community Task Force on Child Abuse; pres. bd. dirs. Hospice of Bloomington, 1980-81. Bd. dirs. Family Service Assn. Monroe County; mem. adv. bd. Families Facing Cancer. Named Social Worker of Yr. for Monroe County Assn. Social Workers, 1979. Mem. Nat. Assn. Social Workers, Nat. Assn. Hosp. Social Work Dirs., Ind. Soc. Hosp. Social Work Dirs. (sec. 1981, pres.-elect 1981-82), Monroe County Social Workers Assn. Methodist (ch. bd. 1980). Home: 111 Park Ridge Rd Bloomington IN 47401 Office: Bloomington Hosp 605 W 2d St Bloomington IN 47402

TALLEY, MELVIN GARY, coll. pres.; b. Westchester, Pa., Feb. 26, 1945; s. Melvin G. and Alberta M. (Faddis) T.; B.S., Pa. State U., 1967; grad. N.Y. Inst. Fin., 1968; children—Kristin Jolene, Mark Gary. Registered rep. DeHaven & Townsend, Crouter & Bodine, Phila., 1967-68; pres. Brown Mackie Coll., Salina, Kans., 1972—; dir. Hilton Hotel, Claymont Savs. and Loan Assn. Bd. dirs. St. Francis Boys' Homes. Served with U.S. Army, 1968-69. Named an Outstanding Young Man Am. Mem. Assn. Ind. Colls. and Schs. (dir.), Kans. Assn. Pvt. Career Schs. (pres.). Presbyterian. Clubs: Rotary, Masons, Shrine. Home: 215 Greenway Salina KS 67401 Office: 126 S Santa Fe Salina KS 67401

TALLMAN, RUSSELL WARRICK, ednl. cons.; b. Ames, Iowa, Aug. 22, 1891: s. Francis Boone and Annette (McKim) T.: A.B., Highland Park Coll., 1916: B.S., Des Moines Coll., 1918; M.A., U. Iowa, 1923, Ph.D., 1925; m. Carrie Nadine Wilson, Aug. 28, 1920. Supt. schs., Coin, Iowa, 1916-17, 1919-20: statistician U. Iowa, 1924-25; prof., head dept. edn. and psychology, chmn. grad. faculty Western State Coll., Colo., 1925-30, v.p., 1928-30; pres. Motivation Charts, Inc., Jewell, Iowa, 1930-52; owner Zippo Bar-Charts, Jewell, 1952-69. Dir. Iowa Emergency Edn., 1934-40; cons. Civilian Conservation Corps, 1934-40; dir. workers edn. tchr. tng., Iowa, Kans., Mo., 1934; Iowa adminstr. Nat. Youth Adminstrn., 1936-40; dir. field service, cons. Iowa State Tchrs. Assn., 1940-41; field rep. Western div. Nat. Policy Commn., Washington, 1942-43; dir. supr. tng., asst. to comdg. officer 842d Specialized Depot, U.S. Army Air Force, Des Moines, 1944-46; chief employee devel. br. tng. officer War Assets Adminstrn., Omaha, 1946-47; tng. specialist, cons. for bus., industry and edn., 1947—; mem. Gov.'s Ednl. Planning Commn. for Iowa; edn. adviser Iowa AFL-CIO. Served with U.S. Army, 1918. Certified trainer Civil Service Commn. Fellow AAAS, Iowa Acad. Sci.; mem. NEA, Nat. Soc. Study Edn., Phi Delta Kappa. Republican. Mem. Federated Ch. Co-author: Guideline-Problem series syllabus and workbook for Principles of Education; Author: Live and Learn?—Learn and Live!. Contbr. articles to profl. pubis. Inventor graph chart forms. Home: 418 S Main St Jewell IA 50130

TAMAN, MAHMOUD SHAWKY, psychiatrist; b. Shebin El-Kom, Egypt, Jan. 6, 1933; s. Abdel-Rahman and Fathia (Yahya) T.; m. Rafia El-Nashar, Mar. 20, 1961; children—Sahar, Mona, Tarik; came to U.S., 1971, naturalized, 1976; M.D., Alexandria U., Egypt, 1957; diploma in psychol. medicine Royal Coll. London (Eng.), 1969. Rotating intern Alexandria U. Hosp., 1957-58; resident gen. medicine Kobba Gen. Hosp., Cairo, 1958-61, resident psychiatry Banstead Hosp., Surrey, Eng., 1966-69; sr. resident High Croft Hosp., Birmingham, Eng., 1969-71; staff psychiatrist and physician in charge alcoholic and drug abuse treatment unit Mental Health Inst., Clarinda, Iowa, 1971-72, chief psychiatrist, 1972-73; pvt. practice psychiatry, Chippewa Falls, Wis., 1973—; med. dir. Chippewa County Guidance Clinic; pres. Chippewa Valley Clinic, 1973—. Mem. AMA, Chippewa County Med. Soc., Am. Psychiat. Assn., Royal Coll. Psychiatrists (Eng.). Club: Rotary of Chippewa Falls. Home: 411 E Wisconsin St Chippewa Falls WI 54729 Office: 705 Bay St Chippewa Falls WI 54729

TAMAROFF, MARVIN MILTON, automobile agy. exec.; b. Detroit, Nov. 17, 1925; s. Louis and Anna (Drapkin) T.; M.Engr., Gen. Motors Inst., 1949; m. Claire Wiesenberg, Aug. 16, 1953; children—Jeffrey Louis, Karen Sue. With, Detroit diesel div. Gen. Motors, 1943-44, 46-49; salesman Wilshire Motors, Detroit, 1950-51, Leo Adler, Inc., Detroit, 1951-52, Pappy's Used Cars, Detroit, 1952-53; owner Marwood Motor Sales, Detroit, 1954-69; pres., gen. mgr., chmn. bd. Tamaroff Buick-Honda, Southfield, Mich., 1969—; pres. Auto Village Fiat-Volvo, Ferndale, Mich., 1979—, Mich. Engine Fgn. Parts, Ferndale, 1979—; treas. MIOH Life Ins. Co., 1979—. Mem. citizens adv. com. Southfield Bd. Edn.; chmn. Gen. Motors Dealers Workmen's Compensation Fund. Served with U.S. Army, 1944-46. Decorated Purple Heart. Mem. Nat. Auto Dealers Assn., Detroit Auto Dealers Assn. (dir. 1979—), Honda Dealers Assn. (treas.), Met. Buick Dealers Assn., Classic Car Club Am., Buick Car Club, Southfield C. of C. (dir.). Clubs: Masons, Shriners, B'nai B'rith. Office: Tamaroff Buick-Honda 28585 Telegraph Rd Southfield MI 48034

TANAZEVICH, ALEXANDER, pharmacist; b. Mansfield, Ohio, Aug. 11, 1925; s. Milivoy and Leposava (Gudurich) T.; student Ohio State U., 1946-48; B.S. in Pharmacy, Ohio No. U., 1951; m. Joyce Faye Crabtree, Apr. 23, 1948; children—Tamara Alexis Bako, Debra Lynn Potts. Mgr., Med. Arts Pharmacy, Mansfield, Ohio, 1951-62; dir. pharmacy Mansfield Gen. Hosp., 1962-66, Martha Jefferson Hosp., Charlottesville, Va., 1967-68, Smyth County Community Hosp., Marion, Va., 1968-69; asst. dir. pharmacy Licking Meml. Hosp., Newark, Ohio, 1969-70, Lorain Community Hosp., Lorain, Ohio, 1971-73; dir. pharmacy Cuyahoga Falls (Ohio) Gen. Hosp., 1973-79, Akron (Ohio) City Hosp., 1979—; pharmacy rep. of health practitioners adv. council, region 6 Peer Rev. Orgn., 1978-79, vice chmn. health practitioners adv. council, 1979—. Served with USAAF, 1943-45. Decorated Air medal with silver oak leaf cluster; recipient Walter Frazier award, 1980; registered pharmacist, Ohio, N.C., Va. Mem. Am. Pharm. Assn., Am. Soc. Hosp. Pharmacists, Nat. Intravenous Therapy Assn., Ohio Soc. Hosp. Pharmacists (v.p. 1981-82), Ohio Pharm. Assn., Northcentral Ohio Pharm. Assn. (past pres.), Am. Soc. for Parenteral and Enteral Nutrition, Akron Soc. Hosp. Pharmacists (past pres.). Club: Masons. Home: 474 Tammery Dr Tallmadge OH 44278 Office: Akron City Hosp 525 E Market St Akron OH 44309

TANDON, JAGDISH SINGH, pollution control co. exec.; b. New Delhi, India, Apr. 3, 1940; s. Mool C. and Vidya V. (Somra) T.; came to U.S., 1961, naturalized, 1973; B.Sc., U. Delhi, 1961; M.S., U. Minn., 1963, postgrad., 1963-67; m. Monika Dettmers, May 12, 1967; 1 son, Hans Peter. Mgr. mech. collector div. Aerodyne Corp., Hopkins, Minn., 1968-69; dir. control systems div. Environ. Research Corp. div. Dart Industries, St. Paul, 1969-70; gen. mgr. pollution control systems div. George A. Hormel & Co., Coon Rapids, Minn., 1970-77; pres. Am. Envirodyne div. Pettibone Corp., Chgo., 1977-78; dir. mktg. MMT Environ. Inc., St. Paul, 1978-80; pres. Environ. Cons., Northbrook, 1980—; instr. U. Minn. Inst. Tech.; vis. scientist Nat. Center Atmospheric Research, Boulder, Colo. Mem. ASCE, Air Pollution Control Assn., Am. Foundry Soc. Contbr. pollution control articles to profl. lit. Home: 1344 Southwind Dr Northbrook IL 60062

TANDON, RAJIV, car rental co. exec.; b. Allahabad, India, May 9, 1944; s. Jagdish Bihari and Vimla Devi (Mehrotra) T.; came to U.S., 1969; B.Tech. with honors, Indian Inst. Tech., 1966; M.S. in Ops. Research, U. Minn., 1972, M.B.A., 1972, postgrad., 1976; m. Priti Khanna, Sept. 21, 1969; children—Ribhu, Veeti. Mgmt. trainee Kumardhubi Engring. Works, Kumardhubi, Bihar, India, 1966-67, prodn. control officer, 1967-69; ops. research analyst Nat. Car Rental Systems, Inc., Mpls., 1971-72, mgr. ops. research, 1972-75, dir. fin. analysis, 1975-77; corporate v.p. Mgmt. Info. Services, 1977-80, corp. v.p., gen. mgr., 1980—; teaching asst. U. Minn., 1970-71, instr., 1971. Mem. Inst. Mgmt. Scis. (sec. Upper Midwest chpt. 1975-76, v.p. 1976-77, pres. 1977-78), Ops. Research Soc. Am., Am. Inst. Decision Scis., Am. Mgmt. Assn., Am. Fin. Assn., N.Am. Soc. Corp. Planners, Planners League (pres. 1979-80). Hindu. Home: 8109 Rhode Island Ave S Bloomington MN 55438 Office: 7700 France Ave S Minneapolis MN 55435

TANEGA, JOSE RESMA, elec. engr.; b. Manila, July 31, 1940; s. Anselmo F. and Estela T. (Resma) T.; came to U.S., 1970, naturalized, 1975; B.S. in Elec. Engring., Mapua Inst. Tech. 1967; m. Conchita M. Salaan, Oct. 2, 1970; children—Joey, Cheryl, Cliff, Jason, Clyde. Elec. estimator Aluminum Products unit Reynolds Aluminum, Manila, 1962-67; acting plant mgr. Impact Corp. Ltd., Manila, 1968-70; asst. telephone engr. GTE Inc., Automatic Electric, North Lake, Ill., 1970-72; elec. designer Castle Engring., Chgo., 1972-74, Macdonald Engring., 1974-76; elec. design engr. Moffett Tech. Center, CPC Internat. Inc., Argo, Ill., 1976-77; sr. elec. engr. Western Electric Co., Chgo., 1977-81; sr. engr. Plexco div. Amsted Industries, Franklin Park, Ill., 1981—. Mem. IEEE, Constrn. Specifications Inst., Philippine Engrs. Scis. Orgn., Nat. Rifle Assn. Roman Catholic. Contbr. articles in field. Home: 4405 Gage Ave Lyons IL 60534 Office: Plexco 3240 N Mannheim Rd Franklin Park IL 60131

TANGEMAN, LARRY ALVIN, coll. pres.; b. Chambers, Nebr., Nov. 14, 1928; s. Alvin and Rachael D. T.; B.S., U. Nebr., 1954, M.A., 1955; Ed.D., U. Colo., 1961; m. Corinne F. Joseph, May 27, 1952; children—John, Jane, Lara. Tchr. rural schs., Nebr., 1946-50; tchr. English and journalism Scottsbluff, Nebr., 1955-57; prin. jr. high sch., Gering, Nebr., 1957-59; v.p. acad. affairs, Chadron, Nebr., 1967-77; cons., Bangladesh, 1964-66; pres. Chadron State Coll., 1973-75, Peru (Nebr.) State Coll., 1977—. Former mem. Profl. Practices Commn. Served with U.S. Army, 1951-53. Mem. NEA, Am. Assn. Sch. Adminstrs., Phi Delta Kappa. Methodist. Clubs: Masons, Kiwanis. Office: Peru State Coll Peru NE 68421

TANGORA, MARTIN CHARLES, mathematician; b. N.Y.C., June 21, 1936; s. Albert and Virginia (Martin) T.; B.S., Calif. Inst. Tech., 1957; M.S., Northwestern U., 1958, Ph.D., 1966; m. Linda F. Perry, June 16, 1973. Mem. tech. staff Aerospace Corp., 1962-64; instr. Northwestern U., 1966-67; instr. U. Chgo., 1967-69; temporary lectr. U. Manchester (Eng.), 1969-70; asst. prof. U. Ill., Chgo., 1970-72, asso. prof., 1972—. Bd. dirs. Landmarks Preservation Council and Service Ill., 1971—, pres. service, 1971-72, pres. council, 1976; mem. adv. com. Commn. on Chgo. Hist. and Archtl. Landmarks, 1974—, chmn., 1978—. Fulbright scholar U. Paris, 1959-60; Sci. Research Council sr. vis. fellow, Oxford, 1973-74; NSF grantee, fellow. Mem. Am. Math. Soc., Math. Assn. Am., Sigma Xi, Tau Beta Pi. Home: 4636 Magnolia Ave Chicago IL 60640 Office: Dept Math Univ Ill Chicago IL 60680

TANKUS, HARRY, engring. exec.; b. Bialystok, Poland, Aug. 23, 1921; s. Isador and Sima (Siegal) T.; came to U.S., 1929; grad. engring. Armour Tech., 1942; student U. Ill., 1946-47; grad. mgmt. course U. Chgo., 1966; m. Lila Beverly Lee, Sept. 9, 1947; children—Rolana, Ilyce. Came to U.S., 1929, naturalized, 1929. Insp. dept. head Buick div. Gen. Motors, Melrose Park, Ill., 1942-44; specification engr. Crane Packing Co., Chgo., 1947-53; chief engr., 1953-62, asst. v.p. engring., Morton Grove, 1962-64, asst. v.p. engring., 1964-71, v.p. seal sales, 1971-76, v.p. product sales, 1976—, also dir. Bd. dirs. Oakton Coll. Ednl. Found., 1979-82, pres., 1979—; bd. dirs. Inst. Indsl. Innovation through Tribology, Ill. Inst. Tech., 1980, chmn. Ill. Inst. Tech., 1970, alumni bd. dirs., 1980-82, mem. Alumni Council of 100; adv. bd. Niles Twp. Sheltered Workshop; bd. dirs. Ill. Right to Work Com.; chmn. Skokie Valley Indsl. div. Crusade of Mercy/United Way, gen. chmn., 1981; bd. dirs. Jr. Engring. Tech. Soc.; active Luth. Social Services of Ill.; trustee Skokie Valley Community Hosp., 1981—. Served with AUS, 1944-46, ETO. Decorated Purple Heart; registered profl. engr., Ill. Fellow Am. Soc. Lubrication Engrs. (pres. 1975-76); mem. Presdl. Council, Soc. Automotive Engrs. (chmn. seal program aerospace conf. 1965), ASME, Am. Soc. Metals (certificate of recognition 1965), Western Soc. Engrs., Am. Soc. Tool and Mfg. Engrs., AAAS, Am. Ordnance Assn., Nat. Conf. on Fluid Power (chmn. 1970, bd. govs. 1967), Nat. Assn. Corrosion Engrs., ASTM (chmn. subcom. carbongraphite 1965), Chgo. Natural History Mus. (asso.). Clubs: Masons, Shriners, Moose. Author articles in field. Patentee in U.S. and fgn. countries. Home: 415 Sunset Dr Wilmette IL 60091 Office: 6400 Oakton Morton Grove IL 60053

TANNEHILL, JOHN CHARLES, engring. educator; b. Salem, Ill., Oct. 14, 1943; s. John Bell and Pearl Hanna (Trulin) T.; B.S., Iowa State U., 1965, M.S., 1967, Ph.D., 1969; m. Marcia Kay George, Jan. 28, 1967; children—Michelle, Johnny. Aerospace engr. NASA Flight Research Center, Edwards, Calif., 1965; mem. tech. staff Aerospace Corp., El Segundo, Calif., 1967; NASA-ASEE fellow NASA Ames Research Center, Moffett Field, Calif., 1970, 71; asst. prof. Iowa State U., Ames, 1969-74, asso. prof. aerospace engring., 1974-79, prof., 1979—; chmn. bd. Engring. Analysis, Inc., Ames, 1976—. NSF trainee, 1965-68; Iowa State U. Research Found. fellow, 1968-69; NASA fellow, 1970-71. Fellow Am. Inst. Aeros. and Astronautics (asso.); mem. Am. Soc. Engring. Edn., Sigma Xi, Sigma Gamma Tau, Tau Beta Pi. Contbr. articles to profl. jours. Home: 2963 Monroe Dr Ames IA 50010 Office: Dept of Aerospace Engring Iowa State U Ames IA 50011

TANNENBERG, DIETER ERNST ADOLF, bus. equipment co. exec.; b. Chevy Chase, Md., Nov. 24, 1932; s. Wilhelm and Margarete (Mundhenk) T.; B.S. in Mech. Engring., Northwestern U., 1959; m. Ruth Hansen, Feb. 6, 1956; 1 dau., Diana. Supervising engr. Flexonics div. Calumet & Hecla, Inc., Chgo., 1959-61, chief engr., 1961-63, program mgr. advanced space systems, 1963-65, dir. mfg. services, 1965-67; dir. mfg. engring. SCM Corp., Cortland, N.Y., 1967-69; tech. dir. internat. Singer Co., N.Y.C., 1969-71; v.p. ops., internat. Addressograph-Multigraph Corp., Cleve., 1971-74; mng. dir. Addressograph Multigraph GmbH, Frankfurt/M., Germany, 1974-78; v.p., gen. mgr. Europe, Middle East and Africa, AM Internat., Inc., Chgo., 1978-79, pres. AM Bruning div., 1979—, corp. v.p., 1981—; chmn. AM Internat. GmbH, Frankfurt. Served with M.I., U.S. Army, 1953-56. Registered profl. engr., Ill., N.Y., N.J., Conn., Ohio, Wis., Ind. Mem. Assn. Reprodn. Materials Mfrs. (dir. 1979—, v.p. 1980—), ASME, Nat. Soc. Profl. Engrs., Pi Tau Sigma. Contbr. chpt. to Handbook of Modern Manufacturing Management, 1970. Patentee machinery. Office: AM Internat 1800 Bruning Dr W Itasca IL 60143

TANNER, LLOYD GEORGE, paleontologist; b. Cozad, Nebr., Oct. 3, 1918; s. George William and Eunice Carolina (Johnson) T.; B.S., U. Nebr., 1951, M.S., 1956; m. Mary Louise Brownfield, Oct. 7, 1971; children—Susan, Ryan; children by previous marriage—Ronald, Jerry. Field asst., U. Nebr. State Mus., 1938-41; supr. fossil excavating U. Nebr., Lincoln, 1939-42; owner, mgr. Paxton Concrete Products (Ill.), 1947-48; asst. cashier Paxton, Farmers Mchts. Nat. Bank, 1947-48; field leader, coordinator field collecting parties U. Nebr., Lincoln, 1959-69, asst. curator vertebrate paleontology, 1956-76, asso. curator, 1976-79, asst. prof. geology, 1976-78, asso. prof., 1978—; cons. mem. expdns. Fayum Province, Egypt, 1965, 66, 67, 77, 78, 79, 80. Served with USAAF, 1942-45. Nebr. Dept. Roads Hwy. Paleontological Salvage program grantee, 1960-81; Ky. col.; fellow U. Nebr. Grad. Coll. Faculty, 1971—. Mem. Nebr. Acad. Sci. (past pres.; life), Nebr. Geol. Soc. (pres. 1978-79), Soc. Vertebrate Paleontology, Terqua-Tertiary-Quaternary Research Group, Sigma Xi, African Geol. Soc. Democrat. Contbr. articles to profl. jours.; author: Evolution of African Mammals, 1979. Office: Mus Vertebrate Paleontology U Nebr Nebr Hall W-436 Lincoln NE 68588

TANSEY, BRIAN ROBERT, health care exec.; b. Cin., Sept. 17, 1932; s. Bernard Joseph and Cecile Marie (Sunman) T.; A.B., Columbia U., 1954; M.Div., Louisville Presbyn. Theol. Sem., 1962; m. Jacqueline M. Henderson, Apr. 19, 1958; children—Stephanie Lynn, Amy Lee, Lori Anne. Ordained to ministry United Presbyterian Ch., 1961; minister, Brownstown, Ind. and Ripley, Ohio, 1961-70; salesman Union Central, Mass. Mut. Life Ins. Cos., Cin., 1970-72; asst. adminstr., adminstr. Oak Pavilion Nursing Home, Cin., 1972-75; adminstr. OakRidge Nursing Home, Mobile, Ala., 1975-77, Brookhaven Convalescent Center, Toledo, 1977-79, Circleville (Ohio) Health Care Center, 1979-80; Americana Lake Shore, Cleve., 1980-81; v.p. Ohio Health Facilities Inc., Toledo, 1981—; mem. Bd. Examiners of Nursing Home Adminstrs., State of Ohio, 1978--. Mem. health techs. adv. com. Owens Tech. Coll., Toledo, 1977-79; chmn. nursing home div., employee group Lucas County United Way Campaign, 1978-79. Served with U.S. Army, 1955-58. Mem. Am. Coll. Nursing Home Adminstrs., Am. Health Care Assn., Ohio Health Care Assn., Toledo Met. Health Care Assn. Republican. Home: 1385 Wildwood Rd Toledo OH 43614 Office: Ohio Health Care Facilities 3700 Holland-Sylvania Rd Toledo OH 43615

TAO, LIANG NENG, engineer, educator; b. Shanghai, China, June 27, 1927; s. Hsieun-Mo and Li-Chien (Chen) T.; came to U.S., 1949, naturalized, 1967; B.S., Chaio Tung U., China, 1949; M.S., U. Ill., 1950, Ph.D., 1953; m. Micheline C. Chao, June 8, 1957; children—Amy Rose, Leonard Michael, Cynthia Mary. Research engr. Worthington Corp., Harrison, N.J., 1953-55; asst. prof. mechs. Ill. Inst. Tech., Chgo., 1955-59, asso. prof., 1959-61, prof., 1961—; cons. in field. Recipient Outstanding New Citizen of Met. Chgo. award, Citizen Council Met. Chgo., 1967. Mem. AAUP, ASME, Soc. Engring. Science, AIAA, Sigma Xi (chpt. pres. 1965-66), Pi Mu Epsilon. Contbr. articles to profl. jours. Home: 6950 N Kilpatrick Ave Lincolnwood IL 60646 Office: 3300 S Federal St Chicago IL 60616

TAPLETT, LLOYD MELVIN, human resources mgmt. cons.; b. Tyndall, S.D., July 25, 1924; s. Herman Leopold and Emiley (Nedvidek) T.; B.A., Augustana Coll., 1949; M.A., U. Nebr., 1958; postgrad. S.D. State U., U. S.D., U. Iowa, Colo. State U.; m. Patricia Ann Sweeney, Aug. 21, 1958; children—Virginia Ann, Sharon Lorraine, Carla Jo, Carolyn Patricia, Catherine Marie, Colleen Elizabeth. Tchr., Sioux Falls (S.D.) public schs., 1952-69; with All-Am. Transport Co., Sioux Falls, 1969-78, Am. Freight System, Inc., Overland Park, Kans., 1978-79; dir. human resources and public relations, corp. affirmative action compliance ofcl. Chippewa Motor Freight Inc., Sioux Falls, 1979-80; human resource and mgmt. cons., 1980—; chmn. Chippewa Credit Union; mem. adv. bd. dirs. Nelson Labs., Sioux Falls, 1981-82. Past bd. dirs. Jr. Achievement, United Way, Sioux Vocat. Sch. for Handicapped; past mem. Gov.'s Adv. Bd. for Community Adult Manpower Planning; chmn. adv. bd. bus. dept. Sioux Falls Public Schs. Served to capt. USMC, 1943-46, 50-52. Recipient Liberty Bell award S.D. Bar Assn., 1967; Sch. Bd. award NEA/Thom McAn Shoe Corp., 1966; named Boss of Yr., Sioux Falls, 1977; cert. tchr. and counselor, S.D. Mem. Am. Soc. for Personnel Adminstrn. (accredited personnel mgr., S.D. dist. dir. 1980-82), Am. Trucking Assn., NEA (life mem., Pacemaker award), S.D. Edn. Assn. (life), Sioux Falls Personnel Assn. (past pres.), Sales and Mktg. Club Sioux Falls, Sioux Falls Traffic Club, VFW (life), Am. Legion. Republican. Roman Catholic. Clubs: Toastmasters (past gov. dist. 41, Disting. Toastmaster award, Outstanding Toastmaster award dist. 41), Elks. Contbr. articles to nat. mags. Office: 2127 S Minnesota Ave Sioux Falls SD 57105

TAPLEY, RICHARD PHILIP, clin./cons. psychologist; b. Chgo., Aug. 23, 1935; s. Philip Anderson and Margaret Elizabeth (Smiley) T.; B.A., Baker U., 1957; M.A., DePaul U., 1964; Ph.D., U. Okla., 1968; m. Carol Jean Zwick, Apr. 11, 1959; children—Anne Elizabeth, Sarah Lynn. Psychology intern Mental Health Center, Chgo., 1967-68; dir. Mobile Home Intervention Team, C.F. Read Zone Center, Chgo., 1970-72; chief psychologist, dir. staff devel. Madden Mental Health Center, Hines, Ill., 1972-76; pvt. practice clin./cons. psychology, Downers Grove, Ill., 1976—. Served with USAR, 1957-64. Mem. Chgo. Transactional Analysis Assn., Assn. DuPage County Psychologists in Profl. Practice, Am. Psychol. Assn., Ill. Psychol. Assn., Internat. Transactional Analysis Assn. Editor: (with Robert A. deVito) A View Into a Modern State-Operated Mental Health Center, the John J. Madden Mental Health Center, 1975; contbr. articles to profl. jours. Address: 625 72d Ct Downers Grove IL 60516

TAPLEY, TERRY CRAIG, educator; b. Streator, Ill., June 19, 1950; s. Carl Theodore and Jean Marie (Derry) T.; B.S. (Ill. scholar 1968-72), Trinity Coll., Hartford, Conn., 1972; M.B.A., Tuck Sch., Dartmouth Coll., 1976; D.B.A., Ind. U., 1980; m. Patricia Marie Boswell, Aug. 16, 1980. Examiner, Fed. Res. Bank Boston, 1972-74; research asso. Tuck Sch., 1978-79; mem. faculty Grad. Sch. Bus., Ind. U., 1979—, asst. prof. fin., 1980—; cons. in field. Mem. Fin. Mgmt. Assn., Am. Fin. Assn., Am. Econ. Assn., Delta Kappa Epsilon, Beta Gamma Sigma. Episcopalian. Author papers, revs. in field. Home: 3209 E 10th St Apt 8E Bloomington IN 47401 Office: Bu370 Ind U Bloomington IN 47405

TAPPENDEN, VIRGINIA JOANNE, educator; b. Altoona, Pa., May 23, 1934; d. Wilbur Paul and Margaret Lena (Thompson) Crider; B.S. in Home Econs., Indiana (Pa.) U., 1956; M.Ed., Pa. State U., 1962; Ph.D., Kent State U., 1982. Tchr. high schs. in Pa. and Ohio, 1956-66; mem. faculty Bowling Green (Ohio) State U., 1966-69; mem. faculty U. Akron (Ohio), 1969—, prof. tchr. edn., 1978—; mem. N. Central Evaluating Teams, 1969—; cons., speaker in field, 1969—. Mem. Am. Home Econs. Assn., Am. Vocat. Assn., Am. Ednl. Scis. Assos., Assn. Tchr. Edn., Assn. Supervision and Curriculum Devel., Nat. Assn. Vocat. Tchr. Educators, Ohio Home Econs. Assn. (Outstanding Home Economist award 1978), Ohio Vocat. Assn., Ohio Assn. Supervision and Curriculum Devel., Buchteles Civic Orgn. Methodist. Clubs: Univ. (Akron); Northfield Flying. Home: 3094 E Edgerton Rd Silver Lake Village Stow OH 44224 Office: 215 A Schrank Hall S Buchtel Ave Akron OH 44325

TAPPER, GORDON ADAMS, human resources cons.; b. Milw., Feb. 20, 1928; s. Harry J. and Orpha Emma T.; student U. Wis., 1947-49; B.S., Milton Coll., 1951; m. Shirley Jayne Kenan, Mar. 15, 1952; children—Jeffrey, Laurel, Sue Ellen, Dianne. Sales engr., mfg. engr. E.L. Essley Machine and Gates Rubber Co., Milw., Chgo., 1952-58; mfg. engr., product mgr. Davis & Thompson Co., Milw., 1958-62; occupational analyst, personnel researcher Employers Assn. Milw., 1962-66; cons. compensation and labor relations Arthur Young & Co., Chgo., 1966-68; mgr. personnel research, cons. Employers Assn. Grand Rapids (Mich.), 1968—; adj. faculty Grand Valley State Coll., U. Minn. Chmn. personnel com. United Fund, 1975; pres. bd. Meth. Community House, 1980—; pres. bd. Grand Valley Assn. for Physically Handicapped, 1976. Served with USNR, 1945-47. Mem. Am. Soc. Personnel Adminstrn. (past dist. dir.), Indsl. Relations Group Grand Rapids (sec.-treas.), Indsl. Relations Research Assn. Presbyn. (elder 1979—). Clubs: Exchange, Press, Masons. Home: 1060 Cadillac Dr SE Grand Rapids MI 49506 Office: 103 Pearl St NW Grand Rapids MI 49503

TARAMAN, KHALIL SHOWKY, educator, engr.; b. Cairo, July 10, 1939; came to U.S., 1967, naturalized, 1975; s. Showky K. and Saadat M. (Ghany) T.; B.Sc. with distinction, Ain Shams U. (Egypt), 1964, M.Sc., 1967; M.Sc., U. Wis., 1969; Ph.D., Tex. Tech U., 1971; m. Sanaa Roushdy, July 4, 1968; children—Shaoky, Sharief. Instr. mech. engring. Ain Shams U., Cairo, 1964-67; research and teaching asst. U. Wis., Madison, 1967-69; research asst. Tex. Tech U., Lubbock, 1969-70, asst. prof., 1970-73; asso. prof. U. Detroit, 1973-77, dir. Mfg. Engring. Inst., 1976—, prof., chmn. dept. mech. engring., 1977—; sr. tech. cons. Bendix Corp., Gen. Electric Co., Ford Motor Co.; supr. research Chrysler, Westinghouse, Gen. Electric, Gen Motors. Mem. Soc. Mfg. Engrs. (sr.; chmn. material removal council 1979—, internat. dir. 1981—), ASME, Am. Soc. Engring. Edn., Am. Soc. Metals, Am. Egyptian Scholars, Pi Tau Sigma, Alpha Pi Mu. Contbr. numerous articles to profl. jours. Office: 4001 W McNichols Univ Detroit Detroit MI 48221

TARAPATA, PETER, architect; b. Detroit, July 24, 1919; s. Elias and Ahafia T.; B.S. in Architecture, U. Mich., 1943, M.Arch., 1947; m. Helen Louise Cook, June 29, 1946; children—Susan Karyl, Karen Ann. Architect, Eberle Smith Assos., Detroit, 1949-56, Tarapata, MacMahon, Paulsen, Inc., Architects, Engrs., Planners, and predecessor, Bloomfield Hills, Mich., 1956—, chmn. bd., 1975—; mem. archtl. adv. panel GSA Region 5, 1970-73. Served to lt. C.E., U.S. Army, 1943-46; CBI. Recipient Progressive Architecture Mag. awards, 1954, 55, 56, 58. Fellow AIA (recipient Merit award for Central Plaza, Canton, Ohio, 1966, master plan for Washtenaw Community Coll., Ann Arbor, Mich. 1971; Gold Medal, Detroit chpt. 1978; mem. Honor Awards jury 1966, 76; chmn. com. on architecture for edn. 1970-74), Engring. Soc. Detroit; mem. Mich. Soc. Architects. Home: 3351 Highmeadow Ct Bloomfield Hills MI 48013 Office: PO Box 289 Bloomfield Hills MI 48013

TARAPATA, PETER, architect; b. Detroit, July 24, 1919; s. Elias and Ahafia T.; B.S. in Architecture, U. Mich., 1943, M.Arch., 1947; m. Helen Louise Cook, June 29, 1946; children—Susan Karyl, Karen Ann. Architect, Eberle Smith Assos., Detroit, 1949-56, Tarapata, MacMahon, Paulsen, Inc., Architects, Engrs., Planners, and predecessor, Bloomfield Hills, Mich., 1956—, chmn. bd., 1975—; mem. archtl. adv. panel GSA Region 5, 1970-73. Served to lt. C.E., U.S. Army, 1943-46; CBI. Recipient Progressive Architecture Mag. awards, 1954, 55, 56, 58. Fellow AIA (recipient Merit award for Central Plaza, Canton, Ohio, 1966, master plan for Washtenaw Community Coll., Ann Arbor, Mich. 1971; Gold Medal, Detroit chpt. 1978; mem. Honor Awards jury 1966, 76; chmn. com. on architecture for edn. 1970-74), Engring. Soc. Detroit; mem. Mich. Soc. Architects. Home: 3351 Highmeadow Ct Bloomfield Hills MI 48013 Office: PO Box 289 Bloomfield Hills MI 48013

TARAZOFF, KENNETH, sales exec.; b. East Chicago, Ind., Sept. 7, 1927; s. Ago and Susan (Avakian) T.; student Purdue U., 1954, U. Wis., 1957; grad. Dale Carnegie, 1959; m. Annalee Bernadette Arzumanian, July 12, 1958; 1 son, Kenneth John. Plant mgr. Lowery Bros., Inc., Chgo., 1948-72; mgr. alloy sales Taylor Chain Co., Hammond, Ind., 1972-76; alloy sales rep. Am. Chain div. Acco Industries, Inc., Melrose Park, Ill., 1976—; cons. in field. Served with USAAF, 1946-47. Mem. Am. Soc. Safety Engrs. Mem. Armenian Apostolic Ch. Clubs: Lions, Masons, Shriners. Home: 7423 W Cashew Dr Orland Park IL 60462 Office: 2040 N Hawthorne Ave Melrose Park IL 60160

TAROSKY, ROBERT EUGENE, cons. engr.; b. New Kensington, Pa., Apr. 29, 1942; s. Frank John and Mary Wanda (Bartos) T.; B.S. in Mech. and Aerospace Engring., Ill. Inst. Tech., 1970; m. Verna May Lucci, Feb. 1, 1964 (dec. 1976); m. 2d, Diane Carol Baran, Feb. 25, 1978; children—Michele Lynn, Renata Elizabeth. With Tuthill Pump Co., Alsip, Ill., 1963-68; with Gen. Environments Corp., Morton Grove, Ill., 1970-75, staff engr., 1970-75, cons. engr., 1975-79; with Hazard Engring. Inc., Morton Grove, 1975—, v.p., 1979—. Registered profl. engr., Ill. Mem. Nat. Soc. Profl. Engrs., Ill. Soc. Profl. Engrs., Soc. Automotive Engrs. Home: 818 N Kennicott Ave Arlington Heights IL 60004 Office: Hazard Engring Inc 6208 Lincoln Ave Morton Grove IL 60053

TARR, DELBERT HOWARD, JR., ednl. adminstr.; b. Aitkin, Minn., June 14, 1934; s. Delbert Howard and Catherine Elizabeth (Boomer) T.; B.A. in Bible, N.Central Bible Coll., 1956; postgrad. Ecole Lemania, Switzerland, 1959-60; M.A. in Communications, U. Minn., 1969, Ph.D. in Communications, 1979; m. Dorothy D. Hill, June 12, 1954; children—Cindy Sharon, Terry Mark, Randel Ray. Ordained to ministry Assemblies of God Ch., 1957; pastor Assemblies of God Ch., Hopkins, Minn., 1956-58; apptd. fgn. missionary Upper Volta, W. Africa, 1960-63; dir. Mossiland Bible Sch., 1964-67; co-founder, dean W. African Advanced Sch. of Theology, Lome, Togo, 1970-73; prof., coordinator cross-cultural communication studies Assemblies of God. Grad. Sch., Springfield, Mo., 1973-77, dean Missions Div., 1977-80, chmn. Missions Dept., 1980—. Mem. Am. Soc. Missiology, Acad. of Evangelism, Soc. for Pentescostal Studies. Club: Flying Ambassadors. Grant-funded researcher African speech mannerisms, 1976-77.

TARTER, BLODWEN, mfg. corp. mktg. ofcl.; b. Sacramento, Dec. 2, 1954; d. Bill and Blodwen Edwards (Coburn) T.; B.A. with distinction, Stanford U., 1976, M.A., 1976; M.B.A., U. Chgo., 1978. Market research intern Bardsley & Haslacher Inc., Palo Alto, Calif., 1977; with Mead Corp., Dayton, Ohio, 1977—, pres.'s M.B.A. intern, 1977, mgr. market research, Mead Products div., 1978-79, asso. mktg. mgr. sch. supplies, 1979-80, mgr. mktg. services Paperboard Products div., 1980—. Trainer, Buckeye Trails council Girl Scouts U.S.A.; vol. Victory Theater. Named Young Career Woman, Dist. XI Ohio Fedn. Bus. and Profl. Women's Clubs, 1981. Mem. Am. Mktg. Assn. Office: Courthouse Plaza NE Dayton OH 45463

TARTER, JOYCE WITTMUSS, ednl. adminstr.; b. Normal, Ill., Sept. 24, 1937; d. Howard A. and Wilma R. (Abner) Wittmuss; B.S. in Edn., Ill. State U., 1959, M.S., 1972; doctoral candidate in vocat. and tech. edn. U. Ill., 1978—; m. Richard D. Tarter, Nov. 23, 1958; children—Gregory Thomas, Jeffery Duane. Tchr. home econs. Moore Twp. High Sch., Farmer City, Ill., 1959-62, Bloomington (Ill.) High Sch., 1962-69; faculty asst. indsl. tech. Ill. State U., Normal, 1971-72, instr. home econs. and indsl. tech., 1972-76, lectr. home econs., 1978-79; team leader vocat. evaluations State of Ill., 1972-73; tchr. home econs. Bloomington Jr. High Sch., 1969-78; tchr.-coordinator Bloomington Area Vocat. Center, 1979—, communications facilitator, 1980-81; cons. Valley View Sch., 1974, Bloomington-Normal Assn. Commerce and Industry, 1978; workshop leader home econs. Unit 5 Schs., Normal, 1974; home econs. rep. Ill. Curriculum Council, 1978—, exec. com., 1980—; project dir. for McLean County CETA Linkage Projects, 1980-81. Mem. St. Joseph Hosp. Aux., 1968—; chmn. Bloomington-Normal Cancer Drive, 1968-69. Mem. NEA (life), Am. Vocat. Assn., Ill. Vocat. Assn. (registration chmn. 1975-78, coordinator program of work 1972), Ill. Edn. Assn., Ill. Vocat. Home Econs. Tchrs. Assn. (mem. adv. council 1975-79), Bloomington Edn. Assn., Ill. Consumer Edn. Assn., Am. Vocat. Home Econs. Tchrs. Assn., Ill. Co-op Vocat. Edn. Coordinators Assn., Am. Bus. Womens Assn., Kappa Delta Phi, Phi Delta Kappa, Phi Kappa Phi. Methodist. Club: Elks. Contbr. evaluation reports of vocat. edn. and programs to profl. publs. Office: Bloomington Area Vocational Center 1202 E Locust Bloomington IL 61701

TARVER, MAE GOODWIN, cons.; b. Selma, Ala., Aug. 9, 1916; d. Hartwell Hill and R. Louise (Wilkins) T.; B.S. in Chemistry, U. Ala., 1939, M.S., 1940. Project supr. container shelflife Continental Can Co., Inc., Chgo., 1941-48, project engr. stats., 1948-54, quality control cons., research statistician, 1954-77; pres., prin. cons. Quest Assos., Ltd., Park Forest, Ill., 1978—; adj. asso. prof. biology dept. Ill. Inst. Tech., Chgo., 1957-81. Bd. dirs. Ash St. Coop., Park Forest, Ill., 1976-81. Fellow Am. Soc. Quality Control (Joe Lisy award 1961, Edward J. Oakley award 1975); mem. Inst. Food Technologists, Soc. Women Engrs., Am. Statis. Assn., Women in Mgmt., Sigma Xi. Home: 130 26th St Park Forest IL 60466 Office: PO Box 182 Park Forest IL 60466

TARVIN, ROBERT EDWARD, coll. adminstr.; b. Covington, Ky., Apr. 16, 1946; s. Fred Irvin and Opal Aliene (McCormick) T.; B.A., Eastern Ky. U., 1968, M.A. (Univ. fellow), 1969; D.Ed., Ind. U., 1972; m. Patty Lynn Anderson, Aug. 7, 1969; children—Tonya Lynn, Shanna Rene. Dir. student activities Eastern Ky. U., Richmond, 1969-72; asso. dean John A. Logan Coll., Carterville, Ill., 1972-73, v.p., 1973-74, pres., 1974—; chmn. Ill. Council Community Coll. Presidents, 1979-80; sec., treas. Ill. Council Community Coll. Presidents, 1978-79; chmn. So. Ill. Colegiate Common Market, 1974-79. Methodist. Home: 318 Lakeview St Marion IL 62959 Office: John A Logan Coll Carterville IL 62918

TARYLE, JOAN CELESTE, bank exec.; b. St. Louis, Oct. 11, 1950; d. George Martin and Helen Marie (Bala) Ivancic; B.A. in Psychology, U. Mo., St. Louis, 1973; m. Gary Travis Taryle, Mar. 18, 1972. Exec. personal banker Mark Twain State Bank, St. Louis, 1973-74; mktg. asst. First Nat. Bank St. Louis, 1974, mktg. coordinator, 1974-75, mktg. asst., 1975-77, asst. mgr. advt. and public relations, 1977-78, advt. mgr., 1978-79; dir. mktg. Gen. Bancshares, St. Louis, 1979; regional dir. mktg. Commerce Bancshares, Inc., St. Louis, 1979—. Adv. dir. Children's Oncology Services, Ronald McDonald House, 1980-81; vol. Craft Alliance Gallery, Orch. and Chorus of St. Louis, 1979-80. Mem. Bank Mktg. Assn., Ill./Mo. Bank Mktg. Assn. Clubs: Advt., Direct Mktg. of St. Louis (bd. dirs.), Press. Home: 12311 N Forty Saint Louis MO 63141 Office: Commerce Bancshares Inc 4019 Chouteau St Saint Louis MO 63110

TATAR, MARTIN LOUIS, advt. and public relations exec.; b. Chgo., July 20, 1915; s. Max Goodman and Jennie (Kahn) T.; student Cornell U., 1933-35, Sarbonne U., 1945; m. Shirley Clubman, Feb. 7, 1943; children—Howard, Jerome. Profl. baseball player, minor and maj. leagues, 1937-39; enlisted in U.S. Army, 1941, commd. 2d lt., 1942, advanced through grades to lt. col., 1968, ret., 1968; tng. officer, 1946-56; tng. officer and bn. comdr., Chgo., 1957-60; bn. and brigade comdr., Chgo., 1960-68; civilian dir. Army schs. U.S. Army, Ft. Sam Houston, Tex., 1968-71, info. officer, 1972-73, dep. chief advt. and info. Midwest recruiting, Skokie, Ill., 1973—; also Jewish lay leader, for U.S. Army; public speaker. Vol., Sr. Adult Activities, Chgo., 1968—; profl. sports ofcl., 1955—; intercollegiate wrestler, 1933-35. Decorated Purple Heart, Bronze Star medal. Mem. Ret. Officers Assn., State Sports Ofcls., Am. Assn. Ethiopian Jews, North Shore Homeowners Assn., Lyric Opera Guild, Phi Epsilon Pi. Democrat. Jewish. Clubs: Chgo. Press, Balt. Orioles Baseball, United Red Carpet, Zionist Orgn., Masons. Contbr. articles to profl. jours. Home: 4851 Davis St Skokie IL 60077 Office: Bldg 84 Fort Sheridan IL 60037

TATE, SHIRLEY ANN, child welfare adminstr.; b. Detroit, Mar. 23, 1943; d. Connie Lee and Bessie (Jennings) Maynard; B.S., Eastern Mich. U., 1965; m. Leonard E. Tate, June 1980; 1 son by previous marriage, Kambui. With State of Mich., 1974—, public welfare adminstr., Detroit, 1978, social services mgr., Taylor, 1978-80, dir. Office Children and Youth Services, Lansing, 1980—; developer Mich. Gen. Assistance Tng. Program; mem. affirmative action adv. council State of Mich.; mem. communications com. Mich. Dept.

Social Services; mem. Mich. Commn. on Youth Employment, Mich. Adv. Com. on Juvenile Justice, Mich. Commn. on Juvenile Justice; del. White House Conf. on Families; chmn. Mich. Conf. on Children and Youth, 1981. Founding mem. Pan-African Congress-U.S.A., 1970. Mem. Am. Mgmt. Assn., Mich. Assn. Childcaring Agys., Child Welfare League Am., Am. Public Welfare Assn., 3203 Monterey Block Club, NAACP, Alpha Kappa Alpha. Office: 300 S Capitol St Lansing MI 48909

TATOOLES, CONSTANTINE JOHN, cardiovascular and thoracic surgeon; b. Chgo., May 7, 1936; B.S., Albion (Mich.) Coll., 1958; M.S. in Physiology, Loyola U., Chgo., 1961, M.D., 1961; m. Betty Ann, Jan. 30, 1960; children—Julie Denise, Anton John, Jon William. Research asst. Loyola U., 1958-59, research asso., 1959-60; intern U. Chgo. Hosps., 1961-62, resident in surgery, 1962-68, instr. in surgery, 1966-68; sr. registrar in surgery Gt. Ormond St. Hosp. for Children, London, 1968-69; practice medicine specializing in cardiovascular and thoracic surgery, Chgo., 1969—; asst. prof. surgery and physiology, Loyola U., 1969-73, attending surgeon, 1969-73; asso. attending surgeon thoracic and cardiovascular surgery Cook County Hosp., Chgo., 1969-73, chmn. dept. cardio-thoracic surgery, 1969-78, attending surgeon, 1970, lectr. in cardiac surgery, 1970; chief cardiovascular and thoracic surgery Abraham Lincoln Sch. Medicine, U. Ill., Chgo., 1973-74, asso. prof. surgery, 1973-76, prof. surgery, 1976; attending surgeon U. Ill., 1973; chmn. dept. cardiothoracic surgery St. Francis Hosp., Evanston, Ill., 1977-78, St. Mary's of Nazareth Hosp., Chgo., 1981; chmn. Chgo. Inst. for Heart and Lung, 1972. Fellow A.C.S., Am. Coll. Cardiology, Am. Coll. Chest Physicians (chmn. motion picture div., 1975-76); mem. Am. Assn. Thoracic Surgery, Am. Heart Assn. (council on cardiovascular surgery), AMA, Am. Thoracic Soc., Assn. for Acad. Surgery, Chgo. Heart Assn. (council on cardiovascular surgery), Chgo. Med. Soc., Chgo. Surg. Soc., Ill. State Med. Soc., Inst. of Medicine Chgo., Royal Soc. Medicine London (Eng.), Soc. Thoracic Surgeons, Chgo. Thoracic Soc. (pres. 1981), Warren J. Cole Soc. Contbr. to films in field, articles to profl. publs. Office: 800 Austin St Evanston IL 60202

TATTER, MILTON ANDREW, assn. exec.; b. Lubbock, Tex., Feb. 2, 1943; s. Gustav and Grace (Balough) T.; B.S. in Gen. Bus., Ball State U., Muncie, Ind., 1965, M.B.A., 1967; postgrad. Rock Valley Coll., Rockford, Ill., 1967-70; m. Karen A. Buxser, May 15, 1976; 1 dau., Terisha Marie. Engaged in retailing, 1958-67; prof. bus. Rock Valley Coll., Rockford, Ill., 1967-70; gen. mgr. Mgmt. Devel. Services, Rockford, 1969-71; sr. account exec. George M. Otto Assos., Chgo., 1971-77; mgr. mktg. communications Standard Publishing Co., Cin., 1977-78; exec. dir. Am. Inst. Plant Engrs., Cin., 1978—; cons. in field. Cert. assn. exec. Mem. Am. Soc. Assn. Execs., Council Engring. and Sci. Socs. Execs., Nat. Platform Speakers Assn., Beta Theta Pi. Republican. Presbyterian. Club: Kosciusko Country (pres. 1961). Author articles in field. Office: 3975 Erie Ave Cincinnati OH 45208

TAUBE, WILLIAM HAROLD, lawyer; b. Kankakee, Ill., Jan. 17, 1934; s. Harold Herman and Cleo Almeda (Rich) T.; B.S., Memphis State U., 1961; J.D., Vanderbilt U., 1963; m. Joanne Joyce Carter, Dec. 12, 1953; children—John William, Janette Elizabeth. Admitted to Tenn. bar, 1963, Ill. bar, 1964; mem. firm Gray, McIntire & Petersen, Kankakee, 1963-68, Ackman, McKnelly, Reagan & Taube, 1968-71, Taube & Judd, 1971-76, Taube & Phipps, 1976—; corp. counsel City of Kankakee, 1965—; spl. asst. state's atty., 1969. Mem. legislative com. Ill. Municipal League, 1971—, vice chmn., 1974, chmn., 1975—. Mem. commercial panel Am. Arbitration Assn., 1975—. Bd. dirs. Kankakee County Heart Fund. Served with USN, 1952-56. Mem. Am., Ill., Kankakee County bar assns., Am. Judicature Soc., Am. Legion, Nat. Inst. Municipal Law Officers (nominating com. 1972-73, resolutions com. 1974, chmn. ordinance and ordinance enforcement com. 1975, Ill. chmn. 1975-79, regional v.p. 1979—). Clubs: Masons, Shriners, Elks; Kankakee Country (dir.), Kankakee County Hundred. Republican. Conglist. Home: 796 S Greenwood Ave Kankakee IL 60901 Office: 359 E Hickory St Kankakee IL 60901

TAUKE, THOMAS J., congressman; b. Dubuque, Iowa, Oct. 11, 1950; B.A., Loras Coll., 1972; J.D., U. Iowa, 1974. Mem. firm Curnan, Fitzsimmons, Schilling and Tauke, 1976-80; mem. Iowa Ho. of Reps., 1975-79; mem. 96th-97th Congresses from 2d Dist. Iowa. Chmn., Dubuque County Republican Com., 1972-74, 2d Congressional Dist. Rep. Com., 1974-77. Mem. Am. Bar Assn., Iowa Bar Assn., Dubuque County Bar Assn., Dubuque C. of C. Roman Catholic. Club: Rotary. Office: 319 Cannon House Office Bldg Washington DC 20515

TAUSCHER, JOHN WALTER, pediatrician; b. La Salle, Ill., Feb. 3, 1929; s. John Robert and Ella (Danz) T.; B.S., U. Ill., 1952, M.D., 1954; m. Mary Claire Cline, June 19, 1954; children—Michael, John, Claire, Mark, Matthew. Intern, Cook County Hosp., Chgo., 1954-55; resident in pediatrics Hurley Hosp., Flint, Mich., 1958-60; practice medicine specializing in pediatrics, Flint, 1960-75; asso. prof. human devel. Mich. State U. Coll. Human Medicine, East Lansing, 1975-80, prof. pediatrics and human devel., 1980—; v.p. After Hours Pediatric Care, P.C., Flint, 1972—; chmn. pediatrics Hurley Med. Center, 1980—. Served with USAF, 1955-58. Recipient Outstanding Teaching award Coll. Human Medicine, Mich. State U., 1977, Clin. Instr. of Yr. award St. Joseph Hosp., 1977; diplomate Am. Bd. Pediatrics. Mem. AMA, Genesee County Med. Soc., Mich. State Med. Soc., Detroit Pediatric Soc., North Eastern Mich. Pediatric Soc., Am. Acad. Pediatrics. Roman Catholic. Club: Elks. Home: 1513 E Court St Flint MI 48503 Office: Mott Childrens Health Center 806 W 6th Ave Flint MI 48503

TAVLARIDES, LAWRENCE LASKARIS, chem. engr.; b. Wilkensburg, Pa., Jan. 8, 1942; s. Laskaris and Mnostula (Doxaki) T.; B.S., U. Pitts., 1963, M.S., 1964, Ph.D., 1968; postgrad. Tech. U. Delft (Netherlands), 1968-69; m. Alexandra H. Pappas, Oct. 15, 1965; children—Mnostula Anna, Phaedra Irene. Mem. faculty Ill. Inst. Tech., 1969—, prof. chem. engring., 1980—; mem. Ill. Engring. Council, 1970-72; cons. to industry. Bd. dirs. Ypapanti Greek Orthodox Ch., East Pittsburgh, Pa., 1965-66. Faculty research fellow Ill. Inst. Tech., 1974-75; grantee NSF, 1971—. Mem. Am. Inst. Chem. Engrs. (cert. of recognition 1976). Author papers in field. Office: 10 W 33d St Chicago IL 60616

TAY, CHENG HIN, anesthesiologist; b. Rangoon, Burma, Mar. 24, 1938; s. Soo Hong and Shiok Kyin (Ho) T.; came to U.S., 1971, naturalized, 1977; M.B.B.S., Inst. Medicine, Rangoon, Burma, 1965; m. Jenny Peh, June 19, 1968; children—Nora PoPo, Ann Belinda, David John. Rotating intern Columbia Cuneo Med. Center, Chgo., 1971; resident in anesthesiology U. Ill. Med. Center, Chgo., 1972-75; anesthesiologist Asso. Anesthesiologists, Peoria, Ill., 1975—; active staff Meth. Med. Center; mem. courtesy staff St. Frances Med. Center, Proctor Community Hosp., 1975—; clin. asso. anesthesia Peoria Sch. Medicine, 1975-77, clin. asst. prof. surgery (anesthesia), 1977—. Mem. AMA, Am. Soc. Anesthesiologists, Gen. Med. Council (Eng.), Ill. State, Peoria med. socs. Home: 111 E Coventry Ln Peoria IL 61614 Office: 416 St Mark Ct Suite 508 Peoria IL 61603

TAY, MICHAEL KIE-SENG, therapeutic radiologist; b. Jakarta, Indonesia, June 3, 1935; s. Pouw Hoet The and Nini Ong; came to U.S., 1969, naturalized, 1974; M.D., U. Indonesia, Jakarta, 1961, Ph.D. in Med. Microbiology, 1965; m. Ingrid Choon-Eng Lim, Sept. 23, 1960; children—Angela Monica, Jonathan Steven, Eugene Michael. Intern, Christ Hosp., Jersey City, 1969-70; resident Kings County Hosp.-Downstate Med. Center, Bklyn., 1970-73; instr. in med. microbiology U. Indonesia, 1961-65, lectr., 1965-69; asst. instr. in radiology SUNY, Bklyn., 1970-73; attending radiation therapist St. Mary's Hosp., Grand Rapids, Mich., 1973-78, cons., mem. staff, 1978—; gen. practice medicine, Jakarta, 1961-69; pvt. practice medicine specializing in therapeutic radiology, Grand Rapids, 1973—; mem. cons. staff West Shore Hosp., Manistee, Mich.; clin. asst. prof. radiology Mich. State U., 1975—. Diplomate Am. Bd. Radiology. Mem. Kent County Med. Soc., Mich. State Med. Soc., AMA, Am. Coll. Radiology, Am. Soc. Therapeutic Radiologists, Mich. Soc. Therapeutic Radiologists, Radiol. Soc. N. Am. Home: 677 Greentree Ln NE Ada MI 49301 Office: 200 Jefferson St SE Grand Rapids MI 49503

TAYIEM, ABDEL KARIM HASAN, surgeon; b. Yazour, Palestine, Mar. 27, 1943; came to U.S., 1964, naturalized, 1977; s. Jasan Tarber and Elishah H. Tayiem; M.D. with honors, Cairo U., 1968; m. Samira A. Razzak, June 27, 1971; children—Niddal, Rania, Lana. Intern, Cairo hosps., 1969, St. Joseph Hosp., Wichita, Kans., 1970; resident in surgery St. Francis Hosp., Wichita, 1971-74; practice medicine specializing in surgery, Atchison, Kans., 1974—; chief surgery Atchison Hosp., 1975—, chief staff, 1979—; cons. VA Hosp., Leavenworth, Kans., Cushing Hosp., Leavenworth; chmn. adv. bd. Lic. Practical Nurse Sch., Atchison. Mem. Internat. Coll. Surgeons, A.C.S., AMA, Indsl. Med. Assn., Southwestern Surg. Congress, Kans. Med. Soc., Islamic Assn. U.S. Club: Atchison Rotary (past dir.). Author papers in field. Home: 904 S 22d St Atchison KS 66002 Office: 122 SW 2d St Atchison KS 66002

TAYLOR, CHARLES AVON, univ. dean; b. Balt., Mar. 23, 1951; s. Ellsworth Howard and Ursula (Watkins) T.; B.A. in Sociology, U. Md., Balt., 1973; M.S. in Edn., Johns Hopkins U., 1976; m. Sheila Vanessa Gibson, Aug. 8, 1975 (div. Apr. 1979); children—Sherri Kearise, Charles Avon. Resident counselor, asst. U. Md., Balt., 1971-73; student activity specialist Catonsville (Md.) Community Coll., 1973-76, asst. soccer coach, 1974-76; asst. dean students, black student adv. Loyola U., Chgo., 1976—. Named Advisor of Yr., Loyola U., Chgo., 1980. Mellon Found. grantee, 1978, 79. Mem. Am. Coll. Unions Internat. (regional rep. com. minority programs), Am. Personnel and Guidance Assn., Nat. Assn. Non-White Concerns, Council Coll. Attendance, Nat. Assn. Equal Opportunity Higher Edn., Ill. Guidance and Personnel Assn., Ill. Assn. Non-White Concerns, Johns Hopkins U. Higher Edn. Club. Home: 6612 S Wood St Chicago IL 60636 Office: 820 N Michigan Ave MC 304 Chicago IL 60611

TAYLOR, DAVID G., banker; b. Charlevoix, Mich., July 29, 1929; s. Frank and Bessie S. Taylor; B.S., Denison U., 1951; M.B.A., Northwestern U., 1953; m. Helen A. Alexander; children—David, Amy Elizabeth, Jeanine. With First Nat. Bank, Chgo., 1953; with Continental Ill. Nat. Bank and Trust Co., 1957—, 2d v.p., 1964-66, v.p., 1966-74, exec. v.p. head bond and money market services, 1974-76, exec. v.p. CICorp., from 1976, dir. Continental Ill. Ltd., 1979, treas., 1980—. Served with USN, 1953-56. Mem. Assn. Primary Dealers U.S. Govt. Securities, Dealer Bank Assn., Public Securities Assn. (vice chmn., dir.), Phi Delta Theta, Kappa Beta Phi. Clubs: Sequanota (Charlevoix); Skokie Country; Bond, Bankers, Economic, Chgo. (Chgo.); Internat. (Washington); World Trade Center (N.Y.C.). Address: 231 S LaSalle St Chicago IL 60693*

TAYLOR, DEBORAH ANN, educator; b. Evansville, Ind., Feb. 6, 1950; d. Norman Henry and Thelma A. Gocker; B.S., Ball State U., 1973; M.S., Purdue U., 1980; m. Kenneth E. Taylor, Mar. 2, 1974. Tchr. home econs. Tippecanoe Sch. Corp., Lafayette, Ind., 1974—. Mem. Am. Vocat. Assn., Nat. Assn. Home Econs. Tchrs., Ind. Vocat. Assn., Ind. Vocat. Home Econs. Assn., Omicron Nu, Psi Iota Xi.

TAYLOR, DENNIS WILLIAM, environ. engr.; b. San Jose, Calif., Apr. 13, 1939; s. Herbert Kenneth and Violet Evelyn T.; B.S. in Civil Engring. (State of Oreg. Edn. grantee), Oreg. State U., 1968, M.S. in Envrion. Engring. (USPHS trainee), 1970; m. Peggy L.; children—Carmelle, Philip, Jessica, Emory, Marty, Linda, Lana. Project engr. research and demonstration U.S. EPA, Corvallis, Oreg., 1970-72; v.p., partner Environ. Assos., Inc., Cons. Engrs., Corvallis, 1973-76; project engr., mem. environ. quality commn. Govt. Am. Samoa, 1976-77; commd. officer USPHS, officer in charge engring. Pine Ridge and Rosebud Sioux Indian Reservations, Martin, S.D., 1977—; dir., co-owner Aqua-Tech Water and Wastewater Lab., Portland, Oreg., 1972—. Pres. Employees Assn., U.S. EPA Research Center, Corvallis, 1972; adminstrn. officer Toastmasters Club, Corvallis, 1972. Served with USN, 1956-62. Named Boss of Yr., Am. Bus. Women's Assn., 1974-75; diplomate Am. Acad. Environ. Engrs.; registered profl. engr., Oreg., S.D. Mem. Conf. Fed. Environ. Engrs., Commd. Officers Assn. USPHS. Democrat. Methodist. Clubs: Oreg. Road Runners, AAU S.D. Contbr. articles on food waste research and treatment. Home: PO Box 284 Martin SD 57551 Office: PO Box F Martin SD 57551

TAYLOR, DONALD, diversified capital goods mfg. co. exec.; b. Worcester, Mass., June 2, 1927; s. John A.B. and Alice M. (Weaver) T.; B.S. in Mech. Engring., Worcester Poly. Inst., 1949; grad. Mgmt. Devel. Program, Northeastern U., 1962, Advanced Mgmt. Program, Harvard U., 1979; m. Ruth L. Partridge, June 2, 1950; children—Linda Taylor Robertson, Donald, Mark, John. Various managerial positions Geo. J. Meyer Mfg. Co., 1951-69; pres. Geo. J. Meyer Mfg. div. A-T-O Inc., 1969; exec. v.p. Nordberg div. Rex Chainbelt, Inc., 1969-73; v.p. ops. Rexnord Inc., 1973-78, pres. Nordberg machinery group, 1973-78, pres., chief operating officer, 1978—; dir. Anatar Industries, Inc., Harnischfeger Corp., Johnson Controls Inc., Marine Corp., Marine Nat. Exchange Bank. Mem. adv. bd. Center for Mgmt. Devel., Northeastern U.; trustee St. Francis Hosp.; bd. dirs., vice chmn. Met. Milw. YMCA; mem. Nat. Council YMCA's; bd. dirs. Milw. Symphony Orch.; div. chmn. Milw. United Way Campaign, 1971, unit chmn., 1972; campaign co-chmn. United Performing Arts Fund, 1976. Served with USNR, 1945-46, 50-54. Registered profl. engr., Mass. Mem. ASME. Clubs: Milw. Country, Milw. Athletic, Town, Univ. (Milw.). Office: Rexnord Inc 3500 First Wisconsin Center 777 E Wisconsin Ave Milwaukee WI 53202

TAYLOR, FANNIE TURNBULL, educator; b. Kansas City, Mo., Sept. 11, 1913; d. Henry King and Fannie (Sills) Turnbull; student Vassar Coll., 1932; B.A., U. Wis., 1938; m. Robert Taylor, Dec. 2, 1938 (div. 1974); children—Kathleen Muir (Mrs. A.R. Isaacs), Anne Kingston (Mrs. Peter R. Wadsack). Dir. Wis. Union Theater, U. Wis.-Madison, 1946-66, prof. social edn., 1952—, now emeritus, asso. dir. arts adminstrn., 1970-72. Mem. Nat. Found. for Arts and Humanities, 1966-67, program dir. music Nat. Endowment for the Arts, 1966-67, dir. program information, 1972-75; co-ordinator, U. Wis. Arts Council, 1967-70, U. Wis., Madison Consortium for Arts; mem. U.S. State Dept. Cultural Exchange team to Yugoslavia, 1971. Bd. dirs., sec. Gov.'s Com. on Arts, 1964-65; bd. dirs. Madison Arts Council, 1965-66, Wis. Arts Found. and Council, 1965-72; bd. dirs. Wis. Nature Conservancy, 1963—, chmn. 1976-77; bd. dirs. Madison Civic Music Assn. (v.p. 1978-82). Mem. Assn. Coll. and Univ. Concert Mgrs. (exec. sec. 1957-70, exec. dir. 1970-72, recipient Fannie Taylor award), Assn. Am. Dance Companies (bd. dirs. 1967-72), Nat. Assn. Regional Ballets (dir. 1975-77), Nat. Guild Community Schs. Arts, Wis. Acad. Arts and Scis., Madison Civics Club (pres. 1969-70), Mortar Board, Theta Sigma Phi. Club: Madison. Editorial bd. Grants mag. Contbr. numerous articles to profl. jours. Home: 1213 Sweet Briar Rd Madison WI 53705 Office: 5525 Humanities Bldg U Wis Madison WI 53706

TAYLOR, GAROLD WAYNE, environ. engr.; b. Canton, Mo., July 19, 1927; s. Harvy Issiac and Audlea Mae (Duncon) T.; student Culver Stockton Coll., 1947; B.S. in Civil Engring., Ind. Inst. Tech., 1958; m. Lavona Williams, June 29, 1951; children—Douglas Wayne, Daphne Ann, Darcy Sue. With Socony Vacuum Oil Co., 1942-44, Minn. Husky Oil Co., 1946; lumber jack Long Bell Lumber Co. (Wash.), 1947; with City Nat. Bank, Kansas City, Mo., 1947-49; draftsman Deere & Co., Moline, Ill., 1949-51; engrs. L.A. Trier, Structural Engrs., Inc., Elkhart, Ind., 1958-62; project engr. NASA, Lewis Research Center, Cleve., 1962-66; project engr. (sr. engr.) Morrison-Knudson Constrn. Co., Vietnam, 1966-67, 70-72; with G.E. Butler Co., cons. engrs., Kansas City, Mo., 1967-70; regional environ. engr. Region VII, HUD, Kansas City, 1972—; tng. officer for nat. disaster Region VII CAUDRI, 1973-79. Pres. Neighborhood Council 14, Independence, 1975-76; scoutmaster Boy Scouts Am., 1949-50, instl. rep., 1955-78; elder, pastor various chs. Reorganized Ch. of Jesus Christ of Latter-day Saints. Served with USNR, 1945-46, 51-55. Recipient Spl. Achievement award HUD, 1977; registered profl. engr., Ohio, Mo. Mem. Am. Water Works Assn. Democrat. Home: 1124 N Liberty St Independence MO 64050 Office: II Gateway Center Suite 818 4th and State Sts Kansas City KS 66101 also 1103 Grand Ave Kansas City MO 64106

TAYLOR, GENE, congressman: b. nr. Sarcoxie, Mo., Feb. 10, 1928; student S.W. Mo. State Coll., Springfield, 1945-46; m. Dorothy Wooldridge, July 26, 1947; children—Linda Kay, Larry Eugene. Mayor, Sarcoxie, 1954-60; automobile dealer, Sarcoxie, 1958-73; mem. 93d-97th Congresses from 7th Mo. Dist. Republican nat. committeeman, 1966-72. Trustee Mo. So. Coll., Joplin. Mem. Mo. N.G., 1948-49. Mem. Mo., Sarcoxie chambers commerce. Methodist. Clubs: Masons, Shriners, Lions. Office: 2430 Rayburn House Office Bldg Washington DC 20515

TAYLOR, GLEN A., state senator; B.S., Mankato State U.; postgrad. Harvard U.; m. Glenda Taylor; children—Teri, Jenn, Mari, Jeff. Pres., Taylor Corp.; mem. Minn. Senate, 1980—. Bd. dirs. Mankato State U., Found., Minn. Jaycee Found.; former pres. YMCA; former chmn. United Way. Mem. C. of C. Republican. Congregationalist. Office: 135 State Office Bldg St Paul MN 55155*

TAYLOR, HARRY MARSHALL, purchasing dir.; b. Bartonville, Ill., June 19, 1920; s. Harry H. and Ruth V. (Church) T.; student public schools; m. Lucille E. Staley, Sept. 4, 1945; children—Ronald Lee, Connie Sue. Apprentice machinist Caterpillar Tractor Co., 1939-42, journeyman machinist, 1942-45; journeyman machinist E.M. Smith & Co., Peoria, Ill., 1945-74, gen. mgr., 1974-78, purchasing dir., 1978—. Served with USMCR, World War II. Mem. Soc. Mfg. Engrs., Nat. Rifle Assn., Travelers Protective Assn., Audubon Soc., Am. Legion (post comdr. 1951-52, 71-72, fin. officer 1972—). Methodist. Clubs: Spoon River Sportsmen Forty and Eight, Wildlife, Franklin, Hamilton. Office: 826 W Detweiller Dr Peoria IL 61615

TAYLOR, HOWARD RICHARD, JR., health care orgn. adminstr.; b. Cleve., Sept. 22, 1919; s. Howard Richard and Ednajean (Wallace) T.; A.B., Allegheny Coll., 1941; m. Barbara MacDonald Shenk, Oct. 18, 1946; children—Margaret Jean Shenk Taylor, Susan McDonald Taylor Scherbel, Lynne Wallace Taylor. Reporter, Butler (Pa.) Eagle, 1941; account exec. Griswold-Eshleman, Cleve., 1946-47; asst. to pres. and v.p. Fenn Coll., Cleve., 1950-56; asst. to pres. Carling Brewing Co., Cleve., 1956-60; owner, pres. Howard Richard Taylor & Assos., Public Relations, Cleve., 1961-71; dir. devel. and public relations Cleve. Clinic Fedn., 1971-79, exec. asst. to chmn. bd. govs., 1979—; dir. Paterson-Leitch Co., Cleve. Trustee, Cleve. Health Mus., 1954-60; trustee Cleve. Center for Alcoholism, 1957-68, pres., 1965-66; trustee Beech Brook, Cleve., 1972—, Fairfax Found., Cleve., 1972—, Center for Human Services, Cleve., 1976-80. Served with USMC, 1941-45, 47-50. Decorated Silver Star, Bronze Star with oak leaf cluster. Mem. Nat. Assn. Hosp. Devel., Am. Mktg. Assn. Republican. Presbyterian. Clubs: Country, Union. Home: 31100 Fairmount Blvd Pepper Pike OH 44124 Office: 9500 Euclid Ave Cleveland OH 44106

TAYLOR, JACK PAUL, supt. schs.; b. Wapakonata, Ohio, Jan. 27, 1931; s. George T. and Frieda (Moeller) T.; B.S., Bowling Green State U., 1953, M.S., 1954; Ph.D., Ohio State U., 1966; m. Berneda Florence Ruck, Dec. 27, 1953; children—Thomas Roberts, Carole Jane. Sr. social studies instr., guidance Perrysburg (Ohio) Schs., 1954-56; high sch. prin. Liberty Center Schs., 1956-59; supt. schs., Crestline, Ohio, 1959-62, Xenia, Ohio, 1964-67, Saginaw, Mich., 1967-76, Shaker Heights, Ohio, 1977—; coordinator Sch. Mgmt. Inst., Columbus, Ohio; vis. prof. Central State U.; adj. prof. Cleve. State U.; cons. grad. faculty Ohio State U. Pres., Future Tchrs. Ohio, 1952; mem. Library Bd., Crestline, 1959-62; mem. Human Relations Commn., Mayor's Com. Concern; chmn. Nat. Consortium on Ednl. Evaluation. Mem. exec. com. Young Republicans Ohio, 1950-54. Bd. dirs. United Fund, Jr. Achievement, YMCA; mem. exec. com. Cuyahoga Council for Handicapped Children; mem. Lt. Gov.'s Task Force on Edn.; pres. Saginaw Symphony Assn.; trustee United Appeal Crestline, Shaker Lake Regional Nature Center; bd. dirs. Ohio Adminstrs. Action Com. Recipient Worth McClure award Am. Assn. Sch. Adminstrs., 1964; E.E. Lewis award in edn. Ohio State U., also Frontier's Internat. service award of year, 1973. Mem. Xenia Area C. of C. (dir.), Distributive Edn. Clubs Am. (past nat. v.p.), Mich. Middle Cities Edn. Assn. (pres.), Bowling Green State U. Alumni Assn. (trustee), Buckeye Assn. Sch. Adminstrs. (legis. com.), Ohio Soc. N.Y., Delta Tau Delta, Omicron Delta Kappa, Pi Sigma Alpha, Phi Delta Kappa. Mem. United Ch. Christ. Rotarian. Club: Edliners (pres.) (Ohio State U.). Home: 21875 S Woodland Rd Shaker Heights OH 44122

TAYLOR, JAMES C., state senator; b. Crawfordsville, Ark., Feb. 8, 1930; student U. Ill., Monticello Coll.; m. Ella; children—Richard, Cassaundra, Cynthia. Hwy. maintenance supr. Stevenson Hwy. and supt. 16th Ward Bur. Sanitation, Chgo.; ward committeeman Democratic Orgn.; del. Dem. Nat. Conv., 1976; former mem. Ill. Ho. of Reps., asst. majority leader; mem. Ill. State Senate. Served with U.S. Army; Korea. Scoutmaster, Boy Scouts Am. Mem. Teamsters Union, Ward Supts. Assn. Roman Catholic. Office: 312 Capitol Bldg Springfield IL 62706*

TAYLOR, JAMES FRANCIS, mktg. and sales exec.; b. Detroit, Sept. 5, 1951; s. Harold James and Mary Frances (Law) T.; B.A. in Polit. Sci., Mich. State U., 1976; postgrad. Thomas Cooley Law Sch., 1979; m. Janet E. Joss, May 21, 1977; children—Jonathan, Jessica. Product mgr. Gen. Aluminum Products, Charlotte, Mich., 1975-77; sales mgr. Empire Metal Products, Columbus, Ohio, 1978; bus. mgr. Paul Martin, Atty., Lansing, Mich., 1978-79; dir. mktg. and sales Feather-Lite Mfg. Co., Troy, Mich., 1979-81; v.p. mktg. and sales Innovative Products Corp., Madison Heights, Mich., 1981—. Home:

693 WHO'S WHO IN THE MIDWEST

13353 Wales St Huntington Woods MI 48070 Office: 31211 Mally Dr Madison Heights MI 48071

TAYLOR, JAMES LEON, social services cons.; b. N.Y.C., May 25, 1948; s. James Furman and Marie Katherine (Fizz) T.; A.A., St. Clair County Community Coll., 1969; B.A. in Sociology, Ky. State U., 1973; M.S.W., U. Mich., 1974, M.A. in Edn., 1975, Ph.D. in Edn., 1977. Conveyorman, machine operator Diamond Crystal Salt Co., St. Clair, Mich., 1968-70; student coordinator, adminstr. Office Career Planning and Placement, Ky. State U., Frankfort, 1971-73; research asst. Sch. Social Work, U. Mich., Ann Arbor, 1974; protective services staff child abuse unit div. children and youth services Mich. Dept. Social Services, Detroit, 1975-77, adult foster care lic. cons. Bur. Regulatory Services, Lansing, 1977—; lectr. adult foster care provider tng. seminars and workshops. NIMH fellow; Minority Opportunity grantee. Mem. Nat. Assn. Social Workers, Nat. Assn. Black Social Workers, Am. Soc. Public Adminstrn., Assn. Mgmt. Analysis in State and Local Govt., Mich. Black Assos. in State Employment, So. Mich. Computer Orgn., U. Mich. Alumni Assn., NAACP, Phi Delta Kappa, Omega Psi Phi (chpt. editor). Office: 2350 W Stadium Blvd Ann Arbor MI 48103

TAYLOR, JAMES ROBERT, chemist; b. Dubuque, Iowa, Apr. 3, 1923; s. Fredrick Karl and Helen Elizabeth (Webster) T.; B.S., U. Dubuque, 1947; m. Betty Jane Thoma, June 19, 1944; children—Robert, David, Richard. Chemist, Swift & Co., Oakbrook, Ill., 1948-52, research chemist 1952-65, 1969-73, supr. routine chemistry, 1969-72, sect. head analytical services, 1973-78, group leader analytical chemistry, 1978—. Served with U.S. Army, 1943-45, 51, 52. Decorated Bronze Star with oak leaf cluster. Mem. Am. Oil Chemist Soc., Am. Chem. Soc., ASTM, Lombard Hist. Soc. Republican. Episcopalian. Contbr. articles to profl. jours. Home: 560 S Fairfield Lombard IL 60148 Office: 1919 Swift Dr Oak Brook IL 60521

TAYLOR, JOYCE GERALDINE, educator; b. Gibsland, Mich., June 16, 1929; d. Lonnie Howard and Beattie (Williams) Lewis; B.S., Mercy Coll., Detroit, 1968; M.Ed., Wayne State U., 1972, Ed.S., 1976; children by previous marriage—Bruce A., Joyce Annette, Gloria, Billy. Tchr. elem. schs., Detroit Public Schs., 1968—. Mem. Detroit Fedn. Tchrs. (bldg. rep. 1981—), Nat. Assn. Supervision and Curriculum Devel., Mich. Assn. Supervision and Curriculum, Am. Fedn. Tchrs. Home: 9655 Whitcomb St Detroit MI 48227 Office: 20601 W Davison St Detroit MI 48223

TAYLOR, MARY JOAN (MRS. EDWARD MCKINLEY TAYLOR, JR.), lawyer; b. Kenton, Ohio, Dec. 24, 1926; d. Maurice A. and Martina (Dolan) McMahon; student St. Mary Springs Coll., 1944-45; Asso. Degree in Bus. Adminstrn. Franklin U., 1946-49; J.D. with high distinction, Ohio No. U., 1951; postgrad., U. Wyo., 1954-56; m. Edward McKinley Taylor, Jr., Apr. 23, 1952; 1 dau., Mary Margaret. Admitted to Ohio bar, 1951; gen practice law, Kenton, 1951-52, Wichita Falls, Tex., 1953—; mem. law firm Taylor and Taylor, Dayton, Ohio, 1957—; law librarian Franklin U., 1948-49. Mem. Ohio Bar Assn., Montgomery County Law Library Assn., Ohio No. U. Alumni Assn. (sec. Miami Valley 1958-60), Ieta Tau Lambda, Kappa Beta Pi. Club: Soroptimist. Home: 7417 N Main St Dayton OH 45415

TAYLOR, MORRIS, analytical chemist; b. St. Louis, July 10, 1922; s. Henry Clay Nathaniel and Georgia Leanna (Kenner) Taylor; B.S. in Chemistry, St. Louis U., 1952; m. Millie B. Fudge, July 17, 1948 (dec. Jan. 2, 1969); children—Morris, Jr., Carla Maria; m. 2d Veonnia J. McDonald, Aug. 4, 1973; children—Dorcas Lynnea, Demetrius Sirrom. Research chemist Universal Match Corp., Ferguson, Mo., 1952-54; mfg. chemist Sigma Chem. Co., St. Louis, 1954; clin. chemist 5th Army Area Med. Lab., St. Louis, 1955-56; with Dept. Agr.-Agrl. Research Service Meat and Poultry Inspection Lab., St. Louis, 1956-79, supervisory chemist, 1967-76, chemist-in-charge, 1976-79; part-time instr. St. Louis Community Coll., Forest Park, 1981—. Mem. Draft Bd. III, 5 years; rating panel mem. Bd. U.S. Civil Service Examiners for Eastern Dist. Mo., Madison and St. Clair Counties, Ill., 1969—; reviewer for Assn. Ofcl. Analytical Chemists; collaborator FDA Labs. on Analytical Methods. Mem. Am. Chem. Soc. (cert.), Assn. Ofcl. Analytical Chemists, St. Louis U. Alumni Chemist Assn., Omega Psi Phi (charter mem. Omicron Sigma chpt.). Recipient Suggestion award Dept. Agr. Animal-Plant Health Inspection Service, Sci. and Tech. Services, Meat and Poultry Inspection Lab. for use of hydrogen generators in lab. to reduce hazard of tanks of hydrogen; participant in group award for analytical proficiency Dept. Agr. Home: 4464 Clarence St St Louis MO 63115 Office: Room 942 1114 Market St St Louis MO 63101

TAYLOR, NORRIS MARVIN, JR., public accountant; b. Wichita, Kans., May 31, 1944; s. Norris Marvin and Doris Louise (Baldwin) T.; B.S., Kans. State U., 1966; children—Lisa Jo, Leslie Gwyn. Acct., Ernst & Ernst, C.P.A.'s, Kansas City, Mo., 1968-73; mgr. auditing dept. Donnelly, Meiners & Jordan Co., Kansas City, Mo., 1973-75, partner, 1976—. Served to 1st lt. U.S. Army, 1966-68. C.P.A. Mem. Kansas City Jaycees, Am. Inst. C.P.A.'s, Mo. Soc. C.P.A.'s, Kans. Soc. C.P.A.'s. Home: 6517 Lowell Dr Merriam KS 66202 Office: One Pershing Sq 2301 Main St Suite 400 Kansas City MO 64108

TAYLOR, ORA CHRISTINE, educator; b. Junction City, La., 1931; d. Jesse Rogers and Ruby Beatrice (Brown) Ross; B.S., U. Ark., 1952; M.Ed., Wayne State U., 1962; summer fellow in math. U. Ill., 1973; m. Tillman Taylor, Jan. 28, 1953; 1 child, Krasne. Tchr. math. Detroit Public Schs., 1952—, supr. middle sch. math., 1969—, dir. metric edn. project, 1978-79, dir./author/contbr. various curriculum materials/projects; part-time faculty Wayne State U., Detroit, 1980-81. Dir., We Care Summer Program, Detroit United Community Services, 1979, 80; dir. Christian edn. Greater St. Mark Baptist Ch.; dir. youth activities Bapt. State Congress, 1979-81, mem. faculty, 1979; also mem. choir, Sunday sch. tchr., leader Bapt. Tng. Union Group local ch. Mem. Nat. Council Tchrs. Math., Assn. Curriculum Supervision and Devel., Nat. Alliance Black Sch. Educators, Mich. Council Tchrs. Math., Mich. Assn. Curriculum Supervision and Devel., Metro Detroit Area Black Sch. Educators, Alpha Kappa Mu. Editor/contbg. author: Alternative Learning Activities, 1974. Home: 18700 Sorrento Detroit MI 48235 Office: 932 Schools Center Bldg 5057 Woodward Ave Detroit MI 48202

TAYLOR, PATRICIA ANN, occupational therapist; b. Allegan, Mich., Sept. 15, 1922; d. John William and Grace Adele (Burnett) Exton; B.S., Milw./Downer Coll., 1944; diploma in Occupational Therapy, Lawrence U., 1945; M.S., U. Mich., 1976; m. Ernest Taylor, Mar. 19, 1954; children—Sally, Carolyn, Steven, David, John. Asst. prof. phys. medicine U. Wis., 1946-49; dir. activity therapy Menninger Found., Topeka, 1949-53; supr. occupational therapy VA, Fayetteville, N.C., 1956-66; coordinator activity therapy Mich. Dept. Mental Health, Northville, 1966-75; clin. instr. Eastern Mich. U. and Wayne State U., 1967-75; curriculum cons. Ohio State U., 1969-70, Wayne State U., 1967-76; rehab. cons. Kans. Dept. Mental Health, Topeka, 1950-54. Civilian occupational therapist U.S. Army Hosps., 1945-46, recreation cons., Korea, 1953; mem. Southeastern Mich. adv. council White House Conf. on Aging, 1981. Recipient Civilian Merit award Hdqrs. Korean Communications Zone, 1953, Mich. Civil Service award, 1968. Mem. Nat. Assn. Retarded Citizens, Mich. Soc. Gerontology, Am. Occupational Therapy Assn. (bd. mgmt. 1950-53). Episcopalian. Contbg. editor Am. Jour. Occupational Therapy, 1950-53. Address: 2551 Sandalwood Circle Ann Arbor MI 48105

TAYLOR, PURCELL, JR., educator; b. Cin., Apr. 20, 1941; s. Purcell and Lucille E. (Partridge) T.; B.A., U. Cin., 1971, M.Ed., 1972, Ed.D., 1977. Cardiovascular pulmonary technician St. Mary's Hosp., Cin., 1964-65; cardiovascular pulmonary technician/inhalation therapist Jewish Hosp., Cin., 1965-71; research asso. div. toxicology, dept. environ. health U. Cin. Med. Sch., 1971-72, research asso. dept. health, 1972-73, asso. prof. psychology, dept. head, 1978—; sch. psychologist Hamilton County Bd. Edn., 1972-73, Cin. Bd. Ed., 1973-74. Commr. Cin. Human Relations Commn., 1981; bd. dirs. Central Community Health Bd., 1980; bd. trustees U. Affiliated Cin. Center for Developmental Disorders, 1978, Cin. Epilepsy Assn., 1978, Cathedral Child Devel. Center, 1978; adv. bd. U. Without Walls/Ohio Cin. Center, 1978. Served with USMC, 1959-65. Danforth fellow, 1971-72; U. Cin. grantee 1973—; cert. sch. psychologist. Mem. Internat. Platform Assn., Nat. Council Research and Devel., Nat. Assn. Sch. Psychologists, Am. Psychol. Assn., Assn. to Advance Ethical Hypnosis, Nat. Black Psychologists Assn., Cin. Black Psychologists Assn., Psi Chi, Phi Delta Kappa. Methodist. Club: Masons (32 deg.). Contbr. articles to profl. jours. Home: 2638 Bellevue Ave Cincinnati OH 45219 Office: 431 French Hall Univ Cin Cincinnati OH 45220

TAYLOR, RALPH ORIEN, JR., developer, builder, investor; b. Kansas City, Mo., Jan. 6, 1919; s. Ralph Orien and Genevieve (Sturgeon) T.; student U. Kansas City, 1936-38; B.S., U. Mo., 1940; m. Betty Boswell, Dec. 7, 1940 (dec. 1959); children—Bradley, Nancy. Partner Sturgeon & Taylor, 1940-42; owner Sturgeon & Taylor, Inc., Kansas City, Mo., 1942—, chmn. bd., 1959—; pres. Sturgeon & Taylor Investment Co., Inc., 1949—, chmn. bd., 1959—; pres. Sturgeon & Taylor Devel. Co., 1950—, chmn. bd., 1959—; pres., chmn. bd. Sturgeon & Taylor Realty Co., Inc., 1955—; pres., chmn. bd. Tiger Constn. Co., Inc., Bengal Homes, Inc., Westbrooke Hotels, Inc., Sturgeon & Taylor Co., Joint Venture; dir., mem. exec. com. Patrons State Bank & Trust, Olathe, Kans. Mem. adv. council U. Mo. Sch. Forestry. Served as lt. comdr. USNR, World War II. Recipient Bronze Star medal. Mem. Home Builders Assn. Greater Kansas City (dir., pres.), Johnson County (Kans.), Kansas City (Mo.) real estate bds., Nat. Assn. Home Builders (life dir.), Phi Delta Theta. Clubs: Indian Hills Country; Lauderdale Yacht, Ft. Lauderdale. Home: 3505 W 71st St Prairie Village KS 66208 Office: 6909 Nall Ave Prairie Village KS 66208

TAYLOR, RANDY RAY, psychologist; b. Miles City, Mont., Mar. 6, 1950; s. Duane Rowland and Elizabeth Frances (Erdelt) T.; B.S., U. Wyo., 1972, M.S., 1973, Ph.D., 1976; m. Susan Lillian Schmidt, Dec. 18, 1975; 1 son, Nicolas Kristen. Clin. psychology intern Northside Community Mental Health Center, Tampa, Fla., 1976-77; dir. psychol. services Gaston-Lincoln Psychiat. Hosp., Gastonia, N.C., 1977-79; pvt. practice family and individual therapy Gastonia, 1978-79, Danville, Ill., 1979—; clin. psychologist VA, Danville, 1979—; pvt. practice individual and family therapy, Danville, 1980—; adj. faculty U. N.C., Charlotte, 1978-79. Bd. dirs. Gaston County Rape Companion Program, 1979. Certified psychologist, N.C., Ill. Mem. Am. Psychol. Assn., N.C. Psychol. Assn., Sigma Xi. Lutheran-Mo. Synod (dir.). Home: Rural Route 5 Box 402 Danville IL 61832 Office: VA Med Center 1900 E Main St Danville IL 61832 also 9 S Griffin St Danville IL 61832

TAYLOR, RAY, state senator; b. Steamboat Rock, Iowa, June 4, 1923; s. Leonard Allen and Mary Delilah (Huffman) T.; student U. No. Iowa, 1940-41, Baylor U., 1948-49; m. Mary Allen, Aug. 29, 1924; children—Gordon, Laura Rae Taylor Hansmann, Karol Ann Taylor Flora, Jean Lorraine Taylor Mahl. Farmer, Steamboat Rock, Iowa, 1943—; mem. Iowa Senate, 1973—; bd. dirs., sec. Am. Legis. Exchange Council, 1979—. Sec., Hardin County Farm Bur., 1970-72; mem. Iowa div. bds. Am. Cancer Soc.; chmn. Am. Revolution Bicentennial Com. Mem. Steamboat Rock Community Sch. Bd., 1955-70; coordinator Republican youth, 1968-72. Bd. dirs. Faith Bapt. Bible Coll.; v.p. Am. Council Christian Chs.; chmn. Iowans for Responsible Govt. Mem. Wildlife Club. Baptist. Address: Steamboat Rock IA 50672

TAYLOR, RAYMOND ELLORY, materials scientist; b. Ames, Iowa, Oct. 19, 1929; s. Alva A. and Maude Marguarite (Crow) T.; B.S., Iowa State U., 1951; M.S., U. Idaho, 1957; Ph.D., (N. Am. fellow), Pa. State U., 1967; m. Elfa Mae Shaffer, Apr. 27, 1952; children—Wayne Alva, David Leo. Research chemist, supr. Gen. Electric Co., Richland, Wash., 1951-57; sr. research N. Am. Rockwell Group., Canoga Park, Calif., 1957-64; asso. sr. research Purdue U., West Lafayette, Ind., 1967-74, sr. researcher, head Properties Research Lab., 1974—. Com. chmn. Boy Scouts Am., 1970-75. NSF grantee. Mem. ASTM, Sigma Xi, Phi Lambda Upsilon. Contbr. articles to profl. jours. Home: 618 Essex St West Lafayette IN 47906 Office: 2595 Yeager Rd West Lafayette IN 47906

TAYLOR, RICHARD LAVERN, computer co. exec.; b. Dayton, Ohio, Mar. 8, 1950; s. William Edward and Beatrice (Long) T.; B.S. (Ill. State scholar), No. Ill. U., 1972; M.B.A., U. Cin., 1973; m. Jacqueline Madigan, Aug. 19, 1972; children—Kristen Nicole, John William. Sr. staff coordinator Muscular Dystrophy Assn., Chgo., 1968-71; asst. buyer fashionwear McAlpins Co., Cin., 1972-73; internat. sales engr. Honeywell Inc., Mpls., 1973-75, mktg. rep., Boston, 1975-77; chief product devel. analyst Ford Motor Corp., Dearborn, Mich., 1977-78, chief program analyst forward model strategy planning, emissions, and fuel economy, 78-80; sr. cons., dir. mktg. industry mfg. Control Data Corp., Mpls., 1980—; dir. Yo Choma, Inc.; cons. Minn. Minority Bus. League; lectr. Hennepin Coll. Asso. adviser explorers council Boy Scouts Am.; mem. Hennepin County CETA Adv. Council, 1980—. U. Cin. fellow, 1972-73. Mem. Am. Mgmt. Assn. Engring. Soc. Detroit, Soc. Automotive Engrs., Am. Mktg. Assn., Assn. MBA Execs., Delta Sigma Pi, Phi Beta Lambda. Democrat. Roman Catholic. Club: Ski Unlimited. Home: 8241 Oregon Rd Bloomington MN 55438 Office: 8100 34th Ave S Minneapolis MN 55440

TAYLOR, ROBERT CARROLL, lawyer, investor, shopping center devel. corp. exec.; b. Phila., Nov. 7, 1925; s. Norman Henry and Helen Blair (Daniel) T.; student Princeton, 1944, Denison U., 1944-45; B.A., U. N.Mex., 1947; LL.B., U. Pa., 1955; m. Barbara Tietzel, July 12, 1958; children—Robert Carroll, Laura Pfeiffer, Sara Daniel. Adminstrv. asst. to regional v.p. Container Corp. Am., Manayunk, Pa., 1948-49; asst. real estate supt. F.W. Woolworth Co., N.Y.C., 1956-61; admitted to N.Y. bar, 1959, Ga. bar, 1968, Ill. bar, 1971; real estate mgr., analyst, atty. J.C. Penney Co., Chgo., 1962, San Francisco, 1963-65, Atlanta, 1966-67, N.Y.C., 1967-68; real estate dir. Hart Schaffner & Marx, Chgo., 1969-71; v.p., dir. Devel. Control Corp., Northfield, Ill., 1971-76; dir. Blaurock-Devel. Control Corp. Realty, Ltd., 1976-78; founder, pres. R.C. Taylor Cos., Inc., Northfield, Ill., 1978—; partner Port Plaza Mall Co., 1974, Rapids Mall Co., 1976, College Hills Mall Co., 1978; guest lectr. real estate devel.; cons. to various ind. retailers in Mid-West. Trustee Arden Shore Home for Boys. Served to lt. comdr. USNR, 1944-46, 47-49, 51-53. Decorated Bronze Star medal with V. Mem. Internat. Council Shopping Centers (state dir. 1976-78), Chgo. Bar Assn., Naval Res. Assn., Kappa Sigma. Republican. Quaker. Home: 860 Melody Rd Lake Forest IL 60045 Office: Suite 259 540 Frontage Rd Northfield IL 60093

TAYLOR, ROBERT ELLSWORTH, ednl. adminstr.; b. Grants Pass, Oreg., Sept. 30, 1927; s. Harold C. and Edith Eleanor (Grace) T.; B.S. cum laude, U. Ariz., 1952, M.S., 1953; Ph.D., Ohio State U., 1961; m. Celianna Isaly, Sept. 20, 1969. Asst. supr. Dept. Edn., State of Ariz., 1952-56, supr., 1956-61; dir. Nat. Center for Agr. Edn., 1962-64; prof. Coll. Agr. and Home Econs. Ohio State U., 1964-65; exec. dir. Nat. Center for Research in Vocat. Edn., Columbus, Ohio, 1964—; asso. dean Coll. Agr. and Home Econs., Ohio State U., Columbus, 1974—; dir. Eric Clearinghouse, Columbus, 1965-73. Served with U.S. Army, 1954-55. Recipient Disting. Service award Tex. Vocat. Agr. Tchrs. Assn., 1965; Centennial medallion Ohio State U., 1970. Mem. Am. Vocat. Assn. (Outstanding Service award 1978), AAAS, Nat. Acad. Scis., Phi Kappa Phi, Phi Delta Kappa, Gamma Sigma Delta, Alpha Zeta, Omicron Tau Theta. Co-author: Career Education: Perspective and Promise, 1972; contbr. articles to profl. jours. Home: 3759 Klondike Rd Delaware OH 43015 Office: 1960 Kenny Rd Columbus OH 42310

TAYLOR, ROBERT ELMER, chem. co. exec.; b. Durango, Colo., Aug. 21, 1935; s. Lloyd B. and Helen Golda (McGee) T.; B.S. in Mktg., Brigham Young U., 1957; m. Dorene Smith, June 20, 1956; children—Shereen, Bryan, David, Dean. Economic analyst, distbn. mgr., mktg. services mgr. El Paso Products Co., 1957-68; dir. diversification No. Natural Gas Co., 1968-69; mktg. mgr. No. Petrochem. Co., Des Plaines, Ill., 1970-73, v.p. petrochems. mktg. div., 1974-81, v.p., bus. dir. petrochems., 1982—; dir. Calcasieu Chem. Corp., Lake Charles, La.; tchr. evening sch. U. Tex., El Paso, 1960-64, Odessa (Tex.) Coll., 1965-68. Mem. Nat. Petroleum Refiners Assn. (bd. dirs., petrochem. com.), Am. Inst. Chem. Engrs., S.W. Chem. Assn. Republican. Mormon. Home: 1559 Elm Northbrook IL 60062 Office: 2350 E Devon Ave Des Plaines IL 60018

TAYLOR, ROBERT MALCOLM, physician; b. Detroit, Sept. 13, 1924; s. Malcolm Edgar and Mary Estelle (Trevarthen) T.; student U. Vt., 1943, Washington U., St. Louis, 1944; M.D., Wayne U., 1948; m. Lorna Elaine Mundt, June 21, 1947; children—Robert Malcolm, Jr., Jill Anne, Sara Jo. Intern, Harper Hosp., Detroit, 1948-49; resident in internal medicine Crile VA Hosp., Cleve., 1950-53; internist Burns Clinic, Petoskey, Mich., 1955—, v.p., 1964-68, 71-74, dir., 1971-74. Mem. Emmet County Rep. Com., 1958-64; del. Mich. Rep. Conv., 1960; elder Presbyterian Ch., Petoskey. Served as capt. M.C., U.S. Army, 1949-50, 53-54. Fellow Am. Coll. Chest Physicians; mem. AMA, Mich. (internal medicine del.), No. Mich. med. socs., A.C.P., Am. Soc. Internal Medicine Mich. Soc. Internal Medicine (pres. 1979). Clubs: Birchwood Country (Harbor Springs, Mich.), DeMolay. Home: 2431 Greenbriar Rd Birchwood Farm Estate Harbor Springs MI 49740 Office: Burns Clinic Petoskey MI 49770

TAYLOR, RONALD LEE, ednl. adminstr.; b. Urbana, Ill., Nov. 11, 1943; s. Lee and Katherine (Becker) T.; A.B. cum laude, Harvard U., 1966; M.B.A., Stanford U., 1971; m. Patricia D. Fitzsimmons, Mar. 10, 1973; children—Jamie, Lara, Meredith, Dana. Sales corr. Moss-Am., St. Louis, 1962-66; group asst. controller Bell & Howell Co., Chgo., 1971-73; pres., dir. Keller Grad. Sch. Mgmt., Chgo., 1973—; dir. Midwest Sintered Products Co., Precision Plastic Co.; cons. Bd. dirs. Robert Crown Center for Health Edn. Served with U.S. Army, 1966-69. Mem. Stanford Alumni Assn. Clubs: Harvard, Hinsdale Golf. Office: 10 S Riverside Plaza Chicago IL 60606

TAYLOR, RUSSELL L., JR., mktg. exec.; b. Umatilla, Fla., Apr. 5, 1937; s. Russell L. and Elizabeth (Williams) T.; B.A. in Bus. Adminstrn. and Econs., Iowa Wesleyan Coll., Mt. Pleasant, 1963; m. Susan Mae Nelson, July 22, 1961; children—William Russell, Andrew Nelson, Elizabeth Diane. Mgr. distbr. services Warner Elec. Brake & Clutch Co., Beloit, Wis., 1968-73, sales rep., 1973-75; nat. accounts mgr. FMC Corp. Power Control Div., Milw., 1975-77, mgr. distbr. mktg., 1977-80; sales mgr. Rockford Dynatorq, Rockford, 1981—. Mem. Rockford (Ill.) Bd. Election Commrs., vice chmn., 1973-79, chmn., 1979—. Served with U.S. Army, 1961-62. Mem. Power Transmission Distbrs. Assn. Republican. Congregationalist. Office: 5173 26th Ave Rockford IL 61109

TAYLOR, SAMUEL GALE, III, physician; b. Elmhurst, Ill., Sept. 2, 1904; s. Samuel Gale, Jr. and Anna Jeffrey (Mead) T.; B.A., Yale, 1927; M.D., U. Chgo., 1931; m. Eleanor Roberts, June 1, 1938 (dec. 1978); children—Constance Taylor Blackwell, John Winthrop, Samuel Gale IV; m. 2d, Jocelyn Pierson, 1979. Intern, Highland Park Hosp., Chgo., 1931; intern Cook County Hosp., Chgo., 1932-33, resident, 1933-35, research fellow metabolic diseases, 1935-40, attending physician, mem. tumor bd., 1963-66; asst., asso., instr., asst. prof. medicine Rush Med. Coll., Chgo., 1933-42, prof. medicine, 1971-77, emeritus, 1977—, dir. Cancer Center Planning Program, 1972-74; asso. dir. Rush Cancer Center, 1975-77; asso. prof. medicine U. Ill. Coll. Medicine, Chgo., 1942-65, mem. Tumor Council, 1948-72, dir. steroid therapy div. Tumor Clinic, 1950-71, prof. medicine, 1965-74, emeritus, 1974—; dir. sect. med. oncology, dept. medicine Presbyn.-St. Lukes Hosp., 1954-71, asso. attending physician, 1961-65, sr. attending, 1965-76, cons., 1976—; chmn. tumor bd. West Side VA Hosp., 1967-72, cons. staff, 1966-72; asst. attending physician Henrotin Hosp., 1935-36, sr. attending physician, 1936-45; asst. attending physician Presbyn. Hosp., 1941-50; attending physician Lake Forest (Ill.) Hosp., 1945-55, cons. staff, 1955—. Mem. Bd. Health, Lake Forest, 1946-58; chmn. med. adv. com. Chgo. Vis. Nurses Assn., 1955-65; pres. Ill. Cancer Council, 1972-74; dir. Ill. Cancer Council Comprehensive Cancer Center Program, 1974-77. Trustee, cancer cons. Nat. Cancer Inst.; mem. adv. com. Cancer Control Program, HEW, 1956-60; liaison mem. cancer commn. A.C.S., 1956-73; cancer adv. com. Ill. Dept. Pub. Health, 1976—. Diplomate Am. Bd. Internal Medicine. Fellow A.C.P. (chmn. com. on cancer 1959-73); mem. Am., Pan Am. med. assns., Ill., Chgo. med. socs., Central Soc. Clin. Research, Soc. Surg. Oncology, Am. Radium Soc., Chgo. Soc. Internal Medicine, Am. Soc. Clin. Oncology, AAAS, Am. Soc. Cancer Research, Am. Cancer Soc. (dir.-at-large, Distinguished Service award), Inst. Medicine Chgo., Am. Diabetes Assn., N.Y. Acad. Scis., Chgo. Soc. Internal Medicine, Am. Coll. Radiology (Commn. on Cancer 1960-76), Sigma Xi. Episcopalian. Clubs: Wausaukee; Univ.; Onwensia. Contbr. articles profl. jours., also chpts. to books. Home: PO Box 646 Lake Forest IL 60045 Office: 36 S Wabash Ave Chicago IL 60603

TAYLOR, STEPHEN LEE, lawyer; b. Cairo, Ill., Sept. 26, 1947; s. Melfred E. and Margaret L. (Mitchell) T.; B.A., S.E. Mo. U., 1969; J.D., Mo. U., 1972; m. Patricia Ann Taylor, Aug. 31, 1968; children—Justin Patrick, Garrett Stephen. Admitted to Mo. bar, 1972; asst. pros. atty. Office of Scott County, Sikeston, Mo., 1973-76; partner firm Gilmore, Gilmore and Taylor, Sikeston, 1976—. Pres. Scott County Young Democrats, 1974-75, Mo. Young Democrats, 1976-77; mem. exec. Mo. Dem. exec. com., Young Dems. Am., 1975-76; state committeeman 27th Senate Dist. Mo. Dem. Com., 1978—. Served to capt. USAR, 1972-81. Recipient Outstanding Service award Mo. Young Democrats, 1976. Mem. Am., Mo., Scott

County bar assns., Mo. Trial Lawyers Assn., Jaycees (named Outstanding Jaycee 1974, Jaycee of Year 1977, Disting. Service award U.S. Jaycees 1978), Phi Delta Phi. Baptist. Home: 801 Vernon St Sikeston MO 63801 Office: 217 S Kingshighway St Sikeston MO 63801

TAYLOR, TIMOTHY DAVID, computer-based tng. co. exec.; b. Akron, Ohio, May 24, 1947; s. John I. and Winnifred F. Taylor; B.A., U. Akron, 1969, M.A., 1971, Ph.D., 1976; m. Gloria Dai-Lin Cheng, July 19, 1978. Tchr., Akron Public Schs., 1974-76; asst. dir. Computer Based Edn. Center, U. Akron, 1976-78, asso. dir., 1978-80, acting dir., 1980-81; mgr. computer-enhanced multimedia tng. devel. Deltak, Inc., Oak Brook, Ill., 1981—; cons. in field. Served with USAR, 1969-77. Mem. Nat. Wildlife Fedn., Am. Forestry Assn., League of Am. Wheelmen, Am. Youth Hostels, Assn. Ednl. Data Systems, Assn. Devel. Computer-Based Instructional Systems, Soc. Applied Learning Technology. Clubs: Sierra, Nat. Audubon Soc., Bikecentennial. Home: PO Box 85 Naperville IL 60566 Office: 1220 Kensington St Oak Brook IL 60521

TAYLOR, WILLIAM JAMES, transp. co. exec.; b. Eddystone, Pa., July 29, 1926; s. William J. and Clara Ella (Harris) T.; A.B., Dickinson Coll., 1949; J.D., U. Pa., 1952; m. Jane Currie, Oct. 18, 1958; children—Deborah Ann, Timothy J., Jeffrey Harris. Admitted to Pa. bar, 1953, N.Y. bar, 1961, also U.S. Supreme Ct. bar; law clk. to chief justice Supreme Ct. Pa., 1952-53; mem. legal dept. Pa. R.R., 1953-61; mem. law dept. REA Express, 1961-62, gen. counsel, 1962-65, v.p., gen. counsel, 1965-66, exec. v.p., gen. counsel, 1966, pres., chief exec. officer, 1966-68, chmn., 1968-69; v.p. Ill. Central R.R., 1969-74; v.p. govtl. affairs Ill. Central Industries, 1969-74, v.p. legal affairs, 1974-76; pres. Ill. Central Gulf R.R., 1978—, chief operating officer, 1976-78, chief exec. officer, 1978—, also dir.; legis. counsel to trustees Penn Central R.R., 1971-74. Trustee Dickinson Coll. Served with USNR, 1944-46. Mem. Am. Bar Assn., Assn. ICC Practitioners, C. of C., Newcomen Soc. N.Am., Sigma Chi, Omicron Delta Kappa. Clubs: Congressional Country, Internat. (Washington); Chgo., Econ. of Chgo.; Barrington Hills (Ill.). Home: 346 Ridge Rd Barrington Hills IL 60010 Office: 233 N Michigan Ave Chicago IL 60601

TAYLOR, WILLIAM MENKE, elec. wiring harnesses co. exec.; b. Logansport, Ind., May 24, 1918; s. William T. and Ethel M. (Menke) T.; student in bus. adminstrn. LaSalle Coll., 1936-40; A.A.F., Elec. Spl. Sch., Lincoln, Nebr., 1942; m. Betty L. Flory, May 8, 1944; children—William M., Alan R. Cost accountant Essex Wire Corp., Logansport, 1935-50, salesman, 1950-55, plant mgr., 1955-56; sales mgr., plant mgr. Airdesign Corp., Norristown, Pa., 1956-60; sales mgr. Dill Products, Inc., Norristown, 1960-73; pres. Tay-Mor Industries Inc., Logansport, 1973—; v.p. Taylor Industries, 1978—; instr. aircraft elec. systems. Served with USAF, 1942-45. Named Ky. Col. Mem. Soc. of Automotive Engrs. Republican. Clubs: Logansport Country, Elks, Masons. Home: 2825 Perrysburg Rd Logansport IN 46947 Office: PO Box 64 Logansport IN 46947

TAYLOR, WINNIFRED JANE, psychologist; b. Akron, Ohio, Aug. 27, 1925; d. Edwin Dain and Jessie Pearl (Keeran) Fletcher; B.S., U. Akron, 1962, M.S., 1965, Ph.D., 1971; m. John Idris Taylor, June 22, 1943; children—John Frederick Taylor, Timothy David Taylor, Kathryn Sue Taylor Cline. Tchr., Akron and Barberton, Ohio, 1959-65; sch. psychologist Akron Pub. Sch., 1965-74; pvt. practice family counseling and psychology, Clinton, Ohio, 1969-74; asst. prof. counselor edn. U. Wis., Superior, 1974—. Recipient Freedom Found. award for Teaching, 1965-66. Mem. Nat. Assn. Sch. Psychologists, Am., Wis. personnel and guidance assns., Am. Soc. Adlerian Psychology, Am. Edn. Research Assn., Am. Sch. Counselors Assn., Assn. Humanistic Psychology, Douglas County Mental Health Assn., Am. Soc. Individual Psychology. Contbr. articles to profl. jours.; syndicated columnist. Home: 3d and Lake Ave Lake Nebagamon WI 54849 Office: U Wis Dept Edn Adminstrn and Counseling Superior WI 54880

TAZELAAR, EDWIN JOSEPH, II, ins. co. exec.; b. Chgo., June 16, 1947; s. Edwin Joseph and Nancy Annette (DeStevens) T.; grad. N.W. Police Acad., 1971; student Harper Coll., 1974-76; children—Bradley James, Marcus Thomas, Edwin Joseph III. Police officer Village of Hoffman Estates (Ill.), 1971-77; asso. Am. Family Life Assurance Co. of Columbus, Ga., 1977; dist. mgr., 1978, regional mgr., Palatine, Ill., 1979—; store mgr. Robert Hall Clothes, Chgo., 1968-71. Served with U.S. Army, 1966-68. Recipient Patrol Achievement award Village of Hoffman Estates, 1973; Fireball award Am. Family Life Assurance Co., 1977, co. awards, 1977, 78, named to President's Club, 1978. Mem. Am. Mgrs. Assn., Am. Family Polit. Action Com. Roman Catholic. Home and Office: 730 N Hicks St Suite 600 Palatine IL 60067

TEACH, GARY LEE, assn. exec.; b. Troy, Ohio, Mar. 2, 1947; s. Lester Edward and Janet Ilene (Hirsch) T.; student Ohio State U., 1965-67; B.S., Bliss Coll., 1969; M.B.A., Xavier U., 1971; m. Glenda LaVerne McKim, May 9, 1969; children—Gary, Sara. Plant acct. Hobart Corp., Troy, 1971-74; treas., gen. mgr. Leisure Lawn Co., Dayton, Ohio, 1974-77, also dir.; dir. fin. and adminstrn. United Way Inc., Dayton, 1977—. Pres., Dollars for Scholars, 1975; treas. Brukner Nature Center, 1975; citywide projects coordinator City of Troy Am. Bicentennial Com., 1976. C.P.A., Ohio. Mem. Troy Jaycees (pres. 1972-74, state dir. 1974-75), Soc. for Advancement Mgmt. (pres. chpt. 1977-78), Nat. Assn. Accts., Inst. Mgmt. Accts. Republican. Presbyterian. Home: 3085 Magnolia Dr Troy OH 45373 Office: 184 Salem Ave Dayton OH 45406

TEAGER, JOHN CARLYLE, chem. co. exec.; b. Dakota City, Nebr., Dec. 19, 1932; s. Mark Carlyle and Eva Matilda (Johnson) T.; B.S. in Bus. Adminstrn., U. Nebr., 1960; m. Patricia Ann Friest, Nov. 29, 1957; children—John, Lisa Ann, Mary Pat. Rate auditor, Maytag Co., Newton, Iowa, 1960-62; buyer Collins Radio Co., Cedar Rapids, Iowa, 1962-65; adminstrv. specialist Fisher Controls Co., Marshalltown, Iowa, 1965-71; purchasing mgr. Hach Chem. Co., Ames, 1971—; owner Teager's Art & Frame Shoppe, Marshalltown, 1972—. Served with USN, 1957-60; Korea. Mem. Profl. Picture Framers Assn., Purchasing Mgmt. Assn. Republican. Home: 1511 Brentwood Terr Marshalltown IA 50158 Office: 100 Dayton Ave Ames IA 50010

TEAGUE, GAIL MARIE, retail mcht.; b. Ft. Fairfield, Maine, Jan. 15, 1942; s. Clarence Clement and Charlotte B. (Miller) Dorsey; student public schs.; m. Gerald David LaPointe, Apr. 4, 1959 (dec. Nov. 1972); children—Linda Ann, Patti Kate, Helen Marie, Stephen David; m. 2d, Jerry Paul Teague, Jan. 26, 1980. Various positions in industry, 1962-64, 71-75; propr. Gail Marie's Apparel, Ft. Fairfield, 1976—. Mem. Ft. Fairfield Charter Revision Commn., 1974-75, Mcpl. Planning Bd., 1976-80. Mem. Ft. Fairfield C. of C. (dir.), VFW Aux. Democrat. Baptist. Home: 13612 Mercury St Omaha NE 68138 Office: 186 Main St Fort Fairfield ME 04742

TEANEY, ROBERT JAMES, food broker; b. Aurora, Ind., Sept. 25, 1925; s. Charles and Mary Elizabeth (Schaefer) T.; B.S. in Chemistry, Xavier U., 1943-47; med. student Ind. U., 1947-51; student bus. Harvard, 1965-67; m. Beverly Ann Bilas; 1 son, Robert James II. Pres., owner Teaney Super Markets, Inc., Aurora, 1951-61, N.J. Janson, Inc., Cin., 1961—; dir. 20th Century Savs. & Loan. Recipient Key to City Cin., 1969; named hon. Ky. Col. Mem. Nat. Food Brokers Assn. (dir.), Nat. Frozen Foods Assn. (dir.), Nat. Canners Assn. (dir.), Greater Cin. C. of C., Ohio Realtors Assn., Coast Guard Aux. Republican. Roman Catholic. Clubs: Bankers, Cin., Dearborn Country, Cin. Grocery Mfrs., K.C., Eagles, Cin., Ky. Adms. Office: 2200 Victory Pkwy Edgecliff Tower Cincinnati OH 45206

TEASDALE, JOSEPH PATRICK, former gov. Mo.; b. Kansas City, Mo., Mar. 29, 1936; s. William B. and Adah Maurine (Downey) T.; student St. Benedicts Coll., 1954-55; B.S. in Lit., Rockhurst Coll., 1957; LL.B., St. Louis U., 1960; m. M. Theresa Ferkenhoff, Oct. 13, 1973; children—William D., John P. Admitted to Mo. bar, 1960; asst. U.S. atty., 1962-66; pros. atty. Jackson County (Mo.), 1966-72; gov. Mo., Jefferson City, from 1977; now atty. Kansas City Mo.; Vice-chmn. com. on agr., mem. com. on human resources Nat. Govs. Assn.; co-chmn. Ozarks Regional Commn. Served with USAFR, 1961-67. Named Outstanding Man of Year, Jr. C. of C., 1969. Mem. Mo. Bar Assn., Kansas City Bar Assn. Democrat. Roman Catholic. Mem. editorial staff St. Louis U. Law Jour., 1958-60. Home: 100 Madison St Jefferson City MO 65101 Office: 1210 Commerce Tower 911 Main St Kansas City MO 64105

TEATER, ROBERT WOODSON, state ofcl.; b. Nicholasville, Ky., Feb. 27, 1927; s. Buford and May (Scott) T.; B.S. in Agr., U. Ky., 1951; M.S. in Agronomy, Ohio State U., 1955, Ph.D., 1957; grad. Command and Gen. Staff Coll., 1964; m. Dorothy Jane Seeth, May 24, 1952; children—David, James, Donald, Andrew. In charge tobacco research program Ohio Agrl. Research and Devel. Center, Columbus, Ohio, 1957-60; exec. asst. to dir. Ohio Dept. Natural Resources, Columbus, 1961-63, asst. dir. dept., 1963-69; asso. dean Coll. Agr. and asst. dir. Ohio Agrl. Research and Devel. Center, 1969-71; asso. dean and dir. Sch. Natural Resources, Ohio State U., Columbus, 1971-75; dir. Ohio Dept. Natural Resources, 1975—. Mem. Army Res. Forces Policy Com., Washington, 1976-80, reserve forces policy bd., Washington, 1980—. Served to maj. gen. Ohio NG, 1954—, comdr. State Area Command, 1979—. Decorated Bronze Star. Mem. Water Mgmt. Assn. Ohio (charter), Soil Conservation Soc. Am., Nature Conservancy, League Ohio Sportsmen, NG Officers Assn., Assn. Ohio Commodores. Republican. Methodist. Office: Fountain Sq Columbus OH 43224

TEDERS, SISTER ELAINE ANN, ednl. adminstr.; b. Garrett, Ind., Oct. 24, 1944; d. Louis Henry and Bernadette Catherine (Meyer) T.; B.A., St. Xavier Coll., 1971; M.S., Purdue U., 1979. Joined Franciscan Sisters of the Sacred Heart, Roman Cath. Ch., 1962; tchr. St. Joseph Sch., Peru, Ill., 1965-69, St. Mary Sch., Mokena, Ill., 1969-70; tchr. St. Mary Sch., Mundelein, Ill., 1971-75, prin., 1975—. Mem. Nat. Cath. Edn. Assn., Assn. Supervision and Curriculum Devel., Archdiocesan Prins. Assn. Address: Route 2 Box 358 Mundelein IL 60060

TEDESCHI, JOHN ALFRED, historian, librarian; b. Modena, Italy, July 17, 1931; s. Caesar George and Piera (Forti) T.; came to U.S., 1939, naturalized, 1944; B.A., Harvard U., 1954, M.A., 1960, Ph.D., 1966; m. Anne Wood Christian, Sept. 8, 1956; children—Martha, Philip, Sara. Bibliographer, European history and lit. Newberry Library, Chgo., 1965—, curator rare books and manuscripts, head dept. spl. collections, 1970—, dir. Center for Renaissance Studies, 1979—; lectr. history U. Chgo., 1969-71; vis. prof. U. Ill., Chgo., 1972-73, adj. prof., 1979—. Served with U.S. Army, 1954-56. Recipient grants Am. Philos. Soc., 1961, Nat. Endowment Humanities, 1967; Old Dominion fellow Harvard U. Center for Renaissance Studies, Florence, Italy, 1967-68; fellow Inst. Research in Humanities, U. Wis., Madison, 1976-77. Mem. Am. Soc. Reformation Research (pres. 1972), Renaissance Soc. Am. (exec. bd. 1971—), Am. Hist. Assn. Editor series Corpus Reformatorum Italicorum, 1968—; editor-in-chief Bibliographie Internat. de L'Humanisme et de la Renaissance, 1977—; contbr. articles to profl. jours. Home: 5021 S Woodlawn Ave Chicago IL 60615 Office: 60 W Walton St Chicago IL 60610

TEEGARDEN, KENNETH LEROY, clergyman; b. Cushing, Okla., Dec. 22, 1921; s. Roy Albert and Eva B. (Swiggart) T.; student Okla. State U., 1938-40; A.B., Phillips U., 1942, M.A., 1945, D.D., 1963; B.D., Tex. Christian U., 1949, D.D., 1976; D.D., Bethany Coll., 1974; LL.D., Lynchburg Coll., 1975; L.H.D., Culver-Stockton Coll., 1975; m. Wanda Jean Strong, May 28, 1944; children—David Kent, Marshall Kirk. Ordained to ministry Christian Ch. (Disciples of Christ), 1940; pastor in Chandler, Okla., 1944-47, Texas City, Tex., 1947-48, Healdton, Okla., 1948-49, Vernon, Tex., 1949-55, Ft. Smith, Ark., 1955-58; exec. minister Christian Ch. in Ark., 1958-65, asst. to pres., Indpls., 1965-69, exec. minister in Tex., 1969-73, gen. minister, pres., Indpls., 1973—. Mem. governing bd. Nat. Council Chs., 1973—; del. 5th Assembly of World Council Chs., Nairobi, Kenya, 1975; rep. Nat. Council Chs. in Exchange of Ch. Leadership with Soviet Union, 1974. Named Distinguished Alumnus, Tex. Christian U., 1973, Phillips U., 1975; Outstanding Citizen, Vernon, Tex., 1954. Author: We Call Ourselves Disciples, 1975. Home: 7232 Highburry Dr Indianapolis IN 46256 Office: 222 S Downey Ave Indianapolis IN 46219

TEEHAN, JANICE KAY, ednl. adminstr.; b. Melrose Park, Ill., Nov. 4, 1948; d. William E. and Lola Faye (Gardner) Harrison; B.S. in Edn., No. Ill. U., 1970; M.A., Governors State U. 1977; m. Harold M. Teehan, III, Apr. 4, 1972; children—Sarah Beth, Timothy Michael. Tchr., Mokena (Ill.) public schs., 1970-76; mem. faculty Governors State U., Park Forest South, Ill., 1976-77; dir. learning resources Mokena public schs., 1977—; cons. on media exploration Tinley Park Crime Prevention Dept., 1976-77. Chmn. Tinley Park Youth Commn., 1975-80. Recipient Commendation, Tinley Park Youth Commn., 1977. Mem. Assn. Ednl. Communications and Tech., Assn. for Supervision and Curriculum Devel., Alpha Phi. Methodist. Contbr. articles to profl. jours. Office: 11331 195th St Mokena IL 60448

TEELE, DORIS CORINNE HEADRICK, real estate broker; b. Springfield, Ill., Feb. 13, 1926; d. John Raymond and Corinne (Burch) Headrick; student Lincoln Land Community Coll., 1970, 71, 73; B.A. in Mgmt., Sangamon State U., 1975; m. Paul Edward Teele, Nov. 27, 1945; children—Cheryl Suzette, Stephan Paul. Real estate salesman Al Sokolis, Springfield, Ill., 1955-57, James D. Call, Realtor, Springfield, 1960-64, Charles Dunseth, Realtor, Springfield, 1964-66; owner Doris Teele, Realtor, Springfield, 1958-60, 66—; owner D'Eleet Residential Rentals, Springfield, 1970—. Chmn., Coalition of Urban Devel., 1975-81. Served with USMCR, 1945. Mem. Women Marines Assn. (past pres. chpt.), Family Motor Coach Assn., Land of Lincoln Coachmen, Marine Corps League, Springfield Art Assn., Ill. Assn. Realtors (Make Am. Better com. 1977-80, chmn. 1980), Luth. Ch. Women, Springfield Bd. Realtors (bd. control Multiple Listing Service, program chmn. 1967, 81, chmn. rules and regulations com., chmn. Make Am. Better com. 1977-80), Coll. Area Homemakers Assn. (pres. 1979), Alpha Omega (past pres.). Lutheran (mem. evangelism com. and fin. com. 1974-81). Home: 4004 Hazelcrest Rd Springfield IL 62703 Office: 430 W Edwards St Springfield IL 62704

TEGELER, DONALD MAURICE, mgmt. cons.; b. Clinton, Iowa, July 17, 1942; s. Maurice and Audrey Marie (Wells) T.; student Evangel Coll., 1960-61, No. Ill. U., 1961-63; B.A., U. Mo., Kansas City, 1976; m. Nancy Marie Wilson, Aug. 31, 1962; children—Donald Maurice. Systems analyst Systec Data Mgmt., Kansas City, Mo., 1969-76; cons. Hewitt Assos., Lincolnshire, Ill., 1976—. Mem. U. Mo. Alumni Assn., Omicron Delta Epsilon. Clubs: Toastmasters, Shriners. Office: 100 Halfday Rd Lincolnshire IL 60015

TEI, TAKURI, accountant; b. Korea, Feb. 25, 1924; s. Gangen and Isun (Song) T.; came to U.S., 1952, naturalized, 1972; diploma Concordia Theol. Sem., 1959; B.D., Eden Theol. Sem., 1965; M.Ed., U. Mo., 1972; m. Maria M. Ottwaska, Dec. 1, 1969; 1 dau., Sun Kyung Lee. Partner, Madeleine Ottwaska & Assos., St. Louis, 1968—; pres. TMS Tei Enterprises Inc., Webster Groves, Mo., 1969—; instr. Forest Park Community Coll. Mem. Am. Coll. Enrolled Agts. (pres. 1976—), Am. Accounting Assn., Am. Taxation Assn., Assn. Asian Studies, NAACP. Republican. Lutheran. Home and office: 7529 Big Bend Blvd Webster Groves MO 63119

TEICH, RALPH DONALD, bus. exec.; b. Chgo., May 24, 1925; s. Curt and Anna (Niether) T.; grad. Lake Forest Acad., 1943; B.S., Northwestern U., 1949; m. Joan Martha Laurine (div. Sept. 1965); children—Deborah, Lawrence, Cheryl, Fred Teich Anderson; m. 2d, Elizabeth Perrizo, Jan. 20, 1968. Vice pres. Curt Tech & Co., Inc., Chgo., 1949-77, pres., 1981; pres. R-Dit Enterprises, Inc., 1976—. Vice pres. Lake Forest Property Owners Assn., 1972—, past deacon, v.p. Luth. Ch. of Holy Spirit; past dir., v.p., pres., interstate bd. govs. Mid-Am. Ballet Found.; past dir., trustee numerous founds. and trusts, active local and nat. historic preservation groups. Mem. Am. Friends Austria (dir.), Field Mus. Natural History (life), Nat. History Mus., Chgo. Hist. Soc., Balzekas Mus. Lithuanian Art, Lake Forest Hist. Soc., Gleassner House, English Speaking Unions, U.S. Power Squadron. Clubs: Executives, University (Chgo.); Michigan Shores (Wilmette, Ill.); Waukegan Swedish Glee, Masons (32 deg. Shriner). Home: 700 S Ridge Rd Lake Forest IL 60045 Office: PO Box 192 Lake Forest IL 60045

TEJWANI, GOPI A., scientist, educator; b. India, Mar. 1, 1946; came to U.S., 1973, permanent U.S. resident; B.S., Nagpur U., 1966, M.S. in Biochemistry, 1968; Ph.D. in Biochemistry, All-India Inst. Med. Scis., New Delhi, 1973; m. Raman; 1 son, Samir. Research asst. Nagpur U., India, 1968-69, All-India Inst. Med. Scis., 1969-73; research asso. dept. microbiology St. Louis U. Sch. Medicine, 1973-74; postdoctoral fellow Roche Inst. Molecular Biology, Nutley, N.J., 1974-76; asst. prof. dept. pharmacology Coll. Medicine, Ohio State U., Columbus, 1977—; vis. prof. U. São Paulo, Brazil, 1978, Moscow (USSR) State U., 1981; cons. Ortho Pharm. Corp., Raritan, N.J. Grantee, Ohio State U., 1979, Distilled Spirits Council U.S., 1979-80, Central Ohio Heart Chpt., 1980-81, Bremer Found., 1980-81, United Cancer Council, 1981, NIH, 1981—, Weight Watchers Found. Inc., 1981—; recipient Marion T. Colwill award, Ohio State U., 1980. Mem. AAAS, Am. Assn. Clin. Chemistry. Referee Archives of Biochemistry and Biophysics, Science, Life Sciences; contbr. writings to profl. publs.; condr. seminars, workshops, symposia; speaker profl. confs. U.S., India, Chile, Brazil. Address: College of Medicine Dept Pharmacology Ohio State Univ Columbus OH 43210

TELETZKE, GERALD HOWARD, pollution control co. exec.; b. Beaver Dam, Wis., Mar. 22, 1928; s. Gerhardt C. and Helen (Mohr) T.; student Mich. Coll. Mining and Tech., 1945-46; B.S.C.E., U. Wis., 1952, M.S.C.E., 1953, Ph.D. in San. Engring., 1956; m. Elaine Mae, June 21, 1952; children—Gary Frances, Barbara Ann. Research asst. U. Wis., Madison, 1952-54, instr., 1954-56; asso. prof. civil engring. Purdue U., 1956-59; dir. san. engring. research Eimco Corp., Palatine, Ill., 1959-61; sales mgr. Zimpro Inc. subs. Sterling Drug Inc., Rothschild, Wis., 1961-64, exec. v.p., 1964-67, pres., 1968—; v.p. Sterling Drug Inc., N.Y.C., 1976—; dir. Gen. Telephone Co. Wis., Sun Prairie, River Valley State Bank, Rothschild. Served with C.E., U.S. Army, 1945-49. Registered profl. engr., Ind. Mem. Am. Acad. Environ. Engrs. (diplomate), ASCE, Water Pollution Control Fedn., Internat. Assn. Water Pollution Research. Office: Zimpro Inc Military Rd Rothschild WI 54474

TELEZYN, NICK, advt. agy. exec.; b. N.Y.C., Sept. 20, 1953; s. Dmytro and Tekla (Lawriw) T.; B.A., Ind. State U., 1974; m. Victoria Lee Aycock, Apr. 2, 1977; 1 son, Michael Dmytro. Account exec. WBOW/WBOQ Radio, Terre Haute, Ind., 1975-79; v.p. G.M. Ideas Inc., Terre Haute, 1979—; guest speaker Ind. State U., 1980, Eastern Ill. U., 1981. Cert. radio mktg. cons. Republican. Roman Catholic. Clubs: Advt. of Indpls. (Addi award 1980); Noon Optimist of Terre Haute (pres. 1978-79). Home: 7030 Carlisle Rd Terre Haute IN 47802 Office: GM Ideas Inc PO Box 2304 Terre Haute IN 47802

TELL, ROBERT, hosp. adminstr.; b. Bklyn., Apr. 4, 1937; s. Samuel and Mildred (Katz) T.; B.A., L.I. U., 1958; M.S., Columbia U., 1962; m. Elaine Fritz, June 10, 1956; children—Celeste Margot, Perry Stuart, Brian Douglas. Planning resident Hosp. Review and Planning Council So. N.Y., 1961; adminstrv. resident Brookdale Hosp. Center, Bklyn., 1961-62; adminstrv. asst. Beth Israel Hosp., N.Y.C., 1962-63; asst. adminstr. Sinai Hosp. Detroit, 1963-68; asso. coordinator N.J. Regional Med. Program, 1968-69; asso. adminstr. L.I. Jewish Med. Center, New Hyde Park, N.Y., 1969-72; asso. dir. Greater Detroit Area Hosp. Council, Inc., 1972-78; exec. dir. Menorah Med. Center, Kansas City, Mo., 1978—; adj. instr. dept. community medicine Wayne State U. Sch. Medicine, 1977—, health adminstrn. and planning program Washington U. Sch. Medicine, 1981-82. Bd. dirs. United Community Services, 1979—; v.p. Coop. Hosp. Services Southeastern Mich., 1976-78; mem. policy council Met. Detroit Cancer Control Program, 1976-78; bd. dirs. Kansas City Hospice, 1979—, Citation, 1980. Recipient awards Mich. Blue Shield, 1965-66. Fellow Am. Coll. Hosp. Adminstrs., Kansas City Area Hosp. Assn. (dir. 1979—), Am. Public Health Assn.; mem. Hosp. Execs. Club N.Y. Contbr. articles to profl. jours. Office: 4949 Rockhill Rd Kansas City MO 64110

TELLER, GERALD ARTHUR, clergyman, ednl. adminstr.; b. Bklyn., May 17, 1940; s. Russell and Belle G. T.; student Bklyn. Coll., 1961; M.H.L., Jewish Theol. Sem., 1966; M.A., U. Detroit, 1971; Ed.D., Wayne State U., 1976; m. Judith Leona Teller, Sept. 2, 1963; children—Shira, Ranon, Aliza. Ordained rabbi, 1966; asst. rabbi, dir. youth and edn. Congregation Shaare Zedek, Southfield, Mich., 1967-79; supt. United Hebrew Schs., Southfield, 1979—; instr. Sch. Edn., Wayne State U. Served with U.S. Army, 1966-67. Mem. Jewish Educators Assembly, Nat. Council Jewish Edn., Assn. Supervision and Curriculum Devel. Office: 21550 W L2 Mile Rd Southfield MI 48076

TELLING, EDWARD RIGGS, retail exec.; b. Danville, Ill., Apr. 1, 1919; s. Edward Riggs and Margaret Katherine (Matthews) T.; Ph.B., Ill. Wesleyan U., 1942, LL.D., 1978; m. Nancy Hawkins, Dec. 29, 1942; children—Edward R. III, Pamela Telling Grimes, Kathryn Telling Bentley, Nancy Telling O'Shaughnessy, Thomas Cole. With Sears, Roebuck & Co., 1946—, store mgr., 1954-59, zone mgr., 1960-64, mgr. met. N.Y.C. area ops., 1965-67, adminstrv. asst. to v.p. Eastern ter., Phila., 1968, v.p. Eastern ter., 1969-74, exec. v.p.

Midwestern ter., Chgo., 1974-75, sr. exec. v.p. field, Chgo., 1976-77, chmn., chief exec. officer, 1978—, also dir.; dir. Allstate Ins. Co., Homart Devel. Co., Kraft, Inc., Sears Roebuck Acceptance Corp., Sears Internat. Fin. Co., Simpsons-Sears Ltd. Bd. dirs. Sears-Roebuck Found.; trustee Savs. and Profit Sharing Fund of Sears Employees, Field Mus. Natural History; mem. Bus. Council, policy com. Bus. Roundtable. Served to lt. USN, 1941-45. Clubs: Chicago, Shoreacres, Old Elm, Commercial. Office: Sears Tower Chicago IL 60684

TELSER, EUGENE, mktg. cons.; b. Chgo., Feb. 24, 1926; s. Samuel David and Belle E. Telser; student Ill. Inst. Tech., 1943-44, De Paul U., 1946-47; B.A., Roosevelt U., 1949; M.A., U. Chgo., 1950; m. Elsa Beck, Aug. 24, 1947 (div.); children—Joanne Telser Breuillier, Margaret, Elizabeth. Exec. v.p. Elrick & Lavidge, Inc., Chgo., 1956-70; v.p. research and planning J. Walter Thompson Co., Chgo., 1971-72; v.p. custom research A.C. Nielsen Co., Northbrook, Ill., 1973-78; pres. Gene Telser, Inc., Evanston, Ill., 1978—; lectr. mktg. research, cons. behavior Internat. Acad. Merchandising. Served with Signal Corps, U.S. Army, 1944-46. Mem. Am. Mktg. Assn., Am. Assn. Public Opinion Research, Midwest Assn. Public Opinion Research. Jewish. Chmn. policy bd. Jour. Consumer Research. Home and Office: 915 Hinman Evanston IL 60202

TEMIN, HOWARD MARTIN, educator; b. Phila., Dec. 10, 1934; B.A., Swarthmore (Pa.) Coll., 1955, D.Sc. (hon.), 1972; Ph.D., Calif. Inst. Tech., 1959, postdoctoral fellow, 1959-60; D.Sc. (hon.), N.Y. Med. Coll., 1972, U. Pa., 1976, Hahnemann Med. Coll., 1976, Lawrence U., 1976, Temple U., 1979, Med. Coll. Wis. Asst. prof. oncology U. Wis., Madison, 1960-64, asso. prof., 1964-69, USPHS research career devel. award Nat. Cancer Inst., 1964-74, prof. oncology, 1969—, Wis. Alumni Research Found. prof. cancer research, 1971-80, H.P. Rusch prof. cancer research, 1980—, Am. Cancer Soc. prof. viral oncology and cell biology, 1974—; mem. virology study sect. NIH, 1971-74, spl. virus cancer program tumor virus detection segment working group Nat. Cancer Inst., 1972-73; Charlton lectr. Tufts U. Med. Sch., 1976; Hoffman-LaRoche lectr. Rutgers U., 1979; mem. adv. com. to dir. NIH, 1978—. sci. adv. Stelton Found., Houston, 1972—. Recipient Warren Triennial prize Mass. Gen. Hosp., 1971, Spl. Commendation, Wis. Med. Soc., 1971, Pap award Papanicolaou Inst., Miami, Fla., 1972, Bertner award M.D. Anderson, Houston, 1972, U.S. Steel Found. award in molecular biology Nat. Acad. Scis., 1972, Waksman award Theobald Smith Soc., 1972, Am. Chem. Soc. award in enzyme chemistry, 1973, Modern Medicine award for distinguished achievement, 1973, Griffuel prize Assn. Devel. Recherche Cancer, Villejuif, 1973, G.H.A. Clowes Lectureship award Am. Assn. for Cancer Research, 1974, Gairdner Found. Internat. award Toronto, 1974, Albert Lasker award in basic med. research, 1974, Nobel prize for physiology or medicine, 1975, Lucy Wortham James award in basic research Soc. Surg. Oncologists, 1976, Alumni Distinguished Service award Calif. Inst. Tech., 1976; New Horizons for Radiologists lectr. Radiol. Soc. N.Am., 1968, Harry Shay Meml. lectr. Fels Inst., Phila., 1973, Dyer lectr. NIH, 1974, Harvey lectr., 1974. Fellow Am. Acad. Arts and Scis.; mem. Nat. Acad. Sci., Am. Philos. Soc., Wis. Acad. Sci., Arts and Letters (hon.). Asso. editor: Jour. of Cellular Physiology, 1966-78, Cancer Research, 1971-74; mem. editorial bd. Jour. of Virology, 1971—, Intervirology, 1972-75, Archives of Virology, 1975-77, Procs. Nat. Acad. Scis., 1975-80. Office: McArdle Lab 450 N Randall St U Wis Madison WI 53706

TEMPLETON, JOHN ALEXANDER, II, diversified co. exec.; b. Chgo., Mar. 31, 1927; s. Phillip Henry and Florence (Moore) T.; B.S., Ind. U., 1950; m. Norma Jane Frazier, Aug. 10, 1949; children—Lori, Linda, Leslie, Sally. Agt., Conn. Mut. Life Ins. Co., Terre Haute, Ind., 1949-51; part owner Miller, Templeton, Scott Ins. Agy., Terre Haute, 1951-64; with Templeton Coal Co., Inc., Terre Haute, 1964—, pres., 1972—; pres. Firman Equipment Corp., Terre Haute, 1958—; Sherwood Templeton Coal Co., Inc., 1968—; chmn. bd. Plumb Supply Co., Des Moines, 1965—; dir. Calvert & Youngblood Coal Co., Inc., Mchts. Nat. Bank Terre Haute. Mem. exec. council Ind. U. Alumni Council, 1953-56. Bd. dirs. Union Hosp., Inc., 1969—, v.p. bd., 1974—; bd. dirs. Ind. State U. Found.; trustee U. Evansville; bd. assos. Rose-Hulman Inst. Tech., 1978—; bd. dirs., v.p. Ind. Asbury Towers, Greencastle, Ind., 1980—. Served with AUS, 1946-48. Mem. Lynch Coal Operators Reciprocal Assn. (dir., chmn. exec. com. 1980), Ind. Coal Assn., Interstate Coal Conf., Ind. Assn. Ins. Agts. (pres. 1959), Ind. C. of C. (dir. 1981—). Methodist (ch. lay leader 1970—). Clubs: Masons (Shriners), Elks, Aero.

TENNANT, OTTO ADDISON, utility exec.; b. Grundy Center, Iowa, Sept. 12, 1918; s. Stanton Edwin and Ernstena Catherine (Beckman) T.; B.S. in Gen. Engring., Iowa State U., 1940; M.A. in Econs., Drake U., Des Moines, 1959; m. Marjorie Mary Doll, Mar. 20, 1944; 1 son, John Otto. Test and design engr. Gen. Electric Co., Schenectady, 1940-42; application engr. Westinghouse Electric Corp., Des Moines, 1945-47; mgr. tech. services Iowa Power & Light Co., Des Moines, 1967—; mem. Des Moines Electric Lic. and Rev. Bd., 1965-77. Mem. solid waste commn. Iowa Dept. Environ. Quality, 1972-77; adv. council Iowa State Center Indsl. Research and Service, 1970-73. Served with USAAF, 1942-45. Decorated D.F.C., Air medal with 2 oak leaf clusters; named Asso. of Year, Homebuilders of Greater Des Moines, 1970; registered profl. engr., Iowa. Mem. Nat. Soc. Profl. Engrs. (pres. 1981-82), IEEE (sr.), ASHRAE, Illuminating Engring. Soc., Iowa Farm Electrification Council, Iowa Engring. Soc. (pres. 1972-73, Anson Marston award 1979). Republican. Lutheran. Clubs: Bohemian, Shriners. Office: 823 Walnut St Des Moines IA 50303

TENNEFOS, JENS, JR., state senator; b. Fargo, N.D., Feb. 15, 1930; s. Jens Peterson and Ivah M. (Gilbraith) T.; student N.D. State U., 1947-49; m. Jeanne P. Quamme, 1960; children—Daniel J., David A., Judie A., Mary J. Pres., Tennefos Constrn. Co., Inc., 1951-75; mem. N.D. Ho. of Reps., 1974-76, N.D. Senate, 1977—. Served with U.S. Army, 1951. Mem. Asso. Gen. Contractors N.D., Am. Legion, Sons of Norway. Lutheran. Club: Elks, Optimist. Office: PO Box 2104 Fargo ND 58107

TENNESSEN, ROBERT JOSEPH, state senator; b. Lismore, Minn., Aug. 24, 1939; s. Alphons and Helen (Klontz) T.; student Fla. State U. extension, 1959-60; B.A., U. Minn., 1965, J.D., 1968; m. Christine Tennessen, 1968; 3 children. Admitted to Minn. Fed. Dist. Ct. and 8th Dist. Ct. of Appeals, 1968; practiced in Mpls. 1968—; mem. Minn. Senate, 1971—. Bd. dirs. Guthrie Theater, Mpls., 1975-81, Mpls. Age and Opportunity Bd.; commn. U.S. Privacy Protection Commn., 1975-77; participant OECD conf., 1977. Mem. Am. Bar Assn., Minn. Bar Assn., Hennepin County Bar Assn. Mem. Democratic-Farmer-Labor party. Office: 309 State Capitol St Paul MN 55155

TENNEY, MARK WILLIAM, environ. engring. cons.; b. Chgo., Dec. 10, 1936; s. William and Frieda (Sanders) T.; B.S., Mass. Inst. Tech., 1958, M.S., 1959, Sc.D., 1965; m. Jane E. Morris, June 1, 1974; children by previous marriage—Scott, Barbara. Design engr. Greeley & Hansen, Engrs., Chgo., 1959-61; asso. prof. civil engring. U. Notre Dame, 1965-73; pres. TenEch Environ. Engrs., Inc., South Bend, Ind., 1973—. Served with C.E., AUS, 1959-60; col. Res. USPHS research fellow, 1961-64. Diplomate Am. Acad. Environ. Engrs. Fellow ASCE; mem. Nat. Soc. Profl. Engrs., Am. Cons. Engrs. Council, Water Pollution Control Fedn., Am. Water Works Assn., Sigma Xi, Chi Epsilon, Phi Delta Theta. Clubs: Ill. Athletic; Lake Macatawa Yacht; Summit. Contbr. articles to profl. jours. Home: 2110 Niles-Buchanan Rd Niles MI 49120 Office: 744 W Washington St South Bend IN 46601

TEPPER, NEAL GARY, counselor; b. Bklyn., Mar. 12, 1951; s. Leon and Bernice Rhoda (Fisher) T.; B.A., State U. N.Y., Potsdam, 1972; M.A., U. N.D., 1973. Group therapist St. Mike's Hosp., Grand Forks, N.D., 1972-73; tchr. courses Center Teaching and Learning, U. N.D., 1973-75, grad. teaching asst. dept. counseling and guidance, 1974-77, intern counselor Counseling Center, 1975-77; practicum guidance counselor Red River High Sch., Grand Forks, 1973-74; mental health clinician IV, Meml. Mental Health and Retardation Center, Mandan, N.D., 1977-79; dir. Children and Family Services for Standing Rock Sioux Tribe, Ft. Yates, N.D., 1978-81; dir. counseling United Tribes Ednl. Tech. Center, 1981—. Mem. Am. Personnel and Guidance Assn., N. Central Assn. Counselor Educators Assns., Mental Health Assn., Assn. Edn. of Young Children, N.D. Conf. Social Welfare. Home: PO Box 2413 Bismarck ND 58501 Office: 3315 S Airport Rd Bismarck ND 58501

TERHUNE, MARIE AMREIN, speech lang. pathologist; b. Chgo., Feb. 16, 1922; d. Andrew Paul and Anna Emily (Machalitzsky) Amrein; B.S., Northwestern U., 1950; m. Richard T. Terhune, Dec. 30, 1950; children—Anne Terhune-Loomis, Richard T. Speech therapist New Trier High Sch., Winnetka, Ill., 1950-52; speech lang. pathologist Bensenville (Ill.) Elementary Schs., 1958-80. Served with US Navy, 1943-46. Mem. Am. (certificate of clin. competence), Ill., DuPage County speech and hearing assns., Delta Kappa Gamma. Presbyterian (elder).

TERKEL, STUDS LOUIS, interviewer, author; b. N.Y.C., May 16, 1912; s. Samuel and Anna (Finkel) T.; Ph.D., U. Chgo., 1932, J.D., 1934; m. Ida Goldberg, July 2, 1939; 1 son, Paul. Stage appearances include Detective Story, 1950, A View From the Bridge, 1958, Light Up the Sky, 1959, The Cave Dwellers, 1960; star TV program Studs Place, 1950-53, radio program Wax Mus., 1945—, Studs Terkel Almanac, 1952—, Studs Terkel Show, Sta. WFMT-FM, Chgo.; master of ceremonies Newport Folk Festival, 1959, 60, Ravinia Music Festival, 1959, U. Chgo. Folk Festival, 1961, others; panel moderator, lectr., narrator films. Program, Wax Museum, winner 1st award as best cultural program in regional radio category Inst. Edn. by Radio-TV, Ohio State U., 1959; recipient Prix Italia, UNESCO award for best radio program East-West Values, 1962; Communicator of Year award U. Chgo. Alumni Assn., 1969, Author: Giants of Jazz, 1956; Division Street America, 1966; (play) Amazing Grace, 1959; Hard Times, 1970; Working, 1974; Talking to Myself, 1977; American Dreams: Lost and Found, 1980. Home: 850 Castlewood Terr Chicago IL 60640 Office: 303 E Wacker Dr Chicago IL 60601

TERMINI, MICHAEL JOSEPH, mfg. co. exec.; b. Kansas City, Mo., Apr. 8, 1948; s. Joseph and Wanda Lee (Givens) T.; B.S. in Mech. and Aerospace Engring., U. Mo., 1970, M.B.A. in Mktg., 1976; m. Patricia Anne, Aug. 30, 1979; children—Kelly Marie, Justin Matthew. Design engr. Pratt & Whitney Aircraft div. United Technologies, Inc., West Palm Beach, Fla., 1970-72; equipment engr. Hallmark Cards, Inc., Kansas City, Mo., 1972-74, ops. analysis and control engr., 1974-76; sr. ops. auditor corp. internal audit Paccar Corp., Bellevue, Wash., 1976-77, material handling mgr. Kenworth Truck div., Kansas City, Mo., 1977-78, material control mgr., 1978-79; div. materials mgr. Combine div. Allis-Chalmers Corp., Independence, Mo., 1979—. Mem. Am. Prodn. and Inventory Control Soc., Internat. Materials Mgmt. Soc., Beta Gamma Sigma. Republican. Presbyterian. Club: Kansas City Engrs. Home: 9908 Belleview St Kansas City MO 64114 Office: PO Box 1099 Cottage and Haywood Sts Independence MO 64051

TERRA, DANIEL JAMES, chem. co. exec., govt. ofcl.; b. Phila., June 8, 1911; s. Louis J. and Mary (DeLuca) T.; B.S., Penn State U., 1931; m. Adeline Evans Richards, Aug. 7, 1937; children—Penny Jane (dec.), James D. Founder, Lawter Chems., Inc., Chgo., 1940, chmn., chief exec. officer, 1964—, also dir.; dir. McLouth Steel Corp., 1st Nat. Bank & Trust Co. Evanston, Stewart-Warner Corp.; ambassador-at-large for cultural affairs Dept. State, 1981—. Bd. dirs. Easter Seal Soc., Chgo. Lyric Opera, Evanston Hosp. Assn., Chgo. Crime Commn.; trustee Chgo. Orchestral Assn., Dickinson Coll., Ill. Inst. Tech., Ravinia Festival Assn., Roycemore Sch.; adv. council Northwestern U. Grad. Sch. Mgmt., mem. Pres.'s Council Nat. Coll. Edn.; mem. Pres.'s club Loyola U.; exec. com. Ill. Inst. Tech. Research Inst.; mem. Chgo. Commn. Trust, Assos. of Northwestern U.; mem. grand council Am. Indian Center Chgo.; citizens bd. U. Chgo.; mem. univ. council Pa. State U.; mem. am. arts com. Art Inst. Chgo. Recipient Winthrop Sears medal Chem. Industry Assn., 1972, Distinguished Alumnus medal Pa. State U., 1976. Mem. Ill. Mfrs. Assn. (dir.). Clubs: Westmoreland Country (Wilmette, Ill.); Kenilworth; Capitol Hill (Washington); Metropolitan, Chicago, Comml., Casino, Mid-Am. (Chgo.); Lauderdale Yacht (Fort Lauderdale, Fla.); Nat. Arts of N.Y.; Links (N.Y.C.). Home: 528 Roslyn Rd Kenilworth IL 60043 also 19 Isla Bahia Dr Ft Lauderdale FL 33361 Office: 990 Skokie Blvd Northbrook IL 60062

TERRELL, CHARLES JOSEPH, aluminum casting foundry exec.; b. Tipton, Ind., Jan. 14, 1908; s. Benjiman Joseph and Hazel (Ogle) T.; student Ball State U., 1926-27; m. Harriet Elizabeth Johnson, Dec. 24, 1928; children—Joanne Terrell Lyons, Joyce Terrell Timmons, Jane Terrell Thompson. Lab. technician Gen. Motors Corp., Anderson, Ind., 1941-43; supt. Apex Elec. Mfg. Foundry, Cleve., 1943-45; asst. supt. Nat. Bronze & Aluminum Foundry, Cleve., 1945-46; owner Washington Aluminum Castings Co., Washington Court House, Ohio, 1946—, pres., 1955—. Mem. nat. adv. bd. Am. Security Council, 1971—; mem. Liberty Lobby Bd. Policy, 1972—. Mem. Bass Fisherman Sportsman's Soc., Fishing Club Am. Republican. Baptist. Club: Nat. Travel. Patentee flower urn. Home: 740 Van Deman St Washington Court House OH 43160 Office: 1011 Mead St Washington Court House OH 43160

TERRELL, WILLIE ANDREW, JR., educator; b. Dayton, Ohio, June 18, 1951; s. Willie A. and Hazel (Wright) T.; B.S., Central State U., Ohio, 1972; Ed.M., Miami U., Ohio, 1977, Wright State U., 1980. Youth advocate Youth Services Bur., Dayton, 1972-76; tchr. social studies Dayton Bd. Edn., 1973-76, 77—; substitute tchr. Hamilton (Ohio) Public Schs., 1977; notary public, Ohio, 1980—. Named Black Man of Yr., Roosevelt Black Awareness Council, 1974. Mem. Assn. for Supervision and Curriculum Devel., Nat. Council Social Studies, NEA, Ohio Council Social Studies, Western Ohio Edn. Assn., Dayton Edn. Assn., Central State U. Alumni Assn., Kappa Delta Pi, Alpha Kappa Mu, Phi Alpha Theta, Omega Psi Phi. Club: Masons. Home: 1721 Radio Rd B-6 Dayton OH 45403 Office: 1313 E 5th St Dayton OH 45403

TERWILLIGER, ROY WILLIAM, banker; b. Winfred, S.D., June 20, 1937; s. Harold C. and Alice Lee T.; B.S., U. S.D., 1960; M.A., U. Iowa, 1961; m. Mary Lou Abner, July 13, 1963; children—Kathryn Mary, Michael Roy, Susan Mary. Asst. to village mgr. Village of Golden Valley (Minn.), 1963; sec. Greater S.D. Assn., Huron, 1964-65; exec. sec., treas. S.D. Bankers Assn., Huron, 1965-68; exec. dir. Am. Bankers Assn., N.Y.C. and Washington, 1968-74; sec.-treas. Internat. Montary Conf., Washington, 1969-74; pres. Suburban Nat. Bank, Eden Prairie, Minn., 1975—; cons. Internat. Realty & Investments, Inc., Washington. Served with U.S. Army, 1961-63. Decorated Army Commendation medal. Mem. Am. Bankers Assn. Republican. Congregationalist. Clubs: Rotary, Elks, Masons, Shriners. Home: 6512 Navaho Trail Edina MN 55435 Office: 8100 Schooner Blvd Eden Prairie MN 55344

TERWOORD, JAMES ANTHONY, fin. exec.; b. Berea, Ohio, Mar. 6, 1947; s. Anthony Francis and Adeline Blanche (Yanke) T.; B.B.A., Ohio U., 1969; M.B.A., Youngstown State U., 1978; m. Cher Waldeck, June 1, 1974. Acct., Arthur Andersen & Co., Cleve., 1973-75; controller Youngstown Coca-Cola Bottling Co. (Ohio), 1975-79; v.p. fin. Agy. Rent-A-Car, Cleve., 1979—; instr. Youngstown State U., 1978-79. Group chmn. United Appeal of Youngstown, 1977-78. Served with USMC, 1970-73. Mem. Am. Inst. C.P.A.'s, Ohio Soc. C.P.A.'s, Nat. Assn. Accts., Am. Mgmt. Assn. Home: 5557 Landover Ct Parma OH 44134 Office: 466 Northfield Rd Bedford OH 44146

TESCHNER, PAUL AUGUST, JR., lawyer, educator; b. Green Bay, Wis., June 20, 1925; s. Paul August and Helen (Boyington) T.; student U. Wis., 1943-44; B.B.A., Northwestern U., 1949; D.J. with distinction, Ind. U., 1953; m. Barbara Malmstone, June 12, 1948; children—Karen Janette, Paul August III, Tammy Jane; m. Anastasia Ferensen, Oct. 15, 1977. Teaching asso. Northwestern U. Sch. Law, Chgo., 1953-54; admitted to Ind., Ill., U.S. Tax Ct. bars, 1953-54, U.S. Ct. of Claims bar, 1963, U.S. Supreme Ct. bar, 1967; employee Pope & Ballard, Chgo., 1954-57; partner firm Pope, Ballard, Uriell, Kennedy, Shepard & Fowle, Chgo., 1958-72; sr. partner Teschner & Teschner, Chgo., 1972-75; chief exec. officer Teschner Profl. Corp., Chgo., 1975—; instr. tax, constl. and bus. law Elmhurst Coll. Evening Div., 1960-73; adj. prof. legal ethics Ind. U. Sch. Law, Bloomington, 1975-76; lectr. in field. Sec., mem. Village of Hinsdale (Ill.) Zoning Bd. of Appeals, 1966-77, Zoning Commn., 1966-77; mem. Ill. Master Plan Com. on Legal Edn., 1968-69. Served with AUS, 1943-46. Decorated Bronze Star with oak leaf cluster. Mem. Am. (com. on standards tax practice of tax sect. 1966-75), Ind., Ill. (com. on specialization 1968-71, 73-77, chmn. legal edn. and admission to bar com. 1970-72, assembly del. 1972-78, 80—, com. profl. ethics 1973—, chmn. 1979—), Chgo. (com. fed. taxation 1958-67, com. legal edn. 1955—, chmn. com. 1967-68, 76-77), also unauthorized practice com., specialization com., chmn. specialization com. 1976-78), Internat. bar assns., World Assn. Lawyers (founder, life), World Peace Through Law Center, Am. Judicature Soc., Selden Soc., Internat. Platform Assn., Order of Coif, Phi Delta Phi, Beta Alpha Psi. Clubs: Monroe (founding life), Execs. Author: Essays Before Watergate, 1977. Contbr. articles to profl. jours. Home: 316 E 6th St Hinsdale IL 60521 Office: 39 S LaSalle St Chicago IL 60603

TESKA, ROBERT BENTS, urban planner; b. Madison, Wis., Oct. 23, 1934; s. Joseph J. and Jessie E. (Bents) T.; B.S. in Civil Engring., U. Wis., 1957, B.S. in City Planning, 1958; M.S. in City Planning, U. Ill., 1961; m. Diane S. Lesinski, June 23, 1962; children—Tracy, Michael, David. Sr. asso. Barton-Aschman Assos., Inc., Chgo., 1961-68, Washington, 1968-71, v.p., Chgo., 1971-75; pres. Robert B. Teska Assos., Inc., Evanston, Ill., 1975—; mem. faculty Northeastern Ill. U., William Rainey Harper Coll.; mem. Evanston Plan Commn., 1964-68; chmn. Evanston Bus. Dist. Redevel. Commn., 1976—; lectr. in field. Served to lt. C.E., U.S. Army, 1958-60. Recipient 1st prize Interam. Planning Soc., 1970. Mem. Am. Inst. Cert. Planners, ASCE, Am. Planning Assn., Urban Land Inst., Coastal Soc., Chgo. Assn. Commerce Industry, Lambda Alpha. Congregationalist. Author column Land Use Mgmt. Trends, Chicagoland Devel. Mag., 1974—; contbr. articles to profl. jours.; planner: Barrington (Ill.) Area (Environ. Monthly citation 1973), Lincoln (Nebr.) Center (Design and Environment award for excellence 1975, Progressive Architecture citation 1976, Am. Soc. Landscape Architects Merit award 1976). Registered profl. engr., Ill. Office: 627 Grove St Evanston IL 60201

TESMER, NANCY ANN STUTLER, librarian; b. Akron, Ohio, Aug. 25, 1934; d. Ernest Lynn and Sophrona Rebecca (Pepper) Stutler; student U. Akron, 1952-54; B.A., Kent State U., 1956; m. Clifford Frank Haines, Aug. 20, 1960 (div.); m. 2d, John A. Tesmer, Sept. 10, 1980. Jr. asst. librarian E. Br. Library, Akron, 1956-59; hosp. librarian VA Hosp., Northampton, Mass., 1959-61; med. librarian VA Hosp., Brecksville, Ohio, 1961-65, chief librarian, 1965-73; asso. chief librarian Cleve. VA Hosp., 1973-75, chief librarian, 1975—. Mem. Med. Library Assn., N.E. Ohio Med. Library Assn., Zeta Tau Alpha. Home: 6558 Brecksville Rd Independence OH 44131 Office: 10701 East Blvd Cleveland OH 44106

TEWFIK, HAMED H., physician, educator; b. Alexandria, Egypt, Feb. 14, 1937; s. Hassan Ahmed and Horeya Mohammed (El-Tabrizi) T.; came to U.S., 1970, naturalized; M.B.Ch.B., Alexandria U. Med. Sch., Egypt, 1959, D.M.R., 1962, D.M., 1967, M.D., 1967; m. Ferial Y. Abbassy, June 9, 1966; children—Sherif, Shahira. Rotating intern Alexandria U. Hosp., 1959-60, resident in radiology, 1960-62; practice medicine, specializing in radiation therapy and nuclear medicine, 1962—; clin. demonstrator radiation therapy and nuclear medicine Alexandria U. Med. Sch., 1962-67, lectr. radiation therapy and nuclear medicine, 1968-70; instr. radiotherapy and nuclear research SUNY, Buffalo, 1970-71, asst. prof., 1971-72; staff radiation therapist E.J. Meyer Meml. Hosp., Buffalo, 1970-72; asso. radiology, radiation therapy sect., asst. prof. Univ. Hosp., Coll. Medicine, Iowa City, 1972-73, asst. prof., 1973-77, asso. prof., 1977-81; prof., chmn. radiation therapy U. Iowa Hosp., also mem. staff, 1972—. Mem. Egyptian Med. Assn., Brit. Inst. Radiologists, Royal Coll. Radiologists, AMA, Iowa Med. Soc., Am. Soc. Therapeutic Radiologists, Radiol. Soc. N.Am., Iowa Radiol. Soc., Am. Coll. Radiology, Am. Soc. Clin. Oncology, Radiation Research Soc. Moslem. Club: Rotary. Contbr. articles to med. jours. Office: Dept Radiation Therapy U Iowa Hosp and Clinics Iowa City IA 52242

TEWS, BRADLEY DEAN, educator; b. Dickinson, N.D., June 1, 1953; s. Clarence and Clara (Jorstad) T.; B.S., N.D. State U., 1975; m. Brenda Fay Johnson, July 2, 1977; 1 dau., Kelli Michelle. Instr. vocat. agr. Bismarck (N.D.) Public Schs., 1975-78, Cando (N.D.) Schs., 1978-79, Dickinson (N.D.) Public Schs., 1979—. Mem. N.D. Vocat. Agr. Tchrs. Assn., Nat. Vocat. Agr. Tchrs. Assn., Am. Vocat. Assn., Future Farmers Am. (hon. farmer Bismarck chpt.), N.D. Edn.

Assn. Lutheran. Home: 1407 17th Ave W Dickinson ND 58601 Office: PO Box 1057 Dickinson ND 58601

THADA, NARONGSAK KIATIKAJORN, physician; b. Saraburi, Thailand, Dec. 12, 1944; s. Amneuy Kiatikajorn and Ooy Kiatikajorn Thada; came to U.S., 1970; naturalized, 1974; M.D., Mahidol U., Thailand, 1969; m. Napaporn Charoenpong, July 25, 1971; children—Monakan and Chatchapol (twins). Intern, Vajira Municipal Hosp., Thailand, 1969-70, Fordham Hosp., Bronx, N.Y., 1970-71; resident in medicine Bronx-Lebanon Hosp. Center, Bronx, N.Y., 1971-73, fellow in hematology, 1973-75; practice medicine specializing in internal medicine and hemato-oncology, Hays, Kans., 1975—; staff St. Anthony and Hadley Regional Med. Center, 1975; vice chief of staff St. Anthony Hosp., Hays, 1977. Diplomate Am. Bd. Internal Medicine. Mem. A.C.P., Kans. State, Central Kans. med. socs. Buddhist. Club: Smoky Hill Country. Home: 3104 Olympic Ln Hays KS 67601 Office: 1201 Fort St Hays KS 67601

THADEN, RONALD THEODORE, area extension farm mgmt. exec.; b. Milbank, S.D., Apr. 18, 1941; s. Theodore and Grace (Hippen) T.; B.S., S.D. State U., 1967, M.S., 1973; m. Linda Muriel Lucas, Aug. 9, 1969; children—Scott, Thomas. Research asst. S.D. State U., Brookings, 1969-73; county extension agt. Extension Service, U.S. Dept. Agr., Philip, S.D., 1973-76, area farm mgmt. specialist extension service, 1976—. Served with USNR, 1967-69. Mem. Am. Soc. Agronomy, Soc. Range Mgmt., Nat. County Agts. Assn., Am. Soc. Farm Mgrs. and Rural Appraisers, Farm House Frat. Home: 1224 4th St NW Watertown SD 57201 Office: 1901 W Kemp Ave Watertown SD 57201

THAIN, JOHN GRIFFITHS, lab. adminstr.; b. Hayes, Middlesex, Eng., Sept. 27, 1937; s. Charles J. and Dilys D. (Griffiths) T.; came to U.S., 1958; student Acton Tech. Coll., 1955-58, Ind. U., 1958-63; A.S. in Bus. Adminstrn., U. New Haven, 1980; m. Jacqueline M. Hart, Nov. 3, 1962; children—Jeremy Guy, Richard Gary, Jennifer Ann. Lab. asst. Castrol Ltd., Hayes, Middlesex, U.K., 1953-58; lab. technician Miles Labs., Inc., Elkhart, Ind., 1958-61, coordinator mfg. records, 1961-67, coordinator packaging devel. and labelling, 1967-72, adminstr. regulatory affairs and inspections, 1972-74, supr. records and auditing, 1974-75, mgr. corp. quality assurance-tng. services, 1976-79, mgr. quality assurance, corp. research, 1979—. Mem. Regulatory Affairs Profl. Soc., Am. Soc. Quality Control. Episcopalian. Home: 59527 Ridgewood Dr Goshen IN 46526 Office: 1127 Myrtle St Elkhart IN 46514

THALMANN, JOAN MARY, sch. adminstr.; b. Evanston, Ill., Dec. 22, 1940; d. Peter Philip and Mary Magdelan (Straub) T.; B.S.Ed., Alverno Coll., 1963; M.Ed., Nat. Coll. Edn., 1977. Tchr., Catholic schs., N.Y.C., Chgo., 1962-66; tchr. Holy Angels Sch., Chgo., 1966-70, Willowbrook Sch., Northbrook Sch. Dist. 30, 1970-80; prin. Madison Sch., Skokie Sch. Dist. 69, Skokie, Ill., 1980—. Mem. Phi Delta Kappa. Home: 746 Locust Rd Wilmette IL 60091 Office: 5100 Madison St Skokie IL 60077

THANE, RUSSELL T., state senator; b. Denver, July 14, 1926; s. Joseph and Bernice (Steere) T.; ed. N.D. State Sch. Sch., 1949, N.D. State U., 1955; m. Betty Jo Chowning, 1952; children—Ronald, Kathleen. Sec.-treas. N.D. Cattle Feeders Assn., Hunter, 1963-70; dir. Home Mut. Ins. Co., Wahpeton, N.D., Red River Valley Beef Growers, Moorhead, N.D.; mem. N.D. State Senate, 1970—. Precinct committeeman, 1964-70. Served with USAF, 1950-54. Mem. Am. Legion. Methodist. Clubs: Shriners, Elks, Masons, Eagles. Office: ND State Senate State Capitol Bismarck ND 58505*

THARP, ROY MICHAEL, mfg. co. exec.; b. Kansas City, Mo., Nov. 19, 1947; s. Roy Elvin and Minnie Louise (Hawkins) T.; B.S. (Elmer F. Pierson scholar), Baker U., 1969; m. Karen Ann Neimeyer, June 7, 1969; 1 dau., Katherine Ann. Advt. copywriter Western Auto Co., Kansas City, Mo., 1970; sr. system analyst Honeywell Co., Mpls., 1979—, tech. publs. system analyst Avionics div., 1976-78. Served with USAF, 1970-76. Recipient Spl. Achievement award Avionics div. Honeywell Co., 1978. Mem. Alpha Psi Omega. Republican. Methodist. Home: 5447 Humboldt Ave N Brooklyn Center MN 55430 Office: 600 2d St NE Hopkins MN 55343

THATCHER, HARRY PEMBERTON, former mfg. co. exec.; b. N.Y.C., Apr. 11, 1913; s. Harry George and Florence Henrietta (Pemberton) T.; B.S., N.Y. U., 1935; M.B.A., Harvard, 1937; m. Barbara Claire Hall, Sept. 20, 1940; children—Randall Hall, Carol Pemberton. With Gen. Electric Co., various locations, 1937-78, mgr. East Central distbn. region lamp div., Cleve., 1957-59, mgr. distbn. service ops., 1960-78, ret., 1978. Home: 4973 Countryside Ln Lyndhurst OH 44124

THATCHER, HUGH KNOX, JR., physician, surgeon; b. Indpls., May 16, 1910; s. Hugh Knox and Mary Elsie (Staneart) T.; A.B., Butler U., 1930; M.D., Ind. U., 1934; m. Mary Lou Briles, May 14, 1938; children—Sandra Sue Gillum, David H., Jane A. Intern, resident Indpls. City Hosp., 1934-36; practice medicine, Indpls., 1936-42, 46—; mem. staff Meth. Hosp., pres., 1974-75; mem. staff Winona Hosp., St. Vincent's Hosp. Chmn. Ind. State Hosp. Licensing Council, 1972—; mem. med. adv. com. Vis. Nursing Assn., 1968-78; mem. joint liaison com. to bd. dirs. Meth. Hosp., 1976—. Served to maj. M.C., AUS, 1942-46; PTO. Named Sagamore of Wabash, 1978. Fellow Am. Acad. Family Practice (charter); mem. Marion County Med. Soc. (dir. 1966-67, pres. 1967-68), Alumni Assn. Butler U. (dir. 1947-49), Ind. Med. Assn. (treas. 1972-75). Mason (Shriner). Home: 11318 Dona Dr Carmel IN 46032 Office: 1010 E 86th St Suite 24 Indianapolis IN 46240

THAXTON, ELIZABETH DYER, clin. social worker; b. Roanoke, Va., Feb. 10, 1932; d. David Allison and Ruth Elizabeth (Laughon) Dyer; A.B., Randolph-Macon Woman's Coll., 1953; M.S.W., U. N.C., Chapel Hill, 1973; children—Cynthia Thaxton Norris, David Robert, Mary Elizabeth. Clin. social worker, team mem. mental health component Adult div. Durham County Dept. Social Services, Durham, N.C., 1973-77; dir. social work dept. Pulaski (Va.) Community Hosp., 1977—; pvt. practice clin. social work, Pulaski, 1979—; adv. council dept. social work Radford Coll.; adv. bd. New River Community Coll.; examiner for licensure Va. Bd. Social Workers, nominee bd. dirs., 1979; dir., chmn. personnel com. Community Counseling Services, Inc. Cert. Acad. Cert. Social Workers; lic. clin. social worker, Va. Mem. Nat. Assn. Social Workers, Soc. Hosp. Social Work Dirs., Phi Mu. Presbyterian. Research on social work intervention in a med. setting. Office: Pulaski Community Hospital PO Box 759 Pulaski VA 24301

THEIMER, AXEL KNUT, educator; b. St. Johann in Tirol, Austria, Mar. 10, 1946; s. Otto and Iris Maria (Zerzawy) T.; came to U.S., 1969; B.A., St. John's U., 1971; M.F.A., U. Minn., 1974. Mem. Vienna Boys Choir, Vienna, Austria, 1956-61; dir. Chorus Viennensis, Vienna, 1967-69; asso. prof. music, dir. choral and vocal activities St. John's U., Collegeville, Minn., 1969—. Vocal soloist Mozart Festivals, Pueblo, Colo., 1971, 75, Alverno Coll., Milw., 1972, Northrup Meml. Auditorium, Mpls., 1973, U. Minn., 1973; clinician/dir. choral and vocal workshops; performing mem. Thursday Musical Mpls. Mem. Am. Choral Found., Am. Choral Dirs. Assn., Coll. Music Soc., Internat. Music Council, Minn. Music Tchrs. Assn., Music Tchrs. Nat. Assn., Nat. Assn. Tchrs. of Singing, Am. Ch. Music Assn. Address: St John's U Collegeville MN 56321

THEIN, ROBERT HUGH, mktg. exec.; b. Rochester, N.Y., Nov. 28, 1933; s. Alfred Raymond and Geneva Helen (Lupien) T.; student U. Notre Dame, 1952-54; B.A., John Carroll U., 1956; M.B.A., Case-Western Res. U., 1969; m. Mary Ann Zickes, Sept. 15, 1962; children—Gregory, David, Laurann. Salesman classified advt. The Plain Dealer, Cleve., 1958-61, salesman retail advt., 1961-63, retail advt. supr., 1963-64, salesman nat. advt., 1964-66, asst. mgr. market research, 1966-81, mgr. market research, 1981—; instr. mktg. Cuyahoga Community Coll., 1981; mem. program com. Advt. Research Found. Indsl. Advt. Conf., 1979-81; mem. mktg. task force Greater Cleve. Growth Assn., 1980-81; mem. mktg. adv. com. Cuyahoga Community Coll., 1979-81. Served with U.S. Army, 1956-58. Mem. Am. Mktg. Assn. (pres. Cleve. chpt. 1978, sec. internat. mktg. conf. 1977), Bus. Economists Club Cleve., Newspaper Research Council. Office: 1801 Superior Ave Cleveland OH 44114

THEIS, FRANK GORDON, judge, past mem. Democratic Nat. Com.; b. Yale, Kans., June 26, 1911; s. Peter F. and Maude (Cook) T.; A.B. cum laude, U. Kans., 1933; LL.B., U. Mich., 1936; m. Marjorie Riddle, Feb. 1, 1939 (dec. 1970); children—Franklin, Roger. Admitted to Kans. bar, 1937, since practiced in Arkansas City; sr. mem. firm Frank G. Theis, 1957—; atty. Kans. Tax Commn., 1937-39; chief counsel OPS for Kans., 1951-52; U.S. dist. judge Dist. Kans., 1967—, chief judge, 1977—. Pres., Young Democrats Kan., 1942-46, Kans. Dem. Club, 1944-46; chmn. Kans. Dem. Com., 1955-60; mem. nat. adv. com. polit. orgn. Dem. Nat. Com., 1956-58, nat. committeeman from Kans., 1957-67; chmn. Dem. Midwest Conf., 1959-60; Dem. nominee for Kans., Supreme Ct. 1950, U.S. Senate, 1960. Mem. Kans. Jr. Bar Conf. (pres. 1942), Am., Kans. bar assns., Phi Beta Kappa. Phi Delta Phi, Sachem. Presbyn. Mason. Office: PO Box 2391 Wichita KS 67201

THELLMANN, EDWARD LOUIS, powder metallurgist; b. Cleve., May 16, 1927; s. Louis and Augusta (Marton) T.; B.S., Cleve. State U., 1959; certificate in metallurgy Fenn Coll., 1963; m. Catherine Ann McCarthy, May 9, 1970; children—Mark, Leah, Kenn, Kim. Project engr. Horizons, Inc., Cleve., 1951-57; process engr. Kennecott Titanium Devel. Corp., Beford, Ohio, 1957-60; group leader materials and process Ocean Systems div. Gould Inc., Cleve., 1960—. Mem. Village of Walton Hills (Ohio) Planning Commn., 1975—. Served with USN, 1945-46. Recipient John C. Vaaler award Chem. Processing Mag., 1966; IR-100 award, 1979. Mem. Am. Soc. Metals (Materials Awards Competition award 1967), Am. Def. Preparedness Assn., Am. Powder Metallurgy Inst. (chmn. local chpt. 1974-75). Clubs: Walton Hills Lake (chmn. 1967-68), Walton Hills Men's (chmn. 1975-76). Contbr. articles to profl. jours.; patentee in field. Home: 18307 Orchard Hill Dr Walton Hills OH 44146 Office: 540 E 105th St Cleveland OH 44108

THENO, DANIEL O'CONNELL, state legislator; b. Ashland, Wis., May 8, 1947; s. Maurice William and Janet Nora (Humphrey) T.; B.S., U. Wis., Madison, 1969; student, Brazil, 1969; m. Sue Burnham, June 16, 1973; children—Scott Patrick, Tad William. Tchr. agr. public schs., Oregon, Wis., 1969-72; mem. Wis. State Senate, 1972—; mem. Wis. Bldg. Commn. Named Superior Hon. Alumni, U. Wis., 1977; recipient Vet. Recognition award, 1978. Mem. Coll. Agr. Alumni Assn., U. Wis. Alumni Assn., Iron Cross Honor Soc. Clubs: Ashland County (Wis.) Republican, Elks, K.C.

THEOBALD, DAVID BUCHAN, cons.; b. Cleve., May 17, 1938; s. Carl J. and Elizabeth (Buchan) T.; B.A. in Econs., Denison U., 1961; m. Anne C. Kennedy, Oct. 3, 1964. With group div. Aetna Life & Casualty Co., 1962-69, asst. regional group annuity supr., 1966-69; with Meidinger & Assos., 1969—, regional v.p., mgr., Cin., 1974-77, corp. v.p., mgr., 1977-79, asst. div. mgr., corp. v.p., 1979—. Served with USAF, 1961-62. Mem. Cin. C. of C., Sigma Chi. Clubs: Rotary (chmn. new mem. com. 1978-79), Cin. Country, Miami Boat, Queen City. Office: 1200 First Nat Bank Center Cincinnati OH 45202

THEOBOLD, JACK CLARENCE, housewares mfg. co. exec.; b. Chgo., Oct. 15, 1927; s. Clarence John and Helen (Jacobson) T.; cert. Ray Vouge Art Sch., Chgo., 1950; B.F.A., Bradley U., 1952; m. M. Carolyn Watton, Mar. 8, 1980; children—Ronald, Paul, David, Nan, Janice, Kathy. With Gen. Outdoor Advt. Co., 1952, Sears Roebuck & Co., 1952-53; with Ekco Housewares Co., Franklin Park, Ill., 1953—, dir. advt. and public relations, 1975—. Publicity chmn., bd. dirs. Republican Orgn. of Elk Grove Twp., 1972-81. Served with USAAF, 1946-47. Club: Chicago Downtown Court. Office: Ekco Housewares Co 9234 W Belmont Ave Franklin Park IL 60131

THIAGARAJAN, DORAI, physician; b. Chingleput, Madras, India, Apr. 15, 1947; s. Dorai and Savarimuthammal Mudaliar; M.B.B.S., U. Madras, 1969; came to U.S., 1971, naturalized, 1979; m. Ranee V. Dass, Aug. 31, 1970; children—Aneetha, Geetha. Intern, Wheeling (W.Va.) Hosp., 1971-72; resident in internal medicine Ohio Valley Med. Center, Wheeling, 1972-74; fellow in hematology W.Va. U. Med. Center, Morgantown, 1974-76; chief hematology Topeka VA Med. Center, 1976-80; clin. instr. Kans. Med. Center, 1977-80; mem. faculty Meninger Sch. Psychiatry, 1977-80; asst. chief hematopathology-oncology Dayton VA Med. Center, 1980—; asst. clin. prof. medicine Wright State U. Med. Sch., Dayton, 1980—. Diplomate Am. Bd. Internal Medicine and Hematology. Fellow ACP; mem. Nat. Assn. VA Physicians, Am. Soc. Hematology. Roman Catholic. Contbr. articles to profl. jours. Home: 1401 Westbrook Rd Dayton OH 45415 Office: VA Med Center 4100 W 3d St Dayton OH 45428

THIEBAUTH, BRUCE EDWARD, advt. exec.; b. Bronxville, N.Y., Oct. 30, 1947; s. Bruce and Margaret Evelyn (Wiederhold) T.; student Colby Coll., Waterville, Maine, 1965-66, Pace Coll., 1971; B.A. magna cum laude in Bus. Adminstrn. and Sociology, Bellevue Coll., 1972; m. Sherry Ann Proplesch, Aug. 31, 1968; 1 son, Bruce Revere. Credit mgr. Gen. Electric Credit Corp., Croton Falls, N.Y., 1971; ops. mgr. Bridal Publs., Inc., Omaha, 1972-73; regional mgr. Bridal Fair, Inc., Omaha, 1973-74, sales mgr., 1974-76, chmn. bd., pres., 1976—; dir. Revere Enterprises, Inc., Multi-Media Group, Inc., Generation Two, Inc. Served with USAF, 1966-70; Vietnam conflict. Recipient Nat. Def. Service medal; Somers League citizenship and pub. service award, Somers, N.Y., 1965. Mem. Nat. Small Bus. Assn., Nat. Radio Broadcasters Assn., Nat. Assn. Broadcasters, Airline Passengers Assn., Bellevue Coll. Alumni Assn. Republican. Congregationalist. Office: 8901 Indian Hills Dr Omaha NE 68114

THIEL, RUTH ELEANOR, real estate broker; b. Chgo., June 11, 1930; d. Frank A. and Lucille L. (Bromm) Dell; A.A., Evanston Twp. Community Coll., 1950; grad. Realtors Inst., 1972; m. Joseph Donald Thiel, Sept. 30, 1950; children—Michael F., Jeffrey D., Patti Thiel Fricks, Mary Beth, Tracy J. Sales asso. Indian Hill Realty, Winnetka, Ill., 1967; v.p., mgr. Mitchell Bros. Realtors, Northbrook, Ill., 1972-75; exec. v.p., gen. mgr. Century 21 Mitchell Bros., Evanston, Ill., 1975—. Mem. State of Ill. Real Estate Examining Com., 1977—, Evanston Econ. Devel. Com., 1979; treas. North Shore Assn. Retarded, 1977-79; mem. instl. rev. com. St. Francis Hosp., 1981—. Recipient Ill. Women's Council of Realtors Woman of the Year award, 1979; Service award City of Hope, North Shore Assn. for Retarded, 1977. Mem. Nat. Assn. Realtors (bd. dirs. 1978—), Ill. Assn. Realtors (exec. com. 1979, bd. dirs. 1977—), North Shore Bd. Realtors (dir. 1970-80), Evanston North Shore Bd. Realtors (pres. 1978), Women's Council Realtors (state pres. 1977), Evanston Bus. and Profl. Women, Women in Real Estate (award 1980). Clubs: Womans of Evanston, Univ., YWCA, Million Dollar, Zonta Internat. Home: 1221 Greenwood St Evanston IL 60201 Office: 2528 Green Bay Rd Evanston IL 60201

THIELING, JOHN RICHARD, accountant; b. St. Paul, Mar. 29, 1944; s. Raymond R. and Lucille A. (Dietz) T.; B.S., Ind. U., 1970; m. Patricia Ann Maldonis, Aug. 23, 1969; children—Amy Katherine, Jennifer Lee, Erik David, Kristin Marie. Acct., Inland Steel Co., East Chicago, Ind., 1967-70; partner McQueen & Thieling, Plymouth, Ind., 1970-81. Dist. commr. Boy Scouts Am., 1973; chmn. Marshall County chpt. March of Dimes, 1976—; pres. Ta Ki Kwa Council Camp Fire Girls, Inc., 1981—; mem. Ind. Estate Planning Council. C.P.A., Ind. Mem. Am. Inst. C.P.A.s (Sells cert. of hon. mention), Ind. C.P.A. Soc. (High Grade award, mgmt. acctg. practice com. 1980—). Club: Kiwanis. Home: 19897 W 12th Rd Plymouth IN 46563

THILL, RICHARD EUGENE, geophysicist; b. St. Paul, June 16, 1934; s. Alphonse James and Marie Irene (Labelle) T.; student Macalester Coll., 1953-54; B.A., U. Minn., 1958, M.S., 1967; m. Patricia Ann Pasket, Mar. 25, 1966; children—Steven Daniel, Jeffrey Scott, Brian Kevin. Curator geol. collections U. Minn., 1962; geophysicist U.S. Bur. Mines, St. Paul, 1963—; instr. geology dept. Macalester Coll., St. Paul, 1959-60. Recipient Invention award U.S. Bur. Mines, 1971. Mem. Soc. Exptl. Stress Analysis (former chmn. Twin City subsect.), Am. Inst. Mining Engrs., Am. Geophys. Union, Twin Cities Geologists Club. Contbr. articles to profl. jours.; patentee in field. Office: US Dept Interior Bur of Mines Twin Cities Research Center Minneapolis MN 55417

THIMLING, STEVEN JON, meteorologist; b. Huntingburg, Ind., Dec. 10, 1951; s. Ambrose Edward and Ruby Amelia (Sickbert) T.; B.S., Purdue U., 1973; m. Kathleen Marie Alt, May 26, 1979. Staff meteorologist Dames & Moore, Park Ridge, Ill., 1973—. Mem. Air Pollution Control Assn. Lutheran. Home: 422 Franklin St Sauk City WI 53583 Office: 800-DS Division St Waunakee WI 53597

THIMOTHEOSE, KADAKAMPALLIL GEEVARGHESE, psychol. counselor; b. Kerala, India, Nov. 7, 1937; s. K.G. and Varghese (Mariamma) Varghese; came to U.S., 1976; M.S. in Ednl. Psychology, U. Kerala, 1966, M.A. in Sociology, 1969, M.A. in History, 1975, Ph.D., 1975; m. P.I. Mariamma, May 20, 1968; children—Geebee, Sonia. Lectr. ednl. psychology, head dept. Tng. Coll., U. Kerala, 1966-76, faculty U. Calicut, 1969-76, hon. dir. Anada Nilayam Orphanage and Widow Center, 1966-76; psychol. counselor Metro Substance Abatement Center, Detroit, 1976—, Ford Hosp., Detroit, 1977-78; clin. dir., Alexandrine House, Inc., Detroit, 1977—; alcoholism therapist Talc Clinic, Detroit, 1977—; exec. dir., chmn. bd. dirs., chief exec. officer Central Therapeutic Services, Inc., Southfield, Mich., 1981—. Mem. adv. bd. Trivadrum Med. Coll. Hosps., 1972-76. Certified social worker, Mich.; cert. tchr. Mich., Ga.; cert. alcoholism-therapist; accredited social psychologist, Mich.; lic. clin. psychologist, Mich. Mem. Am. Am. Psychol. Assn. (div. psychoanalytic psychology), Am. Acad. Psychologists in Marital, Sex and Family Therapy, Mich. Soc. Psychoanalytic Psychology. Author book on ednl. psychology. Home: 21701 Parklawn Oak Park MI 48237

THINNES, ROBERT LOUIS, electronics mfrs. reps. co. exec.; b. Cin., May 24, 1927; s. Elmer Michael and Marie L. (Cook) T.; B.B.A., U. Cin., 1949; student Union Coll., 1945-46; postgrad. U. Dayton, 1967-68; m. Patricia L., May 15, 1955; children—Pamela, Kimberly, Bradley, Sandra. Acct., Continental Electric Equipment Co., Ludlow, Ky., 1949, sales estimator, 1950, sales engr., Cin. and Columbus, Ohio, 1951-53, regional sales mgr., Chgo., 1953; sales engr. Robert O. Whitesell & Assos., Cin., Dayton, Ohio, 1955-69, v.p., Dayton, 1969—, also dir. Bd. dirs. Kettering Tennis Center, 1972—. Served with USNR, 1945-46, 53-55. Mem. Electronic Reps. Assn. (pres. Buckeye chpt. 1976), IEEE, Dayton Sales and Mktg. Execs., Miami Valley Mil. Affairs Orgn. Republican. Clubs: Sycamore Creek Country (pres. 1977), Dayton Agonis. Home: 865 Oakcreek Dr Dayton OH 45429 Office: Robert O Whitesell & Assos 4133 S Dixie Ave Dayton OH 45439

THISTLETHWAITE, PAUL CALVIN, educator; b. Indpls., Nov. 9, 1945; s. Paul Eugene and Berniece Mardelle (Brown) T.; B.S., Ball State U., 1968, M.B.A., 1969; Ph.D., U. Mo. at Columbia, 1975; m. Lindia Lee Schulenberg, Aug. 25, 1968; children—Craig Eric, Ryan Paul. Grad. asst. mktg. and statistics Ball State U., 1968-69; instr. mktg. So. Ill. U., 1969-70; grad. asst. U. Mo. at Columbia, 1970-73; asst. prof. mktg. Western Ill. U., 1973-77, asso. prof. mktg., 1977-81, prof., 1982—; vis. asso. prof. mktg. U. Mo., 1981-82; participant profl. confs. Mem. Am. Mktg. Assn., So. Mktg. Assn., Midwest Mktg. Assn., Ill. Retail Mchts. Assn., Midwest Bus. Adminstrn. Assn. Republican. Methodist (jr. high youth leader 1974-75). Author book; contbr. articles to profl. jours. Home: 1185 Stacey Ln Macomb IL 61455 Office: Dept Mktg Finance Western Ill U Macomb IL 61455

THOLEN, SARAH MARIE, insulation mfg. co. staff mem.; b. Leadville, Colo., Oct. 3, 1950; d. Harold Joseph and Mary Bernadette (Fouhy) Tholen; B.S. in Bus. Adminstrn. (Boettcher Found. scholar), U. Denver, 1974. Northwestern regional dir. Center for Prospective Students, U. Denver, Portland, Oreg., 1974-75; asst. dir. admissions U. Denver, Denver, 1975-77; sales rep. original equipment materials Johns-Manville Corp., Oakbrook, Ill., 1977—. Pres. Republican Assos. of Colo., 1977. Mem. Am. Soc. Gas Engr., Thermal Insulation Mfrs. Assn., Nat. Women's Polit. Caucus, Art Inst. Chgo., Mortar Bd., Sigma Iota Epsilon, Beta Gamma Sigma. Roman Catholic. Club: Colo. Mountain. Home: 17 W 704 Butterfield Rd Oakbrook Terrace IL 60181 Office: 2222 Kensington Ct Oakbrook IL 60521

THOM, JAMES ALEXANDER, novelist, journalist; b. Gosport, Ind., May 28, 1933; s. Jay Webb and Julia Elizabeth (Swain) T.; B.A. in Journalism, Butler U., 1960. Editorial staff mem. Indpls. Star,

1960-64, bus. editor, fin. columnist, 1964-67; writer, editor Nuggets mag. and Post Scripts mag., Indpls., 1967—; sr. editor Saturday Eve. Post Mag., Indpls., 1971; writer Nat. Geog. mag. and Reader's Digest, 1970—; author novels: Let the Sun Shine In, 1976, Spectator Sport, 1978, Long Knife: An Epic Novel of George Rogers Clark, 1979; Follow the River, 1981; mem. journalism faculty Ind. U., 1977-80. Sagamore of Wabash, Ind. Mem. Authors Guild, Authors League.

THOMAN, MARK EDWARD, physician; b. Chgo., Feb. 15, 1936; s. John Charles and Tasula Mark (Petrakis) T.; A.A., Graceland Coll., 1956; B.A., U. Mo., 1958, M.D., 1962; children—Marlisa Rae, Susan Kay, Edward Kim, Nancy Lynn, Janet Lea, David Mark. Intern, U. Mo. at Columbia, 1962-63; resident in pediatrics Blank Meml. Children's Hosp., Des Moines, 1963-65, chief resident, 1964-65, lt. comdr. USPHS, Washington, 1965-66, cons. in toxicology, Res. comdr., 1966-67; chief dept. pediatrics Shiprock (N.Mex.) Navajo Indian Hosp., dir. N.D. Poison Info. Center, also practice medicine, specializing in pediatrics Quain & Ramstad Clinic, Bismarck, N.D., 1967-69; dir. Iowa Poison Info. Center, Des Moines, 1969—; pvt. practice pediatrics, Des Moines, 1969—; sr. aviation med. examiner, accident investigator FAA, 1976—; dir. Cystic Fibrosis Clinic, 1973-82; dir. Mid-Iowa Drug Abuse Program, 1972-76; mem. med. adv. bd. La Leche Leauge Internat., 1965—; pres. Medic-Air Ltd., 1976—. Bd. dirs. Polk County Pub. Health Nurses Assn., 1969-77, Des Moines Speech and Hearing Center, 1974-79. Served with USMCR, 1954-58. Recipient N.D. Gov.'s award of merit, 1969; Cystic Fibrosis Research Found. award, 1975, Am. Psychiat. Assn. Thesis award, 1962. Mem. AMA (del. 1970-79), Polk County Med. Soc., Iowa State Med. Assn., Aerospace Med. Assn., Soc. Adolescent Medicine, Inst. Clin. Toxicology, Internat. Soc. Pediatrics, Am. Acad. Pediatrics, Am. Bd. Pediatrics, Cystic Fibrosis Club, Am. Acad. Clin. Toxicology (trustee 1969—, pres. 1982-84), Am. Assn. Poison Control Centers, Nat. Rifle Assn. (life). Republican. Mem. Reorganized Latter-Day Saints Ch. Clubs: Flying Physicians, Aircraft Owners and Pilots Assn., Nat. Pilots Assn. (Safe Pilot award), Hyperion Field and Country. Editor-in-chief AACTION. Home: 6896 NW Trailridge Dr Des Moines IA 50323 Office: 1426 Woodland Ave Des Moines IA 50309

THOMAS, ALLEN BURKE, civil engr.; b. Tunnel Hill, Ill., Jan. 20, 1943; s. John A. and Mary G. T.; B.S., So. Ill. U., 1969; m. Karen Oshel, June 5, 1964; 1 dau., Sherri L. Engring. technician Ill. Dept. Transp., Carbondale, 1962-67, civil engr., 1969—. Registered profl. engr., Ill. Home: Rural Route 2 Carterville IL 62918 Office: Old Route 13 Carbondale IL 62901

THOMAS, BRUCE LORREY, charitable assn. exec.; b. Boston, Apr. 4, 1930; s. Frank Bryan and Louise Anna Julia (Lorrey) T.; grad. Williston Acad., Easthampton, Mass., 1949; B.A., U. Mass., 1953; M.S.W., U. Conn., 1957; m. Sara Alice Folger, Mar. 18, 1961; children—Richard Folger, Alice Lorrey. Caseworker, Family and Children's Service, Pitts., 1957-59; sr. clin. social worker VA Neuropsychiat. Hosp., Pitts., 1959-63; exec. dir. Western Pa. Multiple Sclerosis Soc., Pitts., 1963-68; exec. dir. United Way of Central Washington County, Washington, Pa., 1968-76, Trumbull County Community Chest and United Way of Trumbull County, Warren, Ohio, 1976—; vol. group chmn. social agys. sect. United Fund Allegheny County, Ptts., 1966-67; mem. citizens participation com. Washington County Planning Commn., 1971-76; field work placement inst. Grad. Sch. Social Work, U. Pitts., 1971-72; mem. Washington County Health Task Force for Long Term Care, 1972-76; treas. Wesley Town, Inc., 1973-76. Bd. dirs., past pres. Washington County-Greene County Community Action Corp.; mem. Trumbull County Welfare Adv. Bd., 1979—. Served with AUS, 1953-55. Mem. Nat. Assn. Social Workers (pres. S.W. Pa. chpt. 1966-69), Acad. Cert. Social Workers, NAACP, Washington County History and Landmarks Soc., Washington C. of C. (co-chmn. legis. action com. 1971), Ohio Council Fund Raising Execs. Presbyn. (elder 1966—). Rotarian. Home: 2866 Crescent Dr NE Warren OH 44483 Office: 415 Washington St NW Warren OH 44482

THOMAS, DALE RICHARD, fin. planner; b. Blue Rapids, Kans., July 11, 1939; s. Lewis H. and Bertha A. T.; C.L.U., Am. Coll. Life Underwriters, 1975; m. Della Marie Falley, Apr. 8, 1966; children—Valerie, Melanie, Mary Ann. Heavy equipment operator, 1957-64; ins. agt. Globe Life & Accident, 1964-67, Woodmen Accident & Life Ins. Co., 1967-81; pres. Tax Qualified Concepts, Inc., Manhattan, Kans., 1981—; instr. Life Underwriters' Tng Council, 1977. Bd. dirs. Meadowlark Hills Retirement Center, Inc. Served with USNR, 1956-57. Life mem. Million Dollar Round Table. Mem. Am. Coll. Life Underwriters, Nat. Assn. Life Underwriters, Fin. Planners Inst. Republican. Methodist. Office: 314 Poyntz Ave Manhattan KS 66502

THOMAS, DAVID CARL, farm assn. exec.; b. Monett, Mo., Sept. 8, 1947; s. Carl M. Thomas; B.S. in Agrl. Edn. with distinction, U. Mo., 1970, M.S., 1978; m. Carla Jolley, May 1976. Mo. agrl. editor, dir. Sta. KRMO, Monett, 1965-69; adminstrv. asst. to dean divisional adminstrn. U. Mo., Columbia, 1969-70; mgmt. intern Eli Lilly Co., Indpls., 1970-71; tchr. vocat. agr. Columbia (Mo.) Public Schs., 1971-72; dir. mgmt. devel. and tng. Mo. Farmers Assn., Inc., Columbia, 1972-75; dir. member relations Midcontinent Farmers Assn., Inc., Columbia, 1975-76, v.p., 1976-79; pres. David C. Thomas & Assos., 1980—; acting asso. vice provost extension div. U. Mo., Columbia, 1980—. Mem. adv. bd. State Fair Community Coll., Sedalia; mem. Luth Ch. Mo. Synod, 1947—; sec. Trinity Luth. Ch., 1977-79; dir. dist. Luth. Ch. Camp, Mo., 1963-66; trustee Mo. 4-H Found., 1976—; chmn. Mo. Farm City Com., 1976-79. Recipient Hon. Am. Farmer degree, 1977. Mem. Nat. Adminstrv. Mgmt. Soc., Am. Soc. Tng. and Devel. (pres. Central Mo. chpt. 1975-76), Nat. Vocat. Tchrs. Assn., Mo. Vocat. Tchrs. Assn., Nat. Vocat. Agr. Tchrs. Assn., Mo. Vocat. Agr. Tchrs. Assn., Columbia Jaycees, Am. Vocat. Assn., Am. Inst. Cooperation (trustee 1977-79), Mo. Inst. Coops. (sec. 1975—), Future Farmers Am. Alumni Assn. (nat. pres. 1976-77, charter pres. Mo. chpt. 1972), Mo. Future Farmers Am. (state v.p. 1966), Phi Delta Kappa, Gamma Sigma Delta, Alpha Tau Alpha, Sigma Rho Sigma, Alpha Zeta, Omicron Delta Kappa. Clubs: Columbia Breakfast, Optimists. Office: 201 S 7th St Columbia MO 65201

THOMAS, DELROY OLIVER, food co. exec.; b. Kingston, Jamaica, Dec. 30, 1939; came to U.S., 1961, naturalized, 1974; B.S., Marquette U., 1965, M.B.A., 1966; m. Doris Oldenberg, Jan. 26, 1963; 1 dau., Debbie. Mktg. mgr. Pillsbury Co., Mpls., 1973-76, Ky. Fried Chicken Corp., Louisville, 1976-78; with Land O'Lakes, Inc., Mpls., 1978—, v.p. new products/mktg. services, 1980—. Office: Land O'Lakes Inc PO Box 116 Minneapolis MN 55440

THOMAS, DON R., psychologist; b. Fredericktown, Mo., Mar. 5, 1939; s. Roy Vernon and Nina Elizabeth (Smallen) T.; m. Carolyn Erickson, Dec. 31, 1971; children—Marilyn, Jeffrey, Donya, Matthew. B.S., U. Ill., 1967, Ph.D., 1972. Program mgr. Englemann-Becker Follow Through Model, Urbana, Ill., 1968-70, asso. dir. Behavior Analysis Follow Through Program, Lawrence, Kans., 1971-73; chief psychologist Minn. Learning Center, Brainerd, 1973, dir., 1973—; clin. practice psychology, 1975—. Coordinator, Dept. Pub. Welfare Task Force Competency Based Certification of Profls. Using Aversive Treatment Procedures, Minn., 1976-78; bd. dirs. Sch. Bd. Minn. Dist. 181, 1978—, chmn., 1981-82; bd. dirs. Human Services Specialists, Inc., 1981—; mem. Minn. Career Exec. Service, 1981—. Lic. cons. psychologist, Minn. Mem. Am. Psychol. Assn., Assn. Advancement of Behavior Therapy, Minn. Assn. Behavior Analysis (pres. 1975-76, mem. certification bd. 1980—), Minn. Psychol. Assn., Assn. Advancement Mental Deficiency, Nat. Assn. Developmental Disabilities Mgrs. Recipient Psi Chi Research award, U. of Ill., 1967. Co-Author: Teaching; A Course in Applied Psychology, 1971; Teaching 1: Classroom Mgmt., 1975; Teaching 2: Cognitive Learning and Instruction, 1975. Home: 432 Tyrol Dr Brainerd MN 56401 Office: Minnesota Learning Center Box 349 Brainerd MN 56401

THOMAS, EDWARD PAUL, allergist, internist; b. Hattiesburg, Miss., July 26, 1920; s. Simon S. and Rosa A. (Henry) T.; student Butler U., 1937-40; M.D., Meharry Med. Coll., 1944; m. Ruby Leah Thomas, May 6, 1944; children—Paul A., Bradford E., Leeland M., Leah Anne. Intern Homer G. Phillips Hosp., St. Louis, 1945; practice medicine specializing in allergies and internal medicine, Indpls.; med. staff Meth. Hosp., Indpls. Served to lt. comdr., M.C., USNR, 1954-56. Mem. Am. Coll. Allergy, Am. Coll. Chest Physicians, Am. Acad. Allergy, Omega Psi Phi, Chi Delta Mu. Home: 1520 Thomas Wood Trail Indianapolis IN 46260 Office: 3450 N Illinois St Indianapolis IN 46208

THOMAS, EUGENE MELVIN, social worker; b. Danville, Ill., Feb. 23, 1933; s. John and Anna Lee (Tate) T.; B.S. (scholar), Eastern Ill. U., 1954; M.S., U. Ill., 1959; M.A. (fellow), U. Chgo., 1971. Tchr. biology Chgo. Public Schs., 1959-61; caseworker Dept. Welfare County of Cook (Ill.), 1961-69; social worker Evanston (Ill.) Schs. Dist. 65, 1970—; psychotherapist Evanston Family Counseling Service, 1974—. Served with U.S. Army, 1955-57. Mem. Nat. Assn. Social Workers (co-chmn. council sch. social work 1979-83), Ill. Assn. Sch. Social Workers (co-chmn. profl. practice com. 1979-80), NEA, Ill. Edn. Assn., Acad. Cert. Social Workers, Nat. Assn. Black Social Workers, Nat. Conf. Social Welfare, U. Ill. Alumni Assn., U. Chgo. Alumni Assn., NAACP. Democrat. Home: 8847 S Dante St Chicago IL 60619 Office: 1314 Ridge Ave Evanston IL 60201

THOMAS, FAYE EVELYN J., educator; b. Summerfield, La., Aug. 3, 1933; d. Reginald Felton and Altee (Hunter) Johnson; B.A., So. U., 1954; student Tuskegee Inst., 1958, 69, U. Detroit, summers, 1961, 62, 63, Central Mich. U., summer 1965; M.S., U. Central Ark., 1971; M.S., Cleve. State U., 1979; m. Archie Taylor Thomas, Sept. 8, 1960; 1 son, Dwayne Andre. Tchr., Cullen (La.) Elem. Sch., 1957; tchr. English and social studies Charles Brown High Sch., Springhill, La., 1957-70; tchr. English, Upward Bound Program, Grambling State U., 1968; tchr. English, Springhill (La.) High Sch., 1970; elem. intermediate tchr. Riveredge Elem. Sch., Berea, Ohio, 1971—. EPDA grantee, 1970-71; Internat. Paper Found. grantee, summers 1958, 60; NDEA grantee, summer 1965. Mem. NEA, Ohio Edn. Assn., Berea Edn. Assn., N.E. Ohio Tchrs. Assn., Assn. for Supervision and Curriculum Devel., Charles Brown Soc. Orgn., People United to Save Humanity, Black Caucus Nat. Edn. Assn., Ohio Motorists Assn. Democrat. Baptist. Mem. Order Eastern Star. Home: 19353 E Bagley Rd Middleburg Heights OH 44130 Office: 224 Emerson Dr Berea OH 44017

THOMAS, FRANCES JONES, social worker; b. St. Louis, Oct. 9, 1942; d. William A. and Sadie B. Jones; A.A., Harris Jr. Coll., 1962; B.S., St. Louis U., 1964, M.S.W., 1968; m. Maurice Thomas, Nov. 30, 1969; 1 son, Darrell Thomas; 1 son by previous marriage, Donovan Banks. Intake specialist Human Devel. Corp., St. Louis, 1965-67; med. social worker St. Louis City Hosp., 1967-75; dir. social services dept. DePaul Community Health Center, Bridgeton, Mo., 1975—; adj. asst. prof. St. Louis U., 1975—; field work instr. social work U. Mo., 1975—, Washington U., 1975—, So. Ill. U., Carbondale, 1977. Bd. dirs. Am. Cancer Soc., 1976-78, service com. chmn., 1976-78; mem. adv. council Helping Other Parents Endure, 1978—; mem. Cardinal Ritter Home Care Adv. Council, 1976—. Mem. Acad. Cert. Social Workers, Nat. Assn. Social Workers, Council on Social Work Edn., St. Louis Soc. Hosp. Social Work Dirs. (pres. 1979-80), Am. Hosp. Assn., Zeta Phi Beta. Democrat. Baptist. Home: 7135 Winchester Dr Northwoods MO 63121 Office: 12303 DePaul Dr Bridgeton MO 63044

THOMAS, FRANCIS ASHE, educator; b. Wilberforce, Ohio, Mar. 16, 1913; s. Alexander Wayman and Frances Adelia (Lee) T.; A.B., Wesleyan U., 1936; M.Div., Yale U., 1939; M.Ed., Miami U., Oxford, Ohio, 1956; Ed.D., Ind. U., 1960; m. Pearlye Toni Lewis, Feb. 14, 1970; children—Helen Wayman. Instr. Wilberforce U. and Payne Sem., Wilberforce, 1940-43, asst. prof., 1944-47; asst. prof. Central State U., Wilberforce, 1947-57, asso. prof., 1958-67, prof., chmn. philosophy and religion, 1967-78, audio-visual dir., 1950-70, prof. emeritus, 1981—; prof. philosophy of religion Payne Sem., Wilberforce, 1978—, acad. dean, 1979—. Bd. dirs. B.F. Lee Health Center. Mem. Am. Philos. Assn., Am. Acad. Religion, AAAS, AAUP, Am. Chem. Soc., Phi Delta Kappa, Alpha Phi Alpha. Mem. A.M.E. Ch. Clubs: Masons, Shriners. Home: PO Box 416 Wilberforce OH 45384 Office: PO Box 474 Wilberforce OH 45384

THOMAS, FRANCIS BRIAN, educator; b. Washington, Dec. 21, 1930; s. Cyrus B. and Carolyn C. (Coates) T.; B.S., U. Cin., 1957; M.A., Kent State U., 1966; m. Diane R. Ruehrwein; children—Teresa Lynn, F. Brian, Leslie Ann, Mark Richard. Prodn. engr. RCA Co., Cin., 1957-59; sci. programmer analyst Lockheed Co., Marietta, Ga., 1959-62; sec. head Applied Computer div. Goodyear Aerospace, Akron, Ohio, 1962-70; dir. computer services U. Akron, 1970—; cons. in field. Served as master sgt. U.S. Army, 1952-54. Decorated Army Commendation medal; recipient Assn. for Systems Mgmt. Systems Man of the Yr. award, 1973, Merit award, 1976, Achievement award, 1978, Disting. Service award, 1981. Mem. Assn. for Systems Mgmt., Assn. for Computing Machinery. Republican. Contbr. articles to profl. jours. Home: 2480 15th St Cuyahoga Falls OH 44223 Office: 302 E Buchtel Ave Akron OH 44325

THOMAS, FRANCIS DARRELL, oil compounder exec.; b. Palestine, Ill., Feb. 11, 1928; s. Odin F. and Dorothy (Carrol) T.; B.S., Butler U., 1951; children—Steven, Bruce, Gail. Regional mgr. Sun Oil Co., Cin., 1955-72; pres. Keenan Oil Co., Cin., 1972-74; gen. mgr. Weatherator Engring. Co., Columbus, Ohio, 1975-76; pres. Nat. Oil and Chem. Co., Hamilton, Ohio, 1976—. Served with USMC, 1946-47. Mem. Ind. Oil Compounders Assn., Assn. Petroleum Re-refiners (past mem. nat. exec. com.), Am. Soc. Lubrication Engrs. (past chmn. Cin. sect.). Republican. Clubs: Clovernook Country, Masons, Shriners. Office: 1000 Forest Ave Hamilton OH 45015

THOMAS, FRANK HOWARD, constrn. co. exec.; b. Wilmington, Del., May 15, 1929; s. Frank Howard and Margaret Sophia (Butler) T.; B.S. in Civil Engring., M.I.T., 1951; m. Patricia Mohr, June 30, 1950; children—William W., Susannah, Jay F., Elizabeth. With Turner Constrn. Co., Chgo., 1951—, gen. supt., 1967-73, v.p., 1973-74, gen. mgr., 1974—. Trustee Bricklayers Union Local 21 Apprenticeship and Tng. Program, Operating Engrs. Local 150 Apprenticeship and Tng. Program, Tech. Engrs. Local 130 Pension Fund. Mem. Builders Assn. Chgo. (dir.), Constrn. Employers Assn. (dir.). Clubs: Tavern, Mid-Am., Execs. (Chgo.). Home: 1146 Wheaton Oaks Dr Wheaton IL 60187 Office: 180 N LaSalle St Chicago IL 60601

THOMAS, GARTH E., data processing exec.; b. Fostoria, Ohio, Aug. 6, 1942; s. Charles E. and Helen M. (Roper) T.; B.S., Ohio State U., 1964; M.S., Xavier U., 1970; m. Jean Thomas, Sept. 16, 1961; children—Timothy, Douglas, Jeffrey, Jennifer. Mgr. systems programming Ohio State U. Hosps., 1966-71; mgr. tech. support U. Mich., Ann Arbor, 1971-78, asst. dir. data systems, 1978—. Asst. scoutmaster Troop 78, Boy Scouts Am., 1965-76. Mem. Am. Mgmt. Assn., Data Processing Mgmt. Assn., Am. Phys. Soc. Home: 9602 Waters Rd Ann Arbor MI 48103 Office: 1005 Greene St Ann Arbor MI 48109

THOMAS, GARY JAMES, constrn. co. exec.; b. Sioux Falls, S.D., June 19, 1929; s. Glen Merle and Gladys Leona (Otelle) T.; student schs. Dinuba, Calif.; m. Lucille Patricia Jones, Aug. 27, 1950; children—Robert D., Linda A., Timothy M. With S.J. Groves Sons Co., Mpls., 1945—, heavy equipment operator, constrn. partsman, maintenance shop foreman, heavy equipment mechanic, equipment supt., equipment mgr., 1960-70, v.p., equipment mgr., 1970—. Mem. Associated Gen. Contractors, Transp. Research Bd., Am. Mgmt. Assn., Exptl. Aircraft Assn. Republican. Methodist. Club: Elks. Contbr. chpt. to handbook in field, paper to profl. conf. Home: 7061 Hickory Dr Fridley MN 55432 Office: 10000 Hwy 55 W Minneapolis MN 55441

THOMAS, GERALD DUANE (JERRY), underground sprinkling and irrigation co. exec.; b. Toledo, Feb. 11, 1931; s. Harold Carl and Doris M. (Bolton) T.; B.B.A., U. Toledo, 1957; m. Betty Jane Kiss, June 9, 1956; children—Andrea Jo, Thomas Edward, Jill Doris. Field sales mgr. Fulton Mfg. Corp., Wauseon, Ohio, 1968-70; nat. sales mgr. Duo Tint Corp., Elk Grove, Ill., 1970-73; gen. mgr. Century Rain Aid Corp., Elk Grove, 1973—. Served with USAF, 1951-54. Recipient V.I.P. award Century Rain Aid Corp., 1978. Mem. Nat. Assn. Home Builders, Irrigation Assn., Golf Course Supts. Assn. Am., Home Builders Assn. Greater Chgo., N.W. Builders Assn., Midwest Inst. Park Execs., Ill. Landscape Contractors Assn., Midwest Assn. Golf Course Supts. Mem. United Ch. Christ. Home: 441 S Windsor Dr Arlington Heights IL 60004 Office: 341 Lively Blvd Elk Grove Village IL 60007

THOMAS, HARVEY MONROE, psychol. cons.; b. Marshall, Mo., Sept. 22, 1925; s. David Monroe and Sue Elizabeth (Eades) T.; A.B., William Jewell Coll., 1947; Ph.D., Washington U., 1953; m. Irene Simon, Dec. 28, 1947; children—Blake David, Kent Monroe, Jonathan Lee. Instr. psychology Washington U., St. Louis, 1947-49; prof. psychology, chmn. dept. psychology William Jewell Coll., Liberty, Mo., 1949-55; staff cons. Nordli, Ogan, Wilson Assos., N.Y.C., 1953-59; pres. Thomas & Assos., Liberty, 1959—; dir. Kans. Nat. Banks, Comml. Bank, Liberty. Trustee, William Jewell Coll., 1958—; dir. Bd. Edn., Liberty, 1957-63; bd. dirs. Arrow Rock Lyceum, 1968—, Liberty Indsl. Commn., 1978—; deacon Second Bapt. Ch., Liberty, 1955—, chmn. bd. deacons, 1975-76. Served with USNR, 1943-46. Washington U. fellow, 1947-49. Mem. Am. Psychol. Assn., Midwest Psychol. Assn., Mo. Psychol. Assn., Sigma Xi. Republican. Baptist. Clubs: Claycrest Country (dir., pres. bd. dirs. 1978-80), Kansas City. Address: 617 Jefferson Circle Liberty MO 64068

THOMAS, IRA DAVID, advt. agy. exec.; b. Youngstown, Ohio, Aug. 15, 1937; s. Ira A. and Laurabell (Williams) T.; B.A. in Econs., Yale U., 1960; m. Frederica Tod Owsley, Aug. 29, 1959; children—Laura Hubbard, Marguerite Owsley. Sales trainee Jones & Laughlin Steel Corp., Pitts. and Detroit, 1960-61, gen. sales, Pitts., 1961-63; acct. exec. Meek & Thomas, Inc., Erie, Pa., 1963-67; pres. Meek & Thomas, Inc., Youngstown, Ohio, 1967-69; pres. Ira Thomas Assos., Inc., Youngstown, 1969—. Trustee, Butler Inst. Am. Art, 1976-80; bd. dirs. Youngstown Symphony Soc., 1976-81, exec. v.p. 1979; vestryman St. John's Episcopal Ch., Youngstown, 1976-79. Mem. Bus. and Profl. Advt. Assn. (cert. bus. communicator; pres. Youngstown chpt. 1971-73), Youngstown C. of C. (dir. 1971-73). Episcopalian. Club: Youngstown Country. Home: 102 Fairway Dr Youngstown OH 44505 Office: 20 Ohltown Rd Youngstown OH 44515

THOMAS, JOHN RUSSELL, profl. football team exec.; b. Griffithsville, W.Va., July 24, 1924; s. Ezra Neri and Ada Elizabeth (Sowards) T.; student Ohio State U., 1943-46; m. Dorothy Snyder, Aug. 3, 1945; children—John, Jim. Player, Detroit Lions, 1946-49, mem. coaching staff, 1952-56, scout, 1952-59, mem. radio broadcasting team, 1960-63, dir. player personnel, 1964-66, exec. v.p., gen. mgr., 1967—; asst. coach St. Bonaventure Coll., Olean, N.Y., 1950-51; dir. NFL Properties; mem. NFL Coaches Pension Plan Com. Office: 1200 Featherstone Rd Box 4200 Pontiac MI 48057

THOMAS, JOHN WILLIAM, cardiothoracic surgeon; b. Normal, Ill., Dec. 29, 1935; s. Raymond Augustus and Mary Alice (Weaner) T.; A.B., Maryknoll Coll., 1957, Wabash Coll., 1960; M.D., St. Louis U., 1964; M.S. in surgery, U. Iowa, 1973; m. Delphine Marie Grzegorczyk, Sept. 18, 1965; children—Rachel, Megan, Sarah, Bridget, Erin. Rotating intern St. Louis U., 1964-65; resident surgery U. Iowa, Iowa City, 1967-73; resident thoracic surgery La. State U., New Orleans, 1973-75; pvt. practice medicine specializing in cardiothoracic surgery, Columbus, Ohio, 1975—; mem. staffs Riverside Meth., Grant hosps., Mt. Carmel Med. Center. Served with AUS, 1965-67. Diplomate Am. Bd. Surgery, Am. Bd. Thoracic Surgery. Fellow A.C.S., Am. Coll. Cardiology, Am. Coll. Chest Physicians; mem. AMA, Ohio State Med. Assn., James D. Rives Surg. Soc., Columbus Surg. Soc., Soc. Thoracic Surgeons, Acad. Medicine of Columbus and Franklin County. Home: 1750 Churchview Ln Columbus OH 43220 Office: 931 Chatham Ln Columbus OH 43221

THOMAS, JON CAYSON, fin. advisor; b. St. Louis, June 22, 1947; s. Jefferson C. and Edna W. Thomas; B.S., U. Mo., 1971; M.B.A., So. Ill. U., 1978; m. Alma DeBasio, Aug. 31, 1968; children—Jennifer Anne, Jon Cayson, II. Div. mgr. pensions and mut. funds Safeco Securities Co./Safeco Life Ins. Co., St. Louis, 1970-74; v.p. fin. planning dept. A.G. Edwards & Sons, Inc., St. Louis, 1974-77; pres. Intermark Fin. Services, Inc., St. Louis, 1978—; founder, 1980, thereafter prin. Monetary Mgmt. Group, St. Louis. Cert. fin. planner. Mem. Nat. Assn. Securities Dealers (registered investment adv.), Internat. Assn. Fin. Planners, Inst. Cert. Fin. Planners, Beta Theta Pi. Office: 232 S Meramac Clayton MO 63105

THOMAS, JOSEPH E., psychologist; b. India, Feb. 11, 1937; s. Ipe and Kunjamma Thomas; m. Chinnamma Kavatt, Nov. 23, 1964; children—Joseph, Kurian, Elizabeth. B.A., Kerala U. (India), 1957, M.A., 1960, Ph.D., 1969. Mem. faculty dept. psychology Kerala U. 1963-72; postdoctoral internship in clin. psychology Northwestern U. Med. Sch., 1971-72, mem. faculty dept. psychiatry, 1972—; psychologist Univ. Health Center, Trivandrum, India, 1964-68; psychologist dept. psychiatry U. Chgo., 1972-74; dir. inpatient psychiat. unit Mental Health Center La Salle County, Ottawa, Ill., 1974; psychologist Northwestern Meml. Hosps., Chgo., 1974-80. Sec. Student Christian Movement of India, Bangalore, 1957-58; treas. St.

Gregorios Orthodox Ch., Evanston, Ill., 1978, 79. Mem. Am. Psychol. Assn., Am. Soc. Clin. Hypnosis. Contbr. articles to profl. jours. Home: 16W731 89th Pl Hinsdale IL 60521 Office: 500 N Michigan Ave Suite 542 Chicago IL 60611

THOMAS, JUDITH BECKER, railcar leasing, maintenance and repair co. exec.; b. Chgo., July 24, 1943; d. Charles Peter and Pearl Jean (Woodrick) Becker; B.B.A., Roosevelt U., 1977; M.B.A., Northwestern U., 1979. Asst. to pres. N.Am. Car Corp., Chgo., 1966-75, asst. dir. personnel, 1975-77, dir. personnel and indsl. relations, 1977-80, v.p. personnel relations, 1980-81, v.p. adminstrn., 1981—. Vol., Planned Parenthood Assn. Mem. Am. Soc. Personnel Adminstrs., Indsl. Relations Assn. Chgo., Soc. Personnel Adminstrn., Internat. Assn. Personnel Women, Ill. Mfrs. Assn. (mem. indsl. relations com. 1979—). Home: 73 E Elm St Chicago IL 60611 Office: 33 W Monroe Chicago IL 60603

THOMAS, LEWIS EDWARD, mktg. exec.; b. Lima, Ohio, May 18, 1913; s. Lewis Edward and Ilma Kathryn (Siebert) T.; B.S., Ohio No. U., 1935; M.S., Purdue U., 1937, postgrad., 1937-40; m. Elinda Patricia Grafton, Dec. 21, 1939; children—Linda (Mrs. John R. Collins), Stephanie (Mrs. Andrew Pawuk), Kathryn (Mrs. James N. Ramsey), Deborah (Mrs. James Masker). Asst. prof. chemistry Va. Mil. Inst., Lexington, 1940-45; devel. engr. Sun Oil Co., Toledo, Ohio, 1945-49, lab. supr., 1950-69, div. supr., 1969-73, lab. mgr., 1973-78; gen. mgr. Toledo Symphony Orch., 1978-80; with mktg. dept. Jones and Henry Labs., Inc., Toledo, 1980—. Dir. First Fed. Savs. & Loan, Toledo. Pres. Harvard Elementary Sch. PTA, 1953-54; mem. Mayor's Indsl. Devel. Com., Toledo, 1963-66. Precinct committeeman, mem. Lucas County Republican Central Com., 1958—. Trustee Toledo Pub. Library, 1966-70, pres., 1969-70; trustee U. Toledo, 1967—, vice chmn. bd., 1971-75; trustee Toledo Lucas County Pub. Library, 1970—, pres., 1973-74; trustee Northwestern Ohio council Girl Scouts U.S., 1981—; mem. Statewide Health Coordinating Council Ohio, 1977-81; mem. adv. bd. St. Charles Hosp., 1972—. Named Chem. Engr. of Yr., Toledo Tech. Council, 1961, 63; Toledo area Engr. of Yr., 1976. Registered profl. engr., Ohio. Mem. Nat., Ohio (chmn. state conv. 1975) socs. profl. engrs., Am. Inst. Chem. Engrs., Am. Chem. Soc. (pres. Toledo chpt. 1960), Nat. Mgmt. Assn. (trustee Toledo chpt. 1962-70, nat. dir. 1968-70), Tech. Socs. Toledo (pres. 1968-69), Assn. Governing Bds. Univs. and Colls., Ohio Acad. Sci. (adv. bd. engring. sect. 1972—), Sigma Xi (asso.), Tau Beta Pi, Nu Theta Kappa, Pi Kappa Alpha. Episcopalian (lay reader). Clubs: Toledo, Toastmasters. Home: 4148 Deepwood Lane Toledo OH 43614 Office: 2000 W Central St Toledo OH 43606

THOMAS, M. LADD, polit. scientist; b. San Francisco, Mar. 19, 1929; s. Albert Melvin and Fern (Ludlow) T.; B.A., U. Utah, 1951, M.A., 1952, postgrad., 1952-53; Ph.D., Fletcher Sch. Law and Diplomacy, Tufts U., 1960. U. Mich. and U. Philippines research fellow, Philippines, 1953-54; instr. in govt. U. Conn., 1957-58; asst. prof. polit. sci. U. Ind. and Thammasat U., Bangkok, Thailand, 1958-60; asst. prof. Ind. U., 1960-61, Rutgers U., 1961-63; asso. prof. No. Ill. U., 1963-66, prof., 1966—, chmn. dept. polit. sci., 1979—, dir. Center S.E. Asian Studies, 1963-71; lectr., cons. in field; mem. World Bank Mission to Thailand, 1979. Asia Soc. SEADAG grantee, Thailand, 1970, 72; Fulbright grantee, Thailand, 1974-75, Philippines, 1978; reviewer grant proposals for research on Asia, Nat. Endowment for Humanities. Mem. Assn. Asian Studies, Midwest Conf. Asian Affairs, Council Thai Studies, Am. Soc. Public Adminstrn., Internat. Studies Assn., Philippine Soc. Public Adminstrn. Club: Rotary (DeKalb, Ill.). Author books, monographs, including: Southeast Asia; A Cultural Region of the World, 1970; Political Violence in Muslim Provinces of South Thailand, 1975; contbr. articles, chpts. to profl. publs. Home: 231 W Royal St DeKalb IL 60115 Office: Dept Polit Sci No Ill U DeKalb IL 60115

THOMAS, O. PENDLETON, rubber co. exec.; b. Forney, Tex., June 14, 1914; s. William Pendleton and Lottye (Trail) T.; B.S., East Tex. State U., 1935, LL.D. (hon.), 1972; M.B.A., U. Tex., 1941; m. Anne Swindell; children—William Pendleton II, Alexander Cole, James Trail. With Sinclair Oil Corp., N.Y.C., 1945-69, pres., 1964-69, chief exec. officer, 1968-69, also dir.; chmn. exec. com. Atlantic Richfield Co., N.Y.C., 1969-71, also dir.; chmn. bd., chief exec. officer, dir. B.F. Goodrich Co., Akron, Ohio, 1971—; dir. Superior Oil Co., Armco, Inc., Westinghouse Electric Corp.; trustee Mut. Life Ins. Co. N.Y. Bd. govs. ARC. Served as lt. USNR, 1942-45. Recipient Distinguished Grad. award U. Tex. Coll. Bus. Adminstrn., 1964; Distinguished Alumnus award U. Tex., 1969. Mem. Am. Petroleum Inst. (hon. dir.), Conf. Bd. (trustee), UN Assn. of U.S.A. (gov., econ. policy council), Rubber Mfrs. Assn. (mem. exec. com.), Bus. Roundtable (policy com.). Clubs: Round Hill (Greenwich, Conn.); River, Links (N.Y.C.); Blind Brook (Portchester, N.Y.); Augusta (Ga.) Nat. Golf; Houston Country; Union (Cleve.); Sharon Golf, Portage Country (Akron); Pepper Pike (O.). Office: B F Goodrich Co 500 S Main St Akron OH 44318

THOMAS, PATRICIA GRAFTON (MRS. LEWIS EDWARD THOMAS), educator; b. Michigan City, Ind., Sept. 30, 1921; d. Robert Wadsworth and Elinda (Oppermann) Grafton; student Stephens Coll., 1936-39, Purdue U., summer 1938; B.Ed. magna cum laude, U. Toledo, 1966; postgrad. (fellow) Bowling Green U., 1968; m. Lewis Edward Thomas, Dec. 21, 1939; children—Linda L. (Mrs. John R. Collins), Stephanie A. (Mrs. Andrew M. Pawuk), I. Kathryn (Mrs. James N. Ramsey), Deborah (Mrs. James E. Masker). Tchr., Toledo Bd. Edn., 1959—, tchr. lang. arts Byrnedale Sch., 1976-81. Dist. capt. Planned Parenthood, 1952-53, ARC, 1954-55; mem. lang. arts curriculum com. Toledo Bd. Edn., 1969, mem. grammar curriculum com., 1974. Mem. Toledo Soc. Profl. Engrs. Aux., Helen Kreps Guild, AAUW, Phi Kappa Phi, Phi Delta Kappa, Kappa Delta Pi, Pi Lambda Theta (chpt. pres. 1978—), Delta Kappa Gamma (chpt. pres. 1976-78, area membership chmn. 1978—). Republican. Episcopalian. Home: 4148 Deepwood Lane Toledo OH 43614 Office: 3645 Glendale St Toledo OH 43614

THOMAS, PHILIP STANLEY, economist, educator; b. Hinsdale, Ill., Oct. 23, 1928; s. Roy K. and Pauline Z. (Grafton) T.; B.A. (Miller scholar) in Econs., Oberlin Coll., 1950; M.A., U. Mich., 1951, Ph.D. in Econs. 1961; postgrad. (Fulbright scholar) Delhi (India) Sch. Econs., 1953-54, (Ford Found. fellow), London Sch. Econs., 1954; m. Carol Morris, Dec. 27, 1950; children—Lindsey Carol, Daniel Kyle, Lauren Louise, Gay Richardson. Instr. dept. econs. U. Mich., Ann Arbor, 1956-57; asst. prof. dept. econs. Grinnell (Iowa) Coll., 1957-63, asso. prof., 1963-65; research advisor Pakistan Inst. Devel. Econs., 1963-65; asso. prof. dept. econs. and bus. Kalamazoo Coll., 1965-68, prof., 1968—; econ. cons. to AID, 1965-68, 71; mem. econ. adv. planning commn. Govt. of Pakistan, 1969-70, ministry of planning Govt. of Kenya, 1980-81; research mgr. Central Bank of Swaziland, 1974-75, acting gov., summer, 1975. Served with U.S. Army, 1954-56. Mem. Am. Econs. Assn., Midwest Econs. Assn. (v.p. 1972-73), Assn. for Asian Studies, Econ. Soc. Mich., AAUP, African Studies Assn., Phi Beta Kappa. Contbr. articles to profl. publs. Home: 1416 Academy St Kalamazoo MI 49007 Office: Kalamazoo College Kalamazoo MI 49007

THOMAS, RALPH HERBERT, engring. exec.; b. Cleve., Nov. 20, 1939; s. Herbert L. and Florence (Novotny) T.; B.S., Case Western Res. U., Cleve., 1961; m. Barbara L. Voth, July 1, 1961; 1 dau., Lauri Ann. Sr. engr., cons. engr. Kliever Devel. Labs., Cleve., 1961-66; product engr. Amelco Semicondr. div. Teledyne, Mountain View, Calif., 1966-67; v.p. Shoptrol ops. Electron, Inc., Cleve., 1967-73; v.p. engring. Comtec, Inc., Twinsburg, Ohio, 1973—; systems cons. Scoutmaster, Boy Scouts Am., 1961-66; pres. Christ Redeemer Ch., 1978-79; cons. Brecksville (Ohio) Sch. Bd., 1979. Mem. IEEE. Republican. Lutheran. Patentee in field. Home: 1148 Cleveland Massillon Rd Bath OH 44313 Office: 1800 Enterprise Pkwy Twinsburg OH 44087

THOMAS, RICHARD L., banker; b. Marion, Ohio, Jan. 11, 1931; s. Marvin C. and Irene (Harruff) T.; B.A., Kenyon Coll., 1953; postgrad U. Copenhagen (Denmark), 1954; M.B.A., Harvard, 1958; m. Helen Moore, June 17, 1953; children—Richard Lee, David Paul, Laura Sue. Pres., dir. First Nat. Bank of Chgo. and First Chgo. Corp.; dir. CNA Fin. Corp., Continental Assurance Co., Continental Casualty Co., Consol. Foods Corp., Chgo. Bd. Options Exchange. Mem. Chgo. Crime Commn.; trustee Orch. Assn., Rush-Presbyn. St. Luke's Med. Center, Northwestern U.; trustee, vice chmn. Kenyon Coll. Served with AUS, 1954-56. Named 1 of 10 Outstanding Young Men, Chgo. Jr. C. of C., 1966. Mem. Harvard Bus. Sch. Assn., Kenyon Coll. Alumni Council, Phi Beta Kappa, Beta Theta Pi. Clubs: Bankers, Casino, Mid-Am., Econ., Comml., Chicago (Chgo.); Indian Hill Country (Winnetka, Ill.); Sunningdale Golf (Berkshire, Eng.); Old Elm (Ft. Sheridan, Ill.). Home: 219 Leicester Rd Kenilworth IL 60043 Office: 1 First Nat Plaza Chicago IL 60670

THOMAS, ROBERT D., educator; b. Plymouth, Ind., Sept. 7, 1939; B.S. in Social Studies, Manchester Coll., 1962; postgrad. NDEA Ednl. Media Inst., Purdue U., Lafayette, Ind., 1965; M.S. in Social Studies, St. Francis Coll., Ft. Wayne, Ind., 1968; married; 3 children. Tchr. grade 6, playground supr. Oregon-Davis Sch. Corp., Grovertown, Ind., 1962-64; audio visual dir. chmn. dept. social studies La Ville Jr.-Sr. High Sch. Lakeville, Ind., 1964-68; audio visual dir. Columbia City (Ind.) Joint High Sch., 1968—, also auditorium mgr., sta. mgr. ednl. FM sta. Mem. NEA (life), Assn. Ind. Media Educators (charter), Ind. Assn. Sch. Broadcasters, Assn. Ednl. Communication and Tech. Cert. in secondary edn., Ind. Home: Route 9 Squawbuck Rd Columbia City IN 46725 Office: Columbia City Joint High Sch 600 N Whitley St Columbia City IN 46725

THOMAS, RONALD LEE, petroleum co. exec.; b. Stella, Mo., May 14, 1943; s. Calvin Herman and Nella Fay (Utter) T.; A.A., Joplin Jr. Coll. (now Mo. So. Coll.), 1963; student Harding U., 1962-63; B.S. in Bus. Adminstrn., Kans. State U., Pitts., 1965; M.B.A., Oklahoma City U., 1976; m. Carol Annetta Sexson, July 2, 1966; children—Craig, Trina, Gretchen, Rhonda, Shane. Acct. Phillips Petroleum Co., Bartlesville, Okla., 1965-68, computer programmer/analyst, 1968-71; systems coordinator Leggett & Platt, Inc., Carthage, Mo., 1971-72; div. controller Baxter Labs., Inc., Mountain Home, Ark., 1972-73; real estate broker Thomas Real Estate, Carthage, 1973-74; systems acct. Mid-Am. Dairymen, Inc., Springfield, Mo., 1973-74; sr. project analyst policies and procedures Champlin Petroleum Co., Enid, Okla., 1974-75, project supr., 1975-76, project mgr. fin. and gen. systems, info. services, 1976-79; controller Pester Refining Co., El Dorado, Kans., 1979-80, v.p., controller, 1980—. Served with Air N.G., 1965-70. Recipient outstanding grad. Sch. Bus. M.B.A. Faculty award, Oklahoma City U., 1976. Mem. Am. Mgmt. Assn., Inst. Mgmt. Acctg., Nat. Auctioneers Assn., Kans. Auctioneers Assn., Am. Quarter Horse Assn. Republican. Mem. Church of Christ. Home: Route 2 El Dorado KS 67042 Office: PO Box 751 El Dorado KS 67042

THOMAS, ROSE M. GREEN, health care adminstr.; b. East Chicago, Ind., Sept. 29, 1936; d. George and Rosalee (Haskins) G.; B.S. in Bus. Adminstrn., Ind. U., 1971, M.S. in Secondary Edn., 1973; cert. in Health Systems Mgmt., Harvard U., 1980. Sec., adminstrv. asst. Chgo. council Girl Scouts U.S.A., 1958-65; tchr. bus. Gary (Ind.) Sch. Corp., 1965-74; clinic adminstr. Med. Center of Gary, Ind., 1974-76; exec. dir. Midwest Assn. Community Health Centers, Inc., Chgo., 1976-80; asst. to asso. vice chancellor Urban Health program U. Ill. at Med. Center, Chgo., 1981—; instr. Ind. Tech. Vocat. Coll. Recipient Am. Cancer Soc. Vol. Service award, 1975. Mem. Nat. Assn. Community Health Centers, Nat. Assn. Health Services Execs., Am. Public Health Assn., Ind. U. Sch. Bus. Alumni Assn., Black Caucus of Health Workers, AAUW, NAACP, Nat. Urban League, League of Black Women, Delta Sigma Theta. Democrat. Clubs: TopNotchers, Inc., Chgo. Idlewilders, Inc. Home: 636 Taft Pl Gary IN 46404 Office: 1737 W Polk St Chicago IL 60612

THOMAS, RUTH, educator; b. Cheshire, Ohio, Oct. 29, 1907; d. Aaron and Laura (Tate) T.; A.B., Ohio U., 1928; M.A., Ohio State U., 1936. High sch. tchr., 1929-36, 54-63; asst. prof. English, Rio Grande (Ohio) Coll., 1964—, acting chmn. div. humanities, 1965-66. Recipient Creative Writing award in non-fiction Marietta (Ohio) Coll. Writers Conf., 1957. Mem. Faculty Assn. Rio Grande Coll. Congregationalist. Club: Philomethean. Author: (poems) Flint and Fireflies, 1942; also articles, revs. Address Dept English Rio Grande Coll Rio Grande OH 45674

THOMAS, RUTH ANN, ednl. adminstr.; b. Morrillton, Ark., Oct. 6, 1916; d. Charles B. and Lula (Byars) Roberts; B.A., Knoxville Coll., 1937; M.A. in Edn., U. Mich., 1945; postgrad. in Math. Edn., U. Toledo; m. William N. Thomas. Tchr., Gary (Ind.) Bd. Edn., 1939-45; tchr. Toledo Bd. Edn., 1947-72, coordinator Title I Math. Labs., 1972—. Co-capt. team United Appeal, 1955. Mem. Ohio, Greater Toledo, Nat. councils tchrs. math., Nat. Council Suprs. of Math., Kappa Delta Pi. Developed diagnostic instrument for use in remediation of ednl. needs in intermediate mathematics. Specialist in mathematics edn., workshops for parents and tchrs. Address: 1060 Lincoln Ave Toledo OH 43607

THOMAS, STEPHEN PAUL, lawyer; b. Bloomington, Ill., July 30, 1938; s. Owen Wilson and Mary Kathryn (Paulsen) T.; B.A., U. Ill., 1959; LL.B., Harvard U., 1962; m. Marie Anne Sauer, Dec. 7, 1963; 1 dau., Catherine. Admitted to Ill. bar, 1962; Lectr., Malawi Inst. Pub. Adminstrn., Blantyre, 1963-65; asso. firm Sidley & Austin and predecessor firms, Chgo., 1965-70, partner, 1970—. Mem. Chgo. Bar Assn., Chgo. Council Lawyers. Democrat. Roman Catholic. Home: 5740 S Harper Chicago IL 60637 Office: 1 1st Nat Plaza Chicago IL 60603

THOMAS, THOMAS STANTON, health planning/mktg. adminstr.; b. Louisiana, Mo., Nov. 3, 1944; s. Glenn S. and Hilda (Gamm) T.; B.A., Westminster Coll., Fulton, Mo., 1966; Ed.M., U. Mo., 1968; m. Nancy Lee Waller, June 7, 1967; 1 son, David Stanton. Adminstrv. asst. Mo. Regional Med. Program, Columbia, 1968-71, asst. dir., 1971-73; asst. dir. Mo. Cancer Control Program, Columbia, 1973-76, adminstrv. dir., 1976-79; div. dir. planning and shared services Boone County Hosp., Columbia, 1979—; cons. HEW region VII Center for Health Planning, 1977-79. Chmn. adv. bd. Columbia Regional Airport, 1977—, sec., 1977-78; chmn. dist. 605, Rotary Info. Inst., 1976, gov.'s aide Rotary Dist. 605; bd. dirs. Friends of Music, U. Mo., 1978—, Phi Gamma Delta Homeowners Assn., Westminster Coll., 1976—; mem. alumni council Westminster Coll.; pres. Mid-Mo. Health Consortium. Recipient Film award Indsl. Mgmt. Soc., 1970. Mem. Soc. of Research Adminstrs., Mo. Public Health Assn., Am. Health Planning Assn., Mo. Assn. for Social Welfare, Phi Delta Kappa. Presbyterian. Club: Rotary (v.p. 1975-76, pres. 1976-77). Contbr. articles on public health to profl. jours. Office: 1600 E Broadway Columbia MO 65201

THOMAS, WILLIAM, educator; b. Cairo, Ill., Jan. 1, 1935; s. William Henry and Claudia Mae (Campbell) T.; B.S., So. Ill. U., 1967, M.S., Purdue U., 1969, Ph.D., 1972; m. Majoice Lewis, Mar. 20, 1967; children—Joyce, Sharon, William, Anjanette, Marcus. Tchr., Gary (Ind.) Schs., 1967-70; adminstrv. asst. Purdue U., 1970-72, asst. prof. ednl. adminstrn., 1973-77, dir. spl. acad. services, 1973-75; asst. prof. DePauw U., 1972-73, dir. black studies, 1972-73; exec. dir. Com. on Instl. Cooperation and Midwest Program for Minorities in Engring., West Lafayette, Ind., 1975-77; v.p. Thomas Distbrs., Chgo., 1977-79; secondary instructional dir. Cairo Sch. Dist. #1, 1979-81, adminstrv. asst. to supt., 1981—. Pres. Dennis Burton Day Care Center, Lafayette, Ind., 1974-76; v.p. Tippecanoe County (Ind.) Child Care, 1977-78; cubmaster Egyptian council Boy Scouts Am., Cairo, 1979—; trustee, treas. So. Med. Center, Cairo, 1981—. Served with USAF, 1954-64. Martin Luther King, Jr. fellow, 1970-71; David Ross fellow, 1971-72. Mem. Assn. Supervision and Curriculum Devel., So. Med. Home and Bldg. Assn. (v.p. 1980—), Phi Delta Kappa. Democrat. Club: Kiwanis. Contbr. articles in field to profl. jours. Home: 2515 Washington Ave Cairo IL 62914 Office: 303 34th St Cairo IL 62914

THOMAS, WILLIAM, JR., pathologist; b. Uniontown, Pa.; s. William and Catherine (Tibbs) T.; B.S. magna cum laude, Springfield Coll., 1951; M.D., Boston U., 1955; m. Elizabeth Ann Driessen, Sept. 17, 1960; children—William C., John J., Christopher P. Intern Detroit Receiving Hosp., Hosp., 1955-56; resident Cin. Gen. Hosp., 1956-60, Henry Ford Hosp., Detroit, 1960-61; practice medicine specializing in pathology, 1961; asst. pathologist Bridgeport (Conn.) Hosp., 1961-64; asso. dir. pathology Michael Reese Hosp., Chgo., 1964-65; asso. pathologist Mt. Sinai Hosp., Chgo., 1965-66, vice-chmn. pathology dept. 1966—; asst. prof. pathology Chgo. Med. Sch., 1965-67, asso. prof., 1967-71, prof., 1971-74; asso. prof. pathology Rush Med. Sch., 1975—; asst. insp. Coll. Am. Pathology, 1974—; cons. alcohol counselor program Gov.'s State U., 1977—. Vice pres. bd. dirs. Haymarket House, 1977-78; bd. dirs. Chgo. Met. Council on Alcoholism, 1973-77; mem. Ill. Citizen's Adv. Com. on Alcoholism, 1974-80, Wilmette Housing Commn., 1978—. Served with USMC, 1945-46. Recipient Certificate of Recognition Chgo. Met. Council on Alcoholism, 1976. Fellow Am. Soc. Clin. Pathologists, Coll. Am. Pathologists, Chgo. Inst. Medicine; mem. AMA, Chgo. Soc. Med. History, Ill. Alcoholism and Drug Dependence Assn., AAUP, Chgo. Pathological Soc., Chgo. Med. Soc., Ill. Med. Soc., Ill. Soc. Pathologists, Sigma Xi, Alpha Omega Alpha. Roman Catholic. Home: 1727 Wilmette Ave Wilmette IL 60091 Office: Mt Sinai Hosp California Ave at 15th St Chicago IL 60608

THOMASETTI, HAROLD PORTER, scrap steel processing co. exec.; b. Wooster, Ohio, Aug. 16, 1952; s. John Harold and Inez Wilma (Amos) T.; B.A., Bluffton Coll., 1974; m. Suzanne Lee Gresser, Dec. 28, 1974. Tchr., asst. football coach Dalton (Ohio) schs., 1974-75; dir. purchasing, maintenance and prodn. Wooster Iron and Metal Co., 1975—; v.p. Duo Dynamics, Inc. Cert. tchr., Ohio. Mem. Inst. Scrap Iron and Steel. Baptist. Office: PO Box 173 Wooster OH 44691

THOMASSON, MARY LOU WAHLERT, radiologist; b. St. Louis, July 1, 1926; d. Ernest Henry and Myrtle Ruth (Jenkins) Wahlert; A.B., Washington U., 1946, M.D., 1951; m. Robert Edgar Thomasson, June 17, 1947; children—Mary Sue Thomasson McSwain, Jeffrey Lee. Intern, St. Louis City Hosp., 1951-52, resident in radiology, 1952-55; practice radiology Luth. Hosp., St. Louis, 1955-60, St. Francois Med. Center, Florissant, Mo., 1960—, Mo. Bapt. Hosp., St. Louis, 1963-65, DePaul Hosp., St. Louis, 1969-76; instr. St. Louis U., 1955-61; pres. St. Francois Med. Center, 1977-79. Diplomate Am. Bd. Radiology. Mem. St. Louis Med. Soc., Mo. Med. Assn., St. Louis Radiol. Soc., Am. Coll. Radiology, Radiol. Soc. N. Am., St. Louis, St. Charles hist. socs., Soc. Preservation of Old Mills, D.A.R. (publicity chmn. Cornelia Greene chpt. 1980-82), Gamma Phi Beta. Club: Eastern Star. Home: 935 Terrill Farms Rd St Louis MO 63124 Office: 525 St Francois Med Center Florissant MO 63031

THOMPSON, ADELL, JR., biologist, educator; b. Kansas City, Kans., June 17, 1932; s. Adell and Gladys (Voorhies) T.; B.S., Philander Smith Coll., 1954; M.S., Kans. State Tchrs. Coll., Pittsburg, 1958; Ph.D., U. Mo., Kansas City, 1974; m. Jacque D. Nichols, Aug. 6, 1955; 1 son, Adell III. Tchr., Kansas City Sch. Dist., 1958-64, chmn. sci. dept. Central High Sch., Kansas City, Mo., 1965-67, sci. cons., 1967-69; instr. sci. edn. and biology U. Mo., Kansas City, 1969-74, asst. prof., 1975-78, asso. prof. sci. edn. and biology, 1978—. State dir. Mo. Jr. Acad. Sci.; active Boy Scouts Am.; bd. dirs. Sci. Pioneers of Greater Kansas City. Served with M.C., U.S. Army, 1955-57. Mem. Nat. Sci. Tchrs. Assn., Nat. Assn. Research in Sci. Teaching, Nat. Assn. Biology Tchrs., Assn. Edn. of Tchrs. Sci., Mo. Coll. Biology Tchrs. Assn., Sci. Tchrs. Mo., Mo. Acad. Sci., Kansas City Sci. Tchrs. Assn. (adv. bd.), Phi Delta Kappa, Alpha Phi Alpha, Alpha Kappa Mu. Baptist. Home: 9700 Winslow Pl Kansas City MO 64131 Office: 5100 Rockhill Rd Univ Mo Kansas City MO 64110

THOMPSON, ALLEN LYLE, health ins. co. exec.; b. Whitehall, Wis., Feb. 1, 1931; s. Antone Clarence and Blanche Marion (Anderson) T.; B.S. in Acctg., Kans. State U., 1964; m. Patricia Ellen Aylward, Dec. 15, 1956; children—Kris Patrick, Paul Allen, Mark Allen. Salesman, Philip Morris Tobacco Co., Manhattan, Kans., 1964-66; with Blue Cross-Blue Shield, Topeka, 1966—, project mgr., 1969-72, mgmt. devel. dir., 1972—. Active local United Fund, PTA. Served to lt. col. U.S. Army, 1950-59. Decorated Bronze Star, Commendation medal. Mem. Am. Soc. Tng. and Devel., Kam Valley Personnel Assn., Am. Legion, Alpha Kappa Psi. Roman Catholic. Clubs: Optimist Boys, K.C. Home: 1804 Campbell St Topeka KS 66604 Office: 1133 Topeka Ave Topeka KS 66629

THOMPSON, ANGELINE CHARLOTTE, village ofcl.; b. Barron County, Wis., 1922; d. Howard and Florence Mable (Kritch) Sheldon; m. Vernon Thompson, June 16, 1941; children—Sandra, Linda, Howard. Village pres. Haugen (Wis.), 1975—. Address: Haugen WI 54841

THOMPSON, CARL WILLIAM, state legislator; b. Washington, Mar. 15, 1914; Ph.D., U. Wis., Madison, 1936, LL.D., 1939; married; 4 children. Admitted to Wis. Bar, 1939; practiced law, Stoughton, Wis., 1939—; real estate broker, 1952—; mem. Wis. Assembly, 1953-59, Wis. Senate, 1959—. Mem. Democratic Nat. Com., 1949-56, presdl. elector, 1948; del. Dem. Nat. Conv., 1952, 56. Served with U.S. Army, 1942-46. Mem. VFW, Am. Legion, Sons of Norway. Club: Rotary. Office: Room 32-A South State Capitol Madison WI 53702

THOMPSON, DALE MOORE, banker; b. Kansas City, Kans., Nov. 19, 1897; s. George Curl and Ruth Anna (Moore) T.; A.B. cum laude, U. Mich., 1920; m. Dorothy Allen Brown, July 2, 1921; 1 son, William

Brown (dec.). Trainee, City Bank of Kansas City (Mo.) (now United Mo. Bank, N.A.), 1920-22, asst. cashier, 1922-27, asst. v.p., 1927-30, v.p., 1930-34; v.p. City Bond & Mortgage Co. Kansas City (now United Mo. Mortgage Co.), 1934-43, exec. v.p., 1943-48, pres., 1948-68, chmn. bd., 1968-74, hon. chmn. bd., 1974—, also dir.; chmn., trustee Central Mortgage & Realty Trust, 1972-76, hon. chmn., 1976—; v.p. Regency Bldg. Co., Kansas City. Lectr. Northwestern U. Sch. Mortgage Banking, also Stanford, 1954-62. Mem. Mo. Gov.' Com. on Arts; chmn. Kansas City campaign United Negro Coll. Fund, 1958-59; mem. Mo. State Bd. Edn., 1966—; pres. Kansas City Philharm. Assn., 1944-54, also trustee; trustee U. Kansas City, Conservatory Music Kansas City, Kansas City Art Inst., Kansas City Children's Mercy Hosp.; treas. Kansas City Truman Med. Center. Served with USN World War I. Recipient citation Kansas City C. of C., 1954, Archbishop's Community Service citation, 1954, citation NCCJ, 1965; Mayor's citation, 1955. Mem. Mortgage Bankers Assn. Am. (nat. pres. 1962-63, Distinguished Service award 1966, life mem. bd. govs.), U. Mich. Alumni Assn. (past dir.), Phi Beta Kappa (pres. Kansas City 1946-49), Trigon, Phi Kappa Psi. Mem. Christian Ch. Clubs: River, University, Indian Hills Country (Kansas City); Monterey Peninsula Country (Pebble Beach, Calif.). Home: 221 W 48th St Kansas City MO 64112 Office: United Mo Bank Bldg Kansas City MO 64106

THOMPSON, DOROTHY BROWN, writer; b. Springfield, Ill., May 14, 1896; d. William Joseph and Harriet (Gardner) Brown; A.B., U. of Kansas, 1919; m. Dale Moore Thompson, July 2, 1921; 1 son, William B. (dec.). Began writing professionally, 1931; contributed verse to nat. magazines and newspapers including Saturday Review, Sat. Eve. Post, Va. Quar. Rev., Poetry, Commonweal, Good Housekeeping and others, author research articles for various historical jours.; poems pub. in over two hundred collections and textbooks; magazines and textbooks pub. in Eng., Australia, New Zealand, Canada, Sweden; twenty-five in Braille. Leader poetry sect. Writers' Conf., U. Kan., 1953-55, McKendree Coll., 1961, 63, Creighton U., Omaha, 1966; lectr. writers' conf. U. Kan., 1965, Am. Poets Series, Kansas City, Mo., 1973; mem. staff Poets Workshop, Central Mo. State U., 1974; poet-in-schs. residency for Mo. State Council of Arts, 1974—. Received Mo. Writers' Guild Award, 1941, Poetry Soc. Am., nat. and local awards. Mem. Diversifiers, Poetry Soc. Am., Nat. Soc. Colonial Dames, First Families of Va. (Burgess for Mo.). Mem. Christian Ch. Clubs: Woman's City, Filson (Louisville). Author: Subject to Change (poems), 1973. Address: 221 W 48th St Apt 1402 Kansas City MO 64112

THOMPSON, EVAN LEWIS, librarian; b. Fall River, Mass., Aug. 26, 1918; s. Alexander Joseph and Mary Ellen (Ankarstran) T.; A.B., Duke U., 1940, M.A. in English Lit., 1942; postgrad. Boston U., 1946, Ohio State U., 1951-54; M.S. in L.S., Simmons Coll., 1955; m. Edith Emily Swift, Feb. 6, 1948; 1 dau., Dianne Alexandra. Instr., Moses Brown Sch., Providence, 1946-47; instr. English, Purdue U., 1947-49, U. Maine, Orono, 1949-51; adult asst. Detroit Public Library, 1955, 1st asst., 1958-60, chief div., Bowen br. librarian, 1960-61, chief dept. lang. and lit. Main Library, 1961-73, asst. dir. Westside brs., 1973—; judge Wayne State U. Annual Playwriting Contest. Bd. dirs., pres. Library Credit Union, Detroit, 1968-70; bd. dirs. Parkside Day Care Center, Detroit, 1969, v.p., 1970, pres., 1971-72. Served with USAF, 1942-46. Mem. ALA, Mich. Library Assn., Detroit Library Staff Assn. (pres. 1959-60), Library Staff Meml. and Fellowship Assn. (treas. 1963, pres. 1964-65), Book Club Detroit (pres. 1970-71), Charles Lamb Soc., Phi Kappa Sigma, Kappa Kappa Psi. Episcopalian. Clubs: Friends of Detroit Public Library; Williams (N.Y.C.). Home: 4261 Bishop Rd Detroit MI 48224 Office: 5201 Woodward Ave Detroit MI 48202

THOMPSON, FRANK HUNT, educator; b. Bellingham, Wash., June 8, 1929; s. Frank Hunt and Ethel (Harold) T.; B.A., Seattle Pacific U., 1951; M.Div., Asbury Theol. Sem., 1962; Th.M. (Woodrow Wilson fellow), Princeton Theol. Sem., 1963; m. Marilyn Louise Rudolph, Nov. 24, 1950; children—Margaret Elizabeth, John Gregory, Anne Catherine. Ordained to ministry Free Methodist Ch., 1950; pastor Free Meth. Chs., National, Wash., 1951-52, Sumner, Wash., 1952-56, Tonasket, Wash., 1956-59; interim supply pastor Plattsburg Presbyterian Ch., Wrightstown, N.J., 1964-67, Carlyle (Ill.) Presbyn. Ch., 1970-74; asso. prof. philosophy and religion Greenville (Ill.) Coll., 1967-77, prof., 1977—, chmn. dept., 1969-77, 78—, dir. spl. acad. sessions, 1976-77, 78—, acting dean, v.p. acad. affairs, 1977-78; Danforth faculty asso., 1969—; instr., speaker ministers and bible confs. Republican committeeman Bond County Central Precinct 2, 1974—; Rep. mem. Bond County Bd., 1976—; del. Ill. Rep. Conv., 1976; chmn. drive Bond County unit ARC, 1977; bd. dirs. Southwestern Ill. Law Enforcement Commn., 1976—, 1st v.p., 1978—, recipient Service award, 1978. Mem. Am. Acad. Religion, Soc. Bibl. Lit., Am. Schs. Oriental Research, Wesleyan Theol. Soc., Ill. Assn. County Bd. Mems., County Commrs. and Suprs. Republican. Club: Kiwanis. Contbr. articles to religious publs. Home: 407 LaDue Pl Greenville IL 62246 Office: Greenville Coll Greenville IL 62246

THOMPSON, GEORGE HARMAN, pediatrician, orthopaedic surgeon; b. San Angelo, Tex., Oct. 8, 1944; s. Rolla George and Bonnie Lee (Harman) T.; B.S., Okla. State U., 1966; M.D., Okla. U., 1970; m. Janice Lynne Ellison, June 9, 1967; children—Brian, Scott, Kathryn, Bradley. Intern, UCLA Med. Center, 1970-71, resident in gen. and orthopaedic surgery, 1971-77; fellow in pediatric orthopaedics U. Toronto, 1978; asst. prof. orthopaedic surgery and pediatrics Case Western Res. U., Cleve., 1979—; dir. pediatric orthopaedics Cleve. Met. Gen. Hosp. Served to maj. M.C., USAF, 1972-74. Named Outstanding Surg. Intern, UCLA, 1970-71; N.Am. Traveling fellow, 1979; diplomate Am. Bd. Orthopaedic Surgery. Mem. Am. Acad. Cerebral Palsy and Devel. Medicine, No. Ohio Pediatric Soc., Cleve. Spine Club, Sigma Xi. Republican. Episcopalian. Editor: (with Robert M. Bilenker and Leslie Rubin) Comprehensive Management in Cerebral Palsy, 1981; (with G.R. Houghton) Problem Fractures in Children, 1982; contbr. articles profl. jours., chpts. in books. Home: 21249 Claythorne Rd Shaker Heights OH 44122 Office: 3395 Scranton Rd Cleveland OH 44109

THOMPSON, GEORGE LEROY, design engr.; b. Elwood, Nebr., Aug. 2, 1952; s. Leonard and Mary (Tillotson) T.; student Kearney State Coll., 1970-72; B.S.M.E., U. Nebr., 1976; postgrad. U. No. Iowa, 1979-80; m. Linda Susan Philo, June 22, 1980. Design engr. Maytag Co., Newton, Iowa, 1977-79; design engr. Doerfer div. Container Corp. Am., Cedar Falls, Iowa, 1979—. Mem. ASME, Pi Tau Sigma. Republican. Methodist. Home: 3708 Eastpark Rd Cedar Falls IA 50613 Office: 201 Washington St Cedar Falls IA 50613

THOMPSON, JAMES FRANK, banker, fin. cons.; b. Chgo., July 3, 1944; s. J. Frank and Lillian Elma Marie (Pitt) T.; B.S., Ind. State U., 1966; M.B.A., Butler U., 1974; m. Priscilla Jane Fountain, Dec. 10, 1980; children—Jason Frank, Amy Jo, Jeremy Miles, Barbara Lynn McGuire, Nelson Metcalfe McGuire III. With Mchts. Nat. Bank & Trust Co. of Indpls., 1966—, v.p., sr. loan rev. officer, div. loan rev., 1971—, v.p. and div. exec., div. comml. banking, asst. v.p., div. loan adminstrn., br. mgr. Kentucky Ave. office; instr. banking Ind. Central U. Served with U.S. Army, 1966-72. Mem. Robert Morris Assos., Nat. Assn. Accts. Clubs: Lions, Masons, Shriners.

THOMPSON, JAMES ROBERT, gov. Ill.; b. Chgo., May 8, 1936; s. J. Robert and Agnes Josephine (Swanson) T.; student U. Ill., Washington U., St. Louis; LL.B., No. U., 1959; m. Jayne Anne Carr, June 19, 1976; 1 dau., Samantha. Admitted to Ill. bar; prosecutor, Cook County States Atty.'s Office, Chgo., 1959-64; asso. prof. Northwestern U. Law Sch., 1964-69; chief dept. law enforcement and pub. protection Atty. Gen.'s Office, 1969-70; asst. U.S. atty. No. Dist. Ill., 1970-71, U.S. atty., 1971-75; gov. Ill., 1977—. Author: Cases in Common on Criminal Procedure; Cases in Common on Criminal Law; Criminal Law and Its Administration. Office: 207 State House Springfield IL 62706

THOMPSON, KENNETH ROY, educator; b. Elgin, Ill., Feb. 8, 1948; s. Glenn R. and Margaret L. (Johnson) T.; B.A., Elmhurst Coll., 1970; M.B.A., No. Ill. U., 1972; Ph.D., U. Nebr., 1977; m. Ann Marie Wesley, June 7, 1980. Teaching asst. No. Ill. U., DeKalb, 1970-71; instr. mgmt. and fin. Ind. State U., Terre Haute, 1972-74; instr. mgmt. U. Nebr., Lincoln, 1974-77; asst. prof. mgmt. U. Notre Dame (Ind.), 1977—; lectr. to various community groups, 1975—; cons. in organizational planning and strategy, 1975—. Recipient Excellence in Teaching award U. Nebr., 1977. Mem. Midwest Acad. Mgmt., Assn. for Bus. Simulation and Exptl. Learning, Am. Inst. for Decision Scis. Mem. United Ch. of Christ. Author: (with R. Pitts) The Supervisor's Survival Guide, 1979; (with F. Luthans and D. Hodgetts) Social Issues in Business, 1980; (with F. Luthans) Organizational Behavior: Instructor's Manual, 1981, Contemporary Readings in Organizational Behavior, 1981; contbr. articles on mgmt. to profl. publs. Home: 52137 Fieldstone Ln Granger IN 46530 Office: College of Bus Adminstrn U Notre Dame Notre Dame IN 46556

THOMPSON, KENRICK STEVEN, sociologist; b. Syracuse, N.Y., May 1, 1946; s. George Greene and Evelyn (Schuyler) T.; B.A., Ohio State U., 1967, M.A., 1970, Ph.D., 1974; m. Christina Jane Thompson; 1 dau., Shelley Lynne. Spl. research asst. Ohio State U., summer 1968, teaching asst. dept. sociology, 1968-70, teaching asso., 1972-74; asst. prof. dept. sociology No. Mich. U., Marquette, 1974-78, asso. prof., 1978—; extension tchr. K.I. Sawyer AFB, Mich., Mich. Dept. Corrections, Marquette Br. Prison. Named Outstanding Young Man of Am., U.S. Jaycees, 1977. Mem. Am., North Central sociol. assns., Midwest Sociol. Soc., Nat. Council on Family Relations, Am. Soc. Criminology, Soc. for Study Social Problems, AAUP, Mich. Assn. U. Profs. Co-author: Social Problems: Divergent Perspectives; The Divorce Profile: Differential Social Correlates in 1952 and in 1972, 1978; contbr. articles to profl. jours. Home: 611 Mesnard St Marquette MI 49855

THOMPSON, LOREN J., supt. public schs.; b. Farwell, Tex., Dec. 19, 1932; s. Charles L. and Ella (Khalden) T.; B.A. in History and English, Eastern N.Mex. U., 1958; M.A. in History, U. Del., 1960, postgrad. 1961-70; Ph.D. in Edn., Ohio State U., 1970; m. Mary Anne Thompson, Jan. 26, 1955; children—Philip Scott, Lisa Dianne. Instr. history and govt. Abilene (Tex.) Christian Coll., 1960-61; tchr. social studies and English, Newark (Del.) Sch. Dist., 1961-67, prin., 1970-75, dir. instrn. 1975-78; grad. asst. philosophy of edn. and curriculum Ohio State U., Columbus, 1969-70, vis. prof., summer, 1972; adminstrv. dir. curriculum New Castle County (Del.) Sch. Dist., 1978-79; supt. schs. Bexley City Sch. Dist., Columbus, 1979—; founder, pres. Lormar Edn. Cons.; cons. curriculum orgn. Lower Merion Sch. Dist., Pa., 1979, Hillsborough County (Fla.) Public Schs., 1979; cons. Ednl. Testing Service, Princeton, N.J., 1981. Bd. dirs. Family Counseling and Crittenton Services. Served with USN, 1951-55; Korea. Recipient Outstanding Young Educator award Del. Jaycees, 1965; Humanitarian award Mayor of Bexley (Ohio), 1981; cert. tchr. and prin., Del.; cert. supt. schs., Del., Ohio. Mem. Am. Assn. Sch. Adminstrs., Am. Ednl. Research Assn., Assn. for Supervision and Curriculum Devel., Phi Delta Theta. Democrat. Club: Rotary. Contbr. articles on learning process and teaching to profl. publs. Home: 137 S Cassingham Rd Columbus OH 43209 Office: 348 S Cassingham Rd Columbus OH 43209

THOMPSON, MARVIN DELMAR, educator; b. New Market, Iowa, Oct. 17, 1920; s. Charles Ivan and Mamie Harriet (Arthur) T.; B.S., Iowa State U., 1947, M.S., 1950, Ph.D., 1955; m. Phyllis Louise Shafer, Sept. 3, 1950; 1 son, Marlin Shafer. Tchr., public schs., Dunlap, Iowa, 1948-50; instr. Iowa State U., 1947, 50-53; asst. prof. agrl. edn. U. Wis., River Falls, 1953-56, asso. prof., 1956-59, prof., 1959—, acting dean Grad. Sch., 1967-68, chmn. dept. agrl. edn., 1961—; cons. AID, Nigeria, 1965. Mem. River Falls Park Bd., 1958-68; mem. Pierce County (Wis.) Selective Service Bd., 1958-72. Served with Signal Corps, U.S. Army, 1943-46. Recipient Disting. Service award Future Farmers Am., 1975, named Hon. Am. Farmer, 1976. Mem. Am. Vocat. Assn., Wis. Assn. Vocat. and Adult Edn., Nat. Vocat. Agr. Tchrs. Assn., Wis. Assn. Vocat. Agr. Instrs., Am. Assn. Tchr. Educators in Agr., Assn. Univ. Wis. Faculties, Gamma Sigma Delta, Phi Kappa Phi, Phi Delta Kappa, Alpha Tau Alpha. Republican. Methodist. Club: Masons. Contbr. articles to profl. jours. Home: 516 Birch St River Falls WI 54022 Office: U Wis River Falls WI 54022

THOMPSON, MICHAEL, lawyer; b. Des Moines, Aug. 2, 1951; s. Harold L. and Carolyn (Yacinich) T.; B.A., U. No. Iowa, 1973; J.D., U. Iowa, 1975, M.A., 1976; m. Barbara Ann Haafke, Oct. 29, 1977. Admitted to Iowa bar, 1976, N.Y. bar, 1978, Mo. bar, 1980; asst. atty. gen. Iowa Dept. Justice, Des Moines, 1976; economist Iowa Commerce Commn., Des Moines, 1976-77; spl. asst. to N.Y. State Public Service Commn., Albany, 1977-80; att. Mo. Pacific R.R. Co., St. Louis, 1980—; adj. instr. in corp. fin. Drake U., 1977. State chmn. Iowa Coll. Young Republicans., 1973. Mem. Am. Bar Assn., N.Y. State Bar Assn., St. Louis Bar Assn., Am. Econ. Assn., Atlantic Econ. Soc. Home: 14 N Kingshwy Blvd Apt 4 Saint Louis MO 63108 Office: Mo Pacific RR 210 N 13th St Saint Louis MO 63103

THOMPSON, MORLEY PUNSHON, mfg. co. exec.; b. San Francisco, Jan. 2, 1927; s. Morley Punshon and Ruth (Wetmore) T.; A.B., Stanford U., 1948; M.B.A., Harvard U., 1950; J.D., Chase Law Sch., 1969; m. Patricia Ann Smith, Jan. 31, 1953; children—Page Elizabeth, Morley Punshon. With Baldwin-United Corp., Cin., 1950—, dir., 1962—, v.p., 1967-70, pres., 1970—; dir. Midland Co., Cin. Milacron Inc., Kroger Co., Cin. Bell, Stearns & Foster, Inc., Anchor Hocking Corp., FMC Corp. Bd. dirs. Cin. Inst. Fine Arts. Served to lt. Supply Corps, USNR, 1952-54. C.P.A., Ohio. Mem. Beta Theta Pi. Office: 1801 Gilbert Ave Cincinnati OH 45202

THOMPSON, ORVILLE KENNETH, steel co. exec.; b. Pikeville, Ky., Nov. 14, 1948; s. Orville and Lillian T. (Scott) T.; student public schs., Pikeville; m. Janice Phillips, Dec. 30, 1978; children—Richard K., Kristen Lynn. Slitter operator Redway Storage Co., Detroit, 1966-73; gen. mgr. Dawson Steel Corp., Roseville, Mich., 1973-76; salesman Franklin Steel Corp., Southfield, Mich., 1976-77; pres. MST Steel Corp., Roseville, 1977—. Home: 11611 Eldorado Sterling Heights MI 48077 Office: MST Steel Corp 21847 Schmeman Warren MI 48077

THOMPSON, PAUL LELAND, artist; b. Buffalo, Iowa, May 20, 1911; s. Buell and Flora Elizabeth (Steen) T.; student Calif. Sch. Fine Arts, 1932-34, Corcoran Sch. Art, 1944-45; m. Phyllis McGregor, June 15, 1953; 1 dau., Leslie Ruth. One-man shows Internat. Galleries, Washington, 1946, M. Knoedler Co. Inc., 1954, Unitarian Ch., Plainfield, N.J., 1975, Cin. Art Club, 1978, others; exhibited group shows Seattle Art Mus., 1937, Honolulu Acad. Art, 1933, Corcoran Biennial Nat. Painting Exhbn., 1945, San Francisco Palace of Legion of Honor, 1948, San Francisco Art Mus., 1948, NAD Nat. Watercolor Exhbn., 1956, Hunterdon County Art Center, Clinton, N.J., 1968; executed two murals Shiloh Baptist Ch., Plainfield, N.J.; represented in permanent collections Barry's Art Gallery, Scotch Plains, N.J., The Heritage Gallery, Cin. Recipient Soc. Washington Artists prize, 1946; Washington Times Herald award, 1947. Mem. Artists Equity N.Y., Artists Equity N.J., N.J. Watercolor Soc., Somerset Art Assn., Cin. McDowell Soc., Am. Inst. Conservation Works of Art, Internat. Inst. Conservation Works of Art, Art Club. Home: 314 Ludlow Ave Cincinnati OH 45220 Office: 3412 Telford St Cincinnati OH 45220

THOMPSON, PHEBE KIRSTEN, physician; b. Glace Bay, N.S., Can., Sept. 5, 1897; d. Peter and Catherine (McKeigan) Christianson; M.D., C.M. Dalhousie U., Halifax, N.S., 1923; m. Willard Owen Thompson, M.D., June 21, 1923 (dec. Mar. 1954); children—Willard Owen, Frederic, Nancy, Donald. Came to U.S., 1923, naturalized, 1937. Intern Children's Hosp., Halifax, N.S., 1922-23; asst. biochemistry, dept. applied physiology Harvard Sch. Pub. Health, 1924-26; asst. and research fellow in medicine thyroid clinic, Mass. Gen. Hosp., Boston, 1926-29; asst. in metabolism dept. (endocrinology) Rush Med. Coll. of U. Chgo. and The Central Free Dispensary Chgo., 1930-46; asso. with husband in practice medicine, Chgo., 1947-54; mng. editor Jour. Clin. Endocrinology and Metabolism, 1954-61, cons. editor, 1961-65; editor Jour. Am. Geriatrics Soc., 1954—; cons. editor Endocrinology, 1961-65; free-lance editor and writer. Recipient Thewlis award Am. Geriatrics Soc., 1966; certificate of appreciation Am. Thyroid Assn., 1966. Fellow Am. Med. Writers' Assn. (adv. com. 1955-60, v.p. Chgo. 1962), Am. Geriatrics Soc., Gerontological Soc. Am.; mem. Endocrine Soc., AAAS, Am. Genetic Assn., Am. Pub. Health Assn., Ill. Pub. Health Assn., Ill. Acad. Scis., Art Inst. Chgo. (life), Chgo. Hist. Soc. (life). Clubs: Univ.; Harvard; Canadian (corr. sec. 1968-73; mem. bd. 1973-76). Address: 2300 Lincoln Park W Chicago IL 60614

THOMPSON, RAYMOND DAVID, computer co. exec.; b. Dawson, Minn., Apr. 20, 1933; s. Peter and Maria (Oslund) T.; B.A., U. Minn., 1961; m. Barbara D. Hofstad, Oct. 16, 1954; children—Michael P., Scott D. With Honeywell Co., Mpls., 1952-68, guidance control coordinator, 1961-66, bus. adminstr., 1966-68; with Sperry Univac, St. Paul, 1968—, mgr. div. govt. liaison, 1976—, also group mgr. Air Force, Army, civilian agys. and internat. contracts, def. systems div. Mem. Longfellow Community Council, 1968; v.p. PTA, 1967; mem. Citizens Com. on Public Edn., 1966-67. Mem. U. Minn. Alumni Assn., Nat. Contract Mgmt. Assn., Electronic Industries Assn., Nat. Security Indsl. Assn. Republican. Lutheran. Home: 17885 Italy Path W Lakeville MN 55044 Office: PO Box 3525 MS U1-J13 St Paul MN 55165

THOMPSON, RENOLD DURANT, mining, transp. and mfg. co. exec.; b. Cleve., July 28, 1926; s. James Renold and Gertrude Goldie (Meyers) T.; B.A., Dartmouth Coll., 1946; B.S., Case Inst. Tech., 1948; m. Shirley Ann Sprague, June 24, 1949; children—Renold Durant, Bradley Sprague, Patricia Sprague. Metallurgist, Am. Steel and Wire div. U.S. Steel Corp., Duluth, Minn., Cleve., 1948-52; salesman ore dept. Oglebay Norton Co., Cleve., 1952-57, asst. mgr. ore sales dept., 1957-59, exec. asst., 1959-61, asst. to pres., 1961-65, sec., asst. to pres., 1965-69, v.p. Oglebay Norton Co., gen. mgr. Ferro Engrng. div., 1969-70, v.p. vessel and mining ops., 1970-72, sr. v.p., 1972-73, exec. v.p. ops., 1973-81, exec. v.p., 1981—; dir. Central Nat. Bank Cleve., Centran Corp., Lubrizol Corp., Oglebay Norton Co.; dir., v.p. Columbia Transp. Co., Eveleth Taconite Co., Locking River Terminal Co., Saginaw Mining Co., Tex. Mining Co.; vice-chmn. mgmt. com. Eveleth Expansion Co. Served with USN, 1944-46. Mem. AIME, Am. Iron Ore Assn., Am. Iron and Steel Inst., Am. Mining Congress, Eastern States Blast Furnace and Coke Oven Assn., Lake Carrier's) Assn. Clubs: Duquesne, Hillbrook, Mayfield Country, Pepper Pike, Tavern, Union. Home: 14883 Hillbrook Dr Hunting Valley Chagrin Falls OH 44022 Office: Suite 2000 1100 Superior Ave Cleveland OH 44114

THOMPSON, RICHARD NEIL, lawyer; b. Newman Grove, Nebr., Nov. 20, 1933; s. Oscar T. and Gladys M. (Olson) T.; student Wayne State Coll., Nebr., 1951-52; B.S. in Law, U. Nebr., 1955, J.D., 1957; m. Dorothy M. Bilson, Aug. 15, 1957; children—Pamela Sue, Richard Neil, Beth Ann. Admitted to Nebr. bar, 1957, asso. firm Cline, Williams, Wright, Johnson & Oldfather, Lincoln, Nebr., 1957-60, mem. firm, 1960-70, Thompson & Sweet, Lincoln, 1970-75; individual practice law, Lincoln, 1975—; sec., dir. Spencer Foods, Inc. (Iowa), 1972-78. Bd. dirs. Lincoln Symphony Assn., 1975-78; trustee Westminster Ch. Found., 1975—, chmn. investment com., 1975—. Served with AUS, 1950-58. Mem. Lincoln, Nebr., Am. (com. fed. regulation securities, 1969—) bar assns., Lincoln C. of C., Phi Delta Phi, Pi Delta Kappa, Phi Gamma Delta. Presbyterian. Clubs: Lincoln U., Lincoln Country, Palmas del mar. Home: 2909 Bonacum Dr Lincoln NE 68592 Office: 968 NBC Center Lincoln NE 68508

THOMPSON, RICHARD WRIGHT, anthropologist; b. Long Branch, N.J., Feb. 16, 1947; s. Richard Ballentine and Wilna Bennett (Wright) T.; B.A., U. Mo., Columbia, 1969, M.A., 1970, Ph.D. in Anthropology, 1973; m. Cheryl J. Martin, Sept. 29, 1967; children—Kenya Elizabeth, Jeremy Lowell, Laura Rebecca. Research asso. Makerere Inst. Social Research, Kampala, Uganda, 1972-73, sr. research asso., 1975-76; vis. asst. prof. anthropology Lawrence U., Appleton, Wis., 1973-74; fellow Inst. African Studies, U. Nairobi, 1976; asst. prof. anthropology U. Ill., Urbana, 1976—. Fellow Am. Anthrop. Assn. Asso. editor Am. Ethnologist, 1979-81; pres. Intermarc, 1979-81. Office: Dept of Anthropology University of Illinois Urbana IL 61801

THOMPSON, ROBERT O'HAIR, ednl. adminstr.; b. Marshall, Mo., Nov. 7, 1925; s. Roy Melvin and Alice Merle (O'Hair) T.; B.A. in Philosophy-Religion, Earlham Coll., Richmond, Ind., 1946; B.D., U. Chgo., 1954, M.A. in Philos. Theology, 1962, Ph.D., 1970; m. Mary Louise Roettger, Sept. 2, 1950; children—Margaret, Ann, Katherine. Instr., Kendall Coll., Chgo., 1961-67, dean, 1967-70, instr., chmn. humanities div., 1971-72, dean, 1972-73; dean U. Wis.-Washington County, West Bend, 1973—. Bd. dirs. Washington County Campus Found., Kettle Moraine YMCA. Mem. Am. Philos. Assn., Am. Acad. Religion. Club: Rotary. Home: 745 Highland View Dr West Bend WI 53095 Office: 400 University Dr West Bend WI 53095

THOMPSON, RONALD KEITH, ednl. adminstr.; b. Fayette County, Ohio, Nov. 26, 1933; s. Daniel H. and Roxie B. (Welsh) T.; B.S., Wilmington Coll., 1957; M.S. Wittenberg U., 1969; postgrad. U. Dayton, Wright State U., Ohio U.; m. Wilma J. Brown, May 2, 1954; 1 dau., Kris Elen. Tchr., public schs., Miami Trace, Ohio, 1957-62, adminstr., 1962-69; prin. elementary sch. Vandalia-Butler City (Ohio) Schs., 1969-74, asst. supt., 1974-80; supt. sch., Washington Court House (Ohio) City Schs., 1980—; dir. Hopewell Spl. Edn. Resource Center; cons. U. Dayton, Wright State U. Mem. Assn. Supervision and Curriculum Devel., Buckeye Assn. Sch. Adminstrs. Presbyterian.

Clubs: Rotary, Masons, Scottish Rite, Shriners. Home: 1006 Briar Ave Washington Court House OH 43160 Office: 323 E Paint St Washington Court House OH 43160

THOMPSON, THOMAS EXCELL, ednl. adminstr.; b. Chgo., June 13, 1949; s. James and Lucille Loretta T.; B.S., U. Ill., 1970, M.Ed., 1974, Ed.D., 1977; m. Joann Williams, Aug. 28, 1971; children—Thomas LaMarr, Brandynne Jonne. Tchr. math, Westinghouse High Sch., Chgo., 1970-74; coordinator, cons. Ednl. Placement Office U. Ill., Champaign, 1974-77; asst. dir. Title VII program Champaign Community Sch. Dist. No.4, 1977; asst. prin. Aldrich High Sch., Beloit, Wis., 1977-80, Beloit Meml. High Sch., 1980—. Bd. dirs. Beloit Boys' Clubs, 1977—, Stateline United Givers, 1979—; mem. exec. bd. Sinnissippi council Boy Scouts Am. B.L. Dodds scholar, 1975. Mem. Black Resources Personnel, Beloit Prins. Assn. (pres. 1981-83), Assn. Supervision and Curriculum Devel., Alpha Phi Alpha, Phi Delta Kappa. Democrat. Baptist. Office: 1225 4th St Beloit WI 53511

THOMPSON, WILLIAM RUTLEDGE, ins. agt.; b. Atlantic City, Aug. 25, 1938; s. William Phillips and Mary (Rutledge) T.; B.A., Ohio Wesleyan U., 1960; m. Sally June Decker, May 18, 1963; children—Douglas, Julia. Underwriter, Ohio Casualty Ins. Group, Hamilton, Ohio, 1960-61; mgr. surety bonds Travelers Ins. Co., Cleve., Mpls., Hartford, Conn. and Cin., 1963-75; partner Brower Ins. Agy., Dayton, Ohio, 1975—. Vice-chmn. ann. fund council Ohio Wesleyan U., 1978—; bd. dirs. Dayton Ballet, Kettering Hosp. Served with USNR, 1961-63. Mem. Nat. Assn. Surety Bond Producers, Asso. Gen. Contractors, Ohio Contractors Assn., Surety Underwriters So. Ohio (pres. 1974), Asso. Bldg. Contractors, Alpha Tau Omega, Methodist. Clubs: Engrs. Dayton, Dayton Racquet, Dayton Country. Home: 3573 Springdale Dr Kettering OH 45419 Office: Brewer Ins Agy 8 N Main St PO Box 37 Dayton OH 45401

THOMPSON-JOHNSON, LAJEWELL SAUNDRA, tng. and computer specialist; b. Chgo., Nov. 20, 1949; d. Maxera and Pearl (Banks) Tolen; A.A., Wilson City Coll., 1969; B.S., Chgo. State U., 1971; M.A., Govs. State U., 1973; m. Clarence Thompson, May 10, 1980; 1 son by previous marriage, Jeffrey S. Johnson. Tng. analyst Oak Forest (Ill.) Hosp., 1969-80; adminstr./asst. Sauk Career Center, Robbins, Ill., 1974—; tng./computer specialist Rehab. Inst. Chgo., 1980—; cons. in field. Mem. Ill. Edn. Assn., United Coalition for Legis. Action, Nat. Assn. Public Adult and Continuing Edn., Public Adult Continuing Edn., NEA, Phi Beta Lambda. Office: 345 E Superior Chicago IL 60611

THOMSON, JOHN WILLIAM, pediatrician, cons.; b. Van Horne, Iowa, July 27, 1913; s. Thomas Lewis and Marguerite (Connell) T.; A.B., Augustana Coll., 1934; M.S., U. Mich., 1937, M.D., 1940, M.P.H., 1962; m. Linda Melita Bauer, Oct. 12, 1940; children—James W., Thomas G., Mary M., Martha A. Intern, U. Mich. Hosp., Ann Arbor, 1940-41, resident, 1946-48; instr. in pediatrics U. Mich., 1947-48; pvt. practice medicine specializing in pediatrics, Grand Rapids, Mich., 1948-61; pediatric cons., med. coordinator Mich. Crippled Children Program, Lansing, 1962-81; asst. clin. prof. human devel., audiology and speech scis. Mich. State U., 1965—. Mem. social concerns com., mem. pastoral affairs commn. Peoples Ch., East Lansing, Mich. Served with USPHS, 1941-46. Diplomate Am. Bd. Pediatrics. Fellow Am. Acad. Pediatrics (Mich. chmn. handicapped com. 1956-60), Am. Public Health Assn. (mem. family planning com. 1968-74); mem. Minn. Public Health Assn. Home: 625 Butterfield Dr East Lansing MI 48823

THOMSON, KENNETH ERVIN, sch. adminstr.; b. Chambers, Nebr., Feb. 14, 1941; s. Willard Ervin and Billie Maxine (Turner) T.; B.A. in Edn., Wayne State Coll., 1962; M.A., U. Nebr., Lincoln, 1974, Ed.D., 1980; m. Sandra Jane Boehler, Aug. 8, 1965; children—Brian Keith, Christopher Ervin. Tchr., coach Cedar Rapids (Nebr.) High Sch., 1962-65; tchr., coach Fremont (Nebr.) Public Schs., 1966-71, adminstr., 1971—. Coach, PeeWee Baseball, Fremont. Mem. Assn. Supervision and Curriculum Devel., Nebr. Council Sch. Adminstrs., Assn. Public Sch. Adminstrs. of Fremont (past pres.), Nat. Assn. Secondary Sch. Prins., Fremont Jaycees, C. of C., Phi Delta Kappa. Democrat. Methodist. Clubs: Elks, Fremont Anglers Assn. Home: 1017 Jones Dr Fremont NE 68025 Office: 130 E 9th St Fremont NE 68025

THOMSON, LESTER GARLAND, veterinarian; b. Sparta, Wis., Apr. 13, 1937; s. Charles Scott and Frances Ruth (Wieland) T.; B.S., U. Ill., 1959, D.V.M., 1961; student Western Ill. U., 1955-57; m. Judith Kay Carson, Feb. 2, 1965; children—Scott, Todd, Lesli, Brett. Regional veterinarian Ill. Dept. Agr., Clinton, 1970-73, asst. adminstr. Bur. Meat and Poultry Insp., Springfield, 1973-78, regional tech. advisor, Champaign, 1978-80, Springfield, 1980—; county rabies control adminstr., veterinarian Am. Humane Assn., Lincoln, Ill. Elder, trustee Jefferson Street Christian Ch., Lincoln, Ill. Served to maj. U.S. Army, 1961-70. Mem. Ill., Central Ill. veterinary med. assns., Ill. Farm Bur., Omega Tau Sigma. Home: 9 Rigg Dr Lincoln IL 62656 Office: State Fairgrounds Springfield IL 62706

THOMSON, RALPH JOHN, data processing co. exec.; b. Salt Lake City, Aug. 15, 1937; s. Ralph and Ruth (Watts) T.; A.B. with honors, U. Utah, 1962; A.M., Fletcher Sch. Law and Diplomacy, Tufts and Harvard univs., 1963, M.A.L.D., 1964, Ph.D., 1968; m. Julienne Allen, June 14, 1962; children—Brook, Kim, Heidi-Noel, Tracy-Ciel, Preston Allen. Asst. to dean Fletcher Sch. Law and Diplomacy, 1963-66; asst. prof. govt. Boston U., 1968-72, co-dir. overseas grad. program in internat. relations, 1968-72; dir. govt. programs Control Data Inst., 1972-73; mgr. govt. programs and ednl. services Control Data Corp., Mpls., 1972-73, regional mgr. edn. services USSR and Eastern Europe, 1973-74, dir. internat. edn. services, 1974-75, gen. mgr., spl. rep. to govts., 1975-78, spl. asst. to chief exec. officer, gen. mgr. corp. strategy implementation, 1978-80, v.p. govt. affairs, 1980—. Mem. bd. curriculum devel. Internat. Bur. Informatics and Internat. Computer Center, Rome, 1973-74; cons. UN, NATO, U.S. Dept. State, Dept. Def. Active Boy Scouts Am. Woodrow Wilson fellow, 1962-63, 65-67; Zellerbach fellow, 1963-65. Mem. Am. Polit. Sci. Assn., Am. Assn. Advancement of Slavic Studies, Inter-Am. Soc., Atlantic Assn., Sigma Chi, Pi Sigma Alpha. Home: 3903 Huntingdon Dr Minnetonka MN 55343 Office: 8100 34th Ave MN 55440

THOMSON, ROBERT JAMES, utility exec.; b. Detroit, Dec. 16, 1927; s. Harold E.J. and Irene (Silsbee) T.; A.B. in Bus. Adminstrn., Mich. State U., 1951, M.B.A., 1967; m. Doris L. Mullen, Sept. 19, 1953; children—Gregory, Susan, Jeffrey, Arthur. Mgr. firm Arthur Andersen & Co., Detroit, 1951-58; with Southeastern Mich. Gas Co., Port Huron, 1958—, v.p., 1961-71, pres., 1971—; also dir.; pres. Southeastern Mich. Gas Enterprises, Inc., Port Huron, 1977—; dir. Mich. Nat. Bank-Port Huron. Bd. dirs. United Way St. Clair County, 1974-81, campaign chmn., 1974; trustee Port Huron Dist. Found., 1972—, pres., 1980—; trustee Port Huron Hosp., 1981—; bd. dirs. Indsl. Devel. Corp., Port Huron, 1972—, pres., 1976-78; pres. St. Martin Luth. Ch., Port Huron, 1976-80; bd. dirs. Jr. Achievement Southeastern Mich., 1979-81. Served with USN, 1946-47. C.P.A., Mich. Mem. Am. Inst. C.P.A.s, Mich. Assn. C.P.A.s, Am. Gas Assn., Am. Mgmt. Assn., Mich. State U. Advt. Mgmt. Program Club, Mich. State C. of C. (dir. 1982—), Greater Port Huron-Marysville C. of C. (v.p. 1973-75, dir.). Clubs: Detroit, Renaissance, Port Huron Golf. Office: 405 Water St Port Huron MI 48060

THONE, CHARLES, gov. of Nebr.; b. Hartington, Nebr., Jan. 4, 1924; J.D., U. Nebr., 1950; m. Ruth Raymond, 1953; children—Ann, Mary, Amy. Admitted to Nebr. bar, 1950, U.S. Supreme Ct. bar, 1956; dep. sec. state State of Nebr., 1950-51; asst. state atty. gen. Nebr., 1951-53; asst. U.S. atty., 1953-55; adminstrv. asst. to Senator Roman L. Hruska of Nebr., 1955-59; practice law, Lincoln, Nebr., 1959-70; mem. 92d-95th Congresses from 1st Nebr. dist., mem. Agr. com., Govt. Ops. com., asst. minority whip; gov. of Nebr., 1979—. Chmn. Republican State Com., Nebr., 1959-61, Lincoln Human Rights Commn., 1967-68; chmn. Old West Regional Council; v.p. Council on State Govts. adv. com. 1981 White House Conf. on Aging; mem. Pres.'s Export Council. Mem. Am., Nebr., Lincoln bar assns., Nebr. Hist. Soc., Nat. Gov.'s Assn. (chmn. com. on agr. 1981—, chmn. agrl. export com.), Nebr. State PTA, U. Nebr. Alumni Assn. (pres. 1961-62), VFW, Am. Legion (past comdr., adj.), Phi Alpha Delta. Club: Elks. Office: Office of Gov State Capitol Lincoln NE 68509

THORN, RODNEY KING, basketball team exec.; b. Princeton, W.Va., May 23, 1941; s. Joseph Davis and Alma Jack (Cheatwood) T.; B.A. in Polit. Sci., U. W.Va., 1963; postgrad. U. Wash., 1972-73; m. Margaret Lois Reynolds, Dec. 28, 1963; children—Jonathan Jared, Amanda Renee and Jessica Lynn (twins). Profl. basketball player Balt. Bullets, 1963-64, Detroit Pistons, 1964-66, St. Louis Hawks, 1966-67; profl. basketball player Seattle Supersonics, 1967-71, asst. coach, 1971-72; asst. coach N.Y. Nets, 1973-75, 76-78; head coach St. Louis Spirits, 1975-76; gen. mgr. Chgo. Bulls, 1978—. Baptist. Club: Elks. Office: 333 N Michigan Ave Chicago IL 60601*

THORNBROUGH, GAYLE, historian; b. Hendricks County, Ind., Oct. 29, 1914; d. Harry C. and Bess (Tyler) T.; A.B., Butler U., Indpls., 1936; A.M., U. Mich., 1942. Editor, Ind. Hist. Soc., 1937-67, dir. publs. and library, 1968-76, exec. sec., 1976—; specialist manuscript div. Library of Congress, 1967-68. Mem. Orgn. Am. Historians, Assn. State and Local History, Manuscript Soc., Ind. Hist. Soc. Editor: Outpost on the Wabash, 1957; Letter Book of the Indian Agency at Fort Wayne, 1961; co-editor: Indianapolis in the Gay Nineties, High School Dairies of Claude G. Bowers, 1964; The Diary of Calvin Fletcher, 1817-1866, 1972—. Office: 315 W Ohio St Indianapolis IN 46202

THORNBURG, RUSSELL CHARLES, photographer, writer, educator; b. Akron, Ohio, June 27, 1953; s. Edwin James and Irma Marie (Wallace) T.; grad. U. Akron, 1977, Olan Mills Tech. Sch. Photography; Editor, Horizon Newspaper, 1976; investigator, photographer guard N. Am. Bur. Investigators, Revenna, Ohio, 1973—; free-lance photographer, Akron, 1974—, free-lance writer, 1976—; asst. photo editor U. Akron Buchtelite, 1976-77; photographer Magic Lantern Photo Studio, 1978, Olan Mills Portrait Studio, 1979; instr. in field. Notary public Summit, Portage (Ohio) Counties, 1974—. Served with USAF Res., 1974-76. Recipient advisor's award, Arnold Air Soc., 1976; membership award, Soc. Am. Military Engrs., 1976. Mem. Am. Def. Preparedness Assn., Wedding Photographers Internat., Photog. Soc. Am., Akron Camera Club, Akron Met. Parks Nature Photography Club, N.E. Ohio Camera Club, AAAS, Soc. Am. Military Engrs., Arnold Air Soc., Soc. Physics Students, Am. Security Council (nat. adv. bd.). Home: 2386 Lakeside Dr Lakemore OH 44250 Office: 2159 22 St NW Suite 16 Akron OH 44314

THORNE, JOSEPH CECIL, JR., Realtor, ret. savs. and loan exec.; b. Willmar, Minn., Sept. 26, 1917; s. Joseph Cecil and Clara Matilda (Johnson) T.; grad. Mpls. Bus. Coll., 1936; extension student U. Minn., 1939-60; m. Marie E. Mercier, Jan. 19, 1952. Gen. credit mgr. retail div. Thompson Yards, Weyerhaeuser Co., 1956-62; pub. relations dir., mgr. home improvement loan dept. First Fed. Savs. & Loan Assn., Mpls., 1962-67, v.p. charge loan activities, 1967-77; owner, pres. Thorne Real Estate and Fin. Services, Inc.; lectr. Realtors Inst., Met. State U., Profl. Ednl. System; tchr. Savs. and Loan Inst. classes; columnist New Homes mag. Past treas., dir. Greater Mpls. Area Bd. Realtors; past dir. Mpls. Builders Assn. Pres., bd. dirs. Hennepin County unit Am. Cancer Soc. Served with USAAF; maj. Res. ret. Am. Legion. Clubs: Toastmasters (past pres.). Home and office: 6802 36th Ave N Crystal MN 55427

THORNHILL, WILLIAM THOMAS, banker; b. Washington, Oct. 14, 1926; s. William Joseph and Gartha Fay (Duncan) T.; student Md. U., 1947; B.C.S., Strayer Coll., 1949, M.C.S., 1950; student Am. U., 1950-51, Richmond U., 1961; m. Janet Marie Eustace, Nov. 23, 1957 (div.); children—Thomas William, Karen Marie; m. 2d, Barbara Jean Allen, Dec. 20, 1969 (div.); m. 3d, Rosemary T. Di Costanzo, Mar. 6, 1976. Sr. auditor Ernst & Ernst, Balt. and Washington, 1950-53; fgn. supervisory auditor Standard-Vacuum Oil Co., White Plains, N.Y., 1953-60; mgmt. trainee Bank Va., Richmond, Va., 1960-61; audit supr. C.I.T. Fin. Corp., N.Y.C., 1961-62; v.p. U.S. Indsl. Corp. and U.S. Indsl. Leasing Corp. subs. U.S. Industries, Inc., N.Y.C., 1962-63, asst. controller U.S. Industries, Inc., 1963-65, gen. mgr. 6 Continents Travel Service subs., 1964-65; exec. controller Central Charge Service, Inc., Washington, 1965-67, treas., asst. sec., 1966-67; asst. v.p. First Nat. Bank, Chgo., 1967-70, v.p., 1970-79; with Arthur Anderson & Co., 1980—. Served with AUS, 1944-46. Mem. Am. Mgmt. Assn. (past mem. fin. planning council), Nat. Assn. Accts., Inst. Internal Auditors, Assn. for Systems Mgmt., Fin. Mgrs. Soc. Savs. Instns., Am. Legion, Phi Theta Pi. Frequent speaker and writer on bus. mgmt.; author: Complete Handbook of Operational and Management Auditing. Home: 220 Pine Crest Circle Barrington IL 60010 Office: One First Nat Plaza Chicago IL 60670

THORNTON, EDMUND BRAXTON, mining co. exec.; b. Chgo., Mar. 9, 1930; s. George A. and Suzanne (Woodward) T.; A.B., Yale U., 1954; children—Jonathan Butler, Thomas Volney, Amanda Braxton, Susan Oakes. With No. Trust Co., Chgo., 1957-59; asst. sec., treas. Ottawa Silica Co. (Ill.), 1959-61, v.p. corp. devel., 1961-62, pres., chief exec. officer, dir., 1962-75, chmn., chief exec. officer, dir. 1975—; v.p., dir. Ottawa Nat. Bank. Adviser, Ill. Nature Preserves Commn., 1969—, chmn. Ill. Hist. Sites Adv. Council, 1969-75; bd. advisers Nat. Trust Historic Preservation, 1970-79; chmn. Nat. Parks Centennial Commn., 1972-73; trustee Nat. Recreation and Parks Assn., 1973-75; bd. dirs., v.p., exec. com. United Republican Fund Ill., 1962-74; del. Rep. Conv., 1968, 80, precinct committeeman, 1978—; chmn. LaSalle County Rep. Central Com., 1980—; trustee Ottawa YMCA, 1974-77. Served to 1st lt. USMCR, 1954-58. Mem. Arctic Inst. N.Am., LaSalle County Hist. Soc., Am. Def. Preparedness Assn., Ill. Mfrs. Assn. (dir. 1969-75, vice chmn. 1975-76, chmn. 1976), Nat. Indsl. Sand Assn. (dir. 1968, 72, 73), Ill. C. of C. (dir. 1969-78), Delta Kappa Epsilon. Congregationalist. Clubs: Chgo., Adventurer's, Univ. (Chgo.); Capitol Hill (Washington); Explorers (N.Y.C.). Home: PO Box 1 Ottawa IL 61350 Office: Boyce Memorial Dr Ottawa IL 61350

THORNTON-TRUMP, WALTER EDMOND, inventor, entrepreneur; b. Edmonton, Alta., Can., Aug. 8, 1918; s. Walter Edward and Olga Wilhelmena Lyntine (Lund) T.-T.; student U. B.C., Vancouver and U. So. Calif., 1939-41; m. Bernice Ruth Boale, Mar. 18, 1942; children—William Hamilton, Alexander Beverly, Belva Lynn, Anne Louise. Pres., Trump, Ltd., Oliver, B.C., 1944-64, Trump Hydraulics, Ltd., Toronto, Can., 1964-70, Trump, Inc., Plattsmouth, Nebr., 1970—; pres. Trump Engrs., Inc., Lillian, Ala., 1976—, Inc., Trump Fabricators, Inc., Plattsmouth, Trump Industries, Lillian; inventor; patentee fire dept. snorkel aerial device, cherry picker, power co. bucket trucks, hot water aircraft ramp deicing, 12 basic hydraulic machines, numerous others. Named Nebraskan of Month, Bus. and Industry Mag., 1976; nominee as Small Businessman of Yr., 1978-79. Served with Can. Army, World War II. Mem. Soc. Automotive Engrs., Aerospace Ground Equipment 2C Com., Plattsmouth C. of C. Club: Rotary (past pres.). Home: 2087 Spanish Cove Lillian AL 36549 Office: PO Box 368 Plattsmouth NE 68048

THORPE, LEYDEN KAYE, family counselor; b. Menominee, Mich., May 13, 1930; s. Royal K. and Matilda T.; A.A., North Park Coll., 1950; B.A., Mich. State U., 1953; M.S.W., U. Nebr., 1966; M.Div., North Park Sem., 1978; m. Esther Frederick, Aug. 11, 1953; children—Peter, David, Joyce. Day care cons. Minn. Dept. Public Welfare, 1966-67; sch. social worker Mound (Minn.) Schs., 1967-71; dir. Community Mental Health Center, Big Stone, Va., 1971; family counselor, dir. Family Health Service, Swedish Covenant Hosp., Chgo., 1971—. Cert. social worker, Ill. Mem. Acad. Cert. Social Workers, Am. Assn. Marriage and Family Therapists, Soc. Tchrs. of Family Practice, Minn. Sch. Social Workers (pres. 1970), Nat. Assn. Christians in Social Work (sec. Midwest chpt. 1979—), Nat. Assn. Social Workers, Covenant Chaplains Assn. Mem. Evang. Covenant Ch. Club: Kiwanis. Office: Family Health Service Swedish Covenant Hosp 5145 N California Ave Chicago IL 60625

THORREZ, CAMIEL EARL, mfg. co. exec.; b. Concord, Mich., Nov. 12, 1948; s. Henry Camiel and Phyllis Joan (Nivison) T.; B.S. in Mech. Engring., Mich. Tech. U., 1970; m. Anne Marie Tarbox, Aug. 30, 1969; children—Christiana, Heather, Holly, Diana, Henry, Bevin, Caroline. Machine operator Concord (Mich.) Mfg. Co., 1964-69, tool designer, 1971-72, plant mgr., 1972—; plant engr., coop. trainee transmission and axle div. Ford Motor Co., Livonia, Mich., 1969-70; tool designer Allied Chucker and Engring. Co., Jackson, Mich., 1970-71; pub., owner Concord News, 1974-80; pres. Belgian Screw Machine Products, Inc., 1979—. dir. Concord Mfg. Co., C. Thorrez Industries, Induction Heating Systems Co. Bd. dirs. Concord Community Sch. Bd., 1972—, sec., 1973-75, 76—; mem. career adv. com. Concord Pub. Schs., Jackson Community Coll., Jackson Career Center; founder Thorrez Found., 1972, pres., 1972-75, adminstr., 1975—. Kellogg Found. fellow, 1973-75; named Outstanding Young Mich. Technol. U. Alumnus, 1975. Mem. Albion Montessori Assn., Nat. Assn. Mfrs., Nat. Fedn. Ind. Bus., Am. Inst. Indsl. Engrs., Mich. Assn. Sch. Bds., Nat. Assn. Sch. Bds., Audubon Soc., Nat. Wildlife Fedn., Hist. Soc. Mich., Jackson County Hist. Soc., Geneal. Soc. Flemish Am., Jackson Geneal. Soc., Am. Forestry Assn., Mich. Mus. Assn., Mich. C. of C. (pvt. enterprise com. 1976—), ASME (treas. 1969), Soc. Mfg. Engrs. (pres. 1969), Concord Heritage Assn. (charter, treas. 1971-73). Club: Concord Lions (dir. 1972). Roman Catholic. Home: 126 Hanover St Concord MI 49237

THORSEN, ROBERT, lawyer; b. Winnetka, Ill., July 8, 1912; s. Henry T. and Catherine (Henrich) T.; B.S.L., Northwestern, 1932; LL.D., U. Chgo., 1934; m. Frances Adele Pierce, Apr. 28, 1935; children—Frances Adele, Robert Lloyd, Richard Pierce. Admitted to Ill., Mo. bars, 1935; br. atty. Nat. Bond Investment Co., St. Louis, 1935-37; asso. with Edward P. Madigan, 1937-40; partner Madigan & Thorsen, Chgo., 1941—; sec. Kerr-Wireryte Co., Kerr Wire Products Co.; v.p., asst. sec., dir. McCormick Commodities Inc.; sec., dir. Tingstol Co. Mem. Am., Ill., Chgo. bar assns., Chgo. Bd. Trade, Chgo. Real Estate Bd., Chgo. Assn. Commerce and Industry. Clubs: University Executives, Westmoreland Country (past pres.), John Henry Wigmore Club (past pres.). Home: 145 Bertling Ln Winnetka IL 60093 Office: Suite 2680 One First Nat Plaza Chicago IL 60603

THRAILKILL, FRANCIS MARIE, coll. pres.; b. San Antonio, Sept. 21, 1937; d. Franklin Eustace and Mary Myrtle (Huggins) T.; B.A., Coll. New Rochelle (N.Y.), 1961; M.A., Marquette U., 1969; Ed.D., Nova U., 1974. Tchr., Ursuline Acad., Dallas, 1961-63; vice prin. Ursuline Acad. High Sch., New Orleans, 1963-70; prin. Ursuline Acad. High Sch., Dallas, 1970-77; now pres. Springfield (Ill.) Coll. Trustee, Coll. New Rochelle, St. Teresa High Sch., Decatur, Ill.; mem. Springfield Urban League, Springfield United Way. Mem. Assn. Supervision and Curriculum Devel., Assn. Cath. Colls. and Univs., N. Central Assn., Fedn. Ind. Ill. Colls. and Univs. Democrat. Office: 1500 N 5th St Springfield IL 62702

THROOP, JAMES WARREN, process engr.; b. Goodrich, Mich., Aug. 26, 1931; s. Warren E. and Mildred (Wolfe) T.; B.M.E., Gen. Motors Inst., 1959; M.S., Mich. State U., 1962; m. Dorothy Lewis (dec.); children—James, Linda Throop Marsh, Cynthia Throop Hufnagel; m. 2d, Ann W. Kinney, Aug. 10, 1968. Supr. plant engring. Fisher Body div. Gen. Motors Corp., Grand Blanc, Mich., 1958-60; instr. agrl. engring. Mich. State U., East Lansing, 1960-62; asst. prof. process engring. Gen. Motors Inst., Flint, Mich., 1962-66, asso. prof., 1966-68, prof., 1968—, Rodes prof., 1976-77; NSF cons., India, 1970. Mem. ASME (profl. devel. com.), Soc. Mfg. Engrs. (chmn. metalworking fluids com.), Computer Aided Mfg. Internat. (vice chmn. standards com.), Am. Soc. Metals, Tau Beta Pi. Unitarian. Author: (with T. Judson) Theory and Practice of Material Removal, 1968; contbr. articles to profl. jours. Home: 6636 Waterford Hill Terr Waterford MI 48095 Office: 1700 W 3d Ave W Flint MI 48502

THRUSH, RANDOLPH STERLING, psychologist; b. Columbus, Ohio, Jan. 24, 1931; s. Martin Valdo and Helen Loretta (Alkire) T.; B.S., Otterbein Coll., 1951; M.A., Bowling Green State U., 1952; Ph.D., Ohio State U., 1958; m. JoAnn Poole, Dec. 13, 1975; children—Valerie Sue, Lisa Lynn. Asst. dir. testing and counseling service U. Mo., Columbia, 1961-65, asst. prof. psychology, 1961-65, asso. prof., 1965; asso. prof., head dept. psychology and sociology Va. Poly. Inst. & State U., Blacksburg, 1965-67; lectr. U. Wis., Madison, 1967-69, asso. prof., 1969-72, prof., 1972—, dir. counseling center, 1967-73; cons. Bur. Hearings and Appeals, Social Security Adminstrn., 1965—, Wis. Dept. Licensing and Regulation, 1973—. Served with U.S. Army, 1952-54. Mem. AAAS, Am. Psychol. Assn., Wis. Psychol. Assn. (mem. exec. council 1980—), Clin. Consulting Psychology (pres. 1980—, mem. bd. govs. 1978—), Am. Personnel and Guidance Assn., Am. Coll. Personnel Assn., Nat. Vocat. Guidance Assn., Wis. Coll. Personnel Assn. (pres. 1972-73, mem. exec. com. 1972-74), Assn. for Measurement and Evaluation in Guidance. Club: Rotary. Contbr. articles in field to profl. jours. Home: 913 County Trunk Hwy JG Rural Route 1 Mt Horeb WI 53572 Office: U Wis Old Edn Bldg Madison WI 53706

THURINGER, CARL BERNARD, surgeon; b. Norman, Okla., Dec. 22, 1922; s. Joseph Mario and Bess LeMarr (Cronim) T.; student St. Johns U., 1942; M.S., U. Okla., 1943, M.D., 1946; m. Mary Ann Hall, June 24, 1945; children—Linda, Brian, Anne, Elizabeth. Intern, St. Anthony Hosp., Oklahoma City, 1946-47; pvt. practice medicine specializing in surgery, St. Cloud, Minn., 1953—; chief surgery St. Cloud Hosp. Served as capt. M.C., U.S.Army, 1947-48. Diplomate Am. Bd. Surgery. Mem. A.C.S., Mayo Alumni Assn., Minn. Surg. Soc., St. Cloud C. of C., AMA, Stearns County Med. Soc., Priestly Soc. Republican. Roman Catholic. Club: Exchange. Home: 104

Dunbar Rd St Cloud MN 56301 Office: 13 and St Germaine Sts St Cloud MN 56301

THURMAN, RICHARD LEE, educator; b. Detroit, Apr. 4, 1940; s. Sylvain Lee and Edna Mary (Scheafer) T.; B.S. in Phys. Edn. and Health, U. Houston, 1962; M.S. in Counselor Edn., So. Ill. U., 1968; Ph.D. in Spl. Edn., St. Louis U., 1974; 1 dau., Tamara Lynn. Substitute tchr. Houston Ind. Sch. Dist., 1962; instr. phys. edn. St. Louis State Hosp., 1963-66, indsl. therapist, 1967-68; substitute tchr. Farmington (Mo.) Public High Sch., 1966; dir. vocat. rehab. St. Louis State Hosp., 1971-72; instr. spl. edn./elem. edn. dept. U. Mo., St. Louis, 1972-73, asst. prof. spl. edn. behavioral studies dept., 1973—; cons. to Mo. State Dept. Edn., Mo. Dept. Mental Health, various sch. dists., 1968—; dir. internat. travel study courses U. Copenhagen, 1975, U. London, 1976-78; neighborhood youth corps counselor Jefferson City, Mo., 1966-67. Bd. dirs. Patio Green Assn., Lake St. Louis, 1977—, pres., 1977—. Served with USAR, 1963. U. Mo. research grantee, 1974-75, 76-77; State of Mo. Elem. and Secondary Edn. Dept. grantee, 1977. Mem. Council for Exceptional Children, Am. Assn. Mental Deficiency, Am. Assn. Sex Educators, Counselors and Therapists. Contbr. articles on spl. edn. to profl. jours. Home: 1227 Weleba St Saint Louis MO 63121 Office: 8001 Natural Bridge Rd Saint Louis MO 63121

THYGERSON, KENNETH JAMES, assn. exec.; b. Chgo., Oct. 1, 1945; s. R. James and Doris L. (Niemann) T.; B.S. with highest distinction, Northwestern U., 1967, Ph.D., 1973; m. Darlene Kay Vernon, June 24, 1967; children—Keith David, Kent James. Instr. mgmt. Northwestern U., Chgo., 1968-70; economist U.S. League Savs. Assns., Chgo., 1970—, chief economist, dir. econs. dept., 1975-79, staff v.p., chief economist, dir. div. econs. and research, 1980—; asso. dir. Office of Policy Coordination, Office of Pres.-Elect, 1980-81; cons. in field; instr. exec. devel. schs. Am. Savs. and Loan Inst., 1970—. Trustee Trinity Lutheran Ch., 1975-77. NDEA fellow, 1967-70. Mem. Am. Statis. Assn. (pres. Chgo. chpt. 1974-75, mem. council 1974-75), Am. Econ. Assn., Am. Fin. Assn., Nat. Assn. Bus. Economists, Am. Real Estate and Urban Econs. Assn. (dir. 1977-80), Phi Sigma Kappa, Delta Sigma Pi. Beta Gamma Sigma. Author: The Effect of Government Housing and Mortgage Credit Programs on Savings and Loan Associations, 1973; Tax Management for Savings and Loan Executives, 1977; Mortgage Portfolio Management, 1978; contbr. articles to profl. jours. Home: 9547 Avers Ave Evanston IL 60203 Office: US League Savs Assns 111 E Wacker Dr Chicago IL 60601

TIANEN, BRUCE JOHN, indsl. engr., health systems cons.; b. Kenosha, Wis., Sept. 20, 1947; s. Roger E. and Helen M. (Pellicori) T.; B.S. in Math., U. Wis., 1971, M.S. in Indsl. Engring., 1978; 1 son, Jason John. Cons., Compucare, Inc., Chgo., 1974-75; sr. systems analyst Meth. Hosp., Madison, Wis., 1975-77; mgr. Medicus Systems Corp., Chgo., 1978—; program planner and coordinator forums Center for Hosp. Mgmt. Engring., Chgo., 1977-78. Wis. Suicide Risk and Therapy research grantee, 1972-74. Mem. Hosp. Mgmt. Systems Soc. (dir. Chgo. 1977-78, nat. dir. 1977-78), Am. Inst. Indsl. Engrs. (mem. health services div. 1974—), Am. Hosp. Assn. Author: Computers and Bio-Medical Research, A Comparison of Models for Predicting the Outcome of Suicide Attempts, 1980-81. Contbr. articles on health systems engring. to profl. publs. Home: 67 Adams Lake Dr Pontiac MI 48054 Office: 880 Woodward Ave Pontiac MI 48053

TICHENOR, ROBERT WOODROW, physician; b. St. Louis, Sept. 1, 1914; s. Robert Anderson and Willie Mae (Wooley) T.; B.S., St. Louis Coll. Pharmacy, 1939; A.B., Washington U., St. Louis, 1941, M.D., 1943; m. Letitia Bernice Youngman, May 20, 1935; children—Trebor Jay, Bruce Harding. Intern, resident St. Louis City Hosp., 1944-45; practice medicine, Sappington, Mo., 1946—; mem. staff St. Joseph, St. Anthony hosps. Served to 1st lt. M.C., AUS, 1945-46. Fellow Am. Acad. Family Physicians; mem. St. Louis (past pres.), Mo., Am. acads. family physicians, Pan-Am., Am. (recognition award for continuing med. edn. 1972), So., Mo., St. Louis med. assns., Royal Soc. Medicine, Am. Geriatric Soc., St. Louis German Shepherd Club (past pres.), Am. Kennel Club (conformation judge), German Shepherd Dog Club Am. (past dir.). Club: Washington University. Home: 175 Misty Manor Rd Fenton MO 63026 Office: 11521 Gravois St Sappington MO 63126

TICHENOR, WILLIAM GEILEY, savs. and loan exec.; b. Terre Haute, Aug. 28, 1917; s. William Taylor and Ause (Geiley) T.; B.S., Ind. State U., 1939; m. Margaret L. Brown, May 4, 1971; 1 son, William Taylor. With Internat. Harvester Co., 1939-41; with Ind. Savs. & Loan, Terre Haute, 1941—, now pres.; dir. Spirit of Terre Haute, Inc., Croy Crest, Inc., Ind. Savs. & Loan. Mem. Terre Haute C. of C., Ind. Savs. and Loan League (past dir.), Terre Haute Bd. Realtors (past sec.-treas.). Clubs: Kiwanis, Shriners, Elks. Office: 100 7th St S Terre Haute IN 47808

TIEDEN, DALE L., state senator; b. Oct. 11, 1922; s. Lewis and Grace (Fisher) T.; grad. Elkader Jr. Coll.; student U. Iowa. Farmer, to 1959; mgr. feed, livestock and fertilizer bus., to 1967; farmer, 1968—; former mem. Iowa Ho. of Reps.; now mem. Iowa Senate; sec. County Farm Bur., Twp. Agr. Com. Mem. Farm Bur., Izaak Walton League, C. of C. Clubs: Masons, Lions. Mem. United Ch. of Christ. Office: State Capitol Des Moines IA 53019*

TIEDGE, LOUIS ALFRED, arbitrator, employee and labor relations cons.; b. South Bend, Ind., June 9, 1913; s. Fred Louis and Anna Maude (Hazen) T.; student Acme Inst. Tech., 1940-42, Notre Dame U., 1943-44, Ind. U.-South Bend, 1954-56; m. Agnes Anna Vogel, Aug. 15, 1930; children—Delores Francis Cleghorn, Geneva Mae Barnes, Sharon Louise Grall, Deborah Ann Peters. Gen. foreman mfg. Bendix Corp., South Bend, 1939-51, staff asst. indsl. relations, 1952-58, mgr. labor relations, 1959-61, dir. indsl. relations, 1962-78; Ind. monitoring officer St. Joseph County CETA, 1979; mgmt. cons. City of South Bend, St. Joseph County and Michiana Area CETA Consortium, 1980—. Mem. South Bend-Mishawaka Labor Mgmt. Commn., 1963—; gen. chmn. United Fund St. Joseph County Campaign, 1966-67; chmn. Ind. Gov.'s Task Force for Employment of Handicapped, 1970-75; mem. hosp. rate rev. com. Ind. Blue Cross, 1978—; trustee St. Joseph Med. Center, South Bend, 1977—. Mem. Am. Soc. Personnel Adminstrn. (accredited exec. personnel), Ind. C. of C. (chmn. labor relations and personnel com. 1975-77), U.S. C. of C. (mem. labor relations com. 1964-69), South Bend-Mishawaka Area C. of C., Inst. Cert. Prof. Mgrs. (accredited cert. mgr.). Republican. Roman Catholic. Club: Rotary (pres. South Bend South 1976-77). Author papers in field. Home: 19400 Sundale Dr South Bend IN 46614

TIELKE, JAMES CLEMENS, retailing co. exec.; b. St. Helena, Nebr., May 15, 1931; s. Joseph Hubert and Catherine Josephine (Schmidt) T.; B.S.B.A., U. S.D., 1959; M.A., 1960; m. Betty Merle Adams, Apr. 18, 1953; children—Patrick James, Michael Jay, Dawn Michelle. Partner, Tielke Motors, Yankton, S.D., 1952-54; owner Fort Collins (Colo.) Motors, 1954-56; grad. asst. U. S.D., 1959-60; with Montgomery Ward and Co., Chgo., 1960—, mdse. devel. mgr., 1969-71, nat. mdse. mgr. paint and wallcoverings, 1971-76, nat. mdse. mgr. TV and radio, 1976-77, inventory mgmt. div. mgr., 1977-78, v.p. mdse. adminstrn., 1978—. Bd dirs., Chgo. Youth Centers, 1980-81; chmn. Ward Polit. Action Com., 1977-78. Served with U.S. Army, 1950-52. Republican. Roman Catholic. Club: Execs. (Chgo.). Office: 2 Montgomery Ward Plaza Chicago IL 60671

TIERNEY, CATHERINE MARIE, librarian; b. Woodbury, N.J., July 11, 1947; d. William John and Marie Cecilia (Oakes) Morgan; B.A. in History, Cardinal Stritch Coll., Milw., 1969; M.L.S., Kent (Ohio) State U., 1974; m. Phillip Arthur Tierney, Aug. 9, 1969. Reference librarian Akron (Ohio) Beacon Jour., 1974-76, chief librarian, 1976—. Mem. Spl. Libraries Assn., Humane Soc. Greater Akron. Republican. Home: 1321 Weather Vane Ln Akron OH 44313 Office: 44 E Exchange St Akron OH 44328

TIERNEY, MARGARET MARIE, state senator; b. Gt. Falls, Mont., Oct. 9, 1938; d. Hamilton Ford and Margaret (Stevenson) Cooley; student U. Mont., 1960-61, 65; B.A., Coll. Gt. Falls, 1965; postgrad. Chapman Coll., 1967-68, N.D. State U., 1977-78; m. John Francis Tierney, 1966; children—Michael, Corette. Tchr. English, Gt. Falls Public Schs., 1965-67, Riverside (Calif.) Sch. Dist., 1967-68, Glen Rock (N.J.) Public Schs., 1969-70, Bismarck (N.D.) Public Schs., 1977—; mem. N.D. State Senate, 1980—. Active ARC. Office: State Capitol Bismarck ND 58505*

TIERNEY, PATRICK JOHN, electronics co. exec.; b. Denver, Oct. 9, 1945; s. Thomas Michael and Betty Ruth (Fairall) T.; B.S., U. Colo., 1967, M.B.A., 1969; postgrad. U. Ariz., 1971; m. Lois B. Anderson, Jan. 1, 1980; children—Chris, Blake. Group v.p. fin. Bunker Ramo Corp., Oak Brook, Ill., 1972-76; pvt. venture capital and bus. cons., 1976-79; group v.p. fin. Gould, Inc., Rolling Meadows, Ill., 1979—. Served with U.S. Army, 1967-68. Home: 417 Valleyview Barrington IL 60010 Office: Gould Inc 10 Gould Center Rolling Meadows IL 60008

TIERNO, MARK JOHN, educator; b. N.Y.C., Apr. 16, 1948; s. Joseph Tierno and Dolores Tierno Walsh; B.A. cum laude (Univ. scholar), Adelphi U., 1970; M.A., Carnegie-Mellon U., 1973, Arts D. (Henry Buhl Jr. Found. fellow), 1975; m. Kathryn Artale, Oct. 5, 1969. Tchr. middle sch. Hauppauge (N.Y.) Public Schs., 1970-71; curriculum research asso. Carnegie-Mellon U., 1972-75; lectr., demonstration tchr. Sch. Edn., U. Pitts., 1975-79; asst. prof. edn., chmn. dept. edn. Lake Forest Coll., 1979—; cons. in field. Bd. dirs. Pitts. Free Clinic, 1978-80. Mem. Am. Ednl. Research Assn., Assn. Supervision and Curriculum Devel., Nat. Middle Schs. Assn., Nat. Council for Social Studies. Home: 7 Faculty Circle Lake Forest IL 60045 Office: Dept Edn Lake Forest Coll Lake Forest IL 60045

TIFFANY, JOSEPH CALVIN, II, surgeon; b. Grand Rapids, Mich., Aug. 12, 1939; s. Joseph Calvin and Dorothy Elizabeth (Yeakey) T.; A.B., Northwestern U., 1961, M.D., 1965; m. Ruth Pauline Luiten, June 15, 1968; children—Dawn Marie, Joseph Calvin. Intern, Cook County Hosp., Chgo., 1965-66; resident in surgery Mayo Grad. Sch. Medicine, Rochester, Minn., 1966-68, Allegheny Gen. Hosp., Pitts., 1969-71, Ross Clinic, Inc. Merrillville, Ind., 1974-80. Served with U.S. Army, 1972-74. Diplomate Am. Bd. Surgery. Fellow A.C.S.; mem. AMA, Racine County Med. Soc., Wis. State Med. Assn. Republican. Presbyterian. Home: 7 Maplewood Ct Racine WI 54302 Office: 3803 Spring St Racine WI 53405

TIGAY, BARRY HAROLD, psychologist; b. Detroit, Aug. 16, 1943; s. Leonard and Ethel (Cooper) T.; B.A., U. Mich., 1968; M.A., Wayne State U., 1973, Ph.D., 1977; m. Judith H. Kay, June 28, 1969; children—Jennifer, Sarah, Donielle, David, Joseph. Chief grad. asst. Lafayette Clinic, Detroit, 1969-70; teaching asst. Wayne State U., Detroit, 1970-71; clin. supr., 1972-73; clin. cons. Children's Center of Wayne County, Detroit, 1973-74, Redford Union Schs., Redford Twp., Mich., 1974-76; clin. psychologist Parent Youth Devel. Service, Farmington, Mich., 1973-78; pres. clin. dir. Psychol. Resources, Inc., Bloomfield Hills, Mich., 1978—; cons. Oakland County Cts., 1978—, Southfield Public Schs., 1979—; USPHS fellow, 1968-69. Mem. Mich. Psychol. Assn. (chmn. ins. com. 1978, v.p. for profl. affairs 1979-81), Assn. for Advancement Psychology, Am. Psychol. Assn., Mich. Interprofl. Assn. on Marriage, Divorce and Family, Mich. Soc. Lic. Psychologists, Psychologists Task Force. Columnist: Mich. Psychol. Assn. Newsletter, 1978—. Contbr. articles in field to profl. jours. Home: 3355 Buckingham Trail West Bloomfield MI 48033 Office: Psychol Resources Inc Suite 301 1575 Woodward Ave Bloomfield Hills MI 48013

TIGGES, JOHN THOMAS, writer, musician; b. Dubuque, Iowa, May 16, 1932; s. John George and Madonna Josephine (Heiberger) T.; student Loras Coll., 1950-52, 57, U. Dubuque, 1960; m. Kathryn Elizabeth Johnson, Apr. 22, 1954; children—Juliana, John, Timothy, Teresa, Jay. Clk. John Deere Tractor Works, Dubuque, Iowa, 1957-61; agt. Penn Mut. Life Inst. Co., Dubuque, 1961-74; bus. mgr. Dubuque Symphony Orch., 1961-68, 71-74; violinist; author novels: The Legend of Jean Marie Cardinal, 1976; Garden of the Incubus, 1982; Rockville Horror (radio play), 1979; plays: No More - No Less, 1979, We Who Are About to Die, 1979; radio plays Valley of Deceit, 1978, The Timid, 1982; editorial asst. Julian Jour.; columnist Memory Lane; tchr. creative writing Northwest Iowa Tech. Inst.; founder Julien Strings, 1972, Northeast Iowa Writers Workshop, 1981; co-host Big Broadcast Radio Program, WDBQ Radio. Founder, bus. mgr. Dubuque Pops Orch., 1957; co-founder, bd. dirs. Dubuque Symphony Orch., 1961-68, 71-74. Recipient Nat. Quality award, 1966-70. Mem. Nat. Writers Club (profl.), Iowa Authors, Am. Fedn. Musicians, Internat. Platform Assn. Roman Catholic. Office: PO Box 902 Dubuque IA 52001-0011

TIGRAK, MEHMET FAUT, structural engr.; b. Istanbul, Turkey, Aug. 26, 1911; s. M. Suleyman and Hediye (Harputlu) T.; Diploma, Mil. Coll., Habiye-Istanbul, 1932; Diploma Mil. Engring., 1934; Certificate, U. Berlin (Germany), 1938; student Technische Hochschule, Berlin, 1938-39; B.S., U. Ill., 1942, M.S., 1943, Ph.D., 1945; m. Mary Louise Evans; children—William M. U., James A.F., Hediye L. Came to U.S., 1958, naturalized. With Turkish Army Corps Engrs., 1934-51, resigned sr. maj., 1951; tech. dir. Turk Yapi Ltd. Co., Ankara, Turkey, 1951; dept. head Metcalf, Hamilton, Grove, Kansas City, Mo., 1951-53; prin. engr. project coordinator Hamilton Co., Kansas City, Mo., 1953-54; owner, operator Tigrak Cons. Engring. Co., Tigrak Constrn. Co., Ankara, 1954-58; prin. partner, mgr. Tigrak & Kolbasi, Engrs.-Contractors, Ankara, 1956-58; asso. in charge structure Clark, Daily, Dietz & Assos., Urbana, Ill., 1958-62; v.p. in charge structure and hwy. div. Clark, Dietz & Assos., Engrs. Inc., Urbana, Ill., 1962-66, v.p. in charge fed. and railroad projects, 1966—. Recipient Honorable Mention award for Findlay Bridge (Shelbyville, Ill.), U.S. Army C.E., 1969. Registered profl. engr., Ill., Ind., Mo., Ky., Tenn., Wis., Turkey; Registered structural engr., Ill., Ky., Turkey. Life mem. ASCE; mem. Ill. Assn. Professions, Nat., Ill. socs. profl. engrs., Am. Concrete Inst., Am. Ry. Engring. Assn. Soc. Am. Mil. Engrs., AAAS, Chamber Architects and Engrs. Turkey, Sigma Xi, Chi Epsilon, Phi Kappa Epsilon. Mason (32 deg., Shriner). Home: 23 Riverview Ln Rural Route 1 Briarcliff Mahomet IL 61853 Office: 211 N Race St Urbana IL 61801

TILLE, CHARLES HERMAN, accountant; b. Decatur, Ill., Aug. 3, 1926; s. Herman Carl and Grace Alice (Cummings) T.; B.S. in Engring. Adminstrn., Millikin U., 1950; m. Alice Elizabeth Wochner, Nov. 25, 1948; m. 2d, Betsy Lou Rucker, May 26, 1973; children—Alice Jean, James E. Acct., Marvel-Schebler Products div. Borg-Warner Corp., Decatur, 1952-54, supr. inventory control, 1954-60, purchasing buyer, 1960-66; sr. acct. Richardson, Karloski, Pinkley & Kuppler, C.P.A.s, Decatur, 1966-76; controller Fleetwood Oil Co. Inc., Moweaqua, Ill., 1976; prin. Charles Tille Acctg. & Tax Service, Decatur, 1976-78; sr. acct. Graves, Moody & Co., C.P.A.s, Decatur, 1978-79, Sleeper, Nalefski & Catlin, C.P.A.s, Decatur, 1979—. Coach, Little League, Decatur, 1960, mgr., 1961, commr., 1962, sec., 1963; mental health vol., Decatur, 1973. Served with USN, 1944-46. Recipient Acctg. award Murphy, Jenne & Jones, 1950. Mem. Am. Legion (county comdr. 1981-82), 40 and 8 Soc. Republican. Club: Elks (audit chmn. 1979-81), Masons (local treas. 1968-78, Shriner). Home: 1735 S Country Club Rd Apt 103 Decatur IL 62521 Office: 600 Citizens Bldg Decatur IL 62523

TILLERY, STEPHEN MATTHEW, lawyer; b. Wood River, Ill., Mar. 9, 1950; s. Donald Lee and Ada Victoria (Waters) T.; B.A., Ill. Coll., 1972; J.D., St. Louis U., 1976; m. Katherine Jean Thompson, Aug. 19, 1972. Student law clk. U.S. Dist. Ct., Eastern Dist. Ill., 1976; admitted to Ill. bar, 1976; law clk. 5th Dist. Ct. Appeals of Ill., Mt. Vernon, 1976-77; partner firm Kassly, Bone, Becker, Dix & Tillery, P.C., Belleville, Ill., 1980—; instr. law St. Louis U., 1977—. SAR fellow, 1968. Mem. Am., Ill., St. Clair County bar assns., Am., Ill. trial lawyers assn., Am. Judicature Soc., Phi Beta Kappa. Presbyterian. Home: 8 Signal Hill Blvd Belleville IL 62223 Office: 7705 W Main Belleville IL 62223

TILLMAN, DONALD LAWRENCE, corp. exec.; b. Toledo, Ohio, July 25, 1930; s. Lambert John and Marie Emily (Rooney) T.; B.S. in Mech. Engring., U. Detroit, 1954; s. Charlene Alice Krugh, Feb. 13, 1965; children—Donald L., Christina Rosevear. Plant engr. Unitcast Corp., Toledo, Ohio, 1956-58; project engr. Toledo Scale Corp. 1958-60; design engr. Ulrich and Assos., Perrysburg, Ohio, 1960-62, 65-66; sales engr. United-McGill Corp., Akron, Ohio, 1962-65; partner Miller, Tillman & Zamis Inc., Perrysburg, 1966-70; pres. Tillman-Unitech Corp., Maumee, Ohio, 1970—; mem. adv. bd. Mid Am. Nat. Bank and Trust; cons. Med. Coll. Ohio, Toledo. Served with U.S. Army, 1954-56. Mem. ASME (past chmn. N.W. Ohio chpt.), Soc. Mfg. Engrs. (past chmn. Toledo chpt.), Soc. Automotive Engrs., Newcomen Soc. N.Am. Republican. Roman Catholic. Club: Brandywine Country. Patentee in field. Home: 6034 N Chanticleer Dr Maumee OH 43537 Office: 420 Holland Rd Maumee OH 43537

TILLMAN, FRANKLIN EDWARD, newspaper automation cons.; b. Larchmont, N.Y., Aug. 12, 1932; s. James A. and Lena S. (Stroll) T.; student Webb Inst. Naval Architecture, 1952-53, N.Y. U., 1956-58; B.S. in Civil Engring., Drexel U., 1963; m. Suzanne Zipes, Oct. 13, 1956 (div. 1979); children—James Robert, Richard Gregory; m. 2d, Barbara Titsch, Aug. 2, 1981. Engr., N.Y. Shipbldg. Corp., Camden, N.J., 1958-63; systems engr. Data Processing div. IBM, Trenton, N.J., 1963-69; mktg. mgr. Tal-Star Computer Systems, Princeton Junction, N.J., 1970-80; pvt. practice cons. newspaper automation, 1980—; group dir. computer ops. for small newspapers, Kankakee, Ill., 1981—; tchr. data processing, programming, 1964-66. Served with Signal Corps, U.S. Army, 1953-54. Mem. Mensa. Home and Office: 1080 Justine Dr Kankakee IL 60901

TILLMAN, JANET MAY, sch. adminstr.; b. Milbank, S.D., July 13, 1941; d. Gerald Joseph and Melba Catherine (Seide) T.; B.A., St. Xavier Coll., Chgo., 1973; M.A., U. Notre Dame, 1978; M.S., No. State Coll., Aberdeen, S.D., 1981. Tchr., pvt. schs., S.D., 1964-71, Chgo., 1971-74, Fort Yates Indian Reservation, N.D., 1974-75; dir. nursing program feasibility study Eagle Butte, Cheyenne River Indian Reservation, N.D., 1978; dir. adult edn. Pierre (S.D.) Assn. for Retarded Citizens, 1978-79; tchr. emotionally disturbed jr. and sr. high sch. students N.D. State Hosp., Jamestown, 1979-80; prin. St. John Acad., Jamestown, 1980—. Lobbyist ARC, Right-to-Life. Mem. Assn. Elem. Sch. Prins. (officer, exec. council), Assn. Supervision and Curriculum Devel., AAUW, Bus. and Profl. Women, Jamestown Edn. Assn., Nat. Catholic Edn. Assn., Council for Exceptional Children, Assn. Retarded Citizens, Cath. Daughters Am., Phi Delta Kappa. Office: 215 5th St SE Jamestown ND 58401

TILLOTSON, JOHN FRANKLIN, physician; b. Delphos, O., Sept. 8, 1915; s. James Richard and Lulu (Friedline) T.; B.A., Oberlin Coll., 1937; M.D., Ohio State U., 1943; M.S., U. Minn., 1950; m. (Mary) Louise Peters, June 20, 1942; children—Christine Louise, Susan Mary, Barbara Lynn, Patricia Anne, Ann Virginia, Cynthia Jane. Intern, Chgo. Presbyn. Hosp., 1943; resident Children's Hosp. of Mich., Detroit, 1947, Mayo Grad. Sch. Medicine, Rochester, Minn., 1948-50; practice medicine specializing in orthopaedic surgery, Lima, O., 1950—; mem. staff St. Rita, Meml. Hosps., Lima; cons. St. Rita, Meml., Joint Twp., Our Lady of Mercy hosps., others. Served with U.S. Army Res., 1939-68, ret. as col., AUS, 1944-46. Decorated Silver Star, Bronze Star, Purple Heart. Diplomate Am. Bd. Orthopaedic Surgeons. Fellow A.C.S., Am. Acad. Orthopaedic Surgeons, Internat. Coll. Surgeons; mem. A.M.A., Phi Rho Sigma. Republican. Methodist. Mason (32 deg., Shriner, Jester), Elk, Optimist (pres. 1963-64). Home: 2227 W High St Lima OH 45805 Office: 658 W Market St Lima OH 45802

TILLOTSON, RAYMOND JENNISON, rancher; b. Shields, Kans., Mar. 1, 1904; s. Warren Jackson and Bessie (Jennison) T.; B.S., Kans. State U., 1929; M.S., Iowa State U., 1931; m. Amy C. Jones, Aug. 28, 1929; children—Don R., Paul J., Betty (Mrs. Kenneth L. Milford), Peggy (Mrs. Edwin J. Tajchman). Rural service engr. Kans. Gas & Elec. Co., Newton, 1929-30; asst. agrl. engr. Soil Conservation Service, U.S. Dept. Agr., Iowa, Mo., Kans., 1934-43; owner, operator ranch, Shields, Kans., 1944—. Mem. dist. bd. Lane County Soil Conservation, 1944-69, chmn., 1949-55; mem. Extension Council Bd., 1966-70, chmn., 1967-70. Mem. Am. Soc. Agrl. Engrs., Am. Soc. Range Mgmt., Kans. Livestock Assn., Kans. Wheat Growers Assn., Lane County Farm Bur. (dir. 1962-66), Kans. Master Farmer (pres. 1971), S.W. Kans. Gem and Mineral Soc. (pres. 1971-72, show chmn. 1977), Kans. Anthrop. Soc. (dir. 1974-76), Lane County Hist. Soc. (pres. 1956-57, dir. 1958—). Methodist. Clubs: Masons, Rotary (pres. 1979-80). Home: Shields KS 67874

TILSON, ROBERT RAY, mfg. co. exec.; b. Asheville, N.C., Apr. 4, 1932; s. Robert Yates and Lena Catherine (Ray) T.; B.S., N.C. State U., 1959; M.B.A., Case Western Res. U., 1971; m. Joan Arlene Murphy, July 18, 1964; children—Robert Burton, John Ray, David Neill. Methods engr. Gen. Electric Co., Cin., 1952-56; devel. engr. TRW, Inc., Cleve., 1959-64; mgr. product planning Reliance Electric Co., Cleve., 1964-71; mgr. corporate projects A. O. Smith, Inc., Milw., 1971-72; dir. mergers and acquisitions and internat. affairs Sundstrand Corp., Rockford, Ill., from 1972, now dir. Corp. devel. and internat. affairs; instr. indsl. engring. N.C. State U., 1957-59; guest lectr. internat. bus. No. Ill. U., DeKalb, 1974-75. Bd. dirs. Community Ednl. Council, Rockford, Ill., 1975-76. Mem. Assn. for Corporate Growth (v.p. 1975), Aerospace Industries Assn., Internat. Trade Club Chgo., Machinery and Allied Products Inst., Am. Mktg. Assn., ASME, World Trade Club No. Ill., U.S.-U.S.S.R. Trade and Econ. Council.

Patentee in field. Home: 6743 Squire Ln Rockford IL 61111 Office: 4751 Harrison Ave Rockford IL 61101

TIMBERLAKE, CHARLES EDWARD, historian, educator; b. South Shore, Ky., Sept. 9, 1935; s. Howard E. and Mabel V. (Collier) T.; B.A. in History, Berea (Ky.) Coll., 1957; cert. Claremont Grad. Sch., 1958; M.A. in History, Claremont Grad. Sch., 1962; Ph.D. (Nat. Defense Fgn. Lang. fellow), U. Washington, Seattle, 1968; m. Patricia Perkins, Dec. 23, 1957; children—Mark B., Daniel E., Eric C. Tchr. history Barstow (Calif.) High Sch., 1959-60, Claremont (Calif.) High Sch., 1960-61; research bibliographer Far Eastern and Russian Inst., U. Wash., Seattle, 1961-62, teaching asst. dept. history, 1962-64; asst. prof. dept. history U. Mo., Columbia, 1967-73, asso. prof., 1973-81, prof., 1981—, editor dept. newsletter, 1972, dir. undergrad. studies, 1973-74, departmental honors dir., 1975—, coordinator honors interdisciplinary program in social and behavioral scis., 1976—; guest lectr. Soviet affairs various schs. and radio TV programs, 1967—. Internat. Research and Exchange Bd. sr. exchange scholar, USSR, 1971; Earhart Found. fellow, 1972, U. Mo. Research Council fellow, 1978; Am. Council Learned Socs. fellow, USSR, 1978; Nat. Endowment for the Humanities grantee, 1979. Mem. Am. Hist. Assn., Am. Assn. for the Advancement of Slavic Studies (dir. 1980—, chmn. council regional affiliates 1981—, rep. Central Slavic Conf. 1979—, pres. Central Slavic Conf. 1976-77), Rocky Mountain Assn. for Slavic Studies. Editor: Essays on Russian Liberalism, 1972; editor, contbr.: Detente: A Documentary Record, 1978; contbr. articles on modern Russian history to periodicals and lit. jours. Home: Route 4 Box 173 Columbia MO 65201 Office: History Dept Univ Missouri Columbia MO 65211

TIMBERLAKE, ROGER DALE, refractories co. exec.; b. South Shore, Ky., May 29, 1949; s. Howard Ellis and Mabel Viola T.; B.B.A., U. Ky., 1971; m. Gloria J. Scherer, Sept. 15, 1971; children—Kristen Rene, Ryan Collier. Dist. sales rep. Taylor Refractories div. N.L. Industries, Cin., 1971-73, dist. sales mgr., Detroit, 1974-77, mgr. indsl. sales mktg., 1978, dir. indsl. mktg. Didier Taylor Refractories Corp., Cin., 1979—. Mem. trends panel Modern Castings mag., 1980—. Mem. Am. Foundrymens Soc. (mem. channel induction com.). Home: 2556 Concord Green Cincinnati OH 45244 Office: PO Box 44040 8361 Broadwell St Cincinnati OH 45244

TIMKEN, W. ROBERT, JR., mfg. co. exec.; b. 1938; B.A., Stanford U., 1960; M.B.A., Harvard U., 1962; married. With Timken Co. (formerly The Timken Roller Bearing Co.), Canton, Ohio, 1962—, asst. to v.p. sales, 1964-65, dir. corp. devel., 1965-68, v.p., 1968-73, vice-chmn. bd., chmn. fin. com., 1973-75, chmn. bd., chmn. fin. com., 1975—, also dir. Office: Timken Co 1835 Dueber Ave SW Canton OH 44706*

TIMM, JEROME JOSEPH, dentist; b. Michigan City, Ind., July 20, 1924; s. Edward Clement and Magdalen Pauline (Wagner) T.; student Ind. U., 1946-48; D.D.S., Loyola U., Chgo., 1952; m. Helen Marie Meers, Nov. 14, 1953; children—Ann Therese, Christopher John, Carol Victoria, Edward Jerome, Mary Elizabeth. Practice gen. dentistry, Michigan City, 1952—; staff dentist Crippled Children Clinic No. Ind., 1971—; mem. staff St. Anthony Hosp., chmn. dental staff, 1968-69. Past bd. dirs., v.p. Meals on Wheels; twice past pres. Marquette High Sch. Booster Club and Found.; pres. Marquette Found. Served with AUS, 1943-46. Fellow Royal Soc. Health; mem. Fedn. Dentaire Internat., ADA, St. Joseph Young Men's Soc., Am. Endodontic Soc., Michigan City C. of C., Ind. Sheriff Assn., Serra Internat. (dist. dep. gov. 1962-63, pres. 1960-61, 69-70, 80-81). Republican. Roman Catholic. K.C. Club: Pottowattomie Country. Home: 208 Robin Trail Michigan City IN 46360 Office: 1232 E Michigan Blvd Michigan City IN 46360

TIMM, RONALD ERIC, nuclear energy research lab. exec.; b. Milw., Feb. 23, 1937; s. Eric Albert and Clara Helen (Vogel) T.; B.S. cum laude, Bradley U., 1964; M.S. in Elec. Engring., U. Colo., 1969; m. Karen Kay Klama, June 20, 1964; children—Julie Renee, Paul David, Rhonda Michelle. Project leader Kaman Nuclear, Colorado Springs, Colo., 1964-69; group leader Argonne Nat. Labs., Lemont, Ill., 1970-77, asso. dir. SAREF Projects, 1977—; guest speaker to civil groups on energy. Chmn. sch. bd. Trinity Luth. Sch., 1977-80. Served with USAF, 1958-62. Mem. Instrument Soc. Am. (sr.). Lutheran. Office: 9700 S Cass Ave Argonne IL 60439

TIMMER, LINDA CHERYL, civil engr.; b. Waynesville, Mo., Dec. 14, 1948; d. Donald Hendrik and Imogene Agnes (Hart) T.; B.S., U. Mo., Columbia, 1970. Structural designer Richland Engring. Ltd., Mansfield, Ohio, 1970-76, transp. engr., 1976-77, project engr., 1977—. Awards chmn. Ohio League of Young Republican Clubs, 1976-77; sec. Richland County Young Republican Club, 1971-72, treas., 1973-75, newsletter editor, 1974-77; Richland County chmn. Youth for Rhodes, 1974; awards chmn. March of Dimes Walk-a-thon, 1978; mem. adv. com. Am. Christian Coll. 1973-75. Registered profl. engr., Ohio. Named Hon. Lt. Gov. Ohio, 1974. Mem. ASCE, Ohio Soc. Profl. Engrs., Nat. Soc. Profl. Engrs., Soc. Women Engrs., Order of the Engr., Nat. Assn. Women in Constrn., Met. Assn. Urban Designers and Environ. Planners, Ohio Hist. Soc., Early Am. Soc., Am. Bible Soc. Republican. Congregationalist. Home: 1800 Washington North Rd Mansfield OH 44903 Office: 2770 Lexington Ave Mansfield OH 44904

TIMMONS, RICHARD WHALEY, publisher; b. South Orange, N.J., June 9, 1930; s. David Jamison and Helen (Taylor) T.; student U. Hartford (Conn.), 1954-57; m. Susan Lovell, Jan. 12, 1973; children—Benjamin, Andrew, Mark, Robert. Advt. salesman Hartford Courant, 1953-63; asst. advt. mgr. The Patriot Ledger, Quincy, Mass., 1967-71, 75-77; mem. nat. advt. staff Christian Sci. Monitor, N.Y.C., 1971-73; advt. dir. The Gazette, Haverhill, Mass., 1975-79; publisher Rhinelander (Wis.) Daily and Sunday News, 1979—. Active Nicolet Male Chorus, Rhinelander. Served with Q.M.C., U.S. Army, 1951-53. Recipient Am. Press Inst. Cert. Columbia U., 1967. Mem. Inland Daily Press Assn., N.E. Newspaper Advt. Bur., Wis. Newspaper Assn. Republican. Christian Scientist. Club: Rotary. Home: 810 Evergreen Ct Rhinelander WI 54501 Office: 314 Courtney St Rhinelander WI 54501

TIMPSON, JEROLD EDWARD, personnel services corp. exec.; b. Grand Rapids, Mich., Nov. 14, 1934; s. John Jacob and Vivian Madelyn (Baird) T.; B.A., Mich. State U., 1957; postgrad. UCLA, 1957-58; m. Patricia JoAnne Swift, Aug. 31, 1937; children—Jerold Brett, Stephen Trent. Vice pres. Timpson Orchard & Storage, Lowell, Mich., 1957-59; mgr. Bowman Assos., Grand Rapids, Mich., 1959-62, chmn. bd. dirs., 1962—; pres., chmn. bd. dirs. Bowman Personnel Services, Inc., Grand Rapids, 1962—; pres. Exec. Services, Inc., Equian Corp., Timpson Properties; v.p. Nat. Personel Associates; condr. seminars Hope Coll., Western Mich. U. Chmn. Citizens' Advisory Counsel to HUD, 1975-79; chmn. various fund raising activities, 1962—. Accredited personnel diplomate. Mem. Nat. Personnel Assn. (dir.), NEA (dir.), Western Mich. Personnel Assn. (dir.), Mich. Edn. Assn. (v.p.), Western Mich. Edn. Assn. (pres.), Pi Kappa Ph. Republican. Presbyterian. Clubs: Peninsular, University. Editor: The Resume, 1973-76. Home: 100 Woodward Ln SE Grand Rapids MI 49506 Office: 1024 Trust Bldg Grand Rapids MI 49503

TINKER, ARTHUR JAMES, hosp. adminstr.; b. Butler, Pa., Oct. 12, 1942; s. Wilkins Z. and C. Ruth (McCandless) T.; student Albion Coll., 1960-62; B.A., U. Mich., 1964, M.H.A., 1967; m. Jean L. Love, July 17, 1965; children—Jennifer, Karen, Kathryn. Adminstrv. resident Wilmington (Del.) Med. Center, 1966-67, asst. adminstr. Del. div., 1967-68, asst. dir., 1968-69; asst. supt. U. Wis. Hosps., Madison, 1969-70, asso. supt., 1970-73, acting supt., 1973-74, asso. supt., 1974-75; Robert Wood Johnson Health Policy fellow Inst. Medicine, Nat. Acad. Scis., Washington, 1975-76; asst. vice chancellor Center Health Scis., U. Wis., Madison, 1976-78; v.p. adminstrn. Oakwood Hosp., Dearborn, Mich., 1978—; mem. subcom. on hosp. bd. trustees New Detroit Health Com., 1979—; v.p. Oakwood Hosp. Found., 1978—. Bd. dirs., exec. com. Southeastern Mich. chpt. ARC, 1980—; bd. dirs. Health Emergency Med. Services, 1980—. Mem. Am. Coll. Hosp. Adminstrs., Am. Hosp. Assn., Am. Public Health Assn., Assn. Univ. Programs Health Adminstrn., Wis. Hosp. Assn. (sec.-treas. So. hosp. dist. 1971-73), Mich. Hosp. Assn. (mem. edn. com. 1979-80, cost containment com. 1980—), Greater Detroit Area Hosp. Council (com. on trustee edn. 1980—, com. on fin. mgmt.), AAAS. Republican. Presbyterian. Clubs: Grosse Ile Golf and Country; Fairlane (Dearborn, Mich.). Home: 21679 Canterbury St Grosse Ile MI 48138 Office: 18101 Oakwood Blvd Dearborn MI 48124

TINKLENBERG, CALVIN EUGENE, constrn. co. exec.; b. Pipestone, Minn., June 16, 1948; d. Gerhart and Christina (Hoek) T.; student Jackson Area Vocat. Tech. Inst., 1966-68; m. Connie Diane Blom, Jan. 1, 1970; children—Kevin Eugene, Lisa Renae, Victoria Sue. Yardman, Solstad's Lumber, Jackson, Minn., 1967-68; carpenter Tinklenberg Constrn., Woodstock, Minn., 1968-72; owner T&R Constrn., Chandler, Minn., 1972—; bldg. cons. Res. officer Pipestone Police, 1970-72; fire chief Chandler Vol. Fire Dept., 1975—; v.p. Chandler Park Bd., 1975-77; mem. Chandler Devel. Commn., 1976; counselor Holland Cadet Club, 1968-70. Pipestone Cadet Club, 1970-72; head counselor Chandler Cadet Club, 1973-77. Recipient Blue Star award, Cadet Club, 1976. Mem. Christian Reformed Church. Club: Rock County Sportsmans. Mem. Nat. Rifle Assn., Minn. State Fire Chiefs Assn., Fire Instrs. Assn. Minn. Designer spl. furniture. Office: T&R Construction Chandler MN 56122

TINNIN, NELSON B., state senator; b. Hornersville, Mo., Oct. 8, 1905; B.S., U. Mo.; m. Lora Bollinger; 1 son, Brent Bollinger. Former prin. elem. sch., Mo.; former tchr. vocat. agr. Hornersville High Sch.; with Hollywood Gin & Elevator Co., Inc., Hornersville; mem. Mo. Senate, 1961—. Chmn. Dunkin County Soil Dist., 1949—; mem. Mo. State Soil Dist. Recipient plaque Hornersville Alumni Assn. for Severely Retarded, 1972; Arrowhead Honor plaque SE Mo. council Boy Scouts Am.; award outstanding work in edn. SE Mo. Tchrs. Assn., 1973; award for service to agr. Gamma Sigma Delta. Methodist. Clubs: Masons, Shriners, Scottish Rite, Order Eastern Star. Office: State Capitol Jefferson City MO 65101*

TIPEI, NICOLAE, elec. and mech. engr.; b. Calarasi, Romania; s. Sever and Elena (Gherghiceanu) T.; came to U.S., 1972; grad. electromechanic engr. Poly. Inst. Bucharest (Romania), 1936, D.Eng., 1968; m. Letitia Radulescu, Apr. 27, 1941; 1 son, Sever. Instr. engring. Poly. Inst. Bucharest, 1936-46, asst. prof., 1946-64, prof. emeritus, 1964-71; chief engr. Romanian Rys. Locomotive Workshops, 1937, Romanian Airlines, 1938; owner, engr. Nicolae Tipei & Co., 1939-43; research worker, corr. mem. Romanian Acad., 1949-71; chief engr. IRMC, Bucharest, 1945-48; sr. research engr. Gen. Motors Tech. Center Research Labs., Warren, Mich., 1972-79, research fellow, 1979—. Served with Romanian Air Force, 1936, 43. Recipient Prize for Sci. Activity, Govt. Romania, 1953, Mayo D. Hersey award ASME, 1980. Mem. Am. Inst. Aeros. and Astronautics, Soc. Applied Math. Mechanics (W.Ger.). Author: Flight Mechanics (Problems and Solutions), 1940; Airports and Civil Aviation, 1942; Theory of Lubrication, 1962; Lagare in Alunecare (Sliding Bearings), 1961; contbr. numerous articles to profl. jours. Home: 1403 E 5th St Royal Oak MI 48067 Office: 12 Mile and Mound Rd Warren MI 48090

TIPPETS, RICHARD JOHNSON, chemist; b. Yuba City, Calif., July 11, 1939; s. McClain Lyman and Kathleen Yvonne (Johnson) T.; B.S., Brigham Young U., 1961; M.S., U. Calif., Davis, 1973; m. Deborah Toni Elkins, Aug. 6, 1978; children—Heather, Kevin, Michael, Theresa. Cons., lab dir. Grow Tech. Inc., Gridley, Calif., 1968-69; cons. Calif. IPA, Gridley, 1969-72; lab dir. Western Ag Tech Inc., Yuba City, 1972-79; chief chemist City St. Joseph (Mo.) Pollution Control, 1980—. Dist. exec. Feather Butte dist. Boy Scouts Am., 1969-72, bd. dirs. Buttes Area council, 1972-75, recipient Dist. Merit award, 1972; J&L Enterprise grantee, 1976. Mem. Water Pollution Control Fedn., Am. Soc. Agronomists. Republican. Mormon. Contbr. articles to profl. jours. Home: 4922 Mockingbird Ln Saint Joseph MO 64506 Office: 3500 Hwy 759 Saint Joseph MO 64504

TIPSHUS, EDWARD CHESTER, data processing specialist, cons.; b. Chgo., Nov. 13, 1929; s. Blase Frank and Tekli (Songaile) T.; B.S., U.S. Naval Acad., 1954; M. Pub. Adminstrn., Am. U., 1968; m. Sondra Leah Bell, June 2, 1962; children—Lisa Ann, John Blase. Served as enlisted man U.S. Marine Corps, 1947-50, commd. 2d lt., 1954, advanced through grades to lt. col., 1969; various assignments in artillery and infantry command and staff, U.S. and overseas, 1954-68; asst. dir. Automated Services Center, Okinawa, 1968-69; dir. automated resources support, Hdqrs. USMC, 1969-70, dir. Automated Services Center, 1971-72; ret., 1972; mgr. data processing dept. Chemical Abstracts Service, Columbus, Ohio, 1972—. Decorated Bronze Star with V, 3 Air Medals, Navy Commendation Medal with V, Vietnamese Gallentry Cross with Silver Star. Mem. U.S. Naval Inst., U.S. Marine Corps Assn., U.S. Naval Acad. Alumni Assn., Ret. Officers Assn., Assn. for Computing Machinery. Republican. Club: Worthington Hills. Home: 8315 Fairway Dr Worthington Hills OH 43085 Office: Box 3012 Columbus OH 43210

TIPTON, CLYDE RAYMOND, JR., research inst. exec.; b. Cin., Nov. 13, 1921; s. Clyde Raymond and Ida Marie (Molitor) T.; B.S., U. Ky., 1946, M.S. (Haggin fellow), 1947; m. Marian Gertrude Beushausen, Aug. 6, 1942; children—Marian Page Cuddy, Robert Bruce. Research engr. Battelle Meml. Inst., Columbus, Ohio, 1947-49, sr. tech. adviser, 1951-62, coordinator corporate communications, 1969-73, v.p. communications, 1973-75, asst. to pres., 1978-79, v.p., corp. dir. communications and public affairs, 1979—; staff mem. Los Alamos Sci. Lab., 1949-51; dir. research Basic, Inc., Bettsville, Ohio, 1962-64; asst. dir. Battelle Pacific N.W. Labs., Richland, Wash., 1964-69; pres., trustee Battelle Commons Co. for Community Urban Redevel., Columbus, 1975-78. Secretariat, U.S. Del., 2d Internat. Conf. on Peaceful Uses Atomic Energy, Geneva, Switzerland, 1958; cons. U.S. AEC in Atoms for Peace Program, Tokyo, Japan, 1959, New Delhi, India, 1959-60, Rio de Janeiro, Brazil, 1961. Bd. dirs., past pres. Pilot Dogs, Central Ohio United Negro Coll. Fund; bd. dirs. Columbus Assn. for Performing Arts, Central Ohio resource bd. CARE; asst. sec.-treas. Pilot Guide Dog Found., 1979—; bd. dirs., pres. Architects Soc. Ohio Found., 1978—; bd. dirs., past pres. Greater Columbus Arts Council. Served with USAAF, 1943. Sr. fellow Otterbein Coll., 1978. Mem. AAAS, Am. Mgmt. Assn., Am. Soc. Metals, Public Relations Soc. Am., Nat., Ohio socs. profl. engrs., Ohio Acad. Sci., Sigma Xi, Alpha Chi Sigma. Episcopalian. Lion. Clubs: Athletic (Columbus, Washington). Editor: Jour. Soc. for Nondestructive Testing, 1953-57; The Reactor Handbook, Reactor Materials, vol. 3, 1955, vol. 1, 1960; Learning to Live on a Small Planet, 1974. Patentee in field. Home: 2354 Dorset Rd Columbus OH 43221 Office: 505 King Ave Columbus OH 43201

TIPTON, GARY LEE, quality control technician; b. Superior, Nebr., Dec. 30, 1952; s. Adelbert Fahy and Ruby Maxine (Woodward) T.; student Creighton U., 1971, U. N.D., 1972; B.S. in Math.-Sci., Mary Coll., 1981; m. Elizabeth Ann Gludt, Jan. 6, 1973; children—Brian Lee, Daniel James. With Melroe div. Clark Equipment Co., Bismarck, N.D., 1974—, material handler, 1975, inventory control clk., 1975-77, prodn. expeditor, 1977, indsl. engring. technician, 1977-80, product design asst. I, 1980, quality control technician, 1980-81, asso. quality control engr., 1981—, chmn. mgmt. devel. com., 1979-81. Mem. Nat. Mgmt. Assn. (chmn. new chpt. promotion com. 1981—). Roman Catholic. Club: Eagles. Home: 1824 E Divide Ave Bismarck ND 58501 Office: 403 Airport Rd PO Box 1215 Bismarck ND 58502

TITCHENAL, OLIVER RAY, packaging co. exec.; b. Parker, Ariz., Mar. 18, 1920; s. Charles Elmer and Dora (Kieth) T.; student Fullerton (Calif.) Jr. Coll., 1937-38; m. Florence Mae Rabourn, Mar. 21, 1948 (div. 1973); children—Stephen Ray, Douglas Wayne, Jeffery Scott. Tooling engr. Douglas Aircraft Co., Santa Monica, Calif., Tulsa, 1938-48; mgr. sales engring. St. Regis Paper Co., Los Angeles, San Francisco, 1948-56, chief engr., 1956-60, gen. mgr. packaging machinery div., 1960-63, dir. packaging engring., 1963-65; asst. dir. research, converted products PKG div. Dow Chem. Co., Midland, Mich., Cleve., 1965-71; founder exec. v.p. Basic Packaging System Inc., Avon Lake, Ohio, 1971—, also dir. Served with USMC, 1944-46. Mem. Am. Assn. Mech. Engrs., Packaging Inst. Registered profl. engr., Calif. Patentee in field. Home: 32795 Brookstone Ln North Ridgeville OH 44039 Office: 583 Miller Rd Avon Lake OH 44012

TITKO, JERRY L., podiatrist; b. Hemlock, Ohio, Feb. 2, 1941; s. Peter E. and Anna M. (Marolt) T.; student Ohio State U., 1958-59; D. Podiatric Medicine, Ohio Coll. Podiatric Medicine, 1963; div.; children—J. Russell, Kristin Kimberly. Intern Cleve. Foot Clinic, 1963-64, Youngstown (Ohio) Foot Clinic, 1964; pvt. practice podiatry, Hamilton, Ohio, 1964—; clin. instr. Ohio Coll. Podiatric Medicine, 1974—. Mem. Am., Ohio, So. Ohio podiatry assns., Acad. Hosp. Podiatry, Internat. Acad. Preventive Medicine, Am. Pub. Health Assn., Acad. Ambulatory Foot Surgery (charter), Ohio Acad. Foot Surgery (charter), Hamilton Investment Club (pres. 1971, 74, 75), Hamilton Jr. C. of C. (v.p. 1967). Presbyterian. Home: 1103 Buckhead Dr Fairfield OH 45014 Office: 25 N F St Hamilton OH 45013

TITMAS, WILLIAM GARY, indsl. systems cons.; b. Patterson, N.J., Dec. 9, 1908; s. Albert and Anna Marie (McGarry) T.; student U. So. Calif., 1935-38, U. Akron (Ohio), 1938-40; m. Clara Black, June 30, 1930 (div.); children—Elizabeth Ann, John, James; m. 2d, Ann Sparks, Nov. 19, 1949. Positions in acctg. with various mfg. cos., 1934-49; controller Republic Stampling and Enameling Co., Canton, Ohio, 1949-51; mgmt. cons. A.T. Kearney Co., Chgo., 1951-52, 56-59; budget mgr. Canton div. E.W. Bliss Co., 1952-56; gen. systems mgr. United Farm Coops., Alliance, Ohio, 1959-64; pres. Data Systems Designers & Cons., indsl. systems cons., Canton, 1964—. Active local Boy Scouts Am. Mem. Nat. Assn. Accountants, Assn. Systems Mgmt. (Merit award 1977). Republican. Episcopalian. Club: Toastmasters. Co-author: How to Adminster Effective Budgets, 1957. Address: 318 Cleveland Ave Canton OH 44702

TITZER, JENNIFER SUSAN, educator; b. Evansville, Ind., May 23, 1957; d. Thomas Leo and Elizabeth Ann (Lutz) T.; B.S., Ball State U., Muncie, Ind., 1980. Tchr., coordinator mktg. and distributive edn. Northrop High Sch., Ft. Wayne (Ind.) Community Schs., 1980—, also volleyball coach, adv. to Distributive Edn. Clubs of Am. Named to Distributive Edn. Clubs of Am. Hall of Fame, 1981. Mem. Am. Vocat. Assn., Ind. Vocat. Assn., Nat. Assn. for Distributive Edn. Tchrs., Ind. Distributive Edn. Assn., Nat. High Sch. Athletic Coaches Assn., Ind. High Sch. Coaches Assn., NEA, Ind. Tchrs. Assn. Home: 5501 N Clinton St Fort Wayne IN 46825 Office: 7001 Coldwater Rd Fort Wayne IN 46825

TIU, ALFONSO LI, internist, cardiologist; b. Cebu, Philippines, Feb. 16, 1943; s. Ching Quiat and Chuti (Li) T.; came to U.S., 1966; A.A. with high honors, U. San Carlos, Cebu City, Philippines, 1960; M.D. with honors, Cebu Inst. Medicine, 1965; m. Lou Divina Taclob, Aug. 25, 1966; children—Chuti Lynn, Alphonse Patrick, Carmelita Anne. Intern, St. Michael Hosp., Milw., 1966; resident in internal medicine Mt. Sinai Hosp., 1967; resident in internal medicine, cardiology fellowship Tulane U. Med. Program, New Orleans, 1968-70; cardiology fellowship Springfield (Mass.) Med. Center, 1970; practice medicine specializing in internal medicine and cardiology, West Allis, Wis., 1971—; med. cons. Allis Chalmers Med. Dept. Diplomate Am. Bd. Internal Medicine, subsplty Bd. Cardiovascular Disease. Fellow Am. Coll. Cardiology, Am. Coll. Chest Physicians, Am. Coll. Angiology, Am. Coll. Internat. Physicians; mem. AMA, A.C.P., Am. Soc. Internal Medicine, Am. Heart Assn. (fellow council on clin. cardiology), Med. Soc. Milw. County, State Med. Soc. Wis., Physicians Martial Arts Assn. Roman Catholic. Office: 10617 W Oklahoma Ave West Allis WI 53227

TOAZ, MILTON WILLIAM, metall. engr.; b. Cleve., Oct. 1, 1930; s. Glenn Alvin and Florence Mabel (Dunham) T.; B.S., Case Inst. Tech., 1954, M.S., 1956; m. Marian Betty Horton, June 26, 1954; children—Todd Horton, Terrell Glenn, Tracy Ellen. Metall. engr. Clevite Research Center, Cleve., 1956-62, engring. mgr. aerospace div., 1962-64, project engr., mech. research div., 1964-68; sr. proejct engr. Gould Lab., Gould, Inc., Cleve., 1968-74, mgr. metallurgy and mechanics, 1974-81, mgr. metallurgy Imperial Clevite Tech. Center, 1981—. Mem. bd. mgrs. Southeast YMCA, 1968—. Mem. Am. Soc. for Metals, Am. Powder Metallurgy Inst., AIME, No. Ohio Swim Ofcls. Assn., Sigma Xi. Republican. Presbyterian. Contbr. articles in field to profl. jours.; patentee. Home: 206 Bexley Dr Bedford OH 44146 Office: Imperial Clevite Tech Center 540 E 105th St Cleveland OH 44108

TOBIN, CALVIN JAY, architect; b. Boston, Feb. 15, 1927; s. David and Bertha (Tanfield) T.; B.Arch., U. Mich., 1949; m. Joan Hope Fink, July 15, 1951; children—Michael Alan, Nancy Ann. Designer, draftsman Arlen & Lowenfish, architects, N.Y.C., 1949-51; with Samuel Arlen, N.Y.C., 1951-53, Skidmore, Owings & Merrill, N.Y.C., 1953; architect Loebl, Schlossman & Bennett, architects, Chgo., 1953-57; v.p. Loebl, Schlossman & Hackl, 1957—. Chmn., Jewish United Fund Bldg. Trades Div., 1969; chmn. AIA and Chgo. Hosp. Council Com. of Hosp. Architecture, 1968-76. Chmn. Highland Park (Ill.) Appearance Rev. Commn., 1972-73; mem. Highland Park Plan Commn., 1972-78; mem. Highland Park City Council, 1974—, mayor pro tem, 1979—; bd. dirs. Young Men's Jewish Council, 1953-67, pres., 1967; bd. dirs. Jewish Community Centers Chgo., 1973-78. Served with USNR, 1945-46. Mem. A.I.A. (2d v.p. Chgo. chpt.), Pi Lambda Phi. Jewish. Archtl. works include Michael Reese Hosp. and Med. Center, 1954—, Prairie Shores Apt. Urban Redevel., 1957-62, Louis A. Weiss Meml. Hosp., Chgo., Chgo. State Hosp., Central Community Hosp., Chgo., Gottlieb Meml. Hosp., Melrose Park, Ill.,

West Suburban Hosp., Oak Park, Ill., Thorek Hosp. and Med. Center, Chgo., Shriners Hosp., Chgo., Water Tower Pl., Chgo., also numerous apt., comml. and community bldgs. Home: 814 Dean Ave Highland Park IL 60035 Office: 845 N Michigan Ave Chicago IL 60611

TOBIN, HELEN MARGUERITE, nursing adminstr.; b. Three Rivers, Mich., Apr. 10, 1922; d. Herman A. and Mary E. (Kirk) T.; B.S. in Nursing, Western Res. U., 1949, M.S., 1957. Staff nurse Three Rivers Hosp., 1943-44, 46; asst. head nurse med. nursing U. Hosps. of Cleve., 1949, head nurse, 1949-52, adminstrv. supr. med.-surg. nursing, 1952-56, asst. dir. nursing, 1960-61, dir. centralized staff devel., 1961—, asst. dir. nursing med.-surg. nursing, 1964-65, 67-68, 70-71; asst. dir. nursing, research and devel. Cleve. Met. Gen. Hosp., 1957-60; lectr. nursing adminstrn. Western Reserve U., Cleve., 1962-63, asst. clin. prof. nursing, 1965-73, asso. clin. prof. nursing, 1973—. Served with U.S. Army Nurse Corps, 1944-46. Recipient Career Women of Achievement Merit award YWCA, 1979, Disting. Alumni award Case-Western Res. U. Sch. Nursing, 1977. Cleve. League Nursing Honor Roll for contbr. to nursing and health care, 1975. Fellow Am. Acad. Nursing; mem. Am. Nurses Assn., Assn. Advancement Nursing Practice, Am. Soc. Tng. Dirs., Sigma Theta Tau. Author: (with P. Yoder, P. Hull, B. Scott) The Process of Staff Development: Components for Change, 1974, 2d edit., 1979; contbr. articles on staff devel. to profl. publs. Home: 3055 Yorkshire Rd Cleveland Heights OH 44118 Office: University Circle Cleveland OH 44106

TOBIN, MICHAEL E., banker; b. Newtown Square, Pa., Jan. 17, 1926; s. Michael Joseph and Emma (Roberts) T.; B.S. in Econs., U. Pa., 1948; m. Judith Anne Brown; children—Michael E., Allegra, Corey. Cons., Philco, RCA, Ebasco Services, Inc., 1950-56; sr. cons. Arthur Young & Co., N.Y.C., 1956-59, Midwest dir. cons. services, Chgo., 1959-68; pres. Midwest Stock Exchange, Chgo., 1968-78; pres. Am. Nat. Bank & Trust Co., Chgo., 1978—, chmn., chief exec. officer, 1979—. Trustee Orchestral Assn. (Chgo. Symphony Orch.); mem. governing bd. Lyric Opera Chgo.; mem. bus. adv. council Chgo. Urban League; bd. dirs. Chgo. Assn. Commerce and Industry. Served in U.S. Army, World War II; ETO. Office: 33 N LaSalle St Chicago IL 60602

TOBOLSKI, FRANCIS PETER, market researcher; b. Chgo., Oct. 20, 1932; s. John Edmund and Stella Dorothy (Lewicki) T.; B.S., Ill. Inst. Tech., 1957, M.S., 1962; fellow Nat. Assn. Ednl. Broadcasters, U. Ill., 1957; m. Callie Mae Christian, Aug. 23, 1958; children—Francis Peter, Carolyn Mary. Asst. supr. radio and TV, Ill. Inst. Tech., 1953-57; research analyst, project leader Container Corp. Am., Chgo., 1957-62; project dir. McCann-Erickson, Inc., Chgo., 1962-63; with design and market research lab. Container Corp. Am., Carol Stream, Ill., 1963—, dir., 1968—; prof. Inst. Mgmt., also instr. M.B.A. program Ill. Benedictine Coll., Lisle, Ill., 1968—. Mem. ednl. adv. com. Roman Cath. Diocese of Joliet (Ill.), 1973; pres. Sts. Peter and Paul Sch. Bd., Naperville, Ill., 1970-71; cons. DuPage council Girl Scouts U.S.A., 1981. Served with AUS, 1954-56. Mem. Soc. Engring. Psychologists (asso.; Div. Cons. Psychologists), Am. Psychol. Assn., Am. Mktg. Assn., Polish Roman Cath. Union, Alpha Sigma Phi, Pi Delta Epsilon. Author articles and chpts. in books. Home: 412 E 12th Ave Naperville IL 60540 Office: 400 E North Ave Carol Stream IL 60187

TODARO, SHERRY ADELE, purchasing exec.; b. Evanston, Ill., Feb. 22, 1929; d. Sherwood and Virginia Mary (Wood) Owen; student public schs., Nauvoo, Ill.; m. Victor Joseph Todaro, Oct. 16, 1965; children—Curtis Fleming, Donald Fleming, Cherie Cottrell, Becky Magley, Bonnie Feikes. Finisher, Howmet Turbine Components Corp., LaPorte, Ind., 1960-68, sec., 1968-73, alloy control clk., 1973-76, sales coordinator, 1976-78, supr. alloy procurement and inventory control, 1978—; sec.-treas. Trader Vic, Ltd., LaPorte, Ind., 1979—. Co-founder Protective Animal League, Inc., LaPorte, 1970; trustee City of Kingsford Heights (Ind.), 1980-84. Mem. Am. Mgmt. Assn. Democrat. Roman Catholic. Clubs: Am. Spaniel, LaPorte County Kennel, Cocker Spaniel N.W. Ind. (founder). Office: 1110 E Lincolnway LaPorte IN 46350

TODD, CURTIS LINN, accountant; b. Ft. Madison, Iowa, June 15, 1948; s. Homer Lee and Iva Parleigh (Faw) T.; B.B.A. in Accounting, U. Iowa, 1970; m. Judith Mae Boltz, June 24, 1972; 1 son, Kieran. Sr. asst. accountant Haskins & Sells, C.P.A.'s, N.Y.C., 1970-72, Omaha, 1973-74; asst. controller Am. Beef Packers, Omaha, 1974-77; staff accountant Buesing & Schleisman, C.P.A.'s, Omaha, 1977; v.p., controller Omaha Steaks Internat., 1977—. Served with U.S. Army, 1970-72. C.P.A., Nebr., Iowa. Mem. Am. Inst. C.P.A.'s, Nebr. Soc. C.P.A.'s, Iowa Soc. C.P.A.'s, Nat. Assn. Accountants (pres. Omaha chpt., 1981—). Home: 14019 Madison Circle Omaha NE 68137 Office: Omaha Steaks Internat 4400 S 96th St Omaha NE 68127

TODD, EUGENIA J. KORCHEVSKY (MRS. ROBERT LOUIS TODD), corp. exec.; b. Newark; d. Joseph and Mary (Leczse) Korchevsky; student Montclair State Tchrs. Coll.; B.S., Jersey City State Tchrs. Coll., 1947; R.N., Jersey City Med. Center, 1947; m. Robert Louis Todd, May 10, 1948; children—Robert Joseph, John Burton. Clk., Irvington (N.J.) Jewish Cemetery, 1938-39; marker Bamberger's Dept. Store, Newark, 1940-41; sec. Graybar Electric Co., Newark, 1942-43, Orbachs Dept. Store, Newark, 1943-44, Montclair State Tchrs. Coll., 1943-44; sec., nurse Jersey City Med. Center, 1944-47; nurse Mountainside Hosp., Montclair, N.J., 1947-49, VA Hosp., Dearborn, Mich., 1949-51; cons. Home and Hawkeye Registry, Burlington, Iowa, 1955-59; v.p., sec., treas. North Hill Med. Bldg. Corp., Burlington, 1960—; journalist Mediapolis New Era; columnist Mediapolis Monitor, Care Center Chatter. Den leader Boy Scouts Am., Burlington, 1955-65. Mem. Art Guild (life, patron), Nat. Wildlife Fedn., Am. Geriatrics Soc., Nat. Parks and Conservation Assn., Smithsonian Assos., Nat. Hist. Soc. Club: Crystal Lake (Ill.); Hen-Co-Hills (Ill.). Office: 608 Prairie St Mediapolis IA 52637

TODD, GARY IRL, radio exec.; b. Walla Walla, Wash., May 8, 1937; s. William Irl and Ruby Alice (Waddington) T.; grad. high sch.; m. Linda May Wolfe, June 21, 1958; children—Teresa Rene, Gary Irl, Scott Robert. Promotion dir. KIMN Radio, Denver, 1965-66, KOL Radio, Seattle, 1967-68; v.p. WIBC Radio, Indpls., 1968—; pres. Gary Todd Co., Inc. Mem. Mayor's Stadium Task Force, 1970—; mem. new events com. 500 Festival Assn., 1970; capt. 150th birthday fund dr. Ind. U., 1970—; mem. pub. relations adv. com. Cath. Youth Orgn., 1970—; radio chmn. Easter Seals, 1969-70, chmn. central Ind.; radio chmn. Ind. Hemophilia Found., 1970—; crusade chmn. Am. Cancer Soc., 1972, bd. dirs. Marion County unit, 1971—; chmn. Central Ind. Christmas Seal Campaign; bd. dirs. Indpls. Christmas Com., 1975-76, Lawrence N. Progress, Inc., 1976-77. Recipient Nat. award of merit Am. Assn. Blood Banks, 1970; Distinguished Service award Indpls. Jr. C. of C., 1971, Speedway Jr. C. of C., 1970; Service to Mankind award Castleton Sertoma, 1976; named Outstanding Young Hoosier, Ind. Jr. C. of C., 1972; Gary Todd Day proclaimed by mayor of Indpls., 1970. Office: 2835 Illinois St Indianapolis IN 46208

TODD, JEFFREY WARREN, county public health ofcl.; b. Oak Park, Ill., May 26, 1949; s. George Litchfield and Mary Jane (McIntosh) T.; student Western Ill. U., 1968-69; B.A., No. Ill. U., 1972; M.S., George Williams Coll., 1979; m. July 22, 1978. Exec. dir. Will County (Ill.) Drug Coordination and Info. Council, Inc., 1972-74; program coordinator mental health div. Will County Health Dept., 1974-76, dir. mental health div., 1976-79; public health adminstr. Grundy County (Ill.) Health Dept., 1979—; bd. dirs. Region IX Health Systems Agy., Inc., 1976-79, 80-81; co-instr. crisis intervention Coll. St. Francis, 1974-76; adj. teaching faculty grad. program in health service adminstrn., 1982. Alderman, City of Morris (Ill.), 1979—. Served with USNR, 1967-68. Mem. Am. Psychol. Assn., Am. Health Planning Assn., Am. Public Health Assn., Am. Personnel and Guidance Assn., Am. Mental Health Counselors Assn., U.S. Conf. City Health Officers, Ill. Public Health Assn., Ill. Assn. Public Health Adminstrs. Democrat. Presbyterian. Club: Lions (Morris). Research on sexual attitudes, knowledge and behavior of rural and urban communities, Grundy County health needs; condr. Morris public opinion survey on cable TV. Home: 408 E High St Morris IL 60450 Office: Grundy County Health Dept 1340 Edwards St Morris IL 60450

TODD, JOHN JOSEPH, justice Minn. Supreme Ct.; b. South St. Paul, Minn., Mar. 16, 1927; student St. Thomas Coll., 1944, 46-47; B.S. in Law, U. Minn., 1949, LL.B., 1950; m. Dolores Shanahan, Sept. 9, 1950; chilren—Richard, Jane, John. Admitted to Minn. bar, 1951; partner firm Thuet & Todd, South St. Paul, 1951-72; asso. justice Minn. Supreme Ct., St. Paul, 1972—; mem. Minn. Tax Ct., 1966-72; chmn. Minn. Fair Trial-Free Press Council. Served with USN, 1945-46. Mem. Minn. Trial Lawyers Assn., First Dist. Bar Assn. Minn. pres. 1969-70), Minn. State Bar Assn. Office: Supreme Ct 225 State Capitol Saint Paul MN 55155

TODD, JOHN ODELL, ins. co. exec.; b. Mpls., Nov. 12, 1902; s. Frank Chisholm and Mary Mable (Odell) T.; A.B., Cornell U., 1924; C.L.U., Am. Coll., 1933; m. Katherine Sarah Cone, Feb. 21, 1925; children—John Odell, George Bennett. Spl. agt. Equitable Life Assurance Soc., Mpls., 1926-28; ins. broker, Mpls., 1928-31; spl. agt. Northwestern Mut. Life Ins. Co., Mpls., 1931-38, Evanston, Ill., 1951—; partner H.S. Vail & Sons, Chgo., 1938-43, Vail and Todd, gen. agts. Northwestern Mut. Life Ins. Co., 1943-44; sole gen. agt., Chgo., 1944-51; pres. Todd Planning and Service Co., life ins. brokers, 1951—; founder prin. John O. Todd Orgn. Inc., Exec. Compensation Specialists and Cons., 1970—; faculty lectr. C.L.U. Insts., U. Conn., 1952-53, U. Wis., 1955-57, U. Calif., 1956, U. Hawaii, 1966; host interviewer ednl. Films Series of the Greats, 1973-74. Pres. Evanston (Ill.) 1st. Ward Non-Partisan Civic Assn., 1956-57; trustee Evanston Hist. Soc., 1973-76. Recipient Golden Plate award Am. Acad. Achievement, 1969; Huebner Gold medal for contbn. to edn., 1978; named Ins. Field Man of Year, Ins. Field Pub. Co., 1965. Mem. Nat. Assn. Life Underwriters (John Newton Russell award 1969), Assn. Advanced Life Underwriters (pres. 1963-64), Am. Coll. Life Underwriters (trustee 1957-78), Chgo. Life Underwriters Assn. (dir. 1938-41), Northwestern Mut. Spl. Agts. Assn. (pres. 1955-56), Life Agy. Mgrs. Assn. (dir. 1945-48), Northwestern Mut. Assn. Agts. (pres. 1957-58), Chgo. Life Trust Council, Psi Upsilon, Sphinx Head. Republican. Clubs: Evanston Univ.; Glen View; Mpls. Author: Taxation, Inflation and Life Insurance, 1950; The Beneficiary in Life Insurance, 1948; Ceiling Unlimited, 1965; contbg. author to text Huebner Foundation, 1951.

TODD, JUANITA MARIE HOUSE, ret. govt. ofcl.; b. St. Louis, June 2, 1922; d. Andrew and Susie (Forrester) House; B.A. in Bus. Adminstrn., Columbia Coll., 1974; M.A. in Mgmt., Webster Coll., 1975; m. Alfred W. Todd, Nov. 22, 1942 (dec. Sept. 1973); children—Pamela Marie Todd Young, Alfred W., Patricia Diane Todd Jones. Clk-typist U.S. Army Troop Support and Aviation Materiel Readiness Command, and predecessors, St. Louis, 1957-58, procurement clk., 1958-62, contract asst., 1962-65, contract specialist, 1965-79. Mem. Nat. Contracts Mgmt. Assn. (certified profl. contracts mgr.). Baptist. Home: 4533 Lexington Ave Saint Louis MO 63115

TODD, MARY ELIZABETH (MRS. ALVA CRESS TODD), coll. ofcl.; b. Lafayette, Ind., Aug. 26, 1920; d. Christian Frederick and Anna Marie (Mahlke) Schelle; diploma Ind. Bus. Coll., 1940; m. Alva Cress Todd, Apr. 17, 1941; children—Richard Schelle, Carol Todd Biegalski, Joanne Todd Horton, Elizabeth Ann Todd Lowry. Sec., Sears Roebuck & Co., Lafayette, 1940, Riley Pountry Farm, Lafayette, 1940-41; treas. Todd Assos., engrs., Villa Park, Ill., 1961-67; co-founder, bus. mgr., treas. Midwest Coll. Engring., Lombard, Ill., 1967—, trustee, 1973—, sec., treas. bd. trustees, 1976, acting pres., 1981—. Mem. Meml. Hosp. Guild, Elmhurst, Ill., 1963—. Mem. Nat. Assn. Coll. and Univ. Bus. Officers, Lombard C. of C., Delta Sigma Kappa. Home: 827 S Summit Ave Villa Park IL 60181 Office: 440 S Finley Rd Lombard IL 60148

TODD, MARYSNOW STONE (MRS. ZANE G. TODD), educator; b. Owensville, Ind., Apr. 6, 1920; d. Clarence Edgar and Mary Pearl (Knowles) Stone; student Lockyear Bus. Coll., 1945-46, Ind. Central Coll., 1958-62; m. Zane G. Todd, Feb. 8, 1950; 1 dau., Betty (Mrs. William Hudson). Bookkeeper, Mo. Valley Bridge & Iron Co., Evansville, Ind., 1942-45, McCrory's Stores, Indpls., 1947-51; asst. editor Research and Rev. Pubs., Inc., Indpls., 1951-55, asso. editor, 1956-58; tchr. Perry Twp. schs., Indpls., 1968—. Counselor in edn., 1965-67. Mem. com. Ind. Symphony Soc., 1960—; area leader Am. Cancer Soc., 1968; mem. Winchester Civic Assn., 1962—, Ind. Hist. Soc., 1959—; volunteer A.R.C., 1970-72; mem. Lions Aux., 1956—. Bd. dirs. Muscular Dystrophy Assn., 1969. Mem. Soc. Comml. Journalists, Internat. Platform Assn. Republican. Presbyn. Clubs: Riviera, Meridian Hills Country, Indianapolis Athletic; La Coquille (Palm Beach, Fla.). Contbr. articles to ins. jours. Home: 7645 Randue Ct Indianapolis IN 46278

TODD, STANTON WESLEY, III, ins. co. exec.; b. Grand Rapids, Mich., Feb. 23, 1941; s. Stanton W. and Rosemary (Hunt) T.; B.A., Lake Forest Coll., 1963; m. Gail B. Walker, Mar. 1, 1969; children—Cortney Walker, Stanton Wesley IV, Kaley Clark, Kathryn Gayl. Salesman, Northwestern Mut. Life Ins. Co., Grand Rapids, 1963-65, N.Y.C., 1965-73; pres. Early Am. Life, St. Paul, 1973-77; sr. mktg. officer, sr. v.p. Globe Life Ins. Co., Chgo., 1978-81; v.p. mktg. U.S. Life Corp., 1981—; also dir. Chmn. bd. govs. Lake Forest (Ill.) Coll.; chmn. leadership council Ravenswood Hosp., Chgo.; mem. Nat. Child Labor Bd., N.Y.C. Mem. Nat. Assn. Life Underwriters. Address: US Life Corp 8501 W Higgins Rd Chicago IL 60631 also 125 Maiden Ln NY

TODD, ZANE GREY, utility exec., elec. engr.; b. Hanson, Ky., Feb. 3, 1924; s. Marshall Elvin and Kate (McCormick) T.; student Evansville Coll., 1948-49; B.S.E.E. summa cum laude, Purdue U., 1951, D. Engring., 1979; postgrad. U. Mich., summer 1965; m. Marysnow Stone, Feb. 8, 1950. Fingerprint classifier FBI, 1942-43; electric system planning engr. Indpls. Power & Light Co., 1951-56, spl. assignments supr., 1956-60, head elec. system planning, 1960-65, head substa. engring., 1965-68, head distbn. engring., 1968-70, asst. to v.p., 1970-72, v.p., 1972-74, exec. v.p., 1974-75, pres., 1975-76, chmn. bd., pres., 1976-81, chmn. bd., chief exec. officer, 1981—, also dir.; gen. mgr. Mooresville Pub. Service Co., Inc. (Ind.), 1956-60; dir. Mchts. Nat. Bank, Am. States Ins. Cos. Mem. adv. bd. St. Vincent Hosp., Salvation Army; bd. dirs. 500 Festival Assos., Commn. for Downtown, United Way of Greater Indpls.; Ind. chmn. U.S. Savs. Bond Program; chmn. bd. trustees Ind. Central U.; bd. govs. Asso. Colls. Ind.; mem. adv. bd., trustee Christian Theol. Sem. Served with AUS, 1943-47. Recipient Distinguished Alumnus award Purdue U., 1976. Fellow IEEE (past chmn. com. application probability methods, past chmn. power systems engring. com.); mem. Indpls. (dir.), Ind. (dir.), Mooresville (past pres.) chambers commerce, Ind. Soc. Profl. Engrs., Am. Mgmt. Assn. (gen. mgmt. council), N.A.M. (dir.), Ind. Electric Assn. (dir., chmn. 1976-77), Eta Kappa Nu, Tau Beta Pi. Rotarian. Clubs: Indianapolis Athletic (bd. dirs.), Meridian Hills Country, Columbia; La Coquille (Palm Beach). Contbr. to tech. jour. Originator probability analysis of power systems reliability. Home: 7645 Randue Ct Indianapolis IN 46278 Office: 25 Monument Circle Indianapolis IN 46204

TOEPFER, LOUIS ADELBERT, lawyer, former univ. pres.; b. Sheboygan, Wis., Aug. 31, 1919; s. Albert and Laura (Reed) T.; B.A., Beloit Coll., 1940; LL.B., Harvard, 1947; m. Alice Mary Willy, Aug. 7, 1942; children—Thomas Michael, Anthony, Daniel, Andrew, John. Asst. dean Law Sch. Harvard, 1947-56, sec., 1956-59, vice dean, 1959-66, dir. admissions, 1947-66, mem. faculty, 1959-66, dean, prof. law Case Western Res. U., Cleve., 1966—, pres., 1971-80; partner-in-charge firm Jones, Day, Reavis & Pogue, Columbus, Ohio, 1980—; dir. Republic Steel Corp. Mem. Ct. Nisi Prius. Served with USNR, 1942-46. Mem. Am., Ohio, Columbus bar assns., Phi Beta Kappa. Office: 50 W Broad St Columbus OH 43215

TOEPPE, JEFFREY JON, metal finishing co. exec.; b. Racine, Wis., Feb. 27, 1956; s. Robert Joseph and Betty M. (Gertz) T.; diploma Gateway Tech. Inst., 1976; diploma Intensive Tng. Course, Am. Electroplaters Soc., 1979, diploma Environ. Compliance course, 1980; diploma Elnic Electroless Nickel Sch., Nashville, 1981; m. Debra Ann Cutts, July 31, 1976. Lab. technician Wis. Plating Works, Racine, part-time, 1973-76, supr., 1976-77, plant supt., 1977-78, plant mgr., 1978-79, v.p., sec., 1979—, also dir. Mem. Am. Electroplaters Soc. (bd. mgrs. 1980-81; chmn. program 1980-81, cert. electroplater). Soc. Mfg. Engrs., World Electroless Nickel Soc. (charter). Republican. Office: Wis Plating Works Racine Inc PO Box 1813 Racine WI 53401

TOEPPER, ROBERT MARVIN, educator; b. Chgo., May 22, 1940; s. Marvin William and Eleanor Marie (Klicman) T.; B.S., Concordia Tchrs. Coll., River Forest, Ill., 1962; M.A., Washington U., St. Louis, 1967, Ph.D. (NDEA fellow), 1978; m. Marilyn Ann Unger, July 28, 1962; children—Michael R., Carolyn G., Christina J., Matthew J. Tchr. social studies, coach Luth. High Sch. S., St. Louis, 1963-69; research asso., instructional environment component NW Regional Ednl. Lab., Tacoma, 1974-76; asst. prof., coordinator student teaching Concordia Coll., Bronxville, N.Y., 1976-78; asso. prof., coordinator secondary edn. Concordia Coll., River Forest, Ill., 1979—. Mem. adv. com. student housing Bethel Sch. Dist., Wash., 1974-75; coach Little League, River Forest, 1979. Experienced Tchr. fellow, 1969-70. Mem. Assn. Supervision and Curriculum Devel., Assn. Tchr. Educators, Dirs. of Student Teaching Group, Chgo. Constorium Colls. and Univs., Ill. Assn. Supervision and Curriculum Devel., Ill. Assn. Tchr. Educators, Ill. Council Social Studies, Lutheran Edn. Assn., Nat. Council Social Studies, Nat. Model R.R. Assn., Phi Delta Kappa. Lutheran. Home: 1107 Monroe Ave River Forest IL 60305 Office: 7400 Augusta St River Forest IL 60305

TOFTNER, RICHARD ORVILLE, environ. mgmt. cons.; b. Warren, Minn., Mar. 5, 1935; s. Orville Gayhart and Cora Evelyn (Anderson) T.; B.A., U. Minn., 1966; M.B.A., Xavier U., 1970; m. Jeanne Bredine, June 26, 1960; children—Douglas, Scott, Kristine, Kimberly, Brian. Sr. economist Federated Dept. Stores, Inc., Cin., 1967-68; dep. dir. EPA, Washington and Cin., 1968-73; mgmt. cons. environ. affairs, products and mktg., 1973-74; prin. PEDCo Environ., Cin., 1974-80; trustee PEDCo trusts, 1974-80; pres. ROTA Mgmt., Inc., Cin., 1980—; adj. prof. U. Cin.; lectr. Grad. fellowship rev. panel Office of Edn., 1978—; advisor, cabinet-level task force Office of Gov. of P.R., 1973; subcom. Nat. Safety Council, 1972. Served with AUS, 1954-57. Mem. Am. Inst. Cert. Planners, Soc. Advancement Mgmt., Water Pollution Control Fedn., Water Resources Council of Ohio. Contbr. articles to mgmt. planning and environ. to periodicals, chpts. in books. Home: 9175 Yellowwood Dr Cincinnati OH 45239 Office: 4700 Lakeview Tower Cincinnati OH 45241

TOKAR, MAUREEN TANSEY, architect; b. Cin., Mar. 4, 1933; d. Bernard Joseph and Cecile Marie (Sunman) Tansey; B.S. in Architecture, U. Cin., 1955; m. Edward Tokar, June 29, 1974. Job capt. Hixson, Tarter & Merkel, Cin., 1964-68; dir. interior architecture Ferry & Henderson, Springfield, Ill., 1968-72; project coordinator Skidmore, Owings & Merrill, Chgo., 1972-76; rev. architect Ill. Capital Devel. Bd., Chgo., 1977—; v.p. Planning and Design Cons., 1975—. Active, Art Inst. Chgo., Field Mus. Mem. AIA, Chgo. Women in Architecture, Alpha Omicron Pi. Club: Chgo. Altrusa. Office: 180 N LaSalle St Chicago IL 60601

TOLBERT, ANTHONY JAMES, III, pub. co. exec., clergyman; b. Martins Ferry, Ohio, Aug. 19, 1932; s. Anthony James and Salome Ann (Morgan) T.; B.F.A., Ohio U., 1954; M.Div., Garrett Theol. Sem., 1960; m. Irene Facklam, July 8, 1962; children—Anthony James IV, Jeffrey Alan, Thomas Andrew. Ordained to ministry United Methodist Ch., 1962; editorial asso. Together mag. United Meth. Pub. House, Park Ridge, Ill., 1960-64, sales mgr. Cokesbury div., north central region, 1964-68, mktg. mgr. Cokesbury div., north central region, 1968-70, regional mgr. Cokesbury div., north central region, 1970—. Bd. dirs. Mt. Prospect (Ill.) Library Bd., 1979—. Served with Signal Corps, U.S. Army, 1954-56. Mem. Chgo. Assn. Commerce and Industry. Park Ridge C. of C. (dir.). Clubs: Rotary (Park Ridge); Masons. Office: Cokesbury Div United Meth Pub House 1661 N Northwest Hwy Park Ridge IL 60068

TOLCH, CHARLES JOHN, univ. dean; b. Sigel, Ill., July 28, 1925; s. Charles William and Lulo Belle (Plummer) T.; B.S. in Edn., Eastern Ill. U., 1949; M.A., Mich. State U., 1950; Ph.D., Ohio State U., 1959; m. Barbara Ruth Taylor, May 31, 1945; children—Jennifer, Johna. Dir. theatre Minot State Tchrs. Coll., 1950-51; tech. dir. Univ. Theatre, U. Nebr., 1951-55; teaching asst., tech. dir. Univ. Theatre, Ohio State U., Columbus, 1955-59; mem. faculty U. Wis., Madison, 1959—, dir. children's theatre, tchr. edn. in theatre and drama, asst. dean in letters and sci., 1965—. Served with USAAF, 1943-45. Mem. Am. Theatre Assn., Children's Theater Assn. Am. (spl. citation for excellence, editor Children's Theatre Rev.), Speech Communication Assn., Wis. Theatre Assn. (spl. citation for excellence), Internat. Assn. Theatre for Children and Young People. Office: Vilas Hall U Wis Madison WI 53706

TOLCZEKI, JOHN, JR., mfg. co. service rep.; b. Cleve., Sept. 16, 1944; s. John and Rose T.; A.A., Cuyahoga Community Coll., 1965, 74. Mem. sales staff W. W. Grainger Co., Cleve., 1971-72; docket clk. Walter Haverfield, et al, Cleve., 1972-74; buyer Westinghouse Apparatus Services, Cleve., 1974-78, customer service rep., 1978—. Capt., CAP, 1976-81. Mem. Am. Walleye Assn. Office: 4600 W 160th St Cleveland OH 44135

TOLENTINO, REBECCA HONG, banker; b. Shanghai, China, Oct. 15, 1934; d. Yung Far and Zung Shu-Chen (Hong) Hong; B.L. magna cum laude, Chu Hai U. (Hong Kong), 1954; M.R.E., Bibl. Sem. N.Y., 1962; M.B.A., N.Y. U., 1964; came to U.S., 1958, naturalized, 1971; m. Teofilo Legaspi Tolentino, Feb. 22, 1964; 1 son, Rudolph. Jr. accountant U.S. Gypsum, Chgo., 1964-65; sr. accountant Harris Bank, Chgo., 1966-68, comml. credit analyst, 1968-73, credit officer, credit adminstrn., 1973-76, asst. v.p. credit adminstrn., 1976-77, asst. v.p. info. systems, 1977-81, asst. v.p. ops. research, 1981—. Presbyterian. Office: Harris Bank 111 W Monroe St Chicago IL 60606

TOLL, DANIEL ROGER, fin. services co. exec.; b. Denver, Dec. 3, 1927; s. Oliver W. and Merle D'Aubigne (Sampson) T.; A.B. magna cum laude, Princeton U., 1949; M.B.A. with distinction (Baker scholar), Harvard U., 1955; m. Sue Andersen, June 15, 1963; children—Daniel Andersen, Matthew Mitchell. Asst. mgr. product supply and distbn. Deep Rock Oil Corp., 1949-51; with Helmerich & Payne, Tulsa, 1955-64, fin. v.p., 1961-64; treas., dir. corp. planning Sunray DX Oil Co., Tulsa, 1964-66, v.p. corp. planning and devel., 1966-68; v.p. Sun Oil Co., 1969; sr. v.p. fin., dir., mem. exec. com. Walter E. Heller Internat. Corp., Chgo., 1970—; exec. v.p. Walter E. Heller & Co., Chgo., 1976—; dir. Brown Group, Inc., Lincoln Nat. Direct Placement Fund, Inc. Vice chmn., mem. budget com. Tulsa Community Chest, 1964-66; v.p., dir. Tulsa Opera, 1960-69; dir., chmn. play choosing and casting coms. Tulsa Little Theatre, 1963-69; chief crusader Chgo. Crusade of Mercy, 1972-76; chmn. Chgo. area council Boy Scouts Am., 1974-76, bd. dirs., 1976—, pack master Kenilworth Cub Scouts, 1972-75; mem. Sch. Bd. Dist. 38, Kenilworth, Ill., 1975—, pres., 1978—, also chmn. fin. com.; chmn. LaSalle St. Dinner Dance. Served to lt. (j.g.) USNR, 1951-52. Mem. Phi Beta Kappa. Clubs: Union League, Economic, Harvard Bus. Sch. (past pres. local chpt., dir. 1971—) (Chgo.); Indian Hill (Winnetka). Home: 125 Abingdon Ave Kenilworth IL 60043 Office: 105 W Adams St Chicago IL 60690

TOLLEFSON, DAVID CHESTER, occupational therapist; b. Mpls., Dec. 20, 1949; s. Chester Rueben and Gladys Marie (Edmundson) T.; student Augsburg Coll., 1968; B.S., U. Minn., 1972; m. Claudia Anne Peterson, June 14, 1970. Chief occupational therapist Marquette (Mich.) Gen. Hosp., 1975—. Mem. Mental Health Bd. Task Force and Long-Term Care Task Force, Upper Peninsula Quality Assurance Program; bd dirs. Stoke Com., Mich. Heart Assn.; bd. dirs. Propylon. Served with USNR, 1972-75. Mem. Occupational Therapy Assn. Am., Mich. Occupational Therapy Assn. Lodge: Sons of Norway. Home: Route 2 Box B2 Bovey MN 55709 Office: 420 W Magnetic St Marquette MI 49855

TOLLEY, WILLIAM RICHARD, assn. exec.; b. Elizabethton, Tenn., Mar. 31, 1939; s. Daniel Luther and Maude (Roberts) T.; A.A., Macomb County Community Coll., 1968; B.B.A., Walsh Inst. Accountancy, 1973; m. Karen Ellen Larsen, Aug. 14, 1970; children—Kimberly Rene, Kelly Denise. Accountant, Ford Motor Credit Corp., Dearborn, Mich., 1962-66; accounting supr. Chrysler Credit Corp., Southfield, Mich., 1966-70; bus. mgr. United Found., Detroit, 1970-74; controller Servomation, Romulus, Mich., 1974-75; dir. adminstrv. services Am. Concrete Inst., Detroit, 1975—; mem. student scholarship com. Inst. Orgn. Mgmt., 1979-81; mem. customer adv. council Blue Cross/Blue Shield, Mich. area, 1980—. Mem. Nat. Accountants Assn., Council Engring. and Sci. Soc. Execs., Detroit Personnel Mgmt. Assn., Detroit Postal Council, Am. Mgmt. Assn. Republican. Methodist. Clubs: Travis Pointe Country; Econ of Detroit. Home: 478 Marlpool Dr Saline MI 48176 Office: 22400 W 7 Mile Rd Detroit MI 48219

TOLMAN, SUZANNE NELSON, psychologist; b. Omaha, Nov. 8, 1931; d. Raymond LeRoy and Lottie (Kerns) Nelson; B.A. with distinction in Spanish, U. Nebr., Omaha, 1951; M.A., U. Nebr., Lincoln, 1952, Ph.D., 1957; m. Dan Edward Tolman, June 8, 1957; 1 dau., Kimberly Suzanne. Research asst. U. Nebr., Lincoln, 1951-52; tchr. Omaha Pub. Schs., 1952-53, counselor, high sch. instr. history and English, 1953-59; instr. psychology U. Nebr., Omaha, 1957-59; social service worker Mayo Clinic, Rochester, Minn., 1959-60; instr. psychology U. Tampa, 1962-63; sch. psychologist Sch. Dist. 535, Rochester, 1966—. Bd. dirs. Jefferson PTA, Rochester, 1966-68; bd. dirs., sec. Family Consultation Center, Rochester, 1970-76; bd. dirs. Olmsted County (Minn.) Council Coordinated Child Care, 1971-75, pres., 1973-75; bd. dirs. Olmsted County Assn. Mental Health; pres. condr.'s com. Rochester Symphony, 1977-78. Mem. Minn., Rochester edn. assns., Minn. Sch. Psychologists, Rochester Civic Music Guild (pres. 1981-82), Am. Psychol. Assn., AAUW, Zumbro Valley Dental Aux. (pres. 1970-71), Phi Delta Kappa, Alpha Lambda Delta, Alpha Delta Kappa, Psi Chi, Chi Omega. Presbyterian. Club: Order Eastern Star. Home: 2709 Merrihills Dr Rochester MN 55901 Office: Ind Sch Dist 535 Rochester MN 55901

TOMALIA, DONALD ANDREW, chem. co. scientist; b. Owosso, Mich., Sept. 5, 1938; s. Andrew Vincent and Mary (Kondel) T.; B.A. in Chemistry, U. Mich., 1961; postgrad. Bucknell U., 1962-63; Ph.D. in Phys. Organic Chemistry, Mich. State U., 1968; m. R. Elizabeth Sellars, June 13, 1959; children—Lynne Marie, Laurel Anne, Donald Andrew, Elizabeth Leigh. Project leader Dow Chem. Co., Midland, Mich., 1966-68, group leader, 1968-71, research mgr., 1971-76, asso. scientist, 1976-79, sr. asso. scientist, 1979—; invited internat. lectr. Polymer Soc. Japan, Tokyo, 1978, Kyoto U. and Internat. Com. Cationic Poly- merization, Japan, 1980. Recipient Indsl. Research award, 1978. Mem. Am. Chem. Soc., Sigma Xi. Author: (with others) Functional Monomers, Vol. 2, 1974; contbr. articles to profl. jours. Holder 56 patents in field. Home: Rt 6 463 W Chippewa River Rd Midland MI 48640 Office: 1710 Bldg Dow Chem Co Midland MI 48640

TOMASEK, HANA, ednl. adminstr.; b. Prague, Czechoslovakia, Apr. 4, 1935; came to U.S., 1972, naturalized, 1978; d. Josef and Jana (Krasna) Krasny; M.S. in Elec. Engring., Tech. U. Prague, 1958, Ph.D., 1967; postgrad. U. Minn., 1975-76; m. Jaroslav Tomasek, Nov. 6, 1959. Mem. faculty Charles U., Prague, 1960-72; supr. indsl. edn. divs., numerous colls. of edn., 1960-72; researcher, instr. U. Minn., Mpls., 1974-76; metrication and curriculum specialist Area Vocat. Tech. Inst. #916, White Bear Lake, Minn., 1976-77, staff devel. specialist, 1977—; cons. on staff devel. Mem. Am. Soc. Tng. and Devel., Minn. Vocat. Assn., Am. Vocat. Assn., U.S. Metric Assn., Minn. Vocat. Personnel Devel. Assn. Club: Tennis, Swim. Contbr. articles to profl. jours.; author textbooks in Czech. Office: 3300 Century Ave N White Bear Lake MN 55110

TOMASEK, JAROSLAV, electronic products co. exec.; b. Trebic, Czechoslovakia, Apr. 26, 1931; came to U.S., 1972, naturalized, 1978; s. Martin and Marie T.; M.S.E.E., Tech. U. Prague, 1956; Ph.D., Czechoslovak Acad. Scis., 1964; m. Hana Krasna, Nov. 6, 1959. Sr. research engr. several research instns., Czechoslovakia, 1956-72; design engr. Electro-Craft Corp., Hopkins, Minn., 1972—, chief engr., 1977—. Mem. IEEE, U.S. Metric Assn. Co-author: (in Czechoslovakian) Semiconductor Switching Devices, 1970; editor: DC Motors, Speed Controls, Servo Systems, 1973; contbr. numerous articles to tech. jours.; patentee electronic switching devices and circuits, high-performance switching servo amplifiers, brushless DC servo systems. Home: 10024 South Shore Dr Plymouth MN 55441 Office: 1600 2d St S Hopkins MN 55343

TOMAZI, GEORGE DONALD, elec. engr.; b. St. Louis, Dec. 27, 1935; s. George and Sophia (Bogovich) T.; B.S. in E.E., U. Mo., Rolla, 1958, Profl. E.E. (hon.), 1970; M.B.A., St. Louis U., 1965, M.S. in E.E., 1971; m. Lois Marie Partenheimer, Feb. 1, 1958; children—Keith, Kent. Project engr. Union Electric Co., 1958-66; dir. corp. planning Gen. Steel Industries, 1966-70; exec. v.p. St. Louis Research Council, 1970-74; exec. v.p. Hercules Constrn. Co., St. Louis, 1974-75; project dir. Mallinckrodt, Inc., St. Louis, 1975—. Active Nat. Kidney Found.; bd. dirs. U. Mo. Devel. Council; elder Lutheran Ch. Served with U.S. Army, 1959-61. Registered profl. engr., Mo., Ill., Wash. Mem. Nat. Soc. Profl. Engr., IEEE, Japan-Am. Soc., AAAS, Am. Inst. Chem. Engrs., Am. Def. Preparedness Assn., U. Mo. Alumni Assn. (dir. 1972-78), Sigma Pi Frat. Clubs: Engrs. (treas. 1981—), Rotary (St. Louis). Author: P-Science: The Role of Science in Society, 1972; The Link of Science and Religion, 1973. Home: 12723 Stoneridge Dr Florissant MO 63033 Office: 675 McDonnell Blvd Saint Louis MO 63134

TOMES, JAMES STEEL, lawyer, mfg. co. exec.; b. Milw., Apr. 30, 1927; s. William Austin and Elizabeth (Steel) T.; B.S., Northwestern U., 1951; LL.B., Chgo. Kent Coll. Law, 1957; m. Joann Witmeyer Raymaley, June 26, 1954; children—Robert Steel, Elizabeth Austin, John Wilson, Julia Hall. Admitted to Ill. bar, 1957; asso. firm Petit, Olin, Overmyer & Fazio, Chgo., 1957-60; asst. counsel Bell & Howell Co., Chgo., 1960-61, counsel, 1961-65, v.p. product mgmt., 1965-67; v.p., gen. mgr. audio visual products div., 1967-69; pres. Ventron Instruments Corp. subs. Ventron Corp., 1969-70; corp. v.p., pres. Internat. group Bell & Howell Co., 1970-72, corp. v.p., pres. consumer products group, 1972-73, sr. corp. v.p., pres. consumer and audiovisual products group, 1973-74; sr. corp. v.p., chief exec. consumer group U.S. Industries, 1975-76; pres., chief exec. officer Filtertek, Inc., Hebron, Ill., 1977-79, dir., 1972-80; pres., chief exec. officer, dir. Bijur Lubricating Corp., Oakland, N.J., 1980—. Bd. dirs. Ill. div. ACLU, 1965-72. Served with AUS, 1945-47; with USAF, 1950-53. Mem. Am., Ill., Chgo. bar assns., Phi Delta Phi. Home: 714 Washington St Wilmette IL 60091 Office: 112 Bauer Dr Oakland NJ 07436

TOMKINS, FRANK SARGENT, physicist; b. Petoskey, Mich., June 24, 1915; s. Charles Frederick and Irene Eugenie (Gouin) T.; B.S., Kalamazoo Coll., 1937; Ph.D. (Parke-Davis fellow), Mich. State U., 1941; m. Mary Ann Lynch, Jan. 6, 1964; 1 son, Frank Sargent. Physicist, Buick Aviation Engine Div., Melrose Park, Ill., 1941-42; scientist Manhattan Project U. Chgo., 1943-45; sr. scientist Argonne (Ill.) Nat. Lab., 1945—, group leader, 1944—; cons. Bendix Corp., Cin., 1963-69; U.S. Dept. State del. 2d Internat. Conf. Peaceful Uses Atomic Energy, Geneva, Switzerland, 1958. John Simon Guggenheim fellow Laboratoire Aime-Cotton, Bellevue, France, 1960-61; Sci. Research Council fellow Imperial Coll., London, 1975; recipient Argonne Universities Assn. Distinguished Appointment, 1975-76. Fellow Optical Soc. Am. (William F. Meggers award 1977); mem. Am. Phys. Soc., Societe Francaise de Physique, N.Y. Acad. Scis., AAAS, Sigma Xi, Research Soc. Am. Contbr. articles to sci. jours. Home: 11714 S 83rd Ave Palos Park IL 60464 Office: 9700 S Cass Ave Argonne IL 60439

TOMLINSON, EUGENE MILLARD, mfg. co. exec.; b. Detroit, June 25, 1932; s. Millard Burr and Mabel Vesta (Schubert) T.; B.S. in Chem. Engring., Wayne State U., 1956, M.S., 1961, M.B.A., 1974; A.A., Ford Community Coll., 1952; m. Dec. 29, 1973; children—Suzanne, Robert, Sheila, John, David, Daniel. Pilot plant engr. ACS div. 3M Co., Detroit, 1956-58; material engr., prin. engr., Advanced Rocket Projects, Liquid Rock Ops., Aerojet Gen. Corp., Sacramento, 1958-65; mgr. advanced rocket systems LTV Aerospace Corp., Sterling Heights, Mich., 1965-77; mgr. vehicle emissions compliance Am. Motors Corp., Detroit, 1977—. Chmn., Wayne State U. Alumni Giving Council, 1979-81. Recipient Engring. Alumni award, Wayne State U., 1979-80; Phoenician Cup, bus. alumni award Alpha Kappa Psi, 1981. Mem. Am. Inst. Chem. Engrs. (sect. chmn. 1962-63), AIAA (sect. chmn. 1972-73), Am. Chem. Soc., Wayne State U. Alumni Assn. (pres. 1974-75), Wayne State U. Bus. Adminstrn. Alumni Assn. (pres. 1980-82), Wayne State U. Coll. Engring. Alumni Assn., Phi Lambda Upsilon. Republican. Congregationalist. Club: Beverly Hills Racquet and Health. Home: 32820 Bassett Woods Ct Birmingham MI 48010 Office: 14250 Plymouth Rd Detroit MI 48232

TOMLINSON, HARRY JUSTIN, pharm. co. exec.; b. Indpls., Mar. 21, 1918; s. Harry M. and Mildred Elizabeth (Sparks) T.; student U. Mex., 1938; B.A., Ind. U., 1939; postgrad. U. Chile, 1940-41, N.Y. U., 1949-51; m. Christina Soulias, Dec. 1, 1951; children—Margaret Anne, Alice Emily, Christina Maria. Corr., UP, 1940-41, N.Y. Herald Tribune, S. Am., 1942-43; with W. R. Grace & Co., 1946-57, dir. public relations, N.Y.C., 1953-57; pres. Cuban-Am. Research & Investment, Havana Cuba, 1957-60; mgr. public relations Upjohn Co., Kalamazoo, 1961-75, adminstr. corp. contbns., 1975—. Served with U.S. Army, 1943-46. Mem. Public Relation Soc. Am., Explorers. Home: 10239 Fox Hollow Portage MI 49081 Office: 7000 Portage Rd Kalamazoo MI 49001

TOMMERAASEN, MILES, coll. pres.; b. Sioux Falls, S.D., Jan. 30, 1923; s. Cornelius and Ester T.; B.A., Morningside Coll., 1943; M.B.A., Northwestern U., 1948; Ph.D., U. Nebr., 1964; m. Marilyn Fladmark, Nov. 23, 1945; children—Marsha, Mark, Miles C. Math. tchr. Ind. Sch. Dist, Canton, S.D., 1943-45; staff accountant Arthur Andersen & Co., Chgo., 1946-50; prof., exec. v.p., dean men, chmn. dept. bus. Morningside Coll., Sioux City, Iowa, 1950-64, pres., 1978—; vice chancellor bus. and finance U. Nebr., Lincoln, 1964-78. Mem. bd. Tax Research Council, 1980—; mem. Lincoln Downtown Adv. Council, 1973-78; mem. Nebr. Coordinating Council for Post-Secondary Edn., 1974-75; fin. sec., council mem. St. Andrew's Ch., Lincoln, Nebr., 1965-72; mem. Sioux City Adult Edn. Council, 1962-64; mem. Sioux City Mayor's Com. for Internat. Visitors, 1960-64; bd. dirs., treas. Siouxland Rehab. Center, 1963-64. C.P.A., Iowa. Mem. Am. Acctg. Assn., Am. Inst. C.P.A.'s, Am. Finance Assn., Fin. Analysts Soc., Inst. Chartered Fin. Analysts, Midwest Bus. Adminstrn. Assn. (pres. 1973-74), Fin. Execs. Inst. (dir. 1974-76), Iowa Soc. C.P.A.'s, Nebr. Soc. C.P.A.'s (dir. 1964-69), C. of C. Lutheran. Home: 1310 Hiawatha Trail Sioux City IA 51106 Office: 1501 Morningside Ave Sioux City IA 51106

TOMPKINS, CARL OSCAR, physician; b. Byers, Kans., Feb. 20, 1922; s. Elmer Lee and Jetta (Alton) T.; B.A., Friends U., 1948; M.D., U. Kans., 1951; m. Violet Van Brocklin, June 14, 1942; children—Gregory Giles, Carolyn Marie, Christa Ellene. Intern, Wesley Hosp., Wichita, Kans., 1951-52; practice gen. medicine Hillsboro, Kans., 1952-53, Newton, Kans., 1953—; mem. med. staff Bethel Hosp., Newton, pres., 1958; staff mem. Coroner, Harvey County, Kans., 1958—; county health officer, 1963-75. Vice chmn. South Central Kans. Comprehensive Health Planning Council, 1969-72, chmn., 1972-75; med. advisor Hospice Council of Harvey County, 1977—, Harvey County Rape Council, 1977—; founder, med. adv. Harvey County Hospice, Newton, 1977—. Served with USCGR, 1942-45. Mem. AMA, Harvey County, Kans. med. socs., Am. Acad. Family Practice, Nat. Assn. Coroners, Am. Public Health Assn. (Crumbine award 1981, state del. to nat. governing council, mem. com. of affiliates 1975—), Kans. Public Health Assn. (chmn. health officers sect. 1965—, pres. 1968—), Kansas Obstet. Soc. Methodist. (chmn. commn. Christian social concerns). Home: 5 Rollin Hills Newton KS 67114 Office: 316 Oak St Newton KS 67114

TOMPKINS, CAROL SUE, educator; b. Oskaloosa, Iowa, July 21, 1944; d. Clayton Leroy and Helen Lucille (Knowler) Kirk; B.A., U. No. Iowa, 1966; M.A., N.E. Mo. State U., 1980; m. Michael Tompkins, Mar. 3, 1979; 1 dau., Stefanie. Tchr., Waterloo (Iowa) Community Schs., 1966—; instr. U. No. Iowa, 1974-77. Named Tchr. of Yr., Waterloo Community Schs., 1973-74. Mem. Iowa Edn. Assn. (state chmn. membership 1974), Assn. Supervision and Curriculum Devel., Nu Sigma Phi, Phi Delta Kappa. Episcopalian. Home: 534 Beverly Hills St Waterloo IA 50701 Office: 1700 Maynard St Waterloo IA 50701

TOMPKINS, CHARLES ARTHUR, pediatrician; b. Washington, Apr. 3, 1925; s. Charles Arthur and Beatrice (Garland) T.; M.D., Howard U., 1948; m. Helen Pediford, June 20, 1948; children—Michael Anthony, Heidi Lynn; m. 2d, Carol Augusta Nelson, July 20, 1979. Intern, then resident in pediatrics Provident Hosp., Chgo., 1949-52; practice medicine specializing in pediatrics, Chgo., 1954—; physician health services med. program Chgo. Bd. Health, 1970-73, 76-80; attending pediatrician Michael Reese Hosp. and Med. Center, 1980—; mem. staff, newborn cons. Roseland Community Hosp., Chgo.; mem. staff Provident, St. Joseph, Mt. Sinai, Tabernacle hosps.; pediatrician King Neighborhood Health Center. Served as officer M.C., AUS, 1952-54. Diplomate Am. Bd. Pediatrics. Fellow Am. Acad. Pediatrics; mem. Midwest Clin. Conf., Chgo. Med. Soc., Chgo. Pediatrics Soc., Chgo. Assn. Children with Learning Disabilities (2d v.p.). Lutheran. Clubs: Saracens, Chgo. Golfers. Office: Woodlawn and Roselawn Community Hosp

TOMPKINS, MARK ALLEN, pediatrician; b. O'Neill, Nebr., Nov. 14, 1949; s. Harvey Alfred and Lois Lenore (Caldwell) T.; B.S. in Biology, Nebr. Wesleyan U., 1971; M.D., U. Nebr., 1974; m. Janice Irene Wellensiek, July 22, 1972; children—Marc Andrew, Jill Elizabeth. Pediatric resident U. Nebr. Med. Center, 1974-77; pediatrician, Grand Island Clinic, Inc. (Nebr.), 1977—; mem. vol. pediatric faculty U. Nebr. Med. Center, 1977—. Diplomate Am. Bd. Pediatrics. Fellow Am. Acad. Pediatrics; mem. AMA, Nebr. Med. Assn., Hall County Med. Assn. Republican. Presbyterian. Home: 2121 Engleman Rd Grand Island NE 68801 Office: 2444 W Faidley Ave Grand Island NE 68801

TOMS, CLINTON LEE, mgmt. cons.; b. Albany, N.Y., May 1, 1928; s. Adrian G. and Ruby (Rymer) T.; student Sampson Coll., 1946-48; B.S. Indsl. Engring., Rutgers U., 1952; m. Clara L. Metcalf, June 26, 1949 (div. Oct. 1980); children—Donna, Scott, Kevin, Laura, Tracey; m. 2d, Barbara Anne Wesener, June 27, 1981. Plant supt. Owens Illinois Co., Columbus, Ohio, 1952-55; dir. inventory control and market research James Lees & Sons, Norristown, Pa., 1955-60; pres. Perkup Co., Pottstown, Pa., 1960-63; co-founder, sr. v.p. K. W. Tunnell Co., Inc., King of Prussia, Pa., 1963-69; pres. Exec. Forums, Inc., Norristown, 1969-74, Center for Applied Mgmt., Inc., Greenfield, Wis., 1974—, Micro Mgmt. Systems, Inc., Milw., 1977—; lectr. numerous univs., colls. Chmn. bd. suprs. Lower Providence Twp., Montgomery County, Pa., 1960-66. Mem. Internat. Materials Mgmt. Soc., Am. Prodn. and Inventory Control Soc. (founding), Inst. Mgmt. Cons. (founding), Am. Inst. Indsl. Engring., Am. Arbitration Assn. Republican. Contbr. numerous articles to profl. jours.; author textbook set, 1960-78; patentee in field.

TONELLA, CLAUDIA, state ofcl.; b. Buenos Aires, Argentina, June 30, 1933; came to U.S., 1957, naturalized, 1963; d. Carlos Cesar and Gabriela Matilde (Raggio) Pineiro; B.B.A., Universidad Nacional de la Plata, Buenos Aires, 1955; M.A.L.S., Rosary Coll., River Forest, Ill., 1973, M.B.A., 1979; children—Andrea Roxana, Jessica Robin. Tchr., Berlitz Sch., Winnetka, Ill., 1969-70; librarian Northwestern U., Evanston, Ill., 1970-73; asst. materials mgr. Materials Mgmt. div., mgr. central info. systems Ill. Tollway Authority, Oak Brook, 1974—. Mem. Am. Mgmt. Assn., ALA, Assn. Records Mgrs. and Adminstrs. Home: 421 Elm St Deerfield IL 60015 Office: 2001 W 22d St Oak Brook IL 60521

TONG, GREGORY YUEH-CHUNG, broadcasting co. exec., newspaper chain exec.; b. China, Oct. 13, 1932; came to U.S., 1968, naturalized, 1979; s. Jick-Sam and Linn Kwai (Yuen) T.; B.A. in Edn., Chung-Hing U., Taiwan, 1955. Producer, Central Broadcasting Sta., Taiwan, 1956-68; pres. Wah Sing Cultural Inst. (Wah Sing Chinese Broadcasting Co.), Chgo., 1980—; dir. Sing Tao Newspapers Chgo. Agy., 1980—; officer Overseas Chinese Affair Com., Taiwan, 1956-59. Pres. Chinese Youth Cultural Assn., N.Y.C. Home and office: 2302 S Princeton Chicago IL 60616

TONI, YOUSSEF TANIOUS, geographer; b. Girga, Egypt, Apr. 2, 1929; s. Tanious Toni and Bahia Andraus (Nemaire) Kawas; immigrated to Can., 1967, naturalized, 1974; B.A., U. Alexandria, 1952; Ph.D., Durham (Eng.) U., 1956; m. Doreen Warbrick, Jan. 26, 1961; children—Kareem, Stephen-Tarek. Asst. prof. U. Damascus (Syria), 1957-60; asso. prof. Ain Shams U., Cairo, 1960-67; prof. geography Laurentian U., Sudbury, Ont., Can., 1967—. Fellow Royal Geog. Soc., Am. Geog. Soc.; mem. Assn. Am. Geographers, Assn. Canadian Geographers, Canadian Population Soc. Coptic Catholic. Author: Phytogeography, 1961; A Dictionary of Geographical Terms, 1964. Home: 1291 Lakewood Dr Sudbury ON SS1 Site 12 Canada Office: Dept Geography Laurentian U Sudbury ON P3E 2O6 Canada

TONIA, CYNTHIA F., sch. prin.; b. Bay Village, Ohio, Aug. 8, 1950; d. Frank L. and Eleanor (Karamus) T.; B.S., Kent State U., 1971; M.A., Carnegie Mellon U., 1975, D.A., 1982. Tchr. social studies Normandy High Sch., Parma, Ohio, 1972-74; tchr. Rocky River (Ohio) High Sch., 1977-80; asst. prin. Orange High Sch., Pepper Pike, Ohio, 1980—. L.D. Beaumont Found. scholar, 1974-76; Carnegie Mellon U. fellow, 1976-77; grantee Carthage Coll. and Kent State U. Mem. Nat. Assn. Secondary Sch. Prins., Ohio Assn. Secondary Sch. Adminstrs., Nat. Council Social Studies. Home: 21037 South Bend Circle Rocky River OH 44116

TOOLE, THOMAS JOHN, chem. co. exec.; b. Detroit, Oct. 4, 1945; s. John Thomas and Gladys (Carter) T.; B.S., Marquette U., 1967; m. Mary Lucille Oakes, Sept. 2, 1967; children—Patrick, Lisa, Kristina. Wage and salary supr. Caterpillar Tractor Co., Milw., 1967-69, mgr. labor relations, 1969-74; dir. indsl. relations Aqua-Chem. Inc. subs. Coca-Cola, Milw., 1974-79, v.p. personnel and indsl. relations, 1979—. Area chmn. United Way Milw., 1978-79; adv. Jr. Achievement, project bus. instr. Served with Air NG, 1967—. Mem. Am. Soc. Personnel Adminstrn., Indsl. Relations Research Assn., Am. Compensation Assn., NAM, Am. Soc. Tng. and Devel., Mgmt. Resources Assn. (exec. com. Mgmt. Club 1979), Marquette U. Sch. Bus. Adminstrn. Alumni Assn. (dir.). Republican. Roman Catholic. Home: 11333 N Saint James Ln Mequon WI 53092 Office: PO Box 421 Milwaukee WI 53201

TOOLEN, VINCENT ALOYSIUS, Jr. state ofcl.; b. St. Louis, Feb. 18, 1937; s. Vincent Aloysius and Marcella A. (O'Connor) T.; B.S., St. Louis U., 1960; M.B.A., U. Ill., 1981; m. Katherine L. Newsom, June 1, 1957; children—Lynn Marie, Carrie, Vincent, Shawn. With Falstaff Brewing Corp., St. Louis, 1964-67, Booz, Allen & Hamilton, Chgo., 1967-69; v.p. Sci. Resources, Inc., Chgo., 1970-71; cons. in data processing, 1970-71; with Motor Vehicle Adminstrn. Office of Sec. of State, State of Ill., Springfield, 1971-72; pres. Am. Mgmt. Resources, Inc., Springfield, 1972-77; dep. dir. Dept. Adminstrv. Services, State of Ill., Springfield, 1977-78, dir., 1978—. Mem. Great Lakes Area Devel. Council, 1981—; chmn. bd. appeals Sangamon County Zoning Bd., 1981; state govt. chmn. United Way, 1980-81; state chmn. Cancer Dr., 1981—; mem. Curran-Gardner Water Dist. Bd., 1980; city councilman City of Bridgeton, 1964-67. Recipient U.S. Dept. Energy's Spl. award for renewable fuels, 1981; United Way Achievement awards, 1979-80. Mem. Nat. Assn. State Info. Systems, Nat. Conf. State Gen. Services Officers, Ill. State Records Commn., Asso. Public Safety Communications Officers, others. Republican. Roman Catholic. Club: Sangamo. Home: 632 Meadowbrook Rd Springfield IL 62707 Office: 715 Stratton Office Bldg Springfield IL 62706

TOOLEY, JOHN ROGER, univ. dean; b. Antigo, Wis., Oct. 31, 1935; s. Harold William and Vera Mae (Schroeder) T.; grad. U. Wis., River Falls, 1955; M.S. in Physics, U. Chgo., 1959; Ph.D. in Elec. Engring. (Texas Instruments Inc. fellow 1966-69), U. Colo., 1969; m. Marguerite Ann Gotz, Feb. 15, 1958; children—Craig Richard, Matthew John, James Sebastian, John William. Mem. tech. staff Tex. Instruments Inc., Dallas, 1959-75; prof. elec. engring., dean engring. U. Evansville (Ind.), 1975—; cons. U.S. Army Sci. Bd., 1978—, Army Sci. Adv. Panel, 1975-78. Mem. IEEE, Am. Soc. Engring. Edn., Phi Beta Kappa, Eta Kappa Nu. Office: EA 291 1800 Lincoln Ave PO Box 329 Evansville IN 47702

TOOLEY, STANLEY DAVID, mfg. co. exec.; b. Oakland City, Ind., Jan. 10, 1947; s. Ralph and Wilma P. Tooley; B.S. in Indsl. Relations, U. Evansville, 1970; M.S. in Human Devel. Counseling, Sangamon State U., 1976; m. Beverly G. Stilwell, Mar. 26, 1970; children—Raegan Elaine, Matthew R. Personnel mgr. Hurst Mfg. Corp., Princeton, Ind., 1970-72; profl. and tech. recruiter Nat. Homes Corp., Lafayette, Ind., 1972-74; supr. employment and tng. Wagner Castings, Decatur, Ill., 1974-77; mgr. human resources Waukesha-Dresser, Waukesha, Wis., 1977—; mem. mgmt. devel. adv. com. U. Wis. Extension. Chmn., WOW Consortium Pvt. Industry Council, 1978-80; mem. exec. com. and state steering com. Job Service Improvement Program, Wis. Recipient commendation Gov. Wis., 1981. Mem. Mgmt. Resources Assn., Am. Soc. Tng. and Devel., Personnel and Indsl. Relations Assn. Republican. Baptist. Clubs: Masons, Shriners. Home: W325 S6943 Westgate Mukwonago WI 53149 Office: Waukesha-Dresser 1000 W St Paul Ave Waukesha WI 53186

TOOMBS, LAWRENCE EDWARD, social worker; b. Kansas City, Kans., Apr. 29, 1941; s. Earl Paul and Dolores C. (Kenney) T.; B.A., U. Kans., 1964; M.S.W., George Williams Coll., Downers Grove, Ill., 1973; m. Rita C. Elam, Oct. 19, 1969; 1 dau., Laura Ann. Social service worker, activity therapies supr. Parsons (Kans.) State Hosp.-Tng. Center, 1966-71; social service coordinator Nevada (Mo.) State Sch.-Hosp., 1973-76; dir. Springfield (Mo.) Regional Center Devel. Disabled, 1976—; cons. Region VI, Council Devel. Disabilities; mem. Greene County Assn. Retarded Children. Mem. Acad. Cert. Social Workers, Nat. Assn. Social Workers, Am. Assn. Mental Deficiency, Greene County Epilepsy Assn. Roman Catholic. Home: 1112 S Fremont St Springfield MO 65804 Office: 1515 E Pythian Springfield MO 65802

TOOT, JOSEPH FREDERICK, JR., mfg. co. exec.; b. Canton, Ohio, 1935; A.B., Princeton U., 1957; postgrad. U. Rochester Sch. Medicine, 1958, Harvard U. Grad. Sch. Bus. Adminstrn., 1961; married. With The Timken Co., Canton, Ohio, 1962—, asst. to v.p. internat. div., 1963-65, gen. mgr. Timken Rollenlager, 1965, dep. mgr. Timken France, 1965-67, v.p. internat. div., 1967-68, corp. v.p., 1968-73, exec. v.p., 1973-79, pres., 1979—, also dir. Office: Timken Co 1835 Dueber Ave SW Canton OH 44706*

TOOTIKIAN, LAWRENCE PETER, mktg. research cons.; b. Cleve., Dec. 18, 1931; s. Jack P. and Marie Tootikian; B.B.S., Northwestern U., 1954; m. Christine Mink, Oct. 7, 1980. Research analyst WGN, Inc., Chgo., 1960-61; research mgr. WBBM-TV, Chgo., 1962-63, WLS-TV, Chgo., 1963-64, Fawcett Pubs., Chgo., 1967-72; pres. Lawrence Tootikian & Assos., Chgo., 1972—. Served with U.S. Army, 1955-57. Mem. Chgo. Bus. Pubs. Assn. (exec. dir. 1979—), Bus./Profl. Advt. Assn. (exec sec. 1979—), Am. Mktg. Assn., Nat. Agrl. Mktg. Assn. Clubs: Execs., Chgo. Press, Chgo. Media Research (pres. 1976-77). Contbr. articles to profl. jours. Office: 919 N Michigan Ave Chicago IL 60611

TOPITZES, NICHOLAS J., advt. agy. exec.; b. Milw., Dec. 24, 1943; s. James William and Despina (Petropoulos) T.; B.S., U. Wis., 1966; m. Judith Emmons, Jan. 23, 1972; 2 children. Asst. dir. World Dairy Expo, 1968-70; exec. dir. Farm Fest U.S.A., 1970-72; account exec. Stephan & Brady, Madison, Wis., 1973-80; pres. Topitzes & Assos., Inc., Madison, 1980—; v.p., treas. Collegiate Confs. Mem. exec. bd. Four Lakes Council Boy Scouts Am., 1980; bd. dirs. So. Wis. dist. Arthritis Found., 1980. Mem. Madison Advt. Fedn., Nat. Agri-Mktg. Assn., Kappa Sigma. Greek Orthodox. Club: Ahepa. Office: 6401 Odana Rd Madison WI 53719

TOPPER, GENE EDWARD, advt. exec.; b. Chgo., June 20, 1948; s. Marvin and Frances May (Rusinoff) T.; B.A., Northwestern U., 1970; M.A., Loyola U., Chgo., 1972, Ph.D. (fellow), 1975, M.B.A., 1979; m. Elisa Freiden, Nov. 22, 1981. Coordinator research and procedures Joint Commn. on Accreditation of Hosps., Chgo., 1975-76; mktg. research mgr. D'Arcy-MacManus & Masius Advt., Chgo., 1976-79; asso. research dir. Campbell Mithun Advt., Chgo., 1979—; adj. faculty Mundelein Coll. Chgo., 1981—. Mem. Am. Psychol. Assn. (chmn. public relations com. div. 23), Assn. Consumer Research, Am. Mktg. Assn., Beta Gamma Sigma. Contbr. articles to profl. jours. Home: 1340 N Dearborn St Apt 3-A Chicago IL 60610 Office: 111 E Wacker Dr Chicago IL 60601

TORDOFF, HARRISON BRUCE, zoologist; b. Mechanicville, N.Y., Feb. 8, 1923; s. Harry F. and Ethel M. (Dormandy) T.; B.S., Cornell U., 1946; M.A., U. Mich., 1949, Ph.D., 1952; m. Jean Van Nostrand, July 3, 1946; children—Jeffrey, James. Curator Inst. of Jamaica, Kingston, 1946-47; instr. U. Kans., Manhattan, 1950-52, asst. prof., 1952-57, asso. prof., 1957; asst. prof. U. Mich., Ann Arbor, 1957-59, asso. prof., 1959-62, prof., 1962-70; dir. Bell Mus. Natural History, prof. ecology, U. Minn., Mpls., 1970—. Served with USAAF, 1942-45. Decorated D.F.C., Air medals (17). Fellow Am. Ornithologists Union (pres. 1978-80); mem. Nature Conservancy (chmn. bd. Minn. chpt. 1975-77), Wilson Cooper Ornithol. Soc. (editor 1952-54), Brit. Ornithologists Union. Contbr. articles to profl. jours. Home: 6 Chickadee Ln North Oaks Saint Paul MN 55110 Office: 10 Church St SE Minneapolis MN 55455

TORELLA, SAMUEL JOSEPH, bowling lanes exec.; b. Lowellville, Ohio, Mar. 23, 1937; s. Roger James and Adeline Marie T.; student George Washington U., 1955-56, Youngstown U., 1957-58; m. Bettie G. Glancy, June 9, 1967; children—Carol, Warren. Clk., Torella Food Market, 1955-58; promotion mgr., instr. Boardman Lanes, Boardman, Ohio, 1958-61; mgr. Circle Lanes, Hampton, Va., 1961-65; mgr. Holiday Bowl, Struthers, Ohio, 1965-70; co-owner, mgr. Classic Bowl, Canton, Ohio, 1970-78; owner, operator Torella Twin Star Lanes, Kent, Ohio, 1978—. Served with U.S. Army, 1961-63. Mem. Profl. Bowling Assn., Portage County Bowling Proprietors Assn., Ohio State Bowling Proprietors Assn. (mem. exec. bd.). Roman Catholic. Clubs: Moose, Elks, Lions. Home: 5382 Cline Rd Kent OH 44240 Office: 2245 State Route 59 Kent OH 44240

TORGELSON, JOHN WINSTON, coll. pres.; b. Benson, Minn., Oct. 16, 1928; s. Julian Forvald and Hilda Othelia (Halvorson) T.; B.A., Luther Coll., Decorah, Iowa, 1950; M.A., U. Minn., 1956, Ph.D., 1963; m. Delores Hanson, June 4, 1955; children—David, Nathan. Prin., Harmony (Minn.) Jr.-Sr. High Sch., 1956-58; asst. prin. Alexander Ramsey Sr. High Sch., Roseville, Minn., 1958-62; prin. Frank B. Kellogg Sr. High Sch., Roseville, 1962-67; pres. Willmar (Minn.) Community Coll., 1967—; vis. prof. edn. Central Wash. State Coll., Ellensburg, summers 1965, 71, Va. Poly. Inst. and State U., 1980. Chmn., Willmar Energy Conservation Bd., 1977—. Served with U.S. Army, 1951-53; col. Res. Decorated Bronze Star medal; recipient Minn. 4-H Alumni award, 1970, Disting. Alumnus award Luther Coll., 1975. Mem. Minn. Assn. Community and Jr. Colls. (sec.-treas.), Minn. 2 Year Coll. Bd. Control for Athletics (chmn.), Res. Officers Assn., Phi Delta Kappa. Lutheran. Club: Lions (dep. gov. Dist. 5-M4, 1978-79). Office: Willmar Community Coll Willmar MN 56201

TORGERSEN, TORWALD HAROLD, architect, interior designer; b. Chgo., Sept. 2, 1929; s. Peder and Hansine Malene (Hansen) T.; student North Central Coll., 1948, Ill. Inst. Tech., 1949; B.S. with honors in Archtl. Engring., U. Ill., 1951; m. Dorothy Darlene Peterson, June 22, 1963. Naval architect Phila. Navy Yard, 1951; partner Coyle and Torgersen, Joliet, Ill., 1955-56; project coordinator Skidmore, Owings and Merrill, Chgo., 1956-60; with Container Corp. Am., Chgo., 1960—, dir. architecture, constrn. and interiors, 1960—. Served with USN, 1952-55, capt. Res. Mem. AIA, Am. Soc. Interior Designers, Nat. Council Archtl. Registration Bds., Found. for Interior Design Edn. Research, Internat. Color Council, Am. Arbitration Assn., Naval Res. Assn., Soc. Am. Mil. Engrs., U. Ill. Alumni Assn., Naval Res. Officers Am. Clubs: Sports Car Am., Rydall Athletic. Home: 3750 N Lake Shore Dr Chicago IL 60613 Office: 500 E North Ave Carol Stream IL 60187

TORGERSEN, TORWALD HAROLD, architect, designer; b. Chgo., Sept. 2, 1929; s. Peder and Hansine Malene (Hansen) T.; B.S. in Archtl. Engring. with honors, U. Ill., 1951; m. Dorothy Darlene Peterson, June 22, 1963. Partner, Coyle & Torgersen Architects-Engrs., Washington, Chgo. and Joliet, Ill., 1955-56; project coordinator Skidmore, Owings & Merrill, Chgo., 1956-60; corp. architect, dir. architecture, constrn. and interiors Container Corp. Am., Chgo., 1960—; guest lectr. U. Wis. Served to capt. USNR, 1951-55. Recipient Top Ten Design award Factory mag., 1964. Registered architect Nat. Council Archtl. Registration Bds. Fellow Am. Soc. Interior Designers; mem. AIA, Naval Res. Assn., Ill. Naval Militia, Am. Arbitration Assn., Am. Soc. Mil. Engrs., Paper Industry Mgmt. Assn. (hon.), Sports Car Club Am., Nat. Eagle Scout Assn. Club: 20 Fathoms. Home: 3750 N Lake Shore Dr Chicago IL 60613 Office: 500 E North Ave Carol Stream IL 60187

TORNABENE, CHARLES AUGUSTUS, food co. exec.; b. Pitts., Dec. 22, 1918; s. Carmelo and Ignazia (Teresi) T.; grad. Wittenberg U., 1940; m. Kathryn Moran, Feb. 11, 1942; children—Charles Augustus, Thomas, Rosemaryl. Gen. sales mgr. Kellogg Co., Battle Creek, Mich., 1958-60, v.p., gen. sales mgr., 1960-67, dir. sales co., 1966-68, pres. sales co., 1968-69, dir. Kellogg Co., 1969—, chmn. bd. sales co., 1969-76, vice-chmn. Kellogg Co., 1976-77, pres. internat., 1977-81, vice-chmn. bd., 1981—. Trustee, Mich. Colls. Found. Served with U.S. Army, 1942-45. Named Man of Yr., Internat. Assn. Chain Stores, 1979. Mem. Conf. Bd. (internat. council). Roman Catholic. Clubs: Asparagus; Illuminators. Office: 235 Porter St Battle Creek MI 49016

TOROK, ANDREW DAVID, pub. co. exec.; b. Detroit, Oct. 14, 1946; s. Andrew and Ethel J. T.; B.A., Mich. State U., 1968; M.B.A., U. Detroit, 1974; m. Susan Katherine Shimp, Oct. 18, 1968; children—Sara, Amy. With Chrysler Corp., 1972-75; inventory mgr. Western Pub. Co., Inc., Racine, Wis., 1975-76, prodn. scheduling and inventory mgr., 1976-77, corp. mgr. mfg. programs, 1977-79, corp. dir. prodn. control, 1979-81, corp. dir. mfg. resource planning, 1981—; adj. asso. prof. U. Wis. (Parkside). Served to capt. inf. AUS, 1968-72. Decorated Army Commendation medal. Mem. Am. Prodn. and Inventory Control Soc. (cert. in prodn. and inventory mgmt.), Prodn. Control Council (pres.), Mfrs. and Employers Assn. of Racine. Home: 1336 S Main St Racine WI 53403 Office: 1220 Mound Ave Racine WI 53404

TORONTO, JOHN JOSEPH, bus. equipment co. exec.; b. Columbus, Ohio, Feb. 2, 1930; s. Larry and Maude (Hoover) T.; student Remington Word Processing Sch., 1976; m. Patricia Shoemaker, Dec. 8, 1978; children—Carol S., James E. City salesman Borden Co., Columbus, 1950-61; dist. mgr. Sperry-Remington, Columbus, 1961-73; founder, pres. Toronto Bus. Equipment, Inc., Columbus, 1973—; cons. Casio, Inc., Remington Bus. Systems, Inc.; mem. dealer adv. council Sperry Remington, 1964, 69, 71, 73, 77, 79, Casio, Inc., 1978, 79. Named Nat. Dealer Sales Leader, Sperry-Remington, 1973, 74, 75, 76, 77, 78. Mem. Nat. Office Machines Dealers Assn. Republican. Clubs: Columbus Maennerchor, Masons, Shriners. Home: 1273 Ducrest Dr S Columbus OH 43220 Office: 1159 W Broad St Columbus OH 43222

TORRES, ANTHONY IGNATIUS, educator; b. Chgo., July 5, 1929; s. Anastasio and Bivina (Garcia) T.; B.S., No. Ill. U., 1954; M.Ed., DePaul U., 1956, Ed.S., 1958; Ed.D., Loyola U., Chgo., 1973. Tchr., Chgo. Public Schs., 1954-66; adminstr. Ill. Office of Edn., 1966-72; prin. Park Ridge (Ill.) Public Schs., 1972-76; dir. personnel Prairie State Coll., Chicago Heights, Ill., 1976-77; supt. schs., River Grove, Ill., 1977-79, Sauk Village, Ill., 1979—. Bd. govs. United Republican Fund; bd. dirs. United Way Suburban Cook County, 1981—. Recipient Those Who Excel award Ill. State Bd. Edn., 1978. Mem. Am. Assn. Sch. Adminstrs., Ill. Assn. Sch. Adminstrs., Am. Assn. U. Adminstrs., Phi Delta Kappa (Service award Loyola U. chpt.). Club: Columbia Yacht (Chgo.). Contbr. articles to profl. jours., column on edn. to local newspapers. Home: 1750 N Wells St Chicago IL 60614

TORRES, EUGENIO, controls engr.; b. San Juan, P.R., May 14, 1950; s. Eugenio and Pura (Agosto) T.; A.E.E., U. P.R., 1971; E.E.T., Wentworth Inst. Tech., Boston, 1973; children—Eugenio F., Herbert. Prodn. supr. Union Carbide, Inc., P.R.; automation specialist Honeywell, Inc., Rio Piedras, P.R.; account mgr. Mal del Caribe, Santurce, P.R.; applications engr. comml. mktg. Carrier Corp., Syracuse, N.Y.; now controls engr. internat. group Rapistan div. Lear Seigler, Grand Rapids, Mich. Served with P.R. Air N.G., 1975-78, USNG, 1978—. Cert. engring. technician. Mem. IEEE, ASHRAE, SIEPR, Delta Phi Theta, Alpha Phi Omega. Roman Catholic. Clubs: Exchange, Nyang NCO, Prang NCO. Home: 2501 Longmeadow NW Grand Rapids MI 49504

TORRES, MARIA ROSEE, owner secretarial service; b. Apr. 18, 1945; Asso. in Bus. Adminstrn., YMCA Coll., Chgo., 1972; B.A. in Polit. Sci., Roosevelt U., 1978; m. Noel Torres, Nov. 6, 1965; children—Noel (dec.), Elisa. Court reporter, 1963-66; legal sec., mgr. law office, 1966-69; owner Legal Secretarial Services, Ltd., Chgo., 1969—; dir. RNT Enterprises Sec. 42d Ward Young Democrats, Chgo., 1973-75; corr. sec. Young Democrats of Cook County, 1974-75. Named Outstanding Young Democrat of Yr., Cook County Young Dems., 1975, Outstanding Woman of Yr., 1975. Mem. Assn. Legal Secs. and Assts. (dir.), Nat. Shorthand Reporters Assn., Assn. Legal Adminstrs., Am. Karate Assn. Democrat. Editor Legal Secretarial News Letter, 1974—. Home: Chicago IL Office: 201 N Wells St Suite 1206 Chicago IL 60602

TORTORIELLO, ANTHONY MICHAEL, oil co. exec.; b. Chgo., June 26, 1933; s. Francis S. and Julia (Agnetti) T.; m. Enis Marie Chimienti, June 11, 1955; children—Julie, Anthony. With Burlington R.R., 1951-53, 55-56, asst. to gen. agt. passenger dept., 1955-56; traffic mgr. Gustafson Oil Co., Chgo., 1956-61; founder, pres., chmn. Torco Oil Co., Chgo., 1961—. Bd. dirs. Spl. Childrens Charities, 1978-80. Served with U.S. Army, 1953-55. Named Man of Year, Chgo. Baseball Cancer Charities, 1979. Mem. Chgo. Traffic Club, Chgo. Oil Men's Club. Roman Catholic. Clubs: Butterfield Country, Oak Brook Polo (Ill.); Ill. Athletic. Office: 624 S Michigan Ave Chicago IL 60605

TORVIK, PATRICIA ANN, hosp. exec.; b. Ivanhoe, Minn., Oct. 3, 1938; d. Carl Elmo and Wilma Gertrude (Wiegert) Nyhus; B.S., Wright State U., 1972, M.Ed., 1977; postgrad. Ohio State U., 1978—; m. Peter John Torvik, Sept. 20, 1958; children—Peter John, Carl Fredric. Tchr. math, middle sch., Dayton, Ohio, 1972-78; teaching supr., program developer forensic psychiat. hosp. Dayton Mental Health Center, 1980—. Pres., LWV, Falcon Heights, Minn., 1963-64; bd. dirs. Met. Chs. United, Dayton. Mem. Philosophy of Edn. Soc., History of Edn. Soc., John Dewey Soc., NEA, Ohio Edn. Assn., Western Ohio Edn. Assn., Ohio Assn. Adult Educators, Am. Ednl. Studies Assn., Assn. Supervision and Curriculum Devel., Ohio Assn. Supervision and Curriculum Devel., Ohio Council Tchrs. of Math., Dayton Council Tchrs. of Math., Kappa Delta Pi, Phi Delta Kappa, Phi Kappa Phi. Democrat. Presbyterian. Home: 2000 Harvard Blvd Dayton OH 45406 Office: 2611 Wayne Ave Dayton OH 45420

TORVIK, PETER JOHN, educator; b. Fergus Falls, Minn., Dec. 6, 1938; s. Freddie Maynard and Esther Lillian (Randall) T.; B.S., U. Minn., 1960, M.S., 1962, Ph.D., 1965; B.A., Wright State U., 1980; m. Patricia Ann Nyhus, Sept. 20, 1958; children—Peter John, Carl Fredric. Teaching asst., fellow, instr. U. Minn., 1960-64; asst. prof. Air Force Inst. Tech., Wright Patterson AFB, Ohio, 1964-67, asso. prof., 1967-73, prof. mechanics, 1973—, head dept., 1980—; vis. prof. Ohio State U., 1979. Served with USAF, 1964-67. Recipient Sci. Achievement award USAF, 1972; Link Found. fellow, 1960-61, NSF fellow, 1961-62, NASA fellow, 1962-64. Asso. fellow AIAA; mem. ASME (chmn. shock and vibration com. 1978-80), Acoustical Soc. Am., Am. Acad. Mechanics, AAUP, Ohio Acad. Sci., Dayton Philharmonic Assn. Contbr. articles to profl. jours. Home: 2000 Harvard Blvd Dayton OH 45406 Office: Dept Aeronautics and Astronautics Air Force Inst Tech Wright Patterson AFB OH 45433

TOSCANO, JAMES VINCENT, med. adminstr.; b. Passaic, N.J., Aug. 8, 1937; s. William V. and Mary A. (DeNigris) T.; B.A., Rutgers U., 1959; M.A., Yale, 1960; m. Sharon Lee Bowers; children—Shawn, Lauren, David Brendan Dania. Lectr., Wharton Sch., U. Pa., 1961-64; chief opinion analyst Pa. Opinion Poll, 1962-64; mng. dir. World Press Inst., Macalester Coll., St. Paul, 1964-68, exec. dir., 1968-72, dir. devel., 1972-74; v.p. for resource devel. and pub. affairs Mpls. Soc. Fine Arts, 1974-79; pres. Minn. Mus. Art, 1979-81; exec. dir. St. Louis Park Med. Center Research Found., 1981—. Ex-officio mem. bd. Minn. Citizens for Arts; sec. bd. dirs. World Press Inst., 1972—; bd. dirs. Minn. World Federalists, Am. Composers Forum, World Affairs Center, Minn. Internat. Center, Citizens Adv. Com. on Cable Communication, St. Paul. Clubs: Minn., Informal, Skylight. Author: The Chief Elected Official in the Penjerdel Region, 1964; author, editor: (with Philip Jacob and others) The Integration of Political Communities, 1964. Office: St Louis Park Med Center Research Found 5000 W 39th St Minneapolis MN 55416

TOSHACH, DANIEL WILKIE, architect; b. Saginaw, Mich., June 28, 1928; s. Clarence Eneas and Charlotte Sellers (Hassett) T.; grad. Phillips Exeter Acad., 1946; B.A., Yale U., 1950, B.Arch., M.Arch., 1953; children (by previous marriage)—Charlotte, Mary, Daniel, Pamela, Katrina; m. 2d, Clarice Oversby, July 30, 1965; children—Duncan, Paul Beard. Architect-in-tng. various archtl. offices, Midland and Saginaw, 1953-57; individual practice architecture, Saginaw, 1957-61; prin. Prine Toshach Spears, Architects and Engrs., Inc., Saginaw, 1961-73, Prine Toshach Assos., Architects and Engrs., Inc., Saginaw, 1973-77; pres. Toshach & Sobczak, Asso. Architects, 1977—. Chmn. adv. com. on archtl. tech. Delta Community Coll., 1965—. Bd. fellows Saginaw Valley State Coll. Mem. Saginaw County Met. Planning Commn., 1966—, chmn., 1976-78. Mem. AIA (pres. Saginaw Valley chpt. 1961, merit award 1966, 72, com. on architecture for commerce and industry), Mich. Soc. Architects (dir. 1964-65), Nat. Council Archtl. Registration Bds. Rotarian. Clubs: Saginaw (pres. 1976-77), Saginaw Valley Torch (pres. 1979-80). Designer Trinity Luth. Ch., Midland, Mich., Univ. Luth. Ch., East Lansing, Mich., Swan Valley High Sch., Saginaw, Career Opportunities Center, Saginaw, 2d Nat. Bank of Saginaw, Pioneer Hall, Saginaw Valley, Bethlehem Luth. Ch., Saginaw, Sta. WNEM-TV, Saginaw. Office: 122 N Washington Ave Saginaw MI 48607

TOSI, OSCAR I., scientist, educator; b. Trento, Italy, June 17, 1929; s. Mario and Ethel (Manescu) T.; came to U.S., 1962, naturalized, 1973; D.Sc. cum laude, Nat. U. Buenos Aires, 1951; Ph.D., Ohio State U., 1965. Asso. prof. physics Nat. U. Buenos Aires, 1952-62; asst. prof. acoustics Mich. State U., East Lansing, 1966-68, asso. prof., 1968-71, prof., 1971—, dir. Speech and Hearing Lab., 1970—, asst. dean (research) Coll. Communication Arts and Scis., 1972-76; expert witness voice identification in fed., state cts., U.S., Can. and Europe; founder, dir. Internat. Assn. Voice Identification, Inc., Lansing, 1971—; mem. com. on evaluation sound spectrograms Nat. Acad. Scis., 1976—. Recipient Certificate of Appreciation, Mich. State Police, 1971, award Spanish Assn. Phoniatrics and Logopedics, 1973. Mem. Internat. Collegium Phonology (sec.-gen.), Internat. Assn. Phoniatrics and Logopedics, Acoustical Soc. Am. (staff mem. tech. com. speech communication 1974-77), Am. Speech and Hearing Assn., Am. Assn. Tchrs. Physics, Internat. Assn. Phonetics, Opera Guild Greater Lansing (founder 1973), Italian Am. Club of Lansing. Author: Physics for Medical Students, 1962; Voice Identification, 1971; contbr. chpts. to Theory of Speech Production and Acoustic Phonetics, 1972, The Problem of Voice Identification and Elimination, 1974, Pausometry, 1974; Voice Identification: Theory and Legal Applications, 1979; Physics for Audiologists and Speech Pathologists, 1981. Contbr. articles to profl. jours. Research dir. voice identification project U.S. Dept. Justice, 1968-71; expert witness for

Italian Govt. to analyze tape recs. related to assassination of Premier Aldo Moro, 1979. Home: 221 Bessemaur East Lansing MI 48823 Office: 370 Communication Bldg Mich State U East Lansing MI 48824

TOSO, MILTON ROBERT, psychologist, personnel ofcl.; b. Graceville, Minn., Dec. 24, 1952; s. Orin Sharold and Mildred Anna T.; B.A. in Psychology, St. Cloud State U., 1975; M.A. in Psychology, Duquesne U., 1976; m. Kristine Mary Jondahl, June 22, 1974; 1 son, Erik Andrew. Psychology asst. Community Mental Health, St. Clairsville, Ohio, 1976-79; psychologist Northland Mental Health, Internat. Falls, Minn., 1979; psychotherapist Abbott-NW Mental Health Clinic, Mpls., 1979-80; prin. employment rep. Sperry Univac, St. Paul, 1980—. Vol. lectr. community groups, 1978-79. Lic. psychologist, Minn. Asso. mem. Am. Psychol. Assn., Minn. Psychol. Assn. Office: Univac Park PO Box 3525 Saint Paul MN 55165

TOSTO, LOUIS FRANK, lumber retail co. exec.; b. Chgo., Mar. 20, 1948; s. Michael Angelo and Eleanor Elizabeth (Caster) T.; student William Penn Coll., Oskaloosa, Iowa, 1966-67, North Park Coll., Chgo., 1967-68, William R. Harper Community Coll., Palatine, Ill., 1968-70. Produce mgr. Jewel Cos. Inc., Chgo., 1964-72; sales rep. Internat. Playtex Corp., N.Y.C., 1972-74; asst. field supr. Southland Corp., Chgo., 1974-75; asst. mgr. Ace Hardware, Elk Grove Village, Ill., 1975-78; asst. store mgr. Edward Hines Lumber Co., Villa Park, Ill., 1978—. Vol. fireman Elk Grove Village Fire Dept., 1969—; bd. dirs. Elk Grove Community Services and Mental Health Bd., 1977-81; founder Elk Grove Village Jayteens, 1977—, Elk Grove Village's Village Fair, 1977—; chmn. Elk Grove Village Youth Services Com., 1978-81; active Boy Scouts Am. Mem. Nat. Retail Hardware Assn., Elk Grove Village Jaycees (dir. 1976-78, pres. 1979-80). Roman Catholic. Club: Elks. Home: 1507 Armstrong Ln Elk Grove Village IL 60007 Office: 600 N Villa Ave Villa Park IL 60181

TOTH, DAVID SCOTT, podiatrist; b. Cleve., Jan. 5, 1952; s. Joseph Francis and Margaret Judy (Kovacs) T.; B.A., Coll. of Wooster, 1973; D.P.M., Ohio Coll. Podiatric Medicine, 1974; m. Donna Georgene Dolch, July 19, 1975; children—David Scott, Jennifer Theresa. Resident Ohio Coll. Podiatric Medicine, 1978; asso. Dr. Marvin Z. Arnold, Maple Heights, Ohio, 1977-78; practice podiatric medicine, Brecksville, Ohio, 1978—; mem. staff Huron Road Hosp., Cleve.; chmn. bd. K.T.E. Found.; lectr. profl. seminars. Recipient Order of Battered Boot award March of Dimes, 1975. Mem. Am. Podiatry Assn., Ohio Podiatry Assn., N.E. Ohio Acad. Podiatric Medicine, Am. Coll. Sports Medicine, Acad. Ambulatory Foot Surgery, Alumni Assn. Ohio Coll. Podiatric Medicine (dir. 1981—), Kappa Tau Epsilon (treas. 1976-77, Outstanding Alumni award), Pi Delta (treas., 1976-77). Roman Catholic. Contbr. articles on foot surgery to profl. jours. Home: 13050 Kenyon Dr Chesterland OH 44026 Office: 7650 Chippewa Rd Suite 205 Brecksville OH 44141

TOTH, MARY JANE, educator; b. Cleve., Mar. 12, 1939; d. Zoltan William and Lucille Agnes (Smith) T.; B.A., Ohio Dominican Coll., 1961; M.A. in Edn., Washington U., St. Louis, 1966; postgrad. Kent State U., 1979—. Tchr. biology and chemistry Kilakala Secondary Sch., Tanzania, 1967-69; tchr. sci. St. Rita Sch., Solon, Ohio, 1970-71; dir. environ. edn. project Maple Heights (Ohio) City Schs., 1976-77; tchr. environ. studies, 1971—; adj. instr. Coll. Urban Affairs, Cleve. State U., 1980—; environ. edn. curriculum cons., 1980-81. Ohio Dept. Edn. grantee, 1979; Environ. Edn. grantee, U.S. Office Edn. grantee, 1976; NSF grantee, 1965. Mem. Nat. Assn. Environ. Edn., Ohio Alliance for Environ. Edn., Ohio Conservation and Outdoor Edn. Assn., Assn. Exptl. Edn., NEA, Ohio Edn. Assn., Northeastern Ohio Tchrs. Assn., Maple Heights Tchrs. Assn., Assn. Supervision and Curriculum Devel., Cleve. Regional Council Sci. Tchrs., Town and Country Planning Assn. Home: 2651 Idlewood Rd Cleveland Heights OH 44118 Office: 5500 Clement Dr Maple Heights OH 44137

TOTTEN, DONALD LEE, cons., state senator; b. Bklyn., Feb. 19, 1933; s. Edgar Lee and Louise (Florentino) T.; B.S.M.E., U. Notre Dame, 1955; m. Joyce Anderson, May 11, 1955; children—Diana, Robert, Kathleen. Plant mgr. Morton Mfg. Co., Farr Co.; asst. to sec. Ill. Dept. Transp.; sales rep. Twin T Co.; rep. Ill. Legislature, 1973-81; cons. Twin T Co., Schaumburg, Ill., 1976—; mem. Ill. State Senate, 1981—. Committeeman Schaumburg Twp., 1966—; chmn. exec. com. Cook County Republican Central Com., 1980-81; mem. transition team Office of Pres.-Elect, 1980, Reagan-Bush Com., 1980, Reagan for Pres. Com., 1980. Roman Catholic. Office: 839 W Higgins St Schaumburg IL 60195*

TOUCHSTONE, FRANK VIRGIL, psychologist; b. London, Ky., July 11, 1927; s. Cary and Mabel Ellen (Thomas) T.; B.A. with honors, So. Methodist U., 1950; M.S., Purdue U., 1952, Ph.D., 1957; m. Dorothy Viola Anderson, Nov. 10, 1961; 1 dau., Ellen Elizabeth. Psychologist, VA, 1956-63; asso. prof. psychology Centenary Coll., Shreveport, 1963-67; asso. prof. edn. Pa. State U., 1967-70; chief psychologist Mental Health Center, Hazard, Ky., 1970-74; dir. psychology Hastings (Nebr.) Regional Center, 1974—; vis. prof. edn. Purdue U., summers 1965, 66; bd. dirs. Caddo Bossier chpt. La. Assn. Mental Health, 1961-67; bd. dirs. Shreveport Child Guidance Center, 1964-65, v.p., 1965; cons. Bur. Hearings and Appeals, Social Security Adminstrn., 1967—. Served with USAAF, 1946-49. Mem. Am. Psychol. Assn., Am. Personnel and Guidance Assn., Am. Rehab. Counseling Assn. (Superior Service award 1976; pres. 1978-79), Nat. Vocat. Guidance Assn., Nat. Rehab. Assn., Nat. Rehab. Counseling Assn., Nebr. Personnel and Guidance Assn. (dir. 1975-81), Psi Chi, Alpha Kappa Delta. Presbyterian. Editor Rehab. Counseling Bull., 1966-70. Home: 2320 W 10th St Hastings NE 68901 Office: Hastings Regional Center Hastings NE 68901

TOVAR, LORENZO, tng. and devel. co. exec.; b. Villagran, Guanajuato, Mex., May 13, 1942; s. Jesus and Eloisa (Flores) T.; came to U.S., 1960; B.B.A., U. Wis., Milw., 1975; M.B.A., U. Chgo., 1980; m. Lourdes Castillo, June 15, 1968; 1 son, Oscar. Vocat. counselor Spanish Speaking Council, Milw., 1970-72; counselor U. Wis., Milw., 1972-74; dir. Inroads/Milw., Inc., 1974-77, v.p., regional dir., 1977—. Bd. dirs. United Way, 1978—; mem. Milw. Forum, 1977; mem. Gov.'s Council on Minority Bus., 1977. Served with U.S. Army, 1964-66. Mem. Am. Mgmt. Assn., Am. Soc. Tng. and Devel., Latin-Am. C. of C. Wis. (pres. 1976-77), U. Chgo. Alumni Assn. Club: U. Chgo. Executive. Home: 8310 N Greenvale Rd Fox Point WI 53217 Office: Inroads/Milw Inc 135 W Wells St Milwaukee WI 53203

TOWER, RAYMOND C., bus. exec.; b. N.Y.C., Feb. 20, 1925; s. Raymond C. and Elinor (Donovan) T.; B.S., Yale U., 1945; m. Jaclyn Bauerline, Feb. 7, 1948; children—Raymond, Patricia, Christopher, Robert, Mary, Michael, Victoria. Research chemist Westvaco Chem. Co., 1946-48; with chem. div. FMC Corp., N.Y.C., 1948-65, v.p., gen. mgr. organic chem. div., 1964-67, exec. v.p., mgr. chem. group, 1967-77, pres. FMC Corp., Chgo., 1977—, also dir.; dir. Marathon Oil Co.; trustee Instl. Liquid Assets. Bd. trustees Drexel U. Served to lt. USNR, 1944-46, 51-53. Mem. Chem. Mfrs. Assn. (dir.), Chgo. Assn. Commerce and Industry (dir.), Ireland-U.S. Council Commerce and Industry, Nat. Safety Council (trustee), Harvard Bus. Sch. Assn., Soc. Chem. Industry, Chgo. Council Fgn. Relations (mem. Chgo. com.), Alpha Chi Sigma. Clubs: Comml., Econ., Mid-Am., Union League (Chgo.); Glen View. Office: 200 E Randolph Dr Chicago IL 60601

TOWLES, ROBERT JOHN, glass and ceramics co. exec.; b. Toledo, Sept. 6, 1936; s. Herman Elwood and Genevieve Dorothy (Kowalski) T.; B.S., U. Toledo, 1962, M.S., 1966; M.B.A., Ohio State U., 1980; m. Sandra Drake Chappelear, July 30, 1960; children—Robert Eric, Christopher Guy, Jeffrey Sean. Technician, Libbey-Owens-Ford, Inc., Toledo, 1959-61; with Owens-Illinois, Inc., Toledo, 1962—, supr. bus. and tech. planning, 1980—. Scoutmaster, Boy Scouts Am., 1973-74, asst. dist. commr., 1974-75. Served with U.S. Army, 1955-61. Recipient Scouters Tng. award Boy Scouts Am., 1973, Mem. Am. Phys. Soc., Am. Ceramic Soc. (pres. 1968), Mensa, Sigma Xi. Roman Catholic. Home: 1796 Valley Way Dr Toledo OH 43614 Office: One Seagate Plaza Toledo OH 43666

TOWNER, JOHN HARDING, realtor; b. Bangor, Maine, July 15, 1922; s. Wayland Dean and Betty (Mills) T.; B.S., Mich. State U., 1948; M.S., U. Ill., 1951; m. Judith E. Dellorto Dec. 16, 1976; children—Alan Edward, Robert Lee, Patricia Ann. Sales dir. Am. Comml. Builders, Park Forest, Ill., 1951-57; owner Town & Country Realty, Inc., Richton Park, Ill., 1957-61; chmn. bd., dir. Thorn Creek Realty, Inc., Chicago Heights, Ill., 1961-75; exec. v.p. Continental Real Estate Inc., Elmhurst, Ill., 1971-74; chmn. bd. Continental Real Estate-South, Chicago Heights, 1975—. Instr. real estate Prairie State Coll., Chicago Heights, 1965—. Mem. sch. bd. dist. 163, Park Forest, 1952-58. Bd. dirs. Harvey (Ill.) Meml. YMCA, 1965-70. Served with USAAF, 1942-45. Mem. Ill. Assn. Real Estate Bds. (dist. v.p. 1969-70, dir. 1977-81, Service medallion 1968), S. Suburban Bd. Realtors (Realtor of Year 1968, pres. 1967-68, 75, 81), Ill. Realtors Inst. (bd. govs. 1972-80), Phi Delta Kappa, Sigma Chi. Moose. Club: Lakes of Four Seasons Property Owners Assn. (pres., bd. dirs., Crown Point, Ind.). Home: 1562 Happy Valley Rd Crown Point IN 46307 Office: 3717 Sauk Trail Richton Park IL 60471

TOWNER, LAWRENCE WILLIAM, historian, librarian; b. St. Paul, Sept. 10, 1921; s. Earl Chadwick and Cornelia (Mallum) T.; B.A., Cornell Coll., Mt. Vernon, Iowa, 1942, L.H.D., 1965; M.A., Northwestern U., 1950, Ph.D. (Hearst Found. fellow), 1955, L.H.D., 1965; LL.D., Lake Forest Coll., 1965; m. Rachel Eleanor Bauman, Nov. 28, 1943; children—Wendy Kay Towner Yanikoski, Kristin Anne Towner Moses, Lawrence Baumann, Elizabeth Gail, Peter Mallum, Michael Chadwick. History master Chgo. Latin Sch., 1946-47; instr., asst. prof. history Mass. Inst. Tech., Cambridge, 1950-55; asso. prof. history Coll. William and Mary, 1955-62; librarian and dir. Newberry Library, Chgo., 1962—, pres., 1975—. Vis. prof. Northwestern U., summer 1957, 68-72; dir. Inst. for Hist. and Archival Mgmt., Radcliffe Coll., Harvard U., 1959; Center for Study History of Liberty In Am. fellow Harvard U. 1961-62. Chmn. Williamsburg Area Interracial Study Group, 1960-61; mem. Ill. Humanities Council, 1974—, chmn., 1976-78; mem. adv. bd. Who's Who in Am.; trustee Grinnell (Iowa) Coll., 1966-72, Chgo. Latin Sch., 1970-72, Mus. Contemporary Art, 1972-75; mem. council Eleutherian Mills-Hagley Found., 1976—, Fedn. Pub. Programs in Humanities, 1977-79; adv. bd. Papers of George Washington, Papers of Benjamin Franklin. Served to 1st lt., pilot AUS, 1943-46. Mem. Am. Hist. Assn. (mem. council 1973-75), Orgn. Am. Historians, Am. Antiquarian Soc., Colonial Soc. Mass., Mass. Hist. Soc., Bibliog. Soc. Am., Modern Poetry Assn. (trustee, pres.). Clubs: Harvard (N.Y.C.); Columbia Yacht, Cosmos, Caxton, Econ., Tavern, Arts. Author: An Uncommon Collection of Uncommon Collections: The Newberry Library, 1970, 76; (with A.N.L. Munby) The Flow of Books and Manuscripts, 1969. Editor: William and Mary Quar.: A Mag. of Early Am. History, 1955-62, A Summary View of the Rights of British America by Thomas Jefferson, 1976; bd. editors Jour. Am. History, 1965-68, America, History and Life, 1965—. Office: 60 W Walton St Chicago IL 60610

TOWNER, LLOYD WESLEY, JR., retail exec.; b. Minn., Oct. 7, 1923; s. Lloyd Wesley and Mable Cecelia T.; student Duluth Jr. Coll., 1941-42; m. Helen Elizabeth Johnson, Aug. 18, 1950; children—Susan Beth Towner Ryder, Nancy Lee. Agt., Conn. Gen. Life Ins. Co., Duluth, Minn.. 1947-51; adminstr. employee benefits Marshall Wells Co., Duluth, 1951-59; v.p. Hunter Agy., Inc., Duluth, 1959-62; v.p. human resources Coast To Coast Stores, Minnetonka, Minn., 1963—. Served with USN, 1943-46. Decorated Purple Heart; accredited exec. in personnel, Minn. Mem. Twin Cities Personnel Assn., Am. Soc. Personnel Adminstrn. Clubs: VFW, Masons. Office: 10801 Red Circle Dr Minnetonka MN 55343

TOWNSEND, EARL CUNNINGHAM, JR., lawyer, author, composer; b. Indpls., Nov. 9, 1914; s. Earl Cunningham and Besse (Kuhn) T.; student De Pauw U., 1932-34; A.B., U. Mich., 1936, J.D., 1939; m. Emily Macnab, Apr. 3, 1947; children—Starr (Mrs. John R. Laughlin), Vicki M. (Mrs. Christopher Ketterjohn), Julia E. (Mrs. Edward Goodrich Dunn, Jr.), Earl Cunningham III, Clyde G. Admitted to Ind. bar, 1939, Mich. bar, 1973, also U.S. Supreme Ct. bar; sr. partner firm Townsend & Townsend, Indpls., 1940-69; sr. partner Townsend, Hovde & Townsend, Indpls., 1970—; individual practice, Roscommon, Mich., 1973—; dep. prosecutor, Marion County, Ind., 1942-44; radio-TV announcer WIRE, WFBM, WFBM-TV, Indpls., 1940-49, 1st TV announcer 500 mile race, 1949, 50; Big Ten basketball referee, 1940-47; lectr. trial tactics U. Notre Dame, Ind. U., U. Mich., 1968-79; owner Tropical Isle Palm Tree Farms, Key Biscayne, Fla., Terney-Townsend Historic House, Roscommon, Mich.; founder, v.p., treas. Am. Underwriters, Inc., Am. Interinsurance Exchange, 1965-70; mem. Com. to Revise Ind. Supreme Ct. Pattern Jury Instructions, 1975—. Founder, life fellow Roscoe Pound Trial Lawyers Found., Cambridge, Mass.; co-founder, dir. Meridian St. Found.; mem. fin. and bldg. coms., bd. dirs., later life trustee Indpls. Mus. Art; trustee Cathedral High Sch., Indpls., Ind. State Mus., Starlight Musicals; fellow Meth. Hosp. Found. Recipient Ind. Univ. Writers Conf. award, 1960; Hanson H. Anderson medal of honor Arsenal Tech. Schs., Indpls., 1971; named to Council Sagamores of Wabash, 1969, Ind. Basketball Hall of Fame; hon. chief Black River-Swan Creek Saginaw-Chippewa Indian tribe, 1971. Fellow Ind. Coll. Trial Lawyers, Internat. Acad. Trial Lawyers, Internat. Soc. Barristers; mem. Ind. Trial Lawyers Assn. (pres. 1963-64), Am. (com. trial techniques 1964-76, com. aviation and space 1977—), Ind. State (del. 1977-79), Indpls., 34th Dist. (Mich.) bar assns., State Bar Mich., Assn. Am. Trial Lawyers (v.p. Ind. 1959-60, bd. govs. 7th jud. circuit 1966-68, asso. editor Jour. 1964—), Bar Assn. 7th Fed. Circuit, Lawyers Assn. Indpls., Ind. Archeol. Soc. (founder, pres.), Genuine Indian Relic Soc. (co-founder, chmn. frauds com.), Ind. Hist. Soc., Trowel and Brush Soc. (hon.), U. Mich. Pres.'s Club, U. Mich. Victors Club (charter), Soc. Mayflower Descs. (gov. 1947-49), Key Biscayne C. of C., Delta Kappa Epsilon, Phi Kappa Phi. Republican. Methodist. Clubs: Players; U. Mich. (local pres. 1950); Columbia; Key Biscayne Yacht; Masons (32 deg., Shriner). Author: Birdstones of the North American Indian, 1959; also articles in legal and archeol. fields; composer Moon of Halloween. Home: 5008 N Meridian St Indianapolis IN 46208 Office: 150 E Market St Indianapolis IN 46204 also 603 Lake St Roscommon MI 48653

TOWNSEND, HAROLD GUYON, JR., pub. co. exec.; b. Chgo., Apr. 11, 1924; s. Harold Guyon and Anne Louise (Robb) T.; A.B., Cornell U., 1948; m. Margaret Jeanne Keller, July 28, 1951; children—Jessica, Julie, Harold Guyon III. Advt. salesman Chgo. Tribune, 1948-51; gen. mgr. Keller-Heartt Co., Clarendon Hills, Ill., 1951-62; pub. Santa Clara (Calif.) Jour., 1962-64; pres., pub. Dispatch-Tribune newspaper Townsend Communications, Inc., Kansas City, Mo., 1964—; dir. United Mo. Bank of Blue Valley. Chmn., Suburban Newspaper Research Commn., 1974—; dir. Certified Audit Bur. of Circulation, 1968-72. del. Rep. Nat. Conv., 1960; chmn. Mission Hills Rep. Com., 1966-77; bd. dirs. Kansas City Jr. Achievement, 1966-68, Kansas City council Girl Scouts U.S.A., 1969-71, Kansas City council Boy Scouts Am., 1974, Kansas City chpt. ARC, 1973-79, Kansas City Starlight Theater, Clay County (Mo.) Indsl. Commn.; treas., trustee Park Coll., Parkville, Mo., 1970-78. Mem. adv. com. North Kansas City Hosp. Served with inf. AUS, World War II. Mem. Kansas City Advt. and Sales Club, Kansas City Press Club, Suburban Press Found. (pres. 1969-71), Suburban Newspapers Am. (pres. 1976-77), Kansas City Printing Industries Assn. (v.p., dir.), Printing Industries of Am. (pres. non-heatset web sect. 1980-82), North Kansas City C. of C. (dir., pres. 1964-70), Sigma Delta Chi, Pi Delta Epsilon, Phi Kappa Psi. Clubs: University (treas. 1977); Indian Hills Country; Hinsdale (Ill.) Golf. Home: 6321 Norwood Rd Mission Hills KS 66208 Office: 7007 NE Parvin Rd Kansas City MO 64117

TOWNSEND, J. RUSSELL, JR., ins. exec.; b. Cedar Rapids, Iowa, Nov. 21, 1910; s. J. Russell and Mabel (Ferguson) T.; B.S., Butler U., 1931; M.B.A., U. Pa., 1933; m. Virginia Holt, Aug. 1, 1938; 1 son, John Holt. Field asst. Equitable Life Ins. Co. Iowa, 1933-50, gen. agt., 1950-69, gen. agt. emeritus, 1969—; mng. asso. J. Russell Townsend & Assos., 1969—; asso. prof. ins. Butler U., Indpls., 1933—; cons. Ind. Dept. Ins., 1948-50; mem. Ind. Ho. of Reps., 1946-48, Ind. Senate, 1956-64; lectr., writer ins. field. Served with USNR, 1942-46; lt. comdr. Res. ret. Chmn. Indpls. Bicentennial Com., 1975-76; pres. Indpls. Jaycees, 1940. Recipient 25-year teaching award Am. Coll. C.L.U.'s, 1960; Alumni Achievement award Butler U., 1979. Mem. Indpls. Chpt. C.L.U.'s (past pres.), Ind. Life Underwriters Assn. (past v.p.), Ret. Officers Assn. (past pres. Indpls. chpt.), Ind. Soc. Assn. Execs., Naval Res. Assn., Navy League U.S., Am. Soc. C.L.U.'s, AAUP, Am. Soc. Risk and Ins., Ind. Acad. Sci., Sales and Marketing Execs. Council, U.S. Naval Inst. Republican. Presbyterian. Clubs: Columbia, Meridian Hills Country, Indpls. Literary, Kiwanis (dir. Ind. Found., lt. gov. Ind. dist. internat. 1975-76), Indpls. Press, Ft. Harrison Officers, Masons, Sojourners (Indpls); Army and Navy (Washington); Crystal Downs Country (Frankfort, Mich.) Contbr. articles to trade mags. Home: 8244 N Pennsylvania St Indianapolis IN 46240 Office: 804 Investors Trust Bldg 107 N Pennsylvania St Indianapolis IN 46204

TOWNSEND, PAUL HENSON, former mfg. exec.; b. Clermont, N.J., Dec. 19, 1889; s. Eli and Frances (Dryburgh) T.; B.A. honoris causa, Yale, 1918; m. Clarissa Marie Davis, Sept. 3, 1920; children—Ann (Mrs. Rodney Wood), Paul H. Tchr. grade schs. Cape May Co., N.J., 1908-10, 13-14; clk. Huron Portland Cement Co., 1919, supt. plants, ships, 1920-39, gen. mgr., 1938-53, v.p., 1942-53, dir., 1944—, pres., 1953-59, chmn. bd., 1959-66; v.p., dir. Detroit Chem. Works, 1937-63, Fed. Motor Truck Co., 1944-49, Nat. Gypsum Co., 1958-64. Dir. adv. com. Great Lakes Protective Assn., 1940-58. Served as capt., 315th F.A., U.S. Army, World War I. Recipient Purple Heart. Mem. Lake Carriers Assn. (dir.), Detroit Bd. Commerce, Detroit Engring. Soc., N.J. Hist. Soc., Detroit Soc. Geneal. Research, Newcomen Soc., Cape May Geog. Soc., Atlantic County Hist. Soc., Mich. Audubon Soc., Newcomen Soc., Alpha Delta Phi. Mem. Grosse Pointe Meml. Ch. Clubs: Propeller, Detroit, University, Yacht (Detroit); Seventy Five; Alpena; Hunter's Creek. Home: 425 Madison Ave Grosse Pointe Farms MI 48236

TOWNSEND, W. WAYNE, state senator; ed. Purdue U. Farmer; mem. Ind. Ho. of Reps., 1959-66, Ind. State Senate, 1971—. Del., Democratic Nat. Conv., 1972, 76; bd. dirs. Marion Gen. Hosp., Grant County Mental Health Assn. Served with U.S. Army, 1954-56. Mem. Friends Ch. Clubs: Masons, Elks. Office: Ind State Capitol Indianapolis IN 46204*

TOWNSEND, WILLIAM BEACH, cons. health and welfare; b. Cleve., Mar. 16, 1910; s. Henry Burton and Helen (Malley) T.; B.A., Western Res. U., 1932, M.A., 1948; m. Colette Marie Sheehan, Dec. 28, 1937; 1 son, Eric Beach. Employment supr. Cleve. Asso. Charities, 1933-40; exec. dir. Cleve. Soc. Crippled Children, 1940-79; adminstr. William B. Townsend Inst. (formerly Heman Rehab. Inst.), 1940-79. Registrar of Camp Cheerful, 1940-79; cons. to aux. Soc. for Crippled Children, 1942-72; cons. Lakewood (Ohio) Draft Bd., 1948— (fed. commendation award for 15 years service); adv. bd. Cuyahoga Assn. Retarded Children; budget com. Health Council; mem. occupational planning com. Ohio Citizens Council for Health and Welfare; v.p. Madonna Hall, 1954-56; pres. Cath. Youth Orgn., 1938-42; trustee Cath. Child Guidance Bur., 1956-62; gov. Lakewood Safety Council; pres. Citizens Juvenile Council; dir. Council Retarded Child, 1952-55, Cleve. Health Council, 1947—, Council Human Relations, 1955—. Treas. Mayor's Com. Employment of Handicapped, 1944-62; adviser F.S.R.C., Rehab. Internat., United Torch Services-Speakers' Bur. Agy.; nat. trustee Nat. Council for Handicapped; mem. Buckeye-Woodland Community Congress, No. Ohio Area Coordinating Com., United Torch Exec. Adv. Com., 1975—; sec.-gen. Stop the Arms Race. Served with Transp. Corps, AUS, 1945-46; PTO. Recipient distinguished service award and Man of year award Cleve. and U.S. Jaycees, 1943; 25-Year commendation U.S. Selective Service, 1973; 1st Ann. Dedicated Service award Nat. Council for Handicapped, 1975; proclamation Mayor of Lakewood, 1975; proclamation of congratulations City of Cleve., 1975; resolution of commendation Ohio Ho. of Reps., 1975; resolution United Way Sers., 1978; plaque Am. Legion, 1978; resolution U.S. Ho. of Reps., others. Mem. Council for Exceptional Children, Nat. Conf. Social Work, Am. Camping Assn. (sec. Ohio sect.), Ohio Rural Health Assn., Easter Seal Execs. Assn., Western Res. U. Alumni Assn., Early Settlers Assn., Advt. Fedn. Am., Cleve. Counsellors Assn. (pres.), Para-Progressives (hon.), Am. Legion, Cleve. Advt. Club, Nat. Publicity Council, Rehab. Internat. (U.S. del. Stockholm Conv. 1951), Cleve. C. of C., Lake Erie Jr. Mus., Ohio Assn. Workers for Blind, Rehab. Internat., Cleve. Council World Affairs, Greater Cleve. Growth Assn., Fedn. for Community Services (rep. assembly), Friends Cleve. Zoo, Cleve. Health Mus., Nat., Ohio (exec. bd. 1958—) rehab. assns., Cleve. Citizens League, Cleve. Mus. Art, Am. Acad., Am. Mus. Natural History, New Eng. Soc. Western Res. (life), Western Res., Lakewood (bd. dirs.), Cleve. hist. socs., League Ohio Sportsmen, Frostville Mus., Cleve. Inst. Music, Human Soc. U.S., Nat. Council Cath. Men, Postal Commemorative Soc., New Eng. Soc. Western Reserve, Smithsonian Instn., Am. Acad. Polit. and Social Sci., Council Rehab. Center Execs., Defenders of Wildlife, Olmsted Hist. Soc. Roman Catholic. Clubs: City, Mid-Day, Communicators, Auto, Rotary (Cleve.). Home: 1107 Nicholson Ave Lakewood OH 44107

TOWNSLEY, CLARENCE PAGE, III, univ. adminstr.; b. Honolulu, May 11, 1924; s. Clarence Page and Elsie (Stuart) T.; A.B., Harvard U., 1946; B.S., U.S. Mcht. Marine Acad., 1945; grad. Advanced Mgmt. Program, Harvard Bus. Sch., 1966; postgrad. N.Y. U. Law Sch., 1950-51; m. Nan Shannon, July 21, 1956; children—Clarence Page, Michael Boley, Darrell Shannon. With Cunard S.S. Co., N.Y.C., Chgo., St. Louis, Dallas, Houston, Cleve., Paris, London, Liverpool,

1949-67; asst. dir. mgmt. programs Northwestern U. Transp. Center, Evanston, Ill., 1967-68, dir. mgmt. programs and lectr., 1968—; transp. cons. Election presiding judge State of Ohio, 1960-64. Served to lt. (j.g.) USNR, 1942-46; ATO; PTO. Lic. marine engr. Mem. Nat Council Phys. Distbn. Mgmt., Am. Econ. Assn., AAUP, Transp. Securities Club of Chgo., Harvard Advanced Mgmt. Assn. Republican. Episcopalian. Clubs: North Shore Fortnightly (pres. 1975-76), Harvard, Harvard Bus. Sch., Speakers, Iroquois. Author: The Steamship Bluebook, 1964; Manual for Bureau Operations Aboard Ship, 1951; editor Cunard Monday Morning News, 1956-58. Home: 110 Girard Ave Wilmette IL 60091 Office: 2001 Sheridan Rd Evanston IL 60201

TOWNSLEY, H. WILLIAM, ins. co. exec.; b. Cin., Jan. 16, 1928; s. Howard Otis and Elsie Mae (Von Seggern) T.; B.A., Ohio Wesleyan U., 1952; M.Ed., Miami U., Oxford, Ohio, 1958; m. M. Virginia Retallick, Mar. 31, 1950; children—Mark William, Gregg Alan. Tng. and devel. advisor Cleve. Electric Illuminating Co., 1960-63; dir. personnel services Mich. Credit Union League, Detroit, 1963-67; v.p. adminstrv. services Mich. Life Ins. Co., Nat. Casualty Co., Southfield, 1967-81, v.p. personnel/corp. services, 1981—; pres. Nat. Casualty Employees Credit Union, 1976-80. Lodge advisor, vigil mem. Order Arrow, Boy Scouts Am. Served to 1st lt. U.S. Army, 1946-48. Fellow Life Mgmt. Inst.; mem. Adminstrv. Mgmt. Soc. (cert. adminstrv. mgr.; Diamond Merit award, dir. Detroit chpt. 1972-77, pres. 1975-76), Am. Mgmt. Assn., Am. Soc. Personnel Adminstrn. (accredited exec. in personnel), SAR, Sigma Chi. Republican. Club: Elks.

TOZZER, JACK CARL, civil engr., surveyor; b. Marion, Ohio, Jan. 5, 1922; s. Carl Henry and Henrietta (Schellenbaum) T.; B.C.E., Ohio No. U., 1944; children—Brent Jack, Hal Jack; m. Aleta C. Lehner, July 14, 1974. Pres. firm Tozzer & Assos. Inc., Marion, 1948—; county engr. Marion County, Ohio, 1964—; city engr. Marion, 1959, Galion, Ohio, 1960—. Cons. civil engr. Mem. consultants bd. Coll. Engring. Ohio No. U., 1970, recipient Order of Engr., 1971; v.p. Marion Community Improvement Corp.; mem. Marion County Regional Planning Commn. Served with USNR, 1944-46. Registered profl. engr., Ohio, Fla., registered surveyor, Ohio. Fellow ASCE; mem. Nat. Soc. Profl. Engrs., Marion C. of C., Cons. Engrs. Ohio, Profl. Land Surveyors Ohio, Ohio, Marion County (past dir.) hist. socs., Delta Sigma Phi. Lutheran (past trustee). Elk. Home: 307 Forest Lawn Blvd Marion OH 43302 Office: 299 Clover Ave Marion OH 43302

TRABULSI, RAYMOND GEORGE, ins. co. exec.; b. Bklyn., Feb. 2, 1937; s. Baseem S. and Valentine (Orfali) T.; B.Mech. Engring., CCNY, 1962; m. Leila Hattab, Jan. 21, 1967; children—Thomas, David. Field engr. Factory Mut., N.Y.C., 1957-65; with Allendale Mut. Ins. Co., 1965—, regional mgr., v.p., Beachwood, Ohio, 1977—. Past trustee St. Nicholas Cathedral, Bklyn., St. George Antiochian Ch., Pitts.; trustee St. George Orthodox Ch., Cleve. Mem. Soc. Fire Protection Engrs., Order St. George (v.p.). Office: 25550 Chagrin Blvd Beachwood OH 44122

TRACHT, VERNON SLOAN, clin. psychologist; b. Chgo., Oct. 26, 1911; s. Frederick Homer and Nora Elaine (Sloan) T.; B.S., U. Chgo., 1943, M.A., 1946; Ph.D., Loyola U., Chgo., 1958. Sr. psychologist dispensary Mercy Hosp., Chgo., 1949-56; psychol. cons. United Cerebral Palsy Greater Chgo., 1955-62; staff clin. psychologist and neuropsychologist Goodwill Industries Rehab. Center, Chgo., 1974—; mem. mobility-limited adv. com. Chgo. Area Transp. Study, 1980—; adv. com. services for handicapped Chgo. Transit Authority; lectr., cons. in field. Recipient various service citations. Mem. Am. Psychol. Assn. (life), Ill. Psychol. Assn. (life), Advocates for Handicapped, Found. Sci. and Handicapped, Nat. Shut-In Soc. (Ill. div.), Ill. Council Congress of Orgns. Physically Handicapped (dir.). Mem. United Ch. Hyde Park. Author articles, reports in field. Office: 120 S Ashland Blvd Chicago IL 60607

TRACY, EUGENE ARTHUR, utility exec.; b. Oak Park, Ill., Dec. 14, 1927; s. Arthur Huntington and Emily Margaret (Groff) T.; B.S. in Bus. Adminstrn., Northwestern U., 1951; M.B.A., DePaul U., Chgo., 1958; m. Irene Walburga Kacin, June 30, 1951; children—Glen Eugene, Diane Emily Tracy Champion, Janet Freda. With Peoples Gas Light & Coke Co., Chgo., 1951-69, 77—, pres., 1977—, chmn., 1981—; with Peoples Gas Co., Chgo., 1969-77, v.p., 1973-77, controller, 1974-77, pres., dir. N. Shore Gas Co., Waukegan, Ill., 1977—, chmn., 1981—; pres., chief exec. officer, chmn. bd., dir. People's Energy Corp., 1981—; dir. First Fed. Savs. & Loan Assn. Chgo. Bd. dirs. Central YMCA Community Coll., Chgo., 1971—, treas., 1972-77, chmn. bd., 1977-79, vice chmn. bd., 1981—; treas. St. David's Episcopal Ch., Glenview, Ill., 1970—; bd. dirs. Civic Fedn. Chgo., 1976-77, Jr. Achievement, Chgo., 1978—; trustee Taxpayers Fedn. Ill., 1973-77, Inst. Gas Tech., Chgo., 1978—, Mus. Sci. and Industry, Chgo., 1981—. Served with U.S. Army, 1946-47. Mem. Am., Midwest gas assns., Chgo. Assn. Commerce and Industry (dir. 1979—, dir. Central Area com. 1981—). Clubs: Economic, University, Chicago (Chgo.); Sunset Ridge Country (Northbrook, Ill.). Office: 122 S Michigan Ave Chicago IL 60603

TRACY, MARY ELIZABETH, librarian; b. Joliet, Ill., Aug. 18, 1922; d. Charles Joseph and Catherine (Fay) Tracy; B.A. cum laude, Coll. St. Francis, 1944; M.A., Rosary Coll., 1958. Tchr., librarian Joliet pub. schs., 1944-52, 54-61, Am. schs., Bremerhaven and Frankfurt, Germany, 1952-54; librarian Central Campus Joliet Twp. High Sch., 1961—; chmn. Joliet Local Archives Com., 1981-82. Sec., v.p., and mem. adv. bd. Alumnae of the Coll. of St. Francis. Mem. Am., Ill. Library Assns., Ill. Assn. for Media in Edn., Ill. Audio-Visual Assn., Will County Library/Media Assn. (pres. 1976), Joliet Jr. Cath. Woman's League (pres. 1950-51). Home: 1010 Glenwood Ave Joliet IL 60435 Office: 201 E Jefferson St Joliet IL 60432

TRAEGER, BARBARA SHIELDS (MRS. JOHN E. TRAEGER), pub. relations exec.; b. Pitts., Oct. 19, 1932; d. Marshall Charles and Margaret Helen (Ward) Shields; B.A. in English, Ripon Coll., 1954; postgrad. U. Chgo., 1971; m. John E. Traeger, Apr. 30, 1971; children by previous marriage—Cynthia, Charles R., Henry. Dir. pub. relations Chgo. unit Am. Cancer Soc., 1964-65; asst. bur. pub. info. Am. Hosp. Assn., Chgo., 1966-68; dir. pub. relations U. Chgo. Hosps. and Clinics, 1968-72; dir. pub. relations Evanston (Ill.) Hosp. Corp., 1972—. Recipient excellence award, Am. Inst. Graphic Arts, 1975, 76, recognition of achievement Nat. Publs. Assn., 1975, MacEachern award, 1972, 73, 74, 75, 79, 80 award Type Dirs. Club, 1970, excellence award Modern Publicity, 1972; Outstanding Editorial Achievement award Chgo. Assn. Bus. Communicators, 1978, 79; Best Internal Publ. award Suburban Press Club, 1979, 80, others. Mem. Assn. Am. Med. Colls., Am. Soc. Hosp. Pub. Relations Dirs. (chmn. mktg. com., mem. accreditation com., chmn. budget com. 1981-82), Acad. Hosp. Pub. Relations (seminar chmn. 1974, dir. 1976, pres. 1978-79, dir. 1980-81), Ill. Hosp. Assn. (ann. meeting com. 1977, 78, 79), Press Council of McGaw Med. Center of Northwestern U., Public Relations Soc. (chmn. mktg. com.) Chgo. Hosp. Council. Club: Publicity (Chgo.). Contbr. articles to Hosps. jour., chpt. to book. Home: PO Box A 3197 Chicago IL 60690 Office: 2650 Ridge Ave Evanston IL 60201

TRAEGER, ROBERT CHARLES, communications co. exec.; b. Chgo., Sept. 2, 1923; s. Charles August and Mary Helen (Murray) T.; student St. Ambrose Coll., 1946-48; m. Elizabeth Jane (Sexton) Fengel, May 22, 1976; children by previous marriage—John, Robert, Barbara, Michael, Patrick, Sally. Salesman, Pillsbury Mills, Chgo., 1948-52, United Film Service, Kansas City, Mo., 1952-57; salesman, local-regional sales mgr. Kans. State Network, Wichita, 1957-79; co-owner, pres. Traeger Advt. & Mktg. Services, Inc., Wichita, 1979-81; gen. sales mgr. Cablevision div. Multimedia, Inc., Wichita, 1981—. Served with AUS, 1942-46. Mem. Wichita Ind. Businessmen's Assn. Roman Catholic. Club: Advt. of Wichita (awards of merit). Office: Multimedia Cablevision Inc 604 N Main St PO Box 3027 Wichita KS 67201

TRAFTON, CHARLES LELAND, sports scientist, educator; b. San Francisco, Feb. 5, 1945; s. William Gilbert and Helen Francis (Sopper) T.; B.S., Oakland City 1967; M.A., U. Evansville, 1974; postgrad. Ind. U., 1973-75; m. Elaine Kennedy, June 3, 1967; children—Shannon Elizabeth, Kelly Rachelle. Tchr., coach English-Sterling Sch. Corp., English, Ind., 1967-69, North Spencer Sch. Corp., Dale, Ind., 1969-71, North Posey Sch. Corp., Poseyville, Ind., 1971-72, Warrick County (Ind.) Sch. Corp., 1973-75; faculty Oakland City (Ind.) Coll., 1975—, asst. prof., head basketball coach, athletic dir., 1979—; nat. tournament dir., sec. Nat. Little Coll. Athletic Assn. Named Coach of Yr., Ky.-Ind. Athletic Conf., 1974. Mem. Nat. Assn Intercollegiate Athletics, NEA, Nat. Little Coll. Athletics Assn. (coach 1980-81 basketball championship team), AAHPER, Nat. Assn. Intercollegiate Athletic Coaches and Athletic Dirs., Ind. Intercollegiate Athletic Assn., Nat. Assn. Collegiate Dirs. of Athletics. Office: Oakland City Coll Oakland City IN 47660

TRAINER, DANIEL OLNEY, univ. adminstr.; b. Chgo., July 13, 1926; s. Daniel Olney and Esther (Frank) T.; B.A., Ripon Coll., 1950; M.S., U. Wis., Madison, 1955, Ph.D., 1960; m. Elizabeth Duggan, June 10, 1955; children—Patricia, Daniel. Researchers, Fromm Labs., 1955-56; pathologist Wis. Dept. Natural Resources, 1956-61; asst. prof. veterinary sci. U. Wis., Madison, 1961-63, asso. prof., 1963-68, prof., 1968-71; dean Coll. Natural Resources U. Wis., Stevens Point, 1971-80, vice chancellor, 1980—. Served with USN, 1944-46. Recipient Disting. Service award Wildlife Disease Assn., 1974. Mem. Wildlife Soc., Am. Inst. Biol. Scis., AAAS, Soc. Am. Foresters, Soil Conservation Soc. (Educator of Yr. 1976), Wildlife Disease Assn., Wildlife Fedn., Wilderness Soc., Audubon Soc., Wis. Acad. Scis., Izaak Walton League (Educator of Yr. 1977), Sigma Xi. Club: Kiwanis. Editor: (with Davis and Karstad) Infectious Diseases of Wild Mammals; Diseases and Parasites of Wild Birds; contbr. 124 articles to profl. jours., popular publs. Office: U Wis Stevens Point WI 54481

TRAINOR, JOHN FELIX, educator; b. Mpls., Dec. 1, 1921; s. James Patrick and Myra Catherine (Pauly) T.; B.A., Coll. St. Thomas, 1943; M.A., U. Minn., 1950; Ph.D., Wash. State U., 1970; m. Margaret Dolores Pudenz, July 3, 1965 (dec. 1977); children—John Anthony, Patrick James. Instr. high sch. Mpls., 1946-47; v.p. Trainor Candy Co., Mpls., 1949-56; instr., asst. prof. econs. Rockhurst Coll., Kansas City, Mo., 1956-62; instr. Wash. State U., Pullman, 1966-67; asst. prof. Moorhead (Minn.) State U., 1967-70, asso. prof. econs., 1971—, chmn. dept. econs., 1981—. Served to lt. (j.g.) USNR, 1943-46; ETO. Mem. Am., Minn. (pres. 1976-77) econ. assns., Assn. Social Econs., AAUP, Minn. Acad. Scis., Interfaculty Assn., NEA, Minn. Edn. Assn., Omicron Delta Epsilon. Democrat. Roman Catholic. Author: (with Frank J. Kottke) The Nursing Home Industry in the State of Washington, 1968. Home: 1333 4th Ave S Moorhead MN 56560 Office: Dept Econs Moorhead State U Moorhead MN 56560

TRANQUILLI, ROLAND ANTHONY, JR., elec. co. exec.; b. Springfield, Ill., May 20, 1941; s. Roland A. and Marian I. (Peters) T.; B.S. in E.E., Wayne State U., 1969; m. Paulette I. Pritula, Mar. 25, 1968; children—Ronald Scott, Tammy Lyn. Engr. printing instrumentation and control Safran Printing Co., Detroit, 1966-70; with Western Electric Co., Naperville, Ill., 1970—, engr. spl. projects devel., 1970-76, sr. engr., 1979-80, project engr. mfg. communication switching systems, 1976-80, mr. engring., 1980—; microprocessor coordinator Western Electric Co., No. Ill. Works, Lisle, 1974-76, vice-chmn. X3T9 standards com. for minicomputers, 1980—. Mktg. and exec. adv. Jr. Achievement, Lisle, 1979-81. Served with USAF, 1960-64. Recipient Spl. Achievement Engring. award Western Electric Co., 1980. Mem. IEEE, Am. Motorcycle Assn., Instrument Soc. Am. Office: Western Electric Co Naperville IL 60566

TRANTER, TERENCE MICHAEL, lawyer; b. Cin., Nov. 26, 1944; s. John Lawrence and Florence Ellen (McGann) T.; A.B., Georgetown U., 1966; J.D., U. Cin., 1969; m. Doris Ann Tepe, June 22, 1968; children—Amy, Terence, Michael, Christopher. Admitted to Ohio bar, 1969, since practiced in Cin.; realtor and ins. solicitor, 1969—; asst. atty. gen. State of Ohio, 1970-71; counsel City of Golf Manor (Ohio), 1971-76; mem. Ohio Gen. Assembly, 1976—. Mem. Cin. Bd. Realtors, Cin. Bar Assn., Cin. Ins. Bd., Ohio Bar Assn., Am. Bar Assn. Democrat. Roman Catholic. Clubs: K.C., Eagles. Home: 7303 Fair Oaks Dr Cincinnati OH 45237 Office: 2540 Kroger Bldg Cincinnati OH 45202

TRAPANI, ANDREW PATRICK, orthodontist; b. Aurora, Mo., Sept. 7, 1944; s. Patrick D. and Helen C. (Chapman) T.; M.S. in Oral Biology, Loyola U., Chgo., 1971; D.D.S., U. Ill., 1969; m. Arleen Carol Widowski, Aug. 27, 1966; children—David Andrew, Amy Colette, Justin Scott. Asso., Drs. Braun and Fleming, Olympia Field, Ill., 1973-74, Dr. Arai, Park Ridge, Ill., 1974-77; pvt. practice orthodontics, Dundee, Ill., 1974—; instr. Dental Coll., U. Ill.; instr., asso. prof. orthodontic dept. Coll. Dentistry Loyola U.; mem. dental staff Sherman Hosp., Elgin, Ill. Chmn. Dundee Days Parade Com., 1974-77; bd. dirs. Dundee Twp. United Way; trustee Elgin Community Coll. Served to capt. Dental Corps, U.S. Army, 1971-73. Recipient certificate of achievement Am. Acad. Oral Medicine. Diplomate Am. Bd. Orthodontics. Mem. ADA, Ill., Fox River Valley (dir.) dental assns., Am., Midwest, Ill. assns. orthodontists, Elgin Dental Soc. (v.p.), Dundee Bus. and Profl. Assn., U. Ill. Alumni Assn., Loyola Alumni Assn., Omicron Kappa Upsilon. Roman Catholic. Clubs: Lions (sec.), St. Catherine's of Sienna Men's, Jaycees (hon.), Sleepy Hollow Service. Home: 59 Oak Hill Dr Dundee IL 60118 Office: 825 Village Quarter Rd Dundee IL 60118

TRASK, OSCAR JOSEPH, agronomist; b. Fort Fairfield, Maine, Sept. 27, 1926; s. Warren William and Katie Maude-Victoria (Wiggins) T.; B.S., U. Maine, 1954, also postgrad.; m. Joyce Martha Dee, July 15, 1950; children—Warren William, Terry Oscar, Dianna Dee, Timothy Lawerence, Oscar Joseph, James Allen. Agr. chemist., sales mgmt. staff, extension agt., agronomist, mgr. agronomy Beacon Feeds, Co. (N.Y.), 1954-63; agt. N.Y. State Extension Service, Millbrook, 1963-65; with Allied Chem. Co., Salt Point, N.Y., 1965-66; agronomist Mass. Farm Bur., Waltham, 1966-68; mgr. Ohio and Va. agronomic services, Royster Co., 1968-80; fertilizer dealer cons., Perrysburg, Ohio, 1980—. Leader, Jr. Achievement; past pres. PTA; com. chmn. Boy Scouts Am. Served with USN, 1944-46; PTO. Mem. Nat. Fertilizer Solutions Assn., Council on Soil Testing and Plant Analysis, Council Agrl. Sci. and Tech., Am. Soc. Agronomy, Soil Sci. Soc. Am., Crop Sci. Soc. Am., North Central Soc. Agronomy, Am. Registry Profls. in Agronomy, Crops and Soils, Alpha Gamma Rho, Alpha Zeta, Phi Kappa Phi. Clubs: Masons, Woodmen. Expert in micronutrients in plant nutrition; pioneer in field devel. fluid lime. Address: 10031 Roachton Rd Perrysburg OH 43551

TRAUTMAN, HENRIETTA (RETTA) CALLERY, mental health adminstr.; b. Pitts., June 20, 1925; d. Edwin King and Henrietta Marie (Hellmann) Callery; ed. Carnegie-Mellon U. (Andrew Mellon scholar), 1944-46, Stanford U., 1946-47; B.A. in Music cum laude, SUNY, Stony Brook, 1970, M.A., 1972; M.S. in Counseling, Health and Rehab., Fla. State U., 1975; m. DeForest Lloyd Trautman, Jr., May 28, 1946; children—Patricia, Edwin, Craig. Music therapist Sagamore Children's Center, Melville, N.Y., 1970-76; asst. dir. clin. services, counselor sch. and day treatment program Med. Coll. Ohio, Toledo, 1976-81, dir., 1981—, asst. prof. dept. psychiatry, 1979—; guest lectr. Adelphi U., Hofstra U. Interviewer for needs survey Services & Facilities for the Disabled & Handicapped, Toledo, 1976; mem. Lucas County (Ohio) Met. Housing Authority Hearing Panel, Toledo, 1976-77; LWV rep. City of Toledo Edn. Coalition Com., 1977-79; trustee Autistic Community of N.W. Ohio, 1979—, treas., 1980—. Recipient commendation for social work activities in ghetto Gov. of Province of Concepcion, Chile, 1969; cert. tchr., N.Y.; cert. clin. mental health counselor. Mem. Am. Assn. Music Therapy (cert. music therapist), Am. Orff-Schulwerk Assn., Am. Personnel and Guidance Assn., Sigma Alpha Iota. Club: Western Square Dancing. Author: (with Vera Moretti) Breaking the Cocoon of Silence, Music and the Autistic Child, 1974. Home: 2625 Middlesex Dr Toledo OH 43606 Office: CS #10008 Toledo OH 43699

TRAVIS, DEMPSEY JEROME, mortgage banker; b. Chgo., Feb. 25, 1920; s. Louis and Mittie (Strickland) T.; B.A., Roosevelt U., 1949; grad. Sch. Mortgage Banking, Northwestern U., 1969; Ph.D. in Econs. (hon.), Olive Harvey Coll.; Ph.D. (hon.), Daniel Hale Williams U.; m. Moselynne Hardwick, Sept. 17, 1949. Pres., Travis Realty Co., 1949—, Travis Ins. Agy., 1951—; pres., owner Sivart Bldg.; pres. Urban Research Inst., Inc.; dir. Sears Bank & Trust Co., Chgo. Pres., Dearborn Real Estate Bd., 1957-59, 70-72; mem. adv. bd. Non-Profit Housing Partnership, Washington; chmn. HUD/PUSH Nat. Housing Task Force, 1975; past mem. adv. bd. Fed. Nat. Mortgage Assn., Washington. Mem. Presdl. Task Force Urban Renewal, 1970—, Mayor's adv. com. Bldg. Code Amendments, 1970—; mem. Mayor's Com. on Rent Control, Ill. Ins. Consumers Adv. Panel, 1970; mem. Presdl. Task Force Inflation, 1974; mem. Fed. Energy Adminstrn.'s Constructive Adv., 1974-75. Life mem. Field Mus. Natural History, Chgo. Art Inst.; mem. adv. com. Urban Am. Bd. dirs. Nat. Housing Conf., Washington, Chgo. Econ. Devel. Corp.; trustee Northwestern Meml. Hosp., Central YMCA Community Coll., 1969—; mem. Mayor's Commn. for Preservation Chgo.'s Hist. Bldgs.; voting mem. Met. Chgo. YMCA. Served with Ordance Corps, AUS, 1942-46. Mem. Mortgage Bankers Assn. Am. (pres.), United Mortgage Bankers Am. (founder 1961, pres. 1961-74), NAACP (pres. Chgo. 1959-60), Nat. Assn. Real Estate Brokers (1st v.p. 1959-60), Am. Soc. Real Estate Counselors, Cosmopolitan C. of C. (dir., vice chmn. ins. com.), Beta Gamma Sigma, Lambda Alpha Internat. Clubs: Executives, Economics, Forty (Chgo.), Cliff Dwellers, Met. Author: Don't Stop Me Now; A 100-Year Odyssey on Black Housing, Chicago, 1900-2000, 1977. Fin. editor Dollars and Sense. Contbr. articles to profl. jours., popular mags. Home: 8001 S Champlain Ave Chicago IL 60619 Office: 840 E 87th St Chicago IL 60619

TRAVIS, JOHN WILLIAM, radiation oncologist; b. Great Falls, Mont., May 12, 1929; s. John Francis Marion and Frances Wilhemina (Wylie) T.; student Colgate U., 1947-49; B.A. with honors, U. Colo., 1951; M.D. with distinction, Northwestern U., 1955, M.S., 1955; m. Mary Ann Faber, June 15, 1954; children—Ann Louise, Peter Faber, John Faber. Intern, Columbia Hosp., Milw., 1955-56; resident, fellow in radiology and nuclear medicine Northwestern U. Med. Center, 1956-59; radiologist asso., Radiology and Nuclear Medicine, P.A., Topeka, 1961—; attending therapeutic radiologist St. Francis, Stormont, Vail and Meml. hosps.; cons. Topeka VA Med. Center; clin. dir. St. Francis Capital Region Radiotherapy Center; clin. asso. prof. U. Kans. Med. Center. Served to lt. comdr. M.C., USNR, 1959-63. Diplomate Am. Bd. Radiology. Fellow A.C.P., Am. Coll. Radiology; mem. AMA, Am. Soc. Therapeutic Radiology (pres. 1980, dir. 1981), Am. Soc. Clin. Oncology, Radiol. Soc. N. Am., Kans. Med. Soc. (pres. 1975), World Med. Assn., Pan Am. Med. Assn., Am. Cancer Soc. (pres. Kans. div. 1969-71), Phi Beta Kappa, Sigma Xi, Alpha Omega Alpha. Republican. Lutheran. Clubs: Shawnee Country, Masons, Shriners. Editor: Practice of Radiology in a Changing Environment, 1974; contbr. articles and revs. to sci. jours. Home: 15 Pepper Tree Ln Topeka KS 66611 Office: 1700 W 7th St Topeka KS 66606

TRAXEL, WILLIAM LOUIS, ophthalmologist; b. Maysville, Ky., Mar. 17, 1939; s. William Louis and Clara Ellen (Brashears) T.; B.A., Northwestern U., 1961; M.D., Vanderbilt U., 1965; postgrad. U. Mich., 1970-72; m. Mary Ann Walker, July 9, 1966; children—Richard Louis, Benjamin Frederick. Intern, Vanderbilt U., Nashville, 1965-66, resident in internal medicine, 1966-67; resident in ophthalmology U. Mich., 1970-72; practice medicine specializing in ophthalmology, Poplar Bluff, Mo., 1973—; mem. staff Doctor's Hosp., Kneibert Clinic. Served to lt. comdr. USN, 1967-69; flight surgeon. Mem. Am. Acad. Ophthalmology, Am., Mo. assns. ophthalmology. Methodist. Contbr. articles to profl. jours. Home: 47 Tomard Trail Poplar Bluff MO 63901 Office: 666 Lester St Poplar Bluff MO 63901

TRAXLER, BOB, congressman; b. Kawkawlin, Mich., July 21, 1931; B.A. in Polit. Sci., Mich. State U., 1953; LL.B., Detroit Coll. Law, 1959; children—Tamara, Brad, Sarah. Admitted to Mich. bar; prosecutor Bay County, Mich., 1960-62; mem. 93d-97th Congresses from 8th Mich. Dist., mem. appropriations com.; mem. Mich. Ho. of Reps., 1962-73. Mem. Am., Mich. bar assns., Bay County Mental Health Soc. Episcopalian. Office: 2448 Rayburn House Office Bldg Washington DC 20515

TRAXLER, EUGENE RICE, mech. engr.; b. Akron, Ohio, Sept. 6, 1912; s. Claude King and Treasure Irene (Hotchkiss) T.; A.B., Kent State U., 1933; B.S. in Mech. Engring., Ohio State U., 1936, M.S. in Engring., 1946; m. Alice Louise Grove, July 14, 1945. With B.F. Goodrich Co., Akron, Ohio, 1935-75, head field engring. group for conveyor belting, 1950-75; cons. Brad. Assos. Inc., Akron, 1978; cons. on belt conveyor design and service problems, Akron, 1978—. Registered profl. engr., Ohio. Mem. ASME, Am. Inst. Mining Engrs. Republican. Mem. Christian Ch. (Disciples of Christ). Clubs: Wampum Investment. Holder 5 patents; contbr. articles to profl. jours. Home and office: 3066 Kent Rd Apt 205-B Stow OH 44224

TRAXLER, JAMES THEODORE, research scientist; b. LeCenter, Minn., Oct. 17, 1929; s. Theodore B. and Mary E. (Butler) T.; B.A., St. John's U., Collegeville, Minn., 1951; Ph.D., U. Notre Dame, 1956; m. Gabrielle Irene Martens, Apr. 7, 1956; children—Lisanne M., Peter R., Martine S., Karen L., Madeleine R. Research chemist, project leader Armour & Co., Chgo., 1955-60; research chemist Am. Cyanamid Co., Stamford, Conn., 1960-62; sect. head organic chemistry Durkee Foods Group (Glidden), Chgo., 1962-66; sr. research chemist Peter Hand Found., Waukegan, Ill., 1966-69; organic research specialist Internat. Minerals & Chems. Corp., Libertyville, Ill., 1969-74; research scientist Velsicol Chem. Corp.,

Chgo., 1974—; lectr. Pres. Dewey Community Conf., 1970-71, bd. dirs., 1966-69. Recipient Outstanding Sr. award Alpha Phi Omega, 1951; Outstanding Sr. award Kiwanis, 1951. Mem. Am. Chem. Soc., AAAS, Sigma Xi. Roman Catholic. Contbr. articles to profl. jours. Patentee in field. Home: 1630 Ashland Ave Evanston IL 60201 Office: 341 E Ohio St Chicago IL 60611

TRAYNOR, MACK VINCENT, JR., internist; b. Devils Lake, N.D., May 31, 1925; s. Mack Vincent and Betty (Dostert) T.; B.A., U. N.D., 1946, B.S., 1947; B.M., Northwestern U., 1949, M.D., 1950; M.S., U. Minn., 1960; m. Rita C. Roach, June 22, 1957; children—Mack Vincent III, Cathy, James, Peggy, Pat. Intern, St. Joseph's Hosp., Chgo., 1949-50; resident in medicine St. Joseph's Hosp., 1952-53, Mayo Clinic, Rochester, Minn., 1953-57; chief of staff St. Luke's Hosp., Fargo, N.D., 1969-72, chief of medicine, 1972—; prof. medicine U. N.D.; adj. prof. medicine N.D. State U. Served to comdr. M.C., USNR, World War II and Korea. Diplomate Am. Bd. Internal Medicine; cert. Am. Bd. Life Ins. Medicine. Fellow ACP; mem. N.D. Med. Assn., 1st Dist. Med. Soc., AMA (N.D. alt. del. to ho. of dels.), Am. Rheumatism Assn. Roman Catholic. Clubs: Elks, K.C., Fargo Country. Home: 1310 9th St S Fargo ND 58102 Office: Box 2067 Fargo ND 58102

TREADWAY, WILLIAM EUGENE, lawyer, educator; b. Bloomington, Ind., Dec. 20, 1901; s. Eugene Theodore and Minnie May (Byerly) T.; A.B., Ind. U., 1924; J.D., George Washington U., 1927; S.J.D., U. Mich., 1933; m. Joyce Winona Asher, July 20, 1927; 1 son, David Armand. Admitted to Ind. bar, 1927, Kans. bar, 1942; gen. law practice Spencer and Indpls., Ind., 1927-41; pros. atty., Owen County, Ind., 1927-29; gen. atty. A.T. & S.F. Ry., Topeka, Kans., 1945-71; lectr. Washburn U. Law Sch., 1946-71, prof., 1971—. Sec. Ind. Commn. on Interstate Cooperation, 1938-41. Pres. bd. trustees Topeka Pub. Library, 1962-70. Judge advocate gen. Kans. Nat. Guard, 1947-62. Mem. Indiana Ho. of Reps., 1934-38. Served from capt. to lt. col. AUS, 1941-45. Mem. Am., Kans., Topeka bar assns., Am. Legion, Nat. Guard Officers Assn., S.A.R. (pres. Topeka chpt. 1958-59). Am. Judicature Soc., Samuel Johnson Soc. Kans. (pres. 1969-70), Kan. Hist. Soc. (pres. 1972-73), Phi Delta Phi, Phi Kappa Phi. Conglist. Mason. Rotarian. Author chpts in books, articles in field. Editor: Kansas Bar Jour., 1947-63. Home: 3500 Avalon Ln Topeka KS 66604 Office: Washburn U Law School Topeka KS 66621

TREADWELL, EDWARD THOMAS, JR., govt. ofcl.; b. Chgo., Mar. 19, 1947; s. Edward Thomas and Maxine Helen (Lippert) T.; B.A., Luther Coll., 1969, postgrad. 1976-77; m. Donna Lynn Bedsworth, June 20, 1970. Instr., Wilmington (Ohio) Coll., 1970-71; asso. dean William Jewell Coll., Liberty, Mo., 1972-76; mgmt. cons., Midwest, 1975—; dir. adminstrn. Mid-Am. Regional Council, Kansas City, Mo., 1976—. Mem. Am. Compensation Assn., Am. Soc. Public Adminstrs., Internat. City Mgrs. Assn. Presbyterian. Home: 908 Jackson Dr Liberty MO 64068 Office: 20 W 9th St Kansas City MO 64105

TREANOR, RICHARD CLIFFORD, physician; b. Chgo., June 14, 1926; s. Bernard and Margaret (Clifford) T.; student Wright Jr. Coll., 1943-44, 46-47; M.D., U. Ill., 1952; m. Helen June Hudon, Aug. 8, 1953; children—Kathi, Terri, Peggy, Paul, Michael, John, Sharon, Thomas. Intern, Cook County Hosp., Chgo., 1952-53; resident in internal medicine Hines (Ill.) Hosp., 1953-56; practice internal medicine, Arlington Heights, Ill., 1956—; asso. med. dir. Universal Oil Products, Des Plaines, Ill., 1956-66, med. dir., 1966—; charter mem. Northwest Community Hosp., 1958—. Mem. Bd. Health Arlington Heights, 1960-67; health dir. Village of Kildeer, 1964—; pres. N.W. Suburban Microfilming Co., 1970—; founder AMICARD physician med. microfilm info. service, 1972—. Served with USAAF, 1944-46. Mem. Chgo. Assn. Commerce and Industry, AMA, Chgo., Ill. med. assns., Chgo. Heart Assn., Indsl. Med. Assn., AMA. Roman Catholic. Club: K.C. (4 deg.). Home: 21539 Boschome Dr W Kildeer IL 60047 Office: 1430 N Arlington Heights Rd Arlington Heights IL 60004

TREBILCOCK, WILLIAM EVERETT, soft drink bottling co. exec.; b. Calumet, Mich., Aug. 13, 1945; s. Everett Robert and Mary Jane (Baccus) T.; B.A., Mich. State U., 1967; M.B.A., Western Mich. U., 1968; m. Ann H. Hoekenga, June 22, 1968; children—Heather, Dereck, Damen. Sales mgr. Coca Cola Bottling of Calif., San Francisco, 1969-71; ops. analyt Wis. Coca Cola Co., Milw., 1971-73; gen. mgr. Coca Cola Pacific, Portland, 1973-78; v.p. sales Coca Cola Bottling Co. of Mich.-Ohio, Lansing, Mich., 1979—. Mem. Mich. Soft Drink Assn. Republican. Conglist. Club: Rotary. Home: 2680 Shadowbrook St Grand Rapids MI 49506 Office: 3300 S Creyts Rd Lansing MI 48917

TREGER, HARVEY, social worker, educator; b. Chgo., July 5, 1924; s. Sam and Lillian (Ertrachter) T.; B.S., Roosevelt U., 1948; M.A., Sch. Social Service Adminstrn. U. Chgo., 1956; certificate Summer Sch. Alcohol Studies Yale U., 1957; certificate child care program Chgo. Inst. Psychoanalysis, 1963; m. Shirley Gladys Feldman, Oct. 24, 1954. Fed. probation officer U.S. Dist. Ct., No. Ill., 1957-65; prof. social work and criminal justice U. Ill., Chgo., 1965—; originator, project dir. police-social work teams, Maywood, Ill., 1974-77, Niles, Ill., 1971-73, Wheaton, Ill., 1970-73; chmn. state and nat. police social work confs.; cons. to minister of justice Lower Saxony, Fed. Republic Germany, 1979. Bd. dirs. Methodist Youth Services, 1979—; vice chmn. profl. adv. council Safer Found., 1977—. Recipient John Howard award, 1973; Key to City, Kansas City, Mo., 1976; Ill. Law Enforcement Commn. grantee, 1970-73, 74-77. Fellow Am. Orthopsychiat. Assn.; mem. Ill. Acad. Criminology (pres. 1969-70, Morris J. Wexler award 1974), Nat. Assn. Social Workers (Social Worker of Yr., Chgo. Area, 1977). Author: The Police Social Work Team, 1975; film project dir.: The Police Social Work Team, 1977 (Helen Cody Baker award). Contbr. articles to profl. jours., ency. Home: 1501 Maple Ave Apt 804 Evanston IL 60201 Office: 4246 ECB Box 4348 Chicago IL 60680

TREICK, EDWARD FREDERICK, mfg. co. mgr.; b. Manitowoc, Wis., Nov. 18, 1939; s. Edward William and Erna Alma (Rodewald) T.; B.S. cum laude, Lawrence U., 1961; M.B.A., U. Wis., 1974; m. Barbara Anne Vogel, May 3, 1969; children—Mark, Kimberly. Actuary, Social Security Adminstrn., Balt., 1961-63; actuarial trainee Northwestern Mut. Life Ins. Co., Milw., 1963-66; sales mgr. Advanced Dakota Products, New Town, N.D., 1966-67; systems analyst W.H. Brady Co., Milw., 1967-69, customer service mgr., 1969, product research supr., 1970-72, mktg. mgr., 1972-74, gen. mgr. computer and drafting products div., 1974-77, gen. mgr. nameplate div., 1977—; undergrad. career cons. Lawrence U., Appleton, Wis., 1981-82. Active, Republican Party, 1964—, mem. Waukesha County Reagan for Pres. com., 1976, 80; mem. fin. com. Ceci for Wis. Supreme Ct., 1979-80; treas. Brookfield Christian Reformed Ch., 1977-78. Named Outstanding Campaigner, N.D. Young Reps., 1967; Outstanding Young Rep., Wis. 9th Congressional Dist. Young Reps., 1969. Mem. Nat. Assn. Nameplate Mfrs., Screen Printing Assn., Beta Gamma Sigma, Phi Kappa Phi. Home: N77 W22266 Wooded Hills Dr Sussex WI 53089 Office: 750 W Glendale Ave Milwaukee WI 53201

TREIMAN, EDWARD M., elec. engr.; b. Toledo, Iowa, July 29, 1910; s. Samuel E. and Dorothy (Walker) T.; B.S. in E.E., Iowa State Coll., 1933, E.E., 1943; m. Selma White, June 24, 1942; children—Paul, Rosalind, Ann. With Western Electric Co., Chgo. and New York, engring., research and transcontinental line experimentations, 1933-37; asst. purchasing agt. Allied Machinery Corp., Feb.-Sept. 1937; with Internat. Western Electric Co., 1938-39; mng. dir. Nat. Electric Light Assn., 1946-52; cons. engr., Chgo., 1952—. Sec. St. Lawrence Commn. of U.S., 1944-46, Second Nat. Radio Conf., 1945. Commd. 1st lt., Signal Corps, U.S. Army, 1937, later capt.; served in U.S. and France. Mem. Am. Inst. Elec. Engrs., Edison Electric Inst., NAM, Tau Beta Pi, Delta Upsilon. Republican. Clubs: Union League, Univ., Recess (N.Y.C.); Univ. (Chgo.). Address: 2918 W Fargo St Chicago IL 60645

TREMBATH, RICHARD DOUGLAS, village ofcl.; b. Oak Park, Ill., July 6, 1943; s. Robert Stevens and Glen Evelyn (Walkley) T.; B.MusicEdn., U. Mich., 1966; postgrad. Mich. State U., 1967-68; m. Elizabeth E. Pierson, Apr. 30, 1966; children—Jeffrey Alan, Jennifer Marie. Band dir. Eau Claire (Mich.) public schs., 1966-68, Tahquamenon area schs., Newberry, Mich., 1968-70; operator wastewater treatment plant Village of Newberry, Mich., 1972-76; supt. wastewater plant and water dept. Village of Lake Odessa, Mich., 1976—, village mgr., 1978. Pres. council on ministries Central United Meth. Ch., Lake Odessa; chmn. supervisory audit com. Govtl. Employees Credit Union Ionia; mem. Western Mich. Regional Planning Commn. Lic. wastewater operator, Mich. Mem. Water Pollution Control Fedn., Am. Water Works Assn., S. Central Mich. Water Assn., LakeLakeshore Operators Assn., W. Mich. Water Works Assn. Methodist. Club: Lions (bd. dirs.). Home: 1033 Washington Blvd Lake Odessa MI 48849 Office: Route 3 Box 190 Lake Odessa MI 48849

TREMBLE, STELLA CRAFT, author, editor, poet; b. Frenchburg, Ky.; d. Levi and Mary (Sexton) Craft; student State Tchrs. Coll., Charleston, 1922, Ypsilanti Tchrs. Coll., 1928; D.Litt., Free U. Asia, 1968; D.Hum., Acad. of Culture, Hull, Eng., 1968; D. Liberal Arts, World U. (Hong Kong); m. Walter Shirley Tremble, Nov. 26, 1925. Tchr. elementary schs., Ashmore, 1922-23, Joliet, 1923-25, Charleston, 1926-34, Royal Oak, Mich., Mattoon, Ill., 1947-50. Author: The Silver Chain, 1953; Thorns and Thistledown, 1954; Wind in the Reed, 1957; Crystal Prism, 1958; Loom and Lyre, 1961; The Prairie Poet Anthology, Vol. II, 1961; Telescope of Time, 1962; Happy Holidays, Vols. I-II, 1963, Vol. II, 1974 (2d place Nat. Fedn. Press Women 1964), Vol. II, 1974; Songs of the Prairie, 1964, 2d edit., 1965; In His Day, 1966; Goodbye, Little Country School, 1966; Bells of Autumn, 1967; From Isles of Silence, 1968 (Mate Palmer award 1969); Center and Circumference, 1968; Paths to Parnassus, 1969; Unmeasured Moments, 1972; Clod and Cloud, 1974; Veering Weathervane, 1975; Peddler's Pack, 1977, Green Branch in the Heart, 1980, Hidden Manna, 1981, From Cats to Kings, 1981, Mother Goose in Politics, 1982, Waste Basket Treasures, 1982, also textbooks; editor, compiler, pub. 35 anthologies; profl. activities include poetry analyst, sec.-treas. Am. Poetry League, 1958-64, pres., 1964—; nat. exec. adviser Am. Poets Fellowship Soc., 1964—, life pres., 1965—. Mem. bd. Nat. Poets Shrine, Hollywood, World Poetry Days Activities; regional dir. Internat. Scambi, Rome. Recipient Book of Year award Am. Poets Fellowship Soc., 1958, gold cup, 1965; 1st prize Nat. Fedn. Press Women (for The Crystal Prism), 1960, George Washington medal Freedoms Found., 1963, Distinguished Alumni award Eastern Ill. U., 1974, numerous other awards. Mem. Ill. Women's Press Assn. (3d v.p. 1967), Ill. State Pen Women (chmn. letters 1967—), Nat. League Am. Penwomen (pres. br.) D.A.R. (chpt. regent, chpt. chaplain, vice chmn. youth work Ill. 1966—), Ill. Poetry Soc. (founding pres. 1973-76), United Poets Soc. Am. (v.p.), Ill. State Poetry Soc. (founding pres. 1971-74), Cosmosynthesis Poetry League Australia (life), Am. Poets, Poets Laureate Internat. Pub., editor: The Am. Poet (2d Mate Palmer award 1964), 1966, 67; founder, editor Prairie Poet, United Poets (mags.); editor Prairie Poet Anthology, 1961, 65, 67; From Sea to Sea in Song (Am. Poetry League anthology), 1965, 66, 67. Home: 902 10th St Charleston IL 61920

TREMEWAN, PAUL GEORGE, educator; b. Flint, Mich., Sept. 9, 1941; s. Edwin and Joyce Tonie (Honig) T.; B.A., U. Mich., 1963; M.A., Eastern Mich. U., 1974; m. Glenda Jean Crawford, June 29, 1963; children—Robert-Paul Crawford, Tracie-Elizabeth. Lectr., Robert T. Longway Planetarium, Flint, 1961-63; tchr. Flint community schs., 1964-76, staff asso. secondary reading and humanities, 1976—; dir. Opportunities for Learning, Flint, 1981—. Mem. Internat. Reading Assn., Assn. Supervision and Curriculum Devel., Nat. Council Social Studies, Urban League Flint, Phi Delta Kappa. Episcopalian. Home: 601 Maxine St Flint MI 48503 Office: 925 S Avon St Flint MI 48503

TRENNT, EVELYN LADENE, educator; b. Miller, Nebr.; d. William Carl and Alura (Chartraw) Trennt; B.A., U. Omaha, 1942; M.A., U. Ill., 1946. Tchr. math. Gaza (Iowa) High Sch., 1942-43, Walnut (Iowa) High Sch., 1943-45; instr. math. Springfield (Ill.) Jr. Coll., 1946-53; tchr. math. Milw.-Downer Sem., 1953-55; asso. prof. math. Monticello Coll., Godfrey, Ill., 1955-71; prof. math. Lewis and Clark Community Coll., Godfrey, 1971—, coordinator of math., 1976. Judge math. div. ann. State Sci. Exposition of Ill. Jr. Acad. Sci., 1958—. Mem. Nat., Ill. (mem. bd. 1960-61) councils tchrs. math., Math. Assn. Am., Ill. Math. Assn. for Community Coll. Tchrs., AAUP, Alton Bus. and Profl. Women's Club, Sigma Pi Phi, Pi Mu Epsilon. Home: 1012 Richard Dr Godfrey IL 62035

TRENT, DONALD MUDRA, scientist; b. Oskaloosa, Ia., June 15, 1922; s. Thomas Wesley and Ruby Leona (Mudra) T.; student Central Coll., 1946-47, Ia. State U., 1948-49; m. Mary Lou Dixon, Aug. 30, 1946; children—Carol Suzanne, Timothy William. Jr. technician Maytag Co., Newton, Ia., 1949-50, sr. technician, 1950-51, process engr., 1951-56, supr. lab., 1956-65, sr. chemist, 1965—. Served with AUS, 1941-46. Decorated Bronze Star medal, Purple Heart medal. Fellow Am. Inst. Chemists; sr. mem. Soc. Plastic Engrs.; mem. North Am. Thermal Analysis Soc., Am. Soc. Metals, Nat. Mgmt. Assn., ASTM. Republican. Congregationalist. Club: Maytag Mgmt. Home: Box 153 Route 1 Newton IA 50208 Office: Maytag Co Newton IA 50208

TRENT, NELLIE JANE, psychologist; b. St. Louis, July 5, 1921; d. Richard Wesley and Helen Elizabeth (Kuhn) Mellow; A.B., Wellesley Coll., 1943; M.A., Washington U., St. Louis, 1944; m. John Brabson Trent, Apr. 9, 1946; children—Elizabeth Mellow (Mrs. Peter D.W. Heberling), John Brabson. Tchr., Mary Inst., St. Louis, 1944-46; grad. asst. psychology Washington U., 1963-65; psychologist Kirkwood (Mo.) Sch. Dist., 1965-75; psychologist, chmn. spl. services Ladue Jr. High Sch., St. Louis, 1975—; lectr. psychology Meramec Community Coll., St. Louis, 1969-70; lectr. spl. edn. St. Louis U., 1970. Founder, pres. Greater St. Louis Women's Assn. of Freedoms Found. at Valley Forge, 1968; residential chmn. St. Louis and St. Louis County United Fund, 1968; v.p. Wellesley Coll. Class of '43, 1973-78. Founder, pres. bd. Ladue Chapel Nursery Sch., 1957-59; mem., sec. long range planning com. Ladue Chapel, 1976-79; bd. dirs. Campbell House, Girls Home, Multiple Sclerosis Soc. St. Louis. Recipient Wellesley Coll. award of year, 1968; Liberty Bowl, Freedoms Found., 1968. Lic. psychologist, Mo. Mem. Am. Psychol. Assn., Mo. Psychol. Assn., Nat. Assn. Sch. Psychologists (charter), Mo. Assn. Sch. Psychologists (charter), Soc. St. Louis Psychologists, Assn. Children with Learning Disabilities, Council Exceptional Children, Am. Personnel and Guidance Assn., St. Louis Jr. League (dir. 1950-53), Mo. Hist. Soc. (pres. women's assn. 1963-64, trustee soc. 1968-71), Kirkwood Community Tchrs. Assn. (dir. 1970-75), Mo. State Tchr. Assn., Ladue Community Tchr. Assn., Nat. Soc. Colonial Dames in Mo. (dir. 1967-69). Presbyn. (deaconess). Clubs: Wellesley Coll. of St. Louis (pres. 1960), St. Louis, Racquet (St. Louis). Contbr. articles to publs. Home: 70 Fair Oaks Saint Louis MO 63124 Office: Ladue Jr High Sch 9701 Conway Rd Saint Louis MO 63124

TRENTA, LOUIS STEPHEN, JR., ednl. adminstr.; b. Barberton, Ohio, Aug. 2, 1939; s. Louis Stephen and Frances Margaret (Arko) T.; A.B., Borromeo Sem., Wickliffe, Ohio, 1962; postgrad. John Carroll U., 1962-63; M.A., Kent (Ohio) State U., 1969, postgrad., 1975-81; m. Mary Joan McCool, Aug. 8, 1964; children—Louis Stephen III, Mary Catherine, Christopher. Tchr., Holy Trinity Sch., Barberton, Ohio, 1962-64; tchr. history and religion St. Vincent High Sch., Akron, Ohio, 1964-66; tchr. history Akron Public Schs., 1966-76, tchr. Latin, 1966-68, unit prin. Central-Hower High, 1976—. Mem. Akron Secondary Prins. Assn., Akron Prins. Assn., Ohio Assn. Secondary Sch. Adminstrs., Nat. Assn. Secondary Sch. Prins., NE Ohio Assn. Supervision and Curriculum Devel., Ohio Assn. Supervision and Curriculum Devel., Assn. Supervision and Curriculum Devel., Akron Prins. Assn. (pres. 1980-81). Home: 4446 Leewood Circle Stow OH 44224 Office: 123 S Forge St Akron OH 44308

TRESCOTT, MARTHA FRANCES MOORE, historian, minister; b. Dallas, Nov. 1, 1941; d. Murray Winn and Frances Marie (McConnell) Moore; student U. Ark., 1960-61; B.S., So. Meth. U., 1964, postgrad., 1964-66, M.A., 1972, doctoral candidate, 1979; postgrad. Perkins Sch. Theology, 1966; m. Paul B. Trescott, Dec. 18, 1971; stepchildren—Jeffrey A., Jill V., Andrew B.; m. James Warren Danley, Jr., Aug. 4, 1981. Chemist, Southwestern Med. Sch., U. Tex., Dallas, 1964-67; tchr. sci. and math. Ursuline Acad., Dallas, 1966; mem. ch. staff Lovers Lane Meth. Ch., Dallas, 1966; literature chemist, searcher Lone Star Gas Co. research and devel. library, Dallas, 1968; lit. researcher, info. scientist, indsl. info. services Sci. and Engring. Library, Southern Meth. U., Dallas, 1968-75; founder, owner Research in Literature of Industry, Dallas, 1973-77; lic. for ministry, Disciples of Christ, 1976, 77; asst. campus minister Ill. Disciples Found., Urbana, 1976-77; research asso. Coll. Engring., U. Ill., Champaign-Urbana, 1978—; program liaison Ill. Humanities Council, 1979. NSF grantee, 1972-74; Rockefeller Found. grantee, 1979-80; Rovensky fellow, 1976-77; recipient Newberry Library award, 1979. Mem. NOW, Soc. History of Tech., Women in Technol. History (founder, sec.), Econ. History Assn., Am. Soc. Engring. Edn., Bus. History Conf., Am. Hist. Assn., Am. Chem. Soc. (history of chemistry div.), Soc. Women Engrs., Women in Bus. and Econ. History (founder, editor, sec.), Nat. Trust for Historic Preservation, Chi Omega, Phi Alpha Theta, Alpha Lambda Delta. Home: 305 S McCullough St Urbana IL 61801 Office: U Ill Urbana IL 61801

TREUER, INGEBORG CONSTANCE, hosp. adminstrv. ofcl.; b. Freiburg, Germany, Dec. 9, 1921; came to U.S., 1949, naturalized, 1954; d. Erich and Mimi (Hagner) T.; ed. German schs. Bookkeeper, St. Louis Shade & Hardware Co., 1950-53, Johannes-Tate Pharmacy, St. Louis, 1953-54; bus. mgr. Shriners Hosp. for Crippled Children, St. Louis, 1954—. Mem. Am. Bus. Women's Assn. (treas. Aditi chpt. 1978, pres. chpt. 1979-80), Hosp. Personnel Dirs. Assn. Greater St. Louis (sec. 1976). Office: 2001 S Lindbergh Blvd Saint Louis MO 63131

TREUTER, CHARLES RICHARD, retail co. exec.; b. Houston, May 19, 1942; s. Richard Oscar and Nellie (Vernon) T.; A.A., Schreiner Inst., 1962; B.S., U. Houston, 1963; m. Lillie Gay, Feb. 16, 1968; children—Shannon Marie, Robert Wayne, Charles Robert. With K-Mart Corp., various locations, 1963—, mgr. Louisville, 1972-73, dist. mgr., Detroit, 1973-77, gen. mgr., Inc., 1977—. Mem. Retail Mchts. Assn., Phi Theta Kappa. Republican. Lutheran. Club: Kiwanis. Home: Rt 7 Box 180-A Evansville IN 47712 Office: 2800 N St Joseph St Evansville IN 47712

TREVATHAN, THOMAS REA, mathematician; b. Jonesboro, Ark., Feb. 25, 1941; s. Denver Lee and Ola June (Rea) T.;B.S.E., Ark. State U. 1962; M.S., Okla. State U., 1963; m. Sandra Mae Wood, Mar. 26, 1960; children—Katherine Michelle, Michael Scott. Instr., Ark. State U., Jonesboro, 1963-66; NASA trainee, teaching asst. U. Okla., Norman, 1966-69; asst. prof. math. Morningside Coll., Sioux City, Iowa, 1969-75, asso. prof., 1975—, chmn. dept. math. and computer sci., 1975-78, dir. devel., 1979-80, v.p. devel., 1981—; vis. lectr. Ark. Acad. Sci. Bd. dirs. Sioux City Art Center, Woodbury County affiliate Am. Heart Assn. Mem. Nat. Council Tchrs. Math., Math. Assn. Am., AAAS, Iowa Council Tchrs. Math., Council on Advancement and Support of Edn., Sioux City C. of C. (bd. dirs.), Iowa Acad. Sci. Democrat. Presbyterian. Clubs: Masons. Home: 2503 S Newton Sioux City IA 51106 Office: 1501 Morningside Ave Sioux City IA 51106

TREXLER, LANCE EMERSON, clin. neuropsychologist; b. Peru, Ind., Sept. 3, 1953; s. Raymond W. and Frances (Hurst) T.; B.A., Ind. U., 1975; M.A., Ball State U., 1976; Ph.D., Purdue U., 1979; m. Carol Ann Barbera, Dec. 28, 1975; children—Christina Frances, Elliott Charles. Cons. research psychologist MSD of Wayne Twp., Indpls., 1976-78; lectr. psychology Marian Coll., Indpls., 1977-78; clin. intern dept. psychiatry Baylor Coll. Medicine, Houston, 1978-79; coordinator neuropsychology services, med. psychology dept. Community Hosp. of Indpls., 1979—; research cons. Meth. Hosp., Indpls., 1980—; clin. asst. prof. Ind. U. Sch. Medicine, Indpls., 1981—. NIMH fellow, Purdue U., 1976-77; State of Ind., Dept. Spl. Edn. grantee, 1975-76, 77-78. Mem. Ind. Psychol. Assn., Am. Psychol. Assn., Internat. Neuropsychology Soc. Contbr. articles to profl. jours.; editor and chief: Cognitive Rehabilitation of Brain Injured, 1981. Office: Med Psychology Dept Community Hosp of Indianapolis 1500 N Ritter Ave Indianapolis IN 46219

TREZEK, THOMAS JAMES, metals co. exec.; b. Chgo., Apr. 19, 1927; s. Joseph and Josephine (Vladika) T.; B.S. in Mech. Engring., U. Ill., 1952; postgrad. Harvard, 1962; m. Jeanette T. Nauss, June 16, 1951; children—Karen, Kristine, Keith, Lisa, Kim. With Central Foundry div. Gen. Motors Corp., 1952—, prodn. mgr., 1961-64, gen. supr., 1964-69, plant mgr., Bedford, Ind., 1969, mgr. Saginaw Malleable Iron Plant (Mich.), 1972, mgr. mfg. services, 1974-76, chief engr., 1976-77, dir. engring. and reliability, 1977-78, gen. mfg. mgr., 1978—. Served with USAAF, 1945-47. Mem. Saginaw County C. of C., Saginaw Mfrs. Assn., Iron Castings Soc. (v.p., dir.), Am. Foundry Soc., Soc. Automotive Engrs. Clubs: K.C., Saginaw Country, Saginaw, Saginaw YMCA Mgmt. Home: 4711 Crutchfield Saginaw MI 48603 Office: 77 W Center Saginaw MI 48605

TRIANA, ARMANDO ROGELIO, educator; b. Santa Clara, Cuba, Aug. 13, 1943; came to U.S., 1960; s. Armando and Estrella M. (Fajardo) T.; B.B.A. in Fin., U. Puerto Rico, 1965; M.B.A. in Internat. Bus., U. Wis., Madison, 1969; Ph.D. in Mgmt., Northwestern U., 1979; m. Maria del Carmen Cabrera, Aug. 11, 1974; 1 son, Armando David. Credit analyst The Chase Manhattan Bank, San Juan, P.R.,

1965-66; div. asst. The No. Trust Bank, Chgo., 1969-71; prof. Governor's State U., Park Forest South, Ill., 1974-79; asst. prof. orgn. behavior and ops. mgmt. De Paul U., Chgo., 1979—; mktg. and mgmt. cons. Nat. chmn. 3d Nat. Symposium on Hispanic Bus. and Economy, 1981. Served with U.S. Army, 1967. Mem. Acad. Mgmt., Latin Am. Studies Assn., Soc. Psychol. Anthropology, Nat. Assn. Hispanic Profs. of Bus. Adminstrn. and Econs. Roman Catholic. Club: Cath. Youth Orgn. Home: 3950 N Lake Shore Dr Chicago IL 60613 Office: 25 E Jackson Blvd Chicago IL 60604

TRICAMO, FRANK PAUL, retail dept. store exec.; b. St. Louis, Nov. 29, 1942; s. Frank and Agnes (Talluto) T.; B.S.C. in Indsl. Relations, St. Louis U., 1964, M.B.A., 1967; m. Vera Anne Echelmeier, July 16, 1975; 1 dau., Melissa Beth. Personnel mgr. Famous Barr Dept. Store div. May Co., St. Louis, 1965-70; wage and salary mgr. Venture Stores, St. Louis, 1970-71, dir. benefits and compensation, 1972-74, dir. employee relations, 1975-76; v.p. personnel Consumers Distributing Co., catalogue stores, Newark, 1976-78; v.p. personnel Carson Pirie Scott Co., Chgo., 1978—. Served with USCG, 1964. Mem. Am. Soc. Personnel Adminstrs. Clubs: Horseless Carriage; Classic Thunderbird; Desoto of America. Home: 1655 Burning Trail Ct Wheaton IL 60187 Office: 1 S State St Chicago IL 60603

TRICOMI, ANTHONY RAYMOND, sales exec.; b. Cleve., Aug. 12, 1951; s. Vincent James and Rose Marie (LaMarca) T.; student Cleve. State U., 1970-71, U. Akron, 1972-73; m. Caroline D'Aveta, Sept. 22, 1973; children—Crista, Vincent. Account exec. Promotional Fixtures, Inc., Rittman, Ohio, 1972-75, v.p., sales mgr., 1975—. Recreation dir. Broadview Heights, Ohio, 1971-72, councilman-at-large, 1973-77. Recipient 1980 Outstanding Merchandising Achievement award Point of Purchase Advt. Inst. Office: 40 Industrial St Rittman OH 44270

TRIEBEL, FRANCES GRANT, assn. exec.; b. Champaign, Ill., Aug. 29, 1916; d. Harry Weston and Laura Alma (Roberts) Grant; student U. Ill., 1934-37; m. Albert Triebel, Jr., Dec. 26, 1937; 1 dau., Marilyn Triebel Burgoyne. Mem. Nat. Soc. DAR (Ill. state officer-registrar 1977-79, Ill. state chmn. public relations 1979-81, Ill. state regent 1981-83, mem. nat. bd. mgrs. 1981-83, mem. adv. bd., trustee Tamassee DAR Sch., S.C. 1981—; mem. endowment com. of bd. trustees Kate Duncan Smith DAR Sch., Grant, Ala. 1981—, area rep. nat. DAR speakers staff 1980-83), Alpha Chi Omega. Presbyterian. Clubs: Rockford Country, Rockford Women's (dir. 1979-81). Home: 3611 Hickory Ln Rockford IL 61107

TRIMAKAS, KESTUTIS ANTANAS, psychologist, priest, editor; b. Kaunas, Lithuania, July 12, 1930; came to U.S., 1948, naturalized, 1955; s. Dionizas and Antanina (Jaksevicius) T.; student Xavier Coll., 1951-53, Boston Coll., 1953-55, 56-61; A.B., Loyola U. Chgo., 1955, M.A., 1956, Lic.Theol., 1961, M.A., 1971, Ph.D., 1972. Ordained priest Roman Catholic Ch., 1960; intern VA Hosp., Downey-North Chgo., 1972, West Side-Chgo., 1972-73; staff psychologist VA Hosp., Hines, Ill., 1973—; clin. instr. dept. psychiatry Stritch Med. Sch., Loyola U., Chgo., 1980—. Mem. Am. Psychol. Assn., Ill. Psychol. Assn., Soc. for Clin. and Exptl. Hypnosis, Ill. Group Psychotherapy Soc., Inst. Lithuanian Studies (chmn. psychology sect. 1981—). Editor-in-chief Laiskai Lietuviams, 1963-67, Ateitis, 1975—; editor Aidai, 1980—. Home: 850 Des Plaines Ave Forest Park IL 60130 Office: VA Hosp Hines IL 60140

TRIMBLE, KAREN ILLINGWORTH, conv. bur. exec.; b. Lafayette, Ind., June 16, 1954; d. Robert LaVerne and Betty Mae (Long) Illingworth; B.S. in Office Adminstrn. cum laude (scholar), Ind. State U., Terre Haute, 1975; postgrad. in bus. adminstrn. Butler U., 1980—; m. Tony L. Trimble, Aug. 30, 1975. Sec. to dir. sales The Studio Press, Inc., Indpls., 1976-78; exec. sec. to pres. Indpls. Conv. and Visitors Bur., 1978-79, conv. services mgr., 1979-80, bus. mgr., 1980—; instr. Clark Coll., Indpls., 1979—. Active United Way campaigns, 1978, 80. Cert. profl. sec. Mem. Am. Bus. Women's Assn. (enrollment event com. 1978, rec. sec. 1979). Roman Catholic. Office: 100 S Capitol Ave Indianapolis IN 46225

TRIPLETT, GLOVER BROWN, JR., agronomist; b. Crawford, Miss., June 2, 1930; s. Glover B. and Louise (Blake) T.; B.S., Miss. State U., 1951; M.S., Miss. State U., 1955; Ph.D., Mich. State U., 1959; m. Imogene Crump, Feb. 4, 1950; 1 dau., Dorinda. With Ohio Agrl. Research and Devel. Center, Wooster, 1959—, asso. prof., 1964-68, prof., 1969—. Served with U.S. Army, 1951-53. Mem. Am. Soc. Agronomy, Crop Sci. Soc., Weed Sci. Soc., Am. Registry Cert. Profls. in Agronomy, Crops and Soils, Internat. Soil Tillage Research Orgn., Sigma Xi. Club: Lions. Contbr. articles to profl. jours. Office: Ohio Agrl Research and Devel Center Wooster OH 44691

TRIPODI, TONY, social worker, author; b. Sacramento, Nov. 30, 1932; s. Nicholas and Christina Maria (Grandinetti) T.; A.B. (scholar), U. Calif., Berkeley, 1954, M.S.W., 1958; D.S.W. (fellow), Columbia U., 1963; m. Roni Ann Roberts, Oct. 28, 1969; children—Lee Anna, Anthony C., Rachel A. Newman (stepdau.), David C., Stephen J. Research technician Calif. Dept. Mental Hygiene, 1958-59; research analyst Calif. Youth Authority, 1959-60; research asst. Columbia U., N.Y.C., 1961-63, asst. prof., 1963-65; research asso. dept. psychology Bklyn. Coll., 1963-65; asst. prof. U. Calif., Berkeley, 1965-66; prof. social work U. Mich., Ann Arbor, 1965—; author: Uses and Abuses of Social Research in Social Work, 1974; co-author: Assessment of Social Research, 1969; Research Techniques for Program Planning, Monitoring and Evaluation, 1977; Differential Social Program Evaluation, 1978; Research Techniques for Clinical Social Workers, 1980; co-editor: Social Workers at Work, 1977; editor-in-chief Social Work Research and Abstracts, 1980-82. Served with USNR, 1954-56. NIMH and NSF research grantee, 1965-66, 71-74; recipient Fulbright-Hays award, 1973-74. Mem. Nat. Assn. Social Workers, Evaluation Research Soc., Am. Psychol. Assn., Council Social Work Edn., AAUP. Home: 330 Hazelwood St Ann Arbor MI 48103 Office: Sch Social Work U Mich Ann Arbor MI 48109

TRIPP, MARIAN BARLOW LOOFE, pub. relations exec.; b. Lodgepole, Nebr., July 26, 1921; d. Lewis Rockwell and Cora Dee (Davis) Barlow; B.S., Iowa State U., 1944; m. James Edward Tripp, Feb. 9, 1957; children—Brendan Michael, Kevin Mark. Writer, editor Dairy Record, St. Paul, 1944-45; head product promotion div. pub. relations dept. Swift & Co., Chgo., 1945-55; account exec. pub. relations dept. J. Walter Thompson Co., N.Y.C., 1955-66, v.p. mgmt. and supervision, Chgo., 1966-73, v.p., dir. consumer affairs, 1973-75; pres. Marian Tripp Communications Inc., Chgo., 1976—. Bd. dirs. Chgo. Conv. and Tourism Bd., 1973-75. Mem. Pub. Relations Soc. Am., Women's Advt. Club Chgo., Am., Ill. home econs. assns., Chgo. Home Economists in Bus. Episcopalian. Club: Fortnightly. Home: 100 E Bellevue Pl Chicago IL 60611 Office: 70 Walton Pl E Chicago IL 60611

TRIPPET, CHARLES KIGHTLY, telephone co. exec.; b. Princeton, Ind., Apr. 14, 1913; s. Sanford and Edith (Kightly) T.; A.B., Wabash Coll., 1936; m. Isabel Key, Sept. 28, 1940; children—Susan, Bruce, Tresa Lynn. Ins. agt. Trippet Ins. Agy., Princeton, 1937—; dir. Princeton Telephone Co., 1947—, treas., 1953-66, pres., 1966—; dir. Gibson County Bank. Trustee Oakland City Coll.; bd. govs. Associated Colls. Ind. Served to 1st lt. U.S. Army, 1942-46. Decorated Bronze Star. Mem. Ind. Telephone Assn. (dir. 1956—, pres. 1977-79), U.S. Ind. Telephone Assn. (dir. 1969—), Am. Legion, VFW. Democrat. Methodist. Clubs: Princeton Rotary (pres. 1954-55), Athletic, Petroleum, Masons, Shriners. Elks. Home: 306 W Spruce St Princeton IN 47670 Office: PO Box 324-315 N Hart St Princeton IN 47670

TROJAN, JACK GERARD, ednl. adminstr.; b. Milw., May 6, 1936; s. Joseph Frances and Francis Gertrude T.; B.S., U. Wis., Platteville, 1958; M.A., U. No. Colo., 1964; postgrad U. Wis., Miw., 1964-65, Platteville, 1968-69, Whitewater, 1970-74; m. Mary Diane Kaltenbach, July 25, 1959. tchr. high sch., Lancaster, Wis., 1959-61, Mayville, Wis., 1962-68; project engr. Maysteel Products Corp., Mayville, 1965-68; prin. high sch., Cuba City, Wis., 1968-70, also curriculum coordinator K-12; dir. instructional services Public Schs., Whitewater, 1970—. Chmn. Wis. Community Action Council for Drug Edn., 1973-74; dir. explorer scouts Boy Scouts Am., 1958-59. Served with AUS, 1958-59, 61-62. Mem. Assn. Supervision and Curriculum Devel., Wis. Assn. Supervision and Curriculum Devel., Nat. Soc. Study Edn., Nat. Council Social Studies, So. Wis. Edn. Assn. (exec. sec. 1968-69). Roman Catholic. Clubs: Lions (dir. 1962-68, 68-70), Kiwanis (pres. 1981-82). Contbr. articles to profl. jours. Home: 1252 Laurel St Whitewater WI 53190 Office: 401 S Elizabeth St Whitewater WI 53190

TROPPITO, CHARLES C., JR., city adminstr.; b. Kansas City, Mo., Sept. 14, 1947; s. Charles C. and Philomene (Magness) T.; B.A., U. Mo., Kansas City, 1970, M.P.A., 1975; m. Mary A. Barthelmass, June 7, 1969; children—Christopher M., Laurie A. Bond underwriter Reliance Ins. Co., Kansas City, Mo., 1969-70; title examiner trainee St. Paul Title Ins. Co., Kansas City, 1970-71; adminstrv. asst. to mayor/plan commn. City of Leawood (Kans.), 1971-75; dir. adminstrn. and budget City of Prairie Village (Kans.), 1975-78; chief adminstrv. officer, budget dir. City of Urbana (Ill.), 1978—; guest lectr. U. Ill., Urbana; mem. adj. faculty public adminstrn. Columbia Coll., Kansas City; treas., bd. dirs. Urbana Promotion Com., 1980-81; mem. planning com. Sch. Adminstrn., U. Mo., Kansas City, 1976; mem. bd. Champaign-Urbana High Tech. Devel. Group, 1980. Recipient various certs. of appreciation. Mem. Internat. City Mgmt. Assn., Mcpl. Fin. Officers Assn., Am. Public Works Assn. Lutheran. Club: Rotary. Author papers, reports in field. Office: 400 S Vine St Urbana IL 61801

TROSSMAN, DON C., mortgage banker; b. Chgo., Sept. 14, 1946; s. Harold and Doris (Cole) T.; B.S. in Psychology, Tulane U., 1968; M.B.A., Loyola U., Chgo., 1971; m. Janis Norman, June 14, 1969; children—Jill Elisabeth, Robert Norman. Asst. v.p. Heitman Mortgage Co., Chgo., 1972-74; loan officer B.B. Cohen & Co., Chgo., 1974-75; v.p., regional mgr. Banco Mortgage Co., Chgo., 1975-81; sr. v.p., dir. Philipsborn Co., 1981—. Served with USAF, 1968-73. Mem. Mortgage Bankers Assn. Am., Assn. Indsl. Real Estate Brokers, Nat. Assn. Office and Indsl. Parks, Internat. Council Shopping Centers, Ill. Mortgage Bankers Assn. Clubs: Standard (Chgo.); Lake Shore Country (Glencoe, Ill.). Office: 115 S LaSalle St 28th Floor Chicago IL 60603

TROUT, WILLIAM HOLLIS, architect; b. Cleve., June 29, 1935; s. William Henry and Margaret Marie (Pauer) T.; B.S. in Architecture, Kent State U., 1960; m. Beverly Heather Law, June 17, 1961; children—William Hollis, Peter Dunsmore, Timothy Pauer. Prin., Trout Architects, Inc., Rocky River, Ohio, 1967—; guest lectr. to various art and archtl. groups, 1970—; major archtl. works include: The Trout House, 1975, The Baron House, 1976, The Desberg House, 1978, The Sciangula House, 1976, The DeBenedetto House, 1968, others. Recipient numerous awards including Nat. Design award Nat. Assn. Home Builders, 1978; Craftsmanship award Cleve. Builders Exchange, 1977; Outstanding Achievement award Cleve. City Council, 1978; Cleve. Arts prize in architecture, 1978; J. Milton Dyer Meml. award; Record House of the Year award Archtl. Record Mag., 1978. Mem. AIA (Design award 1970, 71, 72), Architects Soc. Ohio (Honor award 1976), Am. Underground Space Assn., Delta Tau Delta. Republican. Episcopalian. Home: 299 Yacht Club Dr Rocky River OH 44116 Office: 19063 Lake Rd Rocky River OH 44116

TROWBRIDGE, KAREN SUE, mech. engr.; b. Vermontville, Mich., Nov. 12, 1950; d. Vernon Clifford and Mary Delilah (Viele) T.; B.S. with honors in Mech. Engring., Mich. State U., 1972. Maintenance engr. Johnson & Johnson Corp., Chgo., 1972-73, control supr. facilities and equipment, 1973-75; project engr. Procter & Gamble Corp., Lima, Ohio, 1975, production mgr., 1976-81; project engr. Sohio Vistron Corp., Lima, 1981—. Vol., VA Hosp., Battle Creek, Mich., 1969; troop leader Girl Scouts U.S.A. Beckman Sch. for Retarded, 1969-72; chmn. campus blood drive ARC, 1971-72; advisor Jr. Achievement program, 1975—. Recipient Award for Contributions to Community and Industry Chgo. YWCA, 1974. Mem. ASME, Pi Tau Sigma, Gamma Sigma Sigma. Club: Venture (pres. 1976). Home: 240 Eastown Rd Lima OH 45807 Office: PO Box 1900 Lima OH 45802

TROXEL, LARRY LEE, ready-mixed concrete products co. exec.; b. Battle Creek, Mich., Apr. 18, 1942; s. Emerald V. and Melba Lucille (Church) T.; student Kellogg Community Coll., 1960-62; m. Marilyn Jean Richman, Feb. 2, 1963; children—Jodi Lyn, Karla Sue, Ronna Kay. Mgr., V.E. Troxel & Sons, Inc., Battle Creek, 1960-68, corp. sec., gen. mgr., 1973-81; also dir.; mgr. Lumber div. Wickes Corp., Saginaw, Mich., 1968-73; pres. L-M Troxel Services, Inc., Battle Creek, 1981—; dir. V.E. Troxel & Sons, Inc. Constable, Emmett Twp., 1976-80; mem. Calhoun County Citizens Coalition Against Crime, 1976-79; advisor Jr. Achievement South Central Mich., 1979-80. Recipient Spoke award Battle Creek Jaycees, 1975, Spark Plug award, 1976, 77, 78; named Outstanding Young Man of the Yr., Dale Carnegie, 1977. Mem. Battle Creek Area C. of C. Republican. Baptist. Club: Optimists (pres. 1967-68). Address: 13084 Hoyt Dr Battle Creek MI 49017

TROXELL, JAMES DANE, lawyer, petroleum co. exec.; b. Akron, Ohio, Mar. 5, 1946; s. Delmont and Katherine T.; B.A., U. Akron, 1968, J.D., 1975; m. Sandra L. Coey, June 14, 1969. Trainee, Goodyear Aerospace Co., Akron, Ohio, 1969-70; legal counsel Babcock & Wilcox Co., Barberton, Ohio, 1970-76; admitted to Ohio bar, 1976, U.S. Supreme Ct. bar, 1979; asso. firm Hershey & Browne, Akron, 1976-78; corp. counsel Gen. Tire & Rubber Co., Akron, 1979-80; pres. Ohio Petroleum Energy Co., Cuyahoga Falls, Ohio, 1978—. Past bd. dirs. United Cerebral Palsy of Summit County and Akron. Mem. Am. Bar Assn., Ohio State Bar Assn., Akron Bar Assn., Ohio Oil and Gas Assn., Psi chi. Republican. Club: Cascade (Akron). Office: PO Box 266 Cuyahoga Falls OH 44222

TROXELL, JOHN FRANKLIN, veterinarian; b. Shelbina, Mo., Nov. 25, 1935; s. Clarence Delmar and Eleanor Delano (Smock) T.; B.S., U. Mo., 1963, D.V.M., 1963; m. Mary Elizabeth Shively, July 9, 1964; children—Jason Franklin, Grant Alan. Practice vet. medicine, also cons. to VA Hosp., Martinsburg, W.Va., 1966-68; practice vet. medicine Humane Soc. Mo., St. Louis, 1968; practice vet. medicine, Homewood, Ill., 1968—. Pres., dir. Flossmoor Pet Hosp., Ltd. (Ill.), 1968—; owner Glenwood Village Pet Clinic, Glenwood, Ill.; dir. radio program on vet. edn. WCGO, Chicago Heights, Ill., 1970. Bd. dirs. South Suburban Humane Soc. Served with USNR, 1953-54; served to capt., AUS, 1964-66. Mem. Am., Chgo. vet. med. assns., Toastmasters Internat., Am. Legion, Gamma Sigma Delta, Alpha Zeta. Republican. Methodist. Rotarian. Office: Route 54 and 196th St Homewood IL 60430

TROY, JOHN JOSEPH, corp. exec.; b. Bklyn., May 28, 1949; s. John Joseph and Mary Troy; B.S., St. John's U., 1970; m. Susan Murray Jones, June 7, 1975; 1 dau., Jennifer Anne. Jr. auditor Touche Ross Co., N.Y.C., 1970-71; sr. auditor Clarence Rainess, N.Y.C., 1971-74; regional internal auditor Mobil Oil Co., Phila., 1973-76; corp. internal auditor Ashland (Ky.) Oil Co., 1976-77; corp. controller Hawthorn Mellody Inc., Schaumburg, Ill., 1978—. Served with USNG. C.P.A., Pa. Mem. Am. Inst. C.P.A.'s, Inst. Internal Auditors, Am. Mgmt. Assn., Midwest Planning Assn., Ky. Inst. C.P.A.'s. Office: Hawthorn Mellody Inc 1827 Walden Office Sq Schaumburg IL 60195

TROZZOLO, ANTHONY MARION, chemist, educator; b. Chgo., Jan. 11, 1930; s. Pasquale and Francesca (Vercillo) T.; B.S., Ill. Inst. Tech., 1950; M.S., U. Chgo., 1957, Ph.D., 1960; m. Doris C. Stoffregen, Oct. 8, 1955; children—Thomas, Susan, Patricia, Michael, Lisa, Laura. Asst. chemist Chgo. Midway Labs., 1952-53; asso. chemist Armour Research Found., Chgo., 1953-56; mem. tech. staff Bell Labs., Murray Hill, N.J., 1959-75; Charles L. Huisking prof. chemistry U. Notre Dame, 1975—; chmn. Gordon Research Conf. on Photochemistry, 1964; vis. prof. Columbia U., N.Y.C., 1971. AEC fellow, 1951; NSF fellow, 1957-59; Phillips lectr. U. Okla., 1971; P.C. Reilly lectr. U. Notre Dame, 1972; C. L. Brown lectr., Rutgers, 1975; Sigma Xi lectr., Bowling Green, 1976, Abbott Labs., 1978; M. Faraday lectr. No. Ill. U., 1976; F.O. Butler lectr. S.D. State U., 1978; Plenary lectr. 8th Internat. Symposium on Free Radicals, 1967, 7th Internat. Symposium on Photochemistry, 1978; vis. lectr. Max Planck Inst. Biophysikalische Chemie, Göttingen, Germany, 1978, Staudinger Inst. Makromoleculare Chemie, Freiburg, Germany, 1978; Coronado lectr. Am. Chem. Soc., 1980. Fellow N.Y. Acad. Scis. (chmn. chem. scis. sect. 1969-70, Halpern award 1980), AAAS, Am. Inst. Chemists; mem. Am. Chem. Soc. (Disting. Service award St. Joseph Valley sect. 1979), AAUP, Gordon Research Conf. Council, Sigma Xi. Roman Catholic. Asso. editor Jour. Am. Chem. Soc., 1975-76; editor Chem. Reviews, 1977—; patentee; contbr. articles to profl. jours. Home: 1329 E Washington St South Bend IN 46617 Office: U Notre Dame Notre Dame IN 46556

TRUANT, VINCENT JOHN, brewing co. exec.; b. Balt., Oct. 27, 1947; s. Reno Angelo and Rita Elizabeth T.; B.S. in Psychology magna cum laude, U. Balt., 1970; m. Ida Antoinette, Jan. 11, 1969; 1 dau., Angela Rita. With Eli Lilly & Co., 1970-78, personnel rep., Indpls., 1976-77, market research analyst, 1977-78; personnel mgr. Miller Brewing Co., Milw., 1978-79, mktg. mgr., 1979—. Awarder scholar, 1968-70; Senaotiral scholar, 1968-70. Mem. Am. Mktg. Assn., Antique Automobile Club Am. Home: 1135 Hawthorne Ridge Waukesha WI 53186 Office: 3939 W Highland Blvd Milwaukee WI 53201

TRUE, MARION W. (MRS. LAURENCE M. TRUE), civic worker; b. Franklin, N.H., Feb. 16, 1902; d. Ichabod S. and Mary K. (Dunlap) Williams; B.S. in Chemistry, U. N.H., 1923; m. Laurence M. True, Sept. 3, 1927 (dec.); children—Lavinia (Mrs. Paul H. Plough, Jr.), David, Gilbert, Melbern, Katharine (Mrs. Douglas Logan). Tchr. Sanborn Sem., 1923-24, Braintree High Sch., 1924-27. Active Cleve. Girl Scouts, 1942-69, mem. bd. dirs., mem. regional com. 1951-61, mem. group services council, 1943-61, vice chmn., 1943-58, mem. exec. bd., 1955-58; mem. personnel com. Welfare Fedn. of Cleve., 1954-56; mem. Com. on Older Persons; chmn. Com. on Homes for Aged; alumni dir. U. N.H., 1964-70; pres. Aux. Bapt. Home Ohio; trustee, house chmn., sec. of bd. Judson Park, chmn. work com. Aux., 1973—, co-chmn. gift shop, 1976—; trustee First Baptist Ch., 1958-61, 64-70, 74-76, vice chmn. bd., 1975, chmn. bd., 1976, mem. cabinet, 1970-73, 74-77, stewardship com., 1972-74. Recipient Alumni Meritorious award 1961; Thanks badge, Lake Erie Girl Scouts. Mem. Nat. Soc. New Eng. Women (pres. Cleve. colony, v.p.) New Eng. Soc. Western Res. Daus. Am. Colonists (v.p., vice chmn. 1975-76), ASME (woman's aux.), D.A.R., Alpha Xi Delta. Clubs: College dir.); Canterbury Golf. Home: Jordan-Gardner Tower 2181 Ambleside Rd Cleveland OH 44106

TRUHON, STEPHEN ANTHONY, psychologist, educator; b. N.Y.C., June 19, 1951; s. Anthony Joseph and Beatrice Helen (Kerekes) T.; B.A., Coll. of Holy Cross, 1973; M.A., Mich. State U., 1976, Ph.D., 1978. Instr. psychology Mich. State U., East Lansing, 1978-79; asst. prof. psychology Valparaiso (Ind.) U., 1979—. Mem. Am. Psychol. Assn., Midwestern Psychol. Assn., Soc. for Research in Child Devel., AAUP. Contbr. articles to profl. jours. Home: 156 Andover Ct Apt 18F Valparaiso IN 46383 Office: Dept Psychology Valparaiso U Valparaiso IN 46383

TRULSON, PEARL, educator; b. Parshall, N.D., Oct. 30, 1916; d. Leonard and Mary Elizabeth (Sivear) Colclough; B.S., Minot State Coll., 1969; m. June 15, 1940; 1 son, Ronald Trulson. Tchr., Baldy Sch. Dist. 124, 1936-40, Model Sch. Dist. 9, 1942-49, 51-55, Reservation Sch. Dist., 1961-64, Parshall (N.D.) Public Schs. Dist. 7, 1964-81, 81—. Mem. Assn. Ednl. Data Systems, NEA, N.D. Edn. Assn., N.D. Council Tchrs. Math, Internat. Reading Assn., Am. Legion Aux. Democrat. Episcopalian. Address: PO Box 573 Parshall ND 58770

TRUMBLE, EUGENE FLETCHER, pub. relations exec.; b. Montevideo, Minn., Nov. 8, 1925; s. Eugene Fletcher and Elna Louisa (Gust) T.; B.J., U. Mo., 1950, B.A., 1950; m. Betty Oberlander Jaynes, Nov. 30, 1950; children—Susan (Mrs. Richard M. Chappell, Jr.), Janet (Mrs. Hooman Amiri), Mark, Cynthia, David, John. Program dir. U.S. Jr. C. of C., Tulsa, 1953-55; staff dir. Citizens Com. for Hoover Report, N.Y.C., 1955-56; account exec. Campbell-Mithun Advt., Mpls., 1956-60; dir. pub. relations Apache Corp., Mpls., 1960-66; pres. Trumble & Assos., Inc., Mpls., 1966—. Vice chmn. nat. dist. adv. council SBA, 1972—. Asst. nat. dir. Nixon-Lodge Vols., 1960; Midwest dir. Nixon Campaign Com., 1968; mem. Minn. Republican State Central Com., 1970. Trustee Sumner T. McKnight Found., 1963—, U. Minn. Landscape Arboretum, 1976—, Minn. Outward Bound Sch., 1978—. Served with AUS, 1943-46. Recipient Feature Story of Yr. award U. Mo., 1950. Mem. Pub. Relations Soc. Am., Tau Kappa Epsilon, Sigma Delta Chi. Presbyn. Clubs: Minneapolis, Minn. Press, Hazeltine Nat. Golf. Home: 2025 Audubon Dr Chaska MN 55318 Office: 520 Baker Bldg Minneapolis MN 55402

TRUMFIO, HARRY C., ednl. adminstr.; b. Chgo., Apr. 30, 1941; s. Harry A. and Mary Ann (Porembski) T.; B.S., Loyola U., 1963; M.A., Northwestern U., 1965; Ed.D., Nova U., 1979; m. Lorelei, Dec. 12, 1968; children—Steven, Laura. Tchr., Glenview (Ill.) Jr. High Sch., 1965-68; guidance counselor East Maine Jr. High Sch., Niles, Ill., 1968-70, asst. prin., 1970-71; dir. pupil personnel services Mt. Prospect (Ill.) Schs., 1971-72; prin. Hynes Sch., Morton Grove, Ill., 1972—; cons. on gifted edn. and needs assessment. Mem. Niles Twp. Legis. Coalition, 1980-81. Mem. Niles Twp. Prins. Assn. (past dir.), Ill. Assn. Supervision and Curriculum Devel., Ill. Prins. Assn., Nat.

Assn. Supervision and Curriculum Devel., Phi Delta Kappa, Phi Gamma Mu. Contbr. articles to profl. jours. Home: 116 Bobby Ln Mt Prospect IL 60056 Office: 9000 Bellefort St Morton Grove IL 60053

TRUMMER, AARON JOHN, educator; b. Milw., Sept. 18, 1952; s. John Herman and Ina Agnes (York) T.; B.S. in Edn., U. Wis., Whitewater, 1975, M.Ed., 1981; postgrad. (Hayes-Fulbright scholar to India), Jamia Islamia Amila U., New Delhi, 1978; m. Sally Josephine Michalko, Aug. 2, 1975. Social Studies dir., 8th grade tchr. Templeton Middle Sch., 1975-81; econs. and polit. sci. tchr. Hamilton High Sch., Hamilton Sch. Dist., Sussex, Wis., 1981—; cons., speaker social studies methodology; developer social sci. materials. Active com. on missions, First United Meth. Commn. on Edn. Mem. Assn. Supervision and Curriculum Devel., Nat. Hist. Soc., NEA, United Lakewood Educators (chief negotiator 1975-80), Wis. Edn. Assn., Nat. Social Studies Council, Wis. Social Studies Council, Phi Delta Kappa, Lambda Chi Alpha Alumni Assn. Author: Simulations and Media for Junior High Use, 1979; contbr. writings to mags., papers to profl. confs. Home: 935 N Greenfield Ave Waukesha WI 53186 Office: W220 N 6151 Town Line Bd Sussex WI 53089

TRUSHEIM, H. EDWIN, ins. co. exec.; b. Chgo., 1927; grad. Tchrs. Coll., 1948; student Northwestern U. Pres., chief exec. officer Gen. Am. Life Ins. Co., St. Louis; dir. Angelica Corp. Bd. dirs. Downtown St. Louis, Inc., Urban Redevel. Corp. Office: Gen Am Life Ins Co PO Box 396 Saint Louis MO 63166*

TRUSTY, THOMAS FRANCIS, ins. co. exec.; b. Ft. Dodge, Iowa, Apr. 9, 1931; s. Howard Francis and Mary Henrietta (Maguire) T.; student St. John's U., 1949-50; student Iowa State U., 1954-58; m. Mary Yavonne McDonald, Nov. 15, 1950; children—Thomas J., Catherine M., Mark H., Beth Ann, Lisa M. Data processor Hormel Packing Co., Ft. Dodge, 1950-54; data processing tech. Iowa State U., Ames, 1954-58; sr. systems analyst John Deere & Co., Ankeny, Iowa, 1958-69; sr. v.p. info. systems Am. Republic Ins. Co., Des Moines, 1969—. Mem. data processing adv. com. Ankeny (Ia.) Community Coll., 1972-78; adv. to Des Moines/Polk County Joint Data Processing Center, 1970; pres. Ankeny Library Bd., 1976. Served with USAF, 1951-53. Mem. Greater Des Moines C. of C., Assn. of Systems Mgmt., Data Processing Mgmt. Assn. (chpt. pres. 1968-69, Achievement award 1972). Roman Catholic. Clubs: Des Moines, Hyperion Golf and Field. Home: 308 NW Beechwood St Ankeny IA 50021 Office: 601 6th Ave Des Moines IA 50034

TRUTTER, JOHN THOMAS, telephone co. exec.; b. Springfield, Ill., Apr. 18, 1920; s. Frank L. and Frances (Mischler) T.; A.B., U. Ill., 1942; postgrad. Northwestern U., U. Chgo.; m. Edith English Woods, June 17, 1950; children—Edith English II, Jonathan Woods. With Ill. Bell Telephone Co., Chgo., 1946-55, 58—, gen. traffic mgr., 1959-62, asst. v.p. pub. relations, 1962-65, asst. v.p. suburban ops., 1965-67, gen. mgr. north suburban ops., 1967-69, v.p. pub. relations, 1969-71, v.p. operator services, 1971—; mem. personnel relations staff AT&T, N.Y.C., 1955-58; dir. State Nat. Bank Evanston (Ill.). Lectr. gen. semantics. Mem. City of Evanston Zoning Amendment Bd., 1968-70; exec. v.p., dir. Internat. Visitors Center, Chgo., 1971-72, mem. adv. bd., 1973—; mem. regional bd. NCCJ, Chgo., 1963—, v.p., chmn. exec. com., 1969-73, presiding co-chmn., 1973—, nat. trustee, 1967—, mem. nat. exec. com., 1979—; active Met. Crusade Mercy, 1968-72; mem. adv. bd. Citizenship Council Met. Chgo., 1969—; mem. exec. bd. Chgo. Area council Boy Scouts Am., 1969-75; trustee Children's Home and Aid Soc. Ill., 1970—, v.p., 1975-79, pres., 1979—, also chmn. centennial com.; life trustee Hull House Assn., pres., 1972-74, hon. chmn. 90 Year Fund, 1979—; bd. dirs., exec. com., pres. United Cerebral Palsy Greater Chgo., 1972—, chmn., 1977—; v.p., nat. campaign chmn. United Cerebral Palsy Assns., 1977—, steering com. nat. telethon, 1978-80; bd. dirs. Chgo. Conv. and Tourism Bur., 1979—, exec. com., 1981—; bd. dirs. Chgo. Council Fgn. Relations, 1968-74; bd. dirs. Nat. Minority Purchasing Council, 1976—, nat. treas., 1976-77; mem. com. on case flow Cook County Circuit Ct., 1979-81; chmn. blue ribbon com. truancy in Chgo. schs., 1979-80; task force chmn. Chgo. United Inc., 1971-81, treas., 1981—; mem., Chgo. Crime Commn., dir., 1976—, chmn. membership com., v.p., 1981—, chmn. Chgo. Law Enforcement Week, 1982; bd. dirs. Lyric Opera Chgo., 1976—, mem. 25th Anniversary Com., 1979; hon. vice chmn. Orch. of Ill., 1981—; chmn. bd. dirs. Chgo. City Ballet, 1981—; bd. dirs. North Communities Health Plan, sec., 1979-81; exec. bd. Northwestern U. Library; trustee U. Ill. YMCA, 1970-81. Served to lt. col. AUS, 1942-46; CBI. Recipient Laureate award Lincoln Acad. Ill., 1980-81; Outstanding Exec. Leadership award Nat. Soc. Fund-Raising Execs., 1979; decorated Legion of Merit, China medal. Mem. Sangamon County Hist. Soc. (pres. 1961-62), Pub. Relations Soc. Am., Ill. State Hist. Soc. (v.p. 1978-80), Evanston Current Events Group (chmn. 1978-79), Abraham Lincoln Assn. (dir. 1981—), Alpha Sigma Phi (Nat. award Delta Beta Xi). Clubs: Mid-America, Tavern (bd. govs. 1978-81), Economic (Chgo.). Co-author: Handling Barriers in Communications, 1957; The Governor Takes a Bride, 1977. Contbr. articles to profl. jours. Home: 630 Clinton Pl Evanston IL 60201 Office: 225 W Randolph St Chicago IL 60606

TRUUMAA, AARE, psychologist; b. Tartu, Estonia, Aug. 6, 1926; came to U.S., 1949, naturalized, 1955; s. Peeter and Anna Helene (Lohmus) T.; student in medicine UNRRA U., Munich, Germany, 1946-47, in econs. U. Erlangen (Germany), 1947, in medicine U. Heidelberg (Germany), 1947-48; A.B. in Psychology, Occidental Coll., 1951, M.A. in Psychology, 1952; Ph.D. in Clin. Psychology, Purdue U., Lafayette, Ind., 1957; m. Frances Louise Halbing, Oct. 17, 1959; 1 dau., Karen Louise. Grad. teaching asst. Purdue U., 1952-55; clin. psychology trainee VA Hosp., Ft. Wayne, Ind., 1955-56, VA Hosp., Marion, Ind., 1956-57, VA Mental Health Hygiene Clinic, Indpls., 1957; supr. psychol. services Continued Treatment Service, Beatty Meml. Hosp., Westville, Ind., 1957-58; staff psychologist Riley Child Guidance Clinic, Ind. U. Med. Center, 1958-60, chief clin. psychologist Children's Outpatient and Cons. Services, 1960-70, psychol. cons. Cerebral Palsy Clinic, 1960-63, dir. tng. in clin. psychology, 1970-75, sr. clin. psychologist Children's Outpatient and Cons. Services, 1975—; instr. clin. psychology dept. psychiatry Ind. U. Sch. Medicine, 1958-61, asst. prof. clin. psychology, 1961-66, asso. prof. clin. psychology, 1966-73, prof. clin. psychology, 1973—; psychol. cons. East Central Spl. Services Dist., 1972—. Cert. sch. psychologist, cert. in pvt. practice, Ind. Fellow Am. Orthopsychiat. Assn.; mem. Am. Psychol. Assn., Ind. Psychol. Assn., Central Ind. Psychol. Assn., AAUP, Sigma Xi, Psi Chi. Lutheran. Author: (with E. E. Levitt) The Rorschach Technique with Children and Adolescents: Application and Norms, 1972; contbr. articles to profl. jours. Home: 8330 N Park Ave Indianapolis IN 46240 Office: Riley Child Guidance Clinic Ind U Med Center Indianapolis IN 46223

TRYBER, THOMAS ANTHONY, JR., agriculture and constrn. equipment mfg. co. exec.; b. Rapid City, S.D., May 18, 1943; s. Thomas A. and Rose Mary Tryber; student public schs., Racine, Wis; m. Kathleen M. Kober, May 25, 1963. Supr. cost and budgets J.I. Case, Racine, 1971-74, mgr. cost and budget control, 1974-77, fin. systems analyst, Wichita, Kans., 1977-78, mgr. systems and data processing, 1978—. Mem. Data Processing Mgmt. Assn., Am. Prodn. Inventory Control Soc. Home: 1324 Crestline Wichita KS 67212 Office: J I Case Co 6810 W Kellogg Wichita KS 67209

TRYLOFF, ROBIN SUE, arts adminstr.; b. Mt. Clemens, Mich., July 3, 1951; d. Warren Frederick and Nancy Jane Tryloff; B.A. in Art History and French, U. Mich., 1973; M.A. in Art History, U. Chgo., 1975; m. Ronald C. Roth, Sept. 30, 1978. Program specialist Nat. Endowment for the Arts, 1975-76; dir. Okla. Mus. Assn., 1976-78; asso. dir. Nebr. Arts Council, Omaha, 1978-79, exec. dir., 1979—; mem. artists-in-edn. panel Nat. Endowment for Arts, 1980—, mem. mus. policy panel, 1982—; bd. dirs. Nat. Assembly State Arts Agys., 1981—; vice chmn. Mid-Am. Arts Alliance, 1981-82. Mem. vol. bur. adv. com. United Way, Omaha, 1981—. Office: 1313 Farnam on the Mall Omaha NE 68102-1873

TRYON, MARY MAE, educator; b. Terre Haute, Ind., Apr. 11, 1944; d. Ernest Hubert and Virginia Mae Leach; B.S., Ind. U., 1974, M.S., 1975, Ed.S., 1979; m. Robert Eugene Tryon, Aug. 8, 1965; 1 son, Chad Robert. Tchr., Bartholomew Consol. Sch. Corp., Columbus, Ind., 1975—; instr. Ind. U./Purdue U., 1980—. Mem. Assn. Supervision and Curriculum Devel., Ind. U. Alumni Assn., Pi Lambda Theta. Home: 5760 W Lowell Rd Columbus IN 47201

TSANG, KWONG YOK, immunologist, educator; b. Hong Kong, June 23, 1945; s. Chi Keung and Shui Hing (Lee) T.; came to U.S., 1966, naturalized, 1976; Ph.D., Bowling Green State U., 1974; m. Susan Tarn, May 13, 1972. Research asso. in immunology Med. Coll. Ohio, Toledo, 1974-78, instr., 1975-77, asst. prof., 1977—. Cert. specialist clin. microbiology Am. Acad. Microbiology. Mem. Am. Soc. Microbiologists, Electron Microscopy Soc. N.W. Ohio, Nat. Registry Microbiology, Sigma Xi. Home: 1617 Fallbrook St Toledo OH 43614 Office: Dept Surgery and Orthopedic Surgery Med Coll Ohio Box 6190 Toledo OH 43699

TSAY, CHING SOW, physician; b. Taipei, Taiwan, Jan. 25, 1939; s. Shui Sheng and Len (Chang) T.; came to U.S., 1967, naturalized, 1976; M.D., Kao-Hsiung Med. Coll., Taiwan, 1964; m. Zei-Tsu Chen, Jan. 18, 1964; children—Michael, Cindy, Alice. Intern, St. Vincent's Med. Center of Richmond, S.I., N.Y., 1967-68; resident anesthesia, St. Joseph Hosp., Joliet, Ill., 1968-69, Washington Hosp. Center, Washington, 1969-71; practice medicine, specializing in anesthesiology, 1971—; chief anesthesiology VA Hosp., Kansas City, Mo., 1971-81; from instr. to clin. asst. prof. anesthesia dept. U. Kans. Med. Center, 1971-81; staff in anesthesiology Annapolis Hosp., Wayne, Mich., 1981—. Diplomate Am. Bd. Anesthesiology Fellow Am. Coll. Anesthesiologists; mem. Am., Kans., Mich. socs. anesthesiologists. Home: 3010 Bolgos Circle Ann Arbor MI 48105 Office: 33155 Annapolis Rd Wayne MI 48184

TSCHABOLD, EDWARD EVERTT, research physiologist; b. Wichita Falls, Tex., Dec. 7, 1934; s. Edward Ungles and Thelma Lee (Turner) T.; B.S., Midwestern U., 1957; M.A., Miami U., 1962; Ph.D., Colo. State U., 1967; children—Jennifer Celeste, Randall Edward. Research scientist Eli Lilly Co., Greenfield, Ind., 1967—. Served with U.S. Army, 1957-59. Mem. Growth Regulatory Working Group, Agronomy Soc., Sigma Xi. Office: G-202 Lilly Research Labs Eli Lilly & Co Greenfield IN 46140

TSCHAKERT, ANN CECILIA, ednl. adminstr.; b. Watertown, S.D., May 4, 1954; d. Everett William and Agnes Cecilia (Grygiel) T.; B.S., No. State Coll., Aberdeen, S.D., 1976, vocat. cert., 1978. Mem. secretarial staff No. State Coll., Aberdeen, S.D., 1972-76, Sacred Heart Ch., 1976-78, Milbank (S.D.) Mut. Ins. Co., 1979-80; tchr. bus. and English, Roncalli High Sch., Aberdeen, 1976-78; tchr. distributive edn. Milbank High Sch., 1978-81, tchr. bus. edn., 1981—. Mem. Am. Vocat. Assn., S.D. Vocat. Assn., Nat. Bus. Edn. Assn., S.D. Bus. Edn. Assn., Milbank C. of C. Democrat. Roman Catholic. Home: 111 1/2 S Grant St Milbank SD 57252 Office: Milbank High Sch Milbank SD 57252

TSENGAS, STEVEN, mfg. exec.; b. Athens, Greece, May 26, 1937; s. Nicholas D. and Eugenia S. (Stavrianos) T. (parents U.S. citizens); B.S. in Engring., U. Buffalo, 1960; M.S. in Bus. Adminstrn., U. Rochester, 1965; m. Evangelia K. Maglaras, June 25, 1961; children—Nicholas S., Konstantine S. Sr. indsl. engr. Eastman Kodak Co., 1961-65; asst. to v.p., dir. personnel, mgr. central ops. RF Communications, Inc. subs. Harris Corp., also pres., gen. mgr. Tedford Labs, Inc. subs. RF Communications, 1966-70; asst. dir. corp. planning, Babcock & Wilcox, gen. mgr. ops. Bailey Controls subs., 1970-73; exec. v.p. AMAC Enterprises, 1973-75; founder, chmn. bd., chief exec. officer Naxos Assos., Inc., Advanced Sealing Systems, Inc., APSCO, Inc. and Protel Internat., Inc., Painesville, Ohio, 1976—; instr. Cuyahoga Community Coll.; lectr., speaker, cons. Mem. chmn.'s com. U.S. Senatorial Bus. Adv. Bd.; mem. Council Small Enterprises, AHI Public Affairs Com., Inc., Republican Nat. Com.; adv. com. Cuyahoga Community Coll. Served to lt., USNR, 1960-68. Mem. Ohio Psychol. Assn., Am. Inst. Indsl. Engrs., Beta Gamma Sigma. Eastern Orthodox. Author seminar workbooks. Home: 7768 Litchfield Dr Mentor OH 44060 Office: 1500 W Jackson St Suite 837 Painesville OH 44077

TUBBS, EDWARD LANE, banker; b. Delmar, Iowa, Apr. 17, 1920; s. Clifton Marvin and Mary Ellen (Lane) T.; B.S., Iowa State U., 1941; m. Grace Barbara Dyer, Nov. 27, 1941; children—Steven, Alan, William. With Iowa State U. Agrl. Extension Service, Newton, 1942; farm owner and mgr., 1944—; instr. Vets. On-Farm, DeWitt (Iowa) schs., 1957-58; v.p., dir. Jackson State Bank, Maquoketa, Iowa, 1959-66; chmn., pres., dir., trust officer Maquoketa State Bank, 1966—; pres., dir. Ohnward Bancshares, Inc.; chmn., dir. First Central State Bank, DeWitt; dir. Mid Am. Bankers Service Co., Inc., Iowa Bus. Growth Corp., Iowa Bankers Ins. Services; lectr. banking schs.; Exchange del. USSR, 1959. Pres. Elwood (Iowa) Sch. Bd., 1956-62; treas. City of Maquoketa, 1975-80; mem. Maquoketa Indsl. Devel. Bd., 1970-77; treas. Maquoketa Community Services, 1967-80. Served with AUS, 1942-43. Recipient 4H Club Alumni award, 1962, Century Farm award Iowa Dept. Agr., 1976; named Jaycee Boss of Yr., 1970. Mem. Bank Adminstrn. Inst., Iowa Bankers Assn. (treas. 1978-79, pres. 1980-81), Iowa Transfer System (dir. 1978—), Iowa Ind. Bankers, Am. Legion, Isaac Walton League, Farm Bur., Iowa State U. Alumni Assn., Maquoketa C. of C. (dir. 1966-69), Order of Knoll (Iowa State U.), Internat. Platform Assn., Gamma Sigma Delta. Republican. Mem. United Ch. Christ. Club: Rotary. Author articles in field. Home: 820 Niles St Maquoketa IA 52060 Office: 203 N Main St Maquoketa IA 52060

TUBBS, JERRY RONALD, univ. adminstr.; b. Reed City, Mich., Dec. 12, 1932; s. Roy Walter and Mildred Josephine (Holmquist) T.; B.S. in Acctg., Ferris State Coll., 1961; postgrad. Inst. for Ednl. Mgmt., Harvard U., 1973; M.A. in Ednl. Adminstn., Central Mich. U., 1978; m. Lorraine Bertha Grein, Nov. 21, 1953; children—Deborah Michelle, Michael Roy. Bus. mgr. Ferris State Coll., Big Rapids, Mich., 1960-63; controller Louvers & Dampers, Inc., Somerset, Ky., 1963-64; internal auditor Central Mich. U., Mt. Pleasant, 1964-65; exec. asst. to v.p., bus. and finance, 1965-70, v.p. bus. and finance, 1970—, treas., bd. trustees, 1980—; chmn. Higher Edn. Adminstrn. Referral Service, Washington, 1977—. Mem. supervisory com., bd. dirs. Isabella County Govtl. Employees Credit Union, 1965-70; mem. bd. Isabella County United Way, 1966-74; mem. citizens adv. com. City Mt. Pleasant, 1966-68; trustee, treas. Christ the King Luth. Chapel, 1967-70; treas. Isabella County Commn. Aging, 1975-79, budget com. chmn., 1975-79, mem. exec. com., 1975-79; vice chmn. Isabella County Econ. Devel. Corp., 1978—; mem. President's Club, Central Mich. Univ., 1975—. Served with USN, 1951-54. Mem. Mich. Assn. Colls. and Univ. Bus. Officers, Nat. Assn.Colls. and Univ. Bus. Officers, Central Assn. Coll. and Univ. Bus. Officers, Higher Edn. Adminstrn. Referral Service, Coll. Univ. Personnel Assn., Nat. Assn. Phys. Plant Adminstrs., V.F.W. (life). Lutheran. Home: 4986 W Jordan Rd Weidman MI 48893 Office: 111 Warriner Hall Central Michigan Univ Mount Pleasant MI 48859

TUCHMAN, SIDNEY, service co. exec.; b. Indpls., July 28, 1924; s. Sam and Pearl (Friedman) T.; student Rose Poly. Inst., 1943-44; married; children—Mitchell, Ellen, Kathy. Partner, Tuchman Cleaners, 1947-60, pres., 1960—; keynote speaker Apparelmaster Conv., Atlanta, 1981, Australian and N.Z. Drycleaners Assn., 1981. Vice pres., Better Bus. Bur., Indpls., 1973, Jewish Welfare Fedn., Indpls., 1969; pres. Indpls. Hebrew Congregation, 1977-78. Served with Signal Corps, U.S. Army, 1943-46. Recipient Spirit of Service award Nat. Inst. Dry Cleaners, 1966, 68, 69; Nat. award Am. Inst. Laundering, 1974. Mem. Indpls. Cleaners and Launderers (pres. 1973-74), Ind. Drycleaners and Launderers Assn. (pres. 1978-79), Internat. Roundtable of Drycleaners (pres. 1979-80, Best Ann. Presentation award 1981), Inst. Ind. Launderers, Internat. Fabricare Inst., Am. Mgmt. Assn. Jewish. Clubs: Broadmoor Country, Kiwanis. Contbr. articles to profl. jours. Home: 8145 Ridley Ct Indianapolis IN 46260 Office: 4401 N Keystone Ave Indianapolis IN 46205

TUCKER, BARBARA, safety exec.; b. Mpls., Aug. 21, 1922; d. Ward F. and Miriam L. T.; B.S., U. Minn., 1944. Histology supr. Northwestern Hosp., Mpls., 1945-52, chief adminstrv. technologist, 1953-76, safety dir., 1976—; cons. Norm Steere & Assos. Mem. Am. Soc. for Med. Technologists, Am. Soc. Safety Engrs., Am. Assn. Indsl. Hygienists, Assn. for Advancement of Med. Instrumentation, Nat. Fire Protection Assn., U. Minn. Alumni Assn. Episcopalian. Office: 2727 Chicago Ave Minneapolis MN 55407

TUCKER, DENNIS KEITH, tech. adminstr.; b. Danville, Ill., Apr. 9, 1951; s. Robert Keith and Carol Rose (Henschen) T.; A.S., Danville Jr. Coll., 1971; student U. South Fla., 1971-72; B.S. in Biology, Ill. State U., Normal, 1973; m. Barbara Dale Clay, Dec. 16, 1972; children—Heather Dale, Christopher Keith, Shawna Rose. Devel. technician Lauhoff Grain Co., Danville, 1973-76; instrument analyst A. E. Staley Mfg. Co., Decatur, Ill., 1976-78, asst. chemist, 1978-79, tech. supr., 1979-81, quality control coordinator Des Moines oil refinery, 1981—. Aux. policeman City of Georgetown (Ill.), 1972-74. Mem. Staley Tech. Soc. (exec. com. 1981—). Republican. Developed gas chromatographic method of determining residual hexane in corn and soybean oil. Home: 418 34th St West Des Moines IA 50265 Office: 1940 E Hull Ave PO Box 3071 Des Moines IA 50316

TUCKER, JOYCE ELAINE, lawyer, state human rights adminstr.; b. Chgo., Sept. 20, 1948; d. George M. and Vivian Louise T.; B.S., U. Ill., Urbana, 1970; J.D., John Marshall Law Sch., 1978. Substitute tchr. Chgo. Public Schs., 1970-71; mental health specialist Tinley Park (Ill.) Dept. Mental Health, 1970-74; coordinator Title VII Program, Ill. Dept. Mental Health, Chgo., 1974-76, chief mental health equal employment opportunity officer, 1976-79; acting dir. Ill. Dept. Equal Employment Opportunity, Chgo., 1979-80; dir. Ill. Dept. Human Rights, Chgo., 1980—; admitted to Ill. bar, 1980. Mem. Nat. Bar Assn., Cook County Bar Assn. (Spl. Achievement award 1980), Am. Bar Assn., Chgo. Bar Assn. Mem. African Methodist Episcopal Ch. Office: 179 W Washington St Chicago IL 60601

TUCKER, KENNETH LESLIE, comml. real estate developer; b. Chgo., Apr. 29, 1932; s. Samuel and Mildred (Sonshine) T.; B.S., Roosevelt U., 1954; m. Verba Powell, Apr. 30, 1972; children—Sheryl, Michele, Richard. Partner, Kenroy, Inc., Chgo., 1955-76, pres., 1976; pres., chief exec. officer Ken Tucker & Assos., Skokie, Ill., 1976—. Trustee, Nat. Jewish Hosp., 1978—. Served with USNR, 1950-52. Recipient Torch award City of Hope, 1969; Golda Meier award, State of Israel, 1973. Mem. Internat. Council of Shopping Centers (pres. 1972-73), Urban Land Inst. Jewish. Home: 3220 University St Highland Park IL 60035 Office: 4849 Golf Rd Skokie IL 60077

TUCKER, NICHOLAS JOEL, abrasives mfg. co. exec.; b. Evanston, Ill., Feb. 27, 1951; s. William Ruggles, Jr. and Janet (Boogher) T.; B.A., Monmouth (Ill.) Coll., 1973. Inside domestic sales and service rep. Buehler, Ltd., Evanston, Ill., 1974-77, sales engr., microstructural analyst, Milw., 1977-80; tech. sales rep. CBN products Diamond Abrasives div. Carborundum Co., Niagara Falls, N.Y., 1980-81, abrasive specialist abrasive mktg. N. Am. div., Chgo. regional office, 1981—. Asst. scout master Evanston chpt. Boy Scouts Am., 1967-68. Recipient Eagle Scout award Boy Scouts Am., 1967. Mem. Am. Soc. Metals, Soc. Mfg. Engrs., Abrasive Engrng. Soc., Zeta Beta Tau (chpt. treas., chmn. fin. com. 1972-73), Zeta Beta Tau Alumni Assn. (founding mem. Chgo. chpt.). Republican. Congregationalist. Home: 317 Nora Ave Glenview IL 60025

TUCKER, NORMA JEAN, coll. adminstr.; b. Harrah, Okla., Feb. 11, 1930; d. Jeff Lee and Mary Ellen (Ward) Redwine; B.A. in English, McPherson (Kans.) Coll., 1967; M. Liberal Studies, U. Okla., 1972; Specialist in Edn., Wichita State U., 1979; Ed.D. in Ednl. Adminstrn., U. Kans., 1979; m. Henry Vee Tucker, Dec. 27, 1958; children—Cynthia, Gloria, Pamela, Vanessa. Tchr. English, Buhler (Kans.) High Sch., 1968-71; instr. English and journalism McPherson Coll., 1971-72, asst. prof., dir. publicity, 1972-76, on-campus coordinator Small Coll. Consortium, 1976-77, asso. dean acad. affairs, 1977, dean of the faculty, 1978-81, v.p., 1981—. Pres., Women's Soc., United Methodist Ch., 1963-74. Mem. N.Central Assn. Acad. Deans, McPherson County Fedn. Women's Clubs (pres. 1961-62), P.E.O. Republican. Contbr. articles to profl. jours. and newspapers. Home: 1360 N Walnut St McPherson KS 67460 Office: 1600 E Euclid St McPherson KS 67460

TUCKER, STANLEY EUGENE, bank exec.; b. Liberal, Kans., Nov. 4, 1944; s. Stanley Eugene and Margaret McGinnis (King) T.; B.S. in Mgmt., Murray State U., 1969; m. Keirce Denton, Dec. 27, 1975; children—Michael Lee, Steven Davis. From trainee to controller supt. White Plains (N.Y.) office Aetna Casualty Ins. Co., 1967-72; from counselor to mortgage loan mgr. Avery Fed. Savs. and Loan, Louisville, 1972-81; v.p./loan officer Citizens Bank & Trust Co., Jeffersonville, Ind., 1981—. Bd. dirs. United Way, 1978-80; active Christ Meth. Ch., mem. choir, youth basketball coach; treas. Westmoorland Twp., 1974-76; dir. econ. devel. fund raising Jefferson County Schs., 1979-80. Mem. Louisville Homebuilders Assn., Louisville Condominium Council (asso.), Murray State U. Alumni Assn., Kappa Alpha, Order Ky. Cols. Saxophone player, singer with The Original Tren-dells, 1972-78. Home: 817 Forrest Dr N Sellersburg IN 47172 Office: 460 Spring St Jeffersonville IN 47172

TUCKER, THOMAS GILMORE, regional planning agy. exec.; b. Cape Girardeau, Mo., Feb. 11, 1941; s. Thomas Gilmore and Emma Catherine (Blechle) T.; B.S. in Geography and English, Murray State U., 1967; postgrad. in planning So. Ill. U., Edwardsville, 1967-68; m. Brenda Lou Coy, July 17, 1976; children—Cynthia Lyn Preston, Amy

Catherine. Chief phys. planning East-West Gateway Coordinating Council, St. Louis, 1968-70; exec. dir. S.E. Mo. Regional Planning and Econ. Devel. Commn., Perryville, 1970—; mem. Mo. Gov.'s Adv. Council for Govtl. and Community Services Program, 1975—. Served with USN, 1960-64. Cert. planner-in-charge, Mo. Mem. Mo. Assn. Councils Govt. (vice chmn. exec. dir.'s com.), Am. Legion, Amvets, Internat. City Mgmt. Assn. Roman Catholic. Club: K.C. Author numerous planning reports. Office: 1 W St Joseph St Perryville MO 63775

TUCKER, THOMAS RANDALL, engine co exec.; b. Indpls., Aug. 6, 1931; s. Ovie Allen and Oris Aleen (Robertson) T.; A.B., Franklin Coll., 1953; m. Evelyn Marie Armuth, Aug. 9, 1953; children—Grant, Roger, Richard. Grad. asst. U. Minn., 1953-54; dir. admissions, registrar Franklin Coll., 1954-57; trainee Cummins Engine Co., Inc., Columbus, Ind., 1957-58; supr. community relations, 1958-61, mgr. community relations, 1961-64, mgr. pub. relations, 1964-68, dir. pub. relations, 1968—. Mem. Bd. Sch. Trustees Bartholomew County, Ind., 1966-72, pres., 1968-69; chmn. Bartholomew County Sch. Reorgn. Com., 1964-65; chmn. legislative com. Ind. Sch. Bd. Assn., 1970-71; mem. gen. commn. Ind. State Bd. Edn., 1977—; treas. Bartholomew County Republican Central Com., 1960-80; bd. dirs. Bartholomew County Hosp. Found., 1966-70, pres., 1968; trustee Franklin Coll. Recipient Distinguished Service award Columbus (Ind.) Jr. C. of C., 1965; named One of Five Outstanding Young Men, Ind. Jr. C. of C., 1965. Mem. Pub. Relations Soc. Am., Columbus C. of C., Kappa Tau Alpha, Phi Delta Theta, Sigma Delta Chi. Lutheran. Rotarian. Home: 4380 N Riverside Dr Columbus IN 47201 Office: 1000 5th St Columbus IN 47201

TUDOR, DAVID FREDERICK, lawyer; b. Franklin, Ind., Dec. 22, 1948; s. Lester Leon and Margaret (Wetzel) T.; B.S. in Edn., Ind. U., 1974; J.D., Ind. U.-Indpls. Sch. Law, 1980. With corps. div. Office Sec. State of Ind., 1968; intern, reporter supreme and appellate cts., Indpls., 1969; adminstrv. analyst, research div. Ind. Dept. Revenue, Indpls., 1969, chief auditor, inheritance tax div., 1973-75, asst. adminstr., motor fuel tax div., 1975-77, adminstr. motor fuel tax div., 1977-81; admitted to Ind. bar, 1980; asst. dir. tourism div. Ind. Dept. Commerce, Indpls., 1971, adminstrv. officer div. of planning, 1972; gov. central region N. Am. Gasoline Tax Conf., 1979, exec. com., 1980-81, nat. sec., 1981. State chmn. Ind. Coll. Rep. Fedn., 1970-71; exec. sec. Ind. Young Rep. Fedn., 1971-73; youth activities chmn. Citizens for Carl T. Curtis for U.S. Senator (Nebr.), 1972; mem. exec. com. Young Rep. Nat. Fedn., 1973-75; del. White House Conf. on Youth, 1970; vice chmn. Westfield (Ind.) Bd. Zoning Appeals. Mem. Am. Bar Assn., Nat. Taxpayers Union, Am. Conservative Union, Ind. State Bar Assn., Ind. U. Alumni Assn., Delta Theta Phi, Kappa Delta Rho. Club: Westfield Lions. Home: PO Box 584 Westfield IN 46074 Office: 224 Beechwood Dr Westfield IN

TUFTS, WALTER DAVID, steel co. exec.; b. Cleve., Oct. 16, 1944; s. Elbert and Lelia Beatrice (Williams) T.; A.A., Cuyahoga Community Coll., 1974; student Cleve. State U., 1976—. Relief supr. U.S. Steel, Cleve., 1973-77, sales rep., 1978—. Youth choir dir. Open Door Bapt. Ch., Cleve., 1969—, bldg. and planning bd. chmn., 1972-77, chmn. trustee bd., 1975-77. Served with USAF, 1965-69. Decorated Air Force Commendation medal. Mem. S.E. Cleve. Jr. C. of C. (dir. pub. relations 1970-77). Address: Open Door Bapt Ch 3562 E 140th St Cleveland OH 44120

TUGANDER, DENNIS, broadcasting exec.; b. Bronx, N.Y., July 12, 1949; s. Morris P. and Frances E. T.; student Ohio State U., 1966-68; asso. degree in acctg. Lehman Coll., 1970; m. Diane F. Rinaldi, Sept. 13, 1970; children—Elisa Christine, Andrea Dawn, Laura Beth. Mut. funds adminstr. Bank of N.Y., 1968-70; acct., gen. ledger supr. CBS, Inc., N.Y.C., 1970-72, adminstr. acctg., 1972-74; fin. analyst WBBM-TV, Chgo., 1974-76, mgr. bus. affairs, 1976-78, mgr. budgets/forecasts, 1978-79, dir. bus. affairs, 1979—. Mem. citizens adv. com. E. Maine Twp. Sch. Dist. 63, 1977-78. Mem. Broadcast Fin. Mgmt. Assn., Am. Mgmt. Assn., Broadcast Credit Assn. Jewish. Club: Moose (Des Plaines, Ill.). Home: 8899 Grand St Niles IL 60648 Office: WBBM-TV 630 N McClurg Ct Chicago IL 60611

TULIS, ALLEN JOSEPH, chem. engr.; b. Cicero, Ill., Jan. 28, 1929; s. Anton Francis and Antoinette Amalia (Drtilek) T.; B.S. in Chem. Engring., Ill. Inst. Tech., 1955, B.S. in Math., 1958, M.S. in Chem. Engring., 1963, Ph.D. in Chem. Engring., 1981; m. Elinore Cathaline Maass, May 20, 1951. With Quakers Research Labs., Chgo., 1948; experimentalist Chgo. Vitreous Enamel Corp., Chgo., 1949-51; chem. engr. Inst. Gas Tech., Chgo., 1952-57; sr. chem. engr. Ill. Inst. Tech. Research Inst., Chgo., 1957—. Chmn., chmn. Internat. Pyrotechnics Seminars, 1980, 82. Served with AUS, 1951-52. Mem. Am. Inst. Chem. Engrs., Am. Chem. Soc., AIAA, Soc. Photo-Optical Instrumentation Engring., Internat. Pyrotechnics Soc. (treas.), Combustion Inst., Am. Def. Preparedness Assn., Air Force Assn., U.S. Naval Inst., Sigma Xi. Contbr. to publs. in field. Home: 174 N Country Club Dr Addison IL 60101 Office: 10 W 35th St Chicago IL 60616

TULLY, TERESA ELIZABETH LINNEMAN, computer programmer; b. Maryville, Mo., Mar. 16, 1948; d. Joseph William and Ethel Elizabeth (Edwards) Linneman; diploma Electronic Computer Programming Inst., 1966; m. Michael John Tully, June 2, 1973; 1 son, Cody Alan. Computer programmer R.H. Macy & Co., Kansas City, Mo., 1966-70; computer programmer Medco Jewelry Inc., Kansas City, 1971-72; sr. programmer/analyst McCall Pattern Co., Manhattan, Kans., 1974—. Continuing edn. unit cert., Am. Mgmt. Assn. Home: Rural Route 2 Box 370 Manhattan KS 66502

TUMA, ARTHUR TENNYSON, physician; b. Dickinson, N.D., May 13, 1913; s. John and Mary (Zahradnik) T.; B.S., Dickinson State Tchrs. Coll., 1936; M.S., Mont. State U., 1948; M.S., U. Nebr., 1953; M.D., Creighton U., 1957; m. Kathleen O'Connell, Sept. 25, 1942; children—Arthur D., Edwin D., Darcy O. Navigator, Pan Am. Ferries, Army Transport Command and Trans World Airlines, Washington, 1942-47; physicist AEC, Ames, Iowa, 1948-49; radiol. physicist U. Nebr. Coll. Medicine, 1949-61, instr., then asst. prof., 1950-61; intern Nebr. Meth. Hosp., 1957-58; resident U. Nebr. Coll. Medicine, 1958-61; asst. prof. radiobiology U. Miss. Sch. Medicine, radiologist VA Hosp., Jackson, Miss., 1961-63; practice medicine, specializing in radiology, Poplar Bluff, Mo., 1963—; chief of staff Poplar Bluff Hosp.; staff Ripley County Meml. Hosp.; cons. VA Hosp. Mem. Adv. Com. on Radiation Legislation Neb., 1958-60, Miss., 1961-63. Served with USNR, 1939-40, Diplomate Am. Bd. Radiology. Fellow Am. Geriatrics Soc. (founding); mem. Am. Coll. Radiology, A.M.A., Soc. Nuclear Medicine, U.S. Mil. Engrs., Mo. State, Quad-County (treas. 1964-66, v.p. 1966-67, pres. 1968) med. socs., Radiation Research Soc., Am. Coll. Nuclear Medicine (charter), Radiol. Soc. N. Am., Mo. Radiol. Soc. Address: 1601 Big Bend Rd Poplar Bluff MO 63901

TUMP, ROBERT LEE, mfg. co. exec.; b. Milw., Apr. 5, 1920; s. Adam A. and Hulda (Westphal) T.; evening student U. Wis., Marquette U.; m. Deloris R. Gerondale, May 10, 1947; children—Randall Keith, Ronald Scott. Stationery clk. Briggs & Stratton Corp., Milw., 1939-41, asst. traffic mgr., 1941-62, traffic mgr., 1962-73, corporate traffic mgr., 1973—. Served with AUS, 1943-46; ETO, PTO. Named Wis. Transp. Man of Yr., ICC Practitioners, 1978. Mem. Nat. Indsl. Traffic League, Wis. Met. Milw. Assn. Commerce, Transp. Club of Milw. (past pres.), Milw. Traffic Club (past pres.), Traffic Clubs Internat. (regional v.p.), Wis. Mfrs. and Commerce, Outdoor Power Equipment Inst. Home: 619 S 68th St Milwaukee WI 53214 Office: 3300 N 124th St Milwaukee WI 53201

TUNCA, JOSH COSKUN, physician; b. Istanbul, Turkey, July 19, 1943; came to U.S., 1968, naturalized, 1978; s. Ahmet and Hikmet Emine Tunca; M.D., Cerrahpasa Med. Sch., Istanbul, 1968; m. Nilgun Musoglu, May 1, 1970; 1 son, Alper. Intern, New Hanover Meml. Hosp., Wilmington, N.C., 1968-69; resident in obstetrics and gynecology Bowman-Gray Sch. Medicine, Wake Forest U., Winston-Salem, N.C., 1969-73, chief resident, 1972-73; fellow gynecol. oncology Emory U. Sch. Medicine, Atlanta, Ga., 1973-75; practice medicine specializing in obstetrics and gynecology, Morgantown, W.Va., 1975-77, Madison, Wis., 1977—; dir. gynecol. oncology W.Va. U. Sch. Medicine, 1975-77, asst. prof. obstetrics and gynecology, 1975-77; asst. prof. obstetrics and gynecology U. Wis., Madison, 1977—; mem. staff U. Wis. Center for Health Scis. Am. Cancer Soc. Jr. Faculty Clin. fellow, 1978-79; diplomate Am. Bd. Obstetrics and Gynecology. Mem. Wis. State Med. Soc., Am. Soc. for Colposcopy and Colpomicroscopy, Dane County Obstetrics and Gynecology Soc., AMA. Contbr. articles in field to med. publs. Home: 101 Acadia Dr Madison WI 53717 Office: 600 Higland Ave Madison WI 53792

TUNKS, FREDERICK EDWARD, editor; b. Center Point, Iowa, Feb. 2, 1928; s. Frederick Charles and Lovon Ann (Robertson) T.; B.S. in Tech. Journalism, Iowa State U., 1953; m. Ruth Ann Beckman, June 14, 1953; children—Brian, Lynne, Karen. News editor Independence (Iowa) Newspapers, 1953-54, Monticello (Iowa) Express, 1954-59; markets editor, news editor, mng. editor Feedstuffs, Miller Pub. Co., 1976—, chmn. photography, graphic and editorial coms., 1960—; pres. Tunks, Inc., Mpls. Chmn. promotion com. New Hope (Minn.) Indsl. Commn., 1969-70. Served in USN, 1946-49. Mem. Nat. Agri-Mktg. Assn., Am. Bus. Press, Livestock Merchandising Inst. (trustee), Minn. Press Club, Sigma Delta Chi, Alpha Zeta, Alpha Gamma Rho. Republican. Presbyterian. Clubs: Lions (Monticello); Downtown Kiwanis (Mpls.); Hopewood Internat. Friendship (New Hope); Dairy Shrine (life). Home: 8416 39th Ave N New Hope MN 55427

TUNNEY, JAMES LAWRENCE, JR., appraisal co. exec.; b. Dayton, Ohio, Apr. 20, 1932; s. James Lawrence and Dorothy Ada (Waxler) T.; B. Mech. Engring., Gen. Motors Inst., 1955; M. Engring., U. Dayton, 1972; m. Paula Marie Stelzer, June 14, 1958; children—Susan Marie, James Lawrence III. Supr. test sect. Inland div. Gen. Motors Co., Dayton, 1950-62; v.p. James R. Ahart & Assos., Cons. Engrs., Dayton, 1962-70; mgr. data processing Philips Industries, Inc., Dayton, 1970-74; dir. systems Dayton Press Inc., Dayton, 1974-78; product mgr. Printing Composition Systems, Dayton Sci. Inc., 1978-80; data processing mgr. Sabre Systems and Service Inc., Dayton, 1980—. Mem. Montgomery County Bicentennial Planning Com., 1975-78. Served with U.S. Army; 1956. Registered profl. engr., Ohio. Mem. Assn. Systems Mgmt. Democrat. Roman Catholic. Home: 1636 Spaulding Rd Dayton OH 45432 Office: 900 Meadows Manor Dayton OH 45459

TUOKKO, GEORGE TAPANI, elec. engr.; b. Tempere, Finland, Jan. 24, 1948; came to U.S., 1950, naturalized, 1962; s. Kauno and Kerttu Anne T.; B.S.E.E., Purdue U., 1970; m. Leona Jean, Feb. 14, 1970; children—Timothy George, Matthew James. With Dormeyer Industries, Chgo., 1973—, chief engr., 1977—. Mem. IEEE. Lutheran. Home: 3716 Lee Ave Waukegan IL 60085 Office: 3418 Milwaukee Ave Chicago IL 60641

TUPPER, KENT PHILLIP, lawyer; b. Huron, S.D., July 24, 1931; s. Ezra Lynn and Mildred Virginia (Nason) T.; B.A., U. Minn., 1956; J.D., William Mitchell Coll. Law, St. Paul, 1963; m. Joan McGinley, Dec. 18, 1954; children—Kent Michael, Kay Maria. Indsl. psychologist Chrysler Corp., 1956; ins. claims adjuster and supr. Hardware Mut. Ins. Co., 1957-63; admitted to Minn. bar, 1963, also U.S. Supreme Ct.; pvt. practice, Mpls., 1963-67; dir. legal services project Leech Lake Indian Reservation, 1967-69, chmn. legal services bd., 1969-80; partner firm Tupper Smith and Mattson Ltd., Walker, Minn., 1969—. Tchr. comml. law Am. Inst. Banking, 1972; part-time instr. Indian studies Bemidji (Minn.) State Coll., 1973—; cons. Native Am. Tech. Assistance, Tri-State Indian Community Action Project; evaluator legal services project OEO. Chmn., Shingobee Twp. Democratic Farmer Labor party, 1972, del. Minn. State Conv., 1972. Served with USMC, 1951-53. Mem. Minn., Cass/Hubbard County (pres. 1970-78), 15th Dist. bar assns., Am. Legion, Smithsonian Assos., Tupper Family Assn. Am. Episcopalian. Home: PO Box 146 Walker MN 56484 Office: PO Box 160 Walker MN 56484

TURBEVILLE, GUS, coll. pres.; b. Turbeville, S.C., Jan. 20, 1923; s. William Jasper and Ila Lucile (Morris) T.; B.A., Vanderbilt U., 1944; M.A., La. State U., 1946; Ph.D., Mich. State U., 1948; m. Joanne Beverly Johnson, June 7, 1950; children—David Baxter, William Jackson II, Sara Ellen. Head dept. sociology U. Minn., Duluth, 1948-53; pres. Northland Coll., Ashland, Wis., 1953-61; chmn. dept. sociology and anthropology U. Wis., Superior, 1962-69; pres. Coker Coll., Hartsville, S.C., 1969-74, Emerson Coll., Boston, 1975-78, William Penn Coll., Oskaloosa, Iowa, 1979—. Past bd. dirs. St. Joseph's Hosp., Superior, Mus. Cartoon Art, Port Chester, N.Y. Served with U.S. Army, 1943. Named one of Ten Outstanding Young Men, U.S. Jaycees, 1958, Man of Yr., Ashland, Wis., 1958. Mem. Am. Sociol. Assn., Assn. on Smoking and Health. Quaker. Author: (with T. Lynn Smith) Social Problems, 1955; If You Smoke, What Have You?, 1972; contbr. articles to various jours. Office: William Penn Coll Oskaloosa IA 52577

TURCK, BETTY (ELIZABETH), nurse; b. Holdingford, Minn., July 14, 1938; d. Ernest Mathew and Teresa (Kulig) Smith; R.N., St. Cloud (Minn.) Hosp. Sch. of Nursing, 1958; student St. Cloud State U.; m. William Turck, June 1, 1963; children—Michael Thomas, Brian John, Daniel Edwin, Annemarie. Nurse, St. Cloud Hosp., 1958-59, charge nurse ENT-Urology, 1960-63, ICU-ER, 1963-67, evening nursing service supr., 1967-71, head nurse emergency out-patient dept., 1971-76, dept. head EOP, 1976—, mem. Emergency Med. Care Coordinating Com., 1968—, emergency out-patient med. staff com., 1976—, code blue com., 1977—, product rev. com., 1979—; pediatric staff nurse St. Francis Hosp., Colorado Springs, Colo., 1959-60; staff nurse Melrose (Minn.) Hosp., 1960. Mem. adv. com. on child abuse and neglect Minn. Dept. of Health, 1976-77; mem. Stearns-Benton child abuse and neglect team, 1977—, chmn., 1978-79; mem. gov.'s emergency med. tech. adv. task force, 1974-76; mem. Central Minn. Area Vocat. Inst. EMT and paramedic task force, 1975—; mem. Central Minn. Health Systems Agy. Emergency Med. Services, 1978—; mem. adv. council Stearns County Emergency Med. Services, 1979—. Vice pres. St. Cloud Parents Without Partners, 1974, treas., 1975; bd. dirs. Divorce Awareness program, 1975-78; mem. task force Central Minn. Task Force for Battered Women, 1976—, bd. dirs., 1978—; bd. dirs. Rape Crisis Center, 1977—. Mem. Emergency Dept. Nurses Assn. (state coordinating council 1977—, chmn. 1980-81, sec.-treas. 1978-80), Censota Emergency Dept. Nurses Assn. (pres. 1976-79), Greater Twin Cities Emergency Dept. Nurses Assn. (dir. 1974-76). Roman Catholic. Club: St. Monica's Christian Women. Home: 719 4th St S Sauk Rapids MN 56379 Office: 1406 6th Ave N Saint Cloud MN 56301

TURCOTTE, JEREMIAH GEORGE, physician, educator; b. Detroit, Jan. 20, 1933; s. Vincent Joseph and Margaret Campau (Meldrum) T.; B.S. with high distinction, U. Mich., 1955, M.D. cum laude, 1957; m. Claire Mary Lenz, July 5, 1958; children—Elizabeth Margaret, John Jeremiah, Sarah Lenz, Claire Meldrum. Intern, U. Mich. Med. Center, 1957-58, resident, 1958-60, 61-63; practice medicine specializing in gen. surgery and transplantation, Ann Arbor, Mich., 1963—; mem. faculty dept. surgery U. Mich., Ann Arbor, 1963—, instr., 1963-65, asst. prof., 1965-68, asso. prof., 1968-71, prof., 1971—, chmn. dept. surgery, head sect. gen. surgery, 1974—; mem. sci. adv. bd. Mich. Kidney Found., 1965-81. Recipient Henry Russell award Regents U. Mich., 1970. Diplomate Am. Bd. Surgery. Fellow ACS; mem. Internat. Transplantation Soc., Soc. Surgery Alimentary Tract, Am. Soc. Transplant Surgeons (pres. 1979-80), Frederick A. Coller Soc. (pres.-elect 1981-82), Am. Trauma Soc., Am., Central, Western surg. assns., Soc. Univ. Surgeons, Transplantation Soc. Mich. (pres. 1973-75). Roman Catholic. Mem. editorial bd. Current Surgery, Am. Jour. Surgery; contbr. articles to profl. jours. Home: 769 Heatherway St Ann Arbor MI 48104 Office: 1405 E Ann St Ann Arbor MI 48109

TURCOTTE, MARGARET JANE, nurse; b. Stow, Ohio, May 17, 1927; d. Edward Carlton and Florence Margaret (Hanson) McCauley; R.N., St. Thomas Hosp., Akron, Ohio, 1949; m. Rene George Joseph, Nov. 24, 1961 (div. June 1967); 1 son, Michael Lawrence. Mem. nursing staff St. Thomas Hosp., 1949-50; pvt. duty nurse, 1950-57; polio nurse Akron's Children Hosp., 1953-54; mem. nursing staff Robinson Meml. Hosp., Ravenna, Ohio, 1958-67, head central service, 1963-67; supr. central service Brentwood Hosp., Warrensville Heights, Ohio, 1967, also CPR instr., emergency med. technician. Mem. St. Thomas Hosp. Alumni Assn. Democrat. Roman Catholic. Home: 6037 Highview St Lot 14-F Ravenna OH 44266 Office: 4110 Warrensville Center Rd Warrensville Heights OH 44122

TUREK, STEPHEN, computer specialist; b. St. Louis, Nov. 18, 1941; s. Raymond and Helen Rose (Puzniak) T.; Ph.D., U. Mo., 1972; m. Tarvi Ann Hermann, Aug. 7, 1965. Instr., U. Mo., 1969-73; programmer LTV Aerospace Co., 1973-74; sci. programmer Senturion Scis. Co., Tulsa, 1974-75; systems analyst Kansas City (Mo.) Municipal Ct., 1975-78; sr. data base analyst Hallmark Cards, Kansas City, 1978—. Mem. Math. Assn. Am., Friends of Earth, Phi Delta Kappa. Republican. Home: 7328 Walnut St Kansas City MO 64114 Office: 2501 McGee St Kansas City MO 64108

TURK, FREDERICK GEORGE, educator; b. Cleve., Feb. 11, 1938; s. George and Mary (Huber) T.; B.S., Cleve. State U., 1960; M.A., Case-Western Res. U., 1964; Ph.D., Cath. U. Am., 1974; m. Kay Mae Laswell, Jan. 20, 1968; children—Daniel John, Gregory James, David Matthew, Naomi Jean. Instr., D.C. Tchrs. Coll., Washington, 1969-72; edn. evaluator, OAS, Quito, Ecuador, 1972-74; ednl. planner UNESCO, Santiago, Chile, 1974-75; prof. Universidade Fed. Fluminense, Niterói, Rio de Janeiro, Brazil, 1976-79; prin., dir. religious edn. St. Andrew Parish, Rock Falls, Ill., 1980—; tchr. trainer AID, Guiné-Bissau, W. Africa. Mem. audit adv. com. Sauk Valley Coll. Mem. Comparative and Internat. Edn. Soc., Assn. Supervision and Curriculum Devel., Jean Plaget Soc. Roman Catholic. Author: Teaching Methods, 1975; Inferential Statistics Applied to Educational Problems, 1975; Activities of Piaget for Students of First Year Primary, 1979. Home: 3301 A St Rock Falls IL 61071 Office: St Andrew Parish 701 11th Ave Rock Falls IL 61071

TURKIEWICZ, CAMILLE JOANNE, ednl. adminstr.; b. Chgo.; d. Sigmund and Irene Turkiewicz; student Wright Jr. Coll., 1956, St. Louis Inst. Music, summer, 1956; B.S. in Edn., Northwestern U., 1959, M.A., 1966, postgrad., 1969-76; postgrad. Art Inst. Chgo., 1960-62. Tchr., Wilmette (Ill.) public schs., 1960-66; instr. students, adminstrs. and parents Northwestern U. Demonstration Sch., Evanston, Ill., 1961-67; instr. extension grad. level Nat. Coll. Edn., Evanston, Lombard, Oak Park and River Forest, Ill., 1966—; instr. extension div. Northeastern Ill. U., Chgo. and Elmwood Park, Ill., 1967-80; asst. prin. Mills Sch., Elmwood Park, 1970-77; instr. human potential program Success Motivation Inst., Elmwood Park Schs., 1975-77; exec. dir. instrn. Lombard (Ill.) public schs., 1977—; conf./workshop speaker, 1961—; real estate investor, 1967—. Bd. dirs. Nat. Coll. Edn., 1979—; rep. Waterford Condominium Assn. to environ. div. City of Chgo., 1974-75. Mem. Assn. for Supervision and Curriculum Devel., Ill. Assn. for Supervision and Curriculum Devel. (pres. west suburban br. 1982-83), Internat. Reading Assn., Nat. Council Tchrs. Math., Assn. for Childhood Edn. Internat., Glenbard Curricular Council, DuPage County Curriculum Developers, Phi Delta Kappa, Pi Lambda Theta, Pi Mu. Home: 665 Lake Rd Glen Ellyn IL 60137 Office: 150 W Madison Dr Lombard IL 60148

TURNBULL, CHARLES VINCENT, hosp. adminstr.; b. Mpls., May 13, 1933; s. Charles Vivien and Lucille Frances (Dallas) T.; B.A. in Sociology, U. Minn., 1960, M.S.W., 1962; m. Gloria Marlene Tilley, July 21, 1956; children—Charlene Kay, Charles Vincent, Terry Lucille, Mary Marlene. Unit dir. mental health treatment service Cambridge (Minn.) State Hosp., 1962-67, dir. rehab. therapies, 1967-68, program dir., 1973-74; program dir. Minn. Valley Social Adaptation Center, St. Peter, 1968-73; chief exec. officer Faribault (Minn.) State Hosp., 1974—: program cons. Rochester (Minn.) Social Adaptation Center, 1970-71; cons. St. Louis State Sch. and Hosp., 1973-74. Chmn., United Fund Drive, St. Peter, 1971; scoutmaster Boy Scouts Am., 1973-75; co-chmn. Faribault Bicentennial Horizons Subcom., 1975-76; mem. Minn. Developmental Disabilities Planning Council, 1975, chmn. comprehensive planning subcom., 1977-78; chmn. Cannon River Adv. Council, 1978-79; pres. Riverbend Nature Center, 1981—; mayor Village of Lexington (Minn.), 1962-64; candidate for U.S. Ho. of Reps. from 2d Dist. Minn., 1972, 74. Served with USMC, 1953-56. Mem. Assn. Retarded Children, Am. Assn. Mental Deficiency. Mem. Democratic-Farm-Labor Party. Lutheran. Home: Route 3 Faribault MN 55021 Office: Faribault State Hosp Faribault MN 55021

TURNBULL, GUY ANTHONY, chem. co. design mgr.; b. Rock Island, Ill., July 4, 1944; s. Glenn Owen and Eleanore Genevieve Turnbull; B.F.A. in Indsl. Design, U. Ill., Urbana, 1971; m. Jane Ann Kenney, July 29, 1968; children—Brian William, Jennifer Anne. With Dow Chem. Co., Midland, Mich., 1971—, indsl. designer, 1971-74, design coordinator, 1974-76, package coordinator, 1976-78, sr. package coordinator, 1978-80, mgr. design, 1980—. Served with AUS, 1966-69. Mem. Chem. Mfrs. Assn., Packaging Inst., Chem. Mfrs. Com. Roman Catholic. Patentee bottle design. Office: 2030 Dow Center Midland MI 48640

TURNER, ALLEN MARK, lawyer; b. Chgo., June 27, 1937; s. Myer H. and Madeline G. (Gross) T.; B.B.A., U. Wis., 1958; J.D., U. Chgo., 1961; m. Lynn Sharon Bernberg, Mar. 22, 1959; children—Jennifer Ellen, Christopher Marshall Richard. Admitted to Ill. bar, 1961; since practiced in Chgo.; mem. firm Portes & Green, 1961-64; partner Pritzker & Pritzker, 1965—; dir., chmn. exec. com. Hyatt Internat.

Corp., 1965—; dir., sec., gen. counsel Agrow Industries, Inc., 1965—; chmn. bd. McCall's mag., Working Mother Mag.; dir. McCalls Pub. Co. Lectr. philosophy Chgo. Sch. for Gifted, 1960-61; instr. Chgo. Police Acad., 1966-68. Bd. dirs. Jewish Welfare Fund Met. Chgo., Am. Jewish Com., Jewish Student Service Com.; chmn. bd. dirs. Goodman Theater, Art Inst. Chgo., 1980—, Chgo. Theater Group, 1980—, Victory Gardens Theater, 1975-79. Jewish Fedn. Chgo. travel grantee, 1965. Recipient Glasser award, 1969. Mem. Am., Chgo. bar assns. Club: Standard (Chgo.). Home: 521 Stratford Pl Chicago IL 60657 Office: 2 First Nat Plaza Chicago IL 60670

TURNER, ARTHUR EDWARD, coll. adminstr.; b. Hemlock, Mich., Jan. 31, 1931; s. Alvin S. and Grace E. (Champlain) T.; B.S. (Silliman scholar), Alma (Mich.) Coll., 1952; M.Ed., Wayne State U., 1954; postgrad. Central Mich. U., U. Mich.; LL.D., Ashland Coll., 1968; H.U.D., Colegio Americano de Quito, Ecuador, 1968; m. Johann M. Jordan, May 10, 1953; children—Steven Arthur, Michael Scott, Kathryn Jo. Admissions counselor Alma Coll., 1952-53, dir. admissions, alumni relations, 1953-59; Presbyn. lay minister, 1956-59; organizer Eastminister Presbyn. Ch., Alma, 1956; co-founder Northwood Inst., Alma, 1959, with campuses at Midland, Mich., Cedar Hill, Tex., West Baden, Ind., Quito, Ecuador (extension center), and Bloomfield Hills (Mich.) Acad. (now Bloomfield U. Sch.) (affiliated 1971), 1st pres., 1959-74, chmn., chief exec. officer, trustee, 1974-78, chmn. bd. trustees 1978—. Mem.-at-large Nat. council Boy Scouts Am.; elder Meml. Presbyterian Ch., Midland, 1964—. Recipient People of Peru award, 1966; named One of Ten Outstanding Young Americans, 1965. Mem. Alpha Psi Omega, Phi Phi Alpha. Clubs: Masons (33 deg.), Shriners, Rotary; Detroit; Midland Country; Beach, Poinciana (Palm Beach, Fla.). Home: 4608 Arbor Dr Midland MI 48640 Office: Northwood Inst Midland MI 48640

TURNER, CARL ADAMS, mfg. co. exec.; b. Columbus, Miss., Sept. 21, 1951; s. Roosevelt and Beatrice Estelle T.; B.S. in Bus. Adminstrn., Tenn. State U., 1973; postgrad. Gen. Motors Inst., 1973-74; m. Alfreda Poole, Sept. 24, 1977. Prodn. supr. Buick div. Gen. Motors Corp., Flint, Mich., 1973-74; employee relations mgmt. trainee Gen. Electric Co., Louisville, Erie, Pa., Cin., 1974-77; labor relations supr. Quaker Oats Co., Memphis, 1977-79, employee and community relations mgr., Omaha, 1979—. Active Boy Scouts Am., Big Bros. Mem. Am. Soc. Personnel Adminstrn., Am. Soc. for Tng. and Devel. Democrat. Baptist. Home: 3112 N 77th St Omaha NE 68134 Office: 302 Pierce St Omaha NE 68103

TURNER, FRED L., fast food restaurant co. exec.; b. 1933; B.S., De Paul U., 1952; married. With McDonald's Corp., Oak Brook, Ill., 1956—, exec. v.p., 1967-68, pres., chief adminstrv. officer, 1968-77, chmn. bd., chief exec. officer, 1977—, also dir. Served as 1st lt. U.S. Army, 1943-45. Office: McDonald's Corp One McDonald's Plaza Oak Brook IL 60521*

TURNER, GERALD ALLEN, engring. co. exec.; b. Cleve., Feb. 11, 1948; s. Rudolph Allen and Betty Jean T.; A.S. in E.E. (scholar), Cuyahoga Community Coll., 1968; B.S. in E.E. (scholar), Cleve. State U., 1976; M.B.A., Baldwin-Wallace Coll., 1981. Elec. engr., transmission and distbn. engring. dept. Cleve. Electric Illuminating Co., 1968-78, research and devel. dept., 1977-78; instr. electronics engring. tech. Cuyahoga Community Coll., Cleve., 1976—; instr. electronic tech., elec. power systems design Cleve. State U., 1980—; research cons., instr. parapsychology and biofeedback phenomena New Age Centre, Toronto, Ont., Can., 1978-79; prin., partner Turner & Knight Cons. Engrs., Cleve., 1979—. Served with USN, 1970-71. Registered profl. engr., Ohio. Mem. Nat. Soc. Profl. Engrs., IEEE, Cleve. Engring. Soc., Inst. for Certification Engring. Technicians, Nat. Tech. Assn. Lutheran. Home: 17722 Tarkington Ave Cleveland OH 44128 Office: 24200 Chagrin Blvd Cleveland OH 44122

TURNER, GLENN EVERETT, supt. schs.; b. Plymouth, Nebr., Aug. 10, 1903; s. William A. and Mary (Gerth) T.; student Cotner Coll., 1921-22, Nebr. Wesleyan U., 1922; A.B., U. Nebr., 1933, A.M., 1948, Ph.D., 1959; m. Elizabeth Loos, Dec. 26, 1933; 1 son, Roger. Tchr. public schs., Jefferson County, Nebr., 1922-23, Swanton, Nebr., 1923-24; supt. schs., Garrison, Nebr., 1927-28, Rokeby, Nebr., 1929-40; dir. Nebr. Nat. Youth Adminstrn., 1940-42; supt. schs., Lancaster County, Nebr., 1942—. Pres. Lancaster County Activities Assn., 1932-33, Lincoln (Nebr.) Inter-Civic Council, 1950-51; bd. dirs. Lincoln-Lancaster County Tb Assn., Nebr. State Sch. Bd. Assn., Kiwanis Found. of Lincoln. Recipient Nash Nat. Conservation award, 1953; Merit award DAR, 1965; Kiwanis Vocat. Guidance award, 1966. Mem. NEA (life), Nebr. Acad. Scis. (life), Nebr. State Hist. Soc., Nebr., Am. assns. sch. adminstrs., Lincoln C. of C. (dir.), Nebr. State, Lancaster County (pres. 1930-31) edn. assns., Govtl. Research Inst., Internat. Platform Assn., Phi Delta Kappa. Republican. Conglist. Clubs: Nebr. Schoolmasters, Masons, Scottish Rite (venerable master 1950-51), Shriners (chaplain 1973); Kiwanis (lt. gov. Nebr.-Iowa div. 1965); Order Eastern Star (patron 1969); Lincoln Dinner (sec.-treas. 1951-63), Hiram (pres. 1971), Knife and Fork (pres. 1948-49) (Lincoln). Home: 5030 Washington Lincoln NE 68506 Office: 3234 S 13th St Lincoln NE 68502

TURNER, HARRY EDWARD, state legislator; b. Mt. Vernon, Ohio, Dec. 25, 1927; s. Paul Hamilton and Harriett Ewalt (Kraft) T.; B.A., Baldwin-Wallace Coll., 1951; J.D., Ohio No. U., 1954; m. Shirley Marilyn Eggert, July 8, 1950; children—Harry Edward, Thomas Frederick. Admitted to Ohio bar, 1954; prosecutor Mt. Vernon Mcpl. Ct., 1955-58; solicitor City of Mt. Vernon, 1958-62; pres. Mt. Vernon Bd. Edn., 1964-70; mem. Ohio Ho. of Reps., 1973—. Served with USN 1946-47. Mem. Am., Ohio, Knox County bar assns., Mt. Vernon Area C. of C. (dir. 1973). Home: 400 E Vine St Mount Vernon OH 43050 Office: 118 E High St Mount Vernon OH 43050

TURNER, HERMAN NATHANIEL, JR., educator, mathematician; b. St. Louis, Nov. 6, 1925; s. Herman Nathaniel and Rosie Mae (Williams) T.; B.S., Bradley U., Peoria, Ill., 1951; m. Terrance Diane Parker, Oct. 5, 1980; children by previous marriage—Anthony, Mark, Herman Nathaniel III, Erik; stepchildren—Marian, Mariesta and Melita Simmons. Cartographic aide Aero. Chart and Info. Center, St. Louis 1953-54; mathematician White Sands Proving Ground, N.Mex., 1954-55; tchr. math., Caruthersville, Mo., 1961-62, Phila., 1956-59, East Moline, Ill., 1965-66, N.W. High Sch., St. Louis, 1968—. Served with USMC, 1944-46. Named Tchr. of Yr., N.W. High Sch., 1980; cert. math. tchr., Mo., Ill., N.Y., Pa., N.J.; recipient cert. of appreciation Kiwanis Club of East Moline, 1965; named Tchr. of Month, N.W. High Sch., 1979. Fellow Internat. Biog. Assn., Am. Biog. Inst.; mem. Math. Assn. Am., Am. Math. Soc., Am. Fedn. Tchrs. Democrat. Presbyterian. Club: East Moline Kiwanis. Home: 5917 Emma Ave Saint Louis MO 63136 Office: Northwest High School 5140 Riverview Blvd Saint Louis MO 63120 also PO Box 1028 Saint Louis MO 63188

TURNER, LARRY MORGAN, health and safety exec.; b. Mansura, La., Oct. 9, 1946; s. John Carlton and Edar-belle (Blackman) T.; B.S., Western Ky. U., Bowling Green, 1969; m. Martha Ann Johnson, July 29, 1978; 1 dau., Litisha. Materials supply team mgr. Procter & Gamble Paper Products Co., Cape Girardeau, Mo., 1975-76, Pampers prodn. team mgr., 1976-77, health and safety mgr., 1978-80, Pampers prodn. dept. mgr., 1980—; recruiting coordinator So. U., 1978—. Served with Q.M.C., U.S. Army, 1969-74. Decorated Bronze Star medal; recipient Mfg. Safety award Procter & Gamble Paper Products, 1978; award of honor Nat. Safety Council, 1978. Club: Action for Community Equality Mens Fraternal. Home: 1655 N Spanish St Cape Girardeau MO 63701

TURNER, THOMAS BEDFORD, mgmt. cons.; b. N.Y.C., July 1, 1921; s. John Pickett and Anna Maria Augusta (Zemke) T.; B.E. in Elec. Engring., Yale U., 1942; m. Sally Ann Chambliss, Apr. 18, 1954; children—Thomas Bedford, Henry Hill. With Gen. Electric Co., N.Y.C., 1946-58, with AMLI div. McGraw Edison Co., Cin., 1958-64; asst. mgr. mdse. devel. Montgomery Ward, Inc., Chgo., 1964-66; mgmt. cons. A.T. Kearney, Inc., Chgo., 1966-73; gen. mgr. indsl. products div. Am.-Standard Co., Dearborn, Mich., 1973-74; pres. Midwest div. Case & Co., Inc., 1974—, also dir. Served as lt. (j.g.) USNR, 1943-46. Cert. mgmt. cons. Mem. Inst. Mgmt. Cons., Am. Mgmt. Assn., AAAS, Newcomen Soc., N.Am., Chgo. Council on Fgn. Relations, Assn. for Corp. Growth, Phi Gamma Delta. Clubs: Chgo.; Kenilworth. Office: 2109 Prudential Plaza Chicago IL 60601

TURNER, TIMOTHY D., educator; b. Circleville, Ohio, Apr. 17, 1955; s. Coy W. and Donna J. Cupler; B.S., Ohio State U., 1977. Instr. vocat. agr. East Guernsey Local Schs., Old Washington, Ohio, 1977, Bloom Carroll (Ohio) Local Schs., 1978—; tchr., adv. Future Farmers Am. Mem. Jr. County Fair Bd., 1979—, County Coop. Extension Bd., 1979—. Mem. Ohio Vocat. Agr. Tchrs. Assn., Am., Ohio vocat. assns., Fairfield County Agr. Tchrs. Assn. (pres. 1979—). Mem. Christian Ch. Home: 928 Washington Ave Lancaster OH 43130 Office: Beaver St Carroll OH 43112

TURNER, TIMOTHY THOMAS, physician; b. Kansas City, Mo., Jan. 12, 1947; s. Thomas Arthur and Elizabeth Ann (Egy) T.; A.B., U. Kans., 1968; M.A., U. Mo., Kansas City, 1969; D.O., Univ. for Health Scis., Kansas City, Mo., 1973; m. Cherilyn Louise Hamilton, June 5, 1971; children—Stephen Alex, Stephanie Alicia. Intern, Hillcrest Hosp., Oklahoma City, 1973-74; practice family medicine, Tulsa, 1974-75; pres. Emergency Med. Assos., Tulsa, 1976—; chmn. dept. family practice St. Charles (Mo.) Clinic, 1975-77; emergency physician Christian Hosps.-N.W., St. Louis, 1977—, med. dir. Recovery Center, 1981—; advanced cardiac life support instr. Am. Heart Assn., 1979—. Diplomate Nat. Bd. Med. Examiners, Am. Bd. Family Practice. Fellow Am. Acad. Family Physicians; mem. Am. Coll. Emergency Physicians (councillor nat. council 1976—), Mo. Med. Assn., St. Louis Met. Med. Soc. Republican. Home: 273 Pennington Ln Chesterfield MO 63017 Office: Christian Hosp-NW 11133 Dunn Rd Saint Louis MO 63136

TURNER, VIRGINIA KELLEY (MRS. RICHARD TURNER), media specialist; b. Riverside Calif., Apr. 22, 1919; d. William Eugene and Myrtle Edith (Johnson) Kelley; A.A., Riverside Jr. Coll., 1938; student U. Calif. at Santa Barbara, 1938-40; B.A., Lake Forest Coll., 1954; postgrad. Oriel Coll., Oxford (Eng.) U., summer, 1965; M.A., No. Ill. U., 1967; m. Richard Turner, Feb. 2, 1939; children—Lawrence Kelley, Renee Dorothy (Mrs. Thomas Becker). Tchr. Mundelein (Ill.) Dist. 75, 1948-59, librarian, 1959-70; media coordinator Lincolnshire Prairie View Dist. 103, Prairie View, Ill., 1970—, coordinator instructional services; spl. Ill. grantee for reading program, STEPP metric curriculum; chmn. library groups Area Insts., 1968, 71. Mem. A.L.A., N.E.A., Assn. for Communication and Ednl. Tech., Am. Assn. Sch. Librarians (div. ednl. media and materials), Ill. Edn. Assn., Ill. Audio Visual Assn., Ill. Library Assn., Lake County Curriculum Resource Council (sec. 1978-80). Club: McHenry (Ill.) Country. Home: 3117 Riverstream Dr McHenry IL 60050 Office: Adminstrv Center Dist 103 Prairie View IL 60069

TURNQUIST, DANA DEE, personnel adminstr.; b. Crosby, Minn., Nov. 15, 1943; d. Robert Louis and Valerie June (Lefebvre) Vranish; student U. Minn., Duluth, 1961-63, 74-79; m. Kenneth E. Turnquist, Sept. 14, 1963; children—Christopher Paul, Brett Eric. Dir. Youth Activities Center, Goeppingen, Germany, 1966-67; office mgr. Hickory Lodge, Crosby, 1968; adminstrv. asst. to pres. Key Finders, Inc., St. Paul, 1976-77; personnel adminstr. Gray, Plant, Mooty, Mooty & Bennett, Mpls., 1978—, United Way coordinator, 1978-80. Mem. Minn. Legal Office Adminstrs. Assn. (v.p.), Am. Bus. Women's Assn., Assn. Legal Adminstrs. Lutheran. Home: 3040 Devonshire Dr Woodbury MN 55125 Office: Gray Plant Mooty Mooty Bennett 300 Roanoke Bldg Minneapolis MN 55402

TURRELL, EUGENE SNOW, psychiatrist; b. Hyattsville, Md., Feb. 27, 1919; s. Homer Bassett and Frances Isabelle Glass Turrell; B.S., Ind. U., 1939, M.D., 1947; children—David Hillyer, Gregory Sherman (dec.). Research asst. Ind. U., 1939-41, research asso., 1943-47; research asso. Harvard U., 1941-43; intern Peter Bent Brigham Hosp., Boston, 1947-48; resident physician Kankakee (Ill.) State Hosp., 1948-49, Langley Porter Clinic, San Francisco, 1949-50; psychoanalytic trainee Chgo. Inst. Psychoanalysis, 1960-67; clin. asst. psychiatry U. Calif., San Francisco, 1949-51; asst. prof. psychiatry Ind. U. Sch. Medicine, 1952-53; chief psychiat. consultation service Robert W. Long Hosp., Indpls., 1952-53; asso. prof. psychiatry U. Colo. Sch. Medicine, 1953-58, asst. dean, 1956-57; med. dir. Colo. Psychopathic Hosp., 1953-54; dir. psychiat. services Denver Gen. Hosp., 1957-58; cons. Denver Area Welfare Council, Children's Protective Services, 1956-58; prof., chmn. dept. psychiatry Marquette U. Sch. Medicine, 1958-63, clin. prof. psychiatry, 1963-69; dir. psychiat. services Milw. Sanitarium Found., 1958-69; cons. Columbia Hosp., Milw. Children's Hosp., Hosp. Mental Diseases, Milwaukee County Hosp., VA Hosp., Milw., 1958-69; sr. psychiatrist Center Spl. Problems, San Francisco, 1969-70, dir., 1970-75; lectr. psychiatry U. Calif., San Francisco, 1969-75; mem. cons. faculty Calif. Sch. Profl. Psychology, 1972-75; cons. Human Rights Commn., San Francisco, 1973-75; staff psychiatrist Midtown Community Mental Health Center, Indpls., 1975—; asso. prof. psychiatry Ind. U. Sch. Medicine, Indpls., 1975—; attending physician William N. Wishard Meml. Hosp., Indpls., 1975—, Univ. Hosp., Indpls., 1975—; mem. bd. dirs. Community Addictions Services Agy., Indpls., 1975-79, pres. bd., 1976-77. Served to lt. USNR, 1950-52. Recipient certs. of appreciation Office Sci. Research and Devel., 1945, VA, 1964, Ind. U. Found., 1966. Diplomate Am. Bd. Psychiatry and Neurology. Fellow Am. Psychiat. Assn. (Physician's Recognition award 1978, 79); mem. AMA (Physician's Recognition award 1978, 79), AAAS, Ind. State Med. Assn. (Disting. Mem. 1968-82), Ind. Psychiat. Soc., Marion County Med. Soc., Sigma Xi, Alpha Omega Alpha. Democrat. Episcopalian. Contbr. articles in field to profl. jours. Home: 4000 N Meridian St 6A Indianapolis IN 46208 Office: 1001 W 10th St Indianapolis IN 46202

TURRIFF, CLARENCE JOSEPH, chem. co. exec.; b. Green Bay, Wis., Apr. 22, 1920; s. Charles Henry and Dorinda (Quatsoe) T.; B.S., St. Norbert Coll., 1941; m. Gladys Cecelia Hoenslaar, Apr. 30, 1942; children—Barbara Ann (Mrs. Frederick Shiple III), Thomas Joseph, Susan Clare (Mrs. Harry Leichtman), Terry Lynn, Mary Lee. Buyer, McKesson & Robbins, Inc., Chgo., 1946-48; br. mgr. McKesson Chem. Co., Chgo., 1948-53, dist. mgr., 1953-58; pres., chief exec. TAB Chem. Inc., Chgo., 1958—, owner, chief exec. officer, 1979—; dir. 1st Nat. Bank Western Springs. Served to maj. AUS, 1941-46. Mem. Chgo. Drug and Chem. Assn. (dir. 1963—, pres. 1970). Republican. Roman Catholic. Club: LaGrange (Ill.) Country. Home: 102 Rugeley Rd Western Springs IL 60558 also 228 Live Oak Ln Sugar Mill Country Club Estates New Smyrna Beach FL 32069 Office: 4801 S Austin Ave Chicago IL 60638

TURZINSKI-DUROVY, PATRICIA ANN, personal mgmt. cons.; b. Milw., Nov. 11, 1950; d. Richard James and Doris L. (Smith) Turzinski; student U. Wis., Milw., 1968-69; m. David Michael Durovy, June 25, 1978. Supr. mortgage servicing A.L. Grootemaat & Sons, Milw., 1969-72; legal sec. firm Honeck, Mantyh & Arendt, Milw., 1973; adminstrv. sec. Plastronics Inc., Milw., 1973; mgr. mortgage servicing Universal Mortgage Co., Milw., 1973-74; mgr. Outpost Natural Foods Coop., Milw., 1974-76; owner Genesis, Milw., 1976—; owner, nat. dir., trainer Manifestation Mgmt., Inc., Milw., 1978—; founder Women's Resource Network, 1980—. Bd. dirs. Tai Chi Chuan Center Milw., 1967—; notary public, 1972—. Mem. Rebirth Internat., Am. Soc. Tng. and Devel., Am. Bus. Women's Assn., Nat. Assn. Female Execs., Theta Internat. (co-dir. 1978-80). Author tapes in field. Address: 2437 N Booth St Milwaukee WI 53212

TUSCHMAN, JAMES MARSHALL, steel co. exec., lawyer; b. Toledo, Nov. 28, 1941; s. Chester and Harriet (Harris) T.; B.S. in Bus., Miami U., Oxford, Ohio, 1963; J.D., Ohio State U., 1966; m. Ina S. Cheloff, Sept. 2, 1967; children—Chad Michael, Jon Stephen, Sari Anne. Admitted to Ohio bar, 1966, since practiced in Toledo; partner firm Shumaker, Loop & Kendrick, 1966—; chmn. bd., sec. Tuschman Steel Co., Toledo, 1969-76; vice chmn. bd. Kripke Tuschman Industries, Inc., 1977—; chmn. bd., sec. Toledo Steel Supply Co., 1969—; dir. Superior Cos. Inc., Ft. Wayne, Ind., PIE Mut. Ins. Co., Toledo; partner Starr Ave. Co., Toledo. Mem. Am. (com. law and medicine), Ohio, Toledo bar assns., Nat. Assn. R.R. Trial Counsel, Def. Research Inst., Soc. Hosp. Attys., Zeta Beta Tau, Phi Delta Phi. Jewish (past trustee, v.p., treas. temple). Clubs: Glengary Country, Toledo. Home: 5240 Coldstream Rd Toledo OH 43623 Office: 1000 Jackson St N Courthouse Sq Toledo OH 43624

TUTCHER, CHERYL APPLETON, sch. adminstr.; b. St. Paul, Feb. 7, 1948; d. Robert L. and Elizabeth (O'Neil) Appleton; B.S., Eastern Ill. U., 1972; M.S., No. Ill. U., 1978, Ed.D., 1981; 1 dau., Danielle. Jr. high sch. math. tchr., Overbrook, Kans., 1972-73; elem. tchr., asst. prin. North Sch., Des Plaines, Ill., 1973-79; research asst. Sch. Bus. Mgmt., No. Ill. U., DeKalb, 1979-80, adminstrv. asst., asso. provost, 1980; instr. bus. mgmt., 1979—; bus. mgr. North Chicago Community High Sch., 1980—; workshop instr. classroom mgmt. Nat. Coll., Evanston, Ill., 1978—. Mem. Ill. Assn. Sch. Bus. Ofcls. (workshop coordinator, energy com. co-chmn. 1979-80), Ill. Fin. Acctg. Com.-Sch. Bus. Mgmt., Ill. Women Adminstrs. (charter mem., regional dir. 1978--), Nat. Assn. Women Deans and Counselors, Assn. for Supervision and Curriculum Devel., Ill. Assn. for Supervision and Curriculum Devel., Kappa Kappa Gamma, Phi Delta Kappa, Sigma Sigma Sigma Alumni. Republican. Methodist. Club: Chicago Health. Asst editor state newsletter Ill. Assn. Sch. Bus. Ofcls., 1979-80. Home: 711 Ravine Dr Lake Bluff IL 60044 Office: North Chicago Community High Sch 1717 17th St North Chicago IL 60064

TUTEUR, MURIEL FRIEDMAN, day care adminstr.; b. Chgo., May 17, 1922; d. Morris and Jeanette (Hirschenbein) Friedman; A.B. in Sociology, U. Chgo., 1943; M.S. in Urban Edn. and Early Childhood Edn., Chgo. State U., 1979; m. Charles Anthony Tuteur, Nov. 1, 1942; children—Judith, Peter. With U.S. Steel Works, Chgo., 1942-43, Kaiser Shipyard, Vancouver, Wash., 1943-44; case work aide Cook County (Ill.) Bur. Pub. Welfare, 1946-49; tchr., dir. Hyde Park Jewish Community Center Pre-Sch., Chgo., 1954-59; dir. Garden Valley Jewish Community Center Pre-Sch., Chgo., 1959-70, Amalgamated Child Day Care and Health Center, Chgo., 1970—; lectr. U. Chgo., Oakton Community Coll.; guest lectr. U. Ill.; mem. adv. com. on day care Ill. Dept. Children and Family Services, 1975-80; mem. adv. com. Midwest Women's Center, 1977-79; del., mem. adv. com., chmn. child care work group Ill. White House Conf. on Families, 1980; convenor Ill. Labor Conf. on ERA; bd. dirs. Harper Square Child Care Center, 1973—, Day Care Action Council, 1977-80; Project 1979). Served with WAC, 1944-45; planner, organizer Harper Sq. Child Care Center, 1972-73, bd. dirs., 1973—. Mem. Chgo. Assn. Edn. Young Children (v.p. for program 1978-79), Nat. Assn. Edn. Young Children, Ill. Assn. Edn. Young Children, Day Care and Child Devel. Council Am., Day Care Crisis Council Chgo. Area, Amalgamated Clothing and Textile Workers Union, Coalition of Labor Union Women (steering com. Chgo. chpt. 1974-77, 81, pres. Chgo. chpt. 1977-80, mem. nat. exec. bd. 1977—, co-chmn. nat. child care task force 1977—), Nat. Council Jewish Women, NOW (Outstanding Woman in Ill. award ERA Ratification mem. adv. bd. dept. child devel. Chgo. City-Wide Coll., 1979—; mem. steering com. campaign Child Day Care for Working Families, 1980—; mem. hon. bd. Day Care Action Council Ill., 1980; mem. pre-sch. adv. com. Chgo. State U., 1978-79; mem. steering com. Ill. Women's Agenda, 1980—; mem. adv. bd. Center for Social Policy and Research, U. Ill., Chgo., 1980; mem. adv. com. child devel. program Human Services Inst., City Colls. Chgo., 1978—; mem. nat. implementation task force White House Conf. on Families, 1980; mem. adv. com. Jane Addams Center for Social Policy Research, U. Ill., Chgo., 1980—. Jewish. Home: 1438 W Pratt Blvd Chicago IL 60626 Office: 323 S Ashland Blvd Chicago IL 60607

TUTHILL, JAMES GATES, mfg. co. exec.; b. Chgo., Nov. 12, 1926; s. Gray Butler and Natlan (Gates) T.; B.S., U.S. Mil. Acad., 1948; m. Florence Severance Tornquist, July 28, 1948; children—Sue, James, Ann. With Tuthill Corp., Chgo., 1953-77, Oak Brook, Ill., 1977—, pres., dir., 1955—; dir. Beverly Bank. Served with U.S. Army, 1948-53. Mem. Hydraulic Inst. Republican. Episcopalian. Clubs: Chgo. Athletic Assn., Hinsdale Golf; Econ. (Chgo.). Office: 1415 W 22d St Oak Brook IL 60521

TUTINS, ANTONS, electronics engr.; b. Ludza, Latvia, May 2, 1933; s. Francis and Veronika (Seipulniks) T.; came to U.S., 1950, naturalized, 1963; B.S. in Elec. Engring., Ill. Inst. Tech., 1970; M.B.A., U. Chgo., 1974; m. Raita Snebergs, July 8, 1961; 1 son, Robert. Mfg. mgr. Communications div. Motorola Inc., Chgo., 1964-73; applications engring. supr. Knowles Electronics Inc., Franklin Park, Ill., 1973-77, product engring. mgr., 1977—. Served with USN, 1955-57. Mem. Audio Engring. Soc., Chgo. Audio and Acoustical Group (pres. 1977-78), IEEE, Motorola Engring. Club (pres. 1970-71), Acoustical Soc. Am., Am. Soc. for Quality Control, Midwest Acoustics Exec. Com. (pres. 1980), Latvian Cath. Student Assn. Dzintars (pres. 1979—), Am. Latvian Cath. Assn. (sec. 1975-77). Roman Catholic. Home: 1338 Briar Ct Des Plaines IL 60018 Office: 3100 N Mannheim Rd Franklin Park IL 60131

TUTTLE, JAMES CHARLES, lawyer; b. Des Moines, Mar. 14, 1943; s. Emil Ries and Vera (Sadler) T.; B.S.B.A., Drake U., 1965, J.D., 1967; M.P.A., U. Pitts., 1969; m. Sue Ellen Ball, Dec. 20, 1964; children—Addison L., Jefferson C., Vanessa J. Admitted to Iowa bar, 1967, Mich. bar, 1969, D.C. bar, 1979, N.Y. bar, 1981, U.S. Supreme Ct. bar, 1971, U.S. Customs Ct. bar, 1971; atty. S.S. Kresge Co., Troy,

Mich., 1968—, antitrust and internat. counsel K-mart Corp., 1977—. Internat. Consular Acad. fellow, 1972—. Mem. Am. Bar Assn. (vice chmn. internat. law sect. 1975-80, mem. council 1972—, chmn. internat. legal exchange com. 1979-81), Detroit Bar Assn., Customs and Internat. Trade Bar Assn. Author articles on internat. legal subjects. Editor-in-chief Comml. Treaty Index, 1972, 74, Internat. Law News, 1972-73, Internat. Human Rights: Law and Practice, 1978; co-editor Internat. Ct. Justice Opinion Briefs, 1978. Home: Bloomfield Hills MI 48013 Office: Legal Dept K-mart Corp 3100 W Big Beaver Rd Troy MI 48084

TUTTLE, LINDA LOU, real estate broker; b. McBain, Mich., Apr. 24, 1940; d. Lewis Earl and Vonda Virginia (Cavanagh) Corner; ed. spl. courses Central Mich. U., Ferris State Coll., U. Mich., H. & R. Block income tax course; m. Kenneth Charles Tuttle, July 25, 1971; children by previous marriage—Pamela Rae Friess, Bryce Allen Friess. Sales supr. Sandra Co., 1968-73; sales rep. Avon Products, 1968-77; owner small bus. and individual tax service, 1975—, also real estate sales rep. Accent, Cadillac, Mich., 1977—. Sec.-treas. Cadillac Nursery Sch., 1964, bd. dirs. 1967-68; sec. Franklin PTA, 1969, pres., 1970; active Pal Program, 1972. Mem. Paul Bunyan Realtors Bd. Assn., Cadillac Bus. and Profl. Women. Lutheran. Home: 10901 N Diamond Rd Tustin MI 49688 Office: Parkview Palza Harris St Cadillac MI 49601

TUTTLE, MICHAEL DONALD, educator, author; b. Lansing, Mich., Nov. 6, 1940; s. Donald A. and Harriet Janet (Ristau) T.; A.A., Lansing Community Coll., 1968; B.A., Mich. State U., 1969, M.B.A., 1970; m. Bonnie Marie Kreger, June 25, 1960; children—Kevin John, Tod Alan. Designer, checker Reo div. White Motor Co., Lansing, 1958-60; designer Transicold Corp., Lansing, 1960; sr. layout man Oldsmobile div. Gen. Motors Corp., Lansing, 1960, 61-68, 71; instr. bus. adminstrn. St. Clair County Community Coll., Port Huron, Mich., 1971—; author; books include: Practical Business Math, 1978; (with others) Accounting—A Basic Approach, 1981; speaker profl. assns. Sperry Found. grantee, 1974, 77. Mem. Am. Mktg. Assn., NEA, Mich. Higher Edn. Assn., Distributive Edn. Clubs Am. Republican. Lutheran. Club: South Park Lions. Home: 4614 Lapeer St Port Huron MI 48060 Office: 323 Erie St Port Huron MI 48060

TUTTLE, RALPH TYMESON, contractor; b. Baraboo, Wis., June 2, 1950; s. Ralph T. and Adeline (Slaby) T.; student U. Wis., Sauk County, 1968-69, 69-70, Madison, 1970-71; m. Kathleen A. Haller, June 14, 1975. Carpenter, O.A. Erlandson Constrn. Co., Baraboo, 1968-71; draftsman Valley of Epernay, Spring Green, Wis., 1972; pres. Ralph T. Tuttle Inc., Baraboo, 1973—. Mem. Wis. Bldg. Assn. Home: 233 11th St Baraboo WI 53913 Office: Box 315 Baraboo WI 53913

TUTTLE, VALERIE GALE, radio sales exec.; b. Trion, Ga., Apr. 29, 1946; d. Samuel D. and A. Marie (Bowling) Nix; B.A., Wayne State U.; m. James H. Tuttle, Jan. 18, 1974. Media buyer Ross Roy Advt., Detroit, 1973-75; div. mgr. ABC Radio Spot Sales, Detroit, 1975-77; nat. sales mgr. Sta. WXYZ Radio, Detroit, 1978-81; account exec. Sta. WDIV-TV, Detroit, 1981; v.p., Detroit region mgr. Hillier, Newmark & Wechsler Radio Sales, Birmingham, Mich., 1981—. Mem. Adcraft Club Detroit, Econ. Club Detroit, Am. Mgmt. Assn., Detroit Radio Advt. Group (past sec.). Office: 30800 Telegraph Rd Suite 1922 Birmingham MI 48010

TWEEDY, ROBERT HUGH, equipment co. exec.; b. Mt. Pleasant, Iowa, Mar. 24, 1928; s. Robert and Olatha (Miller) T.; B.S. in Agrl. Engring., Iowa State U., 1952; m. Genevieve Strauss, Aug. 15, 1969; children—Bruce, Mark; 1 stepdau., Mary Ellen Francis. Sr. engr. John Deere Waterloo Tractor Works, Waterloo, Iowa, 1953-64; mktg. rep. U.S. Steel Corp., Pitts., 1964-69; mgr. product planning agrl. equipment div. Allis-Chalmers Corp., Milw., 1969-76, mgr. strategic bus. planning Agrl. Equipment Group, 1976—. Chmn. agrl. research com. Farm and Indsl. Equipment Inst., Chgo., 1974-76, mem. safety policy adv. com., 1972—; mem. farm conf. Nat. Safety Council, Chgo., 1973—. Fellow Am. Soc. Agrl. Engrs. (v.p. 1974-78, pres. 1981-82, gen. chmn. hdqrs. bldg. project 1968-70); mem. Soc. Automotive Engrs. Mason. Patentee in field. Home: 1340 Bonnie Ln Brookfield WI 53005 Office: Allis-Chalmers Corp PO Box 512 Milwaukee WI 53201

TWELLS, DOUGLAS SINCLAIR, automotive parts mfg. co. exec.; b. Ferndale, Mich., June 6, 1924; s. Robert and Margaret (MacKillop) T.; student Ohio State U., 1942; grad. naval aviator U.S. Naval Tng. Coll., 1944; m. Nancy M. MacBurnie, Mar. 19, 1948; children—Bruce Stuart, Leslie Jean, Margaret Jane. Mgr. mfg. engring. Prestolite div. Eltra Corp., 1950-65; engr. div. staff equipment Essex Wire Corp., Detroit, 1965-73; mgr. facilities engring. Holley Carburetor div. Colt Industries, Warren, Mich., 1973-75, engring. dir. staff mfg., 1980—; dir. mfg. services Electro-Wire Products Inc., Troy, Mich., 1976-80. Served with USNR, 1942-45. Mem. ASME, Am. Soc. Metals. Home: 7241 Flamingo Rd Algonac MI 48001 Office: 11955 E Nine Mile Rd Warren MI 48090

TWELLS, JOHN LAWRENCE, mktg. and distbg. co. exec.; b. Flint, Mich., Feb., 1934; s. Robert and Margaret Shaw (MacKillop) T.; B.B.A., U. Toledo, 1957; postgrad. Marquette U., 1975; M.B.A., Columbia Pacific U., 1981; m. Mary Jane Jentzen, Nov., 1961; children—Linda, John Lawrence, Robert William. Lab., terr. mgr., nat. accounts rep. Motorcraft/Autolite div. Ford Motor Co., Dearborn, Mich., 1950-63; regional sales mgr. MOPAR div. Chrysler Corp., Detroit, 1963-67; asst. gen. mgr. NAPA Genuine Parts Co., Atlanta, 1967-68; gen. mgr. John MacKillop & Co., Inc., Poland, Ohio, 1968—; mgr. replacemnt parts Baker Material Handling Corp., a joint venture of Linde AG (W.Ger.) and United Technologies Corp., Cleve., 1976-78, gen. sales mgr. Amweld Bldg. Products div. Am. Welding & Mfg. Co., Niles, Ohio, 1978—; lectr. in field. Deacon, Immanuel Presbyterian Ch., Milw., 1974-76. Served with U.S. Army, 1957-59. Mem. Am. Inst. Indsl. Engring., Constrn. Specifications Inst., Sales and Mktg. Execs. Internat., Am. Def. Preparedness Assn., Am. Legion, VFW. Republican. Club: Rotary. Contbr. articles on microfiche, inventory control, personnel selection, motivation and evaluation to profl. jours. Home: 8996 Sherwood Dr NE Warren OH 44484 Office: PO Box 5214 Poland OH 44514

TWETEN, MALCOLM STUART, state senator; b. Reynolds, N.D., Apr. 30, 1925; s. Sidney Martin and Olga (Syverson) T.; grad. high sch.; m. Helen June Gjelsness, 1951; children—Steven, Erik, William, Elizabeth, Margaret, Daniel, Jonathan. Pres., Tweten Enterprises, Inc.; Nokota Packers, Inc.; mem. N.D. State Senate. Recipient N.D. Agriculturist award N.D. State U., 1974, E. Traill Co. Soil Conservation award, 1976. Mem. Red River Valley Potato Growers Assn. (past dir.), Red River Valley Sugar Beet Growers Assn., Farm Bur. (past state dir.), N.W. Farm Mgrs. Greater N.D. Assn. Lutheran.

TWITCHELL, ERVIN EUGENE, constrn. co. exec.; b. Salt Lake City, Mar. 4, 1932; s. Irvin A. and E. Alberta (Davis) T.; student Brigham Young U., 1954, 55; B.A., Calif. State U., Long Beach, 1959; J.D., UCLA, 1966; m. Joyce Newey, Aug. 9, 1957; children—Laurie, Robert, David, Michael. Contracts adminstr. Rockwell-N. Am. Aviation, Seal Beach, Calif., 1966-68; sr. contracts adminstr. McDonnell Douglas Corp., Long Beach, 1968-73; in-house counsel Albert C. Martin & Assos., Los Angeles, 1973-77; admitted to Mich. bar, 1977; corp. counsel, asst. sec. Barton-Malow Co., Detroit, 1977—; instr. bus. law Golden West Coll., Huntington Beach, Calif., 1973-74. Pres., Corona Musical Theatre Assn., 1976; mem. Internat. Visitors Council Met. Detroit, Inc.; dist. chmn. North Trails dist. Boy Scouts Am., 1978-80; various lay leadership positions Mormon Ch. Served with USAF, 1950-52; Korea. Mem. Am. Bar Assn., Am. Trial Lawyers Assn., Mich. Bar Assn., Oakland County Bar Assn., Detroit Bar Assn., Detroit EEO Forum. Republican. Home: 4069 Middlebury Dr Troy MI 48098 Office: Barton-Malow Co 13155 Cloverdale St Oak Park MI 48237

TWOMBLY, GERALD HENRY, coll. adminstr.; b. York, Maine, Dec. 25, 1944; s. Merrill Everett and Minita Florence (Hawkes) T.; B.A., Miami (Fla.) Christian Coll., 1967; M.Div., Grace Theol. Sem., 1970; m. Sandra Lee Barry, June 18, 1966; children—Christopher Mark, Chad Matthew. Instr., Word of Life Bible Inst., Schroon Lake, N.Y., 1970-74; dir. Word of Life Inn, Schroon Lake, N.Y., 1971-73; dir. Internat. Christian Leadership Soc., Winona Lake, Ind., 1974-75; dir. alumni relations and extension ministries Grace Coll., Winona Lake, 1975—. Mem. Council of Advancement and Support Edn., Evang. Press Assn. Author: An Analytical Survey of the Bible, 1974; A Superman for a total Woman, 1978, Major Themes of the Minor Prophets, 1981; also resource booklets. Home: 304 5th St Winona Lake IN 46590 Office: Grace College and Seminary Winona Lake IN 46590

TYBOUT, ALICE MARIE, educator; b. Ann Arbor, Mich., Dec. 2, 1949; d. Richard Alton and Rita Harris (Holloway) T.; B.A. in Bus. Adminstrn., Ohio State U., 1970, M.A. in Consumer Behavior, 1972; Ph.D. in Mktg., Northwestern U., 1975. Academic counselor Coll. Adminstrv. Scis. Ohio State U., 1970-72; research asst. Northwestern U., Evanston, Ill., 1972-74, asst. prof. mktg. and transp., 1975-81, asso. prof., 1981—, J.J. Kellogg Research prof. Kellogg Grad. Sch. Mgmt., 1980-81; instr. bus. U. Chgo., 1974-75; cons. Charles River Assos. Sears Retailing scholar, 1969. Mem. Am. Mktg. Assn., Assn. Consumer Research. Mem. editorial bd. Jour. Mktg., 1979-81, Jour. Bus. Research, 1980—, Jour. Mktg. Research, 1981—; contbr. articles in field to profl. jours. Office: Department of Marketing 2001 Sheridan Rd Evanston IL 60201

TYER, TRAVIS EARL, librarian; b. Lorenzo, Tex., Oct. 23, 1930; s. Charlie Earl and Juanita (Travis) T.; B.S., Abilene Christian U., 1952; B.S. in L.S., N. Tex. State U., 1959; Ad.M. in L.S., Fla. State U., 1969, postgrad., 1969—; m. Alma Lois Davis, Nov. 6, 1951; children—Alan Ross, Juanita Linn. Librarian, tchr. pub. schs., Gail, Lubbock and Seminole, Tex., 1952-61; with Dallas Public Library, 1961-66, coordinator young adult services, 1962-66; library dir. Lubbock Public Library, 1966; library dir. Lubbock City-County Libraries, 1967-68; mem. faculty Grad. Library Sch., state personnel tng. officer Emporia (Kans.) State U., 1971-72; sr. cons. profl. devel., library devel. group Ill. State Library, Springfield, 1972-80; exec. dir. Gt. River Library System, Quincy, Ill., 1980—. Higher Edn. Act fellow, 1968-72. Mem. ALA (dir. Pub. Library Assn. 1974-79, dir. young adult services div. 1968-69), Continuing Library Edn. Network and Exchange (pres. 1977-78), Ill. Library Assn., Resource Sharing Alliance of West Central Ill. (pres. 1980—), Adult Edn. Assn., N. Tex. State U. Library and Info. Scis. Alumni Assn. (life). Democrat. Mem. Ch. of Christ. Club: Kiwanis. Contbr. articles to library periodicals and profl. jours. Home: 2 Aden Dr Quincy IL 62301 Office: 515 York St Quincy IL 62301

TYLER, ELISABETH WEIR, psychologist; b. Grand Junction Colo., May 29, 1912; B.A., Jamestown Coll., 1935; M.S., Drake U., 1951; M.A., Pepperdine U., 1965; m. Walter A. Tyler, 1937; 3 children. Dir. Fed. Edn. and Recreation Assn., LaMoure County, N.D., 1934-35; prin. Berlin (N.D.) High Sch., 1935-36; tchr. Gackle (N.D.) High Sch., 1936-37, Warren Harding Jr. High, Des Moines, 1949-50, East High Sch., Des Moines, 1950-53; young adult counselor Immanual Presbyn. Ch., Los Angeles, 1953-54, Des Moines Sch. System, 1954-72, Boggs Acad., Keysville, Ga., 1968-69; vol.-in-mission Wasatch Acad., Mt. Pleasant, Utah, also Sheldon Jackson Coll., 1980. Vol., United Presbyn. Ch., Presbyn. Hospitality House, Fairbanks, Alaska, 1972-73, Sheldon Jackson Coll., Sitka, Alaska, 1973-77, adj. prof.-counselor Semester-in-Spain program, 1977. Mem. Iowa, Des Moines ednl. assns., Am., Iowa, Des Moines personnel and guidance assns., Am. Sch. Counselors Assn., Iowa Psychol. Assn. (life), NEA (life), NAACP (life), Psi Chi. Home: The Studio 912 Mandan St Bismarck ND 58501

TYLER, LLOYD JOHN, lawyer; b. Aurora, Ill., May 28, 1924; s. Lloyd J. and Dorothy (Curtis) T.; B.A., Beloit Coll,, 1948; J.D., U. Mich., 1951; m. Inez Chappell Busener, Feb. 25, 1970; children by previous marriage—Barbara Miller, John R., Benjamin C., Robert B., Amy C. Admitted to Ill. bar, 1951; partner Tyler, Solomon & Hughes, Aurora, 1965—. Served with USAAC, 1943-46. Fellow Am. Bar Found.; mem. Ill. Bar Found. (dir. 1968-72, pres. 1972-75), Ill. Bar Assn. (gov. 1970-76, pres. 1978-79), Soc. Trial Lawyers. Contbr. articles to profl. jours. Home: 701 Fargo Blvd Geneva IL 60134 Office: PO Box 1425 Aurora IL 60507

TYLER, STEVEN LAWRENCE, ins. broker; b. Chgo., July 11, 1951; s. Arthur Lawrence and Phyllis Mae (Flanigan) T.; B.A. with distinction, DePauw U., 1973; M.B.A., St. Louis U., 1978; m. Carol Schleiffarth Tyler. Teller supr. First Nat. Bank, Champaign, Ill., 1973-74; personal banking rep. First Nat. Bank, St. Louis, 1974-76, Stadium br. mgr., 1976-78; ins. broker Tyler-Fletcher-Fink-Peterson, Ltd., Champaign, 1978—. Loaned exec. United Way of Greater St. Louis, 1976, mem. Speaker's Bur., 1977. Eagle Scout. Cert. ins. counselor. Mem. Ind. Ins. Agts. of Ill. (chmn. agy. mgmt. com. 1981-82), Aircraft Owners and Pilots Assn., Urbana (Ill.) C. of C. (edn. com. 1980-81), Champaign-Urbana Jaycees (fin. v.p. 1979-81, officer of yr. 1979-80, East region outstanding treas. 1979-80), Phi Delta Theta. Presbyterian. Club: Champaign-Urbana Kiwanis (dir. 1981-82). Home: 108 B Burwash Ave Savoy IL 61874 Office: PO Box 3660 Champaign IL 61820

TYLER, WILLIAM HOWARD, JR., advt. exec.; b. Elizabethton, Tenn., May 21, 1932; s. William Howard and Ethel (Schueler) T.; student Iowa State U., 1950-52, U. Iowa, 1952; A.B., U. Mo., 1958, B.J., 1958, M.A., 1966; m. Margery Ann Moss, Aug. 31, 1957; children—William James, Daniel Moss. Advt. mgr. Rolla (Mo.) Daily News, 1958-59; instr. U. Mo. Sch. Journalism, 1959-61; copywriter D'Arcy Advt. Co., St. Louis, 1961-64, v.p., copy dir., 1964-67; creative supr. Gardner Advt. Co., St. Louis, 1967-69; v.p., creative dir. D'Arcy-MacManus-Masius, St. Louis, 1969-77; sr. v.p., creative dir. Larson Bateman, Inc., Santa Barbara, Calif., 1977-80; v.p., creative dir. Frye-Sills/Y&R, Denver, 1980; v.p. advt. Pizza Hut, Inc., Wichita, Kans., 1980—. Bd. adjustment DesPeres (Mo.) City Govt., 1976-77. Served to 1st lt. USMCR, 1952-55. Mem. Mo. Newspapers Advt. Mgrs. Assn. (v.p. 1959), U. Mo./Columbia Alumni Assn. St. Louis (pres. 1969), Nat. U. Mo. Alumni Assn. (dir. 1969-70), Mensa, Kappa Tau Alpha, Alpha Delta Sigma, Phi Delta Theta. Episcopalian. Home: 715 Stage Coach St Wichita KS 67230 Office: 911 E Douglas St PO Box 428 Wichita KS 67201

TYRRELL, ROBERT EMMETT, JR., editor; b. Chgo., Dec. 14, 1943; s. Robert Emmett and Patricia (Rogers) T.; A.B. in Govt., Ind. U., 1965, M.A. in Am. History, 1967; m. Judy Mathews, Feb. 12, 1972; children—Patrick Daniel, Kathryn Mathews, Anne Elizabeth. Founder, editor The Alternative (later name changed to Am. Spectator), Bloomington, Ind., 1967—, editor-in-chief, 1967—; weekly columnist Washington Post; King Features syndicated columnist. Recipient Am. Eagle award Invest In Am., Inc., 1975, Jefferson award for Greatest Public Service Performed by an Am. 35 Yrs. or Under, Am. Inst. Public Ser., 1975; named 1 of 10 Outstanding Young Men for 1978, U.S. Jaycees. Clubs: Saturday Evening, Pumpkin Papers Irregulars, N.Y. Athletic. Contbr. articles to popular publs., including Harper's, Commentary, N.Y. Mag., Nat. Rev., Wall St. Jour., Washington Post, N.Y. Times; editor: Report on Network News' Treatment of 1972 Democratic Presidential Candidates, 1972, The Future That Doesn't Work: Social Democracy's Failures in Britain, 1975; author Public Nuisances, 1979. Office: 102 W Sixth St PO Box 1969 Bloomington IN 47402

TZANGAS, GEORGE JOHN, lawyer; b. Canton, Ohio, Oct. 1, 1930; s. John M. and Mary (Christian) T.; student Kent State U., 1948-50; B.S.C., Ohio U., 1952; J.D. (Univ. scholar), Washington and Lee U., 1956; m. Venus Mouskondis, Aug. 31, 1952; children—Marianne Tzangas Weiss, John Daniel, Byron George. Office mgr. Minerva (Ohio) plant U.S. Ceramic Tile Co., 1956-58; admitted to Ohio bar, 1957, U.S. Supreme Ct., 1979; individual practice law, Canton, 1957—; dir. numerous cos. Bd. dirs. numerous charitable corps.; co-founder, pres. World Wide Orthodox Renewal for Christ, Inc., Canton; trustee Canton Scholarship Found.; mem. world missions com., spiritual renewal com. Greek Orthodox Ch. of N. Am. and S. Am. Mem. Fed. Bar Assn., Am., Ohio State, Stark County bar assns., Ohio Acad. Trial Lawyers, Assn. Trial Lawyers, Assn. Trial Lawyers Am., Am. Arbitration Assn. (panel 1977), Christian Legal Soc., Phi Alpha Delta. Greek Orthodox. Author: Secrets of Life, 1971; (as John Christian) Have You Talked to Him?, 1974. Home: 1845 Dunkieth Dr NW Canton OH 44708 Office: 454 Citizens Savs Bldg Canton OH 44702

UBBELOHDE, ROBERT ALLEN, coll. dean; b. Sheboygan, Wis., Nov. 9, 1942; s. Robert August and Betty Jane (Heiling) U.; B.S. with honors, U. Wis., 1966, M.S., 1967; Ph.D., U. Wis., Milw., 1972; m. Susan Elise Ortwein, June 19, 1965; children—Donald, Robert. Vis. prof. U. Wis., Madison, summers 1973-75; asso. prof. edn. Memphis State U., 1975-76; asso. prof. edn., dean student devel. Earlham Coll., Richmond, Ind., 1976-81; dean student devel. Northland Coll., Ashland, Wis., 1981—. Sec., bd. dirs. Old Richmond (Ind.), 1975-76; bd. dirs. SPUR, 1978—; chmn. Ind. State Democrats for Ford, 1976. Mem. Assn. for Supervision and Curriculum Devel., Nat. Council for Social Studies, Phi Delta Kappa. Republican. Episcopalian. Contbr. sect. to book. Home: 717 6th Ave W Ashland WI 54806 Office: Northland College Ashland WI 54806

UBEL, JOHN REGINALD, engr., mcpl. ofcl.; b. St. Paul, Sept. 27, 1925; s. John and Ruth Evelyn (Nida) U.; ed. Menomonie (Wis.) public schs., Dunwoodie Indsl. Inst.; m. Mary Adella Lehr, Oct. 2, 1943; children—Heidi Marie, Dina Lee. Owner, Jack's Cafe and Restaurant, 1946-49; partner Ubel & Purvis Hardware, 1950-58; owner Ubel Service Co., 1958-63; pres. Woodward Elec., Inc., 1963-71; dir. utilities City of Menomonie, 1972—; owner Hill Terr Mobile Ct. Mem. Bd. Suprs. Village of Knapp, 1962-66, pres., 1965-69; mem. Dunn County Bd. Suprs., 1967-68; mem. Menomonie Bd. Edn., 1964-70. Registered profl. engr., Wis. Mem. Internat. Assn. Elec. Insps., Internat. Brotherhood Elec. Workers, Wis. Soc. Profl. Designers. Club: Rotary. Home: Box 67 Knapp WI 54749 Office: 800 Wilson Ave Menomonie WI 54751

UCA, LINDA MARIE, edn. center exec.; b. Cleve., Nov. 12, 1945; d. Paul Jacob and Mary (Tasse) U.; B.S., Bowling Green State U., 1966, postgrad., 1967-68. With Burroughs Corp., Cleve., 1969-73, Detroit, 1974—, mgr. Detroit Application Support Center, 1979-81; mgr. Detroit Edn. Devel. Center, 1981—. Mem. Assn. Computing Machinery. Democrat. Greek Orthodox. Home: 1740 Graefield Rd Birmingham MI 48008 Office: 1 Burroughs Pl Detroit MI 48232

UCHIMOTO, TADASHI TED, book binding and mailing firm exec.; b. Stockton, Calif., Feb. 3, 1918; s. Kometaro and Shitsu (Hanaoka) U.; grad. high sch., Hiroshima, Japan, Stockton; m. Hamako Oye, Feb. 11, 1943 (dec. Apr. 1966); 1 son, Dennis Den; m. 2d, Mitsu Miyazaki, Mar. 5, 1967. Founder, Gen. Mailing Service and Sales Co., Inc., Chgo., 1945—. Mem. Japanese Am. Assn. Chgo. (pres.), Chgo. Hiroshima Kenjinkai (pres.). Home: 5515 N Francisco Ave Chicago IL 60625 Office: 2620 W Washington Blvd Chicago IL 60612

UCKO, DAVID A., mus. adminstr.; b. N.Y.C., July 9, 1948; s. Lawrence L. and Helen H. U.; B.A., Columbia U., 1969; Ph.D., M.I.T., 1972; m. Barbara Alice Clark, Aug. 13, 1972; 1 son, Aaron Mark. Asst. prof. chemistry Hostos Community Coll., City U. N.Y., 1972-76; asst. prof. chemistry Antioch Coll., 1976-79, asso. prof., 1979; research coordinator Mus. Sci. and Industry, Chgo., 1979-80, sci. dir., 1981—. Woodrow Wilson fellow, 1969-70; NIH fellow, 1972; NSF, Nat. Endowment Humanities grantee. Mem. Am. Assn. Museums, Am. Chem. Soc., Royal Chem. Soc., AAAS, Sigma Xi, Phi Lambda Upsilon. Author: Living Chemistry, 1977; Basics for Chemistry, 1981; contbr. articles to profl. jours. Office: Mus Sci and Industry 57th St and Lake Shore Dr Chicago IL 60637

UDELL, BRUCE STEPHEN, life ins. co. exec.; b. Youngstown, Ohio, Feb. 3, 1951; s. Aaron J. and Norma R. Udell; B.S., U. Cin., 1973; m. Janet Regina Schwartz, Dec. 26, 1971; 1 son, Jeremy Eric. Agt., life underwriter N.Y. Life Ins. Co., Youngstown, 1973—; sec. Creative Fin. Services, Inc., Youngstown, 1976—. Mem. steering com. Youngstown Jewish Fedn. Young Leadership Group, 1977-78. Mem. Nat. Assn. Life Underwriters (Nat. Quality award 1979, dir. Youngstown), Million Dollar Round Table, Mahoning Valley Estate Planning Council, Am. Soc. Chartered Life Underwriters. Club: N.Y. Life Top. Club: B'nai B'rith (v.p.). Home: 7534 Buchanan Dr Youngstown OH 44512 Office: 1001 City Centre One Bldg East Fed Plaza Youngstown OH 44503

UECKER, ALBERT ELI, psychologist; b. Peru, Ind., Jan. 29, 1917; s. Herman Ludwig and Emma (Givler) U.; B.A., Minot (N.D.) State Coll., 1941; M.A., Columbia Tchrs. Coll., 1946; Ph.D., U. Minn., 1952; m. Cora Frances Dickerson, June 21, 1953; children—Kurt, Nancy, Eric. Psychologist, State Sch. and Hosp., Cambridge, Minn., 1951-54; chief psychologist Longcliff State Hosp., Logansport, Ind., 1956-57; asst. prof. U. No. Iowa, Cedar Falls, 1954-56, 57-59, asso. prof., 1959-62; clin. psychologist, coordinator clin. psychology VA Hosp., St. Cloud, Minn., 1962-66; clin. psychologist, neuropsychologist VA Med. Center, Fort Meade, S.D., 1966—. Mem. S.D. Commn. on Alcoholism, 1973-75, S.D. Bd. Examiners in Psychology, 1979-81. Served with USN, 1942-43. Mem. S.D. Psychol. Assn., Am. Psychol. Assn. Club: Rotary. Editorial referee Jour. Studies on Alcohol, 1975—. Office: 116B VA Med Center Fort Meade SD 57741

UECKER, JAMES CLYDE, engr.; b. Freeport, Ill., Jan. 26, 1942; s. Warren E. and Mary Elizabeth (Hawkins) U.; B.C.E., U. Ill., 1965; m. Barbara Jean Montford, June 30, 1962; children—Jennifer, Jason. Registered profl. engr., Ill. Asst. city engr., Elgin, Ill., 1965-70, dir. engring. and inspection, 1970-72; asso. Alstot, March and Assos., Des Plaines, Ill., 1972-74; pres. J. C. Uecker & Assos., Inc., Elgin, Ill., 1974—; v.p. Guillou & Uecker, Inc., Elgin and Springfield, Ill., 1981—. Mem. council Messiah Luth. Ch., 1970-73; bd. mgrs. Elgin YMCA, 1976—, pres. bd., 1977-79; trustee Midwest Coll. Engring., 1977-78. Mem. Ill. Soc. Profl. Engrs. (sec.-treas. 1974-76, pres. 1979—, nat. dir. 1977-81), ASCE, Am. Public Works Assn., Am. Water Works Assn., Ill. Inst. Traffic Engrs., U. Ill. Alumni Assn. (pres. local club 1977—). Club: Fox Valley Kiwanis (dir. 1975—). Home: 200 S Edison St Elgin IL 60120 Office: 450 Shepard Dr Elgin IL 60120

UEHLING, BARBARA STANER, univ. adminstr.; b. Wichita, Kans., June 12, 1932; d. Roy W. and Mary Elizabeth (Hilt) Staner; B.A. in Psychology, U. Wichita, 1954, Ph.D., 1958; M.A., Northwestern U., 1956; D.H.L. (hon.) Drury Coll., 1978; LL.D. (hon.), Ohio State U., 1980; children—Jeff, David. Mem. faculty, research fellow Emory U., 1964-69; mem. faculty Oglethorpe U., Atlanta, 1959-64; adj. prof. psychology U. R.I., 1969-71; mem. faculty Roger Williams Coll., 1970-71, acad. dean, 1972-74; dean arts and scis. Ill. State U., 1974-76; provost U. Okla., 1976-78, chancellor U. Mo., Columbia, 1978—; dir. Merc. Bancorp. Inc.; adv. dir. Merc. Trust Co.; dir. Meredith Corp. Bd. dirs. United Way, Columbia; trustee Carnegie Council for Advancement Teaching. NIMH fellow, 1966-69. Mem. Am. Assn. Higher Edn. (past pres.), Nat. Council on Ednl. Research (dir.), Am. Council on Edn. (dir.), Sigma Xi. Office: 105 Jesse Hall Univ Mo Columbia MO 65211

UFER, WILLIAM REX, agronomist; b. Wooster, Ohio, Mar. 8, 1939; s. William S. and Elizabeth (Snook) U.; student Ohio State U., 1957-59; B.S., Mich. State U., 1960; children—William R., R. Brent, Melanie R. With Soil Conservation Service, Ohio and Mich., 1956-64; farm planner Ufer Cert. Seed Co., Stryker, Ohio, 1964-70; gen. mgr. Vistron Corp., Lima, Ohio and Jackson, Mich., 1970—, cert. profl. agronomist, Lima, 1979—; owner, mgr. farm, Stryker, 1961—. Served with U.S. Army, 1962. Mem. Am. Soc. Agronomy, Am. Registry Cert. Profls. in Agronomy, Crops and Soils. Home: 1475 Edgewood Dr #5F Lima OH 45805 Office: PO Box 628 Lima OH 45802

UFFELMAN, ROY FREDERICK, mayor; b. Burlington, Iowa, Apr. 17, 1920; s. Roy Herman and Margaret Leah (Hodges) U.; A.A., Burlington Jr. Coll., 1940; m. Margaret Lucille Terry, Jan. 1, 1946; children—Donald Roy, Teri Annette. With Burlington (Iowa) Fire Dept., 1940-75; elec. contractor, Burlington, 1975-80; mayor City of Burlington, 1980—. Served with USNR, 1942-45, 48-50. Office: City Hall Burlington IA 52601

UGAN, CHESTER JOSEPH, mfg. co. exec.; b. Chgo., Feb. 25, 1938; s. Chester S. and Madeline A. (Shenert) U.; B.S. in Mech. Engring., Ill. Inst. Tech., 1961; m. Susan Behrmann, Oct. 6, 1962; children—Robert, David, Karen. Biomed. engr. Baxter Labs., 1959-62; sales engr. Honeywell, Inc., 1962-65; regional sales and applications engr. Rockwell, Inc., 1965-67; constrn. project planner Austin Co., 1967-70; regional sales mgr. Specialty Valve Co., 1970-74; pres. Mechano, Inc., Forest Park, Ill., 1974—; cons. liquid and system applications. Active local Boy Scouts Am., 1970. Served with USMCR. Mem. ASME, Am. Water Works Assn., Ill. Inst. Tech. Alumni Assn. Home: 569 59th St Lisle IL 60532 Office: 21 New Ave Lemont IL 60439

UGOAGWU, MARCEL CHUKWUMA, chem. engr.; b. Nigeria, July 11, 1948; came to U.S., 1970, naturalized, 1978; s. Emmanuel Ukaegbu and Florence (NNoka) U.; B.S.Ch.E. (Dewitt Wallace Found. Merit scholar), Ill. Inst. Tech., 1975, M.S.Ch.E., 1977; m. Barbara Jackson, Aug. 13, 1976. Asst. to dean of students Ill. Inst. Tech., 1976-77, freshman adv., 1977—; process engr. E. I. Dupont DeNemours and Co., East Chicago, Ind., 1977-79, supr. prodn., Cleve., 1979-80; sr. prodn. engr. Henkel Corp., Kankakee, Ill., 1981—. Pres., Fgn. Students Assn., Ill. Inst. Tech., 1971-73. Mem. Am. Inst. Chem. Engrs., Nat. Soc. Profl. Engrs., Dupont Athletic Assn., Brazilian Soccer Club. Democrat. Roman Catholic. Home: 759 Burr Oak Ln Suite 2K Park Forest South IL 60466 Office: Henkel Corp S Kensington Rd Kankakee IL 60901

UHL, KEITH EDWARD, lawyer; b. Mapleton, Iowa, May 27, 1946; s. Ariel Ambrose and Muriel Valentine (Stratton) U.; B.A. with honors, U. S.D., 1968; J.D. with honors (Scottish Rite grad. fellow), George Washington U., 1972; m. Nancy Ann Norman, June 24, 1972. Legis. asst. Congressman Ben Reifel, U.S. Ho. of Reps., Washington, 1968-71; admitted to D.C., Iowa bars, 1972; practiced in Des Moines, 1972—; asst. U.S. atty. So. Dist. Iowa, U.S. Dept. Justice, Des Moines, 1972-76, spl. prosecutor Wounded Knee non-leadership cases, 1975-76; mem. firm Scalise, Scism, Gentry Brick & Brick, 1976—. Mem. commn. Iowa Dept. Environ. Quality, 1981—; legal counsel, bd. dirs. Grassley for U.S. Senate Com., 1979—. Served as 1st lt. AUS, 1973. Mem. Am. (vice chmn. young lawyers com. criminal justice 1973-78, young lawyers exec. council 1976-78; joint com. legal status of prisoners 1974-76, mem. com. econs. of criminal law 1980—), Iowa (chmn. young lawyers disaster relief com. 1972-75; young lawyers ethics seminar Drake U. Law Sch. 1974, young lawyers exec. council 1975-78, chmn. spl. com. criminal law 1976-77; liaison to Am. Bar Assn. criminal law com. 1978—), D.C. bar assns., Am., Iowa trial lawyers assns., Phi Delta Phi, Phi Delta Theta (pres. S.D. Alpha 1966), Omicron Delta Kappa, Pi Sigma Alpha, Phi Eta Sigma (pres. S.D. chpt. 1965). Republican. Methodist. Mason. Home: 3103 Elmwood Dr Des Moines IA 50312 Office: 550 39th St Des Moines IA 50312

UHL, MARY ELIZABETH, educator; b. Mich., Apr. 24, 1945; d. Frances George and Doris Marie (Gearhart) Mida; B.S., Eastern Mich. U., 1967, M.A., 1972; m. Joseph Edward Uhl, Jan. 28, 1967; children—Melissa DeLynn, Joseph Wesley. Tchr. elem. grades Plymouth-Canton (Mich.) Sch. System, 1967—, also former swimming coach; elementary curriculum cons.; mem. dist. adv. com. for talented and gifted; mem. steering com. Parent Reading Conf., 1981; mem. dist. com. Young Author's Conf. Campaign mgr. town clk., 1978, 80; mem. legis. adv. coms. juvenile justice, women's legislation. Mem. AAUW (pres. 1980-82; state legis. chmn. 1977-79), Assn. Supervision and Curriculum Devel., PEO, Alpha Delta Kappa, Plymouth Arts Council, Common Cause, Am. Legion Aux. Presbyterian. Home: 13374 Haverhill St Plymouth MI 48170 Office: Eriksson Elem Sch 1275 Haggerty St Canton MI 48187

UHL, RICHARD ERWIN, pharmacist; b. Blissfield, Mich., Nov. 23, 1934; s. Thurman G. and Ruth A. (Strong) U.; B.S., U. Mich., 1956; m. Janet Mason, July 21, 1956; children—Susan, Stephen. Asst. mgr. Cunningham Drug, Ypsilanti, Mich., 1957; owner Belvil Pharmacy, Belleville, Mich., 1957-60; chief pharmacist Herrick Meml. Hosp., Tecumseh, Mich., 1960; asst. chief pharmacist Freedman Hosp., HEW, Washington, 1961-66; dir. pharmacy Community Health Center Branch County, Coldwater, Mich., 1966—; adj. clin. pharmacy instr. Ferris State U., 1975-76. Treas., Branch County Drug Abuse Com., 1968-73; mem. Bd. Health Occupation Students for Branch County Intermediate Sch., 1971—; co-chmn. Better Schs.-Coldwater Schs., 1972-73; mem. Coldwater Sch. Bd., 1974-78. Recipient Bishop's Cross, Episcopal Ch., 1973; named Employer of Year - Health Occupation, Branch County Intermediate Schs., 1978. Mem. Am. Pharm. Assn., Am. Hosp. Assn., Mich. Pharmacy Assn., Western Mich. Pharmacy Assn., Branch County Pharmacy Assn. (past pres.), U.S. Chess Fedn. Republican. Club: Coldwater Rotary (pres. 1978). Home: 97 Edison Ct Coldwater MI 49036 Office: Community Health Center Branch County 274 E Chicago St Coldwater MI 49036

UHLENHOPP, HARVEY HAROLD, justice Iowa Supreme Ct.; b. Butler County, Iowa, June 23, 1915; s. Henry Harold and Charlotte Ellen Wade (Green) U.; A.B., Grinnell Coll., 1936, LL.D., 1973; J.D., U. Iowa, 1939; m. Elizabeth Christine Elliott, June 20, 1940; children—Elliott Lee, John Cummings. Admitted to Iowa bar, 1939; county atty. Franklin County (Iowa), 1947-50; mem. Iowa Ho. of Reps., 1951-52; dist. judge Iowa, 1953-70; justice Iowa Supreme Ct., Des Moines, 1970—. Served with USCG, 1943-46. Mem. Am., Iowa bar assns., Am. Law Inst., Am. Judicature Soc. (dir. 1965-67), Inst. Jud. Adminstrn. Contbr. articles to legal jours. Active ct. improvement. Office: Box 341 Hampton IA 50441

UHLIR, NORMAN CLARENCE, mgmt. cons.; b. Cleve., Mar. 23, 1937; s. Clarence Stephen and Gladys Katherine (Vanek) U.; B.B.A., Western Res. U., 1960; m. Frances Joan Braun, June 20, 1959; children—Shelly Marie, Dennis John, Scott Michael. Cost, fin. analyst Ford Motor Co., Cleve., 1960-63; asst. div. controller Hupp Corp., Cleve., 1963-65; mgr. fin. analysis TRW, Inc., Cleve., 1965-69; sr. cons. Peat, Marwick, Mitchell & Co., Cleve., 1969-71; corporate controller Huffman Mfg. Co., Dayton, Ohio, 1971-75; controller advanced tech. group Sundstrand Corp., Rockford, Ill., 1975-81; mgmt. cons. Uhlir & Assos., Rockford, 1981—. Mem. Fin. Execs. Inst., Planning Execs. Inst., Am. Mgmt. Assn. Clubs: Masons, Shriners. Home: 1810 Jonquil Circle Rockford IL 61107 Office: 4215 E State St Suite 114 Rockford IL 61108

UHLMAN, CAROL TULLY, sch. psychologist; b. Valparaiso, Ind., Dec. 22, 1942; d. Roger Raymond and Mary Catherine (Shireman) Podell; A.A., Kalamazoo Community Coll., 1973; B.S. cum laude, Western Mich. U., 1975, M.A., 1976, Ed.S., 1978, postgrad. 1978—; children—Jackie Lynne, John Emmett, Janet Carol. Grad. asst. Western Mich. U., Kalamazoo, 1976; sch. psychologist Caledonia (Mich.) Community Schs., 1976—; intern with asst. supt. schs. Kalamazoo, 1980; cons. in field. Mem. Nat. Assn. Sch. Psychologists, Nat. Assn. Supervision and Curriculum Devel., Mich. Assn. Sch. Psychologists, Assn. Supervision and Curriculum Devel. Home: 1232 Alamo Ave Kalamazoo MI 49007 Office: 9770 Duncan Lake Rd Caledonia MI 49316

UHLMAN, HELENE, public health sanitarian/environmentalist; b. Lorain, Ohio; d. Nick and Ida (Toth) Dullos; m. Howard Uhlman, June 29, 1947; 1 dau., Melody. Office mgr. Grade A Milk Program, Gary, Ind., 1948-59; milk coordinator, State of Ind. rep. Calumet Region Milk Sanitation, 1968-70; dir. sanitation Gary (Ind.) Health Dept., 1973-79; health chmn. United Way; guest speaker at high schs., colls.; pres. N.W. Ind. Regional Addiction Authority, 1977. Area chmn. March of Dimes, Gary. Registered profl. sanitarian, Ind., Ill.; cert. grade A plant insp., Ind. Mem. Nat. Environ. Health Assn. (founder and chmn. women's profl. group 1970-71), Merit award 1971), Internat. Assn. Milk, Food and Environ. Sanitarians, Ind. Assn. Sanitarians (pres. local chpt. 1974, (state pres. 1979, Merit award 1975), Ill. Assn. Sanitarians. Lutheran. Home: 1532 W 4th Pl Hobart IN 46342 Office: 824 Broadway Gary IN 46402

UHRIK, STEVEN BRIAN, nephrology social worker, photographer; b. Chgo., June 30, 1949; s. George Steven and Elizabeth Gertrude Beisse (Will) U.; A.A., William Rainey Harper Coll., 1970; B.A., No. Ill. U., 1973; M.S.W., U. Ill., 1980; m. Patricia Ann Bayer, June 5, 1971. Vocat. coordinator O. H. Industries div. Opportunity House, Inc., Sycamore, Ill., 1970-79; clin. social worker, family counselor Rockford (Ill.) Meml. Hosp., 1979-81, co-dir. devel. chronic pain program, 1979-80; social worker West Suburban Kidney Center, S.C., Oak Park, Ill., 1981—; bd. dirs. Children's Learning Center, Dekalb, Ill., 1973-74; public relations cons. Dekalb County Villages, Inc., 1975-76; also freelance photographer. Mem. transp. adv. com. Vol. Action Center, Dekalb, 1974-75; bd. dirs., vol. Ben Gordon Mental Health Center Crisis Line, Dekalb, 1971-74. Recipient award Dekalb-Sycamore Human Relations Commn., 1974; registered athlete AAU. Mem. Nat. Assn. Social Workers, Omicron Delta Kappa, Alpha Kappa Delta. Club: F-Stop. Office: 101 Scoville St Oak Park IL 60304

UICKER, JOHN JOSEPH, JR., educator; b. Derry, N.H., July 11, 1938; s. John Joseph and Elizabeth Josephine (Flint) U.; B.M.E., U. Detroit, 1961; M.S., Northwestern U., 1963, Ph.D., 1965; m. Ann Marie Schumacher, Aug. 12, 1961; children—Theresa Ann, John Joseph, Joseph Michael, Barbara Ann, Dorothy Jean, Joan Elizabeth. Prin. research engr. Ford Motor Co., Dearborn, Mich., 1972-73; asst. prof. mech. engring. U. Wis., 1967-70, asso. prof., 1970-75, prof., 1975—, dir. Computer-Aided Engring. Center, 1980—; sr. Fulbright lectr. Cranfield Inst. Tech., England, 1978-79; cons. in field. Served with U.S. Army, 1965-67. Recipient Soc. Automotive Engrs. Teetor award, 1969. Registered profl. engr., Wis. Mem. ASME, Internat. Fedn. Theory of Machines and Mechanisms, Assn. Computing Machinery, Am. Soc. Engring. Edn., Sigma Xi, Pi Tau Sigma. Roman Catholic. Author: (with J.E. Shigley) Theory of Machines and Mechanisms, 1980; editor: Mechanism and Machine Theory, 1972-77; Computer Program: Integrated Mechanisms Program, 1972—. Contbr. articles to profl. jours. Office: Dept Mech Engring U Wis 1513 University Ave Madison WI 53706

UIHLEIN, HENRY HOLT, refrigeration mfg. co. exec.; b. Milw., Aug. 17, 1921; s. Herman Alfred and Claudia (Holt) U.; B.A., U. Va., 1946; m. Marion Struss, June 13, 1942; children—James Christopher, Richard A., Philip John, Henry Holt. Pres., gen. mgr. Ben Hur Mfg. Co., Milw., 1947-62; pres. Ouictrez Inc., Fond duLac, Wis., 1955-60; pres., gen. mgr., dir. U-Line Corp., Milw., 1962—, chmn. bd., 1977—; pres., dir. Jensen Service Co., 1962—; pres. U-Line Internat. Corp. Bd. dirs. Herman A. Uihlein Found., Inc., 1955—. Served with USMC, 1943-45. Named to Wis. Ice Hockey Hall of Fame, 1978. Christian Scientist. Clubs: Milw., Athletic, Milw. Country. Contbr. articles to profl. jours. Home: 8500 Green Bay Ct N Milwaukee WI 53209 Office: 8900 55th St N Milwaukee WI 53223

ULEVICH, NEAL HIRSH, photojournalist; b. Milw., June 18, 1946; s. Ben and Leah Jean (Klitsner) U.; B.A. in Journalism, U. Wis., 1968; m. Maureen Ann Vaughan, Sept. 25, 1974; 1 son, Jacob Vaughan. Reporter, AP, 1968-69, photographer, photo editor, 1971—; freelance writer, Vietnam, Hong Kong, 1969-71; fellow in journalism U. Wis., Madison, 1971-72. Recipient Pulitzer Prize for news photography, 1976. Jewish. Office: AP 50 Rockefeller Plaza New York NY 10020

ULLAND, JAMES, state senator; B.A., Carleton Coll.; M.B.A., Wharton Sch. Fin. U. Pa.; m. Laurel Donaldson. Christmas tree farmer; mem. faculty U. Minn.-Duluth; former mem. Minn. Ho. of Reps., minority leader, 1975-76; mem. Minn. Senate, 1976—. Chmn. Minn. Gt. Lakes Commn. Mem. Minn. Christmas Tree Growers Assn. Office: 143 State Office Bldg St Paul MN 55155*

ULLRICH, JOHN FREDERICK, mfg. co. exec.; b. Kalamazoo, Aug. 27, 1940; s. Frederick John and Opal Louise (Confer) U.; B.S. in Engring. Physics, U. Mich., 1962, M.S. in Nuclear Engring., 1963, Ph.D., 1967; m. Susan K. Brundage, July 16, 1962; children—Frederick, Kathryn, Amy. Mgr. ignition systems dept. Ford Motor Co., Dearborn, Mich., 1975-76, mgr. vehicle evaluation, 1976-77, exec. engr. elec. and electronics div., 1977-79; v.p. sci. and tech. Internat. Harvester Co., Hinsdale, Ill., 1979—. Mem. guarantors com. Goodman Theatre; mem. corp. relations com., indsl. com. U. Mich.; mem. Mich. Republican State central com., 1971-75; chmn. Reps. of Dearborn, 1972-74; alt. del. Rep. Nat. Conv., 1972. Recipient Ford Community Service award, 1969, 73. Mem. Am. Soc. Agrl. Engrs., Soc. Automotive Engrs., Am. Soc. Engring. Edn., Research Dirs. Assn. Chgo., Indsl. Research Inst., Ill. Sci. Lecture Assn. (dir.), Ill. Council for Energy Research and Devel., Sigma Xi, Tau Beta Pi. Republican. Presbyterian. Home: 828 S Oak St Hinsdale IL 60521 Office: 16 W 260 83d St Hinsdale IL 60521

ULRICH, DENNIS ARTHUR, funeral home exec.; b. Cicero, Ill., Nov. 28, 1943; s. Arthur James and Anne (Vodraska) U.; A.A., Morton Coll., 1963; Ph.D. in Psychology, U. Ill., 1972; Funeral Dir., Worsham Coll., 1977; m. Rosemarie Helen Swartz, Sept. 4, 1965; children—Roseanne, Dennis Arthur II, Kathlene. Gen. mgr. CMD Sports div. Evans Product Corp., Chgo., 1965-76; funeral dir., embalmer Chrastka Funeral Home, Berwyn, Ill., 1978-80; with Ulrich Family Funeral Service, Cicero, 1980—; lectr., instr. funeral service practice; Sanatarian Ill. Dept. Public Health; med. self-help instr. HEW; notary public, Cook County, Ill. Active Chgo. council Boy Scouts Am., 1961—; vol. instr. ARC, 1964—. Mem. Nat. Funeral Dirs. Assn., Ill. Funeral Dirs. Assn., Nat. Rifle Assn., Olympic Shooters Assn., Ill. Police Assn., Chgo. Zool. Soc., Ill. Funeral Dirs. and Embalmers Assn., Worldwide Funeral Service Assn., Fed. Funeral Dirs. Assn., Combined Counties Police Assn., Cicero Policemen's Benevolent Assn., U.S. Govt. Funeral Service Agy. Republican. Roman Catholic. Clubs: Moose, Ind. Order Foresters. Author: Re-Creation through Restorative Art: The Manual; The Funeral Director as a Grief Counselor: The Manual. Home: 2511 S 57th Ave Cicero IL 60650 Office: Ulrich Family Funeral Service 2511 S 57th Ave Cicero IL 60650

UMANS, ALVIN ROBERT, mfg. co. exec.; b. N.Y.C., Mar. 11, 1927; s. Louis and Ethel (Banner) U.; student U. Rochester, 1944-45; m. Nancy Jo Zadek, June 28, 1953 (div.); children—Kathi Lee Umans Lind, Craig Joseph. Sales mgr. Textile Mills Co., Chgo. Chgo., 1954-56; regional sales mgr. Reflector Hardware Corp., Melrose Park, Ill., 1956-58, nat. sales mgr., 1959-62, v.p., 1962-65, pres., treas., dir., 1965—; dir. Concepts, Inc., Charlotte, N.C.; chmn., pres. Garcy Corp., Chgo., v.p., dir. Midland Industries, Inc., Wichita, Kans.; v.p., dir. Goer Mfg. Co., Inc., Charleston Heights, S.C.; pres., treas., dir. Spacemaster Corp., Chgo.; dir. Banner Press, N.Y.C.; v.p., dir. Servicomex S.A., Mexico; pres., dir. Fine Arts Broadcasting, Inc., Chgo., Sharon Broadcasting, Mich., Rinco Corp., Chgo.; pres., treas. Spacemaster-Garcy Corp., Chgo. Trustee, Mt. Sinai Hosp. Med. Center, Chgo., 1972—; bd. dirs. Milton & Rose Zadek Fund, 1965-78. Served with U.S. Army, 1945-46. Mem. Nat. Assn. Store Fixture Mfrs. (dir. 1969-70), Young Pres. Orgn., Chgo. Pres. Orgn. Clubs: Standard (Chgo.). Office: 1400 N 25th Ave Melrose Park IL 60160

UMBEHOCKER, KENNETH SHELDON, pub. relations assn. exec., clergyman; b. Mpls., Sept. 23, 1934; s. Kenneth and Mildred Adeline (Johnson) U.; B.A., Vanderbilt U., 1956; L.Th., Seabury-Western Theol. Sem., 1959; grad. U. Ga. Mgmt. Inst., 1973. Ordained to ministry Episcopal Ch., 1959; pastor chs., Hallock and Virginia, Minn., 1959-65; field rep. Am. Cancer Soc., Mpls., 1965-67; dept. mgr. Rochester (Minn.) Area C. of C., 1967-74; exec. dir. Fargo (N.D.) Parking Authority & Downtown Bus. Assn., 1974—; asst. to dean Gethsemane Epis. Cathedral, Fargo, 1974—, hon. canon, 1979; ch. cons. in communications, adminstrn., 1967—. Dir. Rochester (Minn.) United Fund, 1970-72. Recipient Distinguished Service Award Rochester Jaycees, 1970; named Young Man of Year Rochester, 1970; Seabury fellow Seabury-Western Theol. Sem., 1972. Mem. Am. C. of C. Execs., Internat. Downtown Execs. Assn. Clubs: Mason, Elks, Eagles, Rochester Kiwanis (dir. 1974), Rotary Internat., Mpls. Athletic. Home: 901 8th Ave N Fargo ND 58102 Office: 69 1/2 Broadway Fargo ND 58102

UNDERHILL, GLENN MORIS, educator; b. Trenton, Nebr., Oct. 30, 1925; s. George Frederick and Anna Mabel (Jackson) U.; student McCook Jr. Coll., 1942-44; B.S., Kearney State Coll., 1955; M.A. in Physics, U. Nebr., 1957, Ph.D., 1963; m. F. Susan Ann Day, Dec. 27, 1958; children—G. Mark, Rachel S., Sterling D., Gretchen E., Cynthia A., Enoch M. Grad. asst. U. Nebr., Lincoln, 1955-59, instr., 1960-62; asso. prof. Kearney (Nebr.) State Coll., 1963-67, planetarium dir., 1966—, prof. physics, 1967—, head dept. physics and phys. sci., 1971-77; vis. lectr. various univs.; lectr. in field. Mem. Riverdale (Nebr.) Village Bd., 1978—, chmn. bd., 1978, 79, 80—. Mem. Am. Phys. Soc., Am. Assn. Physics Tchrs., Nebr. Acad. Sci., AAAS, Sigma Xi, Lambda Delta Lambda, Sigma Tau Delta, Kappa Delta Pi. Republican. Mem. Ch. of God. Contbr. articles to profl. jours. Home: PO Box 70 Riverdale NE 68870 Office: Kearney State Coll Kearney NE 68847

UNDERWOOD, ERNEST WADE, business exec.; b. Murray, Ky., Oct. 13, 1935; s. Ernest Alan and Eupha Rubena (Johnson) U.; B.A., Murray State U., 1957, M.A., 1960; Ed.D., U. Akron (Ohio), 1976; m. Jean Heath, June 10, 1959; children—Elizabeth, Mary Jane, Katherine. Tchr. math. Akron City Schs., 1965-68; pres. Akron Edn. Assn., 1968-74; pres. Ohio Edn. Assn., Columbus, 1974-76, exec. sec., 1976-79; pres. Circle Services Ins. Agy., Inc., Circle Services Corp., Circle Services Life Agy., Inc.; pres. Aqua Power Systems, 1981—. Mem. assessment and ann. progress report adv. com. Ohio Dept. Edn., 1976-79; del. Democratic Nat. Conv., 1976. Gen. Electric Co. fellow, 1959, U. Akron fellow, 1973-74. Mem. NEA, Am. Soc. Assn. Execs., Ohio Edn. Assn. (Doers award), Phi Delta Kappa. Baptist. Clubs: Masons; Kiwanis; University. Author: Educator's View of Tax Sheltered Annuities, 1968. Home: 5905 Graessle Rd London OH 43140 Office: Box 2550 225 E Broad St Columbus OH 43216

UNDERWOOD, JACQUELINE MARTIN, computer programmer; b. Knoxville, Tenn., Mar. 23, 1934; d. Ralph Henry and Anna Lou (McMahan) Martin; B.S., Knoxville Coll., 1955; M.S., U. Tenn., 1962, M.M., 1964, Ed.D., 1976; children—Paul, Carla. Tchr., Schutz Sch., Alexandria, Egypt, 1955-58, Vine Jr. High Sch., Knoxville, 1961-65; asso. prof. Knoxville Coll., 1958-60, 65-78; part-time instr. Walters State Community Coll., Morristown, Tenn., 1975-76; computer programmer IBM, Rochester, Minn., 1978-79, asst. to systems assurance lab. mgr., 1979-80, mgr. equal opportunity programs, 1980—; instr. Rochester Community Coll. Vice pres. bd. dirs. Rochester Better Chance, 1980-81; vol. Rapeline, 1979—, Recreation for Mentally Retarded Adults, 1979-80; mem. Rochester Human Rights Commn., 1980—; mem. affirmative action and instrnl. adv. com. Rochester Sch. Bd.; mem. cabinet United Way Campaign. NSF grantee, 1963-64; U.S. Office of Edn. grantee, 1969, 74-76. Mem. Nat. Council Tchrs. Math., Research Council on Diagnostic and

Prescriptive Math., AAUW (dir. 1979-81), LWV (dir. 1979-80), NAACP, Ebon Sisters, Jack and Jill of Am., Alpha Kappa Alpha. Democrat. Presbyterian. Home: 1905 26th Ave NW Apt 213 Rochester MN 55901 Office: IBM Hwy 52 886/003-2 Rochester MN 55901

UNDERWOOD, ROBERT ALLEN, JR., educator; b. Logansport, Ind., Nov. 4, 1942; s. Robert Allen and Betty Jean (Copeland) U.; B.S., Murray State U., 1967, M.A., 1968; Ed.D., Ind. U., 1973; m. Barbara Ann Adams, Aug. 28, 1965; 1 son, Thomas Robert. Asst. prof. bus. edn. Murray (Ky.) State U., 1973-75, dir. grad. programs in bus., 1974-75; chmn. div. bus. edn., 1975-77; mem. faculty N.E. Mo. State U., Maryville, 1975-77; asso. prof. bus. edn. and office adminstrn. Ball State U., Muncie, Ind., 1977—. Mem. Nat. Bus. Edn. Assn., North Central Bus. Edn. Assn., Ind. Bus. Edn. Assn., Am. Bus. Communication Assn., Phi Delta Kappa. Methodist. Club: Kiwanis. Contbr. articles to profl. jours. Home: 2201 W Village Dr Muncie IN 47304 Office: 235 Whitinger Bus Bldg College of Business Ball State Univ Muncie IN 47306

UNDERWOOD, ROBERT CHARLES, justice Supreme Ct. Ill.; b. Gardner, Ill., Oct. 27, 1915; s. Marion L. and Edith L. (Frazee) U.; B.A., Ill. Wesleyan U., 1937; J.D., U. Ill., 1939; grad. appellate judges seminar N.Y. U.; hon. degrees Loyola U., Chgo., Ill. Wesleyan U., Eureka (Ill.) Coll.; m. Dorothy L. Roy, Feb. 2, 1939; 1 dau., Susan Louise. Admitted to Ill. bar, 1939; individual practice law, 1939-46; city atty., Normal, Ill., 1942-43; asst. state's atty., McLean County, Ill., 1942-46, county judge, 1946-62; justice Ill. Supreme Ct., 1962—, chief Justice, 1969-75. Past chmn. bd. 1st Nat. Bank Normal. Del. Golden Anniversary White House Conf. on Children, 1960; vice chmn. Ill. Commn. Children, 1953-55; past mem. law adv. council U. Ill. Coll. Law; adv. council Nat. Center for State Cts. Recipient U.S. C. of C. Disting. Ser. award, 1948, certificate Outstanding Accomplishment Govt., 1953; Ann. citation Ill. Welfare Assn., 1961; Outstanding Citizens award Normal C. of C., 1962; Outstanding Achievement award U. Ill., 1969. Fellow Pa. Mason Juvenile Ct. Inst; mem. Am., Ill. (award of merit 1976), McLean County (past pres) bar assns., Conf. Chief Justices (former vice chmn.), Inst. Jud. Adminstrn, Ill. County and Probate Judges Assn. (past pres.), Am. Judicature Soc. (former trustee), Sigma Chi (Significant Sig award 1971), Sigma Delta Kappa, Pi Kappa Delta. Republican. Methodist. Clubs: Masons (33 deg.), Rotary (hon.), Kiwanis (hon.), Bloomington, Bloomington Country. Ill. Wesleyan U. Century. Office: 300 People's Bank Bldg Bloomington IL 61701

UNDERWOOD, ROBERT LINCOLN, fast food co. exec.; b. Ferndale, Mich., Dec. 6, 1941; s. Herbert Lincoln and Henriette Mae (Huskey) U.; student Northwood Inst., 1961; m. Carolyn E. Rooda, Aug. 16, 1962; children—Barbara, Robert, Scott, Patricia. Asst. foreman Anderson Co., Gary, Ind., 1961-67; salesman Carroll Chevrolet, Crown Point, Ind., 1967-76; mgr. Merrillville (Ind.) Auto License Bur., 1976-78; pres. Lincoln Carry Out Foods, Inc., Gary, 1978—. Mem. Republican Precinct Com., Merrillville, 1961-79; chmn. Ross Twp. (Ind.) Rep. Party, 1973-78; mem. adv. bd. Ross Twp., 1972-76. Named to Chevrolet Legion of Leaders, 1968, 69, 70, 73, 74. Methodist. Office: 400 Fillmore Gary IN 46402

UNGER, ROBERT MICHAEL, dentist; b. Chgo., Nov. 25, 1923; s. Robert and Mary Elizabeth (Janisch) U.; student De La Salle Inst., 1941, Loyola U., 1941-43; D.D.S., Chgo. Coll. Dental Surgery, Loyola U., 1946; m. Dorothy Marion Kinnavy, Apr. 30, 1949; children—Margaret, Marilyn, Robert, James, Richard, Joseph, Dorothy. Pvt. practice dentistry Chgo., 1948—; head dental dept. J.F. Kennedy Jr. Sch. Exceptional Children, 1955-70; cons. in field; bd. dirs. Ill. Dental Service Corp., 1976-80, officer, 1979-81. Bd. dirs. Friends of Austria, 1979-81. Served to capt., Dental Corps, AUS, 1946-48. Recipient Spirit of Life award City of Hope, 1981. Fellow Am., Internat. colls. dentists; mem. Ill. (pres. 1972-73, 79-81, legis. interest com.), Englewood (pres. 1965-66) dental socs., Loyola U. Dental Alumni Assn. (pres. 1972-73), ADA (1st v.p. 1973-74, trustee 1980—), Acad. Gen. Dentistry (v.p. Chgo. 1975-76, pres. 1973-74), Odontographic Soc., Guild St. Appoilona, Fedn. Dentaire Internat., Pierre Fouchard Acad., Redemptorist Club Chgo., Am. Friends Austria. K.C. (4 deg.). Home: 6017 W 55th St Chicago IL 60638 Office: 2656 W 63d St Chicago IL 60629

UNNEWEHR, LEWIS EMORY, elec. engr.; b. Berea, Ohio, Sept. 27, 1925; s. Emory Carl and Ivy May (Lewis) U.; B.S.E.E., Purdue U., 1946; M.S.E.E., U. Notre Dame, 1952; m. L. Jean Affleck, Aug. 22, 1948; children—David, Laura, Janet, Chris. Asso. prof. Valparaiso U. (Ind.), 1949-55; research engr. Franklin Inst., Phila., 1955-57; asso. prof. Villanova (Pa.) U., 1957-61; sr. design engr. Garrett Corp., Los Angeles, 1961-66; mem. research staff Ford Motor Co., Dearborn, Mich., 1966-81; dir. research and devel. Lima Energy Products (Ohio), 1981—. Lay del. Central United Meth. Ch., Detroit, 1978-80. Mem. IEEE (vice-chmn. electronics transformer tech. com.), Sigma Xi. Democrat. Methodist. Author: (with S.A. Nasar) Electromechanics and Electric Machines, 1979; contbr. articles to profl. jours.; patentee in field. Home: 170 Squire Ln Lima OH 45805 Office: 200 E Chapman St Lima OH 45802

UNTENER, KENNETH EDWARD, bishop; b. Detroit, Aug. 3, 1937; B.A., Sacred Heart Sem. Coll., Detroit, 1959; S.T.B., St. John's Provincial Sem., Plymouth, Mich., 1963; S.T.D., Rome, 1971. Ordained priest Roman Cath. Ch., 1963; asst. pastor St. Mary's of Redford Parish, Detroit, 1963-65; asst. chancellor Archdiocese of Detroit, 1965-68, asst. vicar for parishes, 1968-69, asst. to del. for clergy, 1971-77; rector St. John's Provincial Sem., 1977-80; consecrated bishop of Saginaw (Mich.) Diocese, 1980—. Author: Sunday Liturgy Can Be Better, 1980. Office: Chancery Office 5800 Weiss St Saginaw MI 48603

UNZICKER, WILLIAM LUTHER, III, educator; b. Herrin, Ill., Aug. 19, 1946; s. William Luther and Lelle (Baker) U.; student DePauw U., 1964-67, McKendree Coll., 1967-68; B.S., Millikin U., 1969; M.Ed., U. Ill., 1974; m. Patricia Anne Benson, June 14, 1969; children—William Luther IV, Robert Bendick. Tchr. social studies Decatur (Ill.) Public Schs., 1969—; mem. curriculum task force. Mem. Nat. Council for Social Studies, Ill. Consumer Edn. Assn., Assn. Supervision and Curriculum Devel., NEA (life), Phi Delta Kappa, Kappa Delta Pi. Club: Sertoma (life; pres. club 1977-78, chmn. club bd. 1978-79, dist. gov. 1978-79, Disting. Gov. 1979) (Decatur). Home: 482 S Edward Decatur IL 62522 Office: 100 Cerro Gordo Decatur IL 62522

UPSON, MARK, III, mfg. co. exec.; b. Cin., Dec. 15, 1947; s. Mark and Ruth (Smith) U.; B.S.M.E., Cornell U., 1969; M.B.A., Harvard U., 1973; m. Martha Oliver Millan, June 16, 1973; children—Martha Jane, Margot Barnard. With Procter & Gamble, Cin., 1973—, asso. advt. mgr., 1980—. Served with U.S. Army, 1971-73. Club: Camargo. Home: 2590 Grandin Rd Cincinnati OH 45208 Office: PO Box 599 Cincinnati OH 45201

UPTON, LUCILE MORRIS (MRS. EUGENE V. UPTON), writer; b. Dadeville, Mo., July 22, 1898; d. Albert G. and Veda (Wilson) Morris; student Drury Coll., 1915-16, S.W. Mo. State U., 1917-20; m. Eugene V. Upton, July 22, 1936 (dec. July 1947). Pub. sch. tchr., Dadeville Mo., 1917-19, Everton, Mo., 1920-22, Roswell, N.Mex., 1921-23; tchr. creative writing Adult Edn. div. Drury Coll., 1947-52; reporter Denver Express, 1923-24, El Paso (Tex.) Times, 1924-25, Springfield (Mo.) Newspapers, Inc., 1926-64, writer weekly hist. column, 1964—. Mem. Springfield City Council, 1967-71, Springfield Hist. Sites Bd., 1972-78. Recipient Heritage award Mus. of Ozarks, 1978; named Woman of Achievement Woman's div. Springfield C. of C., 1967; named to Greater Ozark Hall of Fame, Sch. of Ozarks, Point Lookout, Mo., 1980. Mem. Mo. Writers Guild (past pres.), State Hist. Soc. Mo. (life), Greene County (Mo.), White River Valley hist. socs., Nat. Fedn. Press Women, Mo. Press Women. Conglist. Author: Bald Knobbers, 1939; (booklet) Battle of Wilson's Creek, 1950; contbr. short stories, articles to mags., newspapers. Home: 1305 S Kimbrough Springfield MO 65807

URBANIAK, DAVID LEE, restaurant exec., microfilm co. exec.; b. Dearborn, Mich., May 5, 1944; s. Joseph Frank and Ethel (Behnke) U.; student Western Mich. U., 1964-65; m. Sally Joanne Dexter, July 25, 1964; children—Matthew James, Bethany Lyn. Foreman, McGraw Edison, Albion, Mich., 1964-70; gen. foreman ITT Hancock, Jackson, Mich., 1970-76; owner Sal's 5th Ave. Restaurant, Michigan Center, Mich., 1976—; founder, pres. Automatic Microfilm Co., Michigan Center, 1978—. Mem. Leoni Bus. Assn. (co-founder 1977, chmn. 1977-81). Lutheran. Home: 484 Ballard St Jackson MI 49201 Office: 115 5th St Michigan Center MI 49254

URBAUER, CRAIG LESTER, urologist; b. Deshler, Nebr., Oct. 28, 1942; s. Lester Leroy and Ruth Gwendolyn (Swanson) U.; B.A., Nebr. Wesleyan U., 1964; M.D., U. Nebr., 1968; m. Arlene Joyce Schoonover, Aug. 12, 1967; children—Stephen Craig, Elizabeth Ann. Intern, Bryan Meml. Hosp., Lincoln, 1968-69; resident in urology U. Iowa, Iowa City, 1971-75; practice urology Urology, P.C., Lincoln, 1975—; mem. staff Bryan Meml. Hosp., St. Elizabeth's Hosp., Lincoln Gen. Hosp.; mem. faculty Lincoln Med. Edn. Found., 1975—. Chmn. service com. Nebr. div. Am. Cancer Soc., 1977-79, pres., 1979-80. Served with U.S. Army, 1969-71, Army N.G., 1977—. Decorated Bronze Star, Air medal, Nat. Cancer Inst. fellow, 1973-74; diplomate Am. Bd. Urology. Mem. AMA (Physicians Recognition award 1979), Lancaster County Med. Assn., Nebr. Med. Assn., Am. Urologic Assn., Aero-space Med. Assn. Republican. Methodist. Club: Univ. Home: 2000 Lawnsdale Dr Lincoln NE 68506 Office: 4740 A St Lincoln NE 68510

URBOM, WARREN KEITH, judge; b. Atlanta, Nebr., Dec. 17, 1925; s. Clarence A. and Anna Myrl (Ireland) U.; A.B., Nebr. Wesleyan U., 1950; J.D., U. Mich., 1953; m. Joyce Crawford, Aug. 19, 1951; children—Kim Marie Urbom Rager, Randall, Allison Lee, Joy R. Admitted to Nebr. bar, 1953; mem. firm Baylor, Evnen, Baylor, Urbom & Curtiss, Lincoln, 1953-70; U.S. dist. judge, 1970—, chief judge Dist. of Nebr., Lincoln, 1972—. Del., Gen. Conf., United Meth. Ch., 1962, 76, 80; pres. Lincoln YMCA, 1965-66; chmn. bd. govs. Nebr. Wesleyan U., 1975-80. Mem. Am., Nebr., Lincoln bar assns., Am. Coll. Trial Lawyers. Clubs: Masons, Shriners. Office: 100 Centennial Mall N Federal Bldg Lincoln NE 68508

URICE, JAMES MCDONALD, advt. sales exec.; b. St. Louis, Dec. 1, 1928; s. John Thomas and Mildred North U.; B.S.C., U. Iowa, 1951; m. Louise Marie Ericsson, June 12, 1959; children—Scott James, Jill Louise. Salesman, Gen. Mills, Inc., Mpls., 1953-55; field sales rep. Farm Jour., Chgo., 1955-66; Midwest advt. mgr. Redbook mag., Chgo., 1966-79; v.p., Midwest sales mgr. Parade Publs., Chgo., 1979—. Mem. Sch. Caucus Bd., Glenview, Ill., 1974-77; dir. Youth Bd., Glenview, 1978-80. Served with USMC, 1951-53. Decorated Purple Heart. Republican. Presbyterian. Clubs: Chgo. Advt., Chgo. Agate; Sunset Ridge Country. Home: 1408 Royal Oak Ln Glenview IL 60025 Office: 401 N Michigan Ave Chicago IL 60611

UROSHEVICH, MIROSLAV, solar energy co. exec.; b. Belgrade, Yugoslavia, Aug. 29, 1933; s. Spasoje and Nevenka (Pretic) Urosevic; B.S. equivalent, U. Belgrade, 1956; postgrad. Beaux Arts and Ecole Polytechnique, Paris, 1957-58; m. Ingrid Schwarzpaul, Dec. 31, 1963; children—Marko, Steven, Yvette, Nicole. Chief designer Panhard et Levassor SA, Paris, 1956-58; chief devel. engr. Keco Industries, Cin., 1958-60; pres. Alpha Designs Inc., cons., Cin., 1960-77; pres. Alpha Solarco Inc., Cin., 1977—; speaker and lectr. on solar energy and related subjects. Mem. Internat. Solar Energy Soc., Solar Energy Industries Assn., Order Ky. Cols. Serbian Orthodox. Patentee in field. Office: 1014 Vine St Suite 2530 Cincinnati OH 45202

URQUHART, RODERICK, advt. exec.; b. Oak Park, Ill., July 2, 1932; s. Roderick M. and Irene W. (Wortman) U.; B.S. in Advt./Mktg., U. Ill., 1953; postgrad. Northwestern U.; 1 son, Kevan A.F. With The Scholl Mfg. Co., Inc., Chgo., 1960-66, Manpower Inc., Milw., 1966-68, Playboy Enterprises, Chgo., 1968-72, Carlson Cos., Mpls., 1972-74, Franklin Mint Internat., London, 1974-77, Wunderman, Ricotta & Kline, Inc., Advt., N.Y.C., 1977-78, Spiegel, Inc., Oak Brook, Ill., 1978-79; v.p. advt. Calhoun's Collectors Soc., Inc., Mpls., 1979-81; lectr. in field. Served with USNR, 1953-55. Recipient Caples 1st pl. award for direct mail, 1980. Mem. Chgo. Council on Fgn. Relations, Chgo. Art Inst. Home: 25 W 677 Flint Creek Rd Wheaton IL 60187

URSETH, WILLIAM A., sales promotion corp. exec.; b. Mpls., June 3, 1949; s. Alvin G. and Beatrice M. U.; B.A., Augsburg Coll., 1971. Vice pres. U.S. Fin. Services, Mpls., 1975—, also dir.; pres., dir. U.S. Communications Corp., Mpls., 1975—, U.S. Entertainment Corp., Mpls., 1976—; dir. Mpls. mag., 1975-79. Chmn. bd. dirs. Mpls. Br. YMCA, 1978-79; bd. dirs. Minn. State Restitution Center. Served with USMC, 1967-70. Producer: Brother Champ, 1978, Nice Faces of 1943, 1976-77. Office: 300 Clifton S Minneapolis MN 55403

USHER, DAVID, pollution control co. exec.; b. Detroit, Dec. 29, 1929; s. Charles and Hannah (Komisaruk) U.; student Admiral Farragut Acad., 1946; m. Althea Marie Dionne; children—Lisa, Ellen, Amy, Charles. Partner Emanon Record Co., 1948—50; pres. Dee Gee Record Co., 1951—54; record producer Chess Producing Co., 1958—60; v.p. Usher Oil Service, Detroit, 1960—; pres. Mich. Tank Cleaning Co., Detroit, 1960—, pres. Marine Services Corp., Detroit, 1961—, Marine Pollution Control Co., Detroit, 1967—. Served with USCG, 1950. Mem. Spill Control Assn. Am. (pres. and founder), Hazardous Materials Control Research Inst. (pres., dir.), Nat. Def. Transp. Assn., Soc. Am. Mil. Engrs., ASTM, Propeller Club. Club: Rotary. Office: 8631 W Jefferson St Detroit MI 48209

UTHLAUT, RALPH, JR., state senator; b. Big Springs, Mo., Dec. 18, 1933; student U. Mo., St. Loius; m. Carol Jean Lattlemann, Dec. 12, 1953; 4 children. Farmer, Florence, Mo.; mem. Mo. Senate, 1962-72, 73—. Served with U.S. Army, 1954-56. Mem. Mo. Farm Bur., Montgomery County C. of C. Republican. Methodist. Home: Route 1 New Florence MO 63363 Office: State Capitol Jefferson City MO 65101*

UZUN-BELDING, N. ESER, health services research scientist; b. Sivas, Turkey, Mar. 23, 1951; came to U.S., 1975; s. Irfan and Hayriye Uzun; B.A., U. Istanbul (Turkey), 1974; M.A., U. Mich., 1977, Ph.D. in Organizational Psychology, 1979. Lectr., mem. research staff dept. psychology and Sch. Bus. Adminstrn., U. Istanbul, 1973-75; teaching asst., student coordinator dept. psychology U. Mich., Ann Arbor, 1975-77, research asso. Inst. for Social Research, 1976-79; health services research scientist VA Med. Center, Ann Arbor, 1979-80; research investigator Inst. Social Research, 1980—. Mem. Acad. Mgmt. Assn., Soc. for Gen. Systems Research, Internat. Council Psychologists, Internat. Assn. Applied Psychology, Am. Public Health Assn. Contbr. articles to profl. jours. Office: Survey Research Center Inst for Social Research U Mich Ann Arbor MI 48109

VACCARO, LOUIS CHARLES, coll. pres.; b. Los Angeles, July 25, 1930; s. Louis Charles and Louise Marie (Vinceguerra) V.; A.A., Los Angeles Valley Coll., 1954; A.B., U. So. Calif., 1957; M.A., Calif. State U., Northridge, 1960; M.Ed., U. So. Calif., 1961; Ph.D., Mich. State U., 1963; postgrad. U. Mich., 1970; Litt.D. (hon.), St. Martin's Coll., 1969; L.H.D. (hon.), Norwich U., 1978; m. Jean Mae Hudak, Jan. 29, 1955; children—Mary, Therese, Victoria, Frances, Michelle, Justin. Exec. trainee Pacific Telephone & Telegraph Co., 1957-59; tchr., coach Montclair Coll. Prep., 1960-61; asst. instr. Calif. State U., Northridge, 1960-61; instr. St. Mary's Coll., Notre Dame, Ind., 1961-62; asst. to v.p. acad. affairs, asst. prof. Marquette U., Milw., 1963-67; v.p. acad. affairs, prof. U. Portland (Oreg.), 1967-70; pres., prof. Marycrest Coll., Davenport, Iowa, 1970-72, Colby-Sawyer Coll., New London, N.H., 1972-77; pres. Siena Heights Coll., Adrian, Mich., 1977—; postdoctroal research fellow U. Oreg., 1966-67; cons. Brazil Fletcher Sch. Law and Diplomacy, Latin Am. Center, Mich. State U., 1974—; vis. prof. Higher Edn. Center, U. Colo., 1974; lectr. Higher Edn. Center, U. Mich., Grad. Sch. Mgmt., U. Dallas, Center Higher Edn., U. Pitts., 1975. Served with USAF, 1951-53. Kellogg fellow Mich. State U., 1962-63. Mem. Delta Epsilon Sigma. Roman Catholic. Club: Rotary. Author, editor five books, including: Reshaping American Higher Education, 1975; Planning in Small Colleges, 1979; contbr. numerous articles in field to profl. jours. Home: 3910 Birnwick Dr Adrian MI 49221 Office: 1247 E Siena Heights Dr Adrian MI 49221

VACHHER, PREHLAD SINGH, psychiatrist; b. Rawalpindi dist., Pakistan, Nov. 30, 1933; s. Thakar Singh and Harbans Kaur (Ghai) V.; came to U.S., 1960, naturalized, 1968; B. Medicine, B.Surgery, Panjab (India) U. Med. Coll. Amritsar, 1956; m. Margaret Begley, Oct. 4, 1963; children—Paul, Sheila, Mary Ann, Eileen, Mark. Intern Worcester (Mass.) City Hosp., 1960-61; resident in psychiatry Rochester (N.Y.) State Hosp., 1962-64, Phila. Gen. Hosp., 1964-65; practice medicine specializing in psychiatry Livonia, Mich., 1966—; staff psychiatrist Trenton (N.J.) State Hosp., 1965-66, Wayne County Gen. Hosp., Eloise, Mich., 1966-68; dir. community psychiatry Northville (Mich.) State Hosp., 1968-72; mem. staff Mercywood Hosp., Ann Arbor, Mich., 1970—; cons. staff Annapolis Hosp., Wayne, Mich., 1966—; cons. psychiatrist St. Joseph Mercy Hosp., Ann Arbor, Mich., 1975. Mem. Am. Psychiat. Assn., Canton C. of C. (v.p. 1972-73, pres. 1973-74). Clubs: Rotary; Econ. of Detroit. Research in use of packed red blood cells in treatment of hepatic cirrhosis. Home: Plymouth MI 48170 Office: Vachher Psychiat Center 32300 Schoolcraft St Livonia MI 48150

VADALABENE, SAM MARTIN, state senator; b. Detroit, July 31, 1914; s. Martin and Anna (Catalano) V.; grad. high sch.; m. Mary Pauline Lesko, 1935; children—William Joseph, Charles Martin, Sam Martin, Patricia Ann Vadalabene Mosby, Martin Joseph. Auditor, Office of Ill. State Supt. Public Instrn., 1959-63; supr. cemetery care Div. Auditor of Public Accts., 1963-67; pres. Edwardsville (Ill.) Twp. Democratic Club, 1963-65; auditor Edwardsville Twp., 196-67; 1965-67; mem. Ill. Ho. of Reps., 1967-71, Ill. State Senate, 1971—. Mgr., Edwardsville Little League, 1956; supr. Edwardsville Recreation Program, 1959-63; co-chmn. Madison County Polio Vaccine Adminstrn. Program. Served in U.S. Army, to 1945; MTO. Recipient 3 commendations Ill. Ho. of Reps.; First Crusade of Courage award Ill. C. of C.; named Outstanding Freshman Legislator, Ill. New Media, 1967; Recognition award Edwardsville C. of C.; Outstanding Legislator award Ill. Assn. Supts. Schs. Mem. Am. Legion, VFW. Clubs: KC (4th deg.), Moose. Roman Catholic. Office: State Capitol Gen Assembly Springfield IL 62706*

VADEN, ALLENE GAY, dietitian, educator; b. Seminole, Okla., Aug. 4, 1937; d. Ezra C. and Ruby (Rogers) Morris; B.S. cum laude, U. Tex. at Austin, 1960; M.S., Tex. Tech. U., 1967; Ph.D., Kans. State U., 1973; m. Richard Ellis Vaden, Nov. 12, 1955; children—Val, Erich. Instr., Tex. Tech. U., Lubbock, 1965-69; foodservice dir. The Matador of University Inns, Lubbock, 1966-67; mgr. Lubbock Women's Club, 1967-69; from instr. to prof. dietetics, restaurant and instl. mgmt., Kans. State U., Manhattan, 1970—, also scientist Agrl. Expt. Sta.; cons. on dietetic edn. and public feeding programs. Mem. com. United Fund, 1974, 79; county chmn. Martha Keys for Congress, 1976. Mem. Assn., Acad. Mgmt., Nat. Restaurant Assn., Am. Dietetic Assn. (chmn. commn. on accreditation 1975-78), Am. Home Econs. Assn., Am. Soc. Allied Health Professions, Am. Soc. Hosp. Foodservice Dirs., Soc. Advancement Foodservice Research, Inst. Food Technologists, Soc. Nutrition Edn. (treas. 1979—), Council on Postsecondary Accreditation (dir. 1979—), Foodservice Systems Mgmt. Edn. Council (chmn. 1977-79), Sigma Xi, Phi Kappa Phi, Omicron Nu, Phi Upsilon Omicron, Gamma Sigma Delta, Phi Gamma Delta. Democrat. Editor: Sch. Foodservice Research Rev., 1977—; Nutrition and the School Age Child. Contbr. articles to profl. jours. Home: 808 Wildcat Ridge Manhattan KS 66502 Office: Dept Dietetics Kans State U Manhattan KS 66506

VAGH, AMRISHKUMAR SURYAPRASAD, physicist; b. Visnagar, India, Jan. 19, 1936; s. Suryaprasad Bapalal and Manglagauri Suryaprasad (Jani) V.; came to U.S., 1968, naturalized, 1974; M.Sc., Gujarat U., 1961; Ph.D. with distinction, S. P. U., 1966; m. Kokila S. Desai, May 18, 1954; 1 son, Avinash. Lectr. Sardar Patel U., 1966-68; postdoctoral fellow State U. N.Y., Buffalo, 1968-69; asst. prof. State U. N.Y., Buffalo, 1969-70, chmn. phys. sci. div., asst. prof. Coop. Community Coll., 1970-71, sr. research physicist, 1971-74; sr. research physicist Ball State U., Muncie, Ind., 1974-75; research physicist NASA, Lewis Research Center, Cleve., 1976—; sr. research fellow Univ. Grant Commn., Govt. India, 1968. Mem. Am. Phys. Soc., Am. Carbon Soc. Contbr. articles to profl. jours. Home: 728 Main St Cincinnati OH 45202

VAGNIERES, ROBERT CHARLES, architect; b. Chgo., Oct. 2, 1932; s. Alfred and Elsa (Krueger) V.; B.Arch., U. Ill., 1955; m. Dorothy Lee Wandrey, June 13, 1953; children—Robert, Krista, Ross, Pam. Draftsman, Robert Soellner, Architect, Park Forest, Ill., 1957-59; asso. mem. firm Joel Robert Hillman, Architect, Chgo., 1959-71; partner Hillman Vagnieres & Assos., Chgo., 1972-75; owner, prin. Robert C. Vagnieres Architect Ltd., Olympia Fields, Ill., 1975-79; cons., 1979—; cons. hotel planning and constrn.; cons. Sheraton Naperville Hotel, 1980, Vista Internat. Hotel, N.Y.C., 1981. Served to lt., C.E., U.S. Army, 1955-57. Mem. AIA. Club: Olympia Fields Country. Architect: Chgo. City Centre, 1976, Sheraton Plaza Hotel, Chgo., 1971, Homewood-Flossmoor (Ill.) High Sch., 1977. Home: 1410 N State Pkwy Chicago IL 60610

VAIL, IRIS JENNINGS, civic worker; b. N.Y.C., July 2, 1928; d. Lawrence K. and Beatrice (Black) Jennings; grad. Miss Porters Sch., Farmington, Conn.; m. Thomas V.H. Vail, Sept. 15, 1951; children—Siri J. Vail Lacey, Thomas V.H. Jr., Lawrence J.W. Exec.

com. Garden Club Cleve., 1962—; mem. womens council Western Res. Hist. Soc., 1960—; mem. jr. council Cleve. Mus. Art, 1953—; chmn. Childrens Garden Fair, 1966-75, Public Square Dinner, 1975; bd. dirs. Garden Center Greater Cleve., 1963-77; trustee Cleve. Zool. Soc., 1971—; mem. Ohio Arts Council, 1974-76, pub. sq. com. Downtown Cleve. Corp., mem. Chagrin Scenic River Adv. Council, Ohio Dept. Natural Resources. Recipient Amy Angell Collier Montague medal Garden Club Am., 1976, Ohio Gov.'s award, 1977. Episcopalian. Clubs: Chagrin Valley Hunt, Cypress Point, Kirtland Country, Union, Colony. Home: Hunting Valley Chagrin Falls OH 44022

VAIL, JOANE RAND, govt. relations exec.; b. Waltham, Mass., Nov. 16, 1928; d. Herbert Smythe and Pauline (Murphy) Rand; R.N., McLean Hosp. Sch. Nursing, 1950; student Boston U., 1945-46, 50-51, U. Md., 1951-54, U. Minn., 1960-61, Met. State U., 1974-77; m. David J. Vail, Nov. 24, 1956; children—David Rand, Garrett Murphy, Sara Jameson, Michael Walsh. Asst. supr. McLean Hosp., 1950-51; dir. nursing edn. Rosewood State Hosp., Owings Mills, Md., 1950-55; staff asst. Office of Gov., State of Minn., St. Paul, 1971-73; dir. legis. service Met. Council, St. Paul, 1973—. Mem. exec. com. Democratic Farmer Labor Party; bd. dirs. Wayside House, Victory House, Vail Pl. Mem. Citizens League, Minn. Hist. Soc., Minn. Govt. Relations Assn. (bd. dirs.). Club: Campedor Bath and Tennis. Home: 127 6th St White Bear Lake MN 55110 Office: 300 Metro Square Saint Paul MN 55101

VAIL, JOE FRANKLIN, mktg. co. exec.; b. Indpls., Mar. 24, 1928; s. Frank Albert and Trixie May (Hawley) V.; B.S., Purdue U., 1951; 1 son, Kevin Joe. Treas., Apex Corp., Indpls., 1953-60; owner, operator Bus. Service Co., Indpls., 1961-63; partner Pulse Publs., Indpls., 1963-64; pres. Unique, Inc., Indpls., 1965-70; owner, operator Mid-Am. Advt. Co., Indpls., 1970-73; pres. Mid-Am. Mktg., Inc., Indpls., 1973—; editor, pub. Land Opportunity Rev., 1970—. Mem. Chgo. Assn. Direct Mktg., Nat. Fedn. Ind. Bus., Am. Bus. Club. Clubs: John Purdue, Masons. Author: Keys to Wealth, 1971; Your Fortune in Mail Order, 1972; How to Get Out of Debt and Live Like a Millionaire, 1977; Money-Where It Is and How To Get It, 1981. Home: 1720 Wellington Ave Indianapolis IN 46219 Office: 1150 N Shadeland Ave Indianapolis IN 46219

VAIL, MARK CHARLES, radio exec.; b. Rochester, Minn., June 25, 1952; s. Robert F. and Doris (Markham) V.; student public schs., Kasson, Minn. Program dir. Agriports, Inc., Rochester, 1974-76; farm dir. KOLM-AM, KWWK-FM, Rochester, 1976-79; farm dir. Rural Am. Farm Network, 1978-79; agr. dir. KROC-AM-FM, Rochester, 1979—; corp. agr. dir. So. Minn. Broadcasting, 1980—. Bd. dirs. S.E. Minn. Citizens Action Council, 1971-77. Mem. Rochester Area C. of C. (chmn. agr. bus. com. 1979-81, dir. 1981), Agr. Council Am. (dir.), Nat. Assn. Farm Broadcasters, Am. Meteorol. Assn., Nat. Agrimktg. Assn. Lutheran. Club: Toastmasters. Home: 2408 18 1/2 Ave NW Rochester MN 55901 Office: 122 4th St SW Rochester MN 55901

VAIL, ROBERT WILLIAM, cons. co. exec.; b. Columbus, Ohio, Oct. 29, 1921; s. Robert David and Dorothy (Mosier) V.; student Ohio State U., 1938-39; m. Martha Henderson, Apr. 7, 1939; children—William N., Veronica Vail Fish, David A., Ashley M., Victor H., Lorelei Meade, Hilary W. Chemist, Barnebey-Cheney Engrng. Co., 1941-44; sr. chemist Pa. Coal Products Co., Petrolia, 1944-51; abrasive engr. Carborundum Co., Niagara Falls, N.Y., 1951-54; tech. sales Allied Chem. Corp., Cleve., 1954-59; head research lab. U.S. Ceramic Tile Co., Canton, Ohio, 1960-62; sales mgr. Ferro Chem. div. Ferro Corp., Walton Hills, Ohio, 1962-70; pres. R. William Vail Inc., Cleve., 1970-72; mgr. tech. services Manpower Inc., Cleve., 1972-74; owner, mgr. Vail, Shaker Heights, Ohio, 1974-78; sr. cons. Hayden, Heman, Smith & Assos., Cleve., 1978—. Recipient Am. Security Council Bus. Citizenship Competition Excellence award, 1967. Mem. Amateur Radio Relay League. Republican. Presbyterian. Club: Masons, Al Koran Shrine. Author: Teardrops Falling, 1963; contbg. author: Ency. of Basic Materials for Plastics, 1967. Home: 1701 E 12th St Apt 20T Cleveland OH 44114 Office: 3260-100 Erieview Plaza Cleveland OH 44114

VAIL, THOMAS VAN HUSEN, publisher, editor; b. Cleve., June 23, 1926; s. Herman Lansing and Delia (White) V.; A.B. cum laude in Polit. Sci., Princeton U., 1949, H.H.D., Wilberforce U., 1964; L.H.D., Kenyon Coll., 1969, Cleve. State U., 1973; m. Iris Jennings, Sept. 15, 1951; children—Siri, Thomas Van Husen, Lawrence J.W. Reporter, Cleve. News, 1949-53, polit. editor, 1953-57; bus. dept. Cleve. Plain Dealer, 1957-61, v.p., 1961-63, pub., editor, 1963—, pres., 1970—, also dir.; pres., dir. Art Gravure Corp., Ohio, AP, 1968-74; mem. U.S. Adv. Commn. on Info., Nat. Adv. Commn. on Health Manpower, Pres.'s Commn. Observance 25th Anniversary UN. Dir., past pres. Cleve. Conv. and Visitors Bur.; chmn. Nat. Brotherhood Week, 1969; bd. dirs. Greater Cleve. Growth Assn.; mem. distbn. com. Cleve. Found.; trustee Cuyahoga unit Am. Cancer Soc., Cleve. Clinic Found., No. Ohio region NCCJ, Downtown Cleve. Corp. Com. for Econ. Devel. Served to lt. (j.g.) USNR, 1944-46. Recipient Nat. Human Relations award NCCJ, 1970, Man of Yr. award Sales and Mktg. Execs. of Cleve. Clubs: Cleve. Athletic, Union (Cleve.); Kirtland Country (Willoughby, Ohio); Cypress Point (Pebble Beach, Calif.); Nat. Press (Washington), Chagrin Valley Hunt. Home: Hunting Valley Chagrin Falls OH 44022 Office: 1801 Superior Ave Cleveland OH 44114

VAISRUB, NAOMI MIRIAM ROSE, biostatistician, educator; b. Winnipeg, Man., Can., Dec. 26, 1949; came to U.S., 1965; d. Samuel and Judith Ida (Maltz) Vaisrub; B.A. in Math., Northwestern U., 1970; M.S. in Biometrics (HEW fellow), Temple U., 1975, Ph.D. (AAUW fellow), 1976; m. Raymond Glassenberg, Jan. 1, 1981; 1 son, Samuel. Research asst. AMA, Chgo., summer 1972; sr. biostatistician G.D. Searle Pharm. Co., Skokie, Ill., 1977-80; biostatistician, dir. biometry unit Diabetes in Pregnancy Center, Center for Endocrinology, Metabolism and Nutrition, Northwestern U. Med. Sch., Chgo., 1980—, asst. prof. dept. community health and preventive medicine, 1980—; biostatis. reviewer-cons. Jour. AMA, Archives Internal Medicine, Archives Dermatology, Archives Otolaryngology, Chest, 1980—. Mem. Am. Statis. Assn., Am. Public Health Assn. Office: Northwestern U Med Sch Center for Endocrinology Metabolism and Nutrition 320 E Superior St Chicago IL 60611

VAISVIL, FRED ANTHONY, coll. adminstr.; b. Chgo., Oct. 21, 1931; s. Frank J. and Bernice (Lauraitis) V.; B.A., U. Ill., 1949; M.A., U. Chgo., 1961; Ed.D., Nova U., 1976; m. Joann E. Zaturski, June 13, 1959; children—Wayne, Christopher, Sandra, Mark. Tchr., High Sch. Dist. 214, Arlington Heights, Ill., 1957-67, vocat. counselor, 1961-67; dir. placement and student aid William Rainey Harper Coll., Palatine, Ill., 1967-73, dir. placement and career devel., 1973-78, dir. student outreach, 1978—; cons. Bell & Howell Scholarship; mem. Coll. Entrance Exam. Bd.; mem. Gould Scholarship Com.; chmn. Eugenia Chapman Scholarship Com.; rep. Nat. Inst. Career Devel. Active Wheeling Township Community Council, Chgo. Govtl. Relations Com., Cook County Council of Govts., 1965-67; bd. dirs. Omni House Youth Services Agy. Served with U.S. Army, 1954-56. Recipient Outgoing Presdl. plaque Ill. Assn. Fin. Aid Adminstrs., 1972; NDEA summer inst. guidance and counseling, 1964. Mem. Am. (mem. career info. systems workshop), Ill., N.W. Suburban personnel and guidance assns., Coll. Placement Council, Midwest Coll. Placement Assn., Placement Assn. Community Colls. and Employers, Am. Assn. Higher Edn. (life), Phi Delta Kappa. Roman Catholic. Clubs: Rotary (past pres. Wheeling), The Right. Contbr. articles to Ill. Guidance and Personnel Quar., Heuristic, Jour. Coll. Placement, 1975—. Home: Route 1 Box 200A Prairie View IL 60069 Office: Algonquin and Roselle Rds Palatine IL 60067

VAKOS, HARRY N., sch. adminstr.; b. Sparta, Greece, Jan. 8, 1927; came to U.S., 1927, naturalized, 1927; s. John P. and Emily C. Vakos; B.S., U. Wis., 1950, M.A., 1953; Ph.D., U. Minn., 1966; m. Cleo T. Vakos, Nov. 25, 1954; 1 son, Gregory. Prin., Edison High Sch., Mpls., 1964-66; asst. supt. Mpls. Public Schs., 1966-73, dep. supt., 1973-75; supt. schs. City of Rochester (Minn.) schs., 1975—. Trustee St. Mary's Hosp., Rochester, Kahler Found., Rochester. Served with U.S. Army, 1945-46. Mem. Am. Assn. Sch. Adminstrs., Minn. Assn. Sch. Adminstrs. Greek Orthodox. Club: Rotary. Office: Coffman Bldg Rochester MN 55901

VALENCIA, HERNAN, real estate fin. co. exec.; b. Cali, Colombia, Nov. 17, 1941; s. Arcesio and Cornelia (Libreros) V.; student Roosevelt U., 1968-72; m. Aliria Maria Orozco, June 7, 1979; children—John, Michael, Vicky. With Tempel Steel Co., Chgo., 1965-72, jr. acct., 1968-72; sr. acct. Heitman Mortgage Co., Chgo., 1972-74; acctg. mgr., controller The Abacus Group, B.B. Cohen Co., Chgo., 1974—. Mem. Ill. Mortgage Bankers Assn., Am. Mgmt. Assn. Club: Lions. Home: PO Box 2318 Chicago IL 60690 Office: 10 S LaSalle St Chicago IL 60603

VALENTINE, BARRY, bishop; b. Shenfield, Essex, Eng., Sept. 26, 1927; s. Harry John and Ethel Margaret (Purkiss) V.; B.A., St. John's Coll., Cambridge (Eng.) U., 1949, M.A., 1952; B.D., McGill U., 1951; L.Th., Montreal Diocesan Theol. Coll., 1951, D.D., 1970; D.D., St. John's Coll., Winnipeg, Man., 1969; m. Mary Currell Hayes, Oct. 4, 1952; children—John Nugent, Lesley Claire, Guy Richard Neville, Michael Hayes. Ordained to ministry Anglican Ch.; curate Christ Ch. Cathedral, Montreal, 1952; incumbent Chateauguay-Beauharnois, 1954; dir. religious edn. Diocese of Montreal, 1957-61; rector St. Lambert Ch., 1961-65; exec. officer Diocese of Montreal, 1965-66, archdeacon, 1966-68; dean of Montreal and rector Christ Ch. Cathedral, 1968-69; coadjutor bishop of Rupert's Land (Winnipeg), 1969-70, bishop, 1970—; chancellor St. John's Coll., Winnipeg, 1970. Office: 935 Nesbitt Bay Winnipeg MB R3T 1W6 Canada

VALENTINE, GLENN VERNON, radio sta. exec.; b. Pampa, Tex., Nov. 1, 1929; s. Lawrence Earl and Myrtle (Roberson) V.; student Inst. Radio Broadcasting, Dallas, 1951-52; m. Marie Foskin, Mar. 12, 1950; children—David L., Teresa M., Timothy J., Toni M. Gen. mgr. Sta. KWBB, Wichita, Kans.; sales mgr. Sta. KTOK, Oklahoma City; program dir. Sta. KBYE, Oklahoma City; gen. mgr. Sta. KYNN, Omaha, 1977—. Served with USAF, 1946-49. Mem. Radio Advt. Bur., Nat. Assn. Broadcasters, Nat. Credit Mgrs. Assn., Omaha C. of C., Council Bluff C. of C. Republican. Office: 615 N 90th St Omaha NE 68114

VALINET, STANLEY, electronic communications equipment mfg. co. exec.; b. Indpls., Nov. 13, 1916; s. Arthur and Mary V.; B.A., Ind. U., Bloomington, 1937; children—Stephen, Pamela, Greg. Founder, Pres. Tru-Lite Research Labs., Indpls., Stanley Realty & Devel., Inc., Indpls., 1950—, Valley Devel. Co., Indpls., 1954—; pres., chmn. bd. NRC Corp., Indpls., 1935—, Lorraine Realty, Inc., Indpls., 1945—, Dundee Realty Corp., Indpls., 1937—. Mem. Profl. Farmers Am., Top Farmers U.S., Ind. Petroleum Assn. Am., Am. Petroleum Inst. Clubs: Indpls. Athletic, Columbia. Home: PO Box 40789 Indianapolis IN 46240

VALINSKY, MARK STEVEN, podiatrist; b. Chgo., May 24, 1951; s. Harry and Beckie (Baker) V.; student Ohio State U., 1969-71, State U. N.Y. at Buffalo, 1971-72; B.S., D. Podiatric Medicine, Ill. Coll. of Podiatric Medicine, 1976; m. Michelle Susan Morgan; 1 dau., Cara Linda. Gen. practice surg. podiatry, Oak Park, Ill., 1977—; active staff Northlake (ill.) Community Hosp.; cons. staff Riveredge Hosp., Forest Park, Ill.; pres., founder Biol. Scis. Research Inst., Inc.; Pres. Aaron Podiatry Assos., P.C., Oak Park; Chief exec. officer Feet R Neat; biol. photographer. Mem. Mayor's Council Sr. Citizens and Handicapped. Certificate of service, Nat. Assn. for Human Devel., 1977; diplomate Nat. Bd. Podiatry Examiners. Mem. Ill. Podiatry Soc. (sec. Zone I, 1980-81, pres. Zone I, 1981-82 del. to bd. dirs. 1980-82), Am. Podiatry Soc., Acad. Ambulatory Foot Surgeons, Biol. Photographers Assn., Smithsonian Inst. Jewish. Club: Am. Karate Assn. Office: 189 S Oak Park Ave Oak Park IL 60302

VALIQUETTE, MARIGENE, state senator; B.A., U. Toledo, J.D. Practice law, Toledo; mem. Ohio Senate, 1969—. Mem. Democratic Nat. Com., 1976—; del. Dem. Nat. Conv., 1980; mem.-at-large Ohio Dem. State Com. Mem. LWV, Bus. and Profl. Women's Club. Office: State Senate Columbus OH 43216*

VALIS, WILLIAM VICTOR, lawyer; b. Cleve., Nov. 23, 1943; s. William John and Anna Frances (Chaplic) V.; B.A. in Econs., St. Vincent Coll., 1965; J.D., Case Western Res. U., 1968; m. Barbara Ann Yeckley, May 21, 1966; children—Kimberly Ann, Kevin William. Admitted to Ohio bar; supr. fin. dept. lamp div. Gen. Electric Corp., Nela Park, Ohio, 1968-69; law clk. for judges of Common Pleas Ct. of Cuyahoga County, Ohio, 1969-71; real estate counsel to Developers Diversified, Beachwood, Ohio, 1971; mem. firm Reminger and Reminger Co., Cleve., 1971-77, partner, 1977—; arbitrator, Am. Arbitration Assn.; panel chmn. Common Pleas Ct. Cuyahoga County Arbitration; v.p., trustee Cleveland Hts. Local Devel. Corp.; instr. bus. law, Cleve. Acad. Profl. Secs., 1969-71. Mem. Ohio State, Am. Bar Assns. Home: 2494 Stratford Rd Cleveland Heights OH 44118 Office: 300 Leader Bldg Cleveland OH 44114

VALLE, RAFAEL FIGUEROA, obstetrician and gynecologist; b. Veracruz, Mex., Sept. 6, 1935; came to U.S., 1966, naturalized, 1979; s. Miguel F. and Beatriz V. V.; M.Ph., U. Comillas, Spain, 1958; M.D., Central U. Madrid, 1965; children—Gabriel, Raquel. Intern, Mt. Sinai Hosp., Mpls., 1966-67, resident in surgery, 1967-69; resident in obstetrics and gynecology U. Minn. Hosp., Mpls., 1969-72, instr. obstetrics and gynecology, 1972-74; attending staff Hennepin County Med. Center, Mpls., 1972-75, also asst. prof. obstetrics and gynecology U. Minn., 1974-76; asst. prof. obstetrics and gynecology Northwestern U., Chgo., 1975-81, asso. prof., 1981—; attending staff Prentice Women's Hosp.; cons. Planned Parenthood of Mpls., 1972-75, Assn. Vol. Sterilization, 1972—, Planned Parenthood Assn. of Chgo., 1976—; cons. obstetrician Maternal Infant Care Projects, Mpls., 1972-75. Mem. Am. Coll. Obstetricians and Gynecologists, Am. Fertility Soc., Central Assn. Obstetricians and Gynecologists, Am. Assn. Gynecol. Laparoscopists, Chgo. Gynecol. Soc., A.C.S., Am. Assn. Planned Parenthood Physians, Minn. Obstetrics-Gynecology Soc. Roman Catholic. Contbr. articles to profl. jours., chpts. in books. Research on new methods of fertility control, new endoscopic methods in gynecology. Office: Suite 150C 333 E Superior St Chicago IL 60611

VALLEE, RUDY G., mfg. co. exec.; b. Barrie, Ont., Can., Aug. 10, 1935; came to U.S., 1951; s. Joseph A. and Marie Agnes (Marchildon) V.; B.A. in Bus. Adminstrn., Bucknell U., Lewisburg, Pa., 1955, B.A. in Applied Psychology, 1955; m. Gail Louise Lightfoot, July 16, 1965; children—Jamie Joseph, Michelle Marie, Christine Suzzane, Nicole Grace. Profl. bowler, Can., 1958-63; nat. sales and mktg. mgr. Tana Co., Montreal, Que., Can., 1963-65; gen. sales mgr. Stein-Hall, Ltd., West Hill, Ont., 1965-68; sales and engring. mgr. Sharples-Stokes div. Pennwalt Corp., Toronto, Ont., 1968-70, regional sales and engring. mgr. midwestern U.S. and Can., gen. mgr. Can. div., Oak Brook, Ill., 1970-81; pres., chmn. bd. Com-Eng, engring. corp., until 1981; v.p. Nilsen U.S.A. Corp. subs. O.J. Nilsen (Australia) Ltd., mem. Nilsen Group, 1981—; past pres. Am. Powder Metallurgy Inst., internat. metallurgy conf. liaison chief. Active sustaining mem. Ill. Republican Club; scout master Boy Scouts Am., 1978. Served with Can. Navy, 1955-58. Recipient Recognition award Golf Digest, 1978; Appreciation award Am. Powder Metallurgy Inst., 1977; Spl. Service award Coll. of DuPage (Ill.), 1978. Mem. Packaging Assn. Can., Advt. and Sales Assn. Toronto, Am. Powder Metal Assn., Am. Pharm. Assn., Aircraft Owner and Pilots Assn. Roman Catholic. Clubs: Kiwanis (Appreciation award 1977), Midland Rotary (hon. mem.). Contbr. articles in psychology to various publs. Home: 23W626 North Ave Wheaton IL 60187 Office: 1793 Bloomingdale Rd Suite 7 Glendale Heights IL 60137

VALONE, RICHARD ANTHONY, anesthetist; b. Warren, Pa., Aug. 31, 1936; s. James Theodore and Jennie Rose (La Duca) V.; B.S. in Biology, Allegheny Coll., Meadville, Pa., 1961; diploma nursing E.J. Meyer Meml. Hosp., Buffalo, 1959; diploma anesthesia St. Francis Hosp. Sch., Pitts., 1963; M.A. in Health Care Adminstrn. (Prudue Frederick fellow 1975), Central Mich. U., 1976; lic. emergency med. technician, 1978; m. Maria Tereza Romeo, Aug. 17, 1963; children—Richard Anthony, Antony James. Staff anesthetist Pitts. Anesthesia Assns., 1963; staff anesthetist Andrew Kaul Meml. Hosp., St. Mary's, Pa., 1963-66; head nurse anesthetist Mercy Hosp., Manistee, Mich., 1968-69; dir. surg. services West Shore Hosp., Manistee, 1969—; bd. dirs. Manistee Mental Health Clinic, 1973-77; program chmn., instr.-coordinator emergency med. technician groups, 1978-79. Co-chmn. heart unit Mich. Heart Assn.; bd. adv., instr. Manistee Childbirth Edn. Assn.; mem. Manistee Planning Commn., 1976—. Served with Nurse Corps, USAR, 1966-68. Recipient citation U.S. Mil. Acad., 1968. Mem. Am. Assn. Nurse Anesthetists, Am. Assn. Respiratory Therapy, Am. Assn. Operating Room Nurses, Mich. Lung Assn. (dir. 1973—), Mich. Assn. Nurse Anesthetists (past dir., trustee region 1976-78, mem. by-laws com. 1978—). Republican. Roman Catholic. Clubs: Rotary, Elks, Civic Players (past dir.). Home: 480 4th St Manistee MI 49660 Office: 1465 E Parkdale Ave Manistee MI 49660

VALTOS, WILLIAM, advt. agy. exec.; b. Scranton, Pa., Aug. 18, 1937; s. James Anthony and Mary (Rukat) V.; student U. Scranton; m. Maria Rosario Cecilia Tolentino Vallarta, Sept. 2, 1959; children—William, Catherine, Anthony, Michael. Copy chief R.H. Macy & Co., N.Y.C., 1959-61; copy chief, v.p., prin. Rockmore, Garfield & Shaub, Inc., 1961-65; creative dir., v.p. Clinton E. Frank, Inc., N.Y.C., 1965-70, v.p., creative dir., Chgo., 1970-75; sr. v.p., creative dir. D'Arcy, MacManus & Masius, Inc., 1975—. Served with USAF, 1955-59. Home: 23241 N High Ridge Rd Barrington IL 60010 Office: 200 E Randolph Chicago IL 60601

VAMOS, ROLAND, violinist, conductor, educator; b. N.Y.C., July 20, 1930; s. Julius and Bertha (Spitzer) V.; B.S. in Violin, Juilliard Sch., 1959, M.S., 1960, D.M.A. in Viola, 1975; M.A. in Music Edn., Columbia U., 1964; m. Almita Hyman, Jan. 31, 1960; children—Seth Andrew, Brandon Jules, Rami Lydell. Violinist, Denver Symphony Orch., 1949, Houston Symphony Orch., 1950, Radio City Music Hall Orchestra, N.Y.C., 1959-64; asst. prof. music Antioch Coll., 1964-67; mem. Columbus (Ohio) Symphony String Quartet, 1967-69; dir. orch. Eastern Ky. U., 1969-72; asso. prof. music Ky. Wesleyan Coll., 1973-74; concert master Owensboro (Ky.) Symphony Orch., 1973-74; asso. prof. music Western Ill. U., 1974—, dir. orchs., 1974—; condr. orch. of Am. Suzuki Assn., Stevens Point, Wis., 1978—. Served with U.S. Army, 1953-55. Mem. Ill. Music Educators Assn., Coll. Music Soc., Am. Fedn. Tchrs., Am. Fedn. Musicians, Phi Mu Alpha. Recs. for violin and viola. Home: 195 Carriage Hill Macomb IL 61455 Office: 128 Browne Hall Western Illinois University Macomb IL 61455

VAN AKEN, CHARLES ROBERT, pharmacist; b. Dexter, Mich., May 31, 1923; s. Addison Dunbar and Maude (Garn) Van A.; B.S., U. Mich., 1961, M.S., 1968; m. Rosemary Mathews, July 2, 1949; children—Thom, Catherine. Tchr., S.W. Art Inst., Dallas, 1946-47; owner Castcraft Co., Dexter, Mich., 1947-48; 2d asst. mgr. Muir Drug Co., Ann Arbor, Mich., 1948-49; clk.-mgr. McLeod Drug, Dexter, 1949-61; shift mgr. Campus Corners Inc., Ann Arbor, 1961-62; staff pharmacist career devel. program VA Hosp., Ann Arbor, 1962-69; dir. pharmacy services Ypsilanti (Mich.) Regional Psychiat. Hosp., 1969—; mem. Mich. Internship Commn., 1973—. Mem. disaster com. Washtenaw County chpt. ARC. Served with USAAF, World War II; ETO. Decorated Air medal; recipient Apothecary award (Smith, Kline & French, 1966; Bicentennial award Bicentennial Commn. Dexter, 1976; various hosp. service awards VA. Mem. Am. Soc. Hosp. Pharmacists, Western Soc. Hosp. Pharmacists, Southeastern Soc. Hosp. Pharmacists, AMA (affiliate), Dexter Area Hist. Assn. Republican. Roman Catholic. Editor: Private Thoughts of the Director of Private Lives, 1977; editor Physicians Hosp. Newsletter, 1977-79, VA Pharmacist Newsletter, 1966-68. Home: 3268 Central St Dexter MI 48130 Office: 3501 Willis St Ypsilanti MI 48197

VAN ANDEL, BETTY JEAN, household products co. exec.; b. Mich., Dec. 14, 1921; d. Anthony and Daisy (Van Dyk) Hoekstra; A.B., Calvin Coll., 1943; m. Jay Van Andel, Aug. 16, 1952; children—Nan Elizabeth, Stephen Alan, David Lee, Barbara Ann. Elementary sch. tchr., Grand Rapids, Mich., 1943-45; service rep. and supr. Mich. Bell Telephone Co., Grand Rapids, 1945-52; dir.-stockholder Amway Corp., Grand Rapids, 1972—. Treas., LWV, 1957-60; chmn. Eagle Forum, Mich., 1975—; bd. dirs. Christian Sch. Ednl. Found., Pine Rest Christian Hosp., W. Mich. Opera Co. Mem. Nat. Trust Hist. Preservation, St. Cecelia Music Soc., Smithsonian Assos. Republican. Club: Women's City of Grand Rapids. Home: 7186 Windy Hill Rd SE Grand Rapids MI 49506 Office: PO Box 172 Ada MI 49301

VAN ARSDELL, STEPHEN COTTRELL, accountant; b. Champaign, Ill., Aug. 28, 1950; s. Paul Marion and Sophia Wilsford (Smith) Van A.; B.S., U. Ill., 1972, M.A.S., 1973. Research asst. Financial Accounting Standards Bd., Stamford, Conn., 1973-74, tech. asst. to chmn., 1974-75, cons., 1976; accountant Deloitte Haskins & Sells, Chgo., 1975-76, 76—; instr. CPA review course DePaul U., Chgo., 1976. Deloitte Haskins and Sells grantee, 1972-73; C.P.A., Ill. Mem. Am. Inst. C.P.A.'s, Am. Accounting Assn., Ill. State Soc. C.P.A.'s, Phi Kappa Phi, Betá Alpha Psi, Beta Gamma Sigma, Sigma Iota Epsilon. Office: 200 E Randolph St Chicago IL 60601

VANASEK, ROBERT E., state legislator; b. New Prague, Minn., Apr. 2, 1949; s. Richard James and Elsie Marie (Kajer) V.; B.A. in Polit. Sci., U. Minn., 1971; m. Mary Wagner, June 2, 1973;

children—Robert, Lora. Engaged in flour milling; mem. Minn. Ho. of Reps., 1972—. Mem. New Prague Vol. Fire Dept.; mem. pastoral council St. Paul Archdiocese, Roman Catholic Ch. Mem. Democratic-Farm-Labor Party. Club: New Prague Sportsman.

VAN ASTEN, MICHAEL GORDON, foodservice mktg. co. exec.; b. Appleton, Wis., Aug. 9, 1953; s. Gordon Henry and Ramona Mae (Litscher) Van A.; B.B.A., St. Norbert Coll., 1975, B.A., 1975; M.B.A. in Mktg., U. Wis., 1980. Gen. mgr. Gordy's Food Fair Stores, Kimberly, Wis., 1975-80; founder, pres. The Sandwich Factory, Kimberly, 1978—, The Big Cheese Pizza Emporium, Kimberly, 1979—; advt. and promotional dir. Sunset Point Plaza, Kimberly, 1979-80; instr. mktg. and retailing Fox Valley Tech. Inst., Appleton, 1976—; pres. Van Asten & Assos., ednl. and travel cons., Appleton, 1979—. Founder, pres. Campaign Excitement, 1972, 76; mem. adv. bd. Appleton Sch. Distributive Edn., 1978—; chmn. Big Bros./Big Sisters Fox Valley, 1979; bd. dirs. Easter Seal Soc. Recipient Public Service award Campaign Excitement, 1976. Mem. Wis. Restaurant Assn. Roman Catholic. Author: Before You Decide to Visit Russia, 1979. Office: 1204 W Kimberly Ave Kimberly WI 54136

VAN AUKEN, RICHARD ANTHONY, architect; b. Cleve., June 16, 1934; s. Lewis Cornell and Loretta (Murphy) Van A.; B.Arch., U. Notre Dame, 1957; m. Susan Duffy, Nov. 10, 1978; children—Bradley, Jacqueline, Mark, Duffy, David, Brian. Project architect Hays & Ruth Architects, Cleve., 1957-58; v.p. Dalton Dalton Assos., Cleve., 1958-68; mng. partner Outcalt-Guenther Partners, Cleve., 1968-70; pres. Van Auken Bridges Inc., Cleve., 1970—; mem. adv. council U. Notre Dame. Trustee St. Alexis Hosp., Ashland Coll.; chmn. Shaker Heights (Ohio) Archtl. Bd. Rev. Served to 2d lt. U.S. Army, 1957-58. Mem. AIA, Architects Soc. Ohio, Ohio Planning Conf., Soc. for Coll. and Univ. Planning, Am. Soc. Planning Ofcls. Roman Catholic. Clubs: Shaker Heights Country, Playhouse, Hidden Valley Country. Home: 5837 Briarwood Ln Solon OH 44139 Office: 5265 Naiman Pkwy Cleveland OH 44139

VAN BEEK, SALLY KAY, registered nurse; b. Minot, N.D., May 19, 1944; d. Arvel Norman and Dorothy Irene (Anderson) Graving; B.S.N., Jamestown Coll., 1967; postgrad. in Patient Care Adminstrn., U. Minn., 1975-77; m. Carter Lee Van Beek, Aug. 12, 1967; children—Stephanie Kay, Kristin Lee. Mental health technician N.D. State Hosp., Jamestown, 1964-65, 67, staff nurse, 1967, 68, asso. dir. nursing service, 1975—; clin. nurse Doctors Plaza, Marshall, Minn., 1967-68; asst. dir. nursing Icenogle Region, N.D. State Hosp., Jamestown, 1968-71, asst. dir. nursing, 1972-75; evening shift coordinator Bernalillo County Mental Health Center, Albuquerque, 1971-72. Mem. Patient Care Adminstrn. Alumni Assn., Am., N.D. State nurses assns., N.D. Nurses Adminstrs. Assn. (co-founder, treas. 1978-79). Republican. Presbyterian. Office: Box 476 Jamestown ND 58401

VAN BERKOM, LAWRENCE PETER, agrl. chem. co. exec.; b. Powers Lake, N.D., Jan. 9, 1933; s. James and Lena Van B.; B.S., N.D. State U., 1955; m. Beverly Ulsrud, July 24, 1955; children—Michelle, Daphne. Technician, mgr. U.S. Soil Conservation Service, N.D. and Minn., 1955-67; salesman N.Y. Life Ins., Battle Lake, Minn., 1967; mgr. agrl. chems. Occidental Chem. Co., Fergus Falls, Minn., 1967-69; mgr. agrl. chems. Thompson Hayward Chem. Co., Mpls., 1969—. Served with AUS, 1956-57. Mem. Minn. Agr. Chems. Assn. (dir. 1974, pres. 1975, com. chmn. 1978-79). Lutheran. Home and office: 718 E Lakeside Dr Fergus Falls MN 56537

VANBOOVEN, PATRICIA SUE, mfg. co. exec.; b. Columbia, Mo., Apr. 23, 1939; d. Vernon L. and Lillian Louise (Claxton) Swanson; student Bakersfield (Calif.) Jr. Coll., 1970, Kay Stevens Bus. Sch., Bakersfield, 1971, Washington U., St. Louis, 1978; m. Ronald John VanBooven, July 26, 1975; children—Cynthia Lynne Thornton, Kevin Dale Thornton. Exec. sec. v.p. sales Gulf Oil Co., Bakersfield, 1971-72; sec. to sales mgr. Allergan Pharms., Irvine, Calif., 1972-73; jr. underwriter Home Life Ins. Co., Columbia, 1973-75; sales adminstr. Toastmaster Inc., Columbia, 1975—. Recipient United Way Public Service award, 1979. Mem. Am. Bus. Women's Assn., Am. Mgmt. Assn., Am. Jogging Assn. Democrat. Methodist. Clubs: Rockbridge High Booster, Columbia Track, Racquetball. Home: 3616 Southland Dr Columbia MO 65201 Office: 1801 Stadium Blvd Columbia MO 65201

VAN BRUNT, MARCIA ADELE, social worker; b. Chgo., Oct. 21, 1937; d. Dean Frederick and Faye Lila (Greim) Slauson; student Moline (Ill.) Pub. Hosp. Sch. Nursing, 1955-57; B.A. with distinguished scholastic record, U. Wis., Madison, 1972, M.S.W. (Fed. tng. grantee), 1973; children—Suzanne, Christine, David. Social worker div. community services Wis. Dept. Health Social Services, Rhinelander, 1973—, regional adoption coordinator, 1973-79, chief No. region adoption and permanent planning sect., 1979—; counselor, pub. speaker, cons. in field. Mem. Nat. Assn. Social Workers, Acad. Cert. Social Workers, Wis. Social Services Assn. Home: Rural Route 1 Box 2262 Rhinelander WI 54501 Office: Box 697 Rhinelander WI 54501

VAN BUSKIRK, EMMETT MOFFITT, artist, educator; b. Ft. Monroe, Va., Oct. 31, 1940; s. Frederick William and Margaret (Moffitt) Van B.; A.B., Middlebury Coll., 1963; M.A.T., Oberlin Coll., 1964; m. Susan Louise Erickson, May 27, 1972; children—Duncan Erickson, Cameron Anderson. Art tchr. Collinwood High Sch., Cleve., 1964; art tchr., supr. Rising Sun (Ind.)-Ohio County Community Schs., 1964-68; instr. art Upper Iowa U., Fayette, 1968-71, asst. prof., 1971-80, asso. prof., chmn. dept. fine arts, 1980—, coordinator Festmahl, 1974, 75; participant in workshops; lectr., judge local art assns. and public schs.; art dir. Fayette Centennial, 1974; contbr. campaign posters for polit. campaigns, 1974, 76, 77, 78. Recipient Spl. citation for service Upper Iowa U., 1978, Sta. KWWL-TV first Iowa TV Art Show purchase award, 1976; first place award watercolor div. N.E. Iowa Art Assn., 1970, Jessie Loomis Meml. Watercolor award, 8th Mcpl. Gallery Show, Waterloo, 1971; juror's spl. mention Charles H. MacNider Mus. Juried Area Show, 1977, Merit award, 1979; Best Painting award N.E. Iowa Competitive Show, Cedar Falls, 1981. Mem. Alpha Psi Omega, Delta Kappa Epsilon. Exhibited Five Iowa Artists Invitational show, Gov.'s Suite, State Capital, Des Moines, 1972-73, 10th Mcpl. Gallery Show, Waterloo, 1974, 26th ann. Iowa Artists Exhbn., Des Moines, 1974; 31st ann. Iowa Artists Exhbn., Des Moines, 1979; one-man shows: Waterloo Art Assn., 1975, Cedar Falls Mcpl. Gallery, 1980, Grant Wood Art Festival, 1978, Mayor's Gallery, Waterloo, Iowa, 1982; artist dust jacket design: The Eagles of Camelot (Reef and Zia Markine), 1976. Office: Art Department Upper Iowa University Fayette IA 52142

VANCE, JOAN EMILY JACKSON (MRS. NORVAL E. VANCE), educator; b. Anderson, Ind., Feb. 25, 1925; d. Virgil S. and Hannah (Hall) Jackson; B.S., Ball State U., 1947, M.A., 1955; m. Norval E. Vance, Aug. 17, 1955; 1 son, Bill E. Tchr. art and phys. edn. Winchester (Ind.) High Sch., 1948-50, 50-52, Wheatfield (Ind.) Elementary and High Sch., 1952-54; tchr. Eaton (Ind.) Elementary and High Sch., 1954—; tchr. elementary art, Elwood, Ind., 1954—, bilingual-bi-cultural migrant sch., summers 1969—; exhibited in group shows at Erica's Gallery, John Herron. Anderson Fine Art Center, state shows, street fairs. Mem. council Hoosier Salon, Indpls. Mus. Art. Recipient First prize Anderson Fine Arts Center show, 1975, 77. Mem. Nat. Art Edn. Assn., Western Art Edn. Assn., Ind Art Edn. Assn. (council), Ind. Art Tchrs. Assn. (mem. council), Anderson Art League (pres. 1967-68, 76—) Anderson Soc. Artists (v.p.), Ind. Weavers Guild, Elwood Art League (pres. 1960-70), Brown County Gallery, Brown County Guild, Delta Kappa Gamma, Delta Theta Tau. Home: Route 1 Box 48 Frankton IN 46044 Office: Elwood Community School State Rd 13 N Elwood IN 46036

VAN CURLER, DONALD EDWARD, architect; b. Pontiac, Mich., Apr. 13, 1931; s. Raymond and Cornelia (Vanderzyl) Van C.; student Port Huron Jr. Coll.; B.Arch., U. Mich., 1960; m. Charlotte Kunzli, Apr. 14, 1956; 1 dau., Claudine. Mem. tool design dept. P.R. Mallory & Co., Indpls., 1951-55; draftsman, designer Charles M. Valentine Architect, Marysville, Mich., 1954-55; draftsman Wyeth & Harmon, Inc., Port Huron, Mich., 1955-56; designer James H. Livingston Architect, Ann Arbor, Mich., 1956-59; partner Hammett Assos. in Architecture, Ann Arbor, 1959-61; prin. Donald E. Van Curler, Architect, Ann Arbor, 1961—; pres. Flying Dutchman Mgmt. Co. Inc., Amsterdam, Inc., Flying Dutchman Motor Inn, Inc.; exec. dir. Ann Arbor Research Inst., Modular Bldg. Research Found. Bd. dirs., v.p. Hwy. Club Systems, Inc. Served with AUS, 1952-54. Registered architect, Mich., Ind., Ohio, Pa., Ill., Ga., Ky., Miss., Wis., Tenn., Ala., Tex., S.C., Ark., Iowa; recipient Best Home for Money award Am. Home Mag., 1962, 63, award of Excellence, Am. Inst. Steel Constrn., 1969. Mem. Soc. Am. Registered Architects, AIA, Nat. Rifle Assn., Soc. Archtl. Historians, Mich. Soc. Architects, Nat. Council Archtl. Registration Bds., Phi Kappa Phi, Tau Sigma Delta. Republican. Baptist. Important works include restaurants, apt. bldgs. shopping centers, municipal bldgs. Office: 2004 Hogback Ann Arbor MI 48104

VAN DE MARK, PAUL LAVERNE, personnel exec.; b. Sterling, Ill., May 31, 1922; s. Fred Vernon and Maureen (Maxfield) Van De M.; B.A., Northeastern Ill. U., 1976; m. Mar jorie Boyle, Apr. 12, 1944; children—Carol Ann Van De Mark Hillary, Jon Douglas, Rebecca S. Position classifier USAF, Dayton, Ohio, 1946-60, personnel officer, 1960-63; personnel officer Air Force Systems Command, Chgo., 1963-65, Def. Logistics Agy., Dept. Def., Chgo., 1965—; spl. assignment on contract adminstrn. nat. planning group Dept. Def., 1965, regional coordinator Stability of Civilian Employment/Priority Placement Program, 1965—. Bd. dirs. N.W. Suburban Headstart Program, 1973; mem. personnel policy forum Bur. Nat. Affairs, 1975—. Served with USAF, 1943-45. Mem. Chgo. Profl. Devel. Assn. (pres. 1972). Recipient Meritorious Civilian Service award USAF, 1964; Meritorious Civilian Service award Def. Logistic Agy., 1966, also Disting. Career Service award, 1980. Home: 601 S Mt Prospect Rd Des Plaines IL 60016 Office: O'Hare Internat Airport PO Box 66475 Chicago IL 60666

VAN DEMARK, ROBERT EUGENE, orthopedic surgeon; b. Alexandria, S.D., Nov. 14, 1913; s. Walter Eugene and Esther Ruth (Marble) Van D.; S.B., U. S.D., 1936; A.B., Sioux Falls (S.D.) Coll., 1937; M.B., Northwestern U., 1938, M.D., 1939; M.S. in Orthopedic Surgery, U. Minn., 1943; m. Bertie Thompson, Dec. 28, 1940; children—Ruth Elaine, Robert, Richard. Interne Passavant Meml. Hosp., Chgo., 1938-39; fellow orthopedic surgery, Mayo Found., 1939-43; 1st asst. orthopedic surgery Mayo Clinic, 1942-43; orthopedic surgeon Sioux Falls (S.D.), 1946—; attending orthopedic surgeon McKennan Hosp., pres. med. staff, 1954, 70, attending orthopedic surgeon Sioux Valley Hosp., pres. staff, 1951-52; clin. prof. orthopedic surgery U. S.D., 1953—; med. dir. Crippled Children's Hosp. and Sch.; chief hand surgery clinic VA Hosp., Sioux Falls. Served from lt. to maj. AUS, 1943-46. Recipient Alumni Achievement award U. S.D., 1977, faculty recognition award Med. Sch., 1980; named Disting. Citizen of Yr., S.D. Press Assn., 1978; diplomate Am. Bd. Orthopedic Surgery. Fellow A.C.S. (pres. S.D. chpt. 1952, 1953); mem. Am. Assn. Med. Colls., Assn. Orthopaedic Chmn., Am. Acad. Orthopedic Surgery, Clin. Orthopedic Soc., Am. Assn. Hand Surgery, Assn. Mil. Surgeons U.S., Am. Acad. Cerebral Palsy, S.D. Med. Assn. (pres. 1974-75), Sioux Falls Dist. Med. Soc., S.A.R., 500 1st Families Am., Sigma Xi, Phi Chi. Lutheran. Clubs: Optimist; Minnehahn Country. Editor S.D. Jour. Medicine. Contbr. to med. jours. Home: 2803 Ridgeview Way Sioux Falls SD 57105 Office: 1701 S Minnesota Ave Sioux Falls SD 57105

VANDENBERG, EDWARD HERMAN, III, banker; b. Kansas City, Kans., Oct. 2, 1946; s. Edward Herman and Vera Jean (Driggs) V.; A.A., Kansas City Community Coll., 1966; student Rockhurst Coll., 1978; m. Charlotte Kay Peters, June 18, 1966; children—Michael, Scott. Mem. audit dept. staff Commerce Bancshares, Inc., Kansas City, Mo., 1966-67, 69-70; asst. controller Commerce Bank of Kansas City (Mo.), 1970-72; controller/cashier Commerce Bank of St. Louis, 1972-77; v.p. Boatmen's North Hills Bank, Kansas City, Mo., 1977—. Served with U.S. Army, 1967-69. Decorated Purple Heart. Fellow Harry S. Truman Library Inst.; mem. Am. Mgmt. Assn., Bank Adminstrn. Inst., Am. Inst. Banking, Greater Kansas City and Northland C. of C. Methodist. Clubs: Hamilton Heights Country, Linden Oaks Racquetball, Masons, Shriners, Eagles. Office: 2728 Vivion Rd Kansas City MO 64119

VANDEPORTAELE, DANIEL D., educator; b. Staden, Belgium, May 16, 1931; s. Maurice and Martha (Decaestecker) V.; A.B., Ypres; St. Vincent's Coll., 1949; Ph.B., Bruges Inst. Philosophy, 1951; M.A., Louvain, Belgium, 1957; Ph.D., U. Chgo., 1968; m. Rogelia A. Napalit, June 18, 1965; 1 dau., Arlene. Came to U.S., 1963, naturalized, 1966. Sr. instr. dept. sociology St. Louis U., Baguio City, P.I., 1959-63; research asst. Population Research and Tng. Center, U. Chgo., 1964-67; asst. prof. sociology Roosevelt U., 1967-68, asst. prof. sociology Ill. Inst. Tech., Chgo., 1968-73, asso. prof., 1973-78, acting chmn. sociology dept., 1970-71, chmn. dept., 1971-75; vis. prof. Office for Population Studies, U. San Carlos, Cebu City, Philippines, 1976-77; UN Fund for Population Activities coordinator for Philippines, 1978-80, coordinator for Turkey, Ankara, 1980-81, UNFPA Dep. Rep. Ankara, 1981—. Cons. forecasting office Ill. Bell Telephone Co., summer, 1966. Mem. Population Assn. Am., Philippine Sociol. Assn., AAAS, Am. Sociol. Assn., Internat. Union Sci. Study Population. Author: A Population Study of Suburban Chicago, Ill., 1966. Contbr. articles in field of demography to profl. jours. Address: UN Fund for Population Activities Daily News Bldg 220 E 42d St New York NY 10017 also UN Devel Programme PO Box 407 Ankara Turkey

VANDER BEE, HARVEY EDWIN, hosp. fin. exec.; b. Grand Rapids, Mich., Oct. 12, 1926; s. John and Minnie (Smit) Vander B.; B.A. in Econs., Calvin Coll., Grand Rapids, 1951; postgrad. U. Mich., 1952-53, Mich. State U., 1954, Ohio State U., 1976-77; m. Ardith Lee Anderson, Aug. 24, 1949; children—Marta Lee, Mark Edwin, Marcy Ann, Caren Jan, Carol John (twins). Acct., Lear-Siegler, Grand Rapids, 1952-62; program acct. Honeywell, Inc., St. Petersburg, Fla., 1962-65; chief acct. Mound Park Hosp., St. Petersburg, 1965-66; controller Meml. Hosp., St. Joseph, Mich., 1966-77; v.p. fin. Meml. Hosp. div. Southwestern Mich. Health Care Assn., St. Joseph, 1977-80; dir. fiscal services St. Mary Hosp., Livonia, Mich., 1980—. Served with USMC, 1944-47, 51-52. Fellow Am. Acad. Med. Adminstrs. (treas., nat. bd. dirs.); mem. Hosp. Fin. Mgmt. Assn. (nat. bd. dirs. 1973-74, pres. Western Mich. chpt. 1971-72, chmn. coordinating council 5 Mich. chpts. 1971-73), Smithsonian Instn., Nat. Audubon Soc. Republican. Mem. Christian Reformed Ch. Home: 11305 Berwick Livonia MI 48150 Office: 36475 Five Mile Rd Livonia MI 48154

VANDER JAGT, GUY, Congressman; b. Cadillac, Mich., Aug. 26, 1931; s. Harry and Marie (Copier) Vander J.; B.A., Hope Coll., 1953; B.D., Yale, 1957; LL.D., U. Mich., 1960; m. Carol Doorn, Apr. 4, 1964; 1 dau., Virginia Marie. Minister, Tustin Presbyn. Ch., 1949-52, Cadillac Congl. Ch., 1957; admitted to Mich. bar, 1960; asso. firm Warner, Norcross & Judd, Grand Rapids, Mich., 1960-64; Mem. Mich. Senate, 1965-66; mem. 89th-97th Congresses from 9th Mich. Dist., mem. ways and means com., chmn. Nat. Republican Congl. Com.; keynote speaker Rep. Nat. Conv., 1980. Named One of 5 Most Outstanding Young Men in Mich., Mich. Jr. C. of C., 1956; Rotary fellow, Bonn, 1955-56. Mem. Mich., Wexford County, Grand Rapids, D.C. bar assns. Republican. Clubs: Masons (33 deg.), Rotary (hon.). Office: 2409 Rayburn House Office Bldg Washington DC 20515

VANDER KOLK, BRUCE WILEY, forensic scientist; b. Allegan, Mich., Mar. 16, 1945; s. Wiley W. and Violet B. VanderK.; B.S., Mich. State U., 1967; M.S., U. Ill., Chgo., 1977; m. Donna S. VanderKolk, Apr. 27, 1968; children—Roger, James. Crime lab analyst Ill. Dept. Law Enforcement, Joliet, 1969-70, lab. supr., Rock Island, 1970-73, lab. supr., Maywood, 1973-77, bur. chief, bur. sci. services, Springfield, 1978—. Served to lt. U.S. Army, 1967-69; maj. Ill. N.G. Decorated Bronze Star, Army Commendation medal with oak leaf cluster; recipient Gov.'s Superior Achievement award, 1971. Mem. Am. Soc. Crime Lab. Dirs., Am. Mgmt. Assn., Am. Acad. Forensic Scis., Midwestern Assn. Forensic Scientists (sec.-treas.). Office: 108 Armory Bldg Springfield IL 62706

VANDER KOLK, KENNETH JAY, obstetrician-gynecologist; b. Zeeland, Mich., Aug. 10, 1928; s. William A. and Johanna (Freriks) Vander K.; B.S., U. Mich., 1950, M.D., 1953; m. Arloa Jean Vander Velde, June 26, 1951; children—Ronald Dale, Kathy Jo, Judy Kay, James Alan. Intern, St. Mary's Hosp., Grand Rapids, Mich., 1953-54; practice medicine specializing in family practice, Petoskey, Mich., 1954-55; resident in obstetrics and gynecology Butterworth Hosp., Grand Rapids, 1957-60, mem. staff, 1960—, dir. obstetrics-gynecology edn., 1966—; practice medicine specializing in obstetrics and gynecology, Grand Rapids, 1960—; prof. Mich. State U. Sch. Human Medicine, 1973—; Mem. central med. adv. bd. Salvation Army; bd. dirs. Planned Parenthood. Mem. consistory Central Ref. Ch., 1975—. Served with MC, USAF, 1955-57. Diplomate Am. Bd. Obstetrics and Gynecology. Fellow Am. Coll. Obstetricians and Gynecologists; mem. AMA, Mich., Kent County med. socs., Am. Assn. Maternal and Infant Health, Central Assn. Obstetricians and Gynecologists, Mich. Soc. Obstetricians and Gynecologists, Central Travel Club Obstetricians and Gynecologists, U. Mich. Alumni Assn. (gov. 1973—). Club: Blythefield Country. Home: 7183 Davies Dr Rockford MI 49341 Office: 21 Michigan St NE Grand Rapids MI 49503

VANDERLAAN, RICHARD B., printing co. exec.; b. Grand Rapids, Mich., Sept. 2, 1931; s. Sieger B. and Helen (Kerr) V.; cert. liberal arts Grand Rapids Jr. Coll., 1952; cert. mech. engring. U.Mich., 1955; cert. indsl. engring. Mich. State U., 1960; m. Charlotte A. Sterling, Aug. 20, 1955; children—Sheryl, Pamella, Brenda. Tool engr. Four Square Mfg. Co., Grand Rapids, 1950-60; sales engr. Ametek, Lansdale, Pa., 1960-63; br. mgr. J.N. Fauver Co., Grand Rapids, 1964-68; v.p. Fauver Co. subs. Sun Oil Co., Grand Rapids 1968-76, exec. v.p., 1976-80; pres. House of Printers, Inc., also dir. bd. dirs. Kent County Cancer Soc.; eagle scout. Mem. Printing Industries Am., Printing Industries Mich., Grand Rapids C. of C., Sales and Mktg. Execs., Grand Rapids Power Squadron. Congregationalist. Clubs: Peninsular, Macatawa Bay Yacht, Cascade Hills Country, East Hills Tennis. Office: Fauver Co 4550 40th St SE Grand Rapids MI 49508

VANDER LAAN, ROBERT, state senator; b. Grand Rapids, Mich., June 4, 1930; s. John R. VanderL.; A.B., Calvin Coll., Mich., 1952; M.A., U. Mich., 1957; m. Mildred Bouman, 1951; children—Linda B., Robert J. Clk., trustee and supr. Paris Twp. (Mich.); mem. Mich. State Senate, 1962—, majority leader, 1970—; v.p., mem. exec. com. Council State Govts.; alt. del. Rep. Nat. Conv., 1972; tchr. history and govt. South Christian High Sch., 7 yrs.; part-time instr. Calvin Coll., 1962. Bd. dirs. South YMCA. Mem. Christian Reformed Ch. Office: Mich Senate State Capital Lansing MI 48903*

VAN DER MEULEN, BARRY EDWIN, energy and securities co. exec., cons.; b. Waukegan, Ill., Jan. 4, 1937; s. George Y. and Adelle (Cary) Van Der M.; B.S. and M.S. in Psychology, Coll. Universal Truth, Chgo. and Los Angeles, 1956, D.D., 1957, Ph.D., 1958; m. Ellen C. Smith, Apr. 1, 1978; children by previous marriage—Cary K., John E., Colette Y. Dist. agt. to dist. mgr. Prudential Ins. Co. Am., 1959-67; v.p. Equity Funding Corp., Los Angeles, 1967-68; founder, organizer Alt Heidelberg Inns, 1969-70; cons., zone v.p. Hamilton Internat. Corp., 1970-71; chmn. bd. Havoco Am., Ltd., Chgo., 1972—, also chmn. bd., chief operating officer subs.'s; mgmt. cons., Indpls., Atlanta, Los Angeles and Detroit, 1968-72. Mem. Internat. Assn. Fin. Planners (adv. bd.), Chgo. Assn. Commerce and Industry, Am. Mgmt. Assn. (president's club), Life Underwriters Assn. Mgmt. Orgn. (v.p., organizer Indpls. chpt. 1966). Office: 155 Harbor Dr Chicago IL 60601

VANDER MEULEN, BONNIE JOYCE, univ. dean, guidance counselor; b. Bklyn., Dec. 12, 1946; d. Walter Herbert and Rosalind (Weiss) Kostin; B.S. in Health, Phys. Edn. and Recreation, Springfield (Mass.) Coll., 1968; M.S. in Counseling and Guidance, U. Wis., Madison, 1970, postgrad., 1970-74; m. David Martin Vander Meulen, Sept. 30, 1973; 1 dau., Nicole. Co-dir. recreation program for retarded and handicapped Madison Public Schs., 1969-73; jr. high sch. guidance counselor, phys. edn. tchr. K-8, Waunakee (Wis.) Public Schs., 1969-70; middle sch. guidance dir. Sauk Prairie Public Schs., Sauk City, Wis., 1970-74; guidance counselor, gymnastics adv. Middleton (Wis.) Public Schs., 1974-76; counselor Coll. Counseling Center, Moorhead (Minn.) State U., 1976-77; instr. phys. edn., head gymnastics coach N.D. State U., Fargo, 1976-77, asst. dean students, dir. spl. student services, 1977-78; instr., counselor edn. dept. U. Wis., Whitewater, 1978—, also liaison adv. Alpha Lambda Delta, Pan-Hellenic adv., dir. spl. student services; counselor, instr. Madison Area Tech. Coll., 1980—; asst. dir. student services U. Wis., Rock County Campus, 1981—. Mem. Old Gals Network, 1977-78, Tri-Coll. Minorities Planning Bd., 1977-78, Madison Theatre Guild, Faculty Wives Assn., Whitewater, 1978—; chairperson Spirit Com., 1977-78. Recipient Best Female Cameo Role award Madison Theatre Guild, 1973. N.D. Com. for Humanities and Public Issues grantee, 1978. Mem. Am. Personnel and Guidance Assn., Am. Coll. Personnel Assn., Kappa Delta Pi. Club: Whitewater Jr. Women's. Home: 244 Ardmor Dr Whitewater WI 53190

VANDERMOLEN, DONALD ROY, electronics engr.; b. Kalamazoo, July 20, 1941; s. Kobe G. and Elizabeth (Rynbrand) V.; B.S. in Elec. Engring., U. Mich., 1964, M.S., 1965; m. Jo-Ann Kalbfleisch, June 13, 1964; children—Kathryn, Janice. Control systems engr., then research engr. thick film microelectronics Whirlpool Corp., Benton Harbor, Mich., 1965-71, sr. research engr.

thick film microelectronics, 1971—. Mem. IEEE, Internat. Soc. Hybrid Microelectronics, Sigma Xi. Club: Twin City Camera. Home: 1837 Williamsburg Dr Stevensville MI 49127 Office: Whirlpool Corp Research and Engring Center Monte Rd Benton Harbor MI 49022

VANDER PLOEG, JOHN, JR., packaging equipment distbr.; b. Grand Rapids, Mich., Nov. 8, 1934; s. John and Henrietta (Bouwkump) V.; student Calvin Coll., 1952-54; m. Margaret Mejeur, Nov. 8, 1954; children—Kathie Vander Ploeg Verbeek, Randall, Michael. Sales mgr. Kalamazoo (Mich.) Rubber Stamp Co., 1954-64; founder Ship-Pac, Inc., Kalamazoo, 1964, pres., 1964—; mem. White House Conf. on Small Bus., 1980, Mich. Gov.'s Conf. on Small Bus., 1981. Pres. Christian Reformed World Relief Com., Grand Rapids, Mich., 1968-72, 78-81; vice mayor City of Kalamazoo, 1981—. Mem. Soc. Packaging and Handling Engrs., Ind. Bus. Assn. (chmn. polit. action com., bd. dirs.). Republican. Club: Rotary. Home: 3632 Woodcliff Dr Kalamazoo MI 49008 Office: 3000 Covington Kalamazoo MI 49001

VANDERPOOL, WARD MELVIN, mgmt. and mktg. cons.; b. Oakland, Mo., Jan. 20, 1915; s. Oscar B. and Clara (McGuire) V.; M.E.E., Tulane U.; m. Lee Kendall, July 7, 1935. Vice pres. charge sales Van Lang Brokerage, Los Angeles, 1934-38; mgr. agrl. div. Dayton Rubber Co., Chgo., 1939-48; pres., gen. mgr. Vee Mac Co., Rockford, Ill., 1948—; pres., dir. Zipout, Inc., Rockford, 1951—, Wife Save Products, Inc., 1959—; chmn. bd. Zipout Internat., Kenvan Inc., 1952—, Shevan Corp., 1951—, Atlas Internat. Corp.; pres. Global Enterprises Ltd., Global Assos. Ltd.; chmn. bd. Atlas Chem. Corp., Merzart Industries Ltd.; trustee Ice Crafter Trust, 1949—; dir. Atlas Chem. Internat. Ltd., Shrimp Tool Internat. Ltd. Mem. adv. bd. Nat. Security Council. Mem. Internat. Swimming Hall of Fame. Mem. Nat. (dir. at large), Rock River (past pres.) sales execs., Sales and Mktg. Execs. Internat. (dir.), Am. Mgmt. Assn., Rockford Engring. Soc., Am. Tool Engrs., Internat. Acad. Aquatic Art (dir.), Am. Inst. Mgmt. (pres. council), Am. Ordnance Assn., Internat. Platform Assn., Ill. C. of C. Clubs: Mason, Shriners, Jesters, Elks, Rockford Swim, Forest Hills Country, Exec., Elmcrest Country, Pyramid, Dolphin, Marlin. Home: 374 Parkland Dr SE Cedar Rapids IA 52403 also 50 Panorama Ct Toronto ON Canada Office: Box 242A Auburn St Rd Rockford IL 61103 also 120 Adelaide St W St W Suite 16 Toronto ON Canada also Panorama Ct Toronto ON Canada

VANDERSTEEN, PAUL RICHARD, dermatologist; b. St. Paul, Sept. 2, 1936; s. Rudolph Richard and Mabel Clare (Tybering) V.; B.S. summa cum laude, Hamline U., 1958; M.D., U. Minn., 1962; m. Bette Jean Nelson, June 16, 1963; children—David, Daniel, Peter, Rachel. Intern, Mpls. Gen. Hosp., 1962-63; resident in dermatology Mayo Clinic, Rochester, Minn., 1967-70, practice gen. medicine, Minot, N.D., 1965-67; staff Med. Arts Clinic, Minot, 1965-67; practice medicine specializing in dermatology Fargo (N.D.) Clinic, 1970—; fellow in dermatology Mayo Clinic, 1967-70; chief div. dermatology, U. N.D. Mem. St Paul Jr. C. of C., Coll. Ct. of Honor. Served with USPHS, 1963-65. Recipient L.A. Brunsting award for outstanding research in dermatology, 1970. Fellow Am. Acad. Dermatology; mem. 1st Dist. Med. Soc., Am., N.D. State med. assns., Minn. Dermatological Soc., N.C., Noah Worcester dermatological socs., Soc. Investigative Dermatology, Dermatologic Therapy Assn., Dermatology Found., Beta Beta Beta, Kappa Phi. Republican. Lutheran. Contbr. numerous articles in field. Home 155 S Woodcrest Dr Fargo NE 58102 Office: Fargo Clinic 737 Broadway Dr Fargo ND 58123

VANDER VELDEN, EDWARD LEENDERT, machine tool sales and environ. equipment mfg. co. exec.; b. Flint, Mich., June 7, 1934; s. Neil Paul and Aileen Jeanette (Cunningham) Vander V.; B.S. in Indsl. Engring., U. Mich., 1957; m. Diane M. Oldenburg, Aug. 30, 1968; children—Anne, Cynthia, Michael, Amy. Sales, engr., office mgr. Allen Bradley Co., Detroit, 1960-65; estimator, project engr. Detroit Broach & Machine Co., 1965; v.p. Valley Tools Sales Inc., Flint, Mich., 1966-74; pres., chmn. bd. Vander Velden, Inc., Grand Blanc, Mich., 1974—, Venturmation, Inc., 1978—. Past mem. Regional Planning Commn., Grand Blanc, Twp. Planning Commn. Served to lt. (j.g.) USN, 1957-60. Mem. Soc. Mfrs. Agts., Nat. Assn. Mfrs. Agts. Club: Warwick Hills Golf and Country. Home: 8498 Bush Hill Ct Grand Blanc MI 48439 Office: G3465 Pollock Rd Grand Blanc MI 48439

VAN DER WEELE, ROBERT ANTHONY, transp. co. exec.; b. Kalamazoo, Jan. 18, 1931; s. Anthony and Meryl Eunice (Ellard) Van Der W.; B.S., Western Mich. U., 1958; m. Marilyn Ruth Martin, Aug. 16, 1953; children—Susan, Brian, Joel. Sta. agt. United Airlines, Toledo, 1958-59; traffic mgr., prodn. control supr. Brown Trailer div. Clark Equipment Co., Michigan City, Ind., 1959-62; truck fleet mgr. J.I. Case Co., Racine, Wis., 1962-67; br. mgr. Saunders Leasing System, Detroit, 1967-74; transp. mgr. Amway Corp., Ada, Mich., 1974-77; dir. transp. Havi Corp., Lemont, Ill., 1977-80; dist. mgr. Lend Lease Transp. Co., Columbus, Ohio, 1980—. Mem. Republican Precinct Com., 1964-67. Served with USAF, 1950-53. Mem. Pvt. Truck Council Am., Ill. Trucking Assn., Pvt. Carrier Conf. Episcopalian. Clubs: Rotary (past v.p.), Masons, Elks. Home: 2045 Keltonshire Blvd Columbus OH 43229 Office: 3710 Lacon Rd Hilliard OH 43026

VAN DERWILL, CALVIN WAYNE, univ. adminstr.; b. Bay City, Mich., Dec. 30, 1925; s. Albert J. and Sarah (Adams) Van D.; student U.S. Mcht. Marine Acad., 1944-46; B.B.A., U. Mich., 1949, M.B.A., 1960; m. Doris L. Koch, June 12, 1948; children—Cathy Doris, Christine Ellen. Sales mgr. Dow Chem. Co., Midland, Mich., also Mexico City, 1950-58; sales trainer Morton Chem. Co., Chgo., 1958-59; supr. corp. suggestion systems Ford Motor Co., Dearborn, Mich., 1960-70; asst. personnel dir. U. Mich., Ann Arbor, 1970—; dir. Allied, Inc., Ann Arbor. Served with U.S. Maritime Service, 1944-47; PTO, ETO. Mem. Nat. Assn. Suggestion Systems (dir.), Coll. and Univ. Personnel Assn. Lutheran. Club: Kiwanis.

VANDE VOORDE, RICHARD RALPH, fin. exec.; b. Clifton Springs, N.Y., Mar. 6, 1944; s. John Peter and Ruth Marie (Becker) Vande V.; B.S., Union Coll., 1966; m. Joyce Louise Weber, Apr. 15, 1972; children—Samantha, Scott. Tchr., Miami Trace High Sch., Washington Court House, Ohio, 1967-69, Lexington (Ohio) High Sch., 1969-71; with Empire Detroit Steel, Mansfield, Ohio, 1971-73; gen. acct. F.E. Myers Co., Ashland, Ohio, 1973-77; fin. analyst North Electric, Galion, Ohio, 1977; asst. controller Mobile Hydraulics div., The Rexroth Corp., Wooster, Ohio, 1977—; faculty Mansfield Bus. Coll., 1973-74. Republican. Roman Catholic. Home: 990 Curtwood Ave Wooster OH 44691 Office: 1700 Old Mansfield Rd Wooster OH 44691

VANDE WALLE, GERALD WAYNE, justice N.D. Supreme Ct.; b. Noonan, N.D., Aug. 15, 1933; s. Jules C. and Blanche Marie (Gits) VandeW.; B.Sc., U. N.D., 1955, J.D., 1958. Admitted to N.D. bar, 1958; spl. asst. atty. gen. State of N.D., Bismarck, 1958-75, 1st asst. atty. gen., 1975-78; justice N.D. Supreme Ct., Bismarck, 1978—; mem. faculty bus. law Bismarck Jr. Coll., 1972-76. Active Bismarck Meals on Wheels; bd. dirs. Bismarck-Mandon Orchestral Assn. Mem. State Bar Assn. N.D., Burleigh County (N.D.) Bar Assn., Am. Bar Assn. N.D. Jud. Council, Am. Contract Bridge League (dir. N.D. unit), Order of Coif, Phi Eta Sigma, Beta Alphi Psi, Beta Gamma Sigma, Phi Alpha Delta. Roman Catholic. Clubs: Elks, K.C. Editor-in-chief N.D. Law Rev., 1957-58. Office: Supreme Ct State Capitol Bismarck ND 58505

VANDIVIER, BARBARA (KIDD), educator; b. Muncie, Ind., Aug. 25, 1929; d. Robert C. and Pauline L. (Sollars) Kidd; B.S., Butler U., 1951, M.S., 1967; also various profl. workshops; m. Robert E. Vandivier, Apr. 20, 1953; children—Blair R., Brian D. Elem. tchr., public schs., Indpls., 1951-53, 64-67, Houston, 1954, Rapid City, S.D., 1954-55; tchr. grades 2/3 Lewis Elem. Sch., Solon, Ohio, 1968—; condr. in-service workshops. Pres. Alpha Chi Latreian, Jr. women's services club 7th Dist., Fedn. Women's Clubs, Indpls. 1961, dir. jr. clubs, 1964-65; coordinator July 4th Bell Ringing for Indpls., 1963. Recipient award for using community for ednl. resource PACE Assn., 1973. Mem. Solon Edn. Assn. (chairperson tchrs. edn. and profl. standards com. 1977-79, cert. service 1969, 74, 79, 81), Solon United Tchrs. Assn. (chairperson com. 1977-79), NEA, Assn. Supervision and Curriculum Devel., North Eastern Ohio Tchrs. Assn., Phi Delta Kappa. Republican. Episcopalian. Club: Pi Beta Phi Alumnae of Cleve. East Dist. Home: 37175 Windy Hill Dr Solon OH 44139 Office: 32345 Cannon Rd Solon OH 44139

VAN DOOIJEWEERT, WILLY NICO, retail luggage co. exec.; b. Tricht, Netherlands, Apr. 17, 1952; came to U.S., 1971; s. Arie and Margaretha (Voet) van D.; A.A. with honors, Netherlands Sch. Bus., 1971; B.A., Mich. State U., 1972, M.B.A. with honors, 1974; m. Linda Joyce Hashimoto, May 27, 1977. Asso. buyer women's moderate sportswear Dayton's Dept. Stores, Mpls., 1974-76, buyer luggage and leather goods, 1976-78; founder, pres. Great Luggage! Inc., St. Paul, 1978—; mem. Nat. Retail Adv. Bd., 1978—, cons. various luggage cos. Mem. U.S. Soccer Assn. (cert. nat. referee), N. Am. Soccer League (profl. referee), Minn. Soccer Referee Assn. (pres. 1979—, soccer referee instr. 1979—), Japan Am. Soc., Friends of St. Paul Chamber Orch., Beta Gamma Sigma. Home: 1112 Benton Way Arden Hills MN 55112 Office: 1120 Maplewood Mall Saint Paul MN 55109

VAN DYKE, GERRIT DONALD, biologist; b. Primghar, Iowa, Apr. 12, 1938; s. Jacob and Bessie (DeVries) Van D.; A.A., Dordt Coll., 1959; B.A., Calvin Coll., 1961; M.A., U. Tex., Austin, 1965; Ph.D., Iowa State U., 1972; m. Laura Beth Haarsma, June 14, 1960; children—Leon Scott, Leslie Dale. Tchr., Western Christian High Sch., Hull, Iowa, 1961-69; tchr. biology Trinity Christian Coll., Palos Heights, Ill., 1972—; tchr. Wheaton Coll. Sci. Sta., Rapid City, S.D., summers 1974—; faculty researcher Argonne Nat. Lab., summer 1979. Served with AUS, 1956-57. Recipient Exceptional Merit award Trinity Christian Coll., 1977-78. Mem. Ecol. Soc. Am., Ill. Acad. Sci., Am. Inst. Biol. Scis., Sigma Xi, Phi Kappa Phi. Mem. Christian Reformed Ch. Author: Investigations of Nematode Trapping Fungi in Iowa, 1968. Home: 12736 S Auburn St Palos Heights IL 60463 Office: 6601 W College Dr Palos Heights IL 60463

VANEK, EUGENIA POPORAD, ednl. cons.; b. Cleve., June 23, 1949; d. George and Anna P. (Dumitru) Poporad; B.S., Case-Western Res. U., 1970; M.A. (fellow), Boston U., 1972; Ed.D., U. Rochester, 1974; m. John Albert Vanek, Aug. 28, 1971; children—Matthew Dumitru, Jessica Petera. Tchr. Cleveland Heights (Ohio) High Sch., 1970; instr. Monroe Community Coll., Rochester (N.Y.) Inst. Tech., 1972-74; asst. prof. med. edn. research Case-Western Res. U., Cleve., 1974-80, asst. prof. family medicine, 1979-80, asst. clin. prof. community dentistry, 1978-81; adj. prof. Goddard Coll., Plainfield, Vt., 1980-81; ednl. cons. 1980—. Chmn. Northeastern Ohio alumni scholarship admissions com. U. Rochester, 1974-76, 1979-80; active N.E. Ohio affiliate Am. Heart Assn., 1977; mem. Task Force on Heart Disease in Young; trustee Oberlin (Ohio) Early Childhood Center, 1980—. Ednl. cons. study fellow, 1977. Mem. Am. Ednl. Research Assn., Am. Assn. Higher Edn., Assn. Supervision and Curriculum Devel., Assn. Tchr. Educators. Author: In Piagetian Research: Compilation and Commentary, Vol. 4, 1976; contbr. numerous articles to various publs. Home and Office: 46 Stewart Ct Oberlin OH 44074

VAN GIESON, WILLIAM RANDOLPH, hosp. adminstr.; b. Columbus, Ohio, Oct. 30, 1942; s. William P. and Wanda L. (Freeland) Van G.; B.S., U. Tulsa, 1967; M.H.A. (Kellogg scholar), Duke U., 1969; m. Dayle Marie Mapes, Aug. 20, 1966; children—Lisa, David. Adminstrv. resident Duke U. Hosp. Adminstrn. Program, 1968-69; asst. adminstr. Bethesda Hosp., Zanesville, Ohio, 1969-72, asso. adminstr., 1972-76, pres., chief exec. officer, 1976—; immediate past pres. bd. Area Six Health Systems Agy.; preceptor Xavier U. Grad. Program in Hosp. and Health Care Adminstrn.; mem. Ohio health and med. leaders People to People Mission to People's Republic of China, 1982. Officer, Mental Health Assn., 1974-76; pres. Home Health Adv. Group, 1974-76; bd. dirs. United Way Muskingum, Perry and Noble Counties, also chmn. long-range planning com.; mem. Blue Cross Contract Rev. Com.; pres. Am. Cancer Soc., 1979-80, crusade chmn., 1978-79; bd. dirs. Muskingum Alcoholism Council, pres., 1973; bd. dirs. Ohio Hosp. Mgmt. Services; mem. adv. bd. Muskingum Area Tech. Coll.; mem. Ohio Citizens Council, Zanesville Indsl. Program. Recipient Rep. DeMolay and Chevalier awards Order DeMolay, 1959, 62. Mem. Am. Coll. Hosp. Adminstrs., Am. Hosp. Assn., Am. Pub. Health Assn., Nat. League Nursing, Am. Acad. Med. Adminstrs., Am. Assn. Hosp. Planning, Nat. Rehab. Assn., Hosp. Fin. Mgmt. Assn., Am. Health Planning Assn., Am. Acad. Health Adminstrn., Group Health Assn. Am., Royal Soc. Health, Am. Assn. Hosp. Planning, Ohio Hosp. Assn. (mem., chmn. various bd. coms.), Ohio Public Health Assn., Ohio Assn. for Alcoholism Programs, Nat. Mgmt. Assn. (pres. Zanesville chpt. 1975), Ohio League Nursing, Central Ohio Health Adminstrs. Assn. (pres. 1979), Zanesville C. of C., Hon. Order Ky. Cols. Methodist. Clubs: Masons; Shriners; Rotary; Order DeMolay (state officer 1962). Contbr. articles to profl. publs. Home: 2550 Douglas Dr Zanesville OH 43701 Office: 2951 Maple Ave Zanesville OH 43701

VAN GILDER, BARBARA JANE DIXON, interior designer, cons.; b. South Bend, Ind., Dec. 6, 1933; d. Vincent Alan and Wanda Anita (Rapell) Dixon; student Mich. State U., 1951-55; postgrad. St. Mary's Coll., 1956-57, N.Y. Sch. Design, 1956-58; m. Erwin Dalton VanGilder, May 25, 1959; children—Eric Dalton, Marc David. Factory color cons. Smith-Alsop Paint Co., Terre Haute, Ind., 1955-56; archtl. design cons., Mishawaka, Ind., 1956-58; residential-comml. designer, South Bend. Chgo., 1958-63; designer industrialized housing industry, Ga., Fla., Ind., Mich., 1962—; design cons. Skyline Corp., Ind., Calif., Pa., 1962-66; v.p. design Treasure Chest Corp., Sturgis, Mich., 1969, also dir.; pres., dir. Sandpiper Art, Inc.; v.p. T.C.I. Ltd.; design cons. C.O. Smith Ind. Peachtree Housing, Moultrie, Ga., Nobility Homes, Ocala, Fla.; head merchandising and design Sandpiper Originals, clothing boutique, 1978—; currently pub. relations ofcl. Am. Mktg. Assn., adj. tchr. Lakeshore Sch. System, also coordinator trade show displays; v.p. Van Gilder Assos., Lakeaire Vending; adviser on merchandising and design Armstrong Corp., Lancaster, Pa.; nat. advt. rep. Studebaker-Packard Corp., Mercedes Benz, Clark Equipment, 1959-63; writer series on decorating for 2 Mich. newspapers, 1961-63; participant TV show Know Your Decorator, Calif. and Maine, 1962, 77. Officer, Shoreham Village (Mich.) Bd. Zoning, 1960-63. Named Woman of Year, Profl. Model's Club, 1952; recipient 1st pl. furniture design hardwoods Nat. Hardwoods Assn., 1956; 1st pl. Best in Show award, Louisville, Atlanta, 1964-65, 66, 69, 70-74, 76; others. Mem. Design Council Industrialized Housing (award 1974), Nat. Soc. Interior Designers, Mich. State U. Alumni Assn., Internat. Platform Assn., Internat. Biog. Assn. Contbg. editor Skyliner mag., 1962-66; permanent guest editor, contbr. Today's Home mag., 1974—. Home: 3630 S Lakeshore Dr Saint Joseph MI 49085 Office: PO Box 244 Stevensville MI 49127 also PO Box 1100 Dunedin FL 33528

VAN GILST, BASTIAN, state senator, farmer; b. Marion County, Iowa, Apr. 14, 1911; s. Peter and Nellie (Klien) Van G.; m. Harriet De Bruin, Nov. 26, 1937; children—Ken, Carl, Elaine, Mark, Diane, Joleen. Mem. Iowa Senate, 1965—, Democratic whip, 1975-76, asst. majority leader, 1977-78; livestock and grain farmer, Oskaloosa, Iowa; dir. VG Farms. Fund dr. chmn. United Community Services; mem. legis. fiscal com. Capitol Planning Commn. Mem. C. of C., Farm Bur. Mem. Christian Reformed Ch. Club: Oskaloosa Lions (past pres.). Office: Iowa State Capitol Des Moines IA 50319

VAN HALSEMA, DICK LUCAS, coll. pres.; b. Grand Rapids, Mich., July 19, 1922; s. Emo F.J. and Nellie (Lucas) Van H.; A.B., Calvin Coll., Grand Rapids, 1943; B.D., Calvin Theol. Sem., 1949; S.T.M., Union Theol. Sem., N.Y.C., 1953, Th.D., 1956; m. Thea Jane Bouma, Mar. 19, 1948; children—David Emo, Nancy Tess, Clark Gerard, Emily Beth, Dick Lucas. Ordained to ministry Christian Reformed Ch., 1949; pastor chs. in N.Y., Fla. and Mich., 1949-57; minister for evangelism Christian Reformed Ch., 1957-63; pres. Reformed Bible Coll., Grand Rapids, 1966—; bd. dirs. World Presbyn. Missions, Samuel Zwemer Inst., Missionary Internship, Fellowship of Faith for Muslims, Middle East Christian Outreach, Christian Witness Tours. Served with AUS, 1943-46; to col. USAR, 1946-78. Decorated Bronze Star with oak leaf cluster, Combat Inf. badge. Mem. Paul Soc. (pres.). Editor Missionary Monthly, 1965—. Composer hymns, anthems. Office: 1869 Robinson Rd Grand Rapids MI 49506

VANHANDEL, RALPH ANTHONY, librarian; b. Appleton, Wis., Jan. 17, 1919; s. Frank Henry and Gertrude Mary (Schmidt) Van H.; B.A., U. Wis., 1946; A.B., U. Mich., 1947; m. Alice Catherine Hogan, Oct. 27, 1945; children—William Patrick, Karen Jean, Mary Jo. Head librarian Lawrence (Kans.) Free Pub. Library, 1947-51, Hibbing (Minn.) Pub. Library, 1951-54; library dir. Gary (Ind.) Pub. Library, 1954-74, Wells Meml. Pub. Library, Lafayette, Inc., 1974—; mem. Ind. Library Certification Bd., 1969—, Ind. Library Expansion Commn., 1973-81. Named Ind. Librarian of Year, 1971. Mem. Anselm Forum (sec. 1964, v.p., 1965), ALA, Ind. (pres. 1963-64), Kans. (v.p. 1951) library assns. Clubs: K.C., Rotary. Home: 3624 Winter St Lafayette IN 47905 Office: 638 North St Lafayette IN 47901

VAN HOOZER, HELEN LUCILLE, instructional designer; b. Shenandoah, Iowa, Jan. 28, 1938; d. George Doak and Hazel Lucille (Burke) Staten; M.A., U. Iowa, 1974; student N.W. Mo. U., N.E. Mo. U., Drake U., Marshalltown Community Coll.; m. Richard Neil Van Hoozer, May 20, 1956; children—Cynthia Diane, Robert Wayne, Randall Gene. Elem. tchr., media dir. Clear Creek Community Schs., Oxford Center, Tiffin, Iowa, 1970-73; media specialist handicapped Midwest Ednl. Resource Center, Coralville, Iowa, 1973-74; instructional designer U. Iowa Coll. Nursing, Iowa City, 1974—. Mem. rules com. John County Democratic Conv., 1976. U. Iowa Fund Spl. Instructional Support grantee, 1978. Mem. Assn. Ednl. Communications and Tech., Iowa Ednl. Media Assn., Assn. Supervision and Curriculum Devel., NOW. Author: (with Alberta A. Tedford) Pharmacology: A Self-Instructional Approach, 1980; contbr. articles to profl. jours. Home: Rural Route 1 Kalona IA 52247 Office: Coll Nursing U Iowa Iowa City IA 52242

VAN HORN, LOUIS HAROLD, realtor; b. Greenville, Mich., Apr. 4, 1928; s. Adrian L. and Mildred (Davis) Van H.; Asso. Scis., Grand Rapids Jr. Coll. 1956, student, 1965; student Mich. State U., 1956-57, U. Mich. Extension, 1958; m. Christina F. Bogden, Oct. 15, 1969 (dec. Jan. 1977); children—Sheila Kay, David Louis; m. 2d, Nancy Ann Van Horn, Oct. 6, 1977. Owner, Koncrete Tile Co., Burbank, Calif., 1946-48; salesman Donald Beardslee Real Estate, Greenville, 1948-50; with Gibson Refrigerator Co., 1952-53; mem. planning and scheduling dept. Gen. Motors 1952, Grand Rapids, 1953-54; builder, realtor, Greenville, 1955—; dir. Realtor Computer Services, subsidiary Nat. Assn. Real Estate Bds., 1971—, v.p., 1972—. City assessor, Greenville, 1958-60; mem. Greenville Zoning Bd., 1958-66, Greenville Planning Commn., 1970-80; Montcalm County chmn. Republican Party, 1976-79. Served with U.S. Army, 1950-52. Decorated Combat Infantry badge. Mem. Montcalm County Bd. Realtors, Farm and Land Brokers (pres. Mich. chpt. 1, 1971), Nat. Inst. Farm and Land Brokers (regional v.p. 1971-72, chmn. spl. services com. 1974, chmn. subcom. computers on real estate 1970, gov. 1975-77). Patentee instant pontoon bridge. Address: PO Box 122 Greenville MI 48838

VAN HORNE, PIETER HAMMOND, lawyer; b. Chgo., Dec. 26, 1941; s. David E. and Marjorie N. (Petersen) van H.; student Williams Coll., 1959-61; B.A., Parsons Coll., 1963; J.D., Northwestern U., 1966; LL.M. in Labor Relations, Wayne State U., 1978; m. Priscilla S. Kruse, Aug. 21, 1965; 1 dau., Jennifer Paige. Admitted to Mich. bar, 1967; atty. N.Y. Central Ry. Co. and successors, Detroit, 1966-71; asso. McInally, Rockwell & Brucker, profl. corp., Detroit, 1971-73, dir., shareholder McInally, Rockwell, Brucker, Newcombe & Wilke, P.C., Detroit, 1974-77; propr. Pieter van Horne, Esq., 1977-78; shareholder English and van Horne, P.C., Detroit, 1979—; dir., gen. counsel R.W.C. Inc. and predecessors, Bay City, Mich., 1973—, Benefit Advisors, Inc., 1978—, Power Magnetics, Inc., 1979—, Johnson Steel Service Inc., 1980—, Midwest Laser Systems Inc., 1980—; gen. counsel Pointe Diversified Services, 1979—; guest lectr. U. Detroit Urban Law Clinic, 1969-70. Com. chmn. U.S. Senator Robert Griffin re-election 14th Congressional Dist., 1972, mem. re-election com. for Mich. Rep. William Bryant, 1972, 74; bd. dirs. Alexandrine House, Inc., Alexandrine House Found., Family Life

Edn. Council, Inc., Detroit br. Multiple Sclerosis Soc. Recipient cert. merit Fed. Defender Program, 1966, cert. of outstanding service Phi Alpha Delta, 1966; named Outstanding Young Man Grosse Pointe Jaycees, 1974, senator Jr. Chamber Internationale, 1975. Mem. Am., Detroit bar assns., State Bar Mich., Am. Trial Lawyers Assn., Immigration and Nationality Lawyers Assn., U.S., Mich. (legal counsel 1973-74), Detroit Philatelic Soc. Methodist (ch. sch. tchr., counsellor 1969-73, mem. adminstrv. bd. 1970-73, 78—, chmn. pastor parish relations com. 1970-73, youth fellowship counsellor 1973-78, fin. com. 1979-81, council on ministries 1979—, chmn. E.M.C. Fund 1969, 78, personnel com. Detroit Conf. 1980—). Home: 791 Lincoln St Grosse Pointe MI 48230 Office: 4472 City Nat Bldg Detroit MI 48226

VAN HOUTEN, JAMES FORESTER, JR., ins. co. exec.; b. Fullerton, Calif., Jan. 13, 1942; s. James Forester and Lois Trout Van H.; A.B. in English, St. Mary's U., 1971; m. Susan Ann Cox; children—Kimberly Evangeline, Lori Lynn. Various mgmt. assignments including regional sales mgr. M.I.C. div. Gen. Motors Corp., 1963-74; v.p. sales and mktg. Volkswagen Ins. Group, St. Louis, 1974-77; profit center v.p. Wausau Ins. Cos., St. Louis, 1977-80, v.p. life and health mktg., Wausau, 1980—; dir. Wausau Underwriters Life Ins. Co.; mem. faculty St. Louis Community Coll. Mem. St. Louis Soc. Mktg. Execs., Soc. C.P.C.U. Office: 2000 Westwood Dr Wausau WI 54401

VAN HOUTEN, VERNE WILLIS, clin. psychologist; b. Modesto, Calif., Nov. 17, 1943; s. Paul and Margaret (Sankey) Van H.; B.A., Calvin Coll., 1967; M.A. (Mich. Dept. Edn. fellow), Central Mich. U., 1969; m. Janice Ruth Mead, Aug. 23, 1968; children—Kimberly Joy, Jason Paul, Laura Beth. Sch. psychologist Isabella County (Mich.) Intermediate Sch. Dist., 1968-69; vocat. rehab. counselor Vocat. Rehab. Services, Grand Rapids, Mich., 1970; clin. psychologist Allegan County (Mich.) Community Mental Health Services, 1970-72, West Shore Mental Health Services, Muskegon, Mich., 1972—; cons. Muskegon County Community Mental Health Services' Partial Hospitalization Program. Bd. dirs. Muskegon Christian Sch., 1974-77, v.p., 1976-77. Served with U.S. Army, 1969. Mem. Community Mental Health Assn. Mich., Am. Psychol. Assn., Mich. Assn. Profl. Psychologists (dir. Region VIII 1979), Mental Health Assn. in Mich. (dir. Muskegon chpt. 1976-77, pres. 1980-81). Mem. Christian Reformed Ch. (deacon 1979, sec.-treas. 1980). Home: 1335 Brookwood Dr Muskegon MI 49441 Office: 2525 Hall Rd Muskegon MI 49442

VAN KERSEN, PHILIP LIONEL, thermometer mfg. co. exec.; b. South Haven, Mich., Nov. 13, 1926; s. Edward Philip and Mildred Irene (Whitney) Van K.; B.A., Western Mich. U., 1949; postgrad. U. Mich., 1949-50; children—Philip William, Christopher Ashley, Melissa Dee, Eric Philip, Matthew Christopher. Field sales rep. Pitman-Moore Co., 1950-62; product promotion mgr. Dow Pharms., 1962-64, product mgr., sr. product mgr., 1964-69; founder, mgr., owner Robert J. Scott Assos., sales promotion agy., Indpls., 1969-73, Temperature Dynamics, mfrs. liquid temperature devices, Indpls., 1973-79; with Clinitemp, Inc., Indpls., 1975—, chmn., 1979—; cons. on sr. citizen needs Indpls. C. of C., 1970-77. Served with Hosp. Corps, USN, 1945-46. Mem. Health Industries Mfrs. Assn., Pharm. Advt. Club N.Y., Midwest Pharm. Advt. Club. Republican. Episcopalian. Author: Aunt Belle's Famous Bread Cookbook, 1980; patentee thermochromic liquid crystal devices; inventor forehead fever detector, bath, wine, yeast thermometers, fever detector for dogs. Home: PO Box 40273 Indianapolis IN 46240 Office: 8549 Zionsville Rd Indianapolis IN 46268

VAN LEUVEN, ROBERT JOSEPH, lawyer; b. Detroit, Apr. 17, 1931; s. Joseph Francis and Olive (Stowell) Van L.; student Albion Coll., 1949-51; B.A. with distinction Wayne State U., 1953; J.D., U. Mich., 1957; m. Holly Goodhue Porter, Dec. 31, 1976; children—Joseph Michael, Douglas Robert, Julie Margaret. Admitted to Mich. bar, 1957, since practiced in Muskegon; partner firm Hathaway, Latimer, Clink & Robb, 1957-68, partner McCroskey, Libner & Van Leuven, 1968-81, Libner, VanLauren & Kortering, 1982—. Bd. dirs. Muskegon Children's Home, 1965-75. Served with AUS 1953-55. Fellow Am. Coll. Trial Lawyers; mem. Am. Bar Assn., State Bar Mich. (past mem. council negligence law sect.), Mich. Assn. Professions, Am. Arbitration Assn., Muskegon Urban League, Delta Sigma Phi. Club: Muskegon Country. Home: 966 Mona Brook Muskegon MI 49445 Office: Huckley Bank Muskegon Mall Muskegon MI 49443

VAN LIEROP, PETER, clergyman, hosp. chaplain; b. Chgo., Apr. 11, 1918; s. Johannes Bernard Henderik and Johanna Kathrina (Hamel) van L.; student Royal Athenaeum of Ghent (Belgium), 1930-36, Ghent Nat. U., Belgium, 1938-40, U. Mich., 1941-42; B.A. in Biology, Hope Coll., 1946; M.Div., Pitts. Theol. Sem., 1949; M.Ed., U. Pitts., 1949, Ph.D., 1955; M.A. in Counseling, Columbia U., 1961; Th.M., Princeton Theol. Sem., 1967; m. Eleanor Catherine Creswell, June 19, 1943; children—Peter Creswell, J. Bernard H., Eleanor J., Martha J., Andrea Margaret. Ordained to ministry United Presbyterian Ch.; missionary to Korea, Fgn. Missions Bd. Presbyn. Ch. in U.S.A., 1949-77; instr. Bible and Christian lit. N. Japan Coll., Sendai, 1951-52; founder Kyung An High Sch., Andong, Korea, 1954, prin., 1954-56; founder Sung-Ro Won Home for ret. Bible women, Andong, Korea, 1953, Good Samaritan Clinic, Andong, 1953; instr. in Bible, Kyung An Bible Inst., Andong, 1952-54, 55-56; prof. Christian edn. and psychology of religion Yonsei U., Seoul, Korea, 1956-76; acting gen. sec. Korea Student Christian Movement, 1957-59; lectr. Presbyn. Sem., Seoul Nat. U., Seoul Women's Coll.; chmn. United Presbyn. Mission in Korea, 1963, 76; founder Christian edn. dept. Yonsei U., Seoul, chmn., 1965-69, 74-76, dir. student union and counseling center, 1967-77, dean Coll. Theology, 1962-66, also dir. clin. pastoral tng. program at United Grad. Sch. Theology, 1973-76; v.p. Korea Human Relations Tng. Assn., 1972-76; dir. Alpha Counseling Services, Villa Park, Ill., 1977-78; chaplain Sheboygan (Wis.) Meml. Hosp., 1979—. Bd. dirs. Kyung Shin High Sch., Seoul, 1958-76, Pierson Bibl. Sem., Seoul, 1960-76, Agape House Coffee House Ministry, Seoul, 1972-76, Korea Bible Soc., 1962-64, Korea Student Christian Fedn., 1959-66, Life Line Telephone Counseling, Seoul, 1975-77. Served with M.C., U.S. Army, 1942-45; ETO. Recipient Human Rights award Korea Bar Assn., 1963; cert. profl. mental health clergy. Mem. Am. Personnel and Guidance Assn., Assn. Mental Health Clergy, Assn. Counselor Edn. and Supervision, Assn. Psychol. and Ednl. Counselors in Asia (standing com. 1976—), Kappa Delta Pi. Republican. Author: Christian Education: Theory and Practice, 1961; Pastoral Counseling, 1977; contbr. numerous articles on Christian edn. to profl. publs.; instrumental in establishment of 120 Bible clubs and ch. schs. in Korea. Home: 2628 N 7th St Sheboygan WI 53081 Office: Chaplain's Office 2629 N 7th St Sheboygan WI 53081

VAN METER, THOMAS ADAMS, state senator; b. Detroit, Apr. 22, 1943; s. Lord Wright and Gwen H. (Paracheck) Van M.; A.B., Ashland Coll., 1965; postgrad. Ohio State U. Law Sch., 1965-66; m. Nancy Josephine Arch, Dec. 18, 1965; children—Margaret, Stephanie. Asst. to Rep. John M. Ashbrook, Washington, 1965-67; mem. staff Ashland County Republican Fin. Com., 1970—; co-exec. chmn., 1970—; mem. Ohio State Senate, 1973—, minority whip, 1977, asst. minority leader, 1978, pres. pro tem, 1981—; asst. registrar Ashland (Ohio) Coll., 1970—, trustee, 1973—; dir. U Brand Corp. of Ashland. Republican candidate for Ohio gov. Served with U.S. Army, 1967-69. Mem. Assn. Ind. Colls. and Univs. (dir.), Midwest Conf., Council of State Govts. Office: State House Columbus OH 43215

VAN MINDEN, MERLE, state legislator; b. Martinsburg, Nebr., June 8, 1926; grad. high sch.; m. Deenette Good, Jan. 23, 1955; children—LeAnn Russell, Scott, Lori. Farmer-feeder; mem. Nebr. Legislature, 1980—. Supr., Dixon County (Nebr.); mem. Region IV Mental Health Bd.; mem. Dixon County Republican Com., chmn. fin. com.; mem. Co-op Elevator Bd.; vol. fireman. Served with U.S. Army; Korea. Mem. Am. Legion, DAV, Farm Bur., Nat. Legis. Council, Am. Legion Press Assn., VFW. Lutheran. Address: Box 127 Allen NE 68710*

VANNELLI, TED MARSHALL, county ofcl.; b. Warren, Ohio, May 16, 1945; s. Emil and Anne (Rudin) V.; student Lewis, Weinberger & Hill Cosmetology Sch., 1964, Kent State U., 1974, Ohio Police Officer Acad., 1975; m. Linda Smith, Mar. 28, 1972; children—Rochelle, Mario, Tina. Pres., Casa de Vannelli Hairstyling, Inc., Southington, Ohio, 1969-81; v.p. Gold Nugget Farms Inc., Southington, 1972—; dep. sheriff County of Trumbull, Ohio, 1972-79, commr., 1979—, pres., 1980—. Chmn. United Appeal, Warren, Ohio, 1980. Cert. police officer, Ohio; Ky. col. Mem. Nat. Assn. Counties (labor relations steering com.), Quarter Horse Racing Assn. (pres. 1975-77). Democrat. Office: 160 High St Warren OH 44481

VAN NORMAN, WILLIS ROGER, clinic exec.; b. Windom, Minn., June 17, 1938; s. Ralph Peter and Thelma Pearl (Bare) Van N.; A.A., Worthington Jr. Coll., 1958; B.S., Mankato State Coll., 1960; m. Irene Anna Penner, Sept. 7, 1959; children—Eric Jon, Brian Mathew, Karin Ruth. Tchr. chemistry, St. Peter, Minn., 1961; tchr., Byron, Minn., 1962, spl. edn., Rochester, Minn., 1963-65; instr. pilots ground sch. Rochester Jr. Coll., 1968-69; with Mayo Clinic, Rochester, 1962—, developer biomed. computer systems, 1974—; instr. Gopher Aviation, 1968-71. Mem. Mankato State Alumni Assn. (dir.), Minn., Nat. ednl. assns., Internat. Flying Farmers, Am. Radio Relay League (mgr. Minn. sect. traffic net), Rochester Amateur Radio Club (pres.). Methodist. Founder, mgr. Van Norman's Flying V Ranch, 1972—, Van Norman Airport, St. Charles, 1977—. Home: Route 3 Box 25 Saint Charles MN 55972 Office: Mayo Clinic Rochester MN 55901

VAN NOSTRAND, DAVID MICHAEL, surgeon, b. Rochester, N.Y., Dec. 29, 1936; s. Manning Eugene and Thyra A. (Gundlach) V.; B.A., Grinnell Coll., 1958; M.D., Boston U., 1962; m. Catharine Marie Herr, July 16, 1960; children—Laura Susan, Catharine Louise, Maren Thyra. Intern, St. Luke's Hosp., Duluth, Minn., 1962-63; resident Hennepin County Gen. Hosp., Mpls., 1963-65, VA Hosp., Mpls., 1965-68; practice medicine specializing gen. surgery, St. Cloud, Minn., 1968—; mem. staffs Paynesville (Minn.) Community Hosp., Milaca (Minn.) Hosp., St. Michael's Hosp., Sauk Center, Minn., St. Gabriel's Hosp., Little Falls, Minn., Meeker County (Minn.) Hosp., Central Minn. Surg. Center, St. Cloud, Monticello-Big Lake (Minn.) Hosp. Vice-pres. YMCA, St. Cloud, 1977-81, pres., 1981—; bd. dirs. Nat. YMCA, 1970—, Camp Olson, Longville, Minn., 1970—. Served to capt. Air N.G., 1963-69. Diplomate Nat. Bd. Med. Examiners; recipient Physicians Recognition award AMA, 1977. Fellow A.C.S.; mem. Minn. Surg. Soc., Aerospace Med. Assn. Contbr. articles to med. jours. Home: 1220 N 13th St St Cloud MN 56301 Office: 2055 N 15th St St Cloud MN 56301

VAN NUYS, JOHN DIXON, physician; b. Chgo., Sept. 15, 1925; s. George Thomas and Marion Esther (Dixon) Van N.; B.S., U. Notre Dame, 1950; M.D., Loyola U., 1955; m. Ann Duginski, May 16, 1959; children—Thomas, Julia, Peter, Timothy, Steven. Intern, Cook County Hosp., Chgo., 1955-56, resident, 1956-57; gen. practice medicine, Chgo., 1957-59; resident ear, nose and throat U. Ill., Hines VA Hosp., 1959-62; practice medicine specializing in ear, nose and throat, Waukegan, Ill., 1962—; mem. attending staff Victory Meml., St. Therese hosps., Waukegan, Ill., 1962—; cons. Condell Meml. hosps., 1963—; mem. asso. staff Lake Forest Hosp., 1965—, Good Shepherd Hosp., Barrington, Ill. Served with USNR, 1944-46. Diplomate Am. Bd. Otolaryngology. Fellow ACS, Am. Acad. Facial Plastic and Reconstructive Surgery; mem. AMA, Am. Acad. Ophthalmology and Otolaryngology, Am. Trauma Soc., Ill. State, Lake County med. socs. Roman Catholic. Clubs: Serra (pres. 1970), Notre Dame (pres. 1969), Elks (Waukegan, Ill.). Home: 511 Cambridge Lane Lake Bluff IL 60044 Office: 609 Greenwood Ave Waukegan IL 60085

VAN RANST, ALFRED FREDERICK, mfg. co. exec.; b. Bklyn., Dec. 18, 1917; s. Milton Garfield and Emelia (Aven) Van R.; B.S., Cornell U., 1939; m. Gladys R. Morse, Nov. 8, 1941; children—Caryl, Alfred Frederick. With Phelps Dodge Copper Products Co., Ft. Wayne, Ind., 1939—, v.p. mktg., 1965-68, pres. Phelps Dodge Magnet Wire Co., 1968-79, chief exec. officer, 1969-80, vice chmn. bd. Phelps Dodge Industries, Inc., N.Y.C., 1980, chmn. bd., 1980—, chief exec. officer Phelps Dodge Copper Products Co., 1980, dir. Phelps Dodge Industries, 1973; dir. Fort Wayne Nat. Bank. Mem. Ind.-Purdue Found. Mem. Am. Mgmt. Assn., Nat. Elec. Mfrs. Assn. (bd. govs.), Fort Wayne C. of C. Clubs: Fort Wayne Country, Summit; Cornell (N.Y.C.). Office: 1302 E Creighton Ave Fort Wayne IN 46803

VANSANT, CARL ALLEN, engring. cons.; b. Clinton, Mo., Feb. 14, 1938; s. Emmett Allen and Mary Elinor (Howell) V.; B.S., U. Mo. at Rolla, 1960; M.S., Purdue U., 1963; m. Margaret Joan Chiabotta, June 15, 1958; children—Lori Elizabeth, John Ayres. Engr., Tex. Instruments, Dallas, 1962-63; phys. metallurgist U.S. AEC, Germantown, Md., 1963-65; systems analyst Operations Research Inc., Silver Spring, Md., 1965-68; systems analyst Vertex Corp., Kensington, Md., 1968-69; energy systems cons., Kensington, 1969-70; systems engr. Value Engring. Co., Alexandria, Va., 1970-71; project mgr. Black & Veatch Cons. Engrs., Kansas City, Mo., 1972—. Served with AUS, 1963-65. Alcoa Found. fellow, 1960-61; NSF fellow, 1961-62. Registered profl. engr., Kans., Ky., Mo., Md., D.C., Wyo., Idaho, Minn., Mont., Oreg., Wash. Mem. Phi Kappa Phi, Tau Beta Pi, Sigma Gamma Epsilon, Alpha Sigma Mu. Lutheran. Patentee in field. Author: Strategic Energy Supply and National Security, 1971. Contbr. articles to profl. jours. Home: 10901 Harrison St Kansas City MO 64131 Office: 1500 Meadow Lake Pkwy Kansas City MO 64114

VAN SANT, JOANNE FRANCES, coll. dean and ofcl.; b. Morehead, Ky., Dec. 29, 1924; d. Lewis L. and Dorothy (Greene) Van Sant; B.A., Denison U., 1946; M.A., Ohio State U., 1953; LL.D., Albright Coll., 1975. Instr. health and phys. edn. Mayfield (Ky.) High Sch., 1946-48, Denison U., 1948; instr. health and phys. edn. Otterbein Coll., 1948-52, asst. prof., 1952-55, asso. prof., 1955—, dean of women, 1952-60, 62-64, v.p. for student affairs, dean of students, 1964—. Bd. dirs. Planned Parenthood Central Ohio, 1976-81, Friends in Action, 1977—; mem. North Area Health and Mental Retardation Bd., 1979—, chmn., 1981-82. Recipient citation for outstanding contbn. to higher edn. Pi Lambda Theta, 1979; named Woman of Year, Otterbein Woman's Club, 1980. Mem. Am., Ohio (chmn. coll. sect. 1963-64) AAUW (dir. 1951-62, 73—), Ohio Assn. Women Deans, Adminstrs. and Counselors (treas., exec. bd. 1972-73), Nat., Ohio assns. student personnel adminstrs., Cap and Dagger, Alpha Lambda Delta, Theta Alpha Phi, Torch and Key. Presbyterian (elder 1967-69, clk. 1968-69, trustee 1975-77). Clubs: Zonta (pres. 1978-80), Walnut Valley Boat, Westerville Women's Music (dance chmn. 1968-74, 76—). Home: 9100 Oakwood Pl Westerville OH 43081 Office: Otterbein Coll Westerville OH 43081

VAN SCYOC-ZIMMERMAN, VERONICA LUCILLE, anthrop. cons.; b. Palmyra, Pa., June 21, 1943; d. James Wayne and Bertha Mary (Gamber) Van Scyoc; A.B., U. Mich., 1979; postgrad. Wayne State U., 1980—; m. Patrick David Zimmerman, Apr. 14, 1962; 1 son, Patrick David. Geneal. research various hist. socs., 1976—; research asst. U. Mich., 1978; anthropol. cons. Dearborn Psychol. Clinic, 1979—. Mem. New Detroit Task Force on Juvenile Delinquency, 1981—. Mem. NOW, Am. Anthrop. Assn., So. Anthrop. Soc., Plains Anthrop. Soc., Pa. Archaeol. Soc. Common Cause. Roman Catholic. Home: 35511 Stephanie St Romulus MI 48174 Office: 23439 Michigan Ave Dearborn MI 48124

VAN SICKLE, ROBERT HOWARD, health center adminstr.; b. Youngstown, Ohio, Feb. 5, 1949; s. Robert E. and Elizabeth A. Van S.; B.S.B.A., Youngstown State U., 1973, M.B.A., 1975; m. Mary Celeste Chesney, Sept. 12, 1970; children—Gretchen, Heather. Br. mgr. Am. Investment Corp., Youngstown, 1968-73; ops. mgr. Trumbull Supply Corp., Youngstown, 1973-76; bus. mgr. Ohio Dept. Mental Retardation, Youngstown, 1976-78; fiscal dir. Child/Adult Mental Health Center, Youngstown, 1978—; exec. dir. Eastern Mahoning County Mental Health Center, 1979-80; operator, owner Little Forest Med. Center, Akron, Ohio, 1980—; owner West Haven (Conn.) Manor Nursing Home, Red Hills Rest Haven, Sumner, Ill.; fin. cons. to parochial schs., group homes for retarded. Treas., Mahoning Valley Gaelic Soc., Youngstown. P.A., Ohio; lic. ins. agt., securities dealer, real estate agt. Mem. Nat. Mgmt. Assn., Nat. Assn. Accts., Nat. Assn. Securities Dealers. Republican. Roman Catholic. Club: Kiwanis. Home: 228 Galluppi Dr Youngstown OH 44436 Office: 1001 Covington St Youngstown OH 44510

VAN SICKLE, ROBERT LEROY, physician; b. Prescott, Mich., May 19, 1934; s. Everett and Imbi (Sipola) V.; student Mich. State U., 1953-56; M.D., U. Mich., 1960; m. Theresa Cecelia Griffin, June 23, 1956; children—Everett John, Anne Marie, Robert Kenneth, Kevin Thomas, Catherine Lynn, Deborah Christine, Stephen Derek. Intern St. Joseph Hosp., Pontiac, Mich., 1960-61, resident, 1961-63; practice medicine specializing in pediatrics, Pontiac, 1965-67, Midland, Mich., 1967—; instr. family practice residency program Midland Hosp. Center, 1967, chief of staff, 1980-81. Served with U.S. Navy, 1963-65. Mem. Midland County Med. Soc. (pres.), Mich. State Med. Soc., AMA, Am. Acad. Pediatrics (fellow). Roman Catholic. Club: Elks. Home: 2405 N Jefferson St Midland MI 48640 Office: 222 N Saginaw Rd Midland MI 48640

VAN SISTINE, JEROME, state senator; b. Milw., Aug. 16, 1926; B.S., Platteville (Wis.) State U., 1952; married; 3 children. Constrn. worker; sch. tchr.; mem. Wis. Senate, 1976—. Mem. archtl. adv. com. NW Tech. Inst.; supr., Brown County (Wis.), 1970-76; mem. Brown County Planning Commn., Brown County Mental Health Bd. Served with USN, World War II. Mem. VFW, United Brotherhood Carpenters and Joiners Am. (sec.), Fox River Valley Council Carpenters (pres.). Democrat. Address: Room 19 South State Capitol Madison WI 53702*

VAN SITTERT, CAROL ANN, communications co. exec.; b. Kansas City, Mo., Dec. 18, 1936; d. Clarence Alfred and Adelaide Harriet (Hurst) Hallberg; student Baker U., 1955-56; A.A., Johnson County Community Coll., 1975; m. Joseph Van Sittert Jr., Mar. 18, 1956; children—Sarah Lynn, Jeanne Marie. Lead programmer Pyramid Life Ins. Co., Mission, Kans., 1965-68; programmer Interstate Securities Corp., Kansas City, Mo., 1968-69; sr. programmer Hercules, Inc., De Soto, Kans., 1969-71; lead programmer Wolf & Co., Kansas City, Mo., 1971-74; datapoint ops. supr., programmer Bayvet div. Cutter Labs., Shawnee, Kans., 1974-79; programmer analyst III, North Supply Co. subs. United Telecommunications, Inc., Lenexa, Kans., 1979—. Mem. Nat. Assn. Female Execs., Data Processing Mgmt. Assn. Home: 12714 W 55th Terrace Shawnee KS 66216 Office: North Supply Co 10951 Lakeview Ave Lenexa KS 66219

VAN STRATEN, GERRIT STANLEY, cons. engr.; b. Balt., July 6, 1932; s. Albert and Dorothy Belle (Patterson) Van S.; diploma Balt. Poly. Inst., 1950; student Johns Hopkins, 1950-53; B.S. in Mech. Engring., Ohio State U., 1959; m. Jane Penrod Shields. Mech. engr. Frank, Lingberg & Maki, Columbus, Ohio, 1956-61; project engr. N.Am. Aviation, Columbus, 1961-66; practice profl. engring. Van Straten Engrs., Columbus, 1966-69; partner, profl. engr. Van Straten & Edwards Engrs., Columbus, 1970-78; owner, pres. Van Straten Engring., 1978; pres. Gerrit S. Van Straten, Inc., 1979—. Mem. U.S. Bicentennial Commn. from Ohio; mem. Ohio Gov.'s Task Force Energy Conservation. Chmn. bd. trustees Republican Glee Club, Columbus, 1973-76, 78, 79, pres., 1977; bd. dirs. Franklin County (Ohio) Forum, 1974-75, sec., 1976, v.p., 1977-79, pres., 1980. Bd. dirs., treas.-sec. T.I.P. Corp., Columbus. Served with AUS. Registered profl. engr., Ohio, Pa., N.Y., W. Va., Md., Del., N.C., Fla., Ky., Mass., Iowa, Ill., Ind., Tenn., Mich., Ga., Va. Mem. Illuminating Engring. Soc., Constrn. Specification Inst., Nat., Ohio socs. profl. engrs., Am. Soc. Heating, Refrigerating and Air Conditioning Engrs. (dir. 1974-75; regional chmn. energy com. 1973-75, sec. Columbus chpt. 1976-78, v.p. 1979, pres. 1981), Cons. Engrs. Council Am., Nat. Council Engring. Examiners, Am. Soc. Plumbing Engrs., Assn. Energy Engrs., Ohio State U. Alumni Assn. (life), Rathcamp Matchcover Soc., Long Beach Matchcover Club, Phi Kappa Psi. Lutheran (mem. steering com. ch. orgn. 1957; fin. sec. 1957-61; elder 1973-75, rep. ecumenical council 1973-75, ch. pres. 1976-79). Kiwanian (club pres. 1970-71; div. chmn. 1972, 74-82, del. internat. conv. 1968, 70-71, 74, 76, 79, Kiwanian of Year 1973). Home: 999 Shetland Ct Worthington OH 43085 Office: 1460 West Lane Ave Columbus OH 43221

VAN TASSEL, LEO M., ret. univ. adminstr.; b. Howard City, Mich., Jan. 28, 1912; s. Louis M. and Lillian (Ranshaw) Van T.; A.C., Grand Rapids Jr. Coll., 1933; A.B., Western Mich. U., 1936; M.A., U. Mich., 1942; postgrad. Columbia, 1949; m. Evelyn Loveridge, Nov. 5, 1938; 1 dau., Marilyn. High sch. tchr., Fennville, Mich., 1936-41, Midland, Mich., 1941-45; pub. accountant Ernst & Ernst, Detroit, 1945-46; prof. accounting No. Mich. U., Marquette, 1946-49, v.p., 1949-77, treas. Univ. Found., 1960-68, devel. fund, 1968-77. Mem. Central, Nat. assns. bus. officers, NEA, Mich. Edn. Assn., Assn. Sch. Bus. Ofcls., Delta Sigma Phi. Mason (Shriner). Home: 710 W Kaye St Marquette MI 49855

VAN TASSEL, NORMAN CHARLES, ins. co. exec.; b. Edwards, Mo., Dec. 8, 1923; s. Arthur John and Maude Elizabeth (Estes) V.; B.B.A., U. Mo., Kansas City, 1976; m. Genevieve Katy, Apr. 15, 1946; children—Marilyn, Susan, John, Jane. Enlisted U.S. Air Force, 1943, advanced to chief master sgt., 1962; air crew protection supt. Carswell AFB, Ft. Worth, 1959-62; flight leader, survival tng. sch. Stead AFB, Nev., 1962-64; ret., 1966; cons. loss control Atwell, Vogel & Sterling, Kansas City, Mo., 1966-80, asst. br. mgr., 1980—. Mem. fund-raising com. YMCA, 1970. Decorated Bronze Battle Star (5); recipient Cert. of Merit for mgmt. cons. services SBA, 1975. Mem. Ins. Underwriters Assn., Ins. Auditors Assn., Am. Soc. Safety Engrs. Republican. Baptist. Clubs: Masons (Warsaw, Mo.); Scottish Rite (Kansas City). Home: 16200 E 38th St Independence MO 64055 Office: PO Box 829 Kansas City MO 64141

VAN THYNE, RAY JOSEPH, steel coating co. exec.; b. Chgo., May 31, 1927; s. Raymond J. and Blanche H. Van T.; B.S., Ill. Inst. Tech., 1950, M.S., 1955; m. Mary Jane Frey, Aug. 27, 1949; children—Cathy, Brian, Keith, Craig. Asst. dir. metals research div. Research Inst., Ill. Inst. Tech., Chgo., 1950-66; founder, pres. Surface Tech. Corp., Stone Park, Ill., 1966—, also dir.; founder, pres. Surfalloy Corp., Stone Park, 1973-76; v.p. Dilex Systems div. Material Scis. Corp., Mt. Prospect, Ill., 1976-81; pres. Van Thyne Assos., Inc., 1981—; tchr. Ill. Inst. Tech.; rep. UN Geneva Atoms for Peace Conf., 1958; chmn. metallographic group U.S. AEC, 1964. Active Boys Scouts Am. Served with A.C., U.S. Navy, 1945-47. Fellow Am. Soc. Metals (Coatings award 1973); mem. AIME, Soc. Mfg. Engrs., Alpha Chi Sigma, Sigma Xi, Tau Beta Pi. Contbr. articles to profl. jours. Patentee in field. Home: 1070 Valley Lake Dr Inverness IL 60067

VAN TIEM, PHILLIP MICHAEL, hosp. ofcl.; b. Grosse Pointe, Mich., Oct. 4, 1935; s. August Gerard and Margaret Mary (Power) Van T.; B.A., Mich. State U., 1963; postgrad. Wayne State U., 1972-73, U. Detroit, 1974-76; M.A. in Public Adminstrn., Central Mich. U., 1968; m. Darlene Miriam Roff, Apr. 4, 1964; children—Bradford, Adrienne. With Gen. Motors Acceptance Corp., 1963-68, credit mgr., 1965-68; comml. sales rep. Goodyear Tire & Rubber Co., 1968-69; mgr. accounts receivable Lansing (Mich.) Gen. Hosp., 1969-70; mgr. patient accounting Sinai Hosp., Detroit, 1971-72, St. John Hosp., Detroit, 1972-79, asst. controller, 1979—. Bd. dirs. Lansing Gen. Hosp. Credit Union, 1969-70, treas., 1970; chmn. supr. com. Sinai Hosp. Credit Union, 1971-72. Vol. social worker Family to Family Movement, 1965-71; mem. vol. program Mich. Dept. Social Services, 1965-71; chmn. publicity Grosse Pointe Park Civic Assn. Served with AUS, 1958-60. Recipient hon. mention for suggestion Mich. Hosp. Assn., 1972; Cost Containment award Hosp. Fin. Mgmt., 1978. Mem. Hosp. Fin. Mgmt. Assn. (membership com. 1975-77, social chmn. 1975-77, awards chmn. 1977-78, public relations chmn. 1978-79, dir. 1979—, chpt. del. for coordinating council 1980—, placement chmn. 1981-82, Follmer award 1979), Grosse Pointe Alumnae Assn. (v.p. 1980-81, pres. 1981-82). Roman Catholic. Home: 1310 Kensington Rd Grosse Pointe MI 48230 Office: 22101 Moross Rd Detroit MI 48236

VAN VLEET, WILLIAM BENJAMIN, JR., lawyer, ins. co. exec.; b. Milw., Dec. 4, 1924; s. William Benjamin and Irene (Peppey) Van V.; student Lawrence Coll., 1943-44; J.D., Marquette U., 1948; m. Marilyn Nilles, Dec. 26, 1946; children—Terese (Mrs. Edward Svetich), Susan (Mrs. Paul Waldo), William Benjamin III, Monica, Mark. Admitted to Wis. bar, 1948, Ill. bar, 1950; gen. counsel George Rogers Clark Mut. Casualty Co., Rockford, Ill., 1948-59; gen. counsel Pioneer Life Ins. Co., Rockford, 1950-59, v.p., gen. counsel, 1959-68; dir., exec. v.p., gen. counsel Pioneer Life Ins. Co. of Ill., Rockford, 1968—; pres., dir. Western Life Ins. Co. Am., 1981—. Mem. Boylan Central Cath. High Sch. Council of Adminstrn., 1965-72; mem. Diocesan Bd. Edn., Rockford, 1970-77, pres., 1970-73; v.p. Nat. Assn. Bds. Edn., 1972-74, pres., 1974-76; bd. dirs. Nat. Catholic Edn. Assn., 1975-78; bd. advisors Marion Coll. of Fond du Lac (Wis.), St. Anthony Hosp., Rockford. Served to lt. (j.g.) USNR, 1944-46. Mem. Am., Ill., Wis. bar assns. Roman Catholic. Home: 811 Coolidge Pl Rockford IL 61107 Office: 127 N Wyman St Rockford IL 61101

VAN WERT, GEORGE RICHARD, linen supply and paper distbn. service co. exec.; b. Vincennes, Ind., June 20, 1926; s. Paul Howland and Helen Ely VanW.; student U. Mich., 1946-48; A.B. magna cum laude in Acctg., Catawba Coll., 1950; M. in mgmt. and acctg. U. Pitts., 1952; m. Wiladine Gilbert, Apr. 25, 1953; children—Thomas, Kim, Karee. Pub. acct. Ernst & Ernst, Cleve., 1952-55; cost engr., fin. analyst Eastman Kodak Co., Rochester, N.Y., 1955-63; asst. to fin. v.p. and systems mgr. Towle Mfg. Co., Newburyport, Mass., 1963-66; asst. corp. controller, group controller Dictaphone Corp., 1966-70; v.p. fin. United Service Co., Youngstown, Ohio, 1970—, also dir.; dir. Franchise Holding Co.; instr. evening div. Rochester Inst. Tech.; pvt. practice acctg. and cons. City recreation dir. City of Emporium (Pa.), 1947-50. Served with U.S. Army, 1943-46; PTO. Mem. Am. Mgmt. Assn., Nat. Assn. Accts., Data Processing Mgmt. Assn., VFW (trustee 1946-47), Am. Legion (vice comdr. 1947-48). Republican. Clubs: Rotary, Kiwanis, Moose, Lions. Office: United Service Co 350 North Ave Youngstown OH 44502

VAN WINKLE, LAWRENCE WILLIAM, coll. adminstr.; b. Newark, Ohio, Mar. 9, 1927; s. John Nicholas and Arda Elizabeth (Smith) Van W.; A.B., Capital U., 1951; m. Martha Jane Sites, Apr. 2, 1950; children—Nicholas A., Richard L., Mike R., Mark S. Accountant, bookstore mgr. Carthage Coll., Kenosha, Wis., 1951-60, acting bus. mgr., 1960-61, bus. mgr., acting treas., 1961-63, controller, 1963-64; v.p. bus. affairs, treas. Iowa Wesleyan Coll., Mount Pleasant, 1964—. Bd. dirs. Indsl. Tng. Center, 1974—, pres., 1976; mem. city council Mount Pleasant, Iowa, 1969-74; commr. Mount Pleasant Low Rent Housing Commn., 1973—. Served with USNR, 1945-46. Mem. Nat. Assn. Coll. and Univ. Bus. Ofcls., Central Assn. Coll. and Univ. Bus. Ofcls., Mount Pleasant C. of C. (pres. 1975). Lutheran. Clubs: Kiwanis (past pres), Masons, Eastern Star. Home: 506 S Pine St Mount Pleasant IA 52641 Office: 601 N Main St Mount Pleasant IA 52641

VAN WYHE, WILLARD EDWIN, mfg. co. exec.; b. Rock Valley, Iowa, July 6, 1939; s. William Edward and Nellie (Verburg) Van W.; student Dordt Coll., 1958; m. Beverly Jean Bechler, June 8, 1962; children—Cynthia Lynette, Sherri Sue. Machinist, Koyker Mfg. Co., Hull, Iowa, 1959-60; with Sudenga Industries, George, Iowa, 1960-61; office mgr. Hele's Supply Co., Worthington, Minn., 1964-65, Sudenga Industries, George, 1965-72; plant mgr. Modern Farm Systems, Inc., Webster City, Iowa, 1974-79; v.p. mfg. Modern Farm Systems, Inc., Webster City, 1980—. Chmn., Airport Commn. Webster City, 1978-80; pres. Trinity Luth. Ch., Webster City, 1977-78. Served with U.S. Army, 1961-64. Decorated Army Commendation medal. Mem. Webster City C. of C. (bd. dirs. 1977-80), Farm and Indsl. Equip. Inst. Lutheran. Club: Lions. Home: 2101 Isa Dr Webster City IA 50595 Office: 1811 W 2d St Webster City IA 50595

VARBLE, DENNIS HAROLD, architect; b. Lebanon, Mo., Nov. 12, 1950; s. Harold Grant and Ruth (Mitchell) V.; student SW Mo. State Coll., 1968-69; B. Arch., U. Ark., 1974. Project architect Migdonio Seidler & Assos., Pittsburg, Kans., 1975-76; asst. instr. bldg. tech. Kans. State Coll., Pittsburg, 1975-76; project architect Allgeier-Martin & Assos., Joplin, Mo., 1976-78, Fullerton Carey & Oman, Kansas City, Mo., 1978—. Registered architect, Kans., Mo.; cert. Nat. Council Archtl. Registration Bds. Mem. AIA (continuing edn. com. Kansas City chpt. 1980, chmn. archtl. exam. study sessions 1981, cert. for outstanding service 1980), U. Ark. Alumni Assn. Designer mcpl. govt. complex city of Galena (Kans.), 1976-77, renovation and remodelling Blue Ridge Mall. Home: Apt 2 3804 Washington Kansas City MO 64111 Office: Fullerton Carey & Oman Suite 2350 1100 Main St Kansas City MO 64105

VARDARIS, RICHARD MILES, educator; b. Lakewood, Ohio, Nov. 28, 1934; s. George Kalos and Florence (Read) V.; B.A. cum laude (NSF fellow), Case Western Res. U., 1962; postgrad. U. Iowa, 1962-64; M.S., U. Oreg., 1967, Ph.D., 1968; m. Kay A. Vatter, June 12, 1970; children—Paul Stephen, Matthew Read. Asst. prof. psychology Kent State U., 1967-71, asso. prof., 1972-78, prof., 1979—; chmn. neurosci. program com., chmn. biopsychology area com., dir., sr. scientist Neurosci. Lab., 1971—, U. fellow, 1971; research prof. neurobiology Northeastern Ohio Univs. Coll. Medicine. NIH grantee, 1972-73, 74—. Mem. Soc. Neurosci., AAAS, Am., Midwestern psychol. assns., Brit. Brain Research Assn. (hon.), European Brain and Behavior Soc. (hon.), Psychonomic Sci., Phi Beta Kappa, Sigma Xi. Reviewer for various sci. jours.; contbr. 4 chpts. to Behavioral Sciences, 1979; editor's cons. Scott, Foresman & Co., 1973—. Contbr. articles to profl. jours. Home: 3175 Bird Dr Ravenna OH 44266 Office: Kent Hall Kent State U Kent OH 44242

VARDI, EMANUEL, conductor; b. Jerusalem, Apr. 21, 1917; U.S. citizen, 1927; student Juilliard Sch., Peabody Conservatory; pupil of father, also Bernard Wagenaar, Tibor Serly. Violinist and violist; condr. S.D. Symphony Orch.; composer: Suite on American Folk Songs for violin or viola and piano; Concerto for solo horn, string quartet, 2 winds, keyboard, 1974; (film scores) Once Before I Die, Diary of Anne Frank (TV spl.); (feature study) Life Study; (electronic score) Devil's Axe. Recipient silver medals for film scores. Address: SD Symphony Orch Suite 218 707 E 41st St Sioux Falls SD 57105*

VARGA, STEVEN CARL, ins. co. exec.; b. Columbus, Ohio, Jan. 19, 1952; s. Stephen Thomas and Eva Jeney Varga; B.A. in Psychology and Philosophy magna cum laude, Carthage Coll., 1977; m. Michelle L. Auld, Nov. 17, 1973; 1 son, Zachary Steven. Service mgr. Chem Law Corp., Columbus, 1972-75; respiratory therapist St. Catherine's Hosp., Kenosha, Wis., 1975-77; policy analyst Nationwide Ins. Cos., Columbus, 1978-79, asst. mgr. Corp. Tng. Center, 1979—, mem. civic action program, 1979—. Mem. Nat. Mental Health Assn., 1972—, v.p. Kenosha County chpt., 1975-77; mem. Franklin County (Ohio) Mental Health Assn., 1978—. Rhodes scholar, 19—. Mem. Am. Soc. for Tng. and Devel., Internat. TV Assn., Am. Assn. Respiratory Therapy, Am. Film Inst., Carthage Coll. Alumni Assn., Phi Beta Kappa, Psi Chi. Home: 1707 E Dunedin Rd Columbus OH 43224 Office: One Nationwide Plaza Columbus OH 43216

VARIAN, DENNIS JOHN, housing mgmt. co. exec.; b. New Rochelle, N.Y., Feb. 23, 1943; s. Henry John and Mary Catherine (Gallin) V.; student U. Detroit, 1961-65, Detroit Inst. Tech., 1965-67; m. Jennifer A. Morris, Apr. 15, 1966; children—Michele Ann, Elaine Marie, Kathleen Alice (triplets). Program engr., asst. v.p., dir. sales FCH Services, Inc., Detroit, 1966-69; govt. programs coordinator Multicon Industries, Inc., Columbus, Ohio, 1969-70; co-founder, sec., treas. Housing & Fin. Assos., Inc., Detroit, 1970—, bd. dirs., 1970—; owner, pres. Plaza Mgmt. Co., Detroit, 1975—; vis. lectr. Oakland Community Coll., 1976-78; exec. dir. Mich. Housing Assos., 1969—. Bd. trustees, exec. v.p., treas. Music Soc. Detroit, 1974-79; bd. dirs., pres. Harbinger Dance Co., 1977-81; bd. dirs., chmn. Colego Concert Series, 1978—; pres. Mich. Assn. Housing Coops., 1968. Mem. Nat. Assn. Housing and Redevel. Ofcls., Mich. Soc. Planning Ofcls. Club: Detroit Boat. Home: 1072 Seminole Detroit MI 48214 Office: 1601 Bradby Dr Detroit MI 48207

VARIN, OMAR GEORGE, R.R. adminstr.; b. Battle Creek, Mich., Sept. 3, 1922; s. William Horton Coleman and Dessie May (Knapp) V.; student U.S. Navy Aviation Machinist Mate Sch., Detroit, 1941-42, U.S. Navy Automatic Pilot Sch., Jacksonville, Fla., 1945, U.S. Naval Res. Instrs. Tng. Sch., Gt. Lakes, Ill., 1964, Grand Trunk R.R. Mgmt. Sems., Gull Lake, Mich., 1973-75; m. Anne Mary Quinn, May 28, 1945; children—Francis William, James Patrick; m. 2d Lucille Margaret Klapper, Sept. 4, 1965. Pressman helper W. K. Kellogg Co., Battle Creek, Mich., 1947; assembler Struthers & Dunn, Phila., 1947; polisher Phila. Rust Proof, 1947; electrician Gradn Trunk R.R., Battle Creek, 1948-72, gang foreman, 1972, enginehouse foreman, 1972—; elec. instr. Served with USN, 1941-47; PTO. Mem. U.S. Naval Inst. (life), Air Force Assn. (life), Am. Def. Preparedness Assn. (life), Am. Police Acad., Am. Fedn. Police, Am. Police Hall of Fame, Police and Firefighters Assn., Mich. Sheriffs Assn., Nat. Rifle Assn., Am. Security Council, America Cause, 52 Assn. Inc., Nat. Audubon Assn., Mich. Audubon Assn., Wildlife Fedn., Cousteau Soc., Met. Opera Guild, Nat. Trust Hist. Preservation, Am. Mus. Natural History, Smithsonian Assos., Early Am. Soc., Nat. Hist. Soc., Mich. Hist. Soc., Bibles for Am. Indians, Nat. Travel Club, Nat. Geog. Soc., Franklin Philatelic Soc., Calhoun's Collectors Soc., Postal Commemorative Soc. Republican. Home: 235 Clarence Blvd Battle Creek MI 49017 Office: 409 Jameston Battle Creek MI 49017

VARKEY, BASIL, pulmonary physician, educator; b. Quilon, India, Feb. 28, 1941; s. Antony V. and Mariamma (Varghese) V.; M.B.B.S., Trivandrum Med. Coll., 1963; m. Sheela Angela Ben, Aug. 17, 1968; children—Anita, Jay Basil. Intern, Saint Michael Hosp., Milw., 1966-67; resident Trumbull Meml. Hosp., Warren, Ohio, 1967-68; resident VA Hosp., Wood, Wis., 1968-70, fellow in pulmonary disease, 1970-72, staff physician, 1972-73, asst. chief pulmonary sect., 1974, acting chief pulmonary sect., 1975, med. dir. respiratory therapy sect., 1975—, chief pulmonary disease sect., 1976—; asst. prof. internal medicine Med. Coll. of Wis., 1973-77, asso. prof., 1977—; cons. pulmonary medicine Milwaukee County Med. Complex; advisor health occupations Milw. Area Tech. Coll. Mem. profl. edn. com. Am. Cancer Soc. Recipient Plaque of Honor, Commn. on Sci. Medicine State Med. Soc. of Wis.; Spl. Performance award VA; diplomate Am. Bd. Internal Medicine (subsplty. bd. pulmonary disease). Fellow Royal Coll. Physicians Can., Am. Coll. Chest Physicians (gov. Wis.); mem. Wis. Respiratory Disease Assn., Am. Thoracic Soc., Am. Fedn. for Clin. Research. Contbr. articles to profl. jours. and books. Home: 2335 Tilton Ct Brookfield WI 53005 Office: 5000 W National Ave Wood WI 53193

VARNER, CHARLEEN LAVERNE MCCLANAHAN (MRS. ROBERT B. VARNER), educator, adminstr., nutritionist; b. Alba, Mo., Aug. 28, 1931; d. Roy Calvin and Lela Ruhama (Smith) McClanahan; student Joplin (Mo.) Jr. Coll., 1949-51; B.S. in Edn., Kans. State Coll. Pittsburg, 1953; M.S., U. Ark., 1958; Ph.D., Tex. Woman's U. 1966; postgrad. Mich. State U., summer, 1955, U. Mo., summers 1952, 62; m. Robert Bernard Varner, July 4, 1953. Apprentice county home agt. U. Mo., summer 1952; tchr. Ferry Pass. Sch., Escambia County, Fla., 1953-54; tchr. biology, home econs. Joplin Sr. High Sch., 1954-59; instr. home econs. Kans. State Coll., Pittsburg, 1959-63; lectr. foods, nutrition Coll. Household Arts and Scis., Tex. Woman's U., 1963-64, research asst. NASA grant, 1964-66; asso. prof. home econs. Central Mo. State U., Warrensburg, 1966-70, adviser to Colhecon, 1966-70, adviser to Alpha Sigma Alpha, 1967-70, 72, mem. bd. advisers Honors Group, 1967-70; prof., head dept. home econs. Kans. State Tchrs. Coll., Emporia, 1970-73; prof., chmn. dept. home econs. Benedictine Coll., Atchison, Kans., 1973-74; prof., chmn. dept. home econs. Baker U., Baldwin City, Kans., 1974-75; owner, operator Diet-Con Dietary Cons. Enterprises, cons. dietitian, 1973—. Mem. Joplin Little Theater, 1956-60. Mem. NEA, Mo., Kans. state tchrs. assns., AAUW, Am., Mo., Kans. dietetics assns., Am., Mo., Kans. home econs. assns., Mo. Acad. Scis., AAUP, U. Ark. Alumni Assn., Alumni Assn. Kans. State Coll. of Pittsburg, Am. Vocat. Assn., Assn. Edn. Young Children, Sigma Xi, Beta Sigma Phi, Beta Beta Beta, Alpha Sigma Alpha, Delta Kappa Gamma, Kappa Kappa Iota, Phi Upsilon Omicron. Methodist (organist). Home: Main PO Box 1009 Topeka KS 66601

VARNER, ROBERT BERNARD, educator; b. Ellsworth, Kans., May 31, 1930; s. Bernard Lafayette and Leota (Campbell) V.; B.S., Kans. State U., Pittsburgh, 1952; M.S., U. Ark., 1959; postgrad. Mich. State U., summer 1955, U. Mo., summer (grantee) U. Kans., 1972-73; m. Charleen LaVerne McClanahan, July 4, 1953. Athletic coach, social sci. tchr. Joplin (Mo.) High Sch., 1956-63; head social sci. dept. R.L. Turner High Sch., Carrollton, Tex., 1963-66; asst. athletic coach, jr. high sch. sci. tchr. Warrensburg, Mo., 1966-70; coach, social sci. tchr., Emporia, Kans., 1970-72; asst. cottage dir., counselor Topeka Youth Center, 1973—; substitute tchr. Topeka Pub. Schs., 1974—. Recreation dir. Carrollton-Farmer's Br. Recreation Center, Dallas County, Tex., 1964-66; city recreation dir., Warrensburg, Mo., 1966-68. Served with USN, 1953-54. Mem. NEA, Kans. State U.-Pittsburgh Alumni Assn., U. Ark. Alumni Assn., Phi Delta Kappa, Sigma Tau Gamma. Democrat. Methodist. Club: Elks. Address: Main PO Box 1009 Topeka KS 66601

VARNER, ROBERT H., aviation corp. exec.; b. Newark, Ohio, May 16, 1921; s. Lester H. and Ethel D. (Lydic) V.; student Bliss Coll., 1942; B.A., Ohio State U., 1955; postgrad. Capital U., 1960, Marion Tech. Coll., 1965; m. Margaret L. Crawford, Apr. 26, 1946; children—Jon, Deborah, Elizabeth. Pres. Lane Aviation Corp., Columbus, Ohio, 1940—, also dir.; dir. Lane Air Services Co.; founder Aviation Consulting Service; instr. Bliss Coll., PFG Assos., Wellesley, Mass. Served with U.S. Army, 1941-44. Recipient Disting. Service award Helicopter Assn. Am., 1973. Mem. Ohio Aviation Congress (adv. bd.), Ohio Aviation Trades Assn. (pres. 1970-71), Columbus Tech. Inst. (aviation adv. bd.), Nat. Air Transp. Assn. (adv. bd.). Contbr. articles to bus. trade jours. Home: 3509 Lancaster Rd Granville OH 43023 Office: 4393 E 17th Ave Columbus OH 43219

VARRICCHIO, CLAUDETTE GOULET, nurse, educator; b. Fall River, Mass., Apr. 13, 1940; d. Joseph Wilfred and Imelda Rose (Barrette) Goulet; B.S., Boston Coll., 1961; M.S., U. Md., 1967; D.S.N., U. Ala., Birmingham, 1982; m. Frederick E. Varricchio, Dec. 29, 1962; children—Nicole, Erika. Staff nurse Univ. Hosp., Balt., 1964; head nurse radiation therapy Memorial-Sloan-Kettering Cancer Center, N.Y.C., 1974-76; clin. instr. Skidmore Coll., Saratoga Springs, N.Y., 1977; asst. prof. Nova U., Ft. Lauderdale, Fla., 1977-78, Northwestern State U. of La., Shreveport, 1978-80; asst. prof., asst. dean Marcella Niehoff Sch. Nursing, Loyola U., Chgo., 1980—; condr. workshops in oncology nursing. Mem. Am. Nurses Assn., Nat. League for Nursing, Oncology Nursing Soc., Ill. Nurses Assn., Sigma Theta Tau. Co-author: The Nurse and Radiotherapy: A Manual of Daily Care, 1979. Office: 6525 N Sheridan Rd Chicago IL 60626

VASEL, FRED J., steel co. exec.; b. St. Louis, Apr. 2, 1929; s. Fred H. and Agnes M. Vasel; A.A., B.A., Columbia Coll. With St. Louis County Police Dept., 1952-75, ret. as major, chief of detectives, 1975; dir. indsl. relations Scullin Steel Co., St. Louis, 1977-78, v.p. mfg., 1978-79, exec. v.p., 1979, chief operating officer, 1979, pres., chief exec. officer, 1979—. Bd. dirs. Laclede's Landing Devel. Corp.; mem. nominating com. Greater St. Louis Health Agy. Served with USMC, World War II, USN, Korea. Mem. Internat. Assn. Chiefs Police, FBI Nat. Acad., Nat. Foundrymen's Assn., Am. Steelcasting Soc., Mo. Police Officers Assn., Chinese Soc., World Council Fgn. Affairs. Roman Catholic. Co-author: Killer Cops, 1980. Home: 12550 Falling Leaves Ct Saint Louis County MO 63141 Office: 6700 Manchester Ave Saint Louis MO 63139

VASILENKO, PETER, III, reproductive physiologist; b. Passaic, N.J., July 25, 1953; s. Peter and Dorothy Catherine (Markert) V., Jr.; B.S. in Biology, Muhlenberg Coll., 1975; Ph.D. in Physiology, Kent State U., 1980; m. Carol Anne Fuller, June 25, 1977. Teaching fellow dept. biol. scis. Kent (Ohio) State U., 1976-80; postdoctoral fellow dept. reproductive biology Sch. Medicine, Case-Western Res. U., Cleve., 1980—; Lalor Found. fellow, 1981-82. Mem. Soc. for Study Reprodn., AAAS, Am. Soc. Zoologists, Sigma Xi (research award 1980). Contbr. articles to profl. jours. Home: 34500 Park East Apt A201 Solon OH 44139 Office: Dept Reproductive Biology MacDonald House-7 2105 Adelbert Rd Cleveland OH 44106

VASIS, ANTHONY CHARLES, educator; b. Chgo., Oct. 2, 1926; s. Anthony Charles and Carolyn Marie (Bergum) V.; B.S., U. Wis., Platteville, 1950; M.S., U. Wis., Stout, 1951; M.Ed., Loyola U., 1962; m. Jewel Collette Sitt, Nov. 20, 1954; children—Julie Anne, Thomas Charles. Tchr. indsl. edn. Wis. Sch. for Boys, Waukesha, 1951; tchr., auto shop Senn High Sch., Chgo., 1951-57; mem. faculty Chgo. State U., 1957—, asso. prof. indsl. edn.; one-man sculpture shows. Served with USNR, 1945-46. Mem. Am. Council on Inds. Arts Tchrs. Edn. (life), Am. Vocat Assn. (life), Am. Indsl. Arts Assn., Ill. Vocat. Assn., Ill. Indsl. Edn. Assn. (dir.), Ill.-Ind. Indsl. Arts Tchr. Edn. Assn., Nat. Assn. Indsl. Tech. (dir.), Ill. Automotive and Aircraft Tchr. Assn., Am. Legion (comdr. 1972), VFW. Contbr. articles to various profl. jours.; research on industries and tech. edn. in 40 countries. Home: 1718 W Thorndale Ave Chicago IL 60660 Office: Chgo State U 95th St at King Dr Chicago IL 60628

VASQUEZ, CESAR LUIS, physician; b. Lima, Peru, Sept. 19, 1935; came to U.S., 1978; s. Eulogio M. and Adelina J. (Soplin) V.; B.S., San Marcos U., 1954, M.D., 1961; m. Mary Margaret MacAulay, Feb. 7, 1964; children—Roberto Luis, Mario Tonyo, Ian Alexander. Asst. prof., research fellow Inst. Andean Biology, Lima, Peru, 1967-72; asso. prof. medicine U. San Marcos, Lima, 1972—, now on leave; med. cons. for Latin Am., Imperial Chem. Industries, Eng., 1969-78; v.p. Vasquez Mgmt. Cons. Internat. Projects Div., Wadsworth, Ill., 1979—. Colo. Heart Assn. fellow, 1963-64. Mem. Peruvian Heart Assn., Am. Heart Assn., N.Y. Acad. Scis., Ill. Med. Soc., AMA. Roman Catholic. Club: Masons. Research on high altitude residents in Peru and Colo., coop. studies on beta-blockers in Latin Am. Home and Office: 38760 Northwoods Dr Wadsworth IL 60083

VATTER, EUGENE WILLIAM, JR., city mgr.; b. Lancaster, Pa., Dec. 18, 1931; s. Eugene William and Erma Mary (Westman) V.; B.A. cum laude, Central Coll., Pella, Iowa, 1972; M.B.A., U. Iowa, 1973; m. Marilyn Sue Green, Aug. 4, 1961; 1 dau., Melissa Anne. Agy. mgr. Lake Ins. Agy., Storm Lake, Iowa, 1959-65; dist. sales mgr. Power Tools, Inc., St. Paul, 1965-70; regional mgr. Western Mortgage Service Co. subs. Evans Products Co., Portland, Oreg., 1974-75; city mgr., Blakesburg, Eddyville, Dallas, Harvey, What Cheer, Melrose, Melcher and Williamson, Iowa, 1975—; panel cons., municipal innovator Drake U., Des Moines. Sunday sch. tchr. Presbyn. Ch., 1975—; pres. Storm Lake Jr. C. of C., 1963-64. Served with USMC,

1951-59. Named Brilliant Financial Innovator, NBC-TV Today Show, 1976. Republican. Club: Masons. Home: 2101 South M Oskaloosa IA 52577 Office: Civic Center Eddyville IA 52553

VAUGHAN, CHARLES WILLIAM, JR., telecommunications co. exec.; b. Cin., Apr. 29, 1927; s. Charles William and Lillian Rose (Lindsley) V.; B.F.A., U. Cin., 1949; M.Ed., Xavier U., 1959; m. Juanita Jane Eckstein, Aug. 16, 1947; children—Linda Jane, Charles David, Kathleen Susan, Robert James. Prodn. mgr. Sta. WLW-TV, Cin., 1948-53; asst. gen. mgr. Sta. WSUN-TV, St. Petersburgh, Fla., 1953-54; night ops. mgr. Sta. WKRC-TV, Cin., 1954-55; program dir. Sta. WCET-TV, Cin., 1955-60, pres., gen. mgr., 1965—; exec. producer Nat. Ednl. TV, N.Y.C., 1960-65; chmn. bd. Central Ednl. Network, 1972; dir. PBS, 1964-72, 75-78. Vice chairperson Greenhills (Ohio) Cable TV Bd., 1981—; chairperson Cin. Arts Mgrs. Council, 1979-80. Served with C.E., U.S. Army, 1944-45. Mem. Public Broadcasting Service. Office: 1223 Central Pkwy Cincinnati OH 45214

VAUGHAN, DAVID JOHN, distbn. co. exec.; b. Detroit, July 17, 1924; s. David Evans and Erma Mildred V.; A.B., U. Ill., 1950; postgrad. U. Chgo., U. Mo.; m. Anne McKeown Miles, Aug. 21, 1975; children by previous marriage—David John, Melissa Ann, Julia Crawford McLaughlin. Chemist, Midland Electric Colleries, 1950-52; pres. Varrco Distbg. Co., Peoria, Ill., 1953—; prin. David J. Vaughan, investment adv., Peoria, 1970—; instr. Carl Sandburg Coll., Peoria, 1968—. Served to lt. USAAF, 1942-46, USAF, 1951-52; Korea. Registered investment adv. Mem. Alpha Tau Omega, Phi Eta Sigma, Phi Alpha Delta. Republican. Presbyterian. Clubs: Peoria Country, Northport Point (Mich.); Peoria Skeet, Racquet, Masons, Shriners, Jesters. Home: 4510 N Miller Ave Peoria IL 61614

VAUGHAN, JOSEPH HARRY, JR., pub. relations exec., journalist; b. Kansas City, Mo., Jan. 12, 1948; s. Joseph H. and Elizabeth McLellan (Wilkinson) V.; A.A., Kansas City (Kans.) Community Coll., 1968; B.S., Kans. U., 1970, postgrad. in polit. sci., 1970-71; m. Karen Lou Reed, Apr. 4, 1981. News dir. Sta. KEWI-KSWT-FM, Topeka, 1971; asst. news dir. WREN, Topeka, 1971-72; newsman Sta. KCKN-AM-FM, Kansas City, Kans., 1972-74; econ. devel. specialist Kansas City (Kans.) Area C. of C., 1974-75; pub. relations asst. United Mo. Bank of Kansas City, 1975-77; newsman Sta. WDAF, Kansas City, Mo., 1977-79, Sta. KFIX-AM, KFIX-FM, Kansas City, Mo., 1979; news dir. KLWN/KLZR, Lawrence, Kans., 1979—; moderator weekly interview program Kansas City (Kans.) cable TV sta., 1975. Elder First United Presbyterian Ch., Kansas City, Kans., 1974—, ruling elder, 1974-77, chmn. Christian Edn. Com., 1975; mem. citadel adv. bd. Kansas City (Kans.) Salvation Army, 1975-81, mem. exec. com., 1978-79; bd. dirs. Project Concern's Greater Kansas City (Mo.) Walk for Mankind, 1975-77, pub. relations chmn. 1976 walk; mem. minority bus. opportunity com. SBA, 1974; mem. pub. relations com. Festival of Progress, 1974; Wyandotte County capt. Easter Seal Telethon, 1975; mem. West Branch YMCA, 1975-77; mem. friends of art Nelson Gallery Art and Atkins Mus., 1976-80; botar escort Belles of Am. Royal, 1976-77; mem. White House motor pool, 1976 Republican Nat. Conv. Recipient Outstanding Young Man of Am. award U.S. Jaycees, 1975. Mem. Assn. News Broadcasters Kans., Kans. Assn. Broadcasters (Newscaster of Yr. award non-metro div. 1980), Kans. U. Alumni Assn. (life), Lawrence C. of C., Kansas City (Kans.) Area Jaycees (sec. corp. bd. dirs. 1973-75, chmn. govtl. affairs com. 1972-75, State Ave. improvement com. 1972-75, named Jaycee-of-Month 1973, 75), Order DeMolay (adv. council Huron chpt. 1974-76, recipient Chevalier Degree award 1973), Am. Mensa, Ltd., Sigma Alpha Epsilon (founder, pres. alumni adv. bd. 1976-79, dir. Greater Kansas City alumni assn. 1975—, treas. 1976-78, pres. 1979-80, mem. house corp. 1973-76, sec. 1973-75, chmn. fund raising com. 1976, Young Alumnus of Yr. award Kans. Alpha chpt. 1979, Order of Phoenix award 1980). Clubs: Kiwanis (dir. 1977-79, v.p. 1978-79), Monkey Table, Bachelors (v.p. 1980), Kansas City Press (Kansas City); Woodside Racquet; Indian Hills Country. Home: 1444 Westbrooke Lawrence KS 66044 Office: 3035 Iowa St Lawrence KS 66044

VAUGHAN, SALLY SEDLAK, state agy. adminstr.; b. Springfield, Ill., Jan. 25, 1942; d. Frank A. and Lorraine (Watts) Sedlak; A.A., Gulf Park Coll., 1961; B.A., MacMurray Coll., 1965; M.A., Sangamon State U., 1973. Tchr. remedial reading and English, Pana (Ill.) Jr. High Sch., 1966-67, Springfield High Sch., 1967-70; coordinator community service center Lincoln Land Community Coll., 1974-77; tng. officer Ill. Dept. Aging, Springfield, 1977—; chmn. health and human services Region V Tng. and Edn. Consortium, 1979. Mem. Am. Soc. for Tng. and Devel., DAR, AAUW, Springfield Art Assn., Jr. League Springfield. Republican. Methodist. Club: Zonta. Office: 421 E Capitol Springfield IL 62706

VAUGHN, CHARLES GEORGE, coll. dean; b. Marshfield, Wis., Nov. 14, 1915; s. Charles George and Dora (Wilcott) V.; student U. Wis., 1936-41; B.S., U. Dayton, 1961; M.S., Miami U., Oxford, Ohio, 1964; m. Noel Janet Wyandt, July 9, 1971; children—Charles George, Jeffrey James, Barbara Jean. Commd. 2d lt. U.S. Army Air Force, 1941, advanced through grades to lt. col., 1964; ret., 1964; dean student personnel Sinclair Community Coll., Dayton, Ohio 1964—. Bd. dirs. YMCA, chmn. phys. com., 1973-81; bd. dirs. Dayton Urban League; mem. mental health bd. Good Samaritan Hosp. Mem. Miami Valley Personnel and Guidance Assn. (past pres.), Am. Coll. Personnel Assn., Nat. Vocat. Guidance Assn., Assn. for Measurement and Evaluation. Democrat. Home: 3700 Wales Dr Dayton OH 45405 Office: 444 3d St W Dayton OH 45402

VAUGHN, CHARLES GORDON, dermatologist; b. Graceville, Minn., Feb. 26, 1926; s. Timothy Charles and Bertha Marie (Haack) V.; B.S., U. Minn., 1944, M.B., 1946, M.D., 1947; m. Mary Ellen Madden, Aug., 1957; children—John, Charles, Peter. Intern, Gen. Hosp., Mpls., 1948-49; resident in dermatology U. Minn. Hosp., Mpls., 1953-56; practice medicine specializing in dermatology, 1956; mem. staffs United, St. Joseph's, Bethesda, Midway St. Paul-Ramsey hosps. (all St. Paul); clin. prof. dermatology U. Minn., 1970—; med. dir. Degree of Honor Ins. Co., St. Paul, 1957—. Served to maj. U.S. Army, 1950-52. Mem. AMA, Minn., Ramsey County med. socs., Am. Acad. Dermatology. Roman Catholic. Home: 200 Mt Curve Blvd Saint Paul MN 55105 Office: 1714 Am Nat Bank Bldg Saint Paul MN 55101

VAUGHN, CHARLES ROBERT, lawyer; b. Olney, Ill., Feb. 17, 1922; s. Charles S. and Elsie B. (Ray) V.; B.S., James Millikin U., 1943; LL.B., U. Ill., 1948; m. Elizabeth Ann Gassmann, Dec. 4, 1943; children—Ann (Mrs. Robert Martin), Carol (Mrs. Robert Schafer), Charles B., Kathleen (Mrs. John Longueville), John R., Allen Z., Ray W., Mary G., Frank E. Admitted to Ill. bar, 1948; practice law, Olney, Ill., 1948—; dir. First Nat. Bank, Olney. States atty., Richland County, Ill., 1952-64, 68-80, asst. states atty., 1948-52. Alt. del. Republican Nat. Conv., 1964. Served with USMCR, 1943-46. Mem. Am. Legion, VFW, Ill. State Attys. Assn., Ill., Richland County bar assns. Roman Catholic. Elk. Home: 507 N Boone St Olney IL 62450 Office: 308 S Kitchell Ave Olney IL 62450

VAUGHN, CLARENCE BENJAMIN, oncologist; b. Phila., Dec. 14, 1928; s. Albert and Aretha (Johnson) V.; B.S., Benedict Coll., 1951; M.S., Howard U., 1955, M.D., 1957; Ph.D., Wayne State U., 1965; m. Sarah Campbell, Sept. 25, 1953; children—Steven, Annette, Carl, Ronald. Intern, D.C. Gen. Hosp., Washington, 1957-58; fellow medicine and allergy, resident Freedman's Hosp., Washington, 1958-59; NIH fellow, 1961-62; NIH spl. research fellow Wayne State U., Detroit, 1962-64, lab. instr., 1963-67; research physician Milton A. Darling Meml. Center, Mich. Cancer Found., Detroit, 1964-70, clin. dir., 1970-72; dir. div. oncology Providence Hosp., Southfield, Mich., 1973—; cons. med. staff, dept. medicine Kirwood Gen. Hosp., Detroit, 1967—, Oakwood Hosp., Dearborn, Mich., 1968—; cons. staff, dept. medicine Detroit Meml. Hosp., 1970, Crittenton Hosp., Rochester, Mich., 1972; courtesy staff Grace Hosp., Detroit, 1973, S.W. Detroit Hosp., 1973; jr. attending Hutzel Hosp., Detroit, 1975—; lab. asst. chemistry Benedict Coll., Columbia, S.C., 1945-51; grad. asst. Howard U., Washington, 1951-52, research asst., 1952-53; chemist Dept. Interior, Washington, 1953-55; lab. instr. Wayne State U., 1963-67, asst. prof. oncology, 1967-78, asso. prof., 1978—, asso. dept. biochemistry, 1967—; med. service liaison office between USAF and Wayne State U., 1960—; med. advisor to comdr. Wilford Hall Med. Center, Lackland AFB, Tex., 1981. Pres. Wayne County unit Am. Cancer Soc. Served to lt. col. USAF, 1959-61; col. Res. Decorated Air Force Commendation medal; recipient Aerospace Physician award Air Force Res., 1974, Outstanding Flight Surgeon award, 1975; named Surgeon of Yr., Air Force Res. Assn., 1980. Fellow Am. Coll. Clin. Pharm.; mem. Am. Cancer Soc. (dir. 1973—), Air Force Assn., Am. Chem. Soc., A.C.P., AAUP, AMA, Am. Radium Soc., Am. Soc. Clin. Oncology, Assn. Mil. Surgeons U.S., Detroit Cancer Club, Detroit Physiol. Soc., Mich. Med. Soc., Mich. Assn. Med. Edn., Nat. Med. Assn. (nat. chmn. aerospace and mil. sect.), N.Y. Acad. Scis., Oakland County Med Soc., Res. Officers Assn. U.S., S.W. Oncology Study Group, Wayne County Med. Soc., Sigma Xi, Alpha Kappa Mu, Beta Kappa Chi, Phi Lambda Upsilon. Contbr. articles to profl. jours. Home: 19410 Canterbury Rd Detroit MI 48221 Office: 16001 W Nine Mile Rd Southfield MI 48075

VAUGHN, JACK LEE, veterinarian; b. Helena, Mo., June 7, 1934; s. Maynard Harte and Hazel Marie (Christy) V.; B.S., U. Mo., 1958, D.V.M., 1958; m. Julie Ann Ramm, June 1, 1975; children—Maynard, David, Judy, Daphne, Pamela. Farmer, 1952—; large animal veterinarian, Columbia, Mo., 1958-63, mixed practice, 1963-67, specialist in small animals, 1967—; dir. Mo. Veterinary Supply Co. Deacon Woodcrest Primitive Bapt. Ch. Mem. Columbia, Central Mo., Mo. veterinary med. assns., AVMA. Republican. Clubs: Forrest Hills Country, Rotary. Home: Route 6 Columbia MO 65201 Office: 400 Nebraska Ave Columbia MO 65201

VAUGHN, LAWRENCE (LARRY) EUGENE, JR., broadcasting exec.; b. Hannibal, Mo., Feb. 14, 1944; s. Lawrence Eugene and Marjorie Gwendolyn (White) V.; grad. Carolina Sch. Broadcasting, 1963; m. Leona Marie Tate, Feb. 8, 1964; children—Link, Lance. Staff announcer Sta. WIST Radio, Charlotte, N.C., 1962-63; news dir. Sta. KWRT Radio, Boonville, Mo., 1963-65; program dir. WDAN Radio, Danville, Ill., 1965-69; sgt. Danville Police Dept., 1969-74; sales mgr. Sta. KCBJ-TV, Columbia, Mo., 1974-75; dir. info. Assn. Mo. Electric Coops., Jefferson City, 1975-77, mgr. coop. advt., 1977-79; comml. mgr. Sta. KCHI-KCHI-FM, Chillicothe, Mo., 1979—; pres. GVC Communications, Inc., 1979-81; lobbyist Mo. Legislature, 1977-79; dir. Bedford & Medicine Creek R.R., 1980—. Mayor City of Holts Summit (Mo.), 1977-79; bd. dirs. Mid-Mo. Council Govts., 1977-79. Lt. col. Mo. State Guard, 1981—. Recipient 1st pl. award spl. projects Nat. Rural Electric Coop. Assn., 1976, spl. award pub. service Mo. Dept. Agr., 1977, Humanitarian award C.A.P., 1977, Disting. Service award, 1979. Mem. Mo. Broadcasters Assn. (spl. award pub. service broadcasting 1976), Pub. Relations Soc. Am., Pub. Utility Communicators Assn., Mo. Pilots Assn., C.A.P. (dep. comdr. Mo. Group III 1978-80). Democrat. Baptist. Club: Lions (pres. Chillicothe 1981—). Home: 1100 Broadway Ave Chillicothe MO 64601 Office: 421 S Washington St Chillicothe MO 64601

VAUGHT, RICHARD LOREN, pediatric urologist; b. Johnson County, Ind., Oct. 28, 1933; s. Loren Judson and Bernice Rose (Bridges) V.; A.B. in Anatomy and Physiology, Ind. U., 1955, M.D., 1958; m. Patricia Sue Lemons, Aug. 28, 1955; children—Megan, Niles, Barbara, Mary. Commd. ensign, M.C., U.S. Navy, 1958, advanced through grades to lt. comdr., 1968; intern U.S. Naval Hosp., St. Albans, N.Y., 1958-59, resident in gen. surgery, 1959-60, resident in urology, 1960-63; spl. fellow in urology Sloan-Kettering Meml. Inst. for Cancer and Allied Diseases, N.Y.C., 1963; observer in pediatric urology Columbia-Presbyterian Babies Hosp., N.Y.C., 1963; head urology U.S. Naval Hosp., Beaufort, S.C., 1963-65; asst. chief urology, head pediatric urology U.S. Naval Hosp., San Diego, 1966-68; ret., 1968; pvt. practice medicine specializing in pediatric urology, Sioux City, Iowa, 1968—; mem. staff St. Luke's Med. Center, Marian Health Center. Pres., Davis Fine Woods, Sioux City. Diplomate Am. Bd. Urology. Fellow Am. Acad. Pediatrics, A.C.S., Am. Pediatric Soc.; mem. AMA, Iowa Med. Soc., Woodbury Med. Soc. (trustee), Am. Urol. Assn., Soc. Pediatric Urology, Internat. Soc. Cryosurgery. Methodist. Clubs: Sertoma, Masons, Heather Highlanders Bagpipe Band. Office: 2928 Hamilton Blvd Sioux City IA 51104

VAYHINGER, JOHN MONROE, clergyman, clin. psychologist, educator; b. Upland, Ind., Jan. 27, 1916; s. Paul J. and Harriett E. (Palmer) V.; A.B., Taylor U., 1937; B.D. cum laude, Drew Theol. Sem., 1940; M.A., Columbia U., 1948, Ph.D., 1956; M.A., Drew U., 1951; m. Ruth Catherine Imler, Sept. 17, 1939; children—John Earl, Karen Lynn. Ordained to minstry United Meth. Ch., 1941; pastor Meth. chs., Ind., N.Y., Conn., Colo., 1938-58; head dept. psychology W.Va. Wesleyan Coll., Buckhannon, 1949-51; chief clin. psychologist Adult and Child Guidance Clinic, South Bend, Ind., 1951-58, Ind. U., 1953-58; prof. pastoral psychology and counseling Garrett Theol. Sem., Northwestern U., Evanston, Ill., 1958-64; prof. psychology of religion and pastoral counseling Iliff Sch. Theology, U. Denver, 1964-67; prof. psychology and pastoral care Anderson (Ind.) Sch. Theology, 1968-81; prof. pastoral care and counseling Asbury Theol. Sem., Wilmore, Ky., 1981—. Bd. dirs. Ind. Council Chs., Life Psychiat. Center, Denver. Served with AUS, 1944-47. Diplomate Am. Bd. Examiners in Profl. Psychology. Fellow Am. Orthopsychiat. Assn., Am. Sci. Affiliation; mem. N.Y. Ann. Conf. United Meth. Ch., Am. Psychol. Assn., Am. Assn. Marriage and Family Therapists Am. Assn. Pastoral Counselors (diplomate), Am. Soc. Psychologists in Family Practice (dir.), Am. Group Psychotherapy Assn., Colo., Ind. psychol. assns., AAUP, Assn. Mil. Chaplains, Acad. Religion and Mental Health, Nat. Congress of Parents and Tchrs., Ind. Congress of Parents and Tchrs., Christian Assn. for Psychol. Studies, Am. Assn. Clin. Pastoral Edn. (sem. rep.). Author: (with others) Casebook of Pastoral Counseling, 1962, In the Beginning of Divorce, 1971. Home: 1235 Favorite St Anderson IN 46013 Office: 1123 E 3d St Anderson IN 46011

VECCHIO, PETER JAMES, food co. exec.; b. Mt. Pleasant, Pa., July 3, 1947; s. Peter and Mary Margaret (Daly) V.; B.B.A., Marshall U., 1969; m. Linda Lou Snyder, Mar. 15, 1968; 1 son, Peter James. Grocery sales rep. H.J. Heinz Co., Pitts., 1969-72, dist. staff asst., 1973-74, area mgr. Cin., 1974-76, broker-mgr. Central region, 1976-77; pres., chmn. bd. Sno Mountain Co., Cin., 1977-80; dist. sales mgr. Borden Inc., Cin., 1980-81; regional sales mgr. Jeno's Inc., 1981—. Trustee Bevis Athletic Assn., 1976. Served with U.S. Army, 1969-71; Vietnam. Decorated Bronze Star. Mem. Nat. Frozen Food Assn., Cin. Grocery Mfrs. Reps. Roman Catholic. Home: 3314 Grovewood Dr Cincinnati OH 45239

VECCHIO, ROBERT PETER, indsl. psychologist, educator; b. Chgo., June 29, 1950; s. Dominick C. and Angeline V.; B.S. summa cum laude, DePaul U., 1972; M.A., U. Ill., 1974, Ph.D., 1976; m. Betty Ann Vecchio, Aug. 21, 1974. Instr., U. Ill., Urbana, 1973-76; mem. faculty dept. mgmt. U. Notre Dame (Ind.), 1976—. Mem. Acad. Mgmt., Am. Psychol. Assn., Assn. Consumer Research, Inst. Mgmt. Scis., Am. Statis. Assn., Am. Inst. Decision Scis., Midwest Acad. Mgmt., Midwest Psychol. Assn., Phi Kappa Phi, Delta Epsilon Sigma, Phi Eta Sigma, Beta Gamma Sigma, Psi Chi. Roman Catholic. Contbr. articles to profl. jours. Home: 52173 Brookview Ct South Bend IN 46637 Office: Dept Mgmt Univ of Notre Dame Notre Dame IN 46556

VECCHIO, THOMAS JAMES, physician, pharm. co. exec.; b. N.Y.C., June 14, 1924; s. James and Mildred (Lepre) V.; B.S., Manhattan Coll., 1944; M.D., Harvard U., 1948; m. Lisa Waslewski, July 16, 1977; children—Karen, Claudia, Theodore, Sarah. Practice medicine specializing in internal medicine, Grand Rapids, Mich., 1954-56; asso. chief internal medicine United Mine Workers Hosp., Williamson, W.Va., 1956-60, chief allergy, 1956-58; cons. Pineville Meml. Hosp., 1956-60; asso. chief internal medicine United Mine Workers Hosp., Middlesboro, Ky., 1958-60; staff physician clin. research Upjohn Co., Kalamazoo, Mich., 1960-62, sect. chief clin. research, 1962, mgr. med. devel., 1964-66, chief med. research Upjohn Internat., Inc., 1966-74, med. mgr. domestic pharm. med. affairs, 1974—; teaching cons. Borgess Hosp., 1963—; med. dir. Kalamazoo Planned Parenthood Fedn., 1970-71. Bd. dirs. Kalamazoo Vis. Nurses Assn. Served with M.C., U.S. Army, 1951-53. Diplomate Am. Bd. Internal Medicine. Fellow ACP; mem. Kalamazoo Acad. Medicine, Mich. Med. Soc., AMA, Am. Diabetes Assn., Am. Soc. Clin. Pharmacology and Therapeutics, Am. Heart Assn. Contbr. articles to med. jours. Office: 7000 Portage Rd Kalamazoo MI 49001*

VEDDER, RICHARD KENT, economist; b. Urbana, Ill., Nov. 5, 1940; s. Byron C. and Kathleen (Fry) V.; B.A., Northwestern U., 1962; A.M., U. Ill., 1963, Ph.D., 1965; m. Karen Pirosko, June 18, 1968; children—Virin Kent, Vanette Kelly. Asst. prof. econs. Ohio U., 1965-69, asso. prof., 1969-74, prof., 1974—, chmn. dept., 1980-81; vis. prof. Claremont Men's Coll., 1979-80, U. Colo., 1979, 80; economist Joint Econ. Com. of Congress, 1981—; trustee Bus. History Conf. Rockefeller-Ford Population Policy Research grantee, 1974-75; grantee, fellow Earhart Found., 1963-70. Mem. Am. Econ. Assn., Econ. History Assn. Republican. Presbyterian. Club: Rotary. Author: The American Economy in Historial Perspective, 1976; editor: (with others) Essays in Economic History, 1975. Home: 295 Beechwood Dr Athens OH 45701 Office: Dept Econs Ohio Univ Athens OH 45701

VEENSTRA, H. ROBERT, cons. engr.; b. Leighton, Iowa, Oct. 21, 1921; s. Henry and Gretta (Vandehaar) V.; B.S. in Civil Engring., Iowa State U., 1947; m. Norena D. Grandia, Sept. 9, 1944; children—Henry Robert, Cynthia L., John N., Mark A. Design engr. Stanley Engring. Co., Muscatine, Iowa, 1947-49, sect. head, 1949-51, project engr., 1951-57, supervising engr., 1957-61; partner Veenstra & Kimm, Engrs. & Planners, West Des Moines, 1961-80; chmn. bd. Veenstra & Kimm, Inc., Engrs. & Planners, West Des Moines, 1980—. Served to capt. AUS, 1942-46. Fellow ASCE, Am. Council Cons. Engrs.; mem. Nat. Soc. Profl. Engrs. (past nat. dir.), Iowa Engring. Soc. (Anson Marston award 1962), Am. Congress on Surveying and Mapping, Cons. Engrs. Council Iowa (past pres.), ASTM, Am. Water Works Assn., Water Pollution Control Fedn., Theta Xi. United Methodist. Club: Masons. Contbr. articles to profl. jours. Office: 300 West Bank Bldg 1601 22nd St West Des Moines IA 50265

VEGA, CONRAD M., state senator; b. June 22, 1938; grad. St. Thomas Coll., 1960; m. Alice Vega; 3 children. Mem. Minn. Senate, 1976—. Mem. Econ. Devel. Authority, South St. Paul. Mem. Minn. Fedn. Tchrs. (past v.p.). Mem. Democratic-Farmer-Labor party. Office: 303 State Capitol St Paul MN 55155*

VEGA, FRANCISCO MIGUEL, cemetery cons.; b. San Antonio, Feb. 28, 1922; s. Lazaro Nava and Sara Lopez Tapia Vega; B.A., Aquinas Coll., Grand Rapids, Mich., 1950; m. Phyllis Jean Lackland, May 10, 1946; children—Susan Louise, Margaret Katherine, Elizabeth Ann. Engaged in cemetery bus., 1950—; gen. sales mgr. Resurrection Cemetery, Grand Rapids, 1953-55; cemetery cons., Grand Rapids, 1954—; pres., treas., co-owner Sunset Meml. Gardens, Ionia, Mich., 1956-70; pres., owner Kent Meml. Gardens Inc., Grand Rapids, 1959—, Pre-Need Kent Plant, Inc., Grand Rapids, 1971—; pres. FaBCo. Inc., Grand Rapids, 1977—. Bd. dirs. Econ. Devel. Corp. Grand Rapids, 1971-72, SER-Jobs for Progress, Inc., 1979-81; pres. Mich. Hispanic Devel. Corp., 1973-75; mem. adv. council SBA, 1968-69; mem. Mich. Adv. Council Spanish Speaking, 1974-75, Grand Rapids Community Relations Commn., 1968-74; mem. bd. Kent County Dept. Social Services, 1977—; pres. Grand Rapids chpt. Latin Am. United Polit. Action, 1966-68; chmn. for Mich., Republican Nat. Hispanic Assembly, 1974; alt. del. Rep. Nat. Conv., 1976; exec. com. 5th Congl. Dist. Rep. Com., 1977-80; mem. citizens adv. com. Kent County Pros. Atty.'s Office, 1977—; co-chmn. adv. com. bi-lingual edn. Grand Rapids Bd. Edn., 1971-74; chmn. Hispanic Reps. Mich., 1976-80. Served with USAAF, 1942-45. Recipient various service awards, certs. of appreciation. Mem. Am. GI Forum, League United Latin Am. Citizens. Roman Catholic. Author articles in field. Home: 1317 Giddings Ave SE Grand Rapids MI 49506 Office: 7101 Clyde Park Ave SW Grand Rapids MI 49509

VEIT, ROBERT JOSEPH, fire chief; b. Grand Rapids, Mich., Mar. 30, 1920; s. Nicholas Joseph and Emma Gertrude (Kirchoff) V.; ed. Grand Rapids public schs.; m. Hilda Gaedert, July 9, 1951. Apprentice pattern maker, 1940-43; firefighter to fire chief Grand Rapids Fire Dept., 1967—, dir. civil def., 1967—. Served with USNR, 19—. Mem. Internat. Assn. Fire Chiefs, Mich. Soc. Fire Chiefs, Metro Chiefs Assn., Western Mich. Fire Chiefs, Internat. Assn. Arson Investigators, Am. Legion. Club: Lions. Office: City Fire Dept Grand Rapids MI 49503

VEKASY, SANDRA CAROLINE, educator; b. Youngstown, Ohio, May 14, 1942; d. Stephen and Mary Caroline (Ravess) V.; B.S. in Edn., Bowling Green State U., 1964, M.A., 1969, postgrad., 1977-78. Tchr. English and geography Warren (Ohio) City Schs., 1964-65; tchr. English, Youngstown (Ohio) Pub. Schs., 1967-68; instr. English, Western Ill. U., Macomb, 1969-70; teaching fellow Bowling Green (Ohio) State U., 1977-78; asst. prof. English, Evangel Coll., Springfield, Mo., 1970—, dir. freshman composition, 1973-76; editorial asst., promotions dept., div. fgn. missions Gospel Pub. House, Springfield, 1974-75. Mem. Mo. Assn. Tchrs. English, Mo. Lang. Arts Dept., Sigma Tau Delta, Kappa Delta Pi. Home: 2124 S Brighton Dr Springfield MO 65804 Office: Evangel Coll 1111 N Glenstone St Springfield MO 65802

VELAER, CHARLES ALFRED, ret. educator; b. Kansas City, Mo., Jan. 25, 1932; s. Charles Alfred and Edna (Bothwell) V.; B.S., Roosevelt U., 1957; M.S., Ill. Inst. Tech., 1960; m. Caryl Ruth Sonnenburg, Nov. 17, 1962; children—Ruth Anne, Charles Alfred. Instr., asst. prof. Roosevelt U., Chgo., 1957-68, asso. prof. physics, 1968-74, ret., 1974; cons. New Horizons Pub., Inc., Chgo. Served with Signal Corps, AUS, 1950-54. Mem. Am. (cons. rosarian 1971—), English, Chgo. Regional (dist. pres. 1966-67, dir. 1968—) rose socs., Am. Inst. Physics. Home: 9636 S Brandt Ave Oak Lawn IL 60453

VELEK, MIROSLAV, psychiatrist; b. Ceské Budejovice, Czechoslovakia, Sept. 14, 1932; s. Josef and Marie (Paroulek) V.; came to U.S., 1977; M.D., Charles U., Prague, Czechoslovakia, 1956; diploma in psychiatry McGill U., Montreal, 1974; m. Nancy Irene Cumming, Oct. 7, 1978; 1 son, David. Psychiatrist-in-chief, outpatient dept. Inst. Nat. Health, Prague, 1962-69; resident McGill U., Montreal, 1970-74; staff psychiatrist Queen Elizabeth Hosp., Montreal, 1974-77; asso. prof. psychiatry Albany (N.Y.) Med. Coll., 1977-80, sr. staff psychiatrist inpatient service, 1977-80; asso. prof. psychiatry, dir. residency tng. So. Ill. U., Springfield, 1980—. Recipient Physicians Recognition award AMA, 1978, 81; cert. in psychiatry, Can.; diplomate Am. Bd. Psychiatry and Neurology. Mem. Am. Psychiat. Assn., Am. Assn. History of Medicine, Can. Psychiat. Assn., Internat. Coll. Psychosomatic Medicine, Assn. for Acad. Psychiatry, Soc. for Neuroscis., Collegium Internationale Neuropsychopharmacologicum. Contbr. articles to profl. jours. Home: 4 Tophill Ln Springfield IL 62704 Office: So Ill U Springfield IL 62708

VENIT, WILLIAM BENNETT, elec. products co. exec.; b. Chgo., May 28, 1931; s. George Bernard and Ida (Schaffel) V.; student U. Ill., Champaign, 1949; m. Nancy Jean Carlson, Jan. 28, 1956; children—Steven Louis, Aprilann. Sales mgr. Coronet, Inc., Chgo., 1952-63, pres., chmn. bd., 1963-74; pres., chmn. bd. Roma Wire Inc., Chgo., 1971-74; pres. Wm. Allen Inc., Chgo., 1972-74; pres., chmn. bd. William Lamp Co., Inc., William Wire Co., Inc., 1974-76; pres., chmn. bd. MSWV, Inc., 1981—; spl. cons. Mac Kinney Co., Hanover Park, Ill., Hartlaub Legs Inc., Mc Sherrystown, Pa., 1978—; cons. Nu Style Lamp Shade, Chgo., Sunbeam Clock Co., Forest, Miss., Greatwestern Lamp Co., Forest City, Iowa, Tex. Lamp Co., Dallas, Moschiano Plating, Chgo., Father and Sons Spinning Co., Chgo. Served with Q.M.C., AUS, 1949-52. Mem. Mfr. Agt. Club, Chgo. Lamp and Shade Inst. (dir.). Home: 4850 N Monticello Ave Chicago IL 60625 Office: 715 N Kedzie Ave Chicago IL 60622

VENTO, BRUCE FRANK, congressman: b. St. Paul, Oct. 7, 1940; s. Frank A. and Ann V. (Sauer) V.; B.A., Wis. State U., River Falls, 1965; postgrad. U. Minn., 1966—; m. Mary Jean Moore, Oct. 24, 1959; children—Michael, Peter, John. Tchr. sci., social studies Mpls. pub. schs., from 1965; mem. Minn. Ho. of Reps. from St. Paul 66A Dist., 1971-76, asst. majority leader, vice chmn. jud. com., 1973-76; mem. 95th-97th Congresses from 4th Minn. Dist. Mem. legis. rev. com. Minn. Commn. on Future. Del., Democratic Farm Labor party Central Com., 1972—, chmn. Ramsey County Com., 1972—. NSF grantee, 1967-68. Mem. Minn. Fedn. Tchrs., Beta Beta Beta, Kappa Delta Phi. Office: 230 Cannon House Office Bldg Washington DC 20515 also 150 Mears Park Place 405 Sibley St Saint Paul MN 55101

VENZKE, NORMAN CHARLES, coast guard officer; b. Balt., Dec. 8, 1927; s. Charles Gottlieb and Florence Amelia (Norris) V.; B.S. in Engring., U.S. Coast Guard Acad., 1950; B.S.E.E., U.S. Naval Postgrad. Sch., 1957; M.S. in Adminstrn., George Washington U., 1974; m. Dolores Elaine Erickson, Apr. 19, 1958 (dec.); 1 dau., Erica Yvette. Commd. ensign U.S. Coast Gurad, 1950, advanced through grades to rear adm., 1977; assigned to extensive polar work with 4 trips to Arctic and Antarctica; served in Vietnam; comdr. 2d Coast Guard Dist., St. Louis, 1979—. Chmn. St. Louis Fed. Exec. Bd. Decorated Legion of Merit with Combat V, Meritorious Service Medal, Navy Commendation Medal. Mem. U.S. Naval Inst., Am. Def. Preparedness Assn., Nat. Def. Transp. Assn. (pres. St. Louis chpt.), Res. Officers Assn. Lutheran. Clubs: Explorers, Masons, Shriners. Home: 16 Chaminade Dr Creve Coeur MO 63141 Office: 1430 Olive St Saint Louis MO 63103

VERAMALLAY, ASHTON ISARDATT, economist, educator; b. Guyana, Mar. 2, 1940; came to U.S., 1967; s. Bonus David and Doris (Jagdeo) V.; B.S., U. Wis., LaCrosse, 1970; M.S., Iowa State U., 1972, Ph.D., 1976; m. Norma S. Madramooto, Apr. 15, 1967; children—Stasia Ashmala, Shayne Ravin. Sr. master Belvedere Govt. Sch., Guyana, 1960-67; research asst. Iowa State U., 1971-74; mem. faculty dept. econs. W.Va. State Coll., 1976-77; prof. econs., dir. Center for Econ. Edn., Ind. U. East, Richmond, 1977—. Mem. Comprehensive Energy Mgmt. Com., City of Richmond. Mem. Am. Econ. Assn., Atlantic Econ. Soc., Midwest Econ. Assn., Ind. Council for Econ. Edn., Joint Council on Econ. Edn., Nat. Council for Social Studies, Soc. Internat. Devel., Comparative and Internat. Edn. Soc. Presbyterian. Club: Kiwanis. Author works in field. Home: 313 S 27th St Richmond IN 47374 Office: 2325 Chester Blvd Richmond IN 47374

VERBONCOUER, JAMES DONNELY, social services adminstr.; b. Green Bay, Wis., Apr. 8, 1952; s. Donnely James and Sophia Angelia (Peer) V.; A.A., Muskegon Community Coll., 1972; B.A. in Social Work, Mich. State U., 1974; M.P.A., Western Mich. U., 1980; m. Joy Lee Cousineau, May 1, 1976. Social services worker Muskegon County Dept. Social Services, Muskegon, Mich., 1974-76; social worker Muskegon Regional Center for Developmental Disabilities, 1976-77, program supr., 1977-79, adminstrv. asst., 1979—; vice chmn. Regional Interagy. Coordinating Com., 1980, chmn., 1981. Trustee, Muskegon Bd. Edn., 1980—. Republican. Baptist. Home: 1285 Ransom St Muskegon MI 49442 Office: 1903 Marquette Ave Muskegon MI 49442

VERDA, DOMINIC JOSEPH, real estate devel. co. exec.; b. St. Louis, Sept. 17, 1947; s. Dominic J. and Dorothy F. (Fuhlage) V.; grad. Florissant Valley Community Coll., 1968; B.S. in Commerce, St. Louis U., 1970; M.B.A., Vanderbilt U., 1973; Ph.D., Sussex U., 1977. Instr. Grad. Sch. Bus. and Adminstrn., U. Tenn., Nashville, 1972-73; fin. exec. Continental Advisors, Coral Gables, Fla., 1973-74; pres. Development By Design Corp., St. Louis, 1974—, chmn. bd., 1974—; cons. fin. and mktg. to various mfg. and bus. firms, 1968-79. Mem. Am. Mktg. Assn., Internat. Police Assn., Ill. Police Assn., St. Louis County Police Comdrs. Assn., Nat. Rifle Assn. Republican. Mem. Christian Ch. Clubs: St. Louis County Pistol, Graduate. Contbr. articles on mgmt. to profl. jours. Address: 16 Pine Valley Dr Saint Louis MO 63124

VERDEGAN, JAMES CLARENCE, restaurateur; b. Kewaunee, Wis., Feb. 22, 1941; s. Clarence John and Helen Doris (Helmer) V.; B.S. in Communications, St. Norbert Coll., 1963; children—Jeffery James, Matthew James, Jennifer Lynne. Salesman, Mut. Benefit Life Ins., Green Bay, Wis., 1965-67; service rep., salesman Wis. Physicians Service, Fox River Valley, 1968-70; salesman northeastern Wis., Xerox, 1970-71; owner, operator Happy's Lobster Place, Kewaunee, Wis., 1972—. Bd. dirs. St. Mary's Hosp., 1971-75; mem. Northeastern Wis. Regional Planning Commn., 1975-76. Served with U.S. Army, 1963-64. Mem. Wis. Restaurant Assn. (Door-Key chpt.). Republican. Club: Northeastern Wis. Gt. Lake Sport Fishermen (pres. 1972-76, service award 1976). Office: 306 Ellis St Kewaunee WI 54216

VERDI, ROBERT WILLIAM, sportswriter; b. Bklyn., Aug. 31, 1946; s. Frank and Anne V.; B.A. in English, Lake Forest Coll., 1967. Sportswriter, Chgo. Tribune, 1967—; cons. to encys. Named Sportswriter of Yr., Nat. Sportscasters and Sportswriters Assn., 1975, 77, 78, 79, 80; Newspaper Fund intern, 1967. Mem. Baseball Writers Assn. Am., Profl. Hockey Writers Assn. Office: 435 N Michigan Ave Chicago IL 60611

VERITY, CALVIN WILLIAM, JR., steel co. exec.; b. Middletown, Ohio, Jan. 26, 1917; s. Calvin William and Elizabeth (O'Brien) V.; grad. Phillips Exeter Acad., 1935; B.A., Yale U., 1939; m. Margaret Burnley Wymond, Apr. 19, 1941; children—Jonathan George, Peggy Wymond (Mrs. John Power), William Wymond. With Armco Steel Corp. (now Armco Inc.), Middletown, 1940—, dir. public relations, 1961-62, asst. to pres., 1962-63, v.p., gen. mgr., 1963-65, exec. v.p., dir., 1965, pres., chief exec. officer, 1965-71, chmn. bd., 1971—; dir. Chase Manhattan Bank, Mead Corp., Dayton, Ohio, Bus. Internat., N.Y.C., First Nat. Bank, Middletown, Boston Co., Taft Broadcasting Co., Cin. Chmn. bd. govs. Ford's Theater. Mem. Middletown C. of C. (past pres.), Cin. Council World Affairs, SAR. Clubs: Brown's Run Country (Middletown); Moraine (Dayton); Laurel Valley (Ligonier, Pa.); Queen City, Camargo (Cin.) Office: Armco Inc 703 Curtis St Middletown OH 45042*

VERMA, SHASHI BHUSHAN, fluid dynamicist and agrl. meteorologist; b. Buxar, Bihar, India, July 27, 1944; came to U.S., 1965, naturalized, 1980; s. Mahadeo P. and Kusum K. (Devi) V.; B.S., Regional Inst. Tech., Jamshedpur, India, 1965; M.S., U. Colo., 1967; Ph.D., Colo. State U., 1971; m. Shefalika Sahai, Mar. 8, 1972; children—Anita, Amit. Research asst. Fluid Dynamics and Diffusion Lab., Colo. State U., Fort Collins, 1967-71, postdoctoral fellow, 1971-72; postdoctoral research asso. agrl. meteorology U. Nebr., Lincoln, 1972-74; staff meteorologist Dames & Moore, San Francisco, 1974; asst. prof. agrl. meteorology sect. dept. agrl. engring. U. Nebr., Lincoln, 1974-78, asso. prof. Center Agrl. Meteorology and Climatology, 1978—. U.S. Dept. Interior Office of Water Resources Research grantee, 1974-75; NSF grantee, 1975—; U.S. Dept. Agr. Sci. and Edn. Adminstrn. grantee, 1979—. Registered profl. engr., Nebr. Mem. Am. Meteorol. Soc., Am. Soc. Agrl. Engrs., Sigma Xi. Contbr. articles in field to profl. jours. Office: Center Agrl Meteorology and Climatology 211 Agrl Engring Bldg U Nebr Lincoln NE 68583

VERNON, DUANE RICHARD, credit bur. exec.; b. Ithaca, Mich., Sept. 3, 1931; s. Wesley Robert and Leah Amelia (Smith) V.; B.A. in Personnel Adminstrn., Mich. State U., 1953; m. Virginia Louise Graff, Apr. 4, 1954 (dec. 1975); children—Rick, Nancy, Mary Jo. Asst. mgr. affiliated divs. Mich. Retailers Assn., Lansing, 1956-59; dir. sales and public relations Credit Bur. Greater Lansing, 1959-74, pres., gen. mgr., 1974—; active in enactment Mich. Equal Credit Opportunity Act, 1977; lectr. Mich. State U., Lansing Community Coll., Cooley Law Sch. Pres., Lansing Jaycees, 1961-62; bd. dirs., capital area div. campaign chmn. United Way, Lansing, 1962-68; pres. Lansing Vol. Bur., 1967-68; bd. dirs. Easter Seal Soc. Mid-Mich., 1975-81, Mich. State U. Devel. Council, 1977-81, Camp Highfields; exec. bd. Chief Okemos council Boy Scouts Am.; charter bd. dirs. Mid-Mich. chpt. Nat. Football Found. and Hall of Fame; Mid-Mich. chmn. Olympathon '79. Served with U.S. Army, 1954-56. Recipient Lansing Jaycees Key Man award, 1960, Lansing Outstanding Young Man of Yr. award, 1963, Jaycee Internat. Senator award, 1978; Outstanding Club Pres.'s award Mich. State U. Alumni Assn., 1969; Disting. Alumni award Delta Tau Delta, 1978, Vandervoort Meml. award Downtown Coaches Club of Lansing, 1978, others. Mem. Asso. Credit Burs. Mich. (pres. 1979-80, Gold Key Leadership award 1978, Exec. Achievement award 1979), Public Relations Assn. Mich., Retail Credit Grantors Assn. Lansing (pres. 1961-62), Mid-Mich. Personnel Assn., Lansing Assn. Credit Mgmt. (bd. dirs. 1977-79), Lansing Regional C. of C. (bd. dirs. 1981—), Mich. State U. Alumni Club (pres. 1969). Methodist. Clubs: Rotary (pres. 1980-81), Downtown Coaches (bd. dirs. 1979-83), Greater Lansing Bull-Pen (pres. 1972), Waverly High Sch. Sideliners Athletic Boosters (pres. 1977-79), Waverly Swim (dir. 1977-79), Box 23 of Lansing (chief 1982). Club: Lansing Rotary (pres. found. 1981-82). Home: 4315 Wagon Wheel St Lansing MI 48917 Office: 520 S Washington St Lansing MI 48901

VERRANT, JOHN ALAN, mfg. co. exec., mech. engr.; b. Hibbing, Minn., Dec. 19, 1951; s. John Carl and Marie (Moudent) Mastell V.; B.M.E., U. Minn., 1974, M.S. in M.E., 1976. Intern engr. Toro Co., Mpls., 1972-74; research and teaching asst. U. Minn., Mpls., 1974-76; research engr. Southwest Research Inst., San Antonio, 1976-77; tech. engring. supr. Donaldson Co., Inc., Mpls., 1977-81; project mgr. Detector Electronics Corp., Mpls., 1981—. Mem. Soc. Automotive Engrs. (Arch T. Colwell Merit award 1978), ASME, Minn. Assn. Farmers-Landowners-Sportsmen. Club: Northwest Racquet. Home: 8308 W 104th St Bloomington MN 55438 Office: 6901 W 110 St Minneapolis MN 55438

VERSIC, RONALD JAMES, research co. exec.; b. Dayton, Ohio, Oct. 19, 1942; s. Charles and Volunta Henrietta (Sherman) V.; B.S., U. Dayton, 1964; M.A., Johns Hopkins U., 1968; Ph.D., Ohio State U., 1969; m. Linda Joan Davies, June 11, 1966; children—Kathryn Clara, Paul Joseph. Sr. physicist GAF Corp., Binghamton, N.Y., 1969-70; program mgr. Systems Research Labs., Dayton, 1970-71; sr. scientist The Standard Register Co., Dayton, 1971-76; dir. chem. research and devel. Monarch Marking Systems, Inc., Dayton, 1976-79; exec. v.p. Ronald T. Dodge Co., Dayton, 1979—. Mem. Citizens' Housing Com., Oakwood, Ohio, 1978—; Precinct I Republican committeeman, Oakwood Ward, 1973—. Named disting. outstanding lt. gov. Ohio Dist. Optimists Internat., 1975-76. Mem. Kettering-Moraine Mus. and Hist. Soc., Am. Chem. Soc., Soc. Photog. Scientists and Engrs., Am. Def. Preparedness Assn., Am. Inst. Physics, Am. Assn. Physics Tchrs., Am. Crystallographic Assn., AAAS, Soc. Photo-Optical Instrumentation Engrs., Air Force Assn., Oakwood Sister Cities, Dayton Art Inst., Nat. Rifle Assn., Sigma Xi. Roman Catholic. Clubs: Johns Hopkins, Kettering Optimists (past pres.), Engrs. of Dayton (gov.), Dayton Execs., Yugoslav of Greater Dayton, Walter P. Chrysler, Inc. Contbr. articles to profl. jours. Home: 1601 Shafor Blvd Dayton OH 45419 Office: PO Box 77 Dayton OH 45409

VERSON, MELVIN DAVID, mfg. co. exec.; b. Chgo., 1927; grad. The Citadel, 1950. Chmn. bd., dir. Verson Allsteel Press Co., Chgo.; dir. Heritage/Pullman Bank, Bank of River Oaks. Office: 1355 E 93d St Chicago IL 60619*

VERTANEN, GEORGE JERRY, engr.; b. Ishpeming, Mich., Apr. 9, 1940; s. William and Hilja V.; m. Nina Marie Ketola, Nov. 28, 1958; children—Mark William, Bruce Karl. With Clinton Engines Corp., Maquoketa, Iowa, 1959-66, design draftsman, 1963-66; jr. project engr. Jacobsen Mfg., Racine, Wis., 1966-68; design engr. Simplicity Mfg., Port Washington, Wis., 1968-73; mgr. product devel. AMF Lawn and Garden, Des Moines, 1973-81, mgr. mfg. engring., 1981—. Republican. Lutheran. Home: 4220 Shawnee Des Moines IA 50310 Office: 3811 McDonald Ave Des Moines IA 50302

VESCOVI, SELVI, pharm. co. exec.; b. N.Y.C., June 14, 1930; s. Antonio and Desolina V.; B.S., Coll. William and Mary, 1951; m. Elma Pasquinelli, Oct. 17, 1954; children—Mark, James, Anne. Salesman, Upjohn Co., N.Y.C., 1954-59, sales supr.,1959-62, product mgr. U.S. domestic pharm. dir., 1962-65, mgr. marketing planning internat. div., 1965-71, v.p. Europe, 1971-74, group v.p. Europe, 1975-77, exec. v.p. Upjohn Internat., Inc., Kalamazoo, Mich., 1978—. Served to 2d lt. M.C., U.S. Army, 1951-53. Mem. Internat. Pharm. Mfrs. Assn. Republican. Roman Catholic. Office: Upjohn Internat 7000 Portage St Kalamazoo MI 49001

VESSEY, JOHN R., mfg. co. exec.; b. Flint, Mich., Oct. 1, 1938; s. John and Marjorie H. (Schultz) V.; A.S. in Engring., Flint Jr. Coll., 1958; B.S.M.E., Gen. Motors Inst., 1962; m. Juliene S. Peters, May 24, 1969; children—John, Karrie, Kellie, Tracy, Susan, Steven. Coop. student A.C. Spark Plug, Flint, 1958-62; sales rep. Purex Corp., Calif., 1963-65; designer Mech. Design & Engring. Co., Flint, 1965-71; with Excel Corp., Fenton, Mich., 1971—, beginning as designer, successively chief engr., gen. mgr., v.p., 1971-76, exec. v.p., chief exec. officer, 1978—. Mem. Am. Mgmt. Assn. Republican. Club: Fenton Lions (pres. 1980-81). Home: 16489 Hi-Land Trail Linden MI 48451 Office: 1101 Copper Ave Fenton MI 48430

VETTER, DALE BENJAMIN, educator; b. Henry County, Ill., Aug. 11, 1908; s. John and Esther (Soliday) V.; A.B., North Central Coll., 1930; A.M., Northwestern U., 1935, Ph.D., 1946; m. Frona A. Tonkinson, Mar. 28, 1932; children—Sharon, Ione, Judith, Rebecca. Prin. Hooppole High Sch., 1932-35; tchr. Harrison Pub. Sch., 1936-37; teacher-librarian Riverside-Brookfield High Sch., 1937-41; prof. English, Ill. State U., 1941-76, prof. emeritus, 1976—. Exec. com. Midwest English Conf., 1962-76. Mem. Am. Assn. U. Profs., Mod. Lang. Assn. Am., Northwestern U. Alumni Assn., Ill. Am. Soc. 18th Century Studies, Newberry Library Assos. Augustan Reprint Soc., Friends of Milner Library, Newberry Library (fellow). Unitarian. Author articles, Bull. of Friends of Milner Library, Ill. State Normal Bull., Modern Language Notes. Home: 214 W Willow St Normal IL 61761

VICARDO, ANTHONY JOSEPH, economist; b. Chgo., Feb. 2, 1944; s. Franklin and Jolana V.; B.A., U. Chgo., 1968, postgrad., 1979—. Fin. analyst to asst. to v.p. fin. Amerline subs. Revlon, Inc., 1965-68; fin. analyst Sinclair Petrochems. subs. Atlantic Richfield, 1968-69, sr. economist mid-continent area, 1970-79; gen. mgr. Mid-Lincoln Investment Co., Inc., Chgo., 1971—. Mem. Chgo. Real Estate Bd. Clubs: Palm Beach Polo and Country, Oak Brook Polo, Sun Valley Ski, Aspen Ski. Home: 180 E Pearson St Chicago IL 60611 Office: 845 N Michigan Ave Chicago IL 60611

VICE, JAMES WILLIAM, JR., univ. exec.; b. Wabash County, Ind., Oct. 7, 1933; s. James William and Lola Loretta (Slusser) V.; M.A., U. Chgo., 1954. Successively dir. housing, dean of freshmen, asst. dean univ. students, lectr. social scis. U. Chgo., 1956-75; dean students Ill. Inst. Tech., 1975-78, dean student life, 1978—. Mem. Nat. Assn. Student Personnel Adminstrs., Phi Beta Kappa, Phi Gamma Delta. Democrat. Office: Ill Inst Tech 3241 S Federal St Chicago IL 60616

VICK, TIMOTHY DOUGALL, geologist, educator; b. Rochester, N.Y., Dec. 5, 1945; s. William Lyon and Louise Elizabeth (Stockard) V.; B.A., Beloit Coll., 1969; M.A.T., U. Wis., River Falls, 1974; m. Jean Louise Inglis, Aug. 19, 1968. Beloit Coll. intern N.Y. Times, 1967-68; reporter Beloit Daily News, 1968-69, Rhinelander (Wis.) Daily News, 1969-71; tchr. earth scis., pub. schs. Rosemount, Minn., 1973-75; tech. supr. geology Carleton Coll., Northfield, Minn., 1975-76, tech. dir. geology, 1976—, Mellon teaching fellow, 1976-77. Mem. Northfield Environ. Quality Commn., 1980—. Served as 1st lt. USAR, 1970-78. Mem. Nat. Assn. Sci. Tchrs., Minn. Acad. Sci., Nat. Assn. Geology Tchrs., Northfield Arts Guild, Audubon Soc., Sigma Xi. Home: 915 Linden St N Northfield MN 55057 Office: Dept Geology Carleton Coll Northfield MN 55057

VICKERS, ERAMUS GILBERT, civil engr.; b. Eagle, Nebr., Aug. 23, 1911; s. John Crosby and Louise Anna (Rockenbach) V.; S.B., Peru State Coll., 1933; B.S. in Civil Engring., U. Nebr., 1934; m. Ida Bernstein, July 17, 1949; 1 dau. by previous marriage, Sibyl. Land Surveyor Lone Star Natural Gas Co., Kans. and Nebr., 1933-36; civil engr. Nebr. Dept. Rds. and Irrigation, Lincoln, 1936-40; service rep. Bucyrus & Erie Co., South Milwaukee, Wis., 1940-41; civil engr. U.S. Public Rds. Adminstrn., Republic of Panama, 1941-42; project engr. earthwork and oilfield contractor and cons. Hobbs, N.Mex., 1945-50; chief insp. Pittsburgh Testing Lab., New Berlin, Wis., 1950—. Servied with U.S. Army, 1943-45. Registered profl. engr., Nebr., Wis. Mem. Nat. Soc. Profl. Engrs., Am. Soc. Mil. Engrs., V.F.W. Republican. Clubs: Masons (32 deg.), Shriners. Home: 220 W 1499 S Springdale Rd Waukesha WI 53186 Office: Pittsburgh Testing Lab 2050 S Calhoun Rd New Berlin WI 53186

VICKERS, GENO THOMAS, farmer, state legislator; b. Gothenburg, Nebr., Mar. 7, 1936; s. George Thomas and Sylvia Violet (Paris) V.; student public schs.; m. Shirley Eileen Messersmith, May 27, 1956; children—Matthew Gene, Mark Dean, Cindy Rae. Farmer, Farnam, Nebr., 1954—; mem. Nebr. Ho. of Reps., 1979—. Bd. dirs. Farmers Coop. Assn., 1971-76, sec., 1971-74, pres., 1975-76; bd. dirs. McCook Public Power Dist., 1972-76. Office: State Capitol Bldg Lincoln NE 68509*

VICKERY, EUGENE LIVINGSTONE, physician; b. Fairmount, Ind., Nov. 27, 1913; s. Lee Otis and Grace (Hawkins) V.; B.S. with distinction, Northwestern U., 1935, M.B., 1940, M.D., 1941; m. Millie Margaret Cox, Dec. 21, 1941; children—Douglas Eugene, Constance Michelle Anita Sue, Jon Livingstone. Intern Evanston (Ill.) Hosp., 1940-41; pvt. practice medicine, Lena, Ill., 1946—; chmn. med. records com. Freeport Meml. Hosp., 1954-64, sec. staff, 1964-67, chairman credentials com., 1964-69, v.p. staff, 1967-69, chief staff, 1969-71, chmn. constn. and bylaws com., 1971-80; mem. staff St. Francis Hosp.; local surgeon Ill. Central R.R.; health officer Lena, 1948—; mem. Stephenson County Bd. Health, 1966-75, v.p., 1969-75; mem. peer rev. policy com. No. Ill. Found. Med. Care. Mem. Lena Sch. Bd., 1951-54; mem. Lena Library Bd., 1958-62; med. dir. Civil Def., rural Stephenson County, Ill., 1961-70; mem. exec. bd. Blackhawk Area council Boy Scouts Am., recipient Silver Beaver award Nat. Council, 1968, Distinguished Eagle award Nat. Council, 1977, mem. nat. council, 1971—; bd. dirs. Stephenson County unit Am. Cancer Soc. Served from 1st lt. to maj. AUS, 1941-46. Decorated Legion of Merit; recipient Lena Community Service award, 1972; named Ill. Family Physician of Yr., 1981. Mem. Stephenson County (pres.), Ill. (chmn. med.-legal council 1976-79) med. socs., AMA, Am. (mental health com. 1981), Ill. (chmn. bd. dirs., pres. 1979) acads. family physicians, Assn. Mil. Surgeons U.S., Blackhawk Area Ind. Practice Assn. (exec. com.), Blackhawk Area Med. Assn. (dir.), AAAS, Ill. Soc. Med. Research, Ill. Assn. of Professions (dir., v.p.), Am. Numis. Assn., Soc. of Medallists, Nat. Rifle Assn., Ill. Gun Collectors Assn., Arctic Inst. N.Am., Am. Legion, Phi Beta Kappa. Republican. Mem. Evang. Free Ch. Lion. Clubs: Apple Canyon, Masons (32 deg.), Shriners. Contbr. articles to numis. publs. Home: 602 Oak St Lena IL 61048 Office: 202 S Schuyler St Lena IL 61048

VIDRICKSEN, BEN EUGENE, food service exec., state senator; b. Salina, Kans., June 11, 1927; s. Henry and Ruby Mae Vidricksen; A.B., Kansas Wesleyan U., 1951; m. Lola Mae Nienke, Jan. 20, 1950; children—Nancy, Janice, Ben, Penelope, Jeffery. Field supt. Harding Creamery div. Nat. Dairy Products, Salina, Kans. and O'Neill, Nebr., 1951-53, mgr., 1953-59; partner Vidricksen's Food Service, Salina, 1959—; cons. in field; mem. Kansas Senate, 1979—. Chmn. Salina Airport Authority, 1976-77; chmn. Republican Central Com., County of Saline, Kans., 1974-79. Served with USN, 1945-46. Mem. North Salina Bus. Assn. (past pres.), Kans. Restaurant Assn. (past pres.), Nat. Restaurant Assn. (dir. 1977—), VFW, Am. Legion. Clubs: Elks, Moose, Eagles, Masons, Shriners. Office: 713 N 11th St Salina KS 67401

VIGGERS, STEPHEN KENNETH, hist. preservationist; b. Des Moines, May 5, 1915; s. Felix and Pearl Almyra (George) V.; student Grinnell Coll., Iowa, 1934; m. Ruth Isabel Foster, Dec. 24, 1950; children—John Stephen, JoEllen Ruth. Rancher, Ariz., 1935-41; farmer, 1946—; hist. preservationist and restorer, 1970—; pres., dir. Jonathan Clark Conger House, Inc., 1972-81; pub. Littler's History of Washington County, 1977. Mem. preservation com. East Central Iowa Council Govts., 1979; v.p. bd. trustees Washington County Hosp., 1973-78. Served with USNR, 1941-45. Recipient Medal of Honor, DAR, 1974. Mem. Washington County Hist. Soc. (pres. 1971-73), Am. Assn. State and Local History, Nat. Soc. Hist. Preservation, Iowa Soc. for Historic Preservation (dir.), Iowa Hist. Soc., Iowa Local Museums Assn. Republican. Presbyterian. Home: Route 3 Washington IA 52353

VIGNIERI, CHARLES JOSEPH, meat packing co. exec.; b. Chgo., Oct. 7, 1924; s. Frank and Rosario (Saporito) V.; student pub. schs., Kenosha, Wis.; m. Lorraine Vander Warn, June 29, 1946; children—Allan, Susan, Dennis, Richard, Patricia, Joseph, Thomas, Daniel, Mark. With Frank Vignieri & Sons, Kenosha, 1936-54; with Kenosha Beef Internat., 1954—, pres., 1960—; pres. Birchwood Meat & Provision, Inc., Kenosha, 1960—; dir. Kenosha Savs. & Loan Assn. Sec., Milw. Meat Council, 1965-67; guest lectr. Carthage Coll., Kenosha, 1970-75, bd. assos., 1970—. Co-chmn. March of Dimes Campaign, Kenosha, 1964; chmn. Paris-Kenosha County Plan Commn., 1965; co-founder, chmn. Kenosha Youth, Inc., 1968-70. Bd. dirs. United Way, Kenosha, 1966-68, 72-75, campaign gen. chmn., 1972, pres., 1973-74; mem. adv. bd. Dominican Sisters of Bethany, Kenosha, 1963-71. Served with AUS, 1943-46; PTO. Mem. Kenosha C. of C. (dir. 1965-68), Nat. Ind. Meat Packers Assn. (dir. 1965-77, v.p. central div. 1974-77, 1st v.p. 1978-80, chmn. bd. 1980—). Roman Catholic (trustee, treas. 1952-66, parish chmn. archibishops fund appeal, 1952-66). Elk, Rotarian (dir. 1965-70, pres. 1967-68). Contbr. articles to profl. jours. Home: 4001 5th Pl Kenosha WI 53142 Office: PO Box 639 Kenosha WI 53141

VILLARREAL, FERNANDO ACOSTA, physician; b. Mexico City, Mex., Sept. 22, 1947; came to U.S., 1950, naturalized, 1974; s. Ignacio Padilla and Rosa Maria (Acosta) V.; B.A., George Washington U., 1969, M.D., 1973; m. Suzanne Rausch, June 5, 1970; children—Christopher, David, Rachel, Jordan. Intern, Good Samaritan Hosp., Dayton, Ohio, 1973-74; practice medicine, specializing in family practice, Dayton, Ohio, 1974-79, Kettering, Ohio, 1979—; asso. clin. prof. dept. family practice Wright State U., Dayton, 1977—; clin. instr. Physician Asst. program, Kettering Coll. Med. Arts, 1973—; mem. staff Good Samaritan Hosp., St. Elizabeth Med. Center, Kettering Med. Center, Sycamore Med. Center. Diplomate Am. Bd. Family Practice; recipient Physicians Recognition award Ohio Med. Assn., AMA, 1980. Fellow Am. Acad. Family Physicians; mem. Montgomery County Med. Soc., Ohio Med. Assn., Ohio Acad. Family Practice, Am. Acad. Family Practice, Smith-Reed-Russell Hon. Soc., Alpha Omega Alpha. Home: 311 Harman Blvd Dayton OH 45419 Office: 3080 Ackerman Blvd Dayton OH 45419

VILLARREAL, MELVIN MILTON, ednl. adminstr.; b. McAllen, Tex., Aug. 8, 1942; s. Ignacio and Angelina (Juarez) V.; B.A., Pan Am. U., 1965; M.A., Mich. State U., 1974, Ph.D., 1982; m. Lee Ellen, Sept. 2, 1980; children—Jeff, Rodney, Kurt, Melissa. Dir. athletics, head football coach Sharyland (Tex.) Ind. Sch. Dist., 1968-73; regional coordinator continuing edn. Lansing (Mich.) Sch. Dist., 1975-80, supr. instrn. and program coordination, 1980-81, asst. in curriculum, planning and staff devel., 1981—; dir. Alternative Counseling Enterprises. Edn. Policy fellow Inst. Ednl. Leadership/George Washington U., 1980-81. Mem. AAUP, Mich. Jail Profl. Services Assn. (exec. bd.), Assn. Supervision and Curriculum Devel., Nat. Assn. Hispanic Placement and Tng. Adminstrs. (Mich. exec. bd.), Phi Delta Kappa. Republican. Roman Catholic. Club: Zach Chandler. Home: 3254 Luroma Dr DeWitt MI 48820

VILONA, RUTH ANN F., banker; b. Long Branch, N.J., Jan. 4, 1939; d. Louis H. and Toba (Vallens) Farb; B.A., Douglass Coll., 1960; m. Bernard D. Vilona. With Fed. Res. Bank of Chgo., 1960—, asso. economist, 1968-71, statis. coordinator, 1971-74, asst. v.p., 1974-79, v.p., 1979—; instr. Am. Inst. Banking, Chgo., 1975-79. Mem. Chgo. Network, Chgo. Fin. Exchange (sec.). Office: 230 S La Salle St Chicago IL 60690

VILTOFT, JORGEN, hotel exec.; b. Copenhagen, Denmark, Feb. 3, 1925; came to U.S., 1946; grad. Danish Hotel Sch.; m. Lucille Viltoft; 4 children. Gen. mgr., regional mgr. Fred Harvey, Chgo., 1957-60; mgr. Edgewater Inn, Mpls., 1960-62; with Marriott Corp., 1962-71, v.p., 1965, sr. v.p., until 1971; pres. Radisson Hotel Corp., Mpls., 1971—. Served with U.S. Army. Clubs: Les Amis D'Escoffier (v.p.), Masons, Scottish Rite. Office: 12805 State Hwy 55 Minneapolis MN 55441

VINCE, THOMAS LOUGHLIN, librarian; b. Cleve., Mar. 13, 1940; s. Joseph Charles and Alice Marie (Drohan) V.; B.A., John Carroll U., 1962; M.A., Ohio State U., 1964; M.S. in Library Sci., Case Western Res. U., 1966. Instr. dept. English, Ohio State U., 1962-64; head fiction dept. Cleve. Public Library, 1966-69; librarian, curator Hudson (Ohio) Library and Hist. Soc., 1969—. Chmn., Hudson Archtl. Study, 1973. Named Outstanding Young Man, C. of C., 1970; recipient award for community service Hudson Jaycees, 1974. Mem. ALA, Ohio Library Assn., Common Cause, Beta Phi Mu. Clubs: Rotary; Rowfant (Cleve.). Editor: Ohio Library Assn. Bull., 1979-82. Home: 49 E Main St Hudson OH 44236 Office: 22 Aurora St Hudson OH 44236

VINCENT, HAL (HAL VINCENT SHUMWAY), organist, mfg. co. exec.; b. Greenfield, Mass., Apr. 9, 1935; s. Allen Leslie and Marietta Alice (King) Shumway; student Juilliard Sch. Music, 1956-57, U. Puget Sound, 1959-60; m. Carole O. McBride; children—Michelle Ona, Alex Vincent; m. 2d, Elise Nannette Mattern, Mar. 29, 1972. Social and entertainment dir. Eastover Resort, Lenox, Mass., 1953-57; organist, pvt. keyboard tchr., Wash., Calif., 1959-67; staff organist, clinician Baldwin Piano & Organ Co., Cin., 1967-69, asst. mgr. organ div., 1969-72, mgr. home organ products, 1972-80; organ product coordinator Kimball Piano & Organ Co., Jasper, Ind., 1980—. Served with AUS, 1957-59. Mem. Nat. Assn. Electronic Organ Mgrs., Amateur Organists Assn. Internat. (dir.), Am. Fedn. Musicians. Recording artist Ad-Rhythm, Jewel and Winmil labels. Office: 1549 Royal St Jasper IN 47546

VINCENT, JACK EDWARD, structural engr.; b. Columbus, Ohio, Jan. 17, 1931; s. Frank Emerson and Gladys Marie (Cline) V.; B.Arch., Ohio State U., 1954; m. Doris Ann McCracken, Feb. 10, 1951; children—Mark, Rochelle, Tracy, Sandra. Bridge engr. Alden E. Stilson & Assos., Columbus, 1954-57, chief bridge engr., Cleve. and Columbus, 1957-68, partner, chief engr. transp. div., 1968-77, partner, mgr., 1977—. Served with Arty., Ohio N.G., 1950-57. Recipient Most Beautiful Bridge award Am. Inst. Steel Constrn., 1965; registered profl. engr., Ohio. Mem. ASCE, Am. Welding Soc., Am. Inst. Steel Constrn., Columbus Engrs. Club, Alpha Rho Chi. Democrat. Methodist. Clubs: Hickory Hills Country, Athletic of Columbus, Ohio State U. Faculty. Instrumental in design of over $100 million of transp. facilities in Midwest. Home: 3927 Monterey Dr Grove City OH 43123 Office: AE Stilson & Assos 170 N High St Columbus OH 43215

VINCENT, M. DIANE, mental health adminstr.; b. Sandusky, Mich., Jan. 20, 1943; d. Frank Sherman and Ethyl Marie (Paige) Reiner; Ph.B., Wayne State U., 1965; M.A., Oakland U., 1978; children—Melissa, Michael, Geoffrey. Caseworker, State of Mich., 1965-66; therapist Project Fresh Start, Dept. Labor Spl. Project, Detroit, 1966-68; probation officer Recorders Ct., Detroit, 1968; dir. Hotline, Birmingham, Mich., 1971-75; adminstrv. dir., v.p., bd. dirs. Square Lake Mental Health Center, P.C., Birmingham, 1975—; dir. Common Ground, Inc., 1975-80; pres. Whethersfield Assos., consultants; mem. coordinators council Oakland County Office of Substance Abuse Services, 1972—; cons. employability programming for women, 1979—; mem. Oakland County Prosecutor's Task Force on Child Molesters, 1978; bd. dirs. Community Action Council. Trainer, empathy trainers; mem. Gov.'s Task Force Substance Abuse Prevention, 1972; sec. bd. dirs. Mich. Assn. Crisis Centers, 1972-75; mem. Substance Abuse Adv. Council, 1980—. Cert. social worker, Mich. Mem. Mich. Assn. Substance Abuse Program Dirs., Am. Personnel and Guidance Assn., Internat. Platform Assn. Co-author: Prosecuters Handbook To Prevent Child Molesting. Home: 1727 Washington St Birmingham MI 48009 Office: 2550 S Telegraph St Bloomfield Hills MI 48013

VINCENT, ROBERT KELLER, geophysicist, geol. cons. co. exec.; b. Bunkie, La., Feb. 6, 1941; s. Edward and Frances L. (Keller) V.; B.A. cum laude, La. Tech. U., 1963, B.S. cum laude in Physics, 1963; M.S. in Physics, U. Md., 1966; postgrad. M.I.T., 1968; Ph.D. in Geology, U. Mich., 1973; m. Dinah Kay Mannerud, June 19, 1978; stepchildren—Kimberley Jane, Hilary Beth, Cory Erwin; children by previous marriage—Derek Andrew, Heather Louise, David Christopher. Engr., Texas Instruments, Inc., summers, 1963-65; research asso. Willow Run Labs., U. Mich., Ann Arbor, 1970-72; research geophysicist Environ. Research Inst. of Mich. (formerly Willow Run Labs.), 1972-74; pres. Geospectra Corp., Ann Arbor, 1974—, chmn. bd., 1974—, cons. to oil and mining cos., 1974—; cons. to NASA Planetary Radar Working Group, 1977-79, U.S. Army Expert Working Group, 1978-80. Served to capt. USAF, 1966-70. Mem. Am. Geophys. Union, Am. Inst. of Physics, Optical Soc. Am., AAAS, Am. Soc. Photogrammetry (chmn. geol. scis. com. 1981—), Sigma Xi, Omicron Delta Kappa, Phi Kappa Phi. Methodist. Club: Masons. Contbr. articles to sci. jours. Home: 1645 Morehead Dr Ann Arbor MI 48103 Office: PO Box 1387 333 Parkland Plaza Ann Arbor MI 48106

VINES, JOHN TALMADGE, civil engr.; b. Durant, Miss., Mar. 16, 1934; s. James Talmadge and Doris Ann (Wigley) V.; B.S., Lamar U., 1960; m. Vera Margaret McGaughey, July 16, 1956; children—Cheree Dawn, Pamela Ann. Survey party chief/insp. La. Dept. Hwys., 1956-60; design engr. Black & Veatch Cons. Engrs., Kansas City, Mo., 1964-68, project engr., 1968-77, constrn. liaison mgr., 1980—; field project mgr. Black & Veatch Internat., Jakarta, Indonesia, 1977-79; cons. water resources, environ. and power engring. Served with AUS, 1953-55. Registered profl. engr., Mo., Kans., Tex., Minn., Utah. Mem. ASCE (chmn. soil mechanics and founds. com. Kansas City chpt. 1973), Nat. Soc. Profl. Engrs., Mo. Soc. Profl. Engrs., Profl. Engrs. in Pvt. Practice, U.S. Com. on Large Dams. Office: 1500 Meadow Lake Pky Kansas City MO 64114

VINKE, HARRY WILLIAM, lumber co. exec.; b. South Holland, Ill., Oct. 14, 1899; s. John L. and Maggie (Gouwens) V.; student Chgo. Met. Bus. Coll., 1915-16; m. Anna Jaynes, Sept. 3, 1921; children—John Louis, Harry William, James Paul. Pres., Wausau Lumber Co., South Holland, 1940—, South Holland Trust & Savs. Bank, 1942-49, also dir., 1940—; dir. South Suburban Savs. & Loan, Harvey, Ill., chmn. bd., 1946-50. Mem. First Ref. Ch. (trustee). Lion. Home: 15915 S Park St South Holland IL 60473 Office: 236 161st Pl South Holland IL 60473

VINKE, JOHN LOUIS, lumber co. exec.; b. Harvey, Ill., July 9, 1924; s. Harry William and Annie (Jaynes) V.; B.A., Coll. of Wooster, 1948; m. Kathryn Mae De Young, June 19, 1946; children—Jill Kathleen, John Louis, Craig Alan, Robert Jaynes, Mary Beth. With Wausau Lumber Co., South Holland, Ill., 1948—, v.p. adminstrv. services, 1953—; v.p. Lansing Lumber & Supply Co., 1964-73; pres., South Holland Loan Assos., 1967—, Illiana Warehouse, Inc., Dixmoor Realty, 1973—; dir. 1st Nat. Bank, Dolton, Ill., Res. Supply Corp., Chgo. Village trustee South Holland, 1951-76; bd. dirs. South Holland Bus. Assn. Served with AUS, 1943-46; ETO. Decorated Silver Star, Bronze Star medal, Combat Infantryman's badge. Mem. South Suburban Geneal. and Hist. Soc., South Holland Hist. Soc., Lumber Trade Assn. Chgo. (v.p.), Am. Legion (comdr. 1954-55). Mem. Ref. Ch. Club: Lions (pres. 1955-56). Home: 525 E 160th Pl South Holland IL 60473 Office: 236 E 161st Pl South Holland IL 60473

VINOKOOROFF, LEONIDE BASIL, former mathematician in planning; b. Kamen, Siberia, Russia, July 18, 1911; came to U.S., 1929, naturalized, 1943; s. Basil Adrianovich and Galina Pavlovna (Kochneff) V.; student Columbia U., 1934; B.A. in Math. and Physics, Albion Coll., 1935; m. Virginia Mann, Feb. 13, 1935 (div. 1937). In various sales positions, 1935-37; Draftsman, Alexander, Decker & Van Stensel, appraisers, Grand Rapids, Mich., 1937-39, J&Q Daverman Co., Architects & Engrs., Grand Rapids, 1940-42; designer, applied mathematician Daverman Assos., Inc., Architects, Engrs., Planners, Grand Rapids, 1946-76; ret., 1976. Served with C.E., U.S. Army, 1942-45; PTO. Decorated Bronze Star. Mem. AAAS, Soc. Gen. Systems Research, N.Y. Acad. Scis., Am. Museum Natural History, Am. Legion, Am. Def. Preparedness Assn., 1st Cav. Div. Assn., Lambda Phi Beta. Russian Orthodox. Clubs: Playboy Internat., Moose. Cartography, airport engring. and zoning, aerial photographs airports and other site analyses, 1946-65, civil engring., 1966-69, econ. analyses and market studies of numerous shopping centers, 1963-70; studies on telephone transmission and power transmission and distbn., 1970-76. Home: 1313 Lewison Ave NE Grand Rapids MI 49505

VINSON, WANDA MAY, youth dir.; b. Kansas City, Mo., Nov. 25, 1916; d. Clarence C. and Maybelle Sarah (Prindle) Vinson; A.B., Baker U., 1938; postgrad. U. Wis., 1938-39; M.A., Kans. U., 1949; D.H.L. (hon.), Baker U., 1979. Prin. Antioch Grade Sch., 1938-39; instr. social sci. Wellsville High Sch., 1939-42; tchr. social sci. and speech Wellington High Sch., 1942-45; instr. social sci. Wichita East High Sch., 1946-47; adminstrv. asst. Kans. High Sch. Activities Assn.; youth dir. Kans. Assn. for Youth, 1946—; dir. speech activities state, 1957-67, dir. student council program, 1950-56. State dir. 2 Kayette Leadership Camps; state citizenship chmn. White House Conf. on Youth; state pres. Kans. Assn. Sch. Health; trustee, Baker U. Recipient Alumni citation Baker U., 1958; nat. citations Cerebral Palsy, CARE, Meals for Millions; nat. citation for outstanding student leadership Nat. Fedn. Activities Assns., 1980; Kans. Teacher's Hall of Fame 1981; Wanda May Vinson Scholarship Fund established by Kays and Kayettes; Wanda May Vinson Seminar Room given to 4-H Citizenship Bldg. by Kays and Kayettes; named Kans. Woman of Year, Cardinal Key Women of KSTC, 1971. Mem. Kans. Assn. Sch. Health (pres. 1976-77, Disting. Service citation 1980), State Tchrs. Assn., AAUW, Pi Lambda Theta, Pi Kappa Delta, Delta Kappa Gamma (1st state v.p. 1971-73). Methodist. Clubs: Topeka Woman's; Kansas Dinner. Home: 1200 College St Topeka KS 66604 Office: 520 W 27th St Topeka KS 66601

VIRGO, JULIE A. CARROLL, assn. exec.; b. Adelaide, South Australia, Australia, June 14, 1944; d. Archibald Henry and Norma Mae (Gillett) Noolan; registration cert. Library Assn. Australia, 1965; A.M. in Librarianship (Univ. fellow, Nat. Library of Medicine fellow), U. Chgo., 1968, Ph.D. in Librarianship, 1974; m. Daniel T. Carroll, 1977. Librarian, Repatriation Dept., South Australia, 1963-66; librarian gen. reading collection U. Chgo., 1966-67, asst. dir. tng. program in med. librarianship Grad. Library Sch., 1969-72, lectr. Grad. Library Sch., 1968—; dir. edn. Med. Library Assn., Chgo., 1972-77; exec. dir. Assn. of Coll. and Research Libraries div. ALA, Chgo., 1977—; bd. dirs. Continuing Library Edn. Network and Exchange. Nat. Library of Medicine research grantee, 1973-75. Mem. Adult Edn. Assn. U.S.A., AAAS, ALA, Am. Soc. Assn. Execs., Am. Soc. for Tng. and Devel., Am. Soc. for Info Sci., Assn. for Ednl. Communications and Tech., Assn. Am. Library Schs., Council on Library Tech., Med. Library Assn., Spl. Libraries Assn., Beta Phi Mu. Office: Assn Coll and Research Libraries 50 E Huron St Chicago IL 60611

VIRNICH, JOHN LEROY, mfg. co. exec.; b. Chgo., July 22, 1948; s. Leroy O. and Sylvia M. Virnich; student Ill. State U., 1966-68; m. Lois Marie Zimmerman, Jan. 31, 1970; children—John Robert, James Leroy. Mgr. customer service Olson div. Acco, Franklin Park, Ill., 1969-71; salesman Wilton Corp., Des Plaines, Ill., 1971-75, dist. mgr., 1975-76; regional mgr. Atlantic Gummed Paper Co., Bklyn., 1976-77; partner Packaging Syndicate, Elk Grove, Ill., 1977-78; midwest regional sales mgr. Wilton Corp., Des Plaines, 1978—; midwest sales mgr. Dynaric Inc., Englewood Cliffs, N.J., 1980—. Active Roselle (Ill.) Blood Bank, 1973—; pres. Season H Homeowners Assn., 1974, 76; active Ronald Reagan for Pres., 1975-76; precinct committee Roselle Rep. Com. Republican. Roman Catholic. Club: Lions. Home: 707 Country Ln S Roselle IL 60172 Office: Dynaric Inc 672 E Irving Park Rd Roselle IL 60172

VIRNICH, S. JOYCE, mktg. exec.; b. Fort Lauderdale, Fla., Apr. 15, 1941; d. James Barney Wetherington and Bonnie Maxine (Hull) Wetherington Murphy; B.S., U. Tulsa, 1963; postgrad. Northwestern U., 1964, DePaul U., 1966; 1 son, Patrick Eugene. Leasing mgr. Apeco Corp., Des Plaines, Ill., 1963-70; regional credit mgr. Bell & Howell Corp., Chgo., 1971; adminstrv. sales mgr. Oce-Industries, Inc., Chgo., 1971-73, product mgr. design and engring. div., 1977—; pres. Genesis Group, Inc., Waukegan, Ill., 1973-77; treas. Lake Forest Condominium Assn., 1981. Mem. Am. Mgmt. Assn., Internat. Entrepreneur's Assn., Nat. Assn. Female Execs. Republican. Home: 1301 North Western Ave #333 Lake Forest IL 60045 Office: 6500 N Lincoln Ave Chicago IL 60645

VIRULHSRI, SUWAT, physician; b. Sukhothai, Thailand, Dec. 26, 1944; came to U.S., 1971; s. Henglai and Sangiam (Lekuthai) Sae Tang; M.D., Mahidol U., 1969; m. Pacharin Incomcrua, Apr. 10, 1973; 1 dau., Pawena. Intern, Meml. Hosp., Albany, N.Y., 1971-72; resident in medicine Bronx (N.Y.)-Lebanon Hosp. Center, 1972-74; fellow in cardiology Kingsbrook (N.Y.) Jewish Med. Center, 1974-76; staff physician VA, Iron Mountain, Mich., 1976—, chief cardiology sect., 1977—. Diplomate Am. Bd. Internal Medicine, Sub-bd. Cardiovascular Disease. Fellow Am. Coll. Internat. Physicians; mem. Am. Coll. Cardiology, A.C.P. Office: VA Hosp Iron Mountain MI 49801

VISNAPUU, HERK, architect; b. Tartu, Estonia, Apr. 26, 1920; s. Eduard and Lilli (Tarri) Y.; student Nomme Jr. Coll., Estonia, 1938-40, Tech. U., Tallinn, Estonia, 1942-43, Tech. Inst., Stockholm, 1947-48; A.B., Oberlin Coll., 1950; B.Arch., Western Res. U., 1953; children—Lilli, Andres; came to U.S., 1948, naturalized, 1957. Architect, City Stockholm, 1945; with Ernst Gronwal, Stockholm, 1946, Ancher, Gate & Lindgren, Stockholm, 1947, H.K. Ferguson Co., Cleve., 1950-54, Garfield, Harris, Robinson, Schafer, Cleve., 1954-56; partner Visnapuu & Gaede Architects & Planners, Cleve., 1956-74; pres. Visnapuu & Assos., Inc., Architects and Planners, 1974—. Mem. fine arts adv. com. City of Cleve.; active Cleve. Mus. Art, YMCA. Bd. dirs. Estonian Nat. Com. U.S.A., Estonian Relief Com., Henrik Visnapuu Lit. Found. Recipient nat. award Ch. Archtl. Guild Am., 1962; merit certificate Ohio Prestressed Concrete Inst., 1963; Honor award Architects Soc. Ohio, 1965; Honor award Greater Cleve. Growth Assn., 1971. Registered architect, Ohio, Pa., Ill., Mass., Ind., N.Y., Mich., Fla., Man., Can. Mem. AIA, Royal Archtl. Inst. Can., Korp Sakala (Estonian frat.), Epsilon Delta Rho. Lutheran. Rotarian. Archtl. work exhibited locally and nationally and pub. in nat. archtl. and trade mags. Home: 2886 Kingsley Rd Shaker Heights OH 44122 Office: One Playhouse Sq Suite 300 Cleveland OH 44115

VISOS, CLARA LOIS KANDARIS (MRS. CHARLES D. VISOS), former advt. co. mgr.; b. Wheeling, W.Va., Oct. 24, 1928; d. Louis E. and Elizabeth (Haniotis) Kandaris; student Straubenmueller Textile High Sch., N.Y.C.; m. Charles Dennis Visos, June 3, 1945; children—John, Larry, Dennis. Various secretarial positions, to 1972; br. mgr. Trading Times, Inc., St. Louis, 1972-75; cons., office mgr. White Glove Systems, comml. cleaning, Kansas City, Mo., 1976; office mgr. R. L. Polk & Co., St. Louis, 1977-80. Mem. Hope Chapel Inter-Faith Fellowship. Home: 817 Big Bend Woods Dr Ballwin MO 63011

VISSER, JOHN EVERT, univ. pres.; b. Orange City, Iowa, Apr. 24, 1920; s. Arthur J. and Frances (Te Paske) V.; B.A., Hope Coll., 1942; M.A., U. Iowa, 1947, Ph.D., 1957; Dr. Honoris Causa, Universided Industrial de Santander, Bucaramanga, Colombia, 1968; m. Virginia Jean Schuyler, May 29, 1946; children—Betty Jean, Mary Frances, Nancy Ann, Martha Ellen. Asst. prof. history Hope Coll., Holland, Mich., 1949-56; asst. registrar Western Mich. U., Kalamazoo, 1956-57; asst. dean Ball State U., Muncie, Ind., 1957-58, exec. asst. to pres., prof. history, 1962-67; dean Grand Rapids (Mich.) Jr. Coll., 1958-62; pres. Emporia (Kans.) State U., 1967—; treas. Am. Assn. State Colls. and Univs., 1971-75. Served with AUS, 1942-46. Mem. Am. Assn. Higher Edn., Nat. Assn. Intercollegiate Athletics (exec. com.), Phi Delta Kappa, Phi Alpha Theta, Blue Key. Presbyterian. Club: Rotary. Home: 1522 Highland St Emporia KS 66801

VITE, FRANK ANTHONY, realtor; b. Aurora, Ill., Feb. 9, 1930; s. Frank A. and Rose (Cosentino) V.; grad. Marmion Mil. Acad., 1948; student Sch. Mgmt., U. Notre Dame, 1958; D.B.A. (hon.), Hillsdale Coll., 1972; m. Barbara Ann Decio, Oct. 23, 1954; children—Bradley Scott, Mark Steven, Michael Lee, Leslie Ann, Lisa Ann. Plant engr. Lyon Metal Products, Aurora, 1951-52, purchasing agt., 1953-54; became sales mgr., exec. v.p., owner, dir. Skyline Homes, Inc., Elkhart, Ind., 1954; pres., owner B&F Realty, Inc., No. Ind. Appraisal Co., Golden Falcon Homes, Inc.; real estate broker; dir. 1st Nat. Bank, Elkhart, Ind. Trustee Hillsdale (Mich.) Coll.; bd. dirs. Ind. Commn. Higher Edn. Served with AUS, 1952-53, Korea. Mem. Elkhart Bd. Realtors, Nat. Sales Execs. Assn., Ind. Real Estate Assn., Nat. Inst. Real Estate Brokers, Holy Name Soc. Republican. Clubs: K.C. (4 deg.), Knight of Malta, Elks. Home: 23236 Shorelane Elkhart IN 46514 Office: 1300 Cassopolis St Elkhart IN 46514

VITEK, RICHARD KENNETH, scientific co. exec.; b. Chgo., Feb. 1, 1935; s. Martin and Mildred (Veverka) V.; A.B., Albion Coll., 1956; M.S., U. Mo., Rolla, 1958; m. Marilyn W. Young, June 23, 1956; children—Christine, Debra, Evelyn. Analytical chemist AEC, Nat. Lead Co., Cin., 1957; asst. instr. chemistry, U. Mass., Amherst, 1958-59; research chemist Allied Chem. Corp., Morristown, N.J., 1959-64; dir. mktg. Aldrich Chem. Co., Inc., Milw., 1964-68; pres. CAMAG Inc., New Berlin, Wis., 1968-78, also dir.; pres., dir. Fotodyne Inc., 1979—; lectr., instr., cons. in field. Mem. ch. bd. deacons; bd. dirs. Council Ind. Mgrs., Wis. Ind. Bus. Assn. Mem. Am. Chem. Soc., Ind. Businessman's Assn. Wis., Milwaukee Astron. Soc., Astron. League. Republican. Club: N.Y. Chemist. Contbr. articles to profl. jours. Office: 16700 W Victor Rd New Berlin WI 53151

VIVONA, DANIEL NICHOLAS, chemist; b. Chgo., Apr. 13, 1924; s. Daniel and Mary Rose (Lamonico) V.; student Chgo. City Coll., 1941-42, 46; B.A., U. Maine, 1951; M.S., Pa. State U., 1953; postgrad. Purdue U., 1953-56; m. Helen Mary Belanger, Sept. 14, 1950; 1 son, Daniel Maurice. Instr. chemistry Purdue U., Lafayette, Ind., 1955-56; with Minn. Mining and Mfg. Co., St. Paul, 1956—, sr. chemist, 1969-79, info. scientist, 1979—. Served with USAAF, 1942-45. Decorated Air medal with oak leaf clusters, D.F.C. Dow Corning fellow, 1952-53. Mem. Am. Chem. Soc., Phi Beta Kappa. Roman Catholic. Club: Toastmasters. Home: 3253 Kraft Circle North Lake Elmo MN 55042 Office: Minn Mining and Mfg Co 235-1E Saint Paul MN 55101

VLASAK, JEFFREY WILLIAM, automotive aftermarket mfg. co. exec.; b. Racine, Wis., Apr. 8, 1954; s. Joseph James and Delores June (Jensen) V.; student U. Wis., LaCrosse, 1974, Gateway Tech. Inst., Racine, 1976-79; m. Jan Zelinger, June 4, 1977. Office mgr. Wis. Bearing Co., Racine, 1975-76; catalog coordinator Walker Mfg. Co., Racine, 1976-78, product coordinator 1978—. Republican. Lutheran. Address: Walker Mfg Co 1201 Michigan Blvd Racine WI 53402

VLASIC, JOSEPH ANTHONY, health care cons.; b. Youngstown, Ohio, Mar. 16, 1930; s. Andrew Matthew and Barbara Frances (Lehpamer) V.; B.E., Youngstown U., 1959; M.B.A., U. So. Calif., 1969; m. Sally Ann Barwicki, July 11, 1959; children—Theresa, Deborah, Christopher. Indsl. engr. U.S. Steel Corp., Youngstown, 1959-63; instr. Youngstown U., 1962-63; systems engr. N.Am. Rockwell, Downey and Anaheim, Calif., 1963-68; dir. systems St. Mary's Long Beach (Calif.) Hosp., 1968-73; cons. Herman Smith Assos., Newport Beach, Calif. and Hinsdale, Ill., 1973—. Served with USN, 1948-52. Registered profl. engr., Calif. Mem. Am. Inst. Indsl. Engrs., Hosp. Mgmt. Systems Soc. of Am. Hosp. Assn. Home: 1652 Swallow St Naperville IL 60540 Office: 120 E Ogden St Hinsdale IL 60521

VLASIS, VICTORIA ELIZABETH TATERKA (VICKI), hosp ofcl., Realtor; b. South St. Paul, Minn.; d. Andrew and Ellen (Hitz) Taterka; R.N., Rochester State Sch. of Nursing; student Moraine Valley Community Coll.; grad. Realtors Inst., 1981; m. George P. Vlasis, Apr. 12, 1942; children—George P. II, Peter George, Sue Ellen. Gen. duty nurse Cook County Hosp., Chgo., 1940-43; pvt. duty nurse, St. Paul and Chgo., 1956-61; vol. chmn. Evangel. Hosp., Chgo., 1956-61; dir. vols. Christ Hosp., Oak Lawn, Ill., 1961—; broker mgr. George Vlasis Realtors, Oak Lawn, 1981—. Pres. Pullman PTA, 1956, 57; health chmn. Dist. 25 PTA, also liaison health chmn. from Dist. 25 to Chgo. Region PTA, 1958, 59; area chmn. Mother's March of Dimes; mem. Field Mus. Natural History, Beverly Art Center, Art Inst. Chgo., Friends of Chgo. Pub. Library, Women's Guild of Balzekas Mus. of Lithuanian Culture, Smithsonian Assos. Recipient cert. of recognition Vol. Service Corp., Vol. Bur. Welfare Council Met. Chgo., 1966; plaque Christ Community Hosp., 1973; cert. of appreciation Oak Lawn C. of C., 1975. Mem. Am. Soc. Dirs. Vol. Services of Am. Hosp. Assn., Ill. Soc. Dirs. of Vol. Services, Assn. Adminstrn. of Vol. Services, Am. Med. Assn. Aux., Women's Aux. Chgo. Med. Soc., Ill. Hosp. Assn. (mem. conf. group on vol. service, Master Auxilian award 1972, chmn. region 2A 1976, 77, dir. region 2A, 1974—, scholarship chmn.; mem. council on vols. 1980—, inservice projects chmn. region 2A, 1981-82; area dir. for regions 2A, 2B and 2C 1978), Am. Soc. Profl. and Exec. Women. Home: 9800 S Kilbourn Ave Oak Lawn IL 60453 Office: Christ Hosp 4440 W 95th St Oak Lawn IL 60453

VOCKEL, RICHARD LANDIS, petroleum co. exec.; b. Harrisburg, Pa., Aug. 8, 1920; s. Stewart Meldred and Miriam Lucille (Landis) V.; B.S. in Mech. Engring., Lehigh U., 1941; m. Barbara Louise Somers, June 27, 1942; children—Constance Lindsay Vockel Ching, Richard Landis, Robert Somers. Mem. tech. service staff Standard Oil Co. (Ohio), 1941-43; with Waverly Oil Works Co., Newark, Ohio, 1946-75, v.p., dir., 1955-65, pres., dir., 1965-75; pres., dir. Waverly Oil, Inc. (subs. Witco Chem. Corp.), Newark, 1975-78, cons., 1978—; vice chmn. bd. exec. com. Central Trust Co.; pres., dir. Granville Resources Corp., 1971-78; mem. Nat. Petroleum Council, 1960-69. Mem. Granville Sch. Bd., 1960-69, pres., 1966-69; mem. Granville Village Council, 1972-73; vice chmn. Granville charter commn., 1963; trustee Licking Meml. Hosp., 1978—, treas., 1979-80, vice chmn., 1981—. Served to 1st lt. USAF, 1943-46. Mem. Ind. Petroleum Assn. (dir., nomination com.), Nat. Stripper Well Assn. (v.p. 1976-80, pres. 1980—), Ohio Oil and Gas Assn. (trustee 1956—, past pres.), Chi Psi, Omicron Delta Kappa, Tau Beta Pi, Pi Delta Epsilon, Pi Tau Sigma. Republican. Episcopalian. Clubs: Moundbuilders Country, Duquesne, Masons. Home: PO Box 457 725 Burg St Granville OH 43023 Office: 1627 Bryn Mawr Dr Newark OH 43055

VOELLER, JOHN GEORGE, III, mech. engr.; b. Denver, Jan. 18, 1949; s. John George and Catherine Eunice (Higgins) V.; B.M.E., Ga. Inst. Tech., 1971; m. Sheila Kay Marriott, June 10, 1972. Field service engr. Westinghouse Electric Corp., N.Y.C., 1971-73, Atlanta, 1973-74; pipe stress analysis engr. Black & Veatch, Kansas City, Mo., 1974-75, computer applications engr., 1975-78; cons. Control Data Corp., Kansas City, 1978-79; computer cons. Black & Veatch Engrs., Kansas City, 1979—; info. cons. on consumer product reliability. Mem. ASME (asso.), AAAS, Consumer Aid Assn. Club: Home Computer. Home: PO Box 12132 Overland Park KS 66212 Office: Overland Park KS

VOELPEL, RAY CARNELL, real estate broker; b. Morton, Ill., Feb. 14, 1922; s. Rae Marion and Ruth Imogene (Grieder) V.; B.S. in Bus. Adminstrn., Marquette U., 1949; postgrad. Law Sch., U. Wis., 1951; grad. Realtors Inst., Ind. U., 1973, Century 21 Internat. Mgmt. Acad., Irvine, Calif., 1981; m. Joyce Marie Burns, May 10, 1952; children—Mark, Thomas, David. Dist. sales mgr. Am. Can Co., Indpls., 1951-64; real estate broker, sales trainer F.C. Tucker Co., Inc., Indpls., 1964-80; v.p. adminstrn., owner Century 21 Realty Group I, Inc., Indpls., 1980-81. Bd. dirs. Devonshire VIII Civic Assn., Indpls. Recipient Disting. Salesman award Sales and Mktg. Execs. Indpls., 1972, Cert. Resdl. Specialist award Realtors Nat. Mktg. Inst., 1978. Real estate Broker, Ind. Mem. Nat. Assn. Realtors, Realtors Nat. Mktg. Inst., Ind. Assn. Realtors, Met. Indpls. Bd. Realtors. Clubs: Exec. Sales, Pres.'s. Home: 6929 Daneby Circle Indianapolis IN 46220 Office: 7172 N Graham Rd Indianapolis IN 46250

VOGE, WILFRED ALLAN, sanitary engr.; b. Racine, Wis., Sept. 28, 1938; s. Verne William and Genivieve Rose (Larson) V.; student U. Wis., 1974, U. Ill., 1975, Internat. Corr. Schs., 1965; m. June Marie Gilbert, Sept. 17, 1966; children—William, Douglas, Wayne, Warren, Sue, Jay, Wesley, Ryan. With Beloit Corp. (Wis.), 1961-65, designer Beloit Passavant Corp., Birmingham, Ala., 1967-71; engr. Peabody Welles Co., Roscoe, Ill., 1971-79; engr. Walker Process div. CBI, Aurora, Ill., 1979-80; chief application engr. Welles Products Inc., Roscoe, Ill., 1980—. Mem. Water Pollution Control Fedn. (asso.). Home: Route 1 Beloit WI 53511 Office: 11765 Main St Roscoe IL 61073

VOGEL, CARL EDWARD, property adminstrn. exec.; b. Chgo., Oct. 21, 1919; s. Eugene E. and Madeline (Keim) V.; student Wilson Jr. Coll., Chgo., 1937-39, Northwestern U., 1940-41; m. Frances Stevens Terrell, Mar. 17, 1945; children—Cynthia, Susan, Meredith, Kirkland. With Nat. Bur. Property Adminstrn., Inc., Chgo., 1939—, chmn. bd., exec. v.p., 1958-63, chmn. bd., pres., 1963—; chmn., bd., pres. Kirkland Corp., Chgo., 1969—. Active in local fund-raising drives. Served to 1st lt. USAAF, 1942-46. Mem. Chgo. Assn. Commerce and Industry, Nat. Assn. Rev. Appraisers, Internat. Assn. Assessing Officers, Nat. Tax Assn., Inst. Property Taxation. Clubs: Executives, Mid-America (Chgo.); North Shore Country (Glenview). Home: 720 Glenayre Dr Glenview IL 60025 Office: 1824 Prudential Plaza Chicago IL 60601

VOGELSANG, WILLIAM R., utility co. exec.; b. Cleve., July 7, 1925; s. William H. and Ann M. (Obrock) V.; B.S. in Edn. and Bus. Adminstrn., Kent State U., 1949; postgrad. Case Western Reserve U. Sch. Advanced Mgmt. and Fin., 1971; m. Oetta E. McAllister, June 11, 1949; children—William R., Nancy L., Richard. Various financial and accounting positions Cleve. Electric Illuminating Co., 1949-74; treas. San Diego Gas and Electric Co., 1974-76, v.p. financial services, 1976-77; asst. v.p., treas. Central Ill. Light Co., Peoria, 1977-78, v.p., treas., 1978-80, v.p., finance, chief fin. officer, 1980—, also dir. dir. Allied Handling Equipment Co., Peoria, 1980—. Bd. dirs. Peoria Symphony Orch., 1980—, Jr. Achievement, 1980—. Home: 93 Forestview Rd Morton IL 61550 Office: 300 Liberty St Peoria IL 61602

VOGT, HERWART CURT, toxicologist; b. Elizabeth, N.J., Sept. 14, 1929; s. Curt George and Dorothea Henriete (Boer) V.; B.S., Northwestern U., 1952; M.S., U. Del., 1954, Ph.D., 1957; M.S., Wayne State U., 1979; m. Nancy E. Behling, Aug. 30, 1958; children—Catherine, Elissa. With BASF Wyandotte Corp., (Mich.), 1959—, mgr. corp. documentation center, 1976-77, corp. toxicologist, 1977—; vis. lectr. Wayne State U., Oakland U. Fire commr. City of Grosse Ile (Mich.), 1966-69; trustee Grosse Ile Sch. Bd., 1969-71; vestryman St. James Episcopal Ch., Grosse Ile, 1975-78, 79—. Wallace H. Carothers research fellow, 1952-57. Mem. Am. Chem. Soc., Chem. Soc. (London), AAAS, Am. Indsl. Hygiene Assn., Sigma Xi. Patentee, publs. in polyurethanes and related isocyanate polymers in chem. reactions; info. retrieval. Office: BASF Wyandotte Corp Toxicology Wyandotte MI 48192

VOICA, RUDOLPH, psychologist; b. East Chicago, Ind., Aug. 6, 1923; s. Jordan and Anna V.; M.S., Inst. State U., Terre Haute, 1952; postgrad. U. Denver, 1956, Ind. U., Bloomington, 1957, Marquette U., 1959, State U. Iowa, 1962, U. Wis., Superior, 1976, U. Wis., Stevens Point, 1977; m. Mary Rita Dusthimer, Sept. 22, 1951; children—Michael, Robert, Joseph. Tchr., counselor Roosevelt High Sch., East Chicago Public Schs., 1952-56; dir. guidance South High Sch., Sheboygan Public Schs., 1957-64; dir. student affairs U. Wis. Center System, Sheboygan, 1964-70; sr. sch. psychologist Stevens Point Area (Wis.) Public Sch. Dist., 1970—. Exec. dir. Portage County chpt. Big Bros. Am., 1972, Sheboygan chpt., 1966-69; instr. evening adult edn. program Hammond (Ind.) Vocat. Tech. High Sch., 1953-56, Sheboygan (Wis.) Vocat.-Tech. Inst., 1959-62; pres. Portage County Assn. Mental Health, 1971-72, exec. com. chmn., 1972-73; v.p. Portage County Council Alcohol and Drug Abuse, 1974-75; bd. dirs. Halfway House, Sheboygan, 1967-68, Head Start Program, Sheboygan, 1967-68; pres. PTA, Wilson Elem. Sch., Sheboygan, 1968-69. Served with U.S. Army, 1943-46, 50-51. Mem. Am. Psychol. Assn., Am. Personnel and Guidance Assn., Council Pupil Personnel Services. Roman Catholic. Home: 714 Maplewood Dr Plover WI 54467 Office: 1900 Polk St Stevens Point WI 54481

VOIGHT, NANCY LEE (MRS. JAY VAN HOVEN), counseling psychologist; b. Kansas City, Mo., Nov. 24, 1945; d. Paul and Leona Alvina (Schultz) V.; B.A., Wittenberg U., 1967; M.A., Ball State U., 1971; Ph.D., Mich. State U., 1975; m. Jay Van Hoven, June 27, 1975; children—Joshua, Janna. Tchr. lang. arts Ashland (Ohio) City Schs., 1967-68; tchr. English, Speedway (Ind.) City Schs., 1969; basic literacy instr. Army Edn. Center, Gelnhausen, W. Ger., 1969-70; individual assistance Bethel Home for Boys, Gaston, Ind., 1970-71; counselor Wittenberg U. Ohio, 1971-72; staff psychologist Ingham County Probate Ct., Lansing, Mich., 1972-74; asst. prof. U. N.C., Chapel Hill, 1975-79, counseling psychologist, 1976-79; psychologist for employee devel. Gen. Telephone Electronics, No. Region Hdqrs., Indpls., 1979-80; behavioral sci. coordinator Family Practice Center, Community Hosp., Indpls., 1980—; media psychologist Sta. WIFE, Indpls., 1981—; asst. dir. Chapel Hill Counseling Center, 1980; advisor Sex Info. and Counseling Center, Chapel Hill, 1977-79. Chmn. housing bd. U. N.C., 1976-79. Office Edn. grantee, 1977-78, 78-80; Spencer Found. young scholars grantee. Mem. Am. Psychol. Assn., Ind. Psychol. Assn., Assn. Advancement Behavior Therapy, Inst. Rational Living, Soc. Behavioral Medicine, Am. Assn. Marriage and Family Therapists. Lutheran. Author: Becoming, 1978; Becoming: Leader's Guide, 1978; Becoming Aware, 1979; Becoming Informed, 1979; Becoming Strong, 1979; also articles. Home: 600 N High School Rd Indianapolis IN 46224 Office: Family Practice Center 5502 E 16th St Indianapolis IN 46218

VOIGT, KATHLEEN JANE, librarian; b. Toledo, Ohio, May 30, 1933; d. Earl H. and Martha M. (Kowalka) Rude; B.A., U. Toledo, 1954; M.A. in Library Sci., U. Mich., 1955; m. Emil Harry Voigt, Dec. 17, 1955; children—Janelyn Dawn, Heidi Hope. Asst. reference librarian art, music and sports div. Toledo-Lucas County Public Library, Ohio, 1955-56, head art librarian, 1958-61, asst. reference librarian (part-time), Sanger br., 1962-63; instr. (part-time) library sci. U. Toledo, 1966-67, asst. reference librarian (part-time), 1967-69, acting head dept. library sci., 1971-72, asst. prof. library sci., 1972-73, asst. prof. library adminstrn., 1973-76, asso. prof. library adminstrn., 1976—, coordinator library programs div., 1978, reference librarian, 1976—; asst. reference librarian Detroit Public Library, 1956-58. Mem. ALA, Acad. Library Assn. Ohio (membership com. 1977-78), AAUP, No. Ohio Tech. Services Librarians, Women Involved in Toledo, Delta Kappa Gamma, Zeta Tau Alpha. Clubs: Order of Eastern Star, Zonta II (Toledo), Order Rainbow Girls. Contbr. book revs. to profl. publs. Home: 2709 Middlesex Dr Toledo OH 43606 Office: Univ of Toledo Carlson Library Toledo OH 43606

VOINOVICH, GEORGE V., mayor of Cleve.; b. Cleve., July 15, 1936; B.A., Ohio U., 1958; J.D., Ohio State U., 1961. Admitted to Ohio bar, 1961, U.S. Supreme Ct. bar, 1968; asst. atty. gen. State of Ohio, 1962-63; mem. Ohio Ho. of Reps., 1967-71; auditor Cuyahoga County (Ohio), 1971-76, county commr., 1977; lt. gov. State of Ohio, 1979; mayor City of Cleve., 1980—. Mem. Omicron Delta Kappa, Phi Alpha Theta, Phi Delta Phi. Office: Office of Mayor City Hall 601 Lakeside Ave E Cleveland OH 44114

VOLANDT, LOUIS CONRAD, aluminum co. exec.; b. Balt., Dec. 10, 1936; s. Louis William and Margaret Doretta (Diehlmann) V.; exec. devel. cert. U. Balt., 1961; B.S. in Bus. Mgmt., 1965; m. Johanne M. Braungart, Apr. 23, 1960; children—Stephen, David, Caroline. With Revere Copper & Brass Inc., 1965-77; with Alcan Aluminum Corp., 1977—, dist. sales mgr., Beechwood, Ohio, 1977—. Served with U.S. Army, 1957-58. Mem. Nat. Aluminum Distbrs. Assn. Republican. Lutheran. Club: Chagrin Valley Racquet. Home: 17365 Wood Acre Trail Chagrin Falls OH 44022 Office: 3659 Green Rd Beachwood OH 44122

VOLIVA, BENJAMIN HARRISON, JR., chem. engr.; b. Monroe County, Ind., July 15, 1936; s. Benjamin Harrison and Margaret Elizabeth (Capshew) V.; B.S., Purdue U., 1958; m. Sharon Lee Grossman, July 23, 1966; children—Annette L., Alan L., Andrea E., Cheryl L., Benjamin Harrison III. Project engr. research and devel. dept. R.R. Donnelley & Sons Co., Chgo., 1958-70, environ. control dept., 1971-76, implementation engring. dept., 1977—, environment, energy and safety engring. group, 1978—. Area fin. chmn. South Cook County council Girl Scouts U.S., 1976. Served with Chem. Corps, U.S. Army, 1958-59, to lt. col. Res. Mem. Chgo. Paint and Coatings Soc., South Suburban Geneal. and Hist. Soc. (pres. 1976-77), Republican. Club: Kiwanis (v.p. Riverdale-Dolton 1977, pres. 1979-80, treas. 1978). Researcher splty. printing inks, 1960-70, catalysts for air pollution control, 1971-73, incorporation heat recovery with pollution control equipment, 1974—. Home: 10 W Sibley Blvd Dolton IL 60419 Office: 2223 S Martin Luther King Dr Chicago IL 60616

VOLK, DAVID LAWRENCE, state treas. S.D.; b. Mitchell, S.D., Apr. 12, 1947; s. Erwin John and Joan M. (Nieses) V.; B.S. in Govt., No. State Coll., Aberdeen, S.D.; postgrad. Augustana Coll., Sioux Falls, S.D. Field rep. Ben Reifel, M.C., 1966-69; state treas. S.D., Pierre, 1972—. Mem. adv. com. U.S. Commn. on Civil Rights; mem. exec. com. Boy Scouts Am., S.D., S.D. Mental Health Assn. Served with U.S. Army, 1969-71. Decorated Bronze Star medal; named Outstanding Young Republican, 1968. Mem. Nat. Assn. State Treas. (pres.), S.D. Investment Soc., VFW, Am. Legion, Jr. C. of C. Roman Catholic. Club: Elks. Office: State Treas Office Capitol Bldg Pierre SD 57501

VOLKART, GREGORY ALBERT, city ofcl.; b. Winona, Minn., May 26, 1950; s. Howard and Gladys (Church) V.; student Winona State U., 1968-72; m. Mary Whingelby, Mar. 10, 1973. Cheese maker Land 'O Lakes, Pine Island, Minn., 1972-73; with Pump, Meter and Tank Service, Rochester, Minn., 1973-74; asst. supt. utilities City of Goodview, Minn., 1974-76, supt. utilities, 1976—. Mem. Goodview Vol. Fire Dept. Mem. Am. Water Works Assn., Goodview Activity Group. Republican. Methodist. Home: Rural Route 1 Winona MN 55987 Office: 4140 5th St Goodview MN 55987

VOLKMER, HAROLD LEE, Congressman; b. Jefferson City, Mo., Apr. 4, 1931; ed. St. Louis U.; LL.B., U. Mo., 1955; m. Shirley Ruth Braskett; children—Jerry Wayne, John Paul, Elizabeth Ann. Admitted to Mo. bar, 1955; individual practice law, Hannibal; pros. atty. Marion County, 1960-66; mem. Mo. Ho. of Reps., 1966-76, chmn. Judiciary com.; mem. 95th-97th Congresses from 9th Mo. Dist., mem. agr. com., Sci. and Tech. com.; asst. atty. gen. Mo. Mem. Mo., 10th Jud. Circuit bar assns. Clubs: K.C., Hannibal Lions. Recipient two awards for meritorious pub. service in Gen. Assembly, St. Louis Globe-Democrat. Office: 1728 Longworth House Office Bldg Washington DC 20515

VOLPE, JAMES ANTHONY, computer co. ofcl.; b. Chgo., June 24, 1954; s. Vincent Francis and Bernice Stella (Piragis) V.; B.S. in Mktg., No. Ill. U., 1975. Br. adminstrv. specialist Four-Phase Systems, Inc., Des Plaines, Ill., 1978-80, central regional adminstrv. mgr., 1980—. Mem. Jammers Athletic Orgn., Phi Sigma Epislon. Roman Catholic. Office: 1111 E Touhy Ave Des Plaines IL 60018

VOLWILER, ERNEST HENRY, chemist; b. Hamilton, Ohio, Aug. 22, 1893; s. Jacob and Dorothea (Tangemann) V.; A.B., Miami U., 1914, D.Sc. (hon.), 1946; Ph.D., U. Ill., 1918, D.Sc. (hon.), 1959; D.Sc. (hon.), Northwestern U., 1949, Phila. Coll. Pharmacy and Sci., 1954, St. Louis Coll. Pharmacy, 1958; Dr. Med. Sci. (hon.), Southwestern U. at Memphis, 1958; LL.D. (hon.), Coe Coll., 1953, Knox Coll., 1954; D.H.L. (hon.), Lake Forest Coll., 1977; m. Lillian F. Huggler, Feb. 23, 1920; children—Doris Volwiler Semler, Marjorie Vowiler Grinnell, Wallace. Teaching asst. in chemistry U. Ill., 1914-17, fellow, 1917-18; research chemist Abbott Labs., 1918-20, chief chemist, 1920, dir. research, 1930-46, v.p., 1933-46, exec. v.p., 1946-50, pres., 1950-58, chmn. bd., 1958-59, also dir.; chmn. bd. Abbott Labs. Internat. Co., 1959-61, cons., 1961—. Bd. regents Nat. Library of Medicine, 1957-61, chmn. div. chem. and chem. tech. NRC, 1958-60; bd. dirs. NSF, 1958-64, McCormick Theol. Sem., 1965-73; v.p. Health Info. Found.; trustee Lake Forest Coll., chmn. bd., 1962-65. Served as maj. Chem. Warfare Research, 1925-38; leader Chem. Warfare Service and med. teams in Germany, 1945. Recipient Modern Pioneers award, 1940; Centennial award Northwestern U., 1951; medal of Soc. Chem. Industry, 1954; medal of Indsl. Research Inst., 1955; Priestley medal, 1958; Sesquicentennial medal Miami U., 1959. Mem. Am. Inst. Chem. Engrs., World Med. Assn. (mem. U.S. com.), Am. Chem. Soc. (pres. 1950, chmn. Chgo. sect. 1924-25, chmn. div. medicinal chemistry 1925, dir. at large, chmn. bd. 1954-55), Am. Pharm. Assn., Am. Drug Mfrs. Assn. (pres. 1956-58), Am. Inst. Chemists (medal 1960), Phi Kappa Tau, Sigma Xi, Alpha Chi Sigma, Gamma Alpha, Phi Beta Kappa, Phi Lambda Upsilon, Beta Gamma Sigma (hon.). Presbyterian. Club: Masons. Clubs: Cosmos (Washington); Chgo. Chemists (pres. 1932); Exmoor, Kiwanis. Editor: Chem. Bull., 1922-24; contbr. to profl. jours and books; patentee in field med. compounds. Home: 900 Lake Rd Lake Forest IL 60045

VOLZ, PAUL ALBERT, educator; b. Ann Arbor, Mich., Mar. 26, 1936; s. Albert Carl and Frieda Clara (Larmee) V.; B.A., Heidelberg Coll., 1958; M.S., Mich. State U., 1962, Ph.D., 1966; postgrad. Ind. U., 1966-68. Asst. prof. biology Purdue U., Indpls., 1968-69; prof.

mycology Eastern Mich. U., Ypsilanti, 1969—; resident research asso. NASA, Johnson Space Center, Houston, 1971-73; vis. prof. mycology and research Nat. Taiwan U., Taipei, 1974—; prin. investigator microbial ecology evaluation device NASA, 1971-74. Am. Soc. Engring. Edn. faculty fellow, 1969-71. Mem. Am. Inst. Biol. Scis., Am. Soc. Microbiology, Mycological Soc. Am., AAAS, Mich. Acad. Sci., Arts and Letters, Assn. for Tropical Biology, Am. Fern Soc., Electron Microscopy Soc. Am., Am. Mus. Natural History, Internat. Soc. for Human and Animal Mycology, Med. Mycological Soc. Ams. Contbr. articles to profl. jours. Home: 1805 Jackson Ave Ann Arbor MI 48103 Office: Dept Biology Eastern Mich U Ypsilanti MI 48197

VON BARGEN, WAYNE JAMES, ednl. adminstr.; b. Chgo., Sept. 9, 1946; s. James Earl and Grace Mary (Dunkel) Von B.; B.S., Ill. Inst. Tech., 1969, M.S., 1970, Ph.D., 1972; m. Cathleen Nora Whisler, Apr. 19, 1969. Clinician, Chgo. Reading and Speech Clinic, 1968-70; cons. psychologist LaSalle County Mental Health Center, Ottawa, Ill., 1970-71; psychologist Valparaiso U., 1971-77, asst. dir. Univ. Counseling Center, 1972-77, part-time asst. prof. psychology, 1972-77; dir. psychophys. therapy Mental Health Center, Fort Wayne, Ind., 1977—; pvt. practice psychology, 1976—; asso. faculty Purdue U., Fort Wayne, 1978-79. Bd. dirs. Allen County Assn. for Retarded, 1978—. Mem. Am., Ind., Midwestern psychol. assns., Biofeedback Soc. Ind., Biofeedback Soc. Am. Contbr. articles to profl. jours. Home: 5030 Twilight Ln Fort Wayne IN 46815 Office: Mental Health Center 909 E Blvd Fort Wayne IN 46805

VON BERG, LOIS HELENE, univ. adminstr.; b. Albert Lea, Minn., Oct. 6, 1932; d. John Phillip and Helene Annette (Oliver) Von B.; B.A., U. No. Iowa, 1955; M.A., U. No. Colo., 1962; postgrad. Springfield Coll., 1966. Tchr. high sch., Madelia, Minn., 1955-56; tchr. jr. high sch., Clinton, Iowa, 1956-59; tchr. high sch., Rochester, N.Y., 1959-61; counselor Douglas High Sch., Ellsworth AFB, S.D., 1962-64; dir. guidance Sch. Nursing, Rochester, Minn., 1964-67; asst. dir. fin. aids State Coll., St. Cloud, Minn., 1967-69; asst. dir. fin. aid U. Wis., Stout, Menomonie, Wis., 1969-71, dir. fin. aid, 1971-81, adminstr. Student Health Center, 1981—; mem. adv. council State Higher Ednl. Aids Bd., 1976-78. Mem. Am. Personnel and Guidance Assn., Am. Coll. Personnel Assn., Nat., Midwest, Wis. (exec. com. 1978—) assns. student fin. aid adminstrs., Assn. U. Wis. Faculties (del. assembly 1972-74), Rochester C. of C. (edn. com. 1965-67), Bus. and Profl. Women's Club (treas. 1968-69), Delta Kappa Gamma (v.p. 1972-76). Home: Rt 7 Box 272A Menomonie WI 54751

VON BESSER, KURT WOLF FREDERICK, chem. products co. exec.; b. N.Y.C., Nov. 25, 1936; s. Verne and Jeannette (Streibaugh) von B.; B.B.A., Lake Forest Coll., 1957; m. Gerlinde Petritsch, July 25, 1966; children—Kurt Friedrich, Kristin Wynn, Kiera Linda. Vice-pres. Middle West Display & Sales, Inc., 1958-65; pres. Middle West Mktg. Co., Chgo., 1965—, Safety Systems, Inc., Chgo., 1972-81, K.B. Recreation Inc., 1981—, Atsko Inc., mfr. Sno-Seal Leather Preservative, 1981—; mfr. Besser ski bindings; chmn. bd. Seattle, 1978-81. Vice-pres. German-Am. Democratic Orgn., 1970-71; chmn. democratic com. German Am. Nat. Congres, 1971. Club: Corinthian Yacht, Chicago Yacht. Developed and formulated chem. weapon formulation known as mace, 1965, developed fogging device for tear gas fog, 1970. Patentee ski bindings. Office: 216-226 S Hoyne St Chicago IL 60612

VON DER RUHR, GERHARD JOSEPH, mfg. co. exec.; b. Elberfeld, Germany, May 10, 1941; s. Herbert J. and Aloysia H. (Straatmann) Von Der R.; B.A., Free U. Berlin, 1963; M.B.A., U. Cologne, 1966; m. Ursula G. Diekmann, July 30, 1965; 1 son, Marc Benjamin. Trainee, Ford Motor Co., Dearborn, Mich. and London, 1966-67, analyst, 1967-68, sr. analyst, 1968-69, project leader, 1969-70; mgr. strategic planning Metra Gen. Electric, Paris and Milw., 1970-72, mgr. internat. studies, 1972-74; v.p. internat. Zimmer/Bristol-Myers, Warsaw, Ind., 1974-76; pres. Biochem Internat. Inc., Milw., 1976—, also dir. Smithsonian fellow, 1975—; Paul Harris fellow. Mem. Am. Mktg. Assn., Am. Mgmt. Assn. Club: Rotary. Address: PO Box 13157 Milwaukee WI 53213

VON EHREN, WARREN RUSSELL, trade assn. exec.; b. Chgo., Mar. 13, 1921; s. Ernest Louis and Nancy Wilheimina (Ramelow) V.; B.S., Northwestern U., 1942, M. Hosp. Adminstrn., 1949; m. Mary Lemon, May 24, 1946; children—Penelope, Daniel. Asst. supt. Bronson Meth. Hosp., Kalamazoo, Mich., 1949-51; adminstrv. asst. AMA, Chgo., 1951-53; adminstr. Bellin Meml. Hosp., Green Bay, Wis., 1953-60; pres. Wis. Hosp. Assn., Madison, 1960—; asst. clin. prof. U. Wis. Med. Sch., Madison, 1967—. Served with U.S. Army, 1942-46. Recipient Award of Merit, Tri-State Hosp. Assembly, 1964; Health Adminstrn. Edn. award U. Wis., 1978. Fellow Am. Coll. Hosp. Adminstrn., Am. Public Health Assn., AAAS; mem. Am. Hosp. Assn. Methodist. Clubs: Rotary, Univ., Madison; Masons, Shriners. Home: 5218 S Hill Dr Madison WI 53705 Office: 5721 Odana Rd Madison WI 53719

VON LANG, FREDERICK WILLIAM, librarian, genealogist; b. Scranton, Pa., May 6, 1929; s. Frederick William and Carrie (Brundage) Baron von Lang zu Leinzell; B.S., Kutztown State Coll., 1951; M.S. in L.S., Syracuse U., 1955; m. Ilsabe von Wackerbarth, July 12, 1960; children—Christoph, Karl Philipp. Librarian, Broughal Jr. High Sch., Bethlehem, Pa., 1951; asst. librarian Bethlehem Public Library, 1952-55; asst. librarian Enoch Pratt Free Library, Balt., 1956-66; library dir. Lehigh County Community Coll., Allentown, Pa., 1966-73, Auburn (Maine) Public Library, 1973-77; dir. St. Joseph (Mo.) Public Library, 1977-79, Hibbing (Minn.) Public Library, 1980—. Founding mem., exec. bd., treas. Friends Bethlehem Public Library, 1964-70; mem. exec. bd. Northampton County Assn. for Blind, 1970-72; bd. dirs. St. Joseph Mental Health Soc.; edn. counselor Lehigh Valley br. Lutheran Brotherhood, 1972-73. Mem. Pa. (treas., exec. bd. Lehigh Valley chpt. 1967-70, chmn. community and jr. coll. sect. 1970-71), Maine (legis. com., editor Legis. Manual), New Eng., Mo., Minn. library assns., ALA (council, fed. relations coordinator to Maine Library Assn.), Bethlehem Jr. C. of C. (past editor, chmn. publs.), S.A.R. (past sec.-treas. bd. mgrs. Valley Forge chpt.), Maine Soc. Mayflower Descs., Soc. Colonial Wars in State Maine, Huguenot Soc. Maine, Bradford Family Compact, Hibbing Hist. Soc. (v.p.), Beta Phi Mu. Clubs: Masons (32 deg.), K.T., Shriners, Elks, Rotary Asso. editor Genealogisches Handbuch des in Bayern immatrikulierten Adels, Vol. 4, 1953. Home: 2129 3d Ave W Hibbing MN 55746 Office: 2020 5th Ave E Hibbing MN 55746

VON SEGGERN, HARLAN CARROLL, safety engr.; b. Scribner, Nebr., Aug. 23, 1924; s. J.H. and G. Bertha (Von Essen) Von S.; B.S., Wayne State U., Nebr., 1948; postgrad. U. Louisville, 1954-55, Drake U., 1964-65; m. Jean Phylis Peters, May 22, 1949; children—Suzanne, Robert J. Tchr. math., physics, chemistry and music Mondamin (Iowa) Consol. Sch. System, 1948-49; high sch. tchr. sci. Sioux City (Iowa) sch. system, 1949-51; journeyman carpenter McCarthy Improvement Co., Ft. Randall, S.D., 1951; shipping and receiving supr. Enterprise Electric, Omaha, 1951-52; chief safety engr. Nebr. Ordinance Plant, Mead, 1952-56; safety and personnel dir. Nat. Gypsum Co., Ft. Dodge, Iowa, 1956-60; safety and plant protection engr. The Maytag Co., Newton, Iowa, 1960-73; mgr. cons. services Safe-Tech Industries, Inc., Des Moines, 1973-74; safety engr. AGC-MBI, Associated Gen. Contractors Iowa-Master Builders Iowa-Constrn. Safety Council, Des Moines, 1974—; charter mem. Iowa Employment Safety Commn., 1965-69. Cert. safety profl. Mem. Am. Soc. Safety Engrs. (treas. Hawkeye chpt. 1973-74, pres. 1978-79), Indsl. Safety Assn. Iowa (dir. 1960—, pres. 1971), Am. Indsl. Hygiene Assn., Nat. Fire Protection Assn., Nat. Safety Council, Iowa Mfrs. Assn. (vice chmn. safety and health com. 1960-81), Aircraft and Pilots Assn., Lambda Delta Lambda. Home: 304 W 14th Sts Newton IA 50208 Office: 221 Park St PO Box 695 Des Moines IA 50303

VON WYSS, MARC ROBERT, cement co. exec.; b. Zurich, Switzerland, Feb. 12, 1931; s. George H. and Mariejenny A. (Burckhardt) von W.; came to U.S., 1971; grad. in mech. engring. and aerodynamics Fed. Inst. Tech., Zurich, 1956; m. Marina V. Gygi, Sept. 4, 1963; children—George M., Martin C. Control systems design engr. Svenska Aeroplan AB, Joenkoeping, Sweden, 1957-60; control systems design engr., asst. dept. head Contraves AG, Zurich, 1961-65; sr. v.p. Holderbank Mgmt. & Cons. Ltd., Holderbank, Switzerland, 1966-71; pres., chief exec. officer Dundee Cement Co. (Mich.), 1971—. Office: PO Box 122 Day Rd Dundee MI 48131

VOSE, DAVID AVERY, economist, univ. adminstr.; b. Gurnee, Ill., Jan. 9, 1937; s. Avery Allen and Thelma Judith (Christensen) V.; B.S. in Agrl. Sci., U. Ill., 1958; Ph.D. in Agrl. Econs., U. Wis., Madison, 1966; m. Roberta Jean Vickers, Dec. 7, 1963; children—Robert James Vickers, Elisebeth Ann. Asst. prof. econs. U. Minn., Duluth, 1966-69, asso. prof., 1969-70, vice provost for acad. adminstrn., 1970-77, dean Sch. of Bus. and Econs., 1977—; chmn. bd. Fond du Lac Mfg. Corp. Served with U.S. Army, 1958-60. Mem. Am. Econ. Assn., Am. Agrl. Econs. Assn. Office: 104 Sch Business and Econs U Minn Duluth MN 55812

VOSMEIER, LEONARD FRANCIS, printing co. exec.; b. Richmond, Ind., Nov. 29, 1925; s. Leonard Henry and Ruth M. (Miller) V.; A.B., Ind. U., 1950; m. Monabelle Romaine Brockmyer, Aug. 26, 1950; children—Valerie, Mark, Mary (dec.), Ned, Matthew. Vice-pres. Mulhaupt Printing Co., Inc., Ft. Wayne, Ind., 1951-55; pres., Ft. Wayne (Ind.) Printing Co., Inc., 1955—; dir., treas. Mulhaupt Printing Co., Inc. Div. chmn. United Way, 1974; co-chmn. patriotism com. Bicentennial Com., 1974-76; admissions rep. U.S. Mil. Acad. Served to col. AUS, 1943-46. Recipient Ind. Commendation medal Mil. Dept. Ind., 1969. Mem. Res. Officers Assn. (pres. 1967, 76), VFW, DAV, Mil. Order World Wars (comdr. Ft. Wayne cadre), Ind. Soc. Sons and Daus. of Pilgrims (pres. 1981), Ind. Soc. SAR (pres. 1981), Am. Legion, Fort Wayne Printing House Craftsman, Allen County-Fort Wayne Hist. Soc., C. of C., Phi Kappa Theta. Republican. Roman Catholic. Clubs: Olympia Country (pres. 1973-75), Serra (Ft. Wayne) (pres. 1976-77), Masons, Shriners. Home: 2705 Whitegate Dr Fort Wayne IN 46805 Office: 340 E Berry St Fort Wayne IN 46802

VOSPER, KENT F., state senator; b. Neche, N.D., Nov. 10, 1921; s. Fred Chester and Nell (Wiley) V.; ed. N.D. Agrl. Coll., N.D. State Sch. Sci.; m. Phyllis Eileen Kelm, 1943; children—Douglas Kent, Mark David, Fred Craid. Mem. N.D. State Senate, 1975—. Served with USAAF, 1943-45; POW, Italy, 1943-45. Decorated Purple Heart, Air medal with clusters. Mem. Am. Ex-Prisoners of War, Am. Legion, VFW. Methodist. Club: Shriners. Address: Neche ND 58265*

VOSS, ALINE JEANETTE, mental health center adminstr.; b. Kankakee, Ill., May. 7, 1926; d. Jesse Eugene and Lillian Ethel Rosendahl; R.N., Ill. Wesleyan U., 1947; B.S., Olivet Nazarene Coll., Bourbonnais, Ill., 1971; M.A. in Health Sci. Adminstrn., Governor State U., Park Forest, Ill., 1973, M.A. in Restorative Nursing, 1975; m. Dec. 3, 1977; children—James, Jaline, Gary, Jesse, Gina, Timothy, J. Richard. With Ill. Dept. Mental Health and Devel. Disabilities, 1952—, dir. nursing Manteno (Ill.) Mental Health Center, 1979—; prof. Governor's State U.; mem. adv. bd. Prairie State Coll., Thornton Community Coll., Kankakee Community Coll. Mem. exec. council troop 295, Girls Scouts U.S.A., Manteno; bd. dirs. United Methodist Ch., Manteno, also ch. tchr. Recipient Gov. of Ill. Superior Achievement award, 1978. Mem. Am. Nurses Assn., Ill. Nurses Assn. (dir. 1977-78), 17th Dist. Nurses Assn. (dir. 1977-78), Assn. Mental Health Adminstrs. Clubs: Manteno Women's Golf Club, Manteno Aux. Sportsman, Am. Legion Aux. Home: N Point Estates Bourbonnais IL 60914 Office: 100 Barnard Rd Manteno IL 60950

VOSS, EDWARD WILLIAM, JR., immunologist; b. Chgo., Dec. 2, 1933; s. Edward William and Lois Wilma (Graham) V.; A.B., Cornell Coll., Iowa, 1955; M.S., Ind. U., 1964, Ph.D., 1966; m. Virginia Hellman, June 15, 1974; children from previous marriage—Cathleen, Valerie. Asst. prof. microbiology U. Ill., Urbana, 1967-71, asso. prof., 1971-74, prof., 1974—. Served with U.S. Army, 1956-58. NIH fellow, 1966-67; NSF fellow, 1975-77, grantee, 1967—. Mem. AAAS, Am. Assn. Immunologists, Am. Assn. Biol. Chemists, Reticuloendothelial Soc., N.Y. Acad. Scis., Nat. Geog. Soc., Am. Chem. Soc., Sigma Xi. Adv. editor Immunochemistry, 1975-78, Molecular Immunology, 1979—; mem. editorial bd. Applied and Environ. Microbiology, 1979—. Contbr. articles to profl. jours. Home: 2207 Boudreau Circle Urbana IL 61801 Office: 217 Burrill Hall Dept Microbiology Univ Ill Urbana IL 61801

VOSS, OMER GERALD, ret. farm equipment co. exec.; b. Downs, Kans., Sept. 14, 1916; s. John and Grace (Bohlen) V.; A.B., Ft. Hays (Kans.) State Coll., 1937; J.D., U. Kans., 1939; m. Annabelle Katherine Lutz, June 20, 1940; children—Jerrol Ann, Omer Gerald. With Internat. Harvester Co., 1936—, v.p. farm equipment div., 1962-66, exec. v.p., dir., 1966—, vice chmn., dir., 1977-79; admitted to Kans. bar, 1939; dir. Ill. Tool Works, Beatrice Foods Co. Served with USAAF, 1943-46. Clubs: Chgo.; Comml.; Westmoreland Country. Office: 9359 N Ridgeway Ave Evanston IL 60203

VOSS, VIRNELLE CRAIG, social worker; b. Roanoke, Mo., Dec. 15, 1916; d. Asa Milton and Martha Cora (Green) Craig; A.B., Central Methodist Coll., 1939; M.S.W., Washington U., St. Louis, 1946; m. Fred August Voss, June 30, 1951; children—Linda, Fred, Martha, Charles. Visitor, Social Security Commn, St. Louis, 1941-43; med. social worker U. Chgo. Clinics, 1946-48; med. social worker, asst. prof. Coll. Medicine, U. Ill., 1948-53, acting dir. dept. social work, 1951-52; field instr. U. Chgo. Social Service Adminstrn., 1948-53; sr. caseworker Child and Family Service, Monroe, Mich., 1967—; field instr. U. Mich. Sch. Social Work, 1972—; acting dir. Child and Family Service, Monroe, 1981; mem. Council for Child Abuse and Neglect, 1978; sect. pres. New Life for Bereaved Orgn.; pres. Alt. Edn. Adv. Bd. Mem. council fin. and adminstrn. Detroit Conf., United Meth. Ch. Mem. Nat. Assn. Social Workers, Acad. Cert. Social Workers, Mental Health Assn. (sect. pres.), Mich. Marriage Counselors Assn. Republican. United Methodist (lay leader). Mem. Order Eastern Star. Clubs: Monroe Garden (pres.), Century Trailer (pres., treas.), Southeastern Mich. Osteo. Aux. (pres.). Home: 7046 N Monroe St Monroe MI 48161 Office: 6 S Monroe Monroe MI 48161

VOSSEN, WAYNE WILLIAM, warehouse exec.; b. St. Paul, Oct. 18, 1949; s. Marvin Hubert and Mary Elaine (Morrissey) V.; A.A., St. Paul Tech. Vocat. Inst., 1971; B.S., U. Minn., 1974; m. Ruth L. Teiken, Nov. 12, 1977; 1 dau., Nicole. Adminstrn. mgr. Murphy Warehouse Co., Mpls., 1974-80; mgr. distbn. systems Econs. Lab., Inc., St. Paul, 1980—. Mem. Am. Mgmt. Assn., Adminstrv. Mgmt. Soc. Democrat. Roman Catholic. Club: Castle Greens. Home: 420 Cretin Ave N Saint Paul MN 55104 Office: Econs Lab Inc Osborn Bldg Saint Paul MN 55102

VOTAW, VERLING MILTON, chemist, church staff exec.; b. Wabash County, Ind., Mar. 20, 1904; s. Joseph Willet and Florence Edna (Barnett) V.; A.B., Ind. U., 1925, M.A. in Chemistry, 1926; m. Mary Elizabeth Mount, Oct. 16, 1926; children—John, Virginia, Alastair, Elizabeth. With Procter & Gamble, Cin., 1926-66, dir. product research, 1955-66; exec. asst. Episcopal Diocese of So. Ohio, Cin., 1966—; councilman City of Wyoming (Ohio), 1952-66; pres. Wyoming Health Assn.; pres. Cin. Public Dental Health Assn., 1974-77; mem. United Appeal allocation com., Cin., 1972—; sr. warden Episcopal Ch., Wyoming, 1952-55. Fellow Royal Soc. Medicine (London) (asso.); mem. ADA (hon. mem.), Cin. Dental Assn., Am. Chem. Soc., AAAS, Sigma Xi, Phi Beta Kappa, Alpha Chi Sigma, Phi Lambda Upsilon, Sigma Alpha Epsilon. Republican. Club: Wyoming. Patentee in field of cooking fats, fluorides in toothpaste. Home: 416 Sugar Maple Ln Maple Knoll Village Cincinnati OH 45246

VOTCA, JOHN ALBERT, educator; b. Mankato, Minn., Sept. 10, 1927; s. Frank and Mary Katherine (Adams) V.; B.S., Mankato State U., 1950, M.S., 1963; m. Charlotte Marschall, June 27, 1953; children—John M., Jane M., Beth A. Cabinet maker Lindsay Sash Co., Mankato, Minn., 1950-51; tchr. public schs., Shakopee, Minn., 1951-52; aeronautics, indsl. edn. tchr. Mankato (Minn.) Area Vocat. Tech. Sch., 1955-60, vocat. coordinator, 1960-65, asst. dir. vocat. edn., 1965-76, dir. vocat. edn., 1976—. Apprenticeship coordinator Jr. Achievement, 1976-81; state adv. com. for vocat. edn., 1976-77; bd. dirs. Mankato United Way, 1980—; mem. council Boy Scouts Am., Mankato, 1972-74; mem. Mankato Arts Council, 1981. Served with USN, 1945-46, 52-55, USNR, 1952—. Recipient United Way Community Service award, 1965; Mankato Area C. of C. Service award, 1980; Mankato State U. Outstanding Alumnus award, 1980. Mem. Mankato Area C. of C. (pres., chmn. bd. dirs. 1979-81), Minn. Vocat. Assn. (pres. 1977-78), Am. Vocat. Assn., Nat. Council of Local Adminstrs. (pres. state chpt. 1961-62), Phi Delta Kappa (pres. 1961-63). Clubs: Serra, Rotary (bd. dirs. 1968-69), K.C. Home: 311 Emerson Ln Mankato MN 56001 Office: 1920 Lee Blvd North Mankato MN 56001

VOTH, HAROLD MOSER, psychiatrist, psychoanalyst; b. Newton, Kans., Dec. 29, 1922; s. Albert Cornelius and Margret (Unruh) V.; B.S., Washburn U., Topeka, 1943; M.D., Kans. U., 1947; m. Patsy Ruth Gardner, Mar. 9, 1946; children—Eric, Gregory, Nicholas. Intern San Diego County Gen. Hosp., 1947-48; resident Menninger Sch. Psychiatry, 1948-50; sr. psychiatrist and psychoanalyst Menninger Found., Topeka, 1957-81; chief staff Topeka VA Hosp., 1981—; cons. surg. gen. USN. Served to rear adm. M.C., USNR. Fellow Am. Coll. Psychoanalysts, Am. Psychiat. Assn. Recipient Wm. C. Menninger Outstanding Tchr. award, 1970; Author: Psychotherapy and the Role of the Environment, 1973; The Castrated Family, 1977. Office: Topeka VA Hosp Topeka KS 66601

VOZAK, FRANK REDIN, III, social worker; b. Alton, Ill., May 12, 1952; s. Frank Henry and Margarita (Redin) V.; B.S. in Social Work, St. Louis U., 1974, cert. environ. studies, 1974, cert. peace studies, 1975, M.S.W., 1975. Clin. social work Edward J. Hines Jr. VA Hosp., Hines, Ill., 1977—; social work officer U.S. Army Med. Dept., 1975-77; instr. field work Jane Addams Sch. Social Work, U. Ill., Chgo., 1980—. Sec., treas. Mo. Public Interest Research Group, 1973-74, pres., 1974-75; adult leader Order of Arrow, Boy Scouts Am. Capt. USAR, 1977—. Cert. social worker, Ill. Mem. Nat. Assn. Social Workers, Ill. Welfare Assn., Acad. Cert. Social Workers, Chgo. and Northwestern Hist. Soc., Nat. Model R.R. Assn., Ill. Ry. Mus., White Pines Model R.R. Club, Gulf Mobile & Ohio Hist. Soc., Air Force Assn., Assn. U.S. Army, Nat. Assn. R.R. Passengers, 20th Century R.R. Club, Oak Park Soc. Model Engrs., Alton Civic Orch. Soc., St. Louis U. Alumni Assn., Alton, Hines & Pacific R.R. Hist. Soc., Frontdriver Club, Alpha Sigma Nu. Unitarian. Home: 1227 S Harlem Berwyn IL 60402 Office: Social Work Service VA Edward J Hines Hospital Hines IL 60141

VRIESMAN, GLORIA RUTH, med. group adminstr.; b. Muskegon, Mich., Feb. 20, 1933; d. Harry and Dena (Kuiper) Bultema; student Muskegon Community Coll., 1978; children—Robert, Laurel A. Hodgson, Lynn E. Caraway, Scott J. With various physicians Muskegon, Mich., 1952-69; with Muskegon Surg. Assocs., P.C., 1969—, med. group adminstr., 1972—; guest instr. Muskegon Bus. Coll., 1978, 81. Mem. Mich. Med. Group Mgmt. Assn. (sec. 1981—), Am. Coll. Med. Group Adminstrs. (cert.), Med. Group Mgmt. Assn., Am. Mgmt. Assn. Berean Ch. Home: 17554 Parkwood Dr Spring Lake MI 49456 Office: W Shore Profl Bldg 1560 E Sherman Blvd Muskegon MI 49444

VRIESMAN, WAYNE RODGER, broadcasting exec.; b. Muskegon, Mich., Apr. 6, 1937; s. John and Henrietta (Poel) V.; B.A., Hope Coll., Holland, Mich., 1959; M.S., Northwestern U., 1960; m. Barbara A. Vannette, Aug. 24, 1957; children—Steven, Sherri, Suzanne. Newswriter, WGN Radio/TV, Chgo., 1960-63, news producer, night mgr. WGN Radio/TV News, 1964-66; news dir., v.p. Sta. KWGN-TV, Denver, 1966-76; v.p., news dir. Radio/TV, WGN Continental Broadcasting Co., Chgo., 1976-78, v.p., sta. mgr. radio, 1978—; instr. Wheaton Coll. Grad. Sch. Communications, 1978—. Vice-chmn. bd. Bethesda Hosp., Denver, 1979—. Mem. Radio TV News Dirs. Assn. (past pres.), Nat. Assn. Broadcasters, Nat. Radio Broadcasters Assn., Chgo. Press Club, Radio Broadcasters Chicagoland, Ill. Broadcasters Assn. Mem. Christian Reformed Ch. Office: 2501 Bradley Pl Chicago IL 60618

VUCKOVICH, DRAGOMIR MICHAEL, neurologist; b. Bileca, Yugoslavia, Oct. 27, 1927; s. Alexander J. and Anka (Ivanisevich) V.; came to U.S., 1957; naturalized, 1962; M.D., U. Birmingham, Eng., 1953; m. Brenda Mary Luther, Aug. 23, 1958; children—John, Nicholas, Adrian. Jr. resident in pediatrics Birmingham Children's Hosp., 1954-55; resident med. officer Princess Beatrice Hosp., London, 1955; house physician Hosp. for Sick Children, London, 1955; resident physician Nat. Hosp., London, 1956-57; rotating intern Columbus Hosp., Chgo., 1957-58; resident in neurology and pediatrics VA Research Hosp., Northwestern U. Med. Sch., Chgo., 1958-59, Wesley Meml. Hosp., Chgo., 1959-60, Children's Hosp., 1960-62; practice medicine specializing in neurology, Chgo., 1962—; asso. attending neurologist Children's Hosp., Chgo., 1968—; head, neurology psychiatry Columbus Hosp., Chgo., 1968-81, head of electroencephalography dept., 1969—; v.p. neurosci. Columbus Cuneo Cabrini Med. Center, Chgo., 1981—; head pediatric neurology Loyola U., Chgo., 1970-79, asso. prof., neurology and pediatrics, 1970-77, prof., 1977—. Served with Royal Yugoslav Army, 1942-44. Diplomate Am. Bd. Psychiatry and Neurology, Am. Bd. Pediatrics, Pan Am. Med. Assn. Fellow Am. Acad. Pediatrics (sect. neurology), Royal Soc. Health; mem. Am. British med. assns., Am. Acad. Neurology, Am. Med. Electroencephalograpic Assn., Royal Coll. Surgeons, Royal Coll. Physicians. Serbian Orthodox. Clubs: Ill. Athletic, Beefeaters, Les Gourmet. Contbr. articles to med. jours.

Home: 755 Kipling Pl Deerfield IL 60015 Office: 104 S Michigan Ave Chicago IL 60603

VUMBACO, JOSEPH ANTHONY, pub. utilities mgr.; b. Meriden, Conn., May 20, 1947; s. Rocco Joseph and Mildred Katherine (Bartley) V.; B.S.M.E., Rose Poly. Inst., 1969; M.B.A., U. Hartford, 1975; m. Linda Mae Maddox, June 19, 1970. Research and devel. engr. Collins Radio Corp., Dallas, 1969-70; exec. asst. elec. div. Dept. Pub. Utilities, Wallingford, Conn., 1971-75, asst. gen. mgr., chief engr., 1975-76; gen. mgr. Hibbing (Minn.) Pub. Utilities, 1976—; owner Vumbaco & Assos. Engring. and Mgmt. Consultants. Registered profl. engr., Conn., Minn. Mem. Minn. Mcpl. Utilities Assn. (dir., past pres.), Northeastern Minn. Mcpl. Power Agy. (dir., pres.), ASME, Am. Pub. Power Assn. (vice chmn. energy services planning com.), Nat., Minn. socs. profl. engrs., Am. Water Works Assn., Am. Public Gas Assn. (dir.). Club: Hibbing Kiwanis. Office: Hibbing Public Utilities 19th St and 6th Ave E Hibbing MN 55746

VYAS, GOPAL MAGH RAJ, engring. and constrn. co. exec.; b. India, Oct. 8, 1945; s. Maghraj A. and Yashoda D. (Purohit) V.; came to U.S., 1968; B.S., Jiwaji U., India, 1966; M.S., Ohio U., 1969; M.B.A., Boston U., 1975; m. Susan Anne McIntosh, Aug. 12, 1971; children—Nisha Anne, Sheila Anne, Raina Anne. Mktg. engr. Greeves Cotton & Co., Ltd., Bombay, India, 1966-68; project engr. research and devel. Digital Info. div. Wang Labs., Lowell, Mass., 1969-71; project mgr. Stewart & Prince, Inc., Danvers, Mass., 1971-77; exec. v.p. Tessier Sheetmetal Works, Inc., Mitchell, S.D., 1977—. Mem. Mitchell Area Arts Council, S.D. Friends Pub. Broadcasting; bd. dirs. Mitchell Area YMCA. Govt. India Merit scholar, 1961-66. Mem. Mitchell Area C. of C., Am. Mgmt. Assn., ASME, ASHRAE. Clubs: Rotary, Elks. Home: 9 Ridge Rd Mitchell SD 57301 Office: 218 E 1st Ave Mitchell SD 57301

VYVERBERG, ROBERT WILLIAM, mental health adminstr.; b. Dubuque, Iowa, Dec. 23, 1940; s. William Pifer and Virginia Thelma (Rutger) V.; B.Ed., Ill. Wesleyan U., 1963; M.S., Ill. State U., 1964; Ed.D., No. Ill. U., 1972; m. Benita Joanne Bushu, June 20, 1964; children—Robert William, Benjamin Rutger. Dir. counseling services Crown High Sch., Carpentersville, Ill., 1964-67; dir. outcare services, children and adolescent unit H. Douglas Singer Mental Health Center, Rockford, Ill., 1969-72, dir. psychiat. rehab. and extended care services, 1972—; region coordinator Services to Elderly, 1978—; lectr. crisis theory and crisis intervention No. Ill. U., 1970—, instr. group counseling and psychotherapy, 1973; cons. Juvenile Justice Personnel Devel. Center, U. Wis., 1977. Mem. social concerns com. Ct. St. United Methodist Ch., Rockford, 1975—; treas. Blackhawk Cub Scout Council, 1977; officer, coach Rockford Ch. League Basketball, 1980—. Mem. Nat. Rehab. Assn., Am. Personnel and Guidance Assn., Am. Rehab. Counselors Assn., Am. Mental Health Counselors Assn., Internat. Assn. Psycho-Social Rehab. Services. Home: 3015 Carriage Ln Rockford IL 61103 Office: H Douglas Singer Mental Health Center 4402 N Main St Rockford IL 61103

WABER, JAMES THOMAS, educator; b. Chgo., Apr. 8, 1920; s. James Warren and Anna May (Cline) W.; B.S., Ill. Inst. Tech., Chgo., 1941, M.S., 1943, Ph.D., 1946; m. Santon Fotheringham, May 12, 1951; children—Lauriene, Sue Berenaise, Gay Ellen (dec.), John James. Research asst. prof. chemistry Ill. Inst. Tech., 1946; staff mem., sect. leader Los Alamos Sci. Lab., 1947-66; prof. materials sci. and engring., nuclear enging. Northwestern U., Evanston, Ill., 1967—; cons. Los Alamos Sci. Lab. Recipient Sr. U.S. Scientist award Alexander von Humbolt Found., 1975, Profl. Achievement award Ill. Inst. Tech. Alumni Assn., 1967, Willis Rodney Whitney award Nat. Assn. Corrosion Engrs., 1961. Fellow Am. Phys. Soc., Inst. Metallurgists (Gt. Britain); mem. Am. Inst. Mining and Metall. Engrs., Am. Soc. Metals. Editor: Compounds of Interest in Nuclear Reactor Technology, 1964; Energy Bands in Metals and Alloys, 1967; Magnetism in Alloys, 1972; contbr. articles to sci. jours.; patentee in field. Home: 310 Linden Ave Wilmette IL 60091 Office: 2145 Sheridan Rd Evanston IL 60201

WACK, JOSEPH PIERRE, mfg. co. exec.; b. Dayton, Ohio, July 11, 1927; s. Edward Paul and Mary Margaret (O'Brien) W.; B.S., U. Dayton, 1949; M.S., St. Louis U., 1952, Ph.D., 1956; children—Catherine, Madonna, Gregory, Joseph Pierre, Monica, Julie, Christine. Sr. instr. dept. pathology St. Louis U., 1956-64; instr. dept. psychology Washington U., St. Louis, 1965; asst. prof. dept. anatomy U. N.D., Grand Forks, 1965-70; instr. Cuyahoga Community Coll., Cleve., 1975-76; with personnel dept. Cleve. Twist Drill Co., 1977-78; mgr. employee assistance program Acme-Cleve. Corp., 1978—. Served with U.S. Army, 1946-47. Mem. Assn. Labor-Mgmt. Adminstrs. and Consultants on Alcoholism (cert. alcoholism counselor). Roman Catholic. Club: K.C. Contbr. articles to med. jours. Home: 7660 Broadview Rd Apt 316 Parma OH 44134 Office: 1127 Euclid Ave Suite 351 Cleveland OH 44115

WACKER, FREDERICK GLADE, JR., mfg. co. exec.; b. Chgo., July 10, 1918; s. Frederick Glade and Grace Cook (Jennings) W.; grad. Hotchkiss Sch., 1936; B.A., Yale, 1940; student Gen. Motors Inst. Tech., 1940-42; m. Ursula Comandatore, Apr. 26, 1958; children—Frederick Glade III, Wendy, Joseph Comandatore. With AC Spark Plug div. Gen. Motors Corp., 1940-43, efficiency engr., 1941-43; with Ammco Tools, Inc., North Chicago, Ill., 1947—, pres., chmn. bd., 1948—; founder, 1954, since pres., chmn. bd. Liquid Controls Corp., North Chicago; partner Francis I. duPont & Co., N.Y.C., 1954-70; dir. Moehlenpah Industries, Inc.; condr. Freddie Wacker and His Orch., 1955-70, orch. appeared on TV and radio, recorded for Dolphin Records, Cadet Records. Mem. World Bus. Council, 1971—; chmn. Chgo. chpt. Young Presidents Orgn., 1965-66. Bd. govs. United Republican Fund Ill., 1952-78; trustee Lake Forest Acad., 1956-71; hon. dir. Chgo. chpt. Multiple Sclerosis Soc.; bd. govs. Warren Wilson Coll.; bd. govs. Lyric Opera Chgo., dir., 1963-66; bd. dirs. Trinity Evang. Div. Sch., 1975—, Ch. League Am., 1977-81, Rockford Inst., 1980—. Served to lt. (j.g.) USNR, 1943-45. Mem. N.A.M., Sports Car Club Am. (pres. 1952-53), Waukegan-North Chgo. C. of C. (dir. 1965-68), Chief Execs. Forum, Chgo. Pres.'s Orgn. (pres. 1972-73), Pres.'s Forum, Am. Motorcycle Assn., Soc. Automotive Engrs., Chgo. Fedn. Musicians (life), Ill. Mfrs. Assn. (dir. 1966—, chmn. bd. 1975), Automotive Orgn. Team (life mem., dir. 1976—). Presbyn. Clubs: Chicago, Racquet (pres. 1960), Econ., Casino, Mid-Am. (Chgo.); Shoreacres (Lake Bluff); Onwentsia (Lake Forest, Ill.); N.Y. Yacht. Home: 1600 Green Bay Rd Lake Bluff IL 60044 Office: 2100 Commonwealth Ave North Chicago IL 60064

WADDELL, ROBERT FOWLER, bearing accessory mfg. co. exec.; b. Lafayette, Ind., Feb. 2, 1926; s. Thomas C. and Mildred M. Waddell; B.S. in Mech. Engring., Purdue U., 1949; m. Marilyn J. Lindemann, Jan. 19, 1962; children—Lynne, Scott, Kathy. Pres., chmn. bd. Standard Locknut & Lockwasher, Inc., Indpls., 1949—, Standard Products Corp., Greenfield, Ill., 1952-70, Carmel Screw Products Corp. (Ind.), 1962-70, Standard Locknut & Lockwasher, Inc., Carmel, 1949—; chmn. bd. Park 100 Foods Inc., Indpls., 1979—. Served with USAAF, 1944-46. Mem. World Bus. Council. Republican. Presbyterian. Office: 1212 S Range Line Rd Carmel IN 46032

WADDICK, WILLIAM ANTHONY, lawyer; b. Chgo., Dec. 7, 1931; s. William Anthony and Mary Elizabeth (Dolan) W.; student Xavier U., 1949-51; B.S. cum laude, U. Notre Dame, 1957; J.D., Ind. U., 1961; m. Clara Maria Taylor, June 13, 1964; children—Maria B., Julia L., Patricia A., Brenda J., Linda J. Admitted to Ind. bar, 1961; mem. firm. Kunz & Kunz, Indpls., 1961—, partner, 1963—. Served with USAF, 1951-54. Mem. Ind., Indpls. bar assns., Ind. Trial Lawyers Assn., St. Thomas More Soc. (pres. 1970-71), Phi Delta Phi. Roman Catholic. Republican. K.C. Clubs: Heather Hills Country (Indpls.), Indianapolis Athletic. Home: 2 Songbird Ct Carmel IN 46032 Office: 320 N Meridian St Indianapolis IN 46204

WADDINGTON, BETTE HOPE (STAGE NAME ELIZABETH CROWDER), violinist; b. San Francisco, July 27, 1921; d. John and Marguerite (Crowder) Waddington; A.B., U. Calif. at Berkeley, 1945, postgrad.; postgrad. (violin scholar) Juilliard Sch. Music, 1950, San Jose State Coll., 1955; M.A., San Francisco State Coll., 1953; life cert. music and art Calif. Jr. Coll. Studied violin with Joseph Fuchs, Felix Rhuner, Naoum Blinder, Eddie Brown, Daniel Bonsack, others. Violinist, St. Louis Symphony, 1958—. Cert. tchr. and librarian, Calif. Mem. U. Calif., San Francisco State Coll., San Jose State U. alumnae assns., Sierra Club, Alpha Beta Alpha. Home: 2800 Olive St Saint Louis MO 63103 Office: Powell Hall Grand Ave and Delmar Blvd Saint Louis MO 63103

WADE, BETTY JEAN, mgmt. cons.; b. Wynne, Ark., Sept. 28, 1929; d. Andrew Lee and Alice Birdie (Stokes) Malone. B.S.E., U. Central Ark., 1965; postgrad. Central Mo. State U., 1971-72, S.W. Mo. State U., 1973-74; m. John Aubrey Wade, Apr. 9, 1950; children—John Aubrey, Carolyn, Elizabeth, Nancy. Student tchr. Sallie-Cone Elem. Sch., Conway, Ark., 1964-65; substitute tchr. Southwood Elem. Sch., Raytown, Mo., 1966-67, 5th grade tchr., 1967-68; tchr. Seoul-Am. Middle Sch., Yongsan, Korea, 1968-70, Westridge Elem. Sch., Raytown, Mo., 1970-72, Logan Elem. Sch., Rogersville, Mo., 1973-75; 4th grade tchr. Galena-Abesville Sch., Galena, Mo., 1976-77; mgmt. cons. Batten, Batten, Hudson & Swab, Des Moines, 1978-82; v.p., mgmt. cons. Wade & Assos., Branson, Mo., 1982—. Mem. exec. bd. local PTAs, 1956-75; leader Brownies, Girl Scouts U.S.A., 1960-62. Mem. Am. Soc. Tng. and Devel., AAUW, Zeta Tau Alpha. Methodist. Home and Office: Star Route 1 Box 1114 Branson MO 65616

WADE, HERBERT ALLEN, solar research scientist; b. Pleasant Hill, Mo., Nov. 28, 1939; s. George N. and Georgia M. (Bunch) W.; B.S., U.S. Naval Acad., 1961; M.B.A., U. R.I., 1967; M.S., No. Ariz. U., 1977; m. Ann Courtney, May 25, 1962; 1 dau., Sarah Ann. Research engr. The Eppley Lab., Newport, R.I., 1965-68; pres. Internat. Sci. Industries, Flagstaff, Ariz., 1968—; prof. mech. engring. No. Ariz. U., Flagstaff, 1974—; asso. dir. Ariz. Solar Energy Research Commn., 1977-78; dir. solar programs Mo. Dept. Natural Resources, 1978—; dir. MASEC Corp. Active Boy Scouts Am. Served USN, 1961-65. Mem. AIAA, Am. Soc. Engring. Mgmt., Internat. Solar Energy Soc., N.Mex., Ariz. solar energy assns. (chmn. Ariz. 1976-77). Designer solar homes and bldgs. in S.W. and midwest; mem. editorial adv. bd. Solar Law Reporter, 1978—.

WADE, JERRY THOMAS, engring. co. exec.; b. Belleville, Ill., Jan. 24, 1940; s. Alfred Yorker and Estel Marie (Gass) W.; student St. Louis U., 1957-60, Belleville Area Coll., 1961-62, U. Ill., 1969; children—Jeffrey, Jay, Joel, Whitney. Surveyor, Wade Engring. Co., Belleville, 1955-62; partner S. G. Randle & Assos., Belleville, 1962-70; partner Thouvenot, Wade and Moerchen, Belleville, 1970—, pres., 1976—; sec. Shilo Valley Devel. Co., Belleville, 1968—; owner sewer systems, pres. Metro East Utility Co., Belleville, 1967—; sec. Testing Analysis & Control, Inc., Belleville, 1969—. Served with U.S. Army, 1957-58. Recipient Gold Heart, Heart Assn., 1974. Mem. Am. Congress Mapping and Plating, Am. Water Works Assn., Central States Water Pollution Control Fedn., Ill. Registered Land Surveyor's Assn., Ill. Water Pollution Control Operators Soc. Roman Catholic. Clubs: Rotary, Racquet Ball (Belleville), Eagles. Office: 2312 Lebanon Ave Belleville IL 62221

WADE, LUCILLE O., tool mfg. co. exec.; b. Hicksville, Ohio, June 9, 1908; d. Ward Cleveland and Daisy Pearl (Osmun) Gingrich; student public schs., Hicksville; m. Gearold C. Wade, Oct. 12, 1933 (dec.); 1 dau., Ann Wade Smith. Operator, chief operator Gen. Telephone Co., Hicksville, 1927-36; co-owner, bookkeeper Wade Machine Co., Mendon, Ohio, 1965-74; bookkeeper Edgerton Tool Co. (Ohio), 1960-74; with Syracuse Tool & Mfg., Inc. (Ind.), 1971—, owner, mgr., 1974—. Methodist. Clubs: Order Eastern Star (past matron) (Hicksville); Shriners. Home: Rural Route 2 Hicksville OH 43526

WADE, MICHAEL ROBERT ALEXANDER, economist; b. N.Y.C., June 29, 1945; s. Burton Jean and Celia (Handleman) W.; student U. Rennes, France, 1964; A.B., U. Chgo., 1967; postgrad. in pub. adminstrn., Am. U., 1967-71; M.B.A. in Fin., N.Y. U., 1975; m. Carole Kay West, Aug. 25, 1974. Program analyst, mgmt. intern HUD, 1967-71; dep. dir. Mgmt. Communications and Briefing Center, U.S. Price Commn., 1972; asst. exec. sec. policy coordination U.S. Cost of Living Council, 1973-74; asso. dir. U.S. Indochina Refugee Program, 1975-76; pres. China Trade Devel. Corp. of Chgo., 1977—; participant with W.R. Grace & Co. in Okla. oil and gas prodn. Recipient Meritorious Service award Exec. Office of the Pres., 1972, Distinguished Service award U.S. Cost of Living Council, 1974. Mem. Soc. Contemporary Art, Internat. Trade Club Chgo. (policy and legis. action com.), Chgo. Council Fgn. Relations. Clubs: U. Chgo. (sec., bd. dirs. Washington 1970-73). Home: 900 Lake Shore Dr Chicago IL 60611 Office: 25 E Washington St Chicago IL 60602

WADE, ROYCE ALLEN, feed co. exec.; b. Medford, Wis., Apr. 30, 1932; s. Charles L. and Mildred H. (Clarin) W.; B.S. (acad. scholar), U. Wis., Stevens Point, 1954; M.Div., Garrett Theol. Sem., Evanston, Ill., 1960; M.S. in Adult Edn., U. Wis., Milw., 1968; postgrad. U. Wis., Madison, 1970-75; m. Corinne Mae Weber, June 30, 1956; children—Suzanne Mae, Debra Ann. Ordained to ministry Methodist Ch., 1960; pastor Richmond (Wis.) Meth. Ch., 1956-58, Asbury United Meth. Ch., Janesville, Wis., 1958-61; tchr., guidance counselor Edgerton (Wis.) High Sch., 1961-62; asso. pastor Community United Meth. Ch., Whitefish Bay, Wis., 1962-66; pastor Simpson and Gardner United Meth. Chs., Milw., 1966-68; asso. pastor St. Luke United Meth. Ch., Sheboygan, Wis., 1968-69; pastor Poynette and Inch United Meth. Chs., 1969-74; dir. Adult Study Center, Portage, Wis., 1974-75; dir. growth and devel., dir. Profl. Products & Services, Inc., Sauk City, Wis., 1976—; curriculum cons. U. Wis. Sch. Nursing, 1974-76, instr. small group seminar, 1974-76, supr. behavioral disabilities student tchrs., 1974-76; adult edn. instr. Wis. Conf. United Meth. Ch., 1964-69. Village trustee, Poynette, 1977-81; mem. Police Aux., Whitefish Bay; bd. dirs. North Shore Council Human Relations, Milw., Inter Faith Council, Milw. Served with C.I.C., AUS, 1954-56. Cert. in pastoral counseling, interpersonal relations. Mem. Adult Edn. Assn., Am. Soc. Tng. and Devel., Phi Delta Kappa. Club: Optimist. Research on participation in adult instrnl. groups using Eriksonian ego-stage theory. Home: 122 E Washington St Poynette WI 53955 Office: 231 Water St Sauk City WI 53583

WADIA, ASPI RUSTOM, aerodynamics design engr.; b. Bombay, India, Apr. 17, 1953; came to U.S., 1975, naturalized, 1980; s. Rustom C. and Tehmi N. (Kanga) W.; B.Tech. with honors, Indian Inst. Tech., 1975; M.S., Cornell U., 1978; Ph.D., U. Tex., 1979; m. Aban Homi Kapadia, Jan. 5, 1976; children—Farah, Shernaz. Trainee positions various airlines and air depots, India, summers 1971-74; research asst. Cornell U., Ithaca, N.Y., 1975-77; teaching asso. U. Tex., Arlington, 1977-79; design engr. Garrett Turbine Engine Co., Phoenix, 1979-81; sr. project engr. Detroit Diesel Allison, Indpls., 1981—; cons. Control Data Corp., Minn., 1979-80. Recipient merit awards AIAA, Sigma Xi. Mem. AIAA, N.Y. Acad. Scis., Sigma Xi, Tau Beta Pi, Sigma Gamma Tau. Zoroastrian. Contbr. articles on aerodynamics to profl. jours. Office: Detroit Diesel Allison Heat Transfer Group PO Box 894 Indianapolis IN 46206

WADSWORTH, GERALD J., machinery co. exec.; b. nr. Grand Blanc, Mich., May 19, 1918; s. William S. and Aethel O. (Beebe) W.; grad. Gen. Motors Tech. Sch., 1940; postgrad. Mich. State Coll., 1943; m. Ruth A. Ackerman, Jan. 10, 1941; children—Jon F., Jo Ann (Mrs. Stephen R. Donahue). Toolroom foreman A.C. Spark Plug Co., Flint, Mich., 1941; toolmaker Indsl. Metal Products Corp., Lansing, Mich., 1942-51, foreman, 1951-52, supt., 1952-68, proposal engr., 1968-69, chief sales engr., 1969-76, advanced planning engr., 1969-76, pres., gen. mgr., 1976—, dir. apprentice tng. program, 1952-68, chmn. joint apprenticeship com., 1974—; pres. Impco Internat., Inc., 1980—. Served with AUS, 1944-46. Mem. Am. Bowling Congress, Am. Mus. Natural History, Indsl. Execs. Republican. Presbyn. Elk. Home: 2810 Delta River Dr Lansing MI 48906 Office: 3417 W St Joseph Rd Lansing MI 48917

WAETJEN, WALTER BERNHARD, univ. pres.; b. Phila., Oct. 16, 1920; s. Walter E. and Marguerite D. (Dettmann) W.; B.S., State Coll., Millersville, Pa., 1942; M.S., U. Pa., 1947; Ed.D., U. Md., 1951; LL.D., Gama Filho U. (Brazil); Litt.D. (hon.) Hanyang U. (Korea); m. Betty Walls, Sept. 28, 1945; children—Walter Bernhard, Kristi (Mrs. Richard Jenkins), Daniel G. Tchr., Sch. Dist. of Phila., 1945-48; research fellow U. Md., 1948-50, mem. faculty, 1950-73, prof. ednl. psychology, 1957-65, dir. Bur. Ednl. Research and Field Services, 1962-65, gen. dir. Interprofl. Research Commn. on Pupil Personnel Services, 1963-65, v.p. adminstrv. affairs, 1965-70, v.p. gen. adminstrn., 1970-73; pres. Cleve. State U., 1973—; dir. Union Commerce Bank, Gray Drug. Bd. dirs. United Way, Cleve. Scholarship Programs, Inc., Cleve. Internat. Program, Cleve. Conv. and Visitors Bur., Cleve. Research Inst. Corp., Cleve. Commn. on Higher Edn., Greater Cleve. Growth Assn., Playhouse Sq. Found., Greater Cleve. Roundtable, Cleanland, Ohio, Ohio World Trade Center, Boy Scouts Am., Downtown Cleve. Corp. Mem. NEA, Assn. for Supervision and Curriculum Devel., Soc. for Research in Child Devel., AAAS, Am. Edn. Research Assn. W.T. Grant Found. fellow, 1960-61; Patty Hill Smith Meml. lectr. U. Louisville, 1964; recipient Disting. Alumni award Pa. State Coll., 1972. Clubs: Mason (33 deg.), 50, Union. Co-author source books in field; contbr. articles to ednl. jours. Home: 14706 Larchmere Blvd Shaker Heights OH 44120 Office: Cleve State U Cleveland OH 44115

WAGGENER, RONALD EDGAR, radiologist; b. Green River, Wyo., Oct. 6, 1926; s. Edgar Fleetwood and Mary Harlene (Hutton) W.; student Colo. A&M U., 1944, Oreg. State U., 1945; B.S., U. Nebr., 1949, M.S., 1952, Ph.D., 1957, M.D. cum laude, 1954, postgrad., 1955-58; postgrad. St. Bartholomew's, London, 1956-57; m. Everina Ann Stalker, Aug. 1, 1948; children—Marta, Nancy, Paul, Daphne. Intern, U. Nebr. Hosp., 1954-55, resident, 1955-56, 57-58; instr. radiology U. Nebr., Omaha, 1958, asst. prof., 1959-61, asso. prof., 1962-80, clin. asso. prof., 1981—; radiation therapist U. Nebr., 1959-65; radiation therapist Nebr. Meth. Hosp., Omaha, 1965-70, dir. Dept. Radiology, 1977-81, dir. cancer fellowship program, 1977—, dir. cancer and radiation therapy, 1970—, chmn. cancer com. 1964—; pres. Highland Assos., Ltd., Omaha, 1960—, R.A. Enterprises, Inc., Omaha, 1960—; mem. cancer com. Children's Meml. Hosp., Omaha, 1970—. Served with C.E., U.S. Army, 1944-46. AEC fellow, 1952-53; Am. Cancer Soc. fellow, 1956-57. Fellow Am. Coll. Radiologists; mem. Midlands Soc. Therapeutic Radiology (founder, pres. 1970-71), Nebr. Med. Assn., Am. Cancer Soc., Nebr. Radiology Soc. (pres. 1963-64), AMA, Am. Soc. Therapeutic Radiology, Radiol. Soc. N.Am., Faculty of Radiologists Gr. Britain, Brit. Inst. Radiology, Am. Radium Soc., Soc. Nuclear Medicine, Am. Assn. Cancer Research, Thoroughbred Owners and Breeders Assn., Horsemen's Benevolent and Protective Assn., Sigma Xi, Alpha Omega Alpha, Phi Nu. Contbr. articles to profl. jours. Home: 1227 S 109 St Omaha NE 68144 Office: 8303 Dodge St Omaha NE 68114

WAGGONER, JEANNE MARIE, ednl. adminstr.; b. St. Louis, July 24, 1937; d. William McDowell and Louise Gertrude (Schnettler) W.; B.S., Notre Dame Coll., 1962; M.Ed. in Pvt. Sch. Adminstrn., U. San Francisco, 1979. Joined Sisters of Notre Dame, Roman Catholic Ch., 1955; tchr. elem. rural, inner-city parochial schs., Albuquerque, 1958-59, Jackson, Mo., 1959-62, Chamois, Mo., 1962-64, St. Louis, 1964-67, Scott City, Mo., 1967-70; adminstr. St. Jude Acad., San Diego, 1976-80, St. Engelbert Elem. Sch., St. Louis, 1980—; mem. Sch. Sisters of Notre Dame's Edn. Council in West, 1970-72; mem. Conf. Religious Dirs. Edn., 1978-80; cons. Title III program, San Diego, 1974. Cert. tchr., Mo., Calif. Mem. Nat. Cath. Edn. Assn., Assn. Supervision and Curriculum Devel. Participant curriculum and program devel. for nongraded, individualized elem. sch., San Diego, 1971-80. Home: 4746 Carter Ave Saint Louis MO 63115 Office: 4720 Carter Ave Saint Louis MO 63115

WAGNER, ALVIN LOUIS, JR., profl. real estate appraiser, cons.; b. Chgo., Dec. 19, 1939; s. Alvin Louis and Esther Jane (Wheeler) W.; student U. Ill., 1958-59; B.A., Drake U., 1962; postgrad. Real Estate Inst., Chgo., 1960-65; m. Susan Carole Fahey, Aug. 14, 1965; children—Alvin Louis III, Robert Percy. Asst. appraiser Oak Park (Ill.) Fed. Savings & Loan Co., 1955-60; v.p. real estate sales A. L. Wagner & Co., Flossmoor, Ill., 1961-63; real estate loan officer, chief appraiser Beverly Bank, Chgo., 1963-67; asso. real estate appraiser C. A. Bruckner & Assos., Chgo., 1967-70; founder, profl. real estate appraiser and cons. A. L. Wagner & Co., Flossmoor, 1970—. Mem. faculty Am. Inst. Real Estate Appraisers, Chgo., 1974—; instr. real estate appraising Prairie State Coll., Chicago Heights, Ill., 1970—; mem. adv. com. Real Estate Sch., 1972—; community prof. Gov.'s State U., 1977—, founding mem. real estate adv. bd. Mem. Rich Township (Ill.) Personal Services Commn., 1973—; v.p., drive chmn. Flossmoor Community Chest, Crusade of Mercy, 1974-75, pres., 1975-76. Auditor, Rich Township, 1973-77. Governing bd. Glenwood (Ill.) Sch. for Boys, 1973—; chmn. bus. edn. occupational adv. com. Homewood-Flossmoor High Sch., 1977. Mem. Am. Inst. Real Estate Appraisers (mem. governing council 1974-75, Profl. Recognition award 1977), Chgo. Assn. Commerce and Industry, Chgo., Homewood-Flossmoor real estate bds., Nat., Ill. assns. realtors, Homewood-Flossmoor Jaycees, Phi Delta Theta (pres. chpt. 1960), Chgo. Phi Delta Theta Alumni Club (pres.), Omega Tau Rho, Lambda Alpha. Clubs: Flossmoor Country, Variety, Rotary, Masons. Mem. editorial bd. Appraisal Jour., 1975—; contbr. articles to real estate jours. Home: 927 Park Dr Flossmoor IL 60422 Office: 2709 Flossmoor Rd Flossmoor IL 60422

WAGNER, CHARLES ALAN, librarian; b. Elkhart, Ind., Apr. 27, 1948; s. C. Arthur and Lydia M. (Stump) W.; B.A., Manchester (Ind.) Coll., 1970; M.L.S., Ind. U., 1973; m. Marilynn B. Dray, Aug. 17, 1971; 1 dau., Wendy. Library dir. Peru Public Library, 1973—. Mem. Ind. Library Assn., Plymouth Club Am. Clubs: Rotary, Hoosier Road Runners. Author articles field. Cartoons have appeared in comic books, newspapers. Address: 102 E Main St Peru IN 46970

WAGNER, DIANE NATALIE, psychologist; b. Chgo., Nov. 8, 1940; d. Frank and Natalie (Gazdik) Dite; B.S. in Edn., No. Ill. U., DeKalb, 1961, M.A., 1968; m. David Wagner, June 23, 1963. Psychologist, DeKalb County Children's Services, 1964-67, Elgin (Ill.) State Hosp., 1967-69, Ben Gordon Community Mental Health Center, DeKalb, 1970-79; cons. for tng. Midwest region Legal Services Corp., Chgo., 1979—; mem. welfare services com. Ill. Dept. Public Aid. Convenor, DeKalb Alliance Against War, 1967-69; mem. bd. Sojourner Bookstore and Women's Center. Mem. Am. Personnel and Guidance Assn., Ill. Group Psychotherapy Assn., Women's Internat. League Peace and Freedom.

WAGNER, DONALD L., state legislator; b. McCook, Nebr., May 31, 1927; ed. public schs.; m. Gertrude E. Tech, May 31, 1948; 15 children. With Reed Engring. Co.; farmer; mem. Nebr. Legislature, 1979—. Mem. Twin Loups Reclamation Dist.; pres. Nebr. Water Reclamation Assn.; vice chmn. Loup Basin Policy Adv. Com.; rural sch. dist. sec. Nebr., Calley County Sch. Reorgn. Com.; pres. Vets. Meml. Bldg. Bd., Water Users Bd. Served with U.S. Army and USAR, World War II. Mem. Ord C. of C., Ducks Unltd., Nat. Rifle Assn., Am. Legion. Clubs: KC, Elks, Karp and Krow. *

WAGNER, DOROTHY MARIE, ct. reporter, service exec.; b. Milw., June 8, 1924; d. Theodore Anthony and Leona Helen (Ullrich) Wagner; grad. Milw. Bus. U., 1944; student Marquette U., U. Wis., Milw. Stenographer, legal sec., Milw., 1942-44; hearing reporter Wis. Workmen's Compensation Dept., 1944-48; ofcl. reporter to judge Circuit Ct., Milw., 1952-53; owner, operator ct. reporting service Dorothy M. Wagner & Assos., Milw., 1948—; asst. ofcl. reporter State of Wis. Recipient Gregg Diamond medal Gregg Pub. Co., 1950. Mem. Nat. (registered profl. reporter, certificate of proficiency), Wis. shorthand reporters assns., Am. Legion Aux. Roman Catholic. Home: 214 Williamsburg Dr Thiensville WI 53092 Office: 135 Wells St Suite 400 Milwaukee WI 53203

WAGNER, FRANK JOSEPH, printing and direct mail co. exec.; b. Detroit, Sept. 20, 1940; s. Carl Joseph and Esther Victoria Wagner; B.S. in Mech. Engring., U. Notre Dame, 1962; M.B.A., Wharton Sch., U. Pa., 1964; m. Susan C. Flinn, Sept. 5, 1970; children—John, Carrie. Mgmt. cons. Touche Ross & Co., C.P.A.'s, Detroit, 1964-68; controller Marbeau Corp., Detroit, 1968-70, Bloch Bros. Corp., Detroit, 1970-79, Robert Silverman Inc., Cleve., 1979—. Mem. Treasurers Club Cleve., Tau Beta Pi. Club: City (Cleve.). Office: 1375 Euclid Ave Cleveland OH 44115

WAGNER, JOHN EDWARD, trucking and warehousing co. exec.; b. Kansas City, Kans., Dec. 17, 1931; s. John Paver and Mary Josophene (Bye) W.; student Kansas City, (Kans.) Jr. Coll., 1949,51, Kansas City U., 1955,57; m. Shirley Jean Nixon, Jan. 27, 1951; children—Pamela Jean, John Edward, Susan Kay, James Kevin. With Wagner Cartage Service, Inc., Kansas City, Mo., 1949—, pres., chief exec. officer, 1965—; owner, pres., chief exec. officer Leonard Bros. Transport, Inc., 1971—. Mem. Am. Trucking Assn. (conf. v.p. 1980—), Am. Warehouseman's Assn., Local and Short Haul Carriers Nat. Conf., Mo. Bus and Truck Assn. (dir. 1976—), Central Indsl. Dist. Assn., U.S. C. of C., Greater Kansas City C. of C., Mid Continent Ind. Small Bus. Assn., Boat Owners Assn. U.S., U.S. Power Squadrons. Republican. Mem. Christian Ch. Clubs: Kansas City, Optimist, Lake of the Ozarks Yacht. Home: 6921 Belinder St Mission Hills KS 66208 Office: Wagner Cartage Service Inc 925 Wyoming St Kansas City MO 64101

WAGNER, LOUIS HERMAN, agronomist; b. Scheller, Ill., July 22, 1938; s. John Frank and Clara (Gajewski) W.; B.S., U. Ill., 1960, M.S., 1965; Tchr. vocat. agr. Neoga High Sch., 1960-65; with Sommer Bros. Seed Co., Pekin, Ill., 1965—, prodn. mgr. hybrid seed corn and soybeans, 1970—. chmn. agrl. extnsion council Tazewell County, 1980—; mem. adv. com. agr. U. Ill., 1979—; mem. adv. com. agr. service, jr. colls. Ill., 1978—. Mem. Am. Soc. Agronomy. Republican. Roman Catholic. Clubs: K.C., Elks. Home: 1022 Washington St Pekin IL 61554 Office: Box 248 Pekin IL 61554

WAGNER, MARY ISABEL WATSON, residential facility adminstr.; b. Urbana, Ohio, Nov. 7, 1920; d. Archibald M. and Catherine L. (O'Brien) Watson; student Nazareth Coll., Borgess Hosp., Kalamazoo; B.S. in Edn., Wayne State U., 1967, M.A. in Spl. Edn., 1971; m. Robert Peter Wagner, July 31, 1943; children—Elizabeth Ann, Yvonne Marie, Roberta Sue, Anthony Peter, James Robert. Tchr. pub. schs., Farmington, Mich., 1965-71; exec. dir. Community Living Centers, Inc., Farmington, 1969—; program cons. Internat. Center for Social Gerontology, Washington, Mich. Housing Devel. Authority, Lansing. Past bd. dirs. YMCA, Farmington. Named Educator of Yr., Oakland County, 1970; Woman of Yr., Wayne State U., 1973. Mem. Nat. Assn. Pvt. Residential Facilities for Mentally Retarded (dir., officer), Nat. Apotolate for Mentally Retarded (dir.), Mich. Assn. for Non-Profit Residential Facilities (dir., officer), Farmington C. of C. (dir., officer), Pi Lambda Theta. Roman Catholic. Home: 35483 Heritage Ln Farmington MI 48024 Office: Community Living Centers Inc 33229 Grand River St Farmington MI 48024

WAGNER, PATRICK A., psychologist; b. Indpls., Feb. 7, 1946; s. Horace Edwin and Maxine (Millikin) W.; student Rose Poly. Inst., 1964-66; A.B., Ind. U., 1969, M.S., 1971, Ph.D., 1976. Staff psychometrist Ind. U. Developmental Tng. Center, 1971-72; sch. psychologist Met. Sch. Dist. Martinsville (Ind.), 1976-77; staff psychologist Marion County Assn. for Retarded Citizens, Indpls., 1977-78; dir. psychol. services New Hope Found. of Ind., Indpls., 1978—; part-time prof. Ind. Central U., 1981; guest lectr. on mental retardation to local univs. Cert. sch. psychologist, Ind. Dept. Pub. Instrn.; cert. pvt. practice psychologist, Ind. Bd. of Examiners. Mem. Am. Psychol. Assn., Ind. Psychol. Assn., Central Ind. Psychol. Assn., Nat. Assn. Sch. Psychologists, Am. Assn. Mental Deficiency, AAAS, Nat. Assn. of Disability Examiners, Biofeedback Soc. Ind. Home: 1710 Centurion Pkwy Indianapolis IN 46260 Office: New Hope Found of Ind 8450 N Payne Rd Indianapolis IN 46268

WAGNER, RICHARD, baseball exec.; b. Central City, Nebr., Oct. 19, 1927; s. John Howard and Esther Marie (Wolken) W.; student public schs., Central City; m. Gloria Jean Larsen, May 10, 1950; children—Randolph Greg, Cynthia Kaye. Gen. mgr. Lincoln (Nebr.) Baseball Club, 1955-58; mgr. Pershing Mcpl. Auditorium, Lincoln, 1958-61; exec. staff Ice Capades, Inc., Hollywood, Calif., 1961-63; gen. mgr. Sta. KSAL, Salina, Kans., 1963-65; dir. promotion and sales St. Louis Nat. Baseball Club, 1965-66; gen. mgr. Forum, Inglewood, Calif., 1966-67; asst. to exec. v.p. Cin. Reds, 1967-70, asst. to pres., 1970-74, v.p. adminstrn., 1975, exec. v.p., 1975-77, exec. v.p., gen. mgr., from 1977 now pres., gen. mgr.; pres., dir. N.Platte (Nebr.) Broadcasting, Inc., 1972—. Served with USNR, 1945-47, 50-52. Named Exec. of Yr., Minor League Baseball, Sporting News, 1958. Mem. Internat. Assn. Arena Mgrs. Republican. Methodist. Office: Cincinnati Reds 100 Riverfront Stadium Cincinnati OH 45202

WAGNER, RICHARD GORDON, orthodontist; b. Primghar, Iowa, Nov. 26, 1926; s. James A. and Iva F. (O'Donnell) W.; D.D.S., U. Iowa, 1951, M.S. in Orthodontics, 1952; m. Dorothy Y. Van Dyke, Sept. 17, 1949; children—Richard Wayne, David Van. Practice dentistry, specializing in orthodontics, Sioux City, 1953—. Head profl. div. United Fund, 1969, head advanced gifts div., 1970-71; adult leader Fellowship Christian Athletes, 1973—. Mem. Sioux City Community Schs. Dist. Bd., 1973-77, pres., 1977-80. Served with USAF, 1952-53. Recipient Outstanding Service award Sertoma, 1957; Disting. Service award Sioux City Jaycees, 1961, Kiwanis Club, 1978. Mem. Sioux City Dental Soc. (pres. 1959—), Iowa Orthodontic Soc. (pres. 1968-69, 74—), Am. Assn. Orthodontists (trustee representing Iowa), Iowa Alumni Assn. Sioux City (co-chmn. 1971—). Clubs: Sertoma (pres. 1959-60), North High Booster (co-chmn. 1972) (Sioux City). Home: 3917 Sylvian Way Sioux City IA 51104 Office: 620 Sioux City Fed Plaza Bldg Sioux City IA 51101

WAGNER, VERNON E., med. assn. exec., state legislator; b. Golden Valley, N.D., June 13, 1926; s. Alex R. and Katie Wagner; B.S., N.D. State U., 1948. Pharmacist, Bismarck, N.D., 1948-67; asst. exec. sec. N.D. Med. Assn., Bismarck, 1967-73, exec. sec., 1972-80, exec. v.p., 1980—; mem. N.D. Ho. of Reps., 1963—. Mem. N.D. Pharm. Assn. (pres. 1962—), Am. Assn. Med. Soc. Execs. Republican. Lutheran. Home: 2102 N Washington St Bismarck ND 58501 Office: PO Box 1198 Bismarck ND 58502

WAGNER, VICTOR GUSTAVE, cons. engr.; b. Waterloo, Wis., Oct. 25, 1925; s. Walter V. and Hilda E. W.; B.S.C.E., U. Wis., Madison, 1949; m. Mary Ann Veith, June 22, 1946; children—Vickie M. Oslos, Richard L., Dianne M. Walls, Steven A., Daniel N., Donald V. Successively asst. san. engr., san. engr., chief water pollution control sect. Ind. Bd. Health, 1949-64; field engr., dir. san. engring. Can-Tex Industries, 1964-70; prin. engr., dir. environ. services mktg. Howard Needles Tammen & Bergendoff, Indpls., 1970—. Former chmn. troop com. Boy Scouts Am.; coach jr. baseball, Little League Football. Served with USNR, 1943-45. Registered profl. engr., Ind.; recipient L.L. Larson Safety award Ind. Water Pollution Control Assn., 1969; diplomate Am. Acad. Environ. Engrs. Fellow ASCE; mem. Am. Water Works Assn., Nat. Soc. Profl. Engrs., Water Pollution Control Fedn. (pres. 1976; Bedell award). Home: 5622 Meadowood Dr Speedway IN 46224 Office: Howard Needles Tammen and Bergendoff 3333 Founders Ln Indianapolis IN 46268

WAHAB, MARY O'HEARN, ednl. cons.; b. Detroit, Mar. 5, 1933; d. Maurice Michael and Genevieve (Clor) O'H.; B.A., Siena Heights Coll., 1960; postgrad. Mich. State U., 1961, Wayne State U., 1963, 65, 66, U. Detroit Coll. Law, 1981—; M.A., Oakland U., 1977, U. Detroit, 1981—; m. Edward Wahab, Aug. 10, 1968. Tchr. English, jr. high sch., Des Moines, 1952-55, Chgo., 1955-62, Warren, Mich., 1962-77; tchr. English, sr. high sch., Warren, 1977-79, lang. arts cons., 1979—. Mem. Am. Bar Assn., NEA, Mich. Edn. Assn., Warren Edn. Assn., Assn. Supervision and Curriculum Devel., Council Basic Edn., Mich. Assn. Affective Edn., NOW, Mensa. Club: Mich. Masters Swimmers. Home: 714 Barclay St Troy MI 48098 Office: 12101 Lachene St Warren MI 48093

WAHBA, GRACE, statistician; b. Washington, Aug. 3, 1934; d. Harry and Anne Goldsmith; B.A., Cornell U., 1956; M.A., U. Md., 1962; Ph.D., Stanford U., 1966; m. A.J. Wahba, 1955 (div. 1964); 1 son, Jeffrey; m. 2d, R.E. Moore, 1972 (div. 1976). Research mathematician Ops. Research, Inc., Silver Spring, Md., 1957-61; systems analyst IBM Corp., 1962-66; postdoctoral research asso. Stanford U., 1967; mem. faculty U. Wis., Madison, 1967—; vis. prof. Stanford U., U. Calif., Santa Cruz, Oxford (Eng.) U., Weizmann Inst. Sci., Israel, Math. Research Center, Madison; fellow St. Cross Coll., Oxford U.; cons. to govt. and industry. Lady Davis fellow Technion, Haifa, Israel. Fellow Inst. Math. Stats. (council 1976-79), Am. Statis. Assn.; mem. Soc. Indsl. and Applied Math. (council 1980—), Am. Math. Soc., Bernouilli Soc., Sigma Xi. Co-developer methods for computerized curve and surface smoothing and model fitting. Address: Dept Statistics U Wis 1210 W Dayton St Madison WI 53706

WAHEED, SHAMAIL, fin. mgmt. co. exec.; b. Pakistan, Sept. 28, 1947; came to U.S., 1972, naturalized, 1980; s. Abdul K. and Saleema W.; B.S.E.E., U. Peshawar (Pakistan), 1969; M.S., Ill. Inst. Tech., 1979; m. Maureen Waheed, Sept. 7, 1974; children—Adam, Aaron. Project mgr. NALCO Chem Co., Northbrook, Ill., 1973-76; mgr. communication systems Chgo. Bd. Options Exchange, 1976-79; mgr. tech. services GATX Corp., Chgo., 1979-80; dir. data processing services ITT Fin. Mgmt. Co., Chippewa Falls, Wis., 1980—. Mem. IEEE, Assn. Computing Machinery. Club: University (Chgo.). Office: PO Box 700 Data Dr Chippewa Falls WI 54729

WAHL, ROSALIE E., state justice; b. Gordon, Kans., Aug. 27, 1924; d. Claude William and Gertrude (Patterson) Erwin; B.A., U. Kans., 1946; J.D., William Mitchell Coll. Law, 1967; m. Roswell W. Wahl, 1946 (div. 1972); children—Christopher Roswell, Sara Emilie, Timothy Eldon, Mark Patterson, Jenny Caroline. Admitted to Minn. bar, 1967; practice in Mpls., 1967-77; asso. justice Minn. Supreme Ct., 1977—; adj. prof. criminal law U. Minn. Law Sch., 1972-73; clin. prof. William Mitchell Coll. Law, 1973-77; instr., lectr. continuing edn. programs. Mem. Nat. Assn. Women Lawyers, Am. Judicature Soc., Am. Bar Assn., Minn. Women Lawyers Assn., Minn. Trial Lawyers Assn., Minn. Bar Assn. Author: Misdemeanors and Moving Traffic Violations Manual, 1973; also handbook. Address: 230 State Capitol Saint Paul MN 55155*

WAISBROT, ANTHONY JOHN, social worker; b. Stevens Point, Wis., Mar. 14, 1943; s. Emil N. and Rose (Wanta) W.; B.S. in Psychology, U. Wis., Madison, 1965; M.S.W., U. Minn., Mpls., 1969; m. Ann Walsh, Aug. 28, 1965; children—James, Paul. Child welfare social worker Portage County Dept. Social Services, Stevens Point, 1965-67; teaching and research asst. U. Minn., 1967-69; spl. project counselor Hennepin County Ct. Services, Mpls., also social worker Head Start, Mpls. Public Schs., 1968-69; juvenile ct. social worker Portage County Dept. Social Services, 1969-70; clin. social worker dept. psychiatry Marshfield (Wis.) Clinic, 1970—. Mental health chmn. Stevens Point Jaycees. Fellow Wis. Soc. Clin. Social Work (pres. 1977-78); mem. Acad. Cert. Social Workers (cert.), Am. Group Psychotherapy Assn., Am. Assn. Marriage and Family Therapists, Nat. Assn. Social Workers (pres. North Central Wis. chpt. 1972-73). Contbr. to Law Enforcement Science and Technology, Vol. 1, 1966. Home: 1141 W Briarwood St Marshfield WI 54449 Office: Dept of Psychiatry Marshfield Clinic 1000 N Oak Ave Marshfield WI 54449

WAITE, LOUIS EDWARD, driver leasing co. exec.; b. Roaring Springs, Pa., Feb. 11, 1926; s. Clarence Earl and Bessie Ruth (Hoover) W.; student Oberlin (Ohio) Coll.; m. Frances Clara Jackson, Dec. 26, 1950; children—Yvonne Bessie, Louis Edward, Duane Douglas, John Thomas. Diesel engr. City of Oberlin, 1948-50; from driver to regional mgr. REA Express, 1950-70; truck transp. mgr. Inland Container Corp., Indpls., 1970-76; v.p. T.L.I. Inc., St. Louis, 1976—, also dir.; dir. I.T.I. Drayage Co., Transco Logistics Co. Served with inf. AUS, 1944-45; ETO. Decorated Combat Inf. badge; named Ky. col., 1972. Mem. Am. Trucking Assn. (dir. pvt. carrier conf.), Driver Leasing Council Am., Mo. Truck and Bus Assn., S.P.E.B.S.Q.A. Republican. Baptist. Clubs: High Hat (life) (Indpls.); Shriners. Home: 2265 Brook Dr Florissant MO 63033 Office: 8 Progress Pkwy Saint Louis MO 63043

WAITKUS, PHILLIP ANTHONY, polymer chemist; b. Sheboygan, Wis., Oct. 27, 1939; s. Felix Anton and Martha Helen (Brotz) W.; B.A., Ripon (Wis.) Coll., 1961; M.A., Wesleyan U., Middletown, Conn., 1963; Ph.D., Tulane U., New Orleans, 1967; m. Audrey Ann Ayo, Jan. 16, 1965; children—Mark Edward, Patrick Anthony. Chemist, Plastics Engring. Co., 1966-70; chief chemist, 1970—. Vice pres., fin. chmn. Sheboygan County Receiving Home, 1970-73; cubmaster, asst. scoutmaster Boy Scouts Am., 1975-79; mem. alumni bd. Ripon Coll., 1970-72. Recipient Scouters Key Boy Scouts Am. Roman Catholic. Club: Sheboygan Noon Optimist (pres. 1969-70). Patentee in field. Home: 2412-A Crosscreek Dr Sheboygan WI 53081 Office: 3518 Lakeshore Rd Sheboygan WI 53081

WAKEMAN, THOMAS GEORGE, engr.; b. Watertown, N.Y., June 28, 1945; s. George Lewis and Naomi Agnes W.; B.S.M.E., Ohio U., 1968; M.S., U. Cin., 1971; m. Connie Anne Wakeman, Aug. 31, 1968; 1 son, Kenneth. Design engr. Gen. Electric Co., Evandale, Ohio, 1968-78, engring. mgr., 1978—. Mem. AIAA, Sigma Xi, Sigma Gamma Tau. Republican. Roman Catholic. Research on high temperature material erosion; patentee in field. Home: 7793 Kennesaw Dr West Chester OH 45069 Office: Newman Way Evendale OH 45215

WALBERT, RICHARD B., stock exchange exec.; b. Milford, Ill., 1916; student Northwestern U. Former pres., dir. Halsey Stuart and Co., Chgo., former vice chmn. exec. com., dir. Bache & Co. Inc.; now chmn. Midwest Stock Exchange, Chgo.; dir. Northwestern Steel and Wire Co. Address: Midwest Stock Exchange 120 S LaSalle St Chicago IL 60603*

WALCHIRK, OSCAR, educator; b. Chgo., Dec. 14, 1919; s. Morris Wolf and Zelda Potash (Goldberg) W.; student Woodrow Wilson Jr. Coll., 1937-39; B.Ed., Ill. State U., 1941; postgrad. Northwestern U., 1942; M.A., U. Chgo., 1946, postgrad. (Kellogg Found. fellow), 1958-59; postgrad. U. Ill., 1974, 80-81; m. Effie Louise Crane, Feb. 23, 1943; children—Judith Deborah Walchirk Kotzin, Susan Hanna Walchirk Wolowitz. Tchr., Sheldon (Ill.) Community High Sch., 1941-42; psychologist VA, Great Lakes, Ill., 1946-48; dir. admissions, records and counseling Chgo. State U., 1948-67; asso. prof. counseling Wilson Jr. Coll., Chgo., 1967-71; prof. counseling Kennedy-King Coll., Chgo., 1971—. Bd. dirs., mem. exec. bd. Henry N. Hart and Hyde Park Jewish Community Center, 1958—, pres., 1964-66; mem. Fifth Ward Citizens Com., 1972—; trustee Rodfei Zedek Congregation, Chgo., 1978—. Served with USAAF, 1942-45. Mem. Am. Personnel and Guidance Assn., Ill. Personnel and Guidance Assn., Student Personnel Assn. for Tchr. Edn., Ill. Assn. Deans and Advisers to Men, Ill. Joint Council on Higher Edn., Cook County Coll. Tchrs. Union, Phi Delta Kappa, Sigma Tau Delta. Home: 5201 S Cornell Ave Chicago IL 60615 Office: Kennedy King College 6800 S Wentworth Ave Chicago IL 60621

WALCUTT, WAYNE W., indsl. engring. cons.; b. Columbus, Ohio, Apr. 15, 1929; s. Eugene W. and Marie A. (Koch) W.; B. Indsl. Engring., Ohio State U., 1952, postgrad., 1962-64; postgrad. Case Inst. Tech., 1954; m. Jo-Ann V. Kaiser, June 14, 1952; children—John W., Richard B., Christina A. Indsl. engr. TRW, Cleve. and Columbus, Ohio, 1953-60; prodn. mgr., asst. to gen. mgr. Ray Data Corp., Columbus, 1960-62; planning engr. Western Electric Co., Columbus, 1962-64; dir. indsl. engring. Roberts Assos., Columbus, 1964-66; staff indsl. engr. Lancaster Colony Corp., Columbus, 1966-70; cons., v.p., asso. Ohio Hosp. Mgmt. Services, Columbus, 1971-80; corp. staff indsl. engr. Ashland Chem. Co., Columbus, 1980—; vis. lectr. Ohio State U., Capital U. Mem. organizing com. East Side High Sch. Sci. Club, Columbus; mem. Columbus Tech. Council, 1981-82, Ohio Engrs. Public Affairs Forum, 1982—. Registered profl. engr., Ohio, W.Va., Calif. Mem. Am. Inst. Indsl. Engrs. (sr. mem., dir. local chpt. 1965-69, 78-80, treas. 1980-81, pres. 1969-70, nat. v.p. 1970-72, state public affairs chmn. 1981-82), Hosp. Mgmt. Systems Soc., Swiss Helvitia Maennerchor, Ohio State U Alumni Assn., Scabbard and Blade, Alpha Pi Mu. Republican. Roman Catholic. Home: 4025 Riverview Dr Columbus OH 43220 Office: Ashland Chemical Co PO Box 2219 Columbus OH 43216

WALDBILLIG, RONALD JOSEPH, retail food co. exec.; b. Dubuque, Iowa, Oct. 29, 1941; s. Carl August and Kathryn (Scholtes) W.; student Indians Hills Community Coll., 1967-68; m. Marcella Rae Miles, Aug. 24, 1968; children—Laura, Brian, Olivia. With Nabisco, Dubuque, Iowa, 1963-67; with Hy-Vee Food Stores Inc., Chariton, Iowa, 1968—, asst. data processing mgr., 1969—. Bd. dirs. Kiddie Kampus Pre-School; mem. Sacred Heart Parish Council. Served with USMC, 1960-63. Mem. Assn. for Systems Mgmt., Central Iowa DOS Users Group. Roman Catholic. Club: K.C. Home: 633 Auburn Ave Chariton IA 50049 Office: 1801 Osceola Ave Chariton IA 50049

WALDEN, JAMES WILLIAM, accountant, educator; b. Jellico, Tenn., Mar. 5, 1936; s. William Evert and Bertha L. (Faulkner) W.; B.S., Miami U., Oxford, Ohio, 1963; M.B.A., Xavier U., Cin., 1966; m. Eva June Selvia, Jan. 16, 1957; 1 son, James William. Tchr. math. Middletown (Ohio) City Sch. Dist., 1963-67, Fairfield (Ohio) High Sch., 1967-69; instr. accounting Sinclair Community Coll., Dayton, Ohio, 1969-72, asst. prof., 1972-75, asso. prof., 1975-78, prof., 1978—; cons., public acct. Active CAP. Served with USAF, 1954-59. Mem. Butler County Torch Club, Pub. Accountants Soc. Ohio (pres. S.W. chpt. 1972-73), Nat. Soc. Pub. Accountants, Greater Hamilton Estate Planning Council, Beta Alpha Psi. Home: 187 Westbrook Dr Hamilton OH 45013 Office: Sinclair Community Coll 444 W 3d St Dayton OH 45402

WALDEN, RAWLS WADDEY, mech. engr.; b. Phila., Aug. 13, 1937; s. James Burrell and Margaret Ellen (Waddey) W.; student Centralia (Ill.) Jr. Coll., 1958; summer student Detroit Edison Inst., 1966; B.S.M.E., U. Ill., 1966, M.S.M.E., 1967, M.B.A., 1980; m. Mary Jane Sievers, Aug. 31, 1962; children—Rawls Waddey II, Leslie, Earl, Joseph. Designer Carroll-Hanneman Cons. Engrs., 1958-66; power plant results engr. Ill. Power Co., Decatur, 1967-71, power plant maintenance engr., 1971-72, environ. engr., 1972-73, environ. affairs supr. air and water pollution control, 1973-77, supr. water quality, 1977—; lectr. in field. Leader Boy Scouts Am., 1967-69, now fund raiser; leader Cub Scouts, 1976-78; treas. Presch. bd., 1968-69; Mem. Mayor's Adv. Com., Mt. Zion, Ill., 1979-81; mem. Mt. Zion Planning Commn., 1980-81; mem. village Bd. Trustees, Mt. Zion, 1981—; fund raiser Jr. Achievement. Served with Arty., AUS, 1955-56. Registered profl. engr., Ill. Mem. ASME (chmn. South Central Ill. group 1975-76), Ill. Soc. Profl. Engrs. (chmn. energy com. 1979-81), Nat. Soc. Profl. Engrs., Chi Gamma Iota. Republican. Presbyterian (deacon). Clubs: Lake Wildwood (Varna, Ill.), Masons, Shriners. Contbr. articles to profl. jours. Home: 1345 Nolan Ct Mount Zion IL 62549 Office: 500 S 27th St Decatur IL 62525

WALDENMYER, DALE RICHARD, real estate exec.; b. Butler, Pa.; s. John Elmer and Evelyn Mae (Eshenbaugh) W.; student Pa. State U., 1941-42, U. Pitts., 1943; 1 son, William Bradford. Owner, Home Engring. Co., Dover, Ohio, 1952-68; pres. D. Waldenmyer, Inc., builder homes and apts., 1958-79; pres. D. & N. Devel., Inc., developer residential subdivs., 1960—; pres. Waldenmyer Realty, Inc., residential and comml. sales, 1965-78. Mem. Community Improvement Corp., 1970—; mem. Tuscarawas County Planning Commn., 1966-78, chmn. subdiv. commn., 1967-71; chmn. Stark County Apt. Council, 1976. Bd. dirs. YMCA, 1958-59. Named Boss of the Yr., Dover Jr. C. of C., 1971, Realtor of Yr. Tuscarawas County, 1972. Mem. Nat. Assn. Home Builders (hon. life dir.), Ohio Home Builders Assn. (hon. life trustee; nat. rep. 1980-81), Ohio Apt. Council (vice chmn. 1977), Ohio Apt. Assn. (sec. 1978), Ohio Developers Council, Urban Land Inst., Tuscarawas County Home Builders (pres. 1962-63), Tuscarawas County C. of C. (pres. 1972), Tuscarawas County Realtors (pres. 1971). Mem. United Ch. of Christ. Mason

(Shriner), Elk. Clubs: Union Country, Schoenbrunn Racquet. Address: 326 E 18th St Dover OH 44622

WALDMAN, PETER DAVID, architect; b. N.Y.C., Sept. 10, 1943; s. Albert Jerome and Elizabeth (Renner) W.; A.B., Princeton U., 1965, M.F.A. in Architecture, 1967; m. Nancy Davila, Dec. 27, 1969; children—Ava Lena, Beth Davila. Vol., Peace Corps, Arequipa, Peru, 1967-69; asst. prof. architecture Princeton U., 1969-80; asso. prof. architecture U. Cin., 1980—; architect Michael Graves, Architect, Princeton, N.J., 1969-73; prin. Peter Waldman, Architect, Princeton, 1974-80, Cin., 1980—; vis. critic R.I. Sch. Design, 1979, U. Va., 1980, U. Miami, 1980. Mem. AIA, N.J. Soc. Architects. Jewish. Home: 254 Elm Ave Cincinnati OH 45215 Office: 715 DAA U Cin Cincinnati OH 45221

WALDMAN, SAUL J., utility exec.; b. Lynbrook, N.Y., Jan. 10, 1931; A.B. in Journalism, Syracuse (N.Y.) U., 1952, postgrad., 1952-53; married; 3 children. Research analyst Prudential Ins. Co. Am., Newark, 1957-61; editor, pub. Hazlet (N.J.) Beacon weekly, 1961-62; sr. writer United Med. Service, N.Y.C., 1962-63; account exec. Ray Josephs Public Relations, Ltd., N.Y.C., 1963-64; asst. mgr. newspaper info. service Am. Newspaper Pubs. Assn., N.Y.C., 1964-68; with Chase Manhattan Bank, N.Y.C., 1968-75, v.p., acting dir. corp. communication, to 1975; mgr. public affairs Detroit Edison Co., 1975-80, asst. v.p. public affairs, 1980-81, v.p. public affairs, 1981—; founder Conf. Corp. House Organ Producers; mem. public affairs com. Atomic Indsl. Forum. Vice pres., chmn. public relations com., pres. Detroit chpt. United Cerebral Palsy Assn. Served to lt. (j.g.) USNR, 1953-57. Mem. Internat. Indsl. TV Assn., Nat. Investor Relations Inst., Public Relations Soc. Am. (dir. Detroit chpt.), Econ. Club Detroit, Sigma Delta Chi. Clubs: Detroit Press, Detroit Athletic.

WALDORF, GENE, state senator; b. Feb. 25, 1936; student Drexel Inst. Tech.; B.E.E., U. Minn.; m. Bernadine Riemer; children—Jeanne, Paul, Bridget, Renee, John, David. Design engrng. specialist 3M Co., St. Paul; mem. Minn. Senate, 1980—. Mem. Phalen Area Community Council, Cursillo Movement, 19—, Archdiocesan Family Life Commn. Roman Catholic. Mem. Democratic-Farmer-Labor party. Office: 235 State Capitol St Paul MN 55155*

WALDORF, LEONARD ANTHONY, computer software co. exec.; b. Detroit, Jan. 4, 1944; s. Clarence Anthony and Rose Agatha (Sauer) W.; student Drake U., 1962-65; m. Janis Lee Person, June 26, 1965; 1 dau., Ann Marie. Bookkeeper, Des Moines Nat. Bank (Iowa), 1963-64; systems mgr. Brenton Banks, Des Moines, 1964-75; mgmt. cons. Wolf & Co., Des Moines, 1975-77; pres. Waldorf Corp., West Des Moines, 1977—. Mem. Assn. Systems Mgmt., Assn. for Computing Machinery. Democrat. Roman Catholic. Developer of Bancado, a set of minicomputer programs for small banks. Home and office: 400 34th St West Des Moines IA 50265

WALDRON, BECKY JOHNSTON, realtor; b. Mpls., Feb. 24, 1920; d. Josiah U. and Myrtle (Harlan) Johnston; student Vassar Coll., 1937-39; B.A., Iowa U., 1941; m. Charles Philip Waldron, Dec. 10, 1941; children—Wendy Churchill Waldron Brandow, Charles Philip. Psychometrist, psychology dept. Iowa State U., Ames, 1945-47; realtor Neil Adamson Co., Inc., Des Moines, 1965-75; realtor, pub. relations dir. Iowa Realty Co. Inc., Des Moines, 1975—. Recipient Americanism award and medal Jewish War Vets., 1962. Mem. Nat. Assn. Real Estate Bds., Am. Jr. League Assn., Nat. Soc. Colonial Dames Am., Kappa Kappa Gamma, Psi Chi. Republican. Episcopalian. Clubs: Wakonda, Embassy, Proteus (Des Moines). Home: 25 35th St Des Moines IA 50312 Office: 2405 Ingersoll Des Moines IA 50312

WALDRON, KENNETH LYNN, lawyer; b. Cape Girardeau, Mo., Oct. 18, 1941; s. Leonard Vernal and Edna Marion (Baskerville) W.; student Westminster Coll., 1959-61; B.S., Mo. U., 1963, J.D., 1966; m. Norma Kay Norwood, Mar. 25, 1967; children—Leonard Andrew, Matthew Cox, Charles Phillips. Salesman, Nat. Biscuit Co., 1963-66; admitted to Mo. bar, 1966; asso. firm Buerkle and Lowes, Jackson, Mo., 1966-71; practiced in Jackson, 1971—; mem. firm Waldron & Turnbow; city atty. Jackson; dir. Stonewall Enterprises, Inc., Scott City Foods, Inc., Heck's Supermarket, Inc., A & V Foods, Inc., Multi-States Sales, Inc., Jackson Kids, Stuffy Ltd., Manassa Sound Systems, Inc., Asso. Inventory Specialists, Inc. Active Boy Scouts Am. Bd. dirs. Southeast Mo. Med. Center, Inc. Served to capt. AUS, 1966-68. Mem. Am. Trial Lawyers Assn., Mo. Trial Attys. Assn., Am. Soc. Law and Medicine, Mo. State Bar, Nat. Inst. Municipal Legal Officers, Jackson Jaycees (past state and regional legal counsel, dir.), Am. Legion (legal counsel). Clubs: Masons, Rotary. Home: 957 Shady Ln Jackson MO 63755 Office: 417 N High St Jackson MO 63755

WALDSMITH, JAMES WALTER, editor, publishing exec.; b. Lake Forest, Ill., July 20, 1951; s. Robert Marlin and Lois Elizabeth (Poppenger) W.; B.A., Miami U., Oxford, Ohio, 1973; m. Marilyn Sue Miller, June 21, 1975; 1 son, Bradley Scott. Reporter, Linden News Pub. Co., Columbus, Ohio, 1973-74, editor Linden-N.E. News and Northland News, 1974-76, news dir. Suburban News Publications, Inc. (formerly Linden News Pub. Co. and Tri-Village Pub. Co.); 1976—, including news dir. 9 Columbus community/suburban newspapers and editor Upper Arlington News, Tri-Village News, Northland News, Beechwold/Clintonville News. Mem. adv. council Franklin County (Ohio) br. Am. Cancer Soc., 1981. Recipient commendation Ohio Eta chpt. Sigma Phi Epsilon, 1973, Northland Jaycees Aux., 1975, Columbus Literacy Council, 1980, Franklin County Campfire Girls, 1978, Northland Community Council, 1975, Columbus No. Lions Club, 1981. Mem. Grandview Area Bus. Assn. (pres. 1980). Office: 919 Old W Henderson Rd Columbus OH 43220

WALDSTEIN, ARNE F., farm mgmt. and appraisal co. exec., state senator; b. Alta, Iowa, Jan. 17, 1925; s. Arthur and Anna Waldstein; B.S., Iowa State U., 1949; m. Marianne Aust, June 17, 1951; children—Fredric, Arne, Elizabeth, Mark. Farm loan rep. Equitable of Iowa Ins. Co., Ft. Dodge, 1950-51; farm mgr., dist. mgr. Opekasit, Inc., Albany, Ga., 1951-54; partner, pres. Stalcup Agrl. Service, Inc., Storm Lake, Iowa, from 1955; mem. Iowa Senate, 1979—. Pres., Storm Lake Park Bd. Served with USAAC, 1944-45. Mem. Am. Soc. Farm Mgrs and Rural Appraisers. Republican. Lutheran. Club: Elks. Office: State Senate Office State Capitol Des Moines IA 50319*

WALENT, STANLEY ANTHONY, safety cons.; b. Chgo., May 12, 1932; s. Stanley and Stella (Rydecki) W.; student Wilson Jr. Coll., 1952-54; B.S., Loyola U., 1960; M.Social and Indsl. Relations, 1964; m. Jacqueline T. Andreski, June 20, 1959; children—Pamela, Michelle, Mark, Christopher, Alyssa, Gregory. Clk. audit dept. 1st Nat. Bank of Chgo., 1956; weather clk. United Airlines, 1956-58; supr. Am. Can Co., 1960-67; safety engr. Aetna Life and Casualty Ins., Chgo., 1967-72; sr. safety engr. Allstate Ins. Co., Northbrook, Ill., 1972-75, CNA Ins. Co., Chgo., 1975; safety cons. M & M Protection Consultants, Chgo., 1975—. Served with C.E., U.S. Army, 1954-56. Recipient Good Hands award Allstate Ins. Co., 1974. Mem. Am. Soc. Safety Engrs., Constrn. Safety Assn. Am. Home: 5243 W 87th St Oaklawn IL 60453 Office: 222 S Riverside Plaza Chicago IL 60606

WALGREEN, CHARLES RUDOLPH, III, retail store exec.; b. Chgo., Nov. 11, 1935; s. Charles Rudolph and Mary Ann (Leslie) W.; B.S. in Pharmacy, U. Mich., 1958; m. Kathleen Bonsignore Allen, Jan. 23, 1977; children—Charles Richard, Tad Alexander, Kevin Patrick, Leslie Ray, Chris Patrick. With Walgreen Co., Chgo., 1952—, adminstrv. asst. to v.p. store ops., 1965-66, dist. mgr., 1967-68, regional dir., 1968-69, v.p., 1969, pres., 1969-75, chmn., 1976—, also dir.; dir. Sanborn Hnos., Mexico City. Mem. bus. adv. council Chgo. Urban League. Bd. dirs. Jr. Achievement Chgo., Chgo. Crime Commn., Internat. Coll. Surgeons Hall Fame and Mus. Surg. Scis.; trustee Nat. Jewish Hosp., Denver. Mem. Am. Found. Pharm. Edn. (chmn., dir. 1971—), Nat. Assn. Chain Drug Stores (dir.), Ill. Retail Mchts. Assn. (dir. 1966—), Young Pres.'s Orgn., Am., Ill. pharm. assns., Delta Sigma Phi. Clubs: Economic, Commercial, Tavern (Chgo.); Great Lakes Cruising; Yacht and Country (Stuart, Fla.); Exmoor Country (Highland Park, Ill.). Office: 200 Wilmot Rd Deerfield IL 60015

WALGREN, ROBERT LOUIS, utilities co. exec.; b. Platte Center, Nebr., Sept. 19, 1934; s. Oliver Edgar and Lucille L. W.; B.S. in Edn., U. Nebr., 1957; m. Shirley E. Irwin, Aug. 20, 1955; children—Charles D., Sue E., Craig I. With Nebr. Public Power Dist., 1959—, asst. treas., 1971-72, wage and salary adminstr., 1972-73, personnel mgr., 1973—. Mem. bd. Platte Center High Sch. Dist., 1960-62, sec., 1963-66; drive chmn. United Fund, 1971-72, pres. bd. dirs., 1974; bd. dirs. Columbus chpt. ARC, 1978—, v.p., 1979-80, pres., 1981—; mem. exec. bd. Mid-Am. council Petah-La-Shauro Dist., Boy Scouts Am., 1974-81, dist. chmn., 1979-80, dr. chmn., 1979-80. Mem. Am. Soc. Personnel Adminstrs., Lincoln Personnel Mgmt. Assn., Am. Mgmt. Assn., Columbus Area Personnel Assn., Columbus Area C. of C. (v.p. 1981-82). Republican. Methodist. Clubs: Lions (past pres.), Elks, Masons, Shriners. Home: 4607 Hill Crest Dr Columbus NE 68601 Office: 1414 15th St Columbus NE 68601

WALI, MOHAN KISHEN, educator; b. Kashmir, India, Mar. 1, 1937; s. Jagan Nath and Somavati (Wattal) W.; came to U.S., 1969, naturalized, 1975; B.Sc., U. Jammu and Kashmir (India), 1957; M.Sc., U. Allahabad (India), 1960; Ph.D., U. B.C. (Can.), 1970; m. Sarla Safaya, Sept. 25, 1960; children—Pamela, Promod. Lectr. S.P. Coll., Srinagar, Kashmir, India, 1963-65; research fellow U. Copenhagen (Denmark), 1965-66; grad. fellow U. B.C., Vancouver, 1967-69; asst. prof. biology U. N.D., Grand Forks, 1969-73, asso. prof., 1973-79, prof., 1979—, Hill research prof., summer 1973, dir. Forest River Biology Area Field Sta., 1970-79; staff ecologist Grand Forks (N.D.) Energy Research Lab., U.S. Dept. Interior, part-time, 1974-75; dir. Project Reclamation, U. N.D., 1975—, spl. asst. to pres. univ., 1977—. Vice chmn. N.D. Air Pollution Adv. Council. Recipient Outstanding Research award, Sigma Xi-U. N.D., 1975; B.C. Gamble Disting. Teaching and Service award, 1977. Mem. Ecol. Soc. Am. (chmn. sect. internat. activities 1980—), British Ecol. Soc., Canadian Bot. Assn. (dir. ecology sect. 1976-79), Torrey Bot. Club, AAAS, Am. Soc. Agronomy, Am. Inst. Biol. Sci., Internat. Assn. Ecology, Internat. Soc. Soil Sci., N.D. Acad. Sci. (chmn. editorial com. 1979-81), Sigma Xi. Contbr. articles to profl. jours. Editor: Some Environmental Aspects of Strip-Mining in North Dakota, 1973; Prairie: A Multiple View, 1975; Practices and Problems of Land Reclamation in Western North America, 1975; Ecology and Coal Resource Development, 1979; sr. editor Reclamation Rev., 1976-80, chief editor, 1980-81; chief editor Reclamation & Revegetation Research, 1982—. Home: 3412 6th Ave N Grand Forks ND 58201

WALKER, ALICE GATES, real estate broker; b. Ill., Feb. 20, 1921; d. Clarence Thomas and Lela (Chenoweth) Gates; student Eastern Ill. U., 1938-41, Rutgers U., 1950; grad. Realtors Inst. Ill., 1973. Sec. to chmn. Civil Service, Rock Island, Ill. and N.Y.C., 1941 Fred Laifer, atty., Newark, 1946-48; exec. sec. to pres. and gen. mgr. Best Mfg. Co., Irvington, N.J., 1948-50; with Glaser-Steers Corp., Newark, 1950-59; real estate sales asso. Anne Sylvester's Realty Corner, Springfield, N.J., 1960-64; real estate broker Robert Carlisle, realtor, Charleston, Ill., 1965-74; owner, mgr. Alice Walker, Realtor, Charleston, 1974—. Bd. dirs. Charleston Community Theatre, 1976—. Mem. Nat., Ill. assns. realtors, Coles County Bd. Realtors (pres. 1977—), Women's Council Realtors, Charleston Bus. and Profl. Woman's Club (legis. chmn. 1977—), Am. Bus. and Profl. Women's Club. Republican. Clubs: Zonta, Women of the Moose. Home and Office: 1408 Division St Charleston IL 61920

WALKER, ARCHIE LEE, dietitian; b. Waco, Tex., June 25, 1927; s. Percy and Esther Pearl (Freeman) W.; B.S., Tuskegee Inst., 1949; postgrad. Prairie View Coll., 1955-56; M.A., Columbia U., 1966; m. Ferdie Louise Miller, Jan. 27, 1951; children—Gayle Louise Walker Richardson, Michael Miller, Sandra LaVonne. Instr. foods Ft. Worth Tex. Inst. Comml. Trades, 1949-51; instr., cafeteria supr. Prairie View (Tex.) Coll., 1953-56; asst. chief dietitian VA Hosp., Ft. Lyon, Colo., 1957-60, Topeka, 1960-65, Ann Arbor, Mich., 1966-67, chief dietitian, St. Louis, 1967—. Mem. Kirkwood (Mo.) R-7 Sch. Bd., 1972-75, also sec., v.p.; trustee Sta. KETC-TV, St. Louis, 1974-79, sec., 1976-79. Served with U.S. Army, 1951-53; col. Res. Mem. Am. Dietetic Assn., Am. Soc. Hosp. Food Service Adminstrs., St. Louis Dietetic Assn., Mo. Dietetic Assn., Omicron Nu, Omega Psi Phi. Democrat. Methodist. Home: 629 Villa Garden Kirkwood MO 63122 Office: Dietetic Service VA Med Center Saint Louis MO 63125

WALKER, C. BROOKS, mktg. research co. exec.; b. Dayton, Ohio, Nov. 22, 1940; s. Stephen Douglas and Marjorie (Brooks) W.; student Miami Univ., Oxford, Ohio, 1958-60; m. Suzanne Schick, Feb. 14, 1970; children—Jon, Dori. Salesman, John Hancock Ins. Co., Dayton, Ohio, 1963-66; field rep. A. C. Nielsen Co., Boston, 1966-67, N.Y.C., 1967-68, Cin., 1968-72, account exec., N.Y.C., 1972-73, Cherry Hill, N.J., 1974-75, sales mgr., Clinton, Iowa, 1975-78, v.p. sales, Northbrook, Ill., 1978—. Served with USAF, 1960-63. Mem. Food Industry Assn. Execs. Republican. Methodist. Home: 1042 Chatham Dr Palatine IL 60067 Office: Nielsen Plaza Northbrook IL 60062

WALKER, CHARLES, JR., chem. co. exec.; b. South Bend, Ind., June 18, 1937; s. Charles and Ollie Mae (Chapman) W.; student Central State U., Wilberforce, Ohio, 1957-61; m. Sue Forney, Dec. 31, 1959; children—Charles Derek, Shaun Lamont, Darin Anthony. Asst. personnel supr. Dow Corning Corp., Hemlock, Mich., 1969-70, personnel supr., Midland, Mich., 1970-71, plant personnel mgr., Hemlock, 1971-73, sales rep., Midland, 1973-74, govt. mktg. mgr., 1974-77, elastomers mktg. mgr., 1977-78, regional sales mgr., Cleve., 1978—. Bd. dirs. Big Bros. Am.; mem. loan exec. program United Fund. Served to capt. U.S. Army, 1962-69; Vietnam. Decorated Bronze Star. Mem. Akron Rubber Group, Am. Def. Preparedness Assn., Soc. Aerospace Materials and Process Engrs., Kappa Alpha Psi. Clubs: Sharon Golf, Tanglewood Country. Office: Dow Corning Corp 3737 Park St E Beachwood OH 44122

WALKER, CHARLES LEON, engrng. co. exec.; b. Calvert City, Ky., Feb. 14, 1933; s. Bennie and Amy Jennie (Qualls) W.; B.S., Murray State Coll., 1960; postgrad. Washington U., 1966-69; m. Neita Faye Harned, Dec. 25, 1958; children—Stephen Charles, Christopher Lee, Leisa Carol. Asst. plant engr. Thoms Industries, Hopkinsville, Ky., 1960-63; designer Bendy Engring. Co., St. Louis, 1964-68, mech. engr., 1969-73, asst. chief mech. engr., 1973-79, project mgr., 1979—. Served with C.E., AUS, 1953-55. Mem. AIME. Home: 1430 Jackson Ln Florissant MO 63031 Office: Bendy Engring Co 4260 Shoreline Dr Earth City MO 63045

WALKER, DAVID BROOKS, osteo. dermatologist; b. Fall River, Mass., Sept. 24, 1935; s. H. Brooks and Mary (Pendlebury) W.; B.A., Wesleyan U., Middletown, Conn., 1957; D.O., Kirksville Coll. Osteo. Medicine, 1963; m. Lois Toner, Jan. 1958; children—Karen Sue, Douglas Brooks, Wesley Todd, Nancy Howland, Michael Howland. Intern, Normandy Osteo. Hosps., St. Louis, 1963-64, mem. staff, 1964—, vice chief staff, 1972-73, chief staff, 1975, 76, 77, cons. dermatologist, 1967—; resident in dermatology Detroit Osteo. Hosp. Group, 1964-67; practice osteo. medicine specializing in dermatology, St. Louis, 1967—; asso. clin. prof. dermatology Kirksville Coll. Osteo. Medicine, 1967—; mem. Adv. Bd. Osteo. Specialists, 1972—, mem. exam. bd. dermatology, 1972—. Trustee Normandy Osteo. Hosps., 1976—. Diplomate Am. Osteo. Bd. Dermatology. Fellow Am. Osteo. Coll. Dermatology (pres. 1974); mem. Am. Osteo. Assn., Mo., St. Louis (sec. 1972—) assns. osteo. physicians and surgeons, Delta Kappa Epsilon. Episcopalian. Club: Nantucket Yacht. Contbr. articles to profl. jours. Home: 12669 Ladue Rd Saint Louis MO 63141 also 10 Walsh St Nantucket MA 02554 Office: 11245 Saint Charles Rock Rd Bridgeton MO 63044

WALKER, DOUGLAS ANTHONY, banker; b. St. Louis, Jan. 6, 1937; s. Douglas James and Anna Bernice (Powell) W.; B.S.C., St. Louis U., 1958, J.D., 1966; postgrad. U. Mo., Kansas City, 1962-65; m. Afra Jean Leavitt, June 18, 1960; children—Mary Elizabeth, Douglas Anthony. Mgmt. trainee Boyd's Inc., St. Louis, 1959-62; claims authorizer Social Security Adminstrn., HEW, Kansas City, Mo., 1962-66; admitted to Mo. bar, 1966; asso. firm Zimbalist, Sachs, Schramm & Branom, Clayton, Mo., 1966-71; partner firm Zimbalist, Schramm, & Walker, Clayton, 1972-75; individual practice law, Brentwood, Mo., 1975; trust officer United Mo. Banks, Kirkwood, 1975—; dir. Aschen Investment Co., Niemeyer Redevelopment Corp. Mcpl. judge, Hillsdale, Mo., 1969-74, Uplands Park, Mo., 1970-74, Margona, Mo., 1971-72; city atty. Velda Village Hills, Mo., 1972-75; dist. atty. Pattonville Bridgeton Terrace Fire Protection Dist., 1972-75. Served with USAR, 1958-59. Mem. Am. Bar Assn., Mo. Bar Assn., Met. St. Louis Bar Assn., St. Louis County Bar Assn., Am. Judicature Soc., Mo. Bankers Assn., Friends of St. Louis Art Mus., Mo. Bot. Garden, Friends of Public TV. Democrat. Roman Catholic. Club: Optimist. Home: 9370 Pine Ave Brentwood MO 63144 Office: 426 N Kirkwood Rd Kirkwood MO 63122

WALKER, DUNCAN EDWARD, air force officer; b. Washington, Aug. 2, 1942; s. Edward John and Katherine Edith (Duncan) W.; B.A. in Indsl. Psychology, N.Mex. State U., 1965; M.S. in Systems Mgmt., U. So. Calif., 1978; M.P.A., Golden Gate U., San Francisco, 1980. Commd. 2d lt. USAF, 1965, advanced through grades to lt. col., 1981; service in Vietnam and Korea; chief devel. and deployment br. Directorate of ICBM Requirements, SAC, Offutt AFB, Nebr., 1981—. Decorated Bronze Star, Meritorious Service medal, Air Force Commendation medal with three oak leaf clusters. Mem. Air Force Assn., Mental Health Assn. Democrat. Unitarian. Home: 1103 Ironwood Ct Apt 196 Bellevue NE 68005 Office: Hdqrs SAC Offutt AFB NE 68113

WALKER, ELVA MAE DAWSON, cons. health, hosps., aging; b. Everett, Mass., June 29, 1914; d. Charles Edward and Mary Elizabeth (Livingston) Dawson; R.N., Peter Bent Brigham Hosp., Boston, 1937; student Simmons Coll., 1935, U. Minn., 1945-48; m. Walter Willard Walker, Dec. 16, 1939 (div. 1969). Supr. nursery Wesson Maternity Hosp., Springfield, Mass., 1937-38; asst. supr. out-patient dept. Peter Bent Brigham Hosp., Boston, 1938-40; supr. surgery and out-patient dept. Univ. Hosps., Mpls., 1945. Chmn. Gov.'s Citizens Council on Aging, Minn., 1960-68, acting dir., 1962-66, Econ. Opportunity Com. Hennepin County, 1964-69; v.p., treas. Nat. Purity Soap & Chem. Co., 1968-69, pres., 1969-76, chmn. bd., 1976—; cons. on aging to Minn. Dept. Pub. Welfare, 1962-67; mem. nat. adv. council for Nurse Tng. Act, 1965-69, Com. Status on Women in Armed Services, 1967-70; dir. Nat. Council on the Aging, 1963-67, sec., 1965-67; dir. Planning Agy. for Hosps. of Met. Mpls., 1963—, United Hosp. Fund of Hennepin County, 1955—, Nat. Council Social Work Edn., 1966-68; vice chmn. Hennepin County Gen. Hosp. Adv. Bd., 1965-68; sec. Hennepin County Health Coalition, 1973; chmn. bd. dirs. Am. Rehab. Found, 1962-68, vice chmn., 1968-70; pres. bd. trustees Northwestern Hosp., 1956-59, Children's Hosp. Mpls., 1961-65; dir. Twin Cities Internat. Program for Youth Leaders and Social Workers, Inc., 1965-67; mem. community adv. council United Community Funds and Council Am., Inc., 1968, Nat. Assembly Social Policy and Devel., Inc., 1968—; mem. priorities determination com. United Fund Mpls., 1971; vice chmn. govt. specifications com. Soap and Detergent Assn., 1972-76, vice-chmn. indsl. and instn. com., 1974-76, chmn., 1976-78, bd. dirs., 1974—; candidate for Congress, 3d Minn. Dist., 1966; trustee Macalester Coll., Archie D. and Bertha H. Walker Found.; chmn. St. Mary's Jr. Coll. Bd., 1970-74, 78—; pres. U. Minn. Sch. Nursing Found., 1958-70. Mem. Am. Pub. Welfare Assn., Mpls. Med. Research Found., Minn. League Nursing (pres. 1971-73), Jr. League Mpls. Democrat. Presbyterian. Home: 3655 Northome Rd Wayzata MN 55391 Office: Nat Purity Soap & Chem Co 110 SE 5th Ave Minneapolis MN 55414

WALKER, FRANK BANGHART, pathologist; b. Detroit, June 14, 1931; s. Roger Venning and Helen Frances (Reade) W.; B.S., Union (N.Y.) Coll., 1951; M.D., Wayne State U., 1955, M.S., 1962; m. Virginia Elinor Granse, June 18, 1955; children—Nancy Anne, David Carl, Roger Osborne, Mark Andrew. Intern Detroit Meml. Hosp., 1955-56; resident Wayne State U. and affiliated hosps., Detroit, 1958-62; asso. pathologist Detroit Meml. Hosp. and Cottage Hosp., Grosse Pointe, Mich., 1962—; pathologist, dir. labs. South Macomb Hosp., Warren, Mich., 1966—; pathologist, dir. labs. Jennings Meml. Hosp., Detroit, 1971-79, Alexander Blain Hosp., Detroit, 1971—. Partner Langston, Walker & Assos., profl. corp., Grosse Pointe, 1968—. Instr. pathology Wayne State U. Med. Sch., Detroit, 1962-72, asst. clin. prof., 1972—. Pres. Mich. Assn. Blood Banks, 1969-70; mem. med. adv. com. ARC, 1972—; mem. Mich. Higher Edn. Assistance Authority, 1975-77. Trustee Alexander Blain Meml. Hosp., Detroit, 1974—, Detroit-Macomb Hosp. Assn., 1975—; bd. dirs. Wayne State Fund, 1971—. Served to capt., M.C., AUS, 1956-58. Diplomate Am. Bd. Pathology. Mem. Wayne State U. Alumni Assn. (bd. govs. 1968-71), Wayne State U. Med. Alumni Assn. (pres. 1969, trustee 1970-75, distinguished alumni award 1974), Coll. Am. Pathologists, Am. Soc. Clin. Pathologists (sec. 1971-77, pres. 1979-80), Mich. Soc. Pathologists (pres. 1980-81), Econ. Club Detroit, AMA, Am., Mich. assns. blood banks, Phi Gamma Delta, Nu Sigma Nu, Alpha Omega Alpha. Republican. Episcopalian. Clubs: Detroit Athletic, Lochmoor; Mid-America (Chgo.). Home and office: 47 DePetris Way Grosse Pointe Farms MI 48236

WALKER, FRED WAYNE, govt. commn. adminstr.; b. Eldorado, Ill., Jan. 25, 1947; s. George F. and Margie O. (Elam) W.; B.A. in Urban Design, So. Ill. U., 1970, postgrad., 1975-76; m. Nancy Walker, 1 dau., Michelle Lynn. Planner, Southeastern Ill. Regional Planning and Devel. Commn., Harrisburg, 1972-73; exec. dir. South Central Ill. Regional Planning and Devel. Commn., Salem, 1973—. Served with U.S. Army, 1970-72. Mem. Am. Planning Assn., Nat. Assn. Regional

Councils, Council for Urban Econ. Devel. Club: Salem Country. Office: Marion County Public Services Bldg Salem IL 62881

WALKER, GEORGE CONWAY, fin. exec.; b. Los Angeles, Oct. 13, 1938; s. Wendell Fellows and Miram Alva (Conway) W.; B.M.E., Stanford U., 1960; m. Patricia Campbell Berry, Nov. 27, 1963; children—Julie Elizabeth, Jennifer Fellows, Charles Berry. Bus. cons. mgr. Arthur Andersen & Co., Milw., 1964-77; v.p. fin., treas. Realist, Inc., Menomonee Falls, Wis., 1977—. Mem. Wis. Gov.'s Mgmt. Fellows Program, 1976; mem. Milw. Exceptional Edn. Task Force, 1975; fin. adv. bd. Fox Point Bayside Sch. Dist., 1972-76; bd. dirs. Wis. Soc. Brain Injured Children, 1969-74; bd. dirs. Milw. Ballet Co., 1976-80. Served as officer USCGR, 1961-64. Mem. ASME, Fin. Execs. Inst., Nat. Investor Relations Inst. Republican. Episcopalian. Clubs: Milwaukee Yacht, North Hills Country. Home: 8029 N Poplar Dr Fox Point WI 53217 Office: Box 67 Menomonee Falls WI 53051

WALKER, GEORGE HERBERT, III, lawyer, investment banking co. exec.; b. St. Louis, Mar. 16, 1931; s. George H. and Mary (Carter) W.; B.A., Yale, 1953; LL.B., Harvard, 1956; m. Sandra E. Canning, Dec. 23, 1955 (div. Oct. 1962); children—Mary Elizabeth, Wendy, Isabelle; m. 2d, Kimberly Gedge, July 27, 1968 (div. Jan. 1977); children—George H. IV, Carter. Admitted to Conn. bar, 1956; registered rep. firm G.H. Walker & Co. (later G.H. Walker, Laird Inc.), St. Louis, 1958-61, gen. partner, 1961-65, founder, mgr. Chgo. office, 1963-71, mng. partner, 1965-71, chmn. exec. com., 1971-73, chmn. bd. dirs., 1973-74; sr. v.p. White, Weld & Co. Inc. (merger G.H. Walker, Laird Inc. with White Weld & Co.), St. Louis, 1974-75, also dir.; exec. v.p. Stifel Nicolaus & Co., 1976-78, pres., chief exec. officer, 1978—, also dir.; dir. Laidlaw Corp. Civilian aide to Sec. U.S. Army for Eastern Mo., 1973—. Bd. dirs. Downtown St. Louis Inc., St. Louis Regional Commerce and Growth Assn., Episcopal Ch. Found., St. Louis Childrens Hosp., Arts and Edn. Council; vice chmn., bd. dirs. Webster Coll. Served with USAF, 1956-58. Mem. Securities Industry Assn. (bd. dirs., exec. com. 1981—), Conn. Bar Assn., Assn. U.S. Army (dir. chpt.). Clubs: Log Cabin, St. Louis Country, Noonday, Racquet, Yale of St. Louis, Yale of N.Y., Links, Univ. of Chgo. Home: 136 S Price Rd Saint Louis MO 63124 Office: 500 N Broadway Saint Louis MO 63102

WALKER, JAMES LEROY, ednl. adminstr.; b. Platte, S.D., June 11, 1932; s. Lynn and Phoebe (Halligan) W.; B.S., So. State Coll., Springfield, S.D., 1959; postgrad. U. S.D., summer 1965; M.Ed., S.D. State U., 1966; m. Audrey June Forgey, Nov. 28, 1952; children—Cindy June Severson, Randy James, Kelli Patrice. Rural sch. tchr., Iona, S.D., 1951-53; acting postmaster, Iona, 1956; elementary and jr. high prin., Ft. Pierre, S.D., 1959-62; jr. high tchr., Brookings, S.D., 1962-63; elementary and jr. high prin., Miller, S.D., 1963-67; coll. tchr. Huron (S.D.) Coll., summer 1965-66; supt schs., Platte, 1967—. Dir., S.E. Ednl. Service Center, Sioux Falls, S.D., 1968-70; mem. S.D. Gov.'s Vocat. Edn. Adv. Council, 1970—. Served with Signal Corps, AUS, 1953-55. Mem. NEA (life), S.D. Edn. Assn. (dir. 1966-71), Platte Tchrs. Assn., Am., S.D. assns. sch. adminstrs. Methodist. Mason. Home: Box 363 Platte SD 57369

WALKER, JESSICA LEE, portrait painter; b. Kansas City, Mo., May 22, 1930; d. Jesse Boone and Mildred (Trueblood) Walker; student San Jose State Coll., 1947-49, Dallas Mus. Fine Arts Sch., 1949-51. Asst. to portrait painter Matteo Sandona, San Francisco, 1952-54; free lance portrait painter, San Jose, Calif., 1955-59, Chgo., 1964—; med. illustrator Consol. Lithograph Co., San Jose, 1960-63; instr. adult art classes, Dallas, 1950-52; painter portraits James Boccardo and family, 1959, Melvin Belli, 1960; represented in collections U.S. and abroad. Winner scholarship Dallas Mus. Fine Arts Sch., 1946. Mem. Am. Soc. Artists. Home: 1730 N McVicker Ave Chicago IL 60639

WALKER, JESSIE, writer, photographer; b. Milw.; d. Stuart Richard and Loraine (Freuler) Walker; B.S., Medill Sch. Journalism, Northwestern U., also M.S. First major feature article appeared in The Am. Home mag., 1950, since contbr. numerous articles in nat. mags. including Am. Heritage's Americana, Better Homes and Gardens, McCall's, House and Garden, Good Housekeeping, others; midwest editor Am. Home mag.; contbg. editor Better Homes & Gardens. Mem. Ill. Opera Guild; mem. N. Shore jr. bd. Northwestern U. Settlement, 1949-59. Recipient Dorothy Dawes award for distinguished journalistic coverage in home furnishing, 1976, 77. Mem. Am. Soc. Interior Designers (press mem.), Women in Communications. Author: How to Plan a Trend Setting Kitchen, 1962; How to Make Window Decorating Easy, 1969; Shaker Design-150-year-old Modern, 1972; Good Design—What Makes It Last?, 1973; Junking Made Easy, 1974; Poster Power, 1976; For Collectors Only, 1977; Bishop Hill-Utopian Community 1978; also articles. Photographer cover photo Better Homes & Gardens, Mar. 1980, Oct. 1980. Address: 241 Fairview Rd Glencoe IL 60022

WALKER, JIMMY NEWTON, bldg. materials co. exec.; b. Eldorado, Okla., Mar. 6, 1924; s. Edward Lee and Ruby Ree (Dixon) W.; B.S., Okla. State U., 1949; M.B.A., U. Chgo., 1963; m. Margaret M. Rice, Sept. 10, 1949; children—Beverly Joan Giberson, Karen Sue. Prodn. foreman U.S. Gypsum Co., Des Plaines, Ill., 1949-51, paint research chemist, 1951-54, plaster and plastics research chemist, 1954-57, mgr. joint systems research and devel., 1958-61, div. mgr. research and devel., 1961-66, dir. research and devel., 1966-77, v.p. research, 1977—. Mem. bd. Lattoff YMCA, 1977—. Served with USAAF, 1943-46. Mem. Am. Chem. Soc., Indsl. Research Inst., Research Dirs. Assn. Chgo. (pres.). Republican. Baptist. Club: Mission Hills Country. Inventor first flat latex paint, epoxy based tooling compounds. Office: 700 N Hwy 45 Libertyville IL 60048

WALKER, KAY L., ins. agt.; b. Rigby, Idaho, Dec. 4, 1942; s. Allen H. and Lora (Taylor) W.; B.S., Brigham Young U., 1967; student So. Ill. U., 1967-68, U. Mo., St. Louis, 1968-69; m. Angela Galloway, Jan. 27, 1966; children—Kara, Kindra, Karsten, Kimber, Kenton, Kayla, Kyle. Agt., N.Y. Life, St. Louis, 1970-77; agt. Paul Revere, St. Louis, 1972—; gen. agt. Nat. Travelers Life, St. Louis, 1976—; gen. agt. Alexander Hamilton Life, 1978—; pres. Walker, Morris & Walker, Inc., St. Louis, 1973—; pres. Nauvoo Devel. Inc., 1977—; sec. St. Louis Tread & Tire Co., Inc.; exec. v.p. Pre Paid Dental Services Inc., 1980—; pres. Halcyon Travel Ltd., 1980—; dir. Continental Security Life Ins. Co., JHLS. Treas., bd. dirs. local PTA, 1977-79; state coordinator Mo. Citizens Council, 1980—. Mem. Nat. Assn. Pension Adminstrs., Life Underwriters Assn., North County C. of C., Million Dollar Round Table, Top of the Table. Republican. Mormon. Kiwanian. Office: 320 Brookes Dr Suite 118 Saint Louis MO 63042

WALKER, MAURICE ANDREW, surgeon; b. Columbus, Kans., Jan. 4, 1904; s. Stephen Lorenzo and Minnie Belle (Mayhew) W.; B.S., Kans. State Tchrs. Coll., Pittsburg, 1923; M.A., U. Kans., 1925; M.D., U. Chgo., 1928; M.S., U. Minn., 1932; m. Marguerite Lescher, Nov. 10, 1928; children—Charles Stephen, Judith Ann. Intern, St. Margaret's Hosp., Kansas City, Kans., 1927-28; resident Trinity Luth. Hosp., Kansas City, 1928; fellow in surgery Mayo Found., 1929-32, U. Kans. St. Margaret's Hosp., 1932-34; gen. practice surgery, Kansas City, 1932—; attending surgeon Bethany Hosp.; cons. in surgery Community Med. Center, Gardner, Kans. Commr. and chmn. or vice-chmn. Urban Renewal Agency of Kansas City, 1955-76; mem. overall devel. plan com. Wyandotte County and Kansas City, 1977—. Served. to col. M.C., U.S. Army, 1942-46. Diplomate Am. Bd. Surgery; recipient Community Citizenship citation C. of C. of Kansas City, 1974. Fellow A.C.S.; mem. AMA, Kansas City S.W. Clin. Soc., Mayo Alumni Assn., Kans. (emeritus), Wyandotte County (hon., award of merit 1972) med. socs., Sigma Xi, Phi Chi. Republican. Methodist. Clubs: Masons, Shriners. Contbr. articles to profl. jours. Home: 1417 S 37th St Kansas City KS 66106 Office: 3214 Strong Ave Kansas City KS 66106

WALKER, NATHAN BELT, state legislator, editor, publisher, farmer; b. Macon, Mo., Apr. 18, 1952; s. Wendell K. and Azalea Ann (Belt) W.; B.S. in Agrl. Journalism, U. Mo., Columbia, 1974, M.S. in Community Devel., 1975. Farmer, Anabel, Mo., 1964—; research analyst Mo. Ho. of Reps., 1976-77, mem. Ho. of Reps., 1981—; owner, pub., editor Macon County Home Press, La Plata, Mo., 1978—. Alt. del. Nat. Republican Conv., Kansas City, Mo., 1976, del., Detroit, 1980. Mem. Missourians Against Hazardous Waste, Community Devel. Soc., Nat. Rifle Assn., Macon C. of C., Jr. C. of C. Mem. Christian Ch. Clubs: Lions, Masons, Elks (Outstanding Leadership award 1970), Commerce (La Plata). Home: Rural Route 1 Anabel MO 63431 Office: Room 101D State Capitol Bldg Jefferson City MO 65101

WALKER, PAUL MONTGOMERY, farm mgr., educator; b. Shawnee, Okla., Aug. 3, 1950; s. Emmett Monroe and Mary Helen (Montgomery) W.; student S.W. Bapt. Coll., 1968-69; B.S. cum laude, U. Mo., 1972, M.S., 1973; Ph.D., U. Ill., 1979; m. Danna Elizabeth Daniels, Apr. 21, 1979. Beef herdsman U. Mo., Columbia, 1969-72, teaching asst., 1972-73; partner Emett Walker & Sons, Manengo, Ill., 1974—; research asst. U. Ill., Urbana, 1976-79; asst. prof. dept. agr. Ill. State U., Normal, 1980—; gen. mgr. Glenview Farms, Inc., 1978-80; cons. Shallow Brook Farm, Bradford, Ill. Cert. Am. Registry Cert. Animal Scientists. Mem. Nat. Cattlemen's Assn., Am. Soc. Animal Sci. (hon.), Sigma Xi, Gamma Sigma Delta, Alpha Zeta. Republican. Baptist. Contbr. articles to profl. jours. Home: 1200 Searle St Normal IL 61761 Office: 149 Turner Hall Ill State U Normal IL 61761

WALKER, PAULINE SCHOENAUER (MRS. MARTIN ELDON WALKER), poet; b. Red Lake Falls, Minn., Apr. 23, 1913; d. Paul Edward and Edythe Mae (Demann) Schoenauer; student MacPhail Coll. Music, 1930-31; m. Martin Eldon Walker, Aug. 2, 1948; 1 son, Martin Paul. Pvt. piano tchr., Plummer, Minn., 1934-41; 45-48, Gonvick, Minn., 1946-49, Oklee, Minn., 1945—; asst. to mgr. music dept. Donaldson's Dept. Store, Mpls., 1942-43; contbr. poems to various mags. including Ideals, Pen, Grit, The Muse, The Am. Bard, Writer's Notes and Quotes, The Farmer, Haiku Highlights, Haiku West, Modern Haiku, On the Line, numerous others. Mem. bd. Northwest Regional Library, Thief River Falls, Minn., 1968—, v.p., 1979. Recipient 2d prize Nat. Camellia Poetry Contest Fed. Chaparral Poets, 1968, spl. mention Haiku West, 1970, award, 1971; hon. mention Modern Haiku, 1970, 73. Mem. Am. Legion Aux. Author: The Things I Love, 1973; Haiku for All Seasons, 1980. Address: PO Box 165 Oklee MN 56742

WALKER, RICHARD OLNEY, JR., civil engr., educator; b. Columbus, Ohio, Sept. 26, 1923; s. Richard O. and Abigail P. (Crayton) W.; B.S. in Engring., Princeton U., 1946, M.S., 1948; m. Marjorie Alice Stearns, Feb. 3, 1951; children—Richard Olney III, David Stearns. Asst. instr. Materials Testing Lab., Princeton (N.J.) U., 1946-48; structural designer Abbott, Merkt & Co., N.Y.C., 1948-51, project coordinator and mgr., 1951-54, asst. to pres., 1954-58, sec., 1958-74, supr. archtl. and structural designs, 1959-74, dir., 1959-74; cons. engr., 1974-78; asso. prof. Sch. Civil Engring., Purdue U., West Lafayette, Ind., 1978—. Vice pres. Lawrence Hosp., Bronxville, 1974-75, mem. bd. govs., 1972-75, chmn. devel. com., 1973-75; mem. Planning Commn., Village of Bronxville, 1965-71; warden Christ Ch., Bronxville, 1970-74, sr. warden, 1971-74; vestryman St. John's Episc. Ch., 1980—; mem. bd. govs. Princeton U. Library in N.Y., 1973—; pres. Princeton U. Class of 1946, 1976-81. Served with U.S. Army, 1942-43. Registered profl. engr., Conn., Md., Mass., N.Y., Pa., Mich., N.J., Wis., Va., Ohio. Fellow ASCE, Am. Cons. Engrs. Council; mem. Am. Inst. Cons. Engrs. (pres. 1967, mem. council 1965-72), Nat. Soc. Profl. Engrs., Ind. Soc. Profl. Engrs. (pres. A.A. Potter chpt. 1980-81), ASTM, Princeton Engring Assn. (mem. exec. com. 1960—), Illuminating Engrs. Soc., Am. Planning Assn., Vets of 7th Regiment, Sigma Xi. Clubs: Princeton of N.Y. (v.p. 1965-69, pres. 1969-72); Field (Bronxville); Nassau; Lafayette Country. Home: 1303 Palmer Dr West Lafayette IN 47907 Office: Sch Civil Engring Purdue U West Lafayette IN 47907

WALKER, THOMAS DAVID, bus. services co. exec.; b. Memphis, Apr. 25, 1942; s. Joseph H. and Ruth (Cooprider) W.; B.A., Tex. Christian U., 1965, M.A., 1967; postgrad. U. London, 1971; m. Danielle Medina Rome; 2 children. Asst. dean Schiller Coll., Paris, 1970-72; edn. dir. Alliance for Franco-Am. Grad. Studies, N.Y.C., 1972-73; tng. coordinator Chase Manhattan Bank, Paris, 1973-77; dir. program adminstrn. Systran Corp., Chgo., 1977-79, dir. proposals, 1979-80, dir. internat. projects, 1980-81, v.p. contract tng., 1981—; prof. English, U. Paris, 1968-69, Coll. des Sciences Sociales et Economiques, Paris, 1974-75, L'Ecole Superieure d'Electricite, Gif-sur-Yvette, France, 1974-76, Institut Francais du Petrole, 1975-76, L'Institut National des Sciences Politiques, Paris, 1976-77. Mem. Nat. Assn. Fgn. Student Affairs, Am. Soc. Tng. and Devel., Phi Alpha Theta. Office: 70 W Hubbard St Chicago IL 60610

WALKER, THOMAS ROSS, fin. cons.; b. Denver, May 9, 1946; s. Howard Ross and Elizabeth Laverne (Weinrich) W.; student Eureka Coll., 1964-65, U. Ill., 1965-66, Walton Coll., 1966-68, Am. Coll., 1976-81; m. Patricia Anna Callen, Dec. 3, 1966; children—Robert Lanny, Deborah Susan. Acct., Sheldon H. Ginsburg & Assos., C.P.A.'s, Skokie, Ill., 1967-71, Shepard Schwartz & Harris, C.P.A.'s, Chgo., 1971-72; salesman N.Y. Life Ins. Co., Chgo., 1972-76; sales mgr. Mut. of N.Y., Chgo., 1976-78; pres. North Shore Fin. Cons., Inc., Highland Park, Ill., 1979—; mem. North Shore Planners, 1980-81. Baseball mgr. Park Dist. of Wheeling, 1975-76; football coach Park Dist. of Highland Park, 1978-79; chmn. Citizens for Dahl Com., 1979. Mem. Nat. Assn. Life Underwriters, Ill. Assn. Life Underwriters, Chgo. Assn. Life Underwriters, N. Suburban Assn. Life Underwriters, Highland Park Jr. C. of C. (pres. 1977-78, Presdl. award 1978). Home: 1921 Sunnyside Highland Park IL 60035 Office: 1866 Sheridan Rd Highland Park IL 60035

WALKER, WALTER WILLARD, real estate and investments exec.; b. Mpls., Dec. 4, 1911; s. Archie Dean and Bertha Willard (Hudson) W.; B.A., Princeton U., 1935; M.D., Harvard U., 1940; postgrad. U. Minn., 1942-48; m. Elva Mae Dawson, Dec. 16, 1939 (div. Oct. 1969); m. Elaine Barbatsis, Mar. 17, 1972. Teaching fellow pathology U. Minn., 1942-48; left medicine, went into bus., 1948; dir. Shasta Forest Co., Redding, Calif., 1951-71, treas., 1954-66, v.p., 1966-71; sec., dir. Barlow Realty Co., Mpls., 1954-67, pres., 1967-77, chmn., 1977-80, sec., 1980—; sec., dir. Walker Pence Co., 1950-72; sec. Penwalk Investment Co., 1958-72, dir., 1943-72; dir. Craig-Hallum Corp., Mpls., 1954—; adv. bd. Lincoln office Northwestern Nat. Bank, Mpls., 1957-74. Bd. dirs. T.B. Walker Found., 1953-76, v.p., 1954-76; bd. dirs. Minn. Opera Co., 1968-73, Archie D. and Bertha H. Walker Found., 1953—, Mpls. Found., 1962-79, Walker Art Center, 1954-76, United Fund, 1966-72; trustee Abbott-Northwestern Hosp., 1969-77; trustee Children's Health Center, Inc., 1968-73, treas., 1969-73; pres. Found. Services, 1967-73; bd. dirs., exec. com. Minn. Charities Review Council, 1965-74; mem. Hennepin County Capital Budgeting Task Force, 1973-74. Mem. Sigma Xi, Nu Sigma Nu. Methodist. Clubs: Minneapolis; Woodhill Country; Princeton (N.Y.C.); U. Minn. Alumni. Home: 1900 Knox Ave S Minneapolis MN 55403 Office: 1121 Hennepin Ave Minneapolis MN 55403

WALKER, WILLIAM RAY, broadcasting exec.; b. Madison, Wis., Aug. 28, 1923; s. William E. and Edna (Blied) W.; B.B.A., U. Wis., 1947, M.S., 1963, Ph.D., 1964; m. Eleanor Bauhs, Jan. 17, 1953; children—Diana (dec.), Thomas, Robert. Advt. agy. account exec. Arthur Towell, Inc., Scott, Inc., 1947-50; radio advt. salesman WMAM, Marinette, Wis., WBEV, Beaver Dam, others, 1950-54; tv sta. mgr. WMBV-TV, Green Bay, Marinette, 1954-56; WRRR, Rockford, Ill., 1956-59, radio sta. mgr. WISM-AM & TFM, Madison, 1956—; dir. United Bank & Trust Madison. Tchr. algebra Holy Name Sem., 1964-77; officer, dir. Midwest Family Radio stas. in Madison, Oshkosh and LaCrosse, Wis., Lansing and St. Joseph, Mich., Rockford, Ill., Springfield, Ill., 1955—; officer, dir. Holiday Acres, Rhinelander, Wis. Past pres. adv. bd. St. Mary's Hosp. and Med. Center, Madison; officer, trustee Pope John XXIII Med.-Moral Research and Edn. Center, St. Louis; trustee Edgewood Coll. Served to capt. AUS, 1943-46. Named knight St. Gregory, 1975. Mem. Am. Council Tchrs. Math., Alpha Delta Phi. Roman Catholic. Clubs: Rotary, Serra (past pres., dist. gov.). Contbr. articles to profl. jours. Home: 1838 Camelot Dr Madison WI 53705 Office: PO Box 2058 Madison WI 53701

WALL, ARTHUR EDWARD PATRICK, editor; b. Jamestown, N.Y., Mar. 12, 1925; s. George Herbert and Doris (Olmstead) W.; student pub. schs.; m. Marcella Joan Petrine, Nov. 5, 1954; children—John Wright, Marie Ann, David Arthur Edward. Copy editor Worcester (Mass.) Telegram, 1958; Sunday editor Hawaii Island Corr., Honolulu Star-Bull., 1958-60; editor Hilo (Hawaii) Tribune-Herald, 1960-63; Sunday editor Honolulu Advertiser, 1963-65, mng. editor, 1971-72; mng. editor Cath. Rev., 1965-66, editor, 1966-71; editor-in-chief Nat. Cath. News Service, Washington, 1972-76; editor, gen. mgr. The New World (name changed to Chgo. Catholic 1977), Chgo., 1976—, pres., 1979—; pres. New World Pub. Co., 1977—; dir. Noll Printing Co., Inc., Huntington, Ind. Dir. bur. info. Archdiocese Balt., 1965-66; mem. fin. com. Archdiocese Chgo., 1979—; mem. council Internat. Cath. Union of Press, Geneva, 1972—, v.p., 1974-77. Chmn., Gov.'s Com. Ednl. TV, Honolulu, 1964-65; regent Chaminade Coll., Honolulu, 1959-65, chmn., 1963-65; trustee St. Mary's Sem. and Univ., Balt., 1975-76; bd. dirs. Our Sunday Visitor, Inc., Huntington, Ind., 1977—; mem. spiritual renewal and devel. com. 41st Internat. Eucharistic Congress, Phila., 1975-76. Named Young Man of Year, Hilo, Hawaii, 1960; recipient St. Francis de Sales award Cath. Press Assn., 1977; Father of Year, Honolulu C. of C., 1964; Spl. award U.S. Cath. Conf., 1980. Mem. Internat. Fedn. Cath. Press Agys. (pres. 1974-77), Internat. Fedn. Cath. Journalists (pres. 1977-80, v.p. 1981—), Cath. Press Assn. U.S. and Can. (bd. dirs. 1978—), Sigma Delta Chi (past chpt. pres.). Roman Catholic. Clubs: Nat. Press (Washington); Overseas Press (N.Y.C.); Chgo. Press. Author: The Big Wave, 1960. Editor: Origins and Catholic Trends, 1972-76. Contbr. articles to mags. Home: 2100 Lincoln Park W Chicago IL 60614 Office: Chicago Catholic 155 E Superior St Chicago IL 60611

WALL, DORIS JANE, educator, counselor; b. Sorento, Ill., Feb. 20, 1935; d. Vivian Henry and Pauline Evelyn (Randle) Bentley; B.S. in Edn., So. Ill. U., 1972, M.S. in Edn., 1975, Edn. Specialist in Counselor Edn., 1978; m. Harry E. Wall, Jr., Jan. 23, 1954; children—Harry Lynn, Larry Gene. Bookkeeper, clk. Citizens Coach Co., Alton Ill., 1953-54; phys. therapist to physician, Alton, Ill., 1955-56; credit mgr. Utlaut Meml. Hosp., Greenville, Ill., 1960-62; sec. to counselors Bond County Community Unit 2 Schs., Greenville, Ill., 1966-69, tchr. English, 1972—, counselor, 1972—; dir. gifted program drama Pocahontas (Ill.) Jr. High Sch., 1974—. Mem. Nat., Ill., Greenville edn. assns., Am. Personnel and Guidance Assn., Ill. Assn. Tchrs. English. Baptist. Club: Eastern Star.

WALL, LARRY LEN, chemist; b. St. Joseph, Mo., Jan. 16, 1943; s. Glen R. and Wanda Maxine (Adkins) W.; B.A., U. Mo., 1965, M.Sc., 1968; m. Sharon Lea Beattie, Aug. 11, 1963; children—Larry Len, Shannon Lea, Shayne Nicole. With Expt. Sta. Chem. Labs., U. Mo., Columbia, 1961—, grad. asst., 1968-72, research specialist, 1972—. Bd. dirs. Daniel Boone Little League, 1976—, pres., 1978-79. Mem. Assn. Ofcl. Analytical Chemists (chmn. com. automated methods 1976—), Am. Chem. Soc., Sigma Xi, Gamma Sigma Delta. Mem. Christian Ch. Club: West Broadway Swim (sec. bd. dirs. 1976-79). Contbr. articles to profl. jours. Home: 2253 Concordia Dr Columbia MO 65201 Office: Room 4 Agrl Bldg U Mo Columbia MO 65201

WALLACE, BILLIE BLAIR, city ofcl.; b. Des Moines, Oct. 6, 1925; s. Charles O. and Iva (Kershaw) W.; B.S. Drake U., 1949; grad. FBI Nat. Acad., 1962; m. Patsy Ruth, Oct. 3, 1945; children—Tamara, Scott, Melody, Lori. With Des Moines Police Dept., 1949—, now chief of police. Served with AC, U.S. Navy, 1943-46. Mem. Iowa State Policeman's Assn., Iowa Chiefs of Police and Peace Officers Assn., Internat. Assn. Chiefs of Police. Club: Echo Valley Country. Office: E 1st St and Court St Des Moines IA 50309*

WALLACE, FRANKLIN SHERWOOD, lawyer; b. Bklyn., Nov. 24, 1927; s. Abraham Charles and Jennie (Etkin) Wolowitz; student U. Wis., 1943-45; B.S. cum laude, U.S. Mcht. Marine Acad., 1950; LL.B., J.D., U. Mich., 1953; m. Eleanor Ruth Pope, Aug. 23, 1953; children—Julia Diane, Charles Andrew. Admitted to Ill. bar, 1954, since practiced in Rock Island; partner firm Winstein, Kavensky, Wallace & Doughty; asst. state's atty. Rock Island County, 1967-68. Bd. dirs. Tri City Jewish Center; trustee United Jewish Charities of Quad Cities. Mem. Am., Ill. (chmn. jud. adv. polls com.), Rock Island County bar assns., Am., Ill. trial lawyers assns., Nat. Assn. Criminal Def. Lawyers, Am. Judicature Soc., Internat. Platform Assn. Democrat. Jewish. Home: 3405 20th St Ct Rock Island IL 61201 Office: Rock Island Bank Bldg Rock Island IL 61201

WALLACE, JAMES DUNCAN, former utility co. exec.; b. Topeka, Kans., Apr. 10, 1914; s. Thomas William and Fay Aleen (Ritchie) W.; B.S. in Elec. Engring., U. Kans., 1936; m. Harriet Elizabeth Johnson, Sept. 5, 1938; 1 son, Douglass William. Jr. engr. Kans. Power & Light Co., 1939-44, div. supt., 1946-52, system elec. engr., 1952-62, mgr. electric ops., 1962-64, v.p. electric ops., 1964-79. Served with USNR, 1944-46. Registered profl. engr., Kans. Mem. Am. Rifle Assn., Kansas City St. Andrew's Soc., Kans., Clan Wallace Soc. (v.p.), Nat. Trust for Scotland. Home: 706 Greenwood St Topeka KS 66606

WALLACE, LARRY JAY, state govt. ofcl.; b. Bellefontaine, Ohio, Oct. 2, 1937; s. Charles Kenneth and Sylvia Lavonna (Myers) W.; A.B., Ind. U., 1960, LL.B., 1962; divorced; children—Daniel G., David C., John J. Admitted to Ind. bar, 1963; practice in Indpls., 1963-74; chmn. Public Service Commn. Ind., 1974—; 1st v.p. Nat. Assn. Regulatory Utility Commns., 1981; chmn. mem. exec. com., chmn. electricity com. State Reps., 1971-72. Republican. Club:

Columbia (Indpls.). Office: 901 State Office Bldg Indianapolis IN 46204

WALLACE, LELAND MORRIS, JR., mfrs. rep.; b. St. Louis, June 15, 1922; s. Leland Morris and Frances I. (Juliuson) W.; B.S., Washington U., St. Louis, 1943; m. Betty J. Elbrecht, Oct. 11, 1947; children—Leland Morris III, Jonathan, Christine, Barbara. Sales engr. Dow Chem. Co., St. Louis, 1946-48; with lamp div. Westinghouse Electric Corp., St. Louis, 1948-57, regional engr., dist. sales mgr., apparatus div., St. Louis, 1957-60; gen. sales mgr. Revere Electric Mfg. Co., Chgo., 1960-65, Joseph Goder, Inc., Chgo., 1966-72; mfrs. rep., 1972—; regional mgr. Kinney-Reese Assos., Inc., N.Y.C., 1975-80; mktg. dir. Major Service Electric, Inc., Chgo., 1978—; asso. Boos & Assos., Inc., Arlington Hts., Ill., 1979-81; asso. The Engrs. Collaborative, Ltd., Chgo., 1982—; v.p. Standards Internat., Inc., Chgo., 1982—. Served to 1st lt. AUS, 1943-45. Decorated Purple Heart. Mem. Sigma Xi, Sigma Chi, Tau Beta Pi, Pi Mu Epsilon, Omicron Delta Kappa. Baptist. Home: 1138 Terrace Ln Glenview IL 60025

WALLACE, RICHARD CHEEVER, sociologist, educator; b. Wayne, Mich., Mar. 5, 1945; s. William Donald and Esther Mae (Belknap) W.; B.S. in Aerospace Engring., U. Mich., 1967; M.A. in Sociology, Temple U., 1971; Ph.D. in Sociology, Yale U., 1976; m. Wendy Jean Drew, Sept. 30, 1966; children—Carey Jean, Mark Cheever. Systems engr. Gen. Electric Co., 1968-70; teaching asst. Temple U., 1970-71; research trainee Yale U., 1971-76, teaching asst., 1974-75; asst. prof. U. Hartford, 1976-78; asst. prof. sociology Hillsdale (Mich.) Coll., 1978—, chmn. behavioral scis. div., 1980—. Mem. Am. Sociol. Assn., AAAS. Quaker. Home: 124 S Howell St Hillsdale MI 49242 Office: Hillsdale College Hillsdale MI 49242

WALLACE, SHERWOOD LEE, financial public relations exec.; b. Chgo., Jan. 25, 1940; s. Paul and Jerry (Crown) W.; B.A. in Journalism and Pub. Relations, State U. Iowa, 1962; postgrad. pub. relations No. Ill. U., 1971-72; m. Lois Terri Takiff, Aug. 9, 1975. Copywriter, Ekco Products Co., Chgo., 1962; polit. reporter Lerner Newspapers, Chgo., 1962; dir. pub. relations Sta. WYNR, Chgo., 1963; account exec. Bud Solk & Assos., Inc., Chgo., 1964-65, Aaron D. Cushman & Assos., Inc., Chgo., 1966-67; sr. v.p. Financial Relations Bd., Chgo., 1967-81; pres. Investor Relations Co., Northbrook, Ill., 1982—; lectr. pub. relations and investor relations to colls. and industry groups. Co-organizer Nat. Alliance for Optional Parenthood, 1971, hon. dir., 1971—; mem. Big Bros. of Met. Chgo., 1974—. Recipient awards for ann. report excellence Fin. World Mag. Mem. Pub. Relations Soc. Am., Publicity Club Chgo. (Golden Trumpet award 1966, 75, 76, certificate of merit 1969), Nat. Investor Relations Inst., State U. Iowa Alumni Assn. (life), Cousteau Soc. Jewish. Home: 1165 County Line Rd Highland Park IL 60035 Office: 633 Skokie Blvd Northbrook IL 60062

WALLACE, THOMAS EDWARD, JR., exec.; b. L.I., N.Y., Dec. 10, 1948; s. Thomas Edward and Antoinette W.; A.A. Cuyahoga Community Coll., 1971; B.S., Lake Erie Coll., 1975. Summer jobs coordinator City of Cleve., 1970-73; sales mgr. Royalty Party Center, Cleve., 1973, 75; mktg. cons., Cleve., 1975-78; gen. mgr. McDonald's Restaurant, Cleve., 1978-79; mgr. Canteen Food Service Corp., 1979—. Mem. Glenville Adv. Commn., 1978—; bd. dirs. Glenville Community Adv. Commn., 1978—; mem. exec. com. Cuyahoga County Dem. Party; candidate for Ohio State Legislature. Mem. NAACP, Am. Mktg. Assn., Cleve. Jr. C. of C., Omega Psi Phi. Democrat. Club: Mason. Home: 10103 N Blvd Cleveland OH 44108

WALLACE, THOMAS FERDINAND, mgmt. cons., educator; b. Cin., Nov. 15, 1935; s. Raymond Joseph and Marie (Madlener) W.; B.S., Marquette U., 1957; M.B.A., Xavier U., 1966; m. Evelyn Marie Ennis, May 30, 1961; children—David, Anne Marie, Mary Clare. With W.G. Seinsheimer & Assos., Cin., 1972-75, v.p., 1973-75; partner Klekamp-Wallace & Co., mgmt. cons., Cin., 1976-80; pres. T.F. Wallace & Co., Specialists in MRP Edn. and Cons., 1980—; v.p. Oliver Wight Video Prodns. Inc., 1980—; affiliate Oliver Wight Edn. Assos., 1979—; speaker to various profl. and tech. socs. Co-founder, pres. Montessori Center Rooms, 1966-69. Served to lt. (j.g.) USNR, 1957-60. Mem. Am. Prodn. and Inventory Control Soc. (pres. Cin. chpt. 1969-70), ASME (Am. nat. standards com.), ACLU, Common Cause, English-Speaking Union. Democrat. Roman Catholic. Club: Cin. Editor, APICS Dictionary of Prodn. and Inventory Mgmt. Terminology. Office: 2929 Wold Ave Cincinnati OH 45206

WALLACE, WAYNE MACAULEY, mfg. corp. exec.; b. Greenfield, Ohio, Apr. 25, 1947; s. Charles Robert and Shirley Ann (Whitfield) W.; B.A., Georgetown Coll., 1970; m. Janice Sue Early, Dec. 19, 1970; 1 dau., Trisha Lynn. Cost estimator, accounts supr. Olinkraft, Inc., Cin., 1970-76, sales service mgr., 1976-79, sales rep., 1979-81; sales rep. Weyerhaeuser Co., Mt. Vernon, Ohio, 1981—. Mem. Am. Mgmt. Assn., Nat. Hist. Soc., Pi Kappa Alpha. Republican. Presbyterian. Home: 6349 Ironwood Dr Loveland OH 45140 Office: Box 151 Mount Vernon OH 43050

WALLACH, JOHN SIDNEY, library adminstr.; b. Steubenville, Ohio, Jan. 6, 1939; s. Arthur Martin and Alice Irene (Smith) W.; B.S. in Edn., Kent State U., 1963; M.L.S., U. R.I., 1968; M.P.A., U. Dayton, 1977; m. Jane Springett Wallach, Sept. 21, 1963; children—John Michael, Wendy Anne, Bethany Lynne, Kristen Michele. Dir. Mercer County (Ohio) Dist. Library, Celina, 1968-70; dir. Greene County (Ohio) Dist. Library, Xenia, 1970-77; asst. dir. Dayton and Montgomery County (Ohio) Library, 1977-78, dir., 1979—. Mem. Ohio Com. for Employer Support of Guard and Res.; mem. adv. com. Sch. L.S., Kent State U.; vice chmn. health div. United Way of Dayton; bd. dirs. Dayton Mus. Natural History; Family Services Assn., Dayton, Ohionet, PAR Council of United Way. Served with U.S. Navy, 1963-68, comdr. Res. Mem. ALA, Ohio Library Assn. (dir. 1971-74, pres.), Naval Res. Assn., Res. Officers Assn., Miami Valley Mil. Affairs Assn. Club: Dayton Discussion. Office: 215 E 3d St Dayton OH 45402

WALLACH, PHILIP, mfg. co. exec.; b. N.Y.C., May 29, 1928; s. Morris and Lillian (Levy) W.; B.S., U.S. Mcht. Marine Acad., 1950; postgrad. N.C. State Grad. Sch. Engring., N.Y. U. Grad. Sch. Bus.; m. Florence O'Neil, Apr. 8, 1951; children—Ruth, Sandra, Louis, David. Sales engr., regional mgr. Nordberg Mfg. Co., 1955-67; v.p. mktg., pres. Engine div. Fairbanks Morse subs. Colt Industries, Inc., Beloit, Wis., 1967-71, corporate v.p., group exec., 1971, group v.p., 1972—; pres. Colt Industries Internat., Inc. Served to lt. USNR, 1953-55. Recipient Outstanding Profl. Achievement award U.S. Mcht. Marine Acad., Marine Man of Yr. award. Mem. Am. Soc. Naval Engrs., Soc. Naval Architects and Marine Engrs. Club: Economic (N.Y.C.). Home: 3211 Montlake Dr Rockford IL 61111 Office: 701 Lawton Ave Beloit WI 53511

WALLENBERG, LOUIS, lawyer; b. Chgo., July 22, 1954; s. Leo Walter and Bernice Constance (Wawrzyniak) W.; B.S. summa cum laude, DePaul U., 1974, J.D., 1977. Admitted to Ill. bar, 1977, Fla. bar, 1977; clk. to Justice John. J. Sullivan, Ill. Appellate Ct., Chgo., 1977-78; atty. Swift & Co., Chgo., 1979-80; atty. Esmark, Inc., Chgo., 1980—. Nat. Endowment for Humanities fellow, 1980. Mem. Am. Bar Assn., Ill. Bar Assn., Chgo. Bar Assn., Fla. Bar Assn., Dade County Bar Assn. Bus. editor DePaul Law Review, 1976-77. Office: Esmark Inc 55 E Monroe St Chicago IL 60603

WALLER, JAMES EDWARD, soft drink bottling co. exec.; b. Sedalia, Mo., Nov. 19, 1937; s. Otis Mack and Viola May W.; B.A. in Acctg., Central Mo. State U., 1959; children—Bucke, Jami. Acct., Haskins & Sells, Kansas City, Kans., 1967; controller Coca-Cola Mid-Am., Lenexa, Kans., 1967-74, exec. v.p., 1974-77, pres., 1977—. Bd. dirs. Jr. Achievement Mid-Am.; Served with U.S. Army, 1959-60. Mem. Kans. Soft Drink Assn., Nat. Soft Drink Assn. (exec. dir.), Coca-Cola Bottlers Assn., Kans. Assn. Commerce and Industry (dir.), Lenexa C. of C. (past pres., dir.), Am. Inst. C.P.A.'s, Fin. Execs. Inst. Clubs: River, Indian Hills Country, Univ. Office: 9000 Marshall Dr Lenexa KS 66215

WALLER, RUSSELL BLISS, publisher; b. St. Paul, May 21, 1907; s. Elza Russell and Grace Evelyn (Bliss) W.; B.A., U. Minn., 1935; m. Mildred Pratt, Jan. 24, 1941; children—Pamela, Dennis, Thomas, Steven, John. Sports reporter St. Paul Pioneer Press, 1925-26; city editor Bemidji (Minn.) Daily Pioneer, 1929-30; news editor Ortonville (Minn.) Ind., 1930-31; pub. Algona (Iowa) Pub. Co., 1932-81, pub. emeritus, 1981—; pres. Midwest Printing & Lithographing Inc., Algona, 1966—. Served with USNR, 1941-45. Mem. Nat., Minn. newspaper assns., Iowa Press Assn. (named Master Editor-Pub. 1979), Ret. Officers Assn., Beta Theta Pi, Sigma Delta Chi, V.F.W., Am. Legion. Club: Masons. Home: 100 E Oak St Algona IA 50511 Office: Algona Pub Co 14 E Nebraska St Algona IA 50511

WALLER, STEVEN SCOBEE, educator; b. Indpls., Aug. 29, 1947; s. Claude Victor and Margaret Ann (Scobee) W.; A.S., Vincennes U., 1967; B.S., Purdue U., 1970; Ph.D., Tex. A & M U., 1975; m. Jessie Ellen Simone, Jan. 24, 1970; children—Christina Dee, Scott Steven. Research fellow Tex. A & M U., 1974-75; asst. prof. animal sci. S.D. State U., 1975-78, asst. to dir. resident, instr., 1977-78; asso. prof. agronomy U. Nebr., Lincoln, 1978—. Served with USAR N.G., 1970-78. Tom Slick Research fellow, 1974-75. Mem. Soc. Range Mgmt. (chmn. Nebr. sect. research com. 1978-82, chmn. membership com. 1978-82, chmn. newsletter 1980-82), Nebr. Forage and Grassland Council (pres. 1981), Nebr. Acad. Sci., Sigma Xi, Phi Sigma, Gamma Sigma Delta, Xi Sigma Pi, Phi Theta Kappa. Methodist. Contbr. articles to profl. jours. Home: 4912 S 63d St Lincoln NE 68516 Office: 347 Keim Hall East Campus Lincoln NE 68583

WALLESTAD, PHILIP WESTON, physician; b. Madison, Wis., May 14, 1922; s. John Oscar and Dorothy Francis (White) W.; B.A., U. Wis., 1947, M.D., 1954; m. Edith Stolle, Jan. 15, 1949 (div. Mar. 1967); children—Kristin Eve, Ingrid Birgitta, Erika Ann; m. 2d, Muriel Annette Moen, June 22, 1968; children—Thomas John, Scott Philip. Intern, Calif. Lutheran Hosp., Los Angeles, 1954, resident in surgery, 1955-56; gen. practice medicine, Fredonia and Port Washington Wis., 1957-72, Libby, Mont., 1972-74; staff physician VA Hosp., Fort Harrison and Helena, Mont., 1974-77, Tomah, Wis., 1977-78, VA Hosp., Iron Mountain, Mich., 1978-81; chief nursing home care unit, 1981—. Served with AUS, 1943-46; lt. col. USAF Res., 1979—. Mem. Exptl. Aviation Assn., Am. Legion, DAV, Assn. Mil. Surgeons U.S., Air Force Assn., Res. Officers Assn., Am. Security Council. Republican. Presbyterian Ch. (elder). Club: Rotary. Home: 1005 Bluff St Kingsford MI 49801 Office: VA Hosp Center H Iron Mountain MI 49801

WALLEY, E. LAWRENCE, exec. search co. exec.; b. Lima, Ohio, Apr. 2, 1942; s. Omar C. and Margaret M. (Smythe) W.; B.S., Ashland Coll., 1966; M.B.A., Washington U., St. Louis, 1968; m. Joanne F. Heitert, Dec. 2, 1967; 1 dau., Mary Patricia. Mgr. sales analysis Appliance div. Tappan Co., Mansfield, Ohio, 1968-77; gen. mgr. Tas-Co Thompson & Sons Co., Crestline, Ohio, 1977-78; mgr. Cooks' Inc. div. Plasticorp, Columbus, Ohio, 1979, corp. adminstr., 1979-81; owner Sanford Rose Assos.-Westerville, Westerville, Ohio, 1981—; lectr. in field. Active Jr. Achievement. Roman Catholic. Home: 45 Tammerlane Ct Westerville OH 43081 Office: 29 W College Ave Westerville OH 43081

WALLHAUSEN, MILDRED CAROLYN, newspaper publisher; b. Bklyn., Apr. 3, 1914; d. James Meroe and Frances (Bronson) Savell; grad. Brown's Bus. Coll., 1932; m. Arthur Louis Wallhausen, Sept. 25, 1936; children—Arthur Louis, Elizabeth Wallhausen Anderson. Sec. to real estate co., N.Y.C., 1932-33; proofreader Daily Am. Republic, Poplar Bluff, Mo., 1933-36; co-owner Enterprise-Courier, Charleston, Mo., 1936-69, pub., 1969—; dir. Cape Central Pub. Co. Mem. Mo. Gov.'s Adv. Council Comprehensive Health Planning, 1969-73, Bootheel Comprehensive Health Planning Council, 1971-77, Community Pub. Health Service Task Force, 1973, Mental Health Task Force, 1973, Regional Planning Commn., 1972-73, Charleston Park and Recreation Bd., 1972-77; mem. bd. Sr. Citizen Housing Project, 1973; mem. rev. team for grants Mo. Div. Mental Health, 1972-75; pres. Eugene Field Sch. PTA, 1948, Charleston High Sch. PTA, 1953; pres. Mississippi County Tb Assn., 1945-53, Mississippi County Child Welfare Council, 1971-77; bd. dirs. Mississippi County Child Devel. Center, 1974-77, Tri-County Counseling Center, 1975—, S.E. Archaeol. Assn., Mississippi County Cancer Soc.; mem. Mississippi County Recreation Assn., SE Mo. Mental Health Adv. Bd., SE Mo. Regional Adv. Council Alcoholism and Drug Abuse, 1976-78; county bd. mem. Sheltered Workshop, 1981—. Recipient various awards for service; named Woman of Year, BPW Club Charleston, 1973. Mem. S.E. Mo. Press Assn. (treas. 1978, sec. 1979, 1st v.p. 1980, pres. 1981), Am. Legion Aux. Clubs: Athena Study (pres. 1955), K. Boone Music (Charleston). Episcopalian (Sunday sch. tchr. 1981). Address: PO Box 69 Charleston MO 63824 Office: 206 S Main St Charleston MO 63824

WALLIN, STEVEN CRAIG, civil engr.; b. Milw., Jan. 2, 1949; s. Elmore Frederick and Marilyn Dorothy (Myrland) W.; B.S. in Civil Engring., U. Ill., 1972; m. Pamela D. Nielsen, Nov. 15, 1980. Project engr. Clyde E. Williams & Assoc., Terre Haute, Ind., 1972-74; project mgr. Clark, Dietz & Assoc., Urbana, Ill., 1974-81; profl. I, Bazzell-Phillips & Assos., Champaign, Ill., 1981—. Registered profl. engr., Ill. Mem. ASCE, Water Pollution Control Fedn., Sigma Phi Epsilon. Home: 210 Spring Circle Urbana IL 61801

WALLIN, WINSTON ROGER, food products co. exec.; b. Mpls., Mar. 6, 1926; s. Carl A. and Theresa (Hegge) W.; B.B.A., U. Minn., 1948; m. Maxine Houghton, Sept. 10, 1949; children—Rebecca, Brooks, Lance, Bradford. With Pillsbury Co., Mpls., 1948—, v.p. commodity ops., 1971-76, exec. v.p., 1976, pres., chief ops. officer, 1977—; dir. Medtronic, Inc., Soo Line R.R., 1st Mpls. Bank. Bd. dirs. United Way, Mpls., 1977, Downtown Council Mpls., 1977. Served with USN, 1944-46. Mem. Chgo. Bd. Trade, Mpls. Grain Exchange (dir. 1977—), Kansas City Bd. Trade. Clubs: Mpls., Interlachen, Minikahda. Office: 608 2d Ave S Minneapolis MN 55402

WALLMAN, CHARLES JAMES, money handling products co. exec.; b. Kiel, Wis., Feb. 19, 1924; s. Charles A. and Mary Ann (Loftus) W.; student Marquette U., 1942-43, Tex. Coll. Mines, 1943-44; B.B.A., U. Wis., 1949; m. Charline Marie Moore, June 14, 1952; children—Stephen, Jeffrey, Susan, Patricia, Andrew. Sales promotion mgr. Brandt, Inc., Watertown, Wis., 1949-65, v.p., 1960-70, exec. v.p., 1970-80, v.p. corp. devel., 1980—, also dir. Mem. exec. bd. Potawatomi council Boy Scouts Am., also former v.p. Trustee, Joe Davies Scholarship Found. Served with armored inf. AUS, 1943-45; ETO. Decorated Bronze Star. Mem. Am. Legion, E. Central Golf Assn. (past pres.), Wis. Alumni Assn. (local past pres.), Phi Delta Theta. Republican. Roman Catholic. Elk (past officer). Club: Watertown Country (past dir.). Home: 700 Clyman St Watertown WI 53094 Office: 705 S 12th St PO Box 200 Watertown WI 53094

WALLOT, ROBERT BRIAN, pharmacist; b. Mt. Vernon, Ohio, June 27, 1948; s. George Armond and Madeleine Elizabeth (Lambillotte) W.; B.S. in Pharmacy, Ohio No. U., 1971; postgrad. Coll. Pharmacy, Butler U., 1971; m. Gwendolyn Sue Sturtevant, Aug. 22, 1970. Pharmacy intern Heckler's Pharmacy, Mt. Vernon, 1969-71; asst. dir. pharmacy Bert W. Martin Meml. Hosp., Mt. Vernon, 1972, dir. pharmacy, 1972-79; pharmacy mgr. Hart's Family Center, Mt. Vernon, 1979—; auditor Martin-Mercy Employees' Fed. Credit Union; moderator Ohio pharm. edn. network Ohio State U., 1972—; preceptor structured externship program Ohio No. U., 1972—. Trustee Knox County Kidney Found., chmn. drug bank, 1979—. Recipient Vol. of Year award Kidney Found., 1975. Mem. Knox County Pharm. Assn. (sec.-treas. 1973—), Nat. Rifle Assn., Ohio Gun Collectors Assn. Methodist. Club: Elks. Home: Route 1 Bellville OH 44813 Office: Hart's Family Center Coshocton Rd Mount Vernon OH 43050

WALLS, BETTY L., psychologist; b. Kansas City, Mo., Oct. 26, 1932; d. Austin T. and Gladys O. (Gillespie) Webb; diploma in nursing Kansas City Gen. Hosp., 1957; B.A. in Psychology, U. Mo., 1967, M.A., 1971, Ph.D. in Psychology, 1974; 1 son, Paul Kevin. Clin. instr. maternity nursing St. Margaret's Hosp., Kansas City, Kans., 1958-60; dir. inservice edn. Research Hosp. Med. Center, Kansas City, Mo., 1962-65; instr. anatomy and physiology Sch. of Record Librarians, Kansas City, Mo., 1965; grad. teaching asst. psychology dept. U. Mo., Kansas City, 1968-69, instr., part-time 1976-80; instr. psychology dept. Park Coll., Parkville, Mo., 1972-73, asst. prof., 1973—, chmn., 1973-75, 78-80; vis. prof. U. Mo., Kansas City, 1981—; cons. to Kansas City Regional Found. for Retardation, 1978—, Cath. Charities, 1980—. Bd. dirs. Inst. for Alcohol Recovery, 1976—; bd. dirs. Sherwood Center for Exceptional Children, 1978—, v.p., 1979—; bd. dirs. Operation Discovery Sch., 1970—, v.p., 1972—. Womens Regional Council fellow, 1974; recipient Service award Kansas City, 1962. Mem. Am. Psychol. Assn., Assn. Behavior Analysts, AAAS, Mo. Psychol. Assn. (mem. com. on research standards 1978-79), N.Y. Acad. Sci., Psi Chi. Democrat. Methodist. Contbr. articles in field to profl. jours.; research in area of human fetal behavior and child behavior. Home: 8019 Kenwood Kansas City MO 64131 Office: U Mo at Kansas City Kansas City MO 64152

WALPOLE, SHERLU RARDIN, broadcasting exec., writer; b. Kirksville, Mo., Mar. 7, 1924; d. Nelson Gailord and Shirley Lou (Humphrey) Rardin; A.A., U. Chgo., 1943, B.A., 1945; M.A., S.W. Mo. State U., 1979; m. Hugh R. Walpole, Sept. 28, 1946 (div. 1954); 1 son, Hugh Nelson. Continuity writer Sta. KWTO, Springfield, Mo., 1951; continuity writer, women's program dir. Sta. KGBX, Springfield, 1952-54; continuity dir. Sta. KTTS-AM-FM-TV, Springfield, 1954-61; promotion mgr., merchandising dir. Sta. KOLR-TV/KTTS-AM-FM-TV, Springfield, 1962-75; account exec., spl. asst. to pres. MAP Advt. Agy., Springfield, 1975-77; promotion dir. Sta. KSMU, Springfield, 1978-80; mem. adj. faculty S.W. Mo. State U., Drury Coll.; feature writer Springfield! mag. Mem. Mo. Press Women, DAR, Mensa, Alpha Epsilon Rho. Democrat. Home: 3237 E Berkeley St Springfield MO 65804

WALSCHINSKI, AARON JAMES, design cons.; b. Green Bay, Wis., Dec. 18, 1935; s. Stanley and Rosalie Ann (Joppe) W.; B.A. in Philosophy, B.A. in Greek, St. Norbert Coll., 1959; M.A. in Classics, U. Wis., 1963; B.F.A., Pratt Inst., 1974, M.S. in Art Edn., 1974. Art asst. WBAY-TV, Green Bay, 1953-54; tchr. St. Norbert High Sch., De Pere, Wis., 1958-59, Bishop Neuman High Sch., Phila., 1964-72, Daylesford Abbey, Paoli, Pa., 1966-68; asst. prof. art and communication arts, campus planning cons., design cons. St. Norbert Coll., De Pere, 1974—, campus photographer, 1979—; design cons. in N.Y.C., Phila.; joined Norbertine Order, 1954, ordained priest, 1962. Recipient Chgo. Tribune award, 1954; Bishop Neumann Art and Drafting award, 1970. Mem. AAUP, Nat. Art Soc. Assn., Nat. Art Dirs. Assn., NEA, Assn. Internat. Photographers (2d prize Washington exhibit 1981), Nat. Coll. Art Tchrs. Assn., Alpha Delta Gamma. Roman Catholic. Exhibited art in shows at Pratt Inst., N.Y.C., U. Wis.-Green Bay Art Faculty Show, Green Bay Blue Print Show, St. Norbert Coll. Art Gallery, Photog '78 at Colby, Kans.; represented in pvt. collections in N.Y., Va., Tex., Wis., Pa., Mass. Home: 103 Grant St De Pere WI 54115 Office: St Norbert Coll De Pere WI 54115

WALSER, RANDAL LOUIS, info. engr.; b. Decatur, Ill., Feb. 20, 1949; s. Bernard Louis and Virginia Selene (Osborn) W.; M.S. in Info. Engring., U. Ill., Chgo., 1975. Research asst. biomed. engring. and neurosurgery Rush-St. Luke's Med. Center, Chgo., 1973-75; research asst. info. engring. U. Ill., Chgo., 1974-77; research systems mgr. Med. Info. Systems Lab., Chgo., 1977-78; research systems mgr. Distributed Image Mgmt. and Projection project Def. Advanced Research Projects Agy., Chgo., 1978-79; pres. Envisioneering, Inc., Chgo., 1979—; cons. in field; research fellow, dept. behavioral sci. Millikin U., 1972-73. Am. Cancer Soc. fellow, 1974. Mem. Assn. for Computing Machinery. Home: 831 W Wrightwood 2 Chicago IL 60614 Office: 2520 N Lincoln Ave Suite 102 Chicago IL 60614

WALSH, BEATRICE PASSAGE, civic worker; b. Schnectady, Mar. 6, 1917; d. William Riley and Jessamine (Littlefield) Passage; student Western Res. U., 1941-42; m. Thomas Joseph Walsh, July 12, 1941; 1 dau., Joan Beatrice Walsh Waltz. Vol. worker A.R.C., 1941-46, 47-53: leader council Cleve. Beachwood (Ohio) Girl Scouts, 1952-57; vol. worker Community Chest, 1947-50; mem. women's com. Cleve. Orch., 1962—; ladies program chmn. Am. Chem. Soc., 1960, Am. Inst. Chem. Engrs., 1961, ladies program conv. com., 1969; mem. Orange Community Arts Council, 1969—, Pepper Pike Civic League, 1966—; ladies program co-chmn. Nat. Heat Transfer Conf., 1964; mem. Shaker Heights League Women Voters, Case Faculty Wives (pres. 1958-59), Western Res. Republican Women's Club, D.A.R. (Shaker chpt., corr. sec. 1962-64, registrar 1964-69, publicity chmn. 1968-70, chaplain 1969-70, del. state conv. 1963, 64, 66, 69, 72, 74, 76, 77, 78, 79, chmn. reception del. nat. conv. 1964, regent 1974-76), Daus. Am. Colonies (vice regent 1977-79, regent 1980—, del. nat. conv. 1979), Magna Carta, Huguenot Soc., Nat. Soc. Colonial Dames XVII Century (parliamentarian 1980—), Order of Crown of Charlemagne, Nat. Soc. New Eng. Women (rec. sec. 1980—). Presbyterian. Clubs: Green Valley Garden, Blackbrook Country, Landerhaven Golf, Moreland Hills Golf, Landerwood Swim, Case-Western Reserve U. Women's. Home: 32555 Creekside Dr Pepper Pike Cleveland OH 44124

WALSH, EDWARD FRANCIS, educator, bus. cons.; b. Chgo., July 11, 1944; s. Patrick J. and Mary J. Walsh; B.B.A., Loyola U., 1967; M.B.A., No. Ill. U., 1969; M.A. in Bus. Adminstrn., Govs. State U., 1976; m. Joan Elizabeth Ambrose, June 26, 1971; children—Erin Ann, Daniel Edward. Teaching asst. No. Ill. U., DeKalb, Ill., 1967-69;

mem. faculty dept. bus. Prairie State Coll., Chicago Heights, Ill., 1969—, prof., 1972—; cons. Allied Tube and Conduit Corp., Harvey, Ill., 1973; acct. Wilkes Besterfield, C.P.A.'s, Olympia Fields, Ill., 1979-80; vis. prof. Govs. State U.; prof. Keller Grad. Sch. Mgmt. C.P.A., Ill. Mem. Ill. C.P.A. Soc., Midwest Bus. Adminstrn. Assn., Blue Key, Sigma Iota Epsilon (pres.), Alpha Beta Gamma (nat. pres. 1979-80). Office: 202 Halsted Chicago Heights IL 60411

WALSH, GLENN WILLIAM, assn. exec.; b. LaCrosse, Kans., Nov. 6, 1928; s. William Peter and Elizabeth (Ickes) W.; student Hutchinson Jr. Coll., 1946-47; m. Marilyn Olive Roberts, June 9, 1957; children—Christine, Douglas. Enlisted USAF, 1954, commd. 2d lt., 1955, advanced through grades to maj., 1966; assigned SAC, 1955-58; stationed Altus AFB, Okla., 1958-63, Lockbourne AFB, Ohio, 1963-68, Ramey AFB, P.R., 1969-71, McConnell AFB, Kans., 1971-74; ret., 1974; chief pilot Charter Serv., Wichita, Kans., 1974-75; exec. dir. Internat. Flying Farmer Orgn., Wichita, 1975—. Decorated DFC, Air medal. Mem. Wichita Area C. of C., Ret. Officers Assn. Republican. Presbyterian. Home: 150 Lochinvar St Wichita KS 67207 Office: PO Box 9124 Wichita KS 67277

WALSH, JAMES PATRICK, JR., ins. cons., actuary; b. Ft. Thomas, Ky., Mar. 7, 1910; s. James Patrick and Minnie Louise (Cooper) W.; comml. engr. degree, U. Cin., 1933; m. Evelyn Mary Sullivan, May 20, 1939. Accountant, Firestone Tire & Rubber Co., also Gen. Motors Corp., 1933-36; rep. ARC, 1937, A.F. of L., 1938-39; dir. Ohio Div. Minimum Wages, Columbus, 1939-42; asst. sec.-treas. union label trades dept. AFL, Washington, 1946-53; v.p. Pension and Group Cons., Inc., Cin., 1953—. Mem. President's Commn. Jud. and Congl. Salaries, 1953, Gov. Ohio Commn. Employment of Negro, 1940, Hamilton (Ohio) County Welfare Bd., 1957—, council long term illness and rehab. Cin. Pub. Health Fedn., 1957-68. Bd. dirs. U. Cin., 1959-67; bd. govs. St. Xavier High Sch., Cin., 1953-65; trustee Newman Fund, Brown Fund; mem. Internat. Found. Employee Benefit Plans, Inc. Served to lt. col. AUS, 1942-46; col. Res. Decorated Legion of Merit, Army Commendation medal with 2 oak leaf clusters; recipient Insignis award St. Xavier High Sch., Cin., 1973, Disting. Alumni award U. Cin.; cert. pension cons. Mem. Am. Acad. Actuaries, English Speaking Union, Res. Officers Assn. (life), Am. Legion (life), Navy League (life), Q.M. Assn., V.F.W., Amvets (life), Nat. Football Found. and Hall of Fame, Mil. Order World Wars (life), Am. Fedn. State, County and Employees Union, Internat. Alliance Theatrical Stage Employees (life mem.; past sgt. at arms), Internat. Hodcarriers, Bldg. and Common Laborers Union, Ins. Workers Internat. Union, Office Employees Internat. Union, Cooks and Pastry Cooks Local, Friendly Sons St. Patrick (past pres.), Covington Latin Sch. Alumni Assn. (past pres.), Soc. for Advancement Mgmt., Def. Supply Assn., Ancient Order Hibernians (past pres.), Assn. U.S. Army, Cursillio, Cin. Council World Affairs, Nat. Hist. Soc., Am. Ordnance Assn., Soc. Am. Mil. Engrs., Am. Arbitration Assn. (nat. community dispute settlement panel, employee benefit claims panel), Order of Alhambra, Allied Constrn. Industries, U. Cin. Alumni Assn. (life), Internat. Assn. Health Underwriters, Health Ins. Council S.W. Ohio, Scabbard and Blade, Greater Cin. Indsl. Relations Research Assn., Zoo Soc., Nat. Council Catholic Men, Archives Assos., Millcreek Valley Assn., Nat. Hist. Soc., Ret. Officers Assn. (past pres. Cin., pres. Ohio council), Am. Assn. Ret. Persons, Men of Milford, CATS, Smithsonian Assos., Inter Am. Soc., Germania Soc., Am. Soc. Pension Actuaries, Alpha Kappa Psi. Catholic. K.C. (4 deg.), Elk. Clubs: St. Antoninus Athletic, Green Twp. Republican, Republican of Hamilton County (life), War Veterans Republican, Newman (Cin.), Cincinnati (past pres.), Queen City, Nat. Travel, American-Irish, Insiders, U.C. Boosters, Xavier U. Musketeer, Bengals Touchdown, Global Sportsman, Military. Home: 5563 Julmar Dr Cincinnati OH 45238 Office: 6 E 4th St Cincinnati OH 45202

WALSH, JEROME LEO, state senator; b. Minot, N.D., Nov. 22, 1932; s. James Leo and Magdalene Mary (Frost) W.; ed. Minot State Coll.; m. Darlene Gail Cecilia Bach, 1952; children—Jerome Mikel, Lloyd Patrik. Owner, operator Walsh Wheat Farm, Minot, 1952—, Walsh Snowmobile Sales, 1968—; mem. N.D. Ho. of Reps., 1970-72, N.D. State Senate, 1975—. Treas., Nedrose Sch. Bd., 1959-69. Named Outstanding Young Farmer, 1962; recipient Wildlife Conservation award Agr. Stblzn. and Conservation, 1967. Mem. Western Snowmobile Assn., N.D. Wildlife Fedn., Farmers Unions. Clubs: Elks, Eagles. Office: State Capitol Bismarck ND 58505*

WALSH, KENNETH ALBERT, chemist; b. Yankton, S.D., May 23, 1922; s. Albert Lawrence and Edna (Slear) W.; B.A., Yankton Coll., 1942; Ph.D., Iowa State U., 1950; m. Dorothy Jeanne Thompson, Dec. 22, 1944; children—Jeanne K., Kenneth Albert, David Bruce, Rhonda Jean, Leslie Gay. Asst. prof. chemistry Iowa State U., Ames, 1950-51; staff mem. Los Alamos Sci. Lab., 1951-57; supr. Internat. Minerals & Chems. Corp., Mulberry, Fla., 1957-60; mgr. Brush Beryllium Co., Elmore, Ohio, 1960-72; asso. dir. tech. Brush Wellman Inc., Elmore, 1972—. Democratic precinct chmn., Los Alamos, 1956, Fremont, Ohio, 1980. Mem. Am. Chem. Soc. (sect. treas. 1956), Am. Soc. for Metals, Am. Ceramic Soc., AIME, AAAS, Theta Xi, Phi Lambda Upsilon. Methodist. Club: Toastmasters Internat. Patentee in field. Home: 2624 Fangboner Rd Fremont OH 43420 Office: Brush Wellman Inc Elmore OH 43416

WALSH, LINDA ELIZABETH, banker; b. Shelbyville, Ill., Jan. 22, 1947; d. Bernard Robert Schaefer and Elizabeth McKinsey; student Gulf Park Coll., 1965-66, U. Madrid, summer 1966; B.S., U. Ariz., 1969; M.B.A., Keller Grad. Sch. Mgmt., 1980. Asst. buyer mgr. Bullocks Dept. Store, Santa Ana, Calif., 1969-70; asst. to dir. Japan Nat. Tourist Orgn., Chgo., 1970-72; asst. mktg. dir. Nat. Security Bank, Chgo., 1972-74; personal banking officer, banking dept. No. Trust Co., Chgo., 1974-80; v.p. in charge mktg. and human resource depts. Heritage County Bank & Trust, Blue Island, Ill., 1981—. Pres. bd. Martha Washington Home for Dependent Crippled Children, 1978—; mem. asso. bd. Chgo. Lung Assn., 1980—; bd. dirs. Children's Meml. Hosp.; bd. dirs., treas. Friends of the Handicapped Riders, 1979-80. Lic. real estate broker, Ill. Mem. Nat. Assn. Bank Women, Women in Mgmt., Am. Soc. Tng. and Devel., Chgo. Fin. Advertisers, Bank Mktg. Assn., Ill. Hunters and Jumpers Assn., English Speaking Union, Alpha Chi Omega. Episcopalian. Club: Lake Shore Center. Home: 1636 N Wells St Chicago IL 60614 Office: 12015 S Western Ave Blue Island IL 60406

WALSH, RICHARD A., state senator; b. Chgo., Nov. 25, 1930; B.S., J.D., Loyola U.; m. Patricia; 6 children. Admitted to Ill. bar, Wis. bar; individual practice law, Chgo., 1960—; mem. Ill. Ho. of Reps., 1962-76, Ill. Senate, 1976—. Served with USNR, 1954-57. Mem. Ill., W. Suburban, Chgo. bar assns. Republican. Office: State Capitol Springfield IL 62706*

WALSH, RITA, ophthalmologist; b. Caguas, P.R., June 11, 1920; d. Clarence Joseph and Mercedes (Chiques) Walsh; B.S., U. P.R., 1939; B.S., Columbia U., 1943; M.D., Loyola U., Chgo., 1950. Clin. fellow, then instr. physiologic optics Dartmouth Eye Inst., Hanover, N.H., 1943-45; intern Hollywood Presbyn. Hosp., Los Angeles, 1950-51; preceptorship ophthalmology Gailey Eye Clinic, Bloomington, Ill., 1951-54, staff ophthalmologist, 1954—; mem. staff Mennonite Hosp. Mem. AMA, Am. Acad. Ophthalmology, Panam. Assn. Ophthalmologists, Internat., Am. colls. surgeons, McLean County (past pres.), Ill. med. socs. Republican. Roman Catholic. Club: Bloomington Country. Contbr. med. jours. Home: 815 N Prairie St Bloomington IL 61701 Office: 1008 N Main St Bloomington IL 61701

WALSH, ROBERT JOSEPH, surgeon; b. Chgo., Dec. 22, 1934; s. Joseph Michael and Iverne Lucille (Griffin) W.; A.B. cum laude, Loyola U. at Chgo., 1957, M.D. cum laude, 1961; m. Catherine Ellen Andersen, June 4, 1960; children—Kevin, Brian, Martin, Carin. Intern, U. Chgo., 1961-62, resident, 1963-66; resident U. Iowa, 1966; practice medicine specializing in orthopedic surgery, Chgo., 1967-71, Arlington Heights, Ill., 1971—; instr. U. Chgo., 1965-66; instr. Northwestern U., 1967-77, asst. prof. clin. orthopedic surgery, 1977—. Chmn. troop com. Boy Scouts Am., 1975. Served to maj., M.C., AUS, 1968-70. Fellow A.C.S.; mem. Chgo., Ill. med. socs., AMA, Am. Acad. Orthopedic Surgeons, Chgo. Com. on Trauma, Chgo., Ill. orthopedic socs., Blue Key, Alpha Sigma Nu. Clubs: Michigan Shores, Meadow. Office: 1120 N Arlington Heights Rd Arlington Heights IL 60004

WALSH, THOMAS J(OSEPH), chem. engr., educator; b. Troy, N.Y., July 17, 1917; s. Thomas Joseph and Anna (Sharp) W.; B.S., Rensselaer Poly. Inst., 1939, M.S., 1941; Ph.D., Case Inst. Tech., 1949; m. Beatrice Metcalfe Passage, July 12, 1941; 1 dau., Joan Beatrice Waltz. Chem. engr. Standard Oil Co. Ohio, 1941-47; prof. Case Inst. Tech., 1947-61; engr. Lewis Flight Propulsion Lab. NACA, 1951-55; cons. Thompson Ramo Wooldridge, 1955-61, sr. staff specialist, requirements mgr. research applications equipment labs. division, 1961-66; process specialist corp. engring. dept. Glidden-Durkee div. SCM Corp., Cleve., 1966-68, mgr. process engring., from 1968, mgr. environ. conservation, energy coordinator, to 1979, mgr. corp. energy conservation, 1979-80; v.p. Consultex, Inc., 1980—; cons. Glascote Products Co., 1954-61, Hukill Chem., Booth Oil Co., ECA, Inc., Argonne Nat. Lab.; adj. prof. chem. engring. Case Western Res. U., 1980—; adj. prof. chem. engring., spl. lectr. Cleve. State U., 1980—. Pres. Northeastern Ohio Science Fair, Inc. Recipient Junior Tech. award Cleve. Tech. Soc. Council, Merit award Cleve. Chem. Profession. Fellow Am. Inst. Chem. Engrs.; mem. AAAS, Am. Chem. Soc. (trustee), ASCE, AAUP, Cleve. Tech. Socs. Council (past pres.), Am. Inst. Aeros and Astronautics, Cleve. Engring. Soc. (gov.). Home: 32555 Creekside Dr Pepper Pike OH 44124 Office: Union Commerce Bldg Cleveland OH 44115

WALSTROM, JOHN ALBERT JAMES, educator; b. Ramsey, Ill., Apr. 25, 1937; s. Gusta Albin and Mary Louise (Dobbs) W.; B.S., Eastern Ill. U., 1960, M.S., 1963; postgrad. North Tex. State U., 1968-69, 71; Ph.D., U. Nebr., 1976; m. Phyllis Kay Peabody, Dec. 21, 1958; children—Kent Alan, Scott Gregory, Brian James. Dir. data processing Eastern Ill. U., 1960-68; prof. data processing Western Ill. U., 1969—; vis. instr. computer sci. U. Nebr., 1974. Cubmaster Cub Scouts Am., 1970-72. Certified data processor. Mem. Data Processing Mgmt. Assn. (dir. exec. bd. East Central Ill. chpt. 1965-68, sec. 1966-68, individual performance award 1968), Assn. Computing Machinery, Ill. Assn. Data Processing Instrs., Soc. Data Educators, Ill. Acad. Sci., Beta Gamma Sigma, Sigma Iota Epsilon, Phi Delta Kappa, Upsilon Pi Epsilon. Contbr. articles to profl. jours. Home: 313 S Verzel Dr Macomb IL 61455

WALT, ALEXANDER JEFFREY, surgeon; b. Cape Town, South Africa, June 13, 1923; came to U.S., 1961, naturalized, 1966; m. Isaac and Lea (Garb) W.; M.B., Ch.B., U. Cape Town, 1948; M.S. in Surgery, U. Minn., 1956; m. Irene Lapping, Dec. 21, 1947; children—John R., Steven D., Lindsay J. Intern, Groote Schuur Hosp., Cape Town, asst. surgeon, 1957-61; resident Mayo Found., Rochester, Minn., 1952-56; asst. chief surgery VA Hosp., Dearborn, Mich., 1961-62; chmn. dept. surgery Wayne State U., Detroit, 1966—, also Penberthy prof. surgery; chief surgery Detroit Receiving Hosp., 1965-80, Harper-Grace Hosps., Detroit, 1972—. Served with South Africa Armed Forces, 1943-45. Diplomate Am. Bd. Surgery (dir.). Fellow Royal Coll. Surgeons (Can.), Royal Coll. Surgeons (Eng.), ACS (gov.); mem. Am. Surg. Assn., Soc. Surgery Alimentary Tract, Am. Assn. Surgery Trauma (pres. 1976-77), AMA, Internat. Soc. Surgery, Central Surg. Assn. (pres. 1977-78), Western Surg. Assn., Alpha Omega Alpha. Author: (with R. F. Wilson) Management of Trauma: Pitfalls and Practice, 1975. Home: 26373 Hendrie St Huntington Woods MI 48070 Office: 540 E Canfield St Detroit MI 48201

WALTER, FRANK SHERMAN, hosp. adminstr.; b. Denver, June 23, 1926; s. Frank J. and Nancy W. (Sherman) W.; B.S., U. Oreg., 1950; M.B.A., U. Chgo., 1951; m. Carolyn May Cox, July 29, 1949; children—Douglas, Steven, Nancy. Adminstrv. resident Grad. Hosp., U. Pa., Phila., 1950-51, adminstrv. asst., 1951-52, asst. dir., 1952-55; adminstr. Meth. Hosp., Phila., 1955-63, St. Barnabas Hosp., Mpls., 1962-70; pres. Met. Med. Center, Mpls., 1970—; trustee Blue Cross/Blue Shield of Minn., 1977—. Bd. dirs. Mpls War Meml. Blood Bank, 1964-70; clin. preceptor U. Minn., 1965—; dir. Downtown Council, 1977—. Served with USAAF, 1944-46. Fellow Am. Coll. Hosp. Adminstrs.; mem. Health Manpower Mgmt. Assn., Upper Midwest Hosp. Assn. (dir. 1977—), Minn. Hosp. Assn. (trustee 1970-78, treas. 1973-74, pres. 1975-76), Twin City Hosp. Assn. (pres. 1970-71). Episcopalian. Club: Kiwanis. Home: 6129 Blake Ridge Rd Edina MN 55436 Office: Met Med Center 900 S 8th St Minneapolis MN 55404

WALTER, FRANKLIN B., state ofc.; b. LaGrange, Ind., Sept. 16, 1929; s. Rollo H. and Lola A. W.; B.S., Manchester Coll., 1951; M.E., Miami U., 1955; Ph.D., Ohio State U., 1965; m. Jane Weber, Dec. 31, 1950; children—Ronald Lynn, Robert Lee. Tchr., Northwestern Local Schs., Springfield, Ohio, 1951-55; prin. New Lebanon High Sch., 1955-56; supt. New Lebanon (Ohio) Schs., 1956-61; research asso. Ohio State U., 1961-63; supt. Westlake (Ohio) City Schs., 1963-68; asst. supt. public instrn. Dept. Edn. State of Ohio, Columbus, 1968-70, dep. supt., 1970-77, supt., 1977—; prof. Nat. Acad. Sch. Execs. Active United Appeal, Boy Scouts Am. Recipient E.E. Lewis Award in Sch. Adminstrn., Centennial award of Coll. Edn. Ohio State U., Miami U. Disting. Service award. Mem. Am. Assn. Sch. Adminstrs., Buckeye Assn. Sch. Adminstrs., Phi Delta Kappa. Lutheran. Contbr. articles to profl. jours. Office: 65 S Front St Columbus OH 43215*

WALTER, GARY A., ins. exec.; b. Manhattan, Kans., May 28, 1948; s. Warren L. and Bonita J. (Gravenstein) W.; B.S. in Bus. Adminstrn., Kans. State U., Manhattan, 1972; m. Jackie L. Grable, June 12, 1971; 1 son, Brian Jeffrey. Life ins. agt. Nat. Life & Accident Ins. Co., Manhattan, 1971-72; advanced sales mgr. Kans. Farm Life Ins. Co., Manhattan, 1972-81, asst. gen. mgr., 1979-81, gen. mgr., 1981—, also asst. sec.; instr. Kans. Bd. Regents Continuing Edn. Chmn. bd. trustees KFB Pension Trust. C.L.U. Mem. Am. Soc. C.L.U.'s Nat. Assn. Life Underwriters, Kans. Life Assn., Am. Council Life Ins., Am. Mgmt. Assn., Manhattan Area Estate Planning Assn. (chmn. 1977), Manhattan C. of C. Republican. Methodist. Clubs: Rotary, Manhattan Country. Contbr. articles in field. Home: 1800 Denholm Dr Manhattan KS 66502 Office: 2321 Anderson Ave Manhattan KS 66502

WALTER, GLEN HERMAN, JR., educator; b. St. Louis, Oct. 19, 1947; s. Glen Herman and Ruth A. (Wunnenburg) W.; B.A., Concordia Tchrs. Coll., River Forest, Ill., 1970; M.S. in Counselor Edn., So. Ill. U., Edwardsville, 1974; Ph.D. in Edn., U. Fla., 1977; m. Jacqueline Ann Dickerson, Sept. 1, 1973; children—Nicholas, Katie. Classroom tchr., Hawaii and Calif., 1968-71; counselor Greenville (Ill.) Sch. Dist., 1974-75; asso. prof. ednl. psychology and guidance Eastern Ill. U., Charleston, 1977—; speaker in field. Bd. dirs. Coles County Parents Against Child Abuse, 1978—. Recipient Outstanding Faculty Merit award Eastern Ill. U., 1979-80. Mem. Assn. Humanistic Edn., Am. Guidance and Personnel Assn., Am. Ednl. Research Assn., Ill. Guidance and Personnel Assn. Roman Catholic. Author: So Where's My Apple: Diary of a First Year Teacher, 1981. Office: Eastern Ill U Charleston IL 61920

WALTER, NOLA JANICE, rental co. exec.; b. Eau Claire, Wis., Mar. 29, 1934; d. Robert Emmet and Adeline Victoria (Johnson) Rossman; student Dist. 1 Tech. Inst., Eau Claire, 1977-78; 1 dau., Rhea Carol. Exec. sec. W.H. Hobbs Supply Co., Eau Claire, 1952-54; jr. accountant C.A. Irwin Co., Eau Claire, 1954-61; legal sec. various attys. in Eau Claire, Mpls., 1963-73; office mgr. Bearson-Steinmetz Rentals, Eau Claire, 1974—; freelance artist, 1980-81. Recipient Gregg Shorthand certificate of merit, 1952, certs. of award in oil painting, 1977, 78; Gold, Silver and Bronze awards in competitive dancing, 1979, 80, 81. Mem. Nat. Wildlife Fedn., Am. Antiques and Crafts Soc., Nat. Trust for Historic Preservation, Mpls. Soc. Fine Arts, Smithsonian Assos., Am. Film Inst. Democrat. Congregationalist. Home: 825 Barland St Eau Claire WI 54701 Office: 315 E Madison St Eau Claire WI 54701

WALTER, RALPH COLLINS, III, investment banking co. exec.; b. Hinsdale, Ill., Nov. 25, 1946; s. Ralph Collins and Ethel Marie (Eustice) W.; B.A., Knox Coll., 1969; M.A., Ind. U., 1972; m. Sharon L. Maretta Koop, Aug. 9, 1980. Instr., Ind. U. Bloomington, 1971-72; with A.G. Becker, Inc., Chgo., 1973—, v.p., 1976—. Served to capt. U.S. Army, 1973. Woodrow Wilson fellow, 1969, Alfred P. Sloan scholar, 1966-69. Mem. Am. Econ. Assn., Am. Fin. Assn., Phi Beta Kappa. Home: 10501 5th Ave Cutoff LaGrange IL 60525 Office: A G Becker Inc 2 First National Plaza Chicago IL 60603

WALTER, TERRY LYNN, cons. psychol. firm exec.; b. Great Bend, Kans., Dec. 23, 1928; s. Clifton William and Helen Naudia (Rusco) W.; B.S., Kans. State U., 1952; M.Ed., U. Mo., 1969, Ph.D., 1979; m. Evelyn Margaret Evans, July 3, 1949; children—Marcia Jeanne, Sandra Alice, Michael Kent, Steven Craig. Chemist, Halliburton Oil Well Cement Co., Great Bend, 1945-47; research asst. U.S. Dept. Agr., Kans. State U., Manhattan, 1948-52; math. and sci. tchr. U. Md. Extension div., Eng., 1953-54; grade sch. tchr. Fairview Sch., Norton, Kans., 1955-56; cons. engr. Walter Cons. Engring. Service, Tribune, Kans., 1954—; pres. Asso. Personnel Technicians, Inc., cons. psychologists; owner, operator Mineral Exploration and Devel. Unltd., 1975—; grad. adminstrv. asst. dir. counseling bur. U. Mo., Columbia, 1968-69, counselor for testing, 1969—, instr. extension div., 1968—; asso. dir. Greeley Coop. Assn., Tribune, 1966-68. Bd. dirs. Wichita Guidance Center; chmn. bd. Christian Community Services, Inc., Wichita Guidance Center; bd. dirs. Am. Bapt. Conv. Served with USAF, 1952-54. Registered profl. engr., Kans. Mem. Am. Personnel and Guidance Assn., Am. Coll. Personnel Assn., Kans. Profl. Engrs., Am. Mgmt. Soc., Am. Soc. Personnel Adminstrs., Am. Psychol. Assn., Wichita Psychol. Assn., Alpha Kappa Lambda. Baptist (dir. Kans. conv. 1962-67). Patentee in field. Home: 6700 Abbotsford Pl Wichita KS 67206

WALTER, VIRGINIA LEE, psychologist; b. Temple, Tex., Oct. 30, 1937; d. Luther Patterson and Virginia Lafayette (Wilkins) Walter; B.S., U. Tex., Austin, 1959, M.Edn., 1967; postgrad. internship program in Spl. Edn. Adminstrn., 1970; Ed.D., U. Houston, 1973; m. Glen Ellis, 1958 (div.); children—Glen Edward, David Walter; m. 2d, Robert Reinehr, 1963 (div.); 1 son, Charles Allen; m. 3d, Robert Bruininks, 1975 (div.). Elem. classroom tchr. Austin Ind. Sch. Dist., 1959-60, Houston Ind. Sch. Dist., 1965; teaching asst. and research asst. dept. ednl. psychology U. Tex., Austin, 1965-66; intern Austin State Hosp., 1967; curriculum specialist Spl. Ednl. Instructional Materials Center, U. Tex., 1967-68; dir. field activities Edn. Personnel Devel., Austin, 1969-70; parent trainer-communications coordinator Edn. Service Center, Austin, 1970-71; grad. asst. U. Houston, 1971-72, teaching fellow, summer 1972, evaluator lab. experiences Tchrs. Inst. Program, 1972-73, grad. asst., advisor in curriculum and instrn. student services center, 1972-73, teaching fellow dept. curriculum and instrn., 1973; prof. ednl. psychology dept. psychoednl. studies U. Minn., Mpls., 1973—; cons. spl. ednl. various sch. dists. Named Minn. Spl. Educator of Yr., 1978; HEW Office of Human Devel. Services grantee, 1976-79; Dept. Edn. grantee, 1980—. Mem. Council for Exceptional Children, Nat. Assn. Children with Learning Disabilities (dir. Minn. chpt. 1978-80), Nat. Assn. Retarded Citizens, AAUP, Assn. Supervision and Curriculum Devel. Editorial cons. Jour. Ednl. Psychology, 1979; asso. editor Exceptional Children, 1979—; contbr. articles to profl. jours., papers to profl. confs. Home: 4914 Arden Ave S Edina MN 55424 Office: 13 Pattee Hall 150 Pillsbury Dr SE University of Minnesota Minneapolis MN 55455

WALTERS, CHARLES WILLIAM, research engr.; b. Indpls., July 2, 1914; s. Harrison and Josephine (Iliff) W.; B.S., Butler U., 1935; postgrad. U. Chgo., 1938-39; m. Marthana McWhir, June 1957; children—David Harrison, Flora Ann. Lectr. inorganic chemistry Butler U., 1935-36; analytical and metall. chemist P.R. Mallory & Co., 1936-38; research engr. electronic components Mallory-Emhart, Indpls., 1946—. Served with USAAF, 1941-46. Mem. Electrochem. Soc. (sec.-treas. Indpls. sect.). Presbyterian. Clubs: Masons, Scottish Rite. Patentee in field. Home: 5934 College Ave Indianapolis IN 46220 Office: Mallory Capacitor Co 101 S Parker Indianapolis IN 46206

WALTERS, DONNA JUNE, interior designer; b. Alva, Okla., June 24, 1937; d. Floyd R. and Elsie Martha (Schick) Paris; B.S., Okla. State U., 1959, postgrad., 1960, 68, 69, Kansas City Art Inst., 1979; children—Terri Sue, Bradford Paris. Tchr. elem. schs., Lakewood, Colo., 1964-65; kindergarten tchr. Dist. 110 Schs., Overland Park, Kans., 1966-67; nat. rep. Chi Omega, 1972-81; founder, owner, designer D.J.'s Interiors, Kansas City, 1973—; exec. bd. Gt. Am. Restaurant Co. Bd. dirs. Kansas City Conv. and Visitors Bur., 1975-78; trustee Country Club Meth. Ch., 1978—, also mem. parsonage com. Recipient Alumnae Achievement award Chi Omega. Mem. Kansas City Panhellenic Assn., Historic Kansas City Soc., Kansas City Womens Philharmonic, PEO, Kansas City Alumnae Chi Omega (exec. bd.), Kansas City Arabian Horse Assn., Internat. Arabian Horse Assn. Democrat. Interior designer Applewood's Restaurant, Oklahoma City, Old Washington St. Sta., The Village Green. Address: 835 W 55th St Kansas City MO 64113

WALTERS, JANE ELLEN, educator; b. Muncie, Ind., Aug. 22, 1928; d. Charles E. and Sarah S. (Culbertson) Stokes; student Hendrix Coll., 1946-47; B.S. in Bus., Washington U., 1950; postgrad. Omaha U., 1952; cert. Mo. U., 1970, M.Ed., 1972; postgrad. Central Mo. State U., summer, 1972; m. Albert F. Walters, Feb. 3, 1951; children—Pamela Lynn, Charles Edwin, Diane Marie. Head stock, infants dept. Stix Baer & Fuller, St. Louis, 1950-51, jr. wear dept. Boston Store, Ft. Smith, Ark., 1952; statis. analyst AT&T, Kansas City, Mo., 1952; customer service rep. Ind. Bell Telephone, Indpls., 1953, Omaha Met. Utilities Dist., 1953; head package food sales orders Gen. Mills Inc., St. Louis, 1954-57; substitute tchr. Rockwood Sch. Dist., St. Louis, 1966-69; tchr., coordinator Pattonville Sch. Dist., St. Louis, 1970-76; dir. Practical Edn. Now pilot projects, St. Louis County, Mo., 1974—; condr. workshops in vocat. and career edn., various sch. dists. in Mo., 1975—. Judge dist. and state competition Future Bus. Leaders Am., 1978-80; vol. worker Cystic Fibrosis, Cancer, Leukemia, Muscular Dystrophy, 1960—; sec. Supt.'s Adv. Com. on Community Resources, 1974. Recipient Service plaque Future Bus. Leaders Am., 1978; Mo. State Outstanding Bus. Educator award, 1976; Cert. of Recognition, Kiwanis Club, 1976, 77. Mem. NEA, Am. Vocat. Assn., Mo. Vocat. Assn., Mo. Edn. Assn., Pattonville Edn. Assn., Delta Gamma. Presbyterian. Contbr. articles to profl. publs.; originator practical edn. program utilized by Mo. Dept. Edn. Office: 11055 St Charles Rock Rd Saint Ann MO 63074

WALTERS, JEFFERSON BROOKS, musician, real estate broker; b. Dayton, Ohio, Jan. 22, 1922; s. Jefferson Brooks and Mildred Frances (Smith) W.; student U. Dayton, 1947; m. Mary Elizabeth Espey, Apr. 6, 1963; children—Dinah Christine Basson, Jefferson Brooks. Composer, cornetist Dayton, 1934—; real estate broker, Dayton, 1948—; founder Am. Psalm Choir, 1965. Served with USCGR, 1942-45; PTO, ETO. Mem. S.A.R., Greater Dayton Antique Study Club (past pres.), Dayton Art Inst., Montgomery County Hist. Soc., Dayton Area Bd. Realtors, Friends of Wright State U. Library (vice chmn.). Presbyterian. Club: Masons (32 deg.). Condr., composer choral, solo voice settings of psalms and poetry Alfred Lord Tennyson; composer Crossing the Bar (meml. performances U.S. Navy band), 1961. Home: 400 Ridgewood Ave Dayton OH 45409 Office: Classics Realty 53 Park Ave Dayton OH 45419

WALTERS, MARGARET CONNOR ARTMAN (MRS. CLARENCE WALTERS), civic worker; b. Chgo., Aug. 27, 1910; d. Joseph Manson and Mildred (Bubenzer) Artman; Ph.B. in Social Service, U. Chgo., 1933, M.A., 1948; m. Clarence Walters, June 20, 1936 (dec. Oct. 1944). Caseworker Pub. Assistance, Chgo., 1938-41; social worker Ch. Fedn. Boys Ct. Service, Chgo., 1943-48; social worker Hines VA Hosp., 1948-51; with state psychiat. clinic, Chgo., 1951-53, dept. psychiatry U. Ill. Coll. Medicine, 1953-55; with Social Service Dept. Cook County Hosp., 1955-61, asst. dir., 1959-61; with mental health div. Chgo. Bd. Health, 1961-70, coordinator tng. and mental health edn., 1967-70. Pres. Internat. House Assn., Chgo., 1953, 54; mem. edn. com. Ill. Gov.'s Commn. Status of Women, 1964-68; mem. Met. Housing and Planning Council, Chgo., 1961—; mem. nutrition adv. council Mayor's Office for Sr. Citizens, Chgo., 1974-76; mem. mental health task force Comprehensive Health Planning, Inc., Chgo., 1974-75; mem. health task force and adv. com. for alcoholism edn. and prevention program MidSouthside Health Planning Orgn., Chgo., 1974-76; active Chgo. Archtl. Found., 1976—, Oriental Inst., 1976—; bd. dirs. Meth. Youth Services, 1978—; mem. health services rev. com. Chgo. Health Systems Agy., 1981—. Fellow Am. Orthopsychiat. Assn (chmn. pub. relations com. 1960); mem. Nat. Assn. Social Workers (chpt. vice chmn. 1962, chpt. dir. 1972), Am. Acad. Certified Social Workers, Ill. Acad. Criminology (sec. 1967-70, archivist 1971, v.p., 1972-73, 75, editor newsletter 1973-76, exec. dir. 1976—), AAAS, Chgo. Acad. Scis., Fedn. Am. Scientists, LWV, Am. Assn. Ret. Persons (chpt. pres. 1975-76, 80-82), Internat. Oceanographic Found., Photog. Soc. Am., Audubon Soc., World Future Soc., Ret. City Employees Club (pres. 1974), Phi Beta Kappa. Democrat. Unitarian-Universalist. Home: 5732 Harper Ave Chicago IL 60637

WALTERS, NANCY ROCKHILL, educator; b. Greencastle, Ind., Apr. 23, 1927; d. Howard and Muriel (Rector) Rockhill; A.B., DePauw U., 1949; M.S., Ind. U., 1951, Ph.D., 1967; m. Elwood Walters, Nov. 22, 1950; children—Mark, Joel, John, Paul, Adam. Tchr. and counselor various sch. dists. in Ind., 1949-64; prof. psychology and counseling Central Mo. State U., Warrensburg, 1967—. Mem. Mo. Del. to White House Conf. on Children, Washington, 1970; mem. Gov.'s Com. for Children and Youth, State of Mo., 1972—; workshop coordinator Gov.'s Conf. Edn., Mo., 1977; mem. Mo. Steering Com. on Sex Equity in Vocat. Edn., 1977—; mem. adminstrn. bd. United Meth. Ch., 1976—. Mem. Mo. Personnel and Guidance Assn. (pres. 1977-78), Am. Personnel and Guidance Assn., Nat. Vocat. Guidance Assn., Nat. Council Family Relations, Am. Psychol. Assn., Mo. Assn. for Specialists in Group Work (pres. 1980-81), Am. Sch. Counselors Assn., Mo. Guidance Assn. (sec. various state coms. 1967—), Phi Delta Kappa. Methodist. Contbr. articles on counseling and edn. to profl. publs. Home: 430 Hamilton St Warrensburg MO 64093 Office: Education 406 Central Missouri Univ Warrensburg MO 64093

WALTERS, THOMAS HARRY, steel co. exec.; b. Youngstown, Ohio, Oct. 23, 1947; s. Robert David and Virginia June Walters; B.S. in Bus. Adminstrn., Youngstown State U., 1971; postgrad. in blast furnace tech. McMaster U., Ont., Can., 1977; m. Patricia Ann Henderson, Mar. 16, 1974; children—Amanda, Joshua. Office asst. Republic Indsl. Edn. Trust, Youngstown, 1964-67; steel coil bundler Indsl. Steel Co., Youngstown, 1967-68; partner painting firm, Youngstown. 1966-68; operator Gen. Motors Assembly div., Lordstown, Ohio, 1968-73; gen. supr. J & L Steel Blast Furnace, East Chicago, Ind., 1973—. Asst. scoutmaster Eagle Scouts, Mahoning Valley council Boy Scouts Am., 1966; mem. Union Vol. Fire Dept., Porter County, Valparaiso, Ind. Mem. Nat. Mgmt. Assn., Western States Blast Furnace and Coke Plant Assn. Democrat. Lutheran. Office: J & L Steel 3100 Dickey Rd East Chicago IN 46312

WALTHER, MICHAEL CHRISTOPHER, lawyer; b. St. Louis, July 30, 1938; s. Adam C. and Alyce K. (Keough) W.; B.S., St. Louis U., 1960, J.D., 1964; m. Alice L. Abel, Nov. 23, 1963; children—Michael Christopher, II, John Charles. Admitted to Mo. bar, 1964; with firm Lashly, Caruthers, Thies, Rava & Hamel, P.C., St. Louis, 1963-80, partner, 1968-80; with Todd & Walther, P.C., St. Louis, 1980—; mcpl. judge City of Hazelwood (Mo.), 1970—; lectr. law St. Louis U. Law Sch., U. Mo. Law Sch. Bd. dirs. St. Louis Jr. C. of C., 1965-70; co-chmn. profls. div. United Way St. Louis, 1974. Fellow Am. Acad. Matrimonial Lawyers (pres. elect Mo. chpt. 1979-80); mem. Am. Bar Assn. (Nat. Conf. Bar Pres.'s), Mo. Bar (gov. 1970, vice chmn. family law sect. 1976—), Bar Assn. Met. St. Louis (pres. 1979-80). Club: Univ. (St. Louis). Author handbook, also articles in field. Home: 35 Crestwood Dr Clayton MO 63105 Office: 212 S Meramec Saint Louis MO 63105

WALTON, HOWARD CHARLES, III, educator; b. Muskogee, Okla., Dec. 13, 1945; s. Howard Charles and Mildred Ruth (Cook) W.; B.S., Auburn U., 1967; M.A., East Tenn. State U., 1970; Ph.D., Fla. State U., 1981; m. Cathryn Spring Jenkins, Mar. 15, 1969. Staff psychologist Bravard Public Sch., Rockledge, Fla., 1970-76; asst. to budget dir. Fla. State U., Tallahassee, 1976-77; adminstr. mgmt. services and research Orange County (Fla.) Public Schs., Orlando, 1977-78, dir. fed. programs, 1978-80; prof. mgmt. Ball State U., Muncie, Ind., 1980—; pres., dir. Comptex, Inc.; dir., exec. v.p. Ind. Inst. Productivity and Growth. Mem. Am. Prodn. Inventory Control Soc., Am. Inst. Decision Scis., Am. Mgmt. Assn., Sigma Iota Epsilon. Presbyterian. Club: Elks. Home: 625 Riley Rd Muncie IN 47304 Office: College of Business Ball State University Muncie IN 47306

WALTON, JAMES RAY, psychologist; b. Kaukauna, Wis., June 2, 1943; s. James Raymond and Harriet Marie W.; B.S., Northeast Mo. State U., 1968, M.A., 1969; Ed.S., U. S.D., 1973; m. Janice Kaye Logli, Feb. 15, 1964; children—Jay, Jon. Tchr., Regional Diagnostic Clinic, Kirksville, Mo., 1968-69; sch. psychologist Kossuth County Bd. Edn., Algona, Iowa, 1969-71; sch. psychologist Lucas and Wayne Counties Bd. Edn., Chariton, Iowa, 1971-73; sch. psychologist Greene County Bed. Edn., Jefferson, Iowa, 1973-75; sch. psychologist Arrowhead Area Edn. Agy., Jefferson, Iowa, 1975—; pvt. practice family and marriage counseling, Jefferson, Iowa, 1978—; human relations-communication trainer. Bd. dirs., Central Iowa Mental Health Center, 1974-77; bd. dirs. Greene County Sheltered Workshop-Activity Center, 1973-78; bd. dirs. Greene County Day Care Center, 1975-78; bd. dirs. Southwest Iowa Family Therapy Systems Project, 1978—; mem. exec. bd. Jefferson Cub Scouts, 1978-79. Cert. sch. psychologist; lic. psychologist, Iowa. Mem. Iowa Psychol. Assn., Nat. Assn. Sch. Psychologists. Roman Catholic. Lions Internat. Office: 218 N Wilson St Jefferson IA 50129

WALTON, LAURENCE ROLAND, info. scientist, librarian; b. Coffeyville, Kans., Mar. 27, 1939; s. Orvile Mac and Zora Laverne Walton; B.A. in Chemistry, Okla. State U., 1965; B.S. in L.S., Washington U., St. Louis, 1972; m. Lucretia Jane Mize, June 1, 1963; 1 son, Laurence Roland. Library asst. Stillwater (Okla.) Public Library, 1957-65; tech. librarian Research and Devel. Center, Pet, Inc., Greenville, Ill., 1965-73, mgr. corp. info. center, 1973—. Mem. Spl. Libraries Assn., Am. Soc. Info. Sci., Inst. Food Technologists, Am. Assn. Cereal Chemists, Am. Soc. Microbiologists. Editor: Food Publication Roundup: A Bibliographic Guide, 1977—. Home: 323 E Winter Greenville IL 62246 Office: Pet Inc 400 S 4th St Saint Louis MO 63166

WALTON, LLOYD BARKER, writer, photographer; b. Indpls., July 30, 1919; s. Frank and Ruby Elizabeth (Barker) W.; student Ind. U., 1944; m. Barbara Jean Fagan, July 31, 1953; children—Bruce Lee, Vicki Sue, Ginger Ann. Photographer Indpls. Times, 1943; chief color photographer, 1945-46, roving reporter-photgrapher, 1947-50, real estate editor, 1951-53, reporter-photographer, 1954-60, chief photographer, 1960-65; lobbyist state legislature, Ind., 1966; copy editor Indpls. Star, 1967-69, writer-photographer Indpls. Star mag., 1969—; lectr. journalism Butler U., 1963-64. Mem. pub. relations com. Marion County chpt. Am. Heart Assn., 1977-80; candidate Ind. Legislature, 1960. Served with AUS, 1940-41. Recipient certificate of merit, Internat. Reading Assn., 1971; Farm writing citation Ind. Farm Bur. Coop., 1972; first place award Nat. Soc. Profl. Engrs., 1973, citations, 1974, 75; Nat. Council for Advancement Edn. Writing award, 1974; Meritorious Service award Ind. Optometric Assn., 1974; Pub. Service award Ind. Podiatry Assn.; Casper award Indpls. Community Service Council, 1975, 78, spl. commendation, 1976; Gold Heart award Am. Heart Assn., 1978, Citation, 1979. Mem. Ind. News Photographers Assn. (founder, sec.-treas. 1957, pres. 1958), Nat. Press Photographers Assn. (President's award 1954, citation 1960), Soc. Profl. Journalists-Sigma Delta Chi. Republican. Methodist. Mason (Shriner). Club: Indpls. Press (sec. 1979, 1st place award for best continuous coverage 1974, Sweepstakes award for 5 1st places 1975, Best Feature Story award 1977). Inventor newspaper color photography printing process, 1946, Maze Word, ednl. game, 1969. Home: 3014 N Richardt Indianapolis IN 46226 Office: Indianapolis Star 307 N Pennsylvania St Indianapolis IN 46206

WALTON, ROBERT EUGENE, agrl. co. exec.; b. Shattuck, Okla., Jan. 15, 1931; s. Lonnie J. and Marguerite (Rose) W.; B.S., Okla. State U., 1952, M.S., 1956; postgrad. Royal Agrl. Coll., Sweden, 1952-53; Ph.D. (Danforth fellow 1956), Iowa State U., 1961; student Program for Mgmt. Devel., Harvard Bus. Sch., 1970; m. Janice Carolyn Graning, Sept. 5, 1959; children—Cynthia Claire, Robert Eugene, John Randolph. Mgr., Westhide Farms, Hereford, Eng., 1953-54; asst. prof. U. Ky., Lexington, 1958-62; geneticist Am. Breeders Service, Inc., DeForest, Wis., 1962-65, dir. marketing and breeding div., 1965-67, exec. v.p., 1967-68, pres., chief exec. officer, 1968—; pres., dir. Simmental Valley, Inc., Walton Bros., Inc.; pres. Cert. Semen Services Inc.; dir. 1st Wis. Nat. Bank. Bd. dirs. World Dairy Expo, Wis. Agri-Bus. Council, Meth. Hosp., Madison, United Way of Dane County. Mem. Am. Dairy Sci. Assn., Am. Soc. Animal Sci., Biometric Soc., Nat. Assn. Animal Breeders (pres., dir.), Farmhouse frat., Sigma Xi, Omicron Delta Kappa, Alpha Zeta (chancellor 1951). Republican. Methodist. Rotarian. Home: 4066 Vinburn Rd DeForest WI 53532 Office: Am Breeders Service Inc DeForest WI 53532

WALTON, ROBERT OWEN, physician; b. Cleve., Feb. 17, 1927; s. Owen M. and Bessie (Van Voorhis) W.; student DePauw U., 1946-48; B.S., U. Pitts., 1951, M.D., 1953; m. 2d, Sally Smith Hawthorne, Feb. 14, 1981; children—Laura Anne, James Robert. Intern, St. Lukes Hosp., Cleve., 1953-54; resident in pediatrics Childrens Hosp., Pitts., 1954-56; practice medicine, specializing in pediatrics, Cleve., 1956-75; asst. prof. pediatrics Case Western Res. U., Cleve., 1975—; dir. dept. pediatrics St. Lukes Hosp., Cleve., 1975—; med. dir. Shaker Heights Sch. System, 1976—; pres. med. staff Health Hill Hosp., 1980—. Trustee, Childrens Services, 1976—, Cleve. Center for Research for Child Devel., 1976—. Served with USNR, 1945-46. Mem. AMA, Ohio Med. Assn., Acad. Medicine Cleve., Am. Acad. Pediatrics, No. Ohio Pediatric Soc., Pasteur Club Cleve., Am. Acd. Med. Dirs. Club: Cleve. Skating. Contbr. articles to profl. jours. Home: 3326 Elsmere Rd Shaker Heights OH 44120 Office: Dept Pediatrics St Lukes Hosp Cleveland OH 44104

WALTON, SHAEN TIMOTHY, mfg. co. exec.; b. Coral Gables, Fla., Sept. 13, 1950; s. Norman Elwood and Pauline Lois (Powell) W.; B.A. in History, Fla. Atlantic U., 1972. Asst. mgr. Captain Orange Restaurant, Miami Beach, Fla., 1970, Fla. Atlantic U. Campus Cafeteria/Tavern/Banquet Hall, Boca Raton, 1972; mgr. installation services Ft. Lauderdale Carpet Gallery (Fla.), 1972-74; asst. mgr. Docktor Pet Center, Dayton, Ohio, 1974-75; nat. and internat. customer service mgr. Shopsmith, Inc., Vandalia, Ohio, 1976-77, adminstrv. asst. to officer of corp., 1977-78, temporary credit dept. mgr., 1977, mgr. printing and mail, 1978-79, mgr. reprographics, 1979, mgr. dir. mktg. collateral, 1979-81, mktg. specialist, 1981— Home: 2970 Stop 8 Road 11 Dayton OH 45414

WALTZ, GERALD DONN, utility engring. exec.; b. Terre Haute, Ind., Feb. 5, 1939; s. George Donald and Ava Lee (Hortin) W.; B.S.E.E., Rose-Hulman Inst. Tech., 1960; M.B.A., Butler U., 1970; m. Vicki Lyn Broyles, Apr. 8, 1961; foster children—Sheryl, Elizabeth, Gregory. Protective relay engr. Indpls. Power & Light Co., 1960-71, dir. elec. system planning dept., 1971-75, chief elec. engr., 1975-78, asst. v.p. engring. and constrn., 1978-79, v.p. engring. and constrn., 1979-81, sr. v.p. engring. and constrn., 1981—; cons. engr., 1967-71. Mem. tech. adv. com. Indpls. Center for Advanced Research. Named Indpls. Man of Day, Sta. WIRE, 1978; registered profl. engr., Ind. Mem. IEEE (past chmn. Central Ind. sect.), Indpls. Sci. and Engring. Found., Air Pollution Control Assn., Nat. Soc. Profl. Engrs., Alpha Tau Omega. Republican. Lutheran. Clubs: Rotary, Indpls. Athletic, Country of Indpls., Columbia (Indpls.). Office: PO Box 1595B Indianapolis IN 46206

WALWORTH, WILLIAM ROGER, educator; b. Lowell, Mass., Oct. 30, 1932; s. Walter Frederick and Madalyn Kathleen (Mayo) W.; B.S., Tufts U., 1954; M.Eng., Yale U., 1957; m. Patricia Anne Walker, Aug. 8, 1959; children—Mary Beth, Karen, Kathleen, Keith, Kevin, Kyle. Instr., Charles Stewart Mott Community Coll., Flint, Mich., 1957-67, 81—, asst. dir. admissions, 1967-70, dir. staff personnel services, 1970-77, interim dean liberal arts and scis., 1976, v.p. bus. and employee relations, 1978-80, provost, 1980-81; cons. Pres., Genesee Intermediate Sch. Dist. Bd. Edn., 1975—; trustee Friends of For-Mar, Inc., 1977—; trustee Kearsley Community Sch. Dist. Bd. Edn., 1969-77, pres., 1970, 73-74. Served with USN, 1954-56; Korea. Contbg. author: Handbook of Faculty Bargaining, 1977; also articles. Home: 1390 Iva Ave Burton MI 48509 Office: 1401 E Court St Flint MI 48503

WAMPLER, LLOYD CHARLES, lawyer; b. Spencer, Ind., Nov. 4, 1920; s. Charles and Vivian (Hawkins) W.; A.B., Ind. U., 1942, J.D., 1947; m. Joyce Ann Hoppenrath, Sept. 28, 1950 (dec. 1954); 1 dau., Natalie Gay. Admitted to Ind. bar, 1947, U.S. Supreme Ct. bar, 1971; instr. bus. law U. Kans., 1947-49; dep. atty. gen. Ind., 1949-50; mem. legal com. Interstate Oil Compact Commn., 1950; asst. public counselor Ind., 1950-53; mem. firm Stevens, Wampler, Travis & Fortin, Plymouth, 1953—. Mem. Ind. Rehab. Services Bd., 1978—; Democratic nominee for judge Ind. Supreme Ct., 1956. Served with USNR, 1942-46. Mem. Am. Judicature Soc., Am., Ind. (bd. mgrs. 1975-77), Marshall County bar assns., Ind. Acad. Sci., Ind. Def. Lawyers Assn. (dir. 1968—, v.p. 1967-71, pres. 1971-72), Ind., Marshall County (dir. 1969—) hist. socs., Assn. Ins. Attys. U.S. and Can., Am. Legion, Phi Delta Phi, Delta Sigma Pi. Club: Moose. Home: 400 S Michigan St Plymouth IN 46563 Office: 119 West Garro St Plymouth IN 46563

WANATICK, MARY ANN, health agy. dir.; b. Detroit, June 12, 1929; d. Samuel Tilden and Cilenore Catherine (Smith) Steedman; B.A., U. Toledo, 1951, B.Ed., 1964; M.P.H., U. Mich., 1975; m. Michael D. Wanatick, Oct. 30, 1958; 1 son, Robert Michael. Instr. computer and related systems Remington Rand, Inc., Toledo, 1951-54; city dir. New Neighbors League, Toledo, 1954-58; area dir. Relax-a-Cizor, Inc., Toledo, 1966-68; elementary tchr. Toledo Pub. Schs., 1962-65; exec. dir. Arthritis Found., Northwestern Ohio chpt., Toledo, 1968—. Mem. Arthritis Found. Profl. Staff Assn., Barrier Free Toledo Com. (adv. com.), N.W. Ohio Rehab. Assn. (bd. dirs.), Nat. Rehab. Assn., Ohio Rehab. Assn., Ohio Pub. Health Assn., Toledo Execs. Forum, Alpha Omicron Pi (pres. Toledo alumni). Club: Zonta (Toledo). Home: 4857 Rudgate Blvd Toledo OH 43623 Office: 4447 Talmadge Rd Toledo OH 43623

WANDEL, JOSEPH FRANK, sales engr.; b. Buffalo, Nov. 28, 1942; s. Joseph Frank and Florence Virginia (Gluszkowski) W.; B.S. in Chemistry, Alliance Coll., 1964; postgrad. St. John's U., N.Y.C., 1964-65; M.B.A., Kent State U.; m. Sally Ann Jessen, Feb. 14, 1976; 1 son, Stephen. Chem. sales rep. Emery Industries, Inc., Cin., 1966-79; tech. rep. Glyco Chem. Co., Greenwich, Conn., 1979—; tech. sales engr. Henkel Corp., chem. spltys. div., Maywood, N.J., 1980—. Adv. merit badges Boy Scouts Am. Served with USAR, 1965-72. Mem. Soc. Plastics Engrs., Am. Chem. Soc., Cleve. Chem. Assn., Akron Rubber Group. Republican. Roman Catholic. Clubs: Walsh Jesuit Boosters, Polish Nat. Alliance. Home: 270 Kennedy Blvd Northfield OH 44067 Office: 255 W Spring Valley Rd Maywood NJ 07607

WANG, EDWARD DEFORD, source data mgmt. systems co. exec.; b. Shanghai, China, May 15, 1935; s. Po-Chun and Elizabeth (Pao) W.; came to U.S., 1951, naturalized, 1962; B.M.E., Syracuse U., 1956, M.B.A., 1971; m. Karin M. Seumenicht, Mar. 19, 1972; children—Aaron, Andrea, Christopher. Mgr. advance product devel. SCM Corp., Syracuse, N.Y., 1957-64; corporate dir. new market devel. Olivetti Corp., Italy, 1964-69; dir. market devel. div. Olivetti Corp. Am., N.Y.C., 1969-71; pres. computer div., corporate v.p. for bus. devel., pres. Bus. Products group Victor Comptometer Corp., Chgo., 1971-75; pres., chmn. Infolink Corp., Northbrook, Ill., 1976—. Mem. Am. Mgmt. Assn., Am. Mktg. Assn. Methodist. Club: Economic (Chgo.). Patentee battery-operated portable electric typewriter; contbr. articles in field to profl. jours. Home: 565 Drexel Ave Glencoe IL 60022 Office: 1925 Holste Rd Northbrook IL 60062

WANG, SUSU, engr., educator; b. Nanking, China, May 10, 1948; s. Chian and Shan-Lin (Tsai) W.; M.S., Nat. Taiwan U., 1970; D.Sc., M.I.T., 1974; m. Nancy N.R. Luh, June 26, 1976. Research asst. M.I.T., 1971-74, research asso., 1974-77; asst. prof. theoretical and applied mechanics U. Ill., Urbana, 1977-80, asso. prof., 1980—; cons. Owens-Corning Fiberglas Co., Naval Research Lab. Mem. Am. Acad. Mechanics, ASME, ASTM, Sigma Xi. Contbr. articles to profl. jours. Home: 2102 S Pond St Urbana IL 61801 Office: 2121 Talbot Lab Univ of Ill Urbana IL 61801

WANG, WAYNE LUNG, nuclear physicist, nuclear engr., software engr.; b. I-Lan City, Taiwan, Jan. 24, 1944; s. Tien-Hai and Ah-Lung (Yu) Wang; m. Ling L. Wang, Oct. 7, 1967; children—Sherman, Morlie. Diploma, Taipei Inst. Tech., Taiwan, 1964; student U. N.H., 1965-66, Rensselaer Poly. Inst., 1966-67; Ph.D., Mass. Inst. Tech., 1971. Research physicist Carnegie-Mellon U., 1971-73; research physicist Lawrence Berkeley Lab., 1973-75; asst. nuclear engr. Argonne (Ill.) Nat. Lab., 1975-78, nuclear engr., 1978-80; software engr. Bell Labs., Naperville, Ill., 1980—. Bd. dirs. Chgo. Formosan Fed. Credit Union, 1979—, pres., 1980. Mem. Am. Phys. Soc., Am. Nuclear Soc., Sigma Xi. Contbr. articles to profl. jours. Home: 814 Albany Ln Darien IL 60559 Office: Bell Labs Naperville IL 60540

WANG, YINPAO, artist, author, educator; b. Soochow, China, Mar. 11, 1915; s. Chuan Chun and Chin Fong (Chiang) W.; M.B.A., U. Pa., 1938; m. Yung Lan Cheng, Jan. 20, 1970. Regional mgr. Farmers Bank of China, 1941-47; prof. Kwansi U., Kweilin, China, 1945-47; prof. S.W. Coll. Finance and Commerce, Kweilin, 1945-47; exec. v.p. Havana Trading Corp., N.Y., 1948-52; product devel. mgr. Garden State Tanning, Inc., Fleetwood, Pa., 1959-62; U.S. rep. Mitsuyu & Co., Osaka, Japan; pres. Parfait Products Corp., 1959—, Harry Wang & Co.; dir. design Pickard, Inc.; cons. automotive, vinyl, ceramic, leather industries; dir. Exchange Control Commn., China, 1941-43; mem. Examination Yuan, Govt. of China, 1942-47. One-man shows at Columbia U., N.Y. World's Fair 1964-65, Detroit Inst. of Art Mus., Ward Eggleston Galleries, Crocker Galleries, Werbe Galleries, Crespie Gallery, Lynn Kottler Galleries, Woodmere Gallery, N.Y. Pub. Library, Nat. Gallery China, many others; represented in permanent collections at Henry Ford Mus., Gracie Mansion, Mus. Fla. Coll., Nat. Mus. China, J.C. Penney Collections. Served to maj. gen. Chinese Army, 1942-45. Recipient Key to City of Harrisburg, Pa., 1964; Internat. awards AID, 1961, 63; Grumbacher Merit award, 1954; ann. award Resources Council, 1973. Fellow Royal Soc. Arts (London); mem. Nat. Press Club, Nat. Soc. Arts and Letters, Phila. Art Alliance, Internat. Platform Assn. (spl. award 1967). Author: The Mysterious Fifth Dimension, 1953; Fundamental Techniques of Chinese Painting, 1968; An Assessment of the New Chinese Landscape, 1971; First Generation, 1975. Home: 714 Dymond Rd Libertyville IL 60048

WANGBERG, LOUIS MURRAY, lt. gov. Minn.; b. Mar. 27, 1941; B.S. in Geography, U. N.D., 1963, M.S., 1964, Ed.D., 1970; m. Jane Ormiston, 1963; children—John Taylor, Carl Clark, Maren Christina. Tchr., Granite Falls (Minn.) High Sch., 1964-66, asst. prin., 1964-66; prin. Cosmos (Minn.) High Sch., 1966-68; asst. supt. schs., Worthington (Minn.), 1970-72; supt. schs., Bemidji (Minn.), 1972-79; lt. gov. of Minn., 1979—. Mem. No. Minn. Public TV Bd., 1972—, Bemidji State U. Found. Recipient Terrance Quirke award Sigma Nu, 1963; Wall Street Jour. fellow, 1964. Mem. Bemidji C. of C., Am. Council Young Polit. Leaders, Nat. Conf. Lt. Govs. (exec. com., Midwest chmn.), Sons of Norway, NAACP, Phi Delta Kappa. Republican. Clubs: Elks, Rotary, Masons, Shriners. Office: Room 122 State Capitol Saint Paul MN 55155

WANGELIN, HARRIS KENNETH, judge; b. Des Moines, May 10, 1913; s. Fred G. and Pearl Clymer (Harris) W.; grad. Iberia Acad. and Jr. Coll., 1932; student Drury Coll., 1932-33; J.D., U. Mo., 1936; m. Freda Alice Buffington, June 27, 1939; 1 dau., Judith Arleen. Admitted to Mo. bar, 1936, since practiced in Poplar Bluff; judge U.S. Dist. Ct., St. Louis, 1970-79, chief judge Eastern Dist. Mo., 1979—. Mem. Mo. Republican State Com., 1952-66, chmn., 1957-62; chmn. Butler County Rep. Central Com., 1950-58; sec.-treas. Rocky Mountain Midwest Rep. State Chmns. Assn., 1958-62; vice chmn. Mo. Senatorial Re-districting Commn., 1965. Trustee U. Mo. Law Sch. Found., 1972-78. Served as lt. USNR, 1942-45. Decorated Silver Star. Mem. Am., Mo. bar assns., VFW, Amvets, Am. Legion, Delta Theta Phi. Conglist. Home: 10374 Chimney Rock Dr Creve Coeur MO 63141 Office: US Court and Custom House 12th and Market Sts Saint Louis MO 63101

WANGSNESS, WAYNE ROGER, farmer; b. Decorah, Iowa, June 20, 1941; s. Elmer Melvin and Hazel (Orleans) W.; Tech. Agr. Degree, Iowa State U., 1965; B.A. in Economics, Luther Coll., 1968; M.A. in Economics (fellow), U. Iowa, 1971; postgrad. (Rotary Found. fellow) Trinity Coll., Dublin, Ireland, 1969-70; m. Cheryl Ann Lee, Feb. 9, 1974; children—Amy Lee, Ryan Wayne. Farmer, cattle raiser, Decorah; pres. Farm Computer Corp.; dir. N.E. Iowa Exptl. Sta.; mem. Agrl. Stblzn. Conservation Twp. Com. Chmn. Washington Prairie Luth. Ch. Congregation. Mem. Iowa Corn Growers Assn. (dir.), Nat. Corn Growers Assn. (dir.). Home and Office: Rural Route 1 Decorah IA 52101

WANKOVSKY, THEODORE ROBERT, ins. co. exec.; b. Chgo., Apr. 11, 1944; s. Morris Edward and Betty Wankovsky; student U. Ill., Chgo., 1962-63, Amundsen Jr. Coll., Chgo., 1963-64, Walton Sch. Commerce, Chgo., 1964-66. Cost acct. Bell & Howell Ditto div., Lincolnwood, Ill., 1966-67; auditor State of Calif. Equalization Bd., Chgo., 1967-69; real estate salesman Kruger & Co., Skokie, Ill., 1969-70; ops. mgr. Programmed Tax Systems Co., Chgo., 1970; gen. mgr. Pants Ranch Inc., Chgo., 1970-76; dist. sales mgr. Nationwide Ins. Co., Wheeling, Ill., 1976—; ins. cons. Omni Ins. Cons., Inc., Northbrook, Ill., 1981—. Mem. Nat. Assn. Life Underwriters. Office: 230 Sumac Rd Wheeling IL 60090

WANNAMAKER, MARY LYMAN, guidance cons.; b. Ft. Collins, Colo., July 29, 1922; d. Jerry Albert and Daisy B. (Burington) Lyman; Mus.B., Colo. State U., 1944; M.A. in Musicology, U. Minn., 1949, M.A. in Ednl. Psychology, 1967; m. John Samuel Wannamaker, Sept. 7, 1946; children—Lois Marie, Daisy Ruth Wannamaker Van Valkenburg. Tchr., Des Moines Pub. Schs., 1958-65; instr., counselor U. Minn., 1966-67; guidance counselor Urbandale (Iowa) Pub. Schs., 1967-75; guidance cons. Area Edn. Agy. XI, Ankeny, Iowa, 1975—; counselor, mem. personnel advisory bd. Drake U., 1974—; pres. career planning service YWCA, 1973-74; clin. assessment counselor Central Assessment Center, Nat. Council on Alcohol, 1981—. Chmn., Nat. Career Guidance Week in Iowa, 1978-79. Nat. Vocat. Guidance grantee, 1966. Mem. Am., Iowa (pres. chpt. 5, exec. dir. 1980) personnel and guidance assns., NEA, Am. Sch. Counselors Assn., AAUW, Profl. Women's League (pres. 1973-74), Royal Neighbors Am., P.E.O. (chmn. chpt. ednl. loan fund), Alpha Delta Kappa, Phi Kappa Phi, Delta Omicron. Club: Altrusa (dir.). Editor: Iowa Personnel and Guidance Bull., 1976—; contbr. articles to profl. jours. Home: 3907 29th St Des Moines IA 50310 Office: 1932 SW 3d St Ankeny IA 50021

WANTZ, JUSTINE CLAIRE, artist, educator; b. Neenah, Wis., Aug. 12, 1943; d. Jack Allan and Ann Elizabeth (Suchy) Mantor; B.F.A., Sch. of Art Inst. Chgo., 1967; M.A., No. Ill. U., 1970, M.F.A., 1971; m. John Allen Wantz, June 28, 1968. Instr. design, art history Coll. DuPage, Glen Ellyn, Ill., 1972; tchr. design-drawing N. Shore Art League, Winnetka, Ill., 1973; asst. prof. drawing, painting, printmaking Loyola U., Chgo., 1971—; dir. Water Tower Gallery, 1975—; lectr. in field, condr. workshops; exhibited one-man shows U. Ill. at Med. Center, Chgo., 1979, Loyola U. Chgo., 1979, Springfield (Ill.) Art Assn., 1979, John Nelson Bergstrom Art Assn. and Mus., Neenah, 1980, ARC Gallery, Chgo., 1981; group shows Aurora Coll. (Ill.), 1979, Colorado X Change, Boulder, 1981, Ill. State Mus., Springfield, 1981; represented in collections at Kemper Group, Long Grove, Ill., Wirth & Daniels Assos. George Snydecker Found. full scholar, 1966-67; Ill. Arts Council Chmn.'s grantee, 1978, Loyola U. and Mellon Found. grantee research in Pre-Columbian art, 1979; Ill. Humanities Council grantee, 1980. Mem. Nat. Art Edn. Assn., World Print Council, Nat. Women's Caucus for Art, Art Inst. Alumni Assn., Artemisia Fund, Chgo. Women's Caucus. Democrat. Methodist. Author catalog Am. Traditional Quilts, Collection of William Hoffman, 1978. Home: 85 N Main St Glen Ellyn IL 60137 Office: Loyola U Chgo 820 N Michigan Ave Chicago IL 60611

WARADY, JOEL DAVID, life ins. exec.; b. Chgo., Nov. 4, 1956; s. John Seymour and Betty Norrine (Hochman) W.; B.A., U. Ill., 1979; grad. Blitz Investment Inst., 1981. Pres., J.D. Warady & Assos., Chgo., 1980—; dir. Rho Corp., Chgo. Mem. Nat. Assn. Life Underwriters, Chgo. Assn. Life Underwriters. Democrat. Jewish. Office: 150 S Wacker Dr 800 Chicago IL 60606

WARCH, RICHARD, univ. pres.; b. Hackensack, N.J., Aug. 4, 1939; s. George William and Belen Anna (Hansen) W.; B.A., Williams Coll., 1961; B.D., Yale U., 1964, Ph.D., 1968; L.H.D. (hon.), Ripon (Wis.) Coll., 1980; m. Margot Lynn Moses, Sept. 8, 1962; children—Stephen Knud, David Preston, Karin. Ordained to ministry United Presbyn. Ch.; asst. prof., then asso. prof. history and Am. studies Yale U., 1968-77, asso. dean coll., dir. summer plans, 1976-77; v.p. acad. affairs Lawrence U., Appleton, Wis., 1977-79, pres., 1979—; dir. 1st Nat. Bank Appleton; cons. in field. Rockefeller Bros. fellow; Morse fellow. Mem. Am. Studies Assn., Soc. Values in Higher Edn. Club: Rotary. Author: School of the Prophets: Yale College, 1701-1740, 1973; editor: John Brown, 1973. Office: Lawrence Univ Box 599 Appleton WI 54912

WARCHOL, CHARLES MICHAEL, gum mfg. co. exec.; b. Lawrence, Mass., Dec. 17, 1941; s. Michael Frank and Julia Alicia (Malek) W.; B.A., Harvard Coll., 1963; M.A., Institut D'Etudes Politiques, Paris, 1965; M.B.A., Stanford U., 1967; m. Tula Rosa Ugarteche, Sept. 4, 1969; children—Michelle Elizabeth, Alexander Frank. Product mgr. The Pillsbury Co., Mpls., 1969-74; product mgr. Chesebrough Ponds, Greenwich, Conn., 1974-79; mktg. dir. William Wrigley Jr. Co., Chgo., 1979—. Served with U.S. Peace Corps, 1967-69. Mem. Am. Mktg. Assn. Clubs: Harvard of Chgo., Fox. Home: 1300 W Deerpath Rd Lake Forest IL 60045 Office: 410 N Michigan Ave Chicago IL 60045

WARD, ALAN JOSEPH, clin. psychologist; b. Boston, May 2, 1936; s. Joseph S. and Rebecca (Myrick) W.; A.B., Brandeis U., 1958; A.M., Temple U., 1960; Ph.D., State U. N.Y., Buffalo, 1965. Caseworker Boston Pub. Welfare Dept., 1959-60; USPHS psychology intern Psychology Clinic, State U. N.Y. at Buffalo, 1960-62; VA psychology intern Neuro-Psychiat. Service, VA Hosp., Buffalo, 1962-64; USPHS postdoctoral fellow in research and clin. psychology Michael Reese Hosp., Psychosomatic and Psychiat. Inst., Chgo., 1964-66; supervising clin. psychologist Eastern State Sch. and Hosp., Trevose, Pa., 1966-70, acting chief psychologist, 1970-71, chief psychologist, 1971-75, dir. autistic children's treatment, tng. and research service, 1966-75; instr. Pa. State U., 1967-68; instr., asso. prof. dept. ednl. psychology Temple U., Phila., 1968-70; pvt. practice psychology, Phila., 1966-75, Chgo., 1975—; instr. dept. psychiatry, children and youth program Jefferson Med. Sch., Phila, 1969—; mem. Gov.'s Adv. Task Force on Mental Health of Children and Youth, 1971-75; dir. Henry Horner Children's Center, Chgo.-Read Mental Health Center, 1975—; chmn. subcom. on children and adolescents, Region 2 Orgnl. Change Task Force, Dept. Mental Health, 1975-77, rep. to Consortium Children's Services Ill., 1976-80, mem. Region 2 Diagnostic Standards of Day Treatment Centers Task Force, 1976-78; asso. prof. dept. psychiatry Abraham Lincoln Sch. Medicine, U. Ill., Chgo., 1976—; chmn. Chgo. Consortium for Children's Mental Health, 1981—. SUNY Buffalo fellow, 1962-63; N.Y. State scholar, 1961-64. Fellow Soc. Projective Techniques, Pa. Psychol. Assn.; mem. AAAS, Am. Soc. Clin. Hypnosis, Am. Assn. Psychiat. Services for Children (program com.), Am., Midwestern, Eastern, Ill. psychol. assns., Mental Health Assn. Southeastern Pa., Phila. Soc. Clin. Hypnosis (mem. exec. bd.), Phila. Soc. Clin. Psychologists (editor newsletter 1968-71, mem. exec. bd. 1970-73), Sigma Xi. Author: Childhood Autism and Structural Therapay, 1976; contbr. articles to profl. jours. Home: Park Tower-Edgewater Plaza 5415 N Sheridan Rd Apt 4301 Chicago IL 60640 Office: 6500 Irving Park Rd Chicago IL 60634

WARD, ALICE MARIE, civic worker; b. New London, Ohio; d. Clyde Eugene and Daisy (White) Ward; B.A., Ohio Wesleyan U., 1932. Sec., asst. treas. C.E. Ward Co., New London, 1937-72, also dir. Mem. Huron County Republican Women's Club. Recipient Rotary Community Service award, 1975; named to Ohio Wesleyan Sports Hall of Fame, 1977. Mem. New London Bus. and Profl. Women's Club (pres. 1967-68, 72—), U.S. Lawn Tennis Assn., Mortar Board, Alpha Xi Delta. Clubs: Medalist, Southwood Tennis. Methodist. Mem. Order Eastern Star (treas.). Composer songs In the Swim, 1959; Tennis for Everyone, 1963; I Hear a Bird Singing, 1963. Home: 139 E Main St New London OH 44851

WARD, BOB-AMNDIH, health system cons.; b. Muskegon, Mich., July 29, 1948; s. William Thomas and Averil Barbara W.; B.A., Carleton Coll., 1970; M.Montessori Ed., St. Nicholas Inst., 1972; postgrad. U.S. Internat. U., 1973-74; cert. Control Data Inst., 1981. Asst. tech. dir. Allenberry Playhouse, Boiling Springs, Pa., 1970; artistic dir. One Flew East Theatre Co., Mpls., 1970-73; ednl. cons., Mpls. and Portland, Oreg., 1973-75; orgn. devel. specialist U. Minn. Hosps., Mpls., 1975-80; sr. asso. Health Systems Cons., Mpls., 1980—; instr. vocat. tech. edn. U. Minn., 1978—; mem. adv. bd. Minn. Employee Assistance Program Planning Force. Pres. bd. dirs. Lasoff & Dean Dance Assos., 1981—; bd. dirs. Center for Wellcare, 1981—; mem. adv. bd. Choreogram Dance Co., 1975-78; bd. dirs. Minn. Tenants Union, 1972-73. Mem. Am. Soc. Tng. and Devel., Am. Soc. Health Care Edn. and Tng. of Am. Hosp. Assn. (state v.p. 1980), Data Processing Mgrs. Assn., OD Network. Author: (with others) Professional Supervision: A Training Program for Health Care Supervisors and Managers, 1979. Home: 3202 Harriet Ave S Minneapolis MN 55408 Office: 3233 Garfield Ave S Minneapolis MN 55408

WARD, CORNELL O'BRYANT, metals co. exec.; b. Florence, Ala., Dec. 31, 1947; guardian Ruby J. Harrison; B.S. in Music Edn., Ala. State U., 1971; M.S. in Administrv. Sci. and Mgmt., U. Ala., 1978; m. Linda F. Stephens, Jan. 6, 1971; children—Gillian Brooke, Cornell O'Bryant II. Profl. musician, 1971-72; mgmt. trainee Reynolds Metals Co., 1972-73, personnel rep., alloys plant, 1973-75, labor relations rep., alloys plant, 1975-77, asst. personnel mgr. Listerhill reduction plant, 1977-79, mgr. labor relations and employee benefits McCook (Ill.) plant, 1979—; pvt. music tchr. Sales adviser Jr. Achievement, 1974; plant campaign chmn. United Way, 1974-76; mem. State of Ala. Adv. Council for Career Edn., 1978—; mem. edn. com. Assn. Industries of Ala., 1978—; mem. Lauderdale County Adv. Bd. for Vocat. Edn., 1978—. Mem. So. Coll. Placement Assn., Ala. Placement Assn., Muscle Shoals Personnel Assn., Cox Creek Jaycees, Alpha Phi Alpha, Phi Mu Alpha. Methodist. Songwriter, composer. Home: 501 Falmore Ln Bolingbrook IL 60439 Office: Reynolds Metals Co PO Box 239 Brookfield IL

WARD, DANIEL PATRICK, state judge; b. Chgo., Aug. 30, 1918; s. Patrick and Jane (Convery) W.; student St. Viator Coll., 1936-38; J.D., DePaul U., 1941, D.H.L. (hon.), 1976; LL.D. (hon.), John Marshall Law Sch., 1972; m. Marilyn Corleto, June 23, 1951; children—Mary Jane, John, Susan, Elizabeth Ward. Admitted to Fed. bar, Ill. bar; asst. prof. law Southeastern U., Washington, 1941-42; pvt. practice law, 1945-48; asst. U.S. atty. No. Dist. of Ill., 1948-54, chief criminal div., 1951-54; with firm Eardley & Ward, Chgo., 1954-55; dean Coll. Law, DePaul U., Chgo., 1955-60; states atty. Cook County, Ill., 1960-66; judge Supreme Ct. Ill., 1966—, chief justice, 1976-79; adj. prof. law DePaul U. Coll. Law, 1979—. Chmn., Ill. Courts Commn., 1969-73. Served with AUS, 1942-45. Mem. Am., Fed., Ill., Chgo. bar assns. Roman Catholic. Home: 11000 Kingston Ave Westchester IL 60153 Office: 3083 Richard J Daley Civic Center Chicago IL 60602

WARD, DONALD EARL, educator; b. Hammond, Ind., Nov. 30, 1946; s. Earl Robert and Dorothy Helen (Foster) W.; B.A. (Edward Rector scholar), DePauw U., 1969; M.S. (NDEA fellow), Purdue U., 1970, Ph.D., 1973; m. Susan Jane Gordon, Nov. 27, 1971; 1 son, Christopher Andrew. Asst. prof., counseling psychologist Ball State U., Muncie, Ind., 1973-76; asst. prof. dept. psychology and counseling, counselor Pittsburg (Kans.) State U., 1976—, dir. Inst. for Career Devel. with The Non-Coll. Bound, 1977. Mem. guidance adv. com. Kans. State Dept. Edn. Mem. Am., Kans. (exec. council, co-chmn. profl. preparation com.), S.E. Kans. (pres.) personnel and guidance assns., Am., Kans. coll. student personnel assn., Am., North Central, Kans. assns. counselor educators and suprs., Kans. Vocat. Guidance Assn., Kans. Assn. Specialists in Group Work (past pres.). Home: 2002 Countryside Dr Pittsburg KS 66762 Office: 303 Hughes Hall Pittsburg State U Pittsburg KS 66762

WARD, DONALD MAXWELL, dentist; b. Detroit, Dec. 21, 1917; s. Harold Bliss and Gertrude Ruth (Wood) W.; student Flint Jr. Coll., 1935-36, Wayne State U., 1936-37; B.A., U. Mich., 1940, D.D.S., 1944; postgrad. Northwestern U., 1958, U. Mich., 1960-72, N.Y. U., 1975; children—Jacquelyn, Wendy (Mrs. Gregory List), Cindy (Mrs. Robert Wickham), Bradley, Wayne. Pvt. practice dentistry, Detroit, 1946-47, Saginaw, Mich., 1947—; treas. Davenside Clinic, Inc., 1963—. Prosthodontist, sec. bd. Saginaw Gen. Hosp. Cleft Palate Team, 1956-67. Sec., Pit and Balcony Inc., Saginaw, Mich., 1949-51. Trustee, sec. Saginaw Twp. Bd. Edn., 1961-62. Served with Dental Corps, USNR, 1944-46. Mem. Saginaw County (past pres.), Saginaw Valley Dist. dental socs., Mich. Assn. Professions, Am., Mich. dental assns., Am. Cleft Palate Assn. (hon. life), Saginaw Bus. and Profl. Men (mem. goodwill tour team to USSR, Czechoslovakia 1959), U. Mich. Union (life), Am. Sunbathing Assn. (life), Mich. United Conservation Clubs, Nat. Wildlife Fedn., Smithsonian Assos., Nat. Geog. Soc., Internat. Platform Assn., Internat. Vasectomy Soc., Delta Sigma Delta (life). Presbyterian. Clubs: Elks (life), Saginaw Ski, Germania, Colony, Knife and Fork, Saginaw Field and Stream, The Wayward Musicians, Mich. Sociables, Cape Coral Yacht and Racquet (charter), Club Mediterranee, Plato's Retreat. Home: 3548 Doncaster Ct S Saginaw MI 48603 Office: 3422 Davenport St Saginaw MI 48602

WARD, FRANK ANTHONY, II, lawyer, archivist; b. Albany, N.Y., Jan. 28, 1939; s. Frank Anthony and Jennette Louise (Skinner) W.; A.B. in Bus. and Indsl. Mgmt., Johns Hopkins U., 1960; J.D., U. Ill., 1963. Admitted to Ill. bar, 1963; v.p., trust officer First Galesburg (Ill.) Nat. Bank & Trust Co., 1964-74, dir., 1975—; individual practice law, Galesburg, 1974-75, 76—; partner firm Ward and Gray, Galesburg, 1975-76; lectr. dept. bus. law Knox Coll., Galesburg, Ill., 1975-78, Carl Sandburg Coll., Galesburg, 1975-76, Nat. Trust for Hist. Preservation, Washington, 1976-78. Treas. Albany Youth Council, 1955-56; deacon First United Presbyn. Ch., Galesburg, 1964-65; mem. council Pilgrim Congl. Ch., Knoxville, Ill., 1966-69, moderator, 1970, deacon, 1971; mem. exec. bd. Prairie council Boy Scouts Am., Galesburg, 1965—, chmn. camp devel. com., 1970-75, chmn. fin. com., 1978-80; chmn. Knox County (Ill.) Sesquicentennial Commn., 1966-68; bd. dirs. Galesburg Community Concert Assn., 1972-76; bd. dirs. United Way of Knox County, 1969-78, 79—, sec. treas., 1970-72; bd. dirs. Knox County United Way Found., 1977-78, 79—, Prairie States Legal Services, 1977-78, Knox County Legal Aid Soc., 1977-78, Knox County Hist. Sites, 1964—, 2d v.p. 1977—; bd. dirs. Galesburg Community Arts Council, 1974-80, pres., 1976. Mem. Ill. Bar Assn., Knox County Bar Assn. (pres. 1970), Ill. Hist. Soc. (v.p. 1977-78), Galesburg Hist. Soc. (pres. 1975—), Kans. Hist. Soc., Carl Sandburg Birthplace Assn. (dir. 1970-77), Assn. Profl. Genealogists, Ill. Geneal. Soc., Knox County Geneal. Soc., Huguenot Soc. Ill., SAR (dir. registrar Gen. Henry Knox chpt. 1973-75), Sons Union Vets. Civil War, War of 1812 Ill. Soc., Loyal Legion Am., Johns Hopkins Alumni Assn., U. Ill. Alumni Assn., Midwestern MG T Register (historian 1979, treas. 1980—), New Eng. MG T Register, Vintage MG Car Club Chgo., Western Ill. Antique Auto Club, Galesburg Area Classic Car Club, Alpha Phi Omega (nat. v.p. 1960-61), Phi Delta Phi. Recipient Disting. Service award Johns Hopkins U., 1958, Galesburg Jaycees, 1970; Outstanding Religious Leader award Knoxville Jaycees, 1971; Thomas B. Herring award Galesburg C. of C., 1979. Author: An Analysis of the Factors Affecting the Desire to Change Geographic Location with Emphasis on Economic and Family Ties, 1770-1960, 1959; Brief Biography of Allen T. Ward, 1963; Thomas Ward and His Descendants, A Genealogical Study, 1963; Striving Backwards or How We Stopped the Ball and Started the Revolution, 1976; contbr. hist. preservation articles to various books. Home: PO Box 224 Rural Route 1 Galesburg IL 61401 Office: 218 Weinberg Arcade Galesburg IL 61401

WARD, HOWARD NELSON, hematologist, oncologist, lawyer; b. Mt. Vernon, Ill., Dec. 30, 1937; s. Harry Seborn and Jenny Willanna (Jeffries) W.; student U. Ill., 1955-58; B.S., Northwestern U., 1959, M.D. with distinction, 1962; J.D. cum laude, Washburn U., 1979; m. Marilyn Jean Strobel, July 13, 1958; children—Martha Lyn, Howard Jeffries. Intern, Chgo. Wesley Meml. Hosp., 1962-63; resident Barnes Hosp., St. Louis, 1963-66, chief resident, 1968-69, fellow in hematology, 1964-65; practice medicine specializing in hematology and oncology, St. Louis, 1969, Topeka, 1969—; mem. staff Stormont-Vail Regional Med. Center, Topeka, chief of staff, 1979-80, trustee, 1980—; mem. staff St. Francis Hosp., Meml. Hosp. (both Topeka); instr. medicine Washington U., 1968, instr. clin. medicine, 1969; asst. prof. medicine U. Kans., 1973—; faculty Menninger Sch. Psychiatry, 1975-77; adj. asst. prof. law Washburn U., 1980—. Trustee, 1st United Meth. Ch., Topeka, 1973-74. Served with USAF, 1966-68. Diplomate Am. Bd. Internal Medicine. Fellow A.C.P.; mem. Am. Soc. Clin. Oncology, Am., Internat. socs. hematology, Kans., Shawnee County med. socs., AMA, Am. Bar Assn., Topeka Bar Assn., Kans. Bar, Am. Soc. Law and Medicine, Am. Coll. Legal Medicine, Nat. Health Lawyers Assn., Alpha Omega Alpha, Omega Beta Pi. Republican. Methodist. Clubs: Rotary, Masons. Contbr. articles to med. jours. Home: 3126 W 15th St Topeka KS 66604 Office: 901 Garfield Topeka KS 66606

WARD, JAMES SHERIDAN, physician; b. Chgo., Apr. 9, 1929; s. William Morgan and Lillian Edna (Sheridan) W.; B.S., State U. Iowa, 1951, M.D., 1956; m. Barbara Jane Jacobs, Nov. 17, 1956; children—Elizabeth, James, Michael, Stephen, Rebecca, Carolyn. Intern, Queen of Angels Hosp., Los Angeles, 1956-57; resident Lafayette Clinic, Detroit, 1957-60; asst. prof. psychiatry U. Iowa, 1962-65; supt. Zeller Zowe Center, Peoria, Ill., 1965-76; pvt. practice psychiatry, Peoria, 1976—; regional adminstr. Ill. Dept. Mental Health, 1971-76. Served to lt. cmdr. USN, 1960-62. Recipient Walter Baer award Illinois Valley Mental Health Assn., 1976. Fellow Am.

Psychiat. Assn.; mem. A.C.P., AMA, Inst. Phys. Medicine and Rehab. (dir.). Republican. Roman Catholic. Home: 606 Scottwood Peoria IL 61615 Office: 515 NE Glen Oak Ave Peoria IL 61603

WARD, MARVIN, automotive ofcl.; b. Palestine, Ark., Sept. 10, 1943; s. Robert, Jr., and Endia Nola (Waitts) W.; B.S., Chgo. State U., 1975; m. Jane A. Jordan, Aug. 13, 1965; children—Maurice L., Michael T., Gerald B. Comml. teller Mut. Nat. Bank, Chgo., 1963-64; insp., supr. Electro Motive div. Gen. Motors Corp., La Grange, Ill., 1970-74, gen. supr., 1978-80, supt. Electro Motive div., Chgo., 1980—. Served with AUS, 1964-66. Baptist. Club: Garden City Lodge. Home: 12100 S Perry St Chicago IL 60628 Office: 900 E 103d St Chicago IL 60628

WARD, PATRICIA SPAIN, historian; b. Davenport, Iowa, Nov. 28, 1931; d. Marceda Ligouri and Nola Ardel (Lensch) Spain; B.A., U. Colo., 1954; M.A., Johns Hopkins U., 1963; m. Robert F. Ward, Aug. 18, 1956 (div. 1973); 1 dau., Lydia. Asst. editor Isis: Internat. Rev. Devoted to History of Sci. and Its Cultural Influences, 1961; mem. academic staff, dept. history of medicine U. Wis., 1976-77, Maurice Richardson fellow, 1976-79, lectr., 1979; research asso. humanistic studies program U. Ill. Med. Center, Chgo., 1979—; centennial historian U. Ill. Coll. Medicine. NIMH grantee, 1958-61; Nat. Library Medicine grantee, 1974-77; Johns Hopkins Centennial scholar, 1976. Mem. Am. Hist. Assn., Orgn. Am. Historians, Soc. Health and Human Values, Am. Assn. for History of Medicine, N.Y. Acad. Sci., AAAS, Chgo. Hist. Soc., Am. Inst. History of Pharmacy, Sigma Xi. Contbr. med. articles to Notable Am. Women, Dictionary Am. Biography, Jour. History of Medicine and Allied Scis., Medicine in Transition: The Centennial of the University of Illinois College of Medicine. others. Home: 1441 W Lexington Chicago IL 60607 Office: Univ Ill Med Center Library of Health Scis 1750 W Polk St Chicago IL 60612

WARD, PHILIP GERALD, community coll. pres.; b. Detroit, Aug. 9, 1935; s. Thomas E. and Vera M. Ward; A.B., Eastern Mich. U., 1958, M.A. in Edn., 1961, M.A. in History, 1963; Ph.D. in Higher Edn. and Adminstrn. (Fulbright fellow 1965, Kellogg fellow 1968-69, Max S. Smith Meml. fellow 1969), Mich. State U., 1971; m. Isabel MacMillen, Jan. 30, 1959; children—Heather, Laurel, Philip. Asst. to dir. Office Community Coll. Coop., Mich. State U., 1968; asst. to pres. Montcalm Community Coll., Sidney, Mich., 1969; dir. div. acad. centers Cleve. State U., 1969-72; dean coll. Rend Lake Coll., Ina, Ill., 1972-76; pres. Glen Oaks Community Coll., Centreville, Mich., 1976—, sec. coll. found., 1965; mem. adv. com. career edn. Mich. Bd. Edn., 1980; mem. Mich. Task Force Adult Edn. Funding, 1980. Chmn. trustees First United Methodist Ch., Sturgis, Mich., 1978; chmn. bd. dirs. Sturgis Arts Council, 1978. Mem. Am. Assn. Higher Edn., Am. Assn. Community and Jr. Colls., Mich. Community Coll. Assn. Clubs: Kiwanis, Elks, Rotary. Office: 62249 Shimmel Rd Centreville MI 49032

WARD, THOMAS GENE, ednl. adminstr.; b. Saginaw, Mich., Aug. 9, 1932; s. Cletus Alphonsus and Bernice Margaret (LaFayette) W.; A.A., Bay City Jr. Coll., 1953; B.A., Mich. State U., 1955; M.Ed., Wayne State U., 1961; m. Therese Ann Solosky, Aug. 6, 1960; children—Thomas M., Jonathan J., Douglas Allan. Profl. actor, 1957; tchr. elementary and secondary schs., Detroit, 1958-69, Saginaw, 1969-70, Sanford, Mich., 1970-74; mem. spl. edn. div. Meridian Pub. Schs., Sanford, 1974—, Title I dir., 1976-80; spl. edn. dir. Bullock Creek-Meridian Schs., 1980—; chmn. Midland County Spl. Edn. Advisory Council; speech cons. Head Start Project, Detroit. Served with USNR, 1955-57. Mem. Am., Mich. speech and hearing assns., NEA, Mich., Meridian (pres.) edn. assns., Council for Exceptional Children, Mich. Reading Assn., Mich. Assn. Adminstrs. in Spl. Edn. Roman Catholic. Home: 2112 Wilmington Dr Midland MI 48640 Office: 3361 N M-30 Sanford MI 48657 also 1519 S Badour Rd Midland MI 48640

WARD, VELMA LEWIS, biochemist; b. Columbus, Ohio, Dec. 27, 1932; foster dau. John Franklin and Anna Clara (Robinson) Lewis; student U. Mich., 1947-49; B.S., Wayne State U., 1953, M.S., 1961; 1 son, Broderick Lewis. Jr. med. technologist Detroit Gen. Hosp., 1953-54; research technologist, dept. medicine Coll. Medicine Wayne State U., 1954-55; supr. med. lab., biochemistry dept. Lafayette Clinic, Detroit, 1956-69, research asso. biochemistry dept., supr. clin. lab., 1960—. Bd. dirs. Detroit Met. Black Arts. Fellow Am. Inst. Chemists; mem. Am. Chem. Soc., Am. Soc. Clin. Pathologists (affiliate mem., registered med. technologist), Am. Soc. Med. Tech., N.Y. Acad. Scis., Detroit Physiol. Soc., Am. Assn. Clin. Chemists, Sigma Xi, Alpha Delta Theta, Alpha Kappa Alpha. Contbr. articles to profl. jours. Home: 18500 Littlefield St Detroit MI 48235 Office: 951 E Lafayette St Detroit MI 48207

WARD, VERNON GRAVES, internist; b. Palisade, Nebr., Mar. 5, 1928; s. Charles Bennett and Mildred Belle (Graves) W.; A.B., Nebr. Wesleyan U., 1948; M.D., U. Nebr., 1954; m. Eleanore Mae Farstveet, Aug. 28, 1952; children—Scott (dec.), Margo, Alison, Barry. Instr. anatomy Columbia U. Coll. Physicians and Surgeons, N.Y.C., 1948-50; intern, resident U. Wis. dept. medicine, Madison, 1954-58, 1961-62; fellow in neurophysiology and psychosomatic medicine U. Okla., Oklahoma City, 1960-61; asso. prof. U. Nebr. Coll. Medicine, Omaha, 1969—; chmn. dept. internal medicine Bishop Clarkson Hosp., Omaha, 1976-78. Served with USN, 1958-60. Nebr. Heart Assn. grantee, 1975; diplomate Am. Bd. Internal Medicine. Mem. AMA, Nebr. Med. Assn., Omaha Med. Soc., Nebr. Soc. Internal Medicine (pres. 1980—), A.C.P. (Hutton traveling scholar 1965), Am. Psychosomatic Soc., Am. Rheumatism Assn., Arthritis Found. Republican. Lutheran. Clubs: Lions (Omaha). Home: 302 N 54th St Omaha NE 68132 Office: 309 Doctors Bldg Omaha NE 68131

WARD, WILLIS WESLEY, mktg. cons.; b. South Bend, Ind., July 14, 1923; s. Charles C. and Grace (Showalter) W.; A.B., DePauw U., 1947; M.B.A., Miami U., 1949; M.A., U. Va., 1951; m. Mary Jane Altman, Nov. 3, 1951; 1 dau., Marsha Jane. Instr., Miami U., 1948-49; extension drama specialist U. Va., 1949-51; mktg. researcher Davee-Koehnlein-Keating, Chgo., 1951-53; merchandising specialist Altman's Cash Feed Stores, Pitts., 1953-56; asst. mgr. Altman Feed Mills, Troy, Ohio, 1956-65; media and research Northlich Stolley, Cin., 1965-71; v.p. research dir. Fahlgren & Ferriss, Inc., 1971-76; mktg. cons., 1976-80; mgr. mktg. and mem. relations Pioneer R.E.C., Inc., Piqua, Ohio, 1980—; lectr., Wright State U., 1966-68, Edison State Coll., 1976-77, U. Dayton, 1978-79. Pres., Troy Bd. Edn., 1963-65; Sesquicentennial narrator, 1963; dir. Troy Civic Theatre. Served with AUS, 1943-46. Mem. Am. Mktg. Assn. (pres. Cin. chpt. 1973-74), Phi Beta Kappa, Lambda Chi Alpha, Phi Eta Sigma, Beta Gamma Sigma, Delta Sigma Rho. Presbyterian (elder). Home: 1131 Fairway Rd Troy OH 45373 Office: PO Box 604 Piqua OH 45356

WARDEN, IVAN LEIGH, clergyman, educator; b. N.Y.C., Aug. 18, 1943; s. Charles Lee and Miriam (Burgess) W.; B.A. in Theology, Oakwood Coll., 1967; M.R.E., N.Y. Theol. Sem., 1970, M.Sacred Theology, 1974; postgrad. Princeton Theol. Sem., 1974—; m. Jean Scantlebury, Feb. 17, 1968; children—Ariel Jeanine, Angela Jeanice. Asst. minister Bethel Seventh-day Adventist Ch., Bklyn., 1967-70; minister S.I. (N.Y.) Seventh-day Adventist Ch., 1970-73; ordained to ministry Seventh-day Adventist Ch., 1972; minister Beth-El Seventh-day Adventist Ch., Jersey City, 1973-75; asst. prof. urban ministry Andrews U., Berrien Springs, Mich., 1976—, Theol. Sem., 1978—. Mem. Vols. in Probation Adv. Bd. of 5th Dist. Ct., State of Mich., 1977—. Recipient award Concerned Citizens Alliance, Jersey City, 1975; Faculty award Andrews U., 1979. Office: Dept Religion Andrews U Berrien Springs MI 49104

WARDNER, CARL ARTHUR, educator; b. Fisher, Minn., July 13, 1904; s. Peder and Janna Sofia (Lindem) W.; B.S., U. N.D., 1927; M.S., 1929; Ph.D., U. Pitts., 1932; m. Alice Flaat, Sept. 10, 1930; children—Alice Joy Wardner Bostrom, Carl Arthur. Research chemist W.H. Daugherty Refining Co. affiliate Wilco Chem. Co., Petrolia, Pa., 1931-35; cons., adv. Flaat Farms, Grand Forks, N.D., 1935-58; prof. chemistry, asso. dir., then dir. NSF program U. N.D., Grand Forks, 1958-71, research asso., cons. limnology, 1971-75, prof. emeritus chemistry, 1971—. Pres. ch. bd. United Luth. Ch., Grand Forks, 1952-53. Recipient Sigma Xi Grad. Research award, 1929; NSF grantee, 1967, 68, 69, 70, 71. Mem. Am. Chem. Soc., N.D. Acad. Sci., Nat. Sci. Tchrs. Assn., AAAS, C. of C. Republican. Lutheran. Contbr. articles to profl. jours. Address: 3720 Cherry St Grand Forks ND 58201

WARE, GEORGE HENRY, botanist; b. Avery, Okla., Apr. 27, 1924; s. Charles and Mildred (Eshelman) W.; B.S., U. Okla., 1945, M.S., 1948; Ph.D., U. Wis., 1955; m. June Marie Gleason, Dec. 21, 1955; children—David, Daniel, Patrick, John. Asst. prof. Northwestern State U. of La., Natchitoches, 1948-56, asso. prof., 1956-62, prof., 1962-67; dir. Conservation Sect., No. La. Supplementary Edn. Center, Natchitoches, 1967-68; dendrologist Morton Arboretum, Lisle, Ill., 1968—, adminstr. research group, 1976—; vis. prof. U. Okla., Norman, summers, 1957, 61, 63, 64; adj. prof. Western Ill. U., 1972—. Trustee nomination caucus Coll. of DuPage, Glen Ellyn, Ill., 1974-78; bd. dirs. Kane-DuPage Soil and Water Conservation Dist., 1969—, DuPage County council Girl Scouts U.S., 1979-80. Served with USN, 1942-46. Mem. AAAS, Ecol. Soc. Am., Soil Conservation Soc. Am., Southwestern Assn. Naturalists, Sigma Xi. Home: 23W 176 Indian Hill Dr Lisle IL 60532 Office: Morton Arboretum Lisle IL 60532

WARE, RICHARD ANDERSON, found. exec.; b. N.Y.C., Nov. 7, 1919; s. John Sayers and Mabelle (Anderson) W.; B.A., Lehigh U., 1941; M. Pub. Adminstrn., Wayne State U., 1943; m. Lucille Henney, Mar. 20, 1942 (div. 1972); children—Alexander W., Janet M., Bradley J., Patricia E.; m. Beverly G. Mytinger, Dec. 22, 1972. Research asst. Detroit Bur. Govt. Research, 1941-42; personnel technician Lend-Lease Adminstrn., Washington, 1942-43; research asso. to asst. dir. Citizens Research Council, Detroit, 1946-56; sec. Earhart and Relm Founds., Ann Arbor, Mich., 1956-70, trustee, pres., 1970—; (on leave) prin. dep. asst. sec. def. Internat. Security Affairs, Washington, 1969-70, cons. Office Asst. Sec. Def., 1970-73. Dir. Ann Arbor Trust Co. Vice pres. Ann Arbor United Fund and Community Services, 1968, pres., 1969; asst. dir. Mich. Joint Legis. Com. on State Reorgn., 1950-52; sec. Gov.'s Com. to Study Prisons, 1952-53; com. to chmn. Ann Arbor City Planning Commn., 1958-67; mem. Detroit Com. on Fgn. Relations, 1971; mem. adv. council Woodrow Wilson Internat. Center for Scholars, 1973—. Polit. analyst Republican Nat. Com., Washington, 1964. Trustee Greenhills Sch., 1973-80; bd. dirs. Liberty Fund, Indpls., 1980—; mem. vis. com. Div. Social Scis., U. Chgo., 1977—; mem. adv. com. The Citadel, 1977—; Ann Arbor Area Found., 1977—; mem. adv. council, internat. security studies program Fletcher Sch., Tufts U., 1981—. Served with USAAF, 1943-46. Recipient Civilian Meritorious Service medal Dept. Def., 1970. Mem. Govtl. Research Asso. (trustee, v.p. 1955-56), Am. Polit. Sci. Assn., Am. Soc. Pub. Adminstrn., Mont Pelerin Soc., Phi Beta Kappa, Phi Alpha Theta. Conglist. Clubs: Ann Arbor; Barton Hills Country, Cosmos (Washington). Home: 16 Haverhill Ct Ann Arbor MI 48105 Office: Plymouth Bldg Suite 204 2929 Plymouth Rd Ann Arbor MI 48105

WARMBROD, CATHARINE PHELPS, educator; b. Lost Nation, Iowa, July 2, 1929; d. Paul Edward and Ruth Dorthea (Langhorst) Phelps; B.A., U. Iowa, 1952; M.S., U. Ill., 1965, advanced cert. edn., 1967; m. James Robert Warmbrod, Jan. 30, 1965. Head supr. student tchrs. in bus. edn. U. Ill., 1966-67; chairperson Columbus Tech. Inst., 1970-77; research specialist, project dir. Nat. Center for Research in Vocat. Edn., Ohio State U., 1977—. U. Ill. summer fellow, 1964. Mem. Am. Vocat. Assn., Nat. Bus. Edn. Assn., Nat. Assn. Industry-Edn. Cooperation, Am. Assn. Community and Jr. Colls., Council Occupational Edn., Delta Pi Epsilon, Phi Delta Kappa. Author: Review and Synthesis of Literature on Residential Schools in Vocational and Technical Education, 1970; Business, Industry, and Labor Inputs in Vocational Education Personnel Development, 1978; Operating a Retirees Volunteer Program in Postsecondary Institutions, 1979; Sharing Resources: Postsecondary Education and Industry Cooperation, 1981; contbr. articles to profl. jours. Home: 3867 Mountview Rd Columbus OH 43220 Office: Nat Center for Research in Vocat Edn Ohio State U 1960 Kenny Rd Columbus OH 43210

WARMBROD, JAMES ROBERT, educator; b. Belvidere, Tenn., Dec. 13, 1929; s. George Victor and Anna Sophia (Zimmerman) W.; B.S., U. Tenn., 1952, M.S., 1954; Ed.D., U. Ill., 1962; m. Catharine P. Phelps, Jan. 30, 1965. Instr. edn. U. Tenn., Knoxville, 1956-57; tchr. high sch., Winchester, Tenn., 1957-59; asst. to asso. prof. U. Ill., Urbana, 1961-67; prof. Ohio State U., Columbus, 1968—, chmn. dept. agrl. edn., 1978—; vis. prof. Pa. State U., 1970, U. Minn., 1971, Iowa State U., 1974. Served with USAF, 1954-56. U. Ill. fellow, 1959-60; recipient Ohio State U. Alumni award distinguished teaching, 1972; distinguished service award Am. Assn. Tchrs. Educators in Agr., 1974; Ohio State U. Gamma Sigma Delta teaching award, 1977. Mem. Am. Vocat. Assn. (v.p. 1976-79), Am. Ednl. Research Assn. (chmn. spl. interest group on vocat. edn. 1972), Am. Vocat. Edn. Research Assn. (pres. 1976), Am. Assn. Tchr. Educators in Agr., Nat. Soc. for Study Edn. Author: Review and Synthesis of Research on the Economics of Vocational Education, 1968; The Liberalization of Vocational Education, 1974. Editor: Agrl. Edn. Mag., 1968-71. Home: 3867 Mountview Rd Columbus OH 43220

WARMINGTON, CATHY A., lawyer; b. Madison, Wis., Oct. 19, 1948; d. Edward M. and Opal C. Huettner; B.S., U. Wis., Madison, 1970, student, Milw., 1969, 71; J.D., Marquette U., 1979; m. Thomas E. Warmington, Aug. 1, 1970. Tchr. biology and sci. New Berlin (Wis.) Pub. Schs., 1970-74; v.p. 20th Century Homes, Inc., Waukesha, Wis., 1974—; office mgr. Fair Oaks Realty Inc., Waukesha, 1974—; v.p. Tomcat Constrn. Corp., Waukesha, 1978—, Homebuilders, Inc., Waukesha, 1978—; admitted to Wis. bar, 1980; prs. Warmington & Warmington, S.C., 1980—. Counselor, Meml. Ch., 1972-73, adminstrv. bd., 1972-75; active YWCA Big Sister Program, 1974-75. Recipient Am. Jurisprudence award, 1980; Wis. Honor scholar, 1966. Mem. Smithsonian Inst., Internat., Nat. wildlife fedns., Phi Delta Phi, Delta Zeta. Office: 152 W Main St Waukesha WI 53186

WARNCKE, RONALD FREDERICK, pub. co. exec.; b. Detroit, Apr. 18, 1943; s. Gilbert John and Fern (Peterson) W.; B.A., Mich. State U., 1970; m. Deborah Adele Wood, Aug. 10, 1969; 1 dau., Amy Ellen Adele. Field rep., Richard D. Irwin and the Dorsey Press, Inc., Detroit, 1970-74; editor The Dorsey Press, Homewood, Ill., 1974-78, exec. editor, 1978—. Active, Izaak Walton League, Homewood, 1979—. Served with USN, 1963-67. Mem. Am. Hist. Assn., Orgn. Am. Historians, Am. Polit. Sci. Assn., Midwest Polit. Sci. Assn., Nat. Geographic Soc., Smithsonian Inst., Nat. Wildlife Fedn. Project editor: A More Perfect Union: Introduction to American Government, 1979, 82; Understanding American Politics, 1982. Office: 1818 Ridge Rd Homewood IL 60430

WARNE, RALPH DICK, ins. co. exec.; b. Hillsboro, Ohio, Dec. 16, 1923; s. James Roy and Mary Jane (Dick) W.; B.S. in Bus. Adminstrn., Ohio State U., 1947; m. Dorothy Louis Brandeberry, June 30, 1957; children—Jane Lynn, Joyce Kay. State agt. Hartford Accident Indemnity Co., Pitts., 1947-51; state mgr. Mass. Bonding and Ins. Co., Columbus, Ohio, 1951-53; pres., chief exec. officer R.D. Warne & Assos., Columbus, 1956—, Columbus Ins. Holding Co. of Wilmington (formerly Conva Indemnity Co.), Columbus, 1969—; pres., chief exec. officer Columbus Ins. Co., Signal Ins. Co. of Austin (Tex.); cons. Ohio Hosp. Assn. Mem. areawide project rev. com. Mid-Ohio Health Planning Fedn., 1976—. Mem. Ohio Health Care Assn., Columbus C. of C., Upper Arlington Civic Assn., Phi Delta Theta. Lutheran. Clubs: Columbus Univ., Ohio State U. Alumni, Scioto Country. Home: 1287 Darcann Dr Columbus OH 43220 Office: 3070 Riverside Dr Columbus OH 43221

WARNEBOLD, GLENN JOSEPH, transp. co. exec.; b. Labadie, Mo., May 15, 1942; s. John C. and Rosaline E. (Unnerstall) W.; B.S.C., St. Louis U., 1964; m. Carolyn Ann Straatmann, June 20, 1964. Controller, United Parcel Service, Nashville and Charlotte, N.C., 1965-78; mgr. adminstrv. services Mo. Pacific Truck Lines, Chesterfield, 1978—. Mem. Alpha Kappa Psi. Roman Catholic. Home: 79 River Bend Dr Chesterfield MO 63017 Office: 210 N 13 St Saint Louis MO 63103

WARNER, BRIAN MARTIN, health and social service exec.; b. Connersville, Ind., Oct. 25, 1947; s. Gilbert Martin and Mary E. (Porter) W.; student Tenn. Temple Coll., 1966-67; B.S. in Secondary Edn., Taylor U., 1970; M.A. in Student Personnel Adminstrn., Ball State U., 1971, M.A. in Pre-Clin. Psychology, 1977; m. Janet Sue Robbins, Dec. 21, 1969; children—Aaron M., Jaren M. Caseworker, Grant County Dept. Public Welfare, Marion, Ind., 1971-72; exec. dir. Family Service Soc., Inc., Marion, 1972—; pastor Ind. Yearly Meeting of Friends, Fairmount, 1971-76; prof. psychology Taylor Univ., Upland, Ind., part-time, 1980-81; psychol. and diagnostic cons. Grant County Dept. Probation and Wabash County Dept. Public Welfare, 1980-81. Mem. Region Six Title Twenty Adv. Com., 1978—, Region Six Ind. State Manpower Planning Council, 1974-75, Region Six Vocational Rehab. Adv. Com. for State of Ind., 1980—. Recipient Disting. Service award Marion Jaycees, 1980; cert. sch. psychometrist, Ind. Mem. Ind. Psychol. Assn., Am. Psychol. Assn. Home: 10360 E 500 South Upland IN 46989 Office: 418 W 3d St Marion IN 46952

WARNER, J. KEITH, bakery cons.; b. Sioux City, Iowa, Mar. 22, 1935; s. Karl R. and Lucille (Shea) W.; B.S., Morningside Coll., 1957; m. Patricia Caldwell, Sept. 3, 1955; children—Linda, Brian, Kevin, Lori, Lisa. With ITT Continental, 1957-74, bakery plant mgr., Wichita, Kans., Milw., 1967-74; exec. v.p. baker div. Heileman Brewery, 1974-75, pres., 1976; pres. Metz Baking Co., Sioux City, Iowa, 1976-81; bakery cons., 1981—. Council pres. Girl Scouts U.S.A., 1978-81. Mem. Am. Inst. Baking (trustee). Republican. Roman Catholic. Club: Rotary.

WARNER, JEROME, state legislator; b. Waverly, Nebr., Nov. 23, 1927; s. Charles J. Warner; B.S., U. Nebr.; m. Betty Person; children—Jamie, Elizabeth. Farmer, breeder Hereford cattle; mem. Nebr. Legislature, 1962—. Chmn., Lancaster County (Nebr.) Com. Reorgn. Sch. Dists.; vice chmn. Young Republican Nat. Fedn.; mem. Lincoln City-Lancaster County Planning and Zoning Commn.; treas. Lancaster County Fair Bd. Served with Nebr. Air NG. Mem. Nebr. State Grange, Farm Bur., Nebr. Livestock Feeders Assn., Nebr. Stockgrowers Assn., Farm House, Gamma Sigma Delta. Alpha Zeta. Clubs: Masons, Shriners, KT, Order Eastern Star. *

WARPEHA, RAYMOND LEONARD, surgeon, clin. dir., educator; b. Mpls., Dec. 5, 1934; s. Frank Joseph and Sophie Helen (Fryzlewicz) W.; B.S., U. Minn., 1956, D.D.S., 1958; M.D., Northwestern U., 1965, Ph.D., 1966; m. Ivy Kloth, Aug. 15, 1975; children—Katherine, John, Joseph, Francis. Instr. anatomy Northwestern U., Chgo., 1963-65, resident in plastic surgery, Med. Sch., 1970-72, professorial lectr. anatomy, 1972—; intern Cook County Hosp., Chgo., 1965-66, resident in surgery, 1966-70; practice medicine specializing in plastic surgery, Maywood, Ill., 1972-75; asst. prof. surgery and anatomy Loyola U. Med. Sch., Maywood, 1972-75, chmn. div. plastic surgery, 1975—, asso. prof., 1975-81, prof., 1981—; dir. burn unit Foster McGaw Hosp., Maywood, 1973—; attending physician Hines (Ill.) VA Hosp., 1972-76, cons. surgery, 1977; chmn. Ill. burn surgeons adv. group Ill. Div. Emergency Med. Services, 1974—; chmn. burn adv. group HEW, 1975—. Diplomate Am. Bd. Surgery, Am. Bd. Plastic Surgery. Fellow A.C.S. Roman Catholic. Contbr. articles to med. jours. Office: Loyola Univ Medical School 2160 S 1st Ave Maywood IL 60153

WARREN, DOROTHY HELEN CAREY, assn. exec.; b. South Bend, Ind., Oct. 31, 1916; d. Harry George and Mary (Heild) Barney; student John Marshall Law Sch., 1945-47, McCormick Coll. Bus., Chgo., 1947-50; m. Francis E. Carey, Sept. 9, 1952 (dec. 1966); 1 dau., Francene Carey Andresen; m. 2d, Benedict O. Warren, May 13, 1976. Exec. sec. Chicagoland Golf Assn., Palos Hills, Ill., 1954—, Sod Growers Assn. Mid-Am., Palos Hills, 1956—, Ill. Turfgrass Found., Palos Hills, 1967-78, Midwest Assn. Golf Course Supts., Palos Hills, 1969—, Central U.S. Distbrs. Equipment Co., Palos Hills, 1974—. Sec., Chgo. Park Dist. Dog Tng. Assn., 1948-54, Sherman Park All Breed Dog Tng., Chgo., 1948-50; organizer, trainer Sherman Park Canine Pal Club, Chgo., 1950-52; organizer, 1st pres. Gage Park All Breed Dog Tng. Group, Chgo., 1951-53; sec. Skokie Valley Kennel Club, 1950-51; organizer Green Acres Riding Club, Hickory Hills, Ill., 1962-63, mem., 1967-75; owner, operator Rocking C Ranch, Orland Park, Ill., 1964-76. Editor Dog Coll. News, 1952-54. Home and office: 11020 S Roberts Rd Palos Hills IL 60465

WARREN, ELIZABETH CURRAN, educator; b. St. Louis, Aug. 23, 1927; d. Maurice Donovan and Florence Elizabeth (Schulte) Curran; B.A., Bryn Mawr Coll., 1949; M.A., U. Kans., 1965; Ph.D., U. Nebr., 1970; m. Geoffrey Spencer Warren, June 26, 1949; children—Kathryn Lloyd, Patricia, Michele, Deborah Perry. Instr. polit. sci. Washburn U., Topeka, Kans., 1968-70; asst. prof. Northwestern U., Chgo., 1970-71, Lake Forest (Ill.) Coll., 1972; adj. prof. Loyola U., Chgo., 1977-79; asst. prof. polit. sci., dir. public affairs program, 1979—. Trustee, Village of Glencoe (Ill.), 1974—. Mem. Am. Polit. Sci. Assn., Am. Soc. Public Adminstrn., Midwest Polit. Sci. Assn., Women's Caucus for Polit. Sci., LWV. Episcopalian. Home: 900 Valley Rd Glencoe IL 60022 Office: Loyola University Political Science Dept 820 N Michigan Ave Chicago IL 60611

WARREN, FOREST GLEN, agrl. cons., economist; b. Kouts, Ind., Dec. 15, 1913; s. Joseph Allen and Mary Imogene (Philpott) W.; B.S., Purdue U., 1937; Ph.D., U. Ill., 1945; m. Olive Louise Lauterbach,

Oct. 17, 1942; children—Mary Anne, Richard Henry. Economist, U.S. Dept. Agr. Chgo., 1941-42, Lend Lease Adminstrn., Washington, 1942-45; U.S. Dept. Commerce, Washington, 1945-59; Export-Import Bank U.S., Washington, 1959-66; U.S. Dept. Agr., Washington, 1966-73; cons. agr., Itasca, Ill. and Valparaiso, Ind., 1973—; pres. Warren Lands, Inc., 1949—. Mem. Am. Econ. Assn., Am. Farm Econs. Assn., Internat. Assn. Agrl. Economists, Sigma Xi. Methodist. Club: Blue Ridge Mountain Country. Contbr. articles to profl. jours. Home and Office: 603 N 50 W Valparaiso IN 46383

WARREN, JOE ELLISON, state senator; b. Silverdale, Kans., Sept. 17, 1912; s. James Edman and Phoebe (Harkelroad) W.; student pub. schs., Arkansas City, Kans.; m. Pauline Goff, Sept. 4, 1931; children—James, Helen Jane. Treas., Spring Creek Twp., 1952-56; mem. Kans. State Senate, 1956—, chmn. soil conservation dist., 1956-78, minority caucus chmn. Senate, 1964-72, chmn. livestock subcom. Senate Com. on agr., 1968-72, vice chmn. legis. facilities com., 1972—, asst. minority leader, 1969-77, caucus chmn., vice chmn. agr. and livestock com., 1974-77; farmer, rancher, Maple City, Kans., 1932—. Mem. sch. bd., Common Sch. Dist., Kans., 1936-57; mem. exec. Council Extension Cowley County, Kan., 1956-58; mem. fed. adv. council Bur. Employment Security, U.S. Dept. Labor; mem. Kans. Legislative Council; mem. Gov.'s Com. on Criminal Adminstrn. Recipient numerous awards in field of soil conservation and edn. Address: Route 1 Maple City KS 67102

WARREN, JOHN CRUIKSHANK, JR., utility exec.; b. St. Paul, Nov. 13, 1940; s. John Cruikshank and Dorothy (Giard) W.; B.A., Coll. St. Thomas, St. Paul, 1963; m. Mary Jo Wickert, Aug. 17, 1963; children—John Cruikshank III, Shanna Marie, Michael Sherman. City editor Mandan (N.D.) Morning Pioneer, 1963-64; news dir. KBOM Radio, Bismarck, N.D., 1964-65; news and pub. affairs dir. Meyer Broadcasting Co., Bismarck, N.D., 1965-70; dir. pub. affairs and devel. St. Mary's Hosp., Rochester, Minn., 1970-80; dir. external affairs Coop. Power Assn., Mpls., 1980—. Chmn. citizens adv. com. Olmsted County CD, 1979-80; bd. dirs. Minn. Citizens Concerned for Life, 1971-76, Cath. Social Services, 1977-78, Rochester Civic Theatre, 1978-79, Rochester Better Chance, 1976-78; mem. public affairs com. Mayo Clinic, 1973-79. Recipient Outstanding TV News award Upper Midwest Radio/TV News, 1968. Past mem. Internat. Assn. Bus. Communicators (Gold Quill award of merit 1979); mem. Nat. Assn. Hosp. Devel. (regional v.p., bd. dirs.), Am. Soc. Hosp. Public Relations, Cath. Hosp. Assn. (mem. spl. commn. on philanthropy 1977-78), Minn. Hosp. Assn. (mem. public relations com.), Rochester Area C. of C. (dir. 1978-80). Club: Rotary (dir. 1978-80) (Rochester, Minn.). Mem. editorial bd. Nat. Assn. Hosp. Devel. Jour., 1973-74; editor Caring mag., 1975-79; past editorial guest writer Rochester Post Bull. Home: 6340 Elm Tree Ave Excelsior MN 55331 Office: Coop Power Assn 3020 Mitchell Rd Eden Prairie MN 55344

WARREN, MYRNA JEAN, newspaper editor; b. Warren, Ohio, July 28, 1936; d. Floyd Elton and Belle Georgia (Baker) Warren; student Ohio State U., 1954-56, Kent (Ohio) State U., 1960-64; grad. Newspaper Inst. Am., 1970. Mem. editorial dept. Warren Tribune Chronicle, 1968-69; pub. relations with Community Hosp., Warren, 1969; adminstrv. asst. Clark Indsl. Supply Co., Warren, 1970-76; editor Western Res. Democrat, Warren, 1976—; instr. journalism John F. Kennedy High Sch., Warren; owner Creative Innovations pub. relations firm; freelance writer syndicated review column Books Today. Mem. Am. Soc. Writers, Mystery Writers Am., Nat., Ohio newspapers assns., Pub. Relations Soc. Am., Women in Communications, Am. Bus. Women's Assn. (past pres.; Woman of Yr. award Warren 1974; Nat. UN fellow 1975), Ohio (pub. relations chmn. 1975-76), Warren (past pres., Gal Friday award 1969) bus. and profl. women's clubs, League Women Voters (publicity chmn. local chpts.), AAUW, ALA, Library Pub. Relations Council, Ohio Women's Polit. Caucus, Ohio Citizens Council for Health and Welfare, Multiple Sclerosis Soc., Columbia Scholastic Press Advisers Assn., Am. Cancer Soc., March of Dimes, Ohio Soc. to Prevent Blindness. Methodist. Home: 1273 State Route 305 NE Cortland OH 44410 Office: 2550 Central Pkwy SE Warren OH 44484

WARREN, ROSS WINSTON, dentist; b. Marshall, Ind., Nov. 7, 1923; s. Bradford and Marcella Pearl (Isaacs) W.; D.D.S., Ind. U., 1945; m. Lyndall Jo Hoopingarner, Dec. 16, 1955; 1 dau., Stacey Ann. Pvt. practice dentistry, Rockville, Ind., 1945-51, Crawfordsville, Ind., 1957—. Instr., Ind. U. Sch. Dentistry, Indpls., 1960-73. Bd. dirs. Sugar Creek Playhouse, Crawfordsville, 1970-73, chmn. bd., 1970-71. Served with AUS, 1943-44, 51-57, now col. Res. Mem. Am., Ind. dental assns., Acad. Gen. Dentistry, Am. Equiliibration Soc. (mem. editorial rev. com. 1970-71, Ben Hur Dental Soc. (pres. 1958-59, 64-65), fellow, Am. Coll. of Dentists, 1976, Delta Sigma Delta, Delta Tau Delta. Republican. Presbyn. (deacon 1961, trustee 1967-70). Mason. Club: Ouiatenon (Crawfordsville). Home: 126 S Davis St Crawfordsville IN 47933 Office: 408 W Market St Crawfordsville IN 47933

WARRICK, PATRICIA SCOTT, educator; b. La Grange, Ind., Feb. 6, 1925; d. Ross B. and DeEtte L. (Ulman) Scott; B.S. in Biochemistry, Ind. U., 1946; B.A. in English, Goshen Coll., 1964; M.A., Purdue U., 1965; Ph.D., U. Wis., Milw., 1977; children—Scott, David, Kristin. Mem. staff bldg. and devel. program L.I. U., Bklyn., 1946-48; dir. technicians med. lab. St. Elizabeth Hosp., Indpls., 1948-52; instr. English, Lawrence U., Appleton, Wis., 1965-66; prof. English U. Wis., Fox Valley, Menasha, 1966—, chmn. English dept., 1976—, dir. 21st century studies, 1977—. Nat. Endowment Humanities fellow, 1973-74; U. Wis. fellow, 1980. Mem. Nat. Council Tchrs. English, Modern Lang. Assn., World Future Soc., Sci. Fiction Research Assn. Author: The Cybernetic Imagination in Science Fiction, 1980. Contbr. articles to profl. jours.; editor numerous works in field. Home: 3308 Scarlet Oak Ln Appleton WI 54911 Office: U Wis Center Menasha WI 54952

WARSHAW, MARTIN RICHARD, educator; b. N.Y.C., Sept. 17, 1924; s. Irving Gregg and Adelaide (Klein) W.; A.B., Columbia U., 1947; M.B.A., U. Mich., 1957, Ph.D., 1960; m. Alice M. Present, Mar. 28, 1948; children—Gregg, Mark, Lynn, Laurie. Salesman, Daniels Jewelry Co., Battle Creek, Mich., 1947-50, store mgr., 1950-55, v.p., dir., Lansing, Mich., 1955-64; instr. bus. adminstrn. U. Mich., 1957-60, asst. prof., 1960-64, asso. prof., 1964-67, prof. mktg., 1967—, chmn. mktg. faculty, 1973-79, 81—; asso. Mgmt. Analysis Center, Cambridge, Mass., 1970—. Served with C.E., U.S. Army, 1943-46. Mem. Am. Mktg. Assn. (past pres. Detroit chpt.). Author: (with Rewoldt and Scott) Introduction To Marketing Management, 4th edit., 1981; (with Engel and Kinnear) Promotional Strategy, 4th edit., 1979. Home: 2279 Mershon Dr Ann Arbor MI 48103 Office: 720 Business Adminstrn U Michigan Ann Arbor MI 48109

WARTA, DENIS JOSEPH, water conditioning dealer; b. New Ulm, Minn., Dec. 20, 1927; s. Henry and Theresa (Hoffmann) W.; student St. John's U., Collegeville, Minn., 1948, U. Minn. Sch. Bus. Adminstrn., 1948-49; m. Dorothy Helen Kraus, Sept. 26, 1950; children—Diann Marie, Dean Michael. With State Bank New Ulm, 1951-54; owner Lindsay Soft Water Co., New Ulm, 1954—. Mem. New Ulm Housing and Redevel. Authority, 1969-72, 81—, Brown County SSS, 1968-73; chmn. Brown-Nicollet Human Services Bd., 1973—; pres. New Ulm Industries, Inc., 1977—; commr. 1st dist. Brown County, 1972-80. Served with USN, 1946-47. Mem. Water Quality Assn., Am. Water Works Assn., Nat. Fedn. Ind. Bus., Minn. Water Conditioning Assn. (past pres.), Minn. Assn. Commerce and Industry, Minn. Social Service Assn., Am. Turners, Am. Legion, VFW, Isaac Walton League, Ducks Unlimited, Minn. Waterfowl Assn., Brown County Hist. Soc. Ind. Republican. Roman Catholic. Clubs: New Ulm Country (dir.), New Ulm Rotary, K.C. Address: 812 S Broadway New Ulm MN 56073

WAS, THOMAS BERNARD, clergyman, cons.; b. South Bend, Ind., Dec. 15, 1936; s. Aloysius and Mary W.; student Menninger Found., 1971-72, George Williams Coll., 1975-79. Ordained priest Roman Catholic Ch., 1964; hosp. chaplain, priest Natchez-Jackson Diocese (Miss.); sch. counselor, Phila.; counselor St. Elizabeth Social Center, Rockford, Ill., Winnebago County Jail, Rockford; asso. dir. pre-novitiate program Tau Frat., Milw., 1978—; personnel dir. Franciscans of Assumption Province, 1981—; cons. orgns.; pvt. counselor. Bd. dirs. Vol. Bur. Greater Rockford, Mental Health Bd. Winnebago County. Recipient Spl. award PALS of Rockford, 1975; cert. of appreciation DuPage County (Ill.) Boy Scouts Am., 1976, 77. Mem. Am. Personnel and Guidance Assn., Am. Psychol. Assn., Assn. for Clin. Pastoral Edn. Designer spl. program for PACE, Cook County (Ill.) Jail, 1977. Home and Office: 645 Irwin Ave Green Bay WI 54301

WASHA, ARTHUR JOHN, bus. exec.; b. Milw., Sept. 23, 1943; s. Arthur Antone and Elizabeth (Harrison) W.; B.S., U. Wis., 1969, M.S., 1971; m. Cheryl Ann Schuepferling, Sept. 2, 1969; children—Andrew John, Wendy Ann, Kristen Ann. Instr., U. Wis. Center System, 1970-71; instr. U. Wis., Milw., 1969-71; investigator Wis. Dept. Justice, 1971; instr. Kenyon Coll. (Ohio), 1971-72; dir. edn., publs. and edn. div. Am. Appraisal Co., Milw., 1972-74; owner, operator Appraisal Assos., West Bend, Wis., 1973-74; exec. dir. edn. Nat. Assn. Ind. Fee Appraisers, St. Louis, 1975-79, Service awards, 1973, 74; pres., dir. Inst. Real Estate Tech., St. Louis, 1979-81; pres. Am. Valuation Services Co., Milw., 1981—; exec. producer, host. television series How To Buy A Home, 1975. Served with USMC, 1962-65. Recipient Hatcher award U. Wis., 1970. Mem. Am. Soc. Appraisers, Am. Soc. for Tng. and Devel., Adult Edn. Council of St. Louis, Inst. Real Estate Tech. Club: Rotary Internat. Author: Residential Real Estate Appraisal: Techniques of Capitalization, 1974; Residential, Commercial and Industrial Building Cost Estimating, 1972. Home: 5617 Kenny Dr West Bend WI 53095

WASHAK, EDWARD ALBERT, JR., advt. co. exec.; b. Lowell, Mass., Mar. 30, 1934; s. Edward Albert and Helen Mary (Keleher) W.; A.A., Boston U., 1954, B.S., 1956; postgrad. Roosevelt U., 1981—; m. Elizabeth Pat Courtney, Sept. 15, 1956; children—Edward Albert III, Courtney Michael, Sean Patrick. Editor, Calumet Index-Beverly, Chgo., 1959-62; reporter Chgo. Daily News, 1962-64; mng. editor Daily Calumet, Chgo., 1964-66; editor Calumet Index-Rev., Chgo., 1966-68; press sec. to candidate for Sec. State of Ill., 1968; founder Ted Ash Advt., Oak Lawn, Ill., 1968—. Bd. dirs. 111th St. YMCA, Taxpayers Assn. Ill.; legis. aide State Rep. J. Theodore Meyer, 1968—. Served with 82d Airborne Div., U.S. Army, 1956, 59. Mem. Ill. Press. Assn. (editor of yr. 1962), Lambda Chi Alpha. Republican. Roman Catholic. Home: 10157 S Forest St Chicago IL 60628 Office: Ted Ash Advertising 5615 W 95th St Oak Lawn IL 60453

WASHAK, ELIZABETH COURTNEY, nurse-practitioner; b. Phila., July 15, 1932; d. Patrick A. and Theresa B. (Cawley) C.; R.N., Carney Hosp. Sch. Nursing, 1949; B.S. in Nursing, Tchrs. Coll., Columbia U., 1952; M.A., Roosevelt U., 1971; M.S., Rush U., 1977; m. Edward A. Washak, Jr., Sept. 15, 1956; children—Edward A. III, Courtney M., Sean P. Tchr.-nurse Chgo. Bd. Edn., 1967-76; nursing instr. Frontier Nursing Service, Hyden, Ky., 1977-78; nurse-practitioner supr. Ill. Dept. Correction, Joliet, 1979-80; ind. nursing practice, 1979—; owner, mgr. Cert. Nurse Practitioner Office, Oak Lawn, Ill., 1979—; instr. Coll. Nursing, Rush U., 1978—; asst. prof. Rush Med. Center, 1980—; cons. Westinghouse Headstart Project, 1979—; mem. task force Chgo. Health Systems Agy. Mem. Chgo. Mayor's Office for Sr. Citizens. Recipient award Chgo. Police Dept. Fellowship Assn., 1966; Kemper Found. Study award, 1964. Registered nurse-practitioner, Ill. Mem. Am. Nurses Assn. (cert. of excellence 1980), Ill. Nurses Assn., Nat. Assn. Primary Nurse Practitioners, Nat. Assn. Women Bus. Owners, NOW, Practitions for Parity (founder-pres. 1980). Office: 5615 W 95th St Suite 200 Oak Lawn IL 60453

WASHBURN, GREGORY GEORGE, printing co. exec.; b. LaGrange, Ill., Jan. 7, 1947; s. George Burton and Doris W.; student U. Notre Dame, 1965-66; B.A. in Bus. Adminstrn., Coe Coll., 1969; married; children—Brian Gregory, Kristin Belle, Clayton Gerard. With mktg. div. Midwest regional office IBM, Chgo., 1969-70; co-owner, v.p. Washburn Graficolor, Inc., Lisle, Ill., 1970—; instr. adult coll. graphic arts program Ill. Benedictine Coll.; co-instr. undergrad. mktg. studies George Williams Coll. Mem. pres.'s adv. council Ill. Benedictine Coll. Recipient award Printing Industry Am., 1972, 76; Outstanding Service award Ill. Benedictine Coll., 1978. Mem. Bus./Profl. Advt. Assn., Phi Kappa Tau. Roman Catholic. Clubs: Kiwanis, Rotary. Office: Washburn Graficolor Inc 1975 University Ln Lisle IL 60532

WASHBURN, JAMES F., hosp. safety ofcl.; b. Lafayette, Ind., Nov. 7, 1925; s. Paul R. and Hazel M. (Miller) W.; student Police Adminstrn., U. Louisville, 1962-63; m. Helen O. Stivers, Sept. 17, 1945; 1 dau., Jamie Jo Washburn Gilliland. With Lafayette Police Dept., 1950-70, traffic engr., 1968-70, ret., 1970; founder safety and security dept. Lafayette Home Hosp., 1970, dir. safety and security, 1981—; chmn. traffic improvement commn. City of Lafayette, 1968-70. Mem. Tippecanoe County CD Adv. Council, def. dir., 1968-70; mem. Lafayette police pension bd., 1955-70; chmn. tech. highway com., 1968-70. Served with Submarine Service, USN, 1943-47. Recipient various service commendations Police Dept. Mem. Am. Soc. Safety Engrs., Internat. Assn. Hosp. Security, Am. Legion, 40 and 8, U.S. Sub Vets World War II, Fraternal Order of Police (life mem., state officer 1963-67). Presbyterian. Clubs: Eagles, Elks. Home: 1012 Kensington Dr Lafayette IN 47905 Office: 2400 South St Lafayette IN 47902

WASHBURN, JOSEPH HULLEY, JR., radiation oncologist; b. Los Angeles, Oct. 15, 1938; s. Joseph Hulley and Viola (Neill) W.; B.A. in Chemistry, Ariz. State U., 1967; M.S. in Exptl. Pathology, Whittier (Calif.) Coll., 1969; M.D., U. Nebr., 1973; m. Ann Marlene Tuttle, Mar. 21, 1967; children—Aimee Elizabeth, Katherine Susan. Intern, St. Joseph Med. Center, Phoenix, 1974; resident in radiation oncology U. Nebr. Med. Center, 1974, asst. prof., 1978; dir. radiation oncology Marian Health Center, Sioux City, Iowa, 1979—; pres. Washburn Radiation Oncology Services, P.C., Sioux City, 1979. Served with USAF, 1960-64. Clin. fellow Am. Cancer Soc., 1975. Mem. AMA, Am. Soc. Clin. Oncology, Am. Coll. Radiology, Am. Coll. Nuclear Physics, Am. Soc. Therapeutic Radiology, Am. Radium Soc., Am. Assn. Cancer Research, Iowa Med. Soc., Midland Soc. Therapeutic Radiology (pres. 1980), Woodbury County Med. Soc. Republican. Home: 20 W Kings Hwy Sioux City IA 51104 Office: 2101 Court St Sioux City IA 51104

WASHBURN, PAUL ARTHUR, bishop; b. Aurora, Ill., Mar. 31, 1911; s. Eliot A. and Lena (Buhrnsen) W.; B.A., N. Central Coll., Naperville, Ill., 1936, L.H.D., 1970; B.D., Evang. Theol. Sem., 1938; D.D., Ind. Central Coll., 1954; D.Cn.L., Westmar Coll., 1972; D.D., Wiley Coll., 1975; m. Kathryn E. Fischer, Jan. 12, 1937; children—Mary Washburn Marks, Jane Washburn Eigenbrodt, Fred, John. Teller, bookkeeper First Nat. Bank, Aurora, Ill., 1929-32; ordained to ministry Evang. Ch., 1938; pastor Eppards Point Evang. Ch., Chenoa, Ill., 1934-39, St. John's Evang. United Brethren Ch., Rockford, Ill., 1939-52; lectr. religion Rockford Coll., 1947-52; pastor First Evang. United Brethren Ch., Naperville, Ill., 1952-64; exec. sec. Commn. on Ch. Union, Evang. United Brethren Ch., 1964-68; bishop Minn. area United Meth. Ch., Mpls., 1968-72, Chgo. area, 1972-80. Directed union of The Meth. Ch. and The Evang. United Brethren Ch.; pres. Bd. Global Ministries, United Meth. Ch., 1972-76. Trustee N. Central Coll., Naperville, 1963—, Garrett-Evang. Theol. Sem., Evanston, Ill., 1954—, Northwestern Meml. Hosp.. Chgo., 1972—. Author: The United Methodist Primer. Home: 413 Parkway Dr Wheaton IL 60187

WASHINGTON, ELOIS DEFRANTZ, educator; b. Los Angeles, Jan. 15, 1949; daughter Louis Lee and Mary Leon Washington; student in art (scholar) Ill. Inst. Tech., 1965-66; B.A., So. Ill. U., 1970, B.A., Western Ill. U., 1973; Ph.D., U. Iowa, 1979. Tchr., Chgo. Public Schs., 1971-76; program coordinator Internat. Adminstrv. Intern Program, U. Iowa, 1976-78, mem. Office of Spl. Support Services Adv. Council, 1978-79; curriculum study coordinator Div. Research and Devel., Test Devel., Am. Coll. Testing Program, Iowa City, Iowa, 1978-79; instr. Nat. Coll. Edn., 1980—; cons. Chgo. Bd. Edn. Dept. Research and Evaluation Bur. Citywide Testing, 1979—; mem. North Central Assn. Evaluation Team, 1979; mem. exec. bd. First Congl. Dist. Edn. Task Force, 1981—. Mem. Am. Ednl. Research Assn., Assn. Supervision and Curriculum Devel., Chgo. Area Alliance Black Sch. Educators, Nat. Alliance Black Sch. Educators, Nat. Council on Measurement in Edn., Phi Delta Kappa, Delta Sigma Theta. Democrat. Methodist. Author reading units and tests. Office: 2021 N Burling Chicago IL 60614

WASHINGTON, HAROLD, congressman; b. Chgo., Apr. 15, 1922; B.A., Roosevelt U., Chgo., 1949; J.D., Northwestern U., 1952. Admitted to Ill. bar, 1953; practice in Chgo., from 1953; asst. city prosecutor Chgo., 1954-58; arbitrator Ill. Indsl. Commn., 1960-64; mem. Ill. Ho. of Reps., 1965-76, chmn. jud. com.; mem. Ill. Senate, 1976-80, chmn. public health, welfare and corrections com.; lectr. urban politics Roosevelt U.; mem. 97th Congress from 1st Dist. Ill. Bd. dirs. Suburban SCLC, Mid-South Mental Health Assn.; founder Washington Youth and Community Orgn. Served with USAAF, 1942-46. Mem. Nat. Bar Assn., Ill. Bar Assn., Cook County Bar Assn., NAACP, Urban League, Black Taxpayers Fedn. (founder, past. pres.). Address: 1610 Longworth House Office Bldg Washington DC 20515*

WASHULESKI, L. ALLAN, occupational safety adminstr.; b. Marinette, Wis., Oct. 18, 1953; s. Frank L. and Pearl L. (Semrau) W.; diploma Ga. State U., 1979; diploma Nat. Safety Council Extension, 1980; A.A., Northeast Wis. Tech. Inst., 1982; m. Lois Nancy Wilson, Apr. 20, 1974; children—Jason Andrew, Brad Allan. Welder, Marinette Marine Corp. (Wis.), 1974-77, safety adv., 1978, supr. safety, 1978—; safety and health cons., 1980—. Vol., County of Marinette Fire Dept., 1974-78; bd. dirs. Marinette County chpt. ARC, 1981—. Mem. Am. Welding Soc., Am. Soc. Safety Engrs. (v.p. Wis. sect. 1981-82), Tri-County Safety Council (dir. 1981—), Nat. Safety Council, Am. Indsl. Hygiene Assn. Republican. Contbr. reports and articles on indsl. safety to profl. publs. Home: 822 Miller St Marinette WI 54143 Office: Marinette Marine Corp Ely St Marinette WI 54143

WASKOW, JOYCE ANN, educator; b. Meriden, Iowa, Aug. 15, 1941; d. Clarence Emory and Lucille Dorothy (Horstman) Smith; B.S., Iowa State U., 1963; m. James Rudolph Waskow, July 6, 1963; children—Susan Jo, Brent James. Tchr. home econs. Collins (Iowa) High Sch., 1963-64; home economist Met. Utilities Dist., Omaha, 1964; tchr. home econs. Dist. 66 Schs., Omaha, 1965-66; home economist The Merchandising Group, N.Y.C., 1972-76; tchr. home econs. Pattonville Sr. High Sch., St. Louis, 1976-79; tchr. home econs. Maplewood-Richmond Heights (Mo.) High Sch., 1979-80; tchr. home econs. Webster Groves (Mo.) High Sch., 1980—. Leader, St. Louis council 860 Girl Scouts U.S.A., 1978-79. Mem. Suburban Home Econs. Tchrs. Assn. (treas. 1980-81, pres.-elect 1981—), Mo. Home Econs. Tchrs. Assn. (chmn. nominating com. 1981—), Mo. Home Econs. Assn. (chmn. nominating com. 1981—), Am. Home Econs. Assn., Am. Vocat. Assn., Mo. Vocat. Assn., Mo. Tchrs. Assn. Republican. Mem. Assembly of God Ch. Author: Tote Along, 1973. Office: 100 Selma St Webster Groves MO 63119

WASMUTH, DUANE LEE, mfg. co. exec.; b. Midland, Mich., Jan. 2, 1939; s. Ralph and Midge Winifred (Mathewson) W.; B.S.E. in Mech. Engring., U. Mich., 1962, M.S.E. in Indsl. Engring., 1963, M.B.A., 1964; m. Gwendolyn Beatrice McKay, Aug. 10, 1963; children—Lisa Anne, Jeffrey Duane. Supt. mfg. Chevrolet Motor Div., General Motors Corp., Detroit, 1964-70; v.p. mfg. Rectrans, Inc., Brighton, Mich., 1970-71; pres. U-Tune, Inc., Madison Heights, Mich., 1971-75; pres. Internat. Husky, Inc., Bloomfield Hills, Mich., 1972-77; v.p. Key Internat., Inc., Southfield, Mich., 1977-78; pres. AIC Internat., Inc., Bloomfield Hills, 1978-80; pres. vehicle group Midas Internat. Corp., Chgo., 1981—; dir. Mills Products, Inc.; Internat. Husky, Inc., IHRRCO, Inc. U.S. Automation Co; cons. Riverside Metal Products Co. Inst. Labor and Indsl. Relations grad. fellow, 1962-63; grad. sch. bus. admni. fellow U. Mich., 1963-64. Mem. Rotary, U. Mich. Alumni Assn., Econic Club Detroit, N. Am. Soc. for Corp. Planning, Tau Beta Pi, Pi Tau Sigma, Alpha Pi Mu, Phi Delta Theta. Republican. Presbyterian. Club: Birmingham Athletic, Bloomfield Hills Country, U. Mich. Pres.'s, U. Mich. Victors, Ocean Reef, Ocean Reef Health and Tennis, Metropolitan. Home: 811 N Sheridan Rd Lake Forest IL 60045

WASSERMAN, GERALD STEWARD, educator; b. Bklyn., Nov. 22, 1937; s. Julius and Bessie (Weissman) W.; m. Louise Janet Mund, June 17, 1962; children—Mark Daniel, Rachel Lynn; B.A., N.Y.U., 1960; Ph.D. (USPHS fellow), Mass. Inst. Tech., 1965. Postdoctoral fellow NIH, 1965-67; asst. prof. U. Wis., Madison, 1967-70, asso. prof., 1970-75; prof. psychobiology Purdue U., West Lafayette, Ind., 1975—. Prin. investigator NSF grant, 1969-73, 79-80, NIH grant, 1975-78. Fellow Optical Soc. Am.; mem. AAAS, Assn. for Research in Vision and Ophthalmology, Midwestern Psychol. Assn., Soc. for Neurosci., Psychonomic Soc. Author: Color Vision, 1978. Editorial bd. Color Research and Application, 1977-80, Behavioral and Brain Scis., 1978—, Contemporary Psychology, 1981—. Contbr. articles to profl. jours. Home: 3512 Capilano Dr West Lafayette IN 47906 Office: Purdue U West Lafayette IN 47907

WASSERMAN, MARVIN, sales and mktg. co. exec.; b. Bklyn., Feb. 16, 1931; s. William and Mary (Moskowitz) W.; A.A., Glendale Coll., 1955; student U. Calif. Extension, Los Angeles, 1964; m. Anita Strain, Jan. 1, 1956 (div. Aug. 1972); children—Steven, Neil, Mark; m. 2d, Mary M. McColgan, Aug. 7, 1981. Machine operator Lockheed Aircraft Co., Burbank, Calif., 1952-55; resident engr., sr. designer Pacific div. Bendix Corp., North Hollywood, Calif., 1955-62, sr. engr. systems div., Ann Arbor, Mich., 1962-64; configuration control coordinator Mich. div. Ling-Temco-Vought, Warren, 1964; sr. gen. engr. liaison Brown Engring. Co., Inc., Huntsville, Ala., 1964-66; sr. tech. asst. IBM Fed. Systems div. Space Systems Center, Huntsville, 1966-67; sr. engring. specialist ARINC Research Corp., Ridgecrest, Calif., 1967-68; prin. devel. engr. Honeywell, Inc., Marine Systems Center, West Covina, Calif., 1968-69; sr. value engr. Aerojet ElectroSystems Co., Azusa, Calif., 1969-74; mgr. value engring. Byron Jackson Pump div. Borg Warner Corp., Vernon Calif., 1974-75; value engr. Ingersoll Rand Co. Proto Tool Div., Fullerton, Calif., 1975-77; v.p. Orosico, Inc., 1976-77; account mgr. McGraw-Hill Pub. Co., Westminster, Calif., 1977-78, regional mgr. Mid-West/Can. region, Chgo., 1978-80; mktg. mgr. aerospace Pyle-Nat., Chgo., 1980; owner, chief exec. officer The Listening Post, 1981—; instr. Grad. Sch. Mgmt., U. Calif. at Los Angeles Extension. Com. chmn. Pack 72, Chikasaw Dist., Tennessee Valley council Boy Scouts Am., 1966-67, mem. awards com. Pack 92, Ridgecrest, 1967-68, mem. spl. projects com. Pack 205, Cypress, Calif., 1969-71. Loaned exec. Jr. Achievement fund raising campaign, 1975. Served with USAF, 1951-52. Recipient Diamond Club award McGraw-Hill Pub. Co., 1978; cert. value specialist. Mem. Soc. Am. Value Engrs. (recipient awards as editor Redstone chpt. newsletter 1966, 67, named Value Engr. of Year 1967, nat. dir. 1967-71, pres. Orange County chpt. 1970-71, nat. v.p. S.W. region 1971-74, gen. chmn. 14th Ann. Nat. Conf. 1974; nat. historian 1976-77), Am. Soc. Performance Improvement (gen. chmn. nat. conf. 1976, v.p. So. Calif. chpt.). Jewish (pres. temple 1971). Contbr. articles to profl. jours. Home: 625 N Fayette St Saginaw MI 48602 Office: The Listening Post 625 N Fayette St Saginaw MI 48602

WASSERMAN, RODGER DEAN, transp.-computer systems cons. co. exec.; b. Detroit, Jan. 14, 1946; s. Alvin and Edith Lorraine (Kavieff) W.; M.A., Mich. State U., 1968; m. Aug. 3, 1969; children—Amy Briar, Kurt Nicholas, Songwriter, pub. Charrington Music Co., Detroit and Notable Music, Inc., N.Y., 1967-69; v.p. Allied Indsl. Contractors, Inc., Detroit, 1969-72; pres. Abacus Corp., Detroit, 1972—; pres. Am. Delivery System, Detroit; dir. Allied Delivery System, Detroit, Rodger Wasserman & Partners, Detroit; cons. v.p. Allied Iron Co., Detroit; cons. computerization and design transp. systems Gen. Motors Parts div. Upjohn Co., Signal Delivery. Jewish. Club: Bloomfield Open Hunt. Designed and developed one of first mini-computer bus. systems in U.S., 1972, first computer system capable performing 100% freight routing, billing, and control, 1974, first commercially feasible computerization of freight rating, 1976. Home: 3951 Shellmarr Bloomfield Hills MI 48013 Office: 300 E Seven Mile Rd Detroit MI 48203

WASSERMAN, STANLEY, statistician; b. Louisville, Aug. 29, 1951; s. Irvin Levitch and Jeanne (Plattus) W.; B.S., U. Pa., 1973, M.A., 1973; M.A., Harvard U., 1974, Ph.D., 1977; m. Sarah Wilson, Feb. 3, 1974; 1 son, Andrew Joseph. Instr., Harvard U., 1976; vis. instr. Carnegie-Mellon U., 1976-77; research asso. Columbia U., 1978; asst. prof. stats. U. Minn., 1977—; cons. Social Sci. Research Council postdoctoral fellow, 1978-79; recipient J. Parker Bursk Meml. award, 1973; NSF grantee, 1979—. Mem. AAAS, Am. Sociol. Assn., Am. Statis Assn., Biometric Soc., Inst. Math. Stats., Sigma Xi. Contbr. articles to statis. and sociol. jours. Home: 4936 Morgan Ave S Minneapolis MN 55409 Office: Dept Applied Statistics U Minn Saint Paul MN 55108

WASSON, WILLIAM BARRY, ins. co. adminstr.; b. Pyote, Tex., Sept. 26, 1944; s. William George and Betty Jean (Irons) W.; B.B.A., Grove City (Pa.) Coll., 1966; cert. Ins. Inst. Am., 1973; m. Carolyn Mary Amore, June 25, 1966; children—Cherie Lynn, Robbin Lee, Nichole Lauran, Grant William Joseph. Claim adjuster trainee Aetna Ins. Co., Hartford, Conn., 1966-67, multi-line claim adjuster, 1967-70, claim supr., Charlotte, N.C., 1970-71, regional claim mgr., Kansas City, Mo., 1971-74, mktg. mgr., 1974-80, br. mgr., Milw., 1980—. Republican committeeman, 1972-74; capt. ins. div. United Way, 1978; mem. Shawnee Planning Commn., 1978—. C.P.C.U. Mem. Old Shawnee Town Hist. Soc., Kansas City Mktg. Mgrs., Blue Goose Internat. Methodist. Club: Masons. Home: Eagle WI 53119 Office: 615 E Michigan Milwaukee WI 53202

WASSON, WILLIAM ELWOOD, educator; b. Coweta, Okla., June 13, 1920; s. William Henry and Cora Anna (Myers) W.; B.S., Okla. State U., 1969, M.S., 1970; postgrad. So. Ill. U., 1971—; m. Betty Rosamond Main, Dec. 26, 1945. Lab. technician Shell Oil Co., Wood River, Ill., 1942-58; owner, operator residential constrn. firm, Birghton, Ill., 1958-67; tchr. constrn. trades Sparta Community Unit Dist. 140, 1970—; condr. workshops; participant U.S. Senate Hearing Com. on Status and Needs of Vocat. Edn., 1976. Served with USAAF, 1943-46; PTO. Mem. Am. Personnel and Guidance Assn., Nat., Am., Ill. vocat. assns., Ill. Vocat. Guidance Assn., Ill. Edn. Assn., Ill. Indsl. Edn. Assn., Vocat. Indsl. Clubs Am., Iota Lambda Sigma. Baptist. Club: Masons. Home: 1812 Swanwick St Chester IL 62233 Office: 200 W Hood St Sparta IL 62286

WATANABE, AUGUST MASARU, physician, educator, scientist; b. Portland, Oreg., Aug. 17, 1941; s. Frank H. and Mary Y. Watanabe; B.S., Wheaton (Ill.) Coll., 1963; M.D., Ind. U., 1967; m. Margaret Whildin Reese, Mar. 14, 1964; children—Nan Reiko, Todd Franklin, Scott Masaru. Intern, Ind. U. Med. Sch., Indpls., 1967-68, resident, 1968-69, 71-72, fellow in cardiology, 1972-74; clin. asso. NIH, 1969-71; clin. instr. medicine Georgetown U. Med. Sch., 1970-71; mem. faculty Ind. U. Med. Sch., Indpls., 1972—, prof. medicine and pharmacology, 1978—; chief cardiology VA Hosp., Inspls.; cons. in field. Served with USPHS, 1969-71. NIH grantee, 1972—; diplomate Am. Bd. Internal Medicine. Fellow Am. Coll. Cardiology, A.C.P.; mem. Am. Soc. Clin. Investigation, Am. Heart Assn., Am. Soc. Pharmacology and Exptl. Therapeutics, Am. Fedn. for clin. Research, Am. Soc. Clin. Pharmacology and Therapeutics, Central Soc. for Clin. Research. Contbr. articles to profl. jours., mem. editorial bds. sci. jours. Office: 1100 W Michigan St Indianapolis IN 46223

WATERS, EDNA M., advt. agy. exec.; b. Downers Grove, Ill., May 17, 1946; d. Walter G. and Helene (Banks) Wilson; B.A., Northwestern U., 1967, M.A., 1968; m. George L. Waters, Aug. 15, 1971; 1 dau., Margaret Anne. Asst. copywriter Clinton E. Frank Advt., Chgo., 1968-72; copywriter Foot, Cone & Belding, Chgo., 1974-78, copy supr., 1978-80, creative dir., 1980—. Active United Way, Girl Scouts U.S. Recipient various advt. awards. Mem. Chgo. Women in Advt. Democrat. Catholic. Home: 8215 S Bishop Chicago IL 60620

WATERS, RAYMOND MICHAEL, govt. ofcl.; b. Chgo., Oct. 7, 1934; s. Bernard Joseph and Rose (Hoban) W.; B.S., Pacific Western U., 1981; m. Rita Mary Skarbowski, July 16, 1960; children—Michael, Kathleen. Service engr. Ozlaid div. Gen. Aniline and Film Corp., Milw., 1957-62; prodn. engr. Welch Sci. Corp., Skokie, Ill., 1963-67; staff indsl. specialist Def. Logistics Agy., U.S. Dept. Def., Chgo., 1967-72, regional coordinator environ. and energy mgmt., 1972-80, chief prodn. ops., 1980—. Served with USAF, 1955-59. Registered profl. engr., Calif.; cert mfg. engr. Soc. Mfg. Engrs.; cert. energy auditor U.S. Dept. Energy; energy profl. Assn. Energy Engrs. Mem. Soc. Logistics Engrs. Roman Catholic. Home: 581 S Mount Prospect Rd Des Plaines IL 60016 Office: PO Box 66475 O'Hare Internat Airport Chicago IL 60666

WATERSTON, WILLIAM DAVID, architect; b. Detroit, Dec. 15, 1949; s. Hugh Miller and Gene Marie (Runke) W.; B.S., U. Mich., 1972, M.Arch. with distinction, 1974; m. Judith Conn, May 29, 1971; children—John William, Mark Vincent. Jr. architect, Smith, Hinchman & Grylls, Detroit, 1973-77; project architect, facilities planner Owens-Corning Fiberglas Corp. Tech. Center, Granville, Ohio, 1977-79, supr. bus.-tech. planning adminstrn., 1979-81, supr. tech. services, insulation operating div., 1981—. Treas., Licking County Young Republicans Club, 1978-80. Mem. AIA, Constrn. Specifications Inst., U. Mich. Alumni Assn., Phi Delta Theta. Presbyterian. Home: 314 Mill Race Granville OH 43023 Office: Fiberglas Tower Toledo OH 43659

WATESKA, LEON PAUL, pharmacist; b. Pitts., Aug. 7, 1944; s. Leo Michael and Stella Joan (Lipinski) W.; B.S., Duquesne U., 1967; M.S., Ohio State U., 1969; m. Madeline Ruth Setele, Apr. 8, 1972; children—David Alan, Cynthia Ruth. Asso. dir. pharmacy Cleve. Clinic Hosp., 1969-72, dir. pharmacy, 1973—. Registered pharmacist, Pa., Ohio. Mem. Am. Pharm. Assn., Am. Soc. Hosp. Pharmacists, Am. Soc. for Parenteral and Enteral Nutrition, Ohio Soc. Hosp. Pharmacists, Cleve. Soc. Hosp. Pharmacists, Duquesne U. Alumni Assn. Cleve. Republican. Presbyterian. Home: 6895 Donna Rae Dr Seven Hills OH 44131 Office: Cleve Clinic Hosp 9500 Euclid Ave Cleveland OH 44106

WATKINS, CAROLYN ANN, nursing educator; b. Canton, Ohio, June 13, 1934; d. Okey J. and Virginia V. (Gotshell) W.; diploma Aultman Hosp. Sch. of Nursing, 1955; B.S. in Nursing Edn., U. Akron, 1964, M.S. in Edn., 1974, postgrad., 1979—. Staff nurse Aultman Hosp., Canton, 1955-56; clin. instr. communicable disease nursing Aultman Hosp. Sch. Nursing, 1956-57, clin. instr. pediatric nursing, 1957-59, instr. obstetric nursing, 1959-68, chmn. maternal child health, 1968-71, curriculum coordinator, 1972-75, asso. dir. acad. affairs, 1976-78, dir., 1978—. Mem. edn. com. Local Cancer Soc., Canton, 1975-77; Sunday sch. tchr. Bethel Luth. Ch., Canton, 1974, chmn. planning com. for re-orgn., 1976-80. Mem. Nat. League Nursing, Assn. Supervision and Curriculum Devel., Council for Diploma Schs., Nat. League Nursing, Ohio Council Diploma Nurse Edn., Aultman Hosp. Alumni Assn., Sigma Theta Tau. Democrat. Home: 2908 6th St SW Canton OH 44710 Office: 2614 6th St SW Canton OH 44710

WATKINS, CURTIS WINTHROP, artist; b. Pontiac, Mich., Apr. 9, 1946; s. Robert James and Arvella Marquitta (Chenoweth) W.; student Ann Arbor Art Center, 1964-66, Kendall Sch. Design, 1966-68, Kraus Hypnosis Center, 1966, 70, Arons Ethical Hypnosis Tng. Center, 1977; m. Gayle Lynn Blom, Dec. 19, 1975; 1 dau., Darcy Ann. Illustrator, instr. Ann Arbor Art Center, 1969-71; owner, dir. Hypno-Art Research Center and Studio, Howell, Mich., 1971—; research on visualization process of subconscious by doing art work under hypnosis; lectr. hypnosis convs. and schs.; one-man shows include: LeVern's Gallery, 1969, Rackham Gallery, 1973, Hartland Gallery, 1974, Platt Gallery, 1975, Detroit Artists Guild Gallery, 1975, Golden Gallery, 1977; bd. dirs. 9th Ann. Hartland Art Show, 1975, Livingston Arts and Crafts Assn., 1977-79, Hartland Art Council, 1974-78. Recipient numerous awards of excellence in art. Mem. Internat. Soc. Artists, Assn. Advance Ethical Hypnosis, Am. Assn. Profl. Hypnologists, Internat. Soc. Profl. Hypnosis, Internat. Platform Assn. Presbyterian. Home and Office: 519 S Michigan Ave Howell MI 48843

WATKINS, DANIEL JOSEPH, cons. civil engr.; b. Albia, Iowa, Dec. 18, 1923; s. Thomas Joseph and Theresa Alice (O'Connor) W.; B.S., Iowa State U., 1947; m. Barbara Lorraine Van Cleve, Sept. 9, 1946; children—Daniel Lawrence, Robert Edward, Alice Elizabeth (Mrs. A.J. Scherzberg), John Vincent, Marianne (Mrs. Paul Horvath), Jeanne Marie (Mrs. Gene Schinstock), Thomas Joseph, James Patrick, Barbara Susan, William Franklin, Margaret Mary, Paul Gerard (dec.), Frances Theresa, David Christopher, Patrick Anthony. Partner, Howard, Needles, Tammen & Bergendoff, cons. engrs., architects, planners, Kansas City, Mo.; incorporator Citizens State Bank, Shawnee Mission, Kans., 1973; dir. United Mo. Bank South, Kansas City. City councilman Prairie Village (Kans.), 1965-71. Bd. dirs. Kansas City Area Hosp. Assn., St. Joseph's Hosp., Kansas City, Mo.; mem. civil engring. adv. bd. Iowa State U. Served to lt. (j.g.), USNR, 1944-46; PTO. Named Councilman of Yr. Prairie Village, 1970. Fellow ASCE, Am. Cons. Engrs. Council; mem. Nat., Mo. (pres. Western chpt. 1965, chmn. state profl. conduct com. 1967-70) socs. profl. engrs., Cons. Engrs. Council Mo. (v.p. 1971-72), Am. Public Works Assn., Am. Road and Transp. Builders Assn., Internat. Bridge, Tunnel and Turnpike Assn., Am. Planning Assn., Transp. Research Bd., Kansas City C. of C. (vice chmn. bd. dirs.), Tau Beta Pi. Roman Catholic. Rotarian. Home: 3511 W 73d St Prairie Village KS 66208 Office: Howard Needles Tammen & Bergendoff 1805 Grand Ave Kansas City MO 64108

WATKINS, DAVID HYDER, surgeon; b. Denver, Nov. 26, 1917; s. David Milroy and Mary Rose (Hyder) W.; A.B., U. Colo., 1937, M.D., 1940; M.S. in Surgery, U. Minn., 1947, Ph.D., 1949; m. Lucile Maxine Pingel, Sept. 27, 1941; children—John David Hyder, Bryan David Pingel. Intern, U. Iowa Hosps., Iowa City, 1940-41; resident Mayo Clinic, Rochester, Minn., 1942-44, asst. surg. staff, 1945-49; instr. surgery Ohio State U., Columbus, 1949-50; asso. prof. surgery U. Colo., Denver, 1951-56, prof., 1956-67; dir. surg. services Denver Gen. Hosp., 1951-67; cons. Fitzsimmons Army Hosp., Denver, 1954-67, cons. emeritus, 1967—; clin. prof. surgery U. Iowa, Iowa City, 1967—; cons. surg. service VA Hosp., Des Moines, 1968—; mem. surg. staff Iowa Meth. Hosp., Des Moines, 1967—; attending staff Broadlawns Hosp., Des Moines, 1968—. Diplomate Am. Bd. Surgery, Am. Bd. Thoracic Surgery. Fellow A.C.S.; mem. Am. Assn. for Thoracic Surgery, Central, Western surg. assns., S.W. Surg. Congress, Soc. Univ. Surgeons, Société Internationale de Chirugie, Am. Heart Assn., Am. Coll. Cardiology, Am. Coll. Chest Physicians, Am. Fedn. for Clin. Research, Am. Geriatrics Soc., Am. Soc. for Artificial Internal Organs., SAR, Phi Beta Kappa, Sigma Xi, Alpha Omega Alpha. Club: University (Denver). Contbr. articles to profl. jours. Home: 6039 N Waterbury Rd Des Moines IA 50312 Office: 1200 Pleasant St Des Moines IA 50308

WATKINS, DEAN EDWARD, city ofcl.; b. Akron, Ohio, July 18, 1946; s. Edward David and Audrey Mae (Ritzman) W.; B.A., U. Cin., 1969, M.A., 1971, postgrad., 1972—; m. Helen Virginia McCoy, June 13, 1970; 1 son, John Gregory. Salesman, Oscar Mayer & Co., Cleve., 1968; research, teaching asst., computer programmer U. Cin., 1969-72; instr. sociology Coll. of Mt. St. Joseph, Cin., 1971; program evaluator Cin. Police Div., 1972-76, supervising mgmt. analyst City of Cin., 1976—. Mem. research task group Urban Appalachian Council, 1974-76. Bd. dirs. Ravine Street Child Care Center, 1971-73. Recipient Danforth award, 1964. Mem. Ops. Research Soc. Am., Inst. Mgmt. Scis., Internat. City Mgrs. Assn., Am. Soc. for Public Adminstrn. Home: 1026 Egan Hills Dr Cincinnati OH 45229 Office: 801 Plum St Cincinnati OH 45202

WATKINS, EDWARD DENNIS, coll. adminstr.; b. Dallas, May 3, 1945; s. Edward Dennis and Virginia Mae (Drake) W.; B.S., S.W. Mo. State U., 1967; M.S., Kans. State U., 1968; m. Janet Bernice Musick, Feb. 28, 1948; children—Brian, Ashlee. Dir. human services, mem. faculty dept. sociology Pembroke (N.C.) State U., 1970-74; dir. 4-County Sr. Citizen's Pilot Project, Joplin, Mo., 1968-69; dir. career devel. center Doane Coll., Crete, Nebr., 1974-78, v.p. life devel., 1980—; exec. dir. Nat. Inst. Career Devel., Crete, 1978—. Founder, Service Opportunities Rendered Through Community Effort, 1972; founder Practical Enterprises for People, 1977. Served with U.S. Army, 1969-70. Congregationalist. Editor, co-author: Preparing Liberal Arts Students for Careers, 1979. Office: Doane Coll Crete NE 68333

WATKINS, EDWIN HERREN, financial exec.; b. Evanston, Ill., Mar. 12, 1924; s. Frank Alonzo and Julia (Herren) W.; B.A., Amherst Coll., 1947; m. Carol Frances Burtis, Nov. 3, 1951; children—Frank, Cynthia, Nancy, Ann, David. With U.S. Gypsum Co., Chgo., 1947-50; time study engr., chief indsl. engr. Mather Stock Car Co., Chgo., 1950-55; steel buyer, div. buyer U.S. Gypsum, Chgo., 1955-59; investment analyst Duff, Anderson & Clark, Chgo., 1959-65; investment mgr. Field Enterprises, Inc., Chgo., 1965-71, v.p., 1971—; dir. Mathers Fund, Inc., Chgo., 1971—; v.p. Amfund, Inc., Chgo., 1972-76, pres., 1976—. Served to ensign USNR, 1945-46. Chartered fin. analyst. Mem. Inst. Chartered Fin. Analysts, Investment Analysts Soc. Chgo., Chgo. Sci. Analysts. Congregationalist. Clubs: East Bank (charter), Univ. (Chgo.); Skokie Country (Glencoe, Ill.). Home: 576 Ash St Winnetka IL 60093 Office: Room 700 401 N Wabash Ave Chicago IL 60611

WATKINS, HIRAM WILLIAM, III, city ofcl.; b. St. Louis, Jan. 24, 1953; s. Hiram William and Mary Therese (Paradise) W.; B.S. in Pub. Adminstrn., U. Mo., 1974, M.S., 1976; m. Kathleen Ann Kibbee, Dec. 29, 1973; children—Kathryne, Carol. Adminstrv. asst. to city mgr. City of Columbia (Mo.), 1974-77; city mgr. City of Newton Falls (Ohio), 1977—. Mem. Internat. City Mgmt. Assn., Ohio City Mgmt. Assn. Club: K.C. Home: 38 Bane Ave Newton Falls OH 44444 Office: 19 N Canal St Newton Falls OH 44444

WATKINS, TERRY GORDON, environ. engr.; b. Tulsa, Oct. 20, 1939; s. Boyd Woodrow and Leona Edna Haines (Temple) W.; B.S., Kans. U., Lawrence, 1963; postgrad. Emporia (Kans.) State U., 1970, Lincoln U., Jefferson City, Mo., 1971. Test engr. Pratt & Whitney, Hartford, Conn., 1963-65; aerospace technologist NASA, Houston, 1965-66; researcher fuel cell devel. NASA, Allis-Chalmers Co., 1967; design engr. Amphenol Conn., Chgo., 1968; tchr., Mokane, Mo., 1971-72; with Kans. Dept. Health and Environ., Topeka, 1972—, environ. engr. II, 1979—; lectr. in field. Lic. profl. engr., Kans. Mem. Tau Beta Pi, Sigma Tau Sigma, Sigma Pi Sigma, Eta Kappa Nu. Mormon. Home: 1107 Western Ave Topeka KS 66604

WATRING, BERENICE ANN LACKEY, cardiovascular specialist; b. Chgo., June 2, 1941; d. Robert Charles Niendorf and Evelyn Dolores (Pecho) Vitarelli; grad. Elgin Community Coll. Sch. Nursing, 1973; student No. Ill. U., 1974, 75, U. Ill., 1959, 60; m. Richard L. Watring, June 7, 1980; children—Sandra Lynn, Patricia Ann. Clin. instr. CCU, Sherman Hosp., Elgin, Ill., 1976-78; staff nurse CCU-ICU, 1973-78; cardiovascular specialist Roche Med. Electronics, Cranbury, N.J., Avco Med. Products, Everett, Mass., 1978; midwest regional coordinator Kontron Cardiovascular Inc., South Holland, Ill., 1978—; speaker cardiovascular symposiums. Registered nurse. Mem. Am. Assn. Critical Care Nurses (cert.), Chgo. Heart Assn., Sigma Kappa, Phi Theta Kappa. Office: 500 W Armory Dr South Holland IL 60473

WATRING, RICHARD LANDON, indsl. relations exec.; b. Akron, Ohio, Jan. 26, 1948; s. Landon Haskett and Dolores Ann (Rapol) W.; B.S. in Indsl. Mgmt., U. Akron, 1974; postgrad. Loyola U., Chgo., 1979—; m. Berenice Ann Niendorf-Lackey, June 7, 1980; step children—Sandra Lynn, Patricia Ann Lackey. Mgr. indsl. relations and personnel Gen. Tire & Rubber Co., Waco, Tex., and Akron, Ohio, 1969-78; regional personnel mgr. Hertz Corp. Truck Div., Chgo. and Dallas, 1978-79; area mgr. indsl. relations Ryder Truck Rental, Chgo., 1979—; tchr. human behavior McLennan Community Coll., Waco. Served with USMC, 1967. Mem. Am. Soc. Personnel Adminstrn., Indsl. Relations Research Assn. Home: 1415 E Central Rd 318C Arlington Heights IL 60005 Office: 350 W Shuman Blvd Naperville IL 60540

WATSON, ANDREW SAMUEL, psychiatrist; b. Highland Park, Mich., May 2, 1920; B.S., U. Mich., 1942; M.D., Temple U., 1950, M.Sc., 1954. Intern, U. Pa. Grad. Hosp., 1950-51; resident Temple U. Hosp., 1951-54; spl. instr. Bryn Mawr Sch. Social Work, 1954-59; asst. prof. psychiatry U. Pa., 1955-57, asso. prof. psychiatry and law, 1957-59; asst. prof. psychiatry, asst. prof. law U. Mich., 1959-62, asso. prof. psychiatry, asso. prof. law, 1962-66, prof. law, prof. psychiatry, 1966-81; mem. adv. com. and faculty for young law tchrs. workshop Am. Assn. Law Sch. Profs., 1969, 71, 73, 77; pres. bd. trustees Washtenaw County br. Mich. Children's Aid Soc., 1964-65; chmn. task force on mental health statues Mich. Dept. lfental Health, 1965-66; mem. med. audit com. Ionia State Hosp. for Criminally Insane, 1966; mem. Mich. Bar Com. to Revise Criminal Code; mem. Mich. Commn. on Law Enforcement and Criminal Justice, 1968-72; mem. Mich. Surgeon Gen.'s Adv. Commn. on TV and Social Behavior, 1969-71; cons. Nat. Conf. Commrs. Uniform State Laws on Divorce and Child Custody; bd. fellows Nat. Center Juvenile Justice, 1973; Robert S. Marx lectr. Coll. Law, U. Cin., 1967; Gifford Meml. speaker U. Syracuse Law Sch., 1969; 100th Ann. speaker Columbus Bar Assn., 1970; Jackson Meml. lectr. Nat. Coll. State Trial Judges, U. Nev., 1971; grad. speaker U. Pitts. Law Sch., 1974; Ford Found. traveling fellow, Eng., 1966-67. Recipient Issac Ray award Am. Psychiat. Assn., 1978. Fellow Am. Psychiat. Assn., Am. Orthopsychiat. Assn., Phila. Psychoanalytic Assn., Am. Coll. Psychiatry. Office: 555 E William 21D Ann Arbor MI 48104

WATSON, BEN CHARLES, chemist, research and devel. exec.; b. Mobile, Ala., Oct. 3, 1944; s. Ben and Bessie (Turner) Watson; m. Mae Johnson, Jan. 31, 1970. B.S., Morehouse Coll., 1967; M.S., Ill. Inst. Tech., 1974, M.B.A., 1978; Ph.D., N.D. State U., 1981. Chemist Applied Research dept. The Sherwin-Williams Co., Chgo., 1968, sr. chemist, 1968-71, group supr., 1971-74, sect. supr., project coordinator, 1974-77, mgr. applied research, 1977-79, tech. dir. Chem. Coatings div., 1981—. Mem. Young Businessmen's Assn., Chgo., 1975-76; mem. Community Devel. Com., 1976. Mem. Am. Chem. Soc., Electrochem. Soc., Chgo. Soc. for Coatings Tech., AAAS. Recipient Outstanding Scientist Yr. award, State of Ga., 1966. Home: 5201 S Cornell Ave Chicago IL 60615 Office: 11541 S Champlain Ave Chicago IL 60628

WATSON, C. GORDON, dentist; b. Rexburg, Idaho, July 2, 1921; grad. Ricks Coll., Rexburg, Brigham Young U.; D.D.S., Northwestern U., 1946; postgrad. U. Chgo., U. Santa Clara; married; 3 sons. Formerly practiced dentistry, San Diego; exec. dir. So. Calif. Dental Assn., 1965-69; exec. dir. Am. Dental Assn., 1970-78; pvt. practice dentistry, Palm Springs, Calif., 1978—. Served with Dental Corps, USNR, 1946-48; capt. Res. Recipient Award of Merit, Northwestern U. Alumni Assn., 1972. Mem. Am., Internat. colls. dentists, Nat. Acad. of Scis. (Inst. of Medicine), Am. Soc. Assn. Execs. (dir. 1969-73; named Certified Assn. Exec. 1971; key award 1972), Am. Pub. Health Assn., Am. Assn. Dental Editors, Alpha Omega. Omicron Kappa Upsilon, Xi Psi Phi (life). Office: 211 E Chicago Chicago IL 60611*

WATSON, DOROTHY MAAHS, restaurant exec.; b. Dayton, Ohio, July 21, 1934; d. Henry H. and Velma J. (Bower) Maahs; student public schs., Dayton, Ohio; m. Harry B. Watson, Sept. 10, 1952; children—Christine Marie, Harry B. Clk., bookkeeper Keowee Sweet Shoppe, Dayton, 1945-54; with Burger Chef of Ohio, Dayton, 1965-68, Rax Roast Beef, Dayton, 1965-68; with Ponderosa System, Inc., Dayton, 1965—, asst. controller, 1970, asst. sec., dir. risk mgmt., 1977—. Mem. Nat. Assn. Accts. (pres. chpt.), Am. Soc. Women Accts. (past pres. chpt., past nat. sec.), Risk and Ins. Mgmt. Soc. (pres. chpt.), Nat. Restaurant Assn., Eintracht Singing Soc. (fin. sec.). Home: 6351 Shull Rd Dayton OH 45424 Office: PO Box 578 Dayton OH 45401

WATSON, GEORGE WILLARD, health educator, adminstr.; b. New Concord, Ohio, July 28, 1909; s. John Willard and Cora Vendella (Ankrum) W.; B.S., Muskingum Coll., 1931; M.S. in Public Health, U. Mich., 1936; m. Mary Ellen Bates, Mar. 17, 1943; children—JoAnne, James Knox, John Kevin. Field statistician Ohio Dept. Health, Columbus, 1939-42; malariologist, U.S. Navy, 1943-46; dir. health edn., Dayton, Ohio, 1948-51; adminstr. Balt. City Health Dept., 1951-56; dir. health edn., Battle Creek, Mich., 1956-60; chief public health educator Ga. Dept. Health, Atlanta, 1960-64; cons. health educator, adminstr., New Concord, 1964—. Served with USNR, 1943-45. Fellow Am. Public Health Assn. Home: 1725 Friendship Dr Route 2 New Concord OH 43762

WATSON, LELAND (LEE) HALE, theatrical lighting designer; b. Charleston, Ill., Feb. 18, 1926; s. Dallas V. and Hazel Emma (Dooley) W.; B.A., State U. Iowa, 1948; M.F.A., Yale U., 1951. Instr., Utah State Agrl. Coll., Logan, 1948-49, Bklyn. Coll., 1952, 54; with CBS-TV, N.Y.C., 1951-55, Polakov Studio Scenic Design, N.Y.C., 1957-62; mem. faculty U. Houston, 1968-71; asst. prof. C.W. Post Coll., L.I.U., 1971-75; guest lectr. Syracuse (N.Y.) U., 1974-75; asso. prof. Purdue U., 1975-81, prof., 1981—; lighting designer Cin. Ballet, 1977-80, also for 27 Broadway prodns. including Diary of Anne Frank, View From the Bridge; numerous Off-Broadway prodns. including The Blacks, Suddenly Last Summer; lighting designer for operas in N.Y.C., Houston, Phila., Balt., Vancouver, Wash., Milw., also dance companies and Seattle World's Fair, 1962; designer sets for 6 Broadway prodns., also prodns. at Washington Arena, indsl. shows. Served with AUS, 1944-45. Decorated Purple Heart; recipient Obie award for Machinal, Show Bus. award 1959. Mem. United Scenic Artists, Internat. Alliance Theatre and Stage Employees, U.S. Inst. Theatre Tech. (pres. 1980—), Soc. Brit. Theatre Designers, Internat. Assn. Lighting Designers, Am. Soc. Lighting Dirs., Illuminating Engring. Soc., Am. Theatre Assn., Phi Beta Kappa. Methodist. Co-author: Theatrical Lighting Practice, 1954; columnist, sr. contbg. editor Lighting Dimensions mag.; contbr. articles magazines. Address: 2501 Soldiers Home Rd Apt 48 West Lafayette IN 47906

WATSON, ROBERT STEPHEN, fin. and ins. co. exec.; b. Evansville, Ind., Dec. 28, 1950; s. Robert Lee and Mary Lou (Stokes) W.; B.A., Purdue U., 1972, M.S., 1973; m. Zelma Beatrice Renfro, Aug. 31, 1974; 1 son, Robert Abraham. Program counselor Alcholic Recovery Center, Evansville, 1974-75; with Credithrift Fin. Mgmt. Corp., Evansville, 1978—, mgr. tng. and devel. nat. hdqrs., 1978—; author tng. programs for govt. and industry. Bd. dirs. Boys Club of Evansville, 1979—, sec., 1980; project bus. cons. Jr. Achievement. Served with U.S. Army, 1975-78. Decorated Meritorious Service Medal. Mem. Am. Soc. Tng. and Devel., Am. Soc. Personnel Adminstrs. Republican. Mem. United Ch. of Christ. Home: 3939 Korressel Rd Evansville IN 47712 Office: 601 NW 2d St Evansville IN 47708

WATT, GARLAND WEDDERICK, ret. judge; b. Elizabeth City, N.C., Feb. 10, 1932; s. Robert L. and Bessie Moore (Wesley) W.; A.B. magna cum laude, N.C. Central U., 1952; postgrad. Harvard, 1952-54; J.D. with honors, DePaul U., 1961; m. Gwendolyn LaNita Canada, Nov. 23, 1958; 1 dau., Marsha. Admitted to Ill. bar, 1961, also U.S. Dist. Ct., No. Dist. Ill., U.S. Ct. Appeals bar; partner firm Turner, Cousins, Gavin & Watt, 1961-65, Cook & Watt, 1965-67, Rivers, Watt & Lockhart, 1967-70, Watt & Holland, Chgo., 1970-74; judge Circuit Ct. Cook County, Chgo., 1975-80; mem. hearing bd., atty. registration and disciplinary com. Supreme Ct. Ill., 1973-75. Mem. bd. advisers Supreme Life Ins. Co. Am., 1971-75. Bd. dirs. Mid-Am. chpt. ARC, 1972-81, Chgo. Hearing Soc., 1970-73, Joint Negro Appeal, 1965-75, Southside Chgo. br. NAACP, 1965-75. Recipient Richard E. Westbrooks award Cook County Bar Assn., 1972, Judicial award, 1975, Judge of Yr. award, 1979. Mem. Am., Ill., Chgo., Cook County, Nat. bar assns., Chgo. Mortgage Attys. Assn., Am. Arbitration Assn., Omega Psi Phi, Alpha Kappa Mu. Democrat. Mem. United Ch. of Christ (dir.). Mason (33 deg.). Clubs: Union League, Economic, Royal Coterie of Snakes, Chgo. Assembly, Harvard of Chgo.; Harvard of N.Y. Bd. editors DePaul Law Rev., 1960-61. Home: 5022 S Greenwood Ave Chicago IL 60615 Office: 400 S Dearborn St Suite 500 Chicago IL 60605

WATTERS, LORAS JOSEPH, bishop; b. Dubuque, Iowa, Oct. 15, 1915; s. Martin James and Carolyn R. (Sisler) W.; B.A., Loras Coll., Dubuque, 1937; S.T.B., Gregorian U., Rome, 1940; S.T.L., Cath. U. Am., 1941, M.A., 1947, Ph.D., 1954. Ordained priest Roman Catholic Ch., 1941; asst. pastor St. Martin's Ch., Cascade, Iowa, 1941-45; mem. faculty Loras Coll., 1945-56; prin. Loras Acad., Dubuque, 1947-52, head edn. dept., 1954-56; spiritual dir. N.Am. Coll., Rome, 1956-60; dir. Am. Martyrs Retreat House, Cedar Falls, Iowa, 1960-65; aux. bishop of Dubuque, 1965-69; pastor Ch. of Nativity, Dubuque, 1965-69; archdiocesan supt. schs., 1967-69; bishop of Winona, Minn., 1969—; mem. bishops com. on priestly formation Nat. Conf. Cath. Bishops, 1970-78, chmn., 1972-75. Office: 55 W Sanborn St Box 588 Winona MN 55987

WATTLES, JOHN CHARLES, banker; b. South Bend, Ind., Jan. 6, 1931; s. Charles P. and Carmen (Irvin) W.; B.B.A., Western Mich. U. 1955; m. Helen Statler Fischer, Feb. 26, 1955; children—Charles, Sara, Katie. Trust officer, v.p. First Nat. Bank & Trust Co. of Mich., Kalamazoo, 1957-69; pres. W.J. Upjohn Mgmt. Co., Kalamazoo, 1969-75; sr. v.p., trust officer Indsl. State Bank & Trust Co., Kalamazoo, 1975—; vice chmn., dir. Wells Mfg. Corp.; dir. APM, Inc., FCF, Inc., Wells-Index Corp. Bd. dirs. Lakeside Children's Home, Inc., Western Mich. U. Found.; trustee YMCA, Howe Mil. Sch.; pres. Civic Auditorium Trustee Corp. Served as 1st lt., Q.M.C., U.S. Army, 1955-57. Mem. Investments Analyst Soc. Chgo. Presbyterian. Club: Park. Office: 151 S Rose St Kalamazoo MI 49007

WATTS, CHARLES HERBERT, pub. offender treatment center exec.; b. Danville, Ind., July 7, 1937; s. Herbert and Harriet LaVada (Scott) W.; M.A. in Human Services, Webster Coll., 1976; m. Anna May Cale, June 5, 1959; 1 son, Charles Blair. Program dir. Westside YMCA, Oklahoma City, 1962-67; exec. dir. South County YMCA, St. Louis, 1967-72, Greater St. Louis Alliance for Shaping a Safer Community, 1972-74; residence dir. Magdala Found., St. Louis, 1974—; part-time instr. corrections Forest Park Community Coll., 1977—; pvt. practice reality therapy. Certified alcohol counselor, Mo. Mem. Am. Correctional Assn., Am. Personnel and Guidance Assn., Internat. Halfway House Assn. Democrat. Mem. Christian Ch. (Disciples of Christ). Office: Saint Louis MO

WATTS, HERSCHEL JAMES, editor; b. Whiteville, N.C., Aug. 25, 1945; s. Horry James and Ora (Godwin) W.; B.S., East Carolina U., 1972; M.B.A., George Mason U., 1977. Acctg. and budget analyst Gen. Services Adminstrn., Washington, 1971-73; bus. edn. dept. chmn. Fairfax (Va.) County Public Schs., 1973-79; editor info. systems South Western Pub. Co., Cin., 1979—; lectr. in field; workshop leader in data processing edn: transition coordinator Presdl. Transition Team, Washington, 1980-81. Served with USAF, 1965-68. Decorated Air Force Commendation medal. Mem. Assn. Ednl. Data Systems, Assn. for Devel. of Computer Based Instrn. Systems, Nat. Bus. Edn. Assn. Republican. Editor: Automated Accounting for the Microcomputer, 1981. Home: 2296 Dana Ave Cincinnati OH 45208 Office: 5101 Madison Rd Cincinnati OH 45227

WATTS, JOHN RANSFORD, univ. adminstr.; b. Boston, Feb. 9, 1930; s. Henry Fowler Ransford and Mary Marion (Macdonald) W.; A.B., Boston Coll., 1950, M.Ed., 1965; M.F.A., Yale U., 1953; Ph.D., Union Grad. Sch., 1978; m. Joyce Lannom, Dec. 20, 1975; 1 son by previous marriage, David Allister. Prof., asst. dean Boston U., 1958-74; prof., dean of fine arts Calif. State U., Long Beach, 1974-79; dean and artistic dir. Goodman Sch. of Drama, DePaul U., Chgo., 1979—; gen. mgr. Boston Arts Festivals, 1955-64; adminstr. Arts Programs at Tanglewood, 1966-69; producing dir. Theatre Co. of Boston, 1973-75. Chmn., Mass. Council on Arts and Humanities, 1968-72; dir., v.p. Long Beach (Calif.) Public Corp. for the Arts, 1975-79; mem. theatre panel, Ill. Arts Council, 1981—. Served with U.S. Army, 1953-55. Mem. Mass. Ednl. Communications Commn., Am. Theatre Assn., Nat. Council on Arts in Edn., Met. Cultural Alliance, League Chgo. Theatres, Phi Beta Kappa. Club: St. Botolph (Boston). Office: 804 N Belden Chicago IL 60614

WATTS, MEREDITH WAYNE, JR., educator, univ. ofcl.; b. Bloomington, Ill., Apr. 14, 1941; s. Meredith Wayne and Leah Lucille (Stiegman) W.; B.A., Lawrence U., 1962; postgrad. No. Ill. U., 1962-63; M.A., Northwestern U., 1964, Ph.D., 1967; m. Leila Fraser, Sept. 22, 1979. children—David, Christopher, Alec. Asst. prof. polit. sci. U. Wis., Milw., 1966-67, 70-74, asso. prof., 1974-78, prof., 1978—, asst. to chancellor, 1977-79, asst. chancellor, 1979—. Active United Way, Future Milw. Served with USAF, 1967-70. Decorated Air Force Commendation medal; Nat. Center for Edn. in Politics fellow, 1964; NSF grantee, 1965-66. Mem. Am. Polit. Sci. Assn., Midwest Polit. Sci. Assn., Internat. Polit. Sci. Assn., Internat. Soc. for Research on Aggression, Internat. Communication Assn., Soc. for Psychophysiol. Research, Internat. Soc. for Human Ethology. Author: (with others) Legislative Roll Call Analysis, 1966, State Legislative Systems, 1968; contbr. articles to profl. jours. Home: 2309 E Menlo Blvd Milwaukee WI 53211 Office: Chapman Hall U Wis Milwaukee WI 53201

WATTS, RALPH S., ch. ofcl.; b. Seoul, Korea, Apr. 15, 1934; s. Ralph S. and Mildred L. (Hoopes) W.; B.A. in Religion, Union Coll., 1956; postgrad. Loma Linda U., Andrews U.; m. Patricia Ann Ortner, Aug. 17, 1952; children—Edie, Marcia, Ralph, Lori. Ordained to ministry Seventh-day Adventist Ch., 1960; evangelist, pastor, Nebr., 1956-61; dir. religious edn. home missions, N.D., 1961-63; dir. religious edn. and relief activities, Korea, 1963-67; dir. religious edn. Far East, 1967-69; pres. S.E. Asia region, 1969-75; pres. N.D. Conf. Seventh-day Adventist Ch., 1975-78; pres. Minn. Conf. Seventh-day Adventist Ch., Mpls., 1978-80, pres. Iowa-Mo. Conf., 1980—. Trustee Union Coll., Adventist Health Systems, Christian Record Braille Found. Office: 1005 Grand Ave West Des Moines IA 50265

WAUGH, GOREE EDWARD, III, computer systems designer; b. Bluefield, W.Va., Mar. 22, 1947; s. Edgar Sleadd and Louise (Stowers) W.; B.B.A., U. Ga., 1970; M.S. in Computer Sci., Ga. Inst. Tech., 1977; m. Pamela Taylor, Aug. 31, 1969; children—Jason Goree, Pamela Louise. Commd. 2d lt. U.S. Army, 1970, advanced through grades to capt., 1977; computer systems designer Automated Logistics Mgmt. Systems Activity, St. Louis, 1977-81; office automation architect Mo. Pacific R.R. Co., St. Louis, 1981—; lectr. on office automation and electronic mail. Mem. Delta Tau Delta, Eureka Jaycees (v.p. 1978-79). Republican. Methodist. Home: 904 Oak Trail Ct Fenton MO 63026 Office: PO Box 1578 Saint Louis MO 63188

WAWRZYNIAK, STEPHEN DAVID, mfg. co. exec.; b. St. Joseph, Mo., Oct. 21, 1949; s. Michael Joseph and Kathryn Maxine(Cook) W.; B.B.A., Mo. Western State Coll., 1973, B.S. in Psychology, 1973; m. Melneta Elizabeth Maschek, June 25, 1975; children—Shannon, Tammy, Lisa, Karrie. Quality control insp. Cannation Co., St. Joseph, 1973-74, plant sanitarian, plant safety coordinator, 1974-76; exec. dir. quality control Doane Products, Joplin, Mo., 1976—. Served with U.S. Army, 1969-70. Lic. and cert. comml. pesticide applicator Mo., Iowa, Calif., Va. Mem. Am. Soc. Quality Control, Inst. Food Technologists, Am. Oil Chemists Soc., Am. Assn. Cereal Chemists, Mo. Pest Control Assn., Nat. Rifle Assn. Republican. Baptist. Clubs: Joplin Rifle and Pistol; Masons, Shriners. Home: 2921 Jefferson St Joplin MO 64801 Office: PO Box 879 Joplin MO 64801

WAXMAN, SHELDON ROBERT, lawyer; b. Chgo., Apr. 22, 1941; s. Henri and Ann (Sokolsky) W.; B.A., U. Ill., 1963; J.D., DePaul U., 1965; m. Katherine Slamski, Aug. 23, 1979; children—Josiah, Zoe. Admitted to Ill. bar, 1965, U.S. Supreme Ct. bar, 1976; staff atty. Argonne (Ill.) Nat. Lab., 1968-71; asst. U.S. State's atty., Chgo., 1971-74; owner firm Shelly Waxman & Assos., Chgo., 1976—. Founder, Libertarian Lawyers Alliance of Ill., People for a Simplified Tax Law, Nukes to the Sun. Mem. Appellate Lawyers Assn. Ill., DePaul Law Rev. Assn. Contbr. articles to profl. jours. Office: 30 W Washington Suite 1115 Chicago IL 60602

WAYESHE, ANTHONY LEE, exec.; b. Northport, Mich., Nov. 8, 1939; s. Charles Louis and Charlotte (Paul) W.; student Loyola U., Chgo., 1971-72; m. Carol Rose Chambers, Nov. 17, 1970; children—Julia, Jo, Dan. Computer operator Atlantic Richfield Co., Chgo., 1963-67; computer programmer Swift & Co., Chgo., 1968-72; computer ops. specialist Central Nat. Bank, Chgo., 1972-76, mgr. computer ops., 1976—. Served with USAF, 1959-62. Republican. Methodist. Home: 479 Saint Charles St Elgin IL 60120 Office: 8550 W Bryn Mawr St Chicago IL 60631

WAYNE, LISLE, II, plastic surgeon; b. N.Y.C., Feb. 9, 1936; s. Ernest Lisle and Teresa (Garcia) W.; B.S., Tex. A&M U., 1957; M.D., U. Tenn., 1962; m. Sheila A. Adkins, Sept. 10, 1977; children—Teresa Terrell, Lisle III, Todd Adkins. Intern, Jackson Meml. Hosp., Miami, Fla., 1962-63; resident in gen. surgery VA Hosp., Memphis, 1963-68; resident in plastic surgery Duke U. Med. Center, 1970-73; chief plastic surgery Trover Clinic and Hopkins County Hosp., Madisonville, Ky., 1973-77; clin. instr. U. Louisville Med. Sch., 1976-77; practice medicine specializing in plastic surgery, Evansville, Ind., 1977—; mem. staff St. Mary's Med. Center, Deaconess, Welborn Baptist hosps. Served as officer M.C., USAF, 1968-70. Decorated Meritorious Service medal; diplomate Am. Bd. Plastic Surgery. Fellow A.C.S.; mem. Am. So. Plastic and Reconstructive Surgeons, Southeastern Soc. Plastic and Reconstructive Surgeons, Ohio Valley Soc. Plastic and Reconstructive Surgery, Bowers Surg. Soc., AMA, Ind. Med. Assn., Vanderburgh County Med. Soc. Presbyterian. Club: Petroleum. Contbr. articles med. jours. Home: 811 Blue Ridge Rd Evansville IN 47715 Office: 3700 Bellemeade Ave Suite 105 Evansville IN 47715

WAYT, WILLIAM ALLEN, educator, economist; b. Moundsville, W. Va., Feb. 20, 1921; s. William Blaine and Margaret (Allen) W.; B.S. in Agr., W. Va. U., 1943; M.S. in Agrl. Econs., Ohio State U., 1947, Ph.D., 1956; m. Gladys Ballard, July 28, 1945. Instr. agrl. econs. Ohio State U., Columbus, 1948-56, asst. prof., 1956-61, asso. prof., 1961-66, prof., 1966-78, prof. emeritus, 1978—; cons. agrl. econs. Bank Raky, Jakarta, Indonesia, 1978. Head dept. agrl. econs. and bus. Coll. Agr., Haile Selassie I U., Ethiopia, 1961-63; research officer Nairobi, Kenya, 1966-67; adviser U. Udaipur, India, 1969; mem. research team Uganda, 1970. Active Am. Red Cross Blood Bank, 1963—. Served with AUS, 1943-45. Recipient Distinguished Internat. Service award Okla. State U., 1969. Mem. Am. Agrl. Econs. Assn., AAUP, Internat. Conf. Agrl. Econs., AAAS, Alpha Zeta, Gamma Sigma Delta. Contbr. articles to profl. jours. Home: 187 E Northwood Ave Columbus OH 43201

WEAKLAND, REMBERT G., archbishop; b. Patton, Pa., Apr. 2, 1927; s. Basil and Mary (Kane) W.; A.B., St. Vincent Coll., 1948; student Julliard Sch. Music, N.Y.C., 1954; grad. studies Sch. Music, Columbia U., 1954-56; L.H.D., Duquesne U., 1964, Belmont Coll., 1964, Cath. U. Am., 1975, St. Joseph's Coll., Rensselaer, Ind., 1979. Joined Benedictines, Roman Cath. Ch., 1945; ordained priest, 1951; mem. faculty music dept. St. Vincent Coll., 1957-63, chmn., 1961-63, chancellor chmn. of bd. of Coll., 1963-67; elected co-adjutor archabbot, 1963, abbot primate Benedictine Confederation, 1967-77; archbishop of Milw., 1977—. Mem. Ch. Music Assn. Am. (pres. 1964-66), Am. Guild Organists. Office: 345 N 95th St Milwaukee WI 53226

WEAR, VERNON ERVIN, plastics co. exec.; b. Dundee, Ill., Aug. 11, 1923; s. George and Alma (Schultz) W.; LL.B., Blackstone Coll., 1950; student Kenyon Coll., 1943-44, Yale, 1944-45; B.B.A., Loyola U., 1953; M.B.A., Ohio Christian Coll., 1971, Ph.D., 1972; m. Betty Charlene Haligas, Dec. 15, 1962; step-children—Patricia Ann, Sharon Marie, Linda Jean, Michael A. Cost accountant Ill. Iron & Bolt Co., Carpentersville, Ill., 1941-43, 46-48; expediter Union Spl. Machine Co., Huntley, Ill., 1948-50; prodn. mgr. Ill. Iron & Bolt Co., Carpentersville, 1950-56; mgmt. cons. Alexander Proudfoot Co., Chgo., 1956-57; controller Revcor, Inc., Carpentersville, 1957-59; office mgr. White Feather Farms div. Hales & Hunter, Dundee, Ill., 1959-62; controller Conolite div. Woodall Industries, Inc., Carpentersville, 1962-77; controller molded products div. LOF Plastics, Inc., Detroit, 1977—. Sec., East Dundee Zoning Commn., 1955-56; trustee Village of East Dundee, 1957-62, East Dundee and Countryside Fire Protection Dist., 1955-56. Served with USAAF, 1943-46. Mem. Nat. Assn. Accountants, Am. Accounting Assn., Am. Mgmt. Assn., Am. Inst. Corp. Controllers, Am. Legion. Lutheran. Home: 2955 Charnwood Dr Troy MI 48098 Office: 7565 E McNichols Rd Detroit MI 48234

WEATHERFORD, JOHN WILLIAM, librarian; b. Decatur, Ill., Jan. 5, 1924; s. E. O. and E. M. (Fields) W.; B.A., Millikin U., 1948; M.A., U. N.Mex., 1949; A.M.L.S., U. Mich., 1954; children—Laura, Alice, John F. Manuscripts librarian Ohio State Museum, Columbus, 1954-57; asst. dir. Miami U. Library, Oxford, Ohio, 1957-70; dir. libraries Central Mich. U., 1970—, asst. provost for faculty contractual relations, 1976-79. Served with U.S. Army, 1943-46. Author: Collective Bargaining and the Academic Librarian, 1976. Office: Central Mich U Mount Pleasant MI 48859

WEATHERHEAD, ALBERT JOHN, III, bus. exec.; b. Cleve., Feb. 17, 1925; s. Albert J. and Dorothy (Jones) W.; A.B., Harvard U., 1950, postgrad., 1951; m. Celia Scott, Jan. 1, 1975; children—Dwight S., Michael H., Mary H. Prodn. mgr. Yale & Towne, Stamford, Conn., 1951-54, Blaw-Knox, Pitts., 1954-56; plant mgr. Weatherhead Co., Cleve., 1957-59, gen. mgr., 1959-61, v.p., gen. mgr., 1962-66, gen. sales mgr., 1962-63, v.p. mfg., 1964-66; v.p., dir. Weatherhead Co. of Can., Ltd. 1960-63, pres., chief exec. officer, dir., 1964-66; pres., dir. Weatherchem Corp., 1971—; dir. Weatherhead Co., Protane Corp., L.P.G. Leasing Corp., Leasepac Corp., Leasepac Can., Ltd., Creative Resources, Inc. Mem. Univ. Sch. Alumni Council, trustee Univ. Sch.; mem. vis. com. Ohio U., Athens; v.p. nat. adv. com. Rollins Coll., Winter Park, Fla.; adv. trustee Pinecrest Sch., Ft. Lauderdale, Fla.; mem. capital campaign steering com. Laurel Sch.; trustee Case Western U., Vocat. Guidance and Rehab. Services, Hwy. Safety Found.; v.p. Weatherhead Found.; mem. com. on univ. resources Harvard U. Served with USAAF, 1943-46. Mem. Am. Newcomen Soc., Beta Gamma Sigma (hon.). Clubs: Union (Cleve.); Country (Shaker Heights, Ohio); Ottawa Shooting (Freemont, Ohio); Ocean (Delray, Fla.); Everglades (Palm Beach, Fla); Codrington (Oxford, Eng.). Author: The New Age of Business, 1965. Home: 19601 Shelburne Rd Shaker Heights OH 44118 Office: 2222 Highland Rd Twinsburg OH 44087

WEATHERS, K. RUSSELL, public relations exec.; b. Harrison County, Mo., June 21, 1942; s. William Kenneth and Mildred Grace (Fitzpatrick) W.; B.S., U. Mo., 1964; m. Judith C. Cain, Aug. 12, 1961; children—Vince S., Kent A., Joy L. Tchr. vocat. agr. N. Platte High Sch., Dearborn, Mo., 1964-66, Centralia (Mo.) Public High Sch., 1966-67; staff asst. and mem. services staff Farmland Industries, Inc., Kansas City, Mo., 1967-69, formerly dir. services div., exec. dir. mem. public relations staff, 198- 0—. Asst. scoutmaster Boy Scouts Am., 1975; chmn. ch. bd. Liberty Christian Ch., 1974-75; co-chmn. Mo-Am. Royal Night, 1980—; chmn. Am. Royal 4-H Conf.; mem. council Kansas City Tomorrow, 1980-81; v.p. Ag Hall of Fame, 1980—; v.p. Earnest Shepherd Youth Center, 1976-78, chmn., 1978-80; bd. dirs., vice chmn. Mo. 4-H Found., 1979—; chmn. Liberty Econ. and Preservation Commn., 1980-81; mem. Liberty City Council, 1977-81; mayor City of Liberty, 1981—, Liberty chmn. County Criminal Justice Center Bond Issue, 1980—; mem. Kansas City FFA adv. com.; mem. ARC Blood Doner's Gallon Club, 1980. Mem. Guest Relations Assn., C. of C. Liberty, Northland C. of C. Club: Internat. Agribus. (v.p. 1979-80, pres. 1980-81). Mem. Christian Ch. Home: 1907 Clay Dr Liberty MO 64068 Office: PO Box 7305 Kansas City MO 64116

WEATHERSBY, GEORGE BYRON, state edn. ofcl.; b. Albany, Calif., Dec. 9, 1944; s. Byron and Fannie A. W.; B.S., U. Calif., Berkeley, 1965, M.S., 1966, M.B.A., 1967; S.M., Harvard U., 1968, Ph.D., 1970; m. Linda Rose W., June 29, 1979; children—Deborah Jane, Geoffrey Byron. Asso. dir. analytical studies U. Calif., Berkeley, 1969-72, also dir. Ford Found. research program, mem. faculty, 1969-72; spl. asst. to U.S. Sec. of State, Washington, 1972-73; dir. research Nat. Commn. on Financing Higher Edn., Washington, 1973-74; asso. prof. mgmt. Harvard U., 1974-78; commr. higher edn. Ind., 1977—. Calif. Regents scholar, 1963-65; NSF fellow, 1966-67; AEC fellow, 1966-67; Kent fellow, 1967-70; White House fellow, 1972-73; named 1 of 100 Outstanding Young Leaders in Higher Edn., Change Mag., 1978, One of Outstanding Young Men of 1976. Mem. Am. Council Edn. Ops. Research Soc. Am., Inst. Mgmt. Scis., Econometrica, Democrat. Author books including: Financing Postsecondary Education in the U.S., 1974; Colleges and Money, 1976; contbr. numerous articles to profl. jours., 1967—; cons. editor

Jour. Higher Edn., 1974—. Office: 143 W Market St Indianapolis IN 46208

WEATHERUP, ROBERT ALEXANDER, aerospace engr.; b. Champion, N.Y., Dec. 19, 1916; s. Garfield Edward and Pearl Rose (McDonald) W.; B.S., U.S. Naval Acad., 1940; B.S. in Aero. Engring., U.S. Naval Postgrad. Sch., 1948; M.S., Calif. Inst. Tech., 1949; m. Kathryn Crites Hesser, Jan. 27, 1943; children—Ann Kathryn, Roy Garfield, John Robert. Commd. ensign U.S. Navy, 1940, advanced through grades to comdr., 1951; comdg. officer Air Antisubmarine Squadron 892, 1951; comdg. officer U.S.S. Burton Island, 1959; ret., 1961; exec. adviser Douglas Aircraft Co., Long Beach, Calif., 1961-69; sr. group engr. McDonnell Aircraft Co., St. Louis, 1970—. Mem. Rolling Hills Estates (Calif.) Planning Commn., 1966-69. Deocrated D.F.C. with cluster, Air medal with 3 clusters, Purple Heart. Asso. fellow AIAA; mem. Mil. Ops. Research Soc., Nat. Security Indsl. Assn. Methodist. Contbr. articles to profl. publs. Patentee in field. Home: 883 Parma Dr Manchester MO 63011 Office: McDonnell Aircraft Co Box 516 St Louis MO 63166

WEAVER, ARTHUR J., banker; b. Falls City, Nebr., Nov. 19, 1912; s. Arthur J. and Maude E. (Hart) W.; m. Harriet Elizabeth Walt; children—Walt F., Arthur, John H., James T. Chmn. bd. Nishna Valley State Bank, Riverton, Iowa; ret. v.p. Alexander & Alexander Inc., N.Y.C.; dir. Comml. Fed. Savs. & Loan Assn., HOC Internat. Ltd., Denver, Kimberly Pines Inc., Davenport, Iowa, N.W. Investors, Inc., Nebrado Ltd., Nassau, Bahamas; spl. U.S. ambassador independence of Republic of Togo, Africa, 1960. Mem. exec. com., v.p. Lancaster chpt. A.R.C.; active YMCA. Trustee U. Nebr. Found; Bd. dirs. Lincoln Found., Lincoln Center Devel. Assn. Mem. City Council of Lincoln, 1939-51, v.p.; chmn. Bd. of Equalization, Utility Tax Com., Post-War Aviation Planning Com.; mem. jud. nominating commn. Supreme Ct. Nebr.; mem. Nebr. State Forestry Adv. Commn. Del.-at-Large Rep. Nat. Conv., 1944, 56, 60. Rep. candidate for Gov. Nebr., 1946; del. at-large, chmn. Nebr. Del. to Rep. Nat. Conv., 1948, 1952. Bd. dirs. Lincoln Found., St. Elizabeth Hosp. Recipient Masters Certificate of Honor and Merit, U. Neb., 1965, Nebr. Builder award, 1971. Mem. Nat. Assn. Ins. Agts., Nebr. Alumni Assn., C. of C., Newcomen Soc. N. Am. Presbyn. Clubs: Lincoln Country, University, Nebraska. Home: 3519 Allendale Dr Lincoln NE 68516 Office: Nishna Valley State Bank Riverton IA 51650

WEAVER, ARTHUR LAWRENCE, physician; b. Lincoln, Nebr., Sept. 3, 1936; s. Arthur J. and Harriet Elizabeth (Walt) W.; B.S. (Regents scholar) with distinction, U. Nebr., 1958; M.D., Northwestern U., 1962; M.S. in Medicine, U. Minn., 1966; m. JoAnn Stonacek, July 6, 1980; children—Arthur Jensen, Anne Christine. Intern U. Mich. Hosps., Ann Arbor, 1962-63; resident Mayo Grad. Sch. Medicine, Rochester, Minn., 1963-66; practice medicine specializing in rheumatology and internal medicine, Lincoln, 1968—; mem. staff Bryan Meml. Hosp., chmn. dept. rheumatology, 1976-78; mem. courtesy staff St. Elizabeths Hosp., Lincoln Gen. Hosp.; mem. cons. staff VA Hosp.; chmn. Juvenile Rheumatoid Arthritis Clinic, 1970—; asso. prof. dept. internal medicine U. Nebr., Omaha, 1976—; med. dir. Lincoln Benefit Life Ins. Co., Nebr., 1972—; mem. exam. bd. Nat. Assn. Retail Druggists. Bd. dirs. Nebr. chpt. Arthritis Found., 1969—; trustee U. Nebr. Found., 1974—. Served to capt., M.C., U.S. Army, 1966-68. Recipient Outstanding Nebraskan award U. Nebr., 1958, also C.W. Boucher award; Philip S. Hench award Rheumatology, Mayo Grad. Sch. Medicine, 1966; diplomate Am. Bd. Internal Medicine. Fellow A.C.P.; mem. Am., Nebr. socs. of internal medicine, Am. Rheumatism Assn., Nebraska Rheumatism Assn., AMA, Nebr. Med. Assn., Lancaster County Med. Soc., Mayo Grad. Sch. Medicine Alumni Assn., Phi Beta Kappa, Sigma Xi, Alpha Omega Alpha, Pi Kappa Epsilon, Phi Rho Sigma. Republican. Presbyterian. Contbr. articles to med. jours. Home: 3600 S 40th St Lincoln NE 68506 Office: 2121 S 56th St Lincoln NE 68506

WEAVER, CLARENCE L(AHR), ret. librarian; b. Delaware, Ohio, Nov. 5, 1904; s. Charles Oscar and Maggie Jane (Betz) W.; B.A., Ohio Wesleyan U., 1926; B.S. in Library Sci., Western Res. U., 1934, M.S. in Library Sci., U. Mich., 1959; m. Gertrude Viola Pratt, May 20, 1926 (dec. May 1970); children—Eleanor Janet (Mrs. Leon Hogan), Kenneth H., Charles A., Carol Lynn (Mrs. Bruce Benton); m. 2d, Marjorie Carr McCready, Nov. 12, 1979. Clk., Order of Bookfellows, Chgo., 1926; apprentice proofreader Lakeside Press, Chgo., 1926-30; landscape gardener Cleve. area, 1931; dairy farmer, South Euclid, O., 1932-33; head cataloger, asso. editor publs. Ohio State Archaeol. and Hist. Soc., Columbus, 1934-46; chief catalog and order dept. Grand Rapids (Mich.) Pub. Library, 1946-69, ret., 1969. Mem. Theosophical Soc. in Grand Rapids (pres. 1971—), Mich. Library Assn., ALA, Mich. Regional Group Catalogers, Bards of Grand Rapids (chaplain 1957-66, yearbook and workshop chmn. 1966-80), Grand Rapids Librarians Club (v.p. 1971-72), Kent Philatelic Soc. Grand Rapids (v.p. 1970-71), Acad. Am. Poets, Poetry Soc. Mich. (v.p. 1971-75, historian, 1975-81), United Amateur Press, World Poetry Soc. Internat., Centro Studi e Scambi Internazionale (Rome). Republican. Author: With All My Love, 1936; A Bard's Prayers, 1967; The Quickened Seed, 1981. Tech. editor.; History of the State of Ohio, 6 vols., 1941-44. Editor, pub. The Quickening Seed, quar. poetry jour., 1933-46, Bardic Echoes, poetry mag., 1960-80, Weave Anthology, 1974; Webs of Loveliness, 2d Weave Anthology, 1975. Originator Weave poetic form. Home: 125 Somerset Dr NE Grand Rapids MI 49503

WEAVER, FLOYD EDWARD, surgeon; b. Dewey, Ill., Jan. 21, 1922; s. Avery Thomas and Magdalena (Ingold) W.; A.B., Goshen Coll., 1954; B.S., Med. Sch., U. Ill., M.D., 1958; m. Edna Mae Stalter, Dec. 22, 1951; children—Sharon Renee, Galen Floyd. Intern, Decatur (Ill.) Gen. Hosp., 1958-59; resident in surgery Hines (Ill.) VA Hosp., 1961-65; chief of staff, St. James Hosp., Pontiac, Ill., 1975-76, chief of surgery, 1968—; surg. cons. Children's Center, Fairburg Hosp.; clin. asso. basic sci. U. Ill. Elder, Mennonite Ch., 1968; regent Winston Churchill Coll., 1968-69; bd. Mental Health Assn., 1970, TB Assn., 1966-70. Diplomate Am. Bd. Surgery. Fellow A.C.S.; mem. Ill. Med. Soc., Ill., Pan-Am., Charles B. Peustow surg. socs., Soc. Abdominal Surgeons, Am. Geriatric Soc., Royal Soc. Physicians. Republican. Contbr. article to profl. jour. Home: 8 Dixie Lane Pontiac IL 61764 Office: 612 E Water St Pontiac IL 61764

WEAVER, GLENN MORRISON, psychiatrist; b. Huntington, W.Va., July 23, 1921; s. John Stanley and Margaret Love (Wallingford) W.; B.S., U. Cin., 1943, M.D., 1945; m. Mary Ellen Roberts, June 22, 1945; children—Pamela Ruth, Margaret Ellen. Intern, St. Louis City Hosp., 1945-46; resident in pathology Cin. Gen. Hosp., 1948-49, in psychiatry Longview State Hosp., 1949-50, Christ Hosp., 1950-51, Cin. Gen. Hosp., 1951-52; practice medicine specializing in psychiatry, Cin., 1952—; mem. staff, dir. dept. neurology and psychiatry Christ Hosp., Cin., 1965—; instr. psychiatry U. Cin., 1952-73, clin. asst. prof., 1973—; cons. AEC, 1952—, Hamilton County Probate Ct., 1956—; mem. Hamilton County Mental Health and Rehab. Bd., 1975—. Served to capt. U.S. Army, 1946-48. Recipient Physician's Recognition award AMA, 1976. Fellow Am. Psychiat. Assn.; mem. Am., Ohio State med. assns., Am. Acad. Psychiatry and Law, Acad. Legal Medicine, Ohio Psychiat. Assn., Cin. Soc. Neurology and Psychiatry, Cin. Acad. Medicine, Keeneland Assn. Presbyterian. Clubs: Univ. (Cin.), Masons, Shriners. Author: Considerations of Multiple Personality, 1965; contbr. articles to med. jour. Home: 323 Warren Ave Cincinnati OH 45220 Office: 250 Wm Howard Taft Rd Cincinnati OH 45219

WEAVER, KENNETH RONALD, hosp. exec.; b. Cass County, Mich., Sept. 19, 1926; s. Clyde D. and Alma L. (Price) W.; B.S., Ball State U., 1953; m. Sharon Kay Kimble, June 15, 1957; children—Laurie Ruth, Jeffrey Kent, Gregory Scott, Michael Gerald. State editor News-Sentinel, Ft. Wayne, Ind., 1953-58; editor Tri-City Progress, Warren, Mich., 1958-60; news editor The Eccentric, Birmingham, Mich., 1960-61, mng. editor, 1961-67; mng. editor Wabash (Ind.) Plain Dealer, 1967-69; mng. editor Community-News-Macomb Group, East Detroit, Mich., 1969-71; publs. editor William Beaumont Hosp., Royal Oak, Mich., 1971, asst. dir. pub. relations, 1971-79; dir. public relations Crittenton Hosp., Rochester, Mich., 1979—. Mem. Ball State Devel. Council, 1954-57. Served with AUS, 1945-46. Recipient Distinguished Service award Ball State U. Alumni, 1967. Mem. Southeastern Mich. (sec. 1973-74), Mich. hosp. pub. relations assns., Internat. Assn. Bus. Communicators/Detroit (dir., treas.), C. of C. Club: Kiwanis. Contbr. articles to mags. Home: 641 Redruth Blvd Clawson MI 48017 Office: Crittenton Hosp Rochester MI 48063

WEAVER, L. RUTH RUNDLE (MRS. C.H. WEAVER), ret. lawyer; b. St. Joseph, Mo.; d. Charles Vail and Anna (Wist) Rundle; B.A., Kearney State Coll., 1923; J.D., Akron U. Coll. Law, 1955; m. Clyde Hulbert Weaver, Feb. 28, 1931 (dec. June 1951). Tchr., Chase County High Sch., Imperial, Nebr., 1923-24, Biwabik (Minn.) High Sch., 1924-25, Child High Sch., Edgerton, Wis., 1925-28, Central High Sch., Akron, Ohio, 1928-30; supr. personnel record sect. Goodyear Tire and Rubber Co., Akron, 1942-47; teller Evans Savs. Assn., Akron, 1951-56; admitted to Ohio bar, 1956, in practice, Akron, to 1980. Bd. dirs. Stan Hywet Found., 1956—, Akron Art Mus., 1981—. Named Woman of Yr., Summit chpt. Am. Bus. Women's Assn., 1961. Mem. Am. Judicature Soc. Fedn. Women's Clubs, Am. (mem. com. cooperation state and local bar groups, taxation sect., 1956-62, com. estate and gift taxes 1962-66, 67-68, gen. practice sect., real property and trust sect., family com. gen. practice sect. 1974-75), Ohio, Akron (mem. public relations com. 1958—, chmn. speakers bur. com. 1965-67, mem. entertainment com. 1965-66, mem. ethics com. 1969-76, mem. probate court com. 1967-69, mem. inquiry com. 1967-76, chmn. welfare and necrology com. 1973-76) bar assns., Ohio Acad. Trial Lawyers, Am. Trial Lawyers Assn., Cuyahoga Falls LWV, Am. Bus. Women's Assn., Nat. Trust Historic Preservation, Western Res. Hist. Soc., Akron Dist. Golf Assn. (tournament chmn. 1939-41, pres. 1941-49), Phi Delta Delta (chpt. pres. 1967-70). Clubs: Quota (membership com. 1961-62, parliamentarian 1962-66, chmn. community service, 1964-65), Woman's City (1st vice chmn. six-thirty sect. 1967-68), Business Women's Current Events (pres. 1964-66). Home: 2453 16th St Cuyahoga Falls OH 44223

WEAVER, LEO, interstate agy. exec.; b. Paterson, N.J., Jan. 4, 1925; s. Forest E. and Bertha H. W.; B.C.E., N.Y. U., 1948; m. Mary Louise Spoonamore, July 2, 1949; children—Lee A., Steven M., Charles E., Michael R., Daniel C., Allison L. Commd. officer USPHS, 1948; san. engr. dir. Nat. Water Quality Network, R.A. Taft Center, Cin., 1960-66, chief Solid Waste Program, 1967, cons. USPHS, 1968, mem. NIH Study Com., 1969-70; dir. research, dir. Washington Office, Am. Public Works Assn., 1968-70; asst. sec. Water Pollution Control Fedn., Washington, 1971-74; exec. dir., chief engr. Ohio River Valley Water Sanitation Commn., Cin., 1974—; cons. U.S. EPA, 1972; mem. adv. com. U.S. Army Biomedical Research Lab. Asst. scoutmaster, dist. committeeman Boy Scouts Am., 1966-74; vice chmn. Montgomery County Environ. Trust, 1969-70. Served with AUS, 1943-46; ETO. Decorated USPHS Commendation medal, 1964; recipient award of merit Boy Scouts Am., 1974. Registered profl. engr., N.Y. Diplomate Am. Acad. Environ. Engrs. Fellow ASCE; mem. Am. Water Works Assn., Water Pollution Control Fedn. (bd. control 1979-82, Bedell award), Nat. Soc. Profl. Engrs. Baptist. Club: Cin. Rotary (v.p. 1980-81). Tech. editor, Refuse Collection Practice, 2d edit., 1958, Municipal Refuse Disposal, 1st edit., 1961. Contbr. tech. articles to profl. jours. Home: 6978 Presidio Ct Cincinnati OH 45244 Office: 414 Walnut St Cincinnati OH 45202

WEAVER, LORIN EUGENE, ednl. adminstr.; b. Ashland, Ohio, Oct. 5, 1940; s. Ralph Clayton and Margaret (Baldwin) W.; B.S., Ohio State U., 1962; M.Edn., Kent State U., 1975; postgrad U. Akron, 1978-80; m. Judy Jane Van Gilder, Aug. 20, 1961; children—Lisa Jane, Brian Tod, Megan Jo. Tchr. vocat. agr. Union Local Schs., Belmont County, Ohio, 1962-63, Warsaw (Ohio) High Sch., 1963-65; agt. Allstate Ins. Co., Ashland, 1965-67; coordinator occupational work experience Hillsdale High Sch., Jeromesville, Ohio, 1967-70; coordinator occupational work experience Wayne County Vocat. Sch. Dist., Smithville, Ohio, 1970-74, supr. occupational work experience, 1974-79, asst. dir., 1979—; dir. adult edn. Hillsdale Local Schs., 1968-70. Supt. Sunday Sch., Grace Brethren Ch., 1975-77, mgr. softball team, 1978—, choir mem. Mem. Wayne County Personnel Assn., Am. Vocat. Assn., Ohio Vocat. Assn., Ohio Edn. Assn. (life), Ohio State U. Alumni Assn., Ohio Assn. Secondary Sch. Adminstrs., Vocat. Indsl. Clubs Am. (North Central Ohio regional adv. 1978-80), Phi Delta Kappa. Home: 209 County Rd 1675 Rt 2 Jeromesville OH 44840 Office: Box 378 Smithville OH 44677

WEAVER, R(ICHARD) DONALD, clergyman; b. St. Louis, Mar. 25, 1926; s. Robert Raymond and Ada Viola (Holz) W.; B.S.C., St. Louis U., 1949; M.Div., Garrett Theol. Sem., 1952; postgrad U. Chgo., 1951-53; M.A., Scarritt Coll., 1979. Ordained to ministry United Methodist Ch., 1951; pastor, Lizton and Salem (Ind.) Meth. Chs., 1951-53, Centenary Meth. Ch., Veedersburg, Ind., 1954-58, Indiana Harbor United Meth. Ch., East Chicago, Ind., 1958-73, 1st United Meth. Ch., Hobart, Ind., 1973-80, 1st United Meth. Ch., Crown Point, Ind., 1980—; lectr. Calumet Coll., Whiting, Ind., 1967—. Pres., United Way, 1974, Twin City Community Services, 1970, Lake County Mental Health Assn., 1963, 64; v.p. Referral and Emergency Services, 1977-78; bd. dirs. No. Ind. Health Systems Agy., 1976-78, Vis. Nurse Assn. N.W. Ind.; pres. Ind. United Meth. Children's Home, 1980-82; mem. East Chicago Housing Commn., 1965; mem. Lake County Community Devel. Com. Served with AUS, 1944-46; ETO. Recipient Community Leadership award Twin City Community Services, 1971. Mem. Am. Soc. Ch. History, Assn. Sociology of Religion, Hymn Soc. Am., Religious Edn. Assn. U.S. and Can., Religious Research Assn., Soc. Sci. Study Religion, Crown Point Ministerial Assn. Club: Rotary. Home: 348 Rose Ellen Dr Crown Point IN 46307 Office: 352 S Main St Crown Point IN 46307

WEAVER, STANLEY B., state senator; b. Harrisburg, Ill., May 23, 1925; student Mich. State Coll., U. Ill.; grad. Ind. Coll. Mortuary Sci.; m. Mary Smith; children—Blake, Sherry. Partner, Weaver-Henderson Funeral Home, Urbana, Ill.; former mem. Ill. Ho. of Reps.; now mem. Ill. Senate; mayor Urbana, 1957-69. Active various civic orgns. Served with USAAF, World War II. Republican: Address: 415 State Capitol Springfield IL 62706*

WEBB, CHARLES HAIZLIP, JR., univ. dean; b. Dallas, Feb. 14, 1933; s. C.H. and Marion E. (Gilker) W.; m. Kenda McGibbon; children—Mark, Kent, Malcolm, Charles; B.A., So. Meth. U., 1955, Mus.M., 1955; Mus.D., Ind. U., 1964; hon. Doctorate, Anderson Coll., 1979. Asst. to dean Sch. Music, So. Meth. U., 1957-58; asso. instr. piano Ind. U., Bloomington, 1958-60, instr. music, mgr. musical attractions, 1960-64, asst. prof. music, 1964-67, asso. prof., 1967, asst. dean, asso. dean Sch. Music, 1964-73, dean, 1973—; dir. Indpls. Symphonic Chorus; chmn. adv. bd. Internat. Festivals, Inc.; commr. Ind. Arts Commn.; adv. panel Music Found.; evaluator challenge grant program Nat. Endowment for Arts; mem. recommendation bd. Avery Fisher Prize Program. Organist, First Meth. Ch., Bloomington, 1959—. Mem. Pi Kappa Lambda, Phi Mu Alpha. Author editor music publs. Home: 648 Woodscrest Dr Bloomington IN 47401

WEBB, JAMES NEIL, metall. engr.; b. Maryville, Tenn., Sept. 6, 1949; s. Harley and Beulah Ann (Webb) W.; B.S. in Metall. Engring., U. Tenn., 1970; postgrad. Ill. Community Coll., 1972-73, Bradley U., 1974-75; m. Paulette Gail Roberts, June 2, 1968; children—James Robert, Elizabeth Gail. With Caterpillar Tractor Co., 1970—, staff metall. engr., Mossville, Ill., 1975, staff welding engr., Davenport, Iowa, 1975, staff metall. quality engr., 1978—. Pres., chmn. bd. North Little League, Davenport. Mem. Chem. Coaters Assn. (sec. Quad Cities chpt.), Am. Soc. Metals, Am. Welding Soc., Metall. Soc. Republican. Baptist. Office: PO Box 2790 Davenport IA 52809

WEBB, JAMES R., economist; b. Granite City, Ill., Apr. 5, 1947; s. Gene and Lucille (Arney) W.; B.S., No. Ill. U., 1972, M.B.A., 1974, postgrad., 1974—. Expediter, Hydroline Mfg. Co., Rockford, Ill., 1967, corr. inside sales, 1967-69, engring. coordinator, 1969-76; analyst corporate systems finance div. Parker Pen Corp., Janesville, Wis., 1976; grad. teaching asst. fin. U. Ill., Urbana-Champaign, 1976-79; asst. prof. real estate fin. Kent (Ohio) State U., 1979—. Mem. Am. Econ. Assn., Am. Fin. Assn., Am. Sociol. Assn., Assn. M.B.A. Execs., others. Home: 477 Park Ridge Dr Munroe Falls OH 44262 Office: Dept Fin Kent State U Kent OH 44242

WEBB, NORMAN FREDERICK, hosp. adminstr.; b. Peoria, Ill., June 8, 1944; s. Norman Frederick and Ruth Ann (Rinker) W.; B.S., U. Ill., 1967; postgrad. Northwestern U., 1967-68; M.A., U. Chgo., 1970; m. Santina Ann Daidone; children—Philip, Joseph. Adminstr., Uptown Community Health Center, Chgo., 1970-71; v.p. profl. services, planning and devel. S. Chgo. Community Hosp., 1972-78; adminstr. Pekin (Ill.) Meml. Hosp., 1978—. Chmn. exec. com. COMPRAND, Chgo., 1976—; mem. com. on planning Chgo. Hosp. Council, 1977-78; mem. adv. bd. State of Ill. Family Practice Residency, 1978—; mem. adv. bd. urban health program U. Ill., 1978—. Mem. Am. Coll. Hosp. Adminstrs., Am. Acad. Med. Adminstrs., Am. Soc. Planning Ofcls., Am. Mgmt. Assn., Ill. Hosp. Assn. Methodist. Club: Masons. Office: Court and 14th Sts Pekin IL 61554

WEBB, PAUL BENEDICT, JR., physician; b. St. Louis, June 28, 1925; s. Paul Benedict and Adela Katherine (Glosemeyer) W.; M.D., St. Louis U., 1952; postgrad. Washington U., 1953-54; m. Bessie Marie Brenneisen, May 2, 1953; children—Paul Benedict III, David, Diane, Steven, Richard, Timothy, Matthew, Kevin, Patricia. Intern St. John's Hosp., 1952-53; resident ophthalmology Ind. U., 1954-56; pvt. practice ltd. to ophthalmology, St. Louis, 1956—; asst. prof. St. Louis U. Merit badge dir. pub. service group Boy Scouts Am. Served with AUS, 1943-46. Diplomate Am. Bd. Ophthalmology. Mem. AMA, Am. Acad. Ophthalmology, St. Louis Ophthalmol. Soc., Mo. Med. Assn., St. Louis Med. Soc., Mo. Ophthalmol. Soc. Home: 6207 Itaska St Saint Louis MO 63109 Office: 6651 Chippewa St Saint Louis MO 63109

WEBB, THELMA ELIZABETH, librarian; b. Bethlehem, Pa., Mar. 24, 1914; d. Ernest and Beatrice Maud (Elwell) Hooper; B.A. cum laude, Baldwin-Wallace Coll., 1936; postgrad. Pestalozzi-Froebel Sch., Chgo., 1962, Concordia Tchrs. Coll., River Forest, 1974-76; M.A. in L.S., Rosary Coll., River Forest, Ill., 1969; m. Harold W. Webb, Sept. 14, 1940; children—Paul Kent, Margaret Eileen Webb St. John. Tchr. pub. schs., Wellington, Ohio, 1936-40, Lincoln Sch., Maywood, Ill., 1961-63; tchr., librarian Jane Addams Sch., Melrose Park, Ill., 1963-74; supr. library media dist. 89 Ill., 1975—. Sec. Irving Sch., Maywood, 1960-61; fin. officer, mgr. Mid-Am. chpt. ARC, 1942-43. Named Outstanding Educator, Phi Delta Kappa, 1980. Mem. Nat., Ill. edn. assns., ALA, Ill. Library Assn., Am. Assn. Sch. Librarians, Ill. Assn. for Media in Edn., Chgo. Suburban Audiovisual Round Table, Assn. Suprs. of Curriculum Devel., Mensa, Bus. and Profl. Women's Club (chpt. treas.), Oak Park (Ill.) PTA (life), Gamma Sigma (treas. 1938-40), Alpha Phi Gamma (v.p. 1939-40), Pi Gamma Mu, Phi Kappa Delta (sec. 1979). Baptist (sec., tchr. Sunday sch.). Home: 913 N 9th Ave Maywood IL 60153 Office: 1133 S 8th Ave Maywood IL 60153

WEBB, WILLIAM DANA, broadcasting exec.; b. Indpls., July 21, 1950; s. William H. and Rosemary (Andrews) W.; B.S., Butler U., Indpls., 1972, M.S., 1973; m. Karen Suzzett Baker, Aug. 27, 1972; children—Curren Scott, Correy Dane. Tchr. music, Julian Music Co., Indpls., 1963-73; announcer Sta WATI, Indpls., 1971; gen. mgr. Sta. WBDG-FM, Indpls., 1973-80; announcer Sta. WIRE, Indpls., 1974—; lectr. in field. Office: 4560 Knollton Rd Indianapolis IN 46208

WEBBER, ARDETH JOANNE, educator; b. Oskaloosa, Iowa, Aug. 18, 1925; d. Albert and Anna Helene (Kienitz) Woodard; B.A., William Penn Coll., 1948; postgrad. Central State U., Wilberforce, Ohio, 1960; M.A., Ohio State U., Columbus, 1967; postgrad. U. Dayton, 1969; m. Warren Loraine Webber, May 31, 1949; children—Carol Lynne, David Leroy, Allen Leigh, Bonny Lanel. Sec., Johnson Abstract Co., Oskaloosa, 1942-48; bus. tchr. Cedar (Iowa) High Sch., 1948-49; sec. Midland Mfg. Co., Monroe, Iowa, 1953-56; vocal instr. Cedar Cliff Pub. Sch., Cedarville, Ohio, 1960-61; instr. bus. edn. Cedarville Coll., 1959-64, asst. prof. bus. edn., 1964-71; asst. prof. bus. edn. Central State U., Wilberforce, 1971—, sec. faculty Coll. Bus., 1971—, adv. com. Coll. Edn., 1977—. Mem. Cedarville Bicentennial Com., Cedarville Bicentennial Community Band, 1975-76; pres. Cedarville Music Boosters Assn., 1976-77, mem. uniform com., 1975-76. Recipient plaque Cedarville Coll., 1970. Mem. Nat. Bus. Edn. Assn., Ohio Bus. Tchrs. Assn., Delta Pi Epsilon. Baptist. Home: 168 Walnut St Cedarville OH 45314 Office: State Route 42 Wilberforce OH 45384

WEBBER, EVERARD LELAND, museum dir.; b. Chgo., Jan. 27, 1920; s. Leland Bacon and Harriet Gaylord (Peck) W.; B.B.A., U. Cin., 1942; C.P.A., U. Ill., 1949; D.H.L., DePaul U., 1980; m. Ellen Gowen Duer, Mar. 30, 1946 (dec. 1974); children—Leland Duer, James Randall, Ellen Robinson; m. 2d, Joan Wray Malloch, Sept. 6, 1975. With Proctor & Gamble Co., Cin., 1939-42, Ernst & Ernst, C.P.A.'s, Chgo., 1945-50; with Field Museum of Natural History, 1950—, exec. asst. to dir., 1951-60, asst. dir., 1960-62, dir., 1962-80, pres., 1976-81, also trustee; dir. Growth Industry Shares; trustee Savs. and Profit Sharing Fund of Sears Employees, 1981—. Bd. dirs. Ill. State Mus., 1966-69; bd. govs. Ill. State Colls. and Univs., 1967-75; mem. Nat. Council on Arts, 1970-76, Nat. 4-H Service Com., 1972-76, Nat. Museum Services Bd., 1977-81. Served to lt. (s.g.) USNR, 1942-45. Mem. AAAS, Am. Assn. Museums (v.p. 1966-70), Beta Theta Pi. Episcopalian. Clubs: Comml., Tavern, Univ., Econ., Caxton, Mich. Shores Arts. Home: 1224 Elmwood Ave Wilmette IL

60091 Office: Field Museum of Natural History Roosevelt Rd and Lake Shore Dr Chicago IL 60605

WEBBER, EVERARD LELAND, mus. ofcl.; b. Chgo., Jan. 27, 1920; s. Leland Bacon and Harriet Gaylord (Peck) W.; B.B.A., U. Cin., 1942; D.H.L., DePaul U., 1980; m. Ellen Gowen Duer, Mar. 30, 1946 (dec. 1974); children—Leland Duer, James Randall, Ellen Robinson; m. 2d Joan Wray Mallaoch, Sept. 6, 1975;. With Proctor & Gamble Co., Cin., 1939-42, Ernst & Ernst, C.P.A.'s, Chgo., 1945-50; with Field Mus. Natural History, Chgo., 1950—, exec. asst. to dir., 1951-60, asst. dir., 1960-62, dir., 1962—, pres., 1976-81, also trustee, 1962—; dir. Growth Industry Shares Bd. dirs. Ill. State Mus., 1966-69; bd. govs. Ill. State Colls and Univs., 1967-75; mem. Nat. Council on Arts, 1970-76, Nat. 4-H Service Com., 1972-76, Nat. Mus. Services Bd., 1977-81; trustee Savs. and Profit-Sharing Fund of Sears Employees, 1981—. Served to lt (s.g.), USNR, 1942-45. Mem. AAAS, Am. Assn. Museums (v.p. 1966-70), Beta Theta Pi. Episcopalian. Clubs: Comml.; Tavern; Univ.; Econ.; Caxton; Mich. Shores Arts. Home: 1224 Elmwood Ave Wilmette IL 60091 Office: Field Mus Natural History Roosevelt Rd and Lake Shore Dr Chicago IL 60605

WEBBER, THOMAS PATRICK, assn. exec.; b. Saginaw, Mich., Mar. 17, 1943; s. Robert W. and Delores A. (DePlonty) W.; B.S., U. Mich., 1966, M.P.H., 1968; m. Sandra S. Hak, Aug. 21, 1965; children—Stephanie, Julie. Public health asst. II, Wayne County Health Dept., Eloise, Mich., 1967; dir. health edn. St. Louis County Health Dept., Duluth, Minn., 1968-71; project dir. Planned Parenthood of Minn., Mpls., 1971, exec. dir., St. Paul, 1971—; guest lectr. Sch. Public Health, U. Minn., 1969-72. Chmn. tech. adv. com. on family planning Minn. Bd. Health, 1972-74. USPHS trainee, 1966-68. Mem. Minn. Human Genetics League (bd. dirs. 1972-77), Minn. Public Health Assn. (pres. 1973), Minn. Heart Assn. (bd. dirs. 1970-71), Minn. Social Services Assn., Am. Public Health Assn., Nat. Exec. Dirs. Council, Planned Parenthood Fedn. Am. (chmn. Gt. Lakes Region exec. dirs. council 1981—). Contbr. articles to profl. jours. Home: 610 Carolyn Ln White Bear Lake MN 55110 Office: 1965 Ford Pkwy Saint Paul MN 55116

WEBER, ARTHUR, publisher; b. Chgo., Feb. 1, 1926; s. Philip and Mary (Arlinsky) W.; student Ill. Inst. Tech., 1943-44; B.S. in Elec. Engring., Northwestern U., 1946; m. Sylvia Zollinger, Aug. 19, 1950; children—Randy, Lori. Elec. design engr. Corn Products Refining Co., 1946-48, Naess & Murphy, architects & engrs., Chgo., 1949-51, Ford Motor Co., 1952-53, Skidmore, Owings & Merill, Chgo., 1954-57, Shaw, Metz & Dolio, Chgo., 1958-59; pub. Consumers Digest mag., Chgo., 1959—, Money Maker mag. Served with USNR, 1944-46. Office: 5705 N Lincoln Ave Chicago IL 60659

WEBER, C(HARLES) EDWARD, educator; b. Chgo., Feb. 21, 1930; s. Edward W. and Augusta (Lonk) W.; student Marquette U., 1948-50; B.A., U. Ill., 1952, M.A. in Labor and Indsl. Relations, 1953; M.A. in Econs. (Hicks fellow), Princeton U., 1954, Ph.D. in Econs., 1958; m. Suzanne Brodseller, Sept. 6, 1952; children—Paul Andrew, Mark Francis. Mem. research staff Princeton, 1954-56; from instr. to asso. prof. bus. U. Pitts., 1956-66, research asso. adminstrv. sci., 1961-63, acting dir. Adminstrv. Sci. Center, 1963-66; prof. policy and mgmt. studies U. Wis.-Milw., 1966—, dean Sch. Bus. Adminstrn., 1966-76; cons. Arthur D. Little, 1964-66; pres. Wis. Cons. Group, 1979—; organizer, dir. Univ. Nat. Bank, Milw., 1970-76; cons. to bus. and govt. Co-chmn. com. to advise on reorgn. Milw. City Govt., 1968-70; commr. public debt City of Milw., 1976—; pres. task force to advise on fire investigation Milw. City Govt.; mem. Citizens Govt. Research Bur., Gov.'s Council Econ. Edn. Ford Found. fellow, 1959-60, 62-63. Mem. Inst. Mgmt. Sci., Am. Econ. Assn., Indsl. Relations Research Assn., Coll. on Orgns, Acad. Mgmt., Met. Milw. Assn. Commerce (vice chmn. com. on legislation), Beta Gamma Sigma. Author: Management Action: Models of Adminstrative Decision, 1969; also articles. Weber Exec. Alumni Assn. of U. Wis., Milw. named in his honor.

WEBER, CAROLYN ANN, city transit ofcl.; b. San Diego, Oct. 7, 1943; d. James C. and Margaret E. Miller; B.S. magma cum laude, Kent State U., 1966, M.A., 1978; children—Todd J., Scott M. Vice pres. Interaction, Inc., Cleveland Heights, Ohio, 1974-77; dir. sch. community relations program Cleve. State U., 1973-74; personnel devel. specialist Greater Cleve. Regional Transit Authority, 1977-78, dir. personnel devel., tng. and safety dept., 1978—; instr. Baldwin-Wallace Coll., 1981, Clevel. State U., 1974. Chmn. bd. dirs. Lakewood (Ohio) YWCA, 1969-71. Urban Mass Transp. Adminstrn. grantee Wharton Sch., 1980. Mem. Organizational Devel. Network, Greater Cleve. Safety Council, Am. Public Transit Assn. (tng. and devel. com. 1981—), Transp. Research Bd., Am. Soc. Tng. and Devel. Home: 3519 Normandy Rd Shaker Heights OH 44120 Office: Greater Cleve Regional Transit Authority 615 Superior Ave NW Cleveland OH 44113

WEBER, DARLENE, restaurant exec.; b. Milw., Jan. 5, 1930; d. Bert B. and Blanche (Corne) Harvey; student public schs., also specialized courses; m. Kurt Weber, Aug. 16, 1964; children—Kim, Jay, Kurt. Engaged in restaurant bus., 1948—; owner-mgr. White Tablecloth Restaurant, Cedarburg, Wis., 1966-69; pres., mgr. The Nantucket, Mequon, Wis., 1969-79; owner, mgr., corp. v.p. Nantucket Shores Restaurant, Milw., 1973—. Regional dir. Milw. Crusade, 1979; mem. council Christ Luth. Ch., Mequon, 1979; pres. Community League, 1960-61. Mem. Wis. Restaurant Assn. (dir., sec. Milw. chpt.), Tempo. Club: Mequon Racquet.

WEBER, EDWARD FORD, congressman; b. Toledo, July 26, 1931; A.B., Denison U., Granville, Ohio, 1953; LL.B., Harvard U., 1956; m. Alice Hammerstrom, 1957; children—Elenore, Ford, Mary. Admitted to Ohio bar, 1956; practiced in Toledo, 1958-80; partner firm Marshall, Melhorn, Cole, Hummer & Spitzer, 1966-80; mem. 97th Congress 9th Dist. Ohio; asst. prof. U. Toledo Law Sch., 1966-79. Trustee, Baptist Theol. Union, 1979—. Served with AUS, 1956-58. Mem. Am. Bar Assn., Ohio Bar Assn., Toledo Bar Assn., NAACP. Republican. Baptist. Address: 512 Cannon House Office Bldg Washington DC 20515

WEBER, ELIZABETH ANN, musician; b. Murphysboro, Ill., Jan. 8, 1941; d. Everett George and Lena Mae (Storey) Weber; student Eastman Sch. Music, 1959-60; Mus.B., Roosevelt U., 1964, B.Mus. Edn., 1964, Mus.M., 1965; D.M.A. (Mu Phi Epsilon doctoral grantee) U. Ill., 1980; m. Gary Wayne Hornik, Dec. 19, 1970 (div. Jan. 30, 1980). Asso. prof. music Chgo. State U., 1972—; instr. music Coe Coll., 1969-72; part-time faculty Roosevelt U., 1972-74; also soprano soloist. Recipient Mary Ganz voice award, 1962; Lola Fletcher Meml. award Chgo. Alumnae chpt. Mu Phi Epsilon, 1964; Chgo. Women's Mus. Club award, 1963; George Woodruff Meml. award, 1963; Oliver Ditson voice scholar, 1963-64, Iowa Arts Council grantee, 1970-71; Mu Phi Epsilon grantee, 1974. Mem. Nat. Assn. Tchrs. of Singing, Soc. Am. Musicians, Music Educators Nat. Conf., Coll. Music Soc., Nat. Assn. Schs. Music, Mu Phi Epsilon, Phi Kappa Phi. Republican. Episcopalian. Office: Music Dept Chgo State U 95th St and King Dr Chicago IL 60628

WEBER, GEORGE RUSSELL, microbiologist; b. Novinger, Mo., Dec. 29, 1911; s. William and Celia Iciphene (Helton) W.; B.S., U. Mo., 1935; Ph.D., Iowa State Coll., 1940; spl. evening student George Washington U., 1944-45, U. Cin., 1948-49; m. Margaret Carrington Cable, Apr. 19, 1947; children—Jeanine Marie, Michael Elwin. Asst. chemist, expt. sta. U. Mo., 1935-36; teaching fellow in bacteriology Iowa State Coll., 1936-38, asst., 1938-39, teaching asst., 1939-40, instr., 1940-42; bacteriologist USPHS, 1946, sr. asst. scientist, 1947, scientist, 1949, chief sanitizing agents unit, 1949-53; research microbiologist Nat. Distillers & Chem. Corp., 1953-63, research project leader, 1963-73, sr. research microbiologist, 1973-75, research asso., 1975, ret., 1977; lectr. in biology U. Cin., 1969-70. Dir. Ky. br. Nat. Chinchilla Breeders of Am., 1955-57, research chmn., 1958-64; pres. Greater Cin. Chinchilla Breeders Assn., 1957-58, 63-64. Served from 1st lt. to maj. AUS, 1942-46; lt. col. AUS (ret.). Recipient War Dept. citation for control of food poisoning and infection, 1946. Fellow Am. Public Health Assn., Royal Soc. Health (Eng.); mem. AAAS, Am. Soc. Microbiology, Am. Inst. Biol. Scis., Ohio Acad. Sci., N.Y. Acad. Scis., Am. Soc. Profl. Biologists (v.p. 1957-58), Smithsonian Assos., Inst. Food Technologists, Research Soc. Am., Res. Officers Assn. U.S. (exec. council Cin. chpt. 1963-65, chpt. pres. 1966-67), Ret. Officers Assn., Mil. Order World Wars, others. Patentee animal feed, biol. metal corrosion control. Home: 1525 Burney Ln Cincinnati OH 45230

WEBER, JUDY MARIE, banker; b. Hays, Kans., Feb. 10, 1944; d. Fred G. and Marie A. (Neuberger) Helget; ed. public and bus. schs., seminars; children—Lori Lee, Deborah Sue, Douglas Joseph, Michael Fred. Loan clk. Assos. Fin. Co., Hays, 1962-65; loan clk., office mgr. Am. Fin. Co., Hays, 1965-67; office mgr. Bryan Inst., Wichita, 1967-72; with Farmers & Mchts. Bank, Colby, Kans., 1971—, sec. to pres., 1974-79, asst. v.p., 1979-81, cashier charge ops., 1981—. Chmn. Colby Recreation Bd.; mem. bd. advisors, dept. bus. Colby Community Coll.; tchr. religion class; Thomas County chmn. for congressional candidate Republican Party. Mem. Nat. Assn. Bank Adminstrs. Republican. Roman Catholic. Home: 1020 E 10th St Colby KS 67701 Office: 240 W 4th St Colby KS 67701

WEBER, MARTHA GESLING, emerita educator; b. Lancaster, Ohio, Apr. 10, 1912; d. William and Sue (Crump) Gesling; A.B., Ohio No. U., 1935, Pd.D. (hon.), 1971; A.M., Ohio State U., 1941; fellow edn. Duke, 1944-46, Ph.D., 1951; m. Dr. Joseph Elliott Weber, Dec. 1956. Tchr. history and music, grad. schs., 1933-40, history, English, debate, high schs., 1940-44; asst. prof. edn., ednl. psychology Bowling Green State U., 1946-49, asso. prof. edn., 1949-53, prof. edn., 1953-75, prof. emerita, 1975—, dir. reading center, 1946-65. Reading cons. basic reading series for slow learners. Recipient Distinguished Alumnus citation Ohio No. U., 1954; Distinguished Faculty award Bowling Gree U., 1963, Coll. of Edn. Outstanding Teaching award, 1968. Mem. Am. Assn. U. Women, Internat. Reading Assn. (pres. Ohio council 1957-58), Am. Ednl. Research Assn., Nat. Soc. Study Edn., Nat. Council Tchrs. English, Coll. Reading Assn. (nat. dir. 1965-68), Mortar Board, Phi Kappa Phi (chpt. pres. 1965-67), Chi Omega, Kappa Delta Pi, Delta Kappa Gamma. Home: 816 E Wooster Bowling Green OH 43402 also 325 3d St N Naples FL 33940

WEBER, MILAN GEORGE, ret. army officer, mgmt. cons.; b. Milw., Oct. 15, 1908; s. Adam George and Frances (Lehrbaumer) W.; B.S., U.S. Mil. Acad., 1931; grad. Coast Arty. and Air Def. Sch., 1938, Nat. War Coll., 1952; m. Mary Agnes Keller, Sept. 2, 1931; 1 son, Milan George. Commd. 2d lt. U.S. Army, 1931, advanced through grades to col., 1944; various army command and staff exec. positions, Philippine Islands, 1932-36, Hawaii, 1938-41, Ft. Monroe, Va., 1936-38; anti-aircraft exec., hdqrs. 3d and 9th armies, U.S., Europe, 1943-45; mem. Gen. Patton's staff, 1944, War Dept. Gen. Staff, 1945-48; mil. adviser to Argentine govt., 1949-51; global strategic planner Joint Chiefs of Staff, 1952-54; comdr. Missile Defense of Norfolk and Hampton Roads, 1954-55; chief of staff advisory group, Japan, 1955-58; dept. comdr. Air Def. Region, Ft. Meade, Md., 1958-60, ret., 1960; mgr. electronic counter measures Loral Electronics Corp., N.Y.C., 1960-62; product mgr. electronic counter measures Hallicrafters Corp. (name changed to Northrop Corp.), Chgo., 1962-64; partner Weber Assos., Mgmt. Cons., Deerfield, Ill., 1964-69; pres. dir. Milan G. Weber Associates, Inc., Deerfield, 1969—; mgmt. cons. to various bus. firms, 1964—; acquisitions and mergers cons. to various corps., 1969—. Chmn. Great Lakes Ecology Assn. Ill., 1974—; chmn. Citizens Com. Honesty in Govt., 1969—; mem. Ill. Drivers Safety Adv. Com., 1975—, Deerfield Library Bd., 1976—, Deerfield Caucus Com., 1978—, Deerfield Energy Adv. Council, 1981—. Decorated Legion of Merit, Bronze Star, Commendation medal with oak leaf cluster. Mem. Assn. Old Crows, West Point Soc. Chgo., Internat. Platform Assn., Assn. Grads. U.S. Mil. Acad., Electronic Counter Measures Assn., Great Lakes Ecology Assn. of the Mil. Clubs: Army Navy, Army Navy Country. Contbr. articles on anti-aircraft arty., air def. and mil. strategy to profl. publs. author of joint strategic capabilities plan; author weekly column on environment, 1977—. Home: 611 Colwyn Terr Deerfield IL 60015 Office: PO Box 81 Deerfield IL 60015

WEBER, NORBERT JOSEPH, physician; b. Defiance, Ohio, Mar. 21. 1923; s. Frank J. and Helen S. (Goller) W.; B.A., Cath. U. Am., 1945; B.S. in Chemistry, Defiance (Ohio) Coll., 1947, B.S. in Edn., 1947; M.D., Stritch Sch. Medicine, Loyola U., Chgo., 1951; m. Mary Kuksta, Sept. 29, 1951; children—Laura Jane, John Joseph. Intern Mercy Hosp., Toledo, 1951-52; resident in surgery, Indpls. Gen. Hosp., 1955-59; practice medicine specializing in surgery, Chgo., 1960—; attending surgeon Holy Cross Hosp., Chgo., 1960—, chmn. dept. surgery, 1972. Served to capt. M.C., AUS, 1953-55. Mem. AMA, Ill., Chgo. med. socs. Roman Catholic. Club: Elks. Home: 10604 S Kolin Ave Oak Lawn IL 60453 Office: 6132 S Kedzie Ave Chicago IL 60629

WEBER, PAUL EGON, physicist, optics engr.; b. Jena, Thurungia, Ger., Nov. 8, 1913; s. Paul Alwin and Barbara B. (Bouffier) W.; came to U.S., 1953, naturalized, 1958; Ingenieur, Höhere Technische Staatslehranstalt, Frankfurt/Main, Germany, 1935; m. Johanna Kühlich, Oct. 30, 1937 (div. 1945); children—Barbara Johanna, Elfriede Margaretha; m. 2d, Gertrud Brüningsen, Nov. 1, 1947; children—Norbert Paul, Dieter Erich; Lab. dir. J.D. Moeller Optical Works, Wedel/Holst, Ger., 1941-45; cons. in optical radiation, Hamburg, Germany, 1945-46, Glücksburg, Ger., 1946-48; physicist H. Steinmetz & Sohn, K.G., Northeim, Hannover, Ger., 1950-53; devel. engr. Am. Optical Co., Buffalo, 1953-54; research engr., Wollensak Optical Co., Rochester, N.Y., 1954-57; physicist Stromberg-Carlson, Rochester, N.Y. 1957-58; staff engr. Avco-Grosley, Cin., 1958-59; prin. engr. Bendix Corp., South Bend, Ind., 1959-60, staff engr. of Bendix Systems Div., Ann Arbor, Mich., 1960-61; scientist Trion Instruments, Inc., Ann Arbor, Mich., 1961-62; mgr. IR Lear Siegler, Inc., Ann Arbor, 1963-65; cons. in optical radiation, Ypsilanti, Mich., 1965-66; physicist Bell & Howell Co., Chgo., 1966-79; cons. physicist Optikal Radiation Physics. Mem. Am. Phys. Soc., Optical Soc. Am. (emeritus), Deutsche Gesellschaft für angewandte Optik. Contbr. articles in optical physics to sci. jours.; patentee optical instruments. Home and office: 921 Bartlet Terr Libertyville IL 60048

WEBER, ROBERT FREDERICK, motor transp. co. exec.; b. La Crosse, Wis., Dec. 2, 1930; s. Arnold E. and Leona L. (Bartz) W.; B.S. in Accounting, U. Wis., 1953; m. Lorraine Ikert, Dec. 27, 1952; children—Robert Frederick, Sandra Kay. Auditor, Baumann, Finney & Co., C.P.A.'s, Chgo., 1953-58; supr. audit group Peat, Marwick, Mitchell & Co., C.P.A.'s, Chgo., 1958-67; fin. v.p., treas. Fruit Belt Motor Service, Inc., Forest Park, Ill., 1967-68; v.p. adminstrn., treas. Signal Delivery Service, Inc., Hinsdale, Ill., 1969-80; v.p., group controller Leaseway Nat. Service Corp., Cleve., 1981—. C.P.A., Ill. Mem. Am. Inst. C.P.A.'s, Ill. Soc. C.P.A.'s, Am. Trucking Assn. (dir. nat. accounting and fin. council), Fin. Execs. Inst., Lutheran Laymen's Movement. Club: Masons. Home: 20670 University Blvd Shaker Heights OH 44122

WEBER, TRUDY REGINA, mathematician; b. Sighisoara, Romania, Dec. 3, 1952; came to U.S., 1969, naturalized, 1977; d. Johann and Regina (Ludwig) W.; B.S. in Math. (grantee), Wayne State U., Detroit, 1976; m. Alex A. Alexandridis, June 21, 1977; 1 dau., Alexis R. Research sci. asso. Gen. Motors Co. Research Labs., Warren, Mich., 1976—. Mem. Am. Statis. Assn. Author research papers in field. Home: 1085 Frankel Ln Bloomfield Hills MI 48013 Office: Gen Motors Research Labs Dept 17 Warren MI 48090

WEBER, VIN, congressman; b. Clayton, Minn., July 24, 1952; ed. U. Minn., 1974; m. Jeanie Lorenz, 1979. Pres., Weber Pub. Co., Clayton; co-pub. Murray County Herald; congressional press sec., 1974-75; senatorial sr. aide, 1979-80; mem. 97th Congress from 6th Dist. Minn. Republican. Address: 514 Cannon House Office Bldg Washington DC 20515*

WEBSTER, BARBARA ANN, dietitian; b. Rockville, Ind., Apr. 13, 1928; d. Robert Harlan and Vallie Irene (Harmless) Strange; B.S., Morehead State U., 1950; postgrad. Ind. State U., 1960-61; m. Ivan Dale Webster, May 25, 1952; children—Valli Jo Howard, Terrence Dale. Tchr. home econs. Newport (Ky.) High Sch., 1950-51; home demonstration agt. Purdue U., Fayette County, Ind., 1951-53; tchr. home econs., Connersville, Ind., 1954-57; 4-H leader, Fayette County, Ind., 1959; theraputic dietitian Meth. Evangelical Hosp., Louisville, 1963-64; head dietary dept. Jackson County Hosp., Seymour, Ind., 1965-71; head dietary Bedford (Ind.) Med. Center, 1971—; cons. dietitian nursing homes, 1965—; mem. adv. com. Area Vocational Sch., 1972—. Mem. Am. Diabetes Assn., Am. Hosp. Soc. Food Service Adminstrn. (bd. dirs., sec.), Am. Heart Assn., Ind. Diabetes Assn. (dir., State Vol. Edn. award). Baptist. Home: 915 W Post Rd Anderson IN 46012 Office: 2900 W 16th St Bedford IN 47421

WEBSTER, JEFFREY LEON, graphic designer; b. Idaho Falls, Idaho, Nov. 23, 1941; s. Leon A. and Marjory M. (McAllister) W.; student Sch. Associated Arts, St. Paul, 1962; m. Judith Kess, Apr. 17, 1965; children—Eric J., Marjorie P. Sci. illustrator Mayo Clinic, Rochester, Minn., 1963-66; layout artist Brown & Bigelow, St. Paul, 1966; graphic designer U. Minn., Mpls., 1966-67, U. Calgary (Alta., Can.), 1967-68; sr. artist Control Data Corp., St. Paul, 1968-70; mem. Idaho State U. Meml. Lectureship Com.; graphic designer Idaho State U., 1978-80; owner, operator studio, Harmony, Minn. Mem. Idaho Civic Symphony Bd. Recipient Profl. citation Library Congress, 1976. Artist pub. ednl. exhibits. Home and Office: Route 1 Harmony MN 55939

WEBSTER, JOHN KIMBALL, investment exec.; b. N.Y.C., June 7, 1934; s. Reginald Nathaniel and Lillian (McDonald) W.; B.A., Yale, 1956; postgrad. Wharton Sch. Finance and Commerce, 1957-58; m. Katherine Taylor Mulligan, Jan. 28, 1967; children—John McDonald, Katherine Kimball. With Dominick & Dominick, N.Y.C., 1961-73, v.p., 1968-73; v.p., sec. Dominick Fund, Inc., Barclay Growth Fund, N.Y.C., 1971-73; v.p. Dominick Mgmt. Corp., N.Y.C., 1971-73; v.p. Monumental Capital Mgmt., Inc., Balt., 1974-75; v.p. Bernstein-Macaulay, Inc., N.Y.C., 1975-78; v.p., dir. Penmark Investments, Inc., Chgo., 1978-79, sr. v.p., 1979-80, exec. v.p., chief operating officer, 1980—; mem. no-load com. Investment Co. Inst., Washington, 1971-73; mem. exec. com. No Load Mut. Fund Assn., N.Y.C., 1971-73, treas., 1972-73. Served to capt. USAF, 1958-61. Mem. No Load Mut. Fund Assn. (exec. com. 1971-73, treas. 1972-73). Episcopalian. Clubs: Church, Yale (N.Y.C.); Rumson (N.J.) Country; Seabright (N.J.) Lawn Tennis; Mid-Day (Chgo.). Home: 1214 Asbury Ave Winnetka IL 60093 Office: Penmark Investments Inc 222 N Dearborn St Chicago IL 60601

WEBSTER, MILDRED ESTHER, ret. educator; b. Webster, N.D., Oct. 16, 1908; d. David E. and Petra Gelena (Lenes) Webster; A.B., Jamestown Coll., 1929; M.A., U. N.D., 1936; postgrad. U. Chgo., summer, 1941, Middlebury Coll., Vt., 1947, (scholarship grantee) Linguistics Inst. Mich. State U., 1965. Tchr. English pub. high schs., Webster, N.D., 1929-31, Tolna, N.D., 1933-35, Clyde, N.D., 1936-38, Luther L. Wright High Sch., Ironwood, Mich., 1938-43; tchr., head dept. English St. Joseph (Mich.) High Sch., 1943-73; guest lectr. Mich. State U., Benton Harbor, 1962-63; instr. evening sch. Lake Mich. Coll., Benton Harbor, 1968-69; mem. exec. bd. of Midwest English Conf., 1952-74; curriculum cons. on English programs, 1968-73. Mem. Nat. (dir. 1946-70, mem. com. on publs. 1968-70, council), Mich. (Charles Carpenter Fries award 1976, Distinguished Service citation 1972, pres. 1950-51, exec. sec. 1964-69) councils of tchrs. English, NEA, Mich. Edn. Assn., Nat. Ret. Tchrs. Assn., Delta Kappa Gamma, AAUW. Mem. Congregational Ch. Contbg. author: Literature of the Americas, 1957; Teaching English: Reflections on the State of the Art, 1979; contbr. articles on teaching of English to profl. jours. Address: 3105 Kevin St Saint Joseph MI 49085

WEBSTER, RICHARD MELTON, state senator; b. Carthage, Mo., Apr. 29, 1922; s. Frank Summers and Christine (Melton) W.; J.D., U. Mo.; m. Janet Whitehead, July 3, 1948; children—Richard Melton, William Lawrence. Admitted to Mo. bar; individual practice law, Carthage and Joplin, Mo., 1948-81; ret., 1981; rep. Mo. Legislature, 1948-55, speaker of house, 1954; mem. Mo. State Senate, 1962—. Served with USCG, 1942-46, with USNR, 1946-76. Mem. Mo. Assn.

Trial Lawyers. Republican. Club: Masons. Office: Senate Post Office Jefferson City MO 65101*

WEDER, DONALD ERWIN, mfg. co. exec.; b. Highland, Ill., Aug. 18, 1947; s. Erwin Henry and Florence Louise (Graham) W.; student U. Ill., 1965-66; B.S. summa cum laude, Bradley U., 1969; m. Phyllis Ann Styron; children—Erwin Michael, Andrew Styron, David August. Pres. Highland Supply Corp. (Ill.), 1969—; exec. v.p. Highland Mfg. & Sales Co., 1970—, also dir.; dir. Seven W Enterprises, Highland Mfg. & Sales Corp. Served to capt., inf. AUS, 1969-71. Mem. Zeta Phi, Phi Kappa Phi. Republican. Kiwanian. Home: 1304 Washington St Highland IL 62249 Office: 1111 6th St Highland IL 62249

WEDER, ERWIN HENRY, corp. exec.; b. Highland, Ill., Dec. 13, 1904; s. August and Julia (Brunner) W.; student public schs.; m. Florence Louise (Graham), July 19, 1938; children—Mary Kay, Dona Lee, Donald Erwin, Wanda May, Janet Marie. Office work Highland Dairy Farms, 1923-25; detective Fla. East Coast Hotel Co., 1927-29; auto salesman, broker L.E. Anderson Co., 1930-32; salesman Metal Goods Corp., 1933-41; product devel., sales mgr., pres., Highland Supply Corp., 1941—; pres., sales and products mgr. Highland Products, Inc., 1948—; pres., sales and products mgr. Highland Mfg. Co., 1944—; mng. partner, sales and products mgr. Highland Mfg. & Sales Co., 1952—; pres. Weder Farms, Inc., 1950—, Quality Motors, Inc., 1946—; sr. partner Seven W. Enterprises, 1958—; owner, operator Six Bar X ranch, Jordan, Mont. Mem. St. Louis Media Club. Republican. Clubs: DX-5; Mo. Athletic; Capitol Hill; Masons. Home: 1304 Washington St Highland IL 62249 Office: 6th and Zschokke Sts Highland IL 62249

WEDGEWORTH, ROBERT, JR., assn. exec.; b. Ennis, Tex., July 31, 1937; s. Robert and Jimmie (Johnson) W.; A.B., Wabash Coll., 1959, Litt.D., 1980; M.S., U. Ill., 1961; Litt.D., Park Coll., 1973; m. Chung Kyun, July 28, 1972; 1 dau., Cicely Veronica. Cataloger, Kansas City Pub. Library, 1961-62; asst. librarian, acting librarian Park Coll., Parkville, Mo., 1962-64; librarian Meramec Community Coll., Kirkwood, Mo., 1964-66; acquisitions librarian Brown U. Library, 1966-69; asst. prof. Rutgers U., 1971-72; exec. dir. A.L.A., Chgo., 1972—. Mem. exec. com. Nat. Book Coms. Bd., Franklin Books Program; mem. Nat. Commn. on New Technol. Uses of Copyrighted Works, 1975-78; mem. biomed. library rev. com. Nat. Library Medicine, 1975-79; bd. visitors Air U., 1977; trustee Newberry Library. Council on Library Resources fellow, 1969. Mem. Am. Soc. Info. Sci., Am. Assn. for Advancement of Humanities (dir. 1979). Editor, Library Resources and Tech. Services, 1971-73, ALA Yearbook, 1976—, ALA World Ency., 1980. Office: 50 E Huron Chicago IL 60611

WEDMORE, JOYCE ANN HOLCOMB, journalist; b. Cromona, Ky., Feb. 12, 1941; d. Virgil and Nola Nora (Isabell) Holcomb; student public schs., Muncie, Ind.; m. Jack Edward Wedmore, Sept. 1, 1961; children—Tracy Allen, Bryan Logan. Producer spl. sects. Muncie (Ind.) Newspapers, Inc., 1969—. Adviser Jr. Achievement; bd. dirs., publicity chmn. Delaware County Hist. Festival; co-chmn. copywriting com. PBS-TV, 1979. Mem. Nat. Fedn. Press Women, Women in Communications, Woman's Press Club of Ind. (3d place award 1976, 80, 81, 1st pl. award 1977, 78, 80, 81, 2d pl. award 1980, 81). Home: 3812 S Ebright St Muncie IN 47302 Office: Muncie Newspapers Inc 125 S High St Muncie IN 47302

WEED, BYRON ELLSWORTH, II, real estate broker; b. Ann Arbor, Mich., June 18, 1938; s. Cecil Max and Hannah (Chappell) W.; B.S., Eastern Mich. U., 1961, M.A., 1963; children—Dalana S., Anissa E. Tchr. high sch. Dearborn Heights, Mich., 1961-63; partner Paige-Weed Realty, Ann Arbor, 1964-69; owner Weed Realty, Ann Arbor, 1969—; sales mgr. new home constrn. Guenther Bldg. Co., 1977-79, gen. sales mgr. for condominium devel., 1981—; dir. sales Candid Realty, Inc., 1979-80, Lectr., instr. U. Mich., Ann Arbor, 1968-80. Served with USNR, 1954-63. Mem. C. of C., Ann Arbor Bd. Realtors (dir., sec. 1973-74), Real Estate Securities and Syndication (dir. 1973), Real Estate Alumni Mich., Phi Sigma Epsilon. Author: Papermaking: A New Process, 1963. Home: 2817 Laurel Hill Ann Arbor MI 48103 Office: 1300 S Main St Ann Arbor MI 48103

WEED, EDWARD REILLY, mfg. co. exec.; b. Chgo., Jan. 25, 1940; s. Cornelius Cahill and Adelaide E. (Reilly) W.; student Fordham U., 1959-61, Loyola U., 1961-62; m. Lawrie Irving Bowes, Feb. 2, 1969. Account exec. Leo Burnett Co., Chgo., 1961-71; pres. GDC Ad Inc., Gen. Devel. Corp., Miami, Fla., 1971-74, corp. asst. v.p., 1971-74; v.p., account supr. D'Arcy Mac Manus & Masius, Chgo., 1975; group v.p. mktg. Hart Schaffner & Marx, Chgo., 1975—; dir. First Nat. Bank So. Miami. Trustee, Latin Sch. Found., 1976—; bd. dirs. North Ave. Day Nursery, 1969-73; pres. Northwestern Mil. and Naval Acad., 1972-74. Served with Ill. N.G. Republican. Roman Catholic. Club: Cliff Dwellers. Office: 101 N Wacker Dr Chicago IL 60606

WEED, MARY THEOPHILOS, psychologist, educator; b. Miami, Fla., Nov. 11, 1928; d. John George and Elizabeth Gundhill (Sodegren) Theophilos; A.B., U. Miami (Fla.), 1953; M.A., U. Chgo., 1960; m. Perry Lewis Weed, Mar. 29, 1963 (div.); 1 dau., Heather. Psychologist, Chgo. Bd. Edn., 1960-62; asst. prof. psychology Chgo. City Colls., Kennedy King Coll., 1962—; pvt. psychologist, Chgo. Cath. Sch. Bd., 1962—, Ill. Bd. Vocat. Rehab., 1969—. Registered psychologist, Ill., Nat. Register Health Service Providers in Psychology. Mem. Am., Ill. psychol. assns. Office: 1525 E 53d St Chicago IL 60615

WEEDON, RONALD RAY, botanist, educator; b. Caldwell, Idaho, May 16, 1939; s. Ralph A. and Mary G. (Stanley) W.; B.S., Coll. Idaho, Caldwell, 1964; M.A., U. Kans., Lawrence, 1969, Ph.D., 1973; postgrad. Idaho State U., 1963, Emporia State U., 1965-66; m. Barbara Kay Nixon, Oct. 4, 1975; 1 dau., Jessica Kay. Tchr. high schs., Euna, Idaho, 1961-62, Leadore, Idaho, 1962-65; grad. asst. Coll. Idaho, 1965-67; asst. instr. U. Kans., 1970, herbarium asst., 1971; vis. asst. prof. Coll. Idaho, 1970; mem. faculty dept. biology Chadron (Nebr.) State Coll., 1971—, asso. prof., 1976—, curator herbarium, 1971—. NDEA fellow, 1967-70. Mem. Internat. Soc. Plant Taxonomy, Am. Soc. Plant Taxonomists, Nebr. Acad. Scis., Greater Nebr. Assn. Tchrs. Sci., AAUP, Torrey Botanical Club, Calif. Botanical Club, Am. Fern Soc., Kans. Acad. Sci., Southwestern Assn. Naturalists, Great Plains Flora Assn., Am. Hort. Soc., Soc. Range Mgmt., Nebr. Statewide Arboretum. Presbyterian. Club: Elks. Contbr. articles to profl. jours. Home: 703 Mears St Chadron NE 69337 Office: Chadron State Coll Chadron NE 69337

WEEKS, MARY CATHERINE, librarian; b. Hampton, Iowa, Sept. 23, 1925; d. Uzziel William and Mary (O'Connor) Weeks; B.A., U. No. Iowa, 1946; M.A., U. Wis., 1952; postgrad. U. Iowa, Iowa State U., U. No. Iowa. Tchr., Britt, Iowa, 1946-48, Colfax, Ia., 1946-50; library asst. Mason City Pub. Library, 1950-51; sch. librarian Long Beach, Calif., 1952-53; reference librarian Kans. State U., 1953-56; library coordinator Iowa Falls Pub. Schs. and Ellsworth Coll., 1956-68, chief librarian Ellsworth Coll., 1956—. Mem. Dubuque Archdiocesan Pastoral Council. Mem. Am., Iowa library assns., Nat., Iowa edn. assns., Bread for the World, Ellsworth Coll. Faculty Assn., Delta Kappa Gamma, Kappa Delta Pi, Pi Gamma Mu. Democrat. Roman Catholic. Home: 116 Meadow Lane Iowa Falls IA 50126 Office: Ellsworth Coll Iowa Falls IA 50126

WEEKS, ROBERT EARL, advt. exec.; b. Yazoo City, Miss., Sept. 17, 1925; s. Dennis H. and Mamie O. (Randolph) W.; student Wilson Jr. Coll., 1947, Latin Am. Inst. Public Relations, 1950, DePaul U., 1952; children—Suzanne Lynn, Robin Denise, Linda, Robert Earl II, Lisa Ann. San. insp. Chgo. Bd. Health, 1965; asso. Pursell Public Relations, Chgo., 1950; br. mgr. King Records, Inc., Chgo., 1948; coordinator Task Force for Community Broadcasting, Chgo. Digest, 1969; pres. Troubadour & Assos., Ltd., Chgo., pub. Troubador Digest Mag., 1976; writer Cablecommunications Resource Center, Washington, 1972. Adminstrv. asst. to Alderman Robert H. Miller, 1966. Served with USAAF, 1944-46. Cert. in sickle cell anemia; registered sanitarian; recipient award Girl Scouts U.S.A. of Chgo.; Tenn. Squire. Mem. Publicity Club Chgo., South Side Community Art Center, Black Media Reps. (v.p. 1976), Hyde Park Improvement Assn. Democrat. Roman Catholic. Club: Clef Social. Author: Cable TV in Chicago, 1976. Home: 5325 S Cottage Grove Ave Chicago IL 60615 Office: 5540 South Shore Dr Suite 203 Chicago IL 60637

WEEKS, SOLAN W., museum curator; b. Detroit, Feb. 2, 1930; s. Otto William and Vera Wanda (Zeller) W.; B.A., Wayne State U., Detroit, 1953, M.Ed., 1960; m. Patricia Kathryn Dolby, May 28, 1954; children—Douglas William, Kathleen Marie, Cynthia Mae. Curator indsl. history Detroit Hist. Mus., 1955-60; dir. Mich. Hist. Mus., Lansing, 1960-66; asst. pres., asso. dir. devel. Old Sturbridge (Mass.) Village, 1967-70, also bd. overseers; dir. hist. dept. City of Detroit, also coordinating dir. Detroit Hist. Soc., 1970—; co-chmn. heritage com. Detroit Bicentennial Commn., 1974-76; treas. Detroit Adventure, 1973—; mem. Detroit Hist. Designation Adv. Bd. Trustee, Detroit Ednl. TV Fund. Mem. Am. Assn. Mus., Am. Assn. State and Local History, Nat. Trust Hist. Preservation, Hist. Soc. Mich. (v.p. 1974-76), Midwest Mus. Conf. (v.p. 1966, 71), Abraham Lincoln Civil War Round Table, Univ. Cultural Center Assn. (treas. 1977—), Gt. Lakes Maritime Inst., Vet. Motor Car Club Am., Assn. Study Afro Am. Life and History. Clubs: Rotary, Torch, Prismatic, Algonquin. Address: Detroit Hist Mus 5401 Woodward Ave Detroit MI 48202*

WEERTMAN, JOHANNES, physicist, educator; b. Fairfield Ala., May 11, 1925; s. Roelof and Christina (van Vlaardingen) W.; student Pa. State Coll., 1943-44; B.S., Carnegie Inst. Tech. (now Carnegie Mellon U.), 1948, D.Sc., 1951; postgrad. Ecole Normale Superieure, Paris, France, 1951-52; m. Julia Ann Randall, Feb. 10, 1950; children—Julia Ann, Bruce Randall. Solid State physicist U.S. Naval Research Lab., Washington, 1952-58, cons., 1960-67; sci. liaison officer U.S. Office Naval Research, Am. Embassy, London, Eng., 1958-59; faculty Northwestern U., Evanston, Ill., 1959—, prof. materials sci. dept., 1961-68, chmn. dept., 1964-68, prof. geol. scis. dept., 1963—, Walter P. Murphy prof. materials sci., 1968—; vis. prof. geophysics Calif. Inst. Tech., 1964, Scott Polar Research Inst., Cambridge (Eng.) U., 1970-71. Cons. U.S. Army Cold Regions Research and Engring. Lab., 1960-75, Oak Ridge Nat. Lab., 1963-67, Los Alamos Sci. Lab., 1967—; co-editor materials sci. books MacMillan Co., 1962-76. Served with USMC, 1943-46. Honored with naming of Weertman Island in Antarctica; recipient Acta Metallurgica Gold medal, 1980. Fulbright fellow, 1951-52; Guggenheim fellow, 1970-71. Fellow Am. Soc. Metals, Am. Phys. Soc., Geol. Soc. Am.; mem. Nat. Acad. Engring., Am. Geophys. Union (Horton award 1962), Am. Inst. Mining, Metall. and Petroleum Engrs. (Mathewson gold medal 1977), Am. Inst. Physics, Internat. Glaciological Soc., AAAS, Arctic Inst., Am. Quaternary Assn., Explorers Club, Sigma Xi, Tau Beta Pi, Phi Kappa Phi, Alpha Sigma Mu, Pi Mu Epsilon. Club: Evanston Running. Author: (with wife) Elementary Dislocation Theory, 1964. Editorial bd. Metal. Trans., 1967-75, Jour. Glaciology, 1972—; Co-editor jour. Mechanics of Materials, 1980—. Contbr. articles to profl. jours. Home: 834 Lincoln St Evanston IL 60201

WEFALD, ROBERT OVROM, lawyer, state ofcl.; b. Excelsior, Minn., July 18, 1942; s. Olav and Walma Jorgine (Ovrom) W.; B.A., U. N.D., 1964; J.D., U. Mich., 1970; m. Susan Elizabeth Benschop, June 21, 1969; children—Sarah Anne, Kathryn Mary, Thomas Olav. Admitted to N.D. bar, 1970; law clk. N.D. Supreme Ct., Bismarck, 1970-71; practiced in Bismarck, 1971-80; mem. firm Wheeler, Wolf, Wefald, Peterson & McDonald, P.C., 1973-80; atty. gen. State of N.D., Bismarck, 1981—. Served with USN, 1964-67; comdr. Res. Mem. Am. Bar Assn., Nat. Assn. Attys. Gen., Am. Legion, VFW, Sons of Norway. Lutheran. Office: State Capitol Bismarck ND 58505

WEGENER, MYRTON O., state senator; b. Woodside Twp., Minn., Nov. 7, 1917; ed. public schs.; m. Hazel Ludtke. Farmer, until 1957; chmn. Bertha Coop. Creamery; mem. Minn. Senate, 1970—. Mem. Bertha (Minn.) Fire Dept.; former mayor, Bertha. Mem. Democratic-Farmer-Labor party. Lutheran. Clubs: Lions, Comml. Office: 328 State Capitol St Paul MN 55155*

WEGMAN, JOSEPH FRANCIS, constrn. co. exec.; b. Cin., Sept. 12, 1942; s. Joseph Francis and Mary Louise (Godar) W.; student Xavier U., 1961, Ohio Coll., 1963-64; m. Sallie Ann Ruff, Oct. 2, 1965; children—Timothy Scott, Melissa Sue, Jennifer Lynn, Kristina Marie. Owner, mgr. Joseph F. Wegman Remodeling, Cin.; now owner, mgr., pres. Wegman Constrn. Co., Inc., Cin. Mem. Asso. Gen. Contractors. Republican. Roman Catholic. Home: 2500 Warsaw St Cincinnati OH 45204 Office: Wegman Construction Co Inc 2725 Falconbridge Cincinnati OH 45238

WEGMAN, MYRON EZRA, health orgn. cons., ret. physician, educator; b. Bklyn., July 23, 1908; s. Max and Nettie (Finkelstein) W.; B.A., CCNY, 1928; M.D., Yale U., 1932; M.P.H., Johns Hopkins U., 1938; m. Isabel Howe, July 4, 1936; children—Judith Wegman Hirst, David Howe, Jane Wegman Dunatchik, Elizabeth Gooding Wegman Petersen. Intern, New Haven Hosp., 1932-33, resident in pediatrics, 1933-36; mem. jr. faculty Yale Med. Sch., 1933-36; pediatric cons. Md. Health Dept., 1936-41; asst. prof. Sch. Tropical Medicine, U. P.R., San Juan, 1941-42; dir. research and tng. N.Y.C. Health Dept., 1942-46; part time faculty mem. Cornell U., Columbia U., Johns Hopkins U., 1939-46; dept. head pediatrics La. State U., 1946-52; dir. edn. and tng. Pan Am. Health Orgn., Washington, 1952-56, sec.-gen., 1957-60; dean Sch. Public Health, U. Mich., Ann Arbor, 1960-74, prof. pediatrics, 1960-78, dean emeritus, prof. emeritus, 1978—; cons. Pan Am. Health Orgn., 1960—, chmn. program com. Pan Am. Health and Edn. Found.; chmn. Comprehensive Health Planning Council S.E. Mich., 1969-74, chmn. bed reduction commn., 1978-80. Recipient Clifford Grulee medal Am. Acad. Pediatrics, 1958; Townsend Harris medal CCNY, 1961; Bronfman prize Am. Public Health Assn., 1967, Sedgwick medal, 1974; Walter Reuther medal UAW, 1974; Disting. Alumnus award Johns Hopkins U. Sch. Hygiene, 1982; elected to Soc. Scholars, Johns Hopkins U., 1975. Fellow Royal Soc. Health (hon.); mem. Am. Pediatric Soc., Soc. Pediatric Research, Am. Assn. World Health (pres. 1982—), Am. Public Health Assn., Sigma Xi, Alpha Omega Alpha, Delta Omega, Phi Kappa Phi. Club: Cosmos (Washington). Editor: Public Health in the People's Republic of China, 1973; contbr. chpts. to books, articles to profl. jours. Office: Sch Public Health Univ of Mich Ann Arbor MI 48109

WEGNER, PATRICIA ANN MALO, genealogist; b. Fairmont, Minn., Feb. 20, 1947; d. Marvin Henry and Betty Jean (Wedoo) Malo; student public schs., Fairmont, 1951-65; m. Dallas J. Wegner, Apr. 8, 1967; children—Wendy Ann, Becky Lynn, Kathy Jean. Nurse's aide Lakeview Home for Elderly, Fairmont, 1972-73; geneal. researcher, 1976—. Leader Girl Scouts U.S.A., 1974-75; tchr. Sunday sch., 1976-77. Mem. Minn. Geneal. Soc., New Eng. Geneal. Soc., Nat. Trust for Hist. Preservation, Sons of Norway. Democrat. Lutheran. Home and Office: 1528 Albion St Fairmont MN 56031

WEHKING, DIANE, real estate asso.; b. Minonk, Ill., Feb. 13, 1939; d. Delbert W. and Sophia (Chromchak) Stokowski; real estate salesman's lic., Midstate Coll., 1974; broker's lic. Bradley U., 1977; m. Wesley P. Wehking, Dec. 16, 1956; children—Mark, Cindy, Colette, Carol, Mike, Cristin. Salesman, Home Realty, Morton, Ill., 1974-77; real estate sales asso. Owen Phillips & Assos., Morton, 1977-81; real estate instr. Lincoln Nat. Realty, Ill. Central Coll., East Peoria. Grad. Real Estate Inst.; cert. residential specialist. Mem. Million Dollar Club (life), Realtors Nat. Mktg. Inst., Ill. Assn. Realtors, (President's Club), Peoria Bd. Realtors, Morton C. of C. Roman Catholic. Home: 433 Fern Wood Morton IL 61550

WEHRMACHER, WILLIAM HENRY, cardiologist; b. Waterloo, Iowa, May 17, 1921; s. William H. and Lulu Ella (Wahlmann) W.; student Wartburg Coll., 1939-41; B.A., State U. Iowa, 1943, M.D., 1945; m. Berdella Larsen; children—William, James, Karen, John, Charles. Intern, U.S. Naval Hosp., Norfolk, Va., 1946; resident VA Hosp. and Wayne U. Med. Sch., Detroit, 1948-50; practice medicine specializing in cardiology, 1950—; instr. Wayne U., 1948-50, State U. Iowa, 1950-51; asso. in medicine Northwestern U., 1951-71; clin. prof. medicine Loyola U., Chgo., 1971—, adj. prof. physiology, 1975—; mem. staffs Loyola, Columbus, St. Joseph hosps., Chgo., Skokie Valley Hosp. Served to lt. comdr. M.C., USN, 1942-44. Diplomate Am. Bd. Internal Medicine. Fellow A.C.P., Am. Coll. Cardiology; mem. Am. Fedn. Clin. Research, AMA, Am. Med. Soc. Vienna, Chgo. Med. Soc., Chgo. Soc. Internal Medcine, Ill. Med. Soc., Inst. Medicine Chgo., Pan Am. Med. Assn., Soc. Med. History in Chgo., Alpha Kappa Kappa, Alpha Omega Alpha, Sigma Xi. Lutheran. Contbr. articles and chpts. to med. jours. and texts. Home: 5706 Capulina Morton Grove IL 60053 Office: 670 N Michigan Ave Chicago IL 60611

WEICHBRODT, JOANNE, bldg. products corp. exec.; b. Berkeley, Calif., Sept. 11, 1937; d. William Ellis and Carol (Brown) Wharton; student Fresno State U., 1957-59; B.A., DePaul U., 1981; m. Henry D. Weichbrodt, June 29, 1980. With Masonite Corp., Chgo., 1969—, salary adminstr., 1974-76, mgr. salary adminstrn., 1976-81, personnel mgr., 1981—; condr. tng. and devel. workshops, career planning, counseling, 1979—. Mem. Am. Compensation Assn., Am. Soc. for Personnel Adminstrn., Exec. Female Assn., Beta Sigma Phi. Club: Eastern Star. Home: 5858 Byron Ave Chicago IL 60634 Office: Masonite Corp 29 N Wacker Dr Chicago IL 60606

WEICKER, JACK EDWARD, educator; b. Woodburn, Ind., June 23, 1924; s. Monald Henry and Helen Mae (Miller) W.; A.B., Ind. U., 1947, M.A. (James Albert Woodburn fellow, All-Univ. fellow), 1951; m. Janet Kathryn Thompson, May 29, 1946; children—John H., Kathryn Ann, Jane Elizabeth, Emily Jo. Tchr. history and English, Harrison Hill Sch., Ft. Wayne, Ind., 1947-48, South Side High Sch., Ft. Wayne, 1951-61; counselor, asst. prin. South Side High Sch., 1961-63, prin., 1963—. Mem. Ind. State Scholarship Commn., 1969-77; mem. exec. com. Midwest regional assembly Coll. Entrance Exam. Bd., 1974-77, chmn. nominating com., 1976-77, mem. nat. nominating com., 1979—. Recipient award for meritorious service Ball State U., 1980; Outstanding Prin. of Yr. award Ind. Secondary Sch. Adminstrs. Assn., 1981. Mem. Ft. Wayne Prins. Assn., Nat. Assn. Secondary Sch. Prins., Ind. Assn. Jr. and Sr. High Sch. Prins., PTA (life), Phi Beta Kappa, Phi Delta Kappa, Phi Alpha Theta. Mem. Disciples of Christ Ch. (moderator of bd. trustees 1975-79). Clubs: Ft. Wayne Rotary (bd. dirs. 1973-76, 79—, pres.-elect 1981-82, pres. 1982-83), Quest (dir. 1979-81), Fortnightly (Ft. Wayne). Author: (with others) Indiana: The Hoosier State, 1959, 63; Due Process and Students Rights/Responsibilities: Two Points of View, 1975; Back to Basics: Language Arts, 1976; College Entrance Exams—Friend or Foe?, 1981. Home: 5200 N Washington Rd Fort Wayne IN 46804 Office: 3601 S Calhoun St Fort Wayne IN 46807

WEIDENHOFER, NEAL, computer co. exec.; b. Chgo., June 18, 1940; s. William Joseph and Pearl Martha (Miller) W.; B.S., U. N.Mex., 1964, M.A., 1965; M.A., Dartmouth Coll., 1967, Ph.D., 1968; children from previous marriage—Mark Raymond, Lisa Marie. Research asst. prof. U. Ill., Urbana, 1968-69; with United Computing Systems, Inc., Kansas City, Mo., 1969—, sr. systems specialist, 1974-79, systems staff cons., 1979-80, mgr. advanced systems dept., 1981—. NASA trainee, 1965-68. Mem. Assn. Computing Machinery, Sigma Xi. Home: 3635 Walnut St 106 Kansas City MO 64111 Office: 2525 Washington St Kansas City MO 64108

WEIGAND, GEORGE ROBERT, internat. trade exec.; b. Wittenberge, Germany, June 16, 1928; s. Kurt Aenderly and Eleonore W.; Canadian citizen; student Bismarck Coll., Germany, 1946-53; diploma bus. mgmt. Centre d'Etudes Industrielles, Geneva, Switzerland, 1964; m. Margarete Bannuscher, Nov. 1, 1955; 1 son, Benjamin. With Plasser Am., Chesapeake, Va., 1964-67; exec. v.p. Ramco/Nationwide Industries, Evanston, Ill., 1967-70; pres. Fedesco, Chgo., 1971—; pres. Lukas American, Inc., Downers Grove, Ill., 1971—; cons. Welt Internat., Frieseke & Hoepfner, W. Germany, Metallwerk Boxdorf, W. Germany. Mem. Am. Railway Engring. Assn., Am. Transit Assn. Home: 353 Huntington Way Bolingbrook IL 60439 Office: 5201 Thatcher Rd Downers Grove IL 60515

WEIGEL, JOHN WILLIAM, urologist; b. Manhattan, Kans., Jan. 15, 1929; s. Paul and Martha Marie (Coons) W.; student U. Kans., 1946-49; B.S., Kans. State U., 1950, M.D., 1954; m. Mary Lou Van Blarcum, Aug. 10, 1953; children—Vicki Sue, John Randall, Teresa Jane. Intern St. Mary's Hosp., Kansas City, Mo., 1954-55; resident in radiology Fitzsimons Army Med. Center, Denver, 1957-58, asst. chief, urology, Fitzsimons Gen. Hosp., 1971-72, chief, urology, 1972-75; resident in gen. surgery DeWitt Army Hosp., Ft. Belvoir, Va., 1961-62; resident in urology Brook Gen. Hosp., San Antonio, Tex., 1962-65; asst. clin. prof. urology, U. Colo., Denver, 1972-75; asso. prof. urology U. Kans., Kansas City, 1975—; chief sect. urology VA Hosp., Kansas City, Mo., 1975-76; practice medicine specializing in urology, Kansas City, Kans., 1975—. Summerfield scholar, 1946. Served with M.C., U.S. Army, 1956-75. Diplomate Am. Bd. Urology. Mem. Am. Urol. Assn., A.C.S., AMA, Assn. Mil. Surgeons, Rocky Mountain Urol. Soc., Western Trauma Assn., Soc. Univ. Urologists, Kansas City Urol. Soc., Beta Theta Pi, Nu Sigma Nu. Decorated Meritorious Service Medal, Order Golden Nephros, Legion of Merit. Contbr. articles to profl. publs. Republican. Presbyterian. Home: 565 Mohawk Lake Quivira Kansas City KS 66106 Office: 39th and Rainbow Blvd Kansas City KS 66103

WEIGEL, PAUL, architect; b. N.Y.C., Aug. 5, 1889; s. Friederich Wilhelm and Wilhelmine (Mueller) W.; B.Arch. (scholar), Cornell U., 1912; m. Martha Marie Coons, June 6, 1926; children—John William, Paul David. Mem. faculty Sch. Architecture, Kans. State U., prof.

emeritus, 1954, head Sch. Architecture, 1924-54; past pres. Collegiate Schs. Architecture; cons. archtl adviser in planning Ataturk U., Turkey, 1957-59; archtl. design staff Panama Canal, 1913-17. Past mem. Manhattan (Kans.) Planning Bd. Served as lt. F.A., U.S. Army, World War I. Hon. fellow emeritus AIA. Presbyterian. Home: 8110 Sagamore Rd Leawood KS 66206

WEIGEL, ROBERT LEWIS, JR., printing co. exec.; b. St. Louis, Sept. 7, 1944; s. Robert Lewis and Georgene Nancy (Walbancke) W.; student St. Petersburg Jr. Coll., 1963-64; m. Mary Ann Davis, Nov. 4, 1967; children—John Christopher, Debra Lynn. Sec.-treas. Creative Interiors, Clearwater, Fla., 1967-69; office mgr. Consol. Hotel Equipment, Clearwater, 1969; store mgr. Am. Nat. Stores, St. Louis, 1970-72; sec.-treas. Weigel Screen Process, Eureka, Mo., 1972-76, pres., 1976—. Served with U.S. Army, 1964-66. Mem. Nat. Space Inst., Screen Printing Assn., Eureka C. of C. (dir.). Episcopalian. Home: PO Box 307 Marthasville MO 63357 Office: 141 S Central Eureka MO 63025

WEIKEL, FRANK KENNETH, metal co. exec.; b. Washington, Mar. 29, 1928; s. Frank and Marjorie (Eisle) W.; B.A., U. Louisville, 1950; m. Carolyn Anderson, Sept. 7, 1951; children—Andrew, Lynne, Steven, Sandra. Asst. mgr. personnel and indsl relations Philip Morris Inc., Louisville, 1965-69; mgr. indsl. relations Peter Eckrich Co., Fremont, Ohio, 1969-72, Bradford-White Corp., Middleville, Mich., 1972-75; v.p. indsl. relations Cast Metal Industries, Cadillac, Mich., 1975—. Served to sgt. U.S. Army, 1950-52. Mem. Cadillac Area Personnel Assn. (founder, pres. 1978—), Hastings Personnel Assn. (pres. 1974), Cadillac C. of C. (dir. 1978-79, pres. 1980-81), Cadillac Area Mfrs. Assn. (sec. 1977, treas. 1978), Am. Soc. Personnel Adminstrn. (dist. rep. No. Mich. 1980-81), Nat. Safety Mgmt. Soc., Indsl. Relations Research Assn., Nat. Foundry Assn., Am. Foundrymen's Soc. Club: Toastmasters (pres. Fremont 1970—). Home: 521 Stimson St Cadillac MI 49601 Office: Cast Metal Industries 230 10th St PO Box 40 Cadillac MI 49601

WEIKER, OSCAR JAMES, former mayor, farmer; b. Republic, Ohio, Nov. 14, 1893; s. Levi and Jane (Schoerger) W.; student Ohio State U., 1914-18; m. Norma Mae Hoppes, June 18, 1919; children—James, Adda Jane, Joan, Eloise. Mgr., U.S. Commn. Upper Sandusky, 1923-37; field rep. Keystone Steel Wire Co., No. Ohio, 1937-63; farmer, 1973—; dir. Elevator Mut. Ins. Assn., 1938-72, pres., 1958-72; incorporator Ohio Farmers Grain Assn., Fostoria, Ohio, 1933, dir., 1937-52. Treas. United Church Home, Upper Sandusky, 1938-64; mayor, Upper Sandusky, 1968-75; pres. Wyandot Sr. Citizens Inc., Wyandot Sr. Village Bldg., 1981. mem. com. merger Evang. and Ref. Ch. and Congregational Ch. in Ohio; mem. com. forming N.W. Assn. United Ch. of Christ in Ohio, moderator N.W. Ohio assn., 1968, del. gen. synod, 1961, 63, 65. Named Pioneer Cooperator Ohio, 1975; recipient Outstanding Sr. Citizen Wyandot County award, 1980, Outstanding Sr. Citizen Upper Sandusky, 1981. Mem. Ohio Grain and Feed Dealer Assn. (past pres.). Mem. United Ch. Christ. Republican. Clubs: Rotary, Masons (32 deg.), Shrine, Elks. Home: 361 W Johnson St Upper Sandusky OH 43351

WEIL, LUIS GARFIUS, JR., plastics co. exec.; b. Winchester, Mass., July 4, 1938; s. Luis G. and Marjorie (Bean) W.; A.B., Bowdoin Coll., 1960; m. Jean Andrea Wallace, Nov. 29, 1959; children—Luis Garfius, III, Jennifer C., Jeffrey W. Sales rep. Am. Cyanamid Co., Indpls., 1963-67, dist. mgr., Detroit, 1967-69; regional sales mgr. Plaskolite, Inc., Columbus, Ohio, 1969-74, v.p. sales, 1974-77, v.p. mktg., 1977—. Industry group chmn. Columbus United Way, 1978; elder Worthington (Ohio) Presbyterian Ch. Served to 1st lt. USMC, 1960-63. Mem. Soc. Plastics Engrs. Office: 1770 Joyce Ave Columbus OH 43219

WEIL, MAX HARRY, physician, educator; b. Baden, Switzerland, Feb. 9, 1927; A.B., U. Mich., 1948; M.D., SUNY, 1952; Ph.D., U. Minn., 1957; m. Marianne Posner, Apr. 9, 1955; children—Susan Margot, Carol Juliet. Intern, 1952-53; resident, 1953-57; chief cardiology City of Hope Med. Center, Duarte, Calif., 1957-59; mem. faculty U. So. Calif. Sch. Medicine, Los Angeles, 1959-81, prof. clin. medicine, 1971-81, prof. clin. biomed. engring., 1972-81, chmn. div. critical care medicine, 1978-81, dir. Inst. Critical Care Medicine, 1974-81; dir. U. So. Calif. Shock Research Unit, 1961-81; sr. attending cardiologist shock research unit, children's div. Los Angeles County Med. Center, 1968-73; cons. physician med. staff Cedars-Sinai Med Center, Los Angeles, 1965-81; dir. U. So. Calif. Center for Critically Ill, Hollywood Presbyn. Med. Center, Los Angeles, 1968-80; prof. medicine Chgo. Med. Sch., U. Health Scis., North Chicago, Ill., 1982—, chmn. dept., 1982—; cons. in acute medicine, physiology, pharmacology and clin. engring. to govt. and industry; mem. Nat. Acad. Sci. Found.; mem. expert adv. panel WHO; chmn. Los Angeles County Commn. on Emergency Med. Care, 1968-73. Bd. dirs. Los Angeles affiliate Am. Heart Assn., 1962-67. Served with U.S. Army, 1946-47. Diplomate Am. Bd. Internal Medicine, Nat. Bd. Med. Examiners. Fellow Am. Coll. Cardiology (chmn. emergency cardiac care com. 1978—), A.C.P.; mem. AMA (Commn. on Emergency Med. Services 1979—), Am. Soc. Pharmacology and Exptl. Therapeutics, Am. Soc. Nephrology, Am. Thoracic Soc., Am. Physiol. Soc., Am. Fedn. Clin. Research, Western Soc. Clin. Research, Soc. Critical Care Medicine (pres. 1970-72), Am. Trauma Soc. (founding mem.), IEEE (sr.), AAUP, Sigma Xi, Alpha Omega Alpha. Co-editor: Diagnosis and Treatment of Shock, 1967; Critical Care Medicine Handbook, 1974; Critical Care Medicine: Current Principles and Practices, 1976; Handbook of Critical Care Medicine, 1978; Manual of Critical Care Medicine, 1978; The Handbook of Critical Care Medicine, 1979; mem. editorial bd. Am. Medicine, 1971-79, Chest, Circulatory Shock, Clin. Engring. Newsletter; contbr. over 400 articles to profl. jours. Office: Dept Medicine U Health Scis/Chgo Med Sch North Chicago IL 60064

WEIL, OSCAR ARNOLD, union exec.; b. Belleville, Ill., Aug. 13, 1925; s. Oscar and Clara (Perschbacher) W.; B.A., McKendree Coll., 1955; M.A., Washington U., 1960; m. Martha Jane Wylie, Mar. 29, 1956; children—Kent Allyn, Laura May. Farmer, Lebanon, Ill., 1941-44; tchr., Roxana (Ill.) High Sch., 1955-63, Bellville Area Coll., 1961-63; mem. exec. bd. Southwestern area council Ill. Fedn. Tchrs., Springfield, 1959-63, exec. dir., 1963-75, legislative dir., 1975—; chmn. com. state fedn. officers Am. Fedn. Tchrs., 1964-66, pres. Union Tchr. Press Assn., 1967-75; mem. Gov's. Commn. on Labor-Mgmt. Relations, 1966-67; mem. Com. on Reorgn., Ill. Office Edn., 1975; mem. Task Force on Edn. Personnel Devel. Served with U.S. Army, 1944-47, 50-52; PTO. Recipient Gen. Excellence award Union Tchr. Press Assn., 1967-68, 71-75, Award of Merit, Internat. Labor Press Assn., 1967, 73. Mem. Am. Fedn. Tchrs., Fund for the Republic. Methodist. Editor, Ill. Union Tchr., 1963-75, Capitol News Roundup, 1963—; contbr. articles to profl. jours. Home: 500 S Walnut St Rochester IL 62563 Office: 914 E Capitol St Springfield IL 62701

WEILAND, STEVEN EDWARD, EDP auditor; b. Chgo., Feb. 27, 1947; s. Jack Nathan and Adeline (Roseburg) W.; B.S. in Mktg., No. Ill. U., 1969; postgrad. Am. U., 1970-71; M.B.A., No. Ill. U., 1972; m. Pamela Ruth Wolin, Aug. 12, 1973; children—Karyn Eileen, Lisa Doreen. Computer cons., mgr. computer services dept. No. Ill. U., DeKalb, 1972-78, instr. bus. edn. and adminstrv. services dept., 1976-78; sr. EDP auditor, auditing dept. Fed. Res. Bank of Chgo., 1978—; mem. faculty Center for Auditor Devel., Fed. Res. System, Atlanta, 1980—; adj. faculty Center for Bus. and Econs., Elmhurst (Ill.) Coll., 1979—; lectr. in field. Served with U.S. Army, 1969-71. Mem. EDP Auditors Assn. (treas. Chgo. chpt.), Ill. Assn. for Ednl. Data Systems. Democrat. Jewish. Home: 9493 N Terrace Pl Des Plaines IL 60016 Office: Fed Res Bank Chgo 230 S LaSalle St Chicago IL 60690

WEIMER, RITA J., educator; b. Boricourt, Kans., Aug. 25, 1933; B.S. in English and Bus., Kans. State Coll., 1956; M.S. in Reading, Curriculum and Instrn., U. Kans., 1964, Ed.D. in Curriculum and Instrn., 1974; m. Robert J. Weimer; children—Robyn, Scott, Wayne, Sandra, Jody, Laura. Instr. Army Edn. Center, Germany, 1956-58; tchr. Washburn Rural High Sch., Topeka, Kans., 1960-66; instr. edn. Kans. State U., Manhattan, 1966-74, asst. prof. edn., 1974—. Mem. AAUP, Internat. Reading Assn., Phi Delta Kappa. Office: Kansas State Univ Coll Edn Manhattan KS 66506

WEINBAUM, BARBARA HYMAN, psychologist; b. Balt., Dec. 23, 1925; d. Emanuel A. and Beatrice (Schwartzman) Hyman; A.B., Goucher Coll., 1946; M.S., Ind. State U., 1972, Ph.D., 1976; m. Jack Gerald Weinbaum, June 16, 1946; children—Marc Eliot, Betty Susan. Med. technologist Terre Haute (Ind.) Med. Lab., 1957-69; instr. psychology Ind. State U., 1972-73, asst. prof., 1973; counselor-cons. Vigo County Sch. Corp., Terre Haute, 1974-75; counselor Student Counseling Center, Ind. State U., Terre Haute, 1975-76; program dir. continuing edn. Katherine Hamilton Mental Health Center, Terre Haute, 1976-77, co-ordinator adult/aging services, 1977-80; pvt. practice clin. psychology and mgmt. cons., 1980—. Founder, pres. Vol. Tutors, Vigo County Sch. Corp., 1965-69; v.p. Nat. Sch. Vol. Program, 1969-71; bd. dirs. Friends of Cunningham Meml. Library, Ind. State U., 1976-80, co-chmn., 1976-77; bd. dirs. Vigo County Mental Health Assn., 1970—, Terre Haute Symphony Bd., Planned Parenthood, 1980—, YWCA, 1981—; bd. dirs. United Hebrew Congregation, 1978—, v.p., 1980—. Cert. biofeedback profl. Mem. Am. Assn. Behavior Therapy, Am. Psychol. Assn., Ind. Biofeedback Soc., ACLU, Ind. Civil Liberties Union (dir. 1976-79), Women's Polit. Caucus (dir. 1977-79), LWV, NOW, NAACP. Jewish. Home and office: 2705 Oak St Terre Haute IN 47803

WEINBERG, ARTHUR, journalist; b. Chgo., Dec. 8, 1915; s. Abraham Morris and Anna (Avedon) W.; A.A., YMCA Coll., Chgo., 1935; diploma journalism Northwestern U., 1938, Ph.B., 1941; m. Lila Shaffer, Jan. 25, 1953; children—Hedy Merrill, Anita Michelle, Wendy Clare. With Hart Schaffner & Marx, Chgo., 1935-39; researcher Ill. Writers Project, Chgo., 1939-41; tech. writer Consol. Aircraft Corp., San Diego, 1941-45; editor Ft. Lewis (Wash.) Flame, 1946; reporter Fairchild Publs., Chgo., 1947—; Midwest bureau chief HFD, 1977-81; Midwest editor Mart, 1981—; lectr. downtown coll. U. Chgo., 1957; moderator radio discussion program Sound-Off, Sta. WXFM, Chgo., 1961; book reviewer Chgo. Daily News, 1962-76, Chgo. Sunday Tribune, 1976—, Women's Wear Daily, Los Angeles Times; faculty Sch. for New Learning, DePaul U., Chgo. Organizer nat. Clarence Darrow Centennial Celebration, 1957, exec. chmn., 1957; chmn. Clarence Darrow Commemorative Com., 1958—; v.p. Clarence Darrow Community Center, Chgo., 1962-64; bd. dirs. Adult Edn. Council Greater Chgo., 1959—, chmn. letters and drama assembly, 1964—. Recipient Chgo. Found. of Lit. award Friends of Lit. Mem. Soc. Midland Authors (pres. 1967-69, award 1981), ACLU, Sigma Delta Chi, Press Club, Headline Club (dir.). Editor: Attorney for the Damned, 1957; (with wife) Lila: The Muckrakers, 1961, Verdicts out of Court, 1963, Instead of Violence, 1963; Passport to Utopia, 1968; Some Dissenting Voices, 1970; Clarence Darrow: Sentimental Rebel, 1980. Home: 5421 Cornell Ave Chicago IL 60615

WEINBERG, MICHAEL NEIL, pathologist; b. Dallas, June 15, 1948; s. Jack and Julia (Pickoff) W.; A.B. magna cum laude, Washington U., St. Louis, 1970; M.D., U. Tex. Southwestern Med. Sch., Dallas, 1974; m. Judy Carolyn Norris Kindinger, Apr. 4, 1976; 1 dau., Jaclyn Whitney. Intern, Parkland Meml. Hosp., Dallas, 1974-75, resident in pathology, 1975-78; asst. prof. pathology U. Tex. Health Sci. Center, Dallas, 1978-80; staff pathologist Parkland Meml. Hosp., Dallas VA Hosp., 1978-80; pathologist Good Samaritan Hosp., Dayton, Ohio, 1980—. Diplomate Am. Bd. Pathology. Mem. AMA, Ohio Med. Assn., Montgomery County Med. Soc., Am. Soc. Clin. Pathologists, Coll. Am. Pathologists, Internat. Acad. Pathology, Buckeye Soc. Cytology, Zionist Orgn. Am., Phi Beta Kappa, Phi Delta Epsilon, Theta Xi. Office: Dept Lab Medicine Good Samaritan Hosp and Health Center 2222 Philadelphia Dr Dayton OH 45406

WEINE, FRANKLIN SCOTT, dentist; b. Chgo., Mar. 5, 1934; s. Herman and Bertha (Levy) W.; B.S., U. Ill., 1953, D.D.S., 1957; M.S.D., Ind. U., 1966; m. Dorothy Ann Strofs, July 7, 1957; children—Perry N., Kenneth M., Allan D. Gen. practice dentistry, Dolton, Ill., 1959-64, ltd. to endodontics, Chgo., 1966—; prof. Ind. U., also prof. Loyola U., 1970—; dir. endodontics Michael Reese Hosp.; minority owner Chgo. White Sox Baseball Club. Served with USNR, 1957-59. Diplomate Am. Bd. Endodontics. Fellow Am. Coll. Dentists, Internat. Coll. Dentists, Am. Coll. Stomatological Surgeons (pres. 1978); mem. E.D. Coolidge (pres. 1972), H.J. Healey (pres. 1971) endodontic study clubs, Odontographic Soc. Chgo. (treas. 1972-78). Author: Endodontic Therapy, 1972, 3d edit., 1981. Home: 20737 Alexander St Olympia Fields IL 60461 Office: 30 N Michigan Ave Chicago IL 60602

WEINER, EGON, sculptor, educator; b. Vienna, Austria, July 24, 1906; s. Moritz and Elsa (Fischer) W.; student Sch. Arts and Crafts, also Acad. Fine Arts (Vienna); m. Margaret Bass, Nov. 19, 1939; children—Peter, Andrew. Came to U.S., 1938, naturalized, 1944. Prof. sculpture and life drawing Art Inst. Chgo., 1945-71, prof. emeritus, 1971—; vis. prof. art Augustana Coll., 1956-71; exhibited one-man shows Art Inst. Chgo., Renaissance Soc. U. Chgo., Chgo. Pub. Library, Ill. Inst. Tech., U. Ill., Evanston Art Center, Augustana Coll., Kunstneres Hus, Oslo, 1973, 75, 76, Am. Embassy, Oslo, 1974, 75, Am. Center, Stockholm, 1974, Hamburg, Germany, 1977, others; group exhibits Art Inst. Chgo., Pa. Acad. Fine Arts, Oakland Art Gallery, Syracuse Mus. Art, Portland (Oreg.) Art Mus., Asso. Am. Artists Gallery, Chgo., Met. Mus. Art, others; represented permanent collections Syracuse Mus. Fine Arts, Augusburg Coll., Mpls., Augustana Coll., Vatican, pvt. collections; works include Monument of Brotherhood, Chgo., Figure of Christ, Luth. Ch., U. Chgo., Prodigal Son at Salem Ch., Chgo., Monument of St. Paul, Luth. Ch. in Mt. Prospect, Ill., portrait bust Otto Behnke, Midway Airport, Chgo., Senator William Benton for Ency. Brit., Dr. Eric Oldberg for Ill. Research Hosp., Willy Brandt for Harvard U., 1972, Ernest Hemingway for Oak Park (Ill.) Library, 1974; monument for Fire Acad. in Chgo., 1961 (AIA Honor award, 1962), Burning Bush of Knowledge, Gary (Ind.) Library, 1966; bronze figure Am. Ch., Oslo, Norway, 1967, Polyphony, St. Joseph Hosp., Chgo., 1972, portrait bust of Henry Kissinger, 1977, portrait head of dau. of Am. ambassador to Norway, 1977; bronze head of former minister of labor Charles Gibson, 1981; others; lectr. modern art in Am. Recipient Grand Prix, Paris, 1925; Blumfeld award, Vienna, 1932-34; Municipal Art League prize, 1948, 69; Logan prize Art Inst. Chgo.; Syracuse Mus. Fine Arts prize, 1949; silver and bronze medal Oakland Art Gallery, 1945, 51; honor award Fine Arts, Vienna, 1955; AIA and Brotherhood award in art Roosevelt U., 1956; ann. award for design in hardwood, 1955, 56, 59; Austrian Cross of Honor for Science and Art, 1st Class, 1977. Hon. fellow Am.-Scandinavian Found.; life fellow Internat. Soc. Arts and Letters, Zurich, Switzerland, Mem. Municipal Art League (dir., Gold medal award 1969), Am. Soc. Ch. Architecture, Nat. Soc. Arts and Letters (adv. council Chgo. 1968-70). Author: Art and Human Emotions, 1975. Home: 835 Michigan Ave Evanston IL 60202 Office: Art Inst Chgo Chicago IL 60603

WEINFURTER, ROBERT WAYNE, cons. co. exec.; b. Appleton, Wis., May 17, 1928; s. George John and Esther Rose (Kumbier) W.; B.S., Lawrence U., 1953, postgrad., 1956; m. Cathryn Janice Masterson, June 20, 1953; children—Erich, Kurt, Karl, Hans. With Bechtel Corp., San Francisco, 1956-59; engr.-in-charge for O'Hare Field Project Soil Testing Services, Inc., Chgo., 1959-62; pres. Soil Testing Services Wis., Green Bay, 1962-70; adminstrv. v.p. Soil Testing Services Inc., Chgo., 1970-74; exec. v.p. Soil Testing Services Iowa, Cedar Rapids, 1974—, also dir.; pres. Soil Testing Services Kans., Kansas City, 1975—, dir., 1962—; prin., dir. Terracon Consultants Inc., Kansas City. Mem. chancellor's bldg. adv. bd. U. Wis., Green Bay, 1968-70. Served with USAF, 1946-49. Registered profl. geologist, Ga., profl. engr., Nev., Wis. Mem. Soc. Mining Engrs. Am. Inst. Metall. Engrs., Am. Concrete Inst., ASTM, Wis. Soc. Profl. Engrs., Assn. Soil and Found. Engrs. (past pres.), Mo. Soc. Profl. Engrs., Assn. Engring. Geologists, Wis. Assn. Professions, Am. Inst. Profl. Geologists, Phi Delta Theta. Republican. Presbyn. (ch. trustee 1967-70, deacon 1973-74). Home: 10063 Hardy Dr Overland Park KS 66212 Office: 8431 Quivira Rd Lenexa KS 66215

WEINGART, MAURICE ALEXANDER, ins. agy. exec.; b. St. Louis, Aug. 14, 1922; s. Joseph and Anna (Greenfield) W.; student Ohio U., 1943-44; m. Freida Dubman, Jan. 12, 1947; children—Sandra Weingart Hertzberg, Sherry Weingart Barenholtz. Broker Joseph Weingart Ins. Agy., University City, Mo., 1947-50, partner, 1950—, owner, 1979—. Mem. Met. Youth Commn., St. Louis and St. Louis County, 1963-65; hon. commr. Mo. Am. Revolution Bicentennial, 1974-76; treas. Creve Coeur-West County Bicentennial Commn., 1974-76. Republican committeeman Creve Coeur (Mo.) Twp., 1967-74; chmn. Mo. 2nd Congl. Dist. Rep. Com., 1970-72; mem. Mo. Rep. State Com., 1972-74. Trustee St. Louis County Retirement Plans, 1967-69, 69-72, 72-75, 76-78; regional adv. bd. Anti-Defamation League, 1973—; v.p., bd. dirs. New Mt. Sinai Cemetery Assn., 1974-78; trustee Central Agy. for Jewish Edn., 1972-75; chmn. Personnel Code Com. City of Creve Coeur, 1976-77. Served to sgt., AUS, 1942-46. Mem. St. Louis Fedn. Reform Temples (pres. 1967), Soc. Chartered Property and Casualty Underwriters (chpt. pres. 1963-64), Jewish War Vets. U.S.A., Creve Coeur Twp. Rep. Men's Club (pres. 1964-65). Jewish religion (pres. congregation 1962-65). Home: 11710 Tarrytown St Creve Coeur MO 63141 Office: 8505 Delmar St University City MO 63124

WEINHOLD, VIRGINIA BEAMER, interior designer; b. Elizabeth, N.J., June 21, 1932; d. Clayton Mitchell and Rosemary (Behrend) Beamer; B.A., Cornell U., 1955; B.A. summa cum laude, Ohio State U., 1969; divorced; children—Thomas Craig, Robert Scott, Amy Linette. Freelance interior designer, 1969-72; interior designer, dir. interior design Karlsberger and Assos. Inc., Worthington, Ohio, 1972—; lectr. indsl. design Ohio State U., 1972, 79-80. Mem. Inst. Bus. Designers (chpt. treas. 1977-79, nat. trustee 1979-81, nat. chmn. contract documents com. 1979-81, chpt. pres. 1981-83): asso. mem. AIA, Am. Soc. Interior Designers. Prin. works include Grands Rapids (Mich.) Osteo. Hosp., Melrose (Mass.) Wakefield Hosp., Christopher Inn, Columbus, John W. Galbreath Hdqrs., Columbus, Guernsey Meml. Hosp., Cambridge, Ohio, Trinity Epis. Ch. and Parish House, Columbus, others. Home: 112 Glen Dr Worthington OH 43085 Office: 180 E Broad St Columbus OH 43215

WEINKAUF, WILLIAM CARL, instructional media co. exec.; b. Fond du Lac, Wis., Apr. 7, 1934; s. Carl Alfred and Erma Gertrude (Lueck) W.; B.A., Ripon Coll., 1955; postgrad. U. Wis., 1954, 57-58; m. Carole Jean Hill, May 3, 1958; children—Carl William, Mary Gretchen, Donald Hill. Dir. Wis. Central Lumber Co., 1959-63; with Carlton Films, Beloit, Wis., 1965-68; founder, pres. IMCO Inc., Green Lake, Wis., 1968—, IMCO Pub. Co., 1978—. Cons. bd. Holy Cross Coll., 1972—. Chmn. council Cub Scouts Am., 1968-69. Mem. county exec. com. Republican party, 1970-71. Served to maj. AUS, 1955-57. Mem. Nat. Audio Visual Assn. (chmn. legis. com. Wis. 1975—), Nat. Sch. Supply and Equipment Assn., U.S. Res. Officers Assn. (chpt. pres. 1966-70), C. of C., Sigma Nu. Mem. United Ch. Christ. (bd. trustees 1965-66). Mason (32 deg., K.T.). Home: 596 Illinois Ave Green Lake WI 54941 Office: 506-510 Mill St Green Lake WI 54941

WEINLANDER, MAX MARTIN, ret. psychologist; b. Ann Arbor, Mich., Sept. 9, 1917; s. Paul and Emma Carol (Lindemann) W.; B.A., Eastern Mich. Coll., 1940; M.A., U. Mich., 1942, Ph.D., 1955; M.A., Wayne U., 1951; m. Albertina Adelheit Abrams, June 4, 1945; children—Bruce, Annette. Psychometrist, VA Hosp., Dearborn, Mich., 1947-51; sr. staff psychologist Ohio Div. Corrections, London, 1954-55; lectr. Dayton and Piqua Centers, Miami U., Oxford, Ohio, 1955-62; chief clin. psychologist Child Guidance Clinic, Springfield, Ohio, 1956-61, acting dir., 1961-65; clin. psychologist VA Center, Dayton, Ohio, 1964-79; cons. Ohio Div. Mental Hygiene; summer guest prof. Miami U., 1957, 58, Wittenberg U., 1958; adj. prof. Wright State U., Dayton, 1975-81; cons. State Ohio Bur. Vocat. Rehab., Oesterlen Home Emotionally Disturbed Children. Pres. Clark County Mental Health Assn., 1960, Clark County Health and Welfare Club, 1961; mem. Community Welfare Council Clark County, 1964; chmn. Comprehensive Mental Health Planning Com. Clark County, 1964; trustee United Appeals Fund, 1960—. Mem. citizens adv. council Columbus Psychiat. Inst., Ohio State U. Served as sgt. AUS, 1942-46. Fellow Ohio Psychol. Assn. (chmn. com. on utilization of pscyhologists; treas., exec. bd. 1968-71); mem. Am. Psychol. Assn., Pi Kappa Delta, Pi Gamma Mu, Phi Delta Kappa. Lutheran. Clubs: Kiwanis; Mitchell Hills Country. Contbr. articles to psychology jours. Home: 17185 Valley Dr Big Rapids MI 49307

WEINMAN, IRVIN ABRAHAM, clin. social worker, educator; b. N.Y.C., Mar. 6, 1922; s. Jacob and Minnie (Feinberg) W.; student U. Ill., 1945, Columbia, 1948; B.S., U. Wis., 1950; M.S.W., U. Denver, 1952; postgrad. Inst. Psychoanalysis, certificate child therapy, 1962; m. Miriam Kniaz, June 4, 1950; children—Natalie Zoe, Richard, Michael (dec.). Caseworker, Jewish Family and Children's Services, Milw., 1952-55, casework supr., 1955-67; lectr. to asst. prof. social welfare U. Wis.-Milw., 1967-71; pvt. practice marriage and family counseling Milw., 1967—; lectr., cons. in field. Bd. dirs. Hope Day Care Center, Elm Grove, Wis., 1970-71. Served with AUS, 1944-46. Mem. Acad. Certified Social Workers, Am. Acad. Psychotherapists, Am. Assn. Marriage and Family Therapists, Wis. Soc. Clin. Social Workers. Club: B'nai B'rith. Home: 8690 N 51st St Milwaukee WI 53223 Office: 6815 W Capitol Dr Milwaukee WI 53216

WEINSTEIN, DAVID, coll. pres.; b. Boston, June 26, 1927; s. Herman and Fanny (Katzoff) W.; B.A., Mass. State Coll., 1950; B.H.L., Hebrew Tchrs. Coll., 1950, M.H.L., 1953; M.Ed., Harvard U., 1952, Ed.D., 1956; m. Sandra Bargad, June 29, 1958; 1 son, Noah. Registrar, Hebrew Tchrs. Coll., 1957-61, prof. lang. edn., 1961-64; pres. Spertus Coll. of Judaica, Chgo., 1964—; cons. Lang. Research

Inst., Harvard U., 1954-64; lang. coordinator Brussels Internat. Fair, 1958; field dir. Harvard U. Lang. Program, Israel, 1959-64. Served in U.S. Army, 1945-47. Author: Essential Hebrew by Examples, 1964; Modern Jewish Educational Thought, 1964; co-author: Hebrew Through Pictures, 1954; First Steps in Reading Hebrew, 1955; Hebrew-English/English-Hebrew Pocket Dictionary, 1961. Office: Spertus Coll Judaica 618 S Michigan Ave Chicago IL 60605

WEINSTEIN, STANLEY HOWARD, real estate exec.; b. N.Y.C., Oct. 27, 1948; s. George and Shirley Beatrice (Greenberg) W.; B.S., U. Ill., 1970; J.D., St. John's Sch. Law, 1973; m. Lenore Marsha Bienenfeld, May 25, 1975; children—Moshe, Ronni Leah. Staff acct. M.J. Weinstein Groothuis & Co., N.Y.C., 1969-70; asst. treas. Nat. Diversified Industries Inc., Great Neck, N.Y., 1970-73; partner Weinstein Assos., N.Y.C. and Milw., 1973—; admitted to N.Y. bar, 1975, D.C. bar, 1979; exec. v.p., sec., owner REIT Property Mgrs., Ltd., Milw., 1975—, also dir.; chmn. bd. RPM/Preiss Real Estate Inc., Milw., 1979—, also dir.; pres. 925 E. Wells Corp., Milw., 1976—, also dir.; pres. Weinstein Assos. Ltd., Milw.; sec. Hudson Valley Corp. Treas., bd. dirs. Hillel Acad., 1978—; bd. dirs. Anshe Sfard Synagogue, Beth Judah Synagogue, Milw. Jewish Community Center; asso. chmn. Acharai II-Fedn. Young Leadership Mission to Israel; mem. budget and planning com. Milw. Jewish Fedn.; mem. Milw. Kosher Restaurant Com. C.P.A., Ill. Mem. Assn. for Torah Advancement (sec., dir.), Am. Inst. C.P.A.'s, N.Y. State Soc. C.P.A.'s, N.Y. State Bar Assn., Assn. Bar City N.Y., Nat. Assn. Rev. Appraisers, Am. Bar Assn., Delta Sigma Pi. Jewish. Office: Weinstein Assos Ltd 925 E Wells St PO Box 92219 Milwaukee WI 53202 also Israel

WEIR, JOHN LEE, state ofcl.; b. Eldorado, Ill., Nov. 13, 1954; s. Jackie Loyal and Eva Jean (Cummings) W.; A.A., Southeastern Ill. Coll., 1974; B.A. in Polit. Sci., So. Ill. U., Carbondale, 1976; m. Julie Ann Mahaffey, June 20, 1981. Placement officer Ill. Dept. Labor Bur. Employment Security at Southeastern Ill. Coll., 1978-80, employment rep., Harrisburg, Ill., 1978—; trustee Local 1048, Am. Fedn. State, County and Mcpl. Employees, AFL-CIO; steward Ill. Dept. Labor. Active campaigner Saline County (Ill.) Young Republicans., 1972—; mem. Pres. Ford Com., 1976; mem. Reagan-Bush Com., 1980; mem. Bush for Pres. Com., 1980. Mem. So. Ill. U. Alumni Assn., Easter Seal Soc. So. Ill., Ill. Farm Bur. Baptist. Home: Route 1 Eldorado IL 62930 Office: Dept Labor Bur Employment Security Parker Plaza Harrisburg IL 62946

WEIR, JOHN PAUL, mining engr.; b. Zeigler, Ill., July 14, 1923; s. Paul and Lura Frances (Hickox) W.; B.S.Ch.E., Purdue U., 1944; B.S. in Mining Engring., Pa. State U., 1949; m. Louise Carolyn Carey, Dec. 19, 1950; children—Mary, John, Sally, Tracy. With Paul Weir Co., cons. mining engrs. and geologists, Chgo., 1949—, exec. v.p., 1970-74, pres., 1974—. Served with USNR, 1943-46. Mem. AIME, Instn. Mining Engrs. (U.K.), Ill. Mining Inst., Am. Cons. Engrs. Council. Republican. Presbyterian. Clubs: Chgo. Athletic, Tower, Skokie Country. Office: 20 N Wacker Dr Chicago IL 60606

WEIR, M. BROCK, trust co. exec.; b. 1921; student Gonzaga U., 1944; B.A., U. Wash., 1947; postgrad. Dartmouth Coll. Grad. Sch. Fin. Mgmt., 1962; married. With Bank of Calif., 1963-72; pres., chief exec. officer AmeriTrust Co., Cleve., 1973-78, chmn. bd., chief exec. officer, 1978—, also dir. Chmn. bd. trustees Cleve. Found. Served to capt. U.S. Army, 1940-45. Office: AmeriTrust Co 900 Euclid Ave Cleveland OH 44101*

WEIS, JACK FRANK, ret. mfg. exec.; b. Columbus, Ohio, Apr. 1, 1902; s. Benjamin and Rose (Wallach) W.; B.S. in Elec. Engring., Ohio State U., 1926. Plant engr. Alloy Steel Casting & Comml. Steel Casting Cos., 1926-29; asst. chief elec. engr. Marion Power Shovel Co., 1929-39; chief elec. engr., 1939-57, chief engr. intermediate and large machines, 1957-67, v.p., 1968-74, cons., 1971-75, ret. Area agt. Ohio State U. Devel. Fund; pres. YMCA Endowment Fund. Mem. Am. Inst. E.E., Ohio State Profl. Engring Soc., Nat. Engring. Soc. Contbr. articles to profl. jours. Home: 758 King Ave Marion OH 43302

WEISBERG, GABRIEL PAUL, mus. curator; b. N.Y.C., May 4, 1942; s. Harry I. and Sarah (Stollak) W.; student Ohio Wesleyan U., 1959-60; B.A., N.Y. U., 1963; M.A., Johns Hopkins U., 1967, Ph.D., 1967; m. Yvonne M. L. Herzog, July 23, 1967. Jr. instr. The Johns Hopkins U., 1963-65; asst. prof. Queens CCNY, 1967; asst. prof. U. N.Mex., 1967-69; vis. asst. prof. N.Y. U., summer 1968; asso. prof. U. Cin., 1969-73, acting head art history dept., summer 1970, 72-73; curator Dept. Art History and Edn., The Cleveland Mus. Art, 1973—; chief reader Advanced Placement Art History, Ednl. Testing Services; cons. NEH; mem. Inst. for Advanced Study Princeton, 1979. Fulbright grantee, 1974; Research on History of 19th Century Decorative Arts Research grantee, Am. Philos. Soc., 1974. Mem. Assn. Am. Museums, Print Club, Print Council Am., Coll. Art Assn. Jewish. Author: Francois Bonvin - His Life and Work, 1979. Contbr. articles to art-oriented periodicals. Home: 2280 Grandview Ave Cleveland OH 44106 OfFice: 11150 East Blvd Cleveland OH 44106

WEISBERG, HARVEY LEONARD, supermarket chain exec.; b. Pitts., July 12, 1924; s. Peter and Clara (Brown) W.; B.A., U. Mich., 1947, J.D., 1950; m. Lucille Judith Birnbaum, June 27, 1948; children—Jeff (dec.), Roger, Danny, Barry. Admitted to Mich. bar, 1950, practiced in Detroit, 1950-53; with Chatham Super Markets, Inc., Warren, Mich., 1950—, exec. v.p., 1968-80, vice chmn. bd., 1980—; adv. com. food distbn. Western Mich. U., 1962—. Bd. dirs. Allied Jewish campaign, Detroit, 1973—, chmn. food div., 1968-70; bd. govs. Jewish Welfare Fedn., Detroit, 1969—; chmn. broadcast div. Jewish Community Council, Detroit, 1972-75, exec. com., 1972-76; nat. commr. for life Anti-Defamation League, B'nai B'rith, 1979—; trustee Congregation Shaarey Zedek, Southfield, Mich., 1961—, exec. com., 1973—, pres., 1981—; trustee Rabbi Morris Adler Meml. Found., 1979—; chmn. divs. United Found., Detroit, 1968-69, 70, adv. bd., 1975—; mem. citizens assembly United Community Services Met. Detroit, 1977—; bd. advisers Wayne State U. Press, Detroit, 1977—. Served to lt. (j.g.) USNR, 1943-46. Mem. Associated Food Dealers (pres. 1969-70, chmn. bd. 1971-73, dir. 1974—), Food Mktg. Inst., Mich. Bar Assn., Mich. Assn. Professions, Detroit Bar Assn., Phi Beta Kappa, Tau Epsilon Rho, Phi Kappa Phi, Delta Sigma Rho, Phi Eta Sigma. Club: Michigauma. Home: 24675 Santa Barbara St Southfield MI 48075 Office: 2300 E Ten Mile Rd Warren MI 48091

WEISBERG, LEONARD R., physicist, govt. ofcl.; b. N.Y.C., Oct. 17, 1929; s. Emmanuel E. and Esther (Raynes) W.; B.A. magna cum laude, Clark U., 1950; M.A., Columbia, 1952; m. Francis Simon, Mar. 23, 1980; children—Glenna Raynes, Orren Beth, Frances Barnett. Research asst. Watson Labs. IBM, N.Y.C., 1953-55; with RCA Labs., Princeton, N.J., 1955-71, mem. tech. staff, 1955-66, head research group, 1966-69, dir. semicondr. device research lab., 1969-71; dir. materials research lab. Itek Corp., Lexington, Mass., 1972-74, v.p., dir. central research lab., 1974-75; dir. electronics tech. Dept. Def., Washington, 1975-79; v.p. sci. and tech. Honeywell Inc., Mpls., 1980—. Fellow IEEE; mem. Am. Phys. Soc., Materials Research Soc., Sigma Xi. Contbr. articles to profl. jours. Home: 1225 LaSalle Ave No 1407 Minneapolis MN 55403 Office: Honeywell Plaza Minneapolis MN 55408

WEISBERG, SEYMOUR WILLIAM, physician; b. Chgo., Aug. 5, 1910; s. Isaac and Eda (Provus) W.; B.S., U. Chgo., 1932; M.D., Rush Med. Coll., 1936; m. Ella Sperling, Oct. 16, 1949; children—Gerald, Louise. Intern Michael Reese Hosp.; resident Cook County Hosp., Chgo.; practice medicine specializing in internal medicine, Chgo., 1940—; asso. prof. medicine U. Ill. Coll. Medicine, Chgo.; asso. attending physician Cook County Hosp., 1940-44; chief resident tng. unit Chgo. Regional Office VA; mem. attending staffs Michael Reese Hosp., Chgo., Louis A. Weiss Meml. Hosp., Chgo. Served with AUS, 1944-47. Diplomate Am. Bd. Internal Medicine. Mem. AMA, Ill. Med. Soc., Phi Beta Kappa, Alpha Omega Alpha. Office: 55 E Washington St Chicago IL 60602

WEISHAAR, MICHAEL FRANCIS, civil engr.; b. St. Louis, Mar. 11, 1939; s. Frank X. and Anastasia Marie (Meives) W.; B.S. in Civil Engring., St. Louis U., 1961; M.S. in Engring. (NIH fellow), U. Mich., 1967, M.P.H., 1967; postgrad. U.S. Army Command and Gen. Staff Coll., 1975, Nat. Def. U., 1978; m. LaVerne R. Eckstein, Aug. 11, 1962; children—Kimberly, Karl, Kevin, Kara. Mgr. environ. affairs Monsanto Co., St. Louis, 1967—. Active, Florrisant (Mo.) Bd. Appeals, 1968, Planning and Zoning Commn., 1969-72, Environ. Quality Commn., 1970-72, troop com. Boy Scouts Am., Mcpl. Adv. Council of Congressman Robert A. Young. Served with Med. Service Corps, U.S. Army, 1962-65, to col. USAR. Jr. Chamber Internat. senator, 1971. Registered profl. engr., sanitarian; diplomate Am. Acad. Environ. Engrs. Mem. ASCE, Water Pollution Control Fedn., Res. Officers Assn., Chem. Industry Council, Mo. Water Pollution Control Assn., Engrs. Club St. Louis, Mo. Jaycees (regional v.p. 1971, state chmn. 1972-75), Phi Kappa Theta. Club: Ky. Cols. Contbr. tech. articles to profl. jours.; patentee in field. Home: 921 Camargo Dr Ballwin MO 63011 Office: 800 N Lindbergh Blvd Saint Louis MO 63166

WEISS, DAVID DONALD, food mfg. co. exec.; b. St. Paul, Mar. 17, 1931; s. Frank N. and Abalona M. W.; B.B.A., U. Minn., 1953; m. Joy Ann Sweeney, Dec. 23, 1953; children—Thomas, Catherine, Mary, Michael. Mgr. internal audit Pillsbury Co., Mpls., 1958-60, area controller-agrl. products, 1960-65, adminstrv. controller info. systems, 1965-69; treas., controller Call-A-Computer Inc., Mpls., 1969-70; dir. audit services Internat. Multifoods Co., South St. Paul, Minn., 1970-72, controller King Foods div., 1972-74, v.p. ops. King Foods div., 1974-79, div. v.p., gen. mgr. King Foods div., 1979-80, corp. dir. risk mgmt., 1980—. Pres. Parent Tchrs. Group Resurrection Sch., Mpls., 1968, T-Ball League, Pearl Park Athletic Assn., Mpls., 1969; v.p. Edina (Minn.) Basketball Assn., 1976-77, pres., 1977-78. Served with USAF, 1954-56. Recipient Outstanding Citizens award City of Edina, 1978. Mem. Inst. Internal Auditors (cert.; sec. 1971-72, v.p. 1972-73, editor letters to editor sect. Internal Auditor 1974-80), U. Minn. Alumni Assn., U. Minn. M Club, Mpls. C. of C. Independent Republican. Roman Catholic. Club: N.W. Racquet and Swim. Office: 1200 Multifoods Bldg 8th and Marquette Minneapolis MN 55402

WEISS, MARTIN E., assn. exec.; b. Cleve., Nov. 22, 1926; s. Samuel B. and Margaret (Freedman) W.; B.A., Columbia U., 1947; children from previous marriage—James L., Andrew R. Dir. advt. and public relations Del. Floor Products, 1948-52; promotion dir. Street & Smith Publs., 1952-56; editor, publisher Westbury (N.Y.) Times, 1956-73; publisher Edn.-Tng. Market Report, Westbury, N.Y., 1973-75; dir. public relations and publs. AAU/USA, Indpls., 1976-79; dir. communications, mktg. Athletics Congress/USA, Indpls., 1979—. Served with AUS, 1944-46. Mem. Ind. Bus. Communicators. Home: 3801 N Meridian St Indianapolis IN 46208 Office: 155 W Washington St Suite 220 Indianapolis IN 46204

WEISSBLATT, ROBERT LEWIS, computer co. exec.; b. N.Y.C., May 22, 1944; s. Norman P. and Gertrude Van Dam (Young) W.; B.B.A., Pace U., 1968; M.E., Bklyn. Coll., 1970; m. Catherine Gabriel, Aug. 22, 1970; children—Maryl Lynn, Paul Norman. Products mgr. mktg. Dunn & Bradstreet, N.Y.C., 1970-72; sales rep. Hyland Labs., N.Y., 1972-73, sales specialist, 1973-75, regional mgr., 1975-76; nat. sales mgr., v.p. The Computer Place, Brooklyn Heights, Ohio, 1976—, also dir.; pres. New Internat. Corp., 1981—. Mem. Computer Dealers Assn., Internat. Word Processing Assn., Data Processing Mgmt. Assn., Small Businessmen's Assn., Nat. Fedn. Ind. Bus., U.S. C. of C. Office: 4595 Van Epps Rd Brooklyn Heights OH 44131

WEISSE, GUENTER, engring. co. exec.; b. Reutlingen, W.Ger., May 22, 1935; s. Kurt and Maria (Haug) W.; came to U.S., 1971; Mech. Engring. Degree, Stuttgart, W.Ger., 1959; m. Solveig Stuetz, Jan. 8, 1971; 1 son, Marcus. Design engr., turbo charger, J. Eberspaeher, W.Ger., 1959-61; design engr., turbocharger and fuel injection, Simms Motor Co., Eng., 1961-63; test engr. tech sales, mgr. tech. sales fuel injection systems Robert Bosch Gmbh, Stuttgart, 1963-71, v.p. prodn. planning and engring. R. Bosch Corp., Broadview, Ill., 1971—. Mem. Soc. Automotive Engrs. Home: 21W545 Glen Valley Dr Glen Ellyn IL 60137 Office: 2800 S 25th Ave Broadview IL 60153

WEISSLER, ARNOLD MERVIN, cardiologist, internist, educator; b. Bklyn., May 13, 1927; s. Soloman F. and Dora W. (Hocheiser) W.; B.A., N.Y. U., 1948; M.D. (Dudley Meml. medal surgery), SUNY, Bklyn., 1953; m. Gloria Lazarus, June 22, 1952; children—Suzanne Robin, Mark Douglas, Leslie Ann, Jonathan Scott. Intern, Maimonides Hosp., N.Y.C., 1953-54; successively asst. resident in medicine Duke U. Hosp., Am. Heart Assn. research fellow, 1955-57, sr. asst. resident, 1957-58, chief resident, 1958-59; chief cardiovascular sect. VA, Durham hosps., 1959-60; asst. prof. medicine U. Tex. Med. Br., Galveston, 1960-61; mem. faculty Ohio State U. Med. Sch., 1961-71, prof. medicine, 1967-71, chief cardiology, 1963-71; prof. medicine, chmn. dept. Wayne State U. Med. Sch., Detroit, 1971-81; chief medicine Harper-Grace Hosps., 1971—; prof. medicine, U. Colo., 1982; chmn. and chief div. of cardiology, Rose Med. Center, 1982. Served with USNR, 1944-45. Recipient Alumni medallion SUNY, Bklyn., 1978; diplomate Am. Bd. Internal Medicine. Fellow A.C.P., Am. Coll. Cardiology, Am. Heart Assn. (council clin. cardiology), Am. Coll. Chest Physicians, Royal Soc. London; mem. Assn. Am. Physicians, Am. Soc. Clin. Investigation, Am. Soc. Pharmacology and Exptl. Therapeutics, Assn. Profs. Medicine, Assn. Univ. Cardiologists, Am. Clin. and Climatol. Soc., Am. Soc. Clin. Pharmacol. Therapeutics, AAAS, AAUP, Central Soc. Clin. Research (pres.-elect 1981), So. Soc. Clin. Research, Mich. Heart Assn., Detroit Heart Club, Detroit Academy of Medicine, Phi Beta Kappa, Sigma Xi, Alpha Omega Alpha. Author: Noninvasive Cardiology, 1974; co-author: Basic and Clinical Parmacology of Digitalis, 1972; Reviews of Contemporary Laboratory Methods, 1980; mem. editorial bds. profl. jours., contbr. articles med. jours. Office: Wayne State Univ Med Sch 540 E Canfield St Detroit MI 48201

WEISSMAN, EUGENE Y., chem. engr.; b. Bucharest, Romania, Sept. 23, 1931; came to U.S., 1958, naturalized, 1967; s. Alfred A. and Paula D. (Braunstein) W.; B.Sc., Israel Inst. Tech., 1953; M.S., U. Mich., 1959; Ph.D. in Chem. Engring., Case Inst. Tech., 1963; M.B.A., U. Chgo., 1972; m. Corinne A. Barzely, Jan. 7, 1958; children—Ian A., Michael L. Project mgr. Israel Atomic Energy Commn., 1953-58; process engr. Hercules Powder Co., 1960-61; sr. engr. Gen. Electric Co., 1963-65, research and devel. mgr., 1965-68; research dept. head Globe-Union, Inc., 1968-73; research dir. B.A.S.F. Wyandotte (Mich.) Corp., 1973—. USPHS fellow, 1959, 62. Registered profl. engr. Mem. Catalysis Soc. New Eng. (dir.), Electrochem. Soc. (mem. nat. membership com.), Am. Inst. Chem. Engrs. (dir. heat transfer and energy conversion div.), Am. Mgmt. Assn. Contbr. articles to profl. jours.; patentee in field. Office: BASF Wyandotte Corp Wyandotte MI 48192

WEISZ, WILLIAM JULIUS, electronics co. exec.; b. Chgo., Jan. 8, 1927; s. George R. and Minnie (Riff) W.; B.S. in Elec. Engring., M.I.T., 1948; D.B.A. (hon.), St. Ambrose Coll., 1976; m. Barbara Becker, Dec. 25, 1947; children—George, Terri, David. With Motorola, Inc., Chgo., then Shaumburg, Ill., 1948—, exec. v.p., 1969-70, pres., 1970—, chief operating officer, 1972—, vice chmn., 1980—, also dir.; pres. Motorola Communications Internat., 1966-69, Motorola Communications and Electronics, Inc., 1966-69. Mem. exec. com. land mobile adv. com. to FCC. Com. chmn. Cub Scout pack Evanston council Boy Scouts Am., 1960-62. Trustee, M.I.T., also chmn. elec. engring. and computer scis. vis. com., mem. Sloan Sch. vis. com.; mem. devel. com. MIT Corp., 1970—. Served with USNR, 1945-46. Recipient award of merit Nat. Electronics Conf., 1970; Freedom Found. of Valley Forge award, 1974. Fellow IEEE (past nat. chmn. vehicular communications group); mem. Electronic Industries Assn. (past chmn. bd. govs.; medal of honor 1981), Econ. Club Chgo., Sigma Xi, Tau Beta Pi, Eta Kappa Nu, Pi Lambda Phi. Clubs: M.I.T. (dir.) (Chgo.). Office: 1303 E Algonguin Rd Schaumburg IL 60196

WEITHERS, JOHN GREGORY, stock exchange exec.; b. Chgo., 1933; ed. U. Notre Dame, 1955, DePaul U., Chgo., 1961. Formerly exec. v.p., now pres., chief operating officer Midwest Stock Exchange, Chgo.; dir. Northwestern Steel and Wire Co.; past vice chmn. exec. com., dir. Bache and Co., Inc. Office: 120 S LaSalle St Chicago IL 60603*

WEITZMAN, JONATHAN, electronics chain exec.; b. Bronx, N.Y., Dec. 13, 1938; s. Leonard and Celia (Hyman) W.; B.A., Hofstra U., 1960, M.A., 1965; m. Anita Marthe DeMille, Dec. 13, 1969; 1 son, Jason Robert. Mgr. career devel. Port Authority of N.Y. and N.J., N.Y.C., 1962-73; mgmt. cons. Felix Lopez & Assos., Port Washington, N.Y., 1973-76; mgr. mgmt. devel. Burger King, Miami, Fla., 1976-77, mgr. region franchising, Mpls., 1977-80; dir. franchising MGM Liquor Warehouse, St. Paul, 1980-81; v.p. franchising Team Electronics, Mpls., 1981—. Mem. Nat. Restaurant Assn., Am. Mgmt. Assn. Democrat. Jewish. Office: 720 29th Ave SE Minneapolis MN 55414

WELBORN, JOHN A., state senator; b. Kalamazoo, Dec. 20, 1932; s. H. Sterling and Elizabeth (Dougherty) W.; grad. high sch.; m. Dorothy Yeomans, Aug. 15, 1952; children—Kayla, Kami, John. Dairy farmer, Cooper Twp., Mich., 1952-68. Twp. supr., Cooper Twp., Kalamazoo County, 1967-71; mem. Mich. Ho. of Reps. from Kalamazoo County, 1972-74, Mich. Senate, 1974—. Dir. local soil conservation dist., 1953-65; mem. Gull Lake Sch. Bd., 1965-72, Kalamazoo County Bd. Suprs., 1967-69; met. council chmn. C. of C. Indsl. Devel., 1970-71; chmn. Kalamazoo Republican com., 1970-72; Mich. chmn. Reagan for Pres. campaign, 1976; del. Rep. Nat. Conv., 1976, 80; Rep. candidate for gov. State of Mich., 1982. Mem. Nat. Tax Assn., Tax Inst. Am. Home: 6304 Riverview Kalamazoo MI 49004 Office: Capitol Lansing MI 48902

WELBORN, WILLIAM CALVERT, JR., lawyer; b. Evansville, Ind., Aug. 2, 1937; s. William Calvert and Georgine Lillydale (Koser) W.; A.B., U. Evansville, 1963; J.D., Ind. U., 1966; m. Mary Elizabeth Jones, Dec. 24, 1956; children—Kathy, William C. III, Dawn, Elizabeth. TV dir. WEHT, WTVW, Evansville, Ind., 1955-59; WFBM, Indpls., 1959-60; admitted to Ind. bar, 1966, Tenn. bar, 1969, U.S. 7th Circuit Ct. bar, 1969; practiced in Evansville, 1966—; asso. firm Merrill Schroeder & Johnson, 1966-67; partner firm Merrill Schroeder, Johnson, Evans & Welborn, 1967-73, Caine & Welborn, 1973-80, Atkinson, Welborn & Bohleber, 1980—; pres. Law-Data Systems, 1978—. dep. prosecutor, Evansville, 1970-72, 80—. Mem. communications and command Civil Air Patrol, Evansville, Ind., 1951-61, 72—; dir. Conrad Baker Found., Evansville, 1967-72. Mem. Ind. State, Evansville (James Bethal Greslam award, 1970, mem. TV com. 1972, v.p. 1974, mem. spl. ct. study com. 1975) bar assns., Mil. Affilaiate Radio Service, Order of Coif. Democrat. Methodist. Contbr. articles to mags.; author various legal and bus. computer programs, 1979—. Editor: Indiana Law Jour., 1965-66, Note in Law Journal, 1966; (with W. Statham, H. Songer, W. Fitzgerald, J. Stone) Crime Study Commission, 1967-69. Home: 9515 W Motz Rd Wadesville IN 47638 Office: 112 NW 7th St Evansville IN 47708

WELCH, EDWARD JOSEPH, food mfg. co. exec.; b. Chgo., Apr. 9, 1949; s. Joseph J. and Laurine (Weldon) W.; B.S., Loyola U., Chgo., 1972; M.B.A., DePaul U., 1978; m. Marsha Matusak, Oct. 8, 1971; children—Jennifer, Brian, Maureen. Acct., Skil Corp., Chgo., 1971-74; cost analyst FMC Corp., Chgo., 1974-77; budget and cost mgr. Ovaltine Products Inc., Villa Park, Ill., 1977-79, brand mgr., 1979—. C.P.A., Ill. Mem. Am. Inst. C.P.A.'s, Ill. C.P.A. Soc.

WELCH, HARVEY, JR., ednl. adminstr.; b. Centralia, Ill., June 5, 1932; s. Harvey and Willie Olivia (James) W.; B.S., So. Ill. U., 1955, M.S., 1958, Ph.D., 1981; children—Harvey C., Gordon P., Karan A., Brian D. Commd. 2d lt. U.S. Air Force, 1955, advanced through grades to col., 1971; served as asst. prof. aerospace studies, Ind. U., 1964-68, admissions officer Air Force Inst. Tech., Wright-Patterson AFB, Ohio, 1968-69, program mgr. interdisciplinary programs, 1969-71, dir. spl. edn. programs, 1973-75, cons. U.S. Mil. Mission for Aid to Turkey, Ankara, 1971-73, ret., 1975; dean of student life So. Ill. U., Carbondale, 1975—. Mem. Carbondale Planning Commn., 1976-78; chmn. Carbondale Police and Fire Commn., 1978—. Decorated Air Force Res. medal; cert. community coll. chief adminstrv. officer, Calif. Mem. Am. Assn. Higher Edn., AAUP, Am. Coll. Personnel Assn. (vice chmn. Commn. I), Am. Personnel and Guidance Assn., Ill. Guidance and Personnel Assn. (pres., 1980-81), Ill. Assn. for Non-White Concerns (pres., 1979-80), Ill. Assn. Student and Fin. Adminstrs., Ill. Coll. Personnel Assn., Ill. State Scholarship Commn. Adv. Com., Nat. Assn. Student Personnel Adminstrs., Mid-Am. Assn. Ednl. Opportunity Program Personnel, Alpha Phi Alpha. Contbr. articles in field to profl. publs. Office: Student Life Office Bldg T-40 So Ill U Carbondale IL 62901

WELCH, JOHN WILEY, home mfg. co. exec.; b. LaCrosse, Wis., June 29, 1928; s. Ralph Oliver and Dorothy Abbott (Tessman) W.; B.S., U. Wis., LaCrosse, 1955; m. Jann Deen Witt, June 21, 1958; children—Kendra Deen, Brent John, James Allen. With Trane Lab., LaCrosse, 1955-56; partner Consol. Builders Supply, LaCrescent, Minn., 1956-68; pres. CBS Homes div., 1968—; owner Brookhill Apts. Chmn., LaCrescent Pool Referendum, 1972, LaCrescent Swimming Pool Com., 1973, LaCrescent Auction and Rummage, 1973-74. Del. Republican State Conv., 1968; bd. dirs. LaCrescent City Recreational Bd., 1974—; bd. dirs. LaCrescent Apple Festival, 1974—, pres., 1976-77; adult Sunday sch. tchr., trustee Bethany Evang. Free Ch. Served with Army Airborne, 1950-52. Named Man of Year, LaCrescent, 1978. Mem. Nat. Assn. Home Builders, N.W. Lumberman's Assn., Nat. Assn. Bldg. Mfrs., LaCrosse Area Home

Builders Assn. (charter; Asso. of Year 1976), Houston County Home Builders (sec. 1961, dir.), Am. Legion (bldg. com. 1969), Internat. Platform Assn., La Crescent C. of C. (pres. 1960, dir. 1960-61), LaCrosse Bus. and Profl. Couples Club (chmn. 1974-76), Lambda Tau Gamma, Eta Phi Alpha. Clubs: Masons (32 deg.), Shriners, K.T.; Gopher Sportsman, LaCrescent Ski. Home: 713 Welshire Dr LaCrescent MN 55947 Office: 184 Main St LaCrescent MN 55947

WELCH, MARTHA JEAN, psychologist, nurse, educator; b. Birmingham, Ala., Nov. 20, 1933; d. Bowman Lavert and Martha Orene (Carpenter) W.; B.S., U. Ala., 1957; M.S., Case Western Res. U., 1968, Ph.D., 1973; M.S., Emory U., 1962. Instr., Univ. Hosp. Sch. Nursing, Birmingham, Ala., 1957-62; instr. Emory U. Sch. Nursing, Atlanta, 1963-66; psychologist Mental Devel. Center, Cleve., part time 1969-75; asst. prof. nursing So. Ill. U., Edwardsville, 1975-81, asso. prof., 1981—; pvt. practice psychology, Cleve., 1972-75, Collinsville, Ill., 1976—. USPHS fellow, 1966-73. Mem. Am., Ill. psychol. assns., Gestalt Inst. Cleve., Soc. Research in Child Devel., Am. Nurses Assn., Sigma Theta Tau. Home: 5 Manor Dr Collinsville IL 62234 Office: Sch Nursing So Ill Univ Edwardsville IL 62026

WELDON, BETTY GOSHORN, publisher, horse breeder; b. Eagle Grove, Iowa, Feb. 20, 1922; d. Robert Charles and Eva Lenore (Rhyno) Goshorn; B.A. cum laude, Mt. Holyoke Coll., 1943; m. William Henry Weldon, July 6, 1956; children—Frank Gifford, Lenore Toncray, Sally Shriver. Founder, owner, pres. Sta. KRCG-TV, 1954-66; co-pub. News Tribune, Jefferson City, Mo., 1958—; horse breeder Callaway Hills Stable, Jefferson City, 1966—; dir. United Mo. Bank; bd. dirs. Am. Saddle Horse Mus. Presbyterian. Home: 1726 Hayselton Dr Jefferson City MO 65101 Office: News Tribune 210 Monroe St Jefferson City MO 65101

WELDON, COURTENAY, lumber co. exec.; b. Indpls., Dec. 4, 1938; s. John J. and Jean (Dinwiddie) W.; B.S., Principia Coll., 1960; postgrad. Harvard Bus. Sch., 1975; m. Emily Ann Stallings, June 23, 1967; children—Heather Emily, Sean Courtenay. Reporter, Indpls. Times, 1960-63; field constrn. supr. Random Homes, Wright-Bachman, Inc., 1963-64, constrn. mgr., 1964-65, 66-70, v.p. W.Va. operation, 1965-66, v.p., Indpls., 1966, div. mgr. Random Homes, 1966-75, gen. mgr. trainee, 1970-76, pres., chief exec. officer, 1976—. Mem. Nat. Lumber Dealers, Nat. Assn. Home Builders, Assn. Gen. Contractors Ind., Home Owners Warranty Corp. Central Ind. (bd. dirs. 1970-75, pres. 1974-75), Ind. Lumber Dealers, Home Builders Ind., Ind. Lumber and Builders Supply Assn., Builders Assn. Greater Indpls. Republican. Club: Indpls. Com. Fgn. Relations. Home: 7920 Fishback Rd Indianapolis IN 46278 Office: 4343 W 71st St PO Box 68130 Indianapolis IN 46268

WELDON, DAVID EUGENE, educator; b. Madelia, Minn., Feb. 3, 1943; s. Fay Buele and Bernice Olive (Morton) W.; A.A., Austin State Jr. Coll., 1962; B.A., U. Minn., 1965; M.A., U. Ill., 1972, Ph.D., 1974; m. Dorothy Rae Benson, Sept. 4, 1965; children—Patrick David, Timothy Harold Hilton. Research asst. U. Ill., Urbana-Champaign, 1969-72, research asso., 1972-73; asst. prof. dept. psychology Washington U., St. Louis, 1973—. Deacon Meml. Presbyterian Ch., St. Louis. Served with U.S. Army, 1965-68; Vietnam. Decorated Army Commendation medal; NSF grantee, 1976-77, 79-81. Mem. Am. Psychol. Assn., Midwest Psychol. Assn., AAUP, Psychonomic Soc. Republican. Contbr. articles in field to profl. jours. Home: 7221 Shaftesbury St Saint Louis MO 63130 Office: Dept Psychology Washington U Saint Louis MO 63130

WELDON, DAVID EUGENE, psychologist, educator; b. Madelia, Minn., Feb. 3, 1943; s. Faye Buele and Bernice Olive (Morton) W.; A.A., Austin State Jr. Coll., 1962; B.A., U. Minn., 1965; M.A., U. Ill., 1972, Ph.D., 1974; m. Dorothy Rae Benson, Sept. 4, 1965; children—Patrick David, Timothy Harold Hilton. Research asst. U. Ill., 1969-72, research asso., 1972-73; asst. prof. dept. psychology Washington U., St. Louis, 1973—; program evaluator Project STAY Soldan High Sch., 1975; cons. Bd. deacons Meml. Presbyterian Ch., St. Louis, 1979—, moderator, 1980. Served with U.S. Army, 1965-68. NSF grantee, 1976-77, 79-80; NSF/Nat. Inst. Edn. grantee, 1979-81. Mem. Am. Psychol. Assn., Midwest Psychol. Assn., AAUP, Psychonomic Soc., Am. Sci. Affiliation, Chi Gamma Iota. Republican. Contbr. articles to profl. jours. Home: 7221 Shaftesbury St Saint Louis MO 63130 Office: Dept Psychology Washington Univ Saint Louis MO 63130

WELDON, MARCUS DUNLAP, agronomist; b. Wood River, Nebr., Nov. 17, 1900; s. James Madison and Margaret Ellen (Dunlap) W.; student Park Coll., Parkville, Mo., 1917-19; A.B., U. Nebr., 1922, M.S., 1926; postgrad. Mich. State U., 1926-30; Ph.D., U. Nebr., 1937; m. Pauline Bancroft, Feb. 11, 1923; children—Doris May, James Marcus. Research asst. U. Nebr., 1923-26, Mich. State U., 1926-30, U. Nebr., 1930-37; instr. U. Nebr., 1935-37, asst. prof., 1937-40, asso. prof., 1940-47, prof., 1947-48, extension prof., 1948-66, extension prof. emeritus, 1966—; cons. Agar-Cross, Inc., Buenos Aires, 1966; agronomist AID, Tanzania, 1968. Former mem. water adv. bd. Lincoln City Council. Served with AUS, 1942-44; ETO; lt. col. Ret. Fellow AAAS; mem. Am. Soc. Agronomy, Soil Sci. Soc. Am., Internat. Soil Sci. Soc., Am. Interprofl. Inst., U. Nebr. Emeriti Assn., The Grange, Lincoln Engrs. Club, Sigma Xi, Gamma Sigma Delta (award of merit 1965). Republican. Clubs: Kiwanis, Lincoln Farmers. Research on chem. nature of soil organic matter; contbr. numerous articles to periodicals. Home: 6335 O St 631 Lincoln NE 68510

WELKER, BRUCE MARVIN, counselor; b. Chgo., Apr. 18, 1939; s. Marvin Frederick and Clara Marion (Peterson) W.; B.Ed., No. Ill. U., 1960; M.Ed., Wash. State U., 1967; m. Beth Lynnell Schlaf, June 17, 1961; children—Kimberly Louise, Kevin Bruce. Tchr. sci., math. Hale Sch., Stillman Valley, Ill., 1961-63; tchr. sci. Lincoln Jr. High Sch., Skokie, Ill., 1963-66; counselor Jason Lee Jr. High Sch., Tacoma, Wash., 1967-68; counselor, tchr. Hillside (Ill.) Sch., 1968-69; career counselor James B. Conant High Sch., Hoffman Estates, Ill., 1969—; resource person counselor edn. courses for career edn. Northeastern Ill. U., also No. Ill. U., 1975—. Dist. chmn. Arlington Heights (Ill.) Crusade of Mercy, 1975. Mem. Am., Ill. (treas. 1978-79), Northwest Suburban Chpt. (dir. 1980-81, pres.-elect 1981—) personnel and guidance assns., Nat., Suburban, Ill. (bd. govs. 1976—, pres.-elect 1979-80), vocat. guidance assns., Am., Ill. fedns. tchrs., Northwest Suburban Assn. Commerce and Industry, Ill. Sch. Counselors Assn., Dist. 211 Edn. Assn. Methodist. Club: United Methodist Men's. Home: 1162 N Hickory St Arlington Heights IL 60004 Office: 700 E Cougar Trail Hoffman Estates IL 60194

WELLER, HARRY DEETS, JR., indsl. mfg. co. exec.; b. Lancaster, Pa., Feb. 26, 1913; s. Harry Deets and Sara Ada (Stively) W.; B.S., Franklin-Marshall Coll., 1934; m. Betty Jane Allenbaugh, Apr. 6, 1940; children—Harry Deets III, Charles D., Judith Lynne. With Firestone Tire & Rubber Co., Akron, Ohio, 1935-48, 49-52; pres. Gengras Motors, Hartford, 1948-49; with White Motor Co., Cleve., 1952—, lease sales div., asst. regional mgr., asst. to v.p. sales, regional mgr., N.Y.C., regional v.p., v.p. sales, v.p. marketing, exec. v.p. sales and product planning; now v.p. procurement White Consol. Industries, Inc., Cleve.; dir. Great Lakes Diesel Corp. Trustee, Cleve. Health Mus. Mem. Pvt. Truck Council Am. (dir.), Am. Ordnance Assn., Soc. Automotive Engrs., Cleve. C. of C., Transp. Assn. Am. (dir.), Phi Kappa Psi. Presbyn. Mason. Clubs: Mayfield Country (past pres.), Union, Pepper Pike Golf, Cleveland Athletic (Cleve.); Pine Lake Trout Farm (Chagrin Falls, Ohio); Sea Pines Plantation (Hilton Head, S.C.). Home: 2728 Claythorne Rd Shaker Heights OH 44120 also 344 Greenwood Dr Hilton Head Island SC 29928 Office: White Consol Industries 11770 Berea Rd Cleveland OH 44111

WELLER, LLOYD WAYNE, engring. firm exec.; b. Kansas City, Kans., Nov. 27, 1921; s. Lloyd Cecil and Maude Buford (Wahlenmaier) W.; B.S. C.E., Kans. State U., 1944; B.S. S.E., U. Ill., 1945; M.S. Environ. Engring., Kans. U., 1966; m. Lorene Grant DeMuth Eherenmann, June 8, 1979; children—Fredrick Wayne, Courtney Ann; stepchildren—Roy Grant DeMuth, William Barry DeMuth, Karol Gwen DeMuth Padget. Engring. designer Consol. Vulta Aircraft Corp., Fort Worth, 1944; engring. designer Black & Veatch, Kansas City, Mo., 1946-51; project engr., 1951-64, partner, prin. engr., 1964—. Cubmaster, Kaw council Boy Scouts Am., 1956, asst. scoutmaster, 1958-61, mem. Eagle Bd. Rev., 1960-70. Served with AUS, 1944-46. Diplomate Am. Acad. Environ. Engrs. Fellow ASCE; mem. Water Pollution Control Fedn., Am. Water Works Assn., Am. Soc. Mil. Engrs., Nat. Soc. Profl. Engrs., Kans. Cons. Engrs. (chmn. 1979-80), Kans. Engring. Soc. (past pres. Eastern chpt., Key Mem. award 1967), Phi Kappa Phi, Sigma Tau, Steel Ring. Republican. Clubs: Homestead Country, Indian Creek Racquet, Woodside Racquet. Contbr. articles to various tech. jours. Home: 5357 Mission Woods Rd Mission Woods KS 66205 Office: Black & Veatch 1500 Meadow Lake Pkwy Kansas City MO 64114

WELLES, NYDIA LELIA CANOVAS, psychologist; b. Buenos Aires, Argentina, Mar. 30, 1935; came to U.S., 1968, naturalized, 1977; d. Artemio Tomás and Pura (Martínez) Canovas; B.A. in Elem. Edn., Nat. Coll. Edn., Evanston, Ill., 1976; M.A. in Counseling Psychology, Northwestern U., 1977, now postgrad.; m. Lorant Welles, Oct. 21, 1967; 1 son, Lorant Esteban. Tchr. in Argentina, 1954-64; pvt. practice psychology, Argentina, 1964-67; social worker Cath. Charities, Chgo., 1971-75; translator SRA, Chgo., 1975; test adminstr. Ednl. Testing Service, 1975-76; Latin Am. Services supr. Edgewater Uptown Community Mental Health Council, Chgo., 1978—; research asst. Center Family Studies, 1978-79. Mem. Ill. Assn. for Hispanic Mental Health (co-founder), Phi Delta Kappa. Roman Catholic. Author papers in field. Home: 5255 W Winona St Chicago IL 60630

WELLIVER, WARREN DEE, lawyer, state supreme ct. justice; b. Butler, Mo., Feb. 24, 1920; s. Carl Winfield and Burdee Marie (Wolfe) W.; B.A., U. Mo., 1945, LL.B., J.D., 1948; m. Ruth Rose Galey, Dec. 25, 1942; children—Gale Dee (Mrs. William B. Stone), Carla Camile Welliver Brooks, Christy Marie. Admitted to Mo. bar, 1948; asst. pros. atty. Boone County, Columbia, Mo., 1948-54; sr. partner firm Welliver, Atkinson and Eng, Columbia; 1960-74; tchr. law U. Mo. Law Sch., 1948-49; mem. Mo. Senate, 1977-79; justice Supreme Ct. Mo., Jefferson City, 1979—. Mem. Gov. Mo. Adv. Council Alcoholism and Drug Abuse, chmn. drug council, 1970-72; chmn. Task Force Revision Mo. Drug Laws, 1970-71; liaison mem. council Nat. Inst. Alcoholism and Alcohol Abuse, 1972—. Bd. dirs. Nat. Assn. Mental Health, 1970—, regional v.p., 1973-75; pres. Mo. Assn. Mental Health, 1968-69, Stephens Coll. Assos., 1965—; pres. Friends of Library, U. Mo., 1978-79. Democratic county chmn., 1954-64; hon. fellow Harry S. Truman Library Inst., 1979—. Served with USNR, 1941-45. Fellow Am. Coll. Trial Lawyers, Am. Bar Found.; mem. Am., Mo. (pres. 1967-68), Boone County (pres. 1970) bar assns., Am. Judicature Soc., Am. Legion (past post comdr.), Order of Coif. Clubs: Country of Mo., Columbia Country (past pres.). Home: RD 1 Hartsburg MO 65039 Office: Supreme Ct Bldg Jefferson City MO 65101

WELLMAN, RONALD DEAN, baseball coach; b. Celina, Ohio, May 2, 1948; s. Karl Frederick and Norma Jean W.; B.S., Bowling Green U., 1970, M.S., 1971; m. Linda Ann Miller, Sept. 20, 1969; children—Angela Jean, Nicole Lynn, Melissa Joy. Mem. faculty Elmhurst (Ill.) Coll., 1971-81, head baseball coach, 1971-81, athletic dir., 1977-81, asso. prof., 1979-81; head baseball coach, asst. prof. athletics Northwestern U., Evanston, Ill., 1981—. Mem. Nat. Assn. Coll. Dirs. Athletics, Nat. Assn. Coll. Baseball Coaches. Club: Lions. Editor: Physical Fitness Digest, 1979. Office: 190 Prospect Elmhurst IL 60126

WELLS, BEN HARRIS, beverage co. exec.; b. Saginaw, Mich., June 11, 1906; s. Ben W. and Florence (Harris) W.; student Ind. U., 1922-25; A.B., U. Mich., 1929, M.A., 1931; L.H.D., Westminster Coll., 1979; m. Katherine Gladney, June 17, 1938; children—Katherine Graves, Ben Gladney. Tchr. John Burroughs Sch., St. Louis County, 1929-31, 33-38; critic tchr. Sch. Edn., U. Mich., 1931-33; copy writer, sales promotion mgr., sales mgr. Seven-Up Co., St. Louis, 1938-43, v.p. sales and advt., 1943-65, pres., chief exec. officer, 1965-74, chmn., 1974-78, chmn. emeritus, 1978—. Bd. dirs. St. Louis council Boy Scouts Am., United Way, St. Louis Conservatory and Schs. for Arts, First Street Forum, Mo. Citizens for Arts, St. Louis Art Mus., Opera Theatre St. Louis, Winston Churchill Meml. and Library, Fulton, Mo., Music Assos. of Aspen (Colo.); dir. emeritus Civic Progress, Inc.; bd. dirs. St. Louis Symphony Soc., pres., 1970-78; chmn. Consumers Research Inst., 1970-78, Com. for Arts in Mo.; trustee John Burroughs Sch., 1954-61, St. Louis Arts and Humanities Commn., Arts and Edn. Council, Community Found.; pres. Laumeier Internat. Sculpture Park, St. Louis County; mem. devel. council U. Mich.; mem. Commn. on Future of Washington U., St. Louis. Mem. Phi Beta Kappa, Sigma Chi. Clubs: Rotary, Media, Bellerive Country, Bogey, Noonday, University, Racquet, Saint Louis. Home: 35 Westmoreland Pl Saint Louis MO 63108 Office: 560 Trinity at Delmar Saint Louis MO 63130

WELLS, DONALD EDWARD, ednl. adminstr.; b. Mauston, Wis., June 3, 1926; s. William Herbert and Fern Edna (Moore) W.; B.S., U. Wis., 1949, M.S., 1950; Ph.D., Mich State U., 1964; m. Anne Marie Wunderlich, Sept. 6, 1947; children—Scott Lawrence, Stevan Donald, Richard Michael. Editor, R.I. Agrl. Expt. Sta., 1950-51; farm dir. A.S. Weill Co., Inc., Buffalo, 1952-53; agrl. editor U. R.I., 1953-58; instr. Mich. State U., 1958-59, 62-63; various positions including dir. Nat. Project Agrl. Communications, Mich. State U., 1959-62; asst. prof., then asso. prof. journalism and mass communication Iowa State U., 1963-70; prof., chmn. dept. communications Wash. State U., Pullman, 1970-79; prof., chmn., dept. information and agrl. journalism, U. Minn., 1979—; mem. journalism edn. com. Western Newspaper Found.; cons. in field. Adv. council Wash. Human Rights Commn.; pres. Pullman United Way, 1976; mem. planning bd., S. Kingstown, R.I. Served with USNR, 1943-46. Mem. Assn. Edn. in Journalism, Agrl. Communicators in Edn., Nat. Agri-Mktg. Assn. Alpha Zeta, Gamma Sigma Delta, Alpha Kappa Delta. Editor books, periodicals, bulls.; editorial bd. Journalism Educator; contbr. articles to profl. publs.

WELLS, EUGENE LEE, ins. co. exec.; b. Waterloo, Iowa, Aug. 9, 1950; s. William L. and Imogene (Beck) W.; student Marion (Ind.) Coll., 1969-71; div. Salesman, Southwestern Book Co., Nashville, 1971; supr. M & D Electric Co., Tipp City, Ohio, 1971-72; sales rep. John Hancock Ins. Co., Dayton, Ohio, 1972-76, sales rep., sales mgr., Columbus, Ohio, 1976-79, sales mgr., 1981—; exec. account rep. Turner & Shepard, Inc., Columbus, 1979-81. Trustee, Columbus Youth Found., Columbus Met. Area Community Action Orgn., Columbus Vols. Orgn.; past state chmn. Hugh O'Brian Youth Found. Mem. Nat. Life Underwriters Assn., Ohio Life Underwriters Assn., Columbus Life Underwriters Assn., Columbus Jaycees (pres. 1981—, dir.; Outstanding Achievement award 1979). Republican. Methodist. Home: 3142 Hayden Rd Columbus OH 43220 Office: 6400 E Main St Reynoldsburg OH 43068

WELLS, EUGENE RALPH, dentist, farmer; b. Hutchinson, Kans., Nov. 5, 1929; s. Ralph H. and Margaret (Crawley) W.; student Hutchinson Jr. Coll., 1947-49, Wichita U., 1949-51; D.D.S., U. Kansas City, 1960; m. Carlene Sturgis, Oct. 16, 1952; children—Melinda, Pam, Julia, Randall, Elizabeth. With Standard Oil Co., 1951-52, N.Y. Life Ins. Co., 1954-56; gen. practice dentistry, Hutchinson, 1960-81. Owner, proprietor cattle ranch and farm, Hutchinson, 1963—; pres. Maropix Oil; v.p. Maropix Inc.; dir. MOD, Inc., Central State Bank, Hutchinson, United Kans. Bank Shares. County co-chmn. Harmon for Gov. com. 1968. Bd. dirs. Hutchinson YMCA, 1970-75. Served with AUS, 1952-54. Mem. ADA (v.p. 1978-79), Kans. Dental Assn. (del., v.p. 1981-82). Elk, Mason (Shriner). Home: 75 Prairie Dr Hutchinson KS 67501 Office: 620 E 30th St Hutchinson KS 67501

WELLS, HERSCHEL JAMES, physician, hosp. adminstr.; b. Kirkland, Ark., Feb. 23, 1924; s. Alymer James and Martha Thelma (Cross) W.; student Emory U., 1941-42, U. Ark., 1942-43; M.D., U. Tenn., 1946; m. Carmen Ruth Williams, Aug. 5, 1946; children—Judith Alliece (Mrs. W.J. Jarecki), Pamela Elliece (Mrs. G. D. McKinven), Joanne Olivia (Mrs. E.M. Meyer). Rotating intern, then resident internal medicine Wayne County Gen. Hosp. and Infirmary, Eloise, Mich., 1946-50, dir. infirmary div., 1955-65, gen. supt., 1965-74, dir. Walter P. Reuther Meml. Long Term Care Facility, 1974-78; rev. physician DDS, SSA, Traverse City, Mich., 1978—. Served to maj. M.C., AUS, 1948-55. Fellow Am. Coll. Nursing Home Adminstrs.; mem. A. M.A., Mich., Wayne County med. socs., Am. Fedn. Clin. Research, Soc. Nuclear Medicine, Mich. Assn. Professions, Alpha Kappa Kappa, Pi Kappa Alpha. Mason (Shriner, 32 deg.). Home: PO Box 305 Mesick MI 49668 Office: PO Box 712 Traverse City MI 49684

WELLS, JOSEPH, aerospace corp. ofcl.; b. Jacksonville, Ill., Mar. 5, 1943; s. Friend and Florence Catherine (Barton) W.; B.S. in Indsl. Engring., Purdue U., 1967; m. Frances Judith Liebelt, Apr. 19, 1969; children—Matthew Joseph, Andrew Michael. With Rockwell Internat., Cedar Rapids, Iowa, 1967—, plating renovation mgr. Interconnect Products, 1977, quality control mgr., 1977—; liaison tng. to several munitions depots U.S. Army, 1967-69. Active Boy Scouts Am., 1952-61; exec. adv. Jr. Achievement, 1976-77. Served with AUS, 1967-69. Mem. Am. Inst. Indsl. Engrs. (region XI dir. 1974-75, pres. Cedar Rapids chpt. 1978-79), Purdue Alumni Assn, Alpha Chi Rho. Editor several tech. manuals, 1967-69, quality systems manual, 1979. Home: Rural Route 4 Box 285 Cedar Rapids IA 52401 Office: Rockwell Internat 400 Collins Rd N E Cedar Rapids IA 52406

WELLS, MAC COLBERT, clergyman; b. Mooers, N.Y., Oct. 14, 1918; s. Myron and Anna Lois (McDowell) W.; B.S., N.Y. U., 1948, M.B.A., 1948; B.D., Princeton Theol. Sem., 1969, Th.M., 1970; m. Mauveleene (Bina) Andrews, Feb. 11, 1945; children—Robert M., Bruce A. Clerical worker U.S. Govt., 1937-40, 41-42; enlisted in USAAF, 1942, commd. 2d lt. 1944, advanced through grades to lt. col. USAF, 1957; service in ETO, Korea; ret., 1965; ordained to ministry United Presbyn. Ch., 1969; bus. mgr., then asst. and asso. pastor First Presbyn. Ch., Princeton, N.J., 1966-75; asso. pastor 2d Presbyn. Ch., Indpls., 1975—. Decorated Purple Heart, Air medal, Air Force Commendation medal (2), Joint Service Commendation medal (2); fellow ch. bus. adminstrn., 1969. Mem. Nat. Assn. Ch. Bus. Adminstrs. (pres. 1980); life mem. Air Force Assn. (charter), Air Force Hist. Assn. Republican. Club: Shriners. Home: 3139 Amherst St Indianapolis IN 46268 Office: 7700 N Meridian St Indianapolis IN 46260

WELLS, ROBERT FRANCIS, guidance counselor; b. Lincoln, Nebr., Aug. 19, 1936; s. Francis Joseph and Ruth Luella (Mills) W.; student Hastings Coll., 1954-57; B.A. in Edn., Nebr. Wesleyan U., 1959; postgrad. U. No. Colo., Greeley, 1964; M.S. in Guidance, U. Nebr., Omaha, 1968, postgrad., 1975-76, Lincoln, 1977—; m. C. Ann Maguire, Dec. 23, 1962; 1 dau., Jane Elizabeth. Tchr., Fairbury (Nebr.) High Sch., Jr. Coll., 1959-62; counselor, tchr. Fremont (Nebr.) Sr. High Sch., 1962-75; counselor Fremont Jr. High Sch., 1975—. Active Dodge County Youth. Served with N.G., Nebr., 1958-64, active duty, 1959. Mem. NEA, Nebr., Fremont edn. assns., Nebr., Am. personnel and guidance assns., Am. Sch. Counselors Assn. Republican. Methodist (sr. choir, commn. on membership and evangelism). Clubs: Eastern Star, Tangier Oriental Band, Masons, Shriners. Home: 2217 Gaeth Fremont NE 68025 Office: 935 Broad St Fremont NE 68025

WELLS, WILEY HAYWARD, mfg. co. exec.; b. South Bend, Ind., July 4, 1945; s. Arthur Lee and Mattie Mae Wells; B.S., Ball State U., 1970; J.D., Valparaiso U., 1978; postgrad. Ind. U., 1979-81. With, Westinghouse Corp., Muncie, Ind., 1964-72; legal researcher firm Mahoney & Stanley, South Bend, 1975-76; dep. Sheriff St. Joseph County Police Dept., 1976-78; admitted to Ind. bar, 1978; mgr. ops. Bendix Corp., South Bend, 1978—. Bd. dirs. St. Joseph County CETA program, 1979—; bd. dirs. Hansel Center, 1979—, chmn. public relations com., 1980—. Served to 2d lt. USAF, 1972-75. Decorated Air Force Commendation medal. Mem. Am. Bar Assn., Ind. Bar Assn., Ind. Am. Vets. Assn., Kappa Alpha Psi. Baptist. Home: 1102 Woodward Ave South Bend IN 46616 Office: Bendix Corp 717 N Bendix Dr South Bend IN 46620

WELLS, WILLIAM RAYMOND, educator; b. Winder, Ga., Nov. 28, 1936; s. Lonnie and Cora Wells; B.S., Ga. Inst. Tech., 1959; M.S., Va. Poly. Inst., 1961, Ph.D., 1968; M.A., Harvard U., 1965; m. Margaret Santen, Sept. 8, 1956; children—Ward, Winston, Richard. Aerospace technologist Langley Research Center, NASA, Hampton, Va., 1959-68; prof. aerospace engring., U. Cin., 1968-77; prof. and chmn. engring., Wright State U., Dayton, Ohio, 1977—; cons. NASA Langley Research Center, USAF Flight Dynamic Lab., Veda, Inc. NASA grantee, 1972-79; USAF grantee, 1977-79. Mem. AAUP, AIAA, Am. Soc. Engring. Edn. (NASA fellow, 1970), Am. Acad. Mechanics. Home: 7223 Crinstead Ct Cincinnati OH 45243 Office: Col Glenn Hwy Dayton OH 45435

WELLS, WILLIAM STEVEN, public relations co. exec.; b. Detroit, Aug. 19, 1945; s. Ronald and Eleanor (Vancea) W.; A.B., Hamilton Coll., 1967; m. Mary Rudolph, Nov. 27, 1969; children—Adam, David. Journalist, New Haven Register, Providence Jour., Detroit Free Press, 1968-75; exec. asst. to Mich. Gov. William Milliken, Lansing, 1975-76; account exec. Fleishman-Hillard, Inc., St. Louis, 1976-78; v.p., mgr. Doremus & Co., Mpls., 1978-80; v.p., mgr. Hill & Knowlton, Inc., Mpls., 1980—. Served with USNR, 1968-69. Mem. Nat. Investor Relations Inst., Public Relations Soc. Am. Republican. Clubs: Minneapolis, Edina Country, Minnesota, Minn. Squash Raquets Assn. Contbr. articles to profl. jours. Office: Hill & Knowlton Inc 490 Pillsbury Center Minneapolis MN 55402

WELLS-DAVIS, MARGIE ELAINE, detergent mfg. co. exec.; b. Marshalltown, Iowa, Apr. 27, 1944; d. Gladstone Eugene and Ida Mae (Marshall) Wells; A.B., Simpson Coll., 1966; M.A., Syracuse U., 1968; Ph.D., U. Cin., 1979; m. Allan Caleb Davis, Oct. 7, 1979; 1 dau., Allana. Tchr., St. Louis Bd. Edn., 1966, Syracuse (N.Y.) public schs., 1967; asst. supr. residence halls Jersey City Job Corps Center for Women, 1968; asst. dean students U. Cin., 1968-70, acting dir. supportive services, 1970-71; ednl. coordinator Narcotics Addiction Program, Cin., 1971-72; sociologist USPHS, Cin., 1972-73; supr. Med. Social Workers Cin. Health Dept., 1973-74, dir. staff, orgn. devel., 1974-76; affirmative action coordinator Procter & Gamble Corp., Cin., 1977—; cons. home health aid services East Harlem Environ. Extension Service, Mont. State U., mental health services No. Jewish Hosp., Cin. Bd. dirs. Cin. Human Relations Commn., 1978, treas., 1979-80; bd. dirs. Newlife for Girls, 1977-79; sec. Central Community Health Bd.; mem. Police Tng. Task Force. Nat. Meth. scholar, 1962; recipient City of Cin. Outstanding Service resolution, 1977. Mem. Am. Mgmt. Assn., Organizational Devel. Network, Am. Soc. Tng. and Devel., Cin. Profl. Women's Network, Phi Beta Kappa, Epsilon Sigma. Methodist. Clubs: Women's City of Cin. (dir.), Womanways. Office: Procter & Gamble Corp PO Box 599 GO South Cincinnati OH 45202

WELSH, HAROLD T. (TOM), credit union exec.; b. LaSalle, Ill., Jan. 1, 1933; s. Harold William and Julia Elizabeth (Nauiokaitis) W.; student public schs., Chgo.; m. Patricia Joan Cobb, Nov. 26, 1955; children—Susan, Steven, Leanne, John, William. Payroll supr. Elec. Utilities Co., LaSalle, Ill., 1950-63; treas. Elec. Utilities Co. Employees Credit Union, LaSalle, 1956-63; mgr. Fed. Paper Bd. Employees Credit Union, Morris, Ill., 1963-68; pres. Gen. Foods Employees Credit Union, Kankakee, Ill., 1968—; v.p. Mid-States Corp. Fed. Credit Union, Oak Brook, Ill., 1975—, chmn. exec. com., 1979—; mem. Ill. Gov.'s Credit Union Adv. Bd. Active Boy Scouts Am., 1970-73, vice chmn. Rainbow council, 1973; mem. ad hoc com. on consumer laws Kankakee Consumer Commn., 1978; treas. Wesley United Meth. Ch., Bradley, Ill., 1981. Served with U.S. Army, 1954-56. Mem. Credit Union Nat. Assn. (treas., dir.), Ill. Credit Union League (chmn. 1977-79, dir., first pres. Found. 1978-79), Ill. Credit Union League Service Corp. (pres.), Nat. Advt. Program Cuna (chmn.), Credit Union Execs. Soc. (dir. Ill. Council 1973-76), Nat. Assn. State Credit Union Suprs. (Ill. rep.), Kankakee County Credit Assn. (pres. 1976-77), World Council Credit Unions (alt. dir.). Club: Lions (dir. club 1975-78). Office: 1495 E Willow St Kankakee IL 60901

WELSH, JOSEPH LEON, investment co. exec.; b. Schuyler County, Mo., Apr. 8, 1944; s. Wallace Leon and Helen Louise W.; B.S. in Econs., U. Mo., 1969; postgrad. U. Pitts., 1970-71, U. Mo., 1973-75; m. Susan DeAnn Dugan, July 24, 1965; children—Melissa Jo, Kelley Ann, Joseph Leon. Engr., Sta. KTVO-TV, Ottumwa, Iowa, 1962-65; sales engr. Gen. Electric Co., Pitts., 1965-72; farmer, businessman, Lancaster, Mo., 1972-77; chief exec. officer Welsh Bros. Investment Co., Lancaster, 1975-81; chief of mktg. ops. Internat. Mktg. Div., Mo. dept. agrl., Jefferson City, 1981—. Chmn., Schuyler County Republican Com., 1978, 79, 80-81. Recipient Outstanding Young Farmer award Future Farmers Am., 1975. Mem. Lancaster Jr. C. of C. (pres. 1973), Young Farmers (pres. 1976). Republican. Baptist. Clubs: Rotary (pres. 1981), Lancaster Community (pres. 1980), Band Boosters, Football Boosters, Masons, Shriners. Home: Rural Route 2 Loesch Rd Jefferson City MO 65101 Office: Jefferson Bldg Jefferson City MO 65102

WELSH, ROBERT WEAVER, bus. exec.; b. Chgo., Mar. 7, 1953; s. Leslie T. and Mary Lee (Weaver) W.; B.S. in Mktg., Pa. State U., 1975. Sales rep. Procter & Gamble Co., Chgo., 1975-77; pres. Boyt div. Welsh Sportings Co., Barrington, Ill., 1977—, Welsh Center Office Complex, Barrington, 1978—; gen. mgr. Shallowbrook Farm, Bradford, Ill., 1977—; sr. partner Welsh Welsh & Vorhees Advt., 1978—; exec. v.p. Leslie T. Welsh Inc., Barrington, 1979—. Mem. Pa. State U. Fund Council, 1981. Recipient Barrash service award Pa. State U., 1975. Mem. Luggage and Leather Goods Mfrs. Assn., Nat. Sporting Goods Assn., Am. Horse Council, Woits Warriors. Republican. Roman Catholic. Clubs: Barrington Hills Country, Chgo., 2400. Home: 33 Lake View Ln Barrington IL 60010 Office: 1300 Grove Ave Barrington IL 60010

WELSHANS, MERLE TALMADGE, utility co. exec.; b. Murphysboro, Ill., June 17, 1918; s. Arthur Isaac and Martha Ellen (Blair) W.; B.Ed., So. Ill. U., 1940; M.A., Washington U., St. Louis, 1947, Ph.D., 1951; m. Mary Katherine Whitenbaugh, June 2, 1942; children—Elizabeth Margaret (Mrs. Samuel Van Steenbergh), Arthur Edmund, Janice Ann. Asst. v.p. Merc. Mortgage Co., Olney, Ill., 1940; exec. officer, dept. bus. adminstrn. George Washington U., 1950-54; prof. fin. Grad. Sch. Bus. Adminstrn., Washington U., 1954-69; v.p. fin. Union Electric Co., St. Louis, 1969—; dir. Union Colliery Co. Trustee McKendree Coll., Deaconess Hosp., Govt. Research Inst., St. Louis Coll. Pharmacy, St. Paul Sch. Theology. Served to capt. AUS, 1942-45. Decorated Bronze Star medal. Mem. Am. Econ. Assn., Am. Fin. Assn., Soc. Fin. Analysts, Fin. Mgmt. Assn., Alpha Kappa Psi, Beta Gamma Sigma, Artus. Methodist. Author: (with R.W. Melicher) Principles of Finance, 5th edit, 1980. Cons. economist, editor Financial Newsletter, 1965-69. Home: 14360 Ladue Rd Chesterfield MO 63017 Office: PO Box 149 Saint Louis MO 63166

WELSTEAD, JEAN MAUDIE, artist, educator; b. Fremont, Nebr., Nov. 22, 1922; d. Edward C. and Irene Elizabeth (Hooper) Olson; student Joslyn Art Mus., Omaha, 1962-64, Midland Luth. Coll., Fremont, 1970-74, St. Mary's Coll., Omaha, 1964-68; m. Marvin Glenn Welstead, Feb. 21, 1942; children—Robert L., Jon A. Legal sec. law firm, Fremont, 1940-42; staff hdqrs. office Northrup Aircraft Co., Hawthorne, Calif., 1943; civil service wartime rationing officer 3d Air Force, U.S. Air Force, Stuttgart, Ark., 1943-46; adminstrv. clk. merit system Dodge County Assistance Office, Fremont, 1946-48; art supr. Fremont Parks and Recreation, 1967-71; pvt. instr. art Fremont, 1967-71; exhibited Sioux City Art Center, 1976-78, 2d Ann. Masters Touch Competitions, 1976, 4th Ann. Printmaking and Drawing Competition, Tulsa, 1977, Elden Gallery, Wesleyan U., 1976-77, Am. Bicentennial Exhbn., 1976; represented in permanent collection Nebr. Artists, Kearney State Coll. Chmn. Art from the Heart Viet Nam Amputees, Oakland Naval Hosp. (Calif.), 1968; active Boy Scouts Am., Republican party; pres. Linden Sch. PTA, 1955. Mem. Assn. Nebr. Art Clubs (award of excellence 1974-75, 76-79, dir. 1974-75), Fremont Art Assn. (charter; organizer, pres. 1965-71), Asso. Artists Omaha, Nat. League Am. Pen Women. Methodist. Club: Order of Eastern Star. Home: 1943 Parkview Dr Fremont NE 68025

WEMHOFF, OWEN CARROLL, social services orgn. adminstr.; b. Decatur, Ind., Sept. 26, 1927; s. Robert and Fanny (Penz) W.; student U. Detroit, 1948-49; B.S., Ball State U., 1952, M.A., 1955; m. Phyllis Collier, June 17, 1960; children—Stacey D., Robin R., Charles D. Tchr., athletic coach public high schs., Ind., 1952-57; exec. dir. Johnny Appleseed Sch. and Tng. Center, Ft. Wayne, Ind., 1957-63; exec. dir. Detroit Met. Adv. Com. for Mentally Retarded, 1963-64; exec. dir. Ind. Assn. for Retarded, 1964-67; asst. exec. dir. Nat. Assn. for Retarded Citizens, N.Y.C., 1967-69; exec. dir. Child Care of Allen County, Ft. Wayne, 1969—. Served with U.S. Army, 1946-48. Mem. Nat. Conf. Agy. Execs. for Retarded Citizens (past pres.), Agy. Adminstrs. of Allen County (pres. 1961-64), Allen County Community Coordinated Child Care (pres. 1960-63), Nat. Assn. Edn. Young Children, Am. Soc. Tng. and Devel., Day Care Council Am., Fort Wayne C. of C. Democrat. Clubs: Sertoma (past pres.), Jaycees (past pres.). Home: 426 W Oakdale Dr Fort Wayne IN 46807 Office: 1021 W Wayne St Fort Wayne IN 46804

WENDEL, GEORGE DORIAN, educator; b. Chgo., Feb. 17, 1928; s. George Peter and Sarah Veronica (Dorian) W.; B.S. with honors, Loyola U., Chgo., 1952; A.M., St. Louis U., 1956, Ph.D., 1960; m. Mary Isabelle Collins, June 28, 1952; children—George Dorian, William Collins, Peter Thomas, Paul John. Instr. polit. sci. St. Louis U., 1956-60, asst. prof., 1960-63, asso. prof., 1963-67, prof., 1967—, dir. Center for Urban Programs, 1968—; asso. Brookings Instn., 1977-81; prof. cons. task force GAO, 1978; spl. cons. on planning to mayors City St. Louis, 1968-77; tech. cons. St. Louis City and County Plan Commns., OEO Community Action Agy., St. Louis, St. Louis and East St. Louis Model Cities Agys. Mem. Mo. Gov.'s Commn. on Reform Local Govt. Law; chmn. Citizens Forum Regional Council Govts., St. Louis; chmn. St. Louis County Suprs. Com. Neighborhood Preservation and Devel.; mem. planning council, chmn. agy. data system com. United Way; bd. dirs. Human Devel. Corp., 1975-79; mem. exec. bd. St. Louis chpt. Interracial Council Bus. Opportunity; mem. State Campaign Fin. Rev. Commn., 1978. Served with Signal Corps, U.S. Army, 1946-48. Nat. Conv. fellow Nat. Center Edn. and Politics and Eagleton Found., Rutgers U., 1964. Mem. Am. Polit. Sci. Assn., AAUP, Am. Soc. Public Adminstrn., Am. Soc. Planning Ofcls., Phi Beta Kappa. Democrat. Roman Catholic. Author: (with H. J. Schmandt and P. G. Steinbicker) Metropolitan Reform in St. Louis, 1961; (with H. J. Schmandt and E. A. Tomey) The Impact of Federal Aid on the City of Saint Louis, 1981. Home: 90 Arundel Pl Clayton MO 63105 Office: Center for Urban Programs St Louis U 221 N Grand Ave Saint Louis MO 63103

WENDELL, HARLAN LEONARD POTTS, auto co. exec.; b. Pottstown, Pa., June 4, 1924; s. James I. and Marjorie P. W.; A.B., Yale U., 1947; M.B.A., Harvard U., 1948; m. Dorothea Richardson, Sept. 10, 1949; children—Harlan Leonard Potts, David R., Thayer. Editor plant publ. E.I. DuPont de Nemours & Co., Inc., Parlin, N.J., 1948-50, editorial asst. pub. affairs dept., Wilmington, Del., 1950-53, mgr. Pacific dist., Menlo Park, Calif., 1954-56, pub. affairs adviser, Wilmington, 1956-63, asst. dir. of pub. affairs dept., 1963-68, asst. dir. pub. affairs, 1968-76, dir. pub. affairs, 1976-78; exec. dir. office of chief exec. communications Ford Motor Co., Dearborn, Mich., 1978—; pub. relations adviser to sec. HEW, Washington, 1953-54. Trustee Tower Hill Sch., Wilmington, Del., 1973, Hill Sch., Pottstown, Pa., 1978. Served with USMCR, 1942-46. Mem. Pub. Relations Soc. Am., Mfg. Chemists Assn. Clubs: Nat. Press, Vicmead Hunt; Rotary, Wilmington, Wilmington Country (Wilmington, Del.). Home: Edgemere Rd Grosse Pointe Farms MI 48236 Office: Ford Motor Co American Rd Dearborn MI 48121

WENDT, GEORGE ROBERT, real estate co. exec.; b. Chgo., Jan. 8, 1923; s. William Henry and Katherine (Crowley) W.; B.S., U. Notre Dame, 1943; m. Loretta M. Howard, Feb. 23, 1946; children—Kathryn (Mrs. Daniel Sudeikis), George Robert, Loretta (Mrs. Gregory Jolivette), Martha (Mrs. Edward Muldoon), Nancy (Mrs. William Healy), Thomas, Paul. With William H. Wendt, Inc., Chgo., 1946—, pres., gen. mgr., dir., 1965—; pres., dir. 1814 Corp., Chgo., 1962—; dir. Beverly Bank Chgo.; mem. Chgo. Real Estate Bd., 1967—. Past trustee Little Company of Mary Hosp., St. Frances de Sales High Sch., Mother McAuley Liberal Arts High Sch.; bd. dirs. Beverly Art Assn. Served to capt. USNR, World War II; companion Ill. Commandery. Recipient Silver Anvil award Pub. Relations Soc. Am., 1959. Mem. Navy League U.S. (Ill. pres. 1964, 65, nat. dir.), Naval Order U.S., Naval Res. Assn. (nat. dir., dist. pres. 1957-60). Clubs: Beverly Country, Tavern, Chgo. Athletic (Chgo.). Home: 9201 S Bell Ave Chicago IL 60620 Office: 9933 S Western Ave Chicago IL 60643

WENDT, MARILYNN SUZANN, ednl. adminstr.; b. Bay City, Mich., Oct. 6, 1939; d. Clarence Henry and Margaret Viola (Rugenstein) W.; A.A., Bay City Jr. Coll., 1959; B.A., Central Mich. U., 1962, M.A., 1964; Ed.D., Wayne State U., 1971. Tchr., teaching prin. Baxman Sch. Dist., Bay City, 1959-62; tchr., elem. curriculum supr., dir. elem. edn. Essexville-Hampton Schs. (Mich.), 1962-66; dir. curriculum research, dir. elem. edn., dir. spl. projects Bloomfield Hills (Mich.) Schs., 1966-75; consortium facilitator exptl. and demonstration centers Mich. Dept. Edn., Lansing, 1975-76; team leader Flexible Learning Alternatives Program, Bloomfield Hills, 1976-78; elem. prin. Waterford (Mich.) Sch. Dist., 1978—; instr. Wayne State U., Detroit, 1971—. Recipient Disting. Service award Bloomfield Hills Schs., 1980. Mem. Assn. Supervision and Curriculum Devel., Nat. Assn. Core Curriculum (dir.), Mich. Assn. Supervision and Curriculum Devel., Mich. Assn. Core Curriculum (past pres.), Wayne Ednl. Options, Waterford Assn. Sch. Adminstrs., Delta Kappa Gamma. Contbr. articles to profl. jours. Home: 5252 Rosamond Ln Pontiac MI 48054

WENDT, VERNON EARL, physician; b. Cleve., Mar. 26, 1931; s. Raymond C. and Esther L. (Naujoks) W.; B.S. in Chemistry and Zoology cum laude, Baldwin Wallace Coll., 1952; M.D., Columbia, 1956; m. Hildegard Moeller, Aug. 14, 1953; children—David, Frederick, Kathy, Beth, Doralyn, James, Vernon Earl. Intern Detroit Receiving Hosp., 1956-57, resident, 1957, 59-62, dir. cardiac lab., 1962-65; USPHS postdoctoral fellow cardiology Wayne State U. Sch. Medicine, 1961, instr. medicine, 1961, asst. prof. medicine, 1962-65, asst. clin. prof. medicine, 1965—; dir. research Blodgett Meml. Hosp., Grand Rapids, Mich., 1965-67; practice medicine specializing in internal medicine and cardiology, Grand Rapids, 1967—; former chief cardiology service, now active staff Butterworth Hosp., Grand Rapids; attending staff Blodgett Meml. Med. Center, Grand Rapids; asso. clin. prof. medicine (cardiology) Mich. State U., 1973—. Past pres. regional bd., trustee, pres. Mich. Lung Assn., past chmn. state profl. edn. and research com.; elder Hope Luth. Ch., Grand Rapids, past pres. Served as capt. M.C., USAF, 1957-59. Fellow Am. Coll. Cardiology, Am. Coll. Angiology; mem. A.M.A., A.C.P., Mich., Kent County, Christian med. socs., Am., Mich. (trustee, past pres. Kent County chpt.) heart assns., AAAS, Western Mich. Critical Care Symposia (bd. dirs.), Am. Fedn. Clin. Research, Western Acad. Medicine, Detroit Physiol. Soc. Author articles clin. and exptl. cardiovascular diseases. Home: 1620 Andover Rd East Grand Rapids MI 49506 Office: 21 Michigan NE Grand Rapids MI 49503

WENGER, J(OHN) C(HRISTIAN), clergyman, author, educator; b. Honey Brook, Pa., Dec. 25, 1910; s. Aaron Martin and Martha A. (Rock) W.; B.A., Goshen Coll., 1934; student Westminster Theol. Sem., 1934-35, 36-37; Th.D., U. Zürich, 1938; postgrad. U. Basel, 1938, U. Chgo., 1941; m. Ruth D. Detweiler, Apr. 3, 1937; children—Daniel M., John Paul, Mary L., Elizabeth A. Ordained to ministry Mennonite Ch., 1944; asso. pastor N. Goshen (Ind.) Mennonite Ch., 1944-49; pastor Olive Mennonite Ch., Jamestown, Ind., 1949-50; bishop, 1951; bishop Olive, Hudson Lake, Pleasant View, Holdeman, Maple Grove, N. Goshen Mennonite chs., 1951—; postdoctoral vis. fellow Princeton Sem., 1964-65; prof. hist. theology Goshen Bibl. Sem., Elkhart, Ind., 1965—; mem. faculty Union Bibl. Sem., Yeotmal, India, 1971, Eastern Mennonite Sem., Harrisonburg, Va., 1971-72; mem. com. on Bible translation, 1965—; moderator Ind.-Mich. Mennonite Conf., 1954-64; mem. Presidium of Mennonite Conf., 1963-72; mem. exec. council Inst. of Mennonite Studies, 1967—. Recipient Alumnus of Yr. award Eastern Mennonite Coll., 1972. Mem. Mennonite Hist. Soc. (pres. 1962-71, 72-73). Author numerous books on theology and history of religion including: Separated unto God, 1951, Introduction to Theology, 1954, God's Word Written, 1966, The Mennonite Church in America, 1967; author numerous booklets; contbr. articles to encys. and various religious publs.; editor: The Complete Writings of Menno Simons, 1956, Conrad Grebel's Programmatic Letters of 1524, 1970; editorial bd. Mennonite Quar. Rev., 1939—, Mennonite Ency., 1946-59, Studies in Anabaptist series, 1946—. Home: 1300 Greencroft Dr Apt 1 Goshen IN 46526 Office: Goshen Bibl Seminary 3003 Benham Ave Elkhart IN 46517

WENNEKER, JAMES EMMETT, publishing exec.; b. Quincy, Ill., Aug. 1, 1935; s. Jacob Emmett and Trula Lurlene (Brockschmidt) W.; student Quincy Coll., 1953-55, LaSalle Extension U., 1967-73; m. Joyce Ann Anderson, Sept. 15, 1956 (div. July 1973); children—Julie Lee, Jeri Ellen. TV dir., TV and radio announcer WGEM AM-FM TV, Quincy, 1953-61; gen. mgr. WZOE-AM, Princeton, Ill.; 1961-67; store mgr. Montgomery Ward, Princeton, Ill., 1967-69; TV dir. WQAD-TV, Moline, Ill., 1969-70; gen. mgr. KSIM-AM Radio, Sikeston, Mo., 1970-76; creative adviser Delta Projects, Inc., Sikeston, 1976—; self-employed piano technician, 1976—. Mem. adv. com. Health Occupations Sikeston pub. schs., 1975—; chmn. Sikeston Bicentennial Commn., 1974-76. Bd. dirs. Ret. Sr. Vol. Program, Scott County, Mo., 1973-76, Sikeston Little Theater, 1970—, Sikeston Council on the Arts, 1973-76. Served with Ill. N.G., 1955-63. Baptist. Mason (32 deg.). Contbg. author Big Bureau and Bright Prairies-History of Bureau County, Ill., 1968. Home: 1911 Oklahoma St Sikeston MO 63801 Office: Sikeston MO 63801

WENNER, HERBERT ALLAN, physician, educator; b. Drums, Pa., Nov. 14, 1912; s. Herbert C. and Verna (Walp) W.; B.S., Bucknell U., 1933; M.D., U. Rochester, 1939; m. Ruth I. Berger, June 27, 1942; children—Peter W., James M., Susan T., Thomas H. Intern pathology U. Colo. Sch. Medicine, Denver, 1939-40, pediatrics Yale Sch. Medicine, 1940-41, asst. resident in pediatrics, 1941-42, instr. preventive medicine, 1944-46; NRC fellow Yale U.-Johns Hopkins U., 1942-43; asst. prof. pediatrics and bacteriology U. Kans. Sch. Medicine, 1946-49; asso. prof. pediatrics and bacteriology U. Kans., 1949-51, research prof. pediatrics, 1951-69, adj. prof., 1975—; Joyce C. Hall Distinguished prof. pediatrics U. Mo., Children's Mercy Hosp., 1969—, adj. prof. Sch. Dentistry, 1970—. Civilian cons. epidemiology Kans. Bd. of Health, USPHS. Recipient Research Career award NIH, 1962. Diplomate Am. Bd. Microbiology, Am. Bd. Pediatrics. Fellow AAAS, Am. Pub. Health Assn., Am. Acad. Pediatrics; mem. Soc. Pediatric Research, Am. Pediatric Soc., Soc. Exptl. Biology and Medicine, Biometrics Soc., Mo. State Med. Assn. AMA, Royal Soc. Health, AAUP, N.Y. Acad. Scis., Am. Soc. for Virology, Am. Epidemiology Soc., Am. Coll. Epidemiology, Infectious Diseases Soc. Am. Episcopalian. Asso. editor Am. Jour. Epidemiology; editorial bd. Intervirology; past mem. editorial adv. bd. Archives Virology; contbr. articles to profl. books, jours. Home: 9711 Johnson Dr Merriam KS 66203 Office: Children's Mercy Hosp 24th at Gillham Rd Kansas City MO 64108

WENSTROM, FRANK AUGUSTUS, state senator, city and county ofcl.; b. Dover, N.D., July 27, 1903; s. James August and Anna Petra (Kringstad) W.; student public schs., Carrington, N.D.; m. Mary Esther Pickett, June 10, 1938. In oil bus., Carrington, 1932-38, Williston, N.D., 1938-45; mgr. Williston C. of C., 1945-51; public relations officer 1st Nat. Bank, Williston, 1951-53, mng. officer real estate mortgage dept., 1953-60; exec. officer Northwestern Fed. Savs. and Loan Assn. Williston, 1964-68; spl. cons. Am. State Bank Williston, 1968-73; mem. N.D. Senate, 1957-60, 67—, pres. pro tem, 1973-74; lt. gov. State of N.D., 1963-64; dir., sec. Williston Community Hotel Co., 1950—; chmn. subscriber's com. N.W. dist. N.D. Blue Cross-Blue Shield, 1972—. Mem. Williston Public Housing Authority, 1951—, Williams County Park Bd., 1951—, N.D. Yellowstone-Ft. Union Commn., 1957-64, Legis. Research Council, 1957-60, Legis. Council, 1969-70; del. N.D. 2d Constl. Conv., 1970, pres., 1971-72; Williams County chmn. U.S. Savs. Bonds Com., 1958-69; bd. dirs. N.D. Easter Seals Soc., 1960-75, state pres., 1970-71; bd. advisors Salvation Army, 1960-75; bd. dirs. Univ. Found., U. N.D., Williston Center, 1965—; mem. joint legis. com. Nat. Assn. Ret. Tchrs.-Am. Assn. Ret. Persons, 1975—, chmn., 1979-80. Recipient Liberty Bell award N.D. Bar Assn., 1977, Disting. Service award Bismarck Jr. Coll., 1981. Mem. Upper Missouri Purebred Cattle Breeders Assn. (sec.-treas. 1947-62), N.D. Wildlife Fedn. (state pres. 1947-48), Greater N.D. Assn. (dir. 1955-56, mem. Roosevelt Nat. Meml. Park com. 1957-63), U.S. Savs. and Loan League (legis. com. 1965-67). Republican. Congregationalist. Clubs: Rotary, Elks, Masons, Shriners, Order Eastern Star. Office: PO Box 187 Williston ND 58801-0002

WENTE, VERGIE D., state ofcl.; b. Decatur County, Kans., Apr. 24, 1936; d. Virgil D. and Hazel (Storer) Wennihan; student Colby Community Coll., 1969; m. Lloyd A. Wente, June 23, 1953 (div. May 1966); children—Allen Charles, Rhonda Marie, Daniel Lloyd, Lynne LaRea. Librarian, N.W. Kans. Library System, Hoxie, Kans., 1968-70; clk. Dist. Ct. Sheridan County, Hoxie, 1971—, chief dist. ct. clk. 15th Jud. Dist., Hoxie, 1977—. Recipient Spl. Recognition, chief Justice Supreme Ct. Kans., 1981. Mem. Kans. Dist. Ct. Clks. Assn. (state sec.-treas. 1978, state pres. 1980), Kans. Assn. Dist. Ct. Clks. and Adminstrs. (legis. chmn. 1981), N.W. Kans. Dist. Ct. Clks. Assn. (pres. 1975-77), Kans. Jud. Adminstrs. (spl. mem. clks. and adminstrs. adv. council 1979, 81-82). Mem. Ch. of Christ. Home: 1417 Sheridan Ave Hoxie KS 67740 Office: Courthouse Hoxie KS 67740

WENTZ, JOHN LEE, steel co. exec.; b. Mishawaka, Ind., Mar. 12, 1936; s. Ray Berl and Violet Ruth W.; B.S. in Indsl. Mgmt., Purdue U., 1974; m. Rachel Ann Cox, Dec. 15, 1956; children—John A., Kevin R., Scott M. Draftsman, U.S. Rubber Co., Mishawaka, 1953-54; buyer Rockwell Standard Corp., Mishawaka, 1959-61; with Midwest Steel div. Nat. Steel Corp., Portage, Ind., 1961—, supr. labor relations, 1967-72, sr. safety engr., 1972—; instr. Purdue U., 1975—. Served with USN, 1954-58. Mem. Am. Soc. Safety Engrs., Am. Iron and Steel Inst., Portage C. of C., Purdue Alumni Assn. Methodist. Home: 2702 Eleanor St Portage IN 46368 Office: Midwest Steel Div US 12 Portage IN 46368

WENZ, HERBERT EMIL, coll. adminstr.; b. Plevna, Mont., July 14, 1931; s. Andrew A. and Mathilda Margaret (Schuetzle) W.; B.A., Yankton Coll., 1953, B.Th., 1954; B.D., M.A., Hartford Sem. Found., 1961; m. Delores Delane Gall, May 31, 1953; children—Chrystal Jean Dorn, Mark Gregory, Jodi Michelle. Ordained to ministry United Ch. of Christ, 1954; pastoral minister, 1954-68; spl. agt. Northwestern Mut. Life Ins. Co., 1968; sales rep. Wallace Labs., 1968-71; successively sales rep., terr. mgr., dist. sales mgr. Beecham Labs., Lincoln, Nebr., and San Francisco, 1971-77; dir. ch. relations, dir. devel., v.p. devel. Yankton Coll., 1977—. Named Dist. Sales Rep. of Yr., Beecham Labs., 1973-74, regional sales rep., 1974-75. Mem. Council Advancement and Support of Edn. (state exec. bd.).

Republican. Clubs: Optimist, Masons. Office: Yankton College 12th and Douglass Sts Yankton SD 57078

WENZEL, FREDERICK JOSEPH, med. clinic adminstr.; b. Marshfield, Wis., Aug. 5, 1930; s. Rudolph Eric and Theresa A. (Kaholka) W.; B.S., Wis. State U., Stevens Point, 1956; postgrad. U. Wis., 1962, 70-71; M.B.A., U. Chgo., 1979; m. Mary Ann Rasmussen, Sept. 6, 1952; children—Ann Frances, Paul Frederick, Ellen Therese, Jane Marie, Thomas Richard, Mary Margaret. Research asst. St. Joseph's Hosp., Marshfield, 1950-53; dir. labs. Marshfield Clinic, 1953-65, exec. dir. clinic, 1976—; exec. dir. Marshfield Med. Found., 1965-77; dir. Central State Bank, Marshfield; chmn. North Central Area Health Planning Assn. regional tech. com. on phys. health, Marshfield, 1973-78, mem. health policy council, research and devel. com., 1974—; mem. com. on drug and alcohol abuse Clinic, Hosp., Found., Marshfield, 1971—, edn. com., 1969—. Mem. gov.'s council for snowmobile recreation, 1971—; chmn. bd. dirs. Mid-State Vocat., Tech. and Adult Edn. Dist., Marshfield, 1968—, vice-chmn. Bds. Assn., 1979—, pres. Wis. Dist. Bds. Assn., 1981; chmn. adv. council St. Joseph's Hosp. Sch. Nursing, Marshfield, 1970-73; bd. dirs. U. Wis. Stevens Point Found., 1973—. Recipient Distinguished Service award Marshfield Jr. C. of C., 1963, First Ann. Distinguished Service award, 1971; citation Wis. Jr. Acad. Sci., 1970, Spl. citation, 1972; Grand award Wis. affiliate Am. Heart Assn., 1977; named Boss of Yr., 1981. Mem. Assn. Community Coll. Trustees, Wis. Heart Assn. (chmn. bd. 1974-76, chmn. research com. 1971-74), Med. Group Mgmt. Assn., Am. Inst. Chemists, Am. Fedn. Clin. Research, N.Y. Acad. Sci., Wis. Acad. Sci., Arts and Letters, Am. Assn. Med. Clinics Found. (dir. 1973—). Roman Catholic (bd. edn. 1967-73). Elk, Rotarian. Contbr. numerous articles to profl. jours. Home: 610 S Sycamore St Marshfield WI 54449 Office: 1000 N Oak Ave Marshfield WI 54449

WERA, ANNE REGINA, ednl. adminstr.; b. Winona, Minn., June 1, 1936; d. Bernard S. and Alvina A. (Kanter) W.; B.A. in Music Edn., Viterbo Coll., LaCrosse, Wis., 1958; M.Mus., U. Minn., Mpls., 1960; Ph.D., U. Iowa, Iowa City, 1969; D. Arts, Nat. Grad. U., Shell Knob, Mo., 1973, Ph.D., 1981; M.A., Loras Coll., Dubuque, Iowa, 1978. Music tchr. Logan Jr. High Sch., LaCrosse, 1958-60; asst. to supr. instrumental music La Crosse Public Schs., 1960-64; acting head music edn. U. Nev., Reno, 1965-66; asst. prof. U. Wis.-Whitewater and River Falls, 1966-67; regional supt. cons. Jo Daviess County, Galena, Ill., 1977-78; secondary adminstrv. intern Sr. High Sch., Dubuque, 1973-74; music specialist Dubuque Public Schs., 1968—; asst. condr. Nat. Youth Symphony & Chorus, Bethel, Pa., summers 1979, 81; cons. in field. Chmn. city crime prevention com. Dubuque C. of C., 1978-81; bd. dirs. Am. Youth Symphony and Chorus, 1979-81, asst. condr., 1979-81; bd. dirs. Dubuque Symphony, 1979-81, Dubuque Girl's Club, 1978-79. Charles Kettering Found. IDEA fellow, 1981; Instrumental Music for Blind, Deaf and Trainable Retarded Children award, 1960-64, 70-79. Mem. Nat. Assn. Secondary Sch. Prins., Am. Assn. Sch. Adminstrs. (nat. minorities com. 1981-82), Assn. Supervision and Curriculum Devel., Nat. Band Assn., Am. Symphony Orch. League, Nat. Women's Band Assn., AAUP, Music Educators Nat. Conf. (life), Music Tchrs. Nat. Assn., AAUW (life), Iowa Edn. Assn. Home: 2688 Marywood Dr Dubuque IA 52001

WERDER, MELISSA ROHDE, public relations exec.; b. Balt., Apr. 29, 1950; d. Walter William and Naomi (Thomas) R.; B.A., Denison U., 1972; M.A., U. Iowa, 1974; m. Albert Werder, June 10, 1972 (div.); 1 dau., Meredith Jane. Asst. dir. public relations Redbook mag., N.Y.C., 1975-78; cons. public relations Scholastics, Inc., N.Y.C., 1978-80; account exec. nat. media relations mgr. Anthony M. Franco, Inc., Public Relations Counselors, Detroit, 1980—. Jr. Miss, State of Ohio, 1968. Mem. Women in Communications, Detroit Press Club. Republican. Congregationalist. Home: 707 Colonial Ct Birmimgham MI 48009 Office: 28 W Adams St Anthony M Franco Inc Detroit MI 48226

WERGOWSKE, WILLIAM GARY, accountant; b. Cin., Sept. 6, 1941; s. William Leslie and Thelma Leah (Clemons) W.; B.B.A., U. Cin., 1963; M.B.A., Xavier U., 1971; m. Mary Helen Kemper, June 7, 1975. Mem. staff Pension Group Cons.'s, Inc., Cin., 1957-63; methods analyst Western and So. Life Ins. Co., Cin., 1965-73; mgr. mgmt. services and accounting services Main Lafrentz and Co., Cin., 1973-77; pvt. practice accounting, Cin., 1977-79; pres. William G. Wergowske & Co., Inc., C.P.A.'s, Cin., 1979—; mem. faculty Coll. Mt. St. Joseph, 1979-80; chmn. bd. Midwest Software, Inc., 1978—; treas. Oil Pit Shop, Inc., 1979-80, Nursing Staff of Louisville, Inc., 1979-80. Treas. home aid service Cin. Community Chest, 1974-77. Served to 1st lt. Signal Corps, U.S. Army, 1963-65. C.P.A., Ohio. Mem. Nat. Assn. Accountants (v.p. 1976-78), Ohio Soc. C.P.A.'s (cons. systems and EDP), Am. Inst. C.P.A.'s, EDP Auditors Assn. Roman Catholic. Club: Cin. (trustee 1977-79, 2d v.p. 1979). Home: 5519 Lucenna Dr Cincinnati OH 45238 Office: 1958 Anderson Ferry Rd Cincinnati OH 45238

WERLE, CHARLES ROBERT, public relations exec.; b. Flint, Mich., Jan. 16, 1936; s. Arthur Willis and Ann Marie (Mascko) W.; B.A., Mich. State U., 1958; postgrad. San Jose State U., 1980; m. Kathleen Mae Wiitanen, June 6, 1959; children—Jeffrey, Mark, David. Mem. advt./editorial staff Lapeer (Mich.) County Press., 1958-59; sports editor LaPorte (Ind.) Herald-Angus, 1961-62; sportswriter Milw. Jour., 1962-66; public relations mgr. Miller Brewing Co., Milw., 1966-72; public relations mgr., dir. AVP-Deltona Corp., Miami, 1972-76; mgmt. supr., dir. creative services public relations div. J. Walter Thompson, Chgo., 1976-78, v.p. public relations, 1977-77; v.p., head creative services div., communications dept. First Nat. Bank, Chgo., 1978—. Sec., trustee United Methodist Homes and Services, Chgo.; public relations adv. council United Way, Chgo. area, U. Fla.; mem. Hinsdale Village Caucus Bd., 1976-78. Served with U.S. Army, 1959-61. Recipient Gold Key award Public Relations News, 1980; Merit award Fin. World mag., 1980. Mem. Public Relations Soc. Am. (co-chmn. nat. public relations com. 1980), Internat. Assn. Bus. Communicators (dir., chmn. mgmt. adv. council Chgo. chpt.), Chgo. Press Club, Milw. Press Club (past treas.). Methodist. Club: Racquet (Hinsdale, Ill.). Office: 2 1st Nat Plaza Chicago IL 60670

WERNER, ELMER LOUIS, JR., ins. co. exec.; b. St. Louis, Nov. 21, 1927; s. Elmer Louis and Helen M. (Kready) W.; A.B., Princeton U., 1948; B.S., Washington U., St. Louis, 1950, LL.B., 1952, J.D., 1952; m. Sandra M. Johnston, Dec. 3, 1966; children—Louis, Eric, Matthew. Admitted to Mo. bar, 1952, U.S. Ct. Mil. Appeals bar, 1963, U.S. Supreme Ct. bar, 1963; asst. v.p. Insurers Service Corp., St. Louis, 1955-59, v.p., gen. counsel, 1959-76, chmn. bd., 1976—; asst. sec. Safety Mut. Casualty Corp., St. Louis, 1955-59, sec.-treas., gen. counsel, 1959-76, exec. v.p., gen. counsel, 1976—; v.p., dir. Butch Baird Enterprises, Inc., 1979—. Bd. dirs. Playgoers of St. Louis, Inc., Better Bus. Bur., St. Louis, Asso. Industries of Mo. Served with JAGC, U.S. Army, 1952-55; ret. col. USAR. Mem. Am. Soc. Charter Property Casualty Underwriters (dir.), Res. Officers Assn. (dir.), Fed. (dir.), Mo. (dir.), St. Louis (dir.) bar assns., Nat. Assn. Safety, Claims Orgns. (dir.), Asso. Industries Mo. Presbyterian (ruling elder 1980). Clubs: Mo. Athletic, St. Louis, Forest Hills Country (sec., dir. 1980), St. Louis Indoor Soccer (dir. 1981), Dome, Ambassadors. Home: 7 Barclay Woods Dr Saint Louis MO 63124 Office: Univ Club Tower 1034 S Brentwood Blvd Saint Louis MO 63117

WERNER, JOHN C., mfg. co. exec.; b. Jamestown, N.D., July 9, 1920; s. Fern C. and Bessie C. (Nord) W.; A.A., Santa Monica City Coll., 1941; m. Persis V. Hite, Oct. 18, 1947 (dec.); children—William J., Wendy P. Production control mgr. Cherry Rivet Co., Los Angeles, 1947-51; supr. tool and production control Bendix Aviation Corp., North Hollywood, Calif., 1951-58; tooling mgr. Cannon Electric Co., Los Angeles, 1959-61; facilities mgr. Martin Marietta Corp., Vandenberg AFB, Calif., 1961-65; production control mgr. Jostens, Inc., Attleboro, Mass., 1965-67; dir. indsl. ops. Performance Tech. Corp., Los Angeles, 1967-70; corporate staff cons. Sunstrand Corp., Rockford, Ill., 1970—; cons. ops. mgmt., cost accounting. Cons. Ill. Gov.'s Commn. on Schs., 1972. Served with USAF, 1942-45; to maj. Res., ret., 1970. Decorated Air medal; certified comml. and multi-engine pilot, USAF, Dept. Transp. Mem. Am. Inst. Indsl. Engrs. (sr. certification, past chpt. dir.), Indsl. Mgmt. Soc., Exptl. Aircraft Assn., Am. Ex-Prisoners of War. Author: Administrative Value Analysis Implementation Program, 1973; Operations Control for Productivity Improvement, 1976; Administrative Planning and Training (APT) Program, 1976; Zero Base Budgeting for Production Oriented Industry, 1977; contbr. Dept. Def. Program Management Criteria, 1967. Home: 215 Shore Ln Rockton IL 61072 Office: 4751 Harrison Ave Rockford IL 61101

WERNING, KENNETH LEE, ins. co. exec.; b. Elgin, Nebr., Apr. 15, 1937; s. John Meinolph and Elizabeth Catherine (Gregor) W.; m. Mary Emma Synder, Apr. 11, 1959; children—Kevin Lyndell, Jeffrey Scott, Robert John. With Mutal of Omaha, 1957—, asst. ops. mgr. internal services adminstrn., 1971-77, asst. v.p., 1978—. Chmn., Bd. of Adjustment, Plattsmouth, Nebr., 1981—; mem. Diocesan Devel. Program, Plattsmouth. Mem. Adminstrv. Mgmt. Soc. (past pres. Omaha chpt., dir.). Roman Catholic. Office: Mutual of Omaha Plaza Omaha NE 68175

WERRELL, TERRY SHERMAN, mfg. engr.; b. Janesville, Wis., Mar. 5, 1936; s. Daniel and Vivian Virginia (Sherman) W.; m. Sandra Ethel Samuelson, July 6, 1957; children—Daniel David, Diana Dawn, Linda Louise, Pamela Leigh. Process engr. Fisher Body Co., Janesville, Wis., 1959-65; process engr. Fisher Body div. Gen. Motors Corp., Lordstown, Ohio, 1965, sr. prodn. engr., 1966-70, maintenance shift supt., 1970-71, Gen. Motors Assembly div., 1971-72, maintenance supt. Vega plant, 1972-74, Vega and Van plants, 1974-76; dir. facilities and processing DeLorean Motor Co., Bloomfield Hills, Mich., 1976-78; asst. gen. mgr. Hardy div. Sheller Globe Corp., Union City, Ind., 1978, div. gen. mgr., 1978-80, chmn. plastic div. product planning com., 1980—; cons. in field. Cert. mfg. engr. Mem. Am. Soc. Electroplated Plastics (dir., pres.), Gen. Motors Alumni Assn., Union City C. of C. Lutheran. Clubs: Masons, Elks. Home: 812 N Columbia St Union City IN 47390 Office: PO Box 109 Union City IN 47390

WERTHEIM, SALLY HARRIS, educator; b. Cleve., Nov. 1, 1931; d. Arthur I. and Anne (Manheim) Harris; B.S., Flora Stone Mather Coll., 1953; M.A., Case Western Res. U., 1967, Ph.D., 1970; m. Stanley E. Wertheim, Aug. 6, 1950; children—Kathryn, Susan, Carole. Mem. staff, social service dept. Univ. Hosps., Cleve., 1953-54; tchr. religion Fairmount Temple Sch., Cleve., 1957-72; instr. edn. John Carroll U., Cleve., 1968-71, asst. prof., 1971-75, asso. prof., 1975-80, prof., 1980—, chmn. dept. edn., 1977—. Pres., Jewish Family Service Assn., 1975-78; trustee Jewish Community Fedn. Bd., 1975—; trustee County Bd. Mental Health, 1977—, sec., 1979—; mem. edn. com. Villa Angela, 1974—, chmn., 1979; pres. Beachwood PTA, 1963-67. Mem. Am. Ednl. Studies Assn. (treas.), History of Edn. Soc., Am. Assn. Colls. Tchr. Edn. (pres. Ohio chpt. 1981), John Dewey Soc., Phi Delta Kappa. Contbr. articles to profl. jours. Office: Dept Edn John Carroll U Cleveland OH 44118

WERTS, MERRILL HARMON, mgmt. cons.; b. Smith Center, Kans., Nov. 17, 1922; s. Mack Allen and Ruth Martha (Badger) W.; B.S., Kans. State U., 1947; M.S., Cornell U., 1948; m. Dorothy Wilson, Mar. 22, 1946; children—Stephen M., Riley J., Todd J., Kelly M. Beef sales mgr. John Morrell & Co., Topeka and Memphis, 1948-53; dir. mktg. Kans. Dept. Agr., Topeka, 1953-55; sec.-treas. Falley's Markets, Inc., Topeka, 1955-58; v.p. S.W. State Bank, Topeka, 1958-65; pres. First Nat. Bank, Junction City, Kans., 1965-78; individual practice mgmt. cons., Junction City, 1978—; mem. Kans. Senate, 1978—; dir. Mid Am. Machine Corp., Ft. Riley (Kans.) Nat. Bank, Smith Drug Stores, Inc., J.C. Housing & Devel., Inc. Mem. Kans. Bank Mgmt. Commn., 1967-71; mem. adv. com. U.S. Comptroller of Currency, 1971-72. Mem. Topeka Bd. Edn., 1957-61; pres. Junction City-Geary County United Fund, 1967-68; pres. Junction City Indsl. Devel., Inc., 1966-72. Trustee Kans. State U. Endowment Assn., Kans. Synod Presbyn. Westminster Found., 1965-72. Served to 1st lt., inf., AUS, 1943-46. Decorated Bronze Star medal, Purple Heart, Combat Inf. badge. Mem. Kans. State U. Alumni Assn. (pres. 1957), Am. Legion, V.F.W., Kans. Bankers Assn., Assn. U.S. Army, U.S., Kans., Junction City (pres. 1975-76) chambers commerce, Kans. Assn. Commerce and Industry (dir. 1979—), Kans. Farm Bur., Kans. Livestock Assn., D.A.V., Sigma Phi Epsilon. Republican. Presbyterian. Clubs: Masons, Shriners, Rotary (dist. gov. 1973-74). Club: Junction City Country (past pres.). Home: 1228 Miller Dr Junction City KS 66441

WERTSCH, JAMES VERNER, educator; b. Mineola, N.Y., May 16, 1947; s. Clifford H. and Mary Louise (Peterson) W.; B.A., U. Ill., 1969; M.A.T., Northwestern U., 1971; Ph.D., U. Chgo., 1975; m. Linda Ann Lenz, June 7, 1969. Postdoctoral researcher Moscow (USSR) State U., 1975-76; asst. prof. linguistics Northwestern U., 1976—. Served with Air N.G., 1969-75. Mem. Linguistic Soc. Am., Am. Psychol. Assn., Soc. Research in Child Devel. Author: Recent Trends in Soviet Psycholinguistics, 1977; The Concept of Activity in Soviet Psychology, 1981; Cognitive Development: A Vygotskian Perspective, in preparation; mem. jour. editorial bds. Home: 210 E Pearson St Chicago IL 60611 Office: Dept Linguistics Northwestern U Evanston IL 60201

WESBURY, STUART ARNOLD, JR., assn. exec.; b. Phila., Dec. 13, 1933; s. Stuart Arnold and Jennie (Glazewska) W.; B.S., Temple U., 1955; M. Hosp. Adminstrn., U. Mich., 1960; Ph.D., U. Fla., 1972; m. June Carol Davis, Feb. 23, 1957; children—Brian, Brent, Bruce, Bradford. Pharmacist, USPHS Hosps., 1955-57; adminstrv. officer, pharmacist USPHS clinic, 1957-58; adminstrv. asst Del. Hosp., 1960-61; asst. adminstr. Bronson Meth. Hosp., 1961-66; asso. dir., asst. prof. U. Fla. Teaching Hosp., 1966-67, dir., asso. prof., 1967-69; v.p. Computer Mgmt. Corp., Gainesville, Fla., 1969-72; dir. prof. Grad. Studies in Health Services Mgmt., U. Mo.-Columbia, 1972-78; pres. Am. Coll. Hosp. Adminstrs., Chgo., 1979—. Active Boy Scouts Am.; chmn. adminstrv. bd. Meth. Ch.; bd. dirs. Boys Clubs, Gainesville. Served with USPHS, 1955-58. Fellow Am. Coll. Hosp. Adminstrs.; mem. Am. Hosp. Assn., Hosp. Mgmt. Systems Soc., Am. Public Health Assn., Assn. Univ. Programs in Health Adminstrn. (chmn. 1977-78). Club: Rotary (past pres.). Contbr. articles to profl. jours. Office: 840 N Lake Shore Dr Chicago IL 60611

WESCOTT, PHILIP CHARLES, advt. agy. exec.; b. Pitts., Oct. 28, 1943; s. Louis S. and Genevieve T. (Flynn) W.; B.A., Wabash Coll., 1965; M.A., Ind. U., 1970; m. Carol Lee Hocker, June 11, 1966; children—Kimberly, Kristen, Philip C. Field pub. relations Gen. Motors Corp., New Eng. States and N.Y., 1965-66; grad. asst. Ind. U., Bloomington, 1969-70; mgr. advt. and promotion Mead Johnson Labs., Evansville, Ind., 1970-73; account supr. Rumrill-Hoyt Advt. Agency, Rochester, N.Y., and Manhattan, N.Y., 1973-74; v.p. adminstrn. Hooker Power Brake Co., Evansville, Ind., 1974-78; v.p., gen. mgr. Creative Advt., Evansville, 1978-80; advt. dir. Mead Johnson Nutritional div. Bristol-Myers Co., Evansville, 1980—; lectr. in field. Served with Adj. Gen.'s Corp, U.S. Army, 1966-69. Mem. Res. Officers Assn. U.S., Automotive Wholesalers Inst., Mktg. Communications Execs. Internat., Sigma Delta Chi (v.p. chpt. 1974-76). Roman Catholic. Clubs: Evansville Kennel, Toastmasters Internat. Home: 7600 Newburgh Rd Evansville IN 47715 Office: 2400 W Pennsylvania Ave Evansville TN 47721

WESELI, ROGER WILLIAM, hosp. adminstr.; b. Cin., Dec. 23, 1932; s. William Henry and Margaret Antoinette (Hoffman) W.; B.A. in Polit. Sci., U. Cin., 1955; M.S. in Hosp. Adminstrn., Northwestern U., 1959; m. Sue Ann Daggett, Sept. 1, 1956; children—Erin, Stacey, Vincent. Adminstrv. asst. Good Samaritan Hosp., Cin., 1959-61, asst. adminstr., 1961-70, asso. adminstr., 1970-75, v.p., adminstr., 1975-78, exec. v.p., adminstr., 1978-79, pres., 1979—; sec. Greater Cin. Hosp. Council, 1978—; chmn.-elect Ohio Hosp. Mgmt. Service, 1981—. Chmn. legislation com. health dept. Ohio Catholic Conf., 1978—; bd. dirs. Friars Boys Club, 1978—. Recipient Alpha Mu Sigma award, 1975; cert. of appreciation Ohio League for Nursing, 1978. Fellow Am. Coll. Hosp. Adminstrs.; mem. Am. Mgmt. Assn., Am. Hosp. Assn., Greater Cin. C. of C., Ohio League for Nursing (v.p. 1977-81), Ohio Hosp. Assn. (trustee, chmn. govt. liaison com. 1978—). Democrat. Roman Catholic. Office: 3217 Clifton Ave Cincinnati OH 45220

WESELY, DONALD RAYMOND, state senator; b. David City, Nebr., Mar. 30, 1954; s. Raymond E. and Irene (Sabata) W.; B.A., U. Nebr., 1977, postgrad., 1978. Grad. asst. U. Nebr., 1977-78; fin. advisor Geis Investments and Ins., Lincoln, 1978-79; mem. Nebr. Legislature, 1979—; researcher S.E. Nebr. Small Farms Action Group, 1980; tchr. SE Nebr. Community Coll. Named an Outstanding Young Man of Am., U.S. Jaycees, 1980; recipient Friend of Edn. award Lincoln Edn. Assn., 1981. Mem. U. Nebr. Alumni Assn., UN Assn. U.S.A., Community Devel. Soc. Am. Roman Catholic. Clubs: Rotary, Lions, Masons. Office: State Capitol Lincoln NE 68509

WESENER, BARBARA ANN, found. adminstr., educator; b. Sheboygan, Wis., Oct. 16, 1948; d. Melvin R. and Delores A. (Wagner) W.; B.A. cum laude, Alverno Coll., Milw., 1970; postgrad. U. Wis., Milw., 1975—; m. Clinton Lee Toms, June 27, 1981. Tchr. English, Pius XI High Sch., Milw., 1970-72; tchr. journalism Divine Savior-Holy Angels High Sch., Milw., 1972-75; teaching asst. U. Wis., Milw., 1975-76; instr. journalism Marquette U., Milw., 1976—, asst. dir. continuing edn., 1976-79; asso. dir. public relations and membership Internat. Found. of Employee Benefit Plans, Brookfield, Wis., 1979—; lectr. Lakeland Coll., Sheboygan. Mem. Alverno Coll. Alumnae Bd. Recipient Merit award Nat. Univ. Extension Assn., 1978. Mem. Women in Communications, Inc. (Southeastern Wis. chpt. pres. 1976-77, v.p. community affairs 1979-80), Public Relations Soc. Am. Contbr. in field; writer poetry. Home: 4918 S Imperial Circle Greenfield WI 53220 Office: PO Box 69 Brookfield WI 53005

WESLEY, JAMES ALOYSIUS, data processing cons.; b. Lakewood, Ohio, Nov. 24, 1945; s. Frank Aloysius and Eleanor Rose (Busato) W.; A. in Data Processing Cuyahoga Community Coll., Cleve., 1977; cert. in Data Processing, Inst. Cert. Computer Profls., Chgo., 1979; m. Barbara Ann James, Feb. 22, 1969; children—Daniel Jason, Nathan Evan. Graphics programmer Univ. Co., Dallas, 1970-71; sr. staff analyst Neoterics, Inc., Cleve., 1971-73; sr. systems software programmer Ferro Corp., Cleve., 1973-76; dir. data processing Medicus Systems Corp., Akron, Ohio, 1976—. Served with U.S. Army, 1965-67. Mem. Assn. Systems Mgmt., Soc. Cert. Data Processors. Episcopalian. Home: 241 Hurd Rd Aurora OH 44202 Office: 525 E Market St Akron OH 44309

WESLEY, LENORA MAE, educator; b. St. Louis, June 13, 1926; d. Matthew Daniel and Willie Mae (Mardis) Brookfield; B.A., St. Louis U., 1970, M.A., 1976; m. Floyd C. Wesley, May 13, 1950; children—Clayvon, Ritchey, Norbert, Mary. Tchr., Archdiocese St. Louis, 1961-69; supr., tchr. Human Devel. Corp., St. Louis, 1962-70; tchr. social studies St. Louis public schs., 1970-81; instr. social studies Northwest High Sch., St. Louis, 1980—; tchr., supr. social services Guardian Angel Settlement, 1962-70. Rec. sec. Hist. Assn. Greater St. Louis, 1978-81. Mem. Mo. Council Social Studies, Mo. Hist. Soc. St. Louis, Assn. Supervision and Curriculum Devel., St. Louis Tchrs. Assn., NEA, Presdl. Classroom for Young Americans, Phi Alpha Theta. Roman Catholic. Home: 7308 Country Club Dr Saint Louis MO 63121 Office: 5140 Riverview Blvd Saint Louis MO 63120

WESLEY, ROLAND EDWARD, social worker; b. Hayti, Mo., Mar. 31, 1937; s. Walter and Alberta (Williams) W.; B.S., Ohio Christian Coll., Columbus, 1969; M.S.W. (Rackham opportunity grantee 1971, minority fellow 1974), U. Mich., Ann Arbor, 1972, A.M., 1973, Ph.D., 1974; m. Carol Jean Washington, Mar. 14, 1957; children—Carleton, Linda, Sharon. Organizer, dir. 1st Youth Service Bur. in N.W. Ind., 1970-71; mem. Mich. Drug Abuse Policy Planning Com., 1972; planner, developer regionalized correctional program for State of Ill., 1973; mem. faculty So. Ill. U., 1975; asso. prof. social work, project dir. ACTION ser. learning program George Williams Coll., Downers Grove, Ill., 1979—; pres. Carlinshar & Assos., applied research corp., 1979—; bd. dirs. Thresholds South, 1977-79; mem. long range planning task force Christian Action Ministry Birth to Three Program, 1977-79; mem. evaluation team day care centers program Christian Action U., 1978-79. Served with USMCR, 1954-56. Grantee Ill. Criminal Justice System, 1973-75, George Williams Coll., 1977—. Mem. Nat. Assn. Social Workers, Nat. Assn. Black Social Workers, Council Social Work Edn., Assn. Sch. Adminstrs., Commn. Human Relations, Nat. Assn. Clin. Social Workers, Nat. Council Juvenile Ct. Judges, Ill. Clin. Assn. Social Workers. Methodist Episcopalian. Author: Aspects of Mental Health: A Guide to Understanding the Meaning of Mental Illness, 1979; contbr. articles to profl. jours. Home: 1159 Quail Run Ave Bolingbrook IL 60439 Office: 555 31st St Downers Grove IL 60515

WESLOH, FERDINAND JOSEPH, priest, ednl. adminstr.; b. St. Louis, Dec. 23, 1938; s. Ferdinand Joseph and Theresa Catherine (Wohlschlaeger) W.; A.B., Cardinal Glennon Coll., 1960; M.Ed., St. Louis U., 1967. Ordained priest Roman Catholic Ch., 1964; guidance dir. Duchesne High Sch., St. Charles, Mo., 1966-74, Mercy High Sch., University City, Mo., 1974-77; adminstr. St. John's High Sch., St. Louis, 1977—; asso. pastor St. Peter Ch., St. Charles, 1964-74, St. Clement Ch., Des Peres, Mo., 1974-77, St. John's Ch., St. Louis, 1977—. Mem. Am., Mo. personnel and guidance assns., Nat. Cath. Guidance Conf. (bd. dirs. 1973-77, sec. 1977-78), St. Louis Cath. Guidance Conf. Clubs: K.C. (chaplain Mo. 1972-74, scholarship and loan chmn. Mo., 1976-78). Editor Nat. Cath. Guidance Newsletter

1973-76. Home: 4200 Delor St Saint Louis MO 63116 Office: 5021 Adkins St Saint Louis MO 63116

WESOLOWSKI, FRANK, county ofcl.; b. Berwyn, Ill., Oct. 16, 1929; s. Frank and Viola (Krochmal) W.; LL.B., DePaul U., 1952; m. Ann Chervinko, Oct. 7, 1956; children—Frank John, Mary Anne, David, Diane, Matthew. Admitted to Ill. bar, 1952; asst. state's atty., Cook County, Ill., 1956-60; asst. state's atty., DuPage County, Wheaton, 1965-67, public defender, 1967—; justice of peace, Town of Cicero, Ill., 1953, 57. Commr., DuPage County Law Enforcement Commn., 1971—, Ill. Law Enforcement Commn., 1972-73, 78—. Mem. adv. bd. Central State Inst., Chgo. Served with AUS, 1953-55. Mem. Ill. Public Defender Assn. (pres. 1973), Am. Trial Lawyers Assn., Ill., DuPage County bar assns. Home: 21W128 Canary Rd Lombard IL 60148 Office: 414 N County Farm Rd Wheaton IL 60187

WESOLOWSKI, STANLEY PETER, physician; b. Warwick, N.Y., Dec. 30, 1914; s. John Paul and Mary Ann (Zagorski) W.; B.S., Fordham U., 1938; M.D., Stritch Sch. Medicine, 1942; m. Ruth E. Swenson, Apr. 8, 1946; children—Patricia Wesolowski Casey, Theresa, Jeanne Wesolowski Darsie, Mary Wesolowski Grebinowski, John, Anne Wesolowski Cosgrove. Intern, St. Francis Hosp., Jersey City, 1942-43; fellow, resident anesthesiology U. Minn., 1946-47; practice medicine, specializing in anesthesiology, Mpls., 1947—; clin. instr. anesthesiology U. Minn. Hosp., 1947-54; chief dept. anesthesiology St. Marys Hosp., 1947-71. Served to capt., M.C., AUS, 1943-46; ETO. Decorated Silver Star medal, D.S.C. Mem. Am. Soc. Anesthesiology, A.M.A., Internat. Anesthesia Research Soc., Minn. Med. Assn., Hennepin County Med. Soc. Roman Catholic. Home: 999 S Fairview Ave St Paul MN 55116 Office: 606 24th Ave S Minneapolis MN 55454

WESSEL, GILBERT ROLAND, obstetrician, gynecologist; b. Ft. Dodge, Iowa, Apr. 25, 1937; s. Roland Henry and Edna Louise (Folkerts) W.; B.A., Wartburg Coll., 1959; M.D., U. Iowa, 1963; m. Mary Alice Reiff, June 23, 1963; children—Susan Ann, James Edward. Intern Hurley Hosp., Flint, Mich., 1963-64; resident in obstetrics and gynecology U. Iowa, Iowa City, 1964-67; individual practice medicine, specializing in obstetrics and gynecology Menasha, Wis., 1969-72, Cedar Rapids, Iowa, 1972—; asso. Riverside Clinic, Menasha, 1969-72; partner Ob-Gyn Assos., Cedar Rapids, 1972—, sec., 1973—; lectr. in field; staff St. Luke's-Mercy Hosp., Cedar Rapids. Served to capt., USAF, 1967-69. Fellow Am. Coll. Obstetricians and Gynecologists; mem. AMA, Iowa, Linn County med. socs., Iowa Alumni Obstet.—Gynecol. Soc. (exec. com. 1976—), Central Assn. Obstetricians and Gynecologists. Lutheran. Club: Cedar Rapids Country. Home: Rural Route 5 Box 205 Cedar Rapids IA 52401 Office: 1201 3d Ave SE Cedar Rapids IA 52406

WESSELS, ARDWIN GILBERT, bus. services co. exec.; b. Clinton, Iowa, Mar. 20, 1933; s. Joseph Bernard and Anna Mary (Dettermann) W.; student pub. schs., Beloit, Wis.; m. Joyce Mary Poupart, Oct. 10, 1953; children—Dominic W., Daniel J., David H., Donald M., Denice J., Dennis J., Darrel A. Service technician Addressograph-Multigraph, Rockford, Ill., 1955-61; asst. supr. printing Beloit Corp., 1961-65, supr., 1965-75, mgr. copy services, 1975-78, sr. buyer, 1978—. Pres. bd. dirs. Colt League, 1963, 64, Pony League, 1968, Boys Baseball Beloit, 1977. Served with USAF, 1951-55. Mem. Assn. Records Mgmt. and Adminstrs., Word Processing Soc. Am., In-Plant Printing Mgmt. Assn. Roman Catholic. Home: 1733 Avon Ct Beloit WI 53511 Office: 1 Saint Lawrence Ave Beloit WI 53511

WESSLER, WILLIAM ERNEST, clergyman; b. Collinsville, Ill., Jan. 8, 1914; s. William H. and Bertha (Washer) W.; grad. St. Pauls Coll. (Concordia, Mo.), 1934; B.D., Concordia Theol. Sem. (St. Louis), 1938; M.A., Washington U., St. Louis, 1948; m. Gertrude C. Henke, June 16, 1940; children—Judith Karen, William Lynn. Ordained to ministry Lutheran Ch., 1939; founding pastor St. Paul's Luth. Ch., Fairview Heights, Ill., 1939-43, Messiah Luth. Ch., Alton, Ill., 1943-51; pastor Trinity Luth. Ch., Gary, Ind., 1951-61; dir. ch. relations Valparaiso (Ind.) U., 1961-68; asst. dir. dept. pub. relations Lutheran Ch.-Mo. Synod, St. Louis, 1968-70, asso. counselor stewardship dept., 1970-79; interim pastor Bethlehem Luth. Ch., St. Louis, 1979—. Chmn. editorial commn. for ofcl. periodicals Luth. Ch.-Mo. Synod, 1959-69, pres. Council Luth. Ministries, 1964-68, Calumet Luth. Mission Assn., 1955-60. Pres., Lake County (Ind.) Assn. for Mental Health, 1957-59; mem. bd. Ind. Assn. for Mental Health. Mem. Luth. Acad. for Scholarship. Editor: Calumet Luth., 1956-62; LutheraNews, 1945-51. Home: 3 Kenstone Ct Florissant MO 63033 Office: 2153 Salisbury St Saint Louis MO 63107

WESSMAN, COLLEEN PATRICIA, food co. exec.; b. Charleroi, Pa., Oct. 17, 1936; d. Paul and Alexandra (Los) Lapcevic; B.S., Carnegie-Mellon U., 1958; M.S., Harvard U., 1971; m. Clarence Wessman, Oct. 3, 1958; children—Scott, Patrick, Cathy. Therapeutic dietitian Letterman Hosp., San Francisco, 1958-60; dir. food service Castro Valley Sch. Dist., Calif., 1960-62, Youth Devel. Center, Waynesburg, Pa., 1966-69, also instr. of nutrition; dir. food service Thera-Care Corp., Boston, 1969-72; chief dietitian St. Joseph Hosp., Elgin, Ill., 1972-74; mgr. product evaluation Quaker Oats Co. Research Center, Barrington, Ill., 1974—; cons. in nutrition, 1972-75. Den mother N.W. Suburban council Cub Scouts Am., 1972-73; pres. PTA, Ellsworth, Pa., 1967-68. Served with Med. Specialists Corps, U.S. Army, 1958-60. Named Outstanding Young Dietitian, Am. Dietetic Assn., 1961. Mem. Inst. Food Technologists, Am. Assn. Cereal Chemists, Am. Dietetic Assn., ASTM. Roman Catholic. Home: 812 Oceola Dr Algonquin IL 60102 Office: 617 W Main St Barrington IL 60010

WEST, BYRON KENNETH, banker; b. Denver, Sept. 18, 1933; s. Willis Byron and Cecil Bernice (Leathers) W.; A.B., U. Ill., 1955; M.B.A., U. Chgo., 1960; m. Barbara Huth, June 25, 1955. With Harris Bank, Chgo., 1957—, investment analyst, 1957-62, asst. cashier, 1962-63, mem. comml. loan div., 1963, asst. v.p., 1964-66, v.p., 1966-76, asst. div. adminstr. Charge Card div., 1967-68, div. adminstr. Corp. Fin. Services div., 1969-72, dep. group exec. Internat. Banking Group, 1972-74, group exec., 1974-76, head banking dept., exec. v.p., 1976, now pres.; dir., Motorola, Inc., Harris Bankcorp, Inc. Mem. Chgo. com. Chgo. Council on Fgn. Relations. Bd. dirs. Rush-Presbyn.-St. Luke's Med Center; governing bd. Chgo. Orchestral Assn. Served with USNR. Mem. Res. City Bankers Assn., Christian Laymen of Chgo., Phi Beta Kappa. Republican. Clubs: Skokie (Ill.) Country; Univ., Chgo., Commonwealth, Comml. (Chgo.). Office: 111 W Monroe St Chicago IL 60603

WEST, DENNIS BLAKE, television broadcasting exec.; b. Rockford, Ill., Aug. 31, 1943; s. Paul Augustus and Betty Jane (Blake) W.; student U. Ill., 1961-63; m. Kathleen Tyra Bovi, Nov. 28, 1964; children—Paul Joseph, Mark Allen. Account exec. sta. WROK, Rockford, Ill., 1964-65, sta. WTVO-TV, Rockford, 1965-67; sales rep. Rockford Newspapers, 1967; account exec. sta. WIFR-TV, Inc., Rockford, 1967-76, nat. sales mgr., 1976-77, gen. sales mgr., 1977-78, pres., gen. mgr., 1980—. Mem. Nat. Broadcast Editorial Assn., Nat. Assn. Broadcasters, Ill. Broadcasters Assn., Rockford Area C. of C., Rockford Jr. C. of C. Clubs: Lions, Toastmasters, Masons, Shriners, Mensa. Home: 1332 Harlem Blvd Rockford IL 61103 Office: 2523 N Meredian Rd Rockford IL 61103

WEST, DOUGLAS XAVIER, chemist; b. Tacoma, June 11, 1937; s. Raymond Idaho and Myrtle Agnes (Sevier) W.; A.B., Whitman Coll., 1959; Ph.D., Wash. State U., 1964; m. Gayl Lee Lucas, June 6, 1964; children—Gregory Joseph, Gabriel Douglas. Instr., Upsala Coll., 1964-65; asst. prof. Central Mich. U., Mt. Pleasant, 1965-68, asso. prof., 1968-72, prof., 1972-75, dir. univ. honors programs, 1970-72; chmn., prof. inorganic chemistry Ill. State U., Normal, 1975—. Mem. Am. Chem. Soc., Chem. Soc., Ill. Acad. Sci., Am. Contract Bridge League (pres. Eastern Mich. unit 1970-72), Sigma Xi, Phi Lambda Upsilon, Phi Kappa Phi. Republican. Contbr. articles to profl. jours. Office: Dept Chemistry Ill State U Normal IL 61761

WEST, GEORGE RUSSELL, architect; b. Indpls., Mar. 28, 1923; s. Frank B. and Tillie (Miller) W.; B.S. in Architecture, U. Cin., 1949; m. Rita A. Reynolds, Nov. 17, 1951; children—Steven Reynolds, Jonathan Reynolds. With McGuire Shook Corp., architects, engrs., planners, 1941—, v.p., 1963-70, pres., 1980—; dir. Noblesville Housing Inc. Mem. Nat. Council Archtl. Registration Bds. Served with inf. AUS, 1943-46. Decorated Silver Star. Mem. Ind. Soc. Architects, AIA, Scarab, Delta Phi Delta, Alpha Tau Omega. Club: Optimist (past pres. Indpls.). Home: 110 Bayley Circle Noblesville IN 46060 Office: Cranbrook Center 7440 N Shadeland Indianapolis IN 46250

WEST, GLENN ALLEN, ins. agt.; b. Columbus, Ohio, Nov. 29, 1946; s. Glenn D. and Edna V. (Blackmore) W.; student Ohio State U., 1964-66, Franklin U., 1966; m. Rosario Garcia Kausin, Aug. 12, 1968; children—Teresa Anne, Glenn Marion. Retread moldman Llewellyn Tire Co., Columbus, 1965; sporting goods salesman F & R Lazarus Co., Columbus, 1965-66; dist. sales mgr. Motorists Ins. Co., Columbus, 1972-75; owner, operator Glenn West Ins. Agy., Westerville, Ohio, 1975—. Served to capt. U.S. Army, 1966-72. Decorated Bronze Star, Air medal with 8 clusters. Named to Motorist Ins. Hall of Fame; recipient Pres.'s award Northland Community Council, 1978. Mem. Northland Jaycees (pres. 1978-79, chmn. bd. 1979-80), Philippine Am. Soc. Central Ohio (pres. 1977-78, chmn. bd. 1978-79). Republican. Methodist. Home and office: 594 Pointview Dr Westerville OH 43081

WEST, JOEL DAN, psychologist; b. Elgin, Ill., July 21, 1934; s. Daniel and Lucille Irene (Sherck) W.; B.A., Manchester Coll., 1956; B.D., Bethany Theol. Sem., 1960; M.A., DePaul U., 1962; Ph.D., U. Md., 1968; m. Jean K. Elder, Jan. 10, 1981; children from previous marriage—Dawn Renee, Brian Joel, Trevor Alan. Mem. faculty No. Mich. U., Marquette, 1968-81, asso. prof. psychology, 1972-78, prof., 1978-81, acting head dept., 1979-80; pvt. clin. practice, 1982—. Mem. Alger Marquette Counties Mental Health Bd., 1980. Grantee Ellen K. Russell Trust, 1980, No. Mich. U. Faculty, 1979. Mem. Am. Psychol. Assn., Midwestern Psychol. Assn., Assn. Behavior Analysis, Mich. Acad. Sci., Arts and Letters. Author: Study Guide for Abnormal Psychology and Modern Life, 5th edit., 1976; contbr. articles on technology of instrn., sex role stereotypes to profl. jours. Home: 3941 Jonquil Ln Okemos MI 48864 Office: Psychol Evaluation and Treatment Center Inc East Lansing MI 48823

WEST, LEE DUVALL, educator; b. Lincoln, Ill., Jan. 29, 1938; s. Paul William and Grace Corinne (Duvall) W.; B.S., U. Ill., 1959, M.Ed., 1962; advanced cert. edn., 1968; m. Anna Marie Detmers, June 22, 1957; children—Kevin, Keith, Leann, Mary. Vocat. agr. tchr., Avon, Ill., 1959-60, Delavan, Ill., 1960-63; vocat. agr. tchr., vocat. dir. Mt. Pulaski (Ill.) Community Unit Schs., 1963—; part-time tchr. Lincoln Land Community Coll., 1978-81. Adviser, Future Farmers Am., 1959-81; treas. St. John's Lutheran Ch., 1969-79; bd. dirs. Mt. Pulaski Pool Found., 1979-81, treas., 1979-81. Recipient Outstanding Young Educator award Logan County Jaycees, 1974. Mem. Am. Vocat. Assn., Ill. Vocat. Assn., Ill. Vocat. Agr. Tchrs. Assn. (20 years service pin 1980). Republican. Clubs: Masons (master 1978-79, high priest 1975-76), K.T. (comdr. 1976-77, scholarship com. 1977—), Order Eastern Star (worthy patron 1974-75). Home: 303 N Vine St Mount Pulaski IL 62548 Office: Mount Pulaski Community Unit Schs Spring and Cooke Sts Mount Pulaski IL 62548

WEST, LLOYD MARVIN, producer, dir., educator; b. McLeansboro, Ill., May 9, 1922; s. Elisha Phillip and Ruth Helen (Wilson) W.; B.F.A., Goodman Theatre, Art Inst. Chgo., 1943, M.F.A., 1947; M.A., Northeastern Ill. U., 1980. Actor, dir. Cleve. Play House, 1945-51; dir., producer John B. Rogers Producing Co., U.S. and Can., 1951-55; asso. CBS-TV, Chgo., 1955-59; prof. speech and theatre City Colls. Chgo., 1959-61, asst. dean Crane Coll., 1961-66, producer, 1966-71, asst. dean Learning Resources Lab. and TV Coll., 1971-73, dean, 1973—; producer series Radio Sta. WIND, 1965-67, Am. Community Coll. series, 1969; exec. producer, narrator Man and His Art, 1970; producer, host The Open Door, Sta. WTTW-TV, 1972-73. Recipient fellowship Art Inst. Chgo., 1943. Author: Effective Communications, 1968. Home: 4863 W Gregory St Chicago IL 60630 Office: 3400 N Austin Ave Chicago IL 60634

WEST, MARGARET LILA WALKER (MRS. VICTOR ROYCE WEST), ednl. adminstr.; b. Gibbon, Neb., Aug. 28, 1905; d. James George and Niema Sybil (Converse) Walker; B.A., U. Neb., 1934; student U. Heidelberg (Germany), 1930-32, 35-36; postgrad. U. Minn., 1948-49, U. Ill., 1952; M.Ed., Nat. Coll. Edn., 1965; m. Victor Royce West, June 3, 1930; children—Sybel West Kimmel, Vicki West Matovic. Tchr. Gibbon (Nebr.) Elem. Sch., 1926-30; tchr. German and Latin Omaha Central High Sch., 1938-40; prin., tchr. Sheltering Arms Hosp. Sch. for Polio Patients, Mpls., 1948-51; supervisory tchr. educable mentally handicapped Evanston (Ill.) Twp. High Sch., 1951-70; supr. student tchrs. in spl. edn. Ill. State U., Normal, 1972—. Bd. dirs. YWCA, Omaha, 1938-40, Evanston, 1965-67, North Shore Assn. for Retarded Children and Shore Tng. Center, Evanston, 1965-67. Am. Assn. Mental Deficiency fellow, 1967. Mem. Internat., Ill. (sec. 1956-58, bd. dirs. 1956-61, chpt. pres. 1960) councils for exceptional children, Am. Assn. Mental Deficiency, Am. Assn. U. Women, Gamma Phi Beta (province dir. 1939-41), Delta Kappa Gamma. Methodist. Home: 9310 Lincolnwood Dr Evanston IL 60203

WEST, PATRICIA ANN, sociologist; b. Birmingham, Ala., Nov. 29, 1945; d. Lucian Winfred and Alice Eugenia (Kirkland) W.; B.S. cum laude, Memphis State U., 1967, M.A., 1969; Ph.D. (Pi Beta Phi fellow), St. Louis U., 1975; m. William Bruce Springer, May 25, 1974; children—Caroline Lee, William Burton, III. Med. sociologist, dept. psychiatry Washington U. Sch. Medicine, St. Louis, 1970-78; project rev. asso. Greater St. Louis Health Systems Agy., 1978-79; vis. asst. prof. dept. sociology U. Mo., St. Louis, 1979-80; pvt. practice health planning and project review cons., St. Louis, 1979—. USPHS fellow, 1975-78. Mem. Am. Sociol. Assn., Midwest Sociol. Soc., Am. Pub. Health Assn., Sigma Xi, Alpha Kappa Delta, Pi Beta Phi. Episcopalian. Home: 24 Willow Hill Rd Saint Louis MO 63124

WEST, PEARL LEONARD, retail music co. exec.; b. Dean, Iowa, Sept. 18, 1914; s. Clarence Aubry and Lydia Ocle (Rachford) W.; student Centerville Jr. Coll., 1935; B.A. in Music, U. Iowa, 1940; m. Eleanor Louise Bosworth, Mar. 15, 1940; children—Shari Ann, Stephen Leonard. With Paul Wendel Music Co., Des Moines, 1939-41; organized West Music Co., Iowa City, 1941; woodwind instr. Iowa City Public Schs., 1942-44; founder, pres. West Music Co., Inc., Coralville, Iowa, 1945-79, chmn. bd., 1980—; v.p. Everett's Music Co., Washington, Iowa, 1977—; dir. Hawkeye State Bank, Iowa City. Mem. Nat. Assn. Music Mchts. (dir.), Nat. Assn. Sch. Music Dealers, U.S. C. of C., Iowa City C. of C., SCORE (Service Corps Ret. Execs.). Democrat. Methodist. Clubs: Rotary, Elks. Home: 1655 Ridge Rd Iowa City IA 52240 Office: West Music Co Inc 1212 5th St Coralville IA 52241

WEST, RICHARD IRVING, financial exec.; b. Racine, Wis., Feb. 10, 1929; s. Byron S. and Ruth (Wilson) W.; B.S., Wis. State U., 1957; M.B.A., Northwestern U., 1966; m. Virginia M. Hansen, Mar. 16, 1957; children—Ruth Ellen, Sharon Marie, David Richard, Benjamin Thomas. Asst. to dir. finance Ill. Agrl. Assn., Chgo., 1957-60; asst. v.p. Chgo. Med. Sch., 1960-63; treas., bus. mgr. George Williams Coll., Downers Grove, Ill., 1963-70; controller Mayer, Brown & Platt, Chgo., 1970-79; pres. real estate mgmt. co., also bus. cons. firm; v.p. Stratum Five Internat., Inc., 1979—. Served with AUS, 1946-49, USAAF, 1950-51. Mem. Downers Grove C. of C. (dir.), Northwestern U. Grad. Bus. Assn. Home: 826 Birch St Downers Grove IL 60515 Office: 921 Curtis St Downers Grove IL 60515

WEST, RONALD LA VERA, mental health adminstr.; b. Tampa, Fla., June 11, 1948; s. Henry and Endiak Julia (Lockett) W.; B.A., Shaw Coll., 1971; M.A., Wayne State U., 1973; m. Linda Marie Ronse, Feb. 27, 1975; children—Shelley Lynn, Julia Lea. With Mich. Dept. Edn., Bur. Rehab., Detroit, 1971-77; with Mich. Dept. Mental Health, Southgate Regional Center, 1977—, counselor, asst. dist. supr., 1977-81, program dir., 1981—, dir. alternative living services, 1981—; mem. adv. council Bur. Rehab. Past chmn. and bd. mem. Riverview (Mich.) Zoning Bd. of Appeals, sec. to bldg. commn., 1978—; chmn. project sales Downriver council Boy Scouts Am., 1978-81; bd. dirs. YMCA, Downriver br. Recipient Meritorious Service award Mich. Rehab. Counseling Assn., 1979; Leadership award, Detroit Rehab. Assn., 1976; cert. social worker, Mich. Mem. Am. Personnel and Guidance Assn., Mich. Personnel and Guidance Assn., Nat. Rehab. Assn., Mich. Rehab. Assn. (dir. 1972—), Detroit Rehab. Assn. (past pres.), Nat. Rehab. Counseling Assn., Great Lakes Region Rehab. Counseling Assn. (past pres.), Mich. Rehab. Counseling Assn. (past pres.), Am. Assn. Mental Deficiency, Omega Psi Phi. Club: Kiwanis (past pres., lt. gov.-elect Mich. Dist. 1981-82, Kiwanian of Yr. award 1981). Home: 14354 Huntington St Riverview MI 48192 Office: 16700 Pennsylvania Rd Southgate MI 48195

WEST, SAM, refrigeration co. exec.; b. Glen Ullen, N.D., Jan. 6, 1916; s. Avedis M. and Jessie (Harris) W.; A.B., State Tchrs. Coll., Mayville, N.D., 1938; M.C.S., Tuck Sch. of Dartmouth, 1947; grad. econ mblzn. course Indsl. Coll. Armed Forces, 1953; m. Ruth Driskill, Aug. 27, 1948; children—Gay Anne West Trottier, Sara Elizabeth West Azarnia, Linda Lee. Instr. comml. subjects schs., McIntosh, Minn., 1938-40, Wadena, Minn., 1941; with Tyler Refrigeration Corp., Niles, Mich., 1947-55, asst. sales mgr., 1955-70, dir. mktg., 1971-76; pres. Tyler Refrigeration Internat., 1977—. Served with USAAF, 1941-45; CBI. Mem. Kappa Sigma. Republican. Presbyterian. Club: Lions. Home: 532 Cedar St Niles MI 49120 Office: 1329 Lake St Niles MI 49120

WEST, SANDRA ARLINE, city ofcl.; b. Detroit, Sept. 15, 1940; d. Walter Ernest and Arlie (Thomas) W.; B.A. (David Wilkie scholar, Inez Robb scholar), Wayne State U., 1963, M.A. candidate. Classified ad writer Detroit Free Press, 1963-66; feature writer Gary (Ind.) Post-Tribune, 1966; reporter UPI, Detroit, 1966-67; publicist City Detroit Pub. Info. Dept., 1967-73, supervising publicist, 1973—. Mem. Mayor's Com. to keep Detroit Beautiful, 1968—; pub. relations rep. Detroit Hist. Soc., 1968-70. Mem. Women in Communications, Assn. Municipal Profl. Women, Wayne State Alumni, Detroit Women's Econ. Club, Women of Wayne. Episcopalian. Home: 2935 E Lafayette Detroit MI 48207 Office: 608 City County Bldg Detroit MI 48226

WEST, WALTER SCOTT, econ. geologist; b. Fayette, Wis., Mar. 12, 1912; s. Frank Edgar and Margaret (Scott) W.; A.B., Cornell Coll., 1934; B.E., Wis. State U., 1935; postgrad. Wis. Inst. Tech., 1935-36; M.S., U. Tenn., 1937; postgrad. U. Iowa, 1938-39, (fellow) U. N.C., 1939-40; m. Dorothy Janet Block, Aug. 30, 1940; children—Walter Scott, Janet Margaret, George LaVergne. Prin., basketball coach, high. sch., Wakenda, Mo., 1937-38; instr. geology N.C. U., 1940-42; engring. aide, cartographer U.S. Geol. Survey, Washington, 1942-46, geologist Alaskan geology br., 1946-54, geologist, sec. geologic names com., 1954-67, geologist and chief Wis. zinc-lead project Eastern mineral resources br., geologic div., Platteville, 1966—; dir. Citizens Nat. Bank, Darlington, Wis. Bd. dirs. Union Grove Cemetery. Recipient awards D.C. Recreation Dept.; 30-Year Service award U.S. Geol. Survey, 1972. Mem. Am. Inst. Mining Engrs., Arctic Inst. N.Am., Washington Acad. Scis., Washington Geol. Soc., Soc. Econ. Geologists, Inst. Lake Superior Geologists, Tri-State Geol. Soc. Contbr. articles to govt. publs. and profl. jours. Home: 601 E Louisa St Darlington WI 53530 Office: US Geol Survey Royce Hall U Wis Platteville WI 53818

WEST, WILMER A., JR., acct., fin. cons.; b. Ashland, Ky., May 28, 1949; s. Wilmer A. and Marguerite E. (English) W.; B.S. (Merit scholar 1973-75), Ind. U., 1975; M.B.A. (Golden State U. Minority Found. Ednl. grantee 1977-79), U. So. Calif., 1979; children—David A., Genine A. Fin. analyst Cummins Engine Co., Columbus, Ind., 1976-77; adminstrv. asst./project coordinator Cummins Service & Sales, Los Angeles, 1977-79, asst. controller, 1979-80; acct. Arthur Andersen & Co., Los Angeles, 1979; controller Mays Chem. Co., Indpls., 1981—; dir. Weskap Corp., Los Angeles; cons. in field. Cons. to Los Angeles council Boy Scouts Am., 1977, Watts Youth Symphony Orch., 1977-78, Quincy Jones Entertainment Workshop, 1977; bd. dirs., fin. staff Ind. Black Expo, 1974-76, So. Christian Leadership Conf.-W., 1979-80; chief acct. Expo Beauty Pageant, 1976; active Big Bros. Greater Los Angeles, 1978-79; bd. dirs. Golden State Minority Found. Alumni, 1979—; coordinating com. Affirmative Action Conf., 1977. Recipient U. So. Calif. Black Student Service award, 1978. C.P.A. Mem. Am. Mgmt. Assn., Nat. Assn. Black Accts., Nat. Black M.B.A. Assn., Ind. Assn. C.P.A.'s, Kappa Alpha Psi, Beta Gamma Sigma. Home: 5829-F Bywood Dr Indianapolis IN 46220 Office: 7202 N Shadeland Suite 111 Indianapolis IN 46250

WESTBROOK, DELOISE ANN BAKER, chemist; b. Marianna, Ark., Apr. 22, 1947; d. Theodore and Kara (Council) Baker; grad. Ark. Mech. and Normal Coll. Vocat. Sch. Practical Nursing, 1966; B.A., U. Ark., Pine Bluff, 1971; postgrad. U. Nebr., Omaha, 1975; children—Kasharri L., Abdul Kareem, Ebony Rashida. Lic. practical nurse Lee Meml. Hosp., Marianna, 1966-67, Ark. Mech. and Normal Coll. Infirmary, Pine Bluff, Ark., 1967-68; lic. practice nurse, asst. instr. lic. practical nurse students Chgo. Osteo. Hosp., 1968-69, 71-76; lab. technician Clarkson Hosp., Omaha, 1976-79; chemist Quarker Oats Chem. Co., Omaha, 1979-80; shift supr. Stauffer Chem. Co., Omaha, 1980—. Vol. worker ARC. Mem. Am. Soc. for Quality Control, Am. Chem. Soc., Alpha Kappa Alpha. Baptist. Office: Stauffer Chem Co 411 Gibson Rd Omaha NE 68107

WESTBROOK, WILLIAM GALE, mfg. co. exec.; b. Columbus, Ohio, Jan. 7, 1927; s. William Gale and Elizabeth Lucille (Loren) W.; student Ohio State U., 1947-48; children—Mark Daniel, Marsha Dee, Miles Hiro, Andrew Shaw, Thomas Ken. With Battelle Meml. Inst., 1950-74, project leader, Bangkok, Thailand, 1967-70, group leader, researcher, Columbus, 1970-74; prodn. mgr. Aerospace Materials Inc., Columbus, 1974-76; v.p., gen. mgr. Clydesbale Aircraft, Inc., aircraft engine remfg., Columbus, 1976—. Mem. Columbus Public TV Task Force, 1974; pres. bd. public affairs City of Hilliard (Ohio), 1954-60, dir. public service, 1960-62. Served with USAAF, 1945-47. Recipient Outstanding Young Man of Yr. award U.S. Jr. C. of C., 1957. Home: 500 Liberty Ln Westerville OH 43081 Office: 3850 E 5th Ave Columbus OH 43219

WESTBURY, IAN DOUGLAS, educator; b. Melbourne, Australia, Jan. 7, 1939; came to U.S., 1968; s. Douglas George and Doris Jean (Tarry) W.; B.A. with honors, U. Melbourne, 1959, diploma of Edn., 1960; postgrad. U. Alta., Can., 1968; m. Susan Alice Hansen, Jan. 13, 1962; children—Brian, David, Andrew. Asst. prof. edn. Ont. Inst. Studies in Edn., Toronto, 1966-68, U. Chgo., 1968-72; prof. secondary edn. U. Ill., Urbana-Champaign, 1972—. Mem. Am. Ednl. Research Assn. Editor: (with Arno A. Bellack) Research into Classroom Processes, 1971; (with Neil J. Wilkof) Science, Curriculum and Liberal Education, 1978; Jour. Curriculum Studies, 1976—. Home: 503 Harding Dr E Urbana IL 61801 Office: 1212 W Springfield St Urbana IL 61801

WESTENFELDER, GRANT ORVILLE, physician; b. Chgo., Jan. 12, 1940; s. Orville L. and Eleanor Jean (Langley) W.; student U. Mich., 1957-60; B.S., Northwestern U. 1961, M.D., 1964; m. Sharon L. Zelesnik, June 22, 1981; children—Mark, Bruce, Natalie. Intern, Evanston (Ill.) Hosp., 1964-65, now sr. attending physician, resident in internal medicine Northwestern U. McGaw Med. Center, 1965-68, fellow in infectious diseases, 1968-70, mem. infectious diseases sect. Med. Sch., 1970—, asst. prof. clin. medicine Northwestern U., 1974-81, asso. prof. clin. medicine, 1981—; asso. chmn. dept. medicine, head div. infectious diseases Evanston Hosp. Corp.; head dept. medicine Glenbrook Hosp., Glenview, Ill. Bd. deacons Trinity Luth. Ch., Evanston, 1970-71. Diplomate Am. Bd. Internal Medicine. Fellow A.C.P., Am. Coll. Chest Physicians; mem. Am. Soc. Microbiology, Am. Fedn. Clin. Research, AMA, Chgo. Soc. Internal Medicine, Alpha Kappa Kappa. Office: 2100 Pfingsten Rd Glenview IL 60025 also 2050 Pfingsten Rd Glenview IL 60025

WESTERHAUS, CATHERINE FRANCES (MRS. GEORGE H. WESTERHAUS), social worker; b. Corydon, Ind., Oct. 13, 1910; d. Anthony J. and Permelia Ann (Mathes) Kannapel; B. Music Edn., Kan. U., 1934; M.S.W., Loyola U., Chgo., 1949; m. George H. Westerhaus, Apr. 15, 1950. Social worker Harvey County Welfare Dept., Newton, Kan., 1934-38, 40-74, welfare dir., 1941-74; adult services supr., regional office Dept. Social and Rehab. Services, Wichita, Kan., 1974-75; social worker Lyon County Welfare Dept., Emporia, Kan., 1938-39; pvt. practice as clin. social worker, Newton, 1976—. Cons. Friendly Acres Home for Aged, Newton, Kans., 1976—. Kans. Christian Home for Intermediate Nursing Care, Newton, 1976-78. Mem. adv. com. Sch. Social Work, Kan. U., Lawrence, 1966—; mem. adv. com. to homemaker service demonstration project, dept. family econs. Kan. State U., Manhattan, 1968-71. Served with USNR, 1945-46. Recipient Kans. Social Worker of Yr. award Wichita chpt. Nat. Assn. Social Workers, 1975. Mem. Acad. Certified Social Workers, Kan. Conf. Social Workers, Am. Legion (dist. child welfare chmn. 1964-77, incentive award Midwestern region 1979, post comdr. 1981-82), Daus. Isabella (regent 1966, 67, 80-82), Legion of Mary (pres. 1976-79, v.p. 1979—). Home: 313 W Broadway Newton KS 67114

WESTGAARD, ODIN EVERETT, instrnl. designer; b. Cody, Wyo., Dec. 9, 1936; s. Olaf and Willie Ruth (Brim) W.; B.A., Western State Coll. of Colo., 1962; M.A., U. No. Colo., 1968, Ed.D., 1970; m. Goldie Jane Schmid, Aug. 15, 1958; children—Olaf, Orville, Oscar. Tchr., Craig (Colo.) Public Schs., 1962-67; instr. U. No. Colo., Greeley, 1967-70; prof. Central Wash. State Coll., Ellensburg, 1970-75; prof. U. Victoria (B.C., Can.), 1976; instrnl. design specialist Advanced Systems, Inc., Chgo., 1976—; cons. Republican Precinct Committeeman, Greeley, Colo., 1968-70. Served with AUS, 1958-62. Continental Oil scholar, 1955-62; recipient Bausch & Lombe Sci. award, 1955. Mem. NEA, Nat. Assn. Performance and Instrn., Am. Soc. Tng. and Devel., Phi Delta Kappa. Republican. Mem. United Ch. Christ. Office: 1601 Tonne Rd Elk Grove Village IL 60007

WESTIN, DAVID ALEXANDER, wholesale distbn. co. exec.; b. Newport, R.I., Jan. 24, 1947; s. George Wilbur and Lillian Hert (Alexander) W.; B.S. B.A. in Engring. and Gen. Bus., U. Denver, 1968, M.B.A. in Mgmt., 1969; m. Mary Virginia Kauffman, Aug. 2, 1969; children—Mark Alexander, David Eric. Mem. audit staff, then cons. mgmt. adv. services Haskins & Sells, C.P.A.'s, Los Angeles, 1969-74; corp. controller Kauffman-Lattimer Co. div. Alco Standard Corp., Columbus, Ohio, 1974-77, v.p., sec.-treas., 1977-79, v.p. fin. and adminstrn., 1979—. Mem. Calif. N.G., 1969-75. C.P.A., Calif. Mem. Nat. Wholesale Druggists Assn. (chmn. fin. mgmt. com. 1979-80), Fin. Execs. Inst. (dir. 1981—), Am. Inst. C.P.A.'s, Drug Wholesalers Legis. Assn. (pres. 1978—), Profl. Ski Instrs. Assn., Nat. Assn. Wholesalers-Distbrs. (trustee 1980—, chmn. young execs. bd. advisors 1981—), Ohio Wholesaler-Distbrs. Assn. (vice chmn. 1977-80), Rocky Mountain Ski Instrs. Assn., Columbus Jaycees (com. chmn. 1974-78). Home: 2358 Brandon Rd Columbus OH 43221 Office: 1200 E 5th Ave Columbus OH 43216

WESTMAN, ROY HERMAN, newspaper exec.; b. Duluth, Minn., Apr. 26, 1913; s. Gustav E. and Henny (Hoglund) W.; B.A., U. Minn., 1938; m. Violet Marie Forsberg, Nov. 12, 1938; children—Karen Shirley (Mrs. David N. Carlson), Linda Marie (Mrs. Calvin Johnson). Advt. salesman Eau Claire (Wis.) News, 1938-39, Evening Telegram, Superior, Wis., 1939-43; advt. mgr. Mesabi Daily News, Virginia, Minn., 1943-50, gen. mgr., 1950-64; gen. mgr. Evening Telegram Co., Superior, 1964-71, exec. v.p., dir., 1971—; sec.-treas. Hibbing (Minn.) Tribune, 1967—; dir. Mesabi Pub. Co., Virginia, Minn., 1958—, v.p., 1969—; sec.-treas., dir. Ashland (Wis.) Pub. Co., 1965—; treas., dir. Wis. Bldg. Co., Superior, 1965—; sec.-treas., dir. Dunedin (Fla.) Times, 1966—, dir. Gulf Sentinel Corp., Largo, Fla., 1967—, West Coast Pub. Co., Pinellas Park, Fla., 1967—, Seminole (Fla.) Pub. Co., 1970—; dir. Apple Valley Broadcasting Co., Yakima, Wash., First Nat. Bank, Virginia, Minn., Nat. Bank of Commerce, Superior, Duluth Sci. Instruments. Chmn., East Range Red Cross, 1960; active Superior Douglas County Devel. Assn., 1966-72, Superior Douglas County United Fund, 1972—. Served with USNR, 1943-46. Mem. Superior C. of C. (pres. 1970), Wis. C. of C. (dir.), N.W. Daily Press Assn. (pres. 1960), Wis. Daily Newspaper League (v.p. 1972-73), V.F.W., Am. Legion. Mason (Shriner). Clubs: Minnesota Press; Kitchi Gammi (Duluth). Home: 2 Highgate St Superior WI 54880 Office: 1226 Ogden Ave Superior WI 54880

WESTON, GALEN W., retail exec. With The Weston Ltd., to 1973; pres., chief exec. officer Nat. Tea Co., Rosemont, Ill., from 1973, now chmn. bd.; chmn. bd., pres. George Weston Ltd.; chmn. bd., chief exec. officer Loblaw Cos. Ltd.; pres. Wittington Investments Ltd. Office: Nat Tea Co 9701 W Higgins Rd Rosemont IL 60018*

WESTON, LLOYD HANAN, newspaper publisher; b. Detroit, Aug. 29, 1942; s. Allan Lewis and Ethel (Rom) W.; student Inst. Allende, Mexico, 1961; A.B. in Journalism, Wayne State U., Detroit, 1964; m. Marilyn Green, June 20, 1971. Reporter, Ypsilanti (Mich.) Daily Press, 1964-65; dir. public relations Jewish Community Center, Detroit, 1965-66; exec. editor Pioneer Press, Inc. subs. Time, Inc., Wilmette, Ill., 1966-71; founder, 1971, since pres., pub., editor Addison Leader Newspaper Corp. (Ill.); dir. Am. Heritage Savs. & Loan Assn., Bloomingdale, Ill., 1969-81, MetroVision Du Page County No. 2, Inc., 1st Du Page Communications, Inc.; pres., pub. Chgo. Daily News, 1979—; mem. Cable Advt. Bur., 1981—. Bd. dirs. Bensenville (Ill.) unit Am. Cancer Soc., 1979, Elmhurst (Ill.) Symphony Orch., 1979—, Addison Public Library, 1969-74; chmn. Addison Sesquicentennial Com., 1968, Addison Cultural Art Devel. Com., 1970-73, Addison Twp. Complete Count Com., 1980; adv. com. local govt. Coll. DuPage, 1969-70; mem. Ill. State Library Adv. Com., 1980—; bd. dirs. DuPage County Family Service Assn., Wheaton, Ill., 1980-82; founder, chmn. DuPage Found., 1980—. Recipient Malcolm Bingay Journalism key Wayne State U., 1964, spl. recognition award Bensenville Community Chest, 1977. Mem. Nat. Newspaper Assn., DuPage County Pubs. Assn., Chgo. Council Fgn. Relations, No. Ill. Newspaper Assn., Suburban Newspapers Am., Ill. Press Assn., Wayne State U. Alumni Assn., Addison C. of C., Addison Indsl. Assn., MacKenzie Honor Soc., Sigma Delta Chi. Jewish. Clubs: Lions, Kiwanis, Chgo. Press, Chgo. Headline, Chgo. Cable, Suburban Press, B'nai B'rith. Home: 262 Lafayette St Wood Dale IL 60191 Office: 130 Army Trail Blvd Addison IL 60101

WESTON, STEVEN PAUL, mktg. exec.; b. Des Moines, Iowa, Jan. 4, 1943; s. Clare Vergel and Polly L. (Lorenze) W.; B.A., Drake U., 1966; m. Susan Ferdon, May 12, 1979. Sr. sales exec. Xerox Corp., Kansas City, Mo., 1971-78; v.p. Techmark Corp., Shawnee Mission, Kans., 1978-80, pres., 1980—; pres. Techmark of Wichita, Inc. (Kans.), 1980—; dir. XMG Corp., 1979—; v.p., dir. Louise Gilliam Lighting Corp., Tulsa, Okla., 1976—. Served to capt. USAF, 1967-71. Decorated Bronze Star medal. Mem. Internat. Word Processing Assn., Exxon Info. Systems Agts. Assn., Animal Protection Assn., Alpha Tau Omega. Republican. Clubs: Woodside Racquet, Spaulding Racquetball. Office: 11855 W 83d Terr Lenexa KS 66214

WESTON, WILLIAM VIRGIL, writer, producer, director; b. Granite City, Ill.; s. Wilbur Herman and Nola Angel (Lindsay) W.; student La Universidad Interamericana, Mexico, 1956; B.S. with honors, U. Ill., Champaign-Urbana, 1958; m. Yuli Weston; 1 dau., Lindsay Nicole. Writer, producer Gardner Advt., St. Louis, 1958-63; free lance fiction writer, Mexico, 1963-64; partner Donnelly & Weston Advt., St. Louis, 1965-67; v.p., mgmt. rep., creative dir. Gardner Advt. Co., St. Louis, 1967-77; pres. Weston Communications, Inc., St. Louis, 1977—. Served with USAF, 1951-55. Recipient over 50 nat. awards for TV commls. and films. Mem. Am. Fedn. Radio and TV Artists. Contbr. short stories and articles to mags. Home: 954 Crick-Hollow Pl Saint Louis MO 63141

WESTPHAL, ROGER ALLEN, grain elevator exec.; b. Hillsboro, Ill., Aug. 5, 1942; s. Clarence Charles and Marguerite Lucille (Brakenhoff) W.; B.S. in Fin., U. Ill., 1971, M.B.A., 1973. With Rieke Elevator & Supply Co., Nokomis, Ill., 1961—; asst. mgr., 1973-77, gen. mgr., chief adminstrv. officer, 1977—. Mem. adv. com. Krannert Center Performing Arts, Urbana, Ill., 1971-73. Served with USAF, 1964-68. Decorated Air Force Commendation medal. Mem. Grain Elevator and Processing Soc., Am. Mgmt. Assn., Assn. M.B.A. Execs., U. Ill. Alumni Assn., Sigma Iota Epsilon. Republican. Lutheran. Home: Route 1 Box 36 Harvel IL 62538 Office: Route 1 Box 108 Nokomis IL 62075

WESTRAN, ROY ALVIN, ins. co. exec.; b. Taft, Oreg., Apr. 30, 1925; s. Carl A. and Mae E. (Barnhardt) W.; B.B.A., Golden Gate Coll., 1955, M.B.A., 1957; m. Dawn M. Oeschger, Oct. 18, 1952; children—Denise, Thomas, Michael, Dawna. Mem. sales staff C.A. Westran Agy., Taft, 1946-49; underwriter Fireman's Fund Group, San Francisco, ins. mgr. Kaiser Aluminum Chem. Oakland, 1952-65; pres., dir. Citizens Ins. Co. Am., Howell, Mich., 1967—, Beacon Ins. Co. Am., Columbus, Ohio, 1967—, Am. Select Ins. Co., Columbus, 1967—; v.p. Hanover Ins. Co.; dir. Worcester (Mass.) Mut. Ins. Co., 1st Nat. Bank, Howell; vice-chmn. Mich. Catastrophe Claims Assn.; dir. Oakland Kaiser Fed. Credit Union, 1957-60. Mem. ins. adv. council Salvation Army, San Francisco, 1957-60, now mem. Howell adv. bd.; chmn. drive United Fund, 1970; mem. adv. council Cleary Coll., Howell, 1981—. Bd. dirs., exec. com. Portage Trails council Boy Scouts Am., 1970-72; bd. dirs. McPherson Health Center; trustee Traffic Safety Assn. Detroit, 1967, Traffic Safety for Mich., 1967; trustee, exec. com. Child and Family Services Mich., 1975. Served with AUS, 1943-46, C.P.C.U. Mem. Ins. Inst. Am., Mich. C. of C. (dir. 1968-71), Am. Soc. Ins. Mgmt. (pres. 1960-62), Soc. C.P.C.U. (nat. pres. 1968-69), Ind. Ins. Agts. Mich. Home: Brighton MI 48116 Office: 645 W Grand River Howell MI 48843

WESTROM, ROBERT GEORGE, microfilm and mosquito control co. exec.; b. Des Moines, Feb. 4, 1925; s. Fred William and Grace Marie (Canady) W.; B.A. in Bus. Adminstrn., N. Central Coll., Naperville, Ill., 1951; m. Thelma Jean Robertson, July 1948; children—Dean Robert, Brad Canady, Lee Francis, Jan Lisa. Supt. personnel dept. Studebaker Corp., Chgo., 1951-55; owner, operator Shoe Tree, West Chicago, Ill., 1955-65, Tifa Sales Corp., West Chicago, 1965-79; owner, pres., dir. Microchem, Inc., West Chicago, 1979—. Mem. Bd. Edn. Dist. 94, West Chicago, 1969-80, pres., 1974-78; dep. chief West Chicago Fire Protection Dist., 1971-74. Served with USN, 1942-45. Named Citizen of Yr., West Chicago C. of C., 1957. Mem. Am. Mosquito Control Assn., Ill. Pest Control Assn., Ill. Mosquito Control Assn., Nat. Micrographics Assn., Ind. Sanitarians, Ind. Vector Control Assn., Ill. Sch. Bds. Assn. Republican. Methodist. Club: Rotary (past pres.). Home: 426 E Washington St West Chicago IL 60185 Office: Microchem Inc 185 W Washington St West Chicago IL 60185

WETHERBEE, RALPH HOUGHTON, JR., brass foundry exec.; b. Pitts., Sept. 20, 1911; s. Ralph Houghton and Ruth May (Bagster) W.; A.B., Miami U., Oxford, Ohio, 1933; m. Corinne Katherine Nolte, Oct. 30, 1947; 1 dau., Katherine Houghton Wetherbee Wildman. Salesman, Samuel Bingham's Son Mfg. Co., Chgo., 1933-35, Sinclair & Valentine Co., N.Y.C., 1935-37, Sigmund Ullman div. Sun Chem. Co., Long Island City, N.Y., 1937-50; pres., treas. Nolte Brass Foundry Co., Springfield, Ohio, 1950—. Chmn. bd. Springfield Art Assn./Center, 1976—. Served to 1st lt. AUS, 1942-46. Mem. Am. Numismatic Assn., SAR (pres. George Rogers Clark chpt. Ohio soc. 1974—), Phi Delta Theta. Republican. Presbyterian. Home: 408 Broadmoor Blvd N Springfield OH 45501 Office: 21 W Jefferson St Springfield OH 45501

WETHERILL, EDWIN D., appliance co. exec.; b. Chilhowee, Mo., Oct. 13, 1928; s. Fred E. and Doris (Espenett) W.; B.S. in Bus. Adminstrn., Gustavus Adolphus Coll., 1950; m. Beverly Jo Hanks, Dec. 29, 1955; children—Dayna Jean, Nancy Jo, Lesley Jane. Acctg. trainee Mpls.-Moline, 1950; with sales and sales promotion Toni Co., Chgo., 1954-55; with Sunbeam Applicance Co., Chgo., 1956—, div. service mgr., 1960, sales stats. supr., 1961-62, systems analyst, 1963-64, mgr. coop. advt., 1965-70, mgr. customer service dept., 1970-75, sr. acctg. exec.-sales, 1976-78, mgr. mktg. services, 1979, dir. distbn., Chgo., 1979—. Mem. Hinsdale Village Caucus, 1967-68, 76-78. Served to lt. U.S. Army, 1951-53. Republican. Lutheran. Clubs: Committee of 100 (Hinsdale); Masons. Home: 518 N Grant St Hinsdale IL 60521 Office: 2001 S York Rd Oak Brook IL 60521

WETHERINGTON, ROBERT EDDIE, power shovel co. exec.; b. La Mesa, Calif., July 27, 1943; s. Eddie Robert and Emma Joanna (Coons) W.; B.S. in M.E., Ohio No. U., 1966; m. Eugenia Faye Fulp, Aug. 29, 1965; 1 son, Anthony Patrick. Jr. engr. United Aircraft Products, Forest, Ohio, 1966-67; engr. Marion Power Shovel Co. (Ohio), 1967-72, sr. engr., 1972-76, design supr. large draglines, 1976-80, chief engr. rotary blast hole drills, 1980—; instr. engring. Marion Tech. Coll., 1979-80. Pres., Bd. dirs. Jr. Achievement Marion, 1976-77; pres. Pleasant Twp. Fire Dept., 1975-76. Registered profl. engr., Ohio. Mem. Am. Mgmt. Assn., PTA. Republican. Baptist. Club: Masons. Home: 3346 Smeltzer Rd Marion OH 43302 Office: PO Box 505 Marion OH 43302

WETHEY, HAROLD EDWIN, educator; b. Port Byron, N.Y., Apr. 10, 1902; s. Charles Edwin and Flora (Keck) W.; A.B., Cornell U., 1923; A.M., Harvard U., 1931, Ph.D., 1934; student U. Paris, summers 1931, 34; m. Alice Luella Sunderland, June 8, 1948; 1 son, David Sunderland. Asst. history of art Harvard U., 1933-34; instr., lectr. then asst. prof. Bryn Mawr (Pa.) Coll., 1934-38; asst. prof. Washington U., St. Louis, 1938-40; asso. prof. U. Mich., Ann Arbor, 1940—, prof. art history, 1946-72, prof. emeritus, 1972—, Henry Russel lectr., 1964-65; vis. prof. U. Tucumán (Argentina), 1943, U. Mex., summer 1960; spl. lectr. Escuela de Estudios Hispano-americanos, La Rabida, Spain, 1948. Recipient Distinguished Faculty Achievement award, 1968; Sheldon fellow Harvard U., 1932-33; Rockefeller fellow, 1944-45; Rackham research grantee, 1948-72; Guggenheim fellow, 1949, 71-72; fellow Am. Council Learned Socs., 1936, 63; Fulbright scholar, Rome, 1958-59; 400th anniversary of death of Titian, speaker U. Venice, 1976. Mem. Hispanic Soc. Am. (Sculpture medal 1962), Coll. Art Assn., Renaissance Soc., Venice com. Internat. Fund for Monuments, Research Club (U. Mich.), Am. Acad. Franciscan History (corr.), Real Acad. de Bellas Artes de San Fernando (Madrid), Soc. Peruana de Historia, Acad. Nacional de Ciencias de Bolivia, Phi Kappa Phi. Author: Gil Siloe and His School, 1936; The Early Works of Bartolomé Ordónez and Diego de Siloe, 1943; Colonial Architecture and Sculpture in Peru (award Soc. Archtl. Historians), 1949; Alonso Cano, Painter, Sculptor and Architect, 1955; Alonso Cano, Pintor, 1958; Arquitectura virreinal en Bolivia, 1961; El Greco and His School, 2 vols., 1962, rev. edit. in Spanish, 1967; editor: (Chandler R. Post) History of Spanish Painting, Vol. XIII, The Schools of Aragon and Navarre in the Early Renaissance, Vol. XIV, The School of Castile in the Later Renaissance, 1966; Titian, Vol. I, The Religious Paintings, 1969, Vol. II, The Portraits, 1971, Vol. III, The Mythological and Historical Paintings, 1975; editor bibliography of Spanish Am. art for Handbook Latin-Am. Studies, 1948-59; editorial bd. Art Bull., 1940-44, 64-71; contbr. to art periodicals (bibliography through 1975 in Hortus Imaginum, Essays in Western Art, pub. in his honor 1975). Home: 1510 Cambridge Rd Ann Arbor MI 48104

WETHINGTON, NORBERT ANTHONY, coll. adminstr.; b. Dayton, Ohio, Sept. 14, 1943; s. Norbert and Sophie Lillian W.; B.A., U. Dayton, 1965; M.A., John Carroll U., 1967; postgrad. Baldwin Wallace Coll., 1968-70; m. Martha M. Vannice, Aug. 13, 1965; children—Paula, Mark, Eric, Kristen, Rebecca, Lisa, Bethany. Grad. asst., teaching asso. John Carroll U., Cleve., 1965-67; English tchr. Padua Franciscan High Sch., Parma, Ohio, 1967-70; instr., chmn. dept. tech. writing and speech N. Central Tech. Coll., Mansfield, Ohio, 1970-74; dir. evening div. Terra Tech. Coll., Fremont, Ohio, 1974-80, dir. public and community service technologies, 1980—. Vice pres. Sandusky County Bd. Health, 1979-80. Mem. Am. Vocat. Assn., Ohio Vocat. Assn., Nat. Council Tchrs. English. Democrat. Roman Catholic. Contbr. articles to profl. jours. Home: 1036 Hazel St Fremont OH 43420 Office: Terra Technical College 1220 Cedar St Fremont OH 43420

WETHINGTON, WILMA ZELLA, artist, gallery dir.; b. Clinton, Iowa, Apr. 15, 1918; d. Marion L. and Marjorie Irene (Huber) Russell; student Marshall U., 1936-37, Wichita State U., 1959-64; m. Bert J. Wethington, Sept. 14, 1938; children—Roberta Ann, Paul L., Richard P. Comml. artist Boeing Airplane Co., Wichita, Kans., 1942-45; comml. artist McCormick-Armstrong, Wichita, 1945-47; tchr., owner, dir. Accent Frame & Gallery, Wichita, 1974—; one-woman shows: Independence (Kans.) Art Mus., Huntsville (Ala.) Civic Art Center, Sandzen Meml. Gallery, Lindsborg, Kans., Philbrook Art Center, Tulsa, Ponca City (Okla.) Art Assn., Community Arts Center, Emporia, Kans., Wichita Art Assn.; dir., tchr. Wethington Studio and Gallery, Wichita, 1964—; mem. faculty Wichita Art Assn. Mem. Hudson Valley Art Assn., Am. Watercolor Soc. (asso.), Ala. Watercolor Soc., So. Watercolor Soc., La. Watercolor Soc., Kans. Watercolor Soc., Wichita Artist Guild. Congregationalist. Home: 2 Linden Dr Wichita KS 67206 Office: 2918 E Central Ave Wichita KS 67214

WETTER, VERNON F., brokerage cons. and tng. exec.; b. Lanesboro, Iowa, Aug. 14, 1924; s. Albert R. and Frances (Sheffield) W.; student Simpson Coll., 1941-43, U. Louisville, 1946-47; m. Geneva Scott, Mar. 28, 1945; children—Larry, Robert, Elizabeth, Kevin, Troy. Salesman, Procter & Gamble Co., Hopkinsville, Ky., 1947-55; salesman Anderson Clayton, Greenview, Ill., 1955-60; salesman Beckly Cardy, Greenview, 1961-64; sec. Monroe St. Securities, Springfield, Ill., 1964; pres. Securities Seminars, Inc., Greenview, 1964—; dir. Middle Atlantic Investment Co.; partner Securities Compliance Assistance, Greenview, 1977—. Pres., Greenview Bd. Edn., 1959. Served with AUS, World War II. Mem. Nat. Assn. Securities Schs. (pres. 1981-83). Mason. Home: 314 S Enterprise St Greenview IL 62642 Office: 322 S Enterprise St Greenview IL 62642

WETTERSTROM, EDWIN, engr.; b. Oak Park, Ill., Dec. 20, 1919; s. Frank and Alma (Ekstrom) W.; bus. diploma Wright Coll., 1940; B.S. in Mech. Engring., Ill. Inst. Tech., 1944; M.S. in Engring. Mechanics, Purdue U., 1947, Ph.D., 1951; m. Betty Barbara Chase. Engr., devel. dept. Continental Can Co., 1944-45; staff mem. engring. mechanics dept. Purdue, 1945-51; analytical research engr. research and devel. dept. Graver Tank & Mfg. Co., 1951, cons., 1952—; asst. prof. civil engring. U. Mo., 1952-55; asso. prof. applied mechanics Mich. State U., 1955-57; prof. mech. engring. N.D. State U., 1957-67, U. Toledo, 1967-70, Ind. Inst. Tech., 1970-72, Tuskegee Inst., 1972-74; sr. analytical engr. Westinghouse Air Brake Co., 1974-80, cons. engr., 1980—. Mem. ASME, Am. Soc. Engring. Edn., Sigma Xi. Lutheran. Contbr. articles tech. press. Home: PO Box 157 Washington IL 61571

WEXLER, SAMUEL, psychologist; b. Chgo., Jan. 7, 1917; s. Benjamin and Emma W.; B.S., U. Ill., 1940, M.S., 1941; Ph.D., Purdue U., 1953; m. Bernice B. Weiner, Dec. 22, 1942; children—Lynne S., Eric Joseph. Psychologist, VA hosps., Long Beach, Calif., 1953-54, Pitts., 1954-56, Downey, Ill., 1956-62; asst. dir. mental health div. Chgo. Bd. Health, 1962-77; psychologist VA Westside Med. Center, Chgo., 1977—; pvt. practice psychotherapy, Chgo., 1958—. Served to capt. AUS, 1942-46. Mem. Am. Psychol. Assn., Sigma Xi, Psi Chi. Office: 259 E Erie St Rm 452 Chicago IL 60611

WEXNER, LESLIE HERBERT, retail chain co. exec.; b. Dayton, Ohio, 1937; B.S., Ohio State U., Columbus, 1959, postgrad. Law Sch., 1959-61. Founder, pres., chmn. bd. Limited Stores, Inc., fashion chain, Columbus, 1963—. Mem. bus. adminstrn. adv. council Ohio State U.; founder Orphan's Day at Ohio State Fair; bd. dirs. Hillel Found., B'nai B'rith; trustee Columbus Jewish Fedn., 1972, Heritage House-Columbus Jewish Home for Aged, 1972, St. Anthony's Hosp., Columbus, 1977, Agudas Achim Synagogue, Columbus; bd. dirs. men's div. Project Hope, 1980. Named Outstanding Young Man, Jaycees, 1971, Man of Yr., Am. Mktg. Assn., 1974. Mem. Young Pres.'s Orgn., Columbus Area C. of C. (dir. 1979-80, 81—), Sigma Alpha Mu. Office: Limited Stores Inc 1 Limited Pkwy Columbus OH 43216

WEYGANDT, JOHN CLIFTON, chemist; b. Akron, Nov. 10, 1934; s. Vernon Foster and Doris Fern (Steffee) W.; B.S., U. Akron, 1956; M.S., Case Western Res. U., 1958; postgrad. (Am. Petroleum Inst. fellow) Ohio State U., 1961-63; Ph.D. (B.F. Goodrich fellow, Goodyear fellow), Kent State U., 1969; m. Bonnie Jean Kaltwasser, Nov. 27, 1960; children—Mark Harold, David John. Chemist, Nylonge Corp., Cleve., 1958-60; instr. Kent (Ohio) State U., 1967-69; mem. faculty Ashland (Ohio) Coll., 1969—, asso. prof. chemistry, 1974-79, prof., 1979—, dean of scis., 1980—; prof. Sohio Research Center, Cleve., summer 1980. Muehlstein scholar, 1955-56; NSF indsl. research grantee, summer 1981. Mem. Am. Chem. Soc. (chmn. Wooster sect.), Sigma Xi, Phi Eta Sigma, Alpha Chi Sigma. Lutheran. Home: 1055 Thomas Dr Ashland OH 44805 Office: Dept Chemistry Ashland Coll Ashland OH 44805

WEYLS, JOHN LAWRENCE, chem. co. exec.; b. Cleve., Oct. 18, 1934; s. W.L. and Emily E. (Lue) W.; student Baldwin Wallace Coll., 1956-68; m. Barbara Ann Wheeler, June 7, 1958; children—John Lawrence, Erik W., Mark T., Daniel C. With Rohco Inc., Cleve., 1955—, exec. v.p., 1966-77, pres., 1977—; exec. v.p. McGea Rohco, Cleve., 1981—. Mem. Am. Electroplaters Soc., Metal Finishing Suppliers Assn. (trustee). Republican. Mason (Shriner). Home: 4166 State Rd Medina OH 44256 Office: 3203 W 71st St Cleveland OH 44102

WEYUKER, BEN, constrn. co. exec.; b. Bklyn., Dec. 24, 1938; s. David and Rose (Secol) W.; student Bklyn. Coll., 1955-57; m. Gail Goldberg, Mar. 26, 1961; children—Mitchell Eric, Beth Lynn. Vice pres. mktg. Levitt & Sons, Inc., Lake Success, N.Y., 1964-71; pres. Bldg. Systems, Inc., Cleve., 1971-75, Pulte Home Corp., Atlanta, 1975-76, Heather Ridge Devel. Co., Gurnee, Ill., 1972-76, Westwood Group, Inc., Vernon Hills, Ill., 1976—. Served with AUS, 1962. Named Man of Yr., State of Israel Bonds, 1979. Mem. Home Builders Assn. Greater Chgo. (Presidents award 1977, George K. Newman award 1979; pres. 1982—), Nat. Assn. Home Builders (dir.), Home Builders Ill. (dir.). Jewish. Office: 300 Butterfield Rd Vernon Hills IL 60061

WHALEY, DIANE BENSON, occupational therapist; b. Bethesda, Md., Dec. 31, 1953; d. LeDell Earl and Adele Marguerite (Borgendale) Benson; B.S. in Occupational Therapy, U. Wis., 1976; m. Charles R.Whaley, III, June 11, 1977. Intern, Abbott Hosp., Mpls., St. Francis Hosp., La Crosse, Wis., 1976-77; occupational therapist River Hills Nursing Home East and South, Milw., 1978-81, supr. occupational therapy students, 1978-79; occupational therapist Curative Rehab. Center, Milw., 1981—. Mem. Am. Occupational Therapy Assn., Wis. Occupational Therapy Assn. Lutheran. Home: 2734 N 46th St Milwaukee WI 53210 Office: 9001 Watertown Plank Rd Milwaukee WI 53226

WHALEY, VERN EDWARD, editor, writer, comml. photographer; b. Valley Junction, Iowa, Nov. 8, 1907; s. Charles Wesley and Jessie Frances (Chaney) W.; student Drake U., 1925; grad. Des Moines U., 1928; m. Mary Whitty, Dec. 2, 1929; children—John, Margaret, Jerry, Robert, Mark, Michael (dec.). Sports writer Des Moines Register, 1925-29; sports columnist, asst. sports editor Chgo. Evening Post, Sunday bulldog editor, rewrite man Chgo. Tribune, 1929-31; asst. sports editor Detroit Mirror, sports promotion dir. Detroit Free Press, news copyreader Detroit Times, 1932-33; gen. reporter, rewrite man Milw. Sentinel, asst. sports editor, picture editor Wis. News, 1933-39; copyreader Chgo. Herald & Examiner, asst. sports editor Chgo. Evening Am., 1939-41; picture editor Chgo. Am. and successor newspapers, also trouble-shooter on photography Hearst chain of newspapers, 1941-62; chmn. bd., chief exec. officer Photo Ideas, Inc., Chgo., 1962—; lectr., cons. Mem. Chgo. Press Vets. Assn., Sigma Delta Chi. Democrat. Roman Catholic. Clubs: Headline, Publicity, Chgo. Press (Chgo.). Home: 4015 N Hamlin Ave Chicago IL 60618 Office: Photo Ideas Inc 804 N Washington Blvd Chicago IL 60607

WHALL, CLIFFORD WILLIAM, JR., physiologist; b. Jamaica, N.Y., June 29, 1946; s. Clifford William and Barbara Ann (DePass) W.; B.A. in Physics, Middlebury Coll., 1968; Ph.D. in Physiology and Biophysics, U. Vt., 1978; m. Monique Jacqueline Davoust, Oct. 9, 1972; children—Mathieu W.D., Stephanie D. Postdoctoral research fellow U. Mich., Ann Arbor, 1978-80; asst. sec. Council on Dental Therapeutics, ADA, Chgo., 1980—. Served with U.S. Army, 1969-71. Decorated Bronze Star, Air medal. NIH and Mich. Heart Assn. postdoctoral fellow. Mem. Internat. Assn. Dental Research, Am. Physiol. Soc., N.Y. Acad. Scis., Sigma Xi. Contbr. articles to profl. jours. Home: 39 S Bodin St Hinsdale IL 60521 Office: 211 E Chicago Ave Chicago IL 60611

WHALLON, EVAN ARTHUR, JR., orch. condr.; b. Akron, Ind., July 24, 1923; s. Evan Arthur and Katharine (Kistler) W.; Mus.B., Eastman Sch. Music, U. Rochester, 1948, Mus.M., 1949; Mus.D. (hon.), Denison U., 1963, Otterbein U., 1969, Ohio Dominican Coll., 1970; m. Jean Pawley Borgman, Aug. 28, 1948; children—Paul Evan, Eric Andrew. Debut with Phila. Orch., 1948; condr. opera The Consul (Menotti), 1950; condr. Springfield Symphony, 1951-56; condr. Columbus (Ohio) Symphony, 1956—; condr. Chautauqua Opera, 1967—; guest condr. Rochester (N.Y.) Opera Under the Stars, N.Y.C. Opera, Spoleto (Italy) Festival, Cleve. Orch., Buffalo Philharmonic, Boston Arts Festival, Budapest Symphony, Prague Symphony. Served to lt. (j.g.) USNR, 1943-46. Clubs: Torch, Rotary. Home: 2993 Shadywood Rd Columbus OH 43221 Office: 101 E Town St Columbus OH 43215

WHANG, KI JUN, urologist; b. Taegu, Korea, Mar. 1, 1939; came to U.S., 1967, naturalized, 1976; s. Bong Kap and Soon Duk (Lee) W.; M.D., Kyungpook Nat. U., 1963, Master, 1967; m. Kae Ja Whang, Apr. 8, 1967; children—Douglas, Edward, Peter. Intern, Detroit Meml. Hosp., 1967-68; resident William Beaumont Hosp., Royal Oak, Mich., 1968-69, U. Iowa Hosp, Iowa City, 1969-72; practice medicine specializing in urology, Beaver Dam, Wis., 1972—. Served to sr. lt. Navy of S. Korea, 1964-67. Diplomate Am. Bd. Urology. Fellow A.C.S.; mem. AMA, Am. Urol. Assn., N. Central sect. Am. Urol. Assn., Wis. Urol. Soc., Dodge County Med. Soc., State Med. Soc. Wis. Republican. Presbyterian. Office: 130 Warren St Beaver Dam WI 53916

WHAPLES, GILMORE THEODORE, architect; b. Oak Park, Ill., Nov. 20, 1943; s. James J. and Jean S. (Mellor) W.; B.A. in Arch. and Structures, U. Ill., 1967; divorced; children—Todd A., Cora L., Darren M. Draftsman, Kleb, Shelp & Assos., Aurora, Ill., 1969; draftsman, architect Frazier, Raferty, Orr & Fairbank, Geneva, Ill., 1970-73; chief architect, asso. Jack D. Pickett & Assos., Burr Ridge, Ill., 1974-76; sr. partner Whaples-Driscoll & Assos., La Grange, Ill., 1976—; prin. works include comml. bldgs., offices, banks and residences. Active La Grange Highlands Youth Sports Program, 1976—; mem. La Grange Highlands Civic Assn., 1978-79. Recipient cert. supply of ednl. material and cons. Coll. of DuPage, 1975; Wood Preservation cert. Osmose, 1976; cert. Nat. Council Archtl. Registration Bds. Mem. Soc. Am. Registered Architects (dir. 1978-80, v.p. 1981), Ind. Architects Assn. Unitarian. Club: La Grange Lions. Home: 5932 Peck Ave La Grange IL 60525 Office: 500 E Ogden Ave Naperville IL 60540

WHARTON, JOHN ROSCOE, mfg. co. exec.; b. Iowa, Nov. 25, 1941; s. Roscoe Oscar and Harriet Jean (Jacobson) W.; Asso. in Elec. Engring., DeVry Inst. Tech., 1962; student Alexander Hamilton Bus. Sch., 1965; m. Mary Patricia Jacobi, Nov. 16, 1963; children—Robin Lisa, Tara Lynn. With Collins Radio Co., Cedar Rapids, Iowa, 1962—, 65; with Wilcox Electric Inc., Kansas City, Mo., 1965—, mgr. internat. sales, 1975—, mgr. advt. and public relations, 1974—; mgmt. cons., 1979—. Bd. dirs., founding pres. Nova Center, Inc., 1980—. Recipient Silver award Air Transport World Mag., 1981. Mem. Kansas City C. of C., Internat. Trade Club Kansas City, Air Traffic Control Assn., Am. Assn. Airport Execs., Nat. Air Transport Assn. Republican. Roman Catholic. Contbr. articles to profl. jours. Home: 10000 Cedar St Overland Park KS 66207 Office: 1400 Chestnut St Kansas City MO 64127

WHEATLEY, CHARLOTTE L., educator; b. Dover, Del., Oct. 14, 1935; d. Harold A. and Ella Lynch; B.S., Salisbury State Coll., 1957; M.S., U. Del., 1966; m. Grayson H. Wheatley, June 29, 1957; 1 son, Grayson H. Tchr., Newark (Del.) Spl. Sch. Dist., 1957-66; instr. Purdue U., West Lafayette, Ind., 1970-77, asst. prof. edn., 1978—, dir. research grants edn. dept. Mem. Assn. Supervision and Curriculum Devel., AAAS, Research Council for Diagnostic and Prescriptive Math., Social Sci. Math. Assn., Nat. Council Tchrs. Math., Ind. Council Tchrs. Math. (adv. bd.). Republican. Presbyterian. Co-author math. texts. Contbr. articles to profl. jours. Home: 2832 Wilshire Ave West Lafayette IN 47906 Office: Ednl Programs PO Box 2345 Purdue U West Lafayette IN 47907

WHEATLEY, KARL JACKSON, editor; b. Bartonville, Ill., Dec. 1, 1924; s. Karl Edward and Anna Wilhelmina (Rury) W.; student Bradley U., 1942-43, 46-47; B.S., Northwestern U., 1950. Reporter, Peoria Transcript, Peoria Jour. Star, 1942-43, 46-52; with Caterpillar Co., Peoria, 1952—, newspaper and mag. editor, 1958-68, coordinator employee information, public affairs, 1968—; mem. faculty Bradley U., 1950-66. Vice pres. Ill. Regional Tourism Commn., 1976-80; pres. Citizens Com. to Preserve Jubilee Coll., 1971—; mem. nat. alumni adv. com. Bradley U., 1975—, pres. chmn. bd., nat. alumni bd., 1973-75; mem. Ill. Bicentennial Commn. Peoria County, 1974-76; pres. Child and Family Service, 1956-57. Served with AUS, 1943-45; ETO. Recipient Freedom Found. award, annually, 1953-56; Outstanding Service award Jubilee Coll., 1981. Mem. Internat. Assn. Bus. Communicators (past pres.), Illinois Valley Press Club (pres. 1965), Nat. Alliance of Businessmen, Internat. Council Indsl. Communicators, Peoria C. of C., Peoria Old Settlers Assn., Peoria Hist. Soc., Lakeview Mus., Sigma Delta Chi, Alpha Delta, Tau Kappa Alpha. Republican. Unitarian-Universalist. Home: Bachaven 1706 W Cedar Hills Dr Dunlap IL 61525 Office: 100 NE Adams St Peoria IL 61629

WHEATON, BURDETTE CARL, educator; b. Mankato, Minn., July 3, 1938; s. Burdette Willard and Elsa (Gramentz) W.; B.S., Mankato State U., 1959; M.A., U. Ia., 1961, Ph.D., 1965; m. Margaret Ann Ehlbeck, June 16, 1968; children—Timothy, Michael John, Julie Ann. Grad. asst. U. Ia., Iowa City, 1959-63; asst. prof. Western Ill. U., Macomb, 1963-65; prof. math. Mankato (Minn.) State U., 1965—. Mem. Nat. Council Tchrs. Math., Am. Math. Soc., Math. Assn. Am., Sigma Xi, Sigma Zeta. Lutheran. Home: 326 Floral Ave Mankato MN 56001 Office: Mankato State U Mankato MN 56001

WHEBY, FRANK TOMAS, cons. engr.; b. Beckley, W.Va., Sept. 7, 1930; s. Albert and Katherine (Hall) W.; B.S. in Geology, Mass. Inst. Tech., 1952; B.S. in Civl Engring., W.Va. U., 1956; M.S. in Civil Engring., Northwestern U., 1961; m. Judith May Oeftering, Apr. 25, 1964; children—Christopher, Jonathan. Geotech. engr. Aluminum Co. of Am., Pitts., 1956, Maryville, Tenn., 1957, Paramaribo, Surinam, S.Am., 1958-59; dept. head Harza Engring. Co., Chgo., 1960-61, Lahore, Pakistan, 1965, Athens, Greece, 1966, Chgo., 1967-73; dept. head R.W. Beck & Assos., Seattle, 1962-64; pvt. practice cons. geotech. engr., Evanston, Ill., 1974—; mem. U.S. Nat. Com. on Tunnelling Tech., 1972-77, Underground Tech. Research Council, 1979—. Mem. Lakefront Recreation Mall Com., Evanston, 1970-72, Environ. Control Bd., Evanston, 1973-74, Pollution and Flood Control Com., Evanston, 1974. Served to 1st lt. U.S. Army, 1952-54. Registered profl. engr., 9 states; certified Nat. Council Engring. Examiners. Mem. ASCE, Assn. Engring. Geologists, Am. Inst. Profl. Geologists. Club: Rotary. Contbr. articles to profl. jours. Home: 1319 Grant St Evanston IL 60201 Office: 1604 Chicago Ave Evanston IL 60201

WHEELER, BARBARA MONICA, lawyer; b. Chgo., Mar. 20, 1947; d. John Benjamin and Elizabeth (Keife) Wheeler; B.A., St. Dominic Coll., 1969; cert. Lewis U. Sch. Paraprofl. Studies, 1976; J.D., DePaul U., 1980. Gen. supt. Md. Manor Devel. Co., Chgo., 1970-74; v.p. Omega Constrn. Co., Chgo., 1974-78; admitted to Ill. bar, 1980; asst. state's atty. State of Ill. Mem. Bd. Edn., Community High Sch. Dist. 99, DuPage County, 1974-76, pres., 1976—. Mem. Ill. Assn. Sch. Bds., dir.-at-large Tri County div., 1976-77, dir. DuPage div., 1977-78; mem. task force on purposes of edn. in eighties Nat. Sch. Bds. Assn. Mem. Am. Bar Assn., Ill. Bar Assn., Chgo. Bar Assn., Am. Mgmt. Assn., Phi Alpha Delta. Roman Catholic. Home: 9 South 230 Landsfield Ct Downers Grove IL 60516 Office: 738 W 43d St Chicago IL 60609

WHEELER, CALVIN WELLINGTON, ins. co. exec.; b. Des Moines, Dec. 26, 1920; s. Walter Arthur and Esther Lydia (Antrim) W.; student Centenary Coll., 1938; J.D., Creighton U., 1947; m. Virginia Grace Brown, Oct. 18, 1942; children—Candace Lynn Wheeler Kommers, Judith Lane Wheeler Collester, Thomas Clinton. Admitted to Nebr. bar, 1948; with Mut. of Omaha Ins. Co., 1947—, asst. v.p., policy counsel, 1959-67, 2d v.p., policy counsel, 1967-68, v.p., policy counsel, 1968-72, v.p. regulatory affairs, 1972—; chmn., dir. N.Mex. Life Ins. Guaranty Assn.; vice chmn. dir. Nebr. Life and Health Ins. Guaranty Assn.; dir. Kans. Life and Health Ins. Guaranty Assn., Ind. Comprehensive Health Ins. Assn., N.D. Comprehensive Health Ins. Assn.; pres. Insurers Action Council, Inc.; vice chmn. Ins. Equity Assn., Inc.; dir. industry adv. com. to Conf. of Ins. Legislators. Co-founder Omaha Zool. Soc., 1951, pres., 1955-57; bd. dirs. Omaha Civic Music Assn., 1960-62; elder Presbyterian Ch. Served to capt. U.S. Army, 1943-46. Decorated Purple Heart; recipient awards Omaha Jr. C. of C.; certs. of appreciation from various agys., civic groups, assns. Mem. Nebr. Bar Assn., Omaha Bar Assn., Health Ins. Assn. Am., Nebr. Assn. Commerce and Industry (dir.), Ins. Fedn. Nebr., Omaha C. of C., Am. Legion, Alpha Sigma Nu. Republican. Clubs: Nebr.; Offutt AFB Officers. Home: 3107 S 104th Ave Omaha NE 68124 Office: Mut of Omaha Ins Co Mutual of Omaha Plaza Omaha NE 68175

WHEELER, ROBERT GRAHAM, former govt. postal adminstr.; b. Wayne City, Ill., Dec. 17, 1915; s. Donald Vernon and Grace Irene (Behymer) W.; student So. Ill. U., 1928; m. Frieda Kathryn French, Dec. 25, 1940; children—Rebecca Ann, Robert Graham. Instr., Lockyears Bus. Coll., 1939-41; auditor C.E., U.S. Army, Louisville, 1941-43; foreman McCall Corp., Dayton, Ohio, 1946-51; mgr. C.A. French Grain Elevator, 1951-54; postmaster U.S. Postal Service, Mill Shoals, Ill., 1954-80; ret., 1980. Served with U.S. Army, 1943-45. Mem. Mill Shoals Ruritan Club, Nat. Assn. Postmasters, Nat. League Postmasters. Republican. Methodist. Clubs: Elks, Masons. Home: PO Box 705 Mill Shoals IL 62862

WHEELER, VIRGINIA ROGERS, educator; b. Columbia, Mo., Oct. 4, 1925; d. John Lewis and Ruby P. (Short) Rogers; B.S. in Elem. Edn., U. Mo., Columbia, 1958, M.Ed. in Elem. Counseling, 1966, Ed.D. in Counseling-Psychology, 1975; m. O.V. Wheeler, Jr., June 7, 1947; children—Jan Leigh Wheeler Nash, Mark Patrick. Elem. tchr. Columbia public schs., 1958-65, tchr. spl. programs, summers 1960-63, psychometrist, summer 1966, elem. counselor, 1966-68; mem. faculty U. Mo., Columbia, 1968—, asst. prof. edn./counseling, 1965—, asst. to dean Coll. Edn., 1976—; rep. NDEA Inst., 1965-67. Cert. tchr., Mo.; lic. psychologist, Mo. Mem. Am. Personnel and Guidance Assn., Nat. Vocat. Guidance Assn., Assn. Humanities Edn. and Devel., Mo. Guidance Assn., Mo. Tchrs. Assn. (past chpt. pres.), Phi Lambda Theta (past chpt. pres.), Phi Delta Kappa, Kappa Delta Pi, Delta Kappa Gamma, Alpha Delta Kappa. Author papers in field. Home: 916 W Ash St Columbia MO 65201 Office: 102 Hill Hall Coll Edn Univ Missouri Columbia MO 65201

WHELAN, JOSEPH L(EO), neurologist; b. Chisholm, Minn., Aug. 13, 1917; s. James Gorman and Johanna (Quilty) W.; student Hibbing Jr. Coll., 1935-38; B.S., U. Minn., 1940, M.B., 1942, M.D., 1943; m. Gloria Ann Rewoldt, June 12, 1948; children—Joseph William, Jennifer Ann. Intern, Detroit Receiving Hosp., 1942-43; fellow neurology U. Pa. Hosp., Phila., 1946-47; resident neurology U. Minn. Hosps., Mpls., 1947-49; chief neurology service VA Hosp., Mpls., 1949; spl. fellow electroencephalography Mayo Clinic, Rochester, Minn., 1951; practice medicine specializing in neurology, Detroit, 1949-73, Petoskey, Mich., 1973—; chief neurology services Grace, St. John's, Bon Secour hosps., Detroit; cons. neurologist No. Mich. Hosps., Petoskey; instr. U. Minn. Med. Sch., 1949; asst. prof. Wayne State U., 1957-63; cons. USPHS, Detroit Bd. Edn. Founder, mem. ad hoc Com. to Force Lawyers Out of Govt.; chmn. Reagan-Bush Campaign, Kalkaska County, Mich., 1980. Served to capt. AUS, 1943-46. Fellow Am. Acad. Neurology (treas. 1955-57), Am. Electroencephalography Soc.; mem. Assn. Research Nervous and Mental Diseases, Soc. Clin. Neurologists, Mich. Neurol. Assn. (sec.-treas. 1967-76), AMA, Mich. Med. Assn., No. Mich. Med. Soc. Club: Grosse Pointe (Mich.). Contbr. to profl. publs. in field. Home: Oxbow Rural Route 2 Mancelona MI 49659 Office: 820 Arlington Dr Petoskey MI 49770

WHIPKEY, KENNETH LEE, educator; b. Cortland, Ohio, June 5, 1932; s. Charles Leigh and Marjorie Opal (Hefner) W.; student Youngstown U., 1950-52; A.B., Kent State U., 1953, M.A., 1958; student French Ministry Edn., summer 1954; student U. Colo., summers 1955, 59, Mich. State U., 1960, Mo. Sch. Mines, 1963; Ph.D., Case Western Res. U., 1969; postgrad. Ariz. State U., 1975, Oxford (Eng.) U., 1975; m. Mary Nell Glaser, Mar. 2, 1962. Instr. math, physics Vernon High Sch., Kinsman, Ohio, 1954-57, asst. prin., 1955-57,; asst. statistician Mallory Sharon Titanium Corp., Niles, Ohio, summer 1955; grad. asst. math. Kent (Ohio) State U., 1957-58; instr. math. Youngstown (Ohio) U., 1957-60, asst. prof., 1960-67; instr. NSF-In-Service Year Inst. Tchrs., Youngstown, 1964-67; workshop instr. Holt, Rinehart & Winston, Youngstown and Canton, Ohio, 1965-66; asst. prof. math. Westminster Coll., New Wilmington, Pa., 1968-69, asso. prof., 1969-76, prof., 1976—. Mem. Danforth Assn., Am. Math. Soc., Math. Assn. Am., Am. Numis. Assn., Kappa Mu Epsilon, Pi Mu Epsilon. Author: The Power of Calculus, 1972, 75, 79; The Power of Mathematics, 2d edit., 1981; The Power of Basic Math, 1977. Home: 456 Bradley Ln Youngstown OH 44504 also Mt View Club RD 2 Brandon Vt 05733 Office: Westminster Coll New Wilmington PA 16142

WHIPPS, EDWARD FRANKLIN, lawyer; b. Columbus, Ohio, Dec. 17, 1936; s. Rusk Henry and Agnes Lucille (Green) W.; B.A., Ohio Wesleyan U., 1958; LL.B., Ohio State U., 1961, J.D., 1968; children—Edward Scott, Rusk Huot, Sylvia Louise, Rudyard Christian. Admitted to Ohio bar, 1961; asso. firm George, Greek, King & McMahon, Columbus, 1961-66; partner firm George, Greek, King, McMahon & McConnaughey, Columbus, 1966-79, McConnaughey, Stradley, Mone & Moul, Columbus, 1979-80, Thompson, Hine & Flory, Columbus, Cleve. and Washington, 1981—; pres. Creative Living Inc., Columbus, 1975—, Community Services Inc., Columbus, 1965—; moderator TV show Upper Arlington Plain Talk, 1980—, Bridging Disability, 1981—. Mem. Upper Arlington Bd. Edn., 1972-80, v.p., 1975, pres., 1976; bd. alumni dirs. Ohio Wesleyan U., 1975—. Mem. Columbus (chmn. municipal ct. com. 1973-75, chmn. common pleas ct. com. 1979-81, chmn. public relations com. 1981—), Am., Ohio bar assns., Assn. Trial Lawyers Am., Ohio Acad. Trial Lawyers, Franklin County Trial Lawyers Assn., Am. Judicature Soc., Upper Arlington Area C. of C. (trustee 1979—). Republican. Methodist. Clubs: Lawyers Columbus, Barristers Columbus, Columbus Athletic, Ohio State U. Faculty, Delta Tau Delta (nat. v.p. 1974-76). Home: 3771 Lyon Dr Columbus OH 43220 Office: 100 E Broad St Columbus OH 43215

WHISLER, CHARLES KEITH, indsl. supply co. exec.; b. Ridgeway, Mo., Apr. 7, 1923; s. Jesse Thomas and Ina Vay (Finegan) W.; B.S. in Bus. Adminstrn., U. Mo., 1948; m. Dorothy Ann Morrison, May 15, 1955; children—Barbara, Janet, Jeff, Brian. Salesman, Gates Rubber Co., 1948-49; salesman, Casper Supply Co., 1949-54; mgr. Johnson Machine, Rapid City, S.D., 1954-56; with Whisler Bearing Co., 1956—, pres., mgr., Rapid City, 1969—; owner, mgr. Rapid Warehouse Co. Pres. Community Service Center, Rapid City, 1959-64, treas., 1974—; com. chmn. Black Hills Area Council Boy Scouts Am., Rapid City, 1976—; pres. United Way, Rapid City, 1980. Served with U.S. Army, 1943-45. Mem. Power Transmission Distributors Assn., Soc. Mining Engrs., Rapid City C. of C. (dir. 1968-71, v.p., 1968-71). Baptist. Clubs: Christian Bus. Mens Com., Lions, Mason, V.F.W., Elks. Home: 2014 West Blvd Rapid City SD 57701 Office: 101 N Maple St Rapid City SD 57701

WHISTON, SHEILA KAY BLATTI, ednl. counselor; b. Urbana, Ill., June 17, 1947; d. William Harold and Vivian Eleanor (Peterson) Blatti; B.A., Elmhurst Coll., 1969; postgrad. SUNY, Plattsburgh, 1976; M.Ed., Wichita State U., 1977, Ed.S., 1981; m. William Clark Whiston, June 7, 1969 (div. Aug. 1980); 1 dau., Nicole Lee. Tech. field rep. Mid-Am. chpt. ARC, Chgo., 1969-70; co-dir. recreation therapy Riverside Hosp., Newport News, Va., 1972-73; chmn. vols.

Plattsburgh (N.Y.) AFB Hosp., 1974-76; research asst. Wichita (Kans.) State U., 1977-78, adminstrv. asst. orientation, 1978, health professions counselor, 1978—; mem. adj. faculty Webster Coll., 1978—. Vol. ARC, 1965—. Mem. Am. Personnel and Guidance Assn., Kans. Personnel and Guidance Assn., Kans. Coll. Personnel Assn. Episcopalian. Home: 202 N Rock Rd Wichita KS 67206 Office: Health Professions Counselor Coll Health Related Professions Wichita State U Box 43 Wichita KS 67208

WHITAKER, NEAL DALE, state legislator; b. Topeka, May 3, 1947; s. Dale W. and Jessie Helen (Neal) W.; B.S. in Psychology, Sterling (Kans.) Coll., 1971; m. Jo Lynn Johnson, Mar. 1, 1969; children—Tracy Lynn. Photojournalist, Hutchinson (Kans.) News, 1964-69; asst. exec. v.p. Kans. Restaurant Assn., Wichita, 1969—; mem. Kans. Ho. of Reps., 1973—, chmn. fed. and state affairs com.; mem. urban devel. com. Nat. Conf. State Legislators; dir. Res. Savs. and Loan Assn., Wichita. Mem. Internat. Soc. Restaurant Assn. Execs., Kans. Soc. Assn. Execs. (pub. handbook 1971). Editor: Kans. Restaurant Mag., 1969—. Home: 2568 Cardinal Dr Wichita KS 67204 Office: 359 S Hydraulic St Wichita KS 67211

WHITAKER, RONALD MARTIN, engr.; b. Fullerton, Nebr., Jan. 30, 1933; s. Leonard Bert and Margaret Mary (Seely) W.; student Central Tech. Community Coll., Hastings, Nebr., 1977, Franklin U., Columbus, Ohio, 1981; m. Janet Louise Spitz, Apr. 12, 1955; children—Mark David, Jeffrey Keith, Wendy Elaine. Mgr. Spitz Foundry Inc., Hastings, Nebr., 1965-78; plant engr. Lattimer Stevens Co., Columbus, Ohio, 1978-80, asst. v.p., chief engr., 1980—; instr. Engr. Center, Ft. Belvoir, Va., 1953. Scoutmaster Overland Trails Council Boy Scouts Am., 1970-78, dist. camping dir., 1975-78, Order of Arrow adv., 1976-78; extraordinary minister Roman Cath. Ch. Served with C.E. U.S. Army, 1953-55. Certified mfg. engr.; registered profl. engr. Mem. Soc. Mfg. Engrs. (vice chmn., sr. mem.), Am. Foundry Soc. (sr.). Republican. Clubs: Nat. Rifle Assn. (endowment mem., certified firearms instr.), Nebr. Rifle and Pistol Assn. (life mem.), Central Ohio Council Internat. Visitors, Nat. Eagle Scout Assn., Am. Photographic Soc. Editorial cons. Plant Engineering mag. Home: 7411 Woodale Dr Carroll OH 43112 Office: 715 Marion Rd Columbus OH 43207

WHITALL, ROBERT WOOD, mech. engr.; b. Phila., Feb. 14, 1924; s. James Dawson and Mary Emma (Ogden) W.; B.S. in Mech. Engring., Pa. State U., 1947; m. Patricia Louise Witherow, Sept. 13, 1947; children—Robert Wood, Susan, Kevin, Scott. Sales engr. Keasbey & Mattison Co., Ambler, Pa., 1947-52; project engr. Amchem Products Inc., Ambler, 1952-62; project engr. R.C. Mahon Co., Detroit, 1962-67; chief engr. Mahon Indsl. Corp., Detroit, 1967-70; chief engr. Haden Schweitzer Corp., Madison Heights, Mich., 1970-77, v.p. engring., 1977—. Mem. Engring. Soc. Detroit, Soc. Mfg. Engrs., Nat. Coil Coaters Assn., Chi Phi, Phi Eta Sigma. Club: Pine Lake Country (Orchard Lake, Mich.). Home: 235 Westwood Dr Birmingham MI 48009 Office: 3220 N Avis Dr Madison Heights MI 48071

WHITCHURCH, CHARLES RANDALL, engring. co. exec.; b. Evanston, Ill., Aug. 29, 1946; s. Charles Goldwin and Jane Dorothy (Christensen) W.; B.A. cum laude in Econs., Beloit Coll., 1968; M.B.A., Stanford U., 1973; m. Jane Ann Neutzling, Feb. 21, 1976; 1 dau., Katherine Jane. Corp. fin. cons. Harris Trust & Savs. Bank, Chgo., 1973-76; chief fin. officer Resinoid Engring. Co., Skokie, Ill., 1976-81; v.p. fin. Corcom, Inc., Libertyville, Ill., 1981—. Served to 1st lt. U.S. Army, 1969-71. Mem. Phi Beta Kappa. Home: 3536 Hillside Rd Evanston IL 60201 Office: 3445 Howard St Skokie IL 60076

WHITCOMB, NIKE SUSAN, fund raising cons.; b. Yuma, Ariz., Feb. 13, 1945; d. William Edward and Martha Louise (Eickhoff) Smyth; B.A., Millikin U., 1966; postgrad. So. Ill. U., U. Ill., 1969. Women's ready-to-wear buyer, Decatur and Springfield, Ill., 1966-68; jr. high sch. music tchr., 1968-69; chief exec. officer United Cerebral Palsy, Springfield, Ill., 1970; public info. officer Revenue, Comprehensive Health depts., Springfield, 1971-73; exec. dir. Am. Diabetes Assn., Chgo./No. Ill., 1973-76; coordinator Internat. Conf. on Fund Raising and Philanthropy, Chgo., 1977; dir. communications, devel. Thorek Hosp. and Med. Center, Chgo., 1977-81; owner, cons. Nike B. Whitcomb Assos., Evanston, Ill., 1981—. Public relations com. ARC, 1974-77; editor Republican state newsletter Trunk Line, 1972; Springfield area pres. Millikin U., 1972-73, Chgo. area alumni pres., 1975-77, named Young Alumnus, 1978; mem. Ill. Council Vol. Health Agys., 1972—, sec.-treas., 1973-75, v.p., 1975-76, pres., 1976-78; bd. dirs. Chgo. council Girl Scouts U.S.A., 1979—. Mem. Nat. Soc. Fund Raising Execs. (dir. 1977—, chmn. public relations com. 1978-79, chmn. chpt. pres.'s council 1979-81, mem. exec. com. 1979-81, dir. Chgo. chpt. 1976—, pres. 1978-80, Pres.'s award 1980, cert. fund raiser 1981), Nat. Assn. for Hosp. Devel. (co-chmn. regional conf. 1978, legis. com. 1977—, cert. 1981), Am. Soc. for Hosp. Public Relations, Delta Delta Delta, Beta Sigma Phi. Club: Publicity of Chgo. (dir. 1975-77). Home and Office: 1113 Lee St Evanston IL 60202

WHITE, ALLEN WILLIAM, sales engr.; b. St. Louis, Mar. 1, 1947; s. William and Marie (Seiler) W.; student St. Louis Jr. Coll., 1964-65, U. Mo., 1970-71; m. Ann Marie Mechler, Dec. 28, 1973; children—Lisa Marie, Allen William, Arin Daniel, Amanda Michelle. Dist. engr. Lamson div. Diebold Inc., St. Louis, 1967-71; project engr. Murphy Co., St. Louis, 1971-73; sales engr. Lamson div. Diebold Inc., Cleve., 1973-74; sales engr. Prodn. Machinery, Inc., Mentor, Ohio, 1974-80; regional sales mgr. Paxson Machine Co., Salem, Ohio, 1980—. Pres., Middle Ridge Communities Assn., 1974-77. Mem. Am. Soc. Metals, Assn. Iron and Steel Engrs., Am. Electroplaters Soc., Assn. Steel Distbrs. Republican. Methodist. Office: 300 Benton Rd Salem OH 44460

WHITE, ARTHUR CLINTON, physician; b. Williamsburg, Ky., Aug. 1, 1925; s. Herman Roy and Ethel Margaret (Goins) W.; B.S., U. Ky., 1948; M.D., Harvard U., 1952; m. Mary Katherine Pope, Dec. 27, 1949; children—Anne, Clinton, Roy. Intern, Vanderbilt Hosp., Nashville, 1952-53, resident in medicine, 1953-57; asst. prof. medicine U. Louisville, 1958-63; asso. prof. medicine Med. Coll. Ga., 1963-67; prof. medicine, dir. infectious disease div. Ind. U. Sch. Medicine, 1967—. Served with USAAF, 1944-45. John and Mary R. Markle scholar. Mem. Infectious Disease Soc. Am., Nat. Acad. Sci. Drug Efficacy Study, Central Soc. Clin. Research. Republican. Presbyterian. Club: Meridian Hills Country. Contbr. articles to sci. jours. and med. textbooks. Home: 6363 Glencoe Dr Indianapolis IN 46260 Office: 1100 W Michigan St Indianapolis IN 46223

WHITE, BILLY FRANCIS, educator; b. Queen City, Mo., Feb. 6, 1923; s. Allen Francis and Freda Dolores (Young) W.; B.S., N.E. Mo. State U., 1956, M.A., 1962; jr. acctg./steno cert. Chillicothe Bus. Coll., 1948; m. Annabelle Buchanan, Aug. 19, 1945; children—Francis DeWayne, David Neil. Instr., dorm supr. Mo. Mil. Acad., Mexico, 1944-45; steno clk. Frisco R.R., Ft. Smith, Ark., Oklahoma City and Tulsa, 1947-48; sec., bus. tchr. Moulton-Udell Community Sch., Moulton, Iowa, 1956-60; bus. tchr., adult edn. dir., coop. occupational edn. coordinator Dallas Center (Iowa)-Grimes Community Sch., 1960—. Mem. Nat. Bus. Edn. Assn., Iowa Bus. Edn. Assn., Am. Vocat. Assn., Iowa Vocat. Assn., NEA, Iowa Edn. Assn., Dallas Center-Grimes Edn. Assn., Pi Omega Pi, Kappa Delta Pi. Mem. Assemblies of God Ch. Home: 1707 Cherry Ave PO Box 23 Dallas Center IA 50063 Office: Dallas Center Grimes Community Sch Dallas Center IA 50063

WHITE, C. THOMAS, justice Supreme Ct. Nebr.; b. Humphrey, Nebr., Oct. 5, 1928; LL.B., Creighton U., Omaha, 1952; m. Joan Jiranek, Oct. 9, 1971; children by previous marriage—Michaela, Thomas, Patrick. Admitted to Nebr. bar, practiced law; judge 21st Dist. Ct. Nebr.; atty. Platte County; justice Supreme Ct. Nebr., 1977—; pres. Nebr. Dist. Ct. Judges Assn. Mem. Alpha Sigma Nu, Delta Theta Phi. Address: Nebr Supreme Ct State Capitol Lincoln NE 68509*

WHITE, CHARLES NORMAN, JR., mfg. co. exec.; b. Chgo., Sept. 11, 1936; s. Charles Norman and Irene Clair (Greby) W.; student Quincy Coll., 1955, Lewis Coll., 1956; m. Joyce Lynne Cameron, Nov. 23, 1962; 1 son, Scott Gordon. Sales staff Gertz Lombard Co., Chgo., 1960-63; sales dist. mgr. Tek Hughes div. Johnson & Johnson, 1963-66; sales div. mgr., key account mgr. Squibb Products Co., N.J., 1966-75, Mich., 1966-71, Chgo., 1971-75; sales mgr. ITT Photo Products Co., Clark, N.J., 1975-78, Chgo., 1975-78; nat. sales mgr. Elgin Waltham Watch Co., Chgo., 1978-80, sales and mktg. mgr. WD-40 Co., San Diego, 1980—; cons. Trebor Co., Chgo., 1976—. Bd. dirs. Greenbrier Home Owners Assn. Served with AUS, 1957-59. Mem. Photo Mktg. Assn. Roman Catholic. Home: 1607 Roanoke Dr Arlington Heights IL 60004 Office: 1061 Cudahy Pl San Diego CA 92110

WHITE, D. JERRY, realtor; b. Springfield, Ill., Nov. 21, 1937; s. George C. and Margaret B. (Kiely) W.; student Springfield Jr. Coll., 1955-56, Northwestern U., 1957-58; B.S., Loyola U., Chgo., 1960; m. Mary Ellen Bahl, June 11, 1960; children—Lynn Ann, Karyn Marie, Mark Jerry. Radio announcer, account exec., disc jockey Radio Sta. WCVS, Springfield, 1954-56; engaged in real estate bus., 1960—; realtor, chief exec. officer, owner Jerry White & Co., Springfield, 1961—; public info. officer Ill. Dept. Children and Family Services. Mem. Chgo. dist. adv. council SBA, 1974—. Commr., Springfield Airport Authority, 1971-72, chmn. land acquisition com., 1971-72; chmn. nat. airlines com. Springfield Airport Authority, 1971-72; commr. Springfield-Sangamon County Regional Plan Commn., 1972—, chmn., 1975-76; mem. UN Day Com., 1975; mem. congressional adv. com. from 20th Dist.; nominee Ill. Senate from 49th Senatorial Dist., 1966. Bd. dirs. Sangamon County His. Soc., 1961-64, v.p., 1961-62; bd. dirs. Sangamon County Sr. Citizens, 1974—. Recipient Loyolan award Loyola U., 1960; certificate of Merit Springfield Airport Authority, 1972; Distinguished Service award UN ambassador Daniel Moynihan, 1976; Key to City of Augusta, Ga., Mayor of Augusta, 1976. Mem. Springfield Greater C. of C., Nat. Assn. Real Estate Bds., Nat. Assn. Real Estate Appraisers (certified), Am. Farm and Land Brokers Assn., Springfield Bd. Realtors, Springfield Art Assn. Roman Catholic. Elk, Eagle. Home: 11 Flossmore Dr Springfield IL 62707 Office: 1 N Old State Capitol Plaza Springfield IL 62706

WHITE, DON LEE, ednl. adminstr.; b. Baxter Springs, Kans., Aug. 31, 1929; s. Harry Garner and Rita Laverne (Rose) W.; B.S., Pittsburg (Kans.) State U., 1962; M.S., 1967; Ph.D., Internat. U., 1978; D.D., Ch. of God Ministry Coll., 1979; m. June Marie Brillhart, May 19, 1948; children—Donna June, Deborah Ann. Tchr., Fairmont Sch., Redfield, Kans., 1958-59, Winfield Scott Sch., Ft. Scott, Kans., 1961-63, Lincoln Sch., Augusta, Kans., 1963-65; coach, prin. Mapleton (Kans.) Elem. Sch., 1959-60; prin. Appleton City (Mo.) Jr. High Sch., 1968-69; head dept. English, Eastside Jr. High Sch., Oswego, Kans., 1969-71; prin. Washington Sch., Baxter Springs, Kans., 1971—. Sec. PTA, 1963. Served with U.S. Army, 1946-47. Recipient Fellowship award Am. Parapsychology Assn., 1978-79; Cert. of Award, Republican Nat. Com., 1978. Mem. Nat. Assn. Elem. Prins., NEA (pres.), Authors Guild, Inc., Authors League Am., Alpha Psi Omega, Phi Delta Kappa. Republican. Author: As On A Darling Plain, 1978. Home: 1719 East Ave Baxter Springs KS 66713

WHITE, GERALD ALOYSIUS, engr.; b. Detroit, June 21, 1925; s. John William and Julia Beatrice (Coffey) W.; B.S., U. Detroit, 1960, postgrad., 1965; m. Shirley Ann Abbott, Nov. 22, 1951; children—John, Ronald, Robert, Joseph, Thomas, Brian. Engring. technician U.S. Rubber Co., Chrysler Corp., Gen. Motors, 1947-49; capt. Yacht Blitzen, Great Lakes, East Coast, and Caribbean, 1949-51; master boat builder Detroit Basinc Inc., 1951-57; staff project engr. computer facilities Gen. Motors Corp., Warren, Mich., 1957—. Served with U.S. Navy, 1943-46. Mem. U.S. Yacht Racing Union, Can. Yachting Assn., Detroit River Yachting Assn. Roman Catholic. Clubs: Crescent Sail Yacht, Offshore Racing of Detroit. Skipper or crew mem. of numerous offshore sail yacht races, 1949—. Inventor automotive devices and engring. systems. Home: 64 Radnor Circle Grosse Pointe Farms MI 48236 Office: Computer Facilities Engring Staff Gen Motors Tech Center Warren MI 48090

WHITE, JAMES EDWARD, microcomputer co. exec.; b. Lynn, Mass., Jan. 15, 1947; s. Herbert Edward and Marie Theresa (Mailloux) W.; student U. Md., 1966, Ind. U., 1968; 1 dau., Linda Dawn. Div. sales mgr. ICS div. Intext, Inc., Scranton, Pa., 1972-75; v.p. mktg. A.V. Products & Programming, Inc., Marblehead, Mass., 1975-78; mktg. mgr. New Eng. br. Value Computing, Inc., Cherry Hill, N.J., 1978-80; dir. mktg. Ednl. Programming Systems, Inc., St. Louis, 1980—. Chmn., Norton Indsl. Devel. Commn., 1976-80; chmn. Mass. Solid Waste Study Com., 1978-79; bd. dirs. Indsl. Devel. Fin. Authority, Inc., Norton, 1978—, Norton Local Devel. Corp., 1979—; chmn. Mass. Citizens Scholarship Fund, 1980—. Notary pub., Mass. Mem. Sales and Mktg. Execs. Internat., Am. Assn. for Computing Machinery, Am. Soc. for Tng. and Devel., U.S. Jaycees. Republican. Roman Catholic. Contbr. articles to profl. jours. Home: 227 Rendina Ln Ellisville MO 63011 Office: 1330 Baur Blvd Saint Louis MO 63132

WHITE, JOE LLOYD, soil scientist; b. Pierce, Okla., Nov. 8, 1921; s. Claud Amos and Alta Maurice (Denney) W.; student Connors State Agrl. Coll., 1940-42; B.S., Okla. State U., 1944, M.S., 1945; Ph.D., U. Wis., 1947; m. Wanita Irene Robertson, May 29, 1945; children—Lerrill, Darla, Ronna, Bren, Janeil. Asst. prof. agronomy Purdue U., West Lafayette, Ind., 1947-51, asso. prof., 1951-57, prof., 1957—; cons. Barcroft Co., William H. Rorer Co., Chattem Chem. Co. NSF fellow, 1965-66; Guggenheim Found. fellow, 1972-73; Fulbright scholar, 1973. Recipient sr. U.S. Scientist award Alexander von Humboldt Found., 1980-81. Fellow Am. Soc. Agronomy, Am. Inst. Chemists, Soil Sci. Soc. Am., Mineral Soc. Am.; mem. AAAS, Am. Chem. Soc., Am. Pharm. Assn., Coblentz Soc., Geochem. Soc., Internat. Soil Sci. Soc., Internat. Zeolite Assn., Soc. Applied Spectroscopy; mem. Sigma Xi, Phi Kappa Phi, Phi Lambda Upsilon. Mem. Ch. of Christ. Patentee in field. Home: 2505 Roselawn Ave Lafayette IN 47904 Office: Dept Agronomy Purdue U West Lafayette IN 47907

WHITE, JOHN JOSEPH, III, physicist; b. Arlington, Mass., Apr. 24, 1939; s. John Joseph and Ruth Edith (Madden) W.; B.S., Coll. William Mary, 1960; Ph.D., U. N.C., 1965; m. Marian Patricia Wagner; children—John, Edmund. Asst. prof. dept. physics and astronomy U. Ga., Athens, 1967-73; sr. engr., applied sci. dept. BDM Corp., Vienna, Va., 1973-74; research scientist Columbus (Ohio) Labs. Battelle Meml. Inst., 1974-78, prin. research scientist, 1978—; mem. design rev. panel landing vehicle assault USN, 1977; dir. Ga. Sci. Engring. Fair, 1973; expert on survivability of mil. structures; cons. tank-automotive tech.; specialist material properties and applications. Served to capt., applied physicist, U.S. Army, 1965-67. Fulbright grantee, 1973. Mem. Ga. Acad. Sci. (chmn. physics engring. sect. 1971), Am. Phys. Soc., Nat. Soc. Profl. Engrs. (nat. public relations com. 1978), ASME, Am. Def. Preparedness Assn., Sigma Xi. Registered profl. engr., Ohio. Contbr. articles to physics and engring. jours. Home: 4865 Arthur Pl Columbus OH 43220 Office: 505 King Ave Columbus OH 43201

WHITE, JON J., public relations counsel; b. Anderson, Ind., July 28, 1955; s. Ozora T. and Maxine G. White; B.A. in Journalism, U. Okla., 1978; M.A. in Radio-TV and Public Relations, Ball State U., 1979. Public affairs writer, compiler Sta. WBST-FM, Muncie, Ind., 1978; grad. asst. Ball State U., Muncie, 1978-79; public info. intern Sta. WIPB-TV, Muncie, 1979; dir. public relations Garrison, Jasper, Rose & Co., Indpls., 1980—. Vice-chmn. public relations com. Ind. affiliate Am. Heart Assn., 1981—. Mem. Public Relations Soc. Am. (asso.), Kappa Tau Alpha. Office: 9240 N Meridian St Indianapolis IN 46240

WHITE, JUDITH ANN, educator; b. Moline, Ill., Nov. 11, 1955; d. Harry Cameron and Jennie Elizabeth (Brackevelt) W.; B.S. in Edn. (Ill. Gen. Assembly scholar), Ill. State U., 1976; postgrad. Quad Cities Grad. Studies Center, 1979—. Tchr. English, United Twp. High Sch., East Moline, Ill., 1976-77, 78—, asst. dir. theatre, 1978—; file-coding clk. Deere and Co., John Deere Ins. Co., Moline, 1977-78; part-time announcer Sta. WQUA-AM, Moline, 1978-79, Sta. WVIK-FM, Rock Island, Ill., 1980-81; map research analyst Rock Island County Voter's Registration, Office of County Clk., 1980-81. Mem. St. Mary's Sch. Bd. Edn.; Class of 1982 sponsor choir St. Mary's Ch.; active community theatres, 1972—; judge Miss Valley Fair, 1979-80; profl. singer. Cert. tchr. grades 6-12, Ill.; 3d class radiotelephone broadcasting lic. FCC. Mem. Am. Assn. for Advancement Humanities, Assn. for Supervision and Curriculum Devel., Council for Basic Edn., Classroom Tchrs. Assn., Ill. Assn. for Supervision and Curriculum Devel., Ill. Assn. Tchrs. English, Ill. Edn. Assn., NEA, Nat. Council Tchrs. English, AAUW, Ill. State U. Alumni Assn., Friends of Arts, Kappa Delta Pi, Rho-Mates of Alpha Gamma Rho, Zeta Tau Alpha. Democrat. Home: 3913 18th Ave Rock Island IL 61201 Office: United Twp High Sch North 1420 18th Ave East Moline IL 61244

WHITE, JUDITH ANN O'RADNIK, social worker; b. St. Paul, Oct. 27, 1943; d. Clarence Edwin and Marcella Ann (Cappelle) O'Radnik; B.A., Quincy Coll., 1965; M.S.W., Ohio State U., 1970; m. Dean H. White, May 22, 1981. Dep. juvenile officer St. Louis Circuit Ct. Juvenile Div., 1965-68; caseworker Ohio Div. Youth Services, Powell, Ohio, 1968-69; supr. intake delinquency juvenile div. St. Louis Circuit Ct., 1970-76, supr. child abuse and neglect unit, 1976—. Bd. dirs. Council on Child Abuse and Neglect of Met. St. Louis, 1979—. Mem. Nat. Council Crime and Delinquency, Ohio State U. Sch. Social Work Alumni Assn. Home: 138 Manlyn Dr Kirkwood MO 63122 Office: 920 N Vandeventer Ave Saint Louis MO 63108

WHITE, KATHY ANN, educator; b. Indpls., Aug. 13, 1944; d. Paul Edwards and Anna Marie (Dziewas) White; B.S., Ball State U., 1966; M.S., Ind. U., 1968. Substitute tchr. Indpls. pub. schs., 1968; mem. faculty of Ind. U.-Purdue U., Indpls., 1970-76; tchr. of bus. edn. North Central High Sch., Washington Twp., Indpls., 1968—; sec. Meth. Hosp., Indpls., summers 1963, 64, 65, 66; mem. faculty ind. study div. Ind. U., 1979—. Rental gallery day chmn. of Indpls. Mus. of Art, 1974—. Mem. Am., Ind. vocat. assns., Adminstrv. Mgmt. Soc. (program dir. 1981-82), Nat. Secs. Assn., Ind. Bus. Edn. Assn. (dir. 1980-82), Indpls. Bus. Edn. Council (sec. 1973, v.p. 1980, pres. 1981-82), North Central Bus. Edn. Assn. (dir. 1982—), Internat. Word Processing (v.p. central Ind. chpt. 1978—), D.A.R., Ind. Bus. Educators, Phi Delta Kappa. Mem. Zions United Ch. of Christ (ch. bd. 1982—). Clubs: Ind. Univ. Alumni, Ball State Alumni. Contbr. articles on bus. edn. to profl. publs. Home: 3025 N Meridian 804 Indianapolis IN 46208

WHITE, LARRY CURTIS, osteo. physician; b. Decatur, Ill., May 1, 1941; s. Gerald Curtis and Elizabeth Jane (Moore) W.; B.S., U. Ill., 1963; D.O., Kirksville Coll. Osteo. Medicine, 1970; m. Mary Ann Savage, Aug. 21, 1965; children—Mark, Michelle, Gerald, Barbara. Intern, Riverside Osteo. Hosp., Trenton, Mich., 1970-71; practice osteo. medicine, pres. Romeo (Mich.) Clinic, 1971—; mem. staff, mem. med. exec. com. Crittenton Hosp., 1977—, chmn. med. records com., 1977, vice chmn. dept. family practice, 1977-79, chmn., 1979—. Diplomate Am. Bd. Family Practice. Mem. Am. Osteo. Assn., Mich. Assn. Osteo. Physicians and Surgeons, Am. Acad. Family Physicians, Am. Assn. Family Practice, U. Ill. Alumni Assn., Psi Sigma Alpha, Alpha Phi Omega, Sigma Sigma Phi, Theta Psi, Alpha Kappa Lambda. Methodist. Clubs: Masons, Shriners, K.T. Home: 2250 E Gunn Rd Rochester MI 48063 Office: 241 N Main St Romeo MI 48065

WHITE, LLOYD RAYMOND, chem. engr.; b. Brainerd, Minn., Jan. 2, 1937; s. Marvin Stewart and Esther Genevieve (Isaacson) W.; B.S. with distinction, U. Minn., 1959; M.S., Columbia U., 1962; Ph.D., U. Minn., 1967; m. Carol Mae Johnson, Aug. 30, 1959; children—Stuart R., Carl D., Paula J., Erika R. Research aide Inst. Paper Chemistry, Appleton, Wis., 1960-63; project scientist Union Carbide Corp., South Charleston, W.Va., 1967-76; project leader Fluidyne Engring. Corp., Mpls., 1976-81; specialist 3M Co., 1981—. Coach, Mpls. Park Bd. Basketball Program; bd. dirs. West Side Activities Council. Mem. Am. Chem. Soc., Am. Inst. Chem. Engrs., AIAA, Sigma Xi. Democrat. Home: 1922 Penn Ave S Minneapolis MN 55405

WHITE, MARVIN, product devel. co. exec.; b. Laud, Ind., Aug. 2, 1937; s. Robert Herold and Margaret Bell (Ward) W.; A.B. in Philosophy, Ind. U., 1963; children—Michelle, Michael. Founder, pres. Genesis Products, Ft. Wayne, Ind., 1979—. Dir. conservation caucus Ind. 4th Congl. Dist., 1977-79; alt. del. to Republican Nat. Conv., 1976; pres. Ft. Wayne chpt. Parents without Partners, 1980-81. Dept. of Energy research grantee, 1979-80. Mem. AAAS, Soc. Mfg. Engrs., Ft. Wayne Astron. Soc., Coptic Fellowship. Republican. Methodist. Patentee in field. Home: 1624 Franklin Ave Fort Wayne IN 46808

WHITE, MARY WINIFRED LEE, counselor; b. N.Y.C., Jan. 18, 1926; d. Charles Henry Jr. and Luella (Simpson) Lee; B.S., Wilberforce U., 1947; M.S., Purdue U., 1974; m. John P. White, Aug. 18, 1946; children—John P., E. Denise White West, Dale E., Leslie L. II. Various positions with USAF, 1948-52; caseworker St. Louis Welfare Dept., 1954-56; social worker Catholic Charities, St. Louis, 1956-57; classroom tchr. St. Louis pub. schs., 1957-71; elementary sch. tchr. Michigan City (Ind.) Area Schs. Corp., 1971-74, sch. counselor, 1974—. Trustee Michigan City Pub. Library, 1972-75. Mem. Am., Ind. personnel and guidance assns., Am. Sch. Counselors Assn., AAUW, LaPorte County Mental Health Assn., Friends of Alfred Adler Inst., Friends of the Library, Festival Players Guild. Alpha Kappa Alpha, Alpha Delta Kappa. Democrat. Roman Catholic. Home: 322 Kenwood Pl Michigan City IN 46360 Office: Barker Jr High School Michigan City IN 46360

WHITE, NEWTON BURGSTRESER, orthopedic surgeon; b. Chgo., Dec. 16, 1927; s. Paul Edmund and Louise Adele (Burgstreser) W.; student Miami U., Oxford, Ohio, 1947-50, U. Chgo. Div. Sch., 1950-52; pre-med. student Roosevelt Coll., U. Ill., 1952-53; M.D., U. Cin., 1957; m. Mary Ann Smith, Apr. 8, 1967; children—Rebecca Louise, Newton Burgstreser, Stephen Paul, Katherine Caroline. Intern, Cook County Hosp., Chgo., 1957-58; asst. resident surgery Surg. Assos., Mason City, Iowa, 1958-59; asst. resident orthopedic surgery Barnes Hosp., St. Louis, 1962-64, resident, 1964; research fellow, instr. orthopedic surgery Washington U. Med. Sch., St. Louis, 1964; resident unit 1 fracture service St. Louis City Hosp., St. Louis Shriners Hosp. for Crippled Children, 1965-66; instr. clin. orthopedic surgery St. Louis U., 1981; gen. practice medicine, Hampton, Iowa, 1959-61; practice medicine specializing in orthopedic surgery, St. Louis, 1966—; pres. St. Louis County Orthopedic Group, Inc., 1969-78, chmn. bd., 1969-80; pres. South County Orthopedics, Inc., St. Louis, 1980—; pres. St. Anthony's Med. Center med. and dental staff, St. Louis, 1978-81, bd. dirs., 1979—; mem. staff Mo. Bapt. Hosp., St. Louis, St. Joseph's Hosp., Kirkwood, Mo., Cardinal Glennon Hosp. for Children, St. Louis. Served with USMC, 1946-47, USN, 1947-49. Diplomate Am. Bd. Orthopaedic Surgery. Mem. A.C.S. (mem. com. on trauma), AMA, Am. Acad. Orthopedic Surgeons, Mo. State Med. Assn., Clin. Orthopedic Soc., St. Louis Orthopedic Soc., St. Louis Med. Soc., St. Louis Rheumatism Soc. (pres. 1979-80), Phi Eta Sigma, Pi Kappa Epsilon. Clubs: University, Washington U. Faculty Conf. Center (St. Louis). Home: 12758 Honeygrove Ct Saint Louis MO 63141 Office: 10004 Kennerly Rd Saint Louis MO 63128

WHITE, NORMAN OAKLEY, air and sound pollution control systems co. exec.; b. Detroit, Apr. 8, 1921; s. Harold M. and Doris Ann (Hatch) W.; B.S. in Mech. Engring., Tri-State U., 1943; m. Betty Ann Brand, June 25, 1943; children—William, Diane, Steven, Barbara. Engr., Curtiss Wright Corp., Patterson, N.J., 1943-44; Kelsey Hayes Wheel, Detroit, 1946-50; engr.-sales, H.M. White, Inc., Detroit, 1950-62, pres., 1962—; chmn. bd. White Environ., Inc. Bd. dirs. YMCA, Farmington, Mich., 1970-72; trustee Tri-State U., 1980—. Recipient Alumni Achievement award Tri-State U., 1978. Mem. Sheet Metal Air Conditioning Nat. Assn. (Air-Pollution Service award 1979). Republican. Methodist. Clubs: Orchard Lake Country, Ocean Reef, Detroit Athletic, 100, Econs. Detroit. Author in field. Patentee air pollution equipment.

WHITE, PENNY ADALYN, ins. inspection co. exec.; b. Calvert, Ala., Aug. 3, 1924; d. Pugh and Willie Ethyl (Green) Henderson; student U. Tex., 1945, Bakersfield (Calif.) Jr. Coll., 1946-47; m. Alva John White, May 26, 1946; children—Brenda, Alva John II. Exec. sec., Boeing Aircraft Co., Wichita, Kans., 1950-53; partner White & White Inspection and Audit Service Inc., Kansas City, Mo., 1953-63, sec. treas., 1963—. Mem. Ins. Women, Nat. Assn. Ind. Ins. Auditors and Engrs. (past pres.), Nat. Soc. Premium Auditors (charter), Personnel Mgmt. Assn., Central Auditors Assn. Democrat. Club: Rockhill Tennis. Home: 8721 Alhambra St Prairie Village KS 66207 Office: PO Box 1215 Kansas City MO 64141

WHITE, R. QUINCY, lawyer; b. Chgo., Jan. 16, 1933; s. Roger Q. and Carolyn Jane (Everett) W.; B.A., Yale U., 1954; J.D., Harvard U., 1960; m. Dorothea Joyce Caldwell, Aug. 4, 1962; children—Cleaver Dorothea, Annelia Everett. Admitted to Ill. bar, 1960; asso. firm Leibman, Williams, Bennett, Baird & Minow (merged to Sidley & Austin 1973), Chgo., 1960-67, partner, 1967—; sec., dir. W.F. McLaughlin & Co., 1964-68; hon. Consul Gen. of Pakistan for Ill., 1978—. Sec. nat. governing bd. The Ripon Soc.; v.p., dir. Juvenile Protective Assn., Chgo., 1965—; chmn. Chgo. Bus. Assn. Com. on Local Govt., 1965-68; pres., co-founder Conf. on Chgo. Govt., 1970-73; exec. com. 43rd and 44th ward regular Republican Orgns., 1970-73; mem. Council on Fgn. and Domestic Affairs, 1970-76. Served to capt. USAF, 1954-56. Mem. Chgo. Council Lawyers, Chgo. Bar Assn. Club: Off-The-Street (dir., counsel 1974—). Home: 316 W Willow St Chicago IL 60614 Office: 1 First National Plaza Chicago IL 60603

WHITE, ROY BERNARD, assn. exec.; b. Cin., July 30, 1926; s. Maurice and Anna (Rudin) W.; B.A., U. Cin., 1949; student U. Miami (Fla.), 1946-47; m. Sally Lee Ostrom, June 17, 1951; children—Maurice Ostrom, Barbara Dee, Daniel Robert. Mem. sales staff Twentieth Century Fox Films, Cin., 1949-52; with Mid-States Theatres, Cin., 1952—, pres., 1962—; mem. Nat. Assn. Theatre Owners, N.Y.C., 1962—, dir., 1966-70, nat. pres., 1971-73, exec. com., 1971—, chmn. bd., 1973-75. Mem. film adv. panel Ohio Arts Council, 1974—; bd. dirs. Will Rogers Meml. Fund, Found. Motion Picture Pioneers, Inc.; mem. media arts panel Nat. Endowment for Arts, 1979—. Served with USAAF, 1944-45. Named Exhibitor of Year, Internat. Film Importers and Distbrs. Am., 1973; Ky. col. Mem. Am. Film Inst. (trustee 1972-75, exec. com. 1972-75), Alpha Epsilon Pi, Phi Eta Sigma. Jewish. Clubs: Masons; B'nai B'rith; Cin., Queen City Racquet; Crest Hills Country; Amberley Village Tennis (pres. 1972-73); Bankers. Home: 3140 N Whitetree Circle Cincinnati OH 45236 Office: 120 E 4th St Suite 750 Cincinnati OH 45202

WHITE, STANTON MCCONNELL, SR., newspaper pub.; b. Oklahoma City, Dec. 7, 1923; s. Stephen S. and Mary M. (McConnell) W.; student public schs., Kankakee, Ill.; m. Marcella M. Girard, Sept. 27, 1945; children—Stanton M., Stephen, Jackie, Rick, Shari. Salesman, Daily Jour., Kankakee, Ill., 1950-53, promotion mgr., 1953-54, asst. ad mgr., 1954-56, advt. mgr., 1956-67, advt. dir., asst. gen. mgr., 1967; with Ottawa (Ill.) Daily Times, 1967—, gen. mgr., 1968-69, pub., 1969—, pres., 1979—; dir. Ottawa Pub. Co.; v.p. Streator (Ill.) Times-Press. Bd. dirs. Greater Ottawa United Fund, Ottawa Downtown Devel. Corp. Served with USN, 1941-46; ETO. Mem. Am. Newspaper Pubs. Assn., Internat. Newspaper Advt. Execs., Inland Press Assn., Ill. Press Assn., Chgo. Press Club, C. of C. and Industry (bd. dirs.). Republican. Clubs: Ottawa Boat, Elks. Home: Rural Route 4 Pine Hills Subdiv Ottawa IL 61350 Office: 110 W Jefferson St Ottawa IL 61350

WHITE, THOMAS JAMES, cons. engr., safety engr.; b. Vicksburg, Mich., Sept. 30, 1944; s. Aubrey James and June Elizabeth (Bates) W.; A.S., Kalamazoo Valley Community Coll., 1971; student No. Mich. U.; spl. courses splty. schs. and tech. schs.; m. Jacquelyn Adele Hancock, Nov. 17, 1962; children—Todd, Jeff. Tech. rep. Home Ins. Co., 1971-74; loss control cons. Kemper Ins. Co., 1974-76; safety engr. White & White Engring., Kansas City, Mo., 1976-80; pres. Thomas J. White, Inc., Grand Rapids, Mich., 1978—, also dir. loss control Total Compensation Services, 1980—, and owner T.J.'s Klothes Kloset. Active Jr. Football League, Little League baseball; bd. dirs. Ottawa/Kent Jr. Football League. Served to sgt., USAF, 1962-66. Cert. product safety mgr., healthcare safety profl. Mem. Nat. Safety Council, Am. Soc. Safety Engrs., Nat. Fedn. Ind. Bus., Am. Indsl. Hygiene Assn. Republican. Methodist. Author trade tng. manuals and client tng. manuals. Home: 11021 Radcliff St Allendale MI 49401 Office: 500 Cascade Pkwy West SE Grand Rapids MI 49501

WHITE, VIRGINIA LOU, twp. ofcl.; b. Barberton, Ohio, Oct. 23, 1932; d. Lucius F. and Edith M. (Carlton) Converse; B.A., Baldwin-Wallace Coll., 1954; m. Neil Mason White, Sept. 8, 1956; children—William Neil, David Converse, Holly Suzanne. Sec. to exec. sec. Adult Edn. Found. (name later Inst. for Civic Edn., U. Akron), 1954-55, office mgr., 1955-57; tchr. bus. edn. Kenmore High Sch., Akron, 1957-59, Elyria (Ohio) Public High Sch., 1959-60; charter twp. clk. Meridian Twp., Okemos, Mich., 1972—. Del., Mich. Republican Conv., 1972, 74, 76, 78, 79, 80, 81; sec. Mich. Rep. Issues Com., 1979-80, vice chmn., 1981, 82—; mem. Ingham County Rep. Exec. Com., 1972—; mem. 6th Congressional Dist. Rep. Exec. Com.; co-leader high sch. youth ch. group. Mem. Internat. Inst. Mcpl. Clks., Mich. Mcpl. Clks., LWV. Mem. Disciples of Christ Ch. Clubs: Zonta Internat. (pres. 1981—), Mich. State U. Women's Sports Booster, Tri-County Bicycle Assn. Home: 1641 Birchwood Dr Okemos MI 48864 Office: 5151 Marsh Rd Okemos MI 48864

WHITE, W. ARTHUR, cons. geologist; b. Sumner, Ill., Dec. 9, 1916; s. Millard Otto and Joy Olive (Atkins) W.; B.S., U. Ill., 1940, M.S., 1947, Ph.D., 1955; m. Alma Evelyn Simonton McCullough, June 21, 1941. With Ill. Geol. Survey, Urbana, 1943-79, geologist, 1955-58, head clay resources and clay mineral technology sect., 1958-72, geologist, 1972-79; pvt. cons. geologist, Urbana, 1979—; prof. geology Fed. U. Rio Grande do Sul, Brazil, 1970. Fellow Geol. Soc. Am., Mineral. Soc. Am., AAAS; mem. Internat. Clay Mineral Soc., Am. Clay Mineral Soc., Ill. Acad. Sci., Mus. Natural History (asso.), Nat. Geog. Soc., Am. Chem. Soc., Mental Health Soc., Am. Ceramic Soc., Colloid Chem. Soc., Geochem. Soc., Soc. Econ. Petrologists and Mineralogists, Sigma Xi. Contbr. articles to profl. jours. Home: 603 Colorado St Urbana IL 61801

WHITE, WILLIAM FRANCIS, newspaper cons.; b. Winona, Minn., Oct. 25, 1923; s. Maxwell H. and Ellnora (Parks) W.; student Carleton Coll., 1941-42, Cornell U., 1942-43; B.A. in Journalism, U. Minn., 1949; m. Dare Lamberton, July 8, 1950; children—Angus, Dana, Andrea. Joined Winona Daily News, 1949, mgr. 1950-61, pub., 1961-80; cons. Lee Enterprises, Inc., 1980—; pres. Republican & Herald Pub. Co., 1961—. Mem. Winona City Planning Commn.; campaign chmn. Winona Community Chest; pres. Winona Indsl. Devel. Assn. Bd. dirs. Winona Goodfellows. Served to capt., 148th Inf. Regt., AUS, 1943-46; PTO; lt. col. Res. Decorated Bronze Star medal, Combat Infantryman's badge. Mem. Winona C. of C. (dir.), Northwest Daily Press Assn. (chmn. bd.), Minn. Heart Assn. (dir.), Graphic Arts Industry Inc. Mpls. (dir.), Minn. Alumni Assn. (dir.), Episcopalian. Clubs: Winona (Minn.) Country; Minn. Press, Mpls. (Mpls.). Home and office: Drumnadrochit Box 70 Winona MN 55987

WHITE, WILLIAM LUTHER, II, mgmt. cons. co. exec.; b. Raleigh, N.C., May 16, 1939; s. William Luther and Wilma Louise (Watrous) W.; student Princeton U., 1957-59; B.A., U. Pitts., 1964; m. Cheryl Nancy Trostrud, children—Suzan, Brent-Kaan, Amie. Mgr. staff selection Am. Can Co., N.Y.C., 1965-69; cons. Booz, Allen & Hamilton, N.Y.C., 1969-71; v.p. Golightly & Co. Internat., N.Y.C., 1971-78; prin. Wyatt Co., Chgo., 1978-81; dir. Hay Assos., Chgo., 1981—. Mem. Turkish-Am. Assn. N.Y., 1975-77. Served with USNR, 1959-61. Mem. Inst. Mgmt. Consultants, Am. Compensation Assn. Republican. Lutheran. Clubs: Princeton, Metropolitan. Author: Capital Accumulation for Executives - A Trade-Off Analysis, 1981. Home: 182 Myrtle St Winnetka IL 60093 Office: Hay Assos 1 E Wacker Dr Chicago IL 60601

WHITE, ZENOBIA MAXINE, educator; b. Cotton Plant, Ark., Feb. 16, 1933; d. Willie Joe and Johnnie (Jones) Reid; B.S., Philander Smith Coll., 1951; postgrad. Drake U., 1971-75; m. Harold White, Nov. 3, 1959; children—Claire, William, June Carol, Harold, Robin, Cris Jon. Exec. sec. Forest Ave Mission, Des Moines, 1960-76; social worker Polk County Dept. Social Services, Des Moines, 1976-77; tchr. public schs. Des Moines Ind. Sch. Dist., 1976—; exec. dir., founder OSACS Inc., 1979—. Mem. adv. com. State Birth Defects Inst., 1970-81. Mem. Assn. Childhood Edn. Am. Office: 1218 1st St Des Moines IA 50311

WHITEAKER, STANLEY CYRIL, accountant; b. Hurdland, Mo., Nov. 24, 1918; s. Roscoe E. and Marie (Surry) W.; evening student Rockhurst U., 1955-58; m. Justine M. Warford, Dec. 25, 1938; 1 dau., Linda J. Accountant Mo. Pub. Service Commn., 1942-51; utility cons., 1951-58; partner Troupe Kehoe, Whiteaker & Kent, C.P.A., offices in Kansas City, Kans. and Mo., 1958—; cons. Kans. Corp. Commn., Mo. Pub. Service Commn., Nat. Energy Bd. Can., and maj. industries in midwest on natural gas usage, also U.S. Air Force; dir. T.K.W. Supply Co., Inc., Bichelmeyer Meat Co. Mem. exec. council Greater Kansas City Council on Alcoholism. Served as sgt. USNR, 1943-45. Mem. C. of C., Kans. State Bd. Accountancy, Am. Inst. C.P.A.'s, Kans. Soc. C.P.A.'s, Nat. Assn. Pub. Accountants, Internat. Platform Assn. Clubs: Odd Fellows, Kansas City, Milburn Golf and Country. Author articles on utility rate making. to profl. publs. Home: 6008 W 86th Terr Overland Park KS 66207 Office: Power and Light Bldg Kansas City MO 64105

WHITED, ROY EDWARD, ins. co. exec.; b. Mt. Vernon, Ohio, Jan. 27, 1946; s. Robert Lee and Virgie May Whited; student Ashland Coll., 1964-66; B.S. in Edn., Ohio State U., 1969; student Life Ins. Mktg. Inst., Purdue U., 1976; m. Judith Ann Dill, July 30, 1967; children—Shelley Sue, Carey Lee. Tchr., Columbus (Ohio) city schs., 1968-72; agt., gen. agt. Golden United Life Ins. Co., Columbus, 1972-73, dir. tng., 1973-76; supt. agencies Greater Ohio Life Ins. Co., Columbus, 1976-77, dir. agy., 1977-78, v.p., agy. dir., 1978—; dir. Life Ins. Seminar, Tampa, Fla.; lectr. in field. Clk., Hilliard Twp., Knox County, Ohio, 1978-80; chmn. Community Good Old Days, 1977. Mem. Columbus Assn. Life Underwriters, Life Inst. Tng. Council, Ohio State U. Alumni Assn., Fraternal Order of Police (asso.), Centerburg Jaycees (dir. 1978—). Democrat. Methodist. Home: 336 Darlene St Centerburg OH 43011 Office: 4740 Reed Rd Columbus OH 43220

WHITEFORD, EMMA MAY BRITTIN, educator; b. Lowder, Ill.; d. George and Katharine (Riley) Brittin: B.S. in Home Econs., N.D. State U., 1938; diploma Pa. Hosp., 1939; M.S., U. Ill., 1951, Ed.D., 1955; m. Clay Pennington Whiteford, July 2, 1940; children—William McConkey, Mary Katharine. Adminstrv. dietitian York (Pa.) Hosp., 1939-40; acting chmn. home econs. Ill. Wesleyan U., Bloomington, 1949-50; dir. homemaking and sch. lunch, Bloomington (Ill.) pub. schs., 1950-53; part-time instr., U. Ill., 1953-55; chmn. dept. home econs. Bowling Green (Ohio) State U., 1955-57; head home econs. edn. dept. Fla. State U., 1957-59; dir. Sch. Home Econs. U. Cin., 1959-66; vis. prof., research asso. U. Ill., 1966-67, prof., chmn. dept. home economics edn. U. Minn., St. Paul, 1967-71, prof., 1971—. Active ARC. Mem. Am., Minn. home econs. assns., Am., Minn. dietetic assns., Am., Minn. vocational assns., Am. Assn. U. Women, Am. Sociol. Soc., Nat. Council on Family Relations, D.A.R., Ill. Sch. Food Service Assn. (regional v.p. 1953-54), PTA, Nat. Minn. edn. assns., Adult Edn. Assn., Am. Assn. U. Profs., Assn. for Higher Edn., Assn. for Student Teaching, Higher Edn. Assn., Council Adminstrs. Home Econs, (treas. 1965-68), Panhellenic, Alpha Phi Gamma, Pi Lambda Theta, Alpha Gamma Delta, Delta Kappa Gamma, Kappa Delta Pi, Omicron Nu, Zonta. Presbyterian. Club: Woman's (Cin.). Home: 902 S Lincoln Ave Apt 202 Urbana IL 61801

WHITEHEAD, DENNIS KEITH, sta. exec.; b. Martin County, Minn., Dec. 24, 1941; s. G. Keith and Helen L. (Martins) W.; student Mankato State U., 1959-60; B.A., Pillsbury Coll., 1964; M.S.T., Central Sem., 1969; m. Sherry Schoeneweiss, July 20, 1963; children—Scott, Lisa, Andrew. With Central Sem. Radio, Mpls., 1968—, now sta. mgr./engr. WCTS; engring. adv. Sta. WAYL, 1974-75, Pillsbury Coll. Radio, 1973—. Recipient cert. of Appreciation, Pillsbury Coll., 1977. Mem. Minn. News Broadcasters (past pres.). Baptist. Clubs: Pillsbury Alumni, Central Sem. Alumni. Home: 1001 25th Ave N Minneapolis MN 55411 Office: 2105 Fremont Ave N Minneapolis MN 55411

WHITEHEAD, H. GEORGE, park dist. adminstr.; b. Ava, Mo., Dec. 16, 1945; s. Hubert C. and J. Leona W.; B.S., So. Ill. U., 1975, postgrad., 1975—; m. Jo Ann Branan, June 14, 1970. Dir. parks and recreation Carbondale (Ill.) Park Dist., 1975—; treas., bd. dirs. So. Ill. Spl. Olympians, Inc. Sec.-treas. Carbondale Park Dist. Bd. Park Commrs., 1976—; notary public; bd. dirs. Carbondale Community Edn., Ill. Park and Recreation Adminstrn. and Fin. Bd., 1980—. Served with AUS, 1965-67. Decorated Army Commendation medal. Mem. Notaries Assn. Ill., Ill. Community Edn. Assn., Nat. Community Edn. Assn., Ill. Park and Recreation Assn. (dir.), Nat. Recreation and Park Assn., So. Ill. Park and Recreation Assn. (past pres.), So. Ill. U. Alumni Assn., Carbondale Jaycees (Community Disting. Service award 1979). Clubs: Rotary, Elks. Home: 2900 Kent Dr Carbondale IL 62901 Office: Carbondale Park Dist Hickory Lodge 1115 W Sycamore St Carbondale IL 62901

WHITEHOUSE, ALTON WINSLOW, JR., oil co. exec.; b. Albany, N.Y., Aug. 1, 1927; s. Alton Winslow and Catherine (Lyda) W.; B.S., U. Va., 1949, LL.B., 1952; m. Helen MacDonald, Nov. 28, 1953; children—Alton, Sarah, Peter. Admitted to Ohio bar, 1953; asso. partner firm McAfree, Hanning, Newcomer, Hazlett & Wheeler, Cleve., 1952-68; v.p., gen. counsel Standard Oil Co. Ohio, Cleve., 1968-69, sr. v.p., 1969-70, pres., chief operating officer, 1970-77, vice chmn. bd., 1977-78, chmn. bd., chief exec. officer, 1978—, also dir., mem. exec. com.; dir. AmeriTrust Co., Midland-Ross Corp., Cleve., Cliffs Iron Co., Brit. Petroleum Co. Ltd. Trustee, Cleve. Clinic Found., Case-Western Res. U., Cleve. Mus. Art, Cleve. Mus. Natural History. Mem. Am. Bar Assn., Ohio Bar Assn., Cleve. Bar Assn., Am. Petroleum Inst. Episcopalian. Office: Standard Oil Co 1750 Midland Bldg Cleveland OH 44115

WHITEHOUSE, ROBERT JOSEPH, physician; b. Milw., May 24, 1948; s. Joseph Arthur and Julia Agnes W.; B.A. with honors, U. Wis., 1970, M.D., 1974; M.A. in Med. Edn., Bradley U., 1979; m. Virginia Rose Bauer, Mar. 1, 1969; children—Ronald, Shelly, Ellen. Resident in family practice Meth. Med. Center of Central Ill., Peoria, 1974-77; practice medicine specializing in family practice, Madison, Wis., 1977—; dir. Madison Geriatric Clinic, 1978—. Fellow Am. Acad. Family Practice; mem. Am. Soc. Sports Medicine, AMA, Dane County Med. Soc. Diplomate Am. Bd. Family Practice. Home: 3102 Lakeland St Madison WI 53704 Office: 3602 Atwood St Madison WI 53714

WHITEHOUSE, WILLIAM ARTHUR, naturalist; b. Youngstown, Ohio, Oct. 9, 1935; s. William Reginald and Rose Marie (Takach) W.; student DePauw U., 1953-54; A.B., Youngstown State U., 1966; m. Marianne Whitehouse. Mus. attendant Mill Creek Park, Youngstown, 1952-54, asst. park naturalist, 1954-70, park naturalist and dir. Ford Nature Edn. Center, 1970—. Cons. Elementary Sci. Field Experiences, a grad. course for tchrs., Sch. Edn., Youngstown State U., 1974—. Merit badge counselor Boy Scouts Am., Youngstown, 1969—. Served with AUS, 1959-60. Mem. Assn. Interpretive Naturalists, Youngstown Nature Club, Grant M. Cook Bird Club. Contbr. to Mill Creek Park Bull., 1970—. Home: 840 Old Furnace Rd Youngstown OH 44511 Office: 816 Glenwood Ave Youngstown OH 44502

WHITEHURST, GROVER JAY, ednl. adminstr.; b. Washington, N.C., Sept. 28, 1944; s. Grover and Dixie (Daniel) W.; A.B., E. Carolina U., 1966; M.A., U. Ill., 1968, Ph.D., 1970; m. Janet Elizabeth Fischel, June 7, 1981. Asst. prof. SUNY, Stony Brook, 1970-74; sr. lectr. U. New South Wales (Australia), 1974-75; asso. prof. SUNY, Stony Brook, 1974-81; v.p. acad. affairs The Merrill-Palmer Inst., Detroit, 1979—; bd. dirs. Early Intellective Devel., Inc., Stony Brook, 1978. Fellow Am. Psychol. Assn.; mem. Soc. Research in Child Devel. Club: Detroit Econ. Editor Developmental Rev., 1980—, Merrill-Palmer Quar. Behavior and Devel., 1979-80; The Functions of Language and Cognition, 1979; author: Child Behavior, 1977. Home: 19120 Parkside St Detroit MI 48221 Office: 71 E Ferry St Detroit MI 48202

WHITESIDE, ROBERT CARL, mfg. co. exec.; b. Deadwood, S.D., Dec. 30, 1942; s. Robert Cecil and Pearl Ramona (Kirsch) W.; A.Indsl.Engring., Internat. Corr. Sch., 1965; postgrad. Manatee Jr. Coll., 1969-70; m. Judith Nightingale, Apr. 19, 1978; 1 dau., Amanda; children by previous marriage—Diane, Lori, stepchildren—Jason, Kerrie. Plant mgr. Tropicana Products, Bradenton, Fla., 1969-71; mfg. engr. Continental Can Co., Chgo., 1971-73; ops. mgr. Thermoline Systems Co., Phoenix, 1973-78; dir. engring. Brown Machine Co., Beaverton, Mich., 1978-81, v.p. engring., 1981—; cons. in field; treas. Thermoline Corp., 1973-77. Active Boy Scouts Am. Mem. Soc. Mfg. Engrs., Am. Mgmt. Assn., Soc. Plastic Engrs., Soc. Plastics Industry. Democrat. Mem. Christian Ch. Contbr. articles to profl. jours.; inventor in field. Home: 5260 W Clarence St Harrison MI 48625 Office: PO Box 434 Beaverton MI 48612

WHITE-WARE, GRACE ELIZABETH, educator; b. St. Louis, Oct. 5, 1921; d. James Eathel, Sr. and Madree (Penn) White; B.A. in Edn., H.B. Stowe Tchrs. Coll., 1943; divorced; 1 son, James Otis Ware II (Oloye Adeyemon). Mgr. advt. Superior Press, St. Louis, 1935-39; tri-owner, v.p. Carolina Oil Co., St. Louis, 1938-42; with pub. relations Triangle Press, St. Louis, 1939-47, sales promotion, 1939-47; account supr. overtime payroll Bell Telephone Labs., Inc., N.Y.C., 1943-46; tchr. Dunbar Elem. Sch., St. Louis, 1946-47, Newberry Elem. Sch., Chgo., 1949, Betsy Ross Elem. Sch., Chgo., 1951, Lincoln Sch., Richmond, Mo., 1951, Dunbar Sch., Kinlock, Mo., 1952, Gladstone Elem. Sch., Cleve., 1954-61, Quincy Elem. Sch., Cleve., 1961-78, head tchr. Head Start program, 1965; tchr. Wm. H. Brett Elem. Sch., Cleve., 1978-79, Euclid Park Elem. Sch., 1979—; adult edn. tchr. Cleve. Public Schs., 1965—; tchr. TV Tonight Sch., lessons for adults, Cleve., 1972; tri-owner, v.p., social editor Style mag., St. Louis, 1947-49; owner/mgr. Wentworth Record Distbrs., Chgo., 1947-51; supr. accounts receivable div. Spiegel, Inc., Chgo., 1947-52; radio panelist Calling All Americans, Cleve., 1957-58; sec. bd. dirs. Hough Pub. Co., also Hough Area Devel. Corp., Cleve., 1968-69. Mem. child devel. parent bd. Greater Cleve. Neighborhood Centers Assn.; mem. fund raising com. Food First Program, co.-chmn. woman's aux. Black Econ. Union, Cleve.; vice chmn. Cleve. com. Youth for Understanding Teenage Program; mem. Cleve. Council Human Relations; mem. Cleve. chpt. Congress Racial Equality; charter mem., financial sec. Tots and Teens, Inc.; treas. Jr. Women's Civic League; mem. Cleve. bd. Afro-Am. Cultural and Hist. Soc.; women's aux. bd. Talbert Clinic and Day Care Center, Cleve.; adv. bd. Langston Hughes Library; mem. Forest City Hosp. Aux. Bd., also Women's Aux. Com. Forest City Hosp.; scholarship com. Women's Allied Arts Assn. Greater Cleve., 1972-74; mem. spl. com. Lake Erie council Girl Scouts U.S.A., 1981—. Named Most Outstanding Vol. of Year, N.Y. Fedn. Settlements, 1944, Leading Tchr. of Community, Cleve. Call and Post, weekly newspaper, 1958; recipient Martha Holden Jennings scholar award Martha Holden Jennings Found., Cleve., 1966-67, Spl. Outstanding Tchrs. award, 1973; Outstanding Service award Black Econ. Union, 1970; certificate appreciation City Cleve., 1973. Mem. Ohio, Cleve. edn. assns., Nat. Assn. Pub. Sch. Adult Edn., NAACP, Phillis Wheatley Assn., Moreland Community Assn., Nat. Council Negro Women, Internat. Platform Assn., Top Ladies of Distinction, Inc. (pres. 1979-81), Eta Phi Beta (chpt. treas. 1977-79, regional treas. 1979—), Phi Delta Kappa (1st v.p. Cleve. 1971-73, Outstanding Achievement award 1975), Delta Sigma Theta (pres. Cleve. 1969-73), Delta Kappa Gamma. Democrat. Clubs: Novelette Bridge (pres. Cleve. 1973-77), Arewa Du-Du Bridge (treas. 1980). Home: 14701 Milverton Rd Cleveland OH 44120

WHITFIELD, ALOUCH, II, mcpl. ofcl.; b. Benton Harbor, Mich., Jan. 22, 1943; s. Alouch and Polly (Inman) W.; student Benton Harbor Community Coll., 1961-63; B.S., Mich. State U., 1965; M.A., Western Mich. U., 1968, student ednl. leadership, 1979; m. Norris Gene Shankle, Dec. 30, 1977; 1 son, Nathan Seymore; children by previous marriage—Celesta, Alouch Jason. Tchr., Benton Harbor High Sch., 1965-68; prof. Lake Mich. Coll., Benton Harbor, 1968-73; dir. Calhoun County Health Dept., Battle Creek, Mich., 1973; dir. alternative edn. Benton Harbor Schs., 1974-78; supt. water plant City of Benton Harbor, 1978-80, dir. public services, 1980—; ednl. liaison Whirlpool Research Labs.; v.p., dir. Peoples Fed. Credit Union, 1969-72. Vice pres. Citizens Adv. Bd., 1976-77; youth adv. community edn., Benton Harbor, 1968-70. Named Tchr. of Yr., Lake Mich. Coll., 1969-70, 70-71; recipient Disting. Alumni award Mich. State U., 1963. Mem. Am. Water Works Assn., Am. Chem. Soc., Mich. Sci. Tchrs. Assn., Nat. Audubon Soc., Mich. United Conservation Clubs, Phi Theta Kappa, Alpha Phi Alpha, Alpha Phi Omega. Episcopalian. Clubs: Hi-Y, Phi-Bio-Che. Research on Gemini fuel cell water, fat metabolism, in-service tng. for water treatment operators. Home: 200 Robbins Ave Benton Harbor MI 49022 Office: PO Box 648 Benton Harbor MI 49022

WHITFIELD, ANTHONY ROY, engring. ofcl.; b. Cleve., June 3, 1951; s. Jack Lemeul and LaVora (Fryer) W.; B.S. in Elec. Engring. Tech., Cleve. State U., 1974; M.B.A., Baldwin-Wallace Coll., 1980. Design engring. asst. Gen. Electric Co., Cleve., 1971-73, plant engring. asst., 1973-74, quality control engr., Memphis, 1974-76; systems engr. Bailey Controls Co., Wickliffe, Ohio, 1976, project engr., 1976-77, project mgr., 1977-78, mgr. process and indsl. contract engring., 1978—; career counselor tech. careers; remedial instr. math. Rawlings Jr. High Sch.; workshop instr. career counseling Inroads, Inc. of Cleve., 1980-81. Adv., Jr. Achievement, 1974-75, 75-76. Recipient cert. of community recognition City of Cleve., 1978. Mem. Am. Inst. Chem. Engrs., IEEE, Instrument Soc. Am., Nat. Soc. Profl. Engrs., Delta Mu Delta, Kappa Alpha Psi. Clubs: U.S. Golf Assn., Toastmasters Internat. Office: 29801 Euclid Ave Wickliffe OH 44092

WHITFIELD, GEORGE POLK, educator; b. Vesta, Nebr., May 11, 1924; s. William Russell and Mary (Ellenberger) W.; student Pa. Mil. Coll., 1943-44, Iowa State Coll., 1944, 49; Mus.B., Eastman Sch. Music, 1948, Mus.M., 1950; Doctor Mus. Arts, U. Mich., 1963; m. Mary Rose Lantz, May 26, 1951 (dec. Aug. 1969); children—Stacy Anne, Lantz David, Stephanie Ellen, Kevin Crispin; m. 2d, Laila Mary Tassava Hansen, July 11, 1970; stepchildren—Michael Douglas Hansen, David Martin Hansen, Andrew Peter Hansen, Robert Gordon Hansen. Grad. asst. Eastman Sch. Music, Rochester, N.Y., 1948-50; mem. faculty Kearney (Nebr.) State Coll., 1950-63, asso. prof. music, 1959-63, mem. ensemble, 1950-63; asso. prof. music No. Mich. U., Marquette, 1963-71, prof. music, 1971—. Music contest adjudicator; dir. piano clinics; soloist, accompanist. Treas. St. Michael's Sch. Bd., Marquette, 1966-67; cub scout leader Boy Scouts Am., Marquette, 1967-68. Served with AUS, 1943-44. Mem. Nat., Mich. assns. higher edn., Marquette Community Concert Assn. (v.p. 1970-71), AAUP, Phi Mu Alpha, Sinfonia. Home: 116 Sandy Ln Marquette MI 49855

WHITLOCK, JOHN JOSEPH, museum dir.; b. South Bend, Ind., Jan. 7, 1935; s. Joseph Mark and Helen Marcella (Cramer) W.; B.S. in Art, Ball State U., 1957, M.A. in Art, 1963; Ed.D., Ind. U., 1971; m. Sue Ann Kirkman, June 10, 1956; children—Kelly Ann, Michele Lynn, Mark. Tchr. art pub. schs., Union City, Ind., 1957-59; tchr. art, art dir. Madison (Ind.) City Schs., 1959-64; prof. art, dir. gallery Hanover (Ind.) Coll., 1964-69; teaching asso. Ind. U., 1969-70; dir., curator Burpee Art Mus., Rockford, Ill., 1970-72; prof. arts and humanities Elgin (Ill.) Community Coll., 1970-72; dir. Brooks Meml. Art Gallery, Memphis, 1972-78; prof. mus. studies Southwestern Coll., Memphis, 1973-78; adj. prof. museology Memphis State U., 1976-78; dir. Univ. Mus. adj. asso. prof. art, mem. grad. faculty So. Ill. U., Carbondale, 1978—. Mem. Human Relation Commn. Rockford, 1971-72; mem. pres.'s council Southwestern Coll., 1972-78. Mem. Am. Assn. Museums, Assn. Art Mus. Dirs., Internat. Council Museums, Midwest Assn. Museums. Office: Univ Museums Southern Ill U Carbondale IL 62901

WHITMORE, ALICE ELIZABETH EMMERT, poet; b. Dixon, Ill., Dec. 8, 1918; d. Howard Elmer and Ruth Ella (McClanahan) Emmert; student Northwestern U., Rockford (Ill.) Coll.; 1 son, Michael Robert Wadsworth. Books of poetry: A Garland of Leis, 1971, Our Singing States, 1973; author plays; contbr. numerous poems and short stories to lit. and popular publs.; writing judge for grade sch. contest. Mem. Ill. Fedn. Women's Clubs (chmn. drama Dixon br.), Rockford Art Assn., Burpee Mus., Mendelssohn Music Club, Nat. League Am. Pen Women, Internat. Platform Assn., Centro Studi e Scambi Internat. (Rome) (hon. v.p. 1976-77, Poet Laureate award 1976).

WHITMORE, BERTHA HARPER, educator; b. Penfield, Ill., June 21, 1923; d. Edward and Lula Josephine (Holt) Harper; B.S., Ill. State U., 1945; M.S., U. Ill., 1946; postgrad., George Peabody Coll. for Tchrs., 1947, Ohio State U., 1951-53; m. Edward Hugh Whitmore, June 11, 1949; children—Stephen Harper, Ann Elizabeth. Instr. math. Metamora (Ill.) Twp. High Sch., 1945; sci. instr. Hall Twp. High Sch., Spring Valley, Ill., 1946-47; instr. phys. scis. Ill. State U., Normal, 1947-51; instr. chemistry West Sr. High Sch., Columbus, Ohio, 1951-54; instr. sci. Mt. Pleasant (Mich.) Jr. High Sch., 1966—, chmn. dept. sci., 1968—. Cons. Gifted Child Program, San Bruno, Calif., 1960-65. Pres. Lab. Sch. P.T.A., Mt. Pleasant, 1966-67, Crestmoor P.T.A., San Bruno, 1961-62; chmn. March of Dimes, San Bruno, 1960-65, City Book Fair, San Bruno, 1961-63; sec. Com. for Better Schs., San Bruno, 1963; chmn. Profl. Study Com., Mt. Pleasant pub. schs., 1970-73, chmn. com. on academically talented students, 1973—, chmn. gifted child com., 1972-76, chmn. profl. study com., 1976—. Recipient Outstanding Sci. Tchr. award Ohio Acad. Sci., 1954. Mem. Nat., Ohio, Mich. sci. tchrs. assns., Ill. Chemistry Tchrs. Assn. (v.p. 1948), Nat., Mich., edn. assns., Nat., Calif. congresses parents and tchrs. (hon. life), Kappa Delta Pi, Kappa Mu Epsilon, Kappa Delta Epsilon, Delta Kappa Gamma. Asst. editor Sci. Tchr., 1948-50. Home: 1105 N Fairfield Mount Pleasant MI 48858 Office: 440 S Bradley Rd Mount Pleasant MI 48858

WHITNEY, CLARENCE W., steel co. exec.; b. Garrison, Kans., July 20, 1925; s. John and Ada (Williams) W.; B.S., Emporia State Tchrs. Coll., 1949; M.A., Columbia U., 1953; children—Robert, Teres, Sarah, Clarisa. Instr. pub. schs., Great Bend, Kans., 1949-53, Shawnee Mission, Kans., 1953-56; dept. chief Western Electric Co., Chgo., 1956-63; dir. systems Interlake, Inc., Chgo., 1963—. Served with USNR, 1943-46. Mem. Steel Industry Systems Assn. (pres. 1974-75), Assn. Systems Mgmt. Club: Masons. Office: Interlake Inc 135th and Perry Sts Chicago IL 60627

WHITNEY, JOHN FREEMAN, JR., city ofcl., educator; b. Balt., Feb. 14, 1944; s. John Freeman and Agnese (Taliaferro) W.; B.A., Baylor U., 1967; M.S., Tex. A. and I. U., 1968; postgrad. Fla. State U., 1971; m. Carolyn Elizabeth Nordyke, Aug. 5, 1966; children—Cristina, Freeman, William. Instr. polit. sci. Lamar U., Beaumont, Tex., 1970, Lincoln Land Coll., Springfield, Ill., 1971—. Parade dir., adminstrv. asst. to state fair mgr. Ill. State Fair Agy., 1973-77; cons. election central NBC News, 1972-74. Campaign mgr. and co-ordinator, various polit. campaigns, 1971—; mem. Ill. Gov.'s Transition Task Force, 1972; alt. del. Democratic Nat. Conv., 1976; mayor City of Chatham (Ill.), 1977—; mem. Springfield-Sangamon County Regional Planning Commn., 1980-82, mem. county zoning com., 1980—; mem. State of Ill. Merit Commn., Office of State Comptroller, 1981—; Democratic precinct committeeman. Recipient Meritorious Achievement award VFW, 1977. Fla. Ford. Found. legis. staff intern Senate Health, Welfare and Instns. Com., 1970; Fla. State U. fellow, 1969. Mem. Am. Polit. Sci. Assn., Midwest, So., Southwestern polit. sci. assns., Ill. Municipal League (state legis. com. 1980—), greater Springfield C. of C., FDR Club, Pi Sigma Alpha. Baptist. Club: Rotary (hon.). Author: The Irony of Democracy Manual, 5th edit., 1981. Editor: Network News, 1981. Contbr. to profl. publs. Home: 18 Pheasant Run Dr Chatham IL 62629 Office: Lincoln Land College Springfield IL 62708

WHITNEY, JOHN JOSEPH, lawyer; b. Phila., Mar. 7, 1926; s. Joseph J. and Margaret (Kelly) W.; A.B., Oberlin Coll., 1947; LL.B., Western Res. U., 1950; m. Joan Durand, July 3, 1948; children—Susan E. Whitney Baab, John Joseph, Nancy C., Laura J. Atty., Goodyear Aircraft Corp., 1950-51; practiced law, Cleve., 1953; mem. firm Ford, Whitney Schulz, 1953—; dir. law City of Berea, Ohio, 1966-68, 72. Gen. chmn. Berea chpt. ARC Fund Campaign, 1958; mem. subcom. on water system Berea Civic Com., 1959; mem. Berea Citizens Adv. Com. on Urban Renewal, 1962-65, Berea Bd. Bldg. Code Appeals, 1962-65; chmn. subcom. on profl. personnel Berea City Sch. Dist. Study Com., 1963-64; mem. adv. com. Deaconess Hosp.; pres. bd. trustees Lake Ridge Acad. Served to lt. USNR, 1946-47, 51-53. Mem. Am., Ohio, Cleve. bar assns., Berea, Ohio, Cleve. chambers commerce. Congregationalist. Club: Rotary. Editor-in-chief Western Res. U. Law Rev., 1949-50. Home: 445 S Rocky River Dr Berea OH 44017 Office: Williamson Bldg Cleveland OH 44114

WHITNEY, WILLIAM ELLIOT, JR., advt. agy. exec.; b. Albany, N.Y., Feb. 22, 1933; s. William Elliot and Louise E. (Goldsmith) W.; B.A. cum laude, Amherst Coll., 1954; M.B.A., Harvard U., 1956; m. Nancy B. Bivings, Mar. 1, 1958; children—Susan, James, Douglas. Account exec. McCann-Erickson, N.Y.C., 1956-58, Marschalk Co., N.Y.C., 1958-60; v.p., sr. v.p. Ogilvy & Mather, N.Y.C., 1960-76, sr. v.p., mng. dir., Chgo., 1976—. Vice-pres., bd. dirs. Chgo. council Boy Scouts Am., 1978-81; bd. dirs. Off the Street Club, 1979-81, Hinsdale Community House, 1981. Mem. Chgo. Advt. Club (dir., pres. 1981). Club: Amherst (v.p.) (Chgo.). Office: 200 E Randolph Dr Chicago IL 60601

WHITSON-SCHMIDT, FRANCES GALE, systems analyst; b. Balt., Oct. 31, 1946; d. Frank Gilson and Frances Elizabeth (Moore) Whitson; B.A., Towson State U., 1967; M.B.A., Northwestern U., 1981; m. Donald Eugene Schmidt. Programmer-analyst Monumental Life Ins., Balt., 1967-72; programmer-analyst United Meth. Bd. of Pensions, Evanston, Ill., 1973-77, sr. systems analyst, 1977—. Treas., bd. dirs. Adult Community OutReach Network, 1979—. Democrat. United Methodist. Home: 628 Sheridan Sq Evanston IL 60202 Office: 1200 Davis St Evanston IL 60201

WHITT, RALPH DUANE, city ofcl.; b. Farina, Ill., Nov. 9, 1948; s. Arnold Adolph and Edna (Carter) W.; A.A.S., Kaskaskia Coll., 1968, postgrad., 1976, 77; m. Kathleen Ann Kocher, Sept. 27, 1969; children—Alan Joseph, Julie Ann. Asst. mgr. Scott Store, Effingham, Ill., 1969-71; salesman, serviceman Prather Mobile Homes, Effingham and Altamont, Ill., 1971-74; self-employed, 1974-76; supt. municipal services City of Farina, 1976—. Master troup Crossroads council Boy Scouts of Am., Farina, 1975-77; mem. Farina Vol. Fire Dept., 1976—. Served with Ill. N.G., 1968-76. Cert. fire fighter. Mem. Am. Water Work Assn., Am. Legion (comdr. 1977—). Roman Catholic. Club: K. C. Home: PO Box 115 Farina IL 62838 Office: PO Box 218 Farina IL 62838

WHITTAKER, ROBERT R., congressman; b. Eureka, Kans., Sept. 18, 1939; student U. Kans., 1957-59, Emporia State Coll., summer 1959; B.S., Ill. Coll. Optometry, 1961, O.D., 1962; m. Marlene Faye Arnold, 1963; children—Steven, Stephanie, Susan. Pvt. practice optometry, 1962-78; dir. Kans. Low Vision Clinic, 1973; mem. Kans. Ho. of Reps., 1974-77; mem. 97th Congress from 5th Dist. of Kans. Precinct committeeman Augusta (Kans.) Republican Com., 1970-74; mem. Augusta City Planning Commn., 1970-74; past chmn., elder, lic. lay minister Christian Ch. Fellow Am. Acad. Optometry; mem. Am. Optometric Assn., Heart of Am. Contact Lens Soc. (past pres.). Office: 516 Cannon House Office Bldg Washington DC 20515

WHITTEMORE, LAURENCE FREDERICK, banker; b. Bangor, Maine, Mar. 7, 1929; s. John Cambridge and Elizabeth Payson (Prentiss) W.; student Balliol Coll., Oxford U., 1950; B.A., Yale U., 1951; M.B.A., Harvard U., 1953; m. Sarah Lee Arnold, Aug. 9, 1958; children—Arianna, Gioia, Lia, Nike. Account mgr. Brown Bros. Harriman & Co., N.Y.C., 1956-72, gen. mgr., 1972-73, partner, 1974—; dir. Manhattan Life Ins. Co., Otto Wolff U.S. Holding Co., Hurricane Industries; mem. fin. com. Uniglobal, Frankfurt, Germany, Guardian Royal Exchange Assurance; mem. Midwest Stock Exchange. Mem. Yale Alumni Fund, 1957—, Am. Trauma Soc., 1976—, Art Inst. Chgo., 1977—, Harvard Bus. Sch. Fund, 1979—. Served to comdr. USNR, 1953-56. Mem. Fin. Analysts Fedn., Investment Analysts Soc. Chgo., N.Y. Soc. Security Analysts. Republican. Episcopalian. Clubs: Econ., Chgo., Attic (Chgo.); Links, 29, Yale (N.Y.C.). Office: Brown Bros Harriman & Co 135 S LaSalle St Chicago IL 60603

WHITTENBERG, JAMES MATTHEW, physician; b. Libertyville, Ill., Jan. 6, 1939; s. Thomas L. and Bessie M. W.; B.A., So. Ill. U., 1960; M.D., U. Ill., 1964; m. Wilma Derringer Walter, Nov. 8, 1979; children—Kimberly, James Matthew II, Jennifer D. Walter. Intern, Springfield (Ohio) City Hosp., 1964-65; practice medicine specializing in family practice, Chester, Ill., 1967—; mem. staff Meml. Hosp. of Chester, Meml. Hosp. of Carbondale; asst. clin. prof. So. Ill. U. Served with M.C., U.S. Army, 1965-67; Vietnam. Decorated Bronze Star, Air medal; diplomate Bd. Med. Examiners. Mem. AMA, Am. Geriatric Soc., Ill. Ob-Gyn Soc., Ill. State Med. Soc., Soc. Contemporary Medicine and Surgery, Am. Acad. Family Practice, Royal Soc. Medicine, VFW (life), Am. Legion. Lutheran. Clubs: Chester Country, Moose. Home: 1211 Henrietta Chester IL 62233 Office: 1650 State St Chester IL 62233

WHOLF, BEVERLY DEAN, real estate broker; b. Omaha, Mar. 14, 1937; d. Everett Lee and Veronica Dean (Wakefield) Gardner; student U. Kans., 1955; m. Emmett Clark Wholf, Oct. 12, 1956; children—Gordon Dean, Stuart Clark, Alan Ray. Sales agt. Brisbois Realtors, Mo., 1961-70; broker, owner E.C. Wholf & Assos., Inc., Realtors, Lee's Summit, Mo., 1976—; dir. Multiple Listing Service Kansas City. Lic. sales agt., Mo.; Grad. Realtors Inst. Mem. Eastern Jackson County Bd. Realtors (dir.), Lee's Summit Area Bd. Realtors (pres. Realtor of Yr. award 1980). Home: 338 SW Marsh Wren Lee's Summit MO 64063 Office: 606 W 3rd St Lee's Summit MO 64063

WHORWELL, JOYCE BARBARA, systems specialist; b. Providence, Feb. 14, 1949; d. Philip John and Helen Elizabeth (Sharkus) Walker; B.S. in Math., Juniata Coll., 1971; m. Edwin Russell Whorwell, May 24, 1975. Tchr. math. Susquehanna Twp. High Sch., Harrisburg, Pa., 1971-72; indsl. engr. Western Elec. Co., Oklahoma City, 1973-74, systems equipment engr., Ballwin, Mo., 1974-75, indsl. engr. switchboard and wired equipment, Ballwin, 1975; statis. methods analyst Aircraft Engine Group, Gen. Electric Co., Cin., 1976-79, systems specialist, maintainability engring., 1979—. Mem. Am. Inst. Indsl. Engrs. (chpt. sec. 1977-79, v.p. programs, newletter editor 1978-80, pres. 1981—), Gen. Elec. Employee Activity Assn. Home: 39 Woodsdale Ave Cincinnati OH 45216 Office: Mail Drop 0-4 General Electric Co Aircraft Engine Group Cincinnati OH 45215

WIBLE, JERRY CRAIG, otolaryngologist; b. Robinson, Ill., Oct. 30, 1947; s. Everest Elmer and Gladys Lorae (Hocker) W.; B.A. in Chemistry, U. Kans., 1969, M.D., 1973; children—Brandt C., Brandi E. Commd. 2d lt. M.C., U.S. Air Force, 1971, advanced through grades to maj., 1976; rotating intern Scott AFB Med. Center, 1973-74; resident in otolaryngology U. Kans., 1974-78; chief of otolaryngology Ehrling-Bergquist Regional Hosp., Offutt AFB, Nebr., 1978—; clin. asst. prof. U. Nebr. Med. Center. Diplomate Am. Bd. Otolaryngology. Fellow Am. Acad. Otolaryngology; mem. AMA, Am. Council Otolaryngology. Republican. Methodist. Office: Doctors Med Bldg Branson MO 65616

WICK, ALICE JOAN MEAD, educator; b. Marshalltown, Iowa, Jan. 7, 1917; d. Edward Joseph and Alice Catherine (Turner) Mead; B.S.C., State U. Iowa, 1938; M.S., St. Cloud State U., 1964; m. Robert Hobbie Wick, Apr. 25, 1942; children—Ann Louise Roettger, Thomas Mead, William Robert. High sch. bus. tchr., Keota, Newton, Iowa, 1938-42; sec., Macon, Ga., 1942-44; instr. bus. edn. St. Cloud (Minn.) State U., 1960—; tchr. night sch., Newton, Iowa, Area Vocat. Sch., St. Cloud. Mem. St. Cloud City Council, 1972-78, St. Cloud Park and Recreation Bd., 1972-78; mem. legis. com. Minn. State League of Cities, 1975-77, mem. exec. search com., 1977, Ludwig award selection com., 1979; trustee Coll. St. Benedict, St. Joseph, Minn., 1977—; bd. dirs. St. Cloud State U. Found., 1979—. Mem. LWV, AAUW, Delta Kappa Gamma. Roman Catholic. Club: St. Cloud Area Genealogists, St. Cloud Reading Room Soc. Home: 1720 N 6th Ave St Cloud MN 56301

WICK, CHAD PHILIP, banker; b. Dayton, Ohio, Aug. 17, 1942; s. Daniel Martin and Louella Elizabeth (Greer) W.; student Gen. Motors Inst. Tech., 1960-62; B.B.A., U. Cin., 1965; M.Internat. Mgmt. with honors, Thunderbird Grad. Sch., 1972; m. Gail Elaine Stichweh, Sept. 19, 1964; children—Christine, Aubrey. With Frigidaire div. Gen. Motors Corp., Dayton, 1960-66; asst. v.p. Winters Nat. Bank, Dayton, 1972-75, v.p., Cin., 1975-79; pres. AmeriTrust of Cin., sr. v.p. AmeriTrust Co., 1979-81; exec. v.p., dir. So. Ohio Bank, Cin., 1981—. Served to capt. USAF, 1966-71. Trustee, Coll. Mt. St. Joseph, 1980—, Cin., Seven Hills Neighborhood Houses, Inc., Minority Bus. Devel. Coalition; bd. dirs. Cin. Council World Affairs, 1978-81; chmn. bd. dirs. World Affairs Inst.; chmn. bd. trustees Program for Cin.; mem. nat. adv. bd. Tools for Tng. Mem. Fgn. Credit Ins. Assn. (Midwest adv. bd.). Unitarian. Clubs: Bankers, Coldstream Country, Queen City. Office: 515 Main St Cincinnati OH 45202

WICK, ROBERT EDWARD, internat. trade exec.; b. Chgo., May 17, 1921; s. Lorenz Henry and Frances Martha (Meine) W.; M.B.A., U. Chgo., 1953; postgrad. Wharton Sch., 1959; M.E., Ill. Inst. Tech., 1946; m. Gladys Eleanor Hanan, June 29, 1952; children—Robert, David, Christopher. Dir. internat. ops. Chgo. Dynamic Industries, 1971-75; pres. Internat. Market Devel. Co., Oak Park, 1974—; internat. mktg. cons. State of Ill., 1977-79; instr. mktg. Elmhurst (Ill.) Coll., 1980. Pres. Village Youth Band, Oak Park, 1977—; pres. Acorn council Boy Scouts Am., 1979; pres. PTA Council; chmn. bd. Community Christian Sch., Chgo., 1979—. Recipient Disting. Service award Hoover Commn., 1954. Mem. Internat. Trade Club. Lutheran. Home: 423 Greenfield St Oak Park IL 60302

WICK, STEPHEN JAMES, JR., radio broadcaster; b. Rio Hondo, Tex., Aug. 17, 1940; s. Stephen James and Leah M. (Taylor) W.; diploma Moody Bible Inst., 1964; student Trinity Coll., 1966-67, Northwestern U., 1968-69; m. Ruth Alice Glerum, July 31, 1965; children—Stephen James II, Carol Beth. Dir. edn. Homewood (Ill.) Baptist Ch., 1964-65; dir. edn. and youth N.W. Bapt. Ch., Chgo., 1965-68; radio producer Stas. WMBI and WMBI-FM, Chgo., 1970-72, supr. prodn., 1972-74, asst. mgr., 1972-74, sta. mgr., program dir., 1974—. Served with USNR, 1960-62. Mem. Nat. Assn. Broadcasters, Nat. Religious Broadcasters. Office: 820 N LaSalle Dr Chicago IL 60610

WICKENDEN, BARBARA HORNER, ednl. adminstr.; b. Rockford, Ill.; d. Forrest A. and Elva (Olander) Lyddon; B.S., Purdue U., 1947; M.S., Akron U., 1968; m. Herbert R. Wickenden, Nov. 21, 1973 (dec. Apr. 1980); children—Robert Horner, Hollace Horner, Charles Horner. Pres., Learning Center, Inc., Akron, Ohio, 1965-75; curriculum dir. Portage County (Ohio) Schs., 1974-81; asst. supt. Crestwood (Ohio) Schs., 1981—; cons., author Ency. Brit. Corp., Chgo., 1969-79. Jennings scholar, 1980-82; ESEA Title IV Devel. grantee, 1979-82. Mem. Internat. Reading Assn., Assn. Supervision and Curriculum Devel., Ohio Sch. Suprs. Assn., Phi Delta Kappa, Delta Kappa Gamma, Pi Delta Theta, Delta Gamma. Congregationalist. Author: Reading Games, 1970; Readiness Math, 1978; Expanding Students Thinking and Comprehension Skills, 1980. Home: 2845 Kent Rd Stow OH 44224 Office: 4565 W Prospect St Mantua OH 44255

WICKERSHAM, JOHN RICHARD, chain restaurant exec.; b. Madison, Wis., Jan. 5, 1946; s. Donald Rex and Vera Elizabeth (Jacobson) W.; A.B., Duke U., 1968; M.I.M., Am. Grad. Sch. Internat. Mgmt., 1972; m. Sydney Biggers, Apr. 28, 1978; 1 dau., Shelley. Asst. internat. officer Citizens and So. Nat. Bank, Atlanta, 1974, internat. officer, 1975, ass. v.p., mgr. S. Am., 1976; mgr. Agronomics Internat., Inc., Atlanta, 1977-78; dir. internat. bus. devel. Pizza Hut, Inc., Wichita, 1978-81, sr. dir. franchsing S. Am., 1981—; guest lectr. Ga. Inst. Tech., Wichita State U. Hon. consul for S.E. U.S., Chile. Served with USNR, 1968-72. Decorated Naval Achievement Medal. Mem. Internat. Bus. Council of Wichita, Ga. Partners of the Americas (dir. 1977-78), Atlanta C. of C., Ga. Internat. Trade Council. Office: PO Box 428 Wichita KS 67201

WICKLUND, MICHAEL ALLEN, mfg. co. exec.; b. St. Louis, Dec. 20, 1942; s. Gerald Raymond and Margie Elizabeth (Pritchard) Brown; B.S. in Metall. Engring., U. Mo., 1965, B.Engring., 1980; m. Barbara Kay Stout, Sept. 1, 1962; children—Michael Allen, Sharon, Liesa, Connie. Co-op student, NASA, Huntsville, Ala., 1963-65; metallurgist Wis. Steel, Chgo., 1965-66, metall. rep., 1968-72, asst. supt. 3 mill, 1972; founder, pres. West Chgo. Forge, West Chicago, Ill., 1972-79; pres. Mo. Forge, Inc., Doniphan, 1979—, chmn. bd. dirs., 1979—. Served to 1st lt., U.S. Army, C.E., 1966-68. Registered profl. engr., Ill.; lic. comml. pilot. Mem. C. of C. of Doniphan, C. of C. of Mo., Am. Soc. Metals, AIME, Forging Industry Assn., Aircraft Owners and Pilots Assn., Pilots Internat. Assn. Republican. Methodist. Club: Kiwanis. Home: Route 3 Box 168 Doniphan MO 63935 Office: PO Box 397 Doniphan MO 63935

WICKMAN, JOHN EDWARD, library exec.; b. Villa Park, Ill., May 24, 1929; s. John E. and Elsie (Voss) W.; A.B., Elmhurst Coll., 1953; M.A., Ind. U., 1958, Ph.D., 1964; m. Shirley Jean Swanson, Mar. 17, 1951; children—Lisa Annette, Eric John. Instr. English, history Hanover (Ind.) Coll., 1959-62; instr. history Ind. U., Jeffersonville, 1962; asst. prof. history N.W. Mo. State Coll., Maryville, 1962-64; faculty fellow Nat. Center Edn. in Politics, 1964-65; asst. prof. history Purdue U., Fort Wayne, Ind., 1965-66; dir. Dwight D. Eisenhower Library, Abilene, Kans., 1966—. Personal asst. to Gov. Kans., 1964-65. Served with AUS, 1953-55. Congl. fellow, Washington, 1975-76. Mem. Oral History Assn. (past pres.), Am. Soc. Pub. Adminstrn., Western History Assn. (council 1972-75), Am., Kans. State (bd. dirs., past pres.) hist. socs. Office: Dwight D Eisenhower Library Abilene KS 67410

WICKS, WILLIAM WITHINGTON, public relations exec.; b. Chgo., Dec. 20, 1923; s. William and Alice M. (Withington) W.; B.N.S., U. Notre Dame, 1944, A.B., 1947; m. Frances M. Horner, Nov. 29, 1947; children—Barbara Ann, Christine Frances. Staff corr. United Press Assn., Milw., 1947; public relations mgr. Internat. Harvester Co., Louisville, 1948-58; mgr. field services-public relations Standard Oil Co. Ind., Chgo., 1959-60; v.p. public relations Griswold-Eshleman Co., Chgo., 1961-68; dir. public relations G. D. Searle & Co., Chgo., 1968-74; v.p. public relations Kimberly-Clark Corp., Neenah, Wis., 1974—. Pres., Jr. Achievement Neenah-Menasha, 1980-81, 78-79. Served to lt. (j.g.) USNR, 1942-46; PTO. Mem. Public Relations Soc. Am. (Silver Anvil award 1963, 2 in 1979), Pharm. Mfrs. Assn. (chmn. public relations sect. 1974), Publicity Club Chgo. (past pres.). Republican. Roman Catholic. Office: Kimberly-Clark Corp Neenah WI 54956

WICKSTROM, LAWRENCE LEE, engring., mfg. and constrn. co. exec.; b. Lander, Wyo., Feb. 7, 1947; s. Lee Worth and Emma Edith (Krone) W.; B.S., U. Wyo., 1970; M.S., Wichita State U., 1980; m. Connie Lynette Burroughs, May 19, 1979; 1 son, Phillip Everett. Product engr. Full Vision, Inc., Newton, Kans., 1973-74; project engr. Farmland Industries SSP, Hutchinson, Kans., 1974-79; chief engr. Superior Equipment Mfg. Co., Mattoon, Ill., 1979-80; dir. engring. Agrl. Bldg. Co., Mendota, Ill., 1980—. Served to 1st lt. U.S. Army, 1970-72. Decorated Bronze Star; registered profl. engr., Ala., Colo., Ill., Ind., Iowa, Kans., Nebr., Ohio, Wyo. Mem. Am. Mgmt. Assn., Am. Soc. Agrl. Engrs. Home: 1713 Sunset Dr Mendota IL 61342 Office: Agricultural Bldg Co Rural Route 2 Box 266 Mendota IL 61342

WIDDIFIELD, DUANE ALDEN, clin. hypnotherapist; b. Fort Wayne, Ind., Apr. 5, 1934; s. Clarence Eugene and Madge Dolores (Graves) W.; D.C., Lincoln Chiropractic Coll., 1959; LL.B., Blackstone Law Sch., 1969; D.D. (hon.), Ridgedale Theol. Sem., 1972, M.Th., 1975; B.S. in Psychology, State U. N.Y. at Albany, 1977; M.A. in Psychology, Calif. Western U., 1976, Ph.D. in Psychology, 1977; postdoctoral Ind. U. Sch. Medicine, Harvard U. Med. Sch.; m. Marlene LaVonne Brown, Mar. 7, 1958; children—Mark Duane, Susan Marlene, Erik Michael, Janice LaVonne. Pres., Indpls. Art Craft, 1958-59; tech. asst. to physician, Indpls., 1962-66, bus. mgr., 1966-69; pvt. practice clin. psychotherapy, Indpls., 1969—. V.p., dir. Medi-Style Inc., Indpls., 1970—; pres., dir. Inst. Clin. Hypnosis, 1977—. Served with U.S. Army, 1959-62. Diplomate Am. Psychotherapy Assn. Recipient various art awards. Ordained Minister Ch. of God; bd. dirs. Faith Assembly. Fellow Am. Inst. Hypnosis (diplomate), Am. Coll. Clin. Adminstrs.; mem. So. Assn. Marriage Counselors, Internat. Transactional Analysis Assn., Hypnotists Exam. Council (cert.), Internat. Soc. Profl. Hypnosis, Nat. Psychol. Assn., Am. Assn. Christian Marriage Counselors, Am. Philos. Assn., Mensa, Intertel, Fraternal Order Police (asso.), Sons Am. Revolution. Contbr. to profl. jours; also poetry. Home: 2501 Redfern Dr Indianapolis IN 46227 Office: 532 Turtle Creek Dr N Indianapolis IN 46227

WIDEMAN, LAWSON GIBSON, chemist; b. Morrellton, Mo., July 17, 1943; s. Joseph and Mabel M. (Hickinbotham) Kargacin; B.S., U. Mo., 1966, M.S., 1967; Ph.D., U. Akron, 1971, postgrad., 1971-73; m. Peggy Jean Carr, June 5, 1965; children—Paula Anne, Mary Elizabeth, Lynn Christine. Staff research chemist Goodyear Tire & Rubber Co., Akron, Ohio, 1967-71, sr. research chemist, 1971—; mem. faculty U. Akron, part-time 1981—. Pres., ch. bd. Emmanuel United Ch. of Christ, Akron, Ohio, 1977-78, elder, 1973—. NSF fellow, 1966-67, NDEA fellow, 1970-71. Mem. Am. Chem. Soc., Akron Chem. Soc., Sigma Xi, Theta Chi. Contbr. articles to profl. jours.; patentee field. Home: 82 N Village View Tallmadge OH 44278 Office: Goodyear Tire & Rubber Co 142 Goodyear Blvd Akron OH 44316

WIDEMAN, ROY LEON, engring. co. exec.; b. Los Angeles, Sept. 4, 1943; s. Walter Leroy and Alice Jane (Smith) W.; B.S., U. Mo., 1968; m. Sherry Lee Lewis, Sept. 7, 1963; children—Eric Leon, Erin Lane, Ryan Lee. Design engr., project engr., estimator Mississippi Valley Structural Steel & Fabricator, St. Louis, 1968-74; pres. Engineered Design, cons. engrs., St. Louis, 1974-76; v.p., treas. Lopinot & Weber, Inc., St. Louis, 1976—. Registered profl. engr., Mo., Ill. Mem. Nat. Soc. Profl. Engrs., Am. Inst. Steel Constrn., Am. Concrete Inst., Mo. Soc. Profl. Engrs. Baptist. Home: Rural Route 3 Box 149A Neff Rd Saint Clair MO 63077 Office: Lopinot & Weber Inc 722 Chestnut St Saint Louis MO 63101

WIDERA, GEORG ERNST OTTO, educator; b. Dortmund, West Germany, Feb. 16, 1938; s. Otto F. and Gertrude A. (Yzermann) W.; came to U.S., 1950, naturalized, 1956; B.S., U. Wis., Madison, 1960, M.S., 1962, Ph.D., 1965; m. Kristel Kornas, June 22, 1974. Instr., U. Wis., 1963-65; asst. prof. engring. mechanics U. Ill., Chgo., 1965-69, asso. prof., 1969-73, prof., 1973—; vis. prof. U. Stuttgart, 1968-69, U. Wis., Milw., 1973-74, Marquette U., Milw., 1978-79; cons. to corps. Grantee NSF, Nat. Acad. Scis., U. Ill.-Chgo. Research Bd.; grad. fellow applied mechs. U. Wis., 1961-63; NASA fellow in space systems engring., 1966; Alexander von Humboldt fellow, 1968-69. Mem. ASCE, Am. Acad. Mechs., ASME (asso. editor Jour. Pressure Vessel Tech. 1977-81, chmn. design and analysis com. PVP div.), Internat. Assn. for Dental Research, Gesellschaft fuer Angewandte Mathematik und Mechanik. Contbr. articles to profl. jours. Home: 345 Greenleaf St Wilmette IL 60091 Office: University of Illinois Box 4348 Chicago IL 60680

WIDLAK, FREDERIC WALTER, research dir.; b. Chgo., June 28, 1940; s. Walter Frederic and Ann Alice (Krajeski) W.; B.S., Ill. Inst. Tech., 1966; M.A., Marquette U., 1971; Ph.D., Purdue U., 1982; m. Prudence Amos, Aug. 12, 1967. Teaching, research asst. Marquette U., 1966-70; research fellow Purdue U., 1970-72, teaching and research asst., 1972-73, adminstrv. asst., 1974; research fellow Northwestern U., 1975-76; instr., program evaluator Ind. U. Med. Center, Indpls., 1975-76, asst. prof., 1976-79; dir. research and evaluation Indpls. Div. Public Health, 1979—; adj. prof. Ind. U. Sch. Nursing, 1981—. Mem. regional planning com. Ind. Heartland Coordinating Commn., 1979-80; mem. Indpls. Zoo Adv. Council, 1976-80. Mem. Am., Midwestern psychol. assns., Am., Midwestern, Ind. ednl. research assns., Nat. Council Measurement in Edn., Midwestern Soc. Multivariate Psychology, Lake Mich. Fedn., Environ. Edn. Assn. Ind. (pres. 1977-78), Ind. Izaak Walton League (pres. 1978-82, environ. edn. chmn. 1975-78), Nat. Izaak Walton League (exec. bd. 1980—), Pi Kappa Phi, Sigma Xi, Psi Chi, Kappa Delta Pi, Pi Nu Epsilon. Club: Toastmasters Internat. Contbr. articles to profl. jours. Home: 4635 N Lesley Ave Indianapolis IN 46226

WIDMAN, PAUL EDWARD, health care exec.; b. Norwalk, Ohio, Jan. 24, 1918; s. Edward Anthony and Josephine (Brown) W.; B.S., U. Toledo, 1941; m. Rose Hoyt, June 21, 1941; children—Jerry Paul, Kathleen Ann. Asst. dir. purchasing Johns Hopkins Hosp., Balt., 1950-51; dir. purchasing Cleve. Clinic Found., 1951-69, dir. adminstrv. services, 1969-76, dir. ops., 1977—. Served with USNR, 1943. Certified purchasing mgr. Nat. Assn. Purchasing Mgmt. Mem. Am. Hosp. Assn. (George R. Gossett award 1967), Am. Coll. Clinic Mgrs., Am. Coll. Hosp. Adminstrs. Home: 745-26 Windward Dr Aurora OH 44202 Office: 9500 Euclid Ave Cleveland OH 44106

WIECHERT, ALLEN LEROY, univ. adminstr.; b. Independence, Kans., Oct. 25, 1938; s. Norman Henry and Serena Johanna (Steinke) W.; B.Arch., Kans. State U., 1962; m. Sandra Swanson, Aug. 19, 1961; children—Kirstin Nan, Brendan Swanson, Megan Ann. Architect in tng. McVey, Peddie, Schmidt & Allen, Wichita, Kans., 1962-63; architect Kivett & Myers, Kansas City, Mo., 1963-68; asst. to vice chancellor plant planning and devel. U. Kans., Lawrence, 1968-74, asso. dir. facilities planning, 1974-78, univ. dir. facilities planning, 1978—; mem. long range phys. planning com. Kans. Bd. Regents, 1971—; designer, archtl. programmer of ednl. facilities; bd. dirs. Kans. U. Fed. Credit Union, 1972-81, pres. bd., 1974. Chmn. horizons com. Lawrence Bicentennial Commn.; designer Kaw River Trail, 1976; mem. Action 80 Com., 1980-81; mem. standing com. Kans. Episcopal Diocese, 1976-80; sr. warden Trinity Episc. Ch., Lawrence, 1978-80; bd. trustees Kans. Sch. Religion, 1973-80; bd. dirs. Trinity Group Care Home, 1973-79. Served to 1st lt. Kans. Air N.G., 1961-67. Lic. architect, Kans.; cert. Nat. Council Archtl. Registration Bds. Mem. AIA, Assn. Univ. Architects, Nat. Hist. Trust. Editor, contbr. to Physical Development Planning Work Book, 1973. Home: 813 Highland Dr Lawrence KS 66044 Office: Office Facilities Planning University of Kansas Lawrence KS 66045

WIECK, GARY DEAN, accountant; b. Palmer, Nebr., Sept. 9, 1941; s. Lawrence H. ahd Lucille L. (Helzer) W.; B.A. in Bus. Adminstrn., Hasting Coll., 1963; m. Nanna Jean Mc Donald, Sept. 16, 1967; children—Trevor, Heather. Accountant, Contryman & Assos., Grand Island, Nebr., 1963-70, partner, 1970—. Mem. adv. bd. electronic data processing Central Nebr. Tech. Coll., 1969—; bd. dirs. Overland Trails council Boy Scouts Am., 1969-73; bd. dirs. Grand Island United Way, 1974-77, asso. campaign chmn., 1973, 75, 77. C.P.A., Nebr.; cert. data processor. Mem. Nebr. Soc. C.P.A.'s (pres. 1981, dir.), Am. Inst. C.P.A.'s, Data Processing Mgmt. Assn. (individual performance award 1976; bd. dirs. Mid-state Nebr. chpt. 1968-74, 76, pres. 1969-70), Central States Acctg. Conf. (dir. 1978—), Countryman Assn. (pres. 1981). Republican. Lutheran. Club: Riverside Golf. Home: 2604 Arrowhead Grand Island NE 68801 Office: 615 W First St Grand Island NE 68801

WIECZOREK, GERALD MICHAEL, fin. exec.; b. Ionia, Mich., Apr. 17, 1948; s. Michael J.C. and Betty Lou (Wheeler) W.; B.A., Mich. State U., 1972. Dir. Counselors Advocate, Inc., Lansing, Mich., 1968—; pres., lobbyist Fed. Legis. Consultants, Inc., Washington, 1972-75; cert. diamond broker Internat. Gems, Ltd., Boston, 1975-76; realtor asso., investment and comml. specialist, 1978-81; instr. investment real estate Lowery & Nickerson. Chmn. bd. dirs. Listening Ear Crisis Intervention Center, East Lansing. Mem. Mich. Assn. Realtors (legis. com.), ACLU, Amnesty Internat., Internat. Commn. of Jurists (Geneva, Switzerland), Council of Internat. Investigators (London, Eng.). Contbr. articles to mags. and profl. jours. Home: 4305 MacDougal Circle Lansing MI 48910

WIED, GEORGE LUDWIG, physician; b. Carlsbad, Czeckoslovakia, Feb. 7, 1921; s. Ernst George and Anna (Travnicek) W.; M.D., Charles U., Prague, 1945; m. Daga M. Graaz, Mar. 19, 1949 (dec. Aug. 1977). Came to U.S., 1953, naturalized, 1960. Intern, County Hosp., Carlsbad, 1945, U. Chgo. Hosps., 1955; resident obstetrics, gynecology U. Munich (Germany), 1946-48; practice medicine, specializing in obstetrics, gynecology, West Berlin, 1948-53, Chgo., 1954—; asst. obstetrics, gynecology Free U., West Berlin, 1948-52; asso. chmn. dept. obstetrics, gynecology Moabit Hosp. Free U., 1953; asst. prof., dir. cytology U. Chgo., 1954-59, asso. prof., 1959-65, prof., 1965—, mem. bd. adult edn., 1964-68, prof. pathology, 1967—, Blum-Riese prof. of obstetrics and gynecology, 1968—, acting chmn. dept. obstetrics and gynecology, 1974-75; hon. dir. Chgo. Cancer Prevention Center, 1959—; chmn. advisory com. cancer control Chgo. Bd. Health, 1961-71; chmn. jury Maurice Goldblatt Cytology award, 1963—. Recipient certificate merit U.S. Surgeon Gen., 1952, Maurice Goldblatt Cytology award, 1961; George N. Papanicolaou award, 1970. Mem. Am. (pres. 1965-66), Mexican (hon.), Spanish (hon.), Brazilian (fgn. corr.), Latin-Am. (hon.), Japanese (hon.), German (hon.), socs. cytology, Internat. Acad. Cytology (pres. 1977-80), Central Soc. Clin. Research, Chgo. Path. Soc., Am. Soc. Cell Biology, German, Bavarian socs. obstetrics and gynecology, German Soc. Endocrinology, Sigma Xi. Contbr. articles to profl. jours.; editor-in-chief: Acta Cytologica, 1957—, Clin. Cytology, 1965—, Introduction to Quantitative Cytochemistry, 1965—, editor: Automated Cell Identification and Cell Sorting; editor-in-chief Jour. Reproductive Medicine, Analytical and Quantitative Cytology. Home: 1640 E 50th St Chicago IL 60615 Office: 5841 S Maryland Ave Chicago IL 60637

WIEDMAN, MARY ELIZABETH, occupational therapist; b. Bonne Terre, Mo., Sept. 12, 1932; d. Edward Carl and Elva (Vinetta) Johnson; student N.W. Okla. State U., 1972-75, postgrad. 1979—; B.S. in Occupational Therapy, U. Okla. Health Sci. Center, 1978; m. Bill B. Wiedman, May 23, 1977; children—Michael Pinkley, Deborah Pinkley Williamson, Mark Pinkley, Susan Pinkley Schneider; stepchildren—Michael Wiedman, Jan Wiedman Schrock, Jill Wiedman Howard. Asst. for tng. Occupational Therapy in Ednl. Mgmt., Oklahoma City and Tulsa, 1981—; pvt. practice pediatric therapy, Kiowa, Kans., 1979—; occupational therapy cons. Achenbach Rehab. Center, Hardtner, Kans., 1979—; occupational therapist Northwestern Okla. Regional Edn. Service Center, Alva, 1978—; guest lectr. N.W. Okla. State U., 1978-79. Mem. World Fedn. Occupational Therapists, Am. Occupational Therapy Assn., Okla. Occupational Therapy Assn., Kans. Occupational Therapy Assn., Am. Occupational Therapy Found., Council Exceptional Children (charter mem. chpt.), Center Study Sensory Integration Dysfunction, AAUW. Republican. Mem. Congregationalist. Home: 1011 Coats Kiowa KS 67070 Office: 1540 Davis St Alva OK 73717

WIEGERT, EMILY (AMY) MARY, educator; b. Valders, Wis., Oct. 23, 1950; d. Harold Andrew and Mabel Elaine (Shimek) Bodart; B.S. in Fashion Merchandising, U. Wis., Stout, 1972; A.Acctg., Lakeshore Tech. Inst., 1980; m. Darrell Wiegert, June 10, 1972; 1 dau., Amanda. Dept. mgr. W.T. Grant, Manitowoc, 1966-69; sales clk. Sears, Roebuck & Co., Manitowoc, 1969-71; clk. Wis. Dept. Social Services, Manitowoc, 1972-76; sec. Red Arrow Products Co., Manitowoc, 1977-79; instr. distributive edn. Lakeshore Tech. Inst., Cleveland, Wis., 1980—. Mem. Am. Vocat. Assn., Wis. Assn. Vocat. and Adult Edn., Am. Legion Aux. Roman Catholic. Home: 216 N Liberty St Valders WI 54245 Office: 1290 N Ave Cleveland WI 53015

WIELAND, REX ALAN, physician; b. Hastings, Mich., Dec. 19, 1948; s. Lawrence Charles and Betty Lou (Canter) W.; B.S. in Biology, Manchester Coll., 1971; M.D., Ind. U., 1975; m. Peggy Sue Becker, Aug. 19, 1972; children—Heather Rae, Kyle Frederick, Heidi Elizabeth. Resident in family practice Meml. Hosp., South Bend, Ind., 1975-78; practice family medicine, North Manchester, Ind., 1978—; mem. staff, chief obstetrical service Wabash County Hosp.; team physician Manchester Coll., Manchester High Sch.; staff cons. patient edn. program Wabash County Hosp.; mem. utilization rev. com. Vernon Manor Children's Home. Bd. dirs. Sycamore Nursery Sch., 1978—, North Manchester Child Devel. Center, 1978—. Diplomate Am. Bd. Family Practice. Mem. Am. Acad. Family Practice, Wabash County Med. Soc. Mem. Ch. of Brethren. Home: 1406 Villa Ct North Manchester IN 46962 Office: 1104 Wayne St North Manchester IN 46962

WIELAND, ROBERT RICHARD, recreation and leisure time products mfg. co. exec.; b. Columbus, Ohio, Jan. 30, 1937; s. Robert Milton and Evelyn Marion (Turner) W.; B.A., Ohio State U., 1958, J.D., 1960; m. Sara J. Gerhart, Dec. 17, 1966; 1 son, Christopher David. Admitted to Ohio bar, 1960, Ill. bar, 1966; atty. Ohio Bell Telephone Co., Cleve., 1960-65, United Air Lines, Inc., Chgo., 1965-67; asst. gen. counsel, asst. sec. Youngstown Sheet and Tube Co. (Ohio), 1967-73, Mead Corp., Dayton, Ohio, 1974-76; v.p., gen. counsel, sec. Huffy Corp., Dayton, 1976—; dir., officer Huffman Mfg. Co., YLC Enterprises, Inc., H.C.A., Inc., Huffy Export Sales, Inc.; sec. Huffy Found., Inc. Trustee Byron R. Lewis Edn. Fund, 1974-80; asso. dir. Dayton Art Inst.; mem. friends bd. Aullwood Center; mem. adminstrv. bd. Christ Meth. Ch., Kettering, Ohio. Served with USAF, 1961-62. Mem. Am. Bar Assn., Ohio State Bar Assn., Dayton Bar Assn., Nat. Interfrat. Council (mem. ho. of dels. 1976-80), Am. Arbitration Assn. (arbitrator panel 1975—), Sigma Pi (nat. pres. 1972-74). Office: Huffy Corp 7701 Byers Rd Miamisburg OH 45342

WIEMANN, MARION RUSSELL, JR., biologist, microscopist; b. Chesterton, Ind., Sept. 7, 1929; s. Marion Russell and Verda (Peek) W.; B.S., Ind. U., 1959; 1 dau., Tamara Lee. Histo-research techician U. Chgo., 1959, research asst., 1959-62, research technician, 1962-64; tchr. sci. Westchester Twp. Sch., Chesterton, Ind., 1964-66; with U. Chgo., 1965-79, sr. research technician, 1967-70, research technologist, 1970-79; prin. Marion Wiemann & Assos., cons. research and devel., Chesterton, Ind., 1979—. Served with USN, 1951-53. McCrone Research Inst. scholar, 1968. Fellow Royal Microscopical Soc.; mem. Soil Sci. Soc. Am., Am. Soc. Agronomy, Crop Sci. Soc. Am. Contbr. articles to profl. jours. Address: PO Box E Chesterton IN 46304

WIERWILLE, DONALD ERNST, ednl. adminstr.; b. Lima, Ohio, Aug. 11, 1940; s. Victor Paul and Dorothea Sarah (Kipp) W.; B.Edn., U. Wis.-Whitewater, 1966; M.S. in Edn., No. Ill. U., 1968; Ed.D. in Ednl. Adminstrn. U. Kans., 1979; m. Wanda May Strohschein, Apr. 14, 1962; children—Laurinda, Ralph, Kristina. Tchr. elementary schs. Winnebago County, Ill., 1962-66; reading specialist pub. schs. Rockton, Ill., 1966-69; elementary prin. schs. Clinton, Wis., 1969-74; v.p. adminstrn., dean Way Coll. of Emporia (Kans.), 1974—; v.p., bd. trustees The Way Internat., New Knoxville, Ohio, 1977—. Mem. NEA, Wis. Elementary Prins., Phi Delta Kappa. Home: PO Box 392 Rural Route 1 New Knoxville OH 45871 Office: PO Box 328 New Knoxville OH 45871

WIERWILLE, VICTOR PAUL, clergyman; b. New Knoxville, Ohio, Dec. 31, 1916; s. Ernst Henry and Emma (Rehn) W.; A.B., Lakeland Coll., 1938; B.D., Mission House Sem., Sheboygan, Wis., 1941; M.Th., Princeton, 1941; Th.D., Pikes Peak Sem., 1948; postgrad. U. Chgo., 1938-40; m. Dorothea Sarah Kipp, July 2, 1937; children—Donald Ernst, Karen Ruth (Mrs. James Kirby Martin), Mary Ellen (Mrs. John Thomas Somerville), Sara Kathryn (Mrs. Kevin Phillips Guigou), John Paul. Ordained to ministry Evang. and Ref. Ch., 1941; pastor Evang. and Ref. Ch., Payne, Ohio, 1941-42, Van Wert, Ohio, 1943-57; founder The Way Internat., bibl. research and teaching center, New Knoxville, 1958—, also pres. and founder, The Way Internat. Fine Arts and Hist. Center, Sidney, Ohio, 1974; founder The Way mag., 1945—. Pres. bd. trustees The Way Coll., Emporia, Kans., 1974—; pres. bd. trustees The Way Coll. of Bibl. Research Ind. Campus, Rome City, 1975—. Author: Victory Through Christ, 1945; Receiving the Holy Spirit Today, 1955, 6th ed., 1972; Power for Abundant Living, 1971; The Bible Tells Me So, 1971; The New, Dynamic Church, 1971; The Word's Way, 1971; Are the Dead Alive Now?, 1971; Jesus Christ is NOT God, 1975; God's Magnified Word, 1977; Jesus Christ Our Passover, 1980. Address: PO Box 328 New Knoxville OH 45871

WIERZBICKI, MARY LOUISE, occupational therapist; b. Milw., May 14, 1951; d. Eugene V. and Evelyn S. (Bykowski) W.; B.S. in Occupational Therapy, U. Wis., Madison, 1972; M.S. in Ednl. Adminstrn. and Supervision, U. Wis., Milw., 1979. Staff occupational therapist Bird S. Coler Meml. Hosp., N.Y.C., 1973-74, sr. occupational therapist, 1974-76; asst. chief occupational therapist Sacred Heart Rehab Hosp., Milw., 1976-78; occupational therapist, owner Willow Rehab. Services, Milw., 1978—; chmn. occupational therapy adv. com. Wis. Bur. Health Care Financing, 1980; lectr., coordinator profl. seminars; cons. adult edn. Recipient award of Merit, Milw. Police Dept., 1979. Mem. Am. Occupational Therapy Assn., Wis. Occupational Therapy Assn. (treas. 1978-79, Bd. Dirs. commendation 1979, S.E. Dist. award appreciation 1981), AAUW, Mensa, Nat. Assn. for Female Execs. Active in promoting passage of health-care delivery bills in Wis. Home and Office: 6661 N Bourbon St Milwaukee WI 53224

WIESE, DANIEL EDWARD, advt. agy. exec.; b. Cedar Rapids, Iowa, June 16, 1936; s. Erwin Edward and Bernice Virginia (Cristy) W.; B.S., Iowa State U., 1958; m. Mary Virginia Smith, Nov. 3, 1958; children—Anne, John, Amy. Research dir. Popular Sci. Pub. Co., N.Y.C., 1965-66; asso. research dir. Readers Digest Assn., N.Y.C., 1966-67; research dir. Successful Farming, Meredith Corp., Des Moines, 1967-75; mgr. Agtrack, Chilton Research Services, Radnor, Pa., 1976-79; v.p., dir. research services Creswell Munsell Fultz & Zirbel Inc., Cedar Rapids, 1980—. Mem. Plymouth Congl. Ch. Nursery Sch., 1967-75, pres., 1975. Served with AUS, 1959. Mem. Advt. Research Found., Nat. Agrimktg. Assn. Home: 625 N 6th St W

Mount Vernon IA 52314 Office: Creswell Munsell Fultz & Zirbel Inc PO Box 2879 4211 Signal Ridge Rd Cedar Rapids IA 52406

WIETHOFF, CLIFFORD ALLEN, surgeon; b. Seymour, Ind., May 12, 1920; s. Clifford Henry and Mary Elizabeth (Rothrock) W.; A.B. in Anatomy, Ind. U., 1942, M.D., 1944; m. Mary Lou Ferguson, June 20, 1943; children—Janet Sue, Richard Allen, Barbara Joanne, John Clifford. Intern U.S. Naval Hosp., Key West, Fla., 1944-45; resident in pathology Ind. U. Med. Center, 1946-47; resident in surgery Indpls. Gen. Hosp., 1947-49; practice medicine specializing in gen. surgery, Seymour, 1950—; me. staffs Jackson County Hosp., Seymour, 1950—, Washington County Hosp., Salem, Ind., 1950—; asst. in surgery, surg. pathology Ind. Med. Center, 1950-51; dir. Fidelity Fed. Savs. and Loan, Seymour. Bd. dirs. Seymour Girls Club, 1953-56. Served to lt. USNR, 1944-46. Diplomate Am. Bd. Surgery. Fellow A.C.S.; mem. Am., Ind. State, Pan-Am. med. assns., Jackson County Med. Soc., Pan-Pacific Surg. Assn., Am. Legion, Seymour C. of C. (dir. 1952-55), Beta Theta Pi, Nu Sigma Nu. Republican. Methodist. Clubs: Seymour Country (dir. 1962-68, pres. 1965), Rotary (pres. 1956) (Seymour); Lake and Forest (Brownstown, Ind.), Elks, Masons, Eagles. Contbr. articles to med. jours. Home: 615 West Dr Sunset Pkwy Seymour IN 47274 Office: 1131 Medical Pl Seymour IN 47274

WIGGINS, HARRY, state senator; b. Kansas City, Mo., Aug. 1, 1932; A.B., Rockhurst Coll.; LL.B., St. Louis U. Former asst. U.S. dist. atty.; mem. Mo. Senate, 1974—. Bd. counselors Avila Coll., Kansas City; bd. dirs. Black Econ. Union; chmn. 911 com. Mid-Am. Regional Council; mem. State Bd. Liquor Control, gen. counsel Mo. Public Service Commn. Served with U.S. Army, 1957-59. Mem. Greater Kansas City Alumni Assn. Alpha Delta Gamma, Phi Delta Phi. Democrat. Roman Catholic. Office: State Capitol Jefferson City MO 65101*

WIGGINS, RONALD DALE, advt. mgr.; b. Peoria, Ill., Jan. 1, 1953; s. Dale E. and Vivian A. (Bennett) W.; B.F.A. with honors (Champion Imagination scholar), Carnegie-Mellon U., 1975; fellow in Printmaking, Exeter (Eng.) Coll. Art, 1972-73; m. Nancy A. Tupa, June 18, 1977; children—Matthew D., Rebecca E. Designer, Bob Juzenas Graphis, Cleve., 1975-76, Epstein & Szilagyi, Cleve., 1976-77; asso. creative dir. Mills Hall Walborn Advt., Cleve., 1977-78; advt. mgr. Childers Products Co., Cleve., 1978—; cons. corp. communications planning Continental Alloy Steel Corp. Mem. Phi Kappa Phi. Roman Catholic. Home: 1655 Crest Rd Cleveland Heights OH 44121 Office: 23350 Mercantile Rd Beachwood OH 44122

WIITALA, STEVE, state legislator; b. Oakland, Calif., Jan. 27, 1942; B.S., No. State Coll., Aberdeen, S.D.; postgrad. U. Nebr., Omaha; m. Sheryl Kerchal, Aug. 18, 1968. Tchr. history Westside High Sch.; mem. Nebr. Legislature, 1980—. Chmn. bd. trustees SID; chmn. bd. dirs. Escalante Hills Property Owners Assn. Office: Westside High Sch 87th and Pacific St Omaha NE 68114*

WIKIERA, EDWARD STANLEY, physician; b. Detroit, Dec. 16, 1918; s. Stanley and Bernice (Kubik) W.; B.S., Wayne State U., 1940, M.D., 1944; m. Josephine Warchol, June 14, 1942. Intern, Woman's Hosp., Detroit, 1944-45; gen. resident Detroit Receiving Hosp., 1947, resident in dermatology, 1949-51; resident dermatology VA Hosp., Detroit, 1948; pvt. practice dermatology, Detroit, 1952-56, Dearborn, Mich., 1956—; cons. dermatology Oakwood Hosp., Alexander Blain Hosp., Annapolis Hosp., Wayne, Mich., Delray Gen. Hosp., Outer Drive Hosp., Ford Motor Co. Mem. Nat. Com. for Immigration Reform, 1966, President's Com. on Immigration Reform. Served to capt. AUS, 1945-47. Diplomate Am. Bd. Dermatology and Syphilology, PanAm. Med. Assn. Fellow Am. Acad. Dermatology and Syphilology, Am. Geriatrics Soc.; mem. AMA, Mich., Wayne County med. socs., N.Y. Acad. Scis., N.Am. Clin. Dermatol. Soc., Internat. Soc. Tropical Dermatology, Assn. Am. Med. Colls., Mich. Assn. Professions, Nat. Med. and Dental Assn. Am., Med. Dental Arts Club, Wayne State Alumni Assn., Phi Beta Pi, Alumni Phi Beta Pi. Clubs: Great Dane of America (Conn.); Deutche-Doggen of Germany; Great Dane of Gt. Britain. Home: 17400 West Outer Dr Dearborn Heights MI 48127 Office: 15120 Michigan Av Dearborn MI 48126

WIKNER, IVAN ARNOLD, agronomist; b. Pipestone, Minn., Feb. 16, 1931; s. Ralph Otto and Elsie Marie (Peterson) W.; B.S., Iowa State U., 1952, M.S., 1959; m. Genevieve K. Wikner, Sept. 14, 1950; children—Susan, Steven, Sandra, Scott. County extension dir. Butler County, Iowa, 1957-59, extension area agronomist Iowa State U., 1959-63; prodn. agronomist Pioneer Hi-Bred Internat., Inc., Johnston, Iowa, 1963-65, area agronomist, 1965-67, agronomist, mgr. agronomy service dept., 1967—; cons. agronomic mgmt. Troop treas. Boy Scouts Am., 1971—; leader, 4H, 1970-75. Served with USAF, 1952-54. Mem. Am. Soc. Agronomy, Alpha Zeta, Epsilon Sigma Phi. Republican. Lutheran. Club: Rotary. Home: 6775 NW Trail Ridge Dr Des Moines IA 50323 Office: 7000 Pioneer Pkwy Johnston IA 50131

WIKOFF, VIRGIL CORNWELL, state legislator, gen. contractor; b. Decatur, Ill., Feb. 6, 1927; s. Virgil L. and Grace (Cornwell) W.; B.S., U. Ill., 1951; m. Ruth Helen Moore, Aug. 23, 1947; children—Terrill Joanne (Mrs. Robert G. Bolduc), Patricia Suzanne (Mrs. Gregory D. Bolton). Formed Lyman-Wikoff, Inc., Champaign, Ill., 1952, pres., 1952—, owner, 1965—; mem. Ill. Ho. of Reps. from 52d Dist., 1976—; former chmn. adv. council Ill. Dept. Local Govt. Affairs; mem. Champaign City Council, 1963-67, mayor, 1967-75; mem. Cities and Villages Municipal Problems Commn. of Ill. Served with USNR, 1945-46, 51-52. Named Outstanding Jaycee in Ill., 1959, Outstanding Jaycee State Dir., 1960, 1 of 10 Outstanding Young Men in Community, 1961, Outstanding Jaycee Nat. Dir., 1963. Mem. Central Ill. Builders Assn. (pres.), Ill. Mcpl. League (v.p. 1968-71, pres. 1972-73, chmn. com. implementation new constn.), Central Ill. Mayors Assn. (treas. 1968, pres. 1970-71), Jr. Chamber Internat. (life), Champaign-Urbana Jr. C. of C. (life), Champaign C. of C. (v.p. 1965), Am. Arbitration Assn. (panelist), Urban League. Presbyterian. Clubs: Hi-12 (Champaign-Urbana); Masons, Shriners, Moose, Kiwanis. Home: 2120 Noel Dr Champaign IL 61820 Office: PO Box 781 Champaign IL 61820

WIKSTROM, MARILYN, educator; b. Defiance, Ohio, Mar. 1, 1935; d. Otho Webster and Orva Mildred (McCague) Mansfield; B.S., Defiance Coll., 1957; M.S., No. State Coll., 1968; Ed.D., U. S.D., 1978; m. Gunnar Wikstrom, Jr., May 16, 1959; children—Jeffrey Alan, Daryl Lyn, Milton Curtis, Byron Kent. Tchr. public schs., Ohio, N.Y., Conn., Ariz., 1955-71; grad. instr. U. S.D., Vermillion, summer, 1975; cons. talented/gifted program Arrowhead Area Edn. Assn., Ft. Dodge, Iowa, 1974-81; mem. faculty Buena Vista Coll., Storm Lake, Iowa, 1972—, asso. prof., 1978—, chmn. edn., psychology and phys. edn., 1980—. Mem. Am. Field Service Com., Storm Lake, 1980—. Colls. of Mid-Am/N.W. Area Project-Evaluations & Redesigned Courses for Adult Learners grantee, 1981—; CMA/Lilly faculty devel. grantee, 1981-82. Mem. Internat. Reading Assn., Iowa Reading Assn., Buena Vista-Cherokee-Pocahantas Reading Assn., Assn. for Supervision and Curriculum Devel., Nat. Council for Social Studies, Iowa Council for Social Studies, Phi Delta Kappa. Democrat. Club: Buena Vista Women. Contbr. articles to profl. jours. and poetry publs. Home: 915 Russell St Storm Lake IA 50588 Office: PO Box 101 Buena Vista Coll Storm Lake IA 50588

WILBANKS, GEORGE DEWEY, obstetrician, gynecologist, gynecologic oncologist, med. coll. adminstr.; b. Gainesville, Ga., Feb. 24, 1931; s. George Dewey and Ruth Lucille (Chamblee) W.; A.B., Duke, 1953, M.D., 1956; m. Evelyn Freeman Rivers, July 31, 1954; children—George Rivers, Wayne Freeman. Resident instr. Duke U. Med. Center, Durham, N.C., 1961-62, asso., 1964-65, asst. prof., 1965-70, asso. prof., 1970—, dir. div. gynecol. oncology, 1968-70; clin. instr. Okla. Sch. Medicine, Oklahoma City, 1963-64; prof., chmn. Rush Med. Coll. Rush Presbyn. St. Lukes Med. Center, Chgo., 1970—; pres. Womens Health Cons. Mem. Assn. Chgo. Gynecol. Oncologists (pres. 1975-77), Am. Soc. Clin. Oncology, Soc. Surg. Oncology, Am. Soc. Colposcopy and Cervical Pathology (pres. 1975-77), Am. Gynecol. Soc., Soc. Gynecol. Oncologists, Soc. Pelvic Surgeons, Am. Assn. Obstetricians Gynecologists, Am. Coll. Obstetricians and Gynecologists, A.C.S. Home: 39 E Elm St Chicago IL 60611 Office: Rush Presbyterian St Lukes Medical Center 1753 W Congress Pkwy Chicago IL 60612

WILBURN, LINNIE THOMAS, JR., hosp. exec.; b. Pocahontas, Va., Dec. 20, 1928; s. Linnie Thomas and Mary Antonia (Suppee) W.; B.S. in Indsl. Engring., Va. Poly. Inst., 1951; m. Sanda Lee Griffith, May 31, 1952; children—Annette Kathleen, Teresa Dawn, Thomas Kevin, Lauri Ann, Casey Shawn. Credit mgr. Universal C.I.T. Credit Corp., N.Y.C., 1951-55; product engr. Allison div. Gen. Motors Corp., Indpls., 1955-59, process engr. Delco div., Rochester, N.Y., 1959-60; indsl. engr. N.Y. Central System, Indpls., 1960-61; various positions to v.p. Community Hosp. of Indpls., Inc., 1961-71; with Bethesda Hosp. and Deaconess Assn., Cin., 1971—, pres., chief exec. officer, 1976—; preceptor Xavier U. Grad. Program; trustee, chmn. policy devel. com. Health Systems Agy.; chmn. planning com. Greater Cin. Hosp. Council; pres. Assn. Home Care Agys., Cin. Chmn. Greater Cin. United Appeal Hosp. Div., 1977; interdist. exec. com. Cath. Archdiocese of Indpls., 1970—; pres. South Dist. Sch. Bd., 1st Parish Council of St. James the Greater Catholic Ch.; co-chmn. Archbishop's Fund Drive, All Saints Ch., Cin., 1978. Recipient William G. Follmer merit award, 1977; named Preceptor of Year, Xavier U. Sch. Hosp. Adminstrn., 1979. Mem. Am. Coll. Hosp. Adminstrs., Am. Hosp. Assn., Ohio Hosp. Assn. (treas.), Am. Inst. Indsl. Engrs., Hosp. Mgmt. Systems Soc., Hosp. Fin. Mgmt. Assn. Democrat. Clubs: Kenwood Country, Rotary, Bankers (Cin.), K.C. Contbr. to Hospital Systems Improvement Through Industrial Engineering, 1963. Home: 4903 Twinbrook Ct Cincinnati OH 45242 Office: 619 Oak St Cincinnati OH 45206

WILCKE, HAROLD LUDWIG, ret. food co. exec.; b. Clinton County, Iowa, Aug. 5, 1906; s. Christian H. and Emily (Peterson) W.; B.S., Iowa State U., 1927, M.S., 1932, Ph.D., 1935; m. Esther Goodwin, June 10, 1930; children—Janet Louise, Carol Esther. With Meridian (Miss.) Grain & Elevator Co., 1927-29; asst. and asso. prof. Iowa State U., Ames, 1929-36, prof., 1936-46; asst. dir. research Ralston Purina, St. Louis, 1946-61, v.p., dir. research, 1961-71, cons., 1971—; pres. Agrl. Research Inst., 1966-67; mem. agr. bd. Nat. Acad. Scis.-NRC, 1966-72. Served with U.S. Army, 1943-46. Fellow AAAS, Am. Soc. Animal Sci., Poultry Sci. Assn.; mem. Am. Inst. Nutrition, Am. Chem. Soc., Am. Oil Chemists Soc., Am. Soc. Animal Sci., N.Y. Acad. Sci., Nat. Cottonseed Products Assn., Poultry Sci., World's Poultry Sci., Sigma Xi, Phi Kappa Phi, Gamma Sigma Delta, Alpha Zeta. Editor or co-editor 4 vols. on food sci.; contbr. articles to profl. jours. Home: 1114 Brookhurst Dr Kirkwood MO 63122

WILCOX, CARL LEE, educator; b. Bassett, Nebr., May 11, 1951; s. Raymond Arthur and Beverly Jean (Johnson) W.; B.S., U. Nebr., 1973, M.S., 1979. Tchr. vocat. agr. Plainview (Nebr.) Jr.-Sr. High Sch., 1973-75; tchr. vocat. agr., adult edn. coordinator Rock County High Sch., Bassett, Nebr., 1975—. Active Bassett Community Improvement Program Com., 1976—. Mem. Am. Vocat. Assn., Nebr. Vocat. Assn., Nat. Vocat. Agr. Assn., Nebr. Vocat. Agr. Assn. (Dist. IV Outstanding Young Mem. 1978, dist. sec.-treas. 1980-82), NEA, Nebr. Edn. Assn. (state communications commn. 1980-82). Clubs: Lions (dist. officer 1980-82, zone officer 1980-81), Masons, Shriners. Home: North Route Newport NE 68759 Office: Rock County High Sch Bassett NE 68714

WILCOX, GARTH EUGENE, educator, investment co. exec.; b. Laona, Wis., Aug. 30, 1923; s. Garth Lewis and Geneva Marie W.; B.S., U. Wis., Stout, 1951, M.S., 1967, postgrad. 1972-79; m. Buelah F. DeLong, Dec. 20, 1946; children—Larry B., Thomas G. Tchr. woodcraft, drafting Tomahawk (Wis.) High Sch., 1951—; community services coordinator Nicolet Coll., Rhinelander, Wis., 1965—; coordinator local vocat. edn., 1972-79; pres. WTP Investment Corp., Tomahawk, Wis., 1976—. Mem. nomination com. Methodist Ch. Served with USMCR, 1941-45; Guam, Bougainville, Iowa Jima. Mem. Tomahawk Edn. Assn., Central Wis. Edn. Assn., Wis. Edn. Assn., NEA, Wis. Indsl. Edn. Assn., Wis. Edn. Assn. (council), Wis. Assn. Secondary Vocat. Adminstrs., Wis. Indsl. Edn. Assn. Adminstrs., Am. Legion, U. Wis. Stout Alumni Assn. (life), Phi Delta Kappa, Epsilon Phi Tau. Home: Route 1 Box 359 Tomahawk WI 54487 Office: High Sch E King's Rd Tomahawk WI 54487

WILCOX, HOWARD SAMUEL, pub. relations cons.; b. Indpls., Feb. 3, 1920; s. Howard Samuel and Kathryn (Dugan) W.; A.B., Ind. U., 1942; m. Joyce; children—Howard S., Donald D., David Warren, Scott Robert. With Indpls., Advt. Agy., 1946-49; exec. dir. Ind. U. Found., Bloomington, 1949-52; dir. personnel and pub. relations Indpls. Star and News, 1952-63; gen. mgr. Ariz. Republic and Phoenix Gazette, Phoenix, 1964-66; pub. relations cons., 1966—; pres. Howard S. Wilcox, Inc., Indpls., 1966—; dir. Unified Mut. Shares, Inc., Unified Funds, Inc., Wabash Life Ins. Co.; pres. sta. WFYI; dir. Gen. Employment Enterprise, Inc. Pres. Nat. Guard Assn. Ind., 1949-51. Trustee Ind. U., 1962-65; bd. dirs. Ind. U. Found., mem. exec. com.; trustee Freedoms Found. at Valley Forge, Indpls. Bar Found., Indpls. Boys Clubs. Served with inf. AUS, 1942-46; maj. gen. Res. Decorated Silver Star, Legion of Merit, Bronze Star with 2 oak leaf clusters, Purple Heart; Brit. Mil. Cross. Mem. Res. Officers Assn. U.S., Nat. Newspapers Promotion and Pub. Relations Assn. (pres. 1957-58), Ind. (dir.), Indpls. (dir.) chambers commerce, Sigma Delta Chi, Alpha Tau Omega. Mason (32 deg., Shriner). Clubs: United States Auto, Indianapolis Athletic (past dir.), Columbia, Indianapolis Press, Meridian Hills Country (Indpls.); Nat. Press. Home: 5335 Whisperwood Ln Indianapolis IN 46226 Office: Guaranty Bldg Indianapolis IN 46204

WILCOX, LAIRD MAURICE, journalist; b. San Francisco, Nov. 28, 1942; s. Laird and AuDeene Helen (Stromer) W.; student Washburn U., 1961-62, U. Kans., 1963-66; m. Eileen Maddocks, 1962 (div. 1967); children—Laird Anthony IV, Elizabeth Leone; m. 2d, Diana Brown, 1978; 1 dau., Carrie Lynn. With Fluor Corp., Ltd., 1960-62; mgr. office supply store U. Kans., 1963; editor Kans. Free Press, 1963-66; owner, operator Maury Wilcox Constrn. Co., Kansas City, Mo., 1967-70; carpenter foreman various employers, 1974—; semi-profl. genealogist, 1975-78; chief investigator Editorial Research Service, Kansas City, Mo., 1977—; lectr. various fields. Dep. sheriff Wyandotte County, Kans., 1971-75. Recipient Liberty award Congress of Freedom, 1969, 70, 71, 73, 75, 77. Fellow Augustan Soc., Acad. Police Sci.; mem. Internat. Brotherhood of Carpenters and Joiners of Am. (officer 1975—, condr. carpenter's local 61 1977—), Nat. Rifle Assn., Mensa, Internat. Legion of Intelligence, SAR, Soc. Mayflower Descs., Mil. Order Loyal Legion of U.S., Nat. Soc. Old Plymouth Colony Descs. Author: Guide To The American Left, 1970; Guide to The American Right, 1970; Psychological Uses of Genealogy, 1976; Astrology, Mysticism and The Occult, 1978; editor Jour. of Superstition and Magical Thinking, 1979—, Wilcox Report, 1979—. Founder Wilcox Collection on Contemporary Polit. Movements, U. Kans. Libraries. Home and Office: PO Box 1832 Kansas City MO 64141

WILCOX, MARK DEAN, lawyer; b. Chgo., May 25, 1952; s. Fabian Joseph and Zeryle Lucille (Tase) W.; J.D., Northwestern U., 1976; B.B.A., U. Notre Dame, 1973. Staff asst. Nat. Dist. Attys. Assn., Chgo., 1974-75; trial asst. Cook County State's Atty.'s Office, Chgo., 1975; intern U.S. Atty.'s Office, Chgo., 1975-76; law clk. Seyfarth, Shaw, Fairweather & Geraldson, Chgo., 1975-76; admitted to Ill. bar, 1976; asso. firm Lord, Bissell & Brook, Chgo., 1976—. Active campaign James Thompson for gov. Ill., 1976; mem. mgmt. com. Hastings YMCA Camp, 1979—; bd. dirs. Irving Park YMCA, 1980—; mem. bd. mgrs. YMCA Met. Chgo., 1980—. Recipient Harvard Book award, 1968, West Point Leadership award, 1969; C.L.U. Mem. Am., Chgo., Ill. bar assns., Coll. Life Underwriters, Beta Gamma Sigma. Episcopalian. Clubs: Execs. Chgo., Nat. Monogram Notre Dame, Chgo. Lions Rugby Football, Trial Lawyers of Chgo., Exec. Sportsmen's, Old Peculiars RFC. Home: 824 Hinman Ave Evanston IL 60202 Office: 115 S LaSalle St Chicago IL 60603

WILCOX, ROGER CLARK, psychologist; b. Zanesville, Ohio, Apr. 1, 1934; s. Clark Lewis and Mildred (O'Hara) W.; B.A., Ohio State U., 1959, M.A. (Nat. Inst. Mental Health fellow), 1960; Ph.D., U. Tenn., 1968; m. Joy Ann Barr, Nov. 2, 1956; children—Beth Hartigan, Wells Lewis, Judd O'Hara. Lectr. Ohio State U., Columbus, 1959-60; instr. psychology Miami U., Oxford, Ohio, 1960-62; asst. prof. Muskingum Coll., 1965-67; U.S. Office Edn. teaching fellow Wilberforce (Ohio) U., 1967-68, asso. prof. psychology, chmn. dept., 1967-69, dir. Ednl. Resources Center, 1967-69; asso. prof., chmn. dept. Calif. State U., San Luis Obispo, 1969-70; prof. psychology Ohio U., Zanesville, 1970-75; dir. adminstrn. and research Muskingum Comprehensive Mental Health Center, 1975-77; pvt. practice, Zanesville, 1977—. NSF vis. scientist Kan. Univs., 1966. Trustee, United Way Am., Goodwill Industries Am. Served with AUS, 1953-56. Mem. Am. Psychol. Assn., Sigma Xi. Author: The Psychological Consequences of Being a Black American. Cons. editor: Psychological Reports, Perceptual and Motor Skills. Contbr. articles to profl. jours. Home and Office: Buckingham Manse 425 Woodlawn Ave Zanesville OH 43701

WILCOX, ROSE MARIE, educator; b. Waterloo, Iowa, May 20, 1938; d. Louis T. and Agnes C. (Frost) O'Brien; B.A. in Bus. Edn., U. No. Iowa, Cedar Falls, 1964; M.A. in Bus. Edn., 1966; m. Rodney Bernard Wilcox, Aug. 11, 1970; children—Valerie Lynn, Jennifer Ann. Adult edn. tchr. Waterloo and Ames (Iowa) Community Schs., 1965-71; tchr. bus. edn. Columbus High Sch., Waterloo, 1964-67; coordinator, tchr. bus. edn. Ames Sr. High Sch., 1967—; mem. North Central Evaluation Team, 1975—. Named Outstanding Young Educator, Ames Jaycees, 1972. Mem. Ames Edn. Assn. (past officer), Iowa Edn. Assn. (past del.), NEA (life), Iowa Vocat. Assn., Am. Vocat. Assn., Iowa Office Edn. Coordinators, Phi Delta Kappa, Delta Pi Epsilon. Roman Catholic. Home: Rural Route 2 Ames IA 50010 Office: Ames High School 20th and Ridgewood Sts Ames IA 50010

WILCOX, WILLIAM HOWARD, sch. adminstr.; b. Columbus, Kans., Dec. 5, 1938; s. Floyd Howard and Opal Katharine (Miller) W.; B.S., Pittsburg State U., 1960, M.S., 1965, Ed.S., 1975; Ed.D., U. Mo., 1981; m. Miriam Catharine Malcolm Cummins, Feb. 8, 1971; children—Denise Catharine, Mary Janis, John Timothy, Miriam Dee. Tchr., Cherokee High Sch., 1960, St. Paul High Sch., 1961-63, Galena High Sch., 1963-65; prin. Cherryvale (Kans.) Jr. High Sch., 1965-68, prin. sr. high sch., 1968-69, supt. schs., 1969-71; prin. high sch. Joplin, Mo., 1971-79; supt. schs. Louisiana, Mo., 1981—; chmn. adv. bd. Franklin Tech. Area Trade Sch., Joplin; asst. state dir. Com. on Accredited Non Public Schs., U. Mo., 1979-81. City chmn. Heart Fund, 1965-71. Mem. Nat. Assn. Secondary Sch. Prins., Mo. Assn. Secondary Sch. Prins., Assn. Supervision and Curriculum Devel., Am. Fedn. Musicians, Nat. Middle Sch. Assn., Assn. Am. Sch. Adminstrs., Phi Delta Kappa, Kappa Delta Pi, Phi Alpha Theta. Republican. Methodist. Clubs: Lions, Exchange, Rotary, Elks. Home: 700 10th St Forest Hill Boonville MO 65233 Office: 218 Hill Hall U Mo Columbia MO 65211

WILDASIN, DAVID EARL, economist, educator; b. Willimantic, Conn., Dec. 2, 1950; s. H.L. and I.M. (Fick) W.; B.A. in Econs., U. Va., 1972; Ph.D. in Econs., U. Iowa, 1976; m. Kathleen Ann Preslin, Aug. 10, 1973; 1 son, Benjamin. Teaching and research asst. econs. U. Iowa, 1972-76; asst. prof. econs. U. Ill., Chgo., 1976-79, Ind. U., Bloomington, 1979—. Mem. Am. Econ. Assn., Econometric Soc., Nat. Tax Assn., Tax Inst. Am. Contbr. articles to profl. jours. Office: Dept of Economics Indiana University Bloomington IN 47405

WILDE, JOHN RAMSEY, III, textile co. exec.; b. Detroit, Oct. 22, 1940; s. John Ramsey, Jr. and Katherine Eleanor (Harrigan) W.; B.S. in Engring., U. Detroit, 1963; M.B.A., Stanford U., 1967; m. Karleen M. Marxen, June 19, 1965; children—Kathleen T., Nicole D., Rachel E. Engr., Martin Marietta Corp., Denver, 1963-65; sr. cons. Touche Ross & Co., Milw., 1967-72; v.p. mktg. Borg Textiles Corp. subs. Bunker Ramo Co., Oakbrook, Ill., 1972—; instr. capital budgeting U. Wis. Exec. Extension. Chmn. publicity com. Mukwanago Sch. Dist. Bd. Edn., 1977-78. Recipient Citizenship and Scholarship award Am. Legion, 1963; Aircraft Design award Bendix Corp., 1963. Home: 524 Walker Hinsdale IL 60521 Office: 900 Commerce Dr Oakbrook IL 60521

WILDER, BILL RALPH, educator; b. Dallas, Aug. 17, 1935; s. Oran Ralph and Dorothy Mae (Tibbetts) W.; B.S., Central Mich. U., 1960, M.A., 1963; postgrad. Mich. State U.; m. Elna Lou Forsten, Sept. 6, 1955; children—Becky, Belnda, Barbara, Michael, Mark. Tchr. math. Public Schs., Weidman (Mich.), 1960-62, Harbor Beach (Mich.), 1962-63; asst. high sch. prin. Public Schs., Pinconning (Mich.), 1963-67; high sch. prin. Public Schs. Tawas (Mich.), 1967-69; high sch. prin. Public Schs. Evart (Mich.), 1969-79, tchr. math., 1979—. Asso. grand guardian Internat. Order Job's Daus., 1979-80; chmn. Recreation Commn., Evart, 1977-79. Served with USAF, 1952-56. Recipient numerous hon. memberships in various chpts. Job's Daus., 1979-80. Mem. Mich. Assn. Secondary Sch. Prins., Nat. Assn. Secondary Sch. Prins., Assn. Supervision and Curriculum Devel. Methodist. Clubs: Lions (pres. 1974-75), Masons (past master), Order of the Eastern Star (past patron), Shriners. Home: 127 N Hemlock Evart MI 49631 Office: 321 N Hemlock Evart MI 49631

WILDER, ETHEL VIRGINIA, food products co. tng. exec.; b. St. Louis, July 13, 1919; d. John Roderick and Nellie O. (Daniel) W.; student U. Mo., 1941, Washington U., St. Louis, 1946-47. Personnel interviewer Ralston Purina Co., St. Louis, 1945-47, sec., 1947-49, pricing specialist, 1949-54, mgr. clerical services, 1954-64, coordinator office planning services, 1964-68, asst. dir. ops. improvement, 1968-72, asst. dir. corp. tng. and devel., 1972-78, mgr. edn. and tng., 1978—; instr. continuing edn. seminars U. Mo., St. Louis, 1970-77, Washington U., St. Louis, 1970-78, Fontbonne Coll.,

1968-69; mem. adv. council South County Tech. High Sch., 1972-78; exec. v.p. Adult Edn. Council, 1979-80. Bd. mem. Vanderschmidt Sch. Mem. Am. Soc. Tng. and Devel., Creative Edn. Found., Women's Commerce Assn., Improvement thru Involvement, Adminstrv. Mgmt. Soc. (pres. 1971-72), Altrusa Internat. Republican. Presbyterian. Office: 835 S 8th St Saint Louis MO 63188

WILDER, JAMES BENJAMIN, pub. co. exec.; b. Hernando, Miss., Aug. 12, 1938; s. Ira and Arzelia (Alexander) W.; B.S., Tenn. State U., 1961; postgrad., Loyola U., Chgo., 1961, Chgo. Tchrs. Coll., 1962-64; M.A., Roosevelt U., 1970; m. Jeadenia G. Nelson, Oct. 10, 1964; children—Jason B., Joan G. Tchr. elem. sch., Chgo., 1961-67; supportive service coordinator and counselor Drake Vocat. Sch., Chgo., 1967-68; sales rep. Follett Ednl. Corp., Chgo. and Washington, 1968-70; sales rep. Ginn and Co./Xerox, Arlington Heights, Ill., 1970-74, sales mgr., 1974-78, mktg. mgr., 1978-80, Midwest regional mgr., 1980—. Pres., Earhart Local Sch. Council, 1967-68. Mem. Profl. Bookmen Am. (treas.), Kappa Alpha Psi (recipient awards 1975-76, 80). Methodist. Address: Ginn and Co 450 W Algonquin Rd Arlington Heights IL 60005

WILDER, JEAN SPAULDING, nurse; b. N.Y.C., Jan. 17, 1920; d. Forrest Brisbin and Genevieve Anderson (Pierson) Spaulding; student Smith Coll., 1937-38; Iowa State U., 1938-40; B.S.N., State U. Iowa, 1970; m. Henry Peacock Wilder, Feb. 22, 1941; children—Priscilla, John Alexander. Margo. Staff nurse Pub. Health Nursing Assn. of Linn County, Cedar Rapids, Iowa, 1970-75; spl. edn. nurse Monroe Developmental Center, Grant Wood area Edn. Agy., Cedar Rapids, Iowa, 1975—. Bd. dirs. YWCA, Cedar Rapids, 1973—, pres., 1976-79; adv. bd. Linn County Assn. for Retarded Citizens' 1977-79; adv. bd. Y-Crest Home, 1976-79. Recipient Service award, Linn County Assn. for Retarded Citizens, 1977. Mem. Am. Nurses Assn., Iowa Nurses Assn., Am. Assn. Mental Deficiency, Grant Wood Edn. Assn., Iowa Edn. Assn., Nat. Assn. Pediatric Nurse Assos./Practitioners. Presbyterian (elder, deacon). Contbr. articles to profl. jours. Home: 163 23d Street Dr SE Cedar Rapids IA 52403 Office: 3200 Pioneer Ave SE Cedar Rapids IA 52403

WILDER, KEVEN CARNEY, ednl. TV exec.; b. Chgo., Jan. 27, 1949; d. William James and Kyle (Adams) Carney; student Smith Coll., 1966-68; A.B. cum laude, Radcliffe Coll., 1970; J.D., Boston U., 1974; m. Nicholas F. Wilder, Sept. 8, 1973. Admitted to Mass. bar, 1974, N.Y. bar, 1976; v.p. Manhattan Cable TV, Inc. subs. Time, Inc., N.Y.C., 1976-79; corp. sec. Field Enterprises, Chgo., 1979-80; asst. to pres. for telecommunications planning WTTW Channel 11, Chgo., 1980—. Recipient Young Women Achievers award N.Y. chpt. YWCA, 1976. Office: 5200 St Louis St Chicago IL 60625

WILDER, ROBERT ANDREW, communications co. exec.; b. Holly, Mich., Nov. 6, 1930; s. Andrew J. and Gladys M. (Skinner) W.; student Depauw U., 1963, Ind. U., 1965-69, Upper Iowa U., 1974-80; cert. U. Mich., 1965. Profl. baseball player Washington Senators, 1950-52; installation technician Western Electric Co., Orlando, Fla., 1953-54; installer foreman Stromberg Carlson div. Gen. Dynamics Corp., Rochester, N.Y., 1954-62, service engr., 1956-58, coordinating supr., 1958-62; gen. mgr. Hendricks Telephone Corp. (name changed to Communications Corp. of Ind.), Roachdale, 1962-75, v.p., dir., 1962-75; regional mgr. Telephone and Data Systems, Inc., Roachdale, 1975—, v.p. ops. of subsidiaries in Ind., Mich. and Ohio, 1975—. Chmn. exec. com. Wabash Valley council Boy Scouts Am., 1964-68; pres. Roachdale Devel. Corp., 1965-72. Served with USN, 1947-50. Mem. Independent Telephone Pioneers Assn., Ind. Telephone Assn. (pres. 1973-75, hon. dir. 1979—), U.S. C. of C., U.S. Independent Telephone Assn. (chmn. ins. com. 1972-74), Ind. Rural Urban Telephone Assn. (pres. 1973-75), Ind. State C. of C., Indpls. Press Club, Ind. Soc. of Chgo., VFW, Am. Legion, Ind. State Sheriff's Assn. Clubs: Masons, Shriners; Lions (pres. 1968-70, Optimists (Roachdale); Order Eastern Star. Democrat. Office: PO Box 248 Roachdale IN 46172

WILDER, WILLIAM CLYDE, educator; b. Dekalb County, Ind., June 23, 1934; s. William Lehr and Berniece Irene (Hart) W.; B.S., Purdue U., 1957; M.S., St. Francis Coll., 1963; m. S. Evelyn Fulmer, June 2, 1962; children—Lisa, David. Instr., Coesse (Ind.) High Sch., 1957-58; instr. vocat. agr., dept. head agr. Columbia City (Ind.) Joint High Sch., 1958—; state chmn. Ind. Jr. Hort. Assn., 1972—. Mem. Am. Vocat. Assn., Nat. Vocat. Agrl. Tchrs. Assn., NEA, Ind. Vocat. Assn., Ind. Vocat. Agr. Tchrs. Assn., Ind. State Tchrs. Assn., Whitley County Tchrs. Assn. Republican. Mem. Ch. of Christ. Club: Kiwanis (dir. 1970-72). Office: 600 N Whitley St Columbia City IN 46725

WILDERMAN, EUGENE JOSEPH, mfg. engr.; b. Evansville, Ind., Apr. 17, 1941; s. Walter Theodore and Cecelia Frances (Sammet) W.; A.A., Allan Hancock Jr. Coll., 1962; B.S.E.E., U. Evansville, 1969; M.B.A., 1973; m. Barbara Theoann Fenner, May 16, 1964; children—Sharon, Raymond, Janeen, Terry. Instrumentation technician Airesearch Mfg. Corp., Los Angeles, 1963-68; electronic engr. Gen. Electric Co., Owensboro, Ky., 1969-75; electronic engr. King Radio Corp., Olathe, Kans., 1975-77; sr. mfg. engr. Harris Corp., Quincy, Ill., 1977—. Served with USAF, 1959-63. Mem. Sigma Pi Sigma, Eta Kappa Nu. Roman Catholic. Clubs: K.C. (fin. sec. 1970-75), United Commercial Travelers. Home: 5006 Sunview Dr Quincy IL 62301 Office: 30th and Wisman Ln Quincy IL 62301

WILDI, BERNARD SYLVESTER, chemist; b. Columbus, Ohio, May 23, 1920; s. Adolph Jasper and Mary Catherine (Meyers) W.; B.S., Ohio State U., 1943, Ph.D., 1948. NRC fellow, Harvard U., Cambridge, Mass., 1948-49; NIH fellow, Bethesda, Md., 1963-64; research chemist Nat. Def. Council, Columbus, 1943-44, Manhattan Project, Los Alamos, N.Mex., 1944-46; asst. prof. chemistry Fla. State U., Tallahassee, 1949-50; research chemist, group leader Monsanto Chem. Co., St. Louis, 1950-63, research mgr., 1964-69, distinguished fellow, 1969—; faculty Wright-Patterson U./Ohio State U. Br., Columbus, 1959-61; cons. in field. Chmn., Dayton sect. Am. Chem. Soc., 1956-57. Served with U.S. Army, 1945-46. Recipient Silver Beaver, Boy Scouts Am., 1967. Mem. Am. Chem. Soc., Royal Soc. Chemistry - London, Swiss Chem. Soc., AAAS, Sigma Xi, Phi Beta Kappa. Roman Catholic. Contbr. articles to profl. jours.; patentee in field. Home: 1234 Folger St Kirkwood MO 63122 Office: 800 N Lindbergh Blvd Saint Louis MO 63146

WILDRIDGE, SHARON KAY, coal co. ofcl.; b. Indpls., Mar. 13, 1950; d. Herbert Oliver and Nora Betty (Shamey) Otterbein; m. Charles Lyman Wildridge, Jr., May 29, 1969. Fin. analyst Ind. Nat. Bank, Indpls., 1972-73; asst. mgr. inventory control Clarklift of Ind., Inc., Indpls., 1973-75; land planning analyst AMAX Coal Co., Indpls., 1975-77, asst. to sr. v.p., 1977—. Co-chmn. Indpls. Bus. Found. Recipient cert. of merit Am. Mgmt. Assn., 1980. Mem. Am. Bus. Women's Assn., Indpls. Mgmt. Assn. Lutheran. Contbr. articles to mags. including Ladies Home Jour., Cosmopolitan, Glamour. Office: 105 S Meridian St Indianapolis IN 46225

WILEMAN, WALLACE KARL, mech. engr.; b. Chgo., Apr. 3, 1919; s. Bernard Thomas and Ethel Evangline (Townsend) W.; M.E., U. Buffalo, 1952; m. Lorene Taressa McMain, June 27, 1959; children—Steven, William, John, Cecil. With Stewart Warner Corp., Chgo., 1950-53; with Nachman Corp., Chgo., 1954-64, gen. supt., 1960-64; with Rowe Industries, Inc., Toledo, 1964-71, indsl. relations dir., 1968-70; chief mfg. engr. Turner Mfg. Co., Chgo., 1971-72; with Northwestern Meml. Hosp., Chgo., 1972-73, dir. plant ops., 1972-73; exec. engr. Meml. Hosp. of Dupage County, Elmhurst, Ill., 1973-80, dir. phys. plant improvement, 1980—. Served with U.S. Army, 1941-45. Recipient Engr. of Yr. award State of Ill., 1981. Mem. Nat. Safety Council (chmn. standard and codes), Midwest Area Health Care Safety (chmn. bd. govs.), Nat. Assn. Power Engrs. (pres. Ill. state assn.), Am. Inst. Plant Engrs., Central Engring. Soc., Assn. Energy Engrs., Nat. Fire Protection Assn., Nat. Inst. for Uniform Licensing Power Engrs. (vice chmn. bd. examiners). Home: 1317 Fargo Ave Chicago IL 60626 Office: 200 Berteau Ave Elmhurst IL 60126

WILEN, WILLIAM WAYNE, educator; b. Phila., Mar. 31, 1943; s. William Harold and Elsie Josephine (Koivisto) W.; B.S. in Edn., Shippensburg (Pa.) State Coll., 1965; M.Ed., Towson (Md.) State Coll., 1969; D.Ed., Pa. State U., 1973; postgrad. U. Akron, 1977; m. Kathryn Lee Nedley, Aug. 14, 1965; children—Leslie Ann, Andrew William. Social studies tchr. N.E. High Sch., Pasadena, Md., 1965-69; instr. edn. Kent (Ohio) State U., 1970-74, asst. prof., 1974-79, asso. prof., 1979—; vis. prof. S.E. Mo. State U., Cape Girardeau, summer 1975, Castleton (Vt.) State Coll., summers 1976-79; speaker, cons. in areas of social studies edn. and instructional methods and analysis. Cert. secondary social studies tchr., Ohio, Pa., Md.; cert. social studies supr., Ohio. Mem. Nat. Council Social Studies, Ohio Council Social Studies (pres. 1979-80), Assn. Tchr. Educators, Assn. Supervision and Curriculum Devel., AAUP, Phi Delta Kappa. Contbr. articles to profl. publs. Home: 607 Yacavona Dr Kent OH 44240 Office: 404 White Hall Kent State U Kent OH 44242

WILENSKY, WOLF, mathematician, educator; b. Chgo., July 24, 1943; s. Aaron and Anna W.; B.S., Roosevelt U., 1967; Asso. Hebrew Lit., Jewish U. Am., Hebrew Theol. Coll., 1977; M.A., Loyola U., Chgo., 1980, also postgrad. Tchr. math. Amundsen High Sch., Chgo., 1969-72, Wells High Sch., Chgo., 1975—; tchr., chmn. math. dept. Cooley Vocat. High Sch., Chgo., 1973-74; ednl. sponsor winners in Chgo. Public Sch. Sci. Fairs. Recipient commendation U.S. Steel Corp., 1975. Mem. Nat. Council Tchrs. Math., Assn. Supervision and Curriculum Devel., Ill. Council Tchrs. Math. Club: B'nai B'rith. Home: 6227 N California Ave Chicago IL 60659

WILETSKY, MARY ELLEN, advt. agy. exec.; b. Milw., Mar. 7, 1939; d. Milton J. and Sara M. (Meyers) Geisenfeld; student U. Wis., 1957; Asso. in Applied Sci. with honors, Waukesha County Tech. Inst., 1979; m. Mary Geisenfeld, May 1, 1965; children—Elizabeth, Mark. Sec., Brust & Brust, Milw.; with Beacon Electronics, Milw.; asst. media coordinator Standard Theatres, Milw.; asso. producer WISN-TV, Milw., to 1965; pres. M & W Advt., Inc., Dousman, Wis., 1980—; account exec. Waukesha Freeman (Wis.), 1981—. Mem. Meml. Hosp. Aux. Corp., Oconomowoc, Wis., 1979-80; mem. aux. bd. Town and Country YMCA, Oconomowoc, 1980. Mem. Altrusa, Wis. Women's Network, Am. Mktg. Assn., C. of C., Waukesha County Tech. Inst. Alumni Assn. Office: Waukesha Freeman 200 Park Pl Waukesha WI 53187

WILEY, GEORGE SCHOTT, mgmt. cons.; b. Cin., May 28, 1935; s. Andrew Foust and Elizabeth (Schott) W.; B.A., Yale U., 1957; postgrad. U. Chgo., 1967-68; m. Sally Pattishall, June 22, 1958; children—Deborah, Michael, Peter. Mgr., Cummins Engine Co., Columbus, Ind., 1957-66; cons. Standard Oil Co. (Ind.), Chgo., 1966—. Mem. Republican Precinct Com., 1970—, chmn. West Deerfield Twp. Com., 1971—, mem. Lake County Rep. Exec. Com., 1974—, alt. del. Rep. Nat. Conv., 1976. Served with U.S. Army, 1958-61. Presbyterian. Clubs: Exmoor Country, Yale, Sturgeon Bay Yacht. Home: 935 Northwoods Dr Deerfield IL 60015 Office: 200 E Randolph Dr Chicago IL 60601

WILEY, VALERIE BAIRD, advt firm exec.; b. Chgo., Oct. 13, 1951; d. Robert Lee and Greta W.; B.A., Bryn Mawr Coll., 1973; m. Timothy Bard Johnson, May 9, 1981. With Leo Burnett Co., Chgo., 1974—, asso. research supr., 1977-78, research supr., 1978-79, asst. account exec., 1979-80, account exec. packaged goods, 1980—. Clubs: Bryn Mawr Coll. Chgo., Women's Athletic. Office: Leo Burnett Co Prudential Plaza Chicago IL 60601

WILGARDE, RALPH L., hosp. adminstr.; b. Phila., Jan. 8, 1928; B.A., U. Pa., 1949, M.B.A., 1954; M.Pub. Adminstrn., Cornell U., 1960. Adminstrv. asst. Jefferson Hosp., Phila., 1956-58; asst. adminstr. Frankford Hosp., 1960-64; adminstr. Irvington (N.J.) Gen. Hosp., 1964-66, Cottage Hosp., Grosse Pointe, Mich., 1966—. Served with AUS, 1950-52. Mem. Am. Hosp. Assn., Am. Coll. Hosp. Adminstrn. Home: 1217 Bishop Rd Grosse Pointe MI 48230 Office: 159 Kercheval St Grosse Pointe MI 48236

WILHELM, LUCILE AGNES, ret. ednl. adminstr.; b. Chgo., Feb. 7, 1920; B.S. in Public Health Nursing, Loyola U., Chgo., 1956, Supr. med.-surg. floor. Oak Park (Ill.) Hosp., 1946-47; staff nurse Met. Life Ins. Co. Vis. Nurse Service, Oak Park, Ill., 1947-52; supr. sch. health service Cook County Ednl. Dist. #88, Bellwood, Ill., 1952—. Mem. Ill. Assn. Sch. Nurses (pres. 1972-74, pres. Lake Shore-Calument Valley div. 1967-71), Ill. Edn. Assn., Am. Sch. Health Assn., Nat. Assn. Sch. Nurses (state sch. nurse dir. 1981—, chmn. editorial com. 1981-82, editor Sch. Nurse). Recipient cert. of recognition for outstanding services and leadership Ill. Office Edn., 1975. Registered nurse, Ill., 1946; certified pub. health nurse, Ill., 1956; certified tchr., nurse, cons., Ill., 1962; certified audiometric technician, Ill. Dept. Pub. Health. Home: 2111 S Kenilworth Ave Berwyn IL 60402

WILHELMY, BETTY ROLLINS, univ. adminstr.; b. Cin., Dec. 15, 1920; d. Otmer William and Anne Laura (Lawrence) Rollins; B.A., U. Cin., 1942; M.A., Tchrs. Coll., Columbia U., 1943; postgrad. Ohio State U., 1969-70; m. Odin Wilhelmy, Jr., Nov. 23, 1945; children—Ann Leslie, Margaret Linn, Janet Lee. Asst. to head of residence Finch Jr. Coll., N.Y.C., 1942-43; asst. to counselor women Cornell U., Ithaca, N.Y., 1943-45, asst. to dean of students, 1945-47; mem. staff personnel dept. Ohio State U. Hosp., Columbus, 1970-72; acad. counselor to graduating srs., pre-theology students Coll. Arts Scis. Ohio State U., Columbus, 1972—. Volunteer worker Columbus State Mental Hosp., 1960-70. Vice pres. Ch. Women United, Columbus and Franklin County, 1968-70; mem. Women's Assn. Columbus Symphony Orch., 1960-70; ruling elder Presbyterian Ch. Recipient certificate in adult edn. Ohio Council of Chs. Mem. Am. Personnel and Guidance Assn., Am. Coll. Personnel Assn., Smithsonian Assn., Ohio Geneal. Soc., Mortar Board, Zeta Tau Alpha, Phi Beta Kappa, Alpha Kappa Delta, Kappa Delta Pi. Clubs: Faculty Women's, Ohio State U. Faculty. Home: 2942 N Star Rd Columbus OH 43221 Office: Rm 128 Denney Hall 164 W 17th Ave Columbus OH 43210

WILKERSON, DAVID J., accountant; b. Lafayette, Ind., June 28, 1946; s. John James and Adena Irene (Booker) W.; B.S. in Acctg., Ind. U., 1972; m. Beth Gruber, Aug. 23, 1970; children—B.J., Cindy. Tax dept. staff Arthur Andersen & Co., Chgo., 1972-73, tax dept. mgr., Indpls., 1973-77; tax dir. Hillenbrand Industries, Inc., Batesville, Ind., 1977-80; tax mgr. Alexander Grant & Co., C.P.A.'s, Louisville, 1981—. Served with U.S. Army, 1966-69. Decorated Army Commendation medal; C.P.A., Ind., Ky. Mem. Am. Inst. C.P.A.'s, Louisville Estate Planning Council, Louisville Employee Benefits Council. Republican. Lutheran. Home: 1300 Glenbrook Anchorage KY 40223 Office: 1409 Citizens Plaza Louisville KY 40202

WILKERSON, JOHN RUSSELL, educator; b. Scotland Neck, N.C., Dec. 18, 1943; s. John R. and Elizabeth (Walston) W.; student Atlantic Christian Coll., 1962-63, Jacksonville U., 1963, U. Md., 1964-65; B.S. magna cum laude, Mankato State U., 1968, M.A. (Coe fellow, teaching asst.), 1970; postgrad. No. Ill. U., 1974-78, Ill. State U., 1975, Nat. Coll. Edn., 1977-79; m. Susan Goldberg, Mar. 25, 1967; 1 son, Michael. Tchr., Maine Twp. High Sch., Dist. 214, Park Ridge, Ill., 1970-72, York Community High Sch., Dist. 205, Elmhurst, Ill., 1972—; cons. Chgo. Area Writing Project, 1978—. Asst. Webelos leader Cub Scouts Am., 1981-82. Served with U.S. Army, 1964-67. Recipient Secondary Edn. award Ill. Council Econ. Edn., 1981. Mem. Am. Fedn. Tchrs. (mem. local exec. bd. 1979-80), Nat. Council Social Studies, Assn. Supervision and Curriculum Dirs., Phi Delta Kappa, Phi Alpha Theta. Jewish. Home: 557 S Fairfield St Lombard IL 60148 Office: 355 W Saint Charles Rd Elmhurst IL 60148

WILKES, DELANO ANGUS, architect; b. Panama City, Fla., Jan. 25, 1935; s. Burnice Angus and Flora Mae (Scott) W.; B.Arch., U. Fla., 1958; m. Dona Jean Murren, June 25, 1960. Designer, Perkins & Will Partnership, Chgo., 1960-63; designer, job capt. Harry Weese, Ltd., Chgo., 1963-66; project architect Fitch Larocca Carrington, Chgo., 1967-69; architect Mittelbusher & Tourtelot, Chgo., 1970-71; asso. Bank Bldg. Corp., Chgo., 1972-75; sr. asso. Charles Edward Stade & Assos., Park Ridge, Ill., 1975-77; sr. architect Consoer Morgan Architect, Chgo., 1977—, mktg. coordinator, 1980—. Design cons. Chamlin & Assos., Peru, Ill., 1969—; cons. Inst. of Crippled and Disabled, N.Y.C., 1978—; guest lectr., field trip guide Coll. DuPage, Glen Ellyn, Ill., 1968-76; guest architect med. adv. com. to Pres.'s Com. for Handicapped, 1977, 78. Mem. Businessmen for Pub. Interest, Folsom Family Assn. Am. (pres. 1978-82), SAR, AIA (chmn. public relations com. 1980), Art Inst. Chgo., Chgo. Lyric Opera Guild, Chgo. Assn. Commerce and Industry (display dir. 1979 meeting), Am. Soc. Interior Design (coordinator Info. Fair 1979), N.C. Geneal. Soc., New Eng. Hist. Geneal. Soc., Putnam County Hist. Soc., Soc. Colonial Wars, Gargoyle. Editor Folsom Bull., 1977-80; producer documentary film The Angry Minority, Menninger Found., 1978. Home: 4040 Harvey Ave Western Springs IL 60558 Office: 303 E Wacker Dr Chicago IL 60601

WILKES, HAROLD LLOYD, clergyman, tool products co. exec.; b. Haskell, Okla., July 9, 1934; s. J.J. and Daisy L. (Williams) W.; student Langston U., 1951-53; M.B.A., U. Mo., 1976; certificate U. Colo., 1970; B.S. in Theology, Midwest Sem., 1969; D.D., Am. Christian Coll., 1969, Moody Bible Coll.; m. Mary Helen Handy, Oct. 22, 1956; children—Patrician L., Cyndy Marie, Jeffrey V. Salesman, Wilkes Music Center, Kansas City, Mo., 1963-65; exec. dir., founder Wilkes & Assos., Inc., Kansas City, Mo., 1969-81; propr., mgr. Midwest K.C. Fastner Co., Kansas City, Mo., 1973—; ordained to ministry Ch. of God, 1965; pastor, Kansas City, 1965-74, 74—; pres. Midwestern Dist. Bishop's and Ministers' Council, Ch. of the Living God, Ky., Ind., Ill., Mo., Kans., 1973-76; dir. Ill. Econ. Opportunity Corp., 1977—. Mem. Govt. Affairs Com. Kans. Served with U.S. Army, 1957-59. Mem. Nat. Small Bus. Assn., Am. Mgmt. Assn., Nat. Urban League, World Council Chs., Nat. Assn. Community Devel., NAACP, Concerned Citizens Assn. (pres. 1977), Police Chaplain Assn., Columbia Alumni Assn. Democrat. Home: 5712 W 99th St Box 2561 Leawood KS 66207 Office: 8120 Holmes Rd Kansas City MO 64131

WILKINS, ARTHUR NORMAN, educator; b. Kansas City, Mo., Sept. 24, 1925; s. Arthur Miller and Jean (DeWitt) W.; A.A., Jr. Coll. of Kansas City, 1947; M.A., U. Chgo., 1950; Ph.D., Washington U., 1953. Grad. asst. Washington U., St. Louis, 1950-52; instr. English, La. State U., Baton Rouge, 1953-56; instr. English, Jr. Coll. of Kansas City, 1956-64, chmn. Dept. English, 1961-64; instr. English Metro. Jr. Coll., Kansas City, Mo., 1964-69, chmn. Dept. English, 1964-68, chmn. Div. Humanities, 1968-69; instr. English, Longview Community Coll., Lee's Summit, Mo., 1969-70, chmn. Dept. Humanities, 1969-70, dean instruction, 1970—. Mem. Mo. State Library planning com., 1980—. Served with U.S. Army, 1943-46. Washington U. fellow, 1952-53. Mem. AAUP, MLA, Nat. Council Tchrs. English, U. Chgo. Library Soc. Author: Mortal Taste, 1965; High Seriousness, 1971; The Lenore Overtures, 1975; contbr. articles to profl. jours. Home: 5724 Virginia Ave Kansas City MO 64110 Office: 500 Longview Rd Lee's Summit MO 64063

WILKINS, GEORGE THOMAS, JR., pediatrician; b. Union County, Ill., Oct. 6, 1932; s. George T. and Mary Alice (Treece) W.; B.S., U. Ill., 1953, M.D., 1957; m. Frances Dee Calvert, Dec. 18, 1955; children—George Thomas III, Geoffrey Todd, Elizabeth Ann, Cheryl Renee. Intern, Presbyn.-St. Luke's Hosp., Chgo., 1957-58; jr. resident Milw. Children's Hosp., 1958-59, sr. resident, 1959-60; practice medicine specializing in pediatrics, Decatur, Ill., 1962-65, Edwardsville, Ill., 1965—; chief of pediatrics St. Elizabeth Hosp., 1970-76; pediatric vis. staff St. Louis Children's Hosp., 1965—; mem. nursery staff St. Louis Maternity Hosp., 1965—; mem. courtesy nursery staff Jewish Hosp., St. Louis, 1968 and after; mem. staff Anderson Hosp., Maryville, Ill., 1975—, chief of staff, 1980-81; asst. instr. pediatrics Med. Sch. Wis., Milw., 1958-60; instr. in pediatrics U. Miami (Fla.) Sch. Medicine, 1960-62; asso. prof. pediatrics Washington Sch. Medicine, St. Louis, 1977—. Served with M.C., USAF, 1960-62. Named Outstanding Young Man of Year, Granite City Jaycees, 1967; diplomate Am. Bd. Pediatrics. Mem. Am. Acad. Pediatrics, Ill. (pres. 1977-78), Tri-City (pres. 1972-75), Madison County, Macon County med. socs., AMA (alt. del. 1975-78, del. 1979—), Am. Coll. Sports Physicians, St. Louis, Central Ill. pediatric socs., Alpha Chi Rho, Alpha Kappa Kappa. Presbyterian. Home: 27 Glen Echo Dr Edwardsville IL 62025 Office: 1 Glen-Ed Profl Park Edwardsville IL 62025

WILKINS, NORMA GALVIN, sch. adminstr.; b. Chgo., Oct. 16, 1930; d. John Maurice and Jean Marie (Allen) Galvin; B.Mus.Edn., Mundelein Coll., 1953; M.Ed., Northwestern U., 1958; m. Harry E. Wilkins, June 30, 1956; children—Anthony, Barry, Harry, Dan, Robert, Marc. With Chgo. Public Schs., 1953—, prin. Leslie Lewis Elem. Sch., 1977—. Active St. Dorothy Sch. Bd., Chgo., Mendal Catholic High Sch. Bd., Chgo. Mem. Assn. Supervision and Curriculum Devel., Ill. Assn. Supervision and Curriculum Devel., Ill. Prins. Assn., Samuel B. Stratton Assn., Chgo. Prins. Assn., Council Basic Edn. Roman Catholic. Office: 1431 N Leamington Ave Chicago IL 60651

WILKINSON, HAROLD WILLIAM, ednl. adminstr.; b. Alton, Ill., May 23, 1930; s. Harold Francis and Esther Matilda (Beaty) W.; student Shurtleff Coll., 1954-57; B.S., So. Ill. U., 1959, M.S. in Edn., 1974; m. Frances A. Aloisi, June 16, 1956; children—Mark Steven, Scott Anthony. Adminstrv. asst. Bunker Hill (Ill.) Community Unit 8, 1963-64, title programs dir., 1964—, asst. supt., 1971-72, prin., 1964—. Mem. Bunker Hill Library Bd., 1970-74; alderman, Bunker Hill, 1975-77. Served with USN, 1948-52. Mem. Assn. Supervision and Curriculum Devel., Nat. Assn. Secondary Sch. Prins., Am. Legion (vice-comdr. 1979-80), Ill. Elem. Sch. Assn. (bd. dirs.), Early Edn. Assn. Ill., Ill. Prins. Assn., Ill. Assn. Supervision and Curriculum

Devel., So. Ill. U.-Edwardsville Alumni Assn. Roman Catholic. Club: Kiwanis, K.C. Home: Box 201 Bunker Hill IL 62014 Office: 504 E Warren St Bunker Hill IL 62014

WILKINSON, JOHN ERCY, lawyer; b. Cherryvale, Kans., July 28, 1931; s. Alva Edward and Virgie Velma (Persinger) W.; A.A., Independence Jr. Coll., 1951; B.S., U. Kans., 1953, J.D., 1958; m. Marianne Anderson, Mar. 30, 1957; children—Thomas Martin, George Edward, Daniel John. Admitted to Kans. bar, 1958; research atty. Kans. Supreme Ct., Topeka, 1959-62; sr. law clk. to Fed. Judge George Templar, Topeka, 1962-67; partner Colmery, McClure, Funk, Letourneau & Wilkinson, Topeka, 1967-77, Wilkinson & Graves, Topeka, 1977-78, John E. Wilkinson, 1978—; franchisee Burger King Corp., 1976—; land commr. Fed. Dist. Ct., Topeka, 1968-79; lectr. appellate practice Washburn U., Topeka, 1967-73. Chmn. Topeka Housing Authority, 1973. Bd. dirs. Channel 11 Club, 1971-74. Served with AUS, 1953-55. Mem. Am., Topeka bar assns., Bar Assn. Kans. (mem. tenure, discipline and retirement of dist. judges com. 1969-74), Phi Delta Phi, Delta Sigma Pi. Lutheran. Mason (Shriner). Home: 1278 Collins St Topeka KS 66604 Office: 214 W 7th St PO Box 1794 Wilkinson Bldg Topeka KS 66601

WILKINSON, LELAND, psychologist, educator; b. Mount Kisco, N.Y., Nov. 5, 1944; s. Kirk Cook and Carolyn Ruth (Gunzer) W.; A.B., Harvard U., 1966, B.D., 1969; Ph.D. (Kent fellow), Yale U., 1975; m. Ruth Elaine VanDemark, June 23, 1967; children—Anne Marie, Caroline Cook. Statis. cons. to VA Hosp., West Haven, Conn., 1973, Yale U. Child Study Center, 1972-76, U. Chgo. project on parent health and infant devel., 1978—; instr. psychology Yale U., 1974-75, lectr. psychology, 1975-76; asst. prof. psychology U. Ill., Chgo., 1976-80, asso. prof., 1980—. Mem. Am. Psychol. Assn., Am. Statis. Assn., Psychometric Soc., Assn. for Computing Machinery. Lutheran. Contbr. articles to profl. jours.; mem. editorial bd. Applied Psycholinguistics, 1980—. Home: 1127 Asbury Ave Evanston IL 60202 Office: Dept Psychology U Illinois PO Box 4348 Chicago IL 60680

WILKINSON, RICHARD ALLEN, pressure sensitive tape mfg. co. exec.; b. Jackson, Mich., June 22, 1937; s. Clark E. and Flossie P. (Stroup) W.; A.S., Jackson Jr. Coll., 1957; B.S.B.A., Mich. State U., 1963; m. Janet Marie Helms, Sept. 12, 1959; children—Christopher, Susan. Sales engr. Walker Mfg. Co., Jackson, Mich., 1958-61; salesman Armour Co., Indpls., 1963-68, dist. sales mgr., 1971-74; sales mgr. Armak Co., Marysville, Mich., 1974-78, nat. sales mgr., 1978—. Served with U.S. Army, 1956-62. Recipient Outstanding Sales Achievement award Armour & Co., 1966. Mem. Am. Mgmt. Assn., Internat. Mgmt. Club. Republican. Roman Catholic. Clubs: K.C., Elks. Home: 3396 Timberline Dr Port Huron MI 48060 Office: 317 Kendall Ave Marysville MI 48040

WILKINSON, THOMAS ALLEN, clin. psychologist; b. Oberlin, Ohio, May 5, 1946; s. Paul Amba and Evelyn Pearl (Rugg) W.; student Ohio State U., 1964-65, John Brown U., 1965-66; B.A., Bethel Coll., 1968; M.A., Kent State U., 1973, Ph.D., 1977; m. Brenda Lou Bos, May 29, 1971; children—Kristen Louann, Alyssa Louise. Psychologist, Pine Rest Christian Hosp., Grand Rapids, Mich., 1970-72, Community House, Kent, Ohio, 1972-77, Psychology Center, Grand Rapids, 1977-80, Psychology Assos., Grand Rapids, 1980—; instr. Mercy Central Sch. Nursing, 1978-80. Mem. Am. Psychol. Assn., Christian Assn. Psychol. Studies. Republican. Mem. Christian Reformed Ch. Home: 1652 Willowbrook Jenison MI 49428 Office: Suite 205 2663 44th St SW Grand Rapids MI 49509

WILLARD, RICHARD WESLEY, motel exec.; b. Pittsburg, Kans., Nov. 4, 1929; s. Russell Orville and Vada (Robertson) W.; B.Gen. Studies, U. Nebr., Omaha, 1970. Pres. Willard & Baughman Inc., Omaha, 1966-73, Starlite and Mansard Motels Inc., Council Bluffs, Iowa, 1973—; regional coordinator Friendship Inns Internat., 1973-79. Served with AUS, 1951-54. Named Man of Year, Friendship Inns Internat., 1976. Mem. Iowa Hotel, Motel and Motor Inn Assn. (dir. 1974-78, 3d v.p. 1976-77, 2d v.p. 1977, 1st v.p. 1978), U. Nebr. Alumni Assn., Iowa Civil Liberties Union, Newberry Library (Chgo.), Am. Hotel and Motel Assn., Omaha Lodging Assn., Council Bluffs C. of C. (chmn. conv. com.). Address: 3545 Grace Saint Louis MO 63116

WILLBRANDT, BARRY WILLIAM, physician; b. Muskegon, Mich., July 22, 1947; s. G. William and Doris Ann (Barrett) W.; B.S., U. Mich., 1969, M.D., 1973; m. Diane K. Wade, May 2, 1969; children—Bradley, Katy. Intern, U. Mich., Ann Arbor, 1973, resident in pediatrics, 1973-76; practice pediatrics Pediatrics Assos., Muskegon, Mich., 1976—; mem. staff Hackley Hosp. Diplomate Am. Bd. Pediatrics. Mem. AMA, Am. Acad. Pediatrics, Phi Beta Kappa. Home: 15994 Harbor Point Spring Lake MI 49456 Office: 1470 Peck St Muskegon MI 49441

WILLEKE, JAMES STANLEY, restaurant exec.; b. Indpls., June 2, 1950; s. Stanley Herbert and Laura Jane (Bratton) W.; student Purdue U., 1972. Restaurant mgr. L-K Enterprises, Mansfield, Ohio, 1972-73; sales rep. CFS Continental, Chgo., 1973-77; v.p. in charge ops. Stan's Family Restaurants, 1977—; dir. Mansfield Restaurants, Inc., 1978—. Notary public, Ohio, 1973—; mem. Red Cross Disaster Action Team, 1978-81. Mem. Nat. Rifle Assn. (life), Fraternal Order Police, Nat. Restaurant Assn., Ohio State Restaurant Assn. (mgmt. awards 1977, 78, 79, 80), Mid-Central Ohio Restaurant Assn. (chmn. legis. com. 1980-81), Fusion Energy Found., Am. Motorcycle Assn. Home: PO Box 874 Mansfield OH 44901 Office: 924 W Fourth St Mansfield OH 44906

WILLET, GERALD L., state senator; b. Duluth, Minn., Oct. 31, 1934; m. Anita; children—Nedra, Noel, Neil, Nona. Mem. Minn. Senate, 1970—. Chmn. Legis. Commn. Minn. Resources, Legis. Audit Commn., Legis. Adv. Commn. Mem. Democratic-Farmer-Labor party. Roman Catholic. Clubs: KC, Eagles. Office: 121 State Capitol St Paul MN 55155*

WILLEY, MICHAEL SCOTT, instrumentation and controls co. exec.; b. Lima, Peru, Mar. 28, 1947 (parents Am. citizens); s. Paul A. and Marie S. (Seminary) W.; B.S., U. Maine, 1970, M.S., 1971; m. Frances Sugar Franklin, June 5, 1970; children—Julia, Mark. Lab. instr. computer sci. U. Maine, 1970-71; mgr. software services Taylor Instrument Co., Rochester, N.Y., 1972-76; mgr. systems engring. Bailey Controls Co., Wickliffe, Ohio, 1976-78, mgr. digital systems engring., 1978-79, v.p. engring., 1979—. Mem. Explorer Adv. Group, 1980-81, vis. com. Fenn Coll. Engring., 1980-81. Served to capt. C.E., AUS, 1972. Registered profl. engr., Calif. Mem. Instrument Soc. Am. (sr.), Am. Inst. Chem. Engrs., TAPPI. Home: 8653 Apple Hill Rd Chagrin Falls OH 44022 Office: Bailey Controls Co 29801 Euclid Ave Wickliffe OH 44092

WILLEY, STEPHEN ARTHUR, paper co. exec.; b. Marion, Ohio, Jan. 1, 1941; s. Robert Arthur and Harriet Ann (Nippert) W.; B.S., Bowling Green (Ohio) State U., 1963; grad. Advanced Mgmt. Program, Harvard U., 1979; m. Georgia Lynne Profusek, Sept. 4, 1965; children—Robert Arthur, II, Stephen Mathew, Laurel Anne. Mgr., Ernst & Whinney, C.P.A.'s, Cleve., 1963-72; successively asst. controller, dir. corp. planning, controller B.F. Goodrich Co., Akron, Ohio, 1972-81; v.p., controller Kimberly-Clark Corp., Neenah, Wis., 1981—. C.P.A., Ohio. Mem. Fin. Execs. Inst. Democrat. Roman Catholic. Club: Cascade. Office: Kimberly-Clark Corp Neenah WI 54956

WILLIAMS, ALFRED BRIAN, mfg. co. exec.; b. Fostoria, Ohio, Oct. 12, 1938; s. Hugh Pennel and Elizabeth (Hall) W.; B.S., Bowling Green State U., 1960; student Ohio State U., 1956-57; m. Dolores J. Shaull, June 18, 1960; children—Jeffrey, Theresa, Michael, Patricia. Market analyst, chief market analyst Republic Steel Corp., Cleve., 1967-71, asst. mgr. Market Research div., Cleve., 1971-73, asst. sales mgr. Stainless and Spl. Metals div., Massillon, Ohio, 1973-77, mgr. prodn. control Enduro div., 1977-79, asst. gen. mgr. order and prodn. planning, Cleve., 1980—. Vice pres. Jackson Twp. Little League, 1976. Presbyterian. Office: PO Box 6778 Cleveland OH 44101

WILLIAMS, ARBOR WAYNE, JR., accountant; b. Cleve., Oct. 22, 1942; s. Arbor Wayne and Jean Eloise (Wilson) W.; B.A., Kent State U., 1965; M.B.A., Case Western Res. U., 1976; m. Susan Jane Lippert, May 7, 1966. Cost analyst Cleve. div. Lamson & Sessions, 1966-70, mgr. cost accounting Bedford Heights div., 1970-76, sr. accountant Bedford Heights div., 1976-79; div. cost acctg. mgr. Ohio Nuclear, 1979—. Pres., Warner-Turney Area Residents Council, 1973-74, finance dir., 1974—. Mem. Nat. Assn. Accts., Aircraft Owners and Pilots Assn. Home: 4620 E 85th St Garfield Heights OH 44125 Office: 59100 Aurora Rd Solon OH 44139

WILLIAMS, BRENDA PAULETTE, TV reporter, anchor; b. St. Louis, July 7, 1946; d. Herman and Hattie Williams; B.J., Ohio U., Athens, 1969; postgrad. U. Mo., Columbia. Newscaster, Sta. KATZ, St. Louis, 1969-70; reporter, talk show producer/host Sta. KPLR-TV, St. Louis, 1973-74, Stas. KSD-TV and Radio, St. Louis, 1974-77; weekend anchor-reporter Sta. KMBC-TV, Kansas City, Mo., 1977—. Recipient Cert. of Appreciation St. Louis Urban League-St. Louis Sentinel, 1975; Human Relaions award Nat. Assn. Colored Women's Clubs, 1975; Documentary Reporting award Mo. Radio and TV Assn., 1979; Consumer Reporting award Mo. Dept. Consumer Affairs, 1979; selected for Am. journalists tour of Israel, Israeli Journalist Assn., 1980; Black Achiever award SCLC, 1981. Mem. Alpha Kappa Alpha (Women of Involvement award 1974).

WILLIAMS, CHARLES D., JR., business exec.; B.S. in Indsl. Personnel Supervision, No. Ill. U., M.S. in Bus. Adminstrn. Indsl. engr. Ekco Products Co., 1964-66; sr. indsl. engr. Motorola, Inc., 1966-68; corp. mgr. indsl. engring. Morton Quality Products, 1968; mgmt. cons. Price Waterhouse & Co., 1968-70; corp. asst. dir. engring. Wells Lamont Corp., 1970-72; corp. spl. projects engr. O'Bryan Bros., Inc., 1972-75; corp. engring. adminstr. Baxter Travenol Labs., Inc., 1975-80; mem. central region staff U.S. Postal Service, 1980—; pres. Chaswil Enterprises, Inc., Arlington Heights, Ill., 1978—; speaker internat. and nat. confs. in field. Mem. Am. Inst. Indsl. Engrs. (sr.; pres. No. Suburban Ill. chpt. 1979-80, chmn. mgmt. div. region VIII 1978-80, v.p. region VIII 1980—), Indsl. Mgmt. Soc., Soc. Mfg. Engrs., Methods Time Measurement Assn., U.S. Jaycees, Sigma Iota Epsilon. Contbr. numerous articles to profl. jours. Office: 2627 N Highland Ave Arlington Heights IL 60004

WILLIAMS, CHARLES VERNON, III, logistician, educator, pilot; b. York, Pa., May 26, 1940; s. Charles Vernon, Jr., and Ruth Irene (Barton) W.; B.G.S. in Bus., U. Nebr., 1974; M.A. in Logistics, Central Mich. U., Mt. Pleasant, 1977; A.A.S. in Religious Instn. Mgmt., Community Coll. of Air Force, 1977; m. Marie Carmal Felix, Mar. 20, 1973; children—Joanne, Monique Marie. Enlisted U.S. Air Force, 1958; exec. 3d AF Staff Chaplain's Office, London, 1969-70; asst. chief fin. and logistics 601 Tactical Control Wing, Wiesbaden, Germany, 1970-73; noncommd. officer-in-charge Hainerberg Chapel, Wiesbaden, 1973-74; chief fin. and logistics 2750th Air Base Wing Installation Chaplain Office, 1974-78; asst. chief budget and logistics Hdqrs. AF Logistics Command Office of Command Chaplain, Wright-Patterson AFB, Ohio, 1978-80; data communications mgr. Mead Corp., Dayton, Ohio, 1980—; mem. faculty bus. tech. Sinclair Community Coll., Capitol U. Organizer, Mil. Com. for Community Action, 1965. Decorated Meritorious Service medal, Bronze Star, AF Commendation medal; cert. profl. photographer. Mem. Am. Mgmt. Assn., Smithsonian Instn., Nat. Geog. Soc., Air Force Assn., Aircraft Owners and Pilots Assn., Internat. Pilots Assn., Internat. Word Processing Assn., S.A.M., Phylaxis Soc., Noncommd. Officers Assn., Noncommd. Officers Acad. Grads. Assn., Nat. Travel Club. Baptist. Clubs: Masons (United Supreme Council 33 deg. Masons), Shriners, Eastern Star, Order of Amaranth. Editor-in-chief, staff photographer European Masonic Quarterly, 1972-74. Home: 2174 Malvern Ave Dayton OH 45406 Office: Mead World Headquarters Courthouse Plaza NE Dayton OH 45463

WILLIAMS, CHARLES WILMOT, former mfg. co. exec., cons.; b. Detroit, Feb. 3, 1916; s. Walter Henry and Frances Preston (Churchill) W.; B.S.E. with highest honors, Princeton U., 1938; M.S.A.E., Chrysler Inst. Engring., 1940; m. Mary Helen Wendel, Oct. 19, 1940; children—James Wendel, Robert Churchill. With Chrysler Corp., Detroit, 1938-61, dir. mfg. Missile div., 1952-61; mgr. product design and mfg. research Fed.-Mogul Corp., Detroit, 1961-69, dir. research, 1969-81, mgr. spl. projects, 1981, ret., 1981; self-employed engring. cons., 1982. Registered profl. engr., Mich. Mem. Nat. Soc. Profl. Engrs., Mich. Soc. Profl. Engrs., Soc. Automotive Engrs., Engring. Soc. Detroit, AIAA. Republican. Episcopalian. Club: Princeton of Mich. Contbr. articles to profl. jours.; patentee in field. Home: 1824 Pine St Birmingham MI 48009 Office: Federal-Mogul PO Box 1966 Detroit MI 48235

WILLIAMS, CLARA JEAN WILSON, dietitian; b. Bay Springs, Miss., May 24, 1942; d. James Ernest Wilson; B.S., U. So. Miss., 1964, M.S., 1968; postgrad. Ind. U., 1976—; children—Tracy René, Terri Lynn. Tchr. secondary sci. Patton Jr. High Sch., Ft. Leavenworth, Kans., 1968-69, Colmer Jr. High Sch., Pascagoula, Miss., 1971-72; nutritionist U.S. Army Hosp., Heidelburg, Germany, 1969-71; dietitian trainee Ind. Sch. for Blind, Indpls., 1972-73, Central State Hosp., Indpls., 1973-74; dir. dept. dietetics Larue D. Carter Meml. Hosp., Ind. U. Med. Center, Indpls., 1974—, dir. dietetic traineeship program, 1976—; cons. Fairbanks Hosp. Inc. Vol. ARC, Heidelburg, 1968-71; leader Protestant Youth of Chapel, Ft. Benjamin Harrison, Ind., 1972-75. Recipient certificate of appreciation U.S. Army, 1973, 75. U. So. Miss. Grad. Ednl. grantee, 1966-67; Ind. Dept. Mental Health Grad. Ednl. grantee, 1976-77. Mem. Am. Dietetic Assn., Ind. Dietetic Assn. (exec. bd. 1975-77), Central Dist. Dietetic Assn., Marion County Mental Health Assn. Club: Sycamore Springs Golf. Office: Larue D Carter Meml Hosp 1315 W 10th St Indianapolis IN 46202

WILLIAMS, DAVID PERRY, automotive co. exec.; b. Detroit, Nov. 6, 1934; s. Marshall Sears Perry and Virginia Ballard (Hayes) W.; B.A., Mich. State U., 1956; M.B.A., Mich. State U., 1964; LL.B., LaSalle, 1978; m. Eleanor Schneider, Aug. 7, 1972; children—Tracy, Perry, David. Vice pres. sales Kelsey Hayes Co., Romulus, Mich., 1958-71; v.p. ITT, N.Y.C. 1971-76; v.p., dir. The Budd Co., Troy, Mich., 1976-79, sr. v.p.-ops., dir., 1979-80, sr. v.p., chief operating officer, dir., 1980—. Served as officer USAF, 1956-58. Mem. Soc. Automotive Engrs., Engrs. Soc. Detroit, Advanced Mgmt. Club of Mich. State U. Beta Gamma Sigma. Republican. Episcopalian. Clubs: Bloomfield Hills Country, Detroit Athletic, Yondotega, Country of Detroit, Internat. Golf (Bolton, Mass.). Home: 333 Lincoln St Grosse Pointe MI 48230 Office: The Budd Co 3155 W Big Beaver Troy MI 48230

WILLIAMS, DONALD CLINTON, mgmt. cons.; b. St. Louis, Feb. 27, 1929; s. R. Arthur and Deborah (Catlin) W.; A.B., Hamilton Coll., 1951; M.B.A., Harvard U., 1953; m. Suzanne Talbot, Aug. 10, 1957; children—Donald Clinton, Bradford H., Bruce T. Sales rep. U.S. Steel Corp., Detroit, 1957-62; gen. mgr. Mich. div. Interstate United Corp., Detroit, 1962-65; with Heidrick & Struggles, Inc., 1965-78, sr. v.p., mgr. Midwest, dir., Chgo., 1973-78; pres. Donald Williams Assos. Inc., Chgo., 1978—; dir. Cavendish Investing Ltd. Served to lt. (j.g.) USNR, 1953-56. Mem. Alpha Delta Phi. Clubs: Glen View; Chicago, Economic, Harvard Bus. Sch. (Chgo.). Home: 222 Leicester St Kenilworth IL 60043 Office: Three First National Plaza Chicago IL 60602

WILLIAMS, EDWARD DONALD, business exec.; b. Chgo., Feb. 5, 1925; s. Edward Joseph and Ann Pauline (Jochum) W.; student Loyola U., Chgo., 1946-48; Ph.B. in Journalism, Marquette U., 1950; M.S. in Journalism, Northwestern U., 1951; m. Dorothy Elizabeth Schroepel, Sept. 18, 1948; children—Lee, Marc, Gregg, Faith, Joy. Reporter-photographer Sheboygan (Wis.) Press, 1951-52; reporter Chgo. Daily News, 1952-58; reporter Chgo.'s Am., 1958-61; reporter-aviation writer Milw. Jour., 1961-74; with dept. pub. relations United Airlines, Chgo., 1974-81; with public affairs dept. Gen. Dynamics, St. Louis, 1981—. Served with USMC, 1942-46. Decorated Air medal, D.F.C. Recipient awards Air Force Assn., 1967, 71, Wis. Wing CAP, 1968, Res. Officers Assn., 1968, Air Force Res., 1973, Wis. Aviation Trades Assn., 1968, Wis. Council on Aeros., 1974. Mem. Headline Club, Chgo. Press Vets., Exptl. Aircraft Assn. (awards 1967, 69), Aircraft Owners and Pilots Assn., Aviation/Space Writers Assn. Contbr. articles to aviation jours. and popular mags.; part-time asso. editor Vintage Airplane Mag. Home: 713 Eastman Dr Mount Prospect IL 60056 Office: Public Affairs Dept Gen Dynamics Pierre Laclede Center Saint Louis MO 63105

WILLIAMS, EMORY, corp. exec., banker; b. Falco, Ala., Oct. 26, 1911; s. William Emory and Nelle (Turner) W.; A.B., Emory U., 1932; m. Janet Hatcher Allcorn, May 15, 1943; children—Nelle (Mrs. Frederick Temple), Janet (Mrs. Lawrence MacNamara), Bliss (Mrs. Howell Browne), Carol (Mrs. James Schroeder), Emory. With Sears, Roebuck & Co., 1933-75, pres. Sears, Roebuck, S.A. (Brazil), 1958-60, pres. Homart Devel. Co., 1960-67, treas. parent co., 1962-64, v.p., treas., 1964-75; chmn. bd., chief exec. officer Sears Bank & Trust Co., 1975-81; chmn. bd. Chgo. Milw. Corp., 1981—; dir. Armstrong Rubber Co., Ft. Dearborn Income Securities Inc., Bobbie Brooks, Inc., Foote Cone Belding Communications, Sears Investment Mgmt. Co., VSI Corp. Div. chmn. Chgo. Crusade of Mercy, 1962-64, gen. chmn., 1966, pres., 1976-78; chmn. Ill. Health Edn. Commn., 1968-70; pres. Adler Planetarium, 1972-75, Ravinia Festival Assn., 1972-78; pres. bd. dirs. Community Fund, 1970-73; trustee Emory U., Chgo. Community Trust, Northwestern Meml. Hosps. Served to lt. col., C.E., U.S. Army, World War II; CBI. Clubs: Piedmont Driving (Atlanta); Chicago, Old Elm, Commercial (Chgo.); Indian Hill (Winnetka, Ill.); Everglades (Palm Beach). Home: 1420 Sheridan Rd Wilmette IL 60091 Office: 401 N Michigan Ave Chicago IL 60611

WILLIAMS, EVAN E., utility exec.; b. Nelsonville, Ohio, Apr. 29, 1920; s. Evan and Harriet Louise (Hemsley) W.; B.S.E.E., Ohio U., 1950; m. Frances Virginia Helsel, June 14, 1942; children—Jeff, Lisa, Andrea, Craig, Brent, Todd. Clk., store mgr. A&P Co., 1939-40; with Columbus & So. Ohio Electric Co., Columbus, 1941—, asst. v.p.-comml., 1965-71, asst. v.p.-rates and valuation, 1971-73, v.p.-rates and valuation, 1973-77, sr. v.p.-adminstrn., 1977—; dir. Dollar Savs. Assn. Vice pres. Columbus Conv. Bur., 1969-73, treas., 1974-76, chmn., 1977-78; treas. Citizens Research, 1976-78, pres., 1980-81; active United Way. Served to capt., Signal Corps, U.S. Army, 1942-45. Presbyterian. Clubs: Kiwanis (past gov.), Masons, Order Eastern Star. Home: 2491 Sherwood Rd Columbus OH 43209 Office: 215 N Front St Columbus OH 43215

WILLIAMS, FLORENCE MILLER, librarian; b. Chgo., Jan. 27, 1934; d. Jerome J. and Florence M. (Attaway) Miller; B.Ed., Chgo. Tchrs. Coll., 1955, M.Ed., 1957; postgrad. DePaul U., 1964-65, U. Chgo., 1965, 68, Peabody Coll., 1959-60; Ph.D., Calif. Western U., Santa Ana, 1980; m. Charles E. Williams, Nov. 29, 1957; children—Ruth Edna, Alice Talise. Mem. faculty Fisk U., Nashville, 1959-60, Roosevelt U., Chgo., 1963-64; tchr.-librarian Chgo. public schs., 1955-76; reference and research librarian, central office library Chgo. Bd. Edn., 1976—. Mem. ALA, Ill. Library Assn., Chgo. Tchrs. Union, NAACP, Urban League, Phi Delta Kappa. Democrat. Methodist. Club: Dentists' Wives (past pres.). Home: 2703 S Michigan Ave Chicago IL 60616 Office: Chgo Bd Edn 228 N LaSalle St Chicago IL 60601

WILLIAMS, FRANK JAMES, JR., retail co. exec.; b. St. Louis, July 2, 1938; s. Frank James and Alberta (Klaus) W.; B.S. in Bus. Adminstrn., Washington U., 1960, J.D., 1963; student Univ. Mo. Grad. Bus. Sch., 1960; m. Alice M. Pairn, Sept. 18, 1965; children—Kimberly Ann, Andrew Scott, Renee Michelle. Admitted to Mo. bar, 1963; asso. gen. counsel May Dept. Stores Co., St. Louis, 1963-66, asst. gen.counsel, 1967-69, v.p., dir. labor relations, 1969-79, v.p. govt. and employee relations, 1979-80, v.p. public affairs, 1980—; atty., corp. sec. dept. Pet, Inc., St. Louis, 1966; lectr. to various legal and trade seminars, 1965—. Recipient Silver Plaque award Nat. Retail Mchts. Assn., 1981. Mem. Am. Bar Assn., St. Louis Met. Bar Assn., Mo. Bar, Am. Retail Fedn. (chmn. com. 1973-76), Nat. Retail Mchts. Assn. (chmn. employee relations com. 1978-79). Roman Catholic. Club: Missouri Athletic (bd. govs., 1st v.p.). Home: 5320 Casa Royale St Saint Louis MO 63129 Office: 611 Olive St Saint Louis MO 63101

WILLIAMS, G. JOSH, tng. and devel. firm exec.; b. N.Y.C., Dec. 16, 1944; s. Hubert M. and Ann (Bernaka) W.; B.A. in Indsl. Psychology, Hofstra U., 1967; M.B.A. in Mktg., Adelphi U., 1971; m. Patricia A. Pellegrino, Jan. 21, 1967; children—Kimberly, Steven, Michael. Nat. sales tng. mgr. and area sales mgr. Xerox Corp., 1967-72; nat. dir. tng. and devel. Savin Bus. Machines Corp., Valhalla, N.Y., 1972-74; nat. dir. sales promotion and advt., gen. sales mgr. Midwest area Western Union Corp., Chgo., 1974-77; gen. mgr. Tratec/McGraw-Hill, Chgo., 1977-80; pres. Skiltec, Inc., Buffalo Grove, Ill., 1980—. Mem. Am. Soc. Tng. and Devel., Am. Mktg. Assn. Republican. Roman Catholic. Club: Toastmasters. Home: 13 Victoria Ln Lincolnshire IL 60015 Office: 1111 Lake Cook Rd Buffalo Grove IL 60090

WILLIAMS, G. MENNEN, justice; b. Detroit, Feb. 23, 1911; s. Henry Phillips and Elma Christina (Mennen) W.; A.B., Princeton, 1933. J.D., Mich. Law Sch., 1936; LL.D., Wilberforce U., Mich. State U., U. Liberia, U. Mich., Aquinas Coll., Ferris Inst., St. Augustine's Coll., Western Mich. U.; H.H.D., Lawrence Inst. Tech.; hon. degree, World U.; m. Nancy Lace Quirk, June 26, 1937; children—Gerhard Mennen, Nancy Quirk (Mrs. Ketterer), Wendy Stock (Mrs. Burns). Atty., Social Security Bd., 1936-38; asst. atty. gen., Mich., 1938-39; exec. asst. to U.S. atty. gen., 1939-40; with criminal div. Dept. Justice,

1940-41; deputy dir. Mich. O.P.A., 1946-47; liquor control commr., Mich., 1948; gov. of Mich., 1949-60; asst. sec. state for African affairs, 1961-66; ambassador to Republic of Philippines, 1968-69; justice Mich. Supreme Ct., 1971—. Served from lt. (j.g.) to lt. comdr. USNR, overseas, 1942-46. Decorated Legion of Merit with Combat V; grand officer Order of Orange Nassau (Netherlands); grand comdr. Royal Order of Phoenix (Greece); Humane Band of African Redemption (Liberia); Polonia Restituta (Polish govt. in exile), also decorations from Niger, Ivory Coast and Philippines. Democrat. Author: Africa for the Africans, 1969. Address: Law Bldg Lansing MI 48901 also 1425 Lafayette Bldg Detroit MI 48226

WILLIAMS, HAZEL BROWNE, educator; b. Kansas City, Mo.; d. John Wesley and Effie Geraldine (Moten) Browne; A.B., U. Kans., 1927, M.A., 1929; M.A., Columbia, 1943; Ph.D., N.Y. U., 1953; m. Claude A. Williams, July 27, 1935 (dec.). Tchr. English high sch., Kansas City, 1927-32, counselor pub. schs., 1942-52; asst. prof. Louisville Municipal Coll., 1932-42; instr. English, N.Y. U., 1948-51; prof. English, Tenn. A & I State U., 1953-56; Fulbright exchange tchr., Vienna, Austria, 1956-57; prof. English edn. U. Mo., Kansas City, 1958-77, prof. emeritus, 1977—. Mem. exec. bd. NAACP, Kansas City, Mo. Recipient Thomas Jefferson award U. Mo., 1977; Alpha Kappa Alpha fgn. fellow, Berlin, 1930-31; faculty grantee U. Mo. Kansas City, 1965, 70. Mem. Inst. Gen. Semantics, Internat. Soc. Gen. Semantics, Nat. Council Tchrs. English (life), MLA, Mo. Tchrs. Assn., Mo. Assn. Tchrs. English, AAUP, Internat. Relations Council, YWCA (life), U. Mo. Kansas City Friends of Library (life), NAACP, Phi Beta Kappa, Phi Delta Kappa, Kappa Delta Pi, Pi Lambda Theta. Mem. A.M.E. Ch. Home: 3606 E 46th St Kansas City MO 64130 Office: Sch Edn U Mo Kansas City MO 64110

WILLIAMS, HERMETTA ELAINE, health care exec.; b. Montgomery, Ala., May 28, 1943; d. Herman and Fannye Mae (Scott) Williams; A.B.A., Central YMCA Coll., 1976; B.A., DePaul U., 1978, M.S., 1979; postgrad. Central Mich. U. Med. asst. Kaplan Med. Center, Chgo., 1963-66, Gerthard Med. Center, Chgo., 1966-67; adminstrv. asst. to dir. labs. Roosevelt Meml. Hosp., Chgo., 1967-81; asst. purchasing adminstr. Milwaukee County; resource cons. Tutorial Center, First Ch. of Deliverance, 1978-79; community resource adv. DePaul U. Sch. for New Learning, 1978-80; coordinator Am. Cancer Soc. summer scholarship program, Roosevelt Meml. Hosp., 1976-80; mem. Ill. Office Edn. Resource and Dissemination Network, 1979-80. Recipient Meritorious Service award, Children's Ch. of First Ch. of Deliverance, 1979; Merit award for leadership, Am. Assn. Med. Personnel, Disting. Citation award, 1974; Service award, Roosevelt Meml. Hosp., 1978; Chgo. Public Schs. Coop. Edn. award, 1976, 77, 78. Fellow Internat. Coll. Med. Tech.; mem. Am. Public Health Assn., Am. Soc. Med. Tech., Nat. Assn. Hosp. Purchasing Mgmt., Hosp. Mgmt. Systems Soc., Am. Registry Med. Assts. (pres. 1972-75, dir. 1972-75), Nat. Socs. Assn., Am. Assn. Med. Assts., Clin. Lab. Mgmt. Assn., Nat. Assn. Female Execs. Editor, Youth Yak newspaper, 1974-77.

WILLIAMS, HUGH ALEXANDER, JR., mech. engr.; b. Spencer, N.C., Aug. 18, 1926; s. Hugh Alexander and Mattie Blanche (Megginson) W.; B.S. in Mech. Engring., N.C. State U., 1948, M.S. in Diesel Engring. (Norfolk So. R.R. fellow), 1950; m. Ruth Ann Gray, Feb. 21, 1950; children—David Gray, Martha Blanche. Jr. engr.-field service engr. Baldwin-Lima Hamilton Corp., Hamilton, Ohio, 1950-52, project engr., 1953-55; project engr. Electro-Motive div. Gen. Motors Corp., La Grange, Ill., 1955-58, sr. project engr., 1958-63, supr. product devel. engine design sect., 1963—. Trustee Downers Grove (Ill.) San. Dist., 1965—, pres., 1974—; pres. Ill. Assn. San. Dists., 1976-77, bd. dirs., 1977—; mem. statewide policy adv. com. Ill. EPA, 1977-79; ruling elder 1st United Presbyn. Ch., Downers Grove. Served with USAAC, 1945. Registered profl. engr., Ill. Mem. ASME (Diesel and Gas Engine Power Div. Speaker award 1968, Div. citation 1977, exec. com. Diesel and Gas Engine Power div. 1981—), Soc. Automotive Engrs. Republican. Club: Masons (32 deg.). Editor: So. Engr., 1947-48; contbr. articles to profl. jours. Patentee in field. Home: 1119 Blanchard St Downers Grove IL 60516

WILLIAMS, JACK RAYMOND, civil engr.; b. Barberton, Ohio, Mar. 14, 1923; s. Charles Baird and Mary (Dean) W.; student Colo. Sch. Mines, 1942-43, Purdue U., 1944-45; B.S., U. Colo., 1946; m. Mary Berneice Jones, Mar. 5, 1947 (dec.); children—Jacqueline Rae, Drew Alan. Gravity and seismograph engr. Carter Oil Co., Western U.S. and Venezuela, 1946-50; with Rock Island R.R., Chgo., 1950-80, structural designer, asst. to engr. bridges, asst. engr. bridges, 1950-63, engr. bridges system, 1963-80; sr. bridge engr. Thomas K. Dyer Inc., 1980—. Served with USMCR, 1943-45. Fellow ASCE; mem. Am. Concrete Inst., Am. Ry. Bridge and Bldg. Assn. (past pres.), Am. Ry. Engring. Assn. Home: 293 Minocqua St Park Forest IL 60466 Office: 310 S Michigan Ave Chicago IL 60604

WILLIAMS, JAMES ALBERT, ins. co. exec.; b. Noblesville, Ind., Feb. 6, 1944; s. Frank E. and Martha B. (Thom) W.; student Purdue U., 1962-65, Butler U., 1977, also various trade schs.; m. Barbara Ann Satterfield, Feb. 15, 1980; children—Camey, Marty. With Statesman Group, Indpls., 1967-75, salesman, 1975-77, v.p. office services, 1977-80; mgr. corp. prodn./underwriting Economy Fire & Casualty Co., Freeport, Ill., 1980—. Mem. Underwriting Exec. Council, Quadrilles. Republican. Clubs: Lions (treas. club 1975), Kiwanis. Home: 1512 W Stephenson St Freeport IL 61032 Office: 500 Economy Ct Freeport IL 61032

WILLIAMS, JAMES HADLEY, geologist; b. Canton, Mo., Nov. 8, 1929; s. Ramoth and Mary Gaile (Hadley) W.; B.A., U. Mo., Columbia, 1951, M.A., 1952; postgrad. Cornell U., Ithaca, N.Y., 1964; Ph.D., U. Mo., Rolla, 1975; m. Marilyn Jane Merrell, Aug. 2, 1953; 1 dau., Mary Lynn Krueger. Geologist, Mo. Geol. Survey, Rolla, 1952-54; chief engring. geology sect. Geology and Land Survey, Rolla, 1960—; lectr. U. Mo., Rolla, 1973-79. Served with USAF, 1954-59. Recipient Employee of Yr. award Mo. Dept. Natural Resources, 1981. Mem. Assn. Engring. Geologists (cert. of Appreciation 1975, 79), U.S. Commn. Large Dams, Am. Inst. Profl. Geologists, Assn. Mo. Geologists, Sigma Xi, Phi Eta Sigma, Phi Kappa Phi. Contbr. articles to profl. jours. Home: Lecoma Star Route Box 31 Rolla MO 65401 Office: PO Box 250 Rolla MO 65401

WILLIAMS, JAMES MERRILL, microbiologist; b. Grand Forks, N.D., Aug. 6, 1928; s. Merrill Leroy and Bertha M. (Zintel) W.; B.S., U. N.D., 1950; M.S., N.D. State U., 1952; m. Ruth A. Kirby, June 20, 1954; children—Peter J., Todd K. Bacteriologist, Rocky Mountain Lab., Hamilton, Mont., 1952-54, Mont. State Bd. Health, Helena, 1954-56, Anchor Serum Co., St. Joseph, Mo., 1956-58, St. Mary's Hosp., Rhinelander, Wis., 1958-60, Ancker Hosp., St. Paul, 1960-62; dir. biology Philips Roxane, 1962-68; dir. bacteriol. research Philips Roxane, Inc., St. Joseph, 1968-78, dir. biol. research, 1978—; affiliate prof. U. Idaho, 1974—. Served with M.C., AUS, 1946-48. Mem. Am. Soc. Microbiology, U.S. Animal Health Assn., Am. Mgmt. Assn. Republican. Methodist. Clubs: Masons, Shriners. Research on staphylococcal mastitis, vibriosis, reproductive, respiratory disease. Patentee brucella canis vaccine. Office: 2621 N Belt St Saint Joseph MO 64502

WILLIAMS, JEAN MARIE, sch. prin.; b. Tulsa, Dec. 17, 1930; d. Theodore and Malysa Armentha (Sexton) Shackelford; B.S., Lincoln U., Mo., 1951; M.Ed., Wichita State U., 1968; Ed.D., U. Kans., 1979; m. Aug. 12, 1952 (div. 1963); children—Denise D. Holden, Janette L. Burton. Clk. typist Ariz. Health Dept., Phoenix, 1951-56; adminstrv. clk. FHA, Phoenix, 1956-63; tchr., asst. prin. Wichita Public Schs., 1964-77, prin. Riverside Elem. Sch., 1977—. Recipient Superior Performance award Fed. Govt., 1959. Mem. Nat. Assn. Elem. Sch. Prins., Wichita Assn. Elem. Sch. Prins. (exec. bd.), Wichita Elem. Mgmt. Assn., Women in Ednl. Mgmt., United Sch. Adminstrs., Assn. Supervision and Curriculum Devel., Kans. PTA, Wichita PTA (bd. mgrs.). Methodist. Home: 2614 N Estelle St Wichita KS 67219 Office: 1001 Porter St Wichita KS 67203

WILLIAMS, JERRY RUTH, telephone co. exec.; b. Bogalusa, La., Sept. 5, 1936; d. Charlie and Procula Marian (Norris) W.; Hutcherson; B.A. magna cum laude, So. U., 1957; M.Ed., U. Mo., St. Louis, 1969; m. Robert P. Williams, Jan. 25, 1959; 1 dau., Michelle Yvette. Tchr. English, New Orleans pub. schs., 1957-59; case worker Mo. Dept. Welfare, St. Louis, 1960-61; tchr. St. Louis pub. schs., 1961-66; counselor Normandy Sch. Dist., St. Louis, 1969-78, dir. alt. learning program, 1975-76; staff trainer Title IX Workshop, 1977; staff supr. service costs Southwestern Bell Telephone Co., St. Louis, 1978-80, customer service supr. bus. installation control, 1980—. Mem. Alliance of Bus. and Service Profls. Metro-Ministry Adv. Council; mem. Dist. Council on Ministries. Mem. United Meth. Women (unit treas., mem. exec. bd.), Phi Delta Kappa, Alpha Kappa Alpha, Kappa Delta Pi, Alpha Kappa Mu. Methodist. Club: Toastmasters. Home: 1967 Willow Lake Dr Chesterfield MO 63017 Office: 720 Olive St Room 2706 Saint Louis MO 63101

WILLIAMS, JOHN DELANE, statistician, educator; b. Ordway, Colo., Oct. 26, 1938; s. John O. and Leila June (Galbraith) W.; A.A., So. Colo. State U., 1958; B.A. in Math., U. No. Colo., 1959, M.A. in Math., 1966, Ph.D. in Stats. and Research Methodology, 1966; postgrad. U. Oreg., 1961-62; m. Jole Ann Wells, July 23, 1980; children—Diane, Brian, Delane. Tchr. math. and sci. Roosevelt Jr. High Sch., Oakland, Calif., 1960-61; grad. teaching asst. math. U. Oreg., 1961-62; instr. math. and stats. Western Wyo. Community Coll., 1962-65; grad. research asst. U. No. Colo., 1965-66; asst. prof. ednl. measurement and stats. U. N.D., Grand Forks, 1966-68, asso. prof., 1968-71, prof., 1971—; statis. cons., 1971—. Recipient Sigma Xi Faculty Award for Outstanding Sci. Research, 1979. Mem. Am. Statis. Assn., Am. Psychol. Assn., Am. Ednl. Research Assn., AAUP, Phi Delta Kappa. Author: Multiple Regression in Educational Research, 1974; Testing and the Testing Industry: A Third View, 1976; Multiple Comparisons by Multiple Linear Regression, 1976; Path Analysis from a Regression Perspective, 1978; Multiple Comparisons in Higher Dimensional Designs, 1980; contbr. numerous articles on ednl. research, psychol. measurement and stats. to profl. jours. Home: 522 Belmont Rd Grand Forks ND 58201 Office: U ND Grand Forks ND 58201

WILLIAMS, JOHN PENNINGTON, clergyman, educator; b. Nanking, China, July 30, 1922; s. Walter Rollin and Myrtle Mae Williams; Th.B., Malone Coll., 1943; A.B., Marion Coll., 1944; M.A., Case Western Res. U., 1951; Ph.D., U. Mich., 1961; m. Geraldine Osborne, Sept. 3, 1943; children—Nancy Jo Davidson, John, Marilyn Sherman, Marjorie Lewis, Margaret Bergert, David, Andy. Ordained to ministry, Evang. Friends Ch., 1944; pastor chs., Ohio, Mich., 1944-53; missionary to China, 1947-48; mem. faculty, adminstr. Malone (Ohio) Coll., 1953-63; adminstr. U. Akron, 1963-66; pastor Stanwood United Ch. of Christ, Massillon, Ohio, 1960-67; dean faculty Buena Vista (Iowa) Coll., 1966-73; acad. dean Friends U., Wichita, Kans., 1973-79; pastor Sterling Evang. Mennonite Ch. (Kans.), 1979-81, Tecumseh (Mich.) Evang. Friends Ch., 1981—; mem. exec. com. Mid-Am. Yearly Meeting of Friends; mem. bd. of home missions Evang. Mennonite Conf. Mem. Iowa Assn. Coll. Deans (past pres.), Mid-Am. Coll. Deans (past chmn.), Phi Delta Kappa. Author: Matching Needs and Facilities for Higher Education, 1961; Three Models for Morality, 1963. Address: 9480 Tecumseh-Clinton Rd Tecumseh MI 49286

WILLIAMS, JOHN TROY, librarian, educator; b. Oak Park, Ill., Mar. 11, 1924; s. Michael Daniel and Donna Marie (Shaffer) W.; B.A., Central Mich. U., 1949; M.A. in Library Science, U. Mich., 1951, M.A., 1954; Ph.D., Mich. State U., 1973. Reference librarian U. Mich., Ann Arbor, 1955-59; instr. Bowling Green (Ohio) State U., 1959-60; reference librarian Mich. State U., East Lansing, 1960-62; 1st asst. reference dept. Flint (Mich.) Pub. Library, 1962-65; head reference services, Purdue U., West Lafayette, Ind., 1965-72; head pub. services No. Ill. U., Dekalb, 1972-75; asst. dean, asst. univ. librarian Wright State U., Dayton, Ohio, 1975-80; vis. scholar U. Mich., Ann Arbor, 1980—; cons. in field. Served with U.S. Army, 1943-46. Mich. State fellow, 1963-64; HEW fellow, 1971-72. Mem. Am. Library Assn., Spl. Libraries Assn., Genessee County Hist. Soc. (dir.), Am. Soc. for Info. Sciences, Am. Sociol. Assn., AAUP, Council on Fgn. Relations. Contbr. articles to profl. jours. Home: 1453 Marlborough Ann Arbor MI 48104

WILLIAMS, JOSEPH EDWARD (REX), social work cons., musician, educator, journalist; b. Panama City, Republic of Panama, Mar. 12, 1927; came to U.S., 1952, naturalized, 1965; s. Edward T. and Stella G. (Westerman) W.; student Nat. Conservatory Music, Panama, 1947-52; student Sherwood Music Sch., Chgo., 1952-55; B. Music Edn., Roosevelt U., Chgo., 1959; M.S.W., Loyola U., Chgo., 1972; postgrad. Northwestern U., 1965; m. Pearl Innis, Feb. 18, 1978. Founder, dir. Cosmopolitan Little Orch., 1949-52; Midwest corr. Panama Tribune, Panama City, 1960-75; violinist Sherwood Symphony Orch., Chgo., 1952-55, various community orchs., 1955-57; instr. piano and violin Mallette Music Sch., Chgo., 1965—, editor newsletter, 1968-69; writer Negro Press Internat., Chgo., 1964-65; caseworker Cook County Dept. Public Aid, Chgo., 1965-68; social worker Lake County (Ind.) Child Welfare, Gary, 1968-69, Ill. Dept. Children and Family Services, Chgo., 1969-71, Central Bapt. Family Services, Chgo., 1975-76, VA West Side Hosp., Chgo., 1976—; social work cons. Harriet Holmes Home Health Care; Chgo. corr. Caribe Horizon newspaper, Montreal, Can., 1970-72; communication specialist Ill. Commn. on Human Relations, Chgo., 1974-76; instr. violin Chgo. State U., Chgo., 1975-78, Urban Gateway-Chgo. Symphony Orch., 1978—. Recipient Feature-Writing award Southtown Economist, 1973. Mem. Nat. Assn. Social Workers, Nat. Sch. Orch. Assn., Suzuki Assn. of the Americas. Clubs: Kiwanis (dir. 1977-80), Masons. Feature editor Bulletin-Booster newspaper, 1965-70; exec. editor North Shore Examiner, 1968-69; asso. editor Southend Rev., 1972-75; columnist Hyde Park Herald, 1972-74.

WILLIAMS, JULIE BELLE, psychiat. social worker; b. Algona, Iowa, July 29, 1950; d. George Howard and Leta Maribelle (Durschmidt) W.; B.A., U. Iowa, 1972, M.S.W., 1973. Social worker Psychopathic Hosp., Iowa City, 1971-72; OEO counselor YOUR, Webster City, Iowa, 1972; social worker Child Devel. Clinic, Iowa City, 1973; group therapist Cedar Manor Nursing Home, Tipton, Iowa, 1973; therapist Mid-Eastern Iowa Community Mental Health Center, Iowa City, 1973; psychiat. social worker Mental Health Center N. Iowa, Mason City, 1974-79, chief psychiat. social worker, 1979-80; asst. dir. Community Counseling Center, White Bear Lake, Minn., 1980—; lectr., cons. in field. NIMH grantee, 1972-73. Mem. Nat. Assn. Social Workers (pres. local chpt.), NOW, Acad. Cert. Social Workers, Am. Orthopsychiat. Assn., Am. Assn. Sex Educators, Counselors and Therapists, Phi Beta Kappa. Democrat. Office: 803 2d St White Bear Lake MN 55110

WILLIAMS, KENNETH R., educator; b. Saxton, Pa., Feb. 14, 1935; s. Kenneth R. and Marian A. (Hunter) W.; A.B., Pa. State U., 1959, M.A., 1961, Ph.D., 1964; m. Linda C. Ladin, Oct. 3, 1980; children—Kenneth R. III, Christopher Joel. Instr. humanities and speech Pa. State U., University Park, 1962-64; asst. prof. speech U. R.I., Kingston, 1964-66, U. Md., College Park, 1966-67; asso. prof. Ohio U., Athens, 1967-77; prof., chmn. dept. communication U. Wis., Stevens Point, 1977—; founder, prin. coordinator Human Development Resources, Inc., Athens, 1973-77. Served with U.S. Army, 1955-57. Recipient distinguished teaching award Ohio U., 1974-75, research grantee, 1972, 79, 81; certified Gold Seal Flight Instr., comml. instrument rated for single and multi-engine landplanes. Mem. Internat., Wis. communication assns., Creative Edn. Found., Speech Communication Assn., Wis. Acad. Arts, Letters, and Scis., Central States Speech Assn., Nat. Assn. Flight Instrs. Contbr. articles on communications, semantics, sociology to jours. Home: 5452 Greenview Ln Stevens Point WI 54481 Office: Dept Communication U Wisconsin at Stevens Point Stevens Point WI 54481

WILLIAMS, LARRY EDWARD, clergyman; b. Danville, Ill., Jan. 30, 1948; s. Robert Eugene and Wilma Jean (Downey) Altman; B.A. in Bible, Central Bible Coll., Springfield, Mo., 1970-73; M.A. in N.T., Wheaton Coll., 1974; student Covenant Theol. Sem., St. Louis, 1974, S.W. Mo. State U., 1977-78, St. Louis U., 1978—; m. Connie Carmin Cox, May 3, 1969; 1 dau., Christa Dawn. Ordained to ministry Gen. Council of Assemblies of God, 1972; pastor Friends Ch., Danville, 1969-70; quality control monitor Tee Pak Corp., Danville, 1968-69; asst. pastor Edwards St. Assembly of God, Alton, Ill., 1974-75; asst. prof. Bibl. studies Evangel Coll., Springfield, Mo., 1975-81; guest lectr., speaker. Served with AUS, 1965-68; Vietnam. Decorated Army Commendation Medal; recipient Merrill Tenney award in N.T., 1974. Mem. Soc. Bibl. Lit., Evang. Theol. Soc., Soc. Pentecostal Studies, Delta Epsilon Chi. Author: Essential Christianity; contbr. articles to religious jours. Home: 2703 E Vincent St Springfield MO 65804 Office: Evangel College 1111 N Glenstone St Springfield MO 65802

WILLIAMS, LOIS JEAN, remedial reading specialist; b. Gerald, Mo., Mar. 30, 1941; d. Leslie Bryan and Gladys Louise (Hollman) Boston; B.S. in Edn., Southwest Mo. State U., 1961; M.Ed., Mo. U., 1967; Reading Specialist Cert., Lincoln U., 1972; m. Jerry Lindell Williams, Aug. 14, 1965; children—Kevin Lindell, Jeffrey Bryan. Tchr. 5th grade Gerald (Mo.) Pub. Schs., 1961-63, tchr. kindergarten, 1963-71, remedial reading tchr., 1971—. Chmn. Gerald chpt. ARC, 1962-66, 77-79; active Cub Scouts. Mem. Mo. State Tchrs. Assn., Nat. Council Tchrs. English, Community Tchrs. Assn., Internat. Reading Assn., Delta Kappa Gamma. Republican. Presbyn. Mem. Order Eastern Star (past matron). Clubs: Jaycee Wives. Contbr. articles to profl. jours. Home: 639 Lincoln St Gerald MO 63037 Office: 600 W Fitzgerald Gerald MO 63037

WILLIAMS, LUTHER STEWARD, biologist; b. Sawyerville, Ala., Aug. 19, 1940; s. Roosevelt and Mattie B. (Wallace) W.; B.A. magna cum laude, Miles Coll., 1961; M.S., Atlanta U., 1963; Ph.D. (NIH fellow), Purdue U., 1968; m. Constance Marie Marion, Aug. 23, 1963; children—Mark Steward, Monique Marie. NSF lab. asst. Spelman Coll., 1961-62; NSF lab. asst. Atlanta U., 1962-63, instr. biology, faculty research grantee, 1963-64, asst. prof. biology, 1969-70; grad. teaching asst. Purdue U., West Lafayette, Ind., 1964-65, grad. research asst., 1965-66, asst. prof. biology, 1970-73, asso. prof., 1973-79, prof., 1979-80, NIH Career Devel. awardee, 1971-75, asst. provost, 1976-80; dean Grad. Sch., prof. biology Washington U., St. Louis, 1980—; Am. Cancer Soc. postdoctoral fellow State U. N.Y., Stony Brook, 1968-69; asso. prof. biology Mass. Inst. Tech., 1973-74; chmn. rev. com. MARC Program, Nat. Inst. Gen. Med. Scis., NIH, 1972-76; grant reviewer NIH, 1971-73, 76, NSF, 1973, 76-80, Med. Research Council of N.Z., 1976. Mem. life scis. screening com. Council for Internat. Scholarly Exchange, 1978-81; mem. recombinant DNA adv. com. HEW, 1979-81; mem. nat. adv. gen. med. sci. council NIH, 1980—. Mem. Am. Soc. Microbiology, Am. Chem. Soc., Am. Soc. Biol. Chemists, AAAS, N.Y. Acad. Scis. Contbr. sci. articles to profl. jours. Home: 7 Birnawoods Ln Olivette MO 63132 Office: 211A South Brookings Hall Washington U Saint Louis MO 63130

WILLIAMS, LYLE, congressman; b. Philippi, W.Va., Aug. 23, 1942; s. Dale and Frankie J.W.; student Molar Barber Coll.; m. Nancie Lee, Oct. 20, 1964; children—Vikki, Diana, Debra, Jason. Mem. bd. zoning appeals, Bloomfield Twp., Ohio; mem. bd. edn. Bloomfield-Sch. Bd., 1970-71; mem. Trumbull County Bd. Commrs., 1973-78; mem. 96th and 97th Congresses from 19th Dist. Ohio. Served with U.S. Army. Club: Optimist (dist. lt. gov. 1970-71). Office: 1004 Longworth House Office Bldg Washington DC 20515

WILLIAMS, MARY BOYKIN, educator; b. Tibbs, Miss., Oct. 28, 1922; d. Mack Lee and Sallie Mae (Smith) Boykin; B.A. in History, U. Miss., 1947, M.A. 1949, Advanced Masters in Reading, 1968; m. Ned Williams; 1 dau., Sally Mae. Tchr. English, Vaiden (Miss.) High Sch., 1957-59, Lafayette Jr. High Sch., Oxford, Miss., 1966-67; remedial reading tchr. Lafayette Elementary Sch., Oxford, 1967-69; dir. reading, Title I dir. Mattoon (Ill.) Community Unit Sch. Dist. 2, 1969—. Mem. NEA, Ill., Mattoon edn. assns., East Central-Eastern Ill. U. (pres. 1971-72), Ill. (rec. sec. 1976-78) reading councils, Internat. Reading Assn., Nat. Council Tchrs. of English, AAUW (pres. Charleston-Mattoon br. 1979—). Certified, Miss., Ill. Club: Charleston Woman's (pres. pot pourri div. 1972-73). Home: 2249 Cortland Dr Charleston IL 61920 Office: 2601 Walnut St Mattoon IL 61938

WILLIAMS, MARY EULALIA, educator; b. East St. Louis, Ill., July 16, 1929; B.S. in Social Studies, Ala. State Coll., Montgomery, 1951, postgrad. in adminstrn.; M.A. in Social Studies, U. Ill., 1971; div. Chmn. dept. Lincoln Sr. High Sch., East St. Louis, 1965-70; coordinator social studies East St. Louis Sch. Dist. 189, 1969—; resource person Ill. Office Edn., 1975—. Mem. Ill. Adv. Council on Multi-Cultural Edn., 1977-78. Mem. Nat., Ill. councils for the social studies, Delta Sigma Theta. NDEA grantee, 1967. Contbr. articles to profl. jours. Office: 240 N 6th St East Saint Louis IL 62201

WILLIAMS, MELVIN DONALD, anthropologist, educator; b. Pitts., Feb. 3, 1933; s. Aaron and Gladys Virginia (Barnes) W.; A.B. in Econs., U. Pitts., 1955, M.A. in Anthropology, 1969, Ph.D., 1973; m. Faye Wanda Strawder, June 20, 1958; children—Aaron Ellsworth, Steven Rodney, Craig Haywood. Propr., operator Wholesale Periodical Distbn. Co., Pitts., 1955-66; from instr. to asst. prof. dept. sociology and anthropology Carlow Coll., Pitts., 1969-75, chmn. dept. sociology and anthropology, 1973-75; asso. prof. anthropology U. Pitts., 1976-79, adj. prof., 1979—; prof. anthropology, dir. African Studies and Research Center, Purdue U., West Lafayette, Ind., 1979—; Olive B. O'Connor prof. Am. instns. Colgate U., 1976-77. Co-chmn. project area com. Urban Redevel. Authority, Pitts., 1972—;

bd. dirs. Cath. Social Service of Allegheny County (Pa.), 1973-76. Served with U.S. Army, 1957-58. NSF grantee, 1969, Community Action Pitts. Research grantee, 1969. Fellow Am. Anthrop. Assn.; mem. Am. Ethnological Soc., Am. Sociol. Assn., Anthrop. Soc. Washington, Council on Anthropology and Edn., AAUP, AAAS, Assn. for Study of Afro-Am. Life and History, Soc. for Psychol. Anthropology, Northeastern Anthrop. Assn., Nat. Council for Black Studies, Soc. for Applied Anthropology, Soc. for Med. Anthropology, Internat. Platform Assn., African Studies Assn., Soc. of Ethnic and Spl. Studies, Sigma Xi, Phi Delta Kappa, Delta Sigma Epsilon. Author: Community in a Black Pentecostal Church, 1974; Selected Readings in Afro-American Anthropology, 1975; On the Street Where I Lived, 1981; contbr. articles to scholarly publs.; asso. editor ethnology Internat. Jour. Cultural and Social Anthropology, 1976-79. Home: 320 Sheetz St West Lafayette IN 47906 Office: 110 Matthews Hall Purdue Univ West Lafayette IN 47907

WILLIAMS, NELLIE JAMES BATT, educator; b. Nashville; d. Ivan C. and Lottie B. (Phillips) James; A.B., Stowe Coll., 1942; M.S., U. Ill., 1945; postgrad. Ill. Inst. Tech., 1959, 64, Oberlin Coll., 1965, St. Louis U., 1962, 63, 67, 68, Rockhurst Coll., 1972; m. Napoleon Williams, July 21, 1973; 1 son by previous marriage, Charles W. Batt, Jr. Tchr. Sumner High Sch., St. Louis, 1949-54, Handly High Sch., 1954-63; tchr., head mathematics dept. Northwest High Sch., St. Louis, 1963-76; instr., dept. head, Acad. Math. and Sci., St. Louis, 1976—; instr., head dept. Harris Teacher Coll., Forest Park Community Coll. Active NAACP, YWCA. NSF grantee, 1959, 62-65, 67, 72. Mem. Math. Club Greater St. Louis, Math. Assn. Am., Assn. Women in Math., Delta Sigma Theta (edn. com.). Methodist. Home: 7584 Amherst St Saint Louis MO 63130

WILLIAMS, OTHA EDSEL, ins. co. exec.; b. Detroit, June 22, 1946; s. Otha and Dessie Venita (Carter) W.; student Tenn. State U., 1966-67; B.A., Wayne State U., 1969-71; m. Geneva Jones, July 19, 1975; 1 dau., Monique Kellie. Reporter, columnist Oakland Press, 1970-72; spl. assignment reporter N.Y. Times, N.Y.C., 1971-72; press rep. Detroit Edison, 1972-74; regional public affairs mgr. Allstate Ins. Co., Southfield, Mich., 1974—. Bd. dirs. Inner City Bus. Improvement Forum, 1981—; bd. dirs. of citizens adv. council Wayne County Community Coll., 1979—. Mem. NAACP, Public Relations Soc. Am., Soc. Consumer Affairs Profls., Detroit C. of C., Nat. Sociol. Honor Soc. Office: Allstate Insurance Co 26801 Northwestern Hwy Southfield MI 48034

WILLIAMS, PHILIP COPELAIN, physician; b. Vicksburg, Miss., Dec. 9, 1917; s. John Oliver and Eva (Copelain) W.; B.S. magna cum laude, Morehouse Coll., 1937; M.D., U. Ill., 1941; m. Constance Sheilda Rhetta, May 29, 1943; children—Philip, Susan Carol, Paul Rhetta. Intern, Cook County Hosp., Chgo., 1942-43, resident in obstetrics and gynecology, 1946-48; resident in gynecology U. Ill., 1948-49; practice medicine specializing in obstetrics and gynecology, Chgo., 1949—; mem. staff St. Joseph Hosp., Augustana Hosp., Cook County Hosp., Mc Gaw Hosp.; clin. prof. Med. Sch. Northwestern U., Chgo. Bd. dirs. Am. Cancer Soc. Chgo. unit and Ill. div. Served with U.S. Army, 1943-45. Recipient Civic award Loyola U., 1970; diplomate Am. Bd. Obstetrics and Gynecology. Fellow A.C.S., Internat. Coll. Surgeons; mem. AMA, Chgo., Ill. med. socs., AMA, Chgo. Gynecol. Soc. (treas. 1975-78, pres. 1980-81), Am. Fertility Soc., Inst. Medicine, N.Y. Acad. Scis., AAAS. Presbyn. Clubs: Ill. Athletic, Carleton, Plaza. Contbr. articles to profl. jours. Home: 1040 N Lake Shore Dr Chicago IL 60611 Office: 200 E 75th St Chicago IL 60619

WILLIAMS, PHILIP GARY, mfg. distbn. exec.; b. Davenport, Iowa, Nov. 29, 1939; s. William Ludman and Betty Jane (Blankenburg) W.; B.A., St. Ambrose Coll., 1966; m. Celia Anne Weaver, Sept. 1, 1961; children—Andrew, David. Mgmt. trainee Aluminum Co. Am., Davenport, 1966-68, supr. traffic office, 1968-70, traffic mgr., 1970-74; corp. traffic mgr. Valmont Industries, Inc., Valley, Nebr., 1974—; Nebr. state chmn. Nat. Transp. Week, 1977, 78. Chmn. bd. dirs. San. Improvement Dist. 6 Saunders County, 1976—; treas. Nebr. Dist. 11 Sch. Bd., 1976-79. Named Transp. Man of Yr., Omaha Transp. Club, 1977; recipient Nat. 1st Pl. award Nat. Transp. Week Competition, 1978. Mem. Omaha Transp. Club, Midwest Shipper Carrier Conf., Nebr. Motor Carrier Assn. (dir.), Nat. Maritime Council (nat. chmn. shippers adv. bd.), Indsl. Traffic Mgrs. Assn., Midwest Internat. Trade Assn., Traffic Clubs Internat. (dir. for Nebr.), Delta Nu Alpha (dir. Omaha chpt.). Republican. Baptist. Clubs: Kiwanis, Masons. Home: Rural Route 5 Douglas Dr Fremont NE 68025 Office: Valmont Industries Inc Hwy 275 Valley NE 68064

WILLIAMS, RALPH THOMAS, hosp. food service adminstr.; b. Detroit, Jan. 4, 1946; s. Ralph Winston and Ruth Evelyn (Jones) W.; A.A., Crowder Coll., 1967; Ph.B., Southwestern Coll., 1981; children—Lara Michelle, Daniel Christopher. Dietary supr. St. John's Hosp., Joplin, Mo., 1967-68; working asst. mgr. Stouffer's Food Corp., St. Louis, 1968-69; mgr. food service Saga Food Service, Bartlesville, Okla., 1969-70; dir. food service William Newton Meml. Hosp., Winfield, Kans., 1970—; co-owner, operator antique shop A Backward Glance, Winfield. Mem. Am. Soc. Hosp. Food Service Adminstrs., Soc. Am. Poets, Winfield Community Theatre. Home: 301 W 9th Ave Winfield KS 67156 Office: William Newton Meml Hosp 1300 E 5th St Winfield KS 67156

WILLIAMS, ROBERT BURGETT, marketing cons.; b. Meadville, Pa., Feb. 28, 1913; s. Emmett A. and Jessie R. Williams; B.B.A., U. Cin., 1937; student Henry Ford Community Coll., 1952-53, Oakland U., 1956-58; m. Elizabeth J. McGuire, 1937 (dec.); children—Richard, Peter, Susan, Michael, Timothy, Stephen. Engaged in brand advt. Procter & Gamble Co., Cin., 1937-43; personnel mgmt. staff Curtiss-Wright Co., Buffalo, 1943-46; promotion and advt. staff Ford Motor Co., Detroit, 1946-79; mktg. cons. Kelly Services, Inc., Detroit, 1979—. Active ARC, Boy Scouts Am., Archdiocesan Devel. Fund; pres. Homeowners Assn. Mem. Delta Tau Delta. Republican. Roman Catholic. Club: Somerset Golf. Office: 999 W Big Beaver Rd Troy MI 48084

WILLIAMS, ROBERT EUGENE, JR., archtl. and engring. firm exec.; b. Milw., May 25, 1948; s. Robert Eugene and Marion Louise (Vanden Breul) W.; A.A.S. in Archtl. & Bldg. Constrn. Engring. Tech., Milw. Sch. Engring., 1969, B.S., 1971, then postgrad.; m. Susan I. Schaefer, June 6, 1970; children—Anne Marie, Rebecca Lynn, Robert Eugene. Vice pres. H.D. Assos., Milw., 1971-75; v.p. Williams, Luepke & Assos., Milw., 1975-77; pres. Threshold Design, Inc., Milw., 1977—, also dir.; instr. Archtl. and Bldg. Constrn. Engring. Tech., Milw. Sch. Engring., 1973-76; bds. dirs. John A. Bauerschmidt Co., W-L Design, Inc. Planning com. Archdiocese of Milw., 1971; dir. CYO St. Agnes Cath. Ch., Butler, Wis., 1972-75. Mem. Nat. Soc. Profl. Engrs., Wis. Soc. Profl. Engrs., ASHRAE, Constrn. Specifications Inst., Urban Land Inst., Am. Planning Assn., Milw. Engrs. and Scientists (housing advisory, 1979), Milw. Sch. Engring Alumni Assn. (bd. dirs., v.p., 1977—, enrollment com., 1973—). Club: Brookfield Jaycees (bd. dirs., 1971). Works include Kogos Buick, Aurora, Ill. (Kirby Bldg. Systems; Nat. Design award, 1977). Home: N57W26289 Mountain Meadows Dr Sussex WI 53089 Office: 1390 Capitol Dr Pewaukee WI 53072

WILLIAMS, ROBERT G., fin. exec.; b. Aug. 24, 1944; B.B.A., U. Mich.; M.B.A. with honors, U. Chgo.; m. Joan Hollenbeck; children—Chad, Ryan, Brandon. Audit staff Arthur Young & Co., 1966-69, tax staff, 1969; asst. dir. taxation Chgo. and Northwestern Ry. Co., 1970-2; mgr. taxes Rand McNally & Co., 1972, dir. fin. services, 1973, treas., 1973-76; sr. v.p. Chgo. Bank of Commerce, 1976-78, exec. v.p., 1978, vice chmn., chief operating officer, 1979, chmn., chief exec. officer, 1981—. C.P.A. Office: 200 E Randolph Dr Chicago IL 60601

WILLIAMS, ROBERT JOHN, psychologist; b. N.Y.C., Jan. 15, 1924; s. Arthur John and Margaret Marie (Ayles) W.; A.B., Columbia U., 1949, M.A., 1950, Ph.D., 1952; m. Marion Beryl Dalhouse, Sept. 8, 1951; children—Kenneth Arthur, Joan Marion, Nancy Ellen. Instr., Columbia U., N.Y.C., 1948-52, asst. prof., 1952-53, asso. prof., 1953-55, prof., 1955-56; exec. v.p. Alfred Politz Research, Inc., N.Y.C., 1956-60; dir. mktg. intelligence Mead Johnson, Inc., Evansville, Ind., 1960-64; sr. research asso. mktg. Dow Chem. Co., Midland, Mich., 1964—. Chmn., Midland Beautification Com., 1969-79; co-chmn. Midland Hist. Com., 1978-79. Served with USAF, 1943-46. Recipient Public Service medallion City of Midland, 1978, 79; cert. psychologist, N.Y., 1952. Mem. Am. Psychol. Assn., AAAS, N.Y. Acad. Sci., Acad. Polit. and Social Sci. Republican. Contbr. articles to profl. jours. Home: 900 Sterling Dr Midland MI 48640 Office: 2020 Abbott Rd Midland MI 48640

WILLIAMS, ROBERT JOSEPH, water supply contractor; b. Klamath Falls, Oreg., Oct. 18, 1931; s. Charles A. and Clementine M. W.; B.A. in Econs., U. Notre Dame, 1954, M.S. in Earth Sci., 1968; m. Mary Ann Grzeszczyk, July 25, 1953; children—Patrick, Diane, James, Michael, Maria, Robert. Vice pres. Layne No. Co., Mishawaka, Ind., 1954-72; pres. Peerless-Midwest, Inc., Granger, Ind., 1972—. Pres., St. Joseph County Park Bd. Served with U.S. Army, 1955. Mem. Am. Water Works Assn. (past pres. Ind. sect.), Nat. Fire Protection Assn., Nat. Water Well Assn. Republican. Roman Catholic. Club: Rotary (dir.). Contbr. articles to profl. jours. Home: 15685 Embers Dr Mishawaka IN 46544 Office: PO Box 26 Granger IN 46530

WILLIAMS, ROBERT K., state senator; b. Dec. 31, 1934; grad. high sch.; m. Aug. 11, 1957; 2 children. With Northwestern Bell Telephone; realtor, Aberdeen, S.D.; mem. S.D. Senate, 1976—. Mem. Aberdeen Realtors Assn. Democrat. Lutheran. Clubs: Elks, Moose. Office: State Capitol Pierre SD 57501*

WILLIAMS, ROGER USHER, city ofcl.; b. Columbus, Ohio, July 8, 1942; s. Gideon Hinkle and Bernice Grace (Usher) W.; student Ohio State U., 1959, Otterbein Coll., 1960-62; B.S., Franklin U., 1970; m. Edith May Turberville, Sept. 6, 1975; children—Shelly Sue, Shawn Gregory, Scott Usher. Asso., Charles A. Reed, Columbus, 1963-64, 67-68; accountant City of Columbus Health Dept., 1967-72; pvt. practice acctg., Columbus, 1972-73; accountant City Columbus Fire Dept., 1973—, bus. mgr., 1978-79; fin. cons. as public accountant, 1971-72; notary public, 1974—. Served with AUS, 1964-67. Registered public acct., Ohio. Republican. Methodist. Home: 6812 Walnut St New Albany OH 43054 Office: City Columbus Fire Dept 200 Greenlawn Ave Columbus OH 43223

WILLIAMS, RONALD FRANKLIN, coll. adminstr.; b. Buffalo, Apr. 25, 1942; s. Franklin C. and Mildred A. Williams; B.S., SUNY, Buffalo, 1965; M.S., SUNY, Oswego, 1967; Ed.D., Ind. U., 1971; m. Suzanne Linzer, Sept. 4, 1965; children—Gregory, Glenn. Dean instrn. for career edn. and adult continuing edn. Sauk Valley Coll., Dixon, Ill., 1974-78; pres. Black Hawk Coll., Kewanee, Ill., 1978—. Dist. chmn. Boy Scouts Am., Kewanee, 1980—. Mem. Am. Community and Jr. Coll. Assn., Phi Delta Kappa. Club: Rotary. Home: 802 Page St Kewanee IL 61443 Office: Black Hawk College PO Box 489 Kewanee IL 61443

WILLIAMS, ROSEMARY MCDONALD, librarian; b. Hamilton County, Ind., June 12, 1920; d. Clarence Carl and Emma Eleanor (Warner) McDonald; B.A., Ball State Tchrs. Coll., 1942, M.A., 1962; m. Thomas Adrian Williams, Nov. 8, 1943; 1 son, Thomas Michael. Tchr., Noblesville (Ind.) High Sch., 1942-44, Middletown (Ind.) High Sch., 1948-55, Highland High Sch., Anderson, Ind., 1955-60; librarian, mem. faculty Ball State U., Muncie, Ind., 1960—, head tech. services ednl. resources, 1968—. Mem. Ind. Library Assn., ALA, Assn. Ednl. Communications and Tech., Kappa Delta Pi, Sigma Tau Delta, Pi Gamma Mu, Pi Lambda Theta. Quaker. Home: Rural Route 8 Box 524 Muncie IN 47302 Office: Bracken Library Ball State Univ Muncie IN 47306

WILLIAMS, SHARON, interior designer; b. Waukegan, Ill., Aug. 23, 1948; d. John Issac and Ruth (Robertson) Williams; B.S. in Bus. Edn. and Interior Design, Western Ill. U., 1970; postgrad. U. Minn., 1975, 79. Interior designer masterplan sales and interior design studio Dayton's Dept. Store, St. Paul, 1973-77; owner, pres., dir. interior design Sherry Williams-Ricks, Studio of Interior Design, Mpls., 1977—; mfrs. rep. contract and furnishings for instns. Recipient design and sales achievement award Dayton's Dept. Store, 1974. Mem. Am. Soc. Interior Designers, Mpls. Soc. Fine Arts, Mpls. Inst. Arts, Nat. Assn. Women Bus. Owners, North Suburban C. of C. Alpha Omicron Phi. Methodist. Home: 343 Ramsey Terr Saint Paul MN 55102 Office: Sta 19 2001 University Ave SE Minneapolis MN 55414

WILLIAMS, THOMAS GARDNER, foods co. exec.; b. Kans. City, Mo., Dec. 16, 1939; s. Thomas Aaron and Viola Emelie (Schloeman) W.; B.S.B.A., U. Mo., 1962; m. Carol Ann Hunt, Sept. 26, 1965; children—Mark Thomas, Mary Elizabeth. Mgmt. trainee Guaranteed Foods, Inc., 1963-64, food sales mgr., 1964-66, non-foods mgr., 1966-67, exec. v.p., gen. sales mgr., 1968-71, v.p., ops. mgr., 1967-68, dir., 1970—, pres., gen. mgr., 1972, pres., chmn. bd., 1974—; dir. Oak Park Nat. Bank, Overland Park, Kans. Bd. commrs., v.p. Kans. Retail Council, 1976—; dir. v.p. Youth Services Bur., 1972-74; mem. Planning Commn., 1978-80; chmn. Heart Fund Campaign, Johnson County Commn., 1974; bd. dirs. City Union Mission, 1979—. Named Outstanding Young Man of Lenexa, 1975. Mem. Am. Assn. Meat Processors, Advt., Mktg. Club, Kans. Assn. Commerce and Industry, Kans. Retail Council, Frozen Food Council (dir.), Lenexa C. of C., Better Bus. Bur., Am. Royal Assn. (bd. govs. 1979—), Delta Tau Delta. Republican. Lutheran. Home: 12100 W 148th St Olathe KS 66062 Office: 8901 Rosehill Rd Lenexa KS 66215

WILLIAMS, THOMAS KAY, counselor; b. Milw., May 16, 1930; s. James Thomas and Pearl June (Ward) W.; B.S., B.A., Andrews U., 1959, M.A., 1960; Ed.D., Western Mich. U., 1970; m. Audrey Eunice Kaatz, June 12, 1955; children—Teresa Kay, Thomas LaMont, Tonyce Ann. Tchr., prin. parochial elementary sch., 1955-57; pastor Seventh-day Adventist Chs., Wis., 1961-62; chaplain Battle Creek (Mich.) Sanitarium, 1962-66; dir. substance abuse services Battle Creek Sanitarium Hosp., 1964—; asso. prof. counseling, dir. splty. program in alcohol and drug abuse Western Mich. U., 1973-78; pres. Sapports, Inc., 1977—; adj. prof. Andrews U. Bd. dirs. Goodwill Industries; mem. State of Mich. Substance Abuse Adv. Com. Served with USN, 1948-52. Mem. Alcohol and Drug Problems Assn. Am., Am. Protestant Hosp. Assn., Am. Personnel and Guidance Assn., Mich. Alcoholism and Addiction Assn., Midwestern Area Alcohol Edn. and Tng. Program, Inc. (dir., exec. com. 1974-77). Author: Winning the Bottle Battle, 1969; co-editor: Basic Curriculum for Substance Abuse Counselors, 1977. Home and Office: 5270 E Halbert Rd Battle Creek MI 49017

WILLIAMS, VEIRL RICHARD, dentist; b. Winchester, Ind., Jan. 10, 1929; s. V. Richard and Geneva Marie (Cage) W.; B.S., Ind. U., 1953, D.D.S., 1955; m. Marilyn Simpson, Jan. 31, 1954; children—Susan, Robert, John, Kate. Pvt. practice dentistry, Winchester, 1957—. Mem. Winchester City Council, 1964-68. Served with USNR, 1955-57. Fellow Internat. Coll. Dentistry; mem. Am. Dental Assn., Ind. (del. 1965), E. Central (pres. 1967-68) dental socs., Ind. Council on Dental Edn., Acad. Gen. Dentistry. Mason. Club: Columbia (Indpls.). Home: Rural Route 2 Winchester IN 47394 Office: 457 Elm St Winchester IN 47394

WILLIAMS, VERNON ANTHONY, architect; b. Chgo., Feb. 23, 1946; s. Herbert G. and Theresa P. W.; B.Arch., U. Ill., 1970, B.A., 1970; postgrad. U. Mich., 1973—; m. Leslie Thompson; 1 dau., Lisa Antoinette. Nat. dir. community design center AIA, Washington, 1970-72; field services dir. Nat. Urban Coalition, Washington, 1972-73; architect Wendell Campbell Assos., Chgo., 1975-77; dir. devel. and adminstrn. Environment Seven, Ltd., Chgo., 1977-79; pres. Amistad Group, Inc., 1980—; instr. Washtenaw Community Coll.; lectr. various colls. and univs.; cons. Afro Am. Bicentennial Commn. Pres., Midwest Assn. for Sickle Cell Anemia, 1976—; bd. dirs. Wabash YMCA, 1978—; pres. South Shore Villa Condominium Assn., 1976-78; dir. Coalition to Save South Shore Country Club. William G. Sheick Research fellow, 1973; Albert Kahn Research fellow, 1974; registered architect, Ill., Mich. Mem. AIA, Nat. Council Archtl. Registration Bds. (cert.), Nat. Orgn. Minority Architects (pres. Ill. chpt. 1978), Interfaith Forum on Religion Art and Architecture, NAACP. Clubs: Saints South, Economic. Office: 154 W Hubbard St Chicago IL 60610

WILLIAMS, WARREN VAIL, psychologist; b. Denver, Apr. 13, 1940; s. Joseph W. and Edna M. (Follin) W.; B.S., Bradley U., 1963, M.A. (fellow), 1964; Ph.D., U. Okla., 1968; m. Linda Williams; children—Ken, Dan, Jeremiah. Research psychologist VA Hosp., Oklahoma City, 1967-68; clin. psychologist adult psychiatry div. Fort Logan Mental Health Center, Denver, 1968-69, dir. evaluation, 1969-74, clin. research psychologist, 1974-75; sr. research asso. Mental Research Inst., Palo Alto, Cal., 1975-78; asso. prof. dept. psychiatry U. S.D. Med. Sch., chief psychology dept., dir. adolescent treatment Human Services Center, Yankton, S.D., 1978—. Adult and adolescent clin. psychologist University Park Psychol. Center, Denver, 1970-75; propr. dir. Social Systems Devel., Assos., Denver, 1970-75; research adv. Fielding Inst., Santa Barbara, Calif., 1977—; lectr. in psychology Arapahoe Community Coll., Littleton, Colo., 1969-71. NIMH grantee, 1973-78. Mem. Am. Psychol. Assn., Colo. Psychol. Assn. (chmn. community psychology 1972-73), S.D. Psychol. Assn., Am. Orthopsychiat. Assn. Club: Denver Athletic. Author: Crisis Intervention in Acute Bereavement: A Model for Primary Prevention. Home: 610 James Pl Yankton SD 57078 Office: U SD Med Sch Human Services Center Box 76 Yankton SD 57078

WILLIAMS, WENDELL STERLING, physicist; b. Lake Forest, Ill., Oct. 27, 1928; s. Sterling Price and Mary Eleanor (Simpson) W.; B.A., Swarthmore Coll., 1951; Ph.D., Cornell U., 1956; m. Dorothy Ellen Watt, June 28, 1952; children—Jennifer Anne, Laura Kathleen. Physicist, Leeds & Northrup Co., Phila., 1951; research physicist Union Carbide Corp., Parma, Ohio, 1956-67; sr. research visitor dept. metallurgy Cambridge (Eng.) U., 1965-66; asso. prof. physics and ceramic engring. U. Ill., Urbana, 1967-69, prof., physics, ceramic engring. and bioengring., 1969—, dir. program ancient technologies and archaeol. materials, 1979—; task coordinator energy related gen. research NSF, Washington, 1974-75, sect. head metallurgy and materials div. materials research, 1977-78. Founder, condr. Southwest Messiah Chorale, Parma, 1960-67; condr. Unitarian-Universalist Ch. choir, Urbana, 1968-73. Recipient grants NSF, ERDA, Dept. Energy. Fellow Am. Phys. Soc., Am. Ceramic Soc.; mem. AAAS, Materials Research Soc., Bioelectric Repair and Growth Soc., Soc. for Bioelectricity. Club: Cosmos (Washington). Contbr. articles to sci. jours. Home: 501 E Mumford Dr Urbana IL 61801 Office: 106 Materials Research Lab Univ Ill Urbana IL 61801

WILLIAMS, WENDY (MRS. BROWNELL VAN ZANDT), writer, author, journalist; b. Evanston, Ill., May 1953; d. Robert Lewis and Patricia Ruth (Brownell) Williams; B.A. in English and French, Lake Forest Coll., 1974; student graphic design Paris, U. Rome, 1972. Owner, Van Zandt Pub. Co., Antioch, Ill., 1974-78; free-lance writer met. newspapers, Boston, Los Angeles, 1975—; developed nightly radio program on travel 108FM, Chgo., 1976-78; author: Skiing the Great Resorts, 1977; Cross Country Ski Waxing and Maintenance, 1977; Starting Your Own Magazine, 1978; Syndicating Your Own Column, 1978; Cinematography: Creating Your Own Film, 1979; Writing Magazine Articles That Sell, 1978; Ice Dancing, 1979; Cross Country in a Day, 1979; The Chicago Symphony Orchestra: 90 Years of Triumph, 1980; 100 Years of Impressionism, 1981; script writer Hollywood films, 1979—; writer film: The Long Shot, 1979. Mem. governing bd. Chgo. Symphony. Nominated Harold Hirsch award, 1977-78. Mem. U.S. Ski Writers (treas. 1976-78), Midwest Travel Writers Assn., U.S. Ski Assn., Alliance Francaise, D.A.R. Republican. Episcopalian. Clubs: Polo, Center. Home and Office: PO Box 258 Antioch IL 60002

WILLIAMS, WESLEY CORRIGAN, bookseller; b. Cleve., June 19, 1940; s. Charles Wesley and Margaret (Corrigan) W.; B.A., Johns Hopkins U., 1963; M.Phil., Yale U., 1968; m. Janet Elizabeth Sandiford, Mar. 18, 1967; children—Geoffrey Brian Corrigan, Lara Trenerry. Lectr., Loyola Coll., Balt., 1964-65; curator history of sci. collection Case Western Res. U., Cleve., 1968-73, curator spl. collections, 1973-79, lectr. history of sci., 1968-79; pres. Trencor, Inc.; asso. curator rare books, mem. adv. council Cleve. Museum Natural History; trustee Glen Oak Sch., Gates Mills, Ohio, 1970-78; trustee Print Club Cleve., 1968-79, 81—, pres., 1977-78; hon. mem. adv. council Univ. Sch. Mem. Bibliog. Soc. Am. (life), Bibliog. Soc. London (life), AAAS (life), Manuscript Soc., Soc. Bibliography Natural History (London), Am. Booksellers Assn., Bibliog. Soc. U. Va. Republican. Episcopalian. Clubs: Rowfant, Cleve. Skating, 13th St. Racquet, Grolier (N.Y.C.); Philos. (pres. 1977-78) (Cleve.). Editor: (with Robert E. Schofield) Man and the Frame of Nature, 1973. Home: 2214 Demington Dr Cleveland Heights OH 44106 Office: 1310 Huron Rd Cleveland OH 44115

WILLIAMS, WILLIAM JAMES, educator; b. Toledo, Mar. 11, 1921; s. William James and Catherine (Curtis) W.; B.S., Okla. State U., 1973, M.S., 1976; m. Rosemary Cucinello, Dec. 8, 1943; 1 dau., Sandra Sarita. Joined U.S. Navy, 1940, advanced through grades to master chief radioman; ret., 1964; rep. Philco Tech., Greenland, 1964-66, tchr. Job Corps, Philco, 1966-74; tchr. indsl. electronics Liberal Area Vocat. Tech. Sch., 1974—. Mem. Am. Vocat. Assn., Vocat. Indsl. Clubs Am., Am. Radio Relay League, Kans. Vocat. Assn., Kans. Indsl. Edn. Assn., Iota Lambda Sigma. Republican. Episcopalian. Clubs: Masons, Shriners, Kiwanis. Home: 1023 S Grant St Liberal KS 67901 Office: PO Box 1599 Liberal KS 67901

WILLIAMS, WILLIAM JOSEPH, holding co. exec.; b. Cin., Dec. 19, 1915; s. Charles F. and Elizabeth (Ryan) W.; student Georgetown Prep. Sch., Garret Park, Md.; A.B., Georgetown U., 1937; postgrad. Harvard U. Bus. Sch., 1938; m. Helen Mary DeCourcy, May 26, 1941; children—Mary F., William Joseph, Richard, Carol., Sharon, Thomas. Agy. dept. Western & So. Life Ins. Co., Cin., 1938-41, v.p., 1939-54, now chmn. bd.; pres. N. Am. Mgmt. & Devel. Co., Inc., personal holding co., Cin., 1954—, Western Industries; sec., dir. Reading Book Concrete Products Co.; dir. Am. Alarm Co., Cin. Equitable Ins. Co., Cin. Bengals; dir., v.p. Cin. Reds, Inc., Columbus Mut. Life Ins. Co. Bd. dirs. Cin. Community Chest, 1953-55; dir. fund campaign Hamilton County chpt. Nat. Found. Infantile Paralysis, chmn. 1953 camp; bd. dirs. Cin. Boys Club; trustee Good Samaritan Hosp.; bd. dirs. Xavier U., Cin. Zool. Soc., Children's Home, Children's Heart Assn. Served to capt. AUS, 1941-45. Decorated Knight of Malta, Knight of Holy Sepulchre. Mem. Cin. Zool. Soc. Clubs: Camargo Queen City, Cin. Country. Office: 212 E 3d St Cincinnati OH 45202

WILLIAMS, WILLIE SAMUEL, psychologist, educator; b. Prattsville, Ala., May 8, 1932; s. Eddie and Iona (Scott) Williams; B.A., U. Wichita, 1958; M. Edn., Xavier U., 1960; Ph.D., Mich. State U., 1970; Kepner-Trego, Govt. Mgmt. Seminar, 1973; diploma Harvard U. Grad. Sch. of Bus. Adminstrn., 1976; m. Marva Flowers, Aug. 22, 1959; children—Kevin, Keith, Karla. Lic. psychologist, Ohio. Sr. counselor and asst. prof. psychology U. Cin., 1970-71; asst. chief psychol. research and training programs NIMH-HEW, Rockville, Md., 1971-74; asso. dean student affairs Case Western Reserve U. Sch. of Medicine, Cleve., 1974—; psychologist Cin. Police Dept., 1970-71. Mem. Am. Personnel and Guidance Assn. (senator), Assn. of Black Psychologists (treas.), Am. Psychol. Assn., Phi Delta Kappa. NSF fellowship, 1961; recipient Merit award, NIMH-HEW, 1972-74. Home: 2690 Green Rd Shaker Heights OH 44122 Office: 2119 Abington Rd Cleveland OH 44106

WILLIAMSON, BARBARA KEARNEY, bank exec.; b. Buffalo, May 8, 1942; d. Norman Loyola and Dorothy Elizabeth (Peters) Kearney; A.B., Webster Coll., 1962; M.B.A., St. Louis U., 1977; grad. Stonier Grad. Sch. Banking, 1979-81; m. Wayne Arland Williamson, May 12, 1979. With First Nat. Bank in St. Louis, 1965—, mgr. cash mgmt., 1980—. Mem. Cash Mgmt. Inst. Republican. Club: St. Louis Ski. Office: First National Bank in St Louis PO Box 267 Saint Louis MO 63166

WILLIAMSON, DONALD RAY, army officer; b. Amarillo, Tex., Oct. 13, 1943; s. Floy Edwin and Dorothy Lorene (Orr) W.; B.S., W.Tex. U., 1966; M.A., Central Mich. U., 1977; student U.S. Army Command and Gen. Staff Coll., 1979-80; m. Beverly Ann Howard, Aug. 31, 1963; children—Rebecca Ann, Catherine Paige. Commd. 2d lt. U.S. Army, 1966, advanced through grades to lt. col., 1981; aero. scout team leader F Troop, 8th Cav., Republic of Viet Nam, 1967-68; flight comdr., instr., Ft. Wolters, Tex., 1969-70; comdg. officer 332d TC Aircraft Maintenance Detachment, Viet Nam, 1971; comdg. officer CSC Co., 2/67 Armor Bn., Ft. Hood, Tex., 1973-74; comdg. officer 2d Aviation Co., Ft. Hood, 1974-75; dep. insp. gen., Ft. Leavenworth, Kans., 1975-78; comdg. officer 213th Aviation Co., Camp Humphreys, Korea, 1978-79; tng. with industry Vought Corp., Dallas, 1980-81; asst. project mgr. Advanced Scout Helicopter, St. Louis, 1981—. Decorated D.F.C. with oak leaf cluster, Bronze Star medal, Meritorious Service medal, Air medal with 36 oak leaf clusters and V device, Army Commendation medal with oak leaf cluster. Mem. Army Aviation Assn. Am., U.S. Armor Assn., Assn. U.S. Army, Lansing Jaycees (pres. 1977-78). Mem. Christian Ch. Author: Battle Tricks, 1979. Home: 50 Orange Hill Chesterfield MO 63017 Office: Advanced Scout Helicopter Project Office 4200 Goodfellow Saint Louis MO

WILLIAMSON, DOROTHY JUNE, artist, educator; b. Mpls., June 13, 1929; d. Louis William and Hazel Irene (Johnson) W.; B.A., Asbury Coll., 1951; M.A., U. Minn., 1963, postgrad., 1969—. Lectr. art Augsburg Coll., Mpls., 1970—; art tchr. Richfield (Minn.) Public Schs., 1954—; cons. fed. art programs HEW; cons. DeCordova Mus., Lincoln, Mass.; cons. spl. program Art for Gifted; nat. judge children's art shows Northwestern Nat. Life Ins. Co., 1969—; judge student show Nat. Luth. Brotherhood Soc., 1981; dir. art program Alt. Learning Program for Handicapped Adults, Augsburg Coll.; exhibited in group shows Minn. Mus. Art, 1975, Fine Arts Exhibit Minn. State Fair, 1965, St. Olaf Coll., 1974, Augsburg Coll., 1975; represented in pvt. collections; mem. Alliance for Arts in Minn.; del. Leadership Conf. Curriculum and Instrn., Washington, 1968. Mem. U.S. Soc. Edn. Through Art (liaison officer), Internat. Soc. Edn. Through Art, Art Educators Minn. (pres. 1966-68), Western Arts Assn., Nat. Art Edn. Assn. (v.p. 1968-70, del. rep. assembly 1967-71, mem. exec. sec. search com.), Citizens for Arts Minn., Minn. Art Therapy Assn., Mpls. Soc. Fine Arts (children's adv. bd.), Walker Art Center, Am. Art Therapy Assn., Delta Kappa Gamma. Mem. editorial bd. Sch. Arts mag., 1978—; contbr. chpts. to books, articles to periodicals; cover photo Sch. Arts mag., Nov. 1980. Home: 4053 21st Ave S Minneapolis MN 55407 Office: Richfield Schs 7451 Oliver Ave S Minneapolis MN 55423 also Augsburg Coll Minneapolis MN 55454

WILLIAMSON, EVALENA, educator; b. Hopkinsville, Ky., Oct. 17, 1919; d. Walter and Lena Alder; B.S., Eastern Mich. U., 1956, M.A., 1960; m. Charles E. Williamson, Sept. 29, 1940; children—Lana Theota, Charles E. Tchr., English, social sci. public schs., Hopkinsville, Ky., 1944-53, Plymouth, Mich., 1954-79; tchr.-counselor Plymouth-Canton Community Schs., 1979-81. Mem. NEA, Mich. Edn. Assn., AAUW.

WILLIAMSON, LAWRENCE L., computer programmer; b. Chgo., June 11, 1941; s. Harley O. and Mildred L. (Ozment) W.; student South Bend Coll. of Commerce, 1963-64, Ind. U., 1975—, IBM Programming courses, 1970—; m. Lottie B. Smith, Feb. 23, 1968; 1 dau., Diana. With automobile rental dept. Hertz Rent-A-Car, South Bend, Ind., 1963-64; computer operator, programmer LaSalle Liquor Corp., South Bend, 1964-72; computer programmer, asst. mgr. data processing Radio Distbg. Co., South Bend, 1973-77, data processing mgr., 1977-81; system analyst/programmer Tucker Freight Lines, South Bend, 1981—. Served with USAF, 1959-63. Home: 520 W Lowell St Mishawaka IN 46544 Office: 1915 N Bendix Dr South Bend IN 46614

WILLIAMSON, RONALD ALAN, planning cons.; b. Chgo., Nov. 9, 1942; s. DeBaun Otto and Elverna Elizabeth (Brockmann) W.; B.S.L.A., Mich. State U., 1965; m. Susan Irene Evans, Aug. 30, 1980; 1 dau., Sanna Jean. Planner, Wichita Segwick County (Kans.) Met. Area Planning Dept., 1965-67; project planner Bucher & Willis, Salina, Kans., 1967-68; landscape designer and contractor, Three Oaks, Mich., 1968-69; chief planner Bucher & Willis, Kansas City, Mo., 1969-74, partner, chief planner, 1974—. Registered landscape architect; cert. planner. Mem. Am. Planning Assn. (pres. Kans. chpt. 1978-80), Am. Inst. Cert. Planners. Home: 5521 W 85 St Overland Park KS 66207 Office: 9140 Ward Pkwy Kansas City MO 64114

WILLIAMSON, THOMAS RAY, architect; b. Memphis, Nov. 11, 1944; s. Henry Wayne and Cecile Alice (McConnell) W.; B.Arch. and Urban Design, U. Kans., 1968; m. Sharon Lynn Farkas, Jan. 17, 1976; children—Sarah Lynn, Robert Wayne, Brian Thomas. Project mgr. Hastings & Chivetta, Architects, St. Louis, 1969-70; architect Fred Kemp & Co., St. Louis, 1970-72; architect Enmark Collaborative, Chesterfield, Mo., 1973-80; mgr., architect facilities div. Parkway Sch. Dist., Chesterfield, 1972—; pres. St. Louis Constrn. Design Group Inc., 1977—; exec. v.p. RFS Inc. subs. Roosevelt Fed. Savs. and Loan Assn., 1980—. Mem. Constrn. Specifications Inst. (Architect of Year award 1972), Am. Mgmt. Assn. Author: School Facility Inventory, 1974; Design Criteria Handbook for Elementary Schools, 1975. Home: 1600 Hickory Knob Rd Glencoe MO 63038 Office: 1601 Clarkson Rd Chesterfield MO 63017

WILLIG, LESLIE AUGUST, photog. equipment mfg. co. exec.; b. Ft. Wayne, Ind., Jan. 29, 1926; s. August Aloysius and Laura Elizabeth W.; B.S., B.N.S. & T., Purdue U., 1947; M.A., U. Louisville, 1951; Ph.D., U. Iowa, 1956; children—Constance J. Willig Roberts, Diana K. Willig Brummer, Larry A., Rosanne M. Willig Johnson, Laura L. Asst. dean of men U. Iowa, Iowa City, 1954-56; asst. dir., asso. prof. Purdue U., Ft. Wayne Center, 1956-60; exec. v.p. Tri-State U., Angola, Ind., 1960-70; v.p., dir. Bankers Investment Corp., Ft. Wayne, 1966-75; chmn. bd., chief exec. officer, pres. Photo Control Corp., Mpls., 1974—; bus. broker and cons. in mgmt., Ft. Wayne, 1970—; sec., dir. North Snow Bay, Inc., 1966—. Chmn., Internat. Sci. Fair Council, 1967; co-founder, bd. dirs. Ind. Sci. Edn. Fund, 1963—. Served to capt. USNR, 1944-47, 51-53. Recipient Disting. Public Service award Navy Dept., 1973; Merit award Naval Res. Assn., 1974. Mem. Am. Psychol. Assn., Midwestern Psychol. Assn., Naval Res. Assn. (nat. pres. 1971-73). Roman Catholic. Club: Summit (Ft. Wayne). Home: Rural Route 1 Box 791 Fremont IN 46737 Office: Photo Control Corp 4800 Quebec Ave N Minneapolis MN 55428

WILLIHNGANZ, CHARLES LEE, educator; b. Beaver Dam, Wis., July 3, 1951; s. Cletus George and Betty Kathryn (Andercheck) W.; B.S., U. Wis., Stout, 1973; m. Michelle J. Gladfelter, Aug. 8, 1981; 1 dau., Katie Helen. Tchr. indsl. arts Lourdes High Sch., Rochester, Minn., 1973—, basketball coach, 1973-79, tennis coach, 1973—, head dept. indsl. arts, 1976—, asst. athletic dir., 1979—; football, basketball and volleyball sports ofcl., 1977—. Mem. Minn. Soc.-AIA, Epsilon Phi Tau. Club: K.C. (com. chmn., youth dir. 1979-81). Home: 839 Memorial Pkwy SW Rochester MN 55901 Office: 700 W Center St Rochester MN 55901

WILLINGHAM, EDWARD BACON, JR., clergyman, religious broadcasting exec.; b. St. Louis, July 27, 1934; s. Edward B. and Harriet (Sharon) W.; B.S. in Physics, U. Richmond, 1956, postgrad. U. Rochester, 1958-59; M.Div., Colgate Rochester Divinity Sch., 1960; m. Angeline Walton Pettit, June 14, 1957; children—Katherine Angeline, Carol Walton. Chief engr. Radio-TV Center, Am. Bapt. Assembly, Green Lake, Wis., summers, 1952-56; various positions WVET-TV, Rochester, N.Y., 1956-60. Ordained to ministry Am. Baptist Ch., 1960; minister Christian edn. Delaware Av. Bapt. Ch., Buffalo, 1960-62; dir. radio and TV Met. Detroit Council Chs., 1962-75, exec. dir. Christian communication council, 1976—. Broadcast cons. Mich. Council Chs., 1965-75; Fed. Republic Germany guest cons. religious broadcasting, 1968; mem. Interfaith Broadcasting Commn. Greater Detroit, 1968—, disc jockey weekly religious mus. show WXYZ, Detroit, 1963-75; mem. cable TV study com. city of Detroit; producer nationally syndicated TV series Choice. Instl. rep. Detroit Ednl. Television Found. Bd. mgrs., exec. com. Broadcasting and Film Commn. Nat. Council of Chs., 1965-73. Recipient Gabriel award UNDA-U.S.A., 1972. Mem. Assn. Regional Religious Communicators (pres. 1969-71), World Assn. Christian Communication (chmn. steering com. N. Am. broadcasting sect. 1970-71, bus. mgr. 1972—, mem. central com. 1973-78), Broadcast Edn. Assn., Phi Gamma Delta, Sigma Pi Sigma. Home: 21440 Lathrup Southfield MI 48075 Office: 1300 Mutual Bldg Detroit MI 48226

WILLIQUETTE, SHIRLEY ANN, educator; b. Oshkosh, Wis., Apr. 12; d. Edward and Anna (Preisinger) W.; B.A., Mt. Mary Coll., 1967; M.A., Cardinal Stritch Coll., 1981. Tchr., Archdiocese of Milw., 1956-68, Milw. public schs., 1968—, directress of jr. high summer program, 1968, Ednl. Telephone Network reading specialist, 1980—, mem. inner-city curriculum com., 1969—, city-wide basal selection com. 1980-81, Title I reading assessment com., 1979-80. Mem. Internat. Reading Assn., Wis. Reading Assn. Roman Catholic. Office: 1503 W Hopkins St Milwaukee WI 53206

WILLIS, MICHEAL WARREN, farmer; b. Liberal, Kans., July 15, 1947; s. Warren Grover and Betty Lee (Hershey) W.; diploma indsl. TV, Wichita Tech. Inst., 1968; m. Kathy Rae Williamson, Dec. 16, 1973; children—Warren Micheal, Jennifer Lynn, Lisa Raylene. Farmer, cattleman, Hugoton, Kans., 1968—; rep. Northrup-King Seed Co., 1976—; TV repairman, 1968—; asso. dir. Farmers Co-op Bd., Hugoton, 1976-79, dir., 1979—. Mem. Stevens County Fair Bd., 1979—; life instr. hunter safety. Served with USAR, 1968-74. Mem. Hugoton Gas Capital Jaycees (Sec. 1972), Am. Bowling Congress. Democrat. Mem. Christian Ch. Address: Star Rte 2 Box 3C Hugoton KS 67951

WILLIS, ROBERT LUTHER, JR., radiologist; b. Toledo, Ohio, Aug. 29, 1927; s. Robert Luther and Eva Tong (Powell) W.; student Kenyon Coll., 1944-47; M.D., Wayne State U., 1951; m. Patricia Jackson, Sept. 7, 1973. Intern, Harper Hosp., Detroit, 1951-52, resident in radiology, 1952-57; practice medicine specializing in radiology Luth. Hosp., Ft. Wayne, Ind.; radiologist Beaumont Hosp., Royal Oak, Mich., 1957-62, Harper Hosp., Detroit, 1962-68, Lutheran Hosp., Fort Wayne, 1968—. Served with USAF, M.C., 1953-55. Diplomate Am. Bd. Radiology. Fellow Am. Coll. Radiology; mem. AMA, Radiol. Soc. N. Am., Ind. State Med. Soc. Republican. Presbyn. Clubs: Fort Wayne Country; LaGorce Country, Palm Bay, Surf (Miami, Fla.). Home: 4701 Covington Rd Fort Wayne IN 46804 Office: 2828 Fairfield Ave Fort Wayne IN 46807

WILLIS, WILLIAM HENRY, otolaryngologist; b. St. Louis, Aug. 1, 1940; s. William Thomas and Faye Irene (White) W.; student St. Louis Coll. Pharmacy, 1958-59, DePauw U., 1959-61; M.D., U. Ill., 1965; m. Jane Rueger, July 6, 1963; children—Peter, Penny. Intern, Henry Ford Hosp., Detroit, 1965-66; resident in gen. surgery Hutzel Hosp., Detroit, 1966-67, resident in otolaryngology N.Y. Eye and Ear Infirmary, N.Y.C., 1967-70, chief resident, 1969-70; practice medicine specializing in otolaryngology Toledo Otolaryngology Group, Inc., 1970—; active staff otolaryngologist St. Vincent's Hosp., Toledo, 1970—, chief dept., 1978—; active staff Toledo Hosp., 1970—; trustee Toledo Hearing and Speech Center, 1971-77; cons. to Parents Hearing Edn. Assn. Toledo Pub. Schs., 1976—. Community health commr., Toledo, 1973-76; council mem. Glenwood Luth. Ch., 1973-76, 79—. Diplomate Am. Bd. Otolaryngology. Fellow A.C.S.; mem. AMA (recipient Physicians' Recognition award 1979—), Ohio State Med. Assn., Alexander Graham Bell Soc. for Deaf, Toledo and Lucas County Acad. Medicine, Am. Acad. Ophthalmology and Otolaryngology, Am. Council Otolaryngology, Deafness Research Found., Pan-Am. Assn. Otorhinolaryngology and Bronchoesophagology, Mich. Otolaryngological Soc., Royal Soc. Medicine. Clubs: Centurion, Toledo. Contbr. articles in field to med. jours. Office: 2743 W Central Ave Toledo OH 43606

WILLMAN, JOHN NORMAN, hosp., lab. and med. equipment mfg. co. exec.; b. St. Joseph, Mo., Jan. 19, 1915; s. John N. and Frances (Potter) W.; student St. Benedict's Coll., 1936; B.A., St. Louis U., 1979; m. Victoria King, May 9, 1941; 1 dau., Victoria. With Am. Hosp. Supply Co., 1940-59; v.p., 1954-59; with Brunswick Corp., St. Louis, 1959-68, v.p., 1961-68, pres. health and sci. div., 1961-68; v.p., dir. Sherwood Med. Industries, Inc., St. Louis, 1961-67, pres., dir., 1967-72, vice chmn., dir. 1972-73; pres., chief exec. officer, dir. IPCO Corp., White Plains, N.Y., 1973-78; mgmt. cons., 1978—; dir. Nat. Patent Devel. Corp., 1980—. Clubs: Noonday, St. Louis, Old Warson Country (St. Louis). Home: 530 N Spoede Rd Creve Coeur MO 63141

WILLMAN, MARTIN LEE, otolaryngologist; b. Louisville, Nov. 18, 1946; s. Walter Michael and Mary Waunita (Gaines) W.; M.D., U. Ky., 1972; m. Mary Linda Warren, June 14, 1969; children—Heather, Stephanie. Intern, St. Louis U. Hosps., 1972-73, resident, 1973-76; practice medicine, specializing in otolaryngology, head and neck surgery, 1976—; asst. clin. prof. St. Louis U., 1976—; pvt. practice otolaryngology St. Charles (Mo.) Clinic, 1978—; mem. staff St. Joseph Hosp., St. Charles, Cardinal Glennon, DePaul, St. Peter's, Firmin Desloge, Bethesda hosps., St. Louis. Diplomate Am. Bd. Otolaryngology. Mem. S. Central Am. Cancer Soc. (bd. dirs. 1979—), A.C.S., St. Louis Med. Soc., Mo. Med. Soc., AMA, Am. Council Otolaryngology, Soc. Univ. Otolaryngologists, Am. Acad. Ophthalmology and Otolaryngology, St. Louis Ears, Nose and Throat Club, Mo. Ear, Nose and Throat Assn. Home: 2304 Todforth Way Saint Louis MO 63131 Office: 2850 W Clay St Saint Charles MO 63301

WILLMOT, ROBERT JOSEPH, publishing and chem. co. exec.; b. Cleve., Feb. 21, 1928; s. Edward Joseph and Laura Mary (Berlyoung) W.; B.S., Kent State U., 1952, M.A., 1958; postgrad Ohio State U., 1964; m. Mary Guerra, Aug. 13, 1955; children—Lorraine, Mary Ellen, Karen. Tchr., audiovisual dir., dir. public relations Massillon (Ohio) Bd. Edn., 1952-65; dir. info., conv. mgr. Nat. Sch. Bds. Assn., Evanston, Ill., 1965-70; dir. public relations Carus Corp., La Salle, Ill., 1970—. Bd. dirs Ill. Valley United Way, 1971-78, pres., 1973-74; bd. dirs. Ill. Valley YMCA, 1976-81. Served with U.S. Navy, 1946-48. Mem. Mfg. Chemists Assn. (pub. relations com.), Public Relations Soc. Am. (accredited), Nat. Sch. Public Relations Assn. (accredited), Ednl. Press Assn. Am., Edn. Writers Assn., Chgo., N.Y.C. publicity clubs, Ill. Valley Area C. of C. (dir. 1973-79, pres. 1975). Club: Rotary (pres. 1975-76) (La Salle). Office: 1500 8th St La Salle IL 61301

WILLMS, JAMES MICHAEL, sch. adminstr.; b. Chgo., Mar. 31, 1942; s. Clarence Emil and Mildred Barbara (Macha) W.; B.S., Ill. State U., 1964; M.S., U. Ill., 1974; m. Marion E. Bartow, Jan. 16, 1971; children—Amanda, J. Kyle, Abby Marie. Tchr. history Palos Jr. High Sch., Palos, Ill., 1964-74, head basketball coach, 1964-77, athletic dir., 1975-77; prin. Independence Jr. High Sch., Palos Heights, Ill., 1977—. Mem. Nat. Assn. Secondary Sch. Prins., Am. Assn. Curriculum Dirs., Ill. High Sch. Assn., South Suburban Prins. Assn., Southwest Suburban Ofcls. Assn. Home: 11902 S 93d Ave Palos Park IL 60464 Office: 6610 W Highland Dr Palos Heights IL 60463

WILLOUGHBY, ERNEST DWIGHT, govt. ofcl.; b. Flint, Mich., Mar. 6, 1932; s. Ernest Clyde and Marion Amelia (Fletcher) W.; B.S., Wayne State U., 1955, postgrad. in Humanities, 1960-65; m. Ann Harper, June 11, 1960; 1 son, Ernest Frank. Various positions occupational research Mich. Employment Security Commn., Detroit, 1959—, mgr. occupational research, 1975—; UN tech. expert occupational research, Tanzania and Ethiopia, 1972-73; lectr. in field. Chairperson, Mich. Combined Episcopal Services Appeal, 1972; career-job placement service adv. bd. Detroit Public Schs., 1977-79; career info. and job analysis cons. to prisons, community agys., schs.; mem. Fed. Occupational Analysis Coordinating Com.; mem. com. on career info. for disabled Mich. Occupational Info. Coordinating Com. Served with U.S. Army, 1955-57; ETO. Recipient resolution Mich. Legislature. Mem. Mensa, Econometric Soc. Author: Occupational Analysis and Classification, Tanzania, 1975; contbr. occupational definitions to Dictionary of Occupational Titles, 1965, 77. Home: 15945 Curtis Ave Detroit MI 48235 Office: Mich Employment Security Commn 7310 Woodward Ave Detroit MI 48202

WILLOUGHBY, RALPH WILLIAM, contractor; b. Anderson, Ind., Dec. 12, 1937; s. William Earl and Dorothy Cleo (Browning) W.; student public schs., also mgmt. tng. classes; m. Shirley Ann Shirley, May 25, 1956; children—David Michael, Christina Lee, Kathleen Sue. Owner, Marathon Service Sta., Anderson, 1963-65; with Delco-Remy div. Gen. Motors Corp., Anderson, 1965-70; carpenter George Stamper Contractor, Carmel, Ind., 1970-71; constrn. foreman Connor Prairie Pioneer Settlement, Noblesville, Ind., 1971-73; owner Creative Carpentry, bldg. remodeling, Pendleton, Ind., 1973—. Pres., Connor Prairie Pioneers, 1972-73. Served with AUS, 1956. Mem. Nat. Home Improvement Council, Nat. Remodelers Assn. Home: Rural Route 1 Box 80 Lapel IN 46051 Office: PO Box 93 Pendleton IN 46064

WILLS, JANE MARIE, educator; b. Fargo, N.D., Apr. 26, 1946; d. W. Hamilton and Lucille A. (Roesler) W.; B.S., N.D. State U., 1968; M.S., U. Minn., 1974; Ph.D., Ohio State U. Jr. and sr. high sch. home econs. instr., Hibbing, Minn., 1968-72; jr. high sch. home cons. instr., Hibbing, 1973-74; textile and clothing instr. home econs. dept. Concordia Coll., Moorhead, Minn., 1974—; energy conservation cons. Minn. State Home Econs. Curriculum Revision Planning Meeting, 1979. Recipient award Concordia Coll. Spl. Awards Summer Sch. Fund, 1978, 79, 80, award Concordia Coll. Spl. Awards Fund, 1979-80; Am. Luth. Ch. future faculty devel. grantee, 1979-80; Gladys Branegan fellow, 1979. Mem. Assn. Coll. Profs. Textiles and Clothing (evaluation com. 1979 conf., proc. com. 1978 conf.), Am. Home Econs. Assn., AAUW, Minn. Educators Assn., Minn. Home Econs. Assn., N.D. Home Econs. Assn. (treas. state conv. 1978), Philanthropic and Ednl. Orgn. for Women, Alpha Lambda Delta, Delta Kappa Gamma, Kappa Delta Pi, Phi Upsilon Omicron, Sigma Alpha Iota. Lutheran. Home: PO Box 72 Casselton ND 58012 Office: PO Box 303 Concordia Coll Moorhead MN 56560

WILLS, MICHAEL EDGAR, advt. agy. exec.; b. Detroit, Sept. 28, 1946; s. Henry and Ursula Constance (Rasko) W.; student Oakland Community Coll., 1970; m. Suzanne Jane Beutel, Apr. 18, 1975. Prodn. mgr. Desmond & Assos. Advt., Oak Park, Mich., 1973-75, asst. account exec., 1976-77; account exec. Kidd & Gilbert Advt., Southfield, Mich., 1977-78, Meldrum & Fewsmith Advt., Southfield, 1978—. Served with U.S. Army, 1968-69. Mem. Bus.-Profl. Advt. Assn. Home: 2681 Calais Pontiac MI 48055 Office: 26011 Evergreen Southfield MI 48076

WILLS, ROBERT HAMILTON, editor; b. Colfax, Ill., June 21, 1926; s. Robert Orson and Ressie May (Hamilton) W.; B.S., M.S., Northwestern U., 1950; m. Sherilyn Lou Nierstheimer, Jan. 16, 1949; children—Robert L., Michael H., Kendall J. Reporter, Duluth (Minn.) Herald & News-Tribune, 1950-51; reporter Milw. Jour., 1951-59, asst. city editor, 1959-62; city editor Milw. Sentinel, 1962-75, editor, 1975—; v.p., dir. The Jour. Co.; sr. v.p., dir. Newspapers, Inc. Pres., Wis. Freedom of Info. Council, 1979—; mem. media-law relations com. State Bar Wis. Served with USNR, 1944-46. Named Wis.

Newsman of the Year, Milw. chpt. Sigma Delta Chi, 1973. Mem. Wis. Newspaper Assn. (dir.), Am. Soc. Newspaper Editors, Internat. Press Inst., Milw. Press Club, Sigma Delta Chi (pres. Milw. chpt. 1979-80), Wis. Asso. Press (pres. 1975-76). Unitarian. Home: 17965 Maple Tree Ln Brookfield WI 53005 Office: Milwaukee Sentinel 918 N 4th Milwaukee MI 53201

WILLSON, BARBARA BURMEISTER, psychologist; b. Walnut, Iowa, Oct. 29, 1927; d. Harry August and Harriet Evelyn (Halden) Burmeister; B.A., U. Nebr., Omaha, 1966, M.A., 1968; m. Philip James Willson, Aug. 24, 1968; children—Victoria Howe, David Hicks. Instr. U. Nebr., Omaha, 1967-70; psychologist Pottawattamie County schs., Council Bluffs, Iowa, 1970-75; pres. Tin Pan Alley, Inc., 1975—; bd. dirs., pres. River Bluffs Mental Health Center; mem. Health Planning Council of Midlands, bd. dirs., v.p. Family Services Agy. Certified psychologist, Iowa. Mem. Am., Midwest, Iowa (licensed psychologist) psychol. assns., Midlands Mall Merchant's Assn. (bd. dirs.), Council Bluffs C. of C. Democrat. Unitarian. Contbr. articles to profl. jours. Home: 548 Cogleywood Ln Council Bluffs IA 51501 Office: 165 Normandy Pl Westroods Omaha NE 68114

WILLSON, SHIRLEY ANNE, ednl. adminstr.; b. Bedford, Ohio, June 15, 1935; d. Axxel Christian and Bernice Rebecca (Dingledine) Jorgensen; B.S. in Elem. Edn., Kent State U., 1956, M.A. in Adminstrn., 1974; m. Reed Allen Willson, Nov. 10, 1956; children—Patricia Anne, Robert Allen, David Eugene, Paul Eric. Tchr. elem. grades Bedford City Schs., 1956-57, Kenston (Ohio) Local Schs., 1957-59, Crestwood (Ohio) Local Schs., 1959-61; tchr. West Geauga Local Schs., Chesterland, Ohio, 1962-76, curriculum dir., elem. edn., 1976—. Supt. Sunday sch. Bainbridge Community United Ch. of Christ, Chagrin Falls, Ohio, 1963-67, Christian edn. dir., 1970-74, chmn. ch. council, 1980—. Mem. Assn. Supervision and Curriculum Devel. Home: 18760 Snyder Rd Chagrin Falls OH 44022 Office: 11844 Caves Rd Chesterland OH 44026

WILMOUTH, ROBERT K(EARNEY), commodities exec.; b. Worcester, Mass., Nov. 9, 1928; s. Alfred F. and Aileen E. (Kearney) W.; B.A., Holy Cross Coll., 1949; M.A., U. Notre Dame, 1950; m. Ellen M. Boyle, Sept. 10, 1955; children—Robert J., John J., James P., Thomas G., Anne Marie. Exec. v.p. First Nat. Bank Chgo., 1972-75, also dir.; pres. chief adminstrv. officer Crocker Nat. Bank, San Francisco, 1975-77; pres., chief exec. officer Chgo. Bd. Trade, 1977—; dir. Victoria Sta., LaSalle Bank, Pvt. Export Funding Corp. Trustee U. Notre Dame; mem. adv. council Grad. Sch. Mgmt., Northwestern U. Served to 2d lt. USAF, 1951-53. Mem. Chgo. Assn. Commerce and Industry (dir.). Clubs: Chgo., Mid-Day (trustee), Economic, Mid-Am. (Chgo.); Barrington Hills Country. Office: 141 W Jackson St Chicago IL 60604

WILMS, WAYNE WILLIAM, biochemist; b. St. Louis, Sept. 28, 1944; s. Charles Edward and Elizabeth (Birnstill) W.; B.S., St. Louis U., 1966; Ph.D. (NDEA fellow), 1974; m. Ruth Ann Witte, Oct. 1, 1966; children—Jeffrey, Clifford. Asst. prof. Simpson Coll., Indianola, Iowa, 1974-75; asst. mgr., analytical chemist, research biochemist Sigma Chem. Co., St. Louis, 1975-81; nuclear/spectro application specialist Beckman Instrument Co., Fullerton, Calif., 1981—. Served with U.S. Army, 1966-69. Mem. AAAS, Am. Soc. Zoologists, Sigma Xi. Roman Catholic. Club: Our Lady of Sorrows Athletic Assn. Home: 4942 Schollmeyer St Saint Louis MO 63109 Office: 1970 Craig Rd Saint Louis MO 63141

WILNER, FREEMAN MARVIN, hematologist, oncologist; b. Detroit, June 14, 1926; s. Jack B. and Bell G. (Goldberg) W.; B.S., Wayne State U., 1950, M.D., 1953; m. Marjorie Louise Tewkesbury, Aug. 29, 1948; children—Jeffrey, Robert, Paul, Laura. Intern and resident in internal medicine and hematology Detroit Gen. Hosp., 1953-57, chief med. resident, 1957; staff mem. VA Hosp., Dearborn, Mich., 1957-58; practice medicine specializing in hematology and oncology, Southfield, Mich., 1958—; chmn. dept. internal medicine Providence Hosp., Southfield, 1963-66; chief sect. hematology-oncology William Beaumont Hosp., Royal Oak, Mich.; clin. asso. prof. medicine Wayne State U. Sch. Medicine; pres. Hematology Assos., Southfield. Served with USAAF, 1944-47. Fellow A.C.P. (counselor Mich. br.); mem. Internat., Am. socs. hematology, Mich. Cancer Found. (vice chmn. bd. trustees 1979-80), Am. Soc. Clin. Oncology, Mich. State, Wayne County, Oakland County med. socs., AMA, Alpha Omega Alpha. Contbr. articles to profl. jours. Office: 20905 Greenfield Rd Suite 501 Southfield MI 48075

WILSON, CHARLES JOHN, dentist; b. Detroit, Oct. 9, 1930; s. Carl John and Marion Ellen (Leathers) W.; A.B., Albion Coll., 1952; D.D.S., Northwestern U., 1956; M.S., Marquette U., 1961. Asst. prof. Marquette U., Milw., 1959-64; pvt. practice specializing in pediatric dentistry, Milw., 1961—; pres. Bio-Research Asso., Inc., Milw., 1965—, Northpoint Dental Group, Ltd., Milw., 1977—; dir., sec. Univ. Nat. Bank, Milw., 1975—, Lampshader, Inc., Milw., 1977—. Trustee, Watertower Landmark Trust, Inc., 1978—. Served to capt. USAR, 1956-58. Fellow AAAS, Internat. Coll. Dentists, Am. Acad. Pedontics, Sigma Xi; mem. ADA, Wis. Dental Assn., Greater Milw. Dental Assn., Am. Soc. Dentistry for Children, Internat. Assn. Dental Research, Am. Acad. Oral Medicine, Wis. Acad. Arts, Scis. and Letters, Delta Sigma Delta. Unitarian. Patentee in field; editorial bd. Jour. Dentistry for Children, 1964—; editor Greater Milw. Dental Bull., 1969-78. Home: 2640 N Terrace Ave Milwaukee WI 53211 Office: 2315 N Lake Dr Milwaukee WI 53211

WILSON, CHARLES STEPHEN, cardiologist; b. Geneva, Nebr., June 14, 1938; s. Robert Butler and Naoma Luella (Norgren) W.; B.A. cum laude, U. Nebr., 1960; M.D., Northwestern U., 1964; m. Linda Stern Walt, Aug. 21, 1960; children—Michael Scott, Amy Lynn, Cynthia Lee. Intern, Fitzsimons Gen. Hosp., Denver, 1964-65; fellow in internal medicine and cardiology Mayo Grad. Sch. Medicine, Rochester, Minn., 1968-72; practice medicine specializing in cardiology, Lincoln, Nebr., 1972—; attending staff Bryan Meml. Hosp., Lincoln, 1972—, chmn. cardiology, 1976-79; attending staff Lincoln Gen. Hosp., 1978—; asst. prof. medicine and cardiology U. Nebr. Med. Center, Omaha; mem. Mayor's Council on Emergency Med. Services, Lincoln, 1974-78; founder, chmn. Nebr. State Hypertension Screening Program; med. dir. Lincoln Mobile Heart Team, 1977—, Lincoln Cardiac Rehab. Program, 1978-79. Served as maj., M.C., USAR, 1963-68. Diplomate Am. Bd. Internal Medicine subsplty. bd. cardiovascular disease, Nat. Bd. Med. Examiners; Gen. Motors Nat. scholar, 1956-60, Nat. Found. Med. scholar, 1960-64, Mead Johnson scholar A.C.P., 1968-71. Fellow A.C.P., Am. Coll. Cardiology, Am. Coll. Chest Physicians, Am. Heart Assn.; mem. Am. Soc. Echocardiography, Mayo Cardiovascular Soc., Nebr. Cardiovascular Soc., Nebr. (dir. 1973-80, pres. 1976-77), Lincoln (dir. 1972-75, pres. 1974-75) heart assns., AMA, Nebr. Med. Assn., Lancaster County Med. Soc., Am. Soc. Internal Medicine, Lincoln Found., Phi Beta Kappa, Sigma Xi, Alpha Omega Alpha, Phi Delta Theta (pres. Nebr. Alpha chpt. 1959-60). Congregationalist. Clubs: Elks, Lincoln Univ. (dir. 1981—). Contbr. articles to profl. jours.; editorial cons. Chest, 1975-76; asst. editor Nebr. Med. Jour., 1981—. Home: 7430 N Hampton Rd Lincoln NE 68506 Office: 2121 S 56th St Lincoln NE 68506

WILSON, CHERYL SUE JONES, accountant; b. Globe, Ariz., June 20, 1948; d. Elton Roland and Shirley Vivian (Scott) Jones; B.S., No. Ariz. U., 1969; m. Gregory S. Wilson, Feb. 14, 1970. Staff accountant Coopers & Lybrand, Chgo., 1970-71, sr. supr., 1972-74, mgr., 1975-77, partner, 1977—, asso. nat. dir. health care services, 1976—. Bd. dirs. Chgo. area Planned Parenthood Assn., 1979—. C.P.A., Ill., Iowa, La., N.C. Mem. Am. Soc. Women C.P.A.'s, Am. Inst. C.P.A.'s, Ill. C.P.A. Soc. (chmn. com. health care instns. 1979-80), Am., Ill. hosp. assns., Hosp. Fin. Mgmt. Assn. (dir. 1980—, chmn. workshops and seminars com. 1979), Chgo. Soc. Assn. Execs. Presbyterian. Home: 36 Fox Trail Lincolnshire IL 60015 Office: Coopers & Lybrand 222 S Riverside Plaza Chicago IL 60606

WILSON, CHESTER HUMPHREY, geologist; b. Detroit, Sept. 9, 1939; s. Chester H. and Mary E. (Humphrey) W.; M.S., Mich. State U., 1967, Ph.D., 1975. Instr., Mott Coll., Flint, Mich., 1967—; dir. geol. studies Omega Inst. Geol. Research, Flint, 1968—. Registered geologist, Calif. Mem. Am. Geophys. Union, Geol. Soc. Am., Soc. Exploration Geophysicists, Michigan Basin Geol. Soc., Sigma Xi, Phi Kappa Phi, Sigma Gamma Epsilon. Author: Geology of Genesee County, 1972. Home: Box 18 Flushing MI 48433 Office: 1401 E Court St Flint MI 48503

WILSON, DONALD EDWARD, physician, educator; b. Worcester, Mass., Aug. 28, 1936; s. Rivers Rivo and Licine (Bradshaw) W.; A.B., Harvard U., 1958; M.D., Tufts U., 1962; m. Patricia Littell; children—Jeffrey D.E., Sean D. Intern, St. Elizabeth Hosp., Boston, 1962-63; resident and research fellow in medicine VA Hosp., Lamuel Shattuck Hosp., Boston, 1963-66; asso. chief gastroenterology Bklyn. Hosp., 1968-71; dir. div. gastroenterology U. Ill. Hosp., Chgo., 1971-73, chief of gastroenterology, 1973—, physician-in-chief, 1976-77; instr. medicine SUNY, Downstate Med. Center, Bklyn., 1968-71; asst. prof. medicine U. Ill., Chgo., 1971-73, asso. prof., 1973-75, prof., 1975—, acting head dept. medicine, 1976-77; vis. prof. medicine U. London, Kings Coll. Med. Sch., 1977-78. Active, Art Inst., Chgo., Chgo. Zool. Soc. Served to capt. M.C., USAF, 1966-68. Recipient Research awards HEW, 1971, 74, John A. Hartford Found., Inc., Distilled Spirits Council of U.S., VA; diplomate Am. Bd. Internal Medicine. Fellow A.C.P.; mem. Am. Gastroenterol. Assn., Am. Fedn. Clin. Research, Central Soc. Clin. Research, Central Research Club, Am. Assn. Study Liver Diseases, Soc. for Exptl. Biology and Medicine, Chgo. Soc. Gastroenterology (pres. 1978-79), Chgo. Soc. Gastrointestinal Endoscopy (pres. 1979-80), Digestive Disease Found. Clubs: Harvard (Chgo.), Midwest Gut. Contbr. numerous articles to profl. jours. Home: 20 E Cedar St Chicago IL 60611 Office: 840 S Wood St Chicago IL 60612*

WILSON, DONALD LEE, govt. ofcl.; b. Covington, Ky., Sept. 23, 1933; s. Charles and Harriet Eleanor (Vogt) W.; B.S., Asso. in Chem. Engring., U. Cin., 1965; m. Maltha Geraldean Knight, June 26, 1965; 1 dau., Jennifer Lee. Editorial clk. Cin. Post, 1951-56; chem. technician Nat. Lead Co. Ohio, Fernald, 1956-65; formulating chemist Interchem. Corp., Cin., 1965; with EPA., Cin., 1965—, phys. scientist Indsl. Environ. Research Lab., 1973—. Mem. Am. Chem. Soc., Am. Inst. Chem. Engrs. Republican. Contbr. articles to profl. jours. Home: 6724 Menz Ln Cincinnati OH 45238 Office: EPA 5555 Ridge Ave Cincinnati OH 45268

WILSON, DOUGLAS DREW, physician; b. Dayton, Ohio, Nov. 15, 1941; s. J. Edwin and Versie Elizabeth (Ellison) W.; B.S., Wright State U., 1969; M.D., George Washington U., 1973; m. Linda D. Shanks, June 21, 1969; children—Michelle Lynn, Sherri Ann. Intern, U. Wis., 1973-74, resident in family practice, 1975-76; mem. Watertown (Wis.) Family Practice Assos., 1976-79, Family Practice Center of Salem, Inc. (Ohio), 1979—; chief of medicine, sec. med. staff Watertown Meml. Hosp. Served with USAF, 1961-65. Recipient Mead-Johnson scholarship award, 1974. Diplomate Am. Bd. Family Practice. Mem. AMA, Wis. Med. Soc., Jefferson County Med. Soc., Am. Acad. Family Physicians, Alpha Omega Alpha, Phi Eta Tau. Home: 1237 Highland Ave Salem OH 44460 Office: 2370 Southeast Blvd Salem OH 44460

WILSON, EDWARD MATTHEW, ednl. adminstr.; b. Jamaica, W.I., Dec. 19, 1937; came to U.S., 1966, naturalized, 1979; s. Ernest E. and Adassa J. (Rose) W.; B.S. in Animal Sci., McGill U., 1964, M.S. in Animal Genetics, 1966, Ph.D. in Dairy Sci., 1969; m. Celia E. Smith, May 19, 1962; children—Mark, JoniLou. Physics instr. McGill U., Can., 1965-66; dir. U.S. AID, Guyana Livestock Mgmt. Program, Tuskegee (Ala.) Inst., 1969-72, asst. prof. animal sci., 1969-73; prin. physiologist Coop. State Research Service, USDA, Washington, 1973-74; dean Coll. Applied Sci. and Tech., dean Coop. Research and Extension, head dept. agr., natural resources and home econs., dir. univ. farms, prof. animal sci. Lincoln U., Jefferson City, Mo., 1974—; mem. Mo. Rural Devel. Exec. Bd., 1980—, Internat. Research Com., Internat. Sci. and Edn. Council, 1981—; U.S. ofcl. agrl. edn. del. to People's Republic of China, 1980; cons. USDA Task Force on Strengthening 1890 LandGrant Instns., 1980, Joint Council on Food and Agrl. Sci., N. Central Region, Mo. rep., 1979. Active, Jefferson City Airport Commn., 1979. Recipient award Nat. Alliance Bus., 1980. Mem. Am. Dairy Sci. Assn., Am. Genetics Assn., Sigma Xi, Gamma Sigma Delta. Methodist. Author: Development of Research at Historically Black Land-Grant Institutes, 1976; contbr. articles to profl. jours. Office: 303 Damel Hall Lincoln U Jefferson City MO 65101

WILSON, ELEANOR MAE, nurse, ednl. coordinator; b. E. Liverpool, Ohio, Nov. 22, 1934; d. Harold Monroe and Arverda Frances (Hunter) W.; diploma nursing E. Liverpool City Hosp., 1957; B.S. in Nursing, Incarnate Word Coll., San Antonio, 1968; M.S. in Edn., So. Ill. U., 1974; M.S. in Pub. Adminstrn., U. So. Calif., 1977. Commd. lt. USAF, 1958, advanced through grades to lt. col., 1974; staff nurse Mountain Home, Idaho, 1958-60; flight nurse, Europe, 1960-63; head nurse Randolph AFB, San Antonio, 1963-69; chief nurse Yokota AFB, Tokyo, 1969-71; ednl. coordinator Scott AFB, Ill., 1971-74, Mather AFB, Calif., 1974-78; adv. selection bd. nursing programs Am. River Coll., 1975-78; mem. advisory com. vocat. nursing Rancho Arroyo Sch. Vocat. Nursing, 1976-78; mem. nursing adv. com. Los Rios Community Coll., 1976-78; mem. occupational adv. com. for Asso. Degree Nursing, Sacramento City Coll., 1976; dir. edn. No. Columbiana County Community Hosp., Salem, Ohio, 1980—; mem. faculty Kent (Ohio) State U. Mem. County Health Commrs. Health and Safety Council; mem. Citizens Adv. Bd.; mem. Four County Mental Retardation Bd.; med. advisor Threshold Residence; chmn. edn. com. Heart Assn. Mem. Am. Nurses Assn., N. Area Inservice Educators, Christian Nurses Fellowship Assn., Alumni Assn. So. Ill. U. Home: 45327 State Rd Lisbon OH 44432

WILSON, FRANCIS SERVIS, JR., securities dealer; b. Chgo., Oct. 7, 1906; s. Francis Servis and Caroline (Seigfried) W.; student Dartmouth Coll., 1925-26; Ph.B., U. Chgo., 1930; m. Kathryn A. Wilson, June 1, 1945; children—Grace E., Francis Servis III, John G., William P., Thomas S. With investment firms, 1930-40; v.p. War Dept., Washington, 1942-43; analyst Standard & Poors Corp., Chgo., 1943-53; chief analyst Bache & Co., Chgo., 1954-63; exec. v.p. Woolard & Co., Chgo., 1963—; dir. Quixote Corp., Chgo., Casualty Ins. Co., Chgo., Stenograph Corp., Skokie, Ill., Spin-Cast Plastics Corp., South Bend, Ind., CIC Fin. Corp., Chgo., Energy Absorption Systems, Chgo. Mem. Delta Kappa Epsilon. Episcopalian. Clubs: Univ., Tavern, Attic (Chgo.); Chikaming Country (Lakeside, Mich.); Everglades, Bath and Tennis (Palm Beach, Fla.). Home: 199 E Lake Shore Dr Chicago IL 60611 Office: 135 S La Salle St Chicago IL 60603

WILSON, GEORGE PICKET, JR., educator; b. Nelson, Va., July 14, 1918; s. George Picket and Helen (Leeson) W.; M.A., U. N.C., 1941; Ph.D., Columbia U., 1958; m. Margaret Fordham, Dec. 19, 1942; children—Anne, George, Edward, Robert, Thomas, Patsy, James. Ednl. dir. WBIG, Greensboro, N.C., 1941-42; dir. radio La Poly. Inst., Ruston, 1942-45; chmn. dept. speech and drama U. Va., Charlottesville, 1958-61, dir. radio TV film div. extension, 1961-62; dir. telecommunicative arts Iowa State U., Ames, 1962-78, prof., 1962—; chmn. adv. com. programming and gen. policy for Iowa Ednl. Broadcasting Network, 1976-77. Pres., Venable PTA, 1959-60, 60-61, Charlottesville. Mem. Speech Communication Assn., Broadcast Edn. Assn., Univ. Film Assn., Nat. Assn. Ednl. Broadcasters, Soc. Motion Picture and TV Engrs., Central States Speech Assn., AAUP, Phi Kappa Phi. Clubs: Actors, Playmakers. Editor Newsletter Nat. Assn. Ednl. Broadcasters, 1974-77. Home: 135 Hazel St N Ames IA 50010 Office: Exhibit Hall Iowa State Univ Ames IA 50011

WILSON, HAROLD KERMIT, mfg. co. exec.; b. Mpls., June 12, 1940; s. Kermit Houchins and Lavina Jesse (Blatterman) W.; student U. Minn., 1958-62; m. Maria Malaya Manalansan, Jan. 7, 1977; children—Leilani, Jocelyn, Sarah; children by previous marriage—Mary Angela, Christopher. With Sico Inc., Mpls., 1962—, regional sales mgr., 1963-64, purchasing mgr., 1964-68, v.p. internat. sales, 1969-72, exec. v.p., 1973-77, pres., chief operating officer, 1977—, also dir.; dir. Nippon Sico K.K. Mem. Edina (Minn.) Homeowners Assn., 1972. Mem. Edina Hist. Soc., Hennepin County Hist. Soc., Minn. Hist. Soc., Young Pres.'s Orgn., Am. Hotel Assn., Am. Mgmt. Assn. Pres.'s Assn., Minn. World Trade Assn. Republican. Clubs: Rotary (dir. 1977-73, dist. internat. youth exchange com. 1972-73), Pony Colt League (co-founder), Edina Hockey Assn. (dir. 1975-77), Wagon Wheel Saddle Club. Office: 7525 Cahill Rd Minneapolis MN 55435

WILSON, HARRY HOWARD, JR., ednl. products co. exec.; b. Blue Island, Ill., Dec. 30, 1926; s. Harry H. and Kathryn Anne (Nicola) W.; B.S., Western Ill. U., 1950; m. Doris Ann Flanary, July 6, 1948; children—Kimberly, Kyle Ann, Kacy. Radio sportscaster WKAI, Macomb, Ill., 1948-50; with Container Corp. Am., Chgo., 1950-52; sales mgr. audio-visual and photog. products Radiant Mfg. Corp., Chgo., 1952-77; pres. H. Wilson Corp., mfg. ednl. audiovisual-products, pub. ednl. materials, South Holland, Ill., 1959—; pres. Wilcom, Inc., South Holland, 1977—; dir. James Metal Products, Chgo. Served with AUS, 1946-47. Mem. Dept. Audio-Visual Instrn., Nat. Audio-Visual Assn. (dir. 1966, chmn. S/S/mgmt. inst.), Nat. Sch. Supply Assn. (dir. 1966-68, exec. com. 1967-68), Am. Soc. Curriculum Dirs., Kappa Delta Pi, Sigma Tau Gamma. Club: Chicago Heights (Ill.) Country. Patentee in field. Home: 651 E Steger Rd Chicago Heights IL 60411 Office: 513 Taft St South Holland IL 60473

WILSON, JAMES BRIAN, hosp. adminstr.; b. N.Y.C., Oct. 19, 1935; s. Thomas Reginald and Winifred Una (Malone) W.; B.S., CCNY, 1958; M.S. Ed., U. Pa., 1961; Ph.D., U. Pitts., 1968; Ph.T. (hon.), Women's Med. Coll. Pa., 1963; m. Janet Marie Goulet, May 9, 1970. Tchr. elem. sch., N.Y.C., 1958-59, Marple Newtown, Pa., 1959-63; asst. prof., dir. tchr. corps, U. Pitts., 1968-69; asso. prof. urban edn. Temple U., Phila., 1969-79; spl. projects coordinator L.E. Phillips Treatment Center, St. Joseph's Hosp., Chippewa Falls, Wis., 1980—; instructional cons. Gen. Learning Corp., Phila. Public Schs., 1968-79; mem. exec. bd. 1st United Meth. Ch. Germantown, Phila., 1973-79, chmn. ecumenical affairs, Growth Group, Men's Group. Served with inf. USAR, 1959-66. Ford Found. grantee, 1965-67; recipient Four Chaplains Service award, 1979. Mem. Am. Ednl. Research Assn., Assn. Supervision and Curriculum Devel., Assn. Humanistic Edn., Scabbard and Blade, Phi Delta Kappa, Alpha Phi Omega. Democrat. Clubs: YMCA, Fellowship Center. Home: Route 8 Box 291 Chippewa Falls WI 54729 Office: St Joseph's Hosp 2661 County Trunk I Chippewa Falls WI 54729

WILSON, JOHN CARL, architect; b. Pittsburg, Kans., Sept. 17, 1935; s. Loxie Bryan and Alvina Jane (Groundwater) W.; student U. Wis., 1953-54; B.S. in Architecture, U. Kans., 1959; m. Barbara Whitney Bell, June 23, 1957; children—Karen Elizabeth, James Mark, Kathy Susan. Draftsman, John Flad & Assos., Madison, Wis., 1959-60; draftsman, job capt. Perkins & Will, Chgo., 1960-62; job capt., project architect Harry Weese & Assos., Chgo., 1962-65; project architect Loebl Schlossman Bennet & Dart, Chgo., 1966-75; owner, prin. John Wilson & Assos., Downers Grove, Ill., 1975-79; asso. Loebl Schlossman & Hackl, Chgo., 1980—. Mem., vice chmn. Downers Grove Plan Commn., 1971-75; Democratic precint committeeman, 1974-75. Served as lt. U.S. Army, 1957-58. Mem. AIA (dir. N.E. Ill. chpt. 1979), Am. Soc. Planning Ofcls., Bldg. Ofcls. and Code Adminstrs. Internat., Chgo. Whitewater Assn. (v.p.). Mem. United Ch. of Christ. Club: Jaycees (past pres. and senator). Home: 238 41st St Downers Grove IL 60515 Office: 845 N Michigan Ave Chicago IL 60611

WILSON, JOHN ROSS, TV exec.; b. Buffalo, May 3, 1946; s. Ross Anderson and June Margaret (Parsons) W.; B.A., Glassboro State Coll., 1968, M.A. (fellow), 1972; m. Kathryn Sanders, Sept. 29, 1979. Community relations dir. Sch. Dist. 151, South Holland, Ill., 1974; asst. TV producer Sta. WTTW, Channel 11, Chgo., 1975-77, mgr. media relations, 1978, dir. info. services, 1978-80, v.p. info. services and advt., 1980—. Served to 1st lt. U.S. Army, 1968-72; Vietnam. Decorated Bronze Star, Army Commendation medal. Mem. Nat. Assn. TV Arts and Scis. Club: Chicago Press. Office: 5400 N St Louis Ave Chicago IL 60625

WILSON, JOHN THOMAS, mfg. co. exec.; b. Chgo., Mar. 22, 1945; s. John Thomas and Marguerite Ann (Meyers) W.; B.S., No. Ill. U., 1972, M.B.A., 1976; m. Janice Lynn Maycan, Oct. 27, 1973. Data base adminstr. P.E.I., Chgo., 1973-75; software mgr. Jewel Foods, Inc., Melrose Park, Ill., 1975-78; tng. mgr. Internat. Harvester Co., Oak Brook, Ill., 1978-79, info. systems services planning mgr., 1979—. Mem. Republican Nat. Com., 1980—. Mem. Am. Mgmt. Assn., Data Processing Mgmt. Assn. Roman Catholic. Home: 468 Nassau Ave Bolingbrook IL 60439 Office: 903 Commerce Dr Oak Brook IL 60521

WILSON, JOHN TODD, educator; b. Punxsutawney, Pa., Mar. 7, 1914; s. Clark Hayes and Alice (Haire) W.; A.B. with distinction, George Washington U., 1941; M.A., State U. Iowa, 1942; Ph.D., Stanford U., 1948; m. Ann B. Camilli, Nov. 23, 1939. Asst. exec. sec. Am. Psychol. Assn., 1948-49; asst. prof. psychology George Washington U., 1949; head personnel and tng. res. br. Office Naval Research, 1949-52; program dir. for psychology NSF, 1952-55, asst. dir. for biol. and med. sci., 1955-61; prof. psychology U. Chgo., 1961—, spl. asst. to pres., 1961-63, v.p., dean faculties, 1968-69, provost, 1969-75, provost, acting pres., 1975, pres., 1975-78, pres. emeritus, prof. edn., 1978—. Served from ensign to lt. comdr. USNR,

1942-46. Mem. AAAS, Phi Beta Kappa, Sigma Xi. Home: 5555 S Everett Ave Chicago IL 60637

WILSON, KERMIT HOUCHINS, mfg. co. exec.; b. Mpls., Mar. 3, 1916; s. Arthur and Grace May (Houchins) W.; student U. Minn., 1946-47; m. LaVonne Esther Bettner, Dec. 31, 1962; children—Harold, LaVaan, Bonnita, Michael, Tereasa. With Cargill Inc., Albany, N.Y. and Mpls, 1934-45; co-founder, partner Waco Steel Scaffolding Co., Mpls., 1945-51; founder, owner SICO, Inc., Mpls., 1951—, chmn. bd., chief exec. officer, 1977—. Chmn. Hennepin County 3rd Dist. Republican Party Neighbor-to-Neighbor campaign, 1964; del. state and county Rep. Party convs., 1968; mem. first trade mission to Eastern Europe and Soviet Union, 1967; chmn. Edina Govtl. Commn., 1973-74; pres. Edina Found., 1978-79; Sunday sch. supt. Fremont Congregational Ch., 1936-38, chmn. bd. trustees, 1938, 62. Recipient Fgn. Trade cert. Dept. Commerce, 1967; Cert. of Appreciation, Govt. Yugoslavia, 1973; Design in Steel award Am. Iron and Steel Inst., 1973; Excellence of Design award Indsl. Design, 1977; Edina C. of C. Bus. award, 1978. Paul Harris fellow Rotary Internat., 1973. Mem. Edina C. of C., Greater Mpls. C. of C., U.S. C. of C. (forums for econ. and polit. discussion 1968), Upper Midwest Council, NAM, Nat. Fedn. Ind. Bus., Nat. Sch. Supply and Equipment Assn. Republican. Clubs: Edina Country, Classic Car of Am., Rotary (founding pres. Edina, 1957), Masons, K.T. Patentee in field. Office: 7525 Cahill Rd Edina MN 55435

WILSON, LANCE RAYMOND, food co. exec.; b. Denver, June 9, 1947; s. Raymond Americus and Mary Evalyne (Young) W.; A.B. with distinction, Calif. State U., San Diego, 1970; M.A., U. Minn., 1972, Ph.D., 1974, postgrad., 1976-77; m. Paula Ann Isberner, Dec. 26, 1971; children—Erich Damon, Erica Isberner, Evan Lance. Teaching asst. dept. sociology U. Minn., Mpls., 1971, mgr. small groups research lab., dept. sociology, 1971-73, research asst., 1970-74, research asso., 1976-77, family impact postdoctoral asso. Family Study Center, 1976-77; research sociologist, mgmt. systems analyst Navy Personnel Research and Devel. Center, San Diego, 1974-77; dir. community planning and research Correctional Service of Minn., Mpls., 1977-79; asst. dir. systems div. Minn. Crime Prevention Center, Mpls., 1979—, mem. bd. dirs., 1979—; systems devel. supr. Land O Lakes, Inc., Mpls., 1980—, forecast mgr., 1981—; cons. for police and mgmt. info. systems. Bd. dirs. Minn. Council on Ex-offender Employment, 1978-79; mem. sex offender treatment adv. bd. Minn. Dept. Corrections, 1978-79; mem. speakers bur. St. Paul United Way, 1978; mem. supportive services unit adv. com. Mpls. United Way, 1979. Mem. Am. Sociol. Assn., Am. Soc. for Info. Systems. Republican. Roman Catholic. Home: 4001 80th Ave N Brooklyn Park MN 55443

WILSON, LAWRENCE FRANCIS, cons. engr.; b. Delbarton, W.Va., May 21, 1933; s. John Henry and Crete (Thompson) W.; B.C.E., Ohio State U., 1960; postgrad. Toledo U., 1961-62; m. Mary June Salmons, Dec. 20, 1952; children—Gerald Anthony, Timothy Dean, Teresa Diane. Rodman Norfolk & Western Ry. Co., Williamson, W.Va. and Portsmouth, Ohio, 1951-53, 55-56; furnace engr. LOF Co., Toledo Tech. Center, 1960-65; mfg. engr. Permaglass Co., Woodville, Ohio, 1965-68; pvt. practice cons. engr., Oregon, Ohio, 1968-75; chief engr. Toledo Testing Lab., 1970-72; chief exec. officer Lawrence F. Wilson Assos., Inc., Oregon, 1975—, Product Analysis & Structural Testing, Inc., 1976—; pres. Product Analysis & Structural Testing Inc., Oregon and Luling, La., 1976—. Mem. Ohio State Bd. Bldg. Appeals, 1980—. Served with Signal Corps, U.S. Army, 1953-55. Registered profl. engr., Ohio, W.Va., Pa., Mich., La., S.D., Ind. Mem. ASCE, Nat., Ohio socs. profl. engrs. Republican. Baptist. Patentee device for drawing sheet glass. Home: 3504 Worden Rd Oregon OH 43616 Office: 4400 Martin-Moline Rd Millbury OH 43447

WILSON, LINDA LOUISE, educator; b. Garnett, Kans., Feb. 5, 1950; d. Paul Jay and Edna Ruth (Mitchell) Boots; B.S. in Edn., Pittsburg (Kans.) State U., 1972; m. James Hermal Wilson, Jr., June 20, 1970; children—Travis James, Derick Paul. Sales rep. KOAM Radio, Pittsburg, 1977-78; psychiat. aide SEK Mental Health, Pittsburg, 1976-76; nursery sch. tchr. Langdon Ln. Sch., Pittsburg, 1969-75; tchr./coordinator home econs. Combination Coop. Vocat. Edn. Program, Frontenac (Kans.) High Sch., 1978—. Active United Way, Pittsburg, 1979-80. Mem. Am. Vocat. Assn., Kans. Vocat. Assn., NEA, Kans. Edn. Assn., Kans. Bus. Occupations Assn., Phi Tau Omega, Parker High Sch. Alumni Assn. (sec. 1978-81). Republican. Methodist. Address: Rural Route 2 Box 297 Pittsburg KS 66762

WILSON, MYRON ROBERT, JR., psychiatrist; b. Helena, Mont., Sept. 21, 1932; s. Myron Robert and Constance (Bultman) W.; B.A. in Humanities, Stanford U., 1954, M.D., 1957. Rotating intern U. Wis. Hosps., Madison, 1957-58; fellow in internal medicine Grad. Sch. Medicine, Mayo Clinic, Rochester, Minn., 1960-61, fellow in gen. psychiatry, 1961-64, fellow in child psychiatry, 1963-65; founder, dir. adolescent psychiat. unit Meth. Hosp., Rochester, 1967-71; cons. psychiatry, 1965-72; prof. psychiatry Carleton Coll., Northfield, Minn., 1970; founder, psychiatrist-in-chief Constance Bultman Wilson Center Edn. and Psychiatry, Faribault, Minn., 1971—, exec. dir., 1972-73, pres., 1973—; attending staff Rice County Dist. I Hosp., Faribault; courtsey staff United Hosps., St. Paul; prof., cons. psychiatry Antioch Coll., Yellow Springs, Ohio. Served to lt. comdr., M.C., USNR, 1958-60. Recipient physician's recognition award AMA, 1973, 76, 79, 81; diplomate Am. Bd. Psychiatry and Neurology. Fellow Am. Psychiat. Assn.; mem. Am. Soc. Adolescent Psychiatry, Am. Coll. Health Assn., Pan Am., Minn., Zumbro Valley med. assns., Am. Acad. Med. Dirs., N.Y. Acad. Scis., Minn. Psychiat. Soc., St. Paul Soc. Psychiatry and Neurology, S.A.R., Sigma Xi. Republican. Episcopalian. Clubs: Minneapolis; Montana (Helena). Contbr. articles to med. jours. Address: Box 917 Faribault MN 55021

WILSON, PAUL DAVID, composer, producer, performer; b. Chgo., Aug. 30, 1952; s. Herbert Liston and Odessa (Steward) W.; B.A. in Music Composition and Theory, De Paul U., 1974; m. Marilyn B., Aug. 12, 1978. Music writer, producer Star Point 7, Chgo., 1974-76; music writer, producer, owner Herschel Comml. Inc., Chgo., 1976—; lectr. Columbia Coll., Chgo. Dir. youth choir Christ Temple Ch. of Christ Holiness, Chgo. Recipient CLIO award N.Y.C., 1978; CEBA award, N.Y.C., 1979. Mem. Nat. Assn. Rec. Arts and Scis. (bd. govs. Chgo. chpt.), Assn. Rec. Musicians (bd. govs. Chgo. chpt.), AFTRA, Screen Actors Guild, Am. Fedn. Musicians. Office: 57 E Walton Chicago IL 60611

WILSON, PAUL EDWIN, educator; b. Quenemo, Kans., Nov. 2, 1913; s. Dale Edwin and Clara (Jacobs) W.; B.A., U. Kans., 1937, M.A., 1938; LL.B., Washburn U., 1940; m. Harriet Eileen Stephens, June 16, 1941; children—Elizabeth, Mary Paulette, Eileen, David. Admitted to Kans. bar, 1940, U.S. Supreme Ct. bar, 1952; individual practice law, Ashland, Kans., 1941-42, Lyndon, Kans., 1946-50; atty. County of Osage (Kans.), 1947-50; gen. counsel Kans. Dept. Social Welfare, 1950-51, asst. atty. gen., 1951-53, 1st asst. atty. gen., 1953-57; asso. prof. law U. Kans., Lawrence, 1957-62, prof., 1962-68, Kane prof., 1968—; cons. in field. Mem. Lawrence Planning Commn., 1962-65; chmn. Bd. Zoning Appeals Lawrence, 1966-67; mem. Kans. Historic Sites Bd. Rev., 1973-77; trustee Ft. Burgwin (N.Mex.) Research Center, 1977—. Served with U.S. Army, 1942-46. Mem. Am. Bar Assn., Kans. Bar Assn., Am. Law Inst., Am. Bar Found., Selden Soc., Nat. Trust Hist. Preservation (bd. advisers 1972-78), Order of Coif, Phi Alpha Delta. Republican. Methodist. Author: Judicial Education in the United States, 1965; (with Reams) Segregation and the Fourteenth Amendment in the States, 1975; Pattern Rules of Court and Code Provisions, 1975; editor Am. Criminal Law Quar., 1963-70; contbr. articles to profl. jours. Home: 2622 W 24th Terr Lawrence KS 66044 Office: New Green Hall U Kans Lawrence KS 66045

WILSON, RALPH COOKERLY, JR., corp. exec.; b. Columbus, Ohio, Oct. 17, 1918; s. Ralph Cookerly and Edith (Cole) W.; A.B., U. Va., 1940; student U. Mich Law Sch., 1940-41; m. Jane Evans, Aug. 30, 1973; children—Christy Cole, Linda Brown, Edith Denise. Pres. Ralph C. Wilson Industries, Inc., ins., trucking mfg., broadcasting and photog. ops., Detroit, 1946—; pres., owner Buffalo Bills Profl. Football Club, 1959—. Served with USNR, 1941-46. Decorated Commendation medal. Presbyn. Clubs: Country of Detroit; Grosse Pointe (Mich.); Bloomfield Hills (Mich.) Country; Buffalo Country; Shriners. Home: 824 Lake Shore Rd Grosse Pointe Shores MI 48236 Office: 400 Renaissance Center Suite 2250 Detroit MI 48243*

WILSON, RICHARD FORREST, instrument co. exec.; b. Fort Wayne, Ind., Sept. 9, 1931; s. Forrest Frazier and Helen Hazel (Miller) W.; B.S., Butler U., 1955; m. Patricia A. Mc Comb, Oct. 22, 1959; children—Peter C., Sarah E. With Honeywell Co., 1957-62; pres. Pyromation Inc., Fort Wayne, Ind., 1962—; v.p. W.C. Grant Co., Ft. Wayne, Ind., 1967-76. Pres., Aboite Township Assn., 1969-70; mem. parent's bd. S.W. Allen County Schs. Served with U.S. Army, 1955-57. Mem. Instrument Soc. Am., Am. Soc. Metals, Fortnightly Hist. Soc. Republican. Clubs: Summit, Tennis. Home: 4225 W Hamilton Rd Fort Wayne IN 46804 Office: 5211 Industrial Rd Fort Wayne IN 46804

WILSON, ROBERT GARROW, JR., weed scientist; b. Lincoln, Nebr., Dec. 14, 1946; s. Robert Garrow and Lois (Hall) W.; B.S., U. Nebr., 1970, M.S., 1971; Ph.D., Wash. State U., 1975; m. Kathyrn A. Jones, Apr. 18, 1971; children—Robert Garrow III, Timothy Andrew. Jr. exec. Monsanto Chem. Co., St. Louis, summers 1968-69; asso. prof. U. Nebr., Scottsbluff, 1971—. Bd. deacons 1st United Presbyterian Ch. Recipient numerous research grants. Mem. Weed Sci. Soc. Am., Am. Soc. Agronomy, N. Central Weed Control Conf. (dir.), Soil Sci. Soc. Am., Council Agrl. Sci. and Tech., Sigma Xi, Gamma Sigma Delta. Republican. Contbr. articles to profl. jours., newspapers and mags. Home: 1100 E 38th St Scottsbluff NE 69361 Office: U Nebr 4502 Ave I Scottsbluff NE 69361

WILSON, ROBERT WILLIAM, pharmacist; b. Aurora, Ill., Mar. 13, 1937; s. Carter Glidden and Catherine (Greiter) W.; B.S., U. Wyo., 1959; m. Marjorie Ann Faltz, June 21, 1958; children—Kathleen Ann, William Robert, Charles Gary, John Raymond, Theresa Marie. Resident in hosp. pharmacy U. Ill., 1971-72; dir. pharmacy services Central DuPage Hosp., Winfield, Ill., 1972-75; dir. pharmacy, rehab. services Central DuPage Hosp., 1973-75; asst. dir. pharmacy St. Mary's Hosp., Rochester, Minn., 1975-76; chief pharmacist MacNeal Meml. Hosp., Berwyn, Ill., 1976—; updated pharmacy services Marianjoy Hosp., Wheaton, Ill., 1974-76; chmn. subcom. for pharmacy group purchasing Chgo. Hosp. Council, 1982—. Pres., Geneva (Ill.) Community Meml. Center, 1970-71; treas. Geneva High Sch. Parent Tchr. Orgn., 1976-79, v.p. Sch. Sports Booster Club, 1977-79. Mem. Am. Soc. Hosp. Pharmacists, Am. Pharm. Assn., Ill. Council Hosp. Pharmacists (dir. 1981—), Ill. Pharm. Assn. (dir. 1981—), No. Ill. Soc. Hosp. Pharmacists, Geneva C. of C. (pres. 1970-71). Roman Catholic. Home: 509 West Ln Geneva IL 60134 Office: MacNeal Meml Hosp 3249 S Oak Park Ave Berwyn IL 60402

WILSON, (JOHN) ROGER, physiol. psychologist; b. Boone, Iowa, Feb. 1, 1944; s. John Raymond and Marjorie Theola (Hiatt) W.; M.S., Kans. State U., 1969; Ph.D., Kent State U., 1973; m. Linda Gail Morrissey, Sept. 14, 1969. NIH predoctoral trainee Kans. State U., Manhattan, 1966-69; predoctoral fellow in psychology Kent (Ohio) State U., 1969-72; NIMH postdoctoral fellow in neurosci. U. Mich. Med. Sch., Ann Arbor, 1972-74, advanced research asso. in psychiatry, 1974-77; asst. prof. psychology U. Man. (Can.), Winnipeg, 1977-81, asso. prof., 1981—. Mem. Neurosci. Soc., Am. Physiol. Soc., AAAS, Am., Midwestern psychol. assns., Psychophysiol. Research Soc., Sigma Xi, Psi Chi. Contbr. articles to profl. jours. Research on brain mechanisms in hypertension, stress, thermoregulation. Office: Dept Psychology U Manitoba Winnipeg MB R3T 2N2 Canada

WILSON, ROGER B., state senator; b. Columbia, Mo., Oct. 10, 1948; B.A., Central Meth. Coll.; m. Patricia M. O'Brien, Mar. 23, 1974; 1 child. Collector, Boone County, Mo., 1976—; mem. Mo. Senate, 1979—. Democrat. Methodist. Office: State Capitol Jefferson City MO 65101*

WILSON, RONALD FRANKLIN, mktg. communications exec.; b. Cin., July 1, 1934; s. Perry Franklin and Sarah Elizabeth (Kendall) W.; B.A., U. Ky., 1958; m. Linda Carol Jacobs, Apr. 15, 1961; children—Roni Lynn, Todd James, Suzanne Elizabeth, Jennifer Leah. Art dir. U.S. Shoe Corp., Cin., 1968-70; owner Insight Advt., Cin., 1970-73; advt. mgr. NCR Corp., Dayton, Ohio, 1973-80; dir. communications Victor Bus. Products, Chgo., 1980—. Served with U.S. Army, 1954-56. Recipient various advt. awards. Mem. Mus. and Profl. Advt. Assn. (Chgo. chpt.), Nat. Indsl. Advt. Assn. Republican. Home: 307 Angela Ct Vernon Hills IL 60061 Office: 3900 N Rockwell Chicago IL 60618

WILSON, RUDOLPH GEORGE, educator; b. River Rouge, Mich., June 17, 1935; s. Randolph and Mary (Oliver) W.; B.A., Los Angeles State Coll., 1963; A.A., Los Angeles City Coll., 1961; M.A., Calif. State U., Los Angeles, 1964; postgrad. Washington U., 1973; m. Sandra L. King, Dec. 20, 1969; children—Trent, James, Dana, Amy. Orderly, Los Angeles Gen. Hosp., 1954-57; counselor Los Angeles Juvenile Hall, 1960-63; tchr., chmn. dept. English, Claremont (Calif.) Unified Sch. Dist., 1963-69; asso. prof. ednl. methods So. Ill. U., Edwardsville, 1969—, dir. Black studies, 1980, adv. coordinator secondary edn., 1979, drug prevention educator, 1973. Pres. bd. dirs. Madison County Council on Alcohol and Drug Dependency; bd. dirs. Edwardsville Unit 7 Sch. Dist., Sr. Citizens, Inc., Hospice, River Bluffs council Girl Scouts U.S.A., Ill. Assn. Alcohol and Drug Dependency Council. Served with U.S. Army, 1957-60. Recipient Gt. Tchr. award Alumni Assn., 1973; Teaching Excellence award So. Ill. U., 1970; award Hudlin Meml. for Humanistic Teaching, 1976; Danforth asso., 1977. Mem. Assn. Supervision and Curriculum Devel., NAACP, Hospice, Inc., Ill. Assn. Alcohol and Drug Abuse, Assn. Council Tchr. Edn., Kappa Alpha Psi. Episcopalian. Club: Goshen Oaks Social. Home: 1237 Gerber Rd Edwardsville IL 62025 Office: So Ill U Edwardsville IL 62025

WILSON, SHARON KAY, planning cons. co. exec.; b. Floyd County, Ind., Mar. 4, 1946; d. Heber and Norma A. (Turner) W.; student Ind. U., 1971-75. Public adminstrn. specialist Kentuckiana Regional Planning and Devel. Agy., Louisville, 1975-76; exec. dir. Clark County Regional Planning Bd., Jeffersonville, Ind., 1976-78; pres., chmn. bd. S.K. Wilson Assos., Inc., Otisco, Ind., 1976—. Pres., Clark County (Ind.) Parks and Recreation Bd., 1979, bd. dirs., 1976-79; organizer Interlocal San. Sewer Commn., Clark County, 1977; bd. dirs. designee Kentuckiana Regional Planning and Devel. Agy., 1976-79; mgmt. cons. Clark County Regional Planning Bd., 1977-79; public adminstrn. cons. Kentuckiana Regional Planning and Devel. Agy., 1976-77. Recipient Cert. of Appreciation, Clark County Superior Ct., 1970. Mem. Nat. Park and Recreation Assn., Am. Planning Assn., Womens Polit. Caucus, Ind. Planning Assn. (bd. dirs. 1975-77), Ind. Park and Recreation Assn. Home: 206 Squire Hill Ct Otisco IN 47163 Office: 506 E Utica St Sellersburg IN 47172

WILSON, SLOAN JACOB, physician; b. Dallas, Jan. 22, 1910; s. Jacob Resor and Estella (Cherrie) W.; A.B., U. Wichita, 1931, M.S., 1932; B.S. in Medicine, U. Kans., 1934, M.D., 1936; m. M. June Bowles, June 14, 1959; children—Sloan Richard, Charles Rook, Nancy Joan, Mark Samuel. Intern, Ohio State U. Hosp., Columbus, 1936-37, resident, 1937-40; practice medicine specializing in internal medicine 1940—; instr. U. Wichita, 1933-34; Ohio State U., 1940; asst. prof. medicine U. Kans., 1946-53, asso. prof., 1954-61, prof., 1962-79, prof. emeritus, 1980—, chief exec. officer, dept. medicine, treas. Med. Assn. Chartered, 1962—; trustee Mutrusco, 1968-71; cons. in field.; bd. dirs. Community Blood Bank Greater Kansas City (Mo.), 1956-59. Mem. Friends of Art, Nelson Gallery of Art, Kansas City, Kans. Served to lt. col. M.C., U.S. Army, 1940-46. Named hon. curator Japanese Art, U. Kans.; recipient Distinguished Service award, dept. medicine, 1976. Diplomate Am. Bd. Internal Medicine. Fellow A.C.P. (gov. Kans., nat. bd. govs. 1964-70), Central Soc. for Clin. Research, Fin. Analysts Fedn., Kansas City Soc. Fin. Analysts, Japan Am. Soc., SAR, Delta Tau Delta, Phi Beta Pi. Presbyterian. Clubs: Homestead Country, Masons. Author: Public Participation in the Stock Market, 1962; The Speculator and the Stock Market, 1962; Introduction to Stock Market Credit Analysis, 1965, Borrowed Money and Stock Market Trends, 1975; Hematology, Basic Rev., 1975; Hematology, Advanced, Rev., 1975; Hematology, Pediatric, Rev., 1975; contbr. articles to profl. jours. Home: 5618 W 62d St Shawnee Mission KS 66202 Office: 39th & Rainbow Blvd Kansas City KS 66103

WILSON, STANLEY NEWELL, osteo. physician; b. Brattleboro, Vt., Sept. 26, 1921; s. August Edward and Harriett Louise (Bemis) W.; student N.E. Mo. State U., 1939-42; D.O., Kirksville Coll. Osteo. Medicine, 1950; m. Doris Esther Burch, June 20, 1943; children—Thomas Newell, Kathryn Helen Wilson Reeves, James Byron. Intern, South Bend (Ind.) Osteo. Hosp., 1950-51; gen. practice osteo. medicine, South Bend, 1951—; mem. staff South Bend Osteo. Hosp., 1951—, chief of staff, 1957, chmn. bd., 1976-78, dir. med. edn., 1974—. Elder, Westminster United Presbyterian Ch., South Bend. Served to 1st lt. U.S. Cavalry, 1944-47. Recipient Med. Edn. award South Bend Osteo. Hosp., 1979. Mem. Ind. Assn. Osteo. Physicians and Surgeons (pres. 1962, Kinsinger plaque 1976), Am. Osteo. Assn. (1st v.p.), Am. Coll. Gen. Practice. Republican. Clubs: Kiwanis (pres. club 1959), Masons. Office: 2505 E Jefferson Blvd South Bend IN 46615

WILSON, THOMAS COLIN, II, med. technologist; b. Topeka, Sept. 5, 1950; s. Thomas Colin and Mary Kathryn (Hoover) W.; B.A., Washburn U., 1974; M.S., Kans. State U., 1977; m. Janet L. Doherty, June 23, 1979. Cert. optician Owens Optical, Topeka, 1970-73; lic. mental health technician Topeka State Hosp., 1973-74; research asst. VA, Topeka, 1974-75; probation officer Shawnee County (Kans.) Juvenile Ct., Topeka, 1974-75; mental health technician Menninger Found., Topeka, 1974-75; staff technologist, 1975—, cons. EEG and neurometrics. Mem. Am. Personnel and Guidance Assn., Kans. Personnel and Guidance Assn., Am. Mental Health Counselors Assn., Assn. Specialists in Group Work. Republican. Roman Catholic. Clubs: W.B. Track (co-founder), Sunflower Runners, Topeka Dive. Home: 333 Courtland Topeka KS 66606 Office: 901 Garfield St Topeka KS 66604

WILSON, THOMAS FREDERICK, economist; b. Pitts., Mar. 4, 1940; s. Glenn Richard and Maybelle Idella (Jennings) W.; B.A., Am. U., 1962; Ph.D., Columbia U., 1970; m. Kay Deitrick, July 6, 1968; children—Darren, Charlotte, Timothy. Economist, Fed. Res. Bank of N.Y., 1968-70; asso. prof. econs. Butler U., Indpls., 1970-80; econs. cons. Am. Fletcher Nat. Bank, 1973—; pres. Wilson Economics, Indpls., 1980—. Fin. chmn. Republican 20th Ward, 1977—. Manpower Adminstrn. grantee, 1966-68. Mem. Am. Econ. Assn., Assn. Study of Grants Economy, Nat. Assn. Bus. Economists, Inst. Mgmt. Scis., Am. Inst. Decision Scis., Phi Kappa Phi, Omicron Delta Epsilon. Republican. Club: Econ. (Indpls.). Editor: (with others) Redistribution Through the Financial System, 1978. Office: PO Box 68735 Indianapolis IN 46268

WILSON, TRUMAN E., state senator; b. St. Joseph, Mo.; student St. Joseph Jr. Coll.; B.S. in Edn., NW Mo. State U.; m. Betty Curtis, June 14, 1952; 3 children. Tchr. public schs. 17 yrs.; now pres. Truman E. Wilson and Assos. Ins. Mktg. Group; former mem. Mo. Ho. of Reps.; mem. Mo. Senate, 1970—. Mem. Mo. State Am. Revolution Bicentennial Commn.; mem. Mo. Gov.'s Conf. Edn.; mem. Commn. for Mo. State Employees Retirement System. Recipient Outstanding Alumni award NW Mo. State U., 1978. Mem. Nat. Conf. Ins. Legislators (exec. com.). Democrat. Baptist. Office: State Capitol Jefferson City MO 65101*

WILSON, W(ALTER) WILLIAM, lawyer; b. Newton, Kans., Dec. 8, 1947; s. Walter Garnet and Mary Elizabeth (Lynsky) W.; B.S., Woodbury U., 1972; J.D., Am. U., 1975; m. Judy Marie Anne Destouet, Jan. 26, 1976; 1 dau., Melissa Marie. Admitted to Mo. bar, 1976; individual practice law, St. Louis, 1975—. Bd. dirs. Orgn. for Missing Americans Abroad, 1976—. Served with U.S. Army, 1967-68. Mem. Am. Bar Assn., Am. Trial Lawyers Assn., St. Louis Bar Assn., Am. Soc. Internat. Law, Inter-Am. Bar Assn., Internat. Anti-Trust Soc., Internat. Bar Assn. Republican. Episcopalian. Home and office: 1126 Basswood Ln Saint Louis MO 63132

WILSON, WAYNE LEONARD, programmer; b. Paducah, Ky., Aug. 28, 1951; s. Leonard and Marion Catherine (Perkins) W.; B.A., Ind. U., 1973; M.S., Purdue U., 1975; M.S. in Applied Stat., So. Meth. U., 1977. Sci. programmer, statistician Gen. Electric, Louisville, 1977-78, sci. programmer, 1978-79; bus. programmer AT&T, Cin., 1979; sci. programmer Upjohn Co., Kalamazoo, 1979—. Ford Found. fellow, 1973-75. Mem. Am. Statis. Assn. Democrat. Office: Upjohn Co Henrietta St 7293-32-2 Kalamazoo MI 49001

WILSON, WILLIAM, JR., metall. engr.; b. Chgo., July 7, 1918; s. William and Myrtle Josephine (Becker) W.; B.S., Ill. Inst. Tech., 1941; M.S., Mo. Sch. Mines, 1943; m. Josephine Novotny, Aug. 29, 1942; 1 son, William. Sr. metall. engr. Armour Research Found., Chgo., 1943-50; supr. metallurgy Ecko Products Co., Chgo., 1951-56; dir. metall. research A. Finkl & Sons Co., Chgo., 1956—; instr. Ill. Inst. Tech., 1943-80. Registered profl. engr., Ill. Mem. Am. Soc. Metals (chmn. Chgo. chpt. 1957-58), Open Die Forging Inst. (chmn. metall. and research com. 1969-71), Steel Soc. Am. Inst. Mining and Metall. Engrs., Brit. Inst. Metals, Sigma Xi, Phi Kappa Phi, Phi Lambda Upsilon. Club: Scottish Rite. Contbr. articles to profl. jours. Home and office: 3308 N New England Ave Chicago IL 60634

WILSON SMITH, NANCY, assn. exec.; b. Oak Park, Ill., July 26, 1946; d. William Y. Wilson and Grace Mary (Dawson) Meeteer; B.S., No. Ill. U., 1968; postgrad. U. Miami, 1969, Keller Grad. Sch. Mgmt., 1979-81; m. Philip Merl Smith, Aug. 24, 1975; stepchildren—Heather Dawn, Ian Sterling. Office mgr. Crow, Pope & Land, Coral Gables, Fla., 1968-72; with Nat. Assn. Realtors, Chgo., 1972—, adminstrv. asst. to pres., 1978-79, asst. to exec. v.p., 1979-80, v.p., 1980—. Mem. Am. Soc. Assn. Execs. Office: 430 N Michigan Ave Chicago IL 60611

WILT, WILLIAM LEWIS, accountant; b. Shelbina, Mo., Jan. 5, 1928; s. Lewis Craig and Willa Mae (Heathman) W.; B.S., U. Mo., 1956, postgrad., 1956; m. Mary Elizabeth Taylor, Sept. 23, 1951; children—Ann Renee, Sandra Kay. Traveling sec. to gen. mgr. CB&Q R.R., 1948-51; staff auditor Arthur Young & Co., Kansas City, Mo., 1956-59; with Wilt & Garrison, pub. accountants, Brookfield, Mo., 1959—, sr. partner, 1963—. Dir., treas. Brookfield Land Corp., 1969—. Treas. A.R.C., Brookfield, 1959-65; auditor Boy Scouts Am., Brookfield, 1972—. Served with USN, 1945-47, 51-53. C.P.A., Mo. Mem. Independent Accountants Soc. Mo. (dir. 1965-75, pres. 1972-73), Nat. Soc. Pub. Accountants, C. of C., Am. Legion, V.F.W. Mem. Christian Ch. (elder 1967—, chmn. bd. 1976-77). Lion (pres. 1966-67), Elk. Club: Brookfield Country (pres. 1963-64). Contbr. articles to profl. jours. Editor Mo. Independent Accountant, 1967—. Editorial com. Nat. Pub. Accountant, 1972—, vice chmn., 1976-77. Home: 19 Markham Estates PO Box 353 Brookfield MO 64628 Office: 108 N Main St Brookfield MO 64628

WILTBERGER, MARY FRANCES SUSAN, employment co. exec.; b. Castleberry, Ala., Nov. 3, 1938; d. Ernest Hampton and Allie B. (Smith) Frazier; A.A., McHenry County Coll., 1974; children—Michael Anthony, Richard David, Anne Elizabeth, Susan Katherine. With Western Casualty & Surety, Crystal Lake, Ill., 1961-65; adminstrv. asst. to state rep. Calvin Skinner Jr., Crystal Lake, 1972-73; asst. reference librarian McHenry County Coll., Crystal Lake, 1973-75; profl. employment cons. to mgr. Computer Centre div. Gen. Employment Enterprises, Palatine, Ill., 1974-79; pres. Computer Personnel, Inc., Schaumburg, Ill., 1979—. Mem. Am. Mgrs. Assn., Nat. Assn. Personnel Cons., Ill. Assn. Personnel Cons., NOW, Nat. Orgn. Women Bus. Owners. Democrat. Clubs: Meadows, Chgo. Exec. Sportsmans, Excambia County Hunt. Office: Computer Personnel Inc 1701 Woodfield Dr Suite 415 Schaumburg IL 60194

WILTSE, DORR NORMAN, ins. exec.; b. Caro, Mich., Sept. 20, 1911; s. Norman Anson and Evie Markham (McCartney) W.; student Eastern Mich. U., 1931-33; teaching cert. Central Mich. U., 1933-37; m. Gladys May Garner, Nov. 11, 1932; children—Dorr Norman, Saire Christina. Tchr., Tuscola County (Mich.) Public Schs., 1931-42; br. mgr. Mich. Mut. Ins. Co., Caro, 1942-75; city assessor, Caro, 1964—, also casualty ins. cons., Caro, 1975-79. Vice pres. Caro Devel. Corp., 1975-79; adv. bd. DeMolay Found. of Mich., 1965-67; founder, pres. Watrousville-Caro Area Hist. Soc., 1972-75, 78; pres. Caro Hist. Commn., 1975-79; chmn. Caro Bicentennial Commn., 1975-76; mem. Com. to Elect Pres. Gerald R. Ford, 1975-76; mem. Indianfields-Caro-Almer Planning Commn., 1972-79. Named Citizen of Year, Caro C. of C., 1975. Mem. Mich. Assessors Assn., Caro Masonic Bldg. Assn., Inc. (pres. 1974-79), Nat. Trust Hist. Preservation, Nat. Hist. Soc., Hist. Soc. Mich., Huguenot Soc. Mich., Saginaw Geneal. Soc., Mich. Archaeol. Soc. Democrat. Presbyterian (elder). Clubs: Caro Lions (pres. 1946), Mich. Mut. Quarter Century, Masons (past master), Shriners. Author: The First Hundred Years, 1978; The Hidden Years of the Master, 1976; The Wiltse Saga, 1980. Home: 708 W Sherman St Box 143 Caro MI 48723 Office: 247 S State St Caro MI 48723

WILTSE, THOMAS R., foundry exec.; b. Bay City, Mich., May 22, 1924; s. Raymond C. and Catherine E. (Teeters) W.; B.S., Gen. Motors Inst., Flint, Mich., 1951; M.S., M.I.T., 1957; m. Jean L. Mertens, Sept. 19, 1952; children—William M., Louise C. Wiltse Rice. With Central Foundry div. Gen. Motors Corp., 1942—, div. works mgr., 1969-74, div. gen. mgr., Saginaw, Mich., 1974—; bd. regents Gen. Motors Inst.; adv. bd. Materials Processing Center, M.I.T.; adv. com. Sch. Sci., Engring. and Tech., Saginaw Valley State Coll.; charter mem. bd. assos. Delta Coll., Saginaw. Vice pres., exec. com. United Way Saginaw County. Served as pilot USN, 1943-46. Decorated Air medal; Sloan fellow, 1956-57. Mem. Internat. Com. Foundry Tech. Assns. (exec. com., past pres.), Am. Foundrymen's Soc. (past pres.), Foundry Ednl. Found., Soc. Automotive Engrs., Iron Castings Soc. (Gold medal 1979), Navy League U.S. Presbyterian. Clubs: Saginaw Country, Saginaw. Office: 77 W Center St Saginaw MI 48605

WIMBUSH, (RUTH) ANNE ENDERS, interior design soc. exec.; b. Benton Harbor, Mich., Mar. 26, 1913; d. Arthur and Lennie Frances (Smith) Enders; student Stephens Coll., 1931; cert. Western Mich. U., 1933; B.A., Eastern Mich. U., 1934; m. Samuel Isaiah Wimbush, June 30, 1934; children—Robert E., Samuel E. High sch. tchr. Coopersville (Mich.) Public Schs., 1960-63; dir., career counselor Med. Bur., Chgo., 1964-67; exec. sec., interior design career counselor Am. Inst. Interior Designers, Chgo., 1967-75; dir. interior design, art career counselor Decorative Arts Personnel, Chgo., 1975-78, dir., 1978—; exec. dir. Am. Soc. Interior Designers, 1978—; cons., speaker in field. Recipient Disting. Service award Am. Inst. Interior Designers, 1972. Christian Scientist. Contbr. articles to mags. including Parents, Surface Design. Home: 210 E Pearson #11-D Chicago IL 60611 Office: ASID 620 Merchandise Mart Chicago IL 60654

WINBINGER, CHARLES LEE, computer co. ofcl.; b. Cuba, Kans., July 26, 1934; s. Leon L. and Frances Ann (Baxa) W.; B.A. in Sociology, Creighton U., 1966, M.S. in Guidance, 1970; m. Kathleen E. Bracht, Feb. 8, 1969; children—Beth, Deborah, Matthew, Kristine, Amy, Gregory. Youth counselor Father Flanagan's Boys Town (Nebr.), 1963-71, head counselor, 1971-73, tchr. high sch., 1973-77; dir. edn. Nebr. Credit Union League, Omaha, 1977-79; fin. counselor Consumer Credit Counseling Service, Omaha, 1979-81; computer operator 1st Data Resources, Omaha, 1981—. Mem. Nat. Personnel Guidance Assn. Roman Catholic. Home: 3404 Augusta Ave Omaha NE 68144

WINBLAD, JAMES NORMAN, surgeon; b. Lindsborg, Kans., May 27, 1927; s. Hjalmar and Nora W.; student Bethany Coll., 1944-45, U.S. Mil. Acad., 1945-46; A.B., U. Kans., 1948; M.A., Kans. U., 1951, M.D., 1953; m. Gloria Danielson, Aug. 16, 1950; children—James Kent, John Mark, Kristin, Ingrid, Sonja. Intern, USPHS Hosp., San Francisco, Detroit, 1954-55, resident Indian Hosp., Phoenix, 1955-56, resident, New Orleans, 1956-62; practice medicine specializing in surgery, Winfield, Kans., 1962—; asso. Snyder Clinic, Winfield, 1962-71, Winfield Med. Arts, P.A., 1971—; mem. staff William Newton Hosp., Arkansas City (Kans.) Meml. Hosp. Diplomate Am. Bd. Surgery. Fellow Am. Coll. Surgeons, Southwestern Surg. Assn., Pan-Am. Surg. Assn.; mem. AMA, Kans., Cowley County med. socs. Episcopalian. Home: 1604 E 12th St Winfield KS 67156 Office: 1211 E 5th St Winfield KS 67156

WINCHELL, CARL CLYDE, sculptor, educator; b. Clinton, Mich., Sept. 4, 1927; s. Hazen B. and Mabel M. (Rudiseler) W.; B.F.A., U. Dayton, 1961; diploma in sculpture, Dayton Art Inst., 1961; M.F.A., Ohio U., 1963; postgrad. Wittenberg U., 1964-66; m. Beatrice Phillips, Feb. 26, 1950. Asst. on Archtl. Commns., Dayton, Ohio, 1957-63; instr. Springfield (Ohio) Art Center, 1963-66; instr. painting, drawing, sculpture Wright Patterson AFB, Dayton, 1964; instr. evening sch. Wittenberg U., Springfield, 1964-67; dir. Springfield Art Center, 1965-66; asst. prof. art Central State U., Wilberforce, Ohio, 1966—; set designer Springfield Civic Opera, 1963-75. Served with USAF, 1953-57. Mem. AAUP, Ohio Art Edn. Assn., Midwest Coll. Art Conf. Methodist. Author: The Patination of Metal Sculpture, 1963. Home: 380 Meadow Ln Springfield OH 45505 Office: Paul Robeson Center Wilberforce OH 45384

WINCHELL, RICHARD, ednl. psychologist; b. Mpls., Aug. 15, 1948; s. George H. and Inez B. W.; B.A., Webster Coll., 1972; M.S., So. Ill. U., Edwardsville, 1974; postgrad. No. Ill. U., 1977—; m. Pamela J. Wolski, Dec. 20, 1975; children—Katherine Michelle, Megan Elizabeth. Sch. psychologist So. Will County Spl. Edn. Coop., Joliet, Ill., 1976-78; psychologist Guardian Angel Home, Joliet, 1978-79; sch. psychologist Kendall County Spl. Edn. Coop., Plano, Ill., 1979—; impartial due process hearing officer State of Ill. Mem. Am. Psychol. Assn., Nat. Assn. Sch. Psychologists, Ill. Assn. Sch. Psychologists. Co-editor: School Psychology in Illinois. Contbr. article to profl. publ. in field. Home: 91 Ingleshire Montgomery IL 60538 Office: 800 Southwest St Plano IL 60545

WINCHELL, RICHARD DEAN, coll. pres.; b. Huron, S.D., June 21, 1929; s. Gerald Jesse and Helene V. (Peterson) W.; B.S., U. Nebr., 1952, M.S. in Ednl. Adminstrn., 1961, M.A. in History, 1962, LL.D., 1976. Tchr., Westside High Sch., Omaha, 1955-67; lectr. history Omaha Univ., 1961-67; mem. faculty Bellevue (Nebr.) Coll., 1968—, prof. history, 1967-68, pres., 1968—; pres. Bellevue Cable TV, 1979—; bd. dirs. First Nat. Bank, Bellevue, 1977—. Served with U.S. Army, 1952-55. Mem. Bellevue C. of C. (v.p. 1977-80), Phi Delta Kappa, Phi Alpha Theta. Republican. Lutheran. Club: Rotary (pres. 1975-77) (Bellevue). Home: 804 Vannornam St Bellevue NE 68005 Office: Bellevue Coll Bellevue NE 68005

WINDELL, VIOLET BRUNER, artist; b. DePauw, Ind., Nov. 1, 1922; d. Emory David and Audra Belle (White) Bruner; A.B., U. Louisville, 1943, M.A., 1958; m. Charles Lester Windell, May 22, 1943; children—Norma Helen, Eugene Kinsey, Lester Ann. Mem. staff advt. dept. Stewart Dry Goods Co., Louisville, 1944-46; instr. English, Ind. U., Jeffersonville, 1958-60; tchr. art North Harrison Schs., Ramsey, Ind., 1965-70; artist in residence Squire Boone Caverns, Corydon, Ind., 1973—; one-woman show: Port-o-Call Gallery, Louisville, 1965, Dist. State Hosp., Madison, Ind., 1980, So. Bapt. Theol. Sem., Louisville, 1981; group shows: State Art Festival, French Lick, Ind., 1966; Salute to Arts Week, Louisville, 1966; Lincoln Hills Ann. Shows, 1966, 77; July Juried Exhibit, New Albany, Ind., 1980; represented in permanent collection: rare books U. Louisville Library. Recipient award Ind. Mental Health Fund Drive, 1978; named Sagamore of the Wabash, 1980. Mem. Lincoln Hills Arts Crafts Assn. (pres. 1973-74), DAR (regent 1968-69, 71-73), Bus. and Profl. Women, Am. Humanist Assn. Republican. Mem. Soc. Friends. Club: Spencer Extension Home Makers. Author: Humen Symbiosis, family biography in 4 vols., 1968-76. Home: Rt 1 Box 108 Ramsey IN 47166 Office: Squire Boone Caverns Rt 1 Box 35A Mauckport IN 47142

WINDSOR, BRUCE ROLAND, chem. co. exec.; b. St. Joseph, Mo., May 2, 1953; s. Paul Noland and Emma Jo W.; B.S., Mo. Western State Coll., 1976; m. Marilyn Sue Deweerdt, Nov. 16, 1973; children—Amanda Nicole, Laura Michelle. Mem. tech. service dept. Hillyard Chem. Co., St. Joseph, Mo., 1976-78, tech. service dir., 1979, product mgr., 1980—, pres. Hillyard Employees Credit Union, 1979—. Mem. Fla. Sch. Plant Mgmt. Assn., Constrn. Specification Inst. Home: 3204 Squire Ln Saint Joseph MO 64506 Office: 302 N 4th St Saint Joseph MO 64504

WINE, DONALD ARTHUR, lawyer; b. Oelwein, Iowa, Oct. 8, 1922; s. George A. and Gladys E. (Lisle) W.; B.A., Drake U., 1946; LL.B., State U. Iowa, 1949; m. Mary L. Schneider, Dec. 27, 1947; children—Mark, Marcia, James. Admitted to Iowa bar, 1949, D.C. bar, 1968; pvt. practice in Newport and Wine, 1949-61; U.S. atty. So. Dist. Iowa, 1961-65; now partner firm Davis, Hockenberg, Wine, Brown & Koehn. Bd. dirs. Des Moines YMCA, 1963-75; bd. dirs. Salvation Army, chmn. advisory bd., 1971; bd. dirs. Davenport YMCA, 1961; bd. dirs. Internat. Assn. Y's Mens, 1957-59, area v.p., 1961. Mem. internat. com. YMCA's U.S. and Can., 1961-75; v.p. Iowa Council Chs.; pres. Des Moines Area Religious Council, 1975; chmn. bd. trustees First Bapt. Ch., 1975. Organizer, Young Democrats, Iowa, 1946; co-chmn. Scott County Citizens for Kennedy, 1960. Served to capt., navigator USAAF, 1943-45. Decorated D.F.C. Mem. Am. (chmn. com. jud. adminstrn. jr. bar sect. 1958), Iowa (pres. jr. bar sect. 1957), Polk County (sec. 1973-74) bar assns., Des Moines C. of C. (chmn. city-state tax com. 1978-80, bd. dirs., chmn. legis. com. 1981—), Order of Coif, Sigma Alpha Epsilon. Clubs: Masons, Kiwanis (pres. Downtown club 1969), Des Moines, Wakonda. Home: 3124 Park Plaza Dr Des Moines IA 50311 Office: Financial Center Bldg Des Moines IA 50309

WINEGARDNER, JAMES MICHAEL, mfg. co. exec.; b. Lima, Ohio, Mar. 6, 1947; s. Weldon Milfred and Jaunita Elizabeth (Van Pelt) W.; B.B.A., U. Notre Dame, 1969; m. Jane Wahl, Apr. 1, 1978. Asst. sales mgr. Surreys Ltd., Ft. Lauderdale, Fla., 1972-77; asst. sales mgr., regional accounts mgr. Superior Metals Products, Lima, 1977—; adv. counsel Range Kleen Mfg., Lima. Served with dog teams M.P., U.S. Army, 1969-70. Mem. Nat. Mgmt. Assn. (youth chmn. Lima chpt., certificate of appreciation, 1980). Republican. Roman Catholic. Clubs: Nat. Monogram, U. Notre Dame, Elks. Office: 625 Victory St Lima OH 45801

WINEMILLER, JAMES D., accountant; b. Sullivan, Ind., July 22, 1944; s. Floyd Maurice and Doris Marie (Lone) W.; A.S., Vincennes U., 1964; B.S., Ind. U., 1966, M.B.A., 1967; m. Nancy Kay Walters, Aug. 10, 1963; 1 dau., Nancy Marie. Accountant, Peat, Marwick, Mitchell & Co., C.P.A.'s, Honolulu, 1967-71; with Blue & Co., C.P.A.'s, Indpls., 1971—, partner-in-charge, 1974-76, mng. partner, 1977—. Grad. teaching asst. dept. accounting Ind. U., Bloomington, 1966-67; instr. accounting Coll. Gen. Studies, U. Hawaii, Honolulu, 1968-69; dir. Poland State Bank (Ind.), 1974-75. Mem. state adv. com. Vincennes U. Recipient Gold Medal for highest grades in state on C.P.A. examination, State Ind., 1966; Elizah Watt Sells Nat. Honorable Mention award, 1966. C.P.A., Ind., Hawaii; Vincennes U. Found. fellow. Mem. Am. Inst. C.P.A.'s, Ind. C.P.A. Soc. (dir. 1980—, treas. 1981-82), Hawaii Soc. C.P.A.'s, Continental Assn. C.P.A. Firms (dir. 1978—), Nat. Assn. Accountants, Am. Acctg. Assn., Ind. U. Well House Soc., Ind. U. Bus. Sch. Deans Assn., Ind. U. Alumni Assn. (life), Ind. U. Varsity-Hoosier Hundred, Vincennes U. Alumni Assn. (life). Presbyterian. Clubs: Rotary (dir. 1973-75, pres. 1974-75, Paul Harris fellow), Indpls. Columbia, Indpls. Econ., Hillcrest Country. Home: 9242 Whitehall Ct Indianapolis IN 46256 Office: 6609 E 82d St PO Box 50920 Indianapolis IN 46250

WINGER, JOSEPH WILLIAM, sch. adminstr.; b. Marion, Ind., Aug. 28, 1945; s. Joseph Ralph and Iola Marie (Burson) W.; B.S. in Edn., Ball State U., 1967, M.A., 1969, postgrad., 1971-72; postgrad. Ind. U., 1970; m. Ann Elizabeth McNair, Aug. 20, 1967; children—Megan Elaine, Whitney Johanna. Tchr., Meridian Sch., Kokomo, Ind., 1967-68; tchr., coach Maple Crest Middle Sch., Kokomo Center Twp. Consol. Sch. Corp., 1968-78; asst. prin. Maple Crest Elem. Middle Sch., Kokomo, 1978—, adminstrv. evaluation com., original mem. gifted and talented com.; active various civic orgns. Mem. Nat. Assn. Sec. Sch. Prins., Assn. for Supervision and Curriculum Devel., Kokomo Prins. Assn., Phi Delta Kappa, Delta Chi. Democrat. Ch. of the Brethren. Author: A Linear Programed Textbook in Electricity, 1969. Home: 1506 W Jefferson St Kokomo IN 46901 Office: 300 W Lincoln Rd Kokomo IN 46902

WINGET, LYNN WARREN, educator; b. Garden City, Kans., July 28, 1926; s. Edwin Arthur and Josephine (Dickerson) W.; B.A., U. Wichita, 1948; M.A., U. Wis., 1949, Ph.D., 1960; student U. Oslo, 1950-51. Instr., Spanish and French, Murray State U., 1954-61; vis. prof. Spanish and French, Ark. State Tchrs. Coll., 1956; prof. Romance langs. Wichita State U., 1961—. Mem. Sister Cities Adv. Bd. Wichita, 1974-81, vice-chmn., 1978, 79; pres. Wichita Choral Soc., 1978-79, dir., 1976-82. Fulbright fellow 1950-51; U. Wis. Markham fellow, 1963-64. Mem. Hispanic Soc. Kans. (dir. 1979—), Am. Assn. Tchrs. Spanish and Portuguese, Modern Lang. Assn., Mediaeval Acad. Am., Linguistic Soc. Am., Kans. Fgn. Lang. Assn., Societat Filologjche Furlane, Alliance Francaise de Wichita. Roman Catholic. Co-author: Spanish for the American Traveler, 1972; 2001 Spanish and English Idioms, 1976; co-editor: The Lapidario of Alfonso el Sabio, 1980. Home: 1730 N Yale Wichita KS 67208 Office: Dept Romance Langs Wichita State U Wichita KS 67208

WINICKER, DOUGLAS ROBERT, architect; b. Ft. Wayne, Ind., Feb. 12. 1950; s. Robert Henry and Ruth (Kiess) W.; B.Arch., U. Cin., 1974. Draftsman, Schenkel, Shultz, and Hodge, Ft. Wayne, Ind., 1970-73; campus planner N.E. Mo. State U., Kirksville, 1974-77, asst. to pres., campus planner, 1978—; project designer Schenkel and Shultz Inc., architects, Ft. Wayne, 1977-78. Mem. facilities task force Mo. Dept. Higher Edn.; adviser merit badge for architecture Boy Scouts Am., 1971, 77; mem. bldg. com. Milan Lutheran Ch., 1976-77; mem. facilities planning com. Kirksville Community Center, 1978. Office: Campus Planner NE Mo State U Kirksville MO 63501

WINKELMAN, STANLEY J., retail exec.; b. Saulte, Ste. Marie, Mich., Sept. 23, 1922; s. Leon G. and Josephine (Rosenblum) W.; B.S. in Chemistry, U. Mich., 1943; m. Margaret Jayne Wallace, Mar. 27, 1943; children—Andra Wallace Winkelman Barr, Marjory Beth Winkelman Epstein, Roger Edward Winkelman. Research chemist Calif. Inst. Tech. and U. Calif., 1943-44; with Winkelman Stores, Inc., Detroit, 1946—, v.p. in charge mdse., 1951-57, sr. v.p., 1957-60, exec. v.p., 1960-65, pres., 1965—, chmn. bd., 1976—, chief exec. officer, 1976—; dir. New Detroit, Inc., 1967—, vice chmn., 1969-70. Pres., Jewish Community Council, 1960-63, exec. com., 1956—; hon. chmn. Mayor's Supported Work Program, 1976—; co-chmn. Citizens Edn. Task Force, Detroit Bd. Edn., 1972-76; mem. Citizens Adv. Com., U. Mich., Dearborn campus, 1970—; bd. dirs. Detroit Round Table of Christians and Jews, 1963—, United Found., 1955—, mem. exec. com., 1969—; bd. govs. Jewish Welfare Fedn., 1956—, v.p., 1969-74; bd. advs. Wayne State U. Press, 1955—; bd. dirs. Wayne State Fund, 1976—, v.p., 1975; bd. dirs. Health Care Inst., Wayne State U., 1977—, Detroit Conv. Bur., 1959-70, v.p., 1966; trustee Temple Beth El, 1st v.p., 1966; trustee Met. NW Detroit Hosps. Corp., 1972—. Served to lt. (j.g.) USN, 1944-46. Recipient Liberty Bell award Detroit Bar Assn., 1968, Am. Jewish Congress Amity award, 1968, U. Detroit Human Relations award, 1968, Wayne State U. Builder award, 1975. Mem. Nat. Retail Mchts. Assn. (v.p. 1978—, chmn. consumer affairs com. 1976—). Democrat. Jewish. Clubs: Standard, Renaissance (Detroit); Franklin Hills Country; Circumnavigators. Home: 1921 Pine Ridge Ln Bloomfield Hills MI 48013 Office: Winkelman Stores Inc 25 Parsons St Detroit MI 48201

WINKELMANN, JOHN PAUL, assn. exec.; b. St. Louis, Sept. 14, 1933; s. Clarence Henry and Alyce Marie (Pierce) W.; B.S., St. Louis U., 1955; B.S. in Pharmacy, St. Louis Coll. Pharmacy, 1960; Sc.D., London Coll. Applied Sci., 1972; m. Margaret Ann Grandy, June 16, 1967; children—John Damian and James Paul (twins), Joseph Peter, Christopher Louis. Pres., chief pharmacist Winkelmann Apothecary, Ltd., St. Louis, 1960-76; pres., Nat. Catholic Pharmacists Guild U.S., 1968-70, 79—, exec. dir., 1970—; historian St. Louis Coll. Pharmacy, 1960—, trustee, 1961—. Served with USAF, 1956-57. Decorated Knight of Malta, 1969, Marian knight of Teutonic Order, 1967; Gold Papal Lateran Cross, 1969, knight St. Maurice and St. Lazarus, 1975, knight Holy Sepulchre, 1980; Pope Paul VI Recognition awards, 1977, 78; Presdl. Sports award Pres. Jimmy Carter, 1977. Fellow Nat. Cath. Pharmacists Guild U.S., Royal Soc. Health, Am. Coll. Apothecaries, Am. Coll. Pharmacists; mem. Am. Acad. Gen. Practice of Pharmacy (charter). Roman Catholic. Author: History of the Saint Louis College of Pharmacy, 1964; Catholic Pharmacy, 1966; editor The Catholic Pharmacist, 1967—. Home and Office: 1012 Surrey Hills Dr Saint Louis MO 63117

WINKLER, HELEN HUTULA, physician; b. Covington, Mich., Jan. 20, 1939; d. Charles August and Dagmar (Kaura) Hutula; student Mich. Tech. U., 1956-57; B.A., Mich. State U., 1959; M.D., Wayne State U., 1963; m. Robert R. Minichelli, Oct. 21, 1978; children by previous marriage—Tanya Marie Powell, Michael Randall Powell. Intern Wayne County Gen. Hosp., Eloise, Mich., 1963-64; instr. anatomy Wayne State U., Detroit, 1964-65; resident in internal medicine Henry Ford Hosp., Detroit, 1965-68; practice medicine specializing in internal medicine, Detroit, 1968-69, 74—; internist Blain Clinic, Detroit, 1969-70, Henry Ford Hosp., Detroit, 1971-74. Diplomate Am. Bd. Internal Medicine. Mem. Am. Occupational Med. Assn., Mich. Indsl. Med. Assn., Mich., Wayne County med. socs., AMA, Am. Med. Women's Assn., A.C.P., Mich. Heart Assn., Finnish Center Assn., Alpha Omega Alpha, Phi Mu, Phi Kappa Phi. Unitarian. Club: Grosse Pointe Hunt. Home: 445 Neff St Grosse Pointe MI 48230 Office: 14616 E Seven Mile St Detroit MI 48205

WINKLER, HENRY RALPH, univ. pres., historian; b. Waterbury, Conn., Oct. 27, 1916; s. Jacob and Ethel (Riegar) W.; A.B., U. Cin., 1938, M.A., 1940; Ph.D., U. Chgo., 1947; hon. degrees Lehigh U., 1974, Rutgers U., 1977, No. Ky. U., 1978, St. Thomas Inst., 1979, Hebrew Union Coll., 1980, Xavier U., 1981, City U. Manila, 1981; m. Clare Sapadin, Aug. 18, 1940; children—Allen Michael, Karen Jean; m. 2d, Beatrice Ross, Jan. 28, 1973. Instr., U. Cin., 1939-40; asst. prof. Roosevelt Coll., 1946-47; mem. faculty Rutgers U., 1947-77, prof. history, 1958-77, chmn. dept., 1960-64, dean faculty liberal arts, 1967, vice provost, 1968-70, acting provost, 1970, v.p. acad. affairs, 1970-72, sr. v.p. acad. affairs, 1972-76, exec. v.p., 1976-77; exec. v.p. U. Cin., 1977, pres., 1977—; mng. editor Am. Hist. Rev., 1964-68; vis. prof. Bryn Mawr Coll., 1959-60, Harvard U. summer, 1964, Columbia U., summer 1967; faculty John Hay Fellows Inst. Humanities, 1960-65; nat. chmn. European history advanced placement com. Coll. Entrance Exam. Bd., 1960-64, council on acad. affairs, 1978-80, trustee, 1979—, vice chmn., 1980—; mem. Nat. Commn. on Humanities in Schs., 1967-68; Am. Assn. Schs. Eastern Asia, 1968; exec. com. Conf. on Brit. Studies, 1968-75; chmn. bd. Nat. Humanities Faculty, 1970-73. Pres., Highland Park (N.J.) Bd. Edn., 1962-63; mem. exec. com. Nat. Assn. State Univs. and Land Grant Colls.; bd. dirs. Am. Council on Edn.; trustee Cin. Mus. Natural

History, 1978. Served with USNR, 1943-46. Mem. Am. Hist. Assn., Phi Beta Kappa, Tau Kappa Alpha, Phi Alpha Theta. Clubs: Queen City, Optimist, Bankers, Cin., Literary, MacDowell, Rotary, Comml. Author: The League of Nations Movement in Great Britain, 1914-19, 1952; Great Britain in the Twentieth Century, 2d edit., 1966. Editor: (with K.M. Setton) Great Problems in European Civilization, 1954, 2d edit., 1966; Twentieth-Century Britain, 1977; editorial bd. Historian, 1958-64; adv. bd. Partisan Rev., 1972-79. Contbr. articles and revs. to profl. jours. Office: U Cincinnati Cincinnati OH 45221

WINKWORTH, DOUGLAS EDWIN, contractor, developer; b. South Bend, Ind., Feb. 27, 1945; s. Edwin Owen and Dorothy Margaret (Barker) W.; B.Arch., U. Detroit, 1969, M.A. in Urban Econs., 1970; m. Mary Elizabeth DiMambro, Dec. 27, 1968; 1 son, Rob Douglas. Market analyst, asst. to v.p. fin. Simone Corp., Detroit, 1969-70; urban designer/planner/analyst Vilican-Leman Assos., Southfield, Mich., 1971-73; corp. sec. DiMambro Constrn., Inc., Oak Park, Mich., 1973—; adminstrv. agt. SETCO & Assos., Ottawa, Ont., 1975—; mng. partner DiMambro Investment Co., Oak Park, 1975—; corp. sec. Conduit Constrn. Corp., Oak Park, 1978—; pres. Northend Properties, Inc.; mng. partner Resource Devel. Group, Campus Devel. Assos., 1981. Bd. dirs. Gateway Montessori House, Inc.; mem. Birmingham (Mich.) City Planning Commn., 1975—. Recipient Titan Ter. award of appreciation U. Detroit, 1977, Service award, 1981, E.D.G.E. Founders award, 1981; named to Outstanding Young Men of Am., U.S. Jaycees, 1978. Mem. Greater Detroit C. of C., Asso. Underground Contractors. Club: Econ. (Detroit). Office: 13000 Northend St Oak Park MI 48237

WINN, BRAD ALAN, med.-tech. firm exec.; b. Peoria, Ill., Dec. 19, 1952; s. Marion Desmond and Mary Louise (Craig) W.; B.S., Ohio State U., 1977; postgrad. Pepperdine U., 1979—; m. Marilyn Jane Brandenburg, Feb. 1, 1974; 1 son, Andrew Ryan. Open heart surg. technician Riverside Meth. Hosp., Columbus, Ohio, 1974-75; circulation technologist U. Mich. Med. Center, Ann Arbor, 1977; circulation technologist Ind. U. Hosps., Indpls., 1977-78, dir. perfusion services, 1980—; product mgr. Bentley Labs., Inc., Irvine, Calif., 1978-80; pres. Extracorporeal Technologies Inc., Indpls., 1980—. Mem. Assn. Circulation Technologists (pres.), Am. Mgmt. Assn., Am. Soc. Extracorporeal Technologists (award for best sci. paper 1977). Office: 1100 W Michigan St Indianapolis IN 46223

WINN, EDWARD LAWRENCE, JR., congressman; b. Kansas City, Mo., Aug. 22, 1919; s. Edward Lawrence and Gertrude (Shepherd) W.; B.A., U. Kans., 1941; m. Joan Ruth Elliott, May 5, 1942; children—Edward Lawrence III, Robert Elliott, Douglas Shepherd, Janet Gay Winn Payne, Cynthia Joan Winn Burr. Sports announcer radio sta. WHB, Kansas City, 1941-42; asst. recreation dir. N.Am. Aviation Co., Kansas City, 1943-44; dir. pub. relations ARC, Kansas City, 1944-45; pvt. builder, Johnson County, Kans., 1946-47; salesman Hamilton-Crawford Realty Co., Johnson County, 1948-49; v.p. Winn-Rau Corp., Overland Park, Kans., 1950—; mem. 90th-97th Congresses from 3d Kans. dist., Sci. and Tech. com., Fgn. Affairs com. Dir. Southgate State Bank, Prairie Village, Kans. Vice pres. Kaw council Boy Scouts Am., 1965-67, rep. Nat. council, 1958-67; mem. adv. bd. Shawnee Mission Hosp., Jr. Achievement Greater Kansas City. Mem. Republican exec. com., State of Kans., 1964-66. Bd. dirs. Community Chest Greater Kansas City, Johnson County United Funds Council. Mem. Kans. Farm Bur., Recipient Silver Beaver award Boy Scouts Am. Mem. Nat. Assn. Home Builders, Home Builders Assn. Greater Kansas City (past v.p.), Sigma Delta Chi, Phi Kappa Psi. Mem. Christian Ch. Club: Rotary. Home: 5405 W 103d Terr Overland Park KS 66207 Office: 2268 Rayburn House Office Bldg Washington DC 20515*

WINN, MAURICE EDWARD, hobby mfg. co. exec.; b. Lucerne, Ind., Oct. 8, 1927; s. Chester B. and Hazel (Kistler) W.; B.S., Purdue U., 1950; postgrad. Butler U., 1951-52; M.A., Academia Hispano Americano, San Miquel De Allende, Guanajuato, Mexico, 1964; m. Mary L. Cline, Jan. 3, 1954; children—Lauren A., M. Douglas. Salesman, Davidsons Lumber Co., Indpls., 1950-52; gen. mgr. Keystone Distbrs., Inc., Indpls., 1952-63; pres. Twinn-K, Inc., Indpls., 1964—; chmn. bd. Twinn-K Internat. Inc., Indpls.; instr. English, Instituto Allende, 1963-64. Served with AUS, 1945-46. Recipient Merit award Gen. Hobby Corp., Phila., 1966-68. Mem. Hobby Industry Assn. Am. (dir. model racing div. 1967-77), Nat. Competition Com. (sec. 1969-78). Republican. Lion (pres. Indpls. 1961), Elk. Clubs: Columbia, Highland Country, World Trade (Indpls.). Contbr. numerous articles to trade mags. Home: 430 S Center St Plainfield IN 46168 Office: 10296 W Washington St PO Box 31228 Indianapolis IN 46231

WINN, RHONDA LEE, psychologist; b. Williamsport, Pa., July 23, 1946; d. James Branch and Juanita Blanche (Dennis) Skeen; A.B., Morris Harvey Coll., U. Charleston, 1968; M.A., W.Va. U., 1971; Ph.D., Northwestern U., 1981. Tchr., Kanawha County Public Schs., Charleston, W.Va., 1968-74; counseling psychologist Job Corps, U.S. Dept. Labor, Charleston, 1974-76; teaching asst., internship supr. M.A.T. program Northwestern U., 1977-79; part-time faculty evening div. Morris Harvey Coll., 1969; lectr. div. edn. U. Wis., Kenosha, 1980—. Mem. Am. Personnel and Guidance Assn., Am. Psychol. Assn., NEA, Kappa Delta Pi, Alpha Lambda Delta, Phi Delta Kappa. Home: 6329 N Albany Ave Chicago IL 60659

WINN, ROBERT CHEEVER, air force officer; b. N.Y.C., Apr. 11, 1939; s. Richard Wilkens and Ella Jane (MacKenzie) W.; B.A., U. Bridgeport, 1962; M.A., Ball State U., 1975; student Squadron Officer's Sch., 1966, Air Command Staff Coll., 1972, Indsl. Coll. Armed Forces, 1976; m. Margery Ellen Irwin, Dec. 22, 1962; children—Elizabeth Jane, Margaret Ruth, Nancy Louise. Commd. 2nd lt. U.S. Air Force, 1963, advanced through grades to maj., 1974; aircraft maintenance officer Brookley AFB, Mobile, Ala., 1964-65, spl. project officer, 1965-66, McClellan AFB, Sacramento, Calif., 1966; officer in charge maintenance support div. Tan Son Nhut Air Base, Saigon, Vietnam, 1967-68; job control officer Beale AFB, Marysville, Calif., 1968-69, officer in charge, 1968-71; officer in charge maintenance control br. RAF Mildenhall, Eng., 1971-74, dep. chief of maintenance, 1974-75; squadron comdr. Minot (N.D.) AFB, 1975-76, maintenance supr., 1976-77, maintenance control officer, 1977; chief acquisition logistics br. Hdqrs. SAC, 1977—. Active PTA, 1972-74, exec. com. chmn., 1972; mem. ch. council Presbyn. Ch., 1973, usher, 1972-77, Sunday sch. leader, 1973-74, lay leader, 1976-77, 81, chmn. evangelism com., 1981, counselor, 1978-81, mem. pastor-parish relations com., 1981-82. Decorated Bronze Star, Meritorious Service medal, Air Force Commendation medal. Mem. Am. Personnel Guidance Assn., Smithsonian Assos., Air Force Assn. Republican. Home: 4915 Dumfries Dr Omaha NE 68157 Office: HQ SAC/LGXX Offutt AFB NE 68113

WINOKUR, GEORGE, psychiatrist; b. Phila., Feb. 10, 1925; s. Louis and Vera P. W.; A.B., Johns Hopkins U., 1944; M.D., U. Md., 1947; m. Betty Stricklin, Sept. 15, 1951; children—Thomas, Kenneth, Patricia. Intern, Ch. Home and Hosp., Balt., 1948-50; resident Seton Inst., Balt., 1948-50, Barnes Hosp., Washington U. Sch. Medicine, 1950-51, St. Louis, research asso. Washington U., asst. prof. psychiatry, 1955-59, asso. prof., 1959-66, prof., 1966-71; prof., head dept. psychiatry U. Iowa, 1971—. Served as capt. USAF, 1952-54. Recipient 1st prize award Anna Monika Stiftung, 1973; Paul Hoch award, 1981; diplomate Am. Bd. Psychiatry and Neurology. Mem. Psychiat. Research Soc., Am. Psychiat. Assn. (Hofheimer prize 1972), Am. Fedn. Clin. Research, Am.Psychopathol. Assn. (pres. 1977, Samuel W. Hamilton award 1977), Am. Soc. Human Genetics, Internat. Group for Study Affective Disorders, Assn. for Research in Nervous and Mental Disorders, Am. Acad. Clin. Psychiatrists, Am. Assn. Chmn. Depts. Psychiatry, Iowa Psychiat. Soc. Author: Manic Depressive Illness, 1969; Determinants of Human Sexual Behavior, 1974; Depression: The Facts, 1981; contbr. numerous articles to profl. jours.; editor Jour. Affective Disorders, 1978—; editorial bd. Archives Gen. Psychiatry, 1975—, Neuropsychobiology, 1975—, Comprehensive Psychiatry, 1977—, Jour. Affective Disorders, 1980—. Office: U Iowa Coll Medicine Dept Psychiatry 500 Newton Rd Iowa City IA 52242

WINQUIST, ALAN HANSON, educator; b. Astoria, N.Y., June 7, 1942; s. Emil Nils and Gertrude Eleanor (Enborg) W.; A.B., Wheaton (Ill.) Coll., 1964; M.A. in Teaching, Northwestern U., 1965; postgrad U. Stockholm, 1965-66; Ph.D., N.Y. U., 1976. Tchr. social studies schools, Northbrook, Ill., 1964-65, Port Washington, N.Y., 1966-67; tchr. history Martin Luther High Sch., Maspeth, N.Y., 1967-69; instr. dept. history Nassau Community Coll., Garden City, N.Y., 1970-74; prof. European history Taylor U., Upland, Ind., 1974—, also chmn. dept. history. Ford Found. scholar: N.Y. U. Travel grantee, 1974; Research grantee Swedish Pioneer Hist. Soc., Assn. Swedish Industries grantee. Mem. Am. Hist. Assn., Swedish Pioneer Hist. Soc., Soc. Advancement of Scandinavian Studies, Conf. Faith and History. Presbyterian. Author: Scandinavians and South Africa, 1976; contbr. articles to profl. jours. Home and Office: Taylor University Upland IN 46989

WINSLOW, ALFRED AKERS, govt. ofcl.; b. Gary, Ind., June 16, 1923; s. Harry Wendell and Lenora (Allen) W.; A.A., Wilson Jr. Coll., 1964; B.B.A., Northwestern U., 1969; m. Maud Esther Franklin, Jan. 15, 1954. With Chgo. Post Office, 1947-66; with U.S. Postal Service, Chgo. Central Region, 1967—, dir. Office Employee Relations, 1973—. Partner Winslow's Apparel Shop, Chgo., 1954-66. Mem. adv. com. on human relations City of Chgo., 1969-73; pres. Cheryl Condominium, Chgo., 1965-67, Evans-Langley Neighborhood Club, Chgo., 1960-64; chmn. Post Office Bd. U.S. Civil Service Examiners Ill., Mich., 1967-71. Served with USCGR, 1943-46. Recipient Outstanding Achievement award, Chgo. Assn. Commerce and Industry, 1969, 70, 68; Great Guy award, Radio Sta. WGRT, 1969. Mem. Northwestern U. Bus. Honor Soc., NAACP bd. dirs. 1968—), Soc. Personnel Adminstrn., Indsl. Relations Assn. Chgo., Am. Legion, Field Mus. Natural History, Chgo. Art Inst., Lyric Opera, Chgo. Ednl. TV Assn., Northwestern U. Alumni Assn.

WINSLOW, EDWARD BYRON, educator, physician; b. London, Ont., Can., Apr. 1, 1942; s. Edward Thompson and Barbara Jean (Knowles) W.; M.D., U. B.C., Can., 1966; m. Rosemarie van Eyck, Apr. 26, 1969; children—Edward Byron, Robert Douglas. Intern, Cook County Hosp., Chgo., 1966-67; resident, cardiology fellow U. Ill. Hosp., 1967-71, asst. prof. medicine 1973-77, asso. prof. clin. medicine, 1977—; dir. coronary care unit VA West Side Hosp., Chgo., 1971-73; dir. med. and coronary care units Ill. Masonic Med. Center, 1973-78; dir. cardiac rehab. Northwestern Meml. Hosp., Chgo., 1979—. Fellow Royal Coll. Physicians, Am. Coll. Cardiology, Am. Coll. Chest Physicians, A.C.P.; mem. Am. Fedn. Clin. Research, Am. Heart Assn. Home: 914 Sheridan Rd Wilmette IL 60091 Office: 250 E Superior St Chicago IL 60610

WINSTEIN, BRUCE DARRELL, physicist, educator; b. Los Angeles, Sept. 25, 1943; s. Saul and Sylvia (Levin) W.; B.A., U. Calif., Los Angeles, 1965; Ph.D., Calif. Inst. Tech., 1970; m. Joan Drucker, Feb. 10, 1979; 1 son, Keith Jonathan. Research physicist Max Planck Inst. Physics Astrophysics, Munich, Germany, 1970-72; sr. research asso. Enrico Fermi Inst., U. Chgo., 1972-76, Arthur H. Compton lectr., 1976, asst. prof. physics, 1976-80, asso. prof., 1980—. NSF grantee, 1976—. Mem. Am. Phys. Soc., Sigma Pi Sigma. Home: 5637 S Harper Ave Chicago IL 60637 Office: 5630 Ellis Ave Chicago IL 60637

WINSTEIN, STEWART ROBERT, lawyer; b. Viola, Ill., May 28, 1924; s. Abram and Esther (Meyer) W.; A.B., Augustana Coll., 1935; J.D., U. Chgo., 1938; m. Dorothy Shock Adams, Nov. 2, 1960; 1 son, Arthur. Admitted to Ill. bar, 1939; sr. partner firm Winstein, Kavensky, Wallace & Doughty, Rock Island, Ill., 1966—; public speaker. Fin. officer State of Ill., 1963-70; del. Democratic Nat. Conv., 1968, 72, Mid-Term Conf., 1974, 78; committeeman 19th Dem. State Central Com., 1970—; vice chmn. Ill. State Central Com., 1973—; public adminstr. Rock Island County, 1974-78; mem. Met. Airport Commn. Trustee, Marycrest Coll. Mem. Rock Island County Bar Assn., Ill. Bar Assn., Am. Bar Assn., Chgo. Bar Assn., Assn. Trial Lawyers Am. Jewish. Club: Elks. Home: 3535 24th St Rock Island IL 61201 Office: PO Box 428 4th Floor Rock Island Bank Bldg Rock Island IL 61201

WINTER, CHARLES KEITH, mfg. co. exec.; b. Logansport, Ind., Aug. 12, 1938; s. James Merriam and Dorothy Verna (Pease) W.; B.S. in Bus. Adminstrn., Andrews U., 1965; m. Janice Ann Taylor, July 7, 1963; children—Erika Sue, Brian Keith. Asst. personnel mgr. Oliver Corp., S. Bend, Ind., 1965-68; mgr. indsl. relations The Weatherhead Co., Columbus, Ohio, 1968-71, Ashland, Ohio, 1971-73; v.p. indsl. relations Simpson Industries, Inc., Litchfield, Mich., 1973—, also sec., trustee Simpson Industries Fund. Mem. NAM, Am. Soc. Personnel Adminstrs., Indsl. Relations Research Assn., Am. Compensation Assn. Republican. Club: Masons. Home: 415 Allen Rd Marshall MI 49068 Office: Simpson Industries Inc 917 Anderson Rd Litchfield MI 49252

WINTER, DUANE WILLIAM, assn. exec.; b. Fitchburg, Mass., Apr. 17, 1944; s. Eino Walter and Lillian Marie (Lundgren) W.; student U. Mass., 1962-63, Suomi Coll., 1963-65; B.S. in Edn., Wayne State U., 1967; M.A. in Edn., U. Mich., 1974; m. Vicky Lynn Rutledge, Aug. 29, 1975; children by previous marriage—Stephen Duane, Kimberly Sue, Melissa Lynn. Elem. sch. tchr. Southfield (Mich.) Public Schs., 1967-71; exec. dir. Lenawee County Edn. Assn., Adrian, Mich., 1971—. Mich. Edn. Assn. staff liaison to State Rep., 40th House Dist., 1971—, to U.S. Congressman, 1976-78. Mem. Profl. Staff Assn., Nat. Staff Orgn., NEA (life), Mich. Edn. Assn. (asso.). Home: 4455 Walnut Hill Ct Route 6 Adrian MI 49221 Office: 227 N Winter St 309 Adrian MI 49221

WINTER, KENNETH MICHAEL, newspaper exec.; b. Lansing, Mich., Aug. 7, 1950; s. Richard G. and Beverly R. (Radcliffe) W.; student (Sigma Delta Chi scholar) Adrian Coll., 1968-69, (Am. Coll. and U. Assn. grantee) Am. U., 1969; B.A., Mich. State U., 1972; postgrad. (Nat. Endowment for Humanities fellow) U. Mich., 1978-79. Reporter, Petoskey (Mich.) News-Rev., 1972, asst. gen. mgr., 1976-79, gen. mgr., 1979—; reported State Jour., Lansing, 1972-73, public service dir., 1973; editor, gen. mgr. Charlevoix (Mich.) Courier, 1974-76, gen. mgr., v.p., 1975—, v.p., dir. Charlevoix Courier Corp., 1976—; sec. Otsego Herald-Times Corp., Gaylord, Mich., 1979—; mem. part-time faculty N. Central Mich. Coll., 1977—. Mem. nat. exploring com. Boy Scouts Am., 1975—, bd. dirs. Scenic Trails council, 1980—; mem. Crooked tree Arts Council, 1976—; vice chmn. Lansing River Devel., 1971-72. Recipient nat., state editorial awards, 1974-76. Mem. Internat. Newspaper Promotion Assn., Nat. Newspaper Assn., Mich. Press Assn., Little Traverse Regional Hist. Soc. (pres., trustee 1975—), Hist. Soc. Mich. (trustee 1979—), Charlevoix C. of C. (treas. 1977—), Sigma Delta Chi. Methodist. Clubs: Charlevoix Yacht; Petoskey Kiwanis (dir.). Home: Box 528 Michigan Shores Dr Petoskey MI 49770 Office: Petoskey News-Rev 319 State St Petoskey MI 49770

WINTER, MAX, profl. football team exec.; b. Ostrava, Austria, June 29, 1904; s. Jacob and Bertha (Ruker) W.; came to U.S., 1913, naturalized, 1920; student Hamline U., 1925-26, U. Chgo., 1927: m. Helen Horovitz, Dec. 5, 1939; children—Susan (Mrs. Robert Diamond), Nancy (Mrs. Dennis Ditlove), Diane (Mrs. Richard Cohen). Co-owner, gen. mgr. Mpls. Lakers Basketball Team, 1947-56; originator Minn. Vikings (Nat. Football League), Mpls., 1960, pres., 1960—; chmn. bd., dir. Viking Enterprises; pres. Max Winter Enterprises, Max Winter Enterprises Hawaii; dir. Downtown Bank St. Paul, Bank of Mpls. Mem. County Park Bd., 1959-64; chmn. Muscular Dystrophy, 1961; mem. Gov.'s Bus. Adv. Com., 1965; chmn. Nat. Govs. Conf., 1965. Recipient Hon. Scout award, 1946, 47, 48. Mem. Mpls. C. of C. (v.p.). Jewish. Clubs: Optimists; Minneapolis Athletic; Oak Ridge Country, Wacalae Country, Outrigger (Honolulu): Rotary. Author: Sports Books for Children, 1957. Office: care Minn Vikings 9520 Viking Dr Eden Prairie MN 55344

WINTEROTH, DORIS LUCILE, home economist, civic worker; b. Jamestown, Kans., Aug. 11, 1924; d. Ralph Wilson and Alice Luana (Christensen) Galloway; B.S. in Vocat. Home Econs. Edn., Kans. State U., 1946; postgrad. Ft. Hays State U., Emporia State Coll.; m. Robert Samuel Winteroth, Aug. 27, 1946; children—Kathleen Winteroth Hursh, Suzanne F. Tchr. home econs. Westmoreland Rural High Sch., 1946-47, Riley Rural High Sch., 1947-49, vocat. home econs. Norton (Kans.) Community High Sch., 1952-53; elem. tchr. Norton Grade Sch., 1957-58; tchr. Norton Jr. High Sch., 1959-67; tchr. vocat. home econs. Norton Jr.-Sr. Community Schs., 1967—. 4-H leader; mem. outreach adv. council Colby Community Coll.; former pres. United Methodist Women; sponsor United Methodist Youth; former pres. Norton chpt. Am. Field Service. Mem. Am. Vocat. Assn., Kans. Vocat. Assn., Kans. Assn. Vocat. Home Econs. Tchrs. (sec.), NEA, Area A Kans. Home Econs. Assn. (sec.-treas.), AAUW (past pres.), Future Homemakers Am. (hon.), Future Farmers Am. (hon.). Republican. Clubs: PEO (past pres.), Mid Century Federated Women's (past pres.). Home: 1109 Eisenhower Dr Norton KS 67654 Office: 706 N Jones St Norton KS 67654

WINTERS, PETER LEE, dermatologist; b. Lockport, N.Y., Dec. 19, 1938; s. Earl Lloyd and Ruby Josephine (Gilmer) W.; B.S., Allegheny Coll., 1960; M.D., Temple U., 1965; m. Christine L. Wells, June 5, 1976; children by previous marriage—Christopher L., Jonathan B. Intern, Meth. Hosp., Indpls., 1965-66, resident in family medicine, 1966-68; resident in dermatology Skin and Cancer Hosp., Phila., 1968-71; practice medicine specializing in dermatology, Indpls., 1971—; instr. dermatology clinic Meth. Hosp. Served to lt. USNR, 1966-68. Recipient physician's recognition award, 1971-73, 73-76, 76-79. Am. Bd. Dermatology, Nat. Bd. Med. Examiners. Mem. AMA, Ind. Med. Soc., Am. Acad. Dermatology (Continuing Med. Edn. award 1977-81), Dermatology Found., Soc. for Investigative Dermatology. Republican. Methodist. Clubs: Riveria Swim, West Indy Racquet. Home: 6969 Warwick Rd Indianapolis IN 46220 Office: 8402 Harcourt Rd Suite 305 Indianapolis IN 46260

WINTERS, STEVEN PAUL, accountant; b. New Castle, Ind., Jan. 10, 1945; s. Paul Henry and Marguerite (Harcourt) W.; cert. in acctg. Ind. U., 1969; B.S., Ball State U., 1972; m. Roberta L. Rahn, 1981; 1 dau., Karen. Audit supr. Coopers & Lybrand, Indpls. and Ft. Wayne, Ind., 1972-77; corp. controller Oxford Devel. Corp., Indpls., 1977-80; real estate tax specialist Kern, Hall, Ford & Co., C.P.A.'s, Indpls., 1980-81; founder Winters & Assos., 1981—. C.P.A., Ind. Mem. Am. Inst. C.P.A.'s, Ind. C.P.A. Soc., Nat. Assn. Accts., Nat. Council Corvette Clubs. Republican. Clubs: Toastmasters Internat. (past corr. sec.), Masons. Home: 8268 N Woodall Dr Indianapolis IN 46268 Office: 9101 Wesleyan Rd Indianapolis IN 46268

WINTERS, SUSAN PATRICIA, audiologist; b. Columbus, Miss., June 28, 1952; d. Everett Louis and Louise (Ivy) W.; B.A.E., U. Miss., 1974; M.A., U. Tenn., 1975. Student tchr. Memphis Public Schs., 1974; clin. audiologist U. Tenn., Knoxville, 1976, Dr. R. E. Flatley's Office, Moline, Ill., 1976—. Mem. Am. Speech and Hearing Assn. (cert. clin. competence in audiology), Quad-Cities Speech and Hearing Assn. Republican. Baptist. Home: 13 Blackhawk Hills Dr Rock Island IL 61201 Office: 829 15th St Moline IL 61265

WINTERSTEEN, GREGORY HAMILTON, psychologist; b. Evanston, Ill., Jan. 4, 1943; s. Clayton Orville and Emma Irene (Hamilton) W.; B.A., No. Ill. U., 1966, M.S., 1968, Ed.D., 1978. Sch. counselor DeKalb Community Unit Dist. No. 428, 1968-78; clin. dir. Youth Service Bur. McHenry County, Woodstock, Ill., 1978—; project dir. Career Edn. Grant, Title III ESEA, 1975. Mem. Am. Personnel and Guidance Assn., Am. Sch. Counselors Assn., Nat. Vocat. Guidance Assn., Ill. Vocat. Guidance Assn. (pres. 1982). Home: 727 Starboard Point Schaumburg IL 60194 Office: Lake Park High Sch 600 S Medinah Rd Roselle IL 60172

WINTON, JEFFREY BLAKE, arbitrator; b. Chgo., Feb. 16, 1945; s. Stanley A. and Phyllis R. (Levin) W.; B.S., U. Ill., 1966, M.S. in Labor Relations, 1968; m. Shoshana Nahmani, 1976. With Midwest Stock Exchange, Chgo., 1968-70; dir. mediation services Office of State Sch. Supt., 1970-73; pres. Radionic Industries, Inc. (formerly Radionic Transformers Corp.), Chgo., 1973—; pres. Jeffrey B. Winton & Assos., Chgo., 1972—. Lectr. labor relations and mgmt. Northwestern U., 1974-78. Campaign aide Senator Adlai E. Stevenson, III, 1966, 70, 74; arbitrator, mediator Fact-Finder Federal Mediation and Conciliation Service, Am. Arbitration Assn., Iowa Public Employment Relations Bd., Wis. Employment Relations Commn., Ind. Edn. Relations Bd., Nat. Mediation Bd. Recipient Gold Key to City of Champaign, Ill., 1968. Mem. Am. Arbitration Assn. (labor panel), Fed. Mediation and Conciliation Service (labor panel), Indsl. Relations Research Assn., Nat. Mediation Bd., Soc. Profls. in Dispute Resolution (v.p.), Chgo. Assn. Commerce. Contbr. articles to profl. publs. Office: Suite 100 2525 W Moffat Chicago IL 60647

WINTZ, JOHN WILLIAM, univ. bookstore mgr.; b. Batesville, Ind., Dec. 9, 1934; s. Aloys Aloysius and Rosella Elizabeth (Heitz) W.; B.S.B.A., Xavier U., 1957, M.B.A., 1965; m. Margaret Louise Parks, Apr. 30, 1960; children—David, John, Thomas, Jane. Bookstore mgr. Xavier U., Cin., 1960—, lectr. mgmt., 1978—. Served with arty. AUS, 1957-59. Mem. Nat. Assn. Coll. Stores (trustee 1974-77), Ohio Assn. Coll. Stores (pres. 1969-70), Corpus Christi Men's Soc. Roman Catholic. Office: Xavier University Dana Ave and Victory Pkwy Cincinnati OH 45207

WIPER, ROBERT ELLS, business exec.; b. Coos Bay, Oreg., Apr. 14, 1929; s. Earl Ells and Alida Berkland (Hage) W.; B.A., Willamette U., 1951, Ed.M., 1957; Ed.D., Oreg. State U., 1969; m. Elizabeth Eileen Alme, Nov. 22, 1966. Instr., Oreg. State U., 1957-61; head dept. bus. edn. and office adminstrn. Utah State U., 1961-65; asst. mgr. ednl. services div. office products IBM, N.Y.C., 1965-67; sr. planner A.B. Dick Co., Chgo., 1967-74; pres. Search Assos. Inc., Mt. Prospect, Ill., 1974—; pres. SAI Graphics Services, Inc., Mt. Prospect, 1976—; cons. in field. Recipient Spl. Recognitionand Commendation, GAO Office Personnel Devel., 1976, Mem. Internat. Word Processing Assn., Internat. Graphic Arts Edn. Assn., Nat. Bus. Edn. Assn., Phi Delta Kappa, Kappa Delta Pi. Republican. Presbyterian. Club: Masons. Contbr. articles to profl. jours. Home: 704 W Regner McHenry IL 60050 Office: 701 W Golf Rd Mount Prospect IL 60056

WIRICK, BETTY JO, welfare adminstr.; b. Bedford, Ind., Jan. 28, 1930; d. Walter Samuel and Mary Edna (Swango) Smith; student Gary (Ind.) Pub. Schs.; m. George Wirick, Sept. 28, 1951; children—Stephen, Paula, Donald. Clk. typist Lake County (Ind.) Welfare Dept., Gary, from 1949, adminstrv. asst., 1968—. Mem. Data Processing Mgmt. Assn., Am. Pub. Welfare Assn., Delta Theta Tau. Lutheran. Home: 9404 Arthur St Crown Point IN 46307 Office: 800 Massachusetts St Gary IN 46402

WIRT, MICHAEL DEAN, educator; b. Saginaw, Mich., Aug. 30, 1938; s. Malcolm Lewis and Ethel Lenore (Honeywell) W.; student Kalamazoo Coll., 1956-57; B.S., Western Mich. U., 1962, M.A., 1965; Ph.D. (NDEA fellow), U. Mich., 1975; m. Karen E. Egly, Jan. 30, 1960; children—Michael Dean II, Andrew Christopher. Grad. asst. Western Mich. U., 1964-66; social worker Mich. Crippled Children Commn., 1963-64; counselor Ferris State Coll., Big Rapids, Mich., 1966-68; research asst. Ednl. Resources Info. Center, Ann Arbor, Mich., 1969-71; counselor U. Alaska, Fairbanks, 1971-72; tchr. cons. Ann Arbor (Mich.) Pub. Schs., 1972-73; dir. counseling Mich. Technol. U., Houghton, 1973-81, coordinator corp. services and coop. edn., 1981—. Vice pres. Copper Country Jr. Hockey Assn., 1975-76, bd. dirs., 1978—; bd. dirs. Portage Lake Multi-Recreational Facility, 1976—, Portage Lake Pioneers Sr. Hockey Club, 1979—. Mem. Am., Mich. personnel and guidance assns., Mich. Coll. Personnel Assn., Assn. for Counselor Edn. and Supervision. Club: Portage Lake Golf (v.p. 1974-76). Home: 30 Peepsock Circle Houghton MI 49931 Office: Mich Technol U Houghton MI 49931

WIRTH, RICHARD MARVIN, educator; b. Grosse Pointe, Mich., Aug. 26, 1929; s. Marvin Oscar and Marion (Maxfield) W.; B.Sc., Wayne State U., 1950, M.A., 1952; postgrad. U. Wis., Western State Coll. Colo., Ball State Tchrs. Coll. Tchr., Warren (Mich.) Consol. Schs., 1951—. Former organist and choir dir. St. John's Evang. United Ch. of Christ, lay minister, 1979; kapellmeister St. John-St. Luke United Ch. Christ. Mem. scholastic writing awards adv. com. SE Mich. Named Vol. of Week, United Found., 1963; recipient Silver Beaver award Boy Scouts Am., 1962; Disting. Educator award Mich. State Fair, 1964; Disting. Tchr. award Mich. Assn. Classroom Tchrs., 1969. Mem. Mich. (pres. dept. classroom tchrs., Tchr. of Yr. 1962, dir. area 6, parliamentarian 1972—, dir.), Ky. (parliamentarian 1974), Kans., Okla. (parliamentarian 1979—) Warren (editor Harbinger, past pres., sr. trustee) edn. assns., Mich. Student Conf. (parliamentarian), Southfield Public Employees, Speech Assn. Am., Nat. Cath. Forensic League (parliamentarian 1979, 82), Nat. Council Tchrs. of English, Mich. League Credit Unions, Mich. League Practical Nurses (parliamentarian), Delta Sigma Rho. Editor of ednl. publs. Contbr. articles to profl. jours. Home: Box 283 Algonac MI 48001 Office: 5460 Arden St Warren MI 48092

WIRTHLIN, LEROY SAMUEL, surgeon; b. N.Y.C., Apr. 11, 1935; s. LeRoy Alvin and Emilie (Stiefel) W.; B.S. in Exptl. Biology, U. Utah, 1955; M.D., Harvard, 1962; m. Mary Louise McEntire, July 7, 1960; children—LeRoy, Richard, Douglas, Bryan, Emily, Michael, Jeffrey, Cheryl, Robert, Mary, Alison, Suzanne Louise, Rebecca Ann, Kathleen. Surg. intern Mass. Gen. Hosp., Boston, 1962-63, asst. resident in surgery, 1963-64, sr. resident, 1966-69, chief resident, 1969-70, asst. in surgery, 1970-73, asst. surgeon, 1973-77; research asst. cardio-respiratory lab. Naval Aerospace Med. Inst., Naval Air Sta., Pensacola, Fla., 1964-66; instr. surgery Harvard Med. Sch., 1970-73, asst. prof. surgery, 1973-77; staff surgeon sect. vascular Surgery Sinai Hosp., Detroit, 1977—, Providence Hosp., Southfield, Mich., 1977—; cancer research trainee Huntington Labs., Mass. Gen. Hosp., 1970-73; clin. asst. Royal Marsden Hosp., London, 1972. Am. Specialists Abroad grantee, Malawi, 1968; Am. Cancer Soc. fellow, 1969-70; Dalton travel award, 1972. Served with USNR, 1964-66. Diplomate Am. Coll. Surgery. Mem. AMA, Mass. Med. Soc., Mich. Med. Soc., Bay State Med. Found., Royal Soc. Medicine, Assn. for Acad. Surgery, A.C.S., Boston Surg. Soc., Internat. Soc. Cardiovascular Surgery, Soc. Surgery Alimentary Tract, Collegium Internat. Chirurgiae Digestives, New Eng. Soc. Vascular Surgery, Midwestern Vascular Soc., Detroit Surg. Assn., Detroit Surg. Acad. Republican. Mormon. Author publs. in field. Office: 15901 W Nine Mile Rd Southfield MI 48075

WIRTZ, ARTHUR M(ICHAEL), real estate and corp. exec.; b. Chgo., Jan. 23, 1901; s. Fredrick C. and Leona (Miller) W.; B.A., U. Mich., 1922; m. Virginia Wadsworth, Mar. 1, 1926; children—Cynthia Wirtz MacArthur, William W., Arthur Michael, Elizabeth V. Founder, 1927, and since chmn., chief exec. officer Wirtz Corp., Chgo.; founder, chmn., chief exec. officer Consol. Enterprises, Inc.; chmn. bd., chief exec. officer Am. Mart, Chgo.; chmn. Chgo. Stadium Corp., Chgo. Blackhawk Hockey Team, Inc., Forman Realty Corp., Chgo., First Nat. Bank of So. Miami (Fla.); co-owner Chgo. Bulls Basketball Team; brought Sonja Henie to U.S., 1936, originator, producer Sonja Henie-Hollywood Ice Revue. Pres., Chgo. Urban Transp. Dist. Mem. Hockey Hall of Fame; named Man of Year, Chgo. Boys Club, 1977. Presbyterian. Clubs: Casino, Racquet, Chgo. Athletic, Saddle and Cycle, Chgo. Yacht, Tavern (Chgo.); Knollwood Country. Home: 1420 Lake Shore Dr Chicago IL 60610 Office: 666 Lake Shore Dr Chicago IL 60611

WIRTZ, DWIGHT C., ret. orthopaedic surgeon; b. Boone, Iowa, May 7, 1902; s. William E. and Carrie (Wickersheim) W.; M.D., U. Iowa, 1928; m. Dorothy M. Edwards, Sept. 4, 1937; children—Paul E., Peter D., Ann M. Intern, Fairview Hosp., Mpls., 1928-29; resident in orthopaedics Gillette State Hosp., St. Paul, 1929-30; practice medicine specializing in orthopaedic surgery, Des Moines, 1930-77; pres. Des Moines Med. Center; chief staff Broadlawns Hosp., Des Moines, 1949-53; chief staff Luth. Hosp., Des Moines, 1959, organizer 1st pvt. polio Kenney treatment clinic in U.S., 1942; pres. Annco Co., 1965—; dir. 1st Fed. State Bank. Trustee United Campaign, 1952-61. Served to capt. USNR, 1942-46. Mem. A.C.S., AMA, Iowa Orthopaedic Soc. (pres. 1949-50), Polk County Med. Soc. (trustee 1948-52, pres. 1953), Iowa Clin. Surgical Soc. (pres. 1963-64), Mid-Central States Orthopaedic Soc. (pres. 1963-64). Republican. Episcopalian. Clubs: Des Moines, Des Moines Golf and Country, Masons, Shriners. Home: 4130 River Oaks Dr Des Moines IA 50312 Office: 3716 Ingersoll St Des Moines IA 50312

WIRTZ, HUBERT, state ofcl.; b. Siegburg, W. Germany, Feb. 27, 1945; came to U.S., 1950, naturalized, 1955; s. Hubert and Anneliese (Schutz) W.; B.A. with distinction (scholar), Purdue U., 1967; M.A., Ohio State U., 1971, M.C.P., 1973, postgrad., 1978—; m. Juanita Sonja Buser, Aug. 6, 1967; children—Jacqueline Michelle, Katherine Renée, Timothy Christopher. Policy analyst Ohio Dept. Econ. and Community Devel., Columbus, 1972-74; mgr. Office of Planning and Policy Analysis, Ohio Dept. Mental Health and Mental Retardation, Columbus, 1974-76, chief Office Planning and Resource Devel., 1977—; panelist various statewide confs., coordinator of statewide workshops. Served with USAF, 1967-72, Res. capt., 1973—. Decorated Air Force Commendation medal; recipient Letters of Commendation, HEW, 1977, Ohio Community Mental Health Bd., 1977. Mem. Am. Soc. Public Adminstrn., Am. Mgmt. Assn., Pi Kappa Phi. Home: 48 Whipple Pl Westerville OH 43081 Office: 30 E Broad St Columbus OH 43215

WIRTZ, VIRGINIA WADSWORTH (MRS. ARTHUR M. WIRTZ), civic worker; b. Cleve., Jan. 30, 1903; d. Charles and Anna (Doyle) Wadsworth; student U. Colo., 1920-21; B.S., Northwestern U., 1924; m. Arthur Michael Wirtz, Mar. 1, 1926; children—Cynthia Wirtz MacArthur, William Wadsworth, Arthur Michael, Jr., Elizabeth Virginia. Mem. Presbyn.-St. Luke's Hosp. Women's Bd., 1926—; mem. women's council Chgo. div. Am. Heart Assn.; women's com. Mental Health Soc. Chgo.; mem. women's bd. Am. Cancer Soc.; trustee Ill. Children's Home and Aid Soc., Am. Opera Soc. Mem. Mortar Bd., Pi Beta Phi. Clubs: Casino, Women's Athletic, Saddle and Cycle, Racquet, Arts; Knollwood Country. Home: 1420 Lake Shore Dr Chicago IL 60610 (summer) Ivanhoe Farm Route 60 Mundelein IL 60060

WIRTZ, WILLIAM WADSWORTH, corp. exec.; b. Chgo., Oct. 5, 1929; s. Arthur Michael and Virginia (Wadsworth) W.; A.B., Brown U., 1950; m. Joan Roney, Dec. 15, 1950; children—William R., Gail W., Karen K., Peter R., Alison M. Pres., Chgo. Blackhawk Hockey Team, Inc., 1966—, Chgo. Stadium Corp., 1966—, Consol. Enterprises, Inc., Chgo., 1966—, Forman Realty Corp., Chgo., 1965—, 333 Building Corp., Chgo., 1966—, Wirtz Corp., Chgo., 1964—. Clubs: Saddle and Cycle, Racquet, Mid-America (Chgo.); Sunset Ridge Country (Northbrook, Ill.); Fin and Feather (Elgin, Ill.). Home: Winnetka IL Office: 666 Lake Shore Dr Chicago IL 60611

WISDOM, GUYRENA KNIGHT, psychologist, educator; b. St. Louis, July 27, 1923; d. Gladys Margaret (Hankins) McCullin; A.B., Stowe Tchrs. Coll., 1945; A.M., U. Ill., 1951; postgrad. St. Louis U., Washington U., St. Louis, Fontbonne Coll., U. Mo., Harris Tchrs. Coll., U. Chgo., Drury Coll. Tchr. elementary sch. St. Louis Pub. Sch. System, 1945-63, psychol. examiner, 1963-68, sch. psychologist, 1968-74, cons. spl. edn., 1974-77, supr. spl. edn. dept., 1977-79, coordinator staff devel. div., 1979—; pvt. tutor, 1971-72; instr. Harris Tchrs. Coll., St. Louis, 1973-74, Harris-Stowe Coll., 1979. Mem. Nat. Staff Devel. Council, Nat. Assn. Sch. Psychologists, Mo. Assn. Children with Learning Disabilities, Council for Exceptional Children, St. Louis Assn. Sch. Adminstrs., United Teaching Profession Orgn., NEA, Mo., St. Louis tchrs. assn., Spl. Edn. Instructional Materials Center, Assn. Supervision and Curriculum Devel., Kappa Delta Pi. Roman Catholic. Home: 5046 Wabada St Saint Louis MO 63113 Office: 5910 Clifton Ave Saint Louis MO 63109

WISE, HENRY SEILER, U.S. judge; b. Mt. Carmel, Ill., July 16, 1909; A.B., LL.B., Washington U., St. Louis, 1933; m. G. Louise Hawkins, Dec. 10, 1938; children—H. Michael, Patricia (Mrs. Stephen Satre), N. Susanne (Mrs. Robert Lang), Marilyn (Mrs. Gerald L. Furnish), David. Admitted to Mo. bar, 1933, Ill. bar, 1934; practice in Danville, Ill., 1934—; mem. firms Jinkins & Jinkins, 1934-37, Meeks & Lowenstein, 1937-42, Meeks & Wise, 1942-51, Graham, Wise, Meyer, Young & Welsch, 1951-66; judge U.S. Dist. Ct., Eastern Dist. Ill., Danville, 1966-78, sr. judge, 1978—. Commr., Ill. Ct. of Claims, 1949-53; mem. Ill. Parole and Pardon Bd., 1961-66. County chmn. Dem. party, 1948-54; del. Dem. nat. conv., 1952, 56, 60, 64. Mem. Am., Ill., Vermilion (Ill.) County bar assns., Am. Judicature Soc., Danville C. of C. K.C. (4), Elk. Club: Danville Country. Home: 406 N Cedarwood Dr PO Box 743 Danville IL 61832 Office: US Dist Ct Danville IL 61832

WISE, PERRY KENNETH, Realtor; b. Lockport, Ill., Feb. 13, 1927; s. Perry Henry and Mable Ruth (Johnson) W.; student public schs., Lockport; m. Wilma Mark, Sept. 5, 1948; children—Douglas Kent, Dennis Mark. Acctg. staff Globe Oil & Refinery Co., Lemont, Ill., 1947-54; editor Naperville (Ill.) Clarion Weekly, 1954-56; advt. mgr., photographer Naperville Sun, 1956-60; salesman Rich Port Realtor, Naperville, 1960-72, v.p., sales mgr., 1972—. Bd. dirs. Naperville Elderly Homes, Inc., 1968—, pres., 1968-75; v.p., sec. Wise Suburban Services, Inc., 1975—. Served with U.S. Mcht. Marine, 1944-46. Mem. DuPage Bd. Realtors (v.p.), DuPage Multiple Listing Service (pres.), Ill. Assn. Realtors (grad. Realtors Inst.), Nat. Assn. Realtors (cert. residential specialist, cert. residential broker). Republican. Lutheran. Home: 7 S 410 Arbor Dr Naperville IL 60540 Office: 933 E Ogden Ave Naperville IL 60540

WISE, RONALD DAVID, dermatologist; b. Hertfordshire, Eng., May 6, 1946; came to U.S., 1953, naturalized, 1962; m. Daly and Bella Phyllis (Kopech) W.; B.S., U. Ill., 1967, M.S. (USPHS trainee), 1970, M.D. (univ. med. student research fellow, univ. med. student scholar), 1974; m. Barbara Ida Selling, June 13, 1976; children—Leon Jacob, Alan Julius. Intern, U. Ill. Med. Center, 1974-75; resident in dermatology Rush-Presbyn.-St. Luke's Hosp., Chgo., 1975-78; practice medicine specializing in dermatology, Chgo. and Skokie, Ill., 1978—; attending physician Grant, Henrotin hosps., Ill. Masonic Med. Center; dermatology examiner Nat. Bd. Podiatric Medicine. Diplomate Nat. Bd. Med. Examiners, Am. Bd. Dermatology. Fellow Am. Acad. Dermatology; mem. AMA, Soc. Investigative Dermatology, Ill. Med. Soc., Chgo. Med. Soc., Chgo. Dermatol. Soc., U. Ill. Alumni Assn., Sigma Xi, Alpha Omega Alpha. Club: Masons. Author articles in field. Office: 30 N Michigan Ave Chicago IL also 4500 W Oakton St Skokie IL 60076

WISE, WILLIAM DEAN, aircraft co. exec.; b. Lebo, Kans., Aug. 30, 1931; s. Frank W. and M. Lucille Wise; B.S.C.E., Kans. State U., 1953; postgrad. in aero. engring. Wichita State U., 1953-59; m. Donna L. Pinon, July 5, 1953; children—Darcie K., David A. Engring. group leader research Cessna Aircraft Co., Wichita, Kans., 1953-59; v.p. advanced tech. Beech Aircraft Corp., Wichita, 1959-79, v.p. commuter div., 1979—; v.p., dir. Beech Aerospace Services, Inc., 1977—; cons. NASA; mem. adv. council aero. engring. dept. Wichita State U., Kans. U. Elder, University Christian Ch., Wichita. Registered profl. engr., Kans. Fellow AIAA (asso.); mem. Soc. Automotive Engrs. (aerospace council), Aerospace Industries Assn. (civil aviation adv. group), Wichita C. of C. (local govt. com. 1975-81). Republican. Club: Masons. Home: 4100 N Parkwood Wichita KS 67220 Office: 9709 E Central Wichita KS 67201

WISEMAN, STEPHEN ARTHUR, mfg. co. exec.; b. Kearney, Nebr., Jan. 13, 1948; s. John Edwin and Esther Vienna (Krause) W.; student Central Nebr. Tech. Coll.; m. Kathleen Ann Desch, Aug. 28, 1976; 1 dau., Christina Lisa. Prodn. supr. Sperry New Holland Co., Grand Island, Nebr., 1967-75; tool and die maker Chief Industries, Grand Island, 1975-76, J&J Castings Co., Hibbing, Minn., 1976-79; prodn. supr. Mesabi ops. Omark Industries, Chisholm, Minn., 1979—. Served with U.S. Army, 1968-70; Vietnam. Decorated Army Commendation medal, Air medal (21). Mem. Am. Soc. Metals. Methodist. Club: Chisholm Curling. Home: 14 SE 6th St Chilsholm MN 55719 Office: PO Box 312 Chisholm MN 55719

WISGOSKI, ALFRED E., coll. exec.; b. Peru, Ill., Mar. 11, 1932; s. Aloysius and Lena (Pioli) W.; B.S., No. Ill. U., 1956, M.S., 1958, Ed.D., 1968; postgrad. Los Angeles State Coll., part-time, 1956-58; m. Rita Ann Grimshaw, Oct. 27, 1951; children—Gregory, Karen. Instr., Jurupa Jr. High Sch., Riverside, Calif., 1956-58, La Salle-Peru Twp. High Sch., Peru, Ill., 1958; instr., counselor Oglesby Jr. Coll., 1958-64; dean students, asst. dean La Salle-Peru-Oglesby Jr. Coll., La Salle, Ill., 1965-67; dean students Ill. Valley Community Coll., Oglesby, 1967-69, adminstrv. dean, 1969-74, pres., 1974—; instr. No. Ill. U. Pres. United Way, 1974-75, bd. dirs., 1968-76. Served with U.S. Army, 1951-53. Mem. V.F.W., Ill. Jr. Coll. Adminstrs. Assn. (dir. 1972-73), Ill. Council Public Community Colls. Presidents (chmn. council 1980-81), Assn. Am. Community/Jr. Colls., Kappa Delta Pi, Phi Delta Kappa. Clubs: Elks, Rotary. Home: 2217 15th St Peru IL 61354 Office: Rural Route 1 Oglesby IL 61348

WISNEWSKI, JEROME EDWARD, farmer, educator; b. Breckenridge, Minn., June 21, 1937; s. Edward F. and Eleanor T. (Witucki) W.; B.S., Ellendale State Coll., 1959; postgrad. S.D. State U., 1960, N.D. State Sch. Sci., 1968-70, U. N.D., 1968, 75-76, Bemidji State Coll., 1971-72, Moorhead State U., 1974; m. Mary C. Bednar, June 25, 1960; children—Jeffrey, Curtis, Craig, Jason. Tchr. indsl. arts public schs., Toronto, S.D., 1959-61, Havana, N.D., 1964-68, Lidgerwood (N.D.) Public Sch., 1968—; grain and livestock farmer, nr. Geneseo, N.D., 1961—; mem. N.D. Adv. Com. for Ednl. Equality in Vocat. Edn. Past mem. Twp. Bd. Suprs. Named N.D. Indsl. Arts Tchr. of Yr., 1977, Lidgerwood Public Sch. Tchr. of Yr., 1981. Mem. NEA, Am. Indsl. Arts Assn., Am. Vocat. Assn., N.D. Farmers Union, N.D. Farm Bur. (dir. 1980—), Sargent County Farm Bur. (dir. 1980—), Lidgerwood Edn. Assn. (past pres.), N.D. Edn. Assn., N.D. Indsl. Arts Assn. (dir. 1974—), N.D. Vocat. Assn. (exec. bd. 1977—), County Crop and Livestock Assn. Roman Catholic. Clubs: K.C., Lions (dir. 1981—). Home: PO Box 325 Geneseo ND 58037

WISSMAN, DONALD JOHN, economist; b. St. Clair County, Mich., Sept. 26, 1937; s. Edwin Karl and Helen Margaret (Crawford) W.; B.S., Mich. State U., 1959, M.S., 1965; m. Janice Ruth Wanklyn, June 28, 1969; children—Scott Donald, Sean David. With Internat. Farm Youth Exchange, Australia, 1959-60; sr. economist Agri div. Dunlap & Assos., Manhattan, Kans., 1965-72; v.p. Devel. Planning & Research Assos., Inc., Manhattan, 1972-80, sr. v.p., prin., 1981—; lectr. Am. Inst. Baking, 1978—. Trustee, Kans. Council on Econ. Edn.; nat. v.p. Internat. Farm Youth Exchange, 1964-65. Served to 1st lt. USAF, 1960-63. Mem. Am. Agrl. Econs. Assn. (industry com.), Am. Econs. Assn., Western Econs. Assn., Assn. of Environ. and Resource Economists, Omicron Delta Epsilon. Baptist. Club: Rotary. Contbr. over 60 articles to profl. jours., also research reports. Home: 313 Fordham Rd Manhattan KS 66502 Office: PO Box 727 200 Research Dr Manhattan KS 66502

WISSMAN, TERRY LEONARD, tool mfg. co. exec.; b. Sidney, Ohio, Mar. 7, 1947; s. Paul Kenneth and Alice Carol (Schmidt) W.; B.M.E., Ohio State U., 1970; M.B.A. (Air Force ROTC scholar), Golden Gate U., 1974; m. Sally Elizabeth Andrews, Sept. 14, 1968; children—Sherri Ann, Tracy Carol. Mfg. engr. Minster Machine Co. (Ohio), 1974-75, master schedula mgr., 1975-77, mgr. computer graphics, 1977-78, mgr. engring., 1978-79, v.p. engring., 1979—; cons. environ. and energy conservation. Served with USAF, 1971-74. Decorated Air Force Commendation medal; recipient appreciation award Boy Scouts Am., 1974; registered profl. engr., Calif., Ohio. Mem. Ohio State Alumni Assn., New Bremen Jr. C. of C. Mem. United Ch. of Christ. Home: 316 Lane St New Bremen OH 45869 Office: Minster Machine Co 240 W 5th St Minster OH 45865

WIT, DANIEL, polit. scientist; b. N.Y.C., 1923; A.B., Union Coll., 1943; A.M., Princeton U., 1948, Ph.D., 1950; postgrad. Yale U., 1943-44, U. Paris, 1945-46; m., 2 children. Instr., Princeton U., 1946-48, Ohio State U., 1948-50; asst. prof. polit. sci. U. Cin., 1950-54; vis. asst. prof. U. Mich., 1954-56; vis. prof. public adminstrn. Inst. Public Adminstrn., Bangkok, Thailand, 1956-58; vis. asso. prof. govt. Ind. U., 1958; professorial lectr. George Washington U., 1959-61; prof. polit. sci. No. Ill. U., DeKalb, 1961—, head dept. polit. sci., 1961-68; prof. fgn. affairs Nat. War Coll., 1963-64; Fulbright prof., chmn. Master of Public Adminstrn. Program, Inst. Social Studies, The Hague, Netherlands, 1966-67; dir. studies div. overseas research and trg., Govtl. Affairs Inst., Washington, 1959, dir. internat. studies, 1959-61; co-dir. Center for S.E. Asian studies No. Ill. U., 1963-68, dir. internat. and spl. programs, 1969-77, dean internat. and spl. programs, 1977—. Mem. master plan com. for grad. edn. in social scis. State of Ill. Bd. Higher Edn., 1968; vice chmn. bd. dirs. Asso. Univs. for Internat. Edn., 1970, bd. chmn., pres., 1970-78; mem. nat. screening com. for Fulbright-Hays Grad. student program, 1975-77, chmn., 1978. Mem. Am. Polit. Sci. Assn. (mem. nat. council 1967-69). Author: Comparative Political Institutions, 1953; Thailand: Another Vietnam?, 1968; (with P.A. Dionisopoulos) Our American Government and Political System, 1972, 2d edit., 1977; 3d edit., 1981; other works. Contbr. articles to profl. jours. Office: Internatl and Special Programs Northern Ill Univ DeKalb IL 60115

WITHERELL, LOUISE ROWAN, educator; b. Toledo, Apr. 18, 1920; d. Stephen Glenn and Marie Wilhelmina (Bristow) Rowan; B.A. summa cum laude in Edn., U. Toledo, 1940; M.A. (Univ. fellow), U. Wis., Madison, 1941, Ph.D. in French, 1948; m. John M. Witherell, Sept. 28, 1945; children—Anne Louise, Jane Marie. Instr. Spanish, Rosary Coll., River Forest, Ill., 1944-45; asst. prof. French, U. Toledo, 1945-47; instr. French and Spanish, U. Wis., Fox Valley, 1951-61, asst. prof., 1961-65, asso. prof., 1965-70; asso. prof. French and edn. U. Wis., Green Bay, 1970-73, prof., 1973—; cons. to Wis. Dept. Public Instrn. Troop leader Girl Scouts U.S.A., 1957-62. Annie Gorham fellow, 1941-42. Mem. Paul Claudel Soc. U.S.A. (v.p. 1969, pres. 1970), Société Paul Claudel (France), Malraux Soc. (sec. 1975—), Am. Assn. Tchrs. French (pres. Wis. chpt. 1975-77), AAUP, MLA, Midwest MLA, Women's Caucus for Modern Langs., Am. Council Tchrs. of Fgn. Langs., Wis. Assn. Fgn. Lang. Tchrs., Bulletin de Récherches et d'Etudes féministes francophones, Phi Kappa Phi, Sigma Delta Pi, Mu Pi Epsilon, Delta Delta Delta. Club: Wednesday Musicale (Appleton, Wis.). Editor: The U.S. and Canada: An Overview, 1970; translator (with H.L. Zillmer): Two Lyric Farces, Exchange, Hostage (Claudel); editorial bd. Claudel Studies, 1976. Home: 850 E Lindbergh Appleton WI 54911 Office: U Wis Green Bay WI 54302

WITHEROW, JUDITH KAY, educator; b. Marion, Ind., Jan. 17, 1943; d. Ivan Brazilla and Bertha Mae (Comer) Seward; B.S. in Edn., Ball State U., 1965, M.A., 1971, Reading Specialist, 1979; m. William David Witherow, Aug. 23, 1964; children—Stephen William, Terri Lyn, Brian David. Elem. tchr. South Madison Community Sch. Corp., Markleville, Ind., 1967-73; tchr. grade 5 No. Community Schs. Tipton County, Windfall, Ind., 1973-79; reading specialist, 1979—. Leader Methodist Youth Fellowship, Vanlue, Ohio. Recipient Tchr. of Yr. award No. Community Schs., 1980, 81. Mem. Internat. Reading Assn., Assn. Supervision and Curriculum Devel., Am. Fedn. Tchrs. Democrat. Home: Rural Route 1 Box 29G-1 Sharpsville IN 46068 Office: No Community Schs Tipton County Oak St Windfall IN 46076

WITHERSPOON, DORIS YVONNE, coll. adminstr.; b. Tuscaloosa, Ala., Apr. 9, 1946; d. Louis and Bessie (Hearns) Witherspoon; B.A., Eastern Mich. U., 1968; M.A., U. Mich., 1976, postgrad., 1981—; 1 son, Chester Allen Beasley. Community occupational therapist Boston State Hosp., 1969-70; sect. chief occupational therapy Ypsilanti (Mich.) State Hosp., 1970-72; dir. occupational therapy Wayne County Community Coll., Detroit, 1972—, acting dir. allied health, 1979-81, instr. 1972—. Mem. task force to rev. sex. edn. Ypsilanti Sch. Dist., 1973; mem. Adv. Bd. on Sch. Age Parents, 1974-81; mem. adv. bd. Detroit Central City Mental Health, 1974-75; cons. Macomb Oakland Residential Treatment Center, 1976; mem. adv. bd. minority recruitment Wayne State U. Occupational Therapy Program, 1976; mem. adv. bd. Washtenaw County United Way, 1976-77, Wayne State U. Occupational Therapy Dept., 1977—; mem. community devel. adv. council City of Ypsilanti, 1979-81, rehab. rev. bd., 1980. Recipient Cert. of Appreciation, Mich. Occupational Therapy Assn., 1979; Certificate of Leadership, Nat. Black Occupational Therapy Caucus, 1980. Mem. Am. Occupational Therapy Assn., Mich. Occupational Therapy Assn., Mich. Council on Edn., Detroit Black Caucus of Health Workers, Nat. Assn. Health Care Execs., Alpha Kappa Alpha. Baptist. Office: 1001 W Fort St Detroit MI 48226

WITHERSPOON, FREDDA LILLY, educator; b. Houston; d. Fred D. and Vanita E. (Meredith) Lilly; A.B., Bishop Coll.; M.S.W., Washington U., 1949, M.A. in Guidance and Counseling, 1954; Ph.D., St. Louis U., 1965; m. Robert L. Witherspoon; children—Robert L., Vanita. Social worker, supr. St. Louis City Welfare Office, Homer G. Phillips Hosp., 1943-50; tchr. English, guidance counselor St. Louis Pub. Schs., 1950-65; prof. student personnel services Forest Park Community Coll., St. Louis, 1965—; cons. Ednl. Testing Service, Princeton, N.J., Head Start program, 1965-68; counseling cons. St. Louis Job Corps Center for Women, 1966-68. Organizer teenage service guild Annie Malone Children's Home, 1964; v.p. St. Louis chpt. NAACP, 1969—, pres. Mo. Conf., 1973—; mem. Challenge of 70's Crime Commn., 1970-75; mem. adv. council Central Inst. for Deaf, 1970—; mem. Mayor's Council Youth, 1970-75; dir. teens fund drive March of Dimes, 1960-72, Lily Day drive for Crippled Children, 1966-72; chpt. chmn., mem. speakers bur. United Way, 1969—. Bd. dirs. children's services City of St. Louis, Mo. Heart Assn., N.A.A.C.P., Social Health Assn., Community Assn. Schs. for Arts, St. Louis Heart Assn., Girl Scouts; pres. St. Louis Met. YWCA, 1978-79, bd. dirs.; bd. dirs., vice-chmn. St. Louis Urban League, 1977—. Named Woman of Year, Greyhound Bus Corp., 1967, St. Louis Argus, 1968, Nat. Outstanding Woman, Iota Phi Lambda, 1970; named Outstanding Woman of Achievement, Globe Dem., 1970, Outstanding Educator of Am., 1971, Nat. Top Lady Distinction, 1974; recipient Negro History award, 1971; George Washington Carver award, 1976; Health and Welfare Council award, 1975. Mem. NAACP (life; Nat. Outstanding Youth Adv. 1977), Am. Personnel and Guidance Assn., AAUP (pres. 1975—), AAUW, Nat. Assn. Women Deans and Counselors, Am. Sch. Counselors Assn., Am. Vocational Guidance Assn., Assn. Measurement and Evaluation in Guidance, Nat. Assn. Jr. Colls., Nat. Faculty Assn. Jr. Colls., League Women Voters, Nat. Council Negro Women, Mo. Assn. Social Welfare, Jack and Jill, Mound City (pres. 1946-49), Nat. (pres. 1951-52) bar auxs., Kappa Delta Pi, Iota Phi Lambda (nat. pres. 1977-81), Sigma Gamma Rho. Research on high sch. drop outs with police records, uses of group guidance techniques in jr. colls. Home: 20 Lewis Pl Saint Louis MO 63113

WITHERSPOON, WILLIAM, investment economist; b. St. Louis, Nov. 21, 1909; s. William Conner and Mary (Houston) W.; student Washington U. Evening Sch., 1928-47; m. Margaret Telford Johanson, June 25, 1938; children—James Tomlin, Jane Witherspoon Peltz, Elizabeth Witherspoon Vodra. Research dept. A. G. Edwards & Sons, 1928-31; pres. Witherspoon Investment Co., 1931-34; head research dept. Newhard Cook & Co., 1934-43; chief price analysis St. Louis Ordnance Dist., 1943-45; head research dept. Newhard Cook & Co., 1945-53; owner Witherspoon Investment Counsel, 1953-64; ltd. partner Newhard Cook & Co., economist, investment analyst, 1965-68; v.p. research Stifel, Nicolaus & Co., 1968-81; lectr. on investments Washington U., 1948-67. Mem. Clayton Bd. of Edn., 1955-68, pres., 1966-67; mem. Clayton Park and Recreation Commn., 1959-60; trustee Ednl. TV, KETC, 1963-64; mem. investment com. Gen. Assembly Mission Bd. Presbyterian Ch. U.S., Atlanta, 1976-79, mem. permanent com. ordination exams, 1979—. Served as civilian Ordnance Dept., AUS, 1943-45. Chartered fin. analyst. Mem. St. Louis Soc. Fin. Analysts (pres. 1949-50). Home: 6401 Ellenwood Clayton MO 63105

WITMER, DAVID ROY, univ. adminstr.; b. Zwingle, Iowa, Feb. 18, 1933; s. Melvin Christopher and Martha Louise (Franz) W.; B.S. magna cum laude, U. Wis.-Madison, 1951, M.S., 1968, Ph.D., 1971; m. Doris Ann Theis, Oct. 29, 1955; children—Mark David, Jeffrey Alvin, Laura Helene. Tchr. geography and English, Public Schs. Stoughton (Wis.), 1960-61, Madison (Wis.), 1961-62; systems analyst Wis. Hwy. Commn., Madison, 1962-64; systems coordinator Bd. of Regents Wis. State Univs., 1964-65, budget officer, 1965-66, adminstrv. officer, 1966-68, dir. instl. studies and acad. planning, 1968-72; asst. chancellor U. Wis.-La Crosse. Mem. Middleton (Wis.) Sch. Bd., 1967-68; mem. Wis. Gov.'s Commn. on Edn., 1970-71; bd. dirs. Cardiac Rehab. Center, United Way of LaCrosse Area. Served with U.S. Army, 1955-60. Mem. Assn. Univ. Wis. Faculty, Am. Assn. Higher Edn., Assn. Instl. Research, Am. Ednl. Research Assn, Nat. Orgn. Legal Problems of Edn., Phi Delta Kappa. Mem. United Ch. of Christ (bd. homeland ministries). Club: Rotary. Contbr. articles to profl. jours. Home: 1815 King St La Crosse WI 54601 Office: 1725 State St La Crosse WI 54601

WITT, DAVID RICHARD, tech. writer, instr.; b. Oshkosh, Wis., Jan. 19, 1934; s. Rueben D. and Josephine O. (Schnieder) W.; student Oshkosh Inst. Tech., 1960-61; m. Carol M. Goyette, Dec. 26, 1953; children—Teresa A., Judith M., Peter D., Rachelle K., Kurt A., Reuben D, II, Martin J. Tech. instr. Giddings and Lewis Machine Tool Co., Fond du Lac, Wis., 1966-78; tech. writer, instr. Giddings and Lewis Electronics Co., Fond Du Lac, 1978—; instr. Moraine Park Tech. Inst., Fond du Lac, 1977-78. Mem. Am. Soc. Tng. and Devel., Nat. Mgmt. Assn., Am. Radio Relay League. Clubs: Fond Du Lac County Republican; Elks. Home: 1828 Bechaud Beach Dr Fond Du Lac WI 54935 Office: 666 S Military Rd Fond Du Lac WI 54935

WITTCOFF, CONSTANCE CLEIN, ednl. psychologist; b. Seattle, Nov. 12, 1931; B.A., Stanford U., 1953; M.A., Washington U., St. Louis, 1977, postgrad., 1978—; m. Raymond H. Wittcoff, June 25, 1958; children—Mark Raymond, Caroline Cynthia. Writer, San Francisco Chronicle, 1953-55; dir. Am. Assn. UN, St. Louis, 1956-60; lectr., program developer St. Louis Art Mus., 1960-71; producer Sta. KETC-TV, pub. broadcasting, St. Louis, 1973-75; instr. dept. edn., counselor for women U. Mo., St. Louis, 1976-78; researcher, clin. asst. dept. psychiatry Med. Sch., Washington U., 1977—; bd. dirs. Adult Edn. Council of Greater St. Louis, 1977—, Com. for Arts and Sr. Citizens, St. Louis. Bd. dirs. women's aux. St. Louis Symphony, 1959-63, Dance Concert Soc., St. Louis, 1974-77; mem. exec. com. Contemporary Art Soc., St. Louis, 1965-70. Recipient pub. service honors for cultural and civic contbns. Mem. Am. Personnel and Guidance Assn., Am. Vocat. Guidance Assn., AAUP, Am. Ednl. Research Assn., Internat. Soc. for Polit. Psychology, Nat. Assn. Ednl. Broadcasters, Am. Soc. Tng., Devel., Assos. Mus. Modern Art, St. Louis Art Mus. (life), Stanford Alumni Assn. (life). Clubs: Stanford of St. Louis, Washington U. Faculty, St. Louis. Author: Effective Learning Skills, 1977; What is Treatment?, 1977; (with Brim and Wetzel) Social Network Characteristics of Hospitalized Depressed Patients, 1979; writer, producer, dir. film: Women and Money: Myths and Realities, 1976. Home: 50 Randelay Dr Saint Louis MO 63124

WITTE, SUSAN BETH, ednl. adminstr.; b. Freeport, Ill., June 26, 1948; d. Fredrick Ralph and Nelda Lauretta (Borcherts) W.; A.A., Highland Community Coll., Freeport, 1968; B.S. in Edn., No. Ill. U., 1971, M.S. in Edn., 1977. Tchr., Rockford (Ill.) Sch. Dist. #205, 1971-79; asst. supt. Regional Office of Edn. Boone-Winnebago Counties (Ill.), Rockford, 1979—; tchr. law-focused edn. project Rockford Public Schs./No. Ill. U., 1975—; instr. creative writing for children Rockford Coll., 1978; test reviewer, evaluator Ill. State Bd. Edn., 1978-79; del. Ill., White House Conf. on Children, 1979-80. Delta Kappa Gamma grantee, 1980. Mem. Assn. Supervision and Curriculum Devel., Ill. Assn. Supervision and Curriculum Devel., Phi Delta Kappa, Delta Kappa Gamma. Contbr. articles to profl. jours. Home: 913 N Main St Apt 1004 Rockford IL 61103 Office: 712 Courthouse Bldg Rockford IL 61101

WITTEMANN, HENRY, consumer products co. exec.; b. Bronx, N.Y., Mar. 20, 1930; s. Henry and Emilie Julie (Preuss) W.; B.S. (Founders Day award), N.Y. U., 1962; m. Marilyn Bobinsky, May 18, 1968; children—Christopher Mark, Carole Lynn. Account exec. Ogilvy & Mather Inc., advt., N.Y.C., 1950-62; v.p., account supr. Compton Advt., Chgo., 1963-65, BBD&O Advt., Chgo., 1965-66; v.p. advt. services Alberto Culver Co., Melrose Park, Ill., 1966—. Served with AUS, 1954-56. Address: Alberto-Culver Co 2525 Armitage Ave Melrose Park IL 60160

WITTENBERG, HARVEY WILLIAM, radio broadcasting exec.; b. Chgo., Sept. 11, 1936; s. Irving and Rose W.; B.A., U. Ill., 1958; children—Sue Ann, Elizabeth, Melissa. Asst. sports editor City News Bur., 1958; asst. news and sports dir. WLS Radio, Chgo., 1958-65; gen. mgr. Sta. WLS-FM, Chgo., 1965-69; sales mgr. Sta. WLOO, Chgo., 1969-79; v.p., sta. mgr. Sta. WLOO, WAIT, Chgo., 1979—; dir. Bedside Network, Chgo. Bd. dirs. Associated Talmud Torahs; trustee Adas Shalom. Jewish. Office: 875 N Michigan Ave Chicago IL 60611

WITTER, RICHARD LAWRENCE, veterinarian; b. Bangor, Maine, Sept. 10, 1936; s. J. Franklin and Verna Harriet (Church) W.; B.S., Mich. State U., 1958, D.V.M., 1960; M.S., Cornell U., 1962, Ph.D., 1964; m. Joan Elizabeth Denny, June 30, 1962; children—Jane Katherine, Steven Franklin. Research veterinarian Regional Poultry Research Lab., Dept. Agr., East Lansing, Mich., 1964—, dir. lab., 1975—; asso. prof. pathology Mich. State U. Mem. AVMA, Am. Assn. Avian Pathologists, Sigma Xi. Club: Okemos Kiwanis (pres. 1977-78). Contbr. articles on avian diseases to profl. jours. Office: Regional Poultry Research Laboratory 3606 E Mount Hope Rd East Lansing MI 48823

WITTIG, RICHARD JOSEPH, business exec.; b. Chgo., July 30, 1943; s. Charles Albert and Marie Margaret (Alston) W.; A.Sci., Ill. Inst. Tech., 1970; B.S. in Bus. summa cum laude, U. Wis., Parkside, 1972, B.S. in Psychology, 1972; M.B.A. in Fin., M.B.A. in Organizational Devel., U. Wis., Madison, 1974; m. Judith Anne Glassman, Sept. 2, 1961; children—Richard Joseph, David Arthur. Field engr., buyer Admiral Corp., 1964-65; with planning dept. Am. Motors, 1965-66; dir. purchases Permonite Mfg. Co., Chgo., 1966-72; with Oshkosh Truck Corp. (Wis.), 1974—, sales mgr., 1975-77, v.p. def. products, 1977—. Served with USN, 1960-64. Sustaining mem. Republican Nat. Com., 1978—. Mem. Nat. Assn. Purchasing Mgmt., Am. Def. Preparedness Assn., Assn. U.S. Army, Air Force Assn., Beta Gamma Sigma. Lutheran. Clubs: Oshkosh Power Boat, Masons, K.T. Author articles. Home: 53 Stoney Beach Rd Oshkosh WI 54901 Office: Oshkosh Truck Corp 2300 Oregon St Oshkosh WI 54903

WITTSTOCK, LAURA WATERMAN, radio programming exec.; b. Cattaraugus, N.Y., Sept. 11, 1937; d. Isaac and Clarinda (Jackson) Waterman; student San Francisco State Coll., 1961, Fla. Jr. Coll., 1964; m. Lloyd Carl Wittstock, Aug. 30, 1970; children by previous marriage—Joe O. Simas III, Tedi Marie Wittstock, Arthur Waterman Simas, James O. Simas, Rose Marie Wittstock. Editor, Legis. Rev., Washington, 1971-73; dir. Project Media, Nat. Indian Edn. Assn., Mpls., 1973-75; exec. dir. Am. Indian Press Assn., Washington, 1975-76; pres., dir. MIGIZI Communications, Mpls., 1976—; ind. cons., 1977-81. Mem. Nat. Commn. Alcoholism and Alcohol Related Problems; patricipant Internat. Women's Yr., 1975; mem. Seminar on Women and Devel.; dir. devel. Juel Fairbanks Aftercare Residence, 1979-80; mem. Am. Indian Policy Rev. Commn. Task Force Urban Indian Concerns, 1976; exec. dir. Am. Indian Press Assn., 1975; adminstr. Red Sch. House, 1976-76. Mem. Nat. Indian Edn. Assn. Mem. Hondenosaunee, People of the Longhouse. Contbr. to Comparative Perspectives of Third World Women, 1980. Home: 917 21st Ave SE Minneapolis MN 55414 Office: 1519 E Franklin Ave Minneapolis MN 55404

WITZEL, JOHN GEORGE, elec. engr.; b. Milw., Aug. 25, 1955; s. George Edgar and Mary Elizabeth (Wagner) W.; student U. Wis., 1977-79; m. Christine M. Bartel, Feb. 3, 1979; 1 dau., Audrey Ann. Owner, mgr. Witzel Electronic Repair and Design, Oshkosh, Wis., 1973-79; research equipment designer U. Wis., Oshkosh, 1978-79; pres. Witzel Electronic Enterprises, Columbia, Md., 1979—. Served with USAF, 1973-77. Mem. Wis. Soc. Profl. Engrs. Address: 8870 Spiral Cut Columbia MD 21045

WITZKE, DONALD BRUCE, psychologist; b. San Francisco, June 5, 1938; s. Otto Clarence and Helmi Hilja (Poutanen) W.; B.A., U. Tex., Austin, 1967, Ph.D., 1975; m. Hazel Evelyn Pittman, Mar. 3, 1972; children—Deborah S. DeShong, Kimberly N. DeShong, Wayne O. Head statis. services Survey Research Center, Inst. Social Sci. Research, UCLA, 1976-78, lectr. dept. edn., 1977; coordinator health sci. edn. research Office Ednl. Resources, Sch. Medicine, U. S.D., Vermillion, 1978-80, co-dir. Office Ednl. Evaluation, Research and Services, 1980—. Served with USAF, 1961-65. Henderson fellow, 1968. Mem. Am. Psychol. Assn., Assn. Am. Med. Colls., Midwestern Psychol. Assn., S.D. Psychol. Assn. Author: (with others) Personality Development in Two Cultures, 1975. Home: 804 E Lewis St Vermillion SD 57069 Office: 119 Lee Medical Bldg University of South Dakota Vermillion SD 57069

WITZKE, PAUL THEODORE, mathematician; b. La Crosse, Wis., Apr. 6, 1919; s. Paul Carl and Martha Mary (Will) W.; B.S., U. Wis., La Crosse, 1941; postgrad. U. Wis., Milw., 1945-48, Marquette U., 1950, U. Wis., Madison, 1953-54; m. Winifred R. Hoppe, July 28, 1945; 1 son, Brian Jon. Clk., First Nat. Bank, La Crosse, 1936-37; partner Bijou Confectionery, La Crosse, 1937-41; prin. insp. U.S. Navy Inspection Service, Milw., 1941-46; tchr. math. and sci. Milw. Area Tech. Coll., 1946—; cons. to pub. cos., including Addison-Wesley Pub. Co. Mem. Math. Assn. Am., Nat. Council Tchrs. Math., Math. Assn. Two-Yr. Colls., Am. Tech. Edn. Assn., Am. Vocat. Assn., Am. Fedn. Tchrs., NEA. Author (with Thomas J. McHale) textbooks, the most recent being: Applied Algebra I, 1979; Applied Algebra II, 1980. Office: 1015 N 6th St Milwaukee WI 53203

WOCHHOLZ, HAROLD FREDERICK, electronics co. exec.; b. Albion, Mich., Mar. 12, 1931; s. Harold Frank Otto and Charlotte Arene (Northrop) W.; B.S.E.E., Mich. State U., 1958, M.S.E.E., 1959; m. Phyllis Jean Newell, Mar. 31, 1951; children—Julie Jean, Harold Frederick. Project engr. Gen. Electric Co., Phoenix, 1959-60, Washington, 1960-63, Daytona Beach, Fla., 1963-66, Somersworth, N.H., 1967; asst. prof. elec. engring. U. N.H., Durham, 1967-71; v.p. engring. N.E. Electronics, Concord, N.H., 1972-77; v.p. engring. McDonnell Douglas Electronics Co., St. Charles, Mo., 1977—; cons. Davidson Rubber Co., Dover, N.H., 1968, Bell Telephone Labs., 1969, N.E. Electronics, 1970-71. Mem. budget com., Durham, N.H., 1969-71; county chmn. Romney for Pres., Strafford County, N.H., 1967; pres. Clarkson Woods Homeowners Assn., Chesterfield, Mo., 1979-81. Served with USN, 1951-55. Alex Dow fellow Mich. State U., 1958-59. Mem. IEEE, Am. Mgmt. Assn., Tau Beta Pi, Eta Kappa Nu, Phi Eta Sigma, Beta Theta Pi. Republican. Patentee in field. Office: PO Box 426 Saint Charles MO 63301

WOCKENFUSS, JAMES HAROLD, performing arts dir., educator; b. Fond du Lac, Wis., Jan. 14, 1930; s. Harold Frederick and Florence Marie (Hanisch) W.; B.A., U. Wis., 1953; m. Lena May Sewell, May 27, 1961; children—Erica Lynn, Kirsten Lee. Theatre mgr. Wis. Union Theater, U. Wis., Madison, 1954-63; dir. La. State U. Union Theater, Baton Rouge, 1963-70; dir. Hancher Auditorium, coordinator Ia. Center for Arts, U. Iowa, Iowa City, 1970—, prof. communication and theatre arts, arts mgmt. program, 1975—. Mem. Urban Renewal Design Com., 1974—; mem. music task force com. Iowa Arts Council, 1974-77. Mem. Assn. Coll., Univ. and Community Arts Adminstrs. (pres. 1972-74, Fannie Taylor award for disting. service to performing arts 1978), Assn. Coll. Unions Internat. (chmn. com. on performing and visual arts 1971-73), Assn. Arts Adminstrn. Educators, Omicron Delta Kappa (faculty sec.). Club: Rotary.

WOEHLKE, PAUL HAMMOND, hosp. exec.; b. N.Y.C., Sept. 12, 1941; s. Louis Paul and Marian (Hammond) W.; B.S., Utah State U., 1967; M.H.A., Washington U., St. Louis, 1969; m. Genoveva E. Dragone, Dec. 21, 1964; children—Erik, Kirk. Adminstrv. asst. Lafayette (Ind.) Home Hosp., 1969-72; asst. adminstr. St. Rita's Med. Center, Lima, Ohio, 1972-77; v.p. Lima Meml Hosp., 1978—. Chmn. crusade Allen County unit Am. Cancer Soc., 1978, 79, 81; membership enrollment chmn. Lima Family YMCA, 1978, 79. Mem. Am. Coll. Hosp. Adminstrs., Am. Hosp. Assn., Ohio Hosp. Assn., West Ohio Hosp. Council. Club: Elks. Home: 2069 High Ridge Rd Lima OH 45805 Office: 1001 Bellefontaine Ave Lima OH 45804

WOELFEL, TERRY ALLAN, assn. exec.; b. Sheboygan, Wis., Mar. 2, 1953; s. Othmar G. and Dolores M. (Schmaling) W.; student Lakeshore Tech. Inst., 1977. With A.A. Laun, Kiel, Wis., 1971-73, Kohler Co. (Wis.), 1973-79; exec. v.p. Wis. Jaycees, Appleton, 1979—. Mem. Nat. Assn. Jaycee Execs., Kiel Jaycees (dir. 1977-79), Wis. Jaycees (dist. dir. 1977-78, regional dir. 1978-79), Eastern Wis. Amateur Basketball League (v.p. 1979—). Roman Catholic. Address: PO Box 1547 Appleton WI 54913

WOELFER, WILMER TOPPER, food equipment mfg. co. exec.; b. St. Louis, Mar. 28, 1938; s. Wilmer Harry and Thelma Ruth (Kowert) W.; B.S., Valparaiso U., 1960; M.S., Eastern Ill. U., 1962; postgrad. Okla. State U., 1964, U. Md., 1967; m. Sarah Jean Gravenhorst, Dec. 27, 1961; children—Jeffrey Scott, Kathryn Jean, Wilmer Todd, Matthew Craig. Tchr., Cleve. and Grayslake, Ill., 1960-70; field rep. dept. public and alumni affairs Valparaiso (Ind.) U., 1970-71; asst. sales mgr. John Boos & Co., Effingham, Ill., 1971-78, exec. v.p. sales, 1978—. Mem. Effingham Bd. Edn., 1974-80, pres., 1978; bd. dirs. Effingham YMCA, 1979—. Mem. Nat. Assn. Food Equipment Mfrs. Lutheran. Home: 1207 Holiday Dr Effingham IL 62401 Office: John Boos & Co 315 S First St Effingham IL 62401

WOELFLE, ARTHUR WILLIAM, food co. exec.; b. Dunkirk, N.Y., Mar. 8, 1920; s. Arthur and Agnes (Johnson) W.; B.S., U. Buffalo, 1943; postgrad. U. Lucerne, Switzerland, 1966, 70, Northwestern U., 1972; m. Ruth A. Godden, Dec. 29, 1943; children—Gretchen, Christine, Ann. Sec.-treas. Bedford Products Co., Dunkirk, 1946-55; sr. v.p. Bedford Products div. Kraft Foods, Dunkirk, 1955-59; div. product mgr. Kraft Foods, 1959-66, chief exec. officer Kraft Foods W. Ger., 1966-69; chmn., mng. dir. Kraft Foods Ltd. in U.K. and Scandinavia, 1969-73; pres., chief operating officer Kraft Inc., Glenview, Ill., 1973—; dir. Santa Fe Industries, Inc., First Nat. Bank Chgo., First Chgo. Corp. Served to lt. USMCR. Mem. Inst. Dirs. (London). Clubs: Chicago; Union League (N.Y.C.); Glenview Golf. Office: Kraft Inc Kraft Court Glenview IL 60025

WOELLHOF, LAWRENCE RAY, social worker; b. Clay Center, Kans., Nov. 28, 1922; s. Jacob F. and Laura M. (Hahn) W.; B.S., Emporia (Kans.) State U., 1949, M.S., 1954; m. Eldene Cook, Sept. 21, 1962; 1 son, Jeffrey. Tchr., Meade (Kans.) Pub. Schs., 1949-53; prin. Lakin (Kans.) Grade Sch., 1953-59; instr. Emporia State U., 1960-63; counselor supr. Kans. State Employment Service, Topeka, 1965-67, asst. mgr., 1967-70; ednl. dir. Kans. Neurol. Inst., Topeka, 1970-72; dir. Foster Grandparent Project, Topeka, 1972-79; counselor Kans. Div. Employment, 1979—; bd. dirs. Community Resources Council, Topeka, 1972—, chmn. aging sect., 1973-74, 77-78; mem. Older Citizens Info. Center, Topeka, 1973-78, pres. bd. dirs., 1977-78; dir. Kans. Citizens Council on Aging, Topeka, 1975—; mem. adv. council Shawnee County (Kans.) Community Mental Health Corp., 1971-72; chmn. Topeka Area Manpower Adv. Planning Council, 1968. Mem. Am. Personnel and Guidance Assn., Nat. Employment Counselors Assn., NEA, Nat. Ret. Tchrs. Assn. Home: 4432 Twilight Dr Topeka KS 66614

WOESTE, GRETCHEN LOUISE, sch. adminstr.; b. Charles City, Iowa, June 10, 1929; d. Hampton T. and Louise (Griffith) Hall; B.S., Iowa State U., 1951; M.S., Kans. State U., 1965; m. Stanley F. Woeste, Oct. 24, 1976. Tchr., Oskaloosa (Iowa) Community Schs., 1957-63; grad. asst. Kans. State U., 1963-64; tchr. Ames (Iowa) Community Schs., 1965-66; supr. home econs. Des Moines Public Schs., 1966—. Mem. Am. Vocat. Assn., Am. Home Econs. Assn., Iowa Home Econs. Assn., Phi Delta Kappa, Delta Kappa Gamma, Omicron Nu, Phi Upsilon Omicron. Home: 304 W Ashland St Indianola IA 50125 Office: 1800 Grand St Des Moines IA 50307

WOHLERS, ARTHUR EUGENE, educator, ednl. facilities cons.; b. Danbury, Ohio, Dec. 10, 1913; s. Henry Edwin and Emma Henrietta (Drickhammer) W.; B.S. in Edn., Bowling Green (Ohio) State U., 1935; M.A., Ohio State U., 1939, Ph.D., 1954; m. Lois Hilda Kemmis, Dec. 24, 1936; children—Janet Lee Wohlers Fillinger, Robert Thad. Tchr. schs. in Ohio, 1935-39; tchr., dir. audio edn., coordinator extracurricular activities Dover (Ohio) Public Schs., 1939-47; high sch. prin., Carey, Ohio, 1947-49, Washington Court House, Ohio, 1947-49; research asst. Ohio State U., 1951-53, research asso., asst. prof., 1953-55; cons. ednl. facility planning Wayne County (Mich.) Intermediate Sch. Dist., 1955-57; lectr. Wayne State U., 1956-57; asso. prof. ednl. facilities unit Ohio State U. Sch. Edn., 1957-61, prof., 1961—, chmn. orgn. and spl. services div., 1961-64, dir. ednl. personnel placement office, 1970-79, ednl. facilities cons., 1979—; cons. ednl. facilities Ohio, other states. Served with USAAF, 1943-46. Mem. NEA, Am. Assn. Sch. Adminstrs., Buckeye Assn. Sch. Adminstrs., Council Ednl. Facility Planners (pres. Great Lakes region), Ohio Assn. Elem. and Secondary Sch. Adminstrs., Nat. Assn. Elem. and Secondary Sch. Adminstrs., Nat. Soc. Study of Edn., Ohio Assn. Supervision and Curriculum Devel., Nat. Assn. Supervision and Curriculum Devel., Ohio Assn. Higher Edn. (pres.), Phi Delta Kappa, Phi Kappa Phi, Kappa Mu Epsilon. Author: Self-Help Manual for Planning Secondary School Buildings, 1954; (with others) Planning Facilities for Higher Education, 1964; contbg. author: The Church School, 1960; Planning Middle School Facilities: The Administrator, 1970; others. Home: 5392 Keeley St Columbus OH 43220 Office: Room 310 Ramseyer Hall Ohio State U 29 W Woodruff Ave Columbus OH 43210

WOHLFEIL, PAUL FREDERICK, psychologist; b. Saginaw, Mich., Aug. 28, 1934; s. Herman Frederick and Rose Elizabeth (Kueffner) W.; B.A., Mich. State U., 1962; M.A., Eastern Mich. U., 1966; Ph.D., Ind. U. Mo.; m. Shirley Jean Setzer, July 20, 1976; children—Paul John, Ondria Rose. Psychologist, Whaley Home for Disturbed Children, Flint, Mich., 1963-67; asst. dir., psychologist Shiawasee Mental Health Clinic, Owosso, Mich., 1967-68; psychologist Bay County Mental Health Clinic, Bay City, Mich., 1968-74; psychologist, Salman Psychiat. Clinic, Bay City, 1974—; dir. counseling Group Health Service of Mich., 1981—; mem. faculty Delta Coll., 1976-77, Central Mich. U., 1969-71. Chmn. bd. Bay County Half Way House for Alcoholics. Served with AUS, 1954-56. Recipient grant Rutgers U., 1974; recipient awards Mich. Assn. Child Agys., 1964, Mich. AP, 1973. Mem. Am., Mich. psychol. assns., Acad. Psychologists in Marital Counseling, Mich. Sch. Psychologists. Lutheran. Club: Riverview Rod and Gun. Author: If I Go See A Shrink Does It Mean I'm Crazy?, 1977; Awareness Counseling. Home: 3102 Sharon Rd Midland MI 48640 Office: 315 S Michigan Saginaw MI 48602

WOHLHUETER, JOHN FREDRICK, mfg. co. exec.; b. Maunie, Ill., Dec. 8, 1923; s. Ralph D. and Emily (Reiling) W.; B.S. in Bus. Adminstrn., Miami U., Ohio, 1946; postgrad. State U. Iowa, 1954, DePaul U., Chgo., 1961; m. Barbara Hodapp, June 23, 1945; children—Ann Krintzline, Joan Powell, Rae Maier. With Belden Corp., Geneva, Ill., 1946—, dir. mfg., 1967-68, asst. v.p. mfg., 1968-70, v.p. mfg., 1970-72, v.p. and gen. mgr. electronic div., 1972-75, group v.p. mfg., 1975-78, exec. v.p. ops., 1978—; dir. 1st Nat. Bank, Geneva. Chmn., United Fund, Wayne County, Ind., 1966, chmn., 1967, pres., 1968; capital fund chmn. YMCA, Richmond, Ind., 1974, membership chmn., 1969. Served to capt. USMC, 1942-46, 51-52. Mem. Am. Mgmt. Assn. Lutheran. Home: 15 N Andover Ln Geneva IL 60134 Office: 2000 S Batavia Ave Geneva IL 60134

WOITO, ROBERT SEVERIN, ednl. orgn. exec.; b. Sioux Falls, S.D., Dec. 13, 1937; s. Harold August and Lois Louise (Severin) W.; B.A., Grinnell Coll., 1960; M.A., U. Calif., Berkeley, 1965, Ph.D., 1976; m. Linda Newman, Aug. 26, 1961; children—Katrina, Andrea, Brian; m. 2d, Jacky Phillips, Oct. 26, 1974; step-children—Jengis, Aaron. With Turn Toward Peace, Berkeley, Calif., 1964-67; dir. publs. World Without War Council, Berkeley, 1967-72, publs. and asso. dir., Chgo., 1972-77, dir. Midwest, 1977—; instr. YMCA Community Coll. Mem. fgn. policy com. Ind. Voters of Ill., 1976-77. Served as info. officer USAF, 1960-63. Recipient first prize short story contest, Air Defense Command, 1961. Mem. Am. Hist. Assn., Conf. on Peace Research in History. Clubs: UN Assn. Greater Chgo. and Ill. (bd. dirs.). Author: To End War, 6th edit., 1981; editor: Vietnam Peace Proposals, Modern Classics of Peace Series, World Hunger Crisis Kit, World Disarmament Kit, Internat. Human Rights Kit. Home: 5441 S Ridgewood Ct Chicago IL 60615 Office: 67 E Madison St Suite 1417 Chicago IL 60603

WOJCIK, CASS, decorative supply co. exec., former city ofcl.; b. Rochester, N.Y., Dec. 3, 1920; s. Emil M. and Casimira C. (Krawiecz) W.; student Lawrence Inst. Tech., 1941-43, Yale, 1943-44, U.S. Sch. for European Personnel, Czechoslovakia, 1945; m. Lilliam Leocadia Lendzion, Sept. 25, 1948; 1 son, Robert Cass. Owner Nat. Florists Supply Co., Detroit, 1948—; owner Nat. Decorative, Detroit, 1950—; co-owner Creation Center, Detroit, 1955-60; cons.-contractor hort.-bot. design auto show displays, TV producers, designers and decorators. Mem. Regional Planning and Evaluation Council, 1969—; city-wide mem. Detroit Bd. Edn., 1970-75; commr. Detroit Pub. Schs. Employees Retirement Commn., until 1975; mem. Area Occupational Ednl. Commn., Ednl. Task Force; chmn., grand marshall Ann. Gen. Pulaski Day Parade, Detroit, 1970, 71, now mem. com., chmn. Pulaski Day Citizens Award Com.; mem. Boys Towns of Italy; del. Detroit Cath. Archdiocese Assembly. Served with AUS, 1944-46. Decorated Bronze Star; recipient citation Polish-Am. Congress, 1971. Mem. S.E. Mich. Council Govts. (exec. com.), Friends of Belle Isle Task Force, Founders Soc. Detroit Inst. Arts, Mich. State Heritage Groups Council, Nat. Small Bus. Assn., Nat. Conf. Am. Ethic Groups, DAV, Central Citizens Com. Detroit, Internat. Platform Assn., Nat. Geog. Soc. Roman Catholic. Clubs: Univ. of Ann Arbor, Polish Century (Detroit). Home: 451 Lodge Dr Detroit MI 48214

WOJCIK, JAMES JOSEPH, univ. adminstr.; b. Detroit, Nov. 23, 1942; s. Mitchell J. and Anne A. (Kulpa) W.; B.S., Central Mich. U., 1965, M.A., 1968; m. Carol L. Humm, June 11, 1966; children—Mark William, Scott James. Sports editor Mount Pleasant Daily Times-News, 1965-66, editor, 1969-71; sports info. dir. Central Mich. U., Mount Pleasant, 1966-68, instr. journalism, 1968-69, asst. dir. devel., 1971-72, dir. student media, 1972—. Chmn. dirs. Central Mich. Community Hosp., 1981, trustee, 1974—. Mem. Nat. Council Collegiate Publs. Advisers, Mount Pleasant Area C. of C. (dir.), Sigma Delta Chi. Roman Catholic. Office: Room 8 Anspach Hall Central Mich U Mount Pleasant MI 48859

WOJTA, GERALD CHARLES, pharm. co. exec.; b. Manitowoc, Wis., Aug. 17, 1930; s. Charles J. and Agnes (Stefl) W.; student U. Wis., 1948-51; children—Pamela, Jerold, Daniel, James, Ann, Kimberly, Melissa. Salesman, Dorsey Labs., Inc., Lincoln, Nebr., 1953-55, asst. sales mgr., 1956, sales mgr., 1957-61; dir. mktg. Philips Roxane Lab., Inc., Columbus, Ohio, 1962-64, v.p., gen. mgr., 1965, pres., 1967—; dir. Mediplex, Inc. Trustee, Coll. Osteo. Medicine and Surgery, Des Moines, Columbus Day U.S.A. Assn. Fellow Am. Coll. Osteo. Obstetricians and Gynecologists; mem. Am., Ohio pharm. assns., Drug Chem. and Allied Trades Assn. Clubs: Scioto Country, Columbus Athletic, Columbus Touchdown. Office: PO Box 16532 Columbus OH 43216

WOLANIN, SOPHIE MAE, civic worker; b. Alton, Ill., June 11, 1915; d. Stephen and Mary (Fijalka) Wolanin; student Pa. State Coll., 1943-44; certificate secretarial sci. U. S.C., 1946, B.S. in Bus. Adminstrn. cum laude, 1948; Ph.D. honoris causa, Colo. State Christian Coll., 1972. Clk., stenographer, sec. Mercer County (Pa.) Tax Collector's Office, Sharon, 1932-34; receptionist, social sec., nurse-technician to doctor, N.Y.C., 1934-37; coil winder, assembler Westinghouse Electric Corp., Sharon, 1937-39, duplicator operator, typist, stenographer, 1939-44, confidential sec., Pitts., 1949-54; exec. sec., charter mem. Westinghouse Credit Corp., Pitts., 1954-72, hdqrs. sr. sec., 1972-80, reporter WCC News, 1967-68, asst. editor, 1968-71, asso. editor, 1971-74; student office sec. to dean U. S.C. Sch. Commerce, 1944-46, instr. math., bus. adminstrn., secretarial sci., 1946-48. Publicity and pub. relations chmn., corr. sec. South Oakland Rehab. Council, 1967-69; mem. nat. adv. bd. Am. Security Council; mem. Friends Winston Churchill Meml. and Library, Westminster Coll., Fulton, Mo. Fellow/patron Intercontinental Biog. Assn. (life), Intercontinental Inst. Community Service (life); mem. Allegheny County Scholarship Assn. (life), Allegheny County League Women voters, AAUW (life), Internat. Fedn. U. Women, N.E. Historic Geneal. Soc. (life), U. S.C. Alumni Assn. Ednl. Found. (Pa. state fund chmn. 1967-68, pres. council 1972—, ofcl. del., rep. inauguration Bethany Coll. pres.), Hypatian Lit. Soc. (hon.), Acad. Polit. Sci. (Columbia) (life), Bus. and Profl. Women's Club Pitts. (bd. dirs. 1963-80, editor Bull. 1963-65, treas. 1965-66, historian 1969-70, pub. relations 1971-76, Woman of Year 1972), Named to Woman's Hall of Fame; recipient numerous prizes Allegheny County Fair, 1952-67, citation Congl. Record, 1969, others. Liturgical Conf. N. Am. (life), Westinghouse Vet. Employees Assn., Nat. Soc. Lit. and Arts, Early Am. Soc., Am. Acad. Social and Polit. Sci., Societe Commemorative de Femmes Celebres, Nat. Trust Historic Preservation, Am. Counselors Soc. (life), Am. Judicature Soc., Am. Mus. Natural History (asso.), Nat. Hist. Soc. (founding mem.), Anglo-Am. Hist. Soc. (charter), Nat. Assn. Exec. Secs., Internat. Platform Assn., Smithsonian Assos., Asso. Nat. Archives, Nat., Pa., Fed. bus. and profl. women's clubs, Mercer County Hist. Soc. (life), Am. Bible Soc., UN Assn. U.S., Am. Counselors Soc. (life), Am. Hort. Soc. Republican. Roman Catholic (mem. Cathedral Altar Soc., patron organ recitals). Clubs: Jonathan Maxcy of U. S.C. (charter); Univ. Catholic of Pitts.; Key of Pa., Fedn. Bus. and Profl. Women (hon.); Coll. (hon.) (Sharon). Contbr. articles to newspapers; Am. corr. Polish radio and TV. Home: 5223 Smith-Stewart Rd SE Girard OH 44420

WOLD, ORPHIE AILEANE, nurse; b. Parshall, N.D., Dec. 1, 1919; d. Lars Nels and Hattie Claudina (Fuglem) Lunde; student Minot State Tchrs. Coll., 1937-38; R.N., Trinity Hosp., Minot, N.D., 1944; m. William Wold, June 22, 1947; 1 son, Michael William. Staff nurse operating room Trinity Med. Center, 1944-47, clin. instr. operating room, 1947-50, head nurse, 1950-59, dept. mgr. operating room, 1959—. Mem. Dist. II Nurses Assn., Am. Nurses Assn., Trinity Alumnae Assn., Assn. Operating Room Nurses. Lutheran. Home: 5 Cedar Country Club Village Minot ND 58701 Office: Trinity Medical Center Minot ND 58701

WOLF, FRANCES LORETA SMITH (MRS. MILTON HARRY WOLF), banker, civic worker; b. Cleve., Sept. 3, 1917; d. Francis William and Laura Barrett (Smitha) Smith; grad. Sch. Public Relations and Mktg., Northwestern U., 1965; m. Milton Harry Wolf, Feb. 14, 1935 (dec. Aug. 1954); children—Henry George II (dec.), Jacqueline Jeanne (Mrs. Ralph Matthew Gruenewald). Writer, visuals, asst. to producer comml. films Ray Waters Inc., 1950-55; adminstrv. asst. to Willard Johnson, NCCJ, 1955-57; craft stylist Chgo. Printed String Co., 1956-59; free lance advt., pub. relations, commls., 1959-60; dir. pub. relations Ave. State Bank (now Ave. Bank & Trust Co. Oak Park), Oak Park, Ill., 1961-68, asst. cashier, pub. relations and advt., 1968-71, asst. v.p. pub. relations, 1971-75, dir. community services and public relations, 1976—. Co-chmn. publicity Santa Claus Event, Oak Park, 1961-69; publicity chmn. Frank Lloyd Wright Festival, Oak Park-River Forest, 1969, chmn. pub. relations com. Frank Lloyd Wright Home and Studio Found., 1974-77; chmn. pub. relations Oak Park-River Forest Antique Show and Sales, 1967-70; bd. mem. Oak Park-River Forest Symphony, 1965-67; incorporator Cultural Arts Center, Oak Park, 1970. Bd. dirs. Sr. Citizens' Oak Park-River Forest; bd. dirs., mem. exec. bd. Thatcher Woods council Boy Scouts Am., 1977—; mem. Camp Shin-Go-Beck Fire Dept., Amundsen Park Community Council, N.W. Austin Community Council. Recipient fund raising award Thatcher Woods council Boy Scouts Am., 1976. Mem. Nat. Assn. Bank Women, Hist. Soc. Oak Park and River Forest (1st v.p., program chmn. 1973-78), Women in Communications (chmn. Jacob Scher awards 1977), Ave.-Lake Plaza Assn. (pres. 1969-70, v.p., treas. 1970-77), Woman's Advt. Club Chgo. (pub. relations com. mem. 1969—), Oak Park-River Forest C. of C. (co-chmn. ann. dinner 1963—), Art Inst. Chgo., Publicity Club Chgo. (dir. 1975-77), Zonta Internat. (dir. Oak Park chpt. 1976-77, chmn. community affairs 1976-77), 19th Century Woman's Club Assn. (spl. events com. 1969-70), D.A.R. (chpt. chaplain 1980-81), Meml. Found. Germanna Colonies in Va. Inc., Ky. Hist. Soc., Am. Clan Gregor Soc., St. Andrew Soc. Ill. Clubs: Chgo. Press, Chgo. Shell, Zonta. Home: 151 N Kenilworth Ave Oak Park IL 60301 Office: 104 N Oak Park Ave Oak Park IL 60303

WOLF, JAMES STUART, banker; b. St. Louis, Jan. 30, 1946; s. Paul Stuart and Edna Marie (Walther) W.; B.A., U. Mo., Columbia, 1972, B.J., 1973; M.B.A., St. Louis U., 1978; m. Mary Martha Yarbrough, Aug. 18, 1973. Documentation analyst First Nat. Bank, St. Louis, 1973-74, sr. documentation analyst, 1974-75, mktg. rep., 1975-76, asst. mktg. planning mgr., 1976; mktg. officer St. Louis County Bank, 1976-80, v.p., 1980—; v.p. County Nat. Bancorp., St. Louis, 1981—; v.p., dir. mktg. St. Louis County Bank, County Nat. Bancorp., 1981—. Bd. dirs. Old Town Clayton Assn., 1977-78, v.p., 1979. Served with USMC, 1969-71. Mem. Bank Mktg. Assn., Mo. Bankers Assn. (mktg. and public relations com.), Ill. Mo. Bank Mktg. Assn. (treas., past dir.), Clayton C. of C. (mktg. com. 1981), U. Mo. Alumni Assn. (dir. St. Louis chpt. 1980-81). Lutheran. Office: 8000 Forsyth Blvd Clayton MO 63105

WOLF, JOHN PHILLIP, univ. adminstr; b. Cleve., Oct. 27, 1940; s. Elden Laufer and Mildred (Pursell) W.; B.A., U. Kans., 1962, M.A., 1966. Instr. philosophy U. Kans.; vis. prof. philosophy Universidad Nacional Autonoma de Honduras, Centro Universitario de Estudios Generales, Tegucigalpa, Honduras, C.A.; regional program prof. philosophy U.S. AID, U.S. Agy. for Internat. Devel., San Jose, Costa Rica, 1966-68; asst. dir. Corbin Coll., U. Kans., 1968-71, asst. to dean and budget officer Coll. Liberal Arts and Scis., 1969—, lectr. philosophy, 1970-79, dir. adminstrv. services, 1974—, asst. to dean div. continuing edn., 1974-79, asst. dean div., 1979—, mem. council internat. programs and chmn. com. service functions, 1981—. Mem. AAUP, Nat. Univ. Extension Assn., Consortium of Univ. Film Centers, Am. Radio Relay League. Home: 435 Maine St Lawrence KS 66044 Office: Div Continuing Edn U Kans Lawrence KS 66045

WOLF, MARLANE LOUISE, advt. exec.; b. St. Paul, June 20, 1945; d. Robert Earl and Natalie Dora Ayers; B.A., U. Minn., 1968; m. Thomas J. Wolf, Jan. 28, 1977. Mktg. research dir. BBDO, Mpls., 1971-75, account exec., 1975-76; mktg. dir. Fisher Nut Co., St. Paul, 1976-80, v.p. mktg., 1980—. Mem. Am. Mgmt. Assn., Am. Mktg. Assn. (dir.), Minn. Advt. Fedn., Minn. Premium and Incentive Club. Contbr. to Am. Mgmt. Assn. Handbook, 1981. Home: 404 S Mississippi River Blvd Saint Paul MN 55105 Office: 2327 Wycliff St Saint Paul MN 55114

WOLF, PAUL JOSEPH, clin. psychologist; b. Quincy, Ill., Mar. 24, 1935; s. John Albert and Florence Anthonette (Scherneck) W.; B.A., St. John's U., Minn., 1958; M.A., Loyola U., Chgo., 1966, Ph.D., 1969; m. Jacqueline Elizabeth Down, June 11, 1966; 1 dau., Kimberly Louise. Staff psychologist Ill. State Madden Zone Center, 1969-70; pvt. practice psychology, Crystal Lake, Ill., 1970-71; staff psychologist Luth. Gen. Hosp., Park Ridge, Ill., 1971-78, chief clin. psychologist for phys. medicine and rehab. unit, 1971-78; pvt. practice psychology, Morton Grove, Ill., 1978—; leader workshops. Active, Roman Catholic Ch. Served with U.S. Army, 1960-62. Cert. clin. psychologist. Mem. Am. Psychol. Assn., Ill. Psychol. Assn., Internat. Neuropsychol. Assn. Home: 153 Asbury St Evanston IL 60202 Office: 5945 W Dempster St Morton Grove IL 60053

WOLF, ROBERT GENE, mech. engr.; b. Minden, Nebr., July 3, 1948; s. Edward William and Leora May (Lienemann) W.; B.S., U. Nebr., 1971; m. Kathleen Sue Mulder, Dec. 12, 1975; children—Christopher Michael, Katee Ellen, Amy Lauren. Design engr. Olsson Assos., Lincoln, Nebr., 1971—; instr. constrn. insp. tng. course Am. Public Works Assn., 1978. Registered profl. engr., Nebr. Mem. ASCE. Republican. Home: 2672 S 13th St Lincoln NE 68502 Office: 611 NBC Center Lincoln NE 68508

WOLFE, ESTEMORE ALVIS, ins. co. exec.; b. Crystal Springs, Miss., Dec. 29, 1919; s. Henry and Vinia (Crump) W.; B.S., Jackson State Coll., 1947; student Fla. Meml. Coll., 1948-49, N.Y. U., 1952-53; M.Ed., Wayne State U., 1951; M.A., Purdue U., 1953; D.Ed., Boston U., 1958; L.H.D., Wilberforce U., 1959; Litt.D., Creighton U., 1961; L.H.D., Syracuse U., 1963; postgrad. Purdue U., 1964; divorced. Dir. med. technicians Detroit Tb Sanitorium, 1947-48; ednl. cons., mass media specialist Detroit Bd. Edn., 1948—; v.p., sec. Wright Mut. Ins. Co., Detroit, 1955—; mem. internat. adv. Hamilton Funding Corp.; dir. Ind. Prodns. Corp., also chmn. nat. edn. com. for educators. Lectr., guest prof. Gt. Lakes Coll., Assumption Coll. (Can.), Wayne U., 1953-56, Jackson State Coll., Bethany Coll., U. Detroit, Wis. State U., Stevens Point, So. U. (La.); writer column Detroit Times; cons. to pres. P. Lenud & Co. Mem. White House Conf. of Children and Youth, 1960; mem. Council on Aging, 1965-66; campaign chmn. Jackson State Coll. Devel. Fund Drive, 1970-71. Organizer, pres. Detroit chpt. Friends of AMISTAD, 1972, nat. v.p., 1972—. Chmn. bd. trustees Detroit Met. Symphony Orch.; trustee Jackson State U. Devel. Fund, Nat. Negro Archives Mus., Washington, Mich. Council Arts, Scis. and Letters, Bethany (W.Va.) Coll. Served with AUS, 1942-46. Recipient Nat. Human Relations award Clark U., 1969, citation Am. Airlines in recognition of contbns. to devel. air transp. and nat. air power, 1969, Presidential citation for performance beyond call of duty, 1945, citation and plaque outstanding service and leadership City of Detroit, 1973; Achievement award Jackson State U. Alumni Assn., also Centennial medallion; plaque Kiwanis Clubs, 1978, Am. Heritage Found. award, 1980, numerous other plaques and citations for leadership in bus., civic orgns., edn. devel.; CASE TWO award Council for Advancement and Support for Higher Edn., 1979; plaque U. Detroit, 1979; 2d Century award Jackson State U., 1979; Spirit of Detroit award, 1980; Key to City of New Orleans, 1980; Outstanding Alumnus award Boston U., 1980; numerous others; named hon. staff col. Gov. Miss., 1977. Mem. NAACP, Nat. Soc. Visual Edn., Nat. Geog. Soc., Am. Acad. Social and Polit. Sci., Nat. Ins. Assn., Detroit Fedn. Tchrs., Detroit Assn. Radio and TV, Detroit Assn. Film Tchrs., Internat. Platform Assn., Detroit Schoolmen's Club, Detroit Roundtable, Nat. Congress Parents and Tchrs., Orgn. Alumni Assn. Wayne State U. (pres.), Nat. Alumni Assn. Jackson State U. (pres. 1976—, regional dir.). Democrat. Methodist (trustee ch.). Office: 2995 E Grand Blvd Detroit MI 48202

WOLFE, GENE, journalist, author; b. N.Y.C., May 7, 1931; s. Roy Emerson and Mary Olivia (Ayres) W.; student Tex. A&M U., 1949-52; B.S.M.E., U. Houston, 1956; postgrad. Miami U., 1970-71; m. Rosemary Frances Dietsch, Nov. 3, 1956; children—Roy, Madeleine, Therese, Matthew. Project engr. Procter & Gamble, Cin., 1956-72; sr. editor Plant Engring. mag., Barrington, Ill., 1972—; books include: Operation Ares, 1970; The Fifth Head of Cerebus, 1972; Peace, 1975; The Devil in a Forest, 1976; The Shadow of the Torturer, 1980; Gene Wolfe's Book of Days, 1981; author more than 150 short stories. Served with inf., AUS, 1952-53. Recipient Nebula award for sci. fiction, 1973, Chgo. Found. for Lit. award for novel, 1977, Rhysling award for poetry, 1978. Mem. Am. Soc. Bus. Press Editors, Am. Welding Soc., Am. Inst. Plant Engrs., Authors Guild, Sci. Fiction Writers Am., World Sci. Fiction Assn., PEN. Roman Catholic. Home: PO Box 69 Barrington IL 60010 Office: 1301 S Grove Ave Barrington IL 60010

WOLFE, GOLDIE BRANDELSTEIN, real estate co. exec.; b. Linz, Austria, Dec. 20, 1945; d. Albert and Regina (Sandman) Brandelstein; student U. Ill., 1963-64; B.S. with honors in Bus. Adminstrn., Roosevelt U., 1967; postgrad. U. Chgo. Grad. Sch. Bus., 1968-69; 1 dau., Alicia Danielle Schuyler. Account research mgr. J. Walter Thompson Advt., Chgo., 1967-71, asso. account exec., 1971-72; account exec. Needham, Harper & Steers, Advt., Chgo., 1972; real estate broker office leasing dept. Arthur Rubloff & Co., Chgo., 1972—, asst. v.p., 1975-77, v.p. office leasing, 1977-80, sr. v.p., 1980—, also dir. Bd. dirs. realty div. Jewish United Fund, 1976-77; bd. dirs. Michael Reese Hosp. Med. Research Inst. Council, 1979—; chmn. services group Chgo. Public TV, 1974-75. Mem. Chgo. Real Estate Bd., Ill. Assn. Realtors, Nat. Assn. Realtors, Am. Mktg. Assn., Young Execs. Club (program v.p. 1980-81). Club: East Bank. Home: 1332 Sutton Pl Chicago IL 60610 Office: Arthur Rubloff & Co 69 W Washington St Chicago IL 60602

WOLFE, JAMES FRANCIS, newspaperman; b. Independence, Mo., Nov. 14, 1925; s. John Claude and Helen (Hifner) W.; student Central Mo. State Coll., 1943-44; m. Lois Lauer, May 1, 1955 (div. 1980); 1 dau., Sherry Jo. Pres. Kansas City Suburban Newspapers, Inc., 1964-74; pub., editor Raytown (Mo.) News, 1965-74; v.p. Little Blue Press, Inc., 1964-80; Jefferson City corr. Joplin Globe and others, 1976—. Mem. Jackson County Bd. Election Commrs., 1965—, sec., 1974-78, chmn., 1978—. Hon. col. staff Gov. Warren E. Hearnes, 1965-73. Mem. Nat. Conf. Editorial Writers, Kansas City Press Club. Democrat. Office: PO Box 1054 Blue Springs MO 64015

WOLFE, JAMES RICHARD, lawyer, railroad exec.; b. Hannibal, Mo., Nov. 7, 1929; s. James Edward and Grace (Kirn) W.; student Georgetown U., 1947-49; B.S., Loyola U., 1951; J.D., DePaul U., 1953; m. Helen Lorraine Rosedale, Dec. 29, 1951; children—Yvonne Bazar, Mary Viano, Theresa Eileen, James E., Michaela Ann, Kathleen Grace, Lorraine Helene. Admitted to Ill. bar, 1953, U.S. Ct. Mil. Appeals bar, 1957, U.S. Supreme Ct. bar, 1961; practiced in Chgo., 1953—; atty. Burlington R.R., Chgo., 1953-55, 58-59; mem. Nat. R.R. Adjustment Bd., Chgo., 1959-63; counsel U.S. R.R.'s, Nat. Labor Cases, 1959-65; gen. atty. Nat. Ry. Labor Conf., 1965-67, gen. counsel, 1967-68; v.p. labor relations Chgo. and Northwestern Transp. Co., 1968-73, v.p. operations, 1973-76, pres., chief operating officer, chief exec. officer, 1976—, also dir., trustee; dir. Nicor, No. Ill.

Gas Co., Nalco Chem. Co., Sears Bank & Trust Co. C. & N.W. subs. cos. Trustee DePaul U., Fenwick High Sch. Served as 1st lt. AUS, 1955-58; capt. Res. Mem. Assn. Am. Rys. (dir. 1976—), Western Ry. Assn. (dir.), Nat. Ry. Labor Conf. (dir.). Clubs: Chicago; Commercial; PGA Nat.; Butler Nat.; Hinsdale Golf; Sombrero Country; Mid-Am., Carlton, Internat. Wine and Food Soc. Home: 422 S Oak St Hinsdale IL 60521 Office: One Northwestern Center Chicago IL 60606

WOLFE, JOHN BINNIE, banker; b. Macomb, Ill., Feb. 25, 1907; s. Edward Clark and Eleanor (Binnie) W.; B.S., Knox Coll., 1930; postgrad. Northwestern U., 1931-32; m. Sara Kramer, Aug. 15, 1936 (dec. Aug. 1969); 1 dau., Mary Eleanor (Mrs. John Satter); m. 2d, Alice Findley Reno, Aug. 22, 1970. Asst. examiner FDIC, 1933-34; bookkeeper, teller Citizens Nat. Bank of Macomb, 1935-36, asst. cashier, 1936-38, cashier, 1938-50, exec. v.p., 1950-51, pres., 1951-73, chmn. bd. dirs., 1966—, also dir. Bd. dirs. Western Ill. U. Found., 1944—, pres., 1973; bd. dirs. Western Ill. Arts Council, 1971-73; bd. dirs. McDonough County chpt. Nat. Found., 1938-77, treas., 1938-77. Recipient award of recognition for service to community and univ. Macomb C. of C.-Western Ill. U. Coll. Bus., 1975. Mem. Macomb C. of C. (dir. 1956-59). Rotarian. Club: Macomb Country. Home: 646 Lincoln Dr Macomb IL 61455 Office: 127 South Side Square Macomb IL 61455

WOLFE, NORMA LEE, constrn. co. exec.; b. Seneca, Mo., Mar. 12, 1932; d. Lawrence L. and Stella Mae Arehart; student Seneca schs.; m. R.E. Wolfe, Mar. 7, 1957; children—Alan E., Deborah L. Corp. sec. Ming of Am. Inc., Prairie Village, Kans., 1969-79, gen. mgr., 1969-75, dir., 1969—; sec.-treas. Alan E. Wolfe Equipment & Constrn. Co., Kansas City, Mo., 1978—; corp. sec., dir., adminstrv. asst. to pres. Tri-City Constrn. Co., Kansas City, Mo., 1973—; commn. officer Joplin (Mo.) Police Dept., supr., 1953-57. Mem. ch. council, treas. Prince of Peace Lutheran Ch., Grandview, Mo., 1970-75; mem. Luth. Ch. Women. Democrat. Office: 3001 E 83d St Kansas City MO 64132

WOLFE, SHEEMON AARON, podiatrist; b. Dayton, Ohio, Oct. 27, 1923; s. Jacob and Fannie (Froug) W.; student U. Dayton, 1942; D.P.M., Ohio Coll. Podiatric Medicine, 1951; m. Rachell Goldrich, Jan. 2, 1960; 1 dau., Andrea Nicole. Med. staff affiliate Good Samaritan Hosp., Dayton, 1955—, chmn. podiatry sect., 1965-72; podiatric surgeon, courtesy staff Greene Meml. Hosp., Xenia, Ohio, 1975—; podiatric surgeon St. Elizabeth Med. Center, Dayton, 1981—; asst. prof. clin. services Ohio Coll. Podiatric Medicine, 1972-76, adj. clin. instr., 1977. Served with 217th F.A., 44th Inf. Div., U.S. Army, 1943-46; ETO. Decorated Bronze Star medal. Diplomate Am. Bd. Podiatric Orthopedics lic. gen. class amateur radio operator, pvt. pilot. Mem. Am. Coll. Foot Surgeons (asso.), Ohio Podiatry Assn. (chmn. bd. trustees, 1978-79, pres., 1979-80, Silver Gavel Club 1980), Am. Podiatry Assn., Am. Acad. Podiatry Sports Medicine, Dayton Amateur Radio Assn., CAP, Quarter Century Wireless Assn., Jewish War Vets. Jewish. Club: Masons. Patentee in field. Home: 180 Burgess Ave Dayton OH 45415 Office: 2422 Salem Ave Dayton OH 45406

WOLFE, WARREN DWIGHT, lawyer; b. Boston, July 30, 1926; s. Louis Julius and Rose (Daniels) W.; B.S. in Journalism, Northwestern U., 1949; M. Internat. Affairs, Columbia U., 1951; J.D. with high honors, U. Toledo, 1959; m. Caroline M. DuMont, Dec. 29, 1973. Reporter, Wilmington (Del.) Record, 1951-52; Sunday editor, asst. news editor Middletown (Ohio) Jour., 1952-55; copy reader, sect. editor Toledo Blade, 1955-60; admitted to Ohio bar, 1959, Mich. bar, 1960; asso. Bugbee & Conkle, Toledo, 1960-64, partner, 1964—. Pres. Health Planning Assn. Northwest Ohio, 1970-73; mem. Comprehensive Health Planning Adv. Council to Ohio Dept. Health, 1972-75; mem. Ohio Gov.'s Task Force on Health, 1973-74. Trustee Toledo Legal Aid Soc., 1968—, pres., 1973-75; trustee Toledo Animal Shelter Assn., 1962-75; trustee Lucas County unit Am. Cancer Soc., 1964—, v.p., 1976-81, pres., 1981; trustee Ohio div., 1969-74. Served with USNR, 1944-46. Mem. Am., Ohio, Lucas County (pres. 1966), Toledo (exec. com. 1969-75) bar assns., State Bar Mich., Am. Trial Lawyers Assn., Law Alumni Assn. U. Toledo Coll. Law (pres. 1965), Sigma Delta Chi. Mason. Club: Toledo Ski (treas. 1972-75, pres. 1975-76). Home: 4562 Westbourne Toledo OH 43623 Office: 1301 Toledo Trust Bldg Toledo OH 43604

WOLFE, WILLIAM KEITH, educator; b. Potosi, Wis., Dec. 9, 1933; s. Vilas Dawson and Jessie May (Schramm) W.; B.S. in Edn., U. Wis., Platteville, 1961, M.S. in Edn., 1965; m. Kathleen Leola Grattan, Oct. 8, 1960; children—Gary, Gretchen, Aaron, Darwyn, Sean. Rural and elem. tchr., Platteville and Potosi, 1952-57; elem. tchr. Cassville (Wis.) Public Schs., 1959-61; elem. prin. Twin Platte and Hanmer Robbins Schs., Platteville, 1961-68; prin. Platteville Middle Sch., 1968-69; instr. communications, chmn. Gen. Edn. div. SW Wis. Vocat.-Tech. Inst., Fennimore, 1969—; mem. Upper Midwest Regional Ednl. Consortium, 1967-69. Actor, Five Flags Theater, Dubuque, Iowa, also Dubuque Fine Arts Soc., 1978-80; lay moderator United Ch. of Christ, Potosi, 1973, 81, clk., 1964-66, choir dir., 1965-79. Served with AUS, 1957-59. Recipient teaching excellence cert. of recognition SW Wis. Assn. Vocat. Educators, 1980; named Outstanding Young Educator, Platteville Jaycees, 1965. Mem. Am. Vocat. Assn., Wis. Assn. Vocat. and Adult Edn. (Profl. Excellence award 1980), NEA, Wis. Edn. Assn., Phi Delta Kappa. Republican. Club: Masons (area adminstr. 1974-76, dist. dep. 1979-82). Author: Articulation of General Education and Occupational Competencies, 1974; Articulation of Adult Basic Education with Career Exploration, 1978; contbr. Wisconsin Curriculum Guide for Career Development, 1977. Home: Box 83 Rt 2 Potosi WI 53820 Office: SW Wis Vocat Tech Inst Bronson Blvd Fennimore WI 53820

WOLFF, DAVID LEE, accountant; b. Sidney, Nebr., Feb. 15, 1953; s. Paul T. and Ardene E. (Clausen) W.; B.A. in Math. and Bus. Adminstrn., Chadron (Nebr.) State Coll., 1975. Accountant, Winterberg's Acctg. Agy., Hot Springs, S.D., 1976-77; partner Winterberg & Wolff, Hot Springs, 1977-78, Nase & Wolff, Hot Springs, 1978—; mem. Accredition Council for Accountancy, 1977—. Bd. dirs. Fall River Assn. for Retarded Citizens, Miss S.D. Pageant. Mem. S.D. Soc. Public Accountants, Hot Springs Jaycees (pres. 1978-79), Sigma Tau Gamma. Democrat. Roman Catholic. Clubs: K.C., Elks. Home: 2025 S 5th St Hot Springs SD 57747 Office: 710 Jennings St Hot Springs SD 57747

WOLFF, GUNTHER ARTHUR, phys. chemist; b. Essen, Germany, Mar. 31, 1918; came to U.S., 1953, naturalized, 1958; s. Joseph and Anna (Breidecker) W.; B.S., Berlin U., 1944, M.S., 1945; Sc.D., Berlin Tech. U., 1948; m. Gertrude Anna Stolte, Feb. 27, 1945; children—Christine, Francis. Research asso. Fritz Haber Inst., Berlin, 1944-50, sci. head, asst., dep. chief crystal kinetics dept., 1950-53; cons. sr. scientist, team leader U.S. Army Signal Corps Research and Devel. Lab., Fort Monmouth, N.J., 1953-60; sr. group leader material research Harshaw Chem. Co., Cleve., 1960-63; dir. material research Erie Tech. Products (Pa.), 1963-64; prin. scientist Tyco Labs., Inc., Waltham, Mass., 1964-70; cons. chemist Lamp Phenomena Research Lab., Lamp Envelope Materials Research Lab., Gen. Electric Co., Cleve., 1970-77; sr. staff engr. Nat. Semicondr. Corp., Hawthorne, Calif., 1977-81, indsl. cons., 1981—. Chmn., Gordon Research Conf. on Chemistry and Metallurgy of Semiconductors, 1965; mem. crystal growth com. Internat. Union Crystallography, 1967-75, mem. Am. com. for crystal growth, 1967-72. Fellow Am. Inst. Chemists, Mineral. Soc. Am.; mem. N.Y. Acad. Sci.; Am. Phys. Soc., Am. Chem. Soc., Electrochem. Soc., Am. Crystallographic Assn., Am. Ceramic Soc. Home and Office: 3776 Northampton Rd Cleveland OH 44121

WOLFF, LINDA M., bus. services co. exec.; b. Chgo., June 30, 1953; d. Calvin and Marian Wolff; B.A. in Psychology, Speech and Theatre, Northeastern Ill. U., 1976. Recruiter, Trans Union Corp., Chgo., 1977-78; compensation adminstr. Am. Res. Corp., Chgo., 1978-79; sr. compensation specialist Bankers Life and Casualty Co., Chgo., 1979-80; dir. human resources IDC Services, Inc., Chgo., 1980—. Mem. Am. Soc. Personnel Adminstrs., Am. Compensation Assn., Soc. Personnel Adminstrs., Am. Soc. Tng. and Devel., Internat. Assn. Personnel Women, Am. Mgmt. Assn., Women in Mgmt. Office: 303 E Ohio St Chicago IL 60611

WOLFF, SIEGFRIED, sex therapist; b. Berlin, Germany, Mar. 14, 1925; came to U.S., 1958, naturalized, 1963; M.S. in Psychology, Erlangen U., 1956; M.A., Johns Hopkins U., 1961, M.P.H., 1964, Cert. of Advanced Study of Edn., 1967; Ph.D., Inst. Advanced Study of Human Sexuality, 1979; m. Edeltraud E. Goetze, June 23, 1955; children—Axel Volker, Xenia Yvette. Dir. dept. sci. Boys Latin Sch., Balt., 1961-64; asso. prof. Community Coll. Balt., 1965-70; dir. planning and adminstrn. So. W.Va. Regional Health Council, 1970-73; health commr. City of West Allis, Wis., 1973-75; dir. health service Loyola U., Chgo., 1975-78; pvt. practice sex therapy, Chgo., 1978—; cons. in field. USPHS grantee, 1963. Fellow Brit. Royal Soc. Health, Am. Public Health Assn., Soc. Advanced Med. Systems; mem. Milwaukee County Med. Soc., Chgo. Med. Soc., Am. Assn. Sex Educators. Author: The Planning Year, 1974. Contbr. articles to profl. jours. Home: 10834 W Hayes Ave Milwaukee WI 53227 Office: 3130 N Broadway St Chicago IL 60657

WOLFGANG, CHARLES HALL, educator; b. Greensburg, Pa., Sept. 14, 1941; s. John Miller and Louise Ruth W.; B.S., Indiana U. Pa., 1964; M.S.Ed., U. So. Calif., 1969; Ph.D., U. Pitts., 1973; m. Mary Ellen Smart, June 9, 1974; 1 dau., Ellen Louise. Tchr., Rhein-Main Am. Elem. Sch., Frankfurt, Germany, 1964-68; high sch. counselor Lakeheath (Eng.) Am. High Sch., 1968-70; tchr., prin. Chaleveston (Eng.) Am. Sch., 1970-71; asst. prin. Alenbury (Eng.) Am. Elem. Sch., 1971-72; asso. prof. early and middle childhood edn. Ohio State U., Columbus, 1973—. Recipient Outstanding Tchr. award Dept. Army, 1969; Outstanding Acad. Book award ALA, 1980-81. Mem. Nat. Assn. Edn. Young Children, Am. Ednl. Research Assn., Assn. Childhood Edn. Author: Helping Aggressive and Passive Preschoolers Through Play, 1977; Solving Discipline Problems: Strategies for Classroom Teachers, 1980; Growing and Learning Through Play, 1981. Home: 1945 High St N 202 Arps Hall Ohio State U Columbus OH 43210

WOLFRAM, DAVID ALAN, motor carrier transp. co. exec.; b. St. Louis, Feb. 3, 1950; s. Vernon John and Vivian Elain (Seevers) W.; B.S. in Mgmt., Valparaiso U., 1972; m. Susan Marjorie Schultz, Aug. 19, 1972; children—Megan, Adam. With Yellow Freight System Inc., 1972—, corp. tng. coordinator, 1977-79, dir. manpower planning and devel., 1979-80, dir. personnel, Overland Park, Kans., 1980—. Bd. dirs. Johnson County United Way, 1978, 2d v.p. 1981; bd. dirs. Heart of Am. United Way, 1981. Mem. Personnel Mgmt. Assn. (dir. 1980), Am. Soc. Tng. and Devel., Am. Soc. Personnel Adminstrn. Republican. Lutheran. Home: 9625 Meadow Ln Leawood KS 66206 Office: 10990 Roe Ave Overland Park KS 66207

WOLFRAM, RALPH EDWIN, bank bldg. corp. exec.; b. St. Louis, Apr. 29, 1925; s. Edwin Fredric and Jeanette A. (Weiss) W.; B.S., U. Mo.-Rolla, 1950; m. Peggy M. Wolfram; children—Marc, Todd, Gwen. Elec. engr. Sverdrup-Parcel Cons. Engrs., 1950-55, Leo A. Daly Co., 1955-56; dir. engring. Bank Bldg. Corp., St. Louis, 1956—; instr., lectr. lighting field, 1965—. Mem. St. Louis Elec. Bd. Served with USAAF, 1943-46. Registered profl. engr., D.C., 20 states. Mem. Nat. Soc. Profl. Engrs., Mo. Soc. Profl. Engrs., Illuminating Engring. Soc. (regional v.p. 1972-76, nat. dir. 1976—), Am. Soc. Hosp. Engrs., Beta Sigma Psi. Lutheran. Club: Engineers of St. Louis. Home: 1405 Starling Dr Crestwood MO 63126 Office: Bank Bldg Corp 1130 Hampton Ave Saint Louis MO 63139

WOLKOWSKI, LESZEK AUGUST, assn. exec.; b. Wilno, Poland, Jan. 14, 1941 (parents Am. citizens); s. John and Halina Teresa (Wankowicz) W.; Baccalaureate, Lycee Polonais de Paris, 1961; student Central Sch. Econs., Warsaw, Poland, 1961-62, U. Warsaw, 1962-65, U. Paris, 1965-67; B.A. with honors, U. Ill., 1969; M.A., Loyola U., Chgo., 1975, Ph.D. in Comparative Internat. Edn., 1979; m. Barbara M. Szlachcic, Mar. 22, 1968; (div.); 1 dau., Grazyna Grace. Instr. modern langs. Loyola U., Chgo., 1969-71; tchr. Notre Dame High Sch., Niles, Ill., 1971-76; instr. Skokie (Ill.) Coll., 1971-79; tchr. modern langs. and debate A. Stevenson High Sch., Lincolnshire, Ill., 1976-78; instr. English Roper IBG Corp., Wheeling, Ill., 1977-78; ins. agt. Mass. Life Ins. Co., Chgo., 1978; real estate broker Gen. Devel. Corp., Chgo., 1978; dist. mktg. dir. U.S. C. of C., Oak Brook, Ill., 1979—. Mem. Polish-Am. Educators Assn., Loyola U. Chgo. Alumni Assn. Home: 927 Amherst Ln Wilmette IL 60091 Office: 1200 Harger Rd Oak Brook IL 60521

WOLL, ROBERT NICOLAS, educator; b. San Jose, Ill., Aug. 3, 1936; s. Robert Henry and Amanda Kathryn (Williams) W.; B.S., Western Ill. U., 1962; M.S., No. Ill. U., 1972, certificate of advanced study in ednl. curriculum and supervision, 1976. Physicist, So. Ill. U., Carbondale, 1961-63; research technician Argonne (Ill.) Nat. Lab., 1963-69; mem. faculty No. Ill. U., DeKalb, 1969-79, faculty asst. allied health professions, 1977-79; asso. prof. electronics tech., program coordinator Moraine Valley Coll., Palos Hills, Ill., 1972-77; dir. tng. Computer Scis. Corp., 1979-80; prin. N. Woll & Co., San Jose, 1955—; tech. tng. cons. to industry and schs. Mem. curriculum adv. com. various orgns. and instns. Post adviser Explorer Scouts Am., 1974-78. Cert. electronics technician, 1973. Mem. IEEE, Ill. Acad. Sci. (mem. exec. council 1976-79), Ill. Indsl. Edn. Assn., Ill. Soc. for Med. Research, Midwest Bio-Med. Soc., Ill. Assn. Elec. and Electronic Educators (pres. 1972-74), Aircraft Owners and Pilots Assn., CAP, Exptl. Aircraft Assn., Flying Huskies No. Ill. U. (pres. 1969-70), Soc. for Applied Learning Tech., Sigma Pi Sigma, Epsilon Pi Tau. Republican. Lutheran. Club: Toastmasters (charter mem. Argonne chpt.). Home: PO Box 154 San Jose IL 62682 Office: N Woll and Co San Jose IL 62682

WOLLMAN, ROGER LELAND, chief justice S.D. Supreme Ct.; b. Frankfort, S.D., May 29, 1934; s. Edwin and Katherine Wollman; B.A., Tabor Coll., Hillsboro, Kans., 1957; J.D. magna cum laude, U. S.D., 1962; LL.M., Harvard, 1964; m. Diane Marie Schroeder, June 21, 1959; children—Steven James, John Mark, Thomas Roger. Admitted to S.D. bar, 1964, practiced in Aberdeen, 1964-71; asso. justice S.D. Supreme Ct., 1971-78, chief justice, 1978—; states atty. Brown County, Aberdeen, 1967-71. Served with AUS, 1957-59. Office: SD Supreme Ct Pierre SD 57501

WOLLMANN, WILLIS JAMES, dentist, mayor; b. Yankton, S.D., May 10, 1925; s. Joseph A. and Elisabeth B. (Ewert) W.; student Bethel Coll., 1943-44, Freeman Jr. Coll., 1946-47, U. S.D., 1947-48; D.D.S., Washington U., St. Louis, 1952; m. Naomi Marie Tiezen, Sept. 9, 1951; children—Wayne Joseph, Janet Marie, Jean Elizabeth, Wilma Joyce, Marilyn Sue. Pvt. practice dentistry, Moundridge, Kans., 1952—. Mem. Moundridge City Council, 1957—, mayor, 1962-65, 77—; mem. McPherson County Airport Bd., 1964—, chmn., 1967-73; chmn. Moundridge City Airport Bd., 1971—, Moundridge Housing Authority, 1968-77. Mem. Kans. (exec. council 1971—), 7th Dist (pres. 1970-71, 79-80) dental socs. Mem. Mennonite Ch. (deacon 1962-79). Club: Lions (pres. 1964). Address: Moundridge KS 67107

WOLLRAB, MARJORIE JUNE, counselor; b. Chgo., Feb. 3, 1937; d. Richard Matthew and Marjorie Dell (Burgess) Fleming; B.S. in Sociology, grad. nurse diploma, Ill. Wesleyan U.; M.A. in Human Devel. Counseling, Sangamon State U., Springfield, Ill., 1978; m. Warren Wollrab, Aug. 20, 1960; children—Warren Louis, Lee Mark, Ross Eric. Tchr., dir. nursing arts dept. Decatur (Ill.) Meml. Hosp.; clin. instr. medicine and surgery Sinai Hosp. Sch. Nursing, Balt.; elementary sch. nurse Decatur public schs.; health services coordinator Sunnyside Center, trainable and severe and profoundly mentally impaired students, Decatur, 1978—. Mem. Decatur Human Relations Commn., Community Commn. on Integration Decatur Sch. Dist.; mem. com. Planned Parenthood Clinic, Decatur. Mem. Am. Personnel and Guidance Assn., Ill. Assn. Sch. Nurses, Ill. Edn. Assn., Decatur Edn. Assn., Ill. Wesleyan U. Alumni Assn., Sangamon State U. Alumni Assn. Republican. Congregationalist.

WOLMAN, J. MARTIN, newspaper pub.; b. Elizabeth, N.J., Mar. 8, 1919; s. Joseph and Dora (Baum) W.; student U. Wis., 1937-42; m. Anne Paley, Sept. 12, 1943; children—Natalie, Jonathan, Ruth Ellen, Lewis. Reporter, Wis. State Jour., Madison, 1937-47, bus. mgr., 1947-68, pub., 1968—; bus. mgr., dir. Madison Newspapers, Inc., 1948-68, pres., 1968—. Trustee Edgewood Coll., 1975; trustee U. Wis. Hosp. and Health Center, 1977—. Served with U.S. Army, 1942-46. Mem. Wis. Newspaper Assn. (past pres., dir.), Inland Press Assn. (dir.), Newspaper Personnel Assn., Nat. Editorial Assn. Clubs: Madison, Rotary. Office: 1901 Fish Hatchery Rd Madison WI 53708

WOLNAK, BERNARD, biochemist, cons.; b. Chgo., Dec. 30, 1918; s. Max and Bessie (Kaplan) W.; B.S., U. Chgo., 1939, M.S., 1940; Ph.D., Ind. U., 1943; m. Frances R. Knoblauch, Aug. 27, 1943; children—Eve K. (Mrs. Ronald Bremen), Laurie R. (Mrs. Craig Steadman). Research chemist Miner Labs., Chgo., 1946-54; pres. Midwest Labs., Chgo., 1954-63, B. Wolnak & Assos., Chgo., 1963—. Mem. Am. Chem. Soc., AAAS, Am. Soc. Microbiology, Inst. Food Technologists. Home: 6101 Sheridan Rd E Chicago IL 60660 Office: 360 N Michigan Ave Suite 706 Chicago IL 60601

WOLPE, HOWARD E., congressman; b. Los Angeles, Nov. 2, 1939; s. Leon and Zelda Wolpe; B.A., Reed Coll., 1960; Ph.D., M.I.T., 1967; m. C. Jeanene Taylor, 1963; 1 son, Michael. Asst. prof. polit. sci. Western Mich. U., 1967-69, asso. prof., 1970-72; cons. Peace Corps, 1966-67, Fgn. Service Inst., U.S. Dept. State, 1967-72; regional rep., state liaison to U.S. Senator Donald Riegle, 1977-78; mem. Mich. Ho. of Reps., 1973-76; city commr. Kalamazoo, 1969-73; mem. 96th and 97th Congresses from 46th dist. Mich; chmn. Fgn. Affairs subcom. on Africa. Democrat. Jewish. Author: Urban Politics in Nigeria: A Study of Port Harcourt, 1974; (with Robert Melson) Nigeria: Modernization and the Politics of Communalism, 1974. Office: 1118 Longworth House Office Bldg Washington DC 20515

WOLPERT, EDWARD ALAN, psychiatrist; b. Chgo., Apr. 22, 1930; s. Sol and Dorothy (Greenwald) W.; B.A., U. Chgo., 1950, M.A. in Psychology, 1954, Ph.D. in Psychology, 1959, M.D., 1960; m. Gloria Adele Yanoff, Mar. 23, 1958; children—Seth I., Andrew O., Edward G. Intern, U. Ill. Research and Ednl. Hosp., Chgo., 1960-61; resident in psychiatry Inst. for Psychosomatic and Psychiat. Research and Tng., Michael Reese Hosp. and Med. Center, Chgo., 1961-64, dir. clin. services, 1966-79, dir. inst., 1979—; grad. Inst. for Psychoanalysis, 1973; practice medicine specializing in psychiatry, Chgo., 1964—; clin. asso. prof. psychiatry Pritzker Sch. Medicine, U. Chgo., 1972-76, clin. prof., 1976—; faculty mem. continuing edn. program for psychiatrists, Chgo. Inst. for Psychoanalysis, 1974—. Served with USNG, 1948-51. Lic. in medicine, Ill., Wis.; cert. in psychology, Ill. Diplomate Am. Bd. Neurology and Psychiatry. Fellow Am. Psychiat. Assn.; mem. AMA, Chgo., Ill. State med. socs., Ill. State Psychiat. Soc., Am. Psychol. Assn., Assn. for Psychophysiol. Study of Sleep, AAAS, N.Y. Acad. Sci., George S. Klein Meml. Psychoanalytic Research Forum, Center for Study of Psychosocial Problems (mem. organizing group), Am. Soc. for Clin. Pharmacology and Therapeutics, Chgo., Am. (cert. in psychoanalysis) psychoanalytic assns., Am. Psychosomatic Soc., Wis. Acad. Arts, Letters, and Scis., Sigma Xi, Alpha Omega Alpha. Home: 727 Elmwood St Wilmette IL 60091 Office: 2959 S Ellis Ave Chicago IL 60616

WOLSIFFER, PATRICIA RAE, ins. co. exec.; b. Indpls., Aug. 15, 1933; d. Charles L. and Dorothy M. (Smith) Bohlsen; student Ind. Central U., 1974-75; m. Edward C. Wolsiffer, Oct. 5, 1956; children—John M. Anderson, Sherry L. Anderson, Edward J. Exec. sec. to pres. The Nicholas Co., Indpls., 1964-69; exec. sec. to v.p. Review Pub. Co., Indpls., 1969-70; exec. sec. to corp. v.p. ARA Services, Inc., Indpls., 1970-71; exec. asst. to sr. v.p. mktg. Blue Cross and Blue Shield of Ind., Indpls., 1971-72, supr. personnel, 1972-76; exec. asst. to pres. Blue Cross of Ind., Indpls., 1976-79, corp. sec., 1979—; dir. Alexander Nat. Group. Mem. Nat. Secs. Assn. Republican. Presbyterian. Clubs: Order Eastern Star, Daus. of Nile, Ladies Oriental Shrine. Home: Rural Route 3 Box 253 Greenfield IN 46140 Office: 120 W Market St Indianapolis IN 46204

WONG, BERNARD PO-WAH, educator; b. Kwangchauwan, China, Feb. 12, 1941; came to U.S., 1969, naturalized, 1977; s. Maurice S. and Teresa S. W.; M.A., U. Wis., Madison, 1971, Ph.D., 1974; m. Rosemarie, Apr. 14, 1973. Instr., Wah Yan Coll., Kowloon, Hong Kong, 1968-69; Ford fellow U. Wis., 1971-73, Inst. S.E. Asian Studies, Singapore, 1978; asso. prof. U. Wis. Center System, Janesville, 1981—, cons. ethnic studies coordinating com., 1978-80. U. Wis.-Madison non-resident scholar, 1970-71, U. Wis.-Madison Ibero-Am. Studies research grantee, 1971, Ford fellow U. Wis.-Madison, 1971-72, Ford Dissertation fellow, 1972-73, NSF doctoral research grantee, 1972-73, Am. Philos. Soc. postdoctoral fellow, 1978, Nat. Endowment for Humanities fellow, 1980. Fellow Am. Anthrop. Assn., Soc. Applied Anthropology; mem. Assn. Asian Studies. Author: A Chinese American Community: Ethnicity and Survival Strategies, 1979; Chinatown-New York, 1981; editor Bridge: An Asian American Perspective, 1978—. Office: U Wis Center Janesville WI 53545

WONG, HAROLD, transp. co. exec.; b. San Francisco, Sept. 26, 1948; s. Harry and Mary (Hom) W.; B.A., Knox Coll., Galesburg, Ill., 1970; M.B.A., DePaul U., Chgo., 1974; m. Barbara Szypkowski, Feb. 25, 1972. With CNA Ins. Co., Chgo., 1970-72, Continental Bank, Chgo., 1972-74; with N. Am. Car Corp., Chgo., 1974—, dir. investor mgmt. program, 1978—. C.P.A., Ill. Mem. Am. Inst. C.P.A.'s, Ill. Soc. C.P.A.'s. Club: University (Chgo.). Office: 33 W Monroe St Chicago IL 60603

WONG, JIMMY PAN, restaurant exec.; b. Canton, China, Oct. 10, 1914; s. Jaw and Toy (Shee) W.; came to U.S., 1923, naturalized, 1923; student pub. schs., Ellensburg, Wash.; m. Cynthia Chan, June 6, 1956; children—Ella, Rosalind, Lisa. Partner, Nan Yan Restaurant, Chgo., 1947-50, owner, mgr., 1950—; owner, mgr. Jimmy Wong's Restaurant, Chgo., 1959—, Jimmy Wong's North, Chgo., 1965—; dir. Bank of Chgo. Adviser Chinese Overseas Commn., Republic China, Taiwan, 1973-74, 75-77, 81-82; developer Chgo.'s New Chinatown. Served with USAAF, W.W. II; ETO. Recipient award recognition Ann. Nat. Restaurant Conv., 1962; Man of Year award Ill. Combined Vets Assn., 1975; award Chgo. Press Photographers Assn., 1973. Mem. Nat. Hip Sing Benevolence Assn. (asst. chmn.), Chew Lun Benevolence Assn. (past Midwest pres.), Am. Vets. Press Assn., VFW (life). Club: Chinese Passenger (pres.) (Chgo.). Home: 9217 N Kenton St Skokie IL 60076 Office: 426 S Wabash Ave Chicago IL 60605

WONG, VICTOR WINGWING, combustion engr.; b. Hong Kong, July 7, 1952; came to U.S., 1971; s. Tin Sik and Kim Yan (Ho) W.; B.A., Dartmouth Coll., 1974; M.S. in Mech. Engring., M.I.T., 1976, Ph.D., 1978; m. Kut Nie Tan, May 28, 1977. Combustion research engr. Detroit Diesel Allison div. Gen. Motors Corp., 1976; group leader research Cummins Engine Co., Columbus, Ind., 1978—. Hon. life guard Royal Life Sav. Soc., Hong Kong, 1969-71. Recipient Bronze medal Royal Life Sav. Soc., 1969; Cummins fellow, 1977. Mem. ASME, Soc. Automotive Engrs., Combustion Inst., Dartmouth Coll. Alumni Assn., M.I.T. Alumni Assn., Phi Beta Kappa, Sigma Xi. Lutheran. Author papers in field. Office: Mail Code 50165 Cummins Engine Co Inc 1000 5th St Columbus IN 47201

WONNELL, WILLIAM HOWARD, transp. co. exec.; b. Columbus, Ohio, Nov. 29, 1920; s. Clarence Edward and Winifred (Van Fossen) W.; student Ohio State U., 1938-39; m. Mary Louise Patterson, June 9, 1944; children—Barbara Ann, Patricia Louise. Supr., mgr. Pa. R.R., Ohio, Ind. and Pa., 1939-68; supt. Penn-Central Co., Cleve., 1969-73; supt., gen. supr. Amtrack, Chgo., 1973-78; mgr. sub ops. C&NW, Chgo., 1978-80; partner LHM Mgmt., Inc., Chgo., 1980—. Served with USMC, 1942-46. Mem. Am. Assn. R.R. Supts., Locomotive Maintenance Officers Assn., Air Brakes Assn., Marine Corps League. Republican. Presbyterian (ruling elder). Clubs: Masons, Elks, Chgo. Diesel. Home: 2000 St Regis Dr Apt 2N Lombard IL 60148

WOOD, EARL HOWARD, physiologist, physician; b. Mankato, Minn., Jan. 1, 1912; s. William Clark and Inez (Goff) W.; B.A. summa cum laude, Macalester Coll., St. Paul, 1934, D.Sc. (hon.), 1950; B.S., U. Minn., 1939, M.S., 1940, M.D., 1941, Ph.D., 1941; m. Ada Peterson, Dec. 20, 1936; children—Phoebe Wood Busch, Mark Goff, Guy Harland, Earl Andrew. Teaching fellow dept. physiology U. Minn., 1936-37, instr., 1939-40; NRC fellow, dept. pharmacology U. Pa. Med. Sch., 1940-41; instr. pharmacology Harvard U. Med. Sch., 1942; research asst. physiology Acceleration Lab., Mayo Aeromed. Unit, 1942-46; sci. cons. to surg. gen. USAF Aeromed. Center, Heidelberg, Germany, 1946; asst. prof. physiology Mayo Grad. Sch., 1943-47, asso. prof., 1947-51; prof. physiology and medicine Mayo Med. Sch., Rochester, Minn., 1951—; cons. physiology Mayo Clinic and Mayo Found., 1946-76; career investigator Am. Heart Assn., 1962—; vis. prof. Physiology Inst., U. Bern, Switzerland, 1965-66; hon. research fellow dept. physiology Univ. Coll., London, 1972-73; chmn. biophys. scis. Unit Mayo Found., 1974-76, sr. cons., biodynamics research unit, 1977—; mem. Pres.'s Sci. Adv. Com., 1962-66; dir. Def. Research and Engring. Adv. Panel on Med. Biol. Scis., 1962-67; mem. ad hoc med. adv. panel NASA SPAMAG, 1964-65; cons. Aerospace Corp., 1964-65; mem. biomed. subcom. sci. and tech. adv. com. NASA, 1967—; mem. med. adv. group USAF Manned Orbital Lab., 1969-74; mem. A.C.P. Med. teaching del. to China, 1979. Recipient Presdl. Cert. of Merit, 1947; AMA award, 1962; Eric Liljencrantz award, 1963; Modern Medicine award, 1963; Alumni award Phi Beta Kappa, 1970; Disting. Citizen award Macalester Coll. Alumni, 1974; Disting. Lectr. Am. Coll. Chest Physicians, 1974. Fellow Am. Coll. Cardiology (hon.), Aerospace Med. Assn.; mem. Am. Physiol. Soc. (Travel award Internat. Congress Physiology, Oxford, Eng. 1947), Biomed. Engring. Soc., Soc. for Exptl. Biology and Medicine (chmn. Minn. sect. 1963), Soc. for Clin. Investigation, Central Soc. for Clin. Research, Minn. Acad. Sci., AAAS, Am. Physiology Soc. (chmn. circulatory group 1963-64, pres. 1980-81, Carl J. Wiggers award 1968), Cardiac Muscle Soc., Am. Inst. Biol. Scis., Nat. Acads. Sci. of Netherlands and Mex. Am. Heart Assn. (Golden Heart award 1980), Minn. Heart Assn. (research com. 1962-65), Federated Am. Soc. for Exptl. Biology (pres. 1981), Sigma Xi, Alpha Omega Alpha, Pi Phi Epsilon. Contbr. articles to med. jours. Home: 1147 2d St NW Rochester MN 55901 Office: 200 1st St NW Rochester MN 55901

WOOD, FRANK E., broadcasting co. exec.; b. Cin., July 19, 1942; s. Frank and Sally (Ross) W.; A.B. cum laude, Harvard U., 1964; J.D., U. Chgo., 196 ; m. Cynthia Van den Burg; children—Phoebe Dangerfield, Peter Birnam. Admitted to Ohio bar, 1967; program dir. Sta. WDAI, Chgo., 1970-71; program dir. Sta. WEBN, Cin., 1971, gen. mgr., 1973—, pres. Circe Communications, Inc., Cin., 1973—; chmn. Sta. WQMF, Louisville, 1981—. Bd. dirs. Contemporary Arts Center, Cin., 1972-76. Mem. Greater Cin. Radio Broadcasters Assn. (pres. 1978-79), Nat. Assn. Broadcasters, Ohio Assn. Broadcasters, Nat. Radio Broadcasters Assn., Louisville Area Radio Stas. Club: Cin. Country. Office: 2724 Erie Ave Cincinnati OH 45208

WOOD, GORDON R., real estate and ins. exec.; b. Mattoon, Ill., Jan. 24, 1934; s. Forrest W. and Phyllis E. (Harshman) W.; B.A., Trinity Coll., Hartford, Conn., 1956; m. Sandra S. Locklar, Dec. 21, 1957; children—Gordon R., Laura L., Gerald R. Commd. 2d lt. USAF, 1956, advanced through grades to capt., 1963; pilot tng., Hondo, Tex., 1957; student Single Engine Jet Pilot Sch., Laredo, Tex., 1957, Weapons Controller Sch., Panama City, Fla., 1958, Squadron Officer Sch., Montgomery, Ala., 1962; resigned, 1963; with Wood Ins. Agy., Inc., Sullivan, Ill., 1964—, pres., 1972—. Counselor, Lincoln Trails council Boy Scouts Am., 1967—; bd. dirs. Moultrie County United Way, pres., 1977-81; trustee Sullivan Fire Protection Dist., 1979-82; trustee Sullivan Ambulance Dist., 1979-82, pres., 1981-82. Mem. Nat. Assn. Real Estate Bds., Nat., Ill. assns. ind. agts., Central Ill. Bd. Realtors, Sullivan C. of C., Illini Quarterback Club (dir.), Moultrie County Area Christian Men's Assn. (past pres. bd.), Kaskaskia Valley Assn. (dir.), Moultrie County Flying Club (sec.-treas.). Methodist (past pres. bd.). Clubs: Sullivan Country (past pres. bd.), Sullivan Sno-N-Go Snowmobile (sec.-treas. 1977-82), Lions (past pres.), Masons, Shriners. Home: Box 157 Sullivan IL 61951 Office: 7 W Harrison St Sullivan IL 61951

WOOD, HOWARD JOHN, III, educator; b. Balt., July 19, 1938; s. Howard John and Cara (Loss) W.; B.A., Swarthmore Coll., 1960; M.A., Ind. U., 1962, Ph.D., 1965; m. Maria Ilona Kovacs, May 20, 1977; 1 son, Andy; children by previous marriage—Cara Loss, Erika Barton. Instr., U. Va., Charlottesville, 1964-65, asst. prof., 1965-69, asso. prof. dept. astronomy, 1969-70; staff astronomer European So. Obs., Santiago, Chile, 1970-75; Fulbright research scholar Vienna (Austria) U. Obs., 1975-77; vis. asst. prof. astronomy Ind. U., Bloomington, 1978-79, research asso., 1979-81; asst. to dir. Cerro Tololo Interam. Obs., La Serena, Chile, 1981—; cons. N.Y. State Dept. Edn., 1968-69. NSF Astronomy research grantee, U. Va., 1965-70, Ind. U., 1979-82. Mem. Am. Astron. Soc., Royal Astron. Soc. (fellow) AAUP, Internat. Astron. Union, Sigma Xi. Contbr. articles to profl. jours.; editor: (with W. Weiss and H. Jenkner) Physics of Ap Stars, 1975. Home: 17 River Hill Rd Louisville KY 40207 Office: Cerro Tololo Interam Obs La Serena Chile

WOOD, JAMES NOWELL, museum ofcl.; b. Boston, Mar. 20, 1941; s. Charles H. and Helen N. (Nowell) W.; diploma U. per Stranieri, Perugia, Italy, 1962; B.A., Williams Coll., 1963; M.A. (Ford Mus. Tng. fellow), N.Y.U., 1966; m. Emese Forizs; children—Lenke Hancock, Rebecca Noel. Asst. to dir. Met. Mus., N.Y.C., 1967-68, asst. curator dept. 20th Century art, 1968-70; curator Albright-Knox Art Gallery, Buffalo, 1970-73, asso. dir., 1973-75; adj. prof. dept. art history SUNY, 1972-75; dir. St. Louis Art Mus., 1975-80, Art Inst. Chgo., 1980—. Mem. Intermuseum Conservation Assn. (pres.). Office: Art Inst Chgo Michigan Ave and Adams St Chicago IL 60603

WOOD, JOHN ROBERT, air force officer, aerospace engr.; b. Montour Falls, N.Y., May 3, 1952; s. Merle Douglas and Janet Arlene (Noble) W.; A.S. in Math. and Sci., Corning Community Coll., 1972; B.S. in Aerospace Engring., SUNY, Buffalo, 1975; postgrad. Air Force Inst. Tech., 1981—. Sci. and sports broadcaster, producer Sta.-WGMF, Watkins Glen, N.Y., 1971-76; substitute tchr., public schs., Odessa, N.Y., 1975-76; commd. 2d lt. U.S. Air Force, 1976, advanced through grades to capt., 1980; chief Satellite Command Generation Team, Air Force Satellite Control Facility, Sunnyvale Air Force Sta., Calif., 1976-78, satellite software engr., 1978, chief Shuttle Ops. Team, VOS, 1978-81; lectr. on shuttle, pres. Co. Grade Officers Council. Discussion leader for Bible study Peninsula Bible Ch., Palo Alto, Calif., 1976-81. Mem. AIAA, Nat. Space Inst. (charter life), Planetary Soc. (charter). Home: 4948 Springfield Pike Dayton OH 45431 Office: AFIT/ENA Box 4188 Wright Patterson AFB OH 45433

WOOD, JON GERALD, travel co. exec.; b. Milw., Apr. 12, 1940; s. John Jack and Cloris V. (Lily) W.; B.S., U. Wis., 1965, postgrad., 1965-69; m. Susan Lee Smith, Sept. 7, 1963; children—Justin William, Nicholas Jon. Sec. to faculty Sch. Nursing, U. Wis., Madison, 1965-69; v.p. sales Odyssey Internat. Travel Service, Milw., 1969-76; dir. charter mktg. and ops. Funway Holidays, Milw., 1976-81; gen. mgr. Funway Holidays Internat., Inc., Chgo., 1981—. Recipient Charter Devel. and Mktg. award Charter div. United Airlines, 1976. Home: 5100 W Elmdale Rd Mequon WI 53092 Office: 8907 N Port Washington Rd Milwaukee WI 53217

WOOD, KATHLEEN ANN STUDT, educator; b. Lansing, Mich., Aug. 20, 1943; d. Robert E. and Georgia (Preston) Studt; B.A., Trevecca Nazarene Coll., 1966; M.A., Wayne State U., 1972, postgrad., 1976—; M.Ed., U. Detroit, 1974; children—Elizabeth, David. Tchr., Southfield (Mich.) Christian Sch., 1972-75; child therapist Met. Guidance Center, Farmington, Mich., 1975-76; instr. John Wesley Coll., Farmington, also dir. lab. sch. for early learners; asst. prof. early childhood edn. Mt. Vernon (Ohio) Nazarene Coll., 1976; guest prof. summer workshops Eastern Nazarene Coll., 1979-80; presenter workshops seminars, 1969—; adviser Head Start and Social Services Day Care and Infant Programs, 1979—. Mem. Am. Assn. Colls. for Tchrs. Edn., Ohio Assn. Colls for Tchr. Edn., Nat. Assn. Edn. Young Children, Council Exceptional Children, Assn. Children with Learning Disabilities, Am. Personnel and Guidance Assn., Nazarene Assn. Tchr. Edn. Office: Mt Vernon Nazarene Coll Mt Vernon OH 43050

WOOD, MICHAEL THOMAS, psychiatrist; b. Mpls., Jan. 8, 1943; s. Dale Charles and Mary Lois (Grabenstein) W.; B.A., St. Olaf Coll., 1965; M.D., Northwestern U., 1969; m. Marylee Palandech, Sept. 8, 1969; children—Jessica, Michael Cory. Intern, Hennepin County Gen. Hosp., Mpls., 1970; resident in psychiatry Psychosomatic and Psychiatric Inst. for Research and Tng., Michael Reese Hosp., Chgo., 1970-73; practice medicine, specializing in psychiatry, Marshfield (Wis.) Clinic, 1973-79, chmn. dept. psychiatry, 1976-77, mem. exec. com., 1978; pvt. practice, Rhinelander, Wis., 1979—; clin. instr. psychiatry U. Wis., Madison, 1975-78; med. dir. Portage County Human Services Bd., Stevens Point, Wis., 1974-77; cons. psychiatrist U. Wis., Stevens Point, 1973-78. Chmn. regional tech. com. mental health developmental disabilities and alcohol and drug abuse N. Central Wis. Area Health Planning Assn., Wausau, 1974-78; chmn. Wood County (Wis.) Health Resource Com., 1978; exec. com. N. Central Area Health Planning Assn., 1978-81, pres., 1979, bd. dirs., 1976-81; med. dir. Oneida Vilas Forest Human Services Bd., 1979—. Mem. AMA, Am. Psychiat. Assn. Home: Route 1 Box 2168 Rhinelander WI 54501 Office: No Wis Psychiatric Asso 21A S Brown St Rhinelander WI 54501

WOOD, MILDRED H., ednl. cons.; b. Alta, Iowa, Apr. 19, 1920; d. Jesse L. and Hazel E. (David) Fisher; B.A., U. No. Iowa, 1956, M.A., 1962, Ed.S., 1963; Ed.D., Ind. U., 1970; m. William O. Wood, June 23, 1940; children—Larry Allan, Donald David. Tchr. pub. schs., Rowley, Iowa, 1939-42; speech and hearing therapist Black Hawk County (Iowa) Sch., 1956-60; tchr. Price Lab. Sch., U. No. Iowa, 1965, instr. spl. edn. dept. edn. and psychology, 1962-65; ednl. cons. and diagnostician Area Edn. Agency Iowa, 1965-69, 70—; chmn. state adv. com. on speech and hearing, 1956-60. Mem. Housing and Community Devel. Task Force, Cedar Falls, 1975—; pres. Human Devel. Commn., Cedar Falls, 1978—; mem. Family Service League exec. bd. Black Hawk County, 1976—; bd. dirs. Cedar Arts Forum, 1977, pres., 1980. Mem. Council Exceptional Children, Iowa Council Exceptional Children (v.p. 1975), Iowa Assn. Retarded Children (chmn. 1960-64), Assn. Children with Learning Disabilities, Iowa Assn. for Children with Learning Disabilities (pres. 1979), Am. Speech and Hearing Assn., Am. Assn. Mental Defiency, Internat. Reading Assn., Assn. Supervision and Curriculum Devel., NSF, Am. Pen Women, Delta Kappa Gamma, Pi Lambda Theta. Baptist. Author 2 books; contbr. articles to profl. jours. Home: 1825 Iowa St Cedar Falls IA 50613 Office: 3712 Cedar Heights Dr Cedar Falls IA 50613

WOOD, RICHARD DONALD, pharm. co. exec.; b. Brazil, Ind., Oct. 22, 1926; s. Howard T. and Dorothy F. (Norfolk) W.; B.S., Purdue U., 1948, LL.D., 1973; M.B.A., U. Pa., 1950; D.Sc., Butler U., 1974; LL.D., DePauw U., 1972, Phila. Coll. Pharmacy and Sci., 1975, Ind. State U., 1978; m. Billie Lou Carpenter, Dec. 29, 1951; children—Catherine Ann, Marjorie Elizabeth. Gen. mgr. ops. in Argentina, Eli Lilly & Co., 1961, dir. ops., Mex. and Central Am., 1962-70, pres. Eli Lilly Internat. Corp., 1970-72, now dir.; pres. Eli Lilly & Co., Indpls., 1972-73, chmn. bd., chief exec. officer, dir., 1973—, also dir.; dir. Elizabeth Arden, Inc., IVAC Corp., Cardiac Pacemakers, Inc., Physio-Control Corp., Elanco Products Co., Chem. N.Y. Corp. & Chem. Bank, Standard Oil Co. (Ind.), Dow Jones & Co. Bd. dirs. Lilly Endowment, Inc., Ind. State Symphony Soc., Indpls. Mus. Art; trustee DePauw U., Am. Enterprise Inst. for Public Policy Research. Mem. Pharm. Mfrs. Assn. (dir.), Council on Fgn. Relations, Com. for Econ. Devel., Internat. C. of C. (trustee U.S. council), Indsl. Conf. Bd. Presbyterian. Clubs: Links (N.Y.C.); Meridian Hills Country (Indpls.). Office: 307 E McCarty St Indianapolis IN 46225

WOOD, RICHARD ROBINSON, real estate exec.; b. Salem, Mass., Nov. 8, 1922; s. Reginald and Irene (Robinson) W.; A.B., Harvard, 1944; postgrad. M.I.T., 1948; m. Pamela Vander Wiele, Mar. 3, 1951; children—Christopher Robinson, Bryant Cornelius, Marcella Jeffries; m. 2d, Jane Philbin Dreyfuss, Sept. 19, 1970. Research and mktg. Godfrey L. Cabot Corp., 1961—, 1948-49; sales promotion asst. Wm. S. Merrell Co., Cin., 1949-55; salesman Macalaster-Bicknell Co., Cambridge, Mass., 1955-59; mgr. investment dept. Hunneman & Co., Boston, 1959-61, v.p. 1961-72, sr. v.p., 1972—; chmn. bd., pres. Continental Real Estate Equities, Inc., 1972-74; exec. v.p. Itel Real Estate Corp., 1975; v.p. Baird & Warner, 1976-80; pres. Richard R. Wood Assos., 1980—; pres. Convest Mgmt.; trustee Suffolk Franklin Savs. Bank. Mem. Beacon Hill Civic Assn., 1958-74; Mayors Adv. Com., Boston, 1965-69; dir. Boston Municipal Research Bur., 1966-74, vice chmn., 1967-70; pres. Boston Republican Com., 1968-72; mem. Mass. State Rep. Com., 1964-72, asst. treas., 1964-72; candidate Mass. Ho. of Reps., 1956. Dir. White Mountain Ski Runners, pres., 1960-62; trustee Mass. Real Estate Investment Trust. Served with U.S. Army, 1944-45. Mem. Boston (dir. 1963-67), Chgo. real estate bds., Rental Housing Assn. (dir. 1961-67), Brokers Inst. (v.p., dir. 1964-67), Nat. Inst. Real Estate Brokers, Mass. Assn. Real Estate Bds. (dir. 1965-70), Calif. Assn. Realtors, Internat. Council Shopping Centers, Real Estate Securities Syndication Inst. (bd. govs. 1973—, v.p. 1974-77, pres. 1977), Nat. Assn. Indsl. and Office Parks. Clubs: Longwood Cricket, Tennis and Racquet, Down Town, Monroe, Comey's Comets Ski. Home: 60 E Scott St Chicago IL 60610 Office: 60 E Scott St Chicago IL 60610

WOOD, ROBERT RAY, machine tool mfg. co. exec.; b. Coffeyville, Kans., Dec. 19, 1942; s. Robert Gould and Geraldine Rosalie (Newman) W.; B.S., U. Wyo., 1966; M.B.A., No. Ill. U., 1974; m. Nola Jean Freouf, June 7, 1964; children—Robert Dean, Todd Ray. With Ingersoll Milling Machine Co., Rockford, Ill., 1966—, controller, 1972-76, v.p. fin., 1976—. Asst. state chief Y-Indian guide program; treas. exec. bd. Blackhawk Area council Boy Scouts Am., 1981; mem. mgmt. adv. bd. Rock Valley Coll.; bd. dirs. Civic League Winnebago County, 1975, Wesley Willows Retirement and Nursing Center, 1975-78, Rockford Community Trust, 1981; bd. dirs. Rockford YMCA, 1976—, treas., 1979-81, 2d v.p., 1981, recipient Vol. of Yr. award, 1975; pres. NW Community Nursery Sch., 1971; chmn. long-range planning com. Christ United Methodist Ch. Mem. Nat. Assn. Accountants, Fin. Council Machine and Allied Products Inst., Fin. Execs. Inst. (charter, 2d v.p. 1978-79, pres. 1979-80), Ill. Mfrs. Assn. (fin. council), Alpha Kappa Psi. Home: 813 Prestwick Pkwy Rockford IL 61107 Office: 707 Fulton Ave Rockford IL 61101

WOOD, SARAH ELDORA, meat processing co. exec.; b. Murdo, S.D., Feb. 22, 1940; d. Howard Arthur and Jessie Eldora (Conger) W.; student Black Hills State Coll., Spearfish, S.D., 1975-75, Metro Tech. Inst., Omaha, 1979; children—Rick, Cindy. with S.S. Kresge Co., Rapid City, S.D., 1962-68, Knecht Industries, Inc., Rapid City, 1968-76; gen. mgr. Rishmore Lighting Center, Rapid City, 1976-78; sr. v.p., gen. mgr. Prime Meat Processors, Inc., Omaha, 1978—, also sec.-treas., dir. Mem. Am. Assn. Credit Women. Club: Highland Country (Omaha). Home: 7820 Read Plaza Omaha NE 68122 Office: 5146 N 90th St Omaha NE 68134

WOODARD, PAUL ELON, hearing aid co. exec.; b. Marshalltown, Iowa, Feb. 24, 1933; s. Harold and Frances W.; B.A., Bethany (W.Va.) Coll., 1954; M.Div., Tex. Christian U., 1959; m. Betty A. Turner, June 12, 1955; children—Bruce P., Dale A., Dawn M. Minister, Christian Ch. (Disciples of Christ), Van Alstyne, Tex., 1957-59, Princeton, Mo., 1959-62; salesman Prudential Ins. Co., Maryville, Mo., 1962-65; mgr. ins. agency Occidental Life of Calif., Chillicothe, Mo., 1965-67; regional supt. agencies Farmers and Bankers Life Ins. Co., Wichita, Kans., 1967-68; hearing aid specialist Woodard Hearing Aid Center, Des Moines, 1969-74, pres., 1974—. Scoutmaster, Boy Scouts Am. Mem. Nat. Hearing Aid Soc. (certified hearing aid audiologist), Iowa Hearing Aid Soc., Am. Auditory Soc. Republican. Methodist. Home: 4120 77th Street Circle Des Moines IA 50322 Office: 309 Shops Bldg Des Moines IA 50309

WOODBRIDGE, HENSLEY CHARLES, librarian, educator; b. Champaign, Ill., Feb. 6, 1923; s. Dudley Warner and Ruby Belle (Mendenhall) W.; A.B., Coll. William and Mary, 1943; M.A., Harvard, 1946; Ph.D., U. Ill., 1950, M.S. in L.S., 1951; student U. Nacional de Mexico, summer 1941, 45; D.Arts, Lincoln Meml. U., 1976; m. Annie Emma Smith, Aug. 28, 1953; 1 dau., Ruby Susan. Corr., Worldover Press, Mexico, 1945; instr. French and Spanish, U. Richmond, 1946-47; teaching asst. U. Ill., 1948-50; reference librarian Ala. Poly. Inst. (now Auburn U.), 1951-53; librarian Murray (Ky.) State Coll. (now Ky. State U.), 1953-65; Latin-Am. bibliographer, asso. prof. modern langs. So. Ill. U., Carbondale, 1965-71, prof., 1971—. Mem. Ky. Folklore Soc., Medieval Soc. Am., Modern Lang. Assn., Am. Assn. Tchrs. Spanish and Portuguese, Bibiog. Soc. Am., Instituto de estudios madrileños. Author: (with Paul Olson) Tentative Bibliography of Ibero-Romance Linguistics, 1952; Jesse Stuart: a bibliography, 1960; (with Gerald Moser) Ruben Dario y el Cojo ilustrado, 1964; (with John London, George Tweney) Jack London: a bibliography, 1966, rev. edit., 1973; Jesse Stuart and Jane Stuart: a bibliography, 1969, rev. edit., 1979; Rubén Darío: A selective critical bibliography, 1975; Rubén Darío: una bibliografía selectiva, clasificada y anotada, 1975; Benito Pérez Galdós: A selective annotated bibliography, 1975; (with L.S. Thompson) Printing in Colonial Spanish America, 1976. Editor: Ky. Library Assn. Bull., 1959-60, Ky. Folklore Record, 1963-64, Am. Assn. Tchrs. Spanish and Portuguese-Scarecrow Press Bibliographical Series; contbg. editor Am. Book Collector, 1965-74; asso. editor Hispania, 1967-81; editor, pub. Jack London Newsletter, 1967—; mem. editorial bd. Modern Lang. Jour. 1971-73; co-editor Basic List of Latin American Materials in Spanish, Portuguese and French, 1975, (with Annie Woodbridge) The Collected Short Stories of Mary Johnston, 1982. Home: 1804 W Freeman Carbondale IL 62901

WOODFORD, CHARLES WALTER, banker; b. Sharon, Wis., Dec. 23, 1931; s. John Chauncey and Pauline Sweet (Goelzer) W.; B.A., Beloit Coll., 1956; postgrad. Northwestern U., 1956-58, U. Chgo., 1958-60, Stanford U., 1969; m. Barbara J. Johnsen, Aug. 25, 1956; children—Mark Mallory, Stuart Allen, Geoffrey James. Investment mgr. Brown Bros. Harriman, Chgo., 1956-66; asst. state treas., Ill., 1967-71, state treas., 1971; v.p., treas. Horace Mann Educators Corp., Springfield, Ill., 1971-75; exec. v.p., head trust and bond depts. Am. Nat. Bank, Chgo., 1975-78; dept. head trust dept., sr. v.p. First Nat. Bank, Chgo., 1978—; pres. Fort Dearborn Income Securities, Chgo., 1978—; chmn. Ill. State Bd. Investment, 1971-74. Trustee Roosevelt U., Children's Home and Aid Soc. Mem. Am. Econ. Assn., Nat. Assn. Bus. Economists, Am. Statis. Assn., Fin. Analysts Fedn. Democrat. Methodist. Clubs: Chicago, Mid-Am., Cliff Dwellers, Tower. Home: 3831 Central Ave Western Springs IL 60558 Office: 1 First Nat Plaza Chicago IL 60670

WOODHALL, JOHN ALEXANDER, JR., constrn. co. exec.; b. Peoria, Ill., Oct. 10, 1929; s. John Alexander and Marion Ellen (Solstad) W.; B.B.A., U. Minn., 1952; m. Donna Irene Simmons, Aug. 21, 1948; children—John Alexander, Susan, Cheryl, Douglas, Robert. Project supt. Central States Constrn. Co., Willmar, Minn., 1953-57, v.p., project mgr., 1957-60; v.p., area mgr. Allied Enterprises, Willmar, 1960-69; exec. v.p. Central Allied Enterprises, Inc., Canton, Ohio, 1969-74, chmn., chief exec. officer, 1974—; chmn. bd. Clark Irrigation Co., Schory Cement Block, Inc.; dir. 1st Nat. Bank Willmar; dir. Road Info. Program. Mem. exec. com. constrn. sect. Nat. Safety

Council; mem. Minn. Gov.'s Occupational Safety Health Adv. Council; bd. dirs., vice-chmn. Minn. Safety Council; pres. W. Central Safety Council, 1979; dist. commr. Viking council Boy Scouts Am., 1969-71. Mem. Am. Mgmt. Assn., Vets. of Safety, Am. Arbitration Assn., Asso. Gen. Contractors Am. (dir.), Asso. Gen. Contractors Minn. (pres. 1977), Lutheran. Clubs: Kiwanis (Willmar); Masons, Shriners, Mpls. Athletic. Home: 190 Lake Ave E Spicer MN 56288 Office: PO Box 1317 Willmar MN 56201 also PO Box 1387 Sta C Canton OH 44708

WOODRESS, FREDERICK ALBERT, writer, cons.; b. St. Louis, Jan. 11, 1923; s. James L. and Jessie (Smith) W.; student Antioch Coll., 1941-43; A.B., 1948; student Washington U., 1946; M.S., U. Ky., 1971; m. Anne Loraine Blackmon, Dec. 31, 1953; 1 dau., Cathy Loraine. Stringer, reporter various Ohio and Mo. newspapers, 1939-48; free-lance writer, 1948-49; public relations asst. Methodist Div. Fgn. Missions, 1949; reporter, columnist, entertainment editor Birmingham (Ala.) Post-Herald, 1949-55; owner Fred Woodress, public relations cons. firm, 1955-69; asst. to chief adminstr. and pub. affairs dir. U. Ala. Med. Center, 1964-69; dir. public relations U. Ky., Lexington 1969-71; public relations cons. Woodress & Myers, Louisville, 1971-74; supr. Pa. Life Ins. Co., Lexington, 1971-74; dir. mktg. Hunter Found. for Health Care, 1974-76; writer-tchr. U. Ky., 1976-79; nat. dir. public relations Am. Legion, Indpls., 1979-82; writer, cons., Indpls., 1982—; tchr. advt. Birmingham So. Coll., 1958; info. specialist U.S. Salvation Army, Haiti, 1963, La., Ark. Salvation Army, New Orleans, 1965. Served with AUS, 1943-46. Mem. Public Relations Soc. Am. (v.p. Ala.-Miss. chpt., Presdl. citation 1968, pres. Ala. chpt., nat. membership chmn.), Nat. Press Club, Sigma Delta Chi. Episcopalian. Author: Impasse pub. in Best One Act Plays, 1949; (with others) 87th Infantry Division History, 1946; Public Relations for Community/Junior Colleges, 1976; contbg. author: Writer's Resource Guide, 1979; 1979 Summer Employment Directory of U.S. Contbr. articles to mags. Home and Office: 5529 Senour Rd Indianapolis IN 46239

WOODRING, DEWAYNE STANLEY, clergyman, ch. ofcl.; b. Gary, Ind., Nov. 10, 1931; s. J. Stanley and Vera Luella (Brown) W.; B.S. with distinction, Northwestern U., 1954, postgrad.; M.Div., Garrett Theol. Sem., 1957; L.H.D., Mt. Union Coll., 1967; D.D., Salem Coll., 1970; m. Donna Jean Wishart, June 15, 1957; children—Judith Lynn, Beth Ellen. YMCA Youth dept. staff, Gary, 1946-50, asso. youth dir., 1950-55; staff mem. radio services dept. Second Assembly, World Council of Chs., Evanston, Ill., 1954; minister edn. Griffith Meth. Ch., Ind., 1955-57; minister adminstrn. and program 1st Meth. Ch., Eugene, Oreg., 1957-59; dir. pub. relations Dakotas Area Meth. Ch., 1959-60, Ohio Area, 1960-64; adminstrv. exec. to bishop, Ohio E. Area, 1964-77; asst. gen. sec. Gen. Council on Fin. and Adminstrn., United Meth. Ch., Evanston, Ill., 1977-79, asso. gen. sec., 1979—; chmn. bd. mgrs. United Meth. Bldg., Evanston. Exec. sec. Ohio Meth. TV, Radio and Film Commn., 1960-72; del. World Meth. Conf., London, Eng., 1966, Dublin, Ireland, 1976, Honolulu, 1981; mem. mass communications com. Meth. N. Central Jurisdiction, 1964-68; chmn. commn. on communications Ohio Council Chs., 1961-65; mem. div. interpretation United Meth. Ch., 1969-72, mem. commn. on gen. conf., 1972—, bus. mgr., exec. dir., 1976—, mem. program com. N. Central Jurisdictional Conf., 1968-76, chmn., 1972-76, mem. council on ministries, 1972-76; exec. com. Assn. United Meth. Founds., 1968-72; participant U.S. Dept. Def. Joint Civilian Orientation Conf., 1970; lectr., cons. on fgn. travel. Trustee, Ohio East Area United Meth. Found, 1967-78, v.p., 1967-76; pres. Guild Travel Assos., 1971—; trustee, v.p. Copeland Oaks Retirement Center Sebring, Ohio, 1969-76. Mem. Am. Soc. Assn. Execs., Public Relations Soc. Am., Meeting Planners Internat., Cert. Meeting Mgrs. (bd. regents), Religious Conv. Mgrs. Assn. (dir.), Def. Orientation Conf. Assn. (dir.). Club: Executives (Chgo.). Editor Ohio East Area News, 1964-73. Home: 205 Enid Ln Northfield IL 60093 Office: 1200 Davis St Evanston IL 60201

WOODRUFF, PHILLIP STEVEN, mgmt. exec., aircraft co. exec., pilot, cons.; b. McLeansboro, Ill., May 8, 1944; s. Max Eugene and Gladys Marguerite (Bell) W.; diploma De Vry Inst. Tech., Chgo., 1966; B.S. in Aviation Mgmt., Embry Riddle Aero. U., 1970; postgrad. Fla. Atlantic U., 1970-71, U. S.C., 1971-72, Okla. State U., 1974-75, Johns Hopkins Sch. Advanced Internat. Studies, 1976, Washburn U. Sch. Law, 1978; m. Betty Sue Allen, Sept. 24, 1966; 1 son, Michael Andrew. Asst. in Coll. Aviation Mgmt., Embry Riddle Aero. U., Daytona Beach, Fla., 1968-71; various engring. and tech. positions in Midwest and So. U.S., AT&T, 1966-68, 71-72; mgr. aviation edn. div. Cessna Aircraft Co., Wichita, Kans., 1972-74, mgr. Africa and Middle East Div., 1974-77, mgr. Internat. Marketing Div., Far East and Pacific, 1977-78; mng. partner Aviation Investment Assos., 1973—; pres. Woodruff Aviation Co., 1978—; tchr. aviation in grad. workshops at various colls. and univs., 1972-75. Trustee Embry Riddle Aero. U. Served with U.S. Army, 1961-64. Recipient Aircraft Distbrs. Mfrs. award, 1975. Mem. Air Force Assn., Nat. Aerospace Edn. Assn. (dir. 1972-73), Gen. Aviation Mfrs. Assn. (chmn. aviation edn. 1974-75), Am. Inst. Aeros. and Astronautics, Aircraft Owners and Pilots Assn., Exptl. Aircraft Assn., Ill. Pilots Assn., World Aerospace Edn. Orgn., Nat. Geog. Soc., Smithsonian Instn., Alpha Eta Rho (hon. life). Republican. Contbr. articles on aviation edn. to profl. publs. Home: 911 Skyline Dr Carbondale IL 62901 Office: One Airport Plaza Box 402 So Ill Airport Carbondale IL 62901

WOODRUFF, ROBERT MARTIN, shoe co. exec.; b. Elmira, N.Y., Mar. 2, 1945; s. Robert John and Emily Marie (Ellis) W.; m. Irene Lois Friedland, July 17, 1965; children—Robert J., Mark, Sarah. Asst. mgr. store planning Endicott Johnson Corp., Endicott, N.Y., 1966-69; asst. mgr. store planning Brown Shoe Co., St. Louis, 1969-74, mgr. store planning, 1974-76, dir. store planning, 1976—. Pres., Glenfield Woods Trustees Assn., 1978—. Mem. Inst. Store Planners (nat. sec., Midwest trustee, St. Louis v.p.). Episcopalian. Office: Brown Shoe Co 8300 Maryland St Saint Louis MO 63105

WOODS, CHARLES HARRISON, chemist; b. Kirwan Heights, Pa., Dec. 10, 1934; s. Leroy Homer and Julia (Voinovich) W.; student Carnegie Inst. Tech., 1952, Muskingum Coll., 1957, Muskingum Area Tech. Coll., 1979-80; m. Ruth Ann Gildea, Oct. 20, 1956; children—Tamara Sue Woods Border, Charles K., Crystal, David. Chief chemist John M. Sherry Labs., Muncie, Ind., 1961-64; chief spectroscopist Vanadium Corp. Am., Cambridge, Ohio, 1965-68; analytical chemist, lab. supr. Foote Mineral Co., Exton, Pa., 1968-70; corporate dir. analytical chemistry Ohio Ferro-Alloys Corp., Philo, Ohio, 1970—. Mem. citizens adv. com. Ohio EPA Muskingum River Basin; mem. data processing tech. adv. com. Muskingum Area Tech. Coll.; loaned exec. United Way, 1978, 79; judge sci. fairs, high sch. Mem. Am. Chem. Soc., Am. Soc. Metals, Nat. Mgmt. Assn. (v.p. Zanesville area 1981). Democrat. Lutheran. Home: 3655 Sunset Circle Zanesville OH 43701 Office: PO Box 158 Philo OH 43771

WOODS, DEBORAH ANNE NAYLOR, chem. mfg. co. ofcl.; b. Euclid, Ohio, Oct. 5, 1956; d. Douglas F. and Eleanor Ruth (Pavlik) Naylor; B.A. in Life Sci. and Econs., U. Pitts., 1978. Advt. mgr. The Pitt News, U. Pitts., 1975-78; jr. exec. Barium and Chems., Inc., Steubenville, Ohio, 1978—. Mem. fin. bd. Martha Manor Home for Aged. Mem. Nat. Assn. Accts., AAUW (chpt. publicity dir. 1979-80), Big Red Booster Club, Antique Collectors Club, Cambridge Glass Club, Am. Fox Terrier Club, Delta Delta Delta. Republican. Presbyterian. Office: PO Box 218 County Rd 44 Steubenville OH 43952

WOODS, EDWARD, JR., ednl. adminstr.; b. Benton Harbor, Mich., Aug. 21, 1945; s. Edward and Lillie Ann (Lee) W.; B.A., Oakwood Coll., 1968; postgrad. Western Mich. U., 1979, Wayne State U., 1980; m. Edith G. Sloan, July 27, 1969; children—Edward, III, Brian Keith, Trishonda Denise. Elem. instr. Benton Harbor Area Schs., 1968-69, community edn. coordinator, 1969-71, asst. prin., coordinator adult edn., 1973-74, coordinator adult and continuing edn., 1974—. Recipient First Thurgood Marshall Grad. fellowship Western Mich. U., 1972. Mem. Assn. Supervision and Curriculum Devel., Berrien/Cass Continuing Edn. Assn. Home: 105 Meadow Ln Berrien Springs MI 49103 Office: 120 E Napier St Benton Harbor MI 49022

WOODS, HARRIETT RUTH, state ofcl.; b. Cleve., June 2, 1927; d. Armin and Ruth (Wise) Friedman; student U. Chgo., 1945; B.A., U. Mich., 1949; m. James B. Woods, Jan. 2, 1953; children—Christopher, Peter, Andrew. Reporter, Chgo. Herald-Am., 1948, St. Louis Globe-Democrat, 1949-51; producer Star. KPLR-TV, St. Louis, 1964-74; moderator, writer Sta. KETC-TV, St. Louis, 1962-64; council mem. University City, Mo., 1967-74; mem. Mo. Hwy. Commn., 1974, Mo. Transp. Commn., 1974-76; mem. Mo. Senate, 1976—. Bd. dirs. LWV of Mo., 1963. Recipient Democracy in Action award Am. Jewish Congress, 1980; Maryville Coll. Civic Service award 1980. Mem. Crusade Against Crime, Orgn. Women Legislators. Jewish. Office: State Capitol Jefferson City MO 65101

WOODS, KENNETH REGINALD, architect; b. Chgo., Apr. 14, 1925; s. Otis Clifford and May (Leeds) W.; B.S., Northwestern U., 1948; m. Betty Jane Seline, Sept. 20, 1946; children—Geoffrey Scott, Candace Lynn, Steven Alan. Pres. Woods & Assos., Inc., Naperville, Ill., 1960—. Mem. Naperville City Council, 1967-71; bd. dirs. Naperville YMCA, 1975-81. Served with A.C., USNR, 1943-47. Mem. AIA, Nat. Soc. Profl. Engrs., Am. Congress for Surveying and Mapping, Ill., Registered Land Surveyors Assn., Sigma Xi. Clubs: Moose, Lions (pres. Naperville noon club 1979-80). Home: 721 Hillside Rd Naperville IL 60540 Office: 112 Water St Naperville IL 60540

WOODS, RICHARD DAVID, civil engr., educator; b. Lansing, Mich., Sept. 4, 1935; s. Andrew M. and Beryl (Evans) W.; B.S.C.E., U. Notre Dame, 1957, M.S.C.E., 1962; Ph.D., U. Mich., 1967; m. Dixie Lee Davis, June 8, 1957; children—Kathleen, Cecilia, Karen. Project engr. Weapons Lab., U.S. Air Force, Albuquerque, 1962-63; instr. civil engring. Mich. Technol. U., Houghton, 1963-64; asst. prof. civil engring. U. Mich., Ann Arbor, 1967-69, asso. prof., 1969-76, prof., 1976—; cons. engring. cos., govt. agys. Served to 1st lt. USMCR, 1957-60. Mem. ASCE (Collingwood prize 1969), ASTM, Am. Soc. Engring. Edn., Seismol. Soc. Am., Sigma Xi, Chi Epsilon. Author: (with F.E. Richart and J.R. Hall) Vibrations of Soils and Foundations, 1970. Home: 700 Mount Pleasant St Ann Arbor MI 48103 Office: 2322 G G Brown Lab U Mich Ann Arbor MI 48104

WOODSON, FLORETTA JEAN, nursing adminstr.; b. Walnut Grove, Mo., Aug. 2, 1930; d. Clarence Harrison and Flora Ola (Bloomer) Dickerson; diploma nursing Springfield Bapt. Hosp., 1951; A.B., Drury Coll., 1954; M.S., Ind. U., 1957; m. Robert Wayne Woodson, Dec. 16, 1961. Staff nurse Springfield (Mo.) Bapt. Hosp., 1951-52, asst. evening supr., 1952, instr. Sch. Nursing, 1953, asst. dir., 1954-55, dir. Sch. Nursing and Nursing Service, 1955-56; asst. dir. Sch. Nursing, Indpls. Meth. Hosp., 1957-60; dir. dept. nursing Mo. State Chest Hosp., Mount Vernon, 1960—; mem. faculty Drury Coll., 1971-72. Pres., Am. Lung Assn. Western Mo., 1976-78. Mem. Council Nursing Facilitators (state chmn.), Am. Nurses Assn. Methodist. Home: PO Box 308 Mount Vernon MO 65712 Office: Mo State Chest Hosp Mount Vernon MO 65712

WOODSON, RILEY D., cons. engr.; b. Penalosa, Kans., Nov. 29, 1908; s. Guy Malcolm and Grace Greenwood (Ogle) W.; B.S.M.E. cum laude, U. Kans., 1935; m. Virginia Marie Anderson, May 31, 1947; children—R. Donald, Marjorie Gayl Woodson Brownlee. With Black and Veatch Cons. Engrs., 1935—, partner, head power div., 1958-78, prin. engr., cons. power div., 1979—. Fellow ASME, Am. Inst. Cons. Engrs.; mem. IEEE, Am. Nuclear Soc., Nat. Soc. Profl. Engrs., Tau Beta Pi, Sigma Tau. Republican. Methodist. Club: Indian Hills Country. Patentee in field. Home: 2012 W 50th Terr Shawnee Mission KS 66205 Office: 11401 Lamar Overland Park KS 66211 also PO Box 8405 Kansas City MO 64114

WOODSON, RILEY DONALD, thoracic and cardiovascular surgeon; b. Winfield, Kans., Dec. 24, 1931; s. Riley Delma and Ruth Philena (Benedict) W.; B.A., U. Kans., 1953, M.D., 1956; children—Riley David, Wade Clinton. Intern, Parkland Meml. Hosp., Dallas, 1956-57, resident in surgery U. Minn. Hosp., Mpls., 1957-63; fellow in cardio-thoracic surgery U. Oreg. Hosp., Portland, 1965-67; mem. staff U. Ill. Hosp., Chgo., 1967-68; asst. prof. surgery U. Ill., Chgo., 1967-68; asso. prof. surgery Med. Coll. Ohio, Toledo, 1969-78; pvt. practice cardiothoracic and vascular surgery, 1978—; mng. partner DJB Enterprises, 1976—. Sec. bd. trustees, med. dir. Regional Emergency Med. Services of N.W. Ohio, 1975—. Served to capt., M.C., USNR, 1963-77. Diplomate Am. Bd. Surgery, Am. Bd. Thoracic Surgery. Fellow A.C.S., Am. Coll. Cardiology, Am. Coll. Chest Physicians; mem. AMA, Pan Am., Undersea med. assns., Soc. Thoracic Surgeons, Am. Thoracic Soc., Internat. Cardiovascular Soc., Soc. Vascular Surgery, Am. Assn. Surgery of Trauma, Am. Trauma Soc., Assn. Mil. Surgeons, Profl. Assn. Diving Instrs., N.W. Ohio Heart Assn. (exec. com., chmn. emergency cardiac care 1975—), Beta Theta Pi, Omicron Delta Kappa, Phi Kappa Phi. Contbr. articles on thoracic and cardiovascular surgery, cardiopulmonary physiology, diving physiology to profl. jours. Office: 6005 Monclova Rd Maumee OH 43537

WOODSON, STEPHEN WILLIAM, collection agy. exec.; b. Kansas City, Mo., May 31, 1950; s. William Albert and Patricia Marguerite (May) W.; A.A., Maple Woods Community Coll., 1977. Asst. mgr. public fin. City of San Pedro (Calif.), 1973-74; asst. to v.p. MOAMCO, Mpls., 1974-75; pres. Regional Collection Services, Inc., Kansas City, Mo., 1975—, Woodson & Assos., credit cons.; collection cons. Blue Valley Fed. Savs. & Loan, 1975—. Active, Big Bros. and Sisters, Kansas City, Mo., 1977—. Served with USN, 1967-70. Recipient Whitehall Found. Scholastic award, 1968. Mem. Internat. Traders Assn., Am. Soc. Profl. Cons., Am. Collectors Assn., Northland C. of C. Democrat. Lutheran. Club: N. Kansas City Breakfast. Home: 4137 NE Davidson Rd Apt 271 Kansas City MO 64116 Office: 4420 NE Chouteau Throughway G-2 Kansas City MO 64117

WOODWARD, JACK CARLTON, pottery co. exec.; b. Roseville, Ohio, July 26, 1923; s. Floyd Harris and Clara Marie (Ungemach) W.; B.B.A., lMeredith Coll., 1942; m. Janice Colleen Harper, Nov. 8, 1962; children—Jon, Jo Ellen, Sharon, Vickie, Jane. With Robinson Ransbottom Pottery Co., Roseville, 1937—, treas., 1970-72, exec. v.p., 1972-78, pres., gen mgr., 1978—, also dir. Mem. Republican Central Com., Zanesville, 1949-53. Served with U.S. Army, 1943-46. Mem. Pottery, China and Glass Assn., Southeastern Ohio Ceramic Assn., U.S. C. of C., Ohio C. of C., Zanesville Area C. of C. (dir. 1976). Presbyterian. Clubs: Elks, Masons (32 deg.), Eagles. Office: Roseville OH 43777

WOODWARD, JAMES KENNETH, pharmacologist; b. Anderson, Mo., Feb. 5, 1938; s. Audley J. and Doris Evelyn (Fields) W.; A.B. in Chemistry, B.S. in Biology, S.W. Mo. State Coll., 1960; postgrad. U. Kans. (USPHS fellow) 1960-62; Ph.D. (USPHS fellow), U. Pa. Sch. Medicine, 1967; m. Kathleen Ruth Winget, June 25, 1960; children—Audley J., Kimie Connette. Pharmacologist, Stine Lab., Newark, Del., 1963-65, research pharmacologist, 1967-71; sr. research pharmacologist Merrell-Nat. Labs., Cin., 1972-73, sect. head, 1973-74, head dept. pharmacology, 1974-78; head dept. pre-clin. pharmacology Merrell Research Center, Merrell Dow Pharms., Inc., 1978—; USPHS post-doctoral fellow U. Pa., 1967. Pres., Golf Manor Recreation Commn., Cin., 1973-75. Mem. Phila. Physiol. Soc., AAAS. Democrat. Baptist. Patentee antisecretory compounds of imidazoline series. Home: 7700 Shadowhill Way Cincinnati OH 45242 Office: 2110 E Galbraith Rd Cincinnati OH 45215

WOODWARD, RAYMOND BERNARD, lawyer; b. Louisville, July 2, 1923; s. Lewis Carl and Loraine Frances (Neff) W.; J.D., U. Louisville, 1948; postgrad. Notre Dame U., John Carroll U., Ind. U.; m. Edna Jean Bowers, Feb. 16, 1946; children—Ronald Lee, Diane (Mrs. Millard Allen Hudson), Gloria. Admitted to Ind. bar, 1948; dep. atty. gen. State of Ind., 1950; dep. prosecutor, Floyd County, Ind., 1955-56; city atty. City of New Albany, Ind., 1956-63; practice law, 1948—, justice of peace New Albany Twp., 1963-76. Trustee Raymond B. Woodward Scholarship Found., 1966-81; bd. dirs. Ind. Masonic Home, 1961-62. Served with USNR, 1943-45, 50-54. Mem. Floyd County Bar Assn. (pres. 1958-59), VFW, Am. Legion (comdr. 1966-76), World Conf. on Local Govts. (U.S. del. 1961), Nat. Soc. Pub. Poets, U.S. Chess Fedn. (past local pres.). Mason. Contbr. articles to profl. jours. Home: 2804 Charleston Rd New Albany IN 47150 Office: 155 E Main St New Albany IN 47150

WOODWARD, ROBERT SIMPSON, IV, educator; b. Easton, Pa., May 7, 1943; s. Robert Simpson and Esther Evans (Thomas) W.; B.A., Haverford Coll., 1965; Ph.D., Washington U., St. Louis, 1972; m. Mary P. Hutton, Feb. 15, 1969; children—Christopher Thomas, Rebecca Marie. Brookings Econ. Policy fellow Dept. HEW, Washington, 1975-76; asst. prof. U. Western Ont. (Can.), London, 1972-77; asst. prof. Sch. Medicine, Washington U., St. Louis, 1978—. Mem. adv. council Mo. Kidney Program, 1980—; coop. mem. Haverford Coll., 1968—. NDEA fellow, 1968-71; Kellogg Nat. fellow, 1981—. Mem. Am. Econs. Assn., Canadian Econs. Assn., Am. Statis. Assn. Contbr. articles to profl. jours. Home: 7050 Westmoreland St University City MO 63130 Office: 724 S Euclid St Saint Louis MO 63110

WOODWARD, WALTER WILLIAM, advt. music prodn. co. exec.; b. Vienna, Austria, June 21, 1949 (parents Am. citizens); s. Jasper Soule and Veronica Joffe (Castle) W.; B.A. with honors in English, U. Fla., 1970; m. Colleen Mary McDonald, May 18, 1974; children—Peter Tyler, Thomas Allan, Michael Francis. Songwriter, Jerry Chesnut Music, Nashville, 1970-72; v.p., copywriter, broadcast producer Griswold Eshleman Co., Cleve., 1972-76; creative dir. Martin Agy., Richmond, Va., 1976-77; pres. Perfect Pitch, Inc., Cleve., 1977—; dir. Audio Recording. Active advt. campaigns for United Way, ARC, Am. Cancer Soc., Cath. Charities, Cleve. Growth Assn., Council for Fin. Aid to Edn., Adult Basic Edn. Ohio. Named Cleve. Advt. Person of Year, Cleve. Advt. Club, 1980, best of show award, 1980; winner 2 Clios, 1979, 3 Clios, 1980. Mem. Cleve. Soc. Communicating Arts (winner best of show, 1980), Soc. Advt. Music Producers, Authors, and Composers, S.E. Soc. Authors and Composers, AFTRA, Am. Fedn. Musicians. Democrat. Roman Catholic. Club: Cleve. Yachting. Composer country music songs: Marty Gray, It Could A'Been Me. Office: 2516 Church Ave Cleveland OH 44116

WOOLF, PRESTON G., lawyer; b. Indpls., Oct. 10, 1906; s. Merritt Edgar and Bertha E. (Stone) W.; B.S., U. Fla., 1928; LL.B., Ind. U., 1932; grad. in material resources Indsl. Coll. Armed Forces; m. Phoebe Ann Cummins, Nov. 9, 1937 (dec. Sept. 12, 1980); m. 2d, Betty Lee Deats, Jan. 2. 1982. Export mgr. Hurty-Peck & Co., Indpls., 1932-36, asst. sec., 1936-47, sec., 1947-76; asst. sec. Hurty-Peck & Co. of Calif., Orange, 1942-46, sec., 1946-76; pres. Am. Beverage and Supply Corp., Indpls., 1945-76, chmn. bd., 1976—; sec. Costa Rican Devel. Co., San Jose, Hurty-Peck Eastern, Inc., Union, N.J., Blanke-Baer Co., St. Louis, Gt. Am. Trading Corp., St. Louis, Mfrs. Fin. Corp., Indpls., Remi Foods Corp., Chgo., Universal Falvors Ill., Chgo., 1959-77; dir. Woolf Internat., Ltd., Hong Kong, 1961—, Ambesco de Mex., S.A. de C.V., Mexico City, Universal Flavors Corp., Universal Flavors, Calif., Inc., Universal Flavors N.J., Inc., Universal Flavors Mo., Inc., 1959-77; spl. fgn. corr. Indpls. Star, 1959—; columnist chain S. Am. newspapers, 1960—; mem. world trade adv. com. U.S. Dept. Commerce, 1958-60, mem. Midwest regional com., 1960-67; dir. Oriental Studies Inst., Oxford U., 1980—. Leader, Republican polit. study mission to Arabian world, 1966; leader Ind. Bankers and Indsl. Leaders study tour around world, 1967, to Africa, 1968, to China, 1976; cons. on Oriental affairs; mem. Trade Missions subcom. Council Fgn. Relations; mem. Ind. Fgn. Lang. Adv. Com.; pres. Indpls. Council World Affairs, 1958-60; dir. Internat. Bldg., Ind. State Fair, 1958-60; dir. Internat. Sch. Bus., Ind. U., 1961-67; mem. adv. council State Ind. Fgn. Lang. Program; 1st v.p. Ind. Econ. Edn. Found., 1965-77; chmn. Ind. Peoples World Affairs Com., 1961—; dir. Citizen's Com. for Free Cuba, 1965—; mem. bd. strategy Episcopal Diocese Indpls., 1961-66. Decorated Gold Cross Merit, 1st class (Fed. Republic of Germany); recipient citation Indpls. C. of C., 1960; Rabbi Stephen S. Wise Meml. citation Am. Jewish Congress, 1959. Mem. English-Speaking Union, Japan Soc., Asia Soc., U.S. C. of C. (world trade com.), Pan-Am. Soc., AIM, Am. Bar Assn., Am. Security Council Washington, Inter-Am. Lawyers Assn. (founder 1935, pres. 1935-38), Am. Legion, Indpls. C. of C. (leader trade missions to Orient 1963, Latin Am. 1965), Delta Chi, Sigma Delta Chi, Sigma Delta Kappa. Republican. Episcopalian. Clubs: Rotary (dir., chmn. internat. contacts com.), Athletic, Press, Literary (Indpls.); Overseas Press (N.Y.C.); Am. (Hong Kong, Singapore); Fgn. Corrs. (Tokyo); Masons. Mem. around-the-world Flight Pan-Am. Airways, 1976, N. and S. Poles Expdn., 1977. Home: 14825 Allisonville Rd Noblesville IN 46060 Office: 5700 W Raymond St Indianapolis IN 46241

WOOLFOLK, MARY JO, sch. adminstr.; b. Warm Springs, Ga., Aug. 5, 1937; d. John Louis and Sarah Alice (Smith) Revell; B.S., Chgo. State Coll., 1970; M.A., Roosevelt U., 1975; m. Fred Woolfolk, June 10, 1956; 1 dau., Debbie. Biller, Allied Radio Corp., Chgo., 1958-65; clk., typist Guardian Electric Mfg. Co., Chgo., 1965-69; receptionist Chgo. State Coll., 1969-70; tchr. Chgo. Public Schs., 1970—, now asst. prin. and counselor. Dir. Christian edn., United Missionary Bapt. Ch. Mem. Chgo. High Sch. Asst. Prins. Assn., Chgo. Elem. Sch. Prins. Assn., Ill. Women Adminstrs., Elem. Counselors Assn., Phi Delta Kappa. Office: 3600 W 5th Ave Chicago IL 60624

WOOLLEY, MERLE EDWARD, mfg. co. exec.; b. Blackwell, Okla., June 29, 1941; s. Edgar Hamilton and Ada Joy (Beck) W.; student public schs., Ponca City, Okla.; m. Patricia Lynn Nicholson, Dec. 20, 1969; children—Mark Alan, Kimberly Kae. Area sales mgr. Mid-Continent Permanent Co., Perry, Okla., 1962-66; sales and mktg. cons., 1966-72; pres., owner S.W. Safety Systems, Inc., Tulsa, 1972-75, Mapakam, Inc., Springfield, Mo., 1976—, MPI Industries Inc., Springfield, 1975—; speaker on motivation, bus. cons., 1972—. Baptist. Home: Route 2 Box 166D Nixa MO 65714 Office: 5121 S Campbell Springfield MO 65807

WOOLSEY, WILLIAM STOVER, printing co. exec.; b. Chgo., Dec. 22, 1917; s. William Robert and Grace (Peck) W.; B.S. in Mech. Engring., U. Mich., 1939, M.S., 1940; m. Doris Marie Neely, Jan. 5, 1946; children—Robert, Mary Woolsey Porter, Carolyn. Engr., Commonwealth Edison Co., Chgo., 1940-55; exec. Neely Printing Co., Chgo., 1955-60, pres., dir., 1960—; pres., dir. Dayanite Corp., Chgo., 1957—, Franklin Offset Litho Co., Chgo., 1960—, N.B.L. Corp., Chgo., 1960—, 917 Bldg. Corp., Chgo., 1960—. Trustee Pressman Sch. Fund; chmn. Lithographer Health and Welfare Fund. Served to lt. col. USAAF, 1940-45. Decorated Bronze Star. Mem. Western Soc. Engrs., Printing Industry of Ill. (dir.), Union Employers Assn. (exec. bd.), Chgo. Lithographers Bd. (dir.), Franklin Assn. (dir.), Printing Industry Am. (exec. bd. union employers sect., planning com.). Clubs: Westmoreland Country; Swedish. Home: 1500 Sheridan Rd Wilmette IL 60091 Office: 871 N Franklin St Chicago IL 60610

WOOLUMS, LARRY LEE, instrument and control engr.: b. Ottumwa, Iowa, Nov. 15, 1935; s. Loren Edward and Neva Adeline (Michael) W.; A.A.S., DeVry Tech. Inst., 1958; m. Delores Ellen Lee, May 27, 1956; children—Sheri Lynn, Lesa Kay, Kristin Lea, Michael Loren. Asso. engr. instrumentation sect. Sundstrand Corp., Rockford, Ill., 1958-62; design engr. instrument and control sect. Central Engring. Center, Am. Can Co., Neenah, Wis., 1962-66; sr. process control engr. process equipment engring. dept. Fair Lawn Engring. Center, Am. Can Co. (N.J.), 1966-68; task force engr. new pulp and paper mill, Halsey, Oreg., 1968; engring. supr. elec. and instrumentation Halsey Pulp and Paper Mill, Am. Can Co., 1969-77; process control systems mgr. process tech. dept. Am. Can Co., Greenwich, Conn., 1977—. Licensed 1st class radio telephone operator FCC. Mem. Instrument Soc. Am. (sr. mem., 1st pres., organizer Pacific Cascade sect.), TAPPI. Contbg. author to Instrumentation in the Process Industries, 1973. Home: 788 Brookwood Circle Oneida WI 54155 Office: 916 Willard Dr PO Box 4040 Green Bay WI 54303

WOON, PAUL SAM, paper co. mgr.; b. Shanghai, China, July 1, 1942; s. Ramon and Rita (Wu) W.; came to U.S., 1959, naturalized, 1968; B.S., U. Iowa, Iowa City, 1965, M.S., 1968; Ph.D. (Indsl. fellow), U. Akron, 1974; m. Lin-Sun Rwan, Dec. 7, 1973; children—Audrey Hui, Eric Chih. Research chemist Clin. Research Center, U. Iowa, Iowa City, 1965-68, PPG Industries, Barberton, Ohio, 1968-71; instr. chemistry Cuyahoga Coll., Cleve., 1972-73; staff research asso. Appleton Papers div. Brit. Am. Tobacco Co., Appleton, Wis., 1974-76; project leader Kimberly-Clark Corp., Neenah, Wis., 1976-79, mgr., 1979—. Fellow Am. Inst. Chemists; mem. Am. Chem. Soc. Contbr. articles to profl. jours.; patentee. Office: Kimberly-Clark Corp W 2100 Winchester Rd Neenah WI 54956

WOOSLEY, BILLY JOE, educator; b. Cin., Nov. 15, 1948; s. William Lewis and Zelma (Wilson) W.; B.S. in Edn., U. Cin., 1971, M.A. in Edn., 1973; m. Janet Lee England, Dec. 13, 1969; children—Amanda Lee, Molly Kathleen. Spl. educator, program supr. Clermont Northeastern schs., Batavia, Ohio, 1971-73; work-study coordinator Hamilton County (Ohio) Office Edn., Cin., 1973-75; spl. educator Oak Hills local schs., Cin., 1975-80; coordinator spl. edn. services Warren County (Ohio) Joint Vocat. Sch. Dist., Lebanon, 1980—; bd. dirs. Clermont County Assn. Retarded Citizens; regional coordinator S.W. Ohio for Spl. Olympics. Joseph P. Kennedy Found. grantee. mem. Council Exceptional Children, Am. Assn. Mental Deficiencies, Ohio Vocat. Assn., Bridgetown Bass Busters, Phi Delta Kappa. Author curriculum materials. Home: 4286 Cider Mill Cincinnati OH 45244 Office: 3525 N State Route 48 Lebanon OH 45036

WOOTEN, BILL MACK, health care center adminstr.; b. San Angelo, Tex., Feb. 25, 1947; s. Billy S. and Maxine C. (Watson) W.; B.A., N. Mex. State U., 1969, M.A., 1976; B.A. in Social Work, St. Cloud State U., 1974; M.S. in Mental Retardation, Mankato (Minn.) State U., 1980; Ph.D., Columbia Pacific U., 1981; m. Linda Ruth Lundgren, Apr. 7, 1973; children—Joshua S., Joseph A. Mental health counselor S.W. Mental Health Center, Alamogordo, N.Mex., 1972-73; exec. dir. REM-Marshall, Inc., Marshall, Minn., 1975—; adj. prof. Mankato State U., 1975—; chmn. Services Industries, Inc., Redwood Falls, Minn., 1977—; cons. MR Services Inc., Edina, Minn., 1975—; behavior analysts Marshall Mental Health Clinic, 1978—. Served with USAF, 1969-73. Mem. Am. Assn. Mental Deficiency, Assn. Advancement of Behavior Therapy, Assn. Behavior Analysis, Minn. Assn. Behavior Analysis (pres. elect 1981-82). Democrat. Unitarian. Club: Kiwanis. Author: (with David C. Pfriem) An Introduction to Behavioral Techniques, 1979; A Rational Approach to Counseling the Mentally Retarded, 1980; contbr. articles in field to profl. jours. Home: 305 E Lyon St Marshall MN 56258 Office: 1005 N 4th St Marshall MN 56258

WOOTEN, BILLY MACK, health care centers adminstr.; b. San Angelo, Tex., Feb. 25, 1947; s. Billy S. and Maxine C. (Watson) W.; B.A. in Psychology, N.Mex. State U., 1969, M.A., 1976; B.A. in Social Work, St. Cloud (Minn.) State U., 1974; M.S. in Mental Retardation, Mankato (Minn.) State U., 1980; Ph.D. in Psychology, Columbia Pacific U., 1981; m. Linda Ruth Lundgren, Apr. 7, 1973; children—Joshua S., Joseph A. Mental health counselor Southwest Mental Health Center, Alamogordo, N.Mex., 1972-73; exec. dir. REM, Inc., Marshall, Minn., 1975—; adj. prof. spl. edn., Mankato State U.; chmn. Services Industries, Inc.; cons. MR Services, Mpls. Served with USAF, 1969-73; behavior analysts Marshall Mental Health Clinic, 1978—. Served with USAF, 1969-73. Mem. Am. Assn. Mental Deficiency (vice chairperson psychology 1977-79, editor Region VIII Newsletter 1979—, Minn. sec.-treas.), Assn. Advancement of Behavior Therapy, Assn. Behavior Analysis, Minn. Assn. for Behavior Analysis (membership chmn., pres.-elect 1981-82). Democrat. Unitarian. Club: Kiwanis. Author: (with David C. Pfriem) An Introduction to Behavioral Techniques, 1979; A Rational Approach to Counseling the Mentally Retarded, 1981; contbr. articles in field to profl. jours. Home: 305 E Lyon St Marshall MN 56258 Office: 1005 N 4th St Marshall MN 56258

WOOTTEN, EDMUND BERNARD, mfg. co. exec.; b. Malvern, Worcester, Eng., June 12, 1929; s. Ernst Dodd and Mary Jane (Waite) W.; B.Sc., Nottingham (Eng.) U., 1954; A.M.P., Harvard Bus. Sch., 1968; m. Linda Mary Allen, Sept. 19, 1955; Sales engr. Goodyear Aviation Div., Wolverhampton, Eng., 1954-57; with Lucas Industries, 1957—, pres., Troy, Mich., 1977—; chmn. Lucas Industries Can., Aris Industries Ltd., Ill.; dir. Siliconix Inc., Calif., Joseph Lucas Ltd., U.K. Served with RAF, 1947-49. Mem. Inst. Mgmt., British Am. C. of C. (dir.), Inst. Mktg., Soc. Automotive Engrs. Clubs: Renaissance, Detroit Athletic, Econ. (Detroit); Royal Air Force, Royal Automobile; Bloomfield Hills (Mich.) Country. Home: 311 Cranbrook Ct Bloomfield Hills MI 48013 Office: 5500 New King St Troy MI 48098

WOOTTEN, GEORGE SIMMONS, JR., data processing and communications profl.; b. Evanston, Ill.; s. George Simmons and Mildred (Knispel) W.; B.S. in Bus. Adminstrn., Northwestern U.; m. Patricia A. Beach; children—George III, Stephanie Lynn. With Union Tank Car Co., Chgo., 1951-60; mgmt. cons. William Kordsiemon & Assos., Chgo., 1960-63; dir. data processing and communications Marquette Cement Co., Chgo., 1966-74; sr. partner Wootten & Assos., Glenview, Ill., 1974—; mgr. info. systems Kinkead Industries, Downers Grove, Ill., 1976-80; v.p., dir. Comprehensive Acctg. Co., Aurora, Ill., 1957-60, data processing cons., 1960—; dir. info. systems A. Finkl & Sons, Chgo., 1980—; v.p., dir. Waterloo Ideas Co. (Iowa), 1963-66. Served with USN, 1948-50. Mem. Assn. Computer Machinery, Internat. Communication Assn., Armed Forces Communications and Electronic Assn., Assn. Systems Mgmt. Mason. Club: Executives (Chgo.). Home: 4200 W Lake Ave Glenview IL 60025

WORDEN, LARRY THOMAS, corp. pilot, business exec.; b. Goshen, Ind., June 21, 1945; s. Wendell Thomas and Velma Darlene (Barrett) W.; B.A., Olivet Coll., 1969; m. Sherilyn Ann Frazier, Mar. 29, 1969; 1 dau., Melissa Jo. Commd. 2d lt. U.S. Air Force, advanced through grades to capt.; ret., 1979; chief pilot Exec. Aircraft Charter Ops., Niles, Mich., 1979; capt. Britt Airlines, Terre Haute, Ind., 1979-80; corp. services analyst Varlen Corp., Rolling Meadows, Ill., 1980—. Decorated Air medal (3), D.F.C. Mem. Aircraft Owners and Pilots Assn., Chgo. Flight Instrs. Assn., Am. Soc. Safety Engrs., Air Force Assn. Republican. Presbyterian. Clubs: Masons, Shriners, Kiwanis. Home: 920 Oxford Rd Glen Ellyn IL 60137 Office: 1 Crossroads of Commerce Rolling Meadows IL 60008

WORK, JAMES HOWARD, JR., tng. and communications co. exec.; b. Hartford, Conn., July 7, 1949; s. James Howard and Florence Harriet (Gilde) W.; B.A., U. N.C., 1971. Mgmt. cons. Wheeler Asso., Nashua, N.H., 1971-72; dealer devel. specialist John Williamson Assos., Birmingham, Ala., 1972-75; account supr. Sandy Corp., Southfield, Mich., 1975-78, account dir. product and service systems, 1978-79, dir. Can. ops., 1980—; dir. Bill Sandy Orgn. Ltd., Toronto, Ont., Can. Mem. Am. Mgmt. Assn. Club: Sports Car Am. Home: 30038 W 12 Mile Rd Farmington Hills MI 48018 Office: Sandy Corp 16025 Northland Dr Southfield MI 48075

WORKMAN, GEORGE HENRY, engring. cons.; b. Muskegon, Mich., Sept. 18, 1939; s. Harvey Merton and Bettie Jane (Meyers) W.; Asso. Sci., Muskegon Community Coll., 1960; B.S.E., U. Mich., 1966, M.S.E., 1966, Ph.D., 1969; m. Vicki Sue Hanish, June 17, 1967; children—Mark, Larry. Prin. engr. Battelle Meml. Inst., Columbus, Ohio, 1969-76; pres. Applied Mechanics Inc., Columbus, 1976—; instr. dept. civil engring. Ohio State U., 1973. Served with USN, 1961-64. Named Outstanding Undergrad. Student, Engring. Mechanics dept. U. Mich., 1965-66, Outstanding Grad. Student, Civil Engring. dept., 1968-69. Registered profl. engr., Ohio. Mem. Am. Acad. of Mechanics, ASME, ASCE, Nat. Soc. Profl. Engrs., Sigma Xi, Chi Epsilon, Phi Kappa Phi, Phi Theta Kappa. Congregationalist. Contbr. tech. papers to nat. and internat. confs. Home and office: 2121 Mc Coy Rd Columbus OH 43220

WORKMAN, GERALD BILLY, fiberglass co. exec.; b. Alliance, Ohio, Jan. 14, 1941; s. Glenn Earl and Margaret Grace (Eells) W.; B.S., Mt. Union Coll., 1964; M.S., St. Francis Coll., Ft. Wayne, Ind., 1969; m. Sharon Kay Mefford, Dec. 23, 1967; children—Douglas Duncan, Brian Glenn. Tchr. math. Atwater (Ohio) schs., 1964-65; tchr. math. Van Wert (Ohio) City Schs., 1965-68, tchr. chemistry, 1968-70; asso. scientist Owens-Corning Fiberglas Co., Granville, Ohio, 1970-72, scientist, 1972-76, advanced scientist, 1976-77, research supr., inorganic analytical lab., 1977—. Mem. Am. Chem. Soc., AAAS. Republican. Presbyterian. Patentee in field. Home: 553 Llanberis Dr Granville OH 43023 Office: Owens-Corning Fiberglas Co Tech Center Granville OH 43023

WORKMAN, JEROME JAMES, JR., research chemist; b. Northfield, Minn., Aug. 6, 1952; s. Jerome James and Louise Mae (Sladek) W.; student St. John's U., 1970-73; B.A. with honors, St. Mary's Coll., 1976, M.A. with distinction, 1980, postgrad., 1980-81; postgrad. U. Minn., 1981; m. Rebecca Marie Workman, Aug. 3, 1974; children—Christina Louise, Stephannie Michelle, Daniel Jerome. Head coach wrestling St. Mary's (Minn.) Coll., 1975-79, adj. instr., 1977-78; lab. mgr., research chemist Watkins Inc., Winona, Minn., 1979—. Scoutmaster Boy Scouts Am., 1976-78. Mem. Am. Chem. Soc., Am. Assn. Cereal Chemists, Am. Assn. Feed Microscopists, Minn. Forage Council, Assn. Ofcl. Analytical Chemists. Republican. Roman Catholic. Contbr. articles to profl. jours. Office: Box 111 1523 Mankoto Mall Mankato MN 56001

WORLOW, ARTHUR ALFRED, JR., drilling co. exec.; b. St. Louis, Oct. 15, 1946; s. Arthur Alfred and Mary Alta Louise (Upton) W.; student public schs., Licking, Mo.; m. Inga Harbo, Dec. 31, 1970; children—Soren, Anthony. With Meadows Drilling Co., Houston, 1965-66, Penrod Drilling Co., Lafayette, La., 1965-67; with Zapata Offshore Co., Houston, 1967-81, supt. Drilling div., until 1981; with Maersk Drilling, Copenhagen, 1981—. Served with U.S. Army, 1970-72. Republican. Baptist. Address: Rural Route 1 Box 206 Raymondville MO 65555

WORMAN, RICHARD W., ins. co. exec., state senator; b. Noble County, Ind., July 3, 1933; s. William D. and Leah M. W.; m. Marna Jo Neuhouser, Sept. 29, 1951; children—Terry Jo, Renay, Denny, Rex, Tammy. Buyer, Neuhouser Poultry, Leo, Ind., 1951-53; salesman Allen Dairy, Ft. Wayne, Ind., 1953-57; with Nationwide Ins. Co., Columbus, Ohio, 1951—, dist. sales mgr.; mem. Ind. Ho. of Reps., 1972-76, Ind. Senate, 1978—; trustee, assessor County of Allen, Ind., 1970-72. C.L.U. Mem. Life Underwriters Assn., Republican. Methodist. Clubs: Lions (past pres.), Mason (past master), Shriner. Office: 909 Coliseum Blvd Fort Wayne IN 46805

WORMER, ANNE GETZ, writer, reporter; b. Detroit, Dec. 22, 1941; d. Edward A. and Elizabeth (Esselstyn) Getz; B.A., U. Mich., 1963, M.A., 1964; postgrad. Loyola U. Law Sch., Chgo., 1966; 1 dau., Anne Marie. Research asst. Time-Life, Inc., N.Y.C., 1964-65; writer, reporter The Chgo. Tribune, 1965-69, The Detroit News, 1969-74; Am. Polit. Sci. Assn. Journalism fellow to U.S. Senate, 1970-71; writer for U.S. Senator John L. McClellan of Ark., Washington, 1970, U.S. Senator Robert P. Griffin of Mich., Washington, 1971; public relations Ford Motor Co. Mem. Young Ams. for Freedom, Ann Arbor, Mich., 1962-64. Mem. Women's Press Assn. Mich., Chgo. Council Fgn. Assn., Sigma Delta Chi. Republican. Presbyterian. Clubs: Detroit Boat, Detroit Press, Univ. (Detroit); Chgo. Press. Home: 1401 Seminole Ave Detroit MI 48214

WORTHAM, JAMES CALVIN, educator; b. Oconee County, Ga., Sept. 12, 1928; s. James Notley and Effie (Cross) W.; B.A., U. Akron, 1957; M.A. (NSF Scholar), Ohio State U., 1969; m. Mary Helena Shelley, Dec. 23, 1953; children—Sharon Elaine, Marilyn Kay, Deborah Louise, James Donald. Tchr. high sch. Akron Pub. Schs., 1956-62, tchr. sr. high sch., 1962-66; math. curriculum specialist Akron (Ohio) Pub. Schs., 1966—; instr. math. U. Akron, 1966—. Served with USAF, 1951-55. Mem. NEA, Ohio Edn. Assn., Math. Assn. Am., Nat., Ohio councils tchrs. of math., Nat. Council Suprs. of Math., Pi Mu Epsilon. Republican. Mem. Ch. of Nazarene. Home: 1665 Wiltshire Rd Akron OH 44313 Office: 70 N Broadway Akron OH 44308

WORTHINGTON, EDWARD EVERETT, mgmt. cons.; b. Cleve., Dec. 12, 1919; s. Edward L. and Ruth (Everett) W.; student Kenyon Coll., 1937-39; B.A., Case Western Reserve U., 1941; postgrad. Cleve. Coll., 1950-57; m. Maryann Wright, Jan. 29, 1944; children—Edward Everett, Ann Ruth, Nathalie. Asst. export mgr. Thompson Products, Inc., Cleve., 1946-52; with Fuller, Smith & Ross, Cleve., 1952-56; sales mgr. Designers for Industry, Cleve., 1960-65; v.p. mktg. Trundle Cons., Inc., Cleve., 1965-73; dir. Booz-Allen & Hamilton, Cleve., 1973-77; chmn. Pres. Counsel, Inc., Cleve., 1977—; cons. to Akron U., Inst. for Futures Studies, 1978—. Served with USAAF, 1942-46. Mem. Cleve. Engring. Soc., Early Settlers Assn. (pres. 1977-79), World Future Soc. (pres. Cleve. chpt. 1970-78). Republican. Presbyterian. Clubs: Cleve. Skating, Cleve. Racquet, Cheshire Cheese, University. Contbr. articles to profl. jours. Home: 7980 Eagle Rd Kirtland OH 44094 Office: 24340 Miles Ave Solon OH 44128 44139

WORTHINGTON, JAMES NORMAN, chem. engr.; b. Seattle, Jan. 25, 1945; s. Robert Edger and Janet Main (Izett) W.; B.S., U. Wash., Seattle, 1967. Sci. asst. Argonne (Ill.) Nat. Lab., Physics div., 1967-74, sci. asso., originator div.'s tech. support group, 1974—; cons. in field. Mem. Downers Grove (Ill.) CD Com., 1968-69. Mem. Am. Inst. Chem. Engrs. Presbyterian. Contbg. author books; contbr. articles to profl. publs. Home: 3455 Regan Rd Joliet IL 60435 Office: 9700 S Cass Ave Argonne IL 60439

WORTHLEY, WARREN WILLIAM, mech. engr., educator; b. Daytona Beach, Fla., Mar. 20, 1935; s. Max L. and Georgianna (Moore) W.; B.S.M.E., Ohio U., 1957; M.S., Mich. State U., 1958; D.Eng., U. Detroit, 1972; m. Donna Jo Gettle, Dec. 23, 1974; children—Susan, Lauren, Cynthia, Michael. Sr. design engr. Pratt & Whitney Aircraft, United, Fla., 1959-66; mem. faculty, chmn. dept. mfg. tech. Ind. U.-Purdue U., Fort Wayne, Ind., 1966—; found. dir. Soc. Mfg. Engrs. Mfg. Engring. Edn. Found., Dearborn, Mich., 1979—. Recipient Mgmt. Achievement award Soc. Mfg. Engrs., 1978. Registered profl. engr., Ind., Wis. Mem. Soc. Mfg. Engrs. (dir. internat.). Republican. Contbr. articles to profl. jours. Office: 2101 Coliseum Blvd E Fort Wayne IN 46805

WORTLEY, CHARLES ALLEN, civil engr.; b. St. Joseph, Mo., May 21, 1934; s. Cabray C. and Janet (Olmsted) W.; B.S., Antioch Coll., 1956; M.S. in Civil Engring., Calif. Inst. Tech., 1957; m. Ardale Dorothy Broch, Aug. 20, 1955; children—Marguerite, Caroline. Partner, Lorenzi, Dodds & Gunnill, cons. engrs., Pitts., 1957-66; v.p., chief engr. Warzyn Engring. Co., cons. engrs., Madison, Wis., 1966-74; asso. prof. engring. U. Wis., Madison, 1974—. Registered profl. engr., Wis. Mem. Wis. Soc. Profl. Engrs. (engr. of year in pvt. practice, 1972, engr. of year Southwest chpt. 1974), Nat. Soc. Profl. Engrs., Am. Soc. Engring. Edn., Internat. Assn. Hydraulic Research. Contbr. articles to profl. jours. Home: 206 Everglade Dr Madison WI 53717 Office: 432 Lake St N Madison WI 53706

WOWK, PAUL IHOR, health care exec.; b. Degendorf, Germany, Aug. 19, 1947; came to U.S., 1953, naturalized, 1956; s. Adam and Iwanna W.; B.S. in Sci., John Carroll U., 1969; M.A. in Health Care Adminstrn., George Washington U., 1973; m. Renee Alda Molina, Nov. 1, 1969; children—Matthew, Stephen. Adminstrv. resident Johns Hopkins Hosp., Balt., 1972-73; asst. adminstr. Kaiser Hosps., Cleve., 1973-75; asst. adminstr. Cin. Gen. Hosp., 1975-78; asst. adminstr. Toledo Hosp., 1978—. Vice chmn. family services ARC, 1977-78. Mem. Am. Coll. Hosp. Adminstrs., Am. Hosp. Assn., George Washington U. Health Care Adminstrs. Alumni Assn. Home: 25696 Brittany Perrysburg OH 43551 Office: 2142 North Cove Blvd Toledo OH 43606

WOYCZYNSKI, WOJBOR ANDRZEJ, educator; b. Czestochowa, Poland, Oct. 24, 1943; s. Eugeniusz and Otylia Sabina (Borkiewicz) W.; came to U.S., 1976; M.Sc. in Elec. Engring., Wroclaw Tech. U., 1966, Ph.D. in Math., 1968; 1 son, Martin Wojbor. Teaching asst. Inst. Math., Wroclaw U., 1966-68, asst. prof., 1968-72, asso. prof., 1972-76, vice dir. sci. affairs, 1975-76; fellow Carnegie-Mellon U., Pitts., 1970-71; asso. prof. math. U. Wis., 1976, Northwestern U., 1976-77; prof. math. Cleve. State U., 1977—, U. S.C., 1979. NSF grantee, 1970, 71, 76, 77, 81. Mem. Am. Math. Soc., Inst. Math. Statistics, Polish Math. Soc. (Great prize 1972). Roman Catholic. Author: Gometry and Martingales in Banach Spaces, Part I, 1975, Part II, 1978. Editor: (with Z. Ciesielski and K. Urbanik) Winter School on Probability, 1975. Dep. editor-in-chief Annals of Polish Math. Soc., 1973-77. Home: 18417 Scottsdale Blvd Shaker Heights OH 44122 Office: Math Dept Cleve State U Cleveland OH 44115

WOZNIAK, SAM, engring. exec.; b. Timblin, Pa., Mar. 6, 1931; s. John and Fenyi (Fedasz) W.; B.S., U. Tulsa, 1971, M.B.A., 1972; m. Shirley J. Johnson, Dec. 28, 1961; children—Susan Rae, John David. Elec. engr. Douglas Aircraft Corp., Long Beach, Calif., 1955; supr. Bell Aircraft Corp., Cleve., 1955-58; supr. and research scientist N.Am. Aviation, Downey, Calif., 1958-61; engring. mgr. Rockwell Internat., Tulsa, 1964-74; dir. div. engring. Brunswick Corp., Skokie, Ill., 1974-76, tech. dir., 1976—; adj. prof. U. Tulsa, 1971-73; spl. adviser to USAF, 1971-74, sci. advisor on ECM, 1977-79. Vice chmn. YMCA, Tulsa, 1968-70. Served with USAF, 1951-55. Mem. Am. Mgmt. Assn., IEEE, Electric Def. Assn., AAAS, Assn. M.B.A. Execs., AIAA, Assn. Old Crows, Assn. for Unmanned Vehicle Systems, Delta Sigma Pi, Pi Sigma Epsilon, Sigma Iota Epsilon, Beta Gamma Sigma. Republican. Presbyterian. Club: Rotary. Author: Guided Missiles Fundamentals, 1953, Radar Systems Manual, 1954, Highly Integrated Defensive Electromagnetic Systems Manual, 1967, Manufacturing Methods for Radar Materials, 1969, Radar Camouflage Benefits, 1975, Army Camouflage Net System, 1975; Peenemunde and Development of V-2 Weapon System, 1979. Office: 1 Brunswick Plaza Skokie IL 60077

WRAY, JAMES RICHARD, polit. party ofcl.; b. Columbus, Ohio, May 14, 1950; s. Louis James and Ruth Eleanor (Chrismer) W.; B.A., Ohio U., 1972; m. Gale Marie Townsend, Feb. 16, 1974; 1 dau., Jennifer Anne. Mgr., Credit Bur., Columbus, 1972-74; regional mgr. Evans Products Co., Columbus, 1974-76; campaign dir. United Way of Franklin County, Columbus, 1976-77; adminstr. CETA Gov.'s Grant State of Ohio, Columbus, 1977-78; field dir. Ohio Republican Com., Columbus, 1978-79, exec. dir., 1979—. Exec. dir. Cuyahoga County Rep. Fin. Com., 1978-79, Ohio Reagan Bush Com., 1980. vice chmn. Ohio League Young Republicans, 1976-77; v.p. Cap City Young Republican Club, 1976-78; mem. Cuyahoga County Rep. Exec. Com., 1978—; mem. Ohio Adv. Council on Vocat. Edn., 1977-78. Recipient Robert A. Taft Service award Ohio League Young Republicans, 1977. Mem. Lakewood Republican Club, Cleve. Area Republicans for Action, Columbus Jaycees. Club: Kiwanis. Home: 10214 Alliston Dr Pickerington OH 43147 Office: 33 N High St Columbus OH 43215

WRAY, LYLE DWIGHT, psychologist, court ofcl.; b. Alta., Can., Jan. 25, 1950; came to U.S., 1979; s. Clarence L. and Mary E. (Hampson) W.; B.A. with honors, U. Man. (Can.), 1972, M.A. in Psychology, 1975, Ph.D. in Psychology, 1980; m. Tsipora Goldberg, Aug. 15, 1978. Researcher verbal devel. with mentally retarded children St. Amant Center, Winnipeg, Man., 1972-78; lectr. dept. psychology U. Man., Winnipeg., 1976-78; co-chmn. program com. Direct Action in Support of Community Homes, Inc., Winnipeg, 1976-78; program dir. Pathway Children's Homes, Winnipeg, 1977-78; dir. mental retardation services dept. social services Govt. of Nfld. (Can.), 1978-79; dir. Bldg. 17 Adult Program Brainerd (Minn.) State Hosp., 1979-80; U.S. Dist. Ct. monitor for Welsch vs. Noot Consent Decree, St. Paul, 1980—; cons. public and community edn. program Ind. Sch. Dist., Brainerd public schs., 1980. Can. Council fellow, 1974-75, Nat. Research Council fellow, 1973-76. Mem. Am. Psychol. Assn., Am. Assn. on Mental Deficiency, Assn. for Advancement of Behavior Therapy. Contbr. articles to profl. publs. Home: 1465 Salem Church Rd Apt 209 Inner Grove Heights MN 55075 Office: 201 Capitol Square 550 Cedar St Saint Paul MN 55101

WRENTMORE, ANITA KAY, educator; b. Logan, Ohio, Dec. 3, 1955; d. Lloyd Earl and Gayle Irene (Daubenmier) W.; B.S. summa cum laude (univ. achievement scholar, Rex Chem. Co. Engring. scholar, Internat. Order Rainbow Girls scholar), Ohio U., Athens, 1978, M.S., 1979. Tchr., Circleville (Ohio) Public Schs., 1979-80; vis. lectr. Denison U., Granville, Ohio, 1980; lectr. math. Ohio State U., Newark, 1980—; guest lectr. Central Ohio Tech. Coll., Newark, 1981—. Life mem. Nat. Council Tchrs. Math., Ohio Council Tchrs. Math., Assn. Tchr. Educators, Kappa Delta Pi, Phi Kappa Phi; mem. Assn. Supervision and Curriculum Devel., Math. Assn. Am., Newark Council Tchrs. Math, Ohio Assn. Two-Yr. Colls., Assn. Individually-Guided Edn., Ohio Math. Assn. of two yr. colls., Council for Basic Edn., Assn. Computing Machinery, Nat. Ret. Tchrs. Assn., Smithsonian Assos., Licking County Bus. and Profl. Woman's Club. Methodist. Club: Order Eastern Star. Home: 1420 Londondale Pkwy Apt 122-C Newark OH 43055 Office: 176 Hopewell Hall University Dr Newark OH 43055

WRIGHT, CHARLES HOWARD, physician; b. Dothan, Ala., Sept. 20, 1918; s. Willie P. and Laura (Florence) W.; B.S., Ala. State Coll., 1939; M.D., Meharry Med. Coll., 1943; m. Louise L. Lovett, Feb. 11, 1950; children—Stephanie Jeanne, Carla Louise. Intern, Harlem Hosp., N.Y.C., 1943-45; asst. resident in pathology Cleve. City Hosp., 1945; resident in obstetrics and gynecology Harlem Hosp., N.Y.C., 1950-53; gen. practice medicine, Detroit, 1946-50, specializing in ob-gyn, 1953—; attending physician Southwest Detroit Hosp.; asst. Grace Hosp., 1954—; attending physician Hutzel Hosp., Detroit, 1953—. Founder, chmn. bd. trustees Afro-Am. Mus. Detroit, Inc.; pres. African Med. Edn. Fund; trustee U. Detroit, until 1975, Hutzel Hosp., 1979, WTVS. Named Omega Man of Year, Omega Psi Phi frat., 1965; recipient cert. Commendation, Mich. Med. Soc., 1967. Diplomate Am. Bd. Obstetrics and Gynecology. Fellow Am. Coll. Obstetricians and Gynecologists; mem. NAACP (life). Contbr. articles to profl. jours. Author, producer: (mus. drama) Were You There?, 1963; exec. producer: (films) This Bank is Open to You, 1969, Segregation in Public Transportation, in Retrospect, 1980, A Proper Sterile Technique for the Surgical Scrub, 1981; producer TV spls.: Were You There?, 1972; Venereal Disease, 1973; writer, narrator radio documentaries: Paul Robeson, 1970; Rosa Parks, 1971; (book) Robeson, Labor's Forgotten Champion, 1975; exec. dir.; (med. recruitment film) You Can Be A Doctor, 1968. Home: 1342 Nicolet Pl Detroit MI 48207

WRIGHT, DALE WALTER, mech. engr.; b. Saginaw, Mich., Apr. 29, 1929; s. Walter Marion and Alice Elizabeth (Hager) W.; B.S. in Indsl. and Mech. Engring., U. Mich., 1951; m. Jane Ann McKee, Dec. 19, 1953; children—Lisa, David, Bethany, John. Chief engr., v.p. Miles Machinery Co., 1955-78; pres., owner Wright Engring. & Design, Saginaw, 1978—. Pres. Young Republicans of Saginaw, 1958; chmn. Harvey for Congress, 1959-60; treas. Saginaw Rep. Party, 1960; mem. Saginaw Twp. Sch. Bd., 1970-71. Served to lt. (j.g.), USNR, 1952-55. Mem. Soc. Mfg. Engrs. Patentee in field. Office: 55 Harrow Ln Saginaw MI 48603

WRIGHT, DONALD CARLYLE, economist, educator; b. Ft. Dodge, Iowa, Sept. 28, 1923; s. Burr Clayton and Gladys Leah (Root) W.; student Dartmouth, 1943-44; B.S., U. Iowa, 1948, M.S., 1949, postgrad., 1958-60; m. Anna Margaret Beebe, July 28, 1946; children—Jacalyn G., Bradley C. Instr. econs. and bus. adminstrn. Washburn U., Topeka, 1949-51, asst. prof., 1951-55, asso. prof., 1955-68, prof., 1968—, acting dean Sch. Bus., 1979-80; mgmt. and govt. cons., 1960—. Mediator Kans. Dept. Labor, 1964. Served with USNR, 1942-45. Mem. Am. Soc. Pub. Adminstrn., Am., S.W. acads. mgmt., Kans. Econ. Assn., Missouri Valley Econ. Assn., Beta Gamma Sigma, Pi Gamma Mu, Phi Kappa Phi, Delta Sigma Pi, Omicron Delta Epsilon. Home: 3719 Munson St Topeka KS 66604

WRIGHT, DUEY EDWARD, communications co. exec.; b. Wausau, Wis., Sept. 28, 1939; s. Duey Ervin and Julia F. W.; B.B.A., U. Wis., 1962; m. Pegge Joy Wright, July 23, 1977; children—Mary Kay, Angela, Michael, Jeffrey. Program dir. Sta. WRIG, Wausau, 1963-65, gen. mgr. Sta. WRIG-AM/FM, 1965-70, pres., gen. mgr. WRIG, Inc., 1970-75; pres. Midwest Communications, Inc., Green Bay, Wis., 1971—; founder, pres. Sta. WROE, Neenah-Menasha, Wis., 1971—; gen. mgr. Sta. WGEE/WIXX, Green Bay, 1975—; pres. Wis. Network, Inc., Wisconsin Rapids, 1978—. Served as capt., Finance Corps, U.S. Army, 1962-63. Mem. Wis. Broadcasters Assn. (dir.). Presbyterian. Club: Elks (past chaplain). Home: 2331 Balsam Way Green Bay WI 54303 Office: 115 S Jefferson St Green Bay WI 54301

WRIGHT, GARY ALAN, toxicologist; b. Lafayette, Ind., Feb. 12, 1950; s. Herman Gordon and Caroline Marie (Haderle) W.; B.S., Purdue U., 1972, M.S., 1976, Ph.D., 1978; m. Kathleen MacDonald, Oct. 3, 1981. Teaching asst. Purdue U., West Lafayette, Ind., 1974-78; sr. research toxicologist Diamond Shamrock Corp., Painesville, Ohio, 1978-81; mgr. environ. affairs Stepan Chem. Co., Northfield, Ill., 1981—. Served with U.S. Army, 1972-74. Mem. Sigma Xi, Rho Chi. Republican. Baptist. Contbr. articles to profl. jours. Office: Stepan Chem Co Northfield IL 60093

WRIGHT, GEORGE FOREST, surgeon; b. Johnstown, Pa., Apr. 16, 1933; s. George Arthur and Vivian Allene (Miller) W.; student Pa. State U., 1951-54; M.D., Temple U., 1958; m. Eva Lynne Best, June 12, 1959; children—George Forest, III, Wendy Ann, Craig Ashley. Intern, Conemaugh Valley Meml. Hosp., Johnstown, 1958-59; resident in gen. surgery Temple U. Med. Center, 1959-63; dep. chief surgery Gallup (N.Mex.) USPHS Indian Hosp., 1964-64; chief of surgery Shiprock (N.Mex.) USPHS Indian Hosp., 1964-65; practice medicine specializing in surgery, Hanover, Pa., 1965-66, Cleve., 1966—; mem. staff Euclid (Ohio) Gen. Hosp., 1966—, chief of surgery, 1973-78; mem. staff Hanover Gen. Hosp., 1965-66; mem. courtesy staff. St. Vincent Charity Hosp.; bd. dirs. Euclid Clinic Found. Served with USPHS, 1963-65. Diplomate Am. Bd. Surgery. Mem. A.C.S., Am., Ohio med. assns., Acad. Medicine of Cleve., Cleve. Surg. Assn., Cleve. Vascular Soc. (founding). Republican. Methodist. Clubs: Lakeside Yacht (Cleve.); Masons. Home: 19801 Edgecliff Dr Euclid OH 44119 Office: 18599 Lake Shore Blvd Cleveland OH 44119

WRIGHT, HAROLD CLINTON, supt. schs.; b. Columbus, Ind., July 12, 1926; s. Edgar Raymond and Mabel Clinton (Sanders) W.; A.B., Ind. Central U., 1953; M.A., Ind. State U., 1956; m. Evelyn Lavely, Oct. 15, 1949; children—William, Kathryn, Jonathan. Tchr. schs. in Ind., 1956-59; prin. Wildcat Twp. (Ind.) Schs., Windfall, Ind., 1959-62; asst. prin. Wheaton (Ill.) North High Sch., 1962-74; regional supt. schs. DuPage County, Ill., 1974-81; regional rep. Region V, U.S. Dept. Edn., Chgo., 1981—; mem. faculty Nat. Coll. Edn., Evanston, Ill., Ill. Benedictine Coll., Lisle. Pres. Sch. Dist. 93 Bd. Edn., 1963-74; exec. com. DuPage sect. Am. Cancer Soc., 1975—; bd. dirs. DuPage-McHenry Lung Assn., 1975—. Served with USNR, 1944-46. Mem. Am. Assn. Sch. Adminstrs., Nat. Assn. Secondary Sch. Prins., Nat. Orgn. Legal Problems in Edn., Assn. Supervision and Curriculum Devel. Republican. Methodist. Office: 300 S Wacker Dr Rm 3214 Chicago IL 60606

WRIGHT, HELEN KENNEDY, editor; b. Indpls., Sept. 23, 1927; d. William Henry and Ida Louise (Crosby) Kennedy; B.A., Butler U., 1945, M.S., 1950; M.S., Columbia U., 1952; m. Samuel A. Wright, Sept. 5, 1970; 1 son, Carl F. Prince II. Reference librarian N.Y. Pub. Library, N.Y.C., 1952-53, Bklyn. Pub. Library, 1953-54; cataloger U. Utah, 1954-57; librarian Chgo. Pub. Library; asst. dir. pub. dept. ALA, Chgo., 1958—, now pub. officer III, editor Reference and Subscription Books Revs. Mem. Phi Kappa Phi, Kappa Delta Pi, Sigma Gamma Rho. Roman Catholic. Contbr. to Ency. of Careers, Ency. of Library and Info. Sci. Home: 1138 W 111th St Chicago IL 60643 Office: 50 E Huron Chicago IL 60611

WRIGHT, HOWARD LELAND, bus. cons.; b. San Jose, Calif., Apr. 2, 1950; s. Howard L. and Marion A. W.; student S.W. Tex. State U., 1969-71, San Jose City Coll., 1972; A.A., W. Valley Coll., 1975; B.S. in Bus., San Jose State U., 1978; postgrad. Sch. Dental Medicine, Washington U., St. Louis, 1979—; m. Glenna Ann Engberg, July 13, 1973. Carpet salesman Carpets of Am., San Antonio, 1969-70, Clayton Moreno Co., 1970; dormitory supt. San Marcos (Tex.) Mil. Acad., 1970-71; night foreman Safeway Stores, Inc., Oklahoma City, 1971; asst. foreman Calif. Canners & Growers, San Jose, 1971; asst. propr. Phillips 66 Oil Co., Gilroy, Calif., 1971; asst. mgr. ops. Bank of Am., San Jose, 1972-75; ins. underwriter N.Y. Life Ins. Co., Santa Clara, Calif., 1975-76; prin. H.L. Wright, task force mktg., bus. cons., San Jose, 1976—. Youth dir. San Jose 1st Baptist Ch., 1973—. Recipient Outstanding Results award Small Bus. Inst., 1977. Mem. Fin. Mgmt. Assn. (pres.), Alpha Gamma Sigma, Beta Alpha Psi, Beta Gamma Sigma, Theta Psi. Republican. Mem. Christian Ch. Address: 1609 Baronet Apt B Manchester MO 63011

WRIGHT, JAMES LYNN, savs. and loan co. exec.; b. Springfield, Ill., Sept. 22, 1940; s. Glenn LaRue and Freida Pearl (Bloomfield) W.; B.S., Ill. Coll., 1963; M. Accounting Sci., U. Ill., 1965, postgrad., 1969-71; m. Karen Ann Barber, Nov. 24, 1976; children—Jeffrey Michael, Timothy Lynn. Staff auditor Arthur Young & Co., Chgo., 1965-66, 68-69; teaching asst. accounting U. Ill., Urbana, 1969-70; instr. accounting Ill. State U., Normal, 1970-71; accountant Bloomington (Ill.) Fed. Savs. & Loan Assn., 1972, asst. treas., 1972-73, dir. data processing, 1974-76, v.p., 1976-78, comptroller, 1976-78, v.p., treas., 1978-81, sr. v.p., treas., 1981—. Served with U.S. Army, 1966-68. Club: Univ. (Chgo.). Home: 308 Vista Dr Bloomington IL 61701 Office: 115 E Washington St Bloomington IL 61701

WRIGHT, JOHN LESLIE, orthopaedic surgeon: b. Normal, Ill., Jan. 8, 1920; s. Frank and Ruth (Bramwell) W.; B.S., Ill. Wesleyan U., 1943; M.D., U. Ill., 1945; m. Shirley Jean Barr, May 13, 1943; children—Judy Lee, Barbara Jean, Patricia Ann, John L., Gretchen Sue. Intern, St. Mary's Mercy Hosp., Gary, Ind., 1945-46; resident VA Hosp., Alexandria, La., 1946-48, La. Meth. Hosp., Peoria, Ill., 1948-49; practice medicine, Minier, Ill., 1949-54; resident in orthopaedics Oschner Found. Hosp. and Clinic, New Orleans, 1954-57; practice medicine specializing in orthopaedics, Bloomington, Ill., 1957—; mem. staffs Mennonite and St. Joseph's hosps., Bloomington, Brokaw Hosp., Normal; clin. asso. Sch. Basic Med. Scis., U. Ill., Urbana-Champaign, 1971—; chmn. adv. bd. Am. Assn. Med. Assts., 1975-79, chmn. adv. bd. Ill. Soc., 1973-80. Served with U.S. Army, M.C., 1946-48. Mem. Ill. Soc. Am. Assn. Med. Assts. (hon.), McLean County, Ill. State med. socs., AMA, Am. Acad. Orthopaedic Surgeons, A.C.S., Oschner Found. Assn., Am. Fracture Assn. (sec.), Tulane Caldwell Orthopaedic Club, Ill. Mid-State Orthopaedic Surgery Club. Methodist. Clubs: Aviation Owners and Pilots Assn., Bloomington, Masons. Contbr. articles to profl. jours. Home: 1010 E Jefferson Bloomington IL 61701 Office: 2416 E Washington St Suite A Bloomington IL 61701

WRIGHT, JOHN LEWIS, educator; b. Brazil, Ind., Nov. 3, 1939; s. John Andrew and Thelma Mae (Winkler) W.; B.S., Ind. State U., Terre Haute, 1967, M.S., 1971, Ph.D., 1972; m. Gianetta Fay Frost, July 12, 1957; children—Denise Helene, Gianetta Kay, Lynn Anne, Esther Elaine. Tchr. English, Staunton (Ind.) High Sch., 1967-69, 71-72; grad. fellow Ind. State U., 1969-71; asso. prof. English, Greenville (Ill.) Coll., 1972-79, prof. English and edn., 1979—; cons. Ill. State Bd. of Edn.; developed workshop in teaching of reading, discipline and motivation for public sch. tchrs.; pastor Woodside Community Ch., Fillmore, Ill., 1978-80. Mem. Ill. Assn. Tchr. Educators, Nat. Council Tchrs. of English, Ill. Assn. Tchrs. of English, Adolescent Lit. Assembly, Assn. Supervision and Curriculum Devel. Author: Footnote to Education, 1970; (with others) A Lesson for Education, 1973, Revolution; The Answer to the Problems in Education, 1973; Learning Objectives and the Teaching of English, 1976; A Footnote to Power Plays Made by Educators, 1976; The Novel as a Device for Motivating Students in Junior High Science Classes, 1979; Discipline: A Definition with Significant Implications for Teachers, 1982. Office: 315 E College St Greenville IL 62246

WRIGHT, JOHNSON KENT, dermatologist; b. Cleve., Sept. 8, 1924; s. J. Kent and Gwendolyn (Santo) W.; B.A., U. Mich., 1948; M.D., Temple U., 1952; m. Katherine Rogan, Dec. 20, 1950; children—Johnson Kent III, Marilyn Kay, James Kevin. Intern, Univ. Hosp., Ann Arbor, Mich., 1952-53, resident in dermatology, 1953-56; practice medicine specializing in dermatology, Traverse City, Mich.; chief of dermatology Munson Med. Center, Traverse City, 1956-72; cons. staff Grand Traverse Med. Care Facility, Traverse City State Hosp. Served with USNR, 1943-45. Diplomate Am. Bd. Dermatology. Mem. AMA, Acad. of Dermatology, Mich. Med. Soc., Grand Traverse-Leelanau-Benzie Med. Soc. Republican. Clubs: Traverse City (Mich.) Golf and Country; Elks, Rotary. Home: 1236 Randall Ct Traverse City MI 49684 Office: 1105 E Front St Traverse City MI 49684

WRIGHT, JOSEPH SUTHERLAND, lawyer, electronics co. exec.; b. Portland, Oreg., Mar. 16, 1911; s. Joseph Alfred and Carrie (Sutherland) W.; LL.B., George Washington U., 1937; m. Ruth Lacklen, Nov. 14, 1936; children—Joseph Sutherland, Susan Jane. Sec., Senator B. K. Wheeler, 1933-36; admitted to D.C. bar, 1934; atty. FTC, 1936-42; asst. gen. counsel, chief compliance, 1947-52; asst. gen. counsel Zenith Radio Corp., Chgo., 1952-53, gen. counsel, dir., 1953-58, v.p., 1951-58, exec. v.p. 1958-59, pres., gen. mgr., 1959-68, chief exec. officer, 1965-76, 79—, chmn., 1968-76, 79—; dir. Standard Oil (Ind.), Bethlehem Steel Corp., Sunbeam Corp., Commonwealth Edison Corp. Trustee U. Chgo., George Washington U., John Crerar Library. Served to lt. comdr. USNR, 1942-45. Mem. Chgo. Bar Assn. Clubs: Comml., Tavern, Chgo., Chgo. Yacht (Chgo.); Met. (Washington); Park Ridge Country. Home: 145 Oxford Rd Kenilworth IL 60043 Office: 1000 Milwaukee Ave Glenview IL 60025

WRIGHT, KATHERYN THORNE, civic worker; b. Ravenswood, Ill., Sept. 19, 1895; d. Albert H. and Sarah (Chapman) Wright; A.B., Mather Coll. (now Western Res. Coll.), 1917, A.M., Case Western Res. U., 1927. Substitute tchr. Cleve. Public Schs., 1917-18; sec. First Meth. Ch., Cleve., 1920; sec. clk.'s office Cleveland Heights (Ohio) Bd. of Edn., 1921-22; sec. Squire, Sanders & Dempsey, Cleve., 1924-62, ret.; also freelance writer, 1962—. Vol., ARC, Am. Cancer Soc., Cleve. Psychiat. Inst.; tutorial program Episcopal Ch. Recipient Cleve. Vol. of Yr. award, 1969; Vol. award Am. Cancer Soc., 1977. Mem. Cleve. Coll. Writers Club, Profl. Secs. Internat. (charter mem. Forest City chpt.), Greater Cleve. Orchid Soc., DAR (Western Res. chpt.), Women's Assn. for Continuing Edn. Episcopalian (lay reader 1973—). Clubs: Quota (charter mem.), College. Home: 2543 Derbyshire Rd Cleveland OH 44106

WRIGHT, KATIE HARPER, ednl. adminstr., journalist; b. Crawfordsville, Ark., Oct. 5, 1923; d. James Hale and Connie Mary (Locke) Harper; B.A., U. Ill., 1944; M.Ed., 1959; Ed.D., St. Louis U., 1979; m. Marvin Wright, Mar. 21, 1952; 1 dau., Virginia (Mrs. Ed Jordan). Elementary and spl. edn. tchr. East St. Louis (Ill.) Pub. Schs., 1944-65, dir. Dist. 189 Instructional Materials Program, 1965-71, dir. spl. edn. Dists. 188, 189, 1971-77, asst. supt. programs, 1977-79; feature writer St. Louis Argus, 1979—; adj. faculty Harris/Stowe State Coll., 1980; cons. to numerous workshops, seminars in field. Mem. Ill. Commn. on Children, 1973—, E. St. Louis Bd. Election Commrs.; pres. bd. dirs. St. Clair Community Mental Health Center, 1970-72; bd. dirs. River Bluff council Girl Scouts, 1979—, United Way, 1979—, Urban League, 1979—; pres. bd. trustees East St. Louis Pub. Library, 1972-77. Recipient Lamp of Learning award East St. Louis Jr. Wednesday Club, 1965; Outstanding Working Woman award Downtown St. Louis, Inc., 1967; Ill. State citation for ednl. document Love is Not Enough, 1974; Delta Sigma Theta citation for document Good Works, 1979; named Woman of Achievement, St. Louis Globe Democrat, 1974, Outstanding Adminstr. So. region Ill. Office Edn., 1975. Mem. Am. Libraries Trustees Assn. (regional v.p. 1978-79, nat. sec. 1979-80, mem. Speakers Bur. 1980—), Ill. Commn. on Children, Mensa, Council for Exceptional Children, Top Ladies of Distinction, Delta Sigma Theta (chpt. pres. 1960-62), Kappa Delta Pi (pres. So. Ill. U. chpt. 1973-74), Phi Delta Kappa, Pi Lambda Theta. Republican. Presbyterian. Club: East St. Louis Women's (pres. 1973-75). Contbr. articles to profl. jours. Home: 733 North 40th St East Saint Louis IL 62205

WRIGHT, KAY MORROW, hosp. exec.; b. Baytown, Tex., Sept. 28, 1942; d. Morris Robinson and Martha (Whiteman) Morrow; B.A. in Mathematics, U. Tex., 1964; m. Terry Frank Wright, June 4, 1966; children—Stephanie Lynn, Stacie Cole. Programmer, The Bankers Life, Des Moines, 1966-68; programmer analyst Enjay Fibers and Laminates Co., Odenton, Md., 1968-69; dir. data processing Mercy Hosp., Des Moines, 1969-75, dir. computer planning and info. services, 1975-78, planning coordinator, 1978-79, computer planning coordinator, 1979-81, systems cons., 1981—. Bd. dirs. Iowa Soc. to Prevent Blindness, 1977—, Mercy Hosp. Credit Union, 1978-80; benefit chmn. Flip for Sight, 1977-81. Mem. Data Processing Mgmt. Assn. (Des Moines chpt.), Iowa Health Computer Assn. (founding pres. 1978-79), Electronic Computing Health Oriented. Democrat. Methodist. Clubs: Delta Zeta Alumnae, Province Alumnae Iowa, Wis. (dir. 1979—), Polk County Attys. Wives. Office: 6th and University Ave Des Moines IA 50314

WRIGHT, RALPH EDWIN, sch. prin.; b. Metropolis, Ill., Feb. 23, 1922; s. Abraham and Mae Nancy (Keel) W.; B.A., Bradley U., 1943, M.A., 1950, Ph.D., 1955; postgrad. U. Minn., 1970-72, U. Calif., San Diego, 1975, UCLA, 1979-80; m. Mary Lorraine Stalter, Apr. 3, 1942; children—Stephen, Jeffry, Alison, Douglas, Cassandra, Timothy. Civil edn. officer Niigata (Japan) Mil. Govt. team, 1946-49; placement officer Bradley U., Peoria, Ill., 1952-53, teaching asst. Coll. Edn., 1950-52; dir. guidance and tchr. social studies Farmington (Ill.) Community High Sch., 1952-54; adminstrv. asst. and guidance dir. Lincoln-Way Community High Sch., New Lenox, Ill., 1954-58; guest instr. Mankato (Minn.) State Coll., 1960-64, Winona (Minn.) State Coll., 1964-65; prin. John Marshall Sr. High Sch., Rochester, Minn., 1958-65, Mayo High Sch., Rochester, Minn., 1965-78, 80—; dir. secondary edn., Rochester, 1978-79, 79-80; chmn. adminstrv. team Rochester (Minn.) public schs., 1972. Lay leader Christ United Meth. Ch., 1963-66; pres. Rochester Area Ch. Council, 1967-68; bd. dirs. YMCA, 1962-68, YMCA Camp Olson, 1972—, v.p., 1980—; bd. dirs. Rochester Found., sec., 1965-81; bd. dirs. Rochester Meth. Hosp., 1965—. Served to 1st lt. U.S. Army, 1943-46; PTO. Recipient Am. Educators medal Freedom Found. at Valley Forge, 1967. Fellow Inst. for Devel. of Ednl. Activities; mem. Headmasters Assn., Nat. Staff Devel. Assn., Rochester Assn. for Study of Transactional Analysis (pres. 1975-80), Collegial Assn. for Devel. and Renewal of Educators, Nat. Assn. Secondary Sch. Prins. (chmn. high sch.-coll. relations com. 1970-74), Minn. Assn Secondary Sch. Prins. (high sch.-coll relations com. 1970-74). Contbr. articles to profl. jours. Home: 726 6th St SW Rochester MN 55901 Office: 1420 11th Ave SE Rochester MN 55901

WRIGHT, ROBERT RICHARD, educator; b. Indpls., May 12, 1942; s. Herbert Harold and Kathleen Elizabeth (Hayworth) W.; A.B., Butler U., 1964; M.S., Ohio State U., 1967, Ph.D., 1975; m. Debbie Kay Mumma, Aug. 28, 1981. Planetarium lectr., asst. to dir. J.I. Holcomb Obs. and Planetarium, Indpls., 1962-64; guest investigator Snow Telescope, Mt. Wilson Obs., Calif., 1964; planetarium lectr., instr. The Center of Sci. and Industry of Columbus, Ohio, 1966; physics and astronomy lectr. Ohio Dominican Coll., 1969-73, asst. dir. admissions, 1978-79; vis. prof. dept. mathematics Ohio Wesleyan U., 1976-77; lectr. dept. math. The Ohio State U., 1973-78, adj. prof. dept. astronomy, 1979—, asst. to dean Coll. Engring., 1979—; cons. mathematics and sci. editor Collegiate Publishing, Inc., Columbus, Ohio, 1971-74. Recipient James E. Hughes scholarship, 1962-64; NDEA fellow, 1964-67. Mem. Am. Astronom. Soc., Am. Soc. Engring. Edn., Am. Inst. Physics, Soc. Automotive Engrs., Math. Assn. Am., Am. Math. Soc. Republican. Co-author (with W. R. Klinger) Basic Algebra, 1972; collaborator: The Professor, 1974; contbr. articles to profl. jours. Home: 280 E Columbus Columbus OH 43206 Office: Coll Engring Ohio State U Columbus OH 43210

WRIGHT, ROBERT W(ILLIAMS), lawyer; b. Elgin, Ill., May 31, 1928; s. Robert Williams and Caroline (Chapman) W.; S.B., Mass. Inst. Tech., 1950; LL.B., Harvard, 1954; m. Nancy Campbell Tucker, Oct. 30, 1954; children—Patricia Jane, Katherine Elizabeth, Robert Tucker. Indsl. engr. Inland Steel Co., East Chicago, Ind., 1950-51; admitted to Ill. bar, 1954, since practiced Chgo.; with firm Keck, Mahin & Cate, 1954—, partner, 1964—. Mem. Am., Ill., Chgo. bar assns., Law and Legal Clubs Chgo., Delta Kappa Epsilon. Clubs: Chicago, Mid-Day (Chgo.). Home: 122 Kenilworth Ave Kenilworth IL 60043 Office: 233 S Wacker Dr Chicago IL 60606

WRIGHT, STANLEY ALLEN, state senator, mayor; b. Stanley, N.D., Feb. 17, 1926; s. James A. and Evelyn (Pace) W.; grad. high sch.; m. Mavis Dalhaug, 1948; children—Pamela Wright Thompson, Joleen, Cheryl. City alderman, Stanley, 1958-70, mayor, 1970—; mem. N.D. State Senate, 1972—. Mem. Legion State band. Served in U.S. Army, 1946-48; Korea. Mem. Am. Legion, Farm Bur. Lutheran. Clubs: Lions, Elks. Address: Box 97 Stanley ND 58784*

WRIGHT, THEO CAROL, nursing home adminstr.; b. Ethel, Mo., Dec. 26, 1927; d. Paul Jones and Zelma Rose (Mitchell) Williams; m. Welford Roscoe Wright, May 18, 1958. Bookkeeper, A.J. Noll Motor Co., Macon, Mo., 1946-56; office mgr. Noll Motors, Inc., Moberly, Mo., 1956-72; warehouse mgr. Williams Energy Co., Moberly, 1973-76; office mgr. Sta. KWIX-KRES, Moberly, 1976-78; asst. adminstr. North Village Manor, Moberly, 1978-81, adminstr., 1981—. Sec., Randolph County Democratic Com., Moberly, 1979-80. Mem. Mo. League Nursing Home Adminstrs. Clubs: Altrusa (past treas.), Randolph County Women's Dem. (program and publicity chmn.). Home: 506 Shumate Moberly MO 65270 Office: 2041 Silva Ln Moberly MO 65270

WRIGHT, WILBUR E., orgn. exec.; b. July 23, 1933; B.S. in Sociology, St. Peter's Coll., 1955; M.S.S. in Psychiat. Social Work, Fordham U., 1958; married, 4 children. Family counselor United Family and Children's Soc., Plainfield, N.J., 1958-59; sr. med. social worker U. Calif., San Diego County Hosp., 1965-66; dir. social worker Scripps Meml. Hosp., LaJolla, Calif., 1966-68; dir. service and rehab. Calif. div. Am. Cancer Soc., San Francisco, 1968-72; cons., dir. resource devel. Orgn. for Bus., Edn., and Community Advancement, Cath. Charities, Archdiocese of San Francisco, 1972-73; dep. head depts. social work and preventive and social medicine Alfred-Monash U. Hosp., Fawkner Park Community Health Center, Prahran, Victoria, Australia, 1973-74; head dept social work Royal Perth Hosp., U. Western Australia, 1974-75; exec. dir. Community Mental Health Bd. Central Fla., Inc., Orlando, 1975-78; sec. gen. Council Internat. Programs, Cleve., 1978-80; mem. internat. case com. San Diego-Tijuana (Mexico) Health Council, Pan-Am. Health Orgn., 1966-68; mem. stroke com. Regional Med. Program, U. Calif., San Diego, 1967-68; mem. Richmond fellowship bd. Community Devel. Center, Western Australia Dept. Mental Hygiene, 1974-75; mem. task force on emotionally disturbed children and adolescents Fla. Dept. Health and Rehabilitative Services, 1976-78; mem. advisory com. Fla. Mental Health/ Health Systems Tng. Program, 1977-78. Commr. Marinwood (Calif.) Community Service Dist., 1971-73; rep. So. region Australian Assistance Plan, Melbourne, 1973-74; mem. Prahran Social Action Com., 1973-74; mem. Blue Ridge Inst., So. Community Services Exec., 1977; mem. exec. com. Council Internat. Fellowship, Bonn, W. Ger., 1978-80. Served with M.C., U.S. Army, 1959-62, USPHS, 1962-65. Fellow Am. Pub. Health Assn., Royal Soc. Health (U.K.); mem. Nat. Assn. Social Workers (chmn. health council San Diego chpt. 1968), Am. Acad. Polit. and Social Sci., Internat. Conf. on Social Welfare (U.S. com.), Internat. Health Soc., Fla. Assn. Dist. Mental Health Bds. (exec. dir. rep. 1976-78). Address: 3393 Daleford Rd Shaker Heights OH 44120

WRIGLEY, WILLIAM, corp. exec.; b. Chgo., Jan. 21, 1933; s. Philip Knight and Helen (Atwater) W.; B.A., Yale U., 1954; m. Alison Hunter, June 1, 1957 (div.); children—Alison, Philip, William. With Wm. Wrigley Jr. Co., Chgo., 1956—, dir., 1960—, pres., chief exec. officer, 1961—; dir. Wrigley Espana S.A. (Spain), The Wrigley Co. Ltd. (U.K.), The Wrigley Co. Pty. Ltd. (Australia), The Wrigley Co. (N.Z.) Ltd., New Zealand, Wrigley Philippines, Inc., Wrigley Co. (H.K.) Ltd. (Hong Kong), Wrigley & Co. Ltd., Japan, Wrigley Co. (East Africa) Ltd. (Kenya), Wrigley N.V. (Netherlands); dir., mem. compensation com. Nat. Blvd. Bank; dir., mem. salary and auditing coms., com. non-mgmt. dirs., spl. com. non-mgmt. dirs., chmn. nominating com. Texaco, Inc.; dir., mem. audit com. Am. Home Products Corp.; dir., v.p., chmn. exec. com. Santa Catalina Island Co.; dir., chmn. exec. com., mem. audit com. Chgo. Nat. League Ball Club, to 1981. Bd. dirs. Wrigley Meml. Garden Found.; bd. dirs., mem. personnel com. Northwestern Meml. Hosp.; trustee Chgo. Latin Sch. Found., 1975—; bd. dirs. Geneva Lake Water Safety Com., 1966—, mem. exec. com., 1968—; mem. adv. bd. Center for Sports Medicine, Northwestern U. Med. Sch., 1976—. Served from ensign to lt. (j.g.) USNR, 1954-56, lt. comdr. Res. ret. Mem. Chgo. Hist. Soc., Field Mus. Natural History, Art Inst. Chgo., Navy League U.S., Wolf's Head Soc., Santa Catalina Island Conservancy (benefactor mem.), Antiquarian Soc. of Art Inst. Chgo., USC Oceanographic Assos., Catalina Island Mus. Soc., Delta Kappa Epsilon. Clubs: Chicago Yacht, Racquet, Saddle and Cycle, Tavern, Commercial (Chgo.); Lake Geneva (Wis.) Country, Lake Geneva Yacht; Brook (N.Y.C.); Catalina Island Gun, Catalina Island Yacht (Calif.); Tuna (Catalina). Office: 410 N Michigan Ave Chicago IL 60611

WROBLEY, RALPH G., lawyer; b. Denver, Sept. 19, 1935; s. Matthew B. and Hedvig (Lyon) W.; B.A., Yale, 1957; J.D., U. Chgo., 1962; m. Madeline C. Kearney, June 13, 1959; children—Kirk Lyon, Eric Lyon, Ann Lyon. With Bell Telephone Co. Pa., Phila., 1957-59; admitted to Mo. bar, 1962; mem. firm Stinson, Mag, & Fizzell, Kansas City, Mo., 1962—, partner, 1965—; sec., dir. Gordon Johnson Industries, Inc., 1976—; dir. Bartlett Agri Enterprises, Inc., RO Corp.; sec., dir. Helzberg's Diamond Shops, Inc., 1978—. Dir. Human Resources Corp., 1971; chmn. Pub. Housing Authority Kansas City, 1971-74; vice chmn. Mayor's Adv. Commn. on Housing, Kansas City, Mo., 1971-74; bd. govs. Citizens Assn., 1965—, mem. adv. com., 1966-69, 75—, mem. exec. com., 1969-75, 78—, vice chmn., 1971-75, chmn., 1978-79; dir. Council on Edn., 1975-81, v.p., 1977-79; mem. Mayor's Commn. on Crime, 1981—; dir., pres. Sam E. and Mary F. Roberts Found., 1974—; trustee Clearinghouse for Midcontinent Founds., 1977—. Recipient Outstanding Mem. award Yale club Kansas City, 1967. Mem. Am. Bar Assn., Mo. Bar, Lawyers Assn. Kansas City. Republican. Presbyterian (deacon). Clubs: Yale (pres. 1969-71), Carriage (Kansas City, Mo.). Home: 1015 W 67th Terr Kansas City MO 64113 Office: Charter Bank Center Kansas City MO 64105

WROBLOWA, HALINA STEFANIA, electrochemist; b. Gdansk, Poland, July 5, 1925; came to U.S., 1960, naturalized, 1970; M.Sc., U. Lodz (Poland), 1949; Ph.D., Warsaw Inst. Tech., 1958; 1 dau., Krystyna Wrobel-Knight. Chmn. dept. prep. studies U. Lodz, 1950-53; adj. Inst. for Phys. Chemistry, Acad. Scis., Warsaw, Poland, 1958-60; dep. dir. electrochemistry lab. U. Pa., Phila., 1960-67, dir. electrochemistry lab. Energy Inst., 1968-75; prin. research scientist Ford Motor Co., Dearborn, Mich., 1978—. Served with Polish Underground Army, 1943-45. Decorated Silver Cross of Merit with Swords. Mem. Assn. Women in Sci., Electrochem. Soc., N.Y. Acad. Scis., Mensa, Sigma Xi. Contbr. chpts. to books, articles to profl. jours. Office: Ford Motor Co SRL S-2079 PO Box 2053 Dearborn MI 48121

WRONSKI, FRANK MARTIN, health care exec.; b. St. Clair, Mich., Sept. 5, 1951; s. Walter and Eleanor (Balinski) W.; B.B.A., Eastern Mich. U., 1972; M.B.A., U. Detroit, 1976; postgrad. Thomas M. Cooley Law Sch., Lansing, Mich., 1980—; m. Lorraine M. Zeglen, Oct. 1, 1976. Exec. adminstr. Livingston Care Center, Inc., Oak Hill Nursing Home, Inc., Livingston Care Center Living Units, 1976—; pres. Mich. Med. Lab., Farmington, 1978—, also dir.; adj. prof. health care adminstrn. Mich. State U., Ferris State U.; mem. exec. com. Southeastern Mich. Health Planning Council, 1977-79. Mem. Am. Coll. Nursing Home Adminstrs., Hosp. Fin. Mgmt. Assn., Health Care Assn. Mich. (public info. com., policy and procedure com., standards and ethics com.), Farmington Jaycees, Delta Sigma Pi (pres. 1972). Office: 23900 Orchard Lake Rd Farmington MI 48024

WRZESINSKI, DOLORES JOSEPHINE, historian; b. Mukwonago, Wis., Sept. 21, 1926; d. Stanley and Marie (Frelichowski) W.; Ph.B., Marquette U., 1948; M.S. U. Wis., Whitewater, 1974. Tchr., Vernon Center Sch., 1948-51, Genesee Sch., 1951-56, prin., 1951-56; tchr. Muskego (Wis.) Elem. Sch., 1956-65, high sch., 1965—. Named Dist. High Sch. Tchr. of Yr., 1980. Mem. Wis. Council Social Studies, Nat. Council Social Studies, Assn. Supervision and Curriculum Devel., United Lakewood East Edn. Assn., NEA, Wis. Edn. Assn. Council, Delta Kappa Gamma. Roman Catholic. Home: W225 S9150 Mt Carmel Dr Big Bend WI 53103 Office: W183 S 8750 Racine Ave Muskego WI 53150

WU, HAI, mech. engr.; b. Tung Hai, Kiangsu, China, Aug. 22, 1936; came to U.S., 1961, naturalized, 1972; s. Shiang-San Wu and Aei-Feng Chen; Ph.D., Case Inst. Tech., 1969; m. Grace Hsiao-lee Ma, Dec. 17, 1966; children—Frank, Carson, Nelson. Research asst., Internat. fellow U. Iowa, 1961-63; research asst. U. Minn., 1963-64; mech. engr. Syska & Hennessy, Engrs., N.Y.C., 1964-65; research asst. Case Inst. Tech., 1965-69; sr. research engr. Ford Motor Co., Dearborn Mich., 1969-76, prin. research engr. asso., 1976-80, prin. staff engr., 1980—; lectr. Detroit Inst. Tech., 1974. Served to 2d lt. Chinese Air Force, 1958-60. Taiwan Cement Co. fellow, 1954-58. Mem. ASME, Detroit Chinese Engrs. Assn. (dir.), Sigma Xi. Contbr. articles to profl. jours. Patentee in field. Home: 50150 Hanford Rd Canton MI 48187 Office: 20000 Rotunda Dr Dearborn MI 48121

WU, HARRY PAO-TUNG, librarian; b. Chinan, Shantung, China, May 1, 1932; s. James Ching-Mei and Elizabeth Hsiao (Lu) W.; B.A., Nat. Taiwan U., Taipei, 1959; student Ohio State U., 1962; M.L.S., Kent State U., 1966; m. Irene I-Len Sun, June 23, 1961; children—Eva Pei-Chen, Walter Pei-Liang. Came to U.S., 1960. Archive and library asst. Taiwan Handicraft Promotion Center, Taipei, 1959-60; student asst. Kent State U. Library, 1960-61; reference librarian Massillon (Ohio) Pub. Library, 1964-65, acting asst. dir., 1965, asst. dir., head adult services, 1966; dir. Flesh Pub. Library, Piqua, Ohio, 1966-68; dir. St. Clair County Library System, Port Huron, Mich., 1968—; founder and dir. Blue Water Library Fedn., Port Huron, 1974—; pres. Mich. Library Film Circuit, Lansing, 1977-79. Mem. Am., Mich. (chmn. library systems roundtable 1974-75) library assns., Am. Mgmt. Assn., Assn. Ednl. Communications and Tech., Detroit Suburban Librarians Roundtable. Clubs: Port Huron Internat., Rotary (dir. 1972-74). Home: 1518 Holland Ave Port Huron MI 48060 Office: 210 McMorran Blvd Port Huron MI 48060

WU, HSIAO HSU, metallurgist; b. Che-Kiang, China, Jan. 7, 1935; s. Jones and Chin (Hsu) W.; came to U.S., 1967, naturalized, 1973; B.Sc., Cheng-Kung U., Taiwan, 1962; M.Eng., N.S. (Can.) Tech. Coll., 1967; m. Amy Yutai Lan, Dec. 30, 1979; 1 son, Alexander. Chemist, M&T Chem. Inc., Ferndale, Mich., 1967-69; metallurgist Anaconda Am. Brass Co., Detroit, 1969-71; chief metallurgist Extruded Metals div. Indian Head Co., Belding, Mich., 1971—. Mem. Am. Soc. Metals, Am. Soc. Quality Control, ASTM, Water Pollution Control Fedn. Patentee in process metallurgy. Home: 7135 Davies St Rockford MI 49341 Office: 302 Ashfield St Belding MI 48809

WU, HSIN-HSIUNG, physician; b. Taiwan, China, Dec. 9, 1938; s. Seng Ping and Wang Yen (Wang) W.; came to U.S., 1967; M.D., Kaohsiung Med. Coll., Taiwan, China, 1964; m. Sally Hsimei, Jan. 1, 1966; children—Richard, Andrew, Nancy. Intern Columbus-Cuneo Med. Center, Chgo., 1967-68; resident in anesthesiology U. Ill., Chgo., 1970-72; fellow in anesthesiology Rush Med. Coll., Chgo., 1972; instr. anesthesiology Med. Coll. of Va., Richmond, 1973-74; chief dept. anesthesiology Annapolis Hosp., Wayne, Mich., 1981—. Diplomate Am. Bd. Anesthesiology. Fellow Am. Coll. Anesthesiologists; mem. Am. Soc. Anesthesiology. Buddhist. Contbr. numerous articles to profl. publs. Office: Dept Anesthesiology Annapolis Hosp Wayne MI 48184

WU, KENNETH KUN-YU, physician; b. Taiwan, July 6, 1941; s. Chuan and Chin-Piau (Yeh) W.; came to U.S., 1967, naturalized, 1976; M.D., Nat. Taiwan U., 1966; M.S. (Research fellow 1967—68), Yale U., 1968; m. Lung-Chin Shih, Mar. 29, 1969; children—Stanley, David. Intern, Bridgeport (Conn.) Hosp., 1968—69; in internal medicine U. Iowa, Iowa City, Washington U., St. Louis, 1969—71; NIH fellow in hematology U. Iowa, 1971—73, asst. prof. medicine, 1974-76; chief and attending physician coagulation and thrombosis unit Rush-Presbyn.-St. Lukes Med. Center, Chgo., 1976—; asso. prof. Rush Med. Coll., 1976—. Served to 2d lt. Republic of China Army, 1966—67. Fellow A.C.P.; mem. Am. Soc. Hematology, Am. Assn. Immunologists, AAAS, Internat. Soc. Hematology, Internat. Soc. Thrombosis and Hemostasis, Cental Soc. Clin. Research, Am. Fedn. Clin. Research. Presbyn. Club: Room 600. Contbr. articles to profl. jours. Home: 1642 Robin Ln Glenview IL 60025 Office: 1753 W Congress Pky Chicago IL 60612

WU, LUNG-CHI, physiologist; b. Taiwan, Jan. 29, 1929; came to U.S., 1972, naturalized, 1979; s. Pee and Tau (Hau) W.; B.S., Nat. Taiwan U., 1953, M.S., 1956; Ph.D., U. Ill., 1959; m. Shu-mei Ting Wu, Oct. 20, 1962; children—Elsie, Dianne, James. Research asso. Mich. State U., East Lansing, 1959-60, asst. prof., 1960-61; asso. prof. Nat. Taiwan U., Taipei, 1961-64, prof., 1964-74; vis. prof. U. Wis., Madison, 1974-76; research scientist Campbell Inst. Agrl. Research, Napoleon, Ohio, 1976-81, in charge mushroom research lab., 1976-81; asso. dir. mushroom research Campbell Inst. for Research and Tech., Napoleon, 1981—; vis. fellow Nat. Acad. Sci. and Asian Found., U.S., 1967, 68; div. chmn., tech. com. on plant protection Ministry of Econ. Affairs, Republic of China, 1969-72; chair of research prof. Nat. Sci. Council, Republic of China, 1965-71; Leverhulme vis. fellow U. Adelaide (Australia), 1972. Mem. Am. Phytopathol. Soc., Am. Soc. Plant Physiologists, Mycol. Soc. Am., Plant Protection Soc. Republic of China (pres. 1972-73), Chinese Soc. Microbiology. Buddhist. Author books including: Introductory Plant Pathology, 1963; Mushrooms, 1972; Fungal Protein, 1975. Home: 1055 Clairmont Ave Napoleon OH 43545 Office: Campbell Inst for Research and Technology Napoleon OH 43545

WU, TAI TE, educator; b. Aug. 2, 1935; M.B., B.S., U. Hong Kong, 1956; B.S. in Mech. Engring., U. Ill., Urbana, 1958; M.S. in Applied Physics, Harvard, 1959, Ph.D. in Engring. (Gordon McKay fellow) 1961; m. Anna Fang. Research fellow in structural mechanics Harvard, 1961-63, research fellow in biol. chemistry Med. Sch., 1964, research asso., 1965-66; research scientist Hydronautics, Inc., Rockville, Md., 1962; asst. prof. engring. Brown U., Providence, 1963-65; asst. prof. biomath. Grad. Sch. Med. Scis., Cornell U. Med. Coll., N.Y.C., 1967-68, asso. prof., 1968-70; asso. prof. physics and engring. scis. Northwestern U., Evanston, Ill., 1970-73, chmn. com. on biophysics, 1972-80, acting chmn. dept. engring. scis., 1973, prof. physics and engring. scis., 1973-74, prof. biochemistry and molecular and cell biology and engring. scis. and applied math., 1974—. Mem. AAAS, Am. Phys. Soc., Am. Soc. Biol. Chemists, Soc. Microbiology, Biophys. Soc., Chgo. Assn. Immunology, N.Y. Acad. Scis., Soc. Indsl. and Applied Math., Sigma Xi, Tau Beta Pi, Pi Mu Epsilon. Recipient Progress award Chinese Engrs. and Scientists Assn. So. Calif., Los Angeles, 1971, Research Career Devel. award USPHS, NIH, 1974-79; C.T. Loo scholar China Inst., N.Y.C., 1959-60; Author: (with E.A. Kabat and H. Bilofsky) Variable Regions of Immunoglobulin Chains, 1976; Sequences of Immunoglobulin Chains, 1979; contbr. articles to profl. jours. Office: Dept Biochemistry and Molecular and Cell Biology Northwestern U Evanston IL 60201

WUERGER, WILLIAM WILFRED, mech. engr.; b. Green Bay, Wis., Apr. 5, 1934; s. Raymond Julius and Hazel Leona (Clark) W.; B.S., U. Wis., Madison, 1957, M.S., 1961; m. Mardelle June Kerkman, Aug. 11, 1956; children—William Wilfred II, Todd R., David S. Evaluation engr. Mpls. Honeywell Corp., 1957; asso. engr. Midwestern Univs. Research Assn., Madison, part-time 1960-61; instr., asst. prof., asso. prof. dept. engring. U. Wis., U. Wis.-Extension, Madison, 1961-79, prof., 1979—, chmn. dept., 1979-80, program dir., 1961—; cons. in field, 1961—. Served with USAF, 1957-60. Recipient Disting. Service award U. Wis.-Extension, 1981; registered profl. engr., Wis. Mem. Nat. Soc. Profl. Engrs., Wis. Soc. Profl. Engrs. (Young Engr. of Yr. award Milw. chpt. 1969, Profl. Engr. in Edn. award 1977, Engr. of Yr. award S.W. chpt. 1981), Am. Soc. Engring. Edn. (treas. continuing profl. devel. div. 1980-81). Editor: (monograph) Continuing Engineering Studies, 1975. Home: 402 Ozark Trail Madison WI 53705 Office: Dept Engring U Wis-Extension 432 N Lake St Madison WI 53706

WUESCHNER, SILVANO ALFONS, educator; b. Fischbach, W. Ger., Sept. 2, 1950; s. Alfons and Caroline (Weber) W.; B.A., Pepperdine U., 1977, M.A. in Human Resource Mgmt., 1979; m. F. Eleanor Mahaffey, Sept. 3, 1971; children—Edward Andrew, Erika Gretchen. Came to U.S., 1961, naturalized, 1966. Instr. psychology, mgmt. Los Angeles Met. Coll., 1979-80; instr. mgmt. devel. Rockwell Internat., Cedar Rapids, Iowa, 1981; mgmt. cons. S.E. Iowa Mgmt. Consultants, Ottumwa, 1981—; mgmt. cons. Ivano Shokai, Ltd., Okinawa, Japan, 1980; guest lectr. philosophy dept. U. Ryukus, Okinawa, 1980; behavioral cons. Tamaki Mental Hosp., Ginowan City, Okinawa, Japan, 1980. Served with USMC, 1971-80. Mem. Am. Mgmt. Assn., Am. Soc. Tng. and Devel., Am. Legion. Home: Rural Route 2 Box 258 Ottumwa IA 52501 Office: SE Iowa Mgmt Consultants Rural Route 2 Ottumwa IA 52501

WULF, GEORGE RICHARD, geologist, oil co. exec.; b. Clinton, Iowa, May 6, 1930; s. Richard Lyle and Bernice Margaret (Thomsen) W.; B.S., S.D. Sch. Mines, 1951, M.S., 1955; Ph.D., U. Mich., 1959, LL.B., 1964; m. Janis Marie Burrows, June 3, 1955; 1 dau., Jennifer. Geophysicist, Mobil Oil Co., Tripoli, Libya, 1955-63; sr. operating geologist Amoco, Casper, Wyo., 1963-64; cons. geologist, Casper, 1964-74; pres., chmn. bd. Wulf Oil Corp., Chadron, Nebr., 1974—; chmn. bd. Bordeaux Petroleum Co., 1979—, 1st Nat. Bank, 1979—, Chadron Energy Corp., 1979—. Served with M.I., U.S. Army, 1952-54. Mobil Oil scholar, 1954; U. Mich. research fellow, 1957-59. Certified profl. geologist. Fellow Geol. Soc. Am.; mem. Am. Assn. Petroleum Geologists, AAAS, Soc. Econ. Paleontologists and Mineralogists, Sigma Xi, Sigma Tau. Democrat. Lutheran. Clubs: Rotary, Elk. Editor Wyo. Geol. Soc. Guidebook, 1968. Contbr. articles on petroleum geology, stratigraphy to profl. publs. Home: 475 Cedar St Chadron NE 69337 Office: PO Box 946 Chadron NE 69337

WULFECK, JAMES ANDREW, JR., ednl. adminstr.; b. Covington, Ky., Nov. 8, 1946; s. James Andrew and Della Mae (Testerman) W.; B.E.S., Thomas More Coll., 1975; postgrad. Xavier U., 1976-77; m. Kathleen Kordenbrock, Oct. 16, 1971; children—Christopher, Daniel. Sales promotion and tng. mgr. Merrell-Nat. Labs., Cin., 1973-76; coporate tng. officer Richardson-Merrell, Inc., Wilton, Conn., 1976-77; exec. v.p. Instructional Techniques Ltd., Manhasset, N.Y., 1977-78; pres. GMP Inst., Cin., 1979—; dir. Rocket Supply, Cin., J. A. Fay & Egan Co., Cin., Coll. and high sch. basketball and football referee. Served with U.S. Army, 1970-71. Mem. Nat. Assn. Sports Ofcls., Am. Soc. Tng. and Devel., Am. Soc. Quality Control. Republican. Roman Catholic. Office: 3823 Pacific Ave Cincinnati OH 45212

WUNDER, DAVID HART, govt. ofcl.; b. Argo, Ill., Dec. 6, 1925; s. Mylton Bowerman and Marion Antoinette (Richcreek) W.; grad. Wabash Coll., 1950; J.D., Chgo. Kent Coll. Law, 1962; m. Mary Ann Koestner, May 9, 1980; children—Rebecca Anne Wunder Thomson, David Hart, Theodore Joseph. Sales rep. Edward Hines Lumber Co., Chgo., 1950-54; sec.-treas. M. Wunder Homes, Inc., Oak Lawn, Ill., 1954-63; enforcement atty., mgr. Chgo. office securities dept. Office of Sec. of State Ill., 1963-72; securities commr. State of Ill., Springfield, 1972—; lectr.; admitted to Ill. bar, 1963. Served with U.S. Army, 1944-46. Recipient various decorations. Mem. Am. Bar Assn., Ill. State Bar (corp. and securities council, chmn. 1978-79), Chgo. Bar Assn., N.Am. Securities Adminstrs. Assn. (pres. 1981-82), Midwest Securities Commrs. Assn. (pres. 1977-78), Central Securities Adminstrs. Council (chmn. 1978-79), SAR, Soc. Mayflower Descs., Am. Legion (dist. comdr. 1971-72), Delta Tau Delta, Delta Theta Phi. Methodist. Office: 151 Bruns Ln Suite 102 Springfield IL 62702

WUNDER, GENE CARROLL, educator, bus. cons.; b. Waterloo, Iowa, Feb. 11, 1939; s. Lloyd Carl and Alice Marie (Reed) W.; B.B.A., U. Iowa, 1969; M.B.A., U. Mo., 1971; postgrad. U. Mo., 1972-75, U. Ark., 1977—; student U. Mo. Sch. Law, Columbia, 1968-70; m. Judy Kay Stone, Dec. 16, 1966; children—Lara Anne, Sara Elizabeth. Agt., Security Mut. Life, 1964-69; mgmt. trainee State Farm Mut. Ins., 1969-71; instr. bus. adminstrn. N.E. Mo. State U., Kirksville, 1972-75, asst. prof. bus. adminstrn., 1976—; cons. in field. Chmn. supervisory com. N.E. Mo. Credit Union, 1976—. Recipient Alpha Kappa Psi Outstanding Alumni award, 1968. Mem. S.W. Fin. Assn., Midwest Fin. Assn., Am. Mktg. Assn., Midwest Mktg. Assn., So. Mktg. Assn., Southwestern Mktg. Assn., Am. Risk Mgmt. Assn., So. Regional Bus. Law Assn., AAUP, Alpha Kappa Psi, Phi Alpha Delta, Phi Delta Kappa. Republican. Methodist. Clubs: Masons (32 deg.), Shriners, Kiwanis, Pachyderms. Contbr. articles to profl. jours. Home: 908 Fairview Dr Kirksville MO 63501 Office: 152 Violette Hall NE Mo State Univ Kirksville MO 63501

WUNDERLICH, PAUL HAROLD, hosp. adminstr.; b. Winfield, Kans., Jan. 5, 1941; s. Lorenz and Mildred (Heger) W.; B.A., Valparaiso U., 1962; M.H.A., Washington U., St. Louis, 1967; m. Sharon Marion Dragschutz, Dec. 29, 1962; children—Jeffrey, Todd. Adminstrv. asst. St. Louis Lutheran Hosp., 1967-69, dir. profl. services, 1969-73; asso. adminstr. St. Lukes Hosp., St. Louis, 1973-74, pres., chief exec. officer, 1974—. Mem. St. Matthews Luth. Ch. Sch. Bd., 1967-69; mem. adv. bd. and corp. assembly St. Louis Blue Cross, 1975—. Served to capt. USMC, 1962-65. Fellow Am. Coll. Hosp. Adminstrs.; mem. Am. Hosp. Assn., Mo. Hosp. Assn. (dir.), Hosp. Assn. Met. St. Louis (dir., mem. bd. exec. com.), Greater St. Louis Health Systems Agy., Am. Legion. Clubs: University, Forest Hills Country (St. Louis). Home: 227 Pennington Ln Chesterfield MO 63017 Office: 5535 Delmar Blvd Saint Louis MO 63112 also 232 S Woods Mill Rd Chesterfield MO 63017

WUOTILA, NORMAN EMERSON, engine components mfg. co. exec.; b. Spokane, Wash., Sept. 15, 1926; s. John Nels and Roberta (Eckley) W.; student U. Wis., 1950-51, bus. adminstrn. and mech. engrng. Purdue U., 1960-65, cost accounting Butler U., 1963; children—Pamela, Patricia. Gen. mgr. Jeffboat, Inc., Jeffersonville, Ind., 1965-68; asst. plant mgr. Erbrich Products, Inc., Indpls., 1968-69; plants engr. Stark-Wetzel, Inc., Indpls., 1969-70; plant mgr. FRP, Inc., Indpls., 1970; plant mgr. Schwitzer div. Wallace-Murray Corp., Elwood, Ind., 1970—. Served with USN, 1944-52. Mem. Soc. Plastic Engrs., Soc. Design Engrs., Ethyl Corp., VFW. Home: 703 Elmwood Circle Noblesville IN 46060 Office: 926 N 9th St Elwood IN 46036

WURTZEL, GEORGE MICHAEL, woodworking co. exec.; b. Saginaw, Mich., June 13, 1954; s. Fred A. and Helen M. (Kratz) W.; student Northwestern Mich. Coll., 1973-74, Grand Valley State Coll., 1974-75; m. Kathleen M. Emig, June 23, 1979. Mechanic, Volkswagen Co., Lansing, Mich., summer 1972; tchr. conversational English schs. Japan, summer 1973; bicycle mechanic Brick Wheels Co., Traverse City, Mich., 1974; bicycle mechanic, ski technician, 1974-75; pres. Wurtzel Woodworking Inc., Traverse City, 1976—. Bd. dirs. Ski for Light, chmn. Internat. Ski for Light, Traverse City, 1980; capt., participant U.S. Disabled Olympic Nordic Team, 1980. Office: 215 E 15th St Traverse City MI 49684

WYATT, ROBERT CHRISTOPHER, sociologist, internat. business exec.; b. Shenandoah, Iowa, Oct. 24, 1944; s. Harold R. and Dorothy (Christopher) W.; student Asbury Coll, 1962-64; B.A., Baylor U., 1966, M.A., 1967; postgrad. St. Paul Sch. Theology, 1975-76; Ph.D., U. Tex., 1976; m. Ann Cherie Edwards, May 15, 1971; 1 son, Edwards Clarke. Research coordinator Action Planning Council, Waco, Tex., 1966; instr. in sociology S.W. Tex. State U., 1967-71; dir. social sci. program East Tex. State U., 1973-75. chmn. dept. sociology Howard Payne U., 1975-77; sr. social systems analyst Midwest Research Inst., Kansas City, Mo., 1977—; pres., chief operating officer Greater Kansas City Fgn.-Trade Zone, Inc., 1981—; adj. prof. U. Mo., Kansas City; mentor Avila Coll. Women's Leadership Inst.; univ. asso. U. Mo., Kansas City; hon. dir. Rockhurst Coll.; dir. Wildwood, Inc. Mem. adv. council Mo. Methodist Found.; lay leader Central United Meth. Ch.; mem. bd. ch. and soc. Mo. W. conf. United Meth. Ch.; chmn. bd. dirs. REACH, Inc., Texarkana, Tex. and Ark., 1973-75. Named Outstanding Tchr., East Tex. State U., 1974; Named to Outstanding Young Men Am., U.S. Jaycees, 1977; NSF grantee, 1978. Mem. Am. Sociol. Assn., Midwest Sociol. Assn., Southwestern Sociol. Assn., S.W. Social Sci. Assn., Internat. Relations Council, Internat. Trade Club. Author: Alternative Futures for Kansas City, 1977; Postsecondary Education Needs in Kansas City, 1978; Decision Oriented Recreation User Information System, 1978; Park College Resource and Market Assessment, 1979; asso. editor Community News Letter; author Mo. Neighborhood Betterment, 1978. Home: 11404 E 69th St Raytown MO 64133 Office: 425 Volker Blvd Kansas City MO 64110

WYATT, ROSEMARY BARBARA SLONE, tax cons.; b. Chgo., Feb. 9, 1927; d. Ben Leo and Martha Dorothea (Bednarski) Slone; student De Paul U., 1949-51; m. J. Frank Wyatt, Jr., Dec. 21, 1951; children—Martha Lee, James Frank III. With F & R Tax Service, Inc., Barrington, Ill., 1973—; v.p., 1976—. Republican committeewoman Barrington Twp., 1962—; pres. Barrington Twp. Rep. Women's Orgn., 1965-68; mem. Rep. candidates' screening com. Second Legis. Dist., 1971, Barrington Twp., 1977; sec. Suburban Committeewomen's Orgn. Cook County, 1974—; bd. dirs. Barrington Twp. Rep. Orgn., 1974—; del. Ill. Rep. Conv., 1972, 76; pres. Episcopal Churchwomen of St. Michael's Episcopal Ch., 1962-64; vetryman St. Michael's Episcopal Ch., 1967-69, treas., 1970—; pres. PTA, Grove Ave Sch., Barrington, 1965-66; Village of Barrington rep. on adminstrv. com. Barrington Area Council Govts., 1972; campaign dir. various elections village trustees and sch. bd. candidates, Barrington, 1963, 67, 71, 75. Home: 625 Concord Pl Barrington IL 60010 Office: 200 Applebee St Barrington IL 60010

WYCISLO, ALOYSIUS JOHN, clergyman; b. Chgo., June 17, 1908; s. Simon Charles and Victoria (Czech) W.; M.A., St. Mary of Lake Sem., Mundelein, Ill., 1933; postgrad. Cath. U. Am., 1939-42. Ordained priest Roman Cath. Ch., 1934; asst. pastor St. Michael's Ch., Chgo., 1934-39; asst. archdiocesan supr. Cath. Charities Chgo., 1939-42; field dir. Cath. Relief Services, Nat. Cath. Welfare Conf., Middle East, India and Africa, 1943-45, supr. resettlement activities for displaced persons, Paris, 1945-47; organizer civilian relief programs Am. Cath. Hierarchy, 1947-48; asst. exec. dir. N.Y. hdqrs. Cath. Relief Services, 1948-49, dir. resettlement programs Europe, Far and Middle East, supr. program in U.S., 1950-59; pastor Immaculate Heart of Mary Ch., Chgo., 1959-68; aux. bishop of Chgo., 1960-68; bishop of Green Bay (Wis.), 1968—; Vatican rep. to UN, 1954-56; mem. Archdiocesan Conservation Council, 1959—, Archdiocesan Bd. Consultors, 1960—; archdiocesan moderator Cath. League Religious Assistance to Poland, 1960—; dir. Chgo. Observance Poland's Millennium of Christianity, 1962; mem. Am. Commns. Lay Apostolate, Missions and Oriental Ch., II Vatican Council, 1962—; chmn. Liturgical Commn., Archdiocese of Chgo., 1964—. Adv. bd. Alexian Bros. Hosp.; bd. dirs. Nat. Conf. Cath. Charities. Named papal chamberlain, 1953, domestic prelate, 1959, knight chaplain Order of Malta, knight Holy Sepulchre; named canon of Primatial Cathedral of Gniezno, Poland, 1960; Man of Yr. Polish Daily News, Chgo., 1964; also numerous fgn. decorations. Address: 1910 S Webster St PO Box 66 Green Bay WI 54305*

WYLIE, CHALMERS PANGBURN, congressman; b. Norwich, Ohio, Nov. 23, 1920; s. Chalmer C. and Margaret (Pangburn) W.; student Otterbein Coll., 1939-40, Ohio State U., 1940-43; LL.B., Harvard, 1948; m. Marjorie Ann Siebold, Sept. 19, 1964; children—Jacquelyn, Bradley. Admitted to Ohio bar, 1948; asst. atty. gen. State of Ohio, 1948; asst. atty. City of Columbus (Ohio), 1949-50, city atty., 1953-57; adminstr. Ohio Bur. Workmen's Compensation, 1957; 1st asst. to gov. Ohio, 1957-58; formerly partner firm Gingher & Christensen, Columbus; mem. Ohio Ho. of Reps., 1961-67; mem. 90th to 97th congresses from 15th Ohio Dist. Past trustee Blue Cross Central Ohio, Inc. Served from pvt. to 1st lt. AUS, World War II. Decorated Silver Star, Bronze Star, Purple Heart, Croix de Guerre (France), Belgian Fouragier. Named One of 10 Men of Year, Columbus Citizen Jour., One of 5 Outstanding Young Men of Ohio, Nat. Jr. C. of C.; recipient Distinguished Service award Columbus Jr. C. of C., 1955. Mem. Ohio, Columbus bar assns., Am. Legion. Republican. Methodist (past trustee). Mason (33 deg.), Kiwanian. Home: 1019 Spring Grove Ln Columbus OH 43085 Office: House of Reps Washington DC 20515

WYLLIE, PETER JOHN, geologist, educator; b. London, Feb. 8, 1930; s. George William and Beatrice Gladys (Weaver) W.; came to U.S., 1961; B.Sc. in Geology and Physics, U. St. Andrews, Scotland, 1952, B.Sc. with 1st class honours in Geology, 1955, Ph.D. in Geology, 1958, D.Sc. (hon.), 1974; m. Frances Rosemary Blair, June 9, 1956; children—Andrew, Elizabeth (dec.), Lisa, John. Glaciologist, Brit. W. Greenland Expdn., 1950, geologist Brit. N. Greenland Expdn., 1952-54; asst. lectr. geology U. St. Andrews, 1955-56; research asst. geochemistry Pa. State U., State College, 1956-58, asst. prof. geochemistry, 1958-59, asso. prof. petrology, 1961-65, acting head, dept. geochemistry mineralogy, 1962-63; research fellow chemistry Leeds (Eng.) U., 1959-60, lectr. exptl. petrology, 1960-61; prof. petrology geochemistry U. Chgo., 1965-77, Homer J. Livingston prof., 1978—, chmn. dept. geophys. scis., 1979—, master phys. scis. collegiate div., asso. dean coll., asso. dean phys. scis. div., 1972-73; chmn. commn. exptl. petrology high pressures temperatures Internat. Union Geol. Scis.; mem. adv. panel earth scis. NSF, 1975-78, chmn. adv. com. earth scis. div., 1979—; mem. U.S. Nat. Com. on Geology, 1978—, U.S. Nat. Com. for Geochemistry, 1981—; mem. U.S. nat. com. Internat. Union Geodesy and Geophysics, 1980—. Served with RAF, 1948-49. Recipient Polar medal H.M. Queen Elizabeth, Eng.; Quantrell award for excellence in undergrad. teaching, 1979. Mem. Mineral. Soc. Am. (award 1965, pres. 1977-78), Internat. Mineral. Assn. (2d v.p. 1978-82), Am. Geophys. Union, Assn. Earth Sci. Editors, Nat. Acad. Scis. (fgn. asso.), Assn. Geoscientists for Internat. Devel., Geol. Soc. Am., Mineral. Soc. (London). Club: Arctic. Author: The Dynamic Earth, 1971; The Way the Earth Works, 1976; editor and contbr.: Ultramafic and Related Rocks, 1967; editor Jour. Geology, 1967—, Series in Intermediate Geology, 1978—; editor-in-chief Minerals Rocks (monograph series), 1967—; contbr. numerous articles to profl. jours. Office: Univ Chicago 5734 S Ellis Ave Chicago IL 60637

WYMAN, PAUL BARTRAM, lawyer; b. Three Rivers, Mich., Oct. 8, 1913; s. Charles Bartram and Bertha (Gesaman) W.; student Kalamazoo Coll., 1932-35; LL.B., Duke U., 1938; m. Louise Cabell Warren, June 10, 1940; children—Warren Bartram, Michael Louis. Admitted to Colo. bar, 1939, Mich. bar, 1943; gen. law practice in Colo., 1939-42; pros. atty, Kalkaska County, Mich., 1943-55; spl. asst. atty. gen. Mich., 1950; asst. pros. atty. Wexford County, Mich., 1955-57, spl. pros. atty., 1962; city atty., City of Cadillac (Mich.), 1959-64; friend of ct. 28th Jud. Circuit of Mich., 1948-81. Pres., Kalkaska Sch. Bd., 1943-46; exec. bd. Scenic Trails council Boy Scouts Am.; bd. dirs. Cadillac Housing Comm., 1978—. Mem. Am., Mich., Wexford-Missankee (past pres.) bar assns., Am. Judicature Soc., Am. Rifle Assn., Mich. Assn. Professions, Mich. Friends of Ct. Assn. (exec. bd. 1977—), Nat. Reciprocal and Family Support Enforcement Assn., Mich. Friends of Ct. Assn. (exec. bd. 1977-80). Clubs: Rotary (pres. 1958-59), Cadillac, Caberfce Ski, Masons (32 deg.). Contbr. articles to profl. publs. Home: 426 Crippen St Cadillac MI 49601

WYNDEWICKE, KIONNE ANNETTE, educator; b. Preston, Miss.; d. Clifton Thomas and Missouria (Jackson) Johnson; student Columbia Coll., Chgo., 1972; B.S., Ill. State Normal U., 1961; postgrad. Williams Coll., Williamstown, Mass., 1972; m. Eugene C. Moorer, Sept. 23, 1961 (div.). Social worker Cook County Dept. Pub. Aid, 1961; tchr. reading Chgo. Bd. Edn., 1961—; asst. to news dir. WCIU-TV, 1972-74; asst. women's editor Chgo. Defender, 1970-72; social sec. Dr. William R. Clarke, 1972—; part-time photog. model, fashion commentator, pub. relations cons., pub. speaker. Co-chmn. installation Profl. Womens Aux., Provident Hosp., 1961, corr. sec., 1969, publicity chmn., 1969-72, 74-77. Selected one of 13 persons in U.S. to attend Innovative Tchr. Tng. Seminar, funded by Henry Luce Found. at Williams Coll., 1972; one of 25 Black women of Chgo. to receive Kizzy award, 1977; recipient Outstanding Community Service award Beatrice Caffrey Youth Service, Inc., 1978. Mem. Ill. Theatre and Speech Assn., WTTW Channel 11 Ednl. TV, Mus. Contemporary Art, Speech Communication Assn. Am., YWCA. Lutheran. Contbr. articles to local newspapers. Home: 533 E 33d Pl Apt 1100 Chicago IL 60616 Office: 707 E 37th St Chicago IL 60653

WYNN, GEORGE ALLAN, orgn. devel. specialist; b. Youngstown, Ohio, Sept. 9, 1945; s. Rudolph George and Marian Eleanor (Repko) W.; student U. Calif., Berkeley, 1963-65, U.S. Mil. Acad., 1965-66; B.S., Ohio State U., 1970, M.A., 1974, Ph.D., 1980; m. Helen Jeanette McGhee-Wynn, Sept. 12, 1970. Instr. drafting and math. Columbus (Ohio) Tech. Coll., 1966-68, asst. to v.p., 1968-73; research asso., program asst. Center for Vocat. Edn., Ohio State U., Columbus, 1973-77; exec. dir. Community Organizational Vocat. Ednl. Devel. Group, Columbus, 1977—; asso. dir. Sch. Studies Council of Ohio, Columbus, 1977-79; sr. ednl. devel. specialist, tng. and curriculum expert Appalachia Ednl. Labs., Charleston, W.Va., 1977; field site dir. Westat Research, U.S. Dept. Labor, 1979; tng. dir. Inst. Effective Integrated Edn., 1980-81; mgr. tng. and devel. R.G. Barry Corp., 1981—. Mem. Am. Ednl. Research Assn., Am. Personnel and Guidance Assn., Am. Coll. Personnel Assn., Nat. Soc. for Performance Instrn., Orgn. Devel. Inst. (chmn. public relations), Porsche Club Am. (pres. Mid-Ohio region), Phi Delta Kappa (exec. com.). Designer, developer orgn. devel. strategies. Home: 2315 Woodbrook Circle N Suite B Columbus OH 43223 Office: 13405 Yarmouth Rd NW Pickerington OH 43147

WYSLOTSKYI, IHOR, engrng. co. exec.; b. Kralovane, Czechoslovakia, Dec. 22, 1930; s. Ivan and Nadia (Alexiew) W.; came to U.S., 1958, naturalized, 1961; M.E., Sch. Aeros., Buenos Aires, Argentina, 1955; m. Maria Czechut, Nov. 22, 1958; children—Katria, Bohdan. Design engr. Kaiser Industries, Buenos Aires, 1955-58; cons. design engr., Newark, 1959-64; chief engr. Universal Tool Co., Chgo., 1964-69; pres. CBC Devel Co., Inc., Chgo., 1969-74; pres. TEC, Inc., Chgo., 1972—; engrng. adviser to bd. Biosystems Assos., Inc., La Jolla, Calif. Chmn. Ukrainian studies com. U. Ill. Mem. Packaging Inst. U.S., Modern Plastics Inst. (mgmt. adv. panel), Am.-Israeli C. of C., Brit. Engrng. Assn. Plate River, Soc. Mfg. Engrs. Clubs: Burnham Harbor Yacht, Michigan City Yacht. Patentee in field. Home: 18630 Golfview Dr Hazel Crest IL 60429 Office: 5328 W 123d Pl Alsip IL 60658

WYSNER, JOHN WILLIAM, tng., communications and human resource devel. co. exec.; b. Highland Park, Mich., Apr. 29, 1945; s. Raymond and Evelyn Julia (Maison) W.; B.A. in Psychology, Wayne State U., 1968; m. Shirley Ann Worth, Mar. 15, 1975; children—Dana Lynn, Kerry Leigh, Catherine Lane. Asso. engr. human factors Chrysler Def. Engring., Centerline, Mich., 1967-69; tng. specialist Bendix Corp., Detroit, 1969-72; supr. customer tng. and publs. Pegasus div. Koehring Co., Troy, Mich., 1972-75; dir. Sandy Corp., Southfield, Mich. Youth athletic dir. YMCA, 1968-70. Recipient award Profl. Service Council, 1980, others. Mem. Soc. Tech. Communications, Am. Mgmt. Assn., Am. Soc. Tng. and Devel., Assn. Supervision and Curriculum Devel., Am. Film Inst., Nat. Assn. Service Mgrs. Roman Catholic. Clubs: Rotary, Kiwanis. Home: 24645 Walden Rd E Southfield MI 48034 Office: 16025 Northland Dr Southfield MI 48075

WYTRWAL, JOSEPH ANTHONY, sch. adminstr.; b. Detroit, Oct. 24, 1924; s. Joseph and Nellie (Kadlof) W.; Ph.B., U. Detroit, 1949, M.Ed., 1950; M.Ed. (Beta Sigma Phi fellow), Wayne State U., 1954, B.A., 1957; M.A., U. Mich., 1955, Ph.D., 1958. Tchr., Cleveland Jr. High Sch., Detroit, 1952-54, Eastern High Sch., Detroit, 1954-60; tchr. Chadsey High Sch., Detroit, 1960-63, counselor, 1963-70, prin. evening sch., 1968-70; asst. prin. Mumford Sr. High Sch., Detroit, 1970-73; prin. Wilson Jr. High Sch., Detroit, 1973—; mem. faculties U. Detroit, 1956-59, Wayne State U., 1959-62; dir. Southeastern Mich. Regional Ethnic Heritage Studies Center, 1968-75; coordinator Wayne County Community Coll., 1968-70; columnist Polish Daily News, English edit., 1974—. Mem. citizens' adv. com. selection gen. supt. Detroit Pub. Schs., 1970; commr. Detroit Commn. on Community Relations, 1969-74; v.p. Polish Am. Congress, 1969-72, recipient certificate of Achievement Mich. div., 1971. Precinct del. 16th Democratic Dist. Orgn., 1971, 80. Served with USNR, 1943-46. Recipient Coe Fellowship award U. Wyo., 1958. Mem. Polish Nat. Alliance, Polish Roman Catholic Union, Assn. Sons of Poland, Polish Falcons, Polish Black Conf. (exec. v.p. 1971-72), Alliance Poles in Am., Polish Hungarian World Fedn., Smithsonian Instn., Schoolmen's Club, Polish Am. Hist. Assn., Phi Delta Kappa, Delta Tau Kappa. Author: America's Polish Heritage (Am. Heritage award), 1961; Poles in American History and Tradition, (Am. Heritage award), 1969; Poles in America, 1969; Behold! The Polish Americans, 1977; Polish/Black Encounters. A History of Polish and Black Relations in America since 1619, 1982; editor-pub. Endurance Press, 1962—; asst. editor Polish American Studies, 1959-62. Home: 5695 Lumley St Detroit MI 48210 Office: 7735 Lane Detroit MI 48209

XAVIER, RAYMOND ARTHUR, oil co. exec.; b. Cleve., May 12, 1926; s. Arthur J. and Ruby P. (Ainslie) X.; B.S., Case-Western Res. U., 1953, M.S., 1962; m. Mary Jane McGann, Aug. 3, 1974; children-Dennis, Donald, Dale, Barbara, Ronald, Richard, Ruth, Robert. Sr. chemist Cleve. Indsl. Research, Euclid, Ohio, 1953-75; sr. chemist Penreco, Cleve., 1975-78; dir. research Transcentral Oil Corp., Chgo., 1978-79; dir. research Westville (Ind.) Oil Co. div. Cam-Or, Inc., 1979—; instr. Cuyahoga Community Coll., 1976-77. Served with AUS, 1944-46. Mem. Am. Chem. Soc., Chgo. Chemists Club, ASTM, Am. Soc. Lubricating Engrs., Am. Soc. Metals, Am. Legion (past post and dist. comdr., Legion Man of Yr. 1964-65), 40 and 8. Club: Masons.

YACOBI, AVRAHAM, pharmacologist; b. Ghasre-Shirin, Iran, Nov. 3, 1945; came to U.S., 1971, naturalized, 1977; m. Yacov and Fahima (Attarzadeh) Y.; M.Pharm. summa cum laude, Hebrew U. Jerusalem, 1970; Ph.D., SUNY, Buffalo, 1975; m. Diana Buckler; children—Oran, Lily-Yonat. Teaching asst. dept. dermatology Hadassah Hosp., Jerusalem, 1969-71; research asso. SUNY, Buffalo, 1975-76; asso. dir. clin. pharmacology, research and med. affairs Am. Critical Care, McGaw Park, Ill., 1976-78, sect. head clin. pharmacology and drug metabolism, 1978—; lectr. Northwestern U., 1978—. Mem. Am. Soc. Clin. Pharmacology and Therapeutics, Am. Pharm. Assn., Ill. Pharm. Assn., Acad. Pharm. Scis., Am. Soc. Pharmacology and Exptl. Therapeutics, Sigma Xi. Jewish. Contbr. numerous articles to profl. jours. Home: 1440 Hazel Ave Deerfield IL 60015 Office: 1600 Waukegan Rd McGaw Park IL 60085

YAGER, JOHN WARREN, lawyer, banker; b. Toledo, Sept. 16, 1920; s. Joseph A. and Edna Gertrude (Pratt) Y.; A.B., U. Mich., 1942, J.D., 1948; m. Dorothy W. Merki, July 25, 1942; children—Julie M., John M. Admitted to Ohio bar, 1948; practiced in Toledo, 1948-64; trust officer Toledo Trust Co., 1964-69; v.p., trust officer, sec. First Nat. Bank, Toledo, 1969—, First Ohio Bancshares, Inc., 1980—. Pres. Toledo Met. Park Dist., 1971—, Neighborhood Health Assn., 1974-75. Councilman, Toledo, 1955-57, 60-61, mayor, 1958-59. Bd. dirs. Toledo-Lucas County Library, 1968-70; past pres. Toledo Legal Aid Soc., Toledo Council Chs., Toledo Municipal League, Econ. Opportunity Planning Assn., Toledo, Com. on Relations with Toledo, Spain. Served to maj. USMC, 1942-46, 50-52. Decorated Bronze Star; named one of 10 outstanding young men, Toledo, 1952, 54, 55. Mem. Ohio, Toledo bar assns., Toledo Estate Planning Council, Toledo Jr. C. of C. (past pres.), Downtown Toledo Assos. (past treas.), Delta Tau Delta. Clubs: Toledo, Belmont Country (Toledo). Home: 4117 Sheraton Rd Toledo OH 43606 Office: First Nat Bank Toledo 606 Madison Ave Toledo OH 43604

YAISH, HASSAN M., pediatric hematologist-oncologist; b. Palestine, Jan. 1, 1937; came to U.S., 1967, naturalized, 1976; s. Murtada S. and Fouziya M. Yaish; B.C.P., Damascus U., 1957, M.D., 1963; m. Nabila Jazairy, June 21, 1966; children—Hala, Dema, Susan, Amjad M., Ayman Danny. House staff officer Augesta Victoria Hosp., Jerusalem, 1962; resident in pediatrics, William Beaumont Hosp., Royal Oak, Mich., 1967-69, resident in hematology, oncology, 1969-71, pediatric hematologist-oncologist, 1971—. Served with Royal Med. Services Jordanian Army, 1963-67. Diplomate Am. Bd. Pediatrics, also Sub-Bd. Pediatric Hematology-Oncology. Mem. Am. Acad. Peditrics, Am. Soc. Hematology, AMA, Am. Soc. Pediatric Hematology-Oncology, Mich. Med. Soc. Contbr. articles to profl. jours. Home: 7301 Mohansic Birmingham MI 48010 Office: William Beaumont Hospital Royal Oak MI 48072

YALOWITZ, JEROME MYER, clin. psychologist; b. Chgo., Oct. 24, 1922; s. Joseph and Mary (Shure) Y.; B.S., U. Ill., 1948, M.S., 1949; divorced; children—Rhoda L., Kenneth G., Jean B. Clin. psychologist Manteno (Ill.) State Hosp., 1949-51; chief psychologist E. Moline (Ill.) State Hosp., 1952-54, Peoria (Ill.) State Hosp., 1954-73; coordinator services for elderly Region 1B, Ill. Dept. Mental Health, also dir. Comprehensive Geriatric Treatment Service, Zeller Mental Health Center, Peoria, 1973—. Served with AUS, 1943-46. Recipient Francis J. Gerty award State of Ill., 1969, 74, 79. Mem. Am. Psychol. Assn., Midwestern Psychol. Assn., Ill. Psychol. Assn. (council 1966-74), Central Ill. Soc. Health Service Providers in Psychology (v.p. 1980-82), Peoria Area Assn. Psychologists (pres. 1956-57, 75-76). Jewish. Editor, Ill. Psychologist, 1966-71. Home: 419 Clybourn Ct Peoria IL 61614 Office: 5407 N University St Peoria IL 61614

YAMAKAWA, ALLAN HITOSHI, ednl. adminstr.; b. San Francisco, Oct. i8, 1938; s. Victor T. and Alice (Sato) Y.; B.S., Roosevelt U., 1962; m. Nancy Ann Habel, Apr. 16, 1977; children—Bryan Allan, David Scott. Exec. dir., dean Britannica Acad. Chgo., 1962-67; dir. curriculum services Newspaper div. Field Enterprises, Chgo., 1967-69; dir. ednl. services Chgo. Tribune Co., 1969-77; dir. tng. services DSI/CCI, N.Y.C., 1977-79; dir. orgn. devel. U. Ill., Chgo. campuses, 1979—; cons. internat. tng.; adj. prof. Govs. State U. Ill., Nat. Coll. Edn., Ill., Pepperdine U., Calif., Eastern Mich. U., Central Mich. U. Instr.-trainer ARC. Mem. Internat. Assn. Human Potential, Am. Soc. Tng. and Devel., Internat. Reading Assn., Nat. Council Social Studies, Soc. Programed and Automated Learning. Club: Toastmasters. Books include: Catalysts for Change, 1970; Population—World in Crisis, 1972; Innovation in Communication, 1974; Survival Teaching, 1974; Stress Management, 1978. Home: 477 Weidner Rd Buffalo Grove IL 60090 Office: Box 4348 706CCC Chicago IL 60680

YANCEY, I(RVING) VICTOR, aero. engr.; b. Boston, Dec. 4, 1927; s. Frederick Howell and Anna (Bosfield) Y.; B.S., Mass. Inst. Tech., 1951; m. Ida Marie Shaw, Nov. 30, 1952 (div. Jan. 31, 1972); children—Gregory Marc, Kim Adele, Allyson Yvonne, Jonathon Victor; m. 2d, Catherine Louise Blake, June 17, 1973. Engr.,

Wright-Patterson AFB, O., 1951-59, aero. engring. mgr., 1964-75, supervisory aero. engr., 1975—; aero. structures devel. engr. Boeing Co., Seattle, 1959-64. Founder, 1st pres. Neighborhood Civic Assn., 1957-59; cub scout leader Miami Valley council Boy Scouts Am., 1958-59, committeeman Chief Seattle council, 1959-63; pres. Music Parents Orgn., 1969-73; pres. bd. trustees Jefferson Regional Water Authority, 1977-80, trustee, 1977—. Served with AUS, 1946-48. Mem. Kappa Alpha Psi. Republican. Episcopalian (vestryman 1961-63, jr. warden 1963, lic. lay reader 1978—). Home: 6592 Farmersville Rd Dayton OH 45418 Office: ASD/TAEF Wright-Patterson AFB OH 45433

YANG WANG, physician; b. Tangshan, China, May 12, 1923; came to U.S., 1949, naturalized, 1954; s. Yu-Shen Wang and Chun-Jung Po; student Yenching U., 1940-41, St. John's U., Shanghai, China, 1942-43; M.B., Nat. Shanghai Med. Coll., 1948; M.D., Harvard U., 1952; m. Helen S. Huang, June 18, 1966; children—Dale, Cynthia, Jennifer, Heather. Resident, Mass. Gen. Hosp., Boston, 1952-57, Paul D. White Cardiology fellow, 1957-58; fellow in physiology Mayo Found., Rochester, Minn., 1958-59; from instr. to prof. medicine, cardiovascular div. U. Minn. Med. Sch., Mpls., 1959—, dir. cardiac catheterization lab., dir. cardiac clinics U. Minn. Hosps.; cons. VA Hosp., Mpls. Served to capt., M.C., USAF, 1954-56. Diplomate Am. Bd. Internal Medicine, Cardiovascular Diseases. Fellow Council on Clin. Cardiology and Council on Circulation of Am. Heart Assn., AAAS, ACP; mem. Assn. Univ. Cardiologists, Central Soc. Clin. Research, Am. Fedn. Clin. Research, Soc. Exptl. Biology in Medicine, Alpha Omega Alpha. Contbr. articles to profl. jours. Office: U Minn Hosp Box 83 Mayo Meml Bldg Minneapolis Mn 55455

YANT, JOHN VIRGIL, retail exec.; b. Minden, Nebr., May 3, 1946; s. Virgil John and Clara Jeanette (Munk) Y.; student Kearney (Nebr.) State Coll., 1966-67, 69-70; grad. Park Bus. Coll., 1966; m. Susan Marie Schwenke, Nov. 30, 1974; children—Brock Jason, Christina Marie. Sales fin. mgr. Dick Hill Ford Co., Kearney, 1970-74, lease mgr., 1972-73; owner, mgr. Yant Motors, Minden, 1975-76; pres. John Yant Ford, Inc., Alma, Nebr., 1976—; chmn. Ford Zone Dealer Council. Lay leader United Meth. Ch., Alma, 1980-81, v.p. Alma United Meth. Men's Group, 1981. Served with AUS, 1967-69; Vietnam. Decorated Purple Heart. Mem. Am. Legion (comdr. 1976), Alma C. of C. (pres. 1979, dir. 1980—), Nat. Auto Dealers Assn., Nebr. New Car and Truck Dealers Assn., V.F.W. Republican. Clubs: Elks, Eagles. Home: 311 N Cumberland St Alma NE 68920 Office: 601 W Main St Alma NE 68920

YANTIS, ETHEL MAY BEATY (MRS. NORVAL K. YANTIS), ednl. adminstr.; b. nr. Howard, Kans., Oct. 1, 1903; d. John S. and Margaret (Patterson) Beaty; B.A., Southwestern Coll., 1959; m. Norval K. Yantis, Apr. 4, 1923; children—John, Sharolyn Kay Yantis Lager. Tchr. elementary schs., Elk County, Kans., 1922-56, supt. schs., 1956-68, dir. sch. dist., dir. fed. projects, 1965-70. Mem. adoption com. Kans. State Reading Circle, 1960-61. Named Kans. Master Tchr., Kans. State Tchrs. COll., 1965. Mem. S.E. Kans. (pres. 1964-67), Kans. . Past (sec.-treas. 1969) county supts. assns., Howard C. of C., N.E.A., Kans. State Tchrs. Assn., Elk County Edn. Assn., P.E.O. (chpt. pres. 1964-66), Delta Kappa Gamma. Republican. Methodist (Sunday Sch. supt. 1940-50). Co-author, editor Elk County History, 1979. Address: 853 Jefferson St Howard KS 67349

YAO, JEFFREY KUOCHING, biochemist; b. China, Sept. 16, 1946; s. Yu-Lun and Lucille (Hsu) Y.; B.Sc., Fu Jen Cath U., Taipei, 1968; Ph.D., U. Detroit, 1972; came to U.S., 1969, naturalized, 1978. Postdoctoral scholar U. Mich., Ann Arbor, 1972-73; research asst. Mayo Clinic, Rochester, Minn., 1973-75, sr. research fellow, 1975-77, asso. cons., 1977—. Mem. Am. Chem. Soc., Am. Oil Chemist Soc., AAAS, Sigma Xi. Contbr. articles to profl. jours. Office: 812 Guggenheim Bldg Mayo Clinic Rochester MN 55901

YAO, JOSEPH HUNG, phys. therapist; b. Hanchu, China, Jan. 8, 1935; s. Stephen C. and Pei-Hsing (Shen) Y.; came to U.S., 1958, naturalized, 1969; B.A., Tamkang Coll., Republic of China, 1955; postgrad. U. Madrid (Spain), 1955-56, U. Barcelona (Spain), 1956-58; B.A., Loras Coll., 1961; certificate phys. therapy U. Iowa Sch. Medicine, 1963; certificate acupuncture China Med. Coll., Republic of China, 1973; m. Jessie Lee Collingsworth, Dec. 26, 1964; children—Dana, David, E. Stephen. Staff phys. therapist Univ. Hosps., Iowa City, 1963-64; chief phys. therapist St. Mary's Hosp., Streator, Ill., 1964-66; dir. phys. therapy dept. St. Therese Hosp., Waukegan, Ill., 1966-70; staff phys. therapy dept. VA Med. Center, North Chicago, Ill., 1970—, dir. phys. therapy dept., 1974—; clin. instr. Northwestern U. Med. Sch., 1975—, Chgo. Med. Coll., 1975—; lectr. on acupuncture to univs., various civic groups; Mem. Am. Phys. Therapy Assn. (ednl. coordinator clin. studies on acupuncture in Peoples Republic of China 1981), Nat. Soc. Crippled Children and Adults, Am. Center Chinese Med. Scis., Acupuncture Research Inst., Am. Acupuncture Assn. Author: The Selected Acupuncture Points, 1972; Acupuncture and T.E.N.S. Techniques, 1978. Home: 808 Paddock Ln Libertyville IL 60048 Office: Phys Therapy Dept VA Med Center North Chicago IL 60064

YAO, TITO GO, physician; b. Manila, May 30, 1943; came to U.S., 1970, naturalized, 1979; s. Vicente and Sin Keng (Go) Y.; M.D., Far Eastern U., Manila, 1969; m. Lilia Ytem, July 3, 1976; 1 son, Robert James. Intern, Evang. Deaconess Hosp., Milw., 1970-71; resident in pediatrics T.C. Thompson Children's Hosp., Chattanooga, 1971-72, Methodist Hosp., Bklyn., 1972-73; fellow St. Christopher Hosp. Children, Phila., 1973-74, Cook County Children's Hosp., Chgo., 1974-75; dir. GSK Med. Center, Chgo., 1976—, RJ Med. Center, Chgo.; mem. staff St. Anne's Loretto and Walther Meml. hosps. Fellow Am. Acad. Pediatrics; mem. AMA (Physician Recognition award 1973—), Assn. Philippine Physicians Practicing in Am., Ill. Med. Assn., Chgo. Med. Soc., Chgo. Pediatric Soc. Office: 5351 W North Ave Chicago IL 60639

YAP, CHONG-BUN, neurologist; b. Amoy, Fukien, China, Apr. 2, 1930; s. Chin-Chay and Ben-Chu (Chua) Y.; came to U.S., 1959, naturalized, 1973; M.D. cum laude, U. Santo Tomas, 1958; m. Le-Kheng Chua; children—Renee Mei, Eric Wei. Intern, Santo Tomas U. Hosp., Manila, Pilippines, 1957-58; resident in neurology U. Louisville Hosp., 1959-62; neurology fellow, Montreal (Que., Can.) Neurol. Inst., 1962-64; instr., Louisville U., 1964-65; asst. prof., Northwestern U., Chgo., 1965-75; chmn. dept. medicine, Henrotin Hosp., 1976-77, pres. med. staff, 1978; dir. EEG dept. Swedish Covenant, Bethesda Hosps. Diplomate Am. Bd. Neurology. Certified Am. Bd. of Qualification in Electroencephalography, Inc. Fellow Am. Acad. Neurology; mem. AMA, Am. Assn. Electromyography and Electrodiagnosis, Am. Epilepsy Soc. Contbr. articles to med. jours. Home: 245 Sheridan Rd Kenilworth IL 60043 Office: 44 Green Bay Rd Winnetka IL 60093

YAP, ENRIQUE TAN, surgeon; b. San Fernando, Philippines, Oct. 9, 1927; s. Intong and Romana Rodriguez (Tan) Y.; A.A., U. Santo Thomas (Manila), 1948, B.S., 1950, M.D., 1953; m. Bette Limestahl, Jan. 27, 1956; children—Elizabeth Ann, Enrique Louis, Mary Leslie. Intern St. Laurence Hosp., Lansing, Mich., 1960-61, resident Maumee Valley Hosp., Toledo, 1955-58, Mo. State Sanitorium, Mt. Vernon, 1958-59, Galesburg (Ill.) Research Hosp., 1960; group practice Hoopeston (Ill.) Med. Center, 1961; practice medicine specializing in surgery, Metropolis, Ill., 1962—; mem. staff Massac Meml. Hosp., Metropolis, pres. med. staff, 1969, 75; mem. staff Western Bapt. Hosp., Lourdes Hosp., Paducah, Ky. Bd. dirs. Massac Mental Health Center, Quadricounty Dept. Pub. Health. Diplomate Am. Bd. Surgery. Fellow A.C.S., Internat. Coll. Surgeons; mem. So. Ill. Surg. Soc., Massac County Med. Soc. (pres. 1968, 79-80), C. of C., Tau Mu Sigma Phi. Republican. Roman Catholic. Elk, Rotarian (v.p. 1968, pres. 1969-70). Club: Metropolis. Home: Rural Route 2 Metropolis IL 62960 Office: 510 W 10th St Metropolis IL 62960

YARGER, WRAY LEROY, sales engr.; b. Massena, Iowa, Oct. 20, 1922; s. Neal Henry and Belva May (Hawks) Y.; B.S., Iowa State U., 1949; m. Helen Ruth Way, Sept. 7, 1940; children—Carolyn Kay, Janet Rae, Diane Lee, Julie Ann. Elec. supr. aircraft plant Glenn L. Martin-Nebr. Co., Omaha, 1942-44; engr. Allen-Bradley Co., Milw., 1949-50; mgr. Yarger Auto Co., Massena, Iowa, 1950-53; engr. sales Kies Electric Supply Co., Waterloo, 1955—. Pres. Massena Pub. Sch. Bd., 1952-53. Served to 2d. lt., USAAF, 1944-45. Names outstanding cons. engr. Jr. Engring. Tech. Soc., 1965. Mem. Illuminating Engring. Soc. (pres. Iowa sect. 1955—), Waterloo Electric League (pres. 1954—), Massena C. of C. (pres. 1951), Iowa Engring. Soc. Republican. Methodist. Clubs: Optimist, Beaver Hills Country, El Mecca, Elks, Masons, Shriners. Home: 1516 Franklin St Cedar Falls IA 50613 Office: 118 Sycamore St Waterloo IA 50704

YASSIN, ROBERT ALAN, art mus. dir.; b. Malden, Mass., May 22, 1941; s. Harold Benjamin and Florence Gertrude (Hoffman) Y.; B.A., Dartmouth Coll., 1962; M.A., U. Mich., 1964; postgrad. Yale U., U. Mich.; m. Marilyn Kramer, June 9, 1963; children—Frederic Giles, Aaron David. Asst. to dir. U. Mich. Mus. Art, 1964-65, asst. dir., 1971-73, asso. and acting dir., 1973; Ford fellow Yale U. Art Gallery, 1966-68; instr. art history U. Mich., 1970-73; chief curator Indpls. Mus. Art, 1973-75, acting dir., 1975, dir., 1975—; adj. prof. Herron Sch. Art, Ind. U., 1976—. Bd. dirs. Indpls. Consortium for Urban Edn., 1976—, Ensemble Music Soc., Indpls., 1976—. Samuel H. Kress Found. fellow, 1968-70. Mem. Am. Assn. Museums, Assn. Art Mus. Dirs., Am. Assn. State and Local History, Midwest Mus. Assn., Am., Midwest coll. art assns., Nat. Trust Historic Preservation. Club: Rotary (Indpls.). Editor Yale U. Art Gallery Bull., 1966-68, U. Mich. Mus. Art Bull., 1970-73; editor: Durer's Cities, Nuremberg and Venice, 1971; Art and the Excited Spirit, 1972; Painting and Sculpture Today, 1980; George Carlson, 1979, others. Home: 2525 Blue Grass Dr Indianapolis IN 46208 Office: 1200 W 38th St Indianapolis IN 46208

YATES, DENNIS LEE, mgmt. co. exec.; b. Wichita, Kans., Nov. 19, 1946; s. Lee Dennis and E. Virginia Yates; B.B.A., Wichita State U., 1978; divorced; children—Robin L., Brian D. Supr., Kans. Air N.G., 1965-76; v.p. Sedgwick State Bank (Kans.), 1976-79, also dir.; personnel officer Reno's Mgmt. Co., Hutchinson, Kans., 1979—, credit mgr., ops. mgr. Reno's Ace Hardward Stores, 1979—; instr. Hutchinson Jr. Coll. Chmn. fin. com. Sedgwick City Council, 1976-79. Served with USAF, 1967-69. Mem. Am. Bankers Assn., Sedgwick Jaycees (v.p. 1977-78), Kans. Jaycees (dir. 1976-77), Hutchinson C. of C. Republican. Clubs: Sedgwick Booster, Rotary. Home: 1705 Wesbrook Hutchinson KS 67501 Office: 215 S Main St Hutchinson KS 67501

YATES, FRANK MARTIN, civil engr.; b. Fulton, Mo., Mar. 7, 1951; s. James Calvin and Audrey Aileen (Clyman) Y.; B.S. in Civil Engring., U. Mo., Rolla, 1973. Peace corps vol., Ghana, West Africa, 1973-76; civil engr. I, Jackson County Pub. Works Dept., Independence, Mo., 1977—. Newsletter editor neighborhood council number 37 Independence Plan for Neighborhood Councils, 1979—; deacon First Presbyterian Ch., Independence. Registered profl. engr., Mo. Mem. ASCE (asso.), Inst. Transp. Engrs. (asso.), Nat. Council Returned Peace Corps Vols., Independence Jaycees (treas.), Chi Epsilon. Office: 306 W Kansas Ave Independence MO 64050

YATES, JAMES HENRY, elec. engr.; b. Dayton, Ohio, Sept. 29, 1951; s. Henry B. and Jessie (Gregory) Y.; B.S. in Elec. Engring., U. Cin., 1974; m. Rebecca M.J. Yates, Sept. 15, 1973. Student engr. Dayton Power & Light Co. (Ohio), 1970-73, asst. planning engr., system planning, 1974-75, asso. planning engr., bulk power planning, 1975-77, coordinator forecasting, planning div., 1977-79, supr. compensation and benefits, employee services div., 1979-80, supr. employee services div., 1980-81; sr. cons. Cresap, McCormick and Paget Inc., N.Y.C., 1981—. Mem. N.Am. Soc. Corp. Planning, Eta Kappa Nu. Club: Engrs. (Dayton). Home: 1916 Far Hills Ave Dayton OH 45419

YATES, SIDNEY R(ICHARD), congressman, lawyer; b. Chgo., Aug. 27, 1909; s. Louis and Ida (Siegel) Y.; Ph.B., U. Chgo., 1931; J.D., 1933; m. Adeline Holleb, June 24, 1935; 1 son, Stephen R. Admitted to Ill. bar, 1933; asst. atty. for Ill. State Bank Receiver, 1935-37; asst. atty. gen. attached to Ill. Commerce Commn. as traction atty., 1937-40; mem. 81st to 87th, 89th to 97th Congresses from 9th Ill. Dist. U.S. del. UN Trusteeship Council with rank of ambassador, 1963-64. Served to lt. USNR, 1944-46. Mem. Am. Ill., Chgo. bar assns., Decalogue Soc. Laws. Democrat. Jewish. Clubs: City, Bryn Mawr Country. Home: 3500 Lake Shore Dr Chicago IL 60657 Office: 2234 Rayburn House Office Bldg Washington DC 20515

YAU, STEPHEN SIK-SANG, elec. engr., computer scientist, educator; b. Wusei, Kiangsu, China, Aug. 6, 1935; s. Pen-Chi and Wing-Chun (Shum) Y.; B.S., Nat. Taiwan U., 1958; M.S., U. Ill., Urbana, 1959, Ph.D., 1961; m. Vickie Liu, June 14, 1964; children—Andrew, Philip. Came to U.S., 1958, naturalized, 1968. Asst. prof. elec. engring. Northwestern U., 1961-64, asso. prof., 1964-68, prof., 1968-70, prof. elec. engring. and computer scis., 1970—, chmn. dept. computer scis., 1972-77, chmn. dept. elec. engring. and computer sci., 1977—. Trustee Nat. Electronics Conf., 1965-68; mem. Joint Computer Conf. Bd., 1972-73; gen. chmn. Nat. Computer Conf., Chgo., 1974. Fellow IEEE (conf. chmn. 1st ann. computer conf. 1967, gen. chmn. 1st internat. conf. on computer software and applications 1977, pres. Computer Soc. 1974-75, dir. 1976-77, chmn. audit com. 1977, editor-in-chief Computer 1981—), Franklin Inst. (Louis E. Levy medal 1963), Am. Fedn. Info. Processing Socs. (dir. 1972—, nominations com. 1973-75, exec. com. 1974-76, 79—); mem. Assn. Computing Machinery, Soc. Indsl. and Applied Math., AAAS, Am. Soc. Engring. Edn., Sigma Xi, Eta Kappa Mu, Pi Mu Epsilon. Contbr. numerous articles to profl. jours. Patentee in field. Office: Dept Elec Engring and Computer Sci Northwestern U Evanston IL 60201

YDE, EDWARD EMIL, switch mfg. co. exec.; b. Freeport, Ill., Aug. 7, 1937; s. Edward Wilmer and Anna Jean (Clayton) Y.; A.A., Freeport Community Coll., 1967; m. Katherine Lucille Ryan, June 29, 1963; children—Matthew Edward, Steven Eugene, Andrea Kaye. Foreman, Structo Mfg. Co., Freeport, 1961-62; with Micro Switch Co., Freeport, 1962—, buyer, 1972-77, sr. buyer, 1977—; value improvement chmn., mech. commodity group Honeywell Inc., 1977—. Active local CBA Basketball, Little League. Served with USAF, 1957-61. Mem. Nat. Assn. Purchasing Mgrs., Ducks Unlimited (treas. Freeport 1977—). Ind. Republican. Roman Catholic. Club: Elks. Home: 404 S Park Blvd Freeport IL 61032 Office: 11 W Spring St Freeport IL 61032

YEAGER, CARSON RANDALL, banker; b. Greensboro, N.C., Nov. 12, 1951; s. Carson Ward and Elizabeth (Dossey) Y.; B.A. in Econs. and Bus., DePauw U., Greencastle (Ind.), 1973; grad. Sch. Banking, U. Wis., Madison, 1979. With First Security Bank Oak Brook (Ill.), 1973—, installment loan officer, 1975-77, asst. v.p. loans, 1977-79, v.p. loans, 1979-81; exec. and profl. banking officer No. Trust Co., Chgo., 1981—. Chmn., Oak Brook Jr. Assn. Found., 1980-81; adv. Explorer post local Boy Scouts Am., 1978—; Republican election judge, 1976—. Mem. Am. Inst. Banking, Bank Adminstrn. Inst., DuPage Bankers Assn., Oak Brook Jaycees (chmn. 1980-81), Oak Brook Exec. Breakfast Club, Oak Brook Assn. Bus. and Industry, Oak Brook Center Assn., Oak Brook Jr. C. of C. and Industry (chmn. 1980-81), Sigma Nu. Mem. United Ch. Christ. Clubs: Shriners, Kiwanis (pres. 1980-81), Illinois. Office: First Security Bank 105 Oak Brook Mall Oak Brook IL 60521

YEAGER, DAVID LEROY, utility co. exec.; b. Youngstown, Ohio, Feb. 12, 1935; s. LeRoy C. and Marjorie (Ballington) Y.; B.E., Youngstown U., 1959; postgrad. Harvard U., 1973; m. Margaret Scott, Feb. 7, 1959; children—David, Karen, Ellen. Supt. electric and steam sales Ohio Edison Co., Youngstown, 1968-70, dir. comml.-indsl. mktg., Akron, 1971-76, mgr. project coordination, 1976-78, asst. to exec. v.p., 1978-79, asst. to pres., 1980—. Pres., Summit County unit Am. Cancer Soc., 1981—. Registered profl. engr., Ohio. Mem. Nat. Soc. Profl. Engrs., ASME, ASHRAE. Home: 2878 Lakeland Pkwy Silver Lake OH 44224 Office: Ohio Edison Co 76 S Main St Akron OH 44308

YEAGER, JOHN ALFRED, ret. chem. co. exec.; b. Hazleton, Pa., Apr. 7, 1918; s. H. Alfred and Agnes D. (Cook) Y.; B.A., Lafayette Coll., 1940. Chief chemist So. Cotton Oil Co., Bayonne, N.J., 1940-43; research chemist GAF, Easton, Pa., 1943-52; project engr. Am. Lava div. Minn. Mining & Mfg. Co., Chattanooga, 1955-57; research chemist Franklin Research div. Purex Co., Phila., 1957-59; with Stepan Chem. Co., Northfield, Ill., 1962-81, mgr. tech. service, 1963-81; Midwest dir. Chem. Industries Council. Mem. Am. Assn. Textile Chemists and Colorists, Am. Oil Chemists Soc. Patentee in field.

YEATON, CHARLES EDWIN, energy mgmt. co. exec.; b. Youngstown, Ohio, June 7, 1934; s. Edwin Rustle and Sylvia O'Brien Y.; student U. Ala., 1953-55; B.E.E., Youngstown U., 1958; m. Janet Williams, Dec. 15, 1957 (dec.); children—Charles Edwin III, Robert, Kenneth; m. 2d, Jane Bolton, Aug. 9, 1975; stepchildren—Leslie, Pamela, Shelley. Apprentice, electrician Internat. Brotherhood Elec. Workers, Youngstown, 1953-59; engr. John Oltean & Assos., Youngstown, 1956-58; with Boyd Electric, Warren, Ohio, 1958-79, v.p., 1971-80; pres. Olympic Cons., Canfield, Ohio, 1971-81; pres., chief exec. officer ME Systems, Inc., Canfield, Ohio, 1978—. Bicentennial chmn., Canfield, 1976. Served with U.S. Army, 1956-58. Named Canfield Man of Yr., 1973. Mem. Assn. Energy Engrs., Nat. Assn. Energy Engrs., Ohio Assn. Energy Engrs. Lutheran. Club: Rotary. Home and Office: 39 Callahan Rd Canfield OH 44406

YEN, SHENG-TIAN, geneticist; b. Taiwan, China, Oct. 25, 1938; came to U.S., 1969, permanent resident, 1978; s. Kuan-Yu and Yu-Mei (Peng) Y.; B.S., Chung-Hsing U., 1961; M.S., U. Philippines, 1967; Ph.D., Iowa State U., 1975; m. Jennie Shou-Mei Hwang, May 31, 1964; children—Tom Yung-Shih, Johnny Yung-I. Research asso. Cornell U., Ithaca, N.Y., 1976-79; plant breeder Dairyland Research Internat., Clinton, Wis., 1979—. Rockefeller Found. scholar, 1965-67. Mem. Am. Soc. Agronomy, Crop Sci. Soc. Am., Council Agrl. Sci. and Tech., AAAS, Sigma Xi. Office: Dairyland Research International Route 1 Box 51 Clinton WI 53525

YENGER, SUE, state senator; b. Ottumwa, Iowa, Aug. 5, 1938; d. James Franklin and Bernice G. (Chapin) Peck; B.A. in Edn., Parsons Coll., Fairfield, Iowa, 1961; m. Jim F. Yenger, Mar. 28, 1959; children—Russell, Laura. Tchr., Ottumwa Public Schs., 1961-71; mgr. Area XV WIN Program, 1973-79; mem. Iowa Senate from 45th Dist., 1979—; commnr. Iowa Commn. Aging, 1979—; del. White House Conf. Aging, 1981. Chmn. bd. Ottumwa Day Care Center, 1975—; bd. dirs. United Way Wapello County, 1973-78, Wapello County Homemaker/Health Aid, 1974—; del. Republican Nat. Conv., 1980; co-chmn. Wapello County Rep. Com., 1969-73. Mem. Am. Legis. Exchange Council, Nat. Order Women Legislators, Iowa Women's Polit. Caucus, Farm Bur., Rep. Women, Rep. Women's Task Force. Mem. Disciples of Christ Ch. (Christian Ch.). Club: Eagles Aux. Office: Iowa Senate Capitol Bldg Des Moines IA 50319

YENNY, FRED ALBERT, tech. coll. pres.; b. Strasburg, Ohio, Dec. 7, 1922; s. Achille J. and Alma Ida (Waldman) Y.; B.S. in Elec. Engring., Case Inst. Tech., 1943, M.S., 1948; m. Dorothy Jane Bichsel, July 13, 1952; children—Thomas, Theodore, Carol. Devel. engr. Gen. Electric Co., Cleve., 1948-49; owner Yenny Electric Co., Strasburg, 1949-65; supr. Canton (Ohio) Area Tech. Sch., 1965-70; founder, 1970, since pres. Stark Tech. Coll., Canton. Vice pres. Buckeye council Boy Scouts Am., 1980—, Strasburg-Franklin Bd. Edn., 1964-72; pres. council St. John United Ch. Christ, Strasburg, 1954, 75; treas. Strasburg Park Devel. Com., 1950-58. Served as officer USNR, 1943-46. Mem. Am. Assn. Community and Jr. Colls. (president's acad.), Ohio Tech. and Community Coll. Orgn., Am. Vocat. Assn., Ohio Orgn. Tech. Colls. (past pres.; award 1977), Ohio Vocat. Assn., Sigma Xi, Tau Beta Pi (past chpt. pres.), Theta Tau (award 1943), Eta Kappa Nu, Phi Delta Kappa. Republican. Home: PO Box 5 Strasburg OH 44680 Office: 6200 Frank Ave NW Canton OH 44720

YESSIOS, CHRIS IOANNIS, architect, planner; b. Edessa, Greece, Aug. 10, 1938; s. Ioannis Christos and Aikaterini (Papachristou) Y.; came to U.S., 1968, naturalized, 1979; degree in law, Aristotelian U., 1962, diploma in architecture, 1967; Ph.D., Carnegie-Mellon U., 1973; m. Alexandra Varsamis, Sept. 1, 1971; children—Ioannis, Katerina, Dorothy. Mem. faculty U. Pitts., 1968-69, Carnegie-Mellon U., 1971-73; asso. prof. architecture and computer aided design Ohio State U., Columbus, 1973—; prin. C.I. Yessios, Archtl. Design, Thessaloniki, Greece, 1967—, Columbus, 1974—; prin. works include single and multi-family homes; cons. computer-aided archtl. design and planning. Mem. Environ. Design and Research Assn., Design Methods Group, Assn. Computing Machinery, Architects Soc. Greece, Columbus Landmarks Found. Mem. Greek Orthodox Ch. Home: 4367 Mumford Dr Columbus OH 43220 Office: 190 W 17th Ave Columbus OH 43210

YETKA, LAWRENCE ROBERT, state supreme ct. justice; b. Cloquet, Minn., Oct. 1, 1924; s. Frank and Martha (Norkowski) Y.; B.S., U. Minn., 1947, J.D., 1948; m. Ellen Marie Fuller, Nov. 11, 1950; children—Frank Barry, Lawrence George, Christopher Hubert. Admitted to Minn. bar, 1949; founder, partner firm Yetka & Newby, Cloquet, 1949-73; spl. mcpl. judge, 1960-64; city atty., Cloquet, 1964-73; atty. Duluth Port Authority, 1957-60; atty. Western Lake Superior San. Dist., 1970-73; asso. justice Minn. Supreme Ct., St. Paul, 1973—; atty., dir. Carlton County Fed. Savs. & Loan Assn., 1958-73; chmn. State Jud. Council, 1974-79, Select Com. on State

Jud. System, 1974-77, State Jud. Planning Agy., 1976—. Del., 12 state Democratic convs., 1948-72, Dem. Nat. Conv., 1956, 64, 68; chmn. Students for Humphrey for Mayor, 1947; Democratic Farmer Labor county officer, 1948-72, 8th Dist., 1962-66; state Dem. vice chmn., 1966-70; mem. Minn. Ho. of Reps., 1951-61, chmn. Ho. Jud. Com., 1955-61, asst. majority leader, 1959-61. Grad., Appellate Judges Seminar sponsored by Inst. Jud. Adminstrn. at N.Y. U. Law Sch., 1976. Mem. Am., Minn., Carlton County (pres. 1963-73) bar assns., Am. Judicature Soc., Inst. Jud. Adminstrn. Lutheran. Office: Supreme Ct Minn 230 State Capitol Saint Paul MN 55155*

YLVISAKER, WILLIAM TOWNEND, mfg. exec.; b. St. Paul, Feb. 25, 1924; s. Lauritz S. and Winifred Jean (Townend) Y.; grad. Lawrenceville Sch., 1943; B.S., Yale U., 1948; m. Jane Penelope Mitchell, May 11, 1972; 1 son, Jon Alastair; children (by previous marriage)—Laurie Ellen, Elizabeth Maren, William Wendell, Amy Townend. Security analyst Bank N.Y., 1948-49; gen. mgr. Lake Forest Motor Sales (Ill.), 1949-52; v.p., gen. mgr. Pheoll Mfg. Co., Chgo., 1952-58; pres. Parker-Kalon div. Gen. Am. Transp. Corp., Clifton, N.J., 1958-61, group v.p., dir. Gen. Am. Transp. Corp., Chgo., 1961-67; chmn. bd., chief exec. officer Gould Nat. Batteries, Inc., 1969-70; pres., dir., chief exec. officer Gould Inc., 1970-75, chmn., pres., chief exec. officer, 1972-75, chmn., chief exec. officer, 1975—; dir. Penske Corp., Piscataway, N.J., Compagnie Francaise D'Electro Chimie, France, Accumuladores Tudor, S.A., Mexico. Bd. dirs. NCCJ, Bush Found., St. Paul, Hwy. Users Fedn., Washington; council Grad. Sch. Bus., U. Chgo.; trustee Lawrenceville (N.J.) Sch., Rush-Presbyn.-St. Luke's Med. Sch., Solomon R. Guggenheim Found., Conf. Bd. Served as ensign USNR, 1943-45. Mem. Chgo. Assn. Commerce and Industry (dir.), Nat. Alliance Businessmen (dir.), U.S. Polo Assn., Northwestern U. Assos. Clubs: Univ., Racquet and Tennis, Links (N.Y.C.); Barrington Hills Country; Oak Brook (Ill.) Polo (gov.); Racquet, Chicago, Yale, Economics (Chgo.); Palm Beach Polo and Country (West Palm Beach, Fla.); Meadow (Rolling Meadows, Ill.); Ocean of Fla. Office: 10 Gould Center Rolling Meadows IL 60008

YNTEMA, VIRGINIA GWIN HEIGHO (MRS. THEODORE OTTE YNTEMA), civic worker; b. Weiser, Idaho; d. Edgar Maurice and Nora (Gwin) Heigho; B.A., Antioch Coll., 1928; m. Theodore Otte Yntema, July 31, 1939; children—Virginia Gwin, Theodore Otte. Trustee, Antioch Coll., 1952-64; life trustee Detroit Inst. Arts, 1966—, trustee, v.p. Detroit Symphony Orch., 1972—, hon. v.p., 1979—; mem. women's bd. U. Chgo., 1965—; bd. assos. Met. Opera, N.Y.C., 1965— Detroit Grand Opera Assn., 1963—, Internat. Inst., Detroit, 1968—; mem. midwest bd. Inst. Internat. Edn., 1967—; adv. bd. United Found., Detroit, 1962—; trustee United Health Orgn., Detroit, 1967—. Mem. Detroit Artists Market. Republican. Episcopalian. Club: Village Woman's. Home: Box 347 Bloomfield Hills MI 48013

YOCHIM, WILLIAM JOSEPH, psychotherapist; b. Erie, Pa., Mar. 13, 1938; s. Eugene Frederick and Marie Elizabeth (McLaughlin) Y.; B.A., St. Mary's U., Balt., 1960; M.S.W., U. Mich., 1965; m. Emilia Ann Tischler, Nov. 2, 1968; children—William Joseph, Stephen E., Jeffrey A. Clin. social worker VA Hosp. Mental Hygiene Clinic, Allen Park, Mich., 1965-66; social service supr. St. Peter's Episcopal Home for Boys, Detroit, 1966-68; social service dir. Kingswood Psychiat. Hosp., Ferndale, Mich., 1968-76; psychiat. social work cons. Glen Eden Hosp., Warren, Mich., 1969—; partner Birmingham Clinic - A Comprehensive Counseling and Learning Center, P.C., Birmingham, Mich., 1975—; lectr. psychology dept. U. Detroit, 1966-69. Bd. dirs. Oakland Mental Health Forum, 1967-71. Served with AUS, 1960-63. Cert. social worker, cert. marriage counselor, Mich. Mem. Nat. Assn. Social Workers, Acad. Cert. Social Workers, Am. Group Psychotherapy Assn., Am. Hosp. Assn., Hosp. Social Work Dirs. (co-chmn. task force on hosp. social work Mich. chpt. 1974-75), Mich. Group Psychotherapy Soc. (bd. dirs., treas. 1974-79, pres. 1981—). Home: 3520 Wards Pointe Dr Orchard Lake MI 48033 Office: Birmingham Clinic 802 S Worth St Birmingham MI 48011

YOCKEY, PEGGY (MARGARET) ELIZABETH, mgmt. scientist, educator; b. Wichita, Kans., July 29, 1945; d. Richard E. and Mary P. (Norris) Stone; B. Liberal Arts and Scis., U. Kans., 1968; m. Dennis W. Yockey, Sept. 29, 1973; 1 dau., Mary Elizabeth. Extension coordinator U. Kans., Wichita Center, 1968-75; dir. Center for Mgmt. Devel., Wichita State U., 1975—. Active Am. Heart Found., Am. Cancer Soc. Arthritis Found., United Fund, Kidney Found., Camp Hyde, Wichita, LVW. Mem. Am. Soc. Personnel Adminstrn. (pres. Wichita chpt. 1975), Assn. Continuing Higher Edn., Kans. Adult Edn. Assn., Am. Soc. Tng. and Devel., Delta Rho Sigma. Democrat. Roman Catholic. Clubs: Kans. C.P.A. Wives, Wichita Racquet. Home: 208 Burr Oak St Wichita KS 67206 Office: Campus Box 86 Wichita State U Wichita KS 67208

YODER, FREDERICK FLOYD, assn. exec.; b. Wilkinsburg, Pa., Oct. 7, 1935; s. Floyd Elvin and Mary Viola (Stahl) Y.; B.S. in Journalism, Ohio U., 1957. Mem. hdqrs. staff Sigma Chi Fraternity, Evanston, Ill., 1957—, coordinator chpt. visitation and installations program, 1964-72, leadership tng. adminstr., 1962-76, editor Mag. of Sigma Chi and Sigma Chi publs., 1972—. Mem. Coll. Fraternity Editors Assn. (past pres.), Am. Soc. Assn. Execs., Chgo. Headline Club, Sigma Chi, Sigma Delta Chi, Omicron Delta Kappa. Editor: The Norman Shield, 1973—; Sigma Chi Membership Directory, 1977. Contbr. articles to interfraternity jours. Home: 2603 Sheridan Rd Evanston IL 60201 Office: 1714 Hinman Ave Box 469 Evanston IL 60204

YOEST, DANIEL CHARLES, educator; b. Tipton, Mo., Dec. 4, 1951; s. Andrew John and Mary Alice (Elmlinger) Y.; student State Fair Community Coll., 1969-70; B.S. in Agr., U. Mo., Columbia, 1973, M.Ed., 1975; m. Susan Catherine Hawkins, Sept. 8, 1973. Tchr. vocat. agr. Salem (Mo.) R-80 Sch. Dist., 1973-74; agr. engring. research asst. U. Mo., Columbia, 1974-75; tchr. vocat. agr., head dept. Gasconade County R-I Sch. Dist., Hermann, Mo., 1975—; mem. com. Mo. Dept. Edn. Mem. Gasconade County Fair Bd.; dir. farm mechanics show Gasconade County Fair; bd. dirs. Historic Herman, Inc.; committeeman Maifest Council. Named Hon. Chpt. Farmer, Herman chpt. Future Farmers Am., 1978. Mem. Am. Vocat. Assn., Mo. Vocat. Assn., Mo. Vocat. Agr. Tchrs. Assn. (pres. S. Central dist. 1978-79, mem. exec. com.), Nat. Vocat. Agr. Tchrs. Assn., C. of C., Hermann Jr. C. of C., Alpha Tau Alpha, Gamma Sigma Delta. Roman Catholic. Home: PO Box 57 Hermann MO 65041 Office: Gasconade County R-I Sch Dist Hwy 100 W Hermann MO 65041

YOHE, RALPH SANDLIN, editor; b. Mt. Erie, Ill., June 27, 1920; s. Irvin Bradhaw and Georgia (Sandlin) Y.; B.S., U. Ill., 1943; postgrad. U. Chgo., 1947-48. Exec. sec. Ill. Poultry Improvement Assn., Chgo., 1946-48; sci. editor, asso. editor Prairie Farmer Pub. Co., Chgo., 1948-57; editor Wis. Agriculturist, Madison, 1957—; v.p., dir. Wis. Farmer Co., Inc.; mem. agrl. com. Nat. Planning Assn., 1958—, mem. com. chaning internat. realities, 1975—, nat. trustee, 1981—; adv. council Coll. Agr., Wis. State U., River Falls, 1968-73; mem. animal disease control adv. council Wis. Dept. Agr., 1972-73. Vice pres., bd. dirs. Nr. Eastern Art Research Center; v.p., trustee Nat. Rug and Textile Found., 1968-76; trustee, sec. Textile Mus., Washington, 1979—. Served with USNR, 1943-46. Mem. Am. Agrl. Editors Assn. (past dir.), United Comml. Travelers Am. (grand counselor Wis. 1971-72), Alpha Zeta. Methodist. Clubs: Shriners, Rotary, Elks. Author: What Our Farmers Can Learn from Other Lands, 1953; (introduction) Don't Forget to Smell the Flowers Along the Way: Portraits of Joseph W. McMulland, 1977; co-author: Exploring the Old World, rev. edit., 1960; Turkish Rugs, 1968; Exploring Regions of the Eastern Hemisphere, 2d edit., 1977; Persian Tribal Rugs, 1971; Cultures in Transition, 1973; Yoruk: The Nomadic Weaving Tradition of the Middle East, 1978; From the Far East, Carpets and Textiles of Morocco. *

YOHN, DAVID STEWART, educator; b. Shelby, Ohio, June 7, 1929; s. Joseph Van and Agnes (Tryon) Y.; B.S., Otterbein Coll., 1951; M.S., Ohio State U., 1953, Ph.D., 1957; M.P.H., U. Pitts., 1960; m. Olivetta McCoy, June 11, 1950; children—Linda Jean, Kathleen Ann, Joseph John, David McCoy, Kristine Renee. Grad. asst. Ohio State U., Columbus, 1951-52, research fellow, 1952-54, research scholar, 1954-56, prof. vet. pathobiology, dept. vet. pathobiology Coll. Vet. Medicine, 1969—, prof. microbiology Colls. Medicine and Biol. Scis., 1970—, dir. Ohio State U. Comprehensive Cancer Center, 1973—; research asso. Grad. Sch. Public Health, U. Pitts., 1956-58, research fellow, 1958-60, asst. research prof. microbiology, 1960-62; asso. cancer research scientist Roswell Park Meml. Inst., 1962-69; asso. research prof. microbiology SUNY, Buffalo, 1962-71; research prof. Niagara U., 1967-69. Bd. dirs. Assn. Am. Cancer Insts.; trustee, mem. exec. com. Hospice of Columbus; mem. steering com. Columbus Center for Health Care Plus. Mem. Internat. Assn. for Comparative Research on Leukemia and Related Diseases (sec. gen), Am. Assn. for Cancer Research, Federated Socs. Immunology, Am. Soc. Microbiology. Presbyterian. Club: Sertoma. Editor: (with Johannes Clemmesen) Comparative Leukemia Research, 1975; (with T.E. Williams and H.E. Wilson) Perspectives in Lung Cancer, 1977; contbr. articles on virology, immunology and oncology to profl. jours. Office: 410 W 12 Ave Suite 302 Columbus OH 43210

YOON, ICK JHIN, research scientist; b. Korea, Oct. 5, 1943; came to U.S., 1969; s. Jang-Ro and Jung Sook (Kim) Y.; M.S., Iowa State U., 1972, Ph.D., 1977; m. Sandy Hyohi Chung, Oct. 27, 1971; 1 son, Kenneth H. Research asst. Engring. Research Inst., Iowa State U., 1970-77; materials scientist Anchor Hocking Corp., Lancaster, Ohio, 1978-79; research scientist Kerr Mfg. Co. div. Sybron, Romulus, Mich., 1979-81; sr. project engr. Zenith Radio Corp., Melrose Park, Ill., 1981—. Mem. Am. Ceramic Soc., Nat. Inst. Ceramic Engrs., Orgn. Am. Nat. Standards, Keramos Fraternity, Sigma Xi.

YORK, BOBBY RAY, power plant exec.; b. Sasakwa, Okla., June 23, 1937; s. Robert Lee and Mary A. (Hill) Y.; student Kirkwood Community Coll., 1976—; m. Ruth Darlene Stewart, Oct. 22, 1960; children—Terry Duane, Jeanette Louise, Sandra Kay. Reactor aux. operator Hallam (Nebr.) Nuclear Power Facility, 1961-63, reactor operator, 1963-69; shift supr. Cooper Nuclear Sta., Brownville, Nebr., 1969-72; ops. supr. Duane Arnold Energy Center, Palo, Iowa, 1972-79, asst. chief engr. ops., 1979—. Served with USAF, 1956-60. Republican. Home: 2128 Evergreen St NE Cedar Rapids IA 52402 Office: Duane Arnold Energy Center Palo IA 52324

YORK, GRACE ANN, librarian; b. Detroit, Jan. 4, 1946; d. John Blase and Ethel Helen (Spear) York; B.A., Wayne State U., Detroit, 1968; M.A. in L.S. (Mich. Inter-Assn. Library scholar 1968-69), U. Mich., 1969. Mem. staff U. Mich. Library, Ann Arbor, 1969—, asst. reference librarian, 1970-75, head documents reference service, 1975—. Mem. ALA, Govt. Documents Round Table Mich. (v.p. 1978-79), Common Cause (dist. membership recruitment chmn. 1975), Phi Beta Kappa, Phi Kappa Phi, Beta Phi Mu (chpt. pres. 1975-77), Sigma Kappa, Gamma Delta (nat. sec. 1966-67). Lutheran. Author: (with others) Documents Handbook, 1973; The American Revolution, 1763-1783: Selected Reference Sources, 1976; Michigan Legislative Histories, 1979. Home: 2927 Shady Ln Ann Arbor MI 48104 Office: Grad Library Univ Mich Ann Arbor MI 48109

YORK, SAMUEL, JR., digital equipment corp. exec.; b. St. Louis, Feb. 24, 1952; s. Samuel and Sallie Emma (Thomas) Y.; B.S.E.E., U. Mo., 1975; m. Karlah J. Ambrose, June 2, 1973: children—Eboni, Amber. Jr. engr. Southwestern Bell Telephone Co., Kansas City, Mo., 1976; engr. Digital Equipment Corp., Nashua, N.H., 1976-79, sales rep., Columbus, Ohio, 1979-81, sales mgr., 1981—; data processing, microprocessor instr. Daniel Webster Coll., summer 1977. Mem. IEEE. Baptist. Designer multiline communications processor for ACS System. Home: 6376 Saddle Ln E Westerville OH 43081 Office: Digital Equipment Corp 6400 E Broad St Columbus OH 43213

YORK, VANCE OWEN, agronomist; b. Odon, Ind., Oct. 12, 1930; s. Owen Cecil and Minnie Beatrice (Bennett) Y.; B.S. in Agr., Purdue U., 1952; m. Reba Ree Strickler, Aug. 19, 1951; children—James Owen, Daniel Eugene, Catherine Marie York Weiss. Dist. sales mgr. eastern div. Pioneer Hi-Bred Internat., Inc., Tipton, Ind., 1954-57, Kernels editor, 1957-64, mgr. sales service dept., 1964-74, sales coordinator, 1974-78, no. regional sales mgr., 1978—. Parade announcer Tipton County Pork Festival, 1972-78; lay leader, choir mem. Kemp United Meth. Ch. Served with U.S. Army, 1952-54. Named Hon. Hoosier and Am. Farmer, Future Farmers Am; recipient award Ind. Vocat. Assn., 1979. Mem. Ind. Forage Council (pres. 1972-73), Am. Forage and Grassland Council (pres. 1982—), Ind. Future Farmers Am. Found. (v.p.), Ind. Seed Trade Assn. (pres. 1979), Ind. Crop Improvement Assn. (dir.), Ind. Young Farmers Assn. (hon.). Clubs: Masons, Scottish Rite, Tipton Rotary (pres. 1965). Home: Rural Route 1 Tipton IN 46072 Office: 1000 W Jefferson Tipton IN 46072

YOULE, (JOHN) CLINTON, writer, financial cons., investment banker; b. Chgo., Apr. 4, 1916; s. John Wilbur and Sadie (Muench) Y.; A.B., Wheaton (Ill.) Coll., 1939. Editor NBC, 1940-50; TV westher commentator, 1949-59; syndicated newspaper columnist, 1952-53; pub. 5 Ill. newspapers, 1949-59; asso. Lehman Bros., investment bankers, 1959-66; v.p., dir. Donald R. Booz & Assos., Inc., 1966-67; pvt. financial cons., 1967—; dir. Safety-Kleen Corp., Madison Kipp Corp., RaiLoc Co., Ariz. Raft Adventures. Mem. Ill. Ho. of Reps., 1964-66; mem. vis. com. Div. Sch. and Div. Social Scis., U. Chgo. With USAF Intelligence, 1942-46. Mem. Am. Meteorol. Soc. Clubs: Chicago; Executives (pres. 1959-60); Dunham Woods Riding (Wayne, Ill.); University. Inventor and mfr. automatic stock gates. Home and Office: Box 187 Scales Mound IL 61075

YOUNG, AMELIA (AMY) MARGARET, jr. coll. dean; b. Sedalia, Mo., Jan. 21, 1934; d. Louis J. and Magdalena (Breuhl) Weller; R.N., St. Mary's Hosp. Sch. Nursing, 1954; B.S., U. Mo., 1974, Ed.M., 1976, Ph.D. in Vocat. Edn., 1979; m. Robert J. Young, July 21, 1955; children—Linda Sue, Gregory Bruce, Sandra Kathrine, Deborah Ann. Nurse, St. Mary's Hosp., Kansas City, Mo., 1954-55; office nurse, Kansas City, Mo., 1955-56; staff nurse St. Luke's Hosp., Kansas City, Mo., 1956-57; indsl. nurse Bendix Corp., Kansas City, 1957-61; staff nurse St. Mary's Hosp., Kansas City, 1961-67, head nurse surg. unit and ICU, 1967-68; coordinator practical nurse program, Marshall, Mo., 1968-70; coordinator pre-service and in-service edn. State Fair Community Coll., Sedalia, Mo., 1970-74, chmn. dept. health occupations edn., 1974-80, dir. health occupations, 1980-81; dean vocat. edn. Moberly (Mo.) Jr. Coll., 1981—; asst. prof. tchr. cert. courses U. Mo., Columbia, 1978-80; cons. Kansas City Tech. Center, Mo., summer, 1978; mem. governing body area II, Health Systems Agy., 1980—. Mem. Am. Vocat. Assn., Mo. Vocat. Assn., Nat. Council Local Adminstrs., Mo. State Assn. Health Occupations Educators (pres.), Mo. Assn. Community Jr. Colls., Mo. Council Local Adminstrs., Am. Cancer Soc. (chairperson public edn. com. Pettis County div. 1981), Phi Kappa Phi. Roman Catholic. Contbr. articles to profl. publs. Office: Moberly Jr Coll College and Rollins Sts Moberly MO 65270

YOUNG, CHRISTOPHER JAMES, systems analyst; b. Bellefontaine, Ohio, May 10, 1952; s. James Franklin and Virginia Alice (Landgraver) Y.; B.S. in Bus. Adminstrn., Bowling Green (Ohio) State U., 1974. Systems analyst NCR Corp., Dayton, Ohio, 1975-79, Marathon Oil Corp., Findlay, Ohio, 1979—; cons. in field. Mem. Assn. Systems Mgmt., Am. Mktg. Assn. Home: 348 E Lincoln St Findlay OH 45840 Office: 539 S Main St Findlay OH 45840

YOUNG, CLIFFORD EUGENE, sales exec.; b. Santa Monica, Calif., Sept. 7, 1939; s. Cleon Buster, Sr., and Evelyn Arlene (Stewart) Y.; student Bethany Bible Coll., 1960; B.S. in Bus. Mgmt., LaSalle U., 1973; m. Mary Kathryn Cox, Jan. 9, 1965; children—Karen Ann, Clifford Eugene, Kathryn Denise. With Stouffer Foods, Solon, Ohio, 1968-75, regional sales mgr., New Eng., 1968-75; v.p. sales Saluto Foods subs. Gen. Mills, 1975-79; pres. Select Products, Inc. Benton Harbor, Mich., 1979—. Mem. chmn.'s com. U.S. Senatorial Bus. Adv. Bd. Mem. Aircraft Owners and Pilots Assn., Airline Passengers Assn., Frozen Food Assn. Nat., Fraternal Order of Police. Republican. Home: 5254 US 33 N Coloma MI 49038 Office: 2654 US 33 N Benton Harbor MI 49022

YOUNG, CLYDE WILLIAM, musicologist; b. Springfield, Mo., Aug. 14, 1919; s. Clyde Anton and Rose Marie (Kiefer) Y.; student Drury Coll., 1937-38; B.S. with high distinction in Edn., diploma in Organ, S.W. Mo. State Coll., 1941; Mus.M. in Organ, U. Mich., 1949; Ph.D. in Musicology, U. Ill., 1957, M.S. in L.S., 1958; postgrad. Union Theol. Sem., 1949; m. Helen Nancy Dinge, Dec. 29, 1962; children—Martha Rose, Anne Marie, William Geoffrey. Clk., St. Louis-San Francisco Ry., Springfield, Mo. and St. Louis, 1941-47; teaching asst., fellow dept. music, dormitory counselor U. Mich., Ann Arbor, 1949-53; dormitory counselor, library asst. U. Ill., Urbana, 1954-58; asst. prof. music State U. N.Y., Cortland, 1958-60; asst. prof., librarian U. Nebr., Lincoln, 1960-61; asst., then asso. prof. music Nebr. Wesleyan U., Lincoln, 1961-64; asso. prof. Wayne State U., Detroit, 1965-73, prof., 1973—. Mem. Am. Musicol. Soc. Mem. United Ch. of Christ. Contbr. articles in field of Renaissance music to profl. jours., Die Musik in Geschichte und Gegenwart, Grove's Dictionary of Music and Musicians, 6th edit.; editor mus. texts. Home: 498 Barrington Rd Grosse Pointe Park MI 48230 Office: Dept Music Wayne State U Detroit MI 48202

YOUNG, COLEMAN ALEXANDER, mayor; b. Tuscaloosa, Ala., May 24, 1918; s. Coleman and Ida Reese (Jones) Y.; LL.D., Eastern Mich. U. Del., Mich. Constl. Conv., 1961-62; mem. Mich. Senate, 1964-73, also Democratic floor leader; mayor of Detroit, 1974—. Del., Dem. Nat. Conv., 1968, 72; Dem. nat. committeeman from Mich.; bd. dirs. Ferndale Coop. Credit Union, Kirwood Hosp., Detroit. Served to 2d lt. USAAF, World War II. Mem. NAACP, Brooker T. Washington Bus. Men's Assn., Trade Union Leadership Council, Assn. for Study Negro Life and History, AFL-CIO Council (spl. rep.). Baptist. Office: Office of Mayor 2 Woodward Ave Detroit MI 48226

YOUNG, CONRAD SCOTLAND, ins. co. exec.; b. Omaha, Nov. 7, 1921; A.B. magna cum laude, Dartmouth Coll., 1943. Health ins. underwriter Mut. of Omaha and United of Omaha, 1948-50, sales div., 1950-52, dir. life ins. tng. United of Omaha, 1952-56, regional sales dir. Gt. Lakes area, 1956-57, dir. field services, 1957-59, officer, 1959-63, v.p., 1963-73, asst. to pres., 1973-74, pres., from 1974, dir., from 1975; now pres. United Benefit Life Ins. Co. and dir. Mut. of Omaha. Mem. Mid-Am. council Boy Scouts Am.; bd. dirs. Lutheran Med. Center, NCCJ, Coll. St. Mary, Riverfront Dvel. Found.; trustee Bishop Clarkson Meml. Hosp., Joslyn Art Mus., U. Nebr. Found.; mem. pres.'s council Creighton U.; past mem. Omaha City Planning Bd.; past chmn. Douglas/Sarpy County Crusade for Cancer and Douglas/Sarpy County Heart Fund Dr.; gen. chmn. United Appeal, United Way Midlands, 1971-72. Mem. Nat. Assn. Securities Dealers (bd. govs.), Delta Tau Delta. Office: United Benefit Life Ins Co Mutual of Omaha Plaza Omaha NE 68175*

YOUNG, ETHEL JEAN, retail sales co. adminstr.; b. Crystal Springs, Miss., July 23, 1955; d. J.W. and Rosie Mae Sturgis; A.S., Internat. Corr. Schs., 1980; student U. Toledo, 1973—; m. George Washington Young, Jr., Nov. 22, 1973; children—Twanna Angeldione, George Henry Damonde, Tammy Jerrell. Sr. sec., Owens Corning Fiberglas Co., Toledo, 1977-79; adminstr., VIP Secretarial and Temp. Services, Toledo, 1977-79; adminstr. The Young Co., Toledo, 1979—. Mem. Nat. Assn. Female Execs. Democrat. Mem. Pentecostal Ch. Club: Hyms. Home: 4354 Deerwood St Toledo OH 43615 Office: PO Box 7006 Toledo OH 43615

YOUNG, GEORGE PATRICK, supt. schs.; b. Butler, Pa., July 17, 1924; s. George Patrick and Mildred Elaine (Fisher) Y.; student Denison U., 1944-45; B.A. in Math., U. Kans., 1947; Ed.M., U. Pitts., 1951; Ed.D., U. Ill., 1960; m. Biloine Whiting, Apr. 1950; children—Robin Ray, Richard Mark, Benjamin Brock, Priscilla Pilar. Tchr., Am. Sch. of Guatemala, 1951-53; dir. guidance, 1952-53, dir. Sch. Boarding House, 1952-53; tchr. Instituto Guatemalteco-Americano, 1951-52; headmaster Colegio Bolivar, Cali, Colombia, 1953-58; grad. asst. Office Field Services, U. Ill., 1958-60; dir. instrn. Urbana (Ill.) Pub. Schs., 1960-64; supt. schs. Gallup-McKinley County, N.Mex., 1964-66, Canton, Ohio, 1966-70, St. Paul, 1970—; lectr. Sch. Adminstrn., U. Minn., 1977—. Spl. adviser sec. edn. Departmento del Valle del Cauca, Colombia, 1956. Chmn., Ill. State Com., Midwest Program on Airborne Television Instrn., 1962, bd. dirs., 1963; mem. Commr. Edn. Adv. Council, State of Minn., 1970—, Gov.'s Adv. Council on Community Schs., 1970—; mem. adminstrs. com. Study Commn. for Higher Edn., 1972—; mem. U. Minn. Coll. Edn. Adv. Group, 1973—. Bd. dirs. Twin City Ednl. TV, Minn. Symphony Orch., Ednl. Research and Devel. Council of Twin City Met. Area; chmn. Minn. Council on Econ. Edn., 1978-79, Large City Sch. Supts. Council, 1978-79, Assn. Orgns. for Tchr. Edn., 1979; mem. exec. bd. Indianhead council Boy Scouts Am. Served to lt. (j.g.) USN, 1942-46. Recipient Ann. Human Relations Council award, 1968, Spl. award Urban League, Canton, 1970; named Distinguished Alumnus Coll. Edn., U. Ill., 1971. Mem. Am., Minn. assns. sch. adminstrs., Nat. Assn. Secondary Sch. Prins., Nat. Assn. Elementary Sch. Prins., U. Ill. Coll. Edn. Alumni Assn. (v.p. 1963), Phi Delta Kappa, Kappa Delta Pi. Rotarian. Author weekly column Young View, St. Paul Dispatch, 1960-73. Contbr. articles to profl. jours. Home: 15 Crocus Hill St Paul MN 55102 Office: 360 Colborne St St Paul MN 55102

YOUNG, H. EDWIN, economist; b. Bonne Bay, Nfld., Can., May 3, 1917; s. William and Annie (McKenzie) Y.; B.S., U. Maine, 1940, M.A., 1942; Ph.D., U. Wis., 1950; m. Phyllis Smart, Feb. 14, 1941; children—Jill, John, Dorothy, Nathan, Barbara. Instr. to asso. prof.

econs. U. Wis., Madison, 1947-55, prof., 1955-65, 68—, Rennebohm prof. applied econs., 1980—, chmn. dept. 1953-61, dean Coll. Letters and Sci., 1961-65, chancellor, 1968-77; pres. U. Wis. System, 1977-80, U. Maine, Orono, 1965-68; pres., chmn. Nat. Assn. State Univ. and Land-Grant Colls., 1978-79; bd. dirs. Am. Univs. Field Staff, 1977—, chmn., 1977-79; bd. govs. East-West Center; dir. Paxall, Inc., 1979—, A.O. Smith Corp., 1980—. Mem. Indsl. Relations Research Assn. Editor: (with M. DAerber) Labor and the New Deal, 1957. Home: 830 Cabot Ln Madison WI 53711 Office: 4123 Helen White 600 N Park St Madison WI 53706

YOUNG, JOAN ELAINE, microbiologist; b. Jersey City, Apr. 9, 1938; d. Edward and Eleanore Marie (Sossong) Johnson; student Jersey City Jr. Coll., 1957-58, Pasadena Jr. Coll., 1960; A.A., Upsala Coll., 1967-68; 1 son, John. Organic chemist Hoffman LaRoche, Nutley, N.J., 1958-60; microbiologist S.B. Penick Co., Jersey City, 1960-62, Hoffman LaRoche, Nutley, N.J., 1962-66; biochemist Warner Lambert Research Inst., Morris Plains, N.J., 1966-67; microbiologist M&M/Mars, Hackettstown, N.J., 1967-73, Airwick Industries, Teterboro, N.J., 1973-80; product registration specialist Tretolite div. Petrolite Corp., St. Louis, 1980. Mem. Am. Soc. Microbiology, Research Soc. Am., ASTM. Clubs: Order of Eastern Star, Camelback Ski. Home: 1651 Wishwood Ct Apt 6 Chesterfield MO 63017 Office: 369 Marshall Ave Saint Louis MO 63119

YOUNG, KENT ALAN, clin. psychologist; b. Tulsa, Dec. 28, 1940; s. Wilson and Naomi (Smyth) Y.; A.B., Oberlin Coll., 1964; postgrad. New Sch. for Social Research, 1964-65; M.A., Western Res. U., 1967, Ph.D., 1972; m. Joan Moore, July 5, 1969; children—Kimberly Allison, Justin Michael, Kevin Matthew. Staff psychologist Lake County Mental Health Center, Mentor, Ohio, 1971-72, coordinator research, 1972-73, asso. dir., 1973—; pvt. practice clin. psychology, Mentor, 1973—; cons. Lake County Ct. Common Pleas, 1976-79. Mem. Lake County Mental Retardation Bd., 1977-78. Mem. Am., Midwestern, Ohio (legis. com. 1973-74, ins. com. 1974-75, trustee 1975-79), Cleve. (chmn. profl. affairs com. 1974-79) psychol. assns., Cleve. Acad. Cons. Psychologists (trustee 1974—, pres. 1976-77, 78-79). Club: Rotary. Home: 8872 Edgehill Rd Mentor OH 44060 Office: Mentor Profl Center 8925 Mentor Ave Mentor OH 44060

YOUNG, MARION RUTH, media cons.; b. Abington, Pa., May 7, 1936; d. Frank Pierce and Agnes Margaret (Roberts) Y.; student Temple U., 1954-60, Beaver Coll., 1959-61, Tyler Sch. Fine Arts, 1961-62; m. William M. Young; children—Richard, Scott, Gregory. Mem. psychol. testing staff Edward N. Hay & Assos., Phila., 1954-55; travel rep. Am. Express Co., Phila., 1955-56; mem. phys. edn. staff Abington (Pa.) YMCA, 1956-58; office mgr. W.G. Knorr, real estate, Glenside, Pa., 1958-59; tchr. retarded and adults Phila. Council of Chs., 1958; tchr. Abington Friends Sch., 1959; asst. dir. admissions Beaver Coll., 1959-61; adult edn. tchr. Dept. Interior, Micronesia, 1965-67; salesperson Vincent Montalto, real estate, Wayne, N.J., 1969-71; exec. v.p. Urban Dynamics, Inc., Oak Park, Ill., 1975—; pres. Studio 909, Inc., Oak Park, 1980—. Trustee, Wilmington Coll., 1978—; Democratic committeewoman, Oak Park, 1976-78; co-dir. Nat. PTA TV Project, 1976-81. Mem. AAUP. Quaker. Clubs: Met., Ill. Athletic. Editor, Televiews, 1976—, PTA TV Rev. Guide, 1976-81, Internat. Assn. Machinists and Aerospace Workers Media Report, 1980—. Office: Studio 909 Inc 909 S Oak Park Ave Oak Park IL 60304

YOUNG, MARVIN OSCAR, coal co. exec., lawyer; b. Union, Mo., Apr. 4, 1929; s. Otto C. and Irene A. Young; B.A., Westminster Coll., 1951; J.D., U. Mich., 1954; m. Sue Carol Mathews, Aug. 23, 1952; children—Victoria Leigh, Kendall Marvin. Admitted to Mo. bar, 1954; asso. firm Thompson & Mitchell, St. Louis, 1954-55, 57-58; atty. Mo. Farmers Assn., Inc., Columbia, 1958-68, v.p. ops., 1967-68; v.p., gen. counsel, sec. Peabody Coal Co., St. Louis, 1968—. Trustee, Westminster Coll., 1977—, 1st vice chmn. bd. trustees, 1979—; trustee Met. St. Louis Sewer Dist., 1974-80, chmn., 1978-79; pres. Clayton Twp. Republican Club, 1973-77; mem. lawyers adv. com. Gt. Plains Legal Found., Kansas City, Mo., 1976—; mem. Boone County Rep. Central Com., 1962-68. Served to capt. USAF, 1955-57. Mem. Am. Bar Assn., Mo. Bar Assn., Bar Assn. Met. St. Louis, Westminster Coll. Alumni Assn. (pres. 1978-80). Episcopalian. Clubs: Mo. Athletic, Rotary, Masons, Round Table of St. Louis. Asso. editor Mich. Law Rev., 1953-54. Office: 301 N Memorial Dr St Louis MO 63102

YOUNG, MICHAEL ALAN, oil corp. exec.; b. Bellefontaine, Ohio, Jan. 16, 1947; s. James Franklin and Virginia Alice Y.; B.S., Bowling Green State U., 1974; A.A.B., Miami-Jacobs Jr. Coll., 1966; m. Dorothy M. Sulivan, Oct. 21, 1967; 1 dau., Alicia Renee. With Marathon Oil Co., Findlay, Ohio, 1966—, system analyst, 1974-75, system coordinator, 1975, refining, mktg. systems coordinator, 1975-76, data mgr., 1976-78, crude oil supply analyst, 1978-79, fgn. coordinator crude oil supply, 1979—. Mem. Explorer adv. bd. Boy Scouts Am., 1969-70; mem. St. Michael's Sch. Bd., 1980-81. Mem. Assn. Systems Mgmt. (cert. of recognition 1976, 78), Pride User Assn. Home: 225 3d St Findlay OH 45840 Office: Marathon Oil Co 539 S Main St Findlay OH 45840

YOUNG, MILTON R., U.S. senator; b. Berlin, N.D., Dec. 6, 1897; s. John Young and Rachel (Zimmerman) Y.; student N.D. State Agr. Coll. and Graceland Coll., Lamoni, Iowa; m. 2d, Patricia M. Byrne, Dec. 27, 1969; children by previous marriage-Wendell M., Duane C., John M. Mem. N.D. Ho. of Reps., 1933-34, N.D. Senate, 1935-45; U.S. Senator from N.D., 1945-81, sec. to Senate Republican Conf. Com., 1946-71, ranking Rep. on Senate Appropriations Com., 1967—, Rep. dean of Senate, mem. Agr., Nutrition and Forestry Com. Home: La Moure ND 58458

YOUNG, ROBERT ANTON, Congressman; b. St. Louis, Nov. 27, 1923; s. Melvin A. and Margaret (Degnan) Y.; student pub. schs., St. Louis; m. Irene Slawson, Nov. 27, 1947; children—Anne Young Lewis, Robert A., Margaret Mary. Mem. 95th-97th Congresses from 2d Mo. Dist., mem. Pub. Works and Transp. Com., Sci. and Tech. Com.; Democratic committeeman Airport Twp., St. Louis County, 1952-77; mem. Mo. Ho. of Reps., 1956-62; mem. Mo. Senate, 1962-76. Mem. Pipefitters Union, Am. Legion, VFW (post comdr.), Amvets (life). Club: St. Ann Lions. Recipient awards for meritorious service St. Louis Globe Democrat, 1972, 74, 76. Office: 4154 Cypress Rd Saint Ann MO 63074 also 1317 Longworth Bldg Washington DC 20515

YOUNG, ROBERT ARTHUR, coal co. exec.; b. Waterloo, Iowa, Sept. 23, 1910; s. J. Arthur and Gertrude M. (Lukhart) Y.; B.S., U. Iowa, 1932; m. Edith Van Houten, Feb. 3, 1932; children—Robert Arthur, James Van. Partner, Young Coal Co., Waterloo, 1932—; pres. Young Lumber Co., Waterloo, 1964—; partner Young Plumbing & Heating Co., Waterloo, 1950-60; v.p. Artificial Ice & Cold Storage, Waterloo, 1960-79; dir. Waterloo Savs. Bank, Black Hawk Broadcasting Co., Keller Apex Loan Co. Mem. Iowa Devel. Commn., 1969-73; mem. Republican Central Com., 1972—; trustee Waterloo Auditorium Commn., 1969-73, Mus. History and Sci., 1969—; chmn. bd. trustees Waterloo YMCA, 1950-76; mem. bd. control athletics U. Iowa, 1966-78; co-trustee McElroy Trust, 1965—; chmn. bd. trustees Grout Mus. History and Sci., 1972—. Mem. Sigma Alpha Epsilon, Beta Gamma Sigma. Congregationalist (chmn. bd. trustees 1945-76). Clubs: Masons, Shriners, Elks, Rotary. Home: 135 Pershing Rd Waterloo IA 50701 Office: 430 W 1st St Waterloo IA 50704

YOUNG, ROBERT LAWRENCE, ophthalmologist; b. Harlem, Mont., Oct. 25, 1918; s. Morris Davis and Esther Rae (Urkov) Yampolsky; B.S., U. Ill., 1940, M.D., 1943; m. Roberta Sternberg, Oct. 10, 1943; children—Fredric, Barbara, James, Michael. Intern, Michael Reese Hosp., Chgo., 1944, resident, 1949-50; resident U. Ill. Hosp., 1948-49, Aspinwall VA Hosp., Pitts., 1950; practice medicine specializing in ophthalmology, Gary, Ind., 1951—; mem. staff, pres. St. Mary of Mercy Hosp., Gary; sr. staff Meth. Hosp., Ind. U. Hosp., both Gary, Community Hosp., Munster, Ind., Our Lady of Mercy Hosp., Dyer, Ind.; mem. adv. com. Ind. U. N.W. br. Med. Sch. Bd. dirs. Munster Community Hosp. Served to capt. M.C., AUS, 1946-48. Diplomate Am. Bd. Ophthalmology. Fellow Internat. Coll. Surgeons; mem. AMA, Assn. Research in Ophthalmology, World Med. Assn., Am. Acad. Ophthalmology, Ind., N.W. Ind., Chgo. ophthalmology socs., AAAS, Ind., Munster chambers commerce, Tau Delta Phi, Phi Delta Epsilon. Democrat. Jewish (temple mens' club). Club: B'nai B'rith. Home: 8809 Crestwood Munster IN 46321 Office: 1646 45th Ave Munster IN 46321

YOUNG, SUMNER BACHELER, ret. lawyer; b. Marion, Mass., Aug. 14, 1898; s. Frank Linnaeus and Minnie Ella (Jones) Y.; A.B., Harvard U., 1920, J.D., 1927; m. Sidney Washburn, Aug. 19, 1925; children—Elisabeth W. Young Krueger, Rosamond, Sidney Young Wear, Sumner S., Jeremiah O'B. Admitted to Minn. bar, 1927, U.S. Supreme Ct. bar, 1950; trainee Frank L. Young Co., Boston, 1920-24, then dir.; with law office Prendergast & Flannery, Mpls., 1928-31; partner Prendergast, Flannery & Young, 1931-37; with law dept. Cargill, Inc., Mpls., 1937-60, asst. sec., 1937-61, v.p., dir., 1961-63, ret., 1963, spl. counsel to exec. com. bd. dirs., 1949-61, with adminstrn. div., 1960-63; counsel Cargill Securities Co., to 1963, now ret. Mayor, Village of Woodland (Minn.), 1949-53. Served as elec. 2/c (R) and elec. 1/c (R) USNRF, 1917-19. Mem. IEEE, Am. Radio Relay League, Am. Polar Soc. Club: Wayzata (Minn.) Country. Contbr. articles to radio mag. Home: 2600 Maplewood Circle East Wayzata MN 55391

YOUNG, SUMNER SULLIVAN, bus. exec.; b. Mpls., Sept. 17, 1932; s. Sumner Bacheler and Sidney (Washburn) Y.; A.B., Brown U., 1955; m. Eris Lundin, Nov. 10, 1962; children—Katherine Dianne, Jennifer Eris. Account exec. Pidgeon Savage Lewis, Inc., 1957-60; advt. and market planning mgr. boat div. Brunswick Corp., 1960-62; account exec. Batten, Barton, Durstine & Osborn, N.Y.C., 1963; v.p. Erle Savage Co., Mpls., 1963-67, pres., 1967-72; chmn. bd. Larson Industries, Inc., Mpls., 1972-76; chmn., chief exec. officer Gen. Boats, Inc., Mpls., 1972—; pres. Advt. Agy., Inc., Mpls., 1975—. Trustee Eitel Hosp., Mpls., 1981—. Served to capt. USAF, spl. agt. Office Spl. Investigations, 1955-57. Mem. N. Central Marine Assn. (dir., pres.), Young Pres.'s Orgn., Minn. Execs. Orgn., Phi Gamma Delta. Clubs: Mpls.; Wayzata (Minn.) Yacht. Home: 2600 Maplewood Circle E Wayzata MN 55391 Office: 2200 Foshay Tower Minneapolis MN 55402

YOUNG, WILLA LOU, occupational therapist; b. Forrest City, Ark., Jan. 26, 1951; d. Johnnie and Maggie Louise Y.; B.S., Manchester Coll., 1973; M.Occupational Therapy, Western Mich. U., 1975. Substitute tchr. Gary (Ind.) public schs., 1973; staff occupational therapist Rush Presbyn. St. Lukes Med. Center, Chgo., 1975-78; supr. rehab. unit occupational therapy sect. Mercy Hosp. and Med. Center, Chgo., 1978—; chmn. Chgo. area Clin. Suprs. Group, 1979-80; mem. Occupational Therapy Licensure Com., 1980. Leader, Girl Scouts U.S.A., 1975-78; mem. alumni bd. dirs. Manchester Coll., 1981—. Thurgood Marshall grad. fellow, 1973. Mem. Am. Occupational Therapy Assn., Ill. Occupational Therapy Assn., Chgo. Area. Clin. Suprs. Group, Delta Sigma Theta. Methodist. Home: 737 Garfield St Apt 1 Oak Park IL 60304

YOUNG, WILLIAM MINEHAN, media cons.; b. Sharon, Pa., Mar. 5, 1933; s. Edward P. and Anna M. (Minehan) Y.; B.S. in Edn., Temple U., 1956, Ed.M., 1956, Ed.D., 1961; postgrad. Northwestern U., 1974; m. Marion R. Young, Jan. 28, 1961; children—Richard, Scott, Gregory. Secondary tchr. Phila. public schs., 1956-59; asst. prof. Temple U., 1959-64; adminstrv. officer, program mgr. Dept. Interior, 1964-67; coordinator profs. City U. Okla., 1967-69; dean spl. programs, prof. edn. William Paterson Coll., Paterson, N.J., 1969-71; dean edn. Chgo. State U., 1971-74; pres. Urban Dynamics, Inc., 1974—; dir. ednl. cons. div. William M. Young & Assos., Oak Park, Ill., 1974—; v.p. Studio 909, Inc., Oak Park, 1980—; pres. New Century Communications, Oak Park, 1978—; co-producer ednl. programs WFLD-TV, Chgo., 1973-74; producer, host radio talk show Young and Educated WGLD-FM, Chgo., 1972-73, weekly edn. show WFYR-FM, Chgo., 1973-74; cons. Internat. Assn. Machinists and Aerospace Workers, Union Operating Engrs., Nat. P.T.A. Bd. dirs. Consortium Colls. and Univs.; mem. profl. adv. bd. Ednl. Facilities Center, Loretto Adult Edn. Center; founder Nat. Urban Deans Biannual Conf. Recipient award Nat. Council Advancement Ednl. Writing, 1974. Mem. NEA (life), Am. Soc. Tng. and Devel., Nat. Assn. TV Program Execs., Ill. Tng. Dirs. Assn., Phi Delta Kappa. Clubs: Metropolitan, Ill. Athletic (Chgo.); Nat. Democratic, University, Nat. Press (Washington); Canadian (N.Y.C.). Author: (with Godfrey Cronin) 400 Navels: The Future of School Health in America, 1979; Single Parents and Their Teenagers, 1968; Talking with Tulsa Teens, 1969; The Paperback Survey: A Model for Urban Change, 1970; editor Challenge, 1972-74. Home: 1035 Wisconsin Ave Oak Park IL 60304 Office: 911 S Oak Park Ave Oak Park IL 60304

YOUNGBERG, SUSAN ANN, educator; b. Iron Mountain, Mich., May 28, 1951; d. Samuel B. and Evelyn Anna Strong; B.S., No. Mich. U., 1975, M.A., 1980; m. Michael Karl Youngberg, Sept. 4, 1971. Sec., Iron Mountain public schs., 1969-72; sec. to v.p. Lake Shore, Inc., Kingsford, Mich., 1973-76; tchr. office simulation Dickinson Area Vocat. Center, Kingsford, 1976—; co-owner Am. Vault Works. Active Dickinson County Spl. Olympics, Dickinson County Humane Soc. Recipient Outstanding Young Educator award Jaycees, 1980. Mem. Am. Bus. Women's Assn. (Woman of Yr., North Land chpt. 1979, past pres.), Am. Vocat. Assn., Nat. Bus. Edn. Assn., Upper Peninsula Bus. Edn. Assn., Mich. Bus. Edn. Assn., Mich. Edn. Assn., Delta Kappa Gamma, Phi Delta Kappa. Republican. Methodist. Club: Lady Elks. Home: 1102 W A St Iron Mountain MI 49801 Office: 300 North Blvd Kingsford MI 49801

YOUNGER, HOWARD WAYNE, container co. exec.; b. Westville, Okla., Aug. 26, 1947; s. Homer and Juanita (Hudson) Y.; A.A., San Joaquin Delta Coll., 1967; B.A., San Francisco State U., 1969, M.A., 1972; m. Ruth Pollard, June 16, 1967; children—Misty, Kevin. Supr., Continental Can Co., San Jose, Calif., 1968-72, dept. supr., Olympia, Wash., 1972-75, engr., 1975-76, project mgr., Chgo., 1976-78, mgr., Milw., 1978—. Served with Green Berets, U.S. Army, 1969-72. Mem. Ch. of Christ. Home: N78 W16398 Carl Ross Dr Menomonee Falls WI 53051 Office: Continental Can Co 4300 N Port Washington Rd Milwaukee WI 53212

YOUNGS, RONALD DEAN, vocat. edn. counselor; b. Bethany, Mo., Sept. 8, 1932; s. Lester Cole and Tula Mae (Davis) Y.; A.A., Trenton Jr. Coll., 1952; B.S. in Edn., N.W. Mo. State U., 1957; postgrad. U. Kans., summer 1959; M.Ed., U. Mo., 1961; postgrad. Central Mo. State U., 1965-66, summers 1966, 72; m. Janet Florene Jarrett, Dec. 23, 1952; children—Tula Denise, Ronald David, James Dale. Social studies tchr., Weston, Mo., 1957-60; counselor Raytown (Mo.) High Sch., 1961-71, Longview Community Coll., Lee's Summit, Mo., 1971-72; coordinator counseling and placement Joe Herndon Area Vocat. Tech. Sch., Raytown, 1972—. Served with USAF, 1952-54. Recipient Spl. Service award Mo. Guidance Assn., 1970, Leadership award Mo. Placement Specialists, 1979. Mem. Raytown Community Tchrs. Assn., NEA, Mo. Tchrs. Assn., Greater Kansas City Guidance Assn., Mo. Vocat. Assn., Am. Vocat. Assn. Republican. Home: 7819 Irwin St Raytown MO 64138 Office: 11501 E 350 Hwy Raytown MO 64138

YOURZAK, ROBERT JOSEPH, owner energy planning and engring. cons. exec.; b. Mpls., Aug. 27, 1947; s. Ruth Phyllis Sorenson; B.C.E., U. Minn., 1969; M.S.C.E., U. Wash., Seattle, 1971, M.B.A., 1975. Surveyor, N.C. Hoium & Assos., Mpls., part-time 1965-68, Lot Surveys Co., Mpls., part-time 1968-69; site layout engr. Sheehy Constrn. Co., St. Paul, 1968; structural engring. aide Dunham Assos., Mpls., part-time 1969; aircraft and aerospace structural engr., program rep. Boeing Co., Seattle, 1969-75; engr., estimator Howard S. Wright Constrn. Co., Seattle, 1976-77; dir. project devel. and adminstrn. DeLeuw Cather & Co., Seattle, 1977-78; sr. mgmt. cons. Alexander Grant & Co., Mpls., 1978-79; mgr. project systems dept., project mgr. Henningson, Durham & Richardson, Mpls., 1979-80; dir. project mgmt., regional offices Ellerbe Assos., Inc., Mpls., 1980-81. Principal, Energy Cons. Corp., St. Paul, 1982—. Lectr. engring. mgmt. U. Wash., part time 1977-78; adj. asst. prof. dept. civil and mineral engring. Inst. Tech., U. Minn., 1979—. Chmn. regional art group experience, Seattle Art Mus., 1975-78, mem. Pacific NW Arts Council, 1977-78, ex-officio adviser Mus. Week, 1976; bd. dirs. Friends of the Rep. Seattle Repertory Theatre, 1973-77; mem. Symphonics Seattle Symphony Orch., 1975-78; Scholar, Boeing Co., 1967-68, Sheehy Constrn. Co., summer 1967. Named an outstanding Young Man of Am., U.S. Jaycees, 1978; registered profl. engr., Wash., Minn. Mem. ASCE (chmn. continuing edn. subcom. Seattle chpt. 1976-79, Minn. chpt. 1979-80, chmn. program com. 1978, mem. transp. and urban planning tech. group 1978, Edmund Friedman Young Engr. award for profl. achievement 1979, chmn. energy com. 1980-81, sec. bd. dirs. 1981—), Sierra Club, Mpls. Soc. Fine Arts, Chi Epsilon (life). Clubs: Rainier (co-chmn. Oktoberfest), Chowder Soc., Mountaineers. Home: 7320 Gallagher Dr 325 Edina MN 55435 Office: 1144 Minnesota Bldg St Paul MN 55101

YOUSE, GLAD ROBINSON, composer; b. Miami, Okla., Oct. 22, 1898; d. James Fountain and Catherine Elizabeth (Green) Robinson; student Stephens Coll., Columbia, Mo., 1918-20; student composition with Tibor Serly, N.Y.C., 1945-52; D.F.A. (hon.), Baker U., Baldwin, Kans., 1976; m. Clarence E. Youse, May 16, 1920; 1 dau., Madolyn (Mrs. Edmund Page Babcock). Composer-dir. Jenkins Music Conf., Kansas City, Mo., 1948-66; nat. chmn. Sigma Alpha Iota Found., Des Moines, 1949-56; nat. music chmn. Nat. League Am. Pen Women, Washington, 1967-68; trustee Baker U., Baldwin, Kans., 1960-68. Recipient Alumnae Achievement citation Stephens Coll., 1955, Matrix Table award Theta Sigma Phi, 1965; Presdl. citation Nat. Fedn. Music Clubs, 1981. Mem. Kans. Authors Club (merit award 1975), ASCAP, Sigma Alpha Iota (hon., Ring of Excellence 1956), Beta Sigma Phi (hon., achievement award 1957). Republican. Methodist. Club: P.E.O. Composer over 200 published songs, choral works; recordings on Golden Crest Records, D/D Record Co. Home and office: 532 E 12th St Baxter Springs KS 66713

YOVICICH, JONES GEORGE STEVEN, civil engr., educator; b. Belgrade, Yugoslavia, June 2, 1927; came to U.S., 1952; s. Steven and Druga (Djurdjevic) Y.; B.S.C.E., Northwestern U., 1951, M.S.C.E., 1956, Ph.D., 1958; Ph.D., Hamilton State U., 1973; Dr.Econs. (hon.), U. Fla., 1972; m. Sofia Sekulic, 1960; 1 son. Civil engr. Hollabird & Root, Chgo., 1956-57; engr., gen. mgr. Arcadia Engring., Internat., Inc., Skokie, Ill., 1956-70, chmn. bd., 1970—; staff overseas and domestic projects U.S. C.E., 1951-54; prof. structural engring. Northwestern U., Evanston, Ill., 1965—; chmn. econs. U. Ill., Chgo., 1966-69. Legis. asst. Ill. Gen. Assembly, 1961-81; chmn. bd. Oakton Coll., 1968-74; pres. Hamilton State U., 1974-76, Tetrakear & Assos., Inc., 1968-79; dir. 1st Skokie Community Hosp. Mem. ASCE, Nat. Soc. Profl. Engrs. Author: "The Pneumatic Tube Goes Modern, 1958; Opportunities in Constrn., 1960; Mgmt. and Labor, 1962; contbr. articles to profl. jours. Home: 5309 Arcadia St Skokie IL 60076 Office: PO Box 712 Skokie IL 60076

YU, ANNE RAMONA WING-MUI, psychologist; b. Hong Kong, Apr. 9, 1948; came to U.S., 1968, naturalized, 1974; d. Hing-wan and Sin-wah (Yau) Yu; B.A. with honors in Psychology, Ohio U., 1971; M.A., So. Ill. U., 1975. Psychologist, Delta Counseling and Guidance Center, Monticello, Ark., 1975-76, Mid-Nebr. Community Mental Health Center, Grand Island, Nebr., 1977—; supr. satellite clinic Loup Valley Mental Health Center, Loup City, Nebr., 1978-79; project dir. Protection from Domestic Abuse, 1978-79; pres. Taskforce on Domestic Violence and Sexual Assault, Grand Island, 1980-82. Mem. mem. Mental Health Bd. Hall County, 1979—. Recipient award of outstanding community service Gov. of Nebr., 1981. Mem. Nebr. Assn. Profl. Psychologists (membership chmn. 1977-78), Am. Psychol. Assn., Am. Assn. for Marriage and Family Therapy (v.p. Nebr. div. 1981-82), Am. Assn. Sex Educators, Counselors, and Therapists, Assn. Women in Psychology, Asian-Am. Psychol. Assn. Club: Bus. and Profl. Women's. Home: Apt 94 1524 Coventry Ln Grand Island NE 68801 Office: Mid-Nebr Community Mental Health Center 914 Baumann Dr Grand Island NE 68801

YUENGER, JAMES LAURY, univ. adminstr.; b. Green Bay, Wis., June 13, 1939; s. David A. and Carol J. (Haines) Y.; B.A., St. Norbert Coll., 1961; m. Blanche Schulz, Nov. 9, 1963; 1 son, Jay N. Reporter, AP, Milw., 1961-62; editor Wis. Rapids (Wis.) Tribune, 1962-63; reporter, editor Chgo. Tribune, 1963-81, Washington corr., 1967-70, Moscow corr., 1970-72, London corr., 1975-76; dir. news and info. U. Chgo., 1981—. Served with U.S. Army, 1957-58. Recipient Golden Key award Ill. Dept. Mental Health, 1965; Edward S. Beck award for disting. fgn. correspondence Chgo. Tribune, 1971, 76. Mem. Am. Kitefliers Assn. Clubs: Quadrangle, Chgo. Press, Chappaquiddick (Mass.) Press. Office: 5801 S Ellis Ave Chicago IL 60637

YUNE, HEUN YUNG, physician; b. Seoul, Korea, Feb. 1, 1929; came to U.S., 1966, naturalized, 1972; s. Sun Wook and Won Eun (Lee) Y.; M.D., Severance Med. Coll., Seoul, 1956; m. Kay Kim, Apr. 12, 1956; children—Jeanny Kim, Helen Kay, Marc Eany. Intern Presbyn. Center, Jeonju, 1956-57, resident in surgery, 1957-60, chief dept. radiology, 1964-66; resident in radiology; Vanderbilt U. Hosp., Nashville, 1960-63; instr. radiology Severance Med. Coll., Korea, 1964-66; instr. radiology Vanderbilt U., 1962-64, asst. prof., 1966-70, asso. prof., 1970-71; prof. radiology Ind. U. Med. Sch., Indpls., 1971—; mem. staff Ind. U. Hosp., Wishard Meml. Hosp., Indpls. VA Hosp. Elder, Presbyn. Ch. Served with Korean Army, 1951-55. Decorated Bronze Star (U.S.); Wharang (Korea). Diplomate Am. Bd. Radiology, Korean Bd. Radiology. Mem. Am. Coll. Radiology, Ind.

Roentgen Soc., Assn. U. Radiologists, Internat. Soc. Lymphology, Radiol. Soc. N. Am., Am. Roentgen Ray Soc., Am. Soc. Head and Neck Radiology (charter), AMA, Ind. Med. Assn., Marion County Med. Soc., Severance Alumni Assn. U.S.A., Ind. U. Friends of Music, Indpls. Mus. Art, Art League Indpls., Fine Arts Soc. Indpls., Alpha Omega Alpha. Clubs: North Willow, Heritage Lake Assn. Contbr. articles to profl. jours.; edit. rev. Am. Jour. Roentgenology, 1975—. Home: 8932 Spicewood Ct Indianapolis IN 46260 Office: 1100 W Michigan St Indianapolis IN 46223

ZABECKI, DAVID TADEUSZ, quality engr.; b. Springfield, Mass., Aug. 8, 1947; s. Julian Tadeusz and Virginia Charlotte (Luthgren) Z.; B.A., Xavier U., 1972, M.A., 1973; M.S., Fla. Inst. Tech., 1976; m. Christine Ann Hellkamp, July 29, 1972; 1 son, Konrad Josef. Patrolman, Xavier U. Campus Police, Cin., 1972-74; quality assurance specialist Rock Island (Ill.) Aresenal, 1974-77; quality engr. Deere & Co., Moline, Ill., 1977—; adj. instr. Fla. Inst. Tech., 1977-79; lectr. in field. Served with U.S. Army, 1966-69; capt. Ill. N.G. Decorated Combat Infantryman's Badge, Bronze Star, Army Commendation medal, others. Mem. Am. Soc. Quality Control (sr. mem., cert. quality and reliability engr.), Res. Officers Assn., Am. Soc. Internat. Law, Am., German philatelic socs., V.F.W., Co. Mil. Historians, Royal Arty. Assn., Nat. Eagle Scouts Assn., Alpha Sigma Nu. Author: Karl Doenitz: A Defense, 1981, also articles; developer contbn. differential concept of quality cost analysis. Home: 29 Oak Ln Davenport IA 52803 Office: John Deere Harvester Works East Moline IL 61244

ZABLOCKI, CLEMENT JOHN, Congressman; b. Milw., Nov. 18, 1912; s. Mathew and Mary (Jankowski) Z.; Ph.B., Marquette U., 1936, LL.D. (hon.), 1966; LL.D., Alverno Coll., 1969, Sogang U., Seoul, Korea, 1974, Alliance Coll., 1975, Jagiellonian U., Cracow, Poland, 1975, U. Notre Dame, 1979; m. Blanche Janic, May 26, 1937 (dec. July 1977); children—Joseph, Jane. High sch. tchr., 1938-39; organist, choir dir., 1932-48; mem. Wis. Senate, 1942-48; mem. 81st to 97th Congresses from 4th Wis. Dist., chmn. fgn. affairs com., chmn. subcom. internat. security and sci. affairs, mem. permanent select com. on intelligence; mem. spl. congressional study mission to West Europe, 1951, S. Asia and Far East, 1953, 54, 63, Poland, 1961; U.S. del. 14th Gen. Assembly UN, 1959; mem. adv. council Center for Strategic Studies, Georgetown U.; congressional adviser U.S. del. Philippine U.S. Commn. Study Vets. Problems; mem. Commn. on Orgn. Govt. for Conduct Fgn. Policy. Mem. Father Marquette Tercentenary Commn. Named Alumnus of Yr., Marquette U., 1979. Mem. Cath. Order of Foresters, St. Vincent Conf., Polish Nat. Alliance, Fedn. Polish Assn. Am., Holy Name Soc. Democrat. Roman Catholic. Home: 3245 W Drury Ln Milwaukee WI 53215 Office: 2183 Rayburn House Office Bldg Washington DC 20515

ZABOROWSKI, ROBERT RONALD JOHN MARIA, archbishop; b. Detroit, Mar. 14, 1946; s. Richard and Bernice Julia (Zaborowski) Kuhlman; student Holy Cross Old Cath. Sem., 1964-68; D.D., St. Ignatius B.M. Old Cath. Sem., 1972, J.C.D., 1974, S.T.D., 1976, Ph.D., 1976, Psy.D., 1977, D.S.S., 1977, D.D.M., 1977, D.Th.D., 1977. Ch. organist, choirmaster Detroit chs., 1962-70; ordained priest Mariavite Old Cath. Ch., 1968, elected bishop, 1971; consecrated Bishop Cum Jure Successionis, 1972, succeeded to Archiepiscopal Dignity, 1972, appointed by Jure Successionis to dignity of Prime Bishop of Mariavite Old Cath. Ch., Province of N. Am., Wyandotte, Mich., 1972—; lectr. in field. Mem. St. Irenaeus Inst. of France. Decorated knight of Grand Cross, Sovereign Order of St. John of Jerusalem, Knights of Malta, knight of justice Sovereign Order of St. John of Jerusalem Knights Hospitaller, prelate of Sovereign Teutonic Order of Levant, Eng., Count of City by St. Stephano Alberto Policastro. Contbr. articles to profl. jours. Address: 2803 10th St Wyandotte MI 48192

ZACCARELLI, BROTHER HERMAN EUGENE, food service expert, author; b. New Castle, Pa., Apr. 11, 1931; s. Frank and Mary (Germaine) Z.; B.S. in Hotel Adminstrn., Cornell U., 1952; student George Washington U. Joined Congregation of Holy Cross, Roman Catholic Ch., 1949; dir. food services Moreau Hall, U. Notre Dame (Ind.), 1954-56, Notre Dame High Sch., Bridgeport, Conn., 1956-60; founder, dir. Internat. Food Research and Ednl. Center, North Easton, Mass., 1956-73; dir. ednl. research and devel. Cahners Books Internat., Boston, 1974—; mgmt. systems editor Chef Instl. mag., N.Y.C., 1974—; vis. prof. Sch. Hotel, Restaurant and Instl. Mgmt., U. Minn., Crookston, 1978; dir. Restaurant, Hotel and Instl. Mgmt. Inst., Purdue U., West Lafayette, Ind., 1978—; faculty Eastern Regional Ednl. Conf., Nat. Assn. Coll. Aux. Services, Cortland, N.Y., 1974; tchr., Nepal, Sri Lanka and Pakistan, 1976. Chmn. nat. food service industry task force Am. Correctional Food Service Assn., 1976; bd. dirs. Permanent Ware Inst.; bd. advisers Culinary Arts Program, Town of Lexington, Mass., Sch. Hotel and Restaurant Adminstrn., U. New Haven (Conn.), Sch. Hotel and Restaurant Mgmt., U. N.Mex., Albuquerque. Mem. Nat. Restaurant Assn., Am. Soc. Tng. and Devel., Am. Sch. Food Service Assn., Council Hotel, Restaurant and Instl. Edn., Soc. Advancement Food Service Research, Catholic Golden Age Assn. (dir. 1974), Internat. Food Service Mfrs. Assn. (mem. nutrition com. 1970). Author: Food Service Manual for School Cafeterias, 1956; The Family Cookbook, 1957; The Institutional Food Manual, 1960; The Cookbook that Tells You How, 1974; food service editor Golf Business, 1976. Contbr. articles in field to profl. jours. Office: Restaurant Hotel and Instl Mgmt Inst Stewart Center Purdue U West Lafayette IN 47907

ZACHEL, KATHERINE ANN, ednl. cons.; b. Toledo, Ohio, Dec. 13, 1949; d. Harry Andrew and Sixta (Cintron) Z.; B.Ed., U. Toledo, 1971, M.Ed., 1974, Ed.S., 1977, postgrad., 1980—. Tchr., Toledo public schs., 1971-74; reading tchr. Oregon (Ohio) city schs., 1974-76; ednl. cons. Lucas County Office Edn., Toledo, 1976—. Recipient Nat. Health and Safety Edn. award ARC, 1981. Mem. Internat. Reading Assn., Nat. Middle Sch. Assn., Assn. Supervision and Curriculum Devel., Ohio Middle Sch. Assn., N.W. Sch. Suprs. Assn., Phi Delta Kappa, Phi Kappa Phi, Delta Kappa Gamma, Pi Lambda Theta, Kappa Delta Pi. Democrat. Roman Catholic. Home: 1817 Dority St Toledo OH 43615 Office: 3350 Collingwood St Toledo OH 43610

ZACHER, ALLAN NORMAN, JR., clergyman, psychologist, lawyer; b. Decatur, Ill., May 23, 1928; s. Allan Norman and Eleanor (Shaw) Z.; student Washington U. Sch. Bus. and Pub. Adminstrn., St. Louis, 1946, 48-50; J.D., Washington U., 1952, Ph.D., 1971; M.Div., Va. Theol. Sem., 1955; S.T.M., Eden Theol. Sem., 1966; m. Estelle Medalie, July 19, 1952; children—Allan Norman III, Mark, John. Admitted to Mo. bar, 1952; asso. firm Fred B. Whalen, St. Louis, 1950-52; ordained to ministry Episcopal Ch., 1955; asst. rector Truro Episcopal Ch., Fairfax, Va., 1955-58; canon counselor Christ Ch. Cathedral, St. Louis, 1958-64; dir. Pastoral Counseling Inst., St. Louis, 1958—; vicar Grace Episcopal Ch., St. Louis, 1958-63; vis. lectr. Eden Sem., St. Louis, Washington U. Sch. Law; chmn. dept. Christian social relations Diocese of Mo., 1959-63, mem. council, 1969-63; cons. to family life, assn. joint family life com. Nat. Council Episcopal Ch., 1962-65; labor arbitrator Fed. Mediation and Conciliation Service, 1959—. Pres. mem. steering com. St. Louis Group Psychotherapy Forum, 1962-65; mem. St. Louis Bd. Edn., 1963-69; pres. Northside Neighborhood Council, St. Louis, 1959-61; treas. Mo. Council Family Relations. Chmn. psychodrama and religion round table, 1st Internat. Congress of Psychodrama, Milan, Italy, 1964, 2d Internat. Congress, Barcelona, Spain, 1966. Bd. dirs. Grace Hill House, St. Louis, chaplain, 1958-63. Served with AUS, 1946-48, Kent fellow, 1968; Community Mental Health Research fellow, 1968; cert. trainer and practitioner in psychodrama and group psychotherapy Am. Bd. Examiners; lic. clin. psychologist, Mo., Ill.; mem. Nat. Register Health Service Providers in Psychology. Fellow Am. Acad. Matrimonial lawyers; mem. St. Louis (family law com.), Am. (family law com. on marriage and family counseling conciliation), Mo. (family law com.), Fed. bar, assns., Am. Soc. Group Psychotherapy and Psychodrama, Episcopal Soc. for Racial Unity (nat. bd.), Am. Assn. Pastoral Counselors (diplomate; mem. funding bd. 1963-65), Am. Assn. Marriage Counselors, Mo. Psychol. Assn., Soc. St. Louis Psychologists (past pres.), Assn. for Clin. Pastoral Edn., Soc. for Religion in Higher Edn. Contbr. articles to religious, psychol. and legal publs. Home: 16 Hortense Pl Saint Louis MO 63108 Office: 8420 Delmar Blvd Saint Louis MO 63124

ZADEREJ, ANDREW, elec. engr.; b. Yampil, Ukraine, July 1, 1921; came to U.S., 1949, naturalized, 1954; s. Jacobs and Olga Z.; E.E., Kiev Poly. Inst., 1942; m. Ludmila Stupina, Sept. 12, 1943; children—Nick, George, Andy, Natalie. Elec. engr. Franklin Elec. Co., Bluffton, Ind., 1950-64; sr. research engr. Magnavox, Ft. Wayne, Ind., 1964-70; v.p. engring. Monitron, South Bend, Ind., 1970-73, Unitron, Elkhart, Ind., 1974-80; dir. research JMJ Electronics, Inc., Mishawaka, Ind., 1980—, pres. Cybernetic Logic Systems, 1981—. Mem. adv. bd. chmn.'s com. U.S. Senate, 1981; co-founder Presdl. Task Force in U.S.A. Mem. AAAS, IEEE, N.Y. Acad. Scis., Fedn. Am. Scientists. Contbr. articles to tech. publs.; patentee in field. Home: 1543 Southbrook St South Bend IN 46614 Office: 4016 N Home St Mishawaka IN 46544

ZAFFKE, VIRGINIA BLANCHE, ednl. adminstr.; b. Backus, Minn., Jan. 17, 1927; d. Aaron, and Blanche Marie (Bloom) Z.; B.S., U. Minn., 1955, M.A., 1969, postgrad., 1970—; m. M. Donald Johnson, Sept. 12, 1946; 1 son, Maurice Johnson Jaffke. High sch. tchr. various cities, Minn., 1955-65; program coordinator Minn. Dept. Public Welfare, 1966-67; dir. child devel. program Minn. Community Coll. System, Brainerd Community Coll., 1967—; condr. workshops, cons. in field. Mem. Minn. Com. on Children and Youth; adv. bd. home econs. program Heartland Vocat. Center, Minn. Learning Center; mem. Minn. Council on Handicapped; chmn. Minn. State Home Econs. Edn. Planning Bd.; mem. Central Minn. Health Manpower Region D Council, Area Health Edn. Planning Council; adult 4-H leader; counselor Camp Jim, Brainerd, Minn.; active Am. Youth Found., YWCA; chmn. Red River Valley Fine Arts Festival, 1964; adv. Future Homemakers Am. Standard Oil scholar, 1945; Readers Digest scholar, 1945; 4-H Nat. Leadership scholar, 1944-45. Mem. AAUW, Bus. and Profl. Women's Club, Minn. Assn. Home Econs., Nat. Assn. Home Econs., Minn. Home Econs. Assn. (counselor Dist. 6 exec. bd.), exec. Am. Youth Found., Minn. Edn. Assn., Community Coll. Faculty Assn. (pres.), Am. Vocat. Edn. Assn., Minn. Vocat. Edn. Assn., Council of Exceptional Children, Am. Assn. Mental Deficiency, Minn. Assn. Retarded Children, Nat. Assn. Retarded Children. Clubs: Christian Women's, Zonta. Contbr. to publs. in field, weekly radio programs, Mpls. and Red River Valley; newspaper columnist. Home: Zaffke Farms Backus MN 56435 Office: Brainerd Community Coll College Dr Brainerd MN 56401

ZAGEL, JAMES BLOCK, state govt. ofcl.; b. Chgo., Mar. 4, 1941; B.A., U. Chgo., 1962, M.A. in Philosophy, 1962; J.D., Harvard U., 1965; m. Margaret Maxwell, May 27, 1979. Admitted to Ill. bar, 1965; asst. state's atty. Cook County (Ill.), 1965-69; asst. atty. gen., chief criminal justice div. State of Ill., 1970-77; chief pros. atty. Ill. Jud. Inquiry Bd., 1973-75; chief asst. atty. gen. State of Ariz., 1975; exec. dir. Ill. Law Enforcement Commn., 1977-79; dir. Ill. Dept. Revenue, 1979-80, Ill. Dept. Law Enforcement, 1980—; chmn. Gov. Ill. Adv. Council Criminal Justice Legislation, 1978—; mem. coms. Supreme Ct. Ill. Mem. Am. Bar Assn., Internat. Assn. Chiefs Police, Ill. Bar Assn., Ill. Assn. Chiefs Police (exec. bd.), Chgo. Bar Assn. Co-author: Criminal Law and Its Administration, 3d edit., 1980; Cases and Comments on Criminal Procedure, 2d edit., 1980. Address: Room 103 Armory Bldg Springfield IL 62706

ZAGOL, STAN, utility co. exec.; b. Chgo., Oct. 26, 1924; s. Frank S. and Caroline (Specht) Z.; B.S., U. Ill., 1949, postgrad., 1949-50; m. Elizabeth Ann Fedrowski, Feb. 9, 1946; children—S. Richard, Steven A., Sharon Elizabeth. Gen. bus. mgr. Council 27, AFSC&ME, AFL-CIO, Mo., 1951-54; v.p., gen. mgr. U.S. Camo Corp., Kansas City, Mo., 1956-58; employment mgr. Toledo Edison Co., 1960-74, indsl. relations dir., 1962-74, Eastern dist. mgr., 1974-79, dir. personnel group, 1979—; chmn. indsl. relations com. Ohio Electric Utility Inst. Vice-pres. United Way of Sandusky County, 1978-79; pres. Lucas County Bd. Edn., 1970-76; mem. Penta County Bd. Edn., 1974-76; mem. citizens com. TAGRA Children's Services Bd.; chmn., moderator YMCA Town Meeting of the Air com., 1970-73. Served with USAAF, 1941-45; ETO. Decorated Air medal. Mem. Toledo Personnel Mgmt. Assn. (past pres.), Indsl. Relations Research Assn., Am. Mgmt. Assn., Sandusky County C. of C. (pres. 1979-80), Toledo C. of C., Edison Electric Inst. Clubs: Toledo; Fremont Rotary. Home: 2420 County Squire Ln Toledo OH 43615 Office: 300 Madison Ave Edison Plaza Toledo OH 43652

ZAIDI, MAHMOOD A., economist; b. India, Dec. 28, 1930; s. Sabir Husain and Naimat (Ali) Z.; B.A. with honors, UCLA, 1957, M.A., 1958; Ph.D. (Ford Found. fellow), U. Calif., Berkeley, 1966. Instr. econs. UCLA, U. Calif., Berkeley, 1958-62; mem. faculty U. Minn., Mpls., 1965—, now prof. econs., dir. grad. study Indsl. Relations Center; vis. prof. U. Western Australia, summer 1974; vis. prof. U. New South Wales (Australia), 1979-80; dir. Internat. Found. for Biosocial Devel. and Human Health, 1978—. Mem. AAUP (trustee 1973-74), Am. Econs. Assn., Royal Econ. Soc., Econometric Soc., Can. Econs. Assn., Indsl. Relations Research Assn., AAAS, Internat. Indsl. Relations Assn. Author: (with Sylvia Ostry) Labour Economics in Canada, 3d edit., 1979; mem. editorial bd. Bioscis. Communications, 1975-78, Health Communications and Computer Scis., 1979—, Eastern Econ. Jour., 1981—. Home: 528 N Mississippi River Blvd Saint Paul MN 55104 Office: Industrial Relations Center U Minn Minneapolis MN 55455

ZAIS, JERROLD C., mfg. co. exec.; b. Kenosha, Wis., Sept. 26, 1945; s. Carmen E. and Valeria R. (Kelnhofer) Z.; student U. Wis., 1977, Marquette U., 1978; children—Lynn, Michael. Prodn. draftsman Marshfield Homes, Inc., Marshfield, Wis., 1963-67; prodn. foreman, asst. plant mgr. Wick Homes, Mazomanie, Wis., 1967-71, plant mgr., Moberly, Mo., 1971-73; material handling mgr. Wausau Homes, Wausau, Wis., 1973-78, service parts distbn. mgr., 1978-80; inventory control mgr. Hoffer's Inc., Wausau, 1980—. Active various charitable orgns. Mem. Am. Prodn. and Inventory Control Soc., Wis. Valley Suprs. Council. Roman Catholic. Home: 805 Flieth St Apt 28 Wausau WI 54401 Office: 310 Bellis St Wausau WI 54401

ZAIS, ROBERT STANLEY, educator; b. Providence, R.I., Dec. 20, 1928; s. Louis and Lena (Baker) Z.; A.B., Brown U., 1950, M.A.T., 1963; Ph.D., U. Conn., 1968; m. Edith Barbara Morein, Sept. 14, 1952; children—Louis Scott, Roberta Susan. Buyer, Fall River (Mass.) Public Markets, Inc., 1950-53; propr. Edith Roberts, Providence, 1955-61; pres. Wayland Sq. Parking Corp., Providence, 1957-60; tchr. English public schs., Warren, R.I., 1963-66; research asst. U. Conn., 1966-68; prof. curriculum and instrn. Kent State U., 1968—. Served with U.S. Army, 1953-55. Mem. NEA, Assn. Supervision and Curriculum Devel., Nat. Soc. Study of Edn., Am. Ednl. Research Assn., Ohio Edn. Assn., AAUP, Phi Delta Kappa. Author: Curriculum: Principles and Foundations, 1976. Contbr. articles to profl. jours. Home: 431 Wilson Ave Kent OH 44240 Office: 407 White Hall Kent State Univ Kent OH 44242

ZALTZMAN, HOWARD ALAN, interior design firm exec.; b. Chgo., June 27, 1948; s. Arthur and Evelyn (Cherman) Z.; B.S., U. Pa., 1970; diploma Harrington Inst. Interior Design, 1977. With customer relations dept. Chesterfield Devel. Corp., Chgo., 1970-79; owner Howard Alan Zaltzman Interior Design, Ltd., Deefield, Ill., 1979—. Served with N.G., 1970-76. Recipient Am. Legion award, 1974. Mem. Am. Soc. Interior Designers (asso.), Kappa Alpha Soc. Address: Howard Alan Zaltzman Interior Design Ltd 1240 Somerset St Deerfield IL 60015

ZAMARRIPA, EDWARD J., ednl. adminstr.; b. Canon City, Colo., Sept. 19, 1941; s. Leo and Helen (Carillo) Z.; B.A., So. Colo. State Coll., 1966; M.S., Fla. State U., 1969; postgrad U. Kans.; m. Mary Ann Moguez, Apr. 21, 1967; children—Gregory Todd, Kevin Patrick. Tchr., prin. Mental Retardation Center, Colo. State Hosp., Pueblo, 1966-67; asst. dir. adminstrn. Bur. Child Research, U. Kans., Lawrence, 1969-72, exec. asst., Center Mental Retardation and Human Devel., 1970-72, asso. dir. adminstrn. Bur. Child Research and Kans. Center Mental Retardation and Human Devel., 1972—. Cubmaster, Boy Scouts Am. Heart of Am. council, 1976—; coach Little League Football, 1979—. Fla. State U. fellow, 1967-69. Mem. Am. Assn. Mental Deficiency, Am. Assn. U. Affiliated Programs for Developmentally Disabled, Mental Retardation Research Centers Dirs. and Adminstrs. Office: Bur Child Research U Kans Lawrence KS 66045

ZAMBRANO, ADOLFO RAUL, research metallurgist; b. Mompos, Colombia, Sept. 27, 1934; came to U.S., 1966; s. Pedro and Zoila (Vanegas-Meza) Z.; B.Sc. in Metallurgy, Nat. U. Colombia, 1961; M.Sc., Colo. Sch. Mines, 1969, Ph.D., 1971; m. Leonor Alicia Serrano, Jan. 4, 1963; children—Luis, Maria, Sylvia, Joseph, Peter. Tchr. math. Lorica High Sch. (Colombia), 1955-56; asst. prof. metallurgy Nat. U. Colombia, Medellin, 1964-66; teaching asst. Colo. Sch. Mines, Golden, 1968-69; research metallurgist, sr. research metallurgist Hanna Mining Co., Nashwauk, Minn., 1970-75, 76-78, sr. supervising research metallurgist, 1979—. Republican. Roman Catholic. Patentee in field. Office: PO Box 67 Nashwauk MN 55769

ZANA, TIBOR LASZLO, dancer, choreographer, educator; b. Budapest, Hungary, Aug. 15, 1936; s. Karoly and Ilona (Matlak) Z.; came to U.S., 1957, naturalized, 1964; B.A., Carroll Coll., 1961; M.F.A. U. Wis., 1964; m. Betty Steffen, Dec. 16, 1961. Mem. Corps de Ballet, Operett Theatre, Budapest, Hungary, 1952-55; soloist Tchaikovsky Concert Hall, Moscow, USSR, 1956; mem. Washington Ballet Co., 1957-58; tchr. Kathryn Hubbard Dance Studio, Madison, Wis., 1959-61; pvt. tchr. ballet, Lake Mills, Wis., 1958-59, Milw., 1958-59, Whitewater, Wis., 1959-60, Sheboygan, Wis., 1959-63; lectr. dept. phys. edn. for women U. Wis., Madison, 1964-68, asst. prof., 1969-71, asso. prof., 1971-77, prof., 1977—; cons. Wis. Idea Theater, 1966-68, Carroll Coll., Wis., 1967, U. Wis. Extension Community Arts Devel., 1968-71, Hungarian Nat. Ballet Sch., Budapest, 1970; choreographer artistic dir. Wis. Ballet Co., 1961-76; adv. on ballet Wis. Dance Council, 1969-70; guest choreographer Cullberg Ballet, Stockholm, 1973, Boston Ballet, 1974, Mich. Ballet Theater, 1974, Omaha Ballet, 1975, Mich. Ballet Theatre, 1975; adjudicator Detroit Dance Festival, 1975; cons. Sta. WHA-TV, 1976; ballet tchr. for Craft of Choreography Conf., New Orleans, 1974, chmn., Madison, 1971. Recipient Gov.'s Award for Excellence in the Arts, 1969; Nat. Endowment for the Arts grantee, 1969-75, Young Audiences Inc. grantee, 1970-75. Mem. Mid-States Regional Ballet Assn. (exec. v.p. 1974-75), Nat. Assn. Regional Ballet (dir. 1978—). Home: 6229 Countryside Ln Madison WI 53705 Office: Univ of Wisconsin Lathrop Hall Madison WI 53706

ZANDER, LLOYD FRED, state govt. ofcl.; b. New Rockford, N.D., July 12, 1923; s. Otto Emil and Clara Zander; student New Rockford schs.; m. June Elizabeth Minnie Proefrock, Oct. 5, 1942; children—David, Tommy, Joyce, Rodney, Richard. Claims examiner VA, 1946-50; claims rep. N.D. Dept. Vets. Affairs, 1950-61, commr., 1961; mem. dean's com. U. N.D. Med. Sch., 1980—. Served with AUS, 1943-46; CBI. Decorated Bronze Star. Mem. Nat. Assn. State Dirs. Vets. Affairs (pres. 1968-69), Internat. War Vets. Alliance (pres. 1970-71), Am. Legion, DAV, VFW. Lutheran. Club: Kiwanis. Office: 1017 4th Ave N Fargo ND 58107

ZAPP, HANS ROLAND, elec. engr.; b. Germany, July 3, 1941; s. Ludwig and Alma (Schafer) Z.; B.S., Mass. Inst. Tech., 1963, M.S., 1965; Ph.D., Stanford U., 1969; m. Roberta Grace Mark, June 12, 1965; children—Alisa Ruth, Jonathan Mark. Mem. tech. staff Lincoln Lab., Mass. Inst. Tech., Lexington, 1968-74, liaison officer aerospace and space and missile systems, San Bernadino, Calif., 1970-71, mem. staff research radar site, Kwajalein, Marshall Islands, 1971-74; asst. prof. elec. engring. and systems sci. Mich. State U., E. Lansing, 1974—; mem. sr. staff Central Solar Energy Research Corp., Detroit, 1977-79; founder, owner Stat Med. Bookstore, 1979—. Den leader local Cub Scouts, 1976-78; Sunday sch. tchr. United Presbyn. Ch., Okemos, Mich., 1976-77. Mem. IEEE, Internat. Solar Energy Soc., Sigma Xi, Eta Kappa Nu, Tau Beta Pi. Contbr. articles to profl. jours. Home: 3617 E Arbutus Okemos MI 48864 Office: Dept Elec Engring and Systems Sci Mich State U East Lansing MI 48824

ZAR, JERROLD H(OWARD), biologist; b. Chgo., June 28, 1941; s. Max and Sarah (Brody) Z.; B.S., No. Ill. U., 1962; M.S., U. Ill., 1964, Ph.D. (NIH fellow), 1967; m. Carol Bachenheimer, Jan. 15, 1967; children—David Michael, Adam Joseph. NSF fellow in marine sci. Duke U. Marine Lab., Durham, N.C., 1965; research asso., dept. zoology, U. Ill., Urbana, 1967-68; asst. prof. dept. biol. scis. No. Ill. U., DeKalb, 1968-71, asso. prof., 1971-78, prof., chmn. dept. biol. scis., 1978—; vis. scientist Argonne Nat. Lab., 1974; cons. U.S. EPA and other govt. agencies and industries; founder, dir. ENCAP, Inc., 1974—. Fellow AAAS; mem. Am. Inst. Biol. Scis., Am. Ornithologists Union, Am. Physiol. Soc., Am. Statis. Assn., Biometric Soc., Cooper Ornithol. Soc., Am. Soc. Zoologists, Internat. Assn. for Ecology, Nat. Assn. Biol. Tchrs., Nat. Assn. Environ. Profls., Wilson Ornithol. Soc. Author: Biostatistical Analysis, 1974; (with J.E. Brower) Field and Laboratory Methods for General Ecology, 1977; contbr. chpts. to books, articles to profl. jours. Office: Dept Biological Sciences Northern Illinois Univ DeKalb IL 60115

ZAREMBA, THOMAS EDMUND BARRY, educator; b. Detroit, May 6; s. Edmund Julius Thiel and Ethel Grace (Barry) Z.; ed. Oakland U., Rochester, Mich., U. Detroit, Wayne State U. Tchr., Center Line (Mich.) Public Schs., Livonia (Mich.) Public Schs.; instr. biol. scis. Wayne State U., Detroit. Mem. AAAS, Mich. Eye Bank, Nat., Mich. funeral dirs. assns., Mich. Prof. Police Assn., Am. Film Inst. (sponsor), Met. Opera Guild, Friends of Detroit Symphony Orch., Founders Soc., Detroit Inst. Arts, Wayne State U. Alumni Assn., Oakland U. Alumni Assn., Detroit Grand Opera Assn. Roman

Catholic. Club: Scarab, Players (Detroit). Office: 217 Farnsworth St Detroit MI 48202 also 5980 Cass Ave Detroit MI 48202

ZAREMSKI, MILES JAY, lawyer; b. Chgo., Aug. 16, 1948; s. Samuel and Ann Zaremski; B.S., U. Ill., 1970; J.D., Case Western Res. U., 1973; m. Elena Cinthia Resnik, July 19, 1970; children—Jason L., Lauren D. Admitted to Ill. bar, 1973; partner firm Fohrman, Lurie, Sklar & Simon, Ltd., 1981—; researcher Law Medicine Center, Case Western Res. Law Sch., Cleve., 1970-73; instr. law Woodlands Acad., Lake Forest, Ill., 1976-77. Organizer of boys baseball programs Evanston, Ill., 1965-70, Cleve., 1970-73; v.p. Village of the Woods Subdiv., Highland Park, Ill., 1978—. Named Outstanding Young Man Am., 1979. Mem. Am. Bar Assn., Ill. State Bar Assn. (1st prize Ann. Lincoln award 1979), Chgo. Bar Assn., Am. Judicature Soc., Scribes-Am. Soc. of Writers on Legal Subjects, Am. Coll. Legal Medicine, Nat. Health Lawyers Assn., Am. Soc. Law and Medicine, Am. Soc. Hosp. Attys., Ill. Soc. Hosp. Attys., Psi Chi. Author: (with others) Introduction to Legal Research and Writing and the Study of Law, 1975; contbr. articles to legal jours.; exec. editor Case Western Res. Jour. Internat. Law, 1972-73; editor-in-chief The Forum, 1979-81, Law, Medicine and Health Care, 1981—; columnist Chicago Daily Law Bull., 1975—. Office: 180 N Michigan Ave Chicago IL 60601

ZARISH, JOSEPH FREDERICK, furniture mfg. co. exec.; b. Chgo., Mar. 13, 1919; s. Michael and Ursula (Petrick) Z.; B.S. in Mktg. Distbn., U. Ill., 1940; postgrad. Northwestern U., Havana Bus. U.; m. Jane Butler, June 21, 1952; children—Janet Ann, Karen Patricia, Barbara Beth, Jeffrey Frederick. Set up export co., Havana, Cuba, 1946; salesman Salmanson & Co., N.Y.C., 1946-48, mgr. Chgo. office, 1947, asst. to pres., 1948; nat. sales and merchandising mgr. Sealy, Inc., Chgo., 1948-53; exec. dir. Spring Air Co., 1953, exec. v.p., 1953-56; became v.p. merchandising Schnadig Corp. and subs.'s, Internat., Karpen, 1956; v.p. mktg., dir. Schnadig Corp., 1958-60, Storkline Corp., 1961-62; pres. Chamberlain Metal Products Co., Frankfort, Mich., 1962-64, also dir.; pres. Canterbury House, Inc., Peru, Ind., 1964—; pres. Flagship Enterprises, 1950-65; pres. Award Exhibits, Inc., 1956-62; cons. in field. Mem. savs. bond div. U.S. Sec. Treasury Staff, 1942-43; steering com. NCCJ, 1953-62; sec. community council Grissom Air Base, 1976, pres., 1978; treas. Peru United Fund, 1974; membership chmn. Mississinewa Reservoir Devel. Assn., 1968-71; chmn. Miami County Heart Fund, 1975; bd. dirs. Clarence Darrow Community Center, Hull House, 1969-74, hon. mem. bd., 1974—; bd. dirs., treas. United Fund, Peru, 1974; bd. dirs. Chgo. chpt. Am. Diabetic Assn., 1975—; treas. Am. Diabetic Assn. Greater Chgo. and N. Affiliates, bd. dirs., chmn. nat. audit com., 1976-77; chmn. indsl. div. Heart Fund, 1971-75, chmn. Ind. div., 1979-81, bd. dirs., 1978. Served from pvt. to maj. Signal Corps, U.S. Army, 1941-46; ETO. Recipient Kimberly Clark Promotional award, 1953. Mem. AIM, Res. Officers Assn., Soc. Gen. Semantics, Peru Circus, Peru C. of C. (dir.), Nat. Assn. Bedding Mfrs., Am. Legion (post chaplain), Nat. Sales Execs. Assn., Furniture Club Am. (pres. 1960), Nat. UN Day Com., Alpha Kappa Psi, Delta Phi (trustee 1975). Clubs: Elks, Execs. Author promotional booklets, articles in sales jours. Home: 1579 Woodvale Deerfield IL 60015 Office: 217 E Canal St Peru IN 46970

ZARSE, LEIGH BRYANT, architect, archtl. engr.; b. Wauwatosa, Wis., Sept. 26, 1930; s. Alfred Henry and Cecile (Moreau) Z.; student U. Wis., Milw., 1948-50, Ohio State U., 1950-52; B. Archtl. Engring., U. Ill., 1954; m. Hannelore Schilling, June 30, 1973. Partner, Zarse & Zarse, Inc., Milw., 1957—, pres., 1967—; mem. municipal planning com. City Club of Milw., 1965—, sec. bd. dirs., 1971. Served to maj. USAFR, 1954-57. Registered architect and profl. engr., Wis.; certified multi-disaster design protection specialist CD Preparedness Agy. Mem. AIA (Top Honor award 1963), ASCE, Am. Concrete Inst., Engrs. and Scientists of Milw., Aircraft Owners Pilots Assn., Alpha Rho Chi, Sigma Delta Omega (pres. local chpt. 1949-50). Designer numerous local, state and fed. govt. bldgs., including: 1500 seat amphitheater for Gen. McCormack, Lackland AFB, San Antonio, 1954, 40 schs. in S.E. Wis., 1957—, Kenosha (Wis. City Hall, 1971, St. Francis (Wis.) City Hall, 1963, Hales Corners (Wis.) City Hall, 1968, FAA and Weather Bur. Bldg. at Gen. Billy Mitchell Field, Milw., 1970, Cathedral Place Condominium, Milw., 1981. Home: 1812 Mountain Ave Wauwatosa WI 53213 Office: 436 W Wisconsin Ave Milwaukee WI 53203

ZAWADZKI, SANDRA M., artist, educator; b. Oak Park, Ill., Mar. 20, 1941; d. Alessandro and Mary (Gallick) Martini; student Art Inst. Chgo., 1959-66; B.A.E., U. Chgo., 1964; M.A., Northwestern U., 1968; m. Felix Zawadzki, Aug. 26, 1961. Tchr. art Argo Community High Sch., 1966-70, Proviso East High Sch., Maywood, Ill., 1970-71; instr. DePaul U., Chgo., 1970-72; founder, instr. art program Iowa State Penitentiary, 1973-76; tchr., art coordinator Fort Madison Community Schs., 1973—; exhibited art in numerous shows. Bd. dirs. Keokuk Art Center, 1973—. Mem. Coll. Art Assn., Nat. Art Edn. Assn., Women's Caucus for the Arts, Iowa Art Educators, Internat. Soc. Artists. Democrat. Roman Catholic. Author: Creactivities, 1979.

ZBILICKI, RICHARD JOSEPH, assn. exec.; b. Milw., Dec. 16, 1941; s. Joseph J. and Stella T. (Ostricki) Z.; student U. Wis.-Milw., 1961-63; m. Mary Ellen A. Schmit, Aug. 28, 1965; children—Therese Marie, Susan Marie, Jeffrey Richard, Jeanne Marie, Sandra Marie, Richard Michael, Julie Anne. Field service technician Allen-Bradley Co., Milw., 1964-67; sr. elec. testing technician Wis. Electric Power Co., Milw., 1967-71; major coordinator John Birch Soc., Belmont, Mass., 1971—. Mem. Am. Mgmt. Assn., Soc. Advancement Mgmt. (exec. v.p.), Slaves Immaculate Heart of Mary (3d order). Roman Catholic. Address: S63 W13178 Windsor Rd Hales Corners WI 53130

ZDAN, RAYMOND LOUIS, oral biologist; b. Omaha, Mar. 18, 1941; s. Ray Walter and Catherine Marie (Mitera) Z.; student Immaculate Conception Sem., 1961-63; B.A., Creighton U., 1971, M.S., 1977; m. Bette Elaine Zoorwill, Oct. 31, 1964; children—Deborah, Andrea, Ruth. Research asst. Creighton U., 1965-67, research asso., 1968-72, asst. instr. Sch. Dentistry, 1973-77, instr., 1977—; histologist, histochemist, cons. Served with Army N.G., 1963-66. Mem. Nebr. Acad. Sci., Internat. Assn. Dental Research. Republican. Roman Catholic. Club: Eagles. Home: 5650 Poppleton Ave Omaha NE 68106 Office: Creighton Dental School 30th and Webster Sts Omaha NE 68178

ZEABART, LEONARD EDWARD, gastroenterologist; b. Lebanon, Ind., Feb. 19, 1949; s. Leo M. and Jean C. Zeabart; B.A., Ind. U., 1971, M.D., 1974; m. Patricia F. Freeman, Nov. 6, 1976; children—Kristine Lynn, Karen Suzanne. Intern U. South Fla., Tampa, 1974-75, resident in internal medicine, 1975-77, resident in gastroenterology, 1977-79; practice medicine specializing in gastroenterology, Muncie, Ind., 1979—; mem. staff, asst. dir. med. edn. Ball Meml. Hosp. Diplomate Am. Bd. Internal Medicine. Mem. A.C.P., Am. Gastroenterology Assn., Am. Soc. Gastrointestinal Endoscopy, Delaware County Med. Soc., Phi Beta Kappa. Club: Delaware Country. Home: 2805 W Petty Rd Muncie IN 47304 Office: 4000 Woodway Dr Muncie IN 47304

ZECK, ROBERT THADDEUS, physician; b. Chgo., Mar. 28, 1946; s. Herbert Charles and Lauretta Dolores (Hickok) Z.; B.S., Loyola U., Chgo., 1968, M.D. cum laude, 1972. Intern, Evanston (Ill.) Hosp., 1972-73; resident in internal medicine Northwestern U. Med. Sch., Chgo., 1973-75, fellow in pulmonary diseases, 1975-77, instr. internal medicine, 1977—; practice medicine specializing in pulmonary medicine, Hinsdale, Ill., 1977—; mem. staff Community Meml. Hosp., LaGrange, Ill., 1977—, med. dir. respiratory therapy, 1977-81; mem. staff Hinsdale San. and Hosp., med. dir. respiratory care, 1981—; pres. Suburban Pulmonary Assos., Ltd., Hinsdale; cons. pulmonary function Argonne (Ill.) Nat. Lab. Diplomate Am. Bd. Internal Medicine. Fellow Am. Coll. Chest Physicians (asso.); mem. A.C.P., Am. Thoracic Soc., AMA, Ill. State Med. Soc., Chgo. Med. Soc., Alpha Omega Alpha. Office: 211 W Chicago Ave Hinsdale IL 60521

ZEEB, JOANIE, business cons.; b. Detroit, Dec. 27, 1936; d. Von Dale and Charlotte Mays (Duffy) Polhemus; student U. Colo., 1954-56; B.S. in Social Sci., Mich. State U., 1975; M.A. in Psychology, Lone Mountain Coll., San Francisco, 1977; children—Katherine, Christopher, Gregory. Personnel dir. Zeeb Animal Hosp., Lansing, Mich., 1970-79; tchr. mgmt. styles adult edn. Okemos (Mich.) public schs., 1977-79; instr. YMCA Career Days, Norman, Okla., 1977; dir. Bus. Cons. Internat.; tchr. transactional analysis in adult edn. classes; tchr. communication and interraction classes, Paris, France, 1980-81. Mem. Internat. Transactional Analysis Assn. Episcopalian. Author: What is T.A., 1977; The T.A. Way To Enjoy Your Work, 1978. Home: Paradise Point Box 103 George Town Exuma Bahamas Office: 13020 US 27 DeWitt MI 48820

ZEGER, PAUL EDWARD, II, packaging corp. exec.; b. Englewood, N.J., Oct. 17, 1947; s. Paul Edward and Marjorie Ellen (McMullen) Z.; B.A., Kans. Wesleyan U., 1970; m. Diane Lynn Gutzeit, Oct. 8, 1977; 1 son, Paul Edward III. Asst. controller Portland Co., Sherwood, Oreg., 1970-71; sales rep. Western Kraft Corp., Chgo., 1971-75; sales rep. Green Bay Packaging, Inc., Chgo., 1975-77, sales mgr., 1977-78, Wausau, Wis., 1978—. Mem. Am. Mgmt. Assn., Fiber Box Assn. Home: 3126 N 13th St Wausau WI 54401 Office: Green Bay Packaging Inc 6845 Packer Dr Wausau WI 54401

ZEHR, MARTIN DALE, psychologist; b. Carthage, N.Y., Sept. 30, 1950; s. Arthur Edward and Ellen Phyllis (Marion) Z.; B.A., SUNY, 1972; M.S., Memphis State U., 1975, Ph.D. in Clin. Psychology, 1979; m. Deborah Ann Borek, Mar. 10, 1977. Clin. predoctoral intern in psychology VA Med. Center, Topeka, Kans., 1978-79, neuropsychologist, 1979—; asst. adj. prof. U. Kans. Med. Sch., Kansas City, 1980—. Mem. Am. Psychol. Assn., Nat. Acad. Neuropsychologists, Am. Assn. Biofeedback Clinicians, Mo. Psychol. Assn., Phi Kappa Phi. Democrat. Club: Kansas City Track. Contbr. articles to profl. jours. Home: 7645 Jarboe St Kansas City MO 64114 Office: Psychology Service VA Med Center 4801 Linwood Blvd Kansas City MO 64128

ZEHRING, JOHN WILLIAM, coll. adminstr.; b. Phila., Sept. 9, 1947; s. C. Ruth (Ackleson) Z.; B.A., Eastern Coll., 1969; M.A., Princeton Theol. Sem., 1971; M.A., Rider Coll., 1971; M.Div., Earlham Sch. Religion, 1981; postgrad. R.I. Coll.; m. Donna Taber, Aug. 3, 1968; children—Micaela Ruth, Jeremiah Donald. Dir. career planning and placement, asst. dean students Barrington (R.I.) Coll., 1971-75; dir. career planning and placement, lectr. in edn. and creative writing Earlham Coll., Richmond, Ind., 1975-81, spl. asst. to pres. for coll. relations, lectr. communications, 1981—; cons. to govt., bus., higher edn., religious orgns.; ordained to ministry United Ch. of Christ; lectr. in field. Mem. Coll. Placement Council, Council for Advancement and Support of Edn., Midwest Coll. Placement Assn., Am. Personnel and Guidance Assn., Am. Coll. Personnel Assn., Nat. Vocat. Guidance Assn. Democrat. Mem. United Ch. of Christ. Author: Get Your Career in Gear: How to Find or Change Your Lifework, 1976; Implications: Case Studies for Ethical and Spiritual Development, 1979; Careers in State and Local Government, 1980; Preparing for Work: Get Ready Now for Life After School, 1981; Making Your Life Count, 1980; contbr. articles to religious, popular and profl. mags.; co-editor: Career Information for College Graduates, 1976; mem. editorial rev. panel Coll. Placement Ann., 1982. Home: 425 S W 16th St Richmond IN 47374 Office: Office of Coll Relations Earlham Coll Richmond IN 47374

ZEITINGER, ROBERT CARL, SR., advt. agy. exec.; b. St. Louis, Aug. 10, 1927; s. Fred Carl and Florence May (Theby) Z.; student Ohio U., 1945; student U. Mo., 1947-48, B.J., 1955; m. Jacquelyn Lillian Read, May 9, 1953; children—Robert Carl, Janice Read. With Moloney Electric Co., St. Louis, 1951, 53, Hebert-Robinson, Inc., 1955-56; with Batz Hodgson Neuwoehner, Inc., St. Louis, 1956—, v.p., 1968-81, exec. v.p., 1981—, also dir.; sec. R.C.H. Aviation, Inc., 1973—. Vice chmn. camping com. St. Louis Area council Boy Scouts Am., 1954-65, mem. Sea Explorer com., 1953-62. Served with USNR, 1945-46, 52-53. Mem. Pub. Utility Communicators Assn., U.S., Md. (past dir.) pilots assns., Bus./Profl. Advertisers Assn. (past gov., past regional dir.), Delta Tau Delta. Contbr. articles on Boy Scouts to nat. mags. Home: 620 Gaslite Ln Kirkwood MO 63122 Office: 910 N 11th St Saint Louis MO 63101

ZEITNER, RICHARD MICHAEL, clin. psychologist; b. Vermillion, S.D., Oct. 21, 1948; s. Waldemar Chris and Inge Antonia (Van Schellenbeck) Z.; B.A., U. S.D., 1970; Ph.D., Brigham Young U., 1975; m. Jane Beatrice Montgomery, Sept. 9, 1971; children—Nicolle Antonia, Aaron Prescott. Commd. 2d lt. U.S. Army, 1972, advanced through grades to capt., 1979; intern Walter Reed Army Med. Center, 1974-75; postdoctoral tng. in family therapy Menninger Found., 1980—; chief psychology service U.S. Army, Fort Leavenworth, Kans., 1975-77; chief psychologist, asst. chief psychiat. service Munson Army Hosp., Fort Leavenworth, 1977-79; ret., 1979; pvt. practice clin. psychology, Leavenworth, Kans., 1977-79; chief spl. services Prime Health Community Group Health Plan, Kansas City, Mo., 1979—; pvt. practice clin. psychology, Blue Springs, Mo., 1979—; clin. instr. U. Kans. Sch. Medicine, 1978-80; mem. staff Menorah Med. Center, St. Mary's Hosp. Mem. adv. council Blue Springs Sch. Bd., 1979-80. Mem. Am. Psychol. Assn., Am. Soc. Clin. Hypnosis, Psychologists Interested in Study of Psychoanalysis, Kansas City Soc. Holistic Health, Psi Chi. Lutheran. Home: 613 Springwood Dr Blue Springs MO 64015 Office: 9150 E 41st Terr Kansas City MO 64133

ZEITOUN, IBRAHIM HANAFI, biologist; b. Egypt, Nov. 26, 1943; came to U.S., 1968, naturalized, 1977; s. Hanafi M. and Aziza M. (El-Mohteseb) Z.; B.S. in Chemistry and Zoology, Alexandria (Egypt) U., 1966; M.S., Mich. State U., 1970, Ph.D., 1973; m. Elaine Sue Keagle, Dec. 22, 1972. Grad. research asst. Inst. of Fisheries, Alexandria, Egypt, 1966-67, asst. dept. oceanography, 1967-68; research asso. Animal Nutrition Lab., Mich. State U., East Lansing, 1973-75; cons. aquatic studies Consumers Power Co., Jackson, Mich., 1975-76, aquatic studies sect. head, dept. environ. services, 1976—. Ford Found. fellow, 1969-73; cert. fisheries scientist, 1977. Mem. Am. Soc. Limnology and Oceanography, Assn. Environ. Profls., Am. Fisheries Soc., Am. Coll. Toxicology, Mich. Acad. Scis., Arts and Letters, Sigma Xi. Moslem. Contbr. articles to sci. jours. Office: Consumers Power Co 1945 Parnall Rd Jackson MI 49201

ZELENKA, VICKIE LOUISE, educator; b. Pawnee City, Nebr., Mar. 2, 1952; d. Carl John and Hildegard Yvonne (Koll) Boehner; B.S. in Edn., U. Nebr., 1974, postgrad., 1976—; m. James William Zelenka, June 5, 1974. Tchr. home econs. Pawnee City Public Schs., 1976—; dist. I advisor State Future Homemakers Am., 1980—. Leader, Pawnee County 4-H, 1981—. Mem. NEA, Nebr. Edn. Assn., Pawnee City Edn. Assn. (v.p. 1978-79, pres. 1979-80, mem. negotiation team 1978-80), Am. Vocat. Assn., Nebr. Vocat. Home Econs. Assn., Nebr. Vocat. Home Econs. Tchrs. Assn. (advisor dist. I, 1978-80), Pawnee County Hosp. Aux., VFW Aux. (pres. 1975), Pawnee County Jaycetts, Am. Legion, Omicron Nu. Republican. Roman Catholic. Home: 743 G St Pawnee City NE 68420 Office: Box 287 Pawnee City NE 68420

ZELEZNIKOW, JOHN, mathematician, educator; b. Paris, France, June 2, 1950; came to U.S., 1979; s. Abram and Masza (Frydman) Z.; B.S. with honors, Monash U. (Australia), 1973, Ph.D., 1980. Tutor, U. Melbourne (Australia), 1976-78; asst. prof. math. No. Ill. U., 1979-80; asst. prof. Mich. State U., 1980—. Bd. dirs. Australian Jewish Welfare and Relief Soc., 1973—; sec. So. Regional Council of Social Devel., Victoria, Australia, 1974-78; councillor City of Caulfield (Australia), 1977-79. Mem. Australian Math. Soc., Am. Math. Soc. Home: 802 109 Cherry Ln East Lansing MI 48823 Office: Dept Math Michigan State U East Lansing MI 48824

ZELINSKI, MICHAEL JAMES, city planner; b. Detroit, Oct. 12, 1947; s. Vincent Francis and Barbara Jean (Keating) Z.; B.Arch., U. Detroit, 1971; M.C.P., U. Pa., 1975. Planning technician City of Oak Park (Mich.), 1968-71; volunteer architect-city planner U.S. Peace Corps, Oujda, Morocco, 1971-73; planner City of Joliet (Ill.), 1975—, planning dir., 1979—; tech. coordinator Peace Corps, Morocco Tng. Group, summer, 1974. State of Mich. scholar, 1965; Mellon fellow, 1974. Mem. Am. Planners Assn., Nat. Trust for Historic Preservation. Home: 257 N Wilcox St 307 Joliet IL 60435 Office: 150 W Jefferson St Joliet IL 60431

ZELL, CARL JOHN, educator, coach; b. St. Louis County, Mo., Sept. 1, 1936; s. George John and Evelyn Grace (Walker) Z.; A.B., Cardinal Glennon Coll., St. Louis, 1958; A.M., St. Louis U., 1963, Ph.D., 1971; m. Joan Benner, June 9, 1962; children—Paul, John. Tchr., St. Mary's High Sch., St. Louis, 1961-64, Ritenour Consol. Sch. Dist., St. Louis, 1964-67, 69-70; asst. prof. Sacred Heart Coll., Belmont, N.C., 1971-73, placement dir., dir. instl. self-study, mem. budget com., 1971-73; tchr. Am. studies, coach Shawnee Mission (Kans.) Sch. Dist., 1973—, mem. long-range planning com., 1980-81; sec.-treas. Marvel Oil Co., St. Louis, 1959-60. Chmn., Overland Park (Kans.) Citizens Com. on Block Grants, 1980—; mem. Overland Park Fair Housing Com., 1977—, Johnson County (Kans.) Human Relations Commn., 1977-79; master of ceremonies Overland Park Town Meeting, 1976; mem. Greenbrier Adv. Council, 1974-77, chmn., 1977; vice-chmn. Kans. Citizens for Ct. Improvement, 1973-74; conferee Citizens Conf. on Kans. Cts, 1973; asst. coach Charlotte Area Soccer Club, 1971-72; camp dir. St. Louis Archdiocesan Youth Council, 1959; bd. dirs. Greenbrier Homes Assn., Inc., Camp Gravois. Mem. Nat. Council Social Studies, NEA (del. nat. conv. 1973, 80), Kans. Council Social Studies (pres. 1980-81), Am. Soc. Public Adminstrn., Piedmont Urban Policy Conf., AAUP, Am. Hist. Assn., Am. Studies Assn., Mecklenburg Hist. Assn., Mo. Hist. Soc., Mo. State Tchrs. Assn., St. Louis Suburban Tchrs. Assn., U.S. Soccer Fedn. (mem. staff state coaches clinics 1981-82, coach Kans. select team under-16, 1981-82), Phi Alpha Theta. Author curriculum materials. Democrat. Roman Catholic. Home: 8622 W 84th Terr Overland Park KS 66212 Office: 12701 W 67 St Shawnee KS 66216

ZELWIN, HARRY, podiatrist; b. Fahrnwald, Germany, Nov. 4, 1947; came to U.S., 1949, naturalized, 1954; s. Samuel and Ida (Duszkin) Z.; student Ohio State U., 1966-69; D.P.M., Ohio Coll. Podiatric Medicine, 1973; m. Deborah Bass, Sept. 1, 1969; children—Tamera Lynn, Gabriel Michael Bass. Practice podiatry, pres. Severance Cirle Foot Center, Inc., Cleveland Heights, Ohio, 1974—; asst. prof. podiatric medicine Ohio Coll. Podiatric Medicine, 1974-77, asso. prof., 1980—. Fellow Ohio Assn. Ambulatory Foot Surgeons, Am. Podiatry Assn.; mem. Am. Assn. Hosp. Podiatrists, Am. Assn. Podiatric Sports Medicine, Nat. Jogging Assn., Am. Assn. Sports Medicine, Internat. Racquetball Assn., Am. Amateur Racquetball Assn., Ohio Podiatry Assn. Club: Jewish Community Center Runners (ednl. v.p.). Office: 5 Severance Circle #804 Cleveland Heights OH 44118

ZEMPER, THEODORE J., sale tng. cons.; b. Pontiac, Mich., Feb. 16, 1939; s. Theodore Wayne and Mildred Regina (Leonard) Z.; B.S.M.E., Mich. State U., East Lansing, 1960; m. F. Anne Ellis, June 13, 1964; children—Karen Anne, Theodore Lowell. Elec. engr. ordnance div. Honeywell, Duarte, Calif., 1962-63, sales rep. EDP div., Los Angeles and N.Y.C., 1963-66; sr. sales rep., sales mgr. info. systems div. Gen. Electric Co., Detroit, 1966-70; sales mgr., dir. sales, dir. systems mgmt. tng. Honeywell Info. Systems, Chgo., 1970-73; v.p. sales devel. div. Fortex Data Corp. subs. D & B, Chgo., 1973-75; pres. Sales Devel. Assos., Inc., Rolling Meadows, Ill., 1975—. Mem. Chgo. Sales Tng. Assn. Office: One Crossroads of Commerce Rolling Meadows IL 60008

ZENDER, ANGELINA ELIZABETH, social services exec.; b. Brighton, Mass., Apr. 19, 1933; d. Sabatino and Giovanina (Beninati) Fantasia; A.S., U. Wis., Madison, 1973, B.S., 1980; m. Frederick Robert Zender, Dec. 30, 1949; children—Richard, Kathryn, James, Nancy, Debra. Waitress, 1955-66; founder Ricky Zender Meml. Home, Inc., Wausau, Wis., 1973, adminstr., daily living coordinator, 1973—; mem. Wis. State Service for Oral Exams, 1974-75. Bd. dirs. Halfway House Fedn. Wis., 1980—. Recipient presdl. citation for community service Apogee, 1975. Mem. Assn. Retarded Citizens (state dir.), Marathon County Assn. Retarded Citizens (treas. 1971, pres. 1973-82), Nat. Assn. Pvt. Residential Facilities for Mentally Retarded (dir.), Nat. Soc. Autistic Children, United Comml. Travelers Aux., United Cerebral Palsy Assn., Wis. Assn. Community Human Services Programs, Am. Assn. Mental Deficiency, Wis. Epilepsy Assn., Wis. Assn. Developmental Disabilities (v.p. 1981), Wausau C. of C. (Personnel Club, chmn. interclub coordinating council). Clubs: Toastmaster, Toastmistress (pres.). Author: (with others) Quality of Life, 1977; mem. rev. com. Guidelines to Community Living Systems for the Developmentally Disabled, 1975. Home: 110 E Moonlite Ave Wausau WI 54401 Office: PO Box 354 Wausau WI 54401

ZENI, BETTY JOY WAGNER, retail co. exec.; b. Chgo., Mar. 3, 1926; d. Percy E. and Elizabeth Cecelia (McGeeney) Wagner; student U. Chgo., 1942-44; B.A., Vassar Coll., 1947; postgrad. U. Zurich, 1947, Katharine Gibbs Sch., 1947-48; m. Ferdinand Joseph Zeni, Nov. 16, 1974. With Marshall Field & Co., Chgo., 1950—, mem. real estate div., 1950-72, mgr. corp. ins., 1972-79, mgr. corp. ins. and property tax, 1979—. Asst. sec. 43d ward Rep. Orgn., 1964-76; bd. dirs. Women's Nat. Rep. Club, Chgo., 1975—, pres., 1976-78; alt. del. Rep. Nat. Conv., 1968; bd. dirs. Lake Shore Condominium Assn., 1975-80; mem. adv. bd. Civic Fedn., 1975—, bd. dirs., 1980—; mem. land valuation com. State St. Council, 1978—. Mem. Vassar Alumnae Assn., Vassar Club Chgo., Katharine Gibbs Alumnae Assn. (past pres.), Risk and Ins. Mgmt. Soc. (dir. 1974-77), Pewter Collectors Club Am., Midwest Pewter Collectors Club, Needlework and Textile Guild Chgo., Lambda Alpha. Home: 1440 N Lake Shore Dr Chicago IL 60610 Office: 25 E Washington St Chicago IL 60602

ZENI, FERDINAND J., JR., lawyer, business exec.; b. DuQuoin, Ill., Oct. 2, 1924; s. Ferdinand J. and Lea E. (Walzer) Z.; B.S., Northwestern U., 1947, J.D., 1950; m. Betty W. Zeni, Nov. 16, 1974. Admitted to Ill. bar, 1950, U.S. Supreme Ct. bar, 1968; asso. firm Ross & O'Keefe, Chgo., 1950-58; gen. atty. Montgomery Ward & Co., Chgo., 1958-78, sr. v.p., sec., gen. counsel, dir. Montgomery Ward Enterprises, Inc., 1978—; dir. Signature Agy., Inc., Montgomery Ward Auto Club, Inc. Chmn., Cook County (Ill.) Young Republican Orgn., 1953-54; committeeman 43d Ward Rep. Com., Chgo., 1964-76; mem. Rep. State Central Com., 1970-74; del. Rep. Nat. Conv., 1972. Mem. Am. Bar Assn., Ill. Bar Assn., Chgo. Bar Assn., Phi Delta Phi, Delta Sigma Rho. Roman Catholic. Club: University (Evanston, Ill.). Office: 2020 W Dempster St Evanston IL 60202

ZENK, GEORGE EDWARD, elec. engr.; b. Erie, Pa., June 8, 1923; s. Otto John and Charlotte (Shafer) Z.; B.A., Westminster Coll., 1949; B.Sc., Carnegie Inst. Tech., 1949, M.Sc., 1950, Ph.D., 1953; m. Irma Rose Haberman, June 13, 1953. Mem. tech. staff Bell Tel. Labs., Whippany, N.J., 1953-61; sr. engr. Honeywell Aero Co., Mpls., 1962-63; cons. Control Data Corp., Mpls., 1964—. Vice pres Found. for Living, Abbott-Northwestern Hosp., Mpls., 1977-78. Served with AUS, 1943-46. NRC fellow, 1950-51; Buhl Found. fellow, 1951-52. Mem. IEEE, Sigma Xi, Tau Beta Pi, Eta Kappa Nu, Phi Kappa Phi. Patentee computer man-machine interface, spacecraft nav. system, electronic filters. Home: 6905 10th Ave S Richfield MN 55423 Office: 2300 E 88th St Bloomington MN 55420

ZENKICH, ELIAS RAMADAN, mech. engr.; b. Kozarac, Yugoslavia, Nov. 14, 1934; s. Ramadan I. and Fata (Kahrimanovich) Z.; came to U.S., 1956, naturalized, 1961; M.E., ICS, Scranton, Pa., 1972; m. Margareta Schall, June 25, 1956; children—Ilias, Ramadan, Ramona. Machine designer Englender Co., 1956-60; pres., owner Zenex Corp., Chgo., 1960—; vice chmn. bd. Washington Nat. Bank of Chgo. Asst. supr. Office of Dep. Sheriff, 1977—. Served with AUS, 1957-59. Mem. Internat. Trade Club of Chgo., Carbide Profl. Engrs., Islamic Cultural Center Chgo., Bosnian Am. Assn. Muslim. Patentee health field. Home: 5156 N Monterey St Norridge IL 60656 Office: 2940 N Halsted St Chicago IL 60657

ZEOLI, WILLIAM JUDSON, motion picture exec.; b. Phila., Sept. 25, 1932; s. Anthony and Elizabeth (Hoffman) Z.; student Phila. Coll. of Bible, 1950-53; B.A., Wheaton Coll., 1955; D.R.E. (hon.), Greenville (Ill.) Coll., 1973; m. Marilyn Zeoli; children—Steven, Patty, David. Exec. dir. Indpls. Youth for Christ, 1955-60; v.p. Youth Films, Inc., Muskegon, Mich., 1960-62; exec. v.p. Gospel Films, Inc., Muskegon, 1962-64, pres., 1964—, dir., 1955—. Exec. sec. Billy Graham Crusade in Greater Indpls., 1958-59. Bd. dirs. Radio Bible House, 1957—, Ch. Centered Evangelism, 1958—, Teen Crusades, Inc., 1967—. Recipient Spl. Service award U.S. Air Force, 1961; Meritorious Service award Army Chaplain Bd., 1966; Community Achievement award Indpls., 1959; Outstanding Achievement award State of Ind., 1959, Ind. Boys Schs., 1959; Key to City of Tacoma, 1960, Key to State of Wash., 1960; Spl. Achievement award for audio-visuals Nat. Film Found. Club: Indianapolis Athletic. Author: Tom Landry and the Dallas Cowboys; Supergoal; God's Got a Better Idea; numerous articles. Home: 944 Rosalie Dr NW Grand Rapids MI 49504 Office: Gospel Films Inc PO Box 455 2735 E Apple Ave Muskegon MI 49443

ZEPHRIES, Z. GEORGE, mfg. co. exec.; b. West Bend, Wis., Nov. 2, 1936; s. Charles and Coconi Zephries; B.B.A., U. Wis., 1960; m. Mary Ellen Gauger, July 11, 1959; children—Scott George, Steven Gauger. With Red Owl Food Stores, Hopkins, Minn., 1959-64; dir. gen. mdse. and sales promotions Kohl's Food Stores, Milw., 1964-69; dir. mktg. J & H Internat., Chgo., 1969-71, v.p. mktg., 1971-72, exec. v.p., 1972-73; v.p., gen. mgr. Ekco Internat., Franklin Park, Ill., 1973-78; pres. Ekco Housewares Co., Franklin Park, 1979—; dir. Kwo Chuan Metal Works, Taichung, Taiwan, Ekco Mex.; pres. Ekco Wood Products, Adams Plastics, Slaymaker Lock Co. Mem. Metal Cookware Mfrs. Assn., Am. Importers Assn. Republican. Roman Catholic. Home: 95 Granville Rd Roselle IL 60172 Office: 9234 W Belmont Ave Franklin Park IL 60131

ZERBI, PAUL GENOESE, thoracic and cardiovascular surgeon; b. Italy, Aug. 2, 1933; s. Domenico Genoese and Rose (Contestabile) Z.; came to U.S., 1962, naturalized, 1972; M.D., U. Modena (Italy), 1960; m. Mary Martha Berring, Jan. 11, 1964; children—Paula, Jayne, Dominic. Intern U. Hosp., U. Modena, 1960; physician with U.S. Army, Germany, 1961; resident in surgery Aultman Hosp., Canton, Ohio, 1962-63, Mercy Hosp., Canton, 1963-65, Columbus Hosp., N.Y.C., 1965-66; resident in thoracic and cardiovascular surgery Emory U. Hosps., Atlanta, 1966-68; chief surgery Central State Hosp., Milledgeville, Ga., 1968-70; practice medicine specializing in thoracic and cardiovascular surgery, Warren, Ohio, 1970—; chief thoracic and cardiovascular surgery Trumbull Meml. Hosp., 1973—. Diplomate Am. Bd. Surgery, Am. Bd. Thoracic Surgery. Fellow A.C.S., Am. Coll. Chest Physicians; mem. Am., Ohio State med. assns., Trumbull County Med. Soc., Cleve. Surg. Soc., Soc. Thoracic Surgeons, Am. Heart Assn. Roman Catholic. Home: 9710 King Graves Rd Warren OH 44484 Office: 3893 E Market St Warren OH 44484

ZEUTHEN, JOHAN PETER FREDERIK, trade assn. exec.; b. Odense, Denmark, Mar. 31, 1948; s. Carl Albert and Ellen Margrethe (Dahlstrom) Z.; came to U.S., 1973, naturalized, 1976; student Aarhus U., 1968-70; B.A., U. Odense, 1971; postgrad. U. Copenhagen, 1971-73; m. Kathleen Ann Giannetto, May 24, 1975; children—Thomas F., Anders F. Export cons. Otto Nielsen Emballage, Lyngby, Denmark, 1971-73; retail mktg. cons. Denmark Cheese Assn., Chgo., 1973-74, gen. mgr., 1974-78, dir., 1978—. Am. Field Service fellow, 1966-67. Mem. Danish Nat. Com., Scandinavian Trade Council (co-founder), Midwest Danish Am. C. of C. (co-founder, exec. sec.). Clubs: Danish (v.p.) (Chgo.); Rotary (Glen Ellyn, Ill.). Lutheran. Office: Denmark Cheese Assn 4415 W Harrison St Hillside IL 60162

ZIBRUN, STEPHEN MICHAEL, telemktg. cons. co. exec.; b. Chgo., Aug. 1, 1945; s. Stephen John and Elizabeth Dolores (Behrendt) Z.; B.A., Elmhurst Coll., 1968; postgrad. Ill. Benedictine Coll., 1982—; m. Carol Ann Salerno, July 19, 1969; children—Michael, Jennifer. With Patten Industries, Elmhurst, Ill., 1968-80, advt. mgr., 1976-79, advt. dir., 1979-80; mgr. corp. communications Mark Controls Corp., Evanston, Ill., 1980-81; pres. S. Michael Assos., Bellwood, Ill., 1981—. Sec., Bellwood Zoning Bd. Appeals, 1977—; mem. Bellwood Commn. on Pornography, 1981—. Served with USNR, 1968-70. Cert. bus. communicator. Mem. Bus. Profl. Advt. Assn. Roman Catholic. Home: 346 S 48th Ave Bellwood IL 60104 Office: PO Box 184 Bellwood IL 60104

ZICCARELLI, SALVATORE FRANCIS, food co. exec.; b. Chgo., May 1, 1936; s. Joseph and Josephine Nancy (Scibilia) Z.; student U. Ill., 1954-58; m. Sheila Mae Weiss, Oct. 28, 1961; children—Mark S., Kathryn J.A., Matthew T., Marina M., John X. Chief chemist Schutter Candy Co., Chgo., 1960-62; quality control mgr. Kitchen Art Foods Co., Chgo., 1962-65; dir. research and devel. Good-N-Rich Foods Co., Chgo., 1965-66; with Newlywed Cracker Co., Chgo., 1966-69; mgr. research and devel. spl. products Beatrice Foods, Chgo., 1969—; cons. in field. Served with USMC, 1959. Mem. Am. Assn. Cereal Chemists, Am. Assn. Dairy Technologists, Am. Assn. Candy Technologists, Assn. Food Technologists. Roman Catholic. Club: Cath. Order Foresters (fin. sec.-treas. 1972—). Inventor in field rapid mfg. chocolate and by-products, coconut flour and process; patentee. Office: 1526 S State St Chicago IL 60605

ZICK, BERNARD HALE, real estate cons.; b. Ft. Worth, July 18, 1944; s. James Mercer and Alice Viola (Hale) Z.; B.S., U. Mo., 1968; M.B.A., Northwestern U., 1969; m. Carol Jean Demuth, Nov. 12, 1977. Portfolio mgr. Stein Roe & Farnham, N.Y.C., 1969-70; cons.; lectr. Real Estate Investors Tng., Inc. Mem. Mayor's Corp. of Progress; mem. adv. bd. Metro Pollution, 1974; mem. Citizens Environ. Council, 1970-75. Mem. Kans. Assn. Realtors, Kansas City Bd. Realtors, Acad. of Real Estate (ACE award), Interex (Cert. Exchangor award), Nat. Assn. Realtors, Nat. Speaker Assn. Club: Kansas City. Author: Money Making Formulas In Creative Real Estate, 1978; Creative Real Estate Financing, Vol. I, 1979, Vol. II, 1981; Creative Formulas Workbook, 1982. Home: 10724 W 108th Terr Overland Park KS 66210 Office: 8500 College St Suite 9 Overland Park KS 66210

ZICK, LEONARD O., mfg. exec., fin. cons., acct.; b. St. Joseph, Mich., Jan. 16, 1905; s. Otto J. and Hannah (Heyn) Z.; student Western State Coll., Kalamazoo; m. Anna Essig, June 27, 1925 (dec. May 1976); children—Rowene Zick Neidow, Arlene Zick Anton, Constance Mae Zick Snell, Shirley Ann Zick Vander Ley (dec.); m. 2d, Genevieve Evans, Nov. 1977. Sr. partner firm Zick, Campbell & Rose, C.P.A.'s, South Bend, Ind., 1928-48; sec.-treas. C. M. Hall Lamp Co., Detroit, 1948-51, pres. 19S1-54, chmn. bd., 1954-56; pres., treas., dir. Allen Group Inc. (formerly Allen Electric & Equipment Co.), Kalamazoo, 1954-57; pres., dir., treas. The Lithibar Co., Holland, Mich., 1956-61; v.p., treas. Crampton Mfg. Co., 1961-63; mgr. corporate fin. dept. Manley, Bennett, McDonald & Co., Detroit, 1963-68; mgr. Leonard O. Zick & Assos., Holland, 1968-81; chmn. fin. com., dir. Eberhard's Foods, Inc., Grand Rapids. Former mem. Mich. Republican Central Com. Mem. Nat. Assn. Accountants (past nat. v.p., dir.), Fin. Execs. Inst., Stuart Cameron McLeod Soc. (past pres.). Lutheran. Clubs: Detroit Athletic, Renaissance (Detroit); East Bay Country (Largo, Fla.); Peninsular (Grand Rapids); Holland Country; Union League (Chgo.); Rotary; Macawtawa Yacht; East Bay Country (Largo, Fla.). Home: 849 Brook Village Holland MI 49423 also 1609 F 225 Country Club Dr Largo FL 33541

ZIDEK, BERNICE LOUISE (MRS. STEPHEN P. ZIDEK), wire mfg. exec.; b. Chgo., Oct. 10, 1906; d. Albert and Bessie (Kaberna) Vonder; diploma Englewood (Ill.) Secretarial Coll., 1923; m. Stephen Paul Zidek, July 22, 1925; children—Louise Ann Zidek Pavlin, Charles Edward. Asst. to asst. mgr. Emerson Drug Co., Chgo., 1923-24; office mgr. Van Dyke Industries, Chgo., 1936-38; partner Midland Metal Products Co., Chgo., 1941—. Troop leader to leader trainer Lone Tree Area council Girl Scouts U.S.A., 1938-68; mem. Ft. Lauderdale Oral Sch. Aux., Holy Cross Hosp. Aux., MacNeal Meml. Hosp. Aux. Recipient Thank You award Girl Scouts U.S.A., 1957. Mem. Nat., Fla. assns. parliamentarians, Am. Inst. Parliamentarians, Am. Guild Flower Arrangers, Fla. Fedn. Garden Clubs (life), Nat. Council State Garden Clubs (life), Nat. Council Flower Show Judges (certified judge), Parliamentary Law Unit Pompano Beach (pres. 1970-71), Coral Springs Cultural Soc., Freedoms Found. at Valley Forge, Moraine Valley Parliamentary Unit (Ill.). Republican. Roman Catholic. Clubs: Bauhinia Garden Circle (pres. 1965-67), Federated Garden Circles of Ft. Lauderdale (pres. 1974-75), Coral Springs Garden, Midwest, Lighthouse Point Bonsai, Amateur Fencers, Ikebana Internat., Women's Civic Coral Ridge Yacht (Ft. Lauderdale); Coral Springs Golf and Tennis; Riverside (Ill.) Golf. Home: 250 N Delaplaine Rd Riverside IL 60546 also: 2791 NW 112th Ave Coral Springs FL 33065

ZIEBARTH, ROBERT CHARLES, mgmt. cons.; b. Evanston, Ill., Sept. 12, 1936; s. Charles Alvin and Marian (Miller) Z.; A.B., Princeton U., 1958; M.B.A., Harvard U., 1964; m. Patience Arnold Kirkpatrick, Aug. 28, 1971; children—Dana Kirkpatrick, Scott Kirkpatrick, Christopher, Nicholas. Mgr. fin. analysis Bell & Howell Co., Chgo., 1964, mgr. fin. planning, 1965-68, controller photo products group, 1968-69, treas., chief fin. exec., 1969-73; mgmt. cons. Ziebarth Co., Chgo., 1973—; mem. dirs. adv. bd. Arkwright Boston Ins. Co., 1969—; dir. Corp Resources Inc., Telemedia, Inc. Asso., Community Renewal Soc., 1969—; trustee Choate Sch., Wallingford, Conn., Latin Sch., Chgo.; bd. dirs. Harvard Bus. Sch. Fund, Chgo. Maternity Center, Prentice Women's Hosp., Gateway House Citizens' Council; mem. Ill. Bd. Higher Edn., Ill. Joint Edn. Commn. Served to lt. USNR, 1959-62. Mem. Naval Hist. Found., Chgo. Hist. Soc., Art Inst., Mus. Modern Art. Clubs: Mid Am., Econ., Execs., Racquet, Saddle and Cycle. Office: 1500 Lake Shore Dr Chicago IL 60610

ZIEN, HERBERT BECKER, mech. contracting co. exec.; b. Milw., Sept. 6, 1947; s. Robert and Blanche (Becker) Z.; B.S. in Mech. Engring., Cornell U., 1969; M.S. (McMullen fellow), Cornell U., 1971; M.S. in Mgmt., M.I.T., 1973; m. Elizabeth Karen Levins, June 22, 1975. Teaching asst. Cornell U., 1969-71; editor Sloan Mgmt. Rev., M.I.T., 1971-73; property mgr. First Realty, Boston, 1973-74; engr. Zien Mech. Contractors, Milw., 1974-77, v.p. Solar Energy and Alt. Heating div., 1977-79, exec. v.p., 1979—; dir. Micro Controls Corp. Lectr., U. Wis., Milw., 1978—. Mem. Wis. State Energy Conservation Adv. Com., 1977—; bd. dirs. Wis. Heritage, 1975-81, pres., 1977; pres. Skylight Comic Opera, 1981—, Theatre X, 1981—. HUD grantee, 1975, 76, Dept. Energy grantee 1977, 80. Mem. Met. Bldrs. Assn. Milw. (adv. bd.), Wis. Bldrs. Assn. (legis. com. 1978—), ASHRAE, Internat. Solar Energy Soc., ASHRAE, Tau Beta Pi, Pi Tau Sigma, Phi Kappa Phi. Research asso. book Building Tomorrow, 1979. Office: 4858 N 35th St Milwaukee WI 53209

ZIENGS, DENNIS J., banker; b. Assen, Netherlands, June 24, 1949; s. Gezinus and Danetta (Everaers) Z.; came to U.S., 1969; diploma Netherlands Sch. Bus., Breukelen, 1969; B.B.A., U. Oreg., 1970, M.B.A., 1971; m. Georgina Emilia Lobos Cerezo, Dec. 4, 1971. With Rotterdam (Netherlands) br. Continental Illinois Nat. Bank and Trust Co. Chgo., 1973-75; with European hdqrs. Continental Bank, London, 1975-76, 2d v.p. multinat. banking dept., Chgo., 1976—. Served to sgt. Dutch Army, 1972-73. Office: 231 S LaSalle St Chicago IL 60693

ZIERDEN, CY, business exec.; b. St. Joseph, Minn., Nov. 10, 1932; s. Norbert G. and Verena Rose (Nathan) Z.; m. Marian Rose Conrad, Nov. 24, 1955; children—Patrick, Pamela, Peggy, Penny. From draftsman to prodn. and gen. mgr. Cold Spring Granite Co. and affiliates, Tex., Calif., N.Y., and Man., Can., 1954-76; owner, pres., chief exec. officer Delano Granite, Inc. (Minn.), 1976—. Served with U.S. Army, 1951-54. Mem. ASTM, Monument Builders N. Am., Nat. Bldg. Granite Quarriers Assn., Bldg. Stone Inst. Roman Catholic. Club: Lions. Home: 406 Lake Blvd Buffalo MN 55313 Office: 265 N River St Delano MN 55328

ZIETTLOW, CARRYL RAYMON, hosp. fund devel. adminstr.; b. Virgil, S.D., Oct. 17, 1920; s. Oscar Frederick and Ella Elvina (Matzke) Z.; B.A., Westmar Coll., 1947; B.D., Garrett-Evang. Theol. Sem., 1950; M.A., U. Mich., 1968; m. Mary Ann Burns, Oct. 28, 1943; children—Janice Lea, Richard Craig. Ordained to Ministry Evang. United Brethren Ch., 1950; pastor chs., Columbus, Mont., 1950-51, Dumont and Story City, Iowa, 1955-61; dir. admissions Westmar Coll., LeMars, Iowa, 1951-55, dir. ch. relations, 1961-63, dir. coll. relations, 1963-67, exec. asst. to pres., 1967-70; dir. resource devel. Iowa Meth. Med. Center, Des Moines, 1970-81; pres. Iowa Meth. Health Found., 1981—; lectr. Nat. Assn. for Hosp. Devel.-U. Wis. Continuing Edn. Program on Devel. Served with USAAF, 1943-46. Named Alumnus of Yr., Westmar Coll., 1972. Fellow Nat. Assn. for Hosp. Devel. Democrat. Methodist. Club: Lions (past pres., past dir.). Home: 2506 54th St Des Moines IA 50310 Office: Iowa Meth Health Found 1405 Woodland Ave Des Moines IA 50309

ZIEVE, CHARLOTTE RUTH, environmentalist; b. Chgo., Sept. 17, 1926; d. Charles and Bessie Cantor; B.S., U. Ill., 1947; M.S., U. Wis., Milw., 1975; m. Edward R. Zieve, June 15, 1947; children—Andrew, Gary, Peter, Wendy, Kathie. Chemist, Farmers Chem. Co., Kalamazoo, 1947-48, Marquette U. Med. Sch., Milw., 1948-49; instr. environ. issues U. Wis., Milw., 1977—; mem. citizens environ. council Wis. Gov.'s Commn. on Environ., 1978-81; chmn. outdoor adv. councils Wis. Dept. Natural Resources, 1977—; mem. consumers adv. council Wis. Electric Power Co., 1980—; legis. chmn. Milw. Audubon Soc., 1975—, pres. Milw. Audubon Soc., 1977—; mem. Milw. Alliance to Save Energy, 1978—; chmn. Citizens for Nine Mile Farm Nature Center, 1969-72; sec. tech. com. S.E. Wis. Coalition for Clean Air, 1970-74. Bd. dirs. Milw. Jewish Council, 1971-77, Environ. Edn. Council Greater Milw., 1975-77, Lake Mich. Fedn., 1978-80, Milw. Jewish Community Center, 1974-80, Planned Parenthood Wis., 1980—, Global Tomorrow Coalition, 1981—; mem. Goals 2000 Land Use Task Force, 1981—; pres. Maple Dale Sch. PTA, 1970-71, Future Milw., 1977-78. Recipient Citizens Activist award Milw. Audubon Soc., 1976, award S.E. Wis. Naturalist Assn., 1978. Mem. Sierra Club, Environ. Decade, Wilderness Soc., Common Cause, Environ. Def. Fund, Zero Population Growth, Nature Conservancy, Population Action Council, Nat. Wildlife Fedn. Address: 9481 N Sequoia Dr Milwaukee WI 53217

ZIGMAN, ROBERT S., public relations exec.; b. Milw., Sept. 22, 1919; s. Walter A. and Becky (Neisser) Z.; student U. Wis., 1947; m. Dorothy T. Traver, Apr. 11, 1953; 1 son, Robert W. Mem. sales staff Milprint, Inc., Milw., 1947-52, mgr. aluminum foil div., 1952-58; chmn. Zigman-Joseph-Skeen PR, Milw., 1959—; dir. Stearns Chem. Corp. Bd. dirs., founder, past pres. U. Wis.-Milw. Found.; founder, past pres., past bd. dirs. Milw. Symphony Orch.; founder, past bd. dirs. United Performing Arts Fund; past bd. dirs. Florentine Opera; past pres., past bd. dirs. Friends of Milw. Pub. Museum; past bd. dirs., bd. curators State Hist. Soc.; past bd. dirs. Gov.'s Council on Arts, Youth Opportunities Unlimited; past bd. dirs., bd. visitors U. Wis. System; trustee U. Wis. Meml. Union. Served with AUS, 1942-46. Decorated Bronze Star medal, Combat Inf. badge; recipient 2 Chinese decorations, Distinguished Service to Music award Wis. Coll. Conservatory Women's League, 1973; Golden Baton awards Milw. Symphony Orch.; citations, County and City Milw. Mem. Milwaukee County Hist. Soc. (past bd. dirs.), Co. Am. Mil. Historians, Wis. State Hist. Soc. (curator 1966—), Scabbard and Blade, Sigma Delta Chi, Beta Gamma Sigma. Home: 6024 N Lake Dr Milwaukee WI 53217 Office: 700 N Water St Milwaukee WI 53202

ZIGO, STEPHEN PAUL, architect; b. Zanesville, Ohio, July 18, 1950; s. Paul P. and Rita F. (Orwig) Z.; B.Arch., U. Cin., 1974; m. Stephanie L. Shook, July 9, 1977; 1 dau., Vanessa. Draftsman, Perkins & Will Partnership, Washington, 1971-72; job capt. T.J. Peabody, architect, Norwalk, Ohio, 1972-74; dist. engr. Spanall Co., Cin., 1975-76; architect C.M. Effinger, architects, Norwalk, 1976—. Chmn. fin. com. Huron County Mental Health Bd.; chmn. planning task force Norwalk Revitalization Com.; bd. dirs. Jr. Achievement, Norwalk Community Center. Mem. AIA, Architects Soc. Ohio, Nat. Trust for Historic Preservation, Firelands Hist. Soc., Norwalk Jaycees (dir. 1979—). Club: Rotary (sec.). Home: 86 W Main St Norwalk OH 44857 Office: C M Effinger 31 Benedict Ave Norwalk OH 44857

ZILLMAN, ROY STUART, social scientist, educator; b. Batavia, N.Y., Mar. 28, 1932; s. Stuart Edward and Winifred Nancy (Dery) Z.; A.B., U. Miami, 1958; M.A. (Falk fellow), U. Calif. at Los Angeles, 1964; Ph.D. (Ford Found. grantee, univ. research grantee), U. Calif. at Riverside, 1971; m. Anne Reymond, Dec. 28, 1972. Vis. research prof. U. Chile, Santiago, 1967-69; asst. prof. polit. sci. Ind. State U., Terre Haute, 1969—, coordinator Latin Am. studies program, 1974—; pres. Calif. Investments, Los Angeles, 1962-64. Served with USAF, 1952-56. U. Chile at Santiago research grantee, 1968. Mem. Inter-Am. Soc., Am. Polit. Sci. Assn., Latin Am., Mid-West Latin Am. studies assns. Home: Box 11 Bowling Green IN 47833

ZIMBERG, HARVEY, photographer; b. Winnipeg, Man., Can., July 19, 1941; s. Joseph and Rose (Okil) Z.; student United Coll., 1962-63. Electronics technician RCAF, Winnipeg, 1963-66; photographer Canadian Grain Commn., Winnipeg, 1966—. Mem. Am., Minn. profl. photographers assns., Winona Sch. Profl. Photography Alumni Assn., Winnipeg (v.p. 1973-76, pres. 1977-79), Man. bowling assns. Club: Bel Acres Golf and Country (dir. 1977—). Home: 202 3916 Grant Ave Winnipeg MB R3R 2W2 Canada Office: 1404-303 Main St Winnipeg MB R3C 3G9 Canada

ZIMMER, GERALD LEE, greeting card co. exec.; b. Cin., Apr. 28, 1943; s. Ralph Nelson and Eleanor Imogene (Eaton) Z.; B.B.A., U. Cin., 1966; M.B.A., Xavier U., 1968; m. Carol Jean Schell, Sept. 1, 1972; children—Wendy Susan, Tyler Alexander. With Procter & Gamble Co., Cin., 1966-73; with Gibson Greeting Cards, Cin., 1973—, gen. credit mgr., dir. credit and adminstrv. services, 1977—. Mem. Nat. Assn. Credit Mgmt., Adminstrv. Mgmt. Soc., Cin. Assn. Credit and Fin. Mgmt. Presbyterian. Home: 2665 Morningridge St Cincinnati OH 45211 Office: Gibson Greeting Cards 2100 Section Rd Cincinnati OH 45237

ZIMMER, JOHN HERMAN, lawyer; b. Sioux Falls, S.D., Dec. 30, 1922; s. John Francis and Veronica (Berke) Z.; student Augustana Coll., Sioux Falls, 1941-42, Mont. State Coll., 1943; LL.B., U. S.D., 1948; m. Deanna Langner, 1976; children by previous marriage—June, Mary Zimmer Levine, Robert Joseph, Judith Maureen. Admitted to S.D. bar, 1948; practice law, Turner County, S.D., 1948—; partner firm Zimmer, Richter & Duncan, Parker, S.D.; states atty. Turner County, 1955-58, 62-64; asst. prof. med. jurisprudence; minority counsel S.D. Senate Armed Services Com. on Strategic and Critical Materials Investigation, 1962-63; chmn. Southeastern Council Govts., 1973-75; mem. U. S.D. Law Sch. adv. council, 1973-74. Chmn. Turner County Republican Com., 1955-56; mem. S.D. Rep. adv. com., 1959-60; alt. del. Rep. Nat. Conv., 1968. Served with AUS, 1943-46; PTO. Decorated Bronze Star, Philippine Liberation ribbon. Mem. Am., Fed., S.D. (commr. 1954-57) bar assns., Am. Trial Lawyers Assn., S.D. Trial Lawyers Assn. (pres. 1967-68), VFW, Am. Legion, Phi Delta Phi. Clubs: Elks, Shriners. Home: Parker SD 57053 Office: Law Bldg Parker SD 57053

ZIMMERMAN, DONALD LEE, photographer; b. Covington, Ohio, Aug. 8, 1935; s. Leslie Loy and Wauneta Waveline (Gephardt) Z.; B.F.A., Ohio U., 1957; postgrad. Ind. U., 1974—, M. Photography; children—Sandra Lynne, Susan Elaine, Stacey Carol. Photographer, Cromer Photos, Covington, 1957-58; studio mgr., photographer Krider Studios, Inc., Lawrenceburg, Ind., 1958-62; photographer Alderman Studios, Inc., High Point, N.C., 1962-67; dir. photography, v.p. H.G. Peters/Format, Indpls., 1967-76; pres. Foto-Graphics, Inc., Indpls., 1976—. Mem. Profl. Photographers Am., Am. Soc. Profl. Photographers. Club: Masons. Home: 6717 Winnock Dr Indianapolis IN 46220 Office: 2402 N Shadeland Ave Indianapolis IN 46219

ZIMMERMAN, GEORGE HERBERT, banker, fin. cons.; b. N.Y.C., Sept. 10, 1895; s. George Henry and Jessie (Browne) Z.; B.C.S., N.Y. U., 1921; D.Sc. (hon.), Assumption U., Windsor, Ont., Can., 1961; m. Mary Helen Campion, July 7, 1926; children—Doris Zimmerman Bato, Elaine Zimmerman Peck, Jessie Zimmerman Hitchens, Georgia Zimmerman Loftus, Louis. Employee N.Y. Edison Co., 1911-16, Guaranty Securities Corp., N.Y.C. and Montreal, 1916-18, Gen. Motors Acceptance Corp., N.Y.C. and Chgo., 1919-26; v.p. Comml. Credit Co., Balt., 1926-28; exec. v.p. Universal Credit Corp., 1928-41; v.p. Universal C.I.T. Credit Corp., Detroit, 1941-50; chmn. bd., pres., dir. Mich. Bank, Detroit, 1944-50; organizer, G. H. Zimmerman Co., bus. and fin. cons., 1950; surveyed econ. and fin. conditions in Australia and New Zealand, 1956; dir. C.I.T. Fin. Corp. (N.Y.C.); cons. Dearborn Motors Credit Corp. (Birmingham, Mich.), Ford Motor Co. Can., Ltd. (Windsor, Ont.); fin. cons. Gar Wood Industries, Inc., Wayne, Mich. Dir., Met. Detroit Bdlg. Found., 1954; pres., trustee Friends Assumption Found., 1955-60. Chmn. fin. com. bd. regents Assumption U., Windsor, Ont., Can., 1953. Chmn. bldg. com. St. Paul Sch. and Convent, Grosse Pointe, Mich., 1950-51. Served with 30th CAC, World War I; war chest Met. Detroit, 1942; U.S. Treasury Dept. war fin. com. for Mich., 1944-45. Recipient Assumption U. Alumni award, 1959. Mem. A.I.M. (charter mem. pres.'s council 1951-56), Fin. Analysts Soc. Detroit, Albert Gallatin Assos. of N.Y. U., N.Y. U. Alumni Detroit (organizer, 1st pres.), Delta Sigma Pi (life). Catholic. Clubs: Grosse Point, Detroit Athletic, Detroit Country, Grosse Pointe Yacht (Detroit); Century (Chgo.); N.Y. University; Surf (Miami Beach, Fla.). Home: 125 Kenwood Rd Grosse Pointe Farms MI 48236 Office: 220 Bagley Ave Detroit MI 48226

ZIMMERMAN, GEORGE RUDOLPH, physician; b. Amana, Iowa, Jan. 7, 1923; s. Karl Henry and Helen (Pecher) Z.; M.D., U. Iowa, 1951; m. Vivian Earp, Sept. 2, 1946 (div. Jan. 1977); children—Karl L., Kent G., Jess K. Intern, resident U. Iowa, 1951-54; resident Gorgas Hosp., C.Z., 1954-55; practice medicine specializing in pathology and nuclear medicine, Iowa City; staff U. Iowa Hosps.; asso. dept. pathology U. Iowa, 1955-56, asst. prof., 1956-61, asso. prof., 1961-68, prof., 1968-70; mem. adv. com. state commr. health Med. Examiner Law, 1962-68. Bd. dirs. Iowa Med. Service, 1967-70. Served with USAAF, 1943-45. Mem. Am. Soc. Exptl. Pathology, Am. Assn. Pathologists and Bacteriologists, Soc. Exptl. Biology and Medicine, AAAS, Coll. Am. Pathologists, Am. Soc. Clin. Pathologists, AMA, Johnson County Med. Soc. (sec.-treas. 1966, pres. 1970), Iowa Assn. Pathologists (exec. council 1965-68), Sigma Xi. Address: 424 North St Burlington IA 52601

ZIMMERMAN, RICHARD LEE, architect, cartoonist; b. Cleve., May 25, 1951; s. Julius Eugene and Shirley Ione (Carter) Z.; B.Arch. magna cum laude, U. Cinn., 1974; m. Penelope Miriam Petti, Sept. 6, 1974. Designer, Damon-Worley-Cady-Kirk Architects, Cleve., 1970-72, Richard L. Bowen & Assos., Architects, Cleve., 1972-74, Baxter, Hoddell, Donnelly, Preston, Architects, Cin., 1974; urban design cons. City of Cin., 1974-77; asso. Richard L. Bowen & Assos., Architects, Cleve., 1977-79, William Dorsky Assos., Architects, Cleve. and Miami, 1979—; works include: Riverfront Park, Cin., Mt. Auburn Urban Design Plan, 5th St. Skywalk Link, Cin., St. Clair Place high-rise housing; comml. bldgs.; published cartoonist. Recipient Achievement medal AIA, 1974, Architects Soc. Ohio, 1973; registered architect, Ohio. Home: 1660 S Belvoir Blvd South Euclid OH 44121 Office: 23200 Chagrin Blvd Cleveland OH 44122

ZIMMERS, NEAL FOSTER, JR., state senator; b. Apr. 15, 1942; s. Neal F. and Annabel (Pierce) Z.; B.A., Denison U.; LL.B., George Washington U.; married. Judge 2d Dist. Ct., Dayton, Ohio, 1968-74; mem. Ohio Senate, 1975—, now asst. minority leader. Del. Democratic Nat. Mid-Term Conf., 1978; mem. Supervisory Council Crime and Delinquency. Recipient Outstanding Young Man award Ohio Jaycees, 1974, Disting. Service award Huber Heights-Wayne Twp., Dayton, 1974. Mem. Am. Bar Assn., Ohio Bar Assn. Presbyterian. Clubs: Dayton Kiwanis, Agonis. Office: State Senate Columbus OH 43216*

ZIMNY, ROBERT WALTER, welding co. exec.; b. Chgo., June 7, 1937; s. Walter William and Francis Clara (Greskowiak) Z.; B.S. in Edn., Chgo. State U., 1971; M.A. in Adminstrn. and Supervision, Govs. State U., 1976; m. Patricia S. Tillema, June 6, 1964; children—Brian Walter, Douglas Robert, Russell Patrick. Welding leadman Elkay Mfg. Co., Broadview, Ill., 1955-63; foreman Stembridge Mfg. Co., Addison, Ill., 1963-65; welding dir. Am. Inst. Engrs., Chgo., 1965-66; welding instr., dept. chmn. Chgo. Vocational High Sch., 1966-70; welding instr. Triton Community Coll., Melrose Park, Ill., 1968-70; welding instr., dept. chmn. Washburne Trade Sch., 1970-78; pres. Zimny Welding Service, Chgo., 1978—; cons. Weldors, Inc., 1970-78. Served with U.S. Army, 1959-61. Mem. Chgo. State U. Alumni Assn., Govs. State U. Alumni Assn., Chgo. Tchrs. Union. Republican. Roman Catholic. Clubs: Downers Grove Sportsman, Salmon Unltd., Ill. Fedn. Sportsmen, Moose. Author: Welding Instructor Handbook, 1971. Office: 3314 W 47th St Chicago IL 60632

ZIMPHER, PAUL RAYMOND, educator; b. Piqua, Ohio, Sept. 10, 1923; s. Raymond Virgil and Jeannette Ruby (Edwards) Z.; student U. Toledo, 1975-81; m. Mary Elizabeth Lawler, Feb. 5, 1944; children—Paul Raymond, Dee Ann. Journeyman, Zimpher Electric Service, Sidney, Ohio, 1949-60; partner, mgr. Zimpher Electric-Elec. Distbrs., Sidney, 1960-70; mgr. Zimpher Electric Supply, Inc., Sidney, 1970-71; with Stolle Corp. Sidney, 1971-75; elec. instr. Upper Valley Joint Vocat. Sch., Piqua, 1975—; cons. Five Oaks Reconstrn. and Renovation, Dayton, 1979—. Mem. Bldg. Code Bd. Appeals, City of Sidney, 1975—. Served with USAAF, 1943-46. Licensed elec. contractor City of Dayton, 1979. Mem. Am. Vocat. Assn., Ohio Vocat. Assn., Jaycees. Baptist. Club: Lions. Home: 128 Edgewood St Sidney OH 45365 Office: 8811 Career Dr Piqua OH 45356

ZINCKE, HORST, surgeon; b. Frankfurt am Main, Germany, Apr. 20, 1937; came to U.S., 1969; s. Kurt M. and Eleonore (Graichen) Z.; M.D., Johann Wolfgang-Goethe U., U. Frankfurt, 1966, Dr. Medicinae, 1967; m. Maren Muenter, Aug. 12, 1966; children—Miriam Tanja, Marian Ivo. Rotating intern, intern in surgery St. Katharinen Hosp., Frankfurt am Main, 1966-68; intern in surgery Univ. Hosp., Iowa City, Iowa, 1969-70; resident in surgery St. Markus Hosp., Frankfurt/Main, Germany, 1968-69; resident in surgery Mayo Clinic, Rochester, Minn., 1970-71, 71-73, resident in urology, transplantation and research fellow, 1973-74, cons. in urology and transplantation surgery, 1975—; asso. prof. urology Mayo Med. Sch., 1979—; mem. adv. bd. Kidney Found. Fellow A.C.S.; mem. Am. Soc. Transplant Surgeons, Internat. Transplantation Soc., Sigma Xi. Office: Mayo Clinic 200 1st St SW Rochester MN 55901

ZINGSHEIM, DAVID LEE, mfr. overhead lifting devices; b. Milw., Aug. 9, 1954; s. Donald James and Shirley Elaine (Andrews) Z.; student public schs.; m. Lois Clara Dorfner, July 10, 1976; children—Joseph David, Angela Marie. With Wis. Lifting Specialists Co., Milw., 1973—, insp. supr., 1975—; cons. in field. Roman Catholic. Home: 2042 N 56th St Milwaukee WI 53208 Office: 2033 W St Paul Ave Milwaukee WI 53201

ZIRBES, SISTER COLETTE MARY, librarian; b. Milw., Nov. 11, 1924; B.A. in English/Edn., Cardinal Stritch Coll., Milw., 1950; M.A. in English Lit., San Francisco Coll. Women, 1957; M.L.S., U. Wis.-Milw., 1970. Asst. librarian U. Wis.-Milw., 1968-70; asso. prof. children's and adolescent lit. Cardinal Stritch Coll., Milw., 1970—, asst. librarian, 1970-76, head librarian, 1976—. Mem. exec. bd., sec. IRA/Signal, Wis. Interlibrary Loan Services, Library Council Met. Milw. Mem. ALA, Wis. Cath. Library Assn. (exec. bd., vice chmn. 1981—, newsletter editor 1981, co-dir. workshop on bibliotherapy 1981), Council Wis. Librarians, Wis. Library Assn., Wis. Assn. Acad. Librarians (publs. com. 1981—). Asso. editor: Hi-Time Trial Series; book reviewer IRA/Signal publ.; contbg. editor Harper & Row Reader Series; spl. editor ALA/Bibliotherapy Newsletter, 1980. Home: 7979 N Port Washington Rd Milwaukee WI 53217 Office: 6801 N Yates Rd Milwaukee WI 53217

ZIRKLE, KENNETH EUGENE, telecommunications engr.; b. Champaign, Ill., Mar. 2, 1945; s. Howard Eugene and Florence Mabel (Dickason) Z.; Asso. in Electronic Tech., So. Ill. U., 1965. Lineman, installer, maintenance Eastern Ill. Telephone Co., 1965-76; traffic engr., dial office adminstr., staff engr. long range planning Mid Continent Telephone Service Corp., Rantoul, Ill., 1976—. Exec. bd. Arrowhead council Boy Scouts Am., 1975—, Dist. Award of Merit, 1977, dist. chmn. No. Dist., 1975-77; pres. Rantoul Beautification Council, 1978. Mem. Ind. Telephone Pioneers Assn. (pres. Pioneers of Ill. chpt. 1981), So. Ill. U. Alumni Assn. (life). Clubs: Champaign County Sports Car, Moose. Office: 300 N Maplewood St Rantoul IL 61866

ZITNIK, RALPH STERLE, cardiologist, internist; b. Chgo., June 24, 1931; s. Charles and Marjorie (Allen) Z.; B.S., Georgetown U., 1953; M.D., Loyola U., Chgo., 1957; m. Ethel Margaret Ladd, June 15, 1957; children—Ralph J., John C., Steven J. Intern, Little Company of Mary Hosp., Evergreen Park, Ill., 1957-58, dir. dept. cardiology, 1972—, sr. attending staff, 1972—; fellow in internal medicine Mayo Grad. Sch. Medicine, Rochester, Minn., 1958-62, asst. prof. internal medicine, 1969-72, dir. heart sta. and cardiac clinics, 1969-72, chmn. cardiac and cardiovascular facilities com., 1971-72; asst. in internal medicine Peter Bent Brigham Hosp., 1962-63; research asst. Harvard Med. Sch., 1962-63; mem. attending staff VA Research Hosp., 1963-65; mem. adj. staff Passavant Meml. Hosp., 1963-65; asst. attending staff Chgo. Wesley Meml. Hosp., 1963-65, asst. dir. heart sta., 1963-65; asso. internal medicine Northwestern U., 1962-63, dir. Cardiac Clinics, 1962-63; asso. clin. prof. medicine U. Chgo., 1972-73; pres. Chgo. Med. Computers, Inc., 1972—; asso. prof. medicine Rush U., Chgo., 1974—; asso. attending staff Rush-Presbyn.-St. Luke's Hosp., Chgo., 1974—; mem. courtesy attending staff Hinsdale (Ill.) Sanitarium and Hosp., 1974—; cons. cardiology Palos Community Hosp., Palos Heights, Ill. Diplomate Am. Bd. Internal Medicine, also sub-bd. Cardiovascular Disease. Fellow Am. Coll. Cardiology, A.C.P., Inst. Medicine Chgo., Am. Heart Assn. Council on Clin. Cardiology; mem. Am. Fedn. Clin. Research, Central Soc. Clin. Research, Assn. Advancement Med. Instrumentation, AAAS, Am. Inst. Ultrasound in Medicine, AMA, Ill. State Med. Soc., Chgo. Med. Soc., South Suburban Heart Assn. (dir. 1974-79, pres. 1975) Chgo. Heart Assn. (dir. 1975—, pres. 1980). Roman Catholic. Clubs: Butterfield Country, Beverly Country, Mid-America. Contbr. articles to profl. jours. Office: 2800 W 95th St Evergreen Park IL 60642 or 120 Oakbrook Center Mall Oak Brook IL 60521

ZOBEL, MILTON MILFORD, contracting and bldg. co. exec.; b. Ida Grove, Iowa, Jan. 22, 1922; s. Louis G. and Anna (Schwenk) Z.; m. Frieda Reuscher, May 20, 1947; 1 dau., Carol Ann. Pres., United Builders, Inc., Ida Grove, 1962—. Served with USAAF, 1942-46. Mem. Master Builders Iowa (pres. 1973), C. of C., Am. Legion. Republican. Lutheran. Clubs: Kiwanis (pres. 1977-78), Med. Arts-Rec. (dir. 1977—). Home: Valley View Dr Ida Grove IA 51445 Office: 200 2d St Ida Grove IA 51445

ZODA, JAMES CHEEVER, commodities co. exec., economist; b. Cedar Rapids, Iowa, Dec. 29, 1941; s. Charles and Dorothy (Cheever) Z.; B.S.E., No. Ill. U., 1965, M.A., 1970, Ph.D. in Econs., 1979. Tchr. math., jr. high sch., Sch. Dist. 95, Cook County, Ill., 1965-73; instr. econs. No. Ill. U., 1973-78; research asst. Ill. Council Econ. Edn., DeKalb, 1977-78; research economist, account exec. Heinold Commodities Inc., Chgo., 1979—. Mem. Ill. Econ. Assn., Am. Econ. Assn., Commodities Futures Trading Commn., Omicron Delta Epsilon. Home: 7400 Grand Ave Downers Grove IL 60516 Office: 250 S Wacker Dr Chicago IL 60606

ZOMAYA, PETER, TV broadcaster; b. Chgo., Jan. 28, 1936; s. Odishoo Joseph and Mary Bebe (Mazur) Z.; student Wright Jr. Coll., 1955; B.A., Northwestern U., 1958; m. Susan Steib, Aug. 15, 1964; children—Mary Rene, Joseph, Andy Paul. Asst. buyer The Fair Store, Chgo., 1955-59; mgr. Time Fin. Co., Chgo., 1959-69; sta. mgr. WCIU-TV, Channel 26, Chgo., 1969—. Recipient awards Am. Cancer Soc., ARC; named Businessman of Yr., Mexican Civic Soc., 1977; hon. mention Mex. Businessmen's Assn., 1978. Mem. Acad. Arts and Scis., Media Club Chgo. Democrat. Eastern Catholic. Office: WCIU 141 W Jackson Blvd Chicago IL 60604

ZONNEVILLE, ROBERT E., trucking co. exec.; b. Williamson, N.Y., Jan. 23, 1925; s. Adrian J. and Matie L. Z.; student U. Buffalo, 1949-52; m. Carol A. Alliger, June 7, 1947; children—Bethann, Robin, Kim, David. Dock worker Associated Transport, Buffalo, 1952-53, terminal mgr., 1960-66; terminal mgr. Spector Redball, Cleve., 1966-68, regional mgr., Wis., Minn. and Ill., 1968-71, v.p. central area, Northfield, Ohio, 1971—. Pres. local Presbyn. Ch., Home Owners Assn.; mem. golf com. City of Euclid, Ohio, 1975, com. to elect mayor of Euclid, 1979. Served with U.S. Army, 1943-45. Decorated Purple Heart with oak leaf cluster, Bronze Star. Recipient awards for community activities, K.C., 1979. Mem. Western Res. Traffic Club. Clubs: Elks, Masons, Scottish Rite, Shriners. Home: 7627 Buchanan Ct Mentor OH 44060 Office: 210 Twinsburg Rd Northfield OH 44067

ZORINSKY, EDWARD, U.S. senator; b. Omaha, Nov. 11, 1928; B.S. in Chemistry and Zoology, U. Nebr., 1949; postgrad. Harvard U., 1966; m. Cece Rottman, 1950; children—Barry, Jeffrey, Susan. Engaged in whlesale tobacco and candy bus.; mayor, Omaha, 1973-77; mem. U.S. Senate, 1977—; mem. Agr., Nutrition and Forestry Com., Fgn. Relations Com.; mem. Omaha Pub. Power Dist. Bd., 1968, Nebr. Jud. Qualifications Commn., 1968; mem. urban econ. policy com. U.S. Conf. Mayors, 1973-76. Served to capt. M.P., U.S. Army. Mem. Internat. Footprinters Assn., Omaha Press Club, Res. Officers Assn. Clubs: Downtown Optimists, Eagles, Elks. Office: 432 Russell Senate Office Bldg Washington DC 20510

ZORKO, MARK ANTHONY, accountant; b. Cleve., Mar. 11, 1952; s. Frank Anton and Dorothy Eileen (Bever) Z.; B.S. in Bus. Adminstrn., Ohio State U., 1976; M.B.A. in Mgmt. Info. Systems, U. Minn., 1977; m. Sue Ann Langdon, Sept. 6, 1975; 1 dau., Jennifer Ann. Teaching asso. U. Minn., 1976-77; sr. staff cons. Arthur Andersen & Co., Mpls., 1978-80; sr. acct. and systems product mgr. Honeywell Inc., Mpls., 1980—; lectr. U. Minn., 1980—; cons. in field. Del., Hennepin County Republican Conv., 1980; bd. dirs. Mpls. Communication Center; chmn. missions commn. Hopkins United Methodist Ch., 1979—. Served as sgt. USMC, 1970-73, C.P.A., Minn. Mem. Am. Inst. C.P.A.'s, Minn. Soc. C.P.A.'s, Minn. Acctg. Aid Soc., Am. Prodn. and Inventory Control Soc. (cert.). Home: 14910 Walker Pl Minnetonka MN 55343 Office: Honeywell Plaza Minneapolis MN 55408

ZORN, ROBERT LYNN, ednl. adminstr.; b. Youngstown, Ohio, Mar. 22, 1938; s. Robert S. and Frances L. Zorn; B.S. Ed., Kent State U., 1959; M.Ed., Westminster Coll., 1964; Ph.D., U. Pitts., 1970; m. Joan M. Wilkos, Apr. 26, 1957; children—Deborah Lynn, Patricia Lynn. Tchr., West Branch (Ohio) Schs., 1961-62; elem. prin. Poland (Ohio) Schs., 1962-67, supt. schs., 1976—; high sch. unit prin. Boardman (Ohio) Schs., 1967-70; dir. adminstrv. services Mahoning County (Ohio) Schs., 1970-73, asst. supt., 1973-76; adj. prof. edn. Youngstown State U., 1970—; chmn. Ohi Adv. Com. to State Dept. Edn.; chmn. McGuffey Hist. Soc. Nat. Educator's Hall of Fame. Chmn. Mahoning County chpt. Am. Cancer Soc.; pres. bd. trustees Poland Methodist Ch.; trustee Mahoning County chpt. Am. Heart Assn. Served to lt. USAF, 1959-61. Mem. Doctoral Assn. Educators (life), Am. Assn. Sch. Adminstrs., Ohio PTA (life; Educator of Yr. 1980-81), Phi Delta Kappa. Republican. Clubs: Fonderlac County, Rotary, Protestant Men's. Author books, the most recent being: Speed Reading, 1980; contbr. articles to profl. jours. Home: 7386 N Lima Rd Poland OH 44514 Office: 53 College St Poland OH 44514

ZORNOW, WILLIAM FRANK, educator; b. Cleve., Aug. 13, 1920; s. William Frederick Emil and Viola (Schulz) Z.; A.B., Western Res. U., 1942, A.M., 1944, Ph.D., 1952. Vice pres., treas. Glenville Coal & Supply Co., Real Value Coal Corp., Zornow Coal Corp., 1941-45; dep. clk. Probate Ct., Cuyahoga County, Ohio, 1941-43; prodn. planning engr. Hickok Elec. Instrument Co., Cleve., 1943-46; teaching asst. Western Res. U., 1944-47; instr. U. Akron, 1946-47, Case Inst. Tech., 1947-50, Washburn U., 1950-51; lectr. Cleve. Coll., 1948-49; asst. prof. Kans. State U., 1951-58; asst. prof. Kent (Ohio) State U., 1958-61, asso. prof., 1961-66, prof. history, 1966—; collection corr. for Berkshire Loan & Fin. Co., Painesville, Ohio, Security Credit Acceptance Corp., Mentor, Ohio, 1951-60; cons. Karl E. Mundt Library Dakota State Coll., Madison, S.D. Mem. Am. Acad. Polit. and Social Sci., Am. Assn. State and Local History (award of merit 1958), Am. Hist. Assn., Orgn. Am. Historians, Ohio Acad. History (chmn. awards com.), Ohio Hist. Soc. (library adv. com. 1969—), Ohio Soc. N.Y., Center for Study of Presidency, Delta Tau Delta, Pi Gamma Mu, Phi Alpha Theta, Phi Delta Kappa. Author: Lincoln and the Party Divided, 1954, 72; Kansas: A History of the Jayhawk State, 1957; America at Mid-Century, 1959; contbr. to Abraham Lincoln: A New Portrait, 1959, Kansas: The First Century, 1956; also articles to encys., profl. jours.; editor: Shawnee County (Kans.) Hist. Bull., 1950-51; abstracter: Am. History and Life, Hist. Abstracts, 1964—. Home: 7893 Middlesex Rd Mentor OH 44060 Office: Kent State U Kent OH 44242

ZOURAS, BILL JAMES, psychologist; b. Chgo., Sept. 15, 1929; s. James and Matina (Kalambokides) Z.; B.S., Roosevelt U., 1951, M.A., 1957; m. Smyrna Tsamouris, Jan. 3, 1970; 1 son, James Bill. Mgmt. cons. John A. Patton Mgmt. Engrs., Inc., Chgo., 1956-59; mgmt. cons. George Fry & Assos., Chgo., 1959-62; dir. psychol. sers. Edward T. Carroll Assos., Chgo., 1962-64; asst. to dir. personnel and adminstrn. Easter Seal Soc., Chgo., 1964-65; pvt. practice psychol. counseling, Chgo., 1965-70; psychologist A.E.R.O. Spl. Edn. Dist., Burbank, Ill., 1970—; psychologist Dubocq & Ross Counseling Assos., Palos Heights, Ill., 1973-80; pvt. practice clin. psychology, Palos Hills, Ill., 1980—. Served with U.S. Army, 1953-55. Mem. Am. Psychol. Assn., Nat. Assn. Sch. Psychologists. Office: 7600 S Mason Ave Burbank IL 60459

ZSIGMOND, ELEMÉR KÁLMÁN, physician; b. Budapest, Hungary, May 16, 1930; s. Elemér Zeykváry and Teréz (Kartori) Z.; came to U.S., 1956, naturalized, 1966; M.D., U. Budapest, 1955; m. Kathryn Fogarasi, Oct. 19, 1953; 1 son, Zoltán William. Intern, Med. Clinics, U. Budapest, 1954-55; intern Allegheny Gen. Hosp., Pitts., 1960-61, resident anesthesiology, 1961-63; resident internal medicine Hosp. Sztálinváros and Cardiac Sanatorium, Balatonfured, Hungary, 1955-56; practice medicine specializing in anesthesiology; cardiologist, dir. lab. Cardiologic Inst., Balatonfured, 1956-57; dir. anesthesia research lab. Mercy Hosp., Pitts., 1957-60; clin. research fellow anesthesiology Allegheny Gen. Hosp., 1963-66, clin. anesthesiologist dir. anesthesiology research labs., 1966-68; prof. anesthesiology U. Mich. Med. Sch., 1968-79, U. Ill. Sch. Medicine, Chgo., 1979—. Diplomate Am. Bd. Anesthesiology. Fellow Am. Coll. Anesthesiologists, Am. Coll. Clin. Pharmacologists; mem. Am. Soc. Anesthesiologists, Internat. Anesthesia Research Soc., N.Y. Acad. Scis., AAAS, AMA, Ill., Chgo. med. socs. Research and publs. in anesthesiology, neuropharmacology, pulmonary physiology. Home: 6609 N LeRoy Ave Lincolnwood IL 60646 Office: 840 S Wood St Chicago IL 60612

ZUBER, BERT LOUIS, biomed. engr.; b. Houston, Oct. 27, 1938; s. Abraham Milton and Stella Evelyn (Marwill) Z.; B.A., U. Pa., 1960, B.S. in Chem. Engring., 1961; M.S. in Biochem. Engring. (Whitney fellow 1961), M.I.T., 1963, Ph.D. in Bioengring., 1965; children—Gregory Neil, Aaron Douglas. Mem. faculty U. Ill., Chgo. Circle, 1965—, prof. bioengring., 1973—, acting head dept., 1970-71, adj. prof. physiology Med. Sch., 1973-78; asst. attending, then asso. attending biomed. engr. Presbyn.-St. Luke's Hosp., Chgo., 1965-76, dir. neurophysiology lab. sect., dept. biomed. engring., 1965-71, dir. biomed. engring. cons. service, 1966-67; biomed. engr. Hines (Ill.) VA

Hosp., 1980—; vis. scientist Bell Labs., Murray Hill, N.J., 1975; lectr. dept. orthopedics Loyola U., 1980—; cons. in field, 1964—. USPHS grantee, 1968-73, NSF grantee, 1974-76. Mem. Nat. Assn. Bioengrs. (dir. 1972-75), IEEE, Am. Physiol. Soc., Internat. Brain Research Orgn., Assn. Research in Vision and Ophthalmology, Biomed. Engring. Soc. Clubs: Chgo. Corinthian Yacht, Heritage Boat. Contbr. numerous articles profl. publs. Office: Bioengring Program Univ Ill Chicago Circle PO Box 4348 Chicago IL 60680

ZUBROFF, LEONARD SAUL, surgeon; b. Minersville, Pa., Mar. 27, 1925; s. Abe and Fannie (Freedline) Z.; B.A., Wayne State U., 1945, M.D., 1949. Intern Garfield Hosp., Washington, 1949-50, resident in surgery, 1951-55, chief resident surgery, 1954-55; practice medicine specializing in surgery, 1958-76; med. dir. Chevrolet Gear and Axle Plant, Chevrolet Forge Plant, Gen. Motors Corp., Detroit, 1977-78, divisional med. dir. Detroit Diesel Allison div., 1978—; mem. staff Hutzel Hosp., Sinai Hosp., Detroit Meml. Hosp. Served with USAF, 1956-58. Diplomate Am. Bd. Surgery. Fellow A.C.S.; mem. AMA, Mich. State, Wayne County med. socs., Acad. Surgery Detroit, Am., Mich. occupational med. assns., Detroit Indsl. Physicians Club, Royal Coll. Medicine, NAACP, Phi Lambda Kappa. Club: Masons (33 deg.). Home: 8701 Kingswood Detroit MI 48221 Office: 13400 W Outer Dr Detroit MI 48228

ZUCCARO, JOHN JOSEPH, ins. exec.; b. Mt. Vernon, Ohio, Oct. 29, 1933; s. John and Frances Rose Z.; B.S. in Bus. Adminstrn., U. Dayton, 1957; m. Sarah A. Harris, Apr. 11, 1961; children—James V., Elizabeth A., Lucia. Sales rep. INA, Chgo., 1957-60, with J.W. Tigh & Son, Mt. Vernon, 1960-64; sales rep. Shelby Mut. Ins. Co., Columbus, 1964-67; sales mgr. Gt. Am. Ins. Co., Columbus, 1967-69; pres. Conva Agy., Inc., Columbus, 1969—; v.p., dir. R.D. Warne & Assos., Inc., Columbus, 1969—; exec. v.p., sec., dir. Conva Indemnity Co., 1972—; sec. Conva Premium Fin. Co., Columbus, 1972—; exec. v.p., sec., dir. Columbus Ins. Holding Co., Wilmington, Del.; asso. Standard Ins. Mgmt., Columbus, 1978—; dir. Signal Mgrs. Inc., Austin, Tex. Home: 2120 Nobleshire Rd Columbus OH 43229 Office: 3070 Riverside Dr Columbus OH 43221

ZUCKER, DAVID K., behavioral neuropathologist; b. Bklyn., May 12, 1948; s. Lawrence and Esta R. (Kawaler) Z.; B.A., Syracuse U., 1969; M.D., Loyola U., Chgo., 1973; m. Hedda H. Smulewicz, Aug. 12, 1973. Intern in surgery Montefiore Hosp., 1973-74; resident in pathology L.I. Jewish Hosp., 1974-76; resident in neuropathology Albert Einstein Coll. Medicine, 1976-78; resident in psychiatry Washington U. Med. Center, St. Louis, 1978-81; instr. pathology SUNY Med. Sch., Stony Brook, 1974-76. Mem. AMA, Soc. Neurosci., Am. Assn. Neuropathologists. Jewish. Author papers in field. Home: 5825 S Dorchester St Chicago IL 60637 Office: Div Biol Scis U Chgo 950 E 59th St Chicago IL 60637

ZUG, ELIZABETH KENDALL, business exec.; b. Boston, Oct. 24, 1954; d. Robert Edward Kendall and Diana (Dana) Fahrney; B.B.A., U. So. Calif., 1976; M.B.A., U. Pa., 1978; m. Graham F. Zug, Sept. 8, 1979. Sales floor mgr. Alroe, Inc., Los Angeles, 1972; asst. editor Jour. Sedimentary Petrology, adminstrv. asst. dept. geology U. So. Calif., 1972-76; acctg. analyst Rockwell Corp., Dallas, 1977; fin. analyst investment analysis group FMC Corp., Chgo., 1978-79, sr. fin. analyst ops. analysis group, 1979, purchasing agt. nat. contracts, 1979—. Bus. and Women's Found. grantee, 1976-78. Mem. Am. Mgmt. Assn., Am. Fin. Assn., Beta Gamma Sigma. Club: The Vincent. Office: FMC Corp 200 E Randolph Dr Chicago IL 60601

ZUIDWEG, DONALD RICHARD, pharm. chem. co. exec.; b. Kalamazoo, Oct. 2, 1936; s. Adrian and Lucille Edna (Mulder) Z.; B.B.A. cum laude, Western Mich. U., 1958; M.B.A., Ind. U., 1960; m. Jean Ann Skidmore, July 21, 1956; children—Scot Richard, Alan Adrian, Lauri Mari. Various mktg., distbn. and fin. positions Upjohn Co., Kalamazoo, 1958-67, v.p. ops., controller, 1967-73, regional distgn. mgr., 1976, corp. acctg. and fin./group mgr., 1976-79, group mgr. corp. acct'g. systems, cost acctg. and mehods and records, 1979-81, group mgr. corp. telecommunications, office automation, methods and records, 1981—; cons. small bus. Active various sch. and ch. orgns. Served to capt. Fin. Corps, U.S. Army, 1960-66. Mem. Kalamazoo Accountants Assn. (pres. 1975), Ind. U. Sch. Bus. Alumni Assn. (life), Assn. M.B.A. Execs., Internat. Communications Assn., Western Mich. U. Alumni Assn. (life). Office: 7000 Portage Rd Kalamazoo MI 49001

ZUPKO, RONALD EDWARD, historian, educator; b. Youngstown, Ohio, Aug. 5, 1938; s. Michael E. and Frances (Bartek) Z.; B.A., Youngstown State U., 1960; M.A., U. Chgo., 1963; Ph.D., U. Wis., 1966; m. Kathleen Monroe, July, 1974; 1 dau., Sarah J. Asst. prof. dept. history Marquette U., Milw., 1966-69, asso. prof., 1969-76, prof., 1976—, asst. chmn. dept. history, 1971-74; mem. Sch. of Hist. Studies, Inst. for Advanced Study, Princeton, N.J., 1975; cons. and field reader U.S. Office Edn., 1977, 78. Recipient Teaching Excellence award Marquette U., 1977; Faculty fellow, 1968, 76; NSF grantee, 1972, 80; Am. Philos. Soc. grantee, 1973, 74; Marquette U. research grantee, 1972-80. Mem. Internat. Soc. History of Sci., Am. Econ. Assn., Am. Metric Assn., Econ. Historians of Wis., Medieval Acad. of Am., Milw. County Hist. Soc., Mid-West Medieval Assn., Inst. for Advanced Study, Sigma Xi, Pi Gamma Mu, Phi Alpha Theta. Author: A Dictionary of English Weights and Measures from Anglo-Saxon Times to the Nineteenth Century, 1968; British Weights and Measures: A History from Antiquity to the Seventeenth Century, 1977; French Weights and Measures Before the Revolution, 1978, others; contbr. articles on history of sci. to scholarly publs. Home: 526 N 77th St Wauwatosa WI 53213 Office: Charles L Coughlin Hall Dept of History Marquette Univ Milwaukee WI 53233

ZWECKER, PENNY LYNN, psychologist; b. Mpls., Sept. 17, 1952; d. Richard Clayton and Lodeema Marie (Zuehlke) Drayer; B.A., Grinnell (Iowa) Coll., 1974; M.S. in Psychology, Trinity U., San Antonio, 1975; m. Jerome Leon Zwecker, Feb. 19, 1977. Dormitory attendant Travis State Sch., Austin, Tex., 1974; psychiat. asst. St. Mary's Hosp., Mpls., 1976; tutor Faribault (Minn.) Area Vocat. Tech. Inst., 1977-78; psychologist Faribault State Hosp., 1976—, Faribault Psychol. Services, P.A., 1979—. Lic. psychologist, Minn. Mem. Am. Assn. Mental Deficiency. Home: 1316 Westwood Dr Faribault MN 55021 Office: Faribault State Hospital Faribault MN 55021

ZWICK, WILLIAM CLARK, sch. adminstr.; b. Columbus, Ohio, June 24, 1947; s. Herman L. and Mary C. Zwick; B.S., Eastern Ky. U., 1970; M.A., Georgetown Coll., 1973; Ed.D., U. Akron, 1981; m. Shirley Linda Ferguson, Aug. 10, 1968; children—Jared Clark, Stacy Laura. Coach, tchr. Jessamine County High Sch., Nicholasville, Ky., 1970-71, Brunswick (Ohio) High Sch., 1971-72; football coach, baseball, phys. edn. instr. Georgetown (Ky.) Coll., 1972-73; prin. Barberton (Ohio) High Sch., 1974-75, 77—; trade and indsl. supr. Polaris Joint Vocat. Sch., Middleburg Heights, Ohio, 1976-77; owner Linwick Constrn. Co., Wadsworth, Ohio, 1974—. Active Republican party Medina County, Ohio, 1972-81; pres. Barberton Area Safety Council, 1979-80; Barberton Sch. chmn. United Way, 1979-80. Mem. Ohio Assn. Secondary Sch. Adminstrs., Ohio Vocat. Assn. Mem. Christian Ch. Club: Elks. Home: 8986 Guilford Rd Seville OH 44273 Office: Barberton High Sch 489 W Hopocan St Barberton OH 44203

ZWIKKER, KEES, graphics co. exec.; mfg. co. exec.; b. Eindhoven, Netherlands, Apr. 29, 1927; s. Cornelius and Johanna Dorothea (Theinert) Z.; M.B.A. with honors, U. Utrecht (Netherlands), 1950; m. Marie Jean Aylward, Dec. 20, 1952 (dec.); children—Robert Kees, Jacqueline Margaret. Advt. prodn. mgr. Lee Donneley Advt. Agy., Cleve., 1952-56; dist. sales mgr. Standard Pub. Co., Cin., 1956-62; advt. mgr. Hess & Clark div. Vick Chem. Corp., Ashland, Ohio, 1962-66; v.p. Topper Assos. Advt. Agy., Ashland, 1966-71; account exec. Cross Assos. Advt., Chagrin Falls, Ohio, 1971-72; mktg. communications mgr. Norton Co., Akron, Ohio, 1972—; chmn. bd. Ashland Graphic Art Co., 1963—. Mem. Aurora (Ohio) City Council, 1977—; sec. Aurora Planning and Zoning Commn., 1974—; bd. dirs. Nat. Trade Show Exhibit Assn., 1978—. Served to capt. Dutch Army, 1947-51. Mem. Nat. Advt. Assn. (cert. public communicator), Nat. Trade Show Exhibit Assn. (dir. 1978—), Indsl. Marketers of Cleve., Bus. and Profl. Advt. Assn., Ad Club. Republican. Roman Catholic. Club: Boating of Aurora Shores. Contbr. articles to profl. jours. Home: 3674 Nautilus Trail Aurora OH 44202 Office: PO Box 350 Akron OH 44309

ZYDLO, STANLEY MATHEW, physician; b. Chgo., Dec. 15, 1933; s. Stanley Mathew and Estelle Helen (Tubilewicz) Z.; B.A., Westminster Coll., 1956; M.D., Loyola U., Chgo., 1960; m. Joyce M. Reid, Aug. 29, 1976; children—Kristi, Sheryl, Scott, Mark, Josh, Matt. Intern, St. Francis Hosp., Evanston, Ill., 1960-61; gen. practice medicine, Wabash, Ind., 1963-69; emergency physician, past pres. Med. Emergency Service Assos., Chgo., now chmn. bd.; founder, co-owner Vernon Manor, home for retarded children, Wabash, 1968—; dir. mobile intensive care unit system N.W. Community Hosp., Arlington Heights, Ill.; med. cons. Nat. Registry Emergency Med. Technicians, 1975-78; del. AMA Commn. Emergency Med. Services, 1975-77. Served with USAF, 1961-63. Mem. Am. Coll. Emergency Physicians (chmn. bd. dirs. Ill. 1971—, past chmn. emergency med. systems com.), Am., Ind., Ill., Chgo. med. assns., Wabash County, Chgo. med. socs., Aerospace Med. Assn., Am. Inst. Aeros. and Astronautics, Air Force Assn., Soc. Flight Surgeons, Am. Profl. Practice Assn., Am. Assn. Physicians and Surgeons, Isaac Walton League, Frat. Order Police. Clubs: Elks, Optimists (charter). Developer, dir. 1st multicommunity mobile intensive care emergency system in 17 N.W. Chgo. suburbs with paramedic level emergency aid. Home: 108 Chicory Ct Rolling Meadows IL 60008 Office: 800 W Central Rd Arlington Heights IL 60005

ZYWICKE, GARON CLEMEN, accountant; b. Milw., Nov. 24, 1933; s. Edward Peter and Elinor Helena (Urbanski) Z.; B.B.A., U. Wis., 1956; m. Virginia Alice Mallinson, Feb. 28, 1976; children—Gregg, Gina, Gayle, Holly. Staff accountant Ernst & Ernst, Chgo., 1958, sr. accountant, 1958-62, supr., 1962-67, supr., Kalamazoo, 1967-70, mgr. tax dept., 1970-75; mgr. Kalamazoo office Doren, Mayhew, Grob & McNamara, 1976; mng. partner Zywicke & Zywicke, Kalamazoo, 1976—. Chmn. acct. sect. Kalamazoo United Way Campaign, 1976, 77. Served with U.S. Army, 1956-58. C.P.A., Ill., Mich. Mem. Am. Inst. C.P.A.'s, Mich. Assn. C.P.A.'s (membership com.), Nat. Assn. Accountants (pres. Kalamazoo chpt.), U. Wis. Alumni Assn. Clubs: Park, Beacon, Am. Businessmen's (2d v.p.) (Kalamazoo). Home and Office: 3405 Tamsin Ave Kalamazoo MI 49008

Who's Who in America

Biographees of the Midwest

The following biographees of the Midwestern region have sketches appearing in the 42nd edition of *Who's Who in America*.

Aaron, Charles
Aaron, Paul R.
Abbey, George Marshall
Abbott, David Henry
Abbott, John David
Abbott, John Sheldon
Abboud, Francois Mitry
Abegg, Martin G.
Abel, Clarence, Jr.
Abel, Harold
Abele, Homer E.
Abeles, Norman
Abell, David Robert
Abelson, Richard D.
Abert, Donald Byron
Abnee, A. Victor, Jr.
Abraham, Paul Leslie
Abrahams, John Hambleton
Abrahamson, Shirley Schlanger
Abramoff, Peter
Abramowicz, Alfred L.
Abrams, Alan Michael
Abrams, Irwin
Abrams, Talbert
Abramson, David Irvin
Abts, Henry William
Abu-Lughod, Janet Louise
Achenbach, Jan Drewes
Achepohl, Keith Anden
Acheson, Allen Morrow
Acker, Duane Calvin
Ackerman, Eugene
Ackerman, James Nils
Ackerman, James Waldo
Ackerman, John Henry
Ackerman, Ora Ray
Ackermann, William Carl
Ackley, (Hugh) Gardner
Ackmann, Lowell Eugene
Adair, John Douglas
Adams, Albert Willie, Jr.
Adams, Algalee Pool
Adams, Arthur Eugene
Adams, Bernard Schroder
Adams, Christopher Steve, Jr.
Adams, David Kenneth
Adams, Edward Franklin
Adams, Jack Ashton
Adams, John Marshall
Adams, John Richard
Adams, Joseph Elkan
Adams, Robert McCormick
Adams, Robert McLean
Adams, Thomas Brooks
Adams, Walter
Adamson, Oscar Charles, II
Adawi, Ibrahim Hasan
Addington, Keene Harwood
Addington, Whitney Wood
Addis, Laird Clark, Jr.
Addy, Frederick Seale
Adelman, Albert Harry
Adelman, R. J.
Adelman, William John
Adelsman, H(arriette) Jean
Adkins, Arthur William Hope
Adkins, Howard Eugene
Adler, Aaron
Adler, Arthur M., Jr.
Adler, Gerald
Adler, Jacob Henry
Adler, Jerome William
Adler, Julius
Adler, Mortimer Jerome
Adler, Philip
Adler, Robert
Adolph, Robert J.
Advani, Sunder Hashmatrai
Aeschbacher, William Driver
Affeldt, John Ellsworth
Agarwal, Paul Dharam
Agee, William M.
Aggarwal, Sundar L(al)
Agnew, William George
Agranoff, Bernard William
Ahlgren, Gilbert Harold
Ahlstrom, Ronald Gustin
Ahmann, John Stanley
Ahmed, Khalil
Ahmed, Nasir
Ahner, Alfred Fredrick
Ahr, Paul Robert
Ahrenholz, H(erman) William
Aikawa, Masamichi
Aird, Kenneth
Aitay, Victor
Akcasu, Ziyaeddin Ahmet
Akin, Ewen Marion, Jr.
Akin, Wallace Elmus
Akos, Francis
Aladjem, Silvio
Alberding, Charles Howard
Albers, Thomas Louis
Alberti, John Robert
Albrecht, Frederick Ivan
Albrecht, Richard Eugene
Albrecht, Ronald Frank
Albright, Jack Lawrence
Albright, Justin W.
Albright, Lyle Frederick
Albright, Penrose Strong
Alcott, James Arthur
Alcox, Michael Thomas
Alden, Raymond Macdonald
Alder, Edwin Francis
Aldrich, Ann
Aldrich, Clyde Frank
Aldrich, Patricia Anne Richardson
Aldridge, Alfred Owen
Aldridge, John Watson
Alexander, Arvin J.
Alexander, Benjamin Harold
Alexander, C. Alex
Alexander, Carl Albert
Alexander, Denton Eugene
Alexander, James Marshall, Jr.
Alexander, John Frank
Alexander, Landon Veltmann
Alexander, Quentin
Alexander, Richard Dale
Alexander, William Henry
Alexis, Marcus
Alexy, R. James
Alfidi, Ralph Joseph
Alfieri, John Joseph
Alfonso, Robert John
Alford, John William
Alford, Lionel Devon
Alger, Chadwick Fairfax
Aliber, Robert Zelwin
Alig, Cornelius O., Jr.
Allard, Jean
Allbee, Robert George
Allen, Charles Eugene
Allen, Charles Joseph, II
Allen, Charles Keller
Allen, Charles Richard
Allen, Darryl Frank
Allen, David Donald
Allen, Durward Leon
Allen, Francis Alfred
Allen, Garland Edward
Allen, Harold Byron
Allen, Harold G.
Allen, James R.
Allen, James Rex, Jr.
Allen, Larry William
Allen, Layman Edward
Allen, Louis G.
Allen, Lyle Wallace
Allen, Maurice Bartelle, Jr.
Allen, Reginald Edgar
Allen, Richard Blose
Allen, Robert Dee
Allen, Robert Hutton
Allen, Ronald Royce
Allen, Sally Lyman
Allen, Wallace Wilbur
Allen, William Cecil
Allerhand, Adam
Alley, William J.
Allinsmith, Wesley
Allison, James Ralph
Allred, Albert Louis
Alltop, James Howard
Allyn, Richard
Almen, Lowell Gordon
Alnes, Ellis Stephen
Alpaugh, Walter George, Jr.
Alper, Albert
Alper, Allen Myron
Alpern, Mathew
Alpers, David Hershel
Alpert, Daniel
Alsaker, Elwood Cecil
Alschuler, Sam
Alsdorf, James William
Alsop, Donald Douglas
Alspach, Philip Halliday
Alspaugh, Robert Odo
Alston, Walter Emmons
Altenau, Alan Giles
Altenbernd, A(ugust) Lynn
Alterman, Irwin Michael
Altheimer, Alan J.
Altis, Harold David
Altman, Arnold David
Altman, Milton Hubert
Altmann, Richard Gustaf
Altner, Peter Christian
Alton, Ralph Taylor
Altschaeffl, Adolph George
Altschul, Alfred Samuel
Altstetter, Carl Joseph
Alverson, William H.
Alvord, William Howard
Al Yasiri, Kahtan Abbass
Alyea, Ethan Davidson, Jr.
Amador, Luis Valentine
Aman, Mohammed Mohammed
Aman, Reinhold Albert
Amann, Peter Henry
Ambrose, Tommy W.
Ambuel, John Philip
Amdahl, Byrdelle John
Amdahl, Douglas Kenneth
Ames, Bruce Charles
Ames, Donald Paul
Ames, John Dawes
Ames, Van Meter
Amick, Charles L(orayne)
Amini, Johari M.
Ammar, Raymond George
Ammerman, Robert Ray
Ammons, Edsel Albert
Amplatz, Kurt
Amstadter, Laurence
Amstutz, Harold Emerson
Amundson, Duane Melvin
Anagnost, Catherine Cook
Anagnostopoulos, Constantine Efthymios
Ancker-Johnson, Betsy
Anderhalter, Oliver Frank
Anders, Edward
Anders, Marion Walter
Andersen, Aksel Robert
Andersen, Elmer L.
Andersen, Harold Wayne
Andersen, Kenneth Benjamin
Andersen, Kenneth Eldon
Anderson, Albert Esten
Anderson, Ansel Cochran
Anderson, Arnold Severen
Anderson, Charles Arner
Anderson, Charles Arnold
Anderson, Charles Samuel
Anderson, Chester Grant
Anderson, Cortland Edwin, Jr.
Anderson, David Daniel
Anderson, Donald Edward
Anderson, Donald George
Anderson, Donald Keith
Anderson, Edwin John
Anderson, Ernest Washington
Anderson, Eugene I.
Anderson, Fletcher Neal
Anderson, Fred Woodrow Wilson
Anderson, Frederic Ducey
Anderson, George Lee (Sparky)
Anderson, Gordon Caldwell
Anderson, Harold Albert
Anderson, Harry Frederick, Jr.
Anderson, Iain Mair
Anderson, J. Joseph
Anderson, James Frederick
Anderson, James George
Anderson, James Henry
Anderson, James Keith
Anderson, Jerry Maynard
Anderson, John Bayard
Anderson, John David
Anderson, John Edward
Anderson, John Robert
Anderson, John Stephen
Anderson, Joseph Norman
Anderson, Kenneth Eugene
Anderson, Kenneth Morse
Anderson, LaVerne Eric
Anderson, Lyle Arthur
Anderson, Marquard John
Anderson, Mary Jane
Anderson, Milton Henry
Anderson, Odin Waldemar
Anderson, Paul F.
Anderson, Richard Paul
Anderson, Richard Paul
Anderson, Richard Todd
Anderson, Robert Ferdinand
Anderson, Robert Marshall
Anderson, Roger E.
Anderson, Stefan Stolen
Anderson, Thomas Harold
Anderson, Thomas P.
Anderson, Thomas Patrick
Anderson, Thomas Ralph
Anderson, Victor Elving
Anderson, Wendell William, Jr.
Anderson, William Breckenridge
Anderson, William Ernest
Anderson, William Hopple
Anderson, William Otis
Andrassy, Timothy Francis
Andre, Paul Dean
Andreano, Ralph Louis
Andreas, Dwayne Orville
Andreas, Lowell Willard
Andreasen, George Fredrick
Andres, Ronald Paul
Andres, William Alfred
Andress, Samuel Coe
Andrew, Gwen
Andrew, Warren
Andrews, Clarence Adelbert
Andrews, Eric Charles Wilson
Andrews, Fletcher Reed
Andrews, Frank Meredith
Andrews, Frederick Newcomb
Andrews, James Lewis
Andrews, Richard Vincent
Andrews, Theodore Francis
Andrews, Wayne
Andrus, Elwin A.
Andrus, John Emory, III
Andry, E. Robert
Anello, John David
Angell, Charles Austen
Angell, Richard Bradshaw
Angelo, Frank
Angst, John Edward
Angus, John Cotton
Ankeny, DeWalt Hosmer, Jr.
Annear, Paul Richard
Anneken, William Bernard
Anno, James Nelson
Anspach, Herbert Kephart
Anthes, Jacob
Anthony, Earl Roderick
Anton, Donald Christ
Antonsen, Elmer Harold
Anvaripour, M.A.
Apostle, Hippocrates George
Appel, John J.
Appel, William Frank
Appelman, Evan Hugh
Appl, Fredric Carl
Appleberry, James Bruce
Applegate, Douglas
Applegate, Malcolm W.
Appleman, Jean
Aprison, Morris Herman
Arakawa, Kasumi
Arbogast, Zollie O., Jr.
Archambault, Bennett
Archer, Dennis Wayne
Archer, John Dale
Archer, Marian Phyllis
Arden, Eugene
Arditti, Fred D.
Areen, Gordon E.
Arena, Angelo Richard
Arenberg, Julius Theodore, Jr.
Arey, Leslie Brainerd
Argento, Dominick
Argirion, Michael
Aris, Rutherford
Armbruster, Kernel Lantin
Armerding, Hudson Taylor
Armour, Laurance Hearne, Jr.
Armour, T. Stanton
Armstrong, Arthur James
Armstrong, Carl Hines
Armstrong, Charles Harry
Armstrong, John Alexander
Armstrong, Neil A.
Armstrong, Neill
Armstrong, Robert Bradley
Armstrong, Robert Eugene
Armstrong, Theodore Morelock
Arnason, Barry Gilbert Wyatt
Arndt, Roger Edward Anthony
Arnesen, Kenneth George
Arneson, George Stephen
Arnett, Harold Edward
Arnheim, Rudolf
Arnoff, E. Leonard
Arnold, David Clement
Arnold, Duane
Arnold, Everett John
Arnold, Harry Bartley
Arnold, James Romer
Arnold, Melvin Chester
Arnold, Paul Beaver
Arnold, Ralph Moffett
Arnold, Richard Thomas
Arnott, Struther
Arnstein, Walter Leonard
Aronson, Howard Isaac
Arpe, John Edwin
Arquilla, Robert
Arthos, John
Arthur, James K.
Arthur, Max
Arthur, Robert Milton
Artis, Jay William
Artner, Alan Gustav
Artz, Frederick Binkerd
Artzt, Edwin Lewis
Arvanites, Demosthenes George
Aschaffenburg, Walter Eugene
Aschauer, Charles Joseph, Jr.
Ashbrook, James Barbour
Ashby, Donald Wayne, Jr.
Ashby, Robert Samuel
Ashcroft, John
Ashe, A.J.
Ashe, Arthur James, III
Ashenhurst, Robert Lovett
Asher, Frederick
Ashford, James Knox
Ashin, Mark
Ashley, Robert Paul, Jr.
Ashman, Allan
Ashton, Sister Mary Madonna
Ashworth, John Lawrence
Askey, Richard Allen
Askins, Wallace Boyd
Asp, William George
Aspen, Marvin Edward
Asplin, Edward William
Astrin, Marvin H.
Atchley, Robert Claude
Atherton, James Dale
Athow, Kirk Leland
Atkin, Rupert Lloyd
Atkinson, Arthur John
Atkinson, Hugh Craig
Atkinson, John William
Atwell, Robert James
Atwood, Donald Jesse, Jr.
Atwood, Gerald Francis
Aubert, Eugene James
Auburn, Norman Paul
Auch, Walter Edward
Aucott, George William
Auer, James Matthew
Auerbach, Carl Abraham
Auerbach, Robert
Aughenbaugh, Nolan Blaine
August, Robert Olin
Auld, Frank
Aurin, Robert James
Ausman, Robert K.
Ausnehmer, Fred Charles
Austin, Arthur Donald, II
Austin, Edwin Charles
Austin, Joseph Allen
Austin, Kenneth Ralph
Austin, Richard Henry
Austin, Spencer Peter
Austin, William Lamont
Autry, Carolyn
Auwers, Stanley John
Avant, Grady, Jr.
Avedisian, Armen G.
Averill, Richard Wood
Avery, James Knuckey
Avery, William Herbert
Avischious, Raymond
Avison, David
Axel, John Werner
Axel, Peter
Axelrad, Norman David
Axford, Roy Arthur
Axinn, George Harold
Aydelotte, Myrtle Kitchell
Aydelotte, William Osgood
Ayer, Mary Jane
Ayers, Donald Howard
Ayers, Donald Walter
Ayers, Thomas G.
Aylward, Ronald Lee
Aymond, Alphonse Henry
Ayres, John Samuel
Ayres, Lyman S.
Ayres, Stephen McClintock
Ayton, Stewart Mitchell
Azarnoff, Daniel Lester
Azneer, J. Leonard
Babb, Ralph W., Jr.
Babbitt, Glenn Day
Babcock, Charles Luther
Babcock, David Edward
Babcock, Richard Felt
Babler, Wayne E.
Bacaner, Marvin Bernard
Bach, Jan Morris
Bachman, John Walter
Bachman, Nathan Dulaney, IV
Backlund, Brandon Haze
Bacon, Charles Langston
Bacon, Vinton Walker
Baddeley, D. Jeffrey
Badeer, Henry Sarkis
Baden, Thomas Arthur
Bader, Alfred Robert
Bader, Kenneth Leroy
Bader, Robert Smith
Badger, Edward William
Badskey, Lorin Justin
Badura-Skoda, Paul
Baehner, Robert Leo
Baer, Charles (Junior)
Baer, Eric
Baer, George Robert
Baer, Joseph Winslow
Baer, Julius Arthur, II
Baer, Kenneth Peter
Baer, Werner
Baerreis, David Albert
Baeumer, Max Lorenz
Baffes, Thomas Gus
Bagan, Thomas P(aul)
Bagby, Frederick Lair, Jr.
Bahlman, William Thorne, Jr.
Bailar, Benjamin Franklin
Bailar, John Christian, Jr.
Bailey, Andrew Dewey, Jr.
Bailey, Cecil Dewitt
Bailey, Charles Waldo, II
Bailey, Dudley
Bailey, Eugene Cary
Bailey, Harold Stevens, Jr.
Bailey, Herman Tracy
Bailey, John Turner
Bailey, Joseph T.
Bailey, Merritt Elton, Jr.
Bailey, Orville Taylor
Bailey, Reeve Maclaren
Bailey, Sturges Williams
Bailey, Wendell
Baillif, Ernest Allen
Bain, Jack Mansfield
Bain, Wilfred Conwell
Bair, Edward Jay
Baird, James Abington
Baird, John Pierson
Baird, Joseph Arthur
Baird, Robert Dahlen
Baird, Roger Allen
Baird, Russell Miller
Bakalar, John Stephen
Baker, Bernard Robert, II
Baker, Chester Bird
Baker, David Hiram
Baker, David Nathaniel, Jr.
Baker, Earl DeWitt
Baker, Edward Martin
Baker, George R.
Baker, George Robert
Baker, Harold Albert
Baker, James Edward
Baker, James Edward Sproul
Baker, John Russell
Baker, Keith Michael
Baker, Michael Harry
Baker, Norman Henderson
Baker, Richard Russell
Baker, Richard Southworth
Baker, Robert Maurice
Baker, Robert Thomas
Baker, Rollin Harold
Baker, Sheridan Warner, Jr.
Baker, Stannard Luther
Baker, William Wallace
Bakker, Cornelis B.
Bakrow, William John
Bakwin, Edward Morris
Balagot, Reuben Castillo
Balbach, Stanley Byron
Balcer, Charles Louis
Balcerzak, Marion John
Baldwin, Benjamin Harrison
Baldwin, Everett Newton
Baldwin, Gordon Brewster
Baldwin, Ralph Belknap
Baldwin, Robert Edward
Baldwin, William Howard
Balentine, Conrad James
Balester, Raymond James
Balfour, William Mayo
Balk, Eugene Norman

Cryderman, William Dale
Cudahy, Richard D.
Cudd, Herschel Herbert
Cudlip, William Byrnes
Culbert, Taylor
Culbertson, John Mathew
Cull, Robert Robinette
Culmer, Marjorie Mehne
Culp, David Albert
Culver, Dwight Wendell
Culver, John C.
Culver, Robert Joseph
Cuming, George Scott
Cummings, Frederick James
Cummings, Larry Lee
Cummings, Richard Howe
Cummings, Walter J.
Cummins, Alfred Byron
Cummins, Delmer Duane
Cummins, Kenneth Burdette
Cunin, John Raymond
Cunningham, C(ecil) Preston
Cunningham, Clark Edward
Cunningham, Glenn Clarence
Cunningham, Harry Blair
Cunningham, Kenneth Wayne
Cunningham, Marcus Eddy
Cunningham, Marilyn Alice Eneix
Cunningham, Pierce Edward
Cunningham, Robert Cyril
Cunningham, Robert Maris, Jr.
Cunningham, William Francis, Jr.
Cunnyngham, Jon
Curatolo, Alphonse Frank
Curfman, Lawrence Everett
Curl, Rane Locke
Curler, Howard J.
Curley, Edwin Munson
Curley, Robert Arnold
Curran, John Charles, Jr.
Curran, Michael Walter
Currie, Allan Baldwin
Currie, David Park
Currie, William Richard
Currier, Frederick Plumer
Curry, Robert Lee
Curti, Merle Eugene
Curtin, David Yarrow
Curtin, John William
Curtis, Douglas Homer
Curtis, James Owen
Curtis, Jerome Nathaniel
Curtis, Kenneth Stewart
Curtis, Philip James
Curtis, Richard Kenneth
Curtis, Samuel Ralston, Jr.
Curtis, William Hall
Curtiss, Charles Francis
Cusack, Anne Millicent
Cushman, Aaron D.
Cushman, Edward L.
Cushman, Lewis Arthur, Jr.
Cuthbert, Marvin Peare
Cuthbert, William Rodger
Cutler, Lynn Germain
Cutler, Richard Woolsey
Cutler, Stephen Joel
Cutler, Warren Gale
Cutlip, Randall Brower
Cutright, Phillips
Cutting, Philip Francis
Cutts, Charles Eugene
Cyphert, Frederick Ralph
Czarnecki, Richard Edward
Czarnik, Marvin Ray
Daane, Adrian Hill
Dabney, Seth Mason, III
Dabovich, Thomas Chris
Dacey, Michael Francis
Dacey, Timothy John, Jr.
Daggett, Duane
Dagley, Stanley
Dagnese, Joseph Martocci
Dahl, Erno Joyce
Dahl, Harry Waldemar
Dahlberg, LeRoy Waldo
Dahler, John Spillers
Dahlgren, Carl Herman Per
Dahlin, Donald C(lifford)
Dahling, Louis Ferdinand
Dahltorp, Bruce Lawrence
Dailey, Donald Earl
Dailey, J. Roberts
Dailey, Thomas Edwin
Daily, James Wallace
Dale, Wesley John
D'Alexander, William Joseph
Daley, Arthur James
Daley, Frank Robert Lee, Jr.
Dallmayr, Winfried (Fred) Reinhard
Dallos, Peter John
Dalrymple, Thomas Lawrence
Dalston, Jeptha William
Dalton, Harry
Dalton, William Matthews
Daly, John Francis
Daly, Leo Anthony
Daly, Maggie (Mrs. Arthur Bazlen)
Daly, Robert Frederic
Daly, Walter Joseph
Dam, Kenneth W.
Dambach, Philip Joseph
D'Ambrosio, Dominick
Dames, Joan Foster (Mrs. Urban L. Dames)
Damman, James Joseph
Dammeyer, Rodney F.
Dampeer, John Lyell
Dancey, Charles Lohman
Danco, Léon Antoine
Danenbarger, William Fowler
Danenberg, Emil Charles
Danford, Ardath Anne
Danforth, David Newton
Danforth, George Edson
Danforth, John Claggett
Danforth, Joseph D.
Danforth, William Henry
Daniel, Robert Woodham
Daniels, Derick January
Daniels, John Hancock
Daniels, Melvin Joe
Daniels, Robert Sanford
Daniels, Terrence David
Danielson, Gordon Charles
Danielson, Gordon Kenneth, Jr.
Danielson, Irvin R.
Danilevicius, Zenonas
Danilov, Victor Joseph
Danis, Peter Godfrey
Dankhoff, Walter Frank
Danly, Donald Robert
Danly, James C.
Danner, Patsy (Pat) Ann
Dante, Harris Loy
Darack, Arthur J.
Darby, Edwin Wheeler
Darby, Harry
Darby, Joseph Branch, Jr.
Darby, William Leonard
Dargene, Carl J.
Dargusch, Carlton Spencer
Dark, Alvin Ralph
Darling, Frank Clayton
Darlington, Oscar Gilpin
D'Arms, John Haughton
Daroff, Robert Barry
Darr, John Walker
Darr, Milton Freeman, Jr.
Darrell, George Albert
Dary, David Archie
Dauch, Richard Eugene
Daughaday, William Hamilton
Dault, Raymond Arthur
Dauphinais, George Arthur
Dautel, Charles Shreve
Davenport, Fred Marshall
Davenport, Horace Willard
Davenport, William Kirk
Davids, Lewis Edmund
Davids, Richard Carlyle
Davidson, Bruce Arthur
Davidson, Charles Henry
Davidson, Gordon Chambers
Davidson, Harvey Justin
Davidson, John Kenneth, Sr.
Davidson, John Lefler, Jr.
Davidson, Richard K.
Davidson, William
Davie, Joseph Myrten
Davies, Alfred Robert
Davies, Michael John
Davies, Robert Holborn
Davies, Ronald N.
Davis, A. Arthur
Davis, Allison
Davis, B. R. Bud
Davis, Bennie Luke
Davis, Bertram George
Davis, Britton Anthony
Davis, Charles Alexander
Davis, Charles Hargis
Davis, Chester R., Jr.
Davis, David
Davis, Earl James
Davis, Edgar Glenn
Davis, Gale Elwood
Davis, Gene Carlton
Davis, Harry Rex
Davis, Howard Ted
Davis, Hubert Eugene
Davis, James (Othello)
Davis, James Cox
Davis, James Robert
Davis, John Bradford, Jr.
Davis, John Christy
Davis, John Dwelle
Davis, John Marcell
Davis, Joseph Lloyd
Davis, Joseph Samuel
Davis, Laurence Laird
Davis, Matthew Dinsdale
Davis, Michael David
Davis, Muller
Davis, O. C.
Davis, Peter Anthony
Davis, Ralph Lanier
Davis, Richard
Davis, Richard Bradley
Davis, Richard Francis
Davis, Richard Josef
Davis, Roger Edwin
Davis, S. Robert
Davis, Sam H.
Davis, Stephen Howard
Davis, Thomas Edward
Davis, Truman A.
Davis, William Eugene
Davisson, Melvin Thomas
Davy, Philip Sheridan
Dawn, Clarence Ernest
Dawson, Clayton Leroy
Dawson, John Frederick
Dawson, William Ryan
Day, Cecil LeRoy
Day, Emerson
Day, Harold John
Day, Jack Grant
Day, John Sidney
Day, Mahlon Marsh
Day, Robert G.
Day, Roland Bernard
Day, Stanley R.
Dayananda, Mysore Ananthamurthy
Dayton, Kenneth Nelson
Deacy, Thomas Edward, Jr.
Deahl, Warren Anthony
Deale, Henry Vail, Jr.
Dean, Burton Victor
Dean, Donald Stewart
Dean, Leland Wilbur
Dean, Robert Hal
Dean, Thomas Floyd
Deaner, R. Milton
DeAntoni, Edward Paul
Dearborn, Delwyn Dayle
Dearden, Douglas Morey
Dearden, John Francis
Deatherage, Fred E.
Deaton, Lowell S.
Deaver, Darwin Holloway
Debacco, Paul L.
De Bardeleben, Arthur
De Bartolo, Edward J., Jr.
Debelak, William F.
De Benko, Eugene
Debicki, Andrew Peter
De Blasi, Anthony Armando
de Blasis, James Michael
De Bloom, Carl George, Jr.
de Boor, Carl
DeBow, Russell Robinson
De Bruler, Roger O.
Debrunner, Peter George
De Bruyn, Peter Paul Henry
De Bruyn, Robert L.
de Bruyn Kops, Julian
Debus, Allen George
de Camara, Richard Paul
DeCamp, Graydon
Decio, Arthur Julius
Decker, Bernard Martin
Decker, David Garrison
Decker, Freeman Bernard
Decker, John Charles
Decker, Oscar Conrad, Jr.
Decker, Richard Knore
Decker, Wayne Leroy
de Coningh, Edward Hurlbut
DeCook, Richard Cyril
DeCook, Richard Cyril
DeCosta, Edwin J.
De Coster, Cyrus Cole
De Crane, Raymond Edward
Dedelow, Duane William
Dedmon, Emmett
Deeb, Gary James
Deep, Ira Washington
Deer, Richard Elliott
Deere, Cyril Thomas
deFiebre, Conrad William
De Francesco, John Blaze, Jr.
De Gaetano, Armand Leonard
De George, Richard Thomas
DeGiusti, Dominic Lawrence
DeGood, Douglas Kent
DeGraaf, Donald Earl
de Gravelles, William Decatur, Jr.
DeGroot, John Darryl
De Guire, Frank C.
DeHaan, Norman Richard
Deikel, Theodore
De Jong, Arthur Jay
De Jong, Meindert
Delakas, Daniel Liudviko
De Lancey, William John
Delaney, Philip Alfred
De Lapp, George Leslie
DeLeone, Carmon
del Greco, Francesco
Delhey, John Donald
Deliyanne, Gregory Louis
Delleur, Jacques William
Dellow, Reginald Leonard
De Long, Roger G.
Delor, Camille Joseph
De Lorenzo, Anthony George
DeLorenzo, David Joseph
De Marco, Thomas Joseph
De Marr, Mary Jean
DeMascio, Robert Edward
Dember, William Norton
Dembo, Lawrence Sanford
Dembowski, Peter Florian
DeMelio, Joseph John
Demetrion, James Thomas
Demetriou, Angelo John
De Micheal, Donald Anthony
Deming, Robert Herschel
Demoff, Samuel Louis
Demorest, Robert Steele
DeMoss, Ralph Dean
Demouth, Robin Madison
Demoz, Abraham
Dempsey, Frank Joseph
Dempsey, James Howard, Jr.
Dempsey, Jerry Edward
Dempsey, John Cornelius
Denham, Daniel Eugene, Jr.
Denkhoff, Elizabeth
Dennen, David Warren
Denner, Melvin Walter
Denney, Arthur Hugh
Denning, Gary R.
Denning, Peter James
Dennis, John L.
Denny, James McCahill
Denomme, Thomas Gerald
Denov, Sam
DeNovo, John August
Denslow, John Stedman
Depew, Charles Gardner
dePeyster, Frederic Augustus
DePorter, Donald James
Deramus, William Neal, III
Derber, Milton
Derby, Stanley Kingdon
Derge, David Richard
Derk, Richard George
Derlacki, Eugene L(ubin)
Derrick, Malcolm
Derwinski, Edward Joseph
Derzon, Gordon M.
De Santis, Anthony
De Santis, Vincent Paul
Desch, Theodore Edward
Deschamps, Georges A.
DeSchweinitz, Karl, Jr.
De Shazor, Ashley Dunn
De Simone, Livio Diego
Desloge, Taylor Stith
Desnoes, Peter
Despres, Leo Arthur
Despres, Leon Mathis
Deters, James Raymond
Detlefsen, Guy-Robert
Detuno, Joseph Edward
Detweiler, Joseph Hall
Detzer, Karl
Deveau, Thomas C.
Devereux, Lawrence Hackett
Devereux, Timothy Edward
Devinatz, Allen
DeVine, (Joseph) Lawrence
Devine, Vaughan P. (Bing)
DeVisé, Pierre Romain
deVito, Robert Alexander
Devitt, Edward James
DeVos, Richard Marvin
DeVries, Bernard Jerin
Dewald, Ernest Leroy
Dewald, Paul Adolph
DeWall, Richard Allison
DeWeese, Marion Spencer
de Wet, Johannes Martanis Jacob
Dewey, Ernest Wayne
Dewey, Lewis William, Jr.
de Windt, Edward Mandell
DeWitt, Clyde Frank
De Witt, Jesse R.
DeWolfe, John Chauncey, Jr.
DeWolfe, John Chauncey, III
Dexter, Donald Harvey
De Young, Dennis Alan
DeYoung, Lillian Jeanette
DeYoung, Melvin Howard
Dhanak, Amritlal Maganlal
Dharmapuri, Vidyasagar
Diamant, Alfred
Diamond, Norma Joyce
Diamond, Seymour
Diamond, Sidney
Diana, Joseph Anthony
Dianis, John Edward
Dible, William Trotter
DiBona, Gerald Frederic
Di Chiera, David
Dick, Albert Blake, III
Dick, Raymond Dale
Dickason, John Hamilton
Dickelman, Howard Clarence
Dickerson, Earl Burrus
Dickerson, Frederick Reed
Dickerson, John McKey
Dickhoner, William Harold
Dickie, George Thomas
Dickie, Helen Aird
Dickinson, Martin Brownlow, Jr.
Dickinson, Richard Donald Nye
Dickinson, William Reynolds
Dicus, Clarence Howard, Jr.
Dicus, John Carmack
DiDio, Liberato John Alphonse
Diebold, Robert Ernest
Diefenbach, Allan Berleman
Diefenbach, Viron Leroy
Diekema, Anthony J.
Dierks, Richard Ernest
Dietch, Henry Xerxes
Dieterle, Donald Lyle
Dietmeyer, Donald Leo
Dietrich, Joseph Jacob
Dietrich, Richard Vincent
Dietrich, William Allen
Dietrich, William Carl
Dietrich, William Gale
Dietz, Albert Arnold Clarence
Dietz, Charlton Henry
Dietz, Earl Daniel
Difford, Winthrop Cecil
DiGangi, Frank Edward
Diggs, Matthew O'Brien, Jr.
Di Girolamo, Joseph
DiLiddo, Bart A.
Dill, Charles Anthony
Dill, William Joseph
Dille, Earl Kaye
Dille, John Flint, Jr.
Dille, Roland Paul
Diller, Theodore Craig
Dillin, Samuel Hugh
Dillman, L. Thomas
Dillon, Gary G.
Dillon, Merton Lynn
Dillon, Paul Wilson
Dillon, Ray E.
Dillon, Richard Wayne
Dillon, W. Martin
DiMascio, William Michael
Dimling, James Sledge
Dimmerling, Harold J.
Dimock, Edward Cameron, Jr.
Dimond, Edmunds Grey
Dimond, Robert Edward
Dineen, Robert Joseph
Ding, Gar Day
Dingeman, James Herbert
Dingman, Maurice J.
Dingman, Reed Othelbert
Dinielli, Nicholas Anthony
Dinitz, Simon
Dinneen, Gerald Paul
Diotte, Alfred Peter
Di Pasquale, Pasquale, Jr.
Di Prima, Frank Peter
Dirks, Lee Edward
Dirvin, Gerald Vincent
Discher, Charles Dale
Dishman, Leonard I.
Dittrich, Raymond Joseph
Divall, Robert Keith
Dively, George Samuel
Dixit, Padmakar Kashinath
Dixon, Arthur George John
Dixon, George Hall
Dixon, Stewart Strawn
Dixon, W(illiam) Robert
Dixon, Wendell Lowell
Dixon, Wesley Moon, Jr.
Dixon, Willie James
Doan, Herbert Dow
Doane, John Philip
Doban, Robert Charles
Dobbins, William Octavius, III
Dobkin, Irving Bern
Dobler, William O.
Doblin, Jay
Dobrovolny, Jerry Stanley
Dobson, William David
Dobyns, Brown McIlvaine
Dockhorn, Robert John
Docking, Robert Blackwell
Doctoroff, Martin Myles
Dodd, Edwin Dillon
Dodd, James Robert
Dodd, Robert Bruce
Dodge, John Vilas
Dodge, Philip Rogers
Dodson, Clifford Lowel
Dodson, Oscar Henry
Dodson, Raymond M.
Doe, Richard Philip
Doelitzsch, Dennis Frank
Doepker, Bernard Edward
Doering, Grace Bernardina (Mrs. John W. McCord)
Doermann, Humphrey
Doermer, Richard T.
Doerr, Howard P.
Doisy, Edward Adelbert
Dolan, John E.
Dolan, Thomas Ironside
Dolch, William Lee
Dole, Robert Paul
Dolibois, John Ernest
Dolin, Albert Harry
Dolph, Charles Laurie
Domino, Edward Felix
Domke, Herbert Reuben
Dommermuth, William P.
Don, Daniel Arthur
Donabedian, Avedis
Donachie, James Ross
Donagan, Alan
Donahey, Gertrude Walton
Donahue, Phil
Donahue, Russell B.
Donahue, Thomas Michael
Donahugh, Robert Hayden
Donald, Larry Watson
Donaldson, Ethelbert Talbot
Donaldson, Frank Arthur, Jr.
Donaldson, Richard Miesse
Donatelle, Edward Patrick
Donath, Fred Arthur
Donati, Robert Mario
Donchin, Emanuel
Dongus, Gustav Herman
Donley, Harvey Edward
Donnell, Edward S.
Donnell, Harold Eugene, Jr.
Donnell, James C., II
Donnell, John Randolph
Donnelley, Gaylord
Donnelly, Charles Francis
Donnelly, Charles Robert
Donnelly, Gerard Kevin
Donnelly, Robert True
Donnem, Roland William
Donohoe, Jerome Francis
Donohue, Carroll John
Donohue, John Patrick
Donovan, Frank William
Donovan, John Anthony
Donovan, Paul V.
Doob, Joseph Leo
Dooley, Donald John
Dooley, Thomas Henry
Doolittle, Robert Frederick
Doolittle, Sidney Newing
Dorati, Antal
Dordal, Erl
Doremus, Robert Barnard
Dorfman, Albert
Dorfman, Isaiah S.
Dorfman, Joel Marvin
Dorfman, Leon Monte
Dorfman, Saul
Dorfmeyer, Robert Edward
Dorgan, Byron Leslie
Dorman, Linneaus Cuthbert
Dorn, Charles Meeker
Dorner, Peter Paul
Dorning, John Joseph
Dorr, John A., Jr.
Dorsey, Gray Lankford
Dorsey, Peter
Dortch, Carl Raymond
Dorton, Joseph La Drue
Dorweiler, John P.
Dosland, William Buehler
Doss, Lawrence Paul
Dossel, William Edward
Dott, Robert Henry, Jr.
Dotts, Harold William
Doty, David Singleton
Doubet, Earl Wesley
Douce, Wayne Richard
Dougan, Arthur Lewis
Dougherty, Charles Joseph
Dougherty, Daniel Joseph
Dougherty, Robert Anthony
Dougherty, Thomas L.
Doughman, Donald James
Douglas, Bruce Lee
Douglas, Kenneth Jay
Douglas, Murray Alanson
Douglas, Paul Louis
Douglas, Robert Ellis
Douglass, Bruce E.
Douvan, Elizabeth
Dovre, Paul John
Dow, Alden Ball
Dow, Dorothy Minerva
Dow, James Wilson
Dow, John Parker
Dow, Peter Anthony
Dow, William Gould
Dowdy, Homer Earl
Dowling, Paul Thomas
Downey, John Charles
Downey, John Wilham
Downey, William Kavanaugh
Downie, Dana
Downing, Joan Forman
Downs, Robert Bingham
Downs, Thomas Joseph
Doyen, Ross Orville
Doyle, Arthur James
Doyle, Daniel Moran
Doyle, Edmund Harold
Doyle, James Alexander
Doyle, James Edward
Doyle, James Joseph
Doyle, Patrick John
Doyle, Richard J.
Drago, Russell Stephen
Drake, George Albert
Drake, John Warren
Drake, Robert Tucker
Drake, William Depue
Drane, Walter Harding
Draper, Freda
Draper, Norman Richard
Drebin, Allan Richard
Dreher, Thomas Haller
Dreifke, Gerald Edmond
Dressel, Paul Leroy
Dresser, Earl George
Drewno, Joanne Meta
Drews. Herbert Richard
Drexler, Lloyd
Dreyer, John Edward
Dreyfus, Lee Sherman
Drickamer, Harry George
Driggs, H. Perry, Jr.
Driggs, Orval Truman, Jr.
Driker, Eugene
Drimmer, Melvin
Drinko, John Deaver
Driscoll, Glen Robert
Driscoll, Justin Albert
Driscoll, Robert Edward, Jr.
Droste, John Brown
Drotning, John Evan
Drown, Gary Kidd
Drucker, Daniel Charles
Drury, Charles Edwin
Drury, Robert Edward
Drvota, Mojmir
Dubes, Richard Charles
Dubin, Alvin
Dubin, Arthur Detmers
Dubin, Howard Victor
Dubin, Martin David
DuBois, Loren Arthur
Du Bois, Philip Hunter
Duchen, Charles
Duchossois, Richard Louis
Duckworth, T.A.
Duckworth, Winston Howard
Ducoff, Howard S.
Duddy, Frank Edward, Jr.
Duderstadt, James Johnson
Dudewicz, Edward John
Dudley, Paul V.
Dudley, Richard David
Dudley, Robert (Walter)
Due, Jean Margaret
Due, John Fitzgerald
Duellman, Joseph Patrick
Duerinck, Louis T.
Duerr, Herman George
Duerre, John Arden
Duesenberg, Richard William
Dufek, Donald Edward
Duff, Ivan Francis
Duff, James George
Duffy, Edward William
Dugan, John Michael
Dugan, Patrick Raymond
Dugan, Paul V(incent)
Dugan, Richard Taylor
Duggan, James Grayson
Duggan, Jerome Timothy
Duggan, John Michael
Duhamel, Joseph O.
Duhme, H(erman) Richard, Jr.
Duke, Richard De La Barre
Duke, Wayne
Dulany, Elizabeth Gjelsness
Dulin, Jacques (James) Matagne
Dumas, Rhetaugh Etheldra Graves
Dumovich, Loretta
Duncan, Carl Porter
Duncan, Charles Howard
Duncan, Clarence Avery, Jr.
Duncan, Donald Pendleton
Duncan, Hearst Randolph
Duncan, James Herbert Cavanaugh
Duncan, Kent Whitney
Duncan, Louis Charles

Flanagan, Carroll Edward
Flanagan, John Theodore
Flanagan, Malachi John
Flanders, Dwight Prescott
Flaskamp, William Davidson
Flaum, Joel Martin
Flavin, Glennon P.
Fleck, Elmer Earl
Flegenheimer, Ernest
Fleischaker, Joseph
Fleming, Arthur Fazzin
Fleming, Douglas G.
Fleming, Elyse S.
Fleming, Ned Nelson
Fleming, Robert John
Fleming, Robert Thomas
Fleming, William Harrison
Flemming, William Norman
Fletcher, Alan Gordon
Fletcher, Edward Abraham
Fletcher, James W.
Fletcher, Jonathan Moss
Fletcher, Robert
Fleuelling, Lewis Edward
Flick, Frank
Fliegel, Frederick Christian
Flikke, Arnold Maurice
Flitcraft, Richard Kirby, II
Floss, Heinz G.
Flower, Joseph Reynolds
Flynn, Colin Peter
Flynn, Donald Francis
Flynn, Edward James
Flynn, Frank Patrick, Jr.
Flynn, James Rourke
Flynn, William Joseph
Foell, Wesley Kay
Foellinger, Helene R.
Foerster, Bernd
Fogarty, Robert Stephen
Fogel, Robert William
Fogg, Richard Lloyd
Foldi, Andrew Harry
Folds, Charles Weston
Foley, Dorance Vincent
Foley, J. Patrick
Foley, James Joseph
Foley, Patrick Joseph
Foley, Raymond William
Folgate, Homer Emmett, Jr.
Follett, Garth B.
Follett, Jean Frances
Follett, Robert John Richard
Folse, John Roland
Fontana, Mars Guy
Fontana, Robert Edward
Fontanne, Lynn
Foote, Barbara Austin
Foote, Joel Lindsley
Foote, Robert Thaddeus
Foran, Thomas Aquinas
Forbes, Franklin Sim
Forbes, Malcolm Holloway
Forbes, Richard E.
Forbes, Richard Mather
Forbis, William Elbert
Ford, Allen Huntington
Ford, Dwain L.
Ford, George Burt
Ford, Henry, II
Ford, James William
Ford, Richard
Ford, Richard Earl
Ford, Richard Flynn
Ford, Richard Irving
Ford, William Clay
Fordham, Sheldon Leroy
Fordyce, Clifton Powell
Forell, George Wolfgang
Foreman, James Davis
Foreman, James Louis
Foresman, Raymond Joseph
Forester, John Everett
Form, William H.
Forman, Phillip Marvin
Forney, Robert Burns
Forni, Patricia Rose
Fornshell, Dave Lee
Forrer, Gordon Randolph
Forrestal, Frank Vincent
Forsell, Lawrence LeRoy
Forst, Marion Francis
Forster, Francis Michael
Forster, Peter H.
Forsyth, George Howard, Jr.
Forsyth, Ilene Haering
Forsythe, Margaret Jeanne
Forsythe, Robert Ames
Fort, Edward Bernard
Fort, Tomlinson, Jr.
Fortinberry, Glen Wood
Fortune, William Lemcke
Fosheim, Jon
Fosholt, Sanford Kenneth
Foss, Harlan Funston
Foss, John Frank
Foss, John William
Foss, Richard Westley
Foss, William Francis
Foster, Alan Herbert
Foster, Donald Lee
Foster, G. William, Jr.
Foster, George Arthur
Foster, Hugh Warren
Foster, John Stuart, Jr.
Foster, Paul David, Jr.
Foulk, William Theodore, Jr.
Fournier, Serge Raymond-Jean
Fowler, Barbara Hughes
Fowler, Earle Cabell
Fowler, Giles Merrill
Fowler, John Russell
Fowler, Noble Owen
Fox, Charles Ephraim
Fox, David Wayne
Fox, Edward Inman
Fox, George
Fox, Hazel Metz (Mrs. Allan E. Fox)
Fox, Jacob Logan
Fox, John Patrick, Jr.
Fox, Karl August
Fox, Kenneth Lee
Fox, Louis
Fox, Noel Peter
Fox, Raymond Bernard
Fox, Robert Kriegbaum
Fox, Robert Phillip
Fox, Robert William
Fox, Ronald Ernest
Fox, Sam
Fox, Samuel
Fox, Thurman Orville
Foy, Norman Ward
Foyt, A(nthony) J(oseph), (Jr.)
Fraedrich, Royal Louis
Fraenkel, Gideon August
Fraenkel, Stephen Joseph
Frager, Norman
Frain, Andrew Dennis
Fraley, Elwin Eugene
Frame, Clarence George
Frame, Ruth Rhea
Frampton, George Thomas
Franch, Glendon Everett, Jr.
Franchot, Douglas Warner
Francis, Dale Lyman
Francis, Marion Smith
Francis, Mary Charee
Franco, Anthony M.
Francois, William Armand
Frank, Clinton Edward
Frank, Eugene Maxwell
Frank, James
Frank, Jerome J.
Frank, Kaye Goodwin
Frank, Richard Calhoun
Franke, Richard James
Frankel, Gerald Alan
Frankel, Marvin
Frankena, William Klaas
Frankforter, Weldon DeLoss
Frankhauser, Wayne Dennis
Franklin, Aretha
Franklin, Charles Benjamin
Franklin, Owen Ellsworth
Franklin, Robert Brewer
Franks, Herman Louis
Frantel, Edward William
Frantz, Welby Marion
Franz, John Matthias
Franz, Richard Peter
Franzen, Earl Theodore
Franzen, Janice Marguerite Gosnell
Fraser, Donald MacKay
Fraser, Douglas Andrew
Fraser, Russell Alfred
Frasier, Ralph Kennedy
Fratcher, William Franklin
Frauenfelder, Hans
Frautschi, Walter Albert
Frawley, Thomas Francis
Frayne, John Patrick
Frazer, John Howard
Frazer, Maurice Doyle
Frazier, Chet June
Frazier, John Warren
Frazier, Robert G.
Frazier, Walt (Walter)
Frechette, Peter Loren
Frederick, Earl James
Frederick, Edward Charles
Frederick, William Sherrad
Fredericks, Marshall Maynard
Fredrickson, (Lawrence) Thomas
Free, John Martin
Freeark, Robert James
Freed, DeBow
Freedman, Daniel X.
Freedman, David Noel
Freedman, Lester
Freedman, Philip
Freedman, Ronald
Freehling, Norman
Freehling, Stanley Maxwell
Freehling, Willard Maxwell
Freeman, Alwyn Vernon
Freeman, Arthur J.
Freeman, Gale Wallace
Freeman, Gaylord
Freeman, Lee Allen, Jr.
Freeman, Ralph McKenzie
Freeman, Rowland Godfrey, III
Freeman, Susan Tax
Freeman, Warren Samuel
Freeman, William Miser
Freinkel, Norbert
Freinkel, Ruth Kimmelstiel
Fremont, Ernest Hoar, Jr.
French, A. James
French, George William, III
French, John Dwyer
French, John Henry, Jr.
French, Lyle Albert
French, Marcus Emmett
French, Robert Houston
Frenkel, Jacob Aharon
Frens, Arthur J.
Frenz, Horst
Freund, Charles Gibson
Freund, Clement Joseph
Freund, Gerald
Freund, William Frederick
Frey, Donald Nelson
Frey, Edward John
Frey, Kenneth John
Frey, Stuart Macklin
Frey, Thomas Lee
Freytag, Donald Ashe
Frick, Ivan Eugene
Frick, William George
Fride, Edward Theodore
Fridley, Russell William
Fried, Josef
Friedberg, Arthur Leroy
Friedberg, Maurice
Frieden, Carl
Frieden, Edward Hirsch
Friederici, Hartmann H.R.
Friedl, Francis Peter
Friedlaender, Fritz Josef
Friedlander, Raymond Nathan
Friedman, Barton Robert
Friedman, Bernard Samuel
Friedman, Gerald Laurence
Friedman, Hans Adolf
Friedman, Harold Edward
Friedman, Jay Kenneth
Friedman, Joyce Barbara
Friedman, Martin
Friedman, Melvin Jack
Friedman, Stanley
Friedman, William Hersh
Friedrich, Stephen Miro
Frieling, Gerald Harvey, Jr.
Fries, Robert Francis
Friese, George Ralph
Frisbie, Jack Michael
Frisque, Alvin Joseph
Friswold, Fred Ravndahl
Fritsche, Ernest Garfield
Fritz, Bruce Morrell
Fritz, Cecil Morgan
Fritz, Harry Garland
Fritz, Michael Henry
Fritz, Roger Jay
Fritzsche, Hellmut
Froehlich, Harold Vernon
Froemming, Herbert Dean
Frohrib, Darrell Albert
Frohring, Paul Robert
Fromm, Arno Henry
Fromm, Erika (Mrs. Paul Fromm)
Fromm, Henry Gordon
Fromm, Paul
Fromme, Alex M.
Frommer, Robert
Froom, William Watkins
Frost, Dee Lloyd
Frost, Earle Wesley
Frost, John Lawrence
Frost, Wilson
Fruehling, Donald Laverne
Fruin, Robert Cornelius
Fry, Bernard Mitchell
Fry, William Frederick
Fryburger, Vernon Ray, Jr.
Fryer, Minot Packer
Frykenberg, Robert Eric
Fu, King-sun
Fucik, Edward Montford
Fuerbringer, Alfred Ottomar
Fuhrman, Charles Andrew
Fujita, Tetsuya Theodore
Fulcher, George Avis
Fulk, Roscoe Neal
Fullagar, William Watts
Fuller, Benjamin Franklin
Fuller, Derek Joseph Haggard
Fuller, Harry Laurance
Fuller, James Chester Eedy
Fuller, Lawrence Robert
Fuller, Marvin Don
Fuller, Mary Margaret Stiehm
Fuller, Perry Lucian
Fuller, Samuel Ashby
Fuller, Stephen Herbert
Fuller, William Richard
Fuller, William Samuel
Fullerton, Charles William
Fullmer, Charles Curtis
Fulton, Robert Lester
Fultz, Clair Ervin
Fulweiler, Howard Wells
Fumagalli, Barbara Merrill
Funk, James (Ellis)
Funk, Roger Lee
Furer, Samuel Henry
Furlow, Mack Vernon, Jr.
Furman, James Merle
Furman, Robert Howard
Furste, Wesley Leonard, II
Fusaro, Ramon Michael
Fussler, Herman Howe
Gaafar, Sayed Mohammed
Gaal, Steven Alexander
Gabinet, Leon
Gabler, Robert Earl
Gabriel, Astrik Ladislas
Gaddes, Richard
Gaddy, Oscar Lee
Gaddy, Robert Joseph
Gadient, Walter G.
Gado, Mokhtar Hishmat
Gaeng, Paul Ami
Gaertner, Richard Francis
Gaffney, Edward J.
Gage, Avery Odell
Gage, Calvin William
Gage, Fred Kelton
Gage, John
Gagen, Franklin Conrad
Gaines, Ervin James
Gaines, Gene Franklin
Gaines, Stanley Noyes
Gainor, Thomas Edward
Gaither, Bill
Galanis, John William
Galati, Frank Joseph
Galbreath, Daniel Mauck
Galbreath, John Wilmer
Gallagher, George Vincent
Gallagher, John Francis, Jr.
Gallagher, John Pirie
Gallagher, Raymond Joseph
Gallaway, Lowell Eugene
Gallman, John Gerry
Gallo, Frank
Galloway, George Harold
Galloway, Robert Lee
Galvin, Robert Terrence
Galvin, Robert W.
Gambal, David
Gambill, John Randolph
Gamble, J. Carr, Jr.
Gamblin, Rodger Lotis
Gamelin, Francis Clifford
Gamson, William Anthony
Gander, John Edward
Gangnes, Alfred V.
Gangwere, George Henry, Jr.
Gann, Gene E.
Gannon, Sister Ann Ida
Gannon, James Patrick
Gannon, Philip Jerome
Gans, Carl
Gantner, George Eugene, Jr.
Gantt, John W.
Gantz, David Martin
Gantz, Wilbur Henry, III
Ganz, (Peter) Felix
Gaples, Harry Seraphin
Gapp, Paul John
Garber, Stanley Thomas
Garbutt, Eugene James
Garcia, David
Gard, Curtis Eldon
Gard, Spencer Agassiz
Gardinier, David Elmer
Gardner, Burleigh Bradford
Gardner, Dan Lewis
Gardner, David Morgan
Gardner, Herbert A.
Gardner, Howard Alan
Gardner, John Crawford
Gardner, John Ridgely
Gardner, Reece Alexander
Gardner, Russell, Jr.
Gardner, William Earl
Gardner, William Michael
Garek, Morris Daniel
Garelick, Martin
Garfield, Sol Louis
Gargan, Edward Thomas
Garinger, Louis Daniel
Garippo, Louis Benjamin
Garland, Charles Raleigh
Garland, Robert Field
Garmezy, Norman
Garn, Stanley Marion
Garner, Columbus Greene
Garnett, Marion Winston
Garnett, Wilson Blanton
Garnier, Robert Charles
Garratt, Charles William
Garretson, Donald Everett
Garrett, Milton Joseph
Garrett, Robert Austin
Garrison, John Raymond
Garrity, Robert Alexander
Garside, John Rushforth, II
Gartenhaus, Solomon
Gartner, Lawrence Mitchel
Gartner, Michael Gay
Garvey, Gerald Thomas
Garvey, John Charles
Garvey, Joseph John
Garvin, John Samuel
Garwood, John Delvert
Garzia, Samuel Angelo
Gasiorowicz, Stephen George
Gasiorowska, Xenia
Gaskell, Charles Thomas
Gass, Clinton Burke
Gass, Raymond William
Gass, Sylvester F.
Gass, William H.
Gasser, Wilbert, Jr.
Gassere, Eugene Arthur
Gassert, Robert George
Gastineau, Clifford Felix
Gates, Crawford Marion
Gates, David Murray
Gates, Jay Rodney
Gates, Richard Daniel
Gates, Robert Maynard
Gatewood, Buford Echols
Gathany, Van R.
Gatherum, Gordon Elwood
Gatto, Louis Constantine
Gault, N.L., Jr.
Gault, Stanley Carleton
Gaur, Krishna Kumar
Gausman, Chester H.
Gauthier, Clarence Joseph
Gauvreau, Paul Richard
Gavan, James Anderson
Gavin, James John, Jr.
Gay, Helen
Gay, Wilson A.
Gayda, Joseph Norbert
Gaylord, Clayton R.
Gayner, Robert Harold
Gazeley, Harold James
Geannopulos, Nick George
Gearhart, Louis Ossman
Gearhart, Thomas Lee
Gearty, Edward Joseph
Geary, John Daniel
Gebhard, Paul Henry
Gecht, Martin Louis
Geddes, Leslie Alexander
Gedgaudas, Eugene
Gee, George Duvall
Gefke, Henry Jerome
Gehling, John Adam
Gehr, Mary
Gehring, Benjamin Robert
Gehring, Frederick William
Gehring, Perry James
Gehrke, Charles William
Gehrz, Robert Gustave
Geier, James Aylward Develin
Geiger, George Raymond
Geiger, Homer Kent
Geis, Norman Winer
Geisinger, Robert Nelson
Geismer, Alan Stearn
Geisser, Seymour
Geitgey, Doris Arlene
Gelatt, Charles Daniel
Gelb, Victor
Gelbach, John A.
Gelfand, Ivan
Gelfand, Lawrence Emerson
Gelfand, Leonard
Gellise, Sister Mary Yvonne
Gellman, William
Gemignani, Michael Caesar
Gemmill, Robert Andrew
Gendell, Gerald Stanleigh
Gendron, Edward Charles
Gengler, Sister M. Jeanne
Gent, Alan Neville
Genther, Charles Booher
Gentles, Roy Allan
Geoffrey, Syed Iqbal (Syed Mohammed Jawaid Iqbal Jafree)
George, Edwin Ordell
George, Emery Edward
George, Newell A.
George, Nicholas Apostolos
George, Raymond Eugene, Jr.
George, Richard Ervin, Jr.
George, William Leo, Jr.
Georgescu, Peter Andrew
Georgi, Carl Eduard
Gephardt, Richard Andrew
Gephardt, Thomas Steuber
Geraci, Joseph Emil
Geraldson, Raymond I.
Gerard, Roy Joseph
Gerber, Eugene J.
Gerber, John Jay
Gerberich, William Warren
Gerbie, Albert Bernard
Gerbracht, Richard Edwin
Gerckens, Laurence Conway
Gerdes, Louis George
Gerdine, Leigh
Gerding, Edward John
Gerhardt, Philipp
Gerholz, Robert Paul
Gerlach, Luther Paul
German, John George
Gerow, Edwin Mahaffey
Gerraughty, Robert Joseph
Gerrie, Robert Bruce
Gerrish, Brian Albert
Gerritz, Ellsworth Melvin
Gershenson, Harry
Gerstacker, Carl Allan
Gerstner, Robert William
Gertler, Alfred Martin
Gerty, Francis Joseph
Gertz, Elmer
Gervais, Sister Generose
Geske, Norman Albert
Gessner, James Walter
Gest, Howard
Gesteland, Robert Charles
Getis, Arthur
Gettler, Benjamin
Gettys, Loyd Bryant
Getz, Lowell Lee
Getz, Oscar
Getzels, Jacob Warren
Getzendanner, Susan
Gewirth, Alan
Ghausi, Mohammed Shuaib
Gherlein, Gerald Lee
Ghiardi, James Domenic
Giampietro, Wayne Bruce
Gibala, Ronald
Gibbs, Clifford Edgar
Giblin, Edward J.
Gibson, Benjamin F.
Gibson, Charles Colmery
Gibson, David Mark
Gibson, Floyd Robert
Gibson, Frank Everett
Gibson, John Robert
Gibson, Ralph Milton
Gibson, Rankin MacDougal
Gibson, Robert William, Jr.
Gibson, Walter Samuel
Gibson, William Merriam
Gidwitz, Gerald
Gielen, Michael Andreas
Giertz, J. Fred
Gies, Thomas Anthony
Gies, Thomas George
Giese, Louis Bernhardt
Giesecke, G(ustav) Ernst
Giesecke, Raymond Henry
Giesen, Frank Hartman
Giesen, Richard Allyn
Giesey, Ralph Edwin
Giesse, Robert C.
Gifford, Harold, Jr.
Gifford, Ray Wallace, Jr.
Gigax, Lester Earl
Gikas, Paul William
Gilbert, Dale Winston
Gilbert, David Heggie
Gilbert, Enid M. Fischer
Gilbert, William James
Gilboe, David Dougherty
Gilbride, William Donald
Gildehaus, Thomas Arthur
Gil de Lamadrid, Jesús
Giles, Eugene
Giles, Homer Wayne
Giles, William Bliss
Giles, William Elmer
Gilfillen, George C., Jr.
Gill, Bernard Ives
Gill, Donald George
Gill, Henry Herr
Gill, William Nelson
Gillam, Basil Early
Gillan, Andrew Steelman
Gilles, Kenneth Albert
Gillespie, Harold Stanley
Gillespie, James Bennett
Gillett, George Nield, Jr.
Gillette, Earle Peter, Jr.
Gillette, Edward Scranton
Gillies, Thomas Daniel
Gillis, Bernard Thomas
Gillis, Frank James
Gillis, Marvin Bob
Gilman, David Alan
Gilman, Henry
Gilman, John Joseph
Gilman, Sid
Gilmore, Artis
Gilmore, Horace Weldon
Gilmore, James Stanley, Jr.
Gilmore, Joseph Patrick
Gilmore, Robert Eugene
Gilmore, Robert Karl
Gilmore, Roger
Gilmore, William Gerard
Gilmour, Allan Dana
Gilpin, Larry Vincent
Gilroy, John
Giltner, Thomas A.
Gimmestad, Victor Edward
Ginger, Leonard George
Gingerich, Vernon Jason
Gingiss, Benjamin Jack
Gingold, Josef
Gingrich, Newell Shiffer
Ginsberg, Donald Maurice
Ginsberg, Edward
Ginsburg, Norton Sydney
Ginsburg, Sigmund G.
Ginty, Daniel F.
Giordano, August T. (Gus)
Giovacchini, Peter Louis
Girouard, Robert Louis
Gislason, Sidney Payson
Gissler, Sigvard (Sig) Gunnar, Jr.
Giusti, Joseph Paul
Givan, Richard Martin
Givens, William Phillip
Givler, Walter M., Jr.
Glaab, Charles Nelson
Glagov, Seymour
Glancy, Alfred Robinson, III
Glaser, Kurt
Glaser, Luis
Glaser, Ronald
Glasser, James J.
Glaves, Donald William
Glaviano, Vincent Valentino
Glavin, John Edmund
Glazier, Robert Carl
Gleason, Douglas
Gleason, Eliza Atkins
Gleason, James Arthur
Gleason, Thomas Daues
Gleisser, Marcus David
Glendening, Everett Austin
Glendening, Everett Austin
Glenister, Brian Frederick
Glenn, Jerry Hosmer, Jr.
Glickman, Carl Davis
Glickman, Louis
Glomset, Daniel Anders
Glower, Donald Duane
Glynn, Thomas Joseph
Gnat, Raymond Earl
Gobin, Leo Calvin
Goble, Paul
Gockenbach, Harold Conrad
Goddard, William Paul
Godwin, William Colin
Goebel, William Mathers
Goelz, George William, Jr.
Goethals, Robert Joseph
Goetsch, Gerald D.
Goetz, John Bullock
Goetzinger, Robert James
Goff, James Matthew
Goffman, William
Goggin, Joseph Robert
Going, William Thornbury
Gold, Aaron Michael
Gold, Bela
Gold, Gerald Seymour
Gold, Ike
Gold, Norman Myron
Goldberg, Arthur Lewis
Goldberg, Bertrand
Goldberg, E(lliott) Marshall
Goldberg, Lawrence Irwin
Goldberg, Leon Isadore
Goldberg, Martin
Goldberg, Samuel
Goldberg, Samuel Irving
Goldberger, Arthur Stanley
Goldblatt, Stanford Jay
Goldenhersh, Joseph Herman
Goldenstein, Erwin Harmon
Goldfarb, Bernard Sanford
Goldfeder, Howard
Goldgar, Bertrand Alvin
Goldhammer, Keith
Goldhor, Herbert
Goldiamond, Israel
Goldin, Sol
Golding, Brage
Goldman, Bernard Marvin
Goldman, Robert David
Goldring, David
Goldring, Norman Max
Goldsborough, Robert Gerald
Goldsholl, Mildred

Goldsmith, Julian Royce
Goldsmith, Myron
Goldsmith, William M.
Goldstein, Bernard
Goldstein, Jerome S.
Goldstein, Melvyn C.
Goldstein, Norman Philip
Goldstein, Richard Jay
Goldstein, Robert
Goldwasser, Edwin Leo
Goldwasser, Eugene
Golightly, Lena Mills
Golightly, Trueman Harlan
Golomski, William Arthur
Goltz, Robert William
Gomberg, Edith Lisansky
Gomberg, Henry Jacob
Gomer, Robert
Gomez, Gustavo Enrique
Gomez, Manuel Rodriguez
Gonser, Thomas Howard
Gonzalez, Richard Florentz
Gooch, Forrest Wendell
Good, Clarence Allen
Good, John Ehrmin
Good, Mary Lowe (Mrs. Billy Jewel Good)
Good, Robert Crocker
Goodger, John Verne
Goodheart, Clyde Raymond
Goodkin, Michael Jon
Goodman, Elliott Irvin
Goodman, Harold S.
Goodman, Oscar R.
Goodman, Robert Norman
Goodman, Stanley
Goodman, Thomas J.
Goodman, William I.
Goodnight, Clarence James
Goodrich, John Bernard
Goodrich, Kenneth Paul
Goodson, Louis Hoffman
Goodwin, Donald William
Goodwin, John Mitchell
Goostree, Robert Edward
Goran, Morris
Gordon, Arnold Mark
Gordon, Bernard
Gordon, Edgar George
Gordon, Edward
Gordon, Ezra
Gordon, Gilbert
Gordon, Howard Scott
Gordon, John Edward
Gordon, Marjorie
Gordon, Melvin Jay
Gordon, Myron Lee
Gordon, Paul
Gordon, Paul John
Gordon, Robert Edward
Gordon, Steven Stanley
Gordon, W. Glenn
Gordon, William Livingston
Gore, Jerome Sidney
Gorecki, Jan
Gorham, Eville
Gorman, Joseph Tolle
Gornick, Alan Lewis
Gorske, Robert Herman
Gorski, Jack
Gorsuch, John Wilbert
Gorton, Thomas Arthur
Goschi, Nicholas Peter
Gosline, Robert Bradley
Gosman, Albert Louis
Goss, Donald E.
Gosselin, John William
Gossett, Philip
Gossett, William Thomas
Gotherman, John E.
Gotoff, Samuel Peter
Gottfried, Leon Albert
Gottheil, Fred Monroe
Gottier, Richard Chalmers
Gottlieb, Gidon Alain Guy
Gottschalk, Alfred
Gotzes, Hubert Richard
Gouke, Cecil Granville
Gould, Benjamin Z.
Gould, Chester
Gould, Edwin Sheldon
Gould, Floyd Jerome
Gould, Fredrick G.
Gould, Harold Alton
Gould, John Philip, Jr.
Gould, Wesley Larson
Goulet, Charles Ryan
Gousha, Richard Paul
Gove, Roger Madden
Gove, Samuel Kimball
Gover, Raymond Lewis
Govindjee
Gowan, Arthur Mitchell
Goy, Robert William
Grabb, William Clarence
Graber, Doris Appel
Graber, Thomas M.
Grabner, George John
Grace, John Eugene
Grace, Oliver Davies
Grace, Richard Edward
Gradison, Willis David, Jr.
Gradwohl, Bernard Sam
Graebel, William Paul
Graessley, William Walter
Graettinger, John Sells
Graf, Donald Lee
Graf, Paul Luther
Graff, George Stephen
Graff, Gerald
Graham, Albert Bruce
Graham, Bruce Douglas
Graham, Charles John
Graham, David Tredway
Graham, Edward Henry
Graham, Elmer Albert
Graham, Erwin Herman
Graham, Evarts Ambrose, Jr.
Graham, Frances Keesler (Mrs. David Tredway Graham)
Graham, Jarlath John
Graham, John Dalby
Graham, Kenneth L.
Graham, Lois
Graham, Richard Marston
Graham, Robert C.
Graham, Robert William
Graham, Walker Ryan Allen
Graham, William B.
Graham, William Butterworth
Graham, William James
Grainger, David William
Gralla, Eugene
Grambsch, Paul Victor
Grampp, William Dyer
Grangaard, Donald R.
Granger, William Woodard, Jr.
Granick, David
Grano, Joseph D.
Grant, Barry Marvin
Grant, Edward
Grant, Gerard Gray
Grant, Peter Raymond
Grant, Robert Allen
Grant, William Downing
Grassmuck, George Ludwig
Gratch, Serge
Grau, Albert A.
Grauer, Allan L.
Graven, Paul Helmer
Graves, Gerald William
Graves, Richard Gordon
Graves, Robert Lawrence
Graves, Wallace Billingsley
Gray, Allen Gibbs
Gray, Charles Elmer
Gray, Franklin Dingwall
Gray, Hanna Holborn
Gray, Helen Theresa Gott
Gray, John Hubert
Gray, John Walker
Gray, Melvin Dean
Gray, Milton Hefter
Gray, Richard George
Gray, Robert Lee
Grayck, Marcus Daniel
Grayhack, John Thomas
Grayson, Richard Carl
Greek, Darold I.
Greeley, Andrew Moran
Greeley, Joseph May
Greeley, Samuel Sewall
Green, Arthur George
Green, Ben Charles
Green, David Ezra
Green, Edward Fairchild
Green, Ernest
Green, Hal Keith
Green, Harry Edward
Green, Jay Patrick, Sr.
Green, Jerome Frederic
Green, Jerome Keith
Green, Lewis Cox
Green, Marguerite
Green, Meyer H.
Green, Morris
Green, Orville Cronkhite, III
Green, Philip Bevington
Green, Ralph J., Jr.
Green, Rebecca McMullan
Green, Richard Calvin
Green, Richard Harold
Green, Richard Reginald
Green, Robert Lee
Green, Robert Thomas
Green, Theodore, III
Green, Warren Harold
Greenawalt, H. Samuel, Jr.
Greenbaum, Stuart I.
Greenberg, Ben Norton
Greenberg, Bernard
Greenberg, Bradley Sander
Greenberg, Frank
Greenberg, Richard Aaron
Greenberger, Ernest
Greenberger, Norton Jerald
Greendyke, William Henry
Greene, Anthony Storm
Greene, Carl Roger
Greene, Charles Cassius
Greene, James Alexander, III
Greene, Jerry George
Greene, Robert Bernard, Jr.
Greenfield, George B.
Greenfield, Lois Broder
Greenfield, Norman Samuel
Greenfield, Richard Kenneth
Greenkorn, Robert Albert
Greenlee, Herbert Breckenridge
Greenman, Martin Allen
Greenough, William Tallant
Greenstein, Julius Sidney
Greenwald, Gerald
Greenwald, Gilbert Saul
Greenwalt, Harlan Edward
Greenwalt, Tibor Jack
Greenwood, Donald Theodore
Greer, Carl Crawford
Greer, Gordon Gregory
Greer, Thomas Hoag
Grefe, Rolland Eugene
Gregg, Duane Lawrence
Gregory, Gustav Robinson
Gregory, Howard Merle
Gregory, Ian Walter
Gregory, Ross
Gregory, Ruth Wilhelmene
Greig, Walter
Greiner, Edward David
Greiner, William Harry
Grenell, James Henry
Greteman, Frank Henry
Grether, Henry Moroni, Jr.
Greville, Thomas N(all) E(den)
Gribbin, John Hawkins
Gribbs, Roman S.
Griem, Melvin Luther
Gries, John Paul
Grieve, Pierson MacDonald
Griffeth, Paul Lyman
Griffin, Claibourne Eugene
Griffin, James Anthony
Griffin, James Bennett
Griffin, James Edward
Griffin, Jerald Lee
Griffin, Leland Milburn
Griffin, Mary
Griffin, Robert P.
Griffin, W(illiam) L(ester) Hadley
Griffing, Joseph Bruce
Griffith, B(ezaleel) Herold
Griffith, Calvin Robertson
Griffith, Clark Calvin, II
Griffith, Donald Raymond
Griffith, Elwin Jabez
Griffith, Frank Wells
Griggs, Douglas Meriwether, Jr.
Griggs, James Henry
Griggs, Leonard LeRoy, Jr.
Grimes, Alden
Grimes, John R.
Grimley, Liam Kelly
Grimm, Edith Rambar
Grimm, Goetz
Grimm, Harold John
Grimm, Reinhold
Grinker, Roy Richard, Jr.
Grinker, Roy Richard, Sr.
Grinnell, Ernest Doane, Jr.
Grip, Carl Manfred, Jr.
Griskey, Richard George
Grissinger, James Adams
Grissom, Donald Bauer
Grissom, Joseph Carol
Grissom, Robert Leslie
Griswold, Bruce
Griswold, Ralph Esty
Grobman, Arnold Brams
Grobman, Hulda Gross (Mrs. Arnold B. Grobman)
Groening, William Andrew, Jr.
Groennert, Charles Willis
Groff, Kenelm A.
Grogan, Hugh
Grogan, Kenneth Augustine
Grogan, Steven James
Grollmes, Eugene E.
Grommesh, Donald Joseph
Groninger, Donald Lynn
Gronvall, John Arnold
Grosh, Richard Joseph
Gros Louis, Kenneth Richard Russell
Gross, John Arthur
Gross, Seymour Lee
Gross, William Joseph
Grosse, Eduard
Grossman, Burton Jay
Grossman, Jerome Barnett
Grossman, Joel Barry
Grossman, Sebastian Peter
Grossweiner, Leonard Irwin
Grotzinger, Laurel Ann
Grove, Ernest L., Jr.
Grove, William Johnson
Groves, Franklin Nelson
Groves, John Taylor, III
Groves, Ray John
Growe, Joan Anderson
Grube, Gerald George
Gruber, William Paul
Gruberg, Martin
Gruen, Gerald Elmer
Gruenewald, Wendell LeRoy
Gruenisen, Allan George
Gruenwald, George Henry
Gruetzmacher, Alfred Henry
Grulee, Clifford Grosselle, Jr.
Gruman, Robert Clayton
Grundstein, Nathan David
Grundy, Kenneth William
Guba, Egon Gotthold
Guelich, Robert Vernon
Guendel, Thomas Joseph
Guenther, Charles John
Guenzel, Paul Walter
Guerri, William G.
Guest, Judith Ann
Guffey, James Roger
Guffy, Robert Ellsworth
Guggenheim, Richard E.
Guidrey, Joseph James
Guillery, Rainer Walter
Guimond, John Patrick
Guin, Russell Lowell
Guindon, Richard Gordon
Guinn, Leslie Wayne
Guinther, Harry Philip
Guion, Robert Morgan
Guisewite, Cathy Lee
Gullickson, Glenn, Jr.
Gunderson, Lee E.
Gunderson, Steve C.
Gunkler, Carl Andrew, Jr.
Gunnerson, Robert Mark
Gunness, Robert Charles
Gunter, Frank Elliott
Gunther, Arthur Gordon
Gupta, Hem Chander
Gupta, Shanti Swarup
Gupta, Suraj Narayan
Guralnick, Sidney Aaron
Gurd, Frank Ross Newman
Guren, Sheldon Bruce
Gurnham, C(harles) Fred(erick)
Gurr, Ted Robert
Gusewelle, Charles Wesley
Guskin, Alan Edward
Gusnard, Raymond Thomas
Gustafson, Charles Donald
Gustafson, Dale Rudolph
Gustafson, James M.
Gustafson, John Emil
Gustafson, Philip Felix
Gustafson, Richard Charles
Gustafson, Stanley Wendell
Gustafson, Winthrop Adolph
Gustafsson, Borje Karl
Gustavson, Carl Gustav
Gutchë, Gene
Guterbock, Hans Gustav
Gutfeld, Norman E.
Guth, John Elias, Jr.
Guth, Sherman Leon
Gutheil, Robert Willoughby
Guthman, Jack
Guthrie, Frank Albert
Guthrie, George Ralph
Guthrie, Louis Charles
Guthrie, Mearl Raymond, Jr.
Guthrie, Richard Alan
Guthrie, William Nelson
Gutmann, Max
Gutowsky, Herbert Sander
Gutridge, David Scott
Gutsche, Carl David
Guttenberg, Albert Ziskind
Gutwirth, Samuel William
Guy, Daniel Sowers
Guy, Ralph B., Jr.
Guy, William Lewis
Guyon, John Carl
Guyton, William James
Guze, Samuel Barry
Guzzetta, Dominic James
Gwinn, Robert P.
Gysbers, Norman Charles
Haag, Everett Keith
Haakenstad, Otto
Haas, Edward Lee
Haas, Felix
Haas, Howard Green
Haas, Kenneth Gregg
Haas, Leonard Clarence
Haas, Robert Green
Haase, William Xavier
Haass, Erwin Herman
Haayen, Richard Jan
Habeck, Irwin John
Habenstein, Robert W.
Haber, Meryl Harold
Haber, Ralph Norman
Haber, William
Habergarten, Charles
Haberman, Frederick William
Haberstroh, Chadwick John
Habig, Anthony P.
Habig, Arnold Frank
Habig, Thomas Louis
Hachten, William Andrews
Hackbirth, David William
Hackel, Emanuel
Hacker, Benjamin Thurman
Hacker, Hilary Baumann
Hackett, John Thomas
Hackett, Roger Fleming
Hackl, Donald John
Hackler, John Byron, III
Hadas, Pamela White
Haddad, George Ilyas
Haddad, George Richard
Haddock, Aubura Glen
Haddox, Benjamin Edward
Hadhazy, Peter
Hadley, Elbert Hamilton
Hadley, Elmer Burton
Hadley, John Michael
Hadley, Marlin LeRoy
Hadley, Stanton Thomas
Haeger, Phyllis Marianna
Haelterman, Edward Omer
Haenicke, Diether Hans
Haensel, Vladimir
Haenszel, William Manning
Haerri, Hermann J. M.
Haertlein, John Belford
Haferbecker, Gordon Milton
Haffner, Charles Christian, III
Hagan, Paul Wandel
Hagedorn, Robert Harry
Hagelman, Charles William, Jr.
Hagen, Charles William, Jr.
Hagen, John William
Hagenah, William John, Jr.
Hager, Joseph Arthur
Hager, Lowell Paul
Haggard, Forrest Deloss
Haggerty, Lawrence George
Haggerty, Raymond Richard
Haglund, Gerhard Oscar
Hagman, Harlan Lawrence
Hagstrom, Warren Olaf
Hagstrum, Jean Howard
Hague, Robert Worst
Hahn, Arvin William
Hahn, George LeRoy
Hahn, Jack Albert Louis
Hahn, Lewis Edwin
Hahn, Richard Ferdinand
Hahn, Richard R.
Hahn, Samuel Wilfred
Hahn, Walter Frederick
Haigh, George Whylden
Haight, Edward Allen
Haight, Gilbert Pierce, Jr.
Haile, H. G.
Haiman, Franklyn Saul
Haiman, Irwin Sanford
Haimann, Theo
Haimes, Yacov Yosseph
Haimo, Deborah Tepper
Haines, Perry Vansant
Haines, Robert Earl
Hainey, Richard Willis
Hainline, Forrest Arthur, Jr.
Hakeem, Michael
Hakimi, S. Louis
Halas, George Stanley
Halcrow, Harold Graham
Haldi, Robert William
Hale, Frank Wilbur, Jr.
Hale, Hamilton Orin
Hale, James Thomas
Hale, Roger Loucks
Hales, David Foster
Haley, George
Hall, Albert Leander, Jr.
Hall, Asaph Hale
Hall, Bernard
Hall, Charles Rudolph
Hall, Dee C., Jr.
Hall, Donald Joyce
Hall, E(ugene) Raymond
Hall, Frederick Leonard
Hall, J. Parker, III
Hall, Joel
Hall, Joyce Clyde
Hall, Larkin Neel
Hall, Marion Trufant
Hall, Philip Barton
Hall, Robert Latané
Hall, Thomas Munroe
Hall, William Delaney
Hall, William Joel
Hallberg, Owen Kenneth
Halleck, Charles A.
Hallene, Alan Montgomery
Haller, Archibald Orben
Halley, James Woods, Jr.
Halliday, William James, Jr.
Hallman, Gary L.
Hallman, George Harlan
Halloran, William Frank
Hallowell, Robert Edward
Halom, James Tibor
Halpern, Jack
Halpern, Norman Gerald
Halporn, James Werner
Halstead, Georgia
Halter, Harold Bernard
Halverson, Wendell Quelprud
Halvorsen, Morrie Edward
Ham, James Richard
Hamady, Jack Ameen
Hamalainen, Pekka Kalevi
Hambleton, Chalkley Jay
Hamburger, Richard James
Hamby, Alonzo Lee
Hamel, Edward Everett
Hamelberg, William
Hamermesh, Bernard
Hamermesh, Daniel Selim
Hamermesh, Morton
Hamerow, Theodore Stephen
Hamill, William Henry
Hamilton, Charles Owen
Hamilton, Clarence Otis
Hamilton, David Whitman
Hamilton, Dennis Dix
Hamilton, Earl Jefferson
Hamilton, Edward Joseph
Hamilton, Fay W.
Hamilton, Harold Philip
Hamilton, Jerald
Hamilton, Stuart
Hamlin, Richard Eugene
Hammar, Lester Everett
Hammer, Charles Lawrence
Hammer, Donald Price
Hammes, George Albert
Hammitt, Frederick Gnichtel
Hammond, Charles Ainley
Hammond, Charles Taylor
Hammond, James Wright
Hammond, Joe Phil
Hamp, Eric Pratt
Hampel, Alvin
Hampton, Kent Bronson
Hampton, Leroy
Hampton, Phillip Michael
Hampton, Verne Churchill, II
Hancock, John Coulter
Hancock, Thomas
Hand, Avery Chapman, Jr.
Handelsman, Harold Samuel
Handler, Jerome Sidney
Handler, Paul
Handy, Charles Brooks
Handy, Richard Lincoln
Hanes, James Henry
Haney, Paul Dunlap
Hanford, William James
Hangen, John, Jr.
Hanifan, James Martin Michael
Hankin, Bernard Jacob
Hanley, Charles
Hanley, Edward Thomas
Hanley, John Thomas
Hanley, John Weller
Hanley, Robert Leo
Hanlin, Hugh Carey
Hanlon, C. Rollins
Hanna, Gordon
Hanna, Jack Bushnell
Hanna, Nessim
Hanna, V. Leonard
Hannah, John Alfred
Hannah, Larry Joseph
Hannon, Bruce M.
Hanold, Terrance
Hanrahan, Robert Paul
Hanratty, Thomas Joseph
Hans, Robert John
Hansen, Andrew Marius
Hansen, Arthur Gene
Hansen, Charles
Hansen, Claire V.
Hansen, Donald W.
Hansen, Francis Eugene
Hansen, Frederick Jacob
Hansen, Grover J.
Hansen, James Roger
Hansen, Kermit Read
Hansen, Lowell C., II
Hansen, Marc Frederick
Hansen, Robert Suttle
Hanson, Alfred Olaf
Hanson, Dick Vincent
Hanson, Eugene Nelson
Hanson, Howard Grant
Hanson, John Bernard
Hanson, Lester Eugene
Hanson, Lyle Eugene
Hanson, Richard Stephen
Hanson, Richard Winfield
Hanson, Robert Alfred
Hanson, Robert Arthur
Hanson, Robert Paul
Hanson, Robert Warren
Hanson, Roger James
Hanson, Walter Edmund
Hanson, William C.
Hanson, William Herbert
Harary, Frank
Harbeck, William James
Harberger, Arnold Carl
Harbourt, Cyrus Oscar
Harden, Edgar Lawrence
Harden, Norman Eugene
Harden, Oleta Elizabeth
Harder, Robert Clarence
Hardesty, Hiram Haines
Hardin, Clifford Morris
Hardin, Dale Wayne
Hardin, David Kimball
Hardin, Fred A.
Hardin, Lowell Stewart
Harding, James Warren
Harding, Victor Mathews
Hardis, Stephen Roger
Hardman, Harold Francis
Hardy, John Edward
Hardy, L. Martin
Hare, Robert Yates
Harger, Arthur James
Hargis, Billy James
Hargrave, Robert Webb
Hargrave, Victoria Elizabeth
Hargreaves, Robert
Harkins, Joseph Francis
Harkness, Bruce
Harl, Neil Eugene
Harlan, Jack Rodney
Harlan, William Robert, Jr.
Harlow, Ivan Frank
Harman, John Royden
Harmet, A(rnold) Richard
Harmon, Merle Reid, Sr.
Harmon, Patrick
Harmon, Robert Lee
Harness, Don Kenneth
Harness, Edward Granville
Harnett, Joseph Durham
Harnischfeger, Henry
Haro, John Calvin
Harper, Alfred Edwin
Harper, Billy Norman
Harper, Charles Michel
Harper, Donald Victor
Harper, Edward O'Neil
Harper, James D., Jr.
Harper, Ramey Wilson
Harper, Ronald Lee
Harper, Roy W.
Harpole, Murray J.
Harpstead, Dale Douglas
Harrell, Everett Richard, Jr.
Harrell, Samuel Runnels
Harriman, Gerald Eugene
Harringer, Olaf Carl
Harrington, David Van
Harrington, Fred Harvey
Harrington, Jean Patrice
Harrington, Jeremy Thomas
Harrington, Robert Warren
Harrington, Roy Victor
Harris, Albert Edward
Harris, Alton Bruce
Harris, Charles Elmer
Harris, Chauncy Dennison
Harris, David John
Harris, David William
Harris, E. Edward
Harris, Everette Bagby
Harris, George Taylor
Harris, Gregory Scott
Harris, Irving
Harris, Irving Brooks
Harris, J(acob) George
Harris, J. Ira
Harris, John William
Harris, John William
Harris, K. David
Harris, Neison
Harris, Randy (Alan)
Harris, Robert Allen
Harris, Stanley Gale, Jr.
Harris, Sydney Justin
Harris, Wayne Webster
Harris, Whitney Robson
Harrison, David Clark
Harrison, Edward James
Harrison, John Alexander
Harrison, Michael Jay
Harrison, Ward Duncan
Harrison, William Henry
Harrod, Scott
Harrold, Bernard
Harsha, Edward Houston
Harshbarger, Kenneth E.
Hart, Alvin Leroy
Hart, Augustin Snow, Jr.

Hart, Buddy Warren
Hart, Craig C.
Hart, David William
Hart, James Warren
Hart, John Fraser
Hart, John Lewis
Hart, William Levata
Harter, Donald Harry
Harter, Robert Hugh
Harth, Phillip
Harthun, Luther Arthur
Hartig, Elmer Otto
Hartigan, Neil F.
Hartje, Robert George
Hartl, Albert Victor
Hartley, Richard Glendale
Hartley, Robert Frank
Hartman, Clinton W.
Hartman, George Edward
Hartman, Glen Walter
Hartman, John Jacob
Hartman, Paul Theodore
Hartman, Robert S.
Hartman, William Vernon
Hartnett, James Patrick
Hartocollis, Peter
Hartsaw, William O.
Hartsuch, Paul Jackson
Hartung, Theodore Eugene
Harvey, Dorothy May
Harvey, Elaine Butler
Harvey, Neil Mowbray
Harvey, Paul
Harvey, Peter Robert
Harvey, Robert Duncan
Harvey, William Franklin
Harwell, William Earnest (Ernie)
Harwood, John Henry
Harwood, Julius J.
Harza, Richard Davidson
Haselhorst, Donald Duane
Haselkorn, Robert
Haselmayer, Louis August
Haseltine, John Burton
Haskell, Albert Russell
Haskell, Harry Ogren
Haskin, Larry Allen
Haskins, Paul Joseph
Hasler, Arthur Davis
Hassan, Ihab Habib
Hassett, Paul Elliot
Hassler, Donald Mackey, II
Hast, Adele
Hast, Malcolm Howard
Hastings, Elizabeth Thomson
Hastings, William Charles
Hatch, Henry Reynolds, III
Hatch, James Alfred
Hatch, Robert Winslow
Hatcher, Gordon Merrell
Hatcher, Richard G.
Hatfield, Elaine Catherine
Hatfield, Paul Harold
Hatie, George Daniel
Hatteberg, Larry Merle
Hatten, William Seward
Hattin, Donald Edward
Haugan, Robert Ellsworth
Haugen, Rolf Eugene
Haugh, Robert James
Haugland, John Clarence
Haun, James William
Haunz, Edgar Alfred
Haurowitz, Felix
Hause, Jesse Gilbert
Hauser, Crane Cheshire
Hauser, Gayelord (Hauser, Helmut Eugene Benjamin Gellert)
Hauser, Jon William
Hauser, Nancy McKnight
Hauser, Philip Morris
Hauserman, William Foley
Hausman, Jerome Joseph
Hausmann, Frank William, Jr.
Hausser, Robert Louis
Havdala, Henri Salomon
Haven, Thomas Kenneth
Haverstick, Edward Everett, Jr.
Havighurst, Robert J.
Hawkins, Brett William
Hawkins, David Rollo
Hawkins, Donald Merton
Hawkins, Eugene Palmer
Hawkins, George Oliver
Hawkins, Joseph Elmer, Jr.
Hawkins, Robert L(ewis), Jr.
Hawkinson, John
Hawkinson, Robert Wayne
Hawley, John Babcock
Hawthorne, Douglas Lawson
Hawthorne, Joseph Campbell
Hay, George Edward
Hay, Peter Heinrich
Hayashi, Tetsumaro
Hayden, Joseph Page, Jr.
Hayden, Martin Scholl
Haydon, Harold Emerson
Hayes, Alice Bourke
Hayes, Douglas Anderson
Hayes, Frank N.
Hayes, John Daniel
Hayes, John Francis
Hayes, Nevin William
Hayes, Paul Gordon
Hayes, Reginald Carroll
Hayes, Richard Johnson
Hayes, Walter (Leopold Arthur)
Hayes, William Aloysius
Hayford, Warren J.
Haygreen, John Grant
Hayles, Alvin Beasley
Haynes, Eugene, Jr.
Haynes, Judith Walton
Haynes, Sherwood Kimball
Haynes, Ulric St. Clair, Jr.
Hayreh, Sohan Singh
Hays, Kathryn
Hays, Robert L.
Hays, Thomas Chandler
Haythorne, Robert E.
Hayton, Jacob William
Hayward, Edward Beardsley
Haywood, Bruce
Haywood, Clarence Robert
Hazard, Frederick Rowland
Hazard, Willis Gilpin
Hazel, David William
Hazen, Stanley Phillip
Hazlett, James Arthur
Hazlett, James Stephen
Heaberlin, David Allen
Head, Patrick James
Headington, John Terence
Headlee, Raymond
Headlee, Richard Harold
Heady, Earl Orel
Heald, James Eudean
Heald, Morrell
Heaney, Gerald William
Heaney, Robert Proulx
Heaphy, John Merrill
Heard, Arthur Bernard
Hearnes, Warren Eastman
Heartney, Matthew Joseph, Jr.
Heath, Edward Charles
Heath, James Edward
Heath, John Clovis
Heath, Thomas Doran
Heavenrich, Robert Maurice
Hebble, William Joseph
Hebel, Anthony Jerome
Heberlein, Garrett Thomas
Hecht, Louis Alan
Hechter, Oscar Milton
Heck, Charles Voisin
Heckel, Richard Wayne
Heckman, James Joseph
Heckmann, Irvin Lee
Heckrodt, Frank H.
Hedberg, Paul Clifford
Hedden, Russell Alfred
Heddesheimer, Walter Jacob
Hedges, Harry George
Hedien, Wayne Evans
Hedrich, William Clifford
Hedrick, Frank Edgar
Heeb, Joseph Alvin
Heffernan, Nathan Stewart
Heffner, Grover Chester
Hefner, Hugh Marston
Hegener, Mark Paul
Hegg, George Lennart
Heggers, John Paul
Heggie, Robert James
Hegre, Theodore A.
Hehemann, Robert Frederick
Hehmeyer, Alexander
Heidel, Charles Macleish
Heidenreich, Douglas Robert
Heidrick, Gardner Wilson
Heilbrun, William C.
Heim, Leo Edward
Heimlich, Henry Jay
Heimlich, Richard Allen
Heimsch, Charles
Heindl, Warren Anton
Heine, Richard Walter
Heineman, Ben Walter
Heineman, Natalie (Mrs. Ben W. Heineman)
Heineman, Paul Lowe
Heinen, Paul A.
Heiney, John Weitzel
Heininger, S(amuel) Allen
Heinrich, Ross Raymond
Heins, Albert Edward
Heins, Allison Edward
Heins, Arthur James
Heinselman, Miron Lee
Heintz, Jack
Heinzerling, Lynn Louis
Heise, George Armstrong
Heise, Richard Allen
Heiser, Charles Bixler, Jr.
Heisler, John Columbus
Heiss, Richard Walter
Heitner, Robert Richard
Heitz, Glenn Edward
Heitzmann, Alfred Otto
Hejna, William Frank
Helbert, Clifford L.
Heldman, Dennis Ray
Helgeland, Glenn Bernard
Helgeson, Arlan Clayton
Helkenn, John Grell
Heller, Alfred
Heller, Charles Andrew, Jr.
Heller, Erich
Heller, Francis Howard
Heller, Paul
Heller, Robert Leo
Heller, Walter Wolfgang
Hellmuth, George Francis
Helm, P. Ralph
Helman, Alfred Blair
Helman, Robert Alan
Helstad, Orrin LaVerne
Hemke, Frederick
Hemmer, Paul Edward
Hemond, Roland
Henderson, Edward Drewry
Henderson, Frank Ellis
Henderson, James Alan
Henderson, John Warren
Henderson, John Woodworth
Henderson, LaVell Merl
Henderson, Lowell Lawrence
Henderson, Paul Audine
Henderson, Robert Arthur
Henderson, William J.
Henderson, William L.
Hendrick, George
Hendrickson, Bruce Carl
Hendrix, Herschel J.
Hengen, William Lincoln
Henken, Willard John
Henle, Robert John
Henley, Fred Louis
Hennessy, William Joseph, II
Henning, Edward Burk
Henning, Harold Walter
Henning, Joel Frank
Henning, Valerian John
Henninger, John George
Hennings, Robert Edward
Henrickson, Eiler Leonard
Henry, Charles Joseph, Jr.
Henry, Hugh Fort
Henry, J. Roy
Henry, John Thomas
Henshall, James Arthur, Jr.
Hensley, Robert Thornton
Henson, Albert Lee
Henson, Paul Harry
Henson, Robert Frank
Henson, Walter Eugene
Hepler, James William
Hepp, K. Kevin
Herbert, Donald Roy
Herbert, Kevin Barry John
Herbert, Michael Kinzly
Herbert, Thomas M.
Herbert, Victor James
Herbertt, Stanley
Herbst, Arthur Lee
Herbst, Jurgen
Herd, Harold Shields
Herfindahl, Lloyd Manford
Hering, Robert Gustave
Herleman, William Nicholas
Herlihy, Horace Murray
Herman, David Theodore
Herman, Harold Wilcox
Herman, Michael Edward
Herman, Stephen Mark
Herman, William Sparkes
Hermann, Donald Harold James
Hermann, Paul David
Hermann, Philip J.
Hermann, Robert Ringen
Hermes, Thomas Joseph
Hernandez, Keith
Herndon, Charles Harbison
Herpich, Wiliam Arthur
Herr, Dan
Herr, Earl Binkley, Jr.
Herrell, Wallace Edgar
Herres, Robert Tralles
Herrick, Allan Adair
Herrick, Kenneth Gilbert
Herrin, Moreland
Herrinton, John Peter
Herrmann, Arthur Dominey
Herrmann, Edward J.
Herron, James Dudley
Herron, Orley Rufus
Hershey, Daniel
Hershey, Falls Bacon
Herstein, Israel Nathan
Hertel, Dennis Mark
Herting, Robert Leslie
Hertz, Richard Cornell
Hertzberg, Paul Stuart
Hertzberg, Stuart Earl
Herzog, Donald Roswell
Herzog, Dorrel Norman Elvert (Whitey)
Herzog, Fred F.
Hesburgh, Theodore Martin
Hesling, Donald Mills
Hess, Eckhard Heinrich
Hess, Evelyn Victorine (Mrs. Michael Howett)
Hess, Sidney J., Jr.
Hessert, Paul Bernard
Hessler, David William
Hessler, Robert Roamie
Hesson, James Marsh
Hesterberg, Gene Arthur
Hetland, James Lyman, Jr.
Hetzel, William Gelal
Heubaum, William Lincoln
Heuer, Arthur Harold
Heuer, Gerald Arthur
Heuer, Michael Alexander
Heuermann, Laura Hall
Heuertz, Matt E.
Hewitt, William Alexander
Hexter, Robert Maurice
Heyburn, Donald Elliott
Heymann, Ralph Edmond
Heyse, Warren John
Hicken, Victor
Hickey, Edward Hutchins
Hickey, Howard Wesley
Hickey, John Thomas
Hickey, John William
Hickey, Matthew Joseph, III
Hickman, Frederic W.
Hickman, James Charles
Hicks, Allan Charles
Hicks, Allen Morley
Hicks, Charles Robert
Hicks, Edwin Hugh
Hicks, Irle Raymond
Hicks, Joseph Robert
Hiegel, Jerry M.
Hiett, Edward Emerson
Higginbotham, William Henry
Higgins, Andrew Jackson
Higgins, Edward Aloysius
Higgins, Geoffrey Trevor
Higgins, James Victor
Higham, Robin
Higuchi, Takeru
Hilborn, Michael G.
Hild, Guy Marvin
Hildebrand, Holly Cheryl
Hildebrand, Roger Henry
Hildreth, Clifford
Hildreth, R(oland) James
Hiler, John Patrick
Hilker, Robert Reuben John
Hill, Alwyn Spencer
Hill, Bennett David
Hill, Bruce Marvin
Hill, Carl Paul
Hill, Delmas Carl
Hill, Draper
Hill, James Stanley
Hill, Knox Calvin
Hill, Lewis Warren
Hill, Luther Lyons, Jr.
Hill, Reuben Lorenzo, Jr.
Hill, Richard Earl
Hill, Theodore Albert
Hill, Winfred Farrington
Hillard, Robert Ellsworth
Hillberry, Ben(ny) M(ax)
Hille, Stanley James
Hillegass, Clifton Keith
Hillestad, Albert William
Hilliard, John Evelyn
Hilliard, Robert John
Hillila, Bernhard Hugo Paul
Hillis, Margaret
Hillman, Douglas Woodruff
Hillman, Stanley Eric Gordon
Hills, George Burkhart, Jr.
Hilpert, Dale William
Hiltner, William Albert
Himmel, Richard Charles
Himmelfarb, John David
Himmelright, Robert John, Jr.
Hind, Joseph Edward, Jr.
Hindman, Hugh David, Jr.
Hinds, William Edward
Hine, Daryl
Hine, Jack
Hiner, Robert L.
Hines, Edward
Hines, Harold H., Jr.
Hines, James Rodger
Hinkle, B. J.
Hinnendael, John Joseph
Hinshaw, Edward Banks
Hinshaw, Virgil Goodman, Jr.
Hinsvark, Inez Genieve
Hinton, Claude Willey
Hinton, Warren S.
Hinze, William James
Hirsch, Elroy Leon
Hirsch, Jay G.
Hirsch, Jerry
Hirsch, Raymond Robert
Hirsch, Robert William
Hirschboeck, Herbert C.
Hirschhorn, Austin
Hirsh, Ira Jean
Hirth, John Price
Hitchcock, Donald Simon
Hitchcock, John Thayer
Hitt, John Charles, Jr.
Hitt, Peter
Hjalmarson, Gordon Ross
Hjellum, John
Hladky, Joseph Frank, Jr.
Hlavacek, Roy George
Hlavka, Edwin J.
Ho, Ping-Ti
Ho, Thomas Inn Min
Hoag, Leverett Paddock
Hoagland, Karl King, Jr.
Hoagland, Laurance Redington, Jr.
Hoak, John Charles
Hoare, Richard David
Hobart, Edward A.
Hobbie, Russell Klyver
Hobbs, James Allen
Hobbs, Lewis Mankin
Hobgood, Burnet McLean
Hoblitzelle, George Knapp
Hoch, Frederic Louis
Hochberg, Joel Morton
Hochgurtel, Jerome Leo
Hochwald, Werner
Hochwalt, Carroll Alonzo
Hockaday, Irvine O., Jr.
Hockeimer, Henry Eric
Hockenbrocht, David William
Hocking, John Gilbert
Hodapp, Leroy Charles
Hodder, William Alan
Hoddy, George Warren
Hoddy, Raymond Arthur
Hodes, Marion Edward
Hodes, Scott
Hodge, Carleton Taylor
Hodge, Gordon Stuart
Hodge, James Campbell
Hodge, James Robert
Hodge, Philip Gibson, Jr.
Hodges, Elmer Burkett
Hodges, Mary Doris
Hodges, Robert Edgar
Hodges, Robert Manley
Hodges, Thomas Kent
Hodgkins, Earl Warner
Hodgkinson, Charles Paul
Hodgson, Charles Arthur
Hodgson, Paul Edmund
Hodgson, Thomas Richard
Hodgson, Voigt Ralph
Hodson, Thomas William
Hoebel, Edward Adamson
Hoeflin, Ruth Merle
Hoeflinger, Norman Charles
Hoeg, Donald Francis
Hoerr, Stanley Obermann
Hoese, Frank Thomas
Hoey, James Joseph
Hofacre, William Marion
Hofeldt, John W.
Hoffer, Robert M.
Hoffman, Alfred John
Hoffman, Gene
Hoffman, James Harvey
Hoffman, James R.
Hoffman, Julius J.
Hoffman, Larry Ronald
Hoffman, Lois Wladis
Hoffman, Richard William
Hoffman, Robert Butler
Hoffman, Warren Eugene
Hoffmann, Charles Wesley
Hoffmann, Donald
Hoffmann, Oswald Carl Julius
Hoffmann, Thomas Russell
Hoffmeister, Donald Frederick
Hofstad, Ralph Parker
Hofstadter, Douglas Richard
Hofstatter, Leopold
Hofstetter, Henry W
Hogan, Joseph Charles
Hogan, Robert F(rancis)
Hogan, Timothy S.
Hogben, Charles Adrian Michael
Hoge, James Fulton, Jr.
Hogenkamp, Henricus Petrus Cornelis
Hogg, Robert Vincent, Jr.
Hoggard, James Clinton
Hoglund, John H.
Hoglund, Peter Klinger
Hognestad, Eivind
Hohnstedt, Leo Frank
Hokenstad, Merl Clifford, Jr.
Hokin, Edwin E.
Hokin, Lowell Edward
Holabird, John Augur, Jr.
Holaday, Allan Gibson
Holbrook, Clyde Amos
Holbrook, Robert Sumner
Holck, Frederick H. George
Holden, Arthur Stone, Jr.
Holden, James F.
Holden, Patrick Cornish
Holden, William Douglas
Holder, Cale James
Holder, Thomas Martin
Holdt, Roy Howard
Hole, William Edward, Jr.
Hole, William Edward, Sr.
Holiday, Harry, Jr.
Holland, Dewey G(eorge)
Holland, Eugene, Jr.
Holland, Eugene, Jr.
Holland, Homer Jay
Holland, Thomas Powell
Hollender, Samuel Sylvan
Hollerman, Charles Edward
Hollett, Byron Pierce
Holley, Gerald Neal
Holley, Jack Karl
Holliday, Barbara Miriam Brooks Gregg
Hollis, Everett Loftus
Hollis, William M.
Holloran, Thomas Edward
Holloway, Joseph Wesley
Holloway, Robert J.
Holloway, William Jimmerson
Holm, Donald Sutherland, Jr.
Holman, J. L. Monte
Holman, Ralph Theodore
Holmberg, Lawrence Oscar
Holmes, Allen Cornelius
Holmes, Arthur Frank
Holmes, Colgate Frederick
Holmes, Jay Thorpe
Holmes, Joseph Patrick
Holmes, Melvin Charles
Holmes, Reed M.
Holmes, Richard Winn
Holmes, Robert Edward
Holmes, Roger Arnold
Holmes, Vernon Harrison
Holmgren, Marvin Edward
Holmgren, Robert Bruce
Holmquist, William Axel
Holonyak, Nick, Jr.
Holowenko, Alfred Richard
Holroyd, Harry James
Holroyd, Louis Vincent
Holschuh, John David
Holsen, Robert Charles
Holshouser, Don Franklin
Holsinger, George Robert, Jr.
Holsinger, Wayne Townsend
Holt, Ivan Lee, Jr.
Holt, (William) Kermit
Holt, Lloyd Eugene
Holt, Robert Theodore
Holten, Tolman Edward
Holter, Don Wendell
Holton, Ira James
Holtz, Harold Frederick
Holtzclaw, Henry Fuller, Jr.
Holtzer, Alfred Melvin
Holtzman, Jerome
Holyoke, Thomas Campbell
Holzwarth, James Carl
Hommel, George Amos
Hong, Richard
Honig, George Raymond
Hoobler, Sibley Worth
Hook, John Burney
Hooper, Blake Howard
Hoopman, Harold DeWaine
Hoover, Charles M.
Hoover, Dwight Wesley
Hoover, Joseph Schiltz
Hopcraft, David L.
Hope, Quentin Manning
Hopfinger, Frank Thomas
Hopkins, Sam
Hopp, Ralph H.
Hopp, William Beecher
Hopper, David Henry
Hopping, Louis Melbert
Hopponen, Raymond Ellwood
Hopps, Howard Carl
Hord, Earl Frederick
Horenstein, Simon
Horgan, James Donald
Horn, Milton
Hornbeak, Harold Lancaster
Hornbruch, Frederick William, Jr.
Hornby, Lesley (Twiggy)
Horner, James Melvin
Horner, John Edward
Horner, Richard Elmer
Horner, Robert David
Horner, Thomas Harvey
Horning, Ross Charles, Jr.
Horns, Howard Lowell
Hornsby, Roger Allen
Hornung, Paul Andrew
Horowitz, Frances Degen
Horr, William Henry
Horsbrugh, Patrick
Horsley, Jack Everett
Horsman, Reginald
Horst, Bruce Everett
Horstmann, James Douglas
Horton, Frank E.
Horton, Frank Elba
Horvath, Ian
Horvay, Frank Dominic
Horwitt, Max Kenneth
Horwitz, Donald Paul
Horwitz, Irwin D.
Hoskins, Charles Ross
Hosler, Russell John
Hostetler, Robert Dalen
Hostettler, Gordon Floyd
Hotchkiss, Eugene, III
Hotze, Charles Wayne
Hough, Gerald Lionel
Hough, Hugh Frederick
Hough, Richard T.
Houghton, David Drew
Houk, James Charles
Houle, Cyril Orvin
Houlton, Lise Rane
Houlton, Loyce J.
Hountras, Peter Timothy
House, Roy C.
Houser, Harold Byron
Houser, Robert Norman
Housewright, Lee Dewey, Jr.
Houston, E. James, Jr.
Houston, John Michael
Hovde, Frederick Lawson
Hoving, John Hannes Forester
Hovnanian, Armen
Hovorka, Frank
Howard, Giles William John
Howard, Howell Hoffman
Howard, James John
Howard, John Addison
Howard, Robert Bruce
Howard, William James
Howdle, John Clayton
Howe, Gary Woodson
Howe, H. Philip
Howe, Herbert Marshall
Howe, Lawrence
Howe, Oscar
Howe, Robert Hsi Lin
Howe, Robert Wilson
Howe, Stanley Merrill
Howe, Wallace Brady
Howell, George Bedell
Howell, John Welsh
Howell, Robert Wayne
Howell, Stephen Haviland
Howell, William Kenneth
Howell, William Smiley
Hower, John, Jr.
Howery, Bill Nelson
Howland, Richard Henry
Howland, Roger Allan
Howlett, Carolyn Svrluga
Howley, Lee Christopher
Howsam, Robert Lee
Howser, Richard Alton
Hoyer, Harvey Conrad
Hoyt, Ben Thomas
Hoyt, Clark Freeland
Hoyt, Lester Harold
Hrdlicka, Richard Franklin
Hrdlicka, Richard Roy
Hruby, Frank M.
Hruby, Norbert Joseph
Hruska, Roman Lee
Hsu, Roger Y. K.
Huang, Eugene Yuching
Huang, Kee Chang
Hubata, Joseph Allen
Hubay, Charles Alfred
Hubbard, Harold Mead
Hubbard, Jesse Donald
Hubbard, Robert Elbert
Hubbard, Stanley Eugene
Hubbard, Stanley Stub
Hubbard, William Neill, Jr.
Hubbell, James Windsor, Jr.
Huber, Sister Alberta
Huber, Joan Althaus
Huber, Robert Frederick
Huber, Thomas Martin
Hubert, Alfred William
Hubertus, Kenneth Leonard
Huck, John Wenzel
Hucker, Charles Oscar
Huckman, Michael Saul
Huddleston, Eugene Lee

Hudec, Robert Emil
Hudnut, Robert Kilborne
Hudnut, William Herbert, III
Hudson, Joseph Lowthian, Jr.
Hudson, Mary
Hudson, Roy Davage
Hudson, William Burchell, Jr.
Huebner, George John, Jr.
Hueg, William Frederick, Jr.
Huff, George Charles
Huff, Robert B.
Huff, Stanley Eugene
Hugghins, Ernest Jay
Huggins, Charles
Huggins, Rollin Charles, Jr.
Hughes, Earl Mulford
Hughes, Fred
Hughes, James A.
Hughes, James John
Hughes, John Russell
Hughes, Kenneth Russell
Hughes, William Franklin, Jr.
Hughes, William Nolin
Hughey, M. Stanley
Huitt, Ralph Kinsloe
Hulbert, Marshall Brandt
Hulburt, Hugh McKinney
Hull, Harvard Leslie
Hull, J(ames) Richard
Hull, John Daniel, Jr.
Hull, Robert Glenn
Hull, Roger Harold
Hull, William Henry
Hulley, Clair Montrose
Hulsebosch, Charles Joseph
Hulsman, Carl Henry
Hulston, John Kenton
Humbard, Rex Emanuel
Humenik, Michael
Hummel, Gene Maywood
Hummer, Donal
Humphrey, Edward William
Humphrey, Edwin Murray
Humphrey, Muriel Fay Buck (Mrs. Hubert Horatio Humphrey)
Humphrey, Neil Darwin
Humphrey, Philip Strong
Humphrey, Robert Clayton
Hunegs, Richard Gene
Hungate, William Leonard
Hungerford, Herbert Eugene
Hunt, Carlton Cuyler, Jr.
Hunt, Charles Brownlow, Jr.
Hunt, Effie Neva
Hunt, J(oseph) McVicker
Hunt, James Robert
Hunt, Joe Harold
Hunt, Lamar
Hunt, Mark Alan
Hunt, Richard
Hunt, Roger Schermerhorn
Hunt, William Alvin
Hunt, William Edward
Hunter, Charles David
Hunter, Donald H.
Hunter, Elmo Bolton
Hunter, Jack Corbett
Hunter, Jack Duval
Hunter, James Alexander
Hunter, Lee
Hunter, Norman L.
Hunter, Thom Hugh
Hunter, William Ray
Hunting, David Dyer
Huntington, David Mack Goode
Huntington, James Cantine, Jr.
Huntress, Keith Gibson
Huntzicker, Harry Noble
Hunzeker, Hubert La Von
Hupp, Robert Paul
Hurd, Carl Bently
Hurd, James Braddock
Hurley, Samuel Clay, III
Hurley, William Joseph
Hurst, Charles Gaines, Jr.
Hurst, James Willard
Hurt, James Riggins
Husky, Ferlin
Hussey, Keith Morgan
Hussung, Melvin Vern, Jr. (Buck)
Husted, Ralph Waldo
Husting, Peter Marden
Huston, Beatrice Louise
Huston, John Lewis
Huston, Margo
Huston, Norman Earl
Hutchens, John Oliver
Hutcheson, Harold Leo
Hutchings, Brian LaMar
Hutchins, John Osborne
Hutchinson, Cary Brown, Jr.
Hutchinson, Madison Curry, Jr.
Hutchinson, Melvin J.
Hutchison, Stanley Philip
Hutson, David Allen
Hutson, Thomas Raymond
Hutterer, Ferenc
Hutton, Edward Luke
Hutton, Robert John
Hutton, William
Huvos, Kornel
Huyser, Robert Ernest
Hvidston, Colburn, III
Hyatt, Gerhardt Wilfred
Hyde, Frederick Wright, Jr.
Hyde, Henry John
Hyde, Lawrence Henry, Jr.
Hyland, Robert Francis, Jr.
Hyman, Irwin Jerome
Hyneman, Charles S.
Hyslop, David Johnson
Iacocca, Lido Anthony (Lee)
Ibarra, Oscar Hererra
Ibele, Warren Edward
Iben, Icko, Jr.
Ibers, James Arthur
Ice, Harry Treese
Ice, Rodney Dean
Ichord, Richard Howard
Idol, James Daniel, Jr.
Idriss, Farouk Salim
Idzerda, Stanley John
Iffland, Don Charles
Igasaki, Masao, Jr.
Iglehart, Robert Leslie
Igleski, Thomas Robert
Ignoffo, Carlo Michael
Ihde, Aaron John
Ikenberry, Stanley Oliver
Ilie, Paul
Iltis, Hugh Hellmut
Imberman, Joseph Charles
Imesch, Joseph Leopold
Imirie, John Frederick, Jr.
Immel, Vincent Clare
Inbau, Fred Edward
Inch, Morris Alton
Incropera, Frank Paul
Ingall, David
Ingersoll, Gary Richard
Inghram, Mark Gordon
Inglehart, Ronald Franklin
Ingram, Robert Palmer
Inhorn, Stanley Lee
Inman, Ross Banks
Inman, William Peter
Instone, Frank Donald
Intons-Peterson, Margaret Jean
Ionescu Tulcea, Cassius
Ireland, Herbert Orin
Ireland, James Duane
Ireland, Ralph Leonard
Ireland, Robert Ebel
Irion, Arthur Lloyd
Iriye, Akira
Irmen, Thomas Leo
Irminger, Eugene Herman
Irons, Lester
Irrgang, William
Irrmann, Robert Henry
Irving, Donald J.
Irwin, H. William
Irwin, Joseph James
Irwin, Richard Dorsey
Irwin, Richard Loren
Isaac, Sol Morton
Isaacs, Roger David
Isaacs, Stephen David
Isaacson, William James
Isbin, Herbert Stanford
Isham, James Livingston
Israelievitch, Jacques Herbert
Issari, Mohammad Ali
Itkin, Bella
Ittmann, Marjorie McCullough
Ivan, Thomas Nathaniel
Iverson, James Richard
Iverson, Robert Lester
Ives, David Homer
Ives, Victor Milo
Ivkovich, Ronald Samuel
Iwasaki, Iwao
Iyengar, Srinivasa
Izant, Robert James, Jr.
Jabara, Francis Dwight
Jache, Albert William
Jack, Nancy Rayford
Jackamonis, Edward George
Jackson, Billy Morrow
Jackson, Clarence Evert
Jackson, Curtis Maitland
Jackson, Don Merrill
Jackson, Frederick Herbert
Jackson, George Gee
Jackson, Herbert Cooper
Jackson, Horace Dwight
Jackson, Jacqueline Dougan
Jackson, James Otis
Jackson, James Sidney
Jackson, Jesse Louis
Jackson, John Howard
Jackson, John Mathews
Jackson, Joseph Harrison
Jackson, LeRoy Eugene
Jackson, Lewis Albert
Jackson, Marion LeRoy
Jackson, Philip Wesley
Jackson, Reginald Sherman
Jackson, Robert Lawrence
Jackson, Thomas Woodrow
Jackson, William Vernon
Jackson, Willis Carl
Jacob, Harry Samuel
Jacob, Herbert
Jacob, Richard Joseph
Jacob, Thomas Bernard
Jacobi, Peter Paul
Jacobs, Burleigh Edmund
Jacobs, Donald P.
Jacobs, Francis Albin
Jacobs, Harvey Collins
Jacobs, Irwin Lawrence
Jacobs, James Najeeb
Jacobs, John Edward
Jacobs, Louis Sullivan
Jacobs, Norman Ernest
Jacobs, Norman G(abriel)
Jacobs, Norman Joseph
Jacobs, Richard Matthew
Jacobs, Robert
Jacobs, William Bruce
Jacobsen, James Conrad
Jacobsen, Robert Fred
Jacobsen, Thomas Warren
Jacobsohn, David Henry
Jacobson, Albert Hillman
Jacobson, Eugene Donald
Jacobson, Harold Karan
Jacobson, Howard
Jacobson, Leon Orris
Jacobson, Milford Eugene
Jacobson, Orville William
Jacobson, Paul Vincent
Jacobson, Robert Manfred
Jacoby, George Alonzo
Jaffe, Hans H.
Jaffe, Lionel Francis
Jagow, Elmer
Jahn, Helmut
Jahnke, Wendell L.
Jaicks, Frederick G.
Jakowatz, Charles V.
Jambor, Robert Vernon
James, Arthur Giangiacomo
James, Carl Clifton
James, Edwin Clark
James, Francis Edward, Jr.
James, Harold Arthur
James, Henry Thomas
James, Patricia Ann
James, Robert Charles
James, Sydney Vincent
James, William Ramsay
Jamieson, John Calhoun
Jamieson, Robert Arthur
Jamrich, John Xavier
Janata, Rudolph
Jancura, Elise Geraldine
Janicki, Robert Stephen
Janke, Otto M.
Janklow, William John
Janovy, David Lee
Janson, Anthony Frederick
Jantzen, Carl Raymond
January, Lewis Edward
Januz, Lauren Robert
Janzow, Walter Theophilus
Jaqua, Richard Allen
Jaros, Dean
Jarosz, Frederick John
Jarrett, Jerry Vernon
Jarvis, David
Jaumot, Frank Edward, Jr.
Javid, Hushang
Javid, Manucher J.
Jay, Burton Dean
Jay, James M(onroe)
Jaye, David Robert, Jr.
Jeannero, Douglas M.
Jebsen, Robert Harry
Jeffay, Henry
Jeffe, Sidney David
Jefferies, Robert Aaron, Jr.
Jeffers, Dean W.
Jeffers, Donald E.
Jefferson, Arthur
Jefferson, John Larry
Jefferson, Thomas Bradley
Jeffrey, Walter Leslie
Jelinek, John Peter
Jellison, Richard Marion
Jencks, Christopher Sandys
Jend, William, Jr.
Jenes, Theodore George, Jr.
Jenkin, Howard Milton
Jenkins, Harold Richard
Jenkins, James Allister
Jenkins, Jerry Bruce
Jenkins, Orville Wesley
Jenkins, Thomas Llewellyn
Jenkins, William Atwell
Jenkins, William Ivy
Jenks, Downing Bland
Jenner, Albert Ernest, Jr.
Jenness, Robert
Jennett, William Armin
Jennings, Burgess Hill
Jennings, Edward Harrington
Jennings, Frank Lamont
Jennings, Leander Warren
Jennings, Lee Byron
Jensen, Adolph Robert
Jensen, Dick Leroy
Jensen, Elwood Vernon
Jensen, George Albert
Jensen, Harold Sherwood
Jensen, James Robert
Jensen, Reuben Rolland
Jensen, Richard Victor
Jensen, Sam
Jensik, Robert Joseph
Jenson, Jon Eberdt
Jerger, Edward William
Jerison, Meyer
Jerome, Joseph Walter
Jerome, Norge Winifred
Jerow, James Edward
Jerrard, Richard Patterson
Jerry, Robert Howard
Jesse, Franklin Culver, Jr.
Jesseph, John Ervin
Jessup, Paul Frederick
Jetton, Girard Reuel, Jr.
Jeuck, John Edward
Jewett, John Rhodes
Jewett, John Roger
Jewson, Ruth Hathaway (Mrs. Vance Jewson)
Joanis, John Weston
Jockusch, Carl Groos, Jr.
Johannes, Wilfred Clemens
Johannsen, Robert Walter
Johanson, Donald Carl
Johanson, Sven Lennart
John, James Edward Albert
Johns, William Davis, Jr.
Johnsen, Alan Ralph
Johnsen, Gordon Norman
Johnson, A(lyn) William
Johnson, Alton Cornelius
Johnson, Arthur Gilbert
Johnson, Benjamin Edgar
Johnson, Carl David
Johnson, Cecil August
Johnson, Charles Edward, II
Johnson, Charles Raymond
Johnson, Chauncey Paul
Johnson, Clifford Francis
Johnson, Clifford R.
Johnson, Curtis Lee
Johnson, David Alfred
Johnson, David Butler
Johnson, David Gale
Johnson, David Lynn
Johnson, David Wolcott
Johnson, Dennis Lester
Johnson, Donald Dodge, Jr.
Johnson, Donald Edward
Johnson, Donald Howard
Johnson, Donald James
Johnson, Donald Joseph
Johnson, Earl Mortimer
Johnson, Earle Bertrand
Johnson, Edgar Frederick
Johnson, Elvis Eugene
Johnson, Eugene Walter
Johnson, Falk Simmons
Johnson, George E.
Johnson, George Robert
Johnson, Gerald Edwin
Johnson, Glenn Thompson
Johnson, Grant Lester
Johnson, Hal Harold Gustav
Johnson, Harold Earl
Johnson, Hollis Ralph
Johnson, Howard Edward
Johnson, Irving Stanley
Johnson, Jack Thomas
Johnson, James Lawrence
Johnson, James Leslie
Johnson, James Robert
Johnson, James Winston
Johnson, Jerry A.
Johnson, John Gray
Johnson, John H.
Johnson, John Irwin, Jr.
Johnson, John Prescott
Johnson, John Warren
Johnson, Joseph Harry
Johnson, Josephine Winslow (Mrs. Grant G. Cannon)
Johnson, Keith Eugene
Johnson, Kenneth Harvey
Johnson, Lael Frederic
Johnson, Leland Parrish
Johnson, Lester Elwin
Johnson, Margaret Kathleen
Johnson, Marvin Melrose
Johnson, Millard Wallace, Jr.
Johnson, Milton Axel
Johnson, Monte Charles
Johnson, Nicholas
Johnson, Paul Oren
Johnson, Philip D.
Johnson, Ray Arvin
Johnson, Richard Louis
Johnson, Richard Merrill
Johnson, Richard Walter
Johnson, Robert Allan
Johnson, Robert Bruce
Johnson, Robert Edward
Johnson, Robert Ivar
Johnson, Robert Lawrence
Johnson, Robert Maurice
Johnson, Robert Reed
Johnson, Robert Royce
Johnson, Robert Willard
Johnson, Roy Ragnar
Johnson, Royal Kenneth
Johnson, Samuel Curtis
Johnson, Sankey Anton
Johnson, Scott William
Johnson, Sidney Malcolm
Johnson, Theodore Oliver, Jr.
Johnson, Virgil Allen
Johnson, Walter
Johnson, Walter Conrad
Johnson, Walter Frank, (Jr.)
Johnson, Walter Heinrick, Jr.
Johnson, Walter Kline
Johnson, Warren C.
Johnson, Warren Donald
Johnson, Wesley Robert
Johnson, William Benjamin
Johnson, William Francis
Johnson, William Howard
Johnson, William Joseph
Johnson, William Roy
Johnson-Masters, Virginia E. (Mrs. William H. Masters)
Johnston, Benjamin Burwell, Jr.
Johnston, Elton E.
Johnston, John Andrew
Johnston, John Clifford, Jr.
Johnston, Marshall W.
Johnston, Percy Walker, Jr.
Johnston, Richard Fourness
Johnston, Samuel Thomas
Johnston, Scott Doran
Joiner, Charles Wycliffe
Jolly, Bruce Dwight
Jonas, Harry S.
Jonasson, Olga
Jondahl, Donald Edward
Jones, Alexander Elvin
Jones, Archer
Jones, Billy Mac
Jones, Bryan J.
Jones, Butler Alfonso
Jones, Charles Edward
Jones, Charles Edward
Jones, Charles Richard
Jones, Clifton Clyde
Jones, Curtis Harvey
Jones, David Charles
Jones, Donald Edward
Jones, E(ben) Bradley
Jones, Edward Cole
Jones, Edwin S.
Jones, Ernest Albin
Jones, Ernest Olin
Jones, Fred Eugene
Jones, Gardner Monore
Jones, Helen Hart
Jones, Howard Aldred
Jones, Howard Wesley
Jones, Howard William
Jones, James Victor
Jones, John Paul
Jones, Joseph Frech
Jones, Kensinger
Jones, Larry Richard
Jones, Lawrence William
Jones, Margaret Eileen Zee
Jones, Mark Elmer, Jr.
Jones, Nathaniel Raphael
Jones, Norma Louise
Jones, Paul Alexander
Jones, Peter d'Alroy
Jones, Philip Alan
Jones, Philip Newton
Jones, Phillip Sanford
Jones, Raymond Edward, Jr.
Jones, Richard M.
Jones, Robert Huhn
Jones, Robert Leon
Jones, Robert Russell
Jones, Russell K.
Jones, Scott
Jones, Shelden Fredrick
Jones, Theodore W.
Jones, Thomas Baker
Jones, Trevor Owen
Jones, Walter Heath
Jones, Wilbur Boardman, Jr.
Jones, William Arnold
Jones, William Augustus, Jr.
Jones, William Catron
Jones, William Hugh
Jones, William Marcellus
Jones, William McKendrey
Jonte, John Haworth
Joravsky, David
Jordan, Charles Morrell
Jordan, Kenneth Allan
Jordan, Lemuel Russell
Jordan, Philip Harding, Jr.
Jordan, Richard Charles
Jordan, Roy Wilcox
Jordan, William Burnap, III
Jordon, Robert Earl
Jorgensen, Chester Neil
Jorgensen, Neal Albert
Jorgenson, William Lloyd
Joseph, Burton M.
Joseph, James Donald
Joseph, David J., Jr.
Joseph, Geri M.
Joseph, Jules K.
Joseph, Ramon Rafael
Joslyn, Jay Thomas
Joslyn, Robert Bruce
Josselson, Jack Bernard
Jouno, Randolph James
Jourdian, George William
Joy, John William
Joyaux, Georges J.
Joyce, Charles Raymond, Jr.
Joyce, Edmund Patrick
Joyce, James Neal
Joyce, Joseph Francis
Joyner, Powell Austin
Joynes, Ralph Carlisle
Juckem, Wilfred Philip
Judd, Robert Carpenter
Judd, William Robert
Judge, Bernard Martin
Judge, John Emmet
Judis, Joseph
Judkins, Donald Ward
Judson, Lyman Spicer Vincent
Judy, Bernard Francis
Judy, John Wayne, Jr.
Juergens, William George
Juettner, Thomas Richard
Julian, Brooks Patton
Julius, Stevo
Juniper, Kerrison, Jr.
Jurgemeyer, Donald William
Juris, Hervey Asher
Justice, Donald Rodney
Justus, Roy Braxton
Juveland, Omar O.
Kaat, James Lee
Kabak, Robert
Kabara, Jon Joseph
Kacek, Don J.
Kachadoorian, Zubel
Kachru, Braj Behari
Kachru, Yamuna
Kadanoff, Leo Philip
Kaegel, Richard James
Kaesberg, Paul Joseph
Kaesler, Roger LeRoy
Kafarski, Mitchell I.
Kagan, Sioma
Kahane, Henry
Kahler, Herbert Frederick
Kahn, Charles Howard
Kahn, Herta Hess (Mrs. Howard Kahn)
Kahn, Paul Frederick
Kahne, Stephen James
Kahrl, Stanley J.
Kainlauri, Eino Olavi
Kaiser, Emil Thomas
Kaiser, George Charles
Kaiser, Leo Max
Kalamaros, Edward Nicholas
Kalbfleisch, Girard Edward
Kales, Robert Gray
Kalisch, Beatrice Jean
Kalkhoff, Ronald Kenneth
Kalman, Andrew
Kalp, Karl Rex
Kamerick, John Joseph
Kaminsky, Manfred Stephan
Kamisar, Yale
Kamm, Herbert
Kamm, Jacob Oswald
Kammash, Terry
Kammholz, Theophil Carl
Kan, Michael
Kanaga, Lawrence Wesley, Jr.
Kancelbaum, Joshua Jacob
Kane, Lucile Marie
Kane, Patricia Lanegran
Kane, Robert Bignal
Kane, Stanley Phillip
Kane, William James
Kanet, Roger Edward
Kanfer, Frederick H.
Kanin, Eugene John
Kanne, Gerald Merle
Kanter, Richard S.
Kantrowitz, Adrian
Kaplan, Bernice Antoville
Kaplan, Burton B.
Kaplan, Harold
Kaplan, Harold Morris
Kaplan, Manuel E.
Kaplan, Michael Irving
Kaplan, Morris Alfred
Kaplan, Morton A.
Kaplan, Phillip
Kaplan, Reuben William
Kaplan, Samuel
Kaplan, Sheldon
Kaplan, Sidney Joseph
Kaplan, Stanley Meisel
Kaplan, Yale Joseph
Kaplansky, Irving
Kapnick, Harvey E., Jr.
Kapp, Ronald Ormond
Kappauf, William Emil, Jr.
Kappes, Philip Spangler
Kapsalis, Thomas
Karaba, Frank Andrew
Karabatsos, Gerasimos John
Karanikas, Alexander
Karavolas, Harry J(ohn)
Karch, George Frederick
Karczmar, Alexander George
Kardas, Barbara Jean
Kardos, Paul James
Kark, Robert M.
Karl, Barry Dean
Karl, Max Henry
Karl, Michael M.
Karlos, Anthony Christ
Karlson, Alfred Gustav
Karman, James Anthony
Karmeier, Delbert Fred
Karnas, George James
Karnes, William Michael
Karol, Nathaniel H.
Karon, Bertram Paul
Karpowicz, Ray Anthony
Karr, John F.
Karr, Lloyd
Karraker, Louis Rendleman
Karrer, Eugene Robert
Karsh, Bernard
Karsten, Orlo Louis, Jr.
Kartalia, Mitchell P.
Kartman, Ben
Kasdorf, Donald Lee
Kaser, David
Kasper, Russell Richard
Kass, Irving
Kass, Leon Richard
Kassabaum, George Edward
Kastenmeier, Robert William
Kastner, Robert George
Kastor, Frank Sullivan
Kasuba, Romualdas
Katon, John Edward
Katona, Peter Geza
Katz, Adrian Izhack
Katz, Daniel
Katz, Dolores Jean
Katz, Harold Ambrose
Katz, Joseph Jacob
Katz, Lewis Robert
Katz, Paul
Katz, Sidney
Katzberg, Allan Alfred
Katzen, Raphael
Katznelson, Ira Isaac
Kauffman, Daniel Erb
Kauffman, Ewing Marion
Kauffmann, Ivan John
Kaufman, Charles Rudolph
Kaufman, Denver
Kaufman, Donald Leroy
Kaufman, Ira Jeffrey
Kaufman, Jerome J.
Kaufman, Karl Lincoln
Kaufman, Leslie Michael
Kauper, Thomas Eugene
Kausler, Donald Harvey
Kautz, Richard Carl
Kavanagh, Preston Breckenridge
Kavanagh, Thomas Giles
Kawalek, Thaddeus P.
Kaye, Norman Joseph
Kazazis, Kostas
Kean, Helen Elizabeth
Keane, Steven Edward
Kearl, Bryant Eastham
Kearney, John Walter
Kearns, Francis Emner
Kearns, Janet Catherine
Kearns, Jerome Barton
Keating, Stephen Flaherty
Keating, William John
Keck, James Moulton
Keck, Robert Clifton
Keck, William
Keckley, James David

Keefe, John Webster
Keefer, William W.
Keehn, Silas
Keel, Sidney Tison
Keele, Harold M.
Keeley, John Lemuel
Keenan, Boyd Raymond
Keesey, Ulker Tulunay
Keesom, Pieter Hendrik
Keettel, William Charles, Jr.
Kefauver, Weldon Addison
Kegerreis, Robert James
Kehoe, Frank Michael
Kehrl, Howard Harmon
Keidan, Fred Hannan
Keisler, Howard Jerome
Keith, Damon Jerome
Keith, Ian Fyvie
Kelalis, Panayotis
Kelb, Norman Ernest
Kelch, Robert Paul
Kellams, Darrell Frank
Keller, Charles Walter
Keller, David Coe
Keller, Eliot Aaron
Keller, Jean Herman
Keller, Kenneth Harrison
Keller, Reed T.
Keller, Robert John
Keller, William Francis
Kellermeyer, Robert William
Kelley, Daniel McCann
Kelley, Donald Hayden
Kelley, Donald William
Kelley, Frank Joseph
Kelley, George Walter
Kelley, John Joseph, Jr.
Kelley, Robb Beardsley
Kelley, Verne Francis, Jr.
Kelley, Wendell J.
Kelley, William Frederick
Kelley, William Nimmons
Kelliher, Peter Maurice
Kelly, Alonzo Hyatt, Jr.
Kelly, Charles J., Jr.
Kelly, Donald Philip
Kelly, Edward James
Kelly, Francis Daniel
Kelly, George P.
Kelly, Matthew Edward
Kelly, Patrick F.
Kelly, Richard Smith
Kelly, Robert Thomas
Kelly, William Crowley
Kelly, William Joseph
Kelm, George
Kelman, Arthur
Kelsey, Myron Plough
Kelson, Allen Howard
Keltner, Raymond Marion, Jr.
Kem, Lawrence R.
Kem, Richard Samuel
Kemble, Ernest Dell
Kemmerer, Donald Lorenzo
Kemp, Robert D.
Kemp, Robert Grant
Kemp, Walter Horace, III
Kempe, Lloyd Lute
Kemper, James Madison, Jr.
Kemper, James Scott, Jr.
Kemper, Rufus Crosby, Jr.
Kemph, John Patterson
Kemple, Joseph Nephi
Kendall, George Preston
Kendall, Leon Thomas
Kende, Hans Janos
Kendzierski, Lottie Henryka
Kenefick, John Cooper
Kenly, Granger Farwell
Kenn, Edward John Littlejohn
Kennard, Edward Cummings
Kennard, Kenneth Clifton
Kennedy, Byrl James
Kennedy, Cornelia Groefsema
Kennedy, Eugene Cullen
Kennedy, Frank Robert
Kennedy, G. Donald
Kennedy, George D.
Kennedy, Grace Harlan
Kennedy, Hayes
Kennedy, John Fisher
Kennedy, John Joseph
Kennedy, Robert Norman
Kenney, Neil Patrick
Kenney, Vincent Paul
Kenrich, John Lewis
Kent, Charles Hadley
Kent, David Guild
Kent, Geoffrey
Kent, James A.
Kent, Raymond Dennis
Kent, Robert Warren
Kepecs, Joseph Goodman
Kerbis, Gertrude Lempp
Kerkvliet, William Cornelius
Kerley, James Joseph
Kern, Ben William
Kern, Byron Mehl
Kern, Franklin Lorenz
Kern, Otto
Kernan, William John, Jr.
Kerr, A(rthur) Stewart
Kerr, Thomas Jefferson, IV
Kerr, William
Kerrigan, (Thomas) Anthony
Kerst, Donald William
Kerwin, Charles Cornelius
Kesler, Clyde Ervin
Kesling, Robert Vernon, Sr.
Kessel, John Howard
Kessler, Joan F.
Kessler, John Whitaker
Kessler, Nathan
Kessler, Richard Howard
Kessler, William Henry
Ketchum, Marshall Dana
Ketchum, Michael Jeremy
Ketchum, Ralph Douglas
Ketner, Wayne Mitchell
Keto, John Edwin
Kettelkamp, Donald Benjamin
Keuler, Roland Leo
Keulks, George William
Kevill, Dennis Neil
Key, Donald
Key, Jack Dayton
Keydel, Frederick Reid
Keye, William R.
Keyes, Daniel
Keyes, Edward Lawrence, Jr.
Keyes, Margaret Naumann
Keys, Samuel Robert
Kezdi, Paul
Kezdy, Ferenc J.
Khan, Fazlur Rahman
Kibbey, Hal Pierce
Kicher, Thomas Patrick
Kidd, William Caughey
Kiddle, Lawrence Bayard
Kidera, George J.
Kiechlin, Robert Jerome
Kieckhefer, James Ferdinand
Kiehl, Elmer Rudolph
Kiesling, Herbert John
Kight, Edward Hill
Kildee, Dale E.
Kilgour, Frederick Gridley
Kilker, Clarence Christian
Killen, Robert Burton
Killenberg, George Andrew
Killian, Donald Joseph
Killian, George Ernest
Killingsworth, Charles Clinton
Killip, Thomas, III
Killpack, James Robert
Kilman, James William
Kilmartin, Edward John
Kilmer, Forrest Junior
Kilmer, Ned Arntz, Jr.
Kilroy, John Muir
Kim, Chin-wu
Kim, Hyung Kon
Kim, Jaegwon
Kim, Moon Hyun
Kimball, Charles Henry Gallwey
Kimball, Charles Newton
Kimball, Spencer LeVan
Kimbrell, Horace Warren
Kimbrough, Robert Alexander, III
Kimbrough, William Joseph
Kimel, William Robert
Kimmel, Carol Frances
Kimmel, Joe Robert
Kimmey, James Richard, Jr.
Kincade, Arthur Warren
Kindig, Fred Eugene
Kindsvater, Carl Edward
Kindt, Glenn William
King, Andre Richardson
King, Donald C.
King, Edward Dunham
King, George Smith, Jr.
King, John Lane
King, Jonathan
King, Leslie Albert
King, Luther Jefferson
King, Lyndel Irene Saunders
King, Morris Kenton
King, Ordie Herbert, Jr.
King, Ray John
King, Richard Allen
King, Richard Harding
King, Robert Charles
King, Robert Cotton
King, Robert Howard
King, Thomas Allen
King, Thomas Van Dyke
King, William Emery
King, Woods, Jr.
Kingdon, Robert McCune
Kinget, G. Marian
Kingman, Henry Selden, Jr.
Kingman, Joseph Ramsdell, III
Kingsbery, Walton Waits, Jr.
Kingsley, James Gordon
Kingsolver, William Scott
Kinnaird, Charles Roemler
Kinnamon, Keneth
Kinneary, Joseph Peter
Kinney, Aldon Monroe, Jr.
Kinney, Earl Robert
Kinney, Eugene McDonald
Kinnison, William Andrew
Kinsella, John James
Kinsella, Ralph Aloysius, Jr.
Kinsinger, Jack Burl
Kinsinger, Robert Earl
Kinsman, Robert Donald
Kinzer, Donald Louis
Kionka, Edward James
Kipnis, David Morris
Kipp, Raymond Joseph
Kipp, Robert Almy
Kirby, Kent Bruce
Kirby, Maurice Helm, Jr.
Kircher, William L.
Kirchner, Edwin James
Kirk, Edgar Lee
Kirk, Russell Amos
Kirk, Sherwood
Kirkegaard, R(aymond) Lawrence, Jr.
Kirkendall, Richard Stewart
Kirkham, Don
Kirkpatrick, Clayton
Kirkpatrick, James C.
Kirkwood, Maurice Richard
Kirmser, Philip George
Kirsch, Charles E.
Kirsch, Edwin Joseph
Kirschbaum, Thomas Harry
Kirschner, Stanley
Kirsner, Joseph Barnett
Kiselewski, Joseph
Kish, Leslie
Kisor, Manown, Jr.
Kissane, James Donald
Kissel, James W.
Kissinger, Harold Arthur
Kister, James Milton
Kistler, Alan Lee
Kitch, Paul Richard
Kitchen, John Milton
Kite, William McDougall
Kittle, Charles Frederick
Kitts, Emmett Harry
Kittsley, Scott Loren
Kivett, Marvin F.
Kivitt, Theodore Tobias
Klagstad, Robert Edgar
Klahr, Saulo
Klapperich, Frank Lawrence, Jr.
Klare, George Roger
Klatt, Albert Arthur
Klatte, Eugene Carl
Klausler, Alfred Paul
Klausmeier, Herbert John
Klawans, Harold Leo
Klayf, Bernard Spencer
Kleckner, Dean Ralph
Kleeman, Jack W.
Kleiman, Bernard
Kleiman, David Harold
Klein, George deVries
Klein, Julius
Klein, Sister M. Rosalie
Klein, Morton Joseph
Klein, Oscar Roy, Jr.
Klein, Robert Michael
Kleinberg, Jacob
Kleinfeld, Erwin
Kleinsmith, Lewis Joel
Kleis, Robert William
Klemens, Roney Walter
Klement, Vera
Klemke, Elmer Daniel
Klemp, Joseph B(ernard)
Kletschka, Harold Dale
Kliebhan, M(ary) Camille
Klimczak, Ernest Joseph
Kline, Daniel L.
Kline, James Edward
Kling, Merle
Kling, William Hugh
Klingler, Eugene Herman
Klipper, Stuart David
Kloap, John Melnick
Kloppenburg, Ralph H.
Kloska, Ronald Frank
Klostermeier, Walter R.
Klotman, Robert Howard
Klotz, Harry Richard
Klotz, Irving Myron
Kluckman, Revone W.
Klugman, Stephan Craig
Kluszewski, Theodore Bernard
Klutznick, Philip M.
Klutznick, Thomas Joseph
Kluwin, John A.
Knabe, Arthur Tompkins
Knabe, George William, Jr.
Knaggs, Nelson Stuart
Knake, Ellery Louis
Knapp, David William
Knauss, Earl L.
Knecht, Loring Dahl
Kneisly, Nathaniel McKay
Kneller, William Arthur
Knepper, George W.
Knepper, William Edward
Knevel, Adelbert Michael
Knieter, Gerard Leonard
Knight, Lester Benjamin
Knight, Robert Montgomery
Knight, V. C.
Knighton, Joseph Raymond
Knighton, Robert Syron
Knights, Norman James
Knilans, Michael Jerome
Knip, John Joseph, Jr.
Knipschild, Robert
Knobe, Rick W.
Knoble, James Keene
Knoch, Win G.
Knoll, Erwin
Knoll, Glenn Frederick
Knott, John Ray, Jr.
Knowles, Warren Perley
Knowlton, Richard Kerr
Knox, Gerald Malm
Knox, Richard Melvin
Knox, Stanley Cramner
Knox, William David
Knudsen, Semon Emil
Knueppel, Arthur Allan
Knutson, Herbert Claus
Knutson, Wayne Shafer
Knutzen, Owen A.
Ko, Hsien Ching
Ko, Wen-Hsiung
Kobacker, Arthur John
Kober, Dieter
Koch, Arthur Louis
Koch, Charles de Ganahl
Koch, Charles Joseph
Koch, James Verch
Koch, Ralph Richard
Koch, Raymond Felt
Koch, Richard Frederick
Koch, Robert Louis
Kocher, Richard Bruce
Kochi, Jay Kazuo
Kochs, Herbert William
Kock, Winston Edward
Kocoras, Charles Petros
Kocur, John Anthony
Koehn, Charles William
Koehnline, William Angus
Koenig, Eldred Miles
Koenig, Jack Leonard
Koenigsberg, Marvin Lee
Koepke, George Henry
Koepsel, Wellington Wesley
Koerber, Lorenz Fred, Jr.
Koessel, Donald Ray
Koester, Robert Gregg
Koff, Richard Myram
Koga, Mary
Kogan, Bernard Robert
Kogan, Herman
Kogut, Maurice David
Kohler, Herbert Vollrath, Jr.
Kohler, Ruth DeYoung
Kohlman, David Leslie
Kohls, Richard Louis
Kohn, Clyde Frederick
Kohn, James Paul
Kohn, Robert Rothenberg
Kohn, William Henry
Kohnen, Ralph Bernard, Jr.
Kohut, Heinz
Kolar, Milton Anton
Kolars, John F.
Kolb, David Allen
Kolb, Gwin Jackson
Kolb, William Lester
Kolbe, James Frank
Kolehmainen, John Ilmari
Kolesnik, Walter Bernard
Kolhoven, John Henry
Kolker, Allan Erwin
Kollaritsch, Felix Paul
Kollat, David Truman
Kollmann, Hilda Hanna
Kollros, Jerry John
Kolmer, Lee Roy
Kolodziej, Edward Albert
Kompass, Edward John
Konhauser, Joseph Daniel Edward
Konopka, Gisela Peiper (Mrs. Erhardt Paul Konopka)
Konrad, John F.
Koontz, Raymond
Koosman, Jerry Martin
Kopel, David
Kopka, Donald Ferris
Koplin, John Lee
Kopp, Carl Robert
Koppang, Henry Oliver
Koppel, Lowell B.
Kopplin, Julius Otto
Koranyi, Adam
Korb, William Brown, Jr.
Korbelik, George Joseph
Korkowski, Robert Joseph
Korn, Roy Joseph
Kornel, Ludwig
Kornguth, Steven Edward
Korotkin, Fred
Korschot, Benjamin Calvin
Korth, Eugene Henry
Kos, Clair Michael
Kosmahl, Henry G.
Kosobud, Richard Francis
Koss, John Charles
Kost, Wayne L.
Kostanski, Thaddeus Anthony
Kostecke, B. William
Kostyo, Jack Lawrence
Kotler, Philip
Kotoske, Roger Allen
Kottke, Frederic James
Kottman, Roy Milton
Kotulak, Ronald
Kotzky, Alex Sylvester
Koumoulides, John Thomas Anastasios
Koury, Aleah George
Kouvel, James Spyros
Kovel, Ralph M.
Kovel, Terry Horvitz (Mrs. Ralph Kovel)
Koven, Howard Richard
Kovler, H. Jonathan
Kowalski, Dennis Allan
Kowalski, Kenneth Lawrence
Kowalsky, Roger Joseph
Kozlowski, Theodore Thomas
Krabbenhoft, Kenneth Lester
Kraegel, Norbert Edward
Kraemer, Paul Wilhelm
Kraft, David Christian
Krahmalkov, Charles Richard
Krainik, Ardis
Krakora, Joseph J.
Kramer, Charles Henry
Kramer, Ferdinand
Kramer, Frank Raymond
Kramer, Gerhardt Theodore
Kramer, Harry Summerfield, Jr.
Kramer, James Joseph
Kramer, John Devitt
Krane, Robert Alan
Krantz, Kermit Edward
Kranz, Norman
Krasney, Samuel Joseph
Kratt, Robert Arthur
Kraus, Joe Walker
Kraus, Mentor A.
Krause, Charles Joseph
Krause, Chester Lee
Krause, Edward Walter
Krause, Harry Dieter
Krause, Norman Lewis
Krause, Paul James
Krause, Ruth Annette
Kraushaar, William Lester
Krausman, Arthur Henry
Krauss, John Barozzi
Kreamer, John Harrison
Kreevoy, Maurice Mordecai
Krehbiel, Frederick August
Krehbiel, John Hammond, Jr.
Kreider, Carl
Krekeler, Carl H.
Krell, Robert Burton
Kreml, Franklin Martin
Krenitsky, Michael V.
Krenitsky, Peter
Krenz, Dean Albert
Kresge, Bruce Anderson
Kresge, Stanley Sebastian
Kress, George F.
Kress, James F.
Kress, Ralph Herman
Kress, Thomas George
Kretzmann, Adalbert Raphael Alexander
Kretzmann, Justus Paul
Krey, Robert Dean
Kreyche, Gerald Francis
Krider, Jake Luther
Krieg, William Henry
Krieger, Irvin Mitchell
Krieger, Leonard
Krier, Herman
Krimm, Samuel
Krisch, Alan David
Krisiloff, Steve
Krislov, Samuel
Kritzer, Hyman William
Krivit, William
Kroc, Raymond A.
Kroch, Carl Adolph
Kroehler, Kenneth
Krogh, Harold Christian
Krogstad, Blanchard Orlando
Krohn, Albertine
Krol, Edward Joseph
Kroll, Barry Lewis
Kroll, George
Kroll, Robert James
Kromm, Franklin Herbert, Jr.
Kromm, Mildred Carolyn
Kropp, David Arthur
Krotine, F(rank) Thomas
Krsul, John Aloysius, Jr.
Krucks, William
Krueger, Everett Heath
Krueger, Maynard Clare
Krueger, Robert James
Kruger, Fred Walter
Kruh, Robert F.
Kruidenier, David
Krulitz, Leo Morrion
Krumm, Daniel John
Krummel, Donald William
Krupansky, Blanche
Krupansky, Robert Bazil
Krupp, David Jean
Krupp, Roland Gerald
Kruse, Edgar Christ
Kruse, John Alphonse
Kruse, Norman Fredrick
Kruse, Paul Walters, Jr.
Krusell, Charles Robert
Kruskal, William Henry
Ksienski, Aharon Arthur
Kubek, Anthony Christopher
Kubly, Herbert
Kucera, Daniel William
Kucharski, Robert Joseph
Kuechle, Urban Theodore
Kuehl, Hal C.
Kuehn, Edmund Karl
Kuehn, James Marshall
Kuehner, Richard Louis
Kuekes, Edward Daniel
Kuenster, John Joseph
Kuethe, James L.
Kuhlmann, Fred L.
Kuhlmann, Fred L.
Kuhlmey, Walter Trowbridge
Kuhn, Albert Joseph
Kuhn, Alfred
Kuhn, Warren Boehm
Kuhnley, Harvey M.
Kukla, Robert John
Kulcinski, Gerald LaVern
Kulla, Raymond James
Kullander, Donald Edward
Kullberg, Duane Reuben
Kullerud, Gunnar
Kultermann, Udo Rainer
Kumar, Romesh
Kumar, Sudhir
Kundert, Alice E.
Kunin, Calvin Murray
Kunkler, Arnold William
Kunze, Ralph Carl
Kunze, Walter Edward, Jr.
Kupcinet, Irv
Kurland, Leonard Terry
Kurland, Philip B.
Kurtis, William (Bill) Horton
Kurtz, Myers Richard
Kurtzman, Allan Roger
Kusik, John Edward
Kutak, Robert Jerome
Kuzma, Joseph Francis
Kwiat, Joseph J.
Kwun, Kyung Whan
Kyle, Richard Erwin
Kyle, William Davidson, Jr.
La Barge, Pierre Lauck, Jr.
LaBelle, Leonard Frank
La Bree, John William
La Budde, Kenneth James
Lacey, Beatrice Cates
Lacey, J.W.
Lach, Alma
Lach, Donald F.
Lachman, Marguerite Leanne
Lachner, Marshall Smith
Lacouture, Paul Edgar
Lacy, Edna Balz
Lacy, Joseph Newton
Lacy, Paul Eston
Ladehoff, Leo William
Ladenson, Alex
La Du, Bert Nichols, Jr.
LaDue, Wendell Richard
Lady, Wendell
Laffoon, Polk, IV
La Follette, Bronson Cutting
Lafontant, Jewel Stradford
Lafore, Laurence Davis
Lagler, Karl Frank
Lagunoff, David
Laha, Radha Govinda
Laidlaw, Robert Richard
Laikin, George Joseph
Lair, Charles R.
Lair, Francis Leo
Lair, Robert Louis
Laird, Roy D.
Lake, Charles William, Jr.
Lake, Fredric David
Lake, Thomas Henry
LaLonde, Bernard Joseph
La Londe, William Salem, 3d
Lamb, Edward
Lambert, Edward Charles
Lambert, Eugene Raymond
Lambert, George Robert
Lambert, Joseph Buckley
Lambert, Marvin Joseph
Lambert, Philip
Lambert, Robert Frank
Lamborn, LeRoy Leslie
Lambros, Thomas Demetrios
Lamey, William Lawrence, Jr.
Lamis, Leroy
LaMore, George Edward, Jr.
Lamoreux, Frederick Holmes
Lampen, Sister Mary Joel
Lampl, Jack Willard, Jr.
Lanahan, John Stevenson
Lance, Dowe Jefferson
Lance, George Milward
Landau, Richard L.
Landau, William Milton
Landecker, Werner Siegmund
Landers, Ann (Mrs. Esther P. Lederer)
Landgrebe, David Allen
Landini, Richard George
Landis, Dan
Landis, Elwood Winton
Landis, Fred
Landon, Robert Gray
Landuyt, Bernard Francis
Landweber, Louis
Landwehr, William Charles
Lane, Aloysius
Lane, Kenneth Edwin
Lane, William James
Lane, William Noble, III
Laner, Richard Warren
Lanford, Luke Dean
Lang, Francis Harover
Lang, H. Jack
Lang, Martha Ann
Langbo, Arnold Gordon
Langdon, Herschel Garrett
Langdon, William Mondeng
Langell, Jerome Edwin
Langenberg, Frederick Charles
Langenheim, Ralph Louis, Jr.
Langer, Lawrence Marvin
Langer, Robert Adolph
Langevin, Thomas Harvey
Langford, Anna Riggs
Langford, George Clement
Langford, James Rouleau
Langhaug, Woodrow Pershing
Langsam, Walter Consuelo
Langsdorf, Alexander, Jr.
Langsley, Donald Gene
Langston, Hiram Thomas
Langworthy, Robert Burton
Lanham, Robert Lee
Lanier, Robert Jerry, Jr.
Lanigan, Robert J.
Lanners, Fred Thomas, Jr.
Lannon, John Joseph
Lano, Charles Jack
Lanterman, Joseph Barney
Lanyon, Ellen (Mrs. Roland Ginzel)
Lanzl, Lawrence Herman
Lapensky, M. Joseph
Lapides, Jack
LaPidus, Jules Benjamin
Lappetito, Paul William
Lardner, Henry Petersen (Peter)
Lardy, Henry Arnold
Large, James Mifflin, Jr.
Larkin, Emmet
Larkin, Eugene David
Larkin, John Day
Larmer, Oscar Vance
LaRoche, Robert Eugene
Laros, Gerald Snyder, II
Larrowe, Charles Patrick
Larsen, Arthur Hoff
Larsen, Edwin Merritt
Larsen, Erik
Larsen, Harold Cecil
Larsen, Joseph Reuben
Larsen, Max Dean
Larsen, Wesley Bernard
Larson, Allan Louis
Larson, Carl Martin
Larson, Carl Theodore
Larson, Clayton Kay
Larson, Curtis Luverne
Larson, Earl Richard
Larson, Gaylen Nevoy
Larson, Jerry L.

Larson, John David
Larson, Maurice Allen
Larson, Philip Allen
Larson, Roy
Larson, Thurston Eric
Larson, Ward Jerome
La Rue, Carl Forman
LaRussa, Anthony, Jr.
Lasansky, Mauricio
Lasater, Donald E.
Lash, Kenneth
Lashly, John Henderson
Lasker, Gabriel Ward
Laskin, Daniel M.
Laskowski, Leonard Francis, Jr.
Laskowski, Michael, Jr.
Lassers, Willard J.
Laster, Howard Joseph
Latimer, George
La Tourette, John Ernest
La Toza, Charles Anton
Latshaw, John
Lattin, Clark Parker, Jr.
Latto, Lewis M., Jr.
Latz, G. Irving, II
Lauck, Anthony Joseph
Lauda, Donald Paul
Lauder, Andrew B.
Lauff, George Howard
Lauffer, Alice A.
Laumann, Edward Otto
Laun, Harold George
Launstein, Howard Cleveland
Laurencelle, Patricia
Lauritzen, John Ronnow
Laursen, Paul Herbert
Laushey, Louis McNeal
Laustsen, David Scott
LaVelle, Arthur
Lavercombe, Robert Rieser
Lavidge, Robert James
Lavin, Bernice E.
Lavin, Leonard H.
Law, Bernard Francis
Law, Cursey Shelby
Lawhorn, Donald Samuel
Lawler, Edmund G.
Lawlis, Merritt Eugene
Lawrence, Charles Harris
Lawrence, Charles Seely, III
Lawrence, David, Jr.
Lawrence, Merle
Lawrence, Wayne Allen
Lawrence, Willard Earl
Lawrence, William Joseph, Jr.
Lawrie, Roy Thomas
Lawson, Donald Elmer
Lawson, William Hogan, III
Lawton, Richard Graham
Lawwill, Theodore
Lawyer, Verne
Lay, Donald Pomeroy
Layde, Durward Charles
Layman, Emma McCloy (Mrs. James W. Layman)
Layton, Wilbur Leslie
Lazarus, Charles Yondorf
Lazarus, David
Lazarus, George Milton
Lazarus, Mell
Lazarus, Ralph
Lazerson, Earl Edwin
Lea, Lorenzo Bates
Lea, William Sentelle
Leabo, Dick Albert
Leach, James Albert Smith
Leach, James Lindsay
Leach, Robert David
Leach, Ronald George
Leader, Robert Wardell
Leahy, Thomas Richard
Leak, David Keith
Leary, Leo William
Leasure, John Keith
Leatherdale, Douglas W.
Leavitt, Lloyd Richardson, Jr.
Lebeck, Warren Wells
Lebedow, Aaron Louis
Lebor, John F(rancis)
Le Boutillier, Philip, Jr.
Lebovitz, Harold Paul
Lebowitz, Albert
Lecker, Abraham
Leckie, Frederick Alexander
Le Duc, Don Raymond
Ledwidge, Patrick Joseph
Lee, Bernard Shing-Shu
Lee, Byron, Jr.
Lee, Carl E.
Lee, Don L. (Haki R. Madhubuti)
Lee, E(ugene) Stanley
Lee, George Hamor
Lee, Gilbert Lamont, Jr.
Lee, Hwa-Wei
Lee, Jack (Jim Sanders Beasley)
Lee, Laurence Raymond
Lee, Leroy William
Lee, Sherman Emery
Lee, Sidney S.
Lee, Tong Hun
Lee, William Craig
Lee, William Marshall
Leech, Charles Russell, Jr.
Leedy, Paul Francis
Leen, Walter Victor
Leepa, Allen
Lees, James Edward
Leeson, Charles Roland
Leet, Richard Hale
Leete, Edward
Lefebvre, Arthur Henry
LeFevre, Perry Deyo
Leffel, Charles Poague
Lefkowitz, Irving
Leftwich, Samuel Gilmer
Legaard, Stuart John
Legg, Wilbur Stephen
Leggett, Glenn
Leggett, Roberta Jean (Bobbi)
Le-Grand, Clay
Lehiste, Ilse
Lehman, John Howard
Lehman, Kieffer Ross
Lehman, Ralph Malcolm
Lehman, Richard Leroy
Lehmann, Charles Frederick
Lehmann, Gilbert Mark
Lehmberg, Stanford Eugene
Lehr, Lewis Wylie
Lehrman, Edgar Harold
Lehrman, Nat
Leibman, Morris Irwin
Leichliter, Van Handlin
Leidel, Frederick Otto
Leidner, Harold Edward
Leighton, George Neves
Leik, Robert K.
Leimkuhler, Ferdinand Francis
Lein, Charles D.
Lein, Malcolm Emil
Leiser, Burton Myron
Leissa, Arthur William
Leith, Emmett Norman
Leland, Austin Porter
Le May, William Edward
Lemberger, August Paul
Lemberger, Louis
Lemcoe, M. Marshall
Lemieux, Joseph H.
Lemon, Henry Martyn
LeMond, Alan Roy
Lemp, Frank Marcus
Lempert, Richard Owen
Lenard, Andrew
Lenardon, Robert Joseph
Lenehan, William Thurman
Lengefeld, Francis Roland
Lenke, Richard Elmer
Lenkoski, Leo Douglas
Lennon, Edward Joseph
Lennon, Sister Mary Isidore
Lenon, Richard Allen
Lens, Sidney
Lentz, James Eugene
Lenzen, Kenneth
Lenzini, Arthur Lee
Leon, Arthur Sol
Leon, Bruno
Leonard, David Henry
Leonard, Eugene Albert
Leonard, Henry Siggins, Jr.
Leonard, Joanne
Leonard, John Walter
Leonard, Nelson Jordan
Leonard, Richard Hart
Leonard, Roy Junior
Leopold, Richard William
Le Page, Frank Albright
Lerman, Albert
Lerner, Albert Martin
Lerner, Alfred
Lerner, Gerda
Lerner, Harry Jonas
Lerner, Nathan Bernard
Lerner, Robert Earl
Leroy, Robert Pierre
Lesar, Hiram Henry
Lesch, Michael
Leslie, James Hill
Leslie, John Hampton
Leslie, Robert Wendell
Leslie, Royal Conrad
Leslie, William Cairns
Lesly, Philip
Lesmeister, John Steven
Lesner, Samuel Joel
L'Esperance, Wilford Louis, III
Less, Clifford Michael
Lesselyoung, Nicholas Jacob, III
Lessiter, Frank Donald
Lester, Wilbur Rufus
LeSuer, William Monroe
Letsinger, Robert Lewis
Lettvin, Theodore
Leuthold, Raymond Martin
Levandowski, Donald William
Leven, Charles Louis
Leventhal, Howard
Levey, Samuel
Levi, Albert William
Levi, Arlo Dana
Levi, Edward Hirsch
Levi, Kurt
Levin, Bertram
Levin, Charles Leonard
Levin, Jack S.
Levin, Jacob Joseph
Levin, Richard Donald
Levine, Donald Nathan
Levine, Edwin Burton
Levine, Myron
Levine, Norman Dion
Levine, Stuart George
Levis, Larry Patrick
Levit, William Harold, Jr.
Levitt, Aaron Louis
Levitt, LeRoy Paul
Levitt, Richard Sander
Levitt, Seymour Herbert
Levy, Charles, Jr.
Levy, Edward Charles, Jr.
Levy, Jack I.
Levy, Matthew Nathan
Levy, Robert Joseph
Levy, Sidney Jay
Levy, Solomon E.
Levy, Stephen Lloyd
Lewert, Robert Murdoch
Lewis, Benjamin Morgan
Lewis, Carl Chandler, Jr.
Lewis, Cary Blackburn, Jr.
Lewis, Charles John
Lewis, Dale Kenton
Lewis, Darrell L.
Lewis, David Lanier
Lewis, David Sloan, Jr.
Lewis, Edmund Jean
Lewis, Edward Earl
Lewis, Gene Dale
Lewis, James Edward
Lewis, James Kirtley
Lewis, James Mose
Lewis, L. Edward
Lewis, L(eo) Rhodes
Lewis, Philip
Lewis, Phillip Harold
Lewis, Robert Lawrence
Lewis, Welbourne Walker, Jr.
Lewy, Ralph I.
Lexau, Henry
Ley, Katherine Louise
Leyh, George Francis
Leymaster, Glen R.
Li, Peter Joseph Ta
Li, Tien-yi
Liberman, Lee Marvin
Licara, Leonard
Licata, Michael J.
Lichstein, Herman Carlton
Lichtenberg, Don Bernett
Lichter, Edward Arthur
Lichter, Paul Richard
Lichtin, J. Leon
Liddell, Leon Morris
Liebelt, Robert Arthur
Lieberman, Laurence J.
Lieberman, Leonard
Liebig, Richard Arthur
Lieblein, Seymour
Liebman, Jerome
Liebman, Jon Charles
Liedholm, Carl Edward
Liener, Irvin Ernest
Lienert, Robert Marcellus
Liepold, Robert Bruce
Lifton, Donald Brian
Liggett, Robert George, Jr.
Liggett, Thomas Jackson
Liggett, William N.
Light, Albert
Light, James Forest
Light, John Caldwell
Light, Kenneth B.
Ligon, Cecil Otis, Jr.
Liljegren, Frank Sigfrid
Lillehei, Clarence Walton
Lilly, David Maher
Lilly, Martin Stephen
Lilly, Sydney Burnam
Lillya, Clifford Peter
Lim, Henry Chol
Limbaugh, Rush Hudson
Lin, Y.K.
Lind, Chester Carl
Lind, Levi Robert
Lindberg, Charles David
Lindberg, Howard Avery
Linde, Ronald Keith
Lindell, Edward Albert
Lindemer, Lawrence Boyd
Linden, Henry Robert
Linder, Lionel
Lindgren, Bernard William
Lindgren, Richard Thomas
Lindholm, Carl Edward
Lindner, Carl H.
Lindner, Kenneth Edward
Lindner, Robert David
Lindquist, John Robert
Lindsay, Charles Rogers, III
Lindsay, Robert
Lindsay, Vaughnie Jean
Lindstrom, Ernest Algot
Lindstrom, Kenneth Albert
Ling, Cyril Curtis
Ling, Joseph Tso-Ti
Lingl, Friedrich Albert
Lingoes, James Charles
Link, Arthur A.
Link, Roger Paul
Linn, James Herbert
Linnell, Albert Paul
Linnenburger, Ralph Leroy
Linowes, David Francis
Linsalata, Frank Natale
Linse, Eugene W.
Linsky, Leonard
Linton, Rodney Curtis
Linton, Roy Nathan
Lipford, Rocque Edward
Lipham, James Maurice
Lipkin, David
Lipking, Lawrence
Lipman, David
Lippe, Melvin Karl
Lippincott, Benjamin Evans
Lipton, Martha
Lis, Edward Francis
Lischer, Ludwig Frederick
List, David Patton
Little, Alan Brian
Little, James Reichard
Little, Robert Andrews
Little, Robert William
Littler, Mark Dunham
Littlewood, Thomas Benjamin
Littner, Ner
Litzsinger, Paul Richard
Liu, Ben-chieh
Liu, Benjamin Young-hwai
Liu, Kuo-Sung
Liu Vi-Cheng
Livingood, Clarence S.
Livingston, Ellis N.
Livingston, Robert Louis
Livingstone, Frank Brown
Lloyd, Fredric Reynolds
Lloyd, John Henry, Jr.
Lo, Irving Yucheng
Lo, Wayne
Loach, Paul Allen
Lobeck, Charles Champlin
Lober, Donald Warring, Jr.
Lober, Paul Hallam
Locher, Ralph S.
Locher, Richard Earl
Lo Chiano, Rocco
Lock, Richard William
Locke, Charles Stanley
Locke, Norton
Lockhart, John Mallory
Lockhart, William Raymond
Lockridge, Ernest Hugh
Lockwood, Ralph Harold
Loder, Dwight Ellsworth
Lodge, James Robert
Lodwick, Gwilym Savage
Loeb, Virgil, Jr.
Loebig, Wilfred (Francis), Jr.
Loeffler, Frank Joseph
Loeschner, Ray B.
Loess, Henry Bernard
Loewe, Leslie F.
Loewenberg, Gerhard
Lofgren, Karl Adolph
Lofquist, Lloyd Henry
Lofton, John Marion
Loftsgard, Laurel Duane
Logan, Henry Vincent
Logan, James C.
Logan, James Kenneth
Logan, John Austin
Loggie, Jennifer Mary Hildreth
Logsdon, Thomas Allen
Loh, Jerome Wei-Ping
Lohman, Victor John (Gus)
Lohman, Walter Rearick
Lohmann, Donald Gene
Lohmar, Douglas William
Lohr, Donald Russell
Lohrman, John J.
Lohwater, A.J.
Loken, Merle Kenneth
Lolich, Mickey Stephen
Lomas, Bernard Tagg
Lomason, William Keithledge
Lombardi, Cornelius Ennis, Jr.
Lombardi, John V.
Long, Alvin William
Long, Charles Franklin
Long, Clarence William
Long, Dennis Patrick
Long, Forrest Edwin
Long, Helen Halter
Long, Herbert Strainge
Long, Isaac Adelbert
Long, John Paul
Long, Lawrence Charles
Long, Robert Eugene
Long, Scott
Long, Theodore Dixon
Longbons, James Leland
Longhorn, Milton
Longmire, John Robinson
Longo, Michael Joseph
Longone, Daniel Thomas
Longworth, Richard Cole
Lonnquist, John Hall
Loomis, Wesley Horace, III
Looney, Marvin Olen
Loop, Floyd D.
Looper, Joseph Henry
Lopata, Helena Znaniecka
Loper, Carl Richard, Jr.
Loppnow, Milo Alvin
LoPrete, James Hugh
Lorand, Laszlo
Lord, Miles Welton
Lore, John Samuel
Lorentzen, Norman Martin
Lorenz, Hugo Albert
Lorenzen, George Arthur
Lorie, James Hirsch
Lorincz, Allan Levente
Lotterman, Hal
Lottes, John William
Loucks, Vernon Reece, Jr.
Loud, Warren Simms
Louis, John Jeffry
Lounsberry, Robert Horace
Lourenco, Ruy Valentim
Love, John, Jr.
Love, Rodney Marvin
Love, Ruth B.
Lovejoy, David Sherman
Lovejoy, Robert Carr
Lovelace, Eldridge Hirst
Lovell, James A., Jr.
Lovell, James Frederick
Lovell, Robert Gibson
Lovely, Howard Eugene
Low, William Hugh
Lowe, Henry Thomas
Lowe, William Henry
Lowengrub, Morton
Lowenstine, Maurice Richard, Jr.
Lowenthal, Henry
Lowery, Paul J.
Lowman, James Thomas
Lowrie, Jean Elizabeth
Lowry, Donald Irwin
Lowry, Gary William
Lowry, Robert James
Lowry, Sheldon Gaylon
Lowther, Gerald Halbert
Lowy, Steven Rudolf
Lubbers, Arend Donselaar
Lubin, Bernard
Lubker, Al
Lubkin, James Leigh
Lucas, Alexander Ralph
Lucas, Billy Lee
Lucas, Ferris Edward
Lucas, George Joseph
Lucas, John Kenneth
Lucas, John Wayne
Lucas, Lawrence Newton
Lucas, Robert Elwood
Lucas, Robert Emerson, Jr.
Lucas, Russell Vail, Jr.
Luce, Walter Arthur
Lucey, Patrick Joseph
Luck, John Virgil
Luckenbach, Carl Frederick
Lucker, Raymond Alphonse
Luckmann, William Henry
Lucow, Milton
Ludington, John Samuel
Ludlow, Charles Henry
Ludwig, Richard Joseph
Luecke, Joseph E.
Luecke, Richard William
Luedtke, Roland Alfred
Luerssen, Frank Wonson
Lueschen, Guenther Rudolf Friedo
Luffler, Ralph Raymond
Luisada, Aldo A.
Luke, Hugh Drummond
Lukens, Donald E. Buz
Lullo, Joseph Williams
Lumry, Rufus Worth, II
Lund, Bert Oscar, Jr.
Lund, Sister Candida
Lund, Lois Ann
Lund, Peter Anthony
Lundberg, James Thomas
Lunde, Harold Irving
Lundeen, Robert West
Lundegaard, Robert Anton
Lundegard, John Thomas
Lunden, Laurence Raymond
Lundgren, Robert Wayne
Lundquist, Carl Harold
Lundy, Joseph Edward
Lunn, Royston Charles
Lunn, William John, Jr.
Lupton, Jeanne Traphagen
Lurie, Melvin
Lurie, Nancy Oestreich
Lurton, H. William
Lusk, William Edward
Luskin, Bert L.
Luther, Clark Edward
Lutwak, Leo
Lutz, Carl Freiheit
Lutz, James
Lutz, Norman Emil
Luzinski, Gregory Michael
Lyall, Katharine C(ulbert)
Lydolph, Paul Edward
Lyke, James Patterson
Lykos, Peter George
Lykoudis, Paul S.
Lyman, William Welles, Jr.
Lynch, Benjamin Leo
Lynch, Beverly Pfeifer
Lynch, David William
Lynch, Donald Eugene
Lynch, Frederick, Jr.
Lynch, Henry Thomson
Lynch, Michael William
Lynch, Ray Joseph
Lynch, William Walmsley, Jr.
Lynn, Arthur Dellert, Jr.
Lynn, Chester Bernard
Lynn, Edward Earl
Lynn, Janet (Janet Lynn Nowicki)
Lynn, Michael Edward, III
Lynn, Naomi Burgos
Lynn, Robert Athan
Lynn, Robert Wood
Lyon, Edward Ellsworth
Lyon, Harvey William
Lyon, James Robert
Lyons, Frederick William, Jr.
Lyons, Jerry Lee
Lyons, M. Arnold
Lysaught, J. Donald
Maas, Duane Harris
Maazel, Lorin
Mabley, Jack
MacAllister, Jack Alfred
Macbeth, William E.
Mac Carthy, John Peters
MacCarty, Collin Stewart
MacCrimmon, Kenneth Robert
Mac Donald, Alan Douglas
MacDonald, Caleb Alan
Macdonald, David Robert
MacDonald, Harld C.
MacDonald, Kenneth
Mac Donald, Leo Hadley, Sr.
Macdonald, Peter McIntyre
MacDonald, Reynold Coleman
Mac Donald, Robert William
MacDonald, Roderick
MacDonald, Walter Howard
Mac Donnell, Wilfred Donald
MacDougal, Gary Edward
MacDougall, Curtis Daniel
Macfarlane, Malcolm Harris
Mac Fie, Clyde Allen
Machol, Robert E.
Macht, Carol Malisoff
MacIlvaine, Chalmers Acheson
MacIver, John Kenneth
Mack, Clifford Glenn
Mack, Eugene Kevin
Mack, Irving
Mack, Raymond Wright
Mack, Robert Emmet
Mack, Wilber H.
Mackal, Roy Paul
Macke, Kenneth A.
MacKendrick, Paul Lachlan
MacKenzie, Gordon Blair
Mackenzie, Kenneth Donald
Mackey, Maurice Cecil
Mackie, Frederick David
Mac Kimm, Margaret (Mardie) Pontius
Mac Kinney, Archie Allen, Jr.
MacKinney, Arthur Clinton, Jr.
Macklin, Philip Alan
MacLane, Saunders
MacLaughlin, Harry Hunter
Macleod, Bruce
MacLeod, Kenneth Authier
MacMaster, Daniel Miller
MacMurray, Charles Gaylord
MacNaughton, Alexander Douglas
Macnee, Alan Breck
Macneil of Barra, Ian Roderick
Mac Nichol, Roland Smith
MacNider, Jack
Macphail, Janetta
MacQueen, James Robert
Macsai, John
Mac Watters, Virginia
Maddex, Myron Brown (Mike)
Maddocks, Robert Allen
Madey, Richard
Madgett, Naomi Long
Madigan, John William
Madigan, Joseph Edward
Madison, Robert P.
Madsen, Charles Clifford
Madsen, Donald George
Madsen, H(enry) Stephen
Maduzia, Edward A.
Maffry, August
Mag, Arthur
Magad, Samuel
Magee, Paul Terry
Magen, Myron Shimin
Maggs, Peter Blount
Magie, William Ashley, Jr.
Magill, Robert Francis
Maginn, Raymond Graham
Magnuson, Keith Arlen
Magnuson, Richard H.
Magnuson, Robert Martin
Magnuson, Warren Roger
Magrath, C. Peter
Maguire, John Patrick
Magyar, Gabriel
Mah, Richard Sze Hao
Mahaffey, Maryann
Mahan, Harold Dean
Mahard, Richard Harold
Maher, Frank Thomas
Maher, Louis James, Jr.
Maher, Robert Francis
Maher, Trafford Patrick
Mahin, Charles Boyd
Mahler, Henry Ralph
Mahmoud, Aly Ahmed
Mahon, Bruce Allan
Mahon, Paul F.
Mahoney, Edward Maurice
Mahoney, Richard John
Mahowald, Mark Edward
Maibach, Ben C., Jr.
Maichel, Joseph Raymond
Maickel, Roger Philip
Maier, Bruce Richard
Maier, Frank Magner
Maier, Henry W.
Maier, Irwin
Maier, Jack Craig
Maier, Paul Luther
Mainous, Bruce Hale
Majerus, Raymond Edward
Majeski, Thomas H.
Major, Jean Armour
Mak, Mankin
Makholm, Mark Henry
Maky, Walter
Malan, Joseph Vernon
Malecki, Henry Raymond
Malicky, Neal
Malina, Marshall Albert
Malis, Louise (Mrs. Louis A. Malis)
Malkasian, George Durand, Jr.
Malkinson, Frederick David
Mallender, Fred, II
Mallender, Milton Fred
Mallinson, George Greisen
Mallory, Arthur Lee
Mallow, Robert William
Malloy, Daniel Victor
Malone, James William
Malone, Robert Roy
Malone, Rowena James
Malone, Thomas Francis
Maloney, David Monas
Maloon, James Harold
Malott, Robert Harvey
Malpass, Leslie Frederick
Malsack, James Thomas
Maltz, J. Herbert
Maltz, Milton Selwyn
Malvern, Donald
Malvin, Richard Lester
Malzahn, Ray Andrew
Mamer, Stuart Mies
Mamet, David Alan
Manatt, Richard
Manchester, Hugh Wallace
Manchester, Robert Asa, II
Mandel, Jack N.
Mandel, Morton Leon
Mandelker, Daniel Robert
Mandelstamm, Jerome Robert
Mandle, Earl Roger
Manella, Daniel John

Maneri, Remo R.
Manes, Milton
Manfred, Carl Lawrence
Manfred, Frederick Feikema
Mangel, Margaret Wilson
Mangold, Grant Douglas
Manheim, Edward
Manheim, Michael
Manilow, Lewis
Manion, Clarence E.
Manley, Robert Edward
Mann, Arthur
Mann, David Scott
Mann, Donald Nathaniel
Mann, Leonard Andrew
Mann, William Richard
Mannering, Gilbert James
Manning, Donald Waddington
Manning, Owen Duncan
Manning, Robert Thomas
Manny, Carter Hugh, Jr.
Manoogian, Richard Alexander
Mansager, Felix Norman
Manson, Samuel Stanford
Mansoor, Menahem
Mantel, Samuel Joseph, Jr.
Manthei, Richard Dale
Mantonya, John Butcher
Maple, Clair George
Mapother, Dillon Edward
Marakas, John Lambros
Marandel, Jean Patrice
Marble, Samuel Davey
Marchello, Joseph Maurice
Marchetti, Jerome John
Marcil, William Christ
Marcoux, Charles Ross, Jr.
Marcoux, William Joseph
Marcovich, Miroslav
Marcum, Joseph LaRue
Marcus, Donald Howard
Marcus, Jacob Rader
Marcus, Joseph
Marcus, Richard Alan
Marcus, Stephen Howard
Mardell, Fred Robert
Marder, Louis
Margerum, Dale William
Margoliash, Emanuel
Margolin, Abraham Eugene
Margolis, Philip Marcus
Marien, Albert Emmett
Mark, Norman Barry
Markert, Wallace, Jr.
Markham, Jordan J.
Markle, Susan Meyer
Markley, Herbert Emerson
Markman, Raymond Jerome
Markman, Ronald
Marko, Harold Meyron
Marks, Bernard Bailin
Marks, Harry Thomas
Markus, Lawrence
Markus, Richard M.
Markus, Robert Michael
Markwardt, Kenneth Marvin
Markwardt, L(orraine) J(oseph)
Marley, Francis Matthias
Marmas, James Gust
Marmon, Owen Holloway
Marovitz, Abraham Lincoln
Marquis, Rollin Park
Marsden, John Hal
Marsden, Ralph Walter
Marsh, Benjamin Franklin
Marsh, Bertrand Duane
Marsh, Don E.
Marsh, Florence Gertrude
Marsh, Robert Charles
Marshall, Charles
Marshall, Dana X.
Marshall, Francis Joseph
Marshall, Gordon Bruce
Marshall, Herbert A.
Marshall, James Frederick
Marshall, Philip Richard
Marshall, Prentice H.
Marshall, Robert Lewis
Marshall, William Robert, Jr.
Marsteller, William A.
Marsters, Ann Pierce (Mrs. Stewart S. Battles)
Marston, Roland F.
Martel, William
Marth, Elmer Herman
Martin, Bernard
Martin, Claude Raymond, Jr.
Martin, Daniel William
Martin, Don Stanley, Jr.
Martin, Donald William
Martin, Edley Wainright, Jr.
Martin, Edwin (John)
Martin, Edwin Webb
Martin, Gordon Mather
Martin, Hugh Jack, Jr.
Martin, James Gilbert
Martin, James Luther, Jr.
Martin, John Bartlow
Martin, John Ellsworth, II
Martin, John Gustin
Martin, Joseph J.
Martin, Judson Phillips
Martin, Lee
Martin, Malcolm Woods
Martin, Maurice John
Martin, Michael McCulloch
Martin, Oscar Thaddeus
Martin, Preston
Martin, Robert Roy
Martin, Ronald Lavern
Martin, Thomas Lyle, Jr.
Martin, Thomas Robert
Martin, William Paxman
Martinek, Otto Charles
Martino, Frank Dominic
Martino, Joseph Paul
Martinovsky, Eugene Simeon
Martins, Heitor Miranda
Martinson, Ida Marie
Marton, George Emil
Marty, Martin Emil
Martyl (Mrs. Alexander Langsdorf, Jr.)
Martz, Bill L.
Martz, George E.
Martz, William Edward
Maruska, Edward Joseph
Marvel, Richard Douglas
Marvin, Henry Howard, Jr.
Marvin, James Conway
Marvin, Philip
Mascho, George Leroy
Maser, Edward Andrew
Mashaw, William Gordon
Masi, Alfonse Thomas
Masko, George
Mason, Edward Archibald
Mason, Edward Eaton
Mason, John Lemear
Mason, Lowell Blake
Mason, Mearle D.
Mason, Ralph Edward
Mason, Rausey Wood
Mason, Richard Dean
Mason, Robert Joseph
Mason, Thomas Lyle
Mason, W. Bruce
Masotti, Louis Henry
Massengale, Martin Andrew
Masserman, Jules Homan
Massey, John
Massey, Vincent
Massey, Walter Eugene
Massman, Virgil Frank
Masters, Edward E.
Masters, Frank Wynne
Masters, William Howell
Masterson, Joe A.
Masterson, John Patrick
Mastin, Thomas William
Mastor, George Constandine
Masur, Ernest Frank
Matejka, Ladislav
Matera, Raymond Ambrose
Matheny, Edward Taylor, Jr.
Mather, Betty Bang
Mather, Charles Harold
Mather, Richard Burroughs
Mathers, Thomas Nesbit
Mathes, John Charles
Matheson, William Angus
Mathews, David
Mathews, Kenneth Pine
Mathews, Robert Edward
Mathewson, Hugh Spalding
Mathis, Byron Claude
Mathis, Harold Fletcher
Mathis, John Samuel
Mathis, Paul Carl
Mathog, Robert Henry
Mathues, Thomas Oliver
Matjasic, Raymond Aloysius
Matkowsky, Bernard Judah
Matlick, Dayton Harris
Matre, Richard Anthony
Matsler, Franklin Giles
Matters, Clyde Burns
Matteson, Albert Denton
Matteson, Robert Eliot
Matthei, Edward Hodge
Mattheis, Duane John
Matthews, Clifford Norman
Matthews, George Tennyson
Matthews, James Benning
Matthews, Luther White, III
Matthey, Louis Woodward
Matthias, Russell Howard
Mattick, Thomas Charles
Mattingly, Richard Francis
Mattox, Clyde Eugene
Mattox, Karl Russell
Mattson, Lawrence Sigfrid
Matzke, Howard Arthur
Mauldin, William H.
Maun, Joseph Angus
Maurer, C. Jackson
Maurer, Evan Maclyn
Maurer, Robert Joseph
Maurer, Wesley Henry
Maurice, Alfred Paul
Mausel, Paul Warner
Mautz, Bernhard
Maves, Paul Benjamin
Mavis, Frederic Theodore
Mawardi, Osman Kamel
Mawby, Russell George
Maxfield, Kenneth Wayne
Maxson, A. L.
Maxwell, Diana Louise
Maxwell, Donald Robert
Maxwell, Jack Erwin
Maxwell, John Bryan
Maxwell, John Ernest
Maxwell, Steven Charles
May, Daniel Francis
May, James C.
May, John Lawrence
Mayeda, Watara
Mayer, Dennis Thomas
Mayer, Harold Max
Mayer, Henry Michael
Mayer, Raymond Richard
Mayer, Robert Wallace
Mayers, Roy Elliot
Mayes, Paul Eugene
Mayfield, Curtis Lee
Mayfield, Demmie Gammon
Mayher, Laurence Thompson
Mayman, Martin
Maynard, H. Glenn
Maynard, Robert Wynfield
Mayne, Lucille Stringer
Mayne, Wiley Edward
Mayo, Gerald Edgar
Mayo, Robert Porter
Mayo, Robert William
Maysent, Harold Wayne
Mazanec, George Lad
Mazer, Henry
Maziarz, Edward Anthony
Mazurek, Keith Peter
Mc Adams, Joe B., Jr.
McAdoo, Bob
Mc Aleece, Donald John
Mc Allister, Lester Belden
McAninch, Harold D.
McArdle, Richard Joseph
Mc Atee, Ott Benton
Mc Auliffe, Michael F.
Mc Avoy, William Charles
Mc Bride, Lloyd Merrill
Mc Bride, Robert Dana
McBride, Robert Terrence
Mc Bride, Robin
Mc Bride, William Leon
Mc Cabe, Brian Francis
McCabe, Charles Law
Mc Cabe, John Charles, III
Mc Cabe, Leo Orvine
McCall, John Patrick
Mc Call, Julien Lachicotte
McCall, Raymond Joseph
McCallum, Francis A.
McCalpin, Francis William
Mc Camman, Ernest Rice
Mc Cammon, David Noel
Mc Camy, James Lucian
McCanles, Michael Frederick
McCann, Thomas Francis
Mc Cardell, Archie Richard
Mc Carragher, Bernard J.
McCartan, Patrick Francis
Mc Carter, C. Ted
McCarter, Charles Chase
Mc Carter, John Wilbur, Jr.
McCarter, William J., Jr.
McCarthy, Daniel J(oseph)
Mc Carthy, Donald Wans
Mc Carthy, Harold Charles
Mc Carthy, John Francis, Jr.
McCarthy, John William
McCarthy, Raymond Malcolm
McCarthy, Walter John
Mc Carthy, Walter John, Jr.
McCartney, Charles Price
Mc Carty, Daniel John
McCarty, Donald James
McCarty, Philip Norman
Mc Carty, Theodore Milson
Mc Carty, Virginia Dill
McCarus, Ernest Nasseph
Mc Cashland, Benjamin William
McCaslin, John Mathers, Jr.
Mc Cauley, Roy Barnard
McClain, Charles James
Mc Clain, William Andrew
Mc Clarren, Robert Royce
McClary, Edith Mae
Mc Clellan, Barbara Lee
Mc Clellan, Catharine
Mc Clellan, William Monson
Mc Clelland, James Craig
McClelland, Lloyd Shaw
McClennan, William Howard, Jr.
Mc Climans, James Dean
Mc Clory, Robert
Mc Clung, Leland Swint
Mc Clure, George Tarrence
Mc Clure, James J., Jr.
Mc Clure, Starling Virgil
Mc Cluskey, Judith
McCobb, Edward Clyde
Mc Collow, Thomas J.
McCollum, Clifford Glenn
McCollum, John Morris
Mc Conagha, Glenn Lowery
Mc Conahey, William McConnell, Jr.
McConkey, Dale Durant
Mc Conkie, George Wilson
Mc Connaughey, George Carlton, Jr.
McConnell, David Graham
McConnell, E. Hoy, II
Mc Connell, James Vernon
McConnell, John Thomas
McConnell, Robert Bruce
McConnell, William Arthur
Mc Conville, Clarence Joseph
Mc Cord, John Harrison
Mc Cormac, John Waverly
McCormack, John Joseph
Mc Cormack, Lawrence John
Mc Cormick, Brooks
McCormick, C(larence) James
Mc Cormick, Edward James, Jr.
Mc Cormick, Hope Baldwin (Mrs. Brooks McCormick)
McCormick, James Loren
Mc Cormick, Mark
Mc Cormick, William Bliss
McCormick, William Edward
McCormick, William Thomas, Jr.
McCown, Hale
Mc Coy, Donald Richard
Mc Coy, Frederick John
Mc Coy, John Bonnet
Mc Coy, John Gardner
Mc Coy, Pressley Crane
Mc Coy, Raymond F.
McCoy, Thomas LaRue
Mc Coy, William Daniel
Mc Cracken, Guy F.
Mc Cracken, Paul Winston
McCray, Billy Quincy
Mc Creary, Robert G., Jr.
Mc Cree, Wade Hampton, Jr.
McCreight, Robert Baker
McCrohon, Maxwell
Mc Crone, Walter Cox
McCubbin, Hamilton, II
McCuen, John Francis, Jr.
Mc Cuistion, Robert Wiley
McCullough, John Jeffrey
McCullough, Louis Garland
McCullough, Richard Lawrence
Mc Cune, Emmett Lee
Mc Curdy, Everett Darling
Mc Curdy, Larry Wayne
Mc Curdy, Patrick Pierre
Mc Curry, Donald Reid
Mc Curry, Paul D.
McCusker, Mary Lauretta
Mc Cutcheon, John Tinney, Jr.
Mc Daniel, Charles-Gene
Mc Daniel, James Edwin
McDaniel, William Lester
Mc David, Virginia Glenn
Mc Dermott, Edward H.
McDill, Thomas Allison
Mc Donagh, Edward Charles
Mc Donald, Alonzo Lowry
Mc Donald, David George
Mc Donald, David William
McDonald, Francis James
Mc Donald, Hugh Joseph
Mc Donald, John Cecil
McDonald, John Garwin
Mc Donald, Patrick Allen
McDonald, William Andrew
Mc Donnell, Michael Eugene
McDonnell, Sanford Noyes
Mc Donough, James Norman
Mc Dougall, Dugald Stewart
Mc Dougall, John
Mc Dowell, Joseph Hampton
Mc Dowell, Robert Charles
Mc Dowell, Robert Hull
Mc Eachen, Edmund David
Mc Elderry, Stanley
Mc Elhaney, James Willson
Mc Elin, Thomas Welsh
Mc Elrath, Gayle William
Mc Elroy, George Spahr
Mc Evers, Robert Darwin
McEvoy, Charles Lucien
McFadden, Harry Webber, Jr.
Mc Fadden, John Volney
Mc Fadden, Joseph Michael
Mc Fadin, Robert Lee
McFall, Kenneth Helicer
Mc Farland, Harold Richard
Mc Farland, Kay Eleanor
Mc Farland, Keith Nielson
McFarland, Richard Donald
Mc Farland, Robert Harold
Mc Farlane, Karen Elizabeth
McFee, William Warren
Mc Gaffey, Jere D.
McGannon, Robert Eugene
Mc Gara, Homer Joseph
Mc Garr, Frank J.
McGarrell, James
Mc Gaw, Foster Glendale
Mc Gaw, Robert Walter
McGee, James Howell
Mc Gee, Joseph John, Jr.
Mc Gehee, H. Coleman, Jr.
Mc Gehee, Nan Elizabeth
Mc Gill, Douglas Brown
Mc Gill, Maurice Leon
McGilley, Sister Mary Janet
Mc Gimpsey, Ronald Alan
Mc Ginn, John Christopher
Mc Ginn, Robert Francis
Mc Ginn, William Donald
Mc Ginnes, Edgar Allen, Jr.
Mc Ginnis, Frank Thomas
Mc Ginnis, George S.
Mc Ginniss, Neil
McGinty, John
Mc Giverin, Arthur A.
Mc Glamery, Marshal Dean
Mc Glasson, Maurice Argyle
Mc Goon, Dwight Charles
McGrath, Brendan
McGrath, John Francis
McGrath, Joseph Edward
Mc Grath, Thomas
Mc Graw, Arthur Garfield, Jr.
Mc Graw, James E.
McGregor, Duncan J(unior)
McGrew, Elizabeth Anne
Mc Grory, Mary
Mc Guire, James T.
McGuire, Timothy James
McHenry, Keith Welles, Jr.
Mc Henry, Powell
Mc Hose, James H.
McHugh, Edward Joseph
Mc Hugh, Richard B.
McIlroy, Robert Stewart
Mc Inally, LeRoy Burdette
McInerney, James Martin
Mc Inerny, Ralph Matthew
Mc Innes, Robert Malcolm
Mc Intire, Richard Lee
Mc Intosh, Harris
Mc Intosh, James Boyd
McIntyre, Bruce Herbert
McIntyre, Charles John
McIntyre, James Charles
Mc Intyre, Robert Walter
McKay, Allan L.
Mc Kay, Neil
Mc Kay, Thomas, Jr.
Mc Keachie, Wilbert James
Mc Keithan, Daniel Franklin, Jr.
McKelvey, James Morgan
Mc Kelvey, John Clifford
Mc Kelvy, Charles Lockhart, Jr.
Mc Kenna, Adrienne Delores
Mc Kenna, Thomas Joseph
McKenna, William J.
McKenzie, Jack Harris
Mc Kenzie, Jeremy Alec
Mc Kenzie, Lloyd William, Jr.
McKeon, James Charles
Mc Keown, James Edward
Mc Keown, Tom
Mc Kibben, William Torrey
Mc Kinley, William Lester
Mc Kinnell, Robert Gilmore
McKinney, E. Kirk, Jr.
Mc Kinney, Frank Edward, Jr.
McKinney, Fred
McKinney, James Edward, Jr.
McKinney, John Benjamin
Mc Kinney, Joseph Crescent
Mc Kinney, Robert Hurley
Mc Kinney, Ross Erwin
Mc Knight, William Warren, Jr.
Mc Kone, Don T.
Mc Lain, John David, Jr.
Mc Laren, John Alexander
Mc Laughlin, (Robert) Fred
Mc Laughlin, Harry Roll
Mc Laughlin, James Francis
Mc Laughlin, Jerry Loren
Mc Laughlin, John Francis
Mc Laughlin, Kathleen
McLaughlin, Matthew Aloysius
McLaughlin, Merlyn
McLaughlin, Ted John
Mc Lean, Malcolm
Mc Lellan, Ronald Douglas
Mc Leod, James Currie
Mc Leran, James Herbert
McMahan, Frederick Joseph
Mc Mahon, John Alexander
McMahon, John Frederick
Mc Manus, Edward Joseph
Mc Manus, Philip Daniel
McManus, William Edward
Mc Master, Howard Maxwell
McMaster, Robert Charles
Mc Meel, John Paul
Mc Mennamin, Michael John
Mc Millan, James
Mc Millan, R(obert) Bruce
Mc Millen, Thomas Roberts
McMillian, Theodore
Mc Million, John Macon
McMorris, Donald Lester
Mc Morrow, Richard Mark
Mc Mullin, Ernan Vincent
Mc Munn, Earl William
Mc Murrin, Lee Ray
Mc Murry, Robert Noleman
McNab, Allan
Mc Nair, Alexander James
Mc Nair, Russell Arthur, Jr.
McNairy, Philip Frederick
McNally, Andrew, III
Mc Nally, Andrew, IV
Mc Nally, Edward Thomas
Mc Nally, William Joseph
Mc Namara, Edward Howard
McNamara, John Francis
McNamara, John Francis
Mc Namara, Lawrence J.
McNamara, William Albinus
McNamee, Catherine
Mc Namee, Maurice Basil
Mc Neal, Harley John
Mc Neal, James Hector, Jr.
Mc Nee, Robert Bruce
Mc Neela, Edward Philip
Mc Neer, Charles Selden
McNeil, David Edward
Mc Neil, Donald Lewis
Mc Neill, David
Mc Neill, William Hardy
Mc Nerney, Walter James
Mc Nicholas, Joseph Alphonsus
Mc Nown, John Stephenson
Mc Nulty, John C.
Mc Pheeters, Thomas S., Jr.
Mc Quillen, Michael Paul
Mc Quistan, Richmond Beckett
Mc Rostie, Clair Neil
McRoy, Paul Furgeson
Mc Sheffrey, Gerald Rainey
Mc Swain, William Adney
Mc Swiney, James Wilmer
McVea, Robert Andrew
McVey, James William
Mc Vey, William Mozart
Mc Vie, Alexander Malcolm
McVoy, Kirk Warren
Mc Whinney, Rodney Owen
Mc Whorter, Clarence Austin
Mead, Beverley Tupper
Mead, Carl David
Mead, George Wilson, II
Mead, Stanton Witter
Mead, William Ramey
Meagher, Cyndi (Cynthia Nash Maza)
Mealman, Glenn Edward
Meaney, Thomas Francis
Means, George Robert
Meathe, Philip James
Mebust, Winston Keith
Mechem, Charles Stanley, Jr.
Mecke, Theodore Hart McCalla, Jr.
Meckstroth, John Robert
Medak, Herman
Medalie, Jack Harvey
Mee, John F.
Meeder, William George
Meehan, William P.
Meehl, Paul Everett
Meek, David Felmley
Meek, Devon Walter
Meek, Edward Stanley
Meek, Russell Charles
Meeker, David Bowyer
Meeks, Everett R.
Meeks, Wilkison Winfield
Meers, Henry W.
Megown, John William
Mehler, Alan Haskell
Mehlinger, Howard Dean
Mehn, W. Harrison
Mehr, Robert Irwin
Mehra, Santosh
Mehus, Oscar Myking
Meider, Elmer Charles, Jr.
Meier, August
Meier, Ben
Meier, Edward Kindt
Meierhenry, Mark V.
Meierhenry, Roy Albert
Meierhenry, Wesley Carl
Meiling, Richard Lewis
Meinert, John Raymond
Meinschein, Warren G.
Meisel, George Ira
Meisel, Jerome
Meisels, Gerhard George
Meissner, David Gifford
Meissner, Edwin Benjamin, Jr.
Melamed, Leo
Meland, Bernard Eugene
Melchior, Louis G.
Meldrum, Alan Hayward
Melhorn, Wilton Newton
Melick, William Frank
Meloy, Harry
Melrose, Kendrick Bascom
Melsen, John P.
Melton, Nancy Lopez
Meltzer, Bernard David
Meltzer, Bernard N(athan)
Meltzer, David Brian
Meltzer, Jack
Melvin, Billy Alfred
Mendelsohn, Joe, III
Mendelson, Alexander
Mendenhall, George Emery
Mendenhall, Robert Vernon
Mendenhall, Rodger Eugene
Mengden, Joseph Michael
Mengel, Robert Morrow
Menger, Karl
Menier, Vincent Joseph
Menke, Allen Carl
Menninger, Karl Augustus
Menninger, Roy Wright
Menninger, William Walter
Menolascino, Frank Joseph
Mentzer, Edward William
Mercer, Elwyn Jarvis
Merchant, Mylon Eugene
Meredith, Edwin Thomas, III
Meredith, James Hargrove
Mergen, Joseph Michael
Mergler, Harry Winston
Merilan, Charles Preston
Merkes, Edward Peter
Merkling, Richard Edwin
Merrell, David John
Merrell, James Lee
Merriam, Robert Edward
Merridew, Reginald P.
Merrill, Kenneth Coleman
Merrill, Lindsey
Merrill, Richard Thomas
Merriman, Joe Jack
Merritt, Lynne Lionel, Jr.
Merritt, Richard Lawrence
Merritt, Walter Davis, Jr.
Merte, Herman, Jr.
Mertz, Edwin Theodore
Mertz, Stuart Moulton
Merwin, Davis Underwood
Merwin, Jack Clifford
Meshii, Masahiro
Mesker, David Warren
Meskin, Lawrence Henry
Messick, Dale
Messinger, William Clifford
Metcalf, Lawrence Eugene
Metcalf, Robert, Clarence
Method, Harold Lambert
Mettler, Ruben Frederick
Metz, Lawrence Anthony
Metz, William Conrad
Metzger, George K.
Metzler, Dwight Fox
Meuser, Fredrick William
Mewissen, Dieudonne Jean
Meyer, Alex Alfred
Meyer, Alfred George
Meyer, Alvin Earl
Meyer, August Christopher
Meyer, August Christopher, Jr.
Meyer, Axel
Meyer, Brud Richard
Meyer, Charles Appleton
Meyer, Charles Edward
Meyer, Daniel Joseph
Meyer, Donald Gordon
Meyer, Duane Gilbert
Meyer, Gene Clinton
Meyer, George Herbert
Meyer, Janet Katherine
Meyer, Karl Heinz
Meyer, Karl William
Meyer, Kenneth M.
Meyer, Leonard Herman

Meyer, Maurice Wesley
Meyer, Maynard William
Meyer, Paul Reims, Jr.
Meyer, Peter
Meyer, Raymond Joseph
Meyer, Richard Charles
Meyer, Richard E(dward)
Meyer, Russel William, Jr.
Meyer, Samuel James
Meyer, Walter
Meyerhoff, Arthur Edward
Meyerhoff, Jack Fulton
Meyers, Arthur Christian, Jr.
Meyers, Cal Yale
Meyers, Gerald Carl
Meyers, Philip Mitchell
Mezera, James Allen
Michael, Alfred Frederick, Jr.
Michael, Floyd Donald
Michael, I. E.
Michael, R. Keith
Michaelides, Constantine Evangelos
Michalski, Thomas Joseph
Micheel, Wayne Edward
Michel, Robert Henry
Micheli, Frank James
Michelson, Irving
Michelson, Richard Albert
Michener, Charles Duncan
Mickelson, Arnold Rust
Mickelson, George Speaker
Mickelson, John Chester
Mickelson, Merlyn Francis
Middaugh, Robert Burton
Miechur, Thomas Frank
Mieher, Robert Lee
Mihalik, Emil John
Mihanovich, Clement Simon
Miklich, Thomas Robert
Mikolajczyk, Henry Louis
Milam, Evelyn Louise
Miles, Frank Charles
Miles, John Bruce
Miles, Wendell A.
Miley, George Hunter
Milford, Frederick John
Milgrim, Franklin Marshall
Milholland, James, Jr.
Milic, Louis Tonko
Militzer, Walter Ernest
Millar, Gordon Halstead
Millar, James Robert
Miller, Allan John
Miller, Arthur LaRue
Miller, Arthur Leonard
Miller, Bruce Louis
Miller, C(harles) Phillip, Jr.
Miller, Charles Joseph
Miller, Charles Williams
Miller, Daniel Weber
Miller, David Hewitt
Miller, Donald Calvin
Miller, Donald Morton
Miller, Duane Leon
Miller, Dwight Whittemore
Miller, Edward B.
Miller, Edward John
Miller, Edward Percival
Miller, Elizabeth Cavert
Miller, Eugene
Miller, Ewing Harry
Miller, Florence Lowden (Mrs. C. Phillip Miller)
Miller, Francis Marion
Miller, Frank William
Miller, Fritz Henry
Miller, George David
Miller, Harold Edward
Miller, Harold James
Miller, Harry George
Miller, Howard C.
Miller, Irving Franklin
Miller, Ivan Lawrence
Miller, J. Duane
Miller, James Alexander
Miller, James Edwin, Jr.
Miller, Jean Roger
Miller, Joel Barry
Miller, John Oscar
Miller, John Pearse
Miller, John Robert
Miller, John William, Jr.
Miller, Joseph Frederick, Jr.
Miller, Joseph Irwin
Miller, Kenneth Edward
Miller, Kenneth Lyall
Miller, Larry Lee
Miller, Lavern Archie
Miller, Leland Bishop, Jr.
Miller, Leslie Haynes
Miller, Lloyd Daniel
Miller, Lloyd Ivan
Miller, Louis Gerard
Miller, Lowell Donald
Miller, Sister Mary Aquin
Miller, Melvin Hull
Miller, Merton Howard
Miller, Morris Folsom
Miller, Pleasant Voorhees, Jr.
Miller, Ralph Dale
Miller, Ralph Paul
Miller, Richard G., Jr.
Miller, Richard Hamilton
Miller, Robert Branson
Miller, Robert Branson, Jr.
Miller, Robert Carl
Miller, Robert Earl
Miller, Robert Haskins
Miller, Robert James
Miller, Robert LaVelle
Miller, Robert Richey Conklin
Miller, Robert Rush
Miller, Robert Stevens, Jr.
Miller, Roland Drew
Miller, Roscoe Earl
Miller, Ross Hays
Miller, Shelby Alexander
Miller, Stanford
Miller, Stephen John
Miller, Thomas J.
Miller, Thomas Milton
Miller, Thomas Williams
Miller, Victor Charles
Miller, Warren Edward
Miller, Wilbur Casteel
Miller, Willard, Jr.
Miller, William H(oward)
Miller, William Jesse, Jr.
Miller, Wilmer Glenn
Millett, John David
Millichap, Joseph Gordon
Milligan, Floyd Wilmer
Milligan, Francis Joseph, Jr.
Milliken, William Grawn
Millman, Ronald Burton
Millner, Arnold John
Mills, Barriss
Mills, Donald Calvin
Mills, Frederick VanFleet
Mills, James Niland
Mills, John Welch
Mills, P. Gerald
Mills, Ralph Joseph, Jr.
Mills, Robert Laurence
Mills, Russell Clarence
Mills-Fischer Shirley Collum
Millstone, Isadore Erwin
Milne, Donald George
Milne, William Gordon
Milner, Harold William
Milnor, Magnus Ryrie
Milton, John Ronald
Minahan, Roger Copp
Minahan, Victor Ivan
Minar, Edwin LeRoy, Jr.
Mindlin, Richard Barnett
Miner, Earl Howard
Miner, Horace Mitchell
Miner, Thomas Hawley
Mingle, John Orville
Minner, Robert Schermerhorn
Minnich, Virginia
Minor, Charles Daniel
Minor, Robert Walter
Minor, Wendell Lafayette
Minow, Josephine Baskin
Minow, Newton Norman
Mints, Thomas M., Jr.
Minty, George James
Mintz, Harry
Mintz, Jerome Richard
Mintzer, David
Mintzer, Olin Wesley, III
Miossi, Alfred F.
Mirabito, Paul S.
Miracle, Gordon Eldon
Miranda, Constancio Fernandes
Mirkin, Bernard Leo
Miron, William L.
Mirsky, Arthur
Misch, Herbert Louis
Mischke, Frederick Charles
Mischler, Harland Louis
Mischley, Walter Anthony
Mishler, Clifford Leslie
Mitby, Norman Peter
Mitchell, Bert Breon
Mitchell, Bryan Henry
Mitchell, Clifford Robert
Mitchell, Edward John
Mitchell, Gerald Benson
Mitchell, Henry Vincent Edwards, III
Mitchell, John Francis
Mitchell, Marion Bonner
Mitchell, Marvin George
Mitchell, Orlan E.
Mitchell, Otis Clinton, Jr.
Mitchell, Robert Arthur
Mitchell, Roger Lowry
Mitchell, Roscoe Edward
Mitchell, Samuel Robert
Mitchell, Stephen Connally
Mitchell, Terence Edward
Mitchell, Thomas
Mitchell, Virgil Allen
Mitchell, William LeRoy
Mithun, Raymond O.
Mitscher, Lester Allen
Mitseff, Carl
Moate, Lester Thomas
Moberg, David Oscar
Modell, Arthur B.
Modell, John
Modersohn, Robert John, III
Modic, Stanley John
Moe, John Howard
Moeckel, Bill Reid
Moede, Gustave Herman, Jr.
Moeller, Carl William
Moellering, Alfred William
Moen, Donald Philip
Moen, Frederick W.
Moersch, Herman John
Moertel, Charles George
Moeser, James Charles
Moffet, Donald Pratt
Moffet, Ernest Beveridge, Jr.
Mogk, John Edward
Mohiuddin, Syed Maqdoom
Mohlenbrock, Robert Herman, Jr.
Mohler, Orren Cuthbert
Mohler, Stanley Ross
Mohlman, Robert Henry
Mohr, Roger John
Mohs, Frederic Edward
Mokodean, Michael John
Moldenhauer, Howard Herman
Moline, Jon Nelson
Molitor, Sister Margaret Anne
Moll, Kenneth Leon
Molloy, Julia Sale
Moltz, Howard
Molzan, Lynn Hopkins
Monasee, Charles Arthur
Monat, William Robert
Monek, Francis Herman
Mongan, James John
Monical, Robert Duane
Monk, Albert Herschel
Monroe, Benjamin Wade
Monroe, James Walter
Monroe, Loren Eugene
Montague, Eugene Bryan
Montgomery, Charles Howard
Montgomery, Donald Joseph
Montgomery, James Winchester
Montgomery, John Albert
Montgomery, Leo Raymond
Montgomery, Rex
Monypenny, Phillip
Moody, Blair, Jr.
Moody, Richard
Moody, Tom
Moog, Florence Emma
Moon, Gordon Ames, II
Moonan, William
Mooney, John Allen
Mooney, Robert Phillip
Mooneyhan, Esther Louise
Moore, Sister Anne Joachim
Moore, Buell Vernon
Moore, Dan Tyler
Moore, David Lowell
Moore, Edward Carter
Moore, Edward Forrest
Moore, Franklin Harkness
Moore, Fred L., Jr.
Moore, George Emerson, Jr.
Moore, Harry Clare
Moore, Harry T.
Moore, Herbert Bell
Moore, John Cordell
Moore, John Duain
Moore, John Newton
Moore, Kenneth Edwin
Moore, Richard Albert
Moore, Richard Kerr
Moore, Robert Etheridge
Moore, Ruth
Moore, Thomas P.
Moore, Ward Wilfred
Moran, Daniel Austin
Moran, James Byron
Moran, John Vincent
Moran, Thomas Joseph
Mordine, Shirley Macaulay
Mordy, Wendell Allen
Morehead, Dwight Hoyt
Morel, Paul Maurice
Moreno, Daniel Henry
Morgan, Arthur Edward
Morgan, David Hadley
Morgan, David Page
Morgan, George Tad
Morgan, Graham James
Morgan, James Alvin
Morgan, Jane Hale
Morgan, John Bruce
Morgan, John Derald
Morgan, June P.
Morgan, Lee Laverne
Morgan, Leger James, Jr.
Morgan, Raleigh, Jr.
Morgan, Ray Ellingwood, Jr.
Morgan, Robert Dale
Morgan, Robert Edward
Morgan, Robert Peter
Morgan, Samuel Huntington
Morgan, William Wilson
Moriarty, Donald William, Jr.
Moriarty, Thomas Edward
Morin, Patrick Joyce
Morin, Robert Edgar
Moritz, Alan Richards
Moritz, Edward
Moritz, Timothy Bovie
Morkovin, Mark Vladimir
Morley, George William
Morley, Harry Thomas, Jr.
Morlock, Carl Grismore
Morneau, Robert Fealey
Morosky, Robert Harry
Morrill, James Frederick
Morrill, John Rhodes
Morris, Alvin Eugene
Morris, Charles Elliot
Morris, Donald Arthur Adams
Morris, Donald Charles
Morris, Donald Fraser
Morris, Earl Franklin
Morris, Edward Lawrence
Morris, G. Ronald
Morris, Harry Leland
Morris, James Haines
Morris, Joan Clair
Morris, John Nelson
Morris, Norval
Morris, Ralph William
Morrison, Clinton
Morrison, David Lee
Morrison, Donal MacLachlan
Morrison, Donald William
Morrison, Gene Erle
Morrison, George
Morrison, Harry
Morrison, John Washburn
Morrison, Karl Frederick
Morrison, Robert Stanley
Morrissette, Bruce Archer
Morrow, George Lester
Morrow, Ralph Ernest
Morse, Erskine Vance
Morse, Grant Wesley
Morse, H(enry) Clifton, IV
Morse, Kenneth Pratt
Morse, Peter Hodges
Morse, Robert Alexander
Morse, William Charles
Mortensen, Dale Thomas
Mortensen, James Merwin
Mortensen, Robert Henry
Morter, Raymond Lione
Mortimer, Edward Albert, Jr.
Mortland, Max Merle
Morton, Joseph Neil
Morton, Richard Arnott
Moscona, Aron Arthur
Moscow, David Hirsh
Moscowitz, Albert Joseph
Moses, Earl Richard
Moses, Fred
Moses, Leon Nathan
Moses, Winfield C., Jr.
Moseson, Darrell D.
Mosher, Gregory Dean
Mosier, Frank Eugene
Moskos, Charles C.
Moskow, Michael H.
Moskowitz, Roland Wallace
Moss, Cruse Watson
Moss, Leonard Wallace
Moss, Robert Drexler
Mosse, Baskett Pershing
Mosse, George L.
Mostert, Paul Stallings
Mott, Charles Stewart Harding
Moulder, James Edwin
Moulder, James William
Moulton, Benjamin
Moulton, Edward Quentin
Moulton, Phillips Prentice
Mount, John Thomas
Mountjoy, Paul Tomb
Mourek, Joseph Edward
Mowery, Bob Lee
Mowrer, Orval Hobart
Mowry, Robert Neil
Moxley, William Mase, Jr.
Moy, Richard Henry
Moyer, Frederick Weaver, Jr.
Mudge, Lewis Seymour
Muehrcke, Robert Carl
Mueller, Alvin William
Mueller, Harold
Mueller, Herbert A.
Mueller, Jack William
Mueller, John Alfred
Mueller, Willard Fritz
Muessig, Raymond Henry
Mugford, Alfred George
Muhammad, Wallace D.
Muhlenbruch, Carl W.
Muirhead, Vincent Uriel
Mulder, Donald William
Mulder, Edwin George
Muldoon, John William
Mulham, Laurence Stanley
Mulheim, Joseph Elbert
Mullan, John Francis
Mullane, Robert E.
Mullaney, Paul Lynch
Mullen, James Gentry
Mullen, Januarius Arthur
Mullenbach, Philip
Mullendore, James Myers
Mullenix, Travis Hubert
Muller, Jans
Muller, Louis Robert
Muller, Sigfrid Augustine
Mulligan, James Joseph
Mulligan, Robert William
Mulligan, Thomas E., Jr.
Mulligan, Thomas Patrick
Mulliken, Robert Sanderson
Mullikin, Thomas Wilson
Mullin, Leo Francis
Mullins, James Patrick
Mulrow, Patrick Joseph
Mulroy, Thomas Robert
Mulvihill, Edward Robert
Mumaw, James Webster
Mundinger, Donald Charles
Mundt, Donald Keith
Munger, Benson Scott
Munger, Elmer Lewis
Munger, Paul Francis
Munnelly, John Patrick
Munro, Donald Jacques
Munro, William Delmar
Munson, Arvid Washburn
Munson, Thomas Lewis
Muntz, Ernest Gordon
Munzer, Cynthia Brown
Murchison, Elisha P.
Murdock, Charles William
Murdock, Robert Mead
Murdock, Stuart Laird
Murphey, Rhoads
Murphy, Charles Francis
Murphy, Charles Francis, Jr.
Murphy, Diana E.
Murphy, Ellis
Murphy, Gordon John
Murphy, Harry Crisman
Murphy, Irene Ellis
Murphy, John Carey
Murphy, Michael Emmett
Murphy, Paul Lloyd
Murphy, Robert Brady Lawrence
Murphy, Terrence J.
Murphy, Thomas Aquinas
Murphy, William A.
Murphy, William Celestin
Murray, George Rathell
Murray, Haydn Herbert
Murray, Hugh Vincent
Murray, John Joseph
Murray, John L.
Murray, Leonard Hugh
Murray, Peter Bryant
Murray, Raymond Gorbold
Murray, Raymond Harold
Murray, Robert Wallace
Murray, Sylvester
Murray, Thomas Dwight
Murrin, Michael Joseph
Murry, Charles Emerson
Murthy, Varanasi Rama
Muschenheim, William Emil
Musha, Jacob Roman
Musial, Stan(ley) (Frank)
Musselman, Peter Rogers
Musson, Noverre
Muth, C. Robert
Muth, John Fraser
Mutz, John Massie
Mutz, Oscar Ulysses
Mydland, Gordon James
Myers, Allen
Myers, Bill Howard
Myers, David N.
Myers, Frances
Myers, Fredrick Sames
Myers, George Elliott
Myers, Harry J., Jr.
Myers, Jesse Jerome
Myers, John Humbird
Myers, John Thomas
Myers, Kenneth Ellis
Myers, Kenneth Melvin
Myers, Malcolm C.
Myers, Malcolm Haynie
Myers, Phillip Samuel
Myers, Phillip Ward
Myers, Ray Franklin
Myers, Raymond Reever
Myers, Richard Gordon
Myers, Robert Gilbert
Myers, Theodore Ash
Myers, William Graydon
Myklebust, Helmer Rudolph
Mylod, Robert Joseph
Myra, Harold Lawrence
Myran, Gunder A(rnold)
Myster, Jay Dudley
Naber, Edward Carl
Nachtrieb, Norman Harry
Nachtsheim, Edward Ernest
Nadel, Eli Maurice
Nader, Robert Alexander
Nadler, Gerald
Nadler, Henry Louis
Nadler, Myron Jay
Naegele, Robert Edwin
Naeve, Milo Merle
Naftalin, Arthur
Nagel, Stuart Samuel
Nagera, Humberto
Nagle, James Lee
Nagy, Andrew Francis
Nagy, Charles Franklin
Nahat, Dennis Fred
Naimoli, Vincent Joseph
Nair, Velayudhan
Najafi, Hassan
Najarian, John Sarkis
Nance, James J.
Nangle, James, Jr.
Nangle, John Francis
Nanne, Louis Vincent
Nanney, David Ledbetter
Nara, Harry Raymond
Narahashi, Toshio
Nartker, Raymond Henry
Nasatir, Maimon
Nash, Curtis Eliot
Nash, Jay Robert, III
Nash, Katherine Elizabeth
Nash, Manning
Nash, Nicholas David
Nash, Robert Fred
Nason, Howard King
Nason, Robert Earl
Nassau, Robert Hamill
Nation, James Edward
Natvig, Paul
Nau, Earl K.
Nault, William Henry
Navarre, Robert Ward
Navin, Louis Edmond
Nawoj, Edward John
Naylor, Arch Waugh, III
Naylor, James Charles
Nazette, Richard Follett
Neathery, Wayne Dwight
Nebel, Henry Martin, Jr.
Nebenzahl, Kenneth
Nebergall, Roger Ellis
Neece, Robert Frederic
Needleman, Philip
Neel, James Van Gundia
Neely, Earl Fisher
Neely, Gartley Atwood
Neese, Elbert Haven
Neff, Frederick Clifton
Neff, John Hallmark
Neff, Robert Carl
Neff, Robert Wilbur
Neff, William Duwayne
Negley, Harold Hoover
Nehrkorn, William Howard
Nehrt, Lee Charles
Neidhardt, Frederick Carl
Neidhardt, Paul Woodrow
Neill, Robert
Neiman, Lionel Joseph
Nein, Lawrence Frederick
Nelsen, William Cameron
Nelson, Alvie Charles
Nelson, Bernard Andrew
Nelson, David Aldrich
Nelson, David Leonard
Nelson, Edwin Clarence
Nelson, Erland Randall
Nelson, Gordon Leon
Nelson, Grant Steel
Nelson, Harry J.
Nelson, John Monninger
Nelson, John Thilgen
Nelson, John Wilton
Nelson, Katherine Greacen
Nelson, Lawrence Evan
Nelson, Leonard
Nelson, Michael Underhill
Nelson, Norbert James
Nelson, Oliver Evans
Nelson, Peter Alan
Nelson, Ralph Alfred
Nelson, Randall Hylman
Nelson, Raymond John
Nelson, Robert Charles
Nelson, Robert Hartley
Nelson, Roger Milton
Nelson, Ronald Harvey
Nelson, Walter Gerald
Nelson, Werner Lind
Nemerov, Howard
Nemeth, Peter John
Nemmers, Erwin Esser
Nequist, John Leonard
Nerlinger, John William
Nerlove, Marc L.
Neroni, Peter Joseph
Nesbit, Mark E., Jr.
Nesbit, Robert Carrington
Nesbitt, Arthur Wallace
Nesbitt, Cecil James
Nesbitt, John Arthur
Nesheim, Robert Olaf
Ness, Ordean Gerhard
Nester, William Raymond, Jr.
Netsch, Walter Andrew, Jr.
Nettels, George Edward, Jr.
Nettl, Bruno
Neubauer, Charles Frederick
Neubert, Theodore John
Neuenschwander, Frederick Phillip
Neugarten, Bernice Levin
Neuhaus, Otto Wilhelm
Neuman, Donald Bernard
Neuman, Howard Jay
Neumann, Forrest Karl
Neuschel, Robert Percy
Nevid, Norbert
Nevill, William Albert
Neville, James Morton
Nevin, John Joseph
Nevins, Albert J.
Nevins, Francis Michael, Jr.
Nevitt, Michael Vogt
Nevling, Lorin Ives, Jr.
Newblatt, Stewart Albert
Newbold, Paul
Newbrough, Edgar Truett
Newcomb, Eldon Henry
Newcombe, Leo Raymond
Newell, Frank William
Newell, Sterling, Jr.
Newey, Paul Davis
Newhard, Harry Wallace
Newman, Andrew Edison
Newman, Bruce Lee
Newman, Eric Pfeiffer
Newman, Gerald
Newman, Leon Theophane
Newman, Louis Benjamin
Newman, M.W.
Newman, Melvin Spencer
Newman, Montelle Gage
Newman, Muriel Kallis Steinberg
Newman, Ralph Geoffrey
Newman, Wade Davis
Newsom, Lionel Hodge
Newton, George Addison
Newton, John Milton
Newton, John Skillman
Newton, Michael
Newton, Niles Rumely
Newton, Robert Chaffer
Newton, Roger Gerhard
Newton, William Allen, Jr.
Nexon, Hubert Henry
Ney, Edward Purdy
Nichol, Fred Joseph
Nicholas, Arthur Soterios
Nicholas, Harold Joseph
Nichols, Donald Arthur
Nichols, Donald Richardson
Nichols, Hugh Conklin
Nichols, John Alden
Nichols, Owen Harvey
Nichols, Robert Lee
Nichols, William Curtis, Jr.
Nicholson, Donald Grant
Nicholson, Francis William
Nicholson, George Albert, Jr.
Nicholson, Gordon J.
Nicholson, Joseph William
Nicholson, Leland R.
Nicholson, Morris Emmons, Jr.
Nicholson, Robert Arthur
Nicholson, Thomas Laurence
Nickerson, John Lester
Nickoley, Keith D.
Nie, Norman H.
Niebank, C(ornelius) George, Jr.
Niebur, Stanley Louis
Niefeld, Jaye Sutter
Niehm, Bernard Frank
Nielsen, Carl Eby
Nielsen, George Lee
Niemeyer, Gerhart
Nier, Alfred Otto Carl
Niezer, Louis Fox
Niles, Frederick Adolph
Nims, John Frederick

Ninneman, Robert Walter
Nisbet, Jerry J.
Nitsche, Johannes Carl Christian
Nix, Edmund Alfred
Nixon, Raymond Blalock
Nixon, Robert Pleasants
Noback, Richardson Kilbourne
Noble, Bernard (Bernie) Baird
Noble, David Watson
Nobles, Laurence Hewit
Nobles, William Scott
Nodine-Zeller, Doris Eulalia
Nolan, John Thomas, Jr.
Nolan, Joseph Thomas
Nolan, Val, Jr.
Noland, James Ellsworth
Noland, Wayland Evan
Nolen, Jerry Aften, Jr.
Nolen, William Anthony
Noll, J(ohn) Douglas
Noll, William Theodore
Nolte, Henry R., Jr.
Nolte, Walter Eduard
Nomura, Masayasu
Nona, Daniel A.
Noonan, Ray John
Norberg, Richard Edwin
Norby, William Charles
Nord, Henry J.
Nordbye, Richard Arthur
Nordin, John Algot
Nordine, Kenneth Edward
Nordland, Gerald
Nordlund, Donald Elmer
Nordman, Christer Eric
Nordstrand, Raymond William
Nordstrom, Carl Clifford
Nordstrom, Robert John
Norins, Arthur Leonard
Norman, Arthur Geoffrey
Norman, Warren Theodore
Norris, Albert Stanley
Norris, Lester J.
Norris, Robert Thomas
Norris, Thomas Gilbert
Norris, William C.
North, Andrew Stewart
North, William Stanley
Northcutt, Richard Glenn
Northrop, Stuart Johnston
Northup, John David
Norton, Daniel John
Norton, John C.
Norton, Peter Bowes
Nosanow, Lewis Harold
Notaro, Michael R.
Nottelmann, Otto Robert
Novak, Alfred
Novak, Dennis Wayne
Novak, Richard Francis
Novales, Ronald Richards
Novick, David Michael
Novotny, Donald Wayne
Noyes, Richard Apps
Nugent, Theodore Anthony
Nugent, Walter Terry King
Nunn, Arthur Sherman, Jr.
Nurmi, Martin Karl
Nurnberger, John Ignatius
Nutt, Thomas Joseph
Nuttli, Otto William
Nye, Russel Blaine
Nyemaster, Ray
Nyhus, Lloyd Milton
Nykiel, Frank Peter
Nyland, John Robert
Nyquist, John Davis
Nyrop, Donald William
Oakes, Robert James
Oasheim, Ralph Irving
Oates, James Franklin, Jr.
Obata, Gyo
Oben, Walter Joseph, Jr.
Obenhaus, Victor
Oberg, Roger Winston
Oberly, James Richard
Obermann, C. Esco
Oberstar, James L.
Obert, Charles Frank
Obert, Edward Fredric
Obert, Paul Richard
O'Boyle, Thomas Patrick
O'Brien, Albert James
O'Brien, (Harold) Dale
O'Brien, Daniel William
O'Brien, Donald Eugene
O'Brien, Elmer John
O'Brien, Frank B.
O'Brien, George Miller
O'Brien, John Harrington
O'Brien, Patrick William
O'Brien, Thomas Francis
O'Brien, William Mahony
O'Brien, William Patrick
O'Bryan, William Hall
Ocasek, Oliver Robert
Ochberg, Frank Martin
Ochiltree, Ned A., Jr.
O'Connell, Daniel Craig
O'Connell, Maurice Daniel
O'Connor, Earl Eugene
O'Connor, Edward Dennis
O'Connor, Francis John
O'Connor, James John
O'Connor, James Patrick
O'Connor, Jerome William
O'Connor, Richard Donald
O'Conor, Vincent John, Jr.
O'Crowley, James Francis, Jr.
Ocvirk, Otto George
Oddi, Raymond David
O'Dea, Paul William
Odell, Gerard Berlage
Odell, Mary Jane
Odom, Herdis Howard
O'Donnell, Cletus Francis
O'Donnell, Edward Joseph
O'Donnell, Joseph William
O'Donnell, Kevin
O'Donnell, William Charles
O'Dowd, Frank Edmund
Oehler, Irving Arthur
Oehlerts, Donald Ervin
Oehme, Reinhard
Oehmke, Robert Harvey
Oesterling, Thomas Ovid
Oetjen, Robert Adrian
Offer, Daniel
Office, Gerald Simms, Jr.
Offner, Franklin Faller
O'Flaherty, Wendy Doniger
Oganovic, Nicholas Joseph
Ogata, Katsuhiko
Ogilvie, Benjamin A.
Ogilvie, Richard Buell
Ogilvie, T(homas) Francis
Ogilvie, William Kay
Ogram, Gordon Fern
Ogura, Joseph H.
O'Halloran, Charles
O'Halloran, Thomas Alphonsus, Jr.
O'Hara, Thomas Edwin
O'Hearne, John Joseph
Ohlrogge, Alvin John
Oinas, Felix Johannes
Ojalvo, Morris
Oka, Takeshi
O'Keefe, Gerald
O'Keefe, James L.
O'Keefe, Thomas Joseph
O'Kelly, Bernard
O'Kelly, Lawrence Ivan
Okita, George T.
Oksenberg, Michel Charles
Oldam, Paul Bernard
Oldberg, Eric
Oldfather, Charles Eugene
Oldham, John William
O'Leary, George Francis
O'Leary, Richard Edwin
O'Leary, Thomas Howard
Olejniczak, Dominic
Olesen, J.M.
Olin, John Merrill
Olin, Spencer Truman
Olins, Robert Abbot
Oliver, Harry Maynard, Jr.
Oliver, John Watkins
Oliver, Robert Clifton
Oliver, William John
Ollerich, Dwayne Adolph
Olmstead, William Edward
Olmsted, Donald Warren
Olmsted, Sterling Pitkin
O'Loughlin, John Kirby
Olsen, Arthur Martin
Olsen, Donal Alan
Olsen, Edward John
Olsen, Gordon Clifford
Olsen, Norman Harry
Olsen, Rex Norman
Olson, Allen Ingvar
Olson, Cal
Olson, Carl William
Olson, Clarence Elmer, Jr.
Olson, Eugene Rudolph
Olson, Frederick Irving
Olson, Gordon Bennie
Olson, Hardin Leonard, Jr.
Olson, Jack B.
Olson, James Clifton
Olson, James Richard
Olson, John H.
Olson, Raymond Verlin
Olson, Richard E.
Olson, Robert Eugene
Olson, Ronald Wayne
Olson, Russell A.
Olson, Stanley William
Olson, Theodore Alexander
Olson, Walter Theodore
Olton, Roy
Olwin, John Hurst
O'Malley, John Daniel
O'Malley, Patrick Lawrence
O'Malley, Paul W.
O'Malley, Thomas Patrick
Oman, Richard Heer
O'Mara, Thomas Patrick
O'Meara, Edward Thomas
O'Meara, Onorato Timothy
O'Melia, Donald C.
O'Morchoe, Charles Christopher Creagh
Ondrejka, Ronald
O'Neal, Dennis Allen
O'Neal, Forest Hodge
O'Neil, John James
O'Neil, Michael Gerald
O'Neil, Robert Marchant
O'Neil, Robert Marchant
O'Neil, Thomas Francis
O'Neill, Arthur J.
O'Neill, Charles Kelly
O'Neill, Edward True
O'Neill, Eugene Milton
O'Neill, Henry Martin, Jr.
O'Neill, John Joseph
O'Neill, Joseph James
O'Neill, Thomas Vincent
O'Neill, William James
O'Neill, William James, Jr.
Ong, John Doyle
Ong, Walter Jackson
Ono, Allen Kenji
Oppedahl, John Fredrick
Opperthauser, Earl Charles
Opre, Thomas Edward
Orava, Raimo Norman
Orben, Robert Allen
Orchin, Milton
Orden, Alex
Oreffice, Paul Fausto
O'Reilly, Charles Terrance
O'Reilly, Daniel Elliott
Orel, Harold
Orfield, Gary Allan
Organ, Claude H., Jr.
Organski, Abramo Fimo Kenneth
Oriani, Richard Anthony
Orland, Frank J.
Orlin, Louis Lawrence
Ornstein, Robert
O'Rourke, Edward William
O'Rourke, Peter Edward
O'Rourke, William Andrew
Orr, George William
Orr, John Michael
Orr, Robert Dunkerson
Orrego-Salas, Juan Antonio
Orthwein, James Busch
Orthwein, William Coe
Orthwein, William Robert, Jr.
Ortman, Eldon E.
Ortman, George Earl
Orvick, George Myron
Osborn, James Marshall, Jr.
Osborn, June Elaine
Osborn, Richard Kent
Osborn, Robert Randolph
Osborn, Steele Bartley
Osborn, William George
Osborne, Arthur Ellsworth, Jr.
Osborne, Jack Cronin
Osborne, James William
Osborne, Richard Hazelet
Osborne, W. Irving, Jr.
Osborne, William Eli
Osburn, James Octavius
Osgood, Charles Egerton
O'Shea, Lynne Edeen
O'Shea, William Michael
Osipow, Samuel Herman
Oskin, Donald Cope
Osment, Frank Carter
Osrin, Raymond Harold
Ostby, Frederick Paul, Jr.
Oster, Clinton Victor
Oster, Merrill James
Ostermeier, Terry Harlan
Osterrieth, Michel M.
Ostrach, Simon
Ostrander, Nancy
Ostrom, Meredith Eggers
Ostrowski, John Edward
Osver, Arthur
Oths, Richard Philip
Otis, James, Jr.
Otis, James Cornish
Ott, James Forgan
Ott, Karl Otto
Ott, Louis John
Otten, Ralph Friedrich
Ottenweller, Albert Henry
Otteson, Schuyler Franklin
Otto, Jean Hammond
Otto, Wayne Raymond
Otwell, Ralph Maurice
Ouweleen, Frederic
Overberg, Paul Joseph
Overberger, Charles Gilbert
Overby, Milton Sidney
Overby, Osmund Rudolf
Overend, John
Overgaard, Mitchell Jersild
Overhauser, Albert Warner
Overseth, Oliver Enoch, Jr.
Overton, Jane Vincent Harper
Oviatt, Ross Hannum
Ovshinsky, Stanford Robert
Owen, Charles Archibald, Jr.
Owen, John Robert
Owens, B(obbie) D(eane)
Owens, Charles Vincent, Jr.
Owens, Frederick Mitchum, Jr.
Ownbey, Gerald Bruce
Owoc, Victor A.
Oxford, Carl J(arvis), Jr.
Oxley, Michael Garver
Oxtoby, Robert Boynton
Oyer, Herbert Joseph
Ozonoff, Ida (Mrs. Jacob B. Ozonoff)
Paauw, Douglas Seymour
Pacala, Leon
Pace, Stanley Carter
Pachman, Daniel J.
Packer, Raymond Allen
Paden, Donald Witt
Paffenbarger, Tom Link
Paffrath, Leslie
Page, Alan Cedric
Page, David Keith
Page, Eleanor
Page, Ernest
Page, John Henry, Jr.
Page, Paul Collins
Page, Ruth
Page, Thomas Cramer
Pagel, Ray Herman
Pagel, William Rush
Paige, Satchel (Leroy Robert)
Paine, Andrew J., Jr.
Paine, Charles William Eliot
Paine, Frederick V.
Painter, John William
Painter, William Hall
Palazzolo, Tom
Palenchar, Robert Edward
Paletta, Francis Xavier
Pallone, Julius Louis
Palluck, Rudolph Edward
Palm, Arthur Cleland
Palm, Bruce Arthur
Palmatier, Robert Allen
Palmer, Adrian B.
Palmer, Charles Milner
Palmer, Cruise
Palmer, David Walter
Palmer, George E.
Palmer, Hazel
Palmer, John Marshall
Palmer, John Robert
Palmer, Lloyd John
Palmer, Patrick Edward
Palmer, Roger Raymond
Paloyan, Edward
Panarese, William C.
Pankow, James Henry
Pantoja, Enrique
Pantuso, Vincent Joseph
Papadakis, Emmanuel Philippos
Papalia-Finlay, Diane Ellen
Paper, Herbert Harry
Paper, Lewis
Papone, Aldo
Papsidero, Joseph Anthony
Paquette, Jack Kenneth
Parch, Grace Dolores
Pardue, Harry Lyle
Paretsky, David
Parfet, Ray T., Jr.
Paridon, Leo James
Parish, John Cook
Parish, Preston S.
Parizek, Eldon Joseph
Park, Gerald Leslie
Park, Philip Mulvena
Park, Thomas
Parke, Wesley Wilkin
Parker, Charles Walter, Jr.
Parker, Clyde Alvin
Parker, Eugene Newman
Parker, Garland Glenwood
Parker, George
Parker, Hampton Brooks
Parker, John Richard
Parker, Paul Lange
Parker, Ralph Halstead
Parker, Robert Frederic
Parkinson, Ethelyn Minerva
Parkinson, George Ambrose
Parkinson, William Charles
Parks, William Robert
Parmelee, David Freeland
Parr, Harry Edward, Jr.
Parriott, James Deforis, Jr.
Parrish, John Bishop
Parrish, Overton Burgin, Jr.
Parrott, Leslie
Parrott, Robert Belgrove
Parsons, Donald James
Parsons, Edward Erskine, Jr.
Parsons, James Benton
Parsons, Jeffrey Robinson
Parsons, Keith I.
Parsons, Russell James
Partain, Edward Allen
Partee, Cecil A.
Parter, Seymour Victor
Pascarella, Perry James
Pasch, Maurice Bernard
Pashigian, Bedros Peter
Pasquariello, Anthony Michael
Passer, Morris H.
Pastalan, Leon
Pasterczyk, William Robert
Patchan, Joseph
Patel, Virendra Chaturbhai
Paterson, Philip Y.
Paterson, Robert Wacker
Patin, Henry A.
Patmos, Adrian Edward
Patner, Marshall
Patrick, John Corbin
Patrick, Robert Merle
Patrick, Ueal Eugene
Patten, Thomas Henry, Jr.
Patterson, Doyle
Patterson, Harlan Ray
Patterson, James Milton
Patterson, Jerome Calvin
Patterson, Merrill Reeves
Patterson, Robert Arthur
Patterson, Robert William
Patterson, Roy
Patterson, Russell
Patterson, Willis Charles
Pattis, S. William
Pattishall, Beverly Wyckliffe
Pattison, Abbott Lawrence
Pattison, John Norwood
Patton, George Thomas, Jr.
Patton, John Barratt
Pattullo, Andrew
Patty, R. Bruce
Pattyn, Remi Caesar
Paul, Ara Garo
Paul, Arthur
Paul, David Lewis
Paul, John Joseph
Paul, Justus Frederick
Paul, Ronald Stanley
Paul, Sherman
Paulin, Henry Sylvester
Paull, Richard Allen
Pauls, Dayton Frank
Paulsen, Norman, Jr.
Paulsen, Serenus Glen
Paulson, Belden Henry
Paulson, James Marvin
Paulson, John Doran
Paulson, Roy Richard
Paulson, William Lee
Paulucci, Jeno Francisco
Paulucci, Michael Jeno
Pavkovic, Ivan
Pavlick, Walter Eugene
Pawlewski, Norman Leonard
Pawley, Thomas Désiré, III
Paxton, Frank, Jr.
Payne, James Leroy
Payne, Kenyon Thomas
Payne, W(illiam) Spencer
Paynter, John Philip
Payton, Walter
Pazik, George James
Peacock, John Edward Dean
Peacock, William Eldred
Peapples, George Alan
Pearce, Donald Joslin
Pearce, James Wishart
Pearlman, Jerry Kent
Pearman, William Robert
Pearsall, Thomas Edward
Pearson, Albert Marchant
Pearson, Allen Day
Pearson, Gerald Leon
Pearson, James Eugene
Pearson, John Earle
Pearson, John Edgar
Pearson, Karl Gustav
Pearson, Larry Lester
Pearson, Olof Hjalmer
Pearson, Paul Guy
Pearson, Paul Hammond
Pearson, Phillip Theodore
Pease, Donald James
Pease, James Lewis, Jr.
Peck, Abraham
Peck, Ben
Peck, Charles Edward
Peck, Donald Vincent
Peck, Franklin Bruce, Sr.
Peck, Garnet Edward
Peck, John W.
Peck, Theresa
Peck, William Arno
Peckham, Ben Miller
Pedace, John Sylvester
Pedersen, Francis D.
Pedersen, Stuart Christian
Pederson, Vernon R.
Pedicini, Louis James
Pedley, John Griffiths
Pedoe, Daniel
Pedrotti, Leno Stephano
Peebles, Carter David
Peerman, Dean Gordon
Pehlke, Robert Donald
Peifer, Edward Lee
Peirson, Walter R.
Peiss, Clarence Norman
Pekow, Eugene
Pell, Wilbur Frank, Jr.
Pella, Milton Orville
Pellett, Thomas Rowand
Peltier, Eugene Joseph
Pelton, John Forrester
Pen, Rudolph Theodore
Pendleton, Barbara Jean
Penick, James Lal, Jr.
Penn, Edwin Allen
Penn, John Clarence
Penniman, Clara
Pennock, George Tennant
Pentecost, Ronald Ray
Peper, Christian Baird
Pepper, John Ennis, Jr.
Peppers, Henry Joseph
Perbix, George Harold
Percas de Ponseti, Helena
Perelman, Melvin
Peretti, Ettore Alex James
Perez, Carlos A.
Perez-Tamayo, Ruheri
Perkins, Bradford
Perkins, Donald Sheldon
Perkins, John Harold
Perkins, John MacIvor
Perkins, Lawrence Bradford
Perkins, Merle Lester
Perkins, Philip Thornton
Perkins, R(ichard) Marlin
Perkins, William H., Jr.
Perkoff, Gerald Thomas
Perkovic, Robert Branko
Perlman, D(avid)
Perlman, Harold Leonard
Perlman, Lawrence
Perlman, Raymond
Perlman, Richard Wilfred
Perlstein, Harris
Perman, Norman Wilford
Perrin, Richard William Edmund
Perrine, Beahl Theodore
Perrucci, Robert
Perry, Anthony John
Perry, Bernard Berenson
Perry, Edmund Franklin
Perry, Harold Otto
Perry, Harold Tyner
Perry, Joseph Samuel
Perry, Kenneth Wilbur
Perry, Paul Alverson
Persavich, Warren Dale
Pershing, Roscoe Louis
Persons, Stow Spaulding
Perutz, Gerald Eric Alexander
Pesch, LeRoy Allen
Pesch, Peter
Peschka, Thomas Alan
Pesek, John Thomas, Jr.
Peshkin, Alan
Peshkin, Murray
Peshkin, Samuel David
Pesmen, Sandra (Mrs. Harold William Pesmen)
Pestillo, Peter John
Petacque, Art
Petchenik, Edward A.
Petering, Ralph Edwin
Peterle, Tony John
Peters, Chester Evan
Peters, Dennis Gail
Peters, Douglas Scott
Peters, Doyle Buren
Peters, Farnsley Lewellyn
Peters, Frank Lewis, Jr.
Peters, Gordon Benes
Peters, Henry Augustus
Peters, Howard Nevin
Peters, Joseph Harlan
Peters, Joseph John
Peters, Michael Bartley
Petersen, Donald Eugene
Petersen, William John
Peterson, Bartlett
Peterson, Bettelou
Peterson, C(arl) Donald
Peterson, Carl L.
Peterson, Charles H.
Peterson, Clifford Lyle
Peterson, Edward Dale
Peterson, Gale Eugene
Peterson, George Lester
Peterson, Harold Oscar
Peterson, Herbert K.
Peterson, J. Dwight
Peterson, J. W.
Peterson, John Booth
Peterson, John Dwight
Peterson, John Lawrence
Peterson, John Marshall
Peterson, Karl Lee
Peterson, Kenneth Gerard
Peterson, Louis Robert
Peterson, Lowell Eugene
Peterson, Martha Elizabeth
Peterson, Mildred Othmer (Mrs. Howard R. Peterson)
Peterson, Paul Kenneth (P.K.)
Peterson, Paul Quayle
Peterson, Richard Elton
Peterson, Richard William
Peterson, Robert Austin
Peterson, Robert L.
Peterson, Spiro
Peterson, Theodore Bernard
Peterson, Wallace Carroll
Peterson, Walter Fritiof
Peterson, Willis Lester
Petfick, Christopher John
Petosa, Jason Joseph
Petrakis, Harry Mark
Petrequin, Harry Joseph, Jr.
Petrich, Beatrice Ann
Petrick, Ernest Nicholas
Petrides, George Athan
Petry, Thomas Edwin
Pettengill, Kroger
Pettersen, George Richard
Pettersen, Rodney Russell
Pettinga, Cornelius Wesley
Petuchowski, Jakob Josef
Petzold, Robert George
Pew, Robert Cunningham, II
Pewitt, Edward Gale
Peyser, Joseph Leonard
Pfannkuch, Robert Blaine
Pfeiffer, Richard Clair
Pfister, Robert Marti
Pflanze, Otto Paul
Pflug, Irving John
Pfunder, Malcolm Gilkey
Phares, E. Jerry
Phelan, John Densmore
Phelan, Martin DuPont
Phelps, David Michael
Phelps, Edwin Rice
Phelps, Hugh Vaughn
Phelps, Paul Michael
Phelps, Richard Frederick
Philipp, Walter Viktor
Philipps, Louis Edward
Philips, Jesse
Philipson, Morris
Philipson, Willard Dale
Phillip, Lee June
Phillippi, Wendell Crane
Phillips, Bert Eugene
Phillips, Charles Dill
Phillips, Clifton J.
Phillips, Daniel Miller
Phillips, David Atlee
Phillips, Elliott Hunter
Phillips, Harvey Gene
Phillips, Ivan Edward
Phillips, James Archibald, Jr.
Phillips, James Linford
Phillips, John Burton
Phillips, Joseph Dexter
Phillips, Ralph Wilbur
Phillips, Ronald Lewis
Phillips, Sidney Frederick
Phillips, Tommy Lee
Phillips, Vel
Phillips, William Dale
Phillips, William George
Phillipson, John Samuel
Philpott, Larry La Fayette
Phipps, John Randolph
Piacsek, Bela Emery
Piccolo, Cosmo Anthony
Piche, LeRoy Francis
Pichler, Joseph Anton
Pickens, Buford Lindsay
Pickens, Robert Bruce
Pickle, Robert Douglas
Pieper, Heinz Paul
Pierce, Daniel Marshall
Pierce, Louis
Pierce, Robert R.
Pierce, William James
Pierpont, Wilbur K.
Pierson, John Theodore, Jr.
Pikaart, Len
Pikarsky, Milton
Pike, Albert Raymond
Pilafian, Suren
Pilarczyk, Daniel Edward

Pile, Robert Bennett
Pilla, Anthony Michael
Pillai, Krishnapillai
  Chennakkadu Sreedharan
Pillet, Roger Albert
Pilliod, Charles Jule, Jr.
Pillsbury, George Sturgis
Pillsbury, John Sargent, Jr.
Pillsbury, Philip Winston
Pincus, Howard Jonah
Pincus, Theodore Henry
Pine, Irving
Pines, David
Pinet, Frank Samuel
Ping, Charles Jackson
Pingel, John Spencer
Pings, Vern Matthew
Pinkert, Joseph S.
Pinkerton, Richard LaDoyt
Pinkham, Mary Ellen
Pinnell, William George
Pinsky, Mark Allan
Pinsof, Nathan
Pipal, Faustin A.
Piper, Henry Dan
Piper, Henry George
Piper, Mark Harry
Piper, Robert Johnston
Pisik, Jay Joseph
Pisney, Raymond Frank
Pistilli, Philip
Pistner, Stephen Lawrence
Pitblado, John M.
Pitkin, Roy Macbeth
Pitner, Samuel Ellis
Pitot, Henry Clement
Pitts, Guy Harvey
Pitzer, Donald Elden
Pizer, Irwin Howard
Place, Geoffrey
Plagenz, George Richard
Plager, Sheldon Jay
Plambeck, Herbert Henry
Plank, Betsy Ann (Mrs.
  Sherman V. Rosenfield)
Plank, Raymond
Plant, Marcus Leo
Plaster, Robert Wayne
Plath, David William
Platou, Carl Nicolai
Platt, Franklin Dewitt
Platts, John H.
Platzman, George William
Plaut, Eric Alfred
Playe, George Louis
Player, Gary Jim
Pletcher, David Mitchell
Pletsch, George Burgess
Pletz, Francis Gregory
Ploeser, Walter Christian
Plonsey, Robert
Plonus, Martin Algirdas
Plotkin, Manuel D.
Plotnick, Harvey Barry
Plotnick, Mark Michael
Plotnik, Arthur
Plucker, Orvin Lowell
Plunkett, Robert
Poboisk, Donald Paul
Pochyly, Donald Frederick
Pocock, Frederick James
Pocock, John William
Podesta, Robert Angelo
Poettcker, Henry
Pohl, Richard Walter
Poinier, Arthur Best
Poinsett, Alexander Caesar
Polesky, Herbert Fred
Poling, Forrest Kenneth
Poling, Harold Arthur
Polk, Louis Frederick
Polk, Ralph Lane, Jr.
Pollack, Gerald Leslie
Pollack, Henry Nathan
Pollack, Norman
Pollack, Richard Martin
Pollard, Braxton
Pollard, Charles William
Pollard, Harry
Pollard, Herman Marvin
Pollard, Morris
Polley, Edward Herman
Polley, Howard Freeman
Pollock, George Howard
Pollock, Robert Elwood
Pollock, Robert John, Jr.
Pomerance, Eugene C.
Pomerantz, Louis
Pomeroy, Lawrence Hitchcock
Pomroy, Jesse Herbert, Jr.
Pond, Alonzo William
Pond, Byron Oliver, Jr.
Pondrom, Lee Girard
Ponitz, David Henry
Ponseti, Ignacio Vives
Pont, John
Poole, John Bayard
Poorman, Paul Arthur
Poorman, Robert Lewis
Popham, Arthur Cobb, Jr.
Popham, Richard Allen
Popham, Wayne Gordon
Poplinger, Louis L.
Poppelbaum, Wolfgang Johann
Porile, Norbert Thomas
Poropat, Anthony Richard
Porter, Arthur Reno
Porter, Barry Lavon
Porter, Barry Schuyler
Porter, Darrell Ray
Porter, David Hugh
Porter, David Stewart
Porter, Dean Alan
Porter, Donald James
Porter, Helen Viney (Mrs.
  Lewis M. Porter, Jr.)

Porter, John Willard
Porter, John Wilson
Porter, Philip Wayland
Porter, Rutherford B.
Porter, Walter Arthur
Porterfield, Neil Harry
Porth, Donald Lester
Porthouse, Cyril Routledge
Portoghese, Philip Salvatore
Posner, Harry A., Jr.
Posnick, Adolph
Poss, Mark Albert
Potchen, Edward James
Pott, Herman Theodore
Potter, Charles Steele
Potter, David Samuel
Potter, Donald Albert
Potter, Robert Joseph
Pottner, M. Richard
Potts, Robert Henderson
Pour-El, Marian Boykan
Poust, John G.
Povish, Kenneth Joseph
Povolny, Mojmir
Powell, Edmund William
Powell, George Everett, Jr.
Powell, James Lawrence
Powell, Max Courtney
Power, Eugene Barnum
Power, F. William
Power, Fremont Alvin
Power, Philip Harwick
Power, Sarah Goddard
Power, William Anthony
Powers, Anne
Powers, Harris Pat
Powers, John R.
Powers, Odell Eugene
Powers, Raymond Edwin, Jr.
Powers, Robert M.
Powers, Robert Throop
Powers, Ronald Clair
Poznanski, Andrew Karol
Poznanski, Elva Orlow
Pozzatti, Rudy Otto
Prager, David
Prager, Stephen
Prange, Henry Carl
Pranses, Anthony Louis
Prasad, Ananda Shiva
Pratt, Dan Edwin
Pratt, Donald Henry
Pratt, Edward Lowell
Pratt, Joseph Hyde, Jr.
Pratt, Philip
Pratt, William Crouch, Jr.
Pray, Lloyd Charles
Preckshot, George William
Preer, John Randolph, Jr.
Prell, Arthur Ely
Prem, Konald Arthur
Prensky, Arthur Lawrence
Prentice, Dixon Wright
Prentiss, Louis Watkins, Jr.
Preparata, Franco Paolo
Preschlack, John Edward
Preska, Margaret Louise
  Robinson
Press, Charles
Preston, David Michael
Preul, Herbert Charles
Preus, David Walter
Preus, Jacob Aall Ottesen
Preus, Robert David
Preuss, Roger E(mil)
Preves, Milton
Price, Charles Harry
Price, Dalias Adolph
Price, David Cecil Long
Price, David Robert
Price, Donald Albert
Price, Edwin Farrow
Price, Harry Steele, Jr.
Price, Jacob Myron
Price, James Gordon
Price, John Leyland
Price, Melvin
Price, Paul Edward
Priestley, William Turk
Primuth, David J.
Prince, Albert Irving
Prince, Kenneth C.
Prince, Thomas Richard
Pringle, Andrew, Jr.
Pringle, Oran Allan
Prinz, John Sebastian, III
Prior, John Alan
Pritchard, Raymond E.
Pritchard, Walter Herbert
Pritikin, Roland I.
Pritsker, A.B.
Pritzker, Abram Nicholas
Pritzker, Jay Arthur
Pritzker, Robert Alan
Priver, Julien
Probst, Walter F.
Prochnow, Herbert Victor
Prochnow, Herbert Victor, Jr.
Proctor, Barbara Gardner
Proctor, Paul Dean
Proctor, William Zinsmaster
Proffer, Ellendea Catherine
Proffitt, Roy Franklin
Prokasy, William Frederick
Proost, Robert Lee
Prosser, Franklin Pierce
Proud, G. O'Neil
Proudfoot, Allin Whitfield
Prouty, Chilton Eaton
Provost, Wally (Wallace B.)
Pruis, John J
Pruitt, Gregory Donald
Pruitt, Raymond Donald
Prus, Francis Vincent
Pruter, Karl Hugo
Pry, Robert Henry

Pry, Robert Henry
Przemieniecki, Janusz
  Stanislaw
Psaltis, John Costas
Puchta, Charles George
Puckett, Robert Hugh
Puffer, Richard Judson
Pugh, Richard Conelley
Pugh, Roderick Wellington
Pulford, Robert Jesse (Bob)
Pulitzer, Emily S. Rauh (Mrs.
  Joseph Pulitzer, Jr.)
Pulitzer, Joseph, Jr.
Pulitzer, Michael Edgar
Pulliam, Eugene Smith
Pulliam, Nina Mason (Mrs.
  Eugene C. Pulliam)
Pumper, Robert William
Punzo, Vincent Christopher
Purcell, James Francis
Purcell, Martin James
Purdy, Charles Robert
Puri, Madan Lal
Purse, James Nathaniel
Purves, Alan Carroll
Putka, Andrew Charles
Putman, Dale Cornelius
Putman, Paul
Putnam, Allan Ray
Putnam, Calvin Richard
Putnam, Frank William
Putnam, Leon Joseph
Putnam, Robert E.
Putney, Mark William
Pyle, Everett Gustav
Pyle, Francis Johnson
Pytell, Robert Henry
Quaal, Ward Louis
Quackenbush, Austin Joseph,
  Jr.
Quade, Quentin Lon
Qualey, Carlton Chester
Quamme, Jack O.
Quarles, Albert Merold
Quarton, William Barlow
Quayle, Calvin King
Quayle, Dan
Queller, Donald Edward
Quellmalz, Frederick
Quenon, Robert Hagerty
Query, Joy Marves Neale
Quie, Albert Harold
Quie, Paul Gerhardt
Quigg, Chris
Quigley, Joseph Milton
Quimby, Robert Sherman
Quinlan, Joseph Edward
Quinlan, Sterling Carroll
Quinn, Bayard Elmer
Quinn, James Leonard
Quinn, Robert Henry
Quinn, Robert Kevin
Quinn, William John
Quintana, Ricardo Beckwith
Quirk, James Patrick
Raab, G. Kirk
Rabahy, Donald Lian
Rabb, George B.
Rabinovich, Sergio
Rachie, Carol
Raclin, Ernestine Morris
Radecki, Anthony Eugene
Radell, Nicholas John
Rademacher, Richard Joseph
Radin, Norman Samuel
Radinsky, Leonard
Radler, Warren S.
Raeburn, Andrew Harvey
Rafelson, Max Emanuel, Jr.
Raffel, Louis Benjamin
Rafferty, Nancy Schwarz
Ragan, Roy Allen
Ragone, David Vincent
Ragsdale, Wilmott
Rahl, James Andrew
Rahman, Yueh-Erh
Rahn, Alvin Albert
Rainsford, George Nichols
Rajki, Walter Albert
Raju, Satyanarayana
  Gottumukkala Venkata
Rakel, Robert Edwin
Rakestraw, Warren Vincent
Rakita, Louis
Rall, Owen
Ralston, Lloyd Stanley
Ramakrishnan, Venkataswamy
Ramaley, Judith Aitken
Ramanauskas-Marconic,
  Helene Maria Apollonia
  Stroecker
Ramberg, Christina
Rambo, James Edmondson
Ramey, Joseph Frederick
Ramirez, Domingo Victor
Ramlow, Donald Eric
Ramsey, Frederick William, II
Ramsey, John Hansberry
Ramsey, Paul Willard
Ramsey, William Lee
Rand, Phillip Gordon
Randall, Clarence A.
Randall, James Edwin
Randall, James R.
Randall, Walter Clark
Randall, William Seymour
Randerson, John Tremper
Randolph, Jennings (Jay), Jr.
Raney, Leon
Rankin, Alfred Marshall, Jr.
Rannells, Will
Ranney, George Alfred
Ranz, Jim
Rao, Nannapaneni Narayana
Raoul-Duval, Michael
Raphaelson, Joel

Rapkin, Joseph E.
Rapoport, Ronald Jon
Rapp, Gerald Duane
Rappaport, Earle Samuel, Jr.
Rappaport, Gary Burton
Rappaport, Roy Abraham
Rapson, Ralph
Rasche, Donald Paul
Rashad, Ahmad (Bobby
  Moore)
Rashid, Moinuddin Sirdar
Rasin, Rudolph Stephen
Raskind, Leo Joseph
Raskosky, Edward J.
Rasmus, Robert Nelson
Rasmusen, Roger Ward
Rasmussen, Glen Russell
Ratcliffe, Myron Fenwick
Rath, Gustave Joseph
Rath, R. John
Rathmann, Franz Heinrich
Rathmann, George Blatz
Ratigan, William
Ratliff, Eugene Field
Ratner, Gerald
Ratner, Lazarus Gershon
Ratner, Milton Dunne
Ratnoff, Oscar Davis
Ratzkin, Jack L.
Rauch, George Washington
Rauen, Arnold John
Rauh, John David
Raup, David Malcolm
Rausch, George Jay, Jr.
Raushenbush, Walter Brandeis
Raven, Peter Hamilton
Ravenhall, David Geoffrey
Rawley, James Albert
Rawski, Conrad H(enry)
Rawson, Merle R.
Rawson, William Robert
Ray, C. Eugene
Ray, Charles Dean
Ray, David Eugene
Ray, Linton Grier, Jr.
Ray, Robert D.
Ray, Robert D.
Ray, Robert Frederick
Ray, Roy Lee
Rayman, Warren Samuel
Raymer, Donald George
Raynor, John Patrick
Rayward, Warden Boyd
Raz, Robert Eugene
Razak, Charles Kenneth
Read, Frank Thompson
Read, John Conyers
Reading, James Edward
Reams, Bernard Dinsmore, Jr.
Reardon, John Edward
Reardon, Leonard Wood
Reavis, John Wallace
Rebeiz, Constantin Anis
Rebenack, John Henry
Reber, William Dewey
Rechholtz, Robert August
Reck, W(aldo) Emerson
Recknagel, Richard Otto
Rector, Gail Wesley
Redden, Jack Allison
Redding, Foster Kinyon
Reder, Melvin W.
Reding, Nicholas Lee
Redman, William Charles
Redmond, Robert Francis
Redmond, Walter T.
Redmond, William Aloysius
Redstone, Louis Gordon
Reed, A(lfred) Byron
Reed, Charles Allen
Reed, Charles Emmett
Reed, Darwin Cramer
Reed, John Frederick
Reed, John Shedd
Reed, John Wesley
Reed, Robert George, III
Reed, Robert Holbrooke
Reed, Ronald Swain, Jr.
Reed, Thomas Ansley
Reed, Walter Dudley
Reeder, Clifton Lee
Reeder, Lee
Reedy, George Edward
Reedy, Jerry Edward
Reedy, John Louis
Rees, Warren James
Reese, Anne Catherine Ohlson
  (Mrs. Edwin Lee Reese)
Reese, Everett D.
Reese, Francis Edward
Reese, John Gilbert
Reeves, Charles Howell
Reeves, J. Douglas
Reeves, James Louis
Refior, Everett Lee
Regan, John K.
Regensteiner, Else Friedsam
  (Mrs. Bertold Regensteiner)
Regnery, Henry
Reh, Carl William
Rehm, Leo Frank
Rehner, Herbert Adrian
Rehnstrom, Vernley Rae
Reice, Charles Thomas
Reich, Edgar
Reich, Jack Egan
Reichard, Hugo Manley
Reichert, David
Reichert, Jack Frank
Reichert, Norman Vernon
Reid, George Williams
Reid, James Sims, Jr.
Reid, John Edward
Reid, Loren Dudley
Reidenbaugh, Lowell Henry
Reidy, John Joseph

Reidy, William Edward
Reiff, Guy Gene
Reiffel, Leonard
Reil, John Edward
Reilly, Frank Kelly
Reilly, Joseph William
Reims, Clifford Waldemar
Reiner, Irving
Reinert, Paul Clare
Reinertsen, Norman
Reingold, Haim
Reinhard, Keith Leon
Reinhardt, Siegfried Gerhard
Reinke, John Henry
Reinke, Ralph Louis
Reinkemeyer, Sister Agnes M.
Reinsdorf, Jerry Michael
Reisman, Arnold
Reitan, Daniel Kinseth
Reitemeier, Richard Joseph
Reiter, Stanley
Reitman, Robert Stanley
Reizen, Maurice S.
Remick, Oscar Eugene
Remington, Frank John
Remini, Robert Vincent
Renda, Randolph Bruce
Rendlen, Albert Lewis
Renken, Henry Algernon
Renner, Robert George
Rennie, Robert Alvin
Reno, Roger
Renshaw, Charles Clark, Jr.
Rensi, Edward Henry
Replinger, John Gordon
Replogle, Frederick Allen
ReQua, Eloise Gallup
Requarth, William Henry
Resch, Glenn Allan
Resch, Joseph Anthony
Resek, Robert William
Reshotko, Eli
Restemeyer, William Edward
Retzler, Kurt Egon
Reuben, Don H.
Reuss, Lloyd Edwin Armin
Reuss, Richard Eugene
Reuss, Robert Pershing
Reusswig, Frederick Webster
Reuter, George Edward
Revzin, Marvin E.
Rexroth, Nancy Louise
Reynolds, A. William
Reynolds, Clarke Eldred
Reynolds, Ellsworth Galbraith
Reynolds, Ernest West
Reynolds, Fred Curtis
Reynolds, John W.
Reynolds, Marc C.
Reynolds, Samuel Williams
Reynolds, Warren Lind
Reynolds, Wynetka Ann
Reynoldson, Walter Ward
Reznikoff, William Stanton
Rhind, James Thomas
Rhoden, Elmer Carl
Rhodes, Ashby Marshall
Rhodes, Charles Kirkham
Rhodes, Irwin Seymour
Rhodes, James Allen
Rice, (Ethel) Ann
Rice, Clare Irwin
Rice, John Rischard
Rice, Raymond Main
Rice, Stuart Alan
Rice, Walter Herbert
Rich, Michael James
Rich, Rosemary
Rich, Travis Dean
Rich, Willis Frank, Jr.
Richard, Bruce Albert
Richards, Gilbert Francis
Richards, John Noble
Richards, Riley Harry
Richards, Roger Claude
Richards, Stanley
Richards, Stanley Harold
Richards, William Frederick
Richardson, David Vivian
Richardson, Dean Eugene
Richardson, Frank Charles
Richardson, John Thomas
Richart, Frank Edwin, Jr.
Richey, Herbert Southall
Richey, Robert Wayne
Richey, Thomas Adam
Richman, Harold Alan
Richman, John Marshall
Richman, Sumner
Ricketts, Gary Eugene
Ricketts, John Adrian
Ricketts, Thomas Roland
Rickey, Martin Eugene
Ricks, Donald Jay
Riddell, Matthew Donald
  Rutherford
Ridder, Bernard Herman, Jr.
Riddle, Donald Husted
Ridenour, Ruth Jean
Ridlen, Julian Leon
Riedy, John K.
Riegle, Gail Daniel
Rielly, John Edward
Ries, Herman Elkan, Jr.
Rigdon, Vernon Drew
Riggs, Byron Lawrence, Jr.
Righter, Walter Cameron
Rigsbee, William Alton
Riley, David Clyde
Riley, Harold Marvin
Riley, James Joseph
Riley, Patrick Gavan Duffy
Riley, Robert Bartlett
Riley, Thomas Austin
Rim, Kwan
Rinder, George Greer

Rinder, Irwin Daniel
Rinehart, Raymond George
Ring, Gerald J.
Ringel, Robert Lewis
Ringler, Ira
Ringo, Boyd Colburn
Ringoen, Richard Miller
Rink, Susan
Rinsley, Donald Brendan
Ripley, Randall Butler
Rippy, Frances Marguerite
  Mayhew
Ris, Hans
Risch, William H.
Risk, J. Fred
Riss, Robert Bailey
Risse, Guenter Bernhard
Risser, Paul Gillan
Ristine, Richard Osborne
Ritchie, Richard Lee
Riter, Vernon Max
Ritschel, Michael Coleman
Ritten, Donald C.
Rittenhouse, Joseph Wilson
Ritts, Roy Ellot, Jr.
River, Louis Philip
Rivette, Gerard Bertram
Rivkin, Ellis
Rixmann, Donald John
Roach, John Robert
Roach, Thomas Adair
Robb, Walter Lee
Robbins, Henry Zane
Robbins, Lawrence Harry
Robbins-Carter, Jane Borsch
Robeck, Gordon G.
Robek, Mary Frances
Robenalt, John Alton
Robert, Henry Flood, Jr.
Roberts, Bruce Everett
Roberts, Burnell Richard
Roberts, Charles Corwin
Roberts, Clyde Francis
Roberts, Edwin Albert, Jr.
Roberts, Harry Vivian
Roberts, Hugh Evan
Roberts, Janet Louise (also
  Louisa Bronte, Rebecca
  Danton, Janette Radcliffe)
Roberts, Leigh Milton
Roberts, Rosalee Ann
Roberts, Seymour M. (Skip)
Roberts, Theodore Harris
Roberts, William B.
Robertson, Abel Alfred
  Lazzarini, Jr.
Robeson, Mark D.
Robinett, Betty Jane
Robins, Eli
Robins, Lee Nelken
Robinson, Alexander
  Cochrane, III
Robinson, Arthur Howard
Robinson, Donald Keith
Robinson, Farrel Richard
Robinson, Gerald Dean
Robinson, Hubert Nelson
Robinson, Jack Albert
Robinson, James Kenneth
Robinson, Jay Luke
Robinson, John Hamilton
Robinson, John Talbot
Robinson, Joseph Albert
Robinson, Larry J.B.
Robinson, Max
Robinson, R(aymond) Wayne
Robinson, Renault Alvin
Robinson, Richard Earl
Robinson, Richard Norman
Robinson, S. Benton
Robinson, Thomas Bullene
Robinson, Walter Stitt, Jr.
Robinson, Wilkes Coleman
Robinson, William Ingraham
Robison, Richard Ashby
Robold, Alice Ilene
Robson, Edwin Albert
Robson, Ernest Sydney, Jr.
Robson, John Edwin
Roby, Donald Franklin
Rocek, Jan
Roche, George Charles, III
Rockwell, Perry Jack, Jr.
Rockwell, R(onald) James, Jr.
Rod, Donald Olaf
Roddick, John William, Jr.
Rode, Arne Robert
Rode, James Dean
Rodehorst, Wayne
Rodenberg, Sidney Dan
Rodin, Ernst Anton
Rodman, George Bush
Rodman, Hugh Burgess
Rodman, James Purcell
Rodriguez-Erdmann, Franz
Roe, Jerrold Melvin
Roe, Richard C.
Roeder, Robert Gayle
Roenigk, Henry Herman
Roesch, Raymond August
Roesner, Peter Lowell
Rogers, A. Robert
Rogers, Bryan Allen
Rogers, Charles B.
Rogers, Charles Edwin
Rogers, Joe E.
Rogers, Justin Towner, Jr.
Rogers, Lawrence H., II
Rogers, Lee Frank
Rogers, Max Tofield
Rogers, Millard Foster, Jr.
Rogers, Richard Dean
Rogers, Richard Hunter
Rogers, Richard Wallace
Rogers, Robert Wentworth
Rogers, Rodney Albert

Rogers, Talmage Gregory, Jr.
Rogers, Vance Donald
Rogers, William Cecil
Rogosheske, Walter Frederick
Rogula, James LeRoy
Rohman, David Gordon
Rohmann, Paul Henry
Rohn, Robert J.
Roig, Lester Clarence
Roizman, Bernard
Roland, Johnny Earl
Rolf, Albert William
Rolfe, Stanley Theodore
Rolfs, Bemiss Alvin
Roll, Marlin Henry
Rolland, Ian McKenzie
Rolls, John Allison
Rom, Irving
Rom, M. Martin
Romani, John Henry
Romanowski, Thomas Andrew
Romans, Donald Bishop
Romney, George
Romzick, Marguerite (Mrs. Vernon C. Romzick)
Ronca, Luciano Bruno
Roney, William Chapoton, Jr.
Rooke, David Lee
Rooks, Raymond Newton
Roomann, Hugo
Rooney, John Edward
Roos, Lawrence K.
Roose, Henry Rasmussen
Root, John O.
Rootes, Charles Wesley
Roper, Raymond Warren, Jr.
Rorick, Alan Green
Rosa, Clarence Henry
Rosavage, A. Richard
Rosberg, Joffre Wesley
Rose, Albert Johnson
Rose, Doyle Lee
Rose, Horace Chapman
Rose, James Turner
Rose, Jerzy Edwin
Rose, Michael Dean
Rose, Noel Richard
Rose, Richard Carlisle
Rose, Robert Carlisle
Rose, Rowland G.
Rose, William Richard
Rosebery, Dean Arlo
Rosegger, Gerhard
Roseliep, Raymond
Roselle, William Charles
Rosen, George
Rosen, Judah Ben
Rosen, Sherwin
Rosen, Simon Peter
Rosenbaum, Irving Joseph
Rosenberg, Hermann Paul
Rosenberg, Irwin Harold
Rosenberg, Milton J.
Rosenberg, Norman Jack
Rosenberg, Robert Brinkmann
Rosenberg, Robert Melvin
Rosenblatt, Judah Isser
Rosenbloom, Alfred A., Jr.
Rosenblum, Victor Gregory
Rosenfeld, Arnold Solomon
Rosenfeld, Mark Kenneth
Rosenheim, Edward Weil
Rosenheim, Howard Harris
Rosenheim, Margaret Keeney
Rosenow, John Henry
Rosenow, Thomas Lloyd
Rosenson, Jay Harold
Rosenthal, Amnon
Rosenthal, Arnold H.
Rosenthal, Bernard Gordon
Rosenthal, Earl Edgar
Rosenthal, Gary
Rosenthal, Ira Maurice
Rosenthal, Leighton A.
Rosenthal, Norman
Rosenthal, Samuel Robert
Rosenzweig, David Lee
Rosenzweig, Saul
Rosett, Richard Nathaniel
Roskam, Jan.
Roskens, Ronald William
Rosloniec, James Joseph
Rosner, Jorge
Rosofsky, Seymour
Ross, Donald Eugene
Ross, Donald Kenneth
Ross, Donald Roe
Ross, Edwin Francis
Ross, Frank Gaylord
Ross, Hugh Alan
Ross, Leonard Ellis
Ross, Louis Robert
Ross, Norman Alexander
Ross, Patrick Conroy
Ross, Russell Marion
Ross, William Edwin
Rosser, John Barkley
Rosser, Richard Franklin
Rossi, Anthony Gerald
Rossi, Harry
Rossman, Elmer Chris
Rossmann, Michael George
Rost, William Joseph
Rostenkowski, Dan
Rostoker, William
Roszkowski, Stanley Julian
Roth, Charles Howell
Roth, Daniel Benjamin
Roth, Edwin Morton Parkin
Roth, Frederic Hull
Roth, Jack Joseph
Roth, Toby
Rothberg, Sol
Rothchild, Irving
Rothe, Kenneth Warren
Rothenberg, Gunther Erich
Rothermich, Norman Oliver
Rothing, Frank John
Rothman, Kenneth Joel
Rothmeier, Steven George
Rothschild, George William
Rothschild, Michael
Rothstein, Morton
Rothwell, Jack C., Jr.
Rothwell, Warren Randall
Rotman, Morris Bernard
Roub, Bryan Roger
Roudebush, George M.
Roulston, Thomas Henry
Rountree, Wilbur Dekle, Jr.
Rouze, Robert Lloyd
Rowan, Gerald Burdette
Rowan, Robert Dale
Rowe, Brian Henry
Rowe, Clair Devere
Rowe, Clarence John
Rowe, David Thomas
Rowe, George Giles
Rowe, Jack Field
Rowe, Max L.
Rowe, Nathaniel Hawthorne
Rowe, Paul Nicholas
Rowe, William Stanhope
Rowell, John Austin
Rowland, Raymond Edgar
Rowland, Robert Edmund
Rowland, Theodore Justin
Rowles, Charles Wesley, Jr.
Rowley, Calvin E.
Rowley, Donald A.
Rowley, Janet Davison
Rownd, Robert Harvey
Roy, Charles Robert
Roy, Ross
Roy, William Robert
Royko, Mike
Rubel, Arthur Joseph
Ruben, Alan Miles
Ruben, Gary A.
Ruben, James Harris
Rubenstein, Albert Harold
Rubenstein, Arthur Harold
Rubenstein, Bernard
Rubin, Abe
Rubin, Alan J.
Rubin, Carl Bernard
Rubin, David Robert
Rubin, Jean Estelle
Rubloff, Arthur
Rubloff, Burton
Ruby, Burton Bennett
Rudd, Dale Frederick
Rudelius, William
Ruder, David Sturtevant
Rudin, Mary Ellen
Rudman, Herbert Charles
Rudney, Harry
Rudo, Milton
Rudolf, Claudia Mignon
Rudolph, Gerald Allen
Rudolph, Karl Henry
Rudolph, Lavere Christian
Rudolph, Lloyd Irving
Rudolph, Richard Hinman
Rudy, Lester Howard
Rudy, Peter
Ruedenberg, Klaus
Ruedisili, Chester Henry
Ruegamer, William Raymond
Ruegsegger, Alcid Devere
Ruehlmann, Eugene Peter
Ruether, Rosemary Radford
Ruffner, Frederick G., Jr.
Ruggiero, Fred F.
Ruggles, Rudy Lamont
Ruhe, C(arl) H(enry) William
Ruhe, Robert Victory
Ruhlin, William Ritter
Ruiter, Michael Thomas
Rumman, Wadi (Saliba)
Rummel, Charles Garman
Rumsfeld, Donald
Rung, Richard Allen
Runge, Donald Edward
Runice, Robert E.
Runke, Darrell M.
Rupert, (Lynn) Hoover
Rupert, John Edward
Rupp, Ralph Russell
Rupp, Robert George
Ruppert, Richard Dale
Rusch, Harold Paul
Rushing, Robert Kyger
Russ, Fritz Junior
Russe, Henry Paul
Russell, David L(awson)
Russell, Francis Garland, Jr.
Russell, Frank E.
Russell, George Albert
Russell, Ralston, Jr.
Russell, Richard Lee
Russell, Robert Gilmore
Russell, Robert William
Russell, Thomas Frank
Russell, Thomas Smith
Russell, Wallace Addison
Russell, William Bruce
Russo, Joseph Robert
Rust, Edward Barry
Rustagi, Jagdish Sharan
Rutford, Robert Hoxie
Ruth, William Edward
Ruthenberg, Donald Burton
Rutherford, Jack Dow
Rutherford, James William
Rutledge, James Albert
Rutledge, William Alvin
Ruttan, Vernon Wesley
Rutterer, Paul James Matthew
Rutz, Donald Edwin
Ruzic, Neil Pierce
Ruzicka, Francis Frederick, Jr.
Ryan, Edwin Leo, Jr.
Ryan, Frances Mary
Ryan, George
Ryan, Howard Chris
Ryan, Jack
Ryan, James Leo
Ryan, John M.
Ryan, John Raymond
Ryan, John William
Ryan, Leo Vincent
Ryan, Michael Allan
Ryan, Michael Beecher
Ryan, Robert John
Ryan, Robert S.
Ryan, Tom Kreusch
Ryan, William Edward
Rybolt, Robert Marsh
Ryckman, DeVere Wellington
Rycroft, Donald Cahill
Ryder, George Conklin
Rydholm, Eber Harwood
Rydholm, Ralph Williams
Rye, Howard Henry
Ryor, John
Ryun, James Ronald
Saada, Adel Selim
Sabates, Felix Nabor
Sabath, Leon David
Sabatini, Frank Carmine
Sabelli, Hector Carlos
Sable, Henry Zodoc
Sable, Martin Howard
Sachs, Alan Arthur
Sachs, Howard F(rederic)
Sachs, Robert Green
Sachtleben, Carl Henry
Sackett, William Tecumseh, Jr.
Sacks, Norman Paul
Saddler, Owen Leslie
Sade, Donald Stone
Sadler, Richard Thomas
Sadler, Robert Edward
Saffels, Dale Emerson
Saffran, Murray
Safran, Hyman
Sagan, Bruce
Sagan, John
Sage, Robert Floyd
Sager, Donald Jack
Sager, Richard James
Sager, William F.
St. Mary, Edward Sylvester
St. Pierre, George Roland, Jr.
St. Pierre, Ronald Leslie
Salamon, Myron Ben
Salamone, Ronald John
Salassa, Robert Maurice
Salci, Larry Eugene
Salem, Lee
Salem, Sam
Saligman, Harvey
Salisbury, Robert Holt
Salkin, Morrey Lee
Sally, Paul Joseph, Jr.
Salmonson, Roland Frank
Salomon, Roger Blaine
Salter, Lewis Spencer
Saltzman, Glenn Alan
Saltzman, Irving Jackson
Saltzman, Maurice
Saltzman, William
Salvendy, Gavriel
Salvino, Carmen Mario
Salvino, S. M.
Samelson, Lincoln Russell
Sammons, James Harris
Samora, Julian
Sample, Sewell Vincent
Sampsell, Robert Bruce
Sampson, Harold Peck
Sampson, Herbert Martin, Jr.
Sampson, Jack Shearer
Sampson, Patsy Hallock
Sampson, Sigved Theodore
Samter, Max
Samuel, Gerhard
Samuelsen, Roy
Sanborn, Theodore
Sances, Anthony, Jr.
Sand, Paul Meinrad
Sandalow, Terrance
Sandblom, Robert Leland
Sandbulte, Arend John
Sandburg, Helga
Sande, Theodore Anton
Sandeen, Ernest Robert
Sandell, Ernest Birger
Sanders, Norman O.
Sanders, W(illiam) Eugene, Jr.
Sanders, Wallace Wolfred, Jr.
Sanders, William Huggins
Sanderson, Edmund Whitford
Sandeson, William Seymour
Sandgren, Find
Sandner, John Francis
Sandor, Gyorgy
Sands, Ernest Monroe
Sanford, Paul Everett
Sang, Elsie Olin (Mrs. Philip David Sang)
Sanner, Royce Norman
Sanstead, Wayne Godfrey
Sant, John Talbot
Santelman, Roger Dean
Santoni, Ronald Ernest
Sargent, Thomas Andrew
Saricks, Ambrose
Sarkesian, Sam Charles
Sarles, William Bowen
Sasenick, Joseph Anthony
Saslow, Daniel L.
Sata, Lindbergh Saburo
Sather, John Henry
Satovsky, Abraham
Satterlee, Lowell Duggan
Sauer, Gordon Chenoweth
Sauer, Harry John, Jr.
Sauerteig, Paul John
Sault, Russell Arthur
Saum, Burnell Frank
Saunders, Doris Evans
Saunders, James Henry
Saunders, John Allen
Saunders, Kenneth D.
Saunders, Warren Phillip, Jr.
Saunders, William Howerton
Sauvey, Donald (Robert)
Savage, Gus
Savin, Samuel Marvin
Sawtell, Stephen M.
Sawyer, John
Sawyer, Robert McLaran
Sawyer, William Dale
Sax, Joseph Lawrence
Sax, Stanley Paul
Saxbe, William Bart
Saxer, Richard Karl
Saxton, William Marvin
Sayad, Homer Elisha
Sayers, Gale
Sayers, Martin Peter
Sayre, Robert Freeman
Scales, Harold Edward
Scalia, Antonin
Scanlon, Charles Franklin
Scanlon, Edward F.
Scanlon, Gerard Thomas
Scanlon, Thomas Michael
Scannell, Dale Paul
Scannell, Francis Xavier
Scantland, Donald Maurice
Scarff, S. Thomas
Scarpelli, Dante Giovanni
Scarpino, Pasquale Valentine
Schaack, Philip Anthony
Schaaf, James Howard
Schacht, Henry Brewer
Schacht, Richard Lawrence
Schaefer, Arnold Albert
Schaefer, Clarence Harold
Schaefer, Edward John
Schaefer, Gordon E.
Schaenen, Lee Joel
Schafer, Michael Frederick
Schaffer, Donald L.
Schaleben, Arville
Schall, Richard Langley
Schaller, Warren Edward
Schanck, Francis Raber
Schanck, Jordan Thomas
Schanda, Royce LaVerne
Schatz, Albert Gerard
Schauer, Wilbert Edward, Jr.
Schaus, Frederick A.
Schechter, Allen E(dward)
Schedler, Thomas Roger
Scheele, Paul Drake
Scheerenberger, Richard Charles
Scheetz, Sister Mary JoEllen
Scheifele, Stuart
Scheig, Henry Frederick
Scheinfeld, James David
Schell, Joseph Otis
Schelske, Claire L.
Schembechler, Glenn Edward
Schenck, Richard Elwood
Schene, Herbert Mauro
Schenk, Boyd Frederick
Schenk, Quentin Frederick
Schenker, Eric
Scher, Jordan Mayer
Scherer, Gordon Harry
Schermerhorn, Kenneth DeWitt
Schick, Thomas Andrew
Schiefelbusch, Richard L.
Schier, Donald Stephen
Schierholz, William Francis, Jr.
Schierl, Paul Julius
Schieve, George Robert
Schiff, Herbert Harold
Schiffer, John Paul
Schiller, Alfred George
Schilpp, Paul Arthur
Schiltz, Evan Bitzer
Schiltz, Richard Joseph
Schinderle, Robert Frank
Schindler, Alfred
Schindler, Marvin Samuel
Schindler, William Stanley
Schirmer, Henry William
Schlack, Alois Leo, Jr.
Schlafly, Phyllis Stewart
Schlechte, Walter August
Schleck, Roth Stephen
Schlegel, Richard
Schlegel, Robert Philip
Schlegel, Walter Lothar, Jr.
Schlesinger, Joseph Abraham
Schleusener, Richard August
Schlickau, George Hans
Schloss, Milton Joseph
Schlosser, George McGarraugh
Schlotfeldt, Rozella May
Schlussel, Mark Edward
Schmid, William Jacob
Schmidt, Albert Daniel
Schmidt, Alexander MacKay
Schmidt, Glenn Walter
Schmidt, Jakob Edward
Schmidt, John Joseph
Schmidt, John Richard
Schmidt, Julius
Schmidt, Milton Otto
Schmidt, Robert
Schmidt, Stephen Christopher
Schmiel, Edgar Herman
Schmitt, Edward Henry
Schmitt, George Frederick, Jr.
Schmitt, Henry Joseph
Schmitt, John Arvid, Jr.
Schmitt, Mark F.
Schnabel, John Henry
Schnabel, Robert Victor
Schnackenberg, Roy
Schnaiberg, Allan
Schneideman, Robert Ivan
Schneider, Arthur Sanford
Schneider, David Murray
Schneider, Donald Frederic
Schneider, Duane Bernard
Schneider, Erwin Henry
Schneider, Harold Joel
Schneider, Harold K.
Schneider, James Gordon
Schneider, Michael Joseph
Schneider, Richard Coy
Schneider, William George
Schneiderman, Howard Allen
Schneiderman, Leonard
Schnoes, Robert Frederick
Schnore, Leo F.
Schober, Glenn E.
Schoellhorn, Robert A.
Schoen, Kenneth Aloys
Schoenberg, Harry Wechsler
Schoenbrunn, Lee Ernst
Schoenfeld, Frederick Paul
Schoenfeld, Hanns-Martin Walter
Schoenherr, Walter Joseph
Schoenke, Richard Warren
Schoepfle, Otto Benjamin, Jr.
Schoepke, Hollis George
Schofield, Robert Edwin
Schofield, William
Scholer, Walter, Jr.
Scholle, Roger Hal
Schönemann, Peter Hans
Schornack, John James
Schornstein, Dave Wilbur
Schorr, Alvin Louis
Schottelkotte, James Edward
Schowen, Richard Lyle
Schrader, Lee Frederick
Schrag, Edward A., Jr.
Schrage, Paul Daniel
Schram, William Clarence
Schramm, David Norman
Schreiber, Arthur Adolphus
Schreiber, George Richard
Schreiber, Joan Emelia
Schreier, John Frank
Schreiner, Albert William
Schreiner, John Christian
Schrey, Jack William
Schrier, Arnold
Schrock, Harold Arthur
Schroeder, Alfred Gustav
Schroeder, Edwin Melvin
Schroeder, Gary Keith
Schroeder, Oliver Charles, Jr.
Schroeder, Robert Anthony
Schroeder, Walter John
Schroer, Edmund Armin
Schuba, Kenneth Florian
Schubert, William Kuenneth
Schuchart, John Albert, Jr.
Schuele, Donald Edward
Schuenke, Donald John
Schuerman, John Richard
Schuessler, Karl Frederick
Schuh, G(eorge) Edward
Schuler, Robert Hugo
Schulian, John Nielsen
Schuller, Ivan Kohn
Schulman, Ivan Albert
Schulman, Sidney
Schulte, David Michael
Schultz, Arthur Warren
Schultz, Carl Herbert
Schultz, Gerald Ernest
Schultz, Jerome Samson
Schultz, Louis William
Schultz, Richard Carlton
Schultz, Richard deWyl
Schultz, Richard Otto
Schultz, Robert James
Schultz, Theodore William
Schultz, William Louis
Schulz, Howard Neff
Schulz, Rockwell Irwin
Schulz, Rudolph Walter
Schulz, Valdyn
Schulze, Arthur Robert, Jr.
Schulze, Erwin Emil
Schulze, Franz, Jr.
Schumacher, Berthold Walter
Schumacher, Gebhard Friederich Bernhard
Schumacher, Robert Kent
Schuman, Harold Leroy
Schuman, Howard
Schuman, Leonard Michael
Schumann, Frederick John
Schumann, Robert William
Schumer, William
Schupp, Paul Eugene
Schur, Leon Milton
Schurman, Donald Glenn
Schurz, Franklin D.
Schurz, Franklin Dunn, Jr.
Schurz, Scott Clark
Schuster, Seymour
Schutt, Walter Eugene
Schutta, Henry Szczesny
Schutte, William Metcalf
Schuyler, Daniel Merrick
Schwab, Bernard
Schwab, Lois Opper (Mrs. Kendall Dreisbach Schwab)
Schwanz, H(erman) Lee
Schwartz, Alan E.
Schwartz, Alfred
Schwartz, Arnold
Schwartz, Carl Edward
Schwartz, Franklin David
Schwartz, Henry Gerard
Schwartz, Irving Donn
Schwartz, Joseph
Schwartz, Michael Robinson
Schwartz, Neena Betty
Schwartz, Robert
Schwartz, Theodore B.
Schwartz, Thomas D.
Schwarz, Egon
Schwarz, Josephine Lindeman
Schwarz, Richard William
Schweickart, Jim
Schweikert, Norman Carl
Schwemm, John Butler
Schweppe, Harry Nelson, Jr.
Schwertfeger, Floyd Edward
Schwier, Frederick Warren
Schwilck, Gene Leroy
Schwimmer, Walter
Scofield, Gordon Lloyd
Scommegna, Antonio
Scotford, David Matteson
Scott, Charles Lewis
Scott, David C.
Scott, Gary Kuper
Scott, George Ernest
Scott, George Matthew
Scott, James White
Scott, Jerome Hayes
Scott, John Paul
Scott, Leslie Wright
Scott, Ralph C.
Scott, Robert Kent
Scott, Theodore R.
Scott, Wallace M., Jr.
Scott, Walter Dill
Scott, Walter O'Daniel
Scott, Will
Scovil, Samuel Kingston
Scoville, James Griffin
Scribner, Gilbert Hilton, Jr.
Scripps, Charles Edward
Scriven, L. E(dward), (II)
Scully, Joseph C.
Seabury, John Ward
Seacrest, Joseph Rushton
Sealy, Albert Henry
Sealy, George Paul
Seaman, Gerald Robert
Seaman, Irving, Jr.
Seaman, William Casper
Searer, R. Floyd
Searle, Daniel Crow
Searle, Rodney Newell
Searle, William Louis
Sears, Ernest Robert
Sears, Walter Edwin
Sease, Gene Elwood
Seaton, Kenneth Duncan
Seaton, Richard Melvin
Seaton, Robert Finlayson
Seaver, James Everett
Seaver, Tom (George Thomas)
Seavitt, Karl L(ouis)
Sebelius, Keith George
Sebeok, Thomas Albert
Sebok, Gyorgy
Sechrist, Chalmers F., Jr.
Secor, Philip Bruce
Secrest, John Cary
Sedelmaier, John Josef
Sedelow, Sally Ann Yeates
Sedelow, Walter Alfred, Jr.
Seder, Arthur Raymond, Jr.
Sedgwick, Ellery, Jr.
Seebohm, Paul Minor
Seefeldt, John Asmus
Seegers, Walter Henry
Seeler, Robert Stanley
Seevers, Charles Junior
Seffrin, John Reese
Segar, William Elias
Seger, Bob
Seghi, Phillip Domenic
Seid, Richard
Seidlin, Oskar
Seidner, Frederic Jay
Seikel, Oliver Edward
Seiler, Robert Eldridge
Seils, William George
Seireg, Ali A(bdel Hay)
Seith, Alex Robert
Seitz, Reynolds C.
Seitzinger, Edward Francis
Sejnost, Richard Leonard
Sekuler, Robert William
Selby, John Douglas
Selden, David Seeley
Self, Madison Allen
Selfridge, George Dever
Selig, Allan H. (Bud)
Selkurt, Ewald Erdman
Sell, George Rubin
Sell, Jackson Harold
Selleck, Robert W.
Sellers, James McBrayer
Sellinger, Francis John
Selonick, James Bennett
Seltzer, Phyllis Estelle
Selzer, Charles Louis
Sember, Michael Daniel
Semler, Bernard Henry
Semple, Robert Baylor
Sen, Ashish Kumar
Sengstacke, John Herman Henry
Senhauser, Donald A(lbert)
Sensenbrenner, Frank James, Jr.
Sepsy, Charles Frank
Sequeira, Luis
Sernett, Richard Patrick
Serrin, James Burton
SerVaas, Beurt Richard
Servaas, Cory Synhorst (Mrs. Beurt R. Servaas)

Sesonske, Alexander
Sessions, William Crighton
Sethna, Patarasp Rustomji
Sevcik, John George
Severa, Gordon
Severino, Dominick Alexander
Severson, Roger Allan
Sevold, Gordon James
Seward, Harry Paul
Sewell, Daniel Keith
Sewell, Phyllis Shapiro
Sewell, William Hamilton
Sexton, Thomas Mackin
Seyfarth, Henry Edward
Seymour, Arthur Hallock
Seymour, Lyle Eugene
Shabat, Oscar E.
Shackelford, Donald Bruce
Shaddle, Alice G.
Shadduck, John Allen
Shade, Nancy Elizabeth
Shaevel, Evelyn Frances
Shafer, B. Lyle
Shafer, Charles Robert
Shafer, Everett Earl
Shaffer, Paul E.
Shaffer, Robert Howard
Shafter, Albert Jene, Jr.
Shaheen, Michael George
Shahidi, Nasrollah Thomas
Shain, Irving
Shalala, Philip David
Shanahan, Edmond M.
Shanas, Ethel
Shane, Harold Gray
Shank, Robert Ely
Shank, Stephen George
Shank, William O.
Shankland, Robert Sherwood
Shannahan, John Henry Kelly
Shannon, Iris Reed
Shannon, James Patrick
Shannon, Larry Joseph
Shannon, Michael Edward
Shannon, Stephen Quinby, Jr.
Shapey, Ralph
Shapira, Michael Stuart
Shapiro, Burton Leonard
Shapiro, Fred David
Shapiro, Fred Louis
Shapiro, Harold Benjamin
Shapiro, Harold Tafler
Shapiro, Henry
Shapiro, Milton
Shapiro, Robert B.
Shapiro, Samuel Harvey
Shapo, Marshall Schambelan
Shappirio, David Gordon
Sharfman, Robert Jay
Sharp, Alexander Edward
Sharp, Allen
Sharp, Robert A.
Sharp, Robert Weimer
Sharpe, John Lee
Sharpstein, Sidney J.
Sharrock, David Bruce
Shattuck, Charles Harlen
Shaver, Robert Harold
Shaw, Donald Hardy
Shaw, Harry Alexander, III
Shaw, Joseph Thomas
Shaw, Kenneth Alan
Shaw, Leroy Robert
Shaw, Michael Allan
Shaw, Paul Dale
Shaw, Raymond Kenneth
Shaw, Stanley Miner
Shawhan, Stanley Dean
Shea, Daniel Bartholomew, Jr.
Shea, Donald Richard
Shea, Francis Raymond
Shea, George Beverly
Shealy, Clyde Norman
Shearing, George Albert
Sheatsley, Paul Baker
Sheehan, Daniel Eugene
Sheehan, Dennis William
Sheehan, John Francis
Sheehy, Howard Sherman, Jr.
Sheetz, David Patrick
Sheetz, Richard Smedley
Sheffel, Irving Eugene
Sheffield, Horace Lindsey
Shehan, Robert Murray
Sheldon, Gilbert Ignatius
Shelley, Walter Brown
Shellow, James Myers
Shemin, David
Shenk, John Christian, Jr.
Shepard, Earl Emanuel
Shepard, Trent Allen
Shepherd, John Calvin
Shepherd, John Herbert
Shepherd, John Thompson
Shepp, Archie
Sheppard, Robert Blair
Shera, Jesse Hauk
Sheran, Robert Joseph
Shere, Dennis
Sheridan, James
Sheridan, James Edward
Sheridan, Leslie William
Sheridan, Martin
Sheridan, Sonia Landy
Sheridan, William Cockburn Russell
Sherman, Saul S.
Sherman, Stuart Holmes, Jr.
Sherman, Vernon Wesley
Shermoen, Richard Eugene
Sherry, Peter Joseph
Shertzer, Bruce Eldon
Shervheim, Lloyd Oliver
Sherwood, Bernath Pardee, Jr.
Sheth, Jagdish Nanchand
Shettle, John Thomas
Shewalter, Charles Ellis
Shewmon, Paul Griffith
Shideman, Frederick Earl
Shield, Richard Thorpe
Shields, Charles Daniel
Shields, John Benedict
Shields, Thomas William
Shields, William Laurie
Shimkin, Demitri Boris
Shindell, Sidney
Shine, Neal James
Shipley, James Ross
Shipman, Robert Jack
Shipp, Barry Eugene
Shirk, Charles Albert
Shive, Thomas M.
Shively, William Phillips
Shkolnick, Rodney
Shoch, David Eugene
Shoquist, Joseph William
Shorb, Eugene Murray
Shore, Thomas Spencer, Jr.
Short, Ray Everett
Shouldice, Kenneth James
Shoup, George Ellsworth, Jr.
Shoup, Harold Arthur
Shoup, Robert John
Shreffler, Donald Cecil
Shriver, Phillip Raymond
Shropshire, Thomas Bailey
Shryock, Russell Webster
Shubik, Philippe
Shuck, Jerry Mark
Shuler, Jack Hayward
Shull, Willard Charles, III
Shultz, Joseph Randolph
Shuman, Nicholas Roman
Shuman, R(obert) Baird
Shurman, Michael Mendelsohn
Shurtleff, Malcolm C.
Shutz, Byron Christopher
Shutz, Byron Theodore
Shwayder, David Samuel
Shy, John Willard
Sibley, Willis Elbridge
Sicherman, Marvin Allen
Sick, Wilson William, Jr.
Sidders, Patrick Michael
Sieben, Harry Albert, Jr.
Sieben, James George
Siebenthaler, Harold Jacob
Sieberger, Willi Friedrich
Siebers, Jack Alan
Siebert, Calvin D.
Siedler, Arthur James
Siegel, George Henry
Siegel, Jeffrey
Siegel, Sid
Siegert, Arnold John Frederick
Siemer, Paul Jennings
Siess, Chester Paul
Sigel, Bernard
Sigler, LeRoy Walter
Sih, Charles John
Sih, Julius Wei Wu
Sikorovsky, Eugene Frank
Silets, Harvey Marvin
Silha, Otto Adelbert
Siljander, Mark
Sill, Webster Harrison, Jr.
Silletto, Charles David
Sillman, Herbert Phillip
Silva, LeRoy Francis
Silver, David Mayer
Silver, Donald
Silver, Gerald
Silver, Howard
Silver, Melvin J.
Silver, Ralph David
Silverman, Albert A.
Silverman, Albert Jack
Silverman, David Wolf
Silverman, Franklin Harold
Silverman, Henry Jacob
Silverman, Theodore N.
Silverstein, Adolph Traub
Silverstein, Stephen Howard
Silverstone, Leon Martin
Silvestri, John Anthony
Silvoso, Joseph Anton
Simcox, Edwin Jesse
Simek, Joseph Ladislav
Simek, Ronald Lee
Simmons, Charles Edward Phillip
Simmons, Edward Dwyer
Simmons, James Edwin
Simmons, John Edwards
Simmons, Merle Edwin
Simmons, Ralph Oliver
Simmons, Ted Lyle
Simon, Bernece Kern
Simon, Jack Aaron
Simon, John Bern
Simon, Julian Lincoln
Simon, Michael Alexander
Simon, Mordecai
Simon, Ralph
Simon, Rita James (Mrs. Julian Simon)
Simon, Roger Mitchell
Simon, Seymour F.
Simon, Steven Cliff
Simon, Todd
Simon, Werner
Simon, William John
Simonet, John Thomas
Simonett, John E.
Simons, Dolph Collins
Simons, Dolph Collins, Jr.
Simons, Leonard Norman Rashall
Simonson, Hugh Melvin
Simonton, Wesley Clark
Simpkin, Lawrence James
Simpkins, Joe
Simpson, David
Simpson, Donald Bruce
Simpson, John Alexander
Simpson, John McLaren
Simpson, Lyle Lee
Simpson, Richard Howard
Simpson, Vinson Raleigh, Jr.
Sims, Philip Stuart
Sims, Richard Lee
Sinclair, George Morton
Sinclair, Stephen John
Sinclair, Warren Keith
Siney, Marion Celestia
Singer, Marcus George
Singer, Marcus Joseph
Singer, Ronald
Sinor, Denis
Sinquefield, Tex. A(ndrew)
Sinsabaugh, Art (Arthur Reeder)
Sinykin, Gordon
Siragusa, Ross David
Siskel, Eugene Kal (Gene)
Sissel, George Allen
Sisson, Everett Arnold
Sitton, Fred Monroe
Sivright, John Avery
Sjoerdsma, Albert
Skadden, Donald Harvey
Skaggs, Harvey Teague
Skantze, Lawrence Albert
Skeggs, Leonard Tucker, Jr.
Skelton, Isaac (Ike) Newton, IV
Skelton, Robert Benjamin
Skendziel, Floyd Raymond
Skernick, Abraham
Skidmore, Howard Franklyn
Skidmore, Thomas Elliott
Skillman, Thomas Grant
Skinner, David Bernt
Skinner, Gordon Sweetland
Skinner, Lloyd Edward
Skinner, Robert Glenn
Skinner, Samuel Knox
Skipper, James Everett
Skok, Richard Arnold
Skoog, Donald Paul
Skoog, Folke Karl
Skoog, Ralph Edward
Skornicka, Joel L.
Skove, Thomas Malcolm
Skramstad, Harold Kenneth, Jr.
Skrebneski, Victor
Skrowaczewski, Stanislaw
Skultety, F(rancis) Miles
Skutt, Vestor Joseph
Slade, Llewellyn Eugene
Slade, Roy
Sladek, Ronald John
Slane, Henry Pindell
Slater, George Richard
Slater, John Greenleaf
Slattery, James Joseph (Joe Slattery)
Slavin, Raymond Granam
Slettebak, Arne
Slichter, Charles Pence
Slife, Harry G.
Sloan, Elaine Frank
Sloan, Herbert Elias
Sloan, James Park
Slotkin, Edward James
Slotkin, Hugo
Slotnick, Daniel Leonid
Slowinski, Emil John
Smale, John Gray
Small, Erwin
Small, Ralph Milton
Small, Stanton Harrison
Smalley, Roy Frederick, III
Smart, Jackson Wyman, Jr.
Smart, William Robertson
Smeds, Edward William
Smisek, Joseph Thomas
Smith, A. Anthes
Smith, Allan Frederick
Smith, Bardwell Leith
Smith, Barnard Elliot
Smith, Bruce Harry
Smith, C. Kenneth
Smith, Charles Henry, Jr.
Smith, Charles Oliver
Smith, Charles Philip
Smith, Charles Roger
Smith, Charles Wallace
Smith, Craig Richey
Smith, D. Richard
Smith, Daniel Richard
Smith, Darwin Eatna
Smith, David Waldo Edward
Smith, Denton Henry
Smith, Donald Cameron
Smith, Donald Kliese
Smith, Edward Arvey
Smith, Edward Byron
Smith, Eldred Reid
Smith, Ephraim Philip
Smith, Ernest Elwood
Smith, Eugene Frederick
Smith, Eugene Preston
Smith, Frank Earl
Smith, Fred George, Jr.
Smith, Frederick Coe
Smith, Frederick Robert, Jr.
Smith, Gerald Allen
Smith, Goff
Smith, Gordon Howell
Smith, Haddon Hartung
Smith, Harold Byron, Jr.
Smith, Harold Philip
Smith, Henry Charles, 3d
Smith, Henry Clay
Smith, Howard Thompson
Smith, J(ames) E(verett) Keith
Smith, J. Thomas
Smith, Jack Carl
Smith, James Gilbert
Smith, James John
Smith, James Norman
Smith, James R.
Smith, Jane Farwell
Smith, John Burnside
Smith, John J.
Smith, Jonathan
Smith, Joseph Aland
Smith, Joseph Victor
Smith, Julian Payne
Smith, Kenneth
Smith, Lacey Baldwin
Smith, Leonard Bingley
Smith, Leonard Charles
Smith, LeRoi Clarence
Smith, Linn Charles
Smith, Lloyd Bruce
Smith, Lucien T.
Smith, Malcolm Norman
Smith, Marion Leroy
Smith, Mary Louise
Smith, Michael John
Smith, Neal Austin
Smith, Norris Kelly
Smith, Otis M.
Smith, Paul Francis
Smith, Philip George
Smith, Ralph Alexander
Smith, Raymond G.
Smith, Raymond Lloyd
Smith, Raymond Thomas
Smith, Richard Lee
Smith, Richey
Smith, Robert
Smith, Robert Angus Kermode, Jr.
Smith, Robert Burns
Smith, Robert Drake
Smith, Robert Nelson
Smith, Roger Bonham
Smith, Roger Dean
Smith, Ronald Lee
Smith, Roy Emerson
Smith, Scott Beecher
Smith, Sherman Allen
Smith, Stewart Gene
Smith, Stewart Worland, Jr.
Smith, Thomas Stevenson
Smith, Victor Earle
Smith, Virginia Dodd (Mrs. Haven Smith)
Smith, Wallace Bunnell
Smith, Ward
Smith, Waverly Graves
Smith, William Keith
Smith, William Wallace
Smith, Worthington LeHuray
Smithburg, William Dean
Smoot, Joseph Grady
Smoot, Thurlow Bergen
Smucker, Paul Highnam
Smuckler, Ralph Herbert
Smull, Ned Willits
Smyth, David John
Smyth, Glen Miller
Smyth, Joseph Vincent
Smythe, Mabel Murphy
Snedaker, Robert Hume, Jr.
Snell, John Raymond
Snider, Delbert Arthur
Snider, Robert Joe
Snitzer, Martin Harry
Snively, William Daniel, Jr.
Snoddy, James Ernest
Snook, John Orla
Snortland, Howard Jerome
Snowbarger, Willis Edward
Snyder, Carl Edward
Snyder, Charles Royce
Snyder, Edward Pheatt
Snyder, George Edward
Snyder, James Newton
Snyder, John William
Snyder, Leon Carleton
Snyder, Lewis Emil
Snyder, Melvin Harold
Snyder, Rachel Frances
Snyder, Robert Henry
Snyder, Robert Owen
Snyder, William Patrick
Sobel, Burton Elias
Sobel, Walter Howard
Sochen, June
Soergel, Konrad Hermann
Soffer, Alfred
Sofield, Harold Augustus
Sogg, Wilton Sherman
Soladay, Charles W.
Solberg, Winton Udell
Solbrig, Nana Shineflug
Soll, A. Ivan
Solley, Thomas Treat
Solo, Robert Alexander
Solomon, Arthur Paul
Solomon, David Eugene
Solomon, Jack Avrum, Jr.
Solomon, Ted Joseph
Soloway, Albert Herman
Solt, Leo Frank
Solti, Georg
Soltow, James Harold
Somers, Louis Robert
Somit, Albert
Sommer, Howard Ellsworth
Sommers, Herbert Myron
Sommers, Lawrence Melvin
Sonderegger, John Forster
Sonkowsky, Robert Paul
Sonneborn, Harry Lee
Sonnecken, Edwin Herbert
Sonnedecker, Glenn Allen
Sonnino, Carlo Benvenuto
Sons, Raymond William
Soo, Shao Lee
Sopranos, Orpheus Javaras
Sorah, Baxter Lee, Jr.
Sorauf, Francis Joseph
Sorby, Donald Lloyd
Sorensen, Leif Boge
Sorensen, Philip Chaikin
Sorkin, Leonard
Sorling, Carl Axel
Soshnik, Joseph
Sosin, Sidney
Sott, Herbert
Souder, Paul Clayton
Souers, Loren Eaton
Soules, Jack Arbuthnott
Southwick, Harry Webb
Sovik, Edward Anders
Sowada, Alphonse Augustus
Sowers, Wesley Hoyt
Sozen, Mete Avni
Spaeth, Raymond Julius
Spaights, Ernest
Spain, James Dorris, Jr.
Spainhower, James Ivan
Spalding, Vernon Benjamin
Spannaus, Warren Richard
Spanton, William Floyd
Spargo, Benjamin H.
Sparks, Earl Edwin
Sparks, Harvey Vise, Jr.
Sparks, Jack David
Sparks, Robert Dean
Sparrow, Ephraim Maurice
Speaks, Donald Wesley
Spear, Richard Edmund
Speas, Raymond Aaron
Specht, Charles Alfred
Spector, Gershon Jerry
Spector, Stanley
Speer, Paul Dee
Speidel, Richard Eli
Speier, John L.
Spellacy, William Nelson
Spelsberg, Thomas Coonan
Speltz, George Henry
Spence, Clark Christian
Spence, Glen Oscar
Spence, John Daniel
Spence, Robert Dean
Spence, William Blair
Spencer, Dale Ray
Spencer, Edson White
Spencer, Lewis Douglas
Spencer, Robert C.
Spengler, William Frederick, Jr.
Sperandio, Glen Joseph
Sperlich, Harold Keith
Sperry, James Edward
Spetrino, Russell John
Spiegel, Edwin John, Jr.
Spier, Robert Forest Gayton
Spiller, Robert Earl
Spina, Anthony
Spingola, Joseph Peter
Spink, Charles Claude Johnson
Spink, Walter Milton
Spink, Wesley W.
Spinner, Frank Kenneth
Spiotta, Raymond Herman
Spitzbart, Abraham
Spitze, Robert George Frederick
Spitzer, John Brumback
Spitzer, Robert Ralph
Spitznagel, William F.
Spivey, Walter Allen
Splane, Beverly Jo
Splinter, William Eldon
Splittstoesser, Walter Emil
Spodek, Bernard
Spohn, Charles L.
Spohn, Herbert Emil
Spokes, Ernest Melvern
Spoor, William Howard
Spradlin, Norman Allen
Sprague, George Frederick
Sprague, Philip Allcock
Sprayregen, Joel Jay
Sprecher, Robert Arthur
Sprenger, Gordon Merril
Spring, John Benham
Spring, Raymond Lewis
Springer, Georg Ferdinand
Springer, George
Springer, William Lee
Sprinkel, Beryl Wayne
Sprinthall, Norman Arthur
Sproger, Charles Edmund
Sproul, Otis Jennings
Sprowl, Charles Riggs
Sprugel, George, Jr.
Sprunk, James Augustus
Spulber, Nicolas
Squires, Robert George
Staba, Emil John
Stack, James Keane
Stack, James Vincent
Stackelberg, Olaf Patrick
Stacy, Bill Wayne
Stade, Charles Edward
Stadtler, Beatrice Horwitz
Staebler, Neil
Staehle, Roger Washburne
Staerkel, William Max
Stafford, John M.
Stafford, Rebecca
Stafford, William Talmadge
Stagl, John Matthew
Stahl, Henry George
Stahmann, Mark Arnold
Stair, Charles William
Staley, Henry Mueller
Stallard, Richard Elgin
Stallings, David William
Stallings, James Otis
Stallmeyer, James Edward
Stalnaker, Armand Carl
Stamey, William Lee
Stamler, Jeremiah
Stamos, John James
Stanczak, Julian
Stander, Joseph William
Standish, Samuel Miles
Stangeland, Arlan Inghart
Stanish, John Richard
Stanisic, Milomir Mirkov
Stanley, Arthur Jehu, Jr.
Stanley, C. Maxwell
Stanley, Justin Armstrong
Stanley, Lawrence Delaney
Stanley, Richard Holt
Stanton, Donald Sheldon
Stanton, Gerald Elroy
Stanton, John William
Stanton, Robert Lee
Stanton, Roger
Stanton, Thomas Mitchell
Stapel, Paul Frederick
Staples, Jack Robison
Stapleton, Harvey James
Stapleton, James Hall
Stark, Camille Rene
Stark, Joan Scism
Starker, Janos
Starr, Bryan Bartlett (Bart)
Starr, Chester G.
Starr, Maurice Kenneth
Starrs, John Richard
Staub, E. Norman
Stauder, William Vincent
Stauffer, Oscar Stanley
Stauffer, Paul Stephen
Stauffer, R. Gary
Stauffer, Stanley Howard
Stauffer, Thomas George
Stauffer, William Albert
Stavitsky, Abram Benjamin
Stavropoulos, D(ionysos) John
Stay, Barbara
Steadman, Jack W.
Stearns, Martin
Steck, Norman Martin
Steck, Theodore Lyle
Steckbeck, Thomas Edward
Steckler, William Elwood
Steefel, Lawrence D., Jr.
Steele, Betty Louise
Steele, Donald Ernest
Steele, Richard Allen
Steele, Walton Wall
Steer, Max David
Stefaniak, Norbert John
Steffen, Walter William
Steigerwaldt, Donna Wolf
Steil, George Kenneth, Sr.
Stein, Bernard Alvin
Stein, Dale F.
Stein, Elliot H.
Stein, Eric
Stein, Herman David
Stein, Howard
Stein, Leon
Stein, Marvin Leonard
Stein, Richard Paul
Stein, Rita F.
Stein, Robert Allen
Stein, Sydney, Jr.
Steinberg, Arthur G(erald)
Steiner, Donald Frederick
Steiner, Jan
Steiner, Peter Otto
Steiner, Wilfred Joseph
Steinhauser, Fredric Robert
Steinhoff, William Richard
Steinmetz, Donald Walter
Stella, Charles Guy, Jr.
Stellman, Samuel David
Stelly, Matthias
Stelmachowicz, Michael Joseph, Jr.
Stelzel, Walter Tell
Stemle, Edward Charles
Stenehjem, Leland Manford
Stenvig, Charles S.
Step, Eugene (Lee)
Stepan, Alfred Charles, Jr.
Stephan, Edmund Anton
Stephan, Robert Downs
Stephan, Robert Taft
Stephanopoulos, Robert George
Stephen, John Erle
Stephens, Norval Blair, Jr.
Stephens, Thomas Maron
Stephens, William Richard
Stephenson, Hugh Edward, Jr.
Stephenson, Roy L.
Stepto, Robert Charles
Sterling, Chandler Winfield
Stern, Clarence Ames
Stern, Ernest
Stern, Gerald Joseph
Stern, Guy
Stern, James Lawrence
Stern, Joseph Smith, Jr.
Stern, Louis William
Stern, Paul George
Stern, Richard Gustave
Stern, Robert Louis
Sternberg, Paul
Sternburg, James Gordon
Sterne, Bobbie
Sterner, Frank Maurice
Sternglass, Ernest Joachim
Stetson, John Benjamin Blank
Stetson, John Charles
Stevens, Dwight Marlyn
Stevens, George Richard
Stevens, Harvey Alonzo
Stevens, John Henry
Stevens, Mark Chancellor

Stevens, Paul Edward
Stevens, Robert Jay
Stevens, Rolland Elwell
Stevens, Story Crandall
Stevens, Thomas Lee
Stevens, William Foster, III
Stevens, William Kenneth
Stevenson, Adlai Ewing, III
Stevenson, Ernest Vail
Stevenson, George Franklin
Stevenson, Harold William
Stevenson, James David
Stewart, Charles Leslie
Stewart, Daniel Robert
Stewart, Donald Edwin
Stewart, Ireland J.
Stewart, Melbourne George, Jr.
Stewart, Norman Lawrence
Stewart, Robert Fletcher
Stewart, Robert Murray, Jr.
Stewart, Warren Earl
Stewart, Wellington Buel
Stichnoth, Dean Roger
Stickler, Fred Charles
Stickler, Gunnar Brynolf
Stievater, James Edward
Stigler, George Joseph
Stiles, John Stephen
Stiles, Stuart Lee
Stillinger, Jack Clifford
Stillings, Frank Stuart
Stillman, Donald Dennis
Stillwell, G(eorge) Keith
Stimson, Frederick Sparks
Stines, Fred, Jr.
Stinson, Patrick Bernard
Stipanowich, Joseph Jean
Stipher, Karl Joseph
Stipp, John Edgar
Stiritz, William P.
Stitt, Don Nelson
Stitt, Jack Reed
Stitzlein, Carl, II
Stivender, Donald Lewis
Stock, Gregg Francis
Stocks, William George
Stockwell, Richard E.
Stoddard, Charles Hatch
Stoecker, David Thomas
Stokely, Alfred Jehu
Stokely, William Burnett, III
Stokes, Carl Burton
Stokes, William Forrest
Stokstad, Marilyn Jane
Stoll, Wilhelm
Stolle, John Fred
Stolley, Alexander
Stollman, Israel
Stolnitz, George Joseph
Stolper, Wolfgang Friedrich
Stoltz, Charles Edward
Stolz, Benjamin Armond
Stone, Alan Jay
Stone, Clement
Stone, Donald Bradford
Stone, Donald James
Stone, Donald Raymond
Stone, Frederick Hamilton
Stone, Harry H.
Stone, Irving I.
Stone, Kirk Haskin
Stone, Marguerite Beverley
Stone, Morris Samuel
Stone, Robert B.
Stone, Robert Frederick
Stone, Roger Warren
Stone, Thomas S.
Stone, W. Clement
Stone, William Harold
Stonehill, Maurice Lewis
Stonehill, Robert Berrell
Stoneking, Danny Alan
Stoneman, William, III
Stoner, Richard Burkett
Stoner, Robert Franklin
Stonich, Timothy Whitman
Storry, Junis Oliver
Storvick, Truman Sophus
Story, William Easton
Stotter, David W.
Stotts, Jack Leven
Stout, Alan Burrage
Stout, Robert Newhart
Stout, William Jewell
Stover, Harry Manning
Stover, John Ford
Stowe, Leland
Strable, Edward George
Strachan, Donald M.
Strachota, Bernard Arthur
Straffon, Ralph Atwood
Strang, Charles Daniel
Strang, Marian Boundy
Strang, Ruth Hancock
Strasburger, Joseph Julius
Strasma, John Drinan
Strasser, Edwin Francis
Strasser, Robert Kenneth
Strassmeyer, Mary
Straumfjord, Jon Vidalin, Jr.
Strauss, Bernard S.
Strauss, John Steinert
Strauss, Karl Martin
Strauss, Walter Adolf
Strawbridge, Herbert Edward
Strawn, Harry Culp
Strecker, Ignatius J.
Street, John Charles
Streeter, Robert Eugene
Streetman, Ben Garland
Streetman, John William, III
Strehlow, Roger Albert
Streichler, Jerry
Stretch, John Joseph
Strickland, Hugh Alfred
Strickland, William Alexander, Jr.
Strickler, Ivan K.
Stringer, Edward Charles
Strobel, Martin Jack
Stroble, Francis Anthony
Strodel, Robert Carl
Strom, Lyle Elmer
Stromberg, Melvin Willard
Stromberg, Roland Nelson
Strominger, Donald B.
Stronach, William Charles
Strong, Cameron Gordon
Strong, Carter Bruce
Strong, Frederick Smith, Jr.
Strong, John William
Strong, Merle Edward
Strothman, Maurice Henry, Jr.
Strotz, Robert Henry
Stroud, Joe Hinton
Stroud, Malcolm Herbert
Strubbe, John Lewis
Strubbe, Thomas R.
Strubel, Richard Perry
Struchen, J Maurice
Struever, Stuart McKee
Struggles, John Edward
Stryker, Clinton Everett
Stryker, Sheldon
Stuart, James
Stuart, James Fortier
Stuart, John McHugh, Jr.
Stuart, Robert
Stuart, Robert Douglas, Jr.
Stuart, Thomas Joseph
Stuart, William Corwin
Stucker, Gilles Alfred Eugene
Stucky, Marvin Wayne
Studenroth, Carl Wilson
Studenroth, Carl Wilson
Studer, William Joseph
Studier, Martin Herman
Studsgaard, Anker Christian
Stuebner, Erwin August
Stukel, James Joseph
Stull, Robert J.
Stults, Allen Parker
Stump, John Edward
Stumpe, Warren Robert
Sturdivant, Frederick David
Stutz, Herbert Walter
Styan, John Louis
Stynes, Stanley Kenneth
Suba, Antonio Ronquillo
Suber, Charles
Sudler, Louis Courtenay
Sugar, Oscar
Sugarman, Nathan
Sugihara, James Masanobu
Suhre, Walter Anthony, Jr.
Suits, Daniel Burbidge
Sullivan, Barry Francis
Sullivan, Daniel Joseph
Sullivan, James Hall
Sullivan, James Stephen
Sullivan, James Thomas
Sullivan, Jeremiah David
Sullivan, John Joseph
Sullivan, John W.
Sullivan, Joseph B.
Sullivan, Joseph Patrick
Sullivan, Patricia Clare
Sullivan, Peggy (Anne)
Sullivan, Thomas Christopher
Sullivan, Thomas Patrick
Sullivan, William Albert, Jr.
Sullivan, William James
Sullivant, Robert Scott
Suloway, Irwin Jerome
Summers, Hollis
Summitt, (William) Robert
Sundberg, R. Dorothy
Sunderland, Robert
Sundquist, Wesley Burton
Super, Robert Henry
Suput, Ray Radoslav
Surdam, Robert McClellan
Surface, Richard Eugene
Surman, William Robert
Sursa, Charles David
Suskind, Raymond Robert
Susman, Millard
Sussman, Alfred Sheppard
Sussman, Sidney X.
Sutera, Salvatore Philip
Sutherland, Donald Wayne
Sutherland, Ronald Roy
Sutphin, Samuel Reid
Sutter, (Howard) Bruce
Sutter, William Paul
Sutton, David B.
Sutton, George Edwin
Sutton, Robert Mize
Suzuki, Hidetaro
Suzuki, Michio
Svec, Frederick Joseph
Svec, Harry John
Svendsbye, Lloyd August
Svetlova, Marina
Svolos, Gus
Swaiman, Kenneth Fred
Swain, O.E.
Swales, William Edward
Swan, James Wesley
Swaney, Russel Alger
Swank, Emory Coblentz
Swanson, Alfred Bertil
Swanson, Bernet Steven
Swanson, Charles Elroy
Swanson, David Shaw
Swanson, Don Richard
Swanson, Donald Frederick
Swanson, Dwight Harold
Swanson, Edward William
Swanson, Gordon Merle
Swanson, Lloyd Oscar
Swanson, Robert Draper
Swanson, Roy Arthur
Swanson, Vernon Andrew
Swanstrom, Thomas Evan
Swarthout, Herbert Marion
Swartz, Donald Everett
Swartz, Robert Dale
Swartz, William John
Swartzendruber, Dale
Swearingen, John Eldred
Sweeley, Charles Crawford
Sweeney, Asher William
Sweeney, James Raymond
Sweeney, (Charles) Leo
Sweeney, Mark Owen
Sweeney, Richard Thomas
Sweet, Bernard
Sweet, Cody
Sweet, David Charles
Sweet, John Wheaton, Jr.
Sweet, Philip W.K., Jr.
Sweeting, George
Swenson, Birger
Swenson, Clayton A.
Swenson, Courtland Sevander
Swenson, George Warner, Jr.
Swenson, Melvin John
Swenson, Sherman Andrew
Swenson, Wendell Monson
Swerdlow, Martin Abraham
Swift, Edward Foster, III
Swift, George Hastings, Jr.
Swift, Hewson Hoyt
Swift, James William
Swigert, James Mack
Swing, Gael Duane
Swisher, Charles F.
Swisher, Scott Neil
Switzer, Robert Lee
Sword, Christopher Patrick
Swygert, Luther Merritt
Sykes, Weathers York
Sylvester, Norbert A.
Symmonds, Richard Earl
Symon, Keith Randolph
Syse, Glenna Marie Lowes
Sytsma, John Frederick
Szabo, Barna Aladar
Szathmáry, Louis István, II
Szesko, Lenore Rundle
Szoka, Edmund Casimir
Szurszewski, Joseph Henry
Szybalski, Waclaw
Szymanski, Frederick John
Taaffe, Edward James
Taaffe, James Griffith
Taaffe, Robert Norman
Tabacchi, Fred Lawrence
Tabakoff, Widen
Tabin, Julius
Tacker, Willis Arnold, Jr.
Taeuber, Karl E(rnst)
Taft, Charles Phelps
Taft, David Dakin
Taft, Dudley Sutphin
Taft, Frederick Lovett
Taft, Robert, Jr.
Taft, William Howard
Tagatz, George Elmo
Taggart, Ross Edgar
Taibleson, Mitchell Herbert
Taibleson, W.B.
Tait, James M.
Talbott, Nelson Strobridge
Talkington, Robert Van
Tallarico, Thomas Michael
Tallchief, Maria
Tallent, William Hugh
Talleur, John Joseph
Talley, Robert Cochran
Talmadge, Robert Louis
Talso, Peter J.
Tamarkin, Robert Allen
Tamcsin, Dennis
Tammeus, William David
Tanaka, Tomoyasu
Tandler, Bernard
Tang, Tom T.
Tang, Wilson Hon-chung
Tankin, Richard Samuel
Tankus, Harry
Tannenbaum, Stanley Irving
Tanner, Paul A.
Tanner, Ralph Melvis
Tanselle, Donald William
Taren, James Arthur
Tarr, Curtis W.
Tarr, David William
Tarvin, Robert Edward
Tarzian, Mary (Mrs. Sarkes Tarzian)
Tassell, Paul Norman
Tatgenhorst, (Charles) Robert
Tatz, Paul Henry
Tauber, Joel David
Tauke, Thomas J(oseph)
Tausch, William Joseph
Tave, Stuart Malcolm
Taw, Dudley Joseph
Tax, Sol
Taylor, Anna Diggs
Taylor, C. James
Taylor, Charles Edward
Taylor, D(arl) Coder
Taylor, David George
Taylor, Donald
Taylor, Donald Arthur
Taylor, George Allen
Taylor, Henry Longstreet
Taylor, James Ronald
Taylor, James Stewart
Taylor, Jay Eugene
Taylor, John Clyde, Jr.
Taylor, John Frank Adams
Taylor, John Richard
Taylor, John Wilkinson
Taylor, Joseph Thomas
Taylor, Kenneth Nathaniel
Taylor, Kenyon Yale
Taylor, Michael Alan
Taylor, Phillip Seyfang
Taylor, Robert William
Taylor, Thomas Hewitt, Jr.
Taylor, William Brooks, II
Taylor, William Clarence
Taylor, William James
Teagan, John Gerard
Teague, Joseph Grant
Teare, Wallace Gleed
Teasdale, Thomas Hennings
Tecklenburg, Harry
Teegarden, Kenneth Leroy
Teerlink, Richard Francis
Teeter, Robert M.
Teets, John Phillip
Teitelbaum, Philip
Te Kolste, Dale
Telleen, John Martin
Telling, Edward Riggs
Telnack, John J.
Telser, Lester Greenspan
Temin, Howard Martin
Templar, George
Temple, Joseph George, Jr.
Temple, Wayne Calhoun
Tennant, Don
Tenney, Merrill Chapin
Tenpas, Garit Henry
Terkel, Studs Louis
Terkhorn, Henry K.
Ternberg, Jessie Lamoin
Terpstra, William Cornelius
Terra, Daniel James
Terracina, Roy David
Terry, Clifford Lewis
Terry, Megan
Terwilliger, Herbert Lee
Tesauro, Dominic Aloysius
Teschner, Richard Rewa
Teska, Gordon Adam
Tessman, Irwin
Tester, John Robert
Testolin, Reno Joseph
Teuscher, George William
Thach, Robert Edwards
Thaden, Edward Carl
Tharp, Melvin Earl
Thatcher, John Sherman
Thayer, Harold Eugene
Thayer, Lee
Theis, Francis William
Theis, Frank Gordon
Theodoroff, B. James
Theus, Lucius
Theus, Reginald W. R.
Thiel, John Charles
Thiemann, Charles Lee
Thiemann, Paul Peter, Jr.
Thieme, Walter Irving
Thies, John Milton
Thiesenhusen, William Charles
Thiss, Charles Scott
Thoele, Charles Edward
Thomas, Arthur Lawrence
Thomas, Beth Eileen Wood (Mrs. Raymond O. Thomas)
Thomas, Bide Lakin
Thomas, Bruce Wallace
Thomas, C(arlton) Dean
Thomas, Charles Allen
Thomas, Christopher Yancey
Thomas, D. Woods
Thomas, Edwin John
Thomas, Elmer Marshall
Thomas, George Sloan
Thomas, (James) Gorman, III
Thomas, James Gladwyn
Thomas, James Samuel
Thomas, Joseph Harruff
Thomas, Julian Johnson, Jr.
Thomas, Mark Stanton
Thomas, Morgan Irwyn
Thomas, Norman Carl
Thomas, Payne Edward Lloyd
Thomas, Philip Stanley
Thomas, R. David
Thomas, Richard L.
Thomas, Robert Jay
Thomas, Russell
Thomas, Todd Edwin
Thomas, William, Jr.
Thomas, William Kernahan
Thompson, Allen Paul
Thompson, Barbara Storck
Thompson, Bert Allen
Thompson, Charles Kenneth
Thompson, Curtis Brooks
Thompson, Dale Moore
Thompson, Daniel T.
Thompson, Edward Charles, Jr.
Thompson, Era Bell
Thompson, Eric Douglas
Thompson, Everett Steven
Thompson, Glenn
Thompson, Herbert Stanley
Thompson, Howard Elliott
Thompson, Hugh Lee
Thompson, James Robert
Thompson, John Douglas
Thompson, Karl Frederick
Thompson, Louis Milton
Thompson, Margaret M.
Thompson, Maynard
Thompson, Morley Punshon
Thompson, Norman Winslow
Thompson, Renold Durant
Thompson, Robert Russell, Jr.
Thompson, Roby Calvin, Jr.
Thompson, Samuel Dean, Jr.
Thompson, Thomas Allert
Thompson, Thomas Henry
Thompson, Warren Bernard
Thompson, Willard Linn
Thompson, William Franklin
Thompson, William Neil
Thomsen, Ib
Thomsen, John G.
Thomson, Bruce Randolph
Thomson, Harry Pleasant, Jr.
Thone, Charles
Thorelli, Hans B.
Thoren, Victor Eugene
Thoresen, Asa Clifford
Thorkelson, Willmar
Thorndal, Herbert Louis
Thorndyke, Lloyd Milton
Thorne, Charles Hugh
Thornton, Frank Eberle
Thornton, Gerald DeWayne
Thornton, Thomas Noel
Thorp, Kenneth Edward
Thorshov, Roy Norman
Thorson, Ralph Edward
Thorson, Reuben
Thorson, Thomas Bertel
Thrailkill, Francis Marie
Thrall, Arthur Alvin
Thrash, Patricia Ann
Throckmorton, Lynn Hiram
Throckmorton, Robert Bentley
Throckmorton, Tom D.
Throdahl, Monte Corden
Thurber, Cleveland, Jr.
Thurber, Donald MacDonald Dickinson
Thurlow, Willard Rowand
Thurman, Christa Charlotte Mayer
Thurston, Robert Ninde
Thwaits, James Arthur
Tibbetts, Arnold MacLean
Tickle, Robert Simpson
Tidmarsh, George Francis
Tiecke, Richard William
Tielke, James Clemens
Tietjen, John Henry
Tiffany, William Lynn
Tigerman, Stanley
Tigges, Kenneth Edwin
Tigrak, Mehmet Faut
Tiley, Sharon Kay
Till, Charles Edgar
Tillinghast, William Cloyd
Tillman, Frank Aubrey
Tillmann, George Lloyd
Tillstrom, Burr
Timothy (Michael Negrepontis)
Tinker, George Henry
Tinstman, Dale Clinton
Tippett, Willis Paul, Jr.
Tipton, Clyde Raymond, Jr.
Tischler, Hans
Tiscornia, Lester Clinton
Tisdale, Stuart Williams
Tishler, William Henry
Toal, Desmond James
Tober, Lester Victor
Tobias, Charles Harrison, Jr.
Tobias, Paul Henry
Tobin, Calvin Jay
Tobin, John Robert, Jr.
Tobin, Michael E.
Tocco, James
Todd, David Arnold, II
Todd, John Joseph
Todd, Kenneth S., Jr.
Todd, William Miller
Todd, Zane Grey
Toepfer, Louis Adelbert
Tofany, Vincent Leon
Toles, Edward Bernard
Toll, Daniel Roger
Tolle, Donald James
Tomanek, Gerald Wayne
Tomasek, Henry John
Tomasini, Wallace J(ohn)
Tomb, Paul David
Tomblinson, James Edmond
Tomkins, Frank Sargent
Tomlinson, Warren E.
Tommeraasen, Miles
Tompkins, Lowell Emerson
Tompson, Marian Leonard
Tondeur, Philippe Maurice
Tone, Kenneth Edward
Tone, Philip Willis
Tongue, William Walter
Toot, J. F., Jr.
Topouzliev, Dometian
Topper, Joseph Ray
Torbett, Mackey Price
Torchiana, Donald Thornhill
Torchinsky, Abe
Tordoff, Harrison Bruce
Torgersen, Torwald Harold
Torgerson, Truman
Torley, John Frederic
Torney-Purta, Judith Vollmar
Torres, Fernando
Torrison, Mandt
Toscano, James Vincent
Tosi, Oscar I.
Totman, Conrad Davis
Toulmin, Stephen Edelston
Touloukian, Yeram Sarkis
Tourlentes, Thomas Theodore
Toussaint, Wayne E.
Towner, Lawrence William
Townley, Preston
Townsend, Earl Cunningham, Jr.
Townsend, Paul Henson
Tozer, Forrest Leigh
Tracy, Eugene Arthur
Tracy, James Donald
Train, Jack Durkee
Traisman, Howard Sevin
Travers, Thomas Joseph
Travis, Dempsey Jerome
Treadway, Lyman Hambright, III
Trebilcott, James Joseph
Treckelo, Richard M.
Treffert, Darold Allen
Treiman, Edward A.
Tremayne, Bertram William, Jr.
Trenkmann, Richard J.
Tresnowski, Bernard Richard
Treumann, William Borgen
Treves, Samuel Blain
Treyz, Joseph Henry
Triandis, Harry Charalambos
Trichel, Gervais William
Trienens, Howard Joseph
Trifa, Valerian D.
Trigg, Paul Reginald, Jr.
Trimble, Marian Alice
Trimble, Paul Edwin
Trinkaus, Charles Edward, Jr.
Trost, Barry Martin
Trotter, John Ellis
Trotter, Mildred
Trova, Ernest Tino
Trow, Robert Charles
Trowbridge, Charles Lambert
Trowbridge, Frederick Newell
Trozzolo, Anthony Marion
Truby, John Louis
Truce, William Everett
Trudeau, Garry B.
Trueblood, David Elton
Truhlar, Donald Gene
Truhlsen, Stanley Marshall
Truran, James Wellington, Jr.
Trussell, Albert Clyde
Trussell, Charles Eugene
Tschappat, Douglas Wilson
Tsou, Tang
Tsuang, Ming Tso
Tsuchiya, Henry Mitsumasa
Tuatay, Hulusi
Tuchman, Joseph
Tucker, Don Eugene
Tucker, Fred C., Jr.
Tucker, Gabriel Frederick, Jr.
Tucker, Robert L.
Tucker, Thomas Allen
Tucker, William Vincent
Tuckey, John Sutton
Tuerkheimer, Frank Mitchel
Tuite, John Francis
Tuite, Patrick Alan
Tull, E. Don
Tully, Richard Lowden
Tulsky, Alex Sol
Turben, Claude Franklin
Turcotte, Jeremiah George
Turk, Leonard Gerald
Turkevich, Anthony Leonid
Turnbull, Charles Vincent
Turner, Allen Mark
Turner, Arthur Edward
Turner, Basil Sidney
Turner, Darwin Theodore Troy
Turner, Fred L.
Turner, Harold Edward
Turner, Harry Edward
Turner, John Elliot
Turner, John Gosney
Turner, Keith Stanley
Turner, Lynne Alison (Mrs. Paul H. Singer)
Turner, Peter Merrick
Turner, Walter James
Turnquest, Byron Whitmore, III
Turnquist, Nels Ernest
Tusken, Roger Anthony
Tussing, Robert Theodore
Tutt, Charles Leaming, Jr.
Twersky, Victor
Twiss, Page Charles
Twyman, Robert Wickliffe
Tyce, Francis Anthony
Tye, Joseph Claire
Tyer, Travis Earl
Tyler, Leslie J.
Tyler, Lloyd John
Tyler, Varro Eugene
Tyner, Neal Edward
Tyree, Alan Dean
Tyree, Donald Andrew
Tyson, Remer Hoyt, Jr.
Ubbelohde, Carl William
Uchendu, Victor Chikezie
Uehling, Barbara Staner
Ueland, Sigurd, Jr.
Uelner, Roy Walter
Ufner, John
Uhlenbeck, Olke Cornelis
Uhlenbrock, Dietrich Albert
Uhlenhopp, Harvey Harold
Uhlenhuth, Eberhard Henry
Ulevich, Neal Hirsh
Ullestad, Harold Norman
Ullman, Pierre Lioni
Ulrich, Benjamin Harrison, Jr.
Ulrich, Werner
Ulstrom, Robert Alger
Ultan, Lloyd
Ultmann, John Ernest
Umans, Alvin Robert
Underkofler, James Russell
Underwood, Robert Charles
Undlin, Charles Thomas
Ungar, Edward William
Unger, Leonard Howard
Unger, Sherman Edward
Untener, Kenneth E.
Uotila, Urho Antti Kalevi
Updegraff, Ralph Brooks
Upshaw, Harry Stephan
Urbanek, James Frank

Urbom, Warren Keith
Urdan, James Alan
Uretz, Robert Benjamin
Urshan, Nathaniel Andrew
Useem, John Hearld
Useem, Ruth Hill
Uselding, Paul John
Utrecht, James C.
Utt, Glenn S., Jr.
Uttal, William R(eichenstein)
Utz, David C.
Utz, Edward Joseph
Uvena, Frank John
Uyeki, Eugene Shigemi
Uygur, Vural
Vacano, Wolfgang
Vail, Thomas Van Husen
Vainstein, Rose
Valdman, Albert
Valk, Robert Earl
Van Aken, William Russell
Van Allen, James Alfred
Van Allen, Maurice Wright
Van Andel, Jay
van Appledorn, E(lizabeth) Ruth
Van Arsdell, Paul Marion
Van Atta, Robert Ernest
Van Bergen, Frederick Hall
Vance, Carl Bruce
Vance, Elbridge Putnam
Vance, Graham Alexander
Vance, James
Vance, John Thomas
Vance, Lee
Vandegrift, Alfred Eugene
Van Demark, Robert Eugene
Vandenburgh, Edward Clinton, III
Vander Clute, Howard Edmund, Jr.
Van der Eb, Henry Gerard
Vanderlind, Merwyn Ray
Vander Velde, John Christian
Van der Voo, Rob
Van der Ziel, Aldert
Vandeveer, Michael D.
VandeWalle, Gerald Wayne
Van Dusen, Bruce Buick
Van Dusen, Richard Campbell
Van Duyn, Mona Jane
Van Dyke, William Duncan, III
Van Gorkom, Jerome William
VanHandel, Ralph Anthony
Van Hauer, Robert
Van Hoeven, L. C., Jr.
Van Housen, Edward Irvin
Van Leeuwen, Gerard
Van Meter, Abram DeBois
Van Meter, Theodore
Vanneman, Edgar, Jr.
Van Ness, James Edward
Van Pelt, Robert
Van Ranst, Alfred Frederick
van Schooneveld, Cornelis Hendrik
Vanselow, Neal Arthur
Van Sickle, Bruce Marion
Vansina, Jan Maria Jozef
Van Tassel, Karl Raymond
Van Til, William
Van Valkenburg, Mac Elwyn
Van Valkenburg, Paul
Van Vlack, Lawrence Hall
Van Wallgehen, Michael J(oseph)
Van Wylen, Gordon John
Van Zante, Shirley Mae
VanZelst, Theodore William
van Zwoll, Cornelius
Varchmin, Thomas Edward
Varco, Richard Lynn
Varg, Paul Albert
Varga, Richard Steven
Vargo, John Franklin
Varian, Hal Ronald
Varner, Barton Douglas
Varner, Sterling Verl
Varro, Barbara Joan
Vass, Guy Boyd
Vassell, Gregory S.
Vaughan, James Herbert, Jr.
Vaughn, Charles Melvin
Vaughn, Dorris Weldon
Vaughn, Robert Allen
Vause, Edwin Hamilton
Vause, Webster Russell
Vecoli, Rudolph John
Vedder, Blair
Vedder, Byron Charles
Veeck, William Louis
Veenker, Claude Harold
Vegeler, Robert Harry
Veis, Arthur
Veit, Fritz
Veit, Werner
Velardo, Joseph Thomas
Velicer, Leland Frank
Veltman, Peter
Veneman, Gerard Earl
Veneziale, Carlo Marcello
Venzke, Norman Charles
Veraldi, Lewis C.
Verber, Richard William
Verdeyen, Joseph Thomas
Verdier, Leonard D'Ooge, Jr.
Verduin, Jacob
Vereen, Robert Charles
Verger, Don Marshall
Verity, C. William, Jr.
Verma, Manindra Kishore
Vernier, Robert Lawrence
Vernon, David Harvey
Verschoor, Curtis Carl
Ver Steeg, Clarence Lester
Vertes, Victor
Vespa, Ned Angelo
Vest, Robert Wilson
Vetter, Eric William
Veysey, Arthur Ernest
Vick, Homer Jerome
Vick, Nicholas A.
Victorin (Victorin Ursache)
Vietor, Harold Duane
Vietti, Teresa Jane
Vilter, Richard William
Vincent, James Louis
Virdon, William Charles
Virgo, Julie Anne Carroll
Virzi, Richard A.
Vischer, Harold Harry
Visek, Willard James
Viskanta, Raymond
Visotsky, Harold Meryle
Visser, John Evert
Viste, Gerald Delmar
Vitaliano, Charles J(oseph)
Vitantonio, Michael N.
Vititoe, William Paul
Vitkus, Richard Francis
Vodovnik, Raymond Frank
Voelker, Larry
Vogel, Arthur Anton
Vogel, Charles Joseph
Vogel, Manfred Henry
Vogel, Michael John
Vogel, Robert
Vogeler, Alan Roth
Voigt, Adolf Frank
Voigt, Keith Marion
Voinovich, George V.
Vojta, Charles John, Jr.
Voketaitis, Arnold Mathew
Voldseth, Edward Victor
Volk, David Lawrence
Volk, Richard Whitcomb
Vollen, Robert Jay
Von Drehle, Ramon Arnold
Vonesh, Raymond James
Von Gierke, Henning Edgar
Von Hoffmann, George
von Lang, Frederick William
Von Rhein, John Richard
Von Tersch, Lawrence Wayne
von Wyss, Marc Robert
Voorhees, John James
Vorbrich, Lynn Karl
Vorys, Arthur Isaiah
Voss, Edward William, Jr.
Voss, Frederick Joseph
Voss, Jack Donald
Voss, Jerrold Richard
Voss, Omer Gerald
Votapek, Ralph James
Vowles, Richard Beckman
Voxman, Himie
Voysey, Frank Ernest
Vrablik, Edward Robert
Wachal, David E.
Wacker, Frederick Glade, Jr.
Wada, Harry Nobuyoshi
Waddington, Raymond Bruce, Jr.
Waddle, Chris
Waddle, John Frederick
Wade, James Francis
Wade, Jay Paul
Wadsworth, Homer Clark
Waetjen, Walter Bernhard
Waggoner, George Ruble
Waggoner, Raymond Walter
Wagman, Frederick Herbert
Wagner, Burton Allan
Wagner, Durrett
Wagner, Harvey Arthur
Wagner, John Addington, Jr.
Wagner, John Garnet
Wagner, Jonathan William
Wagner, Ralph Charles
Wagner, Richard
Wagner, Richard
Wagner, Robert Owen
Wagner, Robert Wayne
Wagner, Thomas Herman
Wagner, Warren Herbert, Jr.
Wagner, William Charles
Wagoner, John Leonard
Wagonseller, James Myrl
Wagstaff, C. Russell
Wagstaff, Robert Wilson
Wahba, Grace
Wahl, Eberhard Wilhelm
Wahl, Jan Boyer
Wahl, Rosalie E.
Wahlberg, Keneth Roger
Wahlen, Edwin Alfred
Wahlert, Robert Henry
Wahlstrom, Lawrence Ferdinand
Waite, Daniel Elmer
Wakeman, Fred Joseph
Wakoski, Diane
Walan, Alfons W.
Walaszek, Edward Joseph
Waldbauer, Gilbert Peter
Walden, Robert Edison
Waldman, Bernard
Waldmeir, Peter Nielsen
Waldo, Laird Douglas
Waldron, Charles Marcian
Waldron, Ellis Leigh
Waldron, Mark A., Jr.
Waldstein, Sheldon Saul
Walgenbach, Paul Henry
Walgreen, Charles Rudolph, III
Walinski, Nicholas Joseph
Walker, Bruce Edward
Walker, Duard Lee
Walker, E. Jerry
Walker, Francis Gene
Walker, Frank Dilling
Walker, George Herbert, III
Walker, Harold Blake
Walker, Howard
Walker, John Andrew
Walker, Richard Harold
Walker, Robert Alander
Walker, Robert Mowbray
Walker, Ronald Edward
Walker, Ronald Frederick
Walker, Russell T.
Walker, Waldo Sylvester
Walker, William Ray
Walker-Hurst, Joan
Wall, Arthur Edward Patrick
Wall, Carroll Edward
Wall, (Hermon) Duncan
Wall, Howard Elden
Wall, Joseph Frazier
Wall, William E.
Wallace, Charles Leslie
Wallace, David Francis
Wallace, Dean Wendell
Wallace, Dwane L.
Wallace, Harry Leland
Wallace, Jane Young (Mrs. Donald H. Wallace)
Wallace, John Francis
Wallace, John Kennard
Wallace, John Malcolm
Wallace, Leon Harry
Wallace, Ralph Howes
Wallace, Richard Lee
Wallace, Robert
Wallace, Robert Francis
Wallach, John S(idney)
Wallach, Luitpold
Wallach, Philip
Waller, George Macgregor
Waller, John Oscar
Wallerstein, David B.
Wallin, Franklin Whittelsey
Wallin, Winston Roger
Wallis, Gaile Ferris
Walls, John William
Wallwork, Gealy Weston
Walsh, Jack B.
Walsh, James Clement
Walsh, James Patrick, Jr.
Walsh, John Charles
Walsh, Loren Melford
Walsh, Michael H.
Walsh, William Francis
Walster, George William
Walt, Alexander Jeffrey
Walt, Dick K.
Walter, Frank Sherman
Walter, Robert Irving
Walters, Donald E.
Walters, Everett
Walters, Robert Eugene
Walters, Waltman
Walters, William LeRoy
Walton, Charles Whitney, III
Walton, Jonathan Taylor
Walton, Lloyd Barker
Walton, Matt Savage
Walton, Robert Wheeler
Walton, Steven Douglas
Walton, William C.
Waltz, Jon Richard
Waltzer, Herbert
Walzl, Florence LeDuc Litchfield (Mrs. Edward McColgan Walzl)
Wanamaker, Robert Joseph
Wanda, Dimitry
Wanderone, Rudolf Walter (Minnesota Fats)
Wanderone, Rudolf Walter (Minnesota Fats)
Wandmacher, Cornelius
Wang, L. Edwin
Wangberg, Lou
Wangelin, Harris Kenneth
Wankelman, Willard Fred
Wanner, James Emerson
Warch, Richard
Ward, Daniel P.
Ward, Donovan Frederick
Ward, Dudley Avery
Ward, George Henry
Ward, Louis Emmerson
Ward, Louis Larrick
Ward, Richard Charles
Ward, Robertson, Jr.
Ward, Sylvan Donald
Ward, Thomas Nelson
Ward, Wallace Dixon
Ward, Warren Hayden
Ware, (Durward) Clifton, Jr.
Ware, Karl Ellis
Ware, Mitchell
Ware, Richard Anderson
Warfield, William Caesar
Warin, Edward George
Waring, Edward Graham, Jr.
Waring, Walter Weyler
Warkany, Josef
Warmbrod, James Robert
Warner, Cecil Francis
Warner, Dwain Willard
Warner, Huber Richard
Warner, J. Keith
Warner, James Daniel
Warner, Marvin Leon
Warner, William Hamer
Warren, James Caldwell
Warren, James Vaughn
Warren, L.D.
Warren, Richard M.
Warren, Robert Willis
Warren, William Gerald
Warrington, John Wesley
Warrington, Willard Glade
Warshaw, Martin Richard
Wartell, C. Robert
Warwick, Ronald Eugene
Wasan, Darsh Tilakchand
Washburn, Paul
Wasiolek, Edward
Wasson, Ted Decker
Watanabe, August Masaru
Waterhouse, John Percival
Waters, Edna A.
Waters, Jack Wesley
Waters, Muddy (McKinley Morganfield)
Waterston, James Rufus
Watkins, Daniel Joseph
Watkins, David Hyder
Watkins, Glenn Elson
Watkins, Lloyd Irion
Watrel, Albert Adam
Watson, Alfred Nelson
Watson, Catherine Elaine
Watson, Dennis Wallace
Watson, Robert Earl
Watson, Roy
Watson, Thomas Sturges
Watt, Andrew J.
Watt, Dean Day
Watt, Stuart George
Wattenberg, Albert
Watters, James I(saac)
Watters, Loras Joseph
Watters, Mortimer Charles
Watterson, Ray Leighton
Watts, Emily Stipes
Wawzonek, Stanley
Waxman, David
Weakland, Rembert G.
Wearstler, Earl Ford
Weary, Daniel Croft
Weatherby, Frank (Buc)
Weathersby, George Byron
Weaver, Franklin Thomas
Weaver, Lawrence Clayton
Weaver, Richard L., II
Webb, Charles Haizlip, Jr.
Webb, Dan K.
Webb, Howard William, Jr.
Webb, James Okrum, Jr.
Webb, Jervis Campbell
Webb, Neil John
Webb, Willard Isaac, III
Webb, William Duncan
Webber, Everard Leland
Webber, Howard Rodney
Webber, Thomas Raymond
Weber, Arthur
Weber, Bertram Anton
Weber, Charles Edward
Weber, Delbert Dean
Weber, Harm Allen
Weber, Morton M.
Weber, Philip Joseph
Weber, Ronald Gilbert
Weber, Roy Edwin
Weber, Walter Jacob, Jr.
Weber, Wendell William
Webster, James Randolph, Jr.
Webster, John Kimball
Webster, Leslie Tillotson, Jr.
Webster, Shirley Alton
Webster, Willis Harry
Wedgeworth, Robert, Jr.
Weed, Ithamar Dryden
Weeden, Morris Skiff
Weeks, Francis William
Weeks, LeRoy Gilbert
Weeks, Paul Martin
Weeks, Richard Elvin
Weeks, Robert Walker
Weeks, Solan William
Weeks, Walter LeRoy
Weening, Richard William, Jr.
Weertman, Johannes
Weese, Benjamin Horace
Weese, Harry M.
Weg, John Gerard
Wegener, Charles William
Wegener, Leander Edward
Wegman, Myron Ezra
Wegner, Karl Heinrich
Wehring, Bernard William
Wehrle, Leroy Snyder
Wehrwein, Austin Carl
Weichlein, William Jesset
Weick, Paul Charles
Weidenaar, Reynold Henry
Weidenthal, Maurice (Bud) David
Weidman, Wallace Reid
Weidner, Edward William
Weil, Herman
Weil, Irwin
Weil, John William
Weil, Louis Arthur, Jr.
Weil, Myron
Weil, Rolf Alfred
Weil, Roman Lee
Weil, William Bachrach, Jr.
Weimer, Arthur Martin
Weinberg, Arthur
Weinberg, Eugene David
Weinberg, Jack
Weinberg, Lila Shaffer
Weinberg, Michael, Jr.
Weinberger, Hans Felix
Weinberger, Jerome A.
Weinberger, Leon Joseph
Weinbrot, Howard David
Weiner, David J.
Weiner, Egon
Weingarten, Herbert N.
Weingartner, Rudolph Herbert
Weinreich, Gabriel
Weinstein, James
Weinstein, Michael Alan
Weinstein, Paul P.
Weinstein, Ronald S.
Weir, Donald Clair
Weir, John Paul
Weir, Morton Webster
Weir, Paul Joseph
Weisbach, Jerry Arnold
Weisblat, David Irwin
Weisbrod, Burton Allen
Weise, Charles Martin
Weisman, Morton Philip
Weisman, Robert Abbie
Weiss, Edward Huhner
Weiss, Harry Joseph
Weiss, James Moses Aaron
Weiss, Morry
Weiss, Morton Louis
Weiss, Robert Francis
Weiss, Robert Orr
Weiss, William Lee
Weissler, Arnold Mervin
Weissman, Herman Benjamin
Weissman, Michael Lewis
Weisstein, Ulrich Werner
Weisz, William Julius
Welch, Fredric Byron
Welch, Patrick Errett
Welch, Ralston B.
Welch, Robert Gibson
Welch, Wayne Willard
Weldon, James Ernest
Weldon, Robert William
Welker, Wallace Irving
Wellborn, Sidney Nelson, Jr.
Weller, John Martin
Wellington, John Adam
Wellington, Robert Hall
Welliver, Warren Dee
Wellman, Carl Pierce
Wells, Ben Harris
Wells, Charles Marion
Wells, Charles William
Wells, Donald Edward
Wells, Herman B
Wells, Herschel James
Wells, James M.
Wells, Joel Freeman
Wells, Joseph Merton
Wells, Robert
Wells, Victor Hugh, Jr.
Welser, John Ralph
Welsh, David John
Welsh, Leslie Thomas
Welsh, Matthew Empson
Welsh, Wiley Alfred
Welton, James Richard
Weltyk, William Harry
Wendt, Kurt Frank
Wendt, Vernon Earl
Wenger, John Christian
Wenner, Gene Charles
Wenner, Herbert Allan
Wennerstrom, Jack Albert
Wenninger, Eugene Paul
Wentland, Otto Paul
Wentland, Paul Scott
Wentworth, Richard Leigh
Wentz, Frederick Kuhlman
Wentz, Robert Earl
Wentz, Walter John
Wenzlau, Thomas Eugene
Wenzler, William Paul
Wenzlick, Roy
Werner, Charles George
Werner, Oswald
Werner, R(ichard) Budd
Wert, Charles Allen
Wert, James William
Wert, Lucille Mathena
Wertz, John Edward
Wesbury, Stuart Arnold, Jr.
Weseli, Roger William
Wessel, Robert Hoover
Wesselmann, Glenn Allen
Wessner, Kenneth Thomas
West, Byron Kenneth
West, Charles Cameron
West, Charles Tyrrell
West, Clark Darwin
West, John Dunham
West, Michael Alan
West, Robert Culbertson
West, Robert MacLellan
West, Thomas Meade
Westbrook, James Edwin
Westerbeck, Kenneth Edward
Westerman, John Harold
Westfall, Ralph Libby
Westfall, Richard Samuel
Westfall, Thomas Creed
Westin, Richard Swan
Westley, John Leonard
Westley, Richard Owen
Westman, Jack Conrad
Weston, Arthur Walter
Weston, Norman Betts
Weston, W. Donald
Westran, Roy Alvin
Westropp, Thomas Champion
Westwater, James William
Wethey, Harold Edwin
Wetmore, Thomas Hall
Wetzel, James Lewis
Wetzel, Robert George
Wexler, Bernard Carl
Wexner, Leslie Herbert
Whale, Arthur Richard
Whalen, Donald Peyton
Whaley, Dallas F(lay), Jr.
Whallon, Evan Arthur, Jr.
Whallon, William
Wharton, Lennard
Wheatley, Paul
Wheaton, Warde Franklin
Wheeler, Charles Bertan
Wheeler, Warren G(age), Jr.
Whelan, Paul Augustine
Whiffen, James Douglas
Whipple, Kenneth
Whisler, Walter William
Whisnant, Jack Page
Whistler, Roy Lester
Whitaker, Gilbert Riley, Jr.
Whitaker, H. Baron
Whitaker, Jack Friel
Whitaker, Meade
Whitby, Kenneth Thomas
Whitcomb, Edgar D.
White, Arthur Clinton
White, David Benjamin
White, Doris Anne
White, Frank, Jr.
White, Fred Rollin, Jr.
White, H. Blair
White, Herbert Spencer
White, James Boyd
White, James Patrick
White, Jimm F.
White, John Wesley, Jr.
White, Philip Butler
White, Robert Allan
White, Robert I.
White, Robert J.
White, Robert M., II
White, Roy Bernard
White, Rufus Elton
White, Terry Ross
White, Thomas
White, Wilbur Lee
White, William
White, William Samuel
White, Willis Sheridan, Jr.
White, Willmon Lee
Whitehead, Donald Francis
Whitehead, John Costello
Whitehead, Richard Francis
Whitehouse, Alton Winslow, Jr.
Whitehouse, Walter MacIntire
Whiteman, Joseph David
Whiteside, Robert Scott
Whitfield, Allen
Whitford, Philip Burton
Whiting, Edmund John
Whitinger, Ralph Judson
Whitlock, John Joseph
Whitman, Donald Ray
Whitman, James Thomas
Whitman, Nathan Thomas
Whitmore, Charles Horace
Whitmore, Edward Hugh
Whitnah, Donald Robert
Whitney, Jack Melville, II
Whitney, John Clarence
Whitney, John Joseph
Whitney, Robert McLaughlin
Whitney, William Chowning
Whitney, William Elliot, Jr.
Whitsel, Robert Malcolm
Whitsitt, Frank Casey
Whitt, Gregory Sidney
Whitten, Eric Harold Timothy
Wickert, Frederic Robinson
Wickesberg, Albert Klumb
Wickhem, John Carroll
Wickman, John Edward
Wicks, Eugene Claude
Widder, Theodore Carl, Jr.
Widder, Willard Graves
Widiss, Alan I.
Widman, Paul Edward
Widmer, Robert H.
Wiebenga, William Martin
Wied, George Ludwig
Wiegner, Edward Alex
Wieland, Robert Richard
Wien, Stuart Lewis
Wiener, Joseph
Wiener, Stanley Lewis
Wier, Patricia Ann
Wiersbe, Warren Wendell
Wierum, Thornton Briggs
Wieser, Charles Edward
Wiet, Mitchell John
Wiggins, Samuel Paul
Wight, Ira Edward
Wijsman, Robert Arthur
Wilbanks, Jan Joseph
Wilber, Laura Ann
Wilbur, Richard Sloan
Wilde, John
Wilder, Keven Carney
Wildermuth, Roger Gregory
Wiley, David Earl
Wiley, Edwin Packard
Wilhelm, Ross Johnston
Wilhelm, William Jean
Wilkerson, James S.
Wilkes, James Oscroft
Wilkey, Richard Ambrose
Wilkie, Leighton Allyn
Wilkie, Michael Leighton
Wilkin, Ed Ray, Jr.
Wilkin, Richard Edwin
Wilkins, George Thomas
Wilkinson, Lois Jean
Wilkinson, Warren Scripps
Wilkinson, William Sherwood
Will, Hubert Louis
Will, Joanne Marie
Will, Robert Erwin
Willard, Glenn Norfleet, Jr.
Willbern, York
Wille, Lois Jean
Wille, Wayne Martin
Willens, Rita Jacobs
Willes, Mark Hinckley
Willet, Richard Allen
Willey, Calvert Livingston
Willey, John Douglas
Willey, Richard Lee
Williams, Alexander Johnston
Williams, Camilla
Williams, Charles Matthew
Williams, Chester Arthur, Jr.

Williams, David Bryan
Williams, David Perry
Williams, Don Stewart
Williams, Douglas Lee
Williams, Dudley
Williams, Earl R.
Williams, Edgar Gene
Williams, Edson Poe
Williams, Edward Joseph
Williams, Emory
Williams, Ernest Eden
Williams, Eugene Flewellyn, Jr.
Williams, Frederick
Williams, G. Mennen
Williams, George Howard
Williams, George James
Williams, Gerald Albert
Williams, Gerald Haliburton
Williams, Gordon Bretnell
Williams, Gordon Bretnell
Williams, Harold Milton
Williams, Harold Roger
Williams, Jack Marvin
Williams, James Patrick
Williams, James R.
Williams, Jim R.
Williams, Karl C.
Williams, Leslie Howard, Jr.
Williams, Martha Ethelyn
Williams, Mason
Williams, Paul Leon
Williams, Robert Fones
Williams, Robert Jene
Williams, Ronald
Williams, Theodore Joseph
Williams, Wallace Cecil
Williams, Walter Jackson, Jr.
Williams, Walter Joseph
Williams, Warner
Williams, Wendell Sterling
Williams, William Joseph
Williams-Ashman, Howard Guy
Williamson, Clarence Kelly
Williamson, Gilbert Pemberton, Jr.
Williamson, John Garrett
Williamson, John Pritchard
Williamson, Warren Pyatt, Jr.
Williamson, William Landram
Willing, Richard Thomas, Jr.
Willis, Betty Jo
Willis, David Edwin
Willis, Edgar Ernest
Willis, George Edmund
Willis, John Steele
Willis, Kenneth Reed
Willis, Paul Gene
Willke, Thomas Aloys
Willman, John Norman
Willman, Vallee Louis
Willmarth, William Walter
Wills, Garry
Wills, John Gordon
Wills, John Harvey
Wills, Robert Hamilton
Wills, Walter Joe
Willson, Fred E.
Willson, Philip James
Wilmeth, Harvey Delbert
Wilmouth, Robert K.
Wilson, Arlene May
Wilson, Christopher William
Wilson, Delbert Ray
Wilson, Francis Servis
Wilson, Francis Servis
Wilson, Gahan
Wilson, Garland, Jr.
Wilson, George Balch
Wilson, George Hugh

Wilson, George Wilton
Wilson, Harold Woodrow
Wilson, Harris Ward
Wilson, Harry B.
Wilson, James Graves
Wilson, Joe Bransford
Wilson, John Alan
Wilson, John Christopher
Wilson, John Rigby
Wilson, John Samuel
Wilson, John Todd
Wilson, Kenneth
Wilson, Lauren Ross
Wilson, Margaret Bush
Wilson, Mark Curtis
Wilson, Sister Mary Lawrence
Wilson, Paul Edwin
Wilson, Ralph Cookerly, Jr.
Wilson, Richard Christian
Wilson, Robert Douglas
Wilson, Robert Thompson
Wilson, Samuel Smith
Wilson, Sloan Jacob
Wilson, Theodore Allen
Wilson, Tom
Wilson, Warner Rushing
Wilson, William Julius
Wilt, James William
Wilton, William Everett
Wimberg, James John
Wimberly, W. Carl
Winchell, Frank Jennings
Winchell, Richard Paul
Winder, Clarence Leland
Windfuhr, Gernot Ludwig
Windle, William Frederick
Wine, Donald Arthur
Wine, Sherwin T.
Winfree, Arthur Taylor
Wing, John Adams
Wingard, Daniel Walter
Winger, Howard Woodrow
Wingerter, Robert George
Winholtz, Howard Messick
Winick, Alfred Zell
Winick, Marvin
Winkelman, Stanley Jay
Winkler, Elmer Louis
Winkler, Henry Ralph
Winkles, Bobby Brooks
Winn, Willis Jay
Winnie, Alon Palm
Winokur, George
Winston, Roland
Winter, Chester Caldwell
Winter, David John
Winter, Max
Winter, Robert Bruce
Winter, William Bergford
Winter, William Earl
Winton, David Michael
Winyard, Leon E.
Wiot, Jerome Francis
Wirszup, Izaak
Wirt, Frederick Marshall
Wirth, Willard Ralph, Jr.
Wirtz, Arthur Michael
Wirtz, William Wadsworth
Wise, Henry Seiler
Wise, John Augustus, Jr.
Wise, William Jerrard
Wiseman, Gordon Gray
Wishner, Maynard Ira
Wishnow, Emanuel
Wissel, Raymond Charles
Wit, Daniel
Witcoff, Sheldon William
Witham, Peter Martin
Withers, W. Russell, Jr.
Witherspoon, D. James
Withrow, John D., Jr.

Withrow, Richard Marshall
Witke, Edward Charles
Witkop, Carl Jacob
Witt, Robert J.
Witt, Robert John
Wittenberg, James Keech
Wittenmeyer, Charles E.
Wittmann, Otto
Witwer, Samuel Weiler
Wobst, Frank Georg
Woelfle, Arthur William
Wogsland, James Willard
Wohlhueter, John Fredrick
Wojcicki, Andrew Adalbert
Wolcott, Alan Thane
Wolf, Don Allen
Wolf, Frederic Eastman
Wolf, Herbert Christian
Wolf, Milton Albert
Wolf, Richard Clarence
Wolf, William Chester
Wolfe, James Richard
Wolfe, John Walton
Wolfe, Ralph Stoner
Wolfe, Sheila
Wolff, Aaron Sidney
Wolfram, Thomas
Wolfson, Albert
Wolfson, Lester Marvin
Wolfson, Robert Lowell
Wolinsky, Emanuel
Wollan, Gerald Casper
Wollman, Roger Leland
Wolman, J. Martin
Wolohan, Richard Vincent
Wolpert, Edward Alan
Wolsiffer, Patricia Rae
Wolter, Jurgen Reimer
Wolterink, Lester Floyd
Womer, Charles Berry
Wommack, Sidney Jackson, Jr.
Wommack, William Walton
Wong, Frank F.
Wong, Warren James
Wood, Arthur MacDougall
Wood, David Charles
Wood, Earl Howard
Wood, Harland Goff
Wood, Harlington, Jr.
Wood, James Nowell
Wood, Lee Blair
Wood, Percy Addison
Wood, Richard Donald
Wood, Robert Edward
Wood, Roy Vaughn
Wood, Steven Pierpont Jeffris
Wood, William Jerome
Woodall, William Leon
Woodard, Gerald Walter
Woodard, Harold Raymond
Woodbridge, Hensley Charles
Woodcock, Leonard
Wooden, Howard Edmund
Woodman, Harold David
Woodring, DeWayne Stanley
Woodroofe, Michael Barrett
Woodruff, Arnold Bond
Woodruff, Neil Parker
Woodruff, Truman Owen
Woods, James Richard
Woods, Joe Darst
Woods, John Dows
Woods, John Lucius
Woods, Paul Harlow
Woods, Robert Archer
Woods, Robert Henry
Woods, Thomas Cochrane, Jr.
Woods, Walter Ralph
Woodside, Howard Bush
Woodson, Riley D.
Woodward, Herbert Norton

Woodworth, James Richard
Wool, Ira Goodwin
Wooldredge, William Dunbar
Woolf, William Blauvelt
Woolley, Eugene Ellsworth
Woolsey, Clarence Olin
Woolson, James Edward
Woolverton, John Jacob, Jr.
Wooten, Cecil Aaron
Workman, Donald Hamilton
Workman, James Clark
Worley, Gordon Roger
Worley, James Clark
Worley, Will J.
Worth, Roger Petrie
Worthy, James Carson
Wotiz, John Henry
Wright, Alfred George James
Wright, Arthur McIntosh
Wright, David Atwood
Wright, Donald Eugene
Wright, Flavel Allen
Wright, Frank Gardner
Wright, George Thaddeus
Wright, Gordon Pribyl
Wright, Harry, III
Wright, Herbert E(dgar), Jr.
Wright, Jackson Atchison
Wright, John
Wright, Joseph Sutherland
Wright, Lafayette Hart
Wright, Marshall
Wright, Robert Joseph
Wright, Scott Olin
Wrigley, William
Wu, Nelson Ikon
Wu, Shien-Ming
Wu, Tai Te
Wuest, Francis Joseph
Wuesthoff, Winfred William
Wuller, James Herman
Wunderlich, Carle Robert
Wurm, John Nicholas
Wurster, Dale Erwin
Wussow, George Carl
Wuthrich, Virgil Eugene
Wyatt, James Frank, Jr.
Wyatt-Brown, Bertram
Wycislo, Aloysius John
Wydman, Perry Byron
Wyllie, Peter John
Wyman, James Thomas
Wyman, Morton
Wynn, Thomas Joseph
Wyse, Marc Allen
Wyss, Walther Erwin
Yaffe, Frank Henry
Yager, John Warren
Yale, Seymour Hershel
Yamasaki, Minoru
Yancey, Philip David
Yanders, Armon Frederick
Yang, Kwang-Tzu
Yankwich, Peter Ewald
Yanney, Michael B.
Yarrington, Blaine J.
Yary, Anthony Ronald
Yashon, David
Yassin, Robert Alan
Yau, Stephen Sik-sang
Yeager, Bruno John
Yeager, Ernest Bill
Yeh, Chai
Yeh, Kung Chie
Yen, William Mao-Shung
Yetka, Lawrence Robert
Yeutter, Clayton Keith
Yih, Chia-Shun
Yinger, J. Milton
Ylvisaker, William Townend
Yngve, Victor Huse

Yocum, Ronald Harris
Yoder, Charles William
Yoder, Douglas O.
Yoder, Frederick Floyd
Yoerger, Roger Raymond
Yohe, Ralph Sandlin
Yohn, David Stewart
Yoho, Lewis Wilbur
Yonkers, Anthony James
Yost, James Everett
Yost, Lyle Edgar
Youker, James E.
Young, Bruce Anderson
Young, Clyde William
Young, Coleman Alexander
Young, Conrad Scotland
Young, Dale Lee
Young, David Pollock
Young, David Wilson
Young, DeForrest Eugene
Young, Dennis Eugene
Young, Don John
Young, Donald E.
Young, Donald Stirling
Young, Edwin Harold
Young, Gail Sellers
Young, George Berkeley
Young, George Haywood, Jr.
Young, George Hooper
Young, George Patrick
Young, Gordon Ellsworth
Young, H. Edwin
Young, Hobart Paul
Young, Jack M.
Young, James Curtis
Young, James Wesley
Young, Jess R.
Young, John Edward
Young, John Paul
Young, Marvin Oscar
Young, Milton R.
Young, Paul Andrew
Young, Paul Helmer, Jr.
Young, Paul Ruel
Young, Ralph Eugene
Young, Richard Alan
Young, Richard Allen
Young, Ronald Faris
Young, William Henry
Youngblood, Richard Neil
Younger, Roy R.
Youngner, Philip Genevus
Youngquist, Alvin Menvid, Jr.
Youngren, Ralph Park
Yovich, Daniel John
Yovicich, George Steven Jones
Yovits, Marshall Clinton
Yozwiak, Bernard James
Yu, George Tzuchiao
Yuan, John Hsun-Kuang
Yudkin, Richard A.
Zabel, Robert Paul
Zablocki, Clement John
Zacks, Gordon Benjamin
Zaffarano, Daniel Joseph
Zafren, Herbert Cecil
Zahner, Victor Henry
Zahniser, Marvin Ralph
Zajonc, Robert B(oleslaw)
Zakin, Jacques Louis
Zalecki, Paul Henry
Zaliouk, Yuval Nathan
Zambie, Allan John
Zander, Alvin Frederick
Zangwill, Willard Ira
Zarafonetis, Chris John Dimiter
Zarnowitz, Victor
Zart, David Paul
Zassenhaus, Hans Julius
Zavala, Donald Charles

Zei, Dino
Zeidler, Frank P.
Zeiger, Martin
Zeisel, Hans
Zekman, Pamela Lois (Mrs. Fredric Soll)
Zeleny, Robert Owen
Zellner, Arnold
Zeltzer, George Meyer
Zemmer, Joseph Lawrence, Jr.
Zeno, Robert S.
Zeps, Valdis Juris
Zerby, Lewis Kenneth
Zetcher, Arnold B.
Zgusta, Ladislav
Zide, Norman Herbert
Ziebarth, E. William
Ziebarth, Robert Charles
Ziegler, Dewey Kiper
Ziegler, Jesse H.
Ziegler, John Augustus, Jr.
Ziegner, Edward Henry
Zietlow, Paul Nathan
Ziffren, Sidney Edward
Zigman, Robert S.
Zigmund, Harold Francis
Zilli, Harry Angelo, Jr.
Zillmann, Robert Edward
Zilly, Margaret Bernice
Zilz, David Arthur
Zimmer, Hans Willi
Zimmer, William H., Jr.
Zimmerman, Austin Manlove
Zimmerman, Gideon K.
Zimmerman, Harry Paul
Zimmerman, Howard Elliot
Zimmerman, John Gustave
Zimmerman, Mary Helen Campion
Zimmerman, Mortimer William
Zimmerman, Paul Albert
Zimmerman, Thomas Fletcher
Zimmerman, William
Zimmerman, William
Zimmermann, Gerhardt
Zimring, Lois Eileen Jacobs
Zintel, Harold Albert
Ziolkowski, Korczak
Zion, Roger H.
Ziperski, James Richard
Zissis, George John
Zlatoff-Mirsky, Everett Igor
Zobrist, Benedict Karl
Zobrist, George Winston
Zografi, George D.
Zolik, Edwin Stanislaus
Zoltai, Tibor Zoltan
Zondervan, Peter John (Pat)
Zonis, Marvin
Zook, Elvin Glenn
Zornow, William Frank
Zowski, Thaddeus
Zsigmond, Elemer Kalman
Zucaro, Aldo Charles
Zucker, Robert A(lpert)
Zuidema, R(einer) Tom
Zulfer, Anthony George, Jr.
Zumwalt, Glen Wallace
Zurheide, Charles Henry
Zuspan, Frederick Paul
Zweifler, Andrew Jonathan